Oxford ... er

Słowni ... olski

... ıgielski

OXFORD
UNIVERSITY PRESS

OXFORD
UNIVERSITY PRESS

Great Clarendon Street, Oxford OX2 6DP

Oxford University Press is a department of the University of Oxford. It furthers the University's objective of excellence in research, scholarship, and education by publishing worldwide in

Oxford New York

Auckland Cape Town Dar es Salaam Hong Kong Karachi Kuala Lumpur Madrid Melbourne Mexico City Nairobi New Delhi Shanghai Taipei Toronto

With offices in

Argentina Austria Brazil Chile Czech Republic France Greece Guatemala Hungary Italy Japan Poland Portugal Singapore South Korea Switzerland Thailand Turkey Ukraine Vietnam

OXFORD and OXFORD ENGLISH are registered trade marks of Oxford University Press in the UK and in certain other countries

First published 2007

2015 2014
12 11 10 9 8 7 6

The British National Corpus is a collaborative project involving Oxford University Press, Longman, Chambers, the Universities of Oxford and Lancaster and the British Library

ISBN 978 0 19 431736 8 (DICTIONARY)
ISBN 978 0 19 431737 5 (CD-ROM)
ISBN 978 0 19 431738 2 (DICTIONARY AND CD-ROM PACK)

Acknowledgements

Third edition edited by: Janet Phillips
Assisted by: Dorota Niewińska, Dorota Hołowiak, Dorota Kotowicz

Illustrations: A Biggs, Anna Brookes, Dave Burroughs, Martin Cox, David Eaton, Angelika Elsebach, Gay Galsworthy, Karen Hiscock, Margaret Jones, Richard Lewington, Vanessa Luff, Kevin Maddison, Coral Mula, Martin Shovel, Mick Stubbs, Technical Graphics Dept, OUP, Harry Venning, Graham White, Michael Woods

Photographs: Corbis A8 (basketball); A16 (spring); Corel A2 (church, monument, ruin, tower, office block, dam, lighthouse, bridge, warehouse), A3 (thatched cottage, castle, stately home), A4 (fisherman), A6 (aeroplane, helicopter, oil tanker, liner, hovercraft, lifeboat, ferry, submarine, yacht), A7 (train, bus, lorry), A8 (cricket, rugby, hockey, boxing, horse racing, show jumping), A9 (skating, fencing, athletics, weightlifting, judo, surfing), A10 (seal), A11 (crocodile, lobster, starfish, lizard, eel, jellyfish), A14 (hamburger, pizza, roast beef, apple pie, teapot, milkshake), A15 (all), A16 (snow); Digital Stock A7 (monorail); Fotosearch A4 (cook, hairdresser, farmer, teacher, nurse, pilot); A5 (fish and chip shop); Getty Images A1 (woman in skirt, woman in pyjamas), A2 (pub, stadium), A5 (grocer's, baker's, optician's, market, butcher, flower stall, dry cleaner's, clothes shop, shopping centre, garden centre), A6 (glider), A7 (underground), A8 (tennis, baseball, ice hockey), A9 (skiing, gymnastics, golf, waterskiing, bungee jumping, abseiling, white-water rafting, windsurfing), A14 (fish and chips, eggs), A16 (autumn, winter, summer, rainbow, sunset, clouds, lightning, rain); Hemera Technologies A1 (man in tie, man in jeans, patterns), A7 (tram, sports car, estate car, hatchback, motorbike, scooter, people carrier, van, coach, taxi), A14 (salad, soup, kebab, pasta, spaghetti, quiche, ice cream, pancake, cheese, honey, waffle, cereal, cup of tea, black coffee); Ingram A10 (dolphin); John Foxx A14 (jam); Punchstock A4 (carpenter, painter), A16 (wind)

Maps © Oxford University Press

Text capture and processing by Oxford University Press
Typeset by Data Standards Limited

Printed in China

Spis treści

Jak korzystać ze słownika

Jak znaleźć hasła

ważne słowa oznaczono kluczem

again /ə'gen; ə'geɪn/ adv. **1** once more; another time: *I'll phone again later.* ◇ *Could you say that again* (powtórzyć), *please?* ◇ *Don't ever do that again!* Nigdy więcej tego nie rób! ▶ **jeszcze raz**, (*zakaz*) **więcej**

pisownię alternatywną podano w nawiasach

organize (also -ise) /'ɔːgənaɪz/ verb **1** [T] to plan or arrange an event, activity, etc. ▶ **organizować 2** [I,T] to put or arrange things into a system or logical order: *Can you decide what needs doing? I'm hopeless at organizing.* ◇ *You need to organize your work more carefully.* ▶ **organizować**

Homonimy są często umieszczone w postaci osobnych haseł, oznaczonych małymi numerami umieszczonymi nad linią wiersza, natomiast poszczególne znaczenia haseł oznaczono numerami na linii wiersza.

bark[1] /bɑːk/ noun **1** [U] the hard outer covering of a tree ▶ **kora 2** [C] the short, loud noise that a dog makes: *The dog next door has a very loud bark.* ▶ **szczekanie**

bark[2] /bɑːk/ verb **1** [I] **bark (at sb/sth)** (used about dogs) to make a loud, short noise or noises ▶ **szczekać** ➲ look at **woof 2** [I,T] **bark (at sb)**; **bark sth (out) (at sb)** to speak to sb in a loud voice in an angry or aggressive way: *The boss came in, barked out some orders and left again.* ▶ **wykrzykiwać**

pisownia amerykańska

centre[1] (US center) /'sentə(r)/ noun **1** [C, usually sing.] the middle point or part of sth: *I work in the centre* (w centrum) *of London.* ◇ *Which way is the town centre* (centrum), *please?* ◇ *She hit the target dead centre.* ▶ **środek** ➲ note at **middle 2** [C] a place where sb/sth is collected together; the point towards which sth is directed: *major urban/industrial centres* ◇ *She always likes to be **the centre of attention*** (w centrum uwagi). ◇ *You should*

Słowa i wyrażenia odnoszące się do głównego hasła

idiomy oznaczono symbolem IDM

Strzałka wskazuje hasło, przy którym należy szukać wyjaśnienia znaczenia danego idiomu.

IDM **(close/near) at hand** (formal) near in space or time: *Help is close at hand.* ▶ **blisko**
be an old hand (at sth) → OLD
by hand 1 done by a person and not by machine: *I had to do all the sewing by hand.* ▶ **ręcznie 2** not by post: *The letter was delivered by hand.* ▶ **doręczony osobiście**

czasowniki złożone (phrasal verbs) oznaczono symbolem PHR V

PHR V **take sb aback** [usually passive] to surprise or shock sb ▶ **zaskakiwać**
take after sb [not used in the continuous tenses] to look or behave like an older member of your family, especially a parent ▶ **być podobnym do kogoś w rodzinie**
take sth apart to separate sth into the different parts it is made of ▶ **rozkładać na części**

wyrazy pochodne (derivatives) oznaczono symbolem ■

Wyrazy pochodne to takie, które:
1 mają tę samą pisownię, ale stanowią różne części mowy;
2 zostały utworzone przez dodanie przyrostka (np. *-ly*, *-ness*) do głównego wyrazu (hasła).

harass /'hærəs; hə'ræs/ verb [T] to annoy or worry sb by doing unpleasant things to them, especially over a long time: *The court ordered him to stop harassing his ex-wife.* ▶ **dręczyć**, **nękać**, **prześladować**
■ **harassment** noun [U]: *She accused her boss of sexual harassment* (molestowanie seksualne). ▶ **gnębienie**

Znaczenie

Definicje słów są napisane przystępną i jasną angielszczyzną.

banger /ˈbæŋə(r)/ noun [C] (Brit., informal) **1** a **sausage** ▶ **kiełbasa 2** an old car that is in very bad condition: *I'm tired of driving around in that old banger.* ▶ **gruchot 3** a small, noisy **firework** ▶ **petarda**

Zdania przykładowe pomagają zrozumieć dane słowo i ilustrują jego poprawne użycie.

below /bɪˈləʊ/ prep. at or to a lower position or level than sb/sth: *Do not write below this line.* ◇ *The temperature fell below freezing* (poniżej zera). ◇ *Her marks in the exam were below average.* ▶ **pod**, **poniżej** OPP **above** ➲ note at **under**
■ **below** adv. at or to a lower position or level: *temperatures of 30° and below* ◇ *I don't live on the top floor – I live on the floor below* (na przedostatnim piętrze). ▶ **poniżej**

wyraz mający to **samo znaczenie**

discontent /ˌdɪskənˈtent/ (also **discontentment** /ˌdɪskənˈtentmənt/) noun [U] the state of being unhappy with sth: *The management could sense growing discontent among the staff.* ▶ **niezadowolenie**, **rozczarowanie**

przenośne użycie wyrazu

dog² /dɒg/ verb [T] (**dogging**; **dogged**) to follow sb closely: *A shadowy figure was dogging their every move.* ◇ (figurative) *Bad luck and illness have dogged her career from the start.* ▶ **śledzić**; **towarzyszyć**

wyraz o tym samym znaczeniu, używany w **angielszczyźnie amerykańskiej**

nappy /ˈnæpi/ noun [C] (pl. **nappies**) (US **diaper** /ˈdaɪəpə(r)/) a piece of soft thick cloth or paper that a baby or very young child wears around its bottom and between its legs: *Does his nappy need changing?* ◇ *disposable* (jednorazowe) *nappies* ▶ **pieluszka**

Gramatyka

część mowy

bellow /ˈbeləʊ/ verb **1** [I,T] **bellow (sth) (at sb)** to shout in a loud deep voice, especially because you are angry: *They bellowed at her to stop.* ▶ **ryczeć 2** [I] to make a deep low sound, like a **bull** ▶ **ryczeć**
■ **bellow** noun [C] ▶ **ryk**; **wrzask**

[C] = **countable noun**
rzeczownik policzalny, tj. taki, od którego można utworzyć liczbę mnogą

[U] = **uncountable noun**
rzeczownik niepoliczalny, tj. taki, od którego nie można utworzyć liczby mnogiej

sing. = **singular noun**
rzeczownik występuje tylko w liczbie pojedynczej

pl. = **plural noun**
rzeczownik występuje tylko w liczbie mnogiej

shadow¹ /ˈʃædəʊ/ noun **1** [C] a dark shape on a surface that is caused by sth being between the light and that surface: *The dog was chasing its own shadow.* ◇ *The shadows lengthened as the sun went down.* ▶ **cień** ➲ picture at **shade 2** [U] an area that is dark because sth prevents direct light from reaching it: *His face was* ***in shadow.*** ▶ **cień** ➲ note at **shade 3** [sing.] a very small amount of sth: *I know without* ***a shadow of doubt*** *that he's lying.* ▶ **cień**
IDM **cast a shadow (across/over sth)** → CAST¹

premises /ˈpremɪsɪz/ noun [pl.] the building and the land around it that a business owns or uses: *Smoking is not allowed* ***on the premises.*** ▶ **budynek z przylegającym terenem**

with sing. or pl. verb
rzeczownik może występować z czasownikiem w liczbie pojedynczej lub mnogiej

committee /kə'mɪti/ noun [C, with sing. or pl. verb] a group of people who have been chosen to discuss sth or decide sth: *to be/sit on a committee* ◇ *The planning committee meets/meet twice a week.* ▶ **komisja**, **zarząd**, **komitet**

nieregularna liczba mnoga

tomato /tə'mɑːtəʊ; US -'meɪ-/ noun [C] (pl. **tomatoes**) a soft red fruit that is often eaten without being cooked in salads, or cooked as a vegetable: *tomato juice/soup/sauce* ▶ **pomidor** ⇨ picture on **page A13**, picture at **salad**

[T] = **transitive verb**
czasownik przechodni – występuje z dopełnieniem

[I] = **intransitive verb**
czasownik nieprzechodni – nigdy nie występuje z dopełnieniem

hide[1] /haɪd/ verb (pt **hid** /hɪd/, pp **hidden** /'hɪdn/) **1** [T] to put or keep sb/sth in a place where they or it cannot be seen; to cover sth so that it cannot be seen: *Where shall I hide the money?* ◇ *You couldn't see Bill in the photo – he was hidden behind John.* ▶ **chować**, **ukrywać** **2** [I] to be or go in a place where you cannot be seen or found: *Quick, run and hide!* ◇ *The child was hiding under the bed.* ▶ **chować się**, **ukrywać się** **3** [T] **hide sth (from sb)** to keep sth secret, especially your feelings: *She tried to hide her disappointment from them.* ▶ **skrywać**

nieregularne formy czasownika

take /teɪk/ verb [T] (pt **took** /tʊk/, pp **taken** /'teɪkən/) **1** to carry or move sb/sth; to go with sb from one place to another: *Take your coat with you – it's cold.* ◇ *Could you take this letter home to your parents?* ◇ *The ambulance took him to hospital.* ◇ *I'm taking the children swimming this afternoon.* ▶ **brać**, **zabierać** ⇨ picture at **bring**

Ostatnią literę czasownika podwaja się przed *-ed* lub *-ing*.

hum /hʌm/ verb (**humming**; **hummed**) **1** [I,T] to sing with your lips closed: *You can hum the tune if you don't know the words.* ▶ **śpiewać mormorando**, **nucić** **2** [I] to make a continuous low noise: *The machine began to hum as I switched it on.* ◇ *The classroom was humming with activity.* W klasie wrzała praca. ▶ **brzęczeć**, **buczeć**
■ **hum** noun [sing.]: *the hum of machinery/distant traffic* ▶ **szum**, **pomruk**, **buczenie**

stopień wyższy (**comparative**)
i najwyższy (**superlative**) przymiotnika

happy /'hæpi/ adj. (**happier**; **happiest**) **1** **happy (to do sth)**; **happy for sb**; **happy that ...** feeling or showing pleasure; pleased: *a happy baby* ◇ *You look very happy today.* ◇ *I was really happy to see Mark again yesterday.* ◇ *Congratulations! I'm very happy for you.* Bardzo się cieszę (np. że coś ci się udało). ▶ **szczęśliwy**, **radosny** OPP **sad**

Podane są tylko formy nieregularne.

good[1] /gʊd/ adj. (**better**; **best**) **1** of a high quality or standard: *a good book/film/actor* ◇ *That's a really good idea!* ◇ *The hotel was quite/pretty good, but not fantastic.* ▶ **dobry** **2** pleasant or enjoyable: *It's good to be home*

Użycie słów

sb = **somebody** (ktoś)
sth = **something** (coś)
uwagi dotyczące stosowania słów w zdaniach, wyboru przyimków i odpowiednich form czasownika oraz użycia w odniesieniu do osób i/lub rzeczy

consider /kən'sɪdə(r)/ verb [T] **1** **consider sb/sth (for/as sth)**; **consider doing sth** to think about sth carefully, often before making a decision: *We're considering going to Spain for our holidays.* ◇ *They are considering him for the part of Romeo.* ◇ *She had never considered nursing as a career.* ▶ **rozważać**, **zastanawiać się (nad czymś)** **2** **consider sb/sth (as/to be) sth**; **consider that ...** to think about sb/sth in a particular way: *He considered the risk (to be) too great.* ◇ *He considered that the risk was too*

unfamiliar /ˌʌnfə'mɪliə(r)/ adj. **1** **unfamiliar (to sb)** that you do not know well: *an unfamiliar part of town* ▶ **nieznany** **2** **unfamiliar (with sb/sth)** not having know-

Przymiotnik nie występuje przed rzeczownikiem. Można go użyć jedynie po czasowniku typu *be, seem*.

asleep /əˈsliːp/ adj. [not before a noun] not awake; sleeping: *The baby is asleep* (śpi). ◇ *It didn't take me long to* ***fall asleep*** (zasnąć) *last night.* ◇ *to be sound/fast asleep* spać twardo (jak zabity) ▶ **we śnie** OPP **awake**

Przymiotnik występuje tylko przed rzeczownikiem.

lone /ləʊn/ adj. [only before a noun] **1** without any other people; alone: *a lone swimmer* ▶ **samotny**, **jedyny**

Oznaczenie słów używanych w określonych sytuacjach

Słowa mogą być oznaczone jako **formal**, tj. używane w formalnej, pisanej angielszczyźnie, **informal**, tj. stosowane w nieformalnych rozmowach i tekstach, **slang**, tj. wyrazy żargonowe albo wulgaryzmy, **written**, tj. spotykane tylko w języku pisanym, **spoken**, tj. używane tylko w języku mówionym lub **old-fashioned**, tj. przestarzałe.

green[1] /griːn/ adj. **1** having the colour of grass or leaves: *dark/light/pale green* ▶ **zielony 2** connected with protecting the environment or the natural world: *the Green Party* Partia Zielonych ◇ *green products* ▶ **zielony**, **ekologiczny 3** (informal) with little experience of life or a particular job: *I'm not so green as to believe that!* ▶ (*niedoś-*

Przekład

Wszystkie słowa i wyrażenia zostały przetłumaczone na język polski. Odpowiedniki polskie umieszczono po podaniu znaczenia w języku angielskim.

directory /dəˈrektəri; dɪ-; daɪ-/ noun [C] (pl. **directories**) **1** a list of names, addresses and telephone numbers in the order of the alphabet: *the telephone directory* książka telefoniczna ◇ *I tried to look up Joe's number but he's* ***ex-directory*** (jego numer jest zastrzeżony). ▶ **spis** (*np. instytucji*) **2** a file containing a group of other files or programs in a computer ▶ **katalog**

Najczęściej zdania przykładowe nie są tłumaczone. Jeżeli jednak zawierają one wyrażenia idiomatyczne trudne do zrozumienia, wówczas podane są ich pełne lub częściowe przekłady.

■ **think** noun [sing.]: *I'm not sure. I'll have to* ***have a think*** *about it.* Będę musiał to sobie przemyśleć. ▶ **rozważanie**

off[1] /ɒf/ adv., prep. **1** down or away from a place or a position on sth: *He fell off the ladder.* ◇ *We got off* (wysiedliśmy z) *the bus.* ◇ *I shouted to him but he just walked off* (odszedł). ◇ *I* ***must be off*** (muszę iść). *It's getting late.* ◇ *When are you off* (wyjeżdżacie) *to Spain?* ◇ (figurative) *We've got off* (zeszliśmy z) *the subject.* ▶ **z 2** (used with verbs that mean 'remove' or 'separate'): *She took her*

Z uwagi na ograniczenie miejsca, dokonując przekładu czasowników angielskich, w słowniku podano ich odpowiedniki polskie tylko w formie niedokonanej. Formy dokonane podano jedynie tam, gdzie nie stosuje się form niedokonanych.

establish /ɪˈstæblɪʃ/ verb [T] **1** to start or create an organization, a system, etc.: *The school was established in 1875.* ◇ *Before we start on the project we should establish some rules.* ▶ **zakładać** (*np. organizację*), **ustalać** (*np. zasady*) **2** to make sth exist (especially a formal relationship with sb/sth): *The government is trying to establish closer links between the two countries.* ▶ **ustanawiać**, **tworzyć 3 establish sb/sth (as sth)** to become

convince /kənˈvɪns/ verb [T] **1 convince sb (of sth/that ...)** to succeed in making sb believe sth: *She convinced him of the need to go back.* ◇ *I couldn't convince her that I was right.* ▶ **przekonać** ➲ look at **persuade 2 convince sb (to**

Rzeczowniki angielskie często występują w znaczeniu przymiotników. Przy hasłach nie podano tłumaczeń odpowiadających im form przymiotnikowych. Natomiast indeks zawiera polskie przymiotniki, które tłumaczy się za pomocą rzeczowników angielskich.

strawberry /ˈstrɔːbəri; US -beri/ noun [C] (pl. **strawberries**) a small soft red fruit with small white seeds on it: *strawberries and cream* ◇ *a wild strawberry* poziomka ▶ **truskawka** ➲ picture on **page A12**

truskawkowy strawberry

Uwagi dotyczące użycia słów

W słowniku są różne rodzaje uwag: uwagi dotyczące gramatyki, uwagi wyjaśniające różnice w użyciu słów o podobnym znaczeniu, informujące o kontekście kulturowym, o słowach pokrewnych itp.

Shade to zacienione miejsce lub obszar, gdzie można schować się przed słońcem. **A shadow** (rzeczownik policzalny) to cień przedmiotu lub osoby utworzony przez odbite światło. **Shadow** (rzeczownik niepoliczalny) oznacza półmrok lub ciemność, w których trudno odróżnić kształty i przedmioty.

gratitude /ˈɡrætɪtjuːd; US -tuːd/ noun [U] **gratitude (to sb) (for sth)** the feeling of being grateful or of wanting to give your thanks: *We should like to express our gratitude to David for all his help.* ▶ **wdzięczność** OPP **ingratitude** ➲ adjective **grateful**

pool[1] /puːl/ noun **1** : *She swims ten lengths of the pool every morning.* = SWIMMING POOL **2** a small area of still water, especially one that has formed naturally: *a rock pool* ▶ **sadzawka** ➲ note at **lake** **3** [C] **a pool (of sth)** a small amount of liquid lying on a surface: *There's a huge pool of water on the kitchen floor.* ▶ **kałuża** (*np. krwi*) ➲ look at **puddle**

Uwagi po angielsku umieszczone w ramkach podają typowe związki wyrazowe i pokrewne słownictwo.

cars
You **fill up** your car with **petrol** (US **gas**) or **diesel** at a **petrol station** (US **gas station**). Many cars run on **unleaded** petrol. If your car **breaks down**, it might need to be **towed** to a **garage** so that you can **have it repaired** by a **mechanic**.

Wymowa

Wymowa każdego słowa podana jest za pomocą symboli fonetycznych stosowanych przez Międzynarodowe Stowarzyszenie Fonetyczne (IPA). Podane są różnice między wymową brytyjską i amerykańską.

ˈ poprzedza sylabę, na którą pada **akcent główny**

ˌ poprzedza sylabę, na którą pada **akcent poboczny**

leisure /ˈleʒə(r); US ˈliːʒər/ noun [U] the time when you do not have to work; free time: *Shorter working hours mean*

ˌ**grass** ˈ**roots** noun [pl.] the ordinary people in an organization, not those who make decisions: *the grass roots of the party* ▶ **zwykli członkowie**

Strona polsko-angielska

Strona polsko-angielska zawiera wyrazy polskie i podaje ich angielskie odpowiedniki. W celu sprawdzenia poprawności użycia słów angielskich, należy je odszukać pod odpowiednimi hasłami w słowniku.

czuł|y 1 (*okazujący czułość*) affectionate, fond, tender[1] **2** (*wrażliwy*) responsive, sensitive; (*słuch itp.*) keen **3** (*fot.*) fast[1] IDM **~e miejsce** a sore point

Numery po stronie polsko-angielskiej odpowiadają numeracji **homonimów** w słowniku.

budzić/o- awake[2], awaken, get sb up, rouse, wake[1] sb (up), waken; ~ **na nowo** revive; ~ **wstręt** repel
□ **budzić/o- się** awake[2], awaken, get up, wake[1] (up), waken; ~ **na nowo** revive

Czasowników polskich należy szukać pod ich **formą niedokonaną**.

brać/wziąć 1 take; (*lekarstwo*) dose[2] yourself with sth; ~ **narkotyki** be on drugs **2** (*kąpiel itp.*) have, take **3** (*odpowiedzialność itp.*) accept; **coś na siebie** take care of sth, take sth on; ~ **na siebie winę** take the blame for

wziąć (się) → BRAĆ (SIĘ)

Słownik angielsko-polski

A a

A, a /eɪ/ noun [C,U] (pl. **As**; **as**; **A's**; **a's** /eɪz/) **1** the first letter of the English alphabet: *'Andy' begins with (an) 'A'.* ▶ **litera a** **2** the highest grade given for an exam or piece of work: *I got an 'A' for my essay.* ▶ **celujący** **3** (used about music) the sixth note in the series of notes called the scale of C major: *A major* A-dur ◇ *A minor* a-moll ◇ *A flat* As, as ◇ *A sharp* Ais, ais ▶ **A/a**

a /ə; strong form eɪ/ (also **an** /ən; strong form æn/) indefinite article ℹ A to przedimek nieokreślony, używany przed rzeczownikami policzalnymi w lp. Często nie tłumaczy się go na polski. Forma **an** występuje przed wyrazami zaczynającymi się na samogłoskę (w wymowie, nie w pisowni!, np. *an uncle*, ale *a university*). **1** one: *A cup of coffee, please.* ◇ *We've got an apple, a banana and two oranges.* ▶ **jeden** **2** (used when you talk about one example of sth for the first time): *I saw a dog chasing a cat this morning. The cat climbed up a tree.* ◇ *Have you got a dictionary?* ➲ look at **the** **3** (used for saying what kind of person or thing sb/sth is): *He's a doctor.* ◇ *She's a Muslim.* ◇ *You are a clever boy.* ◇ *'Is that an eagle?' 'No, it's a falcon.'* **4** (used with sb's name to show that the speaker does not know the person): *There's a Ms Mills to see you.* Jakaś pani Mills chce się z tobą zobaczyć. ▶ **jakiś** **5** (used when you are talking about a typical example of sth) any; every: *An elephant can live for up to eighty years.* ℹ W tym znaczeniu można też użyć rzeczownika w lm: *Elephants can live for up to eighty years.* **6** (used with prices, rates, measurements) each: *I usually drink two litres of water a day.* ◇ *twice a week* ◇ *He was travelling at about 80 miles an hour.* ▶ **za**, **w**, **na** SYN **per** **7** (used with some expressions of quantity): *a lot of money* ◇ *a few cars*

A2 (level) /ˌeɪ ˈtuː (levl)/ noun [C,U] a British exam usually taken in Year 13 of school or college (= the final year) when students are aged 18. Students must first have studied a subject at AS level before they can take an A2 exam. Together AS and A2 level exams form the A-level qualification, which is needed for entrance to universities: *A2 exams* ◇ *She's **doing an A2 (level)** in History.* ▶ **egzamin maturalny**

the AA /ˌeɪ ˈeɪ/ abbr. (in Britain) the **Automobile Association**; an organization for drivers. If you are a member of the AA and your car breaks down, they will send sb to help you: *My car wouldn't start so I called the AA.* ▶ **odpowiednik PZM-otu i Automobilklubu**

A & E = ACCIDENT AND EMERGENCY

aback /əˈbæk/ adv.
PHR V **take sb aback** → TAKE

abacus /ˈæbəkəs/ noun [C] a frame with small balls which slide along wires. It is used as a tool or toy for counting. ▶ **liczydło**

abandon /əˈbændən/ verb [T] **1** to leave sb/sth that you are responsible for, usually permanently: *The bank robbers abandoned the car just outside the city.* ▶ **opuszczać**, **porzucać** **2** to stop doing sth without finishing it or without achieving what you wanted to do: *The search for the missing sailors was abandoned after two days.* ◇ *If I fail this exam, I'll have to **abandon hope** of becoming a doctor.* ▶ **zaniechać**, **rezygnować z czegoś**
■ **abandonment** noun [U] ▶ **opuszczenie**; **zaniechanie**

abandoned /əˈbændənd/ adj. **1** left and no longer wanted, used or needed: *an abandoned car/house* ◇ *The child was found abandoned but unharmed.* ▶ **opuszczony**, **porzucony** **2** (used about people or their behaviour) wild; not following accepted standards: *a wild, abandoned dance* ▶ (*zachowanie itp.*) **zdziczały**, **szalony**

abashed /əˈbæʃt/ adj. [not before a noun] feeling guilty and embarrassed because of sth that you have done: *'I'm sorry,' said Ali, **looking abashed**.* ▶ **zawstydzony**

abate /əˈbeɪt/ verb [I,T] (formal) to become less strong; to make sth less strong: *The storm showed no signs of abating.* ▶ **słabnąć**; **osłabiać**

abattoir (Brit.) = SLAUGHTERHOUSE

abbess /ˈæbes/ noun [C] a woman who is the head of a community of **nuns** ▶ **matka przełożona**

abbey /ˈæbi/ noun [C] a large church together with a group of buildings where **monks** or **nuns** live or lived in the past ▶ **opactwo**

> Zwróć uwagę, że jeden z najsłynniejszych kościołów w Londynie nazywa się **Westminster Abbey**.

abbot /ˈæbət/ noun [C] a man who is the head of a community of **monks** ▶ **opat**

abbreviate /əˈbriːvieɪt/ verb [T] to make sth shorter, especially a word or phrase: *'Kilometre' is usually abbreviated to 'km'.* ▶ **skracać** SYN **shorten** ➲ look at **abridge**

abbreviation /əˌbriːviˈeɪʃn/ noun [C] a short form of a word or phrase: *In this dictionary 'sth' is the abbreviation for 'something'.* ▶ **skrót**

ABC /ˌeɪ biː ˈsiː/ noun [sing.] **1** the alphabet; the letters of English from A to Z ▶ **alfabet** **2** the simple facts about sth: *an ABC of Gardening* ▶ **abecadło**

abdicate /ˈæbdɪkeɪt/ verb **1** [I] to give up being king or queen: *The Queen abdicated in favour of her son.* ▶ **abdykować** **2** [T] to give sth up, especially power or a position: *to **abdicate responsibility*** ▶ **zrzekać się**
■ **abdication** /ˌæbdɪˈkeɪʃn/ noun [C,U] ▶ **abdykacja**; **zrzeczenie się**

abdomen /ˈæbdəmən/ noun [C] a part of your body below the chest, in which the stomach is contained ▶ **brzuch** ➲ picture at **insect**
■ **abdominal** /æbˈdɒmɪnl/ adj. ▶ **brzuszny**

abduct /æbˈdʌkt/ verb [T] to take hold of sb and take them away illegally: *He has been abducted by a terrorist group.* ▶ **uprowadzać**
■ **abduction** noun [C,U] ▶ **uprowadzenie**

aberration /ˌæbəˈreɪʃn/ noun [C,U] (formal) a fact, an action or a way of behaving that is not usual, and that may be unacceptable ▶ **odchylenie od normy**, **dewiacja**

abet /əˈbet/ verb (**abetting**; **abetted**)
IDM **aid and abet** → AID[2]

abhor /əbˈhɔː(r)/ verb [T] (**abhorring**; **abhorred**) to hate sth very much: *All civilized people abhor the use of torture.* ▶ **żywić wstręt**

abhorrence /əbˈhɒrəns/ noun [U] a strong feeling of hate; disgust: *Protesters expressed their **abhorrence of** war.* ▶ **wstręt**

abhorrent /əbˈhɒrənt/ adj. that makes you feel hate or disgust: *The idea of slavery is **abhorrent to** us nowadays.* ▶ **odrażający**

abide /əˈbaɪd/ verb
IDM **can't/couldn't abide sb/sth/doing sth** to hate sb/sth; to not like sb/sth at all ▶ **nie cierpieć kogoś/czegoś** SYN **stand**
PHR V **abide by sth** to obey a law, etc.; to do what sb has decided ▶ **dotrzymywać/przestrzegać czegoś**

abiding /əˈbaɪdɪŋ/ adj. (formal) (used about a feeling or belief) lasting for a long time and not changing: *He is an artist with an abiding concern for humanity.* ▶ **nieprzemijający**

ability /əˈbɪləti/ noun [C,U] (pl. **abilities**) **the ability to do sth** the mental or physical power or skill that makes it possible to do sth: *the ability to make decisions* ◇ *students of mixed abilities* ▶ **umiejętność, zdolność** OPP **inability**

abject /ˈæbdʒekt/ adj. (formal) **1** terrible and without hope: *abject poverty* skrajna bieda ▶ **beznadziejny, nędzny 2** without any pride or respect for yourself: *an abject apology* ▶ **służalczy**

ablaze /əˈbleɪz/ adj. [not before a noun] burning strongly; completely on fire: *Soldiers used petrol to* ***set*** *the building* ***ablaze.*** ◇ (figurative) *The garden was ablaze with colour* (mienił się kolorami). ▶ **w płomieniach**

able /ˈeɪbl/ adj. **1** [used as a modal verb] **be able to do sth** to have the ability, power, opportunity, time, etc. to do sth: *Will you be able to come to a meeting next week?* ◇ *I was able to* (byłem w stanie) *solve the problem quickly.* ◇ *Many men don't* ***feel able*** *to express their emotions.* ▶ **móc** OPP **unable** ℹ W stronie biernej zamiast **be able** używa się **can/could**: *The arrangement can't be changed.* ➲ note at **can**[1] **2** intelligent; good at sth ▶ **zdolny, utalentowany**

■ **ably** /ˈeɪbli/ adv. ▶ **zręcznie, skutecznie**

ˌable-ˈbodied adj. physically healthy and strong; having full use of your body ▶ **zdrowy (fizycznie)**

abnormal /æbˈnɔːml/ adj. different from what is normal or usual, in a way that worries you or that is unpleasant: *I don't want to have children. Is that abnormal?* ◇ *abnormal weather conditions* anomalie pogodowe ▶ **anormalny, odbiegający od normy** OPP **normal**

■ **abnormally** /-məli/ adv.: *abnormally high temperatures* ▶ **anormalnie, w sposób odbiegający od normy**

abnormality /ˌæbnɔːˈmæləti/ noun [C,U] (pl. **abnormalities**) something that is not normal, especially in sb's body: *He was born with an abnormality of the heart.* ▶ **nieprawidłowość, anormalność**

aboard /əˈbɔːd/ adv., prep. on or onto a train, ship, aircraft or bus: *The plane crashed, killing all 158 people aboard.* ◇ *We climbed aboard the train and found a seat.* ◇ *We went aboard the boat.* Weszliśmy na pokład statku. ▶ **w, do, na**

abode /əˈbəʊd/ noun [C, usually sing.] (formal) the place where you live: *They have the right of abode* (prawo stałego pobytu) *in Hong Kong.* ▶ **miejsce zamieszkania**

IDM **(of) no fixed abode/address** → FIXED

abolish /əˈbɒlɪʃ/ verb [T] to end a law or system officially: *When was capital punishment abolished here?* ▶ **znosić**

abolition /ˌæbəˈlɪʃn/ noun [U] the act of ending a law or system officially: *the abolition of slavery in the US* ▶ **zniesienie**

abominable /əˈbɒmɪnəbl/ adj. very bad; shocking: *an abominable crime* ◇ *abominable behaviour* karygodne zachowanie ▶ **ohydny** SYN **disgusting**

■ **abominably** /-əbli/ adv. ▶ **okropnie, karygodnie**

Aboriginal /ˌæbəˈrɪdʒənl/ (also **Aborigine** /ˌæbəˈrɪdʒəni/) noun [C] a member of the race of people who were the first people to live in a country, especially Australia ▶ **aborygen**

■ **aboriginal** adj. ▶ **tubylczy**

abort /əˈbɔːt/ verb [T] **1** to make a **foetus** die before it is born ▶ **przerwać ciążę 2** to end sth before it is complete: *The company aborted the project when they realized it was costing too much.* ▶ **zaniechać**

abortion /əˈbɔːʃn/ noun [C,U] a medical operation that causes a baby to die inside its mother before it is fully developed: *to have an abortion* ◇ *Abortion is illegal in some countries.* ▶ **przerywanie ciąży, aborcja** ➲ look at **miscarriage**

abortive /əˈbɔːtɪv/ adj. not completed successfully; failed: *He made two abortive attempts to escape from prison.* ▶ **nieudany** SYN **unsuccessful**

abound /əˈbaʊnd/ verb [I] to exist in large numbers: *Birds abound in the forest.* W lesie jest wiele ptaków. ◇ *Rumours abound about the actor's arrest.* ▶ **występować w dużej ilości**

PHR V **abound with sth** to contain large numbers of sth: *The lake abounds with fish.* ▶ **obfitować**

about[1] /əˈbaʊt/ adv. **1** (also **around**) a little more or less than: *It's about three miles from here to the city centre.* ◇ *I got home at about half past seven.* ▶ **około, mniej więcej** SYN **approximately 2** (informal) almost; nearly: *Dinner's just about ready.* ▶ **prawie 3** (also **around**) in many directions: *I could hear people moving about upstairs.* ▶ **tam i z powrotem 4** (also **around**) in many places: *Don't leave your clothes lying about all over the floor.* ▶ **tu i tam, po 5** (also **around**) [used after certain verbs] without doing anything in particular: *The kids spend most evenings* ***sitting about,*** *bored.* ▶ **bez celu, tak sobie 6** (also **around**) present in a place; existing: *It was very late and there were few people about.* ◇ *There isn't much good music about these days.* ▶ **obecny**

IDM **be about to do sth** to be going to do sth very soon: *I was just about to explain when she interrupted me.* ◇ *The film's about to start.* Film zaraz się zacznie. ▶ **właśnie mieć zamiar coś zrobić**

about[2] /əˈbaʊt/ prep. **1** on the subject of: *Let's talk about something else.* ◇ *What's your book about?* ◇ *He told me* ***all about*** *his family.* ◇ *I don't like it, but there's nothing I can do about it* (ale nic nie mogę zrobić). ▶ **o 2** in the character of sb/sth: *I like the food, the climate, and everything else about this country.* ◇ *There's something about him* (jest w nim coś, co sprawia) *that I don't quite trust.* ▶ **w kimś/czymś 3** (also **around**) in many directions or places; in different parts of sth: *We wandered about the town for an hour or two.* ◇ *Lots of old newspapers were scattered about the room.* ▶ **po** (*np. mieście*)

IDM **how/what about...? 1** (used when asking for information about sb/sth or for sb's opinion or wish): *How about Ruth? Have you heard from her lately?* ◇ *I'm going to have chicken. What about you?* ▶ **a co słychać u ...?; a ty/on itp.? 2** (used when making a suggestion): *What about going to a film tonight?* A może poszlibyśmy dziś wieczorem do kina? ➲ look at **let**(4), **why not?**

aˌbout-ˈturn (US **aˌbout-ˈface**) noun [C] a complete change of opinion, plan or behaviour: *The government did an about-turn over tax.* ▶ **zwrot o 180°** ➲ look at **U-turn**

above /əˈbʌv/ prep., adv. **1** in a higher place: *The coffee is in the cupboard above the sink.* ◇ *The people in the flat above* (z mieszkania nad nami) *make a lot of noise.* ◇ *He looked up at the sky above.* Popatrzył na niebo nad nim. ▶ **nad, ponad** OPP **below 2** in an earlier part (of sth written): *Contact me at the above address/the address above.* ▶ **wyżej wymieniony** OPP **below 3** more than a number, an amount, a price, etc.: *children aged 11 and above* ◇ *A score of 70 and above will get you a grade B.* ◇ *You must get above 50% to pass.* ◇ *above-average temperatures* ▶ **powyżej, ponad** OPP **below** ➲ look at **over 4** with a higher position in an organization, etc.: *The person above me is the department manager.* ▶ **na wyższym stanowisku** OPP **below 5** too proud to do sth: *He seems to think he's above helping with the cleaning.* On chyba sądzi, że pomaganie w sprzątaniu jest poniżej jego godności. ◇ *She's not above telling a few lies* (pozwala sobie skłamać), *if it makes life easier.* ▶ (*być*) **ponad coś**

IDM **above all** (used to emphasize the main point) most importantly: *Above all, stay calm!* ▶ **przede wszystkim**

above board (used especially about a business deal, etc.) honest and open ▶ **legalny, czysty**

aˌbove-ˈmentioned adj. [only before a noun] mentioned or named earlier in the same letter, book, etc. ▶ **wyżej wspomniany**

abracadabra /ˌæbrəkəˈdæbrə/ exclamation (a word that people say when they do a magic trick, in order to make it successful) ▶ **abrakadabra**

abrasive /ə'breɪsɪv/ adj. **1** rough and likely to scratch: *abrasive kitchen cleaners* ▶ **ostry, ścierny 2** (used about a person) rude and rather aggressive ▶ **szorstki, opryskliwy**

abreast /ə'brest/ adv. **abreast (of sb/sth)** next to or level with sb/sth and going in the same direction: *The soldiers marched two abreast.* ▶ **w jednym rzędzie, ramię w ramię**

IDM **be/keep abreast of sth** to have all the most recent information about sth: *I try to keep abreast of politics.* ▶ **być na bieżąco**

abridge /ə'brɪdʒ/ verb [T] to make sth (usually a book) shorter by removing parts of it ▶ **skracać** ➲ look at **abbreviate**

abroad /ə'brɔːd/ adv. in or to another country or countries: *My mother has never been abroad.* ◇ *She often* ***goes abroad*** *on business.* ◇ *They found it difficult to get used to living abroad.* ▶ **za granic-ą/ę**

abrupt /ə'brʌpt/ adj. **1** sudden and unexpected: *an abrupt change of plan* ▶ **nagły 2** seeming rude and unfriendly ▶ **szorstki, obcesowy**

■ **abruptly** adv. ▶ **nagle; obcesowo** | **abruptness** noun [U] ▶ **nagłość; obcesowość**

abscess /'æbses/ noun [C] a swelling on or in the body, containing **pus** ▶ **ropień**

abscond /əb'skɒnd/ verb [I] (formal) **abscond (from sth) (with sth)** to run away from a place where you should stay, sometimes with sth that you should not take: *to abscond from prison* ◇ *She absconded with all the company's money.* ▶ **zbiec**

abseil /'æbseɪl/ (US **rappel** /ræ'pel/) verb [I] **abseil (down, off, etc. sth)** to go down the side of a very steep, high rock or a building while you are tied to a rope, pushing against the surface with your feet ▶ **spuszczać się po linie** ➲ picture on **page A8**

absence /'æbsəns/ noun **1** [C,U] a time when sb is away from somewhere; the fact of being away from somewhere: *Frequent absences due to illness meant he was behind with his work.* ◇ *I have to make all the decisions in my boss's absence.* ▶ **nieobecność 2** [U] the fact of sth/sb not being there; lack: ***In the absence of*** *a doctor, try to help the injured person yourself.* ◇ *The first thing I noticed about the place was the absence of noise* (kompletna cisza). ▶ **nieobecność, brak** OPP for both meanings **presence**

absent /'æbsənt/ adj. **1 absent (from sth)** not present somewhere: *He was absent from work because of illness.* ▶ **nieobecny** OPP **present 2** thinking about sth else; not paying attention: *an absent stare* ▶ **bezmyślny**

■ **absently** adv. ▶ **bezmyślnie**

absentee /ˌæbsən'tiː/ noun [C] a person who is not in the place where they should be ▶ **nieobecn-y/a**

ˌabsentee 'ballot (US) = POSTAL VOTE

absenteeism /ˌæbsən'tiːɪzəm/ noun [U] the problem of workers or students often not going to work or school ▶ **absencja**

ˌabsent-'minded adj. often forgetting or not noticing things, because you are thinking about sth else ▶ **roztargniony** SYN **forgetful**

■ **absent-mindedly** adv. ▶ **w roztargnieniu** | **ˌabsent-'mindedness** noun [U] ▶ **roztargnienie**

absolute /'æbsəluːt/ adj. **1** complete; total: *The whole trip was an absolute disaster.* ◇ *None of the political parties had* ***an absolute majority*** (bezwzględnej większości głosów). ▶ **całkowity, zupełny 2** not measured in comparison with sth else: *Spending on the Health Service has increased* ***in absolute terms.*** Wydatki brutto na służbę zdrowia wzrosły. ▶ **mierzony w bezwzględnych kategoriach**

absolutely adv. **1** /'æbsəluːtli/ completely: *It's absolutely freezing outside!* Na dworze jest prawdziwy mróz! ◇ *I absolutely refuse to believe that.* W żadnym wypadku nie uwierzę w to. ◇ *He made absolutely no effort* (nawet nie spróbował) *to help me.* ▶ **całkowicie, zupełnie** SYN **totally 2** /ˌæbsə'luːtli/ (used when you are agreeing with sb) yes; certainly: *'It is a good idea, isn't it?' 'Oh, absolutely!'* ▶ **oczywiście**

absolve /əb'zɒlv/ verb [T] **absolve sb (from/of sth)** to say formally that sb does not have to take responsibility for sth: *The driver was absolved of any blame for the train crash.* ▶ **oczyszczać** (*np. z winy*)

absorb /əb'sɔːb; -'zɔːb/ verb [T] **1 absorb sth (into sth)** to take in and hold sth (a liquid, heat, etc.): *a drug that is quickly absorbed into the bloodstream* ◇ *Black clothes absorb the sun's heat.* ▶ **wchłaniać 2 absorb sth (into sth)** to take sth into sth larger, so that it becomes part of it: *Over the years many villages have been absorbed into the city.* ▶ **wchłaniać 3** to take sth into the mind and understand it: *I found it impossible to absorb so much information so quickly.* ▶ **przyswajać sobie 4** to hold sb's attention completely or interest sb very much: *History is a subject that absorbs her.* ▶ **absorbować, pasjonować 5** to reduce the effect of a sudden violent knock, hit, etc.: *The front of the car is designed to absorb most of the impact of a crash.* ▶ **amortyzować**

■ **absorption** /əb'sɔːpʃn; -'zɔːp-/ noun [U] ▶ **wchłanianie; przyswajanie; pochłonięcie**

absorbed /əb'sɔːbd; -'zɔːbd/ adj. **absorbed (in sth)** giving all your attention to sth: *He was absorbed in his work and didn't hear me come in.* ▶ **pochłonięty**

absorbent /əb'sɔːbənt; -'zɔːb-/ adj. able to take in and hold liquid: *an absorbent cloth* ▶ **(dobrze) wchłaniający płyn**

abˌsorbent 'cotton (US) = COTTON WOOL

absorbing /əb'sɔːbɪŋ; -'zɔːb-/ adj. holding all your interest and attention: *an absorbing book* ▶ **pasjonujący**

abstain /əb'steɪn/ verb [I] **1** (in a vote) to say that you are not voting either for or against sth: *Two people voted in favour, two voted against and one abstained.* ▶ **wstrzymywać się** (*od głosu*) ➲ noun **abstention 2** (formal) **abstain (from sth/doing sth)** to stop yourself from doing sth that you enjoy: *The doctor said I should abstain from (drinking) alcohol until I'm better.* ▶ **powstrzymywać się (od czegoś)** ➲ noun **abstinence**

abstemious /əb'stiːmiəs/ adj. (formal) not allowing yourself to have much food or alcohol, or to do things that are enjoyable ▶ **wstrzemięźliwy**

abstention /əb'stenʃn/ noun [C,U] the act of not voting either for or against sth ▶ **wstrzymanie się** (*od głosu*)

abstinence /'æbstɪnəns/ noun [U] (formal) stopping yourself from having or doing sth that you enjoy: *The doctor advised total abstinence from alcohol.* ▶ **powstrzymanie się (od czegoś), abstynencja** ➲ verb **abstain**

abstinent /'æbstɪnənt/ adj. not allowing yourself sth, especially alcoholic drinks, for moral, religious or health reasons ▶ **wstrzemięźliwy, praktykujący abstynencję**

abstract[1] /'æbstrækt/ adj. **1** existing only as an idea, not as a physical thing: *It is hard to imagine an abstract idea like 'eternity'.* ▶ **abstrakcyjny** OPP **concrete 2** (used about art) not showing people and things as they really look: *an abstract painting* ▶ **abstrakcyjny**

abstract[2] /'æbstrækt/ noun [C] **1** an example of **abstract** art ▶ **dzieło sztuki abstrakcyjnej 2** a short piece of writing that tells you the main contents of a book, speech, etc. ▶ **abstrakt, streszczenie** SYN **summary**

IDM **in the abstract** only as an idea, not in real life ▶ **teoretycznie**

abstraction /æb'strækʃn/ noun [C, U] (formal) a general idea not based on any particular real person, thing or situation; the quality of being **abstract** ▶ **abstrakcja, pojęcie abstrakcyjne**

ˌ**abstract 'noun** noun [C] a noun, for example *goodness* or *freedom*, that refers to an idea or a general quality, not to a physical object ▶ **rzeczownik abstrakcyjny** ➲ look at **common noun, proper noun**

absurd /əb'sɜːd/ adj. not at all logical or sensible: *It would be absurd to spend all your money on one pair of shoes.* ◇ *Don't be absurd* (nie bądź śmieszny)! *I can't possibly do all this work in one day.* ◇ *You look absurd* (wyglądasz idiotycznie) *in that hat.* ▶ **absurdalny** SYN **ridiculous**

■ **absurdity** /əb'sɜːdəti/ noun [C,U] (pl. **absurdities**): *When I lost my trousers I had to laugh at the absurdity of the situation.* ▶ **absurd, niedorzeczność** | **absurdly** adv. ▶ **niedorzecznie**

abundance /ə'bʌndəns/ noun [sing., U] a very large quantity of sth: *These flowers grow here* ***in abundance.*** ◇ *There is an abundance of wildlife in the forest.* ▶ **obfitość** SYN **profusion**

abundant /ə'bʌndənt/ adj. existing in very large quantities; more than enough: *abundant supplies of food* ◇ *Fish are abundant in the lake.* ▶ **obfity** SYN **plentiful**

■ **abundantly** adv.: *She made her feelings abundantly clear* (bardzo wyraźnie opisała swoje uczucia) *in the letter.* ▶ **obficie**

🔑 **abuse¹** /ə'bjuːs/ noun **1** [C,U] using sth in a bad or dishonest way: *an abuse of power* ◇ *the dangers of drug abuse* ▶ **nadużywanie 2** [U] bad, usually violent treatment of sb: *He subjected his children to verbal and physical abuse.* ◇ *a victim of sexual abuse* (wykorzystywania seksualnego) ◇ *human rights abuses* łamanie praw człowieka ▶ **krzywdzenie, znęcanie się 3** [U] rude words, used to insult another person: *The other driver leaned out of the car and* ***hurled abuse*** *at me.* ◇ *racial abuse* ▶ **obelgi**

> Uwaga! Rzeczownik **abuse** ma inną wymowę niż czasownik. Końcową spółgłoskę czasownika wymawia się dźwięcznie /z/– rzeczownika bezdźwięcznie /s/.

🔑 **abuse²** /ə'bjuːz/ verb [T] **1** to use sth in a bad or dishonest way: *The politician was accused of abusing* (oskarżony o nadużywanie) *his position in order to become rich.* ▶ **nadużywać 2** to treat sb badly, often violently: *The girl had been sexually abused.* ▶ **krzywdzić 3** to say rude things to sb: *The goalkeeper got a red card for abusing the referee.* ▶ **obrzucać kogoś obelgami** SYN **insult**

abusive /ə'bjuːsɪv/ adj. using rude language to insult sb: *an abusive remark* ▶ **obelżywy**

abysmal /ə'bɪzməl/ adj. very bad; of very poor quality ▶ **beznadziejny**

■ **abysmally** /-məli/ adv. ▶ **beznadziejnie**

abyss /ə'bɪs/ noun [C] a very deep hole that seems to have no bottom ▶ **przepaść, otchłań**

a/c = ACCOUNT¹ (1)

AC /ˌeɪ 'siː/ abbr. **alternating current**; an electric current that changes direction at regular intervals many times a second ▶ **prąd zmienny** ➲ look at **DC**

academia /ˌækə'diːmiə/ noun [U] the world of learning, teaching, research, etc. at universities, and the people involved in it ▶ **środowisko akademickie**

🔑 **academic¹** /ˌækə'demɪk/ adj. **1** connected with education, especially in schools and universities: *The academic year begins in September.* ▶ **akademicki 2** connected with subjects of interest to the mind rather than technical or practical subjects: *academic subjects such as History* ▶ **akademicki, naukowy** OPP **non-academic 3** not connected with reality; not affecting the facts of a situation: *It's academic which one I prefer because I can't have either of them.* ▶ **nieistotny, (czysto) teoretyczny**

■ **academically** /-kli/ adv. ▶ **naukowo**

academic² /ˌækə'demɪk/ noun [C] a person who teaches and/or does research at a university or college ▶ **pracownik naukowy**

academy /ə'kædəmi/ noun [C] (pl. **academies**) **1** a school for special training: *a military academy* ▶ **szkoła, akademia 2** (**Academy**) an official group of people who are important in art, science or literature: *the Royal Academy of Arts* ▶ **akademia**

accede /ək'siːd/ verb (formal) **accede (to sth) 1** [I] to agree to a request, suggestion, etc.: *He acceded to demands for his resignation.* ▶ **przystawać (na coś) 2** [I] to achieve a high position, especially to become king or queen: *Queen Victoria acceded to the throne* (wstąpiła na tron) *in 1837.* ▶ **objąć** (*stanowisko*)

accelerate /ək'seləreɪt/ verb [I,T] to go faster; to make sth go faster or happen more quickly: *The driver slowed down for the bend then accelerated away.* ◇ *The government plans to accelerate the pace of reform.* ▶ **przyśpieszać**

■ **acceleration** /əkˌselə'reɪʃn/ noun [U] ▶ **przyśpieszenie**

accelerator /ək'seləreɪtə(r)/ noun [C] the control in a vehicle that you press with your foot in order to make it go faster: *She put her foot on the accelerator and overtook the bus.* ▶ **pedał gazu** ➲ picture at **car**

🔑 **accent** /'æksent; -sənt/ noun **1** [C,U] a particular way of pronouncing words that is connected with the country, area or social class that you come from: *He speaks with a strong Scottish accent.* ▶ **akcent 2** [C, usually sing.] the particular importance that is given to sth: *In all our products the accent is on quality.* ▶ **nacisk** SYN **emphasis, stress 3** [C] the greater force that you give to a particular word or part of a word when you speak: *In the word 'because' the accent is on the second syllable.* ▶ **akcent** (*wyrazowy*) **4** [C] (in writing) a mark, usually above a letter, that shows that it has to be pronounced in a certain way: *Séance has an accent on the 'e'.* ▶ **znak diakrytyczny**

accented /'æksentɪd/ adj. **1** spoken with a foreign accent: *He spoke heavily accented English.* ▶ **z obcym akcentem 2** spoken with particular emphasis: ***accented vowels/syllables*** ▶ **akcentowany 3** (used about a letter of the alphabet) written or printed with a special mark on it to show it should be pronounced in a particular way: ***accented characters*** ▶ **z akcentem**

accentuate /ək'sentʃueɪt/ verb [T] to make sth easier to notice: *She uses make-up to accentuate her beautiful eyes.* ▶ **podkreślać, uwypuklać**

🔑 **accept** /ək'sept/ verb **1** [I,T] to take willingly sth that is offered; to say 'yes' to an offer, an invitation, etc.: *to accept a bribe* ◇ *She has accepted the job.* ◇ *Thank you for your invitation. I am happy to accept* (przyjmuję z przyjemnością). ◇ *I'd be pleased to accept* (z przyjemnością przyjmę) *your offer of a lift.* ◇ *He asked her to marry him and she accepted.* ▶ **przyjmować** OPP **refuse 2** [T] to receive sth as suitable or good enough: *Will you accept a cheque?* ▶ **przyjmować 3** [T] to agree to or approve of sth: *They accepted the court's decision.* ◇ *Why won't you accept my advice?* ▶ **przyjmować** OPP **reject 4** [T] to admit that you are responsible or to blame for sth: *You have to accept the consequences of your actions.* ◇ *They refused to accept responsibility for the accident.* ▶ **przyjmować (na siebie), brać** (*odpowiedzialność*) **5 accept sth (as sth); accept that...** [T] to believe that sth is true: *She didn't accept that I was telling the truth.* ◇ ***It is generally accepted that*** *people are motivated by success.* ▶ **przyjmować do wiadomości, wierzyć 6 accept sth (as sth); accept that...** [T] to continue in a difficult situation without complaining, because you realize that you cannot change it: *It is hard to accept the death of a child.* ◇ *They accept the risks as part of the job.* ▶ **godzić się (z czymś)** **7 accept sb (into sth) (as sth)** [T] to make sb feel welcome and part of a group: *All children want to be accepted* (zaakceptowane). ▶ **przyjmować** **8 accept sb (into sth) (as sth)** [T] to allow sb to join an organization, attend an institution, use a service, etc.: *The university has accepted me on the course.* ▶ **przyjmować** OPP **reject**

acceptable /ək'septəbl/ adj. **1** that can be allowed: *One or two mistakes are acceptable but no more than that.* ▶ **do przyjęcia** **2** good enough: *We hope that you will consider our offer acceptable.* ▶ **do przyjęcia** SYN **satisfactory** OPP for both meanings **unacceptable**
■ **acceptability** /ək,septə'bɪləti/ noun [U]: *to **gain**/**achieve** acceptability* zostać zaakceptowanym ▶ **możliwość przyjęcia**, **dopuszczalność** | **acceptably** /ək'septəbli/ adv. ▶ **do przyjęcia**

acceptance /ək'septəns/ noun [U,C] the act of accepting or being accepted: *His ready acceptance of the offer surprised me.* ◇ *He quickly **gained acceptance** in the group.* ◇ *acceptance of death* ▶ **przyjęcie**, **pogodzenie się**, **akceptacja**

access[1] /'ækses/ noun [U] **1 access (to sth)** a way of entering or reaching a place: *Access to the garden is through the kitchen.* ▶ **wejście** **2 access (to sth)** the chance or right to use or have sth: *Do you have access to a personal computer?* ▶ **dostęp** **3 access (to sb)** permission, especially legal or official, to see sb: *They are divorced, but he has regular access to the children.* ▶ **widzenie**

access[2] /'ækses/ verb [T] to find information on a computer: *Click on the icon to access a file.* ▶ **otwierać** (*plik komputerowy*)

accessible /ək'sesəbl/ adj. **1** possible to be reached or entered: *The island is only accessible by boat.* ▶ **dostępny** **2** easy to get, use or understand: *This TV programme aims to make history more accessible to children.* ▶ **przystępny** OPP for both meanings **inaccessible**
■ **accessibility** /ək,sesə'bɪləti/ noun [U]: *Computers have given people greater accessibility to information.* ▶ **dostęp**, **dojazd**; **przystępność**

accession /æk'seʃn/ noun [U] the act of taking a very high position, especially as ruler of a country or head of sth ▶ **wstąpienie** (*na tron*), **objęcie** (*urzędu*)

accessorize (also -ise) /ək'sesəraɪz/ verb [I,T] to add fashionable items or extra decorations to sth, especially to your clothes ▶ **wyposażać w dodatkowe akcesoria**

accessory /ək'sesəri/ noun [C] (pl. **accessories**) **1** an extra item that is added to sth and is useful or attractive but not of great importance: *The car has accessories* (akcesoria) *such as an electronic alarm.* **2** [usually pl.] a thing that you wear or carry that matches your clothes, for example a piece of jewellery, a bag, etc. ▶ **dodatki** **3 an accessory (to sth)** (in law) a person who helps sb to do sth illegal ▶ **współwinn-y/a** (*np. zbrodni*)

'access road noun [C] a road used for driving into or out of a particular place ▶ **droga dojazdowa** ➲ look at **slip road**

accident /'æksɪdənt/ noun [C] an unpleasant event that happens unexpectedly and causes damage, injury or death: *I hope they haven't had an accident.* ◇ *a car accident* ◇ *a fatal accident* ◇ *I didn't mean to kick you – it was an accident* (to było niechcący). ▶ **wypadek**
IDM **by accident** by chance; without intending to: *I knocked the vase over by accident as I was cleaning.* ▶ **przypadkiem** OPP **deliberately**

accidental /,æksɪ'dentl/ adj. happening by chance; not planned: *Police do not know if the explosion was accidental or caused by a bomb.* ▶ **przypadkowy**
■ **accidentally** /-təli/ adv.: *As I turned around, I accidentally hit him in the face.* ▶ **przypadkowo**, **nieumyślnie**

,accident and e'mergency (also **casualty**) noun [U] (abbr. **A & E** /,eɪ ənd 'iː/) (US **e'mergency room**) the part of a hospital where people who need urgent treatment are taken, e.g. after a car accident ▶ **izba przyjęć**, **oddział ratownictwa medycznego**

'accident-prone adj. often having accidents ▶ **często ulegający wypadkom**

acclaim /ə'kleɪm/ verb [T, usually passive] **acclaim sb/sth (as sth)** to express a very high opinion of sth/sb: *a **highly acclaimed** new film* ◇ *The novel has been **acclaimed as** a modern classic.* Powieść uznano za klasykę współczesną. ▶ **przyjmować z uznaniem**
■ **acclaim** noun [U]: *The film received widespread critical acclaim.* ▶ **uznanie** (*krytyki*)

acclimatize (also -ise) /ə'klaɪmətaɪz/ verb [I,T] **acclimatize (yourself/sb/sth) (to sth)** to get used to a new climate, situation, place, etc. so that it is not a problem any more: *The team arrived a week early to give the players time to acclimatize to the heat.* ▶ **aklimatyzować (się)**
■ **acclimatization** (also -isation) /ə,klaɪmətaɪ'zeɪʃn; US -tə'z-/ noun [U] ▶ **aklimatyzacja** | **acclimatized** (also -ised) adj. ▶ **zaaklimatyzowany**

accolade /'ækəleɪd/ noun [C] a comment, prize, etc. that you receive which shows people's high opinion of sth you have done: *An Oscar is the highest accolade an actor can receive.* ▶ **dowód/wyrazy uznania**

accommodate /ə'kɒmədeɪt/ verb [T] **1** to provide sb with a place to stay, live or work: *During the conference, you will be accommodated in a nearby hotel.* ▶ **zakwaterowywać** **2** to have enough space for sb/sth, especially for a certain number of people: *Each apartment can accommodate up to six people.* ▶ **mieścić** **3** (formal) to do or provide what sb wants or needs: *Should you have any special requirements, our staff will do their best to accommodate you.* ▶ **zaspokajać** (*czyjeś potrzeby*)

accommodating /ə'kɒmədeɪtɪŋ/ adj. (used about a person) agreeing to do or provide what sb wants: *My boss is very accommodating when I need time off work.* ▶ **usłużny**, **uprzejmy**

accommodation /ə,kɒmə'deɪʃn/ noun [U] a place for sb to live or stay: *We lived in rented accommodation before buying this house.* ◇ *The price of the holiday includes flights and accommodation.* ▶ **dom**, **mieszkanie**, **nocleg**
ℹ **Accommodation** jest rzeczownikiem niepoliczalnym. Nie można powiedzieć ~~*I will help you to find an accommodation*~~. Wówczas mówi się: *I will help you to find somewhere to live/stay.*

accompaniment /ə'kʌmpənimənt/ noun **1** [C,U] music that is played to support singing or another instrument ▶ **akompaniament** **2** [C] something that you eat, drink or use together with sth else: *He only drinks wine as an accompaniment to food.* ▶ **dodatek**
IDM **to the accompaniment of sth** **1** while a musical instrument is being played ▶ **przy akompaniamencie czegoś** **2** while sth else is happening ▶ **przy wtórze czegoś**

accompanist /ə'kʌmpənɪst/ noun [C] a person who plays a musical instrument, especially a piano, while sb else plays or sings the main part of the music ▶ **akompaniator/ka**

accompany /ə'kʌmpəni/ verb [T] (**accompanying**; **accompanies**; pt, pp **accompanied**) **1** to go together with sb/sth: *He went to America accompanied by his wife and three children.* ◇ *Children must be accompanied by an adult* (pod opieką osoby dorosłej). ◇ *Massive publicity accompanied the film's release.* ▶ **towarzyszyć** **2 accompany sb (at/on sth)** to play music for a singer or another instrument: *She accompanied him on the guitar.* ▶ **akompa-**

niować **3** to give or send sth together with sth else, in addition to it ▶ **załączać**

accomplice /əˈkʌmplɪs; US əˈkɑːm-/ noun [C] **an accomplice (to/in sth)** a person who helps sb to do sth bad, especially a crime: *She was charged with being an accomplice to the murder.* ▶ **współwinn-y/a** (*przestępstwa*)

accomplish /əˈkʌmplɪʃ; US əˈkɑːm-/ verb [T] to succeed in doing sth difficult that you planned to do: *I managed to accomplish my goal of writing twenty emails in an evening.* ▶ **osiągać, dokonywać**

accomplished /əˈkʌmplɪʃt; US əˈkɑːm-/ adj. highly skilled at sth: *an accomplished actor* ▶ **znakomity, utalentowany**

accomplishment /əˈkʌmplɪʃmənt; US əˈkɑːm-/ noun **1** [C] something difficult that sb has succeeded in doing or learning ▶ **osiągnięcie, uzdolnienie** SYN **achievement 2** [U] (formal) the act of completing sth successfully: *the accomplishment of a plan* ▶ **osiągnięcie, dokonanie**

accord[1] /əˈkɔːd/ noun [C] an agreement, especially between countries: *the Helsinki accords on human rights* ▶ **porozumienie**

IDM **in accord** in agreement about sth ▶ **zgodny/zgodnie (z czymś)**

of your own accord without being forced or asked: *He wasn't sacked from his job – he left of his own accord.* ▶ **z własnej woli**

accord[2] /əˈkɔːd/ verb (formal) **1** [T] to give sth to sb: *The diplomats were accorded every respect during their visit* (zostali podjęci z wszelkimi należnymi im honorami). ▶ **udzielać, zgotować 2** [I] **accord (with sth)** to match; to agree with: *The information did not accord* (nie była zgodna) *with what I had been told previously.* ▶ **zgadzać się (z czymś)**

accordance /əˈkɔːdns/ noun

IDM **in accordance with sth** in a way that follows or obeys sth: *to act in accordance with instructions* ▶ **zgodny/nie z czymś**

accordingly /əˈkɔːdɪŋli/ adv. **1** in a way that is suitable: *I realized that I was in danger and acted accordingly.* ▶ **odpowiednio 2** (formal) therefore; for that reason ▶ **zatem, dlatego (też)**

according to /əˈkɔːdɪŋ tə/ prep. **1** as stated by sb; as shown by sth: *According to Mick, it's a brilliant film.* ◇ *Standards of living are improving, according to the statistics.* ▶ **według 2** in a way that matches, follows or depends on sth: *Everything went off* ***according to plan.*** ◇ *The salary will be fixed according to experience.* ▶ **zgodnie z czymś, stosownie do czegoś**

accordion /əˈkɔːdiən/ noun [C] a musical instrument that you hold in both hands and play by pulling the two sides apart and then pushing them together, while pressing the keys and/or buttons with your fingers ▶ **akordeon** ➲ look at **concertina**

accost /əˈkɒst/ verb [T] to go up and talk to sb in a way that is surprising or rude ▶ **zaczepiać (kogoś)**

account[1] /əˈkaʊnt/ noun [C] **1** (abbr. **a/c**) the arrangement by which a bank looks after your money for you: *a current/deposit account* ◇ *to open/close an account* ◇ *I have an account with/at Barclays.* ◇ *I paid the cheque into my bank account.* ▶ **konto** ➲ note at **money**

> We use a **current** account to pay for things with a **cheque**. We can save money in a **deposit** or **savings** account.

2 [usually pl.] a record of all the money that a person or business has received or paid out: *If you are self-employed, you have to* ***keep*** *your own* ***accounts*** (prowadzić swoje rachunki). ▶ **rachunek 3** an arrangement with a shop, etc. that allows you to pay for goods or services at a later date: *Most customers* ***settle/pay*** *their* ***account*** *in full every month.* ◇ *Could you charge that to my account?* Proszę to zapisać na mój rachunek. ▶ **kredyt, rachunek 4** sb's report or description of sth that has happened: *She gave the police a full account of the robbery.* ▶ **relacja**

IDM **by all accounts** according to what everyone says: *By all accounts, she's a very good doctor.* ▶ **wszyscy mówią, że**

by your own account according to what you say yourself: *By his own account, Peter was not very good at his job.* ▶ **według czyichś własnych słów**

on account of sth because of sth: *Our flight was delayed on account of bad weather.* ▶ **z powodu czegoś**

on no account; **not on any account** not for any reason: *On no account should you walk home by yourself.* ▶ **pod żadnym pozorem**

take account of sth; **take sth into account** to consider sth, especially when deciding or judging sth: *We'll take account of your comments.* ◇ *We'll take your comments into account.* ▶ **brać coś pod uwagę**

account[2] /əˈkaʊnt/ verb

PHR V **account for sth 1** to explain or give a reason for sth: *How can we account for these changes?* ◇ *I was asked to account for all the money* (wyliczyć się z pieniędzy) *I had spent.* ▶ **wyjaśniać, tłumaczyć 2** to form the amount that is mentioned: *Sales to Europe accounted for 80% of our total sales last year.* ▶ **stanowić**

accountable /əˈkaʊntəbl/ adj. expected to give an explanation of your actions, etc.; responsible: *She is too young to* ***be held accountable*** *for what she did.* ▶ **odpowiedzialny (przed kimś, za coś)**

■ **accountability** /əˌkaʊntəˈbɪləti/ noun [U]: *The new law requires greater accountability from the police.* ▶ **odpowiedzialność**

accountancy /əˈkaʊntənsi/ noun [U] the work or profession of an **accountant** ▶ **księgowość**

accountant /əˈkaʊntənt/ noun [C] a person whose job is to keep or examine the financial accounts of a business, etc. ▶ **księgow-y/a**

accounting /əˈkaʊntɪŋ/ noun [U] the process or work of keeping financial accounts: *a career in accounting* ◇ *accounting methods* ▶ **księgowość**

acˌcounts ˈpayable noun [pl.] money that is owed by a company ▶ **płatności/rachunki do uregulowania**

accreditation /əˌkredɪˈteɪʃn/ noun [U] official approval given by an organization stating that sb/sth has achieved a necessary standard: *a letter of accreditation* ▶ **akredytacja**

accredited /əˈkredɪtɪd/ adj. officially recognized or approved: *a fully accredited course* ▶ **akredytowany, uznany**

accrue /əˈkruː/ verb (formal) **1** [I] **accrue (to sb) (from sth)** to increase over a period of time: *economic benefits accruing to the country from tourism* ◇ *Interest will accrue if you keep your money in a savings account.* ▶ **zwiększać się,** (*odsetki itp.*) **narastać 2** [T] to allow a sum of money or debts to grow over a period of time: *The firm had accrued debts of over $6m.* ▶ **pomnażać** (*np. kapitał*) SYN **accumulate**

■ **accrual** /əˈkruːəl/ noun [U,C] ▶ **przyrost; pomnażanie kapitału**

accumulate /əˈkjuːmjəleɪt/ verb **1** [T] to collect a number or quantity of sth over a period of time: *Over the years, I've accumulated hundreds of books.* ▶ **gromadzić 2** [I] to increase over a period of time: *Dust soon accumulates if you don't clean the house for a week or so.* ▶ **gromadzić się, zbierać się**

■ **accumulation** /əˌkjuːmjəˈleɪʃn/ noun [C,U] ▶ **nagromadzenie (się)**

accurate /ˈækjərət/ adj. exact and correct; without mistakes: *He gave the police an accurate description of the*

robbers. ◇ *That clock isn't very accurate.* ▶ **dokładny** OPP **inaccurate**
■ **accuracy** /'ækjərəsi/ noun [U] ▶ **dokładność** OPP **inaccuracy** | **accurately** adv. ▶ **dokładnie**

accusation /ˌækju'zeɪʃn/ noun [C,U] a statement saying that sb has done sth wrong: *accusations of corruption* ◇ *The player* ***made an accusation*** *of dishonesty against the referee.* ◇ *There was a note of accusation in her voice.* W jej głosie brzmiał wyrzut. ▶ **oskarżenie**

accuse /ə'kju:z/ verb [T] **accuse sb (of sth/doing sth)** to say that sb has done sth wrong or broken the law: *I accused her of cheating.* ◇ *He was accused of murder.* ▶ **oskarżać**
■ **accuser** noun [C] ▶ **oskarżyciel/ka**

the accused /ə'kju:zd/ noun [C] (pl. **the accused**) (used in a court of law) the person who is said to have broken the law ▶ **oskarżon-y/a**

accusing /ə'kju:zɪŋ/ adj. showing that you think sb has done sth wrong: *He gave me an accusing look.* ▶ **oskarżycielski**
■ **accusingly** adv. ▶ **oskarżycielsko**

accustom /ə'kʌstəm/ verb [T] **accustom yourself/sb/sth to sth** to make yourself/sb/sth get used to sth: *It took me a while to accustom myself to working nights.* ▶ **przyzwyczajać się/kogoś/coś do czegoś**

accustomed /ə'kʌstəmd/ adj. **1 accustomed to sth** if you are **accustomed** to sth, you are used to it and it is not strange for you: *She's accustomed to travelling a lot in her job.* ◇ *It took a while for my eyes to get accustomed* (aż moje oczy przyzwyczaiły się) *to the dark room.* ▶ **przyzwyczajony** SYN **used to 2** (formal) usual; regular ▶ **zwyczajowy**

ace /eɪs/ noun [C] **1** a playing card which has a single shape on it. An **ace** has either the lowest or the highest value in a game of cards: *the ace of spades* ▶ **as** ➲ note at **card 2** (in the sport of **tennis**) a **service** that the person playing against you cannot hit back because it is too fast: *to serve an ace* ▶ **as serwisowy**

ache[1] /eɪk/ verb [I] to feel a continuous pain: *His legs ached after playing football for two hours.* Po dwugodzinnej grze w piłkę nożną bolały go nogi. ◇ *She was aching all over.* Wszystko ją bolało. ▶ **boleć**

ache[2] /eɪk/ noun [C] a pain that lasts for a long time: *to have toothache/earache/stomach ache* ▶ **ból**

> **Ache** często występuje w rzeczownikach złożonych, w Br. ang. zwykle bez przedimków **a** lub **an**: *I've got toothache.* (Boli mnie ząb.) Natomiast ze słowem **headache** zawsze używa się przedimka **a**: *I've got a headache.* (Boli mnie głowa.) W Amer. ang. **ache** zwykle używa się z przedimkiem **a** lub **an**, zwł. gdy chodzi o pewien określony atak dolegliwości: *I have an awful toothache.* (Strasznie boli mnie ząb.) ➲ note at **pain**[1]

achieve /ə'tʃi:v/ verb [T] to gain sth, usually by effort or skill; to complete sth by hard work and skill ▶ **osiągać**

achievement /ə'tʃi:vmənt/ noun **1** [C] something that you have done successfully, especially through hard work or skill: *She felt that winning the gold medal was her greatest achievement.* ▶ **osiągnięcie, zdobycie 2** [U] the act or process of of finishing sth successfully: *He enjoys climbing mountains because it gives him* ***a sense of achievement*** (poczucie sukcesu). ▶ **osiągnięcie**

Achilles heel /əˌkɪli:z 'hi:l/ noun [C] a weak point or fault in sb/sth ▶ **pięta Achillesa**

acid[1] /'æsɪd/ noun [C,U] (in chemistry) a liquid substance that can dissolve metal and may burn your skin or clothes. **Acids** have a **pH** value of less than 7: *sulphuric acid* kwas siarkowy ▶ **kwas** ➲ look at **alkali**

acid[2] /'æsɪd/ adj. **1** (also **acidic** /ə'sɪdɪk/) containing an **acid**: *an acid solution* ▶ **kwaśny** OPP **alkaline 2** (used about a fruit, etc.) with a sour taste ▶ **kwaśny**

acidity /ə'sɪdəti/ noun [U] the quality of being **acid**: *to measure the acidity of soil* ▶ **kwasowość**

ˌacid 'rain noun [U] rain that has chemicals in it from factories, etc. and that causes damage to trees, buildings and rivers ▶ **kwaśny deszcz** ➲ note at **environment**

acknowledge /ək'nɒlɪdʒ/ verb [T] **1** to accept or admit that sth is true or exists: *He* ***acknowledged (the fact) that*** *he had made a mistake.* ◇ *It is acknowledged that he is the country's greatest writer./He is acknowledged to be the country's greatest writer.* Jest uznawany za najwybitniejszego pisarza w kraju. ▶ **przyznawać, uznawać 2** to show that you have seen or noticed sb ▶ **pozdrawiać, odkłaniać się**

> Zwróć uwagę, że rodzimi użytkownicy języka angielskiego zazwyczaj nie stosują ukłonu jako formy pozdrowienia.

3 to say that you have received a letter, etc. ▶ **potwierdzać odbiór 4** to publicly express thanks for help you have been given: *The manager sent a card to all the staff to acknowledge their hard work.* ▶ **wyrażać uznanie za coś**

acknowledgement /ək'nɒlɪdʒmənt/ noun **1** [U] the act of showing that you have seen or noticed sb/sth: *The president gave a smile of acknowledgement to the photographers.* ▶ **uznanie 2** [C,U] a letter, etc. that says that sth has been received or noticed: *I haven't received (an) acknowledgement of my job application yet.* ▶ **potwierdzenie odbioru 3** [C] a few words of thanks that an author writes at the beginning or end of a book to the people who have helped them ▶ **podziękowani-e/a**

acne /'ækni/ noun [U] a skin disease that usually affects young people. When you have **acne** you get a lot of spots on your face and neck. ▶ **trądzik**

acorn /'eɪkɔ:n/ noun [C] the small nut of the **oak**, that grows in a base shaped like a cup ▶ **żołądź**

acoustic /ə'ku:stɪk/ adj. **1** connected with sound or the sense of hearing ▶ **akustyczny 2** (of a musical instrument) not electric: *an acoustic guitar* ▶ **akustyczny**

acoustics /ə'ku:stɪks/ noun **1** [pl.] the shape, design, etc. of a room or theatre that make it good or bad for carrying sound: *The theatre has excellent acoustics.* ▶ **akustyka, warunki akustyczne 2** [U] the scientific study of sound ▶ **akustyka**

acquaintance /ə'kweɪntəns/ noun **1** [C] a person that you know but who is not a close friend ▶ **znajom-y/a** ➲ note at **friend 2** [U] **acquaintance with sb/sth** a slight knowledge of sb/sth: *I don't think I've ever* ***made your acquaintance*** *before.* Chyba nie udało się nam wcześniej zawrzeć znajomości. ▶ **znajomość powierzchowna**

acquainted /ə'kweɪntɪd/ adj. [not before a noun] (formal) **1 acquainted with sth** knowing sth: *I went for a walk to* ***get acquainted*** *with my new neighbourhood.* ▶ **zapoznany 2 acquainted (with sb)** knowing sb, but usually not very well ▶ **zaznajomiony**

acquiesce /ˌækwi'es/ verb [I] (formal) **acquiesce in/to sth** to accept sth without argument, although you may not agree with it ▶ **zgadzać się (na coś)**
■ **acquiescence** noun [U] ▶ **przyzwolenie**

acquire /ə'kwaɪə(r)/ verb [T] (formal) to obtain or buy sth: *The company has acquired shares in a rival business.* ◇ *He's acquired a reputation for being difficult to work with.* Wyrobił sobie opinię człowieka, z którym trudno pracować. ◇ *Children do not automatically acquire* (nie otrzymują automatycznie) *British citizenship if they are born in this country.* ▶ **nabywać**

acquisition /ˌækwɪ'zɪʃn/ noun (formal) **1** [U] the act of obtaining or buying sth: *a study of language acquisition* *in children* ▶ **nabywanie 2** [C] something that you have obtained or bought: *This sculpture is the museum's latest acquisition.* ▶ **nabytek**

acquit /ə'kwɪt/ verb [T] (**acquitting**; **acquitted**) **1 acquit sb (of sth)** to state formally that a person is not guilty of a crime: *The jury acquitted her of murder.* ▶ **uniewinniać** OPP **convict 2** (formal) **acquit yourself...** to behave in the way that is mentioned: *He **acquitted himself well** in his first match as a professional.* ▶ **spisywać się**
■ **acquittal** /ə'kwɪtl/ noun [C,U] ▶ **uniewinnienie**

acre /'eɪkə(r)/ noun [C] a measure of land; 0.405 of a **hectare**: *a farm of 200 acres/a 200-acre farm* ▶ **akr**

acrid /'ækrɪd/ adj. having a strong, bitter smell or taste that is unpleasant: *acrid smoke* ▶ **gryzący, ostry**

acrimonious /ˌækrɪ'məʊniəs/ adj. (formal) angry and full of strong feelings and words: *His parents went through an acrimonious divorce.* ▶ **zjadliwy, pełen żółci** SYN **bitter**

acrimony /'ækrɪməni; US -məʊni/ noun [U] (formal) angry bitter feelings or words ▶ **złość, zjadliwość**

acrobat /'ækrəbæt/ noun [C] a person who performs difficult movements of the body, especially in a **circus** ▶ **akrobat(k)a**

acrobatic /ˌækrə'bætɪk/ adj. performing or involving difficult movements of the body ▶ **akrobatyczny**
■ **acrobatically** /-kli/ adv. ▶ **akrobatycznie**

acrobatics /ˌækrə'bætɪks/ noun **1** [pl.] difficult movements of the body ▶ **akrobatyka 2** [U] the art of performing acrobatic acts ▶ **akrobatyka**

acronym /'ækrənɪm/ noun [C] **an acronym (for sth)** a short word that is made from the first letters of a group of words ▶ **skrótowiec**

across /ə'krɒs/ adv., prep. **1** from one side of sth to the other: *He walked across the field.* Przeszedł przez pole. ◇ *The stream was too wide to jump across.* Strumień był zbyt szeroki, żeby go przeskoczyć. ◇ *The river was about 20 metres across.* Rzeka miała 20 metrów szerokości. ◇ *I drew a line across the page.* Narysowałem kreskę w poprzek strony. ◇ *A smile spread across his face.* Uśmiech rozjaśnił mu twarz. ◇ *The bank has 800 branches across the country* (w całym kraju). ▶ **z jednej strony na drugą, przez 2** on the other side of sth: *There's a bank just across the road.* ◇ *The house **across** the road **from** us is for sale.* ▶ **po drugiej stronie**

> W znaczeniu „na drugą stronę" można użyć **across** lub **over**: *I ran across/over the road.* (Przebiegłem przez ulicę.) Jeśli zaś chodzi o pokonywanie wysokiej przeszkody, wówczas używa się **over**: *I can't climb over that wall.* (Nie mogę przejść przez mur.) Ze słowem **room** zwykle stosuje się **across**: *I walked across the room to the door.* (Przeszedłem przez pokój do drzwi.)

IDM **across the board** involving or affecting all groups, members, cases, etc.: *a 10% pay increase across the board* 10-procentowa podwyżka grupowa ▶ **grupowo**

acrylic /ə'krɪlɪk/ noun [C,U] an artificial material that is used in making clothes and paint ▶ **akrylowy**

act[1] /ækt/ noun [C] **1** a thing that you do: *In a typical act of generosity* (z typową dla nich wielkodusznością) *they refused to accept any money.* ◇ *to commit a violent act* ▶ **uczynek**

> **Act** i **action** mogą oznaczać to samo: *It was a brave act/action.* **Act**, ale nie **action**, może łączyć się z przyimkiem **of**: *It was an act of bravery.* (Był to czyn bohaterski.) **Activity** odnosi się do czynności wykonywanych regularnie: *I like outdoor activities* (zajęcia na świeżym powietrzu) *such as walking and gardening.* **Deed** to słowo formalne i nieco przestarzałe; często odnosi się do ważnych wydarzeń: *Robin Hood was famous for his brave deeds.* (Robin Hood słynął ze swych bohaterskich czynów.) Zwykle łączy się z **good**: *I wanted to pay back the good deed he had done.* (Chciałem mu się zrewanżować za ten dobry uczynek.)

2 (often **Act**) a law made by a government: *The government **passed an act** forbidding the possession of guns.* ▶ **akt** (*prawny*), **ustawa 3** behaviour that hides your true feelings: *She seems very happy but she's just **putting on an act*** (udaje). ▶ **gra**, **udawanie 4** (often **Act**) one of the main divisions of a play or an **opera** ▶ **akt 5** a short piece of entertainment, especially as part of a show: *Did you enjoy the clowns' act?* ▶ **punkt programu**, **numer**

IDM **be/get in on the act** become involved in an activity that is becoming popular ▶ **zaangażować się w działalność, która jest modna, przynosi zyski itp.**

get your act together to organize yourself so that you can do sth properly: *If he doesn't get his act together, he's going to lose his job.* ▶ **brać się w garść**

a hard act to follow → HARD[1]

in the act (of doing sth) while doing sth, especially sth wrong: *She caught him in the act of looking through the papers on her desk.* ▶ **w trakcie (robienia czegoś)**; **na gorącym uczynku**

act[2] /ækt/ verb **1** [I] **act (on sth)** to do sth; to take action: *The doctor knew he had to act quickly to save the child.* ◇ *I'm always giving my brother advice but he never acts on it.* ▶ **działać 2** [I] to behave in the way that is mentioned: *Stop **acting like** a child!* ◇ *Although she was trying to act cool, I could see she was really upset.* ◇ *Ali's acting strangely today – what's wrong with him?* ◇ *Don't act like a fool.* Nie udawaj głupiego. ▶ **zachowywać się (jak) 3** [I,T] to perform in a play or film: *I acted in a play at school.* ◇ *He's always wanted to act the part of Hamlet.* ◇ *He hasn't really hurt himself – he's just acting* (tylko udaje)*!* ▶ **grać 4** [I] **act as sth** to perform a particular function: *The elephant's trunk acts as a nose, a hand and an arm.* ◇ *He acted as our guide.* ▶ **pełnić funkcję**

acting[1] /'æktɪŋ/ noun [U] the art or profession of performing in plays or films ▶ **gra**; **sztuka aktorska**

acting[2] /'æktɪŋ/ adj. [only before a noun] doing the job mentioned for a short time: *James will be the acting director while Henry is away.* ▶ **pełniący obowiązki**

action /'ækʃn/ noun **1** [U] doing things, often for a particular purpose: *Now is the time for action.* ◇ *If we don't **take action*** (podejmiemy działania) *quickly, it'll be too late!* ▶ **działanie** OPP **inaction 2** [C] something that you do: *The doctor's quick action saved the child's life.* ◇ *They should be judged by their actions, not by what they say.* ▶ **działanie, czyn** ⊃ note at **act**[1] **3** [C,U] the process of settling an argument in a court of law: *He is going to **take legal action*** (wytoczyć proces) *against the hospital.* ▶ **powództwo 4** [U] fighting in a war: *Their son was **killed in action**.* ▶ **walka**, **bitwa 5** [sing.] the most important events in a story, film or play: *The action takes place in London.* ▶ **akcja 6** [U] exciting things that happen: *There's not much action* (nie ma życia) *in this boring town.* ▶ **akcja 7** [sing.] the effect that one substance has on another: *They're studying the **action of** alcohol **on** the brain.* ▶ **działanie**

IDM **in action** in operation; while working or doing sth: *We shall have a chance to see their new team in action next week.* ▶ **w akcji**, **podczas działania**

into action into operation: *We'll **put** the plan **into action** immediately.* Natychmiast wprowadzimy ten plan w czyn. ◇ *As soon as the security guard left the building, the robbers went/sprang into action* (przystąpili do działania). ▶ **do akcji**

out of action not able to do the usual things; not working: *The coffee machine's out of action again.* ▶ **nieczynny**

'action group noun [C] a group that is formed to work for social or political change: *the Child Poverty Action Group* ▶ **grupa powołana w celu przeprowadzania akcji społecznych lub politycznych**

'action movie noun [C] (Brit. also **'action film**) (informal) a film that has a lot of exciting action and adventure ▶ **film akcji**

'action-packed adj. full of exciting events and activity: *an action-packed weekend* ▶ **pełen ekscytujących wydarzeń**, *(film)* **o wartkiej akcji**

ˌaction 'replay noun [C] (US **ˌinstant 'replay**) part of sth, for example a sports game on television, that is immediately repeated, often more slowly, so that you can see a goal or another exciting or important moment again ▶ **powtórka** *(np. fragmentu meczu zwł. w zwolnionym tempie)*

activate /'æktɪveɪt/ verb [T] to make sth start working: *A slight movement can activate the car alarm.* ▶ **uruchamiać**, **powodować włączenie się**

active /'æktɪv/ adj. **1** involved in activity: *I have a very active social life.* ◇ *My grandfather is very active* (pełen wigoru) *for his age.* ◇ *I was at the meeting but I didn't **take an active part*** (nie brałam czynnego udziału) *in the discussion.* ◇ *He was on active service during the war.* ▶ **czynny** SYN **lively** OPP **inactive** **2** that produces an effect; that is in operation: *an active volcano* ▶ **czynny** **3** (used about the form of a verb or a sentence when the subject of the sentence performs the action of the verb): *In the sentence 'The dog bit him', the verb is active.* ❶ Można też powiedzieć: *The verb is in the active.* ▶ **w stronie czynnej** ➲ look at **passive**
■ **actively** adv.: *She is actively looking for a job.* ▶ **czynnie**

activist /'æktɪvɪst/ noun [C] a person who takes action to cause political or social change, usually as a member of a group: *a protest by environmental activists* ▶ **aktywist(k)a**, **działacz/ka**

activity /æk'tɪvəti/ noun (pl. **activities**) **1** [U] a situation in which there is a lot of action or movement: *The house was full of activity on the morning of the wedding.* ▶ **ruch**, **ożywienie** OPP **inactivity** **2** [C, usually pl.] a thing that you do for interest or pleasure, or in order to achieve a particular aim: *The hotel offers a range of leisure activities.* ◇ ***illegal/criminal activities*** ▶ **zajęcia** *(zazw. rekreacyjne)*, **działalność** ➲ note at **act**[1]

actor /'æktə(r)/ noun [C] a person whose job is to act in a play, film or on TV ▶ **aktor** ➲ note at **theatre**

actress /'æktrəs/ noun [C] a woman whose job is to act in a play, film or on TV ▶ **aktorka** ➲ note at **theatre**

actual /'æktʃuəl/ adj. [only before a noun] real; that happened: *The actual damage to the car was not as great as we had feared.* ◇ *They seemed to be good friends but **in actual fact** they hated each other.* ▶ **rzeczywisty**, **faktyczny**

actually /'æktʃuəli/ adv. **1** really; in fact: *You don't actually believe her, do you?* ◇ *I can't believe that I'm actually going to America!* ▶ **naprawdę** **2** although it may seem strange: *He actually expected me to cook his meal for him!* ▶ **faktycznie**, **prawdę mówiąc**

> **Actually** często używa się w rozmowie, aby przyciągnąć czyjąś uwagę lub grzecznie poprawić czyjś błąd: *Actually, I wanted to show you something. Have you got a minute?* ◇ *We aren't married, actually.* ◇ *I don't agree about the book. I think it's rather good, actually.*
>
> **Actual** i **actually** nie oznaczają, wbrew pozorom, „aktualny"/„aktualnie". W tym znaczeniu stosuje się **current(ly)**, **(at) present** lub **at the moment**: *He's currently working on an article about China.* ◇ *I'm studying for my exams at present.*

acumen /'ækjəmən/ noun [U] the ability to understand and decide things quickly and well: *business/commercial/financial acumen* ▶ **przenikliwość**, **zmysł**

acupuncture /'ækjupʌŋktʃə(r)/ noun [U] a way of treating an illness or stopping pain by putting thin needles into parts of the body ▶ **akupunktura**

acute /ə'kju:t/ adj. **1** very serious; very great: *an acute shortage of food* ◇ *acute pain* ▶ **dotkliwy** **2** (used about an illness) becoming dangerous very quickly: *acute appendicitis* ▶ **ostry** ➲ look at **chronic** **3** (used about feelings or the senses) very strong: *Dogs have an acute sense of smell.* ◇ *acute hearing* ▶ **silny**, **wyczulony** **4** showing that you are able to understand things easily: *The report contains some acute observations.* ▶ **wnikliwy**
■ **acutely** adv. ▶ **dotkliwie**; **wnikliwie**

aˌcute 'angle noun [C] an angle of less than 90° ▶ **kąt ostry** ➲ look at **obtuse angle**, **right angle**

AD /ˌeɪ 'di:/ abbr. (from Latin) **anno domini**; used in the Christian **calendar** to show a particular number of years since the year when Christ was believed to have been born: *AD 44* ▶ **n.e.** ➲ look at **BC**

ad (informal) = ADVERTISEMENT: *I saw your ad in the local paper.*

adage /'ædɪdʒ/ noun [C] a common phrase expressing sth that is always true about people or the world ▶ **powiedzenie**, **przysłowie**

adamant /'ædəmənt/ adj. (formal) very sure; refusing to change your mind: *She was adamant that she would not come.* ▶ **nieugięty**
■ **adamantly** adv. ▶ **niewzruszenie**

Adam's apple /ˌædəmz 'æpl/ noun [C] the lump at the front of the throat that sticks out, particularly in men, and moves up and down when you swallow ▶ **jabłko Adama**

adapt /ə'dæpt/ verb **1** [T] **adapt sth (for sth)** to change sth so that you can use it in a different situation: *The bus was adapted for disabled people.* ◇ *The teacher adapts the coursebook to suit the needs of her students.* ◇ *Tonight's play has been adapted* (zaadaptowana) *for radio from the novel by Charles Dickens.* ▶ **przystosowywać (coś do czegoś)**, **przerabiać (coś na coś)** **2** [I,T] **adapt (yourself) (to sth)** to change your behaviour because the situation you are in has changed: *They were quick to adapt (themselves) to the new system.* ▶ **przystosowywać się**

adaptable /ə'dæptəbl/ adj. able to change to suit new situations ▶ **łatwo przystosowujący się**

adaptation /ˌædæp'teɪʃn/ noun **1** [C] a play or film that is based on a novel, etc.: *a screen adaptation of Jane Austen's 'Pride and Prejudice'* ▶ **adaptacja** **2** [U] the state or process of changing to suit a new situation ▶ **przystoso(wy)wanie (się)**

adapted /ə'dæptɪd/ adj. having all the necessary qualities to do sth: *Chickens are poorly adapted for flight.* ▶ **przystosowany**

adaptor (also **adapter**) /ə'dæptə(r)/ noun [C] **1** a device that allows you to connect more than one piece of electrical equipment to a **socket** ▶ **rozgałęziacz** **2** a device for connecting pieces of electrical equipment that were not designed to be fitted together ▶ **nasadka na wtyczkę umożliwiająca połączenie elektryczne różnych standardów**

add /æd/ verb **1** [I,T] **add (sth) (to sth)** to put sth together with sth else, so that you increase the size, number, value, etc.: *I added a couple more items to the shopping list.* ◇ *The noise of the crowd added to the excitement of* *the race.* ▶ **dodawać 2** [I,T] to put numbers or amounts together so that you get a total: *If you* ***add** 3 **and** 3 **together**, you get 6.* ◇ ***Add** $8 **to** the total, to cover postage and packing.* ◇ *Don't ask me to work it out – I can't add.* ▶ **dodawać** ℹ Przy dodawaniu dwóch liczb często używa się słowa **plus**: *2 plus 2 is 4.* OPP **subtract 3** [T] to say sth more: *'By the way, please don't tell anyone I phoned you,' she added.* ▶ **dodawać**

PHR V **add sth on (to sth)** to include sth: *10% will be added on to your bill* (zostanie wliczone do waszego rachunku) *as a service charge.* ▶ **dodawać**

add up to seem to be a true explanation: *I'm sorry, but your story just doesn't add up* (coś tu nie gra). ▶ **zgadzać się**

add (sth) up to find the total of several numbers: *The waiter hadn't added up the bill correctly.* ▶ **podliczać**

add up to sth to have as a total: *How much does all the shopping add up to?* ▶ **wynosić** (*jakąś kwotę*)

added /ˈædɪd/ adj. in addition to what is usual; extra: *milk with added* (z dodatkiem) *vitamins* ▶ **dodatkowy**

ˈ**added to** prep. in addition to sth; as well as ▶ **(i) w dodatku**

adder /ˈædə(r)/ noun [C] a small poisonous snake ▶ **żmija**

addict /ˈædɪkt/ noun [C] a person who cannot stop taking or doing sth harmful: *a drug addict* narkoman/ka ▶ **nałogowiec**

■ **addicted** /əˈdɪktɪd/ adj. **addicted (to sth)**: *She's addicted to heroin.* ◇ *He's addicted to football.* On jest nałogowym fanem piłki nożnej. ▶ **uzależniony** SYN **hooked** | **addiction** noun [C,U]: *the problem of teenage drug addiction* ▶ **nałóg**

addictive /əˈdɪktɪv/ adj. difficult to stop taking or doing: *a highly addictive drug* ◇ *an addictive game* ▶ **powodujący uzależnienie**

⚷ **addition** /əˈdɪʃn/ noun **1** [U] adding sth, especially two or more numbers: *children learning addition and subtraction* ▶ **dodawanie** ➲ look at **subtraction 2** [C] **an addition (to sth)** a person or thing that is added to sth: *They've got a new addition to the family.* Powiększyła im się rodzina. ▶ **dodatek**

IDM **in addition (to sth)** as well as: *She speaks five foreign languages in addition to English.* ▶ **w dodatku (do czegoś), ponadto**

⚷ **additional** /əˈdɪʃənl/ adj. added: *a small additional charge for the use of the swimming pool* ▶ **dodatkowy** SYN **extra**

■ **additionally** /-ʃənəli/ adv. ▶ **dodatkowo, ponadto**

additive /ˈædətɪv/ noun [C] a substance that is added to sth in small amounts for a special purpose: *food additives* ▶ **dodatek** (*np. barwnik, środek konserwujący*)

ˈ**add-on** noun [C] a thing that is added to sth else: *The company offers scuba-diving as an add-on to the basic holiday price.* ◇ *add-on software* ▶ **dodatkowa usługa/instalacja itp.**

⚷ **address**[1] /əˈdres; US ˈædres/ noun [C] **1** the number of the building and the name of the street and place where sb lives or works: *Let me give you my home/business address.* ◇ *She no longer lives at this address.* ◇ *Please inform the office of any change of address.* ▶ **adres 2** a series of words and/or numbers that tells you where you can find sth using a computer: *What's your email address?* ▶ **adres e-mail 3** a formal speech that is given to an audience: *tonight's televised presidential address* ▶ **przemówienie**

IDM **(of) no fixed abode/address** → FIXED

⚷ **address**[2] /əˈdres/ verb [T] **1 address sth (to sb/sth)** to write the name and address of the person you are sending a letter, etc. to: *The package was returned because it had been wrongly addressed.* ▶ **adresować 2** to make an important speech to an audience: *to address a meeting* ▶ **wygłaszać przemówienie 3** (formal) **address sth to sb** make a comment, etc. to sb: *Kindly address any complaints you have to the manager.* ▶ **kierować (do kogoś) 4 address sb as sth** to talk or write to sb using a particular name or title: *She prefers to be addressed as 'Ms'.* ▶ **tytułować 5** (formal) **address (yourself to) sth** to try to deal with a problem, etc.: *The government is finally addressing the question of corruption.* ▶ **przykładać się do czegoś**

adˈdress book noun [C] **1** a book in which you keep addresses, phone numbers, etc. ▶ **notes na adresy 2** a computer file where you store email and Internet addresses ▶ **książka adresowa, kontakty**

addressee /ˌædreˈsiː/ noun [C] a person that a letter, etc. is addressed to ▶ **adresat/ka**

adenoids /ˈædənɔɪdz/ noun [pl.] pieces of soft **tissue** at the back of the nose and throat, that are part of the body's **immune system** and that can swell up and cause breathing difficulties, especially in children ▶ (*anat.*) **adenoid**

adept /əˈdept/ adj. **adept (at sth)** very good or skilful at sth ▶ **biegły (w czymś)** SYN **skilful** OPP **inept** ℹ W zasadzie nie używa się **adept** przed rzeczownikiem.

⚷ **adequate** /ˈædɪkwət/ adj. **1** enough for what you need: *Make sure you take an adequate supply of water with you.* ▶ **wystarczający 2** just good enough; acceptable: *Your work is adequate but I'm sure you could do better.* ▶ **wystarczający, dostateczny** OPP for both meanings **inadequate**

■ **adequacy** /ˈædɪkwəsi/ noun [U] ▶ **stosowność; adekwatność** | **adequately** adv.: *The mystery has never been adequately explained.* ▶ **wystarczająco; dostatecznie**

adhere /ədˈhɪə(r)/ verb [I] (formal) **adhere (to sth)** to stick firmly to sth: *Make sure that the paper adheres firmly to the wall.* ▶ **przylegać (do czegoś)**

PHR V **adhere to sth** to continue to support an idea, etc.; to follow a rule ▶ **stosować się do czegoś; trzymać się czegoś**

adherent /ədˈhɪərənt/ noun [C] a person who supports a particular idea ▶ **stronni-k/czka** SYN **supporter**

■ **adherence** noun [U] ▶ **stosowanie się; trzymanie się** (*np. zasad, reguł*)

adhesive[1] /ədˈhiːsɪv/ noun [C,U] a substance that makes things stick together: *a fast-drying adhesive* ▶ **środek klejący, przylepiec**

adhesive[2] /ədˈhiːsɪv/ adj. that can stick, or can cause two things to stick together: *He sealed the parcel with adhesive tape.* ▶ **przylepny** SYN **sticky**

ad hoc /ˌæd ˈhɒk/ adj. made or done suddenly for a particular purpose: *They set up an ad hoc committee to discuss the matter.* ◇ *Staff training takes place occasionally* ***on an ad hoc basis.*** ▶ **doraźny, ad hoc**

adjacent /əˈdʒeɪsnt/ adj. **adjacent (to sth)** (used about an area, place or building) next to or close to sth: *She works in the office adjacent to mine.* ◇ *There was a fire in the adjacent building.* ▶ **sąsiedni**

adjectival /ˌædʒekˈtaɪvl/ adj. that contains or is used like an adjective: *The adjectival form of 'smell' is 'smelly'.* ▶ **przymiotnikowy**

adjective /ˈædʒɪktɪv/ noun [C] a word that tells you more about a noun, for example *big* and *clever* in *a big house* and *a clever idea* ▶ **przymiotnik**

adjoining /əˈdʒɔɪnɪŋ/ adj. next to or nearest to sth: *A scream came from the adjoining room.* ▶ **przyległy**

adjourn /əˈdʒɜːn/ verb [I,T] to stop a meeting, trial, etc. for a short time and start it again later: *The meeting adjourned for lunch.* ◇ *The trial was adjourned until the following week.* ▶ **odraczać**

■ **adjournment** noun [C,U] ▶ **odroczenie**

adjudicate /ə'dʒu:dɪkeɪt/ verb [I,T] (formal) to act as an official judge in a competition or to decide who is right when two people or groups disagree about sth ▶ **rozstrzygać**

adjudicator /ə'dʒu:dɪkeɪtə(r)/ noun [C] a person who acts as a judge, for example in a competition ▶ **sędzia, uror/ka**

⚷ **adjust** /ə'dʒʌst/ verb **1** [T] to change sth slightly, especially because it is not in the right position: *The brakes on my bicycle need adjusting.* ▶ **dostosowywać, regulować** **2** [I] **adjust (to sth)** to get used to new conditions or a new situation: *She found it hard to adjust to working at night.* ▶ **przystosowywać się, przyzwyczajać się**
■ **adjustment** noun [C,U]: *We'll just* ***make a few minor adjustments*** *and the room will look perfect.* ▶ **poprawka, dostosowanie (się)**

adjustable /ə'dʒʌstəbl/ adj. that can be **adjusted**: *an adjustable mirror* ▶ **ruchomy; taki, który można dostosować/dostroić/wyregulować itp.**

ad lib /ˌæd 'lɪb/ adj. done or spoken without preparation ▶ **za/improwizowany**
■ **ad lib** adv.: *She had to speak ad lib* (improwizować) *because she couldn't find her notes.* ▶ **bez przygotowania** | **ad lib** verb [I] (**ad libbing**; **ad libbed**): *The singer forgot the words so he had to ad lib.* ▶ **improwizować**

administer /əd'mɪnɪstə(r)/ verb [T] (formal) **1** to control or manage sth ▶ **zarządzać** **2** to give sb sth, especially medicine ▶ **podawać**

administration /ədˌmɪnɪ'streɪʃn/ noun **1** (Brit. also, informal **admin** /'ædmɪn/) [U] the process or act of managing sth, for example a system, an organization or a business: *The administration of a large project like this is very complicated.* ◇ *A lot of the teachers' time is taken up by admin.* ▶ **administracja, zarządzanie** **2** [sing.] the group of people or part of a company that organizes or controls sth: *the hospital administration* ▶ **administracja, zarząd** **3** (often **the Administration**) [C] the government of a country, especially the US: *the Bush Administration* ▶ **rząd**

administrative /əd'mɪnɪstrətɪv; US -streɪt-/ adj. connected with the organization of a country, business, etc., and the way in which it is managed: *London is still the most important administrative centre in Britain.* ▶ **administracyjny**

administrator /əd'mɪnɪstreɪtə(r)/ noun [C] a person whose job is to organize or manage a system, business, etc. ▶ **zarząd-ca/czyni**

admirable /'ædmərəbl/ adj. (formal) that you admire; excellent ▶ **godny podziwu, wspaniały**
■ **admirably** /-əbli/ adv.: *She dealt with the problem admirably.* ▶ **wspaniale**

admiral /'ædmərəl/ noun [C] an official of very high rank in the navy ▶ **admirał**

⚷ **admiration** /ˌædmə'reɪʃn/ noun [U] **admiration (for/of sb/sth)** a feeling of liking and respecting sb/sth very much: *I have great admiration for his work.* Żywię głęboki podziw dla jego pracy. ▶ **podziw**

⚷ **admire** /əd'maɪə(r)/ verb [T] **admire sb/sth (for sth/doing sth)** to respect or like sb/sth very much; to look at sb/sth with pleasure: *Everyone admired the way he dealt with the problem.* ◇ *I've always admired her for being such a wonderful mother.* ◇ *We stopped at the top of the hill to admire the view.* ▶ **podziwiać**

admirer /əd'maɪərə(r)/ noun [C] a person who admires sb/sth: *I've always been a great admirer of her books.* ▶ **wielbiciel/ka**

admiring /əd'maɪərɪŋ/ adj. feeling or expressing admiration ▶ **pełen podziwu**
■ **admiringly** adv. ▶ **z podziwem**

admissible /əd'mɪsəbl/ adj. that can be allowed or accepted, especially in a court of law: *admissible evidence* ▶ **dopuszczalny, do przyjęcia** OPP **inadmissible**

admission /əd'mɪʃn/ noun **1** [C,U] **admission (to sth)** the act of allowing sb to enter a school, club, public place, etc.: *All those who were not wearing a tie were refused admission to the club.* ◇ *Admissions to British universities have increased by 15% this year.* ▶ **wstęp, dostęp** ➲ look at **entrance** **2** [C] a statement that admits that sth is true: *I viewed her silence as* ***an admission of guilt.*** ▶ **przyznanie się** **3** [U] the amount of money that you have to pay to enter a place: *The museum charges half-price admission on Mondays.* ▶ **wstęp, bilet wstępu**

⚷ **admit** /əd'mɪt/ verb (**admitting**; **admitted**) **1** [I,T] **admit sth; admit to sth/doing sth; admit (that ...)** to agree that sth unpleasant is true or that you have done sth wrong: *You should admit your mistake.* ◇ *After trying four times to pass the exam, I finally* ***admitted defeat.*** ◇ *She admitted having broken the computer.* ◇ *He refused to admit to the theft.* ◇ *I have to admit (that) I was wrong.* ▶ **przyznawać się; przyznawać, że** OPP **deny** **2** [T] **admit sb/sth (into/to sth)** to allow sb/sth to enter; to take sb into a place: *He was admitted to hospital with suspected appendicitis.* ▶ **przyjmować, wpuszczać**

admittance /əd'mɪtns/ noun [U] (formal) being allowed to enter a place; the right to enter: *The journalist tried to gain admittance to the minister's office.* ◇ *No admittance.* Wstęp wzbroniony. ▶ **wstęp**

admittedly /əd'mɪtɪdli/ adv. it must be admitted (that ...): *The work is very interesting. Admittedly, I do get rather tired.* ▶ **trzeba przyznać, że**

admonish /əd'mɒnɪʃ/ verb [T] (formal) **admonish sb (for sth/for doing sth)** to tell sb firmly that you do not approve of sth that they have done ▶ **strofować kogoś (za coś)**

ad nauseam /ˌæd 'nɔ:ziæm/ adv. if a person says or does sth **ad nauseam**, they say or do it again and again so that it becomes boring and annoying ▶ **do znudzenia**

ado /ə'du:/ noun
IDM **without further/more ado** (old-fashioned) without delayng; immediately ▶ **bez dalszych ceregieli**

adolescence /ˌædə'lesns/ noun [U] the period of sb's life between being a child and becoming an adult, between the ages of about 13 and 17 ▶ **wiek dojrzewania** SYN **puberty**

adolescent /ˌædə'lesnt/ noun [C] a young person who is no longer a child and not yet an adult, between the ages of about 13 and 18: *the problems of adolescents* (nastolatków) ▶ **młodzieniec, dziewczyna** ➲ look at **teenager**
■ **adolescent** adj.: *an adolescent daughter* ▶ **nastoletni**

⚷ **adopt** /ə'dɒpt/ verb **1** [I,T] to take a child into your family and treat them as your own child by law: *They couldn't have children so they adopted.* ◇ *They're hoping to adopt a child.* ▶ **adoptować** ➲ look at **foster** **2** [T] to take and use sth: *What approach did you adopt when dealing with the problem?* ▶ **przyjmować** ➲ note at **child**
■ **adopted** adj.: *an adopted child* ▶ **adoptowany** | **adoption** noun [C,U] ▶ **adopcja; przyjęcie**

adoptive /ə'dɒptɪv/ adj. (used about parents) having legally taken a child to live with them as part of their family: *the baby's adoptive parents* ▶ (rodzice) **przybrany**

adorable /ə'dɔ:rəbl/ adj. (used about children or animals) very attractive ▶ **rozkoszny, uroczy** SYN **lovely**

adore /ə'dɔ:(r)/ verb [T] **1** to love and admire sb/sth very much; to like sth very much ▶ **uwielbiać**
■ **adoration** /ˌædə'reɪʃn/ noun [U] ▶ **adoracja, uwielbienie** | **adoring** adj.: *his adoring fans* uwielbiający go kibice ▶ **uwielbiający**

adorn /ə'dɔːn/ verb [T] **adorn sth (with sth)** to add sth in order to make a thing or person more attractive or beautiful ▶ **ozdabiać**
■ **adornment** noun [C,U] ▶ **ozdoba**

adrenalin /ə'drenəlɪn/ noun [U] a substance that your body produces when you are very angry, frightened or excited and that makes your heart go faster ▶ **adrenalina**

adrift /ə'drɪft/ adj. [not before a noun] (used about a boat) not tied to anything or controlled by anyone ▶ **unoszony na fali**

adulation /ˌædju'leɪʃn; US ˌædʒə'l-/ noun [U] (formal) admiration for sb, especially when this is greater than is necessary ▶ **schlebianie**

adult /'ædʌlt; ə'dʌlt/ noun [C] a person or an animal that is fully grown ▶ **dorosł-y/a** SYN **grown-up**
■ **adult** adj. ▶ **dorosły**

ˌ**adult edu'cation** (also **conˌtinuing edu'cation**) noun [U] education for adults that is available outside the formal education system, for example at evening classes ▶ **kształcenie dorosłych**

adulterate /ə'dʌltəreɪt/ verb [T, often passive] **adulterate sth (with sth)** to make food or drink less pure by adding another substance to it ▶ **zanieczyszczać, skażać** SYN **contaminate** ➲ look at **unadulterated**
■ **adulteration** /əˌdʌltə'reɪʃn/ noun [U] ▶ **zanieczyszczenie, skażenie**

adulterer /ə'dʌltərə(r)/, **adulteress** /ə'dʌltərəs/ noun [C] (formal) a person who commits **adultery** ▶ **cudzołożnik/ca**

adultery /ə'dʌltəri/ noun [U] (formal) sex between a married person and sb who is not their wife/husband: *He was accused of* ***committing adultery.*** ▶ **cudzołóstwo**
■ **adulterous** /ə'dʌltərəs/ adj.: *an adulterous relationship* ▶ **pozamałżeński**

adulthood /'ædʌlthʊd; ə'dʌlt-/ noun [U] the time in your life when you are an adult ▶ **dorosłość**

advance[1] /əd'vɑːns; US -'væns/ noun **1** [C, usually sing.] forward movement: *the army's advance towards the border* ▶ **posuwanie się naprzód, natarcie** OPP **retreat** **2** [C,U] progress in sth: *advances in computer technology* ▶ **postęp** **3** [C] an amount of money that is paid to sb before the time when it is usually paid: *She asked for an advance on her salary.* ▶ **zaliczka**
IDM **in advance (of sth)** before a particular time or event: *You should book tickets for the concert well in advance.* ▶ **z góry**

advance[2] /əd'vɑːns; US -'væns/ verb **1** [I] to move forward: *The army advanced towards the city.* ▶ **posuwać się naprzód** OPP **retreat** **2** [I,T] to make progress or help sth make progress: *Our research has not advanced much recently.* ▶ **posuwać (się) naprzód**

advance[3] /əd'vɑːns; US -'væns/ adj. [only before a noun] that happens before sth: *There was no* ***advance warning of*** (ostrzeżenia o) *the earthquake.* ◇ *There have been huge* ***advance bookings*** (rezerwacja biletów) *for her latest film.* ▶ **wcześniejszy**

advanced /əd'vɑːnst; US -'vænst/ adj. **1** highly developed: *a country that is not very advanced industrially* ▶ **rozwinięty** **2** of a high level: *an advanced English class* ▶ **zaawansowany**

ad'vanced level (formal) = A LEVEL

advancement /əd'vɑːnsmənt; US -'væns-/ noun (formal) **1** [U,C] the process of helping sth to make progress or succeed; the progress that is made: *the advancement of knowledge/education/science* ▶ **postęp, rozwój** **2** [U] progress in a job, social class, etc.: *There are good opportunities for advancement if you have the right skills.* ▶ **awans**

advantage /əd'vɑːntɪdʒ; US -'væn-/ noun **1** [C] **an advantage (over sb)** something that may help you to do better than other people: *Her experience gave her an advantage over the other applicants.* ◇ *Living abroad means he* ***has the advantage of*** *being fluent in two languages.* ◇ *Some runners try to gain an unfair advantage by taking drugs.* ▶ **przewaga** **2** [C,U] something that helps you or that will bring you a good result: *Each of these systems has its advantages and disadvantages.* ◇ *The traffic is so bad here that* ***there is no advantage in*** *having a car.* ▶ **korzyść** OPP for both meanings **disadvantage** ➲ look at **pro**
IDM **take advantage of sb/sth** **1** to make good or full use of sth: *We should take full advantage of these low prices while they last.* ▶ **skorzystać z czegoś** **2** to make use of sb/sth in a way that is unfair or dishonest in order to get what you want: *You shouldn't let him take advantage of you like this.* ▶ **wykorzystywać kogoś/coś**

advantaged /əd'vɑːntɪdʒd; US -'væn-/ adj. being in a good social or financial situation ▶ **uprzywilejowany** OPP **disadvantaged**

advantageous /ˌædvən'teɪdʒəs/ adj. that will help you or bring you a good result ▶ **korzystny**

advent /'ædvent/ noun **1** [sing.] **the advent of sth/sb** the coming of an important event, person, new technology, etc.: *This area was very isolated before the advent of the railway* (przed nastaniem epoki kolei). ▶ **nastanie, przybycie** **2** (**Advent**) [U] (in the Christian year) the period that includes the four Sundays before Christmas ▶ **adwent**

adventure /əd'ventʃə(r)/ noun [C,U] an experience or event that is very unusual, exciting or dangerous: *She left home to travel, hoping for excitement and adventure.* ◇ *Our journey through the jungle was quite an adventure!* ▶ **przygoda**

adventurer /əd'ventʃərə(r)/ noun [C] **1** (old-fashioned) a person who enjoys exciting new experiences, especially going to unusual places ▶ **poszukiwacz/ka przygód** **2** a person who is willing to take risks or act in a dishonest way in order to gain money or power ▶ **spekulant/ka, kombinator/ka**

adventurous /əd'ventʃərəs/ adj. **1** (used about a person) liking to try new things or have **adventures** ▶ **śmiały, lubiący ryzyko** **2** involving **adventure**: *For a more adventurous holiday try mountain climbing.* ▶ **pełen przygód**

adverb /'ædvɜːb/ noun [C] a word that adds more information about place, time, manner, cause or degree to a verb, an adjective, a phrase or another adverb: *In 'speak slowly', 'extremely funny', 'arrive late' and 'too quickly', 'slowly', 'extremely', 'late' and 'too' are adverbs.* ▶ **przysłówek**
■ **adverbial** /æd'vɜːbiəl/ adj.: *'Very quickly indeed' is an adverbial phrase.* ▶ **przysłówkowy**

adversary /'ædvəsəri/ noun [C] (pl. **adversaries**) (formal) an enemy, or an opponent in a competition ▶ **przeciwnik/czka**

adverse /'ædvɜːs; əd'vɜːs/ adj. (formal) making sth difficult for sb: *Our flight was cancelled because of adverse weather conditions.* ▶ **niesprzyjający** OPP **favourable** ➲ look at **unfavourable**
■ **adversely** adv. ▶ **niesprzyjająco**

adversity /əd'vɜːsəti/ noun [C,U] (pl. **adversities**) (formal) difficulties or problems: *She's always optimistic, even* ***in the face of adversity.*** ▶ **przeciwność** (*losu*)

advert (Brit., informal) = ADVERTISEMENT: *adverts on television*

advertise /'ædvətaɪz/ verb **1** [I,T] **advertise sth (as sth)** to put information in a newspaper, on TV, on a picture on the wall, etc. in order to persuade people to buy sth, to

interest them in a new job, etc.: *a poster advertising a new type of biscuit* ◇ *The job was advertised in the local newspapers.* ◇ *It's very expensive to advertise on TV.* ▶ **reklamować, ogłaszać 2** [I] **advertise (for sb/sth)** to say publicly in a newspaper, on a sign, etc. that you need sb to do a particular job, want to buy sth, etc.: *The shop is advertising for a part-time sales assistant.* ▶ **zamieszczać ofertę, poszukiwać kogoś** (*do pracy*)
■ **advertiser** noun [C] ▶ **ogłoszeniodawca** | **advertising** noun [U]: *The magazine gets a lot of money from advertising.* ◇ *an advertising campaign* ▶ **reklama, reklamowanie**

⚿ **advertisement** /əd'vɜːtɪsmənt; US ˌædvər'taɪz-/ (also informal **ad** /æd/, Brit. also **advert** /'ædvɜːt/) noun [C] a piece of information in a newspaper, on TV, a picture on a wall, etc. that tries to persuade people to buy sth, to interest them in a new job, etc.: *an advertisement for a new brand of washing powder* ◇ *to put an advertisement in a newspaper* ▶ **reklama, ogłoszenie**

⚿ **advice** /əd'vaɪs/ noun [U] an opinion that you give sb about what they should do: *She **took** her doctor's **advice** and gave up smoking.* ◇ *Let me **give** you some **advice** ...* ▶ **rada, porada** ⓘ **Advice** jest rzeczownikiem niepoliczalnym, dlatego nie można powiedzieć ~~an advice~~ ani ~~some advices~~. Można natomiast powiedzieć **a piece of advice** oraz **a lot of advice.**

ad'vice columnist (US) = AGONY AUNT

advisable /əd'vaɪzəbl/ adj. (formal) that is a good thing to do; sensible: *It is advisable to reserve a seat.* ▶ **wskazany, rozsądny** OPP **inadvisable**

⚿ **advise** /əd'vaɪz/ verb **1** [I,T] **advise sb (to do sth); advise (sb) (against sth/against doing sth)** to tell sb what you think they should do: *I would strongly advise you to take the job.* ◇ *They advised us not to travel on a Friday.* ◇ *The newspaper article advised against eating too much meat.* ◇ *He did what the doctor advised.* ◇ *She advises the Government on economic affairs.* ▶ **radzić, doradzać 2** [T] (formal) to officially tell sb sth: *We would like to advise you that the goods are now ready for collection.* SYN **inform** ▶ **informować**

advisedly /əd'vaɪzədli/ adv. (formal) if you say that you are using a word **advisedly**, you mean that you have thought carefully before choosing it ▶ **świadomie, z rozmysłem**

adviser (also **advisor**) /əd'vaɪzə(r)/ noun [C] a person who gives advice to a company, government, etc.: *an adviser on economic affairs* ▶ **dorad-ca/czyni**

advisory /əd'vaɪzəri/ adj. giving advice only; not having the power to make decisions ▶ **doradczy**

advocate¹ /'ædvəkeɪt/ verb [T] (formal) to recommend or say that you support a particular plan or action ▶ **zalecać**

advocate² /'ædvəkət/ noun [C] **1 an advocate (of sth)** a person who supports a particular plan or action, especially in public ▶ **zwolenni-k/czka 2** a lawyer who defends sb in a court of law ▶ **adwokat** ⓘ Zwróć uwagę, że o adwokacie najczęściej mówi się **lawyer.**

aerial¹ /'eəriəl/ (US **antenna**) noun [C] a long metal stick on a building, car, etc. that receives radio or TV signals ▶ **antena**

aerial² /'eəriəl/ adj. from or in the air: *an aerial attack on the city* ◇ *an aerial photograph* (zdjęcie z lotu ptaka) *of the town* ▶ **powietrzny**

aerobics /eə'rəʊbɪks/ noun [U] physical exercises that people do to music: *to **do aerobics*** chodzić na aerobik ▶ **aerobik**

aerodynamics /ˌeərəʊdaɪ'næmɪks/ noun **1** [pl.] the qualities of an object that affect the way it moves through the air: *Research has focused on improving the car's aerodynamics.* ▶ **aerodynamika 2** [U] the scientific study of the way that things move through the air ▶ **aerodynamika**
■ **aerodynamic** adj.: *the aerodynamic design of a racing car* ▶ **aerodynamiczny**

aeroplane /'eərəpleɪn/ (also **plane**; US **airplane** /'eəpleɪn/) noun [C] a vehicle with wings and one or more engines that can fly through the air: *to fly an aeroplane* ▶ **samolot** ⮌ picture on **page A6**

aerosol /'eərəsɒl/ noun [C] a container in which a liquid substance is kept under pressure. When you press a button the liquid comes out in a fine spray. ▶ **aerozol**

aerospace /'eərəʊspeɪs/ noun [U] the industry of building aircraft, vehicles and equipment to be sent into space ▶ **przemysł lotniczy i kosmiczny**

aesthete (US also **esthete**) /'iːsθiːt; 'es-; US 'es-/ noun [C] (formal) a person who has a love and understanding of art and beautiful things ▶ **estet(k)a** ⓘ Czasami wyraża dezaprobatę.

aesthetic¹ (US also **esthetic**) /iːs'θetɪk; es-; US es-/ adj. concerned with beauty or art: *The columns are there for purely aesthetic reasons.* ▶ **estetyczny**
■ **aesthetically** (US also **esthetically**) /-kli/ adv.: *The design is **aesthetically pleasing** as well as practical.* ▶ **estetycznie**

aesthetic² (US also **esthetic**) /iːs'θetɪk; es-; US es-/ noun **1** [C] the **aesthetic** qualities and ideas of sth: *The students debated the aesthetic of the poems.* ▶ **estetyka 2** (**aesthetics**) [U] the branch of philosophy that studies the principles of beauty, especially in art ▶ **estetyka**

afar /ə'fɑː(r)/ adv.
IDM **from afar** (formal) from a long distance away ▶ **z dala**

affable /'æfəbl/ adj. pleasant, friendly and easy to talk to ▶ **przyjazny, skory do rozmowy** SYN **genial**
■ **affably** /-əbli/ adv. ▶ **przyjaźnie**

⚿ **affair** /ə'feə(r)/ noun **1** (**affairs**) [pl.] important personal, business, national, etc. matters: *The organization should have control of its own financial affairs.* ◇ *the minister for foreign affairs* ◇ *current affairs* wydarzenia bieżące ▶ **sprawy 2** [C] an event or situation: *The whole affair has been extremely unpleasant.* ▶ **wydarzenie, sprawa 3** [C] a sexual relationship between two people, usually when at least one of them is married to sb else: *She's **having an affair with** her boss.* ▶ **romans 4** [sing.] something private that you do not want other people to know about: *What happened between us is my affair.* ▶ **sprawa**
IDM **state of affairs** → STATE¹

⚿ **affect** /ə'fekt/ verb [T] **1** make sb/sth change in a particular way; to influence sb/sth: *Her personal problems seem to be affecting her work.* ◇ *This disease affects the brain.* ▶ **oddziaływać na kogoś/coś** ⮌ note at **influence, 2 2** to make sb feel very sad, angry, etc.: *The whole community was affected by the tragedy.* ▶ **dotykać, poruszać**

> Zwróć uwagę, że **affect** to czasownik, zaś **effect** – rzeczownik: *Smoking can affect your health.* ◇ *Smoking can have a bad effect on your health.*

affected /ə'fektɪd/ adj. (used about a person or their behaviour) not natural or sincere ▶ **sztuczny, afektowany** OPP **unaffected**
■ **affectation** /ˌæfek'teɪʃn/ noun [C,U] ▶ **sztuczność, afektacja**

⚿ **affection** /ə'fekʃn/ noun [C,U] **(an) affection (for/towards sb/sth)** a feeling of loving or liking sb/sth: *Mark felt great affection for his sister.* ▶ **przywiązanie, uczucie**

affectionate /ə'fekʃənət/ adj. showing that you love or like sb very much: *a very affectionate child* ▶ **czuły, kochający** SYN **loving**

■ **affectionately** adv. ▶ **czule**

affidavit /ˌæfəˈdeɪvɪt/ noun [C] (technical) a written statement that you swear is true, and that can be used as evidence in court: *to make/swear/sign an affidavit* ▶ **pisemne oświadczenie złożone pod przysięgą**

affiliate /əˈfɪlieɪt/ verb [T, usually passive] **affiliate sth (to sth)** to connect an organization to a larger organization: *Our local club is affiliated to the national association.* ▶ **stowarzyszać**

■ **affiliated** adj. ▶ **stowarzyszony** | **affiliation** /əˌfɪliˈeɪʃn/ noun [C,U] ▶ **powiązanie**

affinity /əˈfɪnəti/ noun [C,U] (pl. **affinities**) **1 (an) affinity (for/with sb/sth)** a strong feeling that you like and understand sb/sth, usually because you feel similar to them or it in some way: *He had always had an affinity for wild and lonely places.* ▶ **sentyment**, **bliskość** (*duchowa*) **2 (an) affinity (with sb/sth)**; **(an) affinity (between A and B)** a similar quality in two or more people or things ▶ **podobieństwo**

affirm /əˈfɜːm/ verb [T] (formal) to say formally or clearly that sth is true or that you support sth strongly: *I can affirm that no one will lose their job.* ◇ *The people affirmed their country's right to independence.* ▶ **twierdzić**, **stwierdzać**; **potwierdzać**, **oświadczać**

■ **affirmation** /ˌæfəˈmeɪʃn/ noun [C,U] ▶ **potwierdzenie**; **oświadczenie**

affirmative /əˈfɜːmətɪv/ adj. (formal) meaning 'yes': *an affirmative answer* ⓘ Można też powiedzieć **an answer in the affirmative.** ▶ **twierdzący** OPP **negative**

affix[1] /ˈæfɪks/ noun [C] a letter or group of letters added to the beginning or end of a word to change its meaning. The **prefix** *un-* in *unhappy* and the **suffix** *-less* in *careless* are both **affixes.** ▶ **afiks**

affix[2] /əˈfɪks/ verb [T, often passive] ~ **sth (to sth)** (formal) to stick or attach sth to sth else: *The label should be firmly affixed to the package.* ▶ **naklejać**; **przymocowywać**

afflict /əˈflɪkt/ verb [T, usually passive] (formal) **afflict sb/sth (with sth)** to cause sb/sth to suffer pain, sadness, etc.: *He has been afflicted with a serious illness* (cierpi na poważną chorobę) *since childhood.* ▶ **dotykać**

■ **affliction** noun [C,U] ▶ **przypadłość**, **nieszczęście**

affluent /ˈæfluənt/ adj. having a lot of money ▶ **zamożny** SYN **wealthy**

■ **affluence** noun [U]: *Increased exports have brought new affluence.* ▶ **zamożność**

⚷ **afford** /əˈfɔːd/ verb [T] [usually after *can, could* or *be able to*] **afford sth/to do sth 1** to have enough money or time to be able to do sth: *We couldn't afford a TV in those days.* ◇ *I've spent more time on this than I can afford.* ▶ **stać (kogoś na coś)**; **pozwalać (sobie na coś)** ➲ note at **loan**, **2** to not be able to do sth or let sth happen because it would have a bad result for you: *The other team is very good so we can't afford to make any mistakes.* ▶ **nie móc (sobie) pozwolić (na coś)**

■ **affordable** adj.: *affordable prices* ▶ (*ceny*) **niewygórowany**, (*produkty*) **niedrogi**

affront /əˈfrʌnt/ noun [C] **an affront (to sb/sth)** something that you say or do that is insulting to sb/sth: *Losing his job was a real affront to Oscar's dignity.* ▶ **obraza**

afield /əˈfiːld/ adv.

IDM **far afield** → FAR[2]

afloat /əˈfləʊt/ adj. [not before a noun] **1** on the surface of the water; not sinking: *A life jacket helps you **stay afloat** if you fall in the water.* ▶ **na wodzie 2** (used about a business, an economy, etc.) having enough money to survive ▶ **w dobrej formie**

afoot /əˈfʊt/ adj. [not before a noun] being planned or prepared: *There are plans afoot to increase taxation.* ▶ **rozważany**, **w toku**

aforementioned /əˌfɔːˈmenʃənd/ (also **aforesaid** /əˈfɔːsed/) adj. [only before a noun] (formal or technical) mentioned before, in an earlier sentence: *The aforementioned person was seen acting suspiciously.* ▶ **wyżej wymieniony**

⚷ **afraid** /əˈfreɪd/ adj. [not before a noun] **1 be afraid (of sb/sth)**; **be afraid (of doing sth/to do sth)** to have or show fear; to be frightened: *Are you afraid of dogs?* ◇ *Ben is afraid of going out after dark.* ◇ *I was too afraid to answer the door.* ▶ **bać się 2 be afraid (that ...)**; **be afraid (of doing sth)** to be worried about sth: *We were afraid that you would be angry.* ◇ *to be afraid of offending somebody* ▶ **obawiać się 3 be afraid for sb/sth** to be worried that sb/sth will be harmed, lost, etc.: *When I saw the gun I was afraid for my life.* ▶ **lękać się o kogoś/coś**

> Por. **afraid** z **frightened. Afraid** występuje tylko po rzeczowniku, podczas gdy **frightened** może występować zarówno przed rzeczownikiem, jak i po nim: *a frightened animal* ◇ *The animal was afraid/frightened.*

IDM **I'm afraid (that ...)** (used for saying politely that you are sorry about sth): *I'm afraid I can't come on Sunday.* ◇ *'Is the factory going to close?' 'I'm afraid so.'* ◇ *'Is this seat free?' 'I'm afraid not/it isn't.'* ▶ **obawiam się (że)**

afresh /əˈfreʃ/ adv. (formal) again, in a new way: *to start afresh* ▶ **od nowa**

ˌ**African Aˈmerican** noun [C] an American citizen whose family was originally from Africa ▶ **Afroamerykan-in/ka**

■ **African American** adj. ▶ **afroamerykański**

Afro-Caribbean /ˌæfrəʊ kærəˈbiːən/ noun [C] a person whose family came originally from Africa, and who was born or whose parents were born in the Caribbean ▶ **Afrokaraib/ka**

■ **Afro-Caribbean** adj. ▶ **afrokaraibski**

⚷ **after**[1] /ˈɑːftə(r); US ˈæf-/ prep. **1** at a later time; following sth in time: *Ian phoned just after 6 o'clock.* ◇ *the week after next* ◇ *I hope to arrive some time after lunch.* ◇ *I went out yesterday morning, and **after that*** (potem) *I was at home all day.* ▶ **po 2 ...after...** repeated many times or continuing for a long time: ***day after day** of hot weather* ◇ *I've told the children **time after time*** (tyle razy dzieciom powtarzam) *not to do that.* ▶ **za 3** following or behind sb/sth: *Shut the door after you.* ◇ *After you.* (w przejściu, puszczając kogoś przodem) Proszę bardzo. ◇ *C comes after B in the alphabet.* ▶ **za**; **po 4** as a result of sth: *After the way he behaved, I won't invite him here again.* ▶ **po 5 be after sb/sth** to be looking for or trying to catch or get sb/sth: *Nicky is after a job in advertising.* ◇ *The police were after him.* ▶ **poszukiwać**, **ścigać 6** (used when sb/sth is given the name of another person or thing): *We called our son William after his grandfather.* ▶ **po kimś**

IDM **after all 1** (used when sth is different in reality to what sb expected or thought): *So you decided to come after all!* ▶ **w końcu**, **jednak 2** (used for reminding sb of a certain fact): *She can't understand. After all, she's only two.* ▶ **w końcu**

after[2] /ˈɑːftə(r); US ˈæf-/ conj. at a time later than sth: *They arrived at the station after the train had left.* ▶ **po**

after[3] /ˈɑːftə(r); US ˈæf-/ adv. at a later time: *That was in April. Soon after, I heard that he was ill.* ◇ *They lived happily ever after.* Żyli długo i szczęśliwie. ▶ **potem** ⓘ Na końcu zdania zwykle używa się słowa **afterwards**, a nie **after**: *We played tennis and then went to Angela's house afterwards.*

ˈ**after-effect** noun [C] an unpleasant result of sth that comes some time later ▶ **następstwo** (*nieprzyjemne*) ➲ look at **effect**, **side effect**

afterlife /ˈɑːftəlaɪf; US ˈæf-/ noun [sing.] a life that some people believe exists after death ▶ **życie po życiu**

aftermath /ˈɑːftəmæθ; -mɑːθ; US ˈæftər-/ noun [sing.] a situation that is the result of an important or unpleasant event: *A lot of rebuilding took place* ***in the aftermath of*** *the war.* ▶ **następstwo**

afternoon /ˌɑːftəˈnuːn; US ˌæf-/ noun [C,U] the part of a day between midday and about 6 o'clock: *I'll see you tomorrow afternoon.* ◇ *What are you doing this afternoon?* ◇ *I studied all afternoon.* ◇ *I usually go for a walk* ***in the afternoon.*** ◇ *He goes swimming every afternoon.* ◇ *She arrived at 4 o'clock in the afternoon.* ◇ *Tom works two afternoons a week.* ◇ *Are you busy* ***on Friday afternoon?*** ◇ *afternoon tea* podwieczorek ▶ **popołudnie** ➲ note at **morning**
IDM **good afternoon** (used when you see sb for the first time in the afternoon) ▶ **dzień dobry** ⓘ Często mówi się tylko **Afternoon**: *'Good afternoon, Mrs Davies.' 'Afternoon, Jack.'*

afters /ˈɑːftəz; US ˈæf-/ noun [U] (Brit., informal) a sweet dish that you eat at the end of a meal ▶ **deser** ➲ look at **dessert**, **pudding**, **sweet**

aftershave /ˈɑːftəʃeɪv; US ˈæf-/ noun [U,C] a liquid with a pleasant smell that men put on their faces after shaving ▶ **płyn po goleniu**

aftertaste /ˈɑːftəteɪst; US ˈæf-/ noun [sing.] a taste (usually an unpleasant one) that stays in your mouth after you have eaten or drunk sth ▶ **posmak**

afterthought /ˈɑːftəθɔːt; US ˈæf-/ noun [C, usually sing.] something that you think of or add to sth else at a later time: *He did the shopping, and then bought some flowers on the way home* ***as an afterthought*** (po namyśle). ▶ **namysł**, **refleksja**

afterwards /ˈɑːftəwədz; US ˈæf-/ (US also **afterward**) adv. at a later time: *He was taken to hospital and died shortly afterwards.* ◇ *Afterwards, I realized I'd made a terrible mistake.* ▶ **później**, **potem**

again /əˈgen; əˈgeɪn/ adv. **1** once more; another time: *I'll phone again later.* ◇ *Could you say that again* (powtórzyć), *please?* ◇ *Don't ever do that again!* Nigdy więcej tego nie rób! ▶ **jeszcze raz**, (*zakaz*) **więcej** ⓘ Czasownik, po którym występuje **again** często tłumaczy się czasownikiem z przedrostkiem „prze-", który wówczas oznacza powtórzenie czynności: *Write the letter out again.* (Przepisz list.) **2** in the place or condition that sb/sth was in before: *It's great to be home again.* ◇ *I hope you'll soon be well again.* ▶ **znowu 3** in addition to sth: *'Is that enough?' 'No, I'd like* ***half as much again*** (jeszcze połowę), *please'.* ▶ **jeszcze**
IDM **again and again** many times: *He said he was sorry again and again, but she wouldn't listen.* ▶ **wielokrotnie**
then/there again (used to say that sth you have just said may not happen or be true): *She might pass her test, but then again she might not.* ▶ **ale z drugiej strony**, **ale przecież**
yet again → YET

against /əˈgenst; əˈgeɪnst/ prep. **1** being an opponent to sb/sth in a game, competition, etc., or an enemy of sb/sth in a war or fight: *We played football against a school from another district.* ▶ **z**, **przeciw 2** not agreeing with or supporting sb/sth: *Are you for or against the plan?* ◇ *She felt that everybody was against her.* ▶ **przeciwko** OPP **for 3** what a law, rule, etc. says you must not do: *It's* ***against the law*** *to buy cigarettes before you are sixteen.* ▶ **wbrew 4** in order to protect yourself from sb/sth: *Take these pills as a precaution against malaria.* ▶ **przed** (*np. chorobą, zimnem*) **5** in the opposite direction to sth: *We had to cycle against the wind* (pod wiatr). ▶ **przeciw 6** touching sb/sth for support: *I put the ladder against the wall.* ▶ **przy**; **o**

agate /ˈægət/ noun [U,C] a hard stone with bands or areas of colour, used in jewellery ▶ **agat**

age[1] /eɪdʒ/ noun **1** [C,U] the length of time that sb has lived or that sth has existed: *Ali is seventeen* ***years of age.*** Ali ma siedemnaście lat. ◇ *She left school* ***at the age of*** *sixteen.* ◇ *Children of all ages will enjoy this film.* ◇ *He needs some friends of his own age.* ▶ **wiek**

> Pytając o czyjś wiek, zazwyczaj mówimy: *How old is she?* Odpowiedź może brzmieć: *She's eighteen* albo: *She's eighteen years old*, (ale nie ~~*She's eighteen years*~~). Oto kilka przykładów mówienia o wieku: *I'm nearly nineteen.* ◇ *a girl of nineteen* ◇ *an eighteen-year-old girl* ◇ *The robber is of medium height and aged about 16 or 17.*

2 [C,U] a particular period in sb's life: *a problem that often develops in* ***middle age*** ◇ *Her sons will look after her in her* ***old age.*** ▶ **wiek 3** [C] a particular period of history: *the computer age* ◇ *the history of art through the ages* ▶ **wiek**, **era 4** [U] the state of being old: *a face lined with age* ◇ *The doctor said she* ***died of old age.*** ▶ **wiek**, **starość** ➲ look at **youth 5** (**ages**) [pl.] (informal) a very long time: *We had to wait (for) ages at the hospital.* ◇ *It's ages since I've done any exercise.* ▶ **(strasznie) długo**
IDM **at a tender age; at the tender age of...** → TENDER[1]
the age of consent the age at which sb can legally agree to have sex ▶ **pełnoletność** (*prawna do rozpoczęcia współżycia seksualnego*)
come of age to become an adult in law: *My father gave me a watch when I came of age.* ▶ **osiągnąć pełnoletność**
feel your age → FEEL[1]
under age not old enough by law to do sth ▶ **nieletni**

age[2] /eɪdʒ/ verb [I,T] (**ageing** or **aging**; pt, pp **aged** /eɪdʒd/) to become or look old; to cause sb to look old: *My father seems to have aged a lot recently.* ◇ *I could see her illness had aged her.* ▶ **starzeć się**; **postarzać (kogoś)**

aged 1 /eɪdʒd/ adj. [not before a noun] of the age mentioned: *The woman, aged 26, was last seen at Victoria Station.* ▶ **w wieku 2** (**the aged**) /ˈeɪdʒɪd/ noun [pl.] very old people: *services for the sick and the aged* ▶ **starsi ludzie**

ˈage group noun [C] people of about the same age: *This club is very popular with the 20-30 age group.* ▶ **przedział wieku**, **grupa wiekowa**

ageing (especially US **aging**) /ˈeɪdʒɪŋ/ noun [U] the process of growing old: *signs of ageing* ▶ **starzenie się**
■ **ageing** adj. [usually before a noun] becoming older and usually less useful, safe, healthy, etc.: *an ageing rock star* ◇ *ageing* (przestarzały) *equipment* ▶ **starzejący się**

ageism (US also **agism**) /ˈeɪdʒɪzəm/ noun [U] unfair treatment of people because they are considered too old ▶ **dyskryminacja z powodu wieku**
■ **ageist** (US also **agist**) /-ɪst/ **1** adj. ▶ **dyskryminujący kogoś z powodu wieku 2** noun [C] ▶ **osoba dyskryminująca kogoś z powodu wieku**

ageless /ˈeɪdʒləs/ adj. (literary) **1** never looking old or never seeming to grow old: *Her beauty appeared ageless.* ▶ **wiecznie młody** SYN **timeless 2** existing for ever; impossible to give an age to: *the ageless mystery of the universe* ▶ **wieczny** SYN **timeless**

ˈage limit noun [C] the oldest or youngest age at which you are allowed to do sth: *the* ***upper/lower age limit*** ▶ **granica wieku**

agency /ˈeɪdʒənsi/ noun [C] (pl. **agencies**) **1** a business that provides a particular service: *an advertising agency* ▶ **agencja 2** (US) a government department: *the Central Intelligence Agency* ▶ **agencja**, **urząd**

agenda /əˈdʒendə/ noun [C] a list of matters that need to be discussed or dealt with: *The first item* ***on the agenda***

at the meeting will be security. ◇ *The government have* ***set an agenda*** *for reform over the next ten years.* ▶ **porządek dzienny**

🔑**agent** /ˈeɪdʒənt/ noun [C] **1** a person whose job is to do business for a company or for another person: *Our company's agent in Rio will meet you at the airport.* ◇ *Most actors and musicians have their own agents.* ◇ *a travel agent* ◇ *an estate agent* ▶ **agent/ka**, **przedstawiciel/ka 2** = SECRET AGENT

aggravate /ˈæɡrəveɪt/ verb [T] **1** to make sth worse or more serious: *She aggravated her bad back by lifting a table.* ▶ **pogarszać 2** (informal) to make sb angry or annoyed: *What aggravates me is that she never listens.* ▶ **denerwować**

■ **aggravation** /ˌæɡrəˈveɪʃn/ noun [C,U] ▶ **pogorszenie**

aggregate /ˈæɡrɪɡət/ noun

IDM **on aggregate** in total: *Our team won 3-1 on aggregate.* ▶ **w sumie**

aggression /əˈɡreʃn/ noun [U] **1** angry feelings or behaviour that make you want to attack other people: *People often react to this kind of situation with fear or aggression.* ▶ **agresja 2** the act of starting a fight or war without reasonable cause ▶ **agresja**

🔑**aggressive** /əˈɡresɪv/ adj. **1** ready or likely to fight or argue: *Some people get aggressive after drinking alcohol.* ▶ **agresywny 2** using or showing force or pressure in order to succeed: *an aggressive salesman* ▶ **natarczywy**

■ **aggressively** adv. ▶ **agresywnie**; **natarczywie**

aggressor /əˈɡresə(r)/ noun [C] a person or country that attacks sb/sth or starts fighting first ▶ **agresor**, **napastni-k/czka**

aggrieved /əˈɡriːvd/ adj. (formal) upset or angry: *I felt aggrieved that I was not chosen for the team.* ▶ **dotknięty**

aggro /ˈæɡrəʊ/ noun [U] (Brit., informal) **1** violent aggressive behaviour: *Don't give me any aggro or I'll call the police.* ▶ **agresja**, **agresywne zachowanie 2** problems and difficulties that are annoying: *I had a lot of aggro at the bank.* ▶ **zamieszanie**

aghast /əˈɡɑːst; US əˈɡæst/ adj. [not before a noun] **aghast (at sth)** filled with great fear and shock when you see or hear sth: *She stared aghast at the amount of blood.* ▶ **przerażony** SYN **horrified**

agile /ˈædʒaɪl; US ˈædʒl/ adj. able to move quickly and easily: *Monkeys are extremely agile.* ▶ **zwinny**, **ruchliwy**, **sprawny**

■ **agility** /əˈdʒɪləti/ noun [U]: *This sport is a test of both physical and mental agility.* ▶ **sprawność**

aging, **agism**, **agist** = AGEING, AGEISM, AGEIST

agitate /ˈædʒɪteɪt/ verb [I] **agitate (for/against sth)** to make other people feel very strongly about sth so that they want to help you achieve it: *to agitate for reform* ▶ **agitować**

agitated /ˈædʒɪteɪtɪd/ adj. worried or excited ▶ **zdenerwowany**

agitation /ˌædʒɪˈteɪʃn/ noun **1** [U] worry and anxiety that you show by behaving in a nervous way ▶ **zdenerwowanie 2** [U,C] **agitation (for/against sth)** public protest in order to achieve political change ▶ **agitacja**

AGM /ˌeɪ dʒiː ˈem/ abbr. (especially Brit.) **Annual General Meeting**; an important meeting which the members of an organization hold once a year ▶ **doroczne walne zgromadzenie**

agnostic /æɡˈnɒstɪk/ noun [C] a person who is not sure if God exists or not ▶ **agnosty-k/czka**

■ **agnostic** adj. ▶ **agnostyczny**

🔑**ago** /əˈɡəʊ/ adv. in the past; back in time from now: *Paul left ten minutes ago.* ◇ *That was* ***a long time ago.*** ◇ ***How long ago*** (jak dawno temu) *did it happen?* ▶ (*okoliczniki czasu*) **temu**

> **Ago** występuje w zdaniach w czasie *simple past*, a nie w *present perfect*: *I arrived in Britain three months ago.* Por. **ago** z **before. Ago** znaczy „temu", a **before** „przedtem" (tj. przed konkretnym momentem w przeszłości): *She married him a year ago.* ◇ *She had left her first husband six years before.* ➲ note at **during**, **since**

agonize (also -ise) /ˈæɡənaɪz/ verb [I] to worry or think about sth for a long time: *to agonize over a difficult decision* ▶ **trapić się**, **dręczyć się**

agonized (also -ised) /ˈæɡənaɪzd/ adj. showing extreme pain or worry: *an agonized cry* ▶ **pełen boleści/zmartwienia**

agonizing (also -ising) /ˈæɡənaɪzɪŋ/ adj. causing extreme worry or pain: *an agonizing choice* ◇ *an agonizing headache* ▶ **dręczący**, **rozdzierający**

agony /ˈæɡəni/ noun [C,U] (pl. **agonies**) great pain or suffering: *to be/scream in agony* ▶ **męczarnia**, **agonia**

ˈ**agony aunt** (masc. ˈ**agony uncle**) (US adˈvice **columnist**) noun [C] a person who writes in a newspaper or magazine giving advice in reply to people's letters about their personal problems ▶ **osoba odpowiadająca na listy czytelników**

agoraphobia /ˌæɡərəˈfəʊbiə/ noun [U] fear of being in public places where there are a lot of people ▶ **chorobliwy lęk przestrzeni**

■ **agoraphobic** adj. ▶ **cierpiący na chorobliwy lęk przestrzeni**

🔑**agree** /əˈɡriː/ verb **1** [I] **agree (with sb/sth)**; **agree (that ...)** to have the same opinion as sb/sth: *'I think we should talk to the manager about this.' 'Yes, I agree.'* ◇ *I agree with Paul.* ◇ *Do you agree that we should travel by train?* ◇ *I'm afraid I don't agree.* ▶ **zgadzać się** OPP **disagree 2** [I] **agree (to sth/to do sth)** to say yes to sth: *I asked my boss if I could go home early and she agreed.* ◇ *Alkis has agreed to lend me his car for the weekend.* ▶ **wyrażać zgodę** OPP **refuse 3** [I,T] **agree (to do sth)**; **agree (on) sth** to make an arrangement or decide sth with sb: *They agreed to meet the following day.* ◇ *Can we agree on a price?* ◇ *We agreed a price of £500.* ▶ **umawiać się**, **zgadzać się 4** [I] **agree with sth** to think that sth is right: *I don't agree with experiments on animals.* ▶ **zgadzać się (na coś)**, **popierać 5** [I] to be the same as sth: *The two accounts of the accident do not agree.* ▶ **wykazywać zgodność**

IDM **not agree with sb** (used about food) to make sb feel ill ▶ (*jedzenie*) **zaszkodzić**

agreeable /əˈɡriːəbl/ adj. **1** pleasant; nice ▶ **miły**, **sympatyczny** OPP **disagreeable 2** [not before a noun] (formal) **be agreeable (to sth)** to be ready to agree: *If you are agreeable, we would like to visit your offices on 21 May.* ▶ **zgadzać się**

■ **agreeably** /-əbli/ adv.: *I was agreeably surprised by the film.* ▶ **przyjemnie**; **mile**

🔑**agreement** /əˈɡriːmənt/ noun **1** [C] a contract or decision that two or more people have made together: *Please sign the agreement and return it to us.* ◇ *The leaders* ***reached an agreement*** *after five days of talks.* ◇ *We never* ***break an agreement.*** ▶ **porozumienie**, **umowa 2** [U] the state of agreeing with sb/sth: *She nodded her head in agreement.* ◇ *We* ***are totally in agreement with*** *what you have said.* ▶ **zgoda** OPP **disagreement**

agriculture /ˈæɡrɪkʌltʃə(r)/ noun [U] keeping animals and growing crops for food; farming ▶ **rolnictwo**

■ **agricultural** /ˌæɡrɪˈkʌltʃərəl/ adj. ▶ **rolniczy**

aground /əˈɡraʊnd/ adv. if a ship **runs/goes aground**, it touches the ground in water that is not deep enough and it cannot move: *The oil tanker* ***ran/went aground*** (osiadł na mieliźnie) *off the Spanish coast.* ▶ **na mieliźnie**

■ **aground** adj. [not before a noun] ▶ **na mieliźnie**

ah /ɑː/ interj. (used for expressing surprise, pleasure, understanding, etc.): *Ah, there you are.* ▶ **ach!**

aha /ɑːˈhɑː/ interj. (used when you suddenly find or understand sth): *Aha! Now I understand.* ▶ **aha!**

ahead /əˈhed/ adv. **ahead (of sb/sth) 1** in front of sb/sth: *I could see the other car about half a mile ahead of us.* ◇ *The path ahead looked narrow and steep.* ◇ *Look straight ahead and don't turn round!* ▶ **przed, z/do przodu 2** before or more advanced than sb/sth: *Inga and Nils arrived a few minutes ahead of us.* ◇ *London is about five hours ahead of New York.* ◇ *The Japanese are* ***way ahead*** *of us* (prześcignęli nas) *in their research.* ▶ **przed, do przodu 3** into the future: *He's got a difficult time ahead of him.* ◇ *We must* ***think ahead*** (z wyprzedzeniem) *and make a plan.* ▶ **przed; naprzód 4** winning in a game, competition, etc.: *The goal* ***put*** *Italy 2-1* ***ahead*** *at half-time.* ▶ **na prowadzenie** ➲ look at **behind**
IDM **ahead of your time** so modern that people do not understand you ▶ **wyprzedzający swoją epokę**
streets ahead → STREET

aid[1] /eɪd/ noun **1** [U] money, food, etc. that is sent to a country or to people in order to help them: *We sent aid to the earthquake victims.* ◇ *economic aid* ▶ **pomoc 2** [U] help: *to walk* ***with the aid of*** *a stick* ◇ *He had to* ***go to the aid of*** *a child* (przyjść z pomocą dziecku) *in the river.* ▶ **pomoc** ➲ look at **first aid 3** [C] a person or thing that helps you: *a hearing aid* aparat słuchowy ◇ *dictionaries and other study aids* ▶ **pomoc; pomocni-k/ca**
IDM **in aid of sb/sth** in order to collect money for sb/sth, especially for a charity: *a concert in aid of Children in Need* ▶ **na rzecz kogoś/czegoś**

aid[2] /eɪd/ verb [T] (formal) to help sb/sth: *Sleep aids recovery from illness.* ▶ **pomagać**
IDM **aid and abet** to help sb to do sth that is not allowed by law ▶ **współuczestniczyć** (*w przestępstwie*)

aide /eɪd/ noun [C] a person who helps another person, especially a politician, in their job ▶ **dorad-ca/czyni**

AIDS (also **Aids**) /eɪdz/ noun [U] **Acquired Immune Deficiency Syndrome**; an illness which destroys the body's ability to fight infection: *He was HIV positive for three years before developing full-blown AIDS.* ◇ *to contract AIDS* ◇ *the AIDS virus* ▶ **AIDS**

ailing /ˈeɪlɪŋ/ adj. not in good health; weak: *an ailing economy* ▶ **chory; kulejący**

ailment /ˈeɪlmənt/ noun [C] (formal) any illness that is not very serious ▶ **choroba**

aim[1] /eɪm/ noun **1** [C] something that you intend to do; a purpose: *Our aim is to open offices in Paris and Rome before the end of the year.* ◇ *His only aim in life is to make money.* ▶ **cel 2** [U] the act of pointing sth at sb/sth before trying to hit them or it with it: *She picked up the gun,* ***took aim*** *and fired.* ◇ *Jo's aim was good and she hit the target.* ◇ *Take aim* (wyceluj) *– fire!* ▶ **cel**

aim[2] /eɪm/ verb **1** [I] **aim to do sth; aim at/for sth** to intend to do or achieve sth: *We aim to leave after breakfast.* ◇ *The company is aiming at a 25% increase in profit.* ◇ *You should always aim for perfection in your work.* ▶ **zamierzać, dążyć 2** [I,T] **aim (sth) (at sb/sth)** to point or direct a weapon, a shot, a kick, etc. at sb/sth: *She aimed (the gun) at the target and fired.* ▶ **celować 3** [T] **aim sth at sb/sth** to direct sth at a particular person or group: *The advertising campaign is aimed at young people.* ▶ **kierować do kogoś/czegoś**
IDM **be aimed at sth/doing sth** to be intended to achieve sth: *The new laws are aimed at reducing heavy traffic in cities.* ▶ **mieć coś na celu**

aimless /ˈeɪmləs/ adj. having no purpose: *an aimless discussion* ▶ **bezcelowy**
■ **aimlessly** adv. ▶ **bezcelowo**

ain't /eɪnt/ (informal) short for **am not; is not; are not; has not; have not** ℹ Wyrażenie **ain't** uważane jest za niepoprawne.

air[1] /eə(r)/ noun **1** [U] the mixture of gases that surrounds the earth and that people, animals and plants breathe: *the pure mountain air* ◇ *Open a window – I need some* ***fresh air.*** ▶ **powietrze 2** [U] the space around and above things: *to throw a ball high* ***into the air*** ◇ ***in the open air*** na wolnym powietrzu ▶ **powietrze 3** [U] travel or transport in an aircraft: *to travel* ***by air*** (samolotem) ◇ *an air ticket* bilet lotniczy ▶ **droga powietrzna, lot 4** [sing.] **an air (of sth)** the particular feeling or impression that is given by sb/sth: *She has a confident air.* ▶ **wrażenie; atmosfera**
IDM **a breath of fresh air** → BREATH
clear the air → CLEAR[2]
be in the air to probably be going to happen soon: *A feeling of change was in the air.* ▶ **zanosić się na coś, wisieć w powietrzu**
in the open air → OPEN[1]
be on (the) air to send out programmes on the radio or TV: *This radio station is on the air 24 hours a day.* ▶ **nadawać**
vanish, etc. into thin air → THIN[1]

air[2] /eə(r)/ verb **1** [I,T] to put clothes, etc. in a warm place or outside in the fresh air to make sure they are completely dry; to become dry in this way: *Put the duvet outside to air.* ▶ **wietrzyć i suszyć (się) 2** [I,T] to make a room, etc. fresh by letting air into it; to become fresh in this way: *Open the window to air the room.* ▶ **wietrzyć (się) 3** [T] to tell people what you think about sth: *The discussion gave people a chance to* ***air their views.*** ▶ **wypowiadać (publicznie), przewentylować** (*np. kwestię*)
■ **airing** /ˈeərɪŋ/ noun [sing.] **1** the expression or discussion of opinions in front of a group of people: *an opportunity to give your views an airing* ◇ *The subject got a thorough airing in the British press.* ▶ **omówienie, dyskusja 2** the act of allowing warm air to make clothes, beds, etc. fresh and dry: *to give the sheets/blankets/clothes an airing* ▶ **przewietrzanie i suszenie**

airbag /ˈeəbæɡ/ noun [C] a device in a car that fills with air if there is an accident. It protects the people sitting in the front. ▶ **poduszka powietrzna**

airbase /ˈeəbeɪs/ noun [C] an airport for military aircraft ▶ **baza lotnicza**

ˈair bed (especially US **ˈair mattress**) noun [C] a large plastic or rubber bag that can be filled with air and used as a bed ▶ **materac nadmuchiwany**

airborne /ˈeəbɔːn/ adj. flying in the air: *Five minutes after getting on the plane we were airborne.* ▶ (*unoszący się*) **w powietrzu**

airbrush /ˈeəbrʌʃ/ noun [C] an artist's tool for spraying paint onto a surface, that works by air pressure ▶ **pistolet natryskowy**
■ **airbrush** verb [T] **airbrush sth (out)** to paint sth with an **airbrush**; to change a detail in a photograph with an **airbrush**: *an airbrushed photograph of a model* ◇ *Somebody had been airbrushed out of the picture.* ▶ **malować pistoletem natryskowym**

ˈair conditioner noun [C] a machine that cools and dries air ▶ **klimatyzator**

ˈair conditioning noun [U] the system that keeps the air in a room, building, etc. cool and dry ▶ **klimatyzacja**
■ **ˈair-conditioned** adj. ▶ **klimatyzowany**

aircraft /ˈeəkrɑːft; US -kræft/ noun [C] (pl. **aircraft**) any vehicle that can fly in the air, for example a plane ▶ **samolot** ➲ picture on **page A6**

ˈaircraft carrier noun [C] a ship that carries military aircraft and that has a long flat area where they can take off and land ▶ **lotniskowiec**

airdrop /ˈeədrɒp/ noun [C] the act of dropping supplies, soldiers, etc. from an aircraft by **parachute**: *The UN has begun making airdrops of food to refugees.* ▶ **zrzut na spadochronie** (*np. żywności*)
■ **airdrop** verb [T] (**airdropping**; **airdropped**) ▶ **zrzucać na spadochronie** (*np. żywność*)

airfare /ˈeəfeə(r)/ noun [C] the money that you pay to travel by plane ▶ **cena biletu lotniczego**

airfield /ˈeəfiːld/ noun [C] an area of land where aircraft can land or take off. An **airfield** is smaller than an airport. ▶ **lądowisko**

ˈair force noun [C, with sing. or pl. verb] the part of a country's military organization that fights in the air ▶ **lotnictwo wojskowe** ➲ note at **war** ➲ look at **army**, **navy**

ˈair freshener noun [C, U] a substance or device for making a place smell more pleasant ▶ **odświeżacz powietrza**

airhead /ˈeəhed/ noun [C] (informal) a stupid person ▶ **przygłup**

ˈair hostess noun [C] (old-fashioned) a woman who looks after the passengers on a plane ▶ **stewardesa** ➲ look at **cabin crew**, **flight attendant**

ˈairing cupboard noun [C] a warm cupboard that you put clothes, etc. in to make sure they are completely dry after being washed ▶ **szafka do wietrzenia i suszenia odzieży**

airless /ˈeələs/ adj. not having enough fresh air: *The room was hot and airless.* ▶ **duszny**

airlift /ˈeəlɪft/ noun [C] an operation to take people, soldiers, food, etc. to or from an area by aircraft, especially in an emergency or when roads are closed or dangerous ▶ **ewakuacja lotnicza**; **dostawa żywności i leków drogą lotniczą** (*np. do miejsc katastrofy*)
■ **airlift** verb [T]: *Two casualties **were airlifted to safety**.* ▶ **ewakuować ludność drogą lotniczą**; **dostarczać żywność/leki drogą lotniczą**

airline /ˈeəlaɪn/ noun [C] a company that provides regular flights for people or goods in aircraft ▶ **linia lotnicza**

airliner /ˈeəlaɪnə(r)/ noun [C] a large plane that carries passengers ▶ **samolot pasażerski**

airmail /ˈeəmeɪl/ noun [U] the system for sending letters, packages, etc. by plane: *I sent the parcel (by) airmail.* ▶ **poczta lotnicza**

ˈair mattress (especially US) = AIR BED

airplane (US) = AEROPLANE

🔑 **airport** /ˈeəpɔːt/ noun [C] a place where aircraft can land and take off and that has buildings for passengers to wait in ▶ **lotnisko** ➲ note at **plane**

ˈair raid noun [C] an attack by military aircraft ▶ **nalot**

airsick /ˈeəsɪk/ adj. feeling sick or **vomiting** as a result of travelling on a plane ▶ (*osoba podróżująca samolotem*) **cierpiący na chorobę lokomocyjną** ➲ look at **carsick**, **seasick**, **travel-sick**

airspace /ˈeəspeɪs/ noun [U] the part of the sky that is above a country and that belongs to that country by law ▶ **przestrzeń powietrzna**

airstrip /ˈeəstrɪp/ (also ˈ**landing strip**) noun [C] a narrow piece of land where aircraft can take off and land ▶ **pas startowy/do lądowania**

airtight /ˈeətaɪt/ adj. that air cannot get into or out of ▶ **szczelny**

ˌair ˌtraffic conˈtroller noun [C] a person whose job is to organize routes for aircraft, and to tell pilots by radio when they can land and take off ▶ **kontroler ruchu powietrznego**

airwaves /ˈeəweɪvz/ noun [pl.] radio waves that are used in broadcasting radio and television: *A well-known voice **came over the airwaves**.* ▶ **fale radiowe**

airy /ˈeəri/ adj. (**airier**; **airiest**) having a lot of fresh air inside ▶ **przewiewny**

ˌairy-ˈfairy adj. (Brit., informal) not clear or practical ▶ **wydumany**, **niedorzeczny** ℹ Wyraża dezaprobatę.

aisle /aɪl/ noun [C] a passage between the rows of seats in a church, theatre, etc., or between rows of shelves in a large shop ▶ **przejście między rzędami krzeseł/ławek**

ajar /əˈdʒɑː(r)/ adj. [not before a noun] (used about a door) slightly open ▶ **uchylony**

aka /ˌeɪ keɪ ˈeɪ/ abbr. **also known as**: *Antonio Fratelli, aka 'Big Tony'* ▶ **alias**

akin /əˈkɪn/ adj. **akin to sth** similar to sth ▶ **pokrewny**

à la carte /ˌɑː lɑː ˈkɑːt/ adj., adv. (used about a meal in a restaurant) where each dish that is available has a separate price and there is not a fixed price for a complete meal ▶ (*wybieranie potraw*) **z jadłospisu**

🔑 **alarm¹** /əˈlɑːm/ noun **1** [U] a sudden feeling of fear or worry: *She jumped up **in alarm**.* ▶ **przerażenie 2** [sing.] a warning of danger: *A small boy saw the smoke and **raised the alarm**.* ▶ **alarm**, **sygnał ostrzegawczy 3** [C] a machine that warns you of danger, for example by ringing a loud bell: *The burglars **set off** the **alarm** when they broke the window.* ◇ *The **burglar alarm** went off at 4 a.m.* ◇ *a **fire alarm*** alarm pożarowy ◇ *a **smoke alarm*** czujnik pożarowy ▶ **urządzenie alarmowe 4** [C] = ALARM CLOCK
IDM **a false alarm** → FALSE

🔑 **alarm²** /əˈlɑːm/ verb [T] to make sb/sth feel suddenly frightened or worried ▶ **trwożyć**, **przerażać**

aˈlarm clock (also **alarm**) noun [C] a clock that you can set to make a noise at a particular time to wake you up: *She set the alarm clock for half past six.* ▶ **budzik**

🔑 **alarmed** /əˈlɑːmd/ adj. [not before a noun] **alarmed (at/by sth)** frightened or worried ▶ **zatrwożony**, **przerażony**

🔑 **alarming** /əˈlɑːmɪŋ/ adj. that makes you frightened or worried ▶ **zatrważający**
■ **alarmingly** adv. ▶ **zatrważająco**

alarmist /əˈlɑːmɪst/ adj. causing unnecessary fear and anxiety ▶ **alarmistyczny**, **panikarski** ℹ Często wyraża dezaprobatę.
■ **alarmist** noun [C] ▶ **alarmist(k)a**, **panika-rz/ra**

alas /əˈlæs/ interj. (formal) (used for expressing sadness about sth) ▶ **niestety**

albatross /ˈælbətrɒs/ noun [C] a very large white bird with long wings that lives in the Pacific and Southern Oceans ▶ **albatros**

albeit /ˌɔːlˈbiːɪt/ conj. (formal) although: *He finally agreed to come, albeit unwillingly.* ▶ **chociaż**

albino /ælˈbiːnəʊ; US -ˈbaɪn-/ noun [C] (pl. **albinos**) a person or an animal with very white skin, white hair and pink eyes ▶ **albinos/ka**

album /ˈælbəm/ noun [C] **1** a book in which you can keep stamps, photographs, etc. that you have collected ▶ **klaser**; **album 2** a collection of songs on one CD, tape, etc.: *The band are about to release a new album.* ▶ **płyta/kaseta** (*zawierająca nagrania jednego artysty*) ➲ note at **pop** ➲ look at **single**

🔑 **alcohol** /ˈælkəhɒl/ noun [U] **1** drinks such as beer, wine, etc. that can make people drunk: *He never drinks alcohol.* ▶ **napoje alkoholowe 2** the clear liquid in drinks such as beer and wine that can make you drunk: *low-alcohol beer* ▶ **alkohol**

alcoholic¹ /ˌælkəˈhɒlɪk/ adj. containing alcohol ▶ **alkoholowy** OPP **non-alcoholic** ⓘ Napoje bezalkoholowe nazywają się też **soft drinks**.

alcoholic² /ˌælkəˈhɒlɪk/ noun [C] a person who regularly drinks too much alcohol and cannot easily stop drinking ▶ **alkoholi-k/czka** ⓘ Abstynent/ka to **teetotaller**.

alcoholism /ˈælkəhɒlɪzəm/ noun [U] a medical condition that is caused by regularly drinking a large amount of alcohol and not being able to stop ▶ **alkoholizm**

alcove /ˈælkəʊv/ noun [C] a small area in a room where one part of the wall is further back than the rest of the wall ▶ **alkowa**

ale /eɪl/ noun [U,C] a type of beer ▶ **rodzaj piwa** ➲ note at **beer**

alert¹ /əˈlɜːt/ adj. **alert (to sth)** watching, listening, etc. for sth with all your attention: *Security guards must be alert at all times.* ◇ *to be alert to possible changes* ▶ **czujny, wyczulony (na coś)**

alert² /əˈlɜːt/ verb [T] **alert sb (to sth)** to warn sb of danger or a problem ▶ **ostrzegać (przed czymś)**

alert³ /əˈlɜːt/ noun [C] a warning of possible danger: *a bomb alert* ▶ **alarm, pogotowie**
IDM **on the alert (for sth)** ready or prepared for danger or an attack ▶ **w gotowości**, *(mieć się)* **na baczności**

ˈA level (also formal **adˈvanced level**) noun [C,U] (in Britain) the qualification that is needed if you want to go to university. It is made up of the AS and A2 level exams which are taken in the last two years of school or college. You usually take A levels in three subjects: *How many A levels have you got?* ◇ *I'm doing my A levels this summer.* ▶ **końcowy egzamin przedmiotowy w szkole średniej** *(odpowiednik matury z określonego przedmiotu)* ➲ look at **AS (level)**, **A2 (level)**, **GCSE**, **SCE**

algae /ˈældʒiː; ˈælgiː/ noun [pl., with sing. or pl. verb] very simple plants that grow mainly in water ▶ **alga**

algebra /ˈældʒɪbrə/ noun [U] a type of mathematics in which letters and symbols are used to represent numbers ▶ **algebra**

alias¹ /ˈeɪliəs/ adv. (used for giving sb's false name): *Norma Jean Baker, alias Marilyn Monroe* ▶ **inaczej (zwany)**

alias² /ˈeɪliəs/ noun [C] a false name, for example one that is used by a criminal: *Castorri is known to the police under several aliases.* ▶ **pseudonim**

alibi /ˈæləbaɪ/ noun [C] (pl. **alibis**) **an alibi (for sth)** evidence that proves that a person was in another place at the time of a crime and so could not have committed it ▶ **alibi**

alien¹ /ˈeɪliən/ adj. **1 alien (to sb)** very strange and completely different from your normal experience ▶ **obcy (komuś)** **2** of another country; foreign: *an alien land* ▶ **obcy**

alien² /ˈeɪliən/ noun [C] **1** (formal) a person who comes from another country ▶ **cudzoziem-iec/ka** **2** a creature that comes from another planet ▶ **przybysz z innej planety**

alienate /ˈeɪliəneɪt/ verb [T] **1** to make people feel that they cannot share your opinions any more: *The Prime Minister's new policies on defence have alienated many of his supporters.* ▶ **zrażać** **2 alienate sb (from sb/sth)** to make sb feel that they do not belong somewhere or are not part of sth ▶ **wyobcowywać**
■ **alienation** /ˌeɪliəˈneɪʃn/ noun [U] ▶ **zrażenie; wyobcowanie**

alight¹ /əˈlaɪt/ adj. [not before a noun] on fire; burning: *A cigarette **set** the petrol **alight*** (zapalił benzynę). ▶ **zapalony, płonący**

Alight może występować tylko po rzeczowniku, ale **burning** można postawić przed rzeczownikiem: *The whole building was alight.* ◇ *a burning building.*

alight² /əˈlaɪt/ verb [I] (formal) **alight (from sth)** to get off a bus, train, etc. ▶ **wysiadać**

align /əˈlaɪn/ verb [T] **align sth (with sth)** to arrange things in a straight line or so that they are parallel to sth else: *The mechanic aligned the wheels of the car* (ustawił zbieżność kół). ▶ **wyrównywać, ustawiać w szeregu**
PHR V **align yourself with sb/sth** to say that you support the opinions of a particular group, country, etc. ▶ **przyjmować zbieżne stanowisko** *(z czyimś stanowiskiem)* ➲ look at **non-aligned**

alignment /əˈlaɪnmənt/ noun **1** [U] arrangement in a straight line or parallel to sth else ▶ **wyrównanie, zbieżność** *(kół)* **2** [C,U] an agreement between political parties, countries, etc. to support the same thing ▶ **zbieżność stanowisk**

alike¹ /əˈlaɪk/ adj. [not before a noun] very similar: *The two children are very alike.* ▶ **podobny; jednakowy**

Alike może występować tylko po rzeczowniku, ale **similar-looking** można postawić przed rzeczownikiem: *The houses in this street are all alike.* ◇ *a street of similar-looking houses.*

alike² /əˈlaɪk/ adv. in the same way; equally: *We try to treat women and men alike in this company.* ◇ *The book is popular with adults and children alike.* ▶ **jednakowo**

alimony /ˈælɪməni; US -məʊni/ noun [U] money that you have to pay by law to your former wife or husband after getting divorced ▶ **alimenty**

ˈA-list adj. (used to describe a group of people who are famous, successful or important): *He only invited **A-list celebrities** to his party.* ▶ **dot. najbardziej znanych postaci z życia publicznego**

alive /əˈlaɪv/ adj. [not before a noun] **1** not dead; living: *The young woman was still alive when the ambulance reached the hospital.* ◇ *He **kept** the kitten **alive*** (utrzymał kociątko przy życiu) *by feeding it warm milk.* ▶ **żywy, żyjący**

Alive może występować tylko po rzeczowniku, ale **living** można postawić przed rzeczownikiem: *Are her parents still alive?* ◇ *Does she have any living relatives?*

2 continuing to exist: *Many old traditions are very much alive in this area of the country.* ▶ **żywy** **3** full of life: *In the evening the town really **comes alive*** (ożywa). ▶ **ożywiony**

alkali /ˈælkəlaɪ/ noun [C,U] a chemical substance that can burn skin when it is dissolved in water. An **alkali** has a **pH** value of more than 7. ▶ **zasada** ➲ look at **acid**
■ **alkaline** adj. ▶ **zasadowy**

all¹ /ɔːl/ determiner, pron. **1** every one of a group: *All (of) my children can swim.* ◇ *My children can all swim.* ◇ *She's read all (of) these books.* ◇ *She's read them all.* ◇ *The people at the meeting all voted against the plan.* ◇ *All of them voted against the plan.* ▶ **wszyscy, wszystkie, każdy** **2** the whole of a thing or of a period of time: *All (of) the food* (całe jedzenie) *has gone.* ◇ *They've eaten all of it.* ◇ *They've eaten it all.* ◇ *This money is all yours.* Te wszystkie pieniądze są twoje. ◇ *All of it is yours.* ◇ *all week/month/year* ◇ *He worked hard all his life.* ▶ **wszystko, cały** **3** everything that; the only thing that: *I wrote down all I could remember.* ◇ *All I've eaten today is one banana.* ▶ **wszystko**
IDM **above all** → ABOVE
after all → AFTER
for all 1 in spite of: *For all her wealth and beauty, she was never very happy.* ▶ **po/mimo** **2** (used to show that sth is not important or of no interest or value to you): ***For all I know**, he's probably remarried by now.* Jak dla

mnie, to on równie dobrze mógł się ponownie ożenić. ➲ note at **altogether**

in all in total: *There were ten of us in all.* ▶ **w sumie**

not all that... not very: *The film wasn't all that good.* ▶ **nie (tak/za) bardzo**

(not) at all in any way: *I didn't enjoy it at all.* ▶ **wcale (nie)** ℹ Można też powiedzieć **not at all** (proszę bardzo) w odpowiedzi na czyjeś podziękowanie.

all² /ɔːl/ adv. **1** completely; very: *He has lived all alone since his wife died.* ◇ *I didn't watch that programme – I forgot all about it.* ◇ *They got all excited about it.* ▶ **całkiem**, **zupełnie**, **bardzo 2** (in sport) for each side: *The score was two all.* ▶ **dla każdego/każdej ze stron**

IDM **all along** from the beginning: *I knew you were joking all along.* ▶ **od początku**

all the better, harder, etc. even better, harder, etc. than before: *It will be all the more difficult with two people missing.* ▶ **jeszcze** (*np. lepiej, trudniej*)

all/just the same → SAME

Allah /ˈælə/ noun [sing.] the Muslim name for God ▶ **Allach**

all-around (US) = ALL-ROUND

allay /əˈleɪ/ verb [T] (formal) to make sth less strong: *The director's optimistic speech **allayed** our **fears** that the company was in trouble.* ▶ **łagodzić**

the ˌ**all-ˈclear** noun [sing.] a signal telling you that a situation is no longer dangerous: *The doctor looked at my tests and **gave** me **the all-clear*** (powiedział, że niebezpieczeństwo minęło). ▶ **odwołanie alarmu**; (*przen.*) **droga wolna**

allege /əˈledʒ/ verb [T] (formal) to say that sb has done sth wrong, but without having any proof that this is true: *The woman alleged that Williams had attacked her with a knife.* ▶ **zarzucać**

■ **allegation** /ˌæləˈɡeɪʃn/ noun [C]: *to **make allegations** of police corruption* ▶ **zarzut** | **alleged** /əˈledʒd/ adj. [only before a noun]: *the alleged criminal* ▶ **domniemany** | **allegedly** /əˈledʒɪdli/ adv. ▶ **przypuszczalnie**

allegiance /əˈliːdʒəns/ noun [U,C] (formal) support for a leader, government, belief, etc.: *Many people **switched allegiance** and voted against the government.* ▶ **wierność, posłuszeństwo** SYN **loyalty**

allegory /ˈæləɡəri; US -ɡɔːri/ noun [C,U] (pl. **allegories**) a story, play, picture, etc. in which each character or event is a symbol representing an idea or a quality, such as truth, evil, death, etc.; the use of such symbols ▶ **alegoria**

■ **allegorical** /ˌæləˈɡɒrɪkl/ adj.: *an **allegorical figure/novel*** ▶ **alegoryczny**

ˌ**all-enˈcompassing** adj. (formal) including everything ▶ **wszechogarniający**

Allen key™ /ˈælən kiː/ (Brit.) (US ˈ**Allen wrench™**) noun [C] a small tool used for turning an **Allen screw** ▶ **klucz do wkrętów z sześciokątnym gniazdkiem**

ˈ**Allen screw™** noun [C] a screw with a hole that has six sides ▶ **wkręt z sześciokątnym gniazdkiem**

allergen /ˈælədʒən/ noun [C] a substance that causes an **allergy** ▶ **alergen**

allergic /əˈlɜːdʒɪk/ adj. **1 allergic (to sth)** having an **allergy**: *I'm allergic to cow's milk.* ▶ **uczulony 2** caused by an **allergy**: *an allergic reaction to house dust* ▶ **uczuleniowy**

allergy /ˈælədʒi/ noun [C] (pl. **allergies**) **an allergy (to sth)** a medical condition that makes you ill when you eat, touch or breathe sth that does not normally make other people ill: *an allergy to cats/shellfish/pollen* ▶ **uczulenie, alergia** ➲ note at **ill** ➲ look at **hay fever**

alleviate /əˈliːvieɪt/ verb [T] to make sth less strong or bad: *The doctor gave me an injection to alleviate the pain.* ▶ **ulżyć**

■ **alleviation** /əˌliːviˈeɪʃn/ noun [U] ▶ **ulga**

alley /ˈæli/ (also **alleyway** /ˈæliweɪ/) noun [C] a narrow passage between buildings ▶ **wąskie przejście**, **wąska uliczka**

alliance /əˈlaɪəns/ noun [C] an agreement between groups, countries, etc. to work together and support each other: *The two parties **formed an alliance**.* ▶ **sojusz** ➲ look at **ally**

allied adj. **1** /ˈælaɪd/ [only before a noun] (used about organizations, countries, etc.) having an agreement to work together and support each other: *allied forces* ▶ **sprzymierzony**, **połączony** (*np. umową*) **2** /əˈlaɪd/ **allied (to sth)** connected with; existing together with: *The newspaper is closely allied to the government.* ▶ **połączony**; **pokrewny**

alligator /ˈælɪɡeɪtə(r)/ noun [C] a large animal with a hard skin covered in scales, a long tail and a big mouth with sharp teeth. **Alligators** live in the lakes and rivers of America and China. ▶ **aligator** ➲ look at **crocodile**

ˌ**all-ˈin** adj. [only before a noun] including everything: *an all-in price* ▶ (*cena*) **łączny**

ˌ**all-inˈclusive** adj. including everything or everyone: *Our trips are all-inclusive* (w ceny naszych wycieczek wliczone są wszystkie opłaty) *– there are no hidden costs.* ▶ **zawierający wszystko/wszystkich**

alliteration /əˌlɪtəˈreɪʃn/ noun [U] (technical) the use of the same letter or sound at the beginning of words that are close together, as in *sing a song of sixpence* ▶ **aliteracja**

allocate /ˈæləkeɪt/ verb [T] **allocate sth (to/for sb/sth)** to give sth to sb as their share or to decide to use sth for a particular purpose: *The government has allocated half the budget for education.* ▶ **przydzielać**

■ **allocation** /ˌæləˈkeɪʃn/ noun [C,U] ▶ **przydział**

allot /əˈlɒt/ verb [T] (**allotting**; **allotted**) **allot sth (to sb/sth)** to give a share of work, time, etc. to sb/sth: *Different tasks were allotted to each member of the class.* ◇ *We all finished the exam in the allotted time.* ▶ **przydzielać**

allotment /əˈlɒtmənt/ noun [C] (Brit.) a small area of land in a town that you can rent for growing vegetables on ▶ **ogródek działkowy**

ˈ**all out** adj. using all your strength, etc.: *an all-out effort* ▶ **całkowity**

■ ˈ**all out** adv.: *We're going all out for the Cup.* ▶ **na całość**

allow /əˈlaʊ/ verb [T] **1 allow sb/sth to do sth**; **allow sth** to give permission for sb/sth to do sth or for sth to happen: *Children under eighteen are not allowed to buy alcohol.* ◇ *I'm afraid we don't allow people to bring dogs into this restaurant.* ◇ *Photography is not allowed* (nie wolno fotografować) *inside the cathedral.* ▶ **pozwalać 2 allow sb sth** to let sb have sth: *My contract allows me four weeks' holiday a year.* ▶ **przyznawać 3** to give permission for sb/sth to be or go somewhere: *No dogs allowed.* Zabrania się wprowadzania psów. ◇ *I'm only allowed out* (wolno mi wychodzić tylko) *on Friday and Saturday nights.* ▶ **pozwalać 4 allow sb/sth to do sth** to make sth possible: *Working part-time would allow me* (pozwoliłoby mi) *to spend more time with my family.* ▶ **pozwalać 5 allow sth (for sb/sth)** to provide money, time, etc. for sb/sth: *You should allow about 30 minutes for each question.* ▶ **przeznaczać**

PHR V **allow for sb/sth** to think about possible problems when you are planning sth and include extra time, money, etc. for them: *The journey should take about two hours, allowing for heavy traffic.* ▶ **uwzględniać**

Por. **allow, permit** i **let. Allow** można używać w formalnej i nieformalnej angielszczyźnie. Bardzo

często używana jest zwłaszcza strona bierna **to be allowed to. Permit** jest słowem formalnym, zwykle stosowanym tylko w pisanej angielszczyźnie.
Let często spotyka się w codziennej, mówionej angielszczyźnie. Mówi się **to allow sb to do sth**, a **to let sb do sth. Let** nie występuje w stronie biernej: *Visitors are not allowed/permitted to smoke in this area.* ◇ *Smoking is not allowed/permitted.* ◇ *I'm not allowed to smoke in my bedroom.* ◇ *My dad won't let me smoke in my bedroom.*

allowable /ə'laʊəbl/ adj. that is allowed, especially by law or by a set of rules ▶ **dozwolony, dopuszczalny**

allowance /ə'laʊəns/ noun [C] **1** an amount of money that you receive regularly to help you pay for sth that you need: *She receives an annual travel allowance in addition to her salary.* ▶ **zasiłek, dodatek** (*do pensji*) **2** an amount of sth that you are allowed: *Most flights have a 20 kg baggage allowance.* ▶ **przydział, dozwolona ilość 3** (especially US) = POCKET MONEY
IDM **make allowances for sb/sth** to judge a person or their actions in a kinder way than usual because they have a particular problem or disadvantage: *You really should make allowances for her. She's very inexperienced.* ▶ **być wyrozumiałym dla kogoś; brać coś pod uwagę**

alloy /'ælɔɪ/ noun [C,U] a metal that is formed by mixing two types of metal together, or by mixing metal with another substance: *Brass is an alloy of copper and zinc.* ▶ **stop**

⚷ **,all 'right** (also informal **alright** /ɔːl'raɪt/) adj., adv., interj. [not before a noun] **1** good enough: *Is everything all right?* ▶ **w porządku 2** safe and well: *I hope the children are all right.* ◇ *Do you feel all right?* ▶ **bezpieczny; zdrowy 3** (showing you agree to do what sb has asked): *'Can you get me some stamps?' 'Yes, all right.'* ▶ **zgoda** SYN for all meanings **OK**

Wyrażenia **That's all right** używa się w odpowiedzi na czyjeś podziękowanie: *'Thanks for the lift home.' 'That's (quite) all right* (proszę bardzo).*'* lub w odpowiedzi na czyjeś przeprosiny: *'I'm so sorry I'm late.' 'That's all right* (nic nie szkodzi).*'*

'all-round (US **,all-a'round**) adj. [only before a noun] able to do many different things well; good in many different ways: *a superb all-round athlete* ◇ *The school aims at the all-round development of the child.* ▶ **wszechstronny**

,all-'rounder noun [C] a person who can do many different things well ▶ **osoba o wszechstronnych umiejętnościach**

,All 'Saints' Day noun [C] a Christian festival in honour of the **saints**, held on 1 November ▶ **Dzień Wszystkich Świętych**

,All 'Souls' Day noun [C] a Christian festival in honour of the dead, held on 2 November ▶ **Zaduszki**

,all-terrain 'vehicle = ATV

'all-time adj. [only before a noun] (used when you are comparing things or saying how good or bad sth is) of any time: *one of the all-time great players* ◇ *Unemployment reached an all-time record of 3 million.* ◇ *Profits are at an* ***all-time high/low*** (na najwyższym/najniższym odnotowanym dotąd poziomie). ▶ **wszech czasów**

allude /ə'luːd/ verb [I] (formal) **allude to sb/sth** to speak about sb/sth in an indirect way ▶ **napomykać**
■ **allusion** /ə'luːʒn/ noun [C,U]: *He likes to* ***make allusions to*** *the size of his salary.* ▶ **napomknięcie**

allure /ə'lʊə(r)/ noun [U] (formal) the quality of being attractive and exciting: *the allure of the big city* ◇ *sexual allure* ▶ **urok**

alluring /ə'lʊərɪŋ/ adj. attractive in an exciting way: *an alluring smile* ▶ **ponętny, kuszący**
■ **alluringly** adv. ▶ **ponętnie, kusząco**

,all-wheel 'drive (especially US) = FOUR-WHEEL DRIVE

⚷ **ally**[1] /'ælaɪ/ noun [C] (pl. **allies**) **1** a country that has an agreement to support another country, especially in a war ▶ **sojusznik** ⮌ look at **alliance 2** a person who helps and supports you, especially when other people are against you: *the Prime Minister's political allies* ▶ **sprzymierzeniec**

⚷ **ally**[2] /ə'laɪ/ verb [T] (**allying**; **allies**; pt, pp **allied**) **ally (yourself) with sb/sth** to give your support to another group or country: *The prince allied himself with the Scots.* ▶ **sprzymierzać się z kimś/czymś**

almighty /ɔːl'maɪti/ adj. **1** having the power to do anything: *Almighty God* ▶ **wszechmogący 2** [only before a noun] (informal) very great: *Suddenly we heard the most almighty crash.* ▶ **przeogromny**

almond /'ɑːmənd/ noun [C] a flat pale nut ▶ **migdał**

⚷ **almost** /'ɔːlməʊst/ adv. nearly; not quite: *By 9 o'clock almost everybody had arrived.* ◇ *Careful! I almost fell into the water then!* ◇ *The film has almost finished.* ◇ *She almost always cycles to school.* ◇ *There's almost nothing left.* ◇ *Almost all the students passed the exam.* ▶ **prawie (że), niemal(że)** SYN **nearly**

aloe vera /,æləʊ 'vɪərə/ noun **1** [U] a substance which comes from a type of **aloe** (= a tropical plant), used in products such as skin creams ▶ **aloes 2** [C] the plant that this substance comes from ▶ **aloes**

⚷ **alone** /ə'ləʊn/ adj. [not before a noun], adv. **1** without any other person: *The old man lives alone.* ◇ *Are you alone? Can I speak to you for a moment?* ◇ *I don't like walking home alone after dark.* ▶ **sam, samotnie 2** [after a noun or pronoun] only: *You alone can help us.* ◇ *The rent alone takes up most of my salary.* ▶ **tylko (sam)**
IDM **go it alone** to start working on your own without the usual help: *He decided to leave the company and go it alone.* ▶ **zacząć pracować samodzielnie/na własny rachunek**
leave sb/sth alone → LEAVE[1]
let alone and certainly not: *We haven't decided where we're going yet, let alone booked the tickets.* ▶ **nie mówiąc już o czymś**

alone
Obydwa słowa **alone** i **lonely** oznaczają przede wszystkim, że nie jest się w towarzystwie innych ludzi. **Lonely** (US **lonesome**) może też oznaczać dokuczliwą samotność, czego **alone** zwykle nie sugeruje. **Alone** nie występuje przed rzeczownikiem. W znaczeniu **alone** można też stosować zwroty **on your own** i **by yourself**. Wyrażenia te są mniej formalne i częściej używa się ich w mówionej angielszczyźnie.

⚷ **along** /ə'lɒŋ/ prep. **1** from one end to or towards the other end of sth: *I walked slowly along the road* (tą ulicą). ◇ *David looked along the corridor* (popatrzył na koniec korytarza) *to see if anyone was coming.* ▶ **po** (*np. ulicy, drodze*), **wzdłuż 2** in a line that follows the side of sth long: *Wild flowers grew along both sides of the river.* ▶ **wzdłuż 3** at a particular point on or beside sth long: *Our house is about halfway along* (jest mniej więcej w połowie) *Hope Street.* ▶ **na, przy**
IDM **all along** → ALL[2]
along with sb/sth together with sb/sth ▶ **razem z kimś/czymś**
go along with sb/sth to agree with sb's ideas or plans: *I don't think I can go along with this scheme.* ▶ **zgadzać się z kimś/czymś**

■ **along** adv. **1** forward: *We moved along slowly with the crowd.* ▶ **naprzód 2** (informal) with sb: *We're going for a walk. Why don't you **come along** too?* ▶ **(razem) z (kimś)**

alongside /əˌlɒŋˈsaɪd/ prep., adv. **1** next to sb/sth or at the side of sth: *The boat moored alongside the quay.* ◇ *Nick caught up with me and rode alongside.* ▶ **obok, wzdłuż 2** together with sb/sth: *the opportunity to work alongside experienced musicians* ▶ **(razem) z**

aloof /əˈluːf/ adj. not friendly or interested in other people: *Her shyness made her seem aloof.* ◇ *The Emperor **kept himself aloof** from the people.* ▶ **trzymający się z daleka (od innych)** SYN **distant**

aloud /əˈlaʊd/ (also ˌ**out** ˈ**loud**) adv. in a normal speaking voice that other people can hear: *to read aloud from a book* ▶ **głośno, na głos** OPP **silently**

alphabet /ˈælfəbet/ noun [C] a set of letters in a fixed order that you use when you are writing a language: *There are 26 letters in the English alphabet.* ▶ **alfabet**

alphabetical /ˌælfəˈbetɪkl/ adj. arranged in the same order as the letters of the alphabet: *The names are listed **in alphabetical order**.* ▶ **alfabetyczny**
■ **alphabetically** /-kli/ adv. ▶ **alfabetycznie**

alphabetize (also -ise) /ˈælfəbətaɪz/ verb [T] to arrange a list of words in alphabetical order ▶ **układać alfabetycznie**

alpine /ˈælpaɪn/ adj. of or found in high mountains: *alpine flowers* ▶ **alpejski**

already /ɔːlˈredi/ adv. **1** (used for talking about sth that has happened before now or before a particular time in the past): *'Would you like some lunch?' 'No, I've already eaten, thanks.'* ◇ *We got there at 6.30 but Marsha had already left.* ◇ *Sita was already awake when I went into her room.* ▶ **już 2** (used in negative sentences and questions for expressing surprise) so early; as soon as this: *Have you finished already?* ◇ *Surely you're not going already!* ▶ **już**

alright (informal) = ALL RIGHT

Alsatian /ælˈseɪʃn/ (especially US ˌ**German** ˈ**Shepherd**) noun [C] a large dog with smooth hair, that is often trained to help the police or as a guard dog ▶ **owczarek niemiecki**

also /ˈɔːlsəʊ/ adv. [not with negative verbs] in addition; too: *He plays several instruments and also writes music.* ◇ *Bring summer clothing and also something warm to wear in the evenings.* ◇ *The food is wonderful, and also very cheap.* ▶ **też, także**
IDM **not only... (but) also** → NOT

> **also**
> **Too** i **as well** są mniej formalne niż **also** i bardzo często stosowane w mówionej angielszczyźnie. **Also** zwykle występuje przed głównym czasownikiem lub po **is**, **are**, **were** itp: *He also enjoys reading* ◇ *He has also been to Australia.* ◇ *He is also intelligent.* **Too** i **as well** zwykle stawia się na końcu zwrotu lub zdania: *I really love this song, and I liked the first one too/as well.*

altar /ˈɔːltə(r)/ noun [C] a high table that is the centre of a religious ceremony ▶ **ołtarz**

alter /ˈɔːltə(r)/ verb [I,T] to make sth different in some way, but without changing it completely; to become different: *We've altered our plan, and will now arrive at 7.00 instead of 8.00.* ◇ *The village seems to have altered very little in the last twenty years.* ▶ **zmieniać (się); przerabiać**

alteration /ˌɔːltəˈreɪʃn/ noun [C,U] **(an) alteration (to/in sth)** a small change in sb/sth: *We want to **make** a few **alterations** to the house before we move in.* ▶ **(drobna) zmiana**

alternate[1] /ˈɔːltəneɪt/ verb **1** [T] **alternate A with B** to cause two types of events or things to happen or follow regularly one after the other: *He alternated periods of work with periods of rest.* ▶ **zmieniać kolejno 2** [I] **alternate with sth**; **alternate between A and B** (used about two types of events, things, etc.) to happen or follow regularly one after the other: *Busy periods in the hospital alternate with times when there is not much to do.* ◇ *She seemed to alternate between hating him and loving him.* ▶ **występować itp. na przemian, oscylować**
■ **alternation** /ˌɔːltəˈneɪʃn/ noun [C,U] ▶ **przemienne występowanie, oscylowanie**

alternate[2] /ɔːlˈtɜːnət; US ˈɔːltər-/ adj. **1** (used about two types of events, things, etc.) happening or following regularly one after the other: *There will be alternate periods of sun and showers tomorrow.* ▶ **przemienny 2** one of every two: *He works alternate weeks.* ▶ **co drugi**
■ **alternately** adv.: *The bricks were painted alternately white and red.* ▶ **przemiennie**

alternative[1] /ɔːlˈtɜːnətɪv/ noun [C] **an alternative (to sth)** one of two or more things that you can choose between: *What can I eat as an alternative to meat?* ◇ *There are several alternatives open to us at the moment.* ▶ **alternatywa**

alternative[2] /ɔːlˈtɜːnətɪv/ adj. [only before a noun] **1** that you can use, do, etc. instead of sth else: *The motorway was closed so we had to find an alternative route.* ▶ **inny 2** different to what is usual or traditional ▶ **niekonwencjonalny, alternatywny**
■ **alternatively** adv. ▶ **ewentualnie**

alˌternative ˈmedicine noun [C, U] any type of treatment that does not use the usual scientific methods of Western medicine, for example one using plants instead of artificial drugs ▶ **medycyna niekonwencjonalna**

although /ɔːlˈðəʊ/ conj. **1** in spite of the fact that: *Although she was tired, she stayed up late watching TV.* ▶ **chociaż 2** and yet; but: *I love dogs, although I wouldn't have one as a pet.* ▶ **chociaż, aczkolwiek**

> Można też użyć **though**, które jest mniej formalne niż **although**. **Even** można użyć razem z **though** (ale nie z **although** w celu nadania emfazy): *She didn't want to go to the party, although/though/even though she knew all her friends would be there.* **Though**, ale nie **although**, może występować na końcu zdania: *She knew all her friends would be there. She didn't want to go, though.*

altitude /ˈæltɪtjuːd; US -tuːd/ noun **1** [sing.] the height of sth above sea level: *The plane climbed to an altitude of 10 000 metres.* ▶ **wysokość 2** [C, usually pl.] a place that is high above sea level: *You need to carry oxygen when you are climbing **at high altitudes*** (na dużych wysokościach). ▶ **wysokość**

Alt key (also **ALT key**) /ˈɔːlt kiː/ noun [C] a key on a computer keyboard which you press while pressing other keys, in order to change their function ▶ (*komput.*) **klawisz Alt**

alto /ˈæltəʊ/ noun [C] (pl. **altos**) the lowest normal singing voice for a woman, the highest for a man; a woman or man with this voice ▶ **kontralt, alt**

altogether /ˌɔːltəˈgeðə(r)/ adv. **1** completely: *I don't altogether agree with you.* ◇ *At the age of 55 he stopped working altogether.* ◇ *This time the situation is altogether different.* ▶ **całkowicie 2** including everything; in total: *How much money will I need altogether?* ◇ *Altogether there were six of us.* ▶ **razem 3** when you consider everything; generally: *Altogether, this town is a pleasant place to live.* ▶ **ogólnie mówiąc/rzecz biorąc**

Altogether nie znaczy to samo co **all together. All together** oznacza „wszystko/wszyscy razem": *Put your books all together on the table.* ◇ *Let's sing. All together now!*

altruistic /ˌæltruˈɪstɪk/ adj. (formal) caring about the needs and happiness of other people more than your own ▶ **altruistyczny**
■ **altruism** /ˈæltruɪzəm/ noun [U] ▶ **altruizm**

aluminium /ˌæljəˈmɪniəm; ˌælə-/ (US **aluminum** /əˈluːmɪnəm/) noun [U] (symbol **Al**) a light silver-coloured metal that is used for making cooking equipment, etc.: *aluminium foil* ▶ **aluminium**

⚷ **always** /ˈɔːlweɪz/ adv. **1** at all times; regularly: *I always get up at 6.30.* ◇ *Why is the train always late when I'm in a hurry?* ▶ **zawsze**; **ciągle 2** all through the past until now: *Tony has always been shy.* ▶ **zawsze**, **od dawna 3** for ever: *I shall always remember this moment.* ▶ **(na) zawsze 4** [only used with continuous tenses] again and again, usually in an annoying way: *She's always complaining about something.* ▶ **stale 5** (used with 'can' or 'could' for suggesting sth that sb could do, especially if nothing else is possible): *If you haven't got enough money, I could always lend you some.* ▶ **zawsze**

Słowo **always** zwykle nie występuje na początku zdania. Zazwyczaj stawia się je przed głównym czasownikiem lub po **is, are, were** itp: *He always wears those shoes* ◇ *I have always wanted to visit Egypt.* ◇ *Fiona is always late.* Można jednak postawić **always** na początku zdania, które jest w formie polecenia: *Always stop and look before you cross the road.*

Alzheimer's disease /ˈæltshaɪməz dɪziːz/ noun [sing.] a disease that affects the brain and makes you become more and more confused as you get older ▶ **choroba Alzheimera**

AM /ˌeɪ ˈem/ abbr. **amplitude modulation**; one of the systems of sending out radio signals ▶ **modulacja amplitudy**

⚷ **a.m.** (US **A.M.**) /ˌeɪ ˈem/ abbr. (from Latin) **ante meridiem**; before midday: *10 a.m.* ▶ **przed południem** ⊃ look at **p.m.**

am /əm; strong form æm/ → BE

amalgam /əˈmælgəm/ noun **1** [C, usually sing.] **amalgam (of sth)** (formal) a mixture or combination of things: *The film script is an amalgam of all three books.* ▶ **mieszanina 2** [U] a mixture of **mercury** and another metal, used especially to fill holes in teeth ▶ **amalgamat** (*zwł. dentystyczny*)

amalgamate /əˈmælgəmeɪt/ verb [I,T] if two organizations **amalgamate** or are **amalgamated**, they join together to form one large organization ▶ **łączyć (się)** SYN **merge**
■ **amalgamation** /əˌmælgəˈmeɪʃn/ noun [C,U] ▶ **połączenie**

amass /əˈmæs/ verb [T] to collect or put together a large quantity of sth: *We've amassed a lot of information on the subject.* ▶ **gromadzić** (*dużą ilość czegoś*)

amateur[1] /ˈæmətə(r)/ noun [C] **1** a person who takes part in a sport or an activity for pleasure, not for money as a job ▶ **amator/ka** OPP **professional 2** (usually used in a critical way) a person who does not have skill or experience when doing sth: *The repair work on this house was clearly done by a bunch of amateurs.* ▶ **amator/ka**

amateur[2] /ˈæmətə(r)/ adj. **1** done, or doing sth, for pleasure (not for money as a job): *an amateur production of a play* ◇ *an amateur photographer* fotograf amator ▶ **amatorski** OPP **professional 2** (also **amateurish** /-rɪʃ/) done without skill or experience: *The painting was an amateurish fake.* ▶ **dyletancki**

⚷ **amaze** /əˈmeɪz/ verb [T] to surprise sb very much; to be difficult for sb to believe: *Sometimes your behaviour amazes me!* ◇ *It amazes me* (nie mogę uwierzyć) *that anyone could be so stupid!* ▶ **zdumiewać**, **zaskakiwać**

⚷ **amazed** /əˈmeɪzd/ adj. **amazed (at/by sb/sth); amazed (to do sth/that ...)** very surprised: *I was amazed by the change in his attitude.* ▶ **zdumiony**, **zaskoczony**

amazement /əˈmeɪzmənt/ noun [U] a feeling of great surprise: *He looked at me* ***in amazement.*** ◇ ***To my amazement****, he remembered me.* ▶ **zdumienie**, **zaskoczenie**

⚷ **amazing** /əˈmeɪzɪŋ/ adj. very surprising and difficult to believe: *She has shown amazing courage.* ◇ *I've got an amazing story to tell you.* ▶ **zdumiewający**, **zaskakujący** SYN **incredible**
■ **amazingly** adv. ▶ **zdumiewająco**, **zaskakująco**

ambassador /æmˈbæsədə(r)/ noun [C] an important person who represents their country in a foreign country: *the Spanish Ambassador to Britain* ▶ **ambasador/ka**

An ambassador lives and works in an **embassy**.

amber /ˈæmbə(r)/ noun [U] **1** a hard clear yellowish-brown substance used for making jewellery or objects for decoration ▶ **bursztyn 2** a yellowish-brown colour: *The three colours in traffic lights are red, amber* (żółty) *and green.* ▶ **kolor bursztynowy**
■ **amber** adj. ▶ **bursztynowy**

ambidextrous /ˌæmbiˈdekstrəs/ adj. able to use the left hand and the right hand equally well ▶ **oburęczny**

ambience (also **ambiance**) /ˈæmbiəns/ noun [sing.] the character and atmosphere of a place: *the relaxed ambience of the city* ▶ **atmosfera**, **nastrój**

ambient /ˈæmbiənt/ adj. **1** [only before a noun] relating to the surrounding area; on all sides: ***ambient temperature/light/conditions*** ▶ **otaczający 2** (especially used about music) creating a relaxed atmosphere: *a compilation of ambient electronic music* ◇ *soft, ambient lighting* ▶ **nastrojowy**

ambiguity /ˌæmbɪˈgjuːəti/ noun [C,U] (pl. **ambiguities**) the possibility of being understood in more than one way; sth that can be understood in more than one way: *We call the two boys 'John A' and 'John B' to avoid ambiguity.* ▶ **dwuznaczność**, **wieloznaczność**

ambiguous /æmˈbɪgjuəs/ adj. having more than one possible meaning ▶ **dwuznaczny**, **wieloznaczny**
■ **ambiguously** adv. ▶ **dwuznacznie**, **wieloznacznie**

⚷ **ambition** /æmˈbɪʃn/ noun **1** [C] **ambition (to do/be sth); ambition (of doing sth)** something that you want to do or achieve very much: *It has always been her ambition to travel the world.* ◇ *He finally* ***achieved*** *his* ***ambition*** *of becoming a doctor.* ▶ **ambicja 2** [U] a strong desire to be successful, to have power, etc.: *One problem of young people today is their lack of ambition.* ▶ **ambicja**

ambitious /æmˈbɪʃəs/ adj. **1 ambitious (to be/do sth)** having a strong desire to be successful, to have power, etc.: *We are ambitious to succeed.* ▶ **ambitny 2** difficult to achieve or do because it takes a lot of work or effort: *The company have announced ambitious plans for expansion.* ▶ **ambitny**

ambivalent /æmˈbɪvələnt/ adj. having or showing a mixture of feelings or opinions about sth or sb ▶ **mający mieszane uczucia**, **ambiwalentny**
■ **ambivalence** noun [C,U] ▶ **mieszane uczucia**, **ambiwalencja**

amble /ˈæmbl/ verb [I] to walk at a slow relaxed speed: *We ambled down to the beach.* ▶ **iść wolnym krokiem** SYN **stroll**

⚷ **ambulance** /ˈæmbjələns/ noun [C] a special vehicle for taking ill or injured people to and from hospital: *the* *ambulance service* ▶ **karetka pogotowia** ➲ note at **hospital**

ambush /ˈæmbʊʃ/ noun [C,U] a surprise attack from a hidden position: *He was killed in an enemy ambush.* ◇ *The robbers were waiting* ***in ambush.*** ▶ **atak z zasadzki**

■ **ambush** verb [T] ▶ **napadać z zasadzki**

ameba (US) = AMOEBA

ameliorate /əˈmi:liəreɪt/ verb [T] (formal) to make sth better ▶ **polepszać**

■ **amelioration** /əˌmi:liəˈreɪʃn/ noun [U] ▶ **polepszenie**

amen /ɑ:ˈmen; eɪˈmen/ interj. a word used at the end of prayers by Christians and Jews ▶ **amen**

amenable /əˈmi:nəbl/ adj. happy to accept sth: *I'm amenable to any suggestions you may have.* ▶ **chętny**, **uległy**

amend /əˈmend/ verb [T] to change sth slightly in order to make it better ▶ **wnosić poprawki**

amendment /əˈmendmənt/ noun **1** [C] a part that is added or a small change that is made to a piece of writing, especially to a law ▶ **poprawka** **2** [U] an act of **amending** sth ▶ **poprawka**

amends /əˈmendz/ noun

IDM **make amends** to do sth for sb, that shows that you are sorry for sth bad that you have done before: *I bought her a present to make amends for the horrible things I had said to her.* ▶ **wynagradzać szkodę**

amenity /əˈmi:nəti; US -ˈmen-/ noun [C] (pl. **amenities**) something that makes a place pleasant or easy to live in: *Among the town's amenities are two cinemas and a sports centre.* ▶ **udogodnienia** ➲ look at **service**[1]

American /əˈmerɪkən/ adj. from or connected with the US: *Have you met Bob? He's American.* ▶ **amerykański**

■ **American** noun [C] ▶ **Amerykan-in/ka**

Aˌmerican ˈfootball (US **football**) noun [U] a game that is played in the US by two teams of eleven players with a ball shaped like an egg. The players wear **helmets** and other protective clothing and try to carry the ball to the end of the field. ▶ **futbol amerykański** ➲ note at **football**

Aˌmerican ˈIndian = NATIVE AMERICAN

Americanize (also -ise) /əˈmerɪkənaɪz/ verb [T] to make sb/sth American in character ▶ **amerykanizować**

■ **Americanization** (also -isation) /əˌmerəkənaɪˈzeɪʃn; US -nəˈz-/ noun [U] ▶ **amerykanizacja**

amethyst /ˈæməθɪst/ noun [C,U] a purple stone, used in making jewellery: *an amethyst ring* ▶ **ametyst**

amiable /ˈeɪmiəbl/ adj. friendly and pleasant ▶ **sympatyczny**, **miły**

■ **amiably** /-əbli/ adv. ▶ **sympatycznie**, **miło**

amicable /ˈæmɪkəbl/ adj. made or done in a friendly way, without argument: *I'm sure we can find an amicable way of settling the dispute.* ▶ **polubowny**, **przyjazny**

■ **amicably** /-əbli/ adv. ▶ **polubownie**, **przyjaźnie**

amid /əˈmɪd/ (also **amidst** /əˈmɪdst/) prep. (formal) in the middle of; among: *Amid all the confusion, the thieves got away.* ▶ **pośród**, **wśród**

amino acid /əˌmi:nəʊ ˈæsɪd/ noun [C] any of the substances that combine to form the basic structure of **proteins** ▶ **aminokwas**

amiss /əˈmɪs/ adj. [not before a noun], adv. wrong; not as it should be: *When I walked into the room I could sense that something was amiss.* ▶ **nie w porządku**, **nie tak**

IDM **not come/go amiss** to be useful or pleasant: *Things are fine, although a bit more money wouldn't come amiss.* ▶ **przydawać się**

take sth amiss to be upset by sth, perhaps because you have understood it in the wrong way: *Please don't take my remarks amiss.* ▶ **brać za złe**

ammonia /əˈməʊniə/ noun [U] (symbol NH_3) a gas with a strong smell; a clear liquid containing **ammonia** used for cleaning ▶ **amoniak**

ammunition /ˌæmjuˈnɪʃn/ noun [U] **1** the supply of bullets, etc. that you need to fire from a weapon ▶ **amunicja** **2** facts or information that can be used against sb/sth ▶ **broń**

amnesia /æmˈni:ziə; US -ˈni:ʒə/ noun [U] loss of memory ▶ **amnezja**, **utrata pamięci**

amnesty /ˈæmnəsti/ noun [C] (pl. **amnesties**) **1** a time when a government forgives political crimes: *The government has announced an amnesty for all political prisoners.* ▶ **amnestia** **2** a time when people can give in illegal weapons without being arrested ▶ **amnestia**

amniocentesis /ˌæmniəʊsenˈti:sɪs/ noun [U, sing.] a medical test that involves taking some liquid from a pregnant woman's **womb** in order to find out if the baby has particular illnesses or health problems ▶ **amniocenteza**

amniotic fluid /ˌæmniɒtɪk ˈflu:ɪd/ noun [U] the liquid that surrounds a baby inside the mother's **womb** ▶ **płyn owodniowy**

amoeba (US also **ameba**) /əˈmi:bə/ noun [C] (pl. **amoebas** or **amoebae** /-bi:/) a very small living creature that consists of only one cell ▶ **ameba**

amok /əˈmɒk/ adv.

IDM **run amok** to suddenly become very angry or excited and start behaving violently, especially in a public place SYN **run riot** ▶ **wpaść w amok**

🔑 **among** /əˈmʌŋ/ (also **amongst** /əˈmʌŋst/) prep. **1** surrounded by; in the middle of: *I often feel nervous when I'm among strangers.* ◇ *I found the missing letter amongst a heap of old newspapers.* ▶ **między**, **pomiędzy**, **wśród**, **pośród** ➲ note at **between** ➲ picture at **between** **2** in or concerning a particular group of people or things: *Discuss it* ***amongst yourselves*** *and let me know your decision.* ◇ *There is a lot of anger among students about the new law.* ◇ ***Among other things,*** *the drug can cause headaches and sweating.* ◇ *She is among the nicest people* (ona jest jedną z najmilszych osób) *I have ever met.* ▶ **między**, **wśród** **3** to each one (of a group): *On his death, his money will be divided among his children.* ▶ **pomiędzy**, **wśród** ➲ note at **between**

amoral /ˌeɪˈmɒrəl/ adj. (used about people or their behaviour) not following any moral rules; not caring about right or wrong ▶ **amoralny** ➲ look at **moral**[1], **immoral**

amorous /ˈæmərəs/ adj. showing sexual desire and love towards sb: *She rejected his amorous advances* (zaloty). ▶ **miłosny**

■ **amorously** adv. ▶ **miłośnie**

amorphous /əˈmɔ:fəs/ adj. [usually before a noun] (formal) having no definite shape, form or structure ▶ **bezkształtny** SYN **shapeless**

🔑 **amount**[1] /əˈmaʊnt/ noun [C] **1** total or sum of money: *You are requested to pay the full amount within seven days.* ▶ **kwota**, **suma** **2** the amount of sth is how much of it there is; quantity: *I spent an enormous amount of time preparing for the exam.* ◇ *a large amount of money* ◇ *I have a certain amount of sympathy with her.* Mam dla niej trochę współczucia. ▶ **ilość**

🔑 **amount**[2] /əˈmaʊnt/ verb [I] **amount to sth** **1** to add up to; to total: *The cost of the repairs amounted to £5000.* ▶ (*suma*) **wynosić** **2** to be the same as: *Whether I tell her today or tomorrow, it amounts to the same thing* (będzie tak samo). ▶ **być równoznacznym**

amp /æmp/ noun [C] **1** (also formal **ampere** /'æmpeə(r); US also -pɪər/) a measure of electric current ▶ **amper 2** (informal) = AMPLIFIER

amphetamine /æm'fetəmiːn/ noun [C,U] a drug, sometimes taken illegally, that makes you feel excited and full of energy. ▶ **amfetamina**

amphibian /æm'fɪbiən/ noun [C] an animal with cold blood that can live on land and in water ▶ **płaz** ➲ look at **reptile** ➲ picture on **page A11**

amphibious /æm'fɪbiəs/ adj. able to live or be used both on land and in water: *amphibious vehicles* ▶ **amfibiotyczny; wodno-lądowy**

amphitheatre (US **amphitheater**) /'æmfɪθɪətə(r); US -θiː-/ noun [C] a round building without a roof and with rows of seats that rise in steps around an open space. **Amphitheatres** were used in ancient Greece and Rome for public entertainment. ▶ **amfiteatr**

ample /'æmpl/ adj. **1** enough or more than enough: *We've got ample time to make a decision.* ◇ *I'm not sure how much the trip will cost, but I should think £500 will be ample.* ▶ **wystarczający, aż nadto 2** large: *an ample car park* ▶ **przestronny, obszerny**

■ **amply** /'æmpli/ adv.: *She was amply rewarded for her work.* ▶ **wystarczająco**

amplifier /'æmplɪfaɪə(r)/ (also informal **amp**) noun [C] a piece of electrical equipment for making sounds louder or signals stronger ▶ **wzmacniacz**

amplify /'æmplɪfaɪ/ verb [T] (**amplifying**; **amplifies**; pt, pp **amplified**) **1** to increase the strength of a sound, using electrical equipment ▶ **wzmacniać** (*dźwięk*) **2** to add details to sth in order to explain it more fully ▶ **rozwijać** (*np. komentarz*)

■ **amplification** /ˌæmplɪfɪ'keɪʃn/ noun [U] ▶ **wzmocnienie** (*dźwięku*); **rozwinięcie** (*np. komentarza*)

amputate /'æmpjuteɪt/ verb [I,T] to cut off sb's arm, leg, etc. for medical reasons: *His leg was so badly injured that it had to be amputated from the knee down.* ▶ **amputować**

■ **amputation** /ˌæmpju'teɪʃn/ noun [C,U] ▶ **amputacja**

⚷ **amuse** /ə'mjuːz/ verb [T] **1** to make sb laugh or smile; to seem funny to sb ▶ **rozbawiać, rozśmieszać 2** to make time pass pleasantly for sb; to stop sb from getting bored: *I've brought a few toys to amuse the children.* ▶ **rozrywać, zabawiać**

⚷ **amused** /ə'mjuːzd/ adj. thinking that sth is funny and wanting to laugh or smile: *You may think it's funny, but I'm not amused* (ale mnie to nie bawi). ◇ *I was amused to hear his account* (rozbawiła mnie jego relacja) *of what happened.* ▶ **rozbawiony**

IDM **keep sb/yourself amused** to do sth in order to pass time pleasantly and stop sb/yourself getting bored ▶ **bawić się; bawić kogoś**

amusement /ə'mjuːzmənt/ noun **1** [U] the feeling caused by sth that makes you laugh or smile, or by sth that entertains you: *Much to the pupils' amusement* (ku wielkiemu rozbawieniu uczniów), *the teacher fell off his chair.* ▶ **rozbawienie, rozweselenie 2** [C] something that makes time pass pleasantly; an entertainment: *The holiday centre offers a wide range of amusements, including golf and tennis.* ▶ **rozrywka, zabawa**

a'musement arcade = ARCADE (2)

a'musement park noun [C] a large park which has a lot of things that you can ride and play on and many different activities to enjoy ▶ **park rozrywki**

⚷ **amusing** /ə'mjuːzɪŋ/ adj. causing you to laugh or smile ▶ **śmieszny, zabawny** ➲ note at **humour**

an → A

anabolic steroid /ˌænəbɒlɪk 'sterɔɪd; 'stɪə-/ noun [C] an artificial **hormone** that increases the size of the muscles. It is sometimes taken illegally by people who play sports. ▶ **steroid anaboliczny, steryd anaboliczny** ➲ look at **steroid**

anachronism /ə'nækrənɪzəm/ noun [C] **1** a person, a custom or an idea that seems old-fashioned and does not belong to the present: *The monarchy is seen by many people as an anachronism in the modern world.* ▶ **anachronizm, przeżytek 2** something that is placed, for example in a book or play, in the wrong period of history: *The book is full of anachronisms which suggests there were parts rewritten in later centuries.* ▶ (*błąd*) **anachronizm**

■ **anachronistic** /əˌnækrə'nɪstɪk/ adj. ▶ **anachroniczny**

anaemia (US **anemia**) /ə'niːmiə/ noun [U] a medical condition in which there are not enough red cells in the blood ▶ **anemia**

■ **anaemic** (US **anemic**) adj. ▶ **anemiczny**

anaesthetic (US **anesthetic**) /ˌænəs'θetɪk/ noun [C,U] a substance that stops you feeling pain, for example when a doctor is performing a medical operation on you: *You'll need to be* ***under anaesthetic*** *for the operation.* ◇ *The dentist gave me a* ***local anaesthetic.*** ◇ *Did you have a* ***general anaesthetic*** *for your operation?* ▶ **środek znieczulający, znieczulenie**

anaesthetist (US **anesthetist**) /ə'niːsθətɪst/ noun [C] a person with the medical training necessary to give **anaesthetic** to patients ▶ **anestezjolog**

anaesthetize (also **-ise**; US **anesthetize**) /ə'niːsθətaɪz/ verb [T] to give an **anaesthetic** to sb ▶ **znieczulać**

anagram /'ænəgræm/ noun [C] a word or phrase that is made by arranging the letters of another word or phrase in a different order ▶ **anagram**

anal /'eɪnl/ adj. **1** connected with the **anus**: *the anal region* ▶ **odbytniczy, analny 2** (also **anal-retentive** /ˌeɪnl rɪ'tentɪv/) caring too much about small details and about how things are organized ▶ **pedantyczny** ⓘ Wyraża dezaprobatę.

analgesic /ˌænəl'dʒiːzɪk/ noun [C] a substance that reduces pain ▶ **środek przeciwbólowy** SYN **painkiller**

analogous /ə'næləgəs/ adj. (formal) **analogous (to/with sth)** similar in some way; that you can compare ▶ **analogiczny, porównywalny**

analogue (US **analog**) /'ænəlɒg/ adj. **1** (used about an electronic process) using a continuously changing range of physical quantities to measure or store data: *an* ***analogue circuit/computer/signal*** ▶ **analogowy 2** (Brit. also **analog**) (used about a clock or watch) showing the time using hands on a **dial** and not with a display of numbers ▶ **analogowy** ➲ look at **digital**

analogy /ə'nælədʒi/ noun [C] (pl. **analogies**) **an analogy (between A and B)** a comparison between two things that shows a way in which they are similar: *You could make an analogy between the human body and a car engine.* ▶ **analogia**

IDM **by analogy** by comparing sth to sth else and showing how they are similar ▶ **przez analogię**

ˌanal-re'tentive = ANAL

⚷ **analyse** (US **analyze**) /'ænəlaɪz/ verb [T] to look at or think about the different parts or details of sth carefully in order to understand or explain it: *The water samples are now being analysed in a laboratory.* ◇ *to analyse statistics* ▶ **analizować**

⚷ **analysis** /ə'næləsɪs/ noun (pl. **analyses** /-siːz/) **1** [C,U] the careful examination of the different parts or details of sth: *Some samples of the water were sent to a laboratory* ***for analysis.*** ◇ *They carried out an analysis of the causes of the problem.* ▶ **analiza 2** [C] the result of a careful examination of sth: *Your analysis of the situation is different from mine.* ▶ **analiza 3** [U] = PSYCHOANALYSIS

analyst /ˈænəlɪst/ noun [C] **1** a person whose job is to examine sth carefully as an expert: *a food analyst ◇ a political analyst* ▶ **analityk 2** = PSYCHOANALYST

analytical /ˌænəˈlɪtɪkl/ (also **analytic** /ˌænəˈlɪtɪk/) adj. using careful examination in order to understand or explain sth ▶ **analityczny**

analyze (US) = ANALYSE

anarchic /əˈnɑːkɪk/ adj. without rules or laws ▶ **anarchiczny**

anarchism /ˈænəkɪzəm/ noun [U] the political belief that there should be no government or laws in a country ▶ **anarchizm**

■ **anarchist** /-ɪst/ noun [C] ▶ **anarchist(k)a**

anarchy /ˈænəki/ noun [U] a situation in which people do not obey rules and laws; a situation in which there is no government in a country: *While the civil war went on, the country was in a state of anarchy.* ▶ **anarchia**

anathema /əˈnæθəmə/ noun [U,C, usually sing.] (formal) a thing or an idea which you hate because it is the opposite of what you believe: *Racial prejudice is (an) anathema to me* (to coś, czego nienawidzę).

anatomy /əˈnætəmi/ noun (pl. **anatomies**) **1** [U] the scientific study of the structure of human or animal bodies ▶ **anatomia 2** [C] the structure of a living thing: *the anatomy of the frog* ▶ **anatomia**

■ **anatomical** /ˌænəˈtɒmɪkl/ adj. ▶ **anatomiczny**

ancestor /ˈænsestə(r)/ noun [C] a person in your family who lived a long time before you ▶ **przodek** ➲ look at **descendant**

■ **ancestral** /ænˈsestrəl/ adj.: *her ancestral* (rodowy) *home* ▶ **odziedziczony po przodkach**

ancestry /ˈænsestri/ noun [C,U] (pl. **ancestries**) all of sb's **ancestors**: *He is of Irish **ancestry**.* Jest z pochodzenia Irlandczykiem. ▶ **przodkowie**, **ród**

anchor[1] /ˈæŋkə(r)/ noun [C,U] a heavy metal object at the end of a chain that you drop into the water from a boat in order to stop the boat moving ▶ **kotwica**

anchor[2] /ˈæŋkə(r)/ verb **1** [I,T] to drop an **anchor**; to stop a boat moving by using an **anchor** ▶ **kotwiczyć 2** [T] to fix sth firmly so that it cannot move: *They anchored the tent with strong ropes.* ▶ **umocowywać**, **kotwiczyć**

anchorman /ˈæŋkəmæn/, **anchorwoman** /ˈæŋkəwʊmən/ noun [C] (pl. **-men** /-men/; **-women** /-wɪmɪn/) a man or woman who presents a radio or television programme and introduces reports by other people ▶ **prezenter/ka telewizyjn-y/a lub radiow-y/a**

anchovy /ˈæntʃəvi; US -tʃəʊ-/ noun [C,U] (pl. **anchovies**) a small fish that has a strong taste of salt ▶ **anchois**

⚷ **ancient** /ˈeɪnʃənt/ adj. **1** belonging to a period of history that is thousands of years in the past: *ancient civilizations ◇ an ancient tradition* ▶ **starożytny**, **starodawny** OPP **modern 2** very old: *I can't believe he's only 30 – he looks ancient* (wygląda bardzo staro)*!* ▶ **bardzo stary**

⚷ **and** /ənd; ən; strong form ænd/ conj. **1** (used to connect words or parts of sentences) also; in addition to: *Come in and sit down. ◇ a boy and a girl* ℹ Jeśli wymieniane rzeczy są blisko ze sobą związane, nie trzeba powtarzać przedimka **a** itp: *a knife and fork ◇ my father and mother.* ▶ **i 2** (used when you are saying numbers in sums) in addition to: *Twelve and six is eighteen.* ▶ **i** SYN **plus** ℹ Przy słownym podawaniu dużych liczb używa się **and** po słowie **hundred**: *We say 2 264 as two thousand, two hundred and sixty-four.* **3** (used instead of 'to' after certain verbs, for example 'go', 'come', 'try'): *Go and answer the door for me, will you? ◇ Why don't you come and stay with us one weekend? ◇ I'll try and find out* (postaram się dowiedzieć) *what's going on.* ▶ **i 4** as a result: *Miss another class and you'll fail.* ▶ **i**, **a 5** (used between repeated words to show that sth is increasing or continuing): *The situation is getting worse and worse. ◇ I shouted and shouted but nobody answered.* ▶ **coraz**, **i 6** (used between repeated words for saying that there are important differences between things of the same kind): *I like city life but there are cities and cities.* ▶ **i**

androgynous /ænˈdrɒdʒənəs/ adj. having both male and female characteristics; looking neither strongly male nor strongly female ▶ **hermafrodytyczny**, **androgeniczny**

android /ˈændrɔɪd/ noun [C] a **robot** that looks like a real person ▶ **android**

anecdotal /ˌænɪkˈdəʊtl/ adj. based on **anecdotes** and possibly not true or accurate: *anecdotal evidence* ▶ **według (ustnych) opowiadań** (*niepotwierdzonych naukowo*)

■ **anecdotally** /-təli/ adv.: *This reaction has been reported anecdotally by a number of patients.* ▶ **według (ustnych) opowiadań** (*niepotwierdzony naukowo*)

anecdote /ˈænɪkdəʊt/ noun [C] a short interesting story about a real person or event ▶ **anegdota**

anemia (US) = ANAEMIA

anesthetic, anesthetist, anesthetize (US) = ANAESTHETIC, ANAESTHETIST, ANAESTHETIZE

anew /əˈnjuː; US əˈnuː/ adv. (formal) again; in a new or different way: *I wish I could start my life anew!* ▶ **znowu**; **na nowo**, **od nowa**

angel /ˈeɪndʒl/ noun [C] **1** a spirit who is believed to carry messages from God. In pictures **angels** are often dressed in white, with wings. ▶ **anioł 2** a person who is very kind: *Be an angel and wash these dishes for me, will you?* ▶ **anioł**

angelic /ænˈdʒelɪk/ adj. looking or acting like an **angel** ▶ **anielski**

■ **angelically** /-kli/ adv. ▶ **anielsko**

⚷ **anger**[1] /ˈæŋgə(r)/ noun [U] the strong feeling that you have when sth has happened or sb has done sth that you do not like: *He could not hide his anger at the news. ◇ She was shaking with anger.* ▶ **gniew** ➲ adjective **angry**

anger[2] /ˈæŋgə(r)/ verb [T] to make sb become angry ▶ **złościć**

⚷ **angle**[1] /ˈæŋgl/ noun [C] **1** the space between two lines or surfaces that meet, measured in degrees: *at an angle of 40° ◇ a **right angle*** kąt prosty *◇ an acute/obtuse angle* kąt ostry/rozwarty ▶ **kąt 2** the direction from which you look at sth: *Viewed from this angle* (patrząc pod tym kątem)*, the building looks bigger than it really is.* ▶ **kąt/punkt** (*np. widzenia*)

IDM **at an angle** not straight: *This hat is meant to be worn at an angle* (na bakier). ▶ **pod (jakimś) kątem**

angle[2] /ˈæŋgl/ verb [T] **1** to put sth in a position that is not straight: *Angle the lamp towards the desk.* ▶ **ustawiać/kierować pod kątem 2 angle sth (at/to/towards sb)** to show sth from a particular point of view; to aim sth at a particular person or group: *The new magazine is angled at young professional people.* ▶ **przedstawiać coś z jakiegoś punktu widzenia**; **kierować (do kogoś)**

PHR V **angle for sth** to try to make sb give you sth, without asking for it in a direct way: *She was angling for an invitation to our party.* ▶ **polować na coś**

ˈ**angle bracket** noun [C, usually pl.] one of a pair of marks, < >, used around words or figures to separate them from the surrounding text ▶ **nawias trójkątny**

angler /ˈæŋglə(r)/ noun [C] a person who catches fish as a hobby ▶ **wędka-rz/rka** ➲ look at **fisherman**

Anglican /ˈæŋglɪkən/ noun [C] a member of the Church of England or of a related church in another English-speaking country ▶ **anglikan-in/ka**

■ **Anglican** adj. ▶ **anglikański**

Anglicize (also -ise) /ˈæŋglɪsaɪz/ verb [T] to make sb/sth English: *Gutmann anglicized his name to Goodman.* ▶ **angielszczyć**

angling /ˈæŋglɪŋ/ noun [U] fishing as a sport or hobby: *He goes angling at weekends.* ▶ **wędkarstwo** ➲ look at **fishing**

Anglo- /ˈæŋgləʊ/ [in compounds] connected with England or Britain (and another country or countries): *Anglo-American relations* ▶ **angielsko-, brytyjsko-**

anglophone /ˈæŋgləʊfəʊn/ noun [C] a person who speaks English, especially in countries where English is not the only language that is spoken ▶ **anglofon**
■ **anglophone** adj. ▶ **anglojęzyczny**

Anglo-Saxon /ˌæŋgləʊ ˈsæksn/ noun **1** [C] a person whose family originally came from England ▶ **osoba angielskiego pochodzenia 2** [C] a person who lived in England before the Norman Conquest ▶ **Anglosas/ka 3** (also ˌOld ˈEnglish) [U] the English language before about 1150 ▶ **język anglosaski**
■ **Anglo-Saxon** adj. ▶ **anglosaski**

angora /æŋˈgɔːrə/ noun **1** [C] a breed of cat, **goat** or **rabbit** that has long smooth hair ▶ *(koza/królik)* **angora 2** [U] a type of soft wool or cloth made from the hair of the **angora goat** or **rabbit**: *an angora sweater* sweter z angory ▶ *(wełna)* **angora**

⚷ **angry** /ˈæŋgri/ adj. (**angrier**; **angriest**) **angry (with sb) (at/about sth)** feeling or showing anger: *My parents will be angry with me if I get home late.* ◇ *Calm down – there's no need to get angry* (nie trzeba się złościć). ▶ **zły, gniewny** SYN **cross**[3] ➲ noun **anger**
■ **angrily** adv. ▶ **gniewnie**

angst /æŋst/ noun [U] a feeling of worry about a situation, or about your life: *teenage angst* ▶ **lęk**

anguish /ˈæŋgwɪʃ/ noun [U] (formal) great mental pain or suffering: *The newspaper told of the mother's anguish at the death of her son.* ▶ **udręka, boleść**
■ **anguished** adj. ▶ **udręczony, cierpiący**

angular /ˈæŋgjələ(r)/ adj. with sharp points or corners: *an angular face* ▶ **kanciasty, kościsty**

⚷ **animal** /ˈænɪml/ noun [C] a living creature that is not a plant; a living creature of this kind, but not including humans: *farm animals* ◇ *He studied the animals and birds of Southern Africa.* ◇ *Humans are social animals* (zwierzętami stadnymi). ◇ *the animal kingdom* ▶ **zwierzę** ❶ Słowa **animal** używa się czasami, gdy mówi się tylko o ssakach. ➲ picture on **page A10**

ˌ**animal ˈrights** noun [pl.] the rights of animals to be treated well, for example by not being hunted or used for medical research: *His research work was attacked by **animal rights activists.*** ▶ **prawa zwierząt**

animate /ˈænɪmət/ adj. (formal) living; having life: *animate beings* ▶ **żywy** OPP **inanimate**

animated /ˈænɪmeɪtɪd/ adj. **1** interesting and full of energy: *an animated discussion* ▶ **ożywiony 2** (used about films) using a process or method which makes pictures or models appear to move: *an animated cartoon* ▶ **rysunkowy**

animation /ˌænɪˈmeɪʃn/ noun [U] **1** the state of being full of energy and enthusiasm ▶ **ożywienie 2** the method of making films, computer games, etc. with pictures or models that appear to move: *computer animation* ▶ **animacja filmowa**

animator /ˈænɪmeɪtə(r)/ noun [C] a person who makes **animated** films ▶ *(film)* **animator/ka**

animosity /ˌænɪˈmɒsəti/ noun [C,U] (pl. **animosities**) **animosity (toward(s) sb/sth)**; **animosity (between A and B)** a strong feeling of disagreement, anger or hatred ▶ **uraza, niechęć** SYN **hostility**

aniseed /ˈænəsiːd/ noun [U] the dried seeds of the **anise** plant, used to give flavour to alcoholic drinks and sweets ▶ **anyż**

⚷ **ankle** /ˈæŋkl/ noun [C] the part of your body where your foot joins your leg: *I tripped and sprained my ankle.* ▶ **kostka** *(u nogi)* ➲ picture at **body**

annex /əˈneks/ verb [T] to take control of another country or region by force ▶ **zawładnąć, anektować**
■ **annexation** /ˌænekˈseɪʃn/ noun [C,U] ▶ **aneksja**

annexe (especially US **annex**) /ˈæneks/ noun [C] a building that is joined to a larger one: *Our classroom is in an annexe to the main building.* ▶ **przybudówka**

annihilate /əˈnaɪəleɪt/ verb [T] to destroy or defeat sb/sth completely: *The army was annihilated in the battle.* ◇ *They weren't just beaten in the match – they were annihilated.* ▶ **unicestwiać, zniszczyć**
■ **annihilation** /əˌnaɪəˈleɪʃn/ noun [U] ▶ **unicestwienie, zniszczenie**

⚷ **anniversary** /ˌænɪˈvɜːsəri/ noun [C] (pl. **anniversaries**) a day that is exactly a year or a number of years after a special or important event: *the hundredth anniversary of the country's independence* ◇ *a wedding anniversary* ▶ **rocznica, jubileusz** ➲ note at **birthday, jubilee**

annotate /ˈænəteɪt/ verb [T] to add notes to a book or text, giving explanations or comments ▶ **opatrywać przypisami/adnotacjami**
■ **annotation** /ˌænəˈteɪʃn/ noun [C,U] ▶ **przypis, adnotacja** | **annotated** adj. ▶ **zaopatrzony w przypisy**

⚷ **announce** /əˈnaʊns/ verb [T] **1** to make sth known publicly and officially: *The winners will be announced in next week's paper.* ▶ **ogłaszać 2** to say sth in a firm or serious way: *She stormed into my office and announced that she was leaving.* ▶ **oznajmiać** *(podniesionym głosem)*

announcement /əˈnaʊnsmənt/ noun **1** [C] a statement that tells people about sth: *Ladies and gentlemen, I'd like to **make an announcement.*** ▶ **ogłoszenie 2** [U] the act of telling people about sth ▶ **ogłoszenie**

announcer /əˈnaʊnsə(r)/ noun [C] a person who introduces or gives information about programmes on radio or TV ▶ **spiker/ka**

⚷ **annoy** /əˈnɔɪ/ verb [T] to make sb angry or slightly angry: *It really annoys me when you act so selfishly.* ◇ *Close the door if the noise is annoying you.* ▶ **irytować** SYN **irritate**

annoyance /əˈnɔɪəns/ noun **1** [U] the feeling of being annoyed: ***Much to my annoyance**, the train had just left when I got to the station.* ▶ **irytacja 2** [C] something that annoys sb: *Low-flying planes are an annoyance in this area.* ▶ **utrapienie**

⚷ **annoyed** /əˈnɔɪd/ adj. **annoyed (with sb) (at/about sth)**; **annoyed that ...** slightly angry: *She's annoyed with herself for making such a stupid mistake.* ▶ **zirytowany, zły** SYN **irritated**

⚷ **annoying** /əˈnɔɪɪŋ/ adj. making you feel angry or slightly angry ▶ **irytujący**

⚷ **annual**[1] /ˈænjuəl/ adj. **1** happening or done once a year or every year: *the company's annual report* ▶ **roczny, coroczny 2** for the period of one year: *What's the average annual salary for a nurse?* ▶ **roczny**
■ **annually** /-juəli/ adv. ▶ **co roku, rocznie**

annual[2] /ˈænjuəl/ noun [C] a book, especially one for children, that is published once each year: *the 2007 Football Annual* ▶ **rocznik**

annuity /əˈnjuːəti; US -ˈnuː-/ noun [C] (pl. **annuities**) a fixed amount of money paid to sb each year, usually for the rest of their life: *She receives a small annuity.* ▶ **dożywotnia roczna renta**

annul /ə'nʌl/ verb [T] (**annulling**; **annulled**) to state officially that sth is no longer legally valid: *Their marriage was annulled after just six months.* ▶ **anulować, unieważniać**
■ **annulment** noun [C,U] ▶ **anulowanie, unieważnienie**

anomalous /ə'nɒmələs/ adj. different from what is normal: *In a few anomalous cases, these drugs have made people ill.* ▶ **nieprawidłowy, odbiegający od normy**

anomaly /ə'nɒməli/ noun [C] (pl. **anomalies**) sth that is different from what is normal or usual: *We discovered an anomaly in the sales figures for August.* ▶ **anomalia, nieprawidłowość**

anon. /ə'nɒn/ abbr. **anonymous**; (used to show that we do not know who did a piece of writing) ▶ **anonimowy**

anonymity /ˌænə'nɪməti/ noun [U] the situation where sb's name is not known ▶ **anonimowość**

anonymous /ə'nɒnɪməs/ adj. **1** (used about a person) whose name is not known or made public: *An anonymous caller told the police that a robbery was going to take place.* ▶ **anonimowy 2** done, written, etc. by sb whose name is not known or made public: *He received an anonymous letter.* ▶ **anonimowy**
■ **anonymously** adv. ▶ **anonimowo**

anorak /'ænəræk/ noun [C] (especially Brit.) **1** a short coat with a covering for your head that protects you from rain, wind and cold ▶ **skafander 2** (slang) a person who enjoys learning boring facts: *He's a real anorak – he can name every player in the World Cup.* ▶ (*przen.*) **kowal**

anorexia /ˌænə'reksiə/ (also **anorexia nervosa** /ˌænəˌreksiə nɜː'vəʊsə/) noun [U] an illness, especially affecting young women, that makes them so afraid of being fat that they do not eat ▶ **anoreksja** ➲ look at **bulimia**
■ **anorexic** adj. ▶ **chory na anoreksję** | **anorexic** noun [C] ▶ **anorekty-k/czka**

🔑**another** /ə'nʌðə(r)/ determiner, pron. **1** one more person or thing of the same kind: *Would you like another drink?* ◇ *They've got three children already and they're having another.* ▶ **jeszcze (jeden) 2** a different thing or person: *I'm afraid I can't see you tomorrow. Could we arrange another day?* ▶ **(jakiś) inny**
IDM **another/a different matter** → MATTER[1]
one after another/the other → ONE[1]
yet another → YET

🔑**answer**[1] /'ɑːnsə(r); US 'æn-/ noun [C] **an answer (to sb/sth) 1** something that you say, write or do as a reply: *The answer to your question is that I don't know.* ◇ *They've made me an offer and I have to **give them an answer** by Friday.* ◇ *I knocked on the door and waited but there was no answer.* ▶ **odpowiedź** SYN **reply 2** a solution to a problem: *I didn't have any money so the only answer was to borrow some.* ▶ **rozwiązanie 3** the correct reply to a question in a test or exam: *What was the answer to question 4?* ▶ **(poprawna) odpowiedź 4** a reply to a question in a test or exam: *How many answers did you get right?* ▶ **odpowiedź**
IDM **in answer (to sth)** as a reply (to sth): *They sent me some leaflets in answer to my request for information.* ▶ **w odpowiedzi (na coś)**

🔑**answer**[2] /'ɑːnsə(r); US 'æn-/ verb [I,T] **1** to say or write sth back to sb who has asked you sth or written to you: *I asked her what the matter was but she didn't answer.* ◇ *I've asked you a question, now please answer me.* ◇ *Answer all the questions on the form.* ◇ *He hasn't answered my letter yet.* ◇ *'No!' he answered angrily.* ▶ **odpowiadać 2** to do sth as a reply: *to **answer the phone*** ◇ *I rang their doorbell but nobody answered.* ▶ **odbierać** (*telefon*), **otwierać** (*drzwi*), **odpowiadać**
PHR V **answer back** to defend yourself against sth bad that has been written or said about you ▶ **bronić się słowami**
answer (sb) back to reply rudely to sb ▶ **odpowiadać niegrzecznie**
answer for sb/sth 1 to accept responsibility for sth/sb: *Somebody will have to answer for all the damage that has been caused.* ▶ **odpowiadać za coś/kogoś 2** to speak in support of sb/sth: *I can certainly answer for her honesty.* ▶ **ręczyć za kogoś/coś**
answer to sb (for sth) to have to explain your actions or decisions to sb ▶ **odpowiadać przed kimś (za coś)**

> **answer**
> **Answer** i **reply** to najczęściej używane czasowniki w sytuacjach, gdy odpowiada się na pytania, listy itp: *I asked him a question but he didn't answer.* ◇ *I sent my application but they haven't replied yet.* Zwróć uwagę, że **answer** używa się bez przyimka: *answer a person, a question or a letter*; a **reply** z przyimkiem **to**: *reply to a letter*. **Respond** jest słowem rzadziej używanym i ma bardziej formalny charakter: *Applicants must respond within seven days.* Częściej używa się go w znaczeniu „reagować w pożądany sposób": *Despite all the doctor's efforts the patient did not respond to treatment.*

answerable /'ɑːnsərəbl; US 'æn-/ adj. [not before a noun] **answerable to sb (for sth)** having to explain and give good reasons for your actions to sb; responsible to sb ▶ **odpowiedzialny przed kimś (za coś)**

'answering machine (Brit. also **answerphone** /'ɑːnsəfəʊn; US 'æn-/) noun [C] a machine that answers the telephone and records messages from the people who call: *I rang him and left a message on his answering machine.* ▶ **automatyczna sekretarka**

ant /ænt/ noun [C] a very small insect that lives in large groups and works very hard ▶ **mrówka** ➲ picture at **insect**

antagonism /æn'tægənɪzəm/ noun [C,U] **antagonism (towards sb/sth)**; **antagonism (between A and B)** a feeling of hate and of being against sb/sth ▶ **antagonizm**
■ **antagonistic** /ænˌtægə'nɪstɪk/ adj.: *Why do you feel so antagonistic towards him?* ▶ **wrogi, nieprzyjazny**

antagonize (also **-ise**) /æn'tægənaɪz/ verb [T] to make sb angry or to annoy sb ▶ **zrażać, antagonizować**

Antarctic /æn'tɑːktɪk/ adj. [only before a noun] connected with the coldest, most southern parts of the world: *an Antarctic expedition* ▶ **antarktyczny** ➲ look at **Arctic**
■ **Antarctic** (**the Antarctic**) noun [sing.] the regions of the world around the South Pole: *the Antarctic Circle* koło podbiegunowe południowe ▶ **Antarktyka** ➲ look at **Arctic**

anteater /'æntiːtə(r)/ noun [C] an animal with a long nose and tongue that eats **ants** ▶ **mrówkojad**

antelope /'æntɪləʊp/ noun [C] (pl. **antelope** or **antelopes**) an African animal with horns and long, thin legs that can run very fast ▶ **antylopa**

antenatal /ˌænti'neɪtl/ adj. [only before a noun] connected with the care of pregnant women: *an antenatal clinic* ◇ *antenatal care* ▶ **prenatalny**

antenna /æn'tenə/ noun [C] **1** (pl. **antennae** /-niː/) one of the two long thin parts on the heads of insects and some animals that live in shells. **Antennae** are used for feeling things. ▶ **czułek** SYN **feeler** ➲ picture at **insect**, picture on **page A11 2** (pl. **antennas**) (US) = AERIAL[1]

anthem /'ænθəm/ noun [C] a song, especially one that is sung on special occasions: *the national anthem* ▶ **hymn**

anthology /æn'θɒlədʒi/ noun [C] (pl. **anthologies**) a book that contains pieces of writing or poems, often on the same subject, by different authors ▶ **antologia**

anthrax /ˈænθræks/ noun [U] a serious disease that affects sheep, cows and sometimes people, and can cause death ▶ **wąglik**

anthropology /ˌænθrəˈpɒlədʒi/ noun [U] the study of humans, especially of their origin, development, customs and beliefs ▶ **antropologia**
■ **anthropological** /ˌænθrəpəˈlɒdʒɪkl/ adj. ▶ **antropologiczny** | **anthropologist** /ˌænθrəˈpɒlədʒɪst/ noun [C] ▶ **antropolog**

anti /ˈænti/ prep. (informal) if sb is **anti** sb/sth, they do not like or agree with that person or thing: *They're completely anti the new proposals.* ▶ **przeciw** ➲ look at **pro**

anti- /ˈænti/ [in compounds] **1** against: *anti-tank weapons* ▶ **anty-, przeciw-** ➲ look at **pro- 2** the opposite of: *anticlimax* rozczarowanie ▶ **przeciwieństwo czegoś 3** preventing: *antifreeze* płyn do chłodnic przeciw zamarzaniu ▶ **przeciwdziałający czemuś**

antibiotic /ˌæntibaɪˈɒtɪk/ noun [C,U] a medicine which is used for destroying bacteria and curing infections ▶ **antybiotyk**

antibody /ˈæntibɒdi/ noun [C] (pl. **antibodies**) a substance that the body produces in the blood to fight disease, or as a reaction when certain substances are put into the body ▶ **przeciwciało**

anticipate /ænˈtɪsɪpeɪt/ verb [T] to expect sth to happen and prepare for it: *to anticipate a problem* ◇ *I anticipate that the situation will get worse.* ▶ **przewidywać, oczekiwać**

anticipation /ænˌtɪsɪˈpeɪʃn/ noun [U] **1** the state of expecting sth to happen (and preparing for it): *The government has reduced tax* ***in anticipation of*** *an early general election.* ▶ **oczekiwanie, przewidywanie 2** excited feelings about sth that is going to happen: *happy/eager/excited anticipation* ▶ **oczekiwanie**

anticlimax /ˌæntiˈklaɪmæks/ noun [C,U] an event, etc. that is less exciting than you had expected or than what has already happened: *When the exams were over we all had a sense of anticlimax.* ▶ **rozczarowanie, zawód**

anticlockwise /ˌæntiˈklɒkwaɪz/ (US **counterclockwise** /ˌkaʊntəˈklɒkwaɪz/) adv., adj. in the opposite direction to the movement of the hands of a clock: *Turn the lid anticlockwise/in an anticlockwise direction.* ▶ **przeciw-nie/ny do ruchu wskazówek zegara** OPP **clockwise**

antics /ˈæntɪks/ noun [pl.] funny, strange or silly ways of behaving ▶ **popisy, błazeństwa**

antidepressant /ˌæntidɪˈpresnt/ noun [C,U] a drug used to treat **depression** ▶ **lek przeciwdepresyjny**

antidote /ˈæntidəʊt/ noun [C] **1** a medical substance that is used to prevent a poison or a disease from having an effect: *an antidote to snake bites* ▶ **odtrutka 2** anything that helps you to deal with sth unpleasant: *Many people find music a marvellous antidote to stress.* ▶ **antidotum**

antifreeze /ˈæntifriːz/ noun [U] a chemical that you add to the water in cars, etc. to stop it from freezing ▶ **płyn do chłodnic przeciw zamarzaniu**

antihistamine /ˌæntiˈhɪstəmiːn/ noun [C,U] a drug used to treat **allergies** such as **hay fever**: *anithistamine cream/injections/shots* ▶ **antyhistamina**

antioxidant /ˌæntiˈɒksɪdənt/ noun [C] a substance such as **vitamin** C or E that removes dangerous **molecules**, etc. from the body ▶ **przeciwutleniacz**

antipathy /ænˈtɪpəθi/ noun [C,U] **antipathy (to/towards sb/sth)** a strong feeling of not liking sb/sth ▶ **niechęć, antypatia** SYN **dislike**

antiperspirant /ˌæntiˈpɜːspərənt/ noun [C,U] a liquid that you use to reduce sweating, especially under your arms ▶ **dezodorant antyperspiracyjny**

antiquated /ˈæntɪkweɪtɪd/ adj. old-fashioned and not suitable for the modern world ▶ **przestarzały**

antique /ænˈtiːk/ adj. very old and therefore unusual and valuable: *an antique vase/table* ◇ *antique furniture/jewellery* ▶ **zabytkowy, antyczny**
■ **antique** noun [C]: *an antique shop* sklep z antykami ▶ **antyk**

> **Antique** (adj.) i **antique** (noun) używa się w odniesieniu do przedmiotów (zwykle mebli), które powstały ponad sto lat temu. Zabytek pochodzący z epoki starożytnej określa się mianem **antiquity**. Porównaj też **ancient**.

antiquity /ænˈtɪkwəti/ noun (pl. **antiquities**) **1** [U] the ancient past, especially the times of the ancient Greeks and Romans ▶ **starożytność 2** [U] the state of being very old or ancient: *priceless objects of great antiquity* bezcenne przedmioty pochodzące z czasów starożytnych ▶ **starość 3** [C, usually pl.] a building or object from ancient times: *Greek/Roman antiquities* ▶ **bezcenny, starożytny przedmiot; antyk**

anti-Semitism /ˌænti ˈsemətɪzəm/ noun [U] unfair treatment of Jewish people ▶ **antysemityzm**
■ **anti-Semitic** /ˌænti səˈmɪtɪk/ adj. ▶ **antysemicki**

antiseptic /ˌæntiˈseptɪk/ noun [C,U] a liquid or cream that prevents a cut, etc. from becoming infected: *Put an antiseptic/some antiseptic on that scratch.* ▶ **środek antyseptyczny** SYN **disinfectant**
■ **antiseptic** adj.: *antiseptic cream* ▶ **antyseptyczny**

antisocial /ˌæntiˈsəʊʃl/ adj. **1** harmful or annoying to other people: *antisocial behaviour* ▶ **aspołeczny 2** not liking to be with other people: *We don't go out much. I suppose we're rather antisocial.* ▶ **nietowarzyski**

antithesis /ænˈtɪθəsɪs/ noun [C,U] (pl. **antitheses** /ænˈtɪθəsiːz/) (formal) **1** the opposite of sth: *Love is the antithesis of hate.* ▶ **antyteza, przeciwieństwo 2** a contrast between two things: *There is an antithesis between the needs of the state and the needs of the people.* ▶ **kontrast**

antler /ˈæntlə(r)/ noun [C, usually pl.] a horn shaped like a branch on the head of some adult male animals: *a pair of antlers* poroże ▶ **róg jelenia** ➲ picture on **page A10**

antonym /ˈæntənɪm/ noun [C] (technical) a word that means the opposite of another word ▶ **antonim** SYN **opposite** ➲ look at **synonym**

anus /ˈeɪnəs/ noun [C] the hole through which solid waste substances leave the body ▶ **odbyt** ➲ picture at **body**

anxiety /æŋˈzaɪəti/ noun [C,U] (pl. **anxieties**) a feeling of worry or fear, especially about the future: *a feeling/state of anxiety* ◇ *There are anxieties over the effects of unemployment.* ▶ **niepokój, lęk**

anxious /ˈæŋkʃəs/ adj. **1 anxious (about/for sb/sth)** worried and afraid: *I'm anxious about my exam.* ◇ *I began to get anxious when they still hadn't arrived at 9 o'clock.* ◇ *an anxious look/expression* ▶ **niespokojny, zaniepokojony** ⓘ **Be/get anxious** często tłumaczy się „niepokoić się". **2** causing worry and fear: *For a few anxious moments we thought we'd missed the train.* ▶ **niespokojny 3 anxious to do sth; anxious for sth** wanting sth very much: *Police are anxious to find* (policji bardzo zależy na odnalezieniu) *the owner of the white car.* ▶ **palący się do czegoś**
■ **anxiously** adv. ▶ **z zaniepokojeniem**

any /ˈeni/ determiner, pron., adv. ⓘ W znaczeniach 1, 2 i 4 **any** często nie tłumaczy się. **1** (used instead of *some* in negative sentences): *We didn't have any lunch.* Nie jedliśmy obiadu. ◇ *I speak hardly any Spanish.* Prawie wcale nie mówię po hiszpańsku. ◇ *I wanted chips but there aren't any.* Chciałem frytki, ale ich nie ma. ◇ *I don't like any of his books.* Nie lubię żadnej z jego książek. ▶ **żaden** ➲ note at **some 2** (used instead of *some* in questions): *Do you have any questions?* ◇ *Have you got any children?* Czy masz dzieci? ◇ *Are there any apples?* Czy są jabłka? ◇ *Do you know any French?* Czy znasz język francuski? ▶ **jakiś** **3** (used for saying that it does not matter which thing or person you choose): *Take any book you want.* ◇ *I'll take any that you don't want.* ▶ **jakikolwiek, którykolwiek, każdy** ➲ look at **any time** **4** [used after *if/whether*] some: *He asked if we had any questions.* Zapytał, czy mamy jakieś pytania. ▶ **jakiś**

IDM **any moment, day, second, etc. (now)** very soon: *She should be home any minute now.* ▶ **lada chwila/minuta/dzień**

■ **any** adv. at all; to any degree: *Is your father any better?* Czy twój ojciec czuje się trochę lepiej? ◇ *I can't run any faster.* Nie mogę biec (jeszcze) szybciej. ▶ **do pewnego stopnia**

anybody /ˈenibɒdi; US also -bʌdi/ (also **anyone** /ˈeniwʌn/) pron. **1** [usually in questions or negative statements] any person: *Is there anybody here who can speak Japanese?* ◇ *Would* ***anybody else*** (ktoś jeszcze) *like to come with me?* ◇ *I didn't know anybody at the party.* ▶ **ktoś; nikt** ⓘ Różnica między **somebody** i **anybody** jest taka sama jak między **some** i **any**. ➲ note at **some**, **somebody** **2** any person, it does not matter who: *Anybody can learn to swim.* ◇ *Can anybody come, or are there special invitations?* ▶ **każdy, ktokolwiek**

anyhow /ˈenihaʊ/ adv. **1** = ANYWAY **2** in a careless way; with no order: *Don't throw your clothes down just anyhow!* ▶ **byle jak**

any 'more (especially US **anymore**) adv. (often used at the end of negative sentences and at the end of questions, to mean 'any longer'): *She doesn't live here any more.* ▶ **już (nie)**

anyone = ANYBODY

anyplace (US) = ANYWHERE

anything /ˈeniθɪŋ/ pron. **1** [in negative sentences] one thing (of any kind): *It was so dark that I couldn't see anything at all.* ◇ *There isn't anything interesting in the newspaper today.* ▶ **(zupełnie) nic** ⓘ Różnica między **something** i **anything** jest taka sama jak między **some** i **any**. ➲ note at **some** **2** [in questions] one thing (of any kind): *Did you buy anything?* ◇ *'I'd like a kilo of apples please.' '****Anything else?****'* ▶ **coś** **3** any thing or things: it does not matter what: *I'm very hungry – I'll eat anything!* ◇ *I'll do anything you say.* ▶ **cokolwiek, obojętnie co**

IDM **anything but** not at all: *Their explanation was anything but clear.* ▶ **wcale nie**

anything like sb/sth at all similar to sb/sth; nearly: *She isn't anything like her sister, is she?* ◇ *This car isn't anything like as fast as mine.* Ten samochód nie jest ani trochę tak szybki jak mój. ▶ **wcale**

as happy, quick, etc. as anything (informal) very happy, quick, etc. ▶ **bardzo szczęśliwy, itd.**

do nothing/not do anything by halves → HALF[1]

like anything → LIKE[1]

not come to anything → COME

'any time (especially US **anytime**) adv. at a time that is not fixed: *Call me any time.* ▶ **kiedykolwiek, o każdej porze**

IDM **anytime soon** (US) (used in negative sentences and questions to refer to the near future): *Will she be back anytime soon?* ▶ **w każdej chwili**

anyway /ˈeniweɪ/ (also **anyhow**) adv. **1** (used to add an extra point or reason) in any case: *I don't want to go out tonight, and anyway I haven't got any money.* ▶ **tak czy owak** SYN **besides** **2** (used when saying or writing sth which contrasts in some way with what has gone before): *I don't think we'll succeed, but anyway we can try.* ◇ *I'm afraid I can't come to your party, but thanks anyway* (niemniej, dziękuję). ▶ **jednak, w każdym razie** **3** (used after a pause in order to change the subject or go back to a subject being discussed before): *Anyway, that's enough about my problems. How are you?* ▶ **w każdym razie** **4** (used for correcting sth you have just said and making it more accurate) at least: *Everybody wants to be rich – well, most people anyway.* ▶ **przynajmniej**

anywhere /ˈeniweə(r)/ (US also **anyplace** /ˈenipleɪs/) adv. **1** [usually in negative sentences or in questions] in, at or to any place: *I can't find my keys anywhere.* ◇ *Is there a post office anywhere near here?* ◇ *You can't buy the book* ***anywhere else*** (nigdzie indziej). ▶ **gdzieś; nigdzie** ⓘ Różnica między **somewhere** i **anywhere** jest taka sama jak między **some** i **any**. ➲ note at **some** **2** any place; it does not matter where: *You can sit anywhere you like.* ▶ **gdziekolwiek, obojętnie gdzie**

AOB /ˌeɪ əʊ ˈbiː/ abbr. **any other business**; the things that are discussed at the end of an official meeting that are not on the **agenda** ▶ **wolne wnioski**

aorta /eɪˈɔːtə/ noun [C] the main **artery** that carries blood from the heart to the rest of the body once it has passed through the **lungs** ▶ **aorta**

apart /əˈpɑːt/ adv. **1** away from sb/sth or each other; not together: *Stand with your feet apart.* ◇ *Plant the potatoes two feet apart.* Sadź ziemniaki co dwie stopy. ◇ *The doors slowly slid apart.* Drzwi wolno się otworzyły. ◇ *I'm afraid our ideas are too far apart.* ▶ **od siebie; osobno** **2** into pieces: *The material was so old that it just* ***fell/came apart*** *in my hands* (po prostu rozsypał się). ◇ *Their relationship was clearly falling apart.* Ich związek najwyraźniej rozlatywał się. ▶ **na części/kawałki**

IDM **take sth apart** to separate sth into pieces: *He took the whole bicycle apart.* ▶ **rozkładać na części**

tell A and B apart → TELL

a'part from (especially US **a'side from**) prep. **1** except for: *There's nobody here apart from me.* ▶ **oprócz** **2** as well as; in addition to: *Apart from music, she also loves painting.* ◇ *You've got to help me. Apart from anything else* (pomijając inne sprawy) *you're my brother.* ▶ **oprócz**

apartheid /əˈpɑːtaɪt; US also -teɪt/ noun [U] the former official government policy in South Africa of separating people of different races and making them live apart ▶ **apartheid**

apartment /əˈpɑːtmənt/ noun [C] **1** (especially US) = FLAT[2] (1) **2** a set of rooms rented for a holiday: *a self-catering apartment* ▶ **apartament**

a'partment block noun [C] (especially US) a large building containing several **apartments** ▶ **blok mieszkalny**

apathetic /ˌæpəˈθetɪk/ adj. lacking interest or desire to act: *Many students are apathetic about politics.* ▶ **apatyczny**

apathy /ˈæpəθi/ noun [U] the feeling of not being interested in or enthusiastic about anything: *There is widespread apathy towards the elections.* ▶ **apatia**

ape[1] /eɪp/ noun [C] a type of animal like a large **monkey** with no tail or only a very short tail ▶ **małpa bezogoniasta, małpa człekokształtna**

ape[2] /eɪp/ verb [T] to copy sb/sth, especially in a ridiculous way ▶ **małpować**

aperitif /əˌperəˈtiːf/ noun [C] an alcoholic drink that you have before a meal ▶ **aperitif**

aperture /ˈæpətʃə(r)/ noun [C] (formal) a small opening in sth, especially one that allows light into a camera ▶ *(fot.)* **przesłona**

apex /ˈeɪpeks/ noun [C, usually sing.] (pl. **apexes**) the top or highest part of sth: *the apex of the roof* ▶ **szczyt, wierzchołek**

aphid /ˈeɪfɪd/ noun [C] a very small insect that is harmful to plants. There are several types of **aphid**. ▶ **mszyca**

aphorism /ˈæfərɪzəm/ noun [C] (formal) a short phrase that says sth true or wise ▶ **aforyzm**

■ **aphoristic** /ˌæfəˈrɪstɪk/ adj. ▶ **aforystyczny**

aphrodisiac /ˌæfrəˈdɪziæk/ noun [C] a food or drug that is said to give people a strong desire to have sex ▶ **afrodyzjak**

apiece /əˈpiːs/ adv. each: *Coates and Owen scored a goal apiece.* ▶ **każdemu po** (*np. złotówce*)

apocalyptic /əˌpɒkəˈlɪptɪk/ adj. **1** describing very serious damage and destruction in past or future events: *an apocalyptic view of history* ▶ **apokaliptyczny 2** like the end of the world: *an apocalyptic scene* ▶ **apokaliptyczny**

apolitical /ˌeɪpəˈlɪtɪkl/ adj. **1** (used about a person) not interested in politics; not thinking politics are important ▶ **apolityczny 2** not connected with a political party ▶ **apolityczny**

apologetic /əˌpɒləˈdʒetɪk/ adj. feeling or showing that you are sorry for sth you have done: *He was most apologetic about* (bardzo przepraszał za) *his son's bad behaviour.* ◇ *I wrote him an apologetic letter.* ▶ **przepraszający, skruszony**

■ **apologetically** /-kli/ adv. ▶ **przepraszająco, ze skruchą**

apologist /əˈpɒlədʒɪst/ noun [C] **apologist (for sb/sth)** a person who tries to explain and defend sth, especially a political system or religious ideas: *apologists for nuclear power* ▶ **apologet(k)a**

⚷ **apologize** (also -ise) /əˈpɒlədʒaɪz/ verb [I] **apologize (to sb) (for sth)** to say that you are sorry for sth that you have done: *You'll have to apologize to your teacher for being late.* ▶ **przepraszać** ⓘ Przepraszając za coś, używa się słów **I'm sorry**. Porównaj **regret²**(2). Tego czasownika używa się w języku formalnym.

apology /əˈpɒlədʒi/ noun [C,U] (pl. **apologies**) **(an) apology (to sb) (for sth)** a spoken or written statement that you are sorry for sth you have done, etc.: *Please accept our apologies for the delay.* ◇ *a letter of apology* ▶ **przeprosiny**

apostle /əˈpɒsl/ noun [C] **1** (**Apostle**) any one of the twelve men that Christ chose to tell people about him and his teachings ▶ **apostoł 2 an apostle (of sth)** (formal) a person who strongly believes in a policy or an idea and tries to make other people believe in it: *an apostle of free enterprise* ▶ **krzewiciel**

apostrophe /əˈpɒstrəfi/ noun [C] **1** the sign (') used for showing that you have left a letter or letters out of a word as in *I'm, can't* or *we'll* ▶ **apostrof 2** the sign (') used for showing who or what sth belongs to as in *John's chair, the boy's room* or *Russia's President* ▶ **apostrof**

app = APPLICATION (3)

appal (US appall) /əˈpɔːl/ verb [T] (**appalling**; **appalled**) [usually passive] to shock sb very much ▶ **wstrząsać, przerażać**

■ **appalled** adj. **appalled (at sth)** feeling or showing horror or disgust at sth unpleasant or wrong: *an* ***appalled expression/silence*** ◇ *They were appalled at the waste of recyclable material.* ▶ **przerażony** SYN **horrified** | **appalling** adj. ▶ **wstrząsający, przerażający** | **appallingly** adv. ▶ **wstrząsająco, przerażająco**

apparatus /ˌæpəˈreɪtəs; US -ˈræt-/ noun [U] the set of tools, instruments or equipment used for doing a job or an activity ▶ **sprzęt**

⚷ **apparent** /əˈpærənt/ adj. **1 apparent (to sb)** clear; easy to see: *It quickly became apparent to us that our teacher could not speak French.* ▶ **oczywisty, widoczny** SYN **obvious 2** [only before a noun] that seems to be real or true but may not be: *His apparent interest in the proposal didn't last very long.* ▶ **pozorny**

⚷ **apparently** /əˈpærəntli/ adv. **1** according to what people say (but perhaps not true): *Apparently, he's already been married twice.* ▶ **podobno 2** according to how sth seems or appears (but perhaps not true): *He was apparently undisturbed by the news.* ▶ **pozornie, najwyraźniej, najwidoczniej**

apparition /ˌæpəˈrɪʃn/ noun [C] the image of a dead person that a living person believes they can see ▶ **zjawa, widmo**

⚷ **appeal¹** /əˈpiːl/ noun **1** [C] a formal request to sb in authority to change a decision: *The judge turned down the defendant's appeal.* ▶ **apelacja 2** [U] the attraction or interesting quality of sth/sb: *I can't understand the appeal of stamp collecting.* ▶ **urok, pociąg (do czegoś) 3** [C] a serious request for sth you need or want very much: *The police have made an urgent appeal for witnesses to come forward.* ▶ **apel, wezwanie 4** [C] **an appeal to sth** a suggestion that tries to influence sb's feelings or thoughts so that they will do what you want: *an appeal to our sense of national pride* ▶ **apel, wezwanie**

⚷ **appeal²** /əˈpiːl/ verb [I] **1 appeal (against/for sth)** to ask sb in authority to make or change a decision: *He decided to appeal against his conviction.* ◇ *The player fell down and appealed for a penalty.* ▶ **wnosić apelację 2 appeal (to sb)** to be attractive or interesting to sb: *The idea of living in the country doesn't appeal to me at all.* ▶ **podobać się,** (*pomysł*) **przemawiać (do kogoś) 3 appeal to sb (for sth)**; **appeal for sth** to make a serious request for sth you need or want very much: *She appealed to the kidnappers to let her son go.* ◇ *Relief workers in the disaster area are appealing for more supplies.* ▶ **zwracać się** (*o pomoc itp.*), **wzywać kogoś do zrobienia czegoś 4 appeal to sth** to influence sb's feelings or thoughts so that they will do sth you want: *We aim to appeal to people's generosity.* ▶ **odwoływać się do czegoś**

appealing /əˈpiːlɪŋ/ adj. **1** attractive or interesting: *The idea of a lying on a beach sounds very appealing!* ▶ **pociągający 2** showing that you need help, etc.: *an appealing look* ▶ **błagalny**

■ **appealingly** adv. ▶ **pociągająco**; **błagalnie**

⚷ **appear** /əˈpɪə(r)/ verb [I] **1 appear to be/do sth**; **appear (that)**... to seem: *She appears* (zdaje się, że ona) *to be very happy in her job.* ◇ *It appears* (zdaje mi się, że) *that you were given the wrong information.* ◇ *'Do you think there will be an election?' 'It appears so/not* (zdaje się, że tak/nie). ▶ **zdawać się** ➲ adjective **apparent 2** to suddenly be seen; to come into sight: *The bus appeared from round the corner.* ▶ **pojawiać się** OPP **disappear 3** to begin to exist: *The disease is thought to have appeared in Africa.* ▶ **pojawiać się 4** to be published or printed: *The article appeared in this morning's paper.* ▶ **ukazywać się 5** to perform or speak where you are seen by a lot of people: *to appear on TV/in a play* ▶ **występować**

⚷ **appearance** /əˈpɪərəns/ noun **1** [U] the way that sb/sth looks or seems: *A different hairstyle can completely change your appearance.* ◇ *He gives the appearance of being extremely confident.* ▶ **wygląd 2** [sing.] the coming of sb/sth: *The crowd was awaiting the appearance of the President.* ◇ *the appearance of TV in the home in the 1950s* ▶ **pojawienie się, początek 3** [C] an act of appearing in public, especially on stage, TV, etc.: *His last appearance before his death was as Julius Caesar.* ▶ **występ**

appease /əˈpiːz/ verb [T] (formal) to give sb what they want in order to make them less angry or to avoid a war ▶ **ułagodzić, udobruchać**

■ **appeasement** noun [U]: *a policy of appeasement* polityka ustępstw ▶ **uspokojenie, udobruchanie**

appendicitis /əˌpendəˈsaɪtɪs/ noun [U] an illness in which your **appendix** becomes extremely painful and usually has to be removed ▶ **zapalenie wyrostka robaczkowego**

appendix /əˈpendɪks/ noun [C] **1** (pl. **appendixes**) a small organ inside your body near your stomach. In humans, the **appendix** has no real function. ▶ **wyrostek robacz-**

kowy ➲ picture at **body** **2** (pl. **appendices** /-dɪsiːz/) a section at the end of a book, etc. that gives extra information ▶ **dodatek**

appetite /ˈæpɪtaɪt/ noun **1** [U,C, usually sing.] physical desire for food: *Some fresh air and exercise should give you an appetite* (powinny ci poprawić apetyt). ◇ *loss of appetite* ▶ **apetyt** **2** [C] **an appetite (for sth)** a natural desire: *The public have an insatiable appetite for scandal.* ◇ *sexual appetites* ▶ **żądza**
IDM **whet sb's appetite** → WHET

appetizer (also **-iser**) = STARTER

appetizing (also **-ising**) /ˈæpɪtaɪzɪŋ/ adj. (used about food, etc.) that looks or smells attractive; making you feel hungry ▶ **apetyczny**, **smakowity**

applaud /əˈplɔːd/ verb **1** [I,T] to hit your hands together many times in order to show that you like sb/sth: *The audience applauded loudly.* ▶ **klaskać**, **bić brawo** **2** [T, usually passive] to express approval of sth: *The decision was applauded* (uzyskała poklask) *by everybody.* ▶ **przyklaskiwać**

applause /əˈplɔːz/ noun [U] the noise made by a group of people hitting their hands together to show their approval and enjoyment: *Let's all give a big* ***round of applause*** *to the cook!* ▶ **oklaski**

⚷ **apple** /ˈæpl/ noun [C,U] a hard, round fruit with a smooth green, red or yellow skin: *apple juice* ◇ *an apple tree* jabłoń ▶ **jabłko** ➲ picture on **page A12**

applet /ˈæplət/ noun [C] a computer program which is run from within another program ▶ **aplet**

appliance /əˈplaɪəns/ noun [C] a piece of equipment for a particular purpose in the house: *washing machines and other domestic appliances* ▶ **urządzenie**, **przyrząd**

applicable /əˈplɪkəbl; ˈæplɪkəbl/ adj. **applicable (to sb/sth)** that concerns sb/sth: *This part of the form is only applicable to* (odnosi się tylko do) *married women.* ▶ **odnoszący się**, **dotyczący** SYN **relevant**

applicant /ˈæplɪkənt/ noun [C] a person who **applies** for sth, especially for a job, a place at a college, university, etc. ▶ **kandydat/ka**

⚷ **application** /ˌæplɪˈkeɪʃn/ noun **1** [C,U] **(an) application (to sb) (for sth)** a formal written request, especially for a job or a place in a school, club, etc.: *Applications for the job should be made to the Personnel Manager.* ◇ *To become a member, fill in the* ***application form.*** ▶ **podanie** ➲ note at **job** **2** [C,U] the practical use (of sth): *the application of technology in the classroom* ▶ **zastosowanie**, **użytek** **3** [C] (abbr. **app**) a computer program designed to do a particular job: *a database application* ▶ **program użytkowy do komputera** **4** [U] hard work; effort: *Success as a writer demands great application.* ▶ **przykładanie się**

applicator /ˈæplɪkeɪtə(r)/ noun [C] a small tool that is used to put a substance onto a surface, or to put sth into an object ▶ **aplikator**

applied /əˈplaɪd/ adj. (used about a subject) studied in a way that has a practical use: *applied mathematics/linguistics* ▶ **stosowany** OPP **pure**

⚷ **apply** /əˈplaɪ/ verb (**applying**; **applies**; pt, pp **applied**) **1** [I] **apply (to sb) (for sth)** to ask for sth in writing: *I've applied to that company for a job.* ◇ *She's applying for a place at university.* ▶ **składać podanie** **2** [T] **apply sth (to sth)** to make practical use of sth: *new technology which can be applied to solving problems in industry* ▶ **stosować** **3** [T] **apply sth (to sth)** to put or spread sth onto sth: *Apply the cream to the infected area twice a day.* ▶ **przykładać**, **smarować** **4** [I] **apply (to sb/sth)** to concern or involve sb/sth: *This information applies to all children born after 2002.* ▶ **odnosić się**, **dotyczyć** **5** [T, usually passive] to use a word, a name, etc. to describe sb/sth: *I don't think the term 'music' can be applied to that awful noise.* Moim zdaniem, nie można określić tego okropnego hałasu mianem muzyki. ▶ **stosować** **6** [T] **apply yourself/sth (to sth/doing sth)** to make yourself give all your attention to sth: *to apply your mind to something* ◇ *He applied himself to his studies.* ▶ **skupiać się nad czymś**, **przykładać się**

⚷ **appoint** /əˈpɔɪnt/ verb [T] **1** **appoint sb (to sth)** to choose sb for a job or position: *The committee have appointed a new chairperson.* ◇ *He's been appointed (as) assistant to Dr McMullen.* ▶ **mianować** **2** (formal) **appoint sth (for sth)** to arrange or decide on sth: *the date appointed for the next meeting* ▶ **wyznaczać**

appointee /əˌpɔɪnˈtiː/ noun [C] a person who has been chosen for a job or position of responsibility: *the new appointee to the post* ▶ **osoba mianowana** (*na stanowisko, posadę*)

⚷ **appointment** /əˈpɔɪntmənt/ noun **1** [C,U] **an appointment (with sb)** an arrangement to see sb at a particular time: *I have an appointment with Dr Sula at 3 o'clock.* ◇ *I'd like to* ***make an appointment*** *to see the manager.* Chciałbym się umówić na spotkanie z kierownikiem. ◇ *I realized I wouldn't be able to* ***keep the appointment*** (dotrzymać terminu spotkania) *so I cancelled it.* ◇ *Visits are by appointment only.* Tylko umówione wizyty. ▶ **umówione spotkanie** **2** [U] **appointment (to sth)** the act of choosing sb for a job ▶ **mianowanie** **3** [C] a job or a position of responsibility: *a temporary/permanent appointment* ▶ **posada**, **stanowisko**

appraisal /əˈpreɪzl/ noun [C,U] (formal) a judgement about the value or quality of sb/sth ▶ **ocena**, **oszacowanie**

appraise /əˈpreɪz/ verb [T] (formal) to judge the value or quality of sb/sth ▶ **oceniać**, **oszacowywać**

appreciable /əˈpriːʃəbl/ adj. noticeable or important ▶ **zauważalny**, **znaczny**

⚷ **appreciate** /əˈpriːʃieɪt/ verb **1** [T] to enjoy sth or to understand the value of sb/sth: *My boss doesn't appreciate me.* ◇ *I don't appreciate good coffee – it all tastes the same to me.* ▶ **doceniać** **2** [T] to be grateful for sth: *Thanks very much. I really appreciate your help.* ▶ **doceniać** **3** [T] to understand a problem, situation, etc.: *I appreciate your problem but I'm afraid I can't help you.* ▶ **zdawać sobie sprawę** **4** [I] to increase in value: *Houses in this area have appreciated faster than elsewhere.* ▶ **podrożeć**

appreciation /əˌpriːʃiˈeɪʃn/ noun [U] **1** understanding and enjoyment of the value of sth: *I'm afraid I have little appreciation of modern architecture.* ▶ **zrozumienie**, **znajdowanie (w czymś) przyjemności** **2** understanding of a situation, problem, etc. ▶ **pojęcie**, **zrozumienie** **3** the feeling of being grateful for sth: *We bought him a present to show our appreciation for all the work he had done.* ▶ **wdzięczność** **4** an increase in value ▶ **wzrost wartości**

appreciative /əˈpriːʃətɪv/ adj. **1** **appreciative (of sth)** grateful for sth: *He was very appreciative of our efforts to help.* ▶ **wdzięczny** **2** feeling or showing pleasure or admiration: *an appreciative audience* ▶ **pochwalny**

apprehend /ˌæprɪˈhend/ verb [T] (formal) (used about the police) to catch sb and arrest them ▶ **zatrzymywać**, **aresztować**

apprehensive /ˌæprɪˈhensɪv/ adj. worried or afraid that sth unpleasant may happen: *to be/feel apprehensive (about sth)* obawiać się ▶ **pełen obaw**
■ **apprehension** /ˌæprɪˈhenʃn/ noun [C,U] ▶ **obawa**

apprentice /əˈprentɪs/ noun [C] a person who works for low pay, in order to learn the skills needed in a particular job: *an apprentice electrician/chef/plumber* ▶ **terminator/ka**, **ucze-ń/nnica**

apprenticeship /ə'prentɪʃɪp/ noun [C,U] the state or time of being an **apprentice**: *He served a two-year apprenticeship as a carpenter.* ▶ **termin** (*nauka rzemiosła*)

approach¹ /ə'prəʊtʃ/ verb **1** [I,T] to come near or nearer to sb/sth: *The day of the exam approached.* ◇ *When you approach the village you will see a garage on your left.* ▶ **zbliżać się, podchodzić (do kogoś/czegoś) 2** [T] to speak to sb usually in order to ask for sth: *I'm going to approach my bank manager about a loan.* ▶ **zwracać się (do kogoś) 3** [T] to begin to deal with a problem, a situation, etc.: *What is the best way to approach this problem?* ▶ **podchodzić** (*np. do problemu*)

approach² /ə'prəʊtʃ/ noun **1** [C] a way of dealing with sb/sth: *Parents don't always know what approach to take with teenage children.* ▶ **podejście 2** [sing.] the act of coming nearer (to sb/sth): *the approach of winter* ▶ **zbliżanie się, podejście 3** [C] a request for sth: *The company has* ***made an approach to us*** (zwróciła się z prośbą) *for financial assistance.* ▶ **propozycja, oferta 4** [C] a road or path leading to sth: *the approach to the village* ▶ **droga dojazdowa, dojście**

approachable /ə'prəʊtʃəbl/ adj. **1** friendly and easy to talk to ▶ **dostępny, przystępny 2** [not before a noun] that can be reached ▶ **dostępny** SYN **accessible**

appropriate¹ /ə'prəʊpriət/ adj. **appropriate (for/to sth)** suitable or right for a particular situation, person, use, etc.: *The matter will be dealt with by the appropriate authorities.* ◇ *I don't think this film is appropriate for young children.* ▶ **odpowiedni** OPP **inappropriate**
■ **appropriately** adv. ▶ **odpowiednio**

appropriate² /ə'prəʊprieɪt/ verb [T] to take sth to use for yourself, usually without permission ▶ **przywłaszczyć sobie**

appropriation /ə,prəʊpri'eɪʃn/ noun **1** [U, sing.] (formal) the act of taking sth which belongs to sb else, especially without permission: *dishonest appropriation of property* ▶ **przywłaszczenie 2** [U, sing.] (formal) the act of keeping or saving money for a particular purpose: *a meeting to discuss the appropriation of funds* ▶ **przeznaczenie, wyasygnowanie 3** [C] (formal) a sum of money to be used for a particular purpose, especially by a government or company: *an appropriation of £20 000 for payment of debts* ▶ **wyasygnowane fundusze/środki**

approval /ə'pru:vl/ noun [U] feeling, showing or saying that you think sth is good; agreement: *Everybody* ***gave*** *their* ***approval to*** *the proposal.* ▶ **pochwała, zgoda** OPP **disapproval**

approve /ə'pru:v/ verb **1** [I] **approve (of sb/sth)** to be pleased about sth; to like sb/sth: *His father didn't approve of him becoming a dancer.* ◇ *Her parents don't approve of her friends.* ▶ **aprobować, pochwalać** OPP **disapprove 2** [T] to agree formally to sth or to say that sth is correct: *We need to get an accountant to approve these figures.* ▶ **zatwierdzać, potwierdzać**

approving /ə'pru:vɪŋ/ adj. showing support or admiration for sth: *'I agree entirely,' he said with an approving smile.* ▶ **aprobujący**
■ **approvingly** adv. ▶ **z aprobatą**

approx (formal) = APPROXIMATE, APPROXIMATELY

approximate /ə'prɒksɪmət/ adj. (abbr. **approx**) almost correct but not completely accurate: *The approximate time of arrival is 3 o'clock.* ◇ *I can only give you an approximate idea of the cost.* ▶ **przybliżony, zbliżony** OPP **exact**

approximately /ə'prɒksɪmətli/ adv. (abbr. **approx**) about ▶ **około** SYN **roughly**

approximation /ə,prɒksɪ'meɪʃn/ noun [C] a number, answer, etc. which is nearly, but not exactly, right ▶ **przybliżona liczba, odpowiedź itp.**

Apr. = APRIL: *2 Apr. 1993*

apricot /'eɪprɪkɒt; US 'æp-/ noun [C] a small, round, yellow or orange fruit with a large stone inside ▶ **morela** ➲ picture on **page A12**

April /'eɪprəl/ noun [U,C] (abbr. **Apr.**) the 4th month of the year, coming after March ▶ **kwiecień** ➲ note at **January**

,April 'Fool noun [C] a person who has a joke or trick played on them on 1 April ▶ **ofiara żartu primaaprilisowego**

,April 'Fool's Day noun [sing.] 1 April ▶ **prima aprilis**

apron /'eɪprən/ noun [C] a piece of clothing that you wear over the front of your usual clothes in order to keep them clean, especially when cooking ▶ **fartuch** ➲ picture at **overall**

apropos /,æprə'pəʊ/ (also **apropos of**) prep. concerning or related to sb/sth: *Apropos (of) what you were just saying...* ▶ **à propos**

apt /æpt/ adj. **1** suitable in a particular situation: *I thought 'complex' was an apt description of the book.* ▶ **trafny 2 apt to do sth** often likely to do sth: *You'd better remind me. I'm rather apt to forget* (często zapominam). ▶ **skłonny**

aptitude /'æptɪtju:d; US -tu:d/ noun [U,C] **aptitude (for sth/for doing sth)** natural ability or skill: *She has an aptitude for learning languages.* ▶ **uzdolnienie**

aptly /'æptli/ adv. in an appropriate way: *The winner of the race was aptly named Alan Speedy.* ▶ **trafnie** SYN **suitably**

aquamarine /,ækwəmə'ri:n/ noun **1** [C,U] a pale greenish-blue **precious** stone ▶ (*kamień*) **akwamaryna 2** [U] a pale greenish-blue colour ▶ (*kolor*) **akwamaryna**
■ **aquamarine** adj. ▶ **niebieskawozielony**

aquarium /ə'kweəriəm/ noun [C] (pl. **aquariums** or **aquaria** /-riə/) **1** a glass container filled with water, in which fish and water animals are kept ▶ **akwarium 2** a building where people can go to see fish and other water animals ▶ **akwarium**

Aquarius /ə'kweəriəs/ noun [C,U] the 11th sign of the **zodiac**, the Water Carrier; a person born under this sign: *I'm an Aquarius.* ▶ **Wodnik; zodiakalny Wodnik**

aquatic /ə'kwætɪk/ adj. living or taking place in, on or near water: *aquatic plants* ◇ *windsurfing and other aquatic sports* ▶ **wodny**

aqueduct /'ækwɪdʌkt/ noun [C] a structure for carrying water, usually one like a bridge across a valley ▶ **akwedukt**

Arab /'ærəb/ noun [C] a member of a people who lived originally in Arabia and who now live in many parts of the Middle East and North Africa ▶ **Arab/ka**
■ **Arab** adj.: *Arab countries* ▶ **arabski**

Arabic /'ærəbɪk/ noun [sing.] the language of Arab people ▶ **język arabski**
■ **Arabic** adj. ▶ **arabski**

arable /'ærəbl/ adj. (in farming) connected with growing crops for sale, not keeping animals: *arable land/farmers* ▶ **orny**

arbiter /'ɑ:bɪtə(r)/ noun [C] **arbiter (of sth)** a person with the power or influence to make judgements and decide what will be done or accepted: *The law is the final arbiter of what is considered obscene.* ◇ *an* ***arbiter of taste/style/fashion*** ▶ **arbiter**

arbitrary /'ɑ:bɪtrəri; 'ɑ:bɪtri; US 'ɑ:rbətreri/ adj. not seeming to be based on any reason or plan: *The choice of players for the team seemed completely arbitrary.* ▶ **arbitralny**
■ **arbitrarily** /,ɑ:bɪ'trerəli; 'ɑ:bɪtrəli; US ,ɑ:rbə't-/ adv. ▶ **arbitralnie**

arbitrate /ˈɑːbɪtreɪt/ verb [I,T] to officially settle an argument between two people or groups by finding a solution that both can accept ▶ **rozsądzać**, **rozstrzygać** (*polubownie*)
■ **arbitration** /ˌɑːbɪˈtreɪʃn/ noun [U]: *The union and the management decided to* ***go to arbitration*** (zdać się na arbitraż). ▶ **arbitraż** | **arbitrator** /ˈɑːbɪtreɪtə(r)/ noun [C] ▶ **rozjemca**

arc /ɑːk/ noun [C] a curved line, part of a circle ▶ **łuk**

arcade /ɑːˈkeɪd/ noun [C] **1** a large covered passage or area with shops along one or both sides: *a shopping arcade* ▶ **pasaż handlowy 2** (also **amusement arcade**) a large room with machines and games that you put coins into to play: *arcade games* gry komputerowe ▶ **salon gier**

arch

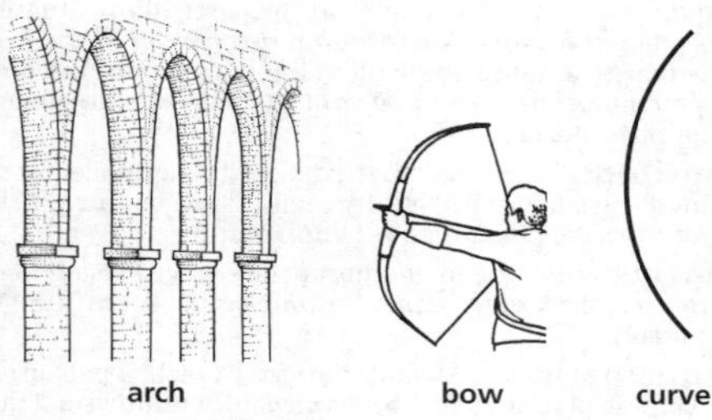

arch¹ /ɑːtʃ/ noun [C] **1** a curved structure with straight sides, often supporting a bridge or the roof of a large building, or it may be above a door or window ▶ **łuk** ➲ look at **archway 2** the curved part of the bottom of your foot ▶ **podbicie**

arch² /ɑːtʃ/ verb [I,T] to make sth into a curve; to form a curve: *The cat arched its back and hissed.* ◇ *Tall trees arched over the path.* ▶ **wyginać (się) w łuk**; **tworzyć łuk**

archaeological (US **archeological**) /ˌɑːkiəˈlɒdʒɪkl/ adj. connected with **archaeology** ▶ **archeologiczny**

archaeologist (US **archeologist**) /ˌɑːkiˈɒlədʒɪst/ noun [C] an expert in **archaeology** ▶ **archeolog**

archaeology (US **archeology**) /ˌɑːkiˈɒlədʒi/ noun [U] the study of the past, based on objects or parts of buildings that are found in the ground ▶ **archeologia**

archaic /ɑːˈkeɪɪk/ adj. very old-fashioned; no longer used ▶ **archaiczny**

archbishop /ˌɑːtʃˈbɪʃəp/ noun [C] a priest with a very high position, in some branches of the Christian Church, who is responsible for all the churches in a large area of a country: *the Archbishop of Canterbury* ▶ **arcybiskup** ➲ look at **bishop**

arched /ɑːtʃt/ adj. in the shape of an **arch** ▶ **łukowaty**, **wygięty w łuk**

ˌarch-ˈenemy noun [C] a person's main enemy ▶ **śmiertelny wróg**

archeological, archeologist, archeology (US) = ARCHAEOLOGICAL, ARCHAEOLOGIST, ARCHAEOLOGY

archer /ˈɑːtʃə(r)/ noun [C] a person who shoots arrows through the air by pulling back a tight string on a **bow** and letting go. In the past this was done in order to kill people, but it is now done as a sport. ▶ **łuczni-k/czka**

archery /ˈɑːtʃəri/ noun [U] the sport of shooting arrows ▶ **łucznictwo**

archetypal /ˌɑːkiˈtaɪpl/ adj. having all the important qualities that make sb/sth a typical example of a particular kind of person or thing ▶ **archetypowy**

architect /ˈɑːkɪtekt/ noun [C] a person whose job is to design buildings ▶ **architekt**

architectural /ˌɑːkɪˈtektʃərəl/ adj. connected with the design of buildings ▶ **architektoniczny**

architecture /ˈɑːkɪtektʃə(r)/ noun [U] the study of designing and making buildings; the style or design of a building or buildings ▶ **architektura**

archive¹ /ˈɑːkaɪv/ noun [C] (also **archives** [pl.]) a collection of historical documents, etc. which show the history of a place or an organization; the place where they are kept: *archive material* (materiały archiwalne) *on the First World War* ▶ **archiw-um/a**

archive² /ˈɑːkaɪv/ verb [T] **1** to put or store a document or other material in an **archive** ▶ **archiwizować 2** to move information that is not often needed to a tape or disk to store it ▶ (*komput.*) **archiwizować**

archivist /ˈɑːkɪvɪst/ noun [C] a person whose job is to develop and manage an **archive** ▶ **archiwist(k)a**

ˌarch-ˈrival noun [C] a person's main opponent ▶ **największy rywal**

archway /ˈɑːtʃweɪ/ noun [C] a passage or entrance with an **arch** over it ▶ **sklepione przejście**

Arctic /ˈɑːktɪk/ adj. [only before a noun] **1** connected with the region around the North Pole (the most northern point of the world) ▶ **arktyczny** ➲ look at **Antarctic 2** (**arctic**) extremely cold ▶ **arktyczny**
■ **Arctic** (**the Arctic**) noun [sing.] the area around the North Pole: *the Arctic Circle* ▶ **koło podbiegunowe północne**; **Arktyka** ➲ look at **Antarctic**

ardent /ˈɑːdnt/ adj. showing strong feelings, especially a strong liking for sb/sth: *an ardent supporter of the Government* ▶ **żarliwy**
■ **ardently** adv. ▶ **żarliwie**

arduous /ˈɑːdjuəs; -dʒu-; US -dʒu-/ adj. full of difficulties; needing a lot of effort: *an arduous journey* ◇ *arduous work* ▶ **uciążliwy**

are /ə(r); strong form ɑː(r)/ → BE

⚷ **area** /ˈeəriə/ noun **1** [C] a part of a town, a country or the world: *Housing is very expensive in the Tokyo area.* ◇ *Forests cover a large area of the country.* ◇ *The high winds scattered litter over a wide area* (na znaczną odległość). ◇ *built-up areas* ▶ **obszar**, **teren 2** [C] a space used for a particular activity: *The restaurant has a non-smoking area.* W tej restauracji jest miejsce dla niepalących. ◇ *the penalty area* pole karne ▶ **rejon**, **strefa 3** [C] a particular part of a subject or an activity: *Training is one area of the business that we could improve.* ▶ **dziedzina 4** [C,U] the size of a surface, that you can calculate by multiplying the length by the width: *The area of the office is 35 square metres.* ◇ *The office is 35 square metres* ***in area.*** ▶ **powierzchnia** ➲ look at **volume**

area
District może stanowić część miasta lub kraju i może mieć konkretne granice: *the district controlled by a council*. **Region** jest większy, na ogół dotyczy części kraju i może nie mieć konkretnych granic: *the industrial regions of the country*. **Area** to określenie najszersze, które może być stosowane do wyrażenia obu powyższych znaczeń: *the poorer areas of a town* ◇ *an agricultural area*. **Part** używa się na ogół do określenia części miasta: *Which part of Paris do you live in?*

ˈarea code noun [C] (especially US) the numbers for a particular area or city, that you use when you are making a telephone call from outside the local area: *The area* *code for New York is 212.* ▶ **numer kierunkowy** ➲ look at **dialling code**

arena /əˈriːnə/ noun [C] **1** an area with seats around it where public entertainments (sports events, concerts, etc.) are held ▶ **arena 2** an area of activity that concerns the public: *She entered the political arena five years ago.* ▶ **scena**

aren't /ɑːnt/ short for **are not**

arguable /ˈɑːgjuəbl/ adj. **1** probably true; that you can give reasons for: *It is arguable that* (można powiedzieć, że) *all hospital treatment should be free.* ▶ **dyskusyjny, prawdopodobny 2** probably not true; that you can give reasons against: *Whether the company should invest so much money is highly arguable.* ▶ **dyskusyjny, sporny** ■ **arguably** /-əbli/ adv.: *'King Lear' is arguably Shakespeare's best play.* „King Lear" jest chyba najlepszą sztuką Szekspira. ▶ **prawdopodobnie**

argue /ˈɑːgjuː/ verb **1** [I] **argue (with sb) (about/over sth)** to say things, often angrily that show that you do not agree with sb about sth: *The couple next door are always arguing.* ◇ *I never argue with my husband about money.* ▶ **sprzeczać się** ➲ look at **fight**[1], **quarrel**[2] **2** [I,T] **argue that ...; argue (for/against sth)** to give reasons that support your opinion about sth: *He argued against buying a new computer.* ▶ **dowodzić, że; argumentować**

argument /ˈɑːgjumənt/ noun **1** [C,U] **an argument (with sb) (about/over sth)** an angry discussion between two or more people who disagree with each other: *Sue **had an argument** with her father* (posprzeczała się z ojcem) *about politics.* ◇ *He accepted the decision without argument* (bez dyskusji). ▶ **sprzeczka, spór** ⓘ Głośna i poważna kłótnia to **row**. **Quarrel** dotyczy zazw. mniej poważnych kwestii. **2** [C] the reason(s) that you give to support your opinion about sth: *What are the **arguments for/against** lower taxes?* ◇ *His argument was that* (twierdził, że) *if they bought a smaller car, they would save money.* ▶ **argument**

argumentative /ˌɑːgjuˈmentətɪv/ adj. often involved in or enjoying arguments ▶ **lubiący dyskutować**

aria /ˈɑːriə/ noun [C] a song for one voice, especially in an **opera** ▶ **aria**

arid /ˈærɪd/ adj. (used about land or climate) very dry; with little or no rain ▶ **suchy, jałowy**

Aries /ˈeəriːz/ noun [C,U] the 1st of the 12 signs of the **zodiac**, the Ram; a person born under this sign: *I'm an Aries* ▶ **Baran; zodiakalny Baran**

arise /əˈraɪz/ verb [I] (pt **arose** /əˈrəʊz/, pp **arisen** /əˈrɪzn/) to begin to exist; to appear: *If any problems arise, let me know.* ▶ **pojawiać się**

aristocracy /ˌærɪˈstɒkrəsi/ noun [C, with sing. or pl. verb] (pl. **aristocracies**) the people of the highest social class who often have special titles ▶ **arystokracja** SYN **nobility**

aristocrat /ˈærɪstəkræt; US əˈrɪst-/ noun [C] a member of the highest social class, often with a special title ▶ **arystokrata**
■ **aristocratic** /ˌærɪstəˈkrætɪk; US əˌrɪstə-/ adj. ▶ **arystokratyczny**

arithmetic /əˈrɪθmətɪk/ noun [U] the kind of mathematics which involves counting with numbers (adding, **subtracting**, multiplying and dividing): ***mental arithmetic*** liczenie w pamięci ▶ **arytmetyka, rachunki**

arm[1] /ɑːm/ noun [C] **1** the long part at each side of your body connecting your shoulder to your hand: *He was carrying a newspaper under his arm.* ▶ **ramię, ręka** ➲ look at **hand**[1] ➲ picture at **body 2** the part of a piece of clothing that covers your arm; a sleeve: *He had a hole in the arm of his jumper.* ▶ **rękaw 3** the part of a chair where you rest your arms ▶ **poręcz**
IDM **arm in arm** with your arm folded around sb else's arm: *The friends walked arm in arm.* ▶ **pod rękę**

arm

arm in arm

arms folded

cross/fold your arms to cross your arms in front of your chest: *James was sitting with his arms crossed* (z założonymi rękami). ▶ **założyć ręce**
twist sb's arm → TWIST[1]
with open arms → OPEN[1]

arm[2] /ɑːm/ verb [I,T] to prepare sb/yourself to fight by supplying or getting weapons ▶ **zbroić (się)** ➲ look at **armed, arms**

armadillo /ˌɑːməˈdɪləʊ/ noun [C] an American animal with a hard shell made of pieces of bone, that eats insects and rolls into a ball if sth attacks it ▶ **pancernik**

armament /ˈɑːməmənt/ noun **1** (**armaments**) [C, usually pl.] weapons, especially large guns, bombs, etc.: *the armaments industry* ▶ **zbrojenia 2** [U] increasing the number of weapons that an army or a country has ▶ **zbrojenie** OPP **disarmament**

armband /ˈɑːmbænd/ noun [C] **1** a piece of cloth that you wear around your arm: *The captain of the team wears an armband.* ▶ **opaska 2** a plastic ring filled with air which you can wear on each of your arms when you are learning to swim ▶ **nadmuchiwany rękawek**

armchair /ˈɑːmtʃeə(r); ɑːmˈtʃeə(r)/ noun [C] a soft comfortable chair with sides which support your arms ▶ **fotel**

armed /ɑːmd/ adj. carrying a gun or other weapon; involving weapons: *All the terrorists were armed.* ◇ *armed robbery* napad z bronią w ręku ◇ *the armed forces* siły zbrojne ◇ (figurative) *They came to the meeting armed with all the latest information.* ▶ **uzbrojony, zbrojny** OPP **unarmed**

armful /ˈɑːmfʊl/ noun [C] the amount that you can carry in your arms ▶ **naręcze**

armhole /ˈɑːmhəʊl/ noun [C] the opening in a piece of clothing where your arm goes through ▶ **pacha**

armistice /ˈɑːmɪstɪs/ noun [C] an agreement between two countries who are at war that they will stop fighting ▶ **zawieszenie broni**

armour (US **armor**) /ˈɑːmə(r)/ noun [U] clothing, often made of metal, that soldiers wore in earlier times to protect themselves: *a suit of armour* ▶ **zbroja**

armoured (US **armored**) /ˈɑːməd/ adj. (used about a vehicle) covered with metal to protect it in an attack ▶ **opancerzony**

armoury (US **armory**) /ˈɑːməri/ noun [C] (pl. **-ies**) a place where weapons and **armour** are kept ▶ **zbrojownia** SYN **arsenal**

armpit /ˈɑːmpɪt/ noun [C] the part of the body under the arm at the point where it joins the shoulder ▶ **pacha** ➲ picture at **body**

armrest /ˈɑːmrest/ noun [C] the part of some types of seat, especially in planes or cars, which supports your arm ▶ **oparcie na rękę**

⚷ **arms** /ɑːmz/ noun [pl.] **1** weapons, especially those that are used in war: *a reduction in nuclear arms* ▶ **broń 2** = COAT OF ARMS

IDM **be up in arms** to protest angrily about sth: *The workers were up in arms over the news that* (byli wzburzeni na wieść o tym, że) *the factory was going to close.* ▶ **zażarcie protestować; być rozjuszonym**

ˈ**arms control** noun [U] international agreements to destroy weapons or limit the number of weapons that countries have ▶ **kontrola zbrojeń**

ˈ**arms race** noun [sing.] a situation in which countries compete to get the most and best weapons ▶ **wyścig zbrojeń**

⚷ **army** /ˈɑːmi/ noun [C, with sing. or pl. verb] (pl. **armies**) **1** the military forces of a country which are trained to fight on land: *the British Army* ◇ *She **joined the army*** (wstąpiła do wojska) *at the age of eighteen.* ◇ *The army is/are advancing towards the border.* ◇ *an army officer* ▶ **wojsko**; **armia** ➲ note at **war** ➲ look at **air force**, **navy** **2** a large number of people, especially when involved in an activity together: *An army of children was helping to pick up the rubbish.* ▶ **armia**

ˈ**A-road** noun [C] (Brit.) a main road, usually not as wide as a **motorway** ▶ **droga pierwszej kategorii**

aroma /əˈrəʊmə/ noun [C] a smell, especially a pleasant one ▶ **zapach**, **aromat** ➲ note at **smell**[2]

■ **aromatic** /ˌærəˈmætɪk/ adj. ▶ **aromatyczny** SYN **fragrant**

aromatherapy /əˌrəʊməˈθerəpi/ noun [U] the use of natural oils with a pleasant smell in order to control pain or make sb feel relaxed ▶ **aromaterapia**

■ **aromatherapist** /-pɪst/ noun [C] ▶ **terapeut(k)a stosujący-y/a aromaterapię**

aromatic /ˌærəˈmætɪk/ adj. having a pleasant noticeable smell: ***aromatic oils/herbs*** ▶ **aromatyczny** SYN **fragrant**

arose past tense of **arise**

⚷ **around**[1] /əˈraʊnd/ adv. **1** (also **about**; **round**) in or to various places or directions: *I don't want to buy anything – I'm just looking around* (tylko oglądam). ◇ *Tom will show you around.* Tom was oprowadzi ▶ **tu i tam 2** (also **round**) moving so as to face in the opposite direction: *Turn around* (odwróć się) *and go back the way you came.* ▶ **w drugą stronę 3** (also **round**) on all sides; forming a circle: *The park has a wall all around.* Park jest otoczony murem. ◇ *Gather around* (zbierzcie się wokoło) *so that you can all see.* ▶ **wokoło 4** (also **round**) near a place: *Is there a bank around here?* ▶ **w pobliżu 5** (also **about**) present or available: *I went to the house but there was nobody around* (ale nikogo nie zastałem). ▶ **obecny**; **dostępny 6** (also **about**) approximately: *I'll see you around seven.* ▶ **około 7** (also **about**) (used for activities with no real purpose): *'What are you doing?' 'Nothing, just lazing around* (leniuchuję).*'* ◇ *I found this pen lying around on the floor* (poniewierające się po podłodze). ◇ *John likes messing around with cars.* John lubi dłubać przy samochodach.

around[2] /əˈraʊnd/ (also **round**) prep. **1** in various directions inside an area; in different places in a particular area: *They wandered around the town, looking at the shops.* ▶ **po** (*np. mieście*) **2** in a circle or following a curving path: *Go around the corner* (skręć za rogiem) *and it's the first house on the left.* ◇ *She had a bandage around her leg.* Miała zabandażowaną nogę. ◇ *We sat down around the table.* ▶ **dookoła**, **wokoło**

aˌ**round-the-ˈclock** = ROUND-THE-CLOCK

arouse /əˈraʊz/ verb [T] to cause a particular reaction in people: *to arouse somebody's curiosity/interest* ▶ **wzbudzać**

■ **arousal** /əˈraʊzl/ noun [U] ▶ **pobudzenie**

arr. abbr. **arrives**: *arr. York 07.15* ▶ **przyj.**

⚷ **arrange** /əˈreɪndʒ/ verb **1** [I,T] **arrange (for) sth**; **arrange to do sth**; **arrange (sth) with sb** to make plans and preparations so that sth can happen in the future: *We're arranging a surprise party for Mark.* ◇ *She arranged for her mother to look after the baby.* ◇ *She arranged to meet Stuart after work.* ◇ *an arranged marriage* małżeństwo kontraktowe ▶ **planować**, **organizować 2** [T] to put sth in order or in a particular pattern: *The books were arranged in alphabetical order.* ◇ *She arranged the flowers in a vase.* ▶ **układać**, **ustawiać**

⚷ **arrangement** /əˈreɪndʒmənt/ noun **1** [C, usually pl.] plans or preparations for sth that will happen in the future: *Come round this evening and we'll **make arrangements** for the party.* ▶ **przygotowanie 2** [C,U] an agreement with sb to do sth: *They **have an arrangement** to share the cost of the food.* ◇ *We both need to use the computer so we'll have to **come to** some **arrangement.*** ◇ *Use of the swimming pool will be **by arrangement** only.* ◇ *They made an arrangement* (uzgodnili, że) *to share the cost of the food.* ◇ *Under the new arrangement* (według nowej umowy) *it will be possible to pay monthly instead of weekly.* ▶ **uzgodnienie**, **umowa 3** [C] a group of things that have been placed in a particular pattern: *a flower arrangement* ▶ **kompozycja**

arranger /əˈreɪndʒə/ noun [C] **1** a person who arranges music that has been written by sb different ▶ (*muz.*) **aranżer/ka 2** a person who arranges things: *arrangers of care services for the elderly* ▶ **organizator/ka**

array /əˈreɪ/ noun [C] a large collection of things, especially one that is impressive and is seen by other people ▶ **ekspozycja**, **wystawa**

arrears /əˈrɪəz/ noun [pl.] money that sb owes that they should have paid earlier ▶ **zaległości**

IDM **be in arrears**; **fall/get into arrears** to be late in paying money that you owe: *I'm in arrears with the rent.* ▶ **mieć zaległości**

be paid in arrears if money or a person is paid **in arrears** for work, the money is paid after the work has been done: *You will be paid monthly in arrears.* ▶ **być opłacanym z dołu**

⚷ **arrest**[1] /əˈrest/ verb [T] when the police arrest sb, they take them prisoner in order to question them about a crime ▶ **aresztować** ➲ note at **crime**

⚷ **arrest**[2] /əˈrest/ noun [C,U] the act of arresting sb: *The police **made** ten **arrests** after the riot.* ◇ *The wanted man is now **under arrest*** (został aresztowany). ▶ **aresztowanie**

⚷ **arrival** /əˈraɪvl/ noun **1** [U] reaching the place to which you were travelling: *On our arrival we were told that our rooms had not been reserved.* ▶ **przybycie**, **przyjazd**, **przylot** OPP **departure 2** [C] people or things that have arrived: *We brought in extra chairs for the late arrivals.* ◇ *I'll look on the arrivals board* (na tablicę przyjazdów/przylotów) *to see when the train gets in.* ▶ **nowo przybyły**

⚷ **arrive** /əˈraɪv/ verb [I] **1 arrive (at/in ...)** to reach the place to which you were travelling: *We arrived home at about midnight.* ◇ *What time does the train arrive in Newcastle?* ◇ *They arrived at the station ten minutes late.* ▶ **przybywać**, **przychodzić**, **przyjeżdżać**

Uwaga! Mówiąc o mieście, kraju itp. używa się **arrive in**, zaś mówiąc o jakimś miejscu, budynku itp. stosuje się **arrive at**.

2 to come or happen: *The day of the wedding had finally arrived.* ◇ *Paula's baby arrived two weeks late.* ▶ **nadchodzić**, **przychodzić na świat**

PHR V **arrive at sth** to reach sth: *We finally arrived at a decision* (podjęliśmy decyzję). ▶ **dochodzić** (*np. do wniosku*)

arrogant /ˈærəɡənt/ adj. thinking that you are better and more important than other people ▶ **arogancki** SYN **self-important**
■ **arrogance** noun [U] ▶ **arogancja** | **arrogantly** adv. ▶ **arogancko**

arrow /ˈærəʊ/ noun [C] **1** a thin piece of wood or metal, with one pointed end and feathers at the other end, that is shot by pulling back the string on a **bow** and letting go: *to fire an arrow at a target* ▶ **strzała** ➲ look at **archer** **2** the sign (→) which is used to show direction: *The arrow is pointing right.* ▶ **strzałka**

arse¹ /ɑːs/ noun [C] (Brit., taboo, slang) **1** (US **ass**) the part of the body that you sit on; your bottom: *Get off your arse!* Rusz tyłek! ▶ **tyłek** **2** [usually following an adjective] a stupid person ▶ **tuman, głupek** ➲ look at **smart alec**
IDM **a pain in the arse/neck** → PAIN

arse² /ɑːs/ verb
IDM **can't be arsed (to do sth)** (Brit., taboo, slang) to not want to do sth because it is too much trouble: *I was supposed to do some work this weekend but I couldn't be arsed.* ▶ **nie mieć ochoty ruszyć tyłka (żeby coś zrobić)**

arsenal /ˈɑːsənl/ noun [C] a large collection of weapons, or a building where they are made or stored ▶ **arsenał**

arsenic /ˈɑːsnɪk/ noun [U] a type of very strong poison ▶ **arszenik**

arson /ˈɑːsn/ noun [U] the crime of setting fire to a building on purpose ▶ **podpalenie**

arsonist /ˈɑːsənɪst/ noun [C] a person who deliberately sets fire to a building ▶ **podpalacz/ka**

art /ɑːt/ noun **1** [U] the activity or skill of producing things such as paintings, designs, etc.; the objects that are produced: *I've never been good at art.* ◇ *an art class* zajęcia plastyczne ◇ *She studied History of Art at university.* ▶ **sztuka** ➲ look at **work of art** **2** [C,U] a skill or sth that needs skill: *There's **an art to** writing a good letter.* Napisanie dobrego listu to sztuka. ▶ **umiejętność, sztuka** **3** (**the arts**) [pl.] activities which involve creating things such as paintings, literature or music: *The government has agreed to spend twice as much on the arts next year.* ◇ *fine art(s)* sztuki piękne ▶ **kultura i sztuka** **4** (**arts**) [pl.] subjects such as history or languages that you study at school or university: *an arts degree* dyplom nauk humanistycznych ◇ *the arts faculty* wydział humanistyczny ▶ **przedmioty/nauki humanistyczne** ℹ **Arts** (lub **arts subjects**) zazw. przeciwstawia się **sciences** (lub **science subjects**).

> **art**
> An **artist** works in a **studio**. A **painter** paints **pictures**, for example **portraits**, **landscapes** or **abstract paintings**. A picture might be a **watercolour** or an **oil painting**. You put a picture in a **frame** and hang it on the wall. A **sculptor** makes **sculptures** of figures or objects in materials such as **marble** or **bronze**. An **exhibition** is a collection of **works of art** which the public can go and see in an **art gallery**. A great work of art is called a **masterpiece**.

artefact /ˈɑːtɪfækt/ noun [C] an object that is made by a person ▶ **artefakt**

artery /ˈɑːtəri/ noun [C] (pl. **arteries**) one of the tubes which take blood from the heart to other parts of the body ▶ **tętnica** ➲ look at **vein**

ˈart form noun **1** [C] a particular type of artistic activity ▶ **forma/rodzaj sztuki** **2** [sing.] an activity that sb does very well and gives them the opportunity to show imagination: *She has elevated the dinner party into an art form.* ▶ (*przen.*) **forma sztuki**

artful /ˈɑːtfl/ adj. clever at getting what you want, sometimes by not telling the truth ▶ **przebiegły, pomysłowy** SYN **crafty**

ˈart gallery = GALLERY

ˈart-house adj. **art-house** films are usually made by small companies and are not usually seen by a wide audience ▶ **studyjny**

arthritis /ɑːˈθraɪtɪs/ noun [U] a disease which causes swelling and pain when you bend your arms, fingers, etc. ▶ **artretyzm**
■ **arthritic** /ɑːˈθrɪtɪk/ adj. ▶ **artretyczny**

artichoke /ˈɑːtɪtʃəʊk/ noun [C] a green vegetable with a lot of thick pointed leaves. You can eat the bottom part of the leaves and its centre. ▶ **karczoch** ➲ picture on **page A13**

article /ˈɑːtɪkl/ noun [C] **1** an object, especially one of a set: *articles of clothing* części garderoby ▶ **przedmiot** **2** a piece of writing in a newspaper or magazine ▶ **artykuł** **3** the words *a*, *an* or *the* ▶ **przedimek** (*nieokreślony/określony*)

articulate¹ /ɑːˈtɪkjuleɪt/ verb [I,T] to say sth clearly or to express your ideas or feelings ▶ **wyraźnie wymawiać, wypowiadać**
■ **articulation** /ɑːˌtɪkjuˈleɪʃn/ noun [U] (formal) **1** the expression of an idea or a feeling in words: *the articulation of his theory* ▶ **sformułowanie** **2** the act of making sounds in speech or music: *The singer worked hard on the clear articulation of every note.* ▶ **wymowa, artykulacja**

articulate² /ɑːˈtɪkjələt/ adj. good at expressing your ideas clearly ▶ **umiejący dobrze się wysławiać** OPP **inarticulate**

articulated /ɑːˈtɪkjuleɪtɪd/ adj. (Brit.) (used about a large vehicle such as a lorry) made of two sections which are joined together ▶ **przegubowy** ➲ picture at **truck**

artifice /ˈɑːtɪfɪs/ noun [U,C] (formal) the clever use of tricks to cheat sb ▶ **sztuczka, podstęp** SYN **cunning**

artificial /ˌɑːtɪˈfɪʃl/ adj. not genuine or natural but made by people ▶ **sztuczny**
■ **artificially** /-ʃəli/ adv. ▶ **sztucznie**

artificial insemination /ˌɑːtɪˈfɪʃl ɪnˌsemɪˈneɪʃn/ noun [U] the process of making a woman or female animal pregnant by an artificial method of putting male **sperm** inside her, and not by sexual activity ▶ **sztuczne zapłodnienie**

ˌartificial inˈtelligence noun [U] (the study of) the way in which computers can be made to copy the way humans think ▶ **sztuczna inteligencja**

artillery /ɑːˈtɪləri/ noun [U] large, heavy guns that are moved on wheels; the part of the army that uses them ▶ **artyleria**

artisan /ˌɑːtɪˈzæn; US ˈɑːrtəzn/ noun [C] (formal) a person who makes things in a skilful way, especially with their hands ▶ **rzemieślnik** SYN **craftsman**

artist /ˈɑːtɪst/ noun [C] a person who produces art, especially paintings or drawings ▶ **artyst(k)a, mala-rz/rka**

artiste /ɑːˈtiːst/ (also **artist**) noun [C] a person whose job is to perform, for example a singer or a dancer ▶ **artyst-a/ka estradow-y/a**

artistic /ɑːˈtɪstɪk/ adj. **1** [only before a noun] connected with art: *the artistic director of the theatre* ▶ **artystyczny** **2** showing a skill in art ▶ **uzdolniony artystycznie**
■ **artistically** /-kli/ adv. ▶ **artystycznie**

arˌtistic diˈrector noun [C] the person in charge of deciding which plays, **operas**, etc. a theatre company will perform, and the general artistic policy of the company ▶ **dyrektor/kierownik artystyczny**

artistry /ˈɑːtɪstri/ noun [U] the skill of an artist ▶ **sztuka, mistrzostwo**

art nouveau (also **Art Nouveau**) /ˌɑː(t) nuːˈvəʊ/ noun [U] a style of decorative art and **architecture** popular in Europe and the US at the end of the 19th century and beginning of the 20th century that uses complicated designs and curved patterns based on natural shapes like leaves and flowers ▶ **secesja**

artwork /ˈɑːtwɜːk/ noun **1** [U] photographs, drawings, etc. that have been prepared for a book or magazine: *a piece of artwork* ▶ **oprawa plastyczna** (*książki, czasopisma*) **2** [C] a work of art, especially one in a museum or a show ▶ **dzieło sztuki**

arty /ˈɑːti/ adj. (informal) seeming or wanting to be very artistic or interested in the arts: *He can't really like all those boring arty films.* ▶ **artystyczny** (*często w sposób pretensjonalny*)

as /əz; strong form æz/ prep., adv., conj. **1** (used for talking about sb/sth's job, role or function): *He works as a train driver.* ◇ *Think of me as your friend, not as your boss.* ◇ *You could use this white sheet as a tablecloth.* ◇ *The robbers were disguised as* (przebrali się za) *security guards.* ▶ **jako**

> **As** czy **like**? **As** przed rzeczownikiem odnosi się do zawodu lub funkcji: *She works as a scientist.* ◇ *I used the jar as a vase.* **Like** oznacza „podobny/podobnie do": *He has blue eyes like his father.* **Like** (lub formalnie **such as**) również oznacza „na przykład": *I love sweet food, like chocolate.*

2 (**as ... as**) (used for comparing people or things): *Ania's almost as tall as me.* ◇ *Ania's almost as tall as I am.* ◇ *It's not as cold as it was yesterday.* ◇ *I'd like an appointment* ***as soon as possible*** (jak najszybciej). ◇ *She earns* ***twice as much as*** *her husband.* Ona zarabia dwa razy tyle, co jej mąż. ◇ *I haven't got as many books as you have.* Nie mam tylu książek, co ty. ▶ **tak ... jak ..., tyle ... co ... 3** while sth else is happening: *As she walked along the road, she thought about her father.* ◇ *The phone rang just as I was leaving the house.* Telefon zadzwonił właśnie kiedy wychodziłem z domu. ▶ **kiedy, gdy, jak 4** in a particular way, state, etc.; like: *Please do as I tell you.* ◇ *Leave the room* ***as it is.*** *Don't move anything.* ▶ **tak jak 5** because: *I didn't buy the dress, as I decided it was too expensive.* ▶ **ponieważ 6** (used at the beginning of a comment about what you are saying): ***As you know,*** *I've decided to leave at the end of the month.* ▶ **jak**

IDM **as for** (used when you are starting to talk about a different person or thing): *Gianni's upstairs. As for Tino, I've no idea where he is.* ▶ **co się tyczy, co do**

as if; **as though** (used for saying how sb/sth appears): *She looks as if/though she's just got out of bed.* Ona wygląda, jak gdyby właśnie wstała z łóżka. ◇ *He behaved as though nothing had happened.* On zachowywał się, jak gdyby nic się nie stało. ▶ **jak gdyby**

as it were (used for saying that sth is only true in a certain way): *She felt, as it were* (do pewnego stopnia), *a stranger in her own house.* ▶ **niejako**

as of; **as from** starting from a particular time: *As from next week, Tim Shaw will be managing this department.* ▶ **od**

as to about a particular thing; concerning: *I was given no instructions as to how to begin.* ▶ **jak**

ASA /ˌeɪ es ˈeɪ/ abbr. (used for indicating the speed of a camera film) ▶ **Amerykański Komitet Normalizacyjny**

AS → AS (LEVEL)

asap /ˌeɪ es eɪ ˈpiː/ abbr. **as soon as possible** ▶ **jak najszybciej**

asbestos /æsˈbestəs/ noun [U] a soft grey material that does not burn and was used in the past to protect against heat ▶ **azbest**

ASBO /ˈæzbəʊ/ noun [C] **antisocial behaviour order**; (in the UK) an order made by a court which says that sb must stop behaving in a harmful or annoying way to other people ▶ **nakaz karny udzielany za zachowanie aspołeczne**

ascend /əˈsend/ verb [I,T] (formal) to go up ▶ **wznosić się; iść w górę** OPP **descend**

■ **ascending** adj.: *The questions are arranged in ascending order of difficulty* (według narastającego stopnia trudności). ▶ **zwiększający się**

ascendancy (also **ascendency**) /əˈsendənsi/ noun [U] (formal) **ascendancy (over sb/sth)** the position of having power or influence over sb/sth: *The opposition party was* ***in the ascendancy*** (zyskiwała przewagę). ▶ **przewaga, dominacja**

Ascension Day noun [U,C] the 40th day after Easter when Christians remember when Jesus left the earth and went into heaven ▶ **Wniebowstąpienie**

ascent /əˈsent/ noun [C] **1** the act of climbing or going up: *the ascent* (zdobycie szczytu) *of Everest* ▶ **wspinaczka 2** a path or hill leading upwards: *There was a steep ascent before the path became flat again.* ▶ **wzniesienie** (*terenu*) OPP for both meanings **descent**

ascertain /ˌæsəˈteɪn/ verb [T] (formal) to find sth out ▶ **stwierdzać, upewniać się (co do czegoś)**

ascribe /əˈskraɪb/ verb [T] **ascribe sth to sb/sth** to say that sth was written by or belonged to sb; to say what caused sth: *Many people ascribe this play to Shakespeare.* ▶ **przypisywać (coś komuś)**

asexual /ˌeɪˈsekʃuəl/ adj. **1** (technical) not involving sex; not having sexual organs: *asexual reproduction* ▶ **bezpłciowy 2** not having sexual qualities; not interested in sex ▶ **aseksualny**

ash /æʃ/ noun **1** [U, pl.] the grey or black powder which is left after sth has burned: *cigarette ash* ◇ *the ashes of a fire* ▶ **popiół 2** (**ashes**) [pl.] what is left after a dead person has been burned ▶ **prochy 3** [C] a type of forest tree that grows in cool countries ▶ **jesion**

ashamed /əˈʃeɪmd/ adj. [not before a noun] **ashamed (of sth/sb/yourself)**; **ashamed that...**; **ashamed to do sth** feeling guilty or embarrassed about sb/sth or because of sth you have done: *She was ashamed of her old clothes.* ◇ *How could you be so rude? I'm ashamed of you* (wstyd mi za ciebie)*!* ◇ *She felt ashamed* (było jej wstyd) *that she hadn't helped him.* ▶ **wstydzić się** OPP **unashamed**

ashen /ˈæʃn/ adj. (used about sb's face) very pale; without colour because of illness or fear ▶ (*cera*) **blady, poszarzały**

ashore /əˈʃɔː(r)/ adv. onto the land from the sea, a river, etc.: *The passengers went ashore for an hour while the ship was in port.* ▶ **na brzeg, na ląd**

ashtray /ˈæʃtreɪ/ noun [C] a small dish for collecting **ash** ▶ **popielniczka**

ˌAsh ˈWednesday noun [U,C] the first day of Lent ▶ **Środa Popielcowa** ➲ look at **Shrove Tuesday**

Asian /ˈeɪʃn; ˈeɪʒn/ noun [C] a person from Asia or whose family was originally from Asia ▶ **Azjat(k)a**

■ **Asian** adj. ▶ **azjatycki**

ˌAsian Aˈmerican noun [C] a person from America whose family come from Asia, especially East Asia ▶ **Amerykan-in/ka pochodzenia azjatyckiego**

■ **ˌAsian-Aˈmerican** adj. ▶ **dot. Amerykanów pochodzenia azjatyckiego**

aside /əˈsaɪd/ adv. **1** on or to one side; out of the way: *We stood aside to let the man go past.* ◇ *She took Richard aside to tell him her secret.* ▶ **na stronę 2** to be kept sep-

arately, for a special purpose: *I try to* ***set aside*** *a little money each month.* ▶ (*odkładać*) **na bok**
■ **aside** noun [C] (in the theatre) something which a character in a play says to the audience, but which the other characters on stage are not intended to hear ▶ **uwaga na stronie**

a'side from (especially US) = APART FROM

ask /ɑːsk; US æsk/ verb **1** [I,T] **ask (sb) (about sb/sth)**; **ask sb sth** to put a question to sb in order to find out some information: *We need to ask about tickets.* ◇ *Can I ask you a question?* ◇ *She asked the little boy his name.* Zapytała chłopczyka, jak się nazywa. ◇ *She asked if I wanted tea or coffee.* ◇ *'What's the time?' he asked.* ◇ *He asked what the time was.* ◇ *He asked me the time.* Zapytał mnie o godzinę. ◇ *I got lost coming here and I had to ask somebody the way* (zapytać kogoś o drogę). ▶ **pytać 2** [I,T] **ask (sb) for sth**; **ask sth (of sb)**; **ask sb to do sth** to request that sb gives you sth or does sth for you: *She sat down and asked for a cup of coffee.* ◇ *Don't ask Joe for money – he hasn't got any.* ◇ *You are asking too much of him* (zbyt wiele od niego wymagasz). ◇ *Ring this number and ask for Mrs Khan.* Zadzwoń pod ten numer i poproś panią Khan. ◇ *I asked him if he would drive me home./I asked him to drive me home.* Poprosiłem go o podwiezienie mnie do domu. ▶ **prosić, żeby ktoś coś zrobił**; **wymagać 3** [I,T] to request permission to do sth: *I'm sure she'll let you go if you ask.* ◇ *Theo asked to use our phone.* ◇ *We asked if we could go home early.* ▶ **prosić (o pozwolenie)**, **pytać 4** [T] **ask sb (to sth)** to invite sb: *They asked six friends to dinner.* ▶ **zapraszać 5** [T] to say the price that you want for sth: *How much are they asking for their car?* ▶ **życzyć sobie** (*pewnej ceny*)
IDM **ask for trouble/it** to behave in a way that will almost certainly cause you problems: *Driving when you're tired is just asking for trouble.* ▶ **szukać nieszczęścia**
if you ask me if you want my opinion ▶ **moim zdaniem**
PHR V **ask after sb** to ask about sb's health or to ask for news of sb: *Tina asked after you today.* ▶ **pytać o kogoś**
ask sb out to invite sb to go out with you, especially as a way of starting a romantic relationship: *Harry's too shy to ask her out.* ◇ *He's asked Eileen out on Saturday.* Umówił się z Eileen na randkę w sobotę. ▶ **zaprosić kogoś na randkę**

askew /ə'skjuː/ adv. not in a straight or level position ▶ **krzywo**
■ **askew** adj. [not before a noun] ▶ **przekrzywiony**

'asking price noun [C] the price that sb wants to sell sth for ▶ **cena ofertowa**

asleep /ə'sliːp/ adj. [not before a noun] not awake; sleeping: *The baby is asleep* (śpi). ◇ *It didn't take me long to* ***fall asleep*** (zasnąć) *last night.* ◇ *to be sound/fast asleep* spać twardo (jak zabity) ▶ **we śnie** OPP **awake**

> Zwróć uwagę, że **asleep** można użyć tylko po rzeczowniku. **Sleeping** może występować zarówno przed, jak i po rzeczowniku: *a sleeping child.* **Be asleep** często tłumaczy się czasownikiem „spać". ➲ note at **sleep**[1]

AS (level) /eɪ 'es levl/ noun [C,U] **Advanced Subsidiary (level)**; a British exam usually taken in the year before the final year of school or college when students are aged 17. Together with A2 levels, AS levels form the A-level qualification, which is needed for entrance to universities: *She's* ***doing an AS (level)*** *in French.* ▶ **rodzaj egzaminu maturalnego** ➲ look at **A level**, **A2 (level)**

asparagus /ə'spærəgəs/ noun [U] a plant with green or white **stems** that you cook and eat as a vegetable ▶ **szparag** ➲ picture on **page A13**

aspect /'æspekt/ noun [C] one of the qualities or parts of a situation, idea, problem, etc. ▶ **aspekt**, **strona**

aspersions /ə'spɜːʃnz; US -ɜːʒnz/ noun [pl.] (formal) critical or unpleasant remarks or judgements: *I wouldn't want to* ***cast aspersions on*** (rzucać oszczerstwa na) *your honesty.* ▶ **oszczerstwo**

asphalt /'æsfælt; US -fɔːlt/ noun [U] a thick black substance that is used for making the surface of roads ▶ **asfalt**

asphyxiate /əs'fɪksieɪt/ verb [I,T] to make sb unable to breathe or to be unable to breathe: *He was asphyxiated by the smoke while he was asleep.* ▶ **dusić (się)**
■ **asphyxiation** /əs,fɪksi'eɪʃn/ noun [U] ▶ **uduszenie (się)**

aspic /'æspɪk/ noun [U] clear jelly which food can be put into when it is being served cold ▶ **galareta**

aspire /ə'spaɪə(r)/ verb [I] (formal) **aspire to sth/to do sth** to have a strong desire to have or do sth: *She aspired to become managing director.* ▶ **dążyć, mieć aspiracje (do czegoś)**
■ **aspiration** /,æspə'reɪʃn/ noun [C,U] ▶ **dążenie**, **aspiracja** | **aspiring** /ə'spaɪərɪŋ/ adj. [only before a noun] wanting to start the career or activity that is mentioned: *Aspiring musicians need hours of practice every day.* ▶ **aspirujący**

aspirin /'æsprɪn; 'æspərɪn/ noun [C,U] a drug used to reduce pain and a high temperature ▶ **aspiryna**

ass /æs/ **1** (US, taboo, slang) = ARSE **2** (Brit., informal) a stupid person ▶ **osioł 3** = DONKEY

assail /ə'seɪl/ verb [T] (formal) **1** to attack sb violently, either physically or with words: *He was assailed with fierce blows to the head.* ◇ *The proposal was assailed by the opposition party.* ◇ (figurative) *A vile smell assailed my nostrils.* ▶ **atakować 2** [usually passive] to disturb or upset sb severely: *to* ***be assailed by worries/doubts/fears*** ▶ (*lęk, problem itp.*) **nękać**

assailant /ə'seɪlənt/ noun [C] (formal) a person who attacks sb ▶ **napastni-k/czka**

assassin /ə'sæsɪn; US -sn/ noun [C] a person who kills a famous or important person for money or for political reasons ▶ **zamachowiec**
■ **assassinate** /ə'sæsɪneɪt; US -sən-/ verb [T] ▶ **dokonywać zamachu (na kogoś)** ➲ note at **kill** | **assassination** /ə,sæsɪ'neɪʃn; US -sə'n-/ noun [C,U] ▶ **zamach**

assault /ə'sɔːlt/ noun [C,U] **assault (on sb/sth)** a sudden attack on sb/sth ▶ **napaść**
■ **assault** verb [T]: *He was charged with assaulting a police officer* (czynne znieważenie policjanta). ▶ **napadać na kogoś**, **atakować**

assemble /ə'sembl/ verb **1** [I,T] to come together or bring sb/sth together in a group: *The leaders assembled in Strasbourg for the meeting.* ◇ *I've assembled all the information I need for my essay.* ▶ **zbierać (się)**, **gromadzić (się) 2** [T] to fit the parts of sth together: *We spent hours trying to assemble our new bookshelves.* ▶ **montować**, **składać**

assembly /ə'sembli/ noun (pl. **assemblies**) **1** [C,U] a large group of people who come together for a particular purpose: *school assembly* apel w szkole ▶ **zgromadzenie 2** [U] the act of fitting the parts of sth together ▶ **montaż**

as'sembly line noun [C] a line of people and machines in a factory that fit the parts of sth together in a fixed order ▶ **taśma montażowa**

assent /ə'sent/ noun [U] (formal) **assent (to sth)** official agreement to sth: *The committee* ***gave their assent*** *to the proposed changes.* ▶ **zgoda**
■ **assent** verb [I] **assent (to sth)** ▶ **wyrażać zgodę**

assert /ə'sɜːt/ verb [T] **1** to say sth clearly and firmly ▶ **twierdzić (stanowczo)**, **zapewniać (o czymś) 2** to behave in a determined and confident way to make people listen to you or to get what you want: *You ought to assert yourself more.* ◇ *to assert your authority* domagać się należnego szacunku ▶ **zachowywać się z pewnością siebie**

assertion /ə'sɜːʃn/ noun **1** [C] a statement that says you strongly believe that sth is true ▶ **zapewnienie, (stanowcze) stwierdzenie 2** [U] the act of showing, using or stating sth strongly: *the assertion of power* demonstracja siły ▶ **domaganie się**

assertive /ə'sɜːtɪv/ adj. expressing your opinion clearly and firmly so that people listen to you or do what you want ▶ **stanowczy**

■ **assertively** adv. ▶ **stanowczo** | **assertiveness** noun [U] ▶ **pewność siebie, stanowczość**

assess /ə'ses/ verb [T] **1** to judge or form an opinion about sth ▶ **szacować 2 assess sth (at sth)** to guess or decide the amount or value of sth: *How much was the value of the house assessed at?* ▶ **szacować**

■ **assessment** noun [C,U]: *I made a careful assessment of the risks involved.* ▶ **ocenianie, oszacowanie** ➲ look at **continuous assessment**

assessor /ə'sesə(r)/ noun [C] **1** an expert in a particular subject who is asked by a court or other official group to give advice ▶ **biegły, rzeczoznawca 2** a person who calculates the value or cost of sth or the amount of money to be paid: *an **insurance/tax assessor*** ▶ **taksator 3** a person who judges how well sb has done in an exam, a competition, etc. ▶ **juror/ka**

asset /'æset/ noun [C] **1 an asset (to sb/sth)** a person or thing that is useful to sb/sth: *She's a great asset to the organization.* ▶ **cenny nabytek, cenna umiejętność 2** [usually pl.] something of value that a person, company, etc. owns ▶ **aktywa**

assiduous /ə'sɪdjuəs; US -dʒuəs/ adj. (formal) working very hard and taking great care that everything is done as well as it can be: *one of the most assiduous members of the team* ▶ **gorliwy, pracowity** SYN **diligent**

■ **assiduously** adv.: *He worked assiduously to earn the money for his son's education.* ▶ **gorliwie, pracowicie**

assign /ə'saɪn/ verb [T] **1 assign sth to sb/sth** to give sth to sb for a particular purpose: *We assigned 20% of our budget to the project.* ▶ **wyznaczać, zadawać 2 assign sb to sth** to give sb a particular job to do: *A detective was assigned to the case.* ▶ **przydzielać, wyznaczać**

assignment /ə'saɪnmənt/ noun [C,U] a job or type of work that you are given to do: *The reporter disappeared while on (an) assignment in the war zone.* ▶ **zadanie**

assimilate /ə'sɪməleɪt/ verb **1** [T] to learn and understand sth: *to assimilate new facts/information/ideas* ▶ **przyswajać sobie 2** [I,T] **assimilate (sb/sth) (into sth)** to become or allow sb/sth to become part of a country, a social group, etc. ▶ **asymilować (się)**

■ **assimilation** /əˌsɪmə'leɪʃn/ noun [U] ▶ **przyswojenie sobie; asymilacja**

🔑 **assist** /ə'sɪst/ verb [I,T] (formal) **assist (sb) in/with sth; assist (sb) in doing sth** to help: *Volunteers assisted in searching for the boy.* ▶ **pomagać**

🔑 **assistance** /ə'sɪstəns/ noun [U] (formal) help or support: *financial assistance for poorer families* ◇ *She shouted for help but nobody came to her assistance.* ◇ *Can I be of any assistance?* Czym mogę służyć? ▶ **pomoc**

🔑 **assistant** /ə'sɪstənt/ noun [C] (abbr. **Asst; asst**) **1** a person who helps sb in a more important position ▶ **asystent/ka 2** (US **clerk**) a person who sells things to people in a shop: *a shop/sales assistant* ▶ **ekspedient/ka**

■ **assistant** adj. [only before a noun]: *the assistant manager* asystent/ka dyrektora ▶ **pomocniczy, zastępujący**

Assoc. = ASSOCIATION

🔑 **associate¹** /ə'səʊʃieɪt; -sieɪt/ verb **1** [T] **associate sb/sth (with sb/sth)** to make a connection between people or things in your mind: *I always associate the smell of the sea with my childhood.* ▶ **kojarzyć** OPP **dissociate 2** [I] **associate with sb** to spend time with sb: *I prefer not to associate with colleagues outside work.* ▶ **obcować 3** [T] **associate yourself with sth** to say that you support sth or agree with sth: *I do not wish to associate myself with any organization that promotes violence.* ▶ **współdziałać, przyłączać się** OPP **dissociate**

associate² /ə'səʊʃiət/ noun [C] a person that you meet and get to know through your work: *a business associate* ▶ **współpracowni-k/czka**

associate³ /ə'səʊʃiət; -siət/ adj. (often used in titles) of a lower rank, having fewer rights in a particular profession or organization ▶ **szeregowy**

associated /ə'səʊʃieɪtɪd; -sieɪt-/ adj. **1** if one thing is **associated with** another, the two things are connected because they happen together or one thing causes the other: *the risks associated with taking drugs* ◇ *Salaries and associated costs have risen substantially.* ▶ **połączony, powiązany** SYN **connected 2** if a person is **associated with** an organization, etc. they support it ▶ **związany** (*np. z partią*) **3** (**Associated**) (used in the name of a business company that is made up of a number of smaller companies): *Associated Newspapers* ▶ (*spółka*) **stowarzyszony**

🔑 **association** /əˌsəʊʃi'eɪʃn; -si'eɪ-/ noun **1** [C] (abbr. **Assoc.**) a group of people or organizations that work together for a particular purpose: *the National Association of Language Teachers* ▶ **stowarzyszenie, związek 2** [U] joining or working with another person or group: *We work **in association with*** (współpracujemy) *our New York office.* ▶ **współpraca 3** [C,U] the act of connecting one person or thing with another in your mind: *The cat soon made the association between human beings and food.* ▶ **skojarzenie, połączenie**

assorted /ə'sɔːtɪd; US -təd/ adj. of different types; mixed: *a bowl of assorted fruit* ▶ **różnorodny**

assortment /ə'sɔːtmənt/ noun [C] a group of different things or of different types of the same thing: *You'll find a wide assortment of gifts in our shop.* ▶ **wybór, mieszanka** SYN **mixture**

Asst (also **asst**) = ASSISTANT

🔑 **assume** /ə'sjuːm; US -'suːm/ verb [T] **1** to accept or believe that sth is true even though you have no proof; to expect sth to be true: *I assume that you have the necessary documents.* ◇ *Everyone assumed Ralph was guilty./Everyone assumed Ralph to be guilty.* ▶ **przypuszczać, zakładać (że) 2** to begin to use power or to have a powerful position: *to assume control of something* ▶ **obejmować** SYN **take 3** to pretend to have or be sb/sth: *to assume a false name* ▶ **przybierać** (*np. nazwisko, tożsamość*)

■ **assuming** conj. **assuming (that...)** (used to suppose that sth is true so that you can talk about what the results might be): *Assuming (that) he's still alive, how old would he be now?* ◇ *I hope to go to college next year, **always assuming** I pass my exams.* ▶ **zakładając (że)**

asˌsumed 'name noun [C] a name that sb uses that is not their real name: *He was living **under an assumed name**.* ▶ **przybrane nazwisko** SYN **pseudonym**

assumption /ə'sʌmpʃn/ noun **1** [C] something that you accept is true even though you have no proof: *We'll work **on the assumption that** guests will be hungry when they arrive.* ◇ *It's unfair to **make assumptions about** somebody's character before you know them.* ◇ *a reasonable/false assumption* ▶ **przypuszczenie 2** [U] **the assumption of sth** the act of taking power or of starting an important job ▶ **objęcie, przejęcie**

assurance /ə'ʃʊərəns; Brit. also -ʃɔːr-/ noun **1** [C] a promise that sth will certainly happen or be true: *They **gave** me **an assurance that** the work would be finished by Friday.*

▶ **zapewnienie** **2** (also ˌself-asˈsurance) [U] the belief that you can do or succeed at sth; confidence ▶ **pewność siebie**

assure /əˈʃʊə(r); Brit. also -ʃɔː(r)/ verb [T] **1** to promise sb that sth will certainly happen or be true, especially if they are worried: *I assure you that it is perfectly safe.* ▶ **zapewniać, gwarantować** **2** to make sth sure or certain: *The success of the new product assured the survival of the company.* ▶ **zapewniać**

assured /əˈʃʊəd; Brit. also əˈʃɔːd/ (also ˌself-asˈsured) adj. believing that you can do sth or succeed at sth; confident: *The doctor had a calm and assured manner.* ▶ **pewny siebie**

asterisk /ˈæstərɪsk/ noun [C] the symbol (*) that you use to make people notice sth in a piece of writing ▶ **gwiazdka, odsyłacz**

asteroid /ˈæstərɔɪd/ noun [C] one of the very large rocks or small planets which go around the sun ▶ **asteroida**

asthma /ˈæsmə; US ˈæz-/ noun [U] a medical condition that makes breathing difficult ▶ **astma**

asthmatic /æsˈmætɪk; US æz'-/ noun [C] a person who has **asthma** ▶ **astmaty-k/czka**
■ **asthmatic** adj. ▶ **astmatyczny**

astigmatism /əˈstɪɡmətɪzəm/ noun [U] a fault in the shape of a person's eye that prevents them from seeing clearly ▶ **astygmatyzm**

astonish /əˈstɒnɪʃ/ verb [T] to surprise sb very much: *She astonished everybody by announcing her engagement.* ▶ **dziwić, zadziwiać** SYN **amaze**
■ **astonished** adj. ▶ **zdziwiony**

astonishing /əˈstɒnɪʃɪŋ/ adj. very surprising ▶ **zadziwiający** SYN **amazing**
■ **astonishingly** adv. ▶ **zadziwiająco**

astonishment /əˈstɒnɪʃmənt/ noun [U] very great surprise: *He stared* ***in astonishment.*** ▶ **zdumienie** SYN **amazement**

astound /əˈstaʊnd/ verb [T, usually passive] to surprise sb very much ▶ **zdumiewać** SYN **amaze**

astounded /əˈstaʊndɪd/ adj. feeling or showing great surprise: *We sat in astounded silence.* ▶ **zdumiony**

astounding /əˈstaʊndɪŋ/ adj. causing sb to feel extremely surprised ▶ **zdumiewający**

astray /əˈstreɪ/ adv.
IDM **go astray** to become lost or be stolen ▶ **gubić się, ginąć**
lead sb astray → LEAD[1]

astride /əˈstraɪd/ prep., adv. with one leg on each side of sth: *to sit astride a horse* ▶ **okrakiem**

astringent /əˈstrɪndʒənt/ adj. (used about a liquid or cream) able to make the skin feel less **oily** or to stop the loss of blood from a cut: *an astringent lotion* ◇ *to have an astringent effect* ▶ (*krem itp.*) **ściągający**
■ **astringency** /-ənsi/ noun [U] ▶ **działanie ściągające**; (*i przen.*) **cierpkość**

astrologer /əˈstrɒlədʒə(r)/ noun [C] a person who is an expert in **astrology** ▶ **astrolog**

astrology /əˈstrɒlədʒi/ noun [U] the study of the positions and movements of the stars and planets and the way that some people believe they affect people and events ▶ **astrologia** ➲ note at **zodiac** ➲ look at **horoscope**

astronaut /ˈæstrənɔːt/ noun [C] a person who works and travels in space ▶ **astronaut(k)a**

astronomer /əˈstrɒnəmə(r)/ noun [C] a person who studies **astronomy** ▶ **astronom**

astronomical /ˌæstrəˈnɒmɪkl/ adj. **1** connected with **astronomy** ▶ **astronomiczny** **2** extremely large: *astronomical house prices* ▶ **astronomiczny**

astronomy /əˈstrɒnəmi/ noun [U] the scientific study of the sun, moon, stars, etc. ▶ **astronomia**

astute /əˈstjuːt; US -ˈstuːt/ adj. very clever; good at judging people or situations ▶ **bystry, wnikliwy**

asylum /əˈsaɪləm/ noun [U] **1** protection that a government gives to people who have left their own country for political reasons: *to give somebody political asylum* ▶ **azyl polityczny** **2** (old-fashioned) a hospital where people who were mentally ill could be cared for, often for a long time ▶ **zakład dla psychicznie chorych**

aˈsylum ˌseeker noun [C] a person who has been forced to leave their own country because they are in danger and who arrives in another country asking to be allowed to stay there ▶ **ubiegający-y/a się o azyl**

asymmetric /ˌeɪsɪˈmetrɪk/ (also **asymmetrical** /ˌeɪsɪˈmetrɪkl/) adj. having two sides or parts that are not the same in size or shape: *Most people's faces are asymmetric.* ▶ **asymetryczny** OPP **symmetrical**
■ **asymmetrically** /-ɪkli/ adv. ▶ **asymetrycznie** | **asymmetry** /ˌeɪˈsɪmətri/ noun [C, U] ▶ **asymetria**

at /ət; strong form æt/ prep. **1** (used to show where sb/sth is or where sth happens): *at the bottom/top of the page* ◇ *He was standing at the door.* ◇ *Change trains at Chester.* ◇ *We were at home all weekend.* ◇ *Are the children at school?* ◇ *'Where's Peter?' 'He's at Sue's.'* ▶ **przy, na, u, w** **2** (used to show when sth happens): *I start work at 9 o'clock.* ◇ *at the weekend* ◇ *at night* ◇ *at Easter* ◇ *She got married at 18* (w wieku 18 lat). ▶ **o, w** **3** in the direction of sb/sth: *What are you looking at?* ◇ *He pointed a gun at the policeman.* ◇ *Don't shout at me!* ▶ **na, do, w** **4** (used to show what sb is doing or what is happening): *They were* ***hard at work.*** ◇ *The two countries were* ***at war*** (w stanie wojny). ▶ **przy** **5** (used to show the price, rate, speed, etc. of sth): *We were travelling at about 50 miles per hour.* ▶ **po, z** (*prędkością*), **w** (*tempie*) **6** because of sth: *We laughed at his jokes.* ◇ *I was surprised at her behaviour.* Byłem zdziwiony jej zachowaniem. ▶ **z** **7** (used with adjectives that show how well sb/sth does sth): *She's not very* ***good at*** *French.* ▶ **w** **8** the symbol (@) used in email addresses ▶ (*komput.*) **znak @, małpa**

ate past tense of **eat**

atheism /ˈeɪθiɪzəm/ noun [U] the belief that there is no God ▶ **ateizm**
■ **atheist** /-ɪst/ noun [C] ▶ **ateist(k)a**

athlete /ˈæθliːt/ noun [C] a person who can run, jump, etc. very well, especially one who takes part in sports competitions, etc. ▶ **lekkoatlet(k)a**

ˌathlete's ˈfoot noun [U] an infectious skin disease that affects the feet, especially between the toes ▶ **grzybica stóp**

athletic /æθˈletɪk/ adj. **1** (used about a person) having a fit, strong, and healthy body ▶ **wysportowany, dobrze zbudowany** **2** [only before a noun] connected with **athletes** or **athletics**: *athletic ability* ▶ **lekkoatletyczny**

athletics /æθˈletɪks/ (US ˌtrack and ˈfield) noun [U] sports such as running, jumping, throwing, etc. ▶ **lekkoatletyka** ➲ note at **sport** ➲ picture on **page A9**

atishoo /əˈtɪʃuː/ interj. (used to represent the sound that you make when you suddenly **sneeze**) ▶ **a psik!**

atlas /ˈætləs/ noun [C] a book of maps: *a road atlas of Europe* ▶ **atlas** ➲ note at **book** ➲ look at **map**

ATM = CASH MACHINE

ˌATˈM card (US) = CASH CARD

atmosphere /ˈætməsfɪə(r)/ noun **1** (**the atmosphere**) [C, usually sing.] the mixture of gases that surrounds the earth or any other star, planet, etc.: *the earth's atmosphere* ▶ **atmosfera** **2** [sing.] the air in a place: *a smoky atmosphere* ▶ **atmosfera, otoczenie** **3** [sing.] the mood or feeling of a place or situation: *The atmosphere of the meeting was relaxed.* ▶ **atmosfera, nastrój**

atmospheric /ˌætməsˈferɪk/ adj. **1** [only before a noun] connected with the earth's atmosphere ▶ **atmosferyczny** **2** creating a particular feeling or emotion: *atmospheric music* ▶ **nastrojowy**

atom /ˈætəm/ noun [C] the smallest part into which an element can be divided: (figurative) *There isn't an atom of* (odrobiny) *truth in these rumours.* ▶ **atom** ➲ look at **molecule**

ˈatom bomb = ATOMIC BOMB

atomic /əˈtɒmɪk/ adj. connected with an atom or atoms: *atomic physics* ◇ *elements with a high/low **atomic number*** ▶ **atomowy** ➲ look at **nuclear**

aˌtomic ˈbomb (also **ˈatom bomb**) noun [C] a bomb that explodes using the energy that is produced when an atom or atoms are split ▶ **bomba atomowa**

aˌtomic ˈenergy noun [U] the energy that is produced when an atom or atoms are split. **Atomic** energy can be used to produce electricity. ▶ **energia jądrowa**

atonal /eɪˈtəʊnl/ adj. (of a piece of music) not written in any particular **key** ▶ **atonalny** OPP **tonal**
■ **atonality** /ˌeɪtəʊˈnæləti/ noun [U] ▶ **atonalność**

atrocious /əˈtrəʊʃəs/ adj. extremely bad: *atrocious weather* ▶ **okropny**, **ohydny** SYN **terrible**
■ **atrociously** adv. ▶ **okropnie**

atrocity /əˈtrɒsəti/ noun [C,U] (pl. **atrocities**) (an action of) very cruel treatment of sb/sth: *Both sides were accused of committing atrocities during the war.* ▶ **okrucieństwo**, **nieludzki czyn**

atrophy /ˈætrəfi/ noun [U] the condition of losing flesh, muscle, strength, etc. in a part of the body because it does not have enough blood: (figurative, formal) *The cultural life of the country will sink into atrophy unless more writers and artists emerge.* ▶ **atrofia**
■ **atrophy** verb (**atrophies**; **atrophying**; **atrophied**; **atrophied**) [I] if a part of the body **atrophies**, it becomes weak because it is not used or because it does not have enough blood: (figurative): *Memory can atrophy through lack of use.* ▶ **popadać w atrofię**

attach /əˈtætʃ/ verb [T] **1 attach sth (to sth)** to fasten or join sth to sth: *I attached a label to each bag.* ▶ **przymocowywać** OPP **detach** **2 attach sth to sb/sth** to think that sth has a particular quality: *Don't attach too much importance to what they say.* ▶ **przywiązywać** **3** [usually passive] **attach sb/sth to sb/sth** to make sb/sth join or belong to sb/sth: *The research centre is attached to the university.* ▶ **przyłączać**, **przydzielać**
IDM **(with) no strings attached**; **without strings** → STRING[1]

attaché case /əˈtæʃeɪ keɪs; US ˌætəˈʃeɪ/ noun [C] a small hard flat case used for carrying business documents ▶ **aktówka** ➲ look at **briefcase**

attached /əˈtætʃt/ adj. [not before a noun] **attached to sb/sth** liking sb/sth very much ▶ **przywiązany do kogoś/czegoś**

attachment /əˈtætʃmənt/ noun **1** [C,U] **attachment (to/for sb/sth)** the feeling of liking sb/sth very much: *emotional attachment* ◇ *I feel a strong attachment to* (jestem głęboko przywiązany do) *this house.* ▶ **przywiązanie (do kogoś/czegoś)** **2** [C] something that you can fit on sth else to make it do a different job: *an electric drill with a range of attachments* ◇ *a bath with a shower attachment* wanna z prysznicem ▶ **przyrząd do przymocowania** **3** [C] a document that you send to sb using email ▶ (*komput.*) **załącznik**

attack[1] /əˈtæk/ noun **1** [C,U] **(an) attack (on sb/sth)** trying to hurt or defeat sb/sth by using force: *The rebel forces launched an attack on the capital.* ◇ *The town was **under attack from*** (było atakowane ze) *all sides.* ▶ **atak**, **szturm** **2** [C,U] **(an) attack (on sb/sth)** an act of saying strongly that you do not like or agree with sb/sth: *an outspoken attack on government policy* ▶ **atak** **3** [C] a short period when you suffer badly from a disease, medical condition, etc.: *an attack of asthma/flu/nerves* ▶ **atak**, **napad** **4** [C] the act of trying to score a point in a game of sport: *The home team went **on the attack*** (przystąpiła do ataku) *again.* ▶ **atak**

attack[2] /əˈtæk/ verb **1** [I,T] to try to hurt or defeat sb/sth by using force: *The child was attacked by a dog.* ▶ **atakować** **2** [T] to say strongly that you do not like or agree with sb/sth: *Steffi attacked Guy's right-wing political views.* ▶ **atakować** **3** [T] to damage or harm sb/sth: *a virus that attacks the nervous system* ▶ **atakować** **4** [I,T] to try to score a point in a game of sport: *This team attacks better than it defends.* ▶ **atakować**

attacker /əˈtækə(r)/ noun [C] a person who tries to hurt sb using force ▶ **napastni-k/czka**

attain /əˈteɪn/ verb [T] to succeed in getting or achieving sth, especially after a lot of effort ▶ **osiągać**

attainable /əˈteɪnəbl/ adj. that can be achieved: *realistically attainable targets* ▶ **osiągalny**

attainment /əˈteɪnmənt/ noun **1** [C] a skill or sth you have achieved: *students with few academic attainments* ▶ **osiągnięcie** **2** [U] the act of achieving sth: *the attainment of the government's objectives* ▶ **osiągnięcie**

attempt[1] /əˈtempt/ noun [C] **1 an attempt (to do sth/at doing sth)** an act of trying to do sth: *The thief **made no attempt*** (nie próbował) *to run away.* ◇ *I failed the exam once but passed **at the second attempt*** (za drugim podejściem). ◇ *They failed **in their attempt** to reach the North Pole.* ▶ **usiłowanie**, **próba** **2 an attempt (on sb/sth)** trying to attack or beat sb/sth: *She hopes to **make an attempt*** (spróbuje pobić) *on the world record in tomorrow's race.* ◇ *an attempt on the President's life* próba zamachu na życie prezydenta ▶ **próba**, **atak na kogoś/coś**
IDM **a last-ditch attempt** → LAST[1]

attempt[2] /əˈtempt/ verb [T] **attempt (to do) sth** to try to do sth that is difficult: *Don't attempt to make him change his mind.* ▶ **usiłować**, **próbować**

attempted /əˈtemptɪd/ [only before a noun] (used about a crime, etc.) that sb has tried to do but without success: *attempted rape/murder/robbery* usiłowanie gwałtu/morderstwa/włamania

attend /əˈtend/ verb **1** [I,T] to go to or be present at a place: *The children attend the local school.* ◇ *We'd like as many people as possible to attend.* ▶ **chodzić (do czegoś/na coś)**; **być (na/w czymś)** **2** [I] (formal) **attend to sb/sth** to give your care, thought or attention to sb/sth or look after sb/sth: *Please attend to this matter immediately.* ▶ **zajmować się kimś/czymś**

attendance /əˈtendəns/ noun **1** [U] being present somewhere: *Attendance at lectures is compulsory.* ▶ **obecność** **2** [C,U] the number of people who go to or are present at a place: *There was a poor attendance at the meeting.* ▶ **frekwencja**

attendant[1] /əˈtendənt/ noun [C] a person whose job is to serve or help people in a public place: *a car park attendant* parkingowy ▶ **członek obsługi**, **dozorca**

attendant[2] /əˈtendənt/ adj. [only before a noun] (formal) that goes together with or results from sth: *unemployment and all its attendant social problems* ▶ **towarzyszący**

attention[1] /əˈtenʃn/ noun [U] **1** watching, listening to or thinking about sb/sth carefully: *I shouted in order to **attract** her **attention**.* ◇ *Shy people hate to be **the centre of attention**.* ◇ *to hold sb's attention* skupiać czyjąś uwagę ▶ **uwaga** **2** special care or action: *The hole in the roof needs urgent attention.* ◇ *to require **medical attention*** ▶ **uwaga**, **opieka** **3** a position in which a sol-

dier stands up straight and still: *to stand/come to attention* ▶ **baczność**
IDM **catch sb's attention/eye** → CATCH[1]
draw (sb's) attention to sth → DRAW[1]
get/have sb's undivided attention; give your undivided attention (to sb/sth) → UNDIVIDED
pay attention → PAY[1]

attention² /ə'tenʃn/ interj. (used for asking people to listen to sth carefully) ▶ **uwaga!**

at'tention deficit disorder (also at,tention ,deficit hyperac'tivity disorder) noun [U] (abbr. **ADD**; **ADHD**) a medical condition, especially in children, that makes it difficult for them to pay attention to what they are doing, to stay still for long and to learn things ▶ **zespół nadpobudliwości psychoruchowej**

attentive /ə'tentɪv/ adj. **attentive (to sb/sth)** watching, listening to or thinking about sb/sth carefully: *The hotel staff were very attentive to our needs.* ▶ **uważny, troskliwy** OPP **inattentive**
■ **attentively** adv.: *to listen attentively to something* ▶ **uważnie**

attest /ə'test/ verb [I] (formal) **attest (to sth)** to show or prove that sth is true: *Her long fight against cancer attests to her courage.* ▶ **potwierdzać**

attic /'ætɪk/ noun [C] the space or room under the roof of a house ▶ **poddasze** ➲ look at **loft**

attire /ə'taɪə(r)/ noun [U] (formal) clothes: *dressed in formal evening attire* ▶ **strój**

attired /ə'taɪəd/ adj. [not before a noun] (formal or literary) dressed in a particular way: *She was fashionably attired in a black evening gown.* ▶ **odziany**

⚷ **attitude** /'ætɪtjuːd; US -tuːd/ noun [C] **an attitude (to/towards sb/sth)** the way that you think, feel or behave: *People's attitude to marriage is changing.* ◇ *She has a positive attitude to her work.* ▶ **stosunek, nastawienie**

attn (also attn.) abbr. (in writing) **for the attention of**: *Sales Dept, attn C Biggs* ▶ (*korespondencja*) **do wiadomości kogoś** (*w celu podjęcia niezbędnych działań*) ➲ look at **FYI**

⚷ **attorney** (US) = LAWYER

At,torney 'General noun [C] (pl. **Attorneys General** or **Attorney Generals**) **1** the most senior legal officer in some countries or states, for example the UK or Canada, who advises the government or head of state on legal matters ▶ **doradca i pełnomocnik prawny rządu** **2** (**the At,torney 'General**) the head of the US Department of Justice and a member of the President's cabinet ▶ **minister sprawiedliwości**

⚷ **attract** /ə'trækt/ verb [T] **1** [usually passive] to cause sb to like sb/sth: *She's attracted to* (ma słabość do) *older men.* ▶ **przyciągać** **2** to cause sb/sth to go to sth or give attention to sth: *I waved to attract the waiter's attention.* ◇ *Moths are attracted to light.* ◇ *The new film has attracted a lot of publicity.* ▶ **przyciągać, wabić**

⚷ **attraction** /ə'trækʃn/ noun **1** [U] a feeling of liking sb/sth: *sexual attraction* ▶ **atrakcyjność, powab, pociąg** **2** [C] something that is interesting or enjoyable: *The city offers all kinds of tourist attractions.* ▶ **atrakcja**

⚷ **attractive** /ə'træktɪv/ adj. **1** (used about a person) beautiful or nice to look at: *He found her very attractive.* ▶ **ładny, przystojny** ➲ note at **beautiful** **2** that pleases or interests you; that you like: *an attractive part of the country* ◇ *an attractive idea* ▶ **interesujący, atrakcyjny** OPP for both meanings **unattractive**
■ **attractively** adv. ▶ **atrakcyjnie** | **attractiveness** noun [U] ▶ **atrakcyjność**

attribute¹ /ə'trɪbjuːt/ verb [T] **attribute sth to sb/sth** to believe that sth was caused or done by sb/sth: *Mustafa attributes his success to hard work.* ◇ *a poem attributed to Shakespeare* ▶ **przypisywać**

attribute² /'ætrɪbjuːt/ noun [C] a quality of sb/sth: *physical attributes* cechy zewnętrzne ▶ **cecha** SYN **feature**

attributive /ə'trɪbjətɪv/ adj. (used about an adjective or a noun) used before a noun to describe it: *In 'the blue sky' and 'a family business', 'blue' and 'family' are attributive.* ▶ **przydawkowy** ➲ look at **predicative**
■ **attributively** adv. ▶ **przydawkowo**

attuned /ə'tjuːnd; US -'tuː-/ adj. [not before a noun] **attuned (to sb/sth)** familiar with sb/sth so that you can understand or recognize them or it and act in an appropriate way: *She wasn't yet attuned to her baby's needs.* ▶ **obeznany (z kimś/czymś)**

ATV /,eɪ tiː 'viː/ abbr. **all-terrain vehicle**; a small open motor vehicle with one seat and four wheels with very thick tyres, designed especially for use on rough ground without roads ▶ **pojazd terenowy** ➲ picture at **car**

atypical /,eɪ'tɪpɪkl/ adj. (formal) not typical of a particular type, group, etc. ▶ **nietypowy** OPP **typical** ➲ look at **untypical**

aubergine /'əʊbəʒiːn/ (US **eggplant** /'egplɑːnt; US -plænt/) noun [C,U] a long vegetable with dark purple skin ▶ **bakłażan** ➲ picture on **page A13**

auburn /'ɔːbən/ adj. (used about hair) reddish-brown ▶ **rudawobrązowy** ➲ look at **chestnut, maroon** ➲ note at **hair**

auction¹ /'ɔːkʃn; Brit. also 'ɒk-/ noun [C,U] a public sale at which items are sold to the person who offers to pay the most money: *The house was sold* ***at/by auction.*** ▶ **aukcja, licytacja**

auction² /'ɔːkʃn; Brit. also 'ɒk-/ verb [T] **auction sth (off)** to sell sth at an **auction** ▶ **wystawiać coś na licytację**

auctioneer /,ɔːkʃə'nɪə(r); Brit. also ,ɒk-/ noun [C] a person who organizes the selling at an **auction** ▶ **licytator, aukcjoner**

audacious /ɔː'deɪʃəs/ adj. (formal) willing to take risks or to do sth shocking ▶ **śmiały, zuchwały** SYN **daring**
■ **audaciously** adv. ▶ **śmiało, zuchwale**

audacity /ɔː'dæsəti/ noun [U] behaviour that shows courage but that is also rude or shocking: *He* ***had the audacity*** (miał czelność) *to say I was too fat.* ▶ **śmiałość, zuchwałość** SYN **nerve**

audible /'ɔːdəbl/ adj. that can be heard: *Her speech was* ***barely audible*** (ledwo słyszalne). ▶ **słyszalny** OPP **inaudible**
■ **audibly** /-əbli/ adv. ▶ **słyszalnie**

⚷ **audience** /'ɔːdiəns/ noun [C] **1** [with sing. or pl. verb] all the people who are watching or listening to a play, concert, speech, the TV, etc.: *The audience was/were wild with excitement.* ▶ **widownia, publiczność** ➲ note at **theatre** **2** a formal meeting with a very important person: *He was granted an audience with the President.* ▶ **audiencja**

audio /'ɔːdiəʊ/ adj. [only before a noun] connected with the recording of sound: *audio equipment* ◇ *audio tape* ▶ **dźwiękowy**

,audio-'visual adj. using both sound and pictures ▶ **audiowizualny**

audit /'ɔːdɪt/ noun [C] an official examination of the present state of sth, especially of a company's financial records: *to carry out an audit* ▶ **kontrola** (*np. ksiąg rachunkowych*), **rewizja**

audition¹ /ɔː'dɪʃn/ noun [C] a short performance by a singer, actor, etc. to find out if they are good enough to be in a play, show, etc. ▶ **przesłuchanie**

audition² /ɔː'dɪʃn/ verb [I,T] **audition (sb) (for sth)** to do or to watch sb do an **audition**: *I auditioned for a part in the* *play.* ▶ **przeprowadzać przesłuchanie**; **uczestniczyć w przesłuchaniu**

auditor /ˈɔːdɪtə(r)/ noun [C] a person whose job is to examine a company's financial records ▶ **rewident**

auditorium /ˌɔːdɪˈtɔːriəm/ noun [C] (pl. **auditoriums** or **auditoria** /-riə/) the part of a theatre, concert hall, etc. where the audience sits ▶ **widownia**, **audytorium**

auditory /ˈɔːdətri; US -tɔːri/ adj. connected with hearing: *auditory stimuli* ▶ **słuchowy**

au fait /ˌəʊ ˈfeɪ/ adj. [not before a noun] **au fait (with sth)** completely familiar with sth: *I'm new here so I'm not completely au fait with the system.* ▶ **obeznany (z czymś)**

Aug. = AUGUST: *10 Aug. 1957*

augment /ɔːɡˈment/ verb [T] (formal) to increase the amount, value, size, etc. of sth ▶ **powiększać**

■ **augmentation** /ˌɔːɡmenˈteɪʃn/ noun [C,U] ▶ **powiększenie**

augur /ˈɔːɡə(r)/ verb

IDM **augur well/ill for sb/sth** (formal) to be a good/bad sign of what will happen in the future ▶ **być dobrą/złą wróżbą**

⚷ **August** /ˈɔːɡəst/ noun [U,C] (abbr. **Aug.**) the 8th month of the year, coming after July ▶ **sierpień** ➲ note at **January**

⚷ **aunt** /ɑːnt; US ænt/ (also informal **auntie**; **aunty** /ˈɑːnti; US ˈænt-/) noun [C] the sister of your father or mother; the wife of your uncle: *Aunt Ellen* ▶ **ciotka**

au pair /ˌəʊ ˈpeə(r)/ noun (Brit.) [C] a person, usually a girl, from another country who comes to live with a family in order to learn the language. An **au pair** helps to clean the house and look after the children. ▶ **cudzoziem-iec/ka zatrudnion-y/a do pomocy w domu i opieki nad dziećmi w zamian za mieszkanie z utrzymaniem** (*celem podjęcia tej pracy jest zazw. pogłębienie znajomości języka obcego*)

aura /ˈɔːrə/ noun [C] (formal) the quality that sb/sth seems to have ▶ **atmosfera**

aural /ˈɔːrəl/ adj. connected with hearing and listening: *an aural comprehension test* test rozumienia ze słuchu ▶ **słuchowy** ➲ look at **oral**

auspices /ˈɔːspɪsɪz/ noun

IDM **under the auspices of sb/sth** with the help and support of sb/sth ▶ **pod auspicjami kogoś/czegoś**

auspicious /ɔːˈspɪʃəs/ adj. that seems likely to be successful in the future: *She made an auspicious start to her professional career when she won her first race.* ▶ **pomyślny** OPP **inauspicious**

Aussie (also **Ozzie**) /ˈɒzi/ noun [C] (informal) a person from Australia ▶ **Australij-czyk/ka**

■ **Aussie** adj. ▶ **australijski**

austere /ɒˈstɪə(r); ɔːˈst-/ adj. **1** very simple; without decoration ▶ **prosty**, **surowy** **2** (used about a person) very strict and serious ▶ **surowy** **3** not having anything that makes your life more comfortable: *The nuns lead simple and austere lives.* ▶ **ascetyczny**, **surowy**

■ **austerity** /ɒˈsterəti; ɔːˈst-/ noun [U] ▶ **surowość**; **prostota**

Australasia /ˌɒstrəˈleɪʃə; -ˈleɪʒə; ˌɔːstrə-/ noun [U] the region including Australia, New Zealand and the islands of the SW Pacific ▶ **Australazja**

■ **Australasian** adj. ▶ **dot. Australazji**

authentic /ɔːˈθentɪk/ adj. **1** that you know is real or genuine: *an authentic Van Gogh painting* ▶ **autentyczny** **2** true or accurate: *an authentic account of life in the desert* ▶ **prawdziwy** **3** made to be exactly the same as the original: *an authentic model of the building* ▶ **dokładny**

■ **authenticity** /ˌɔːθenˈtɪsəti/ noun [U] ▶ **autentyczność**

authenticate /ɔːˈθentɪkeɪt/ verb [T] **authenticate sth (as sth)** to prove that sth is genuine, real or true: *Experts have authenticated the writing as that of Byron himself.* ◇ *The letter has been authenticated by handwriting experts.* ▶ **potwierdzać autentyczność**

■ **authentication** /ɔːˌθentɪˈkeɪʃn/ noun [U] ▶ **potwierdzenie autentyczności**

⚷ **author** /ˈɔːθə(r)/ noun [C] a person who writes a book, play, etc. ▶ **autor/ka**

■ **authorship** noun [U] ▶ **autorstwo**

authorise = AUTHORIZE

authoritarian /ɔːˌθɒrɪˈteəriən; US əˌθɒrəˈt-/ adj. not allowing people the freedom to decide things for themselves: *authoritarian parents* ▶ **apodyktyczny**, **despotyczny**

authoritative /ɔːˈθɒrətətɪv; US əˈθɔːrəteɪtɪv; əˈθɑːr-/ adj. **1** having authority; demanding or expecting that people obey you: *an authoritative tone of voice* ▶ **autorytatywny**, **rozkazujący** **2** that you can trust and respect as true and correct: *They will be able to give you authoritative advice on the problem.* ▶ **wiarygodny**, **miarodajny**

⚷ **authority** /ɔːˈθɒrəti; US əˈθɔːr-; əˈθɑːr-/ noun (pl. **authorities**) **1** [U] the power and right to give orders and make others obey: *Children often begin to question their parents' authority at a very early age.* ◇ *You must get this signed by a person **in authority**.* ▶ **autorytet**, **władza** **2** [U] **authority (to do sth)** the right or permission to do sth: *The police **have the authority** to question anyone they wish.* ◇ *He was sacked for using a company vehicle **without authority**.* ▶ **upoważnienie**, **prawo** **3** [C, usually pl.] a person, group or government department that has the power to give orders, make official decisions, etc.: *I have to report this to the authorities.* ▶ **władza**, **zarząd** **4** [U] the power to influence people because they respect your knowledge or official position: *He spoke with authority and everybody listened.* ▶ **autorytet** **5** [C] **an authority (on sth)** a person with special knowledge ▶ **autorytet**

authorize (also **-ise**) /ˈɔːθəraɪz/ verb [T] to give official permission for sth or for sb to do sth: *He authorized his secretary to sign letters in his absence.* ▶ **aprobować**, **upoważniać**

■ **authorization** (also **-isation**) /ˌɔːθəraɪˈzeɪʃn; US -rəˈz-/ noun [U,C] ▶ **upoważnienie**

autism /ˈɔːtɪzəm/ a mental condition in which a person finds it difficult to communicate or form relationships with other people ▶ **autyzm**

■ **autistic** /ɔːˈtɪstɪk/ adj. ▶ **autystyczny**

autobiography /ˌɔːtəbaɪˈɒɡrəfi/ noun [C,U] (pl. **autobiographies**) the story of a person's life, written by that person ▶ **autobiografia** ➲ note at **book** ➲ look at **biography**

■ **autobiographical** /ˌɔːtəˌbaɪəˈɡræfɪkl/ adj. ▶ **autobiograficzny**

autocracy /ɔːˈtɒkrəsi/ noun (pl. **-ies**) **1** [U] a system of government of a country in which one person has complete power ▶ **autokracja** **2** [C] a country that is ruled by one person who has complete power ▶ **autokracja**

autocrat /ˈɔːtəkræt/ noun [C] **1** a ruler who has complete power ▶ **autokrata** SYN **despot** **2** a person who expects to be obeyed by other people and does not care about their opinions or feelings ▶ **despot(k)a**

■ **autocratic** /ˌɔːtəˈkrætɪk/ adj.: *an autocratic manager* ▶ **autokratyczny**; **despotyczny**

Autocue™ /ˈɔːtəʊkjuː/ (especially US **teleprompter** /ˈtelipr ɒmptə(r)/) noun [C] a device used by people who are speaking in public, especially on television, which displays the words that they have to say ▶ **teleprompter**

autograph /ˈɔːtəɡrɑːf; US -ɡræf/ noun [C] a famous person's name, written by that person and given to sb: *The*

players stopped outside the stadium to ***sign autographs.*** ▶ **autograf**
■ **autograph** verb [T]: *The whole team have autographed the football.* ▶ **podpisywać** (*własne dzieło*), **składać autograf**

autoimmune /ˌɔːtəʊɪˈmjuːn/ adj. [only before a noun] an **autoimmune** disease or medical condition is one which is caused by substances that usually prevent illness: *an autoimmune response* ▶ **autoimmunologiczny**

automate /ˈɔːtəmeɪt/ verb [T, usually passive] to make sth operate by machine, without needing people ▶ **automatyzować**

ˌautomated ˈteller machine = CASH MACHINE

automatic¹ /ˌɔːtəˈmætɪk/ adj. **1** (used about a machine) that can work by itself without direct human control ▶ **automatyczny** **2** done without thinking: *Practise this exercise until it becomes automatic.* ▶ **automatyczny** **3** always happening as a result of a particular action or situation: *All the staff have an automatic right to a space in the car park.* ▶ **automatyczny**
■ **automatically** /-kli/ adv.: *The lights will come on automatically when it gets dark.* ▶ **automatycznie**

automatic² /ˌɔːtəˈmætɪk/ noun [C] an **automatic** machine, gun or car ▶ **samochód z automatyczną skrzynią biegów**; **urządzenie automatyczne**; **broń maszynowa**

automation /ˌɔːtəˈmeɪʃn/ noun [U] the use of machines instead of people to do work ▶ **automatyzacja**

automaton /ɔːˈtɒmətən/ noun [C] (pl. **automatons** or **automata** /-tə/) **1** a person who behaves like a machine, without thinking or feeling anything ▶ (*osoba*) **automat** SYN **robot** **2** a machine that moves without human control; a small **robot** ▶ **automat**

automobile (especially US) = CAR (1)

autonomy /ɔːˈtɒnəmi/ noun [U] the right of a person, an organization, a region, etc. to govern or control their or its own affairs ▶ **autonomia**
■ **autonomous** /ɔːˈtɒnəməs/ adj. ▶ **autonomiczny**

autopsy /ˈɔːtɒpsi/ noun [C] (pl. **autopsies**) an examination of a dead body to find out the cause of death ▶ **sekcja zwłok**

autosave /ˈɔːtəʊseɪv/ noun [sing.] the fact that changes to a document are saved automatically as you work ▶ (*komput.*) **zapisywanie automatyczne**
■ **autosave** verb [T] (*komput.*) ▶ **zapisywać automatycznie**

autumn /ˈɔːtəm/ (US usually **fall**) noun [C,U] the season of the year that comes between summer and winter: *In autumn the leaves on the trees begin to fall.* ▶ **jesień**
➲ picture on **page A16**
■ **autumnal** /ɔːˈtʌmnəl/ adj. ▶ **jesienny**

auxiliary /ɔːɡˈzɪliəri/ adj. [only before a noun] giving extra help: *auxiliary nurses/troops/staff* ▶ **pomocniczy**, **wspomagający**

auˌxiliary ˈverb noun [C] a verb (for example *be*, *do* or *have*) that is used with a main verb to show tense, etc. or to form questions ▶ **czasownik posiłkowy**

avail /əˈveɪl/ noun
IDM **of little/no avail** not helpful; having little or no effect: *All our efforts to persuade her were of little avail.* ▶ **daremny**
to little/no avail without success: *They searched everywhere, but to no avail.* ▶ **daremnie**

availability /əˌveɪləˈbɪləti/ noun [U] the state of being available: *You will receive the colour you order, subject to availability* (jeżeli będzie dostępny). ▶ **dostępność**

available /əˈveɪləbl/ adj. **1 available (to sb)** (used about things) that you can get, buy, use, etc.: *This information is easily available to everyone at the local library.* ◇ *Refreshments are available at the snack bar.* ◇ *Do you know if there are any flats available* (do wynajęcia/na sprzedaż) *in this area?* ▶ **dostępny**, **osiągalny** **2** (used about people) free to be seen, talked to, etc.: *The minister was not available for comment.* ▶ **dostępny**, **osiągalny**

A

avalanche /ˈævəlɑːnʃ; US -læntʃ/ noun [C] a very large amount of snow that slides quickly down the side of a mountain: *Two skiers are still missing after yesterday's avalanche.* ▶ **lawina**

the **avant-garde** /ˌævɒ̃ˈɡɑːd; US -vɑ̃ː- / noun [sing.] extremely modern works of art, music or literature, or the artists who create these ▶ **awangarda**
■ **avant-garde** adj. ▶ **awangardowy**

avarice /ˈævərɪs/ noun [U] (formal) extreme desire to be rich ▶ **chciwość** SYN **greed**
■ **avaricious** /ˌævəˈrɪʃəs/ adj. ▶ **chciwy**

Ave. = AVENUE: *26 Elm Ave.*

avenge /əˈvendʒ/ verb [T] **avenge sth**; **avenge yourself on sb** to punish sb for hurting you, your family, etc. in some way: *He wanted to avenge his father's murder.* ◇ *He wanted to avenge himself on his father's murderer.* ▶ **mścić (się)** ➲ look at **revenge**

avenue /ˈævənjuː; US -nuː/ noun [C] **1** (abbr. **Ave.**) a wide street, especially one with trees or tall buildings on each side: *I live on Kingsdown Avenue.* ▶ **aleja**, **ulica** **2** a way of doing or getting sth: *We must explore every avenue open to us.* ▶ **możliwość**, **ścieżka**

average¹ /ˈævərɪdʒ/ adj. **1** [only before a noun] (used about a number) found by calculating the **average²** (1): *What's the average age of your students?* ▶ **średni**, **przeciętny** **2** normal or typical: *children of* ***above/below average*** *intelligence* ▶ **przeciętny**

average² /ˈævərɪdʒ/ noun **1** [C] the number you get when you add two or more figures together and then divide the total by the number of figures you added: *The average of 14, 3 and 1 is 6.* ◇ *He has scored 93 goals at* ***an average of*** *1.55 per game.* ▶ **średnia** **2** [sing., U] the normal standard, amount or quality: ***On average****, I buy a newspaper about twice a week.* ▶ **średnia**, **przeciętna**

average³ /ˈævərɪdʒ/ verb [T] to do, get, etc. a certain amount as an average: *If we average 50 miles an hour, we should arrive at about 4 o'clock.* ▶ **osiągać średnio**
PHR V **average out (at sth)** to result in an average (of sth) ▶ **wynosić średnio**

averse /əˈvɜːs/ adj. [not before a noun; often with a negative] (formal) **averse to sth** against or not in favour of sth: *He is not averse to trying out new ideas.* ▶ **przeciwko**

aversion /əˈvɜːʃn; US -ʒn/ noun [C, usually sing.] **an aversion (to sb/sth)** a strong feeling of not liking sb/sth: *Some people* ***have an aversion*** *to spiders.* ▶ **awersja**, **niechęć**

avert /əˈvɜːt/ verb [T] to prevent sth unpleasant: *The accident could have been averted.* ▶ **zapobiegać**, **unikać**

avian flu (formal) = BIRD FLU

aviary /ˈeɪviəri; US -vieri/ noun [C] (pl. **aviaries**) a large **cage** or area in which birds are kept ▶ **ptaszarnia**

aviation /ˌeɪviˈeɪʃn/ noun [U] the designing, building and flying of aircraft ▶ **lotnictwo**

avid /ˈævɪd/ adj. **1** very enthusiastic about sth (usually a hobby): *an avid collector of antiques* ▶ **zapalony**, **żądny** SYN **keen** **2 avid for sth** wanting to get sth very much: *Journalists crowded round the entrance, avid for news.* ▶ **żądny czegoś**
■ **avidly** adv.: *He read avidly as a child.* ▶ **z zapałem**

avocado /ˌævəˈkɑːdəʊ/ noun [C] (pl. **avocados**) a tropical fruit that is wider at one end than the other, with a hard green skin and a large stone inside ▶ **awokado**
➲ picture on **page A12**

avoid /ə'vɔɪd/ verb [T] **1 avoid sth/doing sth** to prevent sth happening or to try not to do sth: *He always tried to avoid an argument if possible.* ◇ *She has to avoid eating fatty food.* ▶ **unikać 2** to keep away from sb/sth: *I leave home early to avoid the rush hour.* ▶ **unikać**
■ **avoidance** noun [U] ▶ **unikanie**

avoidable /ə'vɔɪdəbl/ adj. that can be prevented; unnecessary: *We have been asked to cut down on any avoidable expense* (o zredukowanie zbytecznych wydatków). ▶ **możliwy do uniknięcia** OPP **unavoidable**

avowed /ə'vaʊd/ adj. [only before a noun] (formal) that has been admitted or stated in public: *an avowed anti-communist* ◇ *an* ***avowed aim/intention/objective/purpose*** ▶ (*zwolennik itp.*) **zdeklarowany**; (*cel itp.*) **obrany**
■ **avowedly** /ə'vaʊɪdli/ adv. ▶ **zgodnie ze swoją deklaracją, otwarcie**

await /ə'weɪt/ verb [T] (formal) to wait for sb/sth: *We sat down to await the arrival of the guests.* ▶ **czekać, oczekiwać**

awake¹ /ə'weɪk/ adj. [not before a noun] to not be sleeping: *I was sleepy this morning but I'm* ***wide awake*** (zupełnie rozbudzony) *now.* ◇ *They were so tired that they found it difficult to* ***stay/keep awake.*** ◇ *I hope our singing didn't* ***keep*** *you* ***awake*** *last night.* ▶ **nie spać** OPP **asleep**

awake² /ə'weɪk/ verb [I,T] (pt **awoke** /ə'wəʊk/, pp **awoken** /ə'wəʊkən/) **1** to wake up; to make sb/sth wake up: *I awoke to find that it was already 9 o'clock.* ◇ *A sudden loud noise awoke us.* ▶ **budzić (się)** ⓘ Częściej używa się czasownika **wake up**. **2** to make sb have a particular feeling, attitude, etc. ▶ **wzbudzać**

awaken /ə'weɪkən/ verb **1** [I,T] (formal) to wake up; to make sb/sth wake up: *We were awakened by a loud knock at the door.* ▶ **budzić (się)** ⓘ Znacznie częściej używa się czasownika **wake up**. **2** [T] (formal) to produce a particular feeling, attitude, etc. in sb: *The film awakened memories of her childhood.* ▶ **wzbudzać, budzić**
PHR V **awaken sb to sth** to make sb notice or realize sth for the first time: *The letter awakened me to the seriousness of the situation.* ▶ **uświadamiać komuś/sobie, że**

awakening /ə'weɪkənɪŋ/ noun [C, usually sing.] **1** a moment when sb notices or realizes sth for the first time: *It was a* ***rude awakening*** (gorzkie rozczarowanie) *when I suddenly found myself unemployed.* ▶ **budzenie (się)** (*np. uczuć*) **2** the act of starting to feel or understand sth; the start of a feeling, etc.: *the awakening of an interest in the opposite sex* ▶ **przebudzenie**

award¹ /ə'wɔːd/ noun [C] **1** a prize, etc. that sb gets for doing sth well: *This year the awards for best actor and actress went to two Americans.* ▶ **nagroda 2** an amount of money given to sb as the result of a court decision: *She* ***received an award of*** *£5 000 for damages.* ▶ **odszkodowanie**

award² /ə'wɔːd/ verb [T] **award sth (to sb)** to give sth to sb as a prize, payment, etc.: *She was awarded first prize in the gymnastics competition.* ▶ **przyznawać**

aware /ə'weə(r)/ adj. **1** [not before a noun] **aware (of sb/sth)**; **aware (that)** knowing about or realizing sth; conscious of sb/sth: *I am* ***well aware*** *of the problems you face.* ◇ *I suddenly* ***became aware*** *that someone was watching me.* ◇ *There is no other entrance,* ***as far as I am aware.*** ▶ **świadomy** OPP **unaware 2** interested in and knowing about sth: *Many young people are very politically aware.* ▶ **zorientowany**

awareness /ə'weənəs/ noun [U] knowledge or interest: *People's awareness of healthy eating has increased in recent years.* ▶ **świadomość** SYN **consciousness**

awash /ə'wɒʃ/ adj. [not before a noun] **awash (with sth)** covered with water: (figurative) *The city was awash with rumours.* W mieście było pełno plotek. ▶ **zalany wodą**

away /ə'weɪ/ adv. ⓘ **Away** występuje w czasownikach złożonych. Zob. np. **give sth away, take sth away. 1 away (from sth)** at a particular distance from a place: *The village is two miles away from the sea.* ▶ **w odległości, stąd 2** in the future: *Our summer holiday is only three weeks away.* ▶ **w przyszłości, za 3 away (from sb/sth)** to a different place or in a different direction: *Go away* (odejdź)*! I'm busy!* ◇ *I called her name, but she just walked away* (odeszła) *from me.* ◇ *I asked him a question, but he just looked away* (odwrócił wzrok). **4** into a place where sth is usually kept: *Put your books away now.* ◇ *They cleared the dishes away.* Sprzątnęli naczynia ze stołu. ▶ (*odkładać*) **na swoje miejsce** ⓘ Por. **throw sth away** (wyrzucać do kosza). **5 away (from sth)** (used about people) not present: *My neighbours are away on holiday at the moment.* ▶ **nieobecny, poza domem, w terenie** SYN **absent 6** continuously, without stopping: *They chatted away for hours.* Gadali całymi godzinami. ◇ *They worked away* (pracowali zawzięcie) *for two days to get the job finished.* **7** until sth disappears: *The crash of thunder slowly died away* (powoli ucichł). ◇ *The writing has almost faded away* (prawie wyblakło). **8** (used about a football, etc. match) on the other team's ground: *Our team's playing away on Saturday.* ▶ (*występować/grać*) **gościnnie** OPP **at home**
■ **away** adj.: *an away match/game* ▶ (*mecz*) **wyjazdowy**
IDM **do away with sb/sth** to get rid of sb/sth: *The government are going to do away with the tax on fuel.* ▶ **pozbywać się kogoś/czegoś**
right/straight away immediately; without any delay: *I'll phone the doctor right away.* ▶ **natychmiast**

awe /ɔː/ noun [U] feelings of respect and either fear or admiration: *We watched in awe as the rocket took off.* ▶ **szacunek połączony z lękiem lub podziwem**
IDM **be in awe of sb/sth** to admire sb/sth and be slightly afraid of them or it: *As a young boy he was very much in awe of his uncle.* ▶ **być pełnym podziwu dla kogoś/czegoś**

'awe-inspiring adj. causing a feeling of respect and fear or admiration ▶ **wzbudzający jednocześnie szacunek i lęk lub podziw**

awesome /'ɔːsəm/ adj. **1** impressive and sometimes frightening: *an awesome task* ▶ **wzbudzający jednocześnie podziw i lęk 2** (US, informal) very good; excellent ▶ **super**

awestruck /'ɔːstrʌk/ adj. (literary) feeling very impressed by sth ▶ **oniemiały z wrażenia**

awful /'ɔːfl/ adj. **1** very bad or unpleasant: *We had an awful holiday. It rained every day.* ◇ *I feel awful – I think I'll go to bed.* ◇ *What an awful thing to say!* ▶ **okropny, straszny** SYN **terrible** ➲ note at **bad 2** [only before a noun] (informal) very great: *We've got* ***an awful lot*** *of work to do.* ▶ **straszny 3** terrible; very serious: *I'm afraid there's been some awful news.* ▶ **okropny, straszny**

awfully /'ɔːfli/ adv. (informal) very; very much: *I'm awfully sorry.* ▶ **strasznie** SYN **terribly**

awkward /'ɔːkwəd/ adj. **1** embarrassed or embarrassing: *I often feel awkward* (czuję się skrępowany) *in a group of people.* ◇ *There was an awkward silence.* ▶ **krępujący 2** difficult to deal with: *That's an awkward question.* ◇ *You've put me in an awkward position.* ◇ *an awkward customer* ◇ *The box isn't heavy but it's awkward to carry.* ▶ **trudny, grymaśny** SYN **difficult 3** not convenient: *My mother always phones at an awkward time.* ◇ *This tin-opener is very awkward to clean.* ▶ **niedogodny, kłopotliwy, niewygodny** SYN **difficult 4** not using the body in the best way; not elegant or comfort-

able: *I was sitting with my legs in an awkward position.* ▶ **niezgrabny, niezdarny**
■ **awkwardly** adv. ▶ **niezręcznie** | **awkwardness** noun [U] ▶ **niezdarność, skrępowanie**

awning /'ɔːnɪŋ/ noun [C] a sheet of strong cloth that spreads out above a door or window to protect it from the sun or rain ▶ (*zadaszenie*) **markiza**

awoke past tense of **awake²**

awoken past participle of **awake²**

awry /ə'raɪ/ adv. not in the way that was planned: *Our plans always seem to* ***go awry.*** ▶ **krzywo, na opak**
■ **awry** adj. [not before a noun] untidy; in the wrong position: *She rushed out, her hair awry.* ▶ **w nieładzie**

axe¹ (especially US **ax**) /æks/ noun [C] a tool with a wooden handle and a heavy metal head with a sharp edge, used for cutting wood, etc. ▶ **siekiera**

axe² (especially US **ax**) /æks/ verb [T] **1** (used especially in newspapers) to reduce sth by a great amount: *Budgets are to be axed.* ▶ **obcinać, redukować 2** to remove sb/sth: *Hundreds of jobs have been axed.* ▶ **obcinać, redukować**

axiom /'æksiəm/ noun [C] (formal) a rule or principle that most people believe to be true ▶ **aksjomat**

axis /'æksɪs/ noun [C] (pl. **axes** /'æksiːz/) **1** a line we imagine through the middle of an object, around which the object turns: *The earth rotates on its axis.* ▶ **oś 2** a fixed line used for marking measurements on a **graph**: *the horizontal/vertical axis* ▶ **oś**

axle /'æksl/ noun [C] a bar that connects a pair of wheels on a vehicle ▶ **oś**

azure /'æʒə(r); Brit. also 'æzjʊə(r)/ adj. (formal) of a bright blue colour like the sky ▶ **lazurowy**
■ **azure** noun [U] ▶ **lazur**

B b

B, b /biː/ noun [C,U] (pl. **Bs**; **bs**; **B's**; **b's** /biːz/) **1** the second letter of the English alphabet: *'Bicycle' begins with (a) 'B'.* ▶ **litera** ***b*** **2** (used about music) the seventh note in the series of notes called the scale of C major: *B major* H-dur ◇ *B minor* h-moll ◇ *B flat* B/b

b. = BORN: *J S Bach, b. 1685*

BA /ˌbiː 'eɪ/ abbr. **Bachelor of Arts**; the degree that you receive when you complete a university or college course in an arts subject ▶ **bakałarz nauk humanistycznych** ➲ look at **BSc**, **MA**

baa /bɑː/ noun [sing.] the sound that a sheep makes ▶ **beczenie, bek**

babble¹ /'bæbl/ noun [sing.] **1** the sound of many voices talking at the same time: *a babble of voices* ▶ **paplanina 2** talking that is confused or silly and is difficult to understand: *I can't bear his constant babble.* ▶ **paplanina**

babble² /'bæbl/ verb [I] **1** to talk quickly or in a way that is difficult to understand ▶ **paplać 2** to make the sound of water running over stones ▶ **szemrać**

babe /beɪb/ noun [C] **1** (old-fashioned) a baby ▶ **niemowlę 2** (especially US, slang) (used when talking to sb, especially a girl or young woman): *It's OK, babe.* ▶ **dziecinka 3** (slang) an attractive young woman ▶ **laska**

baboon /bə'buːn; US bæ'b-/ noun [C] a large African or Asian **monkey** with a long face like a dog's ▶ **pawian**

🔑 **baby** /'beɪbi/ noun [C] (pl. **babies**) **1** a very young child: *I'm going to* ***have a baby.*** ◇ *When's the baby* ***due?*** ◇ *a baby boy/girl* chłopczyk/dziewczynka ▶ **niemowlę, małe dziecko 2** a very young animal or bird: *a baby rabbit* ▶ **młode 3** (US, slang) a person, especially a girl or young woman, that you like or love ▶ **mała**

> **babies**
>
> You can say about a **pregnant** woman: *She's* ***having/ expecting*** *a baby.* She **gives birth** and the baby **is born**, usually with the help of a **midwife**. If a baby is born early, it is **premature**. If a mother gives birth to two babies at the same time, they are **twins**. Parents **take care of** their baby by feeding it, bathing it and changing its **nappy** (US **diaper**). A woman whose job is to look after other people's babies and children is a **nanny**. A baby sleeps in a **cot** and you take it outside in a **pram**. As a baby grows up and starts to walk it is called a **toddler**.

'baby boom noun [C, usually sing.] a time when more babies are born than usual ▶ **wyż demograficzny**

'baby boomer noun [C] a person born during a baby boom ▶ **osoba urodzona w okresie wyżu demograficznego**

'Baby Buggy™ (Brit.) = BUGGY

'baby carriage (US) = PRAM

ˌbaby 'grand noun [C] a small **grand piano** ▶ **fortepian buduarowy**

Babygro™ /'beɪbigrəʊ/ noun [C] (**-os**) (Brit.) a piece of clothing for babies, usually covering the whole body except the head and hands, made of a type of cloth that stretches easily ▶ (*ubranie*) **pajacyk**

babyish /'beɪbiɪʃ/ adj. suitable for or behaving like a baby: *This book is a bit too babyish for Faruk now.* ▶ **dziecinny** ➲ look at **childish**

babysit /'beɪbisɪt/ verb [I] (**babysitting**; pt, pp **babysat**) to look after a child for a short time while the parents are out: *We have friends who babysit for us if we go out in the evening.* ▶ **opiekować się dzieckiem**
■ **babysitter** noun [C] ▶ **(dochodząca) opiekunka do dziecka** ℹ Również mężczyzna może pracować jako **babysitter**.

bachelor /'bætʃələ(r)/ noun [C] **1** a man who has not yet married ▶ **kawaler** ℹ Obecnie mówiąc o nieżonatym mężczyźnie lub niezamężnej kobiecie najczęściej używa się słowa **single**: *a single man/woman.* ➲ look at **spinster 2** a person who has a first university degree: *a Bachelor of Arts/Science* ▶ **osoba legitymująca się dyplomem wyższej uczelni** (*po trzy-/czteroletnich studiach dyplomowych*) ➲ look at **graduate** ➲ note at **degree**

🔑 **back¹** /bæk/ noun [C] **1** the part of a person's or an animal's body between the neck and the bottom: *Do you sleep* ***on your back*** *or on your side?* ◇ *She was standing* ***with her back to*** *me so I couldn't see her face.* ◇ *A camel has a hump on its back.* ▶ **plecy, grzbiet 2** [usually sing.] the part or side of sth that is furthest from the front: *I sat* ***at the back of*** *the class.* ◇ *The answers are* ***in the back of*** *the book.* ◇ *Write your address* ***on the back of*** *the cheque.* ▶ **tył, koniec 3** the part of a chair that supports your upper body when you sit down: *He put his coat over the back of the chair.* ▶ **oparcie**
IDM **at/in the back of your mind** if sth is **at the back of your mind**, it is in your thoughts but is not the main thing that you are thinking about: *With next week's exam at the back of my mind* (myśląc podświadomie o egzaminie w przyszłym tygodniu), *I couldn't relax and enjoy the film.* ▶ **w podświadomości**
back to back 1 if two people stand **back to back**, they stand with their backs facing or touching each other ▶ **tyłem/plecami do siebie 2** if two or more things happen **back to back**, they happen one after the other ▶ **jeden po drugim**

back to front with the back where the front should be: *Wait a minute – you've got your jumper on back to front.* ▶ **tył na przód, na odwrót** ➲ look at **way**[1] (3)
behind sb's back without sb's knowledge or agreement ▶ **za czyimiś plecami** OPP **to sb's face**
get off sb's back (informal) to stop annoying sb, for example when you keep asking them to do sth ▶ **dawać komuś spokój**
know sth like the back of your hand → KNOW[1]
a pat on the back → PAT[2]
turn your back on sb/sth to refuse to be involved with sb/sth: *He turned his back on his career and went to live in the country.* ▶ **odwracać się od kogoś, porzucać coś**

back to front

back to front

inside out

upside down

back[2] /bæk/ adj. [only before a noun] **1** furthest from the front: *Have you locked the back door?* ◇ *back teeth* ▶ **tylny 2** owed from a time in the past: *back pay/rent* ▶ **zaległy**
IDM **take a back seat** to allow sb to play a more important or active role than yourself in a particular situation ▶ **pozostawać w cieniu, usuwać się na dalszy plan**

back[3] /bæk/ adv. ℹ **Back** występuje w czasownikach złożonych. Zob. np. **keep back**. **1** away from the direction you are facing or moving in: *She walked away without **looking back*** (nie oglądając się za siebie). ◇ *Could everyone **move back*** (cofnąć się) *a bit, please?* OPP **forward 2** away from sth; under control: *The police were unable to **keep** the crowds **back*** (powstrzymać tłumy). ◇ *She tried to **hold back*** (powstrzymać) *her tears.* **3** in or to a place or state that sb/sth was in before: *I'm going out now – I'll **be back*** (wrócę) *about 6 o'clock.* ◇ *It started to rain so I **came back** home* (wróciłem do domu). ◇ ***Go back** to sleep.* Śpij dalej. ◇ *Could I **have** my pen **back**, please?* Czy możesz mi oddać pióro? ◇ *I've got to **take** these books **back*** (odnieść te książki) *to the library.* **4** in or into the past; ago: *I met him a few years back, in Madrid.* ◇ ***Think back*** (sięgnij myślą wstecz) *to your first day at school.* ▶ **w przeszłości, temu 5** in return or in reply: *He said he'd **phone** me **back*** (oddzwoni) *in half an hour.*
IDM **back and forth** from one place to another and back again, all the time: *Travelling back and forth to work takes up a lot of time.* ▶ **tam i z powrotem**

back[4] /bæk/ verb **1** [I,T] to move backwards or to make sth move backwards: *She backed into her office and closed the door.* ◇ *He backed the car into the parking space.* ▶ **cofać (się) 2** [T] to give help or support to sb/sth: *We can go ahead with the scheme if the bank will agree to back us.* ▶ **popierać, wspierać 3** [T] to bet money that a particular horse, team, etc. will win in a race or game: *Which horse are you backing in the 2 o'clock race?* ▶ **stawiać na kogoś/coś** (*pieniądze*)
PHR V **back away (from sb/sth)** to move backwards because you are afraid, shocked, etc.: *He began to back slowly away from the snake.* ▶ **cofać się (przed kimś/czymś)**
back down to stop saying that you are right: *I think you are right to demand an apology. Don't back down now.* ▶ **wycofywać się**
back onto sth (Brit.) to face sth at the back: *Many of the colleges back onto the river.* ▶ (*tyły np. budynku*) **sąsiadować, graniczyć**
back out (of sth) to decide not to do sth that you had promised to do: *You promised to come with me. You just can't back out of it now!* ▶ **wycofywać/wykręcać się (z czegoś)**
back (sth) up to move backwards, especially in a vehicle: *Back up a little so that the other cars can get past.* ▶ **cofać (się)**
back sb/sth up to support sb; to say or show that sth is true: *I'm going to say exactly what I think at the meeting. Will you back me up?* ◇ *All the evidence backed up what she had said.* ▶ **popierać kogoś/coś, potwierdzać coś**
back sth up to make a copy of a computer program, etc. in case the original one is lost or damaged ▶ **robić zapasową kopię**

backache /ˈbækeɪk/ noun [U,C] a continuous pain in the back: (Brit.) *to have (a) backache* ◇ (US) *to have a backache* ▶ **ból krzyża/pleców**

ˌback ˈbench noun [C, usually pl.] (Brit.) a seat in the House of Commons for an ordinary member of Parliament: *to sit on the back benches* ▶ **tylna ławka w Izbie Gmin** (*miejsca, które zajmują zwykli posłowie*)
■ **backbencher** noun [C] ▶ **szeregowy poseł**

backbiting /ˈbækbaɪtɪŋ/ noun [U] unpleasant and unkind talk about sb who is not present ▶ **obgadywanie kogoś za jego plecami**

backbone /ˈbækbəʊn/ noun **1** [C] the row of small bones that are connected together down the middle of your back ▶ **kręgosłup** SYN **spine** ➲ picture at **body 2** [sing.] the most important part of sth: *Agriculture is the backbone of their economy.* ▶ **ostoja**

ˈback-breaking adj. (used about physical work) very hard and tiring ▶ **katorżniczy**

backcloth = BACKDROP

backdate /ˌbækˈdeɪt/ verb [T] to make a document, cheque or payment take effect from an earlier date: *The pay rise will be backdated to 1 April.* ▶ **obowiązywać z wcześniejszą datą**

ˌback ˈdoor noun [C] the door at the back or side of a building ▶ **tylne drzwi**
IDM **by/through the back door** in an unfair or indirect way: *He used his friends to help him get into the civil service by the back door.* ▶ **ukradkiem**

backdrop /ˈbækdrɒp/ (also **backcloth** /ˈbækklɒθ/) noun [C] a painted piece of cloth that is hung at the back of the stage in a theatre ▶ (*teatr*) **zasłona dekoracyjna w głębi sceny**

backer /ˈbækə(r)/ noun [C] a person, an organization or a company that gives support to sb, especially financial support ▶ **osoba udzielająca poparcia, sponsor**

backfire /ˌbækˈfaɪə(r)/ verb [I] **1 backfire (on sb)** to have an unexpected and unpleasant result, often the opposite of what was intended ▶ **osiągać rezultat odwrotny do zamierzonego 2** (used about an engine or a vehicle) to make a sudden noise like an explosion ▶ (*gaźnik*) **strzelać**

backgammon /ˈbækgæmən/ noun [U] a game for two people played by moving pieces around a board marked with long thin triangles ▶ **tryktrak**

background /ˈbækgraʊnd/ noun **1** [C] the type of family and social class you come from and the education and experience you have: *We get on very well together in spite of our different backgrounds.* ▶ **pochodzenie** (*społeczne*) **2** [sing., U] the facts or events that are connected with a situation: *The talks are taking place against a background of increasing tension.* ◇ *background infor-*

mation dodatkowe informacje ▶ **tło 3** [sing.] the part of a view, scene, picture, etc. which is furthest away from the person looking at it: *You can see the mountains **in the background** of the photo.* ▶ **tło, dalszy plan** OPP **foreground 4** [sing.] a position where sb/sth can be seen/heard, etc. but is not the centre of attention: *All the time I was speaking to her, I could hear a child crying **in the background*** (słyszałem dziecko płaczące w dali). ◇ *I like to have **background music** when I'm studying.* Kiedy się uczę, lubię mieć włączoną cicho muzykę. ◇ *The film star's husband prefers to stay in the background* (woli pozostać w cieniu). ▶ **tło**

backhand /ˈbækhænd/ noun [sing.] a way of hitting the ball in sports such as **tennis** that is made with the back of your hand facing forward ▶ **bekhend** OPP **forehand**

backhanded /ˌbækˈhændɪd/ adj. having a meaning that is not directly or clearly expressed, or that is not intended ▶ **dwuznaczny**

IDM **a backhanded compliment**; US also **a left-handed compliment** a remark that seems to express admiration but could also be understood as an insult ▶ **dwuznaczny komplement**

backing /ˈbækɪŋ/ noun [U] help or support to do sth, especially financial support: *financial backing* ▶ **poparcie, wsparcie**

backlash /ˈbæklæʃ/ noun [sing.] a strong negative reaction against a political or social event or development ▶ **gwałtowna reakcja, ostry sprzeciw**

backlog /ˈbæklɒg/ noun [C, usually sing.] an amount of work, etc. that has not yet been done and should have been done already: *Because I've been off sick, I've got a backlog of work to catch up on.* ▶ **zaległości**

backpack¹ /ˈbækpæk/ noun [C] a large bag, often on a metal frame, that you carry on your back when you are travelling ▶ **plecak** SYN **rucksack** ➲ picture at **bag**

backpack² /ˈbækpæk/ verb [I] to go walking or travelling with your clothes, etc. in a **backpack** ▶ **uprawiać turystykę pieszą z plecakiem** ℹ Zwróć uwagę na wyrażenie **go backpacking**: *We went backpacking round Europe last summer.* ➲ note at **holiday**

■ **backpacker** noun [C] ▶ **turyst(k)a uprawiając-y/a wędrówkę z plecakiem**

ˌback-ˈpedal verb (**back-pedalling**; **back-pedalled**; US **back-pedaling**; **back-pedaled**) [I] **1 back-pedal (on sth)** to change an earlier statement or opinion; to not do sth that you promised to do: *The protests have forced the government to back-pedal on the new tax.* ▶ **wycofywać się (z czegoś) 2** to **pedal** backwards on a bicycle; to walk or run backwards ▶ **pedałować do tyłu**

backrest /ˈbækrest/ noun [C] part of a seat that supports sb's back ▶ **oparcie** (*np. krzesła*)

ˌback ˈseat noun [C] a seat at the back of a vehicle ▶ **tylne siedzenie** (*np. w samochodzie*)

IDM **take a back seat** to allow sb else to play a more active and important role in a particular situation than you do ▶ (*przen.*) **usuwać się w cień**

backside /ˈbæksaɪd/ noun [C] (informal) the part of your body that you sit on ▶ **tyłek** SYN **bottom**

backslash /ˈbækslæʃ/ noun [C] a mark (\ ), used in computer commands ▶ (*komput.*) **lewy ukośnik** ➲ look at **forward slash**

backspace /ˈbækspeɪs/ noun [C] the key on the keyboard of a computer or **typewriter** which allows you to move backwards. On a computer keyboard this key also removes the last letter that you typed. ▶ (*komput.*) **klawisz backspace**

■ **backspace** verb [I] to use the **backspace** key on a computer keyboard or on a **typewriter** ▶ (*komput.*) **używać klawisza backspace**

ˈ**back-stabbing** noun [U] the action of criticizing sb when they are not there, while pretending to be their friend at other times ▶ **obgadywanie własn-ego/ej przyjaci-ela/ółki za jego/jej plecami**

backstage /ˌbækˈsteɪdʒ/ adv. in the part of a theatre where the actors get dressed, wait to perform, etc. ▶ **za kulis-y/ami**

backstroke /ˈbækstrəʊk/ noun [U] a style of swimming that you do on your back: *Can you **do backstroke**?* ▶ **styl grzbietowy**

backtrack /ˈbæktræk/ verb [I] **1** to go back the same way you came: *We got lost in the wood and had to backtrack.* ▶ **wracać tą samą drogą 2 backtrack (on sth)** to change your mind about a plan, promise, etc. that you have made: *Unions forced the company to backtrack on its plans to close the factory.* ▶ **zmieniać zdanie/decyzję**

backup /ˈbækʌp/ noun **1** [U] extra help or support that you can get if necessary: *The police officer requested urgent backup from the rest of the team.* ▶ **poparcie, pomoc 2** [C] a copy of a computer disk that you can use if the original one is lost or damaged: *Always make a backup of your files.* ▶ **kopia zapasowa** (*pliku*)

⚷ **backward** /ˈbækwəd/ adj. **1** [only before a noun] directed towards the back: *a backward step* krok do tyłu ◇ *a backward glance* spojrzenie za siebie ▶ **w tył, wstecz** OPP **forward 2** slow to develop or learn ▶ **zacofany**

⚷ **backwards** /ˈbækwədz/ (especially US **backward**) adv. **1** towards a place or a position that is behind: *Could everybody take a step backwards?* ▶ **w tył, do tyłu 2** in the opposite direction to usual: *Can you say the alphabet backwards?* ◇ *In the film they take a journey backwards* (w przeszłość) *through time.* ▶ **odwrotnie** OPP for both meanings **forward**

IDM **backward(s) and forward(s)** first in one direction and then in the other, many times: *The dog ran backwards and forwards, barking loudly.* ▶ **tam i z powrotem**

backwater /ˈbækwɔːtə(r)/ noun [C] a place that is away from the places where most things happen and so is not affected by new ideas or outside events ▶ **cichy zakątek**

backyard /ˌbækˈjɑːd/ noun [C] **1** (Brit.) an area behind a house, with a hard surface and a wall or fence around it ▶ **podwórko** (*za domem*) **2** (US) the whole area behind the house including the grass area and the garden ▶ **teren/ogród z tyłu domu**

bacon /ˈbeɪkən/ noun [U] meat from the back or sides of a pig that has been **cured**, usually served in thin slices ▶ **bekon** ➲ note at **meat** ➲ look at **gammon, ham, pork**

⚷ **bacteria** /bækˈtɪəriə/ noun [pl.] very small living things that can only be seen with a **microscope**. Bacteria exist in large numbers in air, water, soil, plants and the bodies of people and animals. Some bacteria cause disease. ▶ **bakterie** ➲ look at **germ, virus**

⚷ **bad** /bæd/ adj. (**worse** /wɜːs/; **worst** /wɜːst/) **1** not good; unpleasant: *bad weather* ◇ *I'm afraid I've got some bad news for you.* ◇ *It's bad enough losing your job, but to lose your house as well is awful.* ▶ **zły, niedobry 2** of poor quality; of a low standard: *Many accidents are caused by bad driving.* ◇ *This isn't as bad as I thought.* ▶ **zły, kiepski 3 bad (at sth/at doing sth)** not able to do sth well or easily: *a bad teacher/driver/cook* ◇ *I've always been bad at sport.* ▶ **kiepski (w czymś) 4** serious: *That was a very bad mistake!* ◇ *She went home with a bad headache* (z silnym bólem głowy). ◇ *The traffic was very bad* (okropny) *on the way to work.* ▶ **poważny** SYN **severe 5** [only before a noun] difficult or not suitable: *This is a bad time to phone – everyone's out to lunch.* ▶ **nieodpowiedni, niewygodny 6** not good; morally wrong: *He was not a bad man, just rather weak.* ▶ **zły 7** [not before a noun] **bad for sb/sth** likely to damage or hurt sb/sth:

Too many sweets are bad for you (mogą ci zaszkodzić). ▶ **szkodliwy 8** not healthy; painful: *He's always had a bad heart.* ◇ *Keith's off work with a bad back.* ▶ **chory**, **bolący 9** not fresh or suitable to eat: *These eggs will go **bad** if we don't eat them soon.* ▶ **zepsuty** SYN **rotten**
IDM **not bad** (informal) quite good: *'What was the film like?' 'Not bad.'* ◇ *He earned £100 – not bad* (nieźle) *for four hours' work!* ▶ **niezły**
too bad (informal) (used to show that nothing can be done to change a situation): *'I'd much rather stay at home.' 'Well that's just too bad. We've said we'll go.'* ▶ **wielka szkoda!**, **jak nie, to nie**
ℹ **Bad** używa się w innych idiomach, np. **go through a bad patch**. Zob. hasła odpowiednich rzeczowników, przymiotników itp.

bad
Zamiast **very bad** można powiedzieć **awful**, **dreadful** lub **terrible**. **Horrible** opisuje kogoś/coś nieprzyjemnego lub kogoś nieuprzejmego: *He's always saying horrible things to me.* Mówimy również: ***poor** quality* ◇ *an **unpleasant** experience* ◇ *a **disgusting** smell* ◇ *a **serious** accident/illness/problem.*

ˌbad ˈbreath noun [U] breath that smells unpleasant: *Have I got bad breath?* ▶ **nieprzyjemny zapach z ust**

ˌbad ˈdebt noun [C, U] a debt that is unlikely to be paid ▶ **nieściągalny dług**

baddy (also **baddie**) /ˈbædi/ noun [C] (pl. **baddies**) (informal) a bad person in a film, book, etc. ▶ **czarny charakter** OPP **goody**

bade past tense of **bid**

badge /bædʒ/ noun [C] a small piece of metal, cloth or plastic with a design or words on it that you wear on your clothing: *The players all have jackets with the club badge on.* ▶ **odznaka**, **znaczek**

badger /ˈbædʒə(r)/ noun [C] an animal with black and white lines on its head that lives in holes in the ground and comes out at night ▶ **borsuk**

ˌbad ˈhair day noun [C] (informal) a day on which everything seems to go wrong ▶ **pechowy dzień**

ˌbad ˈlanguage noun [U] words that are used for swearing: *You'll get into trouble if you use bad language.* ▶ **brzydkie słowa**

🔑 **badly** /ˈbædli/ adv. (**worse** /wɜːs/; **worst** /wɜːst/) **1** in a way that is not good enough; not well: *'Can you speak French?' 'Only very badly.'* ◇ *She did badly in the exams.* ▶ **źle** OPP **well 2** very much: *He badly needed a holiday.* ▶ **bardzo** (*np. chcieć, potrzebować*) **3** seriously; in a terrible way: *He was badly hurt in* (ciężko ranny) *the accident.* ▶ **poważnie**, **dotkliwie**
IDM **well/badly off** → OFF[1]

badminton /ˈbædmɪntən/ noun [U] a game for two or four people in which players hit a **shuttlecock** over a high net, using a **racket** ▶ **badminton**

ˈbad-mouth verb [T] (informal) to say unpleasant things about sb ▶ **wieszać na kimś psy**

badness /ˈbædnəs/ noun [U] the fact of being morally bad: *There was not a hint of badness in him.* ▶ **zło**

🔑 **ˌbad-ˈtempered** adj. often angry or impatient: *a bad-tempered old man* ▶ **wybuchowy**, **skory do gniewu**

baffle /ˈbæfl/ verb [T] to be impossible to understand; to confuse sb very much: *His illness baffled the doctors.* ▶ **wprawiać w zakłopotanie**
■ **baffled** adj. ▶ **zakłopotany** | **baffling** adj. ▶ **trudny do zrozumienia/rozwiązania**

🔑 **bag[1]** /bæg/ noun **1** [C] a container made of paper or thin plastic that opens at the top; a strong container made from cloth, plastic, leather, etc. usually with one or two handles, used to carry things in when travelling, shopping, etc.: *She brought some sandwiches in a plastic bag.* ◇ *a carrier bag* torba-reklamówka ◇ *a string bag* siatka ◇ *a shopping bag* ◇ *Have you packed your bags yet?* ◇ *She took her purse out of her bag.* ▶ **torba**, **torebka** ➲ picture at **container 2** [C] **a bag (of sth)** the amount contained in a

bags

bag: *She's eaten a whole bag of sweets!* ◇ *a bag of crisps/sugar/flour* ▶ **torebka, opakowanie** **3** [pl.] (Brit.) **bags (of sth)** a lot (of sth); plenty (of sth): *There's no hurry, we've got bags of time.* ▶ **mnóstwo** **4** (**bags**) [pl.] folds of skin under the eyes, often caused by lack of sleep: *I've got terrible bags under my eyes.* ▶ **worki pod oczami** **5** (informal) (especially Brit.) an insulting word for an unpleasant or bad-tempered older woman ▶ **małpa**

bag² /bæg/ verb [T] (**bagging**; **bagged**) (informal) to try to get sth for yourself so that other people cannot have it: *Somebody's bagged the seats by the pool!* ▶ **zaklepywać** ℹ Aby zaznaczyć, że chce się coś zrobić lub bardzo ma się na coś ochotę, często używa się **bags**: *Bags I go first!* Idę pierwszy! Zamawiam!

bagel /ˈbeɪɡl/ noun [C] a type of bread roll in the shape of a ring ▶ **pieczywo w formie obwarzanka, bajgiel** ➲ picture at **bread**

⚷ **baggage** /ˈbæɡɪdʒ/ noun [U] bags, suitcases, etc. used for carrying sb's clothes and things on a journey: *Baggage should be checked in* (odprawiony) *at least an hour before the flight.* ◇ ***excess baggage*** nadbagaż ◇ *We could see the **baggage handlers*** (bagażowych) *loading luggage onto the plane.* ▶ **bagaż** SYN **luggage** ➲ note at **plane**

ˈ**baggage reclaim** (US ˈ**baggage claim**) noun [U] the place at an airport where you get your suitcases, etc. again after you have flown: *I went to wait for my suitcase at baggage reclaim.* ▶ **odbiór bagażu** (*na lotnisku*)

ˈ**baggage room** (US) = LEFT-LUGGAGE OFFICE

baggy /ˈbæɡi/ adj. (**baggier**; **baggiest**) (used about a piece of clothing) big; hanging on the body in a loose way: *a baggy sweater* ▶ **luźny, workowaty** OPP **tight**

ˈ**bag lady** noun [C] a woman who has no home and who walks around carrying her possessions with her ▶ **bezdomna** (*nosząca wszędzie ze sobą swoje rzeczy w torbach*)

ˈ**bag lunch** noun [C] (US) a meal of **sandwiches**, fruit, etc. that you take to school, work, etc. in a bag ▶ **kanapki itp. przygotowane jako drugie śniadanie poza domem** ➲ look at **box lunch**, **packed lunch**

bagpipes /ˈbæɡpaɪps/ noun [pl.] a musical instrument, popular in Scotland, that is played by blowing air through a pipe into a bag and then pressing the bag so that the air comes out of other pipes ▶ **dudy**

bagpipes

baguette /bæˈɡet/ noun [C] **1** a type of bread in the shape of a long thick stick ▶ **bagietka** **2** a small baguette or part of one that is filled with food and eaten as a **sandwich** ▶ **kanapka z części bagietki lub małej podłużnej bułki**

bail¹ /beɪl/ noun [U] **1** money that sb agrees to pay if a person accused of a crime does not appear in court on the day they are called. When **bail** has been arranged, the accused person can go free until that day: *She was **released on bail*** (zwolniona za kaucją) *of £2 000.* ◇ *The judge **set bail*** (wyznaczył kaucję) *at £10 000.* ▶ **kaucja** **2** permission for sb who is accused of a crime to be free until the trial if a sum of money is handed over to the court: *She was **granted bail.*** ◇ *The judge felt that he was a dangerous man and **refused** him **bail.*** ▶ **zwolnienie za kaucją**

bail² /beɪl/ verb [T] to free sb on **bail**

PHR V **bail sb out** **1** to obtain sb's freedom by paying money to the court: *Her parents went to the police station and bailed her out.* ▶ **uzyskać zwolnienie kogoś z więzienia za kaucją** **2** to rescue sb or sth from a difficult situation (especially by providing money): *If you get into trouble, don't expect me to bail you out again!* ▶ **wybawiać kogoś z kłopotu**

bailiff /ˈbeɪlɪf/ noun [C] an officer whose job is to take the possessions and property of people who cannot pay money that they owe ▶ **komornik**

bait /beɪt/ noun [U] **1** food or sth that looks like food that is put onto a hook to catch fish, or to catch animals or birds ▶ **przynęta** **2** something that is used for persuading or attracting sb: *Free offers are often used as bait to attract customers.* ▶ **przynęta, pokusa**

⚷ **bake** /beɪk/ verb [I,T] **1** to cook in an oven in dry heat: *I could smell bread baking in the oven.* ◇ *On his birthday she baked him a cake.* ▶ **wypiekać (się), piec (się) na sucho** ➲ look at **roast** ➲ note at **cook** **2** to become or to make sth hard by heating it: *The hot sun baked the earth.* ▶ **prażyć, spalać (się)**

baked beans noun [pl.] small white **beans** cooked in a tomato sauce and usually sold in cans ▶ **fasolka w sosie pomidorowym** ➲ picture on **page A14**

ˌ**baked poˈtato** = JACKET POTATO

baker /ˈbeɪkə(r)/ noun **1** [C] a person who bakes bread, cakes, etc. to sell in a shop ▶ **piekarz** **2** (**the baker's**) [sing.] a shop that sells bread, cakes, etc.: *Get a loaf at the baker's.* ▶ **piekarnia; cukiernia** ➲ picture on **page A5**

bakery /ˈbeɪkəri/ noun [C] (pl. **bakeries**) a place where bread, cakes, etc. are baked to be sold ▶ **piekarnia; cukiernia**

baking /ˈbeɪkɪŋ/ adj. (also **baking hot**) very hot: *The workers complained of the baking heat in the office.* ▶ **piekielny**

ˈ**baking powder** noun [U] a mixture of powders that is used to make cakes rise and become light as they are baked ▶ **proszek do pieczenia**

ˈ**baking sheet** (also ˈ**baking tray**; US ˈ**cookie sheet**) noun [C] a small sheet of metal used for baking food on ▶ **blacha do pieczenia**

ˈ**baking soda** = SODIUM BICARBONATE

⚷ **balance¹** /ˈbæləns/ noun **1** [sing.] **(a) balance (between A and B)** a situation in which different or opposite things are of equal importance, size, etc.: *The course provides a good balance between academic and practical work.* ◇ *Tourism has upset **the delicate balance of nature** on the island.* ▶ **równowaga** **2** [U] the ability to keep steady with an equal amount of weight on each side of the body: *to **lose** your **balance*** tracić równowagę ◇ *It's very difficult to **keep** your **balance** when you start learning to ski.* ◇ *You need a good **sense of balance** to ride a motorbike.* ▶ **równowaga** **3** [C, usually sing.] the amount that still has to be paid; the amount that is left after some has been used, taken, etc.: *You can pay a 10% deposit now, with the balance due in one month.* ▶ **saldo, reszta** **4** [C] (technical) an instrument used for weighing things ▶ **waga** ➲ look at **scales**

IDM **be, etc. in the balance** to be uncertain: *Following poor results, the company's future hangs in the balance.* ▶ (*losy*) **ważyć się**

(catch/throw sb) off balance (to find or put sb) in a position that is not safe and from which it is easy to fall: *A strong gust of wind caught me off balance and I nearly fell over.* ▶ **sprawiać, że ktoś traci równowagę**

on balance having considered all sides, facts, etc.: *On balance, I've had a pretty good year.* ▶ **wziąwszy wszystko pod uwagę**

strike a balance (between A and B) → STRIKE¹

⚷ **balance²** /ˈbæləns/ verb **1** [I,T] to be or to put sb/sth in a steady position so that their/its weight is not heavier on one side than on the other: *I had to balance on the top* *step of the ladder to paint the ceiling.* ◇ *Carefully, she balanced a glass on top of the pile of plates.* ▶ **utrzymywać równowagę/coś w równowadze** **2** [I,T] **balance (sth) (out) (with sth)** to have or give sth equal value, importance, etc. in relation to other parts: *It's difficult to balance the demands* (pogodzić wymagania) *of a career with caring for an elderly relative.* ◇ *The loss in the first half of the year was balanced out by the profit in the second half.* ◇ *The good and bad effect of any decision will usually balance out.* ▶ **równoważyć** **3** [T] **balance sth against sth** to consider and compare one matter in relation to another: *In planning the new road, we have to balance the benefit to motorists against the damage to the environment.* ▶ **rozważać, brać pod uwagę** **4** [I,T] to have equal totals of money spent and money received: *I must have made a mistake – the accounts don't balance.* ◇ *She is always very careful to balance her weekly budget.* ▶ **bilansować (się)**

balanced /ˈbælənst/ adj. keeping or showing a balance so that different things, or different parts of things, exist in equal or correct amounts: *I like this newspaper because it gives a balanced view.* ◇ *A **balanced diet** plays an important part in good health.* ▶ **wyważony, sprawiedliwy** OPP **unbalanced**

ˌbalance of ˈpayments noun [sing.] the difference between the amount of money one country receives from other countries for things it sells and the amount it pays other countries for things it buys, in a particular period of time ▶ **bilans płatniczy**

ˌbalance of ˈpower noun [sing.] **1** a situation in which political power or military strength is divided between two countries or groups of countries ▶ **równowaga sił** **2** the power that a smaller political party has when the larger parties need its support because they do not have enough votes on their own ▶ **języczek u wagi**

ˈbalance sheet noun [C] a written statement showing the amount of money and property that a company has, and how much has been received and paid out ▶ **zestawienie bilansowe**

balcony /ˈbælkəni/ noun [C] (pl. **balconies**) **1** a platform built on an upstairs outside wall of a building, with a wall or rail around it ▶ **balkon** ➲ look at **patio**, **terrace**, **veranda** **2** (especially US) = CIRCLE[1] (3)

bald /bɔːld/ adj. **1** (used about people) having little or no hair on your head: *to **go bald*** wyłysieć ◇ *He has a **bald patch*** (ma łysinę) *on the top of his head.* ▶ **łysy** ➲ picture at **hair** **2** (used about sth that is said) simple; without extra words: *the bald truth* naga prawda ▶ **prosty**

balding /ˈbɔːldɪŋ/ adj. starting to lose the hair on your head: *a balding man in his fifties* ▶ **łysiejący**

baldly /ˈbɔːldli/ adv. in a few words with nothing extra or unnecessary and without trying to be polite: *'You're lying,' he said baldly.* ▶ **bez ogródek**

bale /beɪl/ noun [C] a large quantity of sth pressed tightly together and tied up: *a bale of hay/cloth/paper* ▶ **bela**

balk (especially US) = BAULK

ball /bɔːl/ noun [C] **1** a round object that you hit, kick, throw, etc. in games and sports: *a tennis/golf/rugby ball* ◇ *a football* ▶ **piłka** **2** a round object or a thing that has been formed into a round shape: *a ball of wool* ◇ *The children threw snowballs at each other.* ◇ *We had meatballs* (pulpety) *for dinner.* ▶ **kula, gałka** **3** one throw, kick, etc. of the ball in some sports: *That was a great ball from the defender.* ▶ **rzut, wykop** **4** (slang) = TESTICLE **5** a large formal party at which people dance ▶ **bal**

IDM **be on the ball** (informal) to always know what is happening and be able to react to or deal with it quickly: *With so many new developments, you really have to be on the ball.* ▶ **być zorientowanym i wyczulonym na nowości**

set/start the ball rolling to start sth (an activity, conversation, etc.) that involves or is done by a group: *I told a joke first, to set the ball rolling.* ▶ **zaczynać, dawać przykład na dobry początek**

ballad /ˈbæləd/ noun [C] a long song or poem that tells a story, often about love ▶ **ballada**

ballast /ˈbæləst/ noun [U] heavy material placed in a ship or **hot-air balloon** to make it heavier and keep it steady ▶ **balast**

ˌball ˈbearing noun [C] one of a number of metal balls put between parts of a machine to make them move smoothly ▶ **łożysko kulkowe**

ballerina /ˌbæləˈriːnə/ noun [C] a woman who dances in ballets ▶ **balerina**

ballet /ˈbæleɪ; US bæˈleɪ/ noun **1** [U] a style of dancing that tells a story with music but without words ▶ **balet** **2** [C] a performance or work that consists of this type of dancing ▶ **balet**

ˈballet dancer noun [C] a person who dances in ballets ▶ **tance-rz/rka baletu**

balletic /bæˈletɪk/ adj. (formal) smooth and elegant, like a movement or a dancer in **ballet** ▶ **baletowy**

ˈball game noun [C] **1** any game played with a ball ▶ **gra, w której używa się piłki** **2** (US) a **baseball** match ▶ **mecz baseballowy**

IDM **a (whole) new/different ball game** something completely new or different: *I'm used to working outside, so sitting in an office all day is a whole new ball game for me.* ▶ **nowa sytuacja**

ballistic /bəˈlɪstɪk/ adj.

IDM **go ballistic** (informal) to become very angry: *He went ballistic when I told him.* ▶ **wściekać się**

ballistic missile noun [C] a **missile** that is fired into the air at a particular speed and angle in order to fall in the right place ▶ **pocisk balistyczny**

balloon /bəˈluːn/ noun [C] **1** a small coloured object that you blow air into and use as a toy or for decoration: *to blow up/burst/pop a balloon* ▶ **balonik** **2** (also **hot-ˈair balloon**) a large **balloon** made of cloth that is filled with gas or hot air so that it can fly through the sky, carrying people in a **basket** underneath it ▶ **balon**

ballot /ˈbælət/ noun **1** [C,U] a secret written vote: *The union will **hold a ballot** on the new pay offer.* ◇ *The committee are elected by ballot every year.* ▶ **tajne głosowanie** **2** (Brit. also **ˈballot paper**) [C] the piece of paper on which sb marks who they are voting for ▶ **karta do głosowania**

■ **ballot** verb [T] **ballot sb (about/on sth)**: *The union is balloting its members on strike action.* ▶ **zapraszać do udziału w tajnym głosowaniu**

ˈballot box noun **1** [C] the box into which people put the piece of paper with their vote on ▶ **urna wyborcza** **2** (**the ballot box**) [sing.] the system of voting in an election: *People will express their opinion through the ballot box.* ▶ **wybory**

ˈballot paper (Brit.) = BALLOT (2)

ballpark /ˈbɔːlpɑːk/ noun [C] a place where the sport of **baseball** is played ▶ **boisko baseballowe**

IDM **in the ballpark** (informal) (used about figures or amounts) that are within the same limits: *All the bids for the contract were in the same ballpark.* ▶ **tego samego rzędu wielkości**

a ballpark figure/estimate a number, amount, etc. that is approximately correct: *We asked the builders for a ballpark figure, to give us an idea of how much it would cost.* ▶ **przybliżona/orientacyjna suma/liczba itp.**

ballpoint /ˈbɔːlpɔɪnt/ (also ˌballpoint ˈpen) noun [C] a pen with a very small metal ball at the end that rolls ink onto paper ▶ **długopis** ➲ look at **Biro** ➲ picture at **stationery**

ballroom /ˈbɔːlruːm; -rʊm/ noun [C] a large room used for dancing on formal occasions ▶ **sala balowa**

ˌballroom ˈdancing noun [U] a formal type of dance in which couples dance together using particular steps and movements ▶ **tradycyjne tańce towarzyskie**

balls¹ /bɔːlz/ noun (taboo, slang) **1** [U] (Brit.) nonsense: *That's a load of balls!* ▶ **bzdury 2** [pl.] courage: *She's got balls, I'll say that for her.* ◇ *It took a lot of balls to do that.* To wymagało dużo odwagi. ▶ **odwaga**

balls²
PHR V **balls sth up** (Brit., taboo, slang) to spoil sth; to do sth very badly ▶ **(s)pieprzyć coś** ⓘ Grzeczniejszą formą tego wyrażenia jest **foul sth up**, **mess sth up** lub **bungle sth**.

balm /bɑːm/ noun [U,C] a liquid, cream, etc. with a pleasant smell, used to make wounds less painful or skin softer: *lip balm* ▶ **balsam**

balmy /ˈbɑːmi/ adj. (used about the air, weather, etc.) warm and pleasant: *a balmy summer evening* ▶ **łagodny** SYN **mild**

baloney /bəˈləʊni/ noun [U] (US, informal) nonsense; lies: *Don't give me that baloney!* ▶ **bzdury**

balsa wood /ˈbɔːlsə wʊd/ (also **balsa**) noun [U] the light wood of a type of tree, used especially for making models ▶ **balsa**

balti /ˈbɔːlti; ˈbɒlti/ noun [C, U] a type of meat or vegetable dish cooked in Pakistani style, usually served in a round metal pan which gives its name to the dish ▶ **potrawa kuchni pakistańskiej przygotowywana w specjalnym garnku**

Baltic /ˈbɔːltɪk/ adj. connected with the Baltic Sea, or the area around it in Northern Europe: *the Baltic States* Republiki Bałtyckie ▶ **bałtycki**

balustrade /ˌbæləˈstreɪd/ noun [C] a row of posts, joined together at the top, built along the edge of a structure such as a bridge, etc. to stop you from falling, or as a decoration ▶ **balustrada** ➲ look at **banister**

bamboo /ˌbæmˈbuː/ noun [C,U] (pl. **bamboos**) a tall tropical plant of the grass family. **Bamboo shoots** can be eaten and the hard parts of the plant are used for making furniture, etc.: *a bamboo chair* ▶ **bambus**

🔑 **ban** /bæn/ verb [T] (banning; banned) **ban sth; ban sb (from sth/from doing sth)** to officially say that sth is not allowed, often by law: *The government has banned the import of products from that country.* ◇ *He was fined £500 and banned from driving for a year.* ▶ **zakazywać** SYN **prohibit**
■ **ban** noun [C] **a ban (on sth)**: *There is a ban on smoking in this building.* ◇ *to impose/lift a ban* ▶ **zakaz**

banal /bəˈnɑːl/ adj. not original or interesting: *a banal comment* ▶ **banalny**

banality /bəˈnæləti/ noun [U,C] (pl. **-ies**) the quality of being **banal**; things, remarks, etc. that are **banal**: *the banality of modern city life* ◇ *They exchanged banalities for a couple of minutes.* ▶ **banał; banalność**

banana /bəˈnɑːnə; US -ˈnæn-/ noun [C,U] a curved fruit with yellow skin that grows in hot countries: *a bunch of bananas* ▶ **banan** ➲ picture on **page A12**

🔑 **band** /bænd/ noun [C] **1** [with sing. or pl. verb] a small group of musicians who play popular music together, often with a singer or singers: *a rock/jazz band* ◇ *He plays the drums in a band.* ◇ *The band has/have announced that it/they is/are going to split up.* ◇ *a brass band* orkiestra dęta ▶ **zespół, grupa** ➲ note at **pop 2** [with sing. or pl. verb] a group of people who do sth together or have the same ideas: *A small band of rebels is/are hiding in the hills.* ▶ **banda 3** a long thin piece or circle of material that is put round things to hold them together: *She rolled up the papers and put an* ***elastic band*** *round them.* ▶ **opaska, gumka, taśma, wstążka 4** a line of colour or material on sth that contrasts with the background: *She wore a red pullover with a green band across the middle.* ▶ **pas, pasek 5** = WAVEBAND

🔑 **bandage** /ˈbændɪdʒ/ noun [C] a long piece of soft white cloth that you tie round a wound or injury ▶ **bandaż**
■ **bandage** verb [T] **bandage sth/sb (up)**: *The nurse bandaged my hand up.* ▶ **bandażować**

Band-Aid™ (US) = PLASTER (3)

bandanna /bænˈdænə/ noun [C] a piece of brightly coloured cloth worn around the neck or head ▶ **chusta** (*na szyję/głowę*)

B and B (also **B & B**)
IDM **bed and breakfast** → BED

bandit /ˈbændɪt/ noun [C] a member of an armed group of thieves who attack people who are travelling ▶ **bandyta**

bandwagon /ˈbændwægən/ noun
IDM **climb/jump on the bandwagon** to copy what other people are doing because it is fashionable or successful ▶ **małpować, naśladować**

bandwidth /ˈbændwɪdθ/ noun [C,U] **1** a band of **frequencies** used for sending electronic signals ▶ **pasmo; szerokość pasma 2** a measure of the amount of information that a group of connected computers or an Internet connection can send in a particular time ▶ **przepustowość łącza**

bandy verb (**bandying**; **bandies**; pt, pp **bandied**)
PHR V **bandy sth about/around** [usually passive] if a name, a word, a story, etc. is **bandied about/around**, it is mentioned frequently by many people: *His name was being bandied about as a future prime minister.* ▶ **wymieniać**

bane /beɪn/ noun [sing.] **the bane of sb/sth** something that causes trouble and makes people unhappy: *The neighbours' kids are the* ***bane of my life.*** ▶ **zmora, przekleństwo**

bang¹ /bæŋ/ verb [I,T] **1** to make a loud noise by hitting sth hard; to close sth or to be closed with a loud noise: *Somewhere in the house, I heard a door bang.* ◇ *He banged his fist on the table* (uderzył pięścią w stół) *and started shouting.* ▶ **trzaskać** (*np. drzwiami*), **walić** SYN **slam 2** to knock against sth by accident; to hit a part of the body against sth by accident: *Be careful not to bang your head on the ceiling. It's quite low.* ◇ *As I was crossing the room in the dark I banged into a table.* ▶ **wpadać na coś, uderzać o/w coś**
PHR V **bang about/around** to move around a place making loud noises: *I could hear him banging about in the kitchen.* ▶ **hałasować**

bang² /bæŋ/ noun [C] **1** a sudden, short, very loud noise: *There was an enormous bang when the bomb exploded.* ▶ **huk 2** a short, strong knock or hit, especially one that causes pain and injury: *a nasty bang on the head* ▶ **uderzenie, cios**
IDM **with a bang** in a successful or exciting way: *Our team's season started with a bang when we won our first five matches.* ▶ (*przen.*) **z wielkim hukiem**

bang³ /bæŋ/ adv. (especially Brit., informal) exactly; directly; right: *Our computers are* ***bang up to date.*** ◇ *The shot was bang on target.* ▶ **właśnie, dokładnie**
IDM **bang goes sth** (informal) (used for expressing the idea that sth is now impossible): *'It's raining!' 'Ah well, bang goes our picnic* (i po pikniku)*!'* ▶ **i już po**

bang⁴ /bæŋ/ interj. (used to sound like the noise of a gun, etc.) ▶ **pif-paf!**

banger /ˈbæŋə(r)/ noun [C] (Brit., informal) **1** a **sausage** ▶ **kiełbasa 2** an old car that is in very bad condition: *I'm tired of driving around in that old banger.* ▶ **gruchot 3** a small, noisy **firework** ▶ **petarda**

bangle /ˈbæŋgl/ noun [C] a circle of metal that is worn round the arm or wrist for decoration ▶ **bransoleta** ➲ picture at **jewellery**

bangs (US) = FRINGE[1] (1)

banish /ˈbænɪʃ/ verb [T] (formal) **1** to send sb away (especially out of the country), usually as a punishment: *They were banished from the country for demonstrating against the government.* ▶ **skazywać na banicję, wypędzać** SYN **exile 2** to make sb/sth go away; to get rid of sb/sth: *She banished all hope of winning from her mind.* ▶ **odganiać, odpędzać** (*myśli*)

banister (also **bannister**) /ˈbænɪstə(r)/ noun [C, often plural] the posts and rail at the side of a set of stairs: *The children loved sliding down the banister* (po poręczy) *at the old house.* ▶ **balustrada**

banjo /ˈbændʒəʊ/ noun [C] (pl. **banjos**) a musical instrument like a **guitar**, with a long thin neck, a round body and four or more strings ▶ **banjo**

🔑 **bank[1]** /bæŋk/ noun [C] **1** an organization which keeps money safely for its customers; the office or building of such an organization. You can take money out, save, borrow or exchange money at a bank: *My salary is paid directly into my bank.* ◇ *I need to go to the bank to get some money out.* ◇ *a bank account/loan* ▶ **bank** ➲ note at **money 2** a store of things, which you keep to use later: *a databank* ◇ *a blood bank in a hospital* ▶ **bank 3** the ground along the side of a river or **canal**: *People were fishing along the banks of the river.* ▶ **brzeg 4** a higher area of ground that goes down or up at an angle, often at the edge of sth or dividing sth: *There were grassy banks on either side of the road.* ▶ **nasyp, wał 5** a mass of cloud, snow, etc.: *The sun disappeared behind a bank of clouds.* ▶ **wał, zaspa**

bank[2] /bæŋk/ verb [I] **bank (with/at ...)** to have an account with a particular bank: *I've banked with HSBC for years.* ▶ **mieć konto w banku**

PHR V **bank on sb/sth** to expect and trust sb to do sth, or sth to happen: *Our boss might let you have the morning off but I wouldn't bank on it.* ▶ **liczyć na kogoś/coś**

ˈbank card noun [C] **1** (Brit.) (also **ˈbanker's card**) a plastic card provided by your bank that may be used as a **cheque card** or **debit card** or to get money from your account out of a machine ▶ **karta bankowa 2** (US) a credit card provided by your bank, that can also be used as a **debit card** and to get money from your account out of a machine ▶ **karta debetowa/płatnicza**

ˈbank draft (also **ˈbanker's draft**) noun [C] a cheque paid by a bank to another bank or to a particular person or organization ▶ **przelew bankowy**

banker /ˈbæŋkə(r)/ noun [C] a person who owns or has an important job in a bank ▶ **bankier**

ˌbank ˈholiday noun [C] (Brit.) a public holiday (not a Saturday or Sunday) ▶ **święto zwyczajowe** (*kiedy banki są zamknięte*)

banking /ˈbæŋkɪŋ/ noun [U] the type of business done by banks: *She decided on a career in banking.* ▶ **bankowość**

banknote = NOTE[1] (4)

bankrupt /ˈbæŋkrʌpt/ adj. not having enough money to pay what you owe: *The company must cut its costs or it will* ***go bankrupt*** (zbankrutuje). ▶ **zbankrutowany**
■ **bankrupt** verb [T]: *The failure of the new product almost bankrupted the firm.* ▶ **doprowadzać do bankructwa**

bankruptcy /ˈbæŋkrʌptsi/ noun [C,U] (pl. **bankruptcies**) the state of being **bankrupt**: *The company* ***filed for bankruptcy*** (wystąpiła o bankructwo) *in 1999.* ◇ *Competition from larger companies drove them to bankruptcy* (doprowadziła ich do bankructwa). ▶ **bankructwo**

ˈbank statement (also **statement**) noun [C] a printed list of all the money going into or out of your bank account during a certain period ▶ **wyciąg z konta**

banner /ˈbænə(r)/ noun [C] a long piece of cloth with words or signs on it, which can be hung up or carried on two poles: *The demonstrators carried banners saying 'Stop the War'.* ▶ **transparent**

bannister = BANISTER

banquet /ˈbæŋkwɪt/ noun [C] a formal meal for a large number of people, usually as a special event at which speeches are made ▶ **bankiet**

banter /ˈbæntə(r)/ noun [U] friendly comments and jokes ▶ **przekomarzanie się**
■ **banter** verb [I] ▶ **przekomarzać się**

baptism /ˈbæptɪzəm/ noun [C,U] a ceremony in which a person becomes a member of the Christian Church by being held underwater for a short time or having drops of water put onto their head. Often they are also formally given a name. ▶ **chrzest** ➲ look at **christening**
■ **baptize** (also **-ise**) /bæpˈtaɪz/ verb [T] ▶ **chrzcić** ➲ look at **christen**

Baptist /ˈbæptɪst/ noun [C] a member of a Protestant Church that believes that **baptism** should only be for people who are old enough to understand the meaning of the ceremony and should be done by placing the person fully underwater ▶ **baptyst(k)a**
■ **Baptist** adj. ▶ (*Kościół*) **baptystów, baptystyczny**

🔑 **bar[1]** /bɑː(r)/ noun [C] **1** a place where you can buy and drink alcoholic and other drinks: *They had a drink in the bar before the meal.* ▶ **bar 2** a long, narrow, high surface where drinks, etc. are served: *She went to the bar and ordered a drink.* ◇ *We sat on stools* ***at the bar.*** ▶ **bar 3** [in compounds] a place where a particular type of

food or drink is the main thing that is served: *a wine bar* ◇ *a coffee bar* ◇ *a sandwich bar* bufet z kanapkami ▶ **bar** **4 a bar (of sth)** a small block of solid material, longer than it is wide: *a bar of soap/chocolate* ▶ **tabliczka**, **kostka**, **baton** **5** a long, thin, straight piece of metal, often placed across a window or door to stop sb from getting through it: *They escaped by sawing through the bars of their prison cell.* ▶ **drążek**, **krata**, **sztaba** **6 a bar (to sth)** a thing that prevents you from doing sth: *Lack of education is not always a bar to success in business.* ▶ **przeszkoda** **7** one of the short, equal units of time into which music is divided: *If you sing a few bars of the song, I might recognize it.* ▶ **takt** ➲ picture at **music**

IDM **behind bars** (informal) in prison: *The criminals are now safely behind bars.* ▶ **za kratami**

> W Wlk. Br. **bar**, w którym sprzedaje się napoje alkoholowe, nie jest osobnym budynkiem (z wyjątkiem **wine bar**) ale zazwyczaj stanowi część pubu, hotelu, restauracji itp. W pubie mogą znajdować się dwa rodzaje barów. **Lounge bar** jest bardziej elegancki (i często droższy) niż **public bar**.

bar² /bɑː(r)/ verb [T] (**barring**; **barred**) **1** [usually passive] to close sth with a **bar¹** (5) or bars: *All the windows were barred.* ◇ *The heavy door was barred and bolted* (zaryglowane). ▶ **zamykać na zasuwę** **2** to block a road, path, etc. so that nobody can pass: *A line of police officers barred the entrance.* ▶ **zagradzać** (*drogę*) **3 bar sb from sth/from doing sth** to say officially that sb is not allowed to do, use or enter sth: *He was barred from the club for fighting.* ▶ **zabraniać**

bar³ /bɑː(r)/ prep. except: *All the seats were taken, bar one.* ▶ **oprócz**

barbarian /bɑːˈbeəriən/ noun [C] a wild person with no culture, who behaves very badly ▶ **barbarzyńca**

barbaric /bɑːˈbærɪk/ adj. very cruel and violent: *barbaric treatment of prisoners* ▶ **barbarzyński**

barbarism /ˈbɑːbərɪzəm/ noun [U] **1** a state of not having any education, respect for art, etc. ▶ **barbarzyństwo**, **barbaryzm** **2** cruel or violent behaviour: *acts of barbarism committed in war* ▶ **barbarzyństwo**

barbarity /bɑːˈbærəti/ noun [C,U] (pl. **barbarities**) behaviour that deliberately causes extreme pain or suffering to others ▶ **barbarzyństwo**

barbarous /ˈbɑːbərəs/ adj. (formal) **1** extremely cruel and shocking: *the barbarous treatment of these prisoners of war* ▶ **barbarzyński** **2** showing a lack of education and good manners ▶ **barbarzyński**

barbecue /ˈbɑːbɪkjuː/ noun [C] (abbr. **BBQ**) **1** a metal frame on which food is cooked outdoors over an open fire ▶ **rożen** **2** an outdoor party at which food is cooked in this way: *Let's **have a barbecue** on the beach.* ▶ **przyjęcie na świeżym powietrzu, na którym serwuje się kiełbaski, hamburgery itp. pieczone na rożnie** ➲ look at **roast**

■ **barbecue** verb [T]: *barbecued steak* ▶ **opiekać na rożnie** ➲ note at **cook**

barbed wire /ˌbɑːbd ˈwaɪə(r)/ noun [U] strong wire with sharp points on it: *a barbed wire fence* ▶ **drut kolczasty**

barber /ˈbɑːbə(r)/ noun **1** [C] a man whose job is to cut men's hair and sometimes to shave them ▶ **fryzjer (męski)** ➲ look at **hairdresser** **2** (**the barber's**) [sing.] (Brit.) a shop where men go to have their hair cut ▶ **zakład fryzjerski męski**

barbiturate /bɑːˈbɪtʃʊrət/ noun [C] any of several types of powerful drug that make you feel calm and relaxed or put you to sleep ▶ **barbituran**

ˈ**bar chart** (also ˈ**bar graph**) noun [C] a diagram which uses narrow bands of different heights to show different amounts, so that they can be compared ▶ **histogram**, **wykres kolumnowy**

ˈ**bar code** noun [C] a pattern of thick and thin lines that is printed on things you buy. It contains information that a computer can read. ▶ **kod kreskowy**

bare /beə(r)/ adj. **1** (used about part of the body) not covered by clothing: *bare arms/feet/shoulders* ▶ **nagi**, **goły** ➲ look at **naked**, **nude** **2** without anything covering it or in it: *They had taken the painting down, so the walls were all bare.* ▶ **goły**, **pusty** **3** [only before a noun] just enough; the most basic or simple: *You won't pass your exams if you just do **the bare minimum**.* ◇ *I don't take much luggage when I travel, just **the bare essentials**.* ◇ *Just give me the **bare facts*** (suche fakty). ▶ **podstawowy**, **główny**

IDM **with your bare hands** without weapons or tools: *She killed him with her bare hands.* ▶ **gołymi rękami**

bareback /ˈbeəbæk/ adj., adv. on a horse without a **saddle** ▶ **na oklep**

barefoot /ˈbeəfʊt/ adj., adv. with nothing (for example shoes, socks, etc.) on your feet: *We walked barefoot along the beach.* ▶ **bosy**; **boso**

barely /ˈbeəli/ adv. [used especially after *can* and *could* to emphasize that sth is difficult to do] only just; almost not: *I was so tired I could barely stand up.* ◇ *I earn barely enough money to pay my rent.* ▶ **ledwie** ➲ look at **hardly**

barf /bɑːf/ verb [I] (US, informal) to **vomit** ▶ **rzygać**

■ **barf** noun [U] ▶ **rzygowiny**

🔑 **bargain¹** /ˈbɑːgən/ noun [C] **1** something that is cheaper or at a lower price than usual: *At that price, it's an absolute bargain!* ◇ *I found a lot of bargains in the sale.* ▶ **okazja** **2** an agreement between people or groups about what each of them will do for the other or others: *Let's **make a bargain** – I'll lend you the money if you'll help me with my work.* ◇ *I lent him the money but he didn't **keep** his **side of the bargain*** (nie dotrzymał słowa). ▶ **umowa**

IDM **into the bargain** (used for emphasizing sth) as well; in addition; also: *They gave me free tickets and a free meal into the bargain.* ▶ **na dodatek**

strike a bargain (with sb) → STRIKE¹

bargain² /ˈbɑːgən/ verb [I] **bargain (with sb) (about/over/for sth)** to discuss prices, conditions, etc. with sb in order to reach an agreement that suits each person: *I'm sure that if you bargain with him, he'll drop the price.* ◇ *They bargained over the price.* ▶ **targować się**

PHR V **bargain for/on sth** [usually in negative sentences] to expect sth to happen and be ready for it: *When I agreed to help him I didn't bargain for how much it would cost me.* ▶ **oczekiwać czegoś**, **liczyć na coś**

ˈ**bargaining power** noun [U] the amount of control a person or group has when trying to reach an agreement with another person or group in a business or political situation ▶ **siła negocjacji**

barge¹ /bɑːdʒ/ noun [C] a long narrow boat with a flat bottom that is used for carrying goods or people on a **canal** or river ▶ **barka** ➲ picture at **boat**

barge² /bɑːdʒ/ verb [I,T] to push people out of the way in order to get past them: *He barged (his way) angrily through the crowd.* ▶ **przepychać się**

baritone /ˈbærɪtəʊn/ noun [C] a male singing voice that is fairly low; a man with this voice ▶ **baryton**

bark¹ /bɑːk/ noun **1** [U] the hard outer covering of a tree ▶ **kora** **2** [C] the short, loud noise that a dog makes: *The dog next door has a very loud bark.* ▶ **szczekanie**

bark² /bɑːk/ verb **1** [I] **bark (at sb/sth)** (used about dogs) to make a loud, short noise or noises ▶ **szczekać** ➲ look at **woof** **2** [I,T] **bark (at sb)**; **bark sth (out) (at sb)** to speak to sb in a loud voice in an angry or aggressive way: *The boss came in, barked out some orders and left again.* ▶ **wykrzykiwać**

'barking mad (also **barking**) adj. (Brit., informal) completely crazy ▶ **stuknięty**

barley /'bɑːli/ noun [U] **1** a plant that produces grain that is used for food or for making beer and other drinks ▶ **jęczmień 2** the grain produced by this plant ▶ **jęczmień**

barmaid /'bɑːmeɪd/ noun [C] (US **bartender** /'bɑːtendə(r)/) a woman who serves drinks from behind a bar in a pub, etc. ▶ **barmanka**

barman /'bɑːmən/ (pl. **-men** /-mən/) (US **bartender**) noun [C] a man who serves drinks from behind a bar in a pub, etc. ▶ **barman**

bar mitzvah /ˌbɑː 'mɪtsvə/ noun [C] a ceremony in the Jewish religion for a boy who is about 13 years old. After the ceremony, he is considered an adult. ▶ (*w religii żydowskiej*) **bar micwa** ➲ look at **bat mitzvah**

barmy /'bɑːmi/ adj. (Brit., informal) slightly crazy ▶ **zbzikowany**

barn /bɑːn/ noun [C] a large building on a farm in which crops or animals are kept ▶ **stodoła**; **stajnia**

barnyard /'bɑːnjɑːd/ noun [C] an area on a farm that is surrounded by farm buildings ▶ **podwórze gospodarskie**

barometer /bə'rɒmɪtə(r)/ noun [C] **1** an instrument that measures air pressure and indicates changes in the weather ▶ **barometr 2** something that indicates the state of sth (a situation, a feeling, etc.): *Results of local elections are often a barometer of the government's popularity.* ▶ **barometr**

baron /'bærən/ noun [C] **1** a man of a high social position ▶ **baron 2** a person who controls a large part of a particular industry or type of business: *drug/oil barons* ▶ **magnat**

baroness /'bærənəs/ noun [C] a woman of a high social position; the wife of a **baron** ▶ **baronowa**

baroque (also **Baroque**) /bə'rɒk; US -'rəʊk/ adj. (used to describe the highly decorated style of European art, buildings and music of the 17th and early 18th centuries): *baroque churches/music* ▶ **barokowy**

barracks /'bærəks/ noun [C, with sing. or pl. verb] (pl. **barracks**) a building or group of buildings in which soldiers live: *Guards were on duty at the gate of the barracks.* ▶ **koszary**

barrage /'bærɑːʒ; US bə'rɑːʒ/ noun [C] **1** a continuous attack on a place with a large number of guns ▶ **ogień zaporowy 2** a large number of questions, comments, etc., directed at a person very quickly: *The minister faced a* ***barrage of questions*** *from reporters.* ▶ **ogień, nawał**

barrel /'bærəl/ noun [C] **1** a large, round, wooden, plastic or metal container for liquids, that has a flat top and bottom and is wider in the middle: *a beer/wine barrel* ◇ *The price of oil is usually given per barrel.* ▶ **beczka, baryłka 2** the long metal part of a gun like a tube through which the bullets are fired ▶ **lufa**

barren /'bærən/ adj. **1** (used about land or soil) not good enough for plants to grow on ▶ **jałowy 2** (used about trees or plants) not producing fruit or seeds ▶ **nieurodzajny**

barricade /ˌbærɪ'keɪd/ noun [C] an object or line of objects that is placed across a road, an entrance, etc. to stop people getting through: *The demonstrators* ***put up barricades*** *to keep the police away.* ▶ **barykada**
■ **barricade** verb [T]
PHR V **barricade yourself in** to defend yourself by putting up a **barricade**: *Demonstrators took over the building and barricaded themselves in.* ▶ **barykadować się**

barrier /'bæriə(r)/ noun [C] **1** an object that keeps people or things separate or prevents them moving from one place to another: *The crowd were all kept behind barriers.* ◇ *The mountains form a natural barrier between the two countries.* ▶ **bariera** ➲ look at **crash barrier 2 a barrier (to sth)** something that causes problems or makes it impossible for sth to happen: *When you live in a foreign country, the* ***language barrier*** *can be a difficult problem to overcome.* ▶ **bariera**

barring /'bɑːrɪŋ/ prep. **1** if there is/are not: *Barring any unforeseen problems* (o ile nie zdarzy się coś nieprzewidzianego), *we'll be moving house in a month.* ▶ **o ile nie zdarzy się 2** except for: *Barring one or two small problems, everything's fine at the moment.* ▶ **oprócz**

barrister /'bærɪstə(r)/ noun [C] (in English law) a lawyer who is trained to speak for you in the higher courts ▶ **adwokat** ➲ note at **lawyer**

barrow /'bærəʊ/ noun [C] **1** (Brit.) a small thing on two wheels on which fruit, vegetables, etc. are moved or sold in the street, especially in markets ▶ **wózek** (*handlarza*) **2** = WHEELBARROW

bartender (US) = BARMAID, BARMAN

barter /'bɑːtə(r)/ verb [I,T] **barter sth (for sth)**; **barter (with sb) (for sth)** to exchange goods, services, property, etc. for other goods, etc. without using money: *The farmer bartered his surplus grain for machinery.* ◇ *The prisoners bartered with the guards for writing paper and books.* ▶ **prowadzić handel wymienny**, **wymieniać**
■ **barter** noun [U] ▶ **handel wymienny**

base¹ /beɪs/ noun [C] **1** the lowest part of sth, especially the part on which it stands or at which it is fixed or connected to sth: *the base of a column/glass* ◇ *I felt a terrible pain* ***at the base of*** *my spine.* ▶ **podstawa 2** an idea, fact, etc. from which sth develops or is made: *With these ingredients* ***as a base****, you can create all sorts of interesting dishes.* ◇ *The country needs a strong economic base.* ▶ **podstawa 3** a place used as a centre from which activities are done or controlled: *This hotel is an ideal base for touring the region.* ▶ **baza 4** a military centre from which the armed forces operate: *an army base* ▶ **baza 5** (in **baseball**) one of the four points that a runner must touch ▶ **baza**, **meta**

base² /beɪs/ verb [T, usually passive] **base sb/sth in ...** to make one place the centre from which sb/sth can work or move around: *I'm based in New York, although my job involves a great deal of travel.* ◇ *a Cardiff-based company* ▶ **zakładać bazę**
PHR V **base sth on sth** to form or develop sth from a particular starting point or source: *This film is based on a true story.* ▶ **opierać** (*np. na faktach*)

baseball /'beɪsbɔːl/ noun [U] a team game that is popular in the US in which players hit the ball with a **bat** and run around the four **bases** to score points ▶ **baseball** ➲ picture on **page A8**

'baseball cap noun [C] a cap with a long **peak**, originally worn by **baseball** players ▶ **baseballówka**

baseless /'beɪsləs/ adj. (formal) not supported by good reasons or facts: *The rumours were completely baseless.* ▶ **bezpodstawny** SYN **unfounded**

basement /'beɪsmənt/ noun [C] a room or rooms in a building, partly or completely below ground level: *a basement flat* ▶ **suterena** ➲ look at **cellar**

bases 1 plural of **basis 2** plural of **base¹**

bash¹ /bæʃ/ verb (informal) **1** [T] to hit sb/sth very hard ▶ **walić kogoś/w coś/o coś 2** [I] to crash into sb/sth: *I didn't stop in time and bashed into the car in front.* ▶ **wpadać na kogoś/coś**, **zderzać się z kimś/czymś 3** [T] to criticize sb/sth strongly: *The candidate continued to bash her opponent's policies.* ▶ **mocno krytykować**

bash² /bæʃ/ noun [C] **1** a hard hit: *He gave Alex a bash on the nose.* ▶ **mocny cios 2** (informal) a large party or celebration: *Are you going to Gary's birthday bash?* ▶ **impreza**

IDM **have a bash (at sth/at doing sth)** (Brit., informal) to try: *I'll get a screwdriver and have a bash at mending the light.* ▶ **próbować (coś robić)**

bashful /ˈbæʃfl/ adj. shy and embarrassed ▶ **nieśmiały, wstydliwy**

basic /ˈbeɪsɪk/ adj. **1** forming the part of sth that is most necessary and from which other things develop: *The basic question is, can we afford it?* ◇ *basic information/facts/ideas* ▶ **podstawowy** **2** of the simplest kind or level; including only what is necessary without anything extra: *This course teaches basic computer skills.* ◇ *The* ***basic pay*** *is £200 a week – with extra for overtime.* ◇ *The rooms in the cheapest hotels are very basic* (bez wygód) *– they have no bathrooms.* ▶ **podstawowy**

basically /ˈbeɪsɪkli/ adv. (used to say what the most important or most basic aspect of sb/sth is): *The two designs are basically the same.* ▶ **w zasadzie** SYN **essentially**

basics /ˈbeɪsɪks/ noun [pl.] the simplest or most important facts or aspects of sth; things that you need the most: *So far, I've only learnt the basics of computing.* ▶ **podstawowe produkty/zasady itp.**

basil /ˈbæzl; US ˈbeɪzl/ noun [C] a **herb** with shiny green leaves that smell sweet and are used in cooking ▶ **bazylia** ➲ picture on **page A12**

basin /ˈbeɪsn/ noun [C] **1** = WASHBASIN ▶ **umywalka** **2** a round open bowl often used for mixing or cooking food ▶ **misa** **3** an area of land from which water flows into a river: *the Amazon Basin* ▶ **basen**

basis /ˈbeɪsɪs/ noun (pl. **bases** /ˈbeɪsiːz/) **1** [sing.] the principle or reason which lies behind sth: *We made our decision* ***on the basis of*** *the reports which you sent us.* ▶ **podstawa** **2** [sing.] the way sth is done or organized: *They meet* ***on a regular basis*** (regularnie). ◇ *to employ somebody* ***on a*** *temporary/voluntary/part-time* ***basis*** (tymczasowo/dobrowolnie/w niepełnym wymiarze godzin) ▶ **3** [C] a starting point, from which sth can develop: *She used her diaries as a basis for her book.* ▶ **podstawa**

bask /bɑːsk; US bæsk/ verb [I] **bask (in sth)** **1** to sit or lie in a place where you can enjoy the warmth: *The snake basked in the sunshine on the rock.* ▶ **wylegiwać się** **2** to enjoy the good feelings you have when other people admire you, give you a lot of attention, etc.: *The team was still* ***basking in the glory*** *of winning the cup.* ▶ **rozkoszować się czymś**

basket /ˈbɑːskɪt; US ˈbæs-/ noun [C] **1** a container for carrying or holding things, made of thin pieces of material that bends easily, such as wood, plastic or wire: *a shopping basket* kosz/yk na zakupy ◇ *a basket of shopping* koszyk pełen zakupów ◇ *a waste-paper basket* ◇ *a clothes/laundry basket* kosz na brudną bieliznę ▶ **koszyk** ➲ picture at **bag** **2** (in **basketball**) a net that hangs from a metal ring high up at each end of a court ▶ **kosz** ➲ picture on **page A8** **3** (in **basketball**) a score of one, two or three points, made by throwing the ball through one of the nets ▶ **kosz**

IDM **put all your eggs in one basket** → EGG[1]

basketball /ˈbɑːskɪtbɔːl; US ˈbæs-/ noun [U] a game for two teams of five players in which you score points by throwing a large ball through the other team's **basket** (2) ▶ **koszykówka** ➲ picture on **page A8**

bass /beɪs/ noun **1** [U] the lowest part in music ▶ **bas** **2** [C] the lowest male singing voice; a singer with this kind of voice ▶ **bas** **3** [C] (also ˌ**bass guiˈtar**) an electric **guitar** which plays very low notes ▶ **gitara basowa** ➲ note at **music** **4** = DOUBLE BASS

■ **bass** adj. [only before a noun]: *a bass drum* ▶ **basowy**

bassoon /bəˈsuːn/ noun [C] a musical instrument that you blow which makes a very deep sound ▶ **fagot** ➲ note at **piano**

bastard /ˈbɑːstəd; ˈbæs-/ noun [C] **1** (taboo, slang) (used to insult sb, especially a man, who has been rude, unpleasant or cruel): *He's a real bastard.* ◇ *You bastard! You've made her cry.* ▶ **sukinsyn** **2** (Brit., slang) (used about or to sb, especially a man, who people feel very sorry for or when they want to have what he has got): *You poor bastard!* Biedak! ◇ *What a lucky bastard!* Szczęściarz! **3** (Brit., slang) (used about sth that causes difficulties or problems): *It's a bastard of a problem.* To jest cholernie trudny problem. **4** (old-fashioned) a person whose parents were not married to each other when they were born ▶ **bękart** ℹ Słowo to może być uznane za obraźliwe. Bardziej neutralne wyrażenie to **an illegitimate child**.

bastardize /ˈbɑːstədaɪz; ˈbæs-/ (also **-ise**) verb [T] (formal) to copy sth, but change parts of it so that it is not as good as the original ▶ **skundlić**

baste /beɪst/ verb [T] to pour liquid fat or juices over meat, etc. while it is cooking ▶ **polewać sosem**

bastion /ˈbæstiən/ noun [C] **1** (formal) a group of people or a system that protects a way of life or a belief when it seems that it may disappear: *a bastion of male privilege* ◇ *a bastion of freedom* ▶ **bastion** **2** a place that military forces are defending ▶ **bastion**

bat[1] /bæt/ noun [C] **1** a piece of wood for hitting the ball in sports such as **table tennis**, **cricket** or **baseball**: *a cricket bat* ▶ **rakietka** (*do tenisa stołowego*), **kij** (*baseballowy lub do krykieta*) ➲ look at **club**, **racket**, **stick** ➲ picture on **page A8** **2** a small animal, like a mouse with wings, which flies and hunts at night ▶ **nietoperz** ➲ picture on **page A10**

IDM **off your own bat** without anyone asking you or helping you ▶ **z własnej inicjatywy**

bat[2] /bæt/ verb [I] (**batting**; **batted**) (used about one player or a whole team) to have a turn hitting the ball in sports such as **cricket** or **baseball** ▶ **wybijać** (*piłkę*) ➲ look at **field**

IDM **not bat an eyelid**; US **not bat an eye** to show no surprise or embarrassment when sth unusual happens ▶ **nie mrugnąć okiem**

batch /bætʃ/ noun [C] a number of things or people which belong together as a group: *The bus returned to the airport for the next batch of tourists.* ▶ **grupa**, **partia**

bated /ˈbeɪtɪd/ adj.

IDM **with bated breath** excited or afraid, because you are waiting for sth to happen ▶ **z zapartym tchem**

bath[1] /bɑːθ; US bæθ/ noun **1** [C] (also **bathtub** /ˈbɑːθtʌb; US bæθ-/) a large container for water in which you sit to wash your body: *Can you answer the phone? I'm in the bath!* ▶ **wanna** **2** [sing.] an act of washing the whole of your body when you sit or lie in a bath filled with water: *to* ***have a bath*** ◇ (especially US) *Would you prefer to* ***take a bath*** (kąpać się) *or a shower?* ▶ **kąpiel** **3** (**baths**) [pl.] (Brit., old-fashioned) a public building where you can go to swim; a public place where people went in past times to have a wash or a bath: *Roman baths* ▶ **basen kryty**; **łaźnia**

bath[2] /bɑːθ; US bæθ/ verb **1** [T] to give sb a bath: *Will you bath the baby?* ▶ **kąpać** **2** [I] (old-fashioned) to have a bath: *I prefer to bath in the mornings.* ▶ **kąpać się** (*w wannie*)

bathe /beɪð/ verb **1** [T] to wash or put part of the body in water, often for medical reasons: *She bathed the wound with antiseptic.* ▶ **przemywać**; **kąpać się** (*np. w morzu, rzece*) **2** [I] (old-fashioned) to swim in the sea or in a lake or river ▶ **kąpać się** (*np. w morzu, rzece*) ➲ look at **sunbathe**

bathed /beɪðd/ adj. (formal) [not before a noun] **bathed in sth** covered with sth: *The room was bathed in moonlight.* ▶ **skąpany**, **zalany** (*światłem*)

bathing /ˈbeɪðɪŋ/ noun [U] the act of swimming in the sea, a river or a lake (not in a swimming pool): *Bathing is possible at a number of beaches along the coast.* ▶ **kąpiel**

bathing cap (especially US) = SWIMMING CAP

ˈ**bath mat** noun [C] **1** a piece of material that you put beside the bath to stand on when you get out ▶ **mata łazienkowa 2** a piece of rubber that you put on the bottom of the bath so that you do not slip ▶ **mata kąpielowa** (*antypoślizgowa*)

bathrobe = DRESSING GOWN

⚷ **bathroom** /ˈbɑːθruːm; -rʊm; US ˈbæθ-/ noun [C] **1** a room where there is a bath and/or a shower, a **washbasin** and often a toilet: *Go and wash your hands in the bathroom.* ▶ **łazienka 2** (US) a room with a toilet: *I have to **go to the bathroom.*** ➲ note at **toilet** ▶ **toaleta, ubikacja**

bathtub = BATH¹ (1)

bat mitzvah /ˌbæt ˈmɪtsvə/ noun [C] a ceremony in the Jewish religion for a girl who is about 13 years old ▶ (*w religii żydowskiej*) **bat micwa** ➲ look at **bar mitzvah**

baton /ˈbætɒn; US bəˈt-/ noun [C] **1** = TRUNCHEON ▶ **batuta 2** a short thin stick used by the person who directs an **orchestra** ▶ **batuta 3** a stick which a runner in a **relay** passes to the next person in the team ▶ **pałeczka sztafetowa**

batsman /ˈbætsmən/ noun [C] (pl. **-men** /-mən/) (in the sport of **cricket**) one of the two players who hit the ball to score **runs** ▶ (*krykiet*) **gracz, który uderza piłkę** ➲ note at **cricket** ➲ picture on **page A8**

battalion /bəˈtæliən/ noun [C] a large unit of soldiers that forms part of a larger unit in the army ▶ **batalion**

batter¹ /ˈbætə(r)/ verb [I,T] to hit sb/sth hard, many times: *The wind battered against the window.* ◇ *He battered the door down.* Staranował drzwi. ◇ *The wind battered against the window* (łomotał oknem). ◇ *High winds battered* (nękały) *Britain again yesterday.* ▶ **walić, maltretować** (*fizycznie*)

batter² /ˈbætə(r)/ noun [U,C] a mixture of flour, eggs and milk used to cover food such as fish, vegetables, etc. before frying them ▶ **ciasto naleśnikowe**

battered /ˈbætəd/ adj. no longer looking new; damaged or out of shape: *a battered old hat* ▶ **zniszczony, zniekształcony**

⚷ **battery** /ˈbætri; -təri/ noun (pl. **batteries**) **1** [C] a device which provides electricity for a toy, radio, car, etc.: *to recharge **a flat battery*** naładować wyczerpaną baterię ▶ **bateria, akumulator 2** [C] (Brit.) a large number of very small **cages** in which chickens, etc. are kept on a farm: *a battery hen/farm* ▶ **kurnik bateryjny** ➲ look at **free-range 3** [U] the crime of attacking sb physically: *He was charged with **assault and battery.*** ▶ **pobicie**

⚷ **battle¹** /ˈbætl/ noun **1** [C,U] a fight, especially between armies in a war: *the battle of Trafalgar* ◇ *to die/be killed **in battle*** ▶ **bitwa, walka 2** [C] **a battle (with sb) (for sth)** a competition, an argument or a fight between people or groups of people trying to win power or control: *a legal battle for custody of the children* ▶ **walka 3** [C, usually sing.] **a battle (against/for sth)** a determined effort to solve a difficult problem or to succeed in a difficult situation: *After three years she lost her battle against cancer.* ▶ **walka**

IDM **a losing battle** → LOSE

battle² /ˈbætl/ verb [I,T] **battle (with/against sb/sth) (for sth)**; **battle (on)** to try very hard to achieve sth difficult or to deal with sth unpleasant or dangerous: *Mark is battling with his maths homework.* ◇ *The little boat battled against the wind.* ◇ *The two brothers were battling for control of the family business.* ◇ *Life is hard at the moment but we're battling on.* ◇ *The teams will **battle it out** in the final next week.* ▶ **walczyć**

battlefield /ˈbætlfiːld/ (also **battleground** /ˈbætlgraʊnd/) noun [C] the place where a battle is fought ▶ **pole bitwy**

battlements /ˈbætlmənts/ noun [pl.] a low wall around the top of a castle with spaces in it that people inside could shoot through ▶ **blankowanie**

battleship /ˈbætlʃɪp/ noun [C] a very large ship with big guns used in war ▶ (*okręt*) **pancernik**

batty /ˈbæti/ adj. (informal) (especially Brit.) (used about people or ideas) slightly crazy, in a harmless way ▶ **zbzikowany**

bauble /ˈbɔːbl/ noun [C] **1** a piece of cheap jewellery ▶ **błyskotka 2** a decoration in the shape of a ball that is hung on a Christmas tree ▶ **bombka** (*na choinkę*)

baulk (especially US **balk**) /bɔːk/ verb [I] **baulk (at sth)** to not want to do or agree to sth because it seems too difficult, dangerous or unpleasant: *She liked horses, but she baulked at riding one.* ▶ **wahać się (przed czymś)**

bawdy /ˈbɔːdi/ adj. (**bawdier**; **bawdiest**) (old-fashioned) (used about songs, plays, etc.) loud, and dealing with sex in an amusing way ▶ **sprośny**

bawl /bɔːl/ verb [I,T] to shout or cry loudly ▶ **wykrzykiwać, wrzeszczeć**

⚷ **bay** /beɪ/ noun [C] **1** a part of the coast where the land goes in to form a curve: *the Bay of Bengal* ◇ *The harbour was in a sheltered bay.* ▶ **zatoka** ➲ look at **gulf 2** a part of a building, an aircraft or an area which has a particular purpose: *a parking/loading bay* ładownia ▶ **część** (*np. budynku lub samolotu o specjalnym przeznaczeniu*), **zatoka**

IDM **hold/keep sb/sth at bay** to stop sb dangerous from getting near you; to prevent a situation or problem from getting worse ▶ **trzymać kogoś z dala**

ˈ**bay leaf** noun [C] the dried leaf of the **bay tree** that is used in cooking as a **herb** ▶ **liść laurowy**

bayonet /ˈbeɪənət/ noun [C] a knife that can be fixed to the end of a gun ▶ **bagnet**

ˌ**bay ˈwindow** noun [C] a window in a part of a room that sticks out from the wall of a house ▶ **okno wykuszowe** ➲ picture on **page A3**

bazaar /bəˈzɑː(r)/ noun [C] **1** (in some eastern countries) a market ▶ **bazar 2** (Brit.) a sale where the money that is made goes to charity: *The school held a bazaar to raise money for the hospital.* ▶ **wenta**

BBC /ˌbiː biː ˈsiː/ abbr. **the British Broadcasting Corporation**; one of the national radio and TV companies in Britain: *a BBC documentary* ◇ *to watch a programme on BBC1* ▶ **brytyjska państwowa sieć radia i telewizji**

BBQ = BARBECUE

BC /ˌbiː ˈsiː/ abbr. **before Christ**; used in dates to show the number of years before the time when Christians believe Jesus Christ was born: *300 BC* ▶ **p.n.e.** ➲ look at **AD**

⚷ **be¹** /bi; strong form biː/ verb ⓘ Formy czasowników **be** podane są w dodatku *Czasowniki nieregularne* na końcu słownika. **1** [T] (**there is/are**) to exist; to be present: *Is there a God?* Czy Bóg istnieje? ◇ *I tried phoning them but there was no answer* (ale nie było odpowiedzi). ◇ *There are some people outside.* Jest kilka osób na zewnątrz. ◇ *There are a lot of trees in our garden.* W naszym ogrodzie rośnie wiele drzew. ▶ **być, istnieć, znajdować się 2** [I] (used to give the position of sb/sth or the place where sb/sth is): *Paula's in her office.* ◇ *He isn't here.* Nie ma go. ◇ *Where are the scissors?* ◇ *The bus stop is five minutes' walk from here.* ◇ *St Tropez is on the south coast.* ▶ **być 3** [I] (used to give the date or age of sb/sth or to talk about time): *My birthday is on April 24th.* ◇ *It's 6 o'clock.* ◇ *It was Tuesday yesterday.* ◇ *It's ages since I last saw him.* ◇ *He's older than Miranda.* ▶ **być**

Zwróć uwagę, że w jęz. ang. określając czyjś wiek używa się czasownika **be**: *Sue is 18.* Sue ma 18 lat. ◇ *He'll be 21 in June.* Skończy 21 lat w czerwcu.

4 [I] (used when you are giving the name of people or things, describing them or giving more information about them): *This is my father, John.* ◇ *I'm Alison.* ◇ *He's Italian. He's* ***from*** *Milan.* ◇ *He's a doctor.* ◇ *What's that?* ◇ *A lion is a mammal.* ◇ *The film was excellent.* ◇ *She's very friendly.* ◇ *'How is your wife?' 'She's fine, thanks.'* ◇ *How much was your ticket?* Ile kosztował twój bilet? ◇ *'What colour is your car* (jakiego koloru jest twój samochód)*?' 'It's green.* (Zielony.)*'* ▶ **być 5** [I] [only used in the perfect tenses] to go to a place (and return): *Have you ever* ***been to*** *Japan?* Czy byłeś kiedyś w Japonii? ▶ **pójść/pojechać dokądś i wrócić** ℹ Por. **has/have been** z **has/have gone**: *Julia's gone to the doctor's.* Julia poszła do lekarza (i jeszcze nie wróciła). ◇ *Julia's been to the doctor's today.* Julia była dzisiaj u lekarza (i już wróciła). ➲ look at **been**

IDM **be yourself** to act naturally: *Don't be nervous; just be yourself and the interview will be fine.* ▶ **być sobą, zachowywać się naturalnie**

-to-be [in compounds] future: *his bride-to-be* ◇ *mothers-to-be* ▶ **przyszły**

be² /bi; strong form biː/ auxiliary verb **1** (used with a past participle to form the passive): *He was killed in the war.* ◇ *Where were they made?* ◇ *The house was still being built.* ◇ *You will be told what to do.* ▶ **być, zostać 2** (used with a present participle to form the continuous tenses): *You're sitting on my book.* Siedzisz na mojej książce. (teraz, w tej chwili) ◇ *I am studying Italian.* Uczę się włoskiego. ◇ *We were chatting* (rozmawialiśmy) *when he arrived.* ◇ *Is he coming?* Czy on przyjdzie? (za chwilę lub w ogóle przy tej okazji) ◇ *How long have we been waiting?* Jak długo już czekamy? (od jakiegoś momentu w przeszłości do chwili obecnej) **3 be to do sth** (used to show that sth must happen or that sth has been arranged): *You are to leave* (masz wyjść) *here at 10 o'clock at the latest.* ◇ *They are to be married* (mają się pobrać) *in June.* ▶ **mieć (koniecznie coś robić) 3 if sb/sth were to do sth** (used to show that sth is possible but not very likely): *If they were to offer me* (gdyby mi zaproponowali) *the job, I'd probably take it.*

beach /biːtʃ/ noun [C] an area of sand or small stones beside the sea: *to sit* ***on the beach*** ▶ **plaża**

beacon /ˈbiːkən/ noun [C] a fire or light on a hill or tower, often near the coast, which is used as a signal ▶ **światło ostrzegawcze**

bead /biːd/ noun [C] **1** a small round piece of wood, glass or plastic with a hole in the middle for putting a string through to make jewellery, etc.: *a string of beads* ▶ **koralik, paciorek 2** (**beads**) [pl.] a necklace made of beads ▶ **korale 3** a drop of liquid: *There were* ***beads of sweat*** *on his forehead.* ▶ **kropla, kropelka**

beady /ˈbiːdi/ adj. (used about eyes) small, round and bright; watching everything closely ▶ *(oczy)* **jak paciorki**

beak /biːk/ noun [C] the hard pointed part of a bird's mouth ▶ **dziób** ➲ picture on **page A11**

beaker /ˈbiːkə(r)/ noun [C] **1** a plastic or paper drinking cup, usually without a handle ▶ **plastikowy/papierowy kubek 2** a glass container used in scientific experiments, etc. for pouring liquids ▶ **zlewka** ➲ picture at **laboratory**

beam¹ /biːm/ noun [C] **1** a line of light: *the beam of a torch* ◇ *The car's headlights were* ***on full beam.*** ◇ *a laser beam* ▶ **snop** *(światła)*, **wiązka** *(promieni)* **2** a long piece of wood, metal, etc. that is used to support weight, for example in the floor or ceiling of a building ▶ **belka 3** a happy smile ▶ **promienny uśmiech**

beam² /biːm/ verb **1** [I] **beam (at sb/sth)** to smile happily: *I looked at Sam and he beamed back at me.* ◇ *Beaming with pleasure* (rozpromieniona) *she stepped forward to receive her prize.* ▶ **uśmiechać się promiennie 2** [T] to send out radio or TV signals: *The programme was beamed live by satellite to many different countries.* ▶ **transmitować 3** [I] to send out light and warmth: *The sun beamed down on them.* ▶ **promieniować, wysyłać promienie**

B

bean /biːn/ noun [C] **1** the seed or **pod** from a climbing plant that is eaten as a vegetable: *green beans* fasolka szparagowa ◇ *soya beans* soja ◇ *broad beans* bób ◇ *runner beans* fasola wielokwiatowa ◇ *haricot beans* fasola zwyczajna ◇ *French beans* fasolka szparagowa ◇ *kidney beans* fasola typu kidney ▶ **fasola** ℹ Zwróć uwagę, że słowo **bean** jest policzalne. ➲ picture on **page A13 2** similar seeds from other plants: *coffee beans* ▶ **ziarnko**

IDM **full of beans/life** → FULL¹

spill the beans → SPILL

beanie /ˈbiːni/ noun [C] a small, round close-fitting hat ▶ **wełniana czapka sportowa** *(w kształcie półpiłki)*

bean sprouts noun [pl.] **bean** seeds that are just beginning to grow, often eaten raw ▶ **kiełek fasoli**

bear¹ /beə(r)/ verb (pt **bore** /bɔː(r)/, pp **borne** /bɔːn/) **1** [T] [(used with *can/could* in negative sentences or in questions)] to be able to accept and deal with sth unpleasant: *I can't bear spiders.* ◇ *She can't bear* (nienawidzi) *waiting for people/ to wait for people.* ◇ *She couldn't bear the thought of anything happening to him.* ◇ *How can you bear to listen to that music?* ◇ *The pain was almost more than he could bear.* ▶ **znosić, cierpieć** SYN **stand, endure 2** [T] **not bear sth/doing sth** to not be suitable for sth; to not allow sth: *These figures won't bear close examination* (nie wytrzymają dokładnej analizy). ◇ *What I would do if I lost my job* ***doesn't bear thinking about*** (strach pomyśleć). **3** [T] (formal) to take responsibility for sth: *Customers will bear the full cost of the improvements.* ▶ **ponosić 4** [T] to have a feeling, especially a negative feeling: *Despite what they did, she* ***bears*** *no* ***resentment*** *towards them.* ◇ *He's not the type to* ***bear a grudge*** *against anyone.* ▶ **żywić** *(uczucia)* **5** [T] to support the weight of sth: *Twelve pillars bear the weight of the roof.* ▶ **dźwigać, utrzymywać 6** [T] (formal) to show sth; to carry sth so that it can be seen: *He still* ***bears the scars*** (nadal ma blizny) *of his accident.* ◇ *She* ***bore a*** *strong* ***resemblance*** (była bardzo podobna) *to her mother.* ◇ *The coins bear* (na monetach jest wybita) *the date and the Queen's head on them.* ◇ *The waiters came in bearing trays of food.* ▶ **nosić ślad czegoś, być naznaczonym; nosić 7** [T] (formal) to give birth to children: *She bore him four children, all sons.* ℹ Częściej używa się wyrażenia **have children**: *She had four children.* ▶ **(u)rodzić**

Kiedy mówisz o czyichś urodzinach, używaj formy **be born**: *Robert was born* (urodził się) *in 1996.* ◇ *The baby will be born* (urodzi się) *in spring.*

8 [I] to turn or go in the direction that is mentioned: *Where the road forks, bear left.* ▶ **skręcać**

IDM **bear the brunt of sth** to suffer the main force of sth: *Her sons usually bore the brunt of her anger.* ▶ **najbardziej ucierpieć od czegoś/z powodu czegoś, skrupiać się na czymś**

bear fruit to be successful; to produce results: *At last our hard work is beginning to bear fruit.* ▶ **przynosić owoce**

bear in mind (that); bear/keep sb/sth in mind → MIND¹

bear witness (to sth) to show evidence of sth: *The burning buildings and empty streets bore witness to a recent attack.* ▶ **być świadectwem (czegoś), świadczyć (o czymś)**

PHR V **bear down (on sb/sth) 1** to move closer to sb/sth in a frightening way: *We could see the hurricane bearing down on the town.* ▶ *(coś strasznego)* **zbliżać się (do**

kogoś/czegoś) **2** to push down hard on sb/sth ▶ **naciskać (coś/kogoś)**
bear sb/sth out to show that sb is correct or that sth is true: *The evidence bears out my theory.* ▶ **potwierdzać czyjeś słowa/zdanie**
bear up to be strong enough to continue at a difficult time: *How is he bearing up after his accident?* ▶ **radzić sobie**
bear with sb/sth to be patient with sb/sth: *Bear with me – I won't be much longer.* ▶ **czekać cierpliwie**

bear[2] /beə(r)/ noun [C] a large, heavy wild animal with thick fur and sharp teeth: *a polar/grizzly/brown bear* ▶ **niedźwiedź** ➲ look at **teddy bear**

bearable /ˈbeərəbl/ adj. that you can accept or deal with, although unpleasant: *It was extremely hot but the breeze made it more bearable.* ▶ **znośny** OPP **unbearable**

⚷ **beard** /bɪəd/ noun [C,U] the hair which grows on a man's cheeks and chin: *I'm going to **grow a beard**.* ▶ **broda** ➲ look at **goatee**, **moustache** ➲ picture at **hair**

bearded /ˈbɪədɪd/ adj. with a beard ▶ **brodaty**

bearer /ˈbeərə(r)/ noun [C] a person who carries or brings sth: *I'm sorry to be the bearer of bad news.* ▶ **okaziciel/ka**, **właściciel/ka**

bearing /ˈbeərɪŋ/ noun **1** [U, sing.] **(a) bearing on sth** a relation or connection to the subject being discussed: *Her comments **had** no **bearing** on our decision.* ▶ **związek z czymś 2** [U, sing.] the way in which sb stands or moves: *a man of dignified bearing* ▶ **postawa**; **sposób poruszania się 3** [C] a direction measured from a fixed point using a **compass** ▶ **położenie**
IDM **get/find your bearings** to become familiar with where you are ▶ **nabierać orientacji**, **zaznajomić się z sytuacją**
lose your bearings → LOSE

ˈ**bear market** noun [C] a period during which people are selling shares, etc. rather than buying, because they expect the prices to fall ▶ **rynek zniżkujący** ➲ look at **bull market**

beast /biːst/ noun [C] (formal) an animal, especially a large one: *a wild beast* ▶ **bestia**, **zwierzę**

beastly (old-fashioned, Brit., informal) very unpleasant ▶ **wstrętny**

⚷ **beat**[1] /biːt/ verb (pt **beat**; pp **beaten** /ˈbiːtn/) **1** [T] **beat sb (at sth)**; **beat sth** to defeat sb; to be better than sth: *He always beats me at tennis.* ◇ *We're hoping to beat the world record.* ◇ *If you want to keep fit, you can't beat* (nie ma nic lepszego niż) *swimming.* ▶ **bić**, **pokonywać 2** [I,T] to hit many times, usually very hard: *The man was beating the donkey with a stick.* ◇ *The rain was beating on the roof of the car.* ▶ **uderzać**, **bić** ➲ note at **hit**[1] **3** [I,T] to make a regular sound or movement: *Her **heart beat** faster as she ran to pick up her child.* ◇ *We could hear the drums beating* (dudnienie bębnów) *in the distance.* ◇ *The bird **beat its wings**.* ▶ **bić**, **brzmieć**, **trzepotać 4** [T] to mix quickly with a fork, etc.: *Beat the eggs and sugar together.* ▶ **ubijać**
IDM **beat about/around the bush** to talk about sth for a long time without mentioning the main point: *Stop beating about the bush and tell me how much money you need.* ▶ **owijać w bawełnę**
(it) beats me (informal) I do not know: *It beats me where he's gone.* ◇ *'Why is she angry?' 'Beats me!'* ▶ **nie mam pojęcia**
beat time (to sth) to move sth (a stick, your foot or your hand) following the rhythm of a piece of music ▶ **wybijać takt (czegoś)**
off the beaten track in a place where people do not often go ▶ **na uboczu**
PHR V **beat sb/sth off** to fight until sb/sth goes away: *The thieves tried to take his wallet but he beat them off.* ▶ **odpierać kogoś/coś**
beat sb to sth to get somewhere or do sth before sb else: *She beat me back to the house.* ◇ *I wanted to ring him first but Kate beat me to it.* ▶ **ubiegać/wyprzedzać kogoś**
beat sb up to attack sb by hitting or kicking them many times: *He was badly beaten up outside the pub last night.* ▶ **pobić kogoś**

⚷ **beat**[2] /biːt/ noun **1** [C] a single hit on sth such as a drum or the movement of sth, such as your heart; the sound that this makes: *Her heart skipped a beat* (przestało na moment bić) *when she saw him.* ▶ **bicie**, **uderzenie 2** [sing.] a series of regular hits on sth such as a drum, or of movements of sth; the sound that this makes: *the beat of the drums* ▶ **bicie** ➲ look at **heartbeat 3** [C] the strong rhythm that a piece of music has: *This type of music has a strong beat to it.* ▶ **takt 4** [sing.] the route along which a police officer regularly walks: *Having more policemen **on the beat** helps reduce crime.* ▶ **rewir policyjny**

beatify /biˈætɪfaɪ/ verb [T] (**beatifying**; **beatifies**; pt, pp **beatified**) (used about the Pope) to give a dead person a special honour by stating officially that he/she is very holy ▶ **beatyfikować**

beating /ˈbiːtɪŋ/ noun [C] **1** a punishment that you give to sb by hitting them: *The boys got a beating when they were caught stealing.* ▶ **bicie**, **lanie 2** a defeat ▶ **porażka**
IDM **take a lot of/some beating** to be so good that it would be difficult to find sth better: *Mary's cooking takes some beating.* Długo byś szukał lepszej kucharki niż Mary. ▶ **być wyjątkowym**

ˌ**beat-ˈup** (also ˌ**beaten-ˈup**) adj. (informal) [usually before a noun] old and damaged: *a beat-up old truck* ▶ **rozklekotany**

beautician /bjuːˈtɪʃn/ noun [C] a person whose job is to improve the way people look with beauty treatments, etc. ▶ **kosmetyczka**

⚷ **beautiful** /ˈbjuːtɪfl/ adj. very pretty or attractive; giving pleasure to the senses: *a beautiful woman* ◇ *The view from the top of the hill was really beautiful.* ◇ *What a beautiful day – the weather's perfect!* ◇ *He has a beautiful voice.* ◇ *A beautiful perfume filled the air.* ▶ **piękny**
■ **beautifully** /-fli/ adv.: *He plays the piano beautifully.* ◇ *She was beautifully dressed.* ▶ **pięknie**

> **Beautiful** (piękna) odnosi się zazw. do kobiet i dziewczynek, podobnie jak **pretty** (ładna). Mówiąc o mężczyznach używa się **handsome** (przystojny). **Good-looking** i **attractive** można użyć zarówno w odniesieniu do mężczyzn, jak i kobiet. **Gorgeous** w języku mówionym opisuje kogoś bardzo atrakcyjnego.

beautify /ˈbjuːtɪfaɪ/ verb [T] (**beautifying**; **beautifies**; pt, pp **beautified**) to make sb/sth beautiful or more beautiful ▶ **upiększać**

⚷ **beauty** /ˈbjuːti/ noun (pl. **beauties**) **1** [U] the quality which gives pleasure to the senses; the state of being beautiful: *I was amazed by the beauty of the mountains.* ◇ *music of great beauty* ▶ **piękno 2** [C] a beautiful woman: *She grew up to be a beauty.* ▶ **piękność**, **ślicznotka 3** [C] a particularly good example of sth: *Look at this tomato – it's a beauty!* ▶ **cudo**

ˈ**beauty salon** (also ˈ**beauty parlour**, US also ˈ**beauty shop**) noun [C] a place where you can pay for treatment to your face, hair, nails, etc., which is intended to make you more beautiful ▶ **salon kosmetyczny**

ˈ**beauty spot** noun [C] **1** (Brit.) a place in the countryside which is famous because it is beautiful ▶ **uroczy zakątek 2** (US also ˈ**beauty mark**) a small dark spot on a woman's face, which used to be thought to make her more beautiful ▶ **pieprzyk**

beaver /ˈbiːvə(r)/ noun [C] an animal with brown fur, a wide, flat tail and sharp teeth. It lives in water and on land and uses branches to build **dams**. ▶ **bóbr**

became past tense of **become**

because /bɪˈkɒz; Brit. also -ˈkəz; US also -ˈkʌz/ conj. for the reason that: *They didn't go for a walk because it was raining.* ▶ **ponieważ** ❶ W języku nieformalnym często opuszcza się pierwszą sylabę **because**. Tak skrócone słowo wymawia się /kɒz; US kəz/, a pisze **'cause**, **cos** lub **coz**.

beˈcause of prep. as a result of; on account of: *They didn't go for a walk because of the rain.* ▶ **z powodu** ➲ note at **due**[1]

beck /bek/ noun

IDM **at sb's beck and call** always ready to obey sb's orders ▶ **na każde skinienie**

beckon /ˈbekən/ verb [I,T] to show sb with a movement of your finger or hand that you want them to come closer: *She beckoned me over to speak to her.* ▶ **skinąć (na kogoś)**

become /bɪˈkʌm/ verb [I] (pt **became** /bɪˈkeɪm/, pp **become**) to begin to be sth: *Mr Saito became Chairman in 1998.* ◇ *She wants to become a pilot.* ◇ *They became friends.* Zaprzyjaźnili się. ◇ *She became nervous as the exam date came closer.* ◇ *He is becoming more like you every day.* ▶ **stawać się**, **zostawać (kimś)**

W tym znaczeniu używa się też często **get**, (zwł. w języku mówionym): *She got nervous as the exam date came closer.* ◇ *He's getting more like you every day.*

PHR V **become of sb/sth** to happen to sb/sth: *What became of Alima? I haven't seen her for years!* ▶ **stać się z kimś/czymś**

BEd /ˌbiː ˈed/ abbr. **Bachelor of Education**; a degree in education for people who want to be teachers and do not already have a degree in a particular subject ▶ **bakałarz nauk pedagogicznych**

bed[1] /bed/ noun **1** [C,U] a piece of furniture that you lie on when you sleep: *The children sleep in* ***bunk beds*** (w piętrowych łóżkach). ◇ *twin beds* dwa jednoosobowe łóżka (w jednym pokoju) ◇ *to* ***make the bed*** słać łóżko ◇ *What time do you usually* ***go to bed?*** ◇ *She was lying* ***on the bed.*** ◇ *When he rang I was already* ***in bed.*** ◇ *It's late. It's* ***time for bed.*** ◇ *to get into/out of bed* ▶ **łóżko** ➲ note at **sleep**[1] **2** (**-bedded**) having the type or number of beds mentioned: *a twin-bedded room* pokój z dwoma jednoosobowymi łóżkami ▶ (*określa liczbę i rodzaj łóżek*) **3** [C] the ground at the bottom of a river or the sea: *the seabed* ▶ **koryto**; **dno 4** [C] = FLOWER BED

IDM **bed and breakfast**; **B and B**; **B & B** /ˌbiː ən ˈbiː/ a place to stay in a private house or small hotel that consists of a room for the night and breakfast; a place that provides this ▶ **(mały hotel, który oferuje) nocleg ze śniadaniem** ➲ note at **hotel**

go to bed with sb (informal) to have sex with sb ▶ **iść z kimś do łóżka**

> **beds**
>
> A bed for one person is called a **single bed** and a bed for a couple to share is a **double bed**. Two single beds next to each other in the same room are called **twin beds**. Rooms in hotels are called **double**, **single** or **twin-bedded** rooms. Two single beds built as a unit with one above the other, used especially by children, are called **bunk beds**. A **futon** is a kind of mattress that can be used for sitting on or rolled out to make a bed.

bed[2] /bed/ verb [T] (**bedding**; **bedded**) to fix sth firmly in sth ▶ **osadzać**

PHR V **bed down** to sleep in a place where you do not usually sleep: *We couldn't find a hotel so we bedded down for the night in the van.* ▶ **znaleźć sobie miejsce do spania**, **przespać się gdzieś**

bedclothes /ˈbedkləʊðz/ (Brit. also **ˈbedcovers**) noun [pl.] the sheets, covers, etc. that you put on a bed ▶ **pościel**

bedding /ˈbedɪŋ/ noun [U] everything that you put on a bed and need for sleeping ▶ **pościel** (*często z materacem i poduszką*)

bedraggled /bɪˈdræɡld/ adj. very wet and untidy or dirty: *bedraggled hair* ▶ **przemoczony i ubłocony/zaszargany**

bedridden /ˈbedrɪdn/ adj. being too old or ill to get out of bed ▶ **przykuty do łóżka**

bedroom /ˈbedruːm; -rʊm/ noun [C] a room which is used for sleeping in: *You can sleep in the* ***spare bedroom.*** ◇ *a three-bedroom house* ▶ **sypialnia**

bedside /ˈbedsaɪd/ noun [sing.] the area that is next to a bed: *She sat at his bedside* (przy jego łóżku) *all night.* ◇ *a* ***bedside table*** szafka nocna ▶ **miejsce przy łóżku**

bedsit /ˈbedsɪt/ (also **ˈbedsitter**) noun [C] (Brit.) a room that a person rents which is used for both living and sleeping in ▶ **wynajęty pokój, używany jako salon i sypialnia**

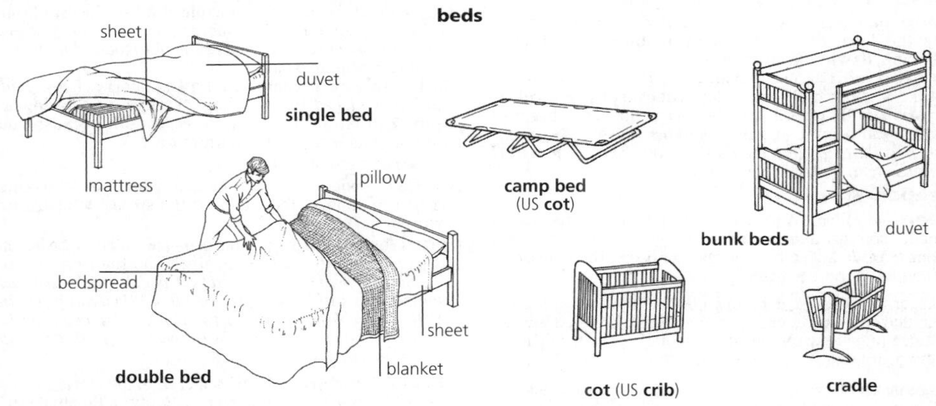

bedspread /'bedspred/ noun [C] an attractive cover for a bed that you put on top of the sheets and other covers ▶ **narzuta** ➲ picture at **bed**

bedtime /'bedtaɪm/ noun [U] the time that you normally go to bed ▶ **pora snu**

bee /bi:/ noun [C] a black and yellow insect that lives in large groups and that makes **honey** ▶ **pszczoła** ➲ look at **beehive**, **wasp**

A large number of bees together is a **swarm**. Bees **buzz** or **hum** when they make a noise. They may **sting** if they are angry.

beech /bi:tʃ/ noun **1** (also 'beech tree) [C] a large tree that produces small nuts with three sides ▶ **buk** **2** [U] the wood from the **beech** tree ▶ **buk**

beef /bi:f/ noun [U] the meat from a cow: *a joint of beef* ◇ *a slice of **roast beef*** ▶ **wołowina** ➲ note at **meat** ➲ picture on **page A14**

beefburger /'bi:fbɜ:gə(r)/ noun [C] **beef** that has been cut up small and pressed into a flat round shape ▶ **kotlet mielony wołowy** ➲ look at **hamburger** ➲ picture on **page A14**

beefy /'bi:fi/ adj. (**beefier**; **beefiest**) having a strong body with big muscles ▶ **dobrze zbudowany**, **umięśniony**

beehive /'bi:haɪv/ (also **hive** /haɪv/) noun [C] a type of box that people use for keeping **bees** in ▶ **ul**

'bee-keeper noun [C] a person who owns and takes care of bees ▶ **pszczelarz**
■ **'bee-keeping** noun [U] ▶ **pszczelarstwo**

beeline /'bi:laɪn/ noun
IDM **make a beeline for sb/sth** (informal) to go straight towards sth/sb as quickly as you can: *As soon as she arrived at the party, she made a beeline for* (ruszyła prosto do) *the food.* ▶ **wybrać najkrótszą drogę**

been /bi:n; bɪn; US bɪn/ past participle of **be**, **go**[1]

Been jest używane jako *past participle* czasowników **be** i **go**: *I've never been seriously ill.* Nigdy nie byłem ciężko chory. ◇ *I've never been to Rome.* Nigdy nie byłem w Rzymie. (= Nigdy nie pojechałem do Rzymu.) **Gone** jest również *past participle* czasownika **go**. Zwróć uwagę na różnicę w znaczeniu: *They've been to the cinema.* Oni byli w kinie. (= Poszli do kina i wrócili.) ◇ *They've gone to the cinema.* Oni poszli do kina. (= Poszli do kina i jeszcze nie wrócili.)

beep /bi:p/ noun [C] a short high noise, for example made by the horn of a car ▶ **krótki charakterystyczny dźwięk**, **dźwięk klaksonu**
■ **beep** verb **1** [I] (used about an electronic machine) to make a short high sound ▶ **wydać krótki charakterystyczny dźwięk** **2** [I,T] when a car horn, etc. **beeps** or when you beep it, it makes a short noise: *I beeped my horn at the dog, but it wouldn't get off the road.* ▶ **trąbić** (*klaksonem*) **3** (US) [T] = BLEEP[2] (2)

beeper (US) = BLEEPER

beer /bɪə(r)/ noun **1** [U] a type of alcoholic drink that is made from grain: *a barrel/bottle/glass of beer* ➲ look at **wine** ▶ **piwo** **2** [C] a type or glass of beer: *We went out for a couple of beers.* ▶ **piwo**

Lager to rodzaj jasnego piwa, które pije się schłodzone. **Ale** to gatunek mocnego, ciemnego piwa, które pije się w temperaturze pokojowej. **Shandy** to piwo zmieszane z lemoniadą.

beeswax /'bi:zwæks/ noun [U] a yellow sticky substance that is produced by **bees** and is used especially for making **candles** and polish for wood ▶ **wosk pszczeli**

beet (US) = BEETROOT ➲ look at **sugar beet**

beetle /'bi:tl/ noun [C] an insect, often large, shiny and black, with a hard case on its back covering its wings. There are many different types of **beetle**. ▶ **chrząszcz** ➲ picture at **insect**

beetroot /'bi:tru:t/ (US **beet** /bi:t/) noun [C,U] a dark red vegetable which is the root of a plant. **Beetroot** is cooked and can be eaten hot or cold. ▶ **burak**

befall /bɪ'fɔ:l/ verb [T] (pt **befell** /bɪ'fel/, pp **befallen** /bɪ'fɔ:lən/) (formal) (used about sth bad) to happen to sb ▶ **przytrafiać się**

befit /bɪ'fɪt/ verb [T] (**befitting**; **befitted**) [used only in the third person and in participles] (formal) to be suitable and good enough for sb/sth: *It was a lavish reception **as befitted** a visitor of her status.* ▶ **przystawać na kogoś/coś**

before[1] /bɪ'fɔ:(r)/ prep. **1** earlier than sb/sth; earlier than the time that: *You can call me any time before 10 o'clock.* ◇ *the week before last* przedostatni tydzień ◇ *They should be here before long* (niedługo). ▶ **przed** **2** (formal) in a position in front of sb/sth: *They knelt before the altar.* ◇ *You will appear before the judge tomorrow.* ▶ **przed** **3** in front of sb/sth (in an order): *'H' comes before 'N' in the alphabet.* ◇ *A very difficult task lies before us.* ◇ *a company that puts profit before safety* ▶ **przed**; **nad**

before[2] /bɪ'fɔ:(r)/ conj. **1** earlier than the time when: *Turn the lights off before you leave* (przed wyjściem). ▶ **zanim** ➲ note at **ago** **2** until: *It may be many years before the situation improves.* Może minąć wiele lat, zanim sytuacja się poprawi. ▶ **zanim** **3** (used to warn or threaten sb that sth bad could happen): *Put that away before it gets broken* (zanim się zepsuje). ▶ **zanim** **4** (formal) rather than: *I'd die before I apologized to him!* Prędzej bym umarł, niż go przeprosił. ▶ **niż**

before[3] /bɪ'fɔ:(r)/ adv. at an earlier time; already: *I think we've met somewhere before.* ◇ *It was fine yesterday but it rained the day before* (przedwczoraj). ▶ **przedtem** ➲ note at **ago**

beforehand /bɪ'fɔ:hænd/ adv. at an earlier time than sth: *If you visit us, phone beforehand to make sure we're in.* ▶ **przedtem**

befriend /bɪ'frend/ verb [T, usually passive] to become a friend of sb, especially sb who needs your help ▶ **zaprzyjaźniać się z kimś**

beg /beg/ verb [I,T] (**begging**; **begged**) **1 beg (sb) for sth**; **beg sth (of/from sb)**; **beg (sb) to do sth** to ask sb for sth strongly, or with great emotion: *He begged for forgiveness.* ◇ *Can I beg a favour of you?* Czy mogę cię prosić o przysługę? ◇ *We begged him to lend us the money.* ▶ **błagać** SYN **entreat**, **implore** ➲ look at **plead** **2 beg (for) sth (from sb)** to ask people for food, money, etc. because you are very poor: *There are people begging for food in the streets.* ▶ **żebrać**, **błagać o coś**
IDM **I beg your pardon** (formal) **1** I am sorry: *I beg your pardon. I picked up your bag by mistake.* ▶ **przepraszam** **2** (used for asking sb to repeat sth because you did not hear it properly) ▶ **słucham?**

began past tense of **begin**

beggar /'begə(r)/ noun [C] a person who lives by asking people for money, food, etc. on the streets ▶ **żebra-k/czka**

begin /bɪ'gɪn/ verb (**beginning**; pt **began** /bɪ'gæn/, pp **begun** /bɪ'gʌn/) **1** [I,T] to start doing sth; to do the first part of sth: *Shall I begin or will you?* ◇ *I began this novel last month and I still haven't finished it.* ◇ *When did he begin his lesson?* ◇ *When do you begin work?* ◇ *We began writing to each other in 1980.* ◇ *The carpet is beginning to look dirty.* ▶ **zaczynać**

Begin i **start** mają podobne znaczenie, ale **start** częściej używa się w języku codziennym. Po obydwu może występować bezokolicznik z **to** albo forma *-ing* czasownika: *The baby began/started to cry/crying.* Kiedy jednak **begin** albo **start** same występują w formie z końcówką *-ing*, wówczas po nich trzeba użyć bezokolicznika z **to**: *The baby was just beginning/starting to cry.* W niektórych kontekstach używa się jedynie **start**: *I couldn't start the car.* ◇ *We'll have to start* (wyruszyć) *early if we want to be in Dover by 8 o'clock.* **Commence** jest słowem o wiele bardziej formalnym niż **begin** i **start** i na ogół nie występuje w języku mówionym.

2 [I] to start to happen or exist, especially from a particular time: *What time does the concert begin?* ▶ **zaczynać się** **3** [I] **begin (with sth)** to start in a particular way, with a particular event, or in a particular place: *My name begins with 'W', not 'V'.* ◇ *The fighting began with an argument about money.* ◇ *This is where the footpath begins.* ▶ **zaczynać się (od czegoś/czymś)**
■ **beginner** noun [C] ▶ **początkując-y/a**
IDM **to begin with 1** at first: *To begin with they were very happy.* ▶ **z początku, najpierw 2** (used for giving your first reason for sth or to introduce your first point): *We can't possibly go. To begin with it's too far and we can't afford it either.* ▶ **po pierwsze**

beginning /bɪˈgɪnɪŋ/ noun [C] the first part of sth; the time when or the place where sth starts: *I've read the article* ***from beginning to end.*** ◇ *We're going away* ***at the beginning of*** *the school holidays.* ▶ **początek**

begonia /bɪˈgəʊniə/ noun [C] a plant with large shiny flowers that may be pink, red, yellow or white, grown indoors or in a garden ▶ **begonia**

begrudge /bɪˈgrʌdʒ/ verb [T] **begrudge (sb) sth 1** to feel angry or upset because sb has sth that you think that they should not have: *He's worked hard. I don't begrudge him his success.* ▶ **żałować czegoś 2** to be unhappy that you have to do sth: *I begrudge paying so much money in tax each month.* ▶ **żałować komuś czegoś**

beguile /bɪˈgaɪl/ verb [T] (formal) **1 beguile sb (into doing sth)** to trick sb into doing sth, especially by being nice to them ▶ **mamić, zwodzić 2** to attract or interest sb: *He was beguiled by her beauty.* ▶ **urzekać**

begun past participle of **begin**

behalf /bɪˈhɑːf; US -ˈhæf/ noun
IDM **on behalf of sb; on sb's behalf** for sb; instead of sb: *Emma couldn't be present so her husband accepted the prize on her behalf.* ◇ *I would like to thank you all on behalf of my colleagues and myself.* ▶ **w imieniu kogoś, na rzecz kogoś**

behave /bɪˈheɪv/ verb **1** [I] **behave well, badly, etc. (towards sb)** to act in a particular way: *Don't you think that Ellen has been behaving very strangely recently?* ◇ *I think you behaved very badly towards your father.* ◇ *He* ***behaves as if/though*** *he was the boss.* ▶ **zachowywać się 2** [I,T] **behave (yourself)** to act in the correct or appropriate way: *I want you to behave yourselves while we're away.* ▶ **zachowywać się** OPP **misbehave 3 (-behaved)** [in compounds] behaving in the way mentioned: *a well-behaved child* dobrze wychowane dziecko ◇ *a badly-behaved class* źle zachowująca się klasa ▶ **(*określa zachowanie*)**

behaviour (US **behavior**) /bɪˈheɪvjə(r)/ noun [U] the way that you act or behave: *He was sent out of the class for bad behaviour.* ▶ **zachowanie**

behead /bɪˈhed/ verb [T] to cut off sb's head, especially as a punishment ▶ **ścinać głowę** SYN **decapitate**

behind[1] /bɪˈhaɪnd/ prep. **1** in, at or to the back of sb/sth: *There's a small garden behind the house.* ◇ *The sun went behind a cloud.* ◇ *Look behind you* (obejrzyj się) *before you drive off.* ▶ **za 2** later or less good than sb/sth; making less progress than sb/sth: *The train is twenty minutes behind schedule.* Pociąg spóźnia się o dwadzieścia minut. ◇ *Jane is behind the rest of the class in maths.* ▶ **za** ➲ look at **ahead 3** supporting or agreeing with sb/sth: *Whatever she decides, her family will be behind her.* ▶ **za 4** responsible for causing or starting sth: *What is the reason behind his sudden change of opinion?* Jaki jest powód jego nagłej zmiany zdania? **5** (used to say that sth is in sb's past): *It's time you* ***put*** *your problems* ***behind you.*** Najwyższy czas, byś pozostawiła już swoje problemy za sobą.

behind[2] /bɪˈhaɪnd/ adv. **1** in, at or to the back of sb/sth: *You go on ahead. I'll follow on behind.* Pójdę za wami. ◇ *He ran off but the police were close behind.* ◇ *Try not to look behind.* Spróbuj nie oglądać się za siebie. ▶ **za 2** in the place where sb/sth is or was: *Oh no! I've* ***left*** *the tickets* ***behind*** (w poprzednim miejscu). **2 behind (with/in sth)** later or less good than sb/sth: *We are a month behind with the rent.* Zalegamy z czynszem za miesiąc. ◇ *Arsenal were behind at half-time.* W połowie meczu Arsenal przegrywał. ▶ **opóźniony** (*z wykonaniem pracy, zapłaceniem czynszu itp.*)

behind[3] /bɪˈhaɪnd/ noun [C] (informal) the part of your body that you sit on ➲ look at **bottom**, **buttock** ▶ **tyłek**

behold /bɪˈhəʊld/ verb [T] (pt, pp **beheld** /bɪˈheld/) to look at or see sb/sth: *Her face was a joy to behold.* ◇ *They beheld a bright star shining in the sky.* ▶ **oglądać; ujrzeć**
ℹ Ten wyraz jest archaiczny lub literacki.

beige /beɪʒ/ adj. of a light brown colour: *a beige coat* ▶ **beżowy**
■ **beige** noun [U] ▶ **beż**

being[1] → BE

being[2] /ˈbiːɪŋ/ noun **1** [U] the state of existing: *When did the organization* ***come into being?*** ▶ **istnienie** SYN **existence 2** [C] a living person or thing: *a human being* ▶ **istota, stworzenie**

belated /bɪˈleɪtɪd/ adj. coming late: *a belated apology* ▶ **spóźniony**
■ **belatedly** adv.: *They have realized, rather belatedly, that they have made a mistake.* ▶ **za późno, poniewczasie**

belch /beltʃ/ verb **1** [I] to let gas out from your stomach through your mouth with a sudden noise SYN **burp**: *He belched.* Odbiło mu się. ▶ **odbijać się (komuś) 2** [T] to send out a lot of smoke, etc.: *The volcano belched smoke and ash.* ▶ **buchać**
■ **belch** noun [C]: *Julia gave a loud belch* (głośno beknęła). ▶ **beknięcie**

beleaguered /bɪˈliːgəd/ adj. **1** (formal) experiencing a lot of criticism and difficulties: *The beleaguered party leader was forced to resign.* ▶ **pod obstrzałem krytyki; nękany kłopotami 2** surrounded by an enemy: *supplies for the beleaguered city* ▶ **oblężony**

belie /bɪˈlaɪ/ verb [T] (**belying**; **belies**; pt, pp **belied**) to give an idea of sth that is false: *His smiling face belied his true feelings.* ▶ **zadawać kłam**

belief /bɪˈliːf/ noun **1** [sing., U] **belief in sb/sth** a feeling that sb/sth is true, morally good or right, or that sb/sth really exists: *She has lost her belief in God.* ▶ **wiara** ➲ look at **disbelief 2** [sing., U] (formal) **belief (that ...)** something you accept as true; what you believe: *It's my belief* (jestem przekonany) *that people are basically good.* ◇ *There is a general belief that things will soon get better.* ◇ *The man was killed* ***in the*** *mistaken* ***belief that*** *he was a member of a terrorist organization.* Mężczyzna został zabity, ponieważ omyłkowo uznano go za członka grupy terrorystycznej. ◇ ***Contrary to popular belief*** (wbrew powszechnej opinii) *the north of the country is not poorer than the south.* ▶ **przekonanie, opinia 3** [C] an idea about religion, politics, etc.: *Divorce is contrary to their religious beliefs.* ▶ **przekonanie**

IDM **beyond belief** (in a way that is) too great, difficult, etc. to be believed: *The amount of money we owe has increased beyond belief.* ▶ **nieprawdopodobnie**

believable /bɪˈliːvəbl/ adj. that can be believed ▶ **wiarygodny** OPP **unbelievable**

believe /bɪˈliːv/ verb [not used in the continuous tenses] **1** [T] to feel sure that sth is true or that sb is telling the truth: *I don't believe you!* ◇ *He said he hadn't taken any money but I didn't believe him.* ◇ *Nobody believes a word she says.* Nikt nie wierzy w to, co ona mówi. ▶ **wierzyć 2** [T] **believe (that)...** to think that sth is true or possible, although you are not certain: *I believe they have moved to Italy.* ◇ *'Does Pat still work there?' 'I* ***believe so.****'* ◇ *The escaped prisoner is believed to be in this area.* Sądzi się, że zbieg przebywa w tej okolicy. ◇ *Four people are still missing, believed drowned.* ▶ **wydawać się (komuś), przypuszczać 3** [T] **believe (that)...** to have the opinion that sth is right or true: *The party believes (that) education is the most important issue facing the government.* ▶ **wierzyć** ➲ note at **think 4** (**don't/can't believe sth**) (used to show anger or surprise at sth): *I can't believe (that) you're telling me to do it again!* ▶ **nie móc uwierzyć w coś 5** [I] to have religious beliefs: *The god appears only to those who believe.* ▶ **wierzyć** ℹ Czasownika **believe** nie używa się w czasach *continuous*. Natomiast często spotyka się go w *present participle* (formie *-ing*): *Believing the house to be empty, she quietly let herself in.*

IDM **believe it or not** it may be surprising but it is true: *Believe it or not, English food can sometimes be quite good.* ▶ **choć trudno w to uwierzyć**

give sb to believe/understand (that) [often passive] to give sb the impression or idea that sth is true: *I was given to believe that I had got the job.* ▶ **pozwolić komuś uwierzyć, dać komuś do zrozumienia**

PHR V **believe in sb/sth** to be sure that sb/sth exists: *Do you believe in God?* ◇ *Most young children believe in Father Christmas.* ▶ **wierzyć w kogoś/coś**

believe in sb/sth; **believe in doing sth** to think that sb/sth is good or right: *They need a leader they can believe in.* ◇ *He doesn't believe in killing animals for their fur.* ▶ **wierzyć w kogoś/coś, popierać kogoś/coś**

believer /bɪˈliːvə(r)/ noun [C] a person who has religious beliefs ▶ **osoba wierząca**

IDM **be a (great/firm) believer in sth** to think that sth is good or right: *He is a great believer in getting things done on time.* ▶ **być (wielk-im/ą) zwolenni-kiem/czką czegoś**

belittle /bɪˈlɪtl/ verb [T] to make sb or the things they do seem unimportant or not very good ▶ **umniejszać**

bell /bel/ noun [C] **1** a metal object, often shaped like a cup, that makes a ringing sound when it is hit by a small piece of metal inside it: *the sound of church bells* ◇ *Her voice came back* ***clear as a bell.*** ▶ **dzwon 2** an electrical device that makes a ringing sound when the button on it is pushed; the sound that it makes: *Ring the doorbell and see if they're in.* ▶ **dzwonek**

IDM **ring a bell** → RING[2]

belligerent /bəˈlɪdʒərənt/ adj. unfriendly and aggressive ▶ **agresywny, wojowniczy**

■ **belligerence** noun [U] ▶ **agresywność, wojowniczość**

bellow /ˈbeləʊ/ verb **1** [I,T] **bellow (sth) (at sb)** to shout in a loud deep voice, especially because you are angry: *They bellowed at her to stop.* ▶ **ryczeć 2** [I] to make a deep low sound, like a **bull** ▶ **ryczeć**

■ **bellow** noun [C] ▶ **ryk; wrzask**

ˈbell pepper (US) = PEPPER[1] (2)

belly /ˈbeli/ noun [C] (pl. **bellies**) the stomach or the front part of your body between your chest and your legs ▶ **brzuch**

ˈbelly button (informal) = NAVEL

belong /bɪˈlɒŋ/ verb [I] to have a right or usual place: *The plates belong in that cupboard.* ◇ *I don't think this paragraph really belongs here.* Myślę, że ten akapit tu nie pasuje. ◇ *It took quite a long time before we felt we belonged in the village* (zanim poczuliśmy się u siebie). ▶ **mieć swoje miejsce**

PHR V **belong to sb** to be owned by sb: *Who does this pen belong to?* ◇ *Don't take anything that doesn't belong to you.* ▶ **należeć**

belong to sth to be a member of a group or organization: *Do you belong to any political party?* ▶ **należeć**

belongings /bɪˈlɒŋɪŋz/ noun [pl.] the things that you own that can be moved, that is, not land and buildings: *They lost all their belongings in the fire.* ▶ **ruchomości, rzeczy**

beloved /bɪˈlʌvd; bɪˈlʌvɪd/ adj. (formal) much loved: *They had always intended to return to their beloved Ireland.* ▶ **u/kochany** ℹ Kiedy **beloved** występuje przed rzeczownikiem, wymawia się /bɪˈlʌvɪd/.

below /bɪˈləʊ/ prep. at or to a lower position or level than sb/sth: *Do not write below this line.* ◇ *The temperature fell below freezing* (poniżej zera). ◇ *Her marks in the exam were below average.* ▶ **pod, poniżej** OPP **above** ➲ note at **under**

■ **below** adv. at or to a lower position or level: *temperatures of 30° and below* ◇ *I don't live on the top floor – I live on the floor below* (na przedostatnim piętrze). ▶ **poniżej**

belt[1] /belt/ noun [C] **1** a thin piece of cloth, leather, etc. that you wear around your waist: *I need a belt to keep these trousers up.* ▶ **pas(ek)** ➲ look at **seat belt** ➲ picture on **page A1 2** a long narrow piece of rubber, cloth, etc. in a circle, that is used for carrying things along or for making parts of a machine move: *The suitcases were carried round on a* ***conveyor belt.*** ◇ *the* ***fan belt*** *of a car* ▶ **pas, taśma 3** an area of land that has a particular quality or where a particular group of people live: ***the green belt*** *around London* (teren, gdzie nie wolno budować) ◇ *the commuter belt* ▶ **pas, strefa**

IDM **below the belt** (informal) unfair or cruel: *That remark was rather below the belt.* ▶ **poniżej pasa**

tighten your belt → TIGHTEN

under your belt (informal) that you have already done or achieved: *She's already got four tournament wins under her belt.* ▶ (*mieć*) **na swoim koncie**

belt[2] /belt/ verb (informal) **1** [T] to hit sb hard ▶ **łoić skórę pasem 2** [I] to run or go somewhere very fast: *I was belting along on my bicycle.* ▶ **pruć**

PHR V **belt sth out** to sing, shout or play sth loudly: *In the restaurant, loudspeakers were belting out Spanish pop music.* ▶ (*przen.*) **ryczeć, bębnić** (*np. na fortepianie*)

belt up 1 to fasten your seat belt in a car ▶ **zapinać pasy 2** (used to tell sb rudely to be quiet): *Belt up! I can't think with all this noise.* ▶ **siedzieć cicho**

bemused /bɪˈmjuːzd/ adj. confused and unable to think clearly ▶ **zakłopotany, zmieszany**

bench /bentʃ/ noun [C] **1** a long wooden or metal seat for two or more people, often outdoors: *a park bench* ▶ **ławka 2** (in the British parliament) the seats where a particular group of politicians sit: *the Government* ***front bench*** ◇ *the Labour* ***back benches*** ▶ **ława 3** a long narrow table that people work at, for example in a factory ▶ **stół montażowy/laboratoryjny**

benchmark /ˈbentʃmɑːk/ noun [C] a standard that other things can be compared to: *These new safety features set a benchmark for other manufacturers to follow.* ▶ **wzór, standard**

bend[1] /bend/ verb (pt, pp **bent** /bent/) **1** [I] to move your body forwards and downwards: *He* ***bent down*** *to tie up his shoelaces.* ▶ **pochylać się 2** [T] to make sth that was straight into a curved shape: *to bend a piece of wire into*

bending down
(also **bending over**)

bending a spoon

an S shape ◇ *It hurts when I bend my knee.* ▶ **zginać** **3** [I] to be or become curved: *The road bends to the left here.* ▶ **skręcać**

IDM **bend the rules** to do sth that is not normally allowed by the rules ▶ **naginać przepisy**

bend² /bend/ noun [C] a curve or turn, for example in a road: *a sharp bend in the road* ▶ **zakręt**

IDM **round the bend** → ROUND²

beneath /bɪ'ni:θ/ prep. **1** in, at or to a lower position than sb/sth; under sb/sth: *The ship disappeared beneath the waves.* ◇ *He seemed a nice person but there was a lot of anger beneath the surface.* Pozornie był sympatyczny, lecz w środku pienił się ze złości. ▶ **poniżej**, **pod** ⊃ note at **under** **2** not good enough for sb: *She felt that washing up for other people was beneath her* (uwłacza jej godności). ▶ **poniżej**

■ **beneath** adv. in, at or to a lower position: *From the top of the tower we gazed down on the city beneath.* ◇ *His calm exterior hid the anger beneath.* ▶ **poniżej**

benefactor /'benɪfæktə(r)/ noun [C] a person who helps or gives money to a person or an organization ▶ **dobroczyńca**, **ofiarodaw-ca/czyni**

beneficial /ˌbenɪ'fɪʃl/ adj. **beneficial (to sb/sth)** having a good or useful effect: *A good diet is beneficial to health.* ▶ **korzystny**

beneficiary /ˌbenɪ'fɪʃəri; US -ʃieri/ noun [C] (pl. **beneficiaries**) **beneficiary (of sth)** **1** a person who gains as a result of sth: *Who will be the main beneficiary of the cuts in income tax?* ▶ **beneficjent/ka** **2** a person who receives money or property when sb dies ▶ **spadkobier-ca/czyni**

benefit¹ /'benɪfɪt/ noun **1** [U,C] an advantage or useful effect that sth has: *A change in the law would be **to** everyone's **benefit*** (wszystkim przyniosłaby korzyści). ◇ *Most parents want to give their children the benefit of a good education* (korzyści płynące z dobrego wykształcenia). ◇ *I can't see **the benefit of** doing things this way.* ◇ *the benefits of modern technology* ▶ **korzyść** **2** [U,C] (Brit.) money that the government gives to people who are ill, poor, unemployed, etc.: *child/sickness/housing benefit* ◇ *I'm not entitled to unemployment benefit.* ▶ **zasiłek** **3** [C, usually pl.] advantages that you get from your company in addition to the money you earn: *a company car and other benefits* ▶ **świadczenie**, **korzyść**

IDM **for sb's benefit** especially to help, please, etc. sb: *For the benefit of the newcomers, I will start again.* ▶ **specjalnie dla kogoś**

give sb the benefit of the doubt to believe what sb says although there is no proof that it is true ▶ **uwierzyć komuś na słowo** (*zgodnie z przywilejem wątpliwości*)

benefit² /'benɪfɪt/ verb (**benefiting**; **benefited** or **benefitting**; **benefitted**) **1** [T] to produce a good or useful effect: *The new tax laws will benefit people on low wages.* ▶ **przynosić korzyść** **2** [I] **benefit (from sth)** to receive an advantage from sth: *Small businesses have benefited from the changes in the law.* ▶ **korzystać**

benevolent /bə'nevələnt/ adj. (formal) kind, friendly and helpful to others ▶ **łaskawy**, **życzliwy**

■ **benevolence** noun [U] ▶ **łaskawość**, **życzliwość**

benign /bɪ'naɪn/ adj. **1** (used about people) kind or gentle: *a benign influence* ▶ **łagodny**, **dobrotliwy** **2** (used about a disease, etc.) not dangerous: *a benign tumour* ▶ **łagodny** OPP **malignant**

bent¹ past tense, past participle of **bend¹**

bent² /bent/ adj. **1** not straight: *Do this exercise with your knees bent.* ◇ *This knife is bent.* ◇ *It was so funny we were **bent double** with laughter.* ▶ **przygarbiony** **2** (Brit., informal) (used about a person in authority) dishonest: *a bent policeman* ▶ **nieuczciwy** SYN **corrupt**

IDM **be bent on sth/on doing sth** to want to do sth very much; to be determined: *They seem bent on moving house, whatever the difficulties.* ▶ **koniecznie chcieć coś zro-bić**

bent³ /bent/ noun [sing.] **a bent for sth/doing sth** a natural skill at sth or interest in sth: *She has a bent for music.* ▶ **talent**

bequeath /bɪ'kwi:ð/ verb [T] (formal) **bequeath sth (to sb)** to arrange for sth to be given to sb after you have died: *He bequeathed £1 000 to his favourite charity.* ▶ **zapisywać** (*w testamencie*) ℹ **Leave** jest częściej używane.

bequest /bɪ'kwest/ noun [C] (formal) something that you arrange to be given to sb after you have died: *He left a bequest to each of his grandchildren.* Zapisał coś każdemu z wnuków. ▶ **zapis** (*w testamencie*)

berate /bɪ'reɪt/ verb [T] (formal) to criticize or speak angrily to sb because you do not approve of sth they have done ▶ **wymyślać (komuś za coś)**

bereaved /bɪ'ri:vd/ adj. having lost a relative or close friend who has recently died ▶ **dotknięty śmiercią bliskiej osoby**

■ **the bereaved** noun [C] (pl. **the bereaved**) a person whose relative or close friend has died recently ▶ **osoba pogrążona w żałobie**

bereavement /bɪ'ri:vmənt/ noun (formal) **1** [U] the state of having lost a relative or close friend who has recently died ▶ **żałoba** **2** [C] the death of a relative or close friend: *There has been a bereavement in the family.* ▶ **utrata bliskiej osoby**

bereft /bɪ'reft/ adj. [not before a noun] (formal) **1** **bereft of sth** completely lacking sth; having lost sth: *bereft of ideas/hope* ▶ **pozbawiony czegoś** **2** (used about a person) sad and lonely because you have lost sth: *He was utterly bereft when his wife died.* ▶ **osamotniony**

beret /'bereɪ; US bə'reɪ/ noun [C] a soft flat round hat ▶ **beret**

berry /'beri/ noun [C] (pl. **berries**) a small soft fruit with seeds: *Those berries are poisonous.* ▶ **jagoda**

berserk /bə'zɜ:k; -'sɜ:rk/ adj. [not before a noun] very angry; crazy: *If the teacher finds out what you've done, he'll **go berserk*** (wpadnie w szał). ▶ **wściekły**

berth /bɜ:θ/ noun [C] **1** a place for sleeping on a ship or train: *a cabin with four berths* ▶ **koja**; **miejsce sypialne** **2** a place where a ship can stop and stay ▶ **miejsce postoju** (*dla statku*)

beseech /bɪ'si:tʃ/ verb [I,T] (pt, pp **besought** /bɪ'sɔ:t/ or **beseeched**) (formal) to ask sb for sth in an anxious way because you want or need it very much: *Let him go, I beseech you!* ▶ **błagać** SYN **beg**, **implore**

beset /bɪ'set/ verb [T] (**besetting**; pt, pp **beset**) (formal) to affect sb/sth in a bad way: *The team has been beset by injuries all season.* ▶ (*nieszczęścia*) **prześladować**

beside /bɪ'saɪd/ prep. at the side of, or next to sb/sth: *Come and sit beside me.* ◇ *He kept his bag close beside him at all times.* ▶ **obok**

IDM **beside the point** not connected with the subject you are discussing ▶ **nie na temat**

be beside yourself (with sth) to not be able to control yourself because of a very strong emotion: *Emily was almost beside herself with grief.* ▶ **nie posiadać się** (*np. z radości*)

besides /bɪˈsaɪdz/ prep. in addition to or as well as sb/sth: *There will be six people coming, besides you and David.* ▶ **oprócz, poza**
■ **besides** adv. in addition; also: *I don't want to go out tonight. Besides, I haven't got any money.* ➲ look at **anyway** ▶ **poza tym**

besiege /bɪˈsiːdʒ/ verb [T] **1** to surround a place with an army ▶ **oblegać 2** [usually passive] (used about sth unpleasant or annoying) to surround sb/sth in large numbers: *The actor was besieged by fans and reporters.* ▶ **oblegać**

besotted /bɪˈsɒtɪd/ adj. [not before a noun] **besotted (with/by sb/sth)** so much in love with sb/sth that you cannot think or behave normally ▶ **ogłupiały** (*z miłości*)

besought past tense, past participle of **beseech**

bespoke /bɪˈspəʊk/ adj. (especially Brit., formal) [usually before a noun] **1** (US usually ˌ**custom-ˈmade**) (used about a product) made specially, according to the needs of an individual customer: *bespoke software* ◇ *a bespoke suit* ▶ **wykonany na indywidualne zamówienie, szyty na miarę** SYN **tailor-made 2** making products specially, according to the needs of an individual customer: *a bespoke tailor* ▶ **wykonujący usługę na miarę/zamówienie**

best¹ /best/ adj. [the superlative of *good*] of the highest quality or level; most suitable: *His latest book is by far his best.* ◇ *I'm going to wear my best shirt to the interview.* ◇ *Who in the class is* ***best at*** *maths?* ◇ ***It's best to*** (najlepiej) *arrive early if you want a good seat.* ◇ *What's the best way* (jak najlepiej) *to get to York from here?* ◇ *The best thing to do is to forget all about it.* Najlepiej o tym zupełnie zapomnieć. ◇ *Who's your* ***best friend?*** ▶ **najlepszy**
IDM **your best bet** (informal) the most sensible or appropriate thing for you to do in a particular situation: *There's nowhere to park in the city centre. Your best bet is to go in by bus.* ▶ **najlepsze, co można zrobić to**
the best/better part of sth → PART¹

best² /best/ adv. [the superlative of *well*] to the greatest degree; most: *He works best in the morning.* ◇ *Which of these dresses do you like best?* ◇ *one of Britain's best-loved TV stars* ▶ **najlepiej, najbardziej**
IDM **as best you can** as well as you can even if it is not perfectly ▶ **jak najlepiej**

best³ /best/ (**the best**) noun [sing.] the person or thing that is of the highest quality or level or better than all others: *When you pay that much for a meal you expect the best* (najwyższej jakości). ◇ *Even the best of us make mistakes sometimes.* ◇ *I think James is the best!* ◇ *I'm not in the best of health.* Nie czuję się najlepiej. ◇ *They are the best of friends.* ◇ *The best we can hope for is that the situation doesn't get any worse.* ▶ **najlepszy** ➲ look at **second best**
IDM **all the best** (informal) (used when you are saying goodbye to sb and wishing them success): *All the best! Keep in touch, won't you?* ▶ **wszystkiego najlepszego!**
at best if everything goes as well as possible; taking the most positive view: *We won't be able to deliver the goods before March, or, at best, the last week in February.* ▶ **w najlepszym razie**
at its/your best in its/your best state or condition: *This is an example of Beckett's work at its best.* ◇ *No one is at their best first thing in the morning.* ▶ **u szczytu formy**
be (all) for the best (used to say that although sth appears bad now, it will be good in the end): *I didn't get the job, but I'm sure it's all for the best.* ▶ **wyjść na dobre**
bring out the best/worst in sb to show sb's best/worst qualities: *The crisis really brought out the best in Tony.* ▶ **wyzwalać najlepsze/najgorsze**
do/try your best to do all or the most that you can: *I did my best to help her.* ▶ **dokładać wszelkich starań**
look your best → LOOK¹
make the best of sth/a bad job to accept a difficult situation and try to be as happy as possible ▶ **zrobić jak najlepszy użytek z czegoś**

ˌ**best-beˈfore date** noun [C] (Brit.) a date printed on a container or package, advising you to use food or drink before this date as it will not be of such good quality after that ▶ **termin przydatności do spożycia**

ˌ**best ˈman** noun [sing.] a man who helps and supports the **bridegroom** at a wedding ▶ **drużba** ➲ note at **wedding**

bestow /bɪˈstəʊ/ verb [T] (formal) **bestow sth (on/upon sb)** to give sth to sb, especially to show how much they are respected: *It was a title bestowed upon him by the king.* ▶ **nadawać (komuś)**

ˌ**best-ˈseller** noun [C] a book or other product that is bought by large numbers of people ▶ **bestseller**
■ ˈ**best-selling** adj. [only before a noun]: *a best-selling novel* ▶ **cieszący się olbrzymim popytem**

bet¹ /bet/ verb [I,T] (**betting**; pt, pp **bet** or **betted**) **1 bet (sth) (on sth)** to risk money on a race or an event by trying to predict the result. If you are right, you win money: *I wouldn't bet on them winning the next election.* ◇ *I bet him £10 he couldn't stop smoking for a week.* ▶ **zakładać się; stawiać** SYN **gamble, put money on sth 2** (informal) (used to say that you are almost certain that sth is true or that sth will happen): *I bet he arrives late – he always does.* ◇ *I bet you're worried about your exam, aren't you?* ▶ **założyć się**
IDM **you bet** (informal) a way of saying 'Yes, of course!': *'Are you coming too?' 'You bet (I am)!'* ▶ **a pewnie!**

bet² /bet/ noun [C] **1** an act of betting: *Did you* ***have a bet*** *on that race?* ◇ *to win/lose a bet* ▶ **zakład 2** an opinion: *My bet is that* (moim zdaniem) *he's missed the train.* ▶ **opinia**
IDM **your best bet** → BEST¹
hedge your bets → HEDGE²

beta version /ˈbiːtə vɜːʃn; vɜːʒn; US ˈbeɪtə vɜːrʒn/ noun [usually sing.] the version of a new product, especially computer software, that is almost ready for the public to buy or use, but is given to a few customers to test first ▶ **wersja beta**

betide /bɪˈtaɪd/ verb
IDM **woe betide sb** → WOE

betray /bɪˈtreɪ/ verb [T] **1** to give information about sb/sth to an enemy; to make a secret known: *She betrayed all the members of the group to the secret police.* ◇ *He refused to betray their plans.* ◇ *to betray your country* ▶ **zdradzać** ➲ note at **traitor 2** to hurt sb who trusts you, especially by not being loyal or faithful to them: *If you take the money, you'll* ***betray*** *her* ***trust.*** ◇ *When parents get divorced the children often* ***feel betrayed.*** ▶ **zdradzać 3** to show a feeling or quality that you would like to keep hidden: *Her steady voice did not betray the emotion she was feeling.* ▶ **zdradzać**
■ **betrayal** /bɪˈtreɪəl/ noun [C,U] ▶ **zdrada**

betrothed /bɪˈtrəʊðd/ adj. (formal or old-fashioned) **betrothed (to sb)** having promised to marry sb ▶ **zaręczony** SYN **engaged**
■ **betrothed** (**sb's betrothed**) noun [sing.] the person that sb has promised to marry ▶ **narzeczon-y/a**

better¹ /ˈbetə(r)/ adj. **1** [the comparative of *good*] **better than sb/sth** of a higher quality or level or more suitable than sb/sth: *I think her second novel was much better than her first.* ◇ *He's far better at English than me.* ◇ *It's a long way to drive. It would be better* (lepiej) *to take the train.* ◇ *You'd be better getting the train* (byłoby lepiej, gdybyś pojechał pociągiem) *than driving.* ▶ **lepszy 2** [the comparative of *well*] less ill; completely healthy again after an illness: *I feel a bit better* (lepiej) *today.* ◇ *You can't go swim-*

ming until you're better (dopóki nie wyzdrowiejesz). ▶ zdrowszy

better² /ˈbetə(r)/ adv. [the comparative of *well*] in a better way; to a greater or higher degree: *I think you could have done this better.* ◇ *Sylvie speaks English better than I do.* ▶ **lepiej**

IDM **(be) better off** [the comparative of *well off*] with more money: *We're much better off now I go out to work too.* ▶ **być dobrze sytuowanym**

(be) better off (doing sth) to be in a more pleasant or suitable situation: *You look terrible. You'd be better off at home in bed.* ▶ **być w lepszej sytuacji** (*jeśli się będzie robić coś innego*)

you, etc. had better you should; you ought to: *I think we'd better go before it gets dark.* ◇ *You'd better take a pen and paper – you might want to take notes.* ▶ **powinien**

ⓘ **Better** używa się w innych idiomach, np. **think better of (doing) sth.** Zob. hasła odpowiednich czasowników, przymiotników itp.

better³ /ˈbetə(r)/ noun [sing.] something that is of higher quality: *the better of the two books* ◇ *The hotel wasn't very good. I must say we'd expected better.* ▶ **lepszy, coś lepszego**

IDM **a change for the better/worse** → CHANGE²

get the better of sb/sth to defeat or be stronger than sb/sth: *When we have an argument she always gets the better of me.* ▶ **wygrać, przewyższyć kogoś**

ˈbetting shop noun [C] a shop where you can go to put money on a race or an event ➲ look at **bookmaker** ▶ **miejsce, gdzie przyjmowane są zakłady**

between

a plant growing between the slabs

a plant growing among the rocks

between /bɪˈtwiːn/ prep. **1 between A and B; in between** in the space in the middle of two things, people, places etc.: *I was sitting between Sam and Charlie.* ◇ *a village between Cambridge and Ely* ◇ *She was standing **in between** the desk **and** the wall.* ▶ **między 2 between A and B; in between** (used about two amounts, distances, ages, times, etc.) at a point that is greater or later than the first and smaller or earlier than the second; somewhere in the middle: *They said they would arrive between 4 and 5 o'clock.* ▶ **między 3** from one place to another and back again: *There aren't any direct trains between here and Manchester.* ▶ **między 4** involving or connecting two people, groups or things: *There's some sort of disagreement between them.* ◇ *There may be a connection between the two crimes.* ▶ **pomiędzy, między 5** choosing one and not the other (of two things): *to choose between two jobs* ◇ *What's the difference between 'some' and 'any'?* ▶ **pomiędzy, między 6** giving each person a share: *The money was divided equally between the two children.* ◇ *We ate all the chocolates between us.* ▶ **między, do spółki**

Between zazw. używa się w odniesieniu do dwóch osób lub rzeczy: *sitting between her mother and father* ◇ *between the ages of 12 and 14.* Jednak czasem można użyć **between**, mówiąc o więcej niż dwóch osobach lub rzeczach, zwłaszcza gdy traktuje się je

indywidualnie, jak np. w znaczeniu numer 6 powyżej: *We drank a bottle of wine between the three of us.* **Among** zawsze używa się w odniesieniu do więcej niż dwóch osób lub rzeczy, traktowanych raczej grupowo niż indywidualnie: *You're among* (wśród) *friends here.*

7 by putting together the actions, efforts, etc. of two or more people: *We've got over a thousand pounds saved up between us* (razem).

■ **between** adv. (also usually **in between**) in the space or period of time separating two or more points, objects, etc. or two dates, events, etc.: *They've got this shirt in size 10 and size 16, but nothing in between.* ▶ **w środku, (po)między**

beverage /ˈbevərɪdʒ/ noun [C] (formal) a drink: *hot and cold beverages* ▶ **napój**

beware /bɪˈweə(r)/ verb [I] [only in the imperative or infinitive] **beware (of sb/sth)** (used for giving a warning) to be careful: *Beware of the dog!* Uwaga, zły pies! ◇ *We were told to beware of strong currents in the sea.* ▶ **wystrzegać się, mieć się na baczności**

bewilder /bɪˈwɪldə(r)/ verb [T] to confuse and surprise: *I was completely bewildered by his sudden change of mood.* ▶ **dezorientować**

■ **bewildered** adj.: *a bewildered expression* ▶ **zdezorientowany** | **bewildering** adj.: *a bewildering experience* ▶ **dezorientujący** | **bewilderment** noun [U]: *to stare at somebody **in bewilderment*** ▶ **konsternacja, osłupienie**

bewitch /bɪˈwɪtʃ/ verb [T] to attract and interest sb very much ▶ **oczarowywać**

beyond /bɪˈjɒnd/ prep. **1** on or to the other side of: *beyond the distant mountains* ▶ **za, poza 2** further than; later than: *Does the motorway continue beyond Birmingham?* ◇ *Most people don't go on working beyond the age of 65.* ▶ **poza, po przekroczeniu 3** more than sth: *The house was **far beyond** what I could afford* (poza zasięgiem moich możliwości). ◇ *I haven't heard anything beyond a few rumours.* ◇ *His success was beyond all our expectations* (przekroczył wszelkie nasze oczekiwania). ▶ **poza, oprócz 4** (used to say that sth is not possible): *The car was completely **beyond repair*** (nie do naprawienia). ◇ *The situation is **beyond** my **control**.* ▶ **poza, nie do zrobienia czegoś 5** too far or too advanced for sb/sth: *The activity was beyond the students' abilities.* ▶ **ponad**

IDM **be beyond sb** (informal) to be impossible for sb to understand or imagine: *Why she wants to go and live there is quite beyond me.* ▶ **przechodzić wszelkie/czyjeś pojęcie/wyobrażenie**

beyond (any) doubt → DOUBT¹

■ **beyond** adv. on the other side; further on: *We could see the mountains and the sea beyond.* ▶ **(położony) dalej, za**

biannual /baɪˈænjuəl/ adj. [only before a noun] happening twice a year ▶ **odbywający się dwa razy do roku** ➲ look at **biennial**

bias¹ /ˈbaɪəs/ noun **1** [C,U] a strong feeling of favour towards or against one group of people, or on one side in an argument, often not based on fair judgement or facts: *a bias against women drivers* ◇ *The BBC has been accused of **political bias**.* ▶ **uprzedzenie; stronniczość 2** [C, usually sing.] an interest in one thing more than others: *a course with a strong scientific bias* ▶ **nastawienie 3** [U, sing.] the **bias** of a piece of cloth is an edge cut **diagonally** across the threads: *The skirt is cut on the bias.* ▶ **skos**

bias² /ˈbaɪəs/ verb [T] (**biasing**; **biased** or **biassing**; **biassed**) to influence sb/sth, especially unfairly; to give an advan-

tage to one group, etc.: *Good newspapers should not be biased towards a particular political party.* ▶ **przychylnie/nieprzychylnie nastawiać**
■ **biased** adj.: *a biased report* ▶ **stronniczy**

bib /bɪb/ noun [C] a piece of cloth or plastic that a baby or small child wears under the chin to protect its clothes while it is eating ▶ **śliniak**

the **Bible** /ˈbaɪbl/ noun [sing.] the book of great religious importance to Christian and Jewish people ▶ **Biblia**
■ **biblical** /ˈbɪblɪkl/ adj. ▶ **biblijny**

bibliography /ˌbɪbliˈɒgrəfi/ noun [C] (pl. **bibliographies**) **1** a list of the books and articles that a writer used when they were writing a particular book or article ▶ **bibliografia 2** a list of books on a particular subject ▶ **bibliografia**

biˌcarbonate of ˈsoda = SODIUM BICARBONATE

bicentenary /ˌbaɪsenˈtiːnəri; US -ˈten-/ noun [C] (pl. **bicentenaries**) (US **bicentennial** /ˌbaɪsenˈteniəl/) the day or the year two hundred years after sth happened or began: *the bicentenary of the French Revolution* ▶ **dwusetna rocznica**

biceps /ˈbaɪseps/ noun [C] (pl. **biceps**) the large muscle at the front of the upper part of your arms ▶ **biceps**

bicker /ˈbɪkə(r)/ verb [I] to argue about unimportant things: *My parents are always bickering about money.* ▶ **kłócić się o drobiazgi**

⚷ **bicycle** /ˈbaɪsɪkl/ (also **bike**) noun [C] a vehicle with two wheels, which you sit on and ride by moving your legs ▶ **rower** ➲ note at **bike**

ˈ**bicycle lane** (US) = CYCLE LANE

⚷ **bid¹** /bɪd/ verb [I,T] (**bidding**; pt, pp **bid**) **bid (sth) (for sth)** to offer to pay a particular price for sth, especially at an **auction**: *I wanted to buy the vase but another man was* ***bidding against*** *me.* ◇ *Somebody bid £5000 for the painting.* ▶ **licytować, składać ofertę**

bid² /bɪd/ verb [I,T] (**bidding**; pt **bade** /beɪd; bæd/, pp **bidden** /ˈbɪdn/) (formal) **bid (sb) good morning, farewell, etc.** to say ‘good morning’, etc. to sb ▶ **życzyć**

⚷ **bid³** /bɪd/ noun [C] **1** an offer by a person or a business company to pay a certain amount of money for sth: *At the auction we* ***made a bid*** *of £100 for the chair.* ◇ *Granada mounted a hostile* ***takeover bid*** *for Forte.* ▶ **oferta 2** (especially US) = TENDER² **3 a bid (for sth); a bid (to do sth)** an effort to do, obtain, etc. sth: *His bid for freedom had failed.* ◇ *Tonight the Ethiopian athlete will* ***make a bid*** *to break the world record.* ▶ **pokuszenie się o coś, usiłowanie** SYN **attempt**
■ **bidder** noun [C]: *The house was sold to the highest bidder* (osobie, która złożyła największą ofertę). ▶ **licytujący, osoba składająca ofertę**

bidding /ˈbɪdɪŋ/ noun [U] **1** the act of offering prices, especially at an **auction**: *There was fast bidding between private collectors and dealers.* ◇ *Several companies remained* ***in the bidding.*** ▶ **licytacja 2** the act of offering to do sth or to provide sth for a particular price: *competitive bidding for the contract* ▶ **licytowanie się 3** (in some card games) the process of stating the number of points that players think they will win ▶ **licytacja 4** (old-fashioned or formal) what sb asks or orders you to do: ***to do sb's bidding*** ▶ **polecenie**

bide /baɪd/ verb
IDM **bide your time** to wait for a good opportunity: *I'll bide my time until the situation improves.* ▶ **uzbrajać się w cierpliwość, czekać stosownego momentu**

bidet /ˈbiːdeɪ; US bɪˈdeɪ/ noun [C] a large bowl in the bathroom that you can sit on in order to wash your bottom ▶ **bidet**

biennial /baɪˈeniəl/ adj. happening once every two years ▶ **dwuletni, dwuroczny**

bifocals /ˌbaɪˈfəʊklz/ noun [pl.] a pair of glasses with each **lens** made in two parts. The upper part is for looking at things at a distance, and the lower part is for looking at things that are close to you. ▶ **okulary dwuogniskowe**
■ **bifocal** adj. ▶ **dwuogniskowy**

⚷ **big** /bɪg/ adj. (**bigger**; **biggest**) **1** large; not small: *a big house/town/salary* ◇ *This dress is too big for me.* OPP **small** ▶ **duży 2** [only before a noun] (informal) older: *a big brother/sister* ▶ **starszy** OPP **little 3** great or important: *They had a big argument yesterday.* ◇ *That was the big-*

bicycle

gest decision I've ever had to make. ◇ *some of the big names in Hollywood* ▶ **wielki**

W odniesieniu do rozmiarów i liczb można użyć zarówno **big**, jak i **large**. **Large** ma znaczenie bardziej formalne i zazw. nie używa się go w odniesieniu do ludzi: *a big/large house* ◇ *a big baby*. **Great** najczęściej stosuje się, mówiąc o ważności lub jakości danej osoby, rzeczy lub wydarzenia: *a great occasion/musician*. Można go też spotkać w zestawieniu z rzeczownikiem niepoliczalnym w języku formalnym, w znaczeniu **a lot of**: *great happiness/care*. **Great**w języku nieformalnym może być stosowane, by zaakcentować przymiotnik określający rozmiar i ilość. Zob. **great**[1](4). Zwróć też uwagę na wyrażenia: *a large amount of* ◇ *a large number of* ◇ *a large quantity of* ◇ *a great deal of* ◇ *in great detail.*

IDM **Big deal!** (informal) (used to say that you think sth is not important or interesting): *'Look at my new bike!' 'Big deal! It's not as nice as mine.'* ▶ **też (mi) coś!, wielka (mi) rzecz!**
a big deal/no big deal (informal) something that is (not) very important or exciting: *Birthday celebrations are a big deal in our family.* ◇ *A 2% pay increase is no big deal.* ▶ **wielkie/małe wydarzenie, coś (nic) ważnego**
a big shot/name an important person ▶ **gruba ryba**
give sb a big hand to hit your hands together to show approval, enthusiasm, etc.: *The audience gave the girl a big hand when she finished her song.* ▶ **nagradzać kogoś gromkimi oklaskami**
in a big/small way → WAY[1]
■ **big** adv. in an impressive way: *We need to think big.* ▶ **z rozmachem, na wielką skalę**

bigamy /ˈbɪɡəmi/ noun [U] the crime of being married to two people at the same time ▶ **bigamia** ➲ look at **monogamy**, **polygamy**
■ **bigamist** /-mɪst/ noun [C] ▶ **bigamist-a/ka** | **bigamous** /-məs/ adj.: *a bigamous relationship* ▶ **bigamiczny**

ˈbig band noun [C] a large group of musicians playing **jazz** or dance music: *the big-band sound* ▶ **big-band**

ˌbig ˈbang noun [sing.] (usually **the big bang**) the single large explosion that some scientists suggest created the universe ▶ **Wielki Wybuch**

ˌbig ˈbusiness 1 large companies which have a lot of power, considered as a group: *links between politics and big business* ▶ **wielki biznes 2** something that has become important because people are willing to spend a lot of money on it: *Health and fitness have become big business.* ▶ **dobry interes**

ˈbig-head noun [C] (informal) a person who thinks they are very important or clever because of sth they have done ▶ **ważniak**
■ **ˌbig-ˈheaded** adj. ▶ (*ironicznie*) **ważny, przemądrzały**

ˈbig mouth noun [C] (informal) a person who talks too much and cannot keep a secret ▶ **gaduła i pleciuch**

bigot /ˈbɪɡət/ noun [C] a person who has very strong and unreasonable opinions and refuses to change them or listen to other people: *a religious/racial bigot* ▶ **fanatyk** ➲ look at **fanatic**
■ **bigoted** adj. ▶ **fanatyczny, nietolerancyjny** | **bigotry** /ˈbɪɡətri/ noun [U] ▶ **fanatyzm**

the **ˈbig time** noun [sing.] success; fame: *an actor who finally **made/hit the big time*** ▶ **wielki sukces, sława**

ˈbig time[1] adv. (especially US, slang) very much: *You screwed up big time, Wayne!* ▶ **okropnie, straszliwie**

ˈbig time[2] adj. [only before a noun] important or famous: *a big time drug dealer/politician* ▶ **ważny; słynny**

big toe noun [C] the largest toe on a person's foot ▶ **wielki palec u nogi**

ˌbig ˈwheel (usually **the Big Wheel**) (especially US **Ferris wheel** /ˈferɪs wiːl/) noun [C] a large wheel which stands in a vertical position at an **amusement park**, with seats hanging at its edge for people to ride in ▶ **diabelski młyn**

🔑 **bike** /baɪk/ noun [C] a bicycle or a motorbike: *Hasan's just learnt to **ride a bike**.* ▶ **rower; motor**

Mówiąc o jeździe rowerem, używa się zwrotów **go on a/your bike** lub **go by bike**. Można też użyć czasowników **ride** i **cycle**. **Cyclist** to osoba, która jeździ na rowerze, natomiast **motorcyclist** to osoba, która jeździ na motocyklu.

bike lane (US, informal) = CYCLE LANE

biker /ˈbaɪkə(r)/ noun **1** a person who rides a motorcycle, usually as a member of a large group ▶ **motocyklist(k)a 2** a person who rides a bicycle, especially a **mountain bike** ▶ **rowerzyst(k)a**

bikini /bɪˈkiːni/ noun [C] (pl. **bikinis**) a piece of clothing, in two pieces, that women wear for swimming ▶ **bikini**

bilateral /ˌbaɪˈlætərəl/ adj. **1** involving two groups of people or two countries: *bilateral relations/agreements/trade/talks* ▶ **dwustronny, bilateralny 2** involving both sides of the body or brain ▶ **obustronny** ➲ look at **multilateral**, **unilateral**
■ **bilaterally** /-rəli/ adv. ▶ **dwustronnie; obustronnie**

bilberry /ˈbɪlbəri; US -ber-/ noun [C] a small dark blue berry that grows on low bushes in Northern Europe ▶ **borówka czarna** ➲ look at **blueberry**

bile /baɪl/ noun [U] **1** a greenish-brown liquid with a bitter unpleasant taste that is produced by your **liver** to help your body break down the fats you eat ▶ **żółć 2** (formal) anger or hatred: *The critic's review of the play was just a paragraph of bile.* ▶ **żółć**

bilingual /ˌbaɪˈlɪŋɡwəl/ adj. **1** able to speak two languages equally well: *Our children are **bilingual in** English and Spanish.* ▶ **dwujęzyczny 2** having or using two languages: *a bilingual dictionary* ▶ **dwujęzyczny** ➲ look at **monolingual**

🔑 **bill**[1] /bɪl/ noun **1** [C] a piece of paper that shows how much money you owe for goods or services: *an electricity bill* ◇ *to pay a bill* ▶ **rachunek 2** (US **check**) [C] a piece of paper that shows how much you have to pay for the food and drinks you have had in a restaurant: *Can I have the bill, please?* ▶ **rachunek** ➲ note at **restaurant 3** [C] (US) = NOTE[1](4): *a ten-dollar bill* ▶ **banknot 4** [C] a plan for a possible new law: *The bill was passed/defeated.* ▶ **projekt ustawy 5** [sing.] the programme of entertainment offered in a show, concert, etc.: *Which bands are **on the bill** at the festival?* ◇ *a **double bill** of films* seans skladający się z dwóch filmów ▶ **program 6** [C] a bird's beak ▶ **dziób** ➲ picture on **page A11**
IDM **foot the bill** → FOOT[2]

bill[2] /bɪl/ verb [T] **1 bill sb (for sth)** to send sb a bill for sth: *Please bill me for the books.* ▶ **wystawiać komuś rachunek 2** [usually passive] **bill sb/sth as sth** to describe sb/sth to the public in an advertisement, etc.: *This young player is being billed as 'the new Pele'.* ▶ **reklamować**

billboard (especially US) = HOARDING

billet /ˈbɪlɪt/ noun [C] a place, often in a private house, where soldiers live temporarily ▶ **kwatera**
■ **billet** verb [T, usually passive]: *The troops were billeted in the town with local families.* ▶ **zakwaterowywać**

billfold (US) = WALLET

billiards /ˈbɪliədz; US -jədz/ noun [U] a game played on a big table covered with cloth. You use a **cue** to hit three balls against each other and into pockets at the corners and sides of the table: *to have a game of/play billiards*

▶ **bilard** ➲ look at **pool**, **snooker** ⓘ Zwróć uwagę, że kiedy **billiard** pojawia się przed innym rzeczownikiem, nie ma 's': *a billiard table* stół do bilarda.

billing /ˈbɪlɪŋ/ noun **1** [U] the position, especially an important one, that sb is advertised or described as having in a show, etc.: *to have **top/star billing*** ▶ **pozycja na afiszu 2** [U] the act of preparing and sending bills to customers ▶ **fakturowanie**

⚷ **billion** /ˈbɪljən/ number 1 000 000 000: *billions of dollars* ▶ **miliard**

Dawniej słowo **billion** znaczyło „milion milionów". Obecnie w tym znaczeniu używa się słowa **trillion**.

Zwróć uwagę, że mówiąc o konkretnych liczbach, używa się słowa **billion** bez **s**: *nine billion pounds.* Więcej informacji o liczbach znajdziesz w dodatku *Wyrażenia liczbowe* na końcu słownika.

billionaire /ˌbɪljəˈneə(r)/ noun [C] an extremely rich person, who has at least a thousand million pounds, dollars, etc. in money or property ▶ **miliarder/ka**

ˌbill of exˈchange noun [C] (pl. **bills of exchange**) (technical) a written order to pay a sum of money to a particular person on a particular date ▶ **weksel**

bill of lading /ˌbɪl əv ˈleɪdɪŋ/ noun [C] (pl. **bills of lading**) (technical) a list giving details of the goods that a ship, etc. is carrying ▶ **list przewozowy**

bill of rights noun [sing.] a written statement of the basic rights of the citizens of a country ▶ **deklaracja praw człowieka**

ˌbill of ˈsale noun [C] (pl. **bills of sale**) (technical) an official document showing that sth has been bought ▶ **akt kupna/sprzedaży**

billow /ˈbɪləʊ/ verb [I] **1** to fill with air and move in the wind: *curtains billowing in the breeze* ▶ **wydymać się, falować 2** to move in large clouds through the air: *Smoke billowed from the chimneys.* ▶ **kłębić się**

ˈbilly goat noun [C] a male **goat** ▶ **kozioł** ➲ look at **nanny goat**

⚷ **bin** /bɪn/ noun [C] **1** a container that you put rubbish in: *to throw something in the bin* ◇ *a litter bin* ◇ *The dustmen come to empty the bins on Wednesdays.* ▶ **pojemnik na śmieci 2** a container, usually with a lid, for storing bread, flour, etc.: *a bread bin* ▶ **pojemnik z przykrywką do przechowywania produktów żywnościowych**

binary /ˈbaɪnəri/ adj. **1** using only 0 and 1 as a system of numbers, used especially by computers: *the **binary system*** ▶ **dwójkowy 2** (technical) based on only two numbers; consisting of two parts ▶ **dwuczłonowy, dwuskładnikowy**
■ **binary** noun [U]: *The computer performs calculations in binary and converts the results to decimal.* ▶ **system dwójkowy**

bind¹ /baɪnd/ verb [T] (pt, pp **bound** /baʊnd/) **1 bind sb/sth (to sb/sth)**; **bind A and B (together)** to tie or fasten with string or rope: *They bound the prisoner's hands behind his back.* ▶ **wiązać, przywiązywać 2 bind A to B**; **bind A and B (together)** to unite people, organizations, etc. so that they live or work together more happily or with better effect: *The two countries are bound together by a common language.* ◇ *They were bound together* (byli zjednoczeni) *by the strength of their beliefs.* ▶ **łączyć (kogoś/coś z kimś/czymś) 3 bind sb (to sth)** to force sb to do sth by making them promise to do it or by making it their duty to do it: *to be bound by a law/an agreement* ◇ *The contract binds you to completion of the work within two years.* ▶ **zobowiązywać 4** [usually passive] to fasten sheets of paper into a cover to form a book: *The book was bound in leather.* ▶ **oprawiać**

bins

waste-paper basket　　litter bins

dustbin
(US **garbage can/trash can**)

bind² /baɪnd/ noun [sing.] (Brit., informal) sth that you find boring or annoying: *I find housework a real bind.* ▶ **coś nieprzyjemnego/nudnego itp., ciężar** SYN **nuisance**

binder /ˈbaɪndə(r)/ noun [C] a hard cover for holding sheets of paper, magazines, etc. together: *a ring binder* ▶ **segregator**

binding¹ /ˈbaɪndɪŋ/ adj. making it necessary for sb to do sth they have promised or to obey a law, etc.: *This contract is **legally binding**.* ▶ **wiążący, obowiązujący**

binding² /ˈbaɪndɪŋ/ noun **1** [C] a cover that holds the pages of a book together ▶ **oprawa 2** [C,U] material that you fasten to the edge of sth to protect or decorate it ▶ **obszycie, lamówka 3** [C] (in **skiing**) a device that fastens your boot to your **ski** ▶ **wiązanie**

binge¹ /bɪndʒ/ noun [C] (informal) a period of eating or drinking too much: *to go **on a binge*** ▶ **obżarstwo, pijatyka**

binge² /bɪndʒ/ verb [I] (**bingeing**; US also **binging**) (informal) **binge (on sth)** to eat or drink too much, especially without being able to control yourself: *When she's depressed she binges on chocolate* ▶ **objadać/opijać się (czymś)**

bingo /ˈbɪŋɡəʊ/ noun [U] a game in which each player has a different card with numbers on it. The person in charge of the game calls numbers out and the winner is the first player to have all the numbers on their card called out. ▶ **bingo**

ˈbin liner noun [C] (Brit.) a plastic bag that is placed inside a container for holding waste ▶ **worek foliowy na śmieci**

binoculars /bɪˈnɒkjələz/ noun [pl.] an instrument with two **lenses** which you look through in order to make objects in the distance seem nearer: ***a pair of binoculars*** ▶ **lornetka** ➲ look at **telescope**

biochemistry /ˌbaɪəʊˈkemɪstri/ noun [U] the study of the chemistry of living things ▶ **biochemia**
■ **biochemist** noun [C] ▶ **biochemik**

biodata /ˈbaɪəʊdeɪtə; US also -dætə/ noun [U, pl.] information about a person and about what they have done in their life ▶ **informacje biometryczne**

biodegradable /ˌbaɪəʊdɪˈɡreɪdəbl/ adj. that can be absorbed back into the earth naturally and so not harm the environment: *Most plastic packaging is not biodegradable* (nie ulega rozkładowi). ▶ **ulegający biodegradacji**

biodegrade /ˌbaɪəʊdɪˈɡreɪd/ verb [I] (used about a substance or chemical) to change back to a harmless natural state by the action of bacteria ▶ **ulegać biodegradacji**

biodiversity /ˌbaɪəʊdaɪˈvɜːsəti/ noun [U] the state of having a large number of different kinds of animals and plants which make a balanced environment ▶ **różnorodność w przyrodzie**

biogas /ˈbaɪəʊɡæs/ noun [U] gas produced by natural waste, that can be used as fuel ▶ **gaz biologiczny**

biographer /baɪˈɒɡrəfə(r)/ noun [C] a person who writes the story of sb else's life ▶ **biograf**

biography /baɪˈɒɡrəfi/ noun [C,U] (pl. **biographies**) the story of sb's life written by sb else: *a biography of Napoleon* ◇ *I enjoy reading science fiction and biography.* ▶ **biografia** ➲ note at **book** ➲ look at **autobiography**
■ **biographical** /ˌbaɪəˈɡræfɪkl/ adj. ▶ **biograficzny**

biological /ˌbaɪəˈlɒdʒɪkl/ adj. **1** connected with the scientific study of animals, plants and other living things: *biological research* ▶ **biologiczny 2** involving the use of living things to destroy or damage other living things: *a biological detergent* ▶ **biologiczny**

ˌbioˌlogical ˈwarfare (also ˌ**germ ˈwarfare**) noun [U] the use of harmful bacteria as weapons of war ▶ **wojna biologiczna**

ˌbioˌlogical ˈweapon noun [C] a weapon of war that uses harmful bacteria ▶ **broń biologiczna**

⚷ **biology** /baɪˈɒlədʒi/ noun [U] the scientific study of living things ▶ **biologia** ➲ note at **science**
■ **biologist** /-dʒɪst/ noun [C] ▶ **biolog**

biopsy /ˈbaɪɒpsi/ noun [C] (pl. **biopsies**) the removal and examination of **tissue** from the body of sb who is ill, in order to find out more about their disease ▶ **biopsja**

biotechnology /ˌbaɪəʊtekˈnɒlədʒi/ (also informal **biotech** /ˈbaɪəʊtek/) noun [U] (technical) the use of living cells and bacteria in industrial and scientific processes ▶ **biotechnologia**

bipartisan /ˌbaɪpɑːtɪˈzæn; US -ˈpɑːtɪzn/ adj. involving two political parties: *a bipartisan policy* ▶ **dwupartyjny**

biplane /ˈbaɪpleɪn/ noun [C] an early type of plane with two sets of wings, one above the other ▶ **dwupłat**

bipolar /ˌbaɪˈpəʊlə(r)/ (also ˌ**manic-deˈpressive**) adj. suffering from or connected with **bipolar disorder** ▶ **maniakalno-depresyjny**
■ **bipolar** (also ˌ**manic-deˈpressive**) noun [C] ▶ **cierpiąc-y/a na psychozę maniakalno-depresyjną**

ˌbiˌpolar disˈorder (also ˌ**biˌpolar afˌfective disˈorder**) noun [U,C] (also ˌ**manic-deˈpression** [U]) a mental illness causing sb to change suddenly from being extremely depressed to being extremely happy ▶ **psychoza maniakalno-depresyjna**

birch /bɜːtʃ/ noun **1** (also **ˈbirch tree**) [C] a type of tree with smooth thin branches ▶ **brzoza 2** [U] the wood from the **birch** tree ▶ **brzoza**

⚷ **bird** /bɜːd/ noun [C] **1** a creature that is covered with feathers and has two wings and two legs. Most birds can fly. ▶ **ptak** ➲ picture on **page A11**

> Birds **fly** and **sing**. They build **nests** and **lay eggs**.

2 (Brit., slang) a word used to refer to a young woman ▶ **lala** ℹ Słowo to bywa czasami obraźliwe.
IDM **kill two birds with one stone** → KILL[1]

ˈbird flu (also formal **avian flu** /ˈeɪviən fluː/) noun [U] a serious illness that affects birds, especially chickens, that can be spread from birds to humans and that can cause death: *Ten new cases of bird flu were reported yesterday.* ▶ **ptasia grypa**

ˌbird of ˈprey noun [C] a bird that kills and eats other birds or small animals ▶ **ptak drapieżny**

birdwatcher /ˈbɜːdwɒtʃə(r)/ noun [C] a person who studies birds in their natural surroundings ▶ **ktoś, kto obserwuje ptaki jako hobby** ℹ Naukowiec zajmujący się ptakami to **ornithologist**.
■ **birdwatching** noun [U] ▶ **obserwowanie ptaków**

Biro™ /ˈbaɪrəʊ/ noun [C] (pl. **Biros**) a plastic pen with a small metal ball at the end that rolls ink onto paper ▶ **rodzaj długopisu** ➲ look at **ballpoint**

⚷ **birth** /bɜːθ/ noun **1** [C,U] being born; coming out of a mother's body: *It was a difficult birth.* ◇ *The baby weighed 3 kilos* ***at birth.*** ◇ *What's your* ***date of birth?*** Jaka jest pana data urodzin? ◇ *My date of birth is the second of the first* (drugiego stycznia), *eighty-eight.* ▶ **poród, narodziny 2** [sing.] the beginning of sth: *the birth of an idea* ▶ **narodziny, początek 3** [U] a person's origin or the social position of their family: *She's always lived in England but she's German* ***by birth*** (jest Niemką z urodzenia). ▶ **urodzenie**
IDM **give birth (to sb)** to produce a baby: *She gave birth to her second child at home.* ▶ **rodzić** ➲ note at **baby**

ˈbirth certificate noun [C] an official document that states the date and place of sb's birth and the names of their parents ▶ **świadectwo urodzenia**

ˈbirth control noun [U] ways of limiting the number of children you have ▶ **kontrola urodzeń** ➲ look at **contraception**, **family planning**

⚷ **birthday** /ˈbɜːθdeɪ/ noun [C] the day in each year which is the same date as the one when you were born: *My birthday's on November 15th.* ◇ *my eighteenth birthday* ◇ *a birthday present/card/cake* ▶ **urodziny**

> **birthdays**
> When it is sb's birthday we say **Happy Birthday!** If we know a person well, we send a special card to them or give them a present. They might have a birthday **party**, and a **birthday cake** with candles, one to represent each year of their age. Your 18th birthday is an important occasion when you legally become an adult.

birthmark /ˈbɜːθmɑːk/ noun [C] a red or brown mark on sb's body that has been there since they were born ▶ (*na skórze*) **znamię**

birthplace /ˈbɜːθpleɪs/ noun **1** [C] the house or town where a person was born ▶ **miejsce urodzenia 2** [sing.] the place where sth began: *Greece is the birthplace of the Olympic Games.* ▶ (*przen.*) **kolebka**

ˈbirth rate noun [C] the number of babies born in a particular group of people during a particular period of time ▶ **liczba urodzeń**

birthright /ˈbɜːθraɪt/ noun [C] a thing that sb has a right to because of the family or country they were born in, or because it is a basic right of all humans: *The property is the birthright of the eldest child* (prawem pierworództwa). ◇ *Education is every child's birthright.* ▶ **prawo przysługujące z urodzenia**

⚷ **biscuit** /ˈbɪskɪt/ (US **cookie** /ˈkʊki/) noun [C] **1** a type of small cake that is thin, hard and usually sweet: *a chocolate biscuit* ◇ *a packet of biscuits* ▶ **herbatnik** ➲ picture at **cake 2** (US) a type of small simple cake that is not sweet ▶ (*niesłodka*) **bułeczka**

bisect /baɪˈsekt/ verb [T] (technical) to divide sth into two equal parts ▶ **przepoławiać**

bisexual /ˌbaɪˈsekʃuəl/ adj. sexually attracted to both men and women ▶ **biseksualny** ➲ look at **heterosexual**, **homosexual**

bishop /ˈbɪʃəp/ noun [C] **1** a priest with a high position in some branches of the Christian Church, who is responsible for all the churches in a city or a district ▶ **biskup** ➲ look at **archbishop** **2** a piece used in the game of **chess** that is shaped like a **bishop's** hat ▶ (*w szachach*) **goniec**

bison /ˈbaɪsn/ noun [C] (pl. **bison**) a large wild animal of the cow family that is covered with hair. There are two types of bison, the North American (also called **buffalo**) and the European ▶ **bizon**; **żubr**

bistro /ˈbiːstrəʊ/ noun [C] (pl. **bistros**) a small informal restaurant that is not very expensive ▶ **bistro**

⚷ **bit**[1] /bɪt/ noun **1** (**a bit**) [sing.] slightly, a little: *I was a bit annoyed with him.* ◇ *I'm afraid I'll be a little bit late tonight.* ◇ *Could you be a bit quieter, please?* ▶ **trochę** **2** (**a bit**) [sing.] a short time or distance: *Could you move forward a bit?* ◇ *I'm just going out for a bit.* ▶ **trochę** **3** (**a bit**) [sing.] (informal) a lot: *It must have rained **quite a bit** during the night.* Musiało nieźle padać. ▶ **sporo** **4** [C] **a bit of sth** a small piece, amount or part of sth: *There were bits of broken glass all over the floor.* ◇ *Could you give me a bit of advice* (doradzić)*?* ◇ *Which bit of the film did you like best?* ▶ **kawałek**, **odrobina**, **trochę** **5** [C] the smallest unit of information that is stored in a computer's memory ▶ **bit** **6** [C] a metal bar that you put in a horse's mouth when you ride it ▶ **wędzidło** ➲ picture at **horse**

IDM **bit by bit** slowly or a little at a time: *Bit by bit we managed to get the information we needed.* ▶ **stopniowo**, **po trochu**

a bit much (informal) annoying or unpleasant: *It's a bit much expecting me to work on Sundays.* ▶ **już za wiele**

a bit of a (informal) rather a: *I've got a bit of a problem.* ▶ **niewielki**, **mały**

bits and pieces (informal) small things of different kinds: *I've finished packing except for a few bits and pieces.* ▶ **drobiazgi**

do your bit (informal) to do your share of sth; to help with sth: *It won't take long to finish if we all do our bit.* ▶ **robić to, co do kogoś należy**

not a bit not at all: *The holiday was not a bit what we had expected.* ▶ **ani trochę**, **wcale nie**

to bits **1** into small pieces: *She angrily tore the letter to bits.* ▶ **na kawałki**, **na strzępy** **2** very much: *I was **thrilled to bits** when I won the competition.* ▶ **strasznie**

bit[2] past tense of **bite**[1]

bitch[1] /bɪtʃ/ verb [I] (informal) **bitch (about sb/sth)** to say unkind and critical things about sb/sth, especially about sb who is not there: *She's not the kind of person who would bitch about you behind your back.* ▶ **obrabiać (kogoś/coś)**

bitch[2] /bɪtʃ/ noun [C] **1** a female dog ▶ **suka** **2** (slang) an offensive way of referring to a woman, especially an unpleasant one ▶ **jędza**, **dziwka**

bitchy /ˈbɪtʃi/ adj. (**bitchier**; **bitchiest**) talking about other people in an unkind way: *a bitchy remark* ▶ **złośliwy**, **jędzowaty**

⚷ **bite**[1] /baɪt/ verb (pt **bit** /bɪt/, pp **bitten** /ˈbɪtn/) **1** [I,T] **bite (into sth)**; **bite (sb/sth)** to cut or attack sb/sth with your teeth: *He picked up the bread and bit into it hungrily.* ◇ *Don't worry about the dog – she never bites.* ◇ *The cat bit me.* ▶ **gryźć** **2** [I,T] (used about some insects and animals) to push a sharp point into your skin and cause pain: *He was bitten by a snake/mosquito/spider.* ▶ **gryźć**, **żądlić**

> Wasps, bees and jellyfish do not **bite** you. They **sting** you.

3 [I] to begin to have an unpleasant effect: *In the South the job losses are starting to bite.* ▶ **dawać się we znaki**

IDM **bite sb's head off** to answer sb in a very angry way ▶ **odpysknąć/odwarknąć komuś**

⚷ **bite**[2] /baɪt/ noun **1** [C] an act of biting: *The dog gave me a playful bite* (lekko mnie ugryzł). ▶ **ugryzienie** **2** [C] a piece of food that you can put into your mouth: *She took a big bite of the apple.* ◇ *Give me a bite* (daj spróbować kawałek) *of your sandwich.* ▶ **kęs** **3** [sing.] (informal) a small meal: *Would you like **a bite to eat*** (coś na ząb) *before you go?* ▶ **coś do jedzenia** SYN **snack** **4** [C] a painful place on the skin made by an insect, snake, dog, etc.: *I'm covered in mosquito bites.* ▶ **ukąszenie**, **ugryzienie** (*i ślad po nim*)

ˈ**bite-sized** (also ˈ**bite-size**) adj. [usually before a noun] small enough to put into the mouth and eat: *Cut the meat into bite-sized pieces.* ▶ **wielkości jednego kęsa**

biting /ˈbaɪtɪŋ/ adj. **1** (used about a wind) very cold and unpleasant ▶ **przenikliwy** **2** (used about remarks) cruel and critical: ***biting sarcasm/wit*** ▶ **kąśliwy**

ˈ**bit part** noun [C] a small part in a film ▶ **epizod**

bitten past participle of **bite**[1]

⚷ **bitter**[1] /ˈbɪtə(r)/ adj. **1** caused by anger or hatred: *a bitter quarrel* ▶ **zażarty**, **zawzięty** **2** **bitter (about sth)** (used about a person) very unhappy or angry about sth that has happened because you feel you have been treated unfairly: *She was very bitter about not getting the job.* ▶ **zgorzkniały**, **rozczarowany** **3** causing unhappiness or anger for a long time; difficult to accept: *Failing the exam was **a bitter disappointment** to him.* ◇ *I've learnt **from bitter experience** not to trust him.* ▶ **gorzki**, **przykry** **4** having a sharp, unpleasant taste; not sweet: *bitter coffee* ▶ **gorzki** ➲ look at **sour** **5** (used about the weather) very cold: *a bitter wind* lodowaty wiatr ▶ **przenikliwie zimny**

■ **bitterness** noun [U] ▶ **gorycz**

bitter[2] /ˈbɪtə(r)/ noun [U,C] (Brit.) a type of dark beer that is popular in Britain: *A pint of bitter, please.* ▶ **piwo ciemne** (*o gorzkim smaku*) ➲ note at **beer**

⚷ **bitterly** /ˈbɪtəli/ adv. **1** in an angry and disappointed way: *'I've lost everything,' he said bitterly.* ▶ **z goryczą** **2** (used for describing strong negative feelings or cold weather) extremely: *bitterly disappointed/resentful* ◇ *a bitterly cold winter/wind* ▶ **strasznie**

bitty /ˈbɪti/ adj. (**bittier**; **bittiest**) made up of a lot of parts which do not seem to be connected: *Your essay is rather bitty.* ▶ **fragmentaryczny**

bitumen /ˈbɪtʃəmən; US bəˈtuː-; -ˈtjuː-/ noun [U] **1** a black sticky substance obtained from oil, used for covering roads or roofs ▶ **bitum** **2** (informal) the surface of a road that is covered with **tar**: *a kilometre and a half of bitumen* ▶ **bitum**

bizarre /bɪˈzɑː(r)/ adj. very strange: *The story had a most bizarre ending.* ▶ **dziwaczny** SYN **weird**

■ **bizarrely** adv.: *bizarrely dressed* ▶ **dziwacznie**

bk (pl. **bks**) = BOOK

blab /blæb/ verb [I,T] (**blabbing**; **blabbed**) **blab (to sb) (about sth)** (informal) to tell sb information that should be kept secret: *Someone must have blabbed to the police.* ▶ **wygadać się**

blabber /ˈblæbə(r)/ verb [I] **blabber (on) (about sth)** (informal) to talk in a way that other people think is silly and annoying: *What was she blabbering on about this time?* ▶ **paplać**

blabbermouth /ˈblæbəmaʊθ/ noun [C] (informal) a person who tells secrets because they talk too much ▶ **papla**

⚷ **black**[1] /blæk/ adj. **1** having the darkest colour, like night or coal: *a shiny black car* ▶ **czarny** **2** belonging to a race of people with dark skins: *a black man/woman* ◇ *the black population of Britain* ◇ *black culture*

▶ **czarny**, **czarnoskóry** **3** (used about coffee or tea) without milk or cream: *black coffee with sugar* ▶ **czarny** **4** very angry: *to give somebody **a black look*** ◇ *to be in **a black mood*** być w wisielczym nastroju ▶ **ponury**, **gniewny** **5** (used about a situation) without hope: *The economic outlook for the coming year is rather black.* ▶ **przygnębiający** SYN **depressing** **6** funny in a cruel or unpleasant way: *The film was **a black comedy**.* ▶ **czarny**

IDM **black and blue** covered with **bruises** because you have been hit by sb/sth ▶ **posiniaczony**

black and white (used about TV, photographs, etc.) showing no colours except black, white and grey ▶ **czarno-biały**

black² /blæk/ noun **1** [U] the darkest colour, like night or coal: *People often **wear black** at funerals.* ▶ **kolor czarny**, **czerń** **2** (usually **Black**) [C] a person who belongs to a race of people with dark skins ▶ **Murzyn/ka** ➲ look at **African American**, **Afro-Caribbean**

Uwaga! W tym znaczeniu używa się **black** zwykle w lm. Ponieważ w lp słowo to może brzmieć obraźliwie, mówi się **a black man/woman**, a w USA również **African American**.

■ **blackness** noun [U] ▶ **czerń**, **ciemność**

IDM **be in the black** (informal) to have some money in the bank ▶ **mieć pieniądze na koncie** OPP **be in the red**

in black and white in writing or in print: *I won't believe we've got the contract till I see it in black and white.* ▶ **czarno na białym**

black³ /blæk/ verb

PHR V **black out** to become unconscious for a short time ▶ **mdleć**, **tracić przytomność** SYN **faint**

blackberry /ˈblækbəri; US -ber-/ (pl. **blackberries**) noun [C] a small black fruit that grows wild on bushes ▶ **jeżyna** ➲ picture on **page A12**

blackbird /ˈblækbɜːd/ noun [C] a common European bird. The male is black with a yellow beak and the female is brown. ▶ **kos**

blackboard /ˈblækbɔːd/ (US **chalkboard** /ˈtʃɔːkbɔːd/) noun [C] a piece of dark board used for writing on with **chalk**, which is used in a class ▶ **tablica szkolna**

blackcurrant /ˈblækˌkʌrənt; ˌblækˈk-; US -ˌkɜːr-; -ˈkɜːr-/ noun [C] a small round black fruit that grows on bushes ▶ **czarna porzeczka**

blacken /ˈblækən/ verb **1** [I,T] to make sth black; to become black ▶ **czernić**; **czernieć** **2** [T] to make sth seem bad, by saying unpleasant things about it: *to blacken somebody's name* ▶ **oczerniać**

ˌblack ˈeye noun [C] an area of dark-coloured skin around sb's eye where they have been hit: *He got a black eye in the fight.* ▶ **podbite oko**

blackhead /ˈblækhed/ noun [C] a small spot on the skin with a black centre ▶ **wągier**

ˌblack ˈhole noun [C] an area in space that nothing, not even light, can escape from, because **gravity** is so strong there: (figurative) *The company viewed the venture as a financial black hole.* ▶ **czarna dziura**

ˌblack ˈice noun [U] ice in a thin layer on the surface of a road ▶ **gołoledź**

blacklist /ˈblæklɪst/ noun [C] a list of people, companies, etc. who are considered bad or dangerous: *to be on somebody's blacklist* ▶ **czarna lista**

■ **blacklist** verb [T]: *She was blacklisted by all the major Hollywood studios.* ▶ **umieszczać na czarnej liście**

ˌblack ˈmagic noun [U] a type of magic that is used for evil purposes ▶ **czarna magia**

blackmail /ˈblækmeɪl/ noun [U] the crime of forcing a person to give you money or do sth for you, usually by threatening to make known sth which they want to keep secret ▶ **szantaż**

■ **blackmail** verb [T] **blackmail sb (into doing sth)** ▶ **szantażować** | **blackmailer** noun [C] ▶ **szantażyst(k)a**

ˌblack ˈmark noun [C] (Brit.) a note, either in writing on an official record, or in sb's mind, of sth you have done or said that makes people think badly of you: *She earned a black mark for opposing company policy.* ◇ *The public scandal was a black mark against him.* ▶ **zła nota**

ˌblack ˈmarket noun [C, usually sing.] the buying and selling of goods or foreign money in a way that is not legal: *to buy/sell something **on the black market*** ▶ **czarny rynek**

blackout /ˈblækaʊt/ noun [C] **1** a period of time during a war, when all lights must be turned off or covered so that the enemy cannot see them ▶ **zaciemnienie** **2** a period when you are unconscious for a short time: *to have a blackout* tracić przytomność ▶ **chwilowa utrata przytomności**

ˌblack ˈsheep noun [usually sing.] a person who is different from the rest of their family or another group, and who is considered bad or embarrassing: *the black sheep of the family* ▶ **czarna owca**

blacksmith /ˈblæksmɪθ/ noun [C] a person whose job is to make and repair things made of iron ▶ **kowal**

blacktop (US) = TARMAC

bladder /ˈblædə(r)/ noun [C] the part of your body where **urine** collects before leaving your body ▶ **pęcherz moczowy** ➲ picture at **body**

blade /bleɪd/ noun [C] **1** the flat, sharp part of a knife, etc. ▶ **ostrze**, **klinga** ➲ note at **tool** **2** one of the flat, wide parts that turn round very quickly on an aircraft, etc.: *the blades of a propeller* ▶ **łopatka** (*śmigła*) ➲ picture on **page A6** **3** a long, thin leaf of grass: *a blade of grass* ▶ **źdźbło**

blag /blæg/ verb [T] (**blagging**; **blagged**) (Brit., informal) to persuade sb to give you sth, or to let you do sth, by talking to them in a clever or amusing way: *I blagged some tickets for the game.* Pogadałem i dostałem bilety na mecz. ◇ *We blagged our way into the reception by saying that we were from the press.* Mówiąc, że jesteśmy z prasy, udało się nam wcisnąć na przyjęcie. ▶ **załatwić coś gadaniem**, **zagadywać**

blah noun [U] (informal) people say **blah, blah, blah** when they do not want to give the exact words that sb has said or written because they think they are not important or are boring: *They said, 'Come in, sit down, blah, blah, blah, sign here.'* ▶ **i tak dalej, i tak dalej**, **ble, ble, ble**

■ **blah** adj. (US, informal) **1** not interesting: *The movie was pretty blah.* ▶ **nudny** **2** not feeling well; feeling slightly unhappy ▶ **rozmamłany**, **rozmamłany psychicznie**

blame¹ /bleɪm/ verb [T] **blame sb (for sth)**; **blame sth on sb/sth** to think or say that a certain person or thing is responsible for sth bad that has happened: *The teacher blamed me for the accident.* ◇ *Some people blame the changes in the climate on pollution.* ▶ **winić**

IDM **be to blame (for sth)** to be responsible for sth bad: *The police say that careless driving was to blame for the accident.* ▶ **być winnym**, **ponosić odpowiedzialność**

I don't blame you/her, etc. (for doing sth) to think that sb is not wrong to do sth; to understand sb's reason for doing sth: *'I'd like to leave school and get a job.' 'I don't blame you* (nie dziwię ci się).*'* ◇ *I don't blame you for feeling fed up.* ▶ **nie mieć komuś za złe**

shift the blame/responsibility (for sth) (onto sb) → SHIFT¹

blame² /bleɪm/ noun [U] **blame (for sth)** responsibility for sth bad: *The government must **take the blame** for the economic crisis.* ◇ *The report **put the blame on** rising prices.* ◇ *Why do I always **get the blame?*** ▶ **wina**

blameless /ˈbleɪmləs/ adj. (formal) not guilty; that should not be **blamed**: *He insisted that his wife was blameless and* *hadn't known about his crimes.* SYN **innocent** ▶ **niewinny**

blanch /blɑːntʃ; US blæntʃ/ verb **1** [I] (formal) **blanch (at sth)** to become pale because you are shocked or frightened ▶ **blednąć 2** [T] to prepare food, especially vegetables, by putting it into boiling water for a short time ▶ **obgotowywać**

bland /blænd/ adj. **1** ordinary or not very interesting: *a rather bland style of writing* ▶ **szary**, **nijaki 2** (used about food) mild or lacking in taste ▶ **bez smaku**, **mdły**, **łagodny 3** not showing any emotion ▶ **obojętny**, **zdawkowy**
■ **blandly** adv. ▶ **bezbarwnie**; **zdawkowo**

blank[1] /blæŋk/ adj. **1** empty, with nothing written, printed or recorded on it: *a blank video/cassette/piece of paper/page* ▶ **czysty**, **niezapisany 2** without feelings, understanding or interest: *a blank expression on his face* ◇ *My mind* ***went blank*** (poczułem zaćmienie umysłu) *when I saw the exam questions.* ▶ **obojętny**, **pusty**
■ **blankly** adv.: *She stared at me blankly, obviously not recognizing me.* ▶ **obojętnie**, **bez wyrazu**

blank[2] /blæŋk/ noun [C] an empty space: ***Fill in the blanks*** *in the following exercise.* ◇ (figurative) *I couldn't remember his name – my mind was a complete blank.* Jego imię wyleciało mi z głowy. ▶ **wolne miejsce**, **luka**
IDM **draw a blank** → DRAW[1]

ˌblank 'cheque noun [C] a cheque that has been signed but that has an empty space so that the amount to be paid can be written in later ▶ **czek in blanco**

blanket[1] /'blæŋkɪt/ noun [C] **1** a cover made of wool, etc. that is put on beds to keep people warm ▶ **koc** ➲ picture at **bed 2** a thick layer or covering of sth: *a blanket of snow* ▶ **pokrywa**
■ **blanket** verb [T, often passive] **blanket sth (in/with sth)**: *The countryside was blanketed in snow.* ▶ **przykrywać**
IDM **a wet blanket** → WET[1]

blanket[2] /'blæŋkɪt/ adj. [only before a noun] affecting everyone or everything: *There is a* ***blanket ban*** *on journalists reporting the case.* ▶ **dotyczący wszystkich lub każdej ewentualności**

ˌblank 'verse noun [U] poetry that has a regular rhythm, usually with ten syllabes and five stresses in each line, but which does not **rhyme** ▶ **biały wiersz**

blare /bleə(r)/ verb [I,T] **blare (sth) (out)** to make a loud, unpleasant noise: *Car horns were blaring in the street outside.* ◇ *The loudspeaker blared out pop music.* ▶ **wyć**, **wydzierać się**
■ **blare** noun [sing.]: *the blare of a siren* ▶ **wycie**

blasé /'blɑːzeɪ; US blɑː'zeɪ/ adj. **blasé (about sth)** not impressed, excited or worried about sth, because you have seen or experienced it many times before ▶ **zblazowany**

blasphemy /'blæsfəmi/ noun [U] writing or speaking about God in a way that shows a lack of respect ▶ **bluźnierstwo**
■ **blasphemous** /'blæsfəməs/ adj. ▶ **bluźnierczy**

blast[1] /blɑːst; US blæst/ noun [C] **1** an explosion, especially one caused by a bomb ▶ **wybuch 2** a sudden strong current of air: *a blast of cold air* ▶ **podmuch** (*powietrza/wiatru*) **3** a loud sound made by a musical instrument, etc.: *The driver gave a few blasts on his horn.* ▶ **zadęcie**

blast[2] /blɑːst; US blæst/ verb [T] **1** to make a hole, a tunnel, etc. in sth with an explosion: *They blasted a tunnel through the mountainside.* ▶ **wysadzać** (*w powietrze*) **2** to criticize sth very strongly: *Union leaders last night blasted the government's proposals.* ▶ **zjechać**
PHR V **blast off** (used about a **spacecraft**) to leave the ground; to take off ▶ **odpalać**

blast[3] /blɑːst; US blæst/ interj. (informal) (especially Brit.) a mild swear word, used to show that you are angry: *Blast! I've cut my finger.* ▶ **o kurczę!**

blasted /'blɑːstɪd; US 'blæs-/ adj. (informal) very annoying: *Can you turn that blasted music down?* ▶ **piekielny**, **przeklęty**

'blast-off noun [U] the time when a **spacecraft** leaves the ground ▶ **odpalenie**

blatant /'bleɪtnt/ adj. (used about actions which are considered bad) done in an obvious and open way without caring if people are shocked: *a blatant lie* ▶ **jawny**, **uderzający** ❶ Wyraża dezaprobatę.
■ **blatantly** adv. ▶ **jawnie**, **uderzająco**

blaze[1] /bleɪz/ verb [I] **1** to burn with bright strong flames ▶ **buchać płomieniem 2 blaze (with sth)** to be extremely bright; to shine brightly: *I woke up to find that the room was blazing with sunshine.* ◇ (figurative) *'Get out!' she shouted, her eyes blazing with anger.* ▶ **błyszczeć**

blaze[2] /bleɪz/ noun **1** [C] a large and often dangerous fire: *It took firefighters four hours to put out the blaze.* ▶ **płomień**, **pożar 2** [sing.] **a blaze of sth** a very bright show of light or colour: *In the summer the garden was a blaze of colour* (mienił się kolorami). ◇ (figurative) *The new theatre was opened in* ***a blaze of publicity*** (przy głośnej kampanii reklamowej). ▶ **blask**

blazer /'bleɪzə(r)/ noun [C] a jacket, especially one that has the colours or symbol of a school, club or team on it: *a school blazer* ▶ **blezer**

blazing /'bleɪzɪŋ/ adj. [only before a noun] **1** (also ˌ**blazing 'hot**) extremely hot: *a blazing hot day* ◇ *blazing heat* nieznośny upał ▶ **upalny 2** extremely angry or full of strong emotion: *She had a* ***blazing row*** *with Eddie and stormed out of the house.* ▶ **gwałtowny**

bleach[1] /bliːtʃ/ verb [T] to make sth white or lighter in colour by using a chemical or by leaving it in the sun: *Her hair had been bleached by the sun.* Słońce rozjaśniło jej włosy. ▶ **wybielać**, **rozjaśniać**

bleach[2] /bliːtʃ/ noun [C,U] a strong chemical substance used for making clothes, etc. whiter or for cleaning things ▶ **wybielacz**

bleak /bliːk/ adj. **1** (used about a situation) bad; without much hope: *a bleak future for the next generation* ▶ **niewesoły 2** (used about the weather) cold and grey: *a bleak winter's day* ▶ **ponury 3** (used about a place) cold, empty and grey: *the bleak Arctic landscape* ▶ **ponury**
■ **bleakly** adv. ▶ **ponuro** | **bleakness** noun [U] ▶ **ponurość**

bleary /'blɪəri/ adj. (used about the eyes) red, tired and unable to see clearly: *We were all rather bleary-eyed after the overnight journey.* ▶ **kaprawy**, **mętny**
■ **blearily** adv. ▶ **niewyraźnie**

bleat /bliːt/ verb **1** [I] to make the sound of a sheep ▶ (*owca, koza*) **beczeć 2** [I,T] to speak in a weak or complaining voice ▶ **bąkać**
■ **bleat** noun [C] ▶ **bek**; **bąknięcie**

bleed /bliːd/ verb [I] (pt, pp **bled** /bled/) to lose blood ▶ **krwawić**
■ **bleeding** noun [U]: *He wrapped a scarf around his arm to stop the bleeding.* ▶ **krwawienie** | **bleeding** adj. (Brit., slang) [only before a noun] = BLOODY (3)

ˌbleeding 'heart noun [C] a person who is too kind and sympathetic towards people that other people think do not deserve kindness: *a bleeding-heart liberal* ▶ **osoba o (zbyt) miękkim sercu** ❶ Wyraża dezaprobatę.

bleep[1] /bliːp/ noun [C] a short, high sound made by a piece of electronic equipment ▶ **krótki, wysoki dźwięk wydawany przez urządzenie elektroniczne**

bleep[2] /bliːp/ verb **1** [I] (used about machines) to make a short high sound: *Why is the computer bleeping?* ▶

(*urządzenie elektroniczne*) **wydawać wysoki dźwięk** **2** (US also **beep**) [T] to attract sb's attention using an electronic machine: *Please bleep the doctor on duty immediately.* ▶ **przywołać kogoś za pomocą brzęczyka**

bleeper /ˈbliːpə(r)/ (US **beeper** /ˈbiːpə(r)/) noun [C] a small piece of electronic equipment that **bleeps** to let a person (for example a doctor) know when sb is trying to contact them ▶ **brzęczyk**, **pager** SYN **pager**

blemish /ˈblemɪʃ/ noun [C] a mark that spoils the way sth looks ▶ **skaza**, **plama**, **wyprysk** (*na skórze*)
■ **blemish** verb [T]: (figurative) *The defect has blemished the team's perfect record.* ▶ **psuć**, **szpecić**

blend[1] /blend/ verb [T] **blend A with B**; **blend A and B (together)** to mix: *First blend the flour and the melted butter together.* ▶ **zmieszać**
PHR V **blend (in) with sth** to combine with sth in an attractive or suitable way: *The new room is decorated to blend in with the rest of the house.* ▶ **pasować**, **współgrać**
blend (into sth) to match or be similar to the surroundings sb/sth is in: *These animals' ability to blend into their surroundings provides a natural form of defence.* ▶ **zlewać się w jedno**, **wpasowywać**

blend[2] /blend/ noun [C] a mixture: *He had the right blend of enthusiasm and experience.* ▶ **mieszanka**

blender /ˈblendə(r)/ (Brit. also **liquidizer**) noun [C] an electric machine that is used for making food into liquid ▶ **mikser** ➲ picture at **mixer**

bless /bles/ verb [T] (pt, pp **blessed** /blest/) to ask for God's help and protection for sb/sth ▶ **błogosławić**
IDM **be blessed with sth/sb** to be lucky enough to have sth/sb: *The West of Ireland is an area blessed with many fine sandy beaches.* ▶ **być obdarzonym czymś/kimś**
Bless you! what you say to a person who has just sneezed ▶ **na zdrowie!**

blessed /ˈblesɪd/ adj. **1** having God's help and protection: *the Blessed Virgin Mary* ▶ **błogosławiony**, **święty** **2** (in religious language) lucky: *Blessed are the pure in heart.* ▶ **błogosławiony**, **szczęśliwy** SYN **fortunate** **3** [only before a noun] (formal) giving great pleasure: *The cool breeze brought **blessed relief** from the heat.* ▶ **błogi** **4** [only before a noun] (old-fashioned, informal) (used to express mild anger) ▶ **niemożliwy**, **przeklęty**

blessing /ˈblesɪŋ/ noun [C] **1** a thing that you are grateful for or that brings happiness: *It's a great blessing that we have two healthy children.* ◇ *Not getting that job was **a blessing in disguise*** (niespodziewaną korzyścią). ◇ *to count your blessings* być zadowolonym z tego, co się ma ▶ **szczęście**, **dobrodziejstwo** **2** [usually sing.] (a prayer asking for) God's help and protection: *The priest said a blessing.* ▶ **błogosławieństwo** **3** [usually sing.] approval or support: *They got married without their parents' blessing.* ▶ **błogosławieństwo**

blew past tense of **blow**[1]

blight[1] /blaɪt/ verb [T] to spoil or damage sth: *His career has been blighted by injuries.* ▶ **nękać**, **niszczyć**

blight[2] /blaɪt/ noun **1** [U,C] any disease that kills plants, especially crops: *potato blight* ▶ **choroba** (*roślin*), **zaraza** **2** [sing., U] **blight (on sb/sth)** something that has a bad effect on a situation, sb's life or the environment: *His death **cast a blight on*** (położyła się cieniem na) *the whole of that year.* ◇ ***urban blight*** ubogie i zaniedbane rejony w mieście ▶ **plaga**

blimey /ˈblaɪmi/ (also **cor blimey**) exclamation (Brit., informal, slang) (used to express surprise or anger) ▶ **(o) kurczę!**

blind[1] /blaɪnd/ adj. **1** unable to see: *a blind person* ◇ *to be completely/partially blind* ▶ **niewidomy**, **ślepy** ℹ O osobach niewidomych mówi się czasami **partially sighted** czy **visually impaired** niż **blind**. **2 blind (to sth)** not wanting to notice or understand sth: *He was completely blind to her faults.* ▶ **ślepy (na coś)** **3** without reason or thought: *He drove down the motorway in **a blind panic**.* ▶ **ślepy**, **całkowity** **4** impossible to see round: *You should never overtake on **a blind corner**.* ▶ **z ograniczoną widocznością**
■ **blindly** adv. ▶ **(na) ślepo** | **blindness** noun [U] ▶ **ślepota**
IDM **turn a blind eye (to sth)** to pretend not to notice sth bad is happening so that you do not have to do anything about it ▶ **przymykać oczy**

blind[2] /blaɪnd/ verb [T] **1** to make sb unable to see: *Her grandfather had been blinded in an accident.* ◇ *Just for a second I was blinded by the sun.* ▶ **oślepiać** **2 blind sb (to sth)** to make sb unable to think clearly or behave in a sensible way ▶ **oślepiać**

blind[3] /blaɪnd/ noun **1** [C] a piece of cloth or other material that you pull down to cover a window ▶ **roleta**, **żaluzja** **2** (**the blind**) noun [pl.] people who are unable to see ▶ **niewidomi**

ˌblind ˈdate noun [C] an arranged meeting between a man and a woman who have never met before to see if they like each other enough to begin a romantic relationship ▶ **randka w ciemno**

blindfold /ˈblaɪndfəʊld/ noun [C] a piece of cloth, etc. that is used for covering sb's eyes ▶ **opaska na oczy**
■ **blindfold** verb [T] ▶ **zawiązać komuś oczy**

blinding /ˈblaɪndɪŋ/ adj. [usually before a noun] very bright; so strong that you cannot see: *a blinding flash of light* ◇ (figurative) *a blinding* (nieznośny) *headache* ▶ **oślepiający**

ˌblind man's ˈbuff (US **ˌblind man's ˈbluff**) noun [U] a children's game in which a player whose eyes are covered with a piece of cloth tries to catch and identify the other players ▶ **ciuciubabka**

ˈblind spot noun [C] **1** the part of the road just behind you that you cannot see when driving a car ▶ **martwy punkt** (*podczas jazdy samochodem*) **2** if you have a **blind spot** about sth, you cannot understand or accept it ▶ **czyjaś słaba strona**

bling-bling /ˌblɪŋ ˈblɪŋ/ (also **bling**) adj. (informal) (used about jewellery) expensive and shiny; (used about clothes) bright and fashionable; (used about a person) wearing such jewellery and clothes in order to attract attention ▶ (*biżuteria*) **drogi i błyszczący**, (*odzież*) **modny i jaskrawy**; **ubrany w takie ciuchy i świecidełka**
■ **bling-bling** (also **bling**) noun [U] ▶ **drogie świecidełka i modne, jaskrawe ciuchy**

blink /blɪŋk/ verb **1** [I,T] to shut your eyes and open them again very quickly: *Oh dear! You blinked just as I took the photograph!* ▶ **mrugać oczami** ➲ look at **wink** ➲ picture on **page 76** **2** [I] (used about a light) to come on and go off again quickly ▶ **migotać**
■ **blink** noun [C] ▶ **mruganie oczami**; **migotanie**

blinker /ˈblɪŋkə(r)/ noun **1** [C] (informal) = INDICATOR (2) **2** (**blinkers**) [pl.] pieces of leather that are placed at the side of a horse's eyes to stop it from looking sideways ▶ **klapki** (*na oczy*)

blinkered /ˈblɪŋkəd/ adj. not considering every aspect of a situation; not willing to accept different ideas about sth: *a blinkered policy/attitude/approach* ▶ **jednotorowy** SYN **narrow-minded**

blip /blɪp/ noun [C] **1** a light flashing on the screen of a piece of equipment, sometimes with a short high sound ▶ **punkt świetlny** (*na ekranie*); **krótki dźwięk wydawany przez urządzenie elektroniczne** **2** a small problem that does not last for long ▶ **potknięcie**

bliss /blɪs/ noun [U] perfect happiness ▶ **rozkosz**, **błogość**
■ **blissful** /ˈblɪsfl/ adj. ▶ **błogi** | **blissfully** /-fəli/ adv. ▶ **błogo**

blister¹ /ˈblɪstə(r)/ noun [C] a small painful area of skin that looks like a bubble and contains clear liquid. **Blisters** are usually caused by rubbing or burning. ▶ **pęcherz**, **bąbel**

blister² /ˈblɪstə(r)/ verb [I,T] **1** to get or cause **blisters** ▶ **pokrywać (się) bąblami 2** to swell and break open or to cause sth to do this: *The paint is starting to blister.* ▶ **odpryskiwać**; **sprawiać, że coś odpryskuje**

blistering /ˈblɪstərɪŋ/ adj. **1** very strong or extreme: *the blistering* (skwarny) *midday heat* ◇ *The runners set off at a blistering pace* (w zawrotnym tempie). ▶ **intensywny 2** very critical: *a blistering attack* ▶ **druzgocący**

blithe /blaɪð/ adj. [usually before a noun] showing you do not care or are not anxious about what you are doing: *He drove with blithe disregard for the rules of the road.* ▶ **beztroski** ℹ Wyraża dezaprobatę.
■ **blithely** adv.: *'It'll be easy,' she said blithely.* ◇ *He was blithely unaware* (w błogiej nieświadomości) *of the trouble he'd caused.* ▶ **beztrosko**

blitz /blɪts/ noun [C, usually sing.] **1** something which is done with a lot of energy: *an* ***advertising/media blitz*** szeroko zakrojona kampania reklamowa ▶ **energiczne zabranie się do czegoś 2 a blitz (on sth)** a sudden attack: (figurative) *The police are planning a blitz on vandalism* (akcję przeciw wandalizmowi). ◇ *I had a blitz on the garden* (ostro zabrałem się do pracy w ogrodzie) *and it's looking quite nice now.* ▶ **szybki atak**, **nalot**

blizzard /ˈblɪzəd/ noun [C] a very bad storm with strong winds and a lot of snow ▶ **zamieć** ➲ note at **storm**

bloated /ˈbləʊtɪd/ adj. unusually large and uncomfortable because of liquid, food or gas inside: *I felt a bit bloated after all that food.* ▶ **opuchnięty**

blob /blɒb/ noun [C] a small piece of a thick liquid: *a blob of paint/cream/ink* ▶ **kropelka** (*gęstej cieczy*)

bloc /blɒk/ noun [C, with sing. or pl. verb] a group of countries that work closely together because they have the same political interests ▶ **blok**

🔑 **block¹** /blɒk/ noun [C] **1** a large, heavy piece of sth, usually with flat sides: *a block of wood* ◇ *huge concrete blocks* ▶ **blok**, **kloc 2** a large building that is divided into separate flats or offices: *a block of flats* ▶ **blok** ➲ look at **apartment block**, **office block** ➲ picture on **page A3 3** a group of buildings in a town which has streets on all four sides: *The restaurant is three blocks away.* ▶ **kwartał 4** a quantity of sth or an amount of time that is considered as a single unit: *The class is divided into two blocks of fifty minutes.* ▶ **blok 5** [usually sing.] a thing that makes movement or progress difficult or impossible: *a block to further progress in the talks* ▶ **przeszkoda**, **blokada** ➲ look at **roadblock**
IDM **have a block (about sth)** to be unable to think or understand sth properly: *I had a complete* ***mental block****. I just couldn't remember his name.* ▶ **doznać zaćmienia pamięci/umysłu**

🔑 **block²** /blɒk/ verb [T] **1 block sth (up)** to make it difficult or impossible for sb/sth to pass: *Many roads are completely blocked by snow.* ▶ **blokować**, **zapychać 2** to prevent sth from being done: *The management tried to block the deal.* ▶ **uniemożliwiać 3** to prevent sth from being seen by sb: *Get out of the way, you're blocking the view!* ▶ **zasłaniać**
PHR V **block sth off** to separate one area from another with sth solid: *This section of the motorway has been blocked off by the police.* ▶ **blokować**, **zagradzać**
block sth out to try not to think about sth unpleasant: *She tried to block out the memory of the crash.* ▶ **wymazać coś z pamięci**

blockade /blɒˈkeɪd/ noun [C] a situation in which a place is surrounded by soldiers or ships in order to prevent goods or people from reaching it ▶ **blokada**
■ **blockade** verb [T] ▶ **blokować**

blockage /ˈblɒkɪdʒ/ noun [C] a thing that is preventing sth from passing; the state of being blocked: *a blockage in the drainpipe* ◇ *There are blockages on some major roads.* ▶ **zatkanie**, **zator**

blockbuster /ˈblɒkbʌstə(r)/ noun [C] a book or film with an exciting story which is very successful and popular ▶ **przebój** ➲ look at **hit²** (2)

ˌ**block ˈcapital** noun [C, usually pl.] a big letter such as 'A' (not 'a'): *Please write your name in block capitals.* ▶ **duża litera**

blog /blɒg/ (also **weblog** /ˈweblɒg/) noun [C] a personal record that sb puts on their website. In their **blogs**, people usually write about things that interest them and about other websites that they have visited. ▶ **blog**
■ **blog** verb [I] (**blogging**; **blogged**) ▶ **blogować** | **blogger** noun [C] ▶ **autor/ka bloga**

bloke /bləʊk/ noun [C] (Brit., informal) a man: *He's a really nice bloke.* ▶ **facet**

🔑 **blonde** /blɒnd/ (also **blond**) adj. (used about hair) pale gold in colour; (used about a person) having **blonde** hair: *Both my sisters have blonde hair.* ▶ **blond**, **jasnowłosy** ℹ Do opisywania mężczyzn używa się pisowni **blond**: *He's tall, slim and blond.*
■ **blonde** noun [C] a woman with hair that is pale gold in colour ▶ **blondynka** ➲ look at **brunette**

🔑 **blood** /blʌd/ noun [U] the red liquid that flows through your body: *The heart pumps blood around the body.* ▶ **krew** ➲ look at **bleed**
IDM **in your blood** a strong part of your character: *A love of the countryside was in his blood.* ▶ **we krwi**
in cold blood → COLD¹
shed blood → SHED²
your (own) flesh and blood → FLESH

ˈ**blood bank** noun [C] a place where blood is kept for use in hospitals, etc. ▶ **bank krwi**

bloodbath /ˈblʌdbɑːθ; US -bæθ/ noun [sing.] an act of violently killing many people ▶ **rozlew krwi**

ˈ**blood-curdling** adj. very frightening: *a blood-curdling scream* ▶ **mrożący krew w żyłach**

ˈ**blood donor** noun [C] a person who gives some of their blood for use in medical operations ▶ **krwiodawca**

ˈ**blood group** (also ˈ**blood type**) noun [C] any of several different types of human blood: *'What blood group are you?' 'O.'* ▶ **grupa krwi**

bloodless /ˈblʌdləs/ adj. **1** without killing or violence: *a bloodless coup* ▶ **bezkrwawy 2** (used about a part of the body) very pale ▶ **blady**

'blood pressure noun [U] the force with which the blood travels round the body: *to have high/low blood pressure* ▶ **ciśnienie krwi**

'blood relation (also 'blood relative) noun [C] a person related to sb by birth rather than by marriage ▶ **krewn-y/a**

bloodshed /'blʌdʃed/ noun [U] the killing or harming of people: *Both sides in the war want to avoid further bloodshed.* ▶ **rozlew krwi**

bloodshot /'blʌdʃɒt/ adj. (used about the white part of the eyes) full of red lines, for example when sb is tired ▶ **nabiegły krwią**

'blood sport noun [C] a sport in which animals or birds are killed ▶ **polowanie**

bloodstain /'blʌdsteɪn/ noun [C] a mark or spot of blood on sth ▶ **krwawa plama**
■ **bloodstained** adj. ▶ **zakrwawiony, krwawy**

bloodstream /'blʌdstri:m/ noun [sing.] the blood as it flows through the body: *drugs injected straight into the bloodstream* ▶ **krwiobieg**

bloodthirsty /'blʌdθɜ:sti/ adj. wanting to use violence or to watch scenes of violence ▶ **krwiożerczy**

'blood transfusion noun [C] the process of putting new blood into sb's body ▶ **transfuzja krwi**

'blood type = BLOOD GROUP

'blood vessel noun [C] any of the tubes in your body which blood flows through ▶ **naczynie krwionośne** ➲ look at **vein**, **artery**

bloody /'blʌdi/ adj. (**bloodier**; **bloodiest**) **1** involving a lot of violence and killing: *a bloody war* ▶ **krwawy** **2** covered with blood: *a bloody knife* ▶ **zakrwawiony** **3** [only before a noun] (Brit., slang) (a swear word used for emphasizing a comment or an angry statement): *The bloody train was late again this morning.* ▶ **cholerny** ⓘ Uwaga! Używanie tego słowa może być uznawane za niegrzeczne.
■ **bloody** adv. (Brit., slang) (a swear word used for emphasizing a comment or an angry statement): *We had a bloody good time.* ◇ *What a bloody stupid thing to say!* ▶ **cholernie** ⓘ Uwaga! Używanie tego słowa może być uznawane za niegrzeczne.

,bloody-'minded adj. (Brit., informal) (used about a person) deliberately difficult; not helpful ▶ **zatwardziały**
■ **bloody-mindedness** noun [U] ▶ **zatwardziałość**

bloom[1] /blu:m/ noun [C] a flower ▶ **kwiat**
IDM **in bloom** with its flowers open: *All the wild plants are in bloom.* ▶ **kwitnący**

bloom[2] /blu:m/ verb [I] to produce flowers: *This shrub blooms in May.* ▶ **kwitnąć**

blossom[1] /'blɒsəm/ noun [C,U] a flower or a mass of flowers, especially on a fruit tree in the spring: *The apple tree is **in blossom*** (rozkwiecone). ▶ **kwiat/y** (*drzew owocowych*)

blossom[2] /'blɒsəm/ verb [I] **1** (used especially about trees) to produce flowers ▶ **kwitnąć** **2 blossom (into sth)** to become more healthy, confident or successful: *This young runner has blossomed into a top-class athlete.* ▶ **rozkwitać**

blot[1] /blɒt/ verb [T] (**blotting**; **blotted**) **1** to remove liquid from a surface by pressing soft paper or cloth on it ▶ **osuszać** (*bibułą*) **2** to make a spot or spots of ink fall on paper ▶ **zrobić kleksa**
PHR V **blot sth out** to cover or hide sth: *Fog blotted out the view completely.* ◇ *She tried to blot out the memory of what happened.* ▶ **zakrywać, wymazywać**

blot[2] /blɒt/ noun [C] **1** a spot of sth, especially one made by ink on paper SYN **stain** ▶ **kleks** **2 a blot on sth** a thing that spoils your happiness or other people's opinion of you ▶ **plama**

blotch /blɒtʃ/ noun [C] a temporary mark or an area of different colour on skin, plants, cloth, etc.: *The blotches on her face showed that she had been crying.* ▶ **plama**
■ **blotchy** (also **blotched**) adj. ▶ **poplamiony**

'blotting paper noun [U] soft paper that you use for drying wet ink after you have written sth on paper ▶ **bibuła**

blouse /blaʊz; US blaʊs/ noun [C] a piece of clothing like a shirt, that women wear ▶ **bluzka** ➲ picture on **page A1**

⚷ **blow**[1] /bləʊ/ verb (pt **blew** /blu:/, pp **blown** /bləʊn/) **1** [I] to send air out of the mouth: *The policeman asked me to blow into the breathalyser.* ▶ **dmuchać** **2** [I,T] (used about wind, air, etc.) to be moving or to cause sth to move: *A gentle breeze was blowing.* ◇ *The wind suddenly blew my hat off* (zwiał mi kapelusz). ▶ **wiać** **3** [I] to move because of the wind or a current of air: *The balloons blew away* (odleciały). ◇ *My papers blew all over the garden.* Wiatr porozwiewał moje papiery po ogrodzie. ▶ **poruszać się na wietrze** **4** [I,T] to produce sound from a musical instrument, etc. by blowing air into it: *The referee's whistle blew for the end of the match.* ◇ *I heard the guard's whistle blow* (usłyszałem gwizdek) *as I ran up the station steps.* ◇ *He blew a few notes on the trumpet.* ◇ *All the drivers were blowing their horns* (trąbili klaksonami). ▶ **grać na instrumencie dętym**; **wydawać dźwięk** **5** [T] to make or shape sth by blowing air out of your mouth: *to blow bubbles/smoke rings* puszczać bańki/kółka z dymu ◇ *to blow (somebody) a kiss* posłać (komuś) całusa ▶ **wydmuchiwać** **6** [I,T] when a **fuse** stops working suddenly because the electric current is too strong: *A fuse has blown.* ◇ *I think the kettle's blown a fuse.* ▶ **przepalać (się)** **7** [T] (informal) **blow sth (on sth)** to spend or waste a lot of money on sth: *She blew all her savings on a trip to China.* ▶ **przepuścić** (*pieniądze*) **8** [T] (informal) to waste an opportunity: *I think I've blown my chances of promotion.* ◇ *You had your chance and you blew it.* ▶ **marnować** (*okazję*) **9** (Brit., informal) (used to show that you are annoyed, surprised or do not care about sth): *Blow it! We've missed the bus.* ▶ **niech to diabli wezmą!**
IDM **blow your nose** to clear your nose by blowing strongly through it into a **handkerchief** or a **tissue** ▶ **wycierać nos**
PHR V **blow (sth) out** to put out a flame, etc. by blowing; (used about a flame, etc.) to be put out by the wind, etc. ▶ **zdmuchiwać**; **zostać zdmuchniętym**
blow over to disappear without having a serious effect: *The scandal will soon blow over.* ▶ **przemijać**
blow up 1 to explode or to be destroyed in an explosion: *The car blew up when the door was opened.* ▶ **wybuchać** **2** to start suddenly and strongly: *A storm blew up in the night.* ◇ *A huge row blew up about money.* ▶ **rozszaleć się**, **wybuchać** (*np. gniewem*)
blow up (at sb) (informal) to become very angry: *The teacher blew up when I said I'd forgotten my homework.* ▶ **wybuchać gniewem**
blow sth up 1 to make sth explode or to destroy sth in an explosion: *The terrorists tried to blow up the plane.* ▶ **wysadzać** (*w powietrze*) **2** to fill sth with air or gas: *to blow up a balloon* ▶ **nadmuchiwać** **3** to make a photograph bigger ▶ **powiększać** (*fotografię*)

⚷ **blow**[2] /bləʊ/ noun [C] **1** a hard hit from sb's hand, a weapon, etc.: *She aimed a blow at me.* ▶ **cios** **2 a blow (to sb/sth)** a sudden shock or disappointment: *It was a blow when I didn't get the job.* ▶ **cios** **3** an act of blowing: *Give your nose a blow!* Wytrzyj nos! ▶ **dmuchnięcie**
IDM **a blow-by-blow account, description, etc. (of sth)** an account, etc. of an event that gives all the exact details of it ▶ **szczegółowe sprawozdanie**

come to blows (with sb) (over sth) to start fighting or arguing (about sth) ▶ **posunąć się do rękoczynów**; **zaczynać kłótnię**
deal sb/sth a blow; **deal a blow to sb/sth** → DEAL[1]

ˈblow-dry verb [T] (pt, pp **blow-dried**) to dry and shape sb's hair using a **hairdryer** and a brush ▶ **modelowanie** (*włosów*)

blowlamp /ˈbləʊlæmp/ (US **blowtorch** /ˈbləʊtɔːtʃ/) noun [C] a tool for directing a very hot flame onto part of a surface, for example to remove paint ▶ **lampa lutownicza**

blown past participle of **blow[1]**

blowout /ˈbləʊaʊt/ noun [C] (informal) **1** a burst tyre: *We had a blow-out* (złapaliśmy gumę) *on the motorway.* ▶ **przebicie/pęknięcie opony** SYN **puncture** **2** [usually sing.] a very large meal at which people eat too much ▶ **wyżerka** **3** (US) a large party or social event ▶ **wielkie przyjęcie**

blowpipe /ˈbləʊpaɪp/ noun [C] **1** a weapon consisting of a long tube through which an arrow is blown ▶ **dmuchawka** (*do wystrzeliwania strzałek*) **2** a long tube for blowing glass into a particular shape ▶ **dmuchawa** (*do wydmuchiwania szkła*)

ˈblow-up noun [C] an **enlargement** of a photograph, picture or design: *Can you do me a blow-up of his face?* ▶ **powiększenie** (*np. zdjęcia*)

blubber[1] /ˈblʌbə(r)/ noun [U] the fat of sea animals, such as **whales** ▶ **tłuszcz** (*np. wielorybi*)

blubber[2] /ˈblʌbə(r)/ verb [I] (informal) to cry noisily ▶ (*płakać*) **beczeć**

bludgeon /ˈblʌdʒən/ verb [T] **1** to hit sb several times with a heavy object ▶ **tłuc** **2 bludgeon sb (into sth/into doing sth)** to force sb to do sth, especially by arguing with them: *They tried to bludgeon me into joining their protest.* ▶ **wymuszać coś na kimś** (*zwłaszcza kłótnią*)

🔑 **blue[1]** /bluː/ adj. **1** having the colour of a clear sky when the sun shines: *His eyes were bright blue.* ◇ *light/dark blue* ◇ *Her hands were blue* (sine) *with cold.* ▶ **niebieski** **2** (informal) (often used in songs) sad: *He'd been feeling blue all week.* ▶ **smutny** **3** (used about films, jokes or stories) connected with sex ▶ **erotyczny**
IDM **black and blue** → BLACK[1]
once in a blue moon → ONCE

🔑 **blue[2]** /bluː/ noun **1** [C,U] the colour of a clear sky when the sun shines: *a deep blue* ◇ *dressed **in blue*** ▶ **kolor niebieski** **2** (**the blues**) [pl.] a type of slow sad music: *a blues singer* ▶ **blues** **3** (**the blues**) [pl.] (informal) feelings of sadness: *to have the blues* ▶ **chandra**
IDM **out of the blue** suddenly; unexpectedly: *I didn't hear from him for years and then this email came out of the blue.* ▶ **znienacka**, **nieoczekiwanie**

bluebell /ˈbluːbel/ noun [C] a plant with blue or white flowers shaped like bells ▶ **dzwonek**

blueberry /ˈbluːbəri; US -beri/ noun [C] a small dark blue berry that grows on low bushes in North America ▶ **borówka amerykańska** ➲ look at **bilberry**

ˌblue-ˈchip adj. [only before a noun] (used about a company, an investment, etc.) safe and likely to make a profit: *blue-chip companies* ▶ (*inwestycja itp.*) **zapewniający zysk**

ˈblue-collar adj. [only before a noun] doing or involving physical work with the hands rather than office work ▶ **dot. pracy fizycznej** ➲ look at **white-collar**

blueish = BLUISH

blueprint /ˈbluːprɪnt/ noun [C] a photograph of a plan, or a description of how to make, build or achieve sth ▶ **podstawy projektu**

blue riband /ˌbluː ˈrɪbənd/ (also ˌ**blue** ˈ**ribbon**) noun [C] an honour (sometimes in the form of a blue **ribbon**) given to the winner of the first prize in a competition ▶ **pierwsza nagroda**

Bluetooth™ /ˈbluːtuːθ/ noun [U] a radio technology that makes it possible for mobile phones, computers and other electronic devices to be linked over short distances, without needing to be connected by wires: *Bluetooth-enabled devices* ▶ **bezprzewodowa technologia komunikacji między różnymi urządzeniami elektronicznymi**

bluff[1] /blʌf/ verb [I,T] to try to make people believe that sth is true when it is not, usually by appearing very confident: *They tried to bluff their parents into believing there was no school that day.* ▶ **blefować**
IDM **bluff your way in, out, through, etc. sth** to trick sb in order to get into, out of a place, etc.: *We managed to bluff our way into the stadium by saying we were journalists.* ▶ **dostać się/wydostać się podstępem**

bluff[2] /blʌf/ noun [U,C] making sb believe that you will do sth when you really have no intention of doing it, or that you know sth when, in fact, you do not know it ▶ **blef**
IDM **call sb's bluff** → CALL[1]

bluish (also **blueish**) /ˈbluːɪʃ/ adj. (informal) slightly blue: *bluish green* ▶ **niebieskawy**

blunder[1] /ˈblʌndə(r)/ noun [C] a stupid mistake: *I'm afraid I've **made a** terrible **blunder**.* ▶ **gafa**

blunder[2] /ˈblʌndə(r)/ verb [I] to make a stupid mistake ▶ **popełnić gafę**
PHR V **blunder about, around, etc.** to move in an uncertain or careless way, as if you cannot see where you are going: *We blundered about in the dark, trying to find the light switch.* ▶ **poruszać się niezdarnie** (*jak po omacku*)

blunt /blʌnt/ adj. **1** (used about a knife, pencil, tool, etc.) without a sharp edge or point: *blunt scissors* ▶ **tępy** OPP **sharp** **2** (used about a person, comment, etc.) very direct; saying what you think without trying to be polite: *I'm sorry to be so blunt, but I'm afraid you're just not good enough.* ▶ **(mówiący) bez ogródek**
■ **blunt** verb [T] ▶ **stępiać** | **bluntly** adv. ▶ **bez ogródek** | **bluntness** noun [U] ▶ **otwartość**, **nietakt**

blur[1] /blɜː(r)/ noun [C, usually sing.] something that you cannot see clearly or remember well: *Without my glasses, their faces were just a blur.* ▶ **mgliste zarysy/wspomnienie**

blur[2] /blɜː(r)/ verb [I,T] (**blurring**; **blurred**) to become or to make sth less clear: *The words on the page blurred as tears filled her eyes.* ▶ **zamglić (się)**, **zamazywać (się)**
■ **blurred** adj. ▶ **zamazany**, (*wzrok, oczy*) **zamglony**

blurb /blɜːb/ noun [C] a short description of a book, a new product, etc., written by the people who have produced it, that is intended to attract your attention and make you want to buy it ▶ **krótki opis reklamowy** (*np. na obwolucie*)

blurt /blɜːt/ verb
PHR V **blurt sth out** to say sth suddenly or without thinking: *We didn't want to tell Mum but Ann blurted the whole thing out.* ▶ **wypaplać**, **wygadać się**

blush /blʌʃ/ verb [I] to become red in the face, especially because you are embarrassed or feel guilty: *She blushed with shame.* ▶ **rumienić się**
■ **blush** noun [C] ▶ **rumieniec**

blusher /ˈblʌʃə(r)/ noun [U,C] a coloured cream or powder that some people put on their cheeks to give them more colour ▶ **róż**

bluster /ˈblʌstə(r)/ verb **1** [I,T] to talk in an aggressive or threatening way, but with little effect ▶ **wrzeszczeć**, **wygrażać** **2** [I] (used about the wind) to blow violently ▶ (*wiatr*) **huczeć**, **dmuchać**
■ **bluster** noun [U] ▶ **wygrażanie**, **odgrażanie się**

blustery /ˈblʌstəri/ adj. (used to describe the weather) with strong winds: *The day was cold and blustery.* ▶ **bardzo wietrzny**

Blu-tack™ /ˈbluː tæk/ noun [U] a blue sticky material used to attach paper to walls ▶ **Blu-tack** (*masa klejąco-mocująca*)

BO = BODY ODOUR

boa constrictor /ˈbəʊə kənstrɪktə(r)/ (also **boa**) noun [C] a large South American snake that kills animals for food by wrapping its body around them and crushing them ▶ **boa**

boar /bɔː(r)/ noun [C] (pl. **boar** or **boars**) **1** a wild pig ▶ **dzik** **2** a male pig ▶ **knur** ➲ note at **pig**

board¹ /bɔːd/ noun **1** [C] a long, thin, flat piece of wood used for making floors, walls, etc.: *The old house needed new* ***floorboards.*** ▶ **deska** **2** [C] a thin flat piece of wood, etc. used for a particular purpose: *an ironing board* ◇ *a surfboard* ◇ *a noticeboard* ◇ *a chessboard* szachownica ▶ **deska, tablica, plansza** **3** [C, with sing. or pl. verb] a group of people who control an organization, company, etc.: *The* ***board of directors*** *is/are meeting to discuss the firm's future.* ◇ *a board meeting* ▶ **zarząd** **4** [U] the meals that are provided when you stay in a hotel, etc.: *The prices are for a double room and* ***full board.*** ▶ **wyżywienie**

IDM **above board** → ABOVE

across the board → ACROSS

on board on a ship or an aircraft: *All the passengers were safely on board.* ▶ **na pokładzie**

board² /bɔːd/ verb **1** [I,T] to get on a plane, ship, bus, etc.: *We said goodbye and boarded the train.* ▶ **wsiadać do czegoś/na coś** **2** (**be boarding**) [I] when a plane or ship is **boarding**, it is ready for passengers to get on: *Flight LH120 to Hamburg is now boarding at Gate 27.* Pasażerowie proszeni są do wyjścia 27 na lot LH120 do Hamburga. **3** to live and take meals in sb's home, in return for payment ▶ **mieszkać i stołować się u kogoś, mieć u kogoś utrzymanie** **4** to live at school during the term ▶ **mieszkać w internacie**

PHR V **board sth up** to cover with **boards¹** (1): *Nobody lives there now – it's all boarded up.* ▶ **zabijać deskami**

boarder /ˈbɔːdə(r)/ noun [C] (Brit.) **1** a child who lives at school and goes home for the holidays. ▶ **mieszkaniec internatu** **2** a person who pays to live at sb's house ▶ **sublokator/ka** ➲ look at **lodger**

ˈ**board game** noun [C] any game played on a board, often using **dice** and small pieces that are moved around ▶ **gra planszowa**

ˈ**boarding card** noun [C] a card that you must show in order to get on a plane or ship ▶ **karta pokładowa**

ˈ**boarding house** noun [C] a private house where you can pay to stay and have meals for a period of time ▶ **pensjonat**

ˈ**boarding school** noun [C] a school that children live at while they are studying, going home only in the holidays ▶ **szkoła z internatem**

boardroom /ˈbɔːdruːm; -rʊm/ noun [C] the room where the **board of directors** meets ▶ **sala konferencyjna**

boardwalk /ˈbɔːdwɔːk/ noun [C] (especially US) a path made of wooden boards, especially on a beach or near water ▶ **promenada nadmorska z desek**

boast /bəʊst/ verb **1** [I] to talk with too much pride about sth that you have or can do: *I wish she wouldn't boast about her family so much.* ▶ **chwalić się** **2** [T] (used about a place) to have sth that it can be proud of: *The town boasts over a dozen restaurants.* ▶ **szczycić się**

■ **boast** noun [C] something that a person talks about in a very proud way, often to seem more important or clear: *Despite his boasts that his children were brilliant, neither of them went to college.* ◇ *It was her* ***proud boast*** *that she had never missed a day's work because of illness.* ▶ **duma; przechwałka**

boastful /ˈbəʊstfl/ adj. (used about a person or the things that they say) showing too much pride ▶ **chełpliwy**

boat /bəʊt/ noun [C] **1** a small vehicle that is used for travelling across water: *The cave can only be reached* ***by boat/in a boat.*** ◇ *a rowing/fishing boat* ▶ **łódź, statek** **2** any ship ▶ **statek, prom**

IDM **rock the boat** → ROCK²

boats

Boat to zazw. łódź mniejsza niż **ship**, choć słowa **boat** można też użyć w odniesieniu do większego statku, zwł. pasażerskiego: *When does the next boat to France sail?* **Liner** oznacza statek do przewożenia pasażerów na długie odległości, wówczas podróż nazywa się **voyage**. **Ferry** przewozi ludzi oraz czasami samochody na krótkich dystansach, które nazywają się

boats and ships

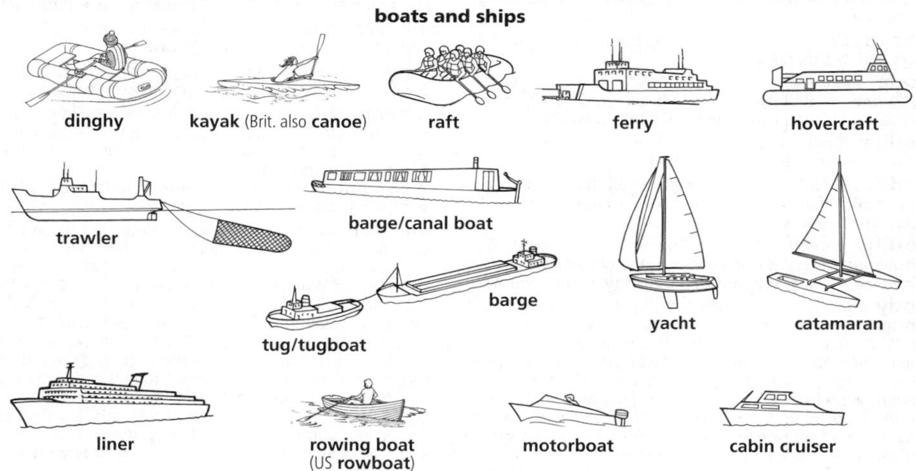

crossings. Statek przewożący ładunek z jednego miejsca na drugie nazywa się **freighter**. Duża łódka żaglowa to **yacht**. **Lifeboat** ma dwa znaczenia: jest to specjalna łódź ratunkowa używana na pełnym morzu do ratowania ludzi; lub łódź ratunkowa na statku, która jest wykorzystywana w sytuacji, gdy statek tonie. Lódź, która porusza się za pomocą wioseł, to **rowing boat** (US **rowboat**). Przednia część łodzi lub statku (dziób) to **bow**, a tylna (rufa) to **stern**. Kiedy stoisz na łodzi twarzą w kierunku dziobu, to prawa strona nazywa się **starboard**, a lewa **port**. Załoga łodzi to **crew**. Osoba dowodząca to **captain**.
➲ picture also on **page A6**

bob[1] /bɒb/ verb [I,T] (**bobbing**; **bobbed**) to move quickly up and down; to make sth do this: *The boats in the harbour were bobbing up and down in the water* (huśtały się na wodzie). ◇ *She bobbed her head nervously.* Nerwowo potrząsnęła głową. ▶ **podskakiwać (jak korek)**
PHR V **bob up** to appear suddenly from behind or under sth: *He disappeared and then bobbed up again on the other side of the pool.* ▶ **nagle się pojawiać**

bob[2] /bɒb/ noun [C] **1** a quick movement down and up of your head and body: *a bob of the head* skinienie głowy ▶ **dygnięcie** **2** a style of a woman's hair in which it is cut the same length all the way around: *She wears her hair in a bob.* ▶ *(fryzura)* **paź** **3** (pl. **bob**) (informal) an old British coin, the **shilling**, worth 12 old pence ▶ **szyling**

bobbed /bɒbd/ adj. (used about hair) cut so that it hangs loosely to the level of the chin all around the back and sides ▶ **ostrzyżony na pazia**

bobbin /ˈbɒbɪn/ noun [C] a small round object which you put thread around, used, for example, in a sewing machine ▶ **szpul(k)a**

bobble /ˈbɒbl/ noun [C] (Brit.) a small, soft ball, usually made of wool, that is used especially for decorating clothes ▶ **pompon** SYN **pompom**

bobby /ˈbɒbi/ noun [C] (old-fashioned, Brit., informal) a policeman: *We need more bobbies on the beat* (policji na ulicach). ▶ **policjant**

ˈ**bobby pin** (US) = HAIRGRIP

bobsleigh /ˈbɒbsleɪ/ (US **bobsled** /ˈbɒbsled/) noun [C] a racing vehicle for two or more people that slides over snow along a track ▶ **bobslej** ➲ look at **sleigh**, **sledge**, **toboggan**

bod /bɒd/ noun [C] (Brit., informal) a person: *She's a bit of an odd bod.* ▶ **facet/ka**

bode /bəʊd/ verb
IDM **bode well/ill (for sb/sth)** to be a sign that sb/sth will have a good/bad future ▶ **wróżyć dobrze/źle**

bodice /ˈbɒdɪs/ noun [C] the top part of a woman's dress, above the waist ▶ **góra sukienki**

bodily[1] /ˈbɒdɪli/ adj. [only before a noun] of the human body; physical: *First we must attend to their bodily needs.* ▶ **fizyczny**, **cielesny**

bodily[2] /ˈbɒdɪli/ adv. by taking hold of the body: *She picked up the child and carried him bodily* (wyniosła je) *from the room.* ▶ **trzymając kogoś** *(np. w ramionach)*

🔑 **body** /ˈbɒdi/ noun (pl. **bodies**) **1** [C] the whole physical form of a person or an animal: *the human body* ▶ **ciało** **2** [C] the part of a person that is not their legs, arms or head: *She had injuries to her head and body.* ▶ **tułów** **3** [C] a dead person: *The police have found a body in the canal.* ▶ **zwłoki** **4** [sing.] the main part of sth: *We agree with the body of the report, although not with certain details.* ▶ **główna część** **5** [C, with sing. or pl. verb] a group of people who work or act together, especially in an official way: *The governing body of the college meets/meet once a month.* ▶ **ciało**, **grupa** **6** [C] (formal) an object: *The doctor removed a foreign body from the child's ear.* ▶ **ciało**, **przedmiot**
IDM **in a body** all together ▶ **jako grupa**

bodybuilding /ˈbɒdibɪldɪŋ/ noun [U] making the muscles of the body stronger and larger by exercise ▶ **kulturystyka**
■ **bodybuilder** noun [C] ▶ **kulturyst(k)a**

bodyguard /ˈbɒdigɑːd/ noun [C] a person or group of people whose job is to protect sb ▶ **ochroniarz**, **ochrona** ℹ Gdy słowo **bodyguard** oznacza grupę ludzi, wówczas może występować w lp lub lm.

ˈ**body language** noun [U] showing how you feel by the way you move, stand, sit, etc., rather than by what you say: *I could tell by his body language that he was scared.* ▶ **mowa ciała**

ˈ**body odour** noun [U] (abbr. **BO** /ˌbiː ˈəʊ/) the unpleasant smell from sb's body, especially of sweat ▶ **zapach potu**

bodywork /ˈbɒdiwɜːk/ noun [U] the main outside structure of a vehicle, usually made of painted metal ▶ **nadwozie**, **karoseria**

boffin /ˈbɒfɪn; US -fən/ noun [C] (Brit., informal) a scientist, especially one doing research ▶ **specjalista**

bog /bɒg/ noun **1** [C,U] an area of ground that is very soft and wet: *a peat bog* ▶ **bagno** **2** (Brit., slang) a toilet ▶ **kibel**

bogey /ˈbəʊgi/ noun [C] **1** something that causes fear, often without reason ▶ **straszydło** **2** (informal) a piece of **mucus** ▶ **smark** ➲ look at **snot**

bogeyman /ˈbəʊgimæn/ noun [C] (US **boogeyman** /ˈbuːgimæn/) (pl. **-men** /-mən/) an imaginary evil spirit that is used to frighten children ▶ **wyimaginowany zły duch straszący dzieci**, **postrach** *(dla dzieci)*

ˌ**bogged** ˈ**down** adj. [not before a noun] **1** (used about a vehicle) not able to move because it has sunk into soft ground ▶ **ugrzęzły** **2** (used about a person) not able to make any progress: *We got bogged down* (utknęliśmy) *in a long discussion.*

boggle /ˈbɒgl/ verb
IDM **sth boggles the mind**; **the mind boggles** (informal) if sth **boggles the mind** or **the mind boggles** at it, it is so unusual that people find it hard do imagine or accept: *'What will happen if his plan doesn't work?' 'The mind boggles* (zdumiewające)*!'* ▶ **zdumiewać (się)** ➲ look at **mind-boggling**

boggy /ˈbɒgi/ adj. (**boggier**; **boggiest**) (used about land) soft and wet, so that your feet sink into it ▶ **bagnisty**

ˌ**bog-**ˈ**standard** adj. (Brit., informal) ordinary; with no special features ▶ **przeciętny** SYN **average**

bogus /ˈbəʊgəs/ adj. pretending to be real or genuine: *a bogus policeman* ▶ **podrobiony**, **fałszywy** SYN **false**

bohemian /bəʊˈhiːmiən/ noun [C] a person, often sb who is involved in the arts, who lives in a very informal way without following the accepted rules of behaviour ▶ **członek cyganerii**
■ **bohemian** adj.: *a* ***bohemian existence/lifestyle*** ▶ **typowy dla cyganerii**

🔑 **boil**[1] /bɔɪl/ verb **1** [I] (used about a liquid) to reach a high temperature where bubbles rise to the surface and the liquid changes to a gas: *Water boils at 100° C.* ◇ *The kettle's boiling.* Woda się gotuje. ▶ **gotować się** **2** [T] to heat a liquid until it boils and let it keep boiling: *Boil all drinking water for five minutes.* ▶ **gotować** **3** [I,T] to cook (sth) in boiling water: *Put the potatoes on to boil, please.* ◇ *to boil an egg* ▶ **gotować (się)** ➲ note at **cook**, **recipe** **4** [I] (used about a person) to feel very angry: *She was boiling with rage.* ▶ **kipieć** *(np. ze złości)*
PHR V **boil down to sth** to have sth as the most important point: *What it all boils down to is that you don't want to spend too much money.* ▶ **sprowadzać się do czegoś**

boil over 1 (used about a liquid) to boil and flow over the sides of a pan: *You let the soup boil over.* ▶ **wykipieć 2** (used about an argument or sb's feelings) to become more serious or angry ▶ **wykipieć**, **unosić się**

boil² /bɔɪl/ noun **1** [sing.] a period of boiling; the point at which a liquid boils: ***Bring** the soup **to the boil*** (doprowadź do wrzenia), *then allow to simmer for five minutes.* ◇ *You'll have to give those shirts a boil* (zagotować koszule) *to get them clean.* ◇ *to **come to the boil*** zagotować się ▶ **gotowanie 2** [C] a small, painful swelling under your skin, with a red or yellow top ▶ **czyrak**

ˌboiled ˈsweet noun [C] (US **hard candy** [U]) a hard sweet made from boiled sugar, often with fruit flavours ▶ **landrynka**

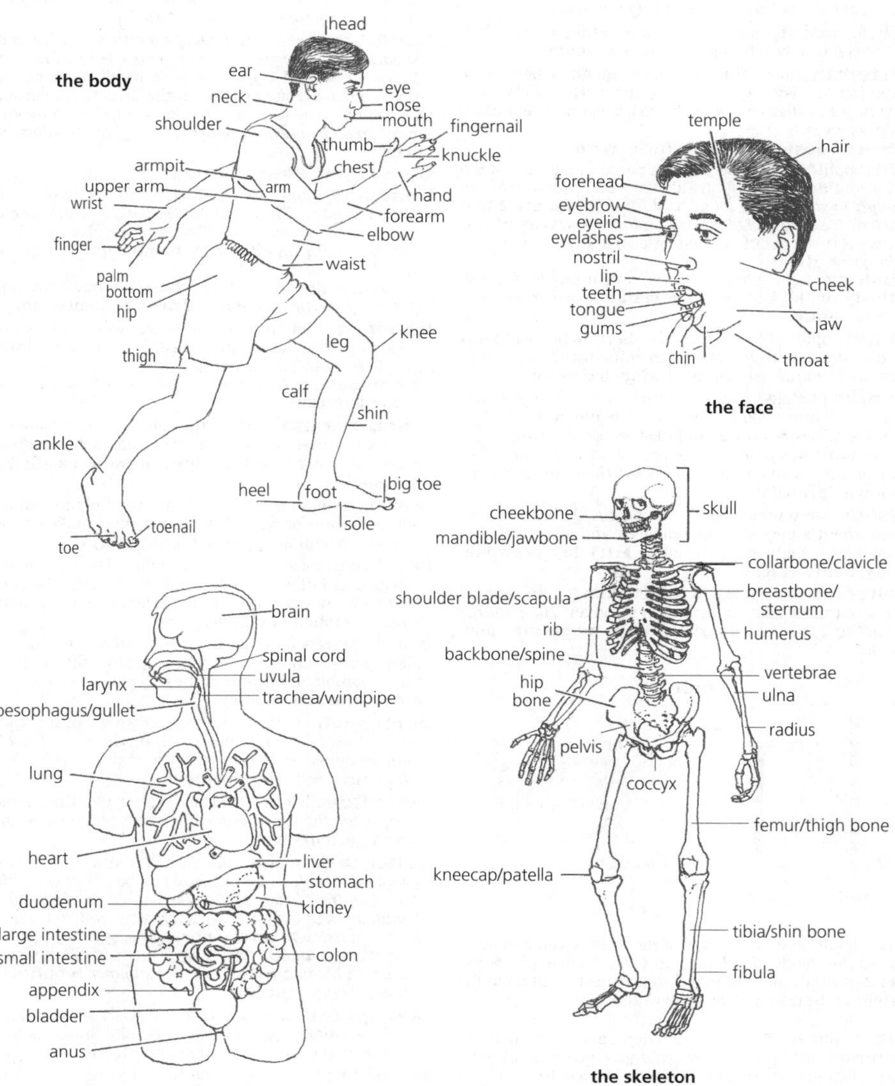

boiler /ˈbɔɪlə(r)/ noun [C] **1** a container in which water is heated to provide hot water or heating in a building ▶ **bojler 2** a container in which water is heated to produce steam in an engine ▶ **kocioł parowy**, **terma**

ˈ**boiler suit** noun [C] (US **coveralls**) a piece of clothing that you wear over your normal clothes to protect them when you are doing dirty work ▶ **kombinezon**

boiling /ˈbɔɪlɪŋ/ (also ˌ**boiling** ˈ**hot**) adj. (informal) very hot: *Open a window – it's boiling hot in here* (można się tu ugotować.). ◇ *Can I open a window? I'm boiling.* Strasznie mi gorąco. ▶ **bardzo gorący** ➲ note at **cold**

ˈ**boiling point** noun [C] the temperature at which a liquid starts to boil ▶ **temperatura wrzenia**

boisterous /ˈbɔɪstərəs/ adj. (used about a person or behaviour) noisy and full of energy: *Their children are very nice but they can get a bit too boisterous.* ▶ **hałaśliwy**, **żywy**

■ **boisterously** adv. ▶ **hałaśliwie**, **żywo**

bold /bəʊld/ adj. **1** (used about a person or their behaviour) confident and not afraid: *Not many people are bold enough to say exactly what they think.* ▶ **śmiały 2** that you can see clearly: *bold, bright colours* ▶ **wyraźny**, **jaskrawy 3** (used about printed letters) in thick, dark type: *bold type* ▶ **tłusty**

■ **bold** noun [U]: *Highlight the important words **in bold**.* ▶ **tłusty druk** | **boldly** adv. ▶ **śmiało** | **boldness** noun [U] ▶ **śmiałość**

bollard /ˈbɒlɑːd; US -ləd/ noun [C] a short thick post that is used to stop motor vehicles from going into an area that they are not allowed to enter ▶ **słupek drogowy**

bollocks /ˈbɒləks/ noun (Brit., taboo, slang) **1** [U] nonsense: *You're talking a load of bollocks!* ▶ **pierdoły 2** [pl.] a man's **testicles** ▶ **jaja 3** (**Bollocks!**) exclamation (used as a swear word when sb is disagreeing with sth, or when they are angry about sth): *Bollocks! He never said that!* ▶ **Gówno prawda!**

bolshie (also **bolshy**) /ˈbɒlʃi; US ˈbəʊl-/ adj. (Brit., informal) (used about a person) bad-tempered and often refusing to do what people ask them to do ▶ **trudny**, **prowokacyjny**, **buntowniczy**

bolster /ˈbəʊlstə(r)/ verb [T] **bolster sb/sth (up)** to support or encourage sb/sth; to make sth stronger: *His remarks did nothing to bolster my confidence.* ▶ **wzmacniać**, **podpierać**

bolt

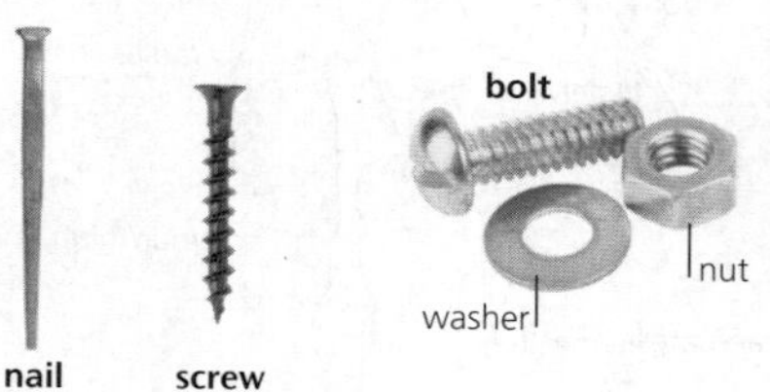

bolt¹ /bəʊlt/ noun [C] **1** a bar of metal that you can slide across the inside of the door in order to fasten it ▶ **rygiel 2** a small piece of metal that is used with a **nut** for fastening things together ▶ **sworzeń**

bolt² /bəʊlt/ verb **1** [T] to fasten a door, etc. with a **bolt¹** (1): *Make sure that the door is locked and bolted.* ▶ **ryglować 2** [T] to fasten one thing to another using a **bolt¹** (2): *All the tables have been bolted to the floor so that nobody can steal them.* ▶ **umacniać sworzniem 3** [I] (used especially about a horse) to run away very suddenly, usually in fear ▶ **wyrywać się 4** [T] **bolt sth (down)** to eat sth very quickly: *She bolted down a sandwich and dashed out of the house.* ▶ **połykać jedzenie (bardzo szybko)**

bolt³ /bəʊlt/ adv.

IDM **bolt upright** sitting or standing very straight ▶ **jakby kij połknął**

bomb¹ /bɒm/ noun **1** [C] a container that is filled with material that will explode when it is thrown or dropped, or when a device inside it makes it explode: *Fortunately, the car bomb failed to **go off**.* ▶ **bomba 2** (**the bomb**) [sing.] nuclear weapons: *How many countries have the bomb now?* ▶ **broń jądrowa 3** (**a bomb**) [sing.] (informal) a lot of money: *That coat must have cost you a bomb* (musiał kosztować fortunę)*!* ▶ **dużo pieniędzy**

bomb² /bɒm/ verb **1** [T] to attack a city, etc. with bombs: *Enemy forces have bombed the bridge.* ▶ **bombardować** ➲ look at **bombard 2** [I] (Brit., informal) **bomb along, down, up, etc.** to move along very fast in the direction mentioned, especially in a vehicle: *He was bombing along at 100 miles an hour when the police stopped him.* ▶ **smarować**, **pruć**

ˈ**bomb alert** (Brit.) = BOMB SCARE

bombard /bɒmˈbɑːd/ verb [T] to attack a place with bombs or guns: *They bombarded the city until the enemy surrendered.* ◇ (figurative) *The reporters bombarded the minister with questions.* ▶ **bombardować** ➲ look at **bomb²**

■ **bombardment** noun [C,U]: *The main radio station has **come under** enemy **bombardment**.* ▶ **bombardowanie**

bombast /ˈbɒmbæst/ noun [U] (formal) words which sound important but have little meaning, used to impress people ▶ (*negatywnie*) **patos**

■ **bombastic** /bɒmˈbæstɪk/ adj.: *a bombastic speaker* ▶ **pompatyczny**

ˈ**bomb disposal** noun [U] the removing or exploding of bombs in order to make an area safe: *a bomb disposal expert* ▶ **usuwanie lub kontrolowane eksplodowanie bomb**

bomber /ˈbɒmə(r)/ noun [C] **1** a type of plane that drops bombs ▶ **bombowiec 2** a person who makes a bomb explode in a public place ▶ **terroryst(k)a**

bombing noun [C,U] an occasion when a bomb is dropped or left somewhere; the act of doing this: *enemy bombing* ◇ *recent bombings in major cities* ▶ **bombardowanie**; **zamach bombowy**

ˈ**bomb scare** (especially US ˈ**bomb threat**; Brit. also ˈ**bomb alert**) noun [C] an occasion when sb says that they have put a bomb somewhere and everyone has to leave the area ▶ **alarm bombowy**

bombshell /ˈbɒmʃel/ noun [C, usually sing.] an unexpected piece of news, usually about sth unpleasant: *The chairman **dropped a bombshell*** (zasunął bombę) *when he said he was resigning.* ▶ **bomba**

bona fide /ˌbəʊnə ˈfaɪdi/ adj. real or genuine: *This car park is for the use of bona fide customers only.* ▶ **prawdziwy**, **autentyczny**

bonanza /bənænzə/ noun [sing.] **1** a situation in which people can make a lot of money or be very successful: *a cash bonanza* (duży gotówkowy zysk) *for investors* ◇ *a bonanza year* (wyjątkowo korzystny rok) *for the computer industry* ▶ **bardzo pomyślna sytuacja** (*zwł. pod względem finansowym*) **2** a large amount of sth pleasant: *the usual bonanza of sport in the summer* ▶ **obfita ilość czegoś przyjemnego**

bon appétit exclamation (used to wish sb an enjoyable meal) ▶ **smacznego!** ℹ Zwrot rzadko stosowany. Najczęściej przed jedzeniem nie mówi się nic.

bond¹ /bɒnd/ noun **1** [C] something that joins two or more people or groups of people together, such as a feeling of friendship: *Our two countries are united by bonds of friendship.* ▶ **więź 2** [C] a certificate that you can buy from a government or company that promises to pay you interest on the money you have given: *government bonds* ▶ **obligacja**

bond² /bɒnd/ verb **1** [I,T] **bond (A and B) (together)**; **bond (A) to B** to join two things together firmly; to join firmly to sth else: *The atoms bond together to form a molecule.* ◇ *This glue cannot be used to bond wood to metal.* ▶ **łączyć (się)**, **spajać (się)** **2** [I] **bond (with sb)** to develop or create a relationship of trust with sb: *Mothers who are depressed sometimes fail to bond with their children.* ▶ **tworzyć emocjonalną więź**

■ **bonding** noun [U] the process of forming a special relationship with sb or with a group of people: *mother-child bonding* ◇ *male bonding* męska przyjaźń ▶ **tworzenie emocjonalnej więzi**

bondage /ˈbɒndɪdʒ/ noun [U] (old-fashioned or formal) the state of being a **slave** or prisoner: (figurative) *women's liberation from the bondage of domestic life* ▶ **niewola** SYN **slavery**

bone¹ /bəʊn/ noun **1** [C] one of the hard parts inside the body of a person or an animal that are covered with muscle, skin, etc.: *He's broken a bone in his hand.* ◇ *This fish has got a lot of bones in it.* ▶ **kość**, **ość** **2** [U] the substance that bones are made of: *knives with bone handles* ▶ **tkanka kostna**

IDM **have a bone to pick with sb** to have sth that you want to complain to sb about ▶ **mieć z kimś na pieńku**

make no bones about (doing) sth to do sth in an open, honest way without feeling nervous or worried about it: *She made no bones about telling him* (powiedziała mu prosto z mostu) *exactly what she thought about him.* ▶ **nie wahać się czegoś zrobić**

bone² /bəʊn/ verb [T] to take the bones out of sth: *to bone a fish* ▶ **obierać mięso z kości/rybę z ości**

ˌbone ˈdry adj. completely dry: *Give that plant some water – it's bone dry.* ▶ **suchy jak pieprz**

ˌbone ˈidle adj. (old-fashioned, Brit., informal) very lazy ▶ **bardzo leniwy**

ˈbone marrow (also **marrow**) noun [U] the soft substance that is inside the bones of a person or an animal ▶ **szpik kostny**

bonfire /ˈbɒnfaɪə(r)/ noun [C] a large fire that you build outside to burn rubbish, as part of a festival, etc. ▶ **ognisko**

ˈBonfire Night noun [C] in Britain, the night of 5 November ▶ **piątego listopada** (*dzień, w którym Brytyjczycy świętują rocznicę nieudanej próby wysadzenia w powietrze Parlamentu przez Guya Fawkesa w 1605 r.*) ℹ W ten dzień puszcza się fajerwerki, a na ognisku pali się kukłę zwaną **guy**.

bong /bɒŋ/ noun [C] **1** the sound made by a large bell ▶ **bim-bom** **2** a long pipe for smoking **cannabis** and other drugs, which passes the smoke through a container of water ▶ **fajka do palenia narkotyków**

bonk /bɒŋk/ noun (Brit., informal) **1** [sing.] an act of sex with sb ▶ (*seks*) **numerek** **2** [C] the act of hitting sb on the head or of hitting your head on sth ▶ **uderzenie (się) w głowę**

■ **bonk** verb **1** [I,T] ▶ **bzykać (się)** **2** [T] ▶ **uderzyć (się) w głowę**

bonkers /ˈbɒŋkəz/ adj. [not before a noun] (slang) crazy: *I'd **go bonkers** if I worked here full-time.* ▶ **świrnięty** SYN **mad**

bonnet /ˈbɒnɪt; US -nət/ noun [C] **1** a type of hat which covers the sides of the face and is fastened with strings under the chin ▶ **czepek** **2** (US **hood**) the front part of a car that covers the engine ▶ **maska samochodu** ➲ picture at **car**, picture on **page A7**

bonny /ˈbɒni/ adj. (**bonnier**; **bonniest**) very pretty; attractive: *a **bonny** baby/**lass*** ▶ **piękny** ℹ Wyraz szkocki.

bonus /ˈbəʊnəs/ noun [C] **1** a payment that is added to what is usual: *All our employees receive an annual bonus.* ▶ **premia** **2** something good that you get in addition to what you expect: *I enjoy my job, and having my own office is **an added bonus**.* ▶ **dodatkowa zaleta**

bon voyage /ˌbɒn vɔɪˈɑːʒ/ exclamation (said to sb who is leaving on a journey, to wish them a good journey) ▶ **szerokiej drogi**

bony /ˈbəʊni/ adj. (**bonier**; **boniest**) so thin that you can see the shape of the bones: *long bony fingers* ▶ **kościsty**

boo /buː/ interj., noun [C] (pl. **boos**) **1** a sound you make to show that you do not like sb/sth: *The minister's speech was met with boos from the audience.* ▶ **buczenie publiczności** (*na znak dezaprobaty*) **2** a sound you make to frighten or surprise sb: *He jumped out from behind the door and said 'boo'* (i huknął). ▶ **huknięcie**

■ **boo** verb [I,T] ▶ **buczeć** (*na znak dezaprobaty*)

boob /buːb/ noun [C] (slang) **1** a woman's breast ▶ **cycek** **2** a silly mistake ▶ **byk**, **gafa** **3** (US) a stupid person ▶ **głupek**

■ **boob** verb [I]: *I'm afraid I've boobed again.* ▶ **strzelić byka**

ˈboob tube noun [C] (Brit., informal) (US **ˈtube top**) a piece of women's clothing that is made of cloth that stretches and covers the chest ▶ **obcisła koszulka damska bez ramiączek**

booby prize /ˈbuːbi praɪz/ (also **wooden spoon**) noun [C] a prize that is given as a joke to the person or team that comes last in a competition ▶ **nagroda pocieszenia**

booby trap /ˈbuːbi træp/ noun [C] a device that will kill, injure or surprise sb when they touch the object that it is connected to ▶ **bomba-pułapka**, **zasadzka**

■ **booby-trap** verb [T] ▶ **urządzać zasadzkę**, **podkładać bombę**

boogie¹ /ˈbuːgi; US ˈbʊgi/ noun (also **ˌboogie-ˈwoogie** /ˈ-wuːgi; US -ˈwʊgi/) [U] a type of blues music played on the piano, with a fast strong rhythm ▶ **muzyka boogie-woogie**

boogie² /ˈbuːgi; US ˈbʊgi/ verb [I] (informal) to dance to fast pop music ▶ **tańczyć w rytmie boogie**

boohoo /ˈbuːhuː; ˌbuːˈhuː/ exclamation (used in written English to show the sound of sb crying) ▶ (*płacz*) **bu** ℹ To słowo jest czasem używane żartobliwie lub przy przedrzeźnianiu.

book¹ /bʊk/ noun **1** [C] a written work that is published as printed pages fastened together inside a cover, or in electronic form: *I'm reading a book on astrology.* ◇ *She's writing a book about her life abroad.* ◇ *Do you have any books by William Golding?* ◇ *hardback/paperback books* ▶ **książka** **2** [C] a number of pieces of paper, fastened together inside a cover, for people to write or draw on: *Please write down all the new vocabulary in your exercise books.* ◇ *a notebook* ◇ *a sketch book* ▶ **zeszyt** **3** [C] a number of things fastened together in the form of a book: *a book of stamps* ◇ *a chequebook* książeczka czekowa ▶ **karnet**, **bloczek** **4** (**books**) [pl.] the records that a company, etc., keeps of the amount of money it spends and receives: *We employ an accountant to **keep the books**.* ▶ **księgi rachunkowe**

IDM **be in sb's good/bad books** (informal) to have sb pleased/angry with you: *He's been in his girlfriend's bad books since he forgot her birthday.* ▶ **mieć plus/krechę u kogoś**

by the book exactly according to the rules: *A policeman must always do things by the book.* ▶ **zgodnie z regulaminem**

(be) on sb's books (to be) on the list of an organization: *The employment agency has hundreds of qualified secretaries on its books.* ▶ **być w rejestrze** (*organizacji*)

books

An **author** is a person who writes a book. The name of a book is its **title**. A **novel** is a book that tells a story, usually divided into **chapters**. The story of sb's life is called a **biography**, or an **autobiography** if a person writes their own life story. You use a **reference book**, for example a **dictionary**, an **atlas** or an **encyclopedia**, to look up information. Reference books usually have a **list of contents** at the front and an **index** at the back, to show you what information the book contains. A **hardback** has a hard **cover** and a **paperback** has a soft cover. Do you prefer reading **fiction** or **non-fiction**?

book² /bʊk/ verb **1** [I,T] to arrange to have or do sth at a particular time: *Have you booked a table, sir?* ◇ *to book a seat on a plane/train/bus* ◇ *I've booked a hotel room for you/I've booked you a hotel room.* ◇ *I'm sorry, but this evening's performance is fully booked.* ▶ **rezerwować** **2** [T] (informal) to officially write down the name of a person who has done sth wrong: *The police booked her for dangerous driving.* ◇ *The player was booked* (otrzymał żółtą kartkę) *for a foul and then sent off for arguing.* ▶ **notować nazwisko**

PHR V **book in** to say that you have arrived at a hotel, etc., and sign your name on a list ▶ **meldować się** (*w hotelu*)

book sb in to arrange a room for sb at a hotel, etc. in advance: *I've booked you in at the George Hotel.* ▶ **rezerwować komuś pokój**

bookbinder /ˈbʊkbaɪndə(r)/ noun [C] a person whose job is fastening the pages of books together and putting covers on them ▶ **introligator/ka**
■ **bookbinding** noun [U] ▶ **introligatorstwo**

bookcase /ˈbʊkkeɪs/ noun [C] a piece of furniture with shelves to keep books on ▶ **regał**

ˈ**book club** noun [C] **1** an organization that sells books cheaply to its members ▶ **klub książki** **2** = BOOK GROUP

ˈ**book group** (also ˈ**book club**; ˈ**reading group**) noun [C] a group of people who meet together regularly to discuss a book they have all read ▶ **dyskusyjny klub książki**

bookie (informal) = BOOKMAKER

booking /ˈbʊkɪŋ/ noun [C,U] the arrangement you make in advance to have a hotel room, a seat on a plane, etc.: *Did you manage to* ***make a booking****?* ◇ *No advance booking is necessary.* ▶ **rezerwacja**

ˈ**booking office** noun [C] an office where you buy tickets ▶ **kasa biletowa**

bookish /ˈbʊkɪʃ/ adj. interested in reading and studying, rather than in more active or practical things ▶ **zainteresowany głównie książkami** ℹ Często wyraża dezaprobatę.

bookkeeper /ˈbʊkkiːpə(r)/ noun [C] a person whose job is to keep an accurate record of the accounts of a business ▶ **księgow-y/a**
■ **bookkeeping** noun [U] ▶ **księgowość**

booklet /ˈbʊklət/ noun [C] a small thin book, usually with a soft cover, that gives information about sth ▶ **broszura**, **książeczka**

bookmaker /ˈbʊkmeɪkə(r)/ (also informal **bookie** /ˈbʊki/) noun **1** [C] a person whose job is to take bets on horse races, etc. ▶ **bukmacher** **2** (**the bookmaker's**) [sing.] a shop, etc. where you can bet money on a race or an event ▶ **punkt bukmacherski**, **biuro bukmacherskie** ➲ look at **betting shop**

bookmark /ˈbʊkmɑːk/ noun [C] **1** a narrow piece of card, etc. that you put between the pages of a book so that you can find the same place again easily ▶ **zakładka** **2** a file from the Internet that you have stored on your computer ▶ (*komputer*) **zakładka**

bookseller /ˈbʊkselə(r)/ noun [C] a person whose job is selling books ▶ **księgarz**

bookshelf /ˈbʊkʃelf/ (pl. **bookshelves** /-ʃelvz/) a shelf that you keep books on ▶ **półka na książki**

bookshop /ˈbʊkʃɒp/ (US **bookstore** /ˈbʊkstɔː(r)/) noun [C] a shop that sells books ▶ **księgarnia**

bookstall /ˈbʊkstɔːl/ (US ˈ**news-stand**) noun [C] a type of small shop, which is open at the front, selling newspapers, magazines and books, for example at a station ▶ **kiosk**

bookstore (US) = BOOKSHOP

ˈ**book token** noun [C] (Brit.) a card, usually given as a gift, that you can exchange for books of a particular value ▶ **bon książkowy**

bookworm /ˈbʊkwɜːm/ noun [C] a person who likes reading books very much ▶ **mól książkowy**

boom¹ /buːm/ noun [C] **1** a period in which sth increases or develops very quickly: *a boom in car sales* ▶ **boom** (*np. gospodarczy*) ➲ look at **slump** **2** [usually sing.] a loud deep sound: *the boom of distant guns* ▶ **grzmot** (*np. armat*)

boom² /buːm/ verb **1** [I,T] **boom (sth) (out)** to make a loud deep sound: *The loudspeaker boomed out instructions to the crowd.* ▶ **grzmieć**; **zabuczeć** **2** [I] to grow very quickly in size or value: *Business is booming in the computer industry.* ▶ **dobrze prosperować**, **rozwijać się pomyślnie**

boomerang /ˈbuːməræŋ/ noun [C] a curved piece of wood that returns to you when you throw it in a particular way ▶ **bumerang**

boon /buːn/ noun [C] a thing that is very helpful and that you are grateful for ▶ **łaska**, **dar**

boorish /ˈbʊərɪʃ; ˈbɔːr-/ adj. (used about people and their behaviour) very unpleasant and rude ▶ **gburowaty**

boost¹ /buːst/ verb [T] to increase sth in number, value or strength: *If we lower the price, that should boost sales.* ◇ *The good exam result boosted her confidence.* ▶ **zwiększać**, **zasilać**

boost² /buːst/ noun [C] something that encourages people; an increase: *The fall in the value of the pound has led to a boost in exports.* ◇ *The president's visit gave a boost to the soldiers' morale.* ▶ **wzrost**; **wzmocnienie**

booster /ˈbuːstə(r)/ noun [C] **1** (also ˈ**booster rocket**) a **rocket** that gives a spacecraft extra power when it leaves the earth, or that makes a **missile** go further ▶ **rakieta nośna** **2** a device that gives extra power to a piece of electrical equipment ▶ **wzmacniacz** **3** an extra small amount of a drug that is given to increase the effect of one given earlier, for example to protect you from a disease for longer: *a tetanus booster* ▶ (*med.*) **dawka przypominająca** **4** a thing that helps, encourages or improves sb/sth: *Her new hairstyle is a real* ***confidence booster.*** Jej nowa fryzura naprawdę dodała jej pewności siebie. ◇ *Mail from home was a much-needed* ***morale booster*** (bardzo potrzebnym wsparciem moralnym) *for the troops.* ▶ **coś, co pomaga, zachęca lub poprawia**

ˈ**booster seat** noun [C] a seat that you put on a car seat, or on a chair at a table, so that a small child can sit higher ▶ **fotelik dziecięcy** (*np. do samochodu*)

boot¹ /buːt/ noun [C] **1** a type of shoe that covers your foot and ankle and often part of your leg: *ski boots* ◇ *walking/climbing boots* ◇ *football boots* ▶ **but z cholewą**, **botek** ➲ picture at **shoe**, picture on **page A1** **2** (US **trunk**) the part of a car where you put luggage, usually at the back: *I'll put the luggage in the boot.* ▶ **bagażnik** ➲ picture at **car**, picture on **page A7**

boot² /buːt/ verb (informal) **1** [T] to kick sth/sb hard: *He booted the ball over the fence.* ▶ **kopać (mocno)** **2** [I,T]

boot (sth) (up) to make a computer ready for use when it is first switched on; to be made ready in this way ▶ **uruchamiać (się)**

PHR V **boot sb/sth out (of sth)** (informal) to force sb/sth to leave a place: *The boys were booted out of the club for fighting.* ▶ **wykopać kogoś/coś (skądś)**

booth /buːð; US buːθ/ noun [C] a small place with thin walls that divide it from the rest of the room or area, where you can do sth that is private: *a phone/photo booth* ◇ *a polling booth* kabina do głosowania ▶ **budka**

bootleg¹ /ˈbuːtleg/ adj. [only before a noun] made and sold illegally: *a bootleg cassette* ▶ **nielegalny**, (*kaseta itp.*) **piracki** ➲ look at **pirate**

■ **bootleg** noun [C]: *a bootleg of the concert* pirackie nagranie koncertu ▶ **nielegalny produkt**

bootleg² /ˈbuːtleg/ (**bootlegging**; **bootlegged**) verb [T] to make or sell goods, especially alcohol, illegally ▶ **produkować lub rozprowadzać nielegalny towar**

■ **bootlegger** noun [C] ▶ **producent lub sprzedawca nielegalnego towaru** | **bootlegging** noun [U] ▶ **produkcja lub sprzedaż nielegalnego towaru**

bootstrap /ˈbuːtstræp/

IDM **pull/drag yourself up by your (own) bootstraps** (informal) to improve your situation yourself, without help from other people ▶ **stanąć na nogi o własnych siłach**

booty /ˈbuːti/ noun [U] things that are taken by thieves or captured by soldiers in a war ▶ **łup** SYN **loot**

booze¹ /buːz/ noun [U] (informal) alcohol ▶ **wóda**

booze² /buːz/ verb [I] (informal) to drink a lot of alcohol: *He went out boozing with some friends on Saturday.* ▶ **chlać**

boozer /ˈbuːzə(r)/ noun [C] (informal) **1** (Brit.) a pub ▶ **pub** **2** a person who drinks a lot of alcohol ▶ **pija-k/czka**

ˈ**booze-up** noun [C] (Brit., informal) an occasion when people drink a lot of alcohol ▶ **popijawa**

bop¹ /bɒp/ noun **1** [C] (Brit., informal) a dance to pop music; a social event at which people dance to pop music ▶ **taniec/impreza przy muzyce pop** **2** [U] a type of **jazz** with complicated rhythms ▶ **odmiana jazzu**

bop² /bɒp/ verb (**bopping**; **bopped**) **1** [I] (Brit., informal) to dance to pop music ▶ **tańczyć do muzyki pop** **2** [T] to hit sb lightly ▶ **uderzać lekko**

⚷ **border¹** /ˈbɔːdə(r)/ noun [C] **1** a line that divides two countries, etc.; the land close to this line: *The refugees escaped* ***across/over the border.*** ◇ *the Moroccan border* ◇ *the border between France and Italy* ◇ *Italy's border with France* ▶ **granica** **2** a band or narrow line around the edge of sth, often for decoration: *a white tablecloth with a blue border* ▶ **brzeg**, **obramowanie**

> **Border** i **frontier** używane są w odniesieniu do linii dzielącej państwa i stany. **Border** zwykle używa się, mówiąc o granicy naturalnej: *The river forms the border between the two countries.* **Boundary** zwykle używa się w odniesieniu do linii dzielącej mniejsze obszary: *the county boundary.*

border² /ˈbɔːdə(r)/ verb [T] to form a border to an area; to be on the border of an area: *The road was bordered* (obsadzona) *with trees.* ▶ **graniczyć**

PHR V **border on sth** **1** to be almost the same as sth: *The dictator's ideas bordered on madness.* ▶ **graniczyć z czymś** **2** to be next to sth: *Our garden borders on the railway line.* ▶ **stykać się z czymś**

borderline /ˈbɔːdəlaɪn/ noun [sing.] the line that marks a division between two different cases, conditions, etc.: *He's* ***a borderline case*** (jest na pograniczu) – *he may pass the exam or he may fail.* ▶ **pogranicze**

⚷ **bore¹** /bɔː(r)/ verb **1** [T] to make sb feel bored, especially by talking too much: *I hope I'm not boring you.* ▶ **nudzić** **2** [I,T] to make a long deep hole with a tool: *This drill can bore (a hole) through solid rock.* ▶ **wiercić** **3** past tense of **bear¹**

bore² /bɔː(r)/ noun **1** [C] a person who talks a lot in a way that is not interesting ▶ **nudzia-rz/ra** **2** [sing.] (informal) something that you have to do that you do not find interesting: *It's such a bore having to learn these lists of irregular verbs.* ▶ **nuda**

⚷ **bored** /bɔːd/ adj. **bored (with sth)** feeling tired and perhaps slightly annoyed because sth is not interesting or because you do not have anything to do: *I'm bored with eating the same thing every day.* ◇ *The children* ***get bored*** *on long journeys.* ◇ *He gave a bored yawn* (ziewnął ze znudzenia). ◇ *The play was awful – we were* ***bored stiff*** (śmiertelnie znudzeni). ▶ **znudzony** ℹ **Be/get bored** często tłumaczy się „nudzić się". Uwaga! **Bored** to „znudzony", a **boring** – „nudny".

boredom /ˈbɔːdəm/ noun [U] the state of being bored: *I sometimes eat out of boredom.* ▶ **nuda**

⚷ **boring** /ˈbɔːrɪŋ/ adj. not interesting; making you feel tired and impatient: *a boring film/job/speech/man* ▶ **nudny** SYN **dull**

⚷ **born¹** /bɔːn/ verb (abbr. **b.**) (**be born**) to come into the world by birth; to start existing: *Where were you born?* ◇ *I was born in London, but I grew up in Leeds.* ◇ *I'm going to give up work after the baby is born.* ◇ *The idea of free education for all was born* (pojawiła się) *in the 19th century.* ◇ *His unhappiness was* ***born out of*** *a feeling of frustration.* ▶ **rodzić się**

born² /bɔːn/ adj. **1** [only before a noun] having a natural ability to do sth: *She's a born leader.* ▶ **urodzony**, **prawdziwy** **2** (**-born**) [in compounds] born in the place or state mentioned: *Samuel Beckett, the Irish-born writer* (z pochodzenia Irlandczyk), *lived in Paris most of his life.* ▶ **urodzony** (*np. w Anglii*)

ˌ**born-aˈgain** adj. [only before a noun] having come to have a strong belief in a particuar religion (especially **evangelical** Christianity) or an idea, and wanting other people to have the same belief: *a born-again Christian* ▶ **odrodzony**

borne past participle of **bear¹**

borough /ˈbʌrə; US ˈbɜːrəʊ/ noun [C] a town, or an area inside a large town, that has some form of local government ▶ **miasto**; **dzielnica**

borrow/lend

She's lending her son some money.

He's borrowing some money from his mother.

⚷ **borrow** /ˈbɒrəʊ/ verb [I,T] **borrow (sth) (from/off sb/sth)** **1** to take or receive sth from sb/sth that you intend to give back, usually after a short time: *I had to borrow from the bank to pay for my car.* ◇ *We'll have to borrow a lot of* *money to buy a car.* ◇ *Could I borrow your pen for a minute?* ◇ *He's always borrowing off his mother.* ◇ *I borrowed a book from the library.* ▶ **pożyczać (od kogoś), wypożyczać**

Uwaga! Nie mylić **borrow** z **lend** (pożyczać komuś): *The bank lent me a thousand pounds.* ◇ *I borrowed a thousand pounds from the bank.*

2 to take sth and use it as your own; to copy sth: *That idea is borrowed from another book.* ▶ **zapożyczać**

borrower /ˈbɒrəʊə(r)/ noun [C] a person who borrows sth ▶ **pożyczający-y/a (od kogoś), dłużnik**

borrowing /ˈbɒrəʊɪŋ/ noun [C,U] the money that a company, an organization or a person borrows; the act of borrowing money: *an attempt to reduce bank borrowings* ◇ *High interest rates help to keep borrowing down.* ▶ **pożyczka; pożyczanie**

bosom /ˈbʊzəm/ noun [sing.] (formal) sb's chest, especially a woman's breasts: *She clutched the child to her bosom.* ▶ **pierś**

IDM **in the bosom of sth** close to; with the protection of: *He was glad to be back in the bosom of his family.* ▶ **na łonie**

ˌbosom ˈfriend noun [C] a very close friend ▶ **serdeczny przyjaciel**

⚷ **boss¹** /bɒs/ noun [C] (informal) a person whose job is to give orders to others at work; an employer; a manager: *I'm going to ask the boss for a day off work.* ◇ *OK. You're the boss.* Dobrze, ty decyduj. ▶ **szef/owa**

boss² /bɒs/ verb [T] **boss sb (about/around)** to give orders to sb, especially in an annoying way: *I wish you'd stop bossing me around.* ▶ **rządzić kimś, narzucać swoją wolę**

bossy /ˈbɒsi/ adj. (**bossier**; **bossiest**) liking to give orders to other people, often in an annoying way: *Don't be so bossy!* ▶ **narzucający swoją wolę**

■ **bossily** adv. ▶ **apodyktycznie** | **bossiness** noun [U] ▶ **apodyktyczność**

botanist /ˈbɒtənɪst/ noun [C] a person who studies plants ▶ **botanik**

botany /ˈbɒtəni/ noun [U] the scientific study of plants ▶ **botanika**

■ **botanical** /bəˈtænɪkl/ adj.: *botanical gardens* ▶ **botaniczny**

botch /bɒtʃ/ verb [T] **botch sth (up)** to do sth badly: *I've completely botched up this typing, I'm afraid.* ▶ **partaczyć** SYN **mess sth up**

⚷ **both** /bəʊθ/ determiner, pron. **1** the two; the one as well as the other: *Both women were French.* ◇ *Both the women were French.* ◇ *Both of the women were French.* ◇ *I liked them both.* ◇ *We were both very tired.* ◇ *Both of us were tired.* ◇ *I've got two sisters. They both live in London/ Both of them live in London.* ℹ Uwaga! Nie można powiedzieć ~~the both sisters~~ ani ~~my both sisters~~. ▶ **obaj, oba** **2 both ... and ...** not only ... but also ...: *Both he and his wife are vegetarian.* ▶ **zarówno ..., jak i ...; i ..., i ...**

⚷ **bother¹** /ˈbɒðə(r)/ verb **1** [I] [usually negative] **bother (to do sth/doing sth)**; **bother (about/with sth)** to make the effort to do sth: *'Shall I make you something to eat?' 'No, don't bother – I'm not hungry.'* ◇ *He didn't even bother* (nawet nie raczył) *to say thank you.* ◇ *Don't bother waiting for me – I'll catch you up later.* ◇ *Don't bother about the washing-up. I'll do it later.* ▶ **fatygować się 2** [T] to disturb or annoy sb: *I'm sorry to bother you, but could I speak to you for a moment?* ◇ *Don't bother Sue with that now* (nie zawracaj Sue teraz tym głowy) *– she's busy.* ▶ **niepokoić, naprzykrzać się** SYN **trouble 3** to worry sb ▶ **martwić**

IDM **can't be bothered (to do sth)** (used to say that you do not want to spend time or energy doing sth): *I can't be bothered to do my homework now. I'll do it tomorrow.* ▶ **nie chcieć zawracać sobie czymś głowy**

not be bothered (about sth) (especially Brit., informal) to think that sth is not important: *'What would you like to do this evening?' 'I'm not bothered really.'* ▶ **być komuś wszystko jedno, być komuś obojętnym**

bother² /ˈbɒðə(r)/ noun [U] trouble or difficulty: *Thanks for all your help. It's saved me a lot of bother.* ▶ **kłopot(y)**

bother³ exclamation (used to express the fact that you are annoyed about sb/sth) ▶ **a niech to ...! o kurczę!**

bothered /ˈbɒðəd/ adj. [not before a noun] worried about sth: *Sam doesn't seem too bothered about losing his job.* ▶ **zmartwiony** ℹ **Be bothered** często tłumaczy się zwrotem „martwić się".

Botox™ /ˈbəʊtɒks/ noun [U] a substance that makes muscles relax. It is sometimes put under the skin around sb's eyes using a needle, in order to remove lines and make the skin look younger. ▶ **botoks**

⚷ **bottle¹** /ˈbɒtl/ noun [C] **1** a glass or plastic container with a narrow neck for keeping liquids in: *a beer bottle* ◇ *an empty bottle* ▶ **butelka 2** the amount of liquid that a bottle can hold: *a bottle of beer* ▶ **butelka** ➲ picture at **container**

bottle² /ˈbɒtl/ verb [T] to put sth into bottles: *After three or four months the wine is bottled.* ◇ *bottled water* woda butelkowana ▶ **rozlewać do butelek, butelkować**

PHR V **bottle sth up** to not allow yourself to express strong emotions: *You'll make yourself ill if you keep your feelings bottled up.* ▶ **dusić coś w sobie**

ˈbottle bank noun [C] a large container in a public place where people can leave their empty bottles so that the glass can be **recycled** ▶ **kontener na butelki do zwrotu**

ˌbottle-ˈgreen adj. (especially Brit.) dark green in colour ▶ **ciemnozielony**

■ **ˌbottle-ˈgreen** noun [U] ▶ **zieleń butelkowa**

bottleneck /ˈbɒtlnek/ noun [C] **1** a narrow piece of road that causes traffic to slow down or stop ▶ **zwężenie jezdni powodujące korek 2** something that makes progress slower, especially in business or industry ▶ **wąskie gardło**

ˈbottle-opener noun [C] a small tool for opening bottles with metal tops, for example beer bottles ▶ **otwieracz do butelek**

⚷ **bottom¹** /ˈbɒtəm/ noun **1** [C, usually sing.] the lowest part of sth: *The house is* ***at the bottom*** *of a hill.* ◇ *I think I've got a pen* ***in the bottom*** *of my bag.* ◇ *The sea is so clear that you can see the bottom.* ▶ **spód, dół, dno** OPP **top 2** [C] the flat surface on the outside of an object, on which it stands: *There's a label* ***on the bottom*** *of the box.* ▶ **spód** OPP **top 3** [sing.] the far end of sth: *The bus stop is* ***at the bottom*** *of the road.* ▶ **koniec** OPP **top 4** [sing.] the lowest position in relation to other people, teams, etc.: *I started* ***at the bottom*** *and now I'm the Managing Director.* ▶ **dół** OPP **top 5** [C] the part of your body that you sit on: *He fell over and landed on his bottom.* ▶ **siedzenie** ➲ picture at **body 6** (**bottoms**) [pl.] the lower part of a piece of clothing that is in two parts: *pyjama bottoms* ◇ *tracksuit bottoms* ▶ **spodnie**

IDM **be at the bottom of sth** to be the cause of sth: *I'm sure Molly Potter is at the bottom of all this* (stoi za tym wszystkim). ▶ **być przyczyną czegoś**

from the (bottom of your) heart → HEART

get to the bottom of sth to find out the real cause of sth ▶ **dochodzić do sedna sprawy**

⚷ **bottom²** /ˈbɒtəm/ adj. [only before a noun] in the lowest position: *the bottom shelf* ◇ *I live on the bottom floor* (na parterze) *of a block of flats.* ▶ **dolny**

bottomless /ˈbɒtəmləs/ adj. very deep; without limit ▶ **bezdenny, niezgłębiony**

ˌbottom ˈline noun [sing.] **1** (**the bottom line**) the most important thing to consider when you are discussing or deciding sth, etc.: *A musical instrument should look and feel good, but the bottom line is how it sounds.* ▶ **sedno sprawy, najważniejszy argument** **2** the final profit or loss that a company has made in a particular period of time ▶ **zysk całkowity, strata całkowita** **3** the lowest price that sb will accept for sth ▶ **cena minimalna**

bough /baʊ/ noun [C] one of the main branches of a tree ▶ **konar, gałąź**

bought past tense, past participle of **buy**[1]

bouillon /ˈbuːjɒn; -jɔ̃/ noun [U,C] a liquid made by boiling meat or vegetables in water, used for making clear soup or sauces ▶ **bulion**

boulder /ˈbəʊldə(r)/ noun [C] a very large rock ▶ **głaz**

boulevard /ˈbuːləvɑːd; US ˈbʊl-/ noun [C] a wide street in a city, often with trees on each side ▶ **bulwar, aleja**

bounce /baʊns/ verb **1** [I,T] (used about a ball, etc.) to move away quickly after it has hit a hard surface; to make a ball do this: *The stone bounced off the wall and hit her on the head.* ◇ *A small boy came down the street, bouncing a ball.* ▶ **odbijać (się)** **2** [I] to jump up and down continuously: *The children were bouncing on their beds.* ▶ **skakać, podskakiwać** ➲ picture at **hop** **3** [I,T] (used about a cheque) to be returned by a bank without payment because there is not enough money in the account ▶ **okazać się bez pokrycia**

■ **bounce** noun [C] ▶ **odbicie (się)**

PHR V **bounce back** to become healthy, successful or happy again after an illness, a failure, or a disappointment ▶ **pozbierać się, wracać do normy**

bouncer /ˈbaʊnsə(r)/ noun [C] a person who is employed to stand at the entrance to a club, pub, etc. to stop people who are not wanted from going in, and to throw out people who are causing trouble inside ▶ **bramkarz** (*np. przed klubem nocnym*)

bouncing /ˈbaʊnsɪŋ/ adj. **bouncing (with sth)** healthy and full of energy: *a bouncing baby boy* ▶ **zdrowy i energiczny**

bouncy /ˈbaʊnsi/ adj. (**bouncier**; **bounciest**) **1** that **bounces** well or that can make things **bounce**: *a bouncy ball/surface* ▶ **dobrze odbijający (się)** **2** (used about a person) full of energy: *She's a very bouncy person.* ▶ **pełen werwy, energiczny** SYN **lively**

⚷ **bound**[1] /baʊnd/ adj. [not before a noun] **1 bound to do sth** certain to do sth: *You've done so much work that you're bound to pass the exam* (na pewno zdasz). ◇ *There are bound to be problems* (na pewno będą problemy) *in a situation like this.* ▶ **z pewnością** **2 bound (by sth) (to do sth)** having a legal or moral duty to do sth: *The company is bound by* (podlega) *UK employment law.* ◇ *She felt bound to refuse the offer.* ▶ **zobowiązany, zmuszony** **3 bound (for...)** travelling to a particular place: *a ship bound for Australia* ▶ **będący w drodze dokądś**

IDM **bound up with sth** closely connected with sth ▶ **związany z czymś**

bound[2] /baʊnd/ verb [I] to run quickly with long steps: *She bounded out of the house to meet us.* ▶ **biec susami**

■ **bound** noun [C]: *With a couple of bounds he had crossed the room.* ▶ **sus**

bound[3] past tense, past participle of **bind**[1]

boundary /ˈbaʊndri/ noun [C] (pl. **boundaries**) a real or imagined line that marks the limits of sth and divides it from other places or things: *national boundaries* ◇ *The road is the boundary between the two districts.* ◇ *Scientists continue to push back the boundaries of human knowledge.* ▶ **granica** ➲ note at **border**

boundless /ˈbaʊndləs/ adj. having no limit: *boundless energy* ▶ **nieograniczony, bezgraniczny**

bounds /baʊndz/ noun [pl.] limits that cannot or should not be passed: *Price rises must be kept within reasonable bounds.* ▶ **granice**

IDM **out of bounds** (used about a place) where people are not allowed to go: *This area is out of bounds to all staff.* Zabrania się wstępu na ten teren wszystkim pracownikom. ▶ **zabroniony**

bountiful /ˈbaʊntɪfl/ adj. (formal) **1** in large quantities; large: *a bountiful supply of food* ▶ **obfity** **2** giving generously: *belief in a bountiful god* ▶ **szczodry** SYN **generous**

bounty /ˈbaʊnti/ noun **1** [U,C] (formal) generous actions; sth provided in large quantities ▶ **hojność; szczodry dar** **2** [C] money given as a reward: *a **bounty hunter*** łowca nagród (za schwytanie poszukiwanych przestępców) ▶ **nagroda pieniężna**

bouquet /buˈkeɪ/ noun [C] a bunch of flowers that is arranged in an attractive way ▶ **bukiet, wiązanka**

bourbon /ˈbɜːbən/ noun [C,U] a type of **whisky** that is made mainly in the US ▶ **rodzaj whisky, burbon**

the **bourgeoisie** /ˌbʊəʒwɑːˈziː/ noun [sing., with sing. or pl. verb] a class of people in society who are interested mainly in having more money and a higher social position ▶ **mieszczaństwo**

■ **bourgeois** /ˈbʊəʒwɑː/ adj.: *bourgeois attitudes/ideas/values* ▶ **mieszczański**

bout /baʊt/ noun [C] **1** a short period of great activity: *a bout of hard work* ▶ **czas** (*poświęcony czemuś*) **2** a period of illness: *I'm just recovering from a bout of flu.* ▶ **atak**

boutique /buːˈtiːk/ noun [C] a small shop that sells fashionable clothes or expensive presents ▶ **butik**

bovine /ˈbəʊvaɪn/ adj. (technical) connected with cows: *bovine diseases* ▶ **bydlęcy, wołowy**

bow[1] /baʊ/ verb [I,T] **bow (sth) (to sb)** to bend your head or the upper part of your body forward and down, as a sign of respect: *The speaker bowed to the guests and left the stage.* ◇ *He bowed his head respectfully.* ▶ **kłaniać się, skłaniać**

PHR V **bow out (of sth/as sth)** to leave an important position or stop taking part in sth: *After a long and successful career, she has decided to bow out of politics.* ◇ *He finally bowed out as chairman after ten years.* ▶ **żegnać się (z czymś)**

bow to sb/sth to accept sth: *They finally bowed to pressure from the public.* ▶ **uginać się przed kimś/czymś**

bow[2] /baʊ/ noun [C] **1** an act of **bowing**[1] (1): *The director of the play came on stage to **take a bow**.* ▶ **ukłon** **2** the front part of a ship ▶ **dziób** OPP **stern** ➲ note at **boat** ➲ picture on **page A6**

bow[3] /bəʊ/ noun [C] **1** a weapon for shooting arrows. A **bow** is a curved piece of wood that is held in shape by a tight string. ▶ **łuk** ➲ picture at **arch** **2** a knot with two loose round parts and two loose ends that you use when you are tying shoes, etc.: *He tied his laces **in a bow**.* ▶ **kokard(k)a** **3** a long thin piece of wood with hair stretched across it that you use for playing some musical instruments: *a violin bow* ▶ **smyczek**

bowel /ˈbaʊəl/ noun [C, usually pl.] one of the tubes that carries waste food away from your stomach to the place where it leaves your body ▶ **jelito, kiszka**

⚷ **bowl**[1] /bəʊl/ noun [C] **1** a deep round dish without a lid that is used for holding food or liquid: *a soup bowl* miseczka do zupy ◇ *a mixing bowl* misa do mieszania ◇ *a sugar bowl* cukiernica ◇ *a salad bowl* salaterka ▶ **miska** ➲ look at **plate** **2** a large plastic container that is used for washing dishes, washing clothes, etc.: *a washing-up bowl* ▶ **miska, miednica** **3** the amount of sth that is in a bowl: *I usually have a bowl of cereal for breakfast.* ▶ **miska, miseczka**

bowl² /bəʊl/ verb [I,T] (in games such as **cricket**) to throw the ball in the direction of the person with the **bat** ▶ **serwować**
PHR V **bowl sb over 1** to knock sb down when you are moving quickly ▶ **przewracać kogoś 2** to surprise sb very much in a pleasant way: *I was absolutely bowled over by the beautiful scenery.* ▶ **zadziwiać kogoś, wprawiać kogoś w podziw**

bow legs /ˌbəʊ ˈlegz/ noun [pl.] legs that curve out at the knees ▶ **kabłąkowate nogi**
■ **bow-legged** /ˌbəʊ ˈlegɪd/ adj. ▶ **o kabłąkowatych nogach**

bowler /ˈbəʊlə(r)/ noun [C] **1** (in the sport of **cricket**) the player who throws the ball in the direction of the person with the **bat** ▶ (*krykiet*) **gracz serwujący piłkę** ➲ note at **cricket** ➲ picture on **page A8 2** (also ˌ**bowler ˈhat**; US **derby**) a round hard black hat, usually worn by men ▶ **melonik**

bowling /ˈbəʊlɪŋ/ noun [U] a game in which you roll a heavy ball down a special track (**lane**) towards a group of wooden objects shaped like bottles (**pins**) and try to knock them all down: *to go bowling* ◇ *a bowling alley* kręgielnia ▶ **gra w kręgle** ➲ look at **skittles**

bowls /bəʊlz/ noun [U] a game in which you try to roll large wooden balls as near as possible to a smaller ball: *to play bowls* ▶ **gra w kule**

bow tie /ˌbəʊ ˈtaɪ/ noun [C] a tie in the shape of a **bow³** (2), that is worn by men, especially on formal occasions ▶ **muszka**

⚷ **box¹** /bɒks/ noun **1** [C] a container made of wood, cardboard, metal, etc. with a flat stiff base and sides and often a lid; a box and the things inside it: *a cardboard box* ◇ *a shoebox* ◇ *a box of chocolates/matches/tissues* ▶ **pudło, pudełko** ➲ picture at **container 2** [C] a small area with walls on all sides that is used for a particular purpose: *a telephone box* ◇ *the jury box* ława przysięgłych ◇ *a witness box* miejsce w sądzie dla świadków obrony lub oskarżenia ▶ **budka 3** [C] a small area in a theatre separated off from where other people sit ▶ **loża 4** [C] an empty square on a form in which you have to write sth: *Write your full name in the box below.* ▶ **ramka 5** (**the box**) [sing.] (Brit., informal) TV: *What's on the box tonight?* ▶ **telewizor, telewizja**

box² /bɒks/ verb **1** [I,T] to fight in the sport of **boxing** ▶ **boksować** ➲ picture on **page A9 2** [T] to put sth into a box ▶ **pakować do pudełka**
PHR V **box sb/sth in** to prevent sb from getting out of a small space: *Someone parked behind us and boxed us in.* ▶ **zablokować**

boxed /bɒkst/ adj. put and/or sold in a box: *a boxed set of original recordings* ▶ (*zestaw*) **w pudełku**

boxer /ˈbɒksə(r)/ noun [C] a person who does **boxing** as a sport ▶ **bokser/ka**

ˈ**boxer shorts** (also **boxers**) noun [pl.] short trousers that men use as underwear ▶ **bokserki**

boxing /ˈbɒksɪŋ/ noun [U] a sport in which two people fight by hitting each other with their hands inside large gloves: *the world middleweight boxing champion* ◇ *boxing gloves* ▶ **boks**

ˈ**Boxing Day** noun [U,C] (Brit.) the day after Christmas Day; 26 December ▶ **drugi dzień Świąt Bożego Narodzenia** ℹ W Anglii i Walii **Boxing Day** jest dniem wolnym od pracy.

ˈ**box lunch** noun [C] (US) a meal of **sandwiches**, fruit, etc. that you take to school, work, etc. in a box ▶ **kanapki itp. przygotowane jako drugie śniadanie do zjedzenia poza domem** (*zapakowane w specjalny pojemnik*) ➲ look at **packed lunch**

ˈ**box number** noun [C] a number used as an address, especially in newspaper advertisements ▶ **numer przydzielany ogłoszeniodawcy, na który są przysyłane oferty**

ˈ**box office** noun [C] the place in a cinema, theatre, etc. where the tickets are sold ▶ **kasa biletowa**

⚷ **boy¹** /bɔɪ/ noun **1** [C] a male child or a young man: *They've got three children – two boys and a girl.* ◇ *I used to play here when I was a boy.* ▶ **chłopiec 2** (**the boys**) [pl.] (informal) a group of male friends who often go out together: *a night out with the boys* ▶ **chłopcy, chłopaki**

boy² exclamation (especially US, informal) (used to express feelings of surprise, pleasure, pain, etc.) ▶ **ojej!**

boycott /ˈbɔɪkɒt/ verb [T] to refuse to buy things from a particular company, take part in an event, etc. because you do not approve of it: *Several countries boycotted the Olympic Games in protest.* ▶ **bojkotować**
■ **boycott** noun [C]: *a boycott of the local elections* ▶ **bojkot**

⚷ **boyfriend** /ˈbɔɪfrend/ noun [C] a man or boy with whom a person has a romantic and/or sexual relationship ▶ **chłopak, sympatia**

boyhood /ˈbɔɪhʊd/ noun [U] the time of being a boy: *My father told me some of his boyhood memories.* ▶ **chłopięce lata**

boyish /ˈbɔɪɪʃ/ adj. like a boy: *a boyish smile* ▶ **chłopięcy**

ˌ**Boy ˈScout** noun [C] (US or old-fashioned) a boy who is a member of the **Scouts** ▶ **skaut**

bra /brɑː/ noun [C] a piece of clothing that women wear under their other clothes to support their breasts ▶ **biustonosz**

brace¹ /breɪs/ noun **1** [C] (US **braces** [pl.]) a metal frame that is fixed to a child's teeth in order to make them straight ▶ **aparat ortodontyczny 2** (**braces**) (US **suspenders**) [pl.] a pair of narrow pieces of **elastic** that go over your shoulders to hold your trousers up ▶ **szelki**

brace² /breɪs/ verb [T] **1 brace yourself (for sth)** to prepare yourself for sth unpleasant: *You'd better brace yourself for some bad news.* ▶ **przygotowywać się (na coś) 2 brace sth/yourself (against sth)** to press your body or part of your body firmly against sth in order to stop yourself from falling ▶ **zbierać się w sobie; zapierać się** (*np. nogami*)

bracelet /ˈbreɪslət/ noun [C] a piece of jewellery, for example a metal chain or band, that you wear around your wrist or arm ▶ **bransoletka** ➲ picture at **jewellery**

bracing /ˈbreɪsɪŋ/ adj. making you feel healthy and full of energy: *bracing sea air* ▶ **orzeźwiający, ożywczy**

bracken /ˈbrækən/ noun [U] a wild plant with large leaves that grows on hills and in woods and turns brown in the autumn ▶ **orlica** (*paproć*)

bracket¹ /ˈbrækɪt/ noun [C] **1** (especially US **parenthesis**) [usually pl.] one of two marks, () or [ ], that you put round extra information in a piece of writing: *A translation of each word is given **in brackets**.* ▶ **nawias 2 age, income, price, etc. bracket** prices, ages, etc. which are between two limits: *to be in a high income bracket* ◇ *The magazine is aimed at people in the 30-40 age bracket* (w przedziale wiekowym 30-40 lat). ▶ **grupa 3** a piece of metal or wood that is fixed to a wall and used as a support for a shelf, lamp, etc. ▶ **podpórka, klamra**

bracket² /ˈbrækɪt/ verb [T] **1** to put a word, number, etc. between **brackets¹** (1) ▶ **brać w nawias 2 bracket A and B (together)**; **bracket A with B** to think of two or more people or things as similar in some way ▶ **łączyć, grupować**

brackish /ˈbrækɪʃ/ adj. (used about water) salty in an unpleasant way ▶ (*woda*) **słonawy**

brag /bræg/ verb [I] (**bragging**; **bragged**) **brag (to sb) (about/of sth)** to talk in a very proud way about sth: *She's always* *bragging to her friends about how clever she is.* ▶ **przechwalać się**

braggart /ˈbræɡət/ noun [C] (old-fashioned) a person who brags ▶ **samochwała**

braid /breɪd/ noun **1** [U] thin coloured rope that is used to decorate military uniforms, etc. ▶ **galon 2** (US) = PLAIT ▶ **warkocz 3** (US) = PIGTAIL

Braille /breɪl/ noun [U] a system of printing, using little round marks that are higher than the level of the paper they are on and which people who cannot see can read by touching them: *The signs were written* ***in Braille.*** ▶ **alfabet Braille'a**

brain /breɪn/ noun **1** [C] the part of your body inside your head that controls your thoughts, feelings and movements: *damage to the brain* ◇ *a brain tumour* ◇ *a brain surgeon* ▶ **mózg** ➲ picture at **body 2** [C,U] the ability to think clearly; intelligence: *She has a very quick brain and learns fast.* ◇ *He hasn't got the brains to be a doctor.* ▶ **umysł, rozum, głowa 3** [C] (informal) a very clever person: *He's one of the best brains in the country.* ▶ **tęga głowa 4** (**the brains**) [sing.] the person who plans or organizes sth: *She's the real brains in the organization.* ▶ **mózg**

IDM **have sth on the brain** (informal) to think about sth all the time: *I've had that song on the brain all day.* Ta piosenka chodzi mi po głowie cały dzień.

rack your brains → RACK²

brainbox /ˈbreɪnbɒks/ noun [C] (Brit., informal) a person who is very intelligent ▶ **tęga głowa**

brainchild /ˈbreɪntʃaɪld/ noun [sing.] the idea, plan, design, etc. of a particular person: *The music festival was the brainchild of a young teacher.* ▶ **(genialny) pomysł, wynalazek**

ˈ**brain damage** noun [U] permanent damage to the brain caused by illness or an accident ▶ **uszkodzenie mózgu** ■ ˈ**brain-damaged** adj. ▶ **z uszkodzeniem mózgu**

ˈ**brain-dead** adj. **1** having serious brain damage and needing a machine to stay alive ▶ **w stanie śmierci mózgowej 2** (informal) unable to think clearly; stupid: *He's brain-dead from watching too much TV.* ▶ (*przen.*) **ogłupiały, głupi**

ˈ**brain drain** noun [sing.] (informal) the movement of highly skilled and qualified people to a country where they can work in better conditions and earn more money ▶ **drenaż mózgów**

brainless /ˈbreɪnləs/ adj. (informal) very silly; stupid ▶ **głupi**

brainpower /ˈbreɪnpaʊə(r)/ noun [U] the ability to think; intelligence ▶ **inteligencja**

brainstorm¹ /ˈbreɪnstɔːm/ noun [C] **1** a moment of sudden confusion: *I* ***had a brainstorm*** *in the exam and couldn't answer any questions.* ▶ **zaćmienie umysłu 2** (US) = BRAINWAVE

brainstorm² /ˈbreɪnstɔːm/ verb [I,T] to solve a problem or make a decision by thinking of as many ideas as possible in a short time: *We'll spend five minutes brainstorming ideas on how we can raise money.* ▶ **przeprowadzać burzę mózgów, dyskutować**

■ **brainstorming** noun [U] a way of making a group of people all think about sth at the same time, often in order to solve a problem or to create good ideas: *a brainstorming session* ▶ **burza mózgów**

ˈ**brain-teaser** noun [C] a problem that is difficult but fun to solve ▶ **łamigłówka**

brainwash /ˈbreɪnwɒʃ/ verb [T] **brainwash sb (into doing sth)** to force sb to believe sth by using strong mental pressure: *TV advertisements try to brainwash people into buying things that they don't need.* ▶ **ogłupiać, mącić komuś w głowie**

■ **brainwashing** noun [U] ▶ **ogłupianie, pranie mózgu**

brainwave /ˈbreɪnweɪv/ (US **brainstorm**) noun [C] (informal) a sudden clever idea: *If I* ***have a brainwave,*** *I'll let you know.* ▶ **natchnienie, genialny pomysł**

brainy /ˈbreɪni/ adj. (**brainier**; **brainiest**) (informal) intelligent ▶ **rozgarnięty**

braise /breɪz/ verb [T] to cook meat or vegetables slowly in a little liquid in a covered dish ▶ **dusić** ➲ note at **cook¹**

brake¹ /breɪk/ noun [C] **1** the part of a vehicle that makes it go slower or stop: *She put her foot on the brake and just managed to stop in time.* ▶ **hamulec** ➲ picture at **bicycle**, **car 2** something that makes sth else slow down or stop: *The Government must try to* ***put a brake on*** *inflation.* ▶ **hamulec**

brake² /breɪk/ verb [I] to make a vehicle go slower or stop by using the **brakes**: *If the driver hadn't braked in time, the car would have hit me.* ▶ **hamować**

ˈ**brake light** (US ˈ**stop light**) noun [C] a red light on the back of a vehicle that comes on when the brakes are used ▶ **światło stopu**

bramble /ˈbræmbl/ noun [C] (Brit.) a wild bush on which **blackberries** grow ▶ **jeżyna**

bran /bræn/ noun [U] the brown outer covering of grains that is left when the grain is made into flour ▶ **otręby** (*np. pszenne*)

branch¹ /brɑːntʃ; US bræn-/ noun [C] **1** one of the main parts of a tree that grows out of the **trunk**: *He climbed the tree and sat on a branch.* ▶ **gałąź 2** an office, shop, etc. that is part of a larger organization: *The company I work for has branches in Paris, Milan and New York.* ▶ **oddział, filia 3** a part of an academic subject: *Psychiatry is a branch of medicine.* ▶ **gałąź, dziedzina**

branch² /brɑːntʃ; US bræn-/ verb

PHR V **branch off** (used about a road) to leave a larger road and go off in another direction: *A bit further on, the road branches off to the left.* ▶ **rozgałęziać się, rozwidlać się**

branch out (into sth) to start doing sth new and different from the things you usually do: *The band has recently branched out into acting.* ▶ **poszerzać działalność**

brand¹ /brænd/ noun [C] **1** the name of a product that is made by a particular company: *a well-known brand of coffee* ▶ **znak firmowy, gatunek 2** a particular type of sth: *a strange brand of humour* ▶ **rodzaj, gatunek**

brand² /brænd/ verb [T] **1 brand sb (as sth)** to say that sb has a bad character so that people have a bad opinion of them: *She was branded as a troublemaker* (została określona mianem wichrzycielki) *after she complained about her long working hours.* ▶ **piętnować 2** to mark an animal with a hot iron to show who owns it ▶ **piętnować**

branded /ˈbrændɪd/ adj. [only before a noun] (used about a product) made by a well-known company and having that company's name on it: ***branded drugs/goods/products*** ▶ **markowy**

branding /ˈbrændɪŋ/ noun [U] the activity of giving a particular name and image to goods and services so that people will be attracted to them and want to buy them ▶ **wyrabianie marki**

brandish /ˈbrændɪʃ/ verb [T] to wave sth in the air in an aggressive or excited way: *The robber was brandishing a knife.* ▶ **wymachiwać, potrząsać**

ˈ**brand name** (also ˈ**trade name**) noun [C] the name given to a product by the company that produces it ▶ **nazwa firmowa**

ˌ**brand ˈnew** adj. completely new ▶ **fabrycznie nowy, nowiutki, nieużywany**

brandy /ˈbrændi/ noun [C,U] (pl. **brandies**) a strong alcoholic drink that is made from wine ▶ **brandy** ➲ look at **cognac**

brash /bræʃ/ adj. too confident and direct: *Her brash manner makes her unpopular with strangers.* ▶ **zuchwały**
■ **brashness** noun [U] ▶ **zuchwałość**

brass /brɑːs; US bræs/ noun **1** [U] a hard yellow metal that is a mixture of **copper** and **zinc**: *brass buttons on a uniform* ▶ **mosiądz 2** [sing., with sing. or pl. verb] the group of musical instruments that are made of **brass**: *the brass section in an orchestra* ◇ *He plays the trumpet in a brass band* (w orkiestrze dętej). ▶ **instrumenty blaszane**
➲ note at **instrument**

ˌ**brassed 'off** adj. (Brit., slang) annoyed ▶ **wkurzony** SYN **fed up**

brasserie /'bræsəri; US ˌbræsə'riː/ noun [C] a type of restaurant, often in a French style, that is not very expensive ▶ **restauracyjka**

brassière /'bræziə(r); US brə'z-/ noun [C] (formal) = BRA

brassy /'brɑːsi; US 'bræs-/ adj. **1** (used about music) loud and unpleasant ▶ **wrzaskliwy 2** (informal) (used about a woman) dressing in a way that makes her sexual attraction obvious, but without style: *the brassy blonde behind the bar* ▶ (*wygląd*) **wyzywający** ⓘ Wyraża dezaprobatę.

brat /bræt/ noun [C] a child who behaves badly and annoys you ▶ **bachor**

bravado /brə'vɑːdəʊ/ noun [U] a confident way of behaving that is intended to impress people, sometimes as a way of hiding a lack of confidence ▶ **brawura**

🔑 **brave**[1] /breɪv/ adj. **1** ready to do things that are dangerous or difficult without showing fear: *the brave soldiers who fought in the war* ◇ *'This may hurt a little, so try and be brave,' said the dentist.* ▶ **odważny 2** needing or showing courage: *a brave decision* ▶ **odważny**
■ **bravely** adv.: *The men bravely defended the town for three days.* ▶ **odważnie**

brave[2] /breɪv/ verb [T] to face sth unpleasant, dangerous or difficult without showing fear: *She braved the rain and went out into the street.* Nie bacząc na deszcz, wyszła na ulicę. ▶ **stawiać czoło**

bravery /'breɪvəri/ noun [U] actions that are **brave**: *After the war he received a medal for bravery.* ▶ **odwaga** SYN **courage**

bravo /ˌbrɑː'vəʊ/ interj. a word that people shout to show that they have enjoyed sth that sb has done, for example a play ▶ **brawo**

bravura /brə'vjʊərə/ noun [U] (formal) great skill and enthusiasm in doing sth artistic: *a bravura performance* brawurowy występ ▶ **brawura**

brawl /brɔːl/ noun [C] a noisy fight among a group of people, usually in a public place ▶ **burda, bijatyka**
■ **brawl** verb [I]: *We saw some football fans brawling in the street.* ▶ **awanturować się**

brawn /brɔːn/ noun [U] physical strength: *To do this kind of job you need more brawn than brain.* ▶ **krzepa, tężyzna**
■ **brawny** adj.: *He folded his brawny arms across his chest.* ▶ **muskularny**

bray /breɪ/ verb **1** [I] when a **donkey brays**, it makes a loud, unpleasant sound ▶ (*osioł*) **ryczeć 2** [I,T] (used about a person) to talk or laugh in a loud, unpleasant voice: *He brayed with laughter.* ▶ **ryczeć** (*np. ze śmiechu*)

brazen[1] /'breɪzn/ adj. without embarrassment, especially in a way which shocks people: *Don't believe a word she says – she's a brazen liar!* ▶ **bezwstydny, bezczelny**
■ **brazenly** adv.: *He brazenly admitted he'd been having an affair.* ▶ **bezwstydnie, bezczelnie**

brazen[2] /'breɪzn/ verb
PHR V **brazen it out** to cope with an embarrassing or difficult situation by behaving as if you are not embarrassed or ashamed: *Now that everyone knew the truth, the only thing to do was to brazen it out.* ▶ **nie okazywać wstydu** (*w żenującej/trudnej sytuacji*)

brazier /'breɪziə(r)/ noun [C] a large metal container that holds a fire and is used to keep people warm when they are outside ▶ **koksownik**

brazil /brə'zɪl/ (also **bra'zil nut**) noun [C] a nut that we eat, with a very hard shell that has three sides ▶ **orzech brazylijski**

breach[1] /briːtʃ/ noun **1** [C,U] **breach (of sth)** an act that breaks an agreement, a law, etc.: *Giving private information about clients is a breach of confidence* (nadużycie zaufania). ◇ *The company was found to be **in breach of** contract.* Odkryto, że firma naruszyła warunki umowy. ▶ **naruszenie 2** [C] a break in friendly relations between people, groups, etc.: *The incident caused a breach between the two countries.* ▶ **zerwanie stosunków 3** [C] an opening in a wall, etc. that defends or protects sb/sth: *The waves made a breach in the sea wall.* ▶ **wyłom, wyrwa**

breach[2] /briːtʃ/ verb [T] **1** to break an agreement, a law, etc.: *He accused the Government of breaching international law.* ▶ **naruszać, gwałcić 2** to make an opening in a wall, etc. that defends or protects sb/sth ▶ **robić wyłom/wyrwę**

🔑 **bread** /bred/ noun [U] a type of food made from flour, water and usually **yeast** mixed together and baked in an oven ▶ **chleb** ⓘ **Bread** jest wyrazem niepoliczalnym, dlatego mówimy **a piece/slice of bread** lub **some bread** (nie ~~*a bread*~~).

ˌ**bread and 'butter** noun [U] **1** slices of bread that have been spread with butter: *a piece of bread and butter* ▶ **chleb z masłem 2** (informal) a person or company's main source of income ▶ **źródło utrzymania**

'**bread bin** (US **breadbox** /'bredbɒks/) noun [C] a wooden, metal or plastic container for keeping bread in so that it stays fresh ▶ **pojemnik na pieczywo**

breadboard /'bredbɔːd/ noun [C] a flat board used for cutting bread on ▶ **deska do krojenia chleba**

breadcrumbs /'bredkrʌmz/ noun [pl.] very small pieces of bread that are used in cooking ▶ **bułka tarta**

breaded /ˈbredɪd/ adj. covered in breadcrumbs ▶ **panierowany**

breadline /ˈbredlaɪn/ noun [sing.] (Brit.) the level of income of very poor people: *Many people without jobs are living **on the breadline*** (na granicy nędzy). ▶ **minimum socjalne**

breadstick /ˈbredstɪk/ noun [C] **1** a long thin piece of bread, which is dry like a biscuit ▶ **twarda pałeczka chlebowa**, **paluszek** (*np. słony, kruchy*) **2** a piece of fresh bread, baked in the shape of a small stick ▶ **miękka pałeczka chlebowa**

breadth /bredθ/ noun [U] **1** the distance between the two sides of sth: *We measured the length and breadth of the garden.* ▶ **szerokość** SYN **width 2** the wide variety of things, subjects, etc. that sth includes: *I was amazed by the breadth of her knowledge* (jej rozległą wiedzą). ▶ **szerokość**, **zasięg** ➲ adjective **broad**
IDM **the length and breadth of sth** → LENGTH

breadwinner /ˈbredwɪnə(r)/ noun [C, usually sing.] the person who earns most of the money that their family needs: *When his dad died, Steve became the breadwinner.* ▶ **żywiciel/ka rodziny**

break[1] /breɪk/ verb (pt **broke** /brəʊk/, pp **broken** /ˈbrəʊkən/) **1** [I,T] to separate, or make sth separate, into two or more pieces: *She dropped the vase onto the floor and it broke.* ◇ *He broke his leg in a car accident.* ▶ **łamać (się)**, **rozbijać (się) 2** [I,T] (used about a machine, etc.) to stop working; to stop a machine, etc. working: *The photocopier has broken.* ◇ *Be careful with my camera – I don't want you to break it.* ▶ **psuć (się) 3** [T] to do sth that is against the law, or against what has been agreed or promised: *to break the law/rules* ◇ *to break a contract* zerwać kontrakt ◇ *Slow down! You're breaking* (przekraczasz) *the speed limit.* ◇ *Don't worry – I never break my promises.* ▶ **naruszać**; **nie dotrzymywać 4** [I,T] to stop doing sth for a short time: *Let's break for coffee now.* ◇ *We decided to break the journey and stop for lunch.* ▶ **przerywać**, **robić przerwę 5** [T] to make sth end: *Suddenly, the silence was broken by the sound of a bird singing.* ◇ *Once you start smoking it's very difficult to **break the habit*** (zerwać z nałogiem). ▶ **przerywać**, **przełamywać 6** [I] to begin: *Day was breaking* (świtało) *as I left the house.* ◇ *We ran indoors when the storm broke* (zerwała się burza). **7** [I] if a piece of news **breaks**, it becomes known: *When the story broke in the newspapers* (kiedy wiadomość ukazała się w gazetach), *nobody could believe it.* ▶ **zostawać rozpowszechnionym 8** [I] (used about a wave) to reach its highest point and begin to fall: *I watched the waves breaking on the rocks.* ▶ **rozbijać się 9** [I] (used about a voice) to change its tone because of emotion: *His voice was breaking with emotion as he told us the awful news.* ▶ **łamać się 10** [I] (used about a boy's voice) to become permanently deeper, usually at about the age of 13 or 14 ▶ **przechodzić mutację 11** [T] to do sth better, faster, etc. than anyone has ever done it before: *She broke the world 100 metres record.* ▶ **pobić rekord** ℹ **Break** używa się w idiomach, np. **break even**. Zob. hasła odpowiednich rzeczowników, przymiotników itp.
PHR V **break away (from sb/sth) 1** to escape suddenly from sb who is holding you ▶ **wyzwalać się**, **uciekać 2** to leave a political party, state, etc. in order to form a new one ▶ **wyłamywać się**, **odłączać się**
break down 1 (used about a vehicle or machine) to stop working: *Akram's car broke down on the way to work this morning.* ▶ **psuć się** ➲ note at **car 2** (used about a system, discussion, etc.) to fail: *Talks between the two countries have completely broken down.* ▶ **załamywać się**, **kończyć się niepowodzeniem 3** to lose control of your feelings and start crying: *He broke down in tears when he heard the news.* ▶ **załamywać się**
break sth down 1 to destroy sth by using force: *The police had to break down the door to get into the house.* ▶ **wyłamywać coś 2** to make a substance separate into parts or change into a different form in a chemical process: *Food is broken down in our bodies by the digestive system.* ▶ **rozkładać coś na czynniki**
break in to enter a building by force, usually in order to steal sth ▶ **włamywać się**
break in (on sth) to interrupt when sb else is speaking: *She longed to break in on their conversation but didn't want to appear rude.* ▶ **wtrącać się** (*np. do rozmowy*)
break into sth 1 to enter a place that is closed: *Thieves broke into his car and stole the radio.* ◇ (figurative) *The company is trying to break into the Japanese market.* ▶ **włamywać się do czegoś 2** to start doing sth suddenly: *She broke into a run/song.* Nagle zaczęła biec/śpiewać. ◇ *He broke into a smile* (nagle uśmiechnął się) *when he heard the good news.* ▶ **nagle zaczynać coś robić**
break off to suddenly stop doing or saying sth: *He started speaking and then broke off in the middle of a sentence.* ▶ **zatrzymywać się**
break (sth) off to remove a part of sth by force; to be removed in this way: *Could you break off another bit of chocolate for me?* ▶ **odłamywać się/coś**
break sth off to end a relationship suddenly: *After a bad argument, they decided to **break off** their **engagement**.* ▶ **zrywać coś**
break out (used about fighting, wars, fires, etc.) to start suddenly ▶ **wybuchać**
break out in sth to suddenly have a skin problem: *I broke out in a rash.* Dostałam wysypki na całym ciele. ◇ *He broke out in a cold sweat.* Oblał go zimny pot. ▶ (*skóra, twarz itp.*) **pokryć się czymś**
break out (of sth) to escape from a prison, etc. ▶ **uciekać z czegoś**
break through (sth) to manage to get past sth that is stopping you: *The protesters were trying to break through the line of police.* ▶ **przedrzeć się (przez coś)**
break up 1 to separate into smaller pieces: *The ship broke up on the rocks.* ▶ **rozbijać się 2** (used about events that involve a group of people) to end or finish: *The meeting broke up just before lunch.* ◇ *My marriage broke up* (rozpadło się) *when I was 35.* ▶ **zakończyć się 3** (Brit.) to start school holidays: *When do you break up for the summer holidays?* ▶ **kończyć naukę przed feriami lub wakacjami**
break sth up 1 to make sth separate into smaller pieces ▶ **podzielić 2** to make people leave sth or stop doing sth, especially by using force: *The police arrived and broke up* (przerwali) *the fight.* ▶ **rozpraszać** (*tłum*)
break up (with sb) to end a relationship with sb: *She's broken up with her boyfriend.* ▶ **zrywać z kimś**
break with sth to end a relationship or connection with sb/sth: *to break with tradition/the past* ▶ **zrywać z czymś**

break[2] /breɪk/ noun [C] **1** a short period of rest: *We worked all day without a break.* ◇ *to **take a break*** zrobić sobie przerwę ▶ **przerwa** ➲ note at **interval 2 break (in sth)**; **break (with sb/sth)** a change from what usually happens or an end to sth: *The incident led to a break in diplomatic relations.* ◇ *She wanted to make a complete break with the past.* ▶ **wyłom**, **zerwanie 3** an opening or space in sth: *Wait for a break in the traffic before you cross the road.* ▶ **przerwa**, **luka 4** a place where sth has been broken: *The X-ray showed there was no break in his leg.* ▶ **złamanie**, **stłuczenie**, **pęknięcie 5** (informal) a piece of good luck: *I got my **lucky break** when I won the 'Young Journalist of the Year' competition.* ▶ **szansa**, **okazja**
IDM **break of day** the time when light first appears in the morning ▶ **brzask**, **świt** SYN **dawn**

B

give sb a break 1 (used to tell sb to stop saying things that are annoying or not true): *Give me a break and stop nagging, OK!* ▶ **zostawiać kogoś w spokoju 2** (especially US) to be fair to sb ▶ **dać komuś szansę**

breakable /ˈbreɪkəbl/ adj. likely to break, easily broken ▶ **łamliwy, łatwo tłukący się**

breakage /ˈbreɪkɪdʒ/ noun [C, usually pl.] something that has been broken: *Customers must pay for any breakages.* ▶ **stłuczka, rozbicie**

breakaway /ˈbreɪkəweɪ/ adj. [only before a noun] (used about a political group, an organization, or a part of a country) that has separated from a larger group or country ▶ **oderwany**
■ **breakaway** noun [sing.] **1** an occasion when members of a political party or an organiazation leave it in order to form a new party, etc. ▶ **wyjście** (*z partii itp.*) **2** a change from an accepted style ▶ **odejście** (*od stylu, przyzwyczajeń itp.*)

ˈ**break-dancing** noun [U] a style of dancing with **acrobatic** movements, often performed in the street ▶ **breakdance**

breakdown /ˈbreɪkdaʊn/ noun [C] **1** a time when a vehicle, machine, etc. stops working: *I hope we don't **have a breakdown** on the motorway.* ▶ **awaria 2** the failure or end of sth: *The breakdown of the talks means that a strike is likely.* ▶ **załamanie się, niepowodzenie 3** a list of all the details of sth: *I would like a full breakdown of how the money was spent.* ▶ **lista, analiza 4** = NERVOUS BREAKDOWN

ˈ**breakdown truck** (US ˈ**tow truck**) noun [C] a truck that is used for taking cars away to be repaired when they have had a breakdown ▶ **samochód pomocy drogowej** ➲ picture at **truck**

breakfast /ˈbrekfəst/ noun [C,U] the meal which you have when you get up in the morning: *to **have breakfast*** jeść śniadanie ◇ *What do you usually have **for breakfast**?* ◇ *to eat a big breakfast* ▶ **śniadanie** ➲ note at **meal**

> W hotelowym lub restauracyjnym jadłospisie **English breakfast** oznacza płatki zbożowe, jajka sadzone, bekon, parówki, pomidory, grzanki itp. **Continental breakfast** oznacza natomiast pieczywo, dżem i kawę.

IDM **bed and breakfast; B & B** → BED[1]

ˈ**break-in** noun [C] the act of entering a building by force, especially in order to steal sth: *The police say there have been several break-ins in this area.* ▶ **włamanie**

ˌ**breaking and ˈentering** noun [U] (US or old-fashioned) the crime of entering a building illegally and using force ▶ **kradzież z włamaniem**

ˈ**breaking point** noun [U] the time when problems become so great that a person, an organization or a system can no longer deal with them: *to **be at/reach breaking point*** ▶ **granica wytrzymałości**

breakneck /ˈbreɪknek/ adj. [only before a noun] very fast and dangerous: *He drove her to the hospital **at breakneck speed*** (na złamanie karku). ▶ **zawrotny**

breakthrough /ˈbreɪkθruː/ noun [C] **a breakthrough (in sth)** an important discovery or development: *Scientists are hoping to **make a breakthrough** in cancer research.* ▶ **przełom**

ˈ**break-up** noun [C] **1** the end of a relationship between two people: *the break-up of a marriage* ▶ **rozpad 2** the process or result of a group or organization separating into smaller parts: *the break-up of the Soviet Union* ▶ **rozpad, rozłam**

breakwater /ˈbreɪkwɔːtə(r)/ noun [C] a wall built out into the sea to protect the **shore** or **harbour** from the force of the waves ▶ **falochron**

breast /brest/ noun [C] **1** one of the two soft round parts of a woman's body that can produce milk: *She put the baby to her breast.* ◇ *breast cancer* ◇ *breast milk* mleko matki ▶ **pierś 2** (a word used especially in literature for the top part of the front of your body, below the neck): *to clasp sb to your breast* ▶ **pierś** SYN **chest 3** the front part of the body of a bird: *breast feathers* ◇ *The robin has a red breast.* ▶ **pierś** ➲ picture on **page A11**

breastbone /ˈbrestbəʊn/ noun [C] the long flat bone in the chest that the seven top pairs of **ribs** are connected to ▶ (*anat.*) **mostek** SYN **sternum** ➲ picture at **body**

breastfeed /ˈbrestfiːd/ verb [I,T] (pt, pp **breastfed**) to feed a baby with milk from the breast ▶ **karmić piersią**

ˌ**breast ˈpocket** noun [C] a pocket on a shirt, or on the outside or inside of the part of a jacket that covers the chest ▶ (*ubranie*) **kieszeń górna**

breaststroke /ˈbreststrəʊk/ noun [U] a style of swimming on your front in which you start with your hands together, push both arms forward and then move them out and back through the water: *to **do (the) breaststroke*** ▶ **styl klasyczny** ➲ look at **backstroke, butterfly, crawl**

breath /breθ/ noun **1** [U] the air that you take into and blow out of your lungs: *to **have bad breath*** (nieprzyjemny zapach z ust) ▶ **oddech, dech 2** [C] an act of taking air into or blowing air out of your lungs: *Take a few deep breaths before you start running.* ▶ **wdech, wydech**
IDM **a breath of fresh air** the clean air which you breathe outside, especially when compared to the air inside a room or building: *Let's go for a walk. I need a breath of fresh air* (muszę się przewietrzyć). ◇ (figurative) *James's happy face is like a breath of fresh air in that miserable place.* ▶ **świeże powietrze; powiew świeżego powietrza**
catch your breath → CATCH[1]
get your breath (again/back) to rest after physical exercise so that your breathing returns to normal ▶ **odsapnąć, wytchnąć**
hold your breath to stop breathing for a short time, for example when you are swimming or because of fear or excitement: *We all held our breath as we waited for her reply.* Czekaliśmy z zapartym tchem na jej odpowiedź. ▶ **wstrzymywać oddech**
out of/short of breath breathing very quickly, for example after physical exercise: *I always get out of breath* (dostaję zadyszki) *when I skip.* ▶ **zadyszany**
say sth, speak, etc. under your breath to say sth very quietly, usually because you do not want people to hear you ▶ **mówić szeptem/półgłosem**
take your breath away to be very surprising or beautiful: *The spectacular view took our breath away.* ▶ **zapierać dech w piersiach** ➲ adjective **breathtaking**
take a deep breath → DEEP[1]
with bated breath → BATED

breathalyse (US **breathalyze**) /ˈbreθəlaɪz/ verb [T] to test the breath of a driver with a **breathalyser** ▶ **badać trzeźwość kierowcy alkomatem**

breathalyser (Brit. **Breathalyzer™**) /ˈbreθəlaɪzə(r)/ noun [C] a device used by the police to measure the amount of alcohol in a driver's breath ▶ **alkomat**

breathe /briːð/ verb [I,T] to take air, etc. into your lungs and blow it out again: ***Breathe out** as you lift the weight and **breathe in** as you lower it.* Na wydechu podnosimy ciężar, a na wdechu obniżamy go. ◇ *I hate having to breathe (in)* (wdychać) *other people's cigarette smoke.* ▶ **oddychać**
■ **breathing** noun [U]: *heavy/irregular breathing* ◇ *These deep breathing exercises will help you relax.* ▶ **oddech, oddychanie**
IDM **(not) breathe a word (of/about sth) (to sb)** to (not) tell sb about sth that is secret: *Don't breathe a word* (nie

piśnij ani słowa) *of this to my mother!* ▶ **nie puszczać pary z ust**

breather /ˈbriːðə(r)/ noun [C] (informal) a short rest: *to **have/take a breather*** zrobić sobie krótką przerwę ▶ **przerwa, chwila wytchnienia**

ˈ**breathing space** noun [C,U] a short rest in the middle of a period of mental or physical effort ▶ **chwila wytchnienia**

breathless /ˈbreθləs/ adj. **1** having difficulty breathing: *I was hot and breathless when I got to the top of the hill.* ▶ **zadyszany 2** not able to breathe because you are so excited, frightened, etc.: *She was breathless with excitement* (zamarła z wrażenia). ▶ **bez tchu**
■ **breathlessly** adv. ▶ **z zadyszką; bez tchu**

breathtaking /ˈbreθteɪkɪŋ/ adj. extremely surprising, beautiful, etc.: *breathtaking scenery* ▶ **zapierający dech w piersiach**

ˈ**breath test** noun [C] a test by the police on the breath of a driver to measure how much alcohol they have drunk ▶ **kontrola trzeźwości kierowcy za pomocą alkomatu** ➲ look at **breathalyse**

breathy /ˈbreθi/ adj. speaking or singing with a noticeable sound of breathing ▶ **posapujący**

ˈ**breech birth** (also ˌ**breech deˈlivery**) noun [C] a birth in which the baby's bottom or feet come out of the mother first ▶ **poród pośladkowy**

breeches /ˈbrɪtʃɪz/ noun [pl.] short trousers fastened just below the knee: *a pair of breeches* ◇ *riding breeches* ▶ **bryczesy**

🔑**breed**[1] /briːd/ verb (pt, pp **bred** /bred/) **1** [I] (used about animals) to have sex and produce young animals: *Many animals won't breed in zoos.* ▶ **rozmnażać się** SYN **mate 2** [T] to keep animals or plants in order to produce young from them: *These cattle are bred to produce high yields of milk.* ▶ **hodować 3** [T] to cause sth: *This kind of thinking breeds intolerance.* ▶ **wywoływać, powodować**
■ **breeding** noun [U] **1** the keeping of animals in order to breed from them ▶ **hodowla 2** the producing of young animals, plants, etc.: *the breeding season* okres rozrodczy ▶ **hodowla reprodukcyjna 3** the family or social background that is thought to result in good manners: *a sign of good breeding* ▶ **dobre wychowanie**

🔑**breed**[2] /briːd/ noun [C] a particular variety of an animal: *a breed of cattle/dog* ▶ **rasa**

breeder /ˈbriːdə(r)/ noun [C] a person who breeds animals or plants: *a dog breeder* ▶ **hodowca**

ˈ**breeding ground** noun [C] **1** a place where wild animals go to breed ▶ **miejsce godów dzikich zwierząt 2** a place where sth can develop: *a breeding ground for crime* ▶ **siedlisko, wylęgarnia**

breeze[1] /briːz/ noun [C] a light wind: *A warm breeze was blowing.* ▶ **wietrzyk**

breeze[2] /briːz/ verb [I] **breeze along, in, out, etc.** to move in a confident and relaxed way: *He just breezed in twenty minutes late without a word of apology.* ▶ **w(y)padać, przemykać**

ˈ**breeze block** (US ˈ**cinder block**) noun [C] a light building block, made of sand, small **cinders** and cement ▶ **pustak**

breezy /ˈbriːzi/ adj. (**breezier**; **breeziest**) **1** with a little wind ▶ **wietrzny 2** happy and relaxed: *You're **bright and breezy** this morning!* ▶ **energiczny, pełen werwy/animuszu**

brethren /ˈbreðrən/ noun [pl.] (old-fashioned) **1** (used to talk to people in church or to talk about members of a male religious group) ▶ **bracia 2** people who are part of the same society as yourself ▶ **brać**

breve /briːv/ noun [C] (used in music) a note that lasts as long as eight **crotchets**, which is rarely used in modern music ▶ **brevis**

breviary /ˈbriːviəri; US -eri/ noun [C] (pl. **breviaries**) a book containing the words of the service for each day in the Roman Catholic church ▶ **brewiarz**

brevity /ˈbrevəti/ noun [U] the state of being short or quick ▶ **krótkotrwałość, zwięzłość** ➲ adjective **brief**

brew /bruː/ verb **1** [T] to make beer ▶ **warzyć** (*piwo*) **2** [T] to make a drink of tea or coffee by adding hot water: *to brew a pot of tea* ▶ **zaparzać 3** [I] (used about tea) to stand in hot water before it is ready to drink: *Leave it to brew for a few minutes.* ▶ **naciągać**
IDM **be brewing** (used about sth bad) to develop or grow: *There's **trouble brewing.*** ▶ **wisieć w powietrzu**

brewer /ˈbruːə(r)/ noun [C] a person or company that makes beer ▶ **piwowar; browar**

brewery /ˈbruːəri/ noun [C] (pl. **breweries**) a place where beer is made ▶ **browar**

briar (also **brier**) /ˈbraɪə(r)/ noun [C] a wild bush with **thorns**, especially a wild **rose** bush ▶ **dzika róża**

bribe /braɪb/ noun [C] money, etc. that is given to sb such as an official to persuade them to do sth to help you that is wrong or dishonest: *to **accept/take bribes*** ▶ **łapówka**
■ **bribe** verb [T] **bribe sb (with sth)**: *They got a visa by bribing an official.* ▶ **przekupywać, dawać łapówkę** | **bribery** /ˈbraɪbəri/ noun [U] ▶ **łapownictwo**

bric-a-brac /ˈbrɪk ə bræk/ noun [U] small items of little value, for decoration in a house ▶ **starocie**

🔑**brick** /brɪk/ noun [C,U] a hard block of baked **clay** that is used for building houses, etc.: *a lorry carrying bricks* ◇ *a house built of red brick* ▶ **cegła**

bricklayer /ˈbrɪkleɪə(r)/ noun [C] a person whose job is to build walls with bricks ▶ **murarz**

brickwork /ˈbrɪkwɜːk/ noun [U] the part of a building that is made of bricks ▶ **murowana część budowli/budynku** (*z cegieł*)

bridal /ˈbraɪdl/ adj. [only before a noun] connected with a **bride**: *the bridal suite* (apartament dla nowożeńców) *in a hotel* ▶ **weselny, ślubny**

bride /braɪd/ noun [C] a woman on or just before her wedding day: *a **bride-to-be*** ▶ **panna młoda** ➲ note at **wedding**

bridegroom /ˈbraɪdɡruːm/ (also **groom**) noun [C] a man on or just before his wedding day ▶ **pan młody** ➲ note at **wedding**

bridesmaid /ˈbraɪdzmeɪd/ noun [C] a woman or girl who helps the **bride** on her wedding day ▶ **druhna** ➲ note at **wedding**

🔑**bridge**[1] /brɪdʒ/ noun **1** [C] a structure that carries a road or railway across a river, valley, road or railway: *a bridge over the River Danube* ◇ *a footbridge* kładka dla pieszych ▶ **most** ➲ picture on **page A2 2** [sing.] the high part of a ship where the captain and the people who control the ship stand ▶ **mostek kapitański 3** [U] a card game for four people ▶ **brydż**

bridge[2] /brɪdʒ/ verb [T] to build a bridge over sth ▶ **budować most**
IDM **bridge a/the gap** to fill a space between two people, groups or things or to bring them closer together: *Baby food bridges the gap between milk and solid food.* ▶ **zbliżać**

bridgework /ˈbrɪdʒwɜːk/ noun [U] **1** artificial teeth and the parts that keep them in place in the mouth ▶ **mostek dentystyczny 2** the work of making these teeth or putting them in place ▶ **wykonywanie lub wstawianie mostka**

bridle¹ /ˈbraɪdl/ noun [C] the narrow pieces of leather that you put around a horse's head so that you can control it when you are riding it ▶ **uzda** ➲ picture at **horse**

bridle² /ˈbraɪdl/ verb **1** [T] to put a **bridle** on a horse ▶ **zakładać uzdę 2** [I] **bridle (at sth)** (formal) to show that you are annoyed and/or offended at sth, especially by moving your head up and backwards in a proud way: *She bridled at the suggestion that she was lying.* ▶ **obruszać się (na coś)**

ˈ**bridle path** (Brit. also **bridleway** /ˈbraɪdlweɪ/) noun [C] a rough path that is suitable for people riding horses or walking, but not for cars ▶ **ścieżka** (*spacerowa lub do jazdy konnej*)

Brie /briː/ noun [U,C] a type of soft French cheese ▶ **ser brie**

⚷ **brief¹** /briːf/ adj. short or quick: *a brief description* ◇ *Please be brief. We don't have much time.* ▶ **krótki, zwięzły** ➲ noun **brevity**

IDM **in brief** using only a few words: *In brief, the meeting was a disaster.* ▶ **w skrócie**

brief² /briːf/ noun [C] instructions or information about a job or task: *He was given the brief of improving the image of the organization.* ▶ **zadanie, obowiązek**

brief³ /briːf/ verb [T] to give sb information or instructions about sth: *The minister has been fully briefed on what questions to expect.* ▶ **informować, instruować**

briefcase /ˈbriːfkeɪs/ noun [C] a flat case that you use for carrying papers, etc., especially when you go to work ▶ **aktówka, teczka** ➲ picture at **bag**, picture on **page A1**

briefing /ˈbriːfɪŋ/ noun [C,U] instructions or information that you are given before sth happens: *a press/news briefing* ▶ **briefing, konferencja prasowa**

⚷ **briefly** /ˈbriːfli/ adv. **1** for a short time; quickly: *She glanced briefly at the letter.* ▶ **krótko, na krótko 2** using only a few words: *I'd like to comment very briefly on that last statement.* ▶ **krótko, zwięźle**

briefs /briːfs/ noun [pl.] men's or women's underwear: *a pair of briefs* ▶ **majtki**

brigade /brɪˈɡeɪd/ noun [C] **1** a large group of soldiers that forms a unit in the army ▶ **brygada 2** a group of people who work together for a particular purpose: *the fire brigade* straż pożarna ▶ **brygada**

brigadier /ˌbrɪɡəˈdɪə(r)/ noun [C] an important officer in the army ▶ **brygadier**

⚷ **bright** /braɪt/ adj. **1** having a lot of light: *a bright* (pogodny), *sunny day* ◇ *eyes bright with happiness* ▶ **jasny, błyszczący 2** strong and easy to see: *a bright yellow jumper* ▶ **jaskrawy, jasny 3** happy: *to feel bright and cheerful* ▶ **ożywiony, pełen werwy/animuszu 4** intelligent; able to learn things quickly: *a bright child* ◇ *a* ***bright idea*** świetny pomysł ▶ **inteligentny, błyskotliwy** ➲ note at **intelligent 5** likely to be pleasant or successful: *The future looks bright.* ▶ **świetlany, pomyślny**

■ **brightly** adv.: *brightly coloured clothes* ▶ **jaskrawo** | **brightness** noun [U] ▶ **blask, żywość, jaskrawość**

IDM **look on the bright side** → LOOK¹

brighten /ˈbraɪtn/ verb [I,T] **brighten (sth) (up)** to become brighter or happier; to make sth brighter: *His face brightened when he saw her.* ◇ *to brighten up somebody's day* ▶ **rozjaśniać (się)**

⚷ **brilliant** /ˈbrɪliənt/ adj. **1** very clever, skilful or successful: *a brilliant young scientist* ◇ *That's a brilliant idea!* ▶ **błyskotliwy, genialny 2** having a lot of light; very bright: *brilliant sunshine* ▶ **błyszczący, olśniewający 3** (informal) very good: *That was a brilliant film!* ▶ **znakomity, świetny** ➲ note at **good**

■ **brilliance** noun [U] ▶ **jasność; znakomitość** | **brilliantly** adv. ▶ **błyszcząco; wspaniale**

brim¹ /brɪm/ noun [C] **1** the top edge of a cup, glass, etc.: *The cup was full to the brim.* ▶ **brzeg 2** the bottom part of a hat that is wider than the rest ▶ **rondo**

brim² /brɪm/ verb [I] (**brimming**; **brimmed**) **brim (with sth)** to be full of sth: *His eyes were brimming with tears.* ▶ **napełniać się**

PHR V **brim over (with sth)** (used about a cup, glass, etc.) to have more liquid than it can hold: *The bowl was brimming over with water.* ◇ (figurative) *to be brimming over with health/happiness* ▶ **przepełniać się; tryskać**

brine /braɪn/ noun [U] salt water that is used especially to keep food in good condition ▶ **zalewa solna**

bring

Bring the newspaper.

Fetch the newspaper.

Take the newspaper.

⚷ **bring** /brɪŋ/ verb [T] (pt, pp **brought** /brɔːt/) **1** to carry or take sb/sth to a place with you: *Is it all right if I bring a friend to the party?* ◇ *Could you bring us some water, please?* ◇ *My sister went to Spain on holiday and brought me back a T-shirt.* ◇ *The prisoner was brought* (został doprowadzony) *into the court by two policewomen.* ◇ (figurative) *He will bring valuable skills and experience to the team.* ▶ **przynosić, przywozić, wnosić 2** to cause or result in sth: *The sight of her brought a smile to his face.* Na jej widok uśmiech zagościł na jego twarzy. ◇ *Money doesn't always bring happiness.* Pieniądze nie zawsze szczęścia dają. ▶ **powodować, przynosić 3** to cause sb/sth to be in a certain place or condition: *Their screams brought people running* (na ich krzyki zbiegli się ludzie) *from all directions.* ◇ *Add water to the mixture and bring it to the boil.* ◇ *An injury can easily* ***bring*** *an athlete's career* ***to an end*** (zakończyć karierę sportowca).

▶ **doprowa-dzać**, **sprowadzać** **4** to move sth somewhere: *She brought the book down* (zdjęła) *off the shelf.* ◇ *Louis brought a photo out of* (wyciągnął) *his wallet and showed it to us.* ▶ **5 bring yourself to do sth** to force yourself to do sth: *The film was so horrible that I couldn't bring myself to watch it.* ▶ **zmuszać się** ⓘ **Bring** używa się w idiomach, np. **bring up the rear**. Zob. hasła odpowiednich rzeczowników, przymiotników itp.

PHR V **bring sth about** to cause sth to happen: *to bring about changes in people's lives* ▶ **powodować/wywoływać coś**

bring sb/sth back to return sb/sth: *Please bring back all library books by the end of the week.* ◇ *He brought me back in his car.* ▶ **oddawać kogoś/coś**; **przywozić kogoś/coś z powrotem**

bring sth back **1** to cause sb to remember sth: *The photographs brought back memories of his childhood.* ▶ **przywodzić coś na myśl** **2** to cause sth that existed before to be introduced again: *Nobody wants to bring back* (nikt nie chce powrotu do) *the days of child labour.* ▶ **przywracać coś**

bring sb sth back; **bring sth back (for sb)** to return with sth for sb: *What did you bring the children back from Italy?* ▶ **przywozić coś** (*wracając z podróży*)

bring sb/sth down to defeat sb/sth; to make sb/sth lose a position of power: *to bring down the government* ▶ **obalać kogoś/coś**

bring sth down to make sth lower in level: *to bring down the price of something* ▶ **obniżać coś**

bring sth forward **1** to move sth to an earlier time: *The date of the meeting has been brought forward by two weeks.* ▶ **przekładać coś na wcześniejszy termin**, **przybliżać coś** OPP **put sth back** **2** to suggest sth for discussion ▶ **przedstawiać** (*np. propozycję*)

bring sb in to ask or employ sb to do a particular job: *A specialist was brought in to set up the new computer system.* ▶ **sprowadzać/zatrudniać kogoś**

bring sth in to introduce sth: *The government have brought in a new law on dangerous dogs.* ▶ **wprowadzać coś**

bring sth off to manage to do sth difficult: *The team brought off an amazing victory.* Drużynie udało się odnieść zdumiewające zwycięstwo. ▶ **zdołać coś zrobić**

bring sth on to cause sth: *Her headaches are brought on by stress.* ▶ **powodować coś**

bring sth out to produce sth or cause sth to appear: *When is the company bringing out its next new model?* ◇ *A crisis can sometimes bring out the best in people* (wyzwolić to, co w ludziach najlepsze). ▶ **wydawać** (*np. książkę*), **wprowadzać coś nowego**

bring sb round to make sb become conscious again: *I splashed cold water on his face to try to bring him round.* ▶ **cucić kogoś**

bring sb round (to sth) to persuade sb to agree with your opinion: *After a lot of discussion we finally brought them round to our point of view.* ▶ **przekonywać kogoś (do czegoś)**

bring sth round to sth to direct a conversation to a particular subject: *I finally brought the conversation round to the subject of money.* ▶ **kierować rozmowę na jakiś temat**

bring sb up to look after a child until they are an adult and to teach them how to behave: *After her parents were killed the child was brought up by her uncle.* ◇ *a well brought up child* dobrze wychowane dziecko ▶ **wychowywać kogoś**

bring sth up **1** to introduce sth into a discussion or conversation: *I intend to bring the matter up at the next meeting.* ▶ **poruszać coś** **2** to be sick so that food comes up from the stomach and out of the mouth ▶ **wymiotować/zwracać coś** SYN **vomit**

brink /brɪŋk/ noun [sing.] **the brink (of sth/doing sth)** if you are on the **brink** of sth, you are almost in a very new, exciting or dangerous situation: *Just when the band were* ***on the brink*** *of becoming famous* (była o krok od sławy), *they split up.* ◇ *She was on the brink of tears.* Była bliska płaczu. ▶ **skraj** (*np. przepaści*)

brinkmanship /ˈbrɪŋkmənʃɪp/ (US also **brinksmanship** /ˈbrɪnks-/) noun [U] the activity, especially in politics, of getting into a situation that could be very dangerous in order to frighten people and make them do what you want ▶ (*polit.*) **gra na przetrzymanie**

brisk /brɪsk/ adj. **1** quick or using a lot of energy; busy: *They set off* ***at a brisk pace.*** ◇ *Trading has been brisk this morning.* ▶ **żwawy**, **ożywiony** **2** confident and practical; wanting to get things done quickly ▶ **energiczny**, **oschły**
■ **briskly** adv. ▶ **żwawo**; **energicznie** | **briskness** noun [U] ▶ **żwawość**; **oschłość**

bristle¹ /ˈbrɪsl/ noun [C] **1** a short thick hair: *The bristles* (szczecina) *on my chin hurt the baby's face.* ▶ **włosek** ➲ picture at **hair** **2** one of the short thick hairs of a brush ▶ **włosie**

bristle² /ˈbrɪsl/ verb [I] **1 bristle (with sth) (at sb/sth)** to show that you are angry ▶ **pienić się** **2** (used about hair or an animal's fur) to stand up straight because of fear, anger, cold, etc. ▶ **jeżyć się**
PHR V **bristle with sth** to be full of sth: *The whole subject bristles with problems.* ▶ **być najeżonym (czymś)**

bristly /ˈbrɪsli/ adj. like or full of **bristles**; rough: *a* ***bristly chin/moustache*** ▶ **pokryty szczeciną**

Brit /brɪt/ noun [C] (informal) a British person ▶ **Brytyjczyk/ka**

Britain = GREAT BRITAIN ➲ note at **United Kingdom**

British /ˈbrɪtɪʃ/ adj. **1** of the United Kingdom (= Great Britain and Northern Ireland): *British industry* ◇ *to hold a British passport* ▶ **brytyjski** **2** (**the British**) noun [pl.] the people of the United Kingdom ▶ **Brytyjczycy**

the ˌBritish ˈIsles noun [pl.] Great Britain and Ireland with all the islands that are near their coasts ▶ **Wyspy Brytyjskie** ⓘ **British Isles** odnosi się do podziału geograficznego, a nie politycznego. ➲ note at **United Kingdom**

Briton /ˈbrɪtn/ noun [C] a person who comes from Great Britain ▶ **Brytyj-czyk/ka**, **obywatel/ka brytyjsk-i/a** ⓘ Wyraz ten jest zazw. używany w prasie lub w odniesieniu do plemienia zamieszkującego niegdyś Wyspy Brytyjskie: *Three Britons killed in air crash.* ◇ *the Ancient Britons.* W pozostałych kontekstach stosuje się **a British man** lub **a British woman**.

brittle /ˈbrɪtl/ adj. hard but easily broken: *The bones become brittle in old age.* ▶ **łamliwy**, **kruchy**

broach /brəʊtʃ/ verb [T] to start talking about a particular subject, especially one which is difficult or embarrassing: *How will you* ***broach the subject*** *of the money he owes us?* ▶ **poruszać** (*delikatny temat*)

ˈB-road noun [C] (in Britain) a road that is not as wide or important as an **A-road** or a **motorway**: *We drove the whole way on B-roads.* ▶ **droga drugiej kategorii**

broad /brɔːd/ adj. **1** wide: *a broad street/river* ◇ *broad shoulders* ◇ *a broad smile* ▶ **szeroki** ➲ noun **breadth** OPP **narrow**

> Mówiąc o odległości między jedną krawędzią a drugą, częściej używa się **wide** niż **broad**: *The gate is four metres wide.* ◇ *The table is too wide to go through the door.* **Broad** często stosuje się w typowo geograficznych opisach: *a broad expanse of desert* oraz w pewnych utartych wyrażeniach: *broad shoulders.*

2 including many different people or things: *We sell a* ***broad range*** *of products.* ◇ *There is broad support for* *the government's policies.* ▶ **powszechny 3** [only before a noun] without a lot of detail; general: *I'll explain the new system* ***in broad terms.*** ▶ **ogólny, ogólnikowy 4** (used about the way sb speaks) very strong: *She has a broad Somerset accent.* ▶ **silny, wyraźny**

IDM **(in) broad daylight** during the day, when it is easy to see: *He was attacked in broad daylight.* ▶ **(w) biały dzień**

broadband /ˈbrɔːdbænd/ noun [U] a way of connecting a computer to the Internet, which allows you to receive information, including pictures, etc., very quickly: *We have broadband at home now.* ▶ (*komput.*) **połączenie typu broadband/szerokopasmowe**

ˌbroad-ˈbased (also **ˌbroadly-ˈbased**) adj. based on a wide variety of people, things or ideas; not limited ▶ **szeroki, powszechny**

ˌbroad ˈbean noun [C] a type of large flat green **bean** that can be cooked and eaten as a vegetable ▶ **bób**

broadcast /ˈbrɔːdkɑːst; US -kæst/ verb [I,T] (pt, pp **broadcast**) to send out radio or TV programmes: *The Olympics are* ***broadcast live*** *around the world.* ▶ **transmitować, nadawać**

■ **broadcast** noun [C] ▶ **audycja, program** | **broadcasting** noun [U] the business of making and sending out radio and television programmes: *to work in broadcasting* ▶ **nadawanie programów w radiu i/lub telewizji**

broadcaster /ˈbrɔːdkɑːstə(r); US -kæst-/ noun [C] a person who speaks on the radio or on TV ▶ **komentator/ka radiow-y/a lub telewizyjn-y/a**

broaden /ˈbrɔːdn/ verb [I,T] **broaden (sth) (out)** to become wider; to make sth wider: *The river broadens out beyond the bridge.* ◇ (figurative) *Travel broadens the mind.* Podróże kształcą. ▶ **poszerzać (się)**

broadly /ˈbrɔːdli/ adv. **1** generally: ***Broadly speaking*** (ogólnie rzecz biorąc), *the scheme will work as follows ...* ▶ **ogólnie 2** (used to describe a way of smiling) with a big, wide smile: *He smiled broadly as he shook everyone's hand.* ▶ **od ucha do ucha**

ˌbroad-ˈminded adj. happy to accept beliefs and ways of life that are different from your own ▶ **tolerancyjny** OPP **narrow-minded**

broadsheet /ˈbrɔːdʃiːt/ noun [C] **1** a newspaper printed on a large size of paper ▶ **gazeta wielkoformatowa 2** a large piece of paper printed on one side only with information or an advertisement ▶ **plakat**

broadside /ˈbrɔːdsaɪd/ noun [C] an aggressive attack in words, whether written or spoken: *The prime minister* ***fired a broadside*** *at his critics.* ▶ **agresywny/ostry atak**

brocade /brəˈkeɪd/ noun [U,C] a type of thick heavy cloth with a raised pattern made especially from gold or silver silk thread ▶ **brokat**

broccoli /ˈbrɒkəli/ noun [U] a thick green plant with green or purple flower heads that can be cooked and eaten as a vegetable ▶ **brokuły** ➲ picture on **page A13**

brochure /ˈbrəʊʃə(r); US -ˈʃʊr/ noun [C] a small book with pictures and information about sth ▶ **prospekt, broszura reklamowa**

broil (especially US) = GRILL² (1)

broke¹ past tense of **break¹**

broke² /brəʊk/ adj. [not before a noun] (informal) having no money: *I can't come out tonight – I'm absolutely broke.* ▶ **spłukany**

broken¹ past participle of **break¹**

broken² /ˈbrəʊkən/ adj. **1** damaged or in pieces; not working: *The washing machine's broken.* ◇ *Watch out! There's broken glass on the floor.* ◇ *a broken leg* ◇ *How did the window* ***get broken****?* ▶ **zepsuty, potłuczony, rozbity, złamany** ➲ picture at **chip²** (1) **2** [usually before a noun] ended or destroyed: ***a broken engagement*** zerwane zaręczyny ◇ ***a broken marriage*** rozbite małżeństwo ▶ **zerwany** ➲ look at **broken home 3** (used about a promise or an agreement) not kept ▶ **niedotrzymany 4** not continuous; interrupted: *a broken line* ◇ *a broken night's sleep* ▶ **przerywany 5** [only before a noun] (used about a foreign language) spoken slowly with a lot of mistakes: *to speak in broken English* ▶ **łamany**

ˌbroken-ˈdown adj. **1** in a very bad condition: *a broken-down old building* ▶ **uszkodzony, rozlatujący się 2** (used about a vehicle) not working: *A broken-down bus was blocking the road.* ▶ **zepsuty**

ˌbroken-ˈhearted = HEARTBROKEN

ˌbroken ˈhome noun [C] a family in which the parents do not live together, for example because they are divorced: *Many of the children came from broken homes.* ▶ **rozbity dom**

broker /ˈbrəʊkə(r)/ noun [C] a person or company that buys and sells things, for example shares, bonds, etc., for other people: *an insurance broker* ▶ **pośrednik, makler** ➲ look at **stockbroker**

ˈbroker-dealer noun [C] a person or company that sells shares, bonds, etc. for other people and for themselves ▶ **makler giełdowy**

brolly (Brit., informal) = UMBRELLA

bronchitis /brɒŋˈkaɪtɪs/ noun [U] an illness of the tubes leading to the lungs **(bronchial tubes)** that causes a very bad cough ▶ **zapalenie oskrzeli**

bronze /brɒnz/ noun **1** [U] a dark brown metal that is made by mixing tin with **copper** ▶ **brąz 2** = BRONZE MEDAL

■ **bronze** adj. ▶ **brązowy, brunatny**

the ˈBronze Age noun [sing.] the period in history between the Stone Age and the Iron Age when people used tools and weapons made of **bronze** ▶ **epoka brązu**

bronzed /brɒnzd/ adj. having skin that has been turned brown, in an attractive way, by the sun ▶ **opalony** ➲ look at **tan**

ˌbronze ˈmedal (also **bronze**) noun [C] a round piece of **bronze** that you get as a prize for coming third in a race or a competition ▶ **brązowy medal** ➲ look at **gold medal, silver medal**

brooch /brəʊtʃ/ noun [C] a piece of jewellery with a pin at the back that women wear on their clothes ▶ **brosz(k)a**

brood¹ /bruːd/ verb [I] **1 brood (on/over/about sth)** to worry, or to think a lot about sth that makes you worried or sad: *to brood on a failure* ▶ **dumać, rozmyślać 2** (used about a female bird) to sit on her eggs ▶ **wysiadywać jaja**

brood² /bruːd/ noun [C] all the young birds that belong to one mother ▶ **lęg**

brooding /ˈbruːdɪŋ/ adj. sad and mysterious or threatening: *dark, brooding eyes* ◇ *a brooding silence* złowroga cisza ▶ **ponury**

broody /ˈbruːdi/ adj. **1** (used about a woman) wanting to have a baby ▶ **z rozbudzonym instynktem macierzyńskim 2** (used about a female bird) ready to have or sit on eggs: *a broody hen* ▶ (*kura*) **kwocząca**

brook¹ /brʊk/ noun [C] a small narrow river ▶ **strumyk** SYN **stream**

brook² /brʊk/ verb [T] **not brook sth/brook no ...** (formal) to not allow sth: *The tone in his voice brooked no argument.* ▶ **nie tolerować, nie znosić**

broom /bruːm/ noun [C] a brush with a long handle that you use for removing dirt from the floor ▶ **miotła** ➲ picture at **brush**

broomstick /ˈbruːmstɪk/ noun [C] the handle of a **broom** ▶ **kij od miotły**

Bros abbr. **Brothers** (used in the name of companies): *Wentworth Bros Ltd* ▶ **bracia**

broth /brɒθ/ noun [U] thick soup: *chicken broth* rosół ▶ (*gęsta*) **zupa**

brothel /ˈbrɒθl/ noun [C] a place where men can go and pay to have sex with a **prostitute** ▶ **burdel**

brother /ˈbrʌðə(r)/ noun [C] **1** a man or boy who has the same parents as another person: *Michael and Jim are brothers.* ◇ *Michael is Jim's brother.* ◇ *a younger/older brother* ▶ **brat** ➲ look at **half-brother**, **stepbrother** ⓘ Zwróć uwagę, że słowo **sibling** (rodzeństwo) jest używane rzadko i tylko w języku formalnym. Najczęściej używa się zwrotu **brothers and sisters**: *Have you got any brothers and sisters?* **2** a man who is a member of a Christian religious community: *Brother Luke* ▶ **brat** **3** (informal) a man who you feel close to because he is a member of the same society, group, etc. as you: *He was greatly respected by his brother officers* (przez towarzyszy oficerów).

brotherhood /ˈbrʌðəhʊd/ noun **1** [U] a feeling of great friendship and understanding between people: *the brotherhood of man* braterstwo narodów ▶ **braterstwo** **2** [C, with sing. or pl. verb] an organization which is formed for a particular, often religious, purpose ▶ **bractwo**

ˈbrother-in-law noun [C] (pl. **brothers-in-law**) **1** the brother of your husband or wife ▶ **szwagier** **2** the husband of your sister ▶ **szwagier**

brotherly /ˈbrʌðəli/ adj. showing feelings of love and kindness that you would expect a brother to show: *brotherly love/advice* ▶ **braterski**

brought past tense, past participle of **bring**

brow /braʊ/ noun [C] **1** = FOREHEAD **2** [usually pl.] = EYEBROW ▶ **czoło** **3** [sing.] the top part of a hill: *Suddenly a car came over the brow of the hill.* ▶ **szczyt**

browbeat /ˈbraʊbiːt/ verb [T] (pt **browbeat**; pp **browbeaten** /ˈbraʊbiːtn/) **browbeat sb (into doing sth)** to frighten or threaten sb in order to make them do sth: *They were browbeaten into accepting the offer.* ▶ **wymuszać**, **zastraszać**

brown[1] /braʊn/ adj. **1** [C,U] of the colour of earth or wood: *brown eyes/hair* ▶ **brązowy** **2** having skin that the sun has made darker: *Although I often sunbathe, I never seem to **go brown**.* ▶ **opalony**

■ **brown** noun [U,C]: *the yellows and browns of the trees in autumn* ◇ *You don't look nice in brown.* ▶ (*kolor*) **brąz**

brown[2] /braʊn/ verb [I,T] to become or make sth become brown: *Brown the meat in a frying pan.* ▶ **brązowieć**, (*kotlety itp.*) **rumienić (się)**, **opalać (się)** ➲ note at **cook**[1]

brownie /ˈbraʊni/ noun [C] **1** a thick, soft, flat cake made with chocolate and sometimes nuts and served in small squares ▶ **rodzaj ciastka czekoladowego** **2** (**Brownie**) a young girl who is a member of the lowest level of the Girl Guides organization ▶ **członkini skautowskiej drużyny dla dziewcząt**

brownish /ˈbraʊnɪʃ/ adj. fairly brown in colour ▶ **brązowawy**, (*oczy*) **piwny**

ˌbrown ˈpaper noun [U] strong, thick paper used for putting round packages, etc.: *I wrapped the books in brown paper and tied the package with string.* ▶ **papier pakowy**

browse /braʊz/ verb **1** [I] to spend time pleasantly in a shop, looking at a lot of things rather than looking for one particular thing: *I spent hours browsing in the local bookshop.* ▶ **rozglądać się**, **oglądać** (*towar*) **2** [I] **browse through sth** to look through a book or magazine without reading every part or studying it carefully: *I enjoyed browsing through the catalogue but I didn't order anything.* ▶ **przeglądać**, **wertować** **3** [T] to look for information on a computer, especially on the Internet: *I've just been browsing the Internet for information on Iceland.* ▶ **przeglądać**

■ **browse** noun [sing.]: *I had a browse through the newspapers* (przejrzałem gazety) *on the plane.* ▶ **wertowanie**, **przeglądanie**

browser /ˈbraʊzə(r)/ noun [C] a computer program that lets you look at words and pictures from other computer systems by receiving information through telephone wires: *an Internet browser* ▶ **przeglądarka**

bruise /bruːz/ noun [C] a blue, brown or purple mark that appears on the skin after sb has fallen, been hit, etc. ▶ **siniak** ⓘ Siniak pod okiem nazywany jest **black eye**.

■ **bruise** verb [I,T]: *I fell over and bruised my arm.* ◇ *Handle the fruit carefully or you'll bruise it.* ◇ *I've got the sort of skin that bruises easily* (podatną na siniaki). ▶ **posiniaczyć**, **obijać (się)**; **nabijać sobie siniaka**

brunch /brʌntʃ/ noun [C, U] a meal that you eat in the late morning as a combination of breakfast and lunch ▶ **połączenie śniadania z lunchem**

brunette /bruːˈnet/ noun [C] a white woman with dark brown hair ▶ **szatynka** ➲ look at **blonde**

brunt /brʌnt/ noun

IDM **bear the brunt of sth** → BEAR[1]

brushes

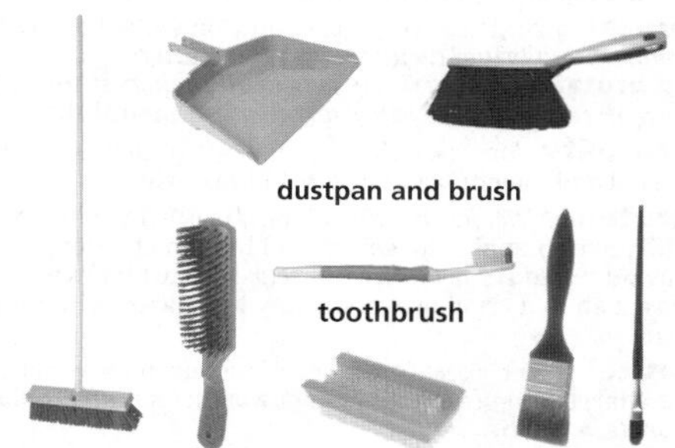

brush[1] /brʌʃ/ noun **1** [C] an object that is used for cleaning things, painting, tidying your hair, etc.: *I took a brush and swept the snow from the path.* ◇ *a toothbrush* szczoteczka do zębów ◇ *a hairbrush* ◇ *a paintbrush* pędzel ▶ **szczotka**, **miotła** **2** [sing.] an act of cleaning, tidying the hair, etc. with a brush: *The floor needs a brush.* ▶ **czyszczenie (szczotką)**, **szczotkowanie** (*włosów*)

IDM **(have) a brush with sb/sth** (to have or almost have) an unpleasant meeting with sb/sth: *My only brush with the law was when I was stopped for speeding.* ▶ **mieć utarczkę z kimś**; **mieć (nieprzyjemny) kontakt z czymś**

brush[2] /brʌʃ/ verb **1** [T] to clean, tidy, etc. sth with a brush: *Make sure you **brush** your **teeth** twice a day.* ◇ ***Brush** your **hair** before you go out.* ▶ **szczotkować**, **czyścić (szczotką)** ➲ note at **clean**[2] **2** [I,T] to touch sb/sth lightly when passing: *Her hand brushed his cheek.* ◇ *Leaves brushed against the car as we drove along the narrow road.* ▶ **muskać**, **ocierać się o coś**

PHR V **brush sb/sth aside** **1** to refuse to pay attention to sb/sth: *She brushed aside the protests and continued with the meeting.* ▶ **ignorować**, **pomijać milczeniem**

2 to push past sb/sth: *He hurried through the crowd, brushing aside the reporters who tried to stop him.* ▶ **odsuwać na bok**
brush sth away; brush sth off (sth) to remove sth with a brush or with the hand, as if using a brush: *I brushed the dust off my jacket.* ▶ **strzepywać, czyścić (szczotką)**
brush sth up/brush up on sth to study or practise sth in order to get back knowledge or skill that you had before and have lost: *She took a course to brush up her Spanish.* ▶ **odświeżać** (*wiedzę*)

'brush-off noun
IDM **give sb the brush-off** (informal) to refuse to be friendly to sb: *I'd ask her to go out with me but I'm scared she'd give me the brush-off* (odprawi mnie z kwitkiem). ▶ **odmowa, odprawa**

brushwood /'brʌʃwʊd/ noun [U] small broken or dead branches of trees, often used to make fires ▶ **chrust**

brushwork /'brʌʃwɜ:k/ noun [U] the particular way in which an artist uses a brush to paint ▶ **technika malarska**

brusque /bru:sk; brʊsk; US brʌsk/ adj. using very few words and sounding rude: *He gave a brusque 'No comment!' and walked off.* ▶ **opryskliwy, obcesowy**
■ **brusquely** adv. ▶ **opryskliwie, obcesowo**

Brussels sprout /ˌbrʌslz 'spraʊt/ (also **sprout**) noun [C, usually pl.] a round green vegetable that looks like a very small **cabbage** ▶ **brukselka** ➲ picture on **page A13**

brutal /'bru:tl/ adj. very cruel and/or violent: *a brutal murder* ◇ *a brutal dictatorship* ▶ **brutalny**
■ **brutally** /-təli/ adv.: *He was brutally honest and told her that he didn't love her any more.* ▶ **brutalnie**

brutality /bru:'tæləti/ noun [C,U] (pl. **brutalities**) very cruel and violent behaviour ▶ **brutalność**

brutalize (Brit. also **-ise**) /'bru:təlaɪz/ verb [T] **1** [usually passive] to make sb unable to feel normal human emotions such as pity: *soldiers brutalized by war* ▶ **brutalizować 2** to treat sb in a cruel or violent way ▶ **traktować brutalnie**

brute¹ /bru:t/ noun [C] **1** a cruel, violent man ▶ **brutal 2** a large strong animal: *That dog of theirs is an absolute brute.* ▶ **bestia**

brute² /bru:t/ adj. [only before a noun] using strength to do sth rather than thinking about it: *I think you'll have to use* ***brute force*** *to get this window open* (będziesz musiał użyć siły, żeby otworzyć to okno). ▶ **brutalny, zwierzęcy**

BSc /ˌbi: es 'si:/ abbr. **Bachelor of Science**; the degree that you receive when you complete a university or college course in a science subject ▶ **bakałarz nauk ścisłych** ➲ look at **BA, MSc**

BSE /ˌbi: es 'i:/ (also informal **mad 'cow disease**) noun [U] **bovine spongiform encephalopathy**; a disease of cows which affects their brains and usually kills them ▶ **gąbczaste zwyrodnienie mózgu** ➲ look at **CJD**

BST /ˌbi: es 'ti:/ noun [U] **British Summer Time**; the time used in Britain between March and October, which is one hour ahead of GMT ▶ **brytyjski czas letni**

BTEC /'bi:tek/ noun [C] **Business and Technology Education Council** (used to refer to any of a large group of British qualifications that can be taken in many different subjects at several levels: *She's doing a BTEC in design.* ▶ **dyplom z dziedziny nauk technicznych i biznesu**

BTW abbr. (used in emails, etc. to mean 'by the way') ▶ **à propos**

bubble¹ /'bʌbl/ noun [C] a ball of air or gas in a liquid, or a ball of air inside a solid substance such as glass: *We knew where there were fish because of the bubbles on the surface.* ▶ **bąbel, bańka**

bubble² /'bʌbl/ verb [I] **1** to produce bubbles or to rise with bubbles: *Cook the pizza until the cheese starts to bubble.* ◇ *The clear water bubbled up out of the ground.* ▶ **bulgotać, kipieć, musować 2 bubble (over) (with sth)** to be full of happy feelings ▶ **tryskać** (*np. entuzjazmem*)

'bubble bath noun [U] a liquid that you can add to the water in a bath to produce a mass of bubbles ▶ **płyn do kąpieli**

bubblegum /'bʌblgʌm/ noun [U] a sticky sweet that you eat but do not swallow and that can be blown into bubbles out of the mouth ▶ **guma balonowa** ➲ look at **chewing gum**

'bubble wrap (US **'Bubble wrap™**) noun [U] a sheet of plastic which has lots of small raised parts filled with air, used for protecting things that are being carried or sent by post/mail ▶ **folia bąbelkowa/pęcherzykowa**

bubbly /'bʌbli/ adj. (**bubblier**; **bubbliest**) **1** full of bubbles ▶ **gazowany, musujący 2** (used about a person) happy and full of energy ▶ **ożywiony, radosny**

buck¹ /bʌk/ noun [C] **1** (US, informal) a US dollar: *Could you lend me a few bucks?* ▶ (*dolar*) **zielony 2** (pl. **buck** or **bucks**) a male **rabbit** or **deer** ▶ **samiec jelenia/królika** ➲ note at **deer**
IDM **pass the buck** → PASS¹

buck² /bʌk/ verb [I] (used about a horse) to jump into the air or to kick the back legs in the air ▶ **stawać dęba**
IDM **buck your ideas up** (Brit., informal) to start behaving in a more acceptable way, so that work gets done better, etc.: *Unless you buck your ideas up* (jeśli nie weźmiesz się w garść), *you'll never pass the exam.*
PHR V **buck (sb/sth) up** (informal) to feel or to make sb feel better or happier: *Drink this – it'll buck you up.* ▶ **nabierać otuchy, odzyskiwać werwę; podnosić kogoś na duchu**

bucket /'bʌkɪt/ noun [C] **1** (also old-fashioned **pail** /peɪl/) a round, open container, usually made of metal or plastic, with a handle, that is used for carrying sth ▶ **wiadro 2** (also **bucketful** /-fʊl/) the amount that a **bucket** contains: *How many buckets of water do you think we'll need?* ▶ **wiadro**
IDM **a drop in the bucket** → DROP²

buckle¹ /'bʌkl/ verb [I,T] **1** to fasten or be fastened with a **buckle** ▶ **zapinać (się), spinać (się) 2** to become crushed or bent because of heat, force, weakness, etc.; to crush or bend sth in this way: *Some railway lines buckled in the heat.* ▶ **wykrzywiać (się)**

buckle² /'bʌkl/ noun [C] a piece of metal or plastic at the end of a belt or other narrow piece of material that is used for fastening it ▶ **klamra, sprzączka, zapinka** ➲ picture at **button**, picture on **page A1**

ˌbuck 'teeth noun [pl.] top teeth that stick forward ▶ **wystające górne zęby**
■ **ˌbuck-'toothed** adj. ▶ **z wystającym zębem**

buckwheat /'bʌkwi:t/ noun [U] small dark grain that is grown as food for animals and for making flour ▶ **gryka**

bud /bʌd/ noun [C] a small lump on a tree or plant that opens and develops into a flower or leaf: *rosebuds* ▶ **pąk**
IDM **nip sth in the bud** → NIP

Buddhism /'bʊdɪzəm/ noun [U] an Asian religion that was started in India by Siddharta Gautama (Buddha) ▶ **buddyzm**

Buddhist /'bʊdɪst/ noun [C] a person whose religion is **Buddhism** ▶ **buddyst(k)a**
■ **Buddhist** adj.: *a Buddhist temple* ▶ **buddyjski**

budding /'bʌdɪŋ/ adj. [only before a noun] wanting or starting to develop and be successful: *Have you got any tips for budding young photographers?* ▶ **obiecujący, dobrze się zapowiadający**

B

buddy /ˈbʌdi/ noun [C] (pl. **buddies**) (informal) a friend, especially a male friend of a man ▶ **kumpel**

budge /bʌdʒ/ verb [I,T] **1** to move or make sth move a little: *I tried as hard as I could to loosen the screw but it simply wouldn't budge* (nawet nie drgnęła). ◇ *We just couldn't budge the car* (nie mogliśmy ruszyć samochodu z miejsca) *when it got stuck in the mud.* ▶ **drgnąć, przesuwać (się) 2** to change or make sb change a firm opinion: *Neither side in the dispute is prepared to budge.* ◇ *Once he's made up his mind, nothing will budge him* (pozostaje nieugięty). ▶ **ustępować**; **nakłonić kogoś do zmiany stanowiska, zmieniać czyjeś zdanie**

budgerigar /ˈbʌdʒərigɑː(r)/ (also informal **budgie** /ˈbʌdʒi/) noun [C] a small, brightly coloured bird that people often keep as a pet in a **cage** ▶ **papużka falista** ➲ note at **pet**

⚷ **budget¹** /ˈbʌdʒɪt/ noun [C,U] **1** a plan of how to spend an amount of money over a particular period of time; the amount of money that is mentioned: *What's your monthly budget for food?* ◇ *a country's defence budget* ◇ *The work was finished on time and* ***within budget.*** ◇ *The builders are already 20%* ***over budget.*** ▶ **budżet 2** (**Budget**) a statement by a government saying how much money it plans to spend on particular things in the next year and how it plans to collect money: *Do you think taxes will go up in this year's budget?* ▶ **budżet**

budget² /ˈbʌdʒɪt/ verb [I,T] **budget (sth) (for sth)** to plan carefully how much money to spend on sth: *The government has budgeted £10 billion for education.* ▶ **asygnować fundusze, przewidywać wydatki**

budget³ /ˈbʌdʒɪt/ adj. [only before a noun] (informal) (used in advertisements) very cheap: *budget holidays* ▶ **na każdą kieszeń**

budgetary /ˈbʌdʒɪtəri; US -teri/ adj. connected with a budget: ***budgetary control/policies/reform*** ▶ **budżetowy**

budgie (informal) = BUDGERIGAR

buff /bʌf/ noun [C] (informal) a person who knows a lot about a particular subject and is very interested in it: *a film/computer buff* ▶ **miłośnik, wielbiciel**

buffalo /ˈbʌfələʊ/ noun [C] (pl. **buffalo** or **buffaloes**) a large wild animal that looks like a cow with long curved horns: *a herd of buffalo* ▶ **bawół**

buffer /ˈbʌfə(r)/ noun [C] **1** a thing or person that reduces the unpleasant effects of sth or prevents violent contact between two things, people, etc.: *UN forces are acting as a buffer between the two sides in the war.* ▶ **bufor 2** a flat round piece of metal with a spring behind it that is on the front or back of a train or at the end of a railway track. **Buffers** reduce the shock when sth hits them. ▶ **bufor, zderzak**

buffet¹ /ˈbʊfeɪ; ˈbʌfeɪ; US bəˈfeɪ/ noun [C] **1** a meal (usually at a party or a special occasion) at which food is placed on a long table and people serve themselves: *Lunch was a cold buffet.* ◇ *a buffet lunch* ▶ **bufet 2** = BUFFET CAR

buffet² /ˈbʌfɪt/ verb [T] to knock or push sth in a rough way from side to side: *The boat was buffeted by the rough sea.* ▶ **miotać, poniewierać**

buffet car /ˈbʊfeɪ kɑː(r); ˈbʌfeɪ; US bəˈfeɪ/ (also **buffet**) noun [C] (Brit.) the part of a train where you can buy sth to eat and drink ▶ **wagon restauracyjny**

buffoon /bəˈfuːn/ noun [C] (old-fashioned) a person who does silly but amusing things ▶ **błazen**

bug¹ /bʌg/ noun **1** [C] (especially US) any small insect ▶ **pluskwa, insekt 2** [C] an illness that is not very serious and that people get from each other: *I don't feel very well – I think I've got the bug that's going round.* ▶ **wirus, zaraza 3** (usually **the ... bug**) [sing.] (informal) a sudden interest in sth: *They've been bitten by the golf bug.* Zarazili się bakcylem golfa. ▶ **namiętne zainteresowanie (czymś) 4** [C] a very small **microphone** that is hidden and used to secretly listen to and record people's conversations ▶ **pluskwa 5** [C] something wrong in a system or machine, especially a computer: *There's a bug in the software.* ▶ **problem, wirus**

bug² /bʌg/ verb [T] (**bugging**; **bugged**) **1** to hide a very small **microphone** somewhere so that people's conversations can be recorded secretly: *Be careful what you say. This room is bugged* (jest na podsłuchu). ▶ **podłożyć pluskwę 2** (informal) to annoy or worry sb: *It bugs him that* (on się gryzie, bo) *he's not as successful as his brother.* ▶ **denerwować**

bugbear /ˈbʌgbeə(r)/ noun [C] (especially Brit.) a thing that annoys people and that they worry about: *Inflation is the government's main bugbear.* ▶ **problem**

bugger¹ /ˈbʌgə(r)/ noun (Brit., taboo, slang) **1** (an offensive word used to insult sb, especially a man, and to show anger or dislike): *You stupid bugger! You could have run me over!* ◇ *Come here, you little bugger!* ▶ **gnojek 2** (used to refer to a person, especially a man, that you like or feel sympathy for): *Poor bugger* (biedaczysko)*! His wife left him last week.* ◇ *He's a tough old bugger* (równy chłop). **3** a thing that is difficult or causes problems: *This door's a bugger to open.* ◇ *Question 6 is a real bugger.* ▶ **męczarnia, coś uciążliwego**

bugger² verb [I,T] **1** (Brit., taboo, slang) (used as a swear word when sb is annoyed about sth or to show that they do not care about sth at all): *Bugger* (niech to szlag)*! I've left my keys at home.* ◇ *Bugger it* (a niech to szlag)*! I've burnt the toast.* ◇ *Oh, bugger the cost* (pieprzmy koszty)*! Let's get it anyway.* ▶ **2** [T] (Brit., taboo slang) to break or ruin sth: *I think I've buggered the computer.* ▶ **pieprzyć**

PHR V **bugger sth up** (Brit., taboo, slang) to do sth badly or spoil sth: *I buggered up the exam.* ◇ *Sorry for buggering up your plans.* ▶ **pieprzyć coś** ⓘ Grzeczniejszym, choć nieformalnym sposobem powiedzenia tego samego jest **foul sth up**, **mess sth up** lub **bungle sth**.

ˌbugger ˈall noun [U] (Brit., taboo, slang) nothing at all; none at all: *There's bugger all on TV tonight.* ▶ **nic a nic**

buggy (Brit.) = PUSHCHAIR

bugle /ˈbjuːgl/ noun [C] a musical instrument like a small **trumpet**, used in the army for giving signals ▶ **trąbka** (*sygnałówka*)

⚷ **build¹** /bɪld/ verb (pt, pp **built** /bɪlt/) **1** [T] to make sth by putting pieces, materials, etc. together: *They've built a new bridge across the river.* ◇ *The house is built of stone.* ▶ **budować 2** [I] to use land for building on: *There's plenty of land to build on around here.* ▶ **budować 3** [T] to develop or increase sth: *The government is trying to build a more modern society.* ◇ *This book claims to help people to build their self-confidence.* ▶ **budować, rozwijać**

PHR V **build sth in/on; build sth into/onto sth** to make sth a part of sth else: *We're planning to build* (dobudować) *two more rooms onto the back of the house.* ◇ *They've made sure that a large number of checks are built into the system.* ▶ **ustanawiać coś częścią czegoś**

build on sth to use sth as a base from which you can make further progress: *Now that we're beginning to make a profit, we must build on this success.* ▶ **budować na czymś**

build sth on sth to base sth on sth: *a society built on the principle of freedom and democracy* ▶ **budować coś** (*np. na bazie*)

build up (to sth) to become greater in amount or number; to increase: *The traffic starts to build up at this time of day.* ▶ **wzrastać do czegoś, wzmagać się do czegoś**

build sth up 1 to make sth seem more important or greater than it really is: *I don't think it's a very serious matter, it's just been built up in the newspapers.* ▶ **rozdmuchiwać coś 2** to increase or develop sth over a period: *You'll need to build up your strength* (będziesz musiał odzyskać siły) *again after the operation.* ▶ **rozwijać/wzmacniać coś**

build² /bɪld/ noun [C,U] the shape and size of sb's body: *She **has a** very athletic **build**.* ▶ **budowa** (*ciała*)

> Por. **build** z **figure**. **Build** zazw. odnosi się do wzrostu, budowy ciała, umięśnienia i siły zarówno kobiet, jak i mężczyzn. **Figure** zazw. opisuje kształt, a szczególnie jego atrakcyjność lub jej brak. Zwykle odnosi się tylko do kobiet.

builder /ˈbɪldə(r)/ noun [C] a person whose job is to build houses and other buildings ▶ **budowniczy**

🔑 **building** /ˈbɪldɪŋ/ noun **1** [C] a structure, such as a house, shop or school, that has a roof and walls: *There are a lot of very old buildings in this town.* ▶ **budynek** **2** [U] the process or business of making buildings: *the building of the school* ◇ *building materials* ◇ *the building industry* ▶ **budownictwo**

ˈbuilding block noun [C] **1** a piece of wood or plastic used as a toy for children to build things with ▶ **klocek** **2** (**building blocks**) [pl.] parts that are joined together in order to make a large thing exist: *Single words are the building blocks of language.* ▶ **podstawa**

ˈbuilding site noun [C] an area of land on which a building is being built ▶ **plac budowy**

ˈbuilding society noun [C] (Brit.) an organization like a bank with which people can save money and which lends money to people who want to buy a house ▶ **kasa oszczędnościowa udzielająca pożyczek hipotecznych**

ˈbuild-up noun [C, usually sing.] **1 a build-up (of sth)** an increase of sth over a period: *The build-up of tension in the area has made war seem more likely.* ▶ **narastanie** **2 a build-up (to sth)** a period of preparation or excitement before an event: *The players started to get nervous in the build-up to the big game.* ▶ **przygotowania**, **końcowe odliczanie** (*przed ważnym wydarzeniem*)

built¹ /bɪlt/ [in compounds] having a body with the shape and size mentioned: *a tall well-built man* ▶ **zbudowany**

built² past tense, past participle of **build**

ˌbuilt-ˈin adj. [only before a noun] that is a part of sth and cannot be removed: *built-in cupboards* ◇ *There is built-in* (naturalna) *unfairness in the system.* ▶ **wbudowany**

ˌbuilt-ˈup adj. covered with buildings: *a built-up area* ▶ **zabudowany**

bulb /bʌlb/ noun [C] **1** (also ˈ**light bulb**) the glass part of an electric lamp that gives out light: *The bulb's gone* (żarówka się przepaliła) *in this lamp – I'll have to put a new one in.* ▶ **żarówka** ➲ picture at **light 2** the round root of certain plants: *a tulip bulb* ▶ **cebulka**

bulbous /ˈbʌlbəs/ adj. fat, round and ugly: *a bulbous red nose* ▶ **bulwiasty**, (*nos*) **kartofelkowaty**

bulge¹ /bʌldʒ/ verb [I] **1 bulge (with sth)** to be full of sth: *His bags were bulging with presents for the children.* ▶ **być wypchanym** **2** to stick out in a lump from sth that is usually flat: *My stomach is starting to bulge. I must get more exercise.* ▶ **wystawać**, **wybrzuszać się**

bulge² /bʌldʒ/ noun [C] a round lump that sticks out on sth ▶ **wypukłość**

bulging /ˈbʌldʒɪŋ/ adj. sticking out: *He had a thin face and rather bulging eyes* (wyłupiaste oczy). ▶ **wypukły**, **wybrzuszony**

bulimia /buˈlɪmiə/ (also **bulimia nervosa** /buˌlɪmiə nɜːˈvəʊsə/) noun [U] an illness in which a person eats too much and then forces himself or herself to **vomit** ▶ **bulimia** ➲ look at **anorexia**

■ **bulimic** /buˈlɪmɪk; bju-; -ˈlɪːmɪk; US / **1** adj. ▶ **bulimiczny** **2** noun [C] ▶ **osoba chora na bulimię**

bulk /bʌlk/ noun **1** [sing.] **the bulk (of sth)** the main part of sth; most of sth: *The bulk of the work has been done, so we should finish this week.* ▶ **ogromna większość** **2** [U] the size, quantity or weight of sth large: *The cupboard isn't especially heavy – it's its bulk that makes it hard to move.* ◇ *He slowly lifted his vast bulk* (cielsko) *out of the chair.* ▶ **masa**, **duży rozmiar**

IDM **in bulk** in large quantities: *If you buy in bulk, it's 10% cheaper.* ▶ **hurtowo**

bulky /ˈbʌlki/ adj. (**bulkier**; **bulkiest**) large and heavy and therefore difficult to move or carry: *a bulky parcel* ▶ **nieporęczny**, **zajmujący dużo miejsca**

bull /bʊl/ noun [C] **1** an adult male of the cow family ▶ **byk** ➲ note at **cow** **2** a male **whale** or **elephant** ▶ **samiec** (*wieloryba/słonia*)

bulldog /ˈbʊldɒg/ noun [C] a strong dog with short legs, a large head and a short, thick neck ▶ **buldog**

ˈBulldog clip™ noun [C] (Brit.) a metal device for holding papers together ▶ **duży spinacz do papieru** (*o walcowatym grzbiecie z dwiema metalowymi wypustkami*)) ➲ picture at **stationery**

bulldoze /ˈbʊldəʊz/ verb [T] to make ground flat or knock down a building with a **bulldozer** ▶ **równać spychaczem**

bulldozer /ˈbʊldəʊzə(r)/ noun [C] a large, powerful vehicle with a wide piece of metal at the front, used for clearing ground or knocking down buildings ▶ **spychacz** ➲ picture at **truck**

🔑 **bullet** /ˈbʊlɪt/ noun [C] a small metal object that is fired from a gun: *The bullet hit her in the arm.* ◇ *a bullet wound* ▶ **kula**, **pocisk**

bulletin /ˈbʊlətɪn/ noun [C] **1** a short news report on TV or radio; an official statement about a situation: *The next **news bulletin** on this channel is at 9 o'clock.* ▶ **komunikat**; **serwis informacyjny** **2** a short newspaper that a club or an organization produces: *As a member of the fan club, she receives a monthly bulletin.* ▶ **biuletyn**, **gazetka**

ˈbulletin board noun [C] **1** (US) = NOTICEBOARD **2** a place in a computer system where you can write or read messages ▶ (*komput.*) **tablica ogłoszeń**

ˈbullet point noun [C] an item in a list in a document, that is printed with a square, diamond or circle in front of it in order to show that it is important. The square, etc. is also called a **bullet point.** ▶ (*kolejny*) **punkt w tekście**, **punktor**

bulletproof /ˈbʊlɪtpruːf/ adj. made of a strong material that stops bullets from passing through it ▶ **kuloodporny**

bullfight /ˈbʊlfaɪt/ noun [C] a traditional public entertainment, especially in Spain, Portugal and Latin America, in which a **bull** is fought and usually killed ▶ **walka byków**

■ **bullfighter** noun [C] ▶ **toreador** | **bullfighting** noun [U] ▶ **walki byków**

bullfinch /ˈbʊlfɪntʃ/ noun [C] a small European bird of the **finch** family, with a strong curved beak and a pink breast ▶ **gil**

bullion /ˈbʊliən/ noun [U] bars of gold or silver: *The dollar price of gold bullion has risen by more than 10%.* ▶ **sztaby złota/srebra**

bullish /ˈbʊlɪʃ/ adj. **1** feeling confident and positive about the future: *in a bullish mood* ▶ **optymistyczny** **2** causing, or connected with, an increase in the price of shares: *a bullish market* ▶ (*giełda*) **zwyżkujący**

ˈbull market noun [C] a period during which share prices are rising and people are buying shares ▶ (*giełda*) **rynek zwyżkujący** ➲ look at **bear market**

bullock /ˈbʊlək/ noun [C] a young **bull** that has been castrated ▶ **wół** ➲ look at **ox**

bullseye /ˈbʊlzaɪ/ noun [C] the centre of the round object that you shoot or throw things at in certain sports; or a shot that hits this ▶ **środek tarczy**; **strzał w dziesiątkę**

bullshit /ˈbʊlʃɪt/ (taboo, slang) noun [U] nonsense ▶ **gówno** ■ **bullshit** verb [I,T] to say things that are not true, especially in order to trick sb: *She's just bullshitting.* ◇ *Don't try to bullshit me!* ▶ **pieprzyć bzdury**

bullshit¹ /ˈbʊlʃɪt/ (also informal **bull**) noun [U] (taboo, slang) nonsense: *That's just bullshit.* ▶ **bzdury**

bullshit² verb [I,T] (**bullshitting**; **bullshitted**) (taboo, slang) to say things that are not true, especially in order to trick sb: *She's just bullshitting.* ◇ *Don't try to bullshit me!* ▶ **wciskać (komuś) kit**
■ **bullshitter** noun [C] ▶ **picer**

bully¹ /ˈbʊli/ noun [C] (pl. **bullies**) a person who uses their strength or power to hurt or frighten people who are weaker ▶ **tyran**, **osoba znęcająca się nad słabszymi**

bully² /ˈbʊli/ verb [T] (**bullying**; **bullies**; pt, pp **bullied**) **bully sb (into doing sth)** to use your strength or power to hurt or frighten sb who is weaker or to make them do sth: *Don't try to bully me into making a decision.* ▶ **znęcać się nad słabszym**; **zmuszać kogoś do czegoś**
■ **bullying** noun [U] ▶ **znęcanie się nad słabszymi**

bulrush (also **bullrush**) /ˈbʊlrʌʃ/ noun [C] a tall plant with long narrow leaves and a long brown head of flowers, that grows in or near water ▶ **sitowie**

bulwark /ˈbʊlwək; US -wɜːk/ noun [C] **1 bulwark (against sth)** (formal) a person or thing that protects or defends sth: *a bulwark against communism* ▶ (*przen.*) **zapora (przed czymś)** **2** a wall built as a defence ▶ **wał obronny**

bum /bʌm/ noun [C] (informal) **1** (Brit.) the part of your body on which you sit ▶ **pupa** SYN **bottom** **2** (especially US) an insulting word for a person who lives on the street ▶ **włóczęga**, **żebrak** **3** (especially US) a lazy or useless person ▶ **próżniak**

bumbag /ˈbʌmbæɡ/ (US **fanny pack** /ˈfæni pæk/) noun [C] (informal) a small bag worn around the waist to keep money, etc. in ▶ **mała torebka noszona przy talii** ➲ picture at **bag**

bumble /ˈbʌmbl/ verb [I] to act or move in an awkward or confused way: *I could hear him bumbling around* (jak hałasował) *in the kitchen.* ▶ **poruszać się niezdarnie**; **być zdezorientowanym**

bumblebee /ˈbʌmblbiː/ noun [C] a large **bee** covered with small hairs that makes a loud noise as it flies ▶ **trzmiel** ➲ picture at **insect**

bumbling /ˈbʌmblɪŋ/ adj. behaving in an awkward confused way, often making careless mistakes ▶ **nieudolny**

bumf (also **bumph**) /bʌmf/ noun [U] (Brit., informal) written information, especially advertisements, official documents, forms, etc., that seem boring or unnecessary: *He threw away my letter, thinking it was just more election bumf.* ▶ **papierki** (*np. nudne dokumenty, reklama*)

bummer /ˈbʌmə(r)/ noun [sing.] (**a bummer**) (informal) a disappointing or unpleasant situation: *It's a real bummer that she can't come.* ▶ **nieprzyjemna sprawa**

bump¹ /bʌmp/ verb **1** [I] **bump against/into sb/sth** to hit sb/sth by accident when you are moving: *She bumped into a lamp post because she wasn't looking where she was going.* ▶ **zderzać się**, **uderzać się o coś** **2** [T] **bump sth (against/on sth)** to hit sth against or on sth by accident: *I bumped my knee on the edge of the table.* ▶ **uderzać czymś o coś** **3** [I] to move along over a rough surface: *The car bumped along the track to the farm.* ▶ **jechać po wyboistej drodze**

PHR V **bump into sb** to meet sb by chance: *I bumped into an old friend on the bus today.* ▶ **wpadać na kogoś**
bump sb off (slang) to murder sb ▶ (*zabić*) **załatwiać kogoś**
bump sth up (informal) to increase or make sth go up: *All this publicity will bump up sales of our new product.* ▶ **spowodować gwałtowny wzrost czegoś**

bump² /bʌmp/ noun [C] **1** the action or sound of sth hitting a hard surface: *She fell and hit the ground with a bump.* ▶ **uderzenie**; **łoskot** **2** a lump on the body, often caused by a hit ▶ **guz** **3** a part of a surface that is higher than the rest of it: *There are a lot of bumps in the road, so drive carefully.* ▶ **wybój**

bumper¹ /ˈbʌmpə(r)/ noun [C] the bar fixed to the front and back of a motor vehicle to protect it if it hits sth ▶ **zderzak** ➲ picture at **car**

bumper² /ˈbʌmpə(r)/ adj. [only before a noun] larger than usual: *The unusually fine weather has produced a bumper harvest this year.* ▶ **rekordowy**

ˈ**bumper sticker** noun [C] a sign that people stick on the **bumper** of their cars with a message on it ▶ **nalepka** (*na tylnym zderzaku*)

bumph = BUMF

bumpkin = COUNTRY BUMPKIN

bumpy /ˈbʌmpi/ adj. (**bumpier**; **bumpiest**) not flat or smooth: *a bumpy road* ◇ *Because of the stormy weather, it was a bumpy flight* (samolot się kołysał). ▶ (*droga*) **wyboisty**, **nierówny** OPP **smooth**

bun /bʌn/ noun [C] **1** a small round sweet cake: *a currant bun* ▶ **słodka bułeczka** **2** a small soft bread roll: *a hamburger bun* ▶ **rodzaj bułki** **3** hair fastened tightly into a round shape at the back of the head: *She wears her hair **in a bun**.* ▶ **kok** ➲ picture at **hair**

⚷ **bunch¹** /bʌntʃ/ noun **1** [C] a number of things, usually of the same type, fastened or growing together: *He bought her a bunch of flowers.* ◇ *a bunch of bananas/grapes* ◇ *a bunch of keys* ▶ **bukiet**, **kiść**, **pęk** ➲ picture at **bar** **2** [C, with sing. or pl. verb] (informal) a group of people: *My colleagues are the best bunch of people I've ever worked with.* ▶ **paczka** **3** (**bunches**) [pl.] long hair that is tied on each side of the head: *She wore her hair in bunches.* ▶ **kucyki** ➲ picture at **hair**

bunch² /bʌntʃ/ verb [I,T] **bunch (sth/sb) (up/together)** to stay together in a group; to form sth into a group or bunch: *The runners bunched up as they came round the final bend.* ◇ *He kept his papers bunched together in his hand.* ▶ **skupiać się**, **ścieśniać się**; **wiązać**

bundle¹ /ˈbʌndl/ noun [C] a number of things tied or folded together: *a bundle of letters with an elastic band round them* ▶ **wiązka**, **plik**

bundle² /ˈbʌndl/ verb [T] to put or push sb or sth quickly and in a rough way in a particular direction: *He was arrested and bundled into a police car.* ▶ **w/wy-pychać**, **ciskać**

PHR V **bundle sth (up)** to make or tie a number of things together: *I bundled up the old newspapers and threw them away.* ▶ **z(a)wiązywać**

bunfight /ˈbʌnfaɪt/ noun [C] (Brit., informal) **1** an impressive or important party or other social event ▶ **impreza** **2** an angry argument or discussion ▶ **sprzeczka**

bung¹ /bʌŋ/ verb [T] (Brit., informal) to put or throw sth somewhere in a rough or careless way: *We bunged the suitcases into the car and drove away.* ▶ **wrzucać**

bung² /bʌŋ/ noun [C] a round piece of wood or rubber that is used for closing the hole in a container such as a **barrel** ▶ **szpunt**, **zatyczka**

bungalow /ˈbʌŋɡələʊ/ noun [C] (Brit.) a house that is all on one level, without stairs ▶ **dom parterowy** ➲ picture on **page A3**

ˌ**bunged ˈup** adj. (informal) blocked, so that nothing can get through: *I feel terrible – I've got a cold and my nose is all bunged up.* ▶ **zablokowany**

bungee jumping /ˈbʌndʒi dʒʌmpɪŋ/ noun [U] a sport in which you jump from a high place, for example a bridge, with a thick **elastic** rope tied round your feet ▶ **skoki na bungee** ➲ picture on **page A8**

bungle /ˈbʌŋɡl/ verb [I,T] to do sth badly or fail to do sth: *The men fled after bungling a raid on a bank* (po nieudanym skoku na bank). ▶ **partaczyć**

bunion /ˈbʌnjən/ noun [C] a painful swelling on the foot, usually on the big toe ▶ **haluks**

bunk /bʌŋk/ noun [C] **1** a bed that is fixed to a wall, for example on a ship or train ▶ **koja 2** (also ˈ**bunk bed**) one of a pair of single beds built as a unit with one above the other ▶ **łóżko piętrowe** ➲ note at **bed**

IDM **do a bunk** (Brit., informal) to run away or escape; to leave without telling anyone ▶ **zwiewać**

bunker /ˈbʌŋkə(r)/ noun [C] **1** a strong underground building that gives protection in a war ▶ **bunkier 2** a hole filled with sand on a **golf course** ▶ (*na polu golfowym*) **bunkier**

bunny /ˈbʌni/ noun [C] (pl. **bunnies**) (used by and to small children) a **rabbit** ▶ **króliczek**

Bunsen burner /ˌbʌnsn ˈbɜːnə(r)/ noun [C] an instrument used in scientific work that produces a hot gas flame ▶ **palnik Bunsena** ➲ picture at **laboratory**

bunting /ˈbʌntɪŋ/ noun [U] coloured flags or paper used for decorating streets and buildings in celebrations ▶ **chorągiewki**

buoy[1] /bɔɪ/ noun [C] a floating object, fastened to the bottom of the sea or a river, that shows the places where it is dangerous for boats to go ▶ **boja**

buoy[2] /bɔɪ/ verb [T] **buoy sb/sth (up) 1** to keep sb happy and confident: *His encouragement buoyed her up during that difficult period.* ▶ **podtrzymywać na duchu 2** to keep sth at a high level: *Share prices were buoyed by news of a takeover.* ▶ **podtrzymywać, utrzymywać** (*np. na wysokim poziomie*)

buoyant /ˈbɔɪənt; US ˈbuːjənt/ adj. **1** (used about business activity, etc.) staying at a high level or increasing, so that people make more money: *Despite the recession, the property market remained buoyant.* ▶ **prężny 2** happy and confident: *The team were in buoyant mood after their win.* ▶ **wesoły 3** (used about a material) floating or able to float ▶ **utrzymujący się na powierzchni wody 4** (used about prices) rising or keeping at a high level ▶ **utrzymujący się na wysokim poziomie; wzrastający**

■ **buoyancy** /-ənsi/ noun [U]: *the buoyancy of the German economy* ◇ *a buoyancy aid* pławik ▶ **prężność; pogoda ducha; pływalność**

burden[1] /ˈbɜːdn/ noun [C] **1** a responsibility or difficult task that causes a lot of work or worry: *Having to make all the decisions is a terrible burden for me.* ◇ *I don't want to be a burden to my children when I'm old.* ▶ **ciężar, brzemię 2** something that is heavy and difficult to carry ▶ **ciężar**

burden[2] /ˈbɜːdn/ verb [T] **burden sb/yourself (with sth)** to give sb/yourself a responsibility or task that causes a lot of work or worry ▶ **obciążać (się), obarczać (się)**

burdensome /ˈbɜːdnsəm/ adj. (formal) causing worry, difficulty or hard work ▶ **uciążliwy**

bureau /ˈbjʊərəʊ/ noun [C] (pl. **bureaux** or **bureaus** /-rəʊz/) **1** (Brit.) a writing desk with drawers and a lid ▶ **sekretarzyk 2** an organization that provides information: *a tourist information bureau* ▶ **biuro 3** (especially US) one of certain government departments: *the Federal Bureau of Investigation* ▶ **biuro**

bureaucracy /bjʊəˈrɒkrəsi/ noun (pl. **bureaucracies**) **1** [U] (often used in a critical way) the system of official rules that an organization has for doing sth, that people often think is too complicated: *Getting a visa involves a lot of unnecessary bureaucracy.* ▶ **biurokracja, formalności 2** [C,U] a system of government by a large number of officials who are not elected; a country with this system ▶ **biurokracja**

■ **bureaucratic** /ˌbjʊərəˈkrætɪk/ adj.: *You have to go through a complex bureaucratic procedure if you want to get your money back.* ▶ **biurokratyczny**

bureaucrat /ˈbjʊərəkræt/ noun [C] (often used in a critical way) an official in an organization or government department ▶ **biurokra(k)a**

bureau de change /ˌbjʊərəʊ də ˈʃɑːnʒ/ noun [C] (pl. **bureaux de change**) (Brit.) an office at an airport, in a hotel, etc. where you can change the money of one country to the money of another country ▶ **kantor wymiany walut**

burette /bjuˈret/ noun [C] a glass tube with measurements marked on it and a tap at one end, used in chemistry ▶ **biureta** ➲ picture at **laboratory**

burgeon /ˈbɜːdʒən/ verb [I] (formal) to begin to grow or develop rapidly ▶ **szybko się rozwijać**

burger = HAMBURGER (1)

-burger /ˈbɜːɡə(r)/ [in compounds] **1** a **hamburger** with sth else on top: *a cheeseburger* ▶ **hamburger** (*różnych rodzajów*) **2** something that is cooked like and looks like a **hamburger**, but is made of sth else: *a veggie burger* ◇ *a fish burger* hamburger rybny ▶ **potrawa w formie hamburgera**

burglar /ˈbɜːɡlə(r)/ noun [C] a person who enters a building illegally in order to steal: *The burglars broke in by smashing a window.* ▶ **włamywacz/ka** ➲ note at **thief**

ˈ**burglar alarm** noun [C] a piece of equipment, usually fixed on a wall, that makes a loud noise if a thief enters a building ▶ **alarm przeciwwłamaniowy**

burglary /ˈbɜːɡləri/ noun [C,U] (pl. **burglaries**) the crime of entering a building illegally in order to steal: *There was a burglary next door last week.* ◇ *He is in prison for burglary.* ▶ **kradzież z włamaniem**

burgle /ˈbɜːɡl/ (US **burglarize** /ˈbɜːɡləraɪz/) verb [T] to enter a building illegally, usually using force, and steal from it: *Our flat was burgled while we were out.* ▶ **włamywać się, okradać**

burgundy /ˈbɜːɡəndi/ noun **1** (**Burgundy**) [U,C] (pl. **Burgundies**) a red or white wine from the Burgundy area of eastern France ▶ (*wino*) **burgund 2** [U] a dark red colour ▶ (*kolor*) **burgund**

■ **burgundy** adj. ▶ (*wino*) **burgundzki**; (*kolor*) **bordowy**

burial /ˈberiəl/ noun [C,U] the ceremony when a dead body is buried in the ground: ▶ **pogrzeb** ➲ note at **funeral**

ˈ**burial ground** noun [C] a place where dead bodies are buried, especially an ancient place ▶ **cmentarzysko**

burka /ˈbɜːkə; Brit. also ˈbʊəkə/ noun a long loose piece of clothing that covers the whole body, including the head and face, worn in public by Muslim women in some countries ▶ **burka**

burly /ˈbɜːli/ adj. (**burlier**; **burliest**) (used about a person or their body) strong and heavy ▶ **krzepki, tęgi**

burn[1] /bɜːn/ verb (pt, pp **burnt** /bɜːnt/ or **burned** /bɜːnd/) **1** [I] to be on fire: *Firemen raced to the burning building.* ▶ **płonąć** ➲ note at **alight 2** [T] to destroy, damage or injure sb/sth with fire or heat: *We took all the rubbish outside and burned it.* ◇ *It was a terrible fire and the whole building was burnt to the ground.* ◇ *If you get too close to the fire, you'll burn yourself.* ▶ **palić, parzyć** **3** [I] to be destroyed, damaged or injured by fire or heat: *If you leave the cake in the oven for much longer, it will burn.* ◇ *I can't spend too much time in the sun because I burn easily.* ◇ *They were trapped by the flames and they burned to death.* ▶ **palić się, przypalać się, parzyć się** **4** [T] to produce a hole or mark in or on sth by burning: *He dropped his cigarette and it burned a hole in the carpet.* ▶ **wypalać** (*np. dziurę*) **5** [T] to use sth as fuel: *an oil-burning lamp* lampa olejowa ▶ **spalać** (*paliwo*) **6** [I] to feel very hot and painful: *You have a temperature – your forehead's burning.* ▶ **być gorącym, odczuwać gorąco** **7** [I] to produce light: *I don't think he went to bed at all – I could see his light burning all night.* ▶ (*światło itp.*) **palić się** **8** [T] to put information onto a CD, etc. ▶ **nagrywać** (*na CD/DVD*) **9** [I] **burn (with sth)** to be filled with a very strong feeling: *She was burning with indignation.* ▶ **płonąć** (*uczuciem*)

IDM **sb's ears are burning** → EAR

PHR V **burn down** (used about a building) to be completely destroyed by fire: *The fire could not be brought under control and the school burned down.* ▶ **spalić się (doszczętnie)**

burn sth down to completely destroy a building by fire: *The house was burnt down in a fire some years ago.* ▶ **spalić (doszczętnie)**

burn (sth) off to remove sth or to be removed by burning ▶ **spalać/wypalać (się/coś)**

burn sth out [usually passive] to completely destroy sth by burning: *the burnt-out wreck of a car* ▶ **wypalać, spalać**

burn (yourself) out to work, etc. until you have no more energy or strength ▶ (*przen: osoba*) **wypalić się**

burn (sth) up to destroy or to be destroyed by fire or strong heat: *The space capsule burnt up on its re-entry into the earth's atmosphere.* ▶ **spalać doszczętnie**

burn² /bɜːn/ noun [C] damage or an injury caused by fire or heat: *He was taken to hospital with **minor burns**.* ◇ *There's a cigarette burn on the carpet.* ▶ **poparzenie, oparzenie**

burner (US) = RING¹ (5)

burning /ˈbɜːnɪŋ/ adj. [only before a noun] **1** (used about a feeling) extremely strong: *a burning ambition/desire* ▶ (*uczucia*) **palący** **2** very important or urgent: *a burning issue/question* ▶ (*problem itp.*) **palący** **3** feeling very hot: *the burning sun* ▶ **palący**

burnout /ˈbɜːnaʊt/ noun [C, U] the state of being extremely tired or ill, either physically or mentally, because you have worked too hard ▶ **wypalenie (się), przemęczenie**

Burns Night noun [U,C] the evening of 25 January when Scottish people celebrate the birthday of the Scottish **poet**, Robert Burns, with traditional Scottish music, **whisky** and dishes such as **haggis** ▶ **święto z okazji urodzin szkockiego poety Roberta Burnsa**

burnt past tense, past participle of **burn**

ˌburnt-ˈout adj. **1** destroyed or badly damaged by fire: *a burnt-out car* ▶ **spalony** **2** feeling as if you have done sth for too long and need to have a rest: *I'm feeling burnt-out at work – I need a holiday.* ▶ **wypalony, przemęczony**

burp /bɜːp/ verb [I] to make a noise with the mouth when air rises from the stomach and is forced out: *He sat back when he had finished his meal and burped loudly.* ▶ **odbijać się, bekać**

■ **burp** noun [C] ▶ **odbicie się** (*po jedzeniu*), **beknięcie**

burrow¹ /ˈbʌrəʊ; US ˈbɜːr-/ verb [I] **1** to dig a hole in the ground, to make a tunnel or to look for sth: *These animals burrow for food.* ▶ **ryć, kopać** (*np. norę*) **2** to search for sth under or among things: *She burrowed in her handbag for her keys.* ▶ **myszkować, szukać**

burrow² /ˈbʌrəʊ; US ˈbɜːr-/ noun [C] a hole in the ground made by certain animals, for example **rabbits**, in which they live ▶ **nora, jama**

bursar /ˈbɜːsə(r)/ noun [C] the person who manages the financial matters of a school, college or university ▶ **kwestor**

bursary /ˈbɜːsəri/ noun [C] (pl. **bursaries**) a sum of money given to a specially chosen student to pay for his or her studies at a college or university ▶ **stypendium** ➲ look at **scholarship**

burst¹ /bɜːst/ verb (pt, pp **burst**) [I,T] to break open suddenly and violently, usually because there is too much pressure inside; to cause this to happen: *The ball burst when I kicked it.* ◇ *You'll burst that tyre if you blow it up any more.* ◇ (figurative) *If I eat any more, I'll burst!* ◇ *If it rains much more, the river will burst its banks.* ▶ **pękać, rozsadzać, rozerwać (się), wylewać**

IDM **be bursting (with sth)** to be very full of sth: *I packed so many clothes that my suitcase was bursting.* ◇ *He was bursting with happiness* (nie posiadał się ze szczęścia) *on his wedding day.* ▶ **pękać (od/z czegoś); tryskać** (*np. radością*)

be bursting to do sth to want to do sth very much: *I'm bursting to tell someone the news but it's a secret.* ▶ **korcić kogoś do czegoś**

burst (sth) open to enter a room or building suddenly and noisily: *Suddenly the doors burst open and five police officers rushed in.* ▶ **gwałtownie (się) otworzyć**

PHR V **burst in; burst into a room, building, etc.** to move suddenly in a particular direction, often using force: *She burst into the manager's office and demanded to speak to him.* ▶ **wdzierać się gdzieś**

burst in on sb/sth to interrupt sb/sth by arriving suddenly: *The police burst in on the gang as they were counting the money.* ▶ **wpadać (gdzieś), wtargnąć**

burst into sth to start doing sth suddenly: *On hearing the news she **burst into tears**.* ◇ *The lorry hit a wall and **burst into flames*** (stanęła w płomieniach). ▶ **wybuchać** (*np. płaczem*)

burst out **1** to start doing sth suddenly: *He looked so ridiculous that I **burst out laughing**.* ▶ **wybuchać** (*np. śmiechem*) **2** to say sth suddenly and with strong feeling: *Finally she burst out, 'I can't stand it any more!'* ▶ **wykrzykiwać**

burst² /bɜːst/ noun [C] **1** a short period of a particular activity, that often starts suddenly: *a burst of energy/enthusiasm/speed* ◇ *a burst of applause/gunfire* ◇ *He prefers to work **in short bursts*** (krótkimi zrywami). ▶ **wybuch** (*np. entuzjazmu*) **2** an occasion when sth bursts or explodes; a crack or hole caused by this: *a burst in a water pipe* ▶ **pęknięcie**

bury /ˈberi/ verb [T] (**burying**; **buries**; pt, pp **buried**) **1** to put a dead body in the ground: *She wants to be buried in the village graveyard.* ▶ **grzebać** **2** to put sth in a hole in the ground and cover it: *Our dog always buries its bones in the garden.* ▶ **zakopywać** **3** [usually passive] to cover or hide sth/sb: *At last I found the photograph, buried at the bottom of a drawer.* ◇ (figurative) *Aisha was buried in a book* (była pochłonięta lekturą) *and didn't hear us come in.* ▶ **przykrywać**

bus /bʌs/ noun [C] a big public vehicle which takes passengers along a fixed route and stops regularly to let people get on and off: *Where do you usually get on/off the bus?* ◇ *We'll have to hurry up if we want to **catch the 9 o'clock bus**.* ◇ *We'd better run or we'll **miss the bus**.* ▶ **autobus** ➲ look at **coach¹** (2) ➲ picture on **page A7 and 104**

buses

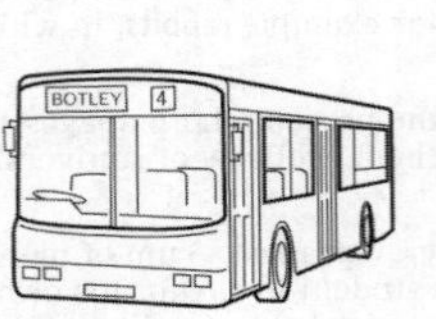

single-decker bus double-decker bus

bus (Brit. also **coach**) minibus

travelling by bus
You can get on or off a bus at a **bus stop** and the place where most bus routes start is the **bus station**. The **bus driver** will probably take the money (your **fare**) and give you your **ticket**, or there may be a **conductor** who collects the fares. You can buy a **single** (=one way) or a **return** (= there and back) ticket. A bus **pass** allows you to travel in a particular area for a fixed period of time. In British English a comfortable bus used for long journeys is called a **coach**. Note that we travel **on the bus** or **by bus**: *'How do you get to work?' 'On the bus.'*

bush /bʊʃ/ noun **1** [C] a plant like a small, thick tree with many low branches: *a rose bush* ▶ **krzak 2** (often **the bush**) [U] wild land that has not been cleared, especially in Africa and Australia ▶ **busz**
IDM beat about/around the bush → BEAT[1]

bushy /bʊʃi/ adj. (**bushier**; **bushiest**) **1** (used about hair or fur) growing closely together in large numbers; thick: *bushy hair/eyebrows* ▶ **gęsty 2** (used about plants) growing thickly, with a lot of leaves ▶ **krzaczasty**

busier, busiest, busily → BUSY[1]

business /ˈbɪznəs/ noun **1** [U] buying and selling as a way of earning money: *She's planning to* ***set up in business*** *as a hairdresser* (otworzyć zakład fryzjerski). ◇ *I'm going to* ***go into business*** (prowadzić działalność gospodarczą) *with my brother.* ◇ *They are very easy to* ***do business with.*** Z nimi bardzo łatwo prowadzi się interesy. ▶ **biznes 2** [U] the work that you do as your job: *The manager will be away* ***on business*** (w podróży służbowej) *next week.* ◇ *a business trip* ▶ **praca 3** [U] the number of customers that a person or company has had: *Business has been good for the time of year.* ▶ **ruch w interesie 4** [C] a firm, a shop, a factory, etc. which produces or sells goods or provides a service: *She aims to* ***start a business*** *of her own.* ▶ **działalność gospodarcza**, **firma 5** [U] something that concerns a particular person: *The friends I choose are my business, not yours.* ◇ *Our business is to collect the information, not to comment on it.* Do nas należy zbieranie informacji, a nie komentowanie. ◇ *'How much did it cost?' 'It's* ***none of your business!'*** ▶ **(czyjaś) sprawa 6** [U] important matters that need to be dealt with or discussed: *First we have some unfinished business from the last meeting to deal with.* ▶ **sprawy 7** [sing.] a situation or an event, especially one that is strange or unpleasant: *The divorce was an awful business.* ◇ *I found the whole business very depressing.* ▶ **sprawa**
IDM get down to business to start the work that has to be done ▶ **zabierać się do pracy/roboty**
go out of business to have to close because there is no more money available ▶ **zwijać interes**
have no business to do sth/doing sth to have no right to do sth ▶ **nie mieć prawa**
mind your own business → MIND[2]
monkey business → MONKEY

ˈ**business administration** noun [U] the study of how to manage a business: *a master's degree in business administration (= an MBA)* ▶ (*przedmiot*) **zarządzanie**

ˈ**business card** noun [C] a small card printed with sb's name and details of their job and company ▶ **wizytówka**

ˈ**business class** (Brit. also ˈ**club class**) noun [U] the part of a plane where passengers have a high level of comfort and service, designed for people travelling on business, and less expensive than first class ▶ **klasa biznes**
■ ˈ**business class** (Brit. also ˈ**club class**) adv.: *I always fly business class.* Zawsze latam klasą biznes.

ˈ**business hours** noun [pl.] the hours in a day that a shop/store or company is open ▶ **godziny urzędowania/pracy**

businesslike /ˈbɪznəslaɪk/ adj. dealing with matters in a direct and practical way, without trying to be friendly: *She has a very businesslike manner.* ▶ **praktyczny**, **rzeczowy, solidny**

businessman /ˈbɪznəsmæn; -mən/, **businesswoman** /ˈbɪznəswʊmən/ noun [C] (pl. **-men** /-men/; **-women** /-wɪmɪn/) **1** a person who works in business, especially in a top position: *a millionaire businessman* ▶ **biznesmen**, **kobieta interesu 2** a person who is skilful at dealing with money: *I should have got a better price for the car, but I'm not much of a businessman.* ▶ **człowiek, który ma dobrą głowę do interesów**

ˈ**business park** noun [C] an area of land that is specially designed for offices and small factories ▶ **centrum biznesowo-przemysłowe**

ˈ**business school** noun [C] a part of a college or university that teaches business, often to **graduates** ▶ **szkoła biznesu**

ˈ**business studies** noun [U] the study of how to control and manage a company ▶ (*studia*) **zarządzanie i administracja**

busk /bʌsk/ verb [I] to sing or play music in the street so that people will give you money ▶ **muzykować na ulicy**

busker /ˈbʌskə(r)/ noun [C] a street musician ▶ **grajek uliczny**

ˈ**bus pass** noun [C] **1** a ticket that allows you to travel on any bus within a particular area for a fixed period of time ▶ **okresowy bilet autobusowy 2** a card that allows people from particular groups (for example, students or old people) to travel free or at a reduced cost ▶ **okresowa legitymacja autobusowa uprawniająca do ulgowych lub darmowych przejazdów** (*np. dla emerytów*)

ˈ**bus shelter** noun [C] a structure with a roof where people can stand while they are waiting for a bus ▶ **wiata autobusowa**

ˈ**bus station** noun [C] the place in a town or city where buses (especially to or from other towns) leave and arrive ▶ **dworzec autobusowy**

bus stop noun [C] a place at the side of a road that is marked with a sign, where buses stop ▶ **przystanek autobusowy**

bust[1] /bʌst/ verb (pt, pp **bust** or **busted**) (informal) **1** [T] to break or damage sth so that it cannot be used ▶ **rozwalać 2** [T] to arrest sb: *He was busted for possession of heroin.* ▶ **przymknąć**

bust² /bʌst/ noun [C] **1** a model in stone, etc. of a person's head, shoulders and chest ▶ **popiersie 2** a woman's breasts; the measurement round a woman's chest: *This blouse is a bit too tight around the bust.* ▶ **biust 3** (informal) an unexpected visit by the police in order to arrest people for doing sth illegal: *a drugs bust* ▶ **nalot**

bust³ /bʌst/ adj. [not before a noun] (informal) broken or not working: *The zip on these trousers is bust.* ▶ **zepsuty**
IDM **go bust** (informal) (used about a business) to close because it has lost so much money: *During the recession thousands of businesses went bust.* ▶ **plajtować** SYN **bankrupt**

bustle¹ /ˈbʌsl/ verb **1** [I,T] to move in a busy, noisy or excited way; to make sb move somewhere quickly: *He bustled about the kitchen making tea.* ◇ *They bustled her out of the room before she could see the body.* ▶ **krzątać się**; **popędzać (kogoś) 2** [I] **bustle (with sth)** to be full of people, noise or activity: *The streets were bustling with shoppers.* ▶ **tętnić życiem**, **roić się**

bustle² /ˈbʌsl/ noun [U] excited and noisy activity: *She loved the bustle of city life.* ▶ **zgiełk**, **bieganina**

bustling /ˈbʌslɪŋ/ adj. ~ **(with sth)** full of people moving about in a busy way: *a bustling city* ◇ *The market was bustling with life.* ▶ **pełen zgiełku**

ˈ**bust-up** noun [C] (informal) an argument: *He had a bust-up with his boss over working hours.* ▶ **draka**

busy¹ /ˈbɪzi/ adj. (**busier**; **busiest**) **1 busy (at/with sth)**; **busy (doing sth)** having a lot of work or tasks to do; not free; working on sth: *Don't disturb him. He's busy.* ◇ *She's busy with her preparations for the party.* ◇ *We're busy decorating the spare room before our visitors arrive.* ▶ **zajęty 2** (used about a period of time) full of activity and things to do: *I've had rather a busy week.* ▶ **pracowity** (*np. dzień, tydzień*) **3** (used about a place) full of people, movement and activity: *The town centre was so busy* (w centrum miasta był taki duży ruch) *that you could hardly move.* ▶ **ruchliwy 4** (especially US) (used about a telephone) being used: *The line's busy at the moment. I'll try again later.* ▶ **zajęty**
■ **busily** adv.: *When I came in she was busily writing something at her desk.* ▶ **pracowicie**
IDM **get busy** to start working: *We'll have to get busy if we're going to be ready in time.* ▶ **zabierać się do pracy**

busy² /ˈbɪzi/ verb [T] (**busying**; **busies**; pt, pp **busied**) **busy yourself with sth**; **busy yourself doing sth** to keep yourself busy; to find sth to do ▶ **zajmować się**

busybody /ˈbɪzibɒdi/ noun [C] (pl. **busybodies**) a person who is too interested in other people's private lives ▶ **wścibsk-i/a**

but¹ /bət; strong form bʌt/ conj. **1** (used for introducing an idea which contrasts with or is different from what has just been said): *The weather will be sunny but cold.* ◇ *Theirs is not the first but the second house on the left.* ◇ *James hasn't got a car but his sister has.* ▶ **ale**, **a 2** however; and yet: *I'd love to come but I can't make it till 8 o'clock.* ▶ **ale (jednak) 3** (used when you are saying sorry for sth): *Excuse me, but is your name David Harries?* ◇ *I'm sorry, but I can't stay any longer.* ▶ **ale 4** (used for introducing a statement that shows that you are surprised or annoyed or that you disagree): *'Here's the book you lent me.' 'But it's all dirty and torn!'* ▶ **ale**, **jednak**
IDM **but then** however; on the other hand: *We could go swimming. But then perhaps it's too cold.* ▶ **zresztą**

but² /bət; strong form bʌt/ prep. except: *I've told no one but you about this.* ◇ *We've had nothing but trouble* (mamy same kłopoty) *with this washing machine!* ▶ **oprócz**
IDM **but for sb/sth** except for or without sb/sth: *We wouldn't have managed but for your help.* ▶ **gdyby nie ktoś/coś**

butcher¹ /ˈbʊtʃə(r)/ noun [C] **1** a person who sells meat ▶ **rzeźnik** ➲ note at **meat 2** (**the butcher's**) [sing.] a shop that sells meat: *She went to the butcher's for some sausages.* ▶ **sklep mięsny** ➲ picture on **page A5 3** a person who kills a lot of people in a cruel way ▶ **morder-ca/czyni**

B

butcher² /ˈbʊtʃə(r)/ verb [T] to kill a lot of people in a cruel way ▶ **dokonywać rzezi**

butchery /ˈbʊtʃəri/ noun [U] cruel killing ▶ **rzeź**

butler /ˈbʌtlə(r)/ noun [C] a person who works in a very large house, whose duties include organizing and serving food and wine ▶ **kamerdyner**

butt¹ /bʌt/ verb [T] to hit sb/sth with the head ▶ **uderzać głową**
PHR V **butt in (on sb/sth)** to interrupt sb/sth or to join in sth without being asked: *I'm sorry to butt in but could I speak to you urgently for a minute?* ▶ **wtrącać się** (*np. do rozmowy*)

butt² /bʌt/ noun [C] **1** the thicker, heavier end of a weapon or tool: *the butt of a rifle* ▶ **grubszy koniec** (*broni lub narzędzia*) **2** a short piece of a cigarette which is left when it has been smoked ▶ **niedopałek 3** (especially US, informal) the part of your body that you sit on; your bottom: *Get up off your butt and do some work!* ▶ **tyłek 4** the act of hitting sb with your head ▶ **uderzenie (kogoś) głową**
IDM **be the butt of sth** a person who is often laughed at or talked about in an unkind way: *Fat children are often the butt of other children's jokes.* ▶ **być ofiarą** (*np. żartu*)

butter¹ /ˈbʌtə(r)/ noun [U] a soft yellow fat that is made from cream and used for spreading on bread, etc. or in cooking ▶ **masło**

butter² /ˈbʌtə(r)/ verb [T] to spread butter on bread, etc.: *I'll cut the bread and you butter it.* ◇ *hot buttered toast* ▶ **smarować masłem**

buttercup /ˈbʌtəkʌp/ noun [C] a wild plant with small shiny yellow flowers that are shaped like cups ▶ **jaskier**

butterfingers /ˈbʌtəfɪŋgəz/ noun [sing.] (informal) a person who often drops things ▶ **niezdara**

butterfly /ˈbʌtəflaɪ/ noun **1** [C] (pl. **butterflies**) an insect with a long, thin body and four brightly coloured wings: *Caterpillars develop into butterflies.* ▶ **motyl** ➲ picture at **insect 2** [sing.] a style of swimming in which both arms are brought over the head at the same time, and the legs move up and down together ▶ **styl motylkowy**
IDM **have butterflies (in your stomach)** (informal) to feel very nervous before doing sth ▶ **mieć tremę**

buttermilk /ˈbʌtəmɪlk/ noun [U] the liquid that is left when butter is separated from milk ▶ **maślanka**

ˈ**butterscotch** /ˈbʌtəskɒtʃ/ noun [U] a type of hard pale brown sweet made by boiling butter and brown sugar together ▶ **cukierek mleczny** (*z brązowego cukru*)

buttock /ˈbʌtək/ noun [C, usually pl.] one of the two parts of your body which you sit on ▶ **pośladek**

button /ˈbʌtn/ noun [C] **1** a small, often round, piece of plastic, wood or metal that you use for fastening your clothes: *One of the buttons on my jacket has come off.* ◇ *This blouse is too tight – I can't fasten the buttons.* ▶ **guzik** ➲ picture on **page A1** ➲ picture on **page 106 2** a small part of a machine, etc. that you press in order to operate sth: ***Press the button** to ring the bell.* ◇ *To dial the same number again, **push the 'redial' button.*** ◇ *Which button turns the volume down?* ◇ *To print a file, simply click on the 'print' button.* ◇ *Double click the right mouse button.* ▶ **guzik** ➲ picture at **handle**

buttons and fasteners

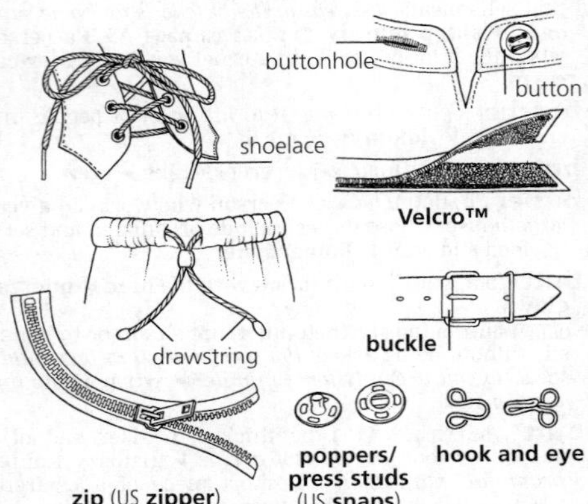

buttonhole[1] /ˈbʌtnhəʊl/ noun [C] **1** a hole in a piece of clothing that you push a button through in order to fasten it ▶ **dziurka** (*od guzika*) ➲ picture at **button 2** (Brit.) a flower worn in the **buttonhole** of a coat or jacket ▶ **kwiat w butonierce**

buttonhole[2] /ˈbʌtnhəʊl/ verb [T] (informal) to make sb stop and listen to you, especially when they do not want to ▶ **zatrzymywać kogoś na rozmowę**

buttress[1] /ˈbʌtrəs/ noun [C] a stone or brick structure that supports a wall ▶ **przypora**

buttress[2] /ˈbʌtrəs/ verb [T] (formal) to support or give strength to sb/sth: *The sharp increase in crime seems to buttress the argument for more police officers on the street.* ▶ **wspierać**; **wzmacniać**

buxom /ˈbʌksəm/ adj. (used about a woman) large in an attractive way, and with large breasts ▶ (*kobieta*) **atrakcyjna i piersiasta**

⚷ **buy[1]** /baɪ/ verb [T] (pt, pp **bought** /bɔːt/) **buy sth (for sb)**; **buy sb sth** to get sth by paying money for it: *I'm going to buy a new dress for the party.* ◇ *We bought this book for you in London.* ◇ *Can I buy you a coffee?* ◇ *He bought the car from a friend.* ◇ *Did you buy your car new or second-hand?* ◇ *He bought the necklace as a present for his wife.* ▶ **kupować** ➲ note at **shopping** OPP **sell**

IDM **buy time** to do sth in order to delay an event, a decision, etc.: *He took a few days' holiday in order to buy some time before giving them his final decision.* ▶ **zyskiwać na czasie**

PHR V **buy sb off** (informal) to pay sb money, especially dishonestly, to stop them from doing sth you do not want them to do: *The construction company tried to buy off the opposition by offering them discounts on the properties they were planning to build.* ▶ **pozyskiwać/kupić kogoś**

buy sb out to pay sb for their share in a house, business, etc. in order to get full control of it yourself: *After the divorce, she bought him out and kept the house for herself.* ▶ **spłacać kogoś**

buy[2] /baɪ/ noun [C] an act of buying sth or a thing that you can buy: *I think your house was a very good buy.* ▶ **zakup**

⚷ **buyer** /ˈbaɪə(r)/ noun [C] **1** a person who is buying sth or may buy sth: *I think we've found a buyer for our house!* ▶ **kupując-y/a** OPP **seller 2** a person whose job is to choose and buy goods to be sold in a large shop ▶ **pracowni-k/ca działu zakupów**

buyout /ˈbaɪaʊt/ noun [C] the act of buying enough or all of the shares in a company in order to get control of it ▶ **wykup** (*akcji przedsiębiorstwa*)

buzz[1] /bʌz/ verb **1** [I] to make the sound that a **bee**, etc. makes when flying: *A large fly was buzzing against the windowpane.* ▶ **bzyczeć**, **brzęczeć 2** [I] **buzz (with sth)** to be full of excitement, activity, thoughts, etc.: *Her head was buzzing* (w głowie jej huczało) *with questions that she wanted to ask.* ◇ *The room was buzzing with activity.* ▶ **tętnić życiem**, **wrzeć jak w ulu 3** [I,T] to call sb by using an electric bell, etc.: *The doctor will buzz for you when he's ready.* ▶ **dzwonić**

buzz[2] /bʌz/ noun **1** [C, usually sing.] the sound that a **bee**, etc. makes when flying: *the buzz of insects* ▶ **bzyk**, **bzyczenie 2** [sing.] the low sound made by many people talking at the same time: *I could hear the buzz of conversation in the next room.* ▶ **gwar 3** [sing.] (informal) a strong feeling of excitement or pleasure: *a buzz of expectation* ◇ *Parachuting **gives me a real buzz.*** ◇ *She **gets a buzz out of** shopping for expensive clothes.* ▶ **odlot**

IDM **give sb a buzz** (informal) to telephone sb ▶ **dzwonić do kogoś**

buzzard /ˈbʌzəd/ noun [C] **1** (Brit.) a large European **bird of prey** of the **hawk** family ▶ **myszołów 2** (US) a large American bird like a **vulture** that eats the flesh of animals that are already dead ▶ **sęp** (*z rodziny Cathartidae*)

buzzer /ˈbʌzə(r)/ noun [C] a piece of equipment that makes a **buzzing** sound: *Press your buzzer if you know the answer to a question.* ▶ **brzęczyk**

buzzword /ˈbʌzwɜːd/ noun [C] a word or phrase, especially one connected with a particular subject, that has become fashionable and popular: *Self-organization is the current buzzword.* ▶ **modne słowo**

⚷ **by** /baɪ/ prep. **1** beside; very near: *Come and sit by me.* ◇ *We stayed in a cottage by the sea* (nad morzem). ▶ **obok**, **przy 2** (used after a passive verb for showing who or what did or caused sth): *The event was organized by local people.* ◇ *She was knocked down by a car.* Potrącił ją samochód. ◇ *I was deeply shocked by the news* (wiadomościami). ◇ *Who was the book written by?/Who is the book by?* Kto napisał tę książkę? ▶ **przez 3** through doing or using sth; by means of sth: *You can get hold of me by phoning this number* (dzwoniąc pod ten numer). ◇ *Will you be paying by cheque* (czekiem)? ◇ *The house is heated by electricity* (elektrycznością). ◇ *'How do you go to work?' 'By train* (pociągiem), *usually.'* ◇ *by bus/car/plane/bicycle* autobusem/samochodem/samolotem/rowerem ◇ *We went in by the back door* (przez tylne drzwi). **4** as a result of sth: *I got on the wrong bus by mistake/accident* (przez pomyłkę). ◇ *I met an old friend by chance* (przypadkowo). ▶ **przez 5** not later than; before: *I'll be home by 7 o'clock.* ◇ *He should have telephoned by now/by this time.* ▶ **do 6** past: *He walked straight by me* (przeszedł tuż koło mnie) *without speaking.* ◇ *We stopped to let the ambulance get by.* ▶ **obok**, **koło 7** [usually without *the*] during a period of time: *By day we covered about thirty miles and by night we rested.* ▶ **w ciągu**, **w 8** [usually without *the*] in a particular situation: *The electricity went off so we had to work by candlelight.* ▶ **przy 9** to the amount mentioned: *Prices have gone up by 10 per cent.* ▶ **o 10** from what sth shows or says; according to sth: *It's 8 o'clock by my watch.* ◇ *By law you have to attend school from the age of five.* ▶ **według 11** (used with a part of the body or an article of clothing) holding: *He grabbed me by the arm.* ▶ **za 12** [often used with *the*] in the quantity or period mentioned: *You can rent a car by the day, the week or the month.* ◇ *Copies of the book have sold by the million.* ◇ *Day by day she was getting better.* ◇ *They came in one by one* (jeden za drugim). ▶ **na**, **w 13** (used for giving more information about where sb comes from, what sb does, etc.): *She's French by birth.* ◇ *He's a doctor by profession.* ▶ **z 14** (used for showing the measurements of an area): *The table is six feet by three feet.*

▶ **na 15** (used for multiplying or dividing): *4 multiplied by 5 is 20.* ◇ *6 divided by 2 is 3.* ▶ **przez**

IDM **by and large** → LARGE

by the way → WAY[1]

close by (sb/sth) → CLOSE

■ **by** adv. past: *We stopped to let the ambulance get by* (przepuścić karetkę). ◇ *If we sit here, we can watch the boats sail by* (jak łodzie przepływają). ◇ *Time seemed to be going by very slowly.* Wydawało się, że czas mija bardzo powoli. ℹ Słowo to często odpowiada polskiemu przedrostkowi, zwł. „prze-".

bye /baɪ/ (also 'bye-bye) interj. (informal) goodbye: *Bye! See you tomorrow.* ▶ **cześć!, pa!**

'by-election noun [C] an election to choose a new Member of Parliament for a particular **constituency**. It is held when the former member has died or left suddenly. ▶ **wybory dodatkowe** ➲ note at **election** ➲ look at **general election**

bygone /'baɪɡɒn/ adj. [only before a noun] that happened a long time ago: *a bygone era* ▶ **miniony**

bygones /'baɪɡɒnz/ noun

IDM **let bygones be bygones** to decide to forget disagreements or arguments that happened in the past ▶ **puścić w niepamięć dawne urazy**

'by-law (also 'bye-law) noun [C] a law that is made by a local authority and that applies only to that area ▶ **rozporządzenie/przepis władz lokalnych**

bypass[1] /'baɪpɑːs/ noun [C] **1** a road which traffic can use to go round a town, instead of through it ▶ **obwodnica** ➲ look at **ring road** **2** an operation on the heart to send blood along a different route so that it does not go through a part which is damaged or blocked: *heart bypass surgery* operacja wszczepienia bypassów ◇ *a triple bypass operation* wszczepienie potrójnego bypassu ▶ **pomostowanie aortalno-wieńcowe**

bypass[2] /'baɪpɑːs/ verb [T] to go around or to avoid sth using a **bypass**: *Let's try to bypass the city centre.* ◇ (figurative) *It's no good trying to bypass the problem.* ▶ **objeżdżać; omijać**

'by-product noun [C] **1** something that is formed during the making of sth else ▶ **produkt uboczny** **2** something that happens as the result of sth else ▶ **skutek uboczny**

bystander /'baɪstændə(r)/ noun [C] a person who is standing near and sees sth that happens, without being involved in it: *Several **innocent bystanders** were hurt when the two gangs attacked each other.* ▶ **przypadkowy świadek**

byte /baɪt/ noun [C] a unit of information stored in a computer, equal to 8 **bits**. Computer memory is measured in **bytes**. ▶ **bajt**

byway /'baɪweɪ/ noun [C] a small road that is not used very much ▶ **boczna droga**

byword /'baɪwɜːd/ noun [C, usually sing.] **1 a byword for sth** a person or a thing that is a typical or well-known example of a particular quality: *A limousine is a byword for luxury.* ▶ **synonim/symbol czegoś** **2** (especially US) a word or phrase that is often used ▶ **powiedzenie**

Cc

C, c /siː/ noun [C,U] (pl. **Cs**; **cs**; **C's**; **c's** /siːz/) **1** the third letter of the English alphabet: *'Car' begins with (a) 'C'.* ▶ **litera c** **2** (used about music) the first note in the series of notes called the scale of C major: *C major* C-dur ◇ *C minor* c-moll ◇ *C sharp* Cis, cis ▶ **C/c**

c /siː/ abbr. **1** (**C**) = CELSIUS, CENTIGRADE: *Water freezes at 0° C.* **2** = CENT, CENTS **3** = CIRCA: *c 1770*

cab /kæb/ noun [C] **1** (especially US) = TAXI[1]: *Let's **take a cab**/ **go by cab.*** **2** the part of a lorry, train, bus, etc. where the driver sits ▶ **kabina kierowcy/maszynisty** ➲ picture on **page A7**

cabaret /'kæbəreɪ; US ˌkæbə'r-/ noun [C,U] entertainment with singing, dancing, etc. in a restaurant or club ▶ **kabaret**

cabbage /'kæbɪdʒ/ noun [C,U] a large round vegetable with thick green, dark red or white leaves: *Cabbages are easy to grow.* ◇ *Do you like cabbage?* ▶ **kapusta** ➲ picture on **page A13**

cabin /'kæbɪn/ noun [C] **1** a small room in a ship or boat, where a passenger sleeps ▶ **kajuta** **2** the part of a plane where the passengers sit ▶ **kabina** ➲ picture at **plane** **3** a small wooden house: *a log cabin* ▶ **chata**

'cabin crew noun [C, with sing. or pl. verb] the people whose job is to take care of passengers on a plane ▶ **załoga samolotu**

cabinet /'kæbɪnət/ noun [C] **1** (**the Cabinet**) [with sing. or pl. verb] the most important ministers in a government, who decide and advise on policy and have regular meetings: *The Cabinet is/are meeting today to discuss the crisis.* ▶ **gabinet, rada ministrów** **2** a cupboard with shelves or drawers, used for storing things: *a medicine cabinet* ◇ *a filing cabinet* ▶ **szafka, gablotka**

cable /'keɪbl/ noun **1** [C] a thick strong metal rope ▶ **lina** ➲ picture at **rope** **2** [C,U] a set of wires covered with plastic, etc., for carrying electricity or signals: *underground/*

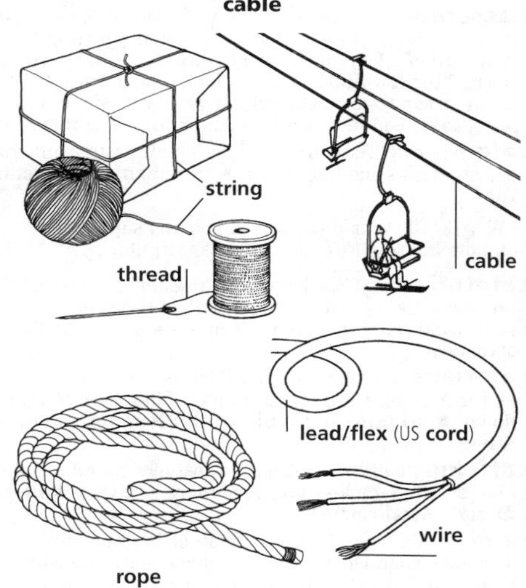

overhead cables ◇ *a telephone cable* ◇ *two metres of cable* ▶ **kabel** ➲ picture at **plug 3** = CABLE TELEVISION

ˈ**cable car** noun [C] a vehicle like a box that hangs on a moving metal cable and carries passengers up and down a mountain ▶ **wagonik kolejki linowej**

ˌ**cable ˈtelevision** (also **cable**) noun [U] a system of sending out TV programmes along wires instead of by radio signals ▶ **telewizja kablowa**

cache[1] /kæʃ/ noun [C] **1** a hidden store of things such as weapons: *an arms cache* ▶ **tajny skład, kryjówka 2** a part of a computer's memory that stores copies of data that is often needed while a program is running. This data can be found very quickly. ▶ (*komput.*) **pamięć podręczna**

cache[2] /kæʃ/ verb [T] **1** to store things in a secret place, especially weapons ▶ **ukrywać 2** to store data in a **cache** on a computer: *This page is cached.* ▶ **zapisywać w pamięci podręcznej/cache**

cackle /ˈkækl/ verb [I] to laugh in a loud, unpleasant way ▶ **rechotać**

■ **cackle** noun [C] **1** the loud sound that a hen makes after laying an egg ▶ **gdakanie 2** a loud, unpleasant laugh ▶ **rechot**

cacophony /kəˈkɒfəni/ noun [U, sing.] (formal) a mixture of loud unpleasant sounds ▶ **kakofonia**

■ **cacophonous** /-nəs/ adj. ▶ **kakofoniczny**

cactus /ˈkæktəs/ noun [C] (pl. **cactuses** or **cacti** /ˈkæktaɪ/) a type of plant that grows in hot, dry areas, especially deserts. A **cactus** has a thick **stem** and sharp points but no leaves. ▶ **kaktus**

cadence /ˈkeɪdns/ noun [C] **1** (formal) the rise and fall of the voice in speaking: *He delivered his words in slow, measured cadences.* ▶ **intonacja 2** the end of a musical phrase ▶ (*muz.*) **kadencja, zakończenie utworu muzycznego**

cadenza /kəˈdenzə/ noun [C] a short passage, usually near the end of a piece of **classical** music, which is played or sung by the **soloist** alone, and intended to show the performer's skill ▶ (*muz.*) **kadencja wirtuozowska**

cadet /kəˈdet/ noun [C] a young person who is training to be in the army, navy, air force or police ▶ **kadet**

Caesarean (also **Caesarian**; US also **cesarean**) /siˈzeəriən/ noun [C] a medical operation in which an opening is cut in a mother's body in order to take out the baby when a normal birth would be impossible or dangerous: *to have a Caesarean* ▶ **cesarskie cięcie** ℹ Używa się też określenia **Caesarean section** lub (w Amer. ang.) **C-section**.

cafe (also **café**) /ˈkæfeɪ/ noun [C] a small restaurant that serves drinks and light meals ▶ **kawiarnia, herbaciarnia**

> W Wlk. Br. w **café** na ogół nie podaje się napojów alkoholowych, które dostępne są w pubie.

cafeteria /ˌkæfəˈtɪəriə/ noun [C] a restaurant, especially one for workers, where people collect their meals themselves and carry them to their tables ▶ **stołówka** ➲ look at **canteen**

cafetière /ˌkæfəˈtjeə(r)/ noun [C] a special glass container for making coffee with a metal **filter** that you push down ▶ **szklane naczynie z tłokiem do parzenia kawy**

caffeine /ˈkæfiːn/ noun [U] the substance found in coffee and tea that makes you feel more active ▶ **kofeina** ➲ look at **decaffeinated**

cage /keɪdʒ/ noun [C] a box made of bars or wire, or a space surrounded by wire or metal bars, in which a bird or an animal is kept so that it cannot escape: *a birdcage* ▶ **klatka**

■ **caged** adj.: *He felt like a caged animal in the tiny office.* ▶ **(trzymany) w klatce**

cagoule /kəˈɡuːl/ noun [C] a long, light jacket with a **hood** that protects you from the rain or wind ▶ **długa kurtka przeciwdeszczowa z kapturem**

cajole /kəˈdʒəʊl/ verb [T,I] **cajole sb (into sth/into doing sth)**; **cajole sth out of sb** to persuade sb to do sth by talking to them and being very nice: *He cajoled me into agreeing to do the work.* ◇ *I managed to cajole their address out of him.* ▶ **skłaniać kogoś do zrobienia czegoś za pomocą pochlebstw i obietnic** SYN **coax**

cake[1] /keɪk/ noun **1** [C,U] a sweet food made by mixing flour, eggs, butter, sugar, etc. together and baking the mixture in the oven: *to make/bake a cake* ◇ *a wedding cake* ◇ *a piece/slice of birthday cake* ➲ picture at **bar**: *Would you like some more cake?* ▶ **ciast(k)o**

> After **making** or **baking** a cake, you often **ice** or (US) **frost** the top and sides of it.

2 [C] a mixture of other food, cooked in a round, flat shape: *fish/potato cakes* ▶ **placek**

IDM **have your cake and eat it** to enjoy the advantages of sth without its disadvantages; to have both things that are available: *You can't go out every night and save for your holiday. You can't have your cake and eat it.* Nie możesz mieć wszystkiego na raz. ▶ **i wilk syty, i owca cała**

a piece of cake → PIECE[1]

cake[2] /keɪk/ verb [T, usually passive] **cake sth (in/with sth)** to cover sth with a thick layer of sth that becomes hard when it dries: *boots caked in mud* ▶ **oblepiać**

calamity /kəˈlæməti/ noun [C,U] (pl. **calamities**) a terrible event that causes a lot of damage or harm ▶ **katastrofa, klęska** SYN **disaster**

calcium /ˈkælsiəm/ noun [U] (symbol **Ca**) a chemical element that is found in food such as milk or cheese. It helps to make teeth and bones strong. ▶ **wapno**

calculate /ˈkælkjuleɪt/ verb [T] **1** to find sth out by using mathematics; to work sth out: *It's difficult to calculate how long the project will take.* ▶ **obliczać 2** to consider or expect sth: *We calculated that the advantages would be greater than the disadvantages.* ▶ **kalkulować**

IDM **be calculated to do sth** to be intended or designed to do sth: *His remark was clearly calculated to annoy me.* ▶ **być zamierzonym, żeby coś wywołać**

calculating /ˈkælkjuleɪtɪŋ/ adj. planning things in a very careful way in order to achieve what you want, without considering other people: *Her cold, calculating approach made her many enemies.* ▶ **wyrachowany**

calculation /ˌkælkjuˈleɪʃn/ noun **1** [C,U] finding an answer by using mathematics: *I'll have to* **do a few calculations** *before telling you how much I can afford.* ◇ *Calculation of the exact cost is impossible.* ▶ **oblicze-**

nie 2 [U] (formal) careful planning in order to achieve what you want, without considering other people: *His actions were the result of deliberate calculation.* ▶ **wyrachowanie**

calculator /ˈkælkjuleɪtə(r)/ noun [C] a small electronic machine used for calculating figures: *a pocket calculator* ▶ **kalkulator**

calendar /ˈkælɪndə(r)/ noun [C] **1** a list that shows the days, weeks and months of a particular year ▶ **kalendarz** ℹ **Calendar** zazwyczaj wisi na ścianie, ma oddzielną stronę na każdy miesiąc i często jest ilustrowany. ➲ look at **diary 2** a list of dates and events in a year that are important in a particular area of activity: *Wimbledon is a major event in the sporting calendar.* ▶ **kalendarz 3** a system for dividing time into fixed periods and for marking the beginning and end of a year: *the Muslim calendar* ▶ **kalendarz**

ˌcalendar ˈmonth = MONTH (1)

ˌcalendar ˈyear = YEAR (1)

calf /kɑːf; US kæf/ noun [C] (pl. **calves** /kɑːvz; US kævz/) **1** the back of your leg, between your ankle and your knee: *I've strained a calf muscle.* ▶ **łydka** ➲ picture at **body 2** a young cow ▶ **cielę** ➲ The meat from a calf is called **veal**. ➲ note at **cow**, **meat**
3 the young of some other animals, for example **elephants** ▶ **młode** (*np. słonia*)

calibre (US **caliber**) /ˈkælɪbə(r)/ noun [sing., U] the quality or ability of a person or thing: *The company's employees are of (a) high calibre.* ▶ **kaliber**

calico /ˈkælɪkəʊ/ noun [U] **1** (especially Brit.) a type of heavy cotton cloth that is usually plain white ▶ **surówka bawełniana 2** (especially US) a type of rough cotton cloth that has a pattern printed on it ▶ **kreton**

CALL /kɔːl/ abbr. **computer-assisted language learning** ▶ **nauka języka wspomagana komputerowo**

🔑 **call¹** /kɔːl/ verb **1** (**be called**) to have as your name: *His wife is called Silvia.* ◇ *What was that village called?* ▶ **nazywać się 2** [T] to name or describe a person or thing in a certain way: *They called the baby Freddie.* ◇ *Are you calling me a liar?* ▶ **nazywać 3** [I,T] **call (out) to sb**; **call (sth) (out)** to say sth loudly or to shout in order to attract attention: *'Hello, is anybody there?' she called.* ◇ *He called out* (wywołał) *the names and the winners stepped forward.* ◇ *I could hear a man calling his dog.* ▶ **wołać**, **krzyczeć 4** [I,T] (especially US) = RING²(1): *Who's calling, please?* ◇ *I'll call you tomorrow.* ◇ *We're just in the middle of dinner. Can I call you back later?* ◇ *Thank you for calling.* Dziękuję za telefon. ▶ **dzwonić** ➲ note at **telephone 5** [T] to order or ask sb to come to a certain place: *Can you call everybody in for lunch?* ◇ *I think we had better call the doctor.* ▶ **wzywać 6** [I] **call (in/round) (on sb/at ...)** to make a short visit to a person or place: *I called in on Mike on my way home.* ◇ *We called at his house but there was nobody in.* ▶ **zaglądać (do kogoś) 7** [I] **call at ...** (used about a train, ship, etc.) to stop at the places mentioned: *This is the express service to London, calling at Manchester and Birmingham.* ▶ **zatrzymywać się** (*w jakimś miejscu/na jakiejś stacji*) **8** [T] to arrange for sth to take place at a certain time: *to call a meeting/an election/a strike* ▶ **ogłaszać**

IDM **bring/call sb/sth to mind** → MIND¹
call it a day (informal) to decide to stop doing sth: *Let's call it a day* (wystarczy na dzisiaj). *I'm exhausted.* ▶ **skończyć coś robić**
call sb's bluff to tell sb to actually do what they are threatening to do (believing that they will not risk doing it) ▶ **sprawdzać kogoś** (*np. czy nie blefuje*)
call sb names to use insulting words about sb ▶ **wymyślać komuś**
call the shots/tune (informal) to be in a position to control a situation and make decisions about what should be done ▶ **nadawać ton**, (*przen.*) **dyrygować (kimś)**

PHR V **call by** (informal) to make a short visit to a place or person as you pass: *I'll call by to pick up the book on my way to work.* ▶ **zaglądać/wpadać (do kogoś)**
call for sb (Brit.) to collect sb in order to go somewhere together: *I'll call for you when it's time to go.* ▶ **przychodzić/przyjeżdżać po kogoś**
call for sth to demand or need sth: *The crisis calls for immediate action.* ◇ *This calls for a celebration!* To trzeba uczcić. ◇ *Their rudeness was not called for.* Ich nieuprzejmość była zupełnie nie na miejscu. ▶ **wymagać**, **wzywać**
call sth off to cancel sth ▶ **odwoływać**
call sb out to ask sb to come, especially to an emergency: *We had to call out the doctor in the middle of the night.* ▶ **wzywać kogoś**
call sb up 1 (especially US) to telephone sb ▶ **zadzwonić do kogoś 2** to order sb to join the army, navy or air force: *All men under 30 were called up to fight in the war.* ▶ **powoływać kogoś** (*np. do wojska*)
call sth up to look at sth that is stored in a computer: *The bank clerk called up my account details on screen.* ▶ **przeglądać** (*dane w komputerze*)

🔑 **call²** /kɔːl/ noun **1** (also ˈ**phone call**) [C] an act of telephoning or a conversation on the telephone: *Were there any calls for me while I was out?* ◇ *I'll* ***give you a call*** (zadzwonię do ciebie) *at the weekend.* ◇ *to* ***make a*** *local* ***call*** zadzwonić pod numer miejscowy ◇ *a long-distance call* rozmowa zamiejscowa/międzynarodowa ▶ **rozmowa telefoniczna**, **telefon 2** [C] a loud sound that is made by a bird or an animal, or by a person to attract attention: *That bird's call is easy to recognize.* ◇ *a call for help* ▶ **śpiew**; **krzyk**; **wołanie 3** [C] a short visit, especially to sb's house: *We could* ***pay a call*** (odwiedzić) *on Dave on our way home.* ◇ *The doctor has several calls to make this morning.* Dziś rano lekarz musi odbyć kilka wizyt domowych. ▶ **wizyta 4** [C] a request or demand for sth: *There have been calls for the President to resign.* ▶ **żądanie 5** [C,U] **call for sth** a need for sth: *The doctor said there was no call for concern.* ▶ **powód do czegoś**

IDM **(be) on call** (to be) ready to work if necessary: *Dr Young will be on call this weekend.* ▶ **na dyżurze**, **w pogotowiu**

ˈcall box = TELEPHONE BOX

ˈcall centre (US ˈ**call center**) noun [C] an office in which many people work using telephones, for example taking customers' orders or answering questions ▶ **centrum telefoniczne**

caller /ˈkɔːlə(r)/ noun [C] a person who telephones or visits sb ▶ **telefonujący/a**; **odwiedzający/a**

calligraphy /kəˈlɪɡrəfi/ noun [U] beautiful **handwriting** that you do with a special pen or brush; the art of producing this ▶ **kaligrafia**
■ **calligrapher** noun [C] ▶ **kaligraf**

ˈcall-in (US) = PHONE-IN

calling /ˈkɔːlɪŋ/ noun [C] **1** a strong desire or feeling of duty to do a particular job, especially one in which you help other people: *He realized that his calling was to preach the gospel.* ▶ **powołanie** (*np. do jakiegoś zawodu*) SYN **vocation 2** (formal) a profession or career: *My father considered engineering one of the highest possible callings.* ▶ **zawód**

callous /ˈkæləs/ adj. not caring about the suffering of other people ▶ **nieczuły**, **bezduszny** SYN **cruel**

🔑 **calm¹** /kɑːm/ adj. **1** not excited, worried or angry; quiet: *Try to* ***keep calm*** (uspokoić się) *– there's no need to panic.* ◇ *She spoke in a calm voice.* ◇ *The city is calm again after last night's riots.* ▶ **spokojny**, **opanowany 2** without big waves: *a calm sea* ▶ **spokojny** OPP **rough 3** without much wind: *calm weather* ▶ **bezwietrzny**

■ **calmly** adv. ▶ **spokojnie** | **calmness** noun [U] ▶ **spokój**

calm² /kɑːm/ verb [I,T] **calm (sb/sth) (down)** to become or to make sb quiet or calm: *Calm down! Shouting at everybody won't help.* ◇ *I did some breathing exercises to calm my nerves.* ▶ **uspokajać (się)**

calm³ /kɑːm/ noun [C,U] a period of time or a state when everything is peaceful: *After living in the city, I enjoyed the calm of country life.* ▶ **spokój**

calorie /ˈkæləri/ noun [C] a measure of the energy value of food: *A fried egg contains about 100 calories.* ◇ *a low-calorie drink/yogurt/diet* ▶ **kaloria**

calves plural of **calf**

camcorder /ˈkæmkɔːdə(r)/ noun [C] a camera that you can carry around and use for recording pictures and sound on a video ▶ **kamera wideo**

came past tense of **come**

camel /ˈkæml/ noun [C] an animal that lives in the desert and has a long neck and either one or two **humps** on its back. It is used for carrying people and goods. ▶ **wielbłąd**

cameo /ˈkæmiəʊ/ noun [C] (pl. **cameos**) **1** a small part in a film or play that is usually played by a famous actor ▶ **mała rola grana przez słynnego aktora** **2** a piece of jewellery that has a design in one colour and a background in a different colour ▶ **kamea**

camera /ˈkæmərə/ noun [C] a piece of equipment that you use for taking photographs or moving pictures: *I need a new film for my camera.* ◇ *a video/TV camera* ▶ **aparat fotograficzny**, **kamera filmowa**

> **cameras**
>
> You use a camera to **take photos** (formal **photographs**). You adjust the **lens** to make sure that the image is **in focus**, not **out of focus**. You need a **zoom lens** to take pictures of things that are a long distance away. If there is not much light or you are indoors, you will probably need to use the **flash**. You take your film to have it **developed**, and **prints** are made from the **negatives**. Many people like to put their photos into **albums** to look at them. **Digital cameras** allow you to take digital photos which you can download and store on your computer. If you want to **pose** for a photo and ask sb to take it with your camera, you can say: *Could you take a photo of me, please?*

cameraman /ˈkæmrəmæn/, **camerawoman** /-wʊmən/ noun [C] (pl. **-men** /-men/; **-women** /-wɪmɪn/) a person whose job is to operate a camera for a film or a TV company ▶ **kamerzyst(k)a** ➲ look at **photographer**

camomile = CHAMOMILE

camouflage /ˈkæməflɑːʒ/ noun [U] **1** materials or colours that soldiers use to make themselves and their equipment difficult to see ▶ **kamuflaż** **2** the way in which an animal's colour or shape matches its surroundings and makes it difficult to see ▶ **kamuflaż**
■ **camouflage** verb [T] ▶ **kamuflować**

camp¹ /kæmp/ noun [C,U] a place where people live in tents or simple buildings away from their usual home: *a refugee camp* ◇ *an army training camp* obóz szkoleniowy dla żołnierzy ◇ *The climbers set up camp* (rozbili obóz) *at the foot of the mountain.* ▶ **obóz**

camp² /kæmp/ verb [I] **camp (out)** to sleep without a bed, especially outside in a tent: *We camped next to a river.* ▶ **biwakować**, **spać pod namiotem** ⓘ W rozmowie o biwakowaniu/kempingowaniu dla przyjemności używa się zwrotu **go camping**: *They went camping in France last year.*

campaign¹ /kæmˈpeɪn/ noun [C] **1** a plan to do a number of things in order to achieve a special aim: *to launch an advertising/election campaign* ▶ **kampania** **2** a planned series of attacks in a war ▶ **kampania**

campaign² /kæmˈpeɪn/ verb [I] **campaign (for/against sb/sth)** to take part in a planned series of activities in order to make sth happen or to prevent sth: *Local people are campaigning for lower speed limits in the town.* ▶ **uczestniczyć w kampanii**, **przeprowadzać kampanię**
■ **campaigner** noun [C]: *an animal rights campaigner* ▶ **uczestni-k/czka kampanii**

ˈ**camp bed** (US **cot**) noun [C] a light, narrow bed that you can fold up and carry easily ▶ **łóżko turystyczne/składane**

camper /ˈkæmpə(r)/ noun [C] **1** a person who stays in a tent on holiday ▶ **biwakowicz/ka** **2** (Brit. also ˈ**camper van**) a motor vehicle in which you can sleep, cook, etc. when you are on holiday ▶ **samochód kempingowy**

camping /ˈkæmpɪŋ/ noun [U] sleeping or having a holiday in a tent: *Camping is cheaper than staying in hotels.* ◇ *to go on a camping holiday* ▶ **biwakowanie**, **spanie w namiocie**

campsite /ˈkæmpsaɪt/ noun [C] a place where you can stay in a tent ▶ **kemping**

campus /ˈkæmpəs/ noun [C,U] the area of land where the main buildings of a college or university are: *About half the students live* **on campus** *– the other half rent rooms in the town.* ▶ **teren uczelni**

can¹ /kən; strong form kæn/ modal verb (negative **cannot** /ˈkænɒt/, short form **can't** /kɑːnt; US kænt/, pt **could** /kəd/ strong form /kʊd/, negative **could not**; short form **couldn't** /ˈkʊdnt/) **1** (used for showing that it is possible for sb/sth to do sth or that sb/sth has the ability to do sth): *Can you ride a bike?* ◇ *He can't speak French.* ▶ **móc**; **umieć**

> **Can** nie występuje w bezokoliczniku ani w formach imiesłowowych. Aby wyrazić czas przyszły lub formy dokonane używa się **be able to**: *One day people will be able to travel to Mars.* **Could have** używa się, aby powiedzieć, że ktoś miał możliwość coś zrobić, ale tego nie zrobił: *She could have passed the exam but she didn't really try.*

2 (used with the verbs 'feel', 'hear', 'see', 'smell', 'taste'): *I can smell something burning.*

> Wyżej wymienionych czasowników (i innych oznaczających postrzeganie za pomocą zmysłów) nie używa się w czasach *continuous*. W sytuacjach, w których wymagane jest użycie tego czasu, zamiast niego często stosuje się **can** + bezokolicznik: *I can smell something burning.* Czuję, że coś się pali.

3 (used to ask for or give permission): *Can I have a drink, please?* ◇ *He asked if he could have a drink.* ▶ **móc**

> Aby wyrazić ogólne pozwolenie w przeszłości, używa się **could**: *I could do anything I wanted when I stayed with my grandma.* Kiedy mówi się o jednej konkretnej sytuacji, wtedy nie używa się **could**: *They were allowed to visit him in hospital yesterday.*

4 (used for offering to do sth): *Can I help at all?* ▶ **móc** **5** (used to ask sb to do sth): *Can you help me carry these books?* ▶ **móc** **6** (used in the negative for saying that you are sure sth is not true): *That can't be Maria – she's in London.* ▶ **móc** **7** (used to talk about sb's typical behaviour or a typical effect): *Wasp stings can be very painful.* ◇ *You can* (potrafisz) *be very annoying.* ▶ **móc**

can² /kæn/ noun [C] **1** a metal or plastic container that is used for holding or carrying liquid: *an oil can* ◇ *a watering can* konewka ▶ **puszka** **2** a metal container in which food or drink is kept without air so that it stays fresh: *a can of beer* ▶ **puszka** ⓘ W Br. ang. częściej używa się słowa **tin. Can** odnosi się do napojów. ➲ picture at **container**

can³ /kæn/ verb [T] (**canning**; **canned**) to put food, drink, etc. into a can in order to keep it fresh for a long time ▶ **puszkować**

■ **canned** adj. **1** (Brit. also **tinned**) (used about food) preserved in a can: *canned food/soup* ▶ **w puszce 2** (**canned laughter/music**) the sound of people laughing or music that has been previously recorded and used in television and radio programmes ▶ (*muzyka, śmiech w programach telewizyjnych/radiowych*) **uprzednio nagrany**

canal /kəˈnæl/ noun [C] **1** a deep cut that is made through land and filled with water for boats or ships to travel along; a smaller cut used for carrying water to fields, crops, etc.: *the Panama Canal* ▶ **kanał 2** one of the tubes in the body through which food, air, etc. passes ▶ **przewód**

caˈnal boat noun [C] a long narrow boat used on **canals** ▶ **barka** ➲ picture at **boat**

canary /kəˈneəri/ noun [C] (pl. **canaries**) a small yellow bird that sings and is often kept in a **cage** as a pet ▶ **kanarek**

⚷ **cancel** /ˈkænsl/ verb [T] (**cancelling**; **cancelled**; US **canceling**; **canceled**) **1** to decide that sth that has been planned or arranged will not happen: *All flights have been cancelled because of the bad weather.* ▶ **odwoływać** ➲ look at **postpone 2** to stop sth that you asked for or agreed to: *to cancel a reservation* ▶ **odwoływać**, **unieważnić**

PHR V **cancel (sth) out** to be equal or have an equal effect: *What I owe you is the same as what you owe me, so our debts cancel each other out.* ▶ **wyrównywać (się)**, **znosić się wzajemnie**

cancellation /ˌkænsəˈleɪʃn/ noun [C,U] the act of cancelling sth: *We had to make a last-minute cancellation.* ▶ **odwołanie**

Cancer /ˈkænsə(r)/ noun [C,U] the 4th sign of the **zodiac**, the Crab; a person born under this sign: *I'm a Cancer.* ▶ **Rak**; **zodiakalny Rak**

⚷ **cancer** /ˈkænsə(r)/ noun [C,U] a very serious disease in which lumps grow in the body: *She has lung cancer.* ▶ **rak**, **nowotwór**

cancerous /ˈkænsərəs/ adj. (used especially about a part of the body or sth growing in the body) having **cancer**: *a cancerous growth* ◇ *cancerous cells* ▶ **nowotworowy**, **rakowy**

candid /ˈkændɪd/ adj. saying exactly what you think: *a candid interview* ▶ **otwarty**, **bezpośredni** ➲ noun **candour** SYN **frank**

■ **candidly** adv. ▶ **otwarcie**, **bezpośrednio**

candidacy /ˈkændɪdəsi/ noun [U] the fact of being a **candidate** ▶ **kandydatura**

⚷ **candidate** /ˈkændɪdət/ noun [C] **1** a person who makes a formal request to be considered for a job or wants to be elected to a particular position ▶ **kandydat/ka** ➲ note at **election 2** a person who is taking an exam ▶ **kandydat/ka**

candle /ˈkændl/ noun [C] a round stick of **wax** with a **wick** through the middle that you can burn to give light: *to light/blow out a candle* ▶ **świeca**

candlelight /ˈkændllaɪt/ noun [U] light that comes from a **candle**: *They had dinner **by candlelight*** (przy świecach). ▶ **światło świec**

candlestick /ˈkændlstɪk/ noun [C] an object for holding a **candle** or **candles**: *a silver candlestick* ▶ **świecznik**

candour (US **candor**) /ˈkændə(r)/ noun [U] the quality of being honest; saying exactly what you think ▶ **otwartość**, **bezpośredniość** ➲ adjective **candid**

⚷ **candy** (US) = SWEET² (1): *You eat too much candy.*

candyfloss /ˈkændiflɒs/ (US ˌ**cotton** ˈ**candy**) noun [U] a type of sweet in the form of a mass of sticky threads made from melted sugar and served on a stick, especially at **fairgrounds** ▶ **wata cukrowa**

cane¹ /keɪn/ noun **1** [C,U] the long central part of certain plants, for example **bamboo**, that is like a tube and is used as a material for making furniture, etc.: *sugar cane* ◇ *a cane chair* ▶ **trzcina 2** [C] a stick that is used to help sb walk ▶ **laska**

cane² /keɪn/ verb [T] to hit a child with a **cane** as a punishment ▶ **chłostać**

canine /ˈkeɪnaɪn/ adj. connected with dogs ▶ **psi**

canister /ˈkænɪstə(r)/ noun [C] a small round metal container: *a gas canister* ▶ **kanister**

cannabis /ˈkænəbɪs/ noun [U] a drug made from **hemp** that some people smoke for pleasure, but which is illegal in many countries ▶ **marihuana**

cannibal /ˈkænɪbl/ noun [C] a person who eats other people ▶ **kanibal**

■ **cannibalism** /ˈkænɪbəlɪzəm/ noun [U] ▶ **kanibalizm**

cannon /ˈkænən/ noun [C] (pl. **cannon** or **cannons**) **1** a large, simple gun that was used in the past for firing large stone or metal balls (**cannon balls**) ▶ **armata 2** a large gun on a ship, army vehicle, aircraft, etc. ▶ **armata**

⚷ **cannot** → CAN¹

canoe /kəˈnuː/ noun [C] a light, narrow boat for one or two people that you can move through the water using a **paddle** ▶ **kajak**, **kanoe** ➲ look at **kayak** ➲ picture at **boat**

■ **canoe** verb [I] (**canoeing**; **canoes**; pt, pp **canoed**): *They canoed down the river.* ▶ **pływać kajakiem** ⓘ Można powiedzieć **He is learning to canoe** lub **They canoed down the river**, ale kiedy mówi się o spędzaniu dłuższego czasu w kajaku, wtedy częściej używa się zwrotu **go canoeing**: *We're going canoeing on the Thames tomorrow.*

canon /ˈkænən/ noun [C] a Christian priest who works in a **cathedral** ▶ **kanonik**

ˈ**can-opener** (especially US) = TIN-OPENER

canopy /ˈkænəpi/ noun [C] (pl. **canopies**) a cover that hangs or spreads above sth: *The highest branches in the rainforest form a dense canopy.* ◇ *a parachute canopy* czasza spadochronu ▶ **baldachim**, **zadaszenie**

can't short for **cannot**

canteen /kænˈtiːn/ noun [C] a place where food and drink are served in a factory, a school, etc.: *the staff canteen* ▶ **stołówka** ➲ look at **cafeteria**

canter /ˈkæntə(r)/ verb [I] (used about a horse and its rider) to run fairly fast but not very ▶ **galopować** ➲ look at **gallop**, **trot**

■ **canter** noun [sing.] ▶ **galop**

canvas /ˈkænvəs/ noun **1** [U] a type of strong cloth that is used for making sails, bags, tents, etc. ▶ **płótno 2** [C] a piece of strong cloth for painting a picture on ▶ **płótno**

canvass /ˈkænvəs/ verb **1** [I,T] **canvass (sb) (for sth)** to try to persuade people to vote for a particular person or party in an election or to support sb/sth: *to canvass for votes* ◇ *He's canvassing for the Conservative Party.* ◇ *The Prime Minister is trying to canvass support for the plan.* ▶ **zabiegać** (*o głosy wyborców*) **2** [T] to find out what people's opinions are about sth ▶ **badać opinie**

canyon /ˈkænjən/ noun [C] a deep valley with very steep sides ▶ **kanion**

⚷ **cap¹** /kæp/ noun [C] **1** a hat that has a part sticking out at the front: *a baseball cap* bejsbolówka ▶ **czapka** (*z daszkiem*) ➲ picture on **page A1 2** a soft hat that is worn for a particular purpose: *a shower cap* ▶ **czapka**, **czepek 3** a hat that is given to a player who is chosen to play for their country: *He won his first cap against France.* Po

C

raz pierwszy został powołany do reprezentacji narodowej na mecz z Francją. **4** a covering for the end or top of sth: *Please put the cap back on the bottle.* ▶ **nakrętka, kapsel, nasadka** ➲ look at **lid** ➲ note at **top**[1] ➲ picture at **container**

cap[2] /kæp/ verb [T] (**capping**; **capped**) **1** to cover the top of sth: *mountains capped with snow* ▶ **pokrywać 2** to limit the amount of money that can be spent on sth ▶ **ograniczać** (*wydatki*) **3** to follow sth with sth bigger or better ▶ **uwieńczyć 4** to choose a player to represent their country in a sport ▶ **wybierać do reprezentacji narodowej**
IDM **to cap it all** as a final piece of bad luck: *I had a row with my boss, my bike was stolen, and now to cap it all I've lost my keys!* ▶ **na domiar złego**

capability /ˌkeɪpəˈbɪləti/ noun [C,U] (pl. **capabilities**) **capability (to do sth/of doing sth)** the quality of being able to do sth: *Animals in the zoo have lost the capability to catch/of catching food for themselves.* ◇ *I tried to fix the computer, but it was* ***beyond*** *my* ***capabilities.*** ◇ *How many countries have nuclear capability* (mają broń jądrową)*?* ▶ **umiejętność, możliwość, zdolność**

capable /ˈkeɪpəbl/ adj. **1 capable of (doing) sth** having the ability or qualities necessary to do sth: *He's capable of passing the exam if he tries harder.* ◇ *That car is capable of 180 miles per hour.* ◇ *I do not believe that she's capable of stealing.* ▶ **zdolny, będący w stanie** (*coś zrobić*) **2** having a lot of skill; good at doing sth: *She's a very capable teacher.* ▶ **sprawny, zdolny, kompetentny** OPP **incapable**
■ **capably** /-əbli/ adv. ▶ **umiejętnie, sprawnie**

capacity /kəˈpæsəti/ noun (pl. **capacities**) **1** [sing., U] the amount that a container or space can hold: *The tank has a capacity of 1 000 litres.* ◇ *The stadium was* ***filled to capacity.*** ▶ **pojemność 2** [sing.] **a capacity (for sth/for doing sth); a capacity (to do sth)** the ability to understand or do sth: *That book is beyond the capacity* (przekracza możliwość zrozumienia) *of young children.* ◇ *a capacity for hard work/for learning languages* ▶ **zdolność (do czegoś) 3** [C] the official position that sb has: ***In his capacity as*** *chairman of the council ...* ▶ **pozycja, stanowisko** SYN **role 4** [sing., U] the amount that a factory or machine can produce: *The power station is working* ***at full capacity.*** ▶ **wydajność**

cape /keɪp/ noun [C] **1** a piece of clothing with no sleeves that hangs from your shoulders ▶ **peleryna** ➲ look at **cloak** ℹ **Cape** jest okryciem krótszym niż **cloak**. **2** a piece of high land that sticks out into the sea: *the Cape of Good Hope* ▶ **przylądek**

capillary /kəˈpɪləri; US ˈkæpəleri/ noun [C] (pl. **capillaries**) any of the smallest tubes in the body that carry blood ▶ **naczynie włoskowate**

capital[1] /ˈkæpɪtl/ noun **1** (also ˌ**capital ˈcity**) [C] the town or city where the government of a country is ▶ **stolica 2** [C] a place that is well known for a particular thing: *Niagara Falls is the honeymoon capital of the world.* ▶ **stolica 3** [U] an amount of money that you use to start a business or to put in a bank, etc. so that you earn interest on it: *When she had enough capital, she bought a shop.* ▶ **kapitał 4** (also ˌ**capital ˈletter**) [C] the large form of a letter of the alphabet: *Write your name in capitals.* ▶ **duża litera** ➲ note at **letter**
IDM **make capital (out) of sth** to use a situation to your own advantage ▶ **obracać coś na swoją korzyść**

capital[2] /ˈkæpɪtl/ adj. **1** [only before a noun] connected with punishment by death: *a capital offence* przestępstwo karane śmiercią ▶ **główny, najwyższy 2** (used about letters of the alphabet) written in the large form ▶ **duży**

ˌ**capital inˈvestment** noun [U] money that a business spends on buildings, equipment, etc. ▶ **inwestycja kapitałowa**

capitalism /ˈkæpɪtəlɪzəm/ noun [U] the economic system in which businesses are owned and run for profit by individuals and not by the state ▶ **kapitalizm**
■ **capitalist** /-ɪst/ **1** noun [C] ▶ **kapitalist(k)a 2** adj. ▶ **kapitalistyczny**

capitalize (also **-ise**) /ˈkæpɪtəlaɪz/ verb
PHR V **capitalize on sth** to use sth to your advantage: *We can capitalize on the mistakes that our rivals have made.* ▶ **wykorzystywać coś** (*do własnych celów*)

ˌ**capital ˈletter** = CAPITAL[1] (4)

ˌ**capital ˈpunishment** noun [U] punishment by death for serious crimes ▶ **kara śmierci** ➲ look at **death penalty, corporal punishment**

capitulate /kəˈpɪtʃuleɪt/ verb [I] (formal) to stop fighting and accept that you have lost; to give in to sb ▶ **kapitulować**
■ **capitulation** /kəˌpɪtʃuˈleɪʃn/ noun [C,U] ▶ **kapitulacja**

caprice /kəˈpriːs/ noun (formal) **1** [C] a sudden change in attitude or behaviour for no obvious reason ▶ **kaprys** SYN **whim 2** [U] the tendency to change your mind suddenly or behave unexpectedly ▶ **kapryśność**

capricious /kəˈprɪʃəs/ adj. changing behaviour suddenly in a way that is difficult to predict: *a capricious actor* ▶ **kapryśny** SYN **unpredictable**

Capricorn /ˈkæprɪkɔːn/ noun [C,U] the 10th sign of the **zodiac**, the Goat; a person born under this sign: *I'm a Capricorn* ▶ **Koziorożec; zodiakalny Koziorożec**

capsize /kæpˈsaɪz; US ˈkæps-/ verb [I,T] (used about boats) to turn over in the water: *The canoe capsized.* ◇ *A big wave capsized the yacht.* ▶ **wywracać (się)**

capsule /ˈkæpsjuːl/ noun [C] **1** a very small closed tube of medicine that you swallow ▶ **kapsułka 2** a container that is closed so that air, water, etc. cannot enter ▶ **kapsuła**

Capt. = CAPTAIN[1]

captain[1] /ˈkæptɪn/ noun [C] (abbr. **capt.**) **1** the person who is in command of a ship or an aircraft: *The captain gave the order to abandon ship.* ▶ **kapitan** ➲ note at **boat 2** a person who is the leader of a group or team ▶ **kapitan 3** an officer at a middle level in the army or navy ▶ **kapitan**

captain[2] /ˈkæptɪn/ verb [T] to be the captain of a group or team ▶ **dowodzić**

caption /ˈkæpʃn/ noun [C] the words that are written above or below a picture, photograph, etc. to explain what it is about ▶ **podpis pod rysunkiem/fotografią**

captivate /ˈkæptɪveɪt/ verb [T] to attract and hold sb's attention ▶ **oczarowywać**
■ **captivating** adj. ▶ **czarujący**

captive[1] /ˈkæptɪv/ adj. kept as a prisoner; (used about animals) kept in a **cage**, etc.: (figurative) *a* ***captive audience*** publiczność mimo woli ▶ **uwięziony; trzymany w klatce/na uwięzi**
IDM **hold sb captive/prisoner** to keep sb as a prisoner and not allow them to escape ▶ **trzymać kogoś w niewoli**
take sb captive/prisoner to catch sb and hold them as your prisoner ▶ **brać kogoś do niewoli**

captive[2] /ˈkæptɪv/ noun [C] a prisoner ▶ **jeniec**

captivity /kæpˈtɪvəti/ noun [U] the state of being kept in a place that you cannot escape from: *Wild animals are often unhappy when kept* ***in captivity.*** ▶ **niewola**

captor /ˈkæptə(r)/ noun [C] a person who takes or keeps a person as a prisoner ▶ **zdobywca; porywacz**

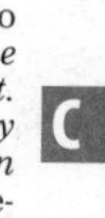

types of car

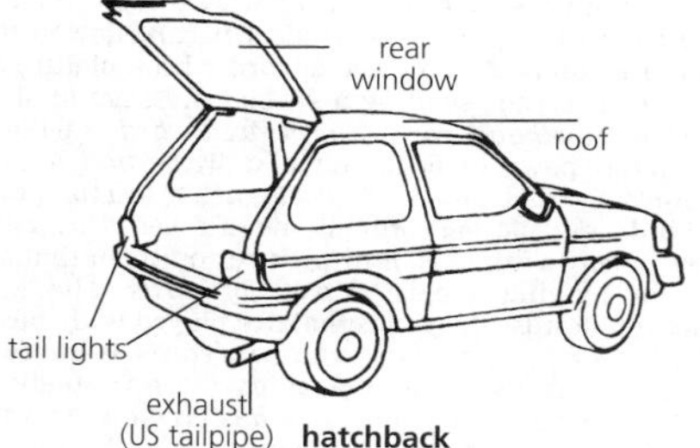

hatchback

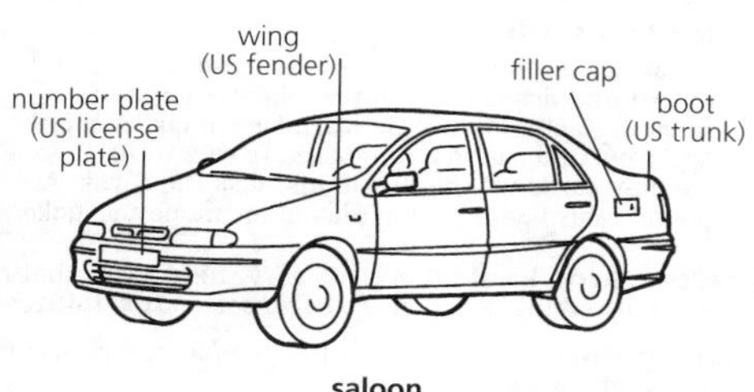

saloon
(US **sedan**)

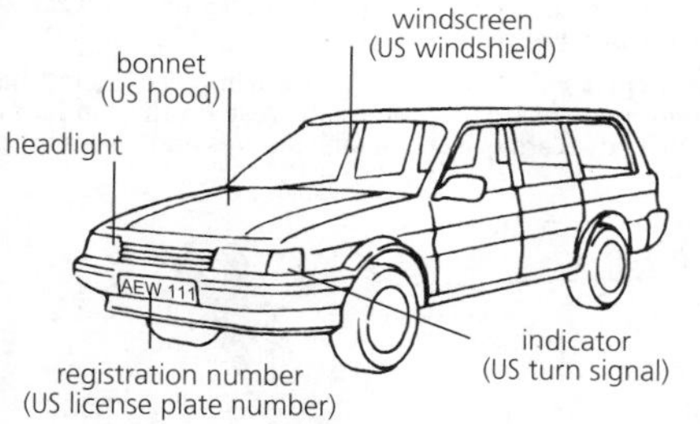

estate car
(US **station wagon**)

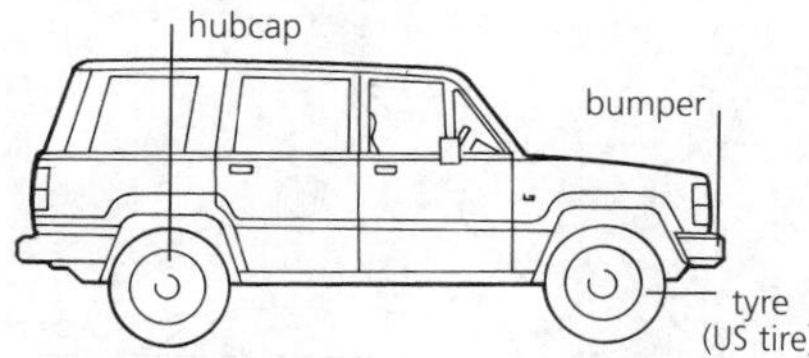

four-wheel drive/all-terrain vehicle (ATV)

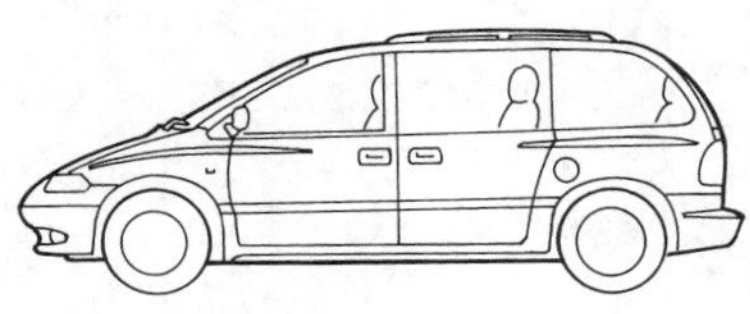

people carrier
(US **minivan**)

capture¹ /ˈkæptʃə(r)/ verb [T] **1** to take a person or an animal prisoner: *The lion was captured and taken back to the zoo.* ▶ **brać do niewoli, pojmać** SYN **catch 2** to take control of sth: *The town has been captured by the rebels.* ◇ *The company has captured 90% of the market.* ▶ **zdobywać 3** to make sb interested in sth: *The story captured the children's imagination/interest/attention* (zafascynowało dzieci). SYN **catch 4** to succeed in representing or recording sth in words, pictures, etc.: *This poem captures the atmosphere of the carnival.* ◇ *The robbery was captured on video.* ▶ **(dobrze) oddawać**

capture² /ˈkæptʃə(r)/ noun [U] the act of capturing sth or being captured ▶ **pojmanie, zdobycie**

car /kɑː(r)/ noun [C] **1** (US also **automobile** /ˈɔːtəməbiːl/) a road vehicle with four wheels that can carry a small number of people: *a new/second-hand car* ◇ *Where can I park the car?* ◇ *They had a car crash.* ◇ *to get into/out of a car* ◇ *an estate car* samochód kombi ▶ **samochód** ℹ Zwróć uwagę, że mówi się **by car** albo **in the car**. Używa się również czasownika **drive**: *I come to work in the car/by car.* ◇ *I drive to work.* ➲ note at **driving**, **parking**, **road** ➲ picture on **page 114 2** (Brit.) a section of a train that is used for a particular purpose: *a dining/sleeping car* ▶ **wagon 3** (US) = CARRIAGE (1)

> **cars**
>
> You **fill up** your car with **petrol** (US **gas**) or **diesel** at a **petrol station** (US **gas station**). Many cars run on **unleaded** petrol. If your car **breaks down**, it might need to be **towed** to a **garage** so that you can **have it repaired** by a **mechanic**.

carafe /kəˈræf/ noun [C] a glass container like a bottle with a wide neck, in which wine or water is served ▶ **karafka**

caramel /ˈkærəmel/ noun **1** [C,U] a type of sticky sweet that is made from boiled sugar, butter and milk ▶ **karmelek 2** [U] burnt sugar that is used to add flavour and colour to food ▶ **karmel**

carat (US **karat**) /ˈkærət/ noun [C] a measure of how pure gold is or how heavy **jewels** are: *a 20-carat gold ring* ▶ **karat**

caravan /ˈkærəvæn/ noun [C] **1** (US **trailer**) a large vehicle that is pulled by a car or a horse. You can sleep, cook, etc. in a **caravan** when you are travelling or on holiday. ▶ **przyczepa kempingowa** ℹ Mówiąc o podróży w **caravan** używa się zwrotu **go caravanning**: *We're going caravanning in Scotland this summer.* **2** a group of people and animals that travel together, for example across a desert ▶ **karawana**

caraway /ˈkærəweɪ/ noun [U] the dried seeds of the **caraway** plant, used to give flavour to food ▶ **kminek** ➲ look at **cumin**

carbohydrate /ˌkɑːbəʊˈhaɪdreɪt/ noun [C,U] one of the substances in food, for example sugar, that gives your body energy: *Athletes need a diet that is high in carbohydrate.* ▶ **węglowodan**

carbon /ˈkɑːbən/ noun [U] (symbol **C**) a chemical substance that is found in all living things, and also in diamonds, coal, petrol, etc. ▶ (*pierwiastek chemiczny*) **węgiel** (*chemiczny*)

ˌcarbon ˈcopy noun [C] **1** a copy of a letter, etc. that was made using **carbon paper** ▶ **kopia przez kalkę 2** an exact copy of sth ▶ **kopia, replika**

ˌcarbon ˈdating (also formal **ˌradiocarbon ˈdating**) noun [U,C] a method of calculating the age of very old objects by measuring the amounts of different forms of carbon in them ▶ (*ustalanie wieku*) **datowanie metodą węgla C14**

carbon dioxide /ˌkɑːbən daɪˈɒksaɪd/ noun [U] (symbol **CO_2**) a gas that has no colour or smell that people and animals breathe out of their lungs ▶ **dwutlenek węgla**

ˌcarbon ˈfootprint noun [C] a measure of the amount of carbon dioxide that is produced by the daily activities of a person, company or an organization, such as driving a vehicle, using gas, electricity, etc.: *a carbon footprint calculator* ◇ ***Offset your carbon footprint** by making donations to companies that produce renewable energy.* Aby zrekompensować wytwarzanie dwutlenku węgla należy wspomagać finansowo zakłady, które produkują odnawialną energię. ▶ **miara emisji dwutlenku węgla** (*przez osobę/firmę*)

carbon monoxide /ˌkɑːbən məˈnɒksaɪd/ noun [U] (symbol **CO**) a poisonous gas. Motor vehicles produce a lot of **carbon monoxide**. ▶ **tlenek węgla**

ˈcarbon paper noun [U] thin paper with a dark substance on one side that you put between two sheets of paper to make a copy of what you are writing ▶ **kalka**

ˌcar ˈboot sale noun [C] an outdoor sale where people sell things they do not want from the back of their cars ▶ **sprzedaż rzeczy używanych z samochodu** ➲ look at **jumble sale**

carburettor (US **carburetor**) /ˌkɑːbəˈretə(r); US ˈkɑːrbəreɪtə(r)/ noun [C] the piece of equipment in a car's engine that mixes petrol and air ▶ **gaźnik**

carcass /ˈkɑːkəs/ noun [C] the dead body of an animal ▶ **padlina** ➲ look at **corpse**

carcinogen /kɑːˈsɪnədʒən/ noun [C] a substance that can cause cancer ▶ **czynnik rakotwórczy**

carcinogenic /ˌkɑːsɪnəˈdʒenɪk/ adj. likely to cause cancer ▶ **rakotwórczy**

card /kɑːd/ noun **1** [U] thick stiff paper: *a piece of card* ▶ **karton 2** [C] a small piece of card or plastic that has information on it: *a business card* wizytówka ◇ *a membership card* legitymacja ◇ *an identity card* dowód tożsamości ▶ **karta 3** [C] a piece of card with a picture on it that you use for sending a special message to sb: *a Christmas/birthday card* ◇ *a get-well card* kartka z życzeniami powrotu do zdrowia ◇ *We've had a card* (pocztówkę) *from Anna in Portugal.* ▶ **karta**, **pocztówka 4** (also **ˈplaying card**) [C] one of a set of 52 small pieces of card with shapes or pictures on them that are used for playing games: *a pack of cards* talia kart ▶ **karta 5** (**cards**) [pl.] games that are played with cards: *Let's play cards.* ◇ *Let's have a game of cards.* ▶ **karty**

IDM **on the cards**; US **in the cards** (informal) likely to happen: *Their marriage break-up has been on the cards for some time now.* ▶ **prawdopodobny**

> **playing cards**
> A **pack** of cards is divided into four **suits**, two red (**hearts** and **diamonds**) and two black (**clubs** and **spades**). Each suit has an **ace**, a **king**, a **queen**, a **jack** and nine other cards, numbered from 2 to 10. Before we play cards we **shuffle**, **cut** and **deal** the cards. A popular card game, often played for money, is **poker**.

cardboard /ˈkɑːdbɔːd/ noun [U] very thick paper that is used for making boxes, etc.: *a cardboard box* ▶ **tektura**

ˈcard game noun [C] a game in which playing cards are used ▶ **gra w karty**

cardiac /ˈkɑːdiæk/ adj. [only before a noun] (formal) connected with the heart: *cardiac surgery* ◇ *a cardiac arrest* zatrzymanie pracy serca ▶ **sercowy**

cardigan /ˈkɑːdɪɡən/ noun [C] a warm piece of clothing, often made of wool, which you wear on the top half of your body. **Cardigans** have long sleeves and fasten at the

car

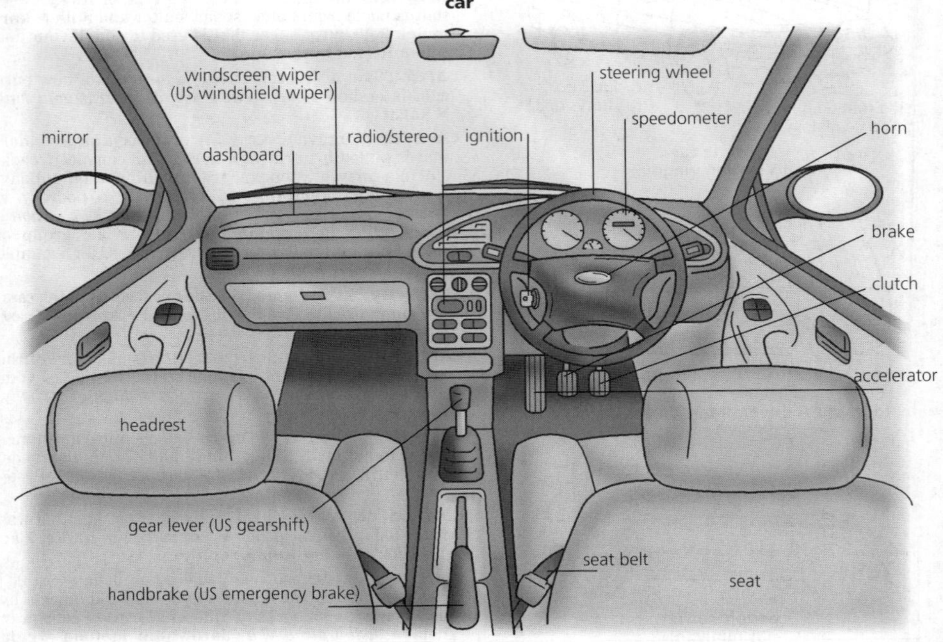

front, usually with buttons ▶ **sweter rozpinany** ➲ note at **sweater**

cardinal /ˈkɑːdɪnl/ noun [C] **1** a priest at a high level in the Roman Catholic Church ▶ **kardynał 2** (also ˌ**cardinal** ˈ**number**) a whole number, for example 1, 2, 3 that shows quantity ▶ **liczebnik główny** ➲ look at **ordinal**

ˈ**card index** (also **index**) a list in order from A to Z of names, books, subjects, etc. written on a series of cards called **index cards** ▶ **kartoteka** ➲ picture at **stationery**

cardiologist /ˌkɑːdiˈɒlədʒɪst/ noun [C] a doctor who studies and treats heart diseases ▶ **kardiolog**
■ **cardiology** /-dʒi/ noun [U] ▶ **kardiologia**

cardiovascular /ˌkɑːdiəʊˈvæskjələ(r)/ adj. connected with the heart and the **blood vessels** ▶ **sercowo-naczyniowy**

cardphone /ˈkɑːdfəʊn/ noun [C] (Brit.) a public telephone in which you use a plastic card (= a **phonecard**) instead of money ▶ **automat telefoniczny na kartę**

ˈ**card swipe** noun [C] an electronic device through which you pass a credit card, etc. in order to record the information on it, open a door, etc. ▶ **czytnik kart magnetycznych**

🔑 **care**[1] /keə(r)/ noun **1** [U] **care (for sb)** the process of looking after sb/sth and providing what they need for their health or protection: *All the children in their care were healthy and happy.* ◇ *This hospital provides free medical care.* ◇ *She's in intensive care* (na oddziale intensywnej terapii). ◇ *skin/hair care products* ▶ **opieka 2** [U] **care (over sth/in doing sth)** thinking about what you are doing so that you do it well or do not make a mistake: *You should* ***take*** *more* ***care*** *over your homework.* ◇ *This box contains glasses – please handle it* ***with care.*** ▶ **staranność, ostrożność 3** [C,U] something that makes you feel worried or unhappy: *Since Charlie retired he* ***doesn't have a care in the world.*** ◇ *It was a happy life, free from care.* ▶ **troska**

IDM **care of sb**; US also **in care of sb** (used when writing to sb at another person's address): *Write to him care of his lawyer.* Napisz do niego na adres jego prawnika. ❶ Na kopertach używa się skrótu **c/o**.

in/into care (Brit.) (used about children) living in a home which is organized by the government, and not with their parents: *They were* ***taken into care*** (byli umieszczeni w ośrodku opiekuńczym) *after their parents died.*

take care (that.../to do sth) to be careful: *Goodbye and take care!* ◇ *Take care that you don't spill your tea.* ◇ *He took care not to arrive too early.* ▶ **uważać** ❶ **Take care** używa się przy pożegnaniu: *Goodbye and take care* (trzymaj się)*!*

take care of sb/sth to deal with sb/sth; to organize or arrange sth: *I'll take care of the food for the party.* ▶ **brać coś na siebie; zajmować się kimś** ➲ note at **care**[2]

take care of yourself/sb/sth to keep yourself/sb/sth safe from injury, illness, damage, etc.; to look after sb/sth: *My mother took care of me when I was ill.* ◇ *She always takes great care of her books.* ▶ **dbać o siebie/kogoś/coś, opiekować się sobą/kimś/czymś**

🔑 **care**[2] /keə(r)/ verb [I,T] **care (about sb/sth)** to be worried about or interested in sb/sth: *Money is the thing that she cares about most.* ◇ *He really cares about his staff.* ◇ *I don't care what you do.* ▶ **dbać, (kogoś) obchodzić**

IDM **I, etc. couldn't care less** (informal) it does not matter to me, etc. at all: *I couldn't care less what Barry thinks.* ▶ **nic mnie (ciebie itp.) to nie obchodzi**

not care/give a damn (about sb/sth) → DAMN[3]

who cares? (informal) nobody is interested; it is not important to anyone: *'I wonder who'll win the match.' 'Who cares?'* ▶ **kogo to obchodzi?**

would you care for.../to do sth (formal) (a polite way to ask if sb would like sth or would like to do sth) ▶ **mieć (na coś) ochotę, życzyć sobie**

PHR V **care for sb 1** to look after sb: *Who cared for her while she was ill?* ▶ **opiekować się kimś 2** to love or like sb very much: *She still cares for Liam although he married someone else.* ▶ **lubić kogoś**

not care for sb/sth (formal) to not like sb/sth: *I don't care for that colour.* Nie podoba mi się ten kolor. ▶ **nie lubić**

> **Care about** czy **take care of**?: *She really* ***cares about*** *the environment.* ◇ *He has to* ***take care of/look after*** *his sick wife.* ◇ *You can borrow my camera, but please* ***take care of/look after it.*** **Take care of** znaczy też „być odpowiedzialnym za": *I'll take care of the travel arrangements.*

🔑 **career**[1] /kəˈrɪə(r)/ noun [C] **1** the series of jobs that sb has in a particular area of work: *Sarah is considering a career in engineering.* ▶ **kariera, zawód 2** the period of your life that you spend working: *She spent most of her career working in India.* ▶ **życie zawodowe, kariera**

career[2] /kəˈrɪə(r)/ verb [I] to move quickly and in a dangerous way: *The car careered off the road and crashed into a wall.* ▶ **pędzić**

careerist /kəˈrɪərɪst/ noun [C] a person whose career is more important to them than anything else: *a careerist politician* ▶ **karierowicz/ka** ❶ Często wyraża dezaprobatę.
■ **careerism** noun [U] ▶ **karierowiczostwo**

carefree /ˈkeəfriː/ adj. with no problems or worries ▶ **beztroski**

🔑 **careful** /ˈkeəfl/ adj. **1 careful (of/with sth); careful (to do sth)** thinking about what you are doing so that you do not have an accident or make mistakes, etc.: ***Be careful!*** *There's a car coming.* ◇ *Please be very careful of the traffic.* ◇ *Be careful with that knife – it's very sharp.* ◇ *That ladder doesn't look very safe. Be careful you don't fall* (uważaj, żebyś nie spadł). ◇ *I was careful not to say* (uważałem, żeby nie powiedzieć) *anything about the money.* ◇ *a careful driver* ▶ **ostrożny, uważny** OPP **careless 2** giving a lot of attention to details to be sure sth is right: *I'll need to give this matter some careful thought.* Będę musiał tę sprawę dokładnie przemyśleć. ◇ *a careful worker* ▶ **dokładny, staranny**
■ **carefully** /-fəli/ adv.: *Please listen carefully.* ▶ **uważnie; dokładnie** | **carefulness** noun [U] ▶ **ostrożność; dokładność**

caregiver (US) = CARER

🔑 **careless** /ˈkeələs/ adj. **1 careless (about/with sth)** not thinking enough about what you are doing so that you make mistakes: *Jo's very careless.* ◇ *The accident was caused by careless driving.* ▶ **nieostrożny, nierozważny** OPP **careful 2** resulting from a lack of thought or attention to detail: *a careless mistake* błąd wynikający z nieuwagi ▶ **niedbały**
■ **carelessly** adv. ▶ **byle jak, niedbale** | **carelessness** noun [U] ▶ **nieostrożność, brak rozwagi; niedbalstwo**

carer /ˈkeərə(r)/ (US **caregiver** /ˈkeəgɪvə(r)/) noun [C] a person who regularly looks after a sick or an old person at home ▶ **opiekun/ka**

caress /kəˈres/ verb [T] to touch sb/sth in a gentle and loving way ▶ **pieścić**
■ **caress** noun [C] ▶ **pieszczota**

caretaker /ˈkeəteɪkə(r)/ (US **janitor** /ˈdʒænɪtə(r)/) noun [C] a person whose job is to look after a large building, for example a school or a block of flats ▶ **dozor-ca/czyni**

cargo /ˈkɑːgəʊ/ noun [C,U] (pl. **cargoes**; US also **cargos**) the goods that are carried in a ship or aircraft: *The tanker began to spill its cargo of oil.* ◇ *the cargo hold of a plane* ładownia w samolocie ◇ *a cargo ship* statek towarowy ▶ **ładunek**

ˈ**cargo pants** (also **cargoes**) noun [pl.] loose trousers that have pockets in various places, for example on the side of the leg above the knee ▶ **luźne spodnie z wieloma kieszeniami w różnych miejscach** (*często powyżej kolan*)

the **Caribbean** /ˌkærɪˈbiən; kəˈrɪbiən/ noun [sing.] the area in the Caribbean Sea where the group of islands called the West Indies is found ▶ **Karaiby**
■ **Caribbean** adj. ▶ **karaibski**

caricature /ˈkærɪkətʃʊə(r)/ noun [C] a picture or description of sb that makes their appearance or behaviour funnier and more extreme than it really is ▶ **karykatura**

caring /ˈkeərɪŋ/ adj. showing that you care about other people: *We must work towards a more caring society.* ▶ **opiekuńczy**

carnage /ˈkɑːnɪdʒ/ noun [U] the violent killing of a large number of people: *a scene of carnage* ▶ **rzeź** SYN **slaughter**

carnal /ˈkɑːnl/ adj. [usually before a noun] (formal or technical) connected with the body or with sex: ***carnal desires/appetites*** ▶ **cielesny**

carnation /kɑːˈneɪʃn/ noun [C] a white, pink or red flower with a pleasant smell ▶ (*kwiat*) **goździk** ➲ picture on **page A15**

carnival /ˈkɑːnɪvl/ noun [C] a public festival that takes place in the streets with music and dancing ▶ **karnawał**

carnivore /ˈkɑːnɪvɔː(r)/ noun [C] any animal that eats meat ▶ **zwierzę mięsożerne** ➲ look at **herbivore**, **omnivore**
■ **carnivorous** /kɑːˈnɪvərəs/ adj. ▶ **mięsożerny**

carol /ˈkærəl/ (also ˌ**Christmas** ˈ**carol**) noun [C] a Christian religious song that people sing at Christmas: *carol singers* kolędnicy ▶ **kolęda**

carousel /ˌkærəˈsel/ noun [C] **1** (US) = MERRY-GO-ROUND **2** a moving belt at an airport that carries luggage for passengers to collect ▶ **taśma do bagaży**

carp /kɑːp/ noun [C] a large **freshwater** fish that is used for food ▶ **karp**

ˈ**car park** (US ˈ**parking lot**) noun [C] an area or building where you can leave your car: *a multi-storey car park* ▶ **parking**

carpenter /ˈkɑːpəntə(r)/ noun [C] a person whose job is to make things from wood ▶ **stolarz** ➲ note at **house** ➲ look at **joiner** ➲ picture on **page A4**

carpentry /ˈkɑːpəntri/ noun [U] the skill or work of a **carpenter** ▶ **stolarka**

carpet /ˈkɑːpɪt/ noun **1** [C,U] (a piece of) thick material that is used for covering floors and stairs: *a square metre of carpet* ◇ *a fitted carpet* wykładzina dywanowa ▶ **dywan** ➲ look at **mat**, **rug** **2** [C] a thick layer of sth that covers the ground: *a carpet of snow* ▶ **pokrywa**, **kobierzec**
■ **carpeted** adj. ▶ **wyłożony dywanami**

ˈ**car phone** noun [C] a telephone that you can use in a car ▶ **telefon komórkowy w samochodzie**

carriage /ˈkærɪdʒ/ noun [C] **1** (also **coach**; US **car**) one of the separate parts of a train where people sit: *a first-class carriage* ▶ **wagon** ➲ look at **coach** **2** a vehicle with wheels that is pulled by horses ▶ **powóz**, **kareta** **3** the act or cost of transporting goods from one place to another ▶ **przewóz**, **transport**

carriageway /ˈkærɪdʒweɪ/ noun [C] (Brit.) one of the two sides of a **motorway** or main road, used by vehicles travelling in one direction only: *the southbound carriageway of the motorway* ▶ **pas ruchu** ➲ look at **dual carriageway**

carrier /ˈkæriə(r)/ noun [C] **1** (in business) a company that transports people or goods: *the Dutch carrier, KLM* ▶ **przewoźnik** **2** a military vehicle or ship that is used for transporting soldiers, planes, weapons, etc.: *an aircraft carrier* ▶ **transportowiec** **3** a person or an animal that can give an infectious disease to others but does not show the signs of the disease: *Some insects are carriers of tropical diseases.* ▶ **nosiciel** **4** (Brit.) = CARRIER BAG

ˈ**carrier bag** (Brit. also **carrier**) noun [C] a plastic or paper bag for carrying shopping ▶ **reklamówka** ➲ picture at **bag**

carrot /ˈkærət/ noun **1** [C,U] a long thin orange vegetable that grows under the ground: *grated carrot* ▶ **marchew** ➲ picture on **page A13** **2** [C] something attractive that is offered to sb in order to persuade them to do sth: *The management have offered them the carrot of a £500 bonus if they agree to work extra hours.* ▶ **zachęta**

carry /ˈkæri/ verb (**carrying**; **carries**; pt, pp **carried**) **1** [T] to hold sb/sth in your hand, arms or on your back while you are moving from one place to another: *Could you carry this bag for me?* ◇ *She was carrying a rucksack on her back.* ▶ **nosić** ℹ W znaczeniu „mieć coś na sobie", np. o odzieży, biżuterii itp. używa się **wear**, a nie **carry**: *He was wearing a black jacket.* **2** [T] to have sth with you as you go somewhere: *I never carry much money with me when I go to London.* ◇ *Do the police carry guns in your country?* ▶ **nosić**, **mieć przy sobie** **3** [T] to transport sb/sth from one place to another: *A train carrying hundreds of passengers crashed yesterday.* ◇ *Strong winds carried the boat off course.* ▶ **przewozić**, **przenosić** **4** [T] to have an infectious disease that can be given to others, usually without showing any signs of the disease yourself: *Rats carry all sorts of diseases.* ▶ **przenosić** **5** [I] (used about a sound) to reach a long distance: *You'll have to speak louder if you want your voice to carry to the back of the room.* ▶ **docierać** **6** [T, usually passive] to officially approve of sth in a meeting, etc., because the largest number of people vote for it: *The motion was carried by 12 votes to 9.* ▶ **przyjmować** (*w głosowaniu*)

IDM **be/get carried away** to be so excited that you forget what you are doing: *I got so carried away watching the race that I forgot how late it was.* ▶ **dawać się ponieść** (*uczuciom*)

carry weight to have influence on the opinion of sb else: *Nick's views carry a lot of weight with our manager.* ▶ **mieć znaczenie**, **liczyć się**

PHR V **carry it/sth off** to succeed in doing sth difficult: *He felt nervous before he started his speech but he carried it off very well.* ▶ **dobrze się spisywać**

carry on (with sth/doing sth); **carry sth on** to continue: *They ignored me and carried on with their conversation.* ◇ *She intends to carry on studying after the course has finished.* ▶ **kontynuować**

carry on sth to do an activity: *to carry on a conversation/a business* ▶ **prowadzić**

carry sth out **1** to do sth that you have been ordered to do: *The soldiers carried out their orders without question.* ▶ **wypełniać**, **wywiązywać się** **2** to do a task, repair, etc.: *to carry out tests/an investigation* ▶ **wykonywać**

carrycot /ˈkærikɒt/ noun [C] a small bed, like a box with handles, that you can carry a baby in ▶ **nosidełko** ➲ picture at **pram**

ˈ**carry-on** noun **1** [usually sing.] (Brit., informal) a display of excitement, anger or silly behaviour over sth unimportant: *What a carry-on!* ▶ **cyrk**, **szopka** **2** (US) [C] a small bag or case that you carry onto a plane with you ▶ **torba/walizka kabinowa**

ˈ**carry-out** (US) = TAKEAWAY

carsick /ˈkɑːsɪk/ adj. feeling sick or **vomiting** as a result of travelling in a car: *to get/feel/be carsick* ▶ (*osoba podróżująca samochodem*) **cierpiący na chorobę lokomocyjną** ➲ look at **airsick**, **seasick**, **travel-sick**

cart[1] /kɑːt/ noun [C] **1** a vehicle with wheels that is used for transporting things: *a horse and cart* ▶ **wóz, fura 2** = TROLLEY (1)

cart[2] /kɑːt/ verb [T] (informal) to take or carry sth/sb somewhere, often with difficulty: *We left our luggage at the station because we didn't want to cart it around all day.* ◇ *Six of the women were carted off* (odwieźli sześć kobiet) *to the police station.* ▶ **taszczyć, nosić**

cartilage /ˈkɑːtɪlɪdʒ/ noun [C,U] a strong substance in the places where your bones join ▶ **chrząstka**

cartographer /kɑːˈtɒɡrəfə(r)/ noun [C] a person who draws or makes maps ▶ **kartograf**

cartography /kɑːˈtɒɡrəfi/ noun [U] the art or process of drawing or making maps ▶ **kartografia**
■ **cartographic** /ˌkɑːtəˈɡræfɪk/ adj. ▶ **kartograficzny**

carton /ˈkɑːtn/ noun [C] a small container made of cardboard or plastic: *a carton of milk/orange juice* ▶ **karton, opakowanie** ➲ picture at **container**

cartoon /kɑːˈtuːn/ noun [C] **1** a funny drawing, especially in a newspaper or magazine ▶ **rysunek, karykatura 2** a film that tells a story by using moving drawings instead of real people and places ▶ **film animowany**

cartoonist /kɑːˈtuːnɪst/ noun [C] a person who draws **cartoons** ▶ **rysownik, karykaturzyst(k)a**

cartridge /ˈkɑːtrɪdʒ/ noun [C] **1** a small tube that contains powder that can explode and a bullet. You put a **cartridge** into a gun when you want to fire it. ▶ **nabój 2** a closed container that holds sth that is used in a machine, for example film for a camera, ink for printing, etc. **Cartridges** can be removed and replaced when they are finished or empty. ▶ **nabój, wkład, kaseta**

cartwheel /ˈkɑːtwiːl/ noun [C] a fast physical movement in which you turn in a circle sideways by putting your hands on the ground and bringing your legs, one at a time, over your head: *to* ***do/turn cartwheels*** ▶ (*sport*) **gwiazda**
■ **cartwheel** verb [I] ▶ **robić gwiazdę**

carve /kɑːv/ verb **1** [I,T] **carve (sth) (out of sth)** to cut wood or stone in order to make an object or to put a pattern or writing on it: *The statue is carved out of marble.* ◇ *He carved his name on the desk.* ▶ **rzeźbić, wycinać 2** [T] to cut a piece of cooked meat into slices ▶ **krajać**

carving /ˈkɑːvɪŋ/ noun [C,U] an object or design that has been **carved**: *There are ancient carvings on the walls of the cave.* ▶ **płaskorzeźba, rzeźba**

ˈ**car wash** noun [C] a place with special equipment, where you can pay to have your car washed ▶ **myjnia samochodowa**

cascade[1] /kæˈskeɪd/ noun [C] **1** a small **waterfall** ▶ **kaskada 2** a large quantity of sth that falls or hangs down: *a cascade of blond hair* ▶ **kaskada**

cascade[2] /kæˈskeɪd/ verb [I] to fall or hang down, especially in large amounts or in stages: *Water cascaded from the roof.* ▶ **opadać kaskadowo**

⚷ **case** /keɪs/ noun **1** [C] a particular situation or example of sth: ***In some cases***, *people have had to wait two weeks for a doctor's appointment.* ◇ *Most of us travel to work by tube – or,* ***in Jim's case***, *by train and tube.* ◇ *Cases of the disease are very unusual in this country.* ▶ **przypadek 2** (**the case**) [sing.] the true situation: *The man said he worked in Cardiff, but we discovered later that this was not the case* (tak nie było). ▶ **stan faktyczny 3** [C] a crime or legal matter: *The police deal with hundreds of murder cases a year.* ◇ *The case will come to court in a few months.* ◇ *a court case* proces sądowy ◇ *to win/lose a case* wygrać/przegrać proces ▶ **sprawa 4** [C, usually sing.] the facts and reasons that support one side in a discussion or legal matter: *She tried to* ***make a case for*** (przedstawić argumenty za) *shorter working hours, but the others disagreed.* ▶ **argumenty 5** [C] [in compounds] a container or cover for sth: *She put her glasses back in the case.* ◇ *a pencil case* piórnik ◇ *a pillowcase* poszewka na poduszkę ◇ *a bookcase* biblioteczka ▶ **futerał, pudełko 6** = SUITCASE: *Would you like me to carry your case?* **7** [C,U] the form of a noun, an adjective or a pronoun in some languages, that shows its relationship to another word: *the nominative/accusative/genitive/dative/locative/instrumental/vocative case* ▶ (*gram.*) **przypadek**
IDM **as the case may be** (used when you are not sure which of two or more possibilities will be true in a particular situation): *There may be an announcement about this tomorrow – or not, as the case may be.* ▶ **zależnie od okoliczności**
(be) a case of sth/doing sth a situation in which sth is needed: *There's no secret to success in this business. It's just a case of hard work* (tu trzeba ciężkiej pracy). ▶ **kwestia czegoś**
in any case whatever happens or has happened: *I don't care how much the tickets cost – I'm going in any case.* ▶ **mimo wszystko, w każdym razie** SYN **anyhow**
(just) in case because sth might happen: *I think I'll take an umbrella in case it rains.* ◇ *I wasn't intending to buy anything but I took my cheque book just in case.* ▶ **na wypadek/w razie czegoś, na wszelki wypadek** ℹ **In case of** czy **if**? W Br. ang. **in case** oraz **if** mają różne znaczenie. Porównaj: *You should buy insurance, in case you are robbed.* ◇ *If you are robbed, you should call the police.*
in case of sth (formal) if sth happens: *In case of fire, break this glass.* ▶ **w razie/wypadku czegoś**
in that case if that is the situation: *'I'm busy on Tuesday.' 'Oh well, in that case we'll have to meet another day.'* ▶ **w takim razie**

ˌ**case** ˈ**history** noun [C] a record of a person's background, past illnesses, etc. that a doctor or **social worker** studies ▶ **historia choroby**

ˈ**case study** noun [C] a detailed study of a person, group, situation, etc. over a period of time ▶ **studium przypadku**

⚷ **cash**[1] /kæʃ/ noun [U] **1** money in the form of coins or notes and not cheques, plastic cards, etc.: *Would you prefer me to pay* ***in cash*** *or by cheque?* ◇ *How much cash have you got with/on you?* ◇ *petty cash* kasa podręczna ▶ **gotówka** ➲ note at **money 2** (informal) money in any form: *I'm a bit short of cash this month so I can't afford to go out much.* ▶ **pieniądze**

cash[2] /kæʃ/ verb [T] to exchange a cheque, etc. for coins and notes ▶ **realizować** (*czek*)
PHR V **cash in (on sth)** to take advantage of a situation ▶ **korzystać z sytuacji**

cashback /ˈkæʃbæk/ noun [U] **1** if you ask for **cashback** when you are paying for goods in some shops with a **debit card**, you get a sum of money in cash, that is added to your bill ▶ **wypłata pieniędzy z konta przy okazji zakupu przy użyciu karty kredytowej** (*w supermarketach w Wlk. Br.*) **2** an offer of money as a present that is made by some banks, companies selling cars, etc. in order to persuade customers to do business with them ▶ **promocyjny zwrot pieniędzy**

ˈ**cash card** (US ˌATˈM card) noun [C] a plastic card given by a bank to its customers so that they can get money from a **cash machine** ▶ **karta do bankomatu** ➲ look at **cheque card**, **credit card**

ˈ**cash crop** noun [C] a crop grown for selling, rather than for use by the person who grows it ▶ **rolna produkcja rynkowa** ➲ look at **subsistence**

'cash desk noun [C] the place in a large shop where you pay for things ▶ **kasa**

'cash dispenser = CASH MACHINE

cashew /ˈkæʃuː; kæˈʃuː/ (also 'cashew nut) noun [C] a small curved nut that we eat ▶ **orzech nerkowca**

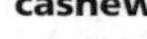

'cash flow noun [sing.] the movement of money into and out of a business as goods are bought and sold: *The company had cash-flow problems and could not pay its bills.* ▶ **przepływ gotówki**

cashier /kæˈʃɪə(r)/ noun [C] the person in a bank, shop, etc. that customers pay money to or get money from ▶ **kasjer/ka**

'cash machine (also 'cash dispenser; Cashpoint™ /ˈkæʃpɔɪnt/, ˌATˈM /ˌeɪ tiː ˈem/) noun [C] a machine inside or outside a bank, etc., that you can get money from at any time of day by putting in a **cash card** ▶ **bankomat** ➲ note at **money**

cashmere /ˈkæʃmɪə(r); ˌkæʃˈm-; US ˈkæʒ-/ noun [U] a type of wool that is very fine and soft ▶ **kaszmir**

'cash register = TILL[2]

casing /ˈkeɪsɪŋ/ noun [C,U] a cover that protects sth: *a camera with a waterproof casing* ▶ **osłona**, **pokrowiec**

casino /kəˈsiːnəʊ/ noun [C] (pl. **casinos**) a place where people play card games, etc. in which they can win or lose money ▶ **kasyno gry**

cask /kɑːsk; US kæsk/ noun [C] a large wooden container in which alcoholic drinks, etc. are stored ▶ **beczka**, **beczułka**

casket (US) = COFFIN

cassava /kəˈsɑːvə/ (also **manioc** /ˈmænɪɒk/) noun [U] **1** a tropical plant with many branches and long roots that you can eat ▶ **maniok 2** the roots of this plant, which can be cooked or made into flour ▶ **maniok**

casserole /ˈkæsərəʊl/ noun **1** [C,U] a type of food made by cooking meat and vegetables in liquid for a long time in the oven: *chicken casserole* ▶ **potrawka 2** [C] a large dish with a lid for cooking **casseroles** in ▶ **garnek żaroodporny** (*z pokrywką*) ➲ picture at **pan**

cassette /kəˈset/ noun [C] a small flat plastic case containing tape for playing or recording music or sound: *to put on/play/listen to a cassette* ▶ **kaseta** SYN **tape**[1] ➲ look at **video**

cas'sette player (also **cas'sette recorder**) noun [C] a machine that you use for recording and playing cassettes ▶ **magnetofon kasetowy**

cast[1] /kɑːst; US kæst/ verb (pt, pp **cast**) **1** [T] to look, smile, etc. in a particular direction: *She cast a welcoming smile in his direction.* ▶ **rzucać** (*np. spojrzenia*) **2** [I,T] to throw a fishing line or net into the water ▶ **zarzucać 3** [T] to throw sb/sth somewhere, especially using force ▶ **ciskać** ℹ Wyrażenie literackie. **4** [T, often passive] to choose an actor for a particular role in a play, film, etc. ▶ **obsadzać** (*w roli*) **5** [T] **cast sth (in sth)** to shape hot liquid metal, etc. by pouring it into a hollow container (called a **mould**) ▶ **odlewać**, **robić odlew**

IDM **cast doubt on sth** to make people less sure about sth: *The newspaper report casts doubt on the truth of the Prime Minister's statement.* ▶ **podawać coś w wątpliwość**

cast an eye/your eye(s) over sb/sth to look at sb/sth quickly ▶ **rzucać okiem**

cast light on sth to help to explain sth: *Can you cast any light on the problem?* ▶ **rzucać (nowe) światło na coś**

cast your mind back to make yourself remember sth: *She cast her mind back to the day she met her husband.* ▶ **wspominać**, **wracać myślami do przeszłości**

cast a shadow (across/over sth) to cause an area of shade to appear somewhere: (figurative) *The accident cast a shadow over the rest of the holiday.* ▶ **rzucać cień**; **kłaść się cieniem**

cast a spell (on sb/sth) to use words that are thought to be magic and have the power to change or influence sb/sth ▶ **rzucać urok (na kogoś/coś)**

cast a/your vote to vote ▶ **oddawać głos**

PHR V **cast around/about for sth** to try to find sth: *Jack cast around desperately for a solution to the problem.* ▶ **szukać czegoś**

cast sb/sth off (formal) to remove or make yourself free of sb/sth ▶ **porzucać**

cast[2] /kɑːst; US kæst/ noun [C, with sing. or pl. verb] all the actors in a play, film, etc.: *The entire cast was/were excellent.* ▶ **obsada**

castaway /ˈkɑːstəweɪ; US ˈkæst-/ noun [C] a person who is left alone somewhere after their ship has sunk ▶ **rozbitek**

caste /kɑːst; US kæst/ noun **1** [C] a social class or group based on your position in society, how much money you have, family origin, etc.: *Hindu society is based on a caste system.* ▶ **kasta 2** [U] the system of dividing people in this way ▶ **system kastowy**

caster (US) = CASTOR

caster sugar (also ˌcastor ˈsugar) noun [U] (Brit.) white sugar in the form of very fine grains, used in cooking ▶ **drobno zmielony cukier** ➲ look at **icing sugar**

ˌcasting 'vote noun [C, usually sing.] the vote given by the person in charge of an official meeting to decide an issue when votes on each side are equal: *You have the casting vote.* ▶ **decydujący głos**

ˌcast 'iron noun [U] a hard type of iron that is shaped by pouring the hot liquid metal into a **mould**: *a bridge made of cast iron* ▶ **żeliwo** ➲ look at **wrought iron**
■ **ˌcast-'iron** adj. made of cast iron: (figurative): *a cast-iron alibi* ▶ **żeliwny**; (*i przen.*) **żelazny**

castle /ˈkɑːsl; US ˈkæsl/ noun [C] **1** a large building with high walls and towers that was built in the past to defend people against attack ▶ **zamek** ➲ picture on **page A3 2** (in the game of **chess**) any of the four pieces placed in the corner squares of the board at the start of the game, usually made to look like a **castle** ▶ **wieża**

'cast-off noun [C, usually pl.] a piece of clothing that you no longer want and that you give to sb else or throw away: *When I was little I had to wear my sister's cast-offs* (musiałam nosić rzeczy po siostrze). ▶ **niepotrzebna część garderoby**

castor (Brit.) (US **caster**) /ˈkɑːstə(r); US ˈkæs-/ noun [C] one of the small wheels fixed to the bottom of a piece of furniture so that it can be moved easily ▶ **kółko** (*np. u fotela*)

ˌcastor 'sugar = CASTER SUGAR

castrate /kæˈstreɪt; US ˈkæstreɪt/ verb [T] to remove part of the sexual organs of a male animal so that it cannot produce young ▶ **kastrować** ➲ look at **neuter**
■ **castration** /kæˈstreɪʃn/ noun [U] ▶ **kastracja**

casual /ˈkæʒuəl/ adj. **1** relaxed and not worried; not showing great effort or interest: *I'm not happy about your casual attitude to your work.* ◇ *It was only a casual remark so I don't know why he got so angry.* ▶ **obojętny**, **niedbały**, **na luzie 2** (used about clothes) not formal: *I always change into casual clothes as soon as I get home from work.* ▶ **codzienny**, **zwyczajny 3** (used about work) done only for a short period; not regular or permanent: *Most of the building work was done by casual labour.* ◇ *a casual job* ▶ **dorywczy**, **sezonowy**

■ **casually** /ˈkæʒuəli/ adv.: *She walked in casually and said, 'I'm not late, am I?'* ◇ *Dress casually – it won't be a formal party.* ▶ **nonszalancko**, **niedbale**, (*ubrany*) **zwyczajnie**

casualty /ˈkæʒuəlti/ noun (pl. **casualties**) **1** [C] a person who is killed or injured in a war or an accident: *After the accident the casualties were taken to hospital.* ▶ **ofiara 2** [C] a person or thing that suffers as a result of sth else: *Many small companies became casualties of the economic crisis.* ▶ **ofiara** SYN **victim 3** [U] (also ˈ**casualty department**) = ACCIDENT AND EMERGENCY

cat /kæt/ noun [C] **1** a small animal with soft fur that people often keep as a pet: *cat food* ▶ **kot** ➲ note at **pet 2** a wild animal of the cat family: *the big cats* ▶ **kot**

> **cats**
>
> A young cat is called a **kitten**. A male cat is called a **tom**. When a cat makes a soft sound of pleasure, it **purrs**. When it makes a louder sound, it **miaows**.

cataclysm /ˈkætəklɪzəm/ noun [C] (formal) a sudden disaster or a violent event that causes change, for example a flood or a war ▶ **kataklizm**

■ **cataclysmic** /ˌkætəˈklɪzmɪk/ adj. [usually before a noun] ▶ **kataklizmowy**

catalogue (US **catalog**) /ˈkætəlɒg/ noun [C] **1** a list of all the things that you can buy, see, etc. somewhere ▶ **katalog 2** a series, especially of bad things: *a catalogue of disasters/errors/injuries* ▶ **seria**

■ **catalogue** verb [T] ▶ **katalogować**

catalyst /ˈkætəlɪst/ noun [C] **1** (in chemistry) a substance that makes a reaction happen faster without being changed itself ▶ **katalizator 2 catalyst (for sth)** a person or thing that causes a change: *I see my role as being a catalyst for change.* ▶ (*przen.*) **katalizator** (*np. przemian*)

catalytic converter /ˌkætəˌlɪtɪk kənˈvɜːtə(r)/ noun [C] a device used in motor vehicles to reduce the damage caused to the environment by poisonous gases ▶ **katalizator**

catapult[1] /ˈkætəpʌlt/ (US **slingshot** /ˈslɪŋʃɒt/) noun [C] a Y-shaped stick with a piece of **elastic** tied to each side that is used by children for shooting stones ▶ **proca**

catapult[2] /ˈkætəpʌlt/ verb [T] to throw sb/sth suddenly and with great force: *When the car crashed the driver was catapulted through the windscreen.* ◇ (figurative) *The success of his first film catapulted him to fame.* ▶ **gwałtownie wyrzucać**; **wynosić kogoś** (*na wysoką pozycję, np. gwiazdy filmowej*)

cataract /ˈkætərækt/ noun [C] a white area that grows over the eye as a result of disease ▶ **katarakta**

catarrh /kəˈtɑː(r)/ noun [U] a thick liquid that forms in the nose and throat when you have a cold ▶ **wydzielina z nosa** (*spowodowana katarem*)

catastrophe /kəˈtæstrəfi/ noun [C] **1** a sudden disaster that causes great suffering or damage: *major catastrophes such as floods and earthquakes* ▶ **katastrofa 2** an event that causes great difficulty, disappointment, etc.: *It'll be a catastrophe if I fail the exam again.* ▶ **katastrofa**

■ **catastrophic** /ˌkætəˈstrɒfɪk/ adj.: *The war had a catastrophic effect on the whole country.* ▶ **katastrofalny**

catch[1] /kætʃ/ verb (pt, pp **caught** /kɔːt/) **1** [T] to take hold of sth that is moving, usually with your hand or hands: *The dog caught the ball in its mouth.* ▶ **łapać 2** [T] to capture sb/sth that you have been following or looking for: *The murderer still hasn't been caught.* ◇ *to catch a fish* ▶ **łapać 3** [T] to notice or see sb doing sth bad: *I caught her taking money from my purse.* ▶ **łapać (kogoś na czymś) 4** [T] to be in time for sth; not to miss sb/sth: *We arrived just in time to catch the beginning of the film.* ◇ *I'll phone her now. I might just catch her before she leaves the office.* ▶ **zdążać** (*na czas*), **łapać 5** [T] to get on a bus, train, plane, etc.: *I caught the bus from Oxford to London.* ▶ **zdążać (na coś)** OPP **miss 6** [T] to get an illness: *to catch a cold/flu/measles* ▶ **nabawić się 7** [I,T] to become or cause sth to become accidentally connected to or stuck in sth: *His jacket caught on a nail and ripped.* ◇ *I caught my finger* (przyciąłem sobie palec) *in the drawer as I shut it.* ◇ *I got caught in the traffic.* Utknąłem w korku. ▶ **zahaczać**, **zaczepiać 8** [T] to hit sb/sth: *The branch caught him on the head.* ▶ **uderzać**, **trafić w kogoś/coś 9** [T] to hear or understand sth that sb says: *I'm sorry, I didn't quite catch what you said. Could you repeat it?* ▶ **dosłyszeć**, **zrozumieć**

IDM **catch sb's attention/eye** to make sb notice sth: *I tried to catch the waiter's eye so that I could get the bill.* ▶ **zwrócić czyjąś uwagę**

catch your breath 1 to breathe in suddenly because you are surprised ▶ **zapierać dech/zaniemówić** (*ze zdumienia*) **2** to rest after physical exercise so that your breathing returns to normal: *I had to sit down at the top of the hill to catch my breath.* ▶ **złapać oddech**

catch your death (of cold) to get very cold: *Don't go out without a coat – you'll catch your death!* ▶ **zmarznąć na kość**, (*przen.*) **zamarznąć na śmierć**

catch fire to start burning, often accidentally: *Nobody knows how the building caught fire.* ▶ **zapalać się**

catch sb red-handed to find sb just as they are doing sth wrong ▶ **złapać kogoś na gorącym uczynku**

catch sight of sb/sth to see sb/sth for a moment ▶ **dostrzegać**, **zobaczyć**

catch the sun (informal) (used about people) to become red or brown because of spending time in the sun ▶ **spiec się** (*na słońcu*)

PHR V **be/get caught up in sth** to be or get involved in sth, usually without intending to: *I seem to have got caught up in a rather complicated situation.* ▶ **być/zostać zamieszanym w coś**

catch on (informal) **1** to become popular or fashionable: *The idea has never really caught on in this country.* ▶ **przyjmować się 2** to understand or realize sth: *She's sometimes a bit slow to catch on.* ▶ **chwytać**, **pojmować**

catch sb out to cause sb to make a mistake by asking a clever question: *Ask me anything you like – you won't catch me out.* ▶ **zaginać**

catch up (with sb); Brit. also **catch sb up 1** to reach sb who is ahead by going faster: *Go on ahead – I'll catch you up in a minute.* ▶ **doganiać 2** to reach the same level or standard as sb who was better or more advanced: *Sharon's missed so much school she'll have to work hard to catch up with the rest of the class.* ▶ **doganiać**

catch up on sth to spend time doing sth that you have not been able to do for some time: *I'll have to go into the office at the weekend to catch up on my work.* ◇ *I phoned my sister to catch up on her news* (żeby dowiedzieć się, co u niej się ostatnio dzieje). ▶ **nadrabiać zaległości**

catch[2] /kætʃ/ noun [C] **1** an act of catching sth, for example a ball ▶ **chwyt**, **złapanie 2** the amount of fish that sb has caught: *The fishermen brought their catch to the harbour.* ▶ **połów 3** a device for fastening sth and keeping it closed: *a window catch* ▶ **zamek**, **zatrzask 4** a hidden disadvantage or difficulty in sth that seems attractive: *It looks like a good offer but I'm sure there must be a catch in it.* ▶ **haczyk**, **pułapka**

catcher /ˈkætʃə(r)/ noun [C] **1** (in **baseball**) the player who stands behind the **batter** and catches the ball if he or she does not hit it ▶ (*sport*) **łapacz 2** [usually in compounds] a person or thing that catches sth: *a rat catcher* łowca szczurów ▶ **wyłapywacz**

catching /ˈkætʃɪŋ/ adj. [not before a noun] (used about a disease or an emotion) passing easily or quickly from one person to another ▶ **zaraźliwy** SYN **infectious**

catchment area /ˈkætʃmənt eəriə/ noun [C] the area from which a school gets its students, a hospital gets its patients, etc. ▶ **rejon** (*np. szkolny*)

catchphrase /ˈkætʃfreɪz/ noun [C] a phrase that becomes famous for a while because it is used by a famous person ▶ **powiedzenie, slogan**

catchy /ˈkætʃi/ adj. (**catchier**; **catchiest**) (used about music or the words of an advertisement) pleasing and easy to remember ▶ (*melodia itp.*) **wpadający w ucho**, (*hasło*) **chwytliwy**

catechism /ˈkætəkɪzəm/ noun [usually sing.] a summary of the main ideas and beliefs of a religion in the form of questions and answers, used for teaching about the religion ▶ **katechizm**

categorical /ˌkætəˈgɒrɪkl/ adj. very definite: *The answer was a categorical 'no'.* ▶ **kategoryczny**
■ **categorically** /-kli/ adv. ▶ **kategorycznie**

categorize (also **-ise**) /ˈkætəgəraɪz/ verb [T] to divide people or things into groups; to say that sb/sth belongs to a particular group ▶ **klasyfikować**

category /ˈkætəgəri; US -gɔːri/ noun [C] (pl. **categories**) a group of people or things that are similar to each other: *These books are* ***divided into categories*** *according to subject.* ◇ *Grammatically, nouns* ***fall into*** *two main* ***categories*** *– countable and uncountable.* ▶ **kategoria**

cater /ˈkeɪtə(r)/ verb [I] **1 cater (for sb/sth)** to provide and serve food and drink at an event or in a place that a lot of people go to: *Our firm caters for the 5 000 staff and visitors at the festival.* ▶ **obsługiwać** (*przyjęcia okolicznościowe*) (*np. dla firm*) **2 cater for sb/sth**; **cater to sth** to provide what sb/sth needs or wants: *We need a hotel that caters for small children* (dysponuje niezbędnymi udogodnieniami dla dzieci). ◇ *The menu caters to all tastes.* ▶ **troszczyć się o kogoś/coś, zaspokajać** (*np. potrzeby*)

caterer /ˈkeɪtərə(r)/ noun [C] a person or business that provides food and drink at events or in places that a lot of people go to ▶ **osoba obsługująca przyjęcia okolicznościowe, firma kateringowa**

catering /ˈkeɪtərɪŋ/ noun [U] the activity or business of providing food and drink at events or in places that a lot of people go to: *Who's going to* ***do the catering*** *at the wedding?* ◇ *the hotel and catering industry* (gastronomia) ▶ **organizacje i/lub obsługa przyjęć okolicznościowych**

caterpillar /ˈkætəpɪlə(r)/ noun [C] a small animal with a long body and a lot of legs, which eats the leaves of plants. A **caterpillar** later becomes a **butterfly** or a **moth** ▶ **gąsienica** ⮊ picture at **insect**

catharsis /kəˈθɑːsɪs/ noun [U,C] (pl. **catharses** /-siːz/) the process of releasing strong feelings, for example through plays or other artistic activities, as a way of providing relief from anger, suffering, etc. ▶ **katharsis**
■ **cathartic** /kəˈθɑːtɪk/ adj.: *It was a cathartic experience.* ▶ **katartyczny**

cathedral /kəˈθiːdrəl/ noun [C] a large church that is the most important one in a district ▶ **katedra**

catheter /ˈkæθɪtə(r)/ noun [C] a thin tube that is put into the body in order to remove liquid such as **urine** ▶ **cewnik** (*do odprowadzania moczu*)

catholic /ˈkæθlɪk/ adj. **1** (**Catholic**) = ROMAN CATHOLIC **2** (formal) including many or most things: *to have catholic tastes* ▶ **wszechstronny**
■ **Catholic** noun [C] = ROMAN CATHOLIC | **Catholicism** /kəˈθɒləsɪzəm/ noun [U] = ROMAN CATHOLICISM

Catseye™ /ˈkætsaɪ/ noun [C] any one of a line of small mirrors in the centre or at the edge of a road as a guide to traffic when it is dark ▶ **światło odblaskowe** (*zatopione w asfalcie na szosie*)

cattle /ˈkætl/ noun [pl.] male and female cows that are kept as farm animals for their milk or meat: *a herd of cattle* ▶ **bydło** ⮊ note at **cow**

catty /ˈkæti/ adj. (informal) (**cattier**; **cattiest**) (used about a woman) saying unkind things about other people: *a catty comment* ▶ **uszczypliwy, jędzowaty** SYN **bitchy, spiteful**
■ **cattiness** noun [U] ▶ **uszczypliwość, jędzowatość**

catwalk /ˈkætwɔːk/ noun [C] the long stage that models walk on during a fashion show: *a* ***catwalk model/show*** ▶ **wybieg dla modelek**

Caucasian noun [C] a member of any of the races of people who have pale skin ▶ **biały człowiek**
■ **Caucasian** adj. ▶ **białej rasy**

caught past tense, past participle of **catch**[1]

cauldron (especially US **caldron**) /ˈkɔːldrən/ noun [C] a large, deep, metal pot that is used for cooking things over a fire ▶ **kocioł** (*do gotowania*)

cauliflower /ˈkɒliflaʊə(r)/ noun [C,U] a large vegetable with green leaves and a round white centre that you eat when it is cooked ▶ **kalafior** ⮊ picture on **page A13**

cause[1] /kɔːz/ noun **1** [C] a thing or person that makes sth happen: *The police do not know the cause of the accident.* ▶ **przyczyna 2** [U] **cause (for sth)** reason for feeling sth or behaving in a particular way: *The doctor assured us that there was no* ***cause for concern.*** ◇ *I don't think you have any real* ***cause for complaint.*** ▶ **powód 3** [C] an idea or organization that a group of people believe in and support: *We are all committed to the cause of racial equality.* ◇ *I don't mind giving money to a good cause.* ▶ **sprawa**
IDM **be for/in a good cause** to be worth doing because it will help other people ▶ **być (zorganizowanym itp.) w szlachetnym celu**
a lost cause → LOST[2]

cause[2] /kɔːz/ verb [T] to make sth happen: *The fire was caused by an electrical fault.* ◇ *Is your leg causing you any pain?* ◇ *High winds caused many trees to fall* (silne wiatry powaliły wiele drzew) *during the night.* ▶ **powodować, sprawiać**

causeway /ˈkɔːzweɪ/ noun [C] a raised road or path across water or wet ground ▶ **droga na grobli**

caustic /ˈkɔːstɪk/ adj. **1** (used about a substance) able to burn or destroy things by chemical action ▶ (*chem.*) **żrący 2** critical in a cruel way: *a caustic remark* ▶ **zjadliwy, kostyczny**

caution[1] /ˈkɔːʃn/ noun **1** [U] great care, because of possible danger: *Any advertisement that asks you to send money should be treated* ***with caution.*** ▶ **uwaga, ostrożność 2** [C] a spoken warning that a judge or police officer gives to sb who has committed a small crime ▶ **ostrzeżenie**

caution[2] /ˈkɔːʃn/ verb **1** [I,T] **caution (sb) against sth** to warn sb not to do sth: *The President's advisers have cautioned against calling an election too early.* ▶ **przestrzegać, ostrzegać 2** [T] to give sb an official warning: *Dixon was cautioned by the referee for wasting time.* ▶ **udzielać pouczenia/napomnienia**

cautionary /ˈkɔːʃənəri; US -neri/ adj. [only before a noun] giving a warning: *The teacher told us a* ***cautionary tale*** *about a girl who cheated in her exams.* ▶ **ostrzegawczy**

cautious /ˈkɔːʃəs/ adj. taking great care to avoid possible danger or problems: *I'm very cautious about expressing my opinions in public.* ▶ **ostrożny**
■ **cautiously** adv. ▶ **ostrożnie**

cavalcade /ˌkævlˈkeɪd/ noun [C] a line of people on horses or in vehicles forming part of a ceremony ▶ **kawalkada**

cavalier /ˌkævəˈlɪə(r)/ adj. [usually before a noun] not caring enough about sth important or about the feelings of other people: *The government takes a **cavalier attitude** to the problems of prison overcrowding.* ▶ **lekceważący, niefrasobliwy**

cavalry /ˈkævlri/ noun [sing., with sing. or pl. verb] **1** the part of the modern army that uses heavily protected vehicles ▶ **kawaleria 2** the group of soldiers who fought on horses in the past ▶ **konnica**

cave¹ /keɪv/ noun [C] a large hole in the side of a **cliff** or hill, or under the ground: *a caveman/cavewoman* jaskiniowiec ▶ **jaskinia**

cave² /keɪv/ verb

PHR V **cave in 1** to fall in: *The roof of the tunnel had caved in and we could go no further.* ▶ **zapadać się 2** to suddenly stop arguing or being against sth: *He finally caved in and agreed to the plan.* ▶ **poddawać się** (*np. w sporze*)

cavern /ˈkævən/ noun [C] a large, deep hole in the side of a hill or under the ground; a big **cave** ▶ **pieczara, jaskinia**

caviar (also **caviare**) /ˈkæviɑː(r)/ noun [U] the eggs of a **sturgeon** that you can eat. Caviar is usually very expensive. ▶ **kawior**

caving /ˈkævɪŋ/ noun [U] the sport or activity of going into caves under the ground ▶ **grotołaztwo** ℹ Zwróć uwagę na zwrot **go caving**.

cavity /ˈkævəti/ noun [C] (pl. **cavities**) **1** an empty space inside sth solid: *a wall cavity* ▶ **wydrążenie, dziura 2** a hole in a tooth: *a cavity in a tooth* ▶ **ubytek**

CBI /ˌsiː biː ˈaɪ/ abbr. **the Confederation of British Industry**; an employers' association ▶ **Konfederacja Brytyjskiego Przemysłu**

cc /ˌsiː ˈsiː/ abbr. **1 carbon copy** (used on business letters and emails to show that a copy is being sent to another person): *to Luke Peters, cc Jane Gold* ▶ **kopia 2 cubic centimetre(s)**: *a 1200cc engine* ▶ **centymetr sześcienny**

CCTV = CLOSED-CIRCUIT TELEVISION

🔑 **CD** /ˌsiː ˈdiː/ (also **compact disc**) noun [C] a small, round, flat piece of hard plastic on which sound or information is recorded. You listen to a CD using a machine called a CD player. ▶ **płyta kompaktowa**

ˌCˈD player noun [C] a machine that you use for playing CDs ▶ **odtwarzacz płyt kompaktowych**

CD-ROM /ˌsiː diː ˈrɒm/ noun [C] a **CD** on which large amounts of information, sound and pictures can be stored, for use on a computer: *a CD-ROM drive* napęd/stacja CD-ROM ▶ **CD-ROM**

🔑 **cease** /siːs/ verb [I,T] (formal) to stop or end: *That organization has ceased to exist.* ◇ *Fighting in the area has now ceased* (ustały). ▶ **(za)przestawać, kończyć się**

ceasefire /ˈsiːsfaɪə(r)/ noun [C] an agreement between two groups to stop fighting each other ▶ **zawieszenie broni** ➲ look at **truce**

ceaseless /ˈsiːsləs/ adj. continuing for a long time without stopping ▶ **nieustanny, nieprzerwany**
■ **ceaselessly** adv. ▶ **nieustannie, nieprzerwanie**

cedar /ˈsiːdə(r)/ noun **1** [C] a tall tree that has hard red wood and wide spreading branches and that stays green all year ▶ **cedr 2** [U] the wood from the **cedar** tree ▶ **drewno cedrowe**

cede /siːd/ verb [T] (formal) to give land or control of sth to another country or person ▶ **cedować**

🔑 **ceiling** /ˈsiːlɪŋ/ noun [C] **1** the top surface of the inside of a room: *a room with a high/low ceiling* ▶ **sufit 2** a top limit: *The Government has put a 10% ceiling on wage increases.* ▶ **pułap**

celeb (informal) = CELEBRITY

🔑 **celebrate** /ˈselɪbreɪt/ verb [I,T] **1** to do sth special and enjoyable on an important day or because of an important event: *When I got the job we celebrated by going out for a meal.* ◇ *Nora celebrated her 90th birthday yesterday.* ▶ **świętować, obchodzić (uroczyście) 2** (used about a priest) to lead a religious ceremony ▶ **odprawiać** (*mszę*)
■ **celebratory** /ˌseləˈbreɪtəri; US ˈseləbrətɔːri/ adj.: *We went out for a celebratory meal after the match.* Aby uczcić zwycięstwo, po meczu poszliśmy na uroczysty obiad. ▶ **dla uczczenia, z okazji**

celebrated /ˈselɪbreɪtɪd/ adj. (formal) famous: *a celebrated poet* ▶ **sławny**

🔑 **celebration** /ˌselɪˈbreɪʃn/ noun [C,U] the act or occasion of doing sth enjoyable because sth good has happened or because it is a special day: *Christmas celebrations* ◇ *I think this is an occasion for celebration!* ▶ **świętowanie; obchody**

celebrity /səˈlebrəti/ (also informal **celeb** /səˈleb/) noun [C] (pl. **celebrities**) a famous person: *a TV celebrity* ▶ **znana osoba, sława** SYN **personality**

celery /ˈseləri/ noun [U] a vegetable with long green and white sticks that can be eaten without being cooked: *a stick of celery* ▶ **seler** ➲ picture on **page A13**

celibate /ˈselɪbət/ adj. (formal) never having sexual relations, often because of religious beliefs ▶ **żyjący w celibacie**
■ **celibacy** /ˈselɪbəsi/ noun [U] ▶ **celibat**

🔑 **cell** /sel/ noun [C] **1** a small room in a prison or police station in which a prisoner is locked ▶ **cela 2** the smallest living part of an animal or a plant: *red blood cells* ▶ **komórka**

cellar /ˈselə(r)/ noun [C] an underground room that is used for storing things ▶ **piwnica** ➲ look at **basement**

cellist /ˈtʃelɪst/ noun [C] a person who plays the **cello** ▶ **wiolonczelist(k)a**

cellmate /ˈselmeɪt/ noun [C] a prisoner with whom another prisoner shares a cell ▶ **współwię-zień/źniarka**

cello /ˈtʃeləʊ/ noun [C] (pl. **cellos**) a large musical instrument with strings. You sit down to play it and hold it between your knees. ▶ **wiolonczela** ➲ note at **music, piano**

Cellophane™ /ˈseləfeɪn/ noun [U] a transparent plastic material used for wrapping things ▶ **celofan**

🔑 **cellphone** (also **ˌcellular ˈphone**) = MOBILE PHONE

cellular /ˈseljələ(r)/ adj. consisting of cells (1): *cellular tissue* ▶ (*biol.*) **komórkowy**

ˌcellular ˈphone = MOBILE PHONE

cellulite /ˈseljulaɪt/ noun [U] a type of fat that some people get below their skin, which stops the surface of the skin looking smooth ▶ **cellulit**

cellulose /ˈseljuləʊs/ noun [U] **1** a natural substance that forms the cell walls of all plants and trees and is used in making plastics, paper, etc. ▶ **celuloza 2** any **compound** of **cellulose** used in making paint, **lacquer**, etc. ▶ **celuloza**

Celsius /ˈselsiəs/ (also **centigrade** /ˈsentɪgreɪd/) adj. (abbr. **C**) of or using a scale of temperature in which water freezes at 0° and boils at 100°: *The temperature tonight will fall to 7° C.* ▶ **Celsjusza** ➲ look at **Fahrenheit**
■ **Celsius** noun [U] ▶ **skala Celsjusza**

Celt /kelt/ noun [C] **1** a member of a race of people from western Europe who settled in ancient Britain before the Romans came ▶ **Celt 2** a person whose **ancestors**

were **Celts**, especially one from Ireland, Wales, Scotland, Cornwall or Brittany ▶ **Celt**

Celtic /ˈkeltɪk/ adj. connected with the Celts or with their culture ▶ **celtycki**

cement[1] /sɪˈment/ noun [U] **1** a grey powder that becomes hard after it is mixed with water and left to dry. It is used in building for sticking bricks or stones together or for making very hard surfaces. ▶ **cement** **2** a type of glue ▶ **rodzaj kleju**

cement[2] /sɪˈment/ verb [T] **1** to join two things together using **cement**, or a strong sticky substance ▶ **spajać, sklejać** **2** to cover sth with cement ▶ **cementować** **3** to make a relationship, agreement, etc. very strong: *This agreement has cemented the relationship between our two countries.* ▶ **utrwalać, cementować**

cemetery /ˈsemətri; US -teri/ noun [C] (pl. **cemeteries**) a place where dead people are buried, especially a place that does not belong to a church ▶ **cmentarz** ➲ look at **graveyard**, **churchyard**

censor[1] /ˈsensə(r)/ noun [C] an official who **censors** books, films, etc.: *All films have to be examined by the board of film censors.* ▶ **cenzor**

censor[2] /ˈsensə(r)/ verb [T] to remove the parts of a book, film, etc. that might offend people or that are considered to be immoral or a political threat ▶ **cenzurować**

■ **censorship** /-ʃɪp/ noun [U] ▶ **cenzura**

censure /ˈsenʃə(r)/ verb [T] (formal) to tell sb, in a strong and formal way, that they have done sth wrong: *The attorney was censured for not revealing the information earlier.* ▶ (*ostro*) **krytykować, karcić**

■ **censure** noun [U]: *a vote of censure* (wotum nieufności) *in parliament* ▶ **dezaprobata**

census /ˈsensəs/ noun [C] an official count of the people who live in a country, including information about their ages, jobs, etc. ▶ **spis ludności**

⚷ **cent** /sent/ noun [C] (abbr. **c**, **ct**) a unit of money that is worth 1% of the main unit of money in many countries, for example of the US dollar or of the euro ▶ **cent** ➲ look at **per cent**

centenary /senˈtiːnəri; US -ˈten-/ noun [C] (pl. **centenaries**) (US **centennial** /senˈteniəl/) the year that comes exactly one hundred years after an important event or the beginning of sth: *2001 was the centenary of Disney's birth.* ▶ **setna rocznica**

center (US) = CENTRE

centigrade = CELSIUS

centilitre (US **centiliter**) /ˈsentiliːtə(r)/ noun [C] (abbr. **cl**) a measure of liquid. There are 100 **centilitres** in a litre. ▶ **centylitr**

⚷ **centimetre** (US **centimeter**) /ˈsentɪmiːtə(r)/ noun [C] (abbr. **cm**) a measure of length. There are 100 centimetres in a metre. ▶ **centymetr**

centipede /ˈsentɪpiːd/ noun [C] a small creature like an insect, with a long thin body and many legs ▶ **pareczník** (*Chilopoda*)

⚷ **central** /ˈsentrəl/ adj. **1** most important; main: *The film's central character is a fifteen-year-old girl.* ▶ **główny** **2** [only before a noun] having control over all other parts: *central government* ◇ *the central nervous system* ▶ **centralny** **3** in the centre of sth: *The flat is in Edgware Road, which is very central* (w śródmieściu). ◇ *a map of central Europe* ▶ **środkowy, znajdujący się blisko/w centrum**

ˌ**central ˈheating** noun [U] a system for heating a building from one main point. Air or water is heated and carried by pipes to all parts of the building. ▶ **centralne ogrzewanie**

centralize (also -ise) /ˈsentrəlaɪz/ verb [T, usually passive] to give control of all the parts of a country or organization to a group of people in one place: *Our educational system is becoming increasingly centralized.* ▶ **centralizować**

■ **centralization** (also -isation) /ˌsentrəlaɪˈzeɪʃn; US -ləˈz-/ noun [U] ▶ **centralizacja**

centrally /ˈsentrəli/ adv. in or from the centre: *a centrally located hotel* hotel położony w śródmieściu ▶ **centralnie**

⚷ **centre**[1] (US **center**) /ˈsentə(r)/ noun **1** [C, usually sing.] the middle point or part of sth: *I work in the centre* (w centrum) *of London.* ◇ *Which way is the town centre* (centrum), *please?* ◇ *She hit the target dead centre.* ▶ **środek** ➲ note at **middle** **2** [C] a place where sb/sth is collected together; the point towards which sth is directed: *major urban/industrial centres* ◇ *She always likes to be* ***the centre of attention*** (w centrum uwagi). ◇ *You should bend your legs to keep a low* ***centre of gravity*** (środek ciężkości). ▶ **centrum** **3** [C] a building or place where a particular activity or service is based: *a sports/health/shopping centre* ◇ *This university is a centre of excellence for medical research.* ▶ **centrum, ośrodek** **4** (usually **the centre**) [sing., with sing. or pl. verb] a political position that is not extreme: *a party of the centre* ◇ *Her views are left of centre.* ▶ **centrum**

centre[2] (US **center**) /ˈsentə(r)/ verb

PHR V **centre on/around sb/sth** to have sb/sth as its centre: *The life of the village centres on the church, the school and the pub.* ▶ **skupiać się na kimś/czymś**

centrefold (US **centerfold**) /ˈsentəfəʊld/ noun [C] **1** a large picture, often of a young woman with few or no clothes on, folded to form the middle pages of a magazine ▶ **rozkładówka** **2** a person whose picture is the **centrefold** of a magazine ▶ **dziewczyna/osoba z rozkładówki**

centrepiece (Brit.) (US **centerpiece**) /ˈsentəpiːs/ noun **1** [sing.] the most important item: *This treaty is the centrepiece of the government's foreign policy.* ▶ **najważniejsza część, główny punkt programu** **2** [C] a decoration for the centre of a table ▶ **dekoracja na środek stołu**

ˌ**centre ˈstage** (US ˌ**center ˈstage**) noun [U] an important position where sb/sth can easily get people's attention: *Education is* ***taking centre stage*** (zaczyna być w centrum uwagi) *in the government's plans.* ◇ *This region continues to* ***occupy centre stage*** *in world affairs.* ▶ **centrum uwagi**

-centric /ˈsentrik/ [in compounds] concerned with or interested in the thing mentioned: *Eurocentric policies* ▶ **-centryczny**

centrifuge /ˈsentrɪfjuːdʒ/ noun [C] a machine with a part that spins around to separate substances, for example liquids from solids, by forcing the heavier substance to the outer edge ▶ **wirówka**

⚷ **century** /ˈsentʃəri/ noun [C] (pl. **centuries**) **1** a particular period of 100 years that is used for giving dates: *We live in the 21st century.* ▶ **wiek** **2** any period of 100 years: *People have been making wine in this area for centuries.* ▶ **stulecie**

IDM **the turn of the century/year** → TURN[2]

CEO = CHIEF EXECUTIVE OFFICER

ceramic /səˈræmɪk/ adj. made of **clay** that has been baked: *ceramic tiles* ▶ **ceramiczny**

■ **ceramic** noun [C, usually pl.] a pot or other object made of clay: *an exhibition of ceramics by Picasso* ▶ **ceramika** | **ceramics** noun [U] the art of making and decorating clay pots, etc. ▶ **ceramika**

cereal /ˈsɪəriəl/ noun [C,U] **1** any type of grain that can be eaten or made into flour, or the grass that the grain comes from: *Wheat, barley and rye are cereals.* ▶ **zboże** **2** a food that is made from grain, often eaten for breakfast with milk: *a bowl of cereal* ▶ **płatki zbożowe** ➲ picture on **page A14**

cerebral /ˈserəbrəl; US səˈriːb-/ adj. of the brain: *He died of a cerebral haemorrhage* (na wylew krwi do mózgu). ▶ **mózgowy**

ˌcerebral ˈpalsy noun [U] a medical condition, usually caused by brain damage before or at birth, that causes the loss of control of the arms and legs ▶ **porażenie mózgowe**

ceremonial /ˌserɪˈməʊniəl/ adj. connected with a ceremony: *a ceremonial occasion* ▶ **uroczysty**, **ceremonialny**
■ **ceremonially** /-niəli/ adv. ▶ **uroczyście**, **ceremonialnie**

ceremonious /ˌserəˈməʊniəs/ adj. (formal) behaving or performed in an extremely formal way: *She unveiled the picture with a ceremonious gesture.* ▶ **(przesadnie) ceremonialny**

ceremony /ˈserəməni/ noun (pl. **ceremonies**) **1** [C] a formal public or religious event: *the opening ceremony of the Olympic Games* ◇ *a wedding ceremony* ▶ **uroczystość**, **ceremonia** **2** [U] formal behaviour, speech, actions, etc. that are expected on special occasions: *The new hospital was opened* ***with great ceremony*** (z wszelkimi honorami). ▶ **ceremonia**

cert /sɜːt/ noun [C] (Brit., informal) a thing that is sure to happen or be successful: *That horse is a* ***dead cert*** *for the next race.* ▶ **pewniak**, **murowany zwycięzca** SYN **certainty**

certain /ˈsɜːtn/ adj. **1 certain (that …)**; **certain (to do sth)** sure to happen or to do sth; definite: *It is almost certain that unemployment will increase this year.* ◇ *We must rescue them today, or they will face certain death.* ◇ *The Director is certain to agree* (na pewno się zgodzi). ▶ **pewny** ➲ note at **sure** **2** [not before a noun] **certain (that …)**; **certain (of sth)** completely sure; without any doubts: *I'm absolutely certain that there was somebody outside my window.* ◇ *I'm certain of one thing – he didn't take the money.* ▶ **pewny**, **przekonany** **3** [only before a noun] (used for talking about a particular thing or person without naming it or them): *You can only contact me at certain times of the day.* ◇ *There are certain reasons why I'd prefer not to meet him again.* ▶ **pewien** **4** [only before a noun] (formal) (used before sb's name to show that you do not know them): *I received a letter from a certain Mrs Berry.* ▶ **pewien**, **jakiś** **5** [only before a noun] some, but not very much: *I suppose I have* ***a certain amount of*** *respect for Mr Law.* ▶ **pewien** **6** [only before a noun] noticeable but difficult to describe: *There was a certain feeling of autumn in the air.* ▶ **pewien**, **jakiś**
■ **certain** pron. (formal) (used for talking about some members of a group of people without giving their names): *Certain of those present were unwilling to discuss the matter further.* ▶ **pewien**, **niektóry**
IDM **for certain** without doubt: *I don't know for certain* (nie jestem pewny) *what time we'll arrive.* ▶ **na pewno**
make certain (that …) **1** to do sth in order to be sure that sth else happens: *They're doing everything they can to make certain that they win.* ▶ **zapewniać (sobie)** **2** to do sth in order to be sure that sth is true: *We'd better phone Akram before we go to make certain he's expecting us.* ▶ **upewniać się**

certainly /ˈsɜːtnli/ adv. **1** without doubt; definitely: *The number of students will certainly increase after 2008.* ◇ *I certainly don't think you should tell him now.* Jestem pewna, że nie należy mu o tym mówić teraz. ▶ **na pewno**, **zdecydowanie** **2** (used in answer to questions) of course: *'Do you think I could borrow your notes?' 'Certainly.'* ▶ **oczywiście**

certainty /ˈsɜːtnti/ noun (pl. **certainties**) **1** [U] the state of being completely sure about sth: *We can't say with certainty that there is life on other planets.* ▶ **pewność** OPP **uncertainty** **2** [C] something that is sure to happen: *It's now almost a certainty our team will win the league.* ▶ **rzecz pewna**

certificate /səˈtɪfɪkət/ noun [C] **1** an official piece of paper that says that sth is true or correct: *a birth/marriage/medical certificate* ▶ **świadectwo** **2** an official document that students gain by successfully completing a course of study or by passing an exam; a qualification obtained after a course of study or an exam: *a Postgraduate Certificate in Education* ▶ **świadectwo**; **dyplom** ➲ note at **degree**

certified /ˈsɜːtɪfaɪd/ adj. having a certificate to show that you have successfully completed a course of training for a particular profession ▶ **wykwalifikowany**

ˌcertified public acˈcountant (US) = CHARTERED ACCOUNTANT

certify /ˈsɜːtɪfaɪ/ verb [T] (**certifying**; **certifies**; pt, pp **certified**) **1** to say formally that sth is true or correct: *We need someone to certify that this is her signature.* ▶ **poświadczać**, **(s)twierdzić** **2** to give sb a certificate to show that they have successfully completed a course of training for a particular profession: *a certified accountant* biegły księgowy ▶ **wystawiać dyplom uprawniający do wykonywania zawodu**, **wykwalifikować**

certitude /ˈsɜːtɪtjuːd; US -tuːd/ noun [U,C] (formal) a feeling of being certain; a thing about which you are certain: *'You will like Rome,' he said, with absolute certitude.* ◇ *the collapse of moral certitudes* ▶ **pewność**; **rzecz pewna/niebudząca wątpliwości**

ˌcervical ˈsmear (Brit.) = SMEAR TEST

cervix /ˈsɜːvɪks/ noun [C] (pl. **cervices** /-vɪsiːz/) the narrow passage at the opening of the **uterus** ▶ **szyjka macicy**
■ **cervical** /ˈsɜːvɪkl; səˈvaɪkl; US / adj. ▶ **szyjny**, **szyjkowy**

cesarean (US) = CAESAREAN

cessation /seˈseɪʃn/ noun [U,C] (formal) the stopping of sth; a pause in sth: *Mexico called for an immediate cessation of hostilities.* ▶ **przerwanie**; **przerwa**

cesspit /ˈsespɪt/ (also **cesspool** /ˈsespuːl/) noun [C] a covered hole or container in the ground for collecting waste from a building, especially from the toilets ▶ **szambo**

cf. abbr. (used in writing) compare ▶ **por.**

CFC /ˌsiː ef ˈsiː/ noun [C,U] **chlorofluorocarbon**; a type of gas, found for example in cans of spray, which is harmful to the earth's atmosphere ▶ (*chem.*) **freon** ➲ look at **ozone layer**

ch = CHAPTER

chador /ˈtʃɑːdɔː(r)/ noun [C] a large piece of cloth that covers a woman's head and upper body so that only the face can be seen, worn by some Muslim women ▶ **czador**

chafe /tʃeɪf/ verb [I,T] if skin **chafes**, or if sth **chafes** it, it becomes sore because the thing is rubbing against it: *Her wrists chafed where the rope had been.* ◇ *The collar was far too tight and chafed her neck.* ▶ (*kołnierz itp.*) **obcierać**

chain[1] /tʃeɪn/ noun **1** [C,U] a line of metal rings that are joined together: *a bicycle chain* ◇ *She was wearing a silver chain round her neck.* ◇ *a length of chain* ▶ **łańcuch**, **łańcuszek** ➲ picture at **bicycle** **2** [C] a series of connected things or people: *a chain of mountains/a mountain chain* ◇ *The book examines the complex* ***chain of events*** (splot wydarzeń) *that led to the Russian Revolution.* ◇ *The Managing Director is at the top of the* ***chain of command*** (na szczycie hierarchii służbowej). ▶ **łańcuch**, **szereg** **3** [C] a group of shops, hotels, etc. that are owned by the same company: *a chain of supermarkets* ◇ *a fast-food chain* ▶ **sieć**

chain² /tʃeɪn/ verb [T] **chain sb/sth (to sth); chain sb/sth (up)** to fasten sb/sth to sth else with a chain: *The dog is kept chained up outside.* ▶ **przykuwać łańcuchem**

ˌchain reˈaction noun [C] **1** a chemical or nuclear change that forms products which themselves cause more changes and new products ▶ **reakcja łańcuchowa 2** a series of events, each of which causes the next: *It set off a chain reaction in the international money markets.* ▶ (*przen.*) **reakcja łańcuchowa**

chainsaw /ˈtʃeɪnsɔː/ noun [C] a tool made of a chain with sharp teeth set in it, that is driven by a motor and used for cutting wood ▶ **piła łańcuchowa**

ˈchain-smoke verb [I,T] to smoke continuously, lighting one cigarette after another ▶ **palić nałogowo** (*jednego papierosa za drugim*)
■ **chain-smoker** noun [C] ▶ **nałogow-y/a palacz/ka** (*paląc-y/a jednego papierosa za drugim*)

ˈchain store noun [C] one of a number of similar shops that are owned by the same company ▶ **sklep danej sieci**

chair¹ /tʃeə(r)/ noun **1** [C] a piece of furniture for one person to sit on, with a seat, a back and four legs. It sometimes has two arms: *a kitchen chair* ◇ *an armchair* fotel ◇ *a wheelchair* wózek inwalidzki ▶ **krzesło 2** [sing.] the person who is controlling a meeting: *Please address your questions to the chair.* ▶ **przewodniczący/a 3** [C] the position of being in charge of a department in a university; the position of a university professor: *She holds the chair of economics* (kieruje katedrą ekonomii) *at London University.* ▶ **katedra**; **profesura**

chair² /tʃeə(r)/ verb [T] to be the **chairperson** of a meeting: *Who's chairing today's meeting?* ▶ **przewodniczyć**

chairlift /ˈtʃeəlɪft/ noun [C] a series of chairs hanging from a moving cable, for carrying people up and down a mountain ▶ **wyciąg krzesełkowy**

chairman /ˈtʃeəmən/, **chairwoman** /ˈtʃeəwʊmən/, **chairperson** /ˈtʃeəpɜːsn/ noun [C] (pl. **-men** /-mən/; **-women** /-wɪmɪn/) **1** a person who controls a meeting ▶ **przewodniczący/a 2** the head of a company or other organization ▶ **prezes**
■ **chairmanship** /-ʃɪp; US / noun [sing.] ▶ **przewodnictwo**; **prezesura**

chalet /ˈʃæleɪ; US ʃæˈl-/ noun [C] a wooden house, especially one built in a mountain area or used by people on holiday ▶ **dom/ek letniskowy** (*zwł. w stylu góralskim*)

chalice /ˈtʃælɪs/ noun [C] a large cup for holding wine, especially one from which wine is drunk in the Christian **Communion** service ▶ **kielich** (*zwł. mszalny*)

chalk¹ /tʃɔːk/ noun **1** [U] a type of soft white rock: *chalk cliffs* ▶ **kreda 2** [C,U] a small stick of soft white or coloured rock that is used for writing or drawing ▶ **kreda**

chalk² /tʃɔːk/ verb [I,T] to write or draw sth with **chalk**: *Somebody had chalked a message on the wall.* ▶ **pisać kredą**
PHR V **chalk sth up** to succeed in getting sth: *The team has chalked up five wins this summer.* ▶ **dorobić się**

chalkboard (US) = BLACKBOARD

challenge¹ /ˈtʃælɪndʒ/ noun [C] **1** something new and difficult that forces you to make a lot of effort: *I'm finding my new job an exciting challenge.* ◇ *The company will have to **face** many **challenges** in the coming months.* ◇ *How will this government **meet the challenge*** (poradzi sobie z wyzwaniem) *of rising unemployment?* ▶ **wyzwanie**, **zadanie** (*wymagające wysiłku*) **2 a challenge (to sb) (to do sth)** an invitation from sb to fight, play, argue, etc. against them: *The Prime Minister should accept our challenge and call a new election now.* ▶ **wyzwanie**

challenge² /ˈtʃælɪndʒ/ verb [T] **1** to question if sth is true, right, etc., or not: *She hates anyone challenging her authority.* ▶ **kwestionować**, **podważać 2 challenge sb (to sth/to do sth)** to invite sb to fight, play, argue, etc. against you: *They've challenged us to a football match this Saturday.* ▶ **rzucać wyzwanie**

challenged /ˈtʃælɪndʒd/ adj. (especially US) [used with an adverb] (a polite way of referring to sb who has a **disability** of some sort): *a competition for physically challenged athletes* ◇ (humorous) *I'm financially challenged* (mam problemy finansowe) *at the moment.* ▶ **niepełnosprawny**

challenger /ˈtʃælɪndʒə(r)/ noun [C] a person who invites you to take part in a competition, because they want to win a title or position that you hold ▶ **rywal/ka**, **pretendent/ka** (*do stanowiska*)

challenging /ˈtʃælɪndʒɪŋ/ adj. forcing you to make a lot of effort: *a challenging job* ▶ **stanowiący wyzwanie**, **wymagający**

chamber /ˈtʃeɪmbə(r)/ noun [C] **1** an organization that makes important decisions, or the room or building where it meets: *a council chamber* ▶ **izba 2** a room that is used for a particular purpose: *a burial chamber* ▶ **sala**, **komnata 3** a closed space in the body, a machine, etc.: *the four chambers of the heart* ▶ **komora**

chambermaid /ˈtʃeɪmbəmeɪd/ noun [C] a woman whose job is to clean and tidy hotel bedrooms ▶ **pokojówka**

ˈchamber music noun [U] a type of **classical music** that is written for a small group of instruments ▶ **muzyka kameralna**

ˌChamber of ˈCommerce noun [C] a group of local business people who work together to help business and trade in a particular town ▶ **Izba Handlowa**

ˈchamber orchestra noun [C] a small group of musicians who play **classical** music together ▶ **orkiestra kameralna**

chameleon /kəˈmiːliən/ noun [C] a small **lizard** that can change colour according to its surroundings ▶ **kameleon**

chamomile (also **camomile**) /ˈkæməmaɪl/ noun [U] a plant with a sweet smell and small white and yellow flowers. Its dried leaves and flowers are used to make tea, medicine, etc.: *chamomile tea* ▶ **rumianek**

champ¹ /tʃæmp/ verb [I,T] (used especially about horses) to bite or eat sth noisily ▶ (*koń*) **gryźć głośno**; **mlaskać**
IDM **champing at the bit** (informal) impatient to do or start doing sth: *Gerry's champing at the bit to go to college.* ▶ **niecierpliwić się**

champ² /tʃæmp/ noun [C] an informal way of referring to a **champion**, often used in newspapers ▶ **mistrz/yni**

champagne /ʃæmˈpeɪn/ noun [U,C] a French white wine which has a lot of bubbles in it and is often very expensive ▶ **szampan**

champion¹ /ˈtʃæmpiən/ noun [C] **1** a person, team, etc. that has won a competition: *a world champion* ◇ *a champion swimmer* ▶ **mistrz/yni 2** a person who speaks and fights for a particular group, idea, etc.: *a champion of free speech* ▶ **orędowni-k/czka** ▶ **bojowni-k/czka (o coś)**

champion² /ˈtʃæmpiən/ verb [T] to support or fight for a particular group or idea: *to champion the cause of human rights* ▶ **być orędownikiem**

championship /ˈtʃæmpiənʃɪp/ noun [C] **1** [often plural] a competition or series of competitions to find the best player or team in a sport or game: *the World Hockey Championships* ▶ **mistrzostwo 2** the position or title of a champion ▶ **mistrzostwo**

chance¹ /tʃɑːns; US tʃæns/ noun **1** [C,U] **a chance of (doing) sth**; **a chance (that ...)** a possibility: *to have a slim/an outside chance of success* ◇ *I think we **stand a** good **chance***

(mamy duże szanse) *of winning the competition.* ◇ *I'm afraid he has very little chance of winning.* ◇ *Is there any chance of getting tickets for tonight's concert?* ◇ *I think there's a good chance* (duże prawdopodobieństwo) *that she'll be the next Prime Minister.* ▶ **szansa 2** [C] **a chance (of doing sth/to do sth)** an opportunity: *If somebody invited me to America, I'd jump at the chance.* ◇ *Be quiet and **give** her **a chance** to explain.* ◇ *I think you should tell him now. You may not **get** another **chance**.* ◇ *The teacher was going to punish Sean, but then decided to give him one more chance* (jeszcze jedną szansę). ▶ **okazja, możliwość** ➲ note at **occasion 3** [C] a risk: *We may lose some money but we'll just have to take that chance.* ◇ *Fasten your seat belt – you shouldn't take (any) chances.* ◇ *I didn't want to **take a chance on** anyone seeing me* (ryzykować, żeby mnie ktoś zobaczył), *so I closed the curtains.* ▶ **ryzyko 4** [U] luck; the way that some things happen without any cause that you can see or understand: *We have to plan every detail – I don't want to **leave** anything **to chance*** (zdawać się na los szczęścia). ◇ *We met **by chance** as I was walking down the street.* ▶ **traf, przypadek**

IDM **by any chance** (used for asking sth politely) perhaps or possibly ▶ **przypadkiem**

the chances are (that)... (informal) it is probable that...: *The chances are that it will rain tomorrow.* ▶ **wygląda na to, że**

no chance (informal) there is no possibility of that happening: *'Perhaps your mother will give you the money.' 'No chance!'* ▶ **wykluczone**

on the off chance in the hope that sth might happen, although it is not very likely: *I didn't think you'd be at home, but I just called in on the off chance.* ▶ **na wszelki wypadek** (*nie spodziewając się, że się uda*)

chance² /tʃɑːns; US tʃæns/ verb **1** [T] (informal) **chance sth/doing sth** to risk sth: *It might be safe to leave the car here, but I'm not going to **chance it**.* ▶ **ryzykować 2** [I] (formal) **chance to do sth** to do sth without planning or trying to do it: *I chanced to see the letter on his desk.* ▶ **zrobić coś przypadkowo**

chance³ /tʃɑːns; US tʃæns/ adj. [only before a noun] not planned: *a chance meeting* ▶ **przypadkowy**

chancellor /ˈtʃɑːnsələ(r); US ˈtʃæns-/ noun [C] **1** the head of the government in some countries: *the German chancellor* ▶ **kanclerz 2** (also ˌ**Chancellor of the Exˈchequer**) (Brit.) the government minister who makes decisions about taxes and government spending ▶ **minister finansów/skarbu**

chandelier /ˌʃændəˈlɪə(r)/ noun [C] a large round frame with many branches for lights or **candles**, that hangs from the ceiling and is decorated with small pieces of glass ▶ **żyrandol**

⚷ **change¹** /tʃeɪndʒ/ verb **1** [I,T] to become different or to make sb/sth different: *This town has changed a lot since I was young.* ◇ *Our plans have changed – we leave in the morning.* ◇ *His lottery win has not changed him at all.* ▶ **zmieniać (się)** SYN **alter 2** [I,T] **change (sb/sth) to/into sth**; **change (from A) (to/into B)** to become a different thing; to make sb/sth take a different form: *They changed the spare bedroom into a study.* ◇ *The new job changed him into a more confident person.* ◇ *The traffic lights changed from green to red.* ▶ **przemieniać (się), zmieniać (się) 3** [T] **change sth (for sth)** to take, have or use sth instead of sth else: *Could I change* (wymienić) *this shirt for a larger size?* ◇ *to change jobs* ◇ *to change a wheel on a car* ◇ *to change direction* ◇ *Can I change my appointment from Wednesday to Thursday?* ▶ **zmieniać 4** [T] [used with a plural noun] **change sth (with sb)** to exchange sth with sb, so that you have what they had, and they have what you had: *The teams change ends at half-time.* ◇ *If you want to sit by the window, I'll change seats with you.* ▶ **zamieniać się, wymieniać się** SYN **swap 5** [I,T] **change (out of sth) (into sth)** to take off your clothes and put different ones on: *He's changed his shoes.* ◇ *I had a shower and changed before going out.* ◇ *She changed out of her work clothes and into a clean dress.* ▶ **przebierać się (w coś)** ⓘ **Get changed** jest często używanym zwrotem, który oznacza „przebierać się": *You can get changed in the bedroom.* **6** [T] to put clean things onto sb/sth: *The baby's nappy needs changing.* ◇ *to change the bed* zmieniać pościel ▶ **zmieniać 7** [T] **change sth (for/into sth)** to give sb money and receive the same amount back in money of a different type: *Can you change a ten-pound note for two fives?* ◇ *I'd like to change fifty pounds into US dollars.* ▶ **rozmieniać, wymieniać**

> Miejsce, gdzie można wymienić pieniądze to **bureau de change**. Rzadko używa się tego zwrotu w języku mówionym. O drogę do kantoru wymiany walut pyta się: *Where can I change money?*

8 [I,T] to get out of one bus, train, etc. and get into another: *Can we get to London direct or do we have to change (trains)?* ▶ **przesiadać się**

IDM **change hands** to pass from one owner to another ▶ **przechodzić z rąk do rąk**

change your mind to change your decision or opinion: *I'll have the green one. No, I've changed my mind – I want the red one.* ▶ **zmieniać zdanie**

change/swap places (with sb) → PLACE¹

change the subject to start talking about sth different ▶ **zmieniać temat**

change your tune (informal) to change your opinion or feelings about sth ▶ **zmieniać front**

change your ways to start to live or behave in a different and better way from before ▶ **zmienić się na lepsze**

chop and change → CHOP¹

PHR V **change over (from sth) (to sth)** to stop doing or using one thing and start doing or using sth else: *The theatre has changed over to a computerized booking system.* ▶ **przechodzić (z czegoś) (do czegoś), zamieniać się (z czegoś) (na coś)**

⚷ **change²** /tʃeɪndʒ/ noun **1** [C,U] **change (in/to sth)** the process of becoming or making sth different: *There was little change in the patient's condition overnight.* ◇ *After two hot summers, people were talking about a change in the climate.* ▶ **zmiana 2** [C] **a change (of sth)** something that you take, have or use instead of sth else: *We must notify the bank of our change of address.* ◇ *I packed my toothbrush and a change of clothes.* ▶ **zmiana 3** [U] the money that you get back if you pay more than the amount sth costs: *If a paper costs 60p and you pay with a pound coin, you will get 40p change.* ▶ **reszta 4** [U] coins of low value: *He needs some change for the phone.* ◇ *Have you got change for a twenty-pound note?* ▶ **drobne** ➲ note at **cash**

IDM **a change for the better/worse** a person, thing or situation that is better/worse than the one before ▶ **zmiana na lepsze/gorsze**

a change of heart a change in your opinion or the way that you feel ▶ **zmiana w sposobie myślenia/patrzenia**

for a change in order to do sth different from usual: *I usually cycle to work, but today I decided to walk for a change.* ▶ **dla odmiany**

make a change (used to say that an activity is enjoyable or pleasant because it is different from what you usually do) ▶ **stanowić miłą odmianę**

changeable /ˈtʃeɪndʒəbl/ adj. likely to change; often changing: *English weather is very changeable.* ▶ **zmienny**

changeover /ˈtʃeɪndʒəʊvə(r)/ noun [C] a change from one system to another ▶ **zmiana**

ˈchanging room noun [C] a room for changing clothes in, for example before or after playing sport ▶ **szatnia, przebieralnia** ➲ look at **fitting room**

channel¹ /ˈtʃænl/ noun [C] **1** a TV station: *Which channel is the film on?* ▶ **kanał, stacja** ➲ look at **station 2** a band of radio waves used for sending out radio or TV programmes: *digital/satellite channels* ▶ **kanał, stacja 3** a way or route along which news, information, etc. is sent: *a channel of communication* ◇ *You have to order new equipment through the official channels.* ▶ **kanał 4** an open passage along which liquids can flow: *drainage channels in the rice fields* ▶ **kanał 5** the part of a river, sea, etc. which is deep enough for boats to pass through: *a cross-channel ferry* ▶ **kanał 6** (**the Channel**) (also **the ˌEnglish ˈChannel**) the sea between England and France ▶ **kanał La Manche**

channel² /ˈtʃænl/ verb [T] (**channelling**; **channelled**; US also **channeling**; **channeled**) to make sth move along a particular path or route: *Water is channelled from the river to the fields.* ◇ (figurative) *You should channel your energies into something constructive.* ▶ **nakierowywać**

the ˌChannel ˈTunnel noun [sing.] the tunnel under the sea that connects England and France ▶ **tunel pod kanałem La Manche**

chant¹ /tʃɑːnt; US tʃænt/ noun **1** [C] a word or phrase that is sung or shouted many times: *A chant of 'we are the champions' went round the stadium.* ▶ **rytmicznie skandowane hasło** (*wykrzykiwane lub śpiewane*) **2** [C,U] a usually religious song with only a few notes that are repeated many times ▶ **pieśń**

chant² /tʃɑːnt; US tʃænt/ verb [I,T] to sing or shout a word or phrase many times: *The protesters marched by, chanting slogans.* ▶ **skandować, śpiewać rytmicznie**

Chanukkah, Chanukah = HANUKKAH

chaos /ˈkeɪɒs/ noun [U] a state of great confusion and lack of order: *The country was* ***in chaos*** *after the war.* ◇ *The heavy snow has* ***caused chaos*** *on the roads.* ▶ **chaos**

chaotic /keɪˈɒtɪk/ adj. in a state of **chaos** ▶ **chaotyczny**

chap /tʃæp/ noun [C] (especially Brit., informal) a man or boy ▶ **facet**

chapel /ˈtʃæpl/ noun **1** [C] a small building or room that is used for Christian worship in a school, prison, large private house, etc.: *a college chapel* ▶ **kaplica 2** [C] a separate part of a large church that can be used for private prayer ▶ **kaplica 3** [C,U] (Brit.) a church for some Protestant groups: *a Methodist chapel* ▶ **kościół, dom modlitwy**

chaperone /ˈʃæpərəʊn/ noun [C] in the past, an older person, usually a woman, who went to public places with a young woman who was not married, to look after her and to make sure that she behaved correctly ▶ **przyzwoitka**
■ **chaperone** verb [T] ▶ **towarzyszyć jako przyzwoitka**

chaplain /ˈtʃæplɪn/ noun [C] a Christian priest who is responsible for the religious needs of people in prison, hospital, the army, etc. ▶ **kapelan** ➲ look at **priest**

chapped /tʃæpt/ adj. (used about the skin or lips) rough, dry and sore, especially because of wind or cold weather ▶ **spierzchnięty**

chapter /ˈtʃæptə(r)/ noun [C] (abbr. **ch**) one of the parts into which a book is divided: *Please read Chapter 2 for homework.* ◇ (figurative) *The last few years have been a difficult chapter in the country's history.* ▶ **rozdział**

character /ˈkærəktə(r)/ noun **1** [C, U] the qualities that make sb/sth different from other people or things; the nature of sb/sth: *The introduction of computers has changed the character of the job.* ◇ *Although they are twins, their characters are quite different.* ◇ *These two songs are very different* ***in character.*** ▶ **charakter 2** [U] strong personal qualities: *The match developed into a test of character rather than just physical strength.* ▶ **charakter 3** [U] qualities that make sb/sth interesting: *Modern houses often seem to lack character.* ▶ **charakter 4** [U] the good opinion that people have of you: *The article was a vicious attack on the President's character.* ◇ *My ex-teacher gave me a* ***character reference*** (referencje) *when I applied for this job.* ▶ **dobre imię, reputacja 5** [C] (informal) an interesting, amusing, strange or unpleasant person: *Neil's quite a character – he's always making us laugh.* ◇ *I saw a suspicious-looking character outside the bank, so I called the police.* ▶ **osobnik; (ciekawa) postać, dziwa-k/czka 6** [C] a person in a book, story, etc.: *The main character* (bohater) *in the book is a boy who meets an alien.* ▶ **postać 7** [C] a letter or sign that you use when you are writing or printing: *Chinese characters* ▶ **litera; znak**
IDM **in/out of character** typical/not typical of sb/sth: *Emma's rude reply was completely out of character.* ▶ **typowy; nietypowy**

characteristic¹ /ˌkærəktəˈrɪstɪk/ adj. **characteristic of (sb/sth)** very typical of sb/sth: *The flat landscape is characteristic of this part of the country.* ▶ **charakterystyczny dla (kogoś/czegoś)** OPP **uncharacteristic**
■ **characteristically** /-kli/ adv. ▶ **charakterystycznie**

characteristic² /ˌkærəktəˈrɪstɪk/ noun [C] **a characteristic of (sb/sth)** a typical feature or quality sth/sb has: *The chief characteristic of fish is that they live in water.* ▶ **cecha**

characterize (also **-ise**) /ˈkærəktəraɪz/ verb [T] (formal) **1** [often passive] to be typical of sb/sth: *the tastes that characterize Indian cooking* ▶ **charakteryzować 2 characterize sb/sth (as sth)** to describe what sb/sth is like: *The President characterized the meeting as friendly and positive.* ▶ **charakteryzować, opisywać**

characterless /ˈkærəktələs/ adj. having no interesting qualities ▶ **bez charakteru**

charade /ʃəˈrɑːd; US -ˈreɪd/ noun **1** [C] a situation or event that is clearly false but in which people pretend to do or be sth: *They pretend to be friends but it's all a charade. Everyone knows they hate each other.* ▶ **gra** (*pozorów*) **2** (**charades**) [U] a party game in which people try to guess the title of a book, film, etc. that one person must represent using actions but not words ▶ **kalambury**

charcoal /ˈtʃɑːkəʊl/ noun [U] a black substance that is produced from burned wood. It can be used for drawing or as a fuel. ▶ **węgiel drzewny**

charge¹ /tʃɑːdʒ/ noun **1** [C,U] the price that you must pay for sth: *The hotel* ***makes a small charge*** (pobiera małą opłatę) *for changing currency.* ◇ *We deliver* ***free of charge.*** Bezpłatna dostawa. ▶ **opłata** ➲ note at **price 2** [C,U] a statement that says that sb has done sth illegal or bad: *He was arrested* ***on a charge of*** *murder.* ◇ *The writer dismissed the charge that his books were childish.* ▶ **oskarżenie, zarzut 3** [U] **be in charge (of sb/sth)** to be in a position of control over sb/sth; to have responsibility for sb/sth: *Who is* ***in charge of*** *the office while Alan's away?* Kto jest odpowiedzialny za biuro podczas nieobecności Alana? ◇ *The assistant manager had to* ***take charge of*** (przejąć kontrolę nad) *the team when the manager resigned.* ▶ **sprawować nadzór 4** [C] the amount of electricity that is put into a battery or carried by a substance: *a positive/negative charge* ▶ **ładunek 5** [C] a sudden attack where sb/sth runs straight at sb/sth else: *He led the charge down the field.* ▶ **szarża**
IDM **bring/press charges (against sb)** to formally accuse sb of a crime so that there can be a trial in a court of law ▶ **wnosić oskarżenie**
reverse the charges → REVERSE¹

charge² /tʃɑːdʒ/ verb **1** [T,I] **charge (sb/sth) for sth** to ask sb to pay a particular amount of money: *We charge £35 per night for a single room.* ◇ *Do you charge for postage and packing?* ▶ **pobierać opłatę, policzyć komuś za coś** ➲ look at **overcharge 2** [T] **charge sb (with sth)** to accuse sb officially of doing sth which is against the law: *Three men have been charged with attempted robbery.* ▶ **oskarżać 3** [I,T] to run straight at sb/sth, or in a particular direction, in an aggressive or noisy way: *The bull put its head down ready to charge (us).* ◇ *The children charged into the room.* ▶ **nacierać na kogoś/coś; szarżować, galopować 4** [T] to put electricity into sth: *to charge a battery* ▶ **ładować** (*np. baterie*) ➲ look at **recharge**
IDM **charge/pay the earth** → EARTH¹

'**charge card** noun [C] a small plastic card provided by a shop which you use to buy goods there, paying for them later ▶ **karta płatnicza stałego klienta** ➲ look at **credit card**

charger /'tʃɑːdʒə(r)/ noun [C] a piece of equipment for loading a battery with electricity: *a mobile phone charger* ▶ **ładowarka do akumulatorów**

chariot /'tʃæriət/ noun [C] an open vehicle with two wheels that was pulled by a horse or horses in ancient times ▶ **rydwan**

charisma /kə'rɪzmə/ noun [U] a powerful personal quality that some people have to attract and influence other people ▶ **charyzma**
■ **charismatic** /ˌkærɪz'mætɪk/ adj. ▶ **charyzmatyczny**

charitable /'tʃærətəbl/ adj. **1** connected with a charity ▶ **charytatywny 2** kind; generous: *Some people accused him of lying, but a more charitable explanation was that he had made a mistake.* ▶ **życzliwy**

charity /'tʃærəti/ noun (pl. **charities**) **1** [C,U] an organization that collects money to help people who are poor, sick, etc. or to do work that is useful to society: *We went on a sponsored walk to **raise money for charity*** (aby zebrać pieniądze na cele dobroczynne). ▶ **organizacja charytatywna** ➲ note at **money 2** [U] kindness towards other people: *to act out of charity* robić coś z dobrego serca ▶ **życzliwość, dobroczynność, miłosierdzie**

'**charity shop** noun [C] a shop that sells clothes, books, etc. given by people to make money for charity ▶ **sklep z tanimi, zwykle używanymi, artykułami** (*na cele dobroczynne*)

charlatan /'ʃɑːlətən/ noun [C] a person who pretends to have knowledge or skills that they do not really have ▶ **szarlatan**

charm¹ /tʃɑːm/ noun **1** [C,U] a quality that pleases and attracts people: *The charm of the island lies in its unspoilt beauty.* ◇ *Alison found it hard to resist Frank's charms.* ▶ **urok 2** [C] something that you wear because you believe it will bring you good luck: *a lucky charm* ▶ **talizman**

charm² /tʃɑːm/ verb [T] **1** to please and attract sb: *Her drawings have charmed children all over the world.* ▶ **zachwycać 2** to protect sb/sth as if by magic: *He has led a charmed life* (miał życie jakby chronione przez czary), *surviving serious illness and a plane crash.* ▶ **zaczarować**

charmer /'tʃɑːmə(r)/ noun [C] a person who acts in a way that makes them attractive to other people, sometimes using this to influence others ▶ **osoba, która potrafi oczarować innych**

charming /'tʃɑːmɪŋ/ adj. very pleasing or attractive: *a charming old church* ▶ **uroczy**
■ **charmingly** adv. ▶ **uroczo**

charred /tʃɑːd/ adj. burnt black by fire ▶ **zwęglony**

chart¹ /tʃɑːt/ noun **1** [C] a drawing which shows information in the form of a diagram, etc.: *a temperature chart* ◇ *This chart shows the company's sales for this year.* ▶ **wykres** ➲ look at **pie chart**, **flow chart 2** [C] a map of the sea or the sky: *navigation charts* ▶ **mapa morska (lub nieba) 3** (**the charts**) [pl.] an official list of the songs or CDs, etc., that have sold the most in a particular week: *The album went straight into the charts at number 1.* ▶ **lista przebojów**

chart² /tʃɑːt/ verb [T] **1** to follow or record sth carefully and in detail: *This TV series charts the history of the country since independence.* ▶ **prześledzić, notować 2** to make a map of one area of the sea or sky: *Cook charted the coast of New Zealand in 1768.* ▶ **sporządzać mapę morską (lub nieba)**

charter¹ /'tʃɑːtə(r)/ noun [C,U] **1** a written statement of the rights, beliefs and purposes of an organization or a particular group of people: *The club's charter does not permit women to become members.* ▶ **statut 2** the renting of a ship, plane, etc. for a particular purpose or for a particular group of people: *a charter airline* ▶ **czarter**

charter² /'tʃɑːtə(r)/ verb [T] **1** to rent a ship, plane, etc. for a particular purpose or for a particular group of people: *As there was no regular service to the island we had to charter a boat.* ▶ **czarterować 2** to give a charter to an organization or a particular group of people ▶ **nadawać prawa** (*np. miejskie*), **rejestrować**

chartered /'tʃɑːtəd/ adj. [only before a noun] (used about people in certain professions) fully trained; having passed all the necessary exams ▶ **dyplomowany**

ˌ**chartered ac'countant** (US ˌ**certified public ac'countant**) noun [C] a fully trained and qualified **accountant** ▶ **biegł-y/a księgow-y/a**

'**charter flight** noun [C] a flight in which all seats are paid for by a travel company and then sold to their customers, usually at a lower price than normal: *Is it a charter flight or a scheduled flight?* ▶ **lot czarterowy**

chase¹ /tʃeɪs/ verb **1** [I,T] **chase (after) sb/sth** to run after sb/sth in order to catch them or it: *The dog chased the cat up a tree.* ◇ *The police car chased after the stolen van.* ▶ **gonić 2** [I] to run somewhere fast: *The kids were chasing around the park.* ▶ **pędzić**

chase² /tʃeɪs/ noun [C] the act of following sb/sth in order to catch them or it: *an exciting car chase* ▶ **pogoń, pościg**
IDM **give chase** to begin to run after sb/sth in order to try to catch them or it: *The robber ran off and the policeman gave chase.* ▶ **rzucić się w pogoń**

chasm /'kæzəm/ noun [C] **1** a deep hole in the ground ▶ **szczelina 2** a wide difference of feelings, interests, etc. between two people or groups ▶ **przepaść**

chassis /'ʃæsi/ noun [C] (pl. **chassis** /-siz/) the metal frame of a vehicle onto which the other parts fit ▶ **podwozie**

chaste /tʃeɪst/ adj. (old-fashioned) **1** never having had a sexual relationship, or only with your husband/wife ▶ **czysty (moralnie) 2** not involving thoughts and feelings about sex: *a chaste kiss on the cheek* ▶ **niewinny** ➲ noun **chastity**

chasten /'tʃeɪsn/ verb [T, often passive] (formal) to make sb feel sorry for sth they have done: *He felt **suitably chastened** and apologized.* ◇ *It was a **chastening experience**.* ▶ **karcić**

chastise /tʃæ'staɪz/ verb [T] (formal) **chastise sb (for sth/for doing sth)** to criticize or punish sb for doing sth wrong ▶ **ganić, udzielać surowej reprymendy**
■ **chastisement** noun [U] ▶ **reprymenda, nagana**

chastity /'tʃæstəti/ noun [U] the state of not having sex with anyone or only having sex with the person you are married to; being **chaste** ▶ **czystość (moralna)** ➲ adjective **chaste**

chat¹ /tʃæt/ verb [I] (**chatting**; **chatted**) **chat (with/to sb) (about sth)** to talk to sb in an informal, friendly way:

The two grandmothers sat chatting about the old days. ▶ **porozmawiać**

PHR V **chat sb up** (Brit., informal) to talk in a friendly way to sb you are sexually attracted to: *John was in the bar chatting up the barmaid.* ▶ **podrywać kogoś przez zagadywanie**

⚷ **chat²** /tʃæt/ noun **1** [C,U] a friendly informal conversation: *I'll **have a chat** with Jim about the arrangements.* ▶ **pogawędka 2** [U,C] a conversation you have on the Internet by exchanging written messages with one or more people: *Log on to the site for live chat and message boards.* ▶ **czat**

ˈ**chat room** noun [C] an area on the Internet where you can join in a discussion ▶ **kanał dyskusyjny w czacie**, **pokój** (*w czacie*) ➲ note at **Internet**

ˈ**chat show** noun [C] a TV or radio programme on which well-known people are invited to talk about themselves ▶ **talk show**

chatter /ˈtʃætə(r)/ verb [I] **1** to talk quickly or for a long time about sth unimportant: *The children were all laughing and chattering excitedly.* ▶ **trajkotać 2** (used about your teeth) to knock together because you are cold or frightened ▶ **szczękać** (*zębami*)

■ **chatter** noun [U] ▶ **trajkotanie**

chatterbox /ˈtʃætəbɒks/ noun [C] (informal) a person who talks a lot, especially a child ▶ **gaduła**

chatty /ˈtʃæti/ adj. (**chattier**; **chattiest**) **1** talking a lot in a friendly way ▶ **gadatliwy 2** in an informal style: *a chatty letter* ▶ **gawędziarski**

ˈ**chat-up** noun [C, U] an occasion when a person is talking to sb in a way that shows they are interested in them sexually: *Is that your best chat-up line?* ▶ **podrywanie przez zagadywanie**

chauffeur /ˈʃəʊfə(r); US -ˈfɜːr/ noun [C] a person whose job is to drive a car for sb else: *a chauffeur-driven limousine* ▶ **szofer**

■ **chauffeur** verb [T] ▶ **wozić (zawodowo) samochodem**

chauvinism /ˈʃəʊvɪnɪzəm/ noun [U] **1** the belief that your country is better than all others ▶ **szowinizm 2** (also **male ˈchauvinism**) the belief that men are better than women ▶ **męski szowinizm**

■ **chauvinist** /-ɪst/ noun [C] ▶ **szowinist-a/ka** | **chauvinistic** /ˌʃəʊvɪˈnɪstɪk; US / adj. ▶ **szowinistyczny**

⚷ **cheap¹** /tʃiːp/ adj. **1** low in price; costing little money: *Computers are getting cheaper all the time.* ▶ **tani** SYN **inexpensive** OPP **expensive 2** charging low prices: *a cheap hotel/restaurant* ▶ **tani 3** low in price and quality and therefore not attractive: *The clothes in that shop look cheap.* ▶ **tandetny**

IDM **dirt cheap** → DIRT

cheap² /tʃiːp/ adv. (informal) for a low price: *I got this coat cheap in the sale.* ▶ **tanio**

IDM **be going cheap** (informal) be on sale at a lower price than usual: *They've got strawberries going cheap at the market.* Na targu są tanie truskawki. ▶ **mieć niską cenę**

cheapen /ˈtʃiːpən/ verb [T] **1** to make sb lose respect for himself or herself: *She felt cheapened by their treatment of her.* ▶ **poniżać 2** to make sth lower in price ▶ **obniżać cenę/wartość 3** to make sth appear to have less value: *The film was accused of cheapening human life.* ▶ **deprecjonować**

⚷ **cheaply** /ˈtʃiːpli/ adv. for a low price ▶ **tanio**

⚷ **cheat¹** /tʃiːt/ verb **1** [T] to trick sb, or to make them believe sth that is not true, especially when that person trusts you: *The shopkeeper cheated customers by giving them too little change.* ▶ **oszukiwać 2** [I] **cheat (at sth)** to act in a dishonest or unfair way in order to get an advantage for yourself: *Paul was caught cheating in the exam.* ◇ *to cheat at cards* ▶ **oszukiwać 3** [I] **cheat (on sb)** to not be faithful to your husband, wife or regular partner by having a secret sexual relationship with sb else ▶ **zdradzać**

PHR V **cheat sb (out) of sth** to take sth from sb in a dishonest or unfair way: *They tried to cheat the old lady out of her savings.* ▶ **wyłudzać coś od kogoś**

⚷ **cheat²** /tʃiːt/ noun [C] a person who cheats ▶ **oszust/ka**

⚷ **check¹** /tʃek/ verb **1** [I,T] **check (sth) (for sth)** to examine or test sth in order to make sure that it is safe or correct, in good condition, etc.: *Check your work for mistakes before you hand it in.* ◇ *The doctor X-rayed me to check for broken bones.* ▶ **sprawdzać 2** [I,T] **check (sth) (with sb)** to make sure that sth is how you think it is: *You'd better check with Tim that it's OK to borrow his bike.* ◇ *I'll phone and check what time the bus leaves.* ▶ **sprawdzać 3** [T] to stop or make sb/sth stop or go more slowly: *She almost told her boss what she thought of him, but checked herself in time.* ◇ *Phil checked his pace as he didn't want to tire too early.* ▶ **powstrzymywać 4** [T] (US) = TICK¹ (2)

PHR V **check in (at …)**; **check into …** to go to a desk in a hotel or an airport and tell an official that you have arrived ▶ **meldować się**, **przechodzić odprawę** ➲ note at **hotel**, **plane**

check sth off to mark names or items on a list: *The boxes were all checked off as they were unloaded.* ▶ **zaznaczać** (*pozycje w spisie*), **zakreślać coś** ➲ look at **tick¹**

check on sb/sth to make sure that there is nothing wrong with sb/sth: *I'll just go and check on the children.* ◇ *My boss comes in once a week to check on progress.* ▶ **sprawdzać kogoś/coś**

check out (of …) to pay for your room, etc. and leave a hotel ▶ **wymeldować się** (*z hotelu*) ➲ note at **hotel**

check sb/sth out 1 to find out more information about sb/sth, especially to find out if sth is true or not: *We need to check out these rumours of possible pay cuts.* ▶ **sprawdzać coś 2** (especially US, slang) to look at sb/sth, especially to find out if you like them or it: *I'm going to check out that new club tonight.* ▶ **popatrzeć na coś**

check up on sb to make sure that sb is doing what they should be doing: *My parents are always checking up on me.* ▶ **kontrolować kogoś**

check up on sth to find out if sth is true or correct: *I need to check up on a few things before I can decide.* ▶ **sprawdzać coś**

⚷ **check²** /tʃek/ noun **1** [C] **a check (on sth)** a close look at sth to make sure that it is safe, correct, in good condition, etc.: *We **carry out/do** regular **checks** on our products to make sure that they are of high quality.* ◇ *I don't go to games, but I like to **keep a check** on my team's results.* ▶ **sprawdzanie**, **kontrola 2** [C,U] a pattern of squares, often of different colours: *a check jacket* ◇ *a pattern of blue and red checks* ▶ (*wzór*) **krat(k)a** ➲ picture on **page A1 3** (US) = BILL¹ (2) **4** [U] the situation in the game of **chess** in which a player must move to protect his or her king: *There, you're in check.* ▶ **szach** ➲ look at **checkmate 5** (US) = CHEQUE **6** (US) = TICK² (1) ➲ look at **rain check**

IDM **hold/keep sth in check** to keep sth under control so that it does not get worse: *government measures to keep inflation in check* ▶ **powstrzymywać**, **hamować**

checkbook (US) = CHEQUEBOOK

checkbox (Brit. also **tickbox** /ˈtɪkbɒks/) noun [C] a small square on a computer screen that you click on with the mouse to choose whether a particular function is switched on or off ▶ (*komput.*) **pole wyboru**

checked /tʃekt/ adj. with a pattern of squares: *a red-and-white checked tablecloth* ▶ **w krat(k)ę**, **kraciasty**

checkers (US) = DRAUGHT¹ (2)

'**check-in** noun [C,U] **1** the place where you check in at an airport ▶ **stanowisko odprawy pasażerów 2** the act of checking in at an airport: *Our check-in time is 10.30a.m.* ▶ **odprawa**

'**checking account** (US) = CURRENT ACCOUNT

checklist /'tʃeklɪst/ noun [C] a list of things that you must do or have ▶ **lista rzeczy do załatwienia**, **spis kontrolny**

'**check mark** (US) = TICK² (1)

checkmate /ˌtʃek'meɪt/ noun [U] the situation in the game of **chess** in which one player cannot protect his or her king and so loses the game ▶ **szach i mat** ➲ look at **check**

checkout /'tʃekaʊt/ noun [C] the place in a large shop where you pay ▶ **kasa**

checkpoint /'tʃekpɔɪnt/ noun [C] a place where all people and vehicles must stop and be checked: *an army checkpoint* ▶ **punkt kontrolny**

'**check-up** noun [C] a general medical examination to make sure that you are healthy: *to* ***go for/have a check-up*** ▶ **badanie lekarskie**

Cheddar /'tʃedə(r)/ noun [U] a type of hard yellow cheese ▶ (*gatunek angielskiego sera*) **cheddar**

⚷ **cheek** /tʃi:k/ noun **1** [C] either side of the face below your eyes: *Tears rolled down her cheeks.* ▶ **policzek** ➲ picture at **body 2** [U, sing.] (Brit.) rude behaviour; lack of respect: *He's got a cheek, asking to borrow money again!* ▶ **tupet**
IDM **(with) tongue in cheek** → TONGUE

cheekbone /'tʃi:kbəʊn/ noun [C] the bone below your eye ▶ **kość policzkowa** ➲ picture at **body**

cheeky /'tʃi:ki/ adj. (**cheekier**; **cheekiest**) (Brit.) not showing respect; rude ▶ **bezczelny**
■ **cheekily** adv. ▶ **bezczelnie**

cheer¹ /tʃɪə(r)/ noun [C] a loud shout to show that you like sth or to encourage sb who is taking part in a competition, sport, etc.: *The crowd* ***gave a cheer*** (zawiwatował) *when the president appeared.* ◇ *Three cheers for the winning team!* Na cześć zwycięskiej drużyny trzykrotne: hip hip hurra! ▶ **wiwat** ➲ look at **hip**

cheer² /tʃɪə(r)/ verb **1** [I,T] to shout to show that you like sth or to encourage sb who is taking part in competition, sport, etc.: *Everyone cheered the winner as he crossed the finishing line.* ▶ **wznosić okrzyki**, **wiwatować 2** [T] to make sb happy or to give sb hope: *They were all cheered by the good news.* ▶ **dodawać otuchy**, **pocieszać**
PHR V **cheer sb on** to shout in order to encourage sb in a race, competition, etc.: *As the runners started the last lap the crowd cheered them on.* ▶ **dopingować**
cheer (sb/sth) up to become or to make sb happier; to make sth look more attractive: *A few pictures would cheer this room up a bit.* ◇ *Cheer up* (głowa do góry)*! Things aren't that bad.* ▶ **rozweselać (się)**

⚷ **cheerful** /'tʃɪəfl/ adj. feeling happy; showing that you are happy: *Caroline is always very cheerful.* ◇ *a cheerful smile* ▶ **pogodny**, **wesoły** ➲ note at **happy**
■ **cheerfully** /-fəli/ adv. ▶ **pogodnie**, **wesoło** | **cheerfulness** noun [U] ▶ **pogoda ducha**

cheerio /ˌtʃɪəri'əʊ/ interj. (Brit., informal) goodbye: *Cheerio! See you later.* ▶ **cześć!** (*na pożegnanie*)

cheerleader /'tʃɪəli:də(r)/ noun [C] (especially in the US) one of a group of girls or women at a sports match who wear special uniforms and shout, dance, etc. in order to encourage people to support the players ▶ **cheerleaderka**

cheers /tʃɪəz/ interj. (informal) **1** (used to express good wishes before having an alcoholic drink): *'Cheers,' she said, raising her wine glass.* ▶ **na zdrowie! 2** (Brit.) goodbye ▶ **cześć!** (*na pożegnanie*) **3** (Brit.) thank you ▶ **dzięki**

cheery /'tʃɪəri/ adj. (**cheerier**; **cheeriest**) happy and smiling: *a cheery remark/wave/smile* ▶ **wesoły**
■ **cheerily** adv. ▶ **wesoło**

⚷ **cheese** /tʃi:z/ noun **1** [U] a type of food made from milk. Cheese is usually white or yellow in colour and can be soft or hard: *a piece of cheese* ◇ *a cheese sandwich* ▶ **ser** ➲ picture on **page A14 2** [C] a type of cheese: *a wide selection of cheeses* ▶ **gatunek sera**

cheesecake /'tʃi:zkeɪk/ noun [C,U] a type of cake that is made from soft cheese and sugar on a **pastry** or biscuit base, often with fruit on top ▶ **sernik**

ˌ**cheesed** '**off** adj. [not before a noun] **cheesed off (with/about sb/sth)** (Brit., informal) annoyed or bored: *He's cheesed off with his job.* ▶ **mający czegoś po dziurki w nosie**

cheesy /'tʃi:zi/ adj. (**cheesier**; **cheesiest**) (informal) of low quality and without style: *an incredibly cheesy love song* ▶ **tandentny**

cheetah /'tʃi:tə/ noun [C] a large wild cat with black spots that can run very fast ▶ **gepard**

chef /ʃef/ noun [C] a professional cook, especially the head cook in a hotel, restaurant, etc. ▶ **szef kuchni**

⚷ **chemical¹** /'kemɪkl/ adj. connected with chemistry; involving changes to the structure of a substance: *a chemical reaction* ▶ **chemiczny**
■ **chemically** /-kli/ adv. ▶ **chemicznie**

⚷ **chemical²** /'kemɪkl/ noun [C] a substance that is used or produced in a chemical process: *Sulphuric acid is a dangerous chemical.* ▶ **substancja chemiczna**

ˌ**chemical** '**weapon** noun [C] a weapon that uses poisonous gases and chemicals to kill and injure people ▶ **broń chemiczna**

⚷ **chemist** /'kemɪst/ noun [C] **1** (also **pharmacist** /'fɑ:məsɪst/; US **druggist** /'drʌgɪst/) a person who prepares and sells medicines ▶ **apteka-rz/rka 2** (**the chemist's**) (US **drugstore** /'drʌgstɔ:(r)/) a shop that sells medicines, soap, camera film, etc.: *I got my tablets from the chemist's.* ▶ **apteka** ⓘ **The chemist's** to zarówno apteka, jak i drogeria. **3** a person who studies chemistry ▶ **chemik**

⚷ **chemistry** /'kemɪstri/ noun [U] **1** the scientific study of the structure of substances and what happens to them in different conditions or when mixed with each other: *We did an experiment in the chemistry lesson.* ▶ **chemia** ➲ note at **science 2** the structure of a particular substance: *The patient's blood chemistry was monitored regularly.* ▶ **skład chemiczny**

chemotherapy /ˌki:məʊ'θerəpi/ noun [U] the treatment of disease, especially cancer, with the use of chemical substances: *a course of chemotherapy* ▶ **chemioterapia**

⚷ **cheque** (US **check**) /tʃek/ noun [C,U] a piece of paper printed by a bank that you sign and use to pay for things: *She* ***wrote out a cheque*** *for £20.* ◇ *to* ***make a cheque out*** *to sb* wypisać czek na kogoś ◇ *I went to the bank to* ***cash a cheque.*** ◇ *Can I* ***pay by cheque?*** ▶ **czek**

chequebook (US **checkbook**) /'tʃekbʊk/ noun [C] a book of cheques ▶ **książeczka czekowa**

'**cheque card** noun [C] (Brit.) a small plastic card that you show when you pay with a cheque as proof that your bank will pay the amount on the cheque ▶ **karta czekowa** ➲ look at **credit card**, **cash card**

chequered (especially US **checkered**) /'tʃekəd/ adj. **1** (**chequered past/history/career**) a person's past, etc. that contains both successful and not successful periods ▶ (*życie itp.*) **burzliwy 2** having a pattern of squares of different colours ▶ (*wzór*) **w szachownicę**

cherish /'tʃerɪʃ/ verb [T] **1** to love sb/sth and look after them or it carefully: *The ring was her most cherished* (najcenniejszą) *possession.* ▶ **dbać o kogoś/coś 2** to keep a thought, feeling, etc. in your mind and think about it often: *a cherished memory* ▶ **żywić** (*np. uczucie*)

cherry /ˈtʃeri/ noun [C] (pl. **cherries**) **1** a small round black or red fruit that has a stone inside it ▶ **wiśnia; czereśnia** ➲ picture on **page A12** **2** (also ˈ**cherry tree**) the tree that produces **cherries** ▶ **wiśnia; czereśnia**

cherub /ˈtʃerəb/ noun [C] (in art) a type of **angel**, shown as an attractive child with wings ▶ **cherubin(ek)**
■ **cherubic** /tʃəˈru:bɪk/ adj. (formal) *a cherubic face* ▶ **jak aniołek, cherubinkowy**

chess /tʃes/ noun [U] a game for two people that is played on a board with 64 black and white squares (**chessboard**). Each player has 16 pieces which can be moved according to fixed rules: *Can you* ***play chess****?* ◇ *Shall we have* ***a game of chess*** (partię szachów)*?* ▶ **szachy**

chest /tʃest/ noun [C] **1** the top part of the front of your body ▶ **pierś, klatka piersiowa** ➲ look at **breast** ➲ picture at **body** **2** a large strong box that is used for storing or carrying things ▶ **skrzynia**
IDM **get sth off your chest** (informal) to talk about sth that you have been thinking or worrying about ▶ **zrzucić ciężar z serca, wygadać się**

chestnut /ˈtʃesnʌt/ noun [C] **1** (also ˈ**chestnut tree**) a tree with large leaves that produces smooth brown nuts in shells with sharp points on the outside ▶ **kasztanowiec, kasztan** **2** a smooth brown nut from the **chestnut** tree. You can eat some **chestnuts.** ▶ **kasztan** (*owoc*) ➲ look at **conker** **3** a deep reddish-brown colour ▶ **kasztan** ➲ look at **auburn, maroon**
■ **chestnut** adj. reddish-brown in colour ▶ **kasztanowy**

ˌ**chest of ˈdrawers** noun [C] a piece of furniture with drawers in it that is used for storing clothes, etc. ▶ **komoda**

chew /tʃu:/ verb [I,T] **1** to break up food in your mouth with your teeth before you swallow it: *You should chew your food thoroughly.* ▶ **żuć** **2** **chew (on) sth** to bite sth continuously with the back teeth: *The dog was chewing on a bone.* ▶ **obgryzać**

ˈ**chewing gum** (also **gum**) noun [U] a sweet sticky substance that you **chew** in your mouth but do not swallow ▶ **guma do żucia** ➲ look at **bubblegum**

chewy /ˈtʃu:i/ adj. (**chewier**; **chewiest**) (used about food) difficult to break up with your teeth before it can be swallowed: *chewy* (żylaste) *meat* ◇ *chewy* (ciągnące się) *toffee* ▶ **trudny do pogryzienia**

chic /ʃi:k/ adj. fashionable and elegant ▶ **szykowny, elegancki**
■ **chic** noun [U] ▶ **szyk, styl**

chick /tʃɪk/ noun [C] **1** a baby bird, especially a young chicken ▶ **pisklę** **2** (old-fashioned, slang) a way of referring to a young woman ▶ **laska, niezła babka**

chicken[1] /ˈtʃɪkɪn/ noun **1** [C] a bird that people often keep for its eggs and its meat: *free-range chickens* ▶ **kurczę, kurczak** **2** [U] the meat of this bird: *chicken soup* ▶ **kurczak**

> Wyrazu **chicken** używa się ogólnie w odniesieniu do ptaka i do mięsa. Samiec to **cock** (US **rooster**), samica to **hen**, a młode to **chick**.

IDM **Don't count your chickens (before they're hatched)** → COUNT[1]

chicken[2] /ˈtʃɪkɪn/ verb
PHR V **chicken out (of sth)** (informal) to decide not to do sth because you are afraid: *Mark chickened out of swimming across the river when he saw how far it was.* ▶ **tchórzyć przed (czymś)**

chickenpox /ˈtʃɪkɪnpɒks/ noun [U] a disease, especially of children. When you have **chickenpox** you feel very hot and get red spots on your skin that make you want to scratch. ▶ **ospa wietrzna**

chickpea /ˈtʃɪk pi:/ noun [C] (especially Brit.) a hard round seed, like a light brown **pea**, that is cooked and eaten as a vegetable ▶ **ciecierzyca**

chicory /ˈtʃɪkəri/ (US **endive** /ˈendaɪv/) noun [U] a small pale green plant with bitter leaves that can be eaten cooked or not cooked ▶ **cykoria**

chide /tʃaɪd/ verb [T] **chide sb (for sth/for doing sth)** (formal) to criticize or blame sb because they have done sth wrong: *She chided herself for being so impatient with the children.* ◇ *'Isn't that a bit selfish?' he chided.* ▶ **łajać** SYN **rebuke**

chief[1] /tʃi:f/ adj. [only before a noun] **1** most important; main: *One of the chief reasons for his decision was money.* ▶ **główny** **2** of the highest level or position: *the chief executive of a company* ▶ **naczelny**

chief[2] /tʃi:f/ noun [C] **1** the person who has command or control over an organization: *the chief* (komendant) *of police* ▶ **szef, kierownik** **2** the leader of a **tribe**: *African tribal chiefs* ▶ **wódz** (*plemienia*)

ˌ**chief eˈxecutive officer** noun [C] (abbr. **CEO** /ˌsi: i: ˈəʊ/) the person in a company who has the most power and authority ▶ **dyrektor naczelny**

chiefly /ˈtʃi:fli/ adv. mostly: *His success was due chiefly to hard work.* Swój sukces zawdzięczał przede wszystkim ciężkiej pracy. ▶ **głównie** SYN **mainly**

chieftain /ˈtʃi:ftən/ noun [C] the leader of a **tribe**: *a 12th-century Scottish chieftain* ▶ **wódz** (*plemienia*)

chiffon /ˈʃɪfɒn; US ʃɪˈf-/ noun [U] a very thin, transparent type of cloth used for making clothes, etc. ▶ **szyfon**

chilblain /ˈtʃɪlbleɪn/ noun [C] a painful red area on your foot, hand, etc. that is caused by cold weather ▶ **(lekkie) odmrożenie** (*palców rąk i nóg*) ➲ look at **frostbite**

child /tʃaɪld/ noun [C] (pl. **children** /ˈtʃɪldrən/) **1** a young boy or girl who is not yet an adult: *A group of children were playing in the park.* ◇ *a six-year-old child* ▶ **dziecko** **2** a son or daughter of any age: *She has two children but both are married and have moved away.* ◇ *an only child* jedyna-k/czka ◇ *a foster child* przybrane dziecko ▶ **dziecko**

> **children**
> An **only child** is a child who has no brothers or sisters. A child whose parents have died is an **orphan**. A person may **adopt** a child who is not his/her own son or daughter. A **foster child** is looked after for a certain period of time by a family that is not his/her own. If your husband or wife has children from a previous marriage, they are your **stepchildren**. Parents are responsible for **bringing up** their children.

ˈ**child abuse** noun [U] the crime of harming a child in a physical, sexual or emotional way ▶ **znęcanie się nad dziećmi; molestowanie dzieci**

child ˈbenefit noun [U] (in Britian) money that the government regularly pays to parents of children up to a particular age ▶ **zasiłek na dziecko**

childbirth /ˈtʃaɪldbɜ:θ/ noun [U] the act of giving birth to a baby: *His wife died* ***in childbirth*** (przy porodzie). ▶ **poród**

childcare /ˈtʃaɪldkeə(r)/ noun [U] the job of looking after children, especially while the parents are at work: *Some employers provide childcare facilities* (żłobek i/lub przedszkole w miejscu pracy). ▶ **opieka nad dziećmi**

childhood /ˈtʃaɪldhʊd/ noun [C,U] the time when you are a child: *Harriet had a very unhappy childhood.* ◇ *childhood memories* wspomnienia z dzieciństwa ▶ **dzieciństwo**

childish /ˈtʃaɪldɪʃ/ adj. like a child ▶ **dziecinny** SYN **immature** OPP **mature** ➲ look at **babyish**

Childish czy **childlike**? Kiedy określa się osobę lub jej zachowanie przymiotnikiem **childlike**, podkreśla się pozytywne cechy dziecka: *childlike innocence* ◇ *His childlike enthusiasm delighted us all.* Natomiast kiedy opisuje się zachowanie dorosłej osoby jako **childish**, krytuje się je, ponieważ uważa się je za niepoważne, dziecinne: *Don't be so childish! You can't always have everything you want.*

■ **childishly** adv. ▶ **jak (małe) dziecko, infantylnie**

childless /ˈtʃaɪldləs/ adj. having no children ▶ **bezdzietny**

childlike /ˈtʃaɪldlaɪk/ adj. like a child ▶ **dziecięcy** ➲ note at **childish**

childminder /ˈtʃaɪldmaɪndə(r)/ noun [C] (Brit.) a person whose job is to look after a child while his or her parents are at work ▶ **opiekun/ka do dziecka, niania**

children plural of **child**

ˈ**children's home** noun [C] an institution where children live whose parents cannot look after them ▶ **dom dziecka**

chili (US) = CHILLI

chill¹ /tʃɪl/ noun **1** [sing.] an unpleasant cold feeling: *There's a chill in the air.* ◇ (figurative) *A chill of fear went down my spine.* ▶ **chłód**; **dreszcz 2** [C] (informal) a common illness that affects your nose and throat; a cold: *to catch a chill* przeziębiać się ▶ **przeziębienie**

chill² /tʃɪl/ verb **1** [I,T] to become or to make sb/sth colder: *It's better to chill white wine before you serve it.* ▶ **chłodzić (się) 2** verb [I] (informal) to spend time relaxing: *We went home and chilled in front of the television.* ▶ **relaksować się**

PHR V **chill out** (informal) to relax and stop feeling angry or nervous about sth: *Sit down and chill out!* ▶ **wyluzować się, zrelaksować się**

chilli (US chili) /ˈtʃɪli/ noun [C,U] (pl. **chillies**; US **chilies**) a small green or red vegetable that has a very strong hot taste: *chilli powder* ▶ **papryka chilli** ➲ picture on **page A13**

chilling /ˈtʃɪlɪŋ/ adj. frightening: *a chilling ghost story* ▶ **mrożący krew w żyłach**

chilly /ˈtʃɪli/ adj. (**chillier**; **chilliest**) **1** (used about the weather) too cold to be comfortable: *It's a chilly morning.* ▶ **zimny 2** (used about people and their behaviour) not friendly: *They gave us a very chilly reception.* ▶ **oziębły**

chime /tʃaɪm/ verb **1** [T] (used about a bell or a clock) to show the time by ringing ▶ **wybijać godziny 2** [I] (used about a bell) to ring ▶ **dzwonić**

■ **chime** noun [C] ▶ **dzwonek, kurant**

PHR V **chime in (with sth)** (informal) to interrupt a conversation and add your own comments ▶ **wtrącać się** (*do rozmowy*)

chimney /ˈtʃɪmni/ noun [C] a pipe through which smoke or steam is carried up and out through the roof of a building ▶ **komin**

ˈ**chimney sweep** noun [C] a person whose job is to clean the inside of **chimneys** with long brushes ▶ **kominiarz**

chimpanzee /ˌtʃɪmpænˈziː/ (also informal **chimp** /tʃɪmp/) noun [C] a small intelligent **ape** which is found in Africa ▶ **szympans**

⚷ **chin** /tʃɪn/ noun [C] the part of your face below your mouth: *He sat listening, his chin resting on his hand.* ◇ *a double chin* podwójny podbródek ▶ **podbródek, broda** ➲ picture at **body**

china /ˈtʃaɪnə/ noun [U] **1** white **clay** of good quality that is used for making cups, plates, etc.: *a china vase* ▶ **porcelana 2** cups, plates, etc. that are made from **china** ▶ **wyroby porcelanowe**

chink¹ /tʃɪŋk/ noun [C] **1** a small narrow opening: *Daylight came in through a chink between the curtains.* ▶ **szpara, szczelina 2** a light ringing sound ▶ **brzęk**

chink² /tʃɪŋk/ [I,T] to make a light ringing sound; to cause this sound, e.g. by knocking two pieces of china or glass together gently ▶ **brzęczeć**; **pobrzękiwać**

chinos /ˈtʃiːnəʊz/ noun [pl.] informal trousers made from strong woven cotton ▶ **rodzaj spodni**

chintz /tʃɪnts/ noun [U] a shiny cotton cloth with a printed design, usually of flowers, which is used for making curtains, covering furniture, etc. ▶ **perkal**

⚷ **chip¹** /tʃɪp/ noun [C] **1** the place where a small piece of stone, glass, wood, etc. has broken off sth: *This dish has a chip in it.* Ten talerz jest wyszczerbiony. ▶ **wyszczerbienie 2** a small piece of stone, glass, wood, etc. that has broken off sth: *chips of wood* ▶ **drzazga, odłamek 3** (especially US ˌ**French** ˈ**fry**; **fry** /fraɪ/, (pl. **fries**) [usually pl.] a thin piece of potato that is fried in hot fat or oil ▶ **frytki** ➲ note at **fish** ➲ picture on **page A14 4** (US) = CRISP² **5** a flat round piece of plastic that you use instead of money when you are playing some games ▶ **żeton 6** = MICROCHIP

IDM **have a chip on your shoulder (about sth)** (informal) to feel angry about sth that happened a long time ago because you think it is unfair: *My dad still has a chip on his shoulder about being thrown out of school.* ▶ **mieć pretensje do całego świata**

chipped

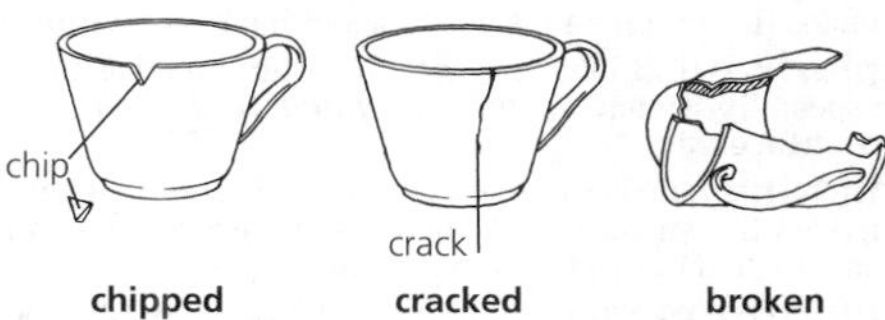

chipped **cracked** **broken**

chip² /tʃɪp/ verb [I,T] (**chipping**; **chipped**) **1** to break a small piece off the edge or surface of sth; to break off in this way: *They chipped* (zdrapali) *the paint trying to get the table through the door.* ◇ *These plates chip easily.* ▶ **wyszczerbiać (się), odłupywać (się) 2** (especially in golf and football) to hit or kick the ball so that it goes high in the air and then lands within a short distance ▶ **wybijać piłkę do góry**

PHR V **chip in (with sth)** (informal) **1** to join in or interrupt a conversation; to add sth to a conversation or discussion: *Pete and Anne chipped in with suggestions.* ▶ **wtrącać się/coś** (*np. do rozmowy*), **przerywać** (*np. rozmowę*) **2** (also ˌ**chip** ˈ**in sth**) to give some money so that a group of people can buy sth together: *If everyone chips in, we'll be able to buy her a really nice present.* ◇ *We each chipped in (with) £5* (zrzuciliśmy się po 5 funtów). ▶ **dorzucać się do czegoś po ileś** SYN **contribute**

ˌ**chip and** ˈ**PIN** (also ˌ**chip and** ˈ**pin**) noun [U] a system of paying for sth with a credit card or **debit card** in which the card has information stored on it in the form of a **microchip** and you prove your identity by typing a number (your PIN) rather than by signing your name ▶ **forma płatności kartą, w której transakcja jest potwierdzona kodem PIN, a nie podpisem**

chipboard /ˈtʃɪpbɔːd/ noun [U] a type of board that is used for building, made of small pieces of wood that are pressed together and stuck with glue ▶ **płyta wiórowa**

ˈ**chip card** noun [C] a plastic card on which information is stored in the form of a **microchip**: *Chip cards will be the money of the future.* ▶ **karta czipowa**

ˈ**chip shop** (Brit., informal **chippy** /ˈtʃɪpi/) noun [C] (in Britain) a shop that cooks and sells fish and **chips** and other fried food to take away and eat ▶ **sklep z rybą i frytkami na wynos**

chiropodist /kɪˈrɒpədɪst/ (US **podiatrist** /pəˈdaɪətrɪst/) noun [C] a person whose job is to look after people's feet ▶ **podiatra**
■ **chiropody** (US **podiatry** /pəˈdaɪətri/) noun [U] ▶ **podiatria**

chirp /tʃɜːp/ verb [I] (used about small birds and some insects) to make short high sounds ▶ **szczebiotać, ćwierkać**
■ **chirp** noun [C] ▶ **szczebiot, ćwierkanie**

chirpy /ˈtʃɜːpi/ adj. (informal) lively and cheerful; in a good mood ▶ **wesoły**
■ **chirpily** adv. ▶ **wesoło** | **chirpiness** noun [U] ▶ **wesołość**

chisel /ˈtʃɪzl/ noun [C] a tool with a sharp end that is used for cutting or shaping wood or stone ▶ **dłuto** ➲ picture at **tool**

ˈ**chit-chat** noun [U] (informal) conversation about things that are not important: *We spent the afternoon in idle chit-chat.* ▶ **pogaduszki** SYN **chat**

chivalry /ˈʃɪvəlri/ noun [U] polite and kind behaviour by men which shows respect towards women ▶ **rycerskość, galanteria**
■ **chivalrous** /ˈʃɪvəlrəs/ adj. ▶ **szarmancki**

chive /tʃaɪv/ noun [C, usually pl.] a long thin green plant that tastes like onion and is used in cooking ▶ **szczypiorek**

chlorinate /ˈklɔːrɪneɪt/ verb [T] to put **chlorine** in sth, especially water: *Is the swimming pool chlorinated?* ▶ **chlorować**

chlorine /ˈklɔːriːn/ noun [U] (symbol **Cl**) a greenish-yellow gas with a strong smell, that is used for making water safe to drink or to swim in ▶ **chlor**

chloroform /ˈklɒrəfɔːm/ noun [U] (symbol $CHCl_3$) a clear liquid used in the past in medicine, etc. to make people unconscious, for example before an operation ▶ **chloroform**

chlorophyll /ˈklɒrəfɪl/ noun [U] the green substance in plants that absorbs light from the sun to help them grow ▶ **chlorofil** ➲ look at **photosynthesis**

choc /tʃɒk/ noun [C] (Brit., informal) a chocolate ▶ **czekoladka**

choccy /ˈtʃɒki/ noun (pl. **-ies**) [U,C] (Brit., informal) chocolate; a sweet made of chocolate ▶ **czekolad(k)a**

chock-a-block /ˌtʃɒk ə ˈblɒk/ adj. [not before a noun] completely full: *The High Street was chock-a-block with shoppers.* ▶ **wypełniony po brzegi**

chock-full /ˌtʃɒk ˈfʊl/ adj. [not before a noun] **chock-full (of sth/sb)** (informal) completely full ▶ **wypełniony po brzegi**

chocoholic /ˌtʃɒkəˈhɒlɪk/ noun [C] a person who loves chocolate and eats a lot of it ▶ **osoba uwielbiająca czekoladę**

🔑 **chocolate** /ˈtʃɒklət/ noun **1** [U] a sweet brown substance made from **cocoa beans** that you can eat as a sweet or use to give flavour to food and drinks: *a bar of* ***milk/plain chocolate*** tabliczka mlecznej/gorzkiej czekolady ▶ **czekolada** ➲ picture at **bar 2** [C] a small sweet that is made from or covered with chocolate: *a box of chocolates* bombonierka ▶ **czekoladka 3** [C,U] a drink made from chocolate powder with hot milk or water: *a mug of* ***hot chocolate*** ▶ **czekolada 4** [U] a dark brown colour ▶ **kolor czekoladowy**
■ **chocolate** adj. **1** made from or covered with chocolate: *a chocolate milkshake* ▶ **czekoladowy 2** dark brown ▶ **czekoladowy**

🔑 **choice**[1] /tʃɔɪs/ noun **1** [C] **a choice (between A and B)** an act of choosing between two or more people or things: *David was forced to* ***make a choice*** (dokonać wyboru) *between moving house and losing his job.* ▶ **wybór 2** [U] the right or chance to choose: *There is a rail strike so we* ***have no choice*** *but to cancel* (nie mamy innego wyboru, jak tylko odwołać) *our trip.* ◇ *to have freedom of choice* ▶ **wybór** ➲ look at **option 3** [C] a person or thing that is chosen: *Barry would be my choice as team captain.* ◇ *What is your choice of colour?* Jaki kolor byś wybrał? ▶ **wybór 4** [C,U] two or more things from which you can or must choose: *This cinema offers a choice of six different films every night.* ▶ **wybór, asortyment** ➲ verb **choose**
IDM **out of/from choice** because you want to; of your own free will: *I wouldn't have gone to America out of choice. I was sent there on business.* ▶ **z (własnego) wyboru**

choice[2] /tʃɔɪs/ adj. [only before a noun] of very good quality: *choice beef* ▶ **wyborowy**

choir /ˈkwaɪə(r)/ noun [C, with sing. or pl. verb] a group of people who sing together in churches, schools, etc. ▶ **chór**

choke[1] /tʃəʊk/ verb **1** [I,T] **choke (on sth)** to be or to make sb unable to breathe because sth is stopping air getting into the lungs: *She was choking on a fish bone.* ◇ *The smoke choked us.* ▶ **dławić (się)** ➲ look at **strangle 2** [T, usually passive] **choke sth (up) (with sth)** to fill a passage, space, etc., so that nothing can pass through: *The roads to the coast were choked with traffic.* ▶ **wypełniać, zatykać**
PHR V **choke sth back** to hide or control a strong emotion: *to choke back tears/anger* ▶ **dławić** (*np. łzy*), **dusić w sobie** (*np. emocje*)

choke[2] /tʃəʊk/ noun [C] **1** a device that controls the amount of air going into the engine of a car, etc. ▶ **ssanie 2** an act or the sound of sb **choking**: *A tiny choke of laughter escaped her.* ▶ **dławienie (się)**

cholera /ˈkɒlərə/ noun [U] a serious disease that causes stomach pains and **vomiting** and can cause death. **Cholera** is most common in hot countries and is carried by water. ▶ **cholera**

cholesterol /kəˈlestərɒl/ noun [U] a substance that is found in the blood, etc. of people and animals. Too much **cholesterol** is thought to be a cause of heart disease ▶ **cholesterol**

chomp /tʃɒmp/ verb [I,T] **chomp (on/through sth)** to eat or bite food noisily: *He chomped his way through two hot dogs.* ◇ *She was chomping away on a bagel.* ▶ **chrupać** SYN **munch**

🔑 **choose** /tʃuːz/ verb [I,T] (pt **chose** /tʃəʊz/, pp **chosen** /ˈtʃəʊzn/) **1 choose (between A and/or B); choose (A) (from B); choose sb/sth as sth** to decide which thing or person you want out of the ones that are available: *Choose carefully before you make a final decision.* ◇ *Amy had to choose between getting a job or going to college.* ◇ *The viewers chose this programme as their favourite.* ▶ **wybierać 2 choose (to do sth)** to decide or prefer to do sth: *You are free to leave whenever you choose* (kiedy tylko zechcesz). ◇ *They chose to resign rather than work for the new manager.* ▶ **decydować się, woleć** ➲ noun **choice**
IDM **pick and choose** → PICK[1]

choosy /ˈtʃuːzi/ adj. (**choosier**; **choosiest**) (informal) (used about a person) difficult to please ▶ **grymaśny, wybredny**

🔑 **chop**[1] /tʃɒp/ verb [T] (**chopping**; **chopped**) **chop sth (up) (into sth)** to cut sth into pieces with a knife, etc.: *Chop the onions up into small pieces.* ◇ *finely chopped herbs* ▶ **rąbać, siekać**
IDM **chop and change** to change your plans or opinions several times ▶ **często zmieniać zdanie**
PHR V **chop sth down** to cut a tree, etc. at the bottom so that it falls down ▶ **ścinać coś**

chop sth off (sth) to remove sth from sth by cutting it with a knife or a sharp tool ▶ **odcinać/odrąbywać coś (od czegoś)**

chop² /tʃɒp/ noun [C] **1** a thick slice of meat with a piece of bone in it ▶ **kotlet** (*z kością*) ➲ look at **steak** **2** an act of cutting sth with a quick downward movement using an **axe** or a knife ▶ **rąbanie** **3** an act of hitting sb/sth with the side of your hand in a quick downward movement: *a karate chop* cios karate ▶ **uderzenie**

chopper /ˈtʃɒpə(r)/ (informal) **1** = HELICOPTER **2** a large heavy knife or small **axe** ▶ **tasak**

ˈchopping board noun [C] a piece of wood or plastic used for cutting meat or vegetables on ▶ **deska do krojenia** ➲ picture at **kitchen**

choppy /ˈtʃɒpi/ adj. (**choppier**; **choppiest**) (used about the sea) having a lot of small waves; slightly rough ▶ (*morze*) **lekko wzburzony**

chopstick /ˈtʃɒpstɪk/ noun [C, usually pl.] either of a pair of thin sticks that are used for eating, especially in some Asian countries ▶ **pałeczka** (*do jedzenia*)

choral /ˈkɔːrəl/ adj. (used about music) that is written for or involving a **choir** ▶ **chóralny**

chorale /kɒˈrɑːl; US kəˈræl; -ˈrɑːl/ noun [C] a piece of church music sung by a group of singers ▶ **chorał**

chord /kɔːd/ noun [C] two or more musical notes that are played at the same time ▶ **akord**

chore /tʃɔː(r)/ noun [C] a job that is not interesting but that you must do: *household chores* prace domowe ▶ **robota**

choreograph /ˈkɒriəgrɑːf; -græf/ verb [T] to design and arrange the movements of a dance ▶ **układać choreografię**

■ **choreographer** /ˌkɒriˈɒgrəfə(r)/ noun [C] ▶ **choreograf**

choreography /ˌkɒriˈɒgrəfi/ noun [U] the arrangement of movements for a dance performance ▶ **choreografia**

chortle /ˈtʃɔːtl/ verb [I,T] to laugh loudly with pleasure or because you are amused: *Gill chortled with delight.* ▶ **rechotać**

■ **chortle** noun [C] ▶ **rechot**, **rechotanie**

chorus¹ /ˈkɔːrəs/ noun **1** [C] the part of a song that is repeated ▶ **refren** SYN **refrain** ➲ look at **verse** **2** [C] a piece of music, usually part of a larger work, that is written for a large **choir** ▶ **utwór chóralny** **3** [C, with sing. or pl. verb] a large group of people who sing together ▶ **chór** **4** [C, with sing. or pl. verb] the singers and dancers in a musical show who do not play the main parts ▶ **chór**, **chórek** **5** [sing.] **a chorus of sth** something that a lot of people say together: *a chorus of cheers/criticism/disapproval* ▶ **chór**

chorus² /ˈkɔːrəs/ verb [T] (used about a group of people) to sing or say sth together: *'That's not fair!' the children chorused.* ▶ **mówić/śpiewać chórem**

ˈchorus girl noun [C] a girl or young woman who is a member of the **chorus** in a musical show, etc. ▶ **dziewczyna, która występuje w zespole wokalno-tanecznym w musicalu**

chose past tense of **choose**

chosen past participle of **choose**

Christ /kraɪst/ (also **Jesus** /ˈdʒiːzəs/, **Jesus Christ**) noun [sing.] the man who Christians believe is the son of God and on whose ideas and beliefs the Christian religion is based ▶ **Chrystus**

christen /ˈkrɪsn/ verb [T] **1** to give a person, usually a baby, a name during a Christian ceremony in which they are made a member of the Church: *The baby was christened Simon Mark.* ▶ **chrzcić** ➲ look at **baptize** **2** to give sb/sth a name: *People drive so dangerously on this stretch of road that they've christened it 'The Mad Mile'.* ▶ **nadawać imię**

christening /ˈkrɪsnɪŋ/ noun [C] the church ceremony in the Christian religion in which a baby is given a name ▶ **chrzciny** ➲ look at **baptism**

Christian /ˈkrɪstʃən/ noun [C] a person whose religion is Christianity ▶ **chrześcijan-in/ka**

■ **Christian** adj. ▶ **chrześcijański**

Christianity /ˌkrɪstiˈænəti/ noun [U] the religion that is based on the ideas taught by Jesus Christ ▶ **chrześcijaństwo**

ˈChristian name noun [C] the name given to a child when they are born; first name ▶ **imię** ➲ note at **name**

Christmas /ˈkrɪsməs/ noun **1** (also ˌ**Christmas ˈDay**) [C] a public holiday on 25 December. It is the day on which Christians celebrate the birth of Christ each year. ▶ **dzień Bożego Narodzenia** **2** [C,U] the period of time before and after 25 December: *Where are you spending Christmas this year?* ▶ **Święta Bożego Narodzenia**

ⓘ **Christmas** czasami jest zapisywane w nieformalnym języku jako **Xmas**.

ˈChristmas cake noun [C, U] a fruit cake covered with **marzipan** and **icing**, traditionally eaten at Christmas ▶ **tradycyjne ciasto bożonarodzeniowe**

ˈChristmas card noun [C] a card with a picture on the front and a message inside that people send to their friends and relatives at Christmas ▶ **kartka świąteczna** (*z okazji Bożego Narodzenia*)

ˌChristmas ˈcarol = CAROL

ˌChristmas ˈcracker = CRACKER (2)

ˌChristmas ˈdinner noun [C] the traditional meal eaten on Christmas Day: *We had a traditional Christmas dinner that year, with roast turkey, Christmas pudding and all the trimmings.* ▶ **tradycyjny bożonarodzeniowy obiad**

ˌChristmas ˈEve noun [C] 24 December; the day before Christmas Day ▶ **Wigilia**

ˌChristmas ˈpudding noun [C,U] a sweet dish made from dried fruit and eaten hot with sauce at Christmas ▶ **tradycyjny bożonarodzeniowy deser**

ˌChristmas ˈstocking noun [C] a long sock which children leave out when they go to bed on Christmas Eve so that it can be filled with presents ▶ **długa skarpeta na prezenty bożonarodzeniowe**

ˈChristmas tree noun [C] a real or an artificial tree, which people bring into their homes and cover with coloured lights and decorations at Christmas ▶ **choinka**

chromatic /krəˈmætɪk/ adj. of the **chromatic scale**, a series of musical notes that rise and fall in **semitones** ▶ **chromatyczny**

chrome /krəʊm/ (also **chromium** /ˈkrəʊmiəm/) noun [U] a hard shiny metal that is used for covering other metals ▶ **chrom**

chromosome /ˈkrəʊməsəʊm/ noun [C] a part of a cell in living things that decides the sex, character, shape, etc. that a person, an animal or a plant will have ▶ **chromosom**

chronic /ˈkrɒnɪk/ adj. (used about a disease or a problem) that continues for a long time: *There is a chronic shortage of housing in the city.* ▶ **przewlekły**, **stały** ➲ look at **acute**

■ **chronically** /-kli/ adv. ▶ **przewlekle**

ˌchronic faˈtigue syndrome = ME

chronicle /ˈkrɒnɪkl/ noun [C, often plural] a written record of historical events describing them in the order in which they happened ▶ **kronika**

chronological /ˌkrɒnəˈlɒdʒɪkl/ adj. arranged in the order in which the events happened: *This book describes*

the main events in his life ***in chronological order.*** ▶ **chronologiczny**
■ **chronologically** /-kli/ adv. ▶ **chronologicznie**

chronology /krəˈnɒlədʒi/ noun [U,C] (pl. **chronologies**) the order in which a series of events happened; a list of these events in order: *Historians seem to have confused the chronology of these events.* ▶ **chronologia**

chrysalis /ˈkrɪsəlɪs/ noun [C] the form of a **butterfly** or a **moth** while it is changing into an adult inside a hard case, which is also called a chrysalis ▶ **poczwarka** ➲ picture at **insect**

chrysanthemum /krɪˈsænθəməm/ noun [C] a large garden flower which is brightly coloured and shaped like a ball ▶ **chryzantema**, **złocień**

chubby /ˈtʃʌbi/ adj. (**chubbier**; **chubbiest**) slightly fat in a pleasant way: *a baby with chubby cheeks* ▶ **pucołowaty**, **pyzaty** ➲ note at **fat**

chuck /tʃʌk/ verb [T] (informal) to throw sth in a careless way: *Chuck that magazine over here.* ◇ *You can chuck those old shoes in the bin.* Możesz wyrzucić te stare buty do kosza. ▶ **ciskać**
PHR V **chuck sth away/out** to throw sth away: *Those old clothes can be chucked out.* ▶ **wyrzucać coś**
chuck sth in to give sth up: *He's chucked his job in because he was fed up.* ▶ **rzucać** (*np. pracę, studia*)
chuck sb out (of sth) to force sb to leave a place ▶ **wyrzucać kogoś (skądś)**

chuckle /ˈtʃʌkl/ verb [I] to laugh quietly: *Bruce chuckled to himself as he read the letter.* ▶ **chichotać** ➲ look at **giggle**
■ **chuckle** noun [C] ▶ **chichot**

chuffed /tʃʌft/ adj. [not before a noun] **chuffed (about sth)** (Brit., informal) very pleased: *He was chuffed to bits to learn that he had won.* Nie posiadał się z radości, gdy się dowiedział, że wygrał. ▶ **bardzo szczęśliwy**

chug /tʃʌg/ verb [I] (**chugging**; **chugged**) **1** (used about a machine or engine) to make short repeated sounds while it is working or moving slowly ▶ **sapać**, **stukać** **2 chug along, down, up, etc.** to move in a particular direction making this sound: *The train chugged out of the station.* ▶ **toczyć się, posapując**

chum /tʃʌm/ noun [C] (old-fashioned, informal) a friend ▶ **kumpel**

chunk /tʃʌŋk/ noun [C] a large or thick piece of sth: *chunks of bread and cheese* ▶ **kawał(ek)**

chunky /ˈtʃʌŋki/ adj. (**chunkier**; **chunkiest**) **1** thick and heavy ▶ (*sweter itp.*) **gruby**, (*biżuteria*) **ciężki** **2** (used about a person) short and strong: *He was a short man with chunky legs.* ▶ **przysadzisty**, **krępy** **3** (used about food) containing thick pieces: *chunky banana milkshake* ▶ **z kawałkami** (*np. owoców*)

🔑 **church** /tʃɜːtʃ/ noun **1** [C,U] a building where Christians go to worship: *Do you go to church regularly?* ▶ **kościół**
ℹ Zwróć uwagę, że w jęz. ang., mówiąc o chodzeniu do kościoła w celu uczestniczenia w praktykach religijnych, nie stosuje się żadnego przedimka – **in church, to church** czy **at church**: *Was Mrs Stevens at church today?*
2 (**Church**) [C] a particular group of Christians: *the Anglican/Catholic/Methodist/Church* ▶ **Kościół** **3** ((**the**) **Church**) [sing., U] the ministers or the institution of the Christian religion: *the conflict between Church and State* ▶ **Kościół**

churchgoer /ˈtʃɜːtʃɡəʊə(r)/ noun [C] a person who goes to church regularly ▶ **osoba religijna/praktykująca**

the ˌ**Church of ˈEngland** (abbr. **C. of E.** /ˌsiː əv ˈiː/) noun [sing.] the Protestant Church, which is the official church in England, whose leader is the Queen or King ▶ **Kościół anglikański** ➲ look at **Anglican**

churchyard /ˈtʃɜːtʃjɑːd/ noun [C] the area of land that is around a church ▶ **dziedziniec kościelny** ➲ look at **cemetery**, **graveyard**

churlish /ˈtʃɜːlɪʃ/ adj. (formal) rude or bad-tempered: *It would be churlish to refuse such a generous offer.* ▶ **grubiański**

churn /tʃɜːn/ verb **1** [I,T] **churn (sth) (up)** to move, or to make water, mud, etc. move around violently: *The dark water churned beneath the huge ship.* ◇ *Vast crowds had churned the field into a sea of mud.* ▶ **wzburzać (się)** **2** [I,T] if your stomach **churns** or sth makes it **churn**, you feel sick because you are disgusted or nervous: *Reading about the murder in the paper made my stomach churn* (robiło mi się niedobrze). ▶ **mdlić**; **przyprawiać o mdłości** **3** [T] to make butter from milk or cream ▶ **ubijać masło**
PHR V **churn sth out** (informal) to produce large numbers of sth very quickly: *Modern factories can churn out cars at an amazing speed.* ▶ **produkować coś szybko i w dużych ilościach**

chute /ʃuːt/ noun [C] a passage down which you can drop or slide things, so that you do not have to carry them: *a laundry/rubbish chute* ◇ *a water chute* zjeżdżalnia (na basenie) ▶ **zsyp**, **rynna**

chutney /ˈtʃʌtni/ noun [U,C] a thick sweet sauce that is made from fruit or vegetables. You eat **chutney** cold with cheese or meat. ▶ **gęsty i ostry sos owocowy lub warzywny do serów lub mięsa**

CIA /ˌsiː aɪ ˈeɪ/ abbr. **the Central Intelligence Agency**; the US government organization that tries to discover secret information about other countries ▶ **Centralna Agencja Wywiadowcza**

ciabatta /tʃəˈbætə/ noun [U,C] a type of heavy Italian bread; a **loaf** of this ▶ **bułka/chlebek ciabatta**

cicada /sɪˈkɑːdə; US -ˈkeɪd-/ noun [C] a large insect with transparent wings, common in hot countries. The male makes a continuous high sound after dark by making two **membranes** on its body **vibrate**. ▶ **cykada**

cider /ˈsaɪdə(r)/ noun [U,C] **1** (Brit.) an alcoholic drink made from apples: *dry/sweet cider* ▶ **jabłecznik**, **cydr** **2** (US) a drink made from apples that does not contain alcohol ▶ **napój jabłkowy**

cigar /sɪˈɡɑː(r)/ noun [C] a thick roll of **tobacco** that people smoke. **Cigars** are larger than cigarettes ▶ **cygaro**

🔑 **cigarette** /ˌsɪɡəˈret/ noun [C] a thin tube of white paper filled with **tobacco** that people smoke: *a packet/pack of cigarettes* ▶ **papieros**

cigaˈrette lighter (also **lighter** /ˈlaɪtə(r)/) noun [C] an object which produces a small flame for lighting cigarettes, etc. ▶ **zapalniczka**

cinch /sɪntʃ/ noun [sing.] (informal) something that is very easy: *The first question is a cinch.* ▶ **pestka**, **łatwizna** SYN **doddle**

cinder /ˈsɪndə(r)/ noun [C] a small piece of **ash** or partly burnt coal, wood, etc. that is no longer burning but may still be hot ▶ **żużel**; **popiół**

🔑 **cinema** /ˈsɪnəmə/ noun **1** [C] (Brit.) a place where you go to see a film: *Let's go to the cinema this evening.* ◇ *What's on at the cinema this week?* ▶ **kino** **2** [U] films in general; the film industry: *one of the great successes of British cinema* ▶ **film**, **kino** ➲ note at **film**

> W Amer. ang. **movie theater** oznacza budynek, w którym są wyświetlane filmy: *There are five movie theaters in this town.* **The movies** używa się, kiedy wybieramy się obejrzeć film: *Let's go to the movies this evening.*

ˈ**cinema-goer** = FILM-GOER

cinematic /ˌsɪnəˈmætɪk/ adj. connected with films and how they are made: *cinematic effects/techniques* ▶ **kinematograficzny**

cinematography /ˌsɪnəməˈtɒɡrəfi/ noun [U] the art or process of making films ▶ **kinematografia**
■ **cinematographic** /ˌsɪnəmætəˈɡræfɪk/ adj. ▶ **kinematograficzny**

cinnamon /ˈsɪnəmən/ noun [U] a sweet brown powder that is used as a spice in cooking ▶ **cynamon** ➲ picture on **page A12**

circa /ˈsɜːkə/ prep. (abbr. **c**) (formal) (used with dates) about; approximately: *The vase was made circa 600 AD.* ▶ **około**

⚷ **circle¹** /ˈsɜːkl/ noun **1** [C] a flat, round area ▶ **koło 2** [C] a round shape like a ring; a line which curves round to form the shape of a ring. Every point on the line is the same distance from the centre: *The children were drawing circles and squares on a piece of paper.* ◇ *We all stood in a circle and held hands.* ▶ **kółko, krąg 3** (**the (dress) circle**) (US **balcony**) [sing.] an area of seats that is upstairs in a cinema, theatre, etc.: *We've booked seats in the front row of the circle.* ▶ **balkon** ❶ Por. **balcony**, który znajduje się wyżej niż **circle. 4** [C] a group of people who are friends, or who have the same interest or profession: *He has a large circle of friends.* ◇ *Her name was well known in artistic circles.* ▶ **koło**
IDM **a vicious circle** → VICIOUS

circle² /ˈsɜːkl/ verb **1** [I,T] to move, or to move round sth, in a circle, especially in the air: *The plane circled the town several times before it landed.* ▶ **krążyć 2** [T] to draw a circle round sth: *There are three possible answers to each question. Please circle the correct one.* ▶ **zakreślać**

circuit /ˈsɜːkɪt/ noun **1** [C] a journey, route or track that forms a circle: *The cars have to complete ten circuits of the track.* ◇ *a racing circuit* ▶ **okrążenie**; **tor**, **bieżnia 2** [C] the complete path of wires and equipment that an electric current flows around ▶ **obwód 3** [sing.] regular events of a particular kind of activity (e.g. a particular type of sport) that are held in different places: *She's one of the best players on the tennis circuit.* To jedna z najlepszych zawodniczek w świecie tenisa. ◇ *He's made a name for himself on the lecture circuit.* Słynie ze swoich wykładów wygłaszanych na całym świecie. ▶ **seria** (*np. rozgrywek sportowych*)

circuitous /səˈkjuːɪtəs/ adj. (formal) (of a route or journey) long and not direct: *He took us on a circuitous route to the hotel.* ▶ (*trasa*) **okrężny** SYN **roundabout**

circular¹ /ˈsɜːkjələ(r)/ adj. **1** round and flat; shaped like a circle: *a circular table* ▶ **okrągły 2** (used about a journey, etc.) moving round in a circle: *a circular tour of Oxford* ▶ **okrężny**

circular² /ˈsɜːkjələ(r)/ noun [C] a printed letter, notice or advertisement that is sent to a large number of people ▶ **okólnik**; **ulotka reklamowa**

circulate /ˈsɜːkjəleɪt/ verb [I,T] **1** (used about a substance) to move or make sth move round continuously: *Blood circulates round the body.* ▶ **krążyć**; **utrzymywać cyrkulację 2** to go or be passed from one person to another: *Rumours were circulating about the Minister's private life.* ◇ *We've circulated a copy of the report to each department.* ▶ **krążyć**; **puszczać w obieg**

circulation /ˌsɜːkjəˈleɪʃn/ noun **1** [U] the movement of blood around the body ▶ **krążenie krwi 2** [U] the passing of sth from one person or place to another: *Old five pence coins are no longer in circulation.* ◇ *the circulation* (przepływ) *of news/information/rumours* ▶ **obieg 3** [C] the number of copies of a newspaper, magazine, etc. that are sold each time it is produced: *This newspaper has a circulation of over a million.* ▶ **nakład**

circumcise /ˈsɜːkəmsaɪz/ verb [T] to cut off the skin at the end of a man's **penis** or to remove part of a woman's **clitoris**, for religious or sometimes (in the case of a man) medical reasons ▶ **obrzezywać**
■ **circumcision** /ˌsɜːkəmˈsɪʒn/ noun [C,U] ▶ **obrzezanie**

circumference /səˈkʌmfərəns/ noun [C,U] the distance round a circle or sth in the shape of a circle: *The Earth is about 40 000 kilometres* ***in circumference.*** ▶ **obwód** ➲ look at **diameter**, **radius**

circumspect /ˈsɜːkəmspekt/ adj. (formal) thinking very carefully about sth before doing it, because there may be risks involved: *He was very circumspect in his financial affairs.* ▶ **ostrożny**, **powściągliwy** SYN **cautious**

⚷ **circumstance** /ˈsɜːkəmstəns; -stɑːns; -stæns; US -stæns/ noun **1** [C, usually pl.] the facts and events that affect what happens in a particular situation: *Police said there were no* ***suspicious circumstances*** *surrounding the boy's death.* ◇ *In normal circumstances I would not have accepted the job, but at that time I had very little money.* ▶ **okoliczność 2** (**circumstances**) [pl.] (formal) the amount of money that you have: *The company has promised to repay the money when its financial circumstances improve.* ▶ **położenie**
IDM **in/under no circumstances** never; not for any reason: *Under no circumstances should you enter my office.* ▶ **w żadnym wypadku**
in/under the circumstances as the result of a particular situation: *It's not an ideal solution, but it's the best we can do in the circumstances.* ◇ *My father was ill at that time, so under the circumstances I decided not to go on holiday.* ▶ **w tych okolicznościach**

circumstantial /ˌsɜːkəmˈstænʃl/ adj. (used in connection with the law) containing details and information that strongly suggest sth is true but are not actual proof of it: *They had only circumstantial evidence.* ▶ **poszlakowy**

circumvent /ˌsɜːkəmˈvent/ verb [T] (formal) **1** to find a way of avoiding a difficulty or a rule: *They found a way of circumventing the law.* ▶ **omijać** (*np. prawo*) **2** to go or travel around sth that is blocking your way ▶ **obchodzić** (*np. przeszkodę*)
■ **circumvention** /ˌsɜːkəmˈvenʃn/ noun [U] ▶ **ominięcie**; **obejście**

circus /ˈsɜːkəs/ noun [C] a show performed in a large tent by a company of people and animals ▶ **cyrk**

cirrhosis /səˈrəʊsɪs/ noun [U] a serious disease of the **liver**, caused especially by drinking too much alcohol ▶ **marskość wątroby**

CIS /ˌsiː aɪ ˈes/ abbr. **the Commonwealth of Independent States** (a group of independent countries that were part of the Soviet Union until 1991) ▶ **Wspólnota Niepodległych Państw**

cistern /ˈsɪstən/ noun [C] a container for storing water, especially one that is connected to a toilet ▶ **zbiornik** (*na wodę*), **rezerwuar klozetowy**

citation /saɪˈteɪʃn/ noun **1** [C] words or lines taken from a book or a speech ▶ **cytat** SYN **quotation 2** [C] an official statement about sth special that sb has done, especially about acts of courage in a war: *a citation for bravery* ▶ **oficjalna pochwała 3** [U] (formal) an act of **citing** or being **cited**: *Space does not permit the citation of any examples.* ▶ **cytowanie**

cite /saɪt/ verb [T] (formal) to mention sth or use sb's exact words as an example to support, or as proof of, what you are saying: *She cited a passage from the President's speech.* ▶ **cytować**

⚷ **citizen** /ˈsɪtɪzn/ noun [C] **1** a person who is legally accepted as a member of a particular country ▶ **obywatel/ka 2** a person who lives in a town or city: *the citizens of Paris* ▶ **mieszkan-iec/ka miasta** ➲ look at **senior citizen**

citizenship /ˈsɪtɪzənʃɪp/ noun [U] the state of being a citizen of a particular country: *After living in Spain for twenty years, he decided to apply for Spanish citizenship.* ▶ **obywatelstwo**

citric /ˈsɪtrɪk/ adj. relating to fruit such as oranges and lemons ▶ **cytrynowy**

citrus /ˈsɪtrəs/ adj. (used to describe fruit such as oranges and lemons) ▶ **cytrusowy**

city /ˈsɪti/ noun (pl. **cities**) **1** [C] a large and important town: *Venice is one of the most beautiful cities in the world.* ◇ *the city centre* ◇ *Many people are worried about housing conditions in Britain's inner cities* (w centralnych dzielnicach brytyjskich miast, które często są siedliskiem problemów społecznych). ▶ **miasto 2** (**the City**) [sing.] the oldest part of London, which is now Britain's financial centre: *a City stockbroker* ▶ **centrum finansowe Londynu**

> **city life**
> Life in the **city** can be **hectic**. People are often **in a hurry** and the **streets** are **crowded** and **noisy**. There is a lot of **traffic** so the air is **polluted**. Many people live in **flats** (US **apartments**), and if you live in the **suburbs**, you spend a lot of time **commuting**. But cities are also **lively** places. There are restaurants, shops, theatres, museums and **sports facilities** (such as stadiums and swimming pools). Many cities are **cosmopolitan**.

civic /ˈsɪvɪk/ adj. officially connected with a city or town: *civic duties/pride* ◇ *Guildford Civic Centre* Urząd Miejski w Guildford ℹ W **civic centre** często znajduje się biblioteka, sala teatralna itp. ▶ **miejski**, **obywatelski**

civil /ˈsɪvl/ adj. **1** [only before a noun] connected with the people who live in a country: *civil disorder* ▶ **społeczny**, **obywatelski 2** [only before a noun] connected with the state, not with the army or the Church: *a civil wedding* ▶ **cywilny 3** [only before a noun] (in law) connected with the personal legal matters of ordinary people, and not criminal law: *civil courts* ▶ **cywilny 4** polite, but not very friendly: *I know you don't like the director, but do try and be civil to him.* ▶ **uprzejmy**, **poprawny**
■ **civilly** /ˈsɪvəli/ adv. ▶ **uprzejmie**

ˌcivil disoˈbedience noun [U] refusal by a large group of people to obey particular laws or pay taxes, usually as a form of peaceful political protest ▶ **nieposłuszeństwo obywatelskie**

ˌcivil engiˈneering noun [U] the design, building and repair of roads, bridges, **canals**, etc.; the study of this as a subject ▶ **inżynieria wodno-lądowa**
■ **ˌcivil engiˈneer** noun [C] ▶ **inżynier budownictwa wodno-lądowego**

civilian /səˈvɪliən/ noun [C] a person who is not in the army, navy, air force or police force ▶ **cywil**

civilization (also **-isation**) /ˌsɪvəlaɪˈzeɪʃn; US -ləˈz-/ noun **1** [U] an advanced state of social and cultural development, or the process of reaching this state: *the civilization of the human race* ▶ **cywilizacja 2** [C,U] a society which has its own highly developed culture and way of life: *the civilizations of ancient Greece and Rome* ◇ *Western civilization* ▶ **cywilizacja 3** [U] all the people in the world and the societies they live in considered as a whole: *Global warming poses a threat to the whole of civilization.* ▶ **ludzkość**

civilize (also **-ise**) /ˈsɪvəlaɪz/ verb [T] to make people or a society develop from a low social and cultural level to a more advanced one ▶ **cywilizować**

civilized (also **-ised**) /ˈsɪvəlaɪzd/ adj. **1** (used about a society) well organized; having a high level of social and cultural development ▶ **cywilizowany 2** polite and reasonable: *a civilized conversation* ▶ **kulturalny**

ˌcivil ˈlaw noun [U] law that deals with the rights of private citizens rather than with crime ▶ **prawo cywilne**

ˌcivil ˈliberty noun [C, usually pl., U] the right of people to be free to say or do what they want while respecting others and staying within the law: *an infringement of our civil liberties* ▶ **swobody obywatelskie**

ˌcivil ˈmarriage noun [C] a marriage with no religious ceremony ▶ **ślub cywilny**

ˌcivil ˈrights noun [pl.] sb's legal right to freedom and equal treatment in society, whatever their sex, race or religion: *the civil rights leader Martin Luther King* ▶ **prawa obywatelskie**

ˌcivil ˈservant noun [C] (especially Brit.) a person who works for **the civil service** ▶ **urzędnik państwowy**

the **ˌcivil ˈservice** noun [sing.] all the government departments (except for the armed forces) and all the people who work in them ▶ **administracja państwowa**; **służba cywilna**

ˌcivil ˈwar noun [C,U] a war between groups of people who live in the same country ▶ **wojna domowa**

CJD /ˌsiː dʒeɪ ˈdiː/ abbr. **Creutzfeldt-Jakob disease**; a disease of the brain caused by eating infected meat ▶ **choroba Creutzfeldta-Jakoba** ➲ look at **BSE**

cl = CENTILITRE

clack /klæk/ verb [I] if two hard objects **clack**, they make a short loud sound when they hit each other: *Her heels clacked on the marble floor.* ▶ **stukać**, **terkotać**
■ **clack** noun [sing.] ▶ **stuk**, **terkot**

clad /klæd/ adj. [not before a noun] (old-fashioned) dressed (in); wearing a particular type of clothing: *The children were warmly clad in coats, hats and scarves.* ▶ **odziany**

claim[1] /kleɪm/ verb **1** [T] **claim (that ...)**; **claim (to be sth)** to say that sth is true, without having any proof: *Colin claims the book belongs to him.* ◇ *The woman claims to be the oldest person in Britain.* ▶ **twierdzić 2** [I,T] **claim (for sth)** to ask for sth from the government, a company, etc. because you think it is your legal right to have it, or it belongs to you: *He is not entitled to claim unemployment benefit.* ◇ *Don't forget to claim for your travel expenses when you get back.* ◇ *The police are keeping the animal until somebody claims it* (dopóki ktoś się po nie nie zgłosi). ◇ (figurative) *No one has claimed responsibility for the bomb attack.* Nikt nie przyznał się do dokonania ataku bombowego. ▶ **ubiegać się (o coś) 3** [T] to cause death: *The earthquake claimed thousands of lives.* ▶ **pochłaniać** (*ofiary*)

claim[2] /kleɪm/ noun [C] **1 a claim (that ...)** a statement that sth is true, which does not have any proof: *I do not believe the Government's claim that they can reduce unemployment by the end of the year.* ▶ **twierdzenie 2 a claim (to sth)** the right to have sth: *You will have to prove your claim to the property in a court of law.* ◇ *a claim* (pretensja) *to the throne* ▶ **prawo (do czegoś)**, **roszczenie 3 a claim (for sth)** a demand for money that you think you have a right to, especially from the government, a company, etc.: *a pay claim* ◇ *to make an insurance claim* ◇ *After the accident he decided to put in a claim for compensation* (złożył wniosek o odszkodowanie). ▶ **wystąpienie o coś**, **roszczenie**
IDM **stake a/your claim** → STAKE[2]

claimant /ˈkleɪmənt/ noun [C] a person who believes they have the right to have sth: *The insurance company refused to pay the claimant any money.* ▶ **osoba zgłaszająca roszczenia**

clairvoyant /kleəˈvɔɪənt/ noun [C] a person who some people believe has special mental powers and can see what will happen in the future ▶ **jasnowidz**

clam[1] /klæm/ noun [C] a **shellfish** that you can eat ▶ **małż jadalny**

clam[2] /klæm/ verb (**clamming**; **clammed**)

PHR V **clam up (on sb)** (informal) to stop talking and refuse to speak, especially when sb asks you about sth ▶ **zamykać się w sobie, przestawać mówić**

clamber /ˈklæmbə(r)/ verb [I] **clamber up, down, out etc.** to move or climb with difficulty, usually using both your hands and feet: *She managed to clamber up and over the wall.* ▶ **wdrapywać się, gramolić się**

clammy /ˈklæmi/ adj. (**clammier**; **clammiest**) damp in an unpleasant way: *clammy hands* ▶ **wilgotny** (*w nieprzyjemny sposób*)

clamour (US **clamor**) /ˈklæmə(r)/ verb [I] **clamour for sth** to demand sth in a loud or angry way: *The public are clamouring for an answer to all these questions.* ▶ **domagać się czegoś podniesionym i/lub rozzłoszczonym głosem**

■ **clamour** (US **clamor**) noun [sing.]: *the clamour of angry voices* ▶ **wrzawa**

clamp¹ /klæmp/ verb [T] **1 clamp A and B (together)**; **clamp A to B** to fasten two things together with a **clamp**: *The metal rods were clamped together.* ◇ *Clamp the wood to the table so that it doesn't move.* ▶ **spinać klamrą, przytwierdzać 2** to hold sth very firmly in a particular position: *Her lips were clamped tightly together.* ▶ **ściskać, zaciskać 3** to fix a metal object to the wheel of a vehicle that has been parked illegally, so that it cannot move: *Oh no! My car's been clamped.* ▶ **nakładać blokadę kół**

PHR V **clamp down on sb/sth** (informal) to take strong action in order to stop or control sth: *The police are clamping down on people who drink and drive.* ▶ **brać się za kogoś/coś**

clamp² /klæmp/ noun [C] **1** a tool that you use for holding two things together very tightly ▶ **klamra 2** (also ˈ**wheel clamp**) (Brit.) a metal object that is fixed to the wheel of a car that has been parked illegally, so that it cannot drive away ▶ **blokada** (*na koła*)

clampdown /ˈklæmpdaʊn/ noun [C] strong action to stop or control sth: *a clampdown on tax evasion* ▶ **zdecydowana akcja (*np. policyjna*) przeciwko komuś/czemuś**

clan /klæn/ noun [C, with sing. or pl. verb] a group of families who are related to each other, especially in Scotland ▶ **klan**

clandestine /klænˈdestɪn/ adj. (formal) secret and often not legal: *a clandestine meeting* ▶ **podziemny, potajemny**

clang /klæŋ/ verb [I,T] to make or cause sth metal to make a loud ringing sound: *The iron gates clanged shut.* ▶ **brzęczeć; szczękać**

■ **clang** noun [C] ▶ **brzęk**

clank /klæŋk/ verb [I,T] to make or cause sth metal to make a loud unpleasant sound: *The lift clanked its way up to the seventh floor.* ▶ **szczękać; pobrzękiwać**

■ **clank** noun [C] ▶ **szczęk**

⚷ **clap¹** /klæp/ verb (**clapping**; **clapped**) **1** [I,T] to hit your hands together many times, usually to show that you like sth: *The audience clapped as soon as the singer walked onto the stage.* ▶ **klaskać 2** [T] to put sth onto sth quickly and firmly: *'Oh no, I shouldn't have said that,' she said, clapping a hand over her mouth.* ▶ **szybko nakładać**

⚷ **clap²** /klæp/ noun [C] **1** an act of **clapping**: *Let's have a big clap for our next performer!* ▶ **oklaski 2** a sudden loud noise: *a clap of thunder* grzmot ▶ **huk**

claret /ˈklærət/ noun **1** [C,U] a red wine from Bordeaux in France ▶ **bordo 2** [U] a dark red colour ▶ **kolor bordo**

clarification /ˌklærəfɪˈkeɪʃn/ noun [U,C] an act of making sth clear and easier to understand: *We'd like some clarification of exactly what your company intends to do.* ▶ **wyjaśnienie** ➲ look at **clarity**

clarify /ˈklærəfaɪ/ verb [T] (**clarifying**; **clarifies**; pt, pp **clarified**) to make sth become clear and easier to understand: *I hope that what I say will clarify the situation.* ▶ **wyjaśniać** ➲ adjective **clear**

clarinet /ˌklærəˈnet/ noun [C] a musical instrument that is made of wood. You play a **clarinet** by blowing through it. ▶ **klarnet** ➲ note at **music**, **piano**

clarity /ˈklærəti/ noun [U] the quality of being clear and easy to understand: *clarity of expression* ▶ **jasność** ➲ look at **clarification**

clash¹ /klæʃ/ verb **1** [I] **clash (with sb) (over sth)** to fight or disagree seriously about sth: *A group of demonstrators clashed with police outside the Town Hall.* ▶ **ścierać się 2** [I] **clash (with sth)** (used about two events) to happen at the same time: *It's a pity the two concerts clash. I wanted to go to both of them.* ▶ **nakładać się na siebie 3** [I] **clash (with sth)** (used about colours, etc.) to not match or look nice together: *I don't think you should wear that tie – it clashes with your shirt.* ▶ **gryźć się, nie pasować do siebie 4** [I,T] (used about two metal objects) to hit together with a loud noise; to cause two metal objects to do this: *Their swords clashed.* ▶ **zderzać (się), dźwięczeć**

clash² /klæʃ/ noun [C] **1** a fight or serious disagreement: *a clash between police and demonstrators* ▶ **starcie 2** a big difference: *a clash of opinions* ◇ *There was a personality clash* (niezgodność charakterów) *between the two men.* ▶ **sprzeczność, konflikt 3** a loud noise, made by two metal objects hitting each other ▶ **brzęk**

clasp¹ /klɑːsp; US klæsp/ verb [T] to hold sb/sth tightly: *Kevin clasped the child in his arms.* ▶ **ściskać**

clasp² /klɑːsp; US klæsp/ noun [C] an object, usually of metal, which fastens or holds sth together: *the clasp on a necklace/brooch/handbag* ▶ **zatrzask, zapinka, zameczek**

⚷ **class¹** /klɑːs; US klæs/ noun **1** [C, with sing. or pl. verb] a group of students who are taught together: *Jane and I are in the same class at school.* ▶ **klasa, grupa 2** [C,U] a lesson: *Classes begin at 9 o'clock in the morning.* ◇ *We watched an interesting video in class yesterday.* ▶ **lekcja, zajęcia 3** [C, with sing. or pl. verb, U] the way that people are divided into social groups; one of these groups: *the working/middle/upper class* ◇ *The idea of class still divides British society.* ◇ *class differences* ▶ **klasa 4** [C] (technical) a group of animals, plants, words, etc. of a similar type ▶ **klasa 5** [U] (informal) high quality or style: *Pele was a football player of great class.* ▶ **klasa 6** [C] [in compounds] of a certain level of quality: *a first-class carriage on a train* ▶ **klasa 7** [C] [in compounds] (Brit.) a mark that you are given when you pass your final university exam: *a first/second/third-class degree* ▶ **stopień końcowy na studiach**

class² /klɑːs; US klæs/ verb [T] **class sb/sth (as sth)** to put sb/sth in a particular group or type: *Certain animals and plants are now classed as 'endangered species'.* ▶ **klasyfikować**

⚷ **classic¹** /ˈklæsɪk/ adj. **1** (used about a book, play, etc.) important and having a value that will last: *the classic film 'Gone With The Wind'* ▶ **klasyczny 2** typical: *It was a classic case of bad management.* ▶ **klasyczny**

⚷ **classic²** /ˈklæsɪk/ noun **1** [C] a famous book, play, etc. which has a value that will last: *All of Charles Dickens' novels are classics.* ▶ **dzieło klasyki 2** (**Classics**) [U] the study of ancient Greek and Roman language and literature: *a degree in Classics* ▶ **filologia klasyczna** ➲ note at **literature**

classical /ˈklæsɪkl/ adj. **1** traditional, not modern: *classical ballet* ▶ **klasyczny 2** connected with ancient Greece or Rome: *classical architecture* ▶ **klasyczny 3** (used about music) serious and having a value that lasts: *I prefer classical music to pop.* ▶ **poważny** ➲ note at **music** ➲ look at **jazz**, **pop**, **rock**

■ **classically** /-kli/ adv. ▶ **klasycznie**

classified /ˈklæsɪfaɪd/ adj. officially secret: *classified information* ▶ **tajny**

ˌ**classified adˈvertisement** (Brit., informal ˌclassified ˈad; ˈsmall ad) noun [C, usually pl.] a small advertisement that you put in a newspaper if you want to buy or sell sth, employ sb, find a flat, etc. ▶ **ogłoszenie drobne**

classify /ˈklæsɪfaɪ/ verb [T] (**classifying**; **classifies**; pt, pp **classified**) **classify sb/sth (as sth)** to put sb/sth into a group with other people or things of a similar type: *Would you classify it as an action film or a thriller?* ▶ **klasyfikować**
■ **classification** /ˌklæsɪfɪˈkeɪʃn/ noun [C,U] ▶ **klasyfikacja**

classmate /ˈklɑːsmeɪt; US ˈklæs-/ noun [C] a person who is in the same class as you at school or college ▶ **kolega**, **koleżanka** (*z klasy/grupy*)

🔑 **classroom** /ˈklɑːsruːm; -rʊm; US ˈklæs-/ noun [C] a room in a school, college, etc. where lessons are taught ▶ **klasa**

classy /ˈklɑːsi; US ˈklæsi/ adj. (**classier**; **classiest**) (informal) of high quality or style; expensive and fashionable: *a classy restaurant* ▶ **wytworny**

clatter /ˈklætə(r)/ verb [I,T] to make or cause sth hard to make a series of short loud repeated sounds: *The horses clattered down the street.* ▶ **stukotać**; **pobrzękiwać**
■ **clatter** noun [usually sing.] ▶ **stukot**, **łoskot**

clause /klɔːz/ noun [C] **1** a group of words that includes a subject and a verb. A **clause** is usually only part of a sentence: *The sentence 'After we had finished eating, we watched a film.' contains two clauses.* ▶ **zdanie** **2** one of the sections of a legal document that says that sth must or must not be done ▶ **klauzula**

claustrophobia /ˌklɔːstrəˈfəʊbiə/ noun [U] fear of being in a small space with walls on all sides ▶ **klaustrofobia**

claustrophobic /ˌklɔːstrəˈfəʊbɪk/ adj. **1** extremely afraid of small spaces with walls on all sides: *Hilary always feels claustrophobic in lifts.* ▶ **cierpiący na klaustrofobię** **2** (used about sth that makes you feel afraid in this way): *a claustrophobic little room* ▶ **klaustrofobiczny**

clavicle (formal) = COLLARBONE

claw¹ /klɔː/ noun [C] **1** one of the long curved nails on the end of an animal's or a bird's foot ▶ **pazur**, **szpon** ➲ picture on **page A10**, **page A11** **2** one of a pair of long, sharp fingers that certain types of **shellfish** and some insects have. They use them for holding or picking things up: *the claws* (kleszcze) *of a crab* ▶ **szczypce** ➲ picture on **page A11**

claw² /klɔː/ verb [I,T] **claw (at) sb/sth** to scratch or tear sb/sth with **claws** or with your nails: *The cat was clawing at the furniture.* ▶ **drapać** (*pazurami*)

clay /kleɪ/ noun [U] heavy earth that is soft and sticky when it is wet and becomes hard when it is baked or dried: *clay pots* ▶ **glina** ➲ picture at **pot**

🔑 **clean¹** /kliːn/ adj. **1** not dirty: *The whole house was beautifully clean.* ◊ *Cats are very clean animals.* ▶ **czysty** OPP **dirty** ➲ noun **cleanliness** **2** (used about humour) not about sex: *a clean joke* ▶ **przyzwoity** OPP **dirty** **3** having no record of offences or crimes: *a clean driving licence* prawo jazdy bez punktów karnych
IDM **a clean sweep** a complete victory in a sports competition, election, etc. that you get by winning all the different parts of it: *The Russians made a clean sweep of all the gymnastics events.* ▶ **całkowita wygrana**

🔑 **clean²** /kliːn/ verb [I,T] to make sth free from dust or dirt by washing or rubbing it: *to clean the windows* ◊ *Don't forget to clean your teeth!* ◊ *Linda comes in to clean* (sprzątać) *after office hours.* ▶ **czyścić**, **myć** ➲ look at **dry-clean**, **spring-clean** ℹ Często zamiast **clean** używa się **do the cleaning**: *I do the cleaning once a week.* Sprzątam raz na tydzień.
PHR V **clean sth out** to clean the inside of sth: *I'm going to clean out all the cupboards next week.* ▶ **wyczyścić** (*wnętrze czegoś*)
clean (sth) up **1** to remove all the dirt from a place that is particularly dirty: *I'm going to clean up the kitchen before Mum and Dad get back.* ▶ **(po)sprzątać (coś)** **2** to remove sth that has just been spilled: *Oh no, you've spilt coffee on the new carpet! Can you clean it up?* ▶ **wyczyścić (coś)**

clean

Clean jest słowem ogólnym i oznacza wszelkie usuwanie brudu z czegoś. **Wash** oznacza czyszczenie za pomocą wody i (często) mydła. **Wipe** oznacza czyszczenie powierzchni przez pocieranie jej wilgotną szmatką; z kolei **dust** to czyszczenie przez pocieranie powierzchni suchą szmatką. Użycie **brush** oznacza, że brud usuwa się szczotką; zaś **sweep** stosuje się wówczas, gdy do czyszczenia używa się miotły (np. do zamiatania podłogi). **Do the housework** oznacza „sprzątać dom".

clean³ /kliːn/ adv. (informal) completely: *I clean forgot it was your birthday.* ▶ **kompletnie**, **całkowicie**
IDM **come clean (with sb) (about sth)** (informal) to tell the truth about sth that you have been keeping secret: *She decided to come clean with Martin about her relationship with Trevor.* ▶ **przyznawać się (do czegoś)**, **wyrzucać coś z siebie**
go clean out of your mind to be completely forgotten ▶ **wypadać komuś z głowy**

cleaner /ˈkliːnə(r)/ noun **1** [C] a person whose job is to clean the rooms and furniture inside a house or other building: *an office cleaner* ▶ **sprzątacz/ka** **2** [C] a substance or a special machine that you use for cleaning sth: *liquid floor cleaners* ◊ *a carpet cleaner* ▶ **substancja lub przyrząd do czyszczenia** ➲ look at **vacuum cleaner** **3** (**the cleaner's**) = DRY-CLEANER'S

ˈ**cleaning lady** (also ˈ**cleaning woman**) noun [C] a woman whose job is to clean the rooms and furniture in an office, a house, etc. ▶ **sprzątaczka**

cleanliness /ˈklenlinəs/ noun [U] being clean or keeping things clean: *High standards of cleanliness are important in a hotel kitchen.* ▶ **czystość**

cleanly /ˈkliːnli/ adv. easily or smoothly in one movement: *The knife cut cleanly through the rope.* ▶ **równo**

cleanse /klenz/ verb [T] to clean your skin or a wound ▶ **oczyszczać** ➲ look at **ethnic cleansing**

cleanser /ˈklenzə(r)/ noun [C,U] a substance that you use for cleaning your skin, especially your face ▶ **płyn do zmywania twarzy**

ˌ**clean-ˈshaven** adj. (used about men) having recently shaved ▶ **gładko ogolony**

🔑 **clear¹** /klɪə(r)/ adj. **1 clear (to sb)** easy to understand; without doubt: *There are clear advantages to the second plan.* ◊ *It was clear to me that he was not telling the truth.* ◊ *She gave me clear directions on how to get there.* ▶ **jasny**, **oczywisty** **2 clear (about/on sth)** (used about a person) sure or definite; without any doubts or confusion: *I'm not quite clear about the arrangements for tomorrow.* ▶ **pewny** ➲ verb **clarify** **3** easy to see or hear: *His voice wasn't very clear on the telephone.* ▶ **wyraźny** **4** easy to see through: *The water was so clear that we could see the bottom of the lake.* ▶ **przejrzysty** **5** free from marks: *a clear sky* bezchmurne niebo ◊ *a clear skin* gładka cera ▶ **bez skazy** **6 clear (of sth)** free from things that are blocking the way: *The police say that most roads are now clear of snow* (odśnieżona). ▶ **wolny (od czegoś)** **7** not guilty: *a clear conscience* ▶ **czysty**

IDM make yourself clear; make sth clear (to sb) to speak so that there can be no doubt about what you mean: *'I do not want you to go to that concert,' said my mother. 'Do I make myself clear?'* ▶ **wyrażać się jasno**

clear² /klɪə(r)/ verb **1** [T] to remove sth that is not wanted or needed: *to clear the roads of snow/to clear snow from the roads* odśnieżać drogi ◇ *It's your turn to clear the table.* ▶ **usuwać, uprzątać 2** [I] (used about smoke, etc.) to disappear: *The fog slowly cleared and the sun came out.* ▶ **rozwiewać się 3** [I] (used about the sky, the weather or water) to become free of clouds, rain, or mud: *After a cloudy start, the weather will clear during the afternoon.* ▶ **przecierać się, rozjaśniać się 4** [T] **clear sb (of sth)** to provide proof that sb is innocent of sth: *The man has finally been cleared of murder.* ▶ **oczyszczać** (*z zarzutów*) **5** [T] to give official permission for a plane, ship, etc. to enter or leave a place: *At last the plane was cleared for take-off.* ▶ **przepuszczać, zezwalać 6** [T] **clear sth (with sb)** to get official approval for sth to be done: *I'll have to clear it with the manager before I can refund your money.* ▶ **uzyskać zgodę przełożonego na coś 7** [I] (used about a cheque) to go through the system that moves money from one account to another: *The cheque will take three days to clear.* ▶ (*czek*) **być zrealizowanym 8** [T] to jump over or get past sth without touching it: *The horse cleared the first jump but knocked down the second.* ▶ **przeskakiwać**

IDM clear the air to improve a difficult or tense situation by talking honestly about worries, doubts, etc. ▶ **oczyścić atmosferę**

clear your throat to cough slightly in order to make it easier to speak ▶ **odchrząkiwać**

PHR V clear off (informal) (used to tell sb to go away) ▶ **spływać, zjeżdżać**

clear sth out to tidy sth and throw away things that you do not want ▶ **wysprzątać coś**

clear up (used about the weather or an illness) to get better: *We can go out for a walk if it clears up later on.* ◇ *The doctor told him to stay at home until his cold cleared up.* ▶ **przecierać się, rozjaśniać się,** (*choroba*) **przechodzić**

clear (sth) up to make sth tidy: *Make sure you clear up properly before you leave.* ▶ **(po)sprzątać (coś)**

clear sth up to find the solution to a problem, cause of confusion, etc.: *There's been a slight misunderstanding but we've cleared it up now.* ▶ **rozwiązywać/wyjaśniać (coś)**

clear³ /klɪə(r)/ adv. **1** in a way that is easy to see or hear: *We can hear the telephone loud and clear from here.* ▶ **wyraźnie 2 clear (of sth)** away from sth; not touching sth: *Stand clear of the doors.* Proszę odsunąć się od drzwi. ▶ **z dala**

IDM keep/stay/steer clear (of sb/sth) to avoid sb/sth because they or it may cause problems: *It's best to keep clear of the town centre during the rush hour.* ▶ **trzymać się z daleka**

clearance /ˈklɪərəns/ noun [U] **1** the removing of sth that is old or not wanted: *The shop is having a clearance sale* (wyprzedaż). ▶ **usunięcie, oczyszczenie 2** the distance between an object and something that is passing under or beside it, for example a ship or vehicle: *There was not enough clearance for the bus to pass under the bridge safely.* ▶ (*miejsce*) **przejazd 3** official permission for sb/sth to do sth: *She was given clearance to work at the nuclear research establishment.* ▶ **zezwolenie**

ˌclear-ˈcut adj. definite and easy to see or understand: *It was a clear-cut case of police corruption.* ▶ **oczywisty**

ˌclear-ˈheaded adj. able to think clearly, especially if there is a problem ▶ **rozważny, roztropny**

clearing /ˈklɪərɪŋ/ noun [C] a small area without trees in the middle of a wood or forest ▶ **polana** ➲ look at **glade**

clearly /ˈklɪəli/ adv. **1** in a way that is easy to see or hear: *It was so foggy that we couldn't see the road clearly.* ▶ **wyraźnie 2** in a way that is sensible and easy to understand: *I'm so tired that I can't think clearly.* ▶ **jasno 3** without doubt: *She clearly* (najwyraźniej) *doesn't want to speak to you any more.* ▶ **oczywiście** **SYN obviously**

ˈclear-out noun [usually sing.] (especially Brit., informal) a process of getting rid of things or people that you no longer want: *to have a clear-out* robić generalne porządki ◇ *A staff clear-out* (zwolnienia pracowników) *is being planned at party headquarters.* ▶ **pozbywanie się czegoś; opróżnianie czegoś**

ˌclear-ˈsighted adj. able to understand situations well and to see what might happen in the future ▶ **trzeźwo/jasno myślący**

cleavage /ˈkliːvɪdʒ/ noun [C,U] the space between a woman's breasts ▶ **miejsce między piersiami kobiety, dekolt**

cleaver /ˈkliːvə(r)/ noun [C] a heavy knife with a broad blade, used for cutting large pieces of meat ▶ **tasak kuchenny**

clef /klef/ noun [C] (in music) a sign (𝄞, 𝄢) at the beginning of a line of written music that shows the area of sound that the notes are in: *the bass/treble clef* ▶ (*muz.*) **klucz** ➲ picture at **music**

ˌcleft ˈlip noun [C] a condition in which sb is born with their upper lip split ▶ **rozszczep wargi**

ˌcleft ˈpalate noun [C] a condition in which sb is born with the roof of their mouth split, making them unable to speak clearly ▶ **rozszczep podniebienia**

clematis /ˈklemətɪs; kləˈmeɪtɪs/ noun [C,U] a climbing plant with white, purple or pink flowers ▶ **powojnik**

clemency /ˈklemənsi/ noun [U] (formal) kindness shown to sb when they are being punished; willingness not to punish sb so severely: *a plea for clemency* prośba o łagodniejszy wymiar kary ▶ **prawo łaski** **SYN mercy**

clementine /ˈkleməntiːn/ noun [C] a type of small orange ▶ **klementynka**

clench /klentʃ/ verb [T] to close or hold tightly ▶ **zaciskać**

clergy /ˈklɜːdʒi/ noun [pl.] the people who perform religious ceremonies in the Christian church: *a member of the clergy* ▶ **duchowieństwo**

clergyman /ˈklɜːdʒimən/ noun [C] (pl. **-men** /-mən/) a male member of the **clergy** ▶ **duchowny** ➲ note at **priest**

clergywoman /ˈklɜːdʒiwʊmən/ noun [C] (pl. **-women** /-wɪmɪn/) a female member of the **clergy** ▶ **kobieta pastor**

clerical /ˈklerɪkl/ adj. **1** connected with the work of a **clerk** in an office: *clerical work* ▶ **biurowy 2** connected with the **clergy** ▶ **duchowny, klerykalny**

clerk /klɑːk; US klɜːk/ noun [C] **1** a person whose job is to do written work or look after records or accounts in an office, bank, court of law, etc.: *an office clerk* ▶ **urzędnik/czka 2** (US) = SHOP ASSISTANT

clever /ˈklevə(r)/ adj. **1** able to learn, understand or do sth quickly and easily; intelligent: *a clever student* ◇ *How clever of you to mend my watch!* Naprawiłeś mój zegarek? Jaki ty jesteś zdolny! ◇ *She's so clever with her hands* (ma tak zręczne ręce) – *she makes all her own clothes.* ▶ **zdolny** ➲ note at **intelligent 2** (used about things, ideas, or sb's actions) showing skill or intelligence: *a clever device* ◇ *We made a clever plan.* ▶ **pomysłowy**

■ **cleverly** adv. ▶ **zręcznie; pomysłowo** | **cleverness** noun [U] ▶ **zręczność; pomysłowość**

cliché /ˈkliːʃeɪ; US kliːˈʃ-/ noun [C] a phrase or idea that has been used so many times that it no longer has any real meaning or interest ▶ **komunał, utarty zwrot**

click¹ /klɪk/ verb **1** [I,T] to make a short sharp sound; to cause sth to do this: *The door clicked shut.* ◇ *He clicked his fingers at the waiter.* ▶ **lekko trzaskać; pstrykać 2** [I,T] **click (on sth)** to press one of the buttons on a computer mouse: *To open a file, click on the menu.* ▶ **klikać 3** [I] (informal) (used about a problem, etc.) to become suddenly clear or understood: *Once I'd found the missing letter, everything **clicked into place.*** ▶ **zaskoczyć, stać się zrozumiałym 4** [I] (Brit., informal) (used about two people) to become friendly immediately: *We met at a party and just clicked.* ▶ **zaprzyjaźnić się (szybko), dogadać się (od razu)**

click

What was that name again?

clicking his fingers

click² /klɪk/ noun [C] **1** a short sharp sound: *the click of a switch* ▶ **trzask, pstryk 2** the act of pressing the button on a computer mouse ▶ **klik**

clickable /ˈklɪkəbl/ adj. if text or an image is **clickable**, you can click on it with the mouse in order to make sth happen ▶ (*komput.*) **na który można kliknąć, aby uruchomić jakąś funkcję**

client /ˈklaɪənt/ noun [C] **1** a person who receives a service from a professional person, for example a lawyer: *to act on behalf of a client* ▶ **klient/ka 2** one of a number of computers that is connected to a **server** ▶ **komputer przyłączony do serwera**

> Uwaga! Słowa **client** nie używa się, mówiąc o ludziach w sklepie czy w restauracji. Tacy ludzie to **customers**. **Clientele** to słowo o znaczeniu ogólnym, używane w języku formalnym. Znaczy zarówno **clients**, jak i **customers**.

clientele /ˌkliːənˈtel; US ˌklaɪ-/ noun [U] all the customers, guests or **clients** who regularly go to a particular shop, hotel, organization, etc. ▶ **klientela** ℹ Mniej formalnymi wyrazami są **customers** i **guests**. ➲ note at **client**

cliff /klɪf/ noun [C] a high, very steep area of rock, especially one next to the sea ▶ **klif**

climactic /klaɪˈmæktɪk/ adj. (formal) (used about an event or a point in time) very exciting; most important ▶ **kulminacyjny, szczytowy**

climate /ˈklaɪmət/ noun [C] **1** the normal weather conditions of a particular region: *a dry/humid/tropical climate* ▶ **klimat 2** the general opinions, etc. that people have at a particular time: *What is the current **climate of opinion*** (nastrój społeczny) *regarding the death penalty?* ◇ *the political climate* ▶ **atmosfera**

climatic /klaɪˈmætɪk/ adj. [only before a noun] connected with the climate (1) ▶ **klimatyczny**

climax /ˈklaɪmæks/ noun [C] the most important and exciting part of a book, play, piece of music, event, etc.: *The novel **reaches a dramatic climax** in the final chapter.* ▶ **punkt kulminacyjny**
■ **climax** verb [I] ▶ **osiągać punkt kulminacyjny**

climb¹ /klaɪm/ verb **1** [I,T] **climb (up) (sth)** to move up towards the top of sth: *to climb a tree/mountain/rope* ◇ *She climbed the stairs to bed.* ◇ *to climb up a ladder* ▶ **wspinać się, wchodzić** (*na górę*) **2** [I] to move, with difficulty or effort, in the direction mentioned: *I managed to climb out of the window.* ▶ **gramolić się, wdrapywać się 3** [I] to go up mountains, etc. as a sport ▶ (*sport*) **wspinać się 4** [I] to rise to a higher position: *The plane climbed steadily.* ◇ *The road climbed steeply up the side of the mountain.* ◇ (figurative) *The value of the dollar climbed against the pound.* ▶ **wspinać się, iść do góry**
IDM **climb/jump on the bandwagon** → BANDWAGON
PHR V **climb down (over sth)** (informal) to admit that you have made a mistake; to change your opinion about sth in an argument ▶ **przyznawać się do błędu; zmieniać zdanie**

climb² /klaɪm/ noun [C] an act of climbing or a journey made by climbing: *The monastery could only be reached by a three-hour climb.* ▶ **wspinaczka, wspinanie się**

climbdown /ˈklaɪmdaʊn/ noun [C] an act of admitting you have been wrong; a change of opinion in an argument: *a government climbdown* ▶ **przyznanie się do błędu; zmiana zdania**

climber /ˈklaɪmə(r)/ noun [C] a person who climbs mountains as a sport ▶ **alpinist(k)a**

climbing /ˈklaɪmɪŋ/ noun [U] the sport or activity of climbing rocks or mountains: *to **go climbing*** uprawiać wspinaczkę ▶ **wspinaczka, alpinizm**

clinch /klɪntʃ/ verb [T] (informal) to finally manage to get what you want in an argument or business agreement: *to clinch a deal* ◇ *to clinch an argument* ▶ **ubijać** (*interes*); **rozstrzygać** (*spór*)

cling /klɪŋ/ verb [I] (pt, pp **clung** /klʌŋ/) **1 cling (on) to sb/sth; cling together** to hold on tightly to sb/sth: *She clung to the rope with all her strength.* ◇ *They clung together for warmth.* Przytulili się mocno do siebie, żeby było im cieplej. ▶ **kurczowo trzymać się czegoś, przywierać 2 cling to sb/sth** to stick firmly to sth: *Her wet clothes clung to her.* ▶ **przylegać 3 cling (on) to sth** to continue to believe sth, often when it is not reasonable to do so: *They were still clinging to the hope that the girl would be found alive.* ▶ **kurczowo trzymać się czegoś**

ˈcling film noun [U] thin transparent plastic used for covering food to keep it fresh ▶ **folia do żywności** ➲ look at **foil¹**

clinging /ˈklɪŋɪŋ/ (also **clingy** /ˈklɪŋi/) adj. **1** (used about clothes or material) sticking to the body and showing its shape: *a clingy sweater* ▶ (*ubranie itp.*) **przylegający, obcisły 2** needing another person too much: *a clingy* (trzymające się rodziców) *child* ▶ **niesamodzielny, bluszczowaty**

clinic /ˈklɪnɪk/ noun [C] **1** a small hospital or a part of a hospital where you go to receive special medical treatment: *He's being treated at a private clinic.* ▶ **klinika, poradnia 2** a time when a doctor sees patients and gives special treatment or advice: *Dr Greenall's clinic is from 2 to 4 on Mondays.* ▶ **godziny przyjęć lekarza**

clinical /ˈklɪnɪkl/ adj. **1** [only before a noun] connected with the examination and treatment of patients at a **clinic** or hospital: *Clinical trials of the new drug have proved successful.* ▶ **kliniczny 2** (used about a person) cold and not emotional ▶ **chłodny, beznamiętny**

clinically /ˈklɪnɪkli/ adv. **1** according to medical examination: *to be clinically dead* ▶ **klinicznie 2** in a cold way; without showing any emotion ▶ **chłodno, bez emocji**

clink /klɪŋk/ noun [sing.] the short sharp ringing sound that objects made of glass, metal, etc. make when they touch each other: *the clink of glasses* ▶ **brzęk**

■ **clink** verb [I,T] ▶ **brzęczeć; pobrzękiwać**

clink

They clinked their glasses.

clip¹ /klɪp/ noun [C] **1** a small object, usually made of metal or plastic, used for holding things together: *a paper clip* spinacz ◇ *a hair clip* spinka ▶ **klips** ➲ picture at **stationery** **2** an act of cutting sth ▶ **przycięcie** **3** a small section of a film that is shown so that people can see what the rest of the film is like ▶ **zwiastun** ➲ look at **trailer** **4** (informal) a quick hit with the hand: *She gave the boy a clip round the ear.* ▶ **kuksaniec, szturchaniec**

clip² /klɪp/ verb (**clipping**; **clipped**) **1** [I,T] to be fastened with a **clip**; to fasten sth to sth else with a **clip**: *Do your earrings clip on?* Czy to są klipsy czy kolczyki? ◇ *Clip the photo to the letter, please.* ▶ **spinać (się), przypinać** (*spinaczem*) **2** [T] to cut sth, especially by cutting small parts off: *The hedge needs clipping.* ▶ **przycinać** **3** [T] to hit sb/sth quickly: *My wheel clipped* (najechało) *the pavement and I fell off my bike.* ▶ **trącić**

ˈ**clip art** noun [U] pictures and symbols that are often included in software packages so that computer users can add them to their documents ▶ **zestaw ilustracji dołączany do programów komputerowych**

clipboard /ˈklɪpbɔːd/ noun [C] a small board with a clip at the top for holding papers, so that you can write while you are standing or moving around ▶ **rodzaj twardej podkładki ze spinaczem u góry do trzymania kartek** ➲ picture at **stationery**

ˈ**clip-on** adj. [only before a noun] fastened to sth with a **clip**: *clip-on earrings* klipsy (biżuteryjne) ◇ *a clip-on bow tie* ▶ **przypinany**

clippers /ˈklɪpəz/ noun [pl.] a small metal tool used for cutting things, for example hair or nails: *a pair of nail clippers* cążki do paznokci ▶ **maszynka do strzyżenia**

clipping (US) = CUTTING¹ (1)

clique /kliːk/ noun [C] a small group of people with the same interests who do not want others to join their group ▶ **klika**

clitoris /ˈklɪtərɪs/ noun [C] the small part of the female sex organs which becomes larger when a woman is sexually excited ▶ **łechtaczka**

cloak /kləʊk/ noun **1** [C] a type of loose coat without sleeves that was more common in former times ▶ **peleryna** ➲ look at **cape** **2** [sing.] a thing that hides sth else: *a cloak of mist* ▶ **maska, osłona**

cloakroom /ˈkləʊkruːm; -rʊm/ (US ˈ**coat check**; **coatroom** /ˈkəʊtruːm; -rʊm/) noun [C] a room near the entrance to a building where you can leave your coat, bags, etc. ▶ **szatnia**

clobber /ˈklɒbə(r)/ verb [T] (Brit., informal) to hit sb hard ▶ **po/bić (kogoś)**

⚷ **clock¹** /klɒk/ noun [C] **1** an instrument that shows you what time it is: *a church clock* ◇ *an alarm clock* budzik ◇ *The clock is five minutes slow* (spóźnia się pięć minut). ◇ *The clock is five minutes fast* (śpieszy się pięć minut). ▶ **zegar** ➲ look at **watch** **2** an instrument in a car that measures how far it has travelled: *My car has only 10 000 miles on the clock.* ▶ **licznik**

IDM **against the clock** to do sth fast in order to finish it before a certain time: *It was a race against the clock* (wyścig z czasem) *to get the building work finished on time.* ▶ **w wielkim pośpiechu, pod presją czasu**

around/round the clock all day and all night: *They are working round the clock to repair the bridge.* ▶ **całą dobę**

put the clock/clocks forward/back to change the time, usually by one hour, at the beginning/end of summer ▶ **przestawiać zegar(y) o godzinę do przodu/tyłu**

clock² /klɒk/ verb

PHR V **clock in/on; clock off** to record the time that you arrive at or leave work, especially by putting a card into a type of clock ▶ **rejestrować godzinę przyjścia do/wyjścia z pracy**

clock sth up to achieve a certain number or total: *Our car clocked up* (przejechał) *over 2 000 miles while we were on holiday.* ▶ **nabić, naliczyć**

clockwise /ˈklɒkwaɪz/ adv. in the same direction as the hands of a clock: *Turn the handle clockwise.* ▶ **zgodnie z kierunkiem ruchu wskazówek zegara** OPP **anticlockwise**, **counterclockwise**

■ **clockwise** adj.: *to move in a clockwise direction* ▶ **zgodny z kierunkiem ruchu wskazówek zegara**

clockwork /ˈklɒkwɜːk/ noun [U] a type of machinery found in certain toys, etc. that you operate by turning a key: *a clockwork toy* ◇ *The plan went **like clockwork**.* Poszło jak w zegarku. ▶ **mechanizm zegarowy**

clod /klɒd/ noun [C] **1** [usually pl.] a lump of earth or **clay**: *clods of earth* ▶ **gruda** (*ziemi*) **2** (informal) a stupid person ▶ **bęcwał**

clog¹ /klɒg/ verb [I,T] (**clogging**; **clogged**) **clog (sth) (up) (with sth)** to block or become blocked: *The drain is always clogging up.* ◇ *The roads were clogged with traffic.* ▶ **zapychać (się)**

clog² /klɒg/ noun [C] a type of shoe made completely of wood or with a thick wooden base ▶ **drewniak**

cloister /ˈklɔɪstə(r)/ noun [C, usually pl.] a covered passage around a square garden, usually forming part of a religious building ▶ **krużganek**

clone /kləʊn/ noun [C] an exact copy of a plant or an animal that is produced from one of its cells by scientific methods ▶ **klon**

■ **clone** verb [T] ▶ **klonować**

⚷ **close¹** /kləʊz/ verb [I,T] **1** to shut: *The door closed quietly.* ◇ *to close a door/window* ◇ *Close your eyes – I've got a surprise.* ▶ **zamykać (się)** **2** to be, or to make sth, not open to the public: *What time do the shops close?* ◇ *The police have closed the road to traffic.* ▶ **zamykać (się)** **3** to end or to bring sth to an end: *The meeting closed at 10pm.* ◇ *Detectives have closed the case on the missing girl.* ▶ **kończyć (się), zamykać (się)** OPP for all meanings **open**

PHR V **close (sth) down** to stop all business or work permanently at a shop or factory: *The factory has had to close down.* ◇ *Health inspectors have closed the restaurant down.* ▶ **zamykać (się), kończyć działalność**

close in (on sb/sth) to come nearer and gradually surround sb/sth, especially in order to attack: *The army is closing in on the enemy troops.* ▶ **zbliżać się** (*zwł. aby zaatakować*)

close sth off to prevent people from entering a place or an area: *The police closed off the city centre because of a bomb alert.* ▶ **zamykać** (*dojazd/wejście*)

close² noun **1** /kləʊz/ [sing.] the end, especially of a period of time or an activity: *the close of trading on the stock market* ◇ *The chairman **brought** the meeting **to a close*** (zakończył zebranie). ◇ *The guests began to leave as the evening **drew to a close*** (zbliżał się do końca). ▶ **koniec** **2** /kləʊs; US / [C] part of the name of a street: *5 Devon Close* ▶ **określenie ulicy** (*zwł. bez wylotu*)

⚷ **close³** /kləʊs/ adj. **1** [not before a noun] **close (to sb/sth)**; **close (together)** near: *The tables are quite close* (blisko) *together.*

◇ *Is our hotel close* (blisko) *to the beach?* ◇ *It's close to midnight.* Zbliża się północ. ▶ **bliski 2** (used about a friend, etc.) known very well and liked: *They invited only close friends to the wedding.* ▶ **bliski 3** [only before a noun] near in a family relationship: *a close relative* ▶ **bliski** OPP **distant 4** careful; thorough: *On close examination, you could see that the banknote was a forgery.* ▶ **dokładny 5** (used about a competition, etc.) only won by a small amount: *a close match* ▶ **z niewielką przewagą** ⮌ note at **near**[1] **6** (used about the weather, etc.) heavy and with little movement of air: *It's so close* (duszno) *today that there might be a storm.* ▶ **duszny**

■ **close** adv. near: *to follow close behind someone* ◇ *I held her close.* Przytuliłem ją do siebie. ▶ **blisko** | **closely** adv.: *to watch somebody closely* ◇ *The insect closely resembles a stick.* ▶ **uważnie**, **dokładnie** | **closeness** noun [U] ▶ **bliskość**

IDM **at close quarters** at or from a position that is very near ▶ **z bliska**

close by (sb/sth) at a short distance from sb/sth: *She lives close by.* ▶ **tuż obok (kogoś/czegoś)**

close/near/dear to sb's heart → HEART

close on nearly; almost: *He was born close on a hundred years ago.* ▶ **niemal**

a close shave/thing a bad thing that almost happened: *I wasn't injured, but it was a close shave.* ▶ **uniknięcie nieszczęścia o mały włos**

close up (to sb/sth) at or from a very short distance to sb/sth: *You can't tell it's a forgery until you look at it close up.* ▶ **z bliska**

come close (to sth/to doing sth) to almost do sth: *We didn't win but we came close.* ▶ **być o włos (od czegoś)**

keep a close watch on sb/sth to watch sb/sth very carefully ▶ **nie spuszczać kogoś/czegoś z oka**

⚷ **closed** /kləʊzd/ adj. not open; shut: *Keep your mouth closed.* ◇ *The supermarket is closed.* ▶ **zamknięty** OPP **open**

ˌ**closed-ˌcircuit 'television** (abbr. **CCTV** /ˌsiː siː tiː 'viː/) noun [C,U] a television system used in a limited area, for example a shopping centre, to protect it from crime ▶ **monitoring wizyjny**

close-fitting /ˌkləʊs 'fɪtɪŋ/ adj. (used about clothes) fitting tightly, showing the shape of the body ▶ *(ubranie)* **obcisły**

close-knit (also ˌclosely-'knit) → KNIT

⚷ **closet** /'klɒzɪt; US -zət/ noun [C] (especially US) a large cupboard that is built into a room ▶ **szafa w ścianie**

close-up /'kləʊs ʌp/ noun [C] a photograph or film of sb/sth that you take from a very short distance away: *Here's a close-up of Mike.* ▶ **zbliżenie**

closing /'kləʊzɪŋ/ adj. [only before a noun] coming at the end of a speech, a period of time or an activity: *his closing remarks* ◇ *the closing stages of the game* końcówka meczu ▶ *(uwagi itp.)* **końcowy** OPP **opening**

■ **closing** noun [U] the act of shutting sth such as a factory, hospital, school, etc. permanently ▶ **zamknięcie**, **zlikwidowanie** OPP **opening**

'**closing time** noun [C] the time when a shop, pub, etc. closes ▶ **godzina zamknięcia**

closure /'kləʊʒə(r)/ noun [C,U] the situation when a factory, school, hospital, etc. shuts permanently: *The firm is threatened with closure.* ▶ **zamknięcie**

clot[1] /klɒt/ noun [C] a lump that is formed when blood dries or becomes thicker: *They removed a blood clot from his brain.* ▶ **skrzep**

clot[2] /klɒt/ verb [I,T] (**clotting**; **clotted**) to form or cause blood to form thick lumps: *a drug that stops blood from clotting during operations* ▶ **ścinać się**; **powodować skrzepnięcie**

⚷ **cloth** /klɒθ/ noun (pl. **cloths** /klɒθs; US -ðz/) **1** [U] a material made of cotton, wool, etc. that you use for making clothes, curtains, etc.: *a metre of cloth* ▶ **materiał**, **tkanina 2** [C] a piece of material that you use for a particular purpose: *Where can I find a cloth to wipe this water up?* ◇ *a tablecloth* obrus ▶ **ścierka**

clothe /kləʊð/ verb [T] (formal) to provide clothes for sb: *to feed and clothe a child* ▶ **ubierać**

clothed /kləʊðd/ adj. **clothed (in sth)** dressed; wearing sth: *He was clothed in leather from head to foot.* ▶ **ubrany**, **odziany**

⚷ **clothes** /kləʊðz; kləʊz/ noun [pl.] the things that you wear, for example trousers, shirts, dresses, coats, etc.: *to put on/ take off your clothes* ◇ *She was wearing new clothes.* ▶ **ubranie** ⮌ look at **garment** ⓘ Pamiętaj, że **clothes** występuje tylko w lm. Do określenia pojedynczej części ubrania używa się **an item/a piece/an article of clothing**: *A kilt is an item of clothing worn in Scotland.*

> **clothes**
>
> Before buying new clothes, you can **try** them **on** to see if they **fit** (are the right shape and **size** for you). **Well-dressed** people **wear** clothes which **suit** them. When we say that a **style** of clothing is **in fashion**, **fashionable** or **trendy** we mean that it is popular at the moment. Many people wear **smart** clothes, such as a suit, at work. Others wear a **uniform**: *a police/school uniform.* People usually **get changed** into **casual** clothes when they come home from work or school.

'**clothes hanger** = HANGER

'**clothes horse** noun [C] (Brit.) a wooden or plastic folding frame that you put clothes on to dry after you have washed them ▶ **rozkładana suszarka do ubrań**

'**clothes line** noun [C] a thin rope that you hang clothes on so that they can dry ▶ **sznur do suszenia bielizny**

'**clothes peg** (US 'clothes pin) = PEG[1] (3)

⚷ **clothing** /'kləʊðɪŋ/ noun [U] the clothes that you wear, especially for a particular activity: *You will need waterproof/outdoor/winter clothing.* ▶ **odzież** ⓘ **Clothing** jest bardziej formalne niż **clothes**.

ˌ**clotted 'cream** noun [U] (Brit.) a type of thick rich cream ▶ **rodzaj gęstej śmietany**

⚷ **cloud**[1] /klaʊd/ noun **1** [C,U] a mass of very small drops of water that floats in the sky and is usually white or grey: *The sun disappeared behind a cloud.* ◇ *A band of thick cloud is spreading from the west.* ▶ **chmura**, **obłok 2** [C] a mass of smoke, dust, sand, etc.: *Clouds of smoke were pouring from the burning building.* ▶ **kłąb**, **tuman**

IDM **every cloud has a silver lining** even a very bad situation has a positive side ▶ **wszystko ma swoje blaski i cienie**

under a cloud with the disapproval of the people around you: *She left her job under a cloud because she'd been accused of stealing.* ▶ **w atmosferze dezaprobaty**

cloud[2] /klaʊd/ verb **1** [T] to make sth less clear or easy to understand: *Her personal involvement in the case was beginning to* ***cloud her judgement.*** ▶ **zaburzać 2** [T] to make sth less enjoyable; to spoil: *Illness has clouded the last few years of his life.* ▶ **psuć**, **mglić 3** [I,T] to become or make sth difficult to see through: *His eyes clouded with tears.* ▶ **mglić (się)**

PHR V **cloud over 1** (used about the sky) to become full of clouds ▶ **zachmurzyć się 2** (used about a person's face) to start to look sad ▶ **zachmurzyć się**

cloudburst /'klaʊdbɜːst/ noun [C] a sudden heavy fall of rain ▶ **oberwanie chmury**

cloudless /'klaʊdləs/ adj. (used about the sky, etc.) clear; without any clouds ▶ **bezchmurny**

cloudy /ˈklaʊdi/ adj. (**cloudier**; **cloudiest**) **1** (used about the sky, etc.) full of clouds ▶ **zachmurzony**, **pochmurny** **2** (used about liquids, etc.) not clear: *cloudy water* ▶ **mętny**

clout /klaʊt/ noun (informal) **1** [U] influence and power: *He's an important man – he has a lot of clout in the company.* ▶ **posłuch** **2** [C] a hard hit, usually with the hand: *to give someone a clout* ▶ **kuksaniec**

clove /kləʊv/ noun [C] **1** the small dried flower of a tropical tree, used as a spice in cooking ▶ (*przyprawa*) **goździk** ➲ picture on **page A12** **2** one of the small separate sections of **garlic** ▶ **ząbek**

clover /ˈkləʊvə(r)/ noun [U] a small plant with pink or white flowers and leaves with three parts to them ▶ **koniczyna**

Znalezienie czterolistnej koniczyny uważane jest za dobry znak również w krajach anglojęzycznych.

clown[1] /klaʊn/ noun [C] **1** a person who wears funny clothes and a big red nose and does silly things to make people (especially children) laugh ▶ **klown** **2** a person who makes jokes and does silly things to make the people around them laugh: *At school, Jan was always the class clown.* ▶ **błazen**

clown[2] /klaʊn/ verb [I] **clown (about/around)** to act in a funny or silly way: *Stop clowning around and get some work done!* ▶ **błaznować**

cloy /klɔɪ/ verb [I] (used about sth pleasant or sweet) to start to become slightly disgusting or annoying, because there is too much of it: *After a while, the rich sauce begins to cloy.* ▶ (*nadmiar słodyczy itp.*) **mdlić**
■ **cloying** adj.: *the cloying sentimentality of her novels* ▶ **mdły**, **przesłodzony**

⚷ **club[1]** /klʌb/ noun **1** [C] a group of people who meet regularly to share an interest, do sport, etc.; the place where they meet: *to join a club* ◇ *to be a member of a club* ◇ *a tennis/football/golf club* ▶ **klub** **2** (also **nightclub** /ˈnaɪtklʌb/) [C] a place where you can go to dance and drink late at night: *the club scene in Newcastle* ▶ **klub nocny** **3** [C] a heavy stick, usually with one end that is thicker than the other, used as a weapon ▶ **maczuga** **4** [C] = GOLF CLUB **5** (**clubs**) [pl.] in a pack of playing cards, the **suit** with black three-leafed shapes on them: *the two/ace/queen of clubs* ▶ **trefle** ➲ note at **card** **6** [C] one of the cards from this suit: *I played a club.* ▶ **trefl**

club[2] /klʌb/ verb (**clubbing**; **clubbed**) **1** [T] to hit sb/sth hard with a heavy object: *to club* (zatłuc) *somebody to death* ▶ **walić ciężkim przedmiotem** **2** [I] **go clubbing** to go dancing and drinking in a club: *She goes clubbing every Saturday.* ▶ **chodzić do nocnych klubów**
PHR V **club together (to do sth)** to share the cost of sth, for example a present: *We clubbed together to buy him a leaving present.* ▶ **składać się** (*na kupno czegoś*)
■ **clubber** noun [C] a person who goes to **nightclubs** regularly; sb visiting a nightclub ▶ **osoba chodząca do klubów nocnych**

ˈ**club car** noun [C] (US) a coach on a train with comfortable chairs and tables, where you can buy sth to eat or drink ▶ **luksusowy wagon restauracyjny**

clubhouse /ˈklʌbhaʊs/ noun [C] the building used by a club, especially a sports club ▶ **budynek klubu**

cluck /klʌk/ noun [C] the noise made by a chicken ▶ **kwokanie**
■ **cluck** verb [I] ▶ **kwokać**

clue /kluː/ noun [C] **a clue (to sth)** a piece of information that helps you solve a problem or a crime, answer a question, etc.: *The police were looking for clues to his disappearance.* ◇ *the clues for solving a crossword puzzle* ▶ **trop**, **wskazówka**
IDM **not have a clue** (informal) to know nothing about sth ▶ **nie mieć pojęcia**

ˌ**clued-**ˈ**up** (US also ˌ**clued-**ˈ**in**) adj. **clued-up (on sth)** knowing a lot about sth: *I'm not really clued-up on the technical details.* ▶ **obeznany**, **na bieżąco**

clueless /ˈkluːləs/ adj. (informal) not able to understand; stupid: *I'm absolutely clueless about computers.* Nie mam pojęcia o komputerach. ▶ **głupi**

clump /klʌmp/ noun [C] a small group of plants or trees, growing together ▶ **kępa**

clumsy /ˈklʌmzi/ adj. (**clumsier**; **clumsiest**) **1** (used about a person) careless and likely to knock into, drop or break things: *I spilt your coffee. Sorry – that was clumsy of me.* ▶ **niezdarny** **2** (used about a comment, etc.) likely to upset or offend people: *He made a clumsy apology.* ▶ **nietaktowny** **3** large, difficult to use, and not attractive in design: *a clumsy piece of furniture* ▶ **niezgrabny**
■ **clumsily** adv. ▶ **niezdarnie**, **nietaktownie** | **clumsiness** noun [U] ▶ **niezdarność**, **nietakt**

clung past tense, past participle of **cling**

cluster[1] /ˈklʌstə(r)/ noun [C] a group of people, plants or things that stand or grow close together: *a cluster of schoolchildren* ▶ **grono**, **kiść**

cluster[2] /ˈklʌstə(r)/ verb
PHR V **cluster around sb/sth** to form a group around sb/sth ▶ **gromadzić się nad kimś/czymś**

ˈ**cluster bomb** noun [C] a type of bomb that throws out smaller bombs when it explodes ▶ **rozpryskowa bomba kasetowa**

clutch[1] /klʌtʃ/ verb [T] to hold sth tightly, especially because you are in pain, afraid or excited: *He clutched his mother's hand in fear.* ▶ **trzymać kurczowo**
PHR V **clutch at sth** to try to take hold of sth: *She clutched at the money but the wind blew it away.* ▶ **starać się uchwycić coś**

clutch[2] /klʌtʃ/ noun **1** [C] the part of a vehicle, etc. that you press with your foot when you are driving in order to change the **gear**; a device in a car that connects and **disconnects** the engine and gears: *to press/release the clutch* ▶ **sprzęgło** ➲ picture at **car** **2** (**clutches**) [pl.] power or control over sb: *He fell **into** the enemy's **clutches**.* ▶ **szpony**

clutter[1] /ˈklʌtə(r)/ verb [T] **clutter sth (up)** to cover or fill sth with a lot of objects in an untidy way: *Don't leave those books there – they're cluttering up the table.* ▶ **zaśmiecać**

clutter[2] /ˈklʌtə(r)/ noun [U] things that are where they are not wanted or needed and make a place untidy: *Who left all this clutter on the floor?* ▶ **rozgardiasz**
■ **cluttered** adj.: *a cluttered desk* ▶ **zaśmiecony**

⚷ **cm** = CENTIMETRE

Co. **1** = COMPANY: *W Smithson & Co.* **2** (formal) = COUNTY: *Co. Down*

c/o abbr. (used for addressing a letter to sb who is staying at another person's house); **care of**: *Andy Kirkham, c/o Mrs Potter* ▶ **na adres kogoś**

co- /kəʊ/ prefix [used in adjectives, adverbs, nouns and verbs] together with: *co-produced* ◇ *cooperatively* ◇ *co-author* ◇ *coexist* ▶ **współ-**

⚷ **coach[1]** /kəʊtʃ/ noun [C] **1** a person who trains people to compete in certain sports: *a tennis coach* ▶ **trener** **2** (Brit.) a comfortable bus used for long journeys: *It's cheaper to travel **by coach** than by train.* ▶ **autokar** ➲ note at **bus** ➲ picture on **page A7** **3** = CARRIAGE (1) **4** a large vehicle with four wheels pulled by horses, used in the past for carrying passengers ▶ **dyliżans** ➲ look at **carriage**, **car**

coach[2] /kəʊtʃ/ verb [I,T] **coach sb (in/for sth)** to train or teach sb, especially to compete in a sport or pass an exam: *She is being coached for the Olympics by a former champion.* ▶ **trenować**

coagulate /kəʊ'ægjuleɪt/ verb [I] (used about a liquid) to become thick and partly solid ▶ **krzepnąć**
■ **coagulation** /kəʊ,ægju'leɪʃn/ ▶ **krzepnięcie**

coal /kəʊl/ noun **1** [U] a type of black mineral that is dug from the ground and burnt to give heat: *a lump of coal* ◇ *a coal fire* ◇ *a coal mine* ▶ **węgiel** ➲ picture at **bar** **2** (**coals**) [pl.] burning pieces of coal ▶ **żarzące się węgle** ➲ picture at **fireplace**

coalesce /,kəʊə'les/ verb [I] **coalesce (into/with sth)** (formal) to come together to form one larger group, substance, etc.: *The puddles had coalesced into a small stream.* ▶ **łączyć się, zlewać się** SYN **amalgamate**
■ **coalescence** /,kəʊə'lesns/ noun [U]: *a remarkable coalescence of opinion* ▶ **z/po-łączenie się, zlanie się**

coalition /,kəʊə'lɪʃn/ noun [C, with sing. or pl. verb] a government formed by two or more political parties working together: *a coalition between the socialists and the Green Party* ▶ **koalicja**

'**coal mine** (also **pit**) noun [C] a place, usually underground, where coal is dug from the ground ▶ **kopalnia węgla** ➲ look at **colliery**

'**coal miner** (also **miner**) noun [C] a person whose job is to dig coal from the ground ▶ **górnik** (*w kopalni węgla*)

coarse /kɔːs/ adj. **1** consisting of large pieces; rough, not smooth: *coarse salt* ◇ *coarse cloth* ▶ **gruboziarnisty; szorstki, chropowaty** OPP **fine, smooth** **2** (used about a person or their behaviour) rude; likely to offend people; having bad manners ▶ **grubiański, prostacki**
■ **coarsely** adv.: *Chop the onion coarsely.* ◇ *He laughed coarsely.* ▶ **grubo; grubiańsko**

coarsen /'kɔːsn/ verb [I,T] to become or to make sth **coarse** ▶ **chropowacieć; stawać się ordynarnym**

coast[1] /kəʊst/ noun [C] the area of land that is next to or close to the sea: *Ipswich is* ***on the east coast.*** ▶ **wybrzeże, brzeg**

coast[2] /kəʊst/ verb [I] **1** to travel in a car, on a bicycle, etc. (especially down a hill) without using power ▶ **zjeżdżać** (*na wolnym biegu*) **2** to achieve sth without much effort: *They coasted to victory.* Zwycięstwo przyszło im bez trudu. ▶ **łatwo dochodzić (do czegoś)**

coastal /'kəʊstl/ adj. on or near a coast: *fishing in coastal waters* ▶ **przybrzeżny**

coastguard /'kəʊstgɑːd/ noun [C] a person or group of people whose job is to watch the sea near the coast in order to help people or ships that are in danger or to stop illegal activities ▶ **służba ochrony wybrzeża**

coastline /'kəʊstlaɪn/ noun [C] the edge or shape of a coast: *a rocky coastline* ▶ **linia brzegowa**

coat[1] /kəʊt/ noun [C] **1** a piece of clothing that you wear over your other clothes to keep warm when you are outside: *Put your coat on – it's cold outside.* ▶ **płaszcz, palto** ➲ look at **overcoat, raincoat** ➲ picture on **page A1** **2** the fur or hair covering an animal's body: *a dog with a smooth coat* ▶ **sierść** ➲ picture on **page A10** **3** a layer of sth covering a surface: *The walls will probably need two coats of paint.* ▶ **warstwa**

coat[2] /kəʊt/ verb [T] **coat sth (with/in sth)** to cover sth with a layer of sth: *biscuits coated with milk chocolate* ▶ **pokrywać, powlekać**

'**coat check** (US) = CLOAKROOM

'**coat hanger** = HANGER

coating /'kəʊtɪŋ/ noun [C] a thin layer of sth that covers sth else: *wire with a plastic coating* ▶ **warstwa, polewa, panierka**

,**coat of 'arms** (pl. **coats of arms**) (also **arms** [pl.]) noun [C] a design that is used as the symbol of a family, a town, a university, etc. ▶ **herb**

coatroom (US) = CLOAKROOM (1)

'**coat stand** noun [C] a stand with hooks for hanging coats and hats on ▶ **wieszak stojący**

coax /kəʊks/ verb [T] **coax sb (into/out of sth/doing sth); coax sth out of/from sb** to persuade sb gently: *The child wasn't hungry, but his mother coaxed him into eating a little.* ◇ *At last he coaxed a smile out of her.* ◇ *They coaxed* (wywabili) *the cat out of the basket.* ▶ **wmówić** (*łagodną perswazją*), **nakłaniać**

cob (especially US) = CORNCOB: *corn on the cob*

cobalt /'kəʊbɔːlt/ noun [U] **1** (symbol **Co**) a hard silver-white metal that is often mixed with other metals and used to give a deep bluish-green colour to glass ▶ **kobalt** **2** (also ,**cobalt 'blue**) a deep bluish-green colour ▶ **kobaltowy błękit**

cobble /'kɒbl/ verb
PHR V **cobble sth together** to make sth or put sth together quickly and without much care ▶ **robić byle jak, klecić**

cobbler /'kɒblə(r)/ noun [C] (old-fashioned) a person who repairs shoes ▶ **szewc**

cobbles /'kɒblz/ (also **cobblestones** /'kɒblstəʊnz/) noun [pl.] small round stones used (in the past) for covering the surface of streets ▶ **kostki brukowe**
■ **cobbled** /'kɒbld; US / adj. ▶ **brukowany**

cobra /'kəʊbrə/ noun [C] a poisonous snake that can spread out the skin at the back of its neck. **Cobras** live in India and Africa. ▶ **kobra**

cobweb /'kɒbweb/ noun [C] a net of threads made by a spider in order to catch insects ▶ **pajęczyna**

Coca-Cola™ /,kəʊkə 'kəʊlə/ (also informal **Coke™** /kəʊk/) noun [U,C] a popular type of **cola** drink ▶ **coca-cola**

cocaine /kəʊ'keɪn/ (also informal **coke**) noun [U] a dangerous drug that some people take for pleasure but which is **addictive** ▶ **kokaina**

coccyx /'kɒksɪks/ noun [C] (pl. **coccyxes** or **coccyges** /'kɒksɪdʒiːz/) the small bone at the bottom of the **spine** ▶ **kość ogonowa** SYN **tailbone** ➲ picture at **body**

cock[1] /kɒk/ noun [C] **1** (US **rooster** /'ruːstə(r)/) an adult male chicken ▶ **kogut** ➲ note at **chicken** **2** an adult male bird of any type ▶ (*ptaki*) **samiec**

cock[2] /kɒk/ verb [T] to hold up a part of the body: *The horse cocked its ears on hearing the noise.* ▶ **nastawiać**
PHR V **cock sth up** (Brit., slang) to do sth very badly and spoil sth ▶ **knocić, partaczyć** ➲ look at **cock-up**

cock-a-doodle-doo /,kɒk ə ,duːdl 'duː/ noun [sing.] the noise made by an adult male chicken ▶ **kukuryku!**

cockerel /'kɒkərəl/ noun [C] a young male chicken ▶ **kogucik**

cockeyed /'kɒkaɪd/ adj. (informal) **1** not level or straight: *Doesn't that picture look cockeyed to you?* ▶ **przekrzywiony** SYN **crooked** **2** not practical; not likely to succeed: *a cockeyed scheme to make people use less water* ▶ **bzdurny**

cockle /'kɒkl/ noun [C] a small **shellfish** that can be eaten ▶ (*mięczak*) **sercówka jadalna**
IDM **warm the cockles (of sb's heart)** → WARM

cockney /'kɒkni/ noun **1** [C] a person who was born and grew up in the East End of London ▶ **rodowity londyńczyk** (*zwł. z dzielnicy wschodniej*) **2** [U] the way of speaking English that is typical of people living in this area: *a cockney* (wschodniolondyński) *accent* ▶ **gwara mieszkańców dzielnicy wschodniej Londynu**

cockpit /'kɒkpɪt/ noun [C] **1** the part of a plane where the pilot sits ▶ **kabina pilota** **2** the part of a racing car where the driver sits ▶ **kabina**

cockroach /ˈkɒkrəʊtʃ/ (US **roach** /rəʊtʃ/) noun [C] a large dark brown insect, usually found in dirty or slightly wet places ▶ **karaluch** ➲ picture at **insect**

cocktail /ˈkɒkteɪl/ noun [C] **1** a drink made from a mixture of alcoholic drinks and fruit juices ▶ **koktajl 2** a mixture of small pieces of food that is served cold: *a prawn cocktail* koktajl z krewetek ▶ **koktajl**

ˈcock-up noun [C] (slang) something that was badly done; a mistake that spoils sth: *What a cock-up you've made of painting that door! You'll have to start again.* ▶ **partanina**

cocky /ˈkɒki/ adj. (**cockier**; **cockiest**) (informal) too confident about yourself in a way that annoys other people ▶ **zarozumiały**, **zbyt pewny siebie**
■ **cockiness** noun [U] ▶ **zarozumiałość**; **nadmierna pewność siebie**

cocoa /ˈkəʊkəʊ/ noun **1** [U] a dark brown powder made from the seeds of a tropical tree and used in making chocolate ▶ **kakao 2** [C,U] a hot drink made from this powder mixed with milk or water; a cup of this drink: *a cup of cocoa* ▶ **kakao**

coconut /ˈkəʊkənʌt/ noun [C,U] a large tropical fruit with a hard shell that is covered with hair ▶ **kokos**, **orzech kokosowy** ➲ picture on **page A12**

cocoon[1] /kəˈkuːn/ noun [C] **1** a covering of silk threads that some insects make to protect themselves before they become adults ▶ **kokon 2** a soft covering that wraps all around sb/sth and keeps them safe: (figurative) *the cocoon of a caring family* ▶ **kokon**; **osłona**

cocoon[2] /kəˈkuːn/ verb [T] **cocoon sb/sth (in sth)** to surround sb/sth completely with sth for protection ▶ **otulać** (*dla ochrony*)

cod /kɒd/ noun [C,U] (pl. **cod**) a large sea fish that lives in the North Atlantic that you can eat ▶ **dorsz**

⚷ **code**[1] /kəʊd/ noun **1** [C,U] a system of words, letters, numbers, etc. that are used instead of the real letters or words to make a message or information secret: *They managed to **break/crack** the enemy **code*** (złamać kod). ◇ *They wrote letters to each other **in code**.* ▶ **szyfr**, **kod** ➲ look at **decode 2** [C] a group of numbers, letters, etc. that is used for identifying sth: *What's the code* (numer kierunkowy) *for Stockholm?* ▶ **kod**, **numer** ➲ look at **bar code 3** [C] a set of rules for behaviour: *a code of practice* kodeks postępowania ◇ *the Highway Code* kodeks drogowy ▶ **kodeks**

code[2] /kəʊd/ verb [T] **1** to use a particular system for identifying things: *The files are colour-coded: blue for Europe, green for Africa.* ▶ **kodować 2** (also **encode** /ɪnˈkəʊd/) to put or write sth in **code**[1] (1): *coded messages* ▶ **kodować** OPP **decode**

ˌcode of ˈpractice noun [C] (pl. **codes of practice**) a set of standards that members of a particular profession agree to follow in their work ▶ **kodeks postępowania zawodowego**

codify /ˈkəʊdɪfaɪ; US ˈkɑːd-/ verb [T] (**codifies**; **codifying**; **codified**; **codified**) to arrange laws, rules, etc. into a system ▶ **kodyfikować**

ˌco-eduˈcational (also informal **coed** /ˌkəʊˈed/) adj. (used about a school) where girls and boys are taught together ▶ **koedukacyjny** SYN **mixed**

coerce /kəʊˈɜːs/ verb [T] (formal) **coerce sb (into sth/doing sth)** to force sb to do sth, for example by threatening them ▶ **zmuszać**
■ **coercion** /kəʊˈɜːʃn/ noun [U] ▶ **przymus**, **wymuszenie**

coexist /ˌkəʊɪɡˈzɪst/ verb [I] to live or be together at the same time or in the same place as sb/sth ▶ **współistnieć**
■ **coexistence** /-ˈzɪstəns/ noun [U] ▶ **współistnienie**

C. of E. = CHURCH OF ENGLAND

⚷ **coffee** /ˈkɒfi/ noun **1** [U] the **roasted** seeds (called **coffee beans**) of a tropical bush; a powder made from them: *Coffee is the country's biggest export.* ◇ *coffee beans* ziarna kawy ▶ **kawa 2** [U] a drink made by adding hot water to this powder: *a cup of coffee* ◇ *instant coffee* kawa rozpuszczalna ◇ *decaffeinated coffee* kawa bezkofeinowa ▶ **kawa 3** [C] a cup of this drink: *Two coffees, please.* ▶ **kawa** ➲ picture on **page A14**

> **coffee**
>
> **Black coffee** is made without milk; **white coffee** is with milk. **Decaffeinated coffee** has had the caffeine taken out. Coffee can be **weak** or **strong**. **Instant coffee** is sold in a jar and made by pouring hot water or milk onto coffee powder in a cup. **Fresh coffee** is made in a coffee pot from coffee beans that have just been ground. **Filter coffee** is made in a special machine. You can buy different kinds of coffee ready to drink at a **coffee bar/shop**.

ˈcoffee bar (also **ˈcoffee shop**) noun [C] (Brit.) a place in a hotel, a large shop, etc. where simple food, coffee, tea and other drinks without alcohol are served ▶ **bar kawowy**

ˈcoffee break noun [C] a short period of rest when you stop working and drink coffee ▶ **przerwa na kawę**

ˈcoffee maker (also **ˈcoffee machine**) noun [C] a small machine for making cups of coffee ▶ **ekspres do kawy**

ˈcoffee pot noun [C] a container in which coffee is made and served ▶ **dzbanek do kawy**

ˈcoffee table noun [C] a small low table for putting magazines, cups, etc., on ▶ **ława**; **niski stolik**

coffin /ˈkɒfɪn/ noun [C] (US **casket** /ˈkɑːskɪt; US ˈkæs-/) a box in which a dead body is buried in the ground or **cremated** ▶ **trumna** ➲ note at **funeral**

cog /kɒɡ/ noun [C] one of a series of teeth on the edge of a wheel that fit into the teeth on the next wheel and cause it to move ▶ (*techn.*) **tryb**

cogent /ˈkəʊdʒənt/ adj. (formal) strongly and clearly expressed in a way that influences what people believe: *She put forward some cogent reasons for abandoning the plan.* ▶ **dobrze przemyślany i wyrażony** SYN **convincing**
■ **cogency** /ˈkəʊdʒənsi/ noun [U] ▶ **umiejętność dobrego przemyślenia i wyrażenia czegoś** | **cogently** adv. ▶ **w sposób przemyślany i dobrze wyrażony**

cognac /ˈkɒnjæk/ noun **1** [U] a type of **brandy** that is made in France ▶ **koniak 2** [C] a glass of this drink ▶ **koniak**

cognitive /ˈkɒɡnətɪv/ adj. [usually before a noun] connected with mental processes of understanding: *a child's cognitive development* ◇ *cognitive psychology* ▶ (*psych.*) **poznawczy**; (*językoznawstwo*) **kognitywny**

cohabit /kəʊˈhæbɪt/ verb [I] (formal) (used about a couple) to live together as if they are married ▶ **żyć w konkubinacie**

coherent /kəʊˈhɪərənt/ adj. clear and easy to understand ▶ **spójny**, **logiczny** OPP **incoherent**
■ **coherence** noun [U] ▶ **spójność**, **logika (wewnętrzna)** | **coherently** adv. ▶ **spójnie**, **logicznie**

cohesion /kəʊˈhiːʒn/ noun [U] the ability to stay or fit together well: *What the team lacks is cohesion – all the players play as individuals.* ▶ **spójność**, **zgranie**

cohesive /kəʊˈhiːsɪv/ adj. (formal) **1** forming a united whole: *a cohesive group* ▶ **spójny 2** causing people or things to become united: *the cohesive power of shared suffering* ▶ **spajający**

coil[1] /kɔɪl/ verb [I,T] to make sth into a round shape: *a snake coiled under a rock* ▶ **zwijać (się) w kłębek**, **okręcać się**

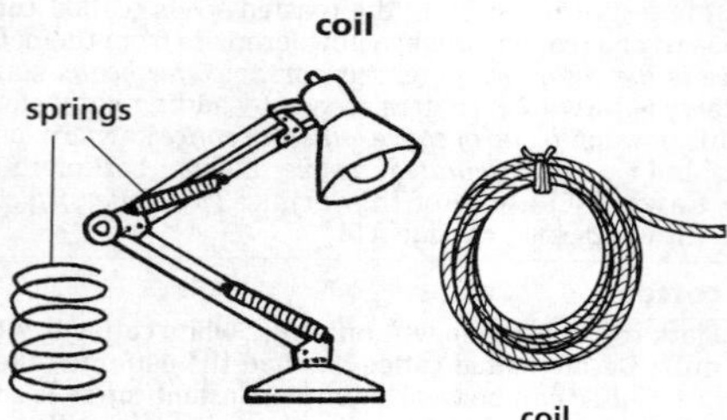

coil² /kɔɪl/ noun [C] **1** a length of rope, wire, etc. that has been made into a round shape: *a coil of rope* ▶ **zwój** **2** = IUD

coin¹ /kɔɪn/ noun [C] a piece of money made of metal: *a pound coin* ▶ **moneta**

coin² /kɔɪn/ verb [T] to invent a new word or phrase: *Who was it who coined the phrase 'a week is a long time in politics'?* ▶ **ukuć** (*np. wyrażenie*)

coincide /ˌkəʊɪnˈsaɪd/ verb [I] **coincide (with sth)** **1** (used about events) to happen at the same time as sth else: *The Queen's visit is timed to coincide with the country's centenary celebrations.* ▶ **zbiegać się (w czasie z czymś)**, **schodzić się** **2** to be exactly the same or very similar: *Our views coincide completely.* ▶ **być zbieżnym**

coincidence /kəʊˈɪnsɪdəns/ noun [C,U] two or more similar things happening at the same time by chance, in a surprising way: *We hadn't planned to meet – it was just (a) coincidence.* ▶ **zbieg okoliczności**

coincidental /kəʊˌɪnsɪˈdentl/ adj. resulting from two similar or related events happening at the same time by chance ▶ **przypadkowy**
■ **coincidentally** /-təli/ adv. ▶ **przypadkowo**

Coke™ /kəʊk/ (informal) = COCA-COLA: *Can I have a Diet Coke?*

coke /kəʊk/ noun [U] **1** (informal) = COCAINE **2** a solid black substance produced from coal and used as a fuel ▶ **koks**

Col. = COLONEL

cola /ˈkəʊlə/ noun [C,U] a brown, sweet cold drink that does not contain alcohol; a glass or can of this ▶ **coca-cola** (*lub inny podobny napój*)

colander /ˈkʌləndə(r)/ noun [C] a metal or plastic bowl with a lot of small holes in it that is used for removing water from food that has been boiled or washed ▶ **cedzak** ➲ picture at **kitchen**

cold¹ /kəʊld/ adj. **1** having a low temperature; not hot or warm: *It's cold outside.* Na dworze jest zimno. ◇ *Shall I put the heating on? I'm cold* (jest mi zimno). ▶ **zimny** **2** (used about food or drink) not heated or cooked; having become cold after being heated or cooked: *a cold drink* ◇ *Have your soup before it gets cold* (zanim wystygnie). ▶ **zimny** **3** (used about a person or sb's behaviour) very unfriendly; not showing kindness, understanding, etc.: *She gave him a cold, hard look.* ▶ **chłodny**, **oziębły**
IDM **get/have cold feet** (informal) to become/be afraid to do sth: *She started to get cold feet as her wedding day approached.* ▶ **bać się**
in cold blood in a cruel way and without pity: *to kill somebody in cold blood* ▶ **z zimną krwią**
in a cold sweat sweating and feeling cold at the same time, usually because of fear or shock ▶ **oblany zimnym potem**

temperature
Por. **cold** z **hot**, **warm** z **cool**. **Hot** określa wysoką temperaturę: *I can't drink this tea yet, it's too hot.* **Warm** oznacza, że coś jest w miarę ciepłe, w przyjemny sposób: *Come and sit by the fire – you'll soon get warm again.* **Boiling (hot)** to nieformalne określenie na „bardzo gorący": *Could you turn the heating down? It's boiling in here!* **Cool** znaczy 'w miarę zimny, szczególnie w przyjemny sposób': *It's hot outside but it's nice and cool in here.* **Freezing (cold)** znaczy 'lodowaty': *It's absolutely freezing outside.* ➲ look at **tepid**

cold² /kəʊld/ noun **1** [sing., U] lack of heat; low temperature; cold weather: *We walked home in the snow, shivering with cold.* ◇ *He rarely wears a coat because he doesn't feel the cold.* ◇ *Come on, let's get out of the cold and go indoors.* ▶ **zimno** **2** [C,U] a common illness of the nose and throat. When you have a cold you have a sore throat and often cannot breathe through your nose: *I think I'm getting a cold.* ◇ *Wear some warm clothes when you go out or you'll **catch cold*** (przeziębisz się). ▶ **przeziębienie** ➲ note at **ill**

ˌcold-ˈblooded adj. **1** cruel; having or showing no pity: *cold-blooded killers* ▶ **bezlitosny** **2** (used about animals, for example fish or snakes) having a blood temperature that changes with the temperature of the surroundings: *Reptiles are cold-blooded.* ▶ **zimnokrwisty** ➲ look at **warm-blooded**

ˌcold-ˈhearted adj. unkind; showing no kindness, understanding, etc. ▶ **zimny**, **nieczuły**

coldly /ˈkəʊldli/ adv. in an unfriendly way; in a way that shows no kindness or understanding ▶ **chłodno**, **ozięble**

coldness /ˈkəʊldnəs/ noun [U] the lack of warm feelings; unfriendly behaviour ▶ **chłód**, **oziębłość**

ˌcold-ˈshoulder verb [T] to treat sb in an unfriendly way ▶ **traktować kogoś ozięble**

ˈcold sore noun [C] a small painful spot on the lips or inside the mouth that is caused by a virus ▶ **opryszczka** (*na wardze*)

ˌcold ˈturkey noun [U] the unpleasant state that drug **addicts** experience when they suddenly stop taking a drug; a way of treating drug **addicts** that makes them experience this state ▶ **głód narkotyczny/nikotynowy itp. odczuwany przez osoby, które rzuciły nałóg z dnia na dzień**
■ **ˌcold ˈturkey** adv.: *I quit smoking cold turkey.* ▶ (*rzucić nałóg*) **z dnia na dzień**

coleslaw /ˈkəʊlslɔː/ noun [U] raw cabbage and carrots, etc., chopped and mixed with mayonnaise and eaten as a salad ▶ **surówka z kapusty i marchwi z majonezem** ➲ look at **sauerkraut**

colic /ˈkɒlɪk/ noun [U] pain in the stomach area, which especially babies get ▶ **kolka**

collaborate /kəˈlæbəreɪt/ verb [I] **1** **collaborate (with sb) (on sth)** to work together (with sb), especially to create or produce sth: *She collaborated with another author on the book.* ▶ **współpracować** **2** **collaborate (with sb)** to help the enemy forces who have taken control of your country ▶ **kolaborować** ❶ Wyraża dezaprobatę.
■ **collaboration** /kəˌlæbəˈreɪʃn/ noun [U] **1** working together to create or produce sth ▶ **współpraca** **2** help given to enemy forces who have taken control of your country ▶ **kolaboracja** | **collaborator** /kəˈlæbəreɪtə(r)/ noun [C] **1** a person who works together with sb else, especially in order to create or produce sth ▶ **współpracowni-k/czka** **2** a person who helps the enemy forces who have taken control of their country ▶ **kolaborant/ka**

collage /ˈkɒlɑːʒ; US kəˈl-/ noun **1** [C] a picture made by fixing pieces of paper, cloth, photographs, etc. onto a surface ▶ **kolaż 2** [U] the art of making a picture like this ▶ **tworzenie kolaży**

collapse¹ /kəˈlæps/ verb [I] **1** to fall down or break into pieces suddenly: *A lot of buildings collapsed in the earthquake.* ▶ **zawalić się, runąć 2** (used about a person) to fall down, usually because you are very ill, and perhaps become unconscious: *The winner collapsed at the end of the race.* ▶ **padać** (*z wyczerpania*) **3** (used about a business, plan, etc.) to fail suddenly or completely ▶ **upadać, bankrutować 4** to fold sth or be folded into a shape that uses less space: *a chair that collapses for easy storage* ▶ (*krzesło itp.*) **składać się**

collapse² /kəˈlæps/ noun **1** [C,U] the sudden or complete failure of sth, such as a business, plan, etc.: *The peace talks were* ***on the brink/verge of collapse.*** ▶ **krach, upadek 2** [sing., U] (used about a building) a sudden fall ▶ **zawalenie się, runięcie 3** [sing., U] (used about a person) a medical condition when a person becomes very ill and suddenly falls down ▶ **załamanie** (*fizyczne lub nerwowe*)

collapsible /kəˈlæpsəbl/ adj. that can be folded into a shape that makes sth easy to store: *a collapsible bed* ▶ (*krzesło itp.*) **składany**

collar¹ /ˈkɒlə(r)/ noun [C] **1** the part of a shirt, coat, dress, etc. that fits round the neck and is often folded over: *a coat with a fur collar* ▶ **kołnierz/yk** ➲ look at **dog collar, blue-collar, white-collar** ➲ picture on **page A1 2** a band of leather that is put round an animal's neck (especially a dog or cat) ▶ **obroża**

collar² /ˈkɒlə(r)/ verb [T] (informal) to catch hold of sb who does not want to be caught: *The police officer collared the thief.* ▶ **dorwać (kogoś)**

collarbone /ˈkɒləbəʊn/ (also formal **clavicle** /ˈklævɪkl/) noun [C] one of the two bones that connect your chest bones to your shoulder ▶ **obojczyk** ➲ picture at **body**

collate /kəˈleɪt/ verb [T] **1** to collect information together from different sources in order to examine and compare it: *to* ***collate data/information/figures*** ▶ **zestawiać** (*np. dane*) **2** to collect pieces of paper or the pages of a book, etc. and arrange them in the correct order ▶ **segregować**
■ **collation** /kəˈleɪʃn/ noun [U]: *the collation of information* ▶ **zestawienie** (*np. danych*); **segregowanie**

collateral /kəˈlætərəl/ noun [U] property or sth valuable that you agree to give if you cannot pay back money that you have borrowed: *They offered their house as collateral on the loan.* ▶ **zastaw, zabezpieczenie spłaty długu**

colleague /ˈkɒliːɡ/ noun [C] a person who works at the same place as you ▶ **kolega** (*z pracy*) ➲ note at **friend**

collect¹ /kəˈlekt/ verb **1** [T] to bring a number of things together: *All the exam papers will be collected at the end.* ▶ **zbierać 2** [T] to get and keep together a number of objects of a particular type over a period of time as a hobby: *to collect stamps* ▶ **zbierać, kolekcjonować 3** [I] to come together: *A crowd collected to see what was going on.* ▶ **gromadzić się** SYN **gather 4** [T] (especially Brit.) to go and get sb/sth from a particular place; to pick sb/sth up: *to collect the children from school* ▶ **odbierać 5** [I,T] to ask for money from a number of people: *to collect for charity* ◇ *The landlord collects the rent at the end of each month.* ▶ **kwestować; pobierać opłaty 6** [T] **collect yourself/sth** to get control of yourself, your feelings, thoughts, etc.: *She collected herself and went back into the room as if nothing had happened.* ◇ *I tried to* ***collect my thoughts*** (pozbierać myśli) *before the exam.* ▶ **opanować (się)**

collect² /kəˈlekt/ adj. (US) (used about a telephone call) to be paid for by the person who receives the call: *a collect call* rozmowa na koszt abonenta ▶ **na rachunek abonenta**
■ **collect** adv.: *She called me collect.* Zadzwoniła do mnie na mój koszt. ▶ **na rachunek abonenta** ⓘ W Br. ang. używa się w tym znaczeniu wyrażeń **make a reverse-charge call** lub **reverse the charges**.

collected /kəˈlektɪd/ adj. [not before a noun] calm and in control of yourself, your feelings, thoughts, etc.: *She felt cool, calm and collected before the interview.* ▶ **opanowany, skupiony**

collection /kəˈlekʃn/ noun **1** [C] a group of objects of a particular type that sb has collected as a hobby: *a stamp collection* ▶ **kolekcja, zbiór 2** [C,U] the act of getting sth from a place or from people: *rubbish collections* wywóz śmieci ▶ **odbiór 3** [C] a group of people or things: *a large collection of papers on the desk* ▶ **grupa; stos 4** [C] a number of poems, stories, letters, etc. published together in one book: *a collection of modern poetry* ▶ **wybór, antologia 5** [C] the act of asking for money from a number of people (for charity, in church, etc.): *a collection for the poor* ▶ **składka, zbiórka pieniędzy 6** [C] a variety of new clothes or items for the home that are specially designed and sold at a particular time: *Armani's stunning new autumn collection* ▶ **kolekcja, zestaw**

collective¹ /kəˈlektɪv/ adj. shared by a group of people together; not individual: *collective responsibility* ▶ **zbiorowy, grupowy**
■ **collectively** adv. ▶ **wspólnie**

collective² /kəˈlektɪv/ noun [C, with sing. or pl. verb] an organization or business that is owned and controlled by the people who work in it ▶ **spółdzielnia**

collector /kəˈlektə(r)/ noun [C] [in compounds] a person who collects things as a hobby or as part of their job: *a stamp collector* kolekcjoner znaczków ◇ *a tax/rent collector* poborca podatkowy/czynszu ◇ *a ticket collector* kontroler biletów ▶ **zbieracz**

college /ˈkɒlɪdʒ/ noun **1** [C,U] an institution where you can study after you leave school (at the age of 16): *a college of further education* szkoła policealna dla dorosłych ◇ *an art college* akademia sztuk pięknych ◇ *a sixth-form college* liceum ▶ **szkoła wyższa, kolegium, uczelnia**

> Jeżeli ktoś uczęszcza do **college** jako student/ka, wówczas przed tym rzeczownikiem nie używa się **the**: *He's at college in York.* ◇ *She's going to college in October.* Jeśli natomiast mowa o **college** jako instytucji czy budynku, wtedy używa się **the**: *I went to an art exhibition at the college last night.*

2 [C] (in the US) a university, or part of one, where students can study for a degree ▶ **szkoła wyższa 3** [C] (in Britain) one of the separate institutions into which certain universities are divided: *King's College, London* ▶ **kolegium**

collide /kəˈlaɪd/ verb [I] **collide (with sb/sth)** to crash; to hit sb/sth very hard while moving ▶ **zderzać się, wpadać (na kogoś/coś)**

collie /ˈkɒli/ noun [C] a dog with long hair and a long pointed nose. Collies are often used for guarding and looking after sheep. ▶ **owczarek szkocki**

colliery /ˈkɒliəri/ noun [C] (pl. **collieries**) (especially Brit.) a coal mine and its buildings ▶ **kopalnia węgla**

collision /kəˈlɪʒn/ noun [C,U] an occasion when things or people **collide**: *It was a* ***head-on collision*** (zderzenie czołowe) *and the driver was killed instantly.* ▶ **zderzenie, kolizja**
IDM **be on a collision course (with sb/sth) 1** to be in a situation which is certain to end in a disagreement or argument: *I'm not surprised they're arguing – they've been on a collision course over money all week.* ▶ **być na krawędzi kłótni 2** to be moving in a direction which is certain to cause a crash: *The ship was on a collision*

course with an iceberg. ▶ **zmierzać nieuchronnie do katastrofy**

collocation /ˌkɒləˈkeɪʃn/ noun **1** [C] a combination of words in a language, that happens very often and more frequently than would happen by chance: *'Resounding success' and 'crying shame' are English collocations.* ▶ **związek wyrazowy 2** [U] the fact that these combinations happen ▶ **łączliwość wyrazów**
■ **collocate** verb [I] (used about words) to be often used together in a language ▶ (*wyrazy*) **występować razem** | **collocate** noun [C] ▶ **kolokacja**

colloquial /kəˈləʊkwiəl/ adj. (used about words, phrases, etc.) used in spoken conversation, not in formal situations ▶ **potoczny**
■ **colloquially** /-kwiəli/ adv. ▶ **potocznie**

colloquialism /kəˈləʊkwiəlɪzəm/ noun [C] a **colloquial** word or phrase ▶ **kolokwializm**

collude /kəˈluːd/ verb [I] **collude (with sb) (in sth/in doing sth)**; **collude (with sb) (to do sth)** (formal) to work together secretly or illegally in order to trick other people: *Several people had colluded in the murder.* ▶ **działać (z kimś) w zmowie**

collusion /kəˈluːʒn/ noun [U] (formal) secret agreement, especially in order to do sth dishonest: *The drugs were brought into the country with the collusion of customs officials.* ▶ **zmowa**

cologne = EAU DE COLOGNE

colon /ˈkəʊlən/ noun [C] **1** the mark (:) used before a list, an explanation, an example, etc. ▶ **dwukropek 2** the lower part of the large **intestine** that carries food away from your stomach to the anus ▶ **okrężnica** ➲ picture at **body**

colonel /ˈkɜːnl/ noun [C] (abbr. **Col.**) an officer of a high level in the army ▶ **pułkownik**

colonial /kəˈləʊniəl/ adj. connected with or belonging to a **colony** ▶ **kolonialny**

colonialism /kəˈləʊniəlɪzəm/ noun [U] the practice by which a powerful country controls another country or countries, in order to become richer ▶ **kolonializm**

colonist /ˈkɒlənɪst/ noun [C] a person who goes to live in a country that has become a **colony** ▶ **kolonizator**

colonize (also -ise) /ˈkɒlənaɪz/ verb [T] to take control of another country or place and make it a **colony** ▶ **kolonizować**
■ **colonization** (also -isation) /ˌkɒlənaɪˈzeɪʃn; US -nəˈz-/ noun [U] ▶ **kolonizacja**

colony /ˈkɒləni/ noun [C] (pl. **colonies**) **1** a country or area that is ruled by another, more powerful country ▶ **kolonia 2** [with sing. or pl. verb] a group of people who go to live permanently in another country but keep their own habits and customs ▶ **kolonia 3** a group of the same type of animals, insects or plants living or growing in the same place: *a colony of ants* ▶ **kolonia**

colossal /kəˈlɒsl/ adj. extremely large: *a colossal building* ◇ *a colossal amount of money* ▶ **kolosalny, olbrzymi**

⚷ **colour**[1] (US color) /ˈkʌlə(r)/ noun **1** [C,U] the fact that sth is red, green, yellow, blue, etc.: *'What colour* (jakiego koloru) *is your car?' 'Red.'* ◇ *a dark/deep colour* ◇ *a bright colour* ◇ *a light/pale colour* ◇ *Those flowers certainly give the room a bit of colour.* ◇ *What colours do the Swedish team play in?* ▶ **kolor, barwa** ⓘ Mówi się **I like the colour blue** a nie ~~*I like blue colour*~~. **2** [U] the use of all the colours, not just black and white: *All the pictures in the book are* ***in colour*** (są kolorowe). ◇ *a colour TV* ▶ **kolor 3** [U] a red or pink colour in your face, particularly when it shows how healthy you are or that you are embarrassed: *You look much better now, you've got a bit more colour.* ◇ *Colour flooded her face when she thought of what had happened.* ▶ **rumieńce, kolory 4** [U,C] the colour of a person's skin, when it shows the race they belong to: *discrimination on the grounds of race, colour or religion* ▶ **kolor skóry, rasa 5** [U] interesting or exciting details: *It's a busy area, full of activity and colour.* ▶ **koloryt**
IDM **off colour** ill ▶ (*czuć się*) **nieswojo, marnie** (*wyglądać*)
with flying colours → FLYING

⚷ **colour**[2] (US color) /ˈkʌlə(r)/ verb [T] **1** to put colour on sth, for example by painting it: *The area coloured yellow on the map is desert.* ▶ **kolorować, malować** (*na jakiś kolor*) **2** to influence thoughts, opinions, etc.: *You shouldn't let one bad experience colour your attitude to everything.* ▶ **wpływać na coś**
PHR V **colour sth in** to fill a shape, a picture, etc. with colour using pencils, paint, etc.: *The children were colouring in pictures of animals.* ▶ **kolorować**

'colour-blind (US 'color-blind) adj. unable to see certain colours, especially red and green: *She is colour-blind.* Ona jest daltonistką. ▶ **cierpiący na daltonizm**

'colour code (US 'color code) noun [C] a system of marking things with different colours so that you can easily identify them ▶ **system segregowania wykorzystujący kolory**
■ **'colour-coded** adj.: *The files have labels that are colour-coded according to subject.* ▶ **posegregowane za wykorzystaniem wybranych kolorów**

⚷ **coloured** (US colored) /ˈkʌləd/ adj. **1** having colour or a particular colour: *brightly coloured lights* ◇ *a coffee-coloured dress* sukienka w kolorze kawowym ▶ **kolorowy, barwny 2** (used about a person) belonging to a race that does not have white skin ▶ (*osoba*) **innej rasy niż biała** ⓘ To słowo jest obecnie uważane za obraźliwe. Powinno się używać określenia **black**, **Asian** itp. **3** (**Coloured**) (in South Africa) having parents who are of different races ▶ (*w Africe Południowej*) **(***określa człowieka, którego rodzice należeli do innych ras***)**

colourful (US colorful) /ˈkʌləfl/ adj. **1** with bright colours; full of colour: *Gary wore a colourful shirt.* ▶ **barwny, kolorowy 2** full of interest or excitement: *He has a rather colourful past* (bujną przeszłość). ▶ **barwny**

colouring (US coloring) /ˈkʌlərɪŋ/ noun **1** [C,U] a substance that is used to give a particular colour to sth, especially food ▶ **barwnik, farbka 2** [U] the colour of a person's hair, skin, etc.: *to have fair/dark colouring* ▶ **karnacja, kolor** (*np. włosów*)

colourless (US colorless) /ˈkʌləĺəs/ adj. **1** without any colour: *a colourless liquid, like water* ▶ **bezbarwny 2** not interesting or exciting ▶ **bezbarwny, nudny** SYN **dull**

'colour scheme (US 'color scheme) noun [C] the way in which colours are arranged, especially in a room ▶ **tonacja kolorystyczna**

colt /kəʊlt/ noun [C] a young male horse ▶ **źrebak**

⚷ **column** /ˈkɒləm/ noun [C] **1** a tall solid vertical post made of stone, supporting or decorating a building or standing alone: *Nelson's Column is a monument in London.* ▶ **kolumna, filar, słup 2** something that has the shape of a column: *a column of smoke* ▶ **kolumna, słup 3** one of the vertical sections into which a printed page, especially in a newspaper, is divided: *a column of text* ▶ **kolumna, szpalta 4** a piece of writing in a newspaper or magazine that is part of a regular series or always written by the same writer: *the travel/gossip column* ▶ **felieton, rubryka 5** a series of numbers written one under the other: *to add up a column of figures* ▶ **kolumna 6** a long line of people, vehicles, etc., one following behind another: *a column of troops* ▶ **kolumna**

columnist /ˈkɒləmnɪst/ noun [C] a journalist who writes regular articles in a newspaper or magazine: *a gossip columnist* ▶ **felietonist(k)a**

coma /ˈkəʊmə/ noun [C] a deep unconscious state, often lasting for a long time and caused by serious illness or injury: *to go into/be in a coma* ▶ **śpiączka**

comatose /ˈkəʊmətəʊs/ adj. **1** deeply unconscious; in a coma ▶ **w stanie śpiączki 2** (informal) deeply asleep: *He had drunk a bottle of vodka and was comatose.* ▶ **śpiący jak zabity, zalany w trupa**

comb¹ /kəʊm/ noun [C] **1** a flat piece of metal or plastic with teeth that you use for making your hair tidy ▶ **grzebień 2** [usually sing.] an act of **combing** the hair: *Give your hair a comb* (uczesz się) *before you go out.* ▶ **czesanie (się)**

comb² /kəʊm/ verb [T] **1** to make your hair tidy using a comb ▶ **czesać 2 comb sth (for sb/sth)** to search an area carefully: *Police are combing the woodland for the murder weapon.* ▶ **przeczesywać**

combat¹ /ˈkɒmbæt/ noun [C,U] a fight, especially in war: *unarmed combat* walka wręcz ▶ **walka**

combat² /ˈkɒmbæt/ verb [T] to fight against sth; to try to stop or defeat sth: *to combat terrorism* ◇ *new medicines to combat heart disease* ▶ **walczyć przeciw czemuś, zwalczać**

combatant /ˈkɒmbətənt/ noun [C] a person who takes part in fighting, especially in war ▶ **osoba walcząca/wojująca**

combative /ˈkɒmbətɪv/ adj. ready and willing to fight or argue: *in a **combative mood/spirit*** ▶ **wojowniczy, napastliwy**

⚷ **combination** /ˌkɒmbɪˈneɪʃn/ noun [C,U] a number of people or things mixed or joined together; a mixture: *The team manager still hasn't found the right combination of players.* ◇ *On this course, you may study French in combination with Spanish or Italian.* ◇ *He left the job for a combination of reasons.* Odszedł z pracy z wielu różnych powodów. ▶ **połączenie, kombinacja**

combiˈnation lock noun [C] a type of lock which can only be opened by using a particular series of numbers or letters ▶ **zamek szyfrowy**

⚷ **combine** /kəmˈbaɪn/ verb **1** [I,T] **combine (sth) (with sb/sth)** to join or mix two or more things together: *The two organizations combined to form one company.* ◇ *Bad planning, combined with bad luck, led to the company's collapse.* ▶ **łączyć (się) 2** [T] **combine A and/with B** to do or have two or more things at the same time: *This car combines speed and reliability.* ◇ *to combine business with pleasure* łączyć przyjemne z pożytecznym ▶ **łączyć**

combined /kəmˈbaɪnd/ adj. done by a number of people joining together, resulting from the joining of two or more things: *The **combined efforts** of the emergency services prevented a major disaster.* ◇ *I use that room as a spare bedroom and office combined* (jako pokoju gościnnego oraz biura). ▶ **połączony**

combine harvester /ˌkɒmbaɪn ˈhɑːvɪstə(r)/ (also **combine**) noun [C] a large farm machine that both cuts a crop and separates the grain from the rest of the plant ▶ **kombajn** ➲ look at **harvest**

combustible /kəmˈbʌstəbl/ adj. able to begin burning easily: *combustible material/gases* ▶ **łatwopalny** SYN **inflammable**

combustion /kəmˈbʌstʃən/ noun [U] the process of burning: *an internal combustion engine* silnik spalinowy ▶ **spalanie**

⚷ **come** /kʌm/ verb [I] (pt **came** /keɪm/, pp **come**) **1** to move to or towards the person who is speaking or the place that sb is talking about: *Come here, please.* ◇ *Come and see what I've found.* ◇ *I hope you can come to my party.* ◇ *They're coming to stay for a week.* ◇ *The children came running* (przybiegły) *into the room.* ▶ **przychodzić, przyjeżdżać 2 come (to...)** to arrive somewhere or reach a particular place or time: *What time are you coming home?* ◇ *The time has come to say goodbye.* ◇ *Has the newspaper come yet?* ◇ *After a few hours in the jungle, we came to a river* ◇ *Her hair comes down to* (sięgają do) *her waist.* ◇ *The water in the pool came up to our knees* (dochodziła nam do kolan). ▶ **przychodzić, nadchodzić 3** to be in a particular position in a series: *March comes after February.* ◇ *I can't wait to find out what comes next in the story.* ◇ *Charlie came second* (był drugi) *in the exam.* ▶ **zajmować określoną pozycję, przychodzić, nadchodzić 4 come in sth** to be available: *Do these trousers come in a larger size?* ▶ **być dostępnym 5** to be produced by or from sth: *Wool comes from sheep.* ▶ **pochodzić z/od czegoś 6** to become open or loose: *Her hair has come untied* (rozwiązały się). ◇ *Your blouse has come undone.* Rozpięła ci się bluzka. **7 come to do sth** (used for talking about how, why or when sth happened): *How did you come to lose your passport?* Jak to się stało, że zgubiłeś swój paszport? **8 come to/into sth** to reach a particular state: *The military government **came to power*** (doszedł do władzy) *in a coup d'état.* ◇ *We were all sorry when the holiday **came to an end*** (skończyły się). ▶ **dochodzić do czegoś**

IDM **come and go** to be present for a short time and then go away: *The pain in my ear comes and goes* (raz jest, raz go nie ma). ▶ **przychodzić i odchodzić**

come easily, naturally, etc. to sb to be easy, natural, etc. for sb to do: *Apologizing does not come easily to her.* ▶ **łatwo przychodzić (komuś)**

come to nothing; not come to anything to fail; to not be successful: *Unfortunately, all his efforts came to nothing.* ▶ **spełznąć na niczym**

come what may in spite of any problems or difficulties you may have ▶ **mimo wszystko**

how come...? (informal) why or how: *How come you're back so early?* ▶ **jak to się stało, że...?**

to come [used after a noun] in the future: *You'll regret it in years to come.* ▶ **w przyszłości**

when it comes to sth/to doing sth when it is a question of sth: *When it comes to value for money, these prices are hard to beat.* ▶ **gdy chodzi o coś/to**

ⓘ **Come** występuje w innych idiomach, np. **come to a head**. Zob. hasła odpowiednich rzeczowników, przymiotników itp.

PHR V **come about** to happen: *How did this situation come about?* ▶ **zdarzać się**

come across/over (as sth) to make an impression of a particular type: *Elizabeth comes across as being rather shy.* ▶ **sprawiać wrażenie**

come across sb/sth to meet or find sb/sth by chance: *I came across this book in a second-hand shop.* ▶ **natykać się na kogoś/coś, napotykać kogoś/coś**

come along 1 to arrive or appear: *An old man was coming along the road.* ▶ **pojawiać się, zbliżać się** (*np. ulicą*) **2** = COME ON (2) **3** = COME ON (3)

come apart to break into pieces: *This old coat is coming apart at the seams.* ▶ **rozpadać się, pruć się**

come away (from sth) to become separated from sth: *The wallpaper is coming away from the wall in the corner.* ▶ **odpadać, odrywać się**

come away with sth to leave a place with a particular opinion or feeling: *We came away with a very favourable impression of Cambridge.* ▶ **odchodzić/odjeżdżać** (*z określonymi wrażeniami*)

come back 1 to return: *I don't know what time I'll be coming back.* ▶ **wracać 2** to become popular or fashionable again: *Flared trousers are coming back again.* ▶ **wracać**

come back (to sb) to be remembered: *When I went to Italy again, my Italian started to come back to me.* ▶ **wracać, przypominać się**

come before sb/sth to be more important than sb/sth else: *Mark feels his family comes before his career.* ▶ **mieć pierwszeństwo, być ważniejszym od czegoś**
come between sb and sb to damage the relationship between two people: *Arguments over money came between the two brothers.* ▶ **poróżnić kogoś z kimś**
come by sth to manage to get sth: *Fresh vegetables are hard to come by in the winter.* ▶ **zdobywać coś**
come down 1 to fall down: *The power lines came down in the storm.* ▶ **walić się, runąć 2** (used about an aircraft, etc.) to land: *The helicopter came down in a field.* ▶ **lądować 3** (used about prices) to become lower: *The price of land has come down in the past year.* ▶ (*ceny*) **obniżać się**
come down to sth/to doing sth (informal) to be able to be explained by a single important point: *It all comes down to having the right qualifications.* ▶ **sprowadzać się do czegoś**
come down with sth to become ill with sth: *I think I'm coming down with flu* (bierze mnie grypa). ▶ **zachorować na coś**
come forward to offer help: *The police are asking witnesses to come forward.* Policja prosi świadków o pomoc w dochodzeniu. ▶ **przychodzić z pomocą**
come from... to live in or have been born in a place: *Where do you come from originally?* ▶ **pochodzić skądś/z jakiegoś miejsca**
come from (doing) sth to be the result of sth: *'I'm tired.' 'That comes from all the late nights you've had.'* ▶ **wynikać z czegoś, być rezultatem czegoś**
come in 1 to enter a place: *Come in and sit down.* ▶ **wchodzić** (*do środka*) **2** (used about the **tides**) to move towards the land and cover the beach: *The tide is coming in.* Nadchodzi przypływ. ➲ look at **tide 3** to become popular or fashionable: *Punk fashions came in in the seventies.* ▶ (*moda itp.*) **przyjąć się 4** (used about news or information) to be received: *Reports are coming in of fighting in Beirut.* ▶ (*wiadomości*) **przychodzić, nadchodzić**
come in for sth to receive sth, especially sth unpleasant: *The government came in for a lot of criticism.* ▶ **być poddanym czemuś, spotykać się** (*np. z ostrą krytyką*)
come of sth/of doing sth to be the result of sth: *We've written to several companies asking for help but nothing has come of it* (nic z tego nie wyszło) *yet.* ▶ **wynikać z czegoś**
come off 1 to be able to be removed: *Does the hood come off?* ▶ **być ruchomym, dawać się zdejmować 2** (informal) to be successful: *The deal seems unlikely to come off.* ▶ **udawać się, wychodzić 3** [before an adverb] (informal) to be in a good, bad, etc. situation as a result of sth: *Unfortunately, Dennis came off worst in the fight.* ▶ **wychodzić na czymś** (*dobrze lub źle*)
come off (sth) 1 to fall off sth: *Kim came off her bicycle and broke her leg.* ▶ **spadać (z czegoś) 2** to become removed from sth: *One of the legs has come off this table.* ▶ **odpadać/odlatywać (z czegoś)**
come off it (informal) (used to say that you do not believe sb/sth or that you strongly disagree with sb): *'I thought it was quite a good performance.' 'Oh, come off it – it was awful!'* ▶ **nie przesadzaj, no co ty!**
come on 1 to start to act, play in a game of sport, etc.: *The audience jeered every time the villain came on.* ◇ *The substitute came on in the second half.* ▶ **pojawiać się, wychodzić** (*np. na scenę*) **2** (also **come along**) to make progress or to improve: *Your English is coming on nicely.* ▶ **postępować, posuwać się (naprzód) 3** (also **Come along!**) (used to tell sb to hurry up, try harder, etc.): *Come on or we'll be late!* ▶ **no dalej!, no wiesz! 4** to begin: *I've got a cold coming on.* ▶ (*choroba*) **brać kogoś**
come out 1 to appear: *The rain stopped and the sun came out.* ▶ **ukazywać się, wychodzić** (*zza chmur*) **2** to be published: *The report came out in 1998.* ▶ **wychodzić** (*drukiem*) **3** to become known: *It was only after David's death that the truth came out.* ▶ **wychodzić na jaw 4** (used about a photograph, etc.) to be produced successfully: *Only one of our photos came out.* ▶ (*zdjęcie*) **wychodzić** (*dobrze*) **5** to no longer hide the fact that you are **homosexual** ▶ **wyjawić, że jest się homoseksualistą**
come out (of sth) to be removed from sth: *Red wine stains don't come out easily.* ▶ (*plama itp.*) **schodzić**
come out against sth to say in public that you do not like or agree with sth: *The Prime Minister came out against capital punishment.* ▶ **wypowiadać się przeciw czemuś**
come out in sth to become covered in spots, etc.: *Heat makes him come out in a rash.* ▶ **dostawać** (*np. wysypki*)
come out with sth to say sth unexpectedly: *The children came out with all kinds of stories.* ▶ **wyrywać się z czymś**
come over = COME ACROSS/OVER (AS STH)
come over (to...) (from...) to visit people or a place a long way away: *They've invited us to come over to Australia for a holiday.* ▶ **przyjeżdżać (dokądś) (skądś)**
come over sb (used about a feeling) to affect sb: *A feeling of despair came over me.* ▶ (*uczucie*) **ogarniać kogoś**
come round 1 (also **come to**) to become conscious again ▶ **odzyskiwać przytomność** OPP **pass out 2** (used about an event that happens regularly) to happen: *The end of the holidays always comes round very quickly.* ▶ **nadchodzić**
come round (to...) to visit a person or place not far away: *Do you want to come round for lunch on Saturday?* ▶ **przychodzić** (*z wizytą*)
come round (to sth) to change your opinion so that you agree with sb/sth: *They finally came round to our way of thinking.* ▶ **przekonać się (do czegoś)**
come through (used about news, information, etc.) to arrive: *The football results are just coming through.* ▶ (*wiadomości itp.*) **nadchodzić**
come through (sth) to escape injury or death in a dangerous situation, illness, etc.: *to come through an enemy attack* ▶ **wychodzić cało z czegoś**
come to = COME ROUND (1)
come to sth 1 to equal or total a particular amount: *The bill for the meal came to £35.* ▶ **wynosić ileś 2** to result in a bad situation: *We will sell the house to pay our debts if we have to but we hope it won't come to that.* ▶ **dochodzić do czegoś** (*złego*)
come under sth to be included in a particular section, department, etc.: *Garages that sell cars come under 'car dealers' in the telephone book.* ▶ **należeć** (*do pewnej kategorii*)
come up 1 (used about a plant) to appear above the soil ▶ (*roślina*) **wschodzić, wyrastać 2** (used about the sun and moon) to rise ▶ (*słońce/księżyc*) **wschodzić 3** to happen or be going to happen in the future: *Something's come up at work* (coś mi wyskoczyło w pracy) *so I won't be home until late tonight.* ◇ *I have an important meeting coming up next week.* ▶ **zdarzać się; zbliżać się 4** to be discussed or mentioned: *The subject of religion came up.* ▶ **wypływać** (*np. w dyskusji*)
come up against sb/sth to find a problem or difficulty that you have to deal with: *I had to stop when I came up against a high fence.* ▶ **natrafiać na kogoś/coś**
come up to sth to be as good as usual or as necessary: *This piece of work does not come up to your usual standard.* ▶ **dorównywać czemuś**
come up with sth to find an answer or solution to sth: *Engineers have come up with new ways of saving energy.* ▶ **znaleźć** (*np. rozwiązanie problemu*)

comeback /ˈkʌmbæk/ noun [C] a return to a position of strength or importance that you had before: *The former world champion is hoping to* ***make a comeback.*** ▶ **powrót** (*np. na scenę*)

comedian /kəˈmiːdiən/ (also **comic**) noun [C] a person whose job is to entertain people and make them laugh, for example by telling jokes ▶ **komik** ⓘ Kobieta komik nazywana jest czasami **comedienne**.

comedown /ˈkʌmdaʊn/ noun [sing.] (informal) a loss of importance or social position: *It's* ***a bit of a comedown*** *for her having to move to a smaller house.* ▶ **obniżenie się stopy życiowej**, **pogorszenie** (*sytuacji*)

comedy /ˈkɒmədi/ noun (pl. **comedies**) **1** [C] an amusing play, film, etc. that has a happy ending: *a romantic comedy* ▶ **komedia** ➲ look at **tragedy** **2** [U] the quality of being amusing or making people laugh: *There is a hint of comedy in all her novels.* ▶ **komizm**, **komedia** SYN **humour**

ˈ**come-on** noun [usually sing.] (informal) an object or action which is intended to attract sb or to persuade them to do sth: *She was definitely giving him the come-on.* Dawała mu zdecydowanie do zrozumienia, że jest nim zainteresowana. ▶ **wabik**, **chwyt** (*np. reklamowy*)

comet /ˈkɒmɪt; US -mət/ noun [C] an object in space that looks like a bright star with a tail and that moves around the sun ▶ **kometa**

comfort¹ /ˈkʌmfət/ noun **1** [U] the state of having everything your body needs, or of having a pleasant life: *Most people expect to live* ***in comfort*** (mieszkać wygodnie) *in their old age.* ◇ *to travel* ***in comfort*** podróżować wygodnie ▶ **komfort**, **wygoda** **2** [U] the feeling of being physically relaxed and in no pain: *This car has been specially designed for extra comfort.* ▶ **wygoda**, **komfort** OPP **discomfort** **3** [U] help or kindness to sb who is suffering: *I tried to offer a few words of comfort.* ▶ **pociecha**, **otucha** **4** [sing.] **be a comfort (to sb)** a person or thing that helps you when you are very sad or worried ▶ **ostoja**, **pociecha** **5** [C] something that makes your life easier or more pleasant: *the comforts of home* ▶ **wygoda** OPP **discomfort**

comfort² /ˈkʌmfət/ verb [T] to try to make sb feel less worried or unhappy: *to comfort a crying child* ▶ **pocieszać**, **podnosić na duchu**

comfortable /ˈkʌmftəbl/ adj. **1** (also informal **comfy** /ˈkʌmfi/) that makes you feel physically relaxed and in no pain; that provides you with everything your body needs: *Sit down and make yourselves comfortable* (rozgośćcie się). ◇ *a comfortable pair of shoes* ◇ *a comfortable temperature* ▶ **wygodny**, **komfortowy** OPP **uncomfortable** **2** not having or causing worry, difficulty, etc.: *He did not feel comfortable* (czuł się nieswojo) *in the presence of so many women.* ▶ **wygodny**, **przyjemny** **3** having or providing enough money for all your needs: *They are not wealthy but they're quite comfortable* (nieźle im się powodzi). ▶ **mający lub zapewniający życie bez problemów finansowych** ➲ look at **convenient**
■ **comfortably** /-əbli/ adv. ▶ **wygodnie**; **bezpiecznie**

comic¹ /ˈkɒmɪk/ adj. that makes you laugh; connected with amusing entertainment ▶ **śmieszny**, **komiczny**

comic² /ˈkɒmɪk/ noun [C] **1** = COMEDIAN **2** (especially US ˈ**comic book**) a magazine for children that tells stories through pictures ▶ **komiks**

comical /ˈkɒmɪkl/ adj. that makes you laugh; funny ▶ **śmieszny**, **komiczny**
■ **comically** /-kli/ adv. ▶ **śmiesznie**, **komicznie**

ˈ**comic strip** (also ˈ**strip cartoon**) noun [C] a short series of pictures that tell a funny story, for example in a newspaper ▶ **historyjka obrazkowa**

coming /ˈkʌmɪŋ/ noun [sing.] the moment when sth new arrives or begins: *The coming of the computer meant the loss of many jobs.* ▶ **przyjście**, **nadejście**, **nastanie**
■ **coming** adj. [only before a noun]: *We've got a lot of plans for the coming year.* ▶ **nadchodzący**, **najbliższy**

comma /ˈkɒmə/ noun [C] the mark (,) used for dividing parts of a sentence or items in a list ▶ **przecinek**

command¹ /kəˈmɑːnd; US -mænd/ noun **1** [C] an order: *The captain's commands must be obeyed without question.* ◇ *I command you to go!* (wypowiedziane przez król-a/ową) ▶ **rozkaz** **2** [U] control over sb/sth: *Who is* ***in command of*** (kto dowodzi) *the expedition?* ◇ ***to take command of*** *a situation* zapanować nad sytuacją ▶ **dowództwo**, **władanie** **3** [sing.] the state of being able to do or use sth well: *She has a good command of French.* Ona dobrze włada francuskim. ▶ **znajomość**
IDM **at/by sb's command** (formal) because you were ordered by sb ▶ **na czyjś rozkaz**
be at sb's command to be ready to obey sb ▶ **być do czyjejś dyspozycji**

command² /kəˈmɑːnd; US -ˈmænd/ verb **1** [I,T] (formal) **command (sb to do sth)** to tell or order sb to do sth: *I command you to leave now!* ▶ **rozkazywać** **2** [T] **command sb/sth** to control or be in charge of sb/sth: *to command a ship/regiment/army* ▶ **dowodzić** **3** [T] to deserve and get sth: *The old man commanded great respect.* ▶ **wzbudzać**

commandant /ˈkɒməndænt/ noun [C] the officer in charge of a particular group of people or institution ▶ **komendant**

commandeer /ˌkɒmənˈdɪə(r)/ verb [T] to take control or possession of sth for military or police use ▶ **rekwirować**

commander /kəˈmɑːndə(r); US -ˈmæn-/ noun [C] **1** a person who controls or is in charge of a military organization or group ▶ **dowódca** **2** (Brit.) an officer at a fairly high level in the navy ▶ **komandor**

commanding /kəˈmɑːndɪŋ; US -ˈmæn-/ adj. **1** [only before a noun] in charge or having control of sb/sth: *Who is your commanding officer?* ▶ **dowodzący** **2** [usually before a noun] strong or powerful: *to speak in a commanding tone of voice* ▶ **władczy**, **imponujący** **3** [only before a noun] if a building is in a **commanding position** or has a **commanding view** you can see the area around very well from it: *The castle occupied a commanding position* (dominował) *at the head of the valley.*

commandment (also **Commandment**) /kəˈmɑːndmənt; US -ˈmæn-/ noun [C] (formal) one of the ten important laws that Christian people should obey ▶ **przykazanie**

commando /kəˈmɑːndəʊ; US -ˈmæn-/ noun [C] (pl. **commandos**) one of a group of soldiers who is trained to make sudden attacks in enemy areas ▶ **komandos**

commemorate /kəˈmeməreɪt/ verb [T] to exist or take place in order to make people remember a special event: *a statue commemorating all the soldiers who died in the last war* ▶ **czcić**; **upamiętniać**
■ **commemoration** /kəˌmeməˈreɪʃn/ noun [C,U]: *The concerts were held* ***in commemoration*** (dla upamiętnienia) *of the 200th anniversary of Mozart's death.* ▶ **uczczenie**

commemorative /kəˈmemərətɪv; US -reɪt-/ adj. intended to help people remember and respect an important person or event in the past: *commemorative stamps* ▶ **pamiątkowy**

commence /kəˈmens/ verb [I,T] (formal) **commence sth/doing sth** to start or begin (sth) ▶ **rozpoczynać** ➲ note at **begin**
■ **commencement** noun [C,U] ▶ **rozpoczęcie**

commend /kəˈmend/ verb [T] (formal) to say officially that sb/sth is very good: *Dean was commended for his excellent work.* ▶ **chwalić**

commendable /kəˈmendəbl/ adj. (formal) that people think is good: *She acted with commendable honesty and fairness.* ▶ **chwalebny, godny polecenia**

🔑**comment¹** /ˈkɒment/ noun [C,U] **comment (on sth)** something that you say or write that gives your opinion or feeling about sth: *I heard someone **make a** rude **comment** about my clothes.* ◇ *The chancellor was not available for comment.* Kanclerz był nieuchwytny, aby udzielić komentarza. ▶ **uwaga, komentarz** ➲ look at **observation, remark**

IDM **no comment** (used in reply to a question when you do not want to say anything at all): *'Mr President, how do you feel about these latest developments?' 'No comment.'* ▶ **bez komentarza**

🔑**comment²** /ˈkɒment/ verb [I] **comment (on sth)** to say what you think or feel about sth: *Several people commented on how ill David looked.* ▶ **komentować, zwracać uwagę**

commentary /ˈkɒməntri/ noun (pl. **commentaries**) **1** [C,U] a spoken description on the radio or TV of sth as it is happening: *a sports commentary* ▶ **sprawozdanie, komentarz 2** [C] a written explanation or discussion of sth such as a book or play: *a critical commentary on the final speech of the play* ▶ **komentarz 3** [C,U] a criticism or discussion of sth: *This drug scandal is a sad commentary on the state of the sport.* ▶ **przykład, komentarz**

commentate /ˈkɒmənteɪt/ verb [I] **commentate (on sth)** to give a spoken description on the radio or TV of sth as it is happening ▶ **komentować**

commentator /ˈkɒmənteɪtə(r)/ noun [C] **1** a person who gives their opinion about sth on the radio, on TV or in a newspaper: *a political commentator* ▶ **komentator/ka 2** a person who gives a spoken description on radio or TV of sth as it is happening: *a sports commentator* ▶ **komentator/ka, sprawozdawca**

commerce /ˈkɒmɜːs/ noun [U] the business of buying and selling things ▶ **handel** ➲ look at **trade**

🔑**commercial¹** /kəˈmɜːʃl/ adj. **1** connected with buying and selling goods and services: *commercial law* ▶ **handlowy 2** selling sth or sold in large quantities to the public: *commercial airlines/products* ▶ **komercyjny 3** [only before a noun] making or trying to make money: *Although it won a lot of awards, the film was not a commercial success.* ▶ **komercyjny**

■ **commercially** /-ʃəli/ adv.: *The factory was closed down because it was no longer commercially viable* (nie była już opłacalna). ▶ **handlowo; komercyjnie**

commercial² /kəˈmɜːʃl/ noun [C] an advertisement on TV or the radio: *a commercial break* przerwa na reklamę ▶ **reklama**

commercialism /kəˈmɜːʃəlɪzəm/ noun [U] the attitude that making money is more important than anything else ▶ **komercjalizm**

commercialize (also -ise) /kəˈmɜːʃəlaɪz/ verb [T] to try to make money out of sth, even if it means spoiling it: *Christmas has become very commercialized over recent years* (bardzo się ostatnio skomercjalizowało). ▶ **komercjalizować**

■ **commercialization** (also -isation) /kəˌmɜːʃəlaɪˈzeɪʃn; US -ʃləˈz-/ noun [U] ▶ **komercjalizacja**

commiserate /kəˈmɪzəreɪt/ verb [I] (formal) **commiserate (with sb) (on/over/for sth)** to feel sorry for and show understanding towards sb who is unhappy or in difficulty: *I commiserated with Debbie over losing her job.* ▶ **wyrażać współczucie**

commiseration /kəˌmɪzəˈreɪʃn/ noun [U,C] (formal) an expression of sympathy for sb who has had sth unpleasant happen to them, especially not winning a competition: *I offered him my commiseration.* ▶ **wyrazy współczucia**

🔑**commission¹** /kəˈmɪʃn/ noun **1** (often **Commission**) [C] an official group of people who are asked to find out about sth: *A Commission was appointed to investigate the causes of the accident.* ▶ **komisja 2** [C,U] money that you get for selling sth: *Agents get 10% commission on everything they sell.* ▶ **prowizja 3** [C,U] money that a bank, etc. charges for providing a particular service: *The bureau de change charges 5% commission.* ▶ **prowizja 4** [C] a formal request to an artist, writer, etc. to produce a piece of work: *He received a commission to write a play for the festival.* ▶ **zamówienie, zlecenie**

🔑**commission²** /kəˈmɪʃn/ verb [T] **commission sb (to do sth); commission sth (from sb)** to ask an artist, writer, etc. to do a piece of work: *to commission an architect to design a building* ▶ **zlecać, zamawiać**

commissioner /kəˈmɪʃənə(r)/ noun [C] the head of the police or of a government department in some countries ▶ **pełnomocnik** (*np. rządu*), **komisarz**

🔑**commit** /kəˈmɪt/ verb [T] (**committing; committed**) **1** to do sth bad or illegal: *to commit suicide/a crime* ▶ **popełniać 2 commit sb/yourself (to sth/to doing sth)** to make a definite agreement or promise to do sth: *I can't commit myself to helping you tomorrow.* ▶ **zobowiązywać (się)** ➲ look at **non-committal 3 commit yourself (on sth)** to make a decision or give an opinion publicly so that it is then difficult to change it: *I'm not going to commit myself on who will win the election.* ▶ **zajmować stanowisko w sprawie, angażować się (w coś)** ➲ look at **non-committal 4** (formal) to decide to use money or time in a certain way: *The government has committed £2 billion to education.* ▶ **przeznaczać, poświęcać 5** (formal) **commit sb to sth** to send sb to a prison, mental hospital, etc.: *She was committed to a psychiatric hospital.* ▶ **uwięzić; umieszczać**

🔑**commitment** /kəˈmɪtmənt/ noun **1** [C,U] a promise or agreement to do sth; a responsibility: *When I **make a commitment*** (kiedy się zobowiążę) *I always stick to it.* ◇ *Helen now works fewer hours because of **family commitments**.* ▶ **zobowiązanie 2** [U] **commitment (to sth)** being prepared to give a lot of your time and attention to sth because you believe it is right or important: *I admire Gary's commitment to protecting the environment.* ▶ **zaangażowanie, poświęcenie**

committed /kəˈmɪtɪd/ adj. **committed (to sth)** prepared to give a lot of your time and attention to sth because you believe it is right or important: *The company is committed to providing quality products.* ▶ **zaangażowany, oddany**

🔑**committee** /kəˈmɪti/ noun [C, with sing. or pl. verb] a group of people who have been chosen to discuss sth or decide sth: *to be/sit on a committee* ◇ *The planning committee meets/meet twice a week.* ▶ **komisja, zarząd, komitet**

commodity /kəˈmɒdəti/ noun [C] (pl. **commodities**) a product or material that can be bought and sold: *Salt was once a very valuable commodity.* ▶ **towar**

🔑**common¹** /ˈkɒmən/ adj. **1** happening or found often or in many places; usual: *The daisy is a common wild flower.* ◇ *Pilot error is the commonest/most common cause of plane crashes.* ◇ *Nowadays it is quite common for people to go abroad* (wiele osób jeździ za granicę) *for their holidays.* ◇ *It is common practice to have security cameras in shops.* Kamery są powszechnie zainstalowane w sklepach. ▶ **powszechny, pospolity** OPP **uncommon 2 common (to sb/sth)** shared by or belonging to two or more people or groups; shared by most or all people: *This type of behaviour is common to most children of that age.* ◇ *We have a common interest in gardening.* ▶ **wspólny 3** [only before a noun] not special; ordinary: *The officers had much better living conditions than the common soldiers.* ▶ **zwyczajny, pospolity** OPP **uncommon 4** (Brit., informal) having or showing a lack of education: *Don't speak like that. It's common!* ▶ **pospolity, prostacki**

IDM **be common/public knowledge** → KNOWLEDGE

common² /ˈkɒmən/ noun [C] an area of open land that anyone can use ▶ **błonie** (*gminne*)

IDM **have sth in common (with sb/sth)** to share sth with sb/sth else: *to have a lot in common with somebody* ▶ **mieć coś wspólnego (z kimś/czymś)**

in common with sb/sth (formal) in the same way as sb/sth else; like sb/sth: *This company, in common with many others* (jak wiele innych), *is losing a lot of money.* ▶ **razem z kimś/czymś**

ˌcommon ˈground noun [U] beliefs, interests, etc. that two or more people or groups share: *They have very little common ground.* Oni mają bardzo niewiele wspólnego. ▶ **wspólne zainteresowania/poglądy itp.**

ˌcommon ˈlaw noun [U] laws in England that are based on decisions that judges have made, not laws that were made by Parliament ▶ **prawo zwyczajowe**

🔑 **commonly** /ˈkɒmənli/ adv. normally; usually ▶ **powszechnie, zwykle**

ˌcommon ˈnoun noun [C] a word such as *table, cat* or *sea* that refers to an object or a thing but is not the name of a particular person, place or thing ▶ **rzeczownik pospolity**

commonplace /ˈkɒmənpleɪs/ adj. not exciting or unusual; ordinary: *Foreign travel has become commonplace* (spowszedniały) *in recent years.* ▶ **zwyczajny, prozaiczny**

ˈcommon room noun [C] a room in a school, university, etc. where students or teachers can go to relax when they are not in class ▶ **świetlica** (*dla uczniów/studentów*), **sala rekreacyjna** (*na uczelni*)

the **Commons** = HOUSE OF COMMONS ➲ note at **Parliament**

ˌcommon ˈsense noun [U] the ability to make good sensible decisions or to behave in a sensible way ▶ **zdrowy rozsądek**

the **Commonwealth** /ˈkɒmənwelθ/ noun [sing.] the group of countries that once formed the British Empire and that work together in a friendly way ▶ **Wspólnota Brytyjska**

commotion /kəˈməʊʃn/ noun [sing., U] great noise or excitement ▶ **zamieszanie, zgiełk**

communal /kəˈmjuːnl; ˈkɒmjənl/ adj. shared by a group of people: *a communal kitchen* ▶ (*pomieszczenie itp.*) **wspólny**

commune /ˈkɒmjuːn/ noun [C, with sing. or pl. verb] a group of people, not from the same family, who live together and share their property and responsibilities ▶ **komuna**

🔑 **communicate** /kəˈmjuːnɪkeɪt/ verb **1** [I,T] to share and exchange information, ideas or feelings with sb: *Parents often have difficulty communicating with their teenage children.* ◇ *Our boss is good at communicating her ideas to the team.* ▶ **porozumiewać się; przekazywać** (*np. wiadomości*) **2** [T, usually passive] (formal) to pass a disease from one person or animal to another ▶ **przenosić** (*np. chorobę*) **3** [I] to lead from one place to another: *two rooms with a communicating door* dwa pokoje w amfiladzie ▶ **łączyć się ze sobą**

🔑 **communication** /kəˌmjuːnɪˈkeɪʃn/ noun **1** [U] the act of sharing or exchanging information, ideas or feelings: *Radio is the only means of communication in remote areas.* ▶ **komunikacja, kontakt, łączność 2** (**communications**) [pl.] the methods that are used for travelling to and from a place or for sending messages between places: *The telephone lines are down so communications are very difficult.* ▶ **łączność, komunikacja 3** [C] (formal) a message: *a communication from head office* ▶ **wiadomość, komunikat**

IDM **be in communication with sb/sth** to be in regular contact with sb/sth: *We are in regular* ***communication with*** *our head office in New York.* ▶ **mieć łączność z kimś/czymś, być w kontakcie z kimś/czymś**

communicative /kəˈmjuːnɪkətɪv; US -keɪt-/ adj. willing and able to talk and share ideas, etc.: *Paolo has excellent communicative skills.* ▶ **rozmowny, komunikatywny**

communion /kəˈmjuːniən/ noun [U] **1** (**Communion**) a Christian church ceremony in which people share bread and wine ▶ **komunia 2** (formal) the sharing of thoughts or feelings ▶ **wspólnota, bliskość, łączność duchowa**

communiqué /kəˈmjuːnɪkeɪ; US kəˌmjuːnəˈkeɪ/ noun [C] (formal) an official statement, especially from a government, a political group, etc. ▶ **komunikat**

communism /ˈkɒmjunɪzəm/ noun [U] the political system in which the state owns and controls all factories, farms, services etc. and aims to treat everyone equally ▶ **komunizm**

communist (also **Communist**) /ˈkɒmjənɪst/ noun [C] a person who believes in or supports **communism**; a member of the **Communist** Party ▶ **komunist(k)a** ℹ Kiedy mówi się o konkretnym społeczeństwie lub partii politycznej, wówczas **Communism** i **Communist** pisze się dużą literą: *He was a member of the Communist Party.*

■ **communist** (also **Communist**) adj. ▶ **komunistyczny**

🔑 **community** /kəˈmjuːnəti/ noun (pl. **communities**) **1** (**the community**) [sing.] all the people who live in a particular place, area, etc. when considered as a group: *Recent increases in crime have disturbed the whole community.* ◇ *community service* praca społeczna ▶ **społeczność, środowisko 2** [C, with sing. or pl. verb] a group of people who have sth in common: *the Asian community in Britain* ◇ *the business community* ▶ **społeczność 3** [U] the feeling of belonging to a group in the place where you live: *There is a strong sense of community in the neighbourhood.* ▶ **wspólnota**

comˈmunity centre (US **comˈmunity center**) noun [C] a building that local people can use for meetings, classes, sports, etc. ▶ **ośrodek kultury**

comˌmunity ˈservice noun [U] work helping people in the local community that sb does without being paid, either because they want to, or because they have been ordered to by a court as a punishment ▶ **praca społeczna** (*wykonywana dobrowolnie lub nakazana wyrokiem sądowym*)

commute /kəˈmjuːt/ verb [I] to travel a long distance from home to work every day: *A lot of people commute to London from nearby towns.* ▶ **dojeżdżać do pracy** ➲ note at **train**

■ **commuter** noun [C] ▶ **dojeżdżając-y/a do pracy**

compact /kəmˈpækt/ adj. small and easy to carry: *a compact camera* ▶ **zajmujący mało miejsca**

ˌcompact ˈdisc = CD

companion /kəmˈpæniən/ noun [C] a person or an animal who you spend a lot of time or go somewhere with: *a travelling companion* ▶ **towarzysz/ka**

companionship /kəmˈpæniənʃɪp/ noun [U] the pleasant feeling of having a friendly relationship with sb and not being alone ▶ **towarzystwo**

🔑 **company** /ˈkʌmpəni/ noun (abbr. **Co.** /kəʊ/) (pl. **companies**) **1** [C, with sing. or pl. verb] a business organization selling goods or services: *The company is/are planning to build a new factory.* ▶ **przedsiębiorstwo, firma** ℹ Nazwy firm pisze się dużą literą. Skrót od **Company** to **Co.**: *the Walt Disney Company* ◇ *Milton & Co.* **2** [C, with sing. or pl. verb] a group of actors, singers, dancers, etc.: *a ballet company* ◇ *the Royal Shakespeare Company* ▶ **trupa tea-**

tralna **3** [U] being with a person: *Jeffrey is very good company.* ▶ **towarzystwo 4** [U] a visitor or visitors: *Sorry, I wouldn't have called if I'd known you had company.* ▶ **goście**

IDM **keep sb company** to go or be with sb so that they are not alone: *She was nervous so I went with her to keep her company.* ▶ **dotrzymywać komuś towarzystwa**

part company → PART[2]

comparable /ˈkɒmpərəbl/ adj. **comparable (to/with sb/sth)** of a similar standard or size; that can be compared with sth: *The population of Britain is comparable to that of France.* ▶ **podobny, porównywalny**

comparative[1] /kəmˈpærətɪv/ adj. **1** that compares things of the same kind: *a comparative study of systems of government* ▶ **porównawczy 2** compared with sth else or with what is usual or normal: *He had problems with the written exam but passed the practical exam with comparative ease.* ▶ **względny 3** (used about the form of an adjective or adverb) expressing a greater amount, quality, size, etc.: *'Hotter' and 'more quickly' are the comparative forms of 'hot' and 'quickly'.* ▶ *(gram.: stopień)* **wyższy**

comparative[2] /kəmˈpærətɪv/ noun [C] the form of an adjective or adverb that expresses a greater amount, quality, size, etc.: *'Bigger' is the comparative of 'big'.* ▶ *(gram.)* **stopień wyższy**

comparatively /kəmˈpærətɪvli/ adv. when compared with sth else or with what is usual; fairly: *Fortunately, the disease is comparatively rare nowadays.* ▶ **względnie, stosunkowo**

🔑 **compare** /kəmˈpeə(r)/ verb **1** [T] (abbr. **cf.**) **compare A and B; compare A with/to B** to consider people or things in order to see how similar or how different they are: *When the police compared the two letters, they realized that they had been written by the same person.* ▶ **porównywać 2** [I] **compare (with/to sb/sth)** to be as good as sb/sth: *There is nothing to compare with* (nic się nie równa) *the taste of bread fresh from the oven.* ◇ *Her last film was brilliant but this one simply doesn't compare* (po prostu mu nie dorównuje). ◇ *This car compares favourably with more expensive models.* Ten samochód wypada korzystnie w porównaniu z droższymi modelami. ▶ **równać się 3** [T] **compare A to B** to say that sb/sth is similar to sb/sth else: *When it was built, people compared the stadium to a spaceship.* ▶ **porównywać, przyrównywać**

IDM **compare notes (with sb)** to discuss your opinions, ideas, experiences, etc. with sb else: *At the beginning of term we met and compared notes about the holidays.* ▶ **wymieniać** *(np. poglądy)*

■ **compared** adj. **compared to/with sb/sth** in comparison with sb/sth; considered in relation to sb/sth: *I'm quite a patient person, **compared with** him.* ◇ ***Compared to** the place where I grew up, this town is exciting.* ▶ **w porównaniu z kimś/czymś**

🔑 **comparison** /kəmˈpærɪsn/ noun [C,U] an act of comparing; a statement in which people or things are compared: *Put the new one and the old one side by side, **for comparison**.* ◇ *It's hard to **make comparisons** between* (trudno porównać) *two athletes from different sports.* ▶ **porównanie**

IDM **by/in comparison (with sb/sth)** when compared: *In comparison with many other people, they're quite well off.* ▶ **w porównaniu (z kimś/czymś)**

compartment /kəmˈpɑːtmənt/ noun [C] **1** one of the separate sections which railway **carriages** are divided into: *a first-class compartment* ▶ **przedział 2** one of the separate sections into which certain containers are divided: *The drugs were discovered in a secret compartment in his suitcase.* ◇ *the **glove compartment*** schowek w samochodzie (np. na mapy) ▶ **przegródka, schowek**

compass /ˈkʌmpəs/ noun [C] **1** an instrument for finding direction, with a needle that always points north: *the **points of the compass*** rumby ▶ **kompas 2 (compasses)** [pl.] a V-shaped instrument that is used for drawing circles: *Use a pair of compasses.* ▶ **cyrkiel**

compassion /kəmˈpæʃn/ noun [U] **compassion (for sb)** understanding or pity for sb who is suffering: *to have/feel/show compassion* ▶ **współczucie**

■ **compassionate** /kəmˈpæʃənət/ adj. ▶ **współczujący**

comˌpassionate ˈleave noun [U] (Brit.) time that you are allowed to be away from work because sb in your family is ill or has died: *She was granted compassionate leave to attend her father's funeral.* ▶ **urlop okolicznościowy** *(np. z powodu śmierci bliskiej osoby)*

compatible /kəmˈpætəbl/ adj. **compatible (with sb/sth)** able to be used together, or to live or exist together: *These two computer systems are not compatible.* ◇ *Janet and Phil found they weren't compatible as soon as they started living together.* ▶ **dopasowany, zgodny, kompatybilny** OPP **incompatible**

■ **compatibility** /kəmˌpætəˈbɪləti/ noun [U] ▶ **zgodność, kompatybilność**

compatriot /kəmˈpætriət; US -ˈpeɪt-/ noun [C] a person who comes from the same country as you ▶ **roda-k/czka**

compel /kəmˈpel/ verb [T] (**compelling; compelled**) (formal) **compel sb to do sth** to force sb to do sth: *I felt compelled to tell her what I really thought of her.* ▶ **zmuszać** ➲ noun **compulsion**

compelling /kəmˈpelɪŋ/ adj. **1** that forces or persuades you to do or to believe sth: *compelling evidence* ▶ **przekonujący; przemożny** ➲ noun **compulsion 2** very exciting; holding your attention ▶ **zajmujący**

compensate /ˈkɒmpenseɪt/ verb **1** [I] **compensate (for sth)** to remove or reduce the bad effect of sth: *His willingness to work hard compensates for his lack of skill.* ▶ **równoważyć 2** [I,T] **compensate (sb) (for sth)** to pay sb money because you have injured them or lost or damaged their property: *The airline sent me a cheque to compensate for losing my luggage.* ▶ **wynagradzać** *(stratę)*

compensation /ˌkɒmpenˈseɪʃn/ noun **1** [U] **compensation (for sth)** money that you pay to sb because you have injured them or lost or damaged their property: *I got £5 000 (in) compensation for my injuries.* ▶ **odszkodowanie 2** [C,U] a fact or action that removes or reduces the bad effect of sth: *City life can be very tiring but there are compensations* (są dobre strony). ▶ **zadośćuczynienie, rekompensata**

compère /ˈkɒmpeə(r)/ noun [C] (Brit.) a person who entertains the audience and introduces the different people who perform in a show ▶ **konferansjer**

■ **compère** verb [T]: *Who compèred the show?* ▶ **prowadzić konferansjerkę**

🔑 **compete** /kəmˈpiːt/ verb [I] **compete (in sth) (against/with sb) (for sth)** to try to win or achieve sth, or to try to be better than sb else: *The world's best athletes compete in the Olympic Games.* ◇ *As children, they always used to compete with each other.* ◇ *Supermarkets have such low prices that small shops just can't compete.* ▶ **współzawodniczyć; rywalizować**

competence /ˈkɒmpɪtəns/ noun [U] the fact of having the ability or skill that is needed for sth: *She quickly proved her competence in her new position.* ▶ **kwalifikacje, umiejętność** OPP **incompetence**

competent /ˈkɒmpɪtənt/ adj. **1** having the ability or skill needed for sth: *a highly competent player* ◇ *Isobel is competent at her job.* ▶ **kompetentny** OPP **incompetent 2** good enough, but not excellent: *The singer gave a competent, but not particularly exciting, performance.* ▶ **dostateczny**

■ **competently** adv. ▶ **kompetentnie**

⚷ **competition** /ˌkɒmpəˈtɪʃn/ noun **1** [U] a situation where two or more people or organizations are trying to achieve, obtain, etc. the same thing or to be better than sb else: *He is* ***in competition with*** (konkuruje z) *three other people for promotion.* ◇ *There was* ***fierce competition*** *among the players for places in the team.* ▶ **rywalizacja**, **konkurencja 2** [C] an organized event in which people try to win sth: *to* ***go in for/enter a competition*** stawać do konkursu ◇ *They* ***hold a competition*** *every year to find the best young artist.* ◇ *He came second in an international piano competition.* ▶ **konkurs 3** (**the competition**) [sing., with sing. or pl. verb] the other people, companies, etc. who are trying to achieve the same as you: *If we are going to succeed, we must offer a better product than the competition.* ▶ **konkurencja**

⚷ **competitive** /kəmˈpetətɪv/ adj. **1** involving people or organizations competing against each other: *The travel industry is a highly competitive business.* ◇ *competitive sports* ▶ **oparty na rywalizacji 2** able to be as successful as or more successful than others: *They are trying to make the company competitive in the international market.* ◇ *Our prices are highly competitive.* ▶ **konkurencyjny 3** (used about people) wanting very much to win or to be more successful than others: *She's a very competitive player.* ▶ **skory do rywalizacji**, **zacięty**
■ **competitively** adv.: *Their products are competitively priced.* ▶ **wyczynowo**; **konkurencyjnie**; **z zacięciem** | **competitiveness** noun [U] ▶ (*produkty*) **konkurencyjność**; (*osoba*) **chęć do współzawodnictwa/rywalizacji**

competitor /kəmˈpetɪtə(r)/ noun [C] a person or organization that is competing against others ▶ **przeciwnik**, **konkurent**

compilation /ˌkɒmpɪˈleɪʃn/ noun **1** [C] a collection of pieces of music, writing, film, etc. that are taken from different places and put together: *A compilation CD of the band's greatest hits.* ▶ **kompilacja**, **składanka 2** [U] the act of **compiling** sth ▶ **kompilowanie**, **opracowanie**

compile /kəmˈpaɪl/ verb [T] to collect information and arrange it in a list, book, etc.: *to compile a dictionary/a report/a list* ▶ **zbierać i porządkować** (*informacje*), **opracować** (*publikację*)

complacent /kəmˈpleɪsnt/ adj. feeling too satisfied with yourself or with a situation, so that you think that there is no need to worry: *He had won his matches so easily that he was in danger of becoming complacent.* ▶ **zadufany** (*we własne siły*), **beztroski**
■ **complacency** /kəmˈpleɪsnsi/ noun [U] ▶ **zadowolenie z siebie**, **zadufanie** | **complacently** adv. ▶ **z (bezpodstawnym) zadowoleniem**

⚷ **complain** /kəmˈpleɪn/ verb [I] **1 complain (to sb) (about sth/that ...)** to say that you are not satisfied with or happy about sth: *We complained to the hotel manager that the room was too noisy.* ◇ *People are always complaining about the weather.* ▶ **po/skarżyć (się)**, **narzekać** ➲ note at **grumble**, **protest 2** (formal) **complain of sth** to say that you have a pain or illness: *He went to the doctor, complaining of chest pains.* ▶ **skarżyć się** (*np. na ból*)

⚷ **complaint** /kəmˈpleɪnt/ noun **complaint (about sth)**; **complaint (that ...) 1** [C] a statement that you are not satisfied with sth: *You should* ***make a complaint*** *to the company that made the machine.* ▶ **zażalenie**, **skarga 2** [U] the act of complaining: *I wrote a* ***letter of complaint*** *to the manager about the terrible service I had received.* ◇ *Jim's behaviour never gave the teachers* ***cause for complaint*** (powodu do narzekań). ▶ **skarga**, **narzekanie 3** [C] an illness or disease: *a serious heart complaint* ▶ **dolegliwość**

complement[1] /ˈkɒmplɪmənt/ noun [C] (formal) **1** a thing that goes together well with sth else: *A cream sauce is the perfect complement to this dessert.* ▶ **uzupełnienie 2** the total number that makes a group complete: *Without a full complement of players, the team will not be able to take part in the match.* ▶ **komplet 3** a word or words, especially a noun or adjective, used after a verb such as 'be' or 'become' and describing the subject of that verb: *In 'He's friendly' and 'He's a fool', 'friendly' and 'fool' are complements.* ▶ **dopełnienie**

complement[2] /ˈkɒmplɪment/ verb [T] to go together well with: *The colours of the furniture and the carpet complement each other.* ▶ **uzupełniać się**

complementary /ˌkɒmplɪˈmentri/ adj. going together well with sb/sth; adding sth which the other person or thing does not have: *They work well together because their skills are complementary: he's practical and she's creative.* ▶ **uzupełniający się**, **dopełniający**

⚷ **complete**[1] /kəmˈpliːt/ adj. **1** [only before a noun] as great as possible; in every way: *It was a complete waste of time.* ◇ *The room is a complete mess.* ▶ **kompletny**, **całkowity** SYN **total 2** having or including all parts; with nothing missing: *I gave a complete list of the stolen items to the police.* ◇ *The book explains the complete history of the place.* ▶ **pełny**, **cały** OPP **incomplete 3** [not before a noun] **complete (with sth)** including sth extra, in addition to what is expected: *The computer* ***comes complete with*** (łącznie z) *instruction manual and printer.* **4** [not before a noun] finished or ended: *The repair work should be complete by Friday.* ▶ **zakończony** OPP **incomplete**
■ **completeness** noun [U] ▶ **całkowitość**

⚷ **complete**[2] /kəmˈpliːt/ verb [T] **1** to finish sth; to bring sth to an end: *When the building has been completed, it will look impressive.* ◇ *He completed his teacher training course in June 2005.* ▶ **zakańczać 2** to write all the necessary information on sth (for example a form): *Please complete the following in capital letters.* ▶ **wypełniać 3** to make sth whole: *We need two more players to complete the team.* ▶ **kompletować**

⚷ **completely** /kəmˈpliːtli/ adv. in every way; fully: *The building was completely destroyed by fire.* ▶ **zupełnie**, **w całości** SYN **totally**

completion /kəmˈpliːʃn/ noun [U] (formal) the act of finishing sth or the state of being finished: *You will be paid on completion of the work.* ◇ *The new motorway is due for completion within two years.* ▶ **zakończenie**, **zrealizowanie**

⚷ **complex**[1] /ˈkɒmpleks; US kəmˈp-/ adj. made up of several connected parts and often difficult to understand; complicated: *a complex problem/subject* ▶ **złożony**, **skomplikowany** SYN **complicated**

complex[2] /ˈkɒmpleks; US kəmˈp-/ noun [C] **1** a group of connected things, especially buildings: *a shopping/sports complex* ▶ **kompleks 2 a complex (about sth)** a mental problem that makes sb worry a lot about sth: *He's got a complex about his height.* ◇ *an inferiority complex* ▶ **kompleks**

complexion /kəmˈplekʃn/ noun [C] **1** the natural colour and quality of the skin on your face: *a dark/fair complexion* ▶ **cera 2** [usually sing.] the general nature or character of sth: *These recent announcements* ***put a different complexion on*** *our situation* (stawiają nas w innym świetle). ▶ **istota** (*rzeczy*)

complexity /kəmˈpleksəti/ noun (pl. **complexities**) **1** [U] the state of being **complex** and difficult to understand: *an issue of great complexity* ▶ **złożoność 2** [C] one of the many details that make sth complicated: *I haven't time to explain the complexities of the situation now.* ▶ **szczegół**, **złożoność**

compliant /kəmˈplaɪənt/ adj. (formal) **compliant (with sth)** working or done in agreement with particular rules, orders, etc.: *All new products must be compliant with EU specifications.* ▶ **zgodny** (*np. z przepisami*)

C

■ **compliance** noun [U]: *A hard hat must be worn at all times* ***in compliance with*** *safety regulations.* ▶ **zgodność** (*np. z przepisami*)

complicate /ˈkɒmplɪkeɪt/ verb [T] to make sth difficult to understand or deal with ▶ **komplikować**

complicated /ˈkɒmplɪkeɪtɪd/ adj. made of many different things or parts that are connected; difficult to understand: *a novel with a very complicated plot* ▶ **skomplikowany** SYN **complex**

complication /ˌkɒmplɪˈkeɪʃn/ noun [C] **1** something that makes a situation hard to understand or to deal with: *Unless there are any unexpected complications, I'll be arriving next month.* ▶ **komplikacja 2** a new illness that you get when you are already ill: *Unless he develops complications, he'll be out of hospital in a week.* ▶ **powikłanie, komplikacja**

complicit /kəmˈplɪsɪt/ adj. **complicit (in/with sb/sth)** involved with other people in sth wrong or illegal: *Several officers were complicit in the cover-up.* ▶ **współwinny**

complicity /kəmˈplɪsəti/ noun [U] (formal) the fact of being involved with sb else in a crime ▶ **współudział**

compliment[1] /ˈkɒmplɪmənt/ noun **1** [C] **a compliment (on sth)** a statement or action that shows admiration for sb: *People often* ***pay her compliments*** *on her piano playing.* ▶ **komplement 2** (**compliments**) [pl.] (formal) (used to say that you like sth or to thank sb for sth): *Tea and coffee are provided with the compliments of the hotel management.* ◇ *My compliments to the chef!* Wyrazy mojego uznania dla szefa kuchni! ▶ **wyrazy szacunku/pozdrowienia** (*np. przy przesyłaniu/darowaniu czegoś w upominku*)

compliment[2] /ˈkɒmplɪment/ verb [T] **compliment sb (on sth)** to say that you think sb/sth is very good: *She complimented them on their smart appearance.* ▶ **prawić komplementy**

complimentary /ˌkɒmplɪˈmentri/ adj. **1** given free of charge: *a complimentary theatre ticket* ▶ **gratisowy, bezpłatny 2** showing that you think sb/sth is very good: *He made several complimentary remarks about her work.* ▶ **pochlebny**

comply /kəmˈplaɪ/ verb [I] (**complying**; **complies**; pt, pp **complied**) (formal) **comply (with sth)** to obey an order or request: *All office buildings must comply with the fire and safety regulations.* ▶ **przestrzegać, spełniać**

component /kəmˈpəʊnənt/ noun [C] one of several parts of which sth is made: *the components of a machine/system* ▶ **część składowa**

■ **component** adj. [only before a noun]: *the component parts of an engine* ▶ **składowy**

compose /kəmˈpəʊz/ verb **1** [T] to be the parts that together form sth: *the parties that compose the coalition government* ▶ **tworzyć** (*całość*) **2** [I,T] to write music ▶ **komponować 3** [T] to produce a piece of writing, using careful thought: *I sat down and composed a letter of reply.* ▶ **układać z namysłem, formułować** (*na piśmie*) **4** [T] to make yourself, your feelings, etc. become calm and under control: *The news came as such a shock that it took me a while to* ***compose myself.*** ▶ **opanowywać się, porządkować** (*myśli*)

composed /kəmˈpəʊzd/ adj. **1 be composed of sth** to be made or formed from several different parts, people, etc.: *The committee is composed of politicians from all parties.* ▶ **składać się z czegoś 2** calm, in control of your feelings: *Although he felt very nervous, he managed to appear composed.* ▶ **opanowany**

composer /kəmˈpəʊzə(r)/ noun [C] a person who writes music ▶ **kompozytor/ka**

composite /ˈkɒmpəzɪt; US kəmˈpɑːzət/ adj. [only before a noun] consisting of different parts or materials ▶ **złożony**

■ **composite** noun [C]: *The document was a composite of information* (był zbiorem informacji) *from various sources.* ▶ **połączenie**

composition /ˌkɒmpəˈzɪʃn/ noun **1** [U] the parts that form sth; the way in which the parts of sth are arranged: *the chemical composition of a substance* ◇ *the composition of the population* ▶ **skład, budowa 2** [C] a piece of music that has been written by sb ➲ note at **music** ▶ **kompozycja, utwór 3** [U] the act of writing a piece of music or text ▶ **komponowanie 4** [U] the skill or technique of writing a piece of music: *She studied both musical theory and composition.* ▶ **kompozycja 5** [C] a short piece of writing done at school, in an exam, etc.: *Write a composition of about 300 words on one of the following subjects.* ▶ **wypracowanie**

compost /ˈkɒmpɒst; US -pəʊ-/ noun [U] a mixture of dead plants, old food, etc. that is added to soil to help plants grow ▶ **kompost**

composure /kəmˈpəʊʒə(r)/ noun [U] the state of being calm and having your feelings under control: *The goalkeeper couldn't regain his composure after his mistake.* ▶ **opanowanie, spokój**

compote /ˈkɒmpɒt; US -pəʊt/ noun [C,U] fruit cooked with sugar ▶ **owoce gotowane z dodatkiem cukru**

> W odróżnieniu od polskiego kompotu (napoju podawanego na deser), angielski **compote** nie jest napojem, lecz daniem. Podaje się go zwykle na zimno, często jako danie śniadaniowe w hotelach.

compound[1] /ˈkɒmpaʊnd/ noun [C] **1** something that consists of two or more things or substances combined together: *a chemical compound* ▶ **związek** (*chemiczny*) **2** a word or phrase consisting of two or more parts that combine to make a single meaning ▶ **wyraz złożony 3** an area of land with a group of buildings on it, surrounded by a wall or fence ▶ **ogrodzony teren zabudowany**

compound[2] /kəmˈpaʊnd/ verb [T] to make sth such as a problem worse ▶ **pogarszać**

comprehend /ˌkɒmprɪˈhend/ verb [T] (formal) to understand sth completely: *She's too young to comprehend what has happened.* ▶ **rozumieć, pojmować**

comprehensible /ˌkɒmprɪˈhensəbl/ adj. easy to understand ▶ **zrozumiały** OPP **incomprehensible**

comprehension /ˌkɒmprɪˈhenʃn/ noun **1** [U] (formal) the ability to understand: *The horror of war is* ***beyond comprehension.*** ◇ *How such a peculiar thing could happen is beyond my comprehension.* Nie mogę pojąć, jak taka dziwna rzecz mogła się wydarzyć. ▶ **zrozumienie, pojmowanie** OPP **incomprehension 2** [C,U] an exercise that tests how well you understand spoken or written language: *a listening comprehension* ▶ **ćwiczenie sprawdzające rozumienie**

comprehensive[1] /ˌkɒmprɪˈhensɪv/ adj. **1** including everything or nearly everything that is connected with a particular subject: *a guide book giving comprehensive information on the area* ▶ **wszechstronny, wyczerpujący 2** (Brit.) (used about education) teaching children of all levels of ability in the same school: *a comprehensive education system* ▶ **ogólnokształcący**

comprehensive[2] /ˌkɒmprɪˈhensɪv/ (also compreˈhensive school) noun [C] (Brit.) a secondary school in which children of all levels of ability are educated ▶ **szkoła średnia ogólnokształcąca**

comprehensively /ˌkɒmprɪˈhensɪvli/ adv. completely ▶ **wszechstronnie, wyczerpująco** SYN **thoroughly**

compress /kəmˈpres/ verb [T] **compress sth (into sth) 1** to press sth together so that it takes up less space: *Divers* *breathe compressed air from tanks.* ▶ **ściskać, skupiać** **2** to express sth briefly or in a shorter form: *He found it hard to compress his ideas into a single page.* ▶ **ujmować zwięźle, streszczać**

■ **compression** /kəmˈpreʃn/ noun [U] ▶ **sprężenie, kompresja; streszczenie**

comprise /kəmˈpraɪz/ verb [T] **1** to consist of; to have as parts or members: *a house comprising three bedrooms, kitchen, bathroom and a living room* ▶ **składać się z czegoś** **2** to form or be part of sth: *Women comprise 62% of the staff.* ▶ **stanowić**

compromise[1] /ˈkɒmprəmaɪz/ noun [C,U] **a compromise (between/on sth)** an agreement that is reached when each person gets part, but not all, of what they wanted: *to **reach a compromise*** ◇ *Both sides will have to be prepared to **make compromises**.* ▶ **kompromis**

compromise[2] /ˈkɒmprəmaɪz/ verb **1** [I] **compromise (with sb) (on sth)** to accept less than you want or are aiming for, especially in order to reach an agreement: *Unless both sides are prepared to compromise, there will be no peace agreement.* ◇ *The company never compromises on the quality of its products.* ▶ **iść na kompromis** **2** [T] **compromise sb/sth/yourself** to put sb/sth/yourself in a bad or dangerous position, especially by doing sth that is not very sensible: *He compromised himself by accepting money from them.* ◇ *She compromised her chances of promotion by missing the meeting.* ◇ *He refused to compromise his principles by signing the letter.* ▶ **kompromitować się; postępować wbrew czemuś, przekreślać** (*szansę*)

compromising /ˈkɒmprəmaɪzɪŋ/ adj. if sth is **compromising**, it shows or tells people sth that you want to keep secret, because it is wrong or embarrassing: *compromising photos* ◇ *They were discovered together in a **compromising situation**.* ▶ **kompromitujący**

compulsion /kəmˈpʌlʃn/ noun **1** [U] the act of forcing sb to do sth or being forced to do sth: *There is no compulsion to take part.* ▶ **przymus** ➲ verb **compel** **2** [C] a strong desire that you cannot control, often to do sth that you should not do: *Tony sometimes felt a strong compulsion to tell lies.* ▶ **pokusa** SYN **urge**

compulsive /kəmˈpʌlsɪv/ adj. **1** (used about a bad or harmful habit) caused by a strong desire that you cannot control: *compulsive eating* ▶ **nałogowy, niepohamowany** **2** (used about a person) having a bad habit that they cannot control: *a compulsive gambler/shoplifter* ▶ **nałogowy** **3** so interesting or exciting that you cannot take your attention away from it: *This book makes compulsive reading.* Nie można się oderwać od tej książki. ▶ **pasjonujący**

■ **compulsively** adv. ▶ **w sposób niepohamowany; nałogowo**

compulsory /kəmˈpʌlsəri/ adj. that must be done, by law, rules, etc.: *Maths and English are compulsory subjects on this course.* ◇ *It is compulsory to wear a hard hat on the building site.* ▶ **obowiązkowy** SYN **obligatory** OPP **voluntary, optional**

compute /kəmˈpjuːt/ verb [T] (formal) to calculate sth ▶ **obliczać**

🔑 **computer** /kəmˈpjuːtə(r)/ noun [C] an electronic machine that can store, find and arrange information, calculate amounts and control other machines: *The bills are all done **by computer**.* ◇ *a computer program* ◇ *a home/personal computer* ◇ *computer software/games* ◇ *First of all, the details are fed into a computer.* ▶ **komputer** ➲ note at **Internet**

> **computers**
>
> Most people use their **computers** for sending and receiving **emails** and for **word processing**. You can also use **the Internet**, play **computer games** or watch **DVDs**. You **log in/on** with your **username** and **password**. You **type in** words on a **keyboard** and **print out** documents on a **printer**. Information is displayed on the **screen** and you select the **icons** using a **mouse**. **Data** is stored in **files** on the **hard disk**, or on a **floppy disk** or **CD-ROM**. The **programs** that are used to operate a computer are called **software**. A computer that you use at work or home is a **PC** or **desktop**. A **laptop** is a small computer that you can carry around with you.

comˈputer game noun [C] a game played on a computer ▶ **gra komputerowa**

computerize (also -ise) /kəmˈpjuːtəraɪz/ verb [T] to use computers to do a job or to store information: *The whole factory has been computerized.* ◇ *We have now computerized the library catalogue.* ▶ **komputeryzować**

■ **computerization** (also -isation) /kəmˌpjuːtəraɪˈzeɪʃn; US -rəˈz-/ noun [U] ▶ **komputeryzacja**

comˌputer-ˈliterate adj. able to use a computer ▶ **znający obsługę komputera**

computing /kəmˈpjuːtɪŋ/ noun [U] the use of computers: *to work in computing* ◇ *She did a course in computing.* ◇ ***educational/network/scientific computing*** ▶ **obsługa komputera, informatyka**

comrade /ˈkɒmreɪd; US -ræd/ noun [C] **1** a person who is a member of the same political party as the person speaking ▶ **towarzysz/ka** **2** (Brit. also ˌcomrade-in-ˈarms) (old-fashioned) a friend or other person that you work with, especially as soldiers during a war: *They were old army comrades.* ▶ **towarzysz** (*np. broni*)

■ **comradeship** noun [U] ▶ **braterstwo, koleżeństwo**

Con = CONSERVATIVE[2] (2)

con[1] /kɒn/ noun [C] (informal) a trick, especially in order to cheat sb out of some money ▶ **oszustwo, naciąganie** (*na pieniądze*)

IDM **the pros and cons** → PRO

con[2] /kɒn/ verb [T] (conning; conned) (informal) **con sb (into doing sth/out of sth)** to cheat sb, especially in order to get money: *He conned her into investing in a company that didn't really exist.* ◇ *The old lady was conned out of her life savings.* ▶ **nabierać kogoś**

concave /kɒnˈkeɪv/ adj. having a surface that curves towards the inside of sth, like the inside of a bowl ▶ **wklęsły** ➲ look at **convex**

conceal /kənˈsiːl/ verb [T] (formal) **conceal sth/sb (from sb/sth)** to hide sb/sth; to prevent sb/sth from being seen or discovered: *She tried to conceal her anger from her friend.* ▶ **ukrywać, skrywać**

■ **concealment** noun [U]: *the concealment of the facts of the case* ▶ **ukrywanie, skrywanie**

concede /kənˈsiːd/ verb [T] (formal) **1** to admit that sth is true although you do not want to: *When it was clear that he would lose the election, he conceded defeat.* ◇ *She conceded that the problem was mostly her fault.* ▶ **przyznawać, uznawać** **2 concede sth (to sb)** to allow sb to take sth although you do not want to: *They lost the war and had to concede territory to their enemy.* ◇ *Despite conceding* (pomimo utraty) *two late goals, they still won.* ▶ **ustępować, przyznawać (komuś prawo do czegoś)** ➲ noun **concession**

conceit /kənˈsiːt/ noun [U] too much pride in yourself and your abilities and importance ▶ **zarozumiałość**

■ **conceited** adj. ▶ **zarozumiały**

conceivable /kənˈsiːvəbl/ adj. possible to imagine or believe: *I made every conceivable effort to succeed in my new career.* ▶ **wyobrażalny** SYN **possible** OPP **inconceivable**

■ **conceivably** /-əbli/ adv.: *She might just conceivably be telling the truth.* Niewykluczone, że ona mówi prawdę. ▶ **możliwe**

conceive /kən'siːv/ verb **1** [T] (formal) to think of a new idea or plan: *He conceived the idea for the novel during his journey through India.* ◇ *I cannot conceive that she would lie to me.* ▶ **mieć pomysł, wyobrażać sobie** **2** [I,T] (formal) **conceive (of) sb/sth (as sth)** to think about sb/sth in a particular way; to imagine: *He started to conceive of the world as a dangerous place.* ▶ **postrzegać** **3** [I,T] to become pregnant: *Tests showed that she was unable to conceive* (nie mogła zajść w ciążę). ▶ **począć** (*dziecko*) ➲ noun **conception**

concentrate /'kɒnsntreɪt/ verb [I,T] **1 concentrate (sth) (on sth/doing sth)** to give all your attention or effort to sth: *I need to concentrate on passing this exam.* ◇ *I tried to concentrate my thoughts on the problem.* ▶ **skupiać (się)** **2** to come together or to bring people or things together in one place: *Most factories are concentrated in one small area of the town.* ▶ **skupiać, koncentrować**

concentrated /'kɒnsntreɪtɪd/ adj. **1** showing determination: *With one concentrated effort we can finish the work by tonight.* ▶ **skoncentrowany** **2** made stronger by removing some liquid: *concentrated orange juice* ▶ **skoncentrowany, stężony**

concentration /ˌkɒnsn'treɪʃn/ noun **1** [U] **concentration (on sth)** the ability to give all your attention or effort to sth: *This type of work requires total concentration.* ◇ *Don't lose (your) concentration or you might make a mistake.* ▶ **skupienie (się)** **2** [C] **concentration (of sth)** a large amount of people or things in one place: *There is a high concentration of chemicals in the drinking water here.* ▶ **stężenie, skupisko**

ˌconcen'tration camp noun [C] a prison (usually a number of buildings inside a high fence) where political prisoners are kept in very bad conditions ▶ **obóz koncentracyjny**

concentric /kən'sentrɪk/ adj. (used about circles of different sizes) having the same centre point ▶ **koncentryczny**

concept /'kɒnsept/ noun [C] **the concept (of sth/that ...)** an idea; a basic principle: *It is difficult to* ***grasp the concept*** *of eternity.* ▶ **pojęcie, zasada**
■ **conceptual** /kən'septʃuəl/ adj. ▶ **pojęciowy**

conception /kən'sepʃn/ noun **1** [U] the process of forming an idea or a plan ▶ **koncepcja** **2** [C,U] **(a) conception (of sth)** an understanding of how or what sth is: *We have no real conception* (nie zdają sobie sprawy) *of what people suffered during the war.* ▶ **koncepcja** **3** [C,U] the moment when a woman or female animal becomes pregnant ▶ **poczęcie** ➲ verb **conceive**

conˌceptual 'art noun [U] art in which the idea which the work of art represents is considered to be the most important thing about it ▶ **sztuka konceptualna**

conceptualize (also -ise) /kən'septʃuəlaɪz/ verb [T] **conceptualize sth (as sth)** (formal) to form an idea of sth in your mind: *These people do not conceptualize hunting as a violent act.* ▶ **konceptualizować; formułować pojęcie**

concern[1] /kən'sɜːn/ verb [T] **1** to affect or involve sb/sth; to be about sth: *This does not concern you. Please go away.* ◇ *The closure of the factory came as a shock* ***to all concerned*** (dla wszystkich zainteresowanych). ◇ *It is important that no risks are taken* ***where*** *safety* ***is concerned.*** ◇ *The main problem concerns the huge cost of the project.* ▶ **dotyczyć, odnosić się (do czegoś)** **2** to worry sb: *What concerns me is that we have no long-term plan.* ▶ **niepokoić** **3 concern yourself with sth** to give your attention to sth: *You needn't concern yourself with the hotel booking. The travel agent will take care of it.* ▶ **troszczyć się (o coś), zajmować się**

IDM **be concerned in sth** to have a connection with or be involved in sth: *She was concerned in a drugs case some years ago.* ▶ **być związanym z czymś, być wplątanym w coś**
be concerned with sth to be about sth: *Tonight's programme is concerned with the effects of the law on ordinary people.* ▶ **dotyczyć czegoś**

concern[2] /kən'sɜːn/ noun **1** [C,U] **concern (for/about/over sb/sth); concern (that ...)** a feeling of worry; sth that causes worry: *The safety officer assured us that there was no* ***cause for concern.*** ◇ *My main concern is that we'll run out of money.* ▶ **obawa, troska** **2** [C] something that is important to you or that involves you: *Financial matters are not my concern.* ▶ **troska, sprawa** **3** [C] a company or business: *a large industrial concern* ▶ **koncern**
IDM **a going concern** → GOING[2]

concerned /kən'sɜːnd/ adj. **concerned (about/for sth); concerned (that ...)** worried and feeling concern about sth: *If you are concerned about your baby's health, you should consult a doctor immediately.* ▶ **zatroskany, zaniepokojony** OPP **unconcerned**

concerning /kən'sɜːnɪŋ/ prep. about; on the subject of: *She refused to answer questions concerning her private life.* ▶ **dotyczący**

concert /'kɒnsət/ noun [C] a performance of music: *The band is on tour doing concerts all over the country.* ▶ **koncert** ➲ look at **recital**
IDM **in concert (with sb/sth)** (formal) working together with sb/sth ▶ **razem (z kimś/czymś)**

concerted /kən'sɜːtɪd/ adj. [only before a noun] done by a group of people working together: *We must all* ***make a concerted effort*** *to finish the work on time.* ▶ **wspólny, zbiorowy**

'concert-goer noun [C] a person who regularly goes to concerts, especially of **classical** music ▶ **bywal-ec/czyni koncertów** (*zwł. muzyki klasycznej*)

concertina /ˌkɒnsə'tiːnə/ noun [C] a musical instrument that you hold in your hands and play by pressing the ends together and pulling them apart ▶ **koncertyna** ➲ look at **accordion** ➲ note at **piano**

concerto /kən'tʃɜːtəʊ/ noun [C] (pl. **concertos**) a piece of music for an **orchestra** and one instrument playing a **solo** ▶ **koncert**

concession /kən'seʃn/ noun **1** [C,U] **(a) concession (to sb/sth)** something that you agree to do in order to end an argument: *Employers have been forced to* ***make concessions*** *to the union.* ▶ **ustępstwo** ➲ verb **concede** **2** [C] a lower price for certain groups of people: *Concessions are available for students and pensioners.* ▶ **zniżka** **3** a special right to do sth that is given or sold to sb/sth ▶ **koncesja**

concessionary /kən'seʃənəri; US -neri/ adj. having a lower price for certain groups of people: *a concessionary fare* ▶ **zniżkowy**

conciliation /kənˌsɪli'eɪʃn/ noun [U] the process of ending an argument or disagreement: *All attempts at conciliation have failed and civil war seems inevitable.* ▶ **pojednanie**

conciliatory /kən'sɪliətəri; US -tɔːri/ adj. that tries to end an argument or disagreement: *a conciliatory speech/gesture* ▶ **pojednawczy, rozjemczy**

concise /kən'saɪs/ adj. giving a lot of information in a few words ▶ **zwięzły, treściwy** SYN **brief**
■ **concisely** adv. ▶ **zwięźle** | **conciseness** noun [U] ▶ **zwięzłość**

conclude /kən'kluːd/ verb **1** [T] **conclude sth from sth** to form an opinion as the result of thought or study: *From the man's strange behaviour I concluded that he was drunk.* ▶ **wnioskować** **2** [I,T] (formal) to end or to bring sth to an end: *May I conclude by thanking* (na zakończenie chciałbym podziękować) *our guest speaker.* ▶ **za-**

kończyć 3 [T] **conclude sth (with sb)** to formally arrange or agree to sth: *to conclude a business deal/treaty* ▶ **zawierać** (*np. umowę*)

conclusion /kən'klu:ʒn/ noun **1** [C] **the conclusion (that ...)** an opinion that you reach after thinking about sth carefully: *After trying to phone Bob for days, I* ***came to the conclusion*** (doszedłem do wniosku) *that he was on holiday.* ◇ *The police were able to* ***draw*** *some* ***conclusions*** (wyciągnąć pewne wnioski) *from the evidence.* ◇ *Have you* ***reached*** *any* ***conclusions*** *from your studies?* Czy wyciągnęliście jakieś wnioski ze swoich badań? ▶ **wniosek 2** [C, usually sing.] (formal) an end to sth: *Let us hope the peace talks* ***reach a*** *successful* ***conclusion.*** ◇ *to bring something to a conclusion* zakończyć coś ▶ **zakończenie 3** [U] an act of arranging or agreeing to sth formally: *The summit ended with the conclusion of an arms-reduction treaty.* ▶ **zawarcie** (*np. umowy, traktatu*)
IDM **a foregone conclusion** → FOREGONE
in conclusion finally ▶ **podsumowując**, **na zakończenie**
jump to conclusions → JUMP¹

conclusive /kən'klu:sɪv/ adj. that shows sth is definitely true or real: *The blood tests gave conclusive proof of Robson's guilt.* ▶ **decydujący**, **rozstrzygający** OPP **inconclusive**
■ **conclusively** adv. ▶ **decydująco**, **autorytatywnie**

concoct /kən'kɒkt/ verb [T] **1** to make sth unusual by mixing different things together ▶ **sporządzać**, **kombinować**, **pichcić 2** to make up or invent sth (an excuse, a story, etc.) ▶ **wymyślać**
■ **concoction** noun [C] ▶ **mikstura**, **sporządzanie**; **wymysł**

concourse /'kɒŋkɔ:s/ noun [C] a large hall or space inside a building such as a station or an airport ▶ **hala** (*np. dworcowa*)

concrete¹ /'kɒŋkri:t/ adj. real or definite; not only existing in the imagination: *Can you give me a concrete example of what you mean?* ▶ **konkretny** OPP **abstract**
■ **concretely** adv. ▶ **konkretnie**

concrete² /'kɒŋkri:t/ noun [U] a hard substance made from **cement** mixed with sand, water and small stones, which is used in building ▶ **beton**

concrete³ /'kɒŋkri:t/ verb [T] **concrete sth (over)** to cover sth with **concrete** ▶ **betonować**

concur /kən'kɜ:(r)/ verb [I] (**concurring**; **concurred**) (formal) to agree ▶ **podzielać czyjeś zdanie**, **zgadzać się**

concurrent /kən'kʌrənt; US -'kɜ:r-/ adj. existing or happening at the same time as sth else ▶ **jednoczesny**
■ **concurrently** adv.: *The semi-finals are played concurrently, so it is impossible to watch both.* ▶ **jednocześnie**

concuss /kən'kʌs/ verb [T, usually passive] to injure sb's brain by hitting their head: *to be badly concussed* doznać poważnego wstrząsu mózgu ▶ **powodować wstrząśnienie/wstrząs mózgu**
■ **concussion** /kən'kʌʃn/ noun [U] ▶ **wstrząśnienie mózgu**

condemn /kən'dem/ verb [T] **1 condemn sb/sth (for/as sth)** to say strongly that you think sb/sth is very bad or wrong: *A government spokesman condemned the bombing as a cowardly act of terrorism.* ▶ **potępiać 2 condemn sb (to sth/to do sth)** to say what sb's punishment will be; to sentence sb: *The murderer was condemned to death.* ◇ (figurative) *Their poor education condemns them to a series of low-paid jobs.* ▶ **skazywać na coś 3 condemn sth (as sth)** to say officially that sth is not safe enough to use: *The building was condemned as unsafe and was demolished.* ▶ **przeznaczać** (*np. do rozbiórki*)

condemnation /ˌkɒndem'neɪʃn/ noun [C,U] the act of **condemning** sth; a statement that **condemns**: *The bombing brought condemnation from all around the world.* ▶ **potępienie**

condensation /ˌkɒnden'seɪʃn/ noun [U] small drops of liquid that are formed when warm air touches a cold surface: *On cold mornings the windows are covered in condensation* (okna są zaparowane). ▶ **skroplenie**

condense /kən'dens/ verb **1** [I,T] to change or make sth change from gas to liquid: *Steam condenses into water when it touches a cold surface.* ▶ **skraplać (się)** ➲ look at **evaporate 2** [T,I] if a liquid **condenses** or you **condense** it, it becomes thicker and stronger because it has lost some of its water: *condensed soup* ▶ **gęstnieć**; **zagęszczać 3** [T] **condense sth (into sth)** to make a piece of writing shorter: *We'll have to condense these three chapters into one.* ▶ **skracać**, **kondensować**

condescend /ˌkɒndɪ'send/ verb [I] **1 condescend (to do sth)** to do sth that you believe is below your level of importance: *Celia only condescends to speak to me when she wants me to do something for her.* ▶ **raczyć (coś robić) 2 condescend (to sb)** to behave towards sb in a way that shows that you think you are better or more important than them ▶ **zniżać się** (*do czyjegoś poziomu*), **traktować (kogoś) protekcjonalnie** SYN **patronize**
■ **condescending** adj.: *a condescending smile* ▶ **protekcjonalny** | **condescension** /ˌkɒndɪ'senʃn/ noun [U] ▶ **protekcjonalność**

condiment /'kɒndɪmənt/ noun [usually pl.] **1** (Brit.) a substance such as salt or pepper that is used to give flavour to food ▶ **przyprawa 2** (especially US) a sauce, etc. that is used to give flavour to food, or that is eaten with food: *hot condiments made from a variety of chili peppers* ▶ **sos**

condition¹ /kən'dɪʃn/ noun **1** [U, sing.] the state that sb/sth is in: *to be in poor/good/excellent condition* ◇ *He looks really ill. He is certainly not in a condition to drive home.* ▶ **stan 2** [C] a medical problem that you have for a long time: *to have a heart condition* chorować na serce ▶ **choroba 3** (**conditions**) [pl.] the situation or surroundings in which people live, work or do things: *The prisoners were kept* ***in*** *terrible* ***conditions.*** ◇ *poor living/housing/working conditions* ▶ **warunki 4** [C] something that must happen so that sth else can happen or be possible: *He said I could borrow his bike* ***on one condition*** *– that I didn't let anyone else ride it.* ▶ **warunek**
IDM **on condition (that ...)** only if ▶ **pod warunkiem, że**
on no condition (formal) not for any reason: *On no condition must the press find out about this.* ▶ **pod żadnym pozorem**
out of condition not physically fit ▶ **nie w formie**, **w złym stanie**

condition² /kən'dɪʃn/ verb [T] **1** to affect or control the way that sb/sth behaves: *Boys are conditioned to feel that they are stronger than girls.* ◇ *to be conditioned by* (zależeć od) *your environment* ▶ **warunkować 2** to keep sth such as your hair or skin in a good condition ▶ **utrzymywać w dobrym stanie**

conditional /kən'dɪʃənl/ adj. **1 conditional (on/upon sth)** that only happens if sth else is done or happens first: *My university place is conditional on my getting good marks in the exams.* ▶ **zależny od czegoś** OPP **unconditional 2** [only before a noun] describing a situation that must exist before sth else can happen. A **conditional** sentence often contains the word 'if': *'If you don't study, you won't pass the exam' is a conditional sentence.* ▶ **warunkowy**
■ **conditionally** /-ʃənəli/ adv. ▶ **warunkowo**

conditioner /kən'dɪʃənə(r)/ noun [C,U] a substance that keeps sth in a good condition: *Do you use conditioner on your hair?* ▶ **odżywka**, **płyn do płukania tkanin**, **krem pielęgnacyjny**

condo (informal) = CONDOMINIUM

condolence /kən'dəʊləns/ noun [pl., U] an expression of how sorry you feel for sb whose relative or close friend has just died: *offer your condolences* ◇ *a message of condolence* ▶ **wyrazy współczucia**

condom /ˈkɒndɒm; US -dəm/ (also informal **rubber**) noun [C] a thin rubber covering that a man wears over his sexual organ during sex to prevent the woman from becoming pregnant or as protection against disease ▶ **prezerwatywa**

condominium /ˌkɒndəˈmɪniəm/ (also informal **condo** /ˈkɒndəʊ/) noun [C] (US) a flat or block of flats owned by the people who live in them ▶ **mieszkanie własnościowe**

condone /kənˈdəʊn/ verb [T] to accept or agree with sth that most people think is wrong: *I can never condone violence – no matter what the circumstances are.* ▶ **aprobować**

conducive /kənˈdjuːsɪv; US -ˈduːs-/ adj. (formal) **conducive (to sth)** helping or making sth happen: *This hot weather is not conducive to* (nie sprzyja) *hard work.* ▶ **sprzyjający**

⚷ **conduct**[1] /kənˈdʌkt/ verb [T] **1** (formal) to organize and do sth, especially research: *to conduct tests/a survey/an inquiry* ▶ **przeprowadzać 2** to stand in front of an **orchestra** and direct the musicians: *the London Symphony Orchestra conducted by Sir Colin Davis* ▶ **dyrygować** (*orkiestrą*) **3** (formal) **conduct yourself well, badly, etc.** to behave in a particular way: *He conducted himself far better than expected.* ▶ **zachowywać się 4** to allow heat or electricity to pass along or through sth: *Rubber does not conduct electricity.* ▶ **przewodzić 5** to lead or guide sb through or around a place: *a conducted tour* (zwiedzanie z przewodnikiem) *of the cathedral* ▶ **oprowadzać**

⚷ **conduct**[2] /ˈkɒndʌkt/ noun [U] **1** sb's behaviour: *a code of conduct* reguły dobrego zachowania ▶ **zachowanie 2** (formal) **conduct of sth** the act of controlling or organizing sth: *She was criticized for her conduct of the bank's affairs.* ▶ **prowadzenie, kierowanie**

conductor /kənˈdʌktə(r)/ noun [C] **1** a person who stands in front of an **orchestra** and directs the musicians ▶ **dyrygent 2** (US) = GUARD[1] (5) **3** (Brit.) a person whose job is to collect money from passengers on a bus or to check their tickets ▶ **konduktor/ka 4** a substance that allows heat or electricity to pass through or along it ▶ **przewodnik**

cone /kəʊn/ noun [C] **1** a shape or an object that has a round base and a point at the top: *Orange cones* (pomarańczowe pachołki) *marked off the area where the roadworks were.* ◇ *an ice cream cone* wafel (w kształcie stożka) ▶ **stożek**; **przedmiot w kształcie stożka** ➲ adjective **conical 2** the hard fruit of a **pine** tree or a **fir** tree ▶ **szyszka** ➲ look at **conifer**

confectionery /kənˈfekʃənəri; US -neri/ noun [U] sweets, cakes, chocolates, etc. ▶ **słodycze, wyroby cukiernicze**

confederacy /kənˈfedərəsi/ noun [C] a group of people, states or political parties with the same aim ▶ **konfederacja**

confederate[1] /kənˈfedərət/ noun [C] a person who helps sb, especially to do sth illegal or secret ▶ **konfederat, wspólni-k/czka** SYN **accomplice**

confederate[2] /kənˈfedərət/ adj. belonging to a **confederacy** ▶ **konfederacki**

confederation /kənˌfedəˈreɪʃn/ noun [C,U] an organization of smaller groups which have joined together: ▶ **konfederacja**

confer /kənˈfɜː(r)/ verb (**conferring**; **conferred**) **1** [I] **confer (with sb) (on/about sth)** to discuss sth with sb before making a decision: *The President is conferring with his advisers.* ▶ **naradzać się 2** [T] (formal) **confer sth (on sb)** to give sb a special right or advantage ▶ **nadawać**

⚷ **conference** /ˈkɒnfərəns/ noun [C] a large official meeting, often lasting several days, at which members of an organization, profession, etc. meet to discuss important matters: *Political parties usually* ***hold a conference*** *once a year.* ◇ *an international conference on global warming* ▶ **konferencja, zjazd**

confess /kənˈfes/ verb [I,T] **1 confess (to sth/to doing sth); confess (sth) (to sb)** to admit that you have done sth bad or wrong: *The young woman confessed to the murder of her boyfriend/to murdering/to having murdered her boyfriend.* ◇ *They confessed to their mother that they had spent all the money on sweets.* ▶ **przyznawać się (do czegoś), wyznawać** ⓘ Mniej formalnym wyrażeniem jest **own up (to sth)**. **2 confess (sth) (to sb)** to tell a priest or God what you have done that is bad or wrong ▶ **spowiadać się**

confession /kənˈfeʃn/ noun [C,U] an act of admitting that you have done sth bad or wrong: *The police persuaded the man to make a full confession.* ▶ **przyznanie się (do czegoś), wyznanie**; **spowiedź**

confessional /kənˈfeʃənl/ noun [C] a private place in a church where a priest listens to people making **confessions** ▶ **konfesjonał**

confetti /kənˈfeti/ noun [U] small pieces of coloured paper that people throw over a man and woman who have just got married ▶ **konfetti**

confide /kənˈfaɪd/ verb [T] **confide sth to sb** to tell sb sth that is secret: *She did not confide her love to anyone – not even to her best friend.* ▶ **zwierzać się komuś z czegoś**
PHR V **confide in sb** to talk to sb that you trust about sth secret or private ▶ **zwierzać się komuś**

⚷ **confidence** /ˈkɒnfɪdəns/ noun [U] **1 confidence (in sb/sth)** trust or strong belief in sb/sth: *The public is losing confidence in the present government.* ◇ *I have every confidence* (głęboko wierzę) *in Edith's ability to do the job.* ▶ **ufność, pewność, zaufanie 2** the feeling that you are sure about your own abilities, opinion, etc.: *I didn't* ***have the confidence*** (nie ośmieliłem się) *to tell her I thought she was wrong.* ◇ *to be* ***full of confidence*** ◇ *'Of course we will win,' the team captain said* ***with confidence.*** ▶ **pewność (siebie)** ➲ look at **self-confidence 3** a feeling of trust in sb to keep sth a secret: *The information was given to me* ***in strict confidence*** (w największej tajemnicy). ◇ *It took a while to* ***win/gain*** *her* ***confidence.*** ◇ *Anne* ***took me into her confidence*** *and told me* (powiedziała mi w zaufaniu) *she was resigning.* ▶ **zaufanie**

ˈ**confidence trick** noun [C] a way of getting money by cheating sb ▶ **oszustwo polegające na wykorzystaniu czyjegoś zaufania**

⚷ **confident** /ˈkɒnfɪdənt/ adj. **confident (of sth/that ...); confident (about sth)** feeling or showing that you are sure about your own abilities, opinions, etc.: *Kate feels confident of passing/that she can pass* (jest przekonana, że zda) *the exam.* ◇ *to be confident of success* ◇ *You should feel confident about your own abilities.* ◇ *Dillon has a very confident manner.* ▶ **pewny (siebie/czegoś)** ➲ look at **self-confident**
■ **confidently** adv.: *She stepped confidently onto the stage and began to sing.* ▶ **pewnie, z pełnym zaufaniem**

confidential /ˌkɒnfɪˈdenʃl/ adj. secret; not to be shown or told to other people: *The letter was marked 'private and confidential'.* ▶ **poufny, tajny**
■ **confidentiality** /ˌkɒnfɪˌdenʃiˈæləti/ noun [U] ▶ **poufność, poufny charakter** | **confidentially** /-ʃəli/ adv. ▶ **w sekrecie, w zaufaniu**

configuration /kənˌfɪɡəˈreɪʃn; US -ɡjəˈr-/ noun [C,U] **1** (formal) the way in which the parts of sth, or a group of things, are arranged ▶ **konfiguracja 2** the equipment and programs that form a computer system and the particular way that these are arranged ▶ **konfiguracja**

⚷ **confine** /kən'faɪn/ verb [T] **1 confine sb/sth/yourself to sth** to stay within the limits of sth: *Please confine your questions to the topic we are discussing.* ▶ **ograniczać (się), poprzestawać na czymś 2 confine sb/sth (in/to sth)** to keep a person or an animal in a particular, usually small, place: *The prisoners are confined to their cells for long periods at a time.* ▶ **ograniczać, zamykać (w czymś)**

⚷ **confined** /kən'faɪnd/ adj. (used about a space) very small ▶ **ograniczony, ścieśniony**

confinement /kən'faɪnmənt/ noun [U] being kept in a small space: *to be kept* ***in solitary confinement*** ▶ **odosobnienie, izolacja**

confines /'kɒnfaɪnz/ noun [pl.] (formal) the limits of sth: *Patients are not allowed beyond the confines of the hospital grounds.* ▶ **obręb, granica**

⚷ **confirm** /kən'fɜːm/ verb [T] **1** to say or show that sth is true; to make sth definite: *Can you confirm that you will be able to attend?* ◇ *Seeing the two of them together confirmed our suspicions.* ▶ **potwierdzać 2** to accept sb as a full member of a Christian Church in a special ceremony ▶ **bierzmować, konfirmować**

■ **confirmation** /ˌkɒnfə'meɪʃn/ noun [C,U] **1** a statement that confirms sth: *We are waiting for confirmation of the report.* ▶ **potwierdzenie 2** a religious service at which a person is confirmed ▶ **bierzmowanie, konfirmacja**

confirmed /kən'fɜːmd/ adj. [only before a noun] fixed in a particular habit or way of life: *a confirmed bachelor* ▶ **zatwardziały, niewzruszony**

confiscate /'kɒnfɪskeɪt/ verb [T] to take sth away from sb as a punishment ▶ **konfiskować**

■ **confiscation** /ˌkɒnfɪ'skeɪʃn/ noun [C,U] ▶ **konfiskata**

⚷ **conflict[1]** /'kɒnflɪkt/ noun [C,U] **1 (a) conflict with sb/sth (over sth)** a fight or an argument: *an armed conflict* konflikt zbrojny ◇ *The new laws have brought the Government* ***into conflict*** *with the unions over pay increases.* ▶ **konflikt, walka 2** a difference between two or more ideas, wishes, etc.: *Many women have to cope with the conflict between their career and their family.* ◇ *a conflict of interests* ▶ **sprzeczność, konflikt**

⚷ **conflict[2]** /kən'flɪkt/ verb [I] **A and B conflict; A conflicts with B** to disagree with or be different from sb/sth: *The statements of the two witnesses conflict.* ◇ *conflicting results* ▶ **być sprzecznym, kolidować**

conform /kən'fɔːm/ verb [I] **conform (to sth) 1** to behave in the way that other people and society expect you to behave: *Children are under a lot of pressure to conform when they first start school.* ▶ **odpowiadać** (*np. normom, wymaganiom*) **2** to obey a rule or law: *This building does not conform to fire regulations.* ▶ **dostosowywać się (do czegoś)**

■ **conformity** /kən'fɔːməti/ noun [U] ▶ **przestrzeganie** (*np. reguł*); **dostosowanie się**

conformist /kən'fɔːmɪst/ noun [C] a person who behaves in the way that people are expected to behave by society ▶ **konformista** OPP **nonconformist**

⚷ **confront** /kən'frʌnt/ verb [T] **1 confront sth; confront sb with sb/sth** to think about, or to make sb think about, sth that is difficult or unpleasant: *to confront a problem/difficulty/issue* ◇ *When the police confronted him with the evidence* (kiedy policja przedstawiła mu dowody), *he confessed.* ▶ **stawać wobec problemu itp. 2** to stand in front of sb, for example because you want to fight them: *The unarmed demonstrators were confronted by a row of soldiers.* ▶ **stawać twarzą w twarz (z kimś/czymś)**

confrontation /ˌkɒnfrʌn'teɪʃn; US -frən-/ noun [C,U] a fight or an argument ▶ **konfrontacja**

confrontational /ˌkɒnfrʌn'teɪʃnl; US -frən-/ adj. tending to deal with people in an aggressive way that is likely to cause arguments, rather than discussing things with them ▶ **konfrontacyjny**

⚷ **confuse** /kən'fjuːz/ verb [T] **1** to make sb unable to think clearly or to know what to do: *He confused everybody with his pages of facts and figures.* ◇ *I'm a bit confused* (nie całkiem rozumiem). *Could you explain that again?* ▶ **mieszać (komuś) w głowie, wikłać 2 confuse A and/with B** to mistake sb/sth for sb/sth else: *I often confuse Lee with his brother. They look very much alike.* ▶ **mylić 3** to make sth complicated: *The situation is confused by the fact that so many organizations are involved.* ▶ **gmatwać, komplikować**

⚷ **confused** /kən'fjuːzd/ adj. **1** not able to think clearly: *When he regained consciousness he was dazed and confused* (nie mógł zebrać myśli). ▶ **zmieszany 2** difficult to understand: *The article is very confused – I don't know what the main point is.* ▶ **pogmatwany, poplątany**

■ **confusedly** /kən'fjuːzɪdli/ adv. ▶ **w stanie zagmatwania, w zamieszaniu**

⚷ **confusing** /kən'fjuːzɪŋ/ adj. difficult to understand: *Her instructions were contradictory and confusing.* ▶ **niejasny, mylący**

■ **confusingly** adv. ▶ **niejasno, myląco**

⚷ **confusion** /kən'fjuːʒn/ noun [U] **1** the state of not being able to think clearly or not understanding sth: *He stared in confusion at the exam paper.* ▶ **zamieszanie, nieporozumienie 2** the act of mistaking sb/sth for sb/sth else: *To avoid confusion, all luggage should be labelled with your name and destination.* ▶ **zamieszanie, pomyłka 3** a lack of order: *Their unexpected visit threw all our plans into confusion* (pogmatwała nasze plany). ▶ **zamieszanie, chaos**

congeal /kən'dʒiːl/ verb [I,T] (used about a liquid) to become solid; to make a liquid solid: *congealed blood* ▶ **krzepnąć, ścinać (się)**

congenial /kən'dʒiːniəl/ adj. (formal) pleasant: *We spent an evening in congenial company.* ▶ **sympatyczny, przyjemny**

congenital /kən'dʒenɪtl/ adj. (used about a disease) beginning at and continuing since birth ▶ **wrodzony**

congested /kən'dʒestɪd/ adj. so full of sth that nothing can move: *The streets of London are congested with traffic.* ▶ **zatłoczony, przeciążony**

■ **congestion** /kən'dʒestʃən/ noun [U]: *severe traffic congestion* ▶ **zatłoczenie, przeciążenie**

conglomerate /kən'glɒmərət/ noun [C] a large firm made up of several different companies ▶ **konglomerat**

conglomeration /kənˌglɒmə'reɪʃn/ noun [C] a group of many different things that have been brought together ▶ **konglomeracja, zbiór, zlepek**

congratulate /kən'græt∫uleɪt/ verb [T] **congratulate sb (on sth)** to tell sb that you are pleased about sth they have done: *Colin congratulated Sue on passing her driving test.* ▶ **gratulować**

⚷ **congratulations** /kənˌgrætʃu'leɪʃnz/ noun [pl.] (used for telling sb that you are pleased about sth they have done): *Congratulations* (gratulacje z okazji) *on the birth of your baby boy!* ▶ **gratulacje**

congregate /'kɒŋgrɪgeɪt/ verb [I] to come together in a crowd or group ▶ **gromadzić się, zbierać się**

congregation /ˌkɒŋgrɪ'geɪʃn/ noun [C, with sing. or pl. verb] the group of people who attend a particular church ▶ **parafianie**

⚷ **congress** /'kɒŋgres; US -grəs/ noun [C, with sing. or pl. verb] **1** a large formal meeting or series of meetings ▶ **kon-**

gres, zjazd **2** (**Congress**) the name in some countries (for example the US) for the group of people who are elected to make the laws: *Congress will vote on the proposals tomorrow.* ▶ **Kongres**

The US Congress to połączone izby parlamentu: **Senate** oraz **House of Representatives**.

congressional /kən'greʃənl/ adj. [only before a noun] connected with a **congress** or **Congress** ▶ **kongresu, kongresowy**

Congressman /'kɒŋgresmən; US -grəs-/, **Congresswoman** /'kɒŋgreswʊmən; US -grəs-/ noun [C] (pl. **-men** /-mən/; **-women** /-wɪmɪn/) (also **Congressperson** /-pɜːsn/) a member of Congress in the US, especially the House of Representatives ▶ **kongresmen/ka**

conical /'kɒnɪkl/ adj. having a round base and getting narrower towards a point at the top ▶ **stożkowy, stożkowaty** ⊃ noun **cone**

conifer /'kɒnɪfə(r); 'kəʊn-/ noun [C] a tree with needles that stays green all through the year and that has **cones** ▶ **drzewo iglaste**

■ **coniferous** /kə'nɪfərəs/ adj. ▶ **iglasty, szpilkowy**

conjecture /kən'dʒektʃə(r)/ verb [I,T] (formal) to guess about sth without real proof or evidence ▶ **domniemywać, snuć domysły**

■ **conjecture** noun [C,U] ▶ **domniemanie, domysł**

conjoined twin (technical) = SIAMESE TWIN

conjugal /'kɒndʒəgl/ adj. [only beforea noun] (formal) connected with marriage ▶ **małżeński**

conjugate /'kɒndʒəgeɪt/ verb [T] to give the different forms of a verb ▶ **odmieniać** (*czasownik*)

■ **conjugation** /ˌkɒndʒu'geɪʃn; US -dʒə-/ noun [C,U] ▶ **odmiana czasownika**

conjunction /kən'dʒʌŋkʃn/ noun [C] a word that is used for joining other words, phrases or sentences ▶ **spójnik**

IDM **in conjunction with sb/sth** together with sb/sth ▶ **w połączeniu z czymś, razem z kimś/czymś**

conjure /'kʌndʒə(r)/ verb [I] to do tricks by clever, quick hand movements, that appear to be magic ▶ **robić sztuczki magiczne**

■ **conjuring** noun [U] ▶ **pokazywanie sztuczek magicznych; sztuczki magiczne**

PHR V **conjure sth up** to cause an image to appear in your mind: *Hawaiian music conjures up images of sunshine, flowers and sandy beaches.* ▶ **wyczarowywać/wywoływać coś**

conjure sth (up) from/out of sth to make sth appear quickly or suddenly: *Mum can conjure up a meal out of almost anything.* ▶ **wyczarowywać coś**

conjuror (also **conjurer**) /'kʌndʒərə(r)/ noun [C] a person who does clever tricks that appear to be magic ▶ **iluzjonista** ⊃ look at **magician**

conk /kɒŋk/ verb

PHR V **conk out** (informal) **1** (used about a machine, etc.) to stop working: *The car conked out halfway up the hill.* ▶ (*urządzenie*) **wysiąść 2** (used about a person) to go to sleep ▶ **kimnąć (się)**

conker (Brit., informal) = HORSE CHESTNUT (2)

'con man noun [C] (informal) a man who tricks others into giving him money, etc. ▶ **oszust/ką, hochsztapler**

⚷ **connect** /kə'nekt/ verb **1** [I,T] **connect (sth) (up) (to/with sth)** to be joined to sth; to join sth to sth else: *The tunnels connect (up) ten metres further on.* ◇ *The printer is connected to the computer.* ◇ *This motorway connects Oxford with Birmingham.* ▶ **łączyć (się) z czymś, podłączać do czegoś** ⊃ look at **disconnect 2** [T] **connect sb/sth (with sb/sth)** to have an association with sb/sth else; to realize or show that sb/sth is involved with sb/sth else: *There was no evidence that she was connected with* (że była zamieszana w) *the crime.* ◇ *Doctors believe that the increase in asthma is connected with* (jest związany z) *pollution levels.* ▶ **wiązać (z kimś/czymś), kojarzyć 3** [I] **connect (with sth)** (used about a bus, train, plane, etc.) to arrive at a particular time so that passengers can change to another bus, train, plane, etc.: *a connecting flight* ▶ **mieć połączenie 4** [T] **connect sb (with sth)** to link sb by telephone ▶ **łączyć**

⚷ **connection** /kə'nekʃn/ noun **1** [C,U] **a connection between A and B; a connection with/to sth** an association or relationship between two or more people or things: *Is there any connection between the two organizations?* ◇ *What's your connection with Brazil? Have you worked there?* ◇ *I'm having problems with my Internet connection.* ▶ **związek, połączenie 2** [C] a place where two wires, pipes, etc. join together: *The radio doesn't work. There must be a loose connection somewhere.* ▶ **kontakt, złącze 3** [C] a bus, train, plane, etc. that leaves soon after another arrives: *Our bus was late so we missed our connection.* ▶ **połączenie 4** [C, usually pl.] a person that you know who is important or of high rank ▶ **koneksja, znajomość**

IDM **in connection with sb/sth** (formal) about or concerning: *I am writing to you in connection with your application.* ▶ **w związku z kimś/czymś, w sprawie kogoś/czegoś**

in this/that connection (formal) about or concerning this/that ▶ **w związku z tym**

connive /kə'naɪv/ verb [I] **1 connive at sth** to do nothing to stop sth that is illegal or wrong ▶ **tolerować, patrzeć przez palce 2 connive (with sb) (to do sth)** to work together with sb to do sth that is wrong: *The two parties connived to get rid of the president.* ▶ **współdziałać** (*np. w zbrodni*)

■ **conniving** adj. behaving in a way that secretly hurts others or deliberately fails to prevent others from being hurt ▶ **potajemnie sprawiający komuś przykrość lub przyzwalający na sprawienie komuś przykrości**

connoisseur /ˌkɒnə'sɜː(r); US -'sʊr/ noun [C] a person who knows a lot about art, good food, wine, music, etc. ▶ **koneser/ka, znaw-ca/czyni**

connotation /ˌkɒnə'teɪʃn/ noun [C] an idea expressed by a word in addition to its main meaning: *'Spinster' means a single woman but it has negative connotations.* ▶ **zabarwienie**

conquer /'kɒŋkə(r)/ verb [T] **1** to take control of a country or city and its people by force, especially in a war: *Napoleon's ambition was to conquer Europe.* ◇ (figurative) *The young singer conquered the hearts of audiences all over the world.* ▶ **podbić, zdobyć 2** to succeed in controlling or dealing with a strong feeling, problem, etc.: *She's trying to conquer her fear of flying.* ▶ **pokonać, podbić**

conqueror /'kɒŋkərə(r)/ noun [C] a person who has **conquered** (1) sth ▶ **zdobyw-ca/czyni**

conquest /'kɒŋkwest/ noun **1** [C,U] an act of **conquering** sth: *the Norman conquest (of England in 1066)* ◇ *the conquest of Mount Everest* ◇ *romantic conquests* podboje sercowe ▶ **podbój 2** [C] an area of land that has been taken in a war ▶ **podbity obszar**

conscience /'kɒnʃəns/ noun [C,U] the part of your mind that tells you if what you are doing is right or wrong: *a clear/a guilty conscience* ▶ **sumienie**

IDM **have sth on your conscience** to feel guilty because you have done sth wrong ▶ **mieć coś na sumieniu**

conscientious /ˌkɒnʃi'enʃəs/ adj. (used about people) careful to do sth correctly and well: *He's a conscientious worker.* ▶ **skrupulatny, sumienny**

■ **conscientiously** adv. ▶ **skrupulatnie, sumiennie**

ˌconscientious ob'jector noun [C] a person who refuses to join the army, etc. because they believe it is morally wrong to kill other people ▶ **człowiek uchylający się od służby wojskowej ze względów moralnych lub religijnych, pacyfist(k)a**

conscious /ˈkɒnʃəs/ adj. **1** [not before a noun] **conscious (of sth/that ...)** noticing or realizing that sth exists: *She didn't seem conscious of the danger.* ◇ *Young people today are very fashion-conscious.* Młodzi ludzie obecnie przywiązują dużą uwagę do mody. ▶ **świadomy** SYN **aware** **2** able to see, hear, feel, etc. things; awake ▶ **przytomny** OPP **unconscious** **3** that you do on purpose or for a particular reason: *We made a conscious effort to treat both children equally.* ▶ **świadomy** ⓘ Wyraz **deliberate** ma podobne znaczenie.
■ **consciously** adv. ▶ **świadomie**

consciousness /ˈkɒnʃəsnəs/ noun **1** [U] the state of being able to see, hear, feel, etc.: *As he fell, he hit his head and* ***lost consciousness.*** ◇ *She* ***regained consciousness*** *after two weeks in a coma.* ▶ **przytomność** **2** [U, sing.] **consciousness (of sth)** the state of realizing or noticing that sth exists: *There is (a) growing consciousness of the need to save energy.* ▶ **świadomość**

conscript¹ /kənˈskrɪpt/ verb [T] to make sb join the army, navy or air force ▶ **powoływać do wojska**
■ **conscription** noun [U] ▶ **pobór** (*do wojska*)

conscript² /ˈkɒnskrɪpt/ noun [C] a person who has been **conscripted** ▶ **poborowy, rekrut** ➲ look at **volunteer**

consecrate /ˈkɒnsɪkreɪt/ verb [T] to state formally in a special ceremony that a place or an object can be used for religious purposes ▶ **święcić**
■ **consecration** /ˌkɒnsɪˈkreɪʃn/ noun [C,U] ▶ **poświęcenie**

consecutive /kənˈsekjətɪv/ adj. coming or happening one after the other: *This is the team's fourth consecutive win.* ▶ **kolejny, z rzędu**
■ **consecutively** adv. ▶ **kolejno, z rzędu**

consensus /kənˈsensəs/ noun [sing., U] **(a) consensus (among/between sb) (on/about sth)** agreement among a group of people: *to* ***reach a consensus*** ◇ *There is no consensus among experts about the causes of global warming.* ▶ **jednomyślność, zgoda**

consent¹ /kənˈsent/ verb [I] **consent (to sth)** to agree to sth; to allow sth to happen ▶ **zgadzać się, pozwalać**

consent² /kənˈsent/ noun [U] agreement; permission: *The child's parents had to give their consent to the operation.* ▶ **zgoda, pozwolenie**
IDM **the age of consent** → AGE¹

consequence /ˈkɒnsɪkwəns; US -sək-/ noun **1** [C] something that happens or follows as a result of sth else: *Many people may lose their jobs* ***as a consequence of*** *recent poor sales.* ▶ **następstwo, skutek** **2** [U] (formal) importance: *It is of no consequence.* ▶ **znaczenie**

consequent /ˈkɒnsɪkwənt/ adj. [only before a noun] (formal) following as the result of sth else: *The lack of rain and consequent poor harvests have led to food shortages.* ▶ **wynikający, następujący**
■ **consequently** adv.: *She didn't work hard enough, and consequently failed the exam.* ▶ **w konsekwencji, wskutek (czegoś)**

conservation /ˌkɒnsəˈveɪʃn/ noun [U] **1** the protection of the natural world: *Conservation groups are protesting against the plan to build a road through the forest.* ▶ **ochrona środowiska, konserwacja** **2** not allowing sth to be wasted, damaged or destroyed: *the conservation of energy* oszczędność energii ▶ **ochrona, konserwacja** ➲ verb **conserve**

conservationist /ˌkɒnsəˈveɪʃənɪst/ noun [C] a person who believes in protecting the natural world ▶ **zwolenni-k/czka ochrony środowiska**

conservatism /kənˈsɜːvətɪzəm/ noun [U] **1** the disapproval of new ideas and change ▶ **konserwatyzm**

2 (usually **Conservatism**) the beliefs of the Conservative Party ▶ **konserwatyzm**

conservative¹ /kənˈsɜːvətɪv/ adj. **1** (**Conservative**) connected with the British Conservative Party: *Conservative voters* ▶ **dot. Partii Konserwatywnej** **2** not liking change; traditional: *He has very conservative tastes.* ▶ **konserwatywny** **3** (used when you are guessing how much sth costs) lower than the real figure or amount: *Even* ***a conservative estimate*** *would put the damage at about £4 000 to repair.* ▶ **ostrożny**
■ **conservatively** adv. ▶ **ostrożnie**

conservative² /kənˈsɜːvətɪv/ noun [C] **1** a person who does not like change ▶ **konserwatyst(k)a** **2** (usually **Conservative**) (abbr. **Con**) a member of the British Conservative Party ▶ **człon-ek/kini Partii Konserwatywnej**

the Conˈservative Party noun [sing., with sing. or pl. verb] one of the main political parties in Britain. The Conservative Party supports a free market and is against the state controlling industry ▶ **Partia Konserwatywna** ➲ note at **party** ➲ look at **Labour Party, Liberal Democrats**

conservatory /kənˈsɜːvətri; US -tɔːri/ noun [C] (pl. **conservatories**) a room with a glass roof and walls often built onto the outside of a house ▶ **szklarnia, cieplarnia**

conserve /kənˈsɜːv/ verb [T] **1** to use as little of sth as possible so that it lasts a long time: *to conserve water* ▶ **oszczędzać** **2** to protect sth and prevent it from being changed or destroyed: *new laws to conserve wildlife in the area* ▶ **chronić, konserwować** ➲ noun **conservation**

consider /kənˈsɪdə(r)/ verb [T] **1 consider sb/sth (for/as sth); consider doing sth** to think about sth carefully, often before making a decision: *We're considering going to Spain for our holidays.* ◇ *They are considering him for the part of Romeo.* ◇ *She had never considered nursing as a career.* ▶ **rozważać, zastanawiać się (nad czymś)** **2 consider sb/sth (as/to be) sth; consider that ...** to think about sb/sth in a particular way: *He considered the risk (to be) too great.* ◇ *He considered that the risk was too great.* ◇ *Jane considers herself an expert on the subject.* ▶ **sądzić, że** **3** to remember or pay attention to sth, especially sb's feelings: *I can't just move abroad. I have to consider my family.* ▶ **brać pod uwagę, mieć wzgląd na coś**

considerable /kənˈsɪdərəbl/ adj. great in amount or size: *A considerable number of people preferred the old building to the new one.* ◇ *We had considerable difficulty* (poważne trudności) *in getting tickets for the flights we wanted.* ▶ **znaczny, spory**
■ **considerably** /-əbli/ adv. ▶ **znacznie**

considerate /kənˈsɪdərət/ adj. **considerate (of sb) (to do sth); considerate (towards sb)** careful not to upset people; thinking of others: *It was very considerate of you* (bardzo ładnie z twojej strony) *to offer to drive me home.* ▶ **uprzejmy, liczący się z innymi** SYN **thoughtful** OPP **inconsiderate**

consideration /kənˌsɪdəˈreɪʃn/ noun **1** [U] (formal) an act of thinking about sth carefully or for a long time: *I have given some consideration to the idea but I don't think it would work.* ▶ **namysł, rozwaga** **2** [C] something that you think about when you are making a decision: *If he changes his job, the salary will be an important consideration.* ▶ **okoliczność, wzgląd** **3** [U] **consideration (for sb/sth)** the quality of thinking about what other people need or feel: *Most drivers show little consideration for cyclists.* ▶ **wzgląd** (*np. na czyjeś uczucia*)
IDM **take sth into consideration** to think about sth when you are forming an opinion or making a decision ▶ **brać coś pod uwagę**

considering /kən'sɪdərɪŋ/ prep., conj. (used for introducing a surprising fact) when you think about or remember sth: *Considering you've only been studying for a year, you speak English very well.* ▶ **zważywszy (na coś)**

consign /kən'saɪn/ verb [T] (formal) **consign sb/sth to sth** to put or send sb/sth somewhere, especially in order to get rid of them or it: *I think I can consign this junk mail straight to the bin.* ▶ **wyrzucać**; **odsyłać**

consignment /kən'saɪnmənt/ noun [C] **1** goods that are being sent to sb/sth ▶ **przesyłka 2** a quantity of goods that are sent or delivered somewhere: *a new consignment of books* ▶ **dostawa**, **wysyłka** (*towaru*)

consist /kən'sɪst/ verb [not used in the continuous tenses]
PHR V **consist in sth** to have sth as its main point: *Her job consisted in welcoming the guests as they arrived.* ▶ **polegać na czymś**
consist of sth to be formed or made up of sth: *The band consists of a singer, two guitarists and a drummer.* ▶ **składać się z czegoś** ℹ Czasownika **consist** nie używa się w czasach *continuous*. Natomiast często spotyka się go w *present participle* (formie *-ing*): *It's a full-time course consisting of fourteen different modules.*

consistency /kən'sɪstənsi/ noun (pl. **consistencies**) **1** [U] the quality of always having the same standard, opinions, behaviour, etc.: *Your work lacks consistency.* ▶ **konsekwencja**, **zgodność** OPP **inconsistency 2** [C,U] how thick or smooth a liquid substance is: *The mixture should have a thick, sticky consistency.* ▶ **konsystencja**, **gęstość**

consistent /kən'sɪstənt/ adj. **1** always having the same opinions, standard, behaviour, etc.; not changing ▶ **konsekwentny 2 consistent (with sth)** agreeing with or similar to sth: *I'm afraid your statement is not consistent with what the other witnesses said.* ▶ **zgodny (z czymś)** OPP for both meanings **inconsistent**
■ **consistently** adv.: *We must try to maintain a consistently high standard.* ▶ **konsekwentnie**, **niezmiennie**

consolation /ˌkɒnsə'leɪʃn/ noun [C,U] a thing or person that makes you feel better when you are sad; a comfort: *It was some consolation to me to know that I wasn't the only one who had failed the exam.* ▶ **pocieszenie**, **pociecha**

console[1] /kən'səʊl/ verb [T] **console sb/yourself (with sth)** to give comfort or sympathy to sb who is unhappy or disappointed: *Nothing could console him when his wife died.* ◇ *Console yourself with the thought that you did your best.* ▶ **pocieszać** SYN **comfort**

console[2] /'kɒnsəʊl/ noun [C] a flat surface which contains all the controls and switches for a machine, a piece of electronic equipment, etc. ▶ **konsola**

consolidate /kən'sɒlɪdeɪt/ verb [I,T] to become or to make sth firmer or stronger: *We're going to consolidate what we've learnt so far by doing some revision exercises today.* ▶ **konsolidować (się)**, **wzmacniać (się)**
■ **consolidation** /kənˌsɒlɪ'deɪʃn/ noun [U] ▶ **konsolidacja**, **wzmocnienie**

consonant /'kɒnsənənt/ noun [C] any of the letters of the English alphabet except *a*, *e*, *i*, *o*, and *u*: *The letters 't', 'm', 's' and 'b' are all consonants.* ➲ look at **vowel**

consortium /kən'sɔːtiəm/ noun [C] (pl. **consortiums** or **consortia** /-tiə/) a group of companies that work closely together for a particular purpose ▶ **konsorcjum**

conspicuous /kən'spɪkjuəs/ adj. easily seen or noticed ▶ **rzucający się w oczy**, **zwracający uwagę** OPP **inconspicuous**
■ **conspicuously** adv. ▶ **w sposób rzucający się w oczy**, **w sposób zwracający uwagę**

conspiracy /kən'spɪrəsi/ noun [C,U] (pl. **conspiracies**) **1** a secret plan by a group of people to do sth bad or illegal: *a conspiracy against the president* ▶ **spisek 2** planning sth, especially a crime, together with other people ▶ **zbrodnicze knowania**, **spisek**

conspirator /kən'spɪrətə(r)/ noun [C] a member of a group of people who are planning to do sth bad or illegal ▶ **spiskowiec**

conspire /kən'spaɪə(r)/ verb [I] **1 conspire (with sb) (to do sth)** to plan to do sth bad or illegal with a group of people: *A group of terrorists were conspiring to blow up the plane.* ▶ **spiskować 2 conspire (against sb/sth)** (used about events) to seem to work together to make sth bad happen: *When we both lost our jobs in the same week, we felt that everything was conspiring against us.* ▶ **sprzysięgać się (przeciwko komuś/czemuś)**

constable = POLICE CONSTABLE

constabulary /kən'stæbjələri; US -leri/ noun [C] (pl. **constabularies**) the police force of a particular area ▶ **policja** (*danego okręgu*)

constant /'kɒnstənt/ adj. **1** happening or existing all the time or again and again: *The constant noise gave me a headache.* ◇ *There were constant interruptions* (ciągle nam przeszkadzano) *so we didn't get the work finished.* ▶ **ciągły**, **nieustanny**, **uporczywy 2** that does not change: *You use less petrol if you drive at a constant speed.* ▶ **stały**, **niezmienny**

constantly /'kɒnstəntli/ adv. always; again and again: *The situation is constantly changing.* ▶ **ciągle**, **stale**

constellation /ˌkɒnstə'leɪʃn/ noun [C] a group of stars that forms a pattern and has a name ▶ **gwiazdozbiór**

consternation /ˌkɒnstə'neɪʃn/ noun [U] a feeling of shock or worry: *We stared at each other **in consternation**.* ▶ **konsternacja**

constipated /'kɒnstɪpeɪtɪd/ adj. not able to empty waste from your body ▶ **cierpiący na zaparcie**
■ **constipation** /ˌkɒnstɪ'peɪʃn/ noun [U]: *to **suffer from/have** constipation* ▶ **zaparcie**

constituency /kən'stɪtjuənsi; US -tʃu-/ noun [C] (pl. **constituencies**) a district and the people who live in it that a politician represents ▶ **okręg wyborczy** ➲ note at **election**

constituent /kən'stɪtjuənt; US -tʃu-/ noun [C] **1** a person who lives, and can vote in a **constituency**: *She has the full support of her constituents.* ▶ **wyborca**, **mieszkaniec okręgu wyborczego 2** one of the parts of sth that combine to form the whole: *Silicon and oxygen are the fundamental constituents of rocks in the earth's crust.* ▶ **część składowa**, **składnik**
■ **constituent** adj. [only before a noun] (formal) forming or helping to make a whole: *to break something up into its **constituent parts/elements*** ▶ (*część itp.*) **składowy**

constitute /'kɒnstɪtjuːt; US -tətuːt/ verb [T] [not used in the continuous tenses] (formal) **1** to be considered as sth; to be equal to sth: *The presence of the troops constitutes a threat to peace.* ▶ **stanowić 2** to be one of the parts that form sth: *Women constitute a high proportion of part-time workers.* ▶ **stanowić** ℹ Czasownika **constitute** nie używa się w czasach *continuous*. Natomiast często spotyka się go w *present participle* (formie *-ing*): *Management has to fix a maximum number of hours as constituting a day's work.*

constitution /ˌkɒnstɪ'tjuːʃn; US -tə'tuː-/ noun **1** [C] the basic laws or rules of a country or organization: *the United States constitution* ▶ **konstytucja 2** [U] the way the parts of sth are put together; the structure of sth: *the constitution of DNA* ▶ **skład 3** [C] (old-fashioned) the way sth is put together ▶ **organizm**

constitutional /ˌkɒnstɪ'tjuːʃənl; US -tə'tuː-/ adj. connected with or allowed by the **constitution** of a country, etc. ▶ **konstytucyjny**

constrain /kən'streɪn/ verb [T] (formal) **1 constrain sb/sth (to do sth)** to force sb/sth to do sth ▶ **przymuszać 2 con-**

strain sb (from doing sth) to limit sb/sth: *The company's growth has been constrained by high taxes.* ▶ **ograniczać, krępować**

constraint /kən'streɪnt/ noun [C,U] something that limits you; a restriction: *There are always some financial constraints on a project like this.* ▶ **ograniczenie, skrępowanie**

constrict /kən'strɪkt/ verb [I,T] **1** to become or make sth tighter, narrower or less: *She felt her throat constrict with fear.* ◇ *The valve constricts the flow of air.* ▶ **ścieśniać (się), kurczyć (się), ograniczać 2** to limit sb's freedom to do sth ▶ **ograniczać**
■ **constriction** noun [C,U] ▶ **skurczenie; ograniczenie**

construct /kən'strʌkt/ verb [T] to build or make sth: *Early houses were constructed out of mud and sticks.* ▶ **konstruować** ⓘ **Construct** jest słowem bardziej formalnym niż **build**.

construction /kən'strʌkʃn/ noun **1** [U] the act or method of building or making sth: *A new bridge is now **under construction*** (w budowie). ◇ *He works in the construction industry* (w budownictwie). ▶ **budowa 2** [C] (formal) something that has been built or made; a building: *The new pyramid was a construction of glass and steel.* ▶ **konstrukcja, budowla 3** [C] the way that words are used together in a phrase or sentence: *a difficult grammatical construction* ▶ **konstrukcja**

constructive /kən'strʌktɪv/ adj. useful or helpful: *constructive suggestions/criticisms/advice* ▶ **konstruktywny**
■ **constructively** adv. ▶ **konstruktywnie**

construe /kən'stru:/ verb [T] (formal) **construe sth (as sth)** to understand the meaning of sth in a particular way: *Her confident manner is sometimes construed as* (jest często odbierany jako) *arrogance.* ▶ **interpretować, rozumieć coś jako coś** ➲ look at **misconstrue**

consul /'kɒnsl/ noun [C] an official who works in a foreign city helping people from his or her own country who are living or visiting there ▶ **konsul**
■ **consular** /'kɒnsjələ(r); US -səl-/ adj. ▶ **konsularny**

consulate /'kɒnsjələt; US -səl-/ noun [C] the building where a **consul** works ▶ **konsulat** ➲ look at **embassy**

consult /kən'sʌlt/ verb **1** [T] **consult sb/sth (about sth)** to ask sb for some information or advice, or to look for it in a book, etc.: *If the symptoms continue, consult your doctor.* ◇ *You can consult your dictionary if you're not sure of a spelling.* ▶ **radzić się; sprawdzać, zaglądać do czegoś 2** [I] **consult with sb** to discuss sth with sb: *Harry consulted with his brothers before selling the family business.* ▶ **naradzać się z kimś**

consultancy /kən'sʌltənsi/ noun (pl. **consultancies**) **1** [C] a company that gives expert advice on a particular subject ▶ **firma konsultingowa 2** [U] expert advice that sb is paid to provide on a particular subject ▶ **konsultacja**

consultant /kən'sʌltənt/ noun [C] **1** a person who gives advice to people on business, law, etc.: *a firm of management consultants* ▶ **konsultant/ka, dorad-ca/czyni 2** (Brit.) a hospital doctor who is an expert in a particular area of medicine: *a consultant psychiatrist* ▶ **lekarz konsultant**

consultation /ˌkɒnsl'teɪʃn/ noun **1** [U] the act of discussing sth with sb or with a group of people before making a decision about it: *The measures were introduced without consultation.* ▶ **naradzanie się 2** [C] a formal meeting to discuss sth: *Diplomats met for consultations on the hostage crisis.* ▶ **konsultacja, narada 3** [C] a meeting with an expert, especially a doctor, to get advice or treatment: *a consultation with a doctor* ▶ **konsultacja, porada 4** [U] the act of looking for information in a book, etc. ▶ **zaglądanie (do czegoś)**

consume /kən'sju:m; US -'su:m/ verb [T] (formal) **1** to use sth such as fuel, energy or time: *This car consumes a lot of petrol.* ▶ **zużywać 2** to eat or drink sth: *Wrestlers can consume up to 10 000 calories in a day.* ▶ **konsumować, spożywać** ➲ noun **consumption 3** (used about an emotion) to affect sb very strongly: *She was consumed by grief* (ogarnął ją żal) *when her son was killed.* ▶ **trawić (kogoś) 4** (used about fire) to destroy sth ▶ *(ogień)* **trawić**

consumer /kən'sju:mə(r); US -'su:-/ noun [C] a person who buys things or uses services ▶ **konsument/ka**

con'sumer goods noun [pl.] goods such as food, clothing, etc. bought by individual customers ▶ **towary konsumpcyjne**

consumerism /kən'sju:mərɪzəm; US -'su:-/ noun [U] **1** the buying and using of goods and services ▶ *(ekon.)* **konsumpcja towarów 2** the belief that it is good for a society or an individual person to buy and use a large quantity of goods and services ▶ **konsumpcjonizm**
■ **consumerist** adj.: *consumerist values* ▶ **konsumpcyjny**

consuming /kən'sju:mɪŋ; US -'su:-/ adj. [only before a noun] that takes up a lot of your time and attention: *Sport is her consuming passion* (jest jej życiową pasją). ▶ **trawiący, pasjonujący**

consummate[1] /'kɒnsəmət/ adj. [only before a noun] (formal) extremely skilled; perfect ▶ **doskonały**

consummate[2] /'kɒnsəmeɪt/ verb [T] (formal) to make a marriage or relationship complete by having sex ▶ **skonsumować**
■ **consummation** /ˌkɒnsə'meɪʃn/ noun [C,U] ▶ **skonsumowanie**

consumption /kən'sʌmpʃn/ noun [U] **1** the act of using, eating, etc. sth: *The meat was declared unfit for human consumption.* ▶ **konsumpcja, spożycie 2** the amount of fuel, etc. that sth uses: *a car with low fuel consumption* ▶ **zużycie** ➲ verb **consume**

cont. (also **contd**) abbr. **continued**: *cont. on p 9* ▶ **cd.**

contact[1] /'kɒntækt/ noun **1** [U] **contact (with sb/sth)** meeting, talking to or writing to sb else: *They are trying to **make contact*** (nawiązać kontakt) *with the kidnappers.* ◇ *I'll **get in contact** with you some time next week.* ◇ *We **keep in contact** with our office in New York.* ◇ *Pat said he'd **be in contact**, but we haven't heard from him yet.* ◇ *It's a pity to **lose contact** with old school friends.* ◇ *I can't help you, but I'll **put** you **in contact** with someone who can.* ▶ **kontakt 2** [U] **contact (with sb/sth)** the state of touching sb/sth: *This product should not **come into contact** with food.* Ten produkt nie powinien znajdować się w pobliżu jedzenia. ◇ *Don't let the wires come into contact with each other.* Nie pozwól, żeby przewody się stykały. ▶ **styczność 3** [C] a person that you know who may be able to help you: *business contacts* ▶ **kontakt, znajomość**

contact[2] /'kɒntækt/ verb [T] to telephone or write to sb: *Is there a phone number where I can contact you?* ▶ **kontaktować się z kimś**

'contact lens noun [C] a small piece of plastic that fits onto your eye to help you to see better ▶ **soczewka kontaktowa**

'contact sport noun [C] a sport in which players have physical contact with each other ▶ **sport kontaktowy** OPP **non-contact sport**

contagious /kən'teɪdʒəs/ adj. (used about a disease) that you can get by touching sb/sth: *Smallpox is a highly contagious disease.* ◇ (figurative) *Her laugh is contagious.* ▶ **zaraźliwy** ➲ look at **infectious**
■ **contagion** /kən'teɪdʒən/ noun [U] ▶ **zakażenie, zaraza**

contain /kən'teɪn/ verb [T] [not used in the continuous tenses] **1** to have sth inside or as part of itself: *Each box contains*

24 tins. ▶ **zawierać** ℹ Czasownika **contain** nie używa się w czasach *continuous*. Natomiast często spotyka się go w *present participle* (formie *-ing*): *petrol containing lead* **2** to keep sth within limits; to control sth: *efforts to contain inflation* ◇ *She found it hard to contain her anger.* ▶ **powstrzymywać**

Por. **contain** z **include. Contain** odnosi się do przedmiotów, w których znajdują się jakieś rzeczy: *a jar containing olives* ◇ *The parcel contained six books.* ◇ *This film contains violent scenes.* **Include** używa się, gdy kilka przedmiotów tworzy pewną całość lub należy do pewnej grupy: *The price of the holiday includes* (w cenę wczasów wliczone jest) *accommodation and evening meals but not lunch.* ◇ *a team of seven people including* (wliczając) *a cameraman and a doctor.*

container /kən'teɪnə(r)/ noun [C] **1** a box, bottle, bag, etc. in which sth is kept: *a plastic container* ▶ **zbiornik, pojemnik, opakowanie 2** a large metal box that is used for transporting goods by sea, road or rail: *a container lorry/ship* ▶ **kontener**

contaminate /kən'tæmɪneɪt/ verb [T] to add a substance which will make sth dirty or harmful: *The town's drinking water was contaminated with poisonous chemicals.* ▶ **skazić, zanieczyszczać**

■ **contamination** /kən,tæmɪ'neɪʃn/ noun [U] ▶ **skażenie, zanieczyszczenie**

contd = CONTINUED

contemplate /'kɒntəmpleɪt/ verb [T] **1** to think carefully about sth or the possibility of doing sth: *Before her illness she had never contemplated retiring.* SYN **consider** ▶ **zastanawiać się nad czymś, rozważać 2** to look at sb/sth, often quietly or for a long time ▶ **kontemplować, przypatrywać się**

■ **contemplation** /,kɒntəm'pleɪʃn/ noun [U] **1** thinking deeply about sth ▶ **rozmyślanie 2** looking at sth quietly ▶ **przypatrywanie się**

contemporary[1] /kən'temprəri; US -pəreri/ adj. **1** belonging to the same time as sb/sth else: *The programme includes contemporary film footage of the First World War.* ▶ **współczesny, ówczesny 2** of the present time: *contemporary music/art/society* ▶ **współczesny, dzisiejszy** SYN **modern**

contemporary[2] /kən'temprəri; US -pəreri/ noun [C] (pl. **contemporaries**) a person who lives or does sth at the same time as sb else ▶ **współczesn-y/a; rówieśni-k/czka/ca**

contempt /kən'tempt/ noun [U] **contempt (for sb/sth)** the feeling that sb/sth does not deserve any respect or is without value: *The teacher treated my question **with contempt**.* ▶ **pogarda**

■ **contemptuous** /kən'temptʃuəs/ adj.: *The boy just gave a contemptuous laugh when I asked him to be quiet.* ▶ **pogardliwy**

contemptible /kən'temptəbl/ adj. (formal) not deserving any respect at all: *contemptible behaviour* ▶ **godny pogardy** SYN **despicable**

con,tempt of 'court noun [U] the crime of refusing to obey an order made by a court; not showing respect for a court or judge: *Any person who disregards this order will be in contempt of court.* ▶ **niezastosowanie się do nakazu sądu; obraza sądu**

contemptuous /kən'temptʃuəs/ adj. **contemptuous (of sb/sth)** feeling or showing that you have no respect for sb/sth: *She gave him a contemptuous look.* ◇ *He was contemptuous of everything I did.* Odnosił się z pogardą do wszystkiego, co robiłem. ▶ **pogardliwy** SYN **scornful**

■ **contemptuously** adv. ▶ **pogardliwie**

contend /kən'tend/ verb **1** [T] (formal) to say or argue that sth is true: *The young man contended that he was innocent.* ▶ **twierdzić, że 2** [I] **contend (for sth)** to compete against sb to win or gain sth: *Two athletes are contending for first place.* ▶ **współzawodniczyć 3** [I] **contend with/against sb/sth** to have to deal with a problem or a difficult situation: *She's had a lot of problems to contend with.* ▶ **walczyć**

containers

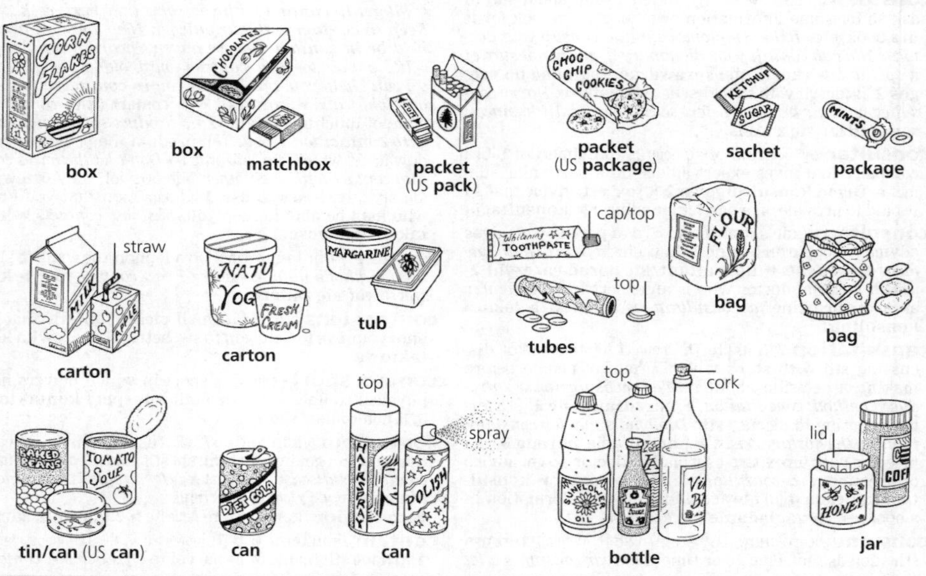

contender /kən'tendə(r)/ noun [C] a person who may win a competition: *There are only two serious contenders for the leadership.* ▶ **zawodni-k/czka, kandydat/ka, pretendent/ka**

content¹ /'kɒntent/ noun **1** (**contents**) [pl.] the thing or things that are inside sth: *Add the contents of this packet to a pint of cold milk and mix well.* ◇ *The contents page* (spis treści) *tells you what is inside a book.* ▶ **zawartość** **2** [sing.] the main subject, ideas, etc. of a book, article, TV programme, etc.: *The content of the essay is good, but there are too many grammatical mistakes.* ▶ **treść** **3** [sing.] the amount of a particular substance that sth contains: *Many processed foods have a high sugar content.* ▶ **zawartość**

content² /kən'tent/ adj. [not before a noun] **content (with sth)**; **content to do sth** happy or satisfied with what you have or do ▶ **zadowolony**

content³ /kən'tent/ verb [T] **content yourself with sth** to accept sth even though it was not exactly what you wanted: *The restaurant was closed, so we had to content ourselves with a sandwich.* ▶ **zadowalać się**

content⁴ /kən'tent/ noun
IDM **to your heart's content** → HEART

contented /kən'tentɪd/ adj. happy or satisfied: *The baby gave a contented chuckle.* ▶ **zadowolony**
■ **contentedly** adv. ▶ **z zadowoleniem**

contention /kən'tenʃn/ noun (formal) **1** [U] arguing; disagreement ▶ **spór, sprzeczka** **2** [C] your opinion; sth that you say is true: *The government's contention is that unemployment will start to fall next year.* ▶ **argument, twierdzenie**
IDM **be in contention (for sth)** to have a chance of winning a competition: *Four teams are still in contention for the cup.* ▶ **rywalizować o coś**

contentious /kən'tenʃəs/ adj. likely to cause argument: *a contentious issue* ▶ **sporny**

contentment /kən'tentmənt/ noun [U] a feeling of happiness and satisfaction ▶ **zadowolenie**

contest¹ /'kɒntest/ noun [C] a competition to find out who is the best, strongest, most beautiful, etc.: *I've decided to **enter** that writing **contest**.* ◇ *The by-election will be a contest* (walką) *between the two main parties.* ▶ **zawody, konkurs**

contest² /kən'test/ verb [T] **1** to take part in a competition or try to win sth: *Twenty-four teams will contest next year's World Cup.* ▶ **walczyć o coś, ubiegać się o coś** **2** to say that sth is wrong or that it was not done properly: *They contested the decision, saying that the judges had not been fair.* ▶ **kwestionować**

contestant /kən'testənt/ noun [C] a person who takes part in a **contest** ▶ **zawodni-k/czka**

context /'kɒntekst/ noun [C,U] **1** the situation in which sth happens or that caused sth to happen: *To **put** our company **in context**, we are now the third largest in the country.* ▶ **kontekst** **2** the words that come before or after a word, phrase or sentence that help you to understand its meaning: *You can often guess the meaning of a word from its context.* ◇ *Taken **out of context**, his comment made no sense.* ▶ **kontekst**

contextualize (also **-ise**) /kən'tekstʃuəlaɪz/ verb [T] (formal) to consider sth in relation to the situation in which it happens or exists ▶ **umieszczać w kontekście**
■ **contextualization** (also **-isation**) /kən,tekstʃuəlaɪz'eɪʃn/ noun [U] ▶ **umieszczenie w kontekście**

continent /'kɒntɪnənt/ noun **1** [C] one of the seven main areas of land on the Earth ▶ **kontynent** **2** (**the Continent**) [sing.] (Brit.) the main part of Europe not including Britain or Ireland: *We're going to spend a weekend on the Continent.* ▶ **Europa**

continental /,kɒntɪ'nentl/ adj. **1** (Brit.) connected with the main part of Europe not including Britain or Ireland: *continental holidays* wakacje w Europie ▶ **europejski** **2** connected with or typical of a continent: *Moscow has a continental climate: hot summers and cold winters.* ▶ **kontynentalny**

,continental 'breakfast noun [C] a breakfast of bread and jam with coffee ▶ **rodzaj lekkiego śniadania europejskiego** ➲ look at **English breakfast**

contingency /kən'tɪndʒənsi/ noun [C] (pl. **contingencies**) a possible future situation or event: *We'd better make **contingency plans*** (plany na ewentualność wypadku itp.) *just in case something goes wrong.* ◇ *We've tried to prepare for every possible contingency.* ▶ **ewentualność, nieprzewidziany wypadek**

contingent /kən'tɪndʒənt/ noun [C, with sing. or pl. verb] **1** a group of people from the same country, organization, etc. who are attending an event: *the Irish contingent at the conference* ▶ **delegacja** **2** a group of armed forces forming part of a larger force ▶ **kontyngent wojsk**

continual /kən'tɪnjuəl/ adj. [only before a noun] happening again and again: *His continual phone calls started to annoy her.* ▶ **ciągły, bezustanny** ➲ look at **incessant**

Por. **continuous. Continuous** używa się do opisania akcji lub stanu, który trwa bez przerwy: *There has been a continuous improvement in his work.* ◇ *After climbing continuously for three hours we were exhausted.* **Continual** używa się do określenia czegoś, co się powtarza, zwłaszcza czegoś denerwującego: *They have had continual problems with the heating.*

■ **continually** /-juəli/ adv. ▶ **ciągle, bezustannie**

continuation /kən,tɪnju'eɪʃn/ noun **1** [sing., U] an act or the state of continuing: *Continuation of the current system will be impossible.* ▶ **kontynuacja, kontynuowanie** **2** [sing.] something that continues sth else or makes it longer: *The team are hoping for a continuation of their recent good form.* ▶ **ciąg dalszy; przedłużenie**

continue /kən'tɪnju:/ verb **1** [I] to keep happening or existing without stopping: *If the pain continues, see your doctor.* ▶ **trwać** **2** [I,T] **continue (doing/to do sth)**; **continue (with sth)** to keep doing sth without stopping: *They ignored me and continued their conversation.* ◇ *He continued working/to work late into the night.* ◇ *Will you continue with the lessons after the exam?* ◇ *He will continue as* (pozostanie) *head teacher until the end of term.* ▶ **kontynuować** **3** [I,T] to go further in the same direction: *The next day we continued our journey.* ▶ **iść/posuwać się dalej; kontynuować** **4** [I,T] to begin to do or say sth again after you had stopped: *The meeting will continue after lunch.* ◇ *I'm sorry I interrupted. Please continue* (mów dalej). ▶ **kontynuować**

continued /kən'tɪnju:d/ (abbr. **cont.**; **contd**) adj. [only before a noun] going on without stopping: *There are reports of continued fighting near the border.* ▶ **ciągły, nieprzerwany**

con,tinuing edu'cation = ADULT EDUCATION

continuity /,kɒntɪ'nju:əti; US -tə'nu:-/ noun [U] the fact of continuing without stopping or of staying the same: *The pupils will have the same teacher for two years to ensure continuity.* ▶ **ciągłość**

continuous /kən'tɪnjuəs/ adj. happening or existing without stopping: *There was a continuous line of cars stretching for miles.* ▶ **ciągły, nieprzerwany** ➲ note at **continual**
■ **continuously** adv. ▶ **nieprzerwanie, ciągle**

con,tinuous as'sessment noun [U] (Brit.) a system of giving a student a final mark based on work done during a course of study rather than on one exam: *Students' marks are based on continuous assessment of their work.*

▶ **ocena końcowa wystawiona na podstawie wyników pracy osiągniętych w całym okresie nauki**

the **con'tinuous tense** (also **the progressive tense**) noun [C] the form of a verb such as 'I am waiting', 'I was waiting' or 'I have been waiting' which is made from a part of 'be' and a verb ending in '-ing' and is used to describe an action that continues for a period of time ▶ **czas ciągły**

continuum /kən'tɪnjuəm/ noun [C] (pl. **continua** /-juə/) a series of similar items in which each is almost the same as the ones next to it but the last is very different from the first ▶ **kontinuum**

contort /kən'tɔːt/ verb [I,T] to move or to make sth move into a strange or unusual shape: *His face contorted/was contorted with pain.* ▶ **wykrzywiać (się)**
■ **contortion** noun [C] ▶ **wykrzywienie**

contour /'kɒntʊə(r)/ noun [C] **1** the shape of the outer surface of sth: *I could just make out the contours of the house in the dark.* ▶ **zarys, kontur 2** (also **'contour line**) a line on a map joining places of equal height: *a contour map* ▶ **warstwica**

contra- /'kɒntrə/ [in nouns, verbs and adjectives] against; opposite: *contradict* zaprzeczać ▶ **kontr(a)-, przeciw-**

contraband /'kɒntrəbænd/ noun [U] goods that are illegally taken into or out of a country: *contraband cigarettes* ◇ *to smuggle contraband* ▶ **przemycany towar**

contraception /ˌkɒntrə'sepʃn/ noun [U] the ways of preventing a woman from becoming pregnant: *a reliable form of contraception* ▶ **antykoncepcja** ➲ look at **birth control, family planning**

contraceptive /ˌkɒntrə'septɪv/ noun [C] a drug or a device that prevents a woman from becoming pregnant ▶ **środek antykoncepcyjny**
■ **contraceptive** adj. [only before a noun] ▶ **antykoncepcyjny**

contract¹ /'kɒntrækt/ noun [C] a written legal agreement: *They* ***signed a*** *three-year* ***contract with*** *a major record company.* ◇ *The company is hoping to* ***win a contract*** *to supply machinery to the government.* ◇ ***Under the terms of the contract,*** *I'm entitled to twenty days annual paid holiday.* ◇ *a temporary contract* ▶ **kontrakt**

contract² /kən'trækt/ verb **1** [I,T] to become or to make sth smaller or shorter: *Metals contract as they cool.* ▶ **kurczyć (się), skracać** OPP **expand 2** [T] to get an illness or disease, especially a serious one: *to contract pneumonia* ▶ **nabawić się 3** [I,T] to make a written legal agreement with sb to do sth: *His firm has been contracted to supply all the furniture for the new building.* ▶ **wynajmować kogoś** (*na podstawie umowy*)
PHR V **contract sth out (to sb)** to arrange for work to be done by sb outside your own company ▶ **zlecać** (*pracę na zewnątrz*)

contraction /kən'trækʃn/ noun **1** [U] the process of becoming or of making sth become smaller or shorter: *the expansion and contraction of a muscle* ▶ **kurczenie (się); zmniejszanie 2** [C] a strong movement of the muscles that happens to a woman as her baby is born ▶ **skurcz porodowy 3** [C] a shorter form of a word or words: *'Mustn't' is a contraction of 'must not'.* ▶ **skrót**

contractor /kən'træktə(r)/ noun [C] a person or company that has a contract to do work or provide goods or services for another company ▶ **wykonawca**

contractual /kən'træktʃuəl/ adj. connected with or included in a contract ▶ **kontraktowy, zawarty w kontrakcie**

contradict /ˌkɒntrə'dɪkt/ verb [T] **1** to say that sth is wrong or untrue; to say the opposite of sth ▶ **zaprzeczać, sprzeciwiać się 2** (used about a statement, fact, etc.) to be different from or opposite to sth: *These instructions seem to contradict previous ones.* ▶ **być sprzecznym**

contradiction /ˌkɒntrə'dɪkʃn/ noun [C,U] a statement, fact or action that is opposite to or different from another one: *There were a number of contradictions in what he told the police.* ◇ *This letter is* ***in complete contradiction to*** *their previous one.* ▶ **sprzeczność, zaprzeczenie**

contradictory /ˌkɒntrə'dɪktəri/ adj. being opposite to or not matching sth else ▶ **sprzeczny**

contraflow /'kɒntrəfləʊ/ noun [C] the system that is used when one half of a wide road is closed for repairs, and traffic going in both directions has to use the other side ▶ **ruch dwukierunkowy na zwężonym odcinku drogi**

contralto /kən'træltəʊ/ noun [C,U] (pl. **contraltos**) the lowest female singing voice; a woman with this voice ▶ **kontralt**

contraption /kən'træpʃn/ noun [C] a strange or complicated piece of equipment: *The first aeroplanes were dangerous contraptions.* ▶ **(nietypowe) urządzenie**

contrapuntal /ˌkɒntrə'pʌntl/ adj. (used about music) having two or more tunes played together to form a whole ▶ (*muz.*) **kontrapunktowy** ➲ look at **counterpoint**

contrary¹ /'kɒntrəri; US -treri/ adj. **1** [only before a noun] completely different: *I thought it was possible, but she took the contrary view.* ▶ **przeciwny** OPP **opposite 2** (**contrary to**) completely different from; opposite to; against: ***Contrary to popular belief*** (wbrew powszechnemu przekonaniu), *not all boxers are stupid.* ▶ **w przeciwieństwie do czegoś**

contrary² /'kɒntrəri; US -treri/ noun
IDM **on the contrary** the opposite is true; certainly not: *'You look as if you're not enjoying yourself.' 'On the contrary, I'm having a great time.'* ▶ **wprost przeciwnie**
to the contrary (formal) saying the opposite: *Unless I hear anything to the contrary, I shall assume that the arrangements haven't changed.* ▶ **inaczej, odwrotnie**

contrast¹ /'kɒntrɑːst; US -træst/ noun **1** [U] comparison between two people or things that shows the differences between them: ***In contrast to*** *previous years, we've had a very successful summer.* ▶ **przeciwieństwo, odróżnienie 2** [C,U] **(a) contrast (to/with sb/sth); (a) contrast (between A and B)** a clear difference between two things or people that is seen when they are compared: *There is a tremendous contrast between the climate in the valley and the climate in the hills.* ▶ **kontrast, zasadnicza różnica 3** [C] something that is clearly different from sth else when the two things are compared: *This house is quite a contrast* (ten dom jest całkiem inny) *to your old one!* ▶ **przeciwieństwo, odmiana**

contrast² /kən'trɑːst; US -'træst/ verb **1** [T] **contrast (A and/with B)** to compare people or things in order to show the differences between them: *The film contrasts his poor childhood with his later life as a millionaire.* ▶ **przeciwstawiać 2** [I] **contrast with sb/sth** to be clearly different when compared: *This comment contrasts sharply with his previous remarks.* ▶ **kontrastować, (silnie) odróżniać się**

contrasting /kən'trɑːstɪŋ; US -'træs-/ adj. very different in style, colour or attitude: *bright, contrasting colours* ◇ *contrasting opinions* ▶ **kontrastujący, kontrastowy**

contravene /ˌkɒntrə'viːn/ verb [T] (formal) to break a law or a rule ▶ **przekraczać, naruszać**
■ **contravention** /ˌkɒntrə'venʃn/ noun [C,U] ▶ **przekroczenie, naruszenie**

contribute /'kɒntrɪbjuːt; kən'trɪbjuːt/ verb **contribute (sth) (to/towards sth) 1** [I,T] to give a part of the total, together with others: *Would you like to contribute* *towards our collection for famine relief?* ◇ *The research has contributed a great deal to our knowledge of cancer.* ▶ **dokładać (się), wnosić (wkład do czegoś)** **2** [I] to be one of the causes of sth: *It is not known whether the bad weather contributed to the accident.* ▶ **wnosić swój udział** **3** [I,T] to write articles for a magazine or newspaper: *She contributed a number of articles to the magazine.* ▶ **pisywać** (*np. artykuły do pisma*)

contribution /ˌkɒntrɪˈbjuːʃn/ noun [C] **a contribution (to/towards sth)** something that you give, especially money or help, or do together with other people: *If we all **make a** small **contribution**, we'll be able to buy Ray a good present.* ▶ **wkład; udział**

contributor /kənˈtrɪbjətə(r)/ noun [C] a person who **contributes** to sth ▶ **osoba przyczyniająca się, współpracowni-k/ca** (*np. pisma*)

contributory /kənˈtrɪbjətəri; US -tɔːri/ adj. helping to cause or produce sth: *Alcohol was a contributory factor in her death.* ▶ **przyczyniający się**

contrite /ˈkɒntraɪt; Brit. also kənˈtraɪt/ adj. (formal) very sorry for sth bad that you have done: *Her expression was contrite.* ▶ **skruszony, odczuwający skruchę**
■ **contritely** adv. ▶ **ze skruchą** | **contrition** /kənˈtrɪʃn/ noun [U]: *a look of contrition* ▶ **skrucha**

contrive /kənˈtraɪv/ verb [T] **1** to manage to do sth, although there are difficulties: *If I can contrive to get off work early, I'll see you later.* ▶ **radzić sobie** (*z trudnym zadaniem*) **2** to plan or invent sth in a clever and/or dishonest way: *He contrived a scheme to cheat insurance companies.* ▶ **wymyślać; kombinować**

contrived /kənˈtraɪvd/ adj. hard to believe; not natural or realistic: *The ending of the film seemed rather contrived.* ▶ **wymyślony, sztuczny**

control[1] /kənˈtrəʊl/ noun **1** [U] **control (of/over sb/sth)** power and ability to make sb/sth do what you want: *Rebels managed to **take control** of* (przejeli kontrolę nad) *the radio station.* ◇ *His anger eventually subsided and he was able to **get control** over himself* (odzyskać panowanie nad sobą). ◇ *Some teachers find it difficult to **keep control** of their class.* Niektórym nauczycielom trudno jest panować nad klasą. ◇ *He **lost control** of the car and crashed.* ◇ *I was late because of circumstances **beyond** my **control*** (z powodu okoliczności niezależnych ode mnie). ▶ **panowanie nad czymś, wpływ** **2** [C,U] **(a) control (on/over sth)** a limit on sth; a way of keeping sb/sth within certain limits: *price controls* ◇ *The faults forced the company to review its **quality control** procedures.* ▶ **regulacja; nadzór** **3** [C] one of the parts of a machine that is used for operating it: *the controls of an aeroplane/a TV* ◇ *a control panel* ◇ *the volume control* przycisk głośności ▶ **urządzenie sterownicze** **4** [sing.] the place from which sth is operated or where sth is checked: *We went through passport control and then got onto the plane.* ▶ **sterownia, punkt kontroli, dyspozytornia**
IDM **be in control (of sth)** to have the power or ability to deal with sth: *The police are again in control of the area following last night's violence.* ▶ **kierować, być u steru**
be/get out of control to be/become impossible to deal with: *The demonstration got out of control and fighting broke out.* ▶ **wymykać się spod kontroli**
under control being dealt with successfully: *It took several hours to bring the fire under control* (aby opanować ogień). ◇ *She finds it difficult to keep her feelings under control.* Z trudem panuje nad swoimi uczuciami. ▶ **pod kontrolą**

control[2] /kənˈtrəʊl/ verb [T] (**controlling**; **controlled**) **1** to have power and ability to make sb/sth do what you want: *One family controls the company.* ◇ *Police struggled to control the crowd.* ◇ *I couldn't control myself any longer and burst out laughing.* ▶ **mieć władzę nad kimś/czymś, panować nad kimś/czymś** **2** to keep sth within certain limits: *measures to control price rises* ▶ **regulować, ograniczać**
■ **controller** noun [C]: *air traffic controllers* ▶ **kontroler, zarządzający**

conˈtrol freak noun [C] (informal) (used in a critical way) a person who always wants to be in control of their own and other people's lives, and to organize how things are done ▶ **osoba lubiąca mieć pełną kontrolę nad swoim życiem, jak i nad innymi ludźmi**

controlled /kənˈtrəʊld/ adj. **1** done or arranged in a very careful way: *a controlled explosion* ▶ **kontrolowany** **2** limited, or managed by law or by rules: *controlled airspace* ▶ **kontrolowany** **3** (**-controlled**) [in compounds] managed by a particular group, or in a particular way: *a British-controlled company* ◇ *computer-controlled systems* systemy sterowane komputerowo ▶ **kontrolowany** **4** remaining calm and not getting angry or upset ▶ **opanowany, spokojny** ➲ look at **uncontrolled**

conˈtrol tower noun [C] a building at an airport from which the movements of aircraft are controlled ▶ **wieża kontrolna**

controversial /ˌkɒntrəˈvɜːʃl/ adj. causing public discussion and disagreement ▶ **kontrowersyjny**

controversy /ˈkɒntrəvɜːsi; kənˈtrɒvəsi/ noun [C,U] (pl. **controversies**) public discussion and disagreement about sth: *The plans for changing the city centre caused much controversy.* ▶ **kontrowersja**

conundrum /kəˈnʌndrəm/ noun [C] **1** a confusing problem or question that is very difficult to solve ▶ **łamigłówka** **2** a question, usually involving a trick with words, that you ask for fun ▶ **zagadka** SYN **riddle**

conurbation /ˌkɒnɜːˈbeɪʃn/ noun [C] a very large area of houses and other buildings where towns have grown and joined together ▶ **konurbacja**

convalesce /ˌkɒnvəˈles/ verb [I] to rest and get better over a period of time after an illness ▶ **powracać do zdrowia** (*np. w sanatorium*)
■ **convalescence** noun [sing., U] ▶ **rekonwalescencja** | **convalescent** /ˌkɒnvəˈlesnt/ adj. ▶ **rekonwalescent/ka**

convene /kənˈviːn/ verb [I,T] (formal) to come together or to bring people together for a meeting, etc. ▶ **gromadzić się; zwoływać**

convenience /kənˈviːniəns/ noun **1** [U] the quality of being easy, useful or suitable for sb: *a building designed **for the convenience of** disabled people* ◇ ***For convenience**, you can pay for everything at once.* ▶ **wygoda** **2** [C] something that makes things easier, quicker or more comfortable: *houses with all the modern conveniences* ▶ **udogodnienie, wygoda** **3** [C] (Brit.) a public toilet ▶ **toaleta publiczna** ➲ note at **toilet**

conˈvenience food noun [C,U] food that you buy frozen or in a box or can, that you can prepare very quickly and easily ▶ **dania gotowe, mrożonki, konserwy**

conˈvenience store noun [C] (especially US) a shop that sells food, newspapers, etc. and often stays open 24 hours a day ▶ **sklep ogólnospożywczy** (*często całodobowy*)

convenient /kənˈviːniənt/ adj. **1** suitable or practical for a particular purpose; not causing difficulty: *I'm willing to meet you on any day that's convenient for you.* ◇ *It isn't convenient to talk at the moment – I'm in the middle of a meeting.* ▶ **dogodny, wygodny** OPP **inconvenient** **2** close to sth; in a useful position: *Our house is convenient for the shops.* ▶ **blisko/dogodnie usytuowany**
■ **conveniently** adv. **1** : *Conveniently* (na szczęście), *a bus was waiting when I got there.* ▶ **wygodnie** **2** : *The*

house is conveniently situated close to the beach. ▶ **dogodnie**

convent /ˈkɒnvənt; US -vent/ noun [C] a place where **nuns** live together in a community ▶ **klasztor (żeński)** ➲ look at **monastery**

convention /kənˈvenʃn/ noun **1** [C,U] a traditional way of behaving or of doing sth: *A speech by the bride's father is one of the conventions of a wedding.* ◇ *The film shows no respect for convention.* ▶ **zwyczaj, obyczaj 2** [C] a large meeting of the members of a profession, political party, etc.: *the Democratic Party Convention* ▶ **zjazd, kongres** SYN **conference 3** [C] a formal agreement, especially between different countries: *the Geneva Convention* ▶ **układ, konwencja**

conventional /kənˈvenʃənl/ adj. always behaving in a traditional or normal way: *conventional attitudes* ▶ **konwencjonalny, stereotypowy**
■ **conventionally** /-ʃənəli/ adv. ▶ **konwencjonalnie, stereotypowo**

converge /kənˈvɜːdʒ/ verb [I] **converge (on sb/sth)** (used about two or more people or things) to move towards each other or meet at the same point from different directions: *Fans from all over the country converge on the village during the annual music festival.* ▶ **skupiać się, zbiegać się** OPP **diverge**

conversant /kənˈvɜːsnt/ adj. (formal) **conversant with sth** knowing about sth; familiar with sth: *All employees should be conversant with basic accounting.* ▶ **biegły/obeznany (w czymś)**

conversation /ˌkɒnvəˈseɪʃn/ noun [C,U] a talk between two or more people: ***I had a** long **conversation** with her about her plans for the future.* ◇ *His job is his only **topic of conversation.*** ◇ *They sat in the corner, deep in conversation* (pogrążeni w rozmowie). ◇ *She finds it difficult to make conversation.* Nie wie, co powiedzieć. ▶ **rozmowa, konwersacja**
IDM **deep in thought/conversation** → DEEP[1]
■ **conversational** /-ʃənl/ adj. **1** not formal; as used in conversation: *a casual and conversational tone* ◇ *I learnt conversational Spanish at evening classes.* ▶ **potoczny; konwersacyjny, swobodny 2** connected with conversation: *Men have a more direct conversational style.* ▶ **konwersacyjny**

converse[1] /kənˈvɜːs/ verb [I] **converse (with sb)** (formal) to talk to sb; to have a conversation with sb: *She conversed with the Czechs in German.* ▶ **rozmawiać, konwersować**

converse[2] /ˈkɒnvɜːs/ (**the converse**) noun [sing.] (formal) the opposite or reverse of a fact or statement: *Building new roads increases traffic and the converse is equally true: reducing the number and size of roads means less traffic.* ▶ **odwrotność**
■ **converse** adj.: *the converse effect* ▶ (*efekt*) **odwrotny, przeciwny**

conversely /ˈkɒnvɜːsli/ adv. (formal) in a way that is opposite to sth: *People who earn a lot of money have little time to spend it. Conversely, many people with limitless time do not have enough money to do what they want.* ▶ **przeciwnie, odwrotnie**

conversion /kənˈvɜːʃn; US -ˈvɜːʒn/ noun [C,U] (a) **conversion (from sth) (into/to sth) 1** the act or process of changing from one form, system or use to another: *a conversion table for miles and kilometres* ◇ *a metric conversion table* tabela przeliczeniowa na system metryczny ▶ **zamiana 2** becoming a member of a different religion ▶ **nawrócenie**

convert[1] /kənˈvɜːt/ verb [I,T] **1 convert (sth) (from sth) (into/to sth)** to change from one form, system or use to another: *a sofa that converts into a double bed* ◇ *How do you convert* (przeliczyć) *pounds into kilos?* ◇ *They're converting* (przebudowują) *the house into four flats.* ▶ **zamieniać (się) 2 convert (sb) (from sth) (to sth)** to change or to persuade sb to change to a different religion: *As a young man he converted to Islam.* ◇ *to convert people to Christianity* ▶ **nawracać (się); przejść** (*na inną wiarę*)

convert[2] /ˈkɒnvɜːt/ noun [C] **a convert (to sth)** a person who has changed their religion ▶ **neofit(k)a, przechrzta**

convertible[1] /kənˈvɜːtəbl/ adj. able to be changed into another form: *convertible currencies* ▶ **rozkładany, wymienialny**

convertible[2] /kənˈvɜːtəbl/ noun [C] a car with a roof that can be folded down or taken off ▶ **kabriolet**

convex /ˈkɒnveks/ adj. having a surface that curves towards the outside of sth, like an eye: *a convex lens* ▶ **wypukły** ➲ look at **concave**

convey /kənˈveɪ/ verb [T] **1 convey sth (to sb)** to make ideas, thoughts, feelings, etc. known to sb: *The film conveys a lot of information but in an entertaining way.* ◇ *Please convey my sympathy to her at this sad time.* ▶ **przekazywać 2** (formal) to take sb/sth from one place to another, especially in a vehicle ▶ **przewozić**

conˈveyor belt noun [C] a moving belt that carries objects from one place to another, for example in a factory ▶ **transporter taśmowy**

convict[1] /kənˈvɪkt/ verb [T] **convict sb (of sth)** to say officially in a court of law that sb is guilty of a crime ▶ **skazywać, zasądzać** OPP **acquit**

convict[2] /ˈkɒnvɪkt/ noun [C] a person who has been found guilty of a crime and put in prison ▶ **skazan-y/a, więzień**

conviction /kənˈvɪkʃn/ noun **1** [C,U] the act of finding sb guilty of a crime in a court of law: *He has several previous convictions for burglary.* ▶ **skazanie, wyrok 2** [C] a very strong opinion or belief: *religious convictions* ▶ **przekonanie, przeświadczenie 3** [U] the feeling of being certain about what you are doing: *He played without conviction and lost easily.* ▶ **przekonanie**

convince /kənˈvɪns/ verb [T] **1 convince sb (of sth/that ...)** to succeed in making sb believe sth: *She convinced him of the need to go back.* ◇ *I couldn't convince her that I was right.* ▶ **przekonać** ➲ look at **persuade 2 convince sb (to do sth)** to persuade sb to do sth: *The salesman convinced them to buy a new cooker.* ▶ **przekonać** ⓘ Według niektórych opinii użycie **convince** w tym znaczeniu jest nieprawidłowe.

convinced /kənˈvɪnst/ adj. [not before a noun] completely sure about sth: *He's convinced of his ability to win.* ▶ **przekonany**

convincing /kənˈvɪnsɪŋ/ adj. **1** able to make sb believe sth: *Her explanation for her absence wasn't very convincing.* ▶ **przekonujący 2** (used about a victory) complete; clear: *a convincing win* ▶ **zdecydowany**
■ **convincingly** adv. ▶ **przekonująco; zdecydowanie**

convivial /kənˈvɪviəl/ adj. happy and friendly: *a convivial evening/atmosphere* ▶ **wesoły, towarzyski** SYN **sociable**

convoke /kənˈvəʊk/ verb [T] (formal) to gather together a group of people for a formal meeting ▶ **zwoływać** (*np. zebranie*) SYN **convene**

convoluted /ˈkɒnvəluːtɪd/ adj. extremely complicated and difficult to follow: ***a convoluted argument/explanation*** ◇ *a book with a convoluted plot* ▶ **zagmatwany**

convoy /ˈkɒnvɔɪ/ noun [C,U] a group of vehicles or ships travelling together: *a convoy of lorries* ◇ *warships travelling **in convoy*** ▶ **konwój**

convulse /kənˈvʌls/ verb [I,T] to make sudden violent movements that you cannot control; to cause sb to move in this way: *He was convulsed with pain.* ▶ **wstrząsać (się), przyprawiać o konwulsje**

convulsion /kənˈvʌlʃn/ noun [C, usually pl.] a sudden violent movement that you cannot control ▶ **konwulsja** ■ **convulsive** /kənˈvʌlsɪv/ adj.: *Her breath came in convulsive gasps.* ▶ **konwulsyjny, spazmatyczny**

coo /kuː/ verb [I] **1** to make a soft low sound like a **dove** ▶ **gruchać 2** to speak in a soft, gentle voice: *He went to the cot and cooed over the baby.* ▶ **gruchać, gaworzyć**

cook[1] /kʊk/ verb **1** [I,T] to prepare food for eating by heating it: *My mother taught me how to cook.* ◇ *The sauce should be cooked on low heat for twenty minutes.* ◇ *He cooked us a meal.* ▶ **gotować 2** [I] (used about food) to be prepared for eating by being heated: *I could smell something delicious cooking in the kitchen.* ▶ **gotować się** ➲ note at **recipe**

PHR V **cook sth up** (informal) to invent sth that is not true: *She cooked up an excuse for not arriving on time.* ▶ **zmyślać coś**

cooking

Food can be cooked in various ways. You can **boil** or **steam** vegetables with water in a **saucepan** and you can **poach** eggs or fish in a small quantity of water or milk. You can **fry** meat, fish and vegetables in oil in a **frying pan**, **sauté** them in a smaller quantity of oil and **stir-fry** them in a **wok**. You **roast** meat and vegetables or **bake** bread and cakes in the **oven**. You can **stew** meat, vegetables, apples, etc. in liquid in a covered pot or **braise** them in a smaller quantity of liquid. You can **grill** meat or fish under the **grill** (US **broil**), but **toast** is usually made in a **toaster**. If you want an easy meal you can **microwave** a **ready meal** in a special oven called a **microwave**. In the summer you can **barbecue** chops, sausages, burgers, etc. on an outside grill, also called a **barbecue**. Meat can also be roasted **on the spit**.

cook[2] /kʊk/ noun [C] a person who cooks ▶ **kucha-rz/rka** ➲ picture on **page A4**

cookbook = COOKERY BOOK

cooker /ˈkʊkə(r)/ noun [C] a large piece of kitchen equipment for cooking using gas or electricity. It consists of an oven, a flat top on which pans can be placed and often a **grill**. ▶ **kuchenka**

cookery /ˈkʊkəri/ noun [U] the skill or activity of preparing and cooking food: *Chinese/French/Italian cookery* ▶ **sztuka kulinarna, kuchnia**

ˈ**cookery book** (also **cookbook** /ˈkʊkbʊk/) noun [C] a book that gives instructions on cooking and contains **recipes** ▶ **książka kucharska**

cookie (US) = BISCUIT

cookie sheet (US) = BAKING SHEET

cooking /ˈkʊkɪŋ/ noun [U] **1** the preparation of food for eating: *Cooking is one of her hobbies.* ◇ *In our house, I do the cleaning and my husband* ***does the cooking.*** ▶ **gotowanie 2** food produced by cooking: *He missed his mother's cooking when he left home.* ▶ **gotowanie**

cool[1] /kuːl/ adj. **1** fairly cold; not hot or warm: *It was a cool evening so I put on a pullover.* ◇ *What I'd like is a long cool drink.* ▶ **chłodny** ➲ note at **cold**[1] **2** calm; not excited or angry: *She always manages to remain cool under pressure.* ▶ **opanowany, spokojny 3** unfriendly; not showing interest: *When we first met, she was rather cool towards me, but later she became friendlier.* ▶ **chłodny, oziębły; obojętny 4** (slang) very good or fashionable: *Those are cool shoes you're wearing!* ▶ **odjazdowy, super**

■ **coolness** noun [U] ▶ **chłód; spokój; rezerwa**

cool[2] /kuːl/ verb **1** [I,T] **cool (sth/sb) (down/off)** to lower the temperature of sth; to become **cool**[1] (1): *Let the soup cool (down).* ◇ *After the game we needed to cool off.* ◇ *A nice cold drink will soon cool you down.* ▶ **stygnąć, chłodzić (się) 2** [I] (used about feelings) to become less strong: *Relations between them have definitely cooled.* ▶ **ochłonąć**

PHR V **cool (sb) down/off** to become or make sb calmer ▶ **uspokajać (się), opanowywać (się)**

cool[3] /kuːl/ noun (**the cool**) [sing.] a cool temperature or place; the quality of being cool: *We sat in the cool of a cafe, out of the sun.* ▶ **chłod, zimno**

IDM **keep/lose your cool** to stay calm/to stop being calm and become angry, nervous, etc. ▶ **zachowywać/tracić spokój**

coolant /ˈkuːlənt/ noun [C, U] a liquid that is used for cooling an engine, a nuclear **reactor**, etc. ▶ **chłodziwo**

ˌ**cooling-ˈoff period** noun [C] a period of time when sb can think again about a decision that they have made ▶ **czas na ochłonięcie i przemyślenie czegoś**

coolly /ˈkuːlli/ adv. **1** in a calm way: *At first she was very angry; then she explained the problem coolly.* ▶ **spokojnie, z opanowaniem 2** without showing much interest or excitement ▶ **chłodno, bez entuzjazmu**

coop /kuːp/ verb

PHR V **coop sb/sth up (in sth)** to keep sb/sth inside a small space: *I've been cooped up in that office* (czuję się zamknięty jak w więzieniu) *all day.* ▶ **zamykać kogoś/zwierzęta w (zbyt) małym pomieszczeniu**

cooperate (Brit. also **co-operate**) /kəʊˈɒpəreɪt/ verb [I] **cooperate (with sb/sth) 1** to work with sb else to achieve sth ▶ **współpracować 2** to be helpful by doing what sb asks you to do: *If everyone cooperates by following the instructions, there will be no problem.* ▶ **współpracować, współdziałać**

cooperation (Brit. also **co-operation**) /kəʊˌɒpəˈreɪʃn/ noun [U] **1 cooperation (with sb)** working together with sb else to achieve sth: *Schools are working in close cooperation with parents to improve standards.* ▶ **współpraca 2** help that you give by doing what sb asks you to do: *The police asked the public for their cooperation in the investigation.* ▶ **współpraca, kooperacja**

cooperative[1] (Brit. also **co-operative**) /kəʊˈɒpərətɪv/ adj. **1** done by people working together: *a cooperative business venture* ▶ **wspólny, spółdzielczy 2** helpful; doing what sb asks you to do: *My firm were very cooperative and allowed me to have time off.* ▶ **pomocny**

cooperative[2] (Brit. also **co-operative**) /kəʊˈɒpərətɪv/ noun [C] a business or organization that is owned and run by all of the people who work for it: *a workers' cooperative* ▶ **spółdzielnia**

coordinate[1] (Brit. also **co-ordinate**) /kəʊˈɔːdɪneɪt/ verb [T] to organize different things or people so that they work together ▶ **koordynować**

coordinate[2] (Brit. also **co-ordinate**) /kəʊˈɔːdɪnət/ noun [C] one of the two sets of numbers and/or letters that are used for finding the position of a point on a map ▶ **współrzędna**

coordination (Brit. also **co-ordination**) /kəʊˌɔːdɪˈneɪʃn/ noun [U] **1** the organization of different things or people so that they work together ▶ **koordynacja, współdziałanie 2** the ability to control the movements of your body properly ▶ **koordynacja** (*ruchów*)

coordinator (Brit. also **co-ordinator**) /kəʊˈɔːdɪneɪtə(r)/ noun [C] a person who is responsible for organizing different things or people so that they work together ▶ **koordynator, prowadząc-y/a**

cop[1] /kɒp/ (also **copper**) noun [C] (informal) a police officer ▶ (*osoba*) **glina**

cop[2] /kɒp/ verb (**copping**; **copped**)

PHR V **cop out (of sth)** (informal) to avoid sth that you should do, because you are afraid or lazy: *She was going* *to help me with the cooking but she copped out at the last minute.* ▶ **wykręcić się (z czegoś)**

cope /kəʊp/ verb [I] **cope (with sb/sth)** to deal successfully with a difficult matter or situation: *She sometimes finds it difficult to cope with all the pressure at work.* ▶ **radzić sobie, podołać** SYN **manage**

copier (especially US) = PHOTOCOPIER

copious /ˈkəʊpiəs/ adj. in large amounts: *She made copious notes at the lecture.* ▶ **obfity**
■ **copiously** adv. ▶ **obficie**

ˈ**cop-out** noun [C] (informal) a way of avoiding sth that you should do ▶ **unik**

copper /ˈkɒpə(r)/ noun **1** [U] (symbol **Cu**) a common reddish-brown metal: *water pipes made of copper* ▶ **miedź** **2** [C] (Brit.) a coin of low value made of brown metal ▶ **miedziak** **3** = COP[1]

co-produce /ˌkəʊprəˈdjuːs/ verb [T] to produce a film, television programme, play, etc. together with another person or company ▶ **koprodukować**

copse /kɒps/ noun [C] a small area of trees or bushes ▶ **zagajnik**

copulate /ˈkɒpjuleɪt/ verb [I] (formal) (used especially about animals) to have sex ▶ **spółkować**
■ **copulation** /ˌkɒpjuˈleɪʃn/ noun [U] ▶ **spółkowanie**

copy[1] /ˈkɒpi/ noun [C] (pl. **copies**) **1** something that is made to look exactly like sth else: *I kept a copy of the letter I wrote.* ◇ *the master copy* oryginał ◇ *to **make a copy** of a computer file* ▶ **kopia** ➲ look at **photocopy** **2** one book, newspaper, record, etc. of which many have been printed or produced ▶ **egzemplarz**

copy[2] /ˈkɒpi/ verb (**copying**; **copies**; pt, pp **copied**) **1** [T] to make sth exactly the same as sth else: *It is illegal to copy videos.* ▶ **kopiować** **2** [T] **copy sth (down/out)** to write down sth exactly as it is written somewhere else: *I copied down the address on the brochure.* ◇ *I copied out the letter more neatly.* ▶ **przepisywać** **3** [T] to draw or paint sth exactly as it is drawn/painted somewhere else: *The children copied pictures from a book.* ▶ **przerysowywać**; **kopiować** (*obraz*) **3** [T] to do or try to do the same as sb else: *She copies everything her friends do.* ▶ **naśladować** SYN **imitate** **4** [I] **copy (from sb)** to cheat in an exam or test by writing what sb else has written: *He was caught copying from another student in the exam.* ▶ **ściągać**, **odpisywać** **5** [T] = PHOTOCOPY

copycat /ˈkɒpikæt/ noun [C] (informal) (used especially by children about and to a person who copies what sb else does because they have no ideas of their own) ▶ (*przen.*) **papuga**
■ **copycat** adj. [only before a noun] (used about a crime) similar to and seen as copying an earlier well-known crime ▶ **papugujący**

ˈ**copy editor** noun [C] a person whose job is to correct and prepare a text for printing ▶ **adiustator/ka**
■ ˈ**copy-edit** verb [T,I] ▶ **adiustować** (*tekst do druku*)

copyright /ˈkɒpiraɪt/ noun [C,U] the legal right to be the only person who may print, copy, perform, etc. a piece of original work, such as a book, a song or a computer program: *Who owns the copyright?* ▶ **prawo autorskie**

coral /ˈkɒrəl/ noun [U] a hard red, pink or white substance that forms in the sea from the bones of very small sea animals: *a coral reef* ▶ **koral**

cord /kɔːd/ noun **1** [C,U] (a piece of) strong, thick string ▶ **sznur** **2** [C,U] (especially US) = FLEX[2] **3** (**cords**) [pl.] trousers made of **corduroy** ▶ **spodnie sztruksowe**

cordial[1] /ˈkɔːdiəl; US -dʒəl/ adj. pleasant and friendly: *a cordial greeting/smile* ▶ **serdeczny**, **życzliwy**
■ **cordially** /-diəli; US -dʒəli/ adv. ▶ **serdecznie**, **życzliwie**

cordial[2] /ˈkɔːdiəl; US -dʒəl/ noun [U,C] (Brit.) a sweet drink that does not contain alcohol, made from fruit juice. It is drunk with water added: *blackcurrant cordial* ▶ **syrop owocowy**

cordless /ˈkɔːdləs/ adj. not connected to its power supply by wires: *a cordless phone/kettle/iron* ▶ **bezprzewodowy**

cordon[1] /ˈkɔːdn/ noun [C] a line or ring of police or soldiers that prevents people from entering an area ▶ **kordon**

cordon[2] /ˈkɔːdn/ verb
PHR V **cordon sth off** to stop people entering an area by surrounding it with a ring of police or soldiers ▶ **otaczać i zamykać kordonem**

corduroy /ˈkɔːdərɔɪ/ noun [U] a thick soft cotton cloth with lines on it, used for making clothes: *a corduroy jacket* ▶ **sztruks**

core /kɔː(r)/ noun **1** [C] the hard centre of certain fruits, containing seeds: *an apple core* ▶ **środek owocu**, **ogryzek** ➲ picture on **page A12** **2** [C] the central part of a planet ▶ **jądro** (*planety*) **3** [sing.] the central or most important part of sth: *the core curriculum* przedmioty obowiązkowe ◇ *What's the core issue* (sednem sprawy) *here?* ▶ **podstawa**, **rdzeń**
IDM **to the core** completely; in every way: *The news shook him to the core.* ▶ **do szpiku kości**

coriander /ˌkɒriˈændə(r)/ noun [U] a plant whose fresh leaves and dried seeds are used in cooking ▶ **kolendra**

cork /kɔːk/ noun **1** [U] a light soft material which comes from the outside of a type of tree: *cork floor tiles* ▶ **korek** **2** [C] a round piece of **cork** that you push into the end of a bottle to close it, especially a bottle of wine ▶ **korek** ➲ picture at **container**

corkscrew /ˈkɔːkskruː/ noun [C] a tool that you use for pulling **corks** out of bottles ▶ **korkociąg** ➲ picture at **kitchen**

corn /kɔːn/ noun **1** [U] (especially Brit.) any plant that is grown for its grain, such as **wheat**; the seeds from these plants: *a field of corn* ◇ *a corn field* ▶ **zboże**; **ziarno** **2** [U] (US) = MAIZE **3** [U] (US) = SWEETCORN **4** [C] a small, painful area of hard skin on the foot, especially the toe ▶ **odcisk**, **nagniotek**

corncob /ˈkɔːnkɒb/ (especially US **cob** /kɒb/) the long hard part of the **maize** plant that the rows of yellow grains grow on ▶ **kolba** (*kukurydzy*)

cornea /ˈkɔːniə/ noun [C] the transparent layer which covers and protects the outer part of the eye ▶ **rogówka**

corner[1] /ˈkɔːnə(r)/ noun [C] **1** a place where two lines, edges, surfaces or roads meet: *Put the lamp **in the corner** of the room* ◇ *Write your address in the top right-hand corner.* ◇ *The shop is **on the corner** of Wall Street and Long Road.* ◇ *He went **round the corner*** (wziął zakręt) *at top speed.* ▶ **kąt**, **róg** **2** a quiet or secret place or area: *a remote corner of Scotland* ▶ **zakątek** **3** a difficult situation from which you cannot escape: *to get yourself into a corner* ▶ **ślepy zaułek**, **sytuacja bez wyjścia** **4** (in football) a free kick from the corner of the field: *to take a corner* ▶ **rzut rożny**

corner

The car is in the corner.

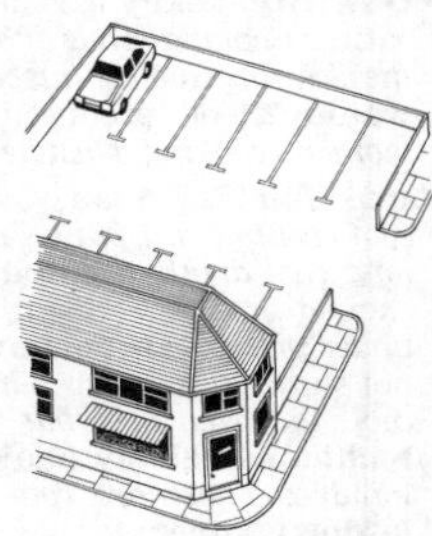

The shop is on the corner.

IDM **cut corners** to do sth quickly and not as well as you should ▶ **robić coś szybko i niedbale**
(just) round the corner very near: *There's a phone box just round the corner.* ▶ **(tuż) za rogiem**

corner² /ˈkɔːnə(r)/ verb [T] **1** to get a person or an animal into a position from which they or it cannot escape: *He cornered me at the party and started telling me all his problems.* ▶ **osaczać, przypierać (kogoś) do muru** **2** to get control in a particular area of business so that nobody else can have any success in it: *That company's really **cornered the market** in health foods.* ▶ **opanowywać**

ˈ**corner shop** noun [C] (Brit.) a small shop that sells food, newspapers, cigarettes, etc., especially one near people's houses ▶ **lokalny sklepik**

cornerstone /ˈkɔːnəstəʊn/ noun [C] **1** (especially US) a stone at the corner of the base of a building, often laid in a special ceremony ▶ **kamień węgielny** **2** the most important part of sth that the rest depends on: *This study is the cornerstone of the whole research programme.* ▶ (*przen.*) **kamień węgielny**

cornflakes /ˈkɔːnfleɪks/ noun [pl.] food made of small pieces of dried **corn** and eaten with milk for breakfast ▶ **płatki kukurydziane**

cornflour /ˈkɔːnflaʊə(r)/ (US **cornstarch** /ˈkɔːnstɑːtʃ/) noun [U] very fine flour often used to make sauces, etc. thicker ▶ **mąka kukurydziana**

cornflower /ˈkɔːnflaʊə(r)/ noun [C] a small plant with blue flowers, that often grows wild ▶ **chaber, bławatek**

ˌ**corn on the** ˈ**cob** noun [U] **corn** (3) that is cooked with all the yellow grains still on the inner part and eaten as a vegetable ▶ **kolba kukurydzy**

cornstarch (US) = CORNFLOUR

corny /ˈkɔːni/ adj. (**cornier**; **corniest**) (informal) too ordinary or familiar to be interesting or amusing: *a corny joke* ▶ **wytarty, wyświechtany**

corollary /kəˈrɒləri; US ˈkɔːrəleri; ˈkɑːr-/ noun [C] (pl. **-ies**) **corollary (of/to sth)** (formal or technical) a situation, an argument or a fact that is the natural and direct result of another one: *In rural areas, the corollary of increased car ownership has been a rapid decline in the provision of public transport.* ▶ **następstwo**

coronary¹ /ˈkɒrənri; US -neri/ adj. connected with the heart: *a coronary artery* ▶ **wieńcowy**

coronary² /ˈkɒrənri; US -neri/ noun [C] (pl. **coronaries**) (also technical ˌ**coronary thromˈbosis**) (informal) a type of heart attack ▶ **zawał serca**

coronation /ˌkɒrəˈneɪʃn/ noun [C] an official ceremony at which sb is made a king or queen ▶ **koronacja**

coroner /ˈkɒrənə(r)/ noun [C] a person whose job is to find out the causes of death of people who have died in violent or unusual ways ▶ **urzędnik sądowy wyjaśniający przyczyny nienaturalnych zgonów**

Corp. (US) = CORPORATION (1): *West Coast Motor Corp.*

corporal /ˈkɔːpərəl/ noun [C] a person at a low level in the army or air force ▶ **kapral**

ˌ**corporal** ˈ**punishment** noun [U] the punishment of people by hitting them, especially the punishment of children by parents or teachers ▶ **kara cielesna** ➲ look at **capital punishment**

corporate /ˈkɔːpərət/ adj. [only before a noun] of or shared by all the members of a group or organization: *corporate responsibility* ▶ **zbiorowy, zespołowy**

corporation /ˌkɔːpəˈreɪʃn/ noun [C, with sing. or pl. verb] **1** (abbr. **Corp.**) a large business company: *multinational corporations* ◇ *the British Broadcasting Corporation* ▶ **korporacja, spółka** **2** (Brit.) a group of people elected to govern a particular town or city ▶ **zarząd miasta**

corps /kɔː(r)/ noun [C, with sing. or pl. verb] (pl. **corps** /kɔːz/) **1** a part of an army with special duties: *the medical corps* ▶ **korpus** **2** a group of people involved in a special activity: *the diplomatic corps* ▶ **korpus**

corpse /kɔːps/ noun [C] a dead body, especially of a person ▶ **zwłoki** ➲ look at **carcass**

corpus /ˈkɔːpəs/ noun [C] (pl. **corpora** /ˈkɔːpərə/ or **corpuses** /-sɪz/) a collection of written or spoken texts: *a corpus of 100 million words of spoken English* ▶ **korpus** (*np. tekstów*)

corpuscle /ˈkɔːpʌsl/ noun [C] any of the red or white cells found in blood: ***red/white corpuscles*** ▶ **krwinka**

⚷ **correct¹** /kəˈrekt/ adj. **1** with no mistakes; right or true: *Well done! All your answers were correct.* ◇ *Have you got the correct time, please?* ▶ **poprawny**; **prawidłowy** **2** (used about behaviour, manners, dress, etc.) suitable, proper or right: *What's the correct form of address for a vicar?* ▶ **właściwy, odpowiedni** OPP for both meanings **incorrect**
■ **correctly** adv. ▶ **poprawnie, prawidłowo; właściwie, odpowiednio** | **correctness** noun [U] ▶ **poprawność, prawidłowość; właściwość, odpowiedniość**

⚷ **correct²** /kəˈrekt/ verb [T] **1** to make a mistake, fault, etc. right or better: *to correct a spelling mistake* ◇ *to correct a test* ▶ **poprawiać** **2** to tell sb what mistakes they are making or what faults they have: *He's always correcting me when I'm talking to people.* ▶ **poprawiać**

correction /kəˈrekʃn/ noun **1** [C] a change that makes a mistake, fault, etc. right or better: *I've made a few small corrections to your report.* ▶ **poprawka** **2** [U] the act or process of correcting sth: *There are some programming errors that need correction.* ▶ **skorygowanie**

corˈrection fluid noun [U] a white liquid that you use to cover mistakes you make when you are writing or typing, and that you can write on top of ▶ **korektor** (*w płynie*) ➲ look at **Tippex** ➲ picture at **stationery**

corrective /kəˈrektɪv/ adj. intended to make sth right that is wrong: *to take corrective action* ▶ **korygujący, korekcyjny**

correlate /ˈkɒrəleɪt/ verb [I,T] to have or to show a relationship or connection between two or more things ▶ **być współzależnym, korelować**
■ **correlation** /ˌkɒrəˈleɪʃn/ noun [C,U]: *There is a correlation between a person's diet and height.* ▶ **współzależność, korelacja**

correspond /ˌkɒrəˈspɒnd/ verb [I] **1 correspond (to/with sth)** to be the same as or equal to sth; to match: *Does the name on the envelope correspond with the name inside the letter?* ◇ *American high schools correspond to British comprehensives.* ▶ **zgadzać się (z czymś); odpowiadać (czemuś)** **2** (formal) **correspond (with sb)** to write letters to and receive them from sb: *They corresponded for a year before they got married.* ▶ **korespondować**

correspondence /ˌkɒrəˈspɒndəns/ noun **1** [U, sing.] (formal) the act of writing letters; the letters themselves: *There hasn't been any correspondence between them for years.* ▶ **korespondencja** **2** [C,U] a close connection or relationship between two or more things: *There is no correspondence between the two sets of figures.* ▶ **zgodność, zbieżność**

correˈspondence course noun [C] a course of study that you do at home, using books and exercises sent to you by post or by email ▶ **kurs korespondencyjny**

correspondent /ˌkɒrəˈspɒndənt/ noun [C] **1** a person who provides news or writes articles for a newspaper, etc., especially from a foreign country: *our Middle East correspondent, Andy Jenkins* ▶ **korespondent/ka zagraniczn-y/a** **2** a person who writes letters to sb ▶ **korespondent/ka**

corresponding /ˌkɒrəˈspɒndɪŋ/ adj. [only before a noun] related or similar to sth: *Sales are up 10% compared with the corresponding period last year.* ▶ **odpowiedni, analogiczny**
■ **correspondingly** adv. ▶ **odpowiednio**

corridor /ˈkɒrɪdɔː(r)/ noun [C] a long narrow passage in a building or train, with doors that open into rooms, etc. ▶ **korytarz**

corroborate /kəˈrɒbəreɪt/ verb [T] (formal) to support a statement, idea, etc. by providing new evidence: *The witness corroborated Mr Patton's statement about the night of the murder.* ▶ **potwierdzać, poświadczać**
■ **corroboration** /kəˌrɒbəˈreɪʃn/ noun [U] ▶ **potwierdzenie, poświadczenie**

corroborative /kəˈrɒbərətɪv; US -reɪt-/ adj. (formal) [usually before a noun] giving support to a statement or theory: *Is there any* ***corroborative evidence*** *for this theory?* ▶ **potwierdzający, poświadczający**

corrode /kəˈrəʊd/ verb [I,T] (used about metals) to become weak or to be destroyed by chemical action; to cause a metal to do this ▶ **korodować**

corrosive /kəˈrəʊsɪv/ adj. **1** tending to destroy sth slowly by chemical action: *the corrosive effects of salt water* ▶ **korozyjny 2** (formal) tending to damage sth gradually: *Unemployment is having a corrosive effect on our economy.* ▶ **niszczący**
■ **corrosion** /kəˈrəʊʒn/ noun [U] ▶ **korozja**

corrugated /ˈkɒrəgeɪtɪd/ adj. (used about metal or cardboard) shaped into folds: *corrugated iron* blacha falista ▶ **fałdowany, karbowany**

corrupt[1] /kəˈrʌpt/ adj. doing or involving illegal or dishonest things in exchange for money, etc.: *corrupt officials who accept bribes* ◇ *corrupt business practices* ▶ **skorumpowany, przekupny**

corrupt[2] /kəˈrʌpt/ verb [T] to cause sb/sth to start behaving in a dishonest or immoral way: *Too many people are corrupted by power.* ◇ *Does TV corrupt the minds of the young?* ▶ **korumpować, demoralizować**

corruption /kəˈrʌpʃn/ noun [U] **1** dishonest or immoral behaviour or activities: *There were accusations of corruption among senior police officers.* ▶ **korupcja, przekupstwo 2** the process of making sb/sth **corrupt**: *the corruption of an innocent young boy* ▶ **korupcja, demoralizacja**

corset /ˈkɔːsɪt/ noun [C] a piece of clothing that some women wear pulled tight around their middle to make them look thinner ▶ **gorset**

cos (also **'cos**) /kɒz; US kəz/ conj. (Brit., informal) because: *I can't see her at all, cos it's too dark.* ▶ **bo**

cosmetic[1] /kɒzˈmetɪk/ noun [usually pl.] a substance that you put on your face or hair to make yourself look more attractive ▶ **kosmetyk** ➲ look at **make-up**

cosmetic[2] /kɒzˈmetɪk/ adj. **1** done in order to improve only the appearance of sth, without changing it in any other way: *changes in government policy which are purely cosmetic* ▶ **powierzchowny 2** (used or done in order to make your face or body more attractive): *cosmetic surgery* ▶ **kosmetyczny**

cosmic /ˈkɒzmɪk/ adj. connected with space or the universe ▶ **kosmiczny**

cosmology /kɒzˈmɒlədʒi/ noun [U] the scientific study of the universe and its origin and development ▶ **kosmologia**
■ **cosmological** /ˌkɒzməˈlɒdʒɪkl/ adj. ▶ **kosmologiczny** | **cosmologist** /kɒzˈmɒlədʒɪst/ noun [C] ▶ **kosmolog**

cosmopolitan /ˌkɒzməˈpɒlɪtən/ adj. **1** containing people from all over the world: *a cosmopolitan city* ▶ **kosmopolityczny, wielonarodowy 2** influenced by the culture of other countries: *a cosmopolitan and sophisticated young woman* ▶ **kosmopolityczny**

the cosmos /ˈkɒzmɒs; US -məs/ noun [sing.] the universe ▶ **kosmos, wszechświat**

⚷ **cost[1]** /kɒst/ noun **1** [C,U] the money that you have to pay for sth: *The cost of petrol has gone up again.* ◇ *The cost of living* (koszty utrzymania) *is relatively high in this country.* ◇ *The hospital was built* ***at a cost of*** *£10 million.* ◇ *The damage will have to be repaired regardless of cost.* ▶ **koszt/y** ➲ note at **price 2** [sing., U] what you have to give or lose in order to obtain sth else: *He achieved great success but only* ***at the cost of*** *a happy family life.* ▶ **cena, koszt 3** (**costs**) [pl.] the amount of money that the losing side has to pay to the winning side in a court of law: *a £250 fine and £100 costs* ▶ **koszty sądowe**
IDM **at all costs/at any cost** using whatever means are necessary to achieve sth: *We must win at all costs.* ▶ **za wszelką cenę**
cover the cost (of sth) → COVER[1]
to your cost in a way that is unpleasant or bad for you: *Life can be lonely at university, as I found out to my cost.* ▶ **na sobie, na własnej skórze**

⚷ **cost[2]** /kɒst/ verb [T] (pt, pp **cost**) **1** to have the price of: *How much does a return ticket to London cost?* ◇ *We'll take the bus – it won't cost much.* ◇ *How much did your bike cost you?* ▶ **kosztować 2** to make you lose sth: *That one mistake cost him his job.* ▶ **kosztować 3** to estimate the price to be asked for some goods, a service, etc.: *Engineers costed the repairs at £2 million.* ▶ **wyceniać, szacować koszt** ⓘ Czas przeszły i imiesłów czasu przeszłego czasownika **cost** w tym znaczeniu to **costed**.
IDM **cost the earth/a fortune** to be very expensive ▶ **kosztować fortunę**

co-star /ˈkəʊstɑː(r)/ verb (**co-starring**; **co-starred**) **1** [T] (used about a film, play, etc.) to have two or more famous actors as its stars: *a film co-starring Leonardo di Caprio and Kate Winslet* ▶ (*film*) **przedstawiać dwie lub więcej gwiazd filmowych 2** [I] (used about actors) to be one of two or more stars in a film, play, etc.: *Kate Winslet co-stars with Leonardo di Caprio in the film.* ▶ **występować wspólnie**
■ **co-star** noun [C] ▶ **współwykonaw-ca/czyni jednej z głównych ról, odtwór-ca/czyni jednej z głównych ról**

ˈcost-benefit noun [U] the relationship between the cost of doing sth and the value of the benefit that results from it: *cost-benefit analysis* ▶ **współzależność między kosztami i korzyściami**

ˈcost-cutting noun [U] the reduction of the amount of money spent on sth, especially because of financial difficulty: *Deliveries of mail could be delayed because of cost-cutting.* ◇ *a* ***cost-cutting*** *exercise/measure/programme* ▶ **obniżanie kosztów, obniżka kosztów**

ˌcost-efˈfective adj. giving the best possible profit or benefits in comparison with the money that is spent: *a cost-effective way to fight crime* ▶ **opłacalny**
■ **ˌcost-efˈfectiveness** noun [U] ▶ **opłacalność**

costing /ˈkɒstɪŋ/ noun [C] an estimate of how much money will be needed for sth: *Here is a detailed costing of our proposals.* ◇ *You'd better do some costings.* ▶ **kosztorys, kalkulacja kosztów**

costly /ˈkɒstli/ adj. (**costlier**; **costliest**) **1** costing a lot of money; expensive: *a costly repair bill* ▶ **drogi, kosztowny 2** involving great loss of time, effort, etc.: *a costly mistake* ▶ **kosztowny**

the ˌcost of ˈliving noun [sing.] the amount of money that people need to pay for food, clothing and somewhere to live: *a steady rise in the cost of living* ◇ *the high cost of living in London* ▶ **koszty utrzymania**

ˌcost ˈprice noun [U] the cost of producing sth or the price at which it is sold without profit: *Copies of the CD can be purchased at cost price.* ▶ **cena produkcji**

costume /ˈkɒstjuːm/ noun [C,U] **1** a set or style of clothes worn by people in a particular country or in a particular historical period: *17th-century costume* ◇ *Welsh national costume* ▶ **strój 2** clothes that an actor, etc. wears in order to look like sth else: *One of the children was dressed in a pirate's costume.* ◇ *The last rehearsal of the play will be done in costume.* ▶ **kostium 3** (Brit.) = SWIMSUIT

cosy (US **cozy**) /ˈkəʊzi/ adj. (**cosier**; **cosiest**) warm and comfortable: *The room looked cosy and inviting in the firelight.* ▶ **przytulny**

cot /kɒt/ noun [C] **1** (US **crib** /krɪb/) a bed with high sides for a baby ▶ **łóżeczko dziecięce 2** (US) = CAMP BED ➲ picture at **bed**

cottage /ˈkɒtɪdʒ/ noun [C] a small and usually old house, especially in the country ▶ **chata**, **chałupa** ➲ picture on page A3

ˌcottage ˈcheese noun [U] a type of soft white cheese in small wet lumps ▶ **serek wiejski**

cotton¹ /ˈkɒtn/ noun [U] **1** a natural cloth or thread made from the thin white hairs of the cotton plant: *a cotton shirt* ◇ *a reel of cotton* ▶ **bawełna**; **nić 2** (US) = COTTON WOOL

cotton² /ˈkɒtn/ verb

PHR V **cotton on (to sth)** (informal) to understand sth: *I suddenly cottoned on to what he was doing.* ▶ **skapować**, **kumać** (*coś*)

ˌcotton ˈcandy (US) = CANDYFLOSS

ˌcotton ˈwool (US **(abˌsorbent) ˈcotton**) noun [U] a soft mass of cotton, used for cleaning the skin, cuts, etc. ▶ **wata**

couch¹ /kaʊtʃ/ noun [C] a long seat, often with a back and arms, for sitting or lying on ▶ **kanapa**, **leżanka**

couch² /kaʊtʃ/ verb [T, usually passive] (formal) to express a thought, idea, etc. in the way mentioned: *His reply was couched in very polite terms.* ▶ **ubierać w słowa**

ˈcouch potato noun [C] (informal) a person who spends a lot of time sitting and watching television ▶ **telemaniak**

cough¹ /kɒf/ verb **1** [I] to send air out of your throat and mouth with a sudden loud noise, especially when you have a cold, have sth in your throat, etc. ▶ **kaszleć** ➲ note at **ill 2** [T] **cough (up) sth** to send sth out of your throat and mouth with a sudden loud noise: *When he started coughing (up) blood* (pluć krwią) *I called the doctor.* ▶ **odkaszlnąć**

■ **coughing** noun [U]: *a fit of coughing* ▶ **kaszel**

PHR V **cough (sth) up** (informal) to give money when you do not want to: *Come on, cough up what you owe me!* ▶ **bulić (na coś)**

cough² /kɒf/ noun [C] **1** an act or the sound of coughing: *He gave a nervous cough before he started to speak.* ▶ **kaszel 2** an illness or infection that makes you cough a lot: *Kevin's got a bad cough.* ▶ **kaszel**

could /kəd; strong form kʊd/ modal verb (negative **could not**; short form **couldn't** /ˈkʊdnt/) **1** (used for saying that sb had the ability or was allowed to do sth): *I could run three miles without stopping when I was younger.* ◇ *She said that she couldn't come* (że nie może przyjść). ◇ *My mother could cook beautifully.* Moja matka świetnie gotowała. ◇ *Ewa said we could stay at her house.* ▶ **mógł itd.**

> Jeśli coś udało się jednorazowo wykonać w przeszłości, wówczas używa się **was/were able to**: *The firemen were able to rescue the children.*
> W zdaniach przeczących można również stosować **could not**: *The firemen couldn't rescue the children.*

2 (used for asking permission politely): *Could I possibly borrow your car?* ▶ **czy mógłbym itd.** ➲ note at **can¹** **3** (used for asking sb politely to do sth for you): *Could you open the door? My hands are full.* ▶ **czy mógłbyś itd. 4** (used for saying that sth may be or may have been possible): *I could* (mogłabym/mogę) *do it now if you like.* ◇ *She could* (może) *be famous one day.* ◇ *10 o'clock is a bit late – couldn't you* (czy nie mógłbyś) *come earlier?* ◇ *He could have gone* (on mógł pójść) *to university but he didn't want to.* ◇ *I can't find my purse. I could have left it* (mogłam zostawić ją) *in the bank.* ◇ *You could have said* (przecież mogłeś powiedzieć, że) *you were going to be late!* ◇ *I could scream, I'm so angry.* Jestem tak wściekły, że mógłbym wrzeszczeć. ◇ *I was so angry I could have screamed.* Byłem taki wściekły, że mogłem wrzeszczeć. ▶ **mógłbym itd.**; **mógłem itd. 5** (used for making a suggestion): *'What do you want to do tonight?' 'We could go to the cinema or we could just stay in.'* ▶ **może(my) 6** (used with the verbs 'feel', 'hear', 'see', 'smell', 'taste') ℹ Czasowniki **feel** itp. nie występują w czasach *continuous*: *We could hear the birds singing* (a nie ~~We were hearing...~~) Słyszeliśmy śpiew ptaków.

IDM **could do with sth** to want or need sth: *I could do with a holiday.* Chętnie wziąłbym urlop.

council (also **Council**) /ˈkaʊnsl/ noun [C, with sing. or pl. verb] **1** a group of people who are elected to govern an area such as a town, city, etc.: *The county council has/have decided to build a new road.* ◇ *My father's on the local council.* ▶ **rada** (*miejska/państwowa*) **2** a group of people chosen to give advice, manage affairs, etc. for a particular organization or activity: *the Arts Council* ▶ **rada**, **zarząd**

ˈcouncil estate noun [C] (Brit.) a large group of houses built by a local council ▶ **osiedle domów komunalnych**

ˈcouncil house (also **ˈcouncil flat**) noun [C] (Brit.) a house or flat rented from the local council ▶ **komunalny dom mieszkalny**

councillor /ˈkaʊnsələ(r)/ noun [C] a member of a **council** ▶ **radn-y/a**

ˈcouncil tax noun [sing., U] (in Britain) a tax charged by local councils, based on the value of a person's home ▶ **podatek komunalny**

counsel¹ /ˈkaʊnsl/ noun [U] **1** (formal) advice ▶ **rada**, **porada 2** a lawyer who speaks in a court of law: *the counsel for the defence/prosecution* ▶ **adwokat**

counsel² /ˈkaʊnsl/ verb [T] (**counselling**; **counselled**; US **counseling**; **counseled**) **1** to give professional advice and help to sb with a problem ▶ **radzić**, **doradzać 2** (formal) to tell sb what you think they should do; to advise: *Mr Dean's lawyers counselled him against* (odradzili mu) *making public statements.* ▶ **radzić**, **doradzać**

counselling (US **counseling**) /ˈkaʊnsəlɪŋ/ noun [U] professional advice and help given to people with problems: *Many students come to us for counselling.* ▶ **porada**, **pomoc psychologa**

counsellor (US **counselor**) /ˈkaʊnsələ(r)/ noun [C] a person whose job is to give advice: *a marriage counsellor* ▶ **(do)radca**

count¹ /kaʊnt/ verb **1** [I] to say numbers one after another in order: *Close your eyes and count (up) to 20.* ▶ **liczyć 2** [T] **count sth** to calculate the total number or amount of sth: *The teacher counted the children as they got on the bus.* ▶ **rachować**, **przeliczać 3** [T] to include sb/sth when you are calculating an amount or number: *There were thirty people on the bus, not counting the driver.* ▶ **wliczać 4** [I] **count (for sth)** to be important or valuable: *I sometimes think my opinion counts for nothing at work.* ▶ **liczyć się 5** [I] **count (as sth)** to be valid or accepted: *The referee had already blown his whistle so the goal didn't count.* ◇ *Will my driving licence count as iden-*

tification? ▶ **liczyć się, być uznawanym 6** [I,T] to consider sb/sth in a particular way: *You should count yourself lucky to have a good job.* ◇ *On this airline, children over 12 count/are counted as adults.* ▶ **uważać za coś**
IDM **don't count your chickens (before they're hatched)** (used to say that you should not be too confident that sth will be successful because sth might still go wrong) ▶ **nie mów hop, dopóki nie przeskoczysz**
PHR V **count against sb** to be considered as a disadvantage: *Do you think my age will count against me?* ▶ **być uznawanym na czyjąś niekorzyść**
count on sb/sth to expect sth with confidence; to depend on sb/sth: *Can I count on you to help me tonight?* ▶ **liczyć na kogoś/coś**
count sb/sth out 1 to count things slowly, one by one: *She carefully counted out the money into my hand.* ▶ **odliczać coś 2** (informal) to not include sb/sth: *If you're going swimming, you can count me out!* ▶ **skreślać kogoś/coś, nie brać kogoś/czegoś pod uwagę**

count² /kaʊnt/ noun [C] **1** [usually sing.] an act of counting or a number that you get after counting: ***At the last count***, *there were nearly 2 million unemployed.* ◇ *On the count of three* (na trzy), *all lift together.* ▶ **obliczanie, rachunek, liczba 2** [usually pl.] a point that is made in a discussion, argument, etc.: *I proved her wrong* ***on all counts*** (pod każdym względem). ▶ **kwestia 3** a title for a man of noble birth in some European countries ▶ **hrabia**
IDM **keep/lose count (of sth)** to know/not know how many there are of sth: *I've lost count of the number of times he's told that joke!* ▶ **prowadzić rachunek czegoś; stracić rachubę**

countable /ˈkaʊntəbl/ adj. that can be counted: *Countable nouns are marked '[C]' in this dictionary.* ▶ **policzalny** OPP **uncountable**

countdown /ˈkaʊntdaʊn/ noun [C] the act of saying numbers backwards to zero just before sth important happens: *the countdown to the lift-off of a rocket* ◇ (figurative) *The countdown to this summer's Olympic Games has started.* ▶ **odliczanie** (*np. czasu*)

countenance¹ /ˈkaʊntənəns/ noun [C] (formal) sb's face or expression ▶ **oblicze; wyraz twarzy**

countenance² /ˈkaʊntənəns/ verb [T] (formal) to support sth or agree to sth happening: *The committee refused to countenance Harding's proposals.* ▶ **popierać, aprobować**

counter- /ˈkaʊntə(r)/ [in compounds] **1** against; opposite: *counterterrorism* ◇ *counter-argument* ▶ **kontr(a)-, przeciw- 2** related or similar to sth: *counterpart* odpowiednik ◇ *to countersign* (kontrasygnować) *sth*

counter¹ /ˈkaʊntə(r)/ noun [C] **1** a long, flat surface in a shop, bank, etc. where customers are served: *The man* ***behind the counter*** *in the bank was very helpful.* ▶ **lada 2** a small object (usually round and made of plastic) that is used in some games to show where a player is on the board ▶ **pionek 3** an electronic device for counting sth: *The needle on the rev counter soared.* ▶ **licznik**

counter² /ˈkaʊntə(r)/ verb [I,T] **1** to reply or react to criticism: *He countered our objections with a powerful defence of his plan.* ▶ **odparowywać 2** to try to reduce or prevent the bad effects of sth: *The shop has installed security cameras to counter theft.* ▶ **usiłować zapobiegać czemuś**

counter³ /ˈkaʊntə(r)/ adv. **counter to sth** in the opposite direction to sth: *The results of these experiments* ***run counter to*** *previous findings.* ▶ **przeciwnie do czegoś, w kierunku odwrotnym**

counteract /ˌkaʊntərˈækt/ verb [T] to reduce the effect of sth by acting against it: *measures to counteract traffic congestion* ▶ **przeciwdziałać**

ˈcounter-attack noun [C] an attack made in reaction to an enemy or opponent's attack ▶ **kontratak**
■ **counter-attack** verb [I,T] ▶ **kontratakować**

counterclockwise (US) = ANTICLOCKWISE

counterfeit /ˈkaʊntəfɪt/ adj. not genuine, but copied so that it looks like the real thing: *counterfeit money* ▶ **podrobiony, fałszywy**

counterfoil /ˈkaʊntəfɔɪl; US -tərfɔɪl-/ noun [C] the part of a cheque, ticket, etc. that you keep when you give the other part to sb else ▶ **odcinek** (*np. czeku*)

counterpart /ˈkaʊntəpɑːt/ noun [C] a person or thing that has a similar position or function in a different country or organization: *the French President and his Italian counterpart* ▶ **odpowiednik**

counterpoint /ˈkaʊntəpɔɪnt/ noun [U] the combination of two or more tunes played together to form a single piece of music: *The two melodies are played in counterpoint.* ▶ **kontrapunkt** ➲ look at **contrapuntal**

counterproductive /ˌkaʊntəprəˈdʌktɪv/ adj. having the opposite effect to the one you want: *It can be counterproductive to punish children.* ▶ **ze skutkiem odwrotnym (do oczekiwanego)** ➲ look at **productive**

ˌcounter-ˌrevoˈlution noun [C, U] opposition to or violent action against a government that came to power as a result of a revolution, in order to destroy and replace it: *to stage a counter-revolution* ▶ **kontrrewolucja**

countersign /ˈkaʊntəsaɪn/ verb [T] (technical) to sign a document that has already been signed by another person ▶ **kontrasygnować** (*np. czek*)

ˌcounter-ˈtenor noun [C] a man who is trained to sing with a very high voice ▶ **kontratenor**

ˌcounter-ˈterrorism noun [U] action taken to prevent the activities of political groups who use violence to try to achieve their aims ▶ **antyterroryzm**
■ **ˌcounter-ˈterrorist** adj. ▶ **antyterrorystyczny**

countess /ˈkaʊntəs; -es/ noun [C] a woman who is married to a count or earl, or who has the same rank as one ▶ **hrabina**

countless /ˈkaʊntləs/ adj. [only before a noun] very many: *I've tried to phone him countless times but he's not there.* ▶ **niezliczony**

country /ˈkʌntri/ noun (pl. **countries**) **1** [C] an area of land with its own people, government, etc.: *There was snow over much of the country during the night.* ▶ **kraj 2** [U] an area of land: *We looked down over miles of open country.* ◇ *hilly country* ▶ **teren, krajobraz** SYN **terrain 3** (**the country**) [sing.] the people who live in a country: *a survey to find out what the country really thinks* ▶ **kraj 4** (**the country**) [sing.] land which is away from towns and cities: *Do you live in a town or* ***in the country?*** ▶ **wieś, prowincja** ➲ note at **scenery** ➲ look at **countryside 5** [U] = COUNTRY AND WESTERN

Wyrażenie **the country** jest używane w celu podkreślenia, że dany obszar znajduje się z dala od miast: *city workers who like to get out into the country at weekends.* Słowo **countryside** również dotyczy obszarów oddalonych od miast, ale podkreśla ich walory przyrodnicze, na przykład wzgórza, rzeki, drzewa itp: *beautiful countryside* ◇ *the destruction of the countryside by new roads.* **Landscape** dotyczy wszystkiego, co widzimy na danym obszarze, bez względu na to, czy jest to teren miejski, czy wiejski: *a dreary landscape of factories and chimneys* ◇ *a landscape of forests and lakes.*

country

Nation to inny wyraz określający kraj lub mieszkańców tego kraju: *The entire nation, it seemed, was watching TV.* **State** stosuje się do określenia kraju jako zorganizowanej społeczności politycznej pod kontrolą jednego rządu. Może również oznaczać sam rząd: *a politically independent state* ◇ *the member states of the EU* ◇ *You get a pension from the state when you retire.* ◇ *state education.* **Land** jest określeniem bardziej formalnym i literackim: *Explorers who set out to discover new lands.*

ˌcountry and ˈwestern (also ˈ**country music**) noun [U] a type of music based on traditional music from the southern and western US ▶ **muzyka country**

country bumpkin /ˌkʌntri ˈbʌmpkɪn/ (also **bumpkin**) noun [C] a person from the country who seems stupid ▶ **(przen.) burak**

ˌcountry ˈhouse noun [C] a large house in the country, usually owned by an important family and often with a lot of land ▶ **rezydencja wiejska**

countryman /ˈkʌntrimən/ noun [C] (pl. **-men** /-mən/) a person from your own country (1): *The Italian Castorri beat his **fellow countryman** Rossi in the final.* ▶ **rodak/czka**

⚷ **the countryside** /ˈkʌntrisaɪd/ noun [U] land which is away from towns and cities, where there are fields, woods, etc.: *From the hill there is a magnificent view of the surrounding countryside.* ▶ **krajobraz wiejski, okolica** ➲ note at **country**, **nature**, **scenery**

⚷ **county** /ˈkaʊnti/ noun [C] (pl. **counties**) (abbr. **Co.** /kəʊ/) an area in Britain, Ireland or the US which has its own local government ▶ **hrabstwo** ➲ look at **province**, **state**

coup /kuː/ noun [C] **1** (also **coup d'état** /ˌkuː deɪˈtɑː/) a sudden, illegal and often violent change of government: *a coup to overthrow the President* ◇ *an attempted coup* nieudany zamach stanu ▶ **zamach stanu** **2** a clever and successful thing to do: *Getting that promotion was a real coup.* ▶ **wyczyn, mistrzowskie posunięcie**

⚷ **couple¹** /ˈkʌpl/ noun [C, with sing. or pl. verb] two people who are together because they are married or in a relationship: *a married couple* małżeństwo ◇ *Is/Are that couple over there part of our group?* ▶ **para** ➲ look at **pair**

IDM **a couple of people, things, etc.** **1** two people, things, etc.: *I need a couple of glasses.* ▶ **para** **2** a few: *I last saw her a couple of months ago.* ▶ **parę**

couple² /ˈkʌpl/ verb [T, usually passive] to join or connect sb/sth to sb/sth else: *The fog, coupled with the amount of traffic on the roads, made driving very difficult.* ▶ **łączyć, wiązać ze sobą**

coupon /ˈkuːpɒn; US also ˈkjuː-/ noun [C] **1** a small piece of paper which you can use to buy goods at a lower price, or which you can collect and then exchange for goods: *a coupon worth 10% off your next purchase* ▶ **talon, kupon** **2** a printed form in a newspaper or magazine which you use to order goods, enter a competition, etc. ▶ **kupon**

⚷ **courage** /ˈkʌrɪdʒ; US ˈkɜːr-/ noun [U] the ability to control fear in a situation that may be dangerous or unpleasant: *It took real courage to go back into the burning building.* ◇ *She **showed** great **courage** all through her long illness.* ▶ **odwaga** SYN **bravery**

■ **courageous** /kəˈreɪdʒəs/ adj. ▶ **odważny**

IDM **pluck up courage** → PLUCK¹

courgette /kʊəˈʒet; kɔːˈʒet/ (especially US **zucchini** /zuˈkiːni/ (pl. **zucchini** or **zucchinis**) noun [C] a long vegetable with dark green skin that is white inside ▶ **cukinia** ➲ picture on **page A13**

courier /ˈkʊriə(r)/ noun [C] **1** a person whose job is to carry letters, important papers, etc., especially when they are urgent: *The package was delivered by motorcycle courier.* ▶ **kurier, goniec** **2** a person whose job is to look after a group of tourists ▶ **pilot/ka wycieczki**

⚷ **course** /kɔːs/ noun **1** [C] **a course (in/on sth)** a complete series of lessons or studies: *I've decided to **enrol on a** computer **course**.* ◇ *I'm going to **take/do a course** in French.* ▶ **kurs** **2** [C,U] the route or direction that sth, especially an aircraft, ship or river, takes: *The hijackers forced the captain to **change course** and head for Cuba.* ◇ *to be **on/off course*** trzymać się kursu/zbaczać z kursu ◇ *The road follows the course of the river.* ◇ (figurative) *I'm on course* (jestem na dobrej drodze do) *to finish this work by the end of the week.* ▶ **kurs** **3** (also ˌ**course of ˈaction**) [C] a way of dealing with a particular situation: *In that situation resignation was the only course open to him.* ▶ **wyjście** (*z sytuacji*), **rozwiązanie** **4** [sing.] the development of sth over a period of time: *events that changed **the course of history*** ◇ *In the normal course of events* (w naturalnej kolei rzeczy) *such problems do not arise.* ▶ **bieg, tryb** **5** [C] the first, second, third, etc. separate part of a meal: *a three-course lunch* ◇ *I had chicken for the **main course**.* ▶ **danie** ➲ look at **dish¹** (3) ➲ note at **restaurant** **6** [C] an area where **golf** is played or where certain types of race take place: *a golf course* ◇ *a racecourse* tor wyścigów konnych ▶ **pole, tor wyścigowy** **7** [C] **a course (of sth)** a series of medical treatments: *The doctor put her on a course of tablets.* ▶ **seria, kuracja**

IDM **be on a collision course (with sb/sth)** → COLLISION

in the course of sth during sth: *He mentioned it in the course of conversation.* ▶ **w trakcie czegoś**

in the course of time when enough time has passed ▶ **z czasem, z upływem czasu** SYN **eventually**

in due course → DUE¹

a matter of course → MATTER¹

of course naturally; certainly: *Of course, having children has changed their lives a lot.* ◇ *'Can I use your phone?' 'Of course (you can).'* ◇ *'You're not annoyed with me, are you?' 'Of course (I'm) not.'* ▶ **oczywiście, naturalnie**

coursebook /ˈkɔːsbʊk/ noun [C] a book for studying from that is used regularly in class ▶ **podręcznik**

ˌcourse of ˈaction = COURSE (3)

coursework /ˈkɔːswɜːk/ noun [U] work that students do during a course of study, not in exams, that is included in their final grade: *Coursework accounts for 40% of the final marks.* ▶ **praca wykonana podczas całego kursu/semestru** (*za którą ocenę włącza się do oceny końcowej ucznia*)

⚷ **court¹** /kɔːt/ noun **1** [C,U] (also ˌ**court of ˈlaw**, pl. **courts of law**; Brit. also ˈ**law court**) the place where legal trials take place and crimes, etc. are judged: *the **civil/criminal** courts* ◇ *A man has been charged and will **appear in court** tomorrow.* ◇ *Bill's company are refusing to pay him so he's decided to **take them to court*** (pozwać ich do sądu). ◇ *a courtroom* sala sądowa ▶ **sąd** **2** (**the court**) [sing.] the people in a court, especially those taking part in the trial: *Please tell the court exactly what you saw.* ▶ **sąd** **3** [C,U] an area where certain ball games are played: *a tennis/squash/badminton court* ◇ *The players have been **on court** for nearly three hours.* ➲ look at **pitch** ➲ picture on **page A8** **4** the official place where kings and queens live ▶ **dwór**

court

The **accused** has the right to a **trial**, which is held in a **court**. All trials have a **judge**, and some have a **jury**, who **try** the **case**. One group of lawyers (the **prosecution**) tries to prove the guilt of the accused, while another group (the **defence**) tries to defend him. They examine the **evidence** to see if there is **proof** that he committed the crime. They may hear evidence from **witnesses**. At the end of the trial the judge or the jury will reach a **verdict** and decide if he is **guilty** or **not guilty**. If the accused is found guilty, he will receive a **sentence**. He may be **fined**, or sent to **jail/prison**.

court² /kɔːt/ verb **1** [T] to try to gain sb's support by paying special attention to them: *Politicians from all parties will be courting voters this week.* ▶ **zabiegać o czyjeś względy, nadskakiwać komuś** **2** [T] to do sth that might have a very bad effect: *Britain is courting ecological disaster if it continues to dump waste in the North Sea.* ▶ **narażać się na coś, igrać (z czymś)** **3** [I] (old-fashioned) (used about two people) to spend time together in a relationship that may lead to marriage ▶ **zalecać się, romansować**

courteous /ˈkɜːtiəs/ adj. polite and pleasant, showing respect for other people ▶ **uprzejmy, grzeczny** OPP **discourteous**

■ **courteously** adv. ▶ **uprzejmie, grzecznie**

courtesy /ˈkɜːtəsi/ noun (pl. **courtesies**) **1** [U] polite and pleasant behaviour that shows respect for other people: *She didn't even* ***have the courtesy*** *to say that she was sorry.* ◇ *If you're going to have a noisy party, you should tell your neighbours* ***out of courtesy.*** ▶ **uprzejmość, kurtuazja** **2** [C] (formal) a polite thing that you say or do when you meet people in formal situations: *The two presidents exchanged courtesies before their meeting.* ▶ **uprzejmość, kurtuazja**

IDM **(by) courtesy of sb** (formal) with the permission or because of the kindness of sb: *These pictures are being shown by courtesy of BBC TV.* ▶ **dzięki uprzejmości, za zgodą kogoś**

courthouse /ˈkɔːthaʊs/ noun [C] **1** (especially US) a building containing courts of law ▶ **gmach sądu** ➲ note at **court** **2** (in the US) a building containing the offices of a county government ▶ **budynek administracji okręgowej**

courtier /ˈkɔːtiə(r)/ noun [C] (in the past) a companion of a king or queen at their court ▶ **dworzanin, dama dworu**

ˌcourt ˈmartial noun [C] a military court that deals with matters of military law; a trial that takes place in such a court: *His case will be heard by a court martial.* ▶ **sąd wojskowy**

■ **court-martial** verb [T] ▶ **oddawać kogoś pod sąd wojskowy**

ˌcourt of ˈlaw = COURT¹ (1)

courtroom /ˈkɔːtruːm; -rʊm/ noun [C] a room in which trials or other legal cases are held ▶ **sala rozpraw**

courtship /ˈkɔːtʃɪp/ noun [C,U] (old-fashioned) the relationship between a man and a woman before they get married ▶ **zaloty, narzeczeństwo**

courtyard /ˈkɔːtjɑːd/ noun [C] an area of ground, without a roof, that has walls or buildings around it, for example in a castle or between houses or flats ▶ **dziedziniec, podwórze**

⚷ **cousin** /ˈkʌzn/ (also **ˌfirst ˈcousin**) noun [C] the child of your aunt or uncle: *Paul and I are cousins.* ▶ **brat/siostra cioteczn-y/a, brat/siostra stryjeczn-y/a**

> Tym samym słowem określa się zarówno brata ciotecznego, jak i siostrę cioteczną. **Second cousin** to dziecko brata ciotecznego lub siostry ciotecznej twojego ojca/twojej matki.

cove /kəʊv/ noun [C] a small area of the coast where the land curves round so that it is protected from the wind, etc.: *a sandy cove* ▶ **zatoczka**

⚷ **cover¹** /ˈkʌvə(r)/ verb **1** [T] **cover sb/sth (up/over) (with sth)** to put sth on or in front of sth to hide or protect it: *Could you cover the food and put it in the fridge?* ◇ *She couldn't look any more and covered her eyes.* ◇ *I covered the floor with newspaper before I started painting.* ◇ (figurative) *Paula laughed to cover* (by ukryć) *her embarrassment.* ▶ **przykrywać, okrywać** OPP **uncover** **2** [T] **cover sb/sth in/with sth** to be on the surface of sth; to make sth do this: *A car went through the puddle and covered me with mud.* ◇ *Graffiti covered the walls.* ◇ *The eruption of the volcano covered the town in a layer of ash.* ▶ **pokrywać** **3** [T] to fill or spread over a certain area: *The floods cover an area of about 15 000 square kilometres.* ▶ **pokrywać, zajmować** **4** [T] to include or to deal with sth: *The course covered both British and European naval history.* ◇ *Part-time workers are not covered by the law.* To prawo nie obejmuje osób pracujących na części etatu. ◇ *All the papers covered* (wszystkie gazety relacjonowały) *the election in depth.* ◇ *I think we've covered* (omówiliśmy) *everything. Now, does anyone have a question?* ◇ *My sales team covers* (działa na) *the north of the country* ▶ **obejmować, uwzględniać** **5** [T] to be enough money for sth: *We'll give you some money to cover your expenses.* ▶ **pokrywać** **6** [T] to travel a certain distance: *We covered about 500 kilometres that day.* ▶ **przebywać, pokonywać** **7** [I] **cover (for sb)** to do sb's job while they are away from work: *Matt's phoned in sick today so we'll have to find someone to cover (for him).* ▶ **zastępować (kogoś)** **8** [T] **cover sb/sth against/for sth** to protect sb/sth with insurance: *The insurance policy covers us for any damage to our property.* ▶ **ubezpieczać**

IDM **cover the cost (of sth)** to have or make enough money to pay for sth: *We made so little money at our school dance that we didn't even cover the cost of the band.* ▶ **pokrywać koszt (czegoś)**

PHR V **cover sth up** to prevent people hearing about a mistake or sth bad: *The police have been accused of trying to cover up the facts of the case.* ▶ **ukrywać coś**

cover up for sb to hide sb's mistakes or crimes in order to protect them: *His wife covered up for him to the police.* ▶ **osłaniać kogoś** (*przed odpowiedzialnością*)

⚷ **cover²** /ˈkʌvə(r)/ noun **1** [C] something that is put on or over sth, especially in order to protect it: *a plastic cover for a computer* ◇ *a duvet cover* poszwa na kołdrę ▶ **pokrywa, przykrycie, osłona** **2** [U] protection from the weather, damage, etc.: *When the storm started we had to* ***take cover*** *in a shop doorway.* ◇ *When the gunfire started everyone* ***ran for cover.*** ▶ **schronienie, osłona** SYN **shelter** **3** [C] the outside part of a book or magazine: *I read the magazine from cover to cover* (od deski do deski). ▶ **okładka** **4** [U] **cover (against sth)** insurance against sth: *The policy* ***provides cover*** *against theft.* ▶ **ubezpieczenie (od czegoś)** **5** (**the covers**) [pl.] the sheets, etc. on a bed: *She threw back the covers and leapt out of bed.* ▶ **przykrycie** **6** [C,U] **a cover (for sth)** something that hides what sb is really doing: *The whole company was just a cover for all kinds of criminal activities.* ◇ *police officers working* ***under cover*** ▶ **parawan, maska** **7** [U] doing sb's job for them while they are away from work: *Joanne's off next week so we'll have to arrange cover.* ▶ **zastępstwo** (*za kogoś*) **8** [C] = COVER VERSION

IDM **under (the) cover of sth** hidden by sth: *They attacked under cover of darkness.* ▶ **pod osłoną czegoś**

coverage /ˈkʌvərɪdʒ/ noun [U] **1** the act or amount of reporting on an event in newspapers, on TV, etc.: *TV coverage of the Olympic Games was excellent.* ▶ **relacja, doniesienie** **2** the amount or quality of information included in a book, magazine, etc.: *The grammar section provides coverage of all the most problematic areas.* ▶ **szczegółowe omówienie**

coveralls (US) **1** = OVERALL² (2) **2** = BOILER SUIT

ˈcover charge noun [C] an amount of money that you pay in some restaurants in addition to the cost of each customer's food and drink ▶ **opłata za wstęp**

⚷ **covered** /ˈkʌvəd/ adj. **1 covered in/with sth** having a layer or a large amount of sth on sb/sth: *She was covered in mud/sweat/dust.* ◇ *nuts covered with chocolate* ▶ **pokryty, przykryty** **2** having a cover, especially a roof: *a covered shopping centre* ▶ **pod dachem, zadaszony**

covering /ˈkʌvərɪŋ/ noun [C] something that covers the surface of sth: *There was a thick covering of dust over everything.* ▶ **pokrywa**

ˌ**covering ˈletter** noun [C] a letter that you send with a package, etc. that gives more information about it: *To apply for the job, send your CV with a covering letter.* ▶ **list przewodni**

covert /ˈkəʊvɜːt; Brit. also ˈkʌvət/ adj. (formal) done secretly: *a covert police operation* OPP **overt** ▶ **tajny**, **zamaskowany**

■ **covertly** adv. ▶ **tajnie**, **ukradkiem**

ˈ**cover-up** noun [C] an act of preventing sth bad or dishonest from becoming known: *Several newspapers have claimed that there has been a government cover-up.* ▶ **zatajenie**, **ukrycie prawdy**

ˈ**cover version** (also **cover**) noun [C] a new recording of an old song by a different band or singer: *a cover version of the 60s pop classic 'The Crying Game'* ▶ (*nowa wersja utworu muzycznego*) **cover**

covet /ˈkʌvət/ verb [T] (formal) to want to have sth very much (especially sth that belongs to sb else) ▶ **pożądać**

cow /kaʊ/ noun [C] **1** a large female animal that is kept on farms to produce milk: *to milk a cow* ▶ **krowa** ➲ note at **meat**

> **Cow** is often used for both male and female animals. A group of cows is a **herd**. The special word for a male is **bull** and a young cow is a **calf**. An **ox** is a male that cannot produce young and which is used for pulling heavy loads. Cows and bulls that are kept as farm animals can be called **cattle**. The noise that cows make is **moo**.

2 the adult female of certain large animals, for example **elephants** ▶ **samica** (*niektórych zwierząt*) **3** (slang) an insulting word for a woman ▶ **małpa**, **jędza**

coward /ˈkaʊəd/ noun [C] a person who has no courage and is afraid in dangerous or unpleasant situations ▶ **tchórz**

■ **cowardly** adj. ▶ **tchórzliwy**

cowardice /ˈkaʊədɪs/ noun [U] a lack of courage; behaviour that shows that you are afraid ▶ **tchórzostwo**

cowboy /ˈkaʊbɔɪ/ noun [C] **1** a man whose job is to look after cows (usually on a horse) in certain parts of the US ▶ **kowboj**, **pastuch** **2** (Brit., informal) a person in business who is not honest or who does work badly: *a cowboy builder* ▶ **partacz**; **naciągacz**

cower /ˈkaʊə(r)/ verb [I] to move back or into a low position because of fear: *The dog cowered under the table when the storm started.* ▶ **kulić się (ze strachu)**

cowslip /ˈkaʊslɪp/ noun [C] a small wild plant with yellow flowers with a sweet smell ▶ **pierwiosnek** (*Primula veris*) ➲ look at **primrose**

coy /kɔɪ/ adj. **1** pretending to be shy or innocent: *a coy smile* ▶ **(pozornie) nieśmiały**, **wstydliwy** **2** not wanting to give information about sth or to answer questions that tell people too much about you: *Don't be coy – tell me* (powiedz mi bez ogródek) *how much you earn.* ▶ **nieskory**, **niechętny** (*np. do rozmowy*)

■ **coyly** adv. ▶ **nieśmiało**, **wstydliwie**, **niechętnie**

cozy (US) = COSY

crab /kræb/ noun **1** [C,U] a sea animal with a flat shell and ten legs that moves sideways. The front two legs have **pincers** on them. ▶ **krab** ➲ picture on **page A11** **2** [U] the meat from a crab ▶ **krab**

crack[1] /kræk/ verb **1** [I,T] to break or to make sth break so that a line appears on the surface, but without breaking into pieces: *Don't put boiling water into that glass – it'll crack.* ◇ *The stone cracked the windscreen but didn't break it.* ▶ **pękać**; **powodować pęknięcie** **2** [T] to break sth open: *Crack two eggs into a bowl.* ▶ **rozbijać**, **rozłupywać** **3** [T] to hit a part of your body against sth; to hit sb with sth: *She stood up and cracked her head on the cupboard door.* ◇ *She cracked the thief over the head with her umbrella.* ▶ **trzaskać**, **walić** **4** [I,T] to make a sudden loud, sharp sound; to cause sth to make this sound: *to crack a whip/your knuckles* ▶ **trzaskać** **5** [I] (used about sb's voice) to suddenly change in a way that is not controlled: *Her voice cracked as she spoke about her parent's death.* ▶ **załamywać się** **6** [I] to no longer be able to deal with pressure and so lose control: *He cracked under the strain of all his problems.* ▶ **załamywać się** **7** [T] (informal) to solve a problem: *to crack a code* ◇ *The police have cracked* (rozbiła) *an international drug-smuggling ring.* ▶ **rozgryźć** **8** [T] to tell or make a joke: *Stop cracking jokes and do some work!* ▶ **zażartować**

IDM **get cracking** (Brit., informal) to start doing sth immediately: *I have to finish this job today so I'd better get cracking* (muszę się zabrać do roboty). ▶ **ruszać się**

PHR V **crack down (on sb/sth)** (used about people in authority) to start dealing strictly with bad or illegal behaviour: *The police have started to crack down on drug dealers.* ▶ **stosować sankcje**; **rozprawić się z kimś**

crack up 1 (informal) to be unable to deal with pressure and so lose control and become mentally ill: *He cracked up when his wife left him.* ▶ **załamywać się** **2** (slang) to suddenly start laughing, especially when you should be serious ▶ **parsknąć śmiechem**

crack[2] /kræk/ noun **1** [C] a line on the surface of sth where it has broken, but not into separate pieces: *a pane of glass with a crack in it* ◇ (figurative) *They had always seemed happy together, but then cracks began to appear* (zaczęło się psuć) *in their relationship.* ▶ **pęknięcie**, **rysa** ➲ picture at **chip**[2] (1) **2** [C] a narrow opening: *a crack in the curtains* ▶ **pęknięcie**, **szpara** **3** [C] a sudden loud, sharp sound: *There was a loud crack as the gun went off.* ▶ **trzask** **4** [C] a hard hit on a part of the body: *Suddenly a golf ball gave him a nasty crack on the head.* ▶ **uderzenie** **5** [U] a dangerous and illegal drug that some people take for pleasure and cannot then stop taking: *a crack addict* ▶ **rodzaj narkotyku** (*odmiana kokainy*) **6** [C] (informal) an amusing, often critical, comment; a joke: *She* ***made a crack*** *about his bald head and he got angry.* ▶ **kpina**

IDM **the crack of dawn** very early in the morning ▶ **blady świt**, **brzask**

have a crack (at sth/at doing sth) (informal) to try to do sth: *I'm not sure how to play but I'll have a crack at it.* ▶ **przymierzać się (do robienia czegoś)**, **spróbować swoich sił (w czymś)**

crack[3] /kræk/ adj. [only before a noun] (used about soldiers or sports players) very well trained and skilful: *crack troops* elitarne oddziały strzeleckie ◇ *He's a crack shot* (strzelcem doborowym) *with a rifle.* ▶ **pierwszorzędny**, **świetny**

crackdown /ˈkrækdaʊn/ noun [C] action to stop bad or illegal behaviour: *Fifty people have been arrested in a police crackdown on street crime.* ▶ **akcja specjalna (przeciw przestępczości)**, **sankcje**

cracked /krækt/ adj. damaged with lines in its surface but not completely broken: *a cracked mirror/mug* ◇ *He suffered cracked ribs and bruising.* ▶ **pęknięty**

cracker /ˈkrækə(r)/ noun [C] **1** a thin dry biscuit that is often eaten with cheese ▶ **krakers** **2** (also

cracker

Christmas cracker

ˌChristmas ˈcracker) a cardboard tube covered in coloured paper and containing a small present. **Crackers** are pulled apart by two people, each holding one end, at Christmas parties. They make a loud noise as they break. ▶ **atrakcja bożonarodzeniowa w kształcie cukierka 3** (Brit., informal) a very good example of sth: *That story he told was a real cracker.* ▶ **coś wspaniałego/bardzo śmiesznego**

crackers /ˈkrækəz/ adj. [not before a noun] (Brit., informal) crazy: *That noise is driving me crackers* (doprowadza mnie do szału). ▶ **stuknięty, szalony**

crackle /ˈkrækl/ verb [I] to make a series of short, sharp sounds: *The radio started to crackle and then it stopped working.* ▶ **trzeszczeć**

■ **crackle** noun [sing.]: *the crackle of dry wood burning* ▶ **trzaskanie**

crackpot /ˈkrækpɒt/ noun [C] (informal) a person with strange or crazy ideas ▶ **świr**

■ **crackpot** adj. [only before a noun]: ***crackpot ideas/theories*** ▶ **szalony, obłąkany**

cradle¹ /ˈkreɪdl/ noun [C] a small bed for a baby. **Cradles** can often be moved from side to side: (figurative) *Greece was the cradle* (kolebką) *of democracy.* ▶ **kołyska** ➲ picture at **bed**

cradle² /ˈkreɪdl/ verb [T] to hold sb/sth carefully and gently in your arms ▶ **trzymać coś ostrożnie, niańczyć**

⚷ **craft** /krɑːft; US kræft/ noun **1** [C,U] a job or activity for which you need skill with your hands: *an arts and crafts exhibition* ◇ *craft, design and technology (CDT)* (przedmiot nauczany w brytyjskich szkołach średnich) ▶ **rzemiosło** ➲ look at **handicraft 2** [C] any job or activity for which you need skill: *He regards acting as a craft.* ▶ **sztuka, kunszt 3** [C] (pl. **craft**) a boat, aircraft or **spacecraft**: *a pleasure craft* ▶ **statek, samolot**

craftsman /ˈkrɑːftsmən; US ˈkræf-/ noun [C] (pl. **-men** /-mən/) a person who makes things in a skilful way, especially with their hands ▶ **rzemieślnik**

craftsmanship /ˈkrɑːftsmənʃɪp; US ˈkræf-/ noun [U] the skill used by sb to make sth of high quality with their hands ▶ **rzemiosło**

crafty /ˈkrɑːfti; US ˈkræf-/ adj. (**craftier**; **craftiest**) clever at getting or achieving things by using unfair or dishonest methods ▶ **przebiegły, chytry**

■ **craftily** adv. ▶ **przebiegle, chytrze**

crag /kræg/ noun [C] a steep, rough rock on a hill or mountain ▶ **turnia**

craggy /ˈkrægi/ adj. **1** having a lot of steep rough rock: *a craggy coastline* ▶ **skalisty, urwisty 2** (used about a man's face) strong and with deep lines, especially in an attractive way ▶ **poorany bruzdami/zmarszczkami** (*w sposób atrakcyjny*)

cram /kræm/ verb (**cramming**; **crammed**) **1** [T] **cram sb/sth in (sth)**; **cram sb/sth into/onto sth** to push people or things into a small space: *I managed to cram all my clothes into the bag but I couldn't close it.* ◇ *We only spent two days in Dublin but we managed to cram a lot of sightseeing in.* ▶ **wpychać, wciskać 2** [I] **cram in (sth)**; **cram into/onto sth** to move, with a lot of other people, into a small space: *He only had a small car but they all managed to cram in.* ▶ **wtłaczać się 3** [I] to study very hard and learn a lot in a short time before an exam: *She's cramming for her exams.* ▶ **wkuwać, kuć**

crammed /kræmd/ adj. very or too full: *That book is crammed with useful information.* ▶ **napchany, zapchany**

cramp /kræmp/ noun [U,C] a sudden pain that you get in a muscle, that makes it difficult to move ▶ **skurcz**

cramped /kræmpt/ adj. not having enough space ▶ **zatłoczony**

cranberry /ˈkrænbəri; US -beri/ noun [C] (pl. **cranberries**) a small round red fruit that tastes sour and is used in cooking: *cranberry sauce* ▶ **żurawina**

crane¹ /kreɪn/ noun [C] a large machine with a long metal arm that is used for moving or lifting heavy objects ▶ **dźwig, żuraw**

crane² /kreɪn/ verb [I,T] to stretch your neck forward in order to see or hear sth: *We all craned forward to get a better view.* ▶ **wyciągać szyję**

cranium /ˈkreɪniəm/ noun [C] (**craniums** or **crania** /ˈkreɪniə/) the bone inside your head; the skull ▶ **czaszka** SYN **skull**

■ **cranial** adj. [only before a noun] ▶ **czaszkowy**

crank /kræŋk/ noun [C] a person with strange ideas or who behaves in a strange way: *Lots of cranks phoned the police confessing to the man's murder.* ▶ **dziwa-k/czka, mania-k/czka**

cranky /ˈkræŋki/ adj. (informal) **1** (Brit.) strange SYN **eccentric**: ***cranky ideas/schemes*** ▶ **dziwaczny 2** (especially US) bad-tempered: *The kids were getting tired and a little cranky.* ▶ **rozdrażniony, marudny**

cranny /ˈkræni/ noun [C] (pl. **crannies**) a small opening in a wall, rock, etc. ▶ **szczelina, szpara**

IDM **every nook and cranny** → NOOK

crap /kræp/ noun (taboo, slang) **1** [U] nonsense: *He's so full of crap.* ◇ *Let's* ***cut the crap*** (przestańmy gadać pierdoły) *and get down to business.* ◇ *You're talking a* ***load of crap!*** Pieprzysz! ▶ **pierdoły 2** [U] something of bad quality: *This work is complete crap.* ◇ *Her latest film is a* ***load of crap.*** ▶ **chała** ℹ Mniej obraźliwe synonimy to **rubbish**, **garbage**, **trash** lub **junk**. **3** [U] criticism or unfair treatment: *I'm not going to take this crap any more.* ▶ **zjeżdżanie, czepianie się 4** [U] solid waste matter from the **bowels** SYN **excrement** ▶ **gówno 5** [sing.] an act of emptying solid waste matter from the **bowels**: *to have a crap* wysrać się ▶ **sranie**

■ **crap** adj. (Brit., taboo, slang) bad; of very bad quality: *a crap band* ▶ **gówniany** | **crap** adv.: *The team played crap yesterday.* ▶ **beznadziejnie**

crappy /ˈkræpi/ adj. (slang) [usually before a noun] of very bad quality: *a crappy novel* ▶ **chłamowaty**

⚷ **crash¹** /kræʃ/ noun [C] **1** an accident when a car or other vehicle hits sth and is damaged: *a car crash* wypadek samochodowy ▶ **zderzenie, katastrofa** (*np. lotnicza*) **2** a sudden loud noise made by sth breaking, hitting sth, etc.: *I heard a crash and ran outside.* ▶ **trzask, łoskot 3** (used about money or business) a sudden fall in the value or price of sth: *the Stock Market crash of 1987* ▶ **krach na giełdzie 4** a sudden failure of a machine, especially a computer ▶ **awaria**

⚷ **crash²** /kræʃ/ verb **1** [I,T] to have an accident in a vehicle; to drive a vehicle into sth: *He braked too late and crashed into the car in front.* ▶ **zderzać się; rozbijać 2** [I] to hit sth hard, making a loud noise: *The tree crashed to the ground.* ▶ **zwalać się/przebijać się z trzaskiem 3** [I] to make a loud noise: *I could hear thunder crashing outside.* ▶ **huczeć, łoskotać 4** [I] (used about money or business) to suddenly lose value or fail: *Share prices crashed to an all-time low yesterday.* ▶ **upadać, bankrutować 5** [I] (used about a computer) to suddenly stop working: *We lost the data when the computer crashed.* ▶ **zepsuć się, nawalić**

crash³ /kræʃ/ adj. [only before a noun] done in a very short period of time: *She did a* ***crash course*** *in Spanish before going to work in Madrid.* ▶ **intensywny**

ˈ**crash barrier** noun [C] a fence that keeps people or vehicles apart, for example when there are large crowds or between the two sides of the road ▶ **bariera**

ˈcrash helmet noun [C] a hard hat worn by motorbike riders, racing drivers, etc. ▶ **kask, hełm**

ˌcrash-ˈland verb [I,T] to land a plane in a dangerous way in an emergency ▶ **lądować w trybie awaryjnym**
■ **ˌcrash ˈlanding** noun [C]: *to make a crash landing* ▶ **lądowanie awaryjne**

crass /kræs/ adj. **1** stupid, showing that you do not understand sth: *It was a crass comment to make when he knew how upset she was.* ▶ **beznadziejnie głupi, bezmyślny 2** extreme: *crass carelessness* ▶ **beznadziejny, bezdenny**

crate /kreɪt/ noun [C] a large box in which goods are carried or stored ▶ **paka, skrzynka**

crater /ˈkreɪtə(r)/ noun [C] **1** the hole in the top of a **volcano**, through which hot gases and liquid rock are forced ▶ **krater 2** a large hole in the ground: *The bomb left a large crater.* ◇ *craters on the moon* ▶ **krater, lej** (*np. po bombie*)

cravat /krəˈvæt/ noun [C] a wide piece of cloth that some men tie around their neck and wear inside the **collar** of their shirt ▶ **fular**

crave /kreɪv/ verb [I,T] **crave (for) sth** to want and need to have sth very much: *Sometimes I really crave for some chocolate.* ▶ **pragnąć czegoś**

craving /ˈkreɪvɪŋ/ noun [C] a strong desire for sth: *When she was pregnant she used to* ***have cravings for*** (miała zachcianki na) *all sorts of peculiar food.* ▶ **pragnienie**

crawl¹ /krɔːl/ verb [I] **1** to move slowly with your body on or close to the ground, or on your hands and knees: *Their baby has just started to crawl* (raczkować). ◇ *An insect crawled across the floor.* ▶ **pełzać, czołgać się** ➲ picture at **kneel 2** (used about vehicles) to move very slowly: *The traffic crawls through the centre of town in the rush hour.* ▶ **wlec się 3** (informal) **crawl (to sb)** to be very polite or pleasant to sb in order to be liked or to gain sth: *He only got promoted because he crawled to the manager.* ▶ **podlizywać się, płaszczyć się przed kimś**
IDM **be crawling with sth** to be completely full of or covered with unpleasant animals: *The kitchen was crawling with insects.* ◇ (figurative) *The village is always crawling with tourists at this time of year.* ▶ **roić się od kogoś/czegoś**

crawl² /krɔːl/ noun **1** [sing.] a very slow speed: *The traffic slowed to a crawl.* ▶ **wleczenie się, żółwie tempo 2** (often **the crawl**) [sing., U] a style of swimming which you do on your front. When you do the **crawl**, you move first one arm and then the other over your head, turn your face to one side so that you can breathe and kick up and down with your legs. ▶ **kraul**

crayon /ˈkreɪən/ noun [C,U] a soft, thick, coloured pencil that is used for drawing or writing, especially by children ▶ **kredka świecowa**
■ **crayon** verb [I,T] ▶ **malować/rysować kredką świecową**

craze /kreɪz/ noun [C] **a craze (for sth) 1** a strong interest in sth, that usually only lasts for a short time: *There was a craze for that kind of music last year.* ▶ **szaleństwo/szał (na punkcie czegoś) 2** something that a lot of people are very interested in: *Pocket TVs are the latest craze among teenagers.* ▶ **szaleństwo/szał na punkcie czegoś**

⚷ **crazy** /ˈkreɪzi/ adj. (**crazier**; **craziest**) (informal) **1** not sensible; stupid: *You must be crazy to turn down such a wonderful offer.* ▶ **szalony, zwariowany 2** very angry: *She* ***goes crazy*** (wścieka się) *when people criticize her.* ▶ **wściekły 3** showing great excitement: *The fans* ***went crazy*** (oszaleli) *when their team scored the first goal.* ▶ **oszalały (z czegoś) 4 crazy about sb/sth** liking sb/sth very much: *He's always been crazy about horses.* ▶ **zwariowany na punkcie czegoś/na czyimś punkcie; zakochany do szaleństwa**
■ **crazily** adv. ▶ **szaleńczo, dziko** | **craziness** noun [U] ▶ **szaleństwo, wariactwo**

creak /kriːk/ verb [I] to make the noise of wood bending or of sth not moving smoothly: *The floorboards creaked when I walked across the room.* ▶ **skrzypieć, zgrzytać**
■ **creak** noun [C] ▶ **skrzyp, zgrzyt**

creaky /ˈkriːki/ adj. **1** making **creaks**: *a creaky old chair* ▶ **skrzypiący, zgrzytający 2** old and not in good condition: *the country's creaky legal machinery* ▶ (*przen.*) **chwiejny**

⚷ **cream¹** /kriːm/ noun **1** [U] the thick yellowish-white liquid that rises to the top of milk: *coffee with cream* ◇ *whipped cream* bita śmietana ▶ **śmietan(k)a** ➲ look at **sour cream** ➲ picture on **page A14 2** [C,U] a substance that you rub into your skin to keep it soft or as a medical treatment: *(an) antiseptic cream* ▶ **krem 3** (**the cream**) [sing.] the best part of sth or the best people in a group: *the cream of New York society* ▶ **śmietanka towarzyska, elita**

⚷ **cream²** /kriːm/ adj. of a yellowish-white colour ▶ **kremowy**
■ **cream** noun [U] ▶ **kolor kremowy**

cream³ /kriːm/ verb
PHR V **cream sb/sth off** to take away the best people or part from sth for a particular purpose: *The big clubs cream off the country's best young players.* ▶ **ściągać śmietankę (towarzyską itp.)**

creamy /ˈkriːmi/ adj. (**creamier**; **creamiest**) **1** containing cream; thick and smooth like cream: *a creamy sauce* ▶ **śmietan(k)owy; gęsty 2** having a light colour like cream: *creamy skin* ▶ **koloru kremowego**

crease¹ /kriːs/ noun [C] **1** an untidy line on paper, material, a piece of clothing, etc. that should not be there: *When I unrolled the poster, there was a crease in it.* ◇ *Your shirt needs ironing – it's full of creases* (jest cała pognieciona). ▶ **zmarszczka, zagięcie 2** a tidy straight line that you make in sth, for example when you fold it: *He had a sharp crease in his trousers.* ▶ **kant, zagięcie** ➲ picture at **fold**

crease² /kriːs/ verb [I,T] to get **creases**; to make sth get **creases**: *Hang up your jacket or it will crease.* ◇ *Crease the paper carefully down the middle.* ▶ **gnieść (się), miąć (się)**

⚷ **create** /kriˈeɪt/ verb [T] to cause sth new to happen or exist: *a plan to create new jobs in the area* ◇ *William created a bad impression* (zrobił złe wrażenie) *at the interview.* ▶ **tworzyć, powodować**

creation /kriˈeɪʃn/ noun **1** [U] the act of causing sth new to happen or exist: *the creation of new independent states* ▶ **u/tworzenie, powołanie (czegoś) do życia, stworzenie 2** [C] something new that sb has made or produced: *This dish is a new creation – I didn't use a recipe.* ▶ **twór, wytwór 3** (usually **the Creation**) [sing.] the act of making the whole universe, as described in the Bible ▶ **stworzenie świata**

creative /kriˈeɪtɪv/ adj. **1** using skill or imagination to make or do new things: *She's a fantastic designer – she's so creative.* ▶ **twórczy, pomysłowy 2** connected with producing new things: *His creative life went on until he was well over 80.* ▶ **twórczy**
■ **creatively** adv. ▶ **twórczo, pomysłowo**

creativity /ˌkriːeɪˈtɪvəti/ noun [U] the ability to make or produce new things using skill or imagination: *We want teaching that encourages children's creativity.* ▶ **zdolności twórcze, pomysłowość**

creator /kriˈeɪtə(r)/ noun **1** [C] a person who makes or produces sth new: *He was the creator of some of the best-known characters in literature.* ▶ **twórca 2** (**the Creator**) [sing.] God ▶ **Stwórca**

creature /ˈkriːtʃə(r)/ noun [C] a living thing such as an animal, a bird, a fish or an insect, but not a plant: *sea creatures* ▶ **stworzenie, istota**

crèche /kreʃ/ noun [C] a place where small children are looked after while their parents are working, shopping, etc. ▶ **żłobek** ➲ look at **nursery**

credentials /krəˈdenʃlz/ noun [pl.] **1** the qualities, experience, etc. that make sb suitable for sth: *He has the perfect credentials for the job.* ▶ **kwalifikacje, przygotowanie zawodowe 2** a document that is proof that you have the training, education, etc. necessary to do sth, or proof that you are who you say you are ▶ **świadectwo, dyplom** (*zawodowy*)

credibility /ˌkredəˈbɪləti/ noun [U] the quality that sb has that makes people believe or trust them: *The Prime Minister had lost all credibility and had to resign.* ▶ **wiarygodność, zaufanie**

credible /ˈkredəbl/ adj. **1** that you can believe: *It's hardly credible that such a thing could happen without him knowing it.* ▶ **wiarygodny** OPP **incredible 2** that seems possible: *We need to think of a credible alternative to nuclear energy.* ▶ **wiarygodny, rzetelny**

credit[1] /ˈkredɪt/ noun **1** [U] a way of buying goods or services and not paying for them until later: *I bought the TV **on credit*** ◇ *interest-free credit* kredyt bez oprocentowania ◇ *Your **credit limit** is now £2 000.* ▶ **kredyt 2** [U] a sum of money that a bank, etc. lends to sb: *The company was not able to get any further credit and went bankrupt.* ▶ **kredyt, pożyczka 3** [U] having money in an account: *No bank charges are made if your account remains **in credit*** (jeśli na koncie są dostępne środki). ◇ *I've run out of credit on my mobile phone.* Skończył mi się limit na karcie komórki. ▶ **saldo dodatnie/kredytowe 4** [C] a payment made into an account: *There have been several credits to her account over the last month.* ▶ **kredyt, wpłata** OPP **debit 5** [U] an act of saying that sb has done sth well: *He **got all the credit*** (zdobył całe uznanie) *for the success of the project.* ◇ *I can't **take** any **credit*** (nie mogę sobie przypisywać jakiejkolwiek zasługi)*; the others did all the work.* ◇ *She didn't do very well but at least **give** her **credit for** trying* (doceń ją za to, że próbowała). ▶ **zasługa, uznanie 6** [sing.] **a credit to sb/sth** a person or thing that you should be proud of: *She is a credit to her school.* ▶ **chluba, duma 7** (**the credits**) [pl.] the list of the names of the people who made a film or TV programme, shown at the beginning or end of the film ▶ **napisy** (*po zakończeniu filmu*) **8** [C] (US) a part of a course at a college or university that a student has completed successfully ▶ **zaliczona część kursu akademickiego**

IDM **do sb credit** (used about sb's qualities or successes) to be so good that people should be proud of them: *His courage and optimism do him credit.* ▶ **przynosić komuś zaszczyt/chlubę**

have sth to your credit to have finished sth that is successful: *He has three best-selling novels to his credit.* ▶ **mieć coś na swoim koncie**

(be) to sb's credit (used for showing that you approve of sth that sb has done, although you have criticized them for sth else): *The company, to its credit* (firma, trzeba jej to przyznać)*, apologized and refunded my money.*

credit[2] /ˈkredɪt/ verb [T] **1** to add money to an account: *Has the cheque been credited to my account* (wpłynął na moje konto) *yet?* ▶ **wpłacać 2 credit sb/sth with sth**; **credit sth to sb/sth** to believe or say that sb/sth has a particular quality or has done sth well: *Of course I wouldn't do such a stupid thing – credit me with a bit more sense than that* (przyznasz chyba, że mam trochę więcej rozumu)*!* ◇ *He credited his success to a lot of hard work.* ▶ **przypisywać, tłumaczyć czymś 3** [usually in negative sentences and questions] to believe sth: *I simply cannot credit that he has made the same mistake again!* ▶ **uwierzyć, zrozumieć**

creditable /ˈkredɪtəbl/ adj. of a quite good standard that cannot be criticized, though not excellent: *It was a creditable result considering that three players were injured.* ▶ **chlubny, chwalebny**

ˈcredit card noun [C] a small plastic card that you can use to buy goods or services and pay for them later: *Can I pay by credit card?* ▶ **karta kredytowa** ➲ look at **cash card, cheque card, debit card**

creditor /ˈkredɪtə(r)/ noun [C] a person or company from whom you have borrowed money ▶ **wierzyciel, kredytodawca**

creditworthy /ˈkredɪtwɜːði/ adj. able to be trusted to pay back money that is owed; safe to lend money to ▶ **mający zdolność kredytową**
■ **creditworthiness** noun [U] ▶ **zdolność kredytowa**

creed /kriːd/ noun [C] a set of beliefs or principles (especially religious ones) that strongly influence sb's life ▶ **kredo, wyznanie**

creek /kriːk/ noun [C] **1** (Brit.) a narrow piece of water where the sea flows into the land ▶ **wąska zatoczka 2** (US) a small river ▶ **strumyk** SYN **stream**

creep[1] /kriːp/ verb [I] (pt, pp **crept** /krept/) **1** to move very quietly and carefully so that nobody will notice you: *She crept into the room so as not to wake him up.* ▶ **skradać się, zakradać się, pełzać 2** to move forward slowly: *The traffic was only creeping along.* ▶ **posuwać się powoli**

IDM **make your flesh creep** → FLESH

PHR V **creep in** to begin to appear: *All sorts of changes are beginning to creep into the education system.* ▶ **pojawiać się, wkradać się**

creep[2] /kriːp/ noun [C] (informal) a person that you do not like because they try too hard to be liked by people in authority ▶ **lizus**

IDM **give sb the creeps** (informal) to make sb feel frightened or nervous: *There's something about the way he laughs that gives me the creeps* (że przechodzą mnie ciarki).

creeper /ˈkriːpə(r)/ noun [C] a plant that grows up trees or walls or along the ground ▶ **pnącze**

creepy /ˈkriːpi/ adj. (**creepier**; **creepiest**) (informal) that makes you feel nervous or frightened ▶ **niesamowity, budzący niepokój** SYN **spooky**

cremate /krəˈmeɪt/ verb [T] to burn the body of a dead person as part of a funeral service ▶ **poddawać kremacji** ➲ note at **funeral**
■ **cremation** /krəˈmeɪʃn/ noun [C,U] ▶ **kremacja**

crematorium /ˌkreməˈtɔːriəm/ noun [C] (pl. **crematoria** /-ˈtɔːriə/ or **crematoriums**) a building in which the bodies of dead people are burned ▶ **krematorium**

Creole (also **creole**) /ˈkriːəʊl/ noun **1** [C] a person of mixed European and African race, especially one who lives in the West Indies ▶ **Kreol/ka 2** [C] a person whose relatives were among the first Europeans to live in the Caribbean and South America, or among the first French or Spanish people to live in the southern states of the US: *the Creole cooking* (kuchnia kreolska) *of New Orleans* ▶ **Kreol/ka 3** [C,U] a language that was originally a mixture of a European language and a local, especially African, language ▶ **język kreolski**

crêpe (also **crepe**) /kreɪp/ noun **1** [U] a type of light thin cloth, made especially from cotton or silk, with a surface that is covered in lines and folds: *a black crêpe dress* ◇ *a crêpe bandage* ▶ (*tkanina*) **krepa 2** [U] a type of strong rubber with a rough surface, used on the bottom of shoes: *crêpe-soled shoes* ▶ (*kauczuk*) **krepa 3** [C] a thin pancake ▶ **cienki naleśnik**

'crêpe paper noun [U] a type of thin brightly coloured paper that stretches and has a surface covered in lines and folds, used especially for making decorations ▶ (*bibuła*) **krepina**

crept past tense, past participle of **creep**[1]

crescendo /krə'ʃendəʊ/ noun [C] (pl. **crescendos**) **1** a gradual increase in how loudly a piece of music is played or sung ▶ **crescendo 2** a gradual increase in noise; the loudest point of a period of continuous noise: *Voices rose in a crescendo and drowned him out.* ◇ (figurative) *The advertising campaign reached a crescendo just before Christmas.* ▶ **wzmagający się hałas**; **kulminacja**

crescent /'kresnt/ noun [C] **1** a curved shape that is pointed at both ends, like the moon in its first and last stages ▶ **sierp księżyca**, **rożek 2** a street that is curved ▶ **ulica w kształcie półkola**

cress /kres/ noun [U] a small plant with very small green leaves that does not need to be cooked and is eaten in salads and **sandwiches** ▶ **rzeżucha**

crest /krest/ noun [C] **1** the top of a hill ▶ **szczyt** (*góry*) **2** the white part at the top of a wave ▶ **grzebień 3** a group of feathers on the top of a bird's head ▶ **grzebień**

crestfallen /'krestfɔːlən/ adj. disappointed or sad because you have failed and did not expect to ▶ **przygnębiony**, **strapiony**

cretin /'kretɪn; US 'kriːtn/ noun [C] (informal) a stupid person ▶ **kretyn/ka**

crevasse /krə'væs/ noun [C] a deep crack in a very thick layer of ice ▶ **szczelina** (*w grubej warstwie lodu*)

crevice /'krevɪs/ noun [C] a narrow crack in a rock, wall, etc. ▶ **szczelina**, **szpara**

crew /kruː/ noun [C, with sing. or pl. verb] **1** all the people who work on a ship, aircraft, etc. ▶ **załoga** ➲ note at **boat 2** a group of people who work together: *a camera crew* ▶ **ekipa**, **zespół**

crib[1] (US) = COT

crib[2] /krɪb/ verb [I,T] (**cribbing**; **cribbed**) **crib (sth) (from/off sb)** to copy sb else's work and pretend it is your own ▶ **odpisywać**, **ściągać (od kogoś)**

crick /krɪk/ noun [sing.] a pain in your neck, back, etc. that makes it difficult for you to move easily ▶ **kurcz**
■ **crick** verb [T]: *I've cricked my neck.* Mam bolesny kurcz w karku ▶ **chwytać**

cricket /'krɪkɪt/ noun **1** [U] a game that is played with a ball and a **bat** on a large area of grass by two teams of eleven players ▶ **krykiet** ➲ picture on **page A8**

> In cricket the **bowler** bowls the ball to the **batsman** who tries to hit it with a **bat** and then score a **run** by running from one end of the pitch to the other.

2 [C] an insect that makes a loud noise by rubbing its wings together ▶ **świerszcz**

cricketer /'krɪkɪtə(r)/ noun [C] a person who plays **cricket** ▶ **gracz w krykieta**

⚷ **crime** /kraɪm/ noun **1** [U] illegal behaviour or activities: *There has been an increase in car crime recently.* ◇ *to fight crime* ▶ **przestępstwo**, **zbrodnia 2** [C] something which is illegal and which people are punished for, for example by being sent to prison: *to **commit a crime*** ▶ **przestępstwo**, **zbrodnia 3** (usually **a crime**) [sing.] something that is morally wrong: *It is a crime to waste food when people are starving.* ▶ **skandal**, **czyn karygodny**

> **crime**
>
> A crime is **illegal** or **against the law**. A person who **commits** a crime is a **criminal**. There are different words for particular crimes and the people who commit them. A **murderer** commits **murder**. A **kidnapper kidnaps** sb. **Terrorists** use violence for political reasons and commit acts of **terrorism**. For example, they sometimes **hijack** planes. **Vandals** commit **vandalism**.
>
> It is the job of the police to **investigate** crimes and try to catch the criminal. If the police think sb may have committed a crime, that person is a **suspect**. When they have enough **evidence** the police can **arrest** and **charge** them **with** the crime. If the suspect **confesses** to the crime, they admit that they did it. If they **deny** the charge, they say that they did not do it.

⚷ **criminal**[1] /'krɪmɪnl/ adj. **1** [only before a noun] connected with crime: *Deliberate damage to public property is a **criminal offence**.* ◇ *criminal law* ▶ **przestępczy**, **karny 2** morally wrong: *a criminal waste of taxpayers' money* ▶ **skandaliczny**, **karygodny**
■ **criminally** /-nəli/ adv.: *criminally insane* ◇ *Not a single officer has been found criminally liable.* Żadnego z policjantów nie pociągnięto do odpowiedzialności karnej. ▶ **kryminalnie**; **karygodnie**

⚷ **criminal**[2] /'krɪmɪnl/ noun [C] a person who has done sth illegal ▶ **przestęp-ca/czyni**, **zbrodnia-rz/rka**

criminalize (also **-ise**) /'krɪmɪnəlaɪz/ verb [T] **1** to make sth illegal by passing a new law: *The use of opium was not criminalized until fairly recently.* ▶ **uznawać coś za niezgodne z prawem przez wprowadzenie nowych przepisów 2** to treat sb as a criminal: *Many gay people felt that they were being criminalized for having relationships.* ▶ **traktować kogoś jak przestępcę**
■ **criminalization** (also **-isation**) /ˌkrɪmɪnəlaɪ'zeɪʃn; US -lə'z-/ noun [U] ▶ **uznanie czegoś za niezgodne z prawem**; **traktowanie kogoś jak przestępcę**

crimson /'krɪmzn/ adj. of a dark red colour ▶ **karmazynowy** ➲ look at **maroon**, **scarlet**
■ **crimson** noun [U] ▶ **karmazyn**

cringe /krɪndʒ/ verb [I] **1** to move away from sb/sth because you are frightened: *The dog cringed in terror when the man raised his arm.* ▶ **kurczyć się**, **kulić się 2** to feel embarrassed: *awful family photographs which **make you cringe** in embarrassment* (wprawiają cię w zażenowanie) ▶ **odczuwać zażenowanie**

crinkle /'krɪŋkl/ verb [I,T] **crinkle (sth) (up)** to have, or to make sth have, thin folds or lines in it: *He crinkled the silver paper up into a ball.* ▶ **miąć (się)**, **marszczyć (się)**, **fałdować (się)** ➲ picture at **fold**
■ **crinkly** /'krɪŋkli/ adj.: *crinkly material* ▶ **marszczony**, **pofałdowany**

cripple[1] /'krɪpl/ verb [T] **1** to damage sb's body so that they are no longer able to walk or move normally ▶ **okaleczać** SYN **disable 2** to damage sth badly: *The recession has crippled the motor industry.* ▶ **paraliżować**, **(poważnie) nadwerężać**

cripple[2] /'krɪpl/ noun [C] (old-fashioned) a person who is unable to walk or move normally because of a disease or injury: (figurative) *He's an emotional cripple.* ▶ **kaleka**
ⓘ Obecnie słowo to jest często uważane za obraźliwe. Zamiast niego lepiej używać **disabled person**.

crippling /'krɪplɪŋ/ adj. that causes very great damage or has a very bad effect: *They had crippling debts and had to sell their house.* ▶ **paraliżujący**, **ciężki**

⚷ **crisis** /'kraɪsɪs/ noun [C,U] (pl. **crises** /-siːz/) a time of great danger or difficulty; the moment when things change and either improve or get worse: *the international crisis* caused by the invasion ◇ a friend you can rely on in times of crisis (w ciężkich czasach) ▶ **kryzys, przełom**

crisp¹ /krɪsp/ adj. **1** pleasantly hard and dry: *Store the biscuits in a tin to keep them crisp.* ▶ **chrupiący, świeży** **2** firm and fresh or new: *a crisp salad/apple* ◇ *a crisp* (szeleszczący) *new £10 note* ◇ *a crisp* (świeżo wyprasowana i (jak gdyby) wykrochmalona) *cotton dress* ▶ **chrupiący, świeży, nowy** **3** (used about the air or weather) cold and dry: *a crisp winter morning* ▶ **świeży, rześki** **4** (used about the way sb speaks) quick, clear but not very friendly: *a crisp reply* ▶ **oschły**
■ **crisply** adv.: *'I disagree,' she said crisply.* ▶ **oschle, cierpko** | **crispy** adj. (informal) = CRISP¹ (1,2)

crisp² /krɪsp/ (Brit. also **po,tato 'crisp**; US **chip**; **po'tato chip**) noun [C] a very thin piece of potato that is fried in oil, then dried and eaten cold. Crisps are sold in small plastic bags and usually have salt or another flavouring on them: *a packet of crisps* ▶ **chips**

crispbread /'krɪspbred/ noun [C,U] a thin crisp biscuit that is usually made from rye and often eaten with cheese ▶ **pieczywo chrupkie**

criss-cross /'krɪs krɒs/ adj. [only before a noun] with many straight lines that cross over each other: *a criss-cross pattern* ▶ **zygzakowaty, krzyżujący się**
■ **criss-cross** verb [I,T]: *Many footpaths criss-cross the countryside in Suffolk.* ▶ **(wielokrotnie) przecinać (się)**

criterion /kraɪ'tɪəriən/ noun [C] (pl. **criteria** /-riə/) the standard that you use when you make a decision or form an opinion about sb/sth: *What are the criteria for deciding who gets a place on the course?* ▶ **kryterium**

critic /'krɪtɪk/ noun [C] **1** a person whose job is to give their opinion about a play, film, book, work of art, etc.: *a film/restaurant/art critic* ▶ **krytyk** **2** a person who says what is bad or wrong with sb/sth: *He is a long-standing critic of the council's transport policy.* ▶ **krytyk**

critical /'krɪtɪkl/ adj. **1 critical (of sb/sth)** saying what is wrong with sb/sth: *The report was very critical of safety standards on the railways.* ▶ **krytyczny** (*np. o uwadze lub w odniesieniu do kogoś/czegoś*) **2** very important; at a time when things can suddenly become better or worse: *The talks between the two leaders have* ***reached a critical stage.*** ▶ **krytyczny, decydujący** **3** dangerous or serious: *The patient is* ***in a critical condition.*** ▶ **krytyczny** **4** [only before a noun] describing the good and bad points of a play, film, book, work of art, etc.: *a critical guide to this month's new films* ▶ **krytyczny**
■ **critically** /-kli/ adv.: *a critically ill patient* pacjent w stanie krytycznym ◇ *It was a critically important* (rozstrzygająca) *decision.* ▶ **krytycznie, poważnie**

criticism /'krɪtɪsɪzəm/ noun **1** [C,U] (an expression of) what you think is bad about sb/sth: *The council has come in for severe criticism* (jest ostro krytykowany) *over the plans.* ◇ *My main criticism* (głównym zarzutem) *is that it is too expensive.* ▶ **krytyka** **2** [U] the act of describing the good and bad points of a play, film, book, work of art, etc.: *literary criticism* ▶ **krytyka**

criticize (also -ise) /'krɪtɪsaɪz/ verb [I,T] **criticize (sb/sth) (for sth)** to say what is bad or wrong with sb/sth: *The doctor was criticized for not sending the patient to hospital.* ▶ **krytykować**

critique /krɪ'ti:k/ noun [C] a piece of writing that describes the good and bad points of sb/sth ▶ **krytyka, recenzja**

croak /krəʊk/ verb [I] to make a rough low sound like a **frog** ▶ **chrypieć**
■ **croak** noun [C] ▶ **rechot, chrypka**

crochet /'krəʊʃeɪ; US krəʊ'ʃ-/ noun [U] a way of making clothes, cloth, etc. by using wool or cotton and a needle with a hook at one end ▶ **szydełkowanie, robótka szydełkowa**
■ **crochet** verb [I,T] (pt, pp **crocheted** /-ʃeɪd/): *My granny crocheted me* (zrobiła mi na szydełku) *this scarf.* ▶ **szydełkować** ➲ look at **knit**

crockery /'krɒkəri/ noun [U] cups, plates and dishes ▶ **porcelana** (*stołowa i kuchenna*) ➲ look at **cutlery**

crocodile /'krɒkədaɪl/ noun [C] a large animal with a hard skin covered in scales, a long tail and a big mouth with sharp teeth. **Crocodiles** live in rivers and lakes in hot countries. ▶ **krokodyl** ➲ look at **alligator** ➲ picture on **page A11** **2** (Brit.) a line of children standing or walking in pairs ▶ **grupa dzieci ustawionych w szeregu lub idących parami**

crocus /'krəʊkəs/ noun [C] a small yellow, purple or white flower that grows in early spring ▶ **krokus**

croissant /'krwæsɒ̃; US krwɑ:'sɑ̃:; krə'sɑ:nt/ noun [C] a type of bread roll, shaped in a curve, that is often eaten with butter for breakfast ▶ **rogalik** ➲ picture at **bread**

crony /'krəʊni/ noun [C] (pl. **cronies**) (informal) (often used in a critical way) a friend ▶ **koleś**

crook /krʊk/ noun [C] **1** (informal) a dishonest person; a criminal ▶ **oszust/ka, przestęp-ca/czyni** **2** (**the crook of your arm/elbow**): the place where your arm bends at the elbow ▶ **zgięcie w łokciu**

crooked /'krʊkɪd/ adj. **1** not straight or even: *That picture is crooked.* ◇ *crooked teeth* ▶ **krzywy, zagięty** **2** (informal) not honest: *a crooked accountant* ▶ **nieuczciwy, sprzedajny**

croon /kru:n/ verb [I,T] to sing sth quietly and gently: *She gently crooned a lullaby.* ◇ *Bobby Darren was crooning 'Dream Lover'.* ▶ **nucić, śpiewać półgłosem**

crop¹ /krɒp/ noun **1** [C, usually pl.] plants that are grown on farms for food: *Rice and soya beans are the main crops here.* ▶ **zboże i inne uprawy** **2** [C] all the grain, fruit, vegetables, etc. of one type that are grown on a farm at one time: *a crop of apples* ◇ *Another year of* ***crop failure*** (nieurodzaju) *would mean starvation for many people.* ▶ **zbiór, plon** **3** [sing.] a number of people or things which have appeared at the same time: *the recent crop of movies about aliens* ▶ **masa, stos**

crop² /krɒp/ verb (**cropping**; **cropped**) **1** [T] to cut sth very short: *cropped hair* ▶ **strzyc na krótko, obcinać bardzo krótko** **2** [I] to produce a **crop¹** (2) ▶ **dawać plony**
PHR V **crop up** to appear suddenly, when you are not expecting it: *We should have finished this work yesterday but some problems cropped up.* ▶ **pojawiać się**

cropper /'krɒpə(r)/ noun
IDM **come a cropper** (informal) **1** to fall over or have an accident ▶ **przewracać się, upadać** **2** to fail ▶ **kończyć się fiaskiem/zawodem itp.**

croquet /'krəʊkeɪ; US -'keɪ/ noun [U] a game that you play on grass. When you play **croquet** you use **mallets** to hit balls through **hoops.** ▶ **krokiet**

cross¹ /krɒs/ noun **1** [C] a mark that you make by drawing one line across another (**x**). The sign is used for showing the position of sth, for showing that sth is not correct, etc.: *I drew a cross on the map to show where our house is.* ◇ *Incorrect answers were marked with a cross.* ▶ **krzyżyk** **2** (**the Cross**) [sing.] the cross that Jesus Christ died on, used as a symbol of Christianity ▶ **krzyż** ➲ look at **crucifix** **3** [usually sing.] **a cross (between A and B)** something (especially a plant or an animal) that is a mixture of two different types of thing: *a fruit which is a cross between a peach and an apple* ▶ **krzyżówka** **4** [C] (in sports such as football) a kick or hit of the ball that goes across the front of the goal: *Beckham's cross was headed into the goal by Heskey.* ▶ **dośrodkowanie** **5** [C] (formal) something that makes you unhappy or worried or that makes your life more difficult ▶ **brzemię, krzyż pański**
IDM **noughts and crosses** → NOUGHT

cross² /krɒs/ verb **1** [I,T] **cross (over) (from sth/to sth)** to go from one side of sth to the other: *to cross the road* ◇ *We crossed from Dover to Calais.* ◇ *I waved and she crossed over.* ▶ **przechodzić (przez), przejeżdżać, przekraczać** (*np. granicę*) **2** [I] (used about lines, roads, etc.) to pass across each other: *The two roads cross just north of the village.* ▶ **przecinać się; rozmijać się 3** [T] to put sth across or over sth else: *to cross your arms* ▶ **zakładać** (*np. nogę na nogę, ręce na piersiach*) **4** [T] to make sb angry by refusing to do what they want you to do: *He's an important man. It could be dangerous to cross him.* ▶ **sprzeciwiać się komuś 5** [T] **cross sth with sth** to produce a new type of plant or animal by mixing two different types ▶ **krzyżować 6** [I,T] (in sports such as football and **hockey**) to pass the ball across the front of the goal: *Owen crossed the ball for Cole to head into the goal.* ▶ **dośrodkowywać** (*piłkę*) **7** [T] **cross yourself** to make the sign of a cross in front of your face and chest as a symbol of the Christian religion ▶ **przeżegnać się**
IDM **cross my heart (and hope to die)** (informal) (used for emphasizing that what you are saying is true): *I won't tell a soul. Cross my heart!* ▶ **jak Boga kocham!**
cross/fold your arms → ARM¹
cross your fingers; keep your fingers crossed → FINGER¹
cross your mind (used about a thought, idea, etc.) to come into your mind: *It never once crossed my mind that she was lying.* ▶ **przychodzić do głowy/na myśl**
PHR V **cross sth off (sth)** to remove sth from a list, etc. by drawing a line through it: *Cross Dave's name off the guest list – he can't come.* ▶ **skreślać coś z czegoś**
cross sth out to draw a line through sth that you have written because you have made a mistake, etc.: *to cross out a spelling mistake* ▶ **skreślać** (*np. z listy*)

cross³ /krɒs/ adj. (informal) **cross (with sb) (about sth)** angry or annoyed: *I was really cross with her for leaving me with all the work.* ▶ **zły (na kogoś)** ℹ **Cross** jest słowem bardziej potocznym niż **angry**.
■ **crossly** adv.: *'Be quiet,' Dad said crossly.* ▶ **ze złością, z irytacją**

crossbar /ˈkrɒsbɑː(r)/ noun [C] **1** the piece of wood over the top of a goal in football, etc. ▶ **poprzeczka 2** the metal bar that joins the front and back of a bicycle ▶ **rama** ➲ picture at **bicycle**

ˌcross-ˈcountry adj. across fields and natural land; not using roads or tracks: *cross-country running/skiing* ▶ **przełajowy**
■ **ˌcross-ˈcountry** adv.: *We walked 10 miles cross-country before we saw a village.* ▶ **na przełaj**

ˌcross-eˈxamine verb [T] to ask sb questions in a court of law, etc. in order to find out the truth about sth ▶ **przesłuchiwać, brać w krzyżowy ogień pytań**
■ **ˌcross-eˌxamiˈnation** noun [C,U] ▶ **przesłuchanie** (*biorąc kogoś w krzyżowy ogień pytań*)

ˈcross-eyed adj. having one or both your eyes looking towards your nose ▶ **zezowaty**

crossfire /ˈkrɒsfaɪə(r)/ noun [U] a situation in which guns are being fired from two or more different directions: *The journalist was killed in crossfire* (podczas strzelaniny). ◇ (figurative) *When my parents argued, I sometimes got **caught in the crossfire*** (znajdowałam się między młotem a kowadłem). ▶ **ogień krzyżowy**

crossing /ˈkrɒsɪŋ/ noun [C] **1** a place where you can cross over sth: *You should cross the road at the pedestrian crossing.* ◇ *a border crossing* ▶ **przejście 2** a journey from one side of a sea or river to the other: *We had a rough crossing.* ▶ **przeprawa, podróż morska 3** a place where roads or railway lines cross each other ▶ **przejazd** (*np. kolejowy*) ➲ look at **level crossing**

cross-legged /ˌkrɒs ˈlegd; -ˈlegɪd/ adv., adj. sitting on the floor with your legs pulled up in front of you and with one leg or foot over the other: *to sit cross-legged* ▶ (*siedzieć*) **po turecku**

cross-legged

cross-legged

with her legs crossed

ˌcross ˈpurposes noun
IDM **be/talk at cross purposes** (used about more than one person) to be confused because you are talking about different things but think you are talking about the same thing: *I think we've been talking at cross purposes* (nie rozumiemy się). *You mean next Saturday but I'm talking about this one.* ▶ **nie rozumieć się nawzajem**

ˌcross ˈreference noun [C] a note in a book that tells you to look in another place in the book for more information ▶ **odnośnik, odsyłacz**

crossroads /ˈkrɒsrəʊdz/ noun [C] (pl. **crossroads**) a place where two or more roads cross each other: *When you come to the next crossroads turn right.* ▶ **skrzyżowanie**

ˈcross section noun [C] **1** a picture of what the inside of sth would look like if you cut through it: *a cross section of the human brain* ▶ **przekrój 2** a number of people, etc. that come from the different parts of a group, and so can be considered to represent the whole group: *The families we studied were chosen to represent a cross section of society.* ▶ **przekrój**

crosswalk (US) = PEDESTRIAN CROSSING

crossword /ˈkrɒswɜːd/ (also **ˈcrossword puzzle**) noun [C] a word game in which you have to write the answers to **clues** in square spaces, which are arranged in a pattern: *Every morning I try to **do the crossword** in the newspaper.* ▶ **krzyżówka**

crotch /krɒtʃ/ (also **crutch**) noun [C] the place where your legs, or the legs of a pair of trousers, join at the top ▶ **krocze**

crotchet /ˈkrɒtʃɪt/ (US **ˈquarter note**) noun [C] (used in music) a type of note ▶ **ćwierćnuta** ➲ picture at **music**

crouch /kraʊtʃ/ verb [I] **crouch (down)** to bend your legs and body so that you are close to the ground: *He crouched down behind the sofa.* ◇ *The cat crouched* (gotował się do skoku) *in front of the hole waiting for the mouse to appear.* ▶ **przykucać, przycupnąć** ➲ picture at **kneel**

crow¹ /krəʊ/ noun [C] a large black bird that makes a loud noise ▶ **wrona**
IDM **as the crow flies** (used for describing distances) in a straight line ▶ **w linii powietrznej**

crow² /krəʊ/ verb [I] **1** to make a loud noise like a **cock** ▶ **piać 2** (informal) to speak in a very proud way about sth ▶ **tokować, przechwalać się** SYN **boast**

crowbar /ˈkrəʊbɑː(r)/ noun [C] a long iron bar that is used for forcing sth open ▶ **łom**

crowd¹ /kraʊd/ noun **1** [C, with sing. or pl. verb] a large number of people in one place: *The crowd was/were extremely noisy.* ◇ *He pushed his way through the crowd.* ▶ **tłum**

2 [C, with sing. or pl. verb] (informal) a group of people who know each other: *John, Linda and Barry will be there – all the usual crowd.* ▶ **paczka 3 (the crowd)** [sing.] ordinary people: *to follow the crowd* naśladować innych ◇ *He wears weird clothes because he wants to* ***stand out from the crowd*** (wyróżniać się). ▶ **tłum**

crowd² /kraʊd/ verb [T] (used about a lot of people) to fill an area: *Groups of tourists crowded the main streets.* ◇ (figurative) *Memories crowded her mind.* ▶ **wypełniać, przepełniać**

PHR V **crowd around/round (sb)** (used about a lot of people) to stand in a large group around sb/sth: *Fans crowded round the singer hoping to get his autograph.* ▶ **tłoczyć się wokół (kogoś)**

crowd into sth; crowd in to go into a small place and make it very full: *Somehow we all crowded into their small living room.* ▶ **wciskać/wpychać się dokądś**

crowd sb/sth into sth; crowd sb/sth in to put a lot of people into a small place: *Ten prisoners were crowded into one small cell.* ▶ **wciskać/wpychać kogoś/coś dokądś/w coś**

crowd sth out; crowd sb out (of sth) to completely fill a place so that nobody else can enter: *Students crowd out the cafe at lunchtimes.* ◇ *Smaller companies are being crowded out* (są wypierane) *of the market.* ▶ **zapełniać coś kimś**

⚷ **crowded** /ˈkraʊdɪd/ adj. full of people: *The town was crowded with* (było pełne) *Christmas shoppers.* ◇ *a crowded bus* ◇ *people living in poor and crowded conditions* ▶ **zatłoczony, przeludniony**

⚷ **crown¹** /kraʊn/ noun **1** [C] a circle made of gold and **jewels**, that a king or queen wears on his or her head on official occasions: *the crown jewels* klejnoty koronne ▶ **korona 2 (the Crown)** [sing.] the state as represented by a king or queen: *an area of land belonging to the Crown* ▶ **Korona** (*monarchia*) **3** [sing.] the top of your head or of a hat ▶ **ciemię; denko** (*kapelusza*) **4** [sing.] the top of a hill ▶ **szczyt** (*góry*)

crown² /kraʊn/ verb [T] **1** to put a **crown** on the head of a new king or queen in an official ceremony: *Elizabeth was crowned in 1952.* ◇ (figurative) *the newly crowned British champion* ▶ **koronować 2** [often passive] **crown sth (with sth)** to have or put sth on the top of sth: *The mountain was crowned with snow.* ◇ (figurative) *Her years of hard work were finally crowned with success.* ▶ **wieńczyć**

IDM **to crown it all** to be the last in a number of lucky or unlucky events ▶ **na dodatek, na domiar złego**

crowning /ˈkraʊnɪŋ/ adj. [only before a noun] the best or most important: *Winning the World Championship was the crowning moment of her career.* ▶ **szczytowy**

ˌCrown ˈprince, ˌCrown prinˈcess noun [C] the person who has the right to become the next king or queen ▶ **następ-ca/czyni tronu**

⚷ **crucial** /ˈkruːʃl/ adj. **crucial (to/for sth)** extremely important: *Early diagnosis of the illness is crucial for successful treatment.* ▶ **decydujący, przełomowy** SYN **vital**

■ **crucially** /-ʃəli/ adv. ▶ **decydująco, przełomowo**

crucible /ˈkruːsɪbl/ noun [C] a pot in which substances are heated to high temperatures, metals are melted, etc. ▶ **tygiel** ➲ picture at **laboratory**

crucifix /ˈkruːsəfɪks/ noun [C] a small model of a cross with a figure of Jesus on it ▶ **krucyfiks**

crucifixion /ˌkruːsəˈfɪkʃn/ noun [C,U] the act of **crucifying** sb: *the Crucifixion of Christ* ▶ **ukrzyżowanie**

crucify /ˈkruːsɪfaɪ/ verb [T] (**crucifying; crucifies**; pt, pp **crucified**) to kill sb by fastening them to a cross ▶ **ukrzyżować**

cruddy /ˈkrʌdi/ adj. (**cruddier; cruddiest**) (informal) (especially US) bad, dirty, or of low quality: *We got really cruddy service in that restaurant last time.* ▶ **paskudny, obrzydliwy**

crude /kruːd/ adj. **1** simple and basic, without much detail, skill, etc.: *The method was crude but very effective.* ◇ *She explained how the system worked* ***in crude terms.*** W bardzo prosty sposób wytłumaczyła, jak ten system działa. ◇ *The paintings seem to be crude representations* (niezdarnym wizerunkiem) *of animals.* ▶ **prymitywny, toporny 2** referring to sex or the body in a way that would offend many people: *He's always telling crude jokes* (słone dowcipy). ▶ **grubiański, obraźliwy 3** in its natural state, before it has been treated with chemicals: *crude oil* ropa naftowa ▶ **surowy, nieoczyszczony**

■ **crudely** adv.: *a crudely drawn face* ▶ **prymitywnie; niedelikatnie**

crudity /ˈkruːdəti/ noun [U,C] (pl. **crudities**) the fact of being **crude**; an example of sth **crude**: *Despite the crudity of their methods and equipment, the experiment was a considerable success.* ◇ *The crudity of her language shocked him.* ▶ **prymitywność; grubiańskość**

⚷ **cruel** /kruːəl/ adj. (**crueller; cruellest**) causing physical or mental pain or suffering to sb/sth: *I think it's cruel to keep animals in cages.* ▶ **okrutny, srogi** OPP **kind**

■ **cruelly** /ˈkruːəli/ adv. ▶ **okrutnie**

cruelty /ˈkruːəlti/ noun (pl. **cruelties**) **1** [U] **cruelty (to sb/sth)** cruel behaviour: *cruelty to children* ▶ **okrucieństwo (wobec kogoś)** OPP **kindness 2** [C, usually pl.] a cruel act: *the cruelties of war* ▶ **okrucieństwo**

cruise¹ /kruːz/ noun [C] a holiday in which you travel on a ship and visit a number of different places: *They're planning to* ***go on a cruise.*** ▶ **rejs, wycieczka morska** ➲ note at **journey, holiday**

cruise² /kruːz/ verb [I] **1** to travel by boat, visiting a number of places, as a holiday: *to cruise around the Caribbean* ▶ **żeglować 2** to stay at the same speed in a car, plane, etc.: *cruising at 80 kilometres an hour* ▶ **jechać z jednakową prędkością, krążyć**

cruiser /ˈkruːzə(r)/ noun [C] **1** a large fast ship used in a war ▶ **krążownik 2** a motorboat which has room for people to sleep in it ▶ **łódź motorowa z kabiną** ➲ picture at **boat**

crumb /krʌm/ noun [C] a very small piece of bread, cake or biscuit ▶ **okruch**

crumble /ˈkrʌmbl/ verb [I,T] **crumble (sth) (up)** to break or make sth break into very small pieces: *The walls of the church are beginning to crumble.* ◇ *We crumbled up the bread and threw it to the birds.* ◇ (figurative) *Support for the government is beginning to crumble.* ▶ **kruszyć (się), rozpadać się**

■ **crumbly** /ˈkrʌmbli/ adj.: *This cheese has a crumbly texture* (rozsypuje się). ▶ **kruchy, rozpadający się**

crummy /ˈkrʌmi/ adj. (**crummier; crummiest**) bad or unpleasant ▶ **lichy, tandetny**

crumpet /ˈkrʌmpət/ noun (Brit.) [C] a flat round type of small cake with holes in the top that you eat hot with butter on it ▶ **rodzaj naleśnika**

crumple /ˈkrʌmpl/ verb [I,T] **crumple (sth) (into sth); crumple (sth) (up)** to be pressed or to press sth into an untidy shape: *The front of the car crumpled when it hit the wall.* ◇ *She crumpled the letter into a ball and threw it away.* ▶ **miąć (się), gnieść (się)** ➲ picture at **fold**

crunch¹ /krʌntʃ/ noun [sing.] an act or noise of **crunching**: *There was a loud crunch as he sat on the box of eggs.* ▶ **chrzęst, skrzypienie**

IDM **if/when it comes to the crunch; if/when the crunch comes** if/when you are in a difficult situation and must make a difficult decision: *If it comes to the crunch, I'll stay and fight.* ▶ **jak przyjdzie co do czego**

crunch² /krʌntʃ/ verb **1** [T] **crunch sth (up)** to make a loud noise when you are eating sth hard: *to crunch an apple* ▶ **chrupać 2** [I] to make a loud noise like the sound of

sth being crushed: *We crunched through the snow.* ▶ **chrzęścić, skrzypieć**
■ **crunchy** adj.: *a crunchy apple* ▶ **chrupiący**

crusade /kruːˈseɪd/ noun [C] **1** a fight for sth that you believe to be good or against sth that you believe to be bad: *Mr Khan is leading a crusade against drugs in his neighbourhood.* ▶ **krucjata** SYN **campaign** **2** (**Crusade**) one of the wars fought in Palestine by European Christians against Muslims in the Middle Ages ▶ **wojna krzyżowa**
■ **crusader** noun [C] ▶ **krzyżowiec**

crush¹ /krʌʃ/ verb [T] **1** to press sb/sth hard so that he/she/it is broken, damaged or injured: *Most of the eggs got crushed when she sat on them.* ◇ *He was crushed to death by a lorry.* ▶ **gnieść, miażdżyć** **2 crush sth (up)** to break sth into very small pieces or a powder: *Crush the garlic and fry in oil.* ▶ **rozgniatać** **3** to defeat sb/sth completely: *The army was quickly sent in to crush the rebellion.* ▶ **tłumić, dławić**
PHR V **crush (sb/sth) into, past, through, etc. sth** (to cause sb/sth) to move into, past, through, etc. a place by pushing or pressing ▶ **wciskać kogoś/coś do czegoś; tłoczyć się do czegoś/w coś**

crush² /krʌʃ/ noun **1** [sing.] a large group of people in a small space: *There was such a crush that I couldn't get near the bar.* ▶ **tłok, ścisk** **2** [C] (informal) **a crush (on sb)** a strong feeling of love for sb that only usually lasts for a short time: *Maria **had a** huge **crush*** (podkochiwała się w) *on her teacher.* ▶ **zakochanie (się)**

crushing /ˈkrʌʃɪŋ/ adj. [only before a noun] that defeats sb/sth completely; very bad: *a crushing defeat* ▶ **druzgocący, miażdżący**

crust /krʌst/ noun [C,U] **1** the hard part on the outside of a piece of bread, a **pie**, etc. ▶ **skórka** ➲ picture at **bread** **2** a hard layer on the outside of sth: *the earth's crust* ▶ **skorupa**

crusty /ˈkrʌsti/ adj. (**crustier**; **crustiest**) **1** (used about food) having a hard part on the outside: *crusty bread* ▶ **chrupiący** **2** (informal) bad-tempered and impatient: *a crusty old man* ▶ **zrzędny, gderliwy**

crutch /krʌtʃ/ noun [C] **1** a type of stick that you put under your arm to help you walk when you have hurt your leg or foot: *She was **on crutches** for two months after she broke her ankle.* ▶ **kula** ➲ look at **walking stick** **2** = CROTCH

crux /krʌks/ noun [sing.] the most important or difficult part of a problem: *The **crux of the matter** is how to stop this from happening again.* ▶ **sedno**

cry¹ /kraɪ/ verb (**crying**; **cries**; pt, pp **cried**) **1** [I] to make a noise and produce tears in your eyes, for example because you are unhappy or have hurt yourself: *The baby never stops crying.* ◇ *The child was crying for her mother.* ◇ *She cried herself to sleep* (płakała, aż sen ją zmorzył) *every night after her father died.* ◇ *They were crying with cold and hunger* (z zimna i głodu). ▶ **płakać** **2** [I,T] **cry (out)** to shout or make a loud noise: *We could hear someone crying for help.* ◇ *'Look,' he cried, 'There they are.'* ◇ *to cry out in pain* (z bólu) ▶ **krzyczeć**
IDM **cry your eyes out** to cry a lot for a long time ▶ **wypłakiwać oczy**
a shoulder to cry on → SHOULDER¹
PHR V **cry out for sth** to need sth very much: *Birmingham is crying out for a new transport system.* ▶ **(aż) się prosić o coś, domagać się czegoś**

cry² /kraɪ/ noun (pl. **cries**) **1** [C] a shout or loud high noise: *the cries of the children in the playground* ◇ *We heard Adam give a cry of pain as the dog bit him.* ◇ (figurative) *Her suicide attempt was really **a cry for help*** (wołaniem o pomoc). ▶ **krzyk** **2** [sing.] an act of **crying¹** (1): *After a good cry* (jak się wypłakałam) *I felt much better.* ▶ **płacz**
IDM **a far cry from sth/from doing sth** → FAR¹
hue and cry → HUE

crying /ˈkraɪɪŋ/ adj. [only before a noun] (used to talk about a bad situation) very great: *There's a crying need for more doctors.* ◇ *It's **a crying shame*** (wielka szkoda) *that so many young people can't find jobs.* ▶ **krzyczący, pilny, naglący**

crypt /krɪpt/ noun [C] a room that is under a church, where people were sometimes buried in the past ▶ **krypta**

cryptic /ˈkrɪptɪk/ adj. having a hidden meaning that is not easy to understand: *a cryptic message/remark/smile* ▶ **tajemniczy, zagadkowy** SYN **mysterious**
■ **cryptically** /-kli/ adv. ▶ **tajemniczo, zagadkowo**

crystal /ˈkrɪstl/ noun **1** [C] a regular shape that some mineral substances form when they become solid: *salt crystals* ▶ **kryształ** **2** [U] a clear mineral that can be used in making jewellery ▶ **kryształ** **3** [U] glass of very high quality: *a crystal vase* ▶ **kryształ**

ˌcrystal ˈball noun [C] a glass ball in which some people say you can see what will happen in the future ▶ **kryształowa kula**

ˌcrystal ˈclear adj. **1** (used about water, glass, etc.) that you can see through perfectly ▶ **krystalicznie czysty** **2** very easy to understand: *The meaning is crystal clear.* ▶ **jasny jak słońce**

crystallize (also **-ise**) /ˈkrɪstəlaɪz/ verb [I,T] **1** (used about thoughts, plans, etc.) to become or to make clear and fixed: *Our ideas began to crystallize into a definite plan.* ◇ *The final chapter crystallizes all the main issues.* ▶ (*przen.*) **krystalizować się** **2** (technical) to form or to make sth form into **crystals**: *The salt crystallizes as the water evaporates.* ▶ **krystalizować się**

cu. = CUBIC: *a volume of 3 cu. ft*

cub /kʌb/ noun **1** [C] a young animal, for example a bear, lion, etc. ▶ **młode lisa/niedźwiedzia/lwa/tygrysa/wilka** ➲ note at **fox** **2** (**the Cubs**) [pl.] the part of the Boy Scout organization that is for younger boys ▶ **organizacja skautowska dla młodszych chłopców** (*podobna do zuchów*) **3** (**Cub**) (also **Cub ˈScout**) [C] a member of the **Cubs** ▶ **zuch, skaut**

cube¹ /kjuːb/ noun [C] **1** a solid shape that has six equal square sides ▶ **sześcian** **2** the number that you get if you multiply a number by itself twice: *The cube of 5 is 125* (= 5 x 5 x 5). ◇ *The cube root* (pierwiastek trzeciego stopnia) *of 64 is 4.* ▶ **trzecia potęga**

cube² /kjuːb/ verb [T, usually passive] to multiply a number by itself twice: *Four cubed is 64* (= 4 x 4 x 4). ▶ **podnosić do trzeciej potęgi**

cubic /ˈkjuːbɪk/ adj. [only before a noun] (abbr. **cu.**) (used to show that a measurement is the **volume** of sth, that is the height multiplied by the length and the width) ▶ **sześcienny**

cubicle /ˈkjuːbɪkl/ noun [C] a small room that is made by separating off part of a larger room ▶ **kabina**

Cub ˈScout = CUB (3)

cuckoo /ˈkʊkuː/ noun [C] (pl. **cuckoos**) a bird which makes a sound like its name and which leaves its eggs in another bird's nest ▶ **kukułka**

cucumber /ˈkjuːkʌmbə(r)/ noun [C,U] a long, thin vegetable with a dark green skin that does not need to be cooked ▶ **ogórek** ➲ look at **gherkin**, **pickle** ➲ picture on **page A13**, picture at **salad**

cuddle /ˈkʌdl/ verb [I,T] to hold sb/sth closely in your arms: *The little girl was cuddling her favourite doll.* ▶ **przytulać się**
■ **cuddle** noun [C]: *He gave the child a cuddle* (przytulił dziecko) *and kissed her goodnight.* ▶ **przytulenie**
PHR V **cuddle up (to/against sb/sth)**; **cuddle up (together)** to move close to sb and sit or lie in a comfortable

C

position: *They cuddled up together for warmth.* ▶ **przytulać (się)**

cuddly /ˈkʌdli/ adj. (**cuddlier**; **cuddliest**) soft and pleasant to hold close to you: *a cuddly toy* ▶ **wywołujący chęć przytulenia**

cue /kjuː/ noun [C] **1** a word or movement that is the signal for sb else to say or do sth, especially in a play: *When Julia puts the tray on the table, that's your cue to come on stage.* ▶ **sygnał 2** a long, thin wooden stick used to hit the ball in the games of **snooker**, **billiards** or **pool** ▶ **kij** (*np. bilardowy*)

IDM **(right) on cue** at exactly the moment expected ▶ **jak na zawołanie**

take your cue from sb/sth to copy what sb else does as an example of how to behave or what to do: *I wasn't sure how to behave at a Japanese wedding, so I took my cue from my hosts.* ▶ **brać przykład z kogoś/czegoś, naśladować kogoś/coś**

cuff¹ /kʌf/ noun [C] **1** the end part of a sleeve, which often fastens at the wrist ▶ **mankiet** ➲ picture on **page A1** **2** (**cuffs**) [pl.] = HANDCUFFS **3** a light hit with the open hand ▶ **szturchaniec, trzepnięcie**

IDM **off the cuff** (used about sth you say) without thought or preparation before that moment: *I haven't got the figures here, but, off the cuff, I'd say the rise is about 10%.* ▶ **z głowy, bez przygotowania**

cuff² /kʌf/ verb [T] to hit sth (especially sb's head) lightly with your open hand

cufflink /ˈkʌflɪŋk/ noun [C, usually pl.] one of a pair of small objects used instead of a button to fasten a shirt sleeve together at the wrist ▶ **spinka do mankietów**

cuisine /kwɪˈziːn/ noun [U] the style of cooking of a particular country, restaurant, etc.: *Italian cuisine* ▶ **kuchnia** ❶ Mniej formalne słowo to **cooking**.

cul-de-sac /ˈkʌl də sæk/ noun [C] (pl. **cul-de-sacs**) a street that is closed at one end ▶ **ślepa uliczka**

culinary /ˈkʌlɪnəri; US -neri/ adj. [only before a noun] (formal) connected with cooking ▶ **kulinarny**

cull¹ /kʌl/ verb [T] to kill a number of animals in a group to prevent the group from becoming too large ▶ **odstrzeliwać (selektywnie)**

PHR V **cull sth from sth** to collect information, ideas, etc., from different places: *I managed to cull some useful addresses from the Internet.* ▶ **zbierać/wybierać coś z czegoś/skądś**

cull² /kʌl/ noun [C] the act of killing some animals in order to stop a group becoming too large: *a deer cull* ▶ **odstrzał/ubój selektywny**

culminate /ˈkʌlmɪneɪt/ verb [I] (formal) **culminate in sth** to reach a final result: *The team's efforts culminated in victory* (doprowadziły do zwycięstwa) *in the national championships.* ▶ **osiągnąć szczyt w czymś, kończyć się czymś**

■ **culmination** /ˌkʌlmɪˈneɪʃn/ noun [sing.]: *The joint space mission was the culmination of years of research.* ▶ **punkt kulminacyjny**

culpable /ˈkʌlpəbl/ adj. (formal) responsible for sth bad that has happened ▶ **winny**; **karygodny**

culprit /ˈkʌlprɪt/ noun [C] a person who has done sth wrong ▶ **winowaj-ca/czyni**

cult /kʌlt/ noun [C] **1** a person or thing that has become popular with a particular group of people: *cult movies* ▶ **przedmiot kultu 2** a type of religion or religious group, especially one that is considered unusual ▶ **kult**

cultivate /ˈkʌltɪveɪt/ verb [T] **1** to prepare and use land for growing plants for food or to sell: *to cultivate the soil* ▶ **uprawiać 2** to grow plants for food or to sell: *Olives have been cultivated for centuries in Mediterranean countries.* ▶ **uprawiać 3** to try hard to develop a friendship with sb: *He cultivated links with colleagues abroad.* ▶ **pielęgnować 4** to try to form a friendship with sb who could be useful to you ▶ **zaskarbiać sobie** (*czyjeś względy*)

■ **cultivation** /ˌkʌltɪˈveɪʃn/ noun [U] ▶ **uprawa**; **pielęgnowanie**; **zaskarbianie sobie względów**

cultivated /ˈkʌltɪveɪtɪd/ adj. **1** well educated, with good manners ▶ **kulturalny 2** (used about land) used for growing plants for food or to sell ▶ **uprawny 3** (used about plants) grown on a farm, not wild ▶ **uprawny**

🔑 **cultural** /ˈkʌltʃərəl/ adj. **1** connected with the customs, ideas, beliefs, etc. of a society or country: *The country's cultural diversity is a result of taking in immigrants from all over the world.* ▶ **kulturowy** ➲ look at **multicultural** **2** connected with art, music, literature, etc.: *The city has a rich cultural life, with many theatres, concert halls and art galleries.* ▶ **kulturalny**

■ **culturally** /-rəli/ adv. ▶ **kulturowo**; **kulturalnie**

🔑 **culture** /ˈkʌltʃə(r)/ noun **1** [C,U] the customs, ideas, beliefs, etc. of a particular society, country, etc.: *the language and culture of the Aztecs* ◇ *people from many different cultures* ▶ **kultura 2** [U] art, literature, music, etc.: *London has always been a centre of culture.* ◇ *a man/woman of culture* światł-y/a mężczyzna/kobieta ▶ **kultura 3** [U] the growing of plants or the keeping of certain types of animals ▶ **uprawa, hodowla**

cultured /ˈkʌltʃəd/ adj. well educated and showing a good knowledge of art, music, literature, etc. ▶ **światły, wyszukany, wyrafinowany**

ˈ**culture shock** noun [U] a feeling of confusion, etc. that you may have when you go to live in or visit a country that is very different from your own ▶ **szok kulturowy**

cum /kʌm/ prep. (used for joining two nouns together) also used as; as well as: *a bedroom-cum-study* sypialnia i pokój do pracy (w jednym pomieszczeniu) ▶ **także używany jako coś**; **razem z czymś**

cumbersome /ˈkʌmbəsəm/ adj. **1** heavy and difficult to carry, use, wear, etc. ▶ **nieporęczny 2** (used about a system, etc.) slow and complicated: *cumbersome legal procedures* ▶ **uciążliwy**

cumin /ˈkɒmɪn/ noun [U] the dried seeds of the **cumin** plant, used in cooking as a spice ▶ **kmin(ek)** ➲ look at **caraway**

cumulative /ˈkjuːmjələtɪv; US -leɪt-/ adj. increasing steadily in amount, degree, etc.: *a cumulative effect* ▶ **kumulacyjny, narastający**

cunning /ˈkʌnɪŋ/ adj. clever in a dishonest or bad way: *He was as cunning as a fox.* ◇ *a cunning trick* ▶ **przebiegły, chytry** SYN **sly, wily**

■ **cunning** noun [U] ▶ **przebiegłość, chytrość** | **cunningly** adv. ▶ **przebiegle, chytrze**

🔑 **cup¹** /kʌp/ noun [C] **1** a small container usually with a handle, used for drinking liquids: *a teacup* ◇ *a cup of coffee* ▶ **filiżanka 2** an object shaped like a cup: *an egg cup* kieliszek do jajek **3** (in sport) a large metal cup given as a prize; the competition for such a cup: *Our team won the cup in the basketball tournament.* ◇ *the World Cup* ▶ **puchar** ➲ picture at **medal**

IDM **not sb's cup of tea** not what sb likes or is interested in: *Horror films aren't my cup of tea.* ▶ **nie być w czyimś guście**

cup² /kʌp/ verb [T] (**cupping**; **cupped**) to form sth, especially your hands, into the shape of a cup; to hold sth with your hands shaped like a cup: *I cupped my hands to take a drink from the stream.* ◇ *to cup your chin in your hands* opierać brodę na dłoniach ▶ **składać w kształt miseczki**; **ujmować** (*w dłoń*)

🔑 **cupboard** /ˈkʌbəd/ noun [C] a piece of furniture, usually with shelves inside and a door or doors at the front, used for storing food, clothes, etc. ▶ **szafa, szafka**

cupful /ˈkʌpfʊl/ noun [C] the amount that a cup will hold: *two cupfuls of water* ▶ **pełna filiżanka (czegoś)**

curable /ˈkjʊərəbl/ adj. (used about a disease) that can be made better ▶ **uleczalny** OPP **incurable**

curate /ˈkjʊərət/ noun [C] a priest at a low level in the Church of England, who helps a more senior priest ▶ **wikary**

curator /kjʊəˈreɪtə(r)/ noun [C] a person whose job is to look after the things that are kept in a museum ▶ **kustosz/ka**

curb¹ /kɜːb/ verb [T] to limit or control sth, especially sth bad: *He needs to learn to curb his anger.* ▶ **hamować, ograniczać**

curb² /kɜːb/ noun [C] **1 a curb (on sth)** a control or limit on sth: *a curb on local government spending* ▶ **hamulec, ograniczenie 2** (especially US) = KERB

curd /kɜːd/ noun [U] (also [pl.] **curds**) a thick soft substance formed when milk turns sour, used in making cheese ▶ **zsiadłe mleko**

curdle /ˈkɜːdl/ verb [I,T] (used about liquids) to turn sour or to separate into different parts; to make sth do this: *I've curdled the sauce.* Sos mi się zwarzył. ◇ (figurative) *The scream made her blood curdle* (ściął jej krew w żyłach). ▶ **warzyć się, zsiadać się** ➲ look at **blood-curdling**

cure¹ /kjʊə(r)/ verb [T] **1 cure sb (of sth)** to make sb healthy again after an illness: *The treatment cured him of cancer.* ▶ **wyleczyć, uzdrawiać 2** to make an illness, injury, etc. end or disappear: *It is still not possible to cure the common cold.* ◇ (figurative) *The plumber cured* (rozwiązał) *the problem with the central heating.* ▶ **wyleczyć 3** to make certain types of food last longer by drying them, or treating them with smoke or salt: *cured ham* ▶ **konserwować**

cure² /kjʊə(r)/ noun [C] **a cure (for sth) 1** a medicine or treatment that can cure an illness, etc.: *There is no cure for this illness.* ▶ **lek 2** a return to good health; the process of being cured: *The new drug brought about a miraculous cure.* ▶ **wyleczenie, uzdrowienie**

curfew /ˈkɜːfjuː/ noun [C] **1** a time after which people are not allowed to go outside their homes, for example during a war: *The government imposed a dusk-to-dawn curfew.* ▶ **godzina policyjna 2** (US) a time when children must arrive home in the evening: *She has a 10 o'clock curfew.* ▶ **obowiązkowa godzina powrotu dzieci do domu**

curiosity /ˌkjʊəriˈɒsəti/ noun (pl. **curiosities**) **1** [U] a desire to know or learn: *I was full of curiosity about their plans.* ◇ ***Out of curiosity**, he opened her letter.* ▶ **ciekawość, zaciekawienie 2** [C] an unusual and interesting person or thing: *The museum was full of historical curiosities.* ▶ **osobliwość, ciekawostka**

curious /ˈkjʊəriəs/ adj. **1 curious (about sth)**; **curious (to do sth)** wanting to know or learn sth: *They were very curious about the people who lived upstairs.* ◇ *He was curious to know how the machine worked.* ▶ **ciekawy, zaciekawiony 2** unusual or strange: *It was curious that she didn't tell anyone about the incident.* ▶ **dziwny, osobliwy 3** too interested in other people's affairs: *Don't be so curious – it's got nothing to do with you.* ▶ **ciekawski**
■ **curiously** adv.: *Curiously enough* (co ciekawe), *we discovered that we had exactly the same name.* ▶ **dziwnie, osobliwie**

curl¹ /kɜːl/ verb **1** [I,T] to form or to make sth form into a curved or round shape: *Does your hair curl naturally?* ◇ *He curled his lip* (wykrzywił usta) *and laughed scornfully.* ▶ **kręcić (się), zawijać (się) 2** [I] to move round in a curve: *The snake curled around his arm.* ◇ *Smoke curled up into the sky.* Spirala dymu unosiła się ku niebu. ▶ **wić się**

PHR V **curl up** to pull your arms, legs and head close to your body: *The cat curled up in front of the fire.* ▶ **zwijać się w kłębek**

curl² /kɜːl/ noun [C] **1** a piece of hair that curves round: *Her hair fell in curls round her face.* ▶ **lok 2** a thing that has a curved round shape: *a curl* (kłąb) *of blue smoke* ▶ **zwój, spirala**

curler /ˈkɜːlə(r)/ noun [C] a small plastic or metal tube that you roll your hair around in order to make it curly ▶ **lokówka, papilot**

curly /ˈkɜːli/ adj. (**curlier**; **curliest**) full of **curls**; shaped like a **curl**: *curly hair* ▶ **kręcony, wijący się** OPP **straight** ➲ picture at **hair**

currant /ˈkʌrənt; US ˈkɜːr-/ noun [C] **1** a very small dried **grape** used to make cakes, etc. ▶ **rodzynek 2** [in compounds] one of several types of small soft fruit: *blackcurrants* ▶ **porzeczka**

currency /ˈkʌrənsi; US ˈkɜːr-/ noun (pl. **currencies**) **1** [C,U] the system or type of money that a particular country uses: *The currency of Argentina is the peso.* ◇ *foreign currency* ◇ *a weak/strong/stable currency* ◇ *a major source of foreign currency* (dewiz) ▶ **waluta 2** [U] the state of being believed, accepted or used by many people: *The new ideas soon gained currency* (szybko się przyjęły). ▶ **powszechny użytek, obieg**

current¹ /ˈkʌrənt; US ˈkɜːr-/ adj. **1** [only before a noun] of the present time; happening now: *current fashions/events* ▶ **aktualny, bieżący 2** generally accepted; in common use: *Is this word still current?* ▶ **powszechnie używany, obiegowy**

current² /ˈkʌrənt; US ˈkɜːr-/ noun **1** [C] a continuous flowing movement of water, air, etc.: *to swim **against/with the current*** ◇ (figurative) *a current* (fala) *of anti-government feeling* ▶ **prąd; nurt 2** [C,U] the flow of electricity through a wire, etc. ▶ **prąd** (*elektryczny*)

ˌcurrent acˈcount (US **ˈchecking account**) noun [C] a bank account that you can take money out of at any time, with a cheque book or **cash card** ▶ **konto bieżące** ➲ look at **deposit account**

ˌcurrent afˈfairs noun [pl.] important political or social events that are happening at the present time ▶ **aktualności**

currently /ˈkʌrəntli; US ˈkɜːr-/ adv. at present; at the moment: *He is currently working in Spain.* ▶ **obecnie, aktualnie** ➲ note at **actually**

curriculum /kəˈrɪkjələm/ noun [C] (pl. **curriculums** or **curricula** /-lə/) all the subjects that are taught in a school, college or university; the contents of a particular course of study: *Latin is not **on the curriculum** at our school.* ▶ **program nauczania** ➲ look at **syllabus**

curriculum vitae = CV

curry /ˈkʌri; US ˈkɜːri/ noun [C,U] (pl. **curries**) an Indian dish of meat, vegetables, etc. containing a lot of spices and usually served with rice: *a hot/mild curry* ▶ (*potrawa*) **curry**
■ **curried** adj.: *curried chicken* ▶ **przyrządzony w sosie curry**

ˈcurry powder noun [U] a fine mixture of strongly flavoured spices that is used to make **curry** ▶ (*przyprawa*) **curry**

curse¹ /kɜːs/ noun [C] **1** a word used for expressing anger; a swear word ▶ **przekleństwo 2** a word or words expressing a wish that sth terrible will happen to sb: *The family seemed to be under a curse* (przeklęta). ▶ **klątwa, urok 3** something that causes great harm: *the curse of drug addiction* ▶ **przekleństwo, klątwa**

curse² /kɜːs/ verb **1** [I,T] **curse (sb/sth) (for sth)** to swear at sb/sth; to use rude language to express your anger: *He* *dropped the box, cursing himself for his clumsiness.* ▶ **kląć, przeklinać 2** [T] to use a magic word or phrase against sb because you wish them harm: *She cursed his family.* ▶ **przeklinać, rzucać klątwę (na kogoś/coś)**

cursor /ˈkɜːsə(r)/ noun [C] a small sign on a computer screen that shows the position you are at ▶ **kursor**

cursory /ˈkɜːsəri/ adj. quick and short; done in a hurry: *a cursory glance* ▶ **pobieżny, powierzchowny**

curt /kɜːt/ adj. short and not polite: *She gave him a curt reply and slammed the phone down.* ▶ **szorstki, lakoniczny**
■ **curtly** adv. ▶ **szorstko, lakonicznie** | **curtness** noun [U] ▶ **szorstkość, lakoniczność**

curtail /kɜːˈteɪl/ verb [T] (formal) to make sth shorter or smaller; to reduce: *I had to curtail my answer as I was running out of time.* ▶ **skracać, ucinać**
■ **curtailment** noun [C,U] ▶ **skracanie, ucięcie**

curtain /ˈkɜːtn/ noun [C] **1** (US also drape) a piece of cloth that you can move to cover a window, etc.: *Could you **draw the curtains*** (zasunąć/odsłonić zasłony), *please?* ◇ *lace curtains* firanki ◇ *The curtain* (kurtyna) *goes up at 7pm.* ▶ **zasłona 2** a thing that covers or hides sth: *a curtain of mist* ▶ (*przen.*) **zasłona, firanka, kurtyna** (*w teatrze*)
PHR V **curtain sth off** to divide a room, etc. with a curtain: *The bed was curtained off from the rest of the room.* ▶ **oddzielać coś zasłoną**

curtsy (also curtsey) /ˈkɜːtsi/ noun [C] (pl. **curtsies** or **curtseys**) a movement made by a woman as a sign of respect, done by bending the knees, with one foot behind the other ▶ **dyg, głęboki ukłon dworski**
■ **curtsy** (also curtsey) verb [I] ▶ **dygać, składać głęboki ukłon**

curve[1] /kɜːv/ noun [C] a line that bends round: *a curve on a graph* ▶ **krzywa, łuk** ➲ picture at **arch**

curve[2] /kɜːv/ verb [I,T] to bend or to make sth bend in a curve: *The bay curved round* (biegła łukiem) *to the south.* ▶ **wyginać (się)**
■ **curved** adj.: *a curved blade* ▶ **wygięty, zakrzywiony**

cushion[1] /ˈkʊʃn/ noun [C] **1** a bag filled with soft material, for example feathers, which you put on a chair, etc. to make it more comfortable ▶ **poduszka** (*ozdobna*) ⓘ Poduszka do spania to **pillow**. **2** something that acts or is shaped like a **cushion**: *A hovercraft rides on a cushion of air* (na poduszce powietrznej). ▶ **poduszka**

cushion[2] /ˈkʊʃn/ verb [T] **1** to make a fall, hit, etc. less painful: *The snow cushioned his fall.* ▶ **amortyzować 2** to reduce the unpleasant effect of sth: *She spent her childhood on a farm, cushioned from the effects of the war.* ▶ **osłaniać, chronić**

cushy /ˈkʊʃi/ adj. (**cushier**; **cushiest**) (informal) too easy, needing little effort (in a way that seems unfair to others): *a cushy job* ciepła posadka ▶ **niewymagający, lekki**

custard /ˈkʌstəd/ noun [U] a sweet yellow sauce made from milk, eggs and sugar. In Britain it is eaten hot or cold with sweet dishes. ▶ **polewa do słodkich potraw**

custodian /kʌˈstəʊdiən/ noun [C] **1** (formal) a person who looks after or protects sth, such as a museum, library, etc. ▶ **kustosz, opiekun/ka 2** (US) = CARETAKER

custody /ˈkʌstədi/ noun [U] **1** the legal right or duty to take care of sb/sth: *After the divorce, the mother **had custody of** the children.* ▶ **opieka, prawo do opieki 2** the state of being guarded, or kept in prison temporarily, especially by the police: *The man was **kept in custody** until his trial.* ▶ **areszt**

custom /ˈkʌstəm/ noun **1** [C,U] a way of behaving which a particular group or society has had for a long time: *It's the custom in Britain for a bride to throw her bouquet to the wedding guests.* ◇ *according to **local custom*** ▶ **obyczaj, zwyczaj** ➲ note at **habit 2** [sing.] (formal) something that a person does regularly: *It's my custom to drink tea in the afternoon.* ◇ *They were walking through the park, as was their custom* (jak mieli w zwyczaju), *when a large dog attacked them.* ▶ **zwyczaj 3** [U] (Brit.) commercial activity; the practice of people buying things regularly from a particular shop, etc.: *The local shop lost a lot of custom* (stracił wielu stałych klientów) *when the new supermarket opened.* ▶ **stałe zaopatrywanie się w danym sklepie** ➲ look at **customs**

customary /ˈkʌstəməri; US -meri/ adj. according to custom; usual: *Is it customary to send cards at Christmas in your country?* ▶ **zwyczajowy, przyjęty**

ˌcustom-ˈbuilt adj. designed and built for a particular person ▶ **zaprojektowany i wybudowany na indywidualne zamówienie**

customer /ˈkʌstəmə(r)/ noun [C] **1** a person who buys goods or services in a shop, restaurant, etc.: *The shop assistant was serving a customer.* ◇ *a regular* (stały) *customer* ▶ **klient/ka** ➲ note at **client 2** [after certain adjectives] (informal) a person: *a tough/an awkward/an odd customer* ▶ **facet, gość**

customize (also -ise) /ˈkʌstəmaɪz/ verb [T] to make or change sth to suit the needs of the owner: *You can customize the software in several ways.* ▶ **dostosowywać do indywidualnych potrzeb użytownika/klienta itp.**
■ **customized** adj.: *a customized car* ▶ **dostosowany do indywidualnych potrzeb użytkownika/klienta itp.**

ˌcustom-ˈmade adj. designed and made for a particular person ▶ **zaprojektowany lub wykonany na indywidualne zamówienie**

customs (also Customs) /ˈkʌstəmz/ noun [pl.] the place at an airport, etc. where government officials check your luggage to make sure you are not bringing goods into the country illegally: *a customs officer* celnik ▶ **odprawa celna** ➲ look at **excise**

cut[1] /kʌt/ verb (**cutting**; pt, pp **cut**) **1** [I,T] to make an opening, wound or mark in sth using a sharp tool, for example a pair of scissors or a knife: *Be careful not to cut yourself on that broken glass!* ◇ *This knife doesn't cut very well.* ◇ *I cut my finger* (skaleczyłem się w palec) *with a vegetable knife.* ▶ **ciąć, kaleczyć (się) 2** [T] **cut sth (from sth)** to remove sth or a part of sth, using a knife, etc.: *She cut two slices of bread (from the loaf).* ▶ **kroić, odkrawać 3** [T] **cut sth (in/into sth)** to divide sth into pieces with a knife, etc.: *She cut the cake into eight (pieces).* ◇ *He cut the rope in two.* ▶ **krajać, przecinać 4** [T] to make sth shorter by using scissors, etc.: *I cut my own hair.* ◇ *to cut the grass* ◇ *to have your hair cut* strzyc się u fryzjera ▶ **obcinać, strzyc 5** [T] to make or form sth by removing material with a sharp tool: *She cut a hole in the card and pushed the string through.* ◇ *They cut a path through the jungle.* ▶ **wycinać 6** [T] to reduce sth or make it shorter; to remove sth: *to cut taxes/costs/spending* ◇ *Several violent scenes in the film were cut.* ▶ **obcinać; wycinać 7** [T] to remove a piece of text from the screen: *Use the **cut and paste** buttons to change the order of the paragraphs.* ▶ (*komput.*) **wycinać 8** [T] (informal) to stop sth: *Cut the chat and get on with your work!* ▶ **zakończyć coś 9** [T] to deeply offend sb or hurt their feelings: *His cruel remarks cut her deeply.* ▶ **ranić** ⓘ **Cut** używa się w innych idiomach, np. **cut corners**. Zob. hasła odpowiednich rzeczowników, przymiotników itp.
PHR V **be cut out for sth**; **be cut out to be sth** to have the qualities needed to do sth; to be suitable for sth/sb: *You're not cut out to be a soldier.* ▶ **być stworzonym dla kogoś/do czegoś, nadawać się do czegoś, być urodzonym** (*np.artystą*)
cut across sth to affect or be true for different groups that usually remain separate: *The question of aid for the*

earthquake victims cuts across national boundaries. ▶ **przekraczać coś**

cut across, along, through, etc. (sth) to go across, etc. sth, in order to make your route shorter: *It's much quicker if we cut across the field.* ▶ **iść na skróty**

cut sth back; cut back (on sth) to reduce sth: *to cut back on public spending* ▶ **obcinać coś**

cut sth down 1 to make sth fall down by cutting it: *to cut down a tree* ▶ **ścinać coś 2** to make sth shorter: *I have to cut my essay down to 2 000 words.* ▶ **skracać coś**

cut sth down; cut down (on sth) to reduce the quantity or amount of sth; to do sth less often: *You should cut down on fatty foods* (ograniczyć spożycie tłustego jedzenia). ▶ **ograniczać/zmniejszać coś**

cut in (on sb/sth) to interrupt sb/sth: *She kept cutting in on our conversation.* ▶ **przerywać (komuś), wtrącać się do czegoś**

cut sb off [often passive] to stop or interrupt sb's telephone conversation: *We were cut off before I could give her my message.* ▶ **rozłączać kogoś**

cut sb/sth off [often passive] to stop the supply of sth to sb: *The electricity/gas/water has been cut off.* ▶ **wyłączać komuś coś**

cut sth off to block a road, etc. so that nothing can pass: *We must cut off all possible escape routes.* ▶ **odcinać coś**

cut sth off (sth) to remove sth from sth larger by cutting: *Be careful you don't cut your fingers off using that electric saw.* ▶ **odcinać coś (czymś)**

cut sb/sth off (from sb/sth) [often passive] to prevent sb/sth from moving from a place or contacting people outside: *The farm was cut off from the village by heavy snow.* ▶ **odcinać kogoś/coś (od kogoś/czegoś)**

cut sth open to open sth by cutting: *She fell and cut her head open* (rozbiła sobie głowę). ▶ **rozcinać coś**

cut sth out 1 to remove sth or to form sth into a particular shape by cutting: *He cut the job advertisement out of the newspaper.* ▶ **wycinać/wykrawać coś (z czegoś) 2** to not include sth: *Cut out all the boring details!* ▶ **opuszczać coś 3** (especially US, informal) to stop saying or doing sth that annoys sb: *Cut that out* (przestań) *and leave me alone!* ▶ **przestawać coś (robić) 4** (informal) to stop doing or using sth: *You'll only lose weight if you cut out sweet things from your diet.* ▶ **rzucać/eliminować coś; zaprzestawać czegoś**

cut sth up to cut sth into small pieces with a knife, etc. ▶ **ciąć coś (na kawałki), siekać coś**

🔑 **cut²** /kʌt/ noun [C] **1** an injury or opening in the skin made with a knife, etc.: *He had a deep cut on his forehead.* ▶ **rana (cięta), cięcie 2** an act of cutting: *to have a cut and blow-dry* ▶ **strzyżenie, cięcie 3 a cut (in sth)** a reduction in size, amount, etc.: *a cut in government spending* ◇ *a power cut* wyłączenie prądu ▶ **cięcie, redukcja 4** (informal) a share of the profits from sth, especially sth dishonest: *They were rewarded with a cut of 5% from the profits.* ▶ **dola, działka 5** a piece of meat from a particular part of an animal: *cheap cuts of lamb* ▶ **płat** ➲ look at **short cut**

ˌcut and ˈdried adj. [not usually before a noun] decided in a way that cannot be changed or argued about: *The inquiry is by no means cut and dried.* ▶ **ustalony, uzgodniony**

cutback /ˈkʌtbæk/ noun [C] a reduction in amount or number: *The management were forced to make cutbacks in staff* (zredukować personel). ▶ **cięcie, redukcja**

cute /kjuːt/ adj. attractive; pretty: *Your little girl is so cute!* ◇ *a cute* (słodki) *smile* ▶ **śliczny, ładniutki**

cuticle /ˈkjuːtɪkl/ noun [C] an area of hard skin at the base of the nails on the fingers and toes ▶ **skórka** (*wokół paznokcia*)

cutlery /ˈkʌtləri/ (US **silverware**) noun [U] the knives, forks and spoons that you use for eating food ▶ **sztućce** ➲ look at **crockery**

cutlet /ˈkʌtlət/ noun [C] a small, thick piece of meat, often with bone in it, that is cooked ▶ **kotlet** (*zwł. z kością*) ➲ look at **rissole**

ˈcut-off noun [C] the level or time at which sth stops: *The cut-off date is* (ostateczny termin upływa) *12 May. After that we'll end the offer.* ▶ **ostateczny/końcowy termin, górna/dolna granica** (*np. wieku*)

ˈcut-price (US **ˈcut-rate**) adj. [only before a noun] sold at a reduced price; selling goods at low prices: *cut-price offers* *a cut-price store* sklep z przecenionym towarem ▶ **przeceniony**

cutters /ˈkʌtəz/ noun [pl.] a tool that you use for cutting through sth, for example metal: *a pair of wire cutters* ▶ **przecinak, nożyce**

ˈcut-throat adj. caring only about success and not worried about hurting anyone: *cut-throat business practices* ▶ **bezwzględny, zmierzający do celu po trupach**

cutting¹ /ˈkʌtɪŋ/ noun [C] **1** (US **clipping** /ˈklɪpɪŋ/) a piece cut out from a newspaper, etc.: *press cuttings* ▶ **wycinek** (*prasowy*) **2** a piece cut off from a plant that you use for growing a new plant ▶ **sadzonka**

cutting² /ˈkʌtɪŋ/ adj. **1** (used about sth you say) unkind; meant to hurt sb's feelings: *a cutting remark* ▶ **uszczypliwy 2** (used about the wind, etc.) cold, strong and unpleasant ▶ **ostry, przejmujący**

ˌcutting ˈedge noun [sing.] **1 the cutting edge (of sth)** the newest, most advanced stage in the development of sth: *working at the cutting edge of computer technology* ▶ **front, czołówka 2** an aspect of sth that gives it an advantage: *We're relying on him to give the team a cutting edge.* ▶ **przewaga**

CV /ˌsiː ˈviː/ (also formal **curriculum vitae** /kəˌrɪkjələm ˈviːtaɪ/, US **résumé** /ˈrezjumeɪ; US -zə-/) noun [C] a formal list of your education and work experience, often used when you are trying to get a new job ▶ **c.v.** (*życiorys*) ➲ note at **job**

cwt. = HUNDREDWEIGHT

cyanide /ˈsaɪənaɪd/ noun [U] a poisonous chemical ▶ **cyjanek**

cybercafe /ˈsaɪbəkæfeɪ/ noun [C] a place with computers where customers can pay to use the Internet ▶ **kawiarenka internetowa** ➲ note at **Internet**

cyberspace /ˈsaɪbəspeɪs/ noun [U] a place that is not real, where electronic messages exist while they are being sent from one computer to another ▶ **przestrzeń internetowa**

🔑 **cycle¹** /ˈsaɪkl/ noun [C] **1** a bicycle or motorbike: *a cycle shop* ▶ **rower; motocykl** SYN **bike 2** a series of events, etc. that happen again and again in the same order: *the life cycle of a frog* ▶ **cykl**

🔑 **cycle²** /ˈsaɪkl/ verb [I] to ride a bicycle: *He usually cycles to school.* ▶ **jeździć na rowerze** ℹ **Go cycling** powszechnie używa się, mówiąc o jeździe rowerem dla rekreacji: *We like to go cycling at weekends.*

ˈcycle lane (US **ˈbicycle lane**) (informal **ˈbike lane**) noun [C] a part of a road that only bicycles are allowed to use ▶ **pas jezdni dla ruchu rowerowego**

cyclic /ˈsaɪklɪk/ (also **cyclical** /ˈsɪklɪkl/) adj. following a repeated pattern ▶ **cykliczny**

cyclist /ˈsaɪklɪst/ noun [C] a person who rides a bicycle ▶ **rowerzyst(k)a, kolarz**

cyclone /ˈsaɪkləʊn/ noun [C] a large, violent storm in which strong winds move in a circle ▶ **cyklon** ➲ note at **storm**

cygnet /ˈsɪɡnət/ noun [C] a young **swan** ▶ **łabędziątko**

cylinder /ˈsɪlɪndə(r)/ noun [C] **1** an object shaped like a tube ▶ **walec 2** a part of an engine shaped like a tube, for example in a car ▶ **cylinder**

■ **cylindrical** /sə'lɪndrɪkl/ adj. ▶ **walcowaty**

cymbal /'sɪmbl/ noun [C, usually pl.] one of a pair of round metal plates used as a musical instrument. **Cymbals** make a loud ringing sound when you hit them together or with a stick. ▶ **czynel**

cynic /'sɪnɪk/ noun [C] a person who believes that people only do things for themselves, rather than to help others ▶ **cynik**
■ **cynical** /-kl/ adj. ▶ **cyniczny** | **cynically** /-kli/ adv. ▶ **cynicznie** | **cynicism** /'sɪnɪsɪzem/ noun [U] ▶ **cynizm**

Cyrillic /sə'rɪlɪk/ noun [U] the alphabet that is used in languages such as Russian ▶ **dot. cyrylicy**

cyst /sɪst/ noun [C] a swelling or a lump filled with liquid in the body or under the skin ▶ **cysta**, **torbiel**

cystic fibrosis /ˌsɪstɪk faɪ'brəʊsɪs/ noun [U] a serious medical condition that some people are born with, in which **glands** in the lungs and other organs do not work correctly. It often leads to infections and can result in early death. ▶ **mukowiscydoza**

czar, czarina = TSAR, TSARINA

Dd

D, d /di:/ noun [C,U] (pl. **Ds**; **ds**; **D's**; **d's** /di:z/) **1** the fourth letter of the English alphabet: *'December' begins with (a) 'D'.* ▶ **litera** *d* **2** (used about music) the second note in the series of notes called the scale of C major: *D major* D-dur ◇ *D minor* d-moll ◇ *D sharp* Dis/dis ◇ *D flat* Des/des ▶ **D/d**

d. abbr. **died**: *W A Mozart, d. 1791* ▶ **zm.**

dab¹ /dæb/ verb [I,T] (**da<u>bb</u>ing**; **da<u>bb</u>ed**) to touch sth lightly, usually several times: *He dabbed the cut with some cotton wool.* ▶ **przecierać (lekko)**
PHR V **dab sth on/off (sth)** to put sth on or to remove sth lightly: *to dab some antiseptic on* (dezynfekować) *a wound* ▶ **wklepywać** (*np. perfumy w skórę*), **zbierać delikatnymi ruchami** (*np. rozlany płyn*)

dab² /dæb/ noun [C] **1** a small quantity of sth that is put on a surface: *a dab of paint/perfume* ▶ **odrobina** **2** a light touch: *She gave her eyes a dab* (lekko przetarła oczy) *with a handkerchief.* ▶ **otarcie** (*np. łez*), **dotknięcie**

dabble /'dæbl/ verb **1** [I] to become involved in sth in a way that is not very serious: *to dabble in politics* ▶ **parać/bawić się (czymś)** **2** [T] to put your hands, feet, etc. in water and move them around: *We sat on the bank and dabbled our toes in the river.* ▶ **pluskać**, **taplać**

dachshund /'dæksnd; US 'dɑ:kshʊnd/ noun [C] a small dog with a long body and short legs ▶ **jamnik**

⚷ **dad** /dæd/ noun [C] (informal) father ▶ **tat-a/o**

daddy /'dædi/ noun [C] (pl. **daddies**) (informal) (used by children) father ▶ **tatuś**

daffodil /'dæfədɪl/ noun [C] a tall yellow flower that grows in the spring ▶ **żonkil** ➲ picture on **page A15**

Daffodil to godło Walii.

daft /dɑ:ft; US dæft/ adj. (informal) silly: *a daft idea* ▶ **głupi**, **stuknięty**

dagger /'dægə(r)/ noun [C] a type of knife used as a weapon, especially in past times ▶ **sztylet**

⚷ **daily¹** /'deɪli/ adj. [only before a noun] done, made or happening every day: *a daily routine/delivery/newspaper* ▶ **codzienny** ➲ note at **routine**
■ **daily** adv.: *Our airline flies to Japan daily.* ▶ **codziennie**

daily² /'deɪli/ noun [C] (pl. **dailies**) (informal) a newspaper that is published every day except Sunday ▶ **dziennik**

dainty /'deɪnti/ adj. (**daintier**; **daintiest**) **1** small and pretty: *a dainty lace handkerchief* ▶ **delikatny**, **zgrabny** **2** (used about sb's movements) very careful in a way that tries to show good manners: *Veronica took a dainty bite of her cucumber sandwich.* ▶ **wykwintny**
■ **daintily** adv. ▶ **delikatnie**, **zgrabnie**; **wykwintnie**

dairy¹ /'deəri/ noun [C] (pl. **dairies**) **1** a place on a farm where milk is kept and butter, cheese, etc. are made ▶ **mleczarnia** **2** a company which sells milk, butter, eggs, etc. ▶ **sklep z nabiałem**, **mleczarnia**

dairy² /'deəri/ adj. [only before a noun] **1** made from milk: *dairy products/produce* nabiał ▶ **mleczny** **2** connected with the production of milk: *dairy cattle* ◇ *a dairy farm* ▶ **mleczny**

dais /'deɪɪs/ noun [C] a stage, especially at one end of a room, on which people stand to make speeches to an audience ▶ **podium**

daisy /'deɪzi/ noun [C] (pl. **daisies**) a small white flower with a yellow centre, which usually grows wild in grass ▶ **stokrotka**

dale /'deɪl/ noun [C] a valley, especially in Northern England ▶ **dolina górska**

Dalmatian /dæl'meɪʃn/ noun [C] a large dog with short white hair marked with dark spots ▶ **dalmatyńczyk**

dam /dæm/ noun [C] a wall built across a river to hold back the water and form a **reservoir** behind it ▶ **tama** ➲ picture on **page A2**
■ **dam** verb [T] ▶ **tamować** (*wodę*), **budować tamę**

⚷ **damage¹** /'dæmɪdʒ/ noun **1** [U] **damage (to sth)** harm or injury caused when sth is broken or spoiled: *Earthquakes can **cause** terrible **damage** in urban areas.* ◇ *It will take weeks to **repair the damage** done by the vandals.* ▶ **szkoda** **2** (**damages**) [pl.] money that you can ask for if sb damages sth of yours or hurts you: *Mrs Rees, who lost a leg in the crash, was awarded damages of £100 000.* ▶ **odszkodowanie**

⚷ **damage²** /'dæmɪdʒ/ verb [T] to spoil or harm sth, for example by breaking it: *The roof was damaged by the storm.* ▶ **uszkadzać**, **psuć** ➲ look at **destroy**
■ **damaging** adj.: *These rumours could be damaging to her reputation.* ▶ **szkodliwy**

dame /deɪm/ noun (**Dame**) [C] (Brit.) a title given to a woman as an honour because of sth special that she has done: *Dame Agatha Christie* ▶ **tytuł przyznawany kobietom za szczególne osiągnięcia**

damn¹ /dæm/ (also **damned** /dæmd/) adj. (slang) **1** (a swear word that people use to show that they are angry): *Some damn fool has parked too close to me.* ▶ **przeklęty**, **cholerny**
■ **damn** adv. (a swear word that people use for emphasizing what they are saying) very: *Read it! It's a damn good book.* ▶ **cholernie**

damn² /dæm/ verb [I,T] **1** (informal) (used for expressing anger or annoyance): *Damn (it!) I've left my money behind.* ▶ **do diabła!** **2** to describe sth as very bad: *The film was damned by all the critics.* ▶ **potępiać** **2** (used about God) to send sb to hell ▶ **skazywać na potępienie**

damn³ /dæm/ noun
IDM **not care/give a damn (about sb/sth)** (slang) not care at all: *I don't give a damn what he thinks about me.* ▶ **mieć kogoś/coś gdzieś**

damnation /dæm'neɪʃn/ noun [U] the state of being in hell; the act of sending sb to hell: *eternal damnation* ▶ **potępienie**

damning /'dæmɪŋ/ adj. that criticizes sth very much: *There was a damning article about the book in the newspaper.* ▶ **potępiający**, **krytyczny**

damp[1] /dæmp/ adj. a little wet: *The house had been empty and felt rather damp.* ▶ **wilgotny**
■ **damp** noun [U]: *She hated the damp and the cold of the English climate.* ▶ **wilgoć** ➲ note at **wet**

damp[2] /dæmp/ verb [T] **damp sth (down) 1** to make sth less strong or urgent: *He tried to damp down their expectations in case they failed.* ▶ (*emocje*) **studzić, tłumić 2** to make a fire burn less strongly or stop burning: *He tried to damp (down) the flames.* ▶ **gasić** (*ogień*)

dampen /ˈdæmpən/ verb [T] **1** to make sth a little wet: *He dampened his hair to try to stop it sticking up.* ▶ **zwilżać 2** to make sth less strong or urgent: *Even the awful weather did not dampen their enthusiasm for the trip.* ▶ **studzić, tłumić** (*emocje*)

dance[1] /dɑːns; US dæns/ noun **1** [C] a series of steps and movements which you do to music ▶ **taniec 2** [U] dancing as a form of art or entertainment: *She's very interested in modern dance.* ▶ **taniec 3** [C] (old-fashioned) a social meeting at which people dance with each other ▶ **tańce, zabawa**

dance[2] /dɑːns; US dæns/ verb **1** [I,T] to move around to the rhythm of music by making a series of steps: *to dance the samba* ◇ *Did you ever see Nureyev dance* (jak tańczy Nuriejew)*?* ▶ **tańczyć 2** [I] to jump and move around with energy: *She was dancing up and down with excitement.* ▶ **skakać, podskakiwać**

dancer /ˈdɑːnsə(r); US ˈdæn-/ noun [C] a person who dances, often as a job: *She's a good dancer.* ◇ *a ballet dancer* ▶ **tance-rz/rka, baletnica**

dancing /ˈdɑːnsɪŋ; US ˈdæn-/ noun [U] the act of moving to music: *I'm hopeless at dancing – I've got no sense of rhythm.* ◇ *Will there be dancing at the party?* ▶ **taniec, tańce**

dandelion /ˈdændɪlaɪən/ noun [C] a small wild plant with a bright yellow flower ▶ **mlecz**

dandruff /ˈdændrʌf/ noun [U] small pieces of dead skin in the hair, that look like white powder ▶ **łupież**

danger /ˈdeɪndʒə(r)/ noun **1** [U,C] the chance that sb/sth may be hurt, killed or damaged or that sth bad may happen: *When he saw the men had knives, he realized his life was* ***in danger.*** ◇ *The men kept on running until they thought they were* ***out of danger*** (nic im nie groziło) ◇ *If things carry on as they are,* ***there's a danger that*** *the factory may have to close.* ◇ *Doctors thought he was going to die, but now he's* ***off the danger list*** (nie jest już w stanie krytycznym). ◇ *Danger* (uwaga)*! Steep hill!* ▶ **niebezpieczeństwo 2** [C] **a danger (to sb/sth)** a person or thing that can cause injury, pain or damage to sb: *Drunk drivers are a danger to everyone on the road.* ▶ **zagrożenie**

dangerous /ˈdeɪndʒərəs/ adj. likely to cause injury or damage: *a dangerous animal/road/illness* ▶ **niebezpieczny, groźny**
■ **dangerously** adv.: *He was standing dangerously close to the cliff edge.* ▶ **niebezpiecznie, groźnie**

dangle /ˈdæŋgl/ verb [I,T] to hang freely; to hold sth so that it hangs down in this way: *She sat on the fence with her legs dangling* (wymachując nogami). ◇ *The police dangled a rope* (zrzuciła sznur) *from the bridge and the man grabbed it.* ▶ **dyndać, zwisać, bujać (się)**

dank /dæŋk/ adj. wet, cold and unpleasant ▶ **zawilgocony, przesiąknięty wilgocią**

dapper /ˈdæpə(r)/ adj. (used about a man) small with a neat appearance and nice clothes ▶ **elegancki**

dappled /ˈdæpld/ adj. marked with spots of colour, or shade: *the dappled light under the trees* ▶ **cętkowany, nakrapiany**

dare[1] /deə(r)/ verb **1** [I] [usually in negative sentences] **dare (to) do sth** to have enough courage to do sth: *I daren't ask her to lend me any more money.* ◇ *We were so frightened that we didn't dare (to) go into the room.* ▶ **śmieć, odważyć się**

> Forma przecząca: **dare not** (zwykle w formie **daren't** /deənt/) lub **do not/does not** (= **don't/doesn't**) **dare.** Forma przecząca w czasie przeszłym: **did not (didn't) dare**, lub (formalnie) **dared not. Dare** zazw. występuje przed bezokolicznikiem bez **to**: *I daren't move.* ◇ *Nobody dared (to) speak.*

2 [T] **dare sb (to do sth)** to ask or tell sb to do sth in order to see if they have the courage to do it: *He dared his friend to put a mouse in the teacher's bag.* ◇ *Can you jump off that wall? Go on, I dare you* (no zrób to)*!* ▶ **wyzywać, nakłaniać**
IDM **don't you dare** (used for telling sb very strongly not to do sth): *Don't you dare tell my parents about this!* ▶ **nie waż się**
how dare you (used when you are angry about sth that sb has done): *How dare you speak to me like that!* ▶ **jak śmiesz**
I dare say (used when you are saying sth is probable): *'I think you should accept the offer.' 'I dare say you're right.'* ▶ **przypuszczam**

dare[2] /deə(r)/ noun [C, usually sing.] something dangerous that sb asks you to do, to see if you have the courage to do it: *'Why did you try to swim across the river?' '****For a dare*** (bo zostałem wyzwany).*'* ▶ **wyzwanie**

daredevil /ˈdeədevl/ noun [C] a person who likes to do dangerous things ▶ **śmiałek, ryzykant**

daring /ˈdeərɪŋ/ adj. involving or taking risks: *a daring attack* ▶ **śmiały, odważny** SYN **brave**
■ **daring** noun [U]: *The climb required skill and daring.* ▶ **śmiałość, odwaga**

dark[1] /dɑːk/ adj. **1** with no light or very little light: *It was a dark night, with no moon.* ◇ *What time does it* ***get dark*** (robi się ciemno) *in winter?* ▶ **ciemny 2** (used about a colour) not light; nearer black than white: *dark blue* ▶ **ciemny, ciemno-** OPP **light, pale 3** (especially Brit.) (used about sb's hair, skin or eyes) brown or black; not fair: *She was small and dark with brown eyes.* ▶ **ciemny 4** [only before a noun] hidden and frightening: *He seemed friendly, but there was a dark side to his character.* ▶ **ciemny, niepokojący 5** [only before a noun] sad; without hope: *the dark days of the recession* ▶ **mroczny**
IDM **keep it/sth dark (from sb)** to keep sth secret ▶ **trzymać coś w tajemnicy (przed kimś)**

dark[2] /dɑːk/ noun (**the dark**) [sing.] the state of having no light: *He's afraid of the dark.* ◇ *Why are you sitting alone* ***in the dark?*** ▶ **ciemność, mrok**
IDM **before/after dark** before/after the sun goes down in the evening ▶ **przed zmrokiem/po zmroku**
(be/keep sb) in the dark (about sth) (be/keep sb) in a position of not knowing about sth: *Don't keep me in the dark. Tell me!* ▶ **nic nie wiedzieć (o czymś); trzymać kogoś w nieświadomości**

the ˈdark ages noun [pl.] **1** (**the Dark Ages**) the period of European history between the end of the Roman Empire and the 10th century AD ▶ **wczesne średniowiecze 2** (often humorous) a period of history or a time when sth was not developed or modern: *Back in the dark ages of computing, in about 1980, they started a software company.* ◇ *You're living in the dark ages* (w ciemnogrodzie)*, Mum!* ▶ **początkowy okres rozwoju,** (*przen.*) **średniowiecze**

ˌdark ˈchocolate noun [U] (Brit. also **ˌplain ˈchocolate**) dark brown chocolate with a slightly bitter taste ▶ **czekolada gorzka**

darken /ˈdɑːkən/ verb [I,T] to become or to make sth darker: *The sky suddenly darkened* (niebo nagle zrobiło się ciemne) *and it started to rain.* ▶ **ściemniać (się), zaciemniać**

ˌ**dark 'glasses** = SUNGLASSES

darkly /'dɑːkli/ adv. **1** in a threatening or unpleasant way: *He hinted darkly that all was not well.* ▶ **złowrogo, ponuro 2** showing a dark colour ▶ **w ciemnym kolorze, ciemno**

darkness /'dɑːknəs/ noun [U] the state of being dark: *We sat **in total darkness**, waiting for the lights to come back on.* ▶ **ciemność, mrok**

darkroom /'dɑːkruːm; -rʊm/ noun [C] a room that can be made completely dark so that film can be taken out of a camera and photographs can be produced there ▶ **ciemnia fotograficzna**

darling /'dɑːlɪŋ/ noun [C] a word that you say to sb you love: *Hello, darling!* Witaj, kochanie! ▶ **ukochan-y/a** ➲ look at **love, 1** (4)

darn¹ /dɑːn/ verb [I,T] to repair a hole in clothes by sewing across it in one direction and then in the other: *I hate darning socks.* ▶ **cerować**

darn² /dɑːn/ (also **darned** /dɑːnd/) adj. (informal) (used as a mild swear word, to emphasize sth): *Why don't you switch the darn thing off and listen to me!* ▶ **cholerny**
■ **darn** adv.: *It's darn cold tonight!* ▶ **cholernie**

dart¹ /dɑːt/ noun **1** [C] an object like a small arrow. It is thrown in a game or shot as a weapon: *The keeper fired a tranquillizer dart into the tiger to send it to sleep.* ▶ **strzałka 2** (**darts**) [U] a game in which you throw **darts** at a a round board with numbers on it (a **dartboard**) ▶ **rzucanie strzałek do tarczy**

dart² /dɑːt/ verb [I,T] to move or make sth move suddenly and quickly in a certain direction: *A rabbit darted across the field.* ◇ *She darted an angry glance at me.* ▶ **rzucać (się), popędzać**

dash¹ /dæʃ/ noun **1** [sing.] an act of going somewhere suddenly and quickly: *Suddenly the prisoner **made a dash for*** (rzucił się do) *the door.* ◇ *When the doors opened, there was a **mad dash** for the seats* (ludzie rzucili się na siedzenia). ▶ **pęd 2** [C, usually sing.] a small amount of sth that you add to sth else: *a dash of lemon juice* ◇ *The rug adds a dash of colour* (nieco koloru) *to the room.* ▶ **kropelka, szczypta 3** [C] a small horizontal line (–) used in writing, especially for adding extra information ▶ **myślnik, pauza** ➲ look at **hyphen**

dash² /dæʃ/ verb **1** [I] to go somewhere suddenly and quickly: *We all dashed for shelter when it started to rain.* ◇ *I must dash – I'm late.* ▶ **biec pędem, dawać susa 2** [I,T] to hit sth with great force; to throw sth so that it hits sth else very hard: *She dashed her racket to the ground.* ▶ **walić; ciskać**
IDM **dash sb's hopes (of sth/of doing sth)** to completely destroy sb's hopes of doing sth: *The accident dashed his hopes of becoming a pianist.* ▶ **rozwiewać** (*nadzieje*)
PHR V **dash sth off** to write or draw sth very quickly: *I dashed off a note to my boss and left.* ▶ **szybko coś napisać/naszkicować**

dashboard /'dæʃbɔːd/ noun [C] the part in a car in front of the driver where most of the switches, etc. are ▶ **tablica rozdzielcza** ➲ picture at **car**

dashing /'dæʃɪŋ/ adj. (old-fashioned) **1** (usually used about a man) attractive, confident and elegant: *a dashing young officer* ▶ **szykowny i pewny siebie 2** (used about a thing) attractive and fashionable: *his dashing red waistcoat* ▶ **fantazyjny, wytworny**

⚷ **data** /'deɪtə; 'dɑːtə; US also 'dætə/ noun [U, pl.] facts or information: *to gather/collect data* ◇ *data capture/retrieval* zbieranie/wyszukiwanie danych ▶ **dane**

Początkowo słowo **data** było formą lm rzeczownika łacińskiego **datum**. Obecnie często używa się go jako rzeczownika niepoliczalnego: *The data we have is not very interesting.*

databank /'deɪtəbæŋk; US also 'dætə-/ noun [C] a large amount of data on a particular subject that is stored in a computer ▶ **bank danych**

database /'deɪtəbeɪs; US also 'dætə-/ noun [C] a large amount of data that is stored in a computer and can easily be used, added to, etc. ▶ **baza danych**

ˌ**data 'processing** noun [U] a series of actions that a computer performs on data to produce an output ▶ **przetwarzanie danych**

ˌ**data pro'tection** noun [U] legal restrictions that keep information stored on computers private and that control who can read it or use it ▶ **ochrona danych**

⚷ **date¹** /deɪt/ noun **1** [C] a particular day of the month or year: *What's the date today?/What date is it today?/What's today's date?* ◇ *What's your **date of birth**?* ◇ *We'd better **fix a date** for the next meeting.* ▶ **data 2** [sing.] a particular time: *We can discuss this **at a later date*** (w późniejszym terminie). ▶ **termin, data** ➲ look at **sell-by date 3** [C] an arrangement to meet sb, especially a boyfriend or girlfriend: *Shall we **make a date** to have lunch together?* Umówimy się na lunch? ◇ *I've got a date with her on Friday night.* ▶ **randka, umówione spotkanie** ➲ look at **blind date 4** [C] (especially US) a boyfriend or girlfriend: *Who's your date?* ▶ **chłopak; dziewczyna 5** [C] a small, sweet, dark brown fruit that comes from a tree which grows in hot countries ▶ **daktyl**
IDM **out of date 1** not fashionable; no longer useful: *out-of-date methods/machinery* ▶ **starej daty, przestarzały 2** no longer able to be used: *I must renew my passport. It's out of date.* ▶ **przeterminowany, nieaktualny**
to date (formal) until now: *We've had very few complaints to date.* ▶ **po dzień dzisiejszy, dotychczas**
up to date 1 completely modern: *The new kitchen will be right up to date, with all the latest gadgets.* ▶ **nowoczesny 2** with all the most recent information; having done everything that you should: *In this report we'll **bring you up to date** with the latest news from the area.* W tym raporcie przedstawiamy państwu aktualne wiadomości z rejonu. ◇ *Are you up to date with your homework?* Czy odrabiasz na bieżąco zadania domowe? ▶ **aktualny, na bieżąco**

⚷ **date²** /deɪt/ verb **1** [T] to write the day's date on sth: *The letter is dated 24 March, 2006.* ▶ **datować, opatrywać datą 2** [T] to discover or guess how old sth is: *The skeleton has been dated at about 3 000 BC.* ▶ **datować, ustalać wiek czegoś 3** [I] to seem, or to make sb/sth seem old-fashioned: *We chose a simple style so that it wouldn't date as quickly.* ▶ **wychodzić z mody 4** [I,T] (especially US, informal) to meet a girlfriend or boyfriend regularly ▶ **chodzić z kimś, spotykać się z kimś**
PHR V **date back to...; date from...** to have existed since ...: *The house dates back to the 17th century.* ◇ *We found photographs dating from before the war.* ▶ **datować się, pochodzić** (*z danego okresu*)

dated /'deɪtɪd/ adj. not fashionable ▶ **niemodny, nie na czasie**

'**dating agency** (also '**dating service**) noun [C] a business or an organization that arranges meetings between single people who want to begin a romantic relationship: *He met his wife through a **computer dating agency**.* ▶ **biuro matrymonialne**

daub /dɔːb/ verb [T] **daub A on B; daub B with A** to spread a lot of a substance such as paint, mud, etc. carelessly onto sth: *The walls of the building were daubed with red paint.* ▶ **mazać** (*np. farbą, błotem*)

⚷ **daughter** /'dɔːtə(r)/ noun [C] a female child ▶ **córka** '**daughter-in-law** noun [C] (pl. **daughters-in-law**) the wife of your son ▶ **synowa**

daunt /dɔːnt/ verb [T, usually passive] to frighten or to worry sb by being too big or difficult: *Don't be daunted by all the controls – in fact it's a simple machine to use.* ▶ **przerażać, niepokoić**
■ **daunting** adj.: *a daunting task* ▶ **przerażający**

dawdle /ˈdɔːdl/ verb [I] to go somewhere very slowly ▶ **marudzić, ociągać się**

dawn¹ /dɔːn/ noun **1** [U,C] the early morning, when light first appears in the sky: *before/at dawn* ◇ *Dawn was breaking* (świtało) *as I set off to work.* ▶ **świt** ➲ look at **sunrise 2** [sing.] the beginning: *the dawn of civilization* ▶ **zaranie**
IDM **the crack of dawn** → CRACK²

dawn² /dɔːn/ verb [I] **1** (formal) to begin to grow light, after the night: *The day dawned bright and cold.* ◇ (figurative) *A new era of peace is dawning* (rozpoczyna się). ▶ **świtać 2 dawn (on sb)** to become clear (to sb): *Suddenly it dawned on her. 'Of course!' she said. 'You're Mike's brother!'* ▶ **zaświtać (komuś) w głowie**

⚷ **day** /deɪ/ noun **1** [C] a period of 24 hours. Seven days make up a week: *'What day is it today?' 'Tuesday.'* ◇ *We're meeting again the day after tomorrow* (pojutrze)/*in two days' time.* ◇ *The next/following day I saw Mark again.* ◇ *I'd already spoken to him the day before/the previous day.* ◇ *the day before yesterday* przedwczoraj ◇ *I have to take these pills twice a day.* ◇ *the day before* poprzedniego dnia/dzień przed ◇ *New Year's Day* Nowy Rok ▶ **dzień, doba 2** [C,U] the time when the sky is light; not night: *The days were warm but the nights were freezing.* ◇ *It's been raining all day (long).* ◇ *Owls sleep* ***by day*** (w dzień) *and hunt at night.* ▶ **dzień** ➲ look at **daily 3** [C] the hours of the day when you work: *She's expected to work a seven-hour day.* ▶ **dzień pracy 4** [C] (often **days**) a particular period of time in the past: *in Shakespeare's day* ◇ *There weren't so many cars in those days* ▶ **czasy**
IDM **at the end of the day** → END¹
break of day → BREAK²
call it a day → CALL¹
day by day every day; as time passes: *Day by day, she was getting a little bit stronger.* ▶ **z dnia na dzień, dzień w dzień**
day in, day out every day, without any change: *Frank sits at his desk working, day in, day out.* ▶ **dzień po dniu, codziennie**
day-to-day happening as a normal part of each day; usual ▶ **codzienny**
from day to day; **from one day to the next** within a short period of time: *Things change so quickly that we never know what will happen from one day to the next.* ▶ **z dnia na dzień**
have a field day → FIELD DAY
it's early days (yet) → EARLY
make sb's day (informal) to make sb very happy ▶ **ucieszyć kogoś**
one day; **some day** at some time in the future: *One day we'll go back and see all our old friends.* ▶ **kiedyś**
the other day → OTHER
the present day → PRESENT¹
these days in the present age ▶ **w dzisiejszych czasach** SYN **nowadays**

daybreak /ˈdeɪbreɪk/ noun [U] the time in the early morning when light first appears ▶ **brzask, świt** SYN **dawn**

'**day care** noun [U] care for small children, or for old or sick people, away from home, during the day: *Day care is provided by the company she works for.* ◇ *a day care centre* ▶ **opieka dzienna**

'**day centre** noun [C] (Brit.) a place that provides care for old or sick people during the day ▶ **dom dziennego pobytu**

daydream /ˈdeɪdriːm/ noun [C] thoughts that are not connected with what you are doing; often pleasant scenes in your imagination: *The child stared out of the window, lost in a daydream* (zatopione w marzeniach). ▶ **marzenia**
■ **daydream** verb [I]: *Don't just sit there daydreaming – do some work!* ▶ **marzyć, śnić na jawie**

daylight /ˈdeɪlaɪt/ noun [U] the light that there is during the day: *The colours look quite different* ***in daylight.*** ◇ *daylight hours* ▶ **światło dzienne**
IDM **(in) broad daylight** → BROAD

ˌ**daylight 'saving time** (also 'daylight time) (US) = SUMMER TIME

day 'off noun [C] (pl. **days off**) a day on which you do not go to work: *I work six days a week. Sunday's my day off.* ▶ **dzień wolny od pracy** ➲ note at **holiday**

ˌ**day re'turn** noun [C] (Brit.) a train or bus ticket for going somewhere and coming back on the same day. It is cheaper than a normal return ticket. ▶ **bilet powrotny ważny jeden dzień**

daytime /ˈdeɪtaɪm/ noun [U] the time when it is light; not night: *These flowers open* ***in the daytime*** (za dnia) *and close again at night.* ◇ *daytime TV* ▶ **dzień, pora dnia**

ˌ**day-to-'day** adj. [only before a noun] **1** planning for only one day at a time: *I have organized the cleaning* ***on a day-to-day basis,*** *until our usual cleaner returns.* ▶ **z dnia na dzień 2** involving the usual events or tasks of each day: *She has been looking after the* ***day-to-day running*** *of the school.* ▶ **codzienny**

daze /deɪz/ noun
IDM **in a daze** unable to think or react normally; confused: *I've been in a complete daze* (całkowicie oszołomiony) *since I heard the news.* ▶ **w oszołomieniu, nieprzytomn-y/ie**

dazed /deɪzd/ adj. unable to think or react normally; confused: *He had a dazed expression on his face.* ▶ **oszołomiony, nieprzytomny**

dazzle /ˈdæzl/ verb [T, usually passive] **1** (used about a bright light) to make sb unable to see for a short time: *She was dazzled by the other car's headlights.* ▶ **oślepiać 2** to impress sb very much: *He had been dazzled by her beauty.* ▶ **olśniewać, oczarowywać**
■ **dazzling** adj.: *a dazzling light* ▶ **oślepiający; olśniewający**

DC /ˌdiː ˈsiː/ abbr. **direct current**; an electric current that flows in one direction ▶ **prąd stały** ➲ look at **AC**

deacon /ˈdiːkən/, **deaconess** /ˌdiːkəˈnes; US ˈdiːkənes/ noun [C] an official who has a rank below a priest, in some Christian churches ▶ **diakon/isa**

deactivate /ˌdiːˈæktɪveɪt/ verb [T] to make sth such as a device or chemical process stop working: *Do you know how to deactivate the alarm?* ▶ **dezaktywować**, (*bomba itp.*) **rozbrajać**

⚷ **dead¹** /ded/ adj. **1** no longer alive: *My father's dead. He died two years ago.* ◇ *Police found a dead body* (trupa) *under the bridge.* ◇ *The man was shot dead* (został śmiertelnie postrzelony) *by a masked gunman.* ◇ *dead leaves* zwiędłe/uschnięte liście ▶ **zmarły; zdechły, martwy** ➲ noun **death**, verb **die 2** no longer used; finished: *Latin is a dead language.* ◇ *We've made our decision so the subject is now dead* (skończony). ▶ **martwy** OPP **living 3** [not before a noun] (used about a piece of equipment) no longer working: *I picked up the telephone but the line was dead.* ◇ *This battery's dead* (wyczerpana). ▶ **zepsuty 4** without movement, activity or interest: *This town is completely dead after 11 o'clock at night.* ▶ **wymarły, senny 5** [not before a noun] (used about a part of the body) no longer able to feel anything: *Oh no, my foot's* ***gone dead*** (zdrętwiała mi noga). ▶ **zdrętwiały, ścierpnięty 6** [only

before a noun] complete or exact: *a dead silence/calm* głucha cisza ◇ *The arrow hit the dead centre of the target* (w sam środek tarczy). ▶ **zupełny**
IDM **a dead end 1** a street that is only open at one end ▶ **droga bez wylotu**, **ślepa uliczka 2** a point, situation, etc. from which you can make no further progress: *a dead-end job* praca bez perspektyw ▶ (*przen.*) **ślepa uliczka**
drop dead → DROP[1]

dead² /ded/ (**the dead**) noun [pl.] people who have died: *A church service was held in memory of the dead.* ▶ **zmarli**
IDM **in/at the dead of night** in the middle of the night, when it is very dark and quiet ▶ **w samym środku nocy**

dead³ /ded/ adv. completely, exactly or very: *The car made a strange noise and then stopped dead.* ◇ *He's dead keen to start work.* ▶ **całkowicie**, **bardzo**

deaden /ˈdedn/ verb [T] to make sth less strong, painful, etc.: *They gave her drugs to try and deaden the pain.* ▶ **łagodzić**, **tłumić**

ˌdead ˈheat noun [C] the result of a race when two people, etc. finish at exactly the same time ▶ **nierozstrzygnięty bieg**

deadline /ˈdedlaɪn/ noun [C] a time or date before which sth must be done or finished: *I usually **set myself a deadline** when I have a project to do.* ◇ *A journalist is used to having to **meet deadlines*** (jest przyzwyczajony do dotrzymywania terminów). ▶ **ostateczny termin**, **nieprzekraczalna granica/data (czegoś)**

deadlock /ˈdedlɒk/ noun [sing., U] a situation in which two sides cannot reach an agreement: *Talks have reached (a) deadlock* (znalazły się w martwym punkcie). ◇ *to try to break the deadlock* (impas) ▶ **martwy punkt**, **sytuacja bez wyjścia**

deadly /ˈdedli/ adj. (**deadlier**; **deadliest**) **1** causing or likely to cause death: *a deadly poison/weapon/disease* ▶ **śmiertelny**, **morderczy 2** [adjective only before a noun] very great; complete: *They're deadly enemies.* ▶ **śmiertelny** ⊃ look at **deathly 3** extremely accurate, so that no defence is possible: *That player is deadly when he gets in front of the goal.* ▶ **morderczy 4** (informal) very boring ▶ **śmiertelnie nudny**
■ **deadly** adv. completely; extremely: *I'm not joking. In fact I'm deadly serious.* ▶ **śmiertelnie**

deadpan /ˈdedpæn/ adj. without any expression on your face or in your voice: *He told the joke with a completely deadpan face.* ▶ **bez wyrazu**

deaf /def/ adj. **1** unable to hear anything or unable to hear very well: *You'll have to speak louder. My father's a bit deaf.* ◇ *to go deaf* ◇ *She's **stone deaf**.* Jest głucha jak pień. ▶ **głuchy 2** (**the deaf**) noun [pl.] people who cannot hear ▶ **głusi 3 deaf to sth** not wanting to listen to sth: *I've told her what I think but she's deaf to my advice.* ▶ **głuchy na coś**
■ **deafness** noun [U] ▶ **głuchota**

deafen /ˈdefn/ verb [T, usually passive] to make sb unable to hear by making a very loud noise: *We were deafened by the loud music.* ▶ **ogłuszać**, **zagłuszać**
■ **deafening** adj. ▶ **ogłuszający**

deal¹ /diːl/ verb (pt, pp **dealt** /delt/) **1** [I,T] **deal (sth) (out)**; **deal (sth) (to sb)** to give cards to players in a game of cards: *Start by dealing seven cards to each player.* ◇ *Whose turn is it to deal?* ▶ **rozdawać 2** [I,T] (informal) to buy and sell illegal drugs ▶ **handlować narkotykami 3** [I] **deal (in sth)**; **deal (with sb)** to do business, especially buying and selling goods: *He deals in second-hand cars.* ◇ *Our firm deals with customers all over the world.* ▶ **handlować czymś**; **prowadzić interesy (z kimś)**
IDM **deal sb/sth a blow**; **deal a blow to sb/sth 1** to give sb a shock, etc.: *This news dealt a terrible blow to my father.* Ta wiadomość była dla ojca strasznym ciosem. ▶ **wywołać szok**, **zadawać komuś/czemuś cios 2** to hit sb/sth: *He was dealt a nasty blow to the head in the accident.* ▶ **wymierzać komuś cios**, **mocno kogoś uderzyć**
PHR V **deal sth out** to give sth to a number of people: *The profits will be dealt out among us.* ▶ **rozdawać coś**
deal with sb to treat sb in a particular way; to handle sb ▶ **postępować z kimś**, **radzić sobie z kimś**
deal with sth 1 to take suitable action in a particular situation in order to solve a problem, complete a task, etc.; to handle sth: *My secretary will deal with my correspondence while I'm away.* ▶ **radzić sobie z czymś**, **zajmować się czymś 2** to have sth as its subject: *This chapter deals with letter-writing.* ▶ **dotyczyć czegoś**, **traktować o czymś**

deal² /diːl/ noun [C] **1** an agreement or arrangement, especially in business: *We're hoping to **do a deal*** (ubić interes) *with an Italian company.* ◇ *Let's **make a deal*** (umówmy się, że) *not to criticize each other's work.* ◇ *'I'll help you with your essay if you'll fix my bike.' 'OK, **it's a deal*** (załatwione)*!'* ▶ **interes**, **transakcja 2** the way that sb is treated: *With high fares and unreliable services, rail users are **getting a raw deal*** (są źle traktowani). ◇ *The new law aims to give pensioners **a fair deal*** (ma na celu sprawiedliwe traktowanie emerytów). ▶ **traktowanie 3** the act of giving cards to players in a card game ▶ **rozdanie** (*kart*)
IDM **a big deal/no big deal** → BIG
a good/great deal (of sth) a lot (of sth): *I've spent a great deal of time on this report.* ▶ **sporo**, **wiele**

dealer /ˈdiːlə(r)/ noun [C] **1** a person whose business is buying and selling things: *a dealer in gold and silver* ◇ *a drug dealer* ▶ **handlowiec**, **handla-rz/rka 2** the person who gives the cards to the players in a game of cards ▶ **rozdając-y/a**

dealing /ˈdiːlɪŋ/ noun **1** (**dealings**) [pl.] relations, especially in business: *We had some dealings with that firm several years ago.* ◇ *The police have had dealings with her before* (miała z nią do czynienia wcześniej). ▶ **interesy 2** [U] buying and selling: *share dealing* obrót akcjami ▶ **handel**

dealt past tense, past participle of **deal¹**

dean /diːn/ noun [C] **1** a priest who is responsible for a large church or a number of small churches ▶ **dziekan 2** an important official at some universities or colleges ▶ **dziekan**

dear¹ /dɪə(r)/ adj. **1 dear (to sb)** loved by or important to sb: *It was a subject that was very dear to him.* ◇ *She's one of my dearest friends.* ▶ **kochany**, **drogi 2** (used at the beginning of a letter before the name or title of the person you are writing to): *Dear Sarah, ...* ◇ *Dear Sir or Madam, ...* ▶ **drogi**, **szanowny 3** [only before a noun] (a word that is used with 'little' or 'old' to express your liking for sb/sth): *Dear old Jane! She always remembers to write at Christmas.* ▶ **(mój) drogi 3** (Brit.) expensive: *How can people afford to smoke when cigarettes are so dear?* ▶ **drogi**
IDM **close/dear/near to sb's heart** → HEART

dear² /dɪə(r)/ interj. (used for expressing disappointment, sadness, surprise, etc.): *Dear me! Aren't you ready?* ▶ **ojej!**

dear³ /dɪə(r)/ noun [C] **1** (Brit., informal) a kind, gentle person: *She's a kind old lady – an absolute dear* (chodząca dobroć). ▶ **dobry/poczciwy człowiek 2** (used when speaking to sb you know well): *Would you like a cup of tea, dear?* ▶ **kochanie 3** (used when speaking to sb in a friendly way, for example by an older person to a young person or a child): *What's your name, dear?* ▶ **kochanie**

dearly /ˈdɪəli/ adv. **1** very much: *I'd dearly like to go there again.* ▶ **bardzo**, **strasznie 2** (formal) in a way that causes damage or suffering, or costs a lot of money: *I've already paid dearly for that mistake.* ▶ **drogo, słono**

dearth /dɜːθ/ noun [sing.] **a dearth (of sb/sth)** a lack of sth; not enough of sth ▶ **niedobór**

death /deθ/ noun **1** [C,U] the end of sb/sth's life; dying: *There were two deaths and many other people were injured in the accident.* ◇ *The police do not know the* ***cause of death.*** ◇ *There was no food and people were* ***starving to death*** (umierali z głodu). ▶ **śmierć, zgon** ➲ adjective **dead**, verb **die 2** [U] the end (of sth): *the death of communism* ▶ **upadek, koniec**

IDM **catch your death (of cold)** → CATCH[1]

a matter of life and/or death → MATTER[1]

put sb to death [usually passive] (formal) to kill sb as a punishment, in past times ▶ **uśmiercić kogoś**

sick to death of sb/sth → SICK[1]

sudden death → SUDDEN

deathly /ˈdeθli/ adj., adv. like death: *There was a deathly silence.* ▶ **śmiertelny** ➲ look at **deadly**

ˈ**death penalty** noun [sing.] the legal punishment of being killed for a crime ▶ **kara śmierci** ➲ look at **capital punishment**

ˌ**death ˈrow** noun [U] the cells in a prison for prisoners who are waiting to be killed as punishment for a serious crime: *prisoners* ***on death row*** ▶ **cele, w których przebywają więźniowie skazani na karę śmierci**

ˈ**death toll** noun [C] the number of people killed in a disaster, war, accident, etc. ▶ **liczba ofiar śmiertelnych**

ˈ**death trap** noun [C] (informal) a building, vehicle, etc. that is dangerous and could cause sb's death ▶ **śmiertelna pułapka**

debase /dɪˈbeɪs/ verb [T, usually passive] (formal) to reduce the quality or value of sth ▶ **obniżać wartość czegoś, deprecjonować**

debatable /dɪˈbeɪtəbl/ adj. not certain; that you could argue about: *It's debatable whether people have a better lifestyle these days.* ▶ **dyskusyjny, sporny**

debate[1] /dɪˈbeɪt/ noun **1** [C] a formal argument or discussion of a question at a public meeting or in Parliament: *a debate on educational reform* ▶ **debata, obrady 2** [U] general discussion about sth expressing different opinions: *There's been a lot of debate about the cause of acid rain.* ▶ **debata, dyskusja**

debate[2] /dɪˈbeɪt/ verb **1** [I,T] to discuss sth in a formal way or at a public meeting: *Politicians will be debating the bill later this week.* ▶ **debatować, obradować 2** [T] to think about or discuss sth before deciding what to do: *They debated whether to go or not.* ▶ **rozważać, zastanawiać się**

debauched /dɪˈbɔːtʃt/ adj. a **debauched** person is immoral in their sexual behaviour, drinks a lot of alcohol, takes drugs, etc. ▶ **rozpustny** SYN **depraved**
■ **debauchery** /dɪˈbɔːtʃəri/ noun [U] ▶ **rozpusta**

debilitate /dɪˈbɪlɪteɪt/ verb [T] (formal) **1** to make sb's body or mind weaker: *The troops were severely debilitated by hunger and disease.* ◇ *She found the heat debilitating.* ◇ *a debilitating disease* ▶ **wycieńczać; wykańczać 2** to make a country, an organization, etc. weaker: *Prolonged strike action debilitated the industry.* ◇ *The economy is now strengthening after a long and debilitating recession.* ▶ **osłabiać**

debit[1] /ˈdebɪt/ noun [C] an amount of money paid out of a bank account ▶ **debet** OPP **credit** ➲ look at **direct debit**

debit[2] /ˈdebɪt/ verb [T] to take an amount of money out of a bank account, etc. usually as a payment; to record this ▶ **debetować** ➲ look at **direct debit**

ˈ**debit card** noun [C] a plastic card that can be used to take money directly from your bank account when you pay for sth ▶ **karta płatnicza** ➲ look at **credit card**

debrief /ˌdiːˈbriːf/ verb [T] **debrief sb (on sth)** to ask sb questions officially, in order to get information about the task that they have just completed: *He was taken to a US airbase to be debriefed on the mission.* ▶ **wysłuchiwać sprawozdania z wypełnionej misji** ➲ look at **brief**
■ **debriefing** noun [U,C]: *a debriefing session* ▶ **wysłuchiwanie sprawozdania z wypełnionej misji**

debris /ˈdebriː; ˈdeɪ-; US dəˈbriː/ noun [U] pieces from sth that has been destroyed, especially in an accident ▶ **szczątki, gruz**

D

debt /det/ noun **1** [C] an amount of money that you owe to sb: *Teresa borrowed a lot of money and she's still paying off the debt.* ▶ **dług** ➲ note at **loan 2** [U] the state of owing money: *After he lost his job, he* ***got into debt*** (popadł w długi). ▶ **zadłużenie 3** [C, usually sing.] (formal) something that you owe sb, for example because they have helped or been kind to you: *In his speech he acknowledged his debt to his family and friends for their support.* ▶ **zobowiązanie, wdzięczność**

IDM **be in/out of debt** to owe/not owe money ▶ **(nie) być zadłużonym**

be in sb's debt (formal) to feel grateful to sb for sth that they have done for you ▶ **mieć dług wdzięczności wobec kogoś**

debtor /ˈdetə(r)/ noun [C] a person who owes money ▶ **dłużnik**

debug /ˌdiːˈbʌɡ/ verb [T] (**debugged**; **debugged**) to look for and remove the faults in a computer program ▶ (*komput.*) **usuwać błędy w oprogramowaniu**

debut (also **début**) /ˈdeɪbjuː; ˈdebjuː; US deɪˈbjuː/ noun [C] a first appearance in public of an actor, etc.: *She* ***made her debut*** (zadebiutowała) *in London in 1959.* ▶ **debiut**

Dec. = DECEMBER: *5 Dec. 1999*

decade /ˈdekeɪd; dɪˈk-/ noun [C] a period of ten years ▶ **dziesięciolecie**

decadence /ˈdekədəns/ noun [U] behaviour, attitudes, etc. that show low moral standards ▶ **upadek, dekadencja**
■ **decadent** /ˈdekədənt/ adj.: *a decadent society* ▶ **schyłkowy, dekadencki**

decaffeinated /ˌdiːˈkæfɪneɪtɪd/ adj. (used about coffee or tea) with most or all of the **caffeine** removed ▶ **bez kofeiny** ➲ note at **coffee**

decapitate /dɪˈkæpɪteɪt/ verb [T] (formal) to cut off sb's head ▶ **ścinać głowę** SYN **behead**

decay[1] /dɪˈkeɪ/ noun [U] the process or state of being slowly destroyed: *tooth decay* ◇ *The old farm was in a terrible state of decay.* ▶ **gnicie, niszczenie; upadek**

decay[2] /dɪˈkeɪ/ verb [I] **1** to go bad or be slowly destroyed: *the decaying carcass of a dead sheep* ▶ **niszczeć, gnić, psuć się** SYN **rot 2** to become weaker or less powerful: *His business empire began to decay.* ▶ **podupadać**
■ **decayed** adj.: *a decayed tooth* ▶ **zepsuty, zgniły**

the **deceased** /dɪˈsiːst/ noun [sing.] (formal) a person who has died, especially one who has died recently: *Many friends of the deceased were present at the funeral.* ▶ **zmarł-y/a**
■ **deceased** adj. ▶ **zmarły**

deceit /dɪˈsiːt/ noun [U] dishonest behaviour; trying to make sb believe sth that is not true ▶ **oszustwo**

deceitful /dɪˈsiːtfl/ adj. dishonest; trying to make sb believe sth that is not true ▶ **oszukańczy, zwodniczy**
■ **deceitfully** /-fəli/ adv. ▶ **oszukańczo, zwodniczo** | **deceitfulness** noun [U] ▶ **zwodniczość**

deceive /dɪˈsiːv/ verb [T] **deceive sb/yourself (into doing sth)** to try to make sb believe sth that is not true: *You're deceiving yourself if you think there's an easy solution to the problem.* ◇ *He deceived his mother into believing that* *he hadn't stolen the money.* ▶ **oszukiwać/zwodzić (kogoś/siebie tak, że/aby)** ➲ noun **deception** or **deceit**

December /dɪˈsembə(r)/ noun [U,C] (abbr. **Dec.**) the 12th month of the year, coming after November ▶ **grudzień** ➲ note at **January**

decency /ˈdiːsnsi/ noun [U] moral or correct behaviour: *She **had the decency to*** (miała na tyle przyzwoitości, żeby) *admit that it was her fault.* ▶ **przyzwoitość**

decent /ˈdiːsnt/ adj. **1** of a good enough standard: *All she wants is a decent job with decent wages.* ▶ **niezły** **2** (used about people or behaviour) honest and fair; treating people with respect ▶ **przyzwoity** **3** not likely to offend or shock sb: *I can't come to the door – I'm not decent* (nie jestem ubrany). ▶ **przyzwoity** OPP **indecent**
■ **decently** adv. ▶ **przyzwoicie**

deception /dɪˈsepʃn/ noun [C,U] making sb believe or being made to believe sth that is not true: *He had obtained the secret papers **by deception**.* ▶ **wprowadzenie w błąd, podstęp** ➲ verb **deceive**

deceptive /dɪˈseptɪv/ adj. likely to make you believe sth that is not true: *The water is deceptive. It's much deeper than it looks.* ▶ **zwodniczy, mylący**
■ **deceptively** adv.: *She made the task sound deceptively easy.* ▶ **pozornie, zwodniczo**

decibel /ˈdesɪbel/ noun [C] a measure of how loud a sound is ▶ **decybel**

decide /dɪˈsaɪd/ verb **1** [I,T] **decide (to do sth)**; **decide against (doing) sth**; **decide about/on sth**; **decide that...** to think about two or more possibilities and choose one of them: *There are so many to choose from – I can't decide!* ◇ *We've decided not to invite Isabel.* ◇ *They decided on a name for the baby.* ◇ *He decided that it was too late to go.* ◇ *She decided against borrowing* (zdecydowała nie pożyczać) *the money.* ◇ *The date hasn't been decided yet.* Jeszcze nie zdecydowano o terminie. ▶ **zdecydować** **2** [T] to influence sth so that it produces a particular result: *Your votes will decide the winner* (zadecydują, kto wygra). ▶ **zadecydować (o czymś)** **3** [T] to cause sb to make a decision: *What finally decided you to leave* (zadecydowało o twoim wyjeździe)*?* ▶ **zadecydować o czymś** ➲ noun **decision**, adjective **decisive**

decided /dɪˈsaɪdɪd/ adj. [only before a noun] clear; definite: *There has been a decided improvement in his work.* ▶ **zdecydowany**
■ **decidedly** adv. ▶ **zdecydowanie**

deciduous /dɪˈsɪdʒuəs/ adj. (used about a tree) of a type that loses its leaves every autumn ▶ **zrzucający liście** ➲ look at **evergreen**

decimal[1] /ˈdesɪml/ adj. based on or counted in units of ten: *decimal currency* dziesiętny system monetarny ▶ **dziesiętny**

decimal[2] /ˈdesɪml/ noun [C] part of a number, written after a **decimal point**: *A quarter expressed as a decimal is 0.25.* ▶ **ułamek dziesiętny**

> Uwaga! W jęz. ang. przed ułamkiem dziesiętnym stawia się kropkę, nie przecinek.

ˌdecimal ˈplace noun [C] the position of a number after a **decimal point**: *The figure is **accurate to two decimal places**.* ▶ **miejsce po przecinku**

ˌdecimal ˈpoint noun [C] a dot or point used to separate the whole number from the tenths, **hundredths**, etc. of a **decimal**, for example in 0.61 ▶ **przecinek dziesiętny**

decimate /ˈdesɪmeɪt/ verb [T] to destroy or badly damage a large number of people or things ▶ **dziesiątkować**

decipher /dɪˈsaɪfə(r)/ verb [T] to succeed in reading or understanding sth that is not clear: *It's impossible to decipher his handwriting.* ▶ **odcyfrowywać, odszyfrowywać**

decision /dɪˈsɪʒn/ noun **1** [C,U] **a decision (to do sth)**; **a decision on/about sth**; **a decision that...** a choice or judgement that you make after thinking about various possibilities: *Have you **made a decision** yet?* ◇ *I realize now that I made the wrong decision.* ◇ *There were good reasons for his decision to leave.* ◇ *I **took the decision** that I believed to be right.* ▶ **decyzja, postanowienie** **2** [U] being able to decide clearly and quickly: *We are looking for someone with decision for this job.* ▶ **zdecydowanie, stanowczość** ➲ verb **decide**

decisive /dɪˈsaɪsɪv/ adj. **1** making sth certain or final: *the decisive battle of the war* ▶ **decydujący** **2** having the ability to make clear decisions quickly: *It's no good hesitating. Be decisive.* ▶ **zdecydowany, stanowczy** OPP **indecisive** ➲ verb **decide**
■ **decisively** adv. ▶ **zdecydowanie, stanowczo** | **decisiveness** noun [U] ▶ **zdecydowanie, stanowczość**

deck /dek/ noun [C] **1** one of the floors of a ship or bus ▶ **pokład, piętro** (*autobusu*) **2** (US) : *a deck of cards* = PACK[2] (6) **3** part of a machine that records and/or plays sounds on a tape or CD: *a cassette/tape deck* ▶ **dek** (*np. odtwarzacza CD*)
IDM **on deck** on the part of a ship which you can walk on outside: *I'm going out on deck for some fresh air.* ▶ **na pokład/pokładzie**

deckchair /ˈdektʃeə(r)/ noun [C] a chair that you use outside, especially on the beach. You can fold it up and carry it. ▶ **leżak**

decking /ˈdekɪŋ/ noun [U] wood used to build a floor (called a **deck**) in the garden next to or near a house ▶ **drewno do zabudowania podłogi altanki/tarasu w ogrodzie przy domu**

declamation /ˌdekləˈmeɪʃn/ noun (formal) **1** [U] the act of speaking or of expressing sth to an audience in a formal way ▶ **deklamacja** **2** [C] a speech or piece of writing that strongly expresses feelings and opinions ▶ **deklaracja**

declamatory /dɪˈklæmətəri; US -tɔːri/ adj. (formal) expressing feelings or opinions in a strong way in a speech or a piece of writing ▶ **deklamatorski**

declaration /ˌdekləˈreɪʃn/ noun **1** [C,U] an official statement about sth: *In his speech he made a strong declaration of support for the rebels.* ◇ *the declaration of war* ▶ **deklaracja, wypowiedzenie** **2** [C] a written statement giving information on goods or money you have earned, on which you have to pay tax: *a customs declaration* ▶ **deklaracja celna**

declare /dɪˈkleə(r)/ verb [T] **1** to state sth publicly and officially or to make sth known in a firm, clear way: *to **declare war** on another country* ◇ *I declare that the winner of the award is Joan Taylor.* ▶ **ogłaszać, wypowiadać** **2** to give information about goods or money you have earned, on which you have to pay tax: *You must declare all your income on this form.* ▶ **deklarować, zgłaszać do oclenia**

declassify /ˌdiːˈklæsɪfaɪ/ verb [T] (**declassifies**; **declassifying**; **declassified**; **declassified**) to state officially that secret government information is no longer secret: *declassified **information/documents*** ▶ **odtajniać** OPP **classify**
■ **declassification** /ˌdiːˌklæsɪfɪˈkeɪʃn/ noun [U] ▶ **odtajnienie**

declension /dɪˈklenʃn/ noun **1** [C] a set of nouns, adjectives, or pronouns that change in the same way to show **case**, number, and **gender** ▶ **deklinacja** **2** [U] the way in which some sets of nouns, adjectives, and pronouns change their form or endings to show **case**, number, or **gender** ▶ **deklinacja**

decline[1] /dɪˈklaɪn/ noun [C,U] **(a) decline (in sth)** a process or period of becoming weaker, smaller or less good: *a* *decline in sales* ◇ *As an industrial power, the country is* ***in decline*** (kraj chyli się ku upadkowi). ▶ **upadek, spadek, pogorszenie, zmniejszanie się**

decline² /dɪ'klaɪn/ verb **1** [I] to become weaker, smaller or less good: *declining profits* ◇ *The standard of education has declined in this country.* ▶ **pogarszać się, zmniejszać się 2** [I,T] (formal) to refuse, usually politely: *Thank you for the invitation but I'm afraid I have to decline.* ◇ *The minister declined to make a statement.* (odmówił wydania oświadczenia) ▶ **odmawiać**

decode /ˌdiː'kəʊd/ verb [T] to find the meaning of a secret message ▶ **odszyfrowywać** OPP **encode**

decoder /ˌdiː'kəʊdə(r)/ noun [C] a device that changes electronic signals into a form that can be understood: *a satellite/video decoder* ▶ **dekoder**

decompose /ˌdiːkəm'pəʊz/ verb [I] to slowly be destroyed by natural chemical processes: *The body was so badly decomposed that it couldn't be identified.* ▶ **rozkładać się**
■ **decomposition** /ˌdiːkɒmpə'zɪʃn/ noun [U] ▶ **rozkład, rozpad**

decongestant /ˌdiːkən'dʒestənt/ noun [C] a medicine that helps sb with a cold to breathe more easily: *a nasal decongestant* ▶ **środek udrożniający górne drogi oddechowe**

deconstruct /ˌdiːkən'strʌkt/ verb [T] (in literature and philosophy) to analyse a text in order to show that there is no fixed meaning within the text but that the meaning is created each time in the act of reading ▶ **przeprowadzać dekonstrukcję**
■ **deconstruction** /ˌdiːkən'strʌkʃn/ noun [U] (in literature and philosophy) a theory that states that it is impossible for a text to have one fixed meaning, and emphasizes the role of the reader in the production of meaning ▶ **dekonstrukcja**

decor /'deɪkɔː(r); US deɪ'kɔːr/ noun [U, sing.] the style in which the inside of a building is decorated ▶ **wystrój**

decorate /'dekəreɪt/ verb **1** [T] **decorate sth (with sth)** to add sth in order to make a thing more attractive to look at: *Decorate the cake with cherries and nuts.* ▶ **ozdabiać, dekorować 2** [I,T] (especially Brit.) to put paint and/or coloured paper onto walls, ceilings and doors in a room or building: *I think it's about time we decorated the living room.* ▶ **malować i/lub tapetować**

decoration /ˌdekə'reɪʃn/ noun **1** [C,U] something that is added to sth in order to make it look more attractive: *Christmas decorations* ▶ **ozdoba, dekoracja 2** [U] the process of decorating a room or building; the style in which sth is decorated: *The house is in need of decoration.* ▶ **malowanie i/lub tapetowanie, wystrój**

decorative /'dekərətɪv; US -reɪt-/ adj. attractive or pretty to look at: *The cloth had a decorative lace edge.* ▶ **ozdobny, dekoracyjny**

decorator /'dekəreɪtə(r)/ noun [C] a person whose job is to paint and decorate houses and buildings ▶ **dekorator/ka wnętrz**

decorous /'dekərəs/ adj. (formal) polite and appropriate in a particular social situation; not shocking: *a decorous kiss* ▶ **godny, stosowny** SYN **proper**
■ **decorously** adv.: *They sipped their drinks decorously.* ▶ **godnie, stosownie**

decorum /dɪ'kɔːrəm/ noun [U] (formal) polite behaviour that is appropriate in a social situation: *a sense of decorum* ▶ **godność, przyzwoitość**

decoy /'diːkɔɪ/ noun [C] a person or object that is used in order to trick sb/sth into doing what you want, going where you want, etc. ▶ **przynęta, wabik**
■ **decoy** verb [T] ▶ **wabić**

decrease¹ /dɪ'kriːs/ verb [I,T] to become or to make sth smaller or less: *Profits have decreased by 15%.* ◇ *Decrease speed when you are approaching a road junction.* ▶ **zmniejszać (się)** OPP **increase**

decrease² /'diːkriːs/ noun [C,U] **(a) decrease (in sth)** the process of becoming or making sth smaller or less; the amount that sth is reduced by: *a 10% decrease in sales* ▶ **spadek, zmniej-szenie/szanie (się)**

decree /dɪ'kriː/ noun [C] an official order given by a government, a ruler, etc. ▶ **rozporządzenie, dekret**
■ **decree** verb [T] (pt, pp **decreed**) ▶ **rozporządzać, zadekretować**

decrepit /dɪ'krepɪt/ adj. (used about a thing or person) old and in very bad condition or poor health ▶ **zniszczony, rozpadający się, zgrzybiały**

decriminalize (also -ise) /diː'krɪmɪnəlaɪz/ verb [T] to change the law so that sth is no longer illegal: *There are moves to decriminalize some soft drugs.* ▶ **zalegalizować** OPP **criminalize**
■ **decriminalization** (also -isation) /diːˌkrɪmɪnəlaɪ'zeɪʃn; US -lə'z-/ noun [U] ▶ **legalizacja**

dedicate /'dedɪkeɪt/ verb [T] **1 dedicate sth to sth** to give all your energy, time, efforts, etc. to sth: *He dedicated his life to helping the poor.* ▶ **poświęcać 2 dedicate sth to sb** to say that sth is specially for sb: *He dedicated the book he had written to his brother.* ▶ **dedykować**

dedicated /'dedɪkeɪtɪd/ adj. giving a lot of your energy, time, efforts, etc. to sth that you believe to be important: *dedicated nurses and doctors* ▶ **zaangażowany (w coś), poświęcający się (czemuś)**

dedication /ˌdedɪ'keɪʃn/ noun **1** [U] the hard work and effort that sb puts into an activity or purpose because they think it is important: *I admire her dedication to her career.* ▶ **zaangażowanie, poświęcenie się (czemuś) 2** [C] a message at the beginning of a book or piece of music saying that it is for a particular person ▶ **dedykacja**

deduce /dɪ'djuːs; US -duːs/ verb [T] to form an opinion using the facts that you already know: *From his name I deduced that he was Polish.* ▶ **wnioskować, dedukować** ➲ noun **deduction**

deduct /dɪ'dʌkt/ verb [T] **deduct sth (from sth)** to take sth such as money or points away from a total amount: *Marks will be deducted for untidy work.* ▶ **odejmować, potrącać**

deduction /dɪ'dʌkʃn/ noun [C,U] **1** something that you work out from facts that you already know; the ability to think in this way: *It was a brilliant piece of deduction by the detective.* ▶ **dedukcja, wniosek** ➲ verb **deduce 2 deduction (from sth)** taking away an amount or number from a total; the amount or number taken away from the total: *What is your total income after deductions?* ▶ **odjęcie, potrącenie** ➲ verb **deduct**

deed /diːd/ noun [C] **1** (formal) something that you do; an action: *a brave/good/charitable deed* ▶ **czyn 2** a legal document that shows that you own a house or building: *The deeds of our house are kept at the bank.* ▶ **akt własności** ➲ look at **act**

deem /diːm/ verb [T] (formal) to have a particular opinion about sth: *He did not even deem it necessary to apologize.* ▶ **uważać, poczytywać za coś**

deep¹ /diːp/ adj. **1** going a long way down from the surface: *to dig a deep hole* ◇ *That's a deep cut.* ◇ *a coat with deep pockets* ▶ **głęboki** ➲ noun **depth 2** going a long way from front to back: *deep shelves* ▶ **głęboki 3** measuring a particular amount from top to bottom or from front to back: *The water is only a metre deep* (basen ma tylko metr głębokości) *here.* ▶ **głęboki** (*na ileś metrów*) **4** low: *a deep voice* ▶ **głęboki, niski 5** dark; strong: *a deep red* ▶ **głęboki, ciemny** OPP **light 6** not easy to wake from: *I was in a deep sleep and didn't hear the phone ringing*

for ages. ▶ **głęboki** OPP **light** **7** strongly felt: *He felt a very deep love for the child.* ▶ **głęboki** **8** dealing with difficult subjects or details: *His books show a deep understanding of human nature.* ▶ **gruntowny, głęboki**
■ **the deep** noun [U]: *She awoke in the deep of the night* (w środku nocy). ◇ *the deep* morze/ocean ❶ Stosuje się tylko w języku literackim. | **deeply** adv.: *a deeply unhappy person* ◇ *to breathe deeply* ▶ **głęboko**
IDM **deep in thought/conversation** thinking very hard or giving sb/sth your full attention: *Irene sat, deep/lost in thought, looking at the old photographs.* ▶ **pogrążony (w czymś)**
take a deep breath to breathe in a lot of air, especially in preparation for doing sth difficult: *He took a deep breath then walked on stage.* ▶ **wziąć głęboki oddech**

deep² /diːp/ adv. a long way down or inside sth: *He gazed deep into her eyes.* ◇ *He dug his hands deep into his pockets.* ▶ **głęboko**
IDM **deep down** in what you really think or feel: *I tried to appear optimistic but deep down I knew there was no hope.* ▶ **w głębi duszy/serca**
dig deep → DIG[1]

deepen /ˈdiːpən/ verb [I,T] to become or to make sth deep or deeper: *The river deepens here.* ▶ **pogłębiać (się)**

ˌdeep ˈfreeze = FREEZER

ˌdeep-ˈrooted (also **ˌdeep-ˈseated**) adj. strongly felt or believed and therefore difficult to change: *deep-rooted fears* ▶ **głęboko zakorzeniony**

ˌdeep vein thromˈbosis noun [C,U] (abbr. **DVT** /ˌdiː viː ˈtiː/) a serious condition caused by a **clot** forming in a tube that carries blood to the heart ▶ **zakrzepica żył głębokich**

deer /dɪə(r)/ noun [C] (pl. **deer**) a large wild animal that eats grass. The male has **antlers** on its head. ▶ **jeleń**

> A male deer is called a **buck** or, especially if it has fully-grown antlers, a **stag**. The female is a **doe** and a young deer is a **fawn**. **Venison** is the meat from deer.

deerstalker /ˈdɪəstɔːkə(r)/ noun [C] a cap with two peaks, one in front and one behind, and two pieces of fabric which are usually tied together on top but can be folded down to cover the ears ▶ **kapelusz myśliwski**

deface /dɪˈfeɪs/ verb [T] to spoil the way sth looks by writing on or marking its surface ▶ **oszpecać**

defamation /ˌdefəˈmeɪʃn/ noun [U,C] (formal) the act of damaging the opinion that people have of sb by saying or writing bad or false things about them: *He sued for defamation of character.* ▶ **zniesławienie, szkalowanie**

defamatory /dɪˈfæmətri; US -tɔːri/ adj. (formal) (used about speech or writing) intended to harm sb by saying or writing bad or false things about them ▶ **zniesławiający, szkalujący**

defame /dɪˈfeɪm/ verb [T] (formal) to harm sb by saying or writing bad or false things about them ▶ **zniesławiać, szkalować**

default¹ /dɪˈfɔːlt/ noun [sing.] a course of action taken by a computer when it is not given any other instruction ▶ (*komput.*) **ustawienie standardowe**
IDM **by default** because nothing happened, not because of successful effort: *They won by default, because the other team didn't turn up.* ▶ **walkowerem**

default² /dɪˈfɔːlt/ verb [I] **1 default (on sth)** to not do sth that you should do by law: *If you default on the credit payments* (jeśli nie zapłacisz rat), *the car will be taken back.* ▶ **nie dotrzymywać prawnego zobowiązania, nie wywiązywać się z płatności** **2 default (to sth)** (used about a computer) to take a particular course of action when no other command is given ▶ (*komputer*) **ustawiać się według parametrów standardowych**

defeat¹ /dɪˈfiːt/ verb [T] **1** to win a game, a fight, a vote, etc. against sb: *The army defeated the rebels after three days of fighting.* ◇ *In the last match France defeated Wales.* ▶ **pokonywać, zwyciężać** SYN **beat** **2** to be too difficult for sb to do or understand: *I've tried to work out what's wrong with the car but it defeats me* (to dla mnie za trudne). ▶ **być zbyt trudnym** **3** to prevent sth from succeeding: *The local residents are determined to defeat the council's building plans.* ▶ **udaremniać**

defeat² /dɪˈfiːt/ noun **1** [C] an occasion when sb fails to win or be successful against sb else: *This season they have had two victories and three defeats.* ▶ **porażka** **2** [U] the act of losing or not being successful: *She refused to **admit defeat** and kept on trying.* ▶ **porażka, niepowodzenie**

defeatism /dɪˈfiːtɪzəm/ noun [U] the attitude of expecting sth to end in failure ▶ **defetyzm**

defeatist /dɪˈfiːtɪst/ adj. expecting not to succeed: *a defeatist attitude/view* ▶ **defetystyczny**
■ **defeatist** noun [C]: *Don't be such a defeatist, we haven't lost yet!* ▶ **defetyst(k)a**

defecate /ˈdefəkeɪt/ verb [I] (formal) to get rid of waste from the body; to go to the toilet ▶ **oddawać stolec**

defect¹ /ˈdiːfekt/ noun [C] sth that is wrong with or missing from sb/sth: *defects in the education system* ◇ *a speech defect* wada wymowy ▶ **wada, mankament**
■ **defective** /dɪˈfektɪv/ adj. ▶ **wadliwy, wybrakowany**

defect² /dɪˈfekt/ verb [I] to leave your country, a political party, etc. and join one that is considered to be the enemy ▶ **uciec z kraju** (*z powodów politycznych*), **przechodzić na stronę wroga**
■ **defection** noun [C,U] ▶ **ucieczka i przyłączenie się do przeciwnika** | **defector** /dɪˈfektə(r)/ noun [C] ▶ **uciekinier/ka polityczn-y/a; osoba, która przeszła z jednej partii politycznej do drugiej; osoba, która przeszła na stronę wroga**

defective /dɪˈfektɪv/ adj. having a fault or faults; not perfect or complete: *defective goods* ◇ *Her hearing was found to be slightly defective.* ▶ **wadliwy** SYN **faulty**
■ **defectively** adv. ▶ **wadliwie** | **defectiveness** noun [U] ▶ **wadliwość**

defence (US **defense**) /dɪˈfens/ noun **1** [U] something that you do or say to protect sb/sth from attack, bad treatment, criticism, etc.: *Would you fight **in defence of** your country?* ◇ *When her brother was criticized she **leapt to his defence*** (pośpieszyła mu z pomocą). ◇ *I must say **in her defence** that I have always found her a very reliable employee.* ▶ **obrona** ➲ look at **self-defence** **2** [C] **a defence (against sth)** something that protects sb/sth from sth, or that is used to fight against attack: *the body's defences against disease* ▶ **system obrony** **3** [U] the military equipment, forces, etc. for protecting a country: *Spending on defence needs to be reduced.* ▶ **obrona** **4** [C] an argument in support of the accused person in a court of law: *His defence was that he was only carrying out orders.* ▶ **obrona** **5** (**the defence**) [sing., with sing. or pl. verb] the lawyer or lawyers who are acting for the accused person in a court of law: *The defence claims/claim that many of the witnesses were lying.* ▶ **obrona, strona pozwana** ➲ note at **court** ➲ look at **prosecution** **6** (usually **the defence**) [sing., U] action to prevent the other team scoring; the players who try to do this: *She plays in defence.* ▶ **obrona; defensywa; obrońcy**

defenceless /dɪˈfensləs/ adj. unable to defend yourself against attack ▶ **bezbronny**

defend /dɪˈfend/ verb **1** [T] **defend sb/sth/yourself (against/from sb/sth)** to protect sb/sth from harm or danger: *Would you be able to defend yourself if someone attacked you in the street?* ▶ **bronić** **2** [T] **defend sb/sth/yourself (against/from sb/sth)** to say or write sth to support sb/sth that has been criticized: *The minister went on TV to defend the government's policy.* ▶ **bronić 3** [I,T] to try to stop the other team or player scoring: *They defended well* (ich defensywa grała bardzo dobrze) *and managed to hold onto their lead.* ▶ **bronić 4** [T] to take part in a competition that you won before and try to win it again: *She successfully defended her title.* ◇ *He is the defending champion.* ▶ **bronić** (*tytułu*) **5** [T] to speak for sb who is accused of a crime in a court of law: *He has employed one of the UK's top lawyers to defend him.* ▶ **bronić, występować w obronie** ➲ look at **prosecute**

defendant /dɪˈfendənt/ noun [C] a person who is accused of a crime in a court of law ▶ **oskarżony, pozwany** ➲ look at **plaintiff**

defender /dɪˈfendə(r)/ noun [C] a person who defends sb/sth, especially in sport ▶ **obroń-ca/czyni**

defense (US) = DEFENCE

defensive¹ /dɪˈfensɪv/ adj. **1** that protects sb/sth from attack: *The troops took up a defensive position.* ▶ **obronny 2** showing that you feel that sb is criticizing you: *When I asked him about his new job, he became very defensive and tried to change the subject.* ▶ **defensywny** OPP **offensive**

defensive² /dɪˈfensɪv/ noun

IDM **on the defensive** acting in a way that shows that you expect sb to attack or criticize you: *My questions about her past immediately put her on the defensive.* ▶ **w defensywie**

defer /dɪˈfɜː(r)/ verb [T] (**deferring**; **deferred**) (formal) to leave sth until a later time: *She deferred her place at university for a year.* ▶ **odraczać**

PHR V **defer to sb/sth** (formal) to agree to accept what sb has decided or what they think about sb/sth because you respect him or her: *We will defer to whatever the committee decides.* ▶ **zastosowywać się do kogoś/czegoś**

deference /ˈdefərəns/ noun [U] polite behaviour that you show towards sb/sth, usually because you respect them ▶ **szacunek, poważanie**

IDM **in deference to sb/sth** because you respect and do not wish to upset sb: *In deference to her father's wishes, she didn't mention the subject again.* ▶ **przez szacunek dla kogoś/czegoś**

defiance /dɪˈfaɪəns/ noun [U] open refusal to obey sb/sth: *an **act of defiance*** ◇ *He continued smoking **in defiance of*** (na przekór) *the doctor's orders.* ▶ **nieposłuszeństwo, bunt** ➲ verb **defy**

defiant /dɪˈfaɪənt/ adj. showing open refusal to obey sb/sth ▶ **buntowniczy, wyzywający** ➲ verb **defy**

■ **defiantly** adv. ▶ **w sposób buntowniczy/wyzywający**

deficiency /dɪˈfɪʃnsi/ noun (pl. **deficiencies**) **deficiency (in/of sth) 1** [C,U] the state of not having enough of sth; a lack: *a deficiency of vitamin C* ▶ **niedobór, niedostatek 2** [C] a fault or a weakness in sb/sth: *The problems were caused by deficiencies in the design.* ▶ **niedoskonałość**

deficient /dɪˈfɪʃnt/ adj. **1 deficient (in sth)** not having enough of sth: *food that is deficient in minerals* ▶ **wykazujący niedobór 2** not good enough or not complete ▶ **niedoskonały, niekompletny**

deficit /ˈdefɪsɪt/ noun [C] the amount by which the money you receive is less than the money you have spent: *a trade deficit* ▶ **deficyt**

defile /dɪˈfaɪl/ verb [T] (formal or literary) to make sth dirty or no longer pure, especially sth that people consider important or holy: *The altar had been defiled by vandals.* ▶ **kalać, bezcześcić**

■ **defilement** noun [U] ▶ **(s)kalanie, (z)bezczeszczenie**

🔑 **define** /dɪˈfaɪn/ verb [T] **1** to say exactly what a word or idea means: *How would you define 'happiness'?* ▶ **definiować 2** to explain the exact nature of sth clearly: *We need to define the problem before we can attempt to solve it.* ▶ **określać**

🔑 **definite** /ˈdefɪnət/ adj. **1** fixed and unlikely to change; certain: *I'll give you a definite decision in a couple of days.* ▶ **ostateczny, definitywny 2** clear; easy to see or notice: *There has been a definite change in her attitude recently.* ▶ **wyraźny** OPP **indefinite**

the ˌ**definite ˈarticle** noun [C] the name used for the word 'the' ▶ **przedimek określony** ➲ look at **indefinite article**

🔑 **definitely** /ˈdefɪnətli/ adv. certainly; without doubt: *I'll definitely consider your advice.* ▶ **na pewno, zdecydowanie**

🔑 **definition** /ˌdefɪˈnɪʃn/ noun [C,U] a description of the exact meaning of a word or idea ▶ **definicja**

definitive /dɪˈfɪnətɪv/ adj. in a form that cannot be changed or that cannot be improved: *This is the definitive version* (wersja ostateczna). ◇ *the definitive performance of Hamlet* najlepsze do tej pory wystawienie „Hamleta" ▶ **ostateczny, szczytowy**

■ **definitively** adv. ▶ **ostatecznie, stanowczo**

deflate /dɪˈfleɪt; ˌdiː-/ verb **1** [I,T] to become or to make sth smaller by letting the air or gas out of it: *The balloon slowly deflated.* Z balonu uszło powietrze. ▶ **wypuszczać powietrze** OPP **inflate 2** [T] to make sb feel less confident, proud or excited: *I felt really deflated when I got my exam results.* ▶ **przygasić**

deflect /dɪˈflekt/ verb **1** [I,T] to change direction after hitting sb/sth; to make sth change direction in this way: *The ball deflected off a defender and into the goal.* ▶ **odbijać (się) i zmieniać kierunek lotu 2** [T] to turn sb's attention away from sth: *Nothing could deflect her from her aim.* ▶ **odwracać** (*uwagę*), **odwodzić**

deflection /dɪˈflekʃn/ noun [C,U] a change of direction after hitting sb/sth ▶ **odchylenie, odbicie, zboczenie**

deforestation /ˌdiːˌfɒrɪˈsteɪʃn/ noun [U] cutting down trees over a large area ▶ **wycinanie lasów** ➲ note at **environment**

deform /dɪˈfɔːm/ verb [T] to change or spoil the natural shape of sth ▶ **zniekształcać, deformować**

deformed /dɪˈfɔːmd/ adj. having a shape that is not normal because it has grown wrongly ▶ **zniekształcony, zdeformowany**

deformity /dɪˈfɔːməti/ noun [C,U] (pl. **deformities**) the condition of having a part of the body that is an unusual shape because of disease, injury, etc. ▶ **zniekształcenie, deformacja**

defraud /dɪˈfrɔːd/ verb [T] **defraud sb (of sth)** to get sth from sb in a dishonest way: *He defrauded the company of millions.* Okradł firmę na miliony. ▶ **oszukiwać**

defrost /ˌdiːˈfrɒst/ verb **1** [I,T] (used about frozen food) to return to a normal temperature; to make food do this: *Defrost the chicken thoroughly before cooking.* ▶ **rozmrażać (się) 2** [T] to remove the ice from sth: *to defrost a fridge* ▶ **odmrażać, rozmrażać** ➲ look at **de-ice**

deft /deft/ adj. (used especially about movements) skilful and quick ▶ **zręczny**

■ **deftly** adv. ▶ **zręcznie**

defunct /dɪˈfʌŋkt/ adj. no longer existing or in use ▶ **zlikwidowany, nieistniejący**

defuse /ˌdiːˈfjuːz/ verb [T] **1** to make a situation calmer or less dangerous: *She defused the tension by changing the subject.* ▶ **rozładowywać 2** to remove part of a bomb so that it cannot explode: *Army experts defused the bomb safely.* ▶ **rozbrajać**

defy /dɪˈfaɪ/ verb [T] (**defying**; **defies**; pt, pp **defied**) **1** to refuse to obey sb/sth: *She defied her parents and continued see-*

ing Brendan. ▶ **przeciwstawiać się, sprzeciwiać się** ➲ adjective **defiant**, noun **defiance** **2 defy sb to do sth** to ask sb to do sth that you believe to be impossible: *I defy you to prove me wrong.* ▶ **wyzy-wać kogoś, żeby coś zrobił** **3** to make sth impossible or very difficult: *It's such a beautiful place that it defies description.* ▶ **być nie do** (*np. opisania*)

degenerate¹ /dɪˈdʒenəreɪt/ verb [I] to become worse, lower in quality, etc.: *The calm discussion degenerated into a nasty argument.* ▶ **ulegać degeneracji, przekształcić się (w coś)**
■ **degeneration** /dɪˌdʒenəˈreɪʃn/ noun [U] ▶ **degeneracja kogoś, żeby coś zrobił**

degenerate² /dɪˈdʒenərət/ adj. having moral standards that have fallen to a very low level ▶ **zdegenerowany**

degradation /ˌdegrəˈdeɪʃn/ noun [U] **1** the act of making sb be less respected; the state of being less respected: *the degradation of being in prison* ▶ **poniżenie** **2** causing the condition of sth to become worse: *environmental degradation* ▶ **degradacja**

degrade /dɪˈgreɪd/ verb [T] to make people respect sb less ▶ **poniżać**
■ **degrading** adj. treating sb as if they have no value, so that they lose their **self-respect** and the respect of other people: *the inhuman and degrading treatment of prisoners* ▶ **poniżający**

⚷ **degree** /dɪˈgriː/ noun **1** [C] a measurement of angles: *a forty-five degree (45°) angle* ◇ *An angle of 90 degrees is called a right angle.* ▶ **stopień** **2** [C] a measurement of temperature: *Water boils at 100 degrees Celsius (100° C).* ◇ *three degrees below zero/minus three degrees (-3°)* ▶ **stopień** **3** [C,U] (used about feelings or qualities) a certain amount or level: *There is always* ***a degree of*** *risk involved in mountaineering.* ◇ *I sympathize with her* ***to some degree.*** ▶ **stopień, miara** **4** [C] an official document that students gain by successfully completing a course at university or college: *Michael's got* ***a degree in*** *Philosophy.* ◇ *to* ***do a*** *Chemistry* ***degree*** ▶ **stopień naukowy**

> **qualifications**
> In Britain **degree** is the usual word for the qualification you get when you complete and pass a university course. You can study for a **diploma** or a **certificate** at other types of college. The courses may be shorter and more practical than degree courses. The best result you can get in a British university degree is a **first**, followed by a **two-one**, a **two-two**, a **third**, a **pass**, and a **fail**.

dehydrate /diːˈhaɪdreɪt; ˌdiːhaɪˈdreɪt/ verb **1** [T, usually passive] to remove all the water from sth: *dehydrated vegetables* suszone warzywa ▶ **odwadniać (się)** **2** [I,T] to lose too much water from your body: *If you run for a long time in the heat, you start to dehydrate.* ▶ **odwadniać (się)**
■ **dehydrated** /ˌdiːhaɪˈdreɪtɪd/ adj.: *Drink lots of water to avoid becoming dehydrated* (aby zapobiec odwodnieniu). ▶ **odwodniony** | **dehydration** /ˌdiːhaɪˈdreɪʃn/ noun [U]: *Several of the runners were suffering from severe dehydration.* ▶ **odwodnienie**

de-ice /ˌdiː ˈaɪs/ verb [T] to remove the ice from sth: *The car windows need de-icing.* ▶ **odmrażać** ➲ look at **defrost**

deign /deɪn/ verb [T] **deign to do sth** to do sth although you think you are too important to do it: *He didn't even deign to look up when I entered the room.* ▶ **raczyć**

deity /ˈdeɪəti/ noun [C] (pl. **deities**) (formal) a god ▶ **bóstwo**

dejected /dɪˈdʒektɪd/ adj. very unhappy, especially because you are disappointed: *The fans went home dejected after watching their team lose once more.* ▶ **strapiony, zniechęcony**
■ **dejectedly** adv. ▶ **ze strapieniem/zniechęceniem** | **dejection** /dɪˈdʒekʃn/ noun [U] ▶ **strapienie, zniechęcenie**

⚷ **delay¹** /dɪˈleɪ/ noun [C,U] a situation or period of time where you have to wait: *Delays are likely on the roads because of heavy traffic.* ◇ *If you smell gas, you should report it without delay.* ▶ **opóźnienie, zwłoka**

⚷ **delay²** /dɪˈleɪ/ verb **1** [T] to make sb/sth slow or late: *The plane was delayed for several hours because of bad weather.* ▶ **opóźniać** **2** [I,T] **delay (sth/doing sth)** to decide not to do sth until a later time: *I was forced to delay the trip until the following week.* ▶ **odkładać (zrobienie czegoś)**

delegate¹ /ˈdelɪgət/ noun [C] a person who has been chosen to speak or take decisions for a group of people, especially at a meeting ▶ **delegat/ka**

delegate² /ˈdelɪgeɪt/ verb [I,T] to give sb with a lower job or position a particular task to do: *You can't do everything yourself. You must learn how to delegate.* ▶ **delegować, zlecać**

delegation /ˌdelɪˈgeɪʃn/ noun **1** [C, with sing. or pl. verb] a group of people who have been chosen to speak or take decisions for a larger group of people, especially at a meeting: *The British delegation walked out of the meeting in protest.* ▶ **delegacja** **2** [U] the process of giving sb work or responsibilities that would usually be yours ▶ **przekazanie uprawnień, delegacja pełnomocnictw**

delete /dɪˈliːt/ verb [T] to remove sth that is written: *'I will/will not be able to attend the meeting. Delete as appropriate* (niepotrzebne skreślić).*'* ▶ **skreślać**
■ **deletion** /dɪˈliːʃn/ noun **1** [U] the act of deleting ▶ **skreślenie, usunięcie** **2** [C] part of sth written or printed (e.g. a word, a sentence, a paragraph, etc.) that is deleted ▶ **skreślenie**

⚷ **deliberate¹** /dɪˈlɪbərət/ adj. **1** done on purpose; planned: *Was it an accident or was it deliberate?* ▶ **celowy** SYN **intentional** **2** done slowly and carefully, without hurrying: *She spoke in a calm, deliberate voice.* ▶ **rozważny, niespieszny**

deliberate² /dɪˈlɪbəreɪt/ verb [I,T] (formal) to think about or discuss sth fully before making a decision: *The judges deliberated for an hour before announcing the winner.* ▶ **deliberować, naradzać się**

⚷ **deliberately** /dɪˈlɪbərətli/ adv. **1** in a way that was planned, not by chance: *I didn't break it deliberately – it was an accident.* ▶ **celowo, rozmyślnie** SYN **purposely** OPP **by accident** **2** slowly and carefully, without hurrying: *He packed up his possessions slowly and deliberately.* ▶ **rozważnie, niespiesznie**

deliberation /dɪˌlɪbəˈreɪʃn/ noun (formal) **1** [C,U] discussion or thinking about sth in detail: *After much deliberation I decided to reject the offer.* ▶ **deliberacja, zastanowienie (się)** **2** [U] the quality of being very slow and careful in what you say and do: *He spoke with great deliberation.* ▶ **rozwaga**

delicacy /ˈdelɪkəsi/ noun (pl. **delicacies**) **1** [U] the quality of being easy to damage or break ▶ **delikatność** **2** [U] great care; a gentle touch: *the delicacy of his touch* ◇ *She played with great delicacy* (grała z wielką wrażliwością). ◇ (figurative) *Be tactful! It's a matter of some delicacy.* ▶ **delikatność** **3** [C] a type of food that is considered particularly good: *Try this dish, it's a local delicacy.* ▶ **delikates, przysmak**

⚷ **delicate** /ˈdelɪkət/ adj. **1** easy to damage or break: *delicate skin* ◇ *the delicate mechanisms of a watch* ▶ **delikatny** **2** often ill or hurt: *He was a delicate child and often in hospital.* ▶ **delikatny, wątły** **3** needing skilful treatment and care: *Repairing this is going to be a very* *delicate operation.* ▶ **wymagający delikatności/precyzji** **4** (used about colours, flavours, etc.) light and pleasant; not strong: *a delicate shade of pale blue* ▶ **delikatny, pastelowy**

■ **delicately** adv. **1** lightly, gently or finely ▶ **delikatnie, subtelnie** **2** with skilful and careful movement: *She stepped delicately over the broken glass.* ▶ **delikatnie, ostrożnie** **3** carefully so as not to offend sb ▶ **delikatnie, ostrożnie**

delicatessen /ˌdelɪkəˈtesn/ noun [C] a shop that sells special, unusual or foreign foods, especially cold cooked meat, cheeses, etc. ▶ **delikatesy** ℹ Zwróć uwagę, że **delicatessen** to rzeczownik w lp.

delicious /dɪˈlɪʃəs/ adj. having a very pleasant taste or smell: *This soup is absolutely delicious.* ▶ **smakowity, pyszny**

⚷ **delight**[1] /dɪˈlaɪt/ noun **1** [U] great pleasure: *She laughed with delight as she opened the present.* ▶ **zachwyt, radość** SYN **joy** **2** [C] something that gives sb great pleasure: *The story is a delight to read.* To opowiadanie czyta się z przyjemnością. ▶ **coś, co zachwyca**

⚷ **delight**[2] /dɪˈlaɪt/ verb [T] to give sb great pleasure: *She delighted the audience by singing all her old songs.* ▶ **zachwycać, radować**

PHR V **delight in sth/in doing sth** to get great pleasure from sth: *He delights in playing tricks on people.* ▶ **uwielbiać coś robić**

⚷ **delighted** /dɪˈlaɪtɪd/ adj. **delighted (at/with/about sth)**; **delighted to do sth/that...** extremely pleased: *She was delighted at getting the job/that she got the job.* ◇ *They're absolutely delighted with their baby.* ◇ *'Would you like to come for dinner?' 'Thanks, I'd be delighted to* (z przyjemnością).*'* ◇ *'How do you feel about winning today?' 'Delighted* (bardzo się cieszę).*'* ▶ **zachwycony** ➲ note at **happy**

delightful /dɪˈlaɪtfl/ adj. very pleasant: *a delightful view of the sea* ▶ **zachwycający, wspaniały**

■ **delightfully** /-fəli/ adv. ▶ **zachwycająco, wspaniale**

delineate /dɪˈlɪnieɪt/ verb [T] (formal) to describe, draw or explain sth in detail: *Our objectives need to be precisely delineated.* ▶ **szczegółowo/dokładnie określać/rysować**

■ **delineation** /dɪˌlɪniˈeɪʃn/ noun [U,C] ▶ **szczegółowy opis**

delinquency /dɪˈlɪŋkwənsi/ noun [U] (formal) bad or criminal behaviour, especially among young people ▶ **przestępczość** (*młodocianych*)

delinquent /dɪˈlɪŋkwənt/ adj. (formal) (usually used about a young person) behaving badly and often breaking the law: *delinquent children* nieletni przestępcy ▶ **naruszający prawo, przestępczy**

■ **delinquent** noun [C]: *a juvenile delinquent* ▶ **(nieletni/a) przestęp-ca/czyni**

delirious /dɪˈlɪriəs/ adj. **1** speaking or thinking in a crazy way, often because of illness ▶ **bredzący, majaczący** **2** extremely happy: *I was absolutely delirious when I passed the exam.* ▶ **uszczęśliwiony, szalejący z radości**

■ **deliriously** adv. ▶ **majacząc, szalejąc z radości**

delirium /dɪˈlɪriəm; Brit. also -ˈlɪəriəm/ noun [U] a mental state where sb becomes **delirious**, usually because of illness ▶ **delirium, maligna**

⚷ **deliver** /dɪˈlɪvə(r)/ verb **1** [I,T] to take sth (goods, letters, etc.) to the place requested or to the address on it: *Your order will be delivered within five days.* ◇ *We deliver free within the local area.* ▶ **dostarczać** **2** [T] (formal) to say sth formally: *to deliver a speech/lecture/warning* ▶ **wygłaszać** **3** [I] (informal) **deliver (on sth)** to do or give sth that you have promised: *The new leader has made a lot of promises, but can he deliver on them* (czy może się z nich wywiązać)*?* ▶ **wywiązywać się (z czegoś), spełniać** (*obietnice*) **4** [T] to help a mother to give birth to her baby: *to deliver a baby* ▶ **przyjmować** (*poród*)

IDM **come up with/deliver the goods** → GOODS

⚷ **delivery** /dɪˈlɪvəri/ noun (pl. **deliveries**) **1** [U] the act of taking sth (goods, letters, etc.) to the place or person who has ordered it or whose address is on it: *Please allow 28 days for delivery.* ◇ *a delivery van* ▶ **doręczenie, dostawa** **2** [C] an occasion when sth is **delivered**: *Is there a delivery here on Sundays?* ▶ **roznoszenie** (*np. poczty*) **3** [C] something (goods, letters, etc.) that is **delivered**: *The shop is waiting for a new delivery of apples.* ▶ **dostawa, poczta** **4** [C] the process of giving birth to a baby: *an easy delivery* ▶ **poród**

delta /ˈdeltə/ noun [C] an area of flat land shaped like a triangle where a river divides into smaller rivers as it goes into the sea ▶ **delta**

delude /dɪˈluːd/ verb [T] to make sb believe sth that is not true: *If he thinks he's going to get rich quickly, he's deluding himself.* ▶ **łudzić, oszukiwać** ➲ noun **delusion**

deluge[1] /ˈdeljuːdʒ/ noun [C] **1** a sudden very heavy fall of rain ▶ **ulewa; potop** SYN **flood** **2 a deluge (of sth)** a very large number of things that happen or arrive at the same time: *The programme was followed by a deluge of complaints from the public.* ▶ **potop**

deluge[2] /ˈdeljuːdʒ/ verb [T, usually passive] to send or give sb/sth a very large quantity of sth, all at the same time: *They were deluged with applications for the job.* ▶ **zasypywać, zalewać**

delusion /dɪˈluːʒn/ noun [C,U] a false belief: *He seems to be **under the delusion** that he's popular.* ▶ **złudzenie** ➲ verb **delude**

de luxe /ˌdə ˈlʌks/ adj. of extremely high quality and more expensive than usual: *a de luxe hotel* ▶ **luksusowy**

delve /delv/ verb [I] to search for sth inside a bag, container, etc.: *She delved into the bag and brought out a tiny box.* ▶ **sięgać**

PHR V **delve into sth** to try hard to find out more information about sth: *We must delve into the past to find the origins of the custom.* ▶ **zagłębiać się w coś**

Dem. = DEMOCRAT, DEMOCRATIC

⚷ **demand**[1] /dɪˈmɑːnd; US -ˈmænd/ noun **1** [C] **a demand (for sth/that...)** a strong request or order that must be obeyed: *a demand for changes in the law* ◇ *I was amazed by their demand that I should leave immediately.* ▶ **żądanie** **2** (**demands**) [pl.] something that sb makes you do, especially sth that is difficult or tiring: *Running a marathon **makes huge demands** on the body* (jest dużym obciążeniem dla organizmu). ▶ **obciążenie, wymagania** **3** [U, sing.] **demand (for sth/sb)** the desire or need for sth among a group of people: *We no longer sell that product because there is no demand for it.* ▶ **popyt, zapotrzebowanie**

IDM **in demand** wanted by a lot of people: *I'm in demand this weekend – I've had three invitations!* ▶ **rozchwytywany, wzięty**

on demand at any time that you ask for it: *This treatment is available from your doctor on demand.* ▶ **na żądanie**

⚷ **demand**[2] /dɪˈmɑːnd; US -ˈmænd/ verb [T] **1 demand to do sth/that...**; **demand sth** to ask for sth in an extremely firm or aggressive way: *I walked into the office and demanded to see the manager.* ◇ *She demanded that I pay her immediately.* ◇ *Your behaviour was disgraceful and I demand an apology.* ▶ **pytać** (*w sposób agresywny*), **żądać, domagać się** **2** to need sth: *a sport that demands skill as well as strength* ▶ **wymagać**

demanding /dɪˈmɑːndɪŋ; US -ˈmæn-/ adj. **1** (used about a job, task, etc.) needing a lot of effort, care, skill, etc.: *It*

D

will be a demanding schedule – I have to go to six cities in six days. ▶ **wymagający 2** (used about a person) always wanting attention or expecting very high standards of people: *Young children are very demanding.* ◇ *a demanding boss* ▶ **wymagający**

demarcate /ˈdiːmɑːkeɪt/ verb [T] (formal) to mark or establish the limits of sth: *Plots of land have been demarcated by barbed wire.* ◇ *The police demarcated the city into eighteen geographical divisions.* ▶ **wyznaczać granicę**

demean /dɪˈmiːn/ verb [T] **1 demean yourself** to do sth that makes people have less respect for you: *I wouldn't demean myself by asking for charity.* ▶ **poniżać się 2** to make people have less respect for sb/sth: *Such images demean women.* ▶ **poniżać** SYN **degrade**

demeanour (US **demeanor**) /dɪˈmiːnə(r)/ noun [U] (formal) the way that sb looks or behaves: *He maintained a professional demeanour throughout.* ▶ **postawa**; **zachowanie się**

demented /dɪˈmentɪd/ adj. **1** (especially Brit.) behaving in a crazy way because you are extremely upset or worried: *I've been nearly demented with worry about you.* ▶ **oszalały**, **bliski obłędu 2** (old-fashioned or technical) having a mental illness ▶ (*med.*) **cierpiący na demencję**
■ **dementedly** adv. ▶ **szaleńczo**

dementia /dɪˈmenʃə/ noun [U] a serious mental **disorder** caused by brain disease or injury, that affects the ability to think, remember and behave normally ▶ **demencja**

demilitarize (also **-ise**) /ˌdiːˈmɪlɪtəraɪz/ verb [T, usually passive] to remove military forces from an area: *a **demilitarized zone*** ▶ **demilitaryzować** OPP **militarize**
■ **demilitarization** (also **-isation**) /ˌdiːˌmɪlɪtəraɪˈzeɪʃn; US -rəˈz-/ noun [U] ▶ **demilitaryzacja**

demise /dɪˈmaɪz/ noun [sing.] **1** the end or failure of sth: *Poor business decisions led to the company's demise.* ▶ **upadek 2** (formal) the death of a person ▶ **zgon**, **śmierć**

demisemiquaver /ˌdemiˈsemikweɪvə(r)/ (US ˌ**thirty-ˈsecond note**) noun [C] (used in music) a note that lasts as long as half a **semiquaver** ▶ (*muz.*) **trzydziestodwójka**

demo /ˈdeməʊ/ noun [C] (pl. **demos**) (informal) **1** (especially Brit.) = DEMONSTRATION (1): *They all went on the demo.* **2** = DEMONSTRATION (2): *I'll **give you a demo**.* **3** a record or tape with an example of sb's music on it: *a demo tape* ▶ **płyta/nagranie demo**

demobilize (also **-ise**) /dɪˈməʊbəlaɪz/ (Brit. also, informal **demob**) verb [T] to release sb from military service, especially at the end of a war ▶ **demobilizować** ➲ look at **mobilize**
■ **demobilization** (also **-isation**) /dɪˌməʊbəlaɪˈzeɪʃn; US -ləˈz-/ noun [U] ▶ **demobilizacja**

democracy /dɪˈmɒkrəsi/ noun (pl. **democracies**) **1** [U] a system in which the government of a country is elected by the people ▶ **demokracja 2** [C] a country that has this system ▶ **demokracja 3** [U] the right of everyone in an organization, etc. to be treated equally and to vote on matters that affect them: *There is a need for more democracy in the company.* ▶ **demokracja**

democrat /ˈdeməkræt/ noun [C] **1** a person who believes in and supports **democracy** ▶ **demokrat-a/ka 2** (**Democrat**) (abbr. **Dem.** /dem/) a member of, or sb who supports, the Democratic Party of the US ▶ **członek lub zwolennik Partii Demokratycznej w USA** ➲ look at **Republican**

democratic /ˌdeməˈkrætɪk/ adj. **1** based on the system of **democracy**: *democratic elections* ◇ *a democratic government* ▶ **demokratyczny** ➲ note at **politics 2** having or supporting equal rights for all people: *a democratic decision* ▶ **demokratyczny 3** (abbr. **Dem.** /dem/) connected with the Democratic Party in the US ▶ **demokratyczny**, **Demokratów**
■ **democratically** /-kli/ adv. ▶ **demokratycznie**

the ˌ**Demoˈcratic Party** noun [sing.] one of the two main political parties of the US ▶ **Partia Demokratyczna** ➲ look at **the Republican Party**

demographics /ˌdeməˈɡræfɪks/ noun [pl.] data relating to the population and different groups within it: *the demographics of radio listeners* ▶ **statystyczne dane demograficzne**

demolish /dɪˈmɒlɪʃ/ verb [T] to destroy sth, for example a building: *The old shops were demolished and a supermarket was built in their place.* ◇ (figurative) *She demolished his argument in one sentence.* ▶ **wyburzać**, **rozbierać**; **obalać**
■ **demolition** /ˌdeməˈlɪʃn/ noun [C,U] ▶ **wyburzenie**, **rozbiórka**

demon /ˈdiːmən/ noun [C] an evil spirit ▶ **demon**, **diabeł**

demonic /diˈmɒnɪk/ adj. connected with, or like, a **demon** ▶ **demoniczny**, **szatański**

🔑 **demonstrate** /ˈdemənstreɪt/ verb **1** [T] **demonstrate sth (to sb)** to show sth clearly by giving proof: *Using this chart, I'd like to demonstrate to you what has happened to our sales.* ▶ **dowodzić**, **demonstrować 2** [I,T] **demonstrate sth (to sb)** to show and explain to sb how to do sth or how sth works: *The crew demonstrated the use of life jackets just after take-off.* ◇ *I'm not sure what you mean – could you demonstrate?* ▶ **demonstrować 3** [I] **demonstrate (against/for sb/sth)** to take part in a public protest for or against sb/sth: *Enormous crowds have been demonstrating against the government.* ▶ **demonstrować** SYN **protest**

demonstration /ˌdemənˈstreɪʃn/ noun **1** (especially Brit., informal **demo**) [C] **a demonstration (against/for sb/sth)** a public protest for or against sb/sth: *demonstrations against a new law* ▶ **manifestacja** ➲ look at **march**[2] **2** (also informal **demo**) [C,U] an act of showing or explaining to sb how to do sth or how sth works: *The salesman gave me a demonstration of what the computer could do.* ▶ **demonstracja 3** [C,U] something that shows clearly that sth exists or is true: *This accident is a clear demonstration of the system's faults.* ▶ **dowód**

demonstrative /dɪˈmɒnstrətɪv/ adj. (used about a person) showing feelings, especially loving feelings, in front of other people ▶ **wylewny**, **otwarty**

demonstrator /ˈdemənstreɪtə(r)/ noun [C] a person who takes part in a public protest ▶ **demonstrant/ka**

demoralize (also **-ise**) /dɪˈmɒrəlaɪz/ verb [T] to make sb lose confidence or the courage to continue doing sth: *Repeated defeats completely demoralized the team.* ▶ **działać demobilizująco**, **zniechęcać do dalszego działania**
■ **demoralization** (also **-isation**) /dɪˌmɒrəlaɪˈzeɪʃn; US also -ləˈz-/ noun [U] ▶ **działanie demobilizujące/zniechęcające** | **demoralizing** (also **-ising**) adj.: *Constant criticism can be extremely demoralizing.* ◇ *the demoralizing effects of unemployment* ▶ **demobilizujący**, **zniechęcający**

demote /ˌdiːˈməʊt/ verb [T] **demote sb (from sth) (to sth)** to move sb to a lower position or less important job, often as a punishment ▶ **degradować** OPP **promote**
■ **demotion** /ˌdiːˈməʊʃn/ noun [C,U] ▶ **degradacja**

demure /dɪˈmjʊə(r)/ adj. (used especially about a girl or young woman) shy, quiet and polite ▶ **skromny** ➲ look at **modest**

den /den/ noun [C] **1** the place where certain wild animals, such as **lions** live ▶ **nora**, **legowisko 2** a secret place, especially for illegal activities: *a den of thieves* ◇ *a gambling den* jaskinia hazardu ▶ **kryjówka**, **melina**

denial /dɪˈnaɪəl/ noun **1** [C] a statement that sth is not true: *The minister issued a denial that he was involved in the scandal.* ▶ **zaprzeczenie**, **wyparcie się 2** [C,U] **(a) denial (of sth)** refusing to allow sb to have or do sth: *a* *denial of personal freedom* ▶ **pozbawienie**, **odmowa** **3** [U] a refusal to accept that sth unpleasant or painful has happened: *He's been* ***in denial*** (odrzuca bolesną prawdę) *ever since the accident.* ▶ **odrzucenie** ➲ verb **deny**

denigrate /ˈdenɪɡreɪt/ verb [T] (formal) to criticize sb/sth unfairly; to say sb/sth does not have any value or is not important: *I didn't intend to denigrate her achievements.* ▶ **oczerniać**; **pomniejszać** SYN **belittle**
■ **denigration** /ˌdenɪˈɡreɪʃn/ noun [U] ▶ **oczernianie**; **pomniejszanie**

denim /ˈdenɪm/ noun [U] a thick cotton cloth (often blue) that is used for making clothes, especially jeans: *a denim jacket* ▶ **materiał dżinsowy**

denomination /dɪˌnɒmɪˈneɪʃn/ noun [C] one of the different religious groups that you can belong to ▶ **wyznanie** (*religijne*)

denote /dɪˈnəʊt/ verb [T] to mean or be a sign of sth ▶ **oznaczać**, **wyznaczać**

denouement (also **dénouement**) /ˌdeɪˈnuːmɒ̃; US ˌdeɪnuːˈmɒ̃/ noun [C] the end of a play, book, etc., in which everything is explained or settled; the end result of a situation ▶ **rozwiązanie akcji**

denounce /dɪˈnaʊns/ verb [T] to say publicly that sth is wrong; to be very critical of a person in public: *The well-known actor has been denounced as a bad influence on young people.* ▶ **potępiać** ➲ noun **denunciation**

dense /dens/ adj. **1** containing a lot of things or people close together: *dense forests* ◇ *areas of dense population* ▶ **gęsty**, **zwarty** **2** difficult to see through: *dense fog* ▶ **gęsty** **3** (informal) not intelligent; stupid ▶ **tępy**
■ **densely** adv.: *densely populated areas* ▶ **gęsto**, **zwarcie**

density /ˈdensəti/ noun (pl. **densities**) **1** [U] the number of things or people in a place in relation to its area: *the density of populaton* ◇ *There is a high density of* (duże zagęszczenie) *wildlife in this area.* ▶ **gęstość** **2** [C,U] (technical) the relation of the weight of a substance to its size: *Lead has a high density.* ▶ **ciężar właściwy**

dent¹ /dent/ verb [T] to damage a flat surface by hitting it but not breaking it: *I hit a wall and dented the front of the car.* ▶ **wginać**

dent² /dent/ noun [C] a place where a flat surface, especially metal, has been hit and damaged but not broken: *This tin's got a dent in it.* ▶ **wgięcie**, **wklęśnięcie**

dental /ˈdentl/ adj. [only before a noun] connected with teeth ▶ **dentystyczny**

ˈ**dental floss** noun [U] a type of thread that is used for cleaning between the teeth ▶ **nić dentystyczna**

⚷ **dentist** /ˈdentɪst/ noun **1** [C] a person whose job is to look after people's teeth: *an appointment with the dentist* ▶ **dentyst(k)a** ➲ note at **tooth** **2** (**the dentist's**) [sing.] the place where a dentist works: *I have to go to the dentist's today.* ▶ **gabinet dentystyczny**

dentistry /ˈdentɪstri/ noun [U] **1** the medical study of the teeth and mouth ▶ **dentystyka** **2** the work of a dentist ▶ **stomatologia**

dentures = FALSE TEETH

denunciation /dɪˌnʌnsiˈeɪʃn/ noun [C,U] an expression of strong disapproval of sb/sth in public ▶ **potępienie** ➲ verb **denounce**

⚷ **deny** /dɪˈnaɪ/ verb [T] (**denying**; **denies**; pt, pp **denied**) **1 deny sth/doing sth**; **deny that…** to state that sth is not true; to refuse to admit or accept sth: *In court he denied all the charges.* ◇ *She denied telling lies/that she had told lies.* ▶ **zaprzeczać**, **wypierać się** OPP **admit** **2** (formal) **deny sb sth**; **deny sth (to sb)** to refuse to allow sb to have sth: *She was denied permission to remain in the country.* ▶ **odmawiać** ➲ noun **denial**

deodorant /diˈəʊdərənt/ noun [C,U] a chemical substance that you put onto your body to prevent bad smells ▶ **dezodorant**

dep. abbr. **departs**: *dep. London 15.32* ▶ **odj.**

depart /dɪˈpɑːt/ verb [I,T] (formal) to leave a place, usually at the beginning of a journey: *Ferries depart for Spain twice a day.* ◇ *The next train to the airport departs from platform 2.* ▶ **odjeżdżać**, **odpływać**, **odlatywać**, **odchodzić** ➲ note at **leave¹** ➲ noun **departure**

⚷ **department** /dɪˈpɑːtmənt/ noun [C] (abbr. **Dept**) **1** one of the sections into which an organization, for example a school or a business, is divided: *the Modern Languages department* ◇ *She works in the accounts department.* ▶ **wydział**, **dział** **2** a division of the government responsible for a particular subject: *the Department of Health* ▶ **ministerstwo** ➲ look at **ministry**

departmental /ˌdiːpɑːtˈmentl/ adj. [only before a noun] connected with a department: *There is a departmental meeting* (zebranie wydziału) *once a month.* ▶ **wydziałowy**, **ministerialny**

deˈpartment store noun [C] a large shop that is divided into sections selling different types of goods ▶ **dom towarowy**

⚷ **departure** /dɪˈpɑːtʃə(r)/ noun [C,U] **1** leaving or going away from a place: *Arrivals and departures are shown on a screen in the station.* ◇ *Kate's sudden departure meant I had to do her job as well as mine.* ◇ *Passengers should check in at least one hour before departure.* ▶ **odjazd**, **odlot**, **odejście** OPP **arrival** ➲ verb **depart** **2 a departure (from sth)** an action which is different from what is usual or expected: *a departure from normal practice* ▶ **odejście** (*od norm*), **odstępstwo**

⚷ **depend** /dɪˈpend/ verb
IDM **that depends**; **it (all) depends** [used alone or at the beginning of a sentence] (used to say that you are not certain of sth until other things have been considered): *'Can you lend me some money?' 'That depends. How much do you want?'* ◇ *I don't know whether I'll see him. It depends what time he gets here.* ▶ **to zależy**
PHR V **depend on sb/sth** to be able to trust sb/sth to do sth: *If you ever need any help, you know you can depend on me.* ◇ *You can't depend on the trains. They're always late.* ◇ *I was depending on getting the money today.* ◇ *You can always depend on him to say what he thinks.* Możesz być pewien, że on zawsze powie to co myśli ▶ **polegać na kimś/czymś**, **liczyć na kogoś/coś** SYN **rely**
depend on sb/sth (for sth) to need sb/sth to provide sth: *Our organization depends on donations from the public.* ▶ **polegać na kimś/czymś**, **być zależnym od kogoś/czegoś**
depend on sth to be decided or influenced by sb/sth: *His whole future depends on these exams.* ▶ **zależeć od czegoś**

dependable /dɪˈpendəbl/ adj. that can be trusted: *The bus service is very dependable.* ▶ **niezawodny**, **pewny** SYN **reliable**

dependant (especially US **dependent**) /dɪˈpendənt/ noun [C] a person who depends on sb else for money, a home, food, etc.: *insurance cover for you and all your dependants* ▶ **osoba będąca na czyimś utrzymaniu**

dependence /dɪˈpendəns/ noun [U] **dependence on sb/sth** the state of needing sb/sth: *The country wants to reduce its dependence on imported oil.* ▶ **zależność** OPP **independence**

dependency /dɪˈpendənsi/ noun [U] the state of being **dependent** on sb/sth; the state of being unable to live without sth, especially a drug ▶ **uzależnienie**

dependent /dɪˈpendənt/ adj. **1 dependent (on sb/sth)** needing sb/sth to support you: *The industry is heavily* *dependent on government funding.* ◇ *Do you have any dependent children?* ▶ **zależny, na czyimś utrzymaniu** **2 dependent on sb/sth** influenced or decided by sth: *The price you pay is dependent on the number in your group.* ▶ **zależny, uzależniony** OPP for both meanings **independent**

depict /dɪˈpɪkt/ verb [T] **1** to show sb/sth in a painting or drawing: *a painting depicting a country scene* ▶ **przedstawiać, dawać obraz** **2** to describe sb/sth in words: *The novel depicts rural life a century ago.* ▶ **opisywać**

deplete /dɪˈpliːt/ verb [T] to reduce the amount of sth so that there is not much left: *Wealthy nations are depleting the world's natural resources.* ▶ **uszczuplać, wyczerpywać**

■ **depletion** /dɪˈpliːʃn/ noun [U]: *the depletion* (zmniejszenie się) *of the ozone layer* ▶ **uszczuplenie, wyczerpanie**

deplorable /dɪˈplɔːrəbl/ adj. (formal) morally bad and deserving disapproval: *They are living in deplorable conditions.* ▶ **zasługujący na potępienie, godny ubolewania**

■ **deplorably** /-əbli/ adv. ▶ **przeraźliwie, odrażająco**

deplore /dɪˈplɔː(r)/ verb [T] (formal) to feel or say that sth is morally bad: *I deplore such dishonest behaviour.* ▶ **potępiać**

deploy /dɪˈplɔɪ/ verb [T] **1** to put soldiers or weapons in a position where they are ready to fight ▶ **rozstawiać** (*wojsko/broń*) **2** to use sth in a useful and successful way ▶ **rozstawiać, ustawiać**

■ **deployment** noun [U,C]: *the deployment of troops* ▶ **rozwinięcie; rozstawienie**

deport /dɪˈpɔːt/ verb [T] to force sb to leave a country because they have no legal right to be there: *A number of illegal immigrants have been deported.* ▶ **deportować**

■ **deportation** /ˌdiːpɔːˈteɪʃn/ noun [C,U] ▶ **deportacja**

depose /dɪˈpəʊz/ verb [T] to remove a ruler or leader from power: *There was a revolution and the dictator was deposed.* ▶ **usuwać ze stanowiska/z tronu**

deposit[1] /dɪˈpɒzɪt/ noun [C] **1 a deposit (on sth)** a sum of money which is the first payment for sth, with the rest of the money to be paid later: *Once you have paid a deposit, the booking will be confirmed.* ▶ **zaliczka** **2** [usually sing.] **a deposit (on sth)** a sum of money that you pay when you rent sth and get back when you return it without damage: *Boats can be hired for £5 an hour, plus £20 deposit.* ▶ **kaucja, zastaw** **3** a sum of money paid into a bank account ▶ **depozyt** **4** a substance that has been left on a surface or in the ground as the result of a natural or chemical process: *mineral deposits* ▶ **osad**

deposit[2] /dɪˈpɒzɪt/ verb [T] **1** to put sth down somewhere: *He deposited his bags on the floor and sat down.* ▶ **składać, umieszczać** **2** (used about liquid or a river) to leave sth lying on a surface, as the result of a natural or chemical process: *mud deposited by a flood* muł naniesiony przez powódź ▶ **pozostawiać coś jako osad** **3** to put money into an account at a bank: *He deposited £20 a week into his savings account.* ▶ **wpłacać** (*na konto*) ➲ look at **withdraw** **4 deposit sth (in sth); deposit sth (with sb/sth)** to put sth valuable in an official place where it is safe until needed again: *Valuables can be deposited in the hotel safe.* ▶ **deponować**

deˈposit account noun [C] (Brit.) a type of bank account where your money earns interest. You cannot take money out of a **deposit account** without arranging it first with the bank. ▶ **konto depozytowe** ➲ look at **current account**

depot /ˈdepəʊ; US ˈdiː-/ noun [C] **1** a place where large amounts of food, goods or equipment are stored ▶ **magazyn, skład** **2** a place where large numbers of vehicles (buses, lorries, etc.) are kept when not in use ▶ **zajezdnia** **3** (US) a small bus or railway station ▶ **dworzec autobusowy lub kolejowy** **4** a place where military supplies are stored ▶ **skład wojskowy**

depraved /dɪˈpreɪvd/ adj. (formal) morally bad ▶ **zdeprawowany** SYN **wicked, evil**

■ **depravity** /dɪˈprævəti/ noun [U] ▶ **zdeprawowanie** SYN **wickedness**

deprecate /ˈdeprəkeɪt/ verb [T] (formal) to feel and express strong disapproval of sth ▶ **potępiać**

■ **deprecating** (also **deprecatory** /ˌdeprəˈkeɪtəri; US ˈdeprɪkətɔːri/) adj.: *a deprecating comment* ▶ **potępiający**

depreciate /dɪˈpriːʃieɪt/ verb [I] to become less valuable over a period of time: *New cars start to depreciate the moment they are on the road.* ▶ **dewaluować się, deprecjonować się**

■ **depreciation** /dɪˌpriːʃiˈeɪʃn/ noun [C,U] ▶ **dewaluacja, deprecjacja**

depress /dɪˈpres/ verb [T] **1** to make sb unhappy and without hope or enthusiasm: *The thought of going to work tomorrow really depresses me.* ▶ **przygnębiać** **2** (used about business) to cause sth to become less successful: *The reduction in the number of tourists has depressed local trade.* ▶ **osłabiać, obniżać** **3** (formal) to press sth down on a machine, etc.: *To switch off the machine, depress the lever.* ▶ **naciskać, przyciskać**

■ **depressing** adj.: *The thought of growing old alone is very depressing.* ▶ **przygnębiający** | **depressingly** adv. ▶ **przygnębiająco**

depressed /dɪˈprest/ adj. **1** very unhappy, often for a long period of time: *He's been very depressed since he lost his job.* ▶ **przygnębiony, w depresji** ➲ note at **sad** **2** (used about a place or an industry) without enough businesses or jobs: *an attempt to create employment in depressed areas* ▶ **dotknięty bezrobociem/kryzysem**

depression /dɪˈpreʃn/ noun **1** [U] a feeling of unhappiness that lasts for a long time. **Depression** can be a medical condition and may have physical signs, for example being unable to sleep, etc.: *clinical/post-natal depression* ▶ **depresja** **2** [C,U] a period when the economic situation is bad, with little business activity and many people without a job: *The country was in the grip of (an) economic depression.* ▶ **stagnacja, kryzys** **3** [C] a part of a surface that is lower than the parts around it: *Rainwater collects in shallow depressions in the ground.* ▶ **obniżenie, wgłębienie**

deprive /dɪˈpraɪv/ verb [T] **deprive sb/sth of sth** to prevent sb/sth from having sth; to take away sth from sb: *The prisoners were deprived of food.* ▶ **pozbawiać**

■ **deprivation** /ˌdeprɪˈveɪʃn/ noun [U] ▶ **pozbawienie; niedostatek, ubóstwo**

deprived /dɪˈpraɪvd/ adj. not having enough of the basic things in life, such as food, money, etc.: *He came from a deprived background.* ▶ **ubogi, potrzebujący**

Dept = DEPARTMENT: *the Sales Dept*

depth /depθ/ noun **1** [C,U] the distance down from the top to the bottom of sth: *The hole should be 3cm in depth.* ▶ **głębokość** **2** [C,U] the distance from the front to the back of sth: *the depth of a shelf* ▶ **głębokość** ➲ picture at **dimension** **3** [U] the amount of emotion, knowledge, etc. that a person has: *He tried to convince her of the depth of his feelings for her.* ▶ **głębia** **4** [C, usually pl.] the deepest, most extreme or serious part of sth: ***in the depths of** winter* w pełni zimy ◇ *to live **in the depths of the country*** (na zapadłej prowincji) ◇ *She was **in the depths of despair*** (w skrajnej rozpaczy). ▶ **głębia** ➲ adjective **deep**

IDM **in depth** looking at all the details; in a thorough way: *to discuss a problem in depth* ◇ *an in-depth report* ◇ *to discuss a problem in depth* (w całej jego złożoności) ▶ **wnikliw-y/ie, szczegółow-y/o**

be/get out of your depth **1** (Brit.) to be in water that is too deep for you to stand up in: *If you're not a very strong swimmer, don't get out of your depth.* ▶ **tracić grunt pod nogami** **2** to be unable to understand sth because it is too difficult; to be in a situation that you cannot control: *He felt totally out of his depth in his new job.* ▶ *(przen.)* **tracić grunt pod nogami**

deputation /ˌdepjuˈteɪʃn/ noun [C, with sing. or pl. verb] a group of people sent to sb to act or speak for others ▶ **delegacja, poselstwo**

deputize (also -ise) /ˈdepjutaɪz/ verb [I] **deputize (for sb)** to act for sb in a higher position, who is away or unable to do sth ▶ **zastępować, działać w zastępstwie kogoś**

deputy /ˈdepjuti/ noun [C] (pl. **deputies**) the second most important person in a particular organization, who does the work of their manager if the manager is away: *the deputy head of a school* ▶ **zastęp-ca/czyni**

derail /dɪˈreɪl/ verb [T] to cause a train to come off a railway track ▶ **wykolejać**

derailment /dɪˈreɪlmənt/ noun [C,U] an occasion when sth causes a train to come off a railway track ▶ **wykolejenie**

deranged /dɪˈreɪndʒd/ adj. thinking and behaving in a way that is not normal, especially because of mental illness ▶ **obłąkany**

derby /ˈdɑːbi; US ˈdɜːbi/ noun [C] (pl. **derbies**) **1** (Brit.) a sports competition between teams from the same area or town: *a **local deby** between the two North London sides* ▶ **lokalne zawody sportowe** **2** a race or sports competition: *a motorcycle derby* ▶ **zawody sportowe** **3** (**the Derby**) (Brit.) a horse race which takes place every year at Epsom ▶ **doroczne wyścigi konne, które odbywają się w Epsom** **4** (US) = BOWLER (2)

deregulate /ˌdiːˈregjuleɪt/ verb [T, often passive] to free a trade, a business activity, etc. from rules and controls: *deregulated financial markets* ▶ **znosić kontrolę, liberalizować**

■ **deregulation** /ˌdiːˌregjuˈleɪʃn/ noun [U] ▶ **zniesienie kontroli, liberalizacja** | **deregulatory** /ˌdiːˈregjələtəri; US -tɔːri/ adj. [only before a noun]: *deregulatory reforms* ▶ **liberalizacyjny**

derelict /ˈderəlɪkt/ adj. no longer used and in bad condition: *a derelict house* ▶ **opustoszały, podupadły**

deride /dɪˈraɪd/ verb [T] to say that sb/sth is ridiculous; to laugh at sth in a cruel way ▶ **wyśmiewać, drwić z kogoś/czegoś**

■ **derision** /dɪˈrɪʒn/ noun [U]: *Her comments were met with derision.* ▶ **wyśmiewanie się, drwina** | **derisive** /dɪˈraɪsɪv/ adj.: *'What rubbish!' he said with a derisive laugh.* ▶ **drwiący, szyderczy**

derisory /dɪˈraɪsəri/ adj. too small or of too little value to be considered seriously: *Union leaders rejected the derisory pay offer.* ▶ **nędzny, (śmiesznie) mały**

derivation /ˌderɪˈveɪʃn/ noun [C,U] the origin from which a word or phrase has developed ▶ **pochodzenie** *(słowa)*

derivative /dɪˈrɪvətɪv/ noun [C] a form of sth (especially a word) that has developed from the original form: *'Sadness' is a derivative of 'sad.'* ▶ **wyraz pochodny**

⚷ **derive** /dɪˈraɪv/ verb **1** [T] (formal) **derive sth from sth** to get sth (especially a feeling or an advantage) from sth: *I derive great satisfaction from my work.* ▶ **czerpać, znajdować w czymś** *(np. przyjemność)* **2** [I,T] (used about a name or word) to come from sth; to have sth as its origin: *The town derives its name from the river* (nazwa miasta pochodzi od rzeki) *on which it was built.* ▶ **wywodzić się od/z czegoś, pochodzić skądś**

dermatitis /ˌdɜːməˈtaɪtɪs/ noun [U] a skin condition in which the skin becomes red, swollen and sore ▶ **zapalenie skóry**

dermatologist /ˌdɜːməˈtɒlədʒɪst/ noun [C] a doctor who studies and treats skin diseases ▶ **dermatolog**

derogatory /dɪˈrɒgətri; US -tɔːri/ adj. expressing a lack of respect for, or a low opinion of sth: *derogatory comments about the standard of my work* ▶ **uchybiający, poniżający**

descant /ˈdeskænt/ noun [C] a tune that is sung or played at the same time as, and usually higher than, the main tune ▶ **wysoki kontrapunkt**

D

ˌ**descant reˈcorder** (US soˌprano reˈcorder) noun [C] the most common size of **recorder**, with a high range of notes ▶ **flet dyszkantowy**

descend /dɪˈsend/ verb [I,T] (formal) to go down to a lower place; to go down sth: *The plane started to descend and a few minutes later we landed.* ◇ *She descended the stairs slowly.* ▶ **obniżać się; schodzić** OPP **ascend**

IDM **be descended from sb** to have sb as a relative in past times: *He says he's descended from a Spanish prince.* ▶ **pochodzić od kogoś**

descendant /dɪˈsendənt/ noun [C] a person who belongs to the same family as sb who lived a long time ago: *Her family are descendants of one of the first Englishmen to arrive in America.* ▶ **potomek** ➲ look at **ancestor**

descent /dɪˈsent/ noun **1** [C] a movement down to a lower place: *The pilot informed us that we were about to begin our descent.* ▶ **obniżenie** *(lotu)*, **zejście** OPP **ascent** **2** [U] a person's family origins: *He is **of** Italian **descent**.* ▶ **pochodzenie**

⚷ **describe** /dɪˈskraɪb/ verb [T] **describe sb/sth (to/for sb)**; **describe sb/sth (as sth)** to say what sb/sth is like, or what happened: *Can you describe the bag you lost?* ◇ *The thief was described as tall, thin, and aged about twenty.* ▶ **opisywać, określać**

⚷ **description** /dɪˈskrɪpʃn/ noun **1** [C,U] a picture in words of sb/sth or of sth that happened: *The man gave the police a detailed description of the burglar.* ▶ **opis; opisywanie** **2** [C] a type or kind of sth: *It must be a tool **of some description*** (jakieś narzędzie), *but I don't know what it's for.* ▶ **rodzaj**

descriptive /dɪˈskrɪptɪv/ adj. that describes sb/sth, especially in a skilful or interesting way: *a piece of descriptive writing* ◇ *She gave a highly descriptive account of the journey.* ▶ **opisowy, szczegółowy**

desecrate /ˈdesɪkreɪt/ verb [T] to damage a thing or place of religious importance or to treat it without respect: *desecrated graves* ▶ **bezcześcić**

■ **desecration** /ˌdesɪˈkreɪʃn/ noun [U] ▶ **(z)bezczeszczenie**

⚷ **desert**[1] /ˈdezət/ noun [C,U] a large area of land, usually covered with sand, that is hot and has very little water and very few plants ▶ **pustynia**

⚷ **desert**[2] /dɪˈzɜːt/ verb **1** [T] to leave sb/sth, usually for ever: *Many people have deserted the countryside and moved to the towns.* ▶ **opuszczać** **2** [I,T] (used especially about sb in the armed forces) to leave without permission: *He deserted because he didn't want to fight.* ▶ **dezerterować**

■ **desertion** noun [C,U] ▶ **porzucenie; dezercja**

⚷ **deserted** /dɪˈzɜːtɪd/ adj. empty, because all the people have left: *a deserted house* ▶ **opuszczony** SYN **abandoned**

deserter /dɪˈzɜːtə(r)/ noun [C] a person who leaves the armed forces without permission ▶ **dezerter/ka**

ˌ**desert ˈisland** noun [C] an island, especially a tropical one, where nobody lives ▶ **bezludna wyspa**

⚷ **deserve** /dɪˈzɜːv/ verb [T] [not used in the continuous tenses] to earn sth, either good or bad, because of sth that you have done: *We've done a lot of work and we deserve a break.* ◇ *He deserves to be punished severely for such a crime.*

▶ **zasługiwać (na coś)** ℹ Czasownika **deserve** nie używa się w czasach *continuous*. Natomiast często spotyka się go w *present participle* (formie *-ing*): *There are other aspects of the case deserving attention.*

deservedly /dɪˈzɜːvɪdli/ adv. in a way that is right because of what sb has done: *He deservedly won the Best Actor award.* ▶ **słusznie, sprawiedliwie**

deserving /dɪˈzɜːvɪŋ/ adj. **deserving (of sth)** that you should give help, money, etc. to: *This charity is a most deserving cause.* ▶ **zasługujący na pomoc**

desiccated /ˈdesɪkeɪtɪd/ adj. **1** (used about food) dried in order to preserve it: *desiccated coconut* ▶ **suszony** **2** completely dry: *treeless and desiccated soil* ▶ **wysuszony**

⚷ **design¹** /dɪˈzaɪn/ noun **1** [U] the way in which sth is planned and made or arranged: *Design faults* (błędy konstrukcyjne) *have been discovered in the car.* ▶ **konstrukcja, projektowanie** **2** [U] the process and skill of making drawings that show how sth should be made, how it will work, etc.: *to study industrial design* ◇ *graphic design* grafika ▶ **projektowanie** **3** [C] **a design (for sth)** a drawing or plan that shows how sth should be made, built, etc.: *The architect showed us her design for the new theatre.* ▶ **projekt czegoś, makieta czegoś** **4** [C] a pattern of lines, shapes, etc. that decorate sth: *a T-shirt with a geometric design on it* ▶ **wzór, deseń** SYN **pattern**

⚷ **design²** /dɪˈzaɪn/ verb **1** [I,T] to plan and make a drawing of how sth will be made: *to design cars/dresses/houses* ▶ **projektować, szkicować** **2** [T] to invent, plan and develop sth for a particular purpose: *The bridge wasn't designed for such heavy traffic.* ▶ **projektować, planować**

designate /ˈdezɪɡneɪt/ verb [T, often passive] (formal) **1 designate sth (as) sth** to give sth a name to show that it has a particular purpose: *This has been designated (as) a conservation area.* ▶ **przeznaczać** **2 designate sb (as) sth** to choose sb to do a particular job or task: *Who has she designated (as) her deputy?* ▶ **mianować** **3** to show or mark sth: *These arrows designate the emergency exits.* ▶ **wskazywać**

designer /dɪˈzaɪnə(r)/ noun [C] a person whose job is to make drawings or plans showing how sth will be made: *a fashion designer* ◇ *designer jeans* dżinsy znanej marki ◇ *I've just sent the text to the designer* (do grafika). ▶ **projektant/ka**

desirable /dɪˈzaɪərəbl/ adj. **1** wanted, often by many people; worth having: *Experience is desirable but not essential for this job.* ▶ **pożądany, mile widziany** OPP **undesirable** **2** sexually attractive ▶ **atrakcyjny**

⚷ **desire¹** /dɪˈzaɪə(r)/ noun [C,U] **(a) desire (for sth/to do sth)** **1** the feeling of wanting sth very much; a strong wish: *the desire for a peaceful solution to the crisis* ◇ *I have no desire to visit that place again.* ▶ **pragnienie** **2** the wish for a sexual relationship with sb: *She felt a surge of love and desire for him.* ▶ **pożądanie**

⚷ **desire²** /dɪˈzaɪə(r)/ verb [T] **1** [not used in the continuous tenses] (formal) to want; to wish for: *They have everything they could possibly desire.* ◇ *The service in the restaurant left a lot to be desired* (pozostawiała wiele do życzenia). ▶ **pragnąć** **2** to find sb/sth sexually attractive: *He still desired her.* ▶ **pożądać** ℹ Czasownika **desire** nie używa się w czasach *continuous*. Natomiast często spotyka się go w *present participle* (formie *-ing*): *Not desiring another argument, she left.*

⚷ **desk** /desk/ noun [C] **1** a type of table, often with drawers, that you sit at to write or work: *The pupils took their books out of their desks.* ◇ *He used to be a pilot but now he has **a desk job*** (pracę biurową). ▶ **biurko** **2** a table or place in a building where a particular service is provided: *an information desk* informacja ◇ *Take your suitcases and tickets to the check-in desk* (do stanowiska odprawy). ▶ **dział, sekcja**

desktop /ˈdesktɒp/ noun [C] **1** the top of a desk ▶ **blat biurka** **2** a computer screen on which you can see **icons** showing the programs, information, etc. that are available to be used ▶ (*ekran monitora*) **pulpit** **3** = DESKTOP COMPUTER

ˌdesktop comˈputer (also **desktop**) noun [C] a computer with a keyboard, screen and main processing unit, that fits on a desk ▶ **komputer stacjonarny** ➲ look at **laptop**, **notebook**

ˌdesktop ˈpublishing noun [U] (abbr. **DTP** /ˌdiː tiː ˈpiː/) the use of a small computer and a machine for printing, to produce books, magazines and other printed material ▶ (*publikacja książek itp.*) **technika DTP**

desolate /ˈdesələt/ adj. **1** (used about a place) empty in a way that seems very sad: *desolate wasteland* ▶ **opustoszały, wyludniony** **2** (used about a person) lonely, very unhappy and without hope ▶ **opuszczony, załamany**
■ **desolation** /ˌdesəˈleɪʃn/ noun [U] **1** the state of being empty because all the people have left: *a scene of desolation.* ▶ **spustoszenie, pustkowie** **2** the feeling of being lonely and without hope: *He felt utter desolation when his wife died.* ▶ **pustka, strapienie**

despair¹ /dɪˈspeə(r)/ noun [U] the state of having lost all hope: *I felt like giving up **in despair**.* ▶ **rozpacz**
■ **despairing** adj.: *a despairing cry* ▶ **zrozpaczony, rozpaczliwy** ➲ look at **desperate**

despair² /dɪˈspeə(r)/ verb [I] **despair (of sb/sth)** to lose all hope that sth will happen: *We began to despair of ever finding somewhere to live.* ▶ **rozpaczać, tracić nadzieję**

despatch (Brit.) = DISPATCH

⚷ **desperate** /ˈdespərət/ adj. **1** out of control and ready to do anything to change the situation you are in because it is so terrible: *She became desperate when her money ran out.* ▶ **zrozpaczony, doprowadzony do rozpaczy** **2** done with little hope of success, as a last thing to try when everything else has failed: *I made a desperate attempt to persuade her to change her mind.* ▶ **rozpaczliwy** **3 desperate (for sth/to do sth)** wanting or needing sth very much: *Let's go into a café. I'm desperate for a drink* (muszę się czegoś napić). ▶ **spragniony (czegoś)** **4** terrible, very serious: *There is a desperate shortage of skilled workers.* ▶ **rozpaczliwy, beznadziejny**
■ **desperately** adv.: *She was desperately unlucky not to win.* ▶ **potwornie, beznadziejnie** | **desperation** /ˌdespəˈreɪʃn/ noun [U] ▶ **rozpacz, desperacja**

despicable /dɪˈspɪkəbl/ adj. very unpleasant or evil: *a despicable act of terrorism* ▶ **nikczemny, zasługujący na pogardę**

despise /dɪˈspaɪz/ verb [T] to hate sb/sth very much: *I despise him for lying to me.* ▶ **gardzić**

⚷ **despite** /dɪˈspaɪt/ prep. without being affected by the thing mentioned: *Despite having very little money, they enjoy life.* ◇ *The scheme went ahead despite public opposition.* ▶ **pomimo, wbrew** SYN **in spite of**

despondent /dɪˈspɒndənt/ adj. **despondent (about/over sth)** without hope; expecting no improvement: *She was becoming increasingly despondent about finding a job.* ▶ **zniechęcony, przygnębiony**
■ **despondency** /dɪˈspɒndənsi/ noun [U] ▶ **zniechęcenie, zwątpienie**

despot /ˈdespɒt/ noun [C] a ruler with great power, especially one who uses it in a cruel way ▶ **despot(k)a**
■ **despotic** /dɪˈspɒtɪk/ adj. ▶ **despotyczny**

dessert /dɪˈzɜːt/ noun [C,U] something sweet that is eaten after the main part of a meal: *What would you like **for dessert** – ice cream or fresh fruit?* ▶ **deser** ➲ note at **restaurant** ➲ look at **pudding**, **sweet**

dessertspoon /dɪˈzɜːtspuːn/ noun [C] a spoon used for eating sweet food after the main part of a meal ▶ **łyżeczka deserowa**

destabilize (also -ise) /ˌdiːˈsteɪbəlaɪz/ verb [T] to make a system, government, country, etc. become less safe and successful ▶ **destabilizować** ➲ look at **stabilize**

destination /ˌdestɪˈneɪʃn/ noun [C] the place where sb/sth is going: *I finally reached my destination two hours late.* ◇ *popular holiday destinations like the Bahamas* ▶ **cel podróży**, **miejsce przeznaczenia**

destined /ˈdestɪnd/ adj. **1 destined for sth/to do sth** having a future that has been decided or planned at an earlier time: *I think she is destined for success* (pisany jest jej sukces). ◇ *He was destined* (było mu pisane, że) *to become one of the country's leading politicians.* ▶ **przeznaczony** **2 destined for…** travelling towards a particular place: *I boarded a bus destined for New York.* ▶ **jadący dokądś**

destiny /ˈdestəni/ noun (pl. **destinies**) **1** [C] the things that happen to you in your life, especially things that you cannot control: *She felt that it was her destiny to be a great singer.* ▶ **przeznaczenie**, **los** **2** [U] a power that people believe controls their lives ▶ **przeznaczenie**, **los** SYN for both meanings **fate**

destitute /ˈdestɪtjuːt; US -tuːt/ adj. without any money, food or a home ▶ **bez środków do życia**
■ **destitution** /ˌdestɪˈtjuːʃn; US -ˈtuː-/ noun [U] ▶ **nędza**

destroy /dɪˈstrɔɪ/ verb [T] **1** to damage sth so badly that it can no longer be used or no longer exists: *The building was destroyed by fire.* ◇ *The defeat destroyed his confidence.* ▶ **niszczyć** ➲ look at **damage** **2** to kill an animal, especially because it is injured or dangerous: *The horse broke its leg and had to be destroyed.* ▶ **dobijać**, **zabijać**

destroyer /dɪˈstrɔɪə(r)/ noun [C] **1** a small ship that is used in war ▶ **niszczyciel** (*okręt*) **2** a person or thing that destroys sth ▶ **niszczyciel/ka**

destruction /dɪˈstrʌkʃn/ noun [U] the act of destroying sth: *The war brought death and destruction to the city.* ◇ *the destruction of the rainforests* ▶ **zniszczenie**

destructive /dɪˈstrʌktɪv/ adj. causing a lot of harm or damage: *destructive weapons* ◇ *the destructive effects of drink and drugs* ▶ **niszczycielski**, **niszczący**

desultory /ˈdesəltri; US -tɔːri/ adj. (formal) going from one thing to another, without a definite plan and without enthusiasm: *I wandered about in a desultory fashion.* ◇ *a desultory conversation* chaotyczna rozmowa ▶ **pozbawiony entuzjazmu i celu**
■ **desultorily** adv. ▶ **bez entuzjazmu i celu**

detach /dɪˈtætʃ/ verb [T] **detach sth (from sth)** to separate sth from sth it is connected to: *Detach the form at the bottom of the page and send it to this address…* ▶ **odrywać**, **odłączać** OPP **attach**

detachable /dɪˈtætʃəbl/ adj. that can be separated from sth it is connected to: *a coat with a detachable hood* ▶ **taki, który można oddzielić/odczepić od czegoś**

detached /dɪˈtætʃt/ adj. **1** (used about a house) not joined to any other house ▶ (*dom*) **wolno stojący** ➲ picture on **page A3** **2** not being or not feeling personally involved in sth; without emotion ▶ **oderwany**, **obojętny**

detachment /dɪˈtætʃmənt/ noun **1** [U] the fact or feeling of not being personally involved in sth ▶ **oderwanie**, **obojętność** **2** [C] a group of soldiers who have been given a particular task away from the main group ▶ **odkomenderowany oddział**

detail¹ /ˈdiːteɪl/ noun [C,U] one fact or piece of information: *Just give me the basic facts. Don't worry about the details.* ◇ *On the application form you should* ***give details of*** (podać szczegółowe informacje dotyczące) *your education and experience.* ◇ *For full details of* (pełne informacje dotyczące) *the offer, contact your local travel agent.* ◇ *The work involves close attention to detail* (zadbania o szczegóły). ▶ **szczegół**
■ **detailed** adj.: *a detailed description* ▶ **szczegółowy**
IDM **go into detail(s)** to talk or write about the details of sth; to explain sth fully: *I can't go into detail now because it would take too long.* ▶ **wdawać się w szczegóły**
in detail including the details: *We haven't discussed the matter in great detail yet.* ▶ **szczegółowo** SYN **thoroughly**

detail² /ˈdiːteɪl/ verb [T] to give a full list of sth; to describe sth completely: *He detailed all the equipment he needed for the job.* ▶ **wyszczególniać**, **podawać szczegóły**

detain /dɪˈteɪn/ verb [T] to stop sb from leaving a place; to delay sb: *A man has been detained by the police for questioning.* ◇ *Don't let me detain you if you're busy.* ▶ **zatrzymywać**, **przetrzymywać** (*w areszcie*) ➲ noun **detention**

detainee /ˌdiːteɪˈniː/ noun [C] a person who is kept in prison, usually because of his or her political opinions ▶ **zatrzyman-y/a** (*zazw. więzień polityczny*)

detect /dɪˈtekt/ verb [T] to notice or discover sth that is difficult to see, feel, etc.: *I detected a slight change in his attitude.* ◇ *Traces of blood were detected on his clothes.* ▶ **dostrzegać**, **wykrywać**
■ **detection** noun [U]: *The crime escaped detection* (nie było wykryte) *for many years.* ▶ **wykrycie**, **wyśledzenie**

detective /dɪˈtektɪv/ noun [C] a person, especially a police officer, who tries to solve crimes ▶ **detektyw**

deˈtective story noun [C] a story about a crime in which sb tries to find out who the guilty person is ▶ **kryminał**

detector /dɪˈtektə(r)/ noun [C] a machine that is used for finding or noticing sth: *a smoke/metal/lie detector* ▶ **wykrywacz**, **czujnik alarmowy**

détente /ˌdeɪˈtɑːnt/ noun [U] (formal) a more friendly relationship between countries that had previously been very unfriendly towards each other ▶ (*polityka*) **odprężenie**

detention /dɪˈtenʃn/ noun [U,C] **1** the act of stopping a person leaving a place, especially by keeping them in prison: *They were kept* ***in detention*** *for ten days.* ▶ **zatrzymanie**, **areszt** **2** the punishment of being kept at school after the other children have gone home ▶ **zostanie po lekcjach** ➲ verb **detain**

deˈtention centre (US deˈtention center) noun [C] **1** a place where young people who have committed offences are kept in **detention** ▶ **dom poprawczy** **2** a place where people are kept in **detention**, especially people who have entered a country illegally ▶ **obóz** (*zwł. dla nielegalnych imigrantów*)

deter /dɪˈtɜː(r)/ verb [T] (**deterring**; **deterred**) **deter sb (from doing sth)** to make sb decide not to do sth, especially by telling them that it would have bad results: *The council is trying to deter visitors from bringing their cars into the city centre.* ▶ **powstrzymywać**, **odstraszać** ➲ noun **deterrent**

detergent /dɪˈtɜːdʒənt/ noun [C,U] a chemical liquid or powder that is used for cleaning things ▶ **środek czyszczący**, **detergent**

deteriorate /dɪˈtɪəriəreɪt/ verb [I] to become worse: *The political tension is deteriorating into* (przeradza się w) *civil war.* ▶ **pogarszać się**
■ **deterioration** /dɪˌtɪəriəˈreɪʃn/ noun [C,U] ▶ **pogorszenie (się)**

determination /dɪˌtɜːmɪˈneɪʃn/ noun [U] **1 determination (to do sth)** the quality of having firmly decided to do sth, even if it is very difficult: *her determination to win* ◇ *You need great determination to succeed in busi-*

ness. ▶ **determinacja** 2 (formal) the process of deciding sth officially: *the determination of future government policy* ▶ **ustalenie**, **określenie**

determine /dɪˈtɜːmɪn/ verb [T] **1** (formal) to discover the facts about sth: *We need to determine what happened immediately before the accident.* ▶ **określać**, **stwierdzać** **2** to make sth happen in a particular way or be of a particular type: *The results of the tests will determine what treatment you need.* ◇ *Age and experience will be* ***determining factors*** *in our choice of candidate.* ▶ **określać**, **decydować** **3** (formal) to decide sth officially: *A date for the meeting has yet to be determined.* ▶ **postanowić**

determined /dɪˈtɜːmɪnd/ adj. **determined (to do sth)** having firmly decided to do sth or to succeed, even if it is difficult: *He is determined to leave school, even though his parents want him to stay.* ◇ *She's a very determined athlete.* ▶ **zdecydowany**, **zdeterminowany**

determiner /dɪˈtɜːmɪnə(r)/ noun [C] a word that comes before a noun to show how the noun is being used: *'Her', 'most' and 'those' are all determiners.* ▶ **określnik**

deterrent /dɪˈterənt; US -ˈtɜːr-/ noun [C] something that should stop you doing sth: *Their punishment will be a deterrent to others.* ▶ **środek odstraszający/zapobiegawczy** ⮌ verb **deter**

■ **deterrent** adj. ▶ **odstraszający**, **zapobiegawczy**

detest /dɪˈtest/ verb [T] to hate or not like sb/sth at all: *They absolutely detest each other.* ▶ **nie cierpieć**, **nienawidzić** SYN **loathe**

detonate /ˈdetəneɪt/ verb [I,T] to explode or to make a bomb, etc. explode ▶ **wybuchać**; **detonować**

detonator /ˈdetəneɪtə(r)/ noun [C] a device for making a bomb explode ▶ **detonator**

detour /ˈdiːtʊə(r)/ noun [C] **1** a longer route from one place to another that you take in order to avoid sth/sb or in order to see or do sth: *Because of the accident we had to make a five-kilometre detour.* ▶ **objazd** **2** (US) = DIVERSION (3)

detox /ˈdiːtɒks/ noun [U] (informal) the process of removing harmful substances from your body by only eating and drinking particular things ▶ **odtruwanie** (*organizmu*), **detoks**

detract /dɪˈtrækt/ verb [I] **detract from sth** to make sth seem less good or important: *These criticisms in no way detract from the team's achievements.* ▶ **umniejszać**, **ujmować**

detriment /ˈdetrɪmənt/ noun

IDM **to the detriment of sb/sth** harming or damaging sb/sth: *Doctors claim that the changes will be to the detriment of patients.* ▶ **ze szkodą/z uszczerbkiem dla kogoś/czegoś**

■ **detrimental** /ˌdetrɪˈmentl/ adj.: *Too much alcohol is* ***detrimental to*** *your health.* ▶ **szkodliwy**

deuce /djuːs; US duːs/ noun [U] a score of 40 points to each player in a game of **tennis** ▶ (*tenis*) **równowaga**

devalue /ˌdiːˈvæljuː/ verb [T] **1** to reduce the value of the money of one country in relation to the value of the money of other countries: *The pound has been devalued against the dollar.* ▶ **dewaluować** **2** to reduce the value or importance of sth: *The refusal of the top players to take part devalues this competition.* ▶ (*przen.*) **dewaluować**

■ **devaluation** /ˌdiːˌvæljuˈeɪʃn/ noun [U] ▶ **dewaluacja**

devastate /ˈdevəsteɪt/ verb [T] **1** to destroy sth or damage it badly: *a land devastated by war* ▶ **niszczyć**, **pustoszyć** **2** to make sb extremely upset and shocked: *This tragedy has devastated the community.* ▶ (*przen.*) **druzgotać**, **załamywać**

■ **devastation** /ˌdevəˈsteɪʃn/ noun [U]: *a scene of total devastation* ▶ **zniszczenie**, **spustoszenie**; **zdruzgotanie**

devastated /ˈdevəsteɪtɪd/ adj. extremely shocked and upset: *They were devastated when their baby died.* ▶ **wstrząśnięty**, **zrozpaczony**

devastating /ˈdevəsteɪtɪŋ/ adj. **1** that destroys sth completely: *a devastating explosion* ▶ **niszczycielski**, **niszczący** **2** that shocks or upsets sb very much: *The closure of the factory was a devastating blow to the men.* ▶ **dotkliwy**, **wstrząsający** **3** impressive and powerful: *his devastating performance* (olśniewający występ) *in the 100 metres* ◇ *a devastating smile* zniewalający uśmiech ◇ *a devastating attack* (miażdżący atak) *on the President's economic record*

■ **devastatingly** adv.: *devastatingly handsome* ▶ **nadzwyczajnie**, **niesłychanie**

develop /dɪˈveləp/ verb **1** [I,T] to grow slowly, increase, or change into sth else; to make sb/sth do this: *to develop from a child into an adult* ◇ *a scheme to help pupils develop their natural talents* ◇ *Scientists have developed* (opracowali) *a drug against this disease.* ◇ *Over the years, she's developed her own unique singing style.* ▶ **rozwijać (się)**, **przeradzać się w coś** **2** [T] to begin to have a problem or disease: *to develop cancer/AIDS* ◇ *The car developed engine trouble* (silnik samochodu się popsuł) *and we had to stop.* ◇ *Her mind had developed an annoying habit of wandering.* ▶ **zachorować (na coś)**, **nabierać** (*przyzwyczajenia/nawyków*) **3** [I] to start to affect sth: *Trouble is developing along the border.* ▶ (*wady, usterki itp.*) **ujawniać się**, (*trudności itp.*) **wynikać** **4** [T] to build houses, shops, factories, etc. on a piece of land: *This site is being developed for offices.* ▶ **eksploatować/zagospodarowywać** (*teren*) **5** [T] to make an idea, a story, etc. clearer or more detailed by writing or talking about it more: *She went on to develop this theme later in the lecture.* ▶ **rozwijać** (*np. temat*) **6** [T] to make pictures from a piece of film by using special chemicals: *to develop a film* ▶ **wywoływać** (*zdjęcia*)

developed /dɪˈveləpt/ adj. of a good level or standard: *a highly developed economy* ▶ **rozwinięty**

developer /dɪˈveləpə(r)/ (also **ˈproperty developer**) noun [C] a person or company that builds houses, shops, etc. on a piece of land ▶ **przedsiębiorca lub agencja zajmująca się zbrojeniem i zabudową terenu**

developing /dɪˈveləpɪŋ/ adj. [only before a noun] (used about a poor country) that is trying to develop or improve its economy: *a developing country* ▶ **rozwijający się**

development /dɪˈveləpmənt/ noun **1** [U] the process of becoming bigger, stronger, better, etc., or of making sb/sth do this: *the development of tourism in Cuba* ◇ *a child's intellectual development* ▶ **rozwój** **2** [U,C] the process of creating sth more advanced; a more advanced product: *She works in* ***research and development*** (w dziale badań i rozwoju) *for a drug company.* ◇ *the latest developments in space technology* ▶ **rozwój**, **postęp** **3** [C] a new event that changes a situation: *This week has seen a number of new developments in the Middle East* (nowy rozwój wypadków). ▶ **(nowe) wydarzenie** **4** [C,U] a piece of land with new buildings on it; the process of building on a piece of land: *a new housing development* (osiedle mieszkaniowe) ◇ *The land has been bought for development.* ▶ **teren zabudowany/pod zabudowę**; **zabudowywanie terenu**

deviant /ˈdiːviənt/ adj. different from what most people consider to be normal and acceptable: ***deviant behaviour/sexuality*** ▶ **odbiegający od normy**, **dewiacyjny**

■ **deviant** noun [C]: *sexual deviants* ▶ **dewiant/ka** | **deviance** /-viəns/ (also **deviancy** /ˈdiːviənsi/) noun [U]: *a study of social deviance and crime* ▶ **odchylenie od normy**, **dewiacja**

deviate /ˈdiːvieɪt/ verb [I] **deviate (from sth)** to change or become different from what is normal or expected: *He never once deviated from his original plan.* ▶ **odchylać się, zbaczać**

deviation /ˌdiːviˈeɪʃn/ noun [C,U] a difference from what is normal or expected, or from what is approved of by society: *a deviation from our usual way of doing things* ◇ *sexual deviation* ▶ **odchylenie, zboczenie**

device /dɪˈvaɪs/ noun [C] **1** a tool or piece of equipment made for a particular purpose: *a security device which detects any movement* ◇ *labour-saving devices such as washing machines and vacuum cleaners* ▶ **przyrząd, urządzenie** ➲ note at **tool 2** a clever method for getting the result you want: *Critics dismissed the speech as a political device for winning support.* ▶ **wybieg**

devil /ˈdevl/ noun [C] **1** (**the Devil**) the most powerful evil being, according to the Christian, Jewish and Muslim religions ▶ **szatan** ➲ look at **Satan 2** an evil being; a spirit ▶ **diabeł, czort, bies 3** (informal) a word used to show pity, anger, etc. when you are talking about a person: *Those kids can be little devils* (diabłami wcielonymi) *sometimes.* ◇ *The poor devil* (biedaczysko) *died in hospital two days later.* ◇ *You're a lucky devil* (szczęściarz)*!* ▶ **facet**

IDM **be a devil** (used to encourage sb to do sth that they are not sure about doing): *Go on, be a devil – buy both of them.* ▶ **zaszalej sobie!**

speak/talk of the devil (used when the person who is being talked about appears unexpectedly) ▶ **o wilku mowa (a wilk tuż)**

devilish /ˈdevəlɪʃ/ adj. **1** cruel or evil: *a devilish conspiracy* ▶ **diaboliczny 2** morally bad, but in a way that people find attractive: *He was handsome, with a devilish charm.* ▶ **diabelski**

ˌdevil's ˈadvocate noun [C] a person who expresses an opinion that they do not really hold in order to encourage a discussion about a subject: *Often the interviewer will need to* ***play devil's advocate*** *in order to get a discussion going.* ▶ **adwokat diabła**

devious /ˈdiːviəs/ adj. clever but not honest or direct: *I wouldn't trust him – he can be very devious.* ◇ *a devious trick/plan* ▶ **przebiegły, podstępny**

■ **deviously** adv. ▶ **przebiegle, chytrze**

devise /dɪˈvaɪz/ verb [T] to invent a new way of doing sth: *They've devised a plan for keeping traffic out of the city centre.* ▶ **wymyślać, wynajdować**

devoid /dɪˈvɔɪd/ adj. (formal) **devoid of sth** not having a particular quality; without sth: *devoid of hope/ambition/imagination* ▶ **pozbawiony**

devolution /ˌdiːvəˈluːʃn; US ˌdev-/ noun [U] the movement of political power from central to local government ▶ **przekazanie władzy** (*samorządom lokalnym*)

devolve /dɪˈvɒlv/ verb

PHR V **devolve on/upon sb/sth** (formal) **1** if property, money, etc. **devolves on/upon** you, you receive it after sb else dies ▶ **przechodzić na kogoś/coś** (*zwł. jako spadek*) **2** if a duty, responsibility, etc. **devolves on/upon** you, it is given to you by sb at a higher level of authority ▶ (*obowiązek itp.*) **przypadać na kogoś/coś**

devolve sth to/on/upon sb to give a duty, responsibility, power, etc. to sb who has less authority than you: *The central government devolved most tax-raising powers to the regional authorities.* ▶ **przekazywać coś komuś**

devote /dɪˈvəʊt/ verb [T] **devote yourself/sth to sb/sth** to give a lot of time, energy, etc. to sb/sth: *Schools should devote more time to science subjects.* ◇ *She gave up work to devote herself full-time to her music.* ▶ **poświęcać (się)**

devoted /dɪˈvəʊtɪd/ adj. **devoted (to sb/sth)** loving sb/sth very much; completely loyal to sb/sth: *Neil's absolutely devoted to his wife.* ▶ **oddany**

devotee /ˌdevəˈtiː/ noun [C] **a devotee (of sb/sth)** a person who likes sb/sth very much ▶ **wielbiciel/ka, entuzjast(k)a**

devotion /dɪˈvəʊʃn/ noun [U] **devotion (to sb/sth) 1** great love for sb/sth: *a mother's devotion to her children* ▶ **oddanie, przywiązanie** SYN **dedication 2** the act of giving a lot of your time, energy, etc. to sb/sth: *devotion to duty* ▶ **poświęcenie (się), przywiązanie** SYN **dedication 3** very strong religious feeling ▶ **pobożność**

devour /dɪˈvaʊə(r)/ verb [T] **1** to eat sth quickly because you are very hungry ▶ **pożerać, pochłaniać 2** to do or use sth quickly and completely: *Lisa devours two or three novels a week.* ▶ **pochłaniać**

devout /dɪˈvaʊt/ adj. very religious: *a devout Muslim family* ▶ **pobożny**

■ **devoutly** adv. ▶ **gorliwie, żarliwie**

dew /djuː; US duː/ noun [U] small drops of water that form on plants, leaves, etc. during the night ▶ **rosa**

dexterity /dekˈsterəti/ noun [U] skill at doing things, especially with your hands ▶ **zręczność, zwinność**

dexterous (also **dextrous**) /ˈdekstrəs/ adj. (formal) skilful with your hands; skilfully done ▶ **zręczny**

■ **dexterously** (also **dextrously**) adv. ▶ **zręcznie**

dextrose /ˈdekstrəʊz; -əʊs/ noun [U] a form of **glucose** (= a type of natural sugar) ▶ **dekstroza**

diabetes /ˌdaɪəˈbiːtiːz/ noun [U] a serious disease in which sb's body cannot control the level of sugar in the blood ▶ **cukrzyca**

diabetic[1] /ˌdaɪəˈbetɪk/ adj. connected with **diabetes** or **diabetics**: *diabetic chocolate* ▶ **cukrzycowy, dla cukrzyków**

diabetic[2] /ˌdaɪəˈbetɪk/ noun [C] a person who suffers from **diabetes** ▶ **cukrzyk**

diacritic /ˌdaɪəˈkrɪtɪk/ noun [C] a mark such as an accent, placed over, under or through a letter in some languages, to show that the letter should be pronounced in a different way from the same letter without a mark ▶ **znak diakrytyczny**

diagnose /ˈdaɪəgnəʊz; -ˈnəʊz; US -ˈnəʊs/ verb [T] **diagnose sth (as sth); diagnose sb as/with sth** to find out and say exactly what illness a person has or what the cause of a problem is: *His illness was diagnosed as bronchitis.* ◇ *I've been diagnosed as (a) diabetic/with diabetes.* ◇ *After a couple of minutes I diagnosed the trouble – a flat battery.* ▶ **stawiać diagnozę, rozpoznawać** (*chorobę*)

diagnosis /ˌdaɪəgˈnəʊsɪs/ noun [C,U] (pl. **diagnoses** /-siːz/) the act of saying exactly what illness a person has or what the cause of a problem is: *to* ***make a diagnosis*** ▶ **diagnoza, rozpoznanie** (*np. choroby, sytuacji*)

diagnostic /ˌdaɪəgˈnɒstɪk/ adj. (technical) connected with identifying sth, especially an illness: *to carry out* ***diagnostic tests*** ▶ **diagnostyczny**

diagonal /daɪˈægənl/ adj. **1** (used about a straight line) joining two sides of sth at an angle that is not 90° or vertical or horizontal: *Draw a diagonal line from one corner of the square to the opposite corner.* ▶ **przekątny 2** (used about a straight line) not vertical or horizontal; sloping ▶ **ukośny**

■ **diagonally** /-nəli/ adv. ▶ **po przekątnej**

diagram /ˈdaɪəgræm/ noun [C] a simple picture that is used to explain how sth works or what sth looks like: *a diagram of the body's digestive system* ▶ **wykres, diagram**

dial[1] /ˈdaɪəl/ noun [C] **1** the round part of a clock, watch, control on a machine, etc. that shows a measurement of time, amount, temperature, etc.: *a dial for showing air pressure* ▶ **tarcza** (*zegara*) **2** the round control on a radio, cooker, etc. that you turn to change sth ▶ **tarcza**

D

(*instrumentu*) **3** the round part with holes in it on some older telephones that you turn to call a number ▶ **tarcza**

dial² /ˈdaɪəl/ verb [I,T] (**dialling**; **dialled**; US **dialing**; **dialed**) to push the buttons or move the **dial** on a telephone in order to call a telephone number: *You can now dial direct* (dzwonić bezpośrednio) *to Singapore.* ◇ *to dial the wrong number* ▶ **wykręcać** (*numer telefoniczny*)

dialect /ˈdaɪəlekt/ noun [C,U] a form of a language that is spoken in one part of a country: *a local dialect* ▶ **dialekt**

ˈ**dialling code** noun [C] (Brit.) (US **code**) the numbers that you must dial for a particular area or country ▶ **numer kierunkowy**

ˈ**dialling tone** noun [C] (US ˈ**dial tone**) the sound that you hear when you pick up a telephone before you begin to dial ▶ **sygnał** (*słyszalny po podniesieniu słuchawki telefonu*)

ˈ**dialog box** (Brit. also ˈ**dialogue box**) noun [C] a box that appears on a computer screen asking the user to choose what they want to do next ▶ (*komputer*) **okno dialogowe**

dialogue (US **dialog**) /ˈdaɪəlɒg/ noun [C,U] **1** (a) conversation between people in a book, play, etc.: *This movie is all action, with very little dialogue.* ◇ *On the tape you will hear a short dialogue between a shop assistant and a customer.* ▶ **dialog 2** (a) discussion between people who have different opinions: *(a) dialogue between the major political parties* ▶ **dialog**

dialysis /ˌdaɪˈæləsɪs/ noun [U] a process for separating substances from a liquid, especially for taking waste substances out of the blood of people with damaged **kidneys**: ***kidney/renal dialysis*** ◇ *a dialysis machine* ▶ **dializa**

diameter /daɪˈæmɪtə(r)/ noun [C] a straight line that goes from one side to the other of a circle, passing through the centre ▶ **średnica** ➲ look at **radius**, **circumference**

⚷ **diamond** /ˈdaɪəmənd/ noun **1** [C,U] a hard, bright **precious** stone which is very expensive and is used for making jewellery. A diamond usually has no colour: *a diamond ring* ▶ **brylant**, **diament 2** [C] a flat shape that has four sides of equal length and points at two ends ▶ **romb 3** (**diamonds**) [pl.] in a pack of playing cards, the **suit** with red shapes like diamonds(2) on them: *the seven of diamonds* ▶ **kara** ➲ note at **card 4** [C] one of the cards from this suit: *I haven't got any diamonds.* ▶ **karo**

ˌ**diamond** ˈ**wedding** noun [C] the 60th anniversary of a wedding ▶ **brylantowe gody** ➲ look at **silver**, **golden**

diaper (US) = NAPPY

diaphragm /ˈdaɪəfræm/ noun [C] **1** the muscle between your lungs and your stomach that helps you to breathe ▶ **przepona 2** a rubber device that a woman puts inside her body before having sex to stop her having a baby ▶ **kapturek**

diarrhoea (US **diarrhea**) /ˌdaɪəˈrɪə; US -ˈriːə/ noun [U] an illness that causes you to get rid of **faeces** from your body very often and in a more liquid form than usual ▶ **biegunka**

⚷ **diary** /ˈdaɪəri/ noun [C] (pl. **diaries**) **1** a book in which you write down things that you have to do, remember, etc.: *I'll just check in my diary to see if I'm free that weekend.* ▶ **kalendarzyk**, **terminarz** ➲ note at **calendar 2** a book in which you write down what happens to you each day: *Do you **keep a diary**?* ▶ **dziennik**, **pamiętnik**

dice /daɪs/ noun [C] (pl. **dice**) a small solid square object with six sides and a different number of spots (from one to six) on each side, used in certain games: ***Throw the dice*** *to see who goes first.* ▶ **kostka do gry**

dichotomy /daɪˈkɒtəmi/ noun [usually sing.] (pl. **-ies**) **dichotomy (between A and B)** (formal) the separation that exists between two groups or things that are completely opposite to and different from each other ▶ **dychotomia**

dictate /dɪkˈteɪt; US ˈdɪkteɪt/ verb **1** [I,T] **dictate (sth) (to sb)** to say sth in a normal speaking voice so that sb else can write or type it: *to dictate a letter to a secretary* ▶ **dyktować 2** [I,T] **dictate (sth) (to sb)** to tell sb what to do in a way that seems unfair: *Parents can't dictate to their children how they should run their lives.* ▶ **dyktować 3** [T] to control or influence sth: *The kind of house people live in is usually dictated by how much they earn.* ▶ **dyktować**

dictation /dɪkˈteɪʃn/ noun [C,U] spoken words that sb else must write or type ▶ **dyktando**

dictator /dɪkˈteɪtə(r); US ˈdɪkteɪt-/ noun [C] a ruler who has total power in a country, especially one who rules the country by force ▶ **dyktator**
■ **dictatorship** noun [C,U] ▶ **dyktatura** | **dictatorial** /ˌdɪktəˈtɔːriəl/ adj.: *dictatorial behaviour* ▶ **dyktatorski**

diction /ˈdɪkʃn/ noun [U] the way that sb pronounces words: *clear diction* ▶ **dykcja**

⚷ **dictionary** /ˈdɪkʃənri; US -neri/ noun [C] (pl. **dictionaries**) **1** a book that contains a list of the words in a language in the order of the alphabet and that tells you what they mean, in the same or another language: *to look up a word in a dictionary* ◇ *a bilingual/monolingual dictionary* ▶ **słownik 2** a book that lists the words connected with a particular subject and tells you what they mean: *a dictionary of idioms* ◇ *a medical dictionary* ▶ **leksykon** ➲ note at **book**

did /dɪd/ past tense of **do**

didactic /daɪˈdæktɪk/ adj. (formal) **1** designed to teach people sth, especially a moral lesson: *didactic art* ▶ **dydaktyczny**, **moralizatorski 2** telling people things rather than letting them find out for themselves ▶ **dydaktyczny**, **pouczający** ⓘ Zwykle wyraża dezaprobatę.
■ **didactically** /-kli/ adv. ▶ **dydaktycznie**

diddle /ˈdɪdl/ verb [T] **diddle sb (out of sth)** (Brit., informal) to get money or some advantage from sb by cheating them ▶ **(o)cyganić kogoś (na coś)** SYN **cheat**

didn't /ˈdɪdnt/ short for **did not**

⚷ **die** /daɪ/ verb (**dying**; **dies**; pt, pp **died**) **1** [I,T] **die (from/of sth)** to stop living: *My father died when I was three.* ◇ *Thousands of people have died from this disease.* ◇ *to die of hunger* ◇ *He died of cancer.* ◇ *to die for what you believe in* ◇ *to die a natural/violent death* ▶ **umierać**, **ginąć** ➲ adjective **dead**, noun **death 2** [I] to stop existing; to disappear: *Our love will never die.* ◇ *The old customs are dying* (wymierają). ▶ **umierać**

IDM **be dying for sth/to do sth** (informal) to want sth/to do sth very much: *I'm dying for a cup of coffee.* ▶ **marzyć o czymś**, **bardzo pragnąć coś robić**

die hard to change or disappear only slowly or with difficulty: *Old attitudes towards women die hard.* ▶ **nie dawać się łatwo wykorzenić**

die laughing to find sth very funny: *I thought I'd die laughing when he told that joke.* ▶ **umierać ze śmiechu**

to die for (informal) if you think that sth is to die for, you really want it and would do anything to get it: *They have a house to die for* (o jakim każdy marzy). ▶ **(być) obiektem pragnień/marzeń**

PHR V **die away** to slowly become weaker before stopping or disappearing: *The sound of the engine died away as the car drove into the distance.* ▶ **cichnąć**, **zanikać**

die down to slowly become less strong: *Let's wait until the storm dies down before we go out.* ▶ **słabnąć**, **cichnąć**

die off to die one by one until there are none left ▶ **wymierać**

die out to stop happening or disappear: *The use of horses on farms has almost died out in this country.* ▶ **zanikać, wymierać**

diesel /ˈdiːzl/ noun **1** [U] a type of heavy oil used in some engines instead of petrol: *a diesel engine* silnik na olej napędowy ◇ *a taxi that runs on diesel* ▶ **olej napędowy** ➲ look at **petrol 2** [C] a vehicle that uses **diesel**: *My new car's a diesel.* ▶ **diesel**

diet[1] /ˈdaɪət/ noun **1** [C,U] the food that a person or an animal usually eats: *The peasants* ***live on a diet of*** (odżywiają się) *rice and vegetables.* ◇ *I always try to have a healthy, balanced diet.* ◇ *Poor diet is a cause of ill health.* ◇ *a balanced diet* pełnowartościowa dieta ▶ **dieta, wyżywienie 2** [C] certain foods that a person who is ill, or who wants to lose weight is allowed to eat: *a low-fat diet* ◇ *a sugar-free diet* ▶ **dieta**
■ **dietary** /ˈdaɪətəri; US -teri/ adj.: *dietary habits/requirements* ▶ **dietetyczny**
IDM **be/go on a diet** to eat only certain foods or a small amount of food because you want to lose weight ▶ **być na diecie, odchudzać się; przechodzić na dietę**

diet[2] /ˈdaɪət/ verb [I] to try to lose weight by eating less food or only certain kinds of food: *You've lost some weight. Have you been dieting?* ▶ **być na diecie, odchudzać się, stosować dietę**

dietitian (also **dietician**) /ˌdaɪəˈtɪʃn/ noun [C] a person whose job is to advise people on what kind of food they should eat to keep healthy ▶ **dietety-k/czka**

differ /ˈdɪfə(r)/ verb [I] **1 differ (from sb/sth)** to be different: *How does this car differ from the more expensive model?* ▶ **różnić się 2 differ (with sb) (about/on sth)** to have a different opinion: *I'm afraid I differ with you on that question.* ▶ **mieć inne zdanie**

difference /ˈdɪfrəns/ noun **1** [C] **a difference (between A and B)** the way that people or things are not the same or the way that sb/sth has changed: *What's the difference between this computer and that cheaper one?* ◇ *From a distance it's hard to* ***tell the difference*** *between* (odróżnić) *the twins.* ▶ **różnica** OPP **similarity 2** [C,U] **difference (in sth) (between A and B)** the amount by which people or things are not the same or by which sb/sth has changed: *There's an age difference of three years between the two children.* ◇ *There's very little difference in price since last year.* ◇ *We gave a 30% deposit and must* ***pay the difference*** (zapłacić resztę) *when the work is finished.* ▶ **różnica 3** [C] a disagreement that is not very serious: *All couples* ***have*** *their* ***differences*** *from time to time.* ◇ *There was* ***a difference of opinion*** *over how much we owed.* ▶ **nieporozumienie, sprzeczka**
IDM **make a, some, etc. difference (to sb/sth)** to have an effect (on sb/sth): *A week's holiday made a lot of difference to her health* (wpłynął dodatnio na jej zdrowie). ▶ **sprawiać/stanowić różnicę**
make no difference (to sb/sth); not make any difference to not be important (to sb/sth); to have no effect: *It makes no difference to us if the baby is a girl or a boy.* ▶ **nie robić różnicy, nie mieć znaczenia**
split the difference → SPLIT[1]

different /ˈdɪfrənt/ adj. **1 different (from/to sb/sth)** not the same: *The play was different from anything I had seen before.* ◇ *The two houses are very different in style.* ◇ *You'd look completely different with short hair.* ◇ *The two houses are very different* (bardzo się różnią) *in style.* ▶ **różny od kogoś/czegoś, inny niż ktoś/coś** OPP **similar** ℹ W Amer. ang. używa się też zwrotu **different than**. **2** [only before a noun] separate; individual: *This coat is available in three different colours.* ▶ **różny** ➲ look at **varied, various**
■ **differently** adv.: *I think you'll feel differently about it tomorrow.* ▶ **inaczej**
IDM **a (whole) new/different ball game** → BALL GAME
another/a different matter → MATTER[1]

differentiate /ˌdɪfəˈrenʃieɪt/ verb **1** [I,T] **differentiate between A and B; differentiate A (from B)** to see or show how things are different: *It is hard to differentiate between these two types of seed.* ▶ **rozróżniać 2** [T] **differentiate sth (from sth)** to make one thing different from another: *The coloured feathers differentiate the male bird from the plain brown female.* ▶ **odróżniać 3** [T] to treat one person or group differently from another: *We don't differentiate between the two groups – we treat everybody alike.* ▶ **wyróżniać** SYN **distinguish**

difficult /ˈdɪfɪkəlt/ adj. **1 difficult (for sb) (to do sth)** not easy to do or understand: *a difficult test/problem* ◇ *I* ***find it difficult to*** (trudno mi) *get up early in the morning.* ◇ *It was difficult for us to hear the speaker.* ◇ *I'm in a difficult situation. Whatever I do, somebody will be upset.* ◇ *Dean found it difficult/It was difficult for Dean to pass the driving test.* Dean miał problemy ze zdaniem egzaminu na prawo jazdy. ▶ **trudny, kłopotliwy 2** (used about a person) not friendly, reasonable or helpful: *a difficult customer* ▶ **trudny, grymaśny, nieuprzejmy** SYN **awkward**

difficulty /ˈdɪfɪkəlti/ noun (pl. **difficulties**) **1** [U,C] **difficulty (in sth/in doing sth)** a problem; a situation that is hard to deal with: *I'm sure you won't* ***have*** *any* ***difficulty*** *getting a visa for America.* ◇ *We* ***had no difficulty*** *selling our car.* ◇ *We found a hotel* ***without difficulty.*** ◇ ***With difficulty,*** *I managed to persuade Alice to lend us the money.* ◇ *I could see someone* ***in difficulty*** (kogoś w tarapatach) *in the water so I went to help them.* ◇ *If you borrow too much money you may* ***get into*** *financial* ***difficulties.*** ▶ **trudność, kłopot 2** [U] how hard sth is to do or to deal with: *The questions start easy and then increase in difficulty.* ▶ **trudność**

diffident /ˈdɪfɪdənt/ adj. not having confidence in your own strengths or abilities: *He has a very diffident manner.* ▶ **nieśmiały, niepewny siebie**
■ **diffidence** noun [U] ▶ **nieśmiałość, brak pewności siebie**

diffract /dɪˈfrækt/ verb [T] to break up a stream of light into a series of dark and light bands or into the different colours of the **spectrum** ▶ (*fiz.*) **uginać**
■ **diffraction** /dɪˈfrækʃn/ noun [U] ▶ **dyfkracja**

diffuse /dɪˈfjuːs/ adj. **1** spread over a wide area: *diffuse light* ◇ *a diffuse community* ▶ **rozproszony 2** not clear or easy to understand; using a lot of words: *a diffuse style of writing* ▶ **rozwlekły, mętny**
■ **diffusely** adv. ▶ **w rozproszony sposób; rozwlekle, mętnie** | **diffuseness** noun [U] ▶ **rozproszenie; rozwlekłość, mętność**

dig[1] /dɪɡ/ verb [I,T] (**digging**; pt, pp **dug** /dʌɡ/) to move earth and make a hole in the ground: *The children are busy digging in the sand.* ◇ *to dig a hole* ▶ **kopać** (*np. łopatą, kilofem*)
IDM **dig deep** to try harder, give more, go further, etc. than is usually necessary: *Charities for the homeless are asking people to dig deep into their pockets in this cold weather.* ▶ **dawać (z siebie) jak najwięcej**
dig your heels in to refuse to do sth or to change your mind about sth: *The union dug its heels in and waited for a better pay offer.* ▶ **uparcie odmawiać zrobienia czegoś**
PHR V **dig (sth) in; dig sth into sb/sth** to push or press (sth) into sb/sth: *My neck is all red where my collar is digging in.* ◇ *He dug his hands deep into his pockets.* ▶ **wbijać się/coś w coś,** (*ubranie*) **obcierać**
dig sb/sth out (of sth) 1 to get sb/sth out of sth by moving the earth, etc. that covers them or it: *Rescue workers dug the survivors out of the rubble.* ▶ **odkopywać coś (z czegoś), wydobywać kogoś/coś (z czegoś)**

2 to get or find sb/sth by searching: *I dug out some old photos from the attic.* ▶ **wygrzebywać/wyszperać coś**
dig sth up **1** to remove sth from the earth by digging: *to dig up potatoes* ▶ **wykopywać/odkopywać coś** **2** to make a hole or take away soil by digging: *Workmen are digging up the road in front of our house.* ▶ **rozkopywać** (*np. ulicę*) **3** to find information by searching or studying: *Newspapers have dug up some embarrassing facts about his private life.* ▶ **wygrzebywać coś**

dig² /dɪg/ [C], noun **1** a hard push: *to give somebody a dig in the ribs* ▶ **szturchnięcie** **2** something that you say to upset sb: *The others kept **making digs** at him because of the way he spoke.* ▶ **docinek, przytyk** **3** an occasion or place where a group of people try to find things of historical or scientific interest in the ground in order to study them: *an archaeological dig* ▶ **wykopalisk-o/a**

digest /daɪˈdʒest/ verb [T] **1** to change food in your stomach so that it can be used by the body: *I'm not going to go swimming until I've digested my lunch.* ▶ **trawić** (*pokarm*) **2** to think about new information so that you understand it fully: *The lecture was interesting, but too much to digest all at once.* ▶ (*przen.*) **przetrawiać**

digestion /daɪˈdʒestʃən/ noun [C,U] the process of changing food in your stomach so that it can be used by the body ▶ **trawienie**

diˈgestive system noun [C] the series of organs inside the body that **digest** food ▶ **układ pokarmowy**

digit /ˈdɪdʒɪt/ noun [C] any of the numbers from 0 to 9: *a six-digit telephone number* ▶ **cyfra, liczba jednocyfrowa**

digital /ˈdɪdʒɪtl/ adj. **1** using an electronic system that uses the numbers 1 and 0 to record sound or store information, and that gives results of a high quality: *a digital camera* ▶ **cyfrowy** **2** showing information by using numbers: *a digital watch* ▶ **elektroniczny**

digitalize (also -ise) = DIGITIZE

ˌdigital reˈcording noun [C, U] a recording in which sounds or pictures are represented by a series of numbers showing that an electronic signal is there or is not there; the process of making a recording in this way ▶ **nagranie cyfrowe**

ˌdigital ˈtelevision noun **1** [U] the system of broadcasting television using **digital** signals ▶ **telewizja cyfrowa** **2** [C] a television set that can receive **digital** signals ▶ **cyfrowy odbiornik telewizyjny**

digitize (also -ise) /ˈdɪdʒɪtaɪz/ (also **digitalize** /ˈdɪdʒɪtəlaɪz/) verb [T] to change data into a **digital** form that can be easily read and processed by a computer: *a digitized map* ▶ **digitalizować**

dignified /ˈdɪgnɪfaɪd/ adj. behaving in a calm, serious way that makes other people respect you: *dignified behaviour* ▶ **pełen godności** OPP **undignified**

dignity /ˈdɪgnəti/ noun [U] **1** calm, serious behaviour that makes other people respect you: *to behave **with dignity*** ▶ **godność** **2** the quality of being serious and formal: *the quiet dignity of the funeral service* ▶ **powaga, dostojeństwo**

digress /daɪˈgres/ verb [I] (formal) to stop talking or writing about the main subject under discussion and start talking or writing about another less important one ▶ **robić dygresję, odchodzić od tematu**
■ **digression** /daɪˈgreʃn/ noun [C,U] ▶ **dygresja**

dike = DYKE

dilapidated /dɪˈlæpɪdeɪtɪd/ adj. (used about buildings, furniture, etc.) old and broken ▶ **rozpadający się, w opłakanym stanie**
■ **dilapidation** /dɪˌlæpɪˈdeɪʃn/ noun [U] ▶ **opłakany stan, ruina**

dilate /daɪˈleɪt/ verb [I,T] to become or to make sth larger, wider or more open: *Her eyes dilated with fear.* ◇ *dilated pupils/nostrils* ▶ **rozszerzać (się)** OPP **contract**
■ **dilation** /daɪˈleɪʃn/ noun [U] ▶ **rozszerzenie**

dilemma /dɪˈlemə/ noun [C] a situation in which you have to make a difficult choice between two or more things: *Doctors **face a** moral **dilemma** of when to keep patients alive artificially and when to let them die.* ◇ *to be **in a dilemma*** ▶ **dylemat**

dilettante /ˌdɪləˈtænti/ noun [C] (pl. **dilettanti** /-tiː/ or **dilettantes**) a person who does or studies sth but is not serious about it and does not have much knowledge ▶ **dyletant/ka**
■ **dilettante** adj.: *a dilettante artist* ▶ **dyletancki**

diligent /ˈdɪlɪdʒənt/ adj. (formal) showing care and effort in your work or duties: *a diligent student/worker* ▶ **pilny, pracowity**
■ **diligently** adv. ▶ **pilnie, pracowicie**

dill /dɪl/ a plant with yellow flowers whose leaves and seeds have a strong taste and are used in cooking as a **herb**. **Dill** is often added to vegetables kept in **vinegar**: *dill pickles* ogórki kiszone ▶ **koper**

dilly-dally /ˈdɪli dæli/ verb (**dilly-dallies**; **dilly-dallying**; **dilly-dallied**; **dilly-dallied**) [I] (old-fashioned, informal) to take too long to do sth, go somewhere or make a decision: *Don't dilly-dally on the way home from school.* ▶ **guzdrać się** SYN **dawdle**

dilute /daɪˈluːt/ verb [T] **dilute sth (with sth)** to make a liquid weaker by adding water or another liquid ▶ **rozcieńczać, rozwadniać**
■ **dilute** adj. ▶ **rozcieńczony, rozwodniony** ⊃ look at **concentrated**

dim¹ /dɪm/ adj. (**dimmer**; **dimmest**) **1** not bright or easy to see; not clear: *The light was too dim to read by.* ◇ *a dim shape in the distance* ◇ *My memories of my grandmother are quite dim.* ▶ **mroczny, niewyraźny, wyblakły** **2** (informal) not very clever; stupid: *He's a bit dim.* ▶ **tępy** **3** (informal) (used about a situation) without much hope: *The prospects of the two sides reaching an agreement look dim.* ▶ **ponury**
■ **dimly** adv. ▶ **niewyraźnie, mętnie**

dim² /dɪm/ verb [I,T] (**dimming**; **dimmed**) to become or make sth less bright or clear: *The lights dimmed.* ◇ *to dim the lights* ▶ **ciemnieć, blaknąć; przyciemniać**

dime /daɪm/ noun [C] a coin used in the US and Canada that is worth ten cents ▶ **moneta dziesięciocentowa**

dimension /daɪˈmenʃn/ noun **1** [C,U] a measurement of the length, width or height of sth ▶ **wymiar** **2** (**dimensions**) [pl.] the size of sth including its length, width and height: *to measure the dimensions of a room* ◇ (figurative) *The full dimensions of this problem are only now being recognized.* ▶ **wymiar; rozmiar** **3** [C] something that affects the way you think about a problem or situation: *to add a new dimension to a problem/situation* ▶ **wymiar, aspekt** **4** (**-dimensional**) /-ʃənl/ [in compounds] having the number of **dimensions** mentioned: *a three-dimensional* (trójwymiarowy) *object* ▶ **wymiarowy**

diminish /dɪˈmɪnɪʃ/ verb [I,T] (formal) to become or to make sth smaller or less important: *The world's rainforests are diminishing fast.* ◇ *The bad news did nothing to diminish her enthusiasm for the plan.* ▶ **pomniejszać (się), zmniejszać (się)** SYN **decrease**

diminutive /dɪˈmɪnjətɪv/ adj. (formal) much smaller than usual ▶ **drobny, niewielki**

dimple /ˈdɪmpl/ noun [C] a round area in the skin on your cheek, etc. which often only appears when you smile ▶ **dołeczek**

ˌdim-ˈwitted adj. (informal) stupid ▶ **tępy**
■ **dimwit** noun [C] ▶ **tępak**

din /dɪn/ noun [sing.] a lot of unpleasant noise that continues for some time ▶ **hałas, harmider**

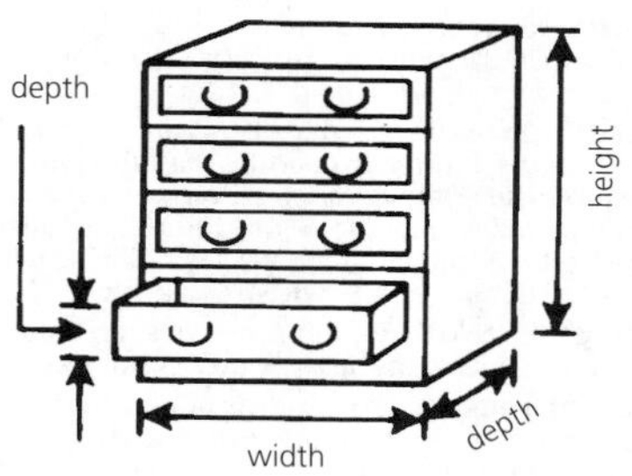

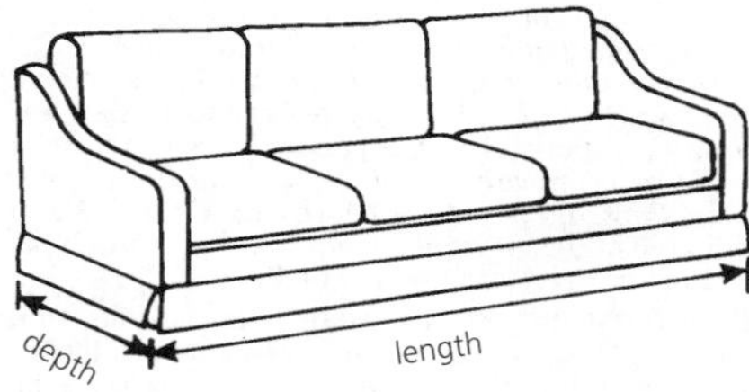

dine /daɪn/ verb [I] (formal) to eat a meal, especially in the evening: *We dined at an exclusive French restaurant.* ◇ *We dined on* (jedliśmy na obiad) *fresh salmon.* ▶ **jeść obiad**

PHR V **dine out** to eat in a restaurant ▶ **jeść obiad w restauracji**

diner /ˈdaɪnə(r)/ noun [C] **1** a person who is eating at a restaurant ▶ **gość (restauracyjny) 2** (US) a restaurant that serves simple, cheap food ▶ **mała tania restauracja**

dinghy /ˈdɪŋgi/ noun [C] (pl. **dinghies**) **1** a small boat that you sail ▶ **łódka** (*z żaglem*) ➲ look at **yacht 2** a small open boat, often used to take people to land from a larger boat ▶ **łódka, szalupa** ➲ picture at **boat**

dingy /ˈdɪndʒi/ adj. (**dingier**; **dingiest**) dirty and dark: *a dingy room/hotel* ▶ **obskurny**

ˈ**dining room** noun [C] a room where you eat meals ▶ **jadalnia**

⚷ **dinner** /ˈdɪnə(r)/ noun **1** [C,U] the main meal of the day, eaten either at midday or in the evening: *Would you like to* ***go out for/to dinner*** *one evening?* ◇ *I never eat a big dinner.* ◇ *What's for dinner, Mum?* ◇ *We have dinner* (jemy obiad) *at 8.00.* ◇ *a dinner service* zastawa obiadowa ◇ *a* ***school dinner*** ▶ **obiad** ➲ note at **meal**

> W różnych częściach kraju, a także w różnych środowiskach, często występują różne nazwy posiłków. Ogólnie można przyjąć, że jeśli w południe jada się **dinner**, wówczas wieczorem spożywany jest lekki posiłek o nazwie **tea** lub **supper**. **Supper** jada się później niż **tea**. **Tea** może także oznaczać podwieczorek. Jeśli **dinner** spożywany jest wieczorem, wówczas lżejszy posiłek, jedzony w południe, określa się mianem **lunch**.

2 [C] a formal occasion in the evening during which a meal is served: *The club is holding its annual dinner next week.* ▶ **bankiet**

ˈ**dinner jacket** (US **tuxedo** /tʌkˈsiːdəʊ/, pl. **tuxedos** /-dəʊz/) (also informal **tux** /tʌks/) noun [C] a black or white jacket that a man wears on formal occasions. A **dinner jacket** is usually worn with a **bow tie**. ▶ **smoking**

ˈ**dinner party** noun [C] a social event at which a small group of people eat dinner at sb's house ▶ **uroczysta kolacja**

dinosaur /ˈdaɪnəsɔː(r)/ noun [C] one of a number of very large animals that became **extinct** millions of years ago: *dinosaur fossils* ▶ **dinozaur**

diocese /ˈdaɪəsɪs/ noun [C] (pl. **dioceses** /-siːz/) an area containing a number of churches, for which a bishop is responsible ▶ **diecezja**

Dip = DIPLOMA

dip[1] /dɪp/ verb (**dipping**; **dipped**) **1** [T] **dip sth (into sth); dip sth (in)** to put sth into liquid and immediately take it out again: *Julie dipped her toe into the pool to see how cold it was.* ▶ **zanurzać 2** [I,T] to go down or make sth go down to a lower level: *The road suddenly dipped down to the river.* ◇ *Sales have dipped disastrously this year.* ◇ *The driver dipped* (przełączył światła mijania) *his headlights when a car came in the opposite direction.* ▶ **zniżać (się), obniżać się**

PHR V **dip into sth 1** to use part of an amount of sth that you have: *Tim had to dip into his savings to pay for his new suit.* ▶ **sięgać do czegoś 2** to read parts, but not all, of sth: *I've only dipped into the book. I haven't read it all the way through.* ▶ **zaglądać do czegoś**

dip[2] /dɪp/ noun **1** [C] (informal) a short swim: *We went for a dip before breakfast.* ▶ **szybka kąpiel** (*np. w morzu*) **2** [C] a fall to a lower level, especially for a short time: *a dip in sales/temperature* ▶ **spadek, obniżenie 3** [C] an area of lower ground: *The cottage was hidden in a dip in the hills.* ▶ **zagłębienie** (*terenu*) **4** [C,U] a thick sauce into which you **dip** biscuits, vegetables, etc. before eating them: *a cheese/chilli dip* ▶ **gęsty sos**

diphtheria /dɪfˈθɪəriə; US ˈdɪp-/ noun [U] a serious disease of the throat that makes it difficult to breathe ▶ **dyfteryt, błonica**

diphthong /ˈdɪfθɒŋ; ˈdɪp-/ noun [C] two vowel sounds that are pronounced together to make one sound, for example the /aɪ/ sound in *fine* ▶ **dyftong**

diploma /dɪˈpləʊmə/ noun [C] (abbr. **Dip**) **a diploma (in sth)** a certificate that you receive when you complete a course of study, often at a college: *I'm studying for a diploma in hotel management.* ▶ **dyplom** ➲ note at **degree**

diplomacy /dɪˈpləʊməsi/ noun [U] **1** the activity of managing relations between different countries: *If diplomacy fails, there is a danger of war.* ▶ **dyplomacja 2** skill in dealing with people without upsetting or offending them: *He handled the tricky situation with tact and diplomacy.* ▶ **takt**

diplomat /ˈdɪpləmæt/ noun [C] an official who represents their country in a foreign country: *a diplomat at the embassy in Rome* ▶ **dyplomat-a/ka**

diplomatic /ˌdɪpləˈmætɪk/ adj. **1** connected with **diplomacy**(1): *to break off diplomatic relations* ▶ **dyplomatyczny 2** skilful at dealing with people: *He searched for a diplomatic reply so as not to offend her.* ▶ **dyplomatyczny** SYN **tactful**

■ **diplomatically** /-kli/ adv. ▶ **dyplomatycznie**

ˌ**diploˈmatic corps** noun (usually **the diplomatic corps**) [C, with sing. or pl. verb] (pl. **diplomatic corps**) all the **diplomats** who work in a particular city or country ▶ **korpus dyplomatyczny**

dippy /ˈdɪpi/ adj. (informal) stupid; crazy ▶ **szalony**

dire /ˈdaɪə(r)/ adj. (formal) very bad or serious; terrible: *dire consequences* ◇ *dire* (skrajna) *poverty* ▶ **poważny; straszny**

IDM be in dire straits to be in a very difficult situation: *The business is in dire straits financially and may go bankrupt.* ▶ **być w tarapatach**

direct¹ /dəˈrekt; dɪ-; daɪ-/ adj. **1** with nobody/nothing in between; not involving anyone/anything else: *The British Prime Minister is* ***in direct contact with*** *the US President.* ◇ *a direct attack on the capital* ◇ *As a* ***direct result*** *of the new road, traffic jams in the centre have been reduced.* ◇ *You should protect your skin from direct sunlight.* ▶ **bezpośredni** OPP **indirect 2** going from one place to another without turning or stopping; straight: *a direct flight to Hong Kong* ▶ **bezpośredni, prosty** OPP **indirect 3** saying what you mean; clear: *She sometimes offends people with her direct way of speaking.* ◇ *Politicians never give a* ***direct answer*** *to a* ***direct question.*** ▶ **bezpośredni, prosty** OPP **indirect 4** [only before a noun] complete; exact: *What she did was in direct opposition* (było dokładnym zaprzeczeniem) *to my orders.* ▶ **kompletny; dokładny**

■ **direct** adv. **1** not turning or stopping; straight: *This bus goes direct to London.* ▶ **bezpośrednio, prosto 2** not involving anybody/anything else ▶ **bezpośrednio, wprost**

direct² /dəˈrekt; dɪ-; daɪ-/ verb [T] **1 direct sth to/towards sb/sth; direct sth at sb/sth** to point or send sth towards sb/sth or in a particular direction: *In recent weeks the media's attention has been directed towards events abroad.* ◇ *The advert is directed at young people.* ◇ *The actor directed some angry words at a photographer.* ▶ **kierować 2** to manage or control sb/sth: *A policeman was in the middle of the road, directing the traffic.* ◇ *to direct a play/film* ▶ **kierować, reżyserować 3** (formal) to tell or order sb to do sth: *Take the tablets as directed by* (według zaleceń) *your doctor.* ▶ **zalecać, polecać 4 direct sb (to ...)** to tell or show sb how to get somewhere: *I was directed to an office at the end of the corridor.* ▶ **kierować** ➲ note at **lead¹** (1)

diˌrect ˈdebit noun [C,U] an order to your bank that allows sb else to take a particular amount of money out of your account on certain dates ▶ **polecenie zapłaty** (*z konta*)

direction /dəˈrekʃn; dɪ-; daɪ-/ noun **1** [C,U] the path, line or way along which a person or thing is moving, looking, pointing, developing, etc.: *A woman was seen running* ***in the direction of*** *the station.* ◇ *We met him coming* ***in the opposite direction.*** ◇ *I think the new speed limit is still too high, but it's* ***a step in the right direction.*** ◇ *I think the wind has* ***changed direction.*** ◇ *I've got such a hopeless* ***sense of direction*** (mam beznadziejną orientację w terenie) *I'm always getting lost.* ▶ **kierunek, strona 2** [C,U] a purpose; an aim: *I want a career that gives me a (sense of) direction in life.* ▶ **cel 3** [usually pl.] information or instructions about how to do sth or how to get to a place: *I'll* ***give you directions*** *to my house.* Wytłumaczę ci, jak trafić do mojego domu. ◇ *We got lost and had to stop and* ***ask for directions*** (spytać się o drogę). ▶ **instrukcje, wskazówki 4** [U] the act of managing or controlling sth: *This department is under the direction of Mrs Walters.* ▶ **kierownictwo, reżyseria**

asking for and giving directions

Excuse me, is there a bank near here?
Can you tell me the way to (czy mógłby mi pan wytłumaczyć, jak dojść do) *the (nearest) station?*
Turn right at the T-junction.
Turn left at the crossroads.
Go straight on (proszę iść prosto) *at the traffic lights.*
Take the third exit at the roundabout.
Take the second left.
It's on the right, next to the museum.
It's opposite the library.
You can't miss it (nie można tego nie zauważyć)*!*

directive /dəˈrektɪv; dɪ-; daɪ-/ noun [C] an official order to do sth: *an EU directive on safety at work* ▶ **dyrektywa, zarządzenie**

directly¹ /dəˈrektli; dɪ-; daɪ-/ adv. **1** in a direct line or way: *The bank is directly opposite the supermarket.* ◇ *He refused to answer my question directly.* ◇ *Lung cancer is directly related to smoking.* ▶ **dokładnie; bezpośrednio** OPP **indirectly 2** immediately; very soon: *Wait where you are. I'll be back directly.* ▶ **wkrótce, zaraz**

directly² /dəˈrektli; dɪ-; daɪ-/ conj. as soon as: *I phoned him directly I heard the news.* ▶ **gdy tylko, skoro**

diˌrect ˈobject noun [C] a noun or phrase that is affected by the act of a verb: *In the sentence 'Anna bought a record', 'a record' is the direct object.* ▶ **dopełnienie bliższe** ➲ look at **indirect object**

director /dəˈrektə(r); dɪ-; daɪ-/ noun [C] **1** a person who manages or controls a company or organization: *She's on the board of directors* (jest w radzie nadzorczej) *of a large computer company.* ◇ *the managing director* (dyrektor naczelny) *of Rolls Royce* ▶ **dyrektor/ka 2** a person who is responsible for a particular activity or department in a company, a college, etc.: *the director of studies of a language school* ▶ **kierowni-k/czka 3** a person who tells the actors, etc. what to do in a film, play, etc.: *a film/theatre director* ▶ **reżyser**

directory /dəˈrektəri; dɪ-; daɪ-/ noun [C] (pl. **directories**) **1** a list of names, addresses and telephone numbers in the order of the alphabet: *the telephone directory* książka telefoniczna ◇ *I tried to look up Joe's number but he's* ***ex-directory*** (jego numer jest zastrzeżony). ▶ **spis** (*np. instytucji*) **2** a file containing a group of other files or programs in a computer ▶ **katalog**

diˌrectory enˈquiries (US **diˌrectory asˈsistance**) noun [U, with sing. or pl. verb] a telephone service that you can use to find out a person's telephone number ▶ **informacja telefoniczna**

diˌrect ˈspeech noun [U] the actual words that a person said ▶ **mowa niezależna** ➲ look at **reported speech**

dirt /dɜːt/ noun [U] **1** a substance that is not clean, such as dust or mud: *His face and hands were covered in dirt.* ◇ *They* ***treat*** *their workers* ***like dirt*** (jak śmieci). ▶ **brud 2** earth or soil: *a dirt track* tor ziemny ▶ **ziemia 3** damaging information about sb: *The press are always trying to* ***dig up dirt*** *on* (wywlekać brudy na temat) *the President's love life.* ▶ (*przen.*) **brudy**

ˌdirt ˈcheap adj., adv. (informal) very cheap: *It was dirt cheap.* ◇ *I got it dirt cheap.* ▶ **tani(o) jak barszcz**

dirty¹ /ˈdɜːti/ adj. (**dirtier; dirtiest**) **1** not clean: *Your hands are dirty. Go and wash them!* ◇ *Gardening is dirty work.* ▶ **brudny** OPP **clean 2** referring to sex in a way that may upset or offend people: *to tell a dirty joke* ▶ **nieprzyzwoity, sprośny 3** unpleasant or dishonest: *He's a dirty player.* ◇ *He doesn't sell the drugs himself – he gets kids to* ***do his dirty work*** *for him* (zwala tę brudną robotę na dzieciaki). ▶ (*przen.*) **brudny, nieuczciwy**

IDM a dirty word an idea or thing that you do not like or agree with: *Work is a dirty word to Frank.* ▶ **brzydkie słowo, obraźliwy termin**

play dirty (informal) to behave or to play a game in an unfair or dishonest way ▶ **grać nieczysto**

dirty² /ˈdɜːti/ verb [I,T] (**dirtying; dirties;** pt, pp **dirtied**) to become or to make sth dirty ▶ **brudzić (się)** OPP **clean**

disability /ˌdɪsəˈbɪləti/ noun (pl. **disabilities**) **1** [C] something that makes you unable to use a part of your body properly: *Because of his disability, he needs constant care.* ▶ **niepełnosprawność, ułomność 2** [U] the state of being unable to use a part of your body properly, usually because of injury or disease: *physical/mental disability* ▶ **niepełnosprawność**

disable /dɪs'eɪbl/ verb [T, often passive] to make sb unable to use part of their body properly, usually because of injury or disease: *Many soldiers were disabled in the war.* ▶ **czynić niepełnosprawnym**

⚷ **disabled** /dɪs'eɪbld/ (also **handicapped** /'hændikæpt/) adj. unable to use a part of your body properly: *A car accident left her permanently disabled.* ▶ **niepełnosprawny, upośledzony**

■ **the disabled** noun [pl.] people who are **disabled**: *The hotel has improved facilities for the disabled.* ▶ **niepełnosprawni**

disabuse /,dɪsə'bju:z/ verb [T] **disabuse sb (of sth)** (formal) to tell sb that what they think is true is, in fact, not true ▶ **wyprowadzać kogoś z błędu (co do czegoś)**

⚷ **disadvantage** /,dɪsəd'vɑ:ntɪdʒ; US -'væn-/ noun [C] **1** something that may make you less successful than other people: *Your qualifications are good. Your main disadvantage is your lack of experience.* ▶ **słaba strona, wada 2** something that is not good or that causes problems: *The main disadvantage of the job is the long hours.* ◇ *What are the advantages and disadvantages of nuclear power?* ▶ **wada** OPP for both meanings **advantage**

IDM **put sb/be at a disadvantage** to put sb or be in a situation where they or you may be less successful than other people: *The fact that you don't speak the language will put you at a disadvantage in France.* ▶ **stawiać kogoś/być w niekorzystnej sytuacji**

to sb's disadvantage (formal) not good or helpful for sb: *The agreement will be to your disadvantage – don't accept it.* ▶ **na czyjąś niekorzyść**

disadvantaged /,dɪsəd'vɑ:ntɪdʒd; US -'væn-/ adj. in a bad social or economic situation; poor: *disadvantaged groups/children* ▶ **nieuprzywilejowany, będący w trudnej sytuacji życiowej**

disadvantageous /,dɪsædvæn'teɪdʒəs/ adj. causing sb to be in a worse situation compared to other people ▶ **niekorzystny (dla kogoś)**

disaffected /,dɪsə'fektɪd/ adj. no longer satisfied with your situation, organization, belief etc. and therefore not loyal to it: *Some disaffected members left to form a new party.* ▶ **zniechęcony**

■ **disaffection** /,dɪsə'fekʃn/ noun [U]: *There are signs of growing disaffection amongst voters.* ▶ **zniechęcenie**

disaffiliate /,dɪsə'fɪlieɪt/ verb [I,T] **disaffiliate (sth) (from sth)** to end the link between a group, a company, or an organization and a larger one ▶ **odłączać (się) (od czegoś), występować** (*np. ze stowarzyszenia*)

■ **disaffiliation** /,dɪsəfɪli'eɪʃn/ noun [U] ▶ **odłączenie (się), wystąpienie** (*np. ze stowarzyszenia*)

⚷ **disagree** /,dɪsə'gri:/ verb [I] **1 disagree (with sb/sth) (about/on sth)** to have a different opinion from sb/sth; to not agree: *Stephen often disagrees with his father about politics.* ◇ *'We have to tell him.' 'No, I disagree. I don't think we should tell him at all.'* ◇ *They strongly disagreed with* (stanowczo sprzeciwiali się) *the idea.* ▶ **nie zgadzać się, sprzeczać się 2** to be different: *These two sets of statistics disagree.* ▶ **nie zgadzać się, być sprzecznym**

PHR V **disagree with sb** (used about sth you have eaten or drunk) to make you feel ill; to have a bad effect on you ▶ (*jedzenie*) **zaszkodzić** OPP **agree**

disagreeable /,dɪsə'gri:əbl/ adj. (formal) unpleasant ▶ **nieprzyjemny, niemiły** OPP **agreeable**

■ **disagreeably** /-əbli/ adv. ▶ **nieprzyjemnie, niemile**

⚷ **disagreement** /,dɪsə'gri:mənt/ noun [U,C] **disagreement (with sb) (about/on/over sth)** a situation in which people have a different opinion about sth and often also argue: *The conference ended in disagreement.* ◇ *It's normal for couples to **have disagreements**.* ◇ *Mandy resigned after a disagreement with her boss.* ▶ **rozbieżność zdań, niezgodność; sprzeczka** OPP **agreement**

disallow /,dɪsə'laʊ/ verb [T] to not allow or accept sth: *The goal was disallowed because the player was offside.* ▶ **unieważniać, odrzucać**

⚷ **disappear** /,dɪsə'pɪə(r)/ verb [I] **1** to become impossible to see or to find: *He walked away and disappeared into a crowd of people.* ◇ *My purse was here a moment ago and now it's disappeared.* ▶ **znikać, ginąć 2** to stop existing: *Plant and animal species are disappearing at an alarming rate.* ▶ **znikać; wymierać** SYN for both meanings **vanish** OPP for both meanings **appear**

D

■ **disappearance** noun [C,U]: *The mystery of her disappearance was never solved.* ▶ **zniknięcie, zaginięcie**

⚷ **disappoint** /,dɪsə'pɔɪnt/ verb [T] to make sb sad because what they had hoped for has not happened or is less good, interesting, etc. than they had hoped: *I'm sorry to disappoint you but I'm afraid you haven't won the prize.* ▶ **rozczarowywać, zawodzić**

⚷ **disappointed** /,dɪsə'pɔɪntɪd/ adj. **disappointed (about/at sth); disappointed (in/with sb/sth); disappointed that...** sad because you/sb/sth did not succeed or because sth was not as good, interesting, etc. as you had hoped: *Lucy was deeply disappointed at not being chosen for the team.* ◇ *We were disappointed with our hotel.* ◇ *I'm disappointed in you. I thought you could do better.* ◇ *They are very disappointed that they can't stay longer.* ◇ *I was disappointed to hear that you can't come to the party.* ▶ **rozczarowany, zawiedziony**

⚷ **disappointing** /,dɪsə'pɔɪntɪŋ/ adj. making you feel sad because sth was not as good, interesting, etc. as you had hoped: *It has been a disappointing year for the company.* ▶ **niezadowalający, przynoszący rozczarowanie/zawód**

■ **disappointingly** adv. ▶ **niezadowalająco**

⚷ **disappointment** /,dɪsə'pɔɪntmənt/ noun **1** [U] the state of being disappointed: *To his great **disappointment** he failed to get the job.* ▶ **rozczarowanie, zawód 2** [C] **a disappointment (to sb)** a person or thing that disappoints you: *She has suffered many disappointments in her career.* ▶ **rozczarowanie, zawód**

⚷ **disapproval** /,dɪsə'pru:vl/ noun [U] a feeling that sth is bad or that sb is behaving badly: *She shook her head **in disapproval**.* ▶ **dezaprobata**

⚷ **disapprove** /,dɪsə'pru:v/ verb [I] **disapprove (of sb/sth)** to think that sb/sth is bad, silly, etc.: *His parents strongly disapproved of him leaving college before he had finished his course.* ▶ **nie aprobować** OPP **approve**

■ **disapproving** adj.: *After he had told the joke there was a disapproving silence.* ▶ **nieprzychylny, krytyczny** | **disapprovingly** adv. ▶ **z dezaprobatą**

disarm /dɪs'ɑ:m/ verb **1** [T] to take weapons away from sb: *The police caught and disarmed the terrorists.* ▶ **rozbrajać 2** [I] (used about a country) to reduce the number of weapons it has ▶ **rozbrajać się 3** [T] to make sb feel less angry: *Jenny could always disarm the teachers with a smile.* ▶ (*przen.*) **rozbrajać**

disarmament /dɪs'ɑ:məmənt/ noun [U] reducing the number of weapons that an army or a country has: *nuclear disarmament* ▶ **rozbrojenie**

disassemble /,dɪsə'sembl/ verb **1** [T] to take apart a machine or structure so that it is in separate pieces: *We had to completely disassemble the engine to find the problem.* ▶ **rozbierać** (*na części*) OPP **assemble 2** [T] to translate sth from computer code into a language that can be read by humans ▶ **tłumaczyć język oprogramowania 3** [I] (formal) (used about a group of people) to move apart and go away in different directions: *The concert ended and the crowd disassembled.* ▶ (*tłum itp.*) **rozchodzić się**

disassociate = DISSOCIATE

disaster /dɪ'zɑːstə(r); US -'zæs-/ noun **1** [C] an event that causes a lot of harm or damage: *earthquakes, floods and other natural disasters* (klęski żywiołowe) ▶ **klęska, katastrofa 2** [C,U] a terrible situation or event: *Losing your job is unpleasant, but it's not a disaster.* ◇ *This year's lack of rain could* ***spell disaster*** (oznacza kastastrofę) *for many farmers.* ▶ **katastrofa 3** [C,U] (informal) a complete failure: *The school play was an absolute disaster.* ▶ **klęska**

disastrous /dɪ'zɑːstrəs; US -'zæs-/ adj. terrible, harmful or failing completely: *Our mistake had disastrous results.* ▶ **fatalny, katastrofalny**
■ **disastrously** adv.: *The plan went disastrously wrong.* Plan okazał się fatalny w skutkach. ▶ **fatalnie, katastrofalnie**

disavow /ˌdɪsə'vaʊ/ verb [T] (formal) to state publicly that you have no knowledge of sth or that you are not responsible for sth/sb: *They disavowed claims of a split in the party.* ▶ **zaprzeczać** (*np. pogłoskom*)
■ **disavowal** /-'vaʊəl/ noun [C, U] ▶ **zaprzeczenie** (*np. pogłoskom*)

disband /dɪs'bænd/ verb [I,T] to stop existing as a group; to separate ▶ **rozwiązywać (się)**

disbelief /ˌdɪsbɪ'liːf/ noun [U] the feeling of not believing sb/sth: *'It can't be true!' he shouted* ***in disbelief.*** ▶ **niedowierzanie**

disbelieve /ˌdɪsbɪ'liːv/ verb [T] to think that sth is not true or that sb is not telling the truth: *I have no reason to disbelieve her.* ▶ **nie wierzyć, nie dowierzać** OPP **believe**

disc (especially US **disk**) /dɪsk/ noun [C] **1** a round flat object: *He wears an identity disc around his neck.* ▶ **krążek, tarcza 2** = DISK (1) **3** one of the pieces of **cartilage** between the bones in your back: *a slipped disc* wypadnięty dysk ▶ **dysk**

discard /dɪs'kɑːd/ verb [T] (formal) to throw sth away because it is not useful ▶ **wyrzucać, wyzbywać się**

discern /dɪ'sɜːn/ verb [T] to see or notice sth with difficulty: *I discerned a note of anger in his voice.* ▶ **dostrzegać, zauważać**
■ **discernible** adj.: *The shape of a house was just discernible through the mist.* ▶ **dostrzegalny**

discerning /dɪ'sɜːnɪŋ/ adj. able to recognize the quality of sb/sth: *The discerning music lover will appreciate the excellence of this recording.* ▶ **wnikliwy, wytrawny**

discharge¹ /dɪs'tʃɑːdʒ/ verb [T] **1** to allow sb officially to leave; to send sb away: *to discharge somebody from hospital* ▶ **wypisywać, zwalniać 2** to send sth out (a liquid, gas, etc.): *Smoke and fumes are discharged from the factory.* ▶ **wypuszczać, wydzielać 3** to do sth that you have to do: *to discharge a duty/task* ▶ **wywiązywać się z czegoś, spełniać**

discharge² /'dɪstʃɑːdʒ/ noun [C,U] **1** a substance that has come out of somewhere: *yellowish discharge from a wound* ▶ **wydzielina, wyciek 2** the act of sending sth out: *The discharge of oil from the leaking tanker could not be prevented.* ▶ **wyciek** (*płynu*) **3** the act of sending sb away: *The wounded soldier was given a medical discharge* (został zwolniony ze względu na stan zdrowia). ▶ **wypisanie** (*np. ze szpitala*), **zwolnienie**

disciple /dɪ'saɪpl/ noun [C] a person who follows a teacher, especially a religious one ▶ **ucze-ń/nnica, zwolenni-k/czka** SYN **follower**

disciplinary /'dɪsəplɪnəri; ˌdɪsə'plɪnəri; US -pləneri/ adj. connected with punishment for breaking rules ▶ **dyscyplinarny**

discipline¹ /'dɪsəplɪn/ noun **1** [U] the practice of training people to obey rules and behave well: *A good teacher must be able to* ***maintain discipline*** *in the classroom.* ▶ **dyscyplina 2** [U] the practice of training your mind and body so that you control your actions and obey rules; a way of doing this: *It takes a lot of* ***self-discipline*** (dyscyplina wewnętrzna) *to study for three hours a day.* ◇ *Having to get up early every day is good discipline for a child.* ▶ **dyscyplina 3** [C] a subject of study; a type of sports event: *Barry's a good all-round athlete, but the long jump is his strongest discipline.* ▶ **dyscyplina**

discipline² /'dɪsəplɪn/ verb [T] **1** to train sb to obey and to behave in a controlled way: *You should discipline yourself to practise the piano every morning.* ▶ **wyrabiać w kimś posłuszeństwo, charakter itp. 2** to punish sb ▶ **karać**

'disc jockey = DJ ▶ **dyskdżokej**

disclaim /dɪs'kleɪm/ verb [T] to say that you do not have sth: *to disclaim responsibility/knowledge* ▶ **wypierać się** SYN **deny**

disclaimer /dɪs'kleɪmə(r)/ noun [C] **1** (formal) a statement in which sb says that they are not connected with or responsible for sth, or that they do not have any knowledge of it ▶ **dementi 2** a statement in which a person says officially that they do not claim the right to do sth ▶ **zrzeczenie się** (*np. pretensji do czegoś*)

disclose /dɪs'kləʊz/ verb [T] (formal) to tell sth to sb or to make sth known publicly: *The newspapers did not disclose the victim's name.* ▶ **ujawniać, podawać do (publicznej) wiadomości** SYN **reveal**

disclosure /dɪs'kləʊʒə(r)/ noun [C,U] making sth known; the facts that are made known: *the disclosure of secret information* ◇ *He resigned following disclosures about his private life.* ▶ **ujawnienie faktów; ujawnione fakty** SYN **revelation**

disco /'dɪskəʊ/ noun [C] (pl. **discos**) (old-fashioned) a place, party, etc. where people dance to recorded music: *Are you going to the school disco?* ▶ **dyskoteka** ➲ look at **club**

discolour (US **discolor**) /dɪs'kʌlə(r)/ verb [I,T] to change or to make sth change colour (often by the effect of light, age or dirt) ▶ **odbarwiać (się), przebarwiać (się)**

discomfort /dɪs'kʌmfət/ noun **1** [U] a slight feeling of pain: *There may be some discomfort after the operation.* ▶ **(lekki) ból 2** [U] a feeling of embarrassment: *I could sense John's discomfort when I asked him about his job.* ▶ **niepokój, skrępowanie 3** [C] something that makes you feel uncomfortable or that causes a slight feeling of pain: *The beauty of the scenery made up for the discomforts of the journey.* ▶ **niewygoda**

disconcert /ˌdɪskən'sɜːt/ verb [T, usually passive] to make sb feel confused or worried: *She was disconcerted when everyone stopped talking and looked at her.* ▶ **niepokoić, wprawiać w zakłopotanie**
■ **disconcerting** adj. ▶ **niepokojący, kłopotliwy** | **disconcertingly** adv. ▶ **niepokojąco**

disconnect /ˌdɪskə'nekt/ verb [T] **1** to stop a supply of water, gas or electricity going to a piece of equipment or a building: *If you don't pay your gas bill, your supply will be disconnected.* ▶ **wyłączać 2** to separate sth from sth: *The brake doesn't work because the cable has become disconnected from the lever.* ▶ **odłączać, odcinać**

disconsolate /dɪs'kɒnsələt/ adj. (formal) very unhappy and disappointed: *The disconsolate players left for home without a trophy.* ▶ **niepocieszony** SYN **dejected**
■ **disconsolately** adv.: *He wandered disconsolately around the town in the pouring rain.* ▶ **ze smutkiem i rozczarowaniem**

discontent /ˌdɪskən'tent/ (also **discontentment** /ˌdɪskən'tentmənt/) noun [U] the state of being unhappy with sth: *The management could sense growing discontent among the staff.* ▶ **niezadowolenie, rozczarowanie**

discontented /ˌdɪskən'tentɪd/ adj. **discontented (with sth)** unhappy because you are not satisfied with your

situation: *He felt discontented with the way his life had turned out.* ◇ *discontented party members* ▶ **niezadowolony, rozgoryczony** SYN **dissatisfied** OPP **contented**
■ **discontentedly** adv. ▶ **z niezadowoleniem**

discontinue /ˌdɪskənˈtɪnjuː/ verb [T] (formal) to stop sth or stop producing sth ▶ **przerywać, zaprzestawać** (*np. produkcji czegoś*)

discord /ˈdɪskɔːd/ noun **1** [U] (formal) disagreement or argument ▶ **rozdźwięk, niezgoda** **2** [C] two or more musical notes that do not sound pleasant when they are played together ▶ **dysonans**

discordant /dɪsˈkɔːdənt/ adj. that spoils a general feeling of agreement: *Her criticism was the only discordant note in the discussion.* ▶ **nieharmonijny, nieprzyjemny**

⚷ **discount**[1] /ˈdɪskaʊnt/ noun [C,U] a lower price than usual: *Staff get 20% discount on all goods.* ◇ *Do you give a discount for cash?* ▶ **zniżka, rabat** SYN **reduction**

discount[2] /dɪsˈkaʊnt/ verb [T] to consider sth not true or not important: *I think we can discount that idea. It's just not practical.* ▶ **pomijać, nie brać w rachubę**

discourage /dɪsˈkʌrɪdʒ; US -ˈkɜːr-/ verb [T] **discourage sb (from doing sth)** to stop sb doing sth, especially by making them realize that it would not be successful or a good idea: *I tried to discourage Jake from giving up his job.* ◇ *Don't let these little problems discourage you.* Nie zrażaj się tymi drobnymi problemami. ▶ **zniechęcać, odradzać komuś (coś)** OPP **encourage**
■ **discouraged** adj.: *After failing the exam again Paul felt very discouraged.* ▶ **zniechęcony, zrezygnowany** | **discouraging** adj.: *Constant criticism can be very discouraging.* ▶ **zniechęcający**

discouragement /dɪsˈkʌrɪdʒmənt; US -ˈkɜːr-/ noun [C,U] a thing that makes you not want to do sth; the act of trying to stop sb from doing sth: *the government's discouragement of smoking* ◇ *High parking charges would be a discouragement to* (zniechęcałyby) *people taking their cars into the city centre.* ▶ **zniechęcanie, odstraszanie; bariera**

discourse /ˈdɪskɔːs/ noun [C,U] (formal) a long and serious discussion of a subject in speech or writing ▶ **poważna dyskusja**

discourteous /dɪsˈkɜːtiəs/ adj. not polite or showing respect for people ▶ **nieuprzejmy** SYN **impolite** OPP **courteous**

⚷ **discover** /dɪˈskʌvə(r)/ verb [T] **1** to find or learn sth that nobody had found or knew before: *Who discovered the lost city of Machu Picchu?* ◇ *Scientists are hoping to discover the cause of the epidemic.* ▶ **odkrywać, wynaleźć** **2** to find or learn sth without expecting to or that sb does not want you to find: *I think I've discovered why the computer won't print out.* ◇ *The police discovered drugs hidden under the floor.* ▶ **odkrywać**
■ **discoverer** noun [C]: *Parkinson's disease was named after its discoverer.* ▶ **odkryw-ca/czyni**

⚷ **discovery** /dɪˈskʌvəri/ noun (pl. **discoveries**) **1** [U] the act of finding sth: *The discovery of X-rays changed the history of medicine.* ▶ **odkrycie, znalezienie** **2** [C] something that has been found: *scientific discoveries* ▶ **odkrycie, wynalazek**

discredit /dɪsˈkredɪt/ verb [T] to make people stop respecting or believing sb/sth: *Journalists are trying to discredit the President by inventing stories about his love life.* ▶ **dyskredytować, kompromitować**
■ **discredit** noun [U] ▶ **zdyskredytowanie, kompromitacja**

discreet /dɪˈskriːt/ adj. careful in what you say and do so as not to cause embarrassment or difficulty for sb ▶ **dyskretny** OPP **indiscreet** ➲ noun **discretion**
■ **discreetly** adv. ▶ **dyskretnie**

discrepancy /dɪsˈkrepənsi/ noun [C,U] (pl. **discrepancies**) a difference between two things that should be the same: *Something is wrong here. There is a discrepancy between these two sets of figures.* ▶ **rozbieżność, sprzeczność**

discrete /dɪˈskriːt/ adj. (formal or technical) independent of other things of the same type: *The organisms can be divided into discrete categories.* ▶ **odrębny** SYN **separate**
■ **discretely** adv. ▶ **odrębnie** | **discreteness** noun [U] ▶ **odrębność**

D

discretion /dɪˈskreʃn/ noun [U] **1** the freedom and power to make decisions by yourself: *You must decide what is best. Use your discretion* (postępuj według swojego uznania). **2** care in what you say and do so as not to cause embarrassment or difficulty for sb: *This is confidential but I know I can rely on your discretion.* ▶ **dyskrecja** ➲ adjective **discreet**
IDM **at sb's discretion** depending on what sb thinks or decides: *Pay increases are awarded at the discretion of the director.* ▶ **według czyjegoś uznania**

discriminate /dɪˈskrɪmɪneɪt/ verb **1** [I,T] **discriminate (between A and B)** to see or make a difference between two people or things: *The immigration law discriminates between political and economic refugees.* ▶ **dostrzegać różnice; rozróżniać** **2** [I] **discriminate (against sb)** to treat one person or group worse than others: *It is illegal to discriminate against any ethnic or religious group.* ▶ **dyskryminować (kogoś)**

discriminating /dɪˈskrɪmɪneɪtɪŋ/ adj. able to judge the good quality of sth: *a discriminating audience/customer* ▶ (*publiczność itp.*) **wyrobiony** SYN **discerning**

discrimination /dɪˌskrɪmɪˈneɪʃn/ noun [U] **1 discrimination (against sb)** treating one person or group worse than others: *sexual/racial/religious discrimination* ◇ *Discrimination against disabled people is illegal.* ▶ **dyskryminacja (kogoś)** **2** (formal) the state of being able to see a difference between two people or things: *discrimination between right and wrong* umiejętność rozróżnienia między dobrem a złem ▶ **rozeznanie**

discus /ˈdɪskəs/ noun **1** [C] a heavy round flat object that is thrown as a sport ▶ **dysk** **2** (**the discus**) [sing.] the sport or event of throwing a **discus** as far as possible ▶ **rzut dyskiem**

⚷ **discuss** /dɪˈskʌs/ verb [T] **discuss sth (with sb)** to talk or write about sth seriously or formally: *I must discuss the matter with my parents before I make a decision.* ▶ **dyskutować, omawiać**

⚷ **discussion** /dɪˈskʌʃn/ noun [C,U] the process of talking about sth seriously or deeply: *After much discussion we all agreed to share the cost.* ◇ *We had a long discussion about art.* ▶ **dyskusja, rozmowa**
IDM **under discussion** being talked about: *Plans to reform the Health Service are under discussion in Parliament.* ▶ **omawiany**

disdain /dɪsˈdeɪn/ noun [U] the feeling that sb/sth is not good enough to be respected: *Monica felt that her boss always **treated** her ideas **with disdain**.* ▶ **lekceważenie, pogarda**
■ **disdainful** /-fl/ adj. ▶ **lekceważący, pogardliwy** | **disdainfully** /-fəli/ adv. ▶ **lekceważąco, pogardliwie**

⚷ **disease** /dɪˈziːz/ noun [C,U] an illness of the body in humans, animals or plants: *an infectious/contagious disease* ◇ *These children **suffer from a** rare **disease**.* ◇ *Rats and flies **spread disease**.* ◇ *Smoking causes heart disease.* ▶ **choroba**
■ **diseased** adj.: *His diseased kidney had to be removed.* ▶ **chory** ➲ note at **ill**

Illness i **disease** mają podobne znaczenie. **Disease** częściej używa się w odniesieniu do konkretnej choroby, charakteryzującej się określonymi objawami. Może być ona wywołana przez bakterie, wirusy itp.; często bywa zakaźna. **Illness** odnosi się do bardziej ogólnych dolegliwości, do bycia chorym w ogóle oraz do okresu czasu, kiedy ktoś nie czuje się dobrze.

disembark /ˌdɪsɪmˈbɑːk/ verb [I] (formal) to get off a ship or an aircraft ▶ **schodzić, wysiadać** OPP **embark**
■ **disembarkation** /ˌdɪsˌembɑːˈkeɪʃn/ noun [U] ▶ **zejście, wysiadanie**

disenchanted /ˌdɪsɪnˈtʃɑːntɪd; US -ˈtʃænt-/ adj. having lost your good opinion of sb/sth: *Fans are already becoming disenchanted with the new team manager.* ▶ **rozczarowany**
■ **disenchantment** noun [U] ▶ **rozczarowanie**

disengage /ˌdɪsɪnˈɡeɪdʒ/ verb **1 disengage (sth/sb) (from sth/sb); disengage yourself (from sb/sth)** [I,T] to free sb/sth from the person or thing that is holding them or it; to become free: *She gently disengaged herself from her sleeping son.* ◇ *to disengage the clutch* zwalniać sprzęgło ◇ *We saw the booster rockets disengage and fall into the sea.* ◇ (figurative) *They wished to disengage themselves from these policies.* ▶ **uwalniać (się/kogoś/coś) (od kogoś/czegoś), rozłączać (się/kogoś/coś) (od kogoś/czegoś)** **2** [I,T] if an army **disengages** or sb **disengages** it, it stops fighting and moves away ▶ (*wojsk.*) **zaprzestawać walki** ➲ look at **engage**
■ **disengagement** noun [U] ▶ **uwolnienie (się), rozłączenie (się)**; (*wojsk.*) **zaprzestanie walki**

disentangle /ˌdɪsɪnˈtæŋɡl/ verb [T] to free sb/sth that had become connected to sb/sth else in a confused and complicated way: *My coat got caught up in some bushes and I couldn't disentangle it.* ◇ (figurative) *Listening to her story, I found it hard to disentangle the truth from the lies* (trudno mi było oddzielić prawdę od kłamstw). ▶ (*i przen.*) **rozplątywać, rozsupływać**

disfigure /dɪsˈfɪɡə(r); US -ɡjər/ verb [T] to spoil the appearance of sb/sth: *His face was permanently disfigured by the fire.* ▶ **zniekształcać**

disgrace¹ /dɪsˈɡreɪs/ noun **1** [U] the state of not being respected by other people, usually because you have behaved badly: *She left the company **in disgrace*** (skompromitowana) *after admitting stealing from colleagues.* ▶ **wstyd, ujma 2** [sing.] **a disgrace (to sb/sth)** a person or thing that gives a very bad impression and makes you feel sorry and embarrassed: *The streets are covered in litter. It's a disgrace!* ◇ *Teachers who hit children are a disgrace to their profession.* ▶ **skandal, wstyd**

disgrace² /dɪsˈɡreɪs/ verb [T] to behave badly in a way that makes you or other people feel sorry and embarrassed: *My brother disgraced himself by starting a fight at the wedding.* ◇ *The disgraced* (skompromitowany) *former leader now works as a cleaner.* ▶ **kompromitować (się)**

disgraceful /dɪsˈɡreɪsfl/ adj. very bad, making other people feel sorry and embarrassed: *The behaviour of the team's fans was absolutely disgraceful.* ▶ **skandaliczny, kompromitujący**
■ **disgracefully** /-fəli/ adv. ▶ **skandalicznie, kompromitująco**

disgruntled /dɪsˈɡrʌntld/ adj. disappointed and annoyed ▶ **niezadowolony, gderliwy**

disguise¹ /dɪsˈɡaɪz/ verb [T] **disguise sb/sth (as sb/sth)** to change the appearance, sound, etc. of sb/sth so that people cannot recognize them or it: *They disguised themselves as fishermen and escaped in a boat.* ◇ (figurative) *His smile disguised his anger.* ▶ **przebierać (za kogoś/coś), zmieniać** (*np. głos, charakter pisma*); **maskować**

disguise² /dɪsˈɡaɪz/ noun [C,U] a thing that you wear or use to change your appearance so that nobody recognizes you: *She is so famous that she has to go shopping **in disguise**.* ◇ *The robbers were wearing heavy disguises so that they could not be identified.* ▶ **przebranie**

⚷ **disgust¹** /dɪsˈɡʌst/ noun [U] **disgust (at sth)** a strong feeling of not liking or approving of sth/sb that you feel is unacceptable, or sth/sb that looks, smells, etc. unpleasant: ***Much to my disgust**, I found a hair in my soup.* ◇ *The film was so bad that we walked out **in disgust*** (wyszliśmy zdegustowani). ▶ **wstręt, oburzenie**

⚷ **disgust²** /dɪsˈɡʌst/ verb [T] **1** to cause a strong feeling of not liking or approving of sb/sth: *Cruelty towards animals absolutely disgusts me.* ▶ **oburzać 2** to make sb feel sick: *The way he eats with his mouth open completely disgusts me* (sprawia, że robi mi się niedobrze). ▶ **napawać wstrętem**

⚷ **disgusted** /dɪsˈɡʌstɪd/ adj. **disgusted (at/with sb/sth)** not liking or approving of sb/sth at all ▶ **oburzony**

⚷ **disgusting** /dɪsˈɡʌstɪŋ/ adj. very unpleasant: *What a disgusting smell!* ▶ **ohydny, odrażający**

disgustingly /dɪsˈɡʌstɪŋli/ adv. **1** extremely (often used to show that you would like to have what sb else has): *Our neighbours are disgustingly rich.* ▶ **obrzydliwie 2** in a way that you do not like or approve of or that makes you feel sick: *The kitchen was disgustingly dirty.* ▶ **ohydnie, odrażająco**

⚷ **dish¹** /dɪʃ/ noun **1** [C] a round container for food that is deeper than a plate ▶ **półmisek, talerz 2** (**the dishes**) [pl.] all the plates, cups, etc. that you use during a meal: *I'll cook and you can wash the dishes.* ▶ **naczynia 3** [C] a type of food prepared in a particular way: *The **main dish*** (na główne danie) *was curry. It was served with a selection of **side dishes*** (zestaw przystawek). ▶ **danie 4** = SATELLITE DISH

dish² /dɪʃ/ verb
PHR V **dish sth out** (informal) to give away a lot of sth: *to dish out advice* ▶ **rozdawać coś**
dish sth up (informal) to serve food ▶ **nakładać potrawy na talerze**

dishcloth /ˈdɪʃklɒθ/ (US **dishrag** /ˈdɪʃræɡ/) noun [C] a cloth for washing dishes ▶ **ścierka do mycia naczyń**

dishearten /dɪsˈhɑːtn/ verb [T, usually passive] to make sb lose hope or confidence ▶ **zniechęcać** OPP **hearten**

disheartened /dɪsˈhɑːtnd/ adj. sad or disappointed ▶ **zniechęcony, przygnębiony**

disheartening /dɪsˈhɑːtnɪŋ/ adj. making you lose hope and confidence; causing disappointment ▶ **zniechęcający, przygnębiający** OPP **heartening**

dishevelled (US **disheveled**) /dɪˈʃevld/ adj. (used about sb's appearance) very untidy ▶ **z rozwichrzonymi włosami, w pomiętym ubraniu** SYN **unkempt**

⚷ **dishonest** /dɪsˈɒnɪst/ adj. that you cannot trust; likely to lie, steal or cheat ▶ **nieuczciwy** OPP **honest**
■ **dishonestly** adv. ▶ **nieuczciwie** | **dishonesty** noun [U] ▶ **nieuczciwość** OPP **honesty**

dishonour¹ (US **dishonor**) /dɪsˈɒnə(r)/ noun [U, sing.] (formal) the state of no longer being respected, especially because you have done sth bad: *Her illegal trading has **brought dishonour on** the company.* ▶ **hańba** OPP **honour**
■ **dishonourable** adj. ▶ **haniebny, nikczemny** OPP **honourable**

dishonour² (US **dishonor**) /dɪsˈɒnə(r)/ verb [T] (formal) to do sth bad that makes people stop respecting you or sb/sth close to you ▶ **okrywać hańbą**

dishrag (US) = DISHCLOTH

dishtowel (US) = TEA TOWEL

dishwasher /ˈdɪʃwɒʃə(r)/ noun [C] a machine that washes plates, cups, knives, forks, etc. ▶ **zmywarka do naczyń**

disillusion /ˌdɪsɪˈluːʒn/ verb [T] to destroy sb's belief in or good opinion of sb/sth ▶ **rozczarowywać**
■ **disillusion** (also **disillusionment** /ˌdɪsɪˈluːʒnmənt/) noun [U]: *I feel increasing disillusion with the government.* ▶ **rozczarowanie**

disillusioned /ˌdɪsɪˈluːʒnd/ adj. disappointed because sb/sth is not as good as you first thought: *She's disillusioned with nursing.* ▶ **rozczarowany**

disillusionment = DISILLUSION

disincentive /ˌdɪsɪnˈsentɪv/ noun [C] a thing that makes sb less willing to do sth: *A low starting salary acts as a strong disincentive to getting back to work for the unemployed.* ▶ **czynnik/środek zniechęcający** OPP **incentive**

disinfect /ˌdɪsɪnˈfekt/ verb [T] to clean sth with a liquid that destroys bacteria: *to disinfect a wound* ▶ **dezynfekować, odkażać**
■ **disinfection** noun [U] ▶ **dezynfekcja, odkażenie**

disinfectant /ˌdɪsɪnˈfektənt/ noun [C,U] a substance that destroys bacteria and is used for cleaning ▶ **środek dezynfekujący/odkażający**

disingenuous /ˌdɪsɪnˈdʒenjuəs/ adj. [not usually before a noun] (formal) not sincere, especially when you pretend to know less about sth than you really do: *It would be disingenuous of me to claim I had never seen it.* ▶ **nieszczery**
■ **disingenuously** adv. ▶ **nieszczerze**

disinherit /ˌdɪsɪnˈherɪt/ verb [T] to prevent sb, especially your son or daughter, from receiving your money or property after your death ▶ **wydziedziczać** ➲ look at **inherit**

disintegrate /dɪsˈɪntɪɡreɪt/ verb [I] to break into many small pieces: *The spacecraft exploded and disintegrated.* ▶ **rozpadać się, rozlatywać się**
■ **disintegration** /dɪsˌɪntɪˈɡreɪʃn/ noun [U]: *the gradual disintegration of traditional values* ▶ **rozpad**

disinterested /dɪsˈɪntrəstɪd/ adj. fair, not influenced by personal feelings: *disinterested advice* ▶ **bezinteresowny, bezstronny** ⓘ Por. **uninterested**, które ma inne znaczenie.

disjointed /dɪsˈdʒɔɪntɪd/ adj. (used especially about ideas, writing or speech) not clearly connected and therefore difficult to follow ▶ **bez związku, nie powiązany**
■ **disjointedly** adv. ▶ **bez związku, bez powiązania**

⚷ **disk** /dɪsk/ noun [C] **1** (especially US) = DISC **2** a flat piece of plastic that stores information for use by a computer ▶ **dysk, dyskietka** ➲ note at **computer** ➲ look at **floppy disk, hard disk**

ˈ**disk drive** noun [C] a piece of electrical equipment that passes information to or from a computer disk ▶ **stacja dysków**

diskette = FLOPPY DISK

⚷ **dislike**[1] /dɪsˈlaɪk/ verb [T] (formal) **dislike (doing) sth** to not like sb/sth: *I really dislike flying.* ◇ *What is it that you dislike about living here?* ▶ **nie lubić** OPP **like** ➲ note at **like**

> **dislike**
>
> **Dislike** to formalny wyraz, dlatego w zwykłych rozmowach raczej używamy **don't like**: *I don't like (doing) sport.* Można też powiedzieć: *I don't **spend much time** doing sport.* ◇ *I'm **not very keen on** (doing) sport.* ◇ *I am **not** very **interested in** sport.* Jeśli bardzo czegoś się nie lubi, można użyć czasownika **hate** lub wyrażeń **really don't like** lub **can't stand**: *I hate/really don't like/can't stand (doing) sport.*

⚷ **dislike**[2] /dɪsˈlaɪk/ noun [U, sing.] (a) **dislike (of/for sb/sth)** the feeling of not liking sb/sth: *She couldn't hide her dislike for him.* ◇ *He seems to have a strong dislike of hard work.* ▶ **niechęć, awersja**
IDM **take a dislike to sb/sth** to start **disliking** sb/sth: *He took an instant dislike to his boss.* ▶ **znienawidzić kogoś/coś, poczuć niechęć do kogoś/czegoś**

dislocate /ˈdɪsləkeɪt; US -ləʊk-; US also dɪsˈləʊ-/ verb [T] to put sth (usually a bone) out of its correct position: *He dislocated his shoulder during the game.* ▶ **zwichnąć, przemieszczać**
■ **dislocation** /ˌdɪsləˈkeɪʃn; US -ləʊ-/ noun [C,U] ▶ **zwichnięcie, przemieszczenie**

dislodge /dɪsˈlɒdʒ/ verb [T] **dislodge sth (from sth)** to make sb/sth move from its correct fixed position: *The strong wind dislodged several tiles from the roof.* ▶ **ruszać z miejsca, usuwać**

disloyal /dɪsˈlɔɪəl/ adj. **disloyal (to sb/sth)** not supporting your friends, family, country, etc.; doing sth that will harm them: *It was disloyal to your friends to repeat their conversation to Peter.* ▶ **nielojalny, niewierny** OPP **loyal**
■ **disloyalty** /-ˈlɔɪəlti/ noun [C,U] (pl. **disloyalties**) ▶ **nielojalność, niewierność**

dismal /ˈdɪzməl/ adj. **1** causing or showing sadness: *dismal surroundings* ▶ **ponury, posępny** SYN **miserable** **2** (informal) of low quality; poor: *a dismal standard of work* ▶ **kiepski, beznadziejny**

dismantle /dɪsˈmæntl/ verb [T] to take sth to pieces; to separate sth into the parts it is made from: *The photographer dismantled his equipment and packed it away.* ▶ **rozkładać na części, rozbierać**

dismay /dɪsˈmeɪ/ noun [U] a strong feeling of disappointment and sadness: *I realized **to my dismay** that I was going to miss the plane.* ▶ **przerażenie, konsternacja**
■ **dismay** verb [T]: *Their reaction dismayed him.* ▶ **przerażać, konsternować** | **dismayed** adj. **dismayed (at/by sth)**; **dismayed to find, hear, see, etc.**: *I was dismayed to find* (z przerażeniem stwierdziłem) *that the train had already left.* ▶ **przerażony czymś**

dismember /dɪsˈmembə(r)/ verb [T] to cut a dead body into pieces ▶ **rozczłonkowywać, rozrywać na części**

⚷ **dismiss** /dɪsˈmɪs/ verb [T] **1 dismiss sb/sth (as sth)** to decide not to think about sth/sb: *He dismissed the idea as nonsense.* Uznał ten pomysł za bzdurę. ◇ *She decided to dismiss her worries from her mind.* Postanowiła przestać myśleć o swoich kłopotach. ▶ **odsuwać od siebie, uznać za nieważne, odrzucać** **2 dismiss sb (from sth)** to order an employee to leave his or her job: *He was dismissed for refusing to obey orders.* ▶ **zwalniać** SYN **fire, sack** ➲ note at **job** **3** to send sb away: *The lesson ended and the teacher dismissed the class.* ▶ **zwalniać** **4** (used in law) to say that a trial or court case should not continue, usually because there is not enough evidence: *The case was dismissed.* ▶ (*prawn.*) **oddalać**
■ **dismissal** /dɪsˈmɪsl/ noun **1** [C,U] ordering sb or being ordered to leave a job: *a case of unfair dismissal* ▶ **zwolnienie** (*pracownika*) **2** [U] refusing to consider sb/sth seriously: *She was hurt at their dismissal of her offer of help.* ▶ **odrzucenie**

dismissive /dɪsˈmɪsɪv/ adj. **dismissive (of sb/sth)** saying or showing that you think that sb/sth is not worth considering seriously: *The boss was dismissive of all the efforts I had made.* ▶ **lekceważący, pogardliwy**
■ **dismissively** adv. ▶ **lekceważąco, pogardliwie**

dismount /dɪsˈmaʊnt/ verb [I] to get off sth that you ride (a horse, a bicycle, etc.) ▶ **zsiadać z czegoś** OPP **mount**

disobedient /ˌdɪsəˈbiːdiənt/ adj. refusing or failing to obey ▶ **nieposłuszny, oporny** OPP **obedient**
■ **disobedience** noun [U] ▶ **nieposłuszeństwo**

disobey /ˌdɪsəˈbeɪ/ verb [I,T] to refuse to do what you are told to do: *He was punished for disobeying orders.* ▶ **sprzeciwiać się, nie słuchać** OPP **obey**

disorder /dɪsˈɔːdə(r)/ noun **1** [U] an untidy, confused or badly organized state: *His financial affairs are* ***in*** *complete* ***disorder.*** ▶ **nieład, nieporządek** OPP **order 2** [U] violent behaviour by a large number of people: *Disorder broke out on the streets of the capital.* ▶ **rozruchy, zamieszki 3** [C,U] an illness in which the mind or part of the body is not working properly: *treatment for* ***eating disorders*** *such as anorexia* ◇ *a kind of* ***mental disorder*** ▶ **zaburzenie, dolegliwość**

disordered /dɪsˈɔːdəd/ adj. untidy, confused or badly organized ▶ **w nieładzie, zaburzony**

disorderly /dɪsˈɔːdəli/ adj. **1** (used about people or behaviour) out of control and violent; causing trouble in public: *They were arrested for being* ***drunk and disorderly.*** ▶ **chuligański 2** untidy ▶ **nieporządny** OPP for both meanings **orderly**

disorganization (also **-isation**) /dɪsˌɔːɡənaɪˈzeɪʃn; US -nəˈz-/ noun [U] a lack of careful planning and order ▶ **dezorganizacja, nieład** OPP **organization**

disorganized (also **-ised**) /dɪsˈɔːɡənaɪzd/ adj. badly planned; not able to plan well ▶ **zdezorganizowany, chaotyczny** OPP **organized**

disorientate /dɪsˈɔːriənteɪt/ (especially US **disorient** /dɪsˈɔːrient/) verb [T] to make sb become confused about where they are: *The road signs were very confusing and I soon became disorientated.* ▶ **dezorientować**

■ **disorientation** /dɪsˌɔːriənˈteɪʃn/ noun [U] ▶ **dezorientacja**

disown /dɪsˈəʊn/ verb [T] to say that you no longer want to be connected with or responsible for sb/sth: *When he was arrested, his family disowned him.* ▶ **wypierać się**

disparage /dɪˈspærɪdʒ/ verb [T] (formal) to talk about sb/sth in a critical way; to say that sb/sth is of little value or importance ▶ **wypowiadać się lekceważąco, dyskredytować**

■ **disparaging** adj.: *disparaging remarks* ▶ **pomniejszający, lekceważący**

disparate /ˈdɪspərət/ adj. (formal) **1** made up of parts or people that are very different from each other: *a disparate group of individuals* ▶ **zróżnicowany 2** (used about two or more things) so different from each other that they cannot be compared or cannot work together: *a critical study that aims to cover such disparate forms as Anglo-Saxon poetry and the modern novel.* ▶ **nieporównywalny, rozbieżny**

disparity /dɪˈspærəti/ noun [U,C] (pl. **disparities**) (formal) a difference, especially one connected with unfair treatment: *the wide disparity between rich and poor* ▶ **nierówność, dysproporcja**

dispassionate /dɪsˈpæʃənət/ adj. not influenced by emotion: *taking a calm, dispassionate view of the situation* ◇ *a dispassionate observer* ▶ **trzeźwy, obiektywny** ❶ Wyraża aprobatę.

■ **dispassionately** adv.: *The case needs to be examined dispassionately at a public inquiry.* ▶ **trzeźwo, obiektywnie**

dispatch (Brit. also **despatch**) /dɪˈspætʃ/ verb [T] (formal) to send sb/sth to a place: *Your order will be dispatched within 7 days.* ▶ **wysyłać, ekspediować**

dispel /dɪˈspel/ verb [T] (**dispelling**; **dispelled**) to make sth, especially a feeling or a belief, disappear: *His reassuring words dispelled all her fears.* ▶ **rozwiewać** (*np. obawy*), **rozpraszać**

dispensable /dɪˈspensəbl/ adj. not necessary: *I suppose I'm dispensable. Anybody could do my job.* ▶ **zbędny** OPP **indispensable**

dispense /dɪˈspens/ verb **1** [T] (formal) to give or provide people with sth: *a machine that dispenses hot and cold drinks* ▶ **wydawać, rozdawać 2** to prepare and give out medicines in a chemist's shop ▶ **sporządzać** (*lekarstwa*), **wykonywać** (*receptę*)

PHR V **dispense with sb/sth** to get rid of sb/sth that is not necessary: *They decided to dispense with luxuries and live a simple life.* ▶ **obywać się bez kogoś/czegoś, pozbywać się kogoś/czegoś**

dispenser /dɪˈspensə(r)/ noun [C] a machine or container from which you can get sth: *a soap dispenser* ◇ *a cash dispenser at a bank* bankomat ▶ **automat** ➲ picture at **stationery**

disperse /dɪˈspɜːs/ verb [I,T] to separate and go in different directions; to make sb/sth do this: *When the meeting was over, the group dispersed.* ◇ *The police arrived and quickly dispersed the crowd.* ▶ **rozpraszać (się), rozchodzić się; rozpędzać**

■ **dispersal** /dɪˈspɜːsl/ noun [U] (formal): *the dispersal of seeds* rozsiewanie ziarna ▶ **rozproszenie**

dispirited /dɪˈspɪrɪtɪd/ adj. having lost confidence or hope ▶ **zniechęcony, przygnębiony** SYN **depressed**

displace /dɪsˈpleɪs/ verb [T] **1** to remove and take the place of sb/sth: *She hoped to displace Seles as the top tennis player in the world.* ▶ **zajmować czyjeś/czegoś miejsce 2** to force sb/sth to move from the usual or correct place: *refugees displaced by the war* ▶ **wysiedlać, przemieszczać**

displacement /dɪsˈpleɪsmənt/ noun (formal) [U] the act of **displacing** sb/sth; the process of being **displaced**: *the largest displacement of civilian population since World War Two* ▶ **wysiedlenie** (*ludności*), **przeniesienie**

⚷ **display**[1] /dɪˈspleɪ/ verb [T] **1** to put sth in a place where people will see it or where it will attract attention: *Posters for the concert were displayed* (były wywieszone) *throughout the city.* ▶ **wystawiać na pokaz 2** to show signs of sth (for example a feeling or a quality): *She displayed no interest in the discussion.* ▶ **okazywać**

⚷ **display**[2] /dɪˈspleɪ/ noun [C] **1** an arrangement of things in a public place for people to see: *a window display in a shop* ▶ **wystawa 2** a public event in which sth is shown in action: *a firework display* ▶ **pokaz, popis 3** behaviour that shows a particular feeling or quality: *a sudden display of aggression* ▶ **demonstrowanie 4** words, pictures, etc. that can be seen on a computer screen ▶ **znak (*tekst, grafika*) wyświetlany na monitorze komputera, wyświetlacz**

IDM **on display** in a place where people will see it and where it will attract attention: *Treasures from the sunken ship were put on display* (zostały wystawione) *at the museum.* ▶ **na wystawie**

displease /dɪsˈpliːz/ verb [T] (formal) to annoy sb or to make sb angry or upset ▶ **urażać, wywoływać niezadowolenie**

■ **displeased** adj. ▶ **niezadowolony** OPP **pleased**

displeasure /dɪsˈpleʒə(r)/ noun [U] (formal) the feeling of being annoyed or not satisfied: *I wrote to express my displeasure at not having been informed sooner.* ▶ **niezadowolenie, irytacja**

disposable /dɪˈspəʊzəbl/ adj. made to be thrown away after being used once or for a short time: *a disposable razor* ▶ **do jednorazowego użytku, jednorazowy**

disposal /dɪˈspəʊzl/ noun [U] the act of getting rid of sth or throwing sth away: *the disposal of dangerous chemical waste* ◇ *bomb disposal* unieszkodliwianie i usuwanie wybuchów ▶ **usunięcie, pozbycie się**

IDM **at sb's disposal** available for sb to use at any time ▶ **do czyjejś dyspozycji**

dispose /dɪˈspəʊz/ verb
PHR V **dispose of sb/sth** to throw away or sell sth; to get rid of sb/sth that you do not want ▶ **usuwać kogoś/coś, pozbywać się kogoś/czegoś**

disposition /ˌdɪspəˈzɪʃn/ noun [C, usually sing.] the natural qualities of sb's character or the way they usually behave: *to have a cheerful disposition* ▶ **usposobienie** SYN **temperament**

dispossess /ˌdɪspəˈzes/ verb [T, usually passive] ~ **sb (of sth)** (formal) to take sb's property, land or house away from them ▶ **wywłaszczać kogoś (z czegoś)**
■ **dispossession** /ˌdɪspəˈzeʃn/ noun [U] ▶ **wywłaszczenie**

disproportionate /ˌdɪsprəˈpɔːʃənət/ adj. **disproportionate (to sth)** too large or too small when compared to sth else: *Her salary is disproportionate to the amount of work she has to do.* ▶ **niewspółmierny, nieproporcjonalny**
■ **disproportionately** adv. ▶ **niewspółmiernie, nieproporcjonalnie**

disprove /ˌdɪsˈpruːv/ verb [T] to show that sth is not true ▶ **odpierać** (*np. wywody*), **obalać** (*np. teorię*) OPP **prove**

dispute[1] /ˈdɪspjuːt; dɪˈspjuːt/ noun [C,U] **(a) dispute (between A and B) (over/about sth)** a disagreement or argument between two people, groups or countries: *a pay dispute* ◇ *There was some dispute between John and his boss about whose fault it was.* ▶ **spór, dysputa**
IDM **be in dispute** to be in a situation of arguing or being argued about: *He is in dispute with the tax office about how much he should pay.* ▶ **być w trakcie sporu; być przedmiotem sporu**

dispute[2] /dɪˈspjuːt/ verb [T] to argue about sth and to question if it is true or right ▶ **kwestionować**

disqualify /dɪsˈkwɒlɪfaɪ/ verb [T] (**disqualifying**; **disqualifies**; pt, pp **disqualified**) **disqualify sb (from sth/doing sth)**; **disqualify sb (for sth)** to officially prevent sb from doing sth or taking part in sth, usually because they have broken a rule or law: *He was disqualified from driving for two years.* ◇ *The team were disqualified for cheating.* ▶ **dyskwalifikować, uznać kogoś za niezdolnego (do czegoś)**
■ **disqualification** /dɪsˌkwɒlɪfɪˈkeɪʃn/ noun [C,U] ▶ **dyskwalifikacja, dyskwalifikowanie**

disquieting /dɪsˈkwaɪətɪŋ/ adj. (formal) causing worry and unhappiness ▶ **niepokojący**

disregard /ˌdɪsrɪˈɡɑːd/ verb [T] to take no notice of sb/sth; to treat sth as unimportant: *These are the latest instructions. Please disregard any you received before.* ▶ **pomijać, ignorować**
■ **disregard** noun [U, sing.] **disregard (for sb/sth)**: *He rushed into the burning building with complete disregard for his own safety.* ▶ **pominięcie, lekceważenie**

disrepair /ˌdɪsrɪˈpeə(r)/ noun [U] the state of being in bad condition because repairs have not been made: *Over the years the building **fell into disrepair*** (uległ zniszczeniu). ▶ **stan zniszczenia, zaniedbanie**

disreputable /dɪsˈrepjətəbl/ adj. not to be trusted; well known for being bad or dishonest: *disreputable business methods* ▶ **podejrzany, niegodziwy** OPP **reputable**

disrepute /ˌdɪsrɪˈpjuːt/ noun [U] the situation when people no longer respect sb/sth: *Such unfair decisions **bring** the legal system **into disrepute*** (dyskredytują system prawny). ▶ **kompromitacja, zła reputacja**

disrespect /ˌdɪsrɪˈspekt/ noun [U] **disrespect (for/to sb/sth)** a lack of respect for sb/sth that is shown in what you do or say ▶ **brak szacunku, lekceważenie** OPP **respect**
■ **disrespectful** /-fl/ adj. ▶ **bez szacunku, lekceważący** OPP **respectful** | **disrespectfully** /-fəli/ adv. ▶ **bez szacunku, lekceważąco**

disrupt /dɪsˈrʌpt/ verb [T] to stop sth happening as or when it should: *The strike severely disrupted flights to Spain.* ▶ **przerywać, wywoływać przerwę**
■ **disruption** noun [C,U] ▶ **przerwanie, zakłócenie** | **disruptive** /dɪsˈrʌptɪv/ adj. ▶ **zakłócający spokój, rozpraszający**

dissatisfaction /ˌdɪsˌsætɪsˈfækʃn/ noun [U] **dissatisfaction (with/at sb/sth)** the feeling of not being satisfied or pleased: *There is some dissatisfaction among teachers with the plans for the new exam.* ▶ **niezadowolenie** OPP **satisfaction**

D

dissatisfied /dɪsˈsætɪsfaɪd/ adj. **dissatisfied (with sb/sth)** not satisfied or pleased: *complaints from dissatisfied customers* ▶ **niezadowolony** OPP **satisfied**

dissect /dɪˈsekt/ verb [T] to cut up a dead body, a plant, etc. in order to study it ▶ **robić sekcję**
■ **dissection** noun [C,U] ▶ **sekcja** (*np. zwłok*)

disseminate /dɪˈsemɪneɪt/ verb [T] (formal) to spread information, knowledge, etc. so that it reaches many people: *Their findings have been **widely disseminated.*** ▶ **rozpowszechniać**
■ **dissemination** /dɪˌsemɪˈneɪʃn/ noun [U] ▶ **rozpowszechnianie**

dissent[1] /dɪˈsent/ noun [U] (formal) disagreement with official or generally agreed ideas or opinions: *There is some dissent within the Labour Party on these policies.* ▶ **różnica zdań, odstępstwo** (*np. od religii*)

dissent[2] /dɪˈsent/ verb [I] (formal) **dissent (from sth)** to have opinions that are different to those that are officially held ▶ **być innego zdania, odstępować** (*np. od religii*)
■ **dissenting** adj.: *dissenting groups/opinions/views* ▶ **różniący się w zapatrywaniach, będący innego zdania**

dissertation /ˌdɪsəˈteɪʃn/ noun [C] a long piece of writing on sth that you have studied, especially as part of a university degree ▶ **rozprawa (naukowa), praca** (*np. magisterska*) ➲ look at **thesis**

disservice /dɪsˈsɜːvɪs/ noun
IDM **do sb a disservice** to do sth that harms sb and the opinion other people have of them: *The minister's comments do the teaching profession a great disservice.* ▶ **wyrządzać szkodę**

dissident /ˈdɪsɪdənt/ noun [C] a person who strongly disagrees with and criticizes their government, especially in a country where it is dangerous to do this: *left-wing dissidents* ▶ **dysydent/ka**
■ **dissidence** noun [U] ▶ **opozycja, niezgoda**

dissimilar /dɪˈsɪmɪlə(r)/ adj. **dissimilar (from/to sb/sth)** not the same; different: *Your situation is **not dissimilar*** (nie różni się) *to mine.* ▶ **niepodobny, różny** OPP **similar**

dissipate /ˈdɪsɪpeɪt/ verb (formal) **1** [I,T] to gradually become or make sth become weaker until it disappears: *Eventually, his anger dissipated.* ◇ *Her laughter soon dissipated the tension in the air.* ▶ **rozpraszać (się), rozwiewać (się)** **2** [T] to waste sth, such as time or money, especially by not planning the best way of using it ▶ **marnować, trwonić** SYN **squander**

dissociate /dɪˈsəʊʃieɪt; -ˈsəʊs-/ (also **disassociate** /ˌdɪsəˈsəʊsieɪt; Brit. also -ˈsəʊʃ-/) verb [T] **dissociate sb/sth/yourself (from sth)** to show that you are not connected with or do not support sb/sth; to show that two things are not connected with each other: *She dissociated herself from the views of the extremists in her party.* ▶ **oddzielać; wyrzekać się związku z czymś, odcinać się od czegoś** OPP **associate**

dissolve /dɪˈzɒlv/ verb [I,T] (used about a solid) to become or to make sth become liquid: *Sugar dissolves in water.* ◇ *Dissolve two tablets in cold water.* ▶ **rozpuszczać (się)**

dissonance /ˈdɪsənəns/ noun **1** [C, U] a combination of musical notes that do not sound pleasant together ▶ (*muz.*) **dysonans** **2** [U] (formal) lack of agreement ▶ **niezgodność, rozdźwięk**
■ **dissonant** /ˈdɪsənənt/ adj.: ***dissonant voices/notes*** ▶ (*muz.*) **dysonansowy**; **rozbieżny**

dissuade /dɪˈsweɪd/ verb [T] **dissuade sb (from doing sth)** to persuade sb not to do sth: *I tried to dissuade her from spending the money, but she insisted.* ▶ **wyperswadować (komuś robienie czegoś), odwodzić kogoś (od robienia czegoś)** OPP **persuade**

distance[1] /ˈdɪstəns/ noun **1** [C,U] the amount of space between two places or things: *The map tells you the distances between the major cities.* ◇ *We can walk home from here – it's no distance* (to nie jest daleko). ◇ *The house is **within walking distance*** (w pobliżu) *of the shops.* ▶ **odległość** **2** [sing.] a point that is a long way from sb/sth: *At this distance I can't read the number on the bus.* ◇ *From a distance the village looks quite attractive.* ▶ **odegłość, oddalenie**
IDM **in the distance** far away: *I could just see Paul in the distance.* ▶ **w oddali**
keep your distance to stay away from sb/sth: *Rachel's got a bad cold so I'm keeping my distance until she gets better.* ▶ **trzymać się z daleka**
within striking distance → STRIKE[1]

distance[2] /ˈdɪstəns/ verb [T] **1 distance sb (from sb/sth)** to make sb feel less friendly towards sb/sth ▶ **oddalać, odsuwać** **2 distance yourself from sb/sth** to show that you are not involved or connected with sb/sth: *She was keen to distance herself from the views of her colleagues.* ▶ **dystansować się, odsuwać się**

distant /ˈdɪstənt/ adj. **1** a long way away in space or time: *travel to distant parts of the world* ◇ *in the not too distant future* wkrótce ▶ **odległy, daleki** **2** [only before a noun] (used about a relative) not closely related: *a distant cousin* ▶ **daleki** **3** not very friendly: *He has a distant manner.* Zachowuje się z rezerwą. ▶ **chłodny, z rezerwą** **4** seeming to be thinking about sth else: *She had a distant look in her eyes* (patrzyła nieobecnym wzrokiem) *and clearly wasn't listening to me.* ▶ **zamyślony, zapatrzony**

distaste /dɪsˈteɪst/ noun [U, sing.] not liking sth; the feeling that sb/sth is unpleasant or offends you: *He looked at the dirty room with distaste.* ▶ **niesmak, niechęć**

distasteful /dɪsˈteɪstfl/ adj. unpleasant or causing offence: *a distasteful remark* ▶ **niesmaczny, przykry**

distil (US **distill**) /dɪˈstɪl/ verb [T] (**distilling**; **distilled**) to make a liquid pure by heating it until it becomes a gas and then collecting the liquid that forms when the gas cools ▶ **destylować**
■ **distillation** /ˌdɪstɪˈleɪʃn/ noun [C,U] ▶ **destylacja**

distillery /dɪˈstɪləri/ noun [C] (pl. **distilleries**) a factory where strong alcoholic drink is made by the process of **distilling** ▶ **gorzelnia**

distinct /dɪˈstɪŋkt/ adj. **1** clear; easily seen, heard or understood: *There has been a distinct improvement in your work recently.* ◇ *I had **the distinct impression** that she was lying.* ▶ **wyraźny, dobitny** **2 distinct (from sth)** clearly different: *Her books fall into two distinct groups: the novels and the travel stories.* ◇ *This region, as distinct* (w odróżnieniu) *from other parts of the country, relies heavily on tourism.* ▶ **oddzielny, odrębny** OPP **indistinct**

distinction /dɪˈstɪŋkʃn/ noun **1** [C,U] **(a) distinction (between A and B)** a clear or important difference between things or people: *We must **make a distinction*** (odróżnić) *between classical and popular music here.* ▶ **rozróżnienie, odróżnienie** **2** [C,U] the quality of being excellent; fame for what you have achieved: *a violinist **of distinction*** wybitny skrzypek ▶ **wyróżnienie, wybitność** **3** [C] the highest mark that is given to students in some exams for excellent work: *James got a distinction in maths.* ▶ **celujący stopień**
IDM **draw a distinction between sth and sth** → DRAW[1]

distinctive /dɪˈstɪŋktɪv/ adj. clearly different from others and therefore easy to recognize: *The soldiers were wearing their distinctive red berets.* ▶ **odmienny, wyróżniający się, charakterystyczny**
■ **distinctively** adv. ▶ **odmiennie, charakterystycznie**

distinctly /dɪˈstɪŋktli/ adv. **1** clearly: *I distinctly heard her say that she would be here on time.* ▶ **wyraźnie, dobitnie** **2** very; particularly: *His behaviour has been distinctly odd recently.* ▶ **dostrzegalnie, wyraźnie**

distinguish /dɪˈstɪŋɡwɪʃ/ verb **1** [I,T] **distinguish between A and B**; **distinguish A from B** to recognize the difference between two things or people: *He doesn't seem able to distinguish between what's important and what isn't.* ◇ *People who are colour-blind often can't distinguish red from green.* ▶ **rozróżniać, odróżniać** SYN **differentiate** **2** [T] **distinguish A (from B)** to make sb/sth different from others: *The power of speech distinguishes humans from animals.* ◇ *distinguishing features* znaki szczególne ▶ **wyróżniać, znamionować** **3** [T] to see, hear or recognize with effort: *I listened carefully but they were too far away for me to distinguish what they were saying.* ▶ **rozpoznawać, zauważać** **4** [T] **distinguish yourself** to do sth which causes you to be noticed and admired: *She distinguished herself in the exams.* ▶ **wyróżniać się**

distinguishable /dɪˈstɪŋɡwɪʃəbl/ adj. **1** possible to recognize as different from sb/sth else: *The male bird is distinguishable from the female by the colour of its beak.* ▶ **rozpoznawalny, dający się rozróżniać** **2** possible to see, hear or recognize with effort: *The letter is so old that the signature is barely distinguishable.* ▶ **dostrzegalny** OPP for both meanings **indistinguishable**

distinguished /dɪˈstɪŋɡwɪʃt/ adj. important, successful and respected by other people: *a distinguished guest* ▶ **wybitny, znakomity**

distort /dɪˈstɔːt/ verb [T] **1** to change the shape or sound of sth so that it seems strange or is not clear: *Her face was distorted with grief.* ◇ *The kidnapper used a device to distort his voice over the telephone.* ▶ **zniekształcać, wykrzywiać** **2** to change sth and show it a way that is not correct or true: *Foreigners are often given a distorted view of this country.* ▶ **zniekształcać, przekręcać**
■ **distortion** noun [C,U] ▶ **zniekształcenie**

distract /dɪˈstrækt/ verb [T] **distract sb (from sth)** to take sb's attention away from sth: *Could you stop talking please? You're distracting me from my work.* ▶ **odwracać czyjąś uwagę, rozpraszać uwagę**

distracted /dɪˈstræktɪd/ adj. unable to give your full attention to sth because you are worried or thinking about sth else ▶ **rozproszony**

distraction /dɪˈstrækʃn/ noun [C,U] something that takes your attention away from what you were doing or thinking about: *I find it hard to work at home because there are so many distractions.* ▶ **rozrywka**; **coś, co powoduje odwrócenie/rozproszenie uwagi**
IDM **to distraction** with the result that you become upset, excited, or angry and unable to think clearly: *The noise of the traffic outside at night is driving me to distraction.* ▶ (*przen.*) **do szaleństwa**

distraught /dɪˈstrɔːt/ adj. extremely sad and upset ▶ **zrozpaczony, zmartwiony**

distress[1] /dɪˈstres/ noun [U] **1** the state of being very upset or of suffering great pain or difficulty: *She was **in such distress** that I didn't want to leave her on her own.* ▶ **rozpacz** **2** the state of being in great danger and needing immediate help: *The ship's captain radioed that it was **in distress**.* ▶ **zagrożenie, niebezpieczeństwo**

distress² /dɪˈstres/ verb [T] to make sb very upset or unhappy: *Try not to say anything to distress the patient further.* ▶ **martwić, unieszczęśliwiać, doprowadzać do rozpaczy**
■ **distressed** adj.: *She was too distressed to talk.* ▶ **zrozpaczony** | **distressing** adj.: *a distressing experience* przykre doświadczenie ◇ *a distressing illness* bolesna choroba ▶ **rozpaczliwy, wstrząsający**

distribute /dɪˈstrɪbjuːt; ˈdɪstrɪbjuːt/ verb [T] **1 distribute sth (to/among sb/sth)** to give things to a number of people: *Tickets will be distributed to all club members.* ◇ *They distributed emergency food supplies to the areas that were most in need.* ▶ **rozdawać, rozdzielać 2** to transport and supply goods to shops, companies, etc.: *Which company distributes this product in your country?* ▶ **rozprowadzać, rozmieszczać 3** to spread sth equally over an area: *Make sure that the weight is* ***evenly distributed.*** ▶ **rozkładać**

distribution /ˌdɪstrɪˈbjuːʃn/ noun **1** [sing., U] the way sth is shared out; the pattern in which sth is found: *The uneven distribution of wealth* (nierówna dystrybucja dóbr) *causes many problems.* ◇ *a map to show the distribution of rainfall in Africa* ▶ **dystrybucja, rozkład 2** [sing., U] the act of giving or transporting sth to a number of people or places: *the distribution of food parcels to the refugees* ▶ **rozdawanie, dystrybucja**

distributor /dɪˈstrɪbjətə(r)/ noun [C] a person or company that transports and supplies goods to a number of shops and companies ▶ **dystrybutor**

district /ˈdɪstrɪkt/ noun [C] **1** a part of a town or country that is special for a particular reason or is of a particular type: *rural districts* ◇ *the financial district of the city* ▶ **okręg, dzielnica 2** an official division of a town or country: *the district council* ◇ *postal districts* ▶ **okręg, dzielnica, obwód** ➲ note at **area**

ˌdistrict ˈnurse noun [C] (in Britain) a nurse who visits patients in their homes ▶ **pielęgniarka środowiskowa**

distrust /dɪsˈtrʌst/ noun [U, sing.] **(a) distrust (of sb/sth)** the feeling that you cannot believe sb/sth; a lack of trust ▶ **nieufność, brak zaufania**
■ **distrust** verb [T]: *She distrusts him because he lied to her once before.* ▶ **nie ufać, nie dowierzać** ➲ look at **mistrust** | **distrustful** /-fl/ adj. ▶ **nieufny, podejrzliwy**

disturb /dɪˈstɜːb/ verb [T] **1** to interrupt sb while they are doing sth or sleeping; to spoil a peaceful situation: *I'm sorry to disturb you but there's a phone call for you.* ◇ *Their sleep was disturbed by a loud crash.* ▶ **przeszkadzać, zakłócać 2** to move sth or change its position: *I noticed a number of things had been disturbed* (niektóre rzeczy były poprzekładane) *and realized that there had been a burglary.* ▶ **zaburzać** (*porządek*) **3** to cause sb to worry: *It disturbed her to think that he might be unhappy.* ▶ **niepokoić, denerwować**

disturbance /dɪˈstɜːbəns/ noun [C,U] **1** something that makes you stop what you are doing, or that upsets the normal condition of sth: *emotional disturbance* zaburzenie emocjonalne ▶ **zakłócenie, przeszkoda 2** an occasion when people behave violently or make a lot of noise in public: *They were arrested for causing a disturbance in the town centre.* ▶ **zamieszki, zakłócenie porządku publicznego**

disturbed /dɪˈstɜːbd/ adj. having mental or emotional problems: *a school for disturbed young people* ▶ **z zaburzeniami (psychicznymi)**

disturbing /dɪˈstɜːbɪŋ/ adj. making you worried or upset: *I found the film about AIDS very disturbing.* ▶ **niepokojący**

disuse /dɪsˈjuːs/ noun [U] the state of not being used any more: *The farm buildings had been allowed to* ***fall into disuse*** (wyjść z użycia). ▶ **nieużywanie**

disused /ˌdɪsˈjuːzd/ adj. not used any more: *a disused railway line* opuszczona linia kolejowa ▶ **nieużywany**

ditch¹ /dɪtʃ/ noun [C] a long narrow hole that has been dug into the ground, especially along the side of a road or field for water to flow along ▶ **rów, kanał**
IDM **a last-ditch attempt** → LAST¹

ditch² /dɪtʃ/ verb [T] (informal) to get rid of or leave sb/sth: *She ditched her old friends when she became famous.* ▶ **rzucać, porzucać**

dither /ˈdɪðə(r)/ verb [I] to be unable to decide sth: *Stop dithering and make up your mind!* ▶ **wahać się, być niezdecydowanym** SYN **hesitate**

ditto /ˈdɪtəʊ/ noun [C] (represented by the mark (") and used instead of repeating the thing written above it) the same ▶ **to samo**
■ **ditto** adv.: *'I'm starving.' 'Ditto.'* ▶ **ja itp. też**

divan /dɪˈvæn; US ˈdaɪvæn/ noun [C] (Brit.) a type of bed with only a thick base to lie on but no frame at either end ▶ **tapczan**

dive¹ /daɪv/ verb [I] (pt **dived**; US also **dove** /dəʊv/; pp **dived**) **1 dive (off/from sth) (into sth)**; **dive in** to jump into water with your arms and head first: *In Acapulco, men dive off the cliffs into the sea.* ◇ *A passer-by dived in and saved the drowning man.* ▶ **skakać do wody, nurkować 2** to swim under the surface of the sea, a lake, etc.: *people diving for pearls* ◇ *I'm hoping to* ***go diving*** *on holiday.* ▶ **nurkować 3** to move quickly and suddenly downwards: *The engines failed and the plane dived.* ▶ **nurkować, pikować 4** to move quickly in a particular direction, especially downwards: *He dived under the table and hid there.* ▶ **rzucać się, dawać nura**
PHR V **dive into sth** to put your hand quickly into a pocket or bag in order to find or get sth: *She dived into her bag and brought out an old photograph.* ▶ **sięgać do czegoś**

dive² /daɪv/ noun [C] **1** the act of **diving** into water ▶ **skok do wody, nurkowanie 2** a quick and sudden downwards movement: *Despite a desperate dive, the goalkeeper couldn't stop the ball.* ▶ **rzucenie się** (*w kierunku czegoś*)

diver /ˈdaɪvə(r)/ noun [C] **1** a person who swims under the surface of water using special equipment ▶ **nurek 2** a person who jumps into water with their arms and head first ▶ **skoczek** (*do wody*)

diverge /daɪˈvɜːdʒ/ verb [I] **diverge (from sth) 1** (used about roads, lines, etc.) to separate and go in different directions: *The paths suddenly diverged and they didn't know which one to take.* ▶ **rozchodzić się, rozbiegać się, rozdzielać się 2** to be or become different: *Attitudes among teachers diverge on this question.* ▶ **różnić się, odchylać się** OPP for both meanings **converge**

diverse /daɪˈvɜːs/ adj. very different from each other: *people from diverse social backgrounds* ◇ *My interests are very diverse.* ▶ **rozmaity, odmienny** ➲ noun **diversity**

diversify /daɪˈvɜːsɪfaɪ/ verb [I,T] (**diversifying**; **diversifies**; pt, pp **diversified**) **diversify (sth) (into sth)** to increase or develop the number or types of sth: *To remain successful in the future, the company will have to diversify.* ◇ *Latin diversified into several different languages.* Z łaciny powstało kilka innych języków. ▶ **rozszerzać** (*np. działalność*)
■ **diversification** /daɪˌvɜːsɪfɪˈkeɪʃn/ noun [C,U] ▶ **rozszerzenie działalności, urozmaicenie**

diversion /daɪˈvɜːʃn/ noun **1** [C,U] the act of changing the direction or purpose of sth, especially in order to solve or avoid a problem: *We made a short diversion* (zjechaliśmy z trasy) *to go and look at the castle.* ◇ *the diversion of government funds to areas of greatest need* ◇ *the diversion of a river* (zmienianie biegu rzeki) *to prevent flood-*

ing ▶ **odwrócenie kierunku 2** [C] something that takes your attention away from sth: *Some prisoners created a diversion while others escaped.* ▶ **coś, co odwraca uwagę 3** [C] (US **detour**) a different route which traffic can take when a road is closed: *For London, follow the diversion.* ▶ **objazd**

diversity /daɪˈvɜːsəti/ noun [U] the wide variety of sth: *cultural and ethnic diversity* ▶ **różnorodność, urozmaicenie**

divert /daɪˈvɜːt/ verb [T] **divert sb/sth (from sth) (to sth); divert sth (away from sth)** to change the direction or purpose of sb/sth, especially to avoid a problem: *During the road repairs, all traffic is being diverted* (cały ruch jest skierowany na objazd). ◇ *Government money was diverted from defence to education.* Rząd zmienił przeznaczenie środków z obrony na oświatę. ◇ *Politicians often criticise each other to divert attention away from* (odwrócić uwagę od) *their own mistakes.* ▶ **odwracać kierunek, skierowywać**

⚷ **divide**[1] /dɪˈvaɪd/ verb **1** [I,T] **divide (sth) (up) (into sth)** to separate into different parts: *The egg divides into two cells.* ◇ *The house was divided up into flats.* ▶ **rozdzielać (się), podzielić (się) 2** [T] **divide sth (out/up) (between/among sb)** to separate sth into parts and give a part to each of a number of people: *The robbers divided the money out between themselves.* ◇ *When he died, his property was divided up among his children.* ▶ **rozdzielać 3** [T] **divide sth (between A and B)** to use different parts or amounts of sth for different purposes: *They divide their time between their two homes.* ▶ **dzielić, rozdzielać 4** [T] to separate two places or things: *The river divides the old part of the city from the new.* ▶ **dzielić, rozdzielać 5** [T] to cause people to disagree: *The question of immigration has divided the country.* ▶ **dzielić, poróżnić** SYN **split 6** [T] **divide sth by sth** to calculate how many times a number will go into another number: *10 divided by 5 is 2.* ▶ **po/dzielić** OPP **multiply**

divide[2] /dɪˈvaɪd/ noun [C] **a divide (between A and B)** a difference between two groups of people that separates them from each other: *a divide between the rich and the poor* ▶ (*przen.*) **przepaść**

diˌvided ˈhighway (US) = DUAL CARRIAGEWAY

dividend /ˈdɪvɪdend/ noun [C] a part of a company's profits that is paid to the people who own shares in the company ▶ **dywidenda**

diˈviding line noun [C] a distinction that is made between two things that are or seem similar: *the dividing line between opinion and fact* ▶ **granica**

divine /dɪˈvaɪn/ adj. connected with God or a god ▶ **boski, boży**

diving /ˈdaɪvɪŋ/ noun [U] the activity or sport of jumping into water or swimming under the surface of the sea, a lake, etc. ▶ **skoki do wody , nurkowanie**

ˈdiving board noun [C] a board at the side of a swimming pool from which people can jump into the water ▶ **trampolina**

divisible /dɪˈvɪzəbl/ adj. [not before a noun] that can be divided: *12 is divisible by 3.* ▶ **podzielny**

⚷ **division** /dɪˈvɪʒn/ noun **1** [U, sing.] **division (of sth) (into sth); division (of sth) (between A and B)** the process or result of separating sth into different parts; the sharing of sth between different people, groups, places, etc.: *an unfair division of the profits* ◇ *There is a growing economic division between the north and south of the country.* ▶ **podział 2** [U] dividing one number by another: *the teaching of multiplication and division* ◇ *long division* ręczne dzielenie przez cyfry wieloliczbowe ▶ **dzielenie 3** [C] **a division (in/within sth); a division (between A and B)** a disagreement or difference of opinion between sb/sth: *deep divisions within the Labour Party* ▶ **podział 4** [C] a part or section of an organization: *the company's sales division* ◇ *the First Division* Pierwsza Liga Piłkarska ▶ **dział, filia 5** [C] a line that separates sth; a border: *The river marks the division between the two counties.* ▶ **podział, granica**

divisive /dɪˈvaɪsɪv/ adj. (formal) likely to cause disagreements or arguments between people: *a divisive policy* ▶ **kontrowersyjny, powodujący podziały**

⚷ **divorce**[1] /dɪˈvɔːs/ noun [C,U] the legal end of a marriage: *to **get a divorce*** rozwodzić się ▶ **rozwód**

⚷ **divorce**[2] /dɪˈvɔːs/ verb **1** [I,T] to legally end your marriage to sb: *She divorced him a year after their marriage.* ◇ *I'd heard they're divorcing.* ▶ **rozwodzić się**

> Częściej niż **to divorce** stosuje się wyrażenie **to get divorced**: *My parents **got divorced** when I was three.* Kiedy jednak tylko jedna strona żąda rozwodu lub gdy podana jest jego przyczyna, wówczas używa się **to divorce**: *She divorced her first husband for mental cruelty.*

2 divorce sb/sth from sth [T] to separate sb/sth from sth: *Sometimes these modern novels seem completely divorced from everyday life* (oderwane od życia). ▶ **oddzielać, rozdzielać**

■ **divorced** adj. ▶ **rozwiedziony** ➲ look at **separated**

divorcé /dɪˌvɔːˈseɪ/ noun [C] (US) a man whose marriage has been legally ended ▶ **rozwodnik**

divorcée /dɪˌvɔːˈseɪ/ noun [C] (US) a woman whose marriage has been legally ended ▶ **rozwódka**

divorcee /dɪˌvɔːˈsiː; US -ˈseɪ/ noun [C] a person who is divorced ▶ **roz-wodnik/wódka**

divulge /daɪˈvʌldʒ/ verb [T] (formal) to tell sth that is secret: *The phone companies refused to divulge details of their costs.* ▶ **wyjawiać**

Diwali /diːˈwɑːli/ noun [sing.] a festival in several Indian religions that takes place in October or November, in which people decorate their homes with lights ▶ (*hinduizm*) **święto ognia**

DIY /ˌdiː aɪ ˈwaɪ/ abbr. **do-it-yourself**; the activity of making, repairing or decorating things in the home yourself, instead of paying sb to do it: *a DIY store* sklep z artykułami do majsterkowania ▶ **zrób to sam** ➲ note at **house**

dizzy /ˈdɪzi/ adj. (**dizzier**; **dizziest**) **1** feeling as if everything is turning round and that you might fall: *I feel/get dizzy in high places.* ▶ **cierpiący na zawroty głowy 2** very great; extreme: *the dizzy pace of life in London* ◇ *The following year, the band's popularity reached **dizzy heights*** (niebosiężny szczyt). ▶ **zawrotny**

■ **dizziness** noun [U] ▶ **zawrót głowy**

DJ /ˈdiː dʒeɪ/ (also **ˈdisc jockey**) noun [C] a person who plays records and talks about music on the radio or in a club ▶ **dyskdżokej**

DNA /ˌdiː en ˈeɪ/ noun [U] the chemical in the cells of animals and plants that controls what characteristics that animal or plant has: *a DNA test* ▶ **DNA**

ˌDNA ˈfingerprinting = GENETIC FINGERPRINTING

⚷ **do**[1] /duː/ verb ⓘ Formy czasowników **do** podane są w dodatku *Czasowniki nieregularne* na końcu słownika. **1** [T] to perform an action, activity or job: *What are you doing?* Co teraz robisz? ◇ *What do you do?* Jaki masz zawód? ◇ *What is the government doing about pollution?* ◇ *Have you done your homework?* Czy odrobiłeś lekcje? ◇ *Did you get your essay done?* Czy napisałeś wypracowanie? ◇ *to do the cooking* gotować ◇ *to do the cleaning* sprzątać ◇ *to do the ironing* prasować ◇ *Do* (uczesz) *your hair before you go out.* ◇ *I do twenty minutes exercise every morning.* Codziennie rano ćwiczę przez dwadzieścia minut. ◇ *to do judo/aerobics/windsurfing* uprawiać judo/aerobik/windsurfing ◇ *What did you do with the keys?* ▶ **robić, czynić 2** [I,T] to make progress or develop;

to improve sth: *'How's your daughter doing at school?' 'She's doing well.'* ▶ **radzić sobie 3** [T] to make or produce sth: *The photocopier does 60 copies a minute.* ◇ *to do a painting/drawing* ▶ **robić**, **wykonywać 4** [T] to study sth or find the answer to sth: *to do French/a course/a degree* ◇ *I can't do question three.* ▶ **robić** (*kurs*), **uczyć się**; **rozwiązać** (*np. zadanie, zagadkę, krzyżówkę*) **5** [T] to travel a certain distance or at a certain speed: *This car does 120 miles per hour.* ◇ *I normally do about five miles when I go running.* Kiedy chodzę biegać, zazwyczaj pokonuję dystans około pięciu mil. ▶ **jechać z określoną prędkością 6** [T] to provide a service: *Do you do eye tests here?* ▶ **wykonywać 7** [I,T] to be enough or suitable: *If you haven't got a pen, a pencil will do.* ▶ **wystarczać 8** [T] to have a particular effect: *A holiday will* ***do you good*** (dobrze ci zrobi). ◇ *The storm did a lot of damage* (wyrządziła wiele szkód). ◇ *Last week's win has* ***done wonders for*** (uczyniła cuda dla) *the team's confidence.* ◇ *This latest scandal will* ***do nothing for*** (zaszkodzi) *this government's reputation.* ▶ **czynić**, **wywierać pewien efekt**

IDM **be/have to do with sb/sth** to be connected with sb/sth: *I'm not sure what Paola's job is, but I think it's something to do with animals.* ◇ *'How much do you earn?' 'It's nothing to do with you* (nie twoja sprawa).*'* ▶ **mieć coś wspólnego z kimś/czymś**

ⓘ **Do** używa się w innych idiomach, np. **do sb credit**. Zob. hasła odpowiednich rzeczowników, przymiotników itp.

PHR V **do away with sth** to get rid of sth: *Most European countries have done away with their royal families.* ▶ **pozbywać się czegoś**, **znosić** (*np. ustawę*)

do sb out of sth to prevent sb having sth in an unfair way; to cheat sb: *They've done me out of my share of the money!* ▶ **pozbawiać kogoś czegoś**

do sth up 1 to fasten a piece of clothing: *Hurry up. Do up your jacket and we can go!* ▶ **zawiązywać coś**, **zapinać coś** (*np. na guziki*), **sznurować** (*buty*) OPP **undo 2** to repair a building and make it more modern: *They're doing up the old cottage.* ▶ **odnawiać**, **restaurować** ➲ note at **house**

do without (sth) to manage without having sth: *If there isn't any tea left, we'll have to do without* (będziemy musieli się bez niej obyć). ▶ **radzić sobie bez czegoś**

do² /də; strong form duː/ auxiliary verb **1** (used with other verbs to form questions and negative sentences, also in short answers and **question tags**): *I don't like fish.* Nie lubię ryby. ◇ *Does she speak Italian?* Czy ona mówi po włosku? ◇ *He doesn't work here, does he* (prawda)*?* ◇ *She works in Paris, doesn't she* (nieprawdaż)*?* ◇ *He didn't say that, did he* (prawda)*?* ▶ **(***bez odpowiednika polskiego***) 2** (used to avoid repeating the main verb): *He earns a lot more than I do* (ode mnie/niż ja). ◇ *She's feeling much better than she did last week* (niż w ubiegłym tygodniu). ▶ **(***bez odpowiednika polskiego***) 3** (used for emphasizing the main verb): *I can't find the receipt now but I'm sure I did pay the phone bill* (jestem przekonana, że na pewno zapłaciłam rachunek telefoniczny). ◇ *'Why didn't you buy any milk?' 'I did buy some* (przecież kupiłem). *It's in the fridge.'* ▶ **(***bez odpowiednika polskiego***)**

do³ /duː/ noun [C] (pl. **dos** /duːz/) (Brit., informal) a party or other social event: *We're having a bit of a do to celebrate Tim's birthday.* ▶ **impreza**

IDM **dos and don'ts** things that you should and should not do: *the dos and don'ts of mountain climbing* ▶ **zalecenia i przestrogi** (*co należy robić, a czego unikać*)

D.O.B. abbr. **date of birth** ▶ **data urodzenia**

docile /ˈdəʊsaɪl; US ˈdɑːsl/ adj. (used about a person or an animal) quiet and easy to control ▶ **uległy**, **posłuszny**

dock¹ /dɒk/ noun **1** [C,U] an area of a port where ships stop to be loaded, repaired, etc. ▶ **dok**, **basen (portowy) 2** (**docks**) [pl.] a group of **docks** with all the buildings, offices, etc. that are around them: *He works down at the docks.* ▶ **doki 3** (US) = JETTY **4** [C, usually sing.] the place in a court of law where the person who is accused sits or stands ▶ **ława oskarżonych**

dock² /dɒk/ verb **1** [I,T] (used about a ship) to sail into a port and stop at the **dock**: *The ship had docked/was docked at Lisbon.* ▶ **wpływać do portu**; **cumować** (*w doku*) **2** [T] to take away part of the money sb earns, especially as a punishment: *They've docked £20 off my wages because I was late.* ▶ **obcinać** (*zarobki*)

D

docket /ˈdɒkɪt/ noun [C] a document or label that shows what is in a package, which goods have been delivered, which jobs have been done, etc. ▶ **opis zawartości** (*np. przesyłki*), **lista** (*np. dostarczonych towarów; wykonanych prac*)

doctor¹ /ˈdɒktə(r)/ noun (abbr. **Dr**) (US, formal **physician** /fɪˈzɪʃn/) **1** [C] a person who has been trained in medicine and who treats people who are ill: *Our family doctor is Dr Laing.* ◇ *I've got a doctor's appointment at 10 o'clock.* ◇ *What time is the doctor's surgery* (godziny przyjęć) *today?* ▶ **lekarz** ➲ note at **disease**, **hospital**, **ill 2** (**the doctor's**) [sing.] a doctor's **surgery**: *I'm going to the doctor's today.* ▶ **przychodnia lekarska** ⓘ Można powiedzieć **go to the doctor** lub **go to the doctor's**. **3** [C] a person who has a **doctorate**: *a Doctor of Philosophy* ▶ **doktor**

going to the doctor

In Britain a **doctor** who looks after general health problems is called a **GP** (/ˌdʒiː ˈpiː/). He/she works in a **surgery** and **sees** or **treats** patients. When you **go to the doctor's**, you describe your **symptoms**: *My head* ***hurts*** ◇ ***I've got*** *a stomach* ***ache***. The doctor may **prescribe** a particular **medicine**. This is written on an official piece of paper called a **prescription**, which you take to a **chemist's** and show when you buy the medicine. If you are feeling very **ill** (US **sick**) or if you are in a lot of **pain**, the doctor may send you to **hospital** for more **treatment**.

doctor² /ˈdɒktə(r)/ verb [T] **1** to change sth that should not be changed in order to gain an advantage: *The results of the survey had been doctored.* ▶ **preparować**, **fałszować 2** to add sth harmful to food or drink ▶ **dodawać coś szkodliwego do jedzenia/napoju**

doctorate /ˈdɒktərət/ noun [C] the highest university degree ▶ **doktorat**

doctrine /ˈdɒktrɪn/ noun [C,U] a set of beliefs that is taught by a church, political party, etc. ▶ **doktryna**

document /ˈdɒkjumənt/ noun [C] **1** an official piece of writing which gives information, proof or evidence: *Her solicitor asked her to read and sign a number of documents.* ▶ **dokument 2** a computer file that contains writing, etc.: *Save the document before closing.* ▶ **dokument**

documentary /ˌdɒkjuˈmentri/ noun [C] (pl. **documentaries**) a film or TV or radio programme that gives facts or information about a particular subject: *Did you see that documentary on Sri Lanka?* ▶ **film/program dokumentalny**

doddle /ˈdɒdl/ noun [sing.] (Brit., informal) something that is very easy to do: *The exam was an absolute doddle!* ▶ **łatwizna**

dodge¹ /dɒdʒ/ verb **1** [I,T] to move quickly in order to avoid sb/sth: *I had to dodge between the cars to cross the road.* ▶ **wymykać się (komuś/czemuś)**, **uchylać się 2** [T] to avoid doing sth that you should do: *Don't try to dodge your responsibilities!* ▶ **unikać**, **wykręcać się (od czegoś)**

dodge² /dɒdʒ/ noun [C] (informal) a clever way of avoiding sth: *a tax dodge* machlojki podatkowe ▶ **wykręt, unik**

dodgy /ˈdɒdʒi/ adj. (**dodgier**; **dodgiest**) (Brit., informal) involving risk; not honest or not to be trusted: *This meat looks a bit dodgy – when did we buy it?* ◇ *a dodgy business deal* ciemny interes ▶ **ryzykowny**; **podejrzany**

doe /dəʊ/ noun [C] a female **deer** or **rabbit** ▶ **łania, królica**; **zajęczyca** ➲ note at **deer**

does /dʌz/ → DO

doesn't /ˈdʌznt/ short for **does not**

⚷ **dog¹** /dɒg/ noun [C] **1** an animal that many people keep as a pet, or for working on farms, hunting, etc.: *dog food* ▶ **pies** ➲ note at **pet 2** a male dog or **fox** ▶ **samiec psa/lisa**

> **dogs**
> **Dog** is used for both male and female animals. The special word for a female is **bitch**. A young dog is called a **puppy**. Dogs that are **trained** to help the blind are called **guide dogs**.When you **take** your dog **for a walk**, you control it with a **lead**. You might put a **muzzle** over its nose and mouth so that it cannot **bite**. When a dog makes a noise it **barks** (written as **woof**), **growls** or **whines**, and when it is excited it **wags** its **tail**.

dog² /dɒg/ verb [T] (**dogging**; **dogged**) to follow sb closely: *A shadowy figure was dogging their every move.* ◇ (figurative) *Bad luck and illness have dogged her career from the start.* ▶ **śledzić**; **towarzyszyć**

ˈdog collar noun [C] (informal) a white band that is worn around the neck by priests in the Christian church ▶ **koloratka**

ˈdog-eared adj. (used about a book or piece of paper) in bad condition with untidy corners and edges because it has been used a lot ▶ **z oślimi uszami**

dogged /ˈdɒgɪd/ adj. refusing to give up even when sth is difficult: *I was impressed by his **dogged determination** to succeed.* ▶ **uparty, wytrwały**
■ **doggedly** adv. ▶ **uparcie**

dogma /ˈdɒgmə/ noun [C,U] a belief or set of beliefs that people are expected to accept as true without questioning ▶ **dogmat**

dogmatic /dɒgˈmætɪk/ adj. being certain that your beliefs are right and that others should accept them, without considering other opinions or evidence ▶ **dogmatyczny**
■ **dogmatically** /-kli/ adv. ▶ **dogmatycznie**

ˈdog-paddle (also **ˈdoggy-paddle**) noun [U] a simple swimming stroke, with short quick movements like those of a dog in the water ▶ (*styl pływacki*) **piesek**

dogsbody /ˈdɒgzbɒdi/ noun [C] (pl. **dogsbodies**) (Brit., informal) a person who has to do the boring or unpleasant jobs that nobody else wants to do and who is considered less important than other people ▶ **popychadło**

ˌdo-it-yourˈself = DIY

the **doldrums** /ˈdɒldrəmz; US ˈdəʊl-/ noun
IDM **in the doldrums 1** unhappy: *He's been in the doldrums ever since she left him.* ▶ **mający chandrę 2** not active or busy: *Business has been in the doldrums recently.* ▶ **w zastoju**

the **dole** /dəʊl/ noun [sing.] (Brit., informal) money that the State gives every week to people who are unemployed: *I lost my job and had to go **on the dole**.* ▶ **zasiłek dla bezrobotnych**

dole /dəʊl/ verb
PHR V **dole sth out** (informal) to give sth, especially food, money, etc. in small amounts to a number of people ▶ **obdzielać coś, rozdzielać coś**

doleful /ˈdəʊlfl/ adj. sad or unhappy: *She looked at him with large doleful eyes.* ▶ **smutny, żałosny**
■ **dolefully** /-fəli/ adv. ▶ **smutno, żałośnie**

doll /dɒl/ noun [C] a child's toy that looks like a small person or a baby ▶ **lalka**

⚷ **dollar** /ˈdɒlə(r)/ noun **1** [C] (symbol **$**) a unit of money in some countries, for example the US, Canada and Australia: *Can I pay in US dollars?* ▶ **dolar**

> There are 100 **cents** in a dollar.

2 [C] a note or coin that is worth one dollar: *a dollar bill* ▶ **jednodolarówka 3** (**the dollar**) [sing.] the value of the US dollar on international money markets: *The dollar closed two cents down.* Na zamknięciu kurs eurodolara spadł o dwa centy. ▶ **dolar amerykański**

dollop /ˈdɒləp/ noun [C] (informal) a lump of sth soft, especially food: *a dollop of ice cream* ▶ **kulka lodów, miarka, łyżka** (*np. śmietanki*)

dolphin /ˈdɒlfɪn/ noun [C] an intelligent animal that lives in the sea and looks like a large fish. **Dolphins** usually swim in **schools**. ▶ **delfin** ➲ picture on **page A10**

domain /dəˈmeɪn; dəʊ-/ noun [C] an area of knowledge or activity: *I don't know – that's outside my domain.* ◇ *This issue is now in the public domain* (została podana do publicznej wiadomości). ▶ **zakres**

dome /dəʊm/ noun [C] a round roof on a building ▶ **kopuła**
■ **domed** adj. having or shaped like a **dome**: *a domed roof/ceiling* ◇ *a domed* (wypukłe) *forehead* ▶ **nakryty kopułą, kopulasty, wysklepiony**

⚷ **domestic** /dəˈmestɪk/ adj. **1** not international; only within one country: *domestic affairs/flights/politics* ▶ **krajowy 2** [only before a noun] connected with the home or family: *domestic chores/tasks* ◇ *the growing problem of **domestic violence*** (przemocy w rodzinie) ◇ *domestic water/gas/electricity supplies* ▶ **domowy 3** (used about a person) enjoying doing things in the home, such as cooking and cleaning: *I'm not a very domestic sort of person.* ▶ **rodzinny, dobrze wykonujący prace domowe 4** (used about animals) kept as pets or on farms; not wild: *domestic animals such as cats, dogs and horses* ▶ **domowy**

domesticated /dəˈmestɪkeɪtɪd/ adj. **1** (used about animals) happy being near people and being controlled by them ▶ **oswojony, udomowiony 2** (used about people) able to do or good at cleaning the house, cooking, etc.: *Men are expected to be much more domesticated* (partnerscy) *nowadays.* ▶ **umiejący dobrze wykonywać prace domowe**

domicile /ˈdɒmɪsaɪl; US also ˈdəʊm-/ noun [C] (formal) the place where sb lives, especially when it is stated for official or legal purposes ▶ **miejsce zamieszkania**

dominance /ˈdɒmɪnəns/ noun [U] control or power: *Japan's dominance of the car industry* ▶ **dominacja**

dominant /ˈdɒmɪnənt/ adj. more powerful, important or noticeable than others: *His mother was the dominant influence in his life.* ◇ *The castle stands in a dominant position above the town* (góruje nad miastem). ▶ **dominujący**

⚷ **dominate** /ˈdɒmɪneɪt/ verb **1** [I,T] to be more powerful, important or noticeable than others: *The Italian team dominated throughout the second half of the game.* ◇ *She always tends to dominate the conversation.* ▶ **dominować 2** [T] (used about a building or place) to be much higher than everything else: *The cathedral dominates the area for miles around.* ▶ **dominować, górować**
■ **domination** /ˌdɒmɪˈneɪʃn/ noun [U] ▶ **dominacja**

domineering /ˌdɒmɪˈnɪərɪŋ; US -məˈn-/ adj. having a very strong character and wanting to control other people ▶ **władczy, despotyczny** SYN **overbearing**

dominion /dəˈmɪniən/ noun (formal) **1** [U] the power to rule and control: *to have dominion over an area* ▶ **zwierzchnictwo 2** [C] an area controlled by one government or ruler ▶ **dominium**

domino /ˈdɒmɪnəʊ; US -mən-/ noun [C] (pl. **dominoes**) one of a set of small flat pieces of wood or plastic, marked on one side with two groups of spots representing numbers, that are used for playing a game called **dominoes** ▶ **kostka do gry w domino**

donate /dəʊˈneɪt; US ˈdəʊn-/ verb [T] **donate sth (to sb/sth)** to give money or goods to an organization, especially one for people or animals who need help ▶ **darować, ofiarować**

donation /dəʊˈneɪʃn/ noun [C] money, etc. that is given to a person or an organization such as a charity, in order to help people or animals in need ▶ **datek, darowizna**

done¹ past participle of **do¹**

done² /dʌn/ adj. [not before a noun] **1** finished: *I've got to go out as soon as this job is done.* ▶ **skończony 2** (used about food) cooked enough: *The meat's ready but the vegetables still aren't done.* ▶ **dogotowany**
IDM **over and done with** completely finished; in the past ▶ **skończony, należący do przeszłości**

done³ /dʌn/ interj. (used for saying that you accept an offer): *'I'll give you twenty pounds for it.' 'Done!'* ▶ **zgoda!**

donkey /ˈdɒŋki/ noun [C] (also ass) an animal like a small horse, with long ears ▶ **osioł**
IDM **donkey's years** (Brit., informal) a very long time: *We've known each other for donkey's years.* ▶ **wieki całe**

donor /ˈdəʊnə(r)/ noun [C] **1** a person who gives money or goods to an organization that helps people or animals ▶ **ofiarodaw-ca/czyni 2** a person who gives blood or a part of their own body for medical use: *a blood donor* krwiodawca ◇ *a kidney donor* ▶ **daw-ca/czyni**

don't /dəʊnt/ short for **do not**

donut (US) = DOUGHNUT

doodle /ˈduːdl/ verb [I] to draw lines, patterns, etc. without thinking, especially when you are bored ▶ **kreślić esy-floresy**
■ **doodle** noun [C] ▶ **esy-floresy**

doom /duːm/ noun [U] death or a terrible event in the future which you cannot avoid: *a sense of impending doom* ◇ *Don't listen to her. She's always full of* ***doom and gloom*** (pełna złych przeczuć). ◇ *In the last scene of the film the villain plunges to his doom in the river* (rzuca się do rzeki na niechybną śmierć). ◇ *a sense of doom* przeczucie katastrofy ▶ **przeznaczenie, zatracenie**
■ **doomed** adj.: *The plan was doomed from the start.* ▶ **skazany na niepowodzenie, przesądzony**

door /dɔː(r)/ noun [C] **1** a piece of wood, glass, etc. that you open and close to get in or out of a room, building, car, etc.: *to open/shut/close the door* ◇ *to answer the door* otworzyć drzwi (w odpowiedzi na pukanie lub dzwonek) ◇ *Have you bolted/locked the door?* ◇ *I could hear someone knocking on the door.* ◇ *the front/back door* ◇ *the fridge door* ▶ **drzwi 2** the entrance to a building, room, car, etc.: *I looked through the door and saw her sitting there.* ▶ **drzwi** ➲ picture on **page A7**
IDM **(from) door to door** (from) house to house: *The journey takes about five hours, door to door.* ◇ *a door-to-door salesman* domokrążca ▶ **od drzwi do drzwi**
next door (to sb/sth) in the next house, room, etc.: *Do you know the people who live next door?* ▶ **obok (kogoś/czegoś), po sąsiedzku**
out of doors outside: *Shall we eat out of doors today?* ▶ **na zewnątrz, na dworze, na świeżym powietrzu** SYN **outdoors** OPP **indoors**

doorbell /ˈdɔːbel/ noun [C] a bell on the outside of a house which you ring when you want to go in ▶ **dzwonek** (*u drzwi*)

doorman /ˈdɔːmən/ noun [C] (pl. **-men** /-mən/) a man, often in uniform, whose job is to stand at the entrance to a large building such as a hotel or a theatre, and open the door for visitors, find them taxis, etc. ▶ **odźwierny** ➲ look at **porter** (3)

doormat /ˈdɔːmæt/ noun [C] **1** a piece of material on the floor in front of a door which you can clean your shoes on before going inside ▶ **wycieraczka 2** (informal) a person who allows other people to treat them badly without complaining ▶ **popychadło**

doorstep /ˈdɔːstep/ noun [C] a step in front of a door outside a building ▶ **próg**
IDM **on your/the doorstep** very near to you: *The sea was right on our doorstep.* ▶ (*przen.*) **tuż za progiem**

doorway /ˈdɔːweɪ/ noun [C] an opening filled by a door leading into a building, room, etc.: *She was standing in the doorway.* ▶ **wejście, drzwi**

dope¹ /dəʊp/ noun (informal) **1** [U] an illegal drug, such as **cannabis** ▶ **narkotyk** (*zwł. marihuana*), **trawka 2** [C] a stupid person ▶ **głupek**

dope² /dəʊp/ verb [T] to give a drug secretly to a person or an animal, especially to make them sleep ▶ **odurzać (podstępnie)**

dopey /ˈdəʊpi/ adj. (**dopier**; **dopiest**) **1** (informal) stupid; not intelligent ▶ **głupawy, nierozgarnięty 2** tired and not able to think clearly, especially because of drugs, alcohol or lack of sleep ▶ **odurzony** (*np. narkotykami*)

dork /dɔːk/ noun [C] (informal) a stupid or boring person that other people laugh at ▶ **głupek**
■ **dorky** adj. ▶ **głupkowaty**

dorm = DORMITORY

dormant /ˈdɔːmənt/ adj. not active for some time: *a dormant* (drzemiący) *volcano* ▶ **uśpiony, będący w zawieszeniu**

dormitory /ˈdɔːmətri; US -tɔːri/ noun [C] (pl. **dormitories**) (also **dorm** /dɔːm/) **1** a large bedroom with a number of beds in it, especially in a school, etc. ▶ **sala sypialna 2** (US) = HALL OF RESIDENCE

dosage /ˈdəʊsɪdʒ/ noun [C, usually sing.] the amount of a medicine you should take over a period of time: *The recommended dosage is one tablet every four hours.* ▶ **dawkowanie**

dose¹ /dəʊs/ noun [C] **1** an amount of medicine that you take at one time: *You should take a large dose of this cough medicine before going to bed.* ▶ **dawka** ➲ look at **overdose 2** an amount of sth, especially sth unpleasant: *a dose of the flu* atak grypy ◇ *I can only stand him in small doses.* ▶ **dawka**

dose² /dəʊs/ verb [T] to give sb/yourself a medicine or drug: *She dosed herself with aspirin and went to work.* ◇ *He was heavily dosed* (był naszpikowany) *with painkillers.* ▶ **podawać/brać** (*lekarstwo*), **dawkować**

doss /dɒs/ verb (Brit., slang)
PHR V **doss about/around** to waste time not doing very much: *We just dossed about in class yesterday.* ▶ **obijać się**
doss down to lie down to sleep, without a proper bed: *Do you mind if I doss down on your floor tonight?* ▶ **przekimać**

dot¹ /dɒt/ noun [C] **1** a small, round mark, like a full stop: *The letters i and j have dots above them.* ◇ *a white dress with black dots* (w czarne groszki) ▶ **kropka**

Słowa **dot** używa się, mówiąc o czyimś adresie e-mailowym. Adres zapisany jako *ann@smithuni.co.uk* czyta się: *Ann at smithuni dot co dot uk.*

2 something that looks like a **dot**: *He watched until the aeroplane was just a dot in the sky.* ▶ **kropka, punkt**
IDM **on the dot** (informal) at exactly the right time or at exactly the time mentioned: *Lessons start at 9 o'clock on the dot* (punkt dziewiąta). ▶ **punktualnie**

dot² /dɒt/ verb [T] (**dotting**; **dotted**) [usually passive] to mark with a **dot** ▶ **kropkować**
IDM **dotted about/around** spread over an area: *There are restaurants dotted about all over the centre of town.* ▶ **rozsiany**
be dotted with to have several things or people spread over an area: *a hillside dotted with sheep* ▶ **cętkowany, upstrzony**

dot-com (also **dotcom**) /ˌdɒt ˈkɒm/ noun [C] a company that sells products and services on the Internet: *The weaker dot-coms have collapsed.* ◇ *a dot-com millionaire* ▶ **sklep internetowy**

dote /dəʊt/ verb [I] **dote on sb/sth** to have or show a lot of love for sb/sth and think he/she/it is perfect: *He's always doted on his eldest son.* ▶ **nie widzieć świata poza kimś**
■ **doting** adj.: *doting parents* ▶ **kochający**

dotted ˈline noun [C] a line of **dots** which show where sth is to be written on a form, etc.: *Sign on the dotted line.* ▶ **linia kropkowana**

double¹ /ˈdʌbl/ adj. **1** twice as much or as many (as usual): *a double helping of ice cream* ▶ **podwójny 2** having two equal or similar parts: *double doors* ◇ *Does 'necessary' have (a) double 's'?* ◇ *My phone number is two four double 0* (zero zero) *four.* ▶ **podwójny 3** made for or used by two people or things: *a double garage* ▶ **podwójny** ➲ note at **bed¹**

double² /ˈdʌbl/ determiner twice as much or as many (as usual): *His income is double his wife's.* ◇ *We'll need double the amount of wine.* ▶ **dwa razy tyle/więcej**

double³ /ˈdʌbl/ adv. in pairs or two parts: *When I saw her with her twin sister I thought I was* ***seeing double*** (myślałem, że dwoi mi się w oczach). ▶ **podwójnie**

double⁴ /ˈdʌbl/ noun **1** [U] twice the (usual) number or amount: *When you work overtime, you get paid double.* ▶ **podwójna stawka/kwota 2** [C] a glass of strong alcoholic drink containing twice the usual amount ▶ **podwójna porcja** (*alkoholu*) **3** [C] a person who looks very much like another: *I thought it was you I saw in the supermarket. You must have a double.* ▶ **sobowtór 4** [C] an actor who replaces another actor in a film to do dangerous or other special things ▶ **dubler/ka 5** [C] = DOUBLE ROOM **6** (**doubles**) [pl.] (in some sports, for example **tennis**) with two pairs playing: *the Men's Doubles final* ▶ **debel** ➲ look at **singles**

double⁵ /ˈdʌbl/ verb **1** [I,T] to become or to make sth twice as much or as many; to multiply by two: *The price of houses has almost doubled.* ◇ *Think of a number and double it.* ▶ **podwajać (się) 2** [I] **double (up) as sth** to have a second use or function: *The small room doubles (up) as a study.* ▶ **być używanym także jako coś**
PHR V **double (sb) up/over** (to cause sb) to bend the body: *to be doubled up with pain/laughter* ▶ **zginać (się)**

ˌdouble ˈagent noun [C] a person who spies for two rival countries at the same time ▶ **podwójny agent**

ˌdouble-ˈbarrelled (US **ˌdouble-ˈbarreled**) adj. [usually before a noun] **1** (used about a gun) having two places where the bullets come out (**barrels**) ▶ **o dwóch lufach 2** (Brit.) (used a family name) having two parts, sometimes joined by a hyphen, for example 'Day-Lewis' ▶ (*nazwisko*) **podwójny**

ˌdouble ˈbass (also **bass**) noun [C] the largest musical instrument with strings, that you can play either standing up or sitting down ▶ **kontrabas**

ˌdouble ˈbed noun [C] a bed made for two people ▶ **łóżko dwuosobowe** ➲ look at **single, twin**

ˌdouble-ˈbreasted adj. (used about a coat or jacket) having two rows of buttons down the front ▶ **dwurzędowy**

ˌdouble-ˈcheck verb [I,T] to check sth again, or with great care ▶ **sprawdzać ponownie/dokładnie**

ˌdouble ˈchin noun [C] a fold of fat under a person's chin, that looks like another chin ▶ **podwójny podbródek**

ˌdouble-ˈclick verb [I,T] **double-click (on sth)** to press one of the buttons on a computer mouse twice quickly: *To run an application, just double-click on the icon.* ▶ (*komput.*) **klikać dwa razy**

ˌdouble-ˈcross verb [T] to cheat sb who believes that they can trust you after you have agreed to do sth dishonest together ▶ **przechytrzyć**

ˌdouble-ˈdealer noun [C] a dishonest person who cheats other people ▶ **dwulicowa osoba**
■ **ˌdouble-ˈdealing** noun [U] ▶ **podwójna gra, dwulicowość**

ˌdouble-ˈdecker noun [C] a bus with two floors ▶ **autobus piętrowy** ➲ picture at **bus**

ˌdouble ˈDutch noun [U] conversation or writing that you cannot understand at all ▶ **chińszczyzna, bezsens**

ˌdouble ˈfigures noun [U] a number that is more than nine: *Inflation is* ***in double figures*** (przekroczyła już 10 procent). ▶ **liczba większa od 10**

ˌdouble ˈglazing noun [U] two layers of glass in a window to keep a building warm or quiet ▶ **podwójne szyby w oknach**
■ **ˌdouble-ˈglazed** adj. ▶ (*okno itp.*) **z podwójną szybą**

ˌdouble-ˈpark verb [I,T] [usually passive] to park a car or other vehicle beside one that is already parked in a street: *A red sports car stood double-parked almost in the middle of the road.* ◇ *I'll have to rush – I'm double-parked.* ▶ **parkować na drugiego**

ˌdouble ˈroom (also **double**) noun [C] a bedroom for two people ▶ **pokój dwuosobowy** ➲ look at **single**

doubly /ˈdʌbli/ adv. **1** more than usually: *Pete made doubly sure that the door was locked.* ▶ **dwukrotnie 2** in two ways: *He was doubly blessed with both good looks and talent.* ▶ **podwójnie**

doubt¹ /daʊt/ noun [C,U] **doubt (about sth)**; **doubt that ...**; **doubt as to sth** a feeling of being uncertain about sth: *If you have any doubts about the job, feel free to ring me and discuss them.* ◇ *There's some doubt that Jan will pass the exam.* ▶ **wątpliwość**
IDM **beyond (any) doubt** in a way that shows that something is completely certain: *The research showed beyond doubt that smoking contributes to heart disease.* ◇ *The prosecution was able to establish* ***beyond reasonable doubt*** *that the woman had been lying.* ▶ **ponad wszelką wątpliwość**
cast doubt on sth → CAST¹
give sb the benefit of the doubt → BENEFIT¹
in doubt not sure or definite ▶ **mający wątpliwości, wątpliwy**
no doubt (used when you expect sth to happen but you are not sure that it will) probably: *No doubt she'll write when she has time.* ▶ **niewątpliwie**
without (a) doubt definitely: *It was, without doubt, the coldest winter for many years.* ▶ **niewątpliwie**

doubt² /daʊt/ verb [T] to think sth is unlikely or to feel uncertain (about sth): *She never doubted that he was telling the truth.* ▶ **wątpić (w coś/o czymś)**

doubtful /ˈdaʊtfl/ adj. **1 doubtful (about sth/about doing sth)** (used about a person) not sure: *John still felt doubt-*

ful about his decision. ▶ **niepewny** **2** unlikely or uncertain: *It's doubtful whether/if we'll finish in time.* ◇ *It was doubtful that he was still alive.* ▶ **wątpliwy**
■ **doubtfully** /-fəli/ adv.: *'I suppose it'll be all right,' she said doubtfully.* ▶ **niepewnie**

doubtless /ˈdaʊtləs/ adv. almost certainly: *Doubtless she'll have a good excuse for being late!* ▶ **niewątpliwie**

dough /dəʊ/ noun [U] **1** a mixture of flour, water, etc. used for baking into bread, etc. ▶ **ciasto** **2** (slang) money ▶ **forsa**

doughnut (US **donut**) /ˈdəʊnʌt/ noun [C] a small cake in the shape of a ball or a ring, made from a sweet **dough** cooked in very hot oil ▶ **pączek**

dour /dʊə(r)/ adj. (used about sb's manner or expression) cold and unfriendly ▶ **oschły, surowy**

douse (also **dowse**) /daʊs/ verb [T] **1 douse sth (with sth)** to stop a fire from burning by pouring liquid over it: *The firefighters managed to douse the flames.* ▶ **ugaszać** **2 douse sb/sth (in/with sth)** to cover sb/sth with liquid: *to douse yourself in perfume* ▶ **oblewać**

dove[1] /dʌv/ noun [C] a type of white bird, often used as a sign of peace ▶ **gołąb (biały)**

dove[2] (US) past tense of **dive**[1]

dowdy /ˈdaʊdi/ adj. (**dowdier**; **dowdiest**) (used about a person or the clothes they wear) not attractive or fashionable ▶ **nieciekawy i bez gustu, niemodny**

down[1] /daʊn/ adv., prep. ⓘ **Down** używa się w czasownikach złożonych. Zob. hasła odpowiednich czasowników, np. **go**, **sit**, **lie**, **turn**, **write**. **1** to or at a lower level or place; from the top towards the bottom of sth: *'Where's Mary?' 'She's down in the basement.'* ◇ *The rain was running down* (spływał po) *the window.* ◇ *The snow began to slide down the mountain.* Śnieg zaczął się zsuwać z góry. ◇ *Her hair hung down her back.* Jej włosy opadały na plecy. ◇ *We watched the sun go down.* Patrzyliśmy na zachód słońca. ◇ *Can you get that book down from the top shelf?* Czy możesz zdjąć tę książkę z górnej półki? ▶ **na dół/dole** **2** from a standing or vertical position to a sitting or horizontal one: *to sit down* siadać ◇ *to lie down* kłaść się **3** (used for showing that the level, amount, strength, etc. of sth is less or lower): *Do you mind if I turn the heating down a bit* (trochę zmniejszę ogrzewanie)*?* ◇ *to turn the radio down* ściszać radio ◇ *to turn the lights down* ściemniać oświetlenie **4** to or in the south: *We went down to Devon for our holiday.* Pojechaliśmy do Devon na wakacje. ▶ **na południ-e/u** **5** (written) on paper: *Put these dates down* (zapisz te daty) *in your diary.* **6** along: *We sailed down the river towards the sea.* Popłynęliśmy z prądem rzeki ku morzu. ◇ *'Where's the nearest garage?' 'Go down this road* (proszę pojechać tą ulicą) *and take the first turning on the right.'* ▶ **wzdłuż** **7 down to sb/sth** even including: *We had everything planned down to the last detail.* ◇ *Everyone was invited from the Director down to the tea ladies* ▶ **aż po kogoś/coś, włącznie z kimś/czymś**
IDM **be down to sb** to be sb's responsibility: *When my father died it was down to me* (na mnie spadł obowiązek) *to look after the family's affairs.* ▶ **zależeć od kogoś**
be down to sth to have only the amount mentioned left: *I can't lend you any money – I'm down to my last* (zostało mi) *£5.* ▶ **mieć zaledwie**
down and out having no money, job or home ▶ **bez grosza, bezdomny i bezrobotny**
down in the dumps unhappy or sad ▶ **przygnębiony**
down under (informal) (in) Australia ▶ **Australia; w Australii**
be/go down with sth to be or become ill with sth: *Simon's gone down with flu* ▶ **za/chorować na coś**

down[2] /daʊn/ verb [T] (informal) to finish a drink quickly: *She* ***downed*** *her drink* ***in one.*** ▶ **wypić do dna**

down[3] /daʊn/ adj. **1** sad: *You're looking a bit down today.* ▶ **smutny, przygnębiony** **2** (used about computers) not working: *I can't access the file as our computers have been down all morning.* ▶ **nie działający, niesprawny** **3** lower than before: *Unemployment figures are down again this month.* ▶ **niższy**

down[4] /daʊn/ noun [U] very soft feathers: *a duvet filled with duck down* ▶ **puch**

ˈdown-and-out noun [C] a person who has got no money, job or home ▶ **rozbitek życiowy**

D

downbeat /ˈdaʊnbiːt/ adj. (informal) **1** dull or depressing; not having much hope for the future: *The overall mood of the meeting was downbeat.* ▶ **przybity, pesymistyczny** OPP **upbeat** **2** not showing strong feelings or enthusiasm ▶ **powściągliwy** (*w okazywaniu uczuć*)

downcast /ˈdaʊnkɑːst; US -kæst/ adj. **1** (used about a person) sad and without hope ▶ **przybity** **2** (used about eyes) looking down ▶ **spuszczony**

downfall /ˈdaʊnfɔːl/ noun [sing.] **1** a loss of power or success: *The government's downfall seemed inevitable.* ▶ **upadek** **2** a thing that causes a loss of power or success: *Greed was her downfall.* ▶ **ruina**

downgrade /ˌdaʊnˈɡreɪd/ verb [T] **downgrade sb/sth (from sth) (to sth)** to reduce sb/sth to a lower level or position of importance: *Tom's been downgraded from manager to assistant manager.* ▶ **przenosić na niższy poziom**

downhearted /ˌdaʊnˈhɑːtɪd/ adj. [not before a noun] sad ▶ **przybity, przygnębiony**

downhill /ˌdaʊnˈhɪl/ adv. (going) downwards; towards the bottom of a hill: *It's an easy walk. The road runs downhill most of the way.* ▶ **w/na dół** OPP **uphill**
IDM **go downhill** to get worse: *Their relationship has been going downhill for some time now.* ▶ **pogarszać się**
■ **downhill** adj.: *downhill skiing* narciarstwo zjazdowe ▶ **w/na dół** OPP **uphill**

download /ˌdaʊnˈləʊd/ verb [T] to copy a computer file, etc. from a large computer system to a smaller one ▶ **ściągać** (*np. muzykę, filmy z internetu*) OPP **upload**
■ **download** /ˈdaʊnləʊd/ noun [C] ▶ **ściągnięt-a/y muzyka/film itp. z internetu** | **downloadable** /ˌdaʊnˈləʊdəbl/ adj. ▶ (*muzyka, film itp.*) **do ściągnięcia z internetu**

downmarket /ˌdaʊnˈmɑːkɪt/ (US **downscale**) adj. cheap and of low quality: *a downmarket newspaper* ▶ **niskiej jakości, niemodny** OPP **upmarket**
■ **downmarket** adv.: *To get more viewers the TV station was forced to* ***go downmarket*** (była zmuszona obniżyć poziom).

ˌdown ˈpayment noun [C] a sum of money that is given as the first part of a larger payment: *We are saving for a down payment on a house.* ▶ **zaliczka, pierwsza rata**

downpour /ˈdaʊnpɔː(r)/ noun [C] a heavy, sudden fall of rain ▶ **ulewa**

downright /ˈdaʊnraɪt/ adj. [only before a noun] (used about sth bad or unpleasant) complete: *The holiday was a downright disaster.* ▶ **całkowity**
■ **downright** adv.: *The way he spoke to me was downright rude!* ▶ **całkowicie**

downs /daʊns/ noun [pl.] an area of low, round hills, especially in the south of England: *the Sussex Downs* ▶ **wyżyny**

downside /ˈdaʊnsaɪd/ noun [C, usually sing.] the disadvantages or negative aspects of sth: *All good ideas have a downside.* ▶ **zła/negatywna strona**

downsize /ˈdaʊnsaɪz/ verb [I,T] to reduce the number of people who work in a company, business, etc. in order to reduce costs ▶ **redukować zatrudnienie** ➲ note at **cut**
■ **downsizing** noun [U] ▶ **redukcja zatrudnienia**

Down's syndrome /ˈdaʊnz sɪndrəʊm/ (US usually **Down syndrome**) noun [U] a condition that a person is born with. People with this condition have a flat, wide face and lower than average intelligence. ▶ **zespół Downa**

downstairs /ˌdaʊnˈsteəz/ adv. **1** down the stairs: *He fell downstairs and broke his arm.* ▶ **w dół** (*schodami*), **ze schodów 2** on or to the ground floor or a lower floor: *Dad's downstairs, in the kitchen.* ▶ **na/w dół; na dole** OPP **upstairs**
■ **downstairs** adj.: *a downstairs toilet* ▶ **na/w dół; na dole** OPP **upstairs**

downstream /ˌdaʊnˈstriːm/ adv. in the direction in which a river flows: *We were rowing downstream.* ▶ **w dół rzeki, z prądem** OPP **upstream**

ˌdown to ˈearth adj. (used about a person) sensible, realistic and practical ▶ **praktyczny, rozsądny**

downtown /ˌdaʊnˈtaʊn/ adv. (especially US) in or towards the centre of a city, especially its main business area: *to go/work downtown* ▶ **do/w centrum miasta**
■ **ˈdowntown 1** adj.: *a downtown store* ▶ **znajdujący się w centrum miasta 2** noun [U]: *a hotel in the heart of downtown* ▶ **centrum miasta**

downtrodden /ˈdaʊntrɒdn/ adj. (used about a person) made to suffer bad treatment or living conditions by people in power, but being too tired, poor, ill, etc. to change this ▶ **sponiewierany**

downturn /ˈdaʊntɜːn/ noun [usually sing.] **a downturn (in sth)** a drop in the amount of business that is done; a time when the economy becomes weaker: *a downturn in sales/trade/business* ▶ **spadek, zmniejszenie** OPP **upturn**

downward /ˈdaʊnwəd/ adj. [only before a noun] towards the ground or a lower level: *a downward movement* ◇ *a downward trend* (tendencja spadkowa) *in house prices* ▶ **w/na dół** OPP **upward**
■ **downwards** /ˈdaʊnwədz/ adv.: *She laid the picture face downwards on the table.* ▶ **na/w dół** OPP **upwards**

dowry /ˈdaʊri/ noun [C] (pl. **dowries**) an amount of money or property which, in some countries, a woman's family gives to the man she is marrying ▶ **posag**

dowse = DOUSE

doz. = DOZEN

doze /dəʊz/ verb [I] to sleep lightly and/or for a short time: *He was dozing in front of the TV.* ▶ **drzemać**
■ **doze** noun [sing.] ▶ **drzemka**
PHR V **doze off** to go to sleep, especially during the day: *I'm sorry – I must have dozed off for a minute.* ▶ **zdrzemnąć się**

dozen /ˈdʌzn/ noun [C] (abbr. **doz.**) (pl. **dozen**) twelve or a group of twelve: *A dozen eggs, please.* ◇ *half a dozen* ◇ *two dozen sheep* ▶ **tuzin**
IDM **dozens (of sth)** (informal) very many ▶ **kilkadziesiąt**

dozy /ˈdəʊzi/ adj. **1** wanting to sleep; not feeling awake: *The wine had made her rather dozy.* ▶ **śpiący 2** (Brit., informal) stupid: not intelligent: *You dozy thing* (ty głupku) *– look what you've done!* ▶ **roztargniony, głupawy**

Dr = DOCTOR[1]

drab /dræb/ adj. not interesting or attractive: *a drab grey office building* ▶ **bezbarwny, nieciekawy**

draconian /drəˈkəʊniən/ adj. (formal) (used about a law, punishment, etc.) extremely cruel and severe: *a call for draconian measures against drug-related crime* ▶ **drakoński**

draft[1] /drɑːft; US dræft/ noun [C] **1** a piece of writing, etc. which will probably be changed and improved; not the final version: *the first draft of a speech/essay* ▶ **zarys, brudnopis 2** a written order to a bank to pay money to sb: *All payments must be made* ***by bank draft.*** ▶ **przelew 3** (US) = DRAUGHT[1] (1)

draft[2] /drɑːft; US dræft/ verb [T] **1** to make a first or early copy of a piece of writing: *I'll draft a letter and show it to you before I type it.* ▶ **pisać na brudno 2** [usually passive] (US) to force sb to join the armed forces: *He was drafted into* (został powołany do) *the army.* ▶ **przeprowadzać pobór** (*do wojska*)

draftsman (US) = DRAUGHTSMAN

drafty (US) = DRAUGHTY

drag[1] /dræg/ verb (**dragging**; **dragged**) **1** [T] to pull sb/sth along with difficulty: *The box was so heavy we had to drag it along the floor.* ▶ **ciągnąć 2** [T] to make sb come or go somewhere: *She's always trying to drag me along to museums, but I'm not interested.* ◇ *Can I drag you away* (odciągnąć) *from the television?* ▶ **wlec 3** [I] **drag (on)** to be boring or to seem to last a long time: *The speeches dragged on for hours.* ▶ **przeciągać się, wlec się 4** [T] to move sth across the screen of the computer using the mouse: *Click on the file and drag it into the new folder.* ▶ **przeciągać**
PHR V **drag sth out** to make sth last longer than necessary: *Let's not drag this decision out – shall we go or not?* ▶ **przedłużać/przeciągać coś**
drag sth out (of sb) to force or persuade sb to give you information ▶ **wyciągać coś (z kogoś)**

drag[2] /dræg/ noun **1** [sing.] (informal) a person or thing that is boring or annoying: *'The car's broken down.' 'Oh no! What a drag!'* ▶ **nuda, kłopot 2** [C] an act of breathing in cigarette smoke: *He took a long drag on his cigarette* (głęboko zaciągnął się). ▶ **zaciągnięcie się** (*papierosem*) **3** [U] clothes that are usually worn by the opposite sex (usually women's clothes worn by men): *men* ***in drag*** ▶ **przebieranie się za kobietę**

dragon /ˈdrægən/ noun [C] (in stories) a large animal with wings, which can breathe fire ▶ **smok**

dragonfly /ˈdrægənflaɪ/ noun [C] (pl. **dragonflies**) an insect with a long thin body and a pair of wings, often seen near water ▶ **ważka** ➲ picture at **insect**

drain[1] /dreɪn/ verb **1** [I,T] to become empty or dry as liquid flows away and disappears; to make sth dry or empty in this way: *The whole area will have to be drained before it can be used for farming.* ◇ *Drain the pasta* (odcedź makaron) *and add the sauce.* ▶ **odwadniać (się) 2** [I,T] **drain (sth) (from/out of sth)**; **drain (sth) (away/off)** to flow away; to make a liquid flow away: *The sink's blocked – the water won't drain away at all.* ◇ *The plumber had to drain the water from the heating system.* ▶ **odprowadzać wodę, odpływać 3** [T] to drink all the liquid in a glass, cup, etc.: *He drained his glass in one gulp.* ▶ **wypić do dna 4** [T] **drain sb/sth (of sth)** to make sb/sth weaker, poorer, etc. by slowly using all the strength, money, etc. available: *Her hospital expenses were slowly draining my funds.* ◇ *The experience left her* ***emotionally drained.*** ▶ **osłabiać, zużywać 5** [I] (used about a feeling) to become weaker and weaker until it disappears: *He felt all his anger begin to drain away.* ▶ (*złość itp.*) **przechodzić**

drain[2] /dreɪn/ noun [C] a pipe or hole in the ground that dirty water, etc. goes down to be carried away ▶ **ściek**
IDM **(go) down the drain** (informal) (to be) wasted: *All that hard work has gone down the drain.* ▶ **marnować się**
a drain on sb/sth something that uses up time, money, strength, etc.: *The cost of travelling is a great drain on our budget.* ▶ **obciążenie** (*np. finansowe*)

drainage /ˈdreɪnɪdʒ/ noun [U] a system used for making water, etc. flow away from a place ▶ **kanalizacja**

ˈdraining board noun [C] the place in the kitchen where you put plates, cups, knives, etc. to dry after washing them ▶ **suszarka do naczyń**

drainpipe /ˈdreɪnpaɪp/ noun [C] a pipe which goes down the side of a building and carries water from the roof into a **drain** ▶ **rynna odpływowa**

drake /dreɪk/ noun [C] a male **duck** ▶ **kaczor** ➲ note at **duck**

drama /ˈdrɑːmə/ noun **1** [C] a play for the theatre, radio or TV: *a contemporary drama* ▶ **dramat**, **sztuka teatralna 2** [U] plays as a form of writing; the performance of plays: *He wrote some drama, as well as poetry.* ▶ **sztuka dramatyczna** ➲ note at **literature 3** [C,U] an exciting event; exciting things that happen: *a real-life courtroom drama* ◇ *Why is there so little drama in my life?* Dlaczego moje życie jest takie nudne? ◇ *...and to add to all the drama* (i na dobitkę), *the lights went out!* ▶ **porywające przeżycie**; **podniecenie**

dramatic /drəˈmætɪk/ adj. **1** noticeable or sudden and often surprising: *a dramatic change/increase/fall/improvement* ▶ **nagły**, **gwałtowny 2** exciting or impressive: *the film's dramatic opening scene* ▶ **dramatyczny 3** connected with plays or the theatre: *Shakespeare's dramatic works* ▶ **dramatyczny 4** (used about a person, sb's behaviour, etc.) showing feelings, etc. in a very obvious way because you want other people to notice you ▶ **dramatyczny**
■ **dramatically** /-kli/ adv. ▶ **dramatycznie**

dramatist /ˈdræmətɪst/ noun [C] a person who writes plays for the theatre, radio or TV ▶ **dramaturg** SYN **playwright**

dramatize (also -ise) /ˈdræmətaɪz/ verb **1** [T] to make a book, an event, etc. into a play: *The novel has been dramatized for TV.* ▶ (*scenicznie*) **adaptować 2** [I,T] to make sth seem more exciting or important than it really is: *The newspaper was accused of dramatizing the facts.* ▶ **dramatyzować**
■ **dramatization** (also -isation) /ˌdræmətaɪˈzeɪʃn/ noun [C,U] ▶ **dramatyzacja**, **adaptacja**

drank past tense of **drink**[2]

drape /dreɪp/ verb [T] **1 drape sth round/over sth** to put a piece of cloth, clothing, etc. on sth in a loose way: *He draped his coat over the back of his chair.* ▶ **zawijać/owijać wokół czegoś 2** [usually passive] **drape sb/sth (in/with sth)** to cover sb/sth (with cloth, etc.): *The furniture was draped in dust sheets.* ▶ **przykrywać** (*np. tkaniną*)
■ **drape** noun [C] (US) = CURTAIN (1)

drastic /ˈdræstɪk/ adj. extreme, and having a sudden very strong effect: *a drastic rise in crime* ▶ **drastyczny**, **ostry**
■ **drastically** /-kli/ adv. ▶ **drastycznie**, **ostro**

draught[1] /drɑːft/ noun **1** (US **draft**) [C] a flow of cold air that comes into a room: *Can you shut the door? There's a draught in here.* ▶ **przeciąg 2** (**draughts**) (US **checkers** /ˈtʃekəz/) [U] a game for two players that you play on a black and white board using round black and white pieces ▶ **warcaby**
■ **draughty** adj. ▶ **z przeciągami**

draught[2] /drɑːft/ adj. (used about beer, etc.) served from a **barrel** rather than a bottle: *draught beer* ▶ (*piwo*) **beczkowy**, **z beczki**

draughtsman /ˈdrɑːftsmən/ (US **draftsman** /ˈdræftsmən/) noun [C] (pl. **-men** /-mən/) a person whose job is to do technical drawings ▶ **kreślarz**

draw[1] /drɔː/ verb (pt **drew** /druː/, pp **drawn** /drɔːn/) **1** [I,T] to make a picture or diagram of sth with a pencil, pen, etc. but not paint: *Shall I draw you a map of how to get there?* ◇ *I'm good at painting but I can't draw.* ▶ **rysować**, **szkicować 2** [T] to pull sth/sb into a new position or in the direction mentioned: *She drew the letter out of* (wyciągnęła list z) *her pocket and handed it to me.* ◇ *The cowboy drew his gun* (wyciągnął broń). ◇ *to draw the curtains* zasuwać/odsłaniać zasłony ◇ *He drew me by the hand into the room.* Wziął mnie za rękę i wprowadził do pokoju. ◇ *Why don't you draw your chair up to the fire?* Przysuń swoje krzesło do ognia. ◇ *The carriage was drawn by six horses.* Powóz ciągnęło sześć koni. ▶ **pociągać 3** [I] to move in the direction mentioned: *The train drew into the station* ◇ *I became more anxious as my exams drew nearer* (zbliżały się egzaminy). ▶ **przyjeżdżać/odjeżdżać 4** [T] **draw sth (from sb/sth)** to get or take sth from sb/sth: *He draws the inspiration for his stories from his family.* Inspirację do pisania powieści czerpie ze swojej rodziny. ▶ **uzyskać 5** [T] **draw sth (from sb)**; **draw sb (to sb/sth)** to make sb react to or be interested in sb/sth: *The advertisement has drawn criticism from people all over the country.* ◇ *The musicians drew quite a large crowd.* ◇ *She had always been drawn to older men.* Zawsze pociągali ją starsi mężczyźni. ▶ **przyciągać 6** [T] **draw sth (from sth)** to learn or decide sth as a result of study, research or experience: *Can we* ***draw*** *any* ***conclusions*** *from this survey?* ◇ *There are important* ***lessons to be drawn*** *from this tragedy.* ▶ **wyciągać 7** [I,T] to finish a game, competition, etc. with equal scores so that neither person or team wins: *The two teams drew.* ◇ *The match was drawn.* Mecz zakończył się remisem. ▶ **remisować**

IDM **bring sth/come/draw to an end** → END[1]

draw (sb's) attention to sth to make sb notice sth: *The article draws attention to the problem of homelessness.* ▶ **zwracać czyjąś uwagę na coś**

draw a blank to get no result or find no answer: *Detectives investigating the case have drawn a blank so far.* ▶ **doznawać zawodu**

draw a distinction between sth and sth to show how two things are different ▶ **odróżniać coś od czegoś**

draw a comparison/a parallel to show how two things compare or are similar: *The programme drew an interesting comparison between Britain and Japan.* ▶ **porównywać**

draw the line at sth/doing sth to say 'no' to sth even though you are happy to help in other ways: *I do most of the cooking but I draw the line at washing up as well* (ale nie ma mowy, abym też zmywał)*!* ▶ **wykluczać coś**

draw lots to decide sth by chance: *They drew lots to see who should stay behind.* ▶ **ciągnąć losy**

PHR V **draw in 1** to get dark earlier as winter arrives: *The days/nights are drawing in.* ▶ **skracać się 2** (used about cars, buses, etc.) to go to the side of the road and stop ▶ **zatrzymywać się**

draw out 1 (used about days) to get longer in the spring ▶ **wydłużać się 2** (used about cars, buses, etc.) to move out from the side of the road where they have stopped ▶ **wyruszać** (*po krótkim postoju*)

draw sth out to take money out of a bank account: *How much cash do I need to draw out?* ▶ **podejmować** (*pieniądze z banku*)

draw up (used about a car, etc.) to drive up and stop in front of or near sth: *A police car drew up outside the building.* ▶ **podjechać**

draw sth up to prepare and write a document, list, etc.: *Our solicitor is going to draw up the contract.* ▶ **sporządzać coś**

draw[2] /drɔː/ noun [C] **1** an act of deciding sth by chance by pulling out names or numbers from a bag, etc.: *a prize draw* ▶ **losowanie 2** a result of a game or competition in which both players or teams get the same score so that neither of them wins: *The match* ***ended in a draw.*** ▶ **remis**

drawback /ˈdrɔːbæk/ noun [C] a disadvantage or problem: *His lack of experience is a major drawback.* ▶ **wada** SYN **disadvantage**

drawer /drɔː(r)/ noun [C] a container which forms part of a piece of furniture such as a desk, that you can pull out to put things in ▶ **szuflada**

D

drawing /ˈdrɔːɪŋ/ noun **1** [C] a picture made with a pencil, pen, etc. but not paint: *He **did a drawing** of the building.* ▶ **rysunek** ➲ note at **painting 2** [U] the art of drawing pictures ▶ **rysowanie**

ˈ**drawing pin** (US **thumbtack** /ˈθʌmtæk/) noun [C] a short pin with a flat top, used for fastening paper, etc. to a board or wall ▶ **pinezka**, **pluskiewka** ➲ picture at **stationery**

ˈ**drawing room** noun [C] (old-fashioned) a living room, especially in a large house ▶ **salon**

drawl /drɔːl/ verb [I,T] to speak slowly, making the vowel sounds very long ▶ (*przy wymawianiu*) **zaciągać**
■ **drawl** noun [sing.]: *to speak with a drawl* ▶ (*typ wymowy*) **zaciąganie**

drawn[1] past participle of **draw**[1]

drawn[2] /drɔːn/ adj. (used about a person or their face) looking tired, worried or ill: *He looked pale and drawn after the long journey.* ▶ **wyczerpany**

ˌ**drawn-ˈout** adj. lasting longer than necessary: *long drawn-out negotiations* ▶ **przeciągający się**

drawstring /ˈdrɔːstrɪŋ/ noun [C] a piece of string that is sewn inside the material at the top of a bag, pair of trousers, etc. that can be pulled tighter in order to make the opening smaller ▶ **sznurek/tasiemka do ściągania** ➲ picture at **button**

dread[1] /dred/ verb [T] to be very afraid of or worried about sth: *I'm dreading the exams.* ◇ *She dreaded having to tell him what had happened.* ◇ *I **dread to think** (boję się pomyśleć) what my father will say.* ▶ **lękać się**
■ **dreaded** adj. ▶ **straszny**

dread[2] /dred/ noun [U, sing.] great fear: *He lived **in dread of** the same thing happening to him.* Żył w ciągłym strachu, że ta sama rzecz znowu mu się nie przydarzy. ▶ **strach**

dreadful /ˈdredfl/ adj. very bad or unpleasant: *I'm afraid there's been a dreadful mistake.* ▶ **okropny** SYN **terrible** ➲ note at **bad**

dreadfully /ˈdredfəli/ adv. **1** very; extremely: *I'm dreadfully sorry – I didn't mean to upset you.* ▶ **strasznie** **2** very badly: *The party went dreadfully* (przyjęcie było okropne) *and everyone left early.* ▶ **okropnie**

dreadlocks /ˈdredlɒks/ noun [pl.] hair worn in long thick pieces, especially by some black people ▶ **dredy** ➲ picture at **hair**

dream[1] /driːm/ noun **1** [C] a series of events or pictures which happen in your mind while you are asleep: *I **had** a strange **dream** last night.* ◇ *That horror film has given me **bad dreams**.* ▶ **sen** ➲ look at **nightmare 2** [C] something that you want very much to happen, although it is not likely: *His dream was to give up his job and live in the country.* ◇ *My dream house would have a huge garden and a swimming pool.* ◇ *Becoming a professional dancer was **a dream come true*** (było spełnieniem marzeń) *for Nicola.* ▶ **marzenie 3** [sing.] a state of mind in which you are not thinking about what you are doing: *You've been in a dream all morning!* Całe przedpołudnie jesteś (myślami) gdzieś indziej! ▶ **oszołomienie**

dream[2] /driːm/ verb (pt, pp **dreamed** /driːmd/ or **dreamt** /dremt/) **1** [I,T] **dream (about sb/sth)** to see or experience pictures and events in your mind while you are asleep: *I dreamt about the house that I lived in as a child.* ◇ *I dreamed that I was running but I couldn't get away.* ▶ **śnić (się)** ➲ look at **daydream 2** [I] **dream (about/of sth/doing sth)** to imagine sth that you would like to happen: *I've always dreamt about winning lots of money.* ▶ **marzyć 3** [I] **dream (of doing sth/that ...)** to imagine that sth might happen: *I **wouldn't dream of*** (nigdy nie przyszłoby mi do głowy) *telling Stuart that I don't like his music.* ◇ *When I watched the Olympics on TV, I **never dreamt** that one day I'd be here competing!* ▶ **marzyć/śnić o zrobieniu czegoś**
PHR V **dream sth up** (informal) to think of a plan, an idea, etc., especially sth strange: *Which of you dreamt up that idea?* ▶ **wymyślać coś**

dreamer /ˈdriːmə(r)/ noun [C] a person who thinks a lot about ideas, plans, etc. which may never happen instead of thinking about real life ▶ **marzyciel/ka**

dreamt past tense, past participle of **dream**

dreamy /ˈdriːmi/ adj. (**dreamier**; **dreamiest**) looking as though you are not paying attention to what you are doing because you are thinking about sth else: *a dreamy look/expression* ▶ **marzycielski**
■ **dreamily** adv. ▶ **marzycielsko**

dreary /ˈdrɪəri/ adj. (**drearier**; **dreariest**) not at all interesting or attractive; boring: *His dreary voice sends me to sleep.* ▶ **ponury**, **nudny**

dredge /dredʒ/ verb [T] to clear the mud, etc. from the bottom of a river, **canal**, etc. using a special machine ▶ **szlamować**, **bagrować**
PHR V **dredge sth up** to mention sth unpleasant from the past that sb would like to forget: *The newspaper had dredged up all sorts of embarrassing details about her private life.* ▶ **wyciągać coś przykrego z przeszłości**

dredger /ˈdredʒə(r)/ noun [C] a boat or machine that is used to clear mud, etc. from the bottom of a river, or to make the river wider ▶ **pogłębiarka**

dregs /dregz/ noun [pl.] **1** the last drops in a container of liquid, containing small pieces of solid waste ▶ **osad**, **fusy 2** the worst and most useless part of sth: *These people were regarded as the dregs of society.* ▶ **męty**

drench /drentʃ/ verb [T, usually passive] to make sb/sth completely wet: *We **got drenched*** (przemokliśmy) *in the storm.* ▶ **przemaczać**

dress[1] /dres/ noun **1** [C] a piece of clothing worn by a girl or a woman. It covers the body from the shoulders to the legs, sometimes reaching to below the knees or to the ankles: *a wedding dress* ▶ **suknia**, **sukienka 2** [U] clothes for either men or women: *formal/casual dress* ◇ *He was wearing Bulgarian national dress* (strój narodowy). ▶ **ubiór**, **ubranie**

dress[2] /dres/ verb **1** [I,T] to put clothes on sb or yourself: *He dressed quickly and left the house.* ◇ *My husband dressed the children while I got breakfast ready.* ◇ *Hurry up! Aren't you dressed yet?* ▶ **ubierać (się)** OPP **undress** ➲ note at **routine** ℹ Powszechnie mówi się **get dressed**, a nie **dress**. **2** [I] to put or have clothes on, in the way or style mentioned: *to dress well/badly/casually* ◇ *to be well dressed/badly dressed/casually dressed* ▶ **ubierać się 3** [T] to put a clean covering on the place on sb's body where they have been hurt: *to dress a wound* ▶ **opatrywać**
IDM **dressed in sth** wearing sth: *The people at the funeral were all dressed in black.* ▶ **ubrany w coś/na czarno itp.**
PHR V **dress up 1** to put on special clothes, especially in order to look like sb/sth else: *The children decided to dress up **as** pirates.* ▶ **przebierać się za kogoś/coś 2** to put on formal clothes, usually for a special occasion: *You don't need to dress up for the party.* ▶ **stroić się**

ˌ**dress ˈcircle** (US usually ˌ**first ˈbalcony**) noun [C] the first level of seats above the ground floor in a theatre ▶ (*teatr*) **pierwszy balkon**

dresser /ˈdresə(r)/ noun [C] **1** (especially Brit.) a piece of furniture with cupboards at the bottom and shelves above. It is used for holding dishes, cups, etc. ▶ **kredens 2** (US) a chest of drawers, usually with a mirror on top ▶ **toaletka**

dressing /ˈdresɪŋ/ noun **1** [C,U] a sauce for food, especially for salads ▶ **sos sałatkowy 2** [C] a covering that you put on a part of sb's body that has been hurt to protect it and keep it clean ▶ **opatrunek** **3** [U] the act or action of putting on clothes ▶ **ubieranie (się)**

'dressing gown (also **bathrobe** /'bɑːθrəʊb; US 'bæθ-/, US **robe**) noun [C] a piece of clothing like a loose coat with a belt, which you wear before or after a bath, before you get dressed in the morning, etc. ▶ **szlafrok**

'dressing table noun [C] a piece of furniture in a bedroom, which has drawers and a mirror ▶ **toaletka**

dressmaker /'dresmeɪke(r)/ noun [C] a person, especially a woman, who makes women's clothes ▶ **krawcowa** ■ **dressmaking** noun [U] ▶ **krawiectwo**

,dress re'hearsal noun [C] the final practice of a play in the theatre, using the clothes and lights that will be used for the real performance: (figurative) *The earlier protests had just been dress rehearsals for full-scale revolution.* ▶ (*i przen.*) **próba generalna**

dressy /'dresi/ adj. (**dressier**; **dressiest**) **1** (used about clothes) elegant and formal ▶ **elegancki**, **szykowny** **2** (used about people) liking to wear elegant or fashionable clothes ▶ **elegancki**, **szykowny**

drew past tense of **draw**[1]

dribble /'drɪbl/ verb **1** [I] to allow **saliva** to run out of the mouth: *Small children often dribble.* ▶ **ślinić się** **2** [I,T] (used about a liquid) to move downwards in a thin flow; to make a liquid move in this way: *The paint dribbled slowly down the side of the pot.* ▶ **kapać**, **sączyć (się)** **3** [I] (used in ball games) to make a ball move forward by using many short kicks or hits ▶ **dryblować**

dried[1] past tense, past participle of **dry**[2]

dried[2] /draɪd/ adj. (used about food) with all the liquid removed from it: *dried milk/fruit* ▶ **suszony**, (*mleko itp.*) **w proszku**

drier = DRYER

drift[1] /drɪft/ noun **1** [C] a slow movement towards sth: *the country's drift into economic decline* ▶ **tendencja**, **dążenie** **2** [C] a pile of snow or sand that was made by wind or water ▶ **zaspa**, **ławica** (*piasku*) **3** [sing.] the general meaning of sth: *I don't understand all the details of the plan but I **get the drift*** (rozumiem, o co chodzi). ▶ **wątek**, **ogólny sens**

drift[2] /drɪft/ verb [I] **1** to move slowly or without any particular purpose: *He drifted from room to room.* ◇ *She drifted into acting* (została aktorką) *almost by accident.* ▶ **chodzić bez celu**, **dryfować** **2** (used about snow or sand) to be moved into piles by wind or water: *The snow drifted up to two metres deep* (nawiało prawie dwa metry śniegu) *in some places.* **3** to be carried or moved along by wind or water: *The boat drifted out to sea.* ▶ **być unoszonym z prądem**, **dryfować**

PHR V **drift apart** to slowly become less close or friendly with sb: *At one time they were close friends, but over the years they've drifted apart.* ▶ (*przen.*) **oddalać się od siebie**

drill[1] /drɪl/ noun **1** [C] a tool or machine that is used for making holes in things: *a dentist's drill* ▶ **wiertarka**, **wiertło** ➲ picture at **tool** **2** [C] something that you repeat many times in order to learn sth ▶ **ćwiczenie** **3** [C,U] practice for what you should do in an emergency: *a fire drill* ▶ **próbny alarm** **4** [U] exercise in marching, etc. that soldiers do ▶ **musztra**

drill[2] /drɪl/ verb [I,T] **1** to make a hole in sth with a **drill**: *to drill a hole in something* ◇ *to drill for oil* ▶ **wiercić** **2** [T] to teach sb by making them repeat sth many times ▶ **ćwiczyć**, **musztrować**

drily (also **dryly**) /'draɪli/ adv. (used about the way sb says sth) in an amusing way that sounds serious ▶ **beznamiętnie**

⚷ **drink**[1] /drɪŋk/ noun [C,U] **1** liquid for drinking: *Can I **have a drink*** (coś do picia) *please?* ◇ *soft drinks* napoje bezalkoholowe ◇ *a drink of milk* kubek mleka ▶ **napój** **2** alcoholic drink: *He's got a drink problem.* Ma problem z alkoholem. ◇ *Shall we **go for a drink**?* Pójdziemy na drinka? ▶ **alkohol**, **trunek**

⚷ **drink**[2] /drɪŋk/ verb (pt **drank** /dræŋk/, pp **drunk** /drʌŋk/) **1** [I,T] to take liquid into your body through your mouth: *Would you like anything to drink?* ◇ *We sat drinking coffee and chatting for hours.* ▶ **pić** **2** [I,T] to drink alcohol: *I never **drink and drive*** (nigdy nie piję alkoholu, kiedy prowadzę samochód) *so I'll have an orange juice.* ◇ *What do you drink – beer or wine?* ◇ *Her father used to **drink heavily*** (pił dużo) *but he's teetotal now.* ▶ **pić** (*alkohol*)

PHR V **drink to sb/sth** to wish sb/sth good luck by holding your glass up in the air before you drink: *We all drank to the future of the bride and groom.* ▶ **pić czyjeś zdrowie**, **wznosić toast za kogoś/coś** ➲ look at **toast**

drink (sth) up to finish drinking sth: *Drink up your tea – it's getting cold.* ▶ **wypić/dopić coś**

,drink-'driver (also **,drunk-'driver**) noun [C] a person who drives after drinking too much alcohol ▶ **pijany kierowca**
■ **drink-driving** noun [U] ▶ **jazda samochodem po pijanemu** ➲ note at **driving**

drinker /'drɪŋkə(r)/ noun [C] a person who drinks a lot of sth, especially alcohol: *I'm not a big coffee drinker.* ◇ *a heavy* (nałogowy) *drinker* ▶ **pija-k/czka**

drinking /'drɪŋkɪŋ/ noun [U] drinking alcohol: *Her drinking became a problem.* ▶ **picie** (*alkoholu*), **pijaństwo**

'drinking water noun [U] water that is safe to drink ▶ **woda pitna**

drip[1] /drɪp/ verb (**dripping**; **dripped**) **1** [I] (used about a liquid) to fall in small drops: *Water is dripping down* (przecieka) *through the roof.* ▶ **kapać** **2** [I,T] to produce drops of liquid: *The tap is dripping.* Kapie z kranu. ◇ *Her finger was dripping blood.* ▶ **kapać**, **sączyć się**

drip[2] /drɪp/ noun **1** [sing.] the act or sound of water **dripping** ▶ **kapanie** **2** [C] a drop of water that falls down from sb/sth: *We put a bucket under the hole in the roof to catch the drips.* ▶ **kropla** **3** [C] a piece of medical equipment, like a tube, that is used for putting liquid food or medicine straight into sb's blood: *She's **on a drip*** (leży pod kroplówką). ▶ **kroplówka**

,drip-'dry adj. made of a type of cloth that will dry quickly without **creases** when you hang it up wet: *a drip-dry shirt* ▶ (*ubranie*) **nie wymagający wyżymania i prasowania**

'drip-feed verb [T] (**drip-fed**; **drip-fed**) to give sb sth in separate small amounts ▶ **(po)dawać coś komuś w małych ilościach**; **odżywiać dożylnie/pozajelitowo**

⚷ **drive**[1] /draɪv/ verb (pt **drove** /drəʊv/, pp **driven** /'drɪvn/) **1** [I,T] to control or operate a car, train, bus, etc.: *Can you drive?* ◇ *to drive a car/train/bus/lorry* ▶ **prowadzić** **2** [I,T] to go or take sb somewhere in a car, etc.: *I usually drive to work.* ◇ *We drove Maki to the airport.* ▶ **jeździć samochodem**; **wozić** **3** [T] to make a machine work, by giving it power: *What drives the wheels in this engine?* ▶ **napędzać** **4** [T] to cause sb to be in a particular state or to do sth: *His constant stupid questions **drive me mad**.* ◇ *to drive somebody to despair* ▶ **doprowadzać do czegoś** **5** [T] to make sb/sth work very hard: *You shouldn't drive yourself so hard.* ▶ **zamęczać** **6** [T] to force people or animals to move in a particular direction: *The dogs drove the sheep into the field.* ▶ **zaganiać**, **kierować** **7** [T] to force sth into a particular position by hitting it: *to drive a post into the ground* ◇ *From the tee, he drove the ball* (posłał piłkę) *into some trees.* ▶ **wbijać**

IDM **be driving at** (informal) to want to say sth; to mean ▶ **zmierzać do czegoś**

drive sth home (to sb) to make sth clear so that people understand it ▶ **wbijać (komuś) coś do głowy**

PHR V **drive off** (used about a car, driver, etc.) to leave ▶ **odjeżdżać**

drive sb/sth off to make sb/sth go away: *They kept a large dog outside to drive off burglars.* ▶ **odpychać kogoś/coś**

drive² /draɪv/ noun **1** [C] a journey in a car: *The supermarket is only a five-minute drive away.* ◇ *Let's* ***go for a drive.*** ▶ **jazda, przejażdżka 2** [U] the equipment in a vehicle that takes power from the engine to the wheels: *a car with four-wheel drive* ◇ *Almost all cars in Britain are left-hand drive* (mają kierownicę po lewej stronie). ▶ **napęd 3** [C] a wide path or short road that leads to the door of a house: *We keep our car on the drive.* ▶ **podjazd 4** [C] a big effort by a group of people in order to achieve sth: *The company is launching a big sales drive.* ▶ **kampania 5** [U] the energy and determination you need to succeed in doing sth: *You need lots of drive to run your own company.* ▶ **energia, zapał 6** [C,U] a strong natural need or desire: *a strong sex drive* (popęd) ▶ **dążność 7** [C] a long hard hit: *This player has the longest drive in golf.* ▶ **silne uderzenie 8** [C] the part of a computer that reads and stores information: *a CD drive* ◇ *a 10 GB hard drive* (twardy dysk) ▶ **napęd, stacja** (*dysków*) ➲ look at **disk drive 9** [C] a street, usually where people live: *They live at 23 Woodlands Drive.* ▶ **ulica**

'drive-by adj. [only before a noun] (US) (used about a shooting) done from a moving car: *drive-by killings* ▶ (*strzelanie*) **z jadącego samochodu**

'drive-in noun [C] (US) a place where you can eat, watch a film, etc. in your car ▶ **restauracja, kino itp. dla zmotoryzowanych, gdzie można korzystać z usług nie wysiadając z samochodu**

drivel /'drɪvl/ noun [U] (informal) silly nonsense: *How can you watch that drivel on TV?* ▶ **bzdury**

driven past participle of **drive¹**

driver /'draɪvə(r)/ noun [C] a person who drives a vehicle: *a bus/train driver* ▶ **kierowca**

driver's test (US) = DRIVING TEST

'drive-through noun [C] (especially US) a restaurant, bank, etc. where you can be served without getting out of your car ▶ **restauracja/bank itp. dla zmotoryzowanych**

driving¹ /'draɪvɪŋ/ noun [U] the action or skill of controlling a car, etc.: *She was arrested for dangerous driving.* ◇ *Joe's having* ***driving lessons.*** ◇ *She works as a* ***driving instructor.*** ◇ *a* ***driving school*** ▶ **jazda** (*samochodem*) ➲ note at **car, road**

IDM **be in the driving seat** to be the person, group, etc. that has the most powerful position in a particular situation ▶ **mieć najsilniejszą pozycję**

> **driving**
>
> You cannot **drive** unless you have passed your **driving test** and have a **driving licence. Motorists** should not **break the speed limit** or **drink and drive.** You can offer to take sb somewhere in your car by asking: *Can I give you a lift?* The **driver** and **passengers** should wear **seatbelts,** in case there is an **accident** /a **crash.** If the road is **congested,** for example during **rush hour,** you will probably find yourself stuck in a **traffic jam.**

driving² /'draɪvɪŋ/ adj. [only before a noun] very strong: *driving ambition* ◇ *Who's the driving force behind this plan?* ◇ *driving* (zacinający) *rain* ▶ **napędowy**

'driving licence (US 'driver's license) noun [C] an official document that shows that you are allowed to drive ▶ **prawo jazdy**

'driving school noun [C] an organization for teaching people to drive a car ▶ **szkoła jazdy**

'driving test (also **'driver's test; 'road test**) noun [C] a test that must be passed before you are qualified to drive a car, etc. ▶ **egzamin na prawo jazdy**

drizzle /'drɪzl/ noun [U] light rain with very small drops ▶ **mżawka**

■ **drizzle** verb [I] ▶ **mżyć** ➲ note at **weather**

drone /drəʊn/ verb [I] to make a continuous low sound: *the sound of the tractors droning away in the fields* ▶ **warczeć, buczeć**

■ **drone** noun [sing.] ▶ **warkot, buczenie**

PHR V **drone on** to talk in a flat or boring voice: *We had to listen to the chairman drone on about sales for hours.* ▶ **mówić monotonnym głosem**

drool /dru:l/ verb [I] **1** to let **saliva** come out from the mouth, usually at the sight or smell of sth good to eat ▶ **ślinić się 2 drool (over sb/sth)** to show in a silly or exaggerated way that you want or admire sb/sth very much: *teenagers drooling over photographs of their favourite pop stars* ▶ **pożerać kogoś/coś wzrokiem**

droop /dru:p/ verb [I] to bend or hang downwards, especially because of weakness or because you are tired: *The flowers were drooping* (więdły) *without water.* ▶ **opadać, omdlewać**

■ **drooping** (also **droopy**) adj.: *a drooping moustache* ▶ **opadający, obwisły**

drop¹ /drɒp/ verb (**dropping; dropped**) **1** [T] to let sth fall: *That vase was very expensive. Whatever you do, don't drop it!* ◇ *The helicopters dropped* (zrzuciły) *food and medicine.* ▶ **upuszczać 2** [I] to fall: *At the end of the race she dropped to her knees exhausted.* ◇ *The parachutist dropped safely* (wylądował szczęśliwie) *to the ground.* ▶ **opadać, zniżać się 3** [I,T] to become lower; to make sth lower: *The temperature will drop to minus 3 overnight.* ◇ *They ought to drop their prices.* ◇ *to drop your voice* ▶ **spadać; obniżać (się), zniżać (się) 4** [T] **drop sb/sth (off)** to stop your car, etc. so that sb can get out, or in order to take sth out: *Drop me off at the traffic lights, please.* ◇ *I'll drop the parcel at your house.* ▶ **wysadzać kogoś z samochodu, podrzucać** (*np. przesyłkę*) **5** [T] **drop sb/sth (from sth)** to no longer include sb/sth in sth: *Joe has been dropped from the team.* ▶ **wyrzucać 6** [T] to stop doing sth: *I'm going to drop geography next term.* ▶ **zarzucać, rzucać**

IDM **drop dead** (informal) to die suddenly ▶ **paść trupem**

drop sb a line (informal) to write a letter to sb: *Do drop me a line when you've time.* ▶ **napisać parę słów do kogoś**

PHR V **drop back; drop behind (sb)** to move into a position behind sb else, because you are moving more slowly: *Towards the end of the race she dropped behind the other runners.* ▶ **pozostawać w tyle**

drop by; drop in (on sb) to go to sb's house on an informal visit or without having told them you were coming: *We were in the area so we thought we'd drop in and see you.* ▶ **wpadać (do kogoś)**

drop off (informal) to fall into a light sleep ▶ **zdrzemnąć się**

drop out (of sth) to leave or stop doing sth before you have finished: *His injury forced him to drop out of the competition.* ◇ *to drop out of college* rzucić szkołę ▶ **rezygnować z czegoś**

drop² /drɒp/ noun **1** [C] a very small amount of liquid that forms a round shape: *a drop of blood/rain* ▶ **kropla** ➲ picture at **bar 2** [C, usually sing.] a small amount of liquid: *I just have a drop of milk in my coffee.* ▶ **kropelka, łyk 3** [sing.] a fall to a smaller amount or level: *The job is much more interesting but it will mean a drop in salary.* ◇ *a drop in prices/temperature* ▶ **spadek, obniżka 4** [sing.] a distance down from a high point to a lower point: *a sheer drop of 40 metres to the sea* ▶ **spadek** (*np. terenu*) **5** (**drops**) [pl.] liquid medicine that you put into your eyes, ears or nose ▶ **krople**

IDM at the drop of a hat immediately; without having to stop and think about it ▶ **natychmiast, bez zastanowienia/wahania**

a drop in the ocean (US **a drop in the bucket**) an amount of sth that is too small or unimportant to make any real difference to a situation ▶ **kropla w morzu**

ˈdrop-dead adv. (informal) (used before an adjective to emphasize how attractive sb/sth is): *She's drop-dead gorgeous.* ▶ **odlotowo**

ˌdrop-down ˈmenu noun [C] a list which appears on your computer screen and that stays there until you choose one of the functions on it ▶ **menu rozwijane**

dropout /ˈdrɒpaʊt/ noun [C] **1** a person who leaves school, university, etc. before finishing their studies: *a university with a high dropout rate* ▶ **ktoś, kto nie skończył szkoły, studiów itp. 2** a person who does not accept the ideas and ways of behaving of the rest of society ▶ **odszczepieniec**

dropper /ˈdrɒpə(r)/ noun [C] a short glass tube that has a rubber end with air in it. A dropper is used for measuring drops of liquids, especially medicines. ▶ **kroplomierz** ➲ picture at **laboratory**

droppings /ˈdrɒpɪŋz/ noun [pl.] waste material from the bodies of small animals or birds ▶ **odchody**

dross /drɒs/ noun [U] **1** something of very low quality; the least valuable part of sth: *mass-produced dross* ▶ (*przen.*) **śmieci 2** a waste substance, especially that separated from a metal when it is melted: *The fire burns away the dross leaving the pure metal.* ▶ **odpady** (*zwł. żużlowe*)

drought /draʊt/ noun [C,U] a long period without rain: *two years of severe drought* ▶ **susza**

drove past tense of **drive**[1]

drown /draʊn/ verb **1** [I,T] to die in water because it is not possible to breathe; to make sb die in this way: *The girl fell into the river and drowned.* ◇ *Twenty people were drowned in the floods.* ▶ **topić (się) 2** [T] **drown sb/sth (out)** (used about a sound) to be so loud that you cannot hear sb/sth else: *His answer was drowned out by the music.* ▶ **zagłuszać**

drowsy /ˈdraʊzi/ adj. (**drowsier**; **drowsiest**) tired and almost asleep: *The heat made me feel drowsy.* ▶ **senny**
■ **drowsily** adv. ▶ **sennie, ospale** | **drowsiness** noun [U] ▶ **senność, ospałość**

drudgery /ˈdrʌdʒəri/ noun [U] hard and boring work ▶ **harówka**

⚷ **drug**[1] /drʌg/ noun [C] **1** a chemical which people use to give them pleasant or exciting feelings. It is illegal in many countries to use drugs: *He doesn't* ***take drugs.*** ◇ *She suspected her son was* ***on drugs*** (bierze narkotyki). ◇ *hard drugs such as heroin and cocaine* ◇ *soft drugs* ▶ **narkotyk 2** a chemical which is used as a medicine: *drug companies* ▶ **lekarstwo, lek**

drug[2] /drʌg/ verb [T] (**drugging**; **drugged**) **1** to give a person or an animal a chemical to make them or it go to asleep or become unconscious ▶ **usypiać 2** to put a drug into food or drink: *I think his drink was drugged.* ▶ **dodawać narkotyku lub środka usypiającego do jedzenia lub napoju**

ˈdrug addict noun [C] a person who cannot stop taking drugs ▶ **narkoman/ka**
■ **ˈdrug addiction** noun [U] ▶ **narkomania**

druggist (US) = CHEMIST (1)

⚷ **drugstore** (US) = CHEMIST (2)

⚷ **drum**[1] /drʌm/ noun [C] **1** a musical instrument like an empty container with plastic or skin stretched across the ends. You play a drum by hitting it with your hands or with sticks: *She plays the drums* (na perkusji) *in a band.* ▶ **bęben** ➲ note at **music 2** a round container: *an oil drum* ▶ **beczka**

drum[2] /drʌm/ verb (**drumming**; **drummed**) **1** [I] to play a drum ▶ **grać na bębnie 2** [I,T] to make a noise like a drum by hitting sth many times: *to drum your fingers on the table* ▶ **bębnić**

PHR V drum sth into sb to make sb remember sth by repeating it many times: *The importance of road safety should be drummed into children from an early age.* ▶ **wbijać komuś coś do głowy**

drum sth up to try to get support or business: *to drum up more custom* ▶ **zjednywać** (*np. klientów*)

drum

drumming her fingers

drummer /ˈdrʌmə(r)/ noun [C] a person who plays a drum or drums ▶ **perkusist-a/ka, dobosz/ka**

drumstick /ˈdrʌmstɪk/ noun [C] **1** a stick used for playing the drums ▶ **pałeczka 2** the lower leg of a chicken or similar bird that we cook and eat ▶ **nóżka** (*np. pieczonego kurczaka*)

⚷ **drunk**[1] /drʌŋk/ adj. [not before a noun] having drunk too much alcohol: *to get drunk* upijać się ▶ **pijany** OPP **sober**
■ **drunk** (also old-fashioned **drunkard** /ˈdrʌŋkəd/) noun [C] a person who often gets drunk ▶ **pija-k/czka (nałogowy/a)**

drunk[2] past participle of **drink**[2]

ˌdrunk ˈdriver (especially US) = DRINK-DRIVER

ˌdrunk ˈdriving (especially US) = DRINK-DRIVING

drunken /ˈdrʌŋkən/ adj. [only before a noun] **1** having drunk too much alcohol: *drunken drivers* ▶ **nietrzeźwy, pijany 2** showing the effects of too much alcohol: *drunken singing* ▶ **pijacki**
■ **drunkenly** adv. ▶ **po pijanemu** | **drunkenness** noun [U] ▶ **pijaństwo**

⚷ **dry**[1] /draɪ/ adj. (**drier**; **driest**) **1** without liquid in it or on it: *The washing isn't dry yet.* ◇ *The paint is dry now.* ◇ *Rub your hair dry* (wytrzyj włosy do sucha) *with a towel.* ◇ *In the summer the stream ran dry* (wysechł). ▶ **suchy** OPP **wet 2** having little or no rain: *a hot, dry summer* ◇ *a dry climate* ▶ **suchy** OPP **wet 3** not having enough natural oil: *a shampoo for dry hair* ▶ **suchy 4** not sweet: *a crisp dry white wine* ▶ **wytrawny 5** (used about what sb says, or sb's way of speaking) amusing, although it sounds serious: *He has a dry sense of humour.* Opowiada dowcipy z poważną miną. ▶ **wypowiedziany z poważną miną 6** not interesting: *dry legal documents* ▶ **nieciekawy, nudny 7** where no alcohol is allowed: *Saudi Arabia is a dry country.* ▶ **przestrzegający prohibicji**
■ **dryness** noun [U] ▶ **suchość; jałowość**
IDM be left high and dry → LEAVE[1]

⚷ **dry**[2] /draɪ/ verb [I,T] (**drying**; **dries**; pt, pp **dried**) to become dry; to make sth dry: *I hung my shirt in the sun to dry.* ◇ *to dry your hands on a towel* ▶ **suszyć (się), wycierać**

PHR V dry (sth) out to become or make sth become completely dry: *Don't allow the soil to dry out.* ▶ **wysychać, suszyć (się)**

dry up 1 (used about a river, etc.) to have no more water in it ▶ **wysychać 2** to stop being available: *Because of the recession a lot of building work has dried up.* ▶ **wyczerpywać się, kończyć się 3** to forget what you were going to say, for example because you are very nervous: *When he came on stage and saw the audience, he dried up completely.* ▶ **zaniemówić**

dry (sth) up to dry plates, knives, forks, etc. with a small piece of cloth after they have been washed ▶ **wycierać** (*naczynia*)

ˌdry-ˈclean verb [T] to clean clothes using special chemicals, without using water ▶ **czyścić chemicznie**

ˌdry-ˈcleaner's (also **cleaner's**) noun [C] the shop where you take your clothes to be cleaned ▶ **pralnia chemiczna** ➲ picture on **page A5**

dryer (also **drier**) /ˈdraɪə(r)/ noun [C] [often in compounds] a machine that you use for drying sth: *a hairdryer* ▶ **suszarka**

ˌdry ˈland noun [U] land, not the sea: *I was glad to be back on dry land again.* ▶ **stały ląd**

dryly = DRILY

DTP = DESKTOP PUBLISHING

dual /ˈdjuːəl; US ˈduː-/ adj. [only before a noun] having two parts: *to have dual nationality* ▶ **podwójny** SYN **double**

ˌdual ˈcarriageway (US **diˌvided ˈhighway**) noun [C] a wide road that has an area of grass or a fence in the middle to separate the traffic going in one direction from the traffic going in the other direction ▶ **droga/szosa szybkiego ruchu, droga dwupasmowa**

ˌdual-ˈpurpose adj. that can be used for two different purposes: *a dual-purpose vehicle* ▶ **dwufunkcyjny**

dub /dʌb/ verb [T] (**dubbing**; **dubbed**) **1** to give sb/sth a new or amusing name: *Bill Clinton was dubbed 'Slick Willy'.* ▶ **przezywać 2 dub sth (into sth)** to change the sound in a film so that what the actors said originally is spoken by actors using a different language: *I don't like foreign films when they're dubbed into English. I prefer subtitles.* ▶ **dubbingować** ➲ look at **subtitle 3** to make a piece of music by mixing different pieces of recorded music together ▶ **miksować** (*muzykę*)

dubious /ˈdjuːbiəs; US ˈduː-/ adj. **1 dubious (about sth/about doing sth)** not sure or certain: *I'm very dubious* (mam poważne wątpliwości) *about whether we're doing the right thing.* ▶ **niepewny 2** that may not be honest or safe: *dubious financial dealings* ▶ **podejrzany**
■ **dubiously** adv. ▶ **z powątpiewaniem, niepewnie**

duchess /ˈdʌtʃəs/ noun [C] a woman who has the same position as a **duke**, or who is the wife of a **duke** ▶ **księżna** ➲ look at **princess**

duck¹ /dʌk/ noun (pl. **ducks** or **duck**) **1** [C] a common bird that lives on or near water. **Ducks** have short legs, **webbed feet** for swimming and a wide beak. ▶ **kaczka**

> **ducks**
> A male duck is called a **drake** and a young duck is a **duckling**. Ducks **waddle** and **quack**. They have **webbed** feet.

2 [C] a female **duck** ▶ **kaczka 3** [U] the meat of a **duck**: *roast duck with orange sauce* ▶ **kaczka**

duck² /dʌk/ verb **1** [I,T] to move your head down quickly so that you are not seen or hit by sb/sth: *The boys ducked out of sight behind a high hedge.* ◇ *I had to duck my head down to avoid the low doorway.* ▶ **robić unik 2** [I,T] (informal) **duck (out of) sth** to try to avoid sth difficult or unpleasant: *She tried to duck out of apologizing.* ◇ *The President is trying to duck responsibility for the crisis.* ▶ **wykręcać się od czegoś 3** [T] to push sb's head underwater for a short time, especially when playing: *The kids were ducking each other in the pool.* ▶ **zanurzać**

duck

He ducked.

duckling /ˈdʌklɪŋ/ noun [C, U] a young **duck**; the meat of a young **duck** ▶ **kaczątko**; (*kulin.*) **kaczka** ➲ note at **duck**

duct /dʌkt/ noun [C] a tube that carries liquid, gas, etc.: *an air duct* przewód wentylacyjny ◇ *tear ducts* gruczoły łzowe ▶ **kanał, przewód**

dud /dʌd/ noun [C] (informal) a thing that cannot be used because it is not real or does not work properly: *a dud cheque* czek bez pokrycia ◇ *a dud coin* fałszywa moneta ◇ *I tried to light the firework but it was a dud* (felerny). ▶ **tandeta**

dude /duːd/ noun [C] (especially US, slang) a man ▶ **facet**

due¹ /djuː; US duː/ adj. **1 due to sb/sth** caused by or because of sb/sth: *His illness is probably due to stress.* ▶ **spowodowany czymś/przez kogoś, z powodu kogoś/czegoś**

> Puryści językowi używają **due to** wyłącznie po czasowniku **to be**: *The strike was due to poor working conditions.* Jednak w praktyce **due to** często używa się w tym samym znaczeniu co **owing to** i **because of**: *Due to/owing to/because of the bad weather many trains have been cancelled.*

2 be due (to do sth) [not before a noun] expected or planned to happen or arrive: *What time is the next train/bus/plane* (przyjeżdża następny pociąg/autobus/przylatuje następny samolot) *due (in)?* ◇ *The baby is due in May.* ◇ *The conference is due to start* (ma się rozpocząć) *in four weeks' time.* ▶ **mieć coś robić, spodziewać się 3** [not before a noun] having to be paid: *The rent is due on the fifteenth of each month.* ▶ **płatny 4 due (to sb)** that is owed to you because it is your right to have it: *Make sure you claim all the benefits that are due to you.* ▶ **należny 5 due for sth** expecting sth or having the right to sth: *I'm due for a pay rise.* Mogę się spodziewać podwyżki. ▶ **należący się komuś 6** [only before a noun] (formal) suitable or right: *After due consideration, I have decided to accept your offer.* ▶ **odpowiedni**
IDM **in due course** at some time in the future, quite soon: *All applicants will be informed of our decision in due course.* ▶ **we właściwym czasie**

due² /djuː; US duː/ adv. [used before *north, south, east* and *west*] exactly: *The aeroplane was flying due east.* ▶ **dokładnie** (*na wschód itp.*)

due³ /djuː; US duː/ noun
IDM **give sb his/her due** to be fair to a person: *She doesn't work very quickly, but to give Sarah her due, she is very accurate.* ▶ **oddawać komuś sprawiedliwość**

duel /ˈdjuːəl; US ˈduː-/ noun [C] a formal type of fight with guns or other weapons which was used in the past to decide an argument between two men ▶ **pojedynek**

duet /djuˈet; US du-/ (also **duo**) noun [C] a piece of music for two people to sing or play ▶ **duet** ➲ look at **solo**

duffel coat (also **duffle coat**) /ˈdʌfl kəʊt/ noun [C] a coat made of thick wool cloth with a **hood**. A duffle coat has **toggles**. ▶ **budrysówka**

dug past tense, past participle of **dig¹**

duke (also **Duke**) /djuːk; US duːk/ noun [C] a man of the highest social position ▶ **książę** ➲ look at **duchess, prince**

dull /dʌl/ adj. **1** not interesting or exciting; boring ▶ **nudny 2** not bright: *a dull and cloudy day* ◇ *The room is painted in dull colours.* ▶ **pochmurny, szary 3** not loud, sharp or strong: *Her head hit the floor with a dull thud.* ◇ *a dull pain* ▶ **tępy, przytłumiony** OPP **sharp**
■ **dullness** noun [U] ▶ **nuda; szarość; otępienie** | **dully** /ˈdʌlli/ adv. **1** in a dull way ▶ **nieciekawie, nudno 2** showing no interest ▶ **tępo, apatycznie**

ˌdull-ˈwitted adj. (old-fashioned) not understanding quickly or easily ▶ (*osoba*) **tępy, nierozgarnięty** SYN **stupid**

duly /ˈdjuːli; US ˈduː-/ adv. (formal) in the correct or expected way: *We all duly assembled at 7.30 as agreed.* Wszyscy zebrali się punktualnie o 7.30, jak ustalono. ▶ **należycie**

dumb /dʌm/ adj. **1** not able to speak: *to be deaf and dumb* ◇ (figurative) *They were **struck dumb*** (zaniemówili) *with amazement.* ▶ **niemy**; **oniemiały** ⓘ **Dumb** w tym znaczeniu może być odebrane jako obraźliwe. Lepiej używać słowa **speech-impaired**. **2** (informal) stupid ▶ **głupi**
■ **dumbly** adv.: *Ken did all the talking, and I just nodded dumbly.* ▶ **milcząco**

dumbfounded /dʌmˈfaʊndɪd/ adj. very surprised ▶ **oniemiały**

dummy /ˈdʌmi/ noun [C] (pl. **dummies**) **1** a model of the human body used for putting clothes on in a shop window or while you are making clothes: *a tailor's dummy* ▶ **manekin** **2** something that is made to look like sth else but that is not the real thing ▶ **atrapa** **3** (informal) a stupid person: *Don't just stand there like a dummy – help me!* ▶ **bałwan** **4** (US **pacifier** /ˈpæsɪfaɪə(r)/) a rubber object that you put in a baby's mouth to keep him/her quiet and happy ▶ **smoczek**
■ **dummy** adj. made to look real, although it is actually a copy which does not work: *dummy bullets* ślepe naboje ▶ **sztuczny**, **podrobiony**

🔑 **dump**¹ /dʌmp/ verb [T] **1** to get rid of sth that you do not want, especially in a place which is not suitable: *piles of rubbish dumped by the side of the road* ◇ *Nuclear waste should not be dumped* (nie wolno zatapiać odpadów nuklearnych) *in the sea.* ◇ (figurative) *I wish you wouldn't keep dumping all the extra work on me.* ▶ **wyrzucać**, (*i przen.*) **po(d)rzucać** **2** to put sth down quickly or in a careless way: *The children dumped their coats and bags in the hall and ran off to play.* ▶ **rzucać coś niedbale** **3** (informal) to get rid of sb, especially a boyfriend or girlfriend: *Did you hear that Laura dumped Chris last night?* ▶ **rzucać kogoś**

🔑 **dump**² /dʌmp/ noun [C] **1** a place where rubbish or waste material from factories, etc. is left: *a rubbish dump* ▶ **wysypisko śmieci** **2** (informal) a place that is very dirty, untidy or unpleasant ▶ **nora** SYN for both meanings **tip**
IDM **down in the dumps** → DOWN¹

ˈ**dumper truck** (US ˈ**dump truck**) noun [C] a lorry that carries material such as stones or earth in a special container which can be lifted up so that the load can fall out ▶ **wywrotka** ➲ picture at **truck**

dumpling /ˈdʌmplɪŋ/ noun [C] a small ball of **dough** that is cooked and usually eaten with meat ▶ **rodzaj kluski/knedla**

dumpy /ˈdʌmpi/ adj. (especially used about a person) short and fat ▶ **przysadzisty**

dune /djuːn; US duːn/ (also ˈ**sand dune**) noun [C] a low hill of sand by the sea or in the desert ▶ **wydma**

dung /dʌŋ/ noun [U] waste material from the bodies of large animals: *cow dung* ▶ **łajno**

dungarees /ˌdʌŋgəˈriːz/ (US **overalls**) noun [pl.] a piece of clothing, similar to trousers, but covering your chest as well as your legs and with narrow pieces of cloth that go over the shoulders: *a pair of dungarees* ▶ **kombinezon**, **spodnie ogrodniczki** ➲ picture at **overall**

dungeon /ˈdʌndʒən/ noun [C] an old underground prison, especially in a castle ▶ **loch**

dunk /dʌŋk/ verb **1** [T] **dunk sth (in/into sth)** to put food quickly into liquid before eating it: *She sat reading a magazine, dunking cookies in her coffee.* ▶ **maczać** (*np. sucharek w herbacie*) **2** [T] (especially US) to push sb underwater for a short time, as a joke; to put sth into water: *The camera survived being dunked in the river.* ▶ **zanurzać**

duo /ˈdjuːəʊ; US ˈduː-/ noun [C] (pl. **duos**) **1** two people playing music or singing together ▶ **duet** **2** = DUET

duodenum /ˌdjuːəˈdiːnəm/ noun [C] the first part of the small intestine, next to the stomach ▶ **dwunastnica** ➲ picture at **body**

dupe /djuːp; US duːp/ verb [T] to lie to sb in order to make them believe sth or do sth: *The woman was duped into carrying the drugs.* Kobieta została podstępem wciągnięta do przewożenia narkotyków. ▶ **wmieszać kogoś w coś wbrew jego woli**

D

duplicate¹ /ˈdjuːplɪkeɪt; US ˈduː-/ verb [T] **1** to make an exact copy of sth ▶ **powielać**, **kopiować** **2** to do sth that has already been done: *We don't want to duplicate the work of other departments.* ▶ **powielać**, **dublować**
■ **duplication** /ˌdjuːplɪˈkeɪʃn; US ˌduː-/ noun [U] ▶ **powielanie**

duplicate² /ˈdjuːplɪkət; US ˈduː-/ noun [C] something that is exactly the same as sth else ▶ **kopia**
■ **duplicate** adj. [only before a noun]: *a duplicate key* dorobiony klucz ▶ **identyczny**
IDM **in duplicate** with two copies (for example of an official piece of paper) that are exactly the same: *The contract must be in duplicate.* ▶ **w dwóch egzemplarzach**

durable /ˈdjʊərəbl; US ˈdʊər-/ adj. that can last a long time: *a durable fabric* ▶ **trwały**, **wytrzymały**
■ **durability** /ˌdjʊərəˈbɪləti/ noun [U] ▶ **trwałość**, **wytrzymałość**

duration /djuˈreɪʃn; US du-/ noun [U] the time that sth lasts: *Please remain seated for the duration of the flight.* ▶ **czas trwania (czegoś)**

duress /djuˈres; US du-/ noun [U] threats or force that are used to make sb do sth: *He signed the confession **under duress**.* ▶ **przymus**

🔑 **during** /ˈdjʊərɪŋ; US ˈdʊər-/ prep. within the period of time mentioned: *The audience must remain seated during the performance.* ◇ *During the summer holidays we went swimming every day.* ◇ *Grandpa was taken ill during the night* (w nocy). ▶ **podczas**

> Zwróć uwagę, że **during** używa się, by powiedzieć, kiedy coś się wydarzyło. Do określenia, jak długo coś trwało, używa się **for**: *I went shopping during my lunch break. I was out for about 25 minutes.* ➲ note at **ago**, **since**

dusk /dʌsk/ noun [U] the time in the evening when the sun has already gone down and it is nearly dark ▶ **zmierzch** ➲ look at **dawn**, **twilight**

🔑 **dust**¹ /dʌst/ noun [U] very small pieces of dry dirt, sand, etc. in the form of a powder: *a thick layer of dust* ◇ *chalk/coal dust* ◇ *The tractor came up the track in a cloud of dust.* ◇ *a speck of dust* pyłek ▶ **kurz**, **pył**
■ **dusty** adj. (**dustier**; **dustiest**) ▶ **zakurzony**

🔑 **dust**² /dʌst/ verb [I,T] to clean a room, furniture, etc. by removing dust with a cloth ▶ **ścierać kurze (z czegoś)**, **wycierać (coś) z kurzu** ➲ note at **clean**²

dustbin /ˈdʌstbɪn/ (US ˈ**garbage can**; ˈ**trash can**) noun [C] a large container for rubbish that you keep outside your house ▶ **(duży) pojemnik na śmieci** ➲ picture at **bin**

dustcart /ˈdʌstkɑːt/ (US ˈ**garbage truck**) noun [C] a vehicle for collecting rubbish from outside houses, etc. ▶ **śmieciarka**

duster /ˈdʌstə(r)/ noun [C] a soft dry cloth that you use for cleaning furniture, etc. ▶ **ścierka do kurzu**

dustman /ˈdʌstmən/ noun [C] (pl. **-men** /-mən/) a person whose job is to take away the rubbish that people put in **dustbins** ▶ **śmieciarz**

dustpan /ˈdʌstpæn/ noun [C] a flat container with a handle into which you brush dirt from the floor: *Where do* *you keep your* ***dustpan and brush?*** ▶ **szufelka** ➲ picture at **brush**

dutiful /ˈdjuːtɪfl; US ˈduː-/ adj. happy to respect and obey sb: *a dutiful son* ▶ **posłuszny**; **obowiązkowy**
■ **dutifully** /-fəli/ adv. ▶ **posłusznie**, **obowiązkowo**

⚷ **duty** /ˈdjuːti; US ˈduː-/ noun (pl. **duties**) **1** [C,U] something that you have to do because people expect you to do it or because you think it is right: *A soldier must* ***do*** *his* ***duty.*** ◇ *a sense of moral duty* ▶ **obowiązek 2** [C,U] the tasks that you do when you are at work: *the duties of a policeman* ◇ *Which nurses are on night duty this week?* ▶ **obowiązek**, **służba**, **dyżur 3** [C] a tax that you pay, especially on goods that you bring into a country: *import duty* ▶ **cło**
IDM **on/off duty** (used about doctors, nurses, police officers, etc.) to be working/not working: *The porter's on duty from 8 till 4.* ◇ *What time does she go off duty?* O której godzinie ona kończy dyżur? ▶ **na/po dyżurze**

ˌ**duty-ˈfree** adj. (used about goods) that you can bring into a country without paying tax: *an airport duty-free shop* ▶ **wolnocłowy**
■ **duty-free** adv.: *I bought this wine duty-free.* ▶ **bez cła** ➲ look at **tax-free**

duvet /ˈduːveɪ/ noun [C] a thick cover filled with feathers or another soft material that you sleep under to keep warm in bed ▶ **kołdra**, **pierzyna** ➲ look at **eiderdown**, **quilt** ➲ picture at **bed**

DVD /ˌdiː viː ˈdiː/ noun [C] **digital videodisc** or **digital versatile disc**; a disk on which large amounts of information, especially photographs and video, can be stored, for use on a computer or DVD player: *Is it available* ***on DVD*** *yet?* ◇ *a DVD-ROM drive* ▶ **DVD**

DVT = DEEP VEIN THROMBOSIS

dwarf[1] /dwɔːf/ noun [C] (pl. **dwarfs** or **dwarves** /dwɔːvz/) **1** (in children's stories) a very small person ▶ **krasnoludek**, **ka-rzełek/rliczka 2** a person, animal or plant that is much smaller than the usual size ▶ **ka-rzeł/rlica**, **miniatura** (*zwierzę lub roślina*)

dwarf[2] /dwɔːf/ verb [T] (used about a large object) to make sth seem very small in comparison: *The skyscraper dwarfs all the other buildings around.* ▶ **pomniejszać**, **przytłaczać**

dwell /dwel/ verb [I] (pt, pp **dwelt** /dwelt/ or **dwelled**) (old-fashioned, formal) to live or stay in a place ▶ **mieszkać**, **rezydować**
PHR V **dwell on/upon sth** to think or talk a lot about sth that it would be better to forget: *I don't want to dwell on the past. Let's think about the future.* ▶ **rozwodzić się nad czymś**

dweller /ˈdwelə(r)/ noun [C] [in compounds] a person or an animal that lives in the place mentioned: *city dwellers* ▶ **mieszkan-iec/ka**

dwelling /ˈdwelɪŋ/ noun [C] (formal) the place where a person lives; a house ▶ **mieszkanie**, **dom**

dwelt past tense, past participle of **dwell**

dwindle /ˈdwɪndl/ verb [I] **dwindle (away)** to become smaller or weaker: *Their savings dwindled away to nothing* (skurczyły się do zera). ▶ **zmniejszać się**; **słabnąć**

dye[1] /daɪ/ verb [T] (**dyeing**; **dyes**; pt, pp **dyed**) to make sth a different colour: *Does she dye her hair?* ◇ *I'm going to dye this blouse black.* ▶ **farbować**

dye[2] /daɪ/ noun [C,U] a substance that is used to change the colour of sth ▶ **farba**

⚷ **dying** present participle of **die**

dyke (also **dike**) /daɪk/ noun [C] **1** a long thick wall that is built to prevent the sea or a river from covering low land with water ▶ **grobla**, **tama 2** (especially Brit.) a long narrow space dug in the ground and used for taking water away from land ▶ **rów odwadniający**

dynamic /daɪˈnæmɪk/ adj. **1** (used about a person) full of energy and ideas; active ▶ **prężny 2** (used about a force or power) that causes movement ▶ **dynamiczny**
■ **dynamism** /ˈdaɪnəmɪzəm/ noun [U] ▶ **prężność** (*działania*)

dynamics /daɪˈnæmɪks/ noun **1** [pl.] the way in which people or things behave and react to each other in a particular situation ▶ (*przen.*) **dynamika 2** [U] the scientific study of the forces involved in movement: *fluid dynamics* ▶ **dynamika**

dynamite /ˈdaɪnəmaɪt/ noun [U] **1** a powerful substance which can explode ▶ **dynamit 2** a thing or person that causes great excitement, shock, etc.: *His news was dynamite.* ▶ **dynamit**, **bomba**

dynamo /ˈdaɪnəməʊ/ noun [C] (pl. **dynamos**) a device that changes energy from the movement of sth such as wind or water into electricity ▶ **dynamo** (*maszyna*), **prądnica**

dynasty /ˈdɪnəsti; US ˈdaɪ-/ noun [C] (pl. **dynasties**) a series of rulers who are from the same family ▶ **dynastia**

dysentery /ˈdɪsəntri; US -teri/ noun [U] a serious disease which causes you to have **diarrhoea** and to lose blood ▶ **czerwonka**, **dyzenteria**

dyslexia /dɪsˈleksiə/ noun [U] a difficulty that some people have with reading and spelling ▶ **dysleksja**
■ **dyslexic 1** noun [C] ▶ **dyslekty-k/czka 2** adj. ▶ **dyslektyczny**

Ee

E, e /iː/ noun [C,U] (pl. **Es**; **es**; **E's**; **e's** /iːz/) **2** the fifth letter of the English alphabet: *'Egg' begins with (an) 'E'.* ▶ **litera** *e* **2** (used about music) the third note in the series of notes called the scale of C major: *E major* E-dur ◇ *E minor* e-moll ◇ *E flat* Es, es ▶ **E/e**

E abbr. = EAST[1], EASTERN (1): *E Asia*

e- /iː/ [in compounds] connected with the use of electronic communication, especially the Internet, for sending information, doing business, etc.: *e-commerce* ◇ *e-business* ▶ **elektroniczny**

⚷ **each** /iːtʃ/ determiner, pron. (abbr. **ea**) every individual person or thing: *Each lesson lasts an hour.* ◇ *Each of the lessons lasts an hour.* ◇ *The lessons each last an hour.* ◇ *These T-shirts are £5 each.* ▶ **każdy**

⚷ ˌ**each ˈother** pron. (used for saying that A does the same thing to B as B does to A): *Emma and Dave love each other very much.* ◇ *We looked at each other.* ▶ **się**, **siebie**, **sobie (nawzajem)**

eager /ˈiːɡə(r)/ adj. **eager (to do sth)**; **eager (for sth)** full of desire or interest: *We're all eager to start work on the new project.* ◇ *eager for success* ▶ **ochoczy**, **chętny** SYN **keen**
■ **eagerly** adv. ▶ **ochoczo**, **chętnie** | **eagerness** noun [U] ▶ **zapał**, **gorliwość**

eagle /ˈiːɡl/ noun [C] a very large bird that can see very well. It eats small birds and animals. ▶ **orzeł**

EAP /ˌiː eɪ ˈpiː/ abbr. **English for Academic Purposes** ▶ **specjalistyczny angielski do celów naukowych**

⚷ **ear** /ɪə(r)/ noun **1** [C] one of the two parts of the body of a person or an animal that are used for hearing: *He pulled his hat down over his ears.* ▶ **ucho** ➲ picture at **body** ➲ picture on **page A10 2** [sing.] **an ear (for sth)** an ability to recognize and repeat sounds, especially in music or language: *Kimiko has a good ear for languages.* ▶ **słuch**, **(muzykalne) ucho 3** [C] the top part of a plant that produces grain: *an ear of corn* ▶ **kłos**

IDM **sb's ears are burning** (used when a person thinks that other people are talking about them, especially in an unkind way) ▶ **palą kogoś uszy**
go in one ear and out the other (used about information, etc.) to be forgotten quickly: *Everything I tell him seems to go in one ear and out the other.* ▶ **wpadać jednym uchem, wypadać drugim**
play (sth) by ear to play a piece of music that you have heard without using written notes: *She can read music, but she can also play by ear.* ▶ **grać ze słuchu**
play it by ear to decide what to do as things happen, instead of planning in advance: *We don't know what Alan's reaction will be, so we'll just have to play it by ear.* ▶ **improwizować**
prick up your ears → PRICK[1]

earache /ˈɪəreɪk/ noun [U] a pain in your ear: *I've got earache.* ▶ **ból u-cha/szu** ➲ note at **ache**

eardrum /ˈɪədrʌm/ noun [C] a thin piece of skin inside the ear that is tightly stretched and that allows you to hear sound ▶ **błona bębenkowa**

earl /ɜːl/ noun [C] a British man of a high social position ▶ **hrabia** ℹ Kobieta nosząca tytuł hrabiowski to **countess**.

ˈear lobe noun [C] the round soft part at the bottom of your ear ▶ **płatek** (*ucha*)

early[1] /ˈɜːli/ adj. (**earlier**; **earliest**) **1** near the beginning of a period of time, a piece of work, a series, etc.: *I think John's in his early twenties.* ◇ *The project is still only in its early stages.* ▶ **wczesny, początkowy 2** before the usual or expected time: *Spring is early* (przyszła za wcześnie) *this year.* ▶ **wczesny** OPP for both meanings **late**
IDM **at the earliest** not before the date or time mentioned: *I can repair it by Friday at the earliest.* ▶ **najwcześniej, najprędzej**
the early hours very early in the morning in the hours after midnight ▶ **wczesne godziny (poranne)**
an early/a late night → NIGHT
an early riser a person who usually gets up early in the morning ▶ **ranny ptaszek**
it's early days (yet) (used to say that it is too soon to know how a situation will develop) ▶ **jest za wcześnie** (*by coś wiedzieć itp.*)

early[2] adv. **1** near the beginning of a period of time, a piece of work, a series, etc.: *I have to get up early on weekday mornings.* ◇ *The tunnel will be finished early next year* (na początku przyszłego roku). ▶ **wcześnie 2** before the usual or expected time: *She arrived five minutes early for her interview.* ▶ **(za) wcześnie** OPP for both meanings **late**
IDM **early on** soon after the beginning: *He achieved fame early on in his career.* ▶ **na/z początku**

earmark /ˈɪəmɑːk/ verb [T] **earmark sb/sth (for sth/sb)** to choose sb/sth to do sth in the future: *Everybody says Ania has been earmarked as the next manager.* ▶ **przeznaczać, wyznaczać**

earn /ɜːn/ verb [T] **1** to get money by working: *How much does a dentist earn?* ◇ *I earn £20 000 a year.* ◇ *It's hard to* ***earn a living*** (zarabiać na życie) *as an artist.* ▶ **zarabiać, utrzymywać się (z czegoś) 2** to get money as profit or interest on money you have in a bank, lent to sb, etc.: *How much interest will my savings earn* (jakie będzie oprocentowanie moich oszczędności) *in this account?* ▶ **przynosić** (*np. procent, zysk*) **3** to win the right to sth, for example by working hard: *The team's victory today has earned them* (zapewniło im) *a place in the final.* ▶ **zapracowywać/zasługiwać na coś**

earnest /ˈɜːnɪst/ adj. serious or determined: *They were having a very earnest discussion.* ▶ **poważny, przejęty**
■ **earnestly** adv. ▶ **poważnie**
IDM **in earnest 1** happening more seriously or with more force than before: *After two weeks work began in earnest on the project.* ▶ **poważnie, (na) serio 2** serious and sincere about what you are going to do: *He was in earnest about wanting to leave university.* ▶ **poważnie, (na) serio**

earnings /ˈɜːnɪŋz/ noun [pl.] the money that a person earns by working ▶ **zarobki**

earphones /ˈɪəfəʊnz/ noun [pl.] a piece of equipment that fits over or in the ears and is used for listening to music, the radio, etc. ▶ **słuchawki**

earpiece /ˈɪəpiːs/ noun [C] the part of a telephone or piece of electrical equipment that you hold next to or put into your ear so that you can listen ▶ **głośnik** (*zwł. w słuchawce telefonu*), **słuchawka** (*zwł. wkładana do ucha*)

ˈear-piercing[1] adj. [only before a noun] very high, loud and unpleasant: *an ear-piercing scream* ▶ (*dźwięk*) **przenikliwy, rozdzierający**

ˈear-piercing[2] noun [U] the practice of making small holes in sb's ears so jewellery can be put in them ▶ **przekłuwanie uszu**

earplug /ˈɪəplʌɡ/ noun [usually pl.] a piece of soft material that you put into your ear to keep out noise or water ▶ **zatyczka do ucha**

earring /ˈɪərɪŋ/ noun [C] a piece of jewellery that is worn in or on the lower part of the ear: *Are these clip-on earrings or are they for pierced ears?* ▶ **kolczyk, klips**

earshot /ˈɪəʃɒt/ noun
IDM **(be) out of/within earshot** where a person cannot/can hear: *Wait until he's out of earshot before you say anything about him.* ▶ **(być) poza zasięgiem/w zasięgu słuchu**

earth[1] /ɜːθ/ noun **1** (**the earth**; **the Earth**) [sing.] the world; the planet on which we live: *life on earth* ◇ *The earth goes round the sun.* ▶ **ziemia, Ziemia** ➲ note at **space 2** [sing.] the surface of the world; land: *The spaceship fell towards earth.* ◇ *I could feel the earth shake when the earthquake started.* ▶ **ziemia 3** [U] the substance that plants grow in; soil: *The earth around here is very fertile.* ▶ **ziemia, gleba** ➲ note at **ground 4** [C, usually sing.] (US **ground**) a wire that makes a piece of electrical equipment safer by connecting it to the ground: *The green and yellow wire is the earth.* ▶ **uziemienie** ➲ picture at **plug**
IDM **charge/pay the earth** (informal) to charge/pay a very large amount of money: *Dan must have paid the earth for that new car.* ▶ **słono (za coś) policzyć/płacić**
cost the earth/a fortune → COST[2]
how/why/where/who etc. on earth (informal) (used for emphasizing sth or expressing surprise): *Where on earth have you been?* ▶ **gdzie/dlaczego itp. na litość boską ...?**

earth[2] /ɜːθ/ (US **ground**) verb [T] to make a piece of electrical equipment safer by connecting it to the ground with a wire: *Make sure the plug is earthed.* ▶ **uziemiać**

earthenware /ˈɜːθnweə(r)/ adj. made of very hard baked **clay** ▶ **ceramiczny**
■ **earthenware** noun [U] ▶ **wyroby ceramiczne**

earthly /ˈɜːθli/ **1** adj. (often in questions or negatives) possible: *There's* ***no earthly reason*** *why* (nie ma najmniejszego powodu, dla którego) *you shouldn't go.* ◇ *What earthly use is a gardening book to me* (po kiego licha mi książka o ogrodnictwie)*? I haven't got a garden!* ▶ **możliwy 2** connected with this world, not heaven ▶ **ziemski**

earthquake /ˈɜːθkweɪk/ (also informal **quake**) noun [C] sudden, violent movement of the earth's surface ▶ **trzęsienie ziemi**

earthworm /ˈɜːθwɜːm/ noun [C] a small, long, thin animal with no legs or eyes that lives in the soil ▶ **dżdżownica**

earthy /ˈɜːθi/ adj. (**earthier**; **earthiest**) **1** concerned with the body, sex, etc. in an open and direct way that some people find rude or embarrassing: *an earthy sense of humour* ▶ (*osoba*) **prostolinijny**, (*dowcip, komentarz itp.*) **pikantny 2** of or like earth or soil: *earthy colours* ▶ **ziemisty**
■ **earthiness** noun [U] ▶ **prostolinijność**, **pikanteria**; **ziemistość**

ease¹ /iːz/ noun [U] a lack of difficulty: *She answered the questions **with ease**.* ▶ **łatwość**
IDM **(be/feel) at (your) ease** to be/feel comfortable, relaxed, etc.: *They were all so kind and friendly that I felt completely at ease.* ▶ **być/czuć się spokojnym**, **być zrelaksowanym** ➲ adjective **easy**

ease² /iːz/ verb **1** [T] to move sth slowly and gently: *He eased* (ostrożnie wsunął) *the key into the lock.* ▶ **przesuwać ostrożnie 2** [I,T] to become or make sth less painful or serious: *The pain should ease by this evening.* ◇ *This money will ease their financial problems a little.* ▶ **zelżeć**; **łagodzić** ➲ adjective **easy**
IDM **ease sb's mind** to make sb feel less worried: *The doctor tried to ease her mind about her son's illness.* ▶ **uspokajać kogoś**
PHR V **ease off** to become less strong or unpleasant: *Let's wait until the rain eases off.* ▶ **zelżeć**, **popuszczać**
ease up to work less hard: *Ease up a bit or you'll make yourself ill!* ▶ **przyhamować**

easel /ˈiːzl/ noun [C] a wooden frame that holds a picture while it is being painted ▶ **sztaluga**

easily /ˈiːzəli/ adv. **1** without difficulty: *I can easily ring up and check the time.* ▶ **z łatwością**, **łatwo 2 easily the best, worst, nicest, etc.** without doubt: *It's easily his best novel.* ▶ **z pewnością**, **bez wątpienia**
■ **easiness** noun [U] ▶ **łatwość**

east¹ /iːst/ noun [sing.] (abbr. **E**) **1** (also **the east**) the direction you look towards in order to see the sun rise; one of the **points of the compass**: *Which way is east?* ◇ *a cold wind from the east* ◇ *Which county is **to the east of** Oxfordshire?* ▶ **wschód 2** (**the east**; **the East**) the part of any country, city, etc. that is further to the east than the other parts: *Norwich is in the east of England.* ▶ **wschód 3** (**the East**) the countries of Asia, for example China and Japan ▶ **Wschód** ➲ look at **Far East**, **Middle East**

east² /iːst/ adj. **1** (also **East**) [only before a noun] in the east: *the east coast* ▶ **wschodni 2** (used about a wind) coming from the east ▶ **wschodni**, **ze wschodu**
■ **east** adv. to or towards the east: *They headed east.* ◇ *We live east of the city.* ◇ *Is London east of Oxford?* ▶ **na wschód/wschodzie**

eastbound /ˈiːstbaʊnd/ adj. travelling or leading towards the east: *the eastbound carriageway of the motorway* ▶ (*jadący/idący itp.*) **w kierunku wschodnim/na wschód**

the ˌEast ˈEnd noun [U] (Brit.) an area of East London traditionally connected with the working class ▶ **część wschodniego Londynu**

Easter /ˈiːstə(r)/ noun [U] a festival on a Sunday in March or April when Christians celebrate Christ's return to life; the time before and after **Easter** Sunday: *the Easter holidays* ◇ *Are you going away **at Easter**?* ▶ **Wielkanoc**

ˈEaster egg noun [C] an egg, usually made of chocolate, that you give as a present at **Easter** ▶ **jajko wielkanocne**

easterly /ˈiːstəli/ adj. **1** [only before a noun] towards or in the east: *They travelled in an easterly direction.* ▶ **wschodni 2** (used about winds) coming from the east: *cold easterly winds* ▶ **wschodni**, **ze wschodu**

eastern (also **Eastern**) /ˈiːstən/ adj. **1** [only before a noun] (abbr. **E**) of, in or from the east of a place: *Eastern Scotland* ◇ *the eastern shore of the lake* ▶ **wschodni 2** from or connected with the countries of the East: *Eastern cookery* ▶ **wschodni**

eastwards /ˈiːstwədz/ (also **eastward**) adv. towards the east: *The Amazon flows eastwards.* ▶ **na wschód**
■ **eastward** adj.: *to travel in an eastward direction* ▶ **wschodni**

easy¹ /ˈiːzi/ adj. (**easier**; **easiest**) **1** not difficult: *an easy question* ◇ *It isn't easy to explain the system./The system isn't easy to explain.* Tego systemu nie da się łatwo wytłumaczyć. ▶ **łatwy** OPP **hard 2** comfortable, relaxed and not worried: *an easy life* ◇ *My mind's easier now.* ▶ **spokojny** OPP **uneasy** ➲ noun, verb **ease**
IDM **free and easy** → FREE¹
I'm easy (informal) (used to say that you do not have a strong opinion when sb offers you a choice): *'Do you want to watch this or the news?' 'I'm easy. It's up to you.'* ▶ **wszystko mi jedno**

easy² /ˈiːzi/ adv. (**easier**, **easiest**)
IDM **easier said than done** (informal) more difficult to do than to talk about: *'You should get her to help you.' 'That's easier said than done.'* ▶ **łatwo powiedzieć**
go easy on sb/on/with sth (informal) **1** to be gentle or less strict with sb: *Go easy on him* (bądź dla niego wyrozumiały) – *he's just a child.* ▶ **traktować kogoś łagodnie/wyrozumiale 2** to avoid using too much of sth: *Go easy on the salt – it's bad for your heart.* ▶ **nie przesadzać z czymś**
take it/things easy to relax and not work too hard or worry too much ▶ **nie przejmować się**

ˌeasy ˈchair noun [C] a large comfortable chair with arms ▶ **rodzaj fotela**

ˌeasy-ˈgoing adj. (used about a person) calm, relaxed and not easily worried or upset by what other people do: *Her parents are very easy-going. They let her do what she wants.* ▶ **niefrasobliwy**, **łatwy w pożyciu** SYN **laidback**

eat /iːt/ verb (pt **ate** /et/, pp **eaten** /ˈiːtn/) **1** [I,T] to put food into your mouth, then bite and swallow it: *Who ate all the biscuits?* ◇ *She doesn't eat properly. No wonder she's so thin.* ◇ *Eat your dinner up* (zjedz wszystko, co masz na talerzu), *Joe.* ▶ **jeść 2** [I] to have a meal: *What time shall we eat?* ▶ **jeść** (*np. obiad*)
IDM **have sb eating out of your hand** to have control and power over sb ▶ **sprawić, by inni jedli komuś z ręki**
have your cake and eat it → CAKE¹
PHR V **eat sth away/eat away at sth** to damage or destroy sth slowly over a period of time: *The sea had eaten away at the cliff.* ▶ **podmywać**, **wyżerać**
eat out to have a meal in a restaurant: *Would you like to eat out tonight?* ▶ **jeść na mieście**

eater /ˈiːtə(r)/ noun [C] a person who eats in a particular way: *We're not great meat eaters in our family.* W naszej rodzinie rzadko jemy mięso. ◇ *My uncle's a big eater* (lubi dużo zjeść). ◇ *She's a fussy eater.* Jest wybredna w jedzeniu. ▶ **osoba, która je coś w jakiś sposób**

eau de cologne /ˌəʊ də kəˈləʊn/ (also **cologne**) noun [U] a type of **perfume** that is not very strong ▶ **woda kolońska**

eaves /iːvz/ noun [pl.] the edges of a roof that stick out over the walls: *There's a bird's nest under the eaves.* ▶ **okap**

eavesdrop /ˈiːvzdrɒp/ verb [I] (**eavesdropping**; **eavesdropped**) **eavesdrop (on sb/sth)** to listen secretly to other people talking: *They caught her eavesdropping on their conversation.* ▶ **podsłuchiwać**

the ebb /eb/ noun [sing.] the time when sea water flows away from the land ▶ **odpływ**

> The movement of sea water twice a day is called the **tide**. The opposite of **ebb tide** is **high tide**.

IDM **the ebb and flow (of sth)** (used about a situation, noise, feeling, etc.) a regular increase and decrease in the progress or strength of sth ▶ **wzloty i upadki**

ebb /eb/ verb [I] **1** (used about sea water) to flow away from the land, which happens twice a day ▶ (*morze*) **odpływać** SYN **go out 2 ebb (away)** (used about a feeling, etc.) to become weaker: *The crowd's enthusiasm began to ebb.* ▶ **słabnąć**

ebony /'ebəni/ noun [U] a hard black wood ▶ **heban**

ebullient /ɪ'bʌliənt; -'bʊl-/ adj. (formal) full of confidence, energy and good humour: *The Prime Minister was in ebullient mood.* ▶ **pełen entuzjazmu i energii**
■ **ebullience** /-əns/ noun [U]: *I put her remarks down to youthful ebullience.* ▶ **entuzjazm i energiczność** | **ebulliently** adv. ▶ **z energią i entuzjazmem**

'e-cash noun [U] a system for sending and receiving payments using the Internet ▶ **system dokonywania płatności przez internet**

eccentric /ɪk'sentrɪk/ adj. (used about people or their behaviour) strange or unusual ▶ **dziwaczny**, **ekscentryczny**
■ **eccentric** noun [C]: *She's just an old eccentric.* ▶ **dziwak**, **ekscentryk** | **eccentricity** /ˌeksen'trɪsəti/ noun [C,U] (pl. **eccentricities**) ▶ **dziwactwo**, **ekscentryczność**

ecclesiastical /ɪˌkliːzi'æstɪkl/ adj. connected with or belonging to the Christian Church: *ecclesiastical law* ▶ **kościelny**, **duchowny**

echelon /'eʃəlɒn/ noun [C, usually pl.] a rank or position of authority in an organization or a society: *the **lower / upper / top / higher echelons** of the Civil Service* ▶ **szczebel** (*w hierarchii*)

echo¹ /'ekəʊ/ noun [C] (pl. **echoes**) a sound that is repeated as it is sent back off a surface such as the wall of a tunnel ▶ **echo**

echo² /'ekəʊ/ verb **1** [I] (used about a sound) to be repeated; to come back as an **echo**: *Their footsteps echoed in the empty church.* ▶ (*dźwięk*) **odbijać się 2** [I,T] **echo sth (back)**; **echo (with/to sth)** to repeat or send back a sound; to be full of a particular sound: *The tunnel echoed back their calls.* ◇ *The hall echoed with their laughter.* ▶ **odbijać się** (*np. echem*), **rozbrzmiewać** (*np. śmiechem*) **3** [T] to repeat what sb has said, done or thought: *The child echoed everything his mother said.* ◇ *The newspaper article echoed my views completely* (całkowicie odzwierciedlał mój pogląd). ▶ **powtarzać** (*jak echo*), **odbijać** (*dźwięki*)

eclair /ɪ'kleə(r)/ noun [C] a type of long thin cake, usually filled with cream and covered with chocolate ▶ (*ciastko*) **ekler**

eclectic /ɪ'klektɪk/ adj. (formal) not following one style or set of ideas but choosing from or using a wide variety: *She has very eclectic tastes in literature.* ▶ **eklektyczny**
■ **eclectically** /-tɪkli/ adv.: *Her work draws eclectically on psychoanalysis and mythology.* ▶ **eklektycznie** | **eclecticism** /ɪ'klektɪsɪzəm/ noun [U] ▶ **eklektyzm**

eclipse¹ /ɪ'klɪps/ noun **1** [C] an occasion when the moon or the sun seems to completely or partly disappear, because one of them is passing between the other and the earth: *a total/partial eclipse of the sun* ▶ **zaćmienie 2** [sing., U] the loss of a person's importance, success, etc. ▶ **usunięcie w cień**, **przyćmienie**

eclipse² /ɪ'klɪps/ verb [T] **1** (used about the moon, etc.) to cause an **eclipse** of the sun, etc. ▶ **zaćmiewać 2** (used about a person) to make another person seem less interesting, important, etc. ▶ **przyćmiewać (kogoś)**

eco-friendly /'ikəʊ frendli/ adj. not harmful to the environment: *eco-friendly products/fuel* ▶ **przyjazny środowisku**

ecologist /i'kɒlədʒɪst/ noun [C] a person who studies or is an expert in **ecology** ▶ **ekolog**

ecology /i'kɒlədʒi/ noun [U] the relationship between living things and their surroundings; the study of this subject ▶ **ekologia**
■ **ecological** /ˌiːkə'lɒdʒɪkl/ adj.: *The oil spill caused an ecological disaster.* ▶ **ekologiczny** | **ecologically** /-kli/ adv. ▶ **ekologicznie**

economic /ˌiːkə'nɒmɪk; ˌekə-/ adj. **1** [only before a noun] connected with the supply of money, business, industry, etc.: *The country faces growing economic problems.* ▶ **ekonomiczny**, **gospodarczy 2** producing a profit: *The mine was closed because it was not economic.* ▶ **rentowny**, **przynoszący zysk** OPP **uneconomic** ℹ Por. **economical**, które ma inne znaczenie.

economical /ˌiːkə'nɒmɪkl; ˌekə-/ adj. that costs or uses less time, money, fuel, etc. than usual: *The new model is a very economical car to run.* ▶ (*urządzenie itp.*) **oszczędny** OPP **uneconomical** ℹ Por. **economic**, które ma inne znaczenie.
■ **economically** /-kli/ adv.: *The train service could be run more economically.* ▶ **oszczędnie**, **gospodarnie**

economics /ˌiːkə'nɒmɪks; ˌekə-/ noun [U] the study or principles of the way money, business and industry are organized: *a degree in economics* ◇ *the economics of a company* ▶ **ekonomia**, **ekonomika**

economist /ɪ'kɒnəmɪst/ noun [C] a person who studies or is an expert in **economics** ▶ **ekonomista**

economize (also -ise) /ɪ'kɒnəmaɪz/ verb [I] **economize (on sth)** to save money, time, fuel, etc.; to use less of sth ▶ **oszczędzać**, **oszczędnie gospodarować**

economy /ɪ'kɒnəmi/ noun (pl. **economies**) **1** (**the economy**) [C] the operation of a country's money supply, commercial activities and industry: *There are signs of improvement in the economy.* ◇ *the economies of America and Japan* ▶ **gospodarka**, **ekonomia 2** [C,U] careful spending of money, time, fuel, etc.; trying to save, not waste sth: *Our department is **making economies** in the amount of paper it uses.* ◇ *economy class* druga klasa ▶ **oszczędność**

ecosystem /'iːkəʊsɪstəm/ noun [C] all the plants and living creatures in a particular area considered in relation to their physical environment ▶ **ekosystem**

ecotourism /'iːkəʊtʊərɪzəm; Brit. also -tɔːr-/ noun [U] organized holidays that are designed so that the environment is damaged as little as possible, especially when some of the money the tourists pay is used to protect the local environment ▶ **ekoturystyka**
■ **ecotourist** /-ɪst; Brit. also -tɔːr-/ noun [C] ▶ **ekoturyst(k)a**

ecstasy /'ekstəsi/ noun [C,U] **1** (pl. **ecstasies**) a feeling or state of great happiness: *to be **in ecstasy*** ◇ *She **went into ecstasies*** (oszalała z zachwytu) *about the ring he had bought her.* ▶ **ekstaza**, **zachwyt 2** (**Ecstasy**) [U] an illegal drug, taken especially by young people at parties, clubs, etc. ▶ **Ecstasy**

ecstatic /ɪk'stætɪk/ adj. extremely happy ▶ **pełen zachwytu**, **w ekstazie**

ecu (also **ECU**) /'ekjuː/ noun [C] (pl. **ecus**; **ecu**) **European Currency Unit**; (until 1999) money used for business and commercial activities between member countries of the European Union ▶ **europejska jednostka monetarna**

ecumenical /ˌiːkjuː'menɪkl; ˌekjuː-/ adj. connected with the idea of uniting all the different parts of the Christian Church ▶ **ekumeniczny**

eczema /'eksɪmə; US ɪg'ziːmə/ noun [U] a disease which makes your skin red and dry so that you want to scratch it ▶ **egzema**

ed. = EDITION (1), EDITOR

eddy /'edi/ noun [C] (pl. **eddies**) a movement of air, water or dust in a circle ▶ **wir, zawirowanie**

edge¹ /edʒ/ noun [C] **1** the place where sth, especially a surface, ends: *the edge of a table* ◇ *I stood at the water's edge.* ▶ **krawędź, brzeg 2** the sharp cutting part of a knife, etc. ▶ **ostrze**

IDM **an/the edge on/over sb/sth** a small advantage over sb/sth: *She knew she had the edge over the other candidates.* ▶ **przewaga nad kimś/czymś**

(be) on edge to be nervous, worried or quick to become upset or angry: *I'm a bit on edge because I get my exam results today.* ▶ **być zdenerwowanym, być rozdrażnionym** ℹ Por. **edgy**, które ma podobne znaczenie.

edge² /edʒ/ verb **1** [I,T] **edge (your way/sth) across, along, away, back, etc.** to move yourself/sth somewhere slowly and carefully: *We edged closer to get a better view.* ◇ *She edged her chair up to the window.* ▶ **posuwać (się) ostrożnie/pomału 2** [T, usually passive] **edge sth (with sth)** to put sth along the edge of sth else: *The cloth was edged with lace.* ▶ **obszywać, wysadzać** (*np. drogę drzewami*)

edgeways /'edʒweɪz/ (also **edgewise** /-waɪz/) adv.

IDM **not get a word in edgeways** → WORD¹

edgy /'edʒi/ adj. (**edgier**; **edgiest**) (informal) nervous, worried or quick to become upset or angry ▶ **zdenerwowany, rozdrażniony**

edible /'edəbl/ adj. good or safe to eat ▶ **jadalny** OPP **inedible**

edict /'i:dɪkt/ noun [U,C] (formal) an official order or statement given by sb in authority ▶ **edykt** SYN **decree**

edifice /'edɪfɪs/ noun [C] (formal) a large impressive building ▶ **gmach**

edifying /'edɪfaɪɪŋ/ adj. (formal or humorous) likely to improve your mind or your character: *edifying literature* ◇ *Watching soccer fans howling racist remarks was not an edifying sight.* ▶ **budujący** (*np. moralnie*), **pouczający**

edit /'edɪt/ verb [T] **1** to prepare a piece of writing to be published, making sure that it is correct, the right length, etc. ▶ **redagować 2** to make changes to text or data on screen on a computer ▶ **edytować 3** to prepare a film, TV or radio programme by cutting and arranging recorded material in a particular order ▶ **montować, redagować 4** to be in charge of a newspaper, magazine, etc. ▶ **redagować**

edition /ɪ'dɪʃn/ noun [C] **1** (abbr. **ed.**) the form in which a book is published; all the books, newspapers, etc. published in the same form at the same time: *a paperback/hardback edition* ◇ *the morning edition of a newspaper* ▶ **wydanie, edycja 2** one of a series of newspapers, magazines, TV or radio programmes: *And now for this week's edition of 'Panorama'...* ▶ **wydanie, audycja 3** the number of copies of a book, etc. that are printed at the same time ▶ **nakład**

editor /'edɪtə(r)/ noun [C] (abbr. **ed.**) **1** the person who is in charge of all or part of a newspaper, magazine, etc. and who decides what should be included: *the financial editor* ◇ *Who is the editor of 'The Times'?* ▶ **redaktor/ka (naczeln-y/a) 2** a person whose job is to prepare a book to be published by checking for mistakes and correcting the text ▶ **redaktor/ka 3** a person whose job is to prepare a film, TV programme, etc. for showing to the public by cutting and putting the recorded material in the correct order ▶ **montażyst(k)a**

editorial /ˌedɪ'tɔ:riəl/ noun [C] an article in a newspaper, usually written by the **editor**, giving an opinion on an important subject ▶ **artykuł wstępny**

educate /'edʒukeɪt/ verb [T] to teach or train sb, especially in school: *Young people should be educated to care for their environment.* ◇ *All their children were educated at private schools.* ▶ **kształcić, edukować**

educated /'edʒukeɪtɪd/ adj. having studied and learnt a lot of things to a high standard: *a highly educated woman* ▶ **wykształcony**

education /ˌedʒu'keɪʃn/ noun [C, usually sing., U] the teaching or training of people, especially in schools: *primary/secondary/higher/adult education* ◇ *She received an excellent education.* ▶ **wykształcenie** ➲ note at **school**, **study**

■ **educational** /-ʃənl/ adj.: *an educational toy/visit/experience* ▶ **kształcący, budujący**

eel /i:l/ noun [C] a long fish that looks like a snake ▶ **węgorz** ➲ picture on **page A11**

eerie (also **eery**) /'ɪəri/ adj. strange and frightening: *an eerie noise* ▶ **pełen grozy, przeraźliwy**

■ **eerily** adv. ▶ **strasznie, przeraźliwie** | **eeriness** noun [U] ▶ **groza**

effect¹ /ɪ'fekt/ noun **1** [C,U] **(an) effect (on sb/sth)** a change that is caused by sth; a result: *the effects of acid rain on the lakes and forests* ◇ *Her shouting **had little or no effect** on him.* ◇ *Despite her terrible experience, she seems to have suffered no **ill effects**.* ▶ **skutek, wrażenie** ➲ note at **affect** ➲ look at **after-effect**, **side effect 2** [C,U] a particular look, sound or impression that an artist, writer, etc. wants to create: *How does the artist **create the effect of** moonlight?* ◇ *He likes to say things just for effect* (na pokaz). ▶ **wrażenie, efekt 3** (**effects**) [pl.] (formal) your personal possessions: *The insurance policy covers all baggage and personal effects.* ▶ **dobytek, ruchomości**

IDM **bring/put sth into effect** to cause sth to come into use: *The recommendations will soon be put into effect.* ▶ **wprowadzać coś w życie**

come into effect (used especially about laws or rules) to begin to be used ▶ **wchodzić w życie**

in effect 1 in fact; for all practical purposes: *Though they haven't made an official announcement, she is, in effect, the new director.* ▶ **w istocie, w rzeczywistości 2** (used about a rule, a law, etc.) in operation; in use: *The new rules will be in effect from next month.* ▶ **obowiązujący**

take effect 1 (used about a drug, etc.) to begin to work; to produce the result you want: *The anaesthetic took effect immediately.* ▶ **zadziałać, skutkować 2** (used about a law, etc.) to come into operation: *The ceasefire takes effect from midnight.* ▶ **nabierać mocy, wchodzić w życie**

to this/that effect with this/that meaning: *I told him to leave her alone, or words to that effect.* ▶ **o podobnej treści**

effect² /ɪ'fekt/ verb [T] (formal) to cause sth to happen; to have sth as a result: *to effect a change* ▶ **dokonywać, uskuteczniać** ℹ Por. **affect**, które ma inne znaczenie.

effective /ɪ'fektɪv/ adj. **1** successfully producing the result that you want: *a medicine that is effective against the common cold* ▶ **skuteczny** OPP **ineffective 2** making a pleasing impression: *That picture would look more effective on a dark background.* ▶ **efektowny 3** [only before a noun] real or actual, although perhaps not official: *The soldiers gained effective control of the town.* ▶ **faktyczny, efektywny**

■ **effectiveness** noun [U] ▶ **skuteczność**

effectively /ɪ'fektɪvli/ adv. **1** in a way that successfully produces the result you wanted: *She dealt with the situation effectively.* ▶ **skutecznie 2** in fact; in reality: *It meant that, effectively, they had lost.* ▶ **w rezultacie, w rzeczywistości**

effeminate /ɪ'femɪnət/ adj. (used about a man or his behaviour) like a woman ▶ **zniewieściały**

effervescent /ˌefə'vesnt/ adj. **1** (used about people and their behaviour) excited, enthusiastic and full of energy

▶ **ożywiony, tryskający energią** SYN **bubbly 2** (used about a liquid) having or producing small bubbles of gas ▶ **musujący** SYN **fizzy**
■ **effervescence** noun [U] ▶ **ożywienie; musowanie**

efficient /ɪˈfɪʃnt/ adj. able to work well without making mistakes or wasting time and energy: *Our secretary is very efficient.* ◇ *You must find a more efficient way of organizing your time.* ▶ **kompetentny, wydajny, skuteczny** OPP **inefficient**
■ **efficiency** /ɪˈfɪʃnsi/ noun [U] ▶ **wydajność, rentowność, skuteczność** | **efficiently** adv. ▶ **wydajnie; oszczędnie, skutecznie**

effigy /ˈefɪdʒi/ noun [C] (pl. **effigies**) **1** a statue of a famous or religious person, often shown lying down: *stone effigies in the church* ▶ **posąg** (*przedstawiający osobę zazw. w pozycji leżącej*) **2** a model of a person that makes them look ugly: *The demonstrators burned a crude effigy of the president.* ▶ **kukła**

effluent /ˈefluənt/ noun [U] liquid waste, especially chemicals produced by factories ▶ **ścieki**

effort /ˈefət/ noun **1** [U] the physical or mental strength or energy that you need to do sth; sth that takes a lot of energy: *They have* ***put a lot of effort into*** *their studies this year.* ◇ *He* ***made no effort*** *to contact his parents.* ▶ **wysiłek, trud 2** [C] **an effort (to do sth)** something that is done with difficulty or that takes a lot of energy: *It was a real effort to stay awake in the lecture.* ▶ **wysiłek, trud** SYN **struggle**

effortless /ˈefətləs/ adj. needing little or no effort so that sth seems easy ▶ **łatwy, (pozornie) nie wymagający wysiłku**
■ **effortlessly** adv. ▶ **bez wysiłku**

effusive /ɪˈfjuːsɪv/ adj. showing much or too much emotion: *an effusive welcome* ◇ *He was effusive in his praise.* ▶ **wylewny**
■ **effusively** adv. ▶ **wylewnie**

EFL /ˌiː ef ˈel/ abbr. **English as a Foreign Language** ▶ **nauka języka angielskiego jako języka obcego**

e.g. /ˌiː ˈdʒiː/ abbr. **for example**: *popular sports, e.g. football, tennis, swimming* ▶ **np.**

egalitarian /iˌɡælɪˈteəriən/ adj. (used about a person, system, society, etc.) following the principle that everyone should have equal rights ▶ **egalitarny**

egg¹ /eɡ/ noun **1** [C] an almost round object with a hard shell that contains a young bird, insect or **reptile**: *crocodile eggs* ▶ **jajko** ➲ picture at **insect**

> A female bird **lays** her eggs, often in a **nest**, and then **sits on** them until they **hatch**. ➲ picture on **page A11**

2 [C,U] a bird's egg, especially one from a chicken, etc. that we eat: *egg yolks/whites* ◇ *boiled* (gotowane)/*fried* (sadzone)/*poached* (w koszulkach, gotowane bez skorupki)/*scrambled eggs* (jajecznica) ▶ **jajko** ➲ picture on **page A1ł 3** [C] (in women and female animals) the small cell that can join with a **sperm** to make a baby: *an egg donor* ▶ **komórka jajowa**
IDM **put all your eggs in one basket** to risk everything by depending completely on one thing, plan, etc. instead of giving yourself several possibilities ▶ **stawiać wszystko na jedną kartę**

egg² /eɡ/ verb
PHR V **egg sb on (to do sth)** to encourage sb to do sth that he or she should not do ▶ **namawiać/podjudzać kogoś (do robienia czegoś)**

ˈ**egg cup** noun [C] a small cup for holding a boiled egg ▶ **kieliszek do jajek**

eggplant (US) = AUBERGINE

eggshell /ˈeɡʃel/ noun [C,U] the hard outside part of an egg ▶ **skorupka jajka**

ˈ**egg timer** noun [C] a device that you use to measure the time needed to boil an egg ▶ **minutnik do jajek**

ego /ˈiːɡəʊ; ˈeɡəʊ/ noun [C] (pl. **egos**) the (good) opinion that you have of yourself: *It was a blow to her ego when she lost her job.* ▶ **poczucie własnej wartości**

egocentric /ˌeɡəʊˈsentrɪk; ˌiːɡ-/ adj. thinking only about yourself and not what other people need or want ▶ **samolubny** SYN **selfish**

egoism /ˈeɡəʊɪzəm; ˈiːɡ-/ (also **egotism** /ˈeɡətɪzəm; ˈiːɡ-; US -ɡəʊ-/) noun [U] the fact of thinking that you are better or more important than anyone else ▶ **egoizm**
■ **egoist** /ˈeɡəʊɪst; ˈiːɡəʊɪst/ (also **egotist** /ˈeɡətɪst; ˈiːɡə-/) noun [C]: *I hate people who are egoists.* ▶ **egoist(k)a** | **egoistic** /ˌeɡəʊˈɪstɪk; ˌiːɡ-/ (also **egotistical** /ˌeɡəˈtɪstɪkl; ˌiːɡə-/) adj. ▶ **samolubny**

E

egomania /ˌeɡəʊˈmeɪniə; ˌiːɡəʊ-/ noun [U] a mental condition in which sb is interested in themselves or concerned about themselves in a way that is not normal ▶ **skrajny egotyzm**
■ **egomaniac** /ˌeɡəʊˈmeɪniæk; ˌiːɡəʊ-/ noun [C] ▶ **(skrajn-y/a) egotyst(k)a**

ˈ**ego trip** noun [C] an activity that sb does because it makes them feel good and important: *To possess power is the ultimate ego trip for most people.* ▶ **czynność/działalność itp. będąca źródłem egoistycznej satysfakcji oraz poczucia ważności** ℹ Zwykle wyraża dezaprobatę.

eh /eɪ/ interj. (Brit., informal) **1** (used for asking sb to repeat sth): *'Did you like the film?' 'Eh?' 'I asked if you liked the film!'* ▶ **co? 2** (used for asking sb to agree with you): *'Good party, eh?'* ▶ **(no) nie?**

Eid (also **Id**) /iːd/ noun [sing.] any of several Muslim festivals, especially one that celebrates the end of Ramadan ▶ (*religia muzułmańska*) **święto, zwł. na zakończenie ramadanu**

eiderdown /ˈaɪdədaʊn/ noun [C] a covering for a bed filled with soft feathers, usually used on top of other coverings for the bed ▶ **pierzyna** ➲ look at **duvet**

eight /eɪt/ number **1** 8 ▶ **osiem** ➲ note at **six 2** (**eight-**) [in compounds] having eight of sth: *an eight-sided shape* ▶ **ośmio-**

eighteen /ˌeɪˈtiːn/ number 18 ▶ **osiemnaście** ➲ note at **six**
■ **eighteenth** /ˌeɪˈtiːnθ/ **1** ordinal number 18th ▶ **osiemnasty** ➲ note at **sixth 2** noun [C] 1/18; one of eighteen equal parts of sth ▶ **(jedna) osiemnasta**

eighth /eɪtθ/ ordinal number 8th ▶ **ósmy** ➲ note at **sixth**
■ **eighth** noun [C] ⅛; one of eight equal parts of sth ▶ **(jedna) ósma**

ˈ**eighth note** (US) = QUAVER

eighty /ˈeɪti/ number 80 ▶ **osiemdziesiąt** ➲ note at **sixty**
■ **eightieth** /ˈeɪtiəθ/ **1** ordinal number 80th ▶ **osiemdziesiąty** ➲ note at **sixth 2** noun [C] 1/80; one of eighty equal parts of sth ▶ **(jedna) osiemdziesiąta**

either¹ /ˈaɪðə(r); ˈiːðə(r)/ determiner, pron. **1** one or the other of two; it does not matter which: *You can choose either soup or salad, but not both.* ◇ *You can ask either of us for advice.* ▶ **jeden (lub drugi), którykolwiek (z dwóch),** (*zdania przeczące*) **żaden (z dwóch)** ℹ **Either** łączy się zasadniczo z czasownikiem w lp, jednak w potocznej angielszczyźnie po **either of** można też użyć czasownika w lm, jeśli rzeczownik lub zaimek osobowy występuje w lm: *Either of us are willing to help.* **2** both: *It is a pleasant road, with trees on either side* (po obu stronach). ▶ **obaj, oboje itp.**

either² /ˈaɪðə(r); ˈiːðə(r)/ adv. **1** [used after two negative statements] also: *I don't like Pat and I don't like Nick much either.* ◇ *'I can't remember his name.' 'I can't either* (ani ja).*'* ▶ **też, także** ℹ Można też powiedzieć **neither can I**. Por. **too**, aby zobaczyć konstrukcję podobnych wyrażeń w twierdzeniach. **2** (used for emphasizing a negative statement): *The restaurant is quite good. And it's not expensive either.* ▶ **ponadto**, **wcale (nie)** ➲ note at **neither**, **too**

either³ /ˈaɪðə(r); ˈiːðə(r)/ conj. **either ... or ...** (used when you are giving a choice, usually of two things): *I can meet you either Thursday or Friday.* ◇ *Either you leave or I do.* ▶ **albo ... albo**

ejaculate /iˈdʒækjuleɪt/ verb **1** [I] to send out **semen** from the **penis** ▶ **mieć wytrysk** (*nasienia*) **2** [I,T] (old-fashioned) to say sth suddenly ▶ **nagle coś powiedzieć**, **wykrzykiwać**

■ **ejaculation** /iˌdʒækjuˈleɪʃn/ noun [C,U] ▶ **wytrysk** (*nasienia*); **okrzyk**

eject /iˈdʒekt/ verb **1** [T, often passive] (formal) **eject sb (from sth)** to push or send sb/sth out of a place (usually with force): *The protesters were ejected from the building.* ▶ **usuwać**, **wyrzucać** **2** [I] to escape from an aircraft that is going to crash ▶ **katapultować się** **3** [I,T] to remove a tape, disk, etc. from a machine, usually by pressing a button: *To eject the CD, press this button.* ◇ *After recording for three hours the video will eject automatically.* ▶ **wysuwać (się)**

eke /iːk/ verb

IDM **eke out a living** to manage to live with very little money ▶ **z trudem wiązać koniec z końcem**

PHR V **eke sth out** to make a small amount of sth last a long time ▶ **sztukować/rozciągać coś**

elaborate¹ /ɪˈlæbərət/ adj. very complicated; done or made very carefully: *an elaborate pattern* ◇ *elaborate plans* ▶ **skomplikowany**, **wypracowany**

■ **elaborately** adv.: *an elaborately decorated room* ▶ **misternie**, **wymyślnie**

elaborate² /ɪˈlæbəreɪt/ verb [I] (formal) **elaborate (on sth)** to give more details about sth: *Could you elaborate on that idea?* ▶ **omawiać coś szczegółowo**

elapse /ɪˈlæps/ verb [I] (formal) (used about time) to pass ▶ **upływać**

elastic¹ /ɪˈlæstɪk/ noun [U] material with rubber in it which can stretch ▶ **gumka** (*np. u majtek*)

elastic² /ɪˈlæstɪk/ adj. **1** (used about material, etc.) that returns to its original size and shape after being stretched ▶ **elastyczny** **2** that can be changed; not fixed: *Our rules are quite elastic.* ▶ **elastyczny**

elasticated /ɪˈlæstɪkeɪtɪd/ (Brit.) (US **elasticized** /ɪˈlæstɪsaɪzd/) adj. (used about clothing, or part of a piece of clothing) made using **elastic** material that can stretch: *a skirt with an elasticated waist* ▶ (*ubranie*) **elastyczny**

eˌlastic ˈband = RUBBER BAND

elasticity /ˌiːlæˈstɪsəti; ˌelæ-; ɪˌlæ-/ noun [U] the quality that sth has of being able to stretch and return to its original size and shape ▶ **elastyczność**

elated /iˈleɪtɪd/ adj. very happy and excited ▶ **podniecony**, **pijany** (*np. szczęściem*)

■ **elation** /iˈleɪʃn/ noun [U] ▶ **podniecenie**, **uniesienie**

🔑 **elbow¹** /ˈelbəʊ/ noun [C] **1** the place where the bones of your arm join and your arm bends: *She jabbed him with her elbow.* ▶ **łokieć** ➲ picture at **body** **2** the part of the sleeve of a coat, jacket, etc. that covers the elbow: *His old jacket was worn at the elbows.* ▶ **łokieć**

elbow² /ˈelbəʊ/ verb [T] to push sb with your elbow: *He elbowed her out of the way.* Odepchnął ją z drogi. ▶ **rozpychać się łokciami** ➲ look at **nudge**

ˈelbow room noun [U] enough space to move freely ▶ **(wolne) miejsce**, **przestrzeń**

elder¹ /ˈeldə(r)/ adj. [only before a noun] older (of two members of a family): *My elder daughter is at university now.* ◇ *an elder brother/sister* ▶ **starszy**

elder² /ˈeldə(r)/ noun **1** (**the elder**) [sing.] the older of two people: *Who is the elder of the two?* ▶ **starsz-y/a** **2** (**my, etc. elder**) [sing.] a person who is older than me, etc.: *He is her elder by several years.* ▶ **starsz-y/a** **3** (**elders**) [pl.] older people: *Do children still respect the opinions of their elders?* ▶ **starsi** **4** [C] a small tree with white flowers with a sweet smell (**elderflowers**) and bunches of black berries (**elderberries**) ▶ **dziki bez**

elderberry /ˈeldəberi/ (pl. **elderberries**) noun [C] the fruit of an elder tree ▶ **owoc czarnego bzu**

elderflower /ˈeldəflaʊə(r)/ noun [C] the flower of the **elder** tree, used to make wines and other drinks: *elderflower cordial* ▶ **kwiat dzikiego bzu**

🔑 **elderly** /ˈeldəli/ adj. (used about a person) old: *elderly relatives* ▶ **w podeszłym wieku** ℹ Jest to słowo grzecznościowe używane zamiast **old**.

■ **the elderly** noun [pl.] old people in general: *The elderly need special care in winter.* ▶ **ludzie starsi** ➲ look at **old**

eldest /ˈeldɪst/ adj., noun [C] (the) oldest (of three or more members of a family): *Their eldest child is a boy.* ▶ **najstarsz-y/a**

🔑 **elect** /ɪˈlekt/ verb [T] **1 elect sb (to sth)**; **elect sb (as sth)** to choose sb to have a particular job or position by voting for them: *He was elected to Parliament in 1970.* ▶ **wybierać** **2** (formal) **elect to do sth** to decide to do sth: *Many people elect to work from home.* ▶ **postanawiać coś zrobić**

🔑 **election** /ɪˈlekʃn/ noun [C,U] (the time of) choosing a Member of Parliament, President, etc. by voting: *In America, presidential elections are held every four years.* ◇ *If you're interested in politics, why not* ***stand for election*** *yourself?* ▶ **wybory** ➲ note at **politics**

> **elections**
>
> In Britain, **general elections** are held about every five years. Sometimes **by-elections** are held at other times. In each region (**constituency**) voters must choose one person from a list of **candidates**.

elective /ɪˈlektɪv/ noun [C] (especially US) a course or subject at a college or school which a student can choose to do ▶ **kurs/przedmiot do wyboru**

elector /ɪˈlektə(r)/ noun [C] a person who has the right to vote in an election ▶ **wyborca** ℹ Częściej używa się słowa **voter**.

■ **electoral** /ɪˈlektərəl/ adj.: *the electoral register/roll* spis wyborców ▶ **wyborczy**

electorate /ɪˈlektərət/ noun [C, with sing. or pl. verb] all the people who can vote in a region, country, etc. ▶ **elektorat**

🔑 **electric** /ɪˈlektrɪk/ adj. **1** producing or using electricity: *an electric current* ◇ *an electric kettle* ➲ picture at **kettle** ▶ **elektryczny** ➲ look at **electrical** **2** very exciting: *The atmosphere was electric.* ▶ **pełen napięcia**, **elektryzujący**

🔑 **electrical** /ɪˈlektrɪkl/ adj. of or about electricity: *an electrical appliance* ◇ *an electrical engineer* inżynier elektryk ▶ **elektryczny** ➲ look at **electric**

the eˌlectric ˈchair noun [sing.] a chair used in some countries for killing criminals with a very strong electric current ▶ **krzesło elektryczne**

electrician /ɪˌlekˈtrɪʃn/ noun [C] a person whose job is to make and repair electrical systems and equipment ▶ **elektryk** ➲ note at **house**

🔑 **electricity** /ɪˌlekˈtrɪsəti/ noun [U] a type of energy that we use to make heat, light and power to work machines, etc. ▶ **prąd**, **elektryczność**

> Electricity is usually **generated** in **power stations**. It may also be produced by **generators** or by **batteries**.

e͵lectric ˈrazor = SHAVER

e͵lectric ˈshock (also **shock**) noun [C] a sudden painful feeling that you get if electricity goes through your body ▶ **porażenie** (*prądem*)

electrify /ɪˈlektrɪfaɪ/ verb [T] (**electrifying**; **electrifies**; pt, pp **electrified**) **1** to supply sth with electricity: *The railways are being electrified.* ▶ **elektryfikować 2** to make sb very excited: *Ronaldo electrified the crowd with his pace and skill.* ▶ **elektryzować**

electrocute /ɪˈlektrəkjuːt/ verb [T] to kill sb with electricity that goes through the body ▶ **razić (śmiertelnie) prądem elektrycznym**
■ **electrocution** /ɪ͵lektrəˈkjuːʃn/ noun [U] ▶ **(śmiertelne) porażenie prądem elektrycznym**

electrode /ɪˈlektrəʊd/ noun [C] one of two points where an electric current enters or leaves a battery, etc. ▶ **elektroda**

electromagnetic /ɪ͵lektrəʊmægˈnetɪk/ adj. having both electrical and **magnetic** characteristics (or **properties**): *an* ***electromagnetic wave/field*** ◇ ***electromagnetic radiation*** ▶ **elektromagnetyczny**

electron /ɪˈlektrɒn/ noun [C] part of an atom, that carries a negative electric charge ▶ **elektron** ➲ look at **neutron**, **proton**

⚷ **electronic** /ɪ͵lekˈtrɒnɪk/ adj. **1** using **electronics**: *electronic equipment* ◇ *This dictionary is available in electronic form.* ▶ **elektroniczny 2** done using a computer: *electronic banking/shopping* ▶ **przez internet**, **internetowy**
■ **electronically** /-kli/ adv. ▶ **elektronicznie**

electronics /ɪ͵lekˈtrɒnɪks/ noun [U] the technology used to produce computers, radios, etc.: *the electronics industry* ▶ **elektronika**

⚷ **elegant** /ˈelɪgənt/ adj. having a good or attractive style ▶ **elegancki** SYN **stylish**
■ **elegance** noun [U] ▶ **elegancja** | **elegantly** adv. ▶ **elegancko**

elegy /ˈelədʒi/ noun [C] (pl. **elegies**) a poem or song that expresses sadness, especially for sb who has died ▶ **elegia**

⚷ **element** /ˈelɪmənt/ noun **1** [C] one important part of sth: *Cost is an important element when we're thinking about holidays.* ▶ **część**, **element 2** [C, usually sing.] **an element of sth** a small amount of sth: *There was an element of truth* (ziarnko prawdy) *in what he said.* ▶ **element 3** [C] people of a certain type: *The criminal element at football matches causes a lot of trouble.* ▶ **element 4** [C] one of the simple chemical substances, for example iron, gold, etc. ▶ **pierwiastek 5** [C] the metal part of a piece of electrical equipment that produces heat: *The kettle needs a new element.* ▶ **grzałka 6** (**the elements**) [pl.] (bad) weather: *exposed to the elements* wydany na pastwę żywiołów ▶ **żywioły**
IDM **in/out of your element** in a situation where you feel comfortable/uncomfortable: *Bill's in his element speaking to a large group of people, but I hate it.* ▶ **(nie) w swoim żywiole**

elementary /͵elɪˈmentri/ adj. **1** connected with the first stages of learning sth: *an elementary course in English* ◇ *a book for elementary students* ▶ **podstawowy 2** basic; not difficult: *elementary physics* ▶ **elementarny**

͵eleˈmentary school noun [C] (US) a school for children aged 6 to 11 ▶ **szkoła podstawowa**

elephant /ˈelɪfənt/ noun [C] a very large grey animal with big ears, two **tusks** and a **trunk** ▶ **słoń** ➲ picture on **page A10**

elevate /ˈelɪveɪt/ verb [T] (formal) to move sb/sth to a higher place or more important position: *an elevated platform* ◇ *an elevated railway* kolej nadziemna ◇ *He was elevated to the Board of Directors.* ▶ **wynosić**; **podnosić** SYN **raise**

elevating adj. (formal) improving the mind; educating: *an elevating book* ▶ **umoralniający**

elevation /͵elɪˈveɪʃn/ noun **1** [C,U] (formal) the process of moving to a higher place or more important position: *his elevation to the presidency* ▶ **wyniesienie**; **wzniosłość 2** [C] the height of a place above sea level: *The city is* ***at an elevation of*** *2000 metres.* ▶ **wysokość** (*nad poziomem morza*)

⚷ **elevator** (US) = LIFT² (1)

⚷ **eleven** /ɪˈlevn/ number 11 ▶ **jedenaście** ➲ note at **six**
■ **eleventh** /ɪˈlevnθ/ **1** ordinal number 11th ▶ **jedenasty** ➲ note at **sixth 2** noun [C] 1/11; one of eleven equal parts of sth ▶ **(jedna) jedenasta**

elf /elf/ noun [C] (pl. **elves** /elvz/) (in stories) a small creature with pointed ears who has magic powers ▶ **elf**

elicit /iˈlɪsɪt/ verb [T] (formal) **elicit sth (from sb)** to manage to get information, facts, a reaction, etc. from sb ▶ **wydobywać**

eligible /ˈelɪdʒəbl/ adj. **eligible (for sth/to do sth)** having the right to do or have sth: *In Britain, you are eligible to vote when you are eighteen.* ◇ *an eligible young man* dobra partia ▶ **uprawniony do czegoś**; **nadający się** OPP **ineligible**

eliminate /ɪˈlɪmɪneɪt/ verb [T] **1** to remove sb/sth that is not wanted or needed: *We must try and eliminate the problem.* ▶ **usuwać**, **wykluczać 2** [often passive] to stop sb going further in a competition, etc.: *The school team was eliminated in the first round of the competition.* ▶ **eliminować**
■ **elimination** /ɪ͵lɪmɪˈneɪʃn/ noun [U] ▶ **usunięcie**; **eliminacja**

elite /eɪˈliːt/ noun [C, with sing. or pl. verb] a social group that is thought to be the best or most important because of its power, money, intelligence, etc.: *an intellectual elite* ▶ **elita**
■ **elite** adj.: *an elite* (stanowiąca elitę) *group of artists* ▶ **elitarny**

elitism /eɪˈliːtɪzəm/ noun [U] the belief that some people should be treated in a special way ▶ **elitaryzm**
■ **elitist** /-ɪst/ noun [C], adj. ▶ **zwolenni-k/czka elitaryzmu**; **elitarny**

elk /elk/ (US **moose** /muːs/) noun [C] a very large **deer** with large flat horns on its head ▶ **łoś**

ellipse /ɪˈlɪps/ noun [C] (technical) a regular **oval** shape ▶ **elipsa**

elliptical /ɪˈlɪptɪkl/ adj. **1** with a word or words left out of a sentence deliberately: *He made an elliptical remark.* ▶ (*przen.*) **eliptyczny 2** (also **elliptic** /ɪˈlɪptɪk/) connected with or in the form of an **ellipse** ▶ **eliptyczny**
■ **elliptically** /-kli/ adv.: *to speak/write elliptically* ▶ **eliptycznie**

elm /elm/ (also ˈ**elm tree**) noun [C] a tall tree with large leaves ▶ **wiąz**

elocution /͵eləˈkjuːʃn/ noun [U] the ability to speak clearly and correctly, especially in public ▶ **dykcja**, **krasomówstwo**

elongate /ˈiːlɒŋgeɪt; US ɪˈl-/ verb [I,T] to become longer; to make sth longer ▶ **wydłużać (się)** SYN **lengthen**

elongated /ˈiːlɒŋgeɪtɪd; US ɪˈl-/ adj. long and thin ▶ **wydłużony**

elope /ɪˈləʊp/ verb [I] **elope (with sb)** to run away secretly to get married ▶ **uciekać z ukochan-ym/ą z zamiarem pobrania się**

E

eloquent /ˈeləkwənt/ adj. (formal) able to use language and express your opinions well, especially when you speak in public ▶ **wymowny**
■ **eloquence** noun [U] ▶ **wymowność, umiejętność wysławiania się** | **eloquently** adv. ▶ **elokwentnie**

else /els/ adv. [used after words formed with *any-*, *every-*, *no-*, *some-* and after question words] another, different person, thing or place: *Does anybody else* (czy ktoś jeszcze) *know about this?* ◇ *This isn't mine. It must be* ***someone else's*** (kogoś innego). ◇ ***Everybody else*** *is allowed* (pozostałym wolno) *to stay up late.* ◇ *Was it you who phoned me, or* ***somebody else?*** ◇ *You'll have to pay.* ***Nobody else*** (nikt inny) *will.* ◇ *There's nothing on the television. Let's find* ***something else*** (coś innego) *to do.* ◇ ***What else*** *would you like?* ◇ *I'm tired of that cafe – shall we go* ***somewhere else*** *for a change?* ▶ **jeszcze, inny, oprócz (mnie itp.)**;
IDM **or else** otherwise; if not: *You'd better go to bed now or else you'll be tired in the morning.* ◇ *He either forgot or else decided not to come.* ▶ **bo w przeciwnym razie, bo jak nie; albo**

elsewhere /ˌelsˈweə(r)/ adv. in or to another place: *He's travelled a lot – in Europe and elsewhere* (i innych kontynentach). ▶ **gdzie indziej**

ELT /ˌiː el ˈtiː/ abbr. **English Language Teaching** ▶ **nauka języka angielskiego dla obcokrajowców**

elucidate /iˈluːsɪdeɪt/ verb [I,T] (formal) to make sth clearer by explaining it more fully: *He elucidated a point of grammar.* ◇ *I will try to elucidate what I think the problems are.* ◇ *Let me elucidate.* ▶ **wyjaśniać, objaśniać**
SYN **explain**
■ **elucidation** /iˌluːsɪˈdeɪʃn/ noun [U,C] ▶ **wyjaśnienie, objaśnienie**

elude /iˈluːd/ verb [T] (formal) **1** to manage to avoid being caught: *The escaped prisoner eluded the police for three days.* ▶ **uchodzić, wymykać się** **2** to be difficult or impossible to remember: *I remember his face but his name eludes me* (ale nie mogę sobie przypomnieć, jak się nazywa). ▶ **umykać (z pamięci)**

elusive /iˈluːsɪv/ adj. not easy to catch, find or remember ▶ **nieuchwytny**

elves plural of **elf**

emaciated /ɪˈmeɪʃieɪtɪd/ adj. extremely thin and weak because of illness, lack of food, etc. ▶ **wychudzony**
■ **emaciation** /ɪˌmeɪsiˈeɪʃn/ noun [U] ▶ **wychudzenie**

email (also **e-mail**) /ˈiːmeɪl/ noun **1** [U] a way of sending electronic messages and data from one computer to another: *to send a message by email* ▶ **poczta elektroniczna** **2** [C,U] a message or messages sent by email: *I'll* ***send you an email*** *tomorrow.* ▶ **e-mail**
■ **email** verb [T]: *I'll email the information to you.* ▶ **przesyłać pocztą elektroniczną**

emanate /ˈeməneɪt/ verb [T] (formal) to produce or show sth: *He emanates confidence.* ▶ **emanować**
PHR V **emanate from sth** to come from sth or somewhere: *The sound of loud music emanated from the building.* ▶ **pochodzić/dochodzić skądś**

emancipate /ɪˈmænsɪpeɪt/ verb [T] (formal) to give sb the same legal, social and political rights as other people ▶ **emancypować**
■ **emancipation** /ɪˌmænsɪˈpeɪʃn/ noun [U] ▶ **emancypacja**

embalm /ɪmˈbɑːm/ verb [T] to prevent a dead body from being slowly destroyed by treating it with special substances ▶ **balsamować**
■ **embalmer** noun [C] ▶ **balsamist(k)a**

embankment /ɪmˈbæŋkmənt/ noun [C] a wall of stone or earth that is built to stop a river from spreading into an area that should be dry or to carry a road or railway ▶ **nabrzeże, nasyp**

embargo /ɪmˈbɑːɡəʊ/ noun [C] (pl. **embargoes**) an official order to stop doing business with another country: *to impose an embargo on arms sales* ◇ *to lift/remove an embargo* ▶ **zakaz** (*importu, wywozu*)

embark /ɪmˈbɑːk/ verb [I] to get on a ship: *Passengers with cars and caravans must embark first.* ▶ **wsiadać na statek** OPP **disembark**
■ **embarkation** /ˌembɑːˈkeɪʃn/ noun [C,U] ▶ **wejście na statek**
PHR V **embark on sth** (formal) to start sth (new): *I'm embarking on a new career.* ▶ **rozpoczynać coś**

embarrass /ɪmˈbærəs/ verb [T] to make sb feel uncomfortable or shy: *Don't ever embarrass me in front of my friends again!* ▶ **żenować, wprawiać w zakłopotanie**

embarrassed /ɪmˈbærəst/ adj. **embarrassed (about/at sth)**; **embarrassed (to do sth)** feeling uncomfortable or shy because of sth silly you have done, because people are looking at you, etc.: *She's embarrassed about her height.* ▶ **zakłopotany, zażenowany**

embarrassing /ɪmˈbærəsɪŋ/ adj. making you feel uncomfortable or shy: *an embarrassing question/mistake* ▶ **żenujący, wprawiający w zakłopotanie**
■ **embarrassingly** adv. ▶ **żenująco, kłopotliwie**

embarrassment /ɪmˈbærəsmənt/ noun **1** [U] the feeling you have when you are embarrassed: *I nearly died of embarrassment when he said that.* ▶ **zażenowanie, zakłopotanie** **2** [C] a person or thing that makes you embarrassed ▶ **ktoś/coś, kto/co przynosi wstyd lub wprawia w zakłopotanie**

embassy /ˈembəsi/ noun [C] (pl. **embassies**) (the official building of) a group of **diplomats** and the **ambassador**, who represent their government in a foreign country ▶ **ambasada** ➲ look at **consulate**

embed /ɪmˈbed/ verb [T] (**embedding**; **embedded**) [usually passive] to fix sth firmly and deeply (in sth else): *The axe was embedded in the piece of wood.* ▶ **wbijać, wmurowywać**

embellish /ɪmˈbelɪʃ/ verb [T] (formal) **1** to make sth more beautiful by adding decoration to it ▶ **ozdabiać** SYN **decorate** **2** to make a story more interesting by adding details that are not always true ▶ (*przen.*) **upiększać, ubarwiać**
■ **embellishment** noun [U,C] ▶ **ozdabianie, ozdobienie; upiększ-anie/enie**

ember /ˈembə(r)/ noun [C, usually pl.] a piece of wood or coal that is not burning, but is still red and hot after a fire has died ▶ **żarzące się węgle, żar**

embezzle /ɪmˈbezl/ verb [T] to steal money that you are responsible for or that belongs to your employer ▶ **sprzeniewierzać, defraudować**
■ **embezzlement** noun [U] ▶ **sprzeniewierzenie, defraudacja**

embittered /ɪmˈbɪtəd/ adj. angry or disappointed about sth over a long period of time: *a sick and embittered old man* ▶ **zgorzkniały, rozgoryczony**

emblem /ˈembləm/ noun [C] an object or symbol that represents sth ▶ **godło, symbol**

embody /ɪmˈbɒdi/ verb [T] (**embodying**; **embodies**; pt, pp **embodied**) (formal) **1** to be a very good example of sth: *To me she embodies all the best qualities of a teacher.* ▶ **uosabiać, ucieleśniać** **2** to include or contain sth: *This latest model embodies many new features.* ▶ **zawierać, posiadać**
■ **embodiment** noun [C]: *She is the embodiment of a caring mother.* ▶ **uosobienie, ucieleśnienie**

emboss /ɪmˈbɒs/ verb [T, usually passive] **emboss A with B**; **emboss B on A** to put a raised design or piece of writing on paper, leather, etc. ▶ **wytłaczać wzór**

embrace /ɪmˈbreɪs/ verb **1** [I,T] to put your arms around sb as a sign of love, happiness, etc. ▶ **obejmować** **2** [T] (formal) to accept sth with enthusiasm: *She embraced Christianity in her later years.* ▶ **przyjmować** **3** [T] (formal) to include: *His report embraced all the main points.* ▶ **zawierać**

■ **embrace** noun [C]: *He held her in a warm embrace.* ▶ **uścisk, objęcie**

embroider /ɪm'brɔɪdə(r)/ verb **1** [I,T] to decorate cloth by sewing a pattern or picture on it: *an embroidered blouse* ▶ **haftować** **2** [T] to add details that are not true to a story to make it more interesting ▶ **upiększać**

■ **embroidery** /ɪm'brɔɪdəri/ noun [U] ▶ **haftowanie; wyszywanka**

embroil /ɪm'brɔɪl/ verb [T, often passive] **embroil sb/yourself (in sth)** (formal) to involve sb/yourself in an argument or a difficult situation: *He became embroiled in a dispute with his neighbours.* ▶ **wplątywać kogoś/się (w coś)**

embryo /'embriəʊ/ noun [C] (pl. **embryos** /-əʊz/) a baby, an animal or a plant in the early stages of development before birth ▶ **embrion** ➲ look at **foetus**

embryonic /ˌembri'ɒnɪk/ adj. [usually before a noun] **1** (formal) in an early stage of development: *The plan, as yet, only exists in embryonic form.* ▶ (*przen.*) **zarodkowy** **2** of an **embryo**: *embryonic cells* ▶ **embrionalny**

emerald /'emərəld/ noun [C] a bright green **precious** stone ▶ **szmaragd**

■ **emerald** (also ˌemerald 'green) adj.: *an emerald green dress* ▶ (*kolor*) **szmaragdowy**

⚷ **emerge** /i'mɜːdʒ/ verb [I] **emerge (from sth)** **1** to appear or come out from somewhere: *A man emerged from the shadows.* ◇ (figurative) *The country emerged from the war in ruins.* ▶ **wyłaniać się; wychodzić** (*np. z opresji*) **2** to become known: ***It emerged that*** *she was lying about her age.* ▶ **okazać się**

■ **emergence** noun [U]: *the emergence of* (pojawienie się) *AIDS in the 1980s* ▶ **wyłonienie się**

⚷ **emergency** /i'mɜːdʒənsi/ noun [C,U] (pl. **emergencies**) a serious event that needs immediate action: *In an emergency* (w razie wypadku) *phone 999 for help.* ◇ *to declare **a state of emergency*** (stan wyjątkowy) ◇ *an emergency exit* wyjście awaryjne ◇ *emergency measures* środki nadzwyczajne ◇ *to undergo emergency surgery* przejść natychmiastową operację ▶ **nagły wypadek, awaria, krytyczna sytuacja**

e'mergency brake (US) = HANDBRAKE

e'mergency room [C] (abbr. **ER**) (US) = ACCIDENT AND EMERGENCY

e'mergency services noun [pl.] (Brit.) the public organizations that deal with emergencies: the police, fire, ambulance and coastguard services ▶ **służby ratownicze**

emergent /i'mɜːdʒənt/ adj. [usually before a noun] new and still developing: ***emergent nations/states*** ▶ **wyłaniający się**

emigrant /'emɪgrənt/ noun [C] a person who has gone to live in another country ▶ **emigrant/ka** ➲ look at **immigrant**

emigrate /'emɪgreɪt/ verb [I] **emigrate (from ...) (to ...)** to leave your own country to go and live in another ▶ **emigrować** ➲ look at **migrate**

■ **emigration** /ˌemɪ'greɪʃn/ noun [C,U] ▶ **emigracja** ➲ look at **immigration**

émigré /'emɪgreɪ/ noun [C] a person who has left their own country, usually for political reasons ▶ **emigrant/ka** (*zwł. polityczny*) SYN **exile**

eminent /'emɪnənt/ adj. (formal) (used about a person) famous and important: *an eminent scientist* ▶ **wybitny, sławny**

eminently /'emɪnəntli/ adv. (formal) very; extremely: *She is eminently suitable for the job.* ▶ **oczywiście, znakomicie**

emit /i'mɪt/ verb [T] (**emitting**; **emitted**) (formal) to send out sth, for example a smell, a sound, smoke, heat or light: *The animal emits a powerful smell when scared.* ▶ **emitować**

■ **emission** /i'mɪʃn/ noun [C,U]: *sulphur dioxide emissions from power stations* ▶ **emisja**

emoticon /ɪ'məʊtɪkɒn/ noun [C] a symbol that shows your feelings when you send an email or text message. For example :-) represents a smiling face. ▶ **emotikon**

⚷ **emotion** /ɪ'məʊʃn/ noun [C,U] a strong feeling such as love, anger, fear, etc.: *to control/express your emotions* ◇ *His voice was filled with emotion.* ◇ *Brown showed no emotion as the police took him away.* ▶ **uczucie, wzruszenie**

⚷ **emotional** /ɪ'məʊʃənl/ adj. **1** connected with people's feelings: *emotional problems* ▶ **uczuciowy, emocjonalny** **2** causing strong feelings: *Kelly gave an emotional speech.* ▶ **poruszający** **3** having strong emotions and showing them in front of people: *She always **gets** very **emotional*** (bardzo się wzrusza) *when I leave.* ▶ **uczuciowy**

■ **emotionally** /-ʃənəli/ adv.: *She felt physically and emotionally drained after giving birth.* ▶ **uczuciowo, emocjonalnie**

emotive /i'məʊtɪv/ adj. causing strong feelings: *emotive language* ◇ *an emotive issue* ▶ **wzruszający**

empathy /'empəθi/ noun [U] **empathy (with/for sb/sth); empathy (between A and B)** the ability to imagine how another person is feeling and so understand their mood: *Some adults **have** (a) great **empathy** with children.* ▶ **empatia, wczuwanie się**

■ **empathize** (also -ise) /'empəθaɪz/ verb [I] **empathize (with sb/sth)**: *He's a popular teacher because he empathizes with his students.* ▶ **utożsamiać się, wczuwać się** (*w czyjąś sytuację*)

emperor /'empərə(r)/ noun [C] the ruler of an empire ▶ **cesarz**

⚷ **emphasis** /'emfəsɪs/ noun [C,U] (pl. **emphases** /-siːz/) **1 emphasis (on sth)** (giving) special importance or attention (to sth): *There's a lot of emphasis on science at our school.* ◇ *You should **put** a greater **emphasis** on quality rather than quantity when you write.* ▶ **nacisk** **2** the force that you give to a word or phrase when you are speaking; a way of writing a word to show that it is important: *In the word 'photographer' the emphasis is on the second syllable.* ◇ *I underlined the key phrases of my letter for emphasis.* ▶ **nacisk, emfaza** SYN for both meanings **stress**[1]

⚷ **emphasize** (also -ise) /'emfəsaɪz/ verb [T] **emphasize (that ...)** to put **emphasis** on sth: *They emphasized that healthy eating is important.* ◇ *They emphasized the importance of healthy eating.* ▶ **podkreślać, kłaść nacisk na coś** SYN **stress**

emphatic /ɪm'fætɪk/ adj. said or expressed in a strong way: *an emphatic refusal/denial* ▶ **stanowczy, emfatyczny**

■ **emphatically** /-kli/ adv. ▶ **stanowczo, emfatycznie**

emphysema /ˌemfɪ'siːmə/ noun [U] a condition that affects the lungs, making it difficult to breathe ▶ **rozedma płuc**

⚷ **empire** /'empaɪə(r)/ noun [C] **1** a group of countries that is governed by one country: *the Roman Empire* ▶ **cesarstwo, imperium** ➲ look at **emperor, empress** **2** a very large company or group of companies: *a business empire* ▶ **imperium**

empirical /ɪm'pɪrɪkl/ adj. (formal) based on experiments and practical experience, not on ideas: *empirical evidence* ▶ **empiryczny, namacalny**

⚷ **employ** /ɪm'plɔɪ/ verb [T] **1 employ sb (in/on sth); employ sb (as sth)** to pay sb to work for you: *They employ 600 workers.* ◇ *He is employed as a lorry driver.* ▶ **zatrudniać**

➲ look at **unemployed 2** (formal) **employ sth (as sth)** to use: *In an emergency, an umbrella can be employed as a weapon.* ▶ **stosować**

employee /ɪm'plɔɪiː/ noun [C] a person who works for sb: *The factory has 500 employees.* ▶ **pracowni-k/ca** ➲ note at **job**

employer /ɪm'plɔɪə(r)/ noun [C] a person or company that employs other people ▶ **pracodaw-ca/czyni**

employment /ɪm'plɔɪmənt/ noun [U] **1** the state of having a paid job: *to be in/out of employment* ◇ *This bank can **give employment to** ten extra staff.* ◇ *It is difficult to **find employment** in the north of the country.* ▶ **zatrudnienie** ➲ note at **work** ➲ look at **unemployment 2** (formal) the use of sth: *the employment of force* ▶ **zastosowanie**

em'ployment agency noun [C] a company that helps people to find work and other companies to find workers ▶ **biuro pośrednictwa pracy, urząd pracy**

empower /ɪm'paʊə(r)/ verb [T, usually passive] (formal) to give sb power or authority (to do sth) ▶ **upoważniać, umożliwiać**

■ **empowerment** noun [U] ▶ **upoważnienie**

empress /'emprəs/ noun [C] **1** a woman who rules an empire ▶ **cesarzowa 2** the wife of an **emperor** ▶ **cesarzowa**

empty[1] /'empti/ adj. (**emptier**; **emptiest**) **1** having nothing or nobody inside it: *an empty box* ◇ *The bus was half empty.* ▶ **pusty, opustoszały 2** without meaning or value: *It was an empty threat.* ◇ *My life feels empty now the children have left home.* ▶ **pusty, czczy** SYN **hollow**

■ **emptiness** noun [U] ▶ **pustka**

empty[2] /'empti/ verb (**emptying**; **empties**; pt, pp **emptied**) **1** [T] **empty sth (out/out of sth)** to remove everything that is inside a container, etc.: *I've emptied a wardrobe for you to use.* ◇ *Luke emptied everything out of his desk and left.* ▶ **opróżniać; wylewać, wyrzucać, opróżniać 2** [I] to become empty: *The cinema emptied very quickly once the film was finished.* ▶ **opróżniać się, pustoszeć**

,empty-'handed adj. without getting what you wanted; without taking sth to sb: *The robbers fled empty-handed.* ▶ (*wrócić skądś*) **z pustymi rękami**

EMU /,iː em 'juː/ abbr. **Economic and Monetary Union** (of the countries of the European Union) ▶ **Unia Ekonomiczna i Monetarna** ➲ look at **euro**

emulate /'emjuleɪt/ verb [T] (formal) to try to do sth as well as, or better than, sb ▶ **(starać się) dorównać komuś/prześcignąć kogoś** ⓘ Mniej formalnym słowem jest **copy**.

emulsify /ɪ'mʌlsɪfaɪ/ verb [I,T] (**emulsifying**; **emulsifies**; pt, pp **emulsified**) if two liquids of different thicknesses **emulsify** or **are emulsified**, they combine to form a smooth mixture ▶ **emulgować (się)**

emulsion /ɪ'mʌlʃn/ noun [C,U] **1** a mixture of liquids that do not normally mix together, such as oil and water ▶ **emulsja 2** (also **e'mulsion paint**) (Brit.) a type of paint used on walls and ceilings that dries without leaving a shiny surface ▶ **farba emulsyjna**

enable /ɪ'neɪbl/ verb [T] **enable sb/sth to do sth** to make it possible for sb/sth to do sth: *The software enables you to access the Internet in seconds.* ▶ **umożliwiać** SYN **allow**

enact /ɪ'nækt/ verb [T] **1** [often passive] to pass a law: *legislation enacted by parliament* ▶ **uchwalać 2** [often passive] (formal) to perform a play or act a part in a play: *scenes from history enacted by local residents* ▶ **odgrywać, (za)grać 3** [T] (**be enacted**) (formal) to take place: *They seemed unaware of the drama being enacted a few feet away from them.* ▶ (*scena, akcja itp.*) **rozgrywać się**

enamel /ɪ'næml/ noun [U] **1** a hard, shiny substance used for protecting or decorating metal, etc.: *enamel paint* ▶ **emalia 2** the hard white outer covering of a tooth ▶ **szkliwo, emalia**

enc. = ENCL.

encapsulate /ɪn'kæpsjuleɪt/ verb [T] **encapsulate sth (in sth)** (formal) to express the most important parts of sth in a few words, a small space or a single object: *The poem encapsulates many of the central themes of her writing.* ▶ **ujmować zwięźle, podsumowywać** SYN **sum up**

enchant /ɪn'tʃɑːnt; US -'tʃænt/ verb [T] **1** (formal) to attract sb strongly and make them feel very interested, excited, etc.: *The happy family scene had enchanted him.* ▶ **oczarowywać** SYN **delight 2** to place sb/sth under a magic spell ▶ **rzucać czary/urok na kogoś/coś** SYN for both meanings **bewitch**

enchanted /ɪn'tʃɑːntɪd; US -'tʃæn-/ adj. **1** (in stories) affected by magic powers ▶ **zaczarowany 2** (formal) pleased or very interested: *The audience was enchanted by her singing.* ▶ **oczarowany, zachwycony**

enchanting /ɪn'tʃɑːntɪŋ; US -'tʃænt-/ adj. very nice or pleasant; attractive ▶ **czarujący, zachwycający** SYN **delightful**

encircle /ɪn'sɜːkl/ verb [T] (formal) to make a circle round sth; to surround: *London is encircled by the M25 motorway.* ▶ **otaczać, okrążać**

encl. (also **enc.**) abbr. **enclosed**; used on business letters to show that another document is being sent in the same envelope ▶ **w załączniku**

enclave /'enkleɪv/ noun [C] an area of a country or city where the people have a different religion, culture or **nationality** from those who live in the country or city that surrounds it ▶ **enklawa**

enclose /ɪn'kləʊz/ verb [T] **1** [usually passive] **enclose sth (in sth)** to surround sth with a wall, fence, etc.; to put one thing inside another: *He gets very nervous in enclosed spaces* (w zamkniętej przestrzeni). ◇ *The jewels were enclosed* (były zamknięte) *in a strong box.* ▶ **ogradzać, otaczać** (*ogrodzeniem*) **2** to put sth in an envelope, package, etc. with sth else: *Can I enclose a letter with this parcel?* ◇ ***Please find enclosed** a cheque for £100.* ▶ **przesyłać w załączeniu**

enclosure /ɪn'kləʊʒə(r)/ noun [C] **1** a piece of land inside a wall, fence, etc. that is used for a particular purpose: *a wildlife enclosure* ▶ **teren ogrodzony 2** something that is placed inside an envelope together with the letter ▶ **załącznik**

encode = CODE[2] (2)

encore[1] /'ɒŋkɔː(r)/ noun [C] a short, extra performance at the end of a concert, etc. ▶ **bis**

encore[2] /'ɒŋkɔː(r)/ interj. called out by an audience that wants the people who perform in a concert, etc. to sing or play sth extra ▶ **bis!**

encounter[1] /ɪn'kaʊntə(r)/ verb [T] **1** to experience sth (a danger, difficulty, etc.): *I've never encountered any discrimination at work.* ▶ **doświadczać, spotykać (się) (z czymś)** SYN **meet with sth 2** (formal) to meet sb unexpectedly; to experience or find sth unusual or new: *She was the most remarkable woman he had ever encountered.* ▶ **niespodziewanie spotykać kogoś/się z czymś, doświadczać** ➲ look at **come across sb/sth**

encounter[2] /ɪn'kaʊntə(r)/ noun [C] **an encounter (with sb/sth)**; **an encounter (between A and B)** an unexpected (often unpleasant) meeting or event: *I've had a number of **close encounters** with bad drivers.* ▶ **nieoczekiwanie i nieprzyjemne spotkanie**

encourage /ɪn'kʌrɪdʒ; US -'kɜːr-/ verb [T] **1 encourage sb/sth (in sth/to do sth)** to give hope, support or confidence to sb: *The teacher encouraged her students to ask questions.* ▶ **zachęcać, popierać** OPP **discourage** ⓘ Zwróć uwagę, że mówi się **discourage sb from doing sth**: *The teacher discouraged her students from asking questions.* **2** to make sth happen more easily: *The government wants to encourage new businesses.* ▶ **popierać, zachęcać** OPP for both meanings **discourage**

■ **encouragement** noun [C,U] ▶ **zachęta, poparcie** | **encouraging** adj. ▶ **zachęcający**

encroach /ɪnˈkrəʊtʃ/ verb [I] (formal) **encroach (on/upon sth)** to use more of sth than you should: *I do hope that I am not encroaching too much upon your free time.* ▶ **nadużywać** (*np. czyjegoś czasu*), **wtargnąć** (*na czyjąś ziemię*), **naruszać** (*prawa, prywatność*)

encrypt /ɪnˈkrɪpt/ verb [T] to put information into a special code, especially in order to prevent people from looking at it without authority ▶ **szyfrować**

■ **encryption** /ɪnˈkrɪpʃn/ noun [U] ▶ **szyfrowanie**

encumber /ɪnˈkʌmbə(r)/ verb [T, usually passive] **encumber sb/sth (with sth)** (formal) **1** to make it difficult for sb to do sth or for sth to happen: *The police operation was encumbered by crowds of reporters.* ◇ *The business is encumbered with debt* (jest obciążony długami). ▶ **przeszkadzać, utrudniać 2** to be large and/or heavy and make it difficult for sb to move: *The frogmen were encumbered by their diving equipment.* ▶ **obciążać, obarczać**

encyclopedia (also **encyclopaedia**) /ɪnˌsaɪkləˈpiːdiə/ noun [C] (pl. **encyclopedias**) a book or set of books that gives information about very many subjects, arranged in the order of the alphabet (= from A to Z); a similar collection of information on a CD-ROM ▶ **encyklopedia** ➲ note at **book**

end¹ /end/ noun [C] **1** the furthest or final part of sth; the place or time where sth stops: *My house is* ***at the end of*** *the street.* ◇ *I live in the end house* (w ostatnim domu). ◇ *the end seat* ostatnie miejsce (z tyłu autobusu itp.) ◇ *There are some seats* ***at the far end of*** *the room.* ◇ *I'm going on holiday* ***at the end of*** *October.* ◇ *He promised to give me an answer by the end of the week.* ◇ *She couldn't wait to hear the end of the story.* ◇ *The man on the other end of the phone spoke so quietly that I didn't catch his name.* ▶ **koniec**

> **In the end** czy **at the end**? Wyrażenie **in the end** odnosi się do czasu i oznacza „wreszcie", „w końcu": *We were too tired to cook, so in the end* (ostatecznie) *we decided to eat out.* **At the end of sth** odnosi się do ostatniej części książki, filmu, lekcji itp., do chwili, gdy książka (film, lekcja itp.) zbliżają się ku końcowi: *At the end of the meal* (pod koniec posiłku) *we had an argument about who should pay for it.*
>
> Por. rzeczownik **finish**, który oznacza to samo co **end** tylko w kontekście zawodów czy wyścigów.

2 (formal) an aim or purpose: *They were prepared to do anything to achieve their ends.* ▶ **cel 3** a little piece of sth that is left after the rest has been used: *a cigarette end* niedopałek papierosa ▶ **końcówka, resztka**

IDM **at an end** (formal) finished or used up: *Her career is at an end.* ▶ **skończony**

at the end of the day (Brit., informal) (used to say the most important fact in a situation): *At the end of the day, you have to make the decision yourself.* ▶ **w ostatecznym rachunku**

at the end of your tether feeling that you cannot deal with a difficult situation any more, because you are too tired, worried, etc. ▶ **u kresu wytrzymałości**

at a loose end → LOOSE¹

at your wits' end → WIT

bring sth/come/draw to an end (to cause sth) to finish: *His stay in England was coming to an end.* ▶ **kończyć (się)**

a dead end → DEAD¹

end to end in a line with the ends touching: *They put the tables end to end.* ▶ **na styk**

in the end at last; finally: *He wanted to get home early but in the end it was midnight before he left.* ▶ **w końcu**

make ends meet to have enough money for your needs: *It's hard for us to make ends meet.* ▶ **wiązać koniec z końcem**

make sb's hair stand on end → HAIR

a means to an end → MEANS

no end of sth (informal) too many or much; a lot of sth: *She has given us no end of trouble.* ▶ **mnóstwo, bez końca, bez liku**

odds and ends → ODDS

on end (used about time) continuously: *He sits and reads for hours on end.* ▶ **całymi** (*godzinami, dniami itp.*)

put an end to sth to stop sth from happening any more ▶ **położyć kres**

end² /end/ verb [I,T] **end (in/with sth)** (to cause sth) to finish: *The road ends here.* ◇ *How does this story end?* ◇ *The match ended in a draw.* ◇ *I think we'd better end this conversation now.* ▶ **kończyć (się)**

PHR V **end up (as sth)**; **end up (doing sth)** to find yourself in a place/situation that you did not plan or expect: *We got lost and ended up in the centre of town.* ◇ *She had always wanted to be a writer but ended up as a teacher.* ◇ *There was nothing to eat at home so we ended up going out* (w końcu stanęło na tym, że poszliśmy) *for fish and chips.* ▶ **skończyć (na czymś/jako coś), wylądować**

endanger /ɪnˈdeɪndʒə(r)/ verb [T] to cause danger to sb/sth: *Smoking seriously endangers your health.* ▶ **zagrażać, narażać na niebezpieczeństwo**

endangered /ɪnˈdeɪndʒəd/ adj. (used about animals, plants, etc.) in danger of becoming **extinct**: *The giant panda is* ***an endangered species.*** ▶ **zagrożony wyginięciem** ➲ note at **environment**

endear /ɪnˈdɪə(r)/ verb [T] (formal) **endear sb/yourself to sb** to make sb/yourself liked by sb: *She managed to endear herself to everybody by her kindness.* Dzięki swojej dobroci zdobyła ogólną sympatię. ▶ **zdobywać sympatię**

■ **endearing** adj.: *an endearing habit* ▶ **ujmujący, uroczy** | **endearingly** adv. ▶ **ujmująco, uroczo**

endeavour (US **endeavor**) /ɪnˈdevə(r)/ verb [I] (formal) **endeavour (to do sth)** to try hard: *She endeavoured to finish her work on time.* ▶ **usiłować, starać się**

■ **endeavour** noun [C,U] ▶ **usiłowanie, wysiłek, zabiegi**

endemic /enˈdemɪk/ adj. **endemic (in/to ...)** regularly found in a particular place or among a particular group of people and difficult to get rid of: *Malaria is endemic in many hot countries.* ◇ *the endemic problem of racism* ▶ **endemiczny**

ending /ˈendɪŋ/ noun [C] **1** the end (of a story, play, film, etc.): *That film made me cry but I was pleased that it had* ***a happy ending.*** ▶ **zakończenie 2** the last part of a word, which can change: *When nouns end in -ch or -sh or -x, the plural ending is -es not -s.* ▶ **końcówka**

endive (US) = CHICORY

endless /ˈendləs/ adj. **1** very large in size or amount and seeming to have no end: *The possibilities are endless.* ▶ **nieograniczony 2** lasting for a long time and seeming to have no end: *Our plane was delayed for hours and the wait seemed endless* (zdawało się, że oczekiwanie nie ma końca). ▶ **nie kończący się, ciągły** SYN **interminable**

■ **endlessly** adv. ▶ **ciągle, bez końca**

endocrine /ˈendəʊkrɪn; -kraɪn; US ˈendəkrɪn/ adj. connected with **glands** that put **hormones** and other products directly into the blood: *the endocrine system* ▶ (*med.*) **dokrewny**

endocrinology /ˌendəʊkrɪˈnɒlədʒi; US -krəˈn-/ noun [U] the part of medicine concerning the **endocrine** system and **hormones** ▶ **endokrynologia**

■ **endocrinologist** /-dʒɪst/ noun [C] ▶ **endokrynolog**

endorse /ɪn'dɔːs/ verb [T] **1** to say publicly that you give official support or agreement to a plan, statement, decision, etc.: *Members of all parties endorsed a ban on firearms.* ▶ **popierać 2** [usually passive] (Brit.) to add a note to sb's **driving licence** to say that the driver has broken the law ▶ **umieszczać w prawie jazdy adnotację o popełnieniu wykroczenia 3** to write your name on the back of the cheque ▶ **podpisywać się na odwrocie czeku**

■ **endorsement** noun [C,U] ▶ **potwierdzenie**; **adnotacja w prawie jazdy o popełnieniu wykroczenia**; **aprobata**

endow /ɪn'daʊ/ verb [T] to give a large sum of money to an institution such as a school or college: *In her will, she endowed a scholarship* (ufundowała stypendium) *in the physics department.* ▶ **zapisywać darowiznę na rzecz instytucji edukacyjnej**

PHR V **be endowed with sth** to naturally have a particular characteristic, quality, etc.: *She was endowed with intelligence and wit.* ▶ **być obdarzonym** (*np. talentem*)

endowment /ɪn'daʊmənt/ noun [C,U] money that is given to a school, college, etc.; the act of giving this money ▶ **darowizna**; **fundowanie**

'**end product** noun [C] something that is produced by a particular process or activity ▶ **produkt końcowy**

endurance /ɪn'djʊərəns; US -'dʊr-/ noun [U] the ability to continue doing sth painful or difficult for a long period of time without complaining ▶ **wytrzymałość**, **cierpliwość**

endure /ɪn'djʊə(r); US -'dʊr/ verb (formal) **1** [T] to suffer sth painful or uncomfortable, usually without complaining: *She endured ten years of loneliness.* ▶ **cierpieć**, **przetrzymywać** ⓘ Słowo **endure** jest często używane w przeczeniach: *My parents can't endure pop music.* W tym znaczeniu stosuje się też wyrażenia **can't bear** lub **can't stand**, które są mniej formalne. SYN **bear 2** [I] to continue ▶ **trwać** SYN **last**

■ **enduring** adj. ▶ **trwały**, **stały**

enemy /'enəmi/ noun (pl. **enemies**) **1** [C] a person who hates and tries to harm you: *They used to be friends but became* ***bitter enemies.*** ◇ *He has* ***made*** *several* ***enemies*** *during his career.* ▶ **wróg** ➲ look at **enmity 2** (**the enemy**) [sing., with sing. or pl. verb] the army or country that your country is fighting against: *The enemy is/are approaching.* ◇ *enemy forces* ▶ **wróg**

energetic /ˌenə'dʒetɪk/ adj. full of or needing energy and enthusiasm: *Jogging is a very energetic form of exercise.* ▶ **pełny/wymagający energii**, **energiczny**

■ **energetically** /-kli/ adv. ▶ **energicznie**

energize (also -ise) /'enədʒaɪz/ verb [T] **1** to make sb enthusiastic about sth ▶ **rozbudzać czyjś entuzjazm 2** to give sb more energy, strength, etc.: *a refreshing and energizing fruit drink* ▶ **pobudzać**, **wzmacniać**

energy /'enədʒi/ noun (pl. **energies**) **1** [U] the ability to be very active or do a lot of work without getting tired: *Children are usually* ***full of energy.*** ▶ **energia**, **siła 2** (**energies**) [pl.] the effort and attention that you give to doing sth: *She devoted her energies to helping others.* ▶ **energia**, **siły 3** [U] the power that comes from coal, electricity, gas, etc. that is used for producing heat, driving machines, etc.: *nuclear energy* ▶ **energia**

enforce /ɪn'fɔːs/ verb [T] to make people obey a law or rule or do sth that they do not want to: *How will they enforce the new law?* ▶ **egzekwować**, **wprowadzać w życie**, **wymuszać**

■ **enforced** adj.: *enforced redundancies* ▶ **wymuszony**, **przymusowy** | **enforcement** noun [U] ▶ **egzekwowanie**, **narzucanie**, **wprowadzanie w życie**

enfranchise /ɪn'fræntʃaɪz/ verb [T, usually passive] (formal) to give sb the right to vote in an election ▶ **nadawać komuś prawo wyborcze**

■ **enfranchisement** /ɪn'fræntʃɪzmənt/ noun [U] ▶ **nadanie komuś prawa wyborczego**

engage /ɪn'geɪdʒ/ verb (formal) **1** [T] to interest or attract sb: *You need to engage the students' attention right from the start.* ▶ **zajmować**, **angażować 2** [T] **engage sb (as sth)** to give work to sb: *They engaged him as a cook.* ▶ **zatrudniać 3** [I,T] when a part of a machine **engages**, or when you **engage** it, it fits together with another part of the machine and the machine begins to work: *One cogwheel engages* (zazębia się) *with the next.* ◇ *Engage the clutch* (naciśnij sprzęgło) *before selecting a gear.* ▶ **włączać (się)**

PHR V **engage in sth** to take part in sth: *I don't engage in that kind of gossip!* ▶ **zajmować się czymś**, **brać udział w czymś**

engaged /ɪn'geɪdʒd/ adj. **1** (formal) **engaged (in/on sth)** (used about a person) busy doing sth: *I'm afraid I can't come. I'm* ***otherwise engaged*** (mam inne zobowiązania). ◇ *They are engaged in talks* (prowadzą rozmowy) *with the Irish government.* ▶ **zajęty 2 engaged (to sb)** having agreed to get married: *Susan is engaged to Jim.* ◇ *We've just* ***got engaged.*** Właśnie się zaręczyliśmy. ▶ **zaręczony 3** (especially US **busy**) (used about a telephone) in use: *I can't get through – the line is engaged.* ▶ **zajęty 4** (used about a toilet) in use ▶ **zajęty** OPP **vacant**

engagement /ɪn'geɪdʒmənt/ noun [C] **1** an agreement to get married; the time when you are **engaged**: *He broke off their engagement.* ▶ **zaręczyny**, **narzeczeństwo 2** (formal) an arrangement to go somewhere or do sth at a fixed time: *I can't come on Tuesday as I have a* ***prior engagement.*** ▶ **umówione spotkanie**, **zajęcie** SYN **appointment**

en'gagement ring noun [C] a ring, usually with **precious** stones in it, that a man gives to a woman when they agree to get married ▶ **pierścionek zaręczynowy**

engender /ɪn'dʒendə(r)/ verb [T] (formal) to make a feeling or situation exist: *The issue engendered controversy.* ◇ *problems engendered* (spowodowane) *by the restructuring of the company* ▶ **rodzić**, **być źródłem**

engine /'endʒɪn/ noun [C] **1** the part of a vehicle that produces power to make the vehicle move: *This engine runs on diesel.* ◇ *a car/jet engine* ▶ **silnik**, **motor** ➲ note at **motor 2** (also **locomotive** /ˌləʊkə'məʊtɪv/) a vehicle that pulls a railway train ▶ **lokomotywa**

'**engine driver** (also '**train driver**; US **engineer**) noun [C] a person whose job is to drive a railway engine ▶ **maszynista**

engineer[1] /ˌendʒɪ'nɪə(r)/ noun [C] **1** a person whose job is to design, build or repair engines, machines, etc.: *a chemical/electrical/mechanical engineer* inżynier chemik/elektryk/mechanik ◇ *a civil engineer* inżynier budownictwa wodno-lądowego ▶ **inżynier**, **technik 2** (US) = ENGINE DRIVER

engineer[2] /ˌendʒɪ'nɪə(r)/ verb [T] (formal) to arrange for sth to happen by careful secret planning: *Her promotion was engineered by her father.* ▶ **aranżować w tajemnicy**, **przeprowadzać z ukrycia** (*np. akcję*)

engineering /ˌendʒɪ'nɪərɪŋ/ noun [U] (the study of) the work that is done by an **engineer**: *mechanical/civil/chemical engineering* ▶ **inżynieria**, **technika**, **mechanika**

English[1] /'ɪŋglɪʃ/ noun **1** [U] the language that is spoken in Britain, the US, Australia, etc.: *Do you speak English?* ◇ *I've been learning English for 5 years.* ◇ *I am studying English at Warsaw University* Studiuję anglistykę na Uniwersytecie Warszawskim. ▶ **język angielski 2** (**the English**) [pl.] the people of England ▶ **Anglicy**

English[2] /'ɪŋglɪʃ/ adj. belonging to England, the English people, the English language, etc. ▶ **angielski**

Uwaga! Mieszkańcy Szkocji **the Scots** i Walii **the Welsh** nie są Anglikami, lecz Brytyjczykami. ➲ note at **United Kingdom**

ˌEnglish ˈbreakfast noun [C] a breakfast that consists of cereals, cooked bacon and eggs, toast and marmalade and tea or coffee, etc. ▶ **tradycyjne angielskie śniadanie** ➲ look at **continental breakfast**

the **ˌEnglish ˈChannel** = CHANNEL[1] (6)

Englishman /ˈɪŋɡlɪʃmən/, **Englishwoman** /ˈɪŋɡlɪʃwʊmən/ noun [C] (pl. **-men** /-mən/; **-women** /-wɪmɪn/) a person who comes from England or whose parents are English ▶ **Anglik**, **Angielka**

Anglicy zwykle mówią o sobie **I'm English**, (a nie ~~*I'm an Englishman*~~). O kobiecie Angielce można powiedzieć **an Englishwoman**, ale nie jest to forma często stosowana.

ˌEnglish ˈmuffin (US) = MUFFIN (1)

engrave /ɪnˈɡreɪv/ verb [T] **engrave B on A**; **engrave A with B** to cut words or designs on metal, stone, etc.: *His name is engraved on the cup.* ◇ *The cup is engraved with his name.* ▶ **grawerować**, **wy/ryć**

engraving /ɪnˈɡreɪvɪŋ/ noun [C,U] a design that is cut into a piece of metal or stone; a picture made from this ▶ **grawiura**, **rycina**

engross /ɪnˈɡrəʊs/ verb [T] if sth **engrosses** you, it is so interesting that you give it all your attention and time: *As the business grew, it totally engrossed him.* ▶ **pochłaniać**, **absorbować**
■ **engrossing** /ɪnˈɡrəʊsɪŋ/ adj. ▶ **absorbujący**

engrossed /ɪnˈɡrəʊst/ adj. **engrossed (in/with sth)** so interested in sth that you give it all your attention: *She was completely engrossed in her book.* ▶ **pochłonięty**, **zaabsorbowany**

engulf /ɪnˈɡʌlf/ verb [T] (formal) **1** to surround or to cover sb/sth completely: *He was engulfed by a crowd of reporters.* ◇ *The vehicle was **engulfed in flames**.* ▶ **otaczać**, (*przen.*) **zatapiać** **2** to affect sb/sth very strongly: *Fear engulfed her.* ▶ (*uczucie itp.*) **ogarniać**

enhance /ɪnˈhɑːns; US -ˈhæns/ verb [T] (formal) to improve sth or to make sth look better ▶ **polepszać**; **uwydatniać**

enigma /ɪˈnɪɡmə/ noun [C] (pl. **enigmas**) a person, thing or situation that is difficult to understand ▶ **enigma**, **zagadka**
■ **enigmatic** /ˌenɪɡˈmætɪk/ adj. ▶ **enigmatyczny**, **zagadkowy**

⚷ **enjoy** /ɪnˈdʒɔɪ/ verb [T] **1 enjoy sth/enjoy doing sth** to get pleasure from sth: *I really enjoyed that meal.* ◇ *He enjoys listening to music while he's driving.* ▶ **lubić**, **podobać się**, **smakować** ➲ note at **like** **2 enjoy yourself** to be happy; to have a good time: *I enjoyed myself at the party last night.* ▶ **dobrze się bawić**, **miło spędzać czas**

⚷ **enjoyable** /ɪnˈdʒɔɪəbl/ adj. giving pleasure ▶ **przyjemny**, **miły**

⚷ **enjoyment** /ɪnˈdʒɔɪmənt/ noun [U,C] pleasure or a thing which gives pleasure: *She gets a lot of enjoyment from teaching.* Uczenie sprawia jej dużo przyjemności. ◇ *One of her main enjoyments is foreign travel.* ▶ **przyjemność**, **zadowolenie**

enlarge /ɪnˈlɑːdʒ/ verb [I,T] to make sth bigger or to become bigger: *I'm going to have this photo enlarged.* ▶ **powiększać (się)**, **rozszerzać (się)**
PHR V **enlarge on sth** to say or write more about sth ▶ **rozwijać** (*temat, myśl*)

enlargement /ɪnˈlɑːdʒmənt/ noun [U,C] making sth bigger or sth that has been made bigger: *an enlargement of a photo* ▶ **powiększenie**, **rozszerzenie** SYN **reduction**

enlighten /ɪnˈlaɪtn/ verb [T] (formal) to give sb information so that they understand sth better ▶ **oświecać**, **objaśniać**

enlightened /ɪnˈlaɪtnd/ adj. having an understanding of people's needs, a situation, etc. that shows a modern attitude to life ▶ (*osoba*) **światły**, (*sytuacja*) **nowoczesny**, **oświecony**

enlist /ɪnˈlɪst/ verb **1** [T] to get help, support, etc.: *We need to enlist your support.* ▶ **uzyskiwać**, **zjednywać** (*poparcie*) **2** [I,T] to join the army, navy or air force; to make sb a member of the army, etc.: *They enlisted as soon as war was declared.* ▶ **wstępować do wojska**; **werbować**

enliven /ɪnˈlaɪvn/ verb [T] (formal) to make sth more interesting or more fun ▶ **ożywiać**, **uczynić coś ciekawszym/weselszym itp.**

en masse /ˌɒ̃ ˈmæs/ adv. all together, and usually in large numbers: *The young folk were emigrating en masse.* ▶ **masowo**

enmity /ˈenməti/ noun [U] the feeling of hatred towards an enemy ▶ **wrogość**

enormity /ɪˈnɔːməti/ noun [sing.] (formal) the very great size, effect, etc. of sth; the fact that sth is very serious: *the enormity of a task/decision/problem* ▶ **ogrom**; **potworność** (*np. zbrodni*)

⚷ **enormous** /ɪˈnɔːməs/ adj. very big or very great: *an enormous building* ◇ *enormous pleasure* ▶ **ogromny**, **olbrzymi** SYN **huge**
■ **enormously** adv. ▶ **ogromnie**, **wielce**

⚷ **enough**[1] /ɪˈnʌf/ determiner, pron. **1** as much or as many of sth as necessary: *We've saved enough money to buy a computer.* ◇ *Not everybody can have a book – there aren't enough.* ◇ *If enough of you are interested, we'll arrange a trip to the theatre.* ▶ **wystarczająca (ilość/liczba)**, **wystarczająco dużo**, **dosyć** **2** as much or as many as you want: *I've had enough of living in a city.* ◇ *Don't give me any more books. I've got **quite enough** already.* ▶ **dosyć**, **wystarczająco dużo**

⚷ **enough**[2] /ɪˈnʌf/ adv. [used after verbs, adjectives and adverbs] **1** to the necessary amount or degree: *You don't practise enough.* ◇ *He's not old enough to travel alone.* ◇ *Does she speak Italian well enough to get the job?* ▶ **dostatecznie**, **wystarczająco** SYN **sufficiently** **2** quite, but not very: *She plays well enough, for a beginner.* ▶ **dosyć**, **całkiem**
IDM **fair enough** → FAIR[1]
funnily, strangely, etc. enough it is funny, etc. that...: *Funnily enough, I thought exactly the same myself.* ▶ **a co najśmieszniejsze, najdziwniejsze itp., to ...**
sure enough → SURE

enquire (also **inquire**) /ɪnˈkwaɪə(r)/ verb [I,T] (formal) **enquire (about sb/sth)** to ask for information about sth: *Could you enquire when the trains to Cork leave?* ◇ *We need to enquire about hotels in Vienna.* ▶ **pytać (się)**, **dowiadywać się**
PHR V **enquire after sb** to ask about sb's health ▶ **pytać o czyjeś zdrowie**
enquire into sth to study sth in order to find out all the facts: *The journalist enquired into the politician's financial affairs.* ▶ **dociekać czegoś**, **wnikać w coś**

enquirer (also **inquirer**) /ɪnˈkwaɪərə(r)/ noun [C] (formal) a person who asks for information ▶ **informując-y/a się**, **pytając-y/a**

enquiring (also **inquiring**) /ɪnˈkwaɪərɪŋ/ adj. **1** interested in learning new things: *We should encourage children to have enquiring minds.* ▶ **dociekliwy**, **wnikliwy** **2** asking for information: *He gave me an enquiring look.* ▶ **badawczy**
■ **enquiringly** (also **inquiringly**) adv. ▶ **pytająco**, **badawczo**

⚷ **enquiry** (also **inquiry**) /ɪnˈkwaɪəri/ noun (pl. **enquiries**) **1** [C] (formal) **an enquiry (about/concerning/into sb/sth)** a question that you ask about sth: *I'll **make** some **enquiries** into* (zasięgnę informacji na temat) *English language courses* in Oxford. ▶ **prośba o informację, zasięganie informacji** **2** [U] the act of asking about sth: *After weeks of enquiry he finally found what he was looking for.* ▶ **dowiadywanie się, zapytanie** **3** [C] **an enquiry (into sth)** an official process to find out the cause of sth: *After the accident there was an enquiry into safety procedures.* ▶ **dochodzenie, śledztwo**

enrage /ɪnˈreɪdʒ/ verb [T] (formal) to make sb very angry ▶ **rozwścieczyć, rozzłościć**

enrapture /ɪnˈræptʃə(r)/ verb [T, usually passive] (formal) to give sb great pleasure or joy ▶ **zachwycać, oczarowywać** SYN enchant

enrich /ɪnˈrɪtʃ/ verb [T] **1** to improve the quality, flavour, etc. of sth: *These cornflakes are enriched with vitamins.* ▶ **wzbogacać** **2** to make sb/sth rich or richer ▶ **wzbogacać, polepszać** (*np. jakość*) OPP impoverish
■ **enrichment** noun [U] ▶ **wzbogacenie**

enrol (US **enroll**) /ɪnˈrəʊl/ verb [I,T] (**enrolling**; **enrolled**) to become or to make sb a member of a club, school, etc.: (Brit.) *I've enrolled on an Italian course.* ◇ (US) *to enrol in a course* ◇ *They enrolled 100 new students last year.* ▶ **zapisywać (się)**
■ **enrolment** (US **enrollment**) noun [U] ▶ **zapisy (na coś/do czegoś), zgłoszenia**

en route /ˌɒ̃ ˈruːt; US also ˌɒn/ adv. **en route (from ...) (to ...)**; **en route (for...)** on the way; while travelling from/to a place ▶ **w drodze (dokądś)**

ensemble /ɒnˈsɒmbl/ noun **1** [C, with sing. or pl. verb] a small group of musicians, dancers or actors who perform together: *a brass/wind/string ensemble* ◇ *The ensemble is/are based in Lyon.* ▶ **zespół muzyczny/taneczny/aktorski** **2** [C, usually sing.] a set of clothes that are worn together ▶ **strój**

enslave /ɪnˈsleɪv/ verb [T, usually passive] to make sb a **slave** ▶ **czynić kogoś niewolnikiem**
■ **enslavement** noun [U] ▶ **uczynienienie kogoś niewolnikiem**

ensue /ɪnˈsjuː; US -ˈsuː/ verb [I] (formal) to happen after (and often as a result of) sth else ▶ **wynikać, być następstwem czegoś**

en suite /ˌɒ̃ ˈswiːt/ adj. (used about a bathroom) joined onto a bedroom and for use only by people in that bedroom ▶ **połączony z czymś**
■ **en suite** adv.: *The bedroom has a bathroom en suite.* To sypialnia z łazienką.

🔑 **ensure** (US **insure**) /ɪnˈʃʊə(r); Brit. also -ˈʃɔː(r)/ verb [T] to make sure that sth happens or is definite: *Please ensure that the door is locked before you leave.* Zanim wyjdziesz, upewnij się, czy drzwi są zamknięte na klucz. ▶ **zapewniać, gwarantować**

entail /ɪnˈteɪl/ verb [T] (formal) to make sth necessary; to involve sth: *The job sounds interesting but I'm not sure what it entails.* ▶ **pociągać za sobą, wymagać**

entangled /ɪnˈtæŋgld/ adj. caught in sth else: *The bird was entangled in the net.* ◇ (figurative) *She didn't want to get emotionally entangled with him.* Nie chciała się z nim wiązać emocjonalnie. ◇ *I've got myself entangled* (uwikłałem się) *in some financial problems.* ▶ **zaplątany, uwikłany**

🔑 **enter** /ˈentə(r)/ verb **1** [I,T] (formal) to come or go into a place: *Don't enter without knocking.* ◇ *They all stood up when he entered the room.* ▶ **wchodzić (do czegoś); wkraczać** ℹ Zwróć uwagę, że czasownik **enter** występuje bez przyimka. Bardziej potocznymi odpowiednikami tego słowa są **come into** i **go into**. ➲ nouns **entrance**, **entry** **2** [T] to become a member of sth, especially a profession or an institution: *She entered the legal profession in 1998.* ◇ *to enter school/college/university* ▶ **wstępować (do czegoś), rozpoczynać działalność, obierać** (*zawód*) ➲ noun **entrant** **3** [T] to begin or become involved in an activity, a situation, etc.: *When she entered the relationship, she had no idea he was already married.* ◇ *We have just entered* (wkroczyliśmy w) *a new phase in international relations.* ▶ **zapoczątkować** **4** [I,T] **enter (for) sth**; **enter sb (in/for sth)** to put your name or sb's name on the list for an exam, race, competition, etc.: *I entered a competition in the Sunday paper and I won £20!* ▶ **zgłaszać udział, przystępować** **5** [T] **enter sth (in/into/on/onto sth)** to put names, numbers, details, etc. in a list, book, computer, etc.: *Enter your password and press return.* ◇ *I've entered all the data onto the computer.* ▶ **wpisywać, zapisywać**
PHR V **enter into sth** **1** to start to think or talk about sth: *I don't want to enter into details now.* ▶ **wchodzić w coś, zagłębiać się w coś** **2** to be part of sth; to be involved in sth: *This is a business matter. Friendship doesn't enter into it.* ▶ **mieć związek z czymś**
enter into sth (with sb) to begin sth: *The government has entered into negotiations with the unions.* ▶ **rozpoczynać coś (z kimś), przystępować** (*np. do negocjacji (z kimś)*)

enterprise /ˈentəpraɪz/ noun **1** [C] a company or business: *a new industrial enterprise* ▶ **przedsiębiorstwo** **2** [C] a large project, especially one that is difficult: *It's a very exciting new enterprise.* ▶ **przedsięwzięcie, inicjatywa** **3** [U] the development of businesses by the people of a country rather than by the government: *grants to encourage enterprise in the region* ◇ *private enterprise* ▶ **przedsiębiorstwo** **4** [U] the ability to think of new projects or create new businesses and make them successful: *We need men and women of enterprise and energy.* ▶ **inicjatywa, przedsiębiorczość**

enterprising /ˈentəpraɪzɪŋ/ adj. having or showing the ability to think of new projects or new ways of doing things and make them successful ▶ **przedsiębiorczy**

🔑 **entertain** /ˌentəˈteɪn/ verb **1** [I,T] to welcome sb as a guest, especially to your home; to give sb food and drink: *They entertain a lot.* ◇ *They do a lot of entertaining.* ▶ **podejmować gości** **2** [T] **entertain (sb) (with sth)** to interest and amuse sb in order to please them: *I find it very hard to keep my class entertained on a Friday afternoon.* ▶ **bawić, zabawiać**

🔑 **entertainer** /ˌentəˈteɪnə(r)/ noun [C] a person whose job is to amuse people, for example by singing, dancing or telling jokes: *a street entertainer* ▶ **osoba zawodowo zajmująca się rozrywką, konferansjer**

🔑 **entertaining** /ˌentəˈteɪnɪŋ/ adj. interesting and amusing ▶ **rozrywkowy, zabawny**

🔑 **entertainment** /ˌentəˈteɪnmənt/ noun [U,C] film, music, etc. used to interest and amuse people: *There isn't much entertainment for young people in this town.* ◇ *There's a full programme of entertainments every evening.* ◇ *Entertainments Guide* dział w gazecie informujący o programach kin, teatrów itp. ▶ **rozrywka**

enthral (US **enthrall**) /ɪnˈθrɔːl/ verb [T] (**enthralling**; **enthralled**) to hold sb's interest and attention completely: *He was enthralled by her story.* ▶ **oczarowywać, pochłaniać (uwagę)**
■ **enthralling** adj. ▶ **zajmujący**

enthrone /ɪnˈθrəʊn/ verb [T, usually passive] when a king, queen or important member of a Church is **enthroned**, they sit on a **throne** in a ceremony to mark the beginning of their rule: *The painting depicts the enthroned* (siedzącą na tronie) *Madonna and Child.* ▶ **intronizować**
■ **enthronement** noun [U,C] ▶ **intronizacja**

enthuse /ɪnˈθjuːz; US -θuːz/ verb **1** **enthuse (about/over sth/sb)** [I,T] to talk in an enthusiastic and excited way about sth: *The article enthused about the benefits that the new system would bring.* ◇ *'It's a wonderful idea', he enthused.* ▶ **entuzjazmować się** **2** [T, usually passive] **enthuse sb (with sth)** to make sb feel very interested and excited: *Everyone* *present was enthused by the idea.* ▶ **zarażać kogoś entuzjazmem**

enthusiasm /ɪn'θju:ziæzəm; US -'θu:-/ noun [U] **enthusiasm (for/about sth/doing sth)** a strong feeling of excitement or interest in sth and a desire to become involved in it: *Jan showed great enthusiasm for the new project.* ◇ *There wasn't much enthusiasm* (nie wywołało to większego entuzjazmu) *when I mentioned the trip to the museum.* ▶ **entuzjazm**

enthusiast /ɪn'θju:ziæst; US -'θu:-/ noun [C] a person who is very interested in an activity or subject ▶ **entuzjast(k)a**

enthusiastic /ɪn,θju:zi'æstɪk; US -,θu:-/ adj. **enthusiastic (about sth/doing sth)** full of excitement and interest in sth ▶ **entuzjastyczny**, **pełen zapału**
■ **enthusiastically** /-kli/ adv. ▶ **entuzjastycznie**

entice /ɪn'taɪs/ verb [T] **entice sb (into sth/doing sth)** to persuade sb to do sth or to go somewhere by offering them sth nice: *Advertisements try to entice people into buying more things than they need.* ▶ **kusić**, **wabić**
■ **enticement** noun [C,U] ▶ **pokusa**

enticing /ɪn'taɪsɪŋ/ adj. attractive and interesting ▶ **kuszący**, **ponętny**

entire /ɪn'taɪə(r)/ adj. [only before a noun] whole or complete: *He managed to read the entire book in two days.* ▶ **cały**, **całkowity** ⓘ Słowo **entire** ma mocniejszy wydźwięk niż **whole**. SYN **whole**
■ **entirely** adv.: *I entirely agree with Michael.* ▶ **całkowicie** | **entirety** /ɪn'taɪərəti/ noun [U]: *We must consider the problem in its entirety* (we wszystkich aspektach). ▶ **całość**

entitle /ɪn'taɪtl/ verb [T, usually passive] **entitle sb (to sth)** to give sb the right to have or do sth: *I think I'm entitled* (mam prawo) *to a day's holiday – I've worked hard enough.* ▶ **uprawniać**, **upoważniać**

entitled /ɪn'taɪtld/ adj. (used about books, plays, etc.) with the title ▶ **zatytułowany**, **pod tytułem**

entitlement /ɪn'taɪtlmənt/ noun (formal) **1** [U] **entitlement (to sth)** the official right to have or do sth: *This may affect your entitlement to compensation.* ▶ **prawo do czegoś** **2** [C] something that you have an official right to; the amount that you have the right to receive: *Your contributions will affect your pension entitlements.* ▶ **uprawnienie**

entity /'entəti/ noun [C] (pl. **entities**) something that exists separately from sth else and has its own identity: *The kindergarten and the school are in the same building but they're really* ***separate entities.*** ▶ **jednostka**, **istota**

entrance /'entrəns/ noun **1** [C] **the entrance (to/of sth)** the door, gate or opening where you go into a place: *I'll meet you at the entrance to the theatre.* ▶ **wejście**, **wjazd** ⓘ W Amer. ang. używa się w tym samym znaczeniu słowa **entry**. OPP **exit** **2** [C] **entrance (into/onto sth)** the act of coming or going into a place, especially in a way that attracts attention: *He made a dramatic entrance onto the stage.* ▶ **wejście** ⓘ W tym samym znaczeniu można użyć słowa **entry**. SYN **entry** OPP **exit** **3** [U] **entrance (to sth)** the right to enter a place: *an entrance fee* ◇ *They were refused entrance* (odmówiono im prawa wstępu) *to the club.* ▶ **wstęp** SYN **entry** ⓘ W tym samym znaczeniu używa się też słowa **entry**. ➲ look at **admission**, **admittance** **4** [U] **entrance (into/to sth)** permission to join a club, society, university, etc.: *You don't need to take an entrance exam to get into university.* ▶ **wstęp** ➲ look at **admission**

entrant /'entrənt/ noun [C] a person who enters a profession, competition, exam, university, etc. ▶ **początkujący/a** (*w zawodzie*), **uczestni-k/czka**; **kandydat/ka**; **rozpoczynając-y/a studia**

entrap /ɪn'træp/ verb (**entrapping**; **entrapped**) [T, often passive] (formal) **1** to put or catch sb/sth in a place or situation from which they cannot escape: *She felt entrapped by her family's expectations.* ▶ (*przen.*) **złapać w pułapkę** SYN **trap** **2** **entrap sb (into doing sth)** to trick sb, and encourage them to do sth, especially to commit a crime, so that they can be arrested for it ▶ **podstępnie zachęcić kogoś do popełnienia nielegalnego czynu, którego konsekwencją będzie zaaresztowanie**

entreat /ɪn'tri:t/ verb [T] (formal) to ask sb to do sth, often in an emotional way ▶ **upraszać**, **błagać** SYN **beg**

entrepreneur /,ɒntrəprə'nɜ:(r)/ noun [C] a person who makes money by starting or running businesses, especially when this involves taking financial risks ▶ **przedsiębiorca**
■ **entrepreneurial** /,ɒntrəprə'nɜ:riəl/ adj. ▶ **przedsiębiorczy**

entrust /ɪn'trʌst/ verb [T] (formal) **entrust A with B/entrust B to A** to make sb responsible for sth: *I entrusted Rachel with the arrangements for the party.* ◇ *I entrusted the arrangements for the party to Rachel.* ▶ **powierzać**

entry /'entri/ noun (pl. **entries**) **1** [C] the act of coming or going into a place: *The thieves forced entry* (włamali się) *into the building.* ▶ **wejście**, **wkroczenie** SYN **entrance** **2** [U] **entry (to/into sth)** the right to enter a place: *an entry visa* ◇ *The immigrants were refused entry* (odmówiono imigrantom zezwolenia na wjazd) *at the airport.* ◇ *The sign says 'No Entry'* (wstęp wzbroniony). ▶ **wstęp**, **wjazd** SYN **entrance** ➲ look at **admission**, **admittance** **3** [U] the right to take part in sth or become a member of a group: *countries seeking entry into the European Union* ▶ **wejście** **4** [C] a person or thing that is entered for a competition, etc.: *There were fifty entries for the Eurovision song contest.* ◇ *The winning entry is number 45!* ▶ **zgłoszenie** **5** [C] one item that is written down in a list, account book, dictionary, etc.: *an entry in a diary* ◇ *You'll find 'ice-skate' after the entry for 'ice'.* ▶ **pozycja**; **hasło**, **zapis** **6** [C] (US) a door, gate, passage, etc. where you enter a building, etc. ▶ **wejście**, **wjazd** ⓘ W Amer. ang. można też użyć słowa **entrance**, które jednak jest jedynym słowem używanym w tym znaczeniu w Br. ang. SYN **entrance**

entwine /ɪn'twaɪn/ verb [T, usually passive] **1** **entwine sth (with/in/around sth)** to twist or wind sth around sth else: *They strolled through the park, with arms entwined* (ze splecionymi rękami). ◇ *The balcony was entwined with roses* (opleciony różami). ▶ **splatać**, **oplatać** **2** (**be entwined (with sth)**) to be very closely involved or connected with sth: *Her destiny was entwined with his.* Jej los był spleciony z jego losem. ◇ *Their lives are entwined.* ▶ **splatać**

enumerate /ɪ'nju:məreɪt; US ɪ'nu:-/ verb [T] (formal) to name things on a list one by one: *She enumerated the main points.* ▶ **wyliczać**, **wymieniać**
■ **enumeration** /ɪ,nju:mə'reɪʃn; US ɪ,nu:-/ noun [U,C] ▶ **wyliczanie**, **wymienianie**

enunciate /ɪ'nʌnsieɪt/ verb [I,T] to say or pronounce words clearly: *She enunciated each word slowly and carefully.* ▶ **wyraźnie wymawiać**
■ **enunciation** /ɪ,nʌnsi'eɪʃn/ noun [U] ▶ **wyraźna wymowa**

envelop /ɪn'veləp/ verb [T] (formal) to cover or surround sb/sth completely (in sth): *The hills were enveloped in mist.* ▶ **spowijać**, **okrywać**

envelope /'envələʊp; 'ɒn-/ noun [C] the paper cover for a letter ▶ **koperta** ➲ look at **stamped addressed envelope**

> After writing a letter, you **address** the envelope, **seal** it and **stick a stamp** in the top right-hand corner. Sometimes when you answer an advertisement you are asked to send an **SAE**. This is a **stamped addressed envelope**, addressed to yourself.

enviable /ˈenviəbl/ adj. (used about sth that sb else has and that you would like) attractive ▶ **godny pozazdroszczenia** ➲ verb, noun **envy**

envious /ˈenviəs/ adj. **envious (of sb/sth)** wanting sth that sb else has: *She was envious of her sister's success.* ▶ **zazdrosny** SYN **jealous** ➲ verb, noun **envy**
■ **enviously** adv. ▶ **zazdrośnie**

environment /ɪnˈvaɪrənmənt/ noun **1** [C,U] the conditions in which you live, work, etc.: *a pleasant working environment* ▶ **otoczenie**, **środowisko 2** (**the environment**) [sing.] the natural world, for example the land, air and water, in which people, animals and plants live: *We need stronger laws to protect the environment.* ▶ **środowisko naturalne** ➲ look at **surroundings**
■ **environmental** /ɪnˌvaɪrənˈmentl/ adj.: *environmental science* nauka o środowisku ▶ **środowiskowy**, **dotyczący/wywołany wpływem środowiska/otoczenia** | **environmentally** /-təli/ adv.: *environmentally-damaging* (szkodliwe dla środowiska naturalnego) *forms of transport* ◇ *environmentally-sensitive* (ekologicznie znaczące) *coastal areas* ◇ *environmentally conscious* świadomy znaczenia środowiska naturalnego ▶ **środowiskowo**, **ekologicznie**, (*ważny, szkodliwy itp.*) **dla środowiska**

> **the environment**
> The environment is being damaged by air and water **pollution**. Many **species** of wildlife are **endangered** as a result of **deforestation** and **acid rain**. **Environmentalists** are also concerned about **global warming** and the hole in the **ozone layer**.
> We can **conserve** the Earth's **resources** by **recycling** more **waste**, and by using **renewable energy** such as **solar power** and **hydroelectric power**.

environmentalist /ɪnˌvaɪrənˈmentəlɪst/ noun [C] a person who wants to protect the environment ▶ **zwolenni-k/czka działań na rzecz ochrony środowiska naturalnego**

enˌvironmentally ˈfriendly (also **enˌvironment-ˈfriendly**) adj. (used about products) not harming the environment: *environmentally-friendly packaging* ▶ **ekologiczny**, **przyjazny środowisku**

environs /ɪnˈvaɪrəns/ noun [pl.] (formal) the area around a place, especially a town: *Berlin and its environs* ▶ **okolica**

envisage /ɪnˈvɪzɪdʒ/ verb [T] (formal) to think of sth as being possible in the future; to imagine: *I don't envisage any problems with this.* ▶ **wyobrażać sobie**

envoy /ˈenvɔɪ/ noun [C] a person who is sent by a government with a message to another country ▶ **wysłanni-k/czka**

envy[1] /ˈenvi/ noun [U] **envy (of sb)**; **envy (at/of sth)** the feeling that you have when sb else has sth that you want: *It was difficult for her to hide her envy of her friend's success.* ▶ **zazdrość** ➲ look at **enviable**, **envious**
IDM **be the envy of sb** to be the thing that causes sb to feel **envy**: *The city's transport system is the envy of many of its European neighbours.* ▶ **obiekt/przedmiot zazdrości**

envy[2] /ˈenvi/ verb [T] (**envying**; **envies**; pt, pp **envied**) **envy (sb) (sth)** to want sth that sb else has; to feel **envy**: *I've always envied your good luck.* ◇ *I don't envy you that job.* ▶ **zazdrościć**

enzyme /ˈenzaɪm/ noun [C] (technical) a substance, produced by all living things, that helps a chemical change happen or happen more quickly, without being changed itself ▶ **enzym**

ephemeral /ɪˈfemərəl/ adj. (formal) lasting or used for only a short time ▶ **efemeryczny**, **krótkotrwały** SYN **short-lived**

epic /ˈepɪk/ adj. very long and exciting: *an epic struggle/journey* ▶ **epicki**
■ **epic** noun [C]: *The film 'Glory' is an American Civil War epic.* ▶ **epopeja**

epicure /ˈepɪkjʊə(r)/ noun [C] (formal) a person who enjoys food and drink of high quality and knows a lot about it ▶ **smakosz/ka**

epidemic /ˌepɪˈdemɪk/ noun [C] a large number of people or animals suffering from the same disease at the same time ▶ **epidemia**

epilepsy /ˈepɪlepsi/ noun [U] a disease of the brain that can cause a person to become unconscious (sometimes with violent movements that they cannot control) ▶ **epilepsja**, **padaczka**

epileptic /ˌepɪˈleptɪk/ noun [C] a person who suffers from **epilepsy** ▶ **epilepty-k/czka**
■ **epileptic** adj.: *an epileptic fit* ▶ **epileptyczny**

epilogue /ˈepɪlɒɡ/ noun [C] a short piece that is added at the end of a book, play, etc. and that comments on what has gone before ▶ **epilog** ➲ look at **prologue**

Epiphany /ɪˈpɪfəni/ noun [C] a Christian festival, held on the 6 January, in memory of the time when the three wise men (**the Magi**) came to see the baby Jesus at Bethlehem ▶ **święto Trzech Króli**

episode /ˈepɪsəʊd/ noun [C] **1** one separate event in sb's life, a novel, etc.: *That's an episode in my life I'd rather forget.* ▶ **epizod 2** one part of a TV or radio story that is shown or told in several parts ▶ **odcinek** (*serialu*)

epitaph /ˈepɪtɑːf; US -tæf/ noun [C] words that are written or said about a dead person, especially words written on a stone where they are buried ▶ **epitafium**

epitome /ɪˈpɪtəmi/ noun [sing.] **the epitome (of sth)** a perfect example of sth: *Her clothes are the epitome of good taste.* ▶ **najlepszy/najbardziej typowy przykład**

epitomize (also **-ise**) /ɪˈpɪtəmaɪz/ verb [T] to be typical of sth: *This building epitomizes modern trends in architecture.* ▶ **stanowić typowy przykład**

epoch /ˈiːpɒk; US ˈepək/ noun [C] a period of time in history (that is important because of special events, characteristics, etc.) ▶ **epoka**

equal[1] /ˈiːkwəl/ adj. **1 equal (to sb/sth)** the same in size, amount, value, number, level, etc.: *They are equal in weight.* ◇ *They are of equal weight.* ◇ *Divide it into two equal parts.* ▶ **równy**, **jednakowy** OPP **unequal 2** having the same rights or being treated the same as other people: *This company has an equal opportunities policy.* ◇ *We've appointed an Equal Opportunities Officer* (urzędnika do spraw równouprawnienia). ▶ **równorzędny**, **o równych prawach 3** (formal) **equal to sth** having the strength, ability, etc. to do sth: *I'm afraid Bob just isn't equal to the job.* ▶ **zdolny zmierzyć się** (*np. z zadaniem*)
IDM **be on equal terms (with sb)** to have the same advantages and disadvantages as sb else ▶ **na równych prawach**

equal[2] /ˈiːkwəl/ noun [C] a person who has the same ability, rights, etc. as you do: *to treat somebody as an equal* ▶ **równ-y/a sobie**

equal[3] /ˈiːkwəl/ verb [T] (**equalling**; **equalled**; US **equaling**; **equaled**) **1** (used about numbers, etc.) to be the same as sth: *44 plus 17 equals 61 is written: 44 + 17 = 61.* ▶ **równać się 2** to be as good as sb/sth: *He ran an excellent race, equalling the world record.* ▶ **dorównywać**

equality /iˈkwɒləti/ noun [U] the situation in which everyone has the same rights and advantages: *racial equality* ▶ **równouprawnienie** OPP **inequality**

equalize (also -ise) /ˈiːkwəlaɪz/ verb [I] (in sport) to reach the same number of points as your opponent ▶ **remisować**

equally /ˈiːkwəli/ adv. **1** to the same degree or amount: *They both worked equally hard.* ▶ **równo, jednakowo 2** in equal parts: *His money was divided equally between his children.* ▶ **równo 3** (formal) (used when you are comparing two ideas or commenting on what you have just said) at the same time; but/and also: *I do not think what he did was right. Equally, I can understand why he did it.* ▶ **jednocześnie, jednakże**

equate /iˈkweɪt/ verb [T] **equate sth (with sth)** to consider one thing as being the same as sth else: *Some parents equate education with exam success.* ▶ **zrównywać, uważać za identyczne/podobne**

equation /ɪˈkweɪʒn/ noun [C] (in mathematics) a statement that two quantities are equal: *2x + 5 = 11 is an equation.* ▶ **równanie**

the **equator** (also **the Equator**) /ɪˈkweɪtə(r)/ noun [sing.] the imagined line around the earth at an equal distance from the North and South Poles: *north/south of the Equator* ◇ *The island is on the equator.* ▶ **równik**
■ **equatorial** /ˌekwəˈtɔːriəl/ adj. near the **equator** or typical of a country that is near the **equator**: *equatorial rainforests* ◇ *an equatorial climate* ▶ **równikowy**

equestrian /ɪˈkwestriən/ adj. (formal) connected with horse riding ▶ **jeździecki**

equilibrium /ˌiːkwɪˈlɪbriəm; ˌek-/ noun [U, sing.] **1** a state of balance, especially between opposite forces or influences: *The point at which the solid and the liquid are* ***in equilibrium*** *is called the freezing point.* ◇ *We have achieved economic equilibrium.* ▶ **równowaga 2** a calm state of mind and a balance of emotions ▶ **równowaga**

equinox /ˈiːkwɪnɒks; ˈek-/ noun [C] one of the two times in the year (around 20 March and 22 September) when day and night are of equal length: *the spring/autumn equinox* ▶ **równonoc** ➲ look at **solstice**

equip /ɪˈkwɪp/ verb [T] (**equipping**; **equipped**) **equip sb/sth (with sth) 1** [usually passive] to supply sb/sth with what is needed for a particular purpose: *The schools in France are much better equipped than ours.* ◇ *The flat has a* ***fully-equipped*** (z pełnym wyposażeniem) *kitchen.* ◇ *We shall equip all schools with new computers over the next year.* ▶ **wyposażać, zaopatrywać 2** to prepare sb for a particular task: *The course equips students with all the skills necessary to become a chef.* ▶ **przygotowywać kogoś do wykonania określonego zadania**

equipment /ɪˈkwɪpmənt/ noun [U] the things that are needed to do a particular activity: *office/sports/computer equipment* ▶ **wyposażenie, ekwipunek** ⓘ **Equipment** jest rzeczownikiem niepoliczalnym. Mówiąc o jednym przedmiocie używa się zwrotu **a piece of equipment**: *a very useful piece of kitchen equipment.*

equitable /ˈekwɪtəbl/ adj. (formal) fair and reasonable; treating everyone in an equal way: *an equitable distribution of resources* ▶ **sprawiedliwy** SYN **fair**
■ **equitably** /-bli/ adv. ▶ **sprawiedliwie**

equity /ˈekwəti/ noun **1** [U] the value of the shares issued by a company: *He controls seven per cent of the equity.* ▶ **wartość akcji przedsiębiorstwa 2** (**equities**) [pl.] ordinary stocks and shares that carry no fixed interest: *to invest in equities* ◇ *the equities market* ▶ **akcje nieuprzywilejowane** (*przynoszące dywidendę*) **3** [U] the money value of a property after all the charges on it, e.g. those relating to a mortgage, have been paid ▶ **wartość majątku netto** (*po potrąceniu zobowiązań*)

equivalent /ɪˈkwɪvələnt/ adj. **equivalent (to sth)** equal in value, amount, meaning, importance, etc.: *The British House of Commons is roughly equivalent to the American House of Representatives.* ▶ **równorzędny, odpowiadający**
■ **equivalent** noun [C]: *There is no English equivalent to the French 'bon appétit'.* ▶ **odpowiednik**

ER /ˌiː ˈɑː(r)/ abbr. (US) **emergency room** = ACCIDENT AND EMERGENCY

er /ɜː(r)/ interj. (used in writing to show the sound that sb makes when they cannot decide what to say next) ▶ **hm**

era /ˈɪərə; US ˈerə/ noun [C] a period of time in history (that is special for some reason): *We are living in the era of the computer.* ▶ **era**

eradicate /ɪˈrædɪkeɪt/ verb [T] (formal) to destroy or get rid of sth completely: *Some diseases, such as smallpox, have been completely eradicated.* ▶ **wykorzeniać, wytępić**
■ **eradication** /ɪˌrædɪˈkeɪʃn/ noun [U] ▶ **wytępienie**

erase /ɪˈreɪz; US -ˈreɪs/ verb [T] (formal) to remove sth completely (a pencil mark, a recording on tape, a computer file, etc.): (figurative) *He tried to erase the memory of those terrible years from his mind.* ▶ **wymazywać** ⓘ Jeżeli chodzi o wymazywanie czegoś, co zostało napisane ołówkiem, w Br. ang. używa się częściej czasownika **rub out**.
■ **eraser** (especially US) = RUBBER (2)

erect[1] /ɪˈrekt/ adj. **1** standing straight up: *He stood with his head erect.* ▶ **prosty, podniesiony 2** (used about the male sexual organ) hard and standing up because of sexual excitement ▶ **w stanie erekcji**

erect[2] /ɪˈrekt/ verb [T] (formal) to build sth or to stand sth straight up: *Huge TV screens were erected above the stage.* ◇ *to erect a statue* ▶ **budować, wznosić**

erection /ɪˈrekʃn/ noun **1** [C] if a man has an **erection**, his **penis** becomes hard and stands up because he is sexually excited: *to get/have an erection* ▶ **erekcja 2** [U] (formal) the act of building sth or standing sth straight up ▶ **budowa, montaż**

ergonomic /ˌɜːɡəˈnɒmɪk/ adj. designed to improve people's working conditions and to help them work more efficiently: *ergonomic design* ▶ **ergonomiczny**
■ **ergonomically** adv. ▶ **ergonomicznie**

ermine /ˈɜːmɪn/ noun [U] the white winter fur of a stoat, that is sometimes used on the clothes worn by judges, etc. ▶ **futro gronostajowe**

erode /ɪˈrəʊd/ verb [T, usually passive] (used about the sea, the weather, etc.) to destroy sth slowly: *The cliff has been eroded by the sea.* ▶ **erodować, wyżerać; podkopywać** (*np. znaczenie czegoś*)
■ **erosion** /ɪˈrəʊʒn/ noun [U]: *the erosion of rocks by the sea* ▶ **erozja; podkopywanie**

erotic /ɪˈrɒtɪk/ adj. causing sexual excitement: *an erotic film/poem/dream* ▶ **erotyczny**

erotica /ɪˈrɒtɪkə/ noun [U] books, pictures, etc. that are intended to make sb feel sexual desire ▶ **książki/rysunki itp. o tematyce erotycznej**

err /ɜː(r); US er/ verb [I] (formal) to be or do wrong; to make mistakes ▶ **popełniać błąd**
IDM **err on the side of sth** to do more of sth than is necessary in order to avoid the opposite happening: *It is better to* ***err on the side of caution*** (być zbyt przezornym). ▶ **grzeszyć nadmiarem czegoś**

errand /ˈerənd/ noun [C] (old-fashioned) a short journey to take or get sth for sb, for example to buy sth from a shop ▶ **załatwianie spraw (dla kogoś)** (*np. zakupów*)

erratic /ɪˈrætɪk/ adj. (used about sb's behaviour, or about the quality of sth) changing without reason; that you can never be sure of: *Marc Jones is a talented player but he's very erratic.* ▶ **nieprzewidywalny, niezrównoważony**
■ **erratically** /-kli/ adv. ▶ **w sposób nieprzewidywalny, nieregularnie, na wszystkie strony**

erroneous /ɪˈrəʊniəs/ adj. (formal) not correct; based on wrong information: *erroneous conclusions* ▶ **błędny**

■ **erroneously** adv. ▶ **błędnie**

error /'erə(r)/ noun **1** [C] (formal) a mistake: *The telephone bill was too high due to a* ***computer error.*** ◇ *an* ***error of judgement*** mylny osąd ◇ *to* ***make an error*** ▶ **błąd, pomyłka** ➲ note at **mistake**

Error jest słowem bardziej formalnym niż **mistake**. W niektórych wyrażeniach można użyć tylko słowa **error**, np. **error of judgement, human error**.

2 [U] the state of being wrong: *The letter was sent to you* ***in error.*** ◇ *The accident was the result of* ***human error.*** ▶ **błąd**

IDM **trial and error** → TRIAL

erudite /'erudaɪt/ adj. (formal) having or showing great knowledge that is gained from academic study ▶ **erudycyjny, uczony** SYN **learned**

erupt /ɪ'rʌpt/ verb [I] **1** (used about a **volcano**) to explode and throw out fire, burning rocks, smoke, etc. ▶ **wybuchać 2** (used about violence, shouting, etc.) to start suddenly: *The demonstration erupted into violence.* ▶ **wybuchać 3** (used about a person) to suddenly become very angry: *George erupted when he heard the news.* ▶ **wybuchać**

■ **eruption** noun [C,U]: *a volcanic eruption* ▶ **wybuch**

escalate /'eskəleɪt/ verb [I,T] **1 escalate (sth) (into sth)** (to cause sth) to become stronger or more serious: *The demonstrations are escalating into violent protest in all the major cities.* ◇ *The terrorist attacks escalated tension in the capital.* ▶ **wzrastać, wzmagać (się) 2** (to cause sth) to become greater or higher; to increase: *The cost of housing in the south has escalated in recent years.* ▶ **wzmagać (się)**

■ **escalation** /ˌeskə'leɪʃn/ noun [C,U] ▶ **eskalacja**

escalator /'eskəleɪtə(r)/ noun [C] moving stairs that carry people between different floors of a shop, etc. ▶ **schody ruchome**

escapade /ˌeskə'peɪd/ noun [C] an exciting experience that may be dangerous ▶ **eskapada**

escape¹ /ɪ'skeɪp/ verb **1** [I] **escape (from sb/sth)** to manage to get away from a place where you do not want to be; to get free: *They managed to escape from the burning building.* ◇ *Two prisoners have escaped.* ▶ **uciekać 2** [I,T] to manage to avoid sth dangerous or unpleasant: *David Smith escaped injury when his car skidded off the road.* ◇ *to escape criticism/punishment* ◇ *The two men in the other car escaped unhurt* (uszli cało). ▶ **unikać 3** [T] to be forgotten or not noticed by sb: *His name escapes me.* ◇ *to escape somebody's notice* ▶ **uchodzić** (*uwadze*) **4** [I] (used about gases or liquids) to come or get out of a container, etc.: *There's gas escaping somewhere.* ▶ **ulatniać się, przeciekać**

■ **escaped** adj.: *The police have caught escaped prisoner.* ▶ **zbiegły**

escape² /ɪ'skeɪp/ noun **1** [C,U] **escape (from sth)** the act of escaping(1,2): *There have been twelve escapes from the prison this year.* ◇ *She had* ***a narrow/lucky escape*** (o włos uniknęła nieszczęścia) *when a lorry crashed into her car.* ◇ *When the guard fell asleep they were able to* ***make their escape.*** ▶ **ucieczka, wyciek, uniknięcie** ➲ look at **fire escape 2** [U, sing.] something that helps you forget your normal life: *For him, listening to music is a means of escape.* ◇ *an escape from reality* ▶ **ucieczka**

escapism /ɪ'skeɪpɪzəm/ noun [U] an activity, a form of entertainment, etc. that helps you avoid or forget unpleasant or boring things: *For John, reading is a* ***form of escapism.*** ▶ **eskapizm**

■ **escapist** /-ɪst/ adj. ▶ **eskapistyczny**

escort¹ /'eskɔːt/ noun [C] **1** [with sing. or pl. verb] one or more people or vehicles that go with and protect sb/sth, or that go with sb/sth as an honour: *an armed escort* ◇ *He arrived* ***under police escort.*** ▶ **eskorta, konwój, straż 2** (formal) a person who takes sb to a social event ▶ **osoba towarzysząca 3** a person, especially a woman, who is paid to go out socially with sb: *an escort agency* ▶ **osoba towarzysząca** (*często dziewczyna z agencji towarzyskiej*)

escort² /ɪs'kɔːt/ verb [T] to go with sb to protect them or to show them the way: *The President's car was escorted by several police cars.* ◇ *Philip escorted her to the door.* ▶ **eskortować; towarzyszyć**

Eskimo /'eskɪməʊ/ noun [C] (pl. **Eskimo** or **Eskimos**) a member of a race of people from northern Canada, and parts of Alaska, Greenland and Siberia. ▶ **Eskimos/ka**

Uwaga! Eskimosi wolą, gdy nazywa się ich **Inuits**.

ESL /ˌiː es 'el/ abbr. **English as a Second Language** ▶ **nauka języka angielskiego jako drugiego języka**

esophagus (US) = OESOPHAGUS

esoteric /ˌesə'terɪk; ˌiːsə-/ adj. (formal) likely to be understood or enjoyed by only a few people with a special knowledge or interest: *a programme of music for everyone, even those with the most esoteric taste* ▶ **ezoteryczny**

ESP abbr. /ˌiː es 'piː/ **English for Specific/Special Purposes**; the teaching of English to people who need it for a special reason, such as scientific study, a technical job, etc. ▶ **nauka języka angielskiego na użytek specjalny**

esp. = ESPECIALLY (1)

especial /ɪ'speʃl/ adj. [only before a noun] (formal) not usual; special: *This will be of especial interest to you.* ▶ **wyjątkowy, szczególny**

especially /ɪ'speʃəli/ adv. **1** (abbr. **esp.**) more than other things, people, situations, etc.; particularly: *She loves animals, especially dogs.* ◇ *Teenage boys especially can be very competitive.* ◇ *He was very disappointed with his mark in the exam, especially as he had worked so hard for it.* ▶ **zwłaszcza, szczególnie** SYN **particularly 2** for a particular purpose or person: *I made this especially for you.* ▶ **specjalnie** ℹ W tym znaczeniu można też stosować słowo **specially**. Jest ono mniej formalne. **3** very (much): *It's not an especially difficult exam.* ◇ *'Do you like jazz?' 'Not especially.'* ▶ **szczególnie** SYN **particularly**

espionage /'espiənɑːʒ/ noun [U] the act of finding out secret information about another country or organization ▶ **szpiegostwo** ➲ verb **spy**

espouse /ɪ'spaʊz/ verb [T] (formal) to give your support to a belief, policy etc.: *They espoused the notion of equal opportunity for all in education.* ▶ **opowiadać się za czymś, wspierać**

■ **espousal** /ɪ'spaʊzl/ noun [U, sing.] **espousal of sth** ▶ **wsparcie, poparcie**

Esq. abbr. (especially Brit., formal) **Esquire**; (used when you are writing a man's name on an envelope): *Edward Hales, Esq.* ℹ Ta forma jest staromodna. Częściej pisze się: *Mr Edward Hales.* ▶ **odpowiednik JWP**

essay /'eseɪ/ noun [C] **an essay (on/about sth)** a short piece of writing on one subject: *a 1 000-word essay on tourism* ▶ **wypracowanie, esej**

essayist /'eseɪɪst/ noun [C] a person who writes essays to be published ▶ **eseist(k)a**

essence /'esns/ noun **1** [U] the basic or most important quality of sth: *The essence of the problem is that there is not enough money available.* ◇ *Although both parties agree* ***in essence,*** *some minor differences remain.* ▶ **istota (czegoś) 2** [C,U] a substance (usually a liquid) that is taken from a plant or food and that has a strong smell or taste of that plant or food: *coffee/vanilla essence* ▶ **esencja**

essential /ɪ'senʃl/ adj. completely necessary; that you must have or do: *essential services* ◇ *essential medical* *supplies* ◊ *Maths is essential for a career in computers.* ◊ *It is essential that all school-leavers should have a qualification.* ▶ **niezbędny, konieczny, istotny** ➲ note at **important**

■ **essential** noun [C, usually pl.]: *food, and other essentials such as clothing and heating* ▶ **rzecz niezbędna/istotna**

🔑 **essentially** /ɪˈsenʃəli/ adv. when you consider the basic or most important part of sth: *The problem is essentially one of money.* ▶ **zasadniczo** SYN **basically**

🔑 **establish** /ɪˈstæblɪʃ/ verb [T] **1** to start or create an organization, a system, etc.: *The school was established in 1875.* ◊ *Before we start on the project we should establish some rules.* ▶ **zakładać** (*np. organizację*), **ustalać** (*np. zasady*) **2** to make sth exist (especially a formal relationship with sb/sth): *The government is trying to establish closer links between the two countries.* ▶ **ustanawiać, tworzyć 3 establish sb/sth (as sth)** to become accepted and recognized as sth: *She has been trying to establish herself as a novelist for years.* ▶ **ustalać 4** to discover or find proof of the facts of a situation: *The police have not been able to establish the cause of the crash.* ▶ **ustalać**

establishment /ɪˈstæblɪʃmənt/ noun **1** [C] (formal) an organization, a large institution or a hotel: *an educational establishment* placówka oświatowa ▶ **zakład; firma 2** (**the Establishment**) [sing.] the people in positions of power in a country, who usually do not support change ▶ **establishment 3** [U] the act of creating or starting a new organization, system, etc.: *the establishment of new laws on taxes* ▶ **założenie**

🔑 **estate** /ɪˈsteɪt/ noun [C] **1** a large area of land in the countryside that is owned by one person or family: *He owns a large estate in Scotland.* ▶ **posiadłość, majątek 2** (Brit.) an area of land that has a lot of houses or factories of the same type on it: *an industrial estate* osiedle przemysłowe ◊ *a housing estate* osiedle mieszkaniowe ▶ **osiedle 3** all the money and property that sb leaves when they die: *Her estate was left to her daughter.* ▶ **majątek**

esˈtate agent (US **realtor** /ˈriːəltə(r)/, **ˈreal estate agent**) noun [C] a person whose job is to buy and sell houses and land for other people ▶ **pośrednik sprzedaży nieruchomości** ➲ note at **house**

esˈtate car (US **station wagon**) noun [C] a car with a door at the back and a long area for luggage behind the back seat ▶ **kombi** ➲ picture at **car**, picture on **page A7**

esteem /ɪˈstiːm/ noun [U] (formal) great respect; a good opinion of sb ▶ **szacunek**

esthete, esthetic (US) = AESTHETE, AESTHETIC

🔑 **estimate¹** /ˈestɪmət/ noun [C] **1 an estimate (of sth)** a guess or judgement about the size, cost, etc. of sth, before you have all the facts and figures: *Can you give me* ***a rough estimate*** *of how many people will be at the meeting?* ◊ ***At a conservative estimate,*** *the job will take six months to complete.* ▶ **oszacowanie** (*w przybliżeniu*) **2 an estimate (for sth/doing sth)** a written statement from a person who is going to do a job for you, for example a builder, telling you how much it will cost: *They gave me an estimate for repairing the roof.* ▶ **kosztorys** ➲ look at **quotation**

IDM **a ballpark figure/estimate** → BALLPARK

🔑 **estimate²** /ˈestɪmeɪt/ verb [T] **estimate sth (at sth); estimate that...** to calculate the size, cost, etc. of sth approximately, before you have all the facts and figures: *The police estimated the crowd at 10 000.* ◊ *She estimated that the work would take three months.* ▶ **oszacować (w przybliżeniu), obliczać**

estimation /ˌestɪˈmeɪʃn/ noun [U] (formal) opinion or judgement: *Who is to blame,* ***in your estimation?*** ▶ **opinia; osąd, ocena**

estranged /ɪˈstreɪndʒd/ adj. **1** no longer living with your husband/wife: *her estranged husband* ▶ **żyjący w separacji 2 estranged (from sb)** no longer friendly or in contact with sb who was close to you: *He became estranged from his family following an argument.* ◊ *She felt estranged from her sister.* Czuła, że z siostrą stały się już sobie obce. ▶ **obcy sobie**

estrogen (US) = OESTROGEN

estuary /ˈestʃuəri; US -eri/ noun [C] (pl. **estuaries**) the wide part of a river where it joins the sea ▶ **ujście** (*rzeki*)

ETA /ˌiː tiː ˈeɪ/ abbr. **estimated time of arrival**; the time at which an aircraft, a ship, etc. is expected to arrive ▶ **przewidywany czas przyjazdu/przylotu** ➲ look at **ETD**

🔑 **etc.** /ˌet ˈsetərə/ abbr. **et cetera**; and so on, and other things of a similar kind: *sandwiches, biscuits, cakes, etc.* ▶ **itd., itp.**

etch /etʃ/ verb **etch A (with B); etch B (in/into/on A)** [I,T] to cut lines into a piece of glass, metal etc. in order to make words or a picture: *a glass tankard with his initials etched on it/a glass tankard etched with his initials* szklany kufel z wyrytymi jego inicjałami ▶ **wytrawiać, (wy)ryć**

etching /ˈetʃɪŋ/ noun [C, U] a picture that is printed from an **etched** piece of metal; the art of making these pictures ▶ **akwaforta**

ETD /ˌiː tiː ˈdiː/ abbr. **estimated time of departure**; the time at which an aircraft, ship, etc. is expected to leave ▶ **przewidywany czas odjazdu/odlotu** ➲ look at **ETA**

eternal /ɪˈtɜːnl/ adj. **1** without beginning or end; existing or continuing for ever: *Some people believe in eternal life.* ▶ **wieczny 2** [only before a noun] happening too often; seeming to last for ever: *I'm tired of these eternal arguments!* ▶ **wieczny**

■ **eternally** /-nəli/ adv.: *I'll be* ***eternally grateful*** *if you could help.* ▶ **wiecznie, na wieki**

eternity /ɪˈtɜːnəti/ noun **1** [U] time that has no end; the state or time after death ▶ **wieczność 2** (**an eternity**) [sing.] (informal) a period of time that never seems to end: *It seemed like an eternity before the ambulance arrived.* ▶ **nieskończoność**

ethanol /ˈeθənɒl; US -nəʊl/ noun [U] the type of alcohol in alcoholic drinks, also used as a fuel or **solvent** ▶ **etanol**

ether /ˈiːθə(r)/ noun [U] **1** a clear liquid made from alcohol, used in industry as a **solvent** and, in the past, in medicine to make people unconscious before an operation ▶ **eter 2** (**the ether**) (old-fashioned or literary) the upper part of the sky: *Her words disappeared into the ether.* ▶ **eter, niebo 3** (**the ether**) the air, when it is thought of as the place in which radio or electronic communication takes place ▶ (*fale radiowe itp.*) **eter**

ethereal /iˈθɪəriəl/ adj. (formal) extremely delicate and light; seeming to belong to another, more spiritual, world: *ethereal music* ▶ **pozaziemski, eteryczny**

ethic /ˈeθɪk/ noun **1** (**ethics**) [pl.] moral principles that control or influence a person's behaviour: ***professional/business/medical ethics*** ◊ *to draw up a* ***code of ethics*** ▶ **etyka 2** [sing.] a system of moral principles or rules of behaviour: *a strongly defined work ethic* ▶ **etyka 3** (**ethics**) [U] the branch of philosophy that deals with moral principles ▶ **etyka**

ethical /ˈeθɪkl/ adj. **1** connected with beliefs of what is right or wrong: *That is an ethical problem.* ▶ **etyczny 2** morally correct: *Although she didn't break the law, her behaviour was certainly not ethical.* ▶ **etyczny**

■ **ethically** /-kli/ adv. ▶ **etycznie**

ethnic /ˈeθnɪk/ adj. connected with or typical of a particular race or religion: *ethnic food/music/clothes*

E

◇ *ethnic minorities* mniejszości narodowe ▶ **charakteryzujący daną grupę etniczną**

ˌethnic ˈcleansing noun [U] the policy of forcing people of a certain race or religion to leave an area or country ▶ **czystki etniczne**

ethnicity /eθˈnɪsəti/ noun [U] the fact of belonging to a particular race ▶ **przynależność etniczna/rasowa**

ˌethnic miˈnority noun [C] a group of people from a particular culture or of a particular race living in a country where the main group is of a different culture or race ▶ **mniejszość etniczna**

ethnography /eθˈnɒgrəfi/ noun [U] the scientific description of different races and cultures ▶ **etnografia**
■ **ethnographic** /ˌeθnəˈgræfɪk/ adj.: *ethnographic research* ▶ **etnograficzny**

ethnology /eθˈnɒlədʒi/ noun [U] the scientific study and comparison of human races ▶ **etnologia**
■ **ethnological** /ˌeθnəˈlɒdʒɪkl/ adj. ▶ **etnologiczny** | **ethnologist** /eθˈnɒlədʒɪst/ noun [C] ▶ **etnolog**

ethos /ˈiːθɒs/ noun [sing.] (formal) the moral ideas and attitudes that belong to a particular group or society: *an ethos of public service* ▶ **etos**

etiquette /ˈetɪket/ noun [U] the rules of polite and correct behaviour: *professional etiquette* ▶ **etykieta**

etymology /ˌetɪˈmɒlədʒi/ noun (pl. **etymologies**) **1** [U] the study of the origins and history of words and their meanings ▶ **etymologia** **2** [C] an explanation of the origin and history of a particular word ▶ **etymologia**

EU = EUROPEAN UNION

eucalyptus /ˌjuːkəˈlɪptəs/ noun [C,U] (pl. **eucalyptuses** or **eucalypti** /-taɪ/) (also **eucaˈlyptus tree**) a tall straight tree with leaves that produce an oil with a strong smell, that is used in medicine. There are several types of **eucalyptus** and they grow especially in Australasia. ▶ **eukaliptus**

eulogy /ˈjuːlədʒi/ noun [C, U] (pl. **-eulogies**) **1 eulogy (of/to sb/sth)** a speech or piece of writing praising sb/sth very much: *a eulogy to marriage* ▶ **panegiryk** **2 eulogy (for/to sb)** (especially US) a speech given at a funeral praising the person who has died ▶ **mowa pogrzebowa**

euphemism /ˈjuːfəmɪzəm/ noun [C,U] using a polite word or expression instead of a more direct one when you are talking about sth that is unpleasant or embarrassing; a word used in this way: *'Pass away' is a euphemism for 'die'.* ▶ **eufemizm**
■ **euphemistic** /ˌjuːfəˈmɪstɪk/ adj. ▶ **eufemistyczny**

euphoria /juːˈfɔːriə/ noun [U] (formal) a feeling of great happiness ▶ **euforia**
■ **euphoric** /juːˈfɒrɪk/ adj.: *My euphoric mood could not last.* ▶ **euforyczny**

Euro- /ˈjʊərəʊ/ [in compounds] connected with Europe or the European Union: *a Euro-MP* poseł do Parlamentu Europejskiego ◇ *Euro-elections* ▶ **euro-**

⚷ **euro** /ˈjʊərəʊ/ noun [C] (symbol €) (pl. **euros** or **euro**) (since 1999) a unit of money used in several countries of the European Union: *The price is given in dollars or euros.* ▶ **euro** ➲ look at **EMU**

Eurocheque /ˈjʊərəʊtʃek/ noun [C] a cheque that can be used in many European countries ▶ **euroczek**

European¹ /ˌjʊərəˈpiːən/ adj. of or from Europe: *European languages* ▶ **europejski**

European² /ˌjʊərəˈpiːən/ noun [C] a person from a European country ▶ **Europej-czyk/ka**

the ˌEuroˌpean ˈUnion noun [sing.] (abbr. **EU** /ˌiː ˈjuː/) an economic and political association of certain European countries ▶ **Unia Europejska**

ˌEuro-ˈsceptic noun [C] a person, especially a British politician, who is opposed to closer links with the European Union ▶ **eurosceptyk**
■ **ˌEuro-ˈsceptic** adj. ▶ **eurosceptyczny**

euthanasia /ˌjuːθəˈneɪziə; US -ˈneɪʒə/ noun [U] the practice (illegal in most countries) of killing without pain sb who wants to die because they are suffering from a disease that cannot be cured ▶ **eutanazja**

evacuate /ɪˈvækjueɪt/ verb [T] to move people from a dangerous place to somewhere safer; to leave a place because it is dangerous: *Thousands of people were evacuated from the war zone.* ◇ *The village had to be evacuated when the river burst its banks.* ▶ **ewakuować**
■ **evacuation** /ɪˌvækjuˈeɪʃn/ noun [C,U] ▶ **ewakuacja**

evade /ɪˈveɪd/ verb [T] **1** to manage to escape from or to avoid meeting sb/sth: *They managed to evade capture and escaped to France.* ▶ **unikać** **2** to avoid dealing with or doing sth: *to evade responsibility* ◇ *I asked her directly, but she evaded the question.* ▶ **uchylać się od czegoś** ➲ noun **evasion**

evaluate /ɪˈvæljueɪt/ verb [T] (formal) to study the facts and then form an opinion about sth: *We evaluated the situation very carefully before we made our decision.* ▶ **oceniać**
■ **evaluation** /ɪˌvæljuˈeɪʃn/ noun [C,U] ▶ **ocena**

evangelical /ˌiːvænˈdʒelɪkl/ adj. (used about certain Protestant churches) believing that religious ceremony is not as important as belief in Jesus Christ and study of the Bible ▶ **ewangelicki**

evaporate /ɪˈvæpəreɪt/ verb [I] **1** (used about a liquid) to change into steam or gas and disappear: *The water evaporated in the sunshine.* ▶ **wyparować** ➲ look at **condense** **2** to disappear completely: *All her confidence evaporated when she saw the exam paper.* ▶ **znikać**
■ **evaporation** /ɪˌvæpəˈreɪʃn/ noun [U] ▶ **wyparowanie; zniknięcie**

evasion /ɪˈveɪʒn/ noun [C,U] **1** the act of avoiding sth that you should do: *He has been sentenced to two years' imprisonment for* ***tax evasion.*** ◇ *an evasion of responsibility* ▶ **uchylanie się** **2** a statement that avoids dealing with a question or subject in a direct way: *The President's reply was full of evasions* (pełna wymijających odpowiedzi). ▶ **unik** ➲ verb **evade**

evasive /ɪˈveɪsɪv/ adj. trying to avoid sth; not direct: *Ann gave an evasive answer.* ▶ **wymijający**

eve /iːv/ noun [C] the day or evening before a religious festival, important event, etc.: *New Year's Eve* ◇ *He injured himself* ***on the eve of*** *the final.* ▶ **wigilia, przeddzień**

⚷ **even¹** /ˈiːvn/ adj. **1** flat, level or smooth: *The game must be played on an even surface.* ▶ **równy, gładki** OPP **uneven** **2** not changing; regular: *This wine must be stored at an even temperature* ▶ **równomierny** **3** (used about a competition, etc.) equal, with one side being as good as the other: *The contest was very even until the last few minutes of the game.* ▶ **wyrównany** OPP **uneven** **4** (used about numbers) that can be divided by two: *2, 4, 6, 8, 10, etc. are even numbers.* ▶ **parzysty** OPP **odd**
IDM **be/get even (with sb)** (informal) to hurt or harm sb who has hurt or harmed you ▶ **wyrównać z kimś rachunki, policzyć się z kimś**
break even to make neither a loss nor a profit ▶ **wyjść na zero/czysto**

⚷ **even²** /ˈiːvn/ adv. **1** (used for emphasizing sth that is surprising): *It isn't very warm here even in summer.* ◇ *He didn't even open the letter.* ▶ **nawet** **2 even more, less, bigger, nicer, etc.** (used when you are comparing things, to make the comparison stronger): *You know even less about it than I do.* ◇ *It is even more difficult than I expected.* ◇ *We are even busier than yesterday.* ▶ **jeszcze**
IDM **even if** (used for saying that what follows 'if' makes no difference): *I wouldn't ride a horse, even if you paid*

me (choćbyś mi zapłacił) *a thousand pounds.* ▶ **choćby, nawet gdyby/jeśli**

even so (used for introducing a new idea, fact, etc. that is surprising) in spite of that: *There are a lot of spelling mistakes; even so it's quite a good essay.* ▶ **mimo to** SYN **nevertheless**

even though although: *I like her very much even though she can be very annoying.* ▶ **chociaż, mimo że** ➲ note at **although**

even³ /ˈiːvn/ verb

PHR V **even out** to become level or steady, usually after varying a lot: *House prices keep rising and falling but they should eventually even out.* ▶ **wyrównywać się**

even sth out to spread things equally over a period of time or among a number of people: *He tried to even out the distribution of work among his employees.* ▶ **wyrównywać coś**

ˌeven-ˈhanded adj. completely fair, especially when dealing with different groups of people: *He had an even-handed approach to the negotiations.* ▶ **bezstronny, sprawiedliwy**

evening /ˈiːvnɪŋ/ noun [C,U] the part of the day between the afternoon and the time that you go to bed: *What are you doing this evening* (dziś wieczorem)*?* ◇ *We were out yesterday evening.* ◇ *I went to the cinema on Saturday evening.* ◇ *Tom usually goes swimming on Wednesday evenings.* ◇ *Most people watch TV **in the evening**.* ▶ **wieczór** ➲ note at **morning**

IDM **good evening** (used when you see sb for the first time in the evening) ▶ **dobry wieczór** ℹ Często mówi się tylko **Evening**: *'Good evening, Mrs Wilson.' 'Evening, Mr Mills.'*

ˈevening class noun [C] a course of study for adults in the evening: *an evening class in car maintenance* ▶ **kurs wieczorowy**

ˈevening dress noun **1** [U] elegant clothes worn for formal occasions in the evening ▶ **strój wieczorowy 2** [C] a woman's usually long formal dress ▶ **suknia wieczorowa**

evenly /ˈiːvnli/ adv. in a smooth, regular or equal way: *The match was very evenly balanced.* ◇ *Spread the cake mixture evenly in the tin.* ▶ **równo**

event /ɪˈvent/ noun [C] **1** something that happens, especially sth important or unusual: *a historic event* ◇ *The events of the past few days have made things very difficult for the Government.* ▶ **wydarzenie** ➲ look at **happening 2** a planned public or social occasion: *a fund-raising event* ▶ **impreza 3** one of the races, competitions, etc. in a sports programme: *The next event is the 800 metres.* ▶ **punkt programu, konkurencja**

IDM **at all events/in any event** whatever happens: *I hope to see you soon, but in any event I'll phone you on Sunday.* ▶ **na wszelki wypadek**

in the event of sth (formal) if sth happens: *In the event of fire, leave the building as quickly as possible.* ▶ **w razie czegoś**

ˌeven-ˈtempered adj. not easily made angry or upset: *He's very even-tempered – in fact I've never seen him angry.* ▶ **zrównoważony**

eventful /ɪˈventfl/ adj. full of important, dangerous, or exciting things happening ▶ **bogaty w wydarzenia, urozmaicony**

eventual /ɪˈventʃuəl/ adj. [only before a noun] happening as a result at the end of a period of time or of a process: *It is impossible to say what the eventual cost will be.* ▶ **końcowy, ostateczny** ℹ Uwaga! Słowo **eventual** nie oznacza „ewentualny". „Ewentualny" to **possible**.

eventually /ɪˈventʃuəli/ adv. in the end; finally: *He eventually managed to persuade his parents to let him buy a motor bike.* ▶ **w końcu, ostatecznie** ℹ Uwaga! Słowo **eventually** nie oznacza „ewentualnie". „Ewentualnie" to **if necessary**. SYN **finally**

eventuate /ɪˈventʃueɪt/ verb [I] (formal) to happen as a result of sth ▶ **wynikać z czegoś**

ever /ˈevə(r)/ adv. **1** (used in questions and negative sentences, when you are comparing things, and in sentences with *if*) at any time: *Do you ever wish you were famous?* ◇ *She **hardly ever*** (rzadko kiedy) *goes out.* ◇ *Today is hotter **than ever**.* ◇ *This is the best meal I have ever had.* ◇ *If you ever visit England, you must come and stay with us.* ◇ *Nobody ever* (nikt nigdy) *comes to see me.* ▶ **kiedykolwiek, kiedy 2** (used in questions with verbs in the perfect tenses) at any time up to now: *Have you ever been to Spain?* ▶ **kiedykolwiek** ℹ Zwróć uwagę, że w odpowiedzi na tak zadane pytanie nie stosuje się **ever**, lecz **Yes, I have** lub **No, I haven't** albo **No, never. 3** (used with a question that begins with 'when', 'where', 'who', 'how', etc. to show that you are surprised or shocked): ***What ever*** (o czymże) *were you thinking about when you wrote this?* ◇ ***How ever*** (jakim cudem) *did he get back so quickly?* ◇ ***Why ever*** (czemuż) *did you agree?* ➲ look at **whatever, whenever, however**

IDM **(as) bad, good, etc. as ever** (as) bad, good, etc. as usual or as always: *In spite of his problems, Andrew is as cheerful as ever.* ▶ **zły/dobry itp. jak zawsze**

ever after (used especially at the end of stories) from that moment on for always: *The prince married the princess and they lived happily ever after* (długo i szczęśliwie). ▶ **już na zawsze**

ever since ... all the time from ... until now: *She has had a car ever since she was at university.* ▶ **odkąd, od momentu kiedy**

ever so/ever such (a) (Brit., informal) very: *He's ever such a kind man.* Jest takim dobrym mężczyzną. ◇ *He's ever so kind* (taki (strasznie) dobry). ▶ **bardzo, strasznie**

for ever → FOREVER

ever- /ˈevə(r)/ [in compounds] always; continuously: *the ever-growing problem of pollution* ▶ **ciągle, wciąż**

evergreen /ˈevəgriːn/ noun [C], adj. (a tree or bush) with green leaves all through the year ▶ *(drzewo)* **wiecznie zielony** ➲ look at **deciduous**

everlasting /ˌevəˈlɑːstɪŋ; US ˈlæst-/ adj. (formal) continuing for ever; never changing: *everlasting life/love* ▶ **wieczny, nieskończony**

every /ˈevri/ determiner **1** [used with singular nouns] all of the people or things in a group of three or more: *She knows every student in the school.* ◇ *There are 200 students in the school, and she knows every one of them.* ◇ *I've read every book in this house.* ◇ *You were out every time I phoned.* ▶ **każdy 2** all that is possible: *You have every chance of success.* ◇ *She had every reason to be angry.* ▶ **wszelki, każdy 3** (used for saying how often sth happens): *We see each other **every day*** (codziennie). ◇ *Take the medicine every four hours.* ◇ *The milkman comes **every other day*** (co drugi dzień). ◇ ***One in every** three marriages ends in divorce.* ◇ *every now and then* co jakiś czas ▶ **co (jakiś czas), każdy**

> **Everyone** odnosi się wyłącznie do ludzi. Nie występuje po nim **of**. **Every one** oznacza „każda osoba lub rzecz" i często po nim występuje **of**: ***Every one of** his records has been successful.* Zob. też uwaga przy **somebody**.

everybody /ˈevribɒdi; US -bʌdi/ (also **everyone** /ˈevriwʌn/) pron. [with sing. verb] every person; all people: *Is everybody here?* ◇ *The police questioned everyone who was at the party.* ◇ *I'm sure everybody else* (wszyscy inni) *will agree with me.* ▶ **każdy, wszyscy** ➲ note at **somebody**

everyday /ˈevrideɪ/ adj. [only before a noun] normal or usual: *The computer is now part of everyday life.* ▶ **codzienny, powszedni**

everyone = EVERYBODY

everyplace (US) = EVERYWHERE

everything /ˈevriθɪŋ/ pron. [with sing. verb] **1** each thing; all things: *Sam lost everything in the fire.* ◇ *Everything is very expensive in this shop.* ◇ *We can leave* ***everything else*** (resztę) *until tomorrow.* ▶ **wszystko 2** the most important thing: *Money isn't everything.* ▶ **wszystko**

everywhere /ˈevriweə(r)/ (also **everyplace** /ˈevripleɪs/) adv. in or to every place: *I've looked everywhere.* ▶ **wszędzie**

evict /ɪˈvɪkt/ verb [T] to force sb (officially) to leave the house or land which they are renting: *They were evicted for not paying the rent.* ▶ **eksmitować**
■ **eviction** noun [C,U] ▶ **eksmisja**

evidence /ˈevɪdəns/ noun [U] **evidence (of/for sth)**; **evidence that ...** the facts, signs, etc. that make you believe that sth is true: *There was no evidence of a struggle in the room.* ◇ *You have absolutely no evidence for what you're saying!* ◇ *There was not enough evidence to prove him guilty.* ◇ *Her statement to the police was* ***used in evidence*** *against him.* ◇ *The witnesses to the accident will be asked to* ***give evidence*** *in court.* ▶ **dowód**, **świadectwo** ➲ note at **court** ➲ look at **proof**
IDM **(to be) in evidence** that you can see; present in a place: *When we arrived there was no ambulance in evidence* (nie było śladu karetki). ▶ **(być) widocznym**
ℹ Zwróć uwagę, że **evidence** jest rzeczownikiem niepoliczalnym. Kiedy chodzi o pojedyncze przedmioty stanowiące dowód, stosuje się słowo **piece**: *One piece of evidence is not enough to prove somebody guilty.*

evident /ˈevɪdənt/ adj. clear (to the eye or mind); obvious: *It was evident that the damage was very serious.* ▶ **jasny**, **oczywisty**

evidently /ˈevɪdəntli/ adv. **1** clearly; that can be easily seen or understood: *She was evidently extremely shocked at the news.* ▶ **wygląda na to, że 2** according to what people say: *Evidently he has decided to leave.* ▶ **najwyraźniej**; **jasne, że**

evil[1] /ˈiːvl/ adj. morally bad; causing trouble or harming people: *In the play, Richard is portrayed as an evil king.* ▶ **zły** OPP **good**

Inny przymiotnik o tym samym znaczeniu to **wicked**. Oba są mocnymi wyrażeniami. Na niegrzeczne dzieci mówi się **naughty** lub **mischievous**.

evil[2] /ˈiːvl/ noun [U,C] a force that causes bad or harmful things to happen: *Drugs and alcohol are two of the evils of modern society.* ◇ *The play is about the good and evil in all of us.* ▶ **zło** OPP **good**
IDM **the lesser of two evils** → LESSER

evocative /ɪˈvɒkətɪv/ adj. **evocative (of sth)** making you think of or remember a strong image or feeling, in a pleasant way: *evocative smells/sounds/music* ◇ *Her new book is wonderfully evocative of village life.* ▶ **ewokacyjny**, **przywodzący coś na myśl**

evoke /ɪˈvəʊk/ verb [T] (formal) to produce a memory, feeling, etc. in sb in a pleasant way: *For me, that music always evokes hot summer evenings.* ◇ *Her novel evoked a lot of interest.* ▶ **przywoływać**, **wywoływać**

evolution /ˌiːvəˈluːʃn; ˌev-/ noun [U] **1** the development of plants, animals, etc. over many thousands of years from simple early forms to more advanced ones: *Darwin's theory of evolution* ▶ **ewolucja 2** the process of change and development of sth that happens gradually: *Political evolution is a slow process.* ▶ **rozwój**

evolutionary /ˌiːvəˈluːʃənri; ˌev-; US -neri/ adj. connected with **evolution**; connected with gradual development and change: *evolutionary theory* ◇ *evolutionary change* ▶ **ewolucyjny**

evolve /iˈvɒlv/ verb **1** [I,T] (formal) to develop or to make sth develop gradually, from a simple to a more advanced form: *His style of painting has evolved gradually over the past 20 years.* ▶ **rozwijać (się) 2** [I] **evolve (from sth)** (used about plants, animals, etc.) to develop over many thousands of years from simple forms to more advanced ones ▶ **rozwijać się**

ewe /juː/ noun [C] a female sheep ▶ **samica owcy** ➲ note at **sheep**

ex- /eks/ [in nouns] former: *ex-wife* ◇ *ex-president* ▶ **były**

exacerbate /ɪgˈzæsəbeɪt/ verb [T] (formal) to make sth worse, especially a disease or problem: *The symptoms may be exacerbated by certain drugs.* ▶ **pogarszać**, **zaostrzać** SYN **aggravate**
■ **exacerbation** /ɪgˌzæsəˈbeɪʃn/ noun [C,U] ▶ **pogorszenie**, **zaostrzenie**

exact[1] /ɪgˈzækt/ adj. **1** (completely) correct; accurate: *I can't tell you the exact number of people who are coming.* ◇ *She's* ***the exact opposite*** *of her sister.* ◇ *He's in his mid-fifties. Well, 56* ***to be exact*** (ściśle mówiąc). ▶ **dokładny 2** able to work in a way that is completely accurate: *You need to be very exact when you calculate the costs.* ▶ **dokładny**
■ **exactness** noun [U] ▶ **dokładność**

exact[2] /ɪgˈzækt/ verb [T] (formal) **exact sth (from sb)** to demand and get sth from sb ▶ **wymagać**

exacting /ɪgˈzæktɪŋ/ adj. needing a lot of care and attention; difficult: *exacting work* ▶ **wymagający**

exactly /ɪgˈzæktli/ adv. **1** (used to emphasize that sth is correct in every way) just: *You've arrived at exactly the right moment.* ◇ *I found exactly what I wanted.* ▶ **dokładnie 2** (used to ask for, or give, completely correct information): *He took exactly one hour to finish.* ▶ **dokładnie** SYN **precisely 3** (informal) (used for agreeing with a statement) yes; you are right: *'I don't think she's old enough to travel on her own.' 'Exactly.'* ▶ **właśnie**
IDM **not exactly** (informal) **1** (used when you are saying the opposite of what you really mean) not really; not at all: *He's not exactly the most careful driver I know.* ▶ **niezupełnie**, **nie całkiem 2** (used as an answer to say that sth is almost true): *'So you think I'm wrong?' 'No, not exactly, but ...'* ▶ **niezupełnie**

exaggerate /ɪgˈzædʒəreɪt/ verb [I,T] to make sth seem larger, better, worse, etc. than it really is: *Don't exaggerate. I was only two minutes late, not twenty.* ◇ *The problems have been greatly exaggerated.* ▶ **przesadzać**, **wyolbrzymiać**
■ **exaggerated** adj.: *exaggerated claims* ▶ **przesadzony**, **wyolbrzymiony** | **exaggeration** /ɪgˌzædʒəˈreɪʃn/ noun [C,U]: *It's rather an exaggeration to say that all the students are lazy.* ▶ **przesada**

exalted /ɪgˈzɔːltɪd/ adj. **1** (formal or humorous) of high rank, position or great importance: *She was the only woman to rise to such an exalted position.* ▶ **wysoko postawiony 2** (formal) full of great joy and happiness ▶ **wniebowzięty**, **pełen radości**

exam /ɪgˈzæm/ (also formal **examination**) noun [C] a written, spoken or practical test of what you know or can do: *an English exam* ◇ *the exam results* ◇ *to* ***revise for an exam*** ◇ *to* ***do/take/sit an exam*** zdawać egzamin ◇ *to* ***pass*** (zdać)/***fail*** (oblać) ***an exam*** ▶ **egzamin** ➲ note at **pass**, **study**

Test oznacza zazwyczaj mniej ważny i krótszy egzamin (np. kolokwium, sprawdzian, klasówka).

examination /ɪgˌzæmɪˈneɪʃn/ noun **1** [C] (formal) = EXAM **2** [C,U] the act of looking at sth carefully, especially to see if there is anything wrong or to find the cause of a problem: *a medical examination* ◇ *On close examination, it was found that the passport was false.* ▶ **badanie**, **inspekcja**

examine /ɪɡˈzæmɪn/ verb [T] **1** to consider or study an idea, a subject, etc. very carefully: *These theories will be examined in more detail later on in the lecture.* ▶ **badać, analizować 2 examine sb/sth (for sth)** to look at sb/sth carefully in order to find out sth: *The detective examined the room for clues.* ▶ **badać, sprawdzać 3** (formal) **examine sb (in/on sth)** to test what sb knows or can do: *You will be examined on everything that has been studied in the course.* ▶ **egzaminować/sprawdzać kogoś (z czegoś)**

examiner /ɪɡˈzæmɪnə(r)/ noun [C] a person who tests sb in an exam ▶ **egzaminator/ka**

example /ɪɡˈzɑːmpl; US -ˈzæmpl/ noun [C] **1 an example (of sth)** something such as an object, a fact or a situation which shows, explains or supports what you say: *I don't quite understand you. Can you* ***give me an example of*** *what you mean?* ◇ *This is* ***a typical example of*** *a Victorian house.* ▶ **przykład 2 an example (to sb)** a person or thing or a type of behaviour that is good and should be copied: *Joe's bravery should be an example to us all.* ▶ **przykład, wzór**

IDM **follow sb's example/lead** → FOLLOW

for example; e.g. (used for giving a fact, situation, etc. which explains or supports what you are talking about): *In many countries, Italy, for example, family life is much more important than here.* ▶ **na przykład** ⓘ Forma skrócona **for example** to **e.g.**

set a(n) (good/bad) example (to sb) to behave in a way that should/should not be copied: *Parents should always take care when crossing roads in order to set a good example to their children.* ▶ **dawać (komuś) (dobry/zły) przykład**

exasperate /ɪɡˈzæspəreɪt/ verb [T] to make sb angry; to annoy sb very much: *This lack of progress exasperates me.* ▶ **rozdrażniać**

■ **exasperated** adj.: *She was becoming exasperated with all their questions.* Drażniły ją te ich wszystkie pytania. ▶ **rozdrażniony** | **exasperating** adj.: *an exasperating problem* ▶ **drażniący** | **exasperation** /ɪɡˌzæspəˈreɪʃn/ noun [U]: *She finally threw the book across the room* ***in exasperation.*** ▶ **rozdrażnienie**

excavate /ˈekskəveɪt/ verb [I,T] to dig in the ground to look for old objects or buildings that have been buried for a long time; to find sth by digging in this way: *A Roman villa has been excavated in a valley near the village.* ▶ **prowadzić wykopaliska; odkopywać** (*coś w czasie prac wykopaliskowych*)

■ **excavation** /ˌekskəˈveɪʃn/ noun [C,U]: *Excavations on the site have revealed Saxon objects.* ▶ **prace wykopaliskowe, wydobywanie**

excavator /ˈekskəveɪtə(r)/ noun [C] a large machine that is used for digging and moving earth ▶ **koparka** ➲ picture at **truck**

exceed /ɪkˈsiːd/ verb [T] **1** to be more than a particular number or amount: *The weight should not exceed 20 kilos.* ▶ **przekraczać, przewyższać 2** to do more than the law, a rule, an order, etc. allows you to do: *He was stopped by the police for exceeding the speed limit.* ▶ **przekraczać** ➲ look at **excess, excessive**

exceedingly /ɪkˈsiːdɪŋli/ adv. (formal) very: *an exceedingly difficult problem* ▶ **niezmiernie, nadmiernie**

excel /ɪkˈsel/ verb (**excelling; excelled**) (formal) **1** [I] **excel (in/at sth/doing sth)** to be very good at doing sth: *Regina excels at sports.* ▶ **celować w czymś 2** [T] (Brit.) **excel yourself** to do sth even better than you usually do: *Rick's cooking is always good but this time he really excelled himself.* ▶ **przechodzić samego siebie**

excellence /ˈeksələns/ noun [U] the quality of being very good: *The head teacher said that she wanted the school to be a centre of academic excellence.* ▶ **znakomitość, świetność**

excellent /ˈeksələnt/ adj. very good; of high quality: *He speaks excellent French.* ▶ **znakomity, świetny** ➲ note at **good**

■ **excellently** adv. ▶ **znakomicie, świetnie**

except[1] /ɪkˈsept/ prep. **except (for) sb/sth; except that ...** not including sb/sth; apart from the fact that: *The museum is open every day except Mondays.* ◇ *I can answer all of the questions except for the last one.* ◇ *It was a good hotel except that it was rather noisy.* ▶ **oprócz, poza, prócz tego**

except[2] /ɪkˈsept/ verb [T, often passive] (formal) **except sb/sth (from sth)** to leave sb/sth out; to not include sb/sth: *Nobody is excepted from helping with the housework.* ▶ **wyłączać, wykluczać**

■ **excepting** prep.: *I swim every day excepting Sundays.* ▶ **wyłączając, wyjąwszy**

exception /ɪkˈsepʃn/ noun [C] a person or thing that is not included in a general statement: *Most of his songs are awful but this one is an exception.* ◇ *Everybody was poor as a student and I was* ***no exception.*** ▶ **wyjątek**

IDM **make an exception (of sb/sth)** to treat sb/sth differently: *We don't usually allow children under 14 but we'll make an exception in your case.* ▶ **zrobić (dla kogoś) wyjątek**

with the exception of except for; apart from: *He has won every major tennis championship with the exception of Wimbledon.* ▶ **z wyjątkiem czegoś**

without exception in every case; including everyone/everything: *Everybody without exception must take the test.* ▶ **bez wyjątku**

exceptional /ɪkˈsepʃənl/ adj. very unusual; unusually good: *You will only be allowed to leave early in exceptional circumstances.* ◇ *We have had a really exceptional summer.* ▶ **wyjątkowy** SYN **outstanding**

■ **exceptionally** /-ʃənəli/ adv.: *The past year has been exceptionally difficult for us.* ▶ **wyjątkowo**

excerpt /ˈeksɜːpt/ noun [C] a short piece taken from a book, film, piece of music, etc. ▶ **fragment, urywek**

excess[1] /ɪkˈses/ noun [sing.] **an excess (of sth)** more of sth than is necessary or usual; too much of sth: *An excess of fat in your diet can lead to heart disease.* ▶ **nadmiar**

IDM **in excess of** more than: *Her debts are in excess of £1 000.* ▶ **ponad** ➲ verb **exceed**

excess[2] /ˈekses/ adj. [only before a noun] more than is usual or allowed; extra: *Cut any excess fat off the meat.* ◇ *excess baggage* nadbagaż ▶ **nadmierny, przekraczający normę** ➲ verb **exceed**

excessive /ɪkˈsesɪv/ adj. too much; too great or extreme: *He was driving at excessive speed when he crashed.* ▶ **wygórowany, nadmierny**

■ **excessively** adv. ▶ **nadmiernie, przesadnie**

exchange[1] /ɪksˈtʃeɪndʒ/ noun **1** [C,U] giving or receiving sth in return for sth else: *a useful exchange of information* ◇ *We can offer free accommodation* ***in exchange for*** (w zamian za) *some help in the house.* ▶ **wymiana, zamiana 2** [U] the relation in value between kinds of money used in different countries: *The* ***exchange rate*** (kurs) *is one pound to 250 yen.* ◇ *What's the* ***exchange rate/rate of exchange*** *for dollars?* ◇ *Most of the country's* ***foreign exchange*** (dewiz) *comes from oil.* ▶ **wymiana** ➲ look at **stock exchange 3** [C] a visit by a group of students or teachers to another country and a return visit by a similar group from that country: *She went on an exchange to Germany when she was sixteen.* ▶ **wymiana 4** [C] an angry conversation or argument: *She had a* ***heated exchange*** *with her neighbours about the noise the night before.* ▶ **(ostra) wymiana zdań 5** = TELEPHONE EXCHANGE

E

exchange² /ɪksˈtʃeɪndʒ/ verb [T] **exchange A for B; exchange sth (with sb)** to give or receive sth in return for sth else: *I would like to exchange this skirt for a bigger size.* ◇ *Claire and Molly exchanged addresses with the boys.* ◇ *They exchanged glances.* ▶ **wymieniać, zamieniać** ➲ note at **shopping**

excise /ˈeksaɪz/ noun [U] a government tax on certain goods that are produced or sold inside a country, for example cigarettes, alcohol, etc. ▶ **akcyza, podatek akcyzowy** ➲ look at **customs**

excitable /ɪkˈsaɪtəbl/ adj. easily excited ▶ **pobudliwy**

excite /ɪkˈsaɪt/ verb [T] **1** to make sb feel happy and enthusiastic or nervous: *Don't excite the baby too much or we'll never get him off to sleep.* ▶ **pobudzać, podniecać 2** to make sb react in a particular way: *The programme excited great interest.* ▶ **wzbudzać**

excited /ɪkˈsaɪtɪd/ adj. **excited (about/at/by sth)** feeling or showing happiness and enthusiasm; not calm: *Are you getting excited about your holiday?* ◇ *We're all very excited at the thought of moving house.* ▶ **podniecony**
■ **excitedly** adv. ▶ **z podnieceniem**

excitement /ɪkˈsaɪtmənt/ noun [U] the state of being excited, especially because sth interesting is happening or will happen: *There was **great excitement** as the winner's name was announced.* ◇ *The match was **full of excitement** until the very last minute.* ▶ **podniecenie**

exciting /ɪkˈsaɪtɪŋ/ adj. causing strong feelings of pleasure and interest: *That's very exciting news.* ◇ *Berlin is one of the most exciting cities in Europe.* ▶ **podniecający**

exclaim /ɪkˈskleɪm/ verb [I,T] to say sth suddenly and loudly because you are surprised, angry, etc.: *'I just don't believe it!' he exclaimed.* ▶ **wykrzykiwać**

exclamation /ˌekskləˈmeɪʃn/ noun [C] a short sound, word or phrase that you say suddenly because of a strong emotion, pain, etc.: *'Ouch!' is an exclamation.* ▶ **okrzyk** SYN **interjection**

ˌexclaˈmation mark (US **ˌexclaˈmation point**) noun [C] a mark (!) that is written after an **exclamation** ▶ **wykrzyknik**

exclude /ɪkˈskluːd/ verb [T] [not used in the continuous tenses] **1** to leave out; not include: *The price excludes all extras such as drinks or excursions.* ▶ **wykluczać, usuwać** OPP **include 2 exclude sb/sth (from sth)** to prevent sb/sth from entering a place or taking part in sth: *Women are excluded from* (nie mają wstępu do) *the temple.* ◇ *Jake was excluded from the game for cheating.* ▶ **wykluczać** OPP **include 3** to decide that sth is not possible: *The police had **excluded the possibility** that the child had run away.* ▶ **nie wliczać, nie uwzględniać**

excluding /ɪkˈskluːdɪŋ/ prep. leaving out; without: *Lunch costs £10 per person excluding drinks.* ▶ **z wyjątkiem, bez** OPP **including**

exclusion /ɪkˈskluːʒn/ noun [U] keeping or leaving sb/sth out ▶ **wykluczenie**

exclusive¹ /ɪkˈskluːsɪv/ adj. **1** [only before a noun] only to be used by or given to one person, group, etc.; not to be shared: *This car is for the Director's exclusive use.* ◇ *Tonight we are showing an exclusive interview with the new leader of the Labour Party.* ▶ **wyłączny 2** expensive and not welcoming people who are thought to be of a lower social class: *an exclusive restaurant* ◇ *a flat in an exclusive part of the city* ▶ **ekskluzywny 3 exclusive of sb/sth** not including sb/sth; without: *Lunch costs £7 per person exclusive of drinks.* ▶ **nie licząc kogoś/czegoś, bez**

exclusive² /ɪkˈskluːsɪv/ noun [C] a newspaper story that is given to and published by only one newspaper ▶ **wydarzenie opublikowane wyłącznie w jednej gazecie**

exclusively /ɪkˈskluːsɪvli/ adv. only; not involving anyone/anything else: *The swimming pool is reserved exclusively for members of the club.* ▶ **wyłącznie**

excommunicate /ˌekskəˈmjuːnɪkeɪt/ verb [T] **excommunicate sb (for sth)** to punish sb by officially stating that they can no longer be a member of a Christian Church, especially the Roman Catholic Church ▶ **ekskomunikować**
■ **excommunication** /ˌekskəˌmjuːnɪˈkeɪʃn/ noun [U,C] ▶ **ekskomunika**

excrement /ˈekskrɪmənt/ noun [U] (formal) the solid waste material that you get rid of when you go to the toilet ▶ **kał** SYN **faeces**

excrete /ɪkˈskriːt/ verb [T] (formal) to get rid of solid waste material from the body ▶ **oddawać kał**

excruciating /ɪkˈskruːʃieɪtɪŋ/ adj. extremely painful ▶ **rozdzierający**

excursion /ɪkˈskɜːʃn/ noun [C] a short journey or trip that a group of people make for pleasure: *to **go on an excursion** to the seaside* ▶ **wycieczka** ➲ note at **travel**

excusable /ɪkˈskjuːzəbl/ adj. that you can forgive: *an excusable mistake* ▶ **wybaczalny** OPP **inexcusable**

excuse¹ /ɪkˈskjuːs/ noun [C] **an excuse (for sth/doing sth)** a reason (that may or may not be true) that you give in order to explain your behaviour: *There's **no excuse for** rudeness.* ◇ *He always **finds an excuse** for not helping with the housework.* ◇ *to **make an excuse*** ▶ **usprawiedliwienie, wymówka**

excuse² /ɪkˈskjuːz/ verb [T] **1 excuse sb/sth (for sth/for doing sth)** to forgive sb for sth they have done wrong that is not very serious: *Please excuse the interruption but I need to talk to you.* ▶ **wybaczać 2** to explain sb's bad behaviour and make it seem less bad: *Nothing can excuse such behaviour.* ▶ **usprawiedliwiać 3 excuse sb (from sth)** to free sb from a duty, responsibility, etc.: *She excused herself and left the meeting early.* ▶ **zwolnić kogoś/się (z czegoś)**

> Wyrażenie **excuse me** ma zastosowanie w sytuacjach, kiedy przerywa się czyjąś rozmowę lub zwraca się do kogoś obcego: *Excuse me* (przepraszam pana/panią), *can you tell me the way to the station?*
> W Amer. ang. i czasami w Br. ang. **excuse me** występuje również, jeśli się kogoś przeprasza za drobne przewinienie: *Did I tread on your toe? Excuse me.*

execute /ˈeksɪkjuːt/ verb [T] **1** [usually passive] **execute sb (for sth)** to kill sb as an official punishment: *He was executed for murder.* ▶ **stracić kogoś, wykonać na kimś wyrok 2** (formal) to perform a task, etc. or to put a plan into action ▶ **wykonywać, przeprowadzać**
■ **execution** /ˌeksɪˈkjuːʃn/ noun [C,U] ▶ **stracenie (kogoś); wykonanie**

executioner /ˌeksɪˈkjuːʃənə(r)/ noun [C] a person whose job is to **execute** criminals ▶ **kat**

executive¹ /ɪɡˈzekjətɪv/ noun **1** [C] a person who has an important position as a manager of a business or organization: *She's a senior executive in a computer company.* ▶ **pracownik na kierowniczym stanowisku 2** [C, with sing. or pl. verb] the group of people who are in charge of an organization or a company: *The executive has/have yet to reach a decision.* ▶ **pracownik na kierowniczym stanowisku 3 (the executive)** [sing., with sing. or pl. verb] the part of a government responsible for putting new laws into effect ▶ **władza wykonawcza** ➲ look at **judiciary, legislature**

executive² /ɪɡˈzekjətɪv/ adj. [only before a noun] **1** (used in connection with people in business, government, etc.) concerned with managing, making plans, decisions, etc.: *executive decisions/jobs/duties* ◇ *an executive director of the company* dyrektor firmy ▶ **wykonawczy**

2 (used about goods, buildings, etc.) designed to be used by important business people: *an executive briefcase* ▶ **dla ludzi biznesu, biznesowy**

exemplary /ɪɡˈzempləri/ adj. very good; that can be an example to other people: *exemplary behaviour* ▶ **wzorowy**

exemplify /ɪɡˈzemplɪfaɪ/ verb [T] (**exemplifying**; **exemplifies**; pt, pp **exemplified**) to be a typical example of sth ▶ **ilustrować, być przykładem**

exempt¹ /ɪɡˈzempt/ adj. [not before a noun] **exempt (from sth)** free from having to do sth or pay for sth: *Children under 16 are exempt from dental charges.* ▶ **zwolniony (z czegoś)**
■ **exemption** noun [C,U] ▶ **zwolnienie, ulga**

exempt² /ɪɡˈzempt/ verb [T] (formal) **exempt sb/sth (from sth)** to say officially that sb does not have to do sth or pay for sth ▶ **zwalniać (z czegoś)**

exercise¹ /ˈeksəsaɪz/ noun **1** [U] physical or mental activity that keeps you healthy and strong: *The doctor advised Sebastian to **take regular exercise**.* ◇ *Swimming is a good form of exercise.* ▶ **gimnastyka, ćwiczenie 2** [C, often plural] a movement or activity that you do in order to stay healthy or to become skilled at sth: *I **do** keep-fit **exercises** every morning.* ◇ *breathing/stretching/relaxation exercises* ▶ **gimnastyka, ćwiczenie gimnastyczne 3** [C] a piece of work that is intended to help you learn or practise sth: *an exercise on phrasal verbs* ▶ **ćwiczenie 4** [U] (formal) **exercise of sth** the use of sth, for example a power, right, etc.: *the exercise of patience/judgement/discretion* ▶ **korzystanie (z czegoś) 5** [C] **an exercise in sth** an activity or a series of actions that have a particular aim: *The project is an exercise in getting the best results at a low cost.* ▶ **zadanie 6** [C, usually pl.] a series of activities by soldiers to practise fighting: *military exercises* ▶ **ćwiczenia wojskowe**

exercise² /ˈeksəsaɪz/ verb **1** [T] to make use of sth, for example a power, right, etc.: *You should exercise your right to vote.* ▶ **korzystać z czegoś 2** [I] to do some form of physical activity in order to stay fit and healthy: *It is important to exercise regularly.* ▶ **zażywać ruchu**

ˈexercise bike noun [C] a bicycle that does not move forward but is used for getting exercise indoors ▶ **rower treningowy**

ˈexercise book noun [C] **1** (US **notebook**) a small book for students to write their work in ▶ **zeszyt** (*do ćwiczeń*) **2** (US) = WORKBOOK

exert /ɪɡˈzɜːt/ verb [T] **1** to make use of sth, for example influence, strength, etc., to affect sb/sth: *Parents exert a powerful influence on their children's opinions.* ▶ **wywierać 2 exert yourself** to make a big effort: *You won't make any progress if you don't exert yourself a bit more.* ▶ **wysilać się**

exertion /ɪɡˈzɜːʃn/ noun [U,C] using your body in a way that takes a lot of effort; sth that you do that makes you tired: *At his age physical exertion was dangerous.* ◇ *I'm tired after the exertions of the past few days.* ▶ **wytężenie, wysiłek**

exhale /eksˈheɪl/ verb [I,T] (formal) to breathe out so that the air leaves your lungs ▶ **wydychać** OPP **inhale**
■ **exhalation** /ˌekshəˈleɪʃn/ noun [C,U] ▶ **wydech**

exhaust¹ /ɪɡˈzɔːst/ noun **1** [U] the waste gas that comes out of a vehicle, an engine or a machine: *car exhaust fumes/emissions* ▶ **rura wydechowa 2** [C] (also **exhaust pipe**; US **tailpipe** /ˈteɪlpaɪp/) a pipe (particularly at the back of a car) through which waste gas escapes from an engine or machine ▶ **spaliny** ➲ picture at **car**, picture on **page A7**

exhaust² /ɪɡˈzɔːst/ verb [T] **1** to make sb very tired: *The long journey to work every morning exhausted him.* ▶ **wyczerpywać 2** to use sth up completely; to finish sth: *All the supplies of food have been exhausted.* ▶ **zużyć 3** to say everything you can about a subject, etc.: *Well, I think we've exhausted that topic.* ▶ **wyczerpywać**

exhausted /ɪɡˈzɔːstɪd/ adj. very tired ▶ **wyczerpany**

exhausting /ɪɡˈzɔːstɪŋ/ adj. making sb very tired: *Teaching young children is exhausting work.* ▶ **wyczerpujący**

exhaustion /ɪɡˈzɔːstʃən/ noun [U] the state of being extremely tired ▶ **wyczerpanie, przemęczenie**

exhaustive /ɪɡˈzɔːstɪv/ adj. including everything possible: *This list is certainly not intended to be exhaustive.* ▶ **wyczerpujący**

exˈhaust pipe = EXHAUST¹ (2)

exhibit¹ /ɪɡˈzɪbɪt/ verb [T] **1** to show sth in a public place for people to enjoy or to give them information: *His paintings have been exhibited in the local art gallery.* ▶ **wystawiać (na pokaz) 2** (formal) to show clearly that you have a particular quality, feeling, etc.: *The refugees are exhibiting signs of exhaustion and stress.* ▶ **okazywać**

exhibit² /ɪɡˈzɪbɪt/ noun [C] an object that is shown in a museum, etc. or as a piece of evidence in a court of law ▶ **eksponat**; (*prawn.*) **dowód rzeczowy**

exhibition /ˌeksɪˈbɪʃn/ noun **1** [C] a collection of objects, for example works of art, that are shown to the public: *an exhibition of photographs* ◇ *Her paintings will be **on exhibition** in London for the whole of April.* ▶ **wystawa 2** [C] an occasion when a particular skill is shown to the public: *We saw an exhibition of Scottish dancing last night.* ▶ **pokaz, przedstawienie 3** [sing.] (formal) the act of showing a quality, feeling, etc.: *The game was a superb exhibition of football at its best.* ▶ **pokaz, widowisko**

exhibitionist /ˌeksɪˈbɪʃənɪst/ noun [C] a person who likes to make other people notice him or her ▶ **ekshibicjonist(k)a** ⓘ Zwykle wyraża dezaprobatę.

exhibitor /ɪɡˈzɪbɪtə(r)/ noun [C] a person, for example an artist, a photographer, etc. who shows their work to the public ▶ **wystawca**

exhilarate /ɪɡˈzɪləreɪt/ verb [T, usually passive] to make sb feel very excited and happy: *We felt exhilarated by our walk along the beach.* ▶ **ożywiać, radować**
■ **exhilarating** adj. very exciting and enjoyable ▶ **ekscytujący, emocjonujący** | **exhilaration** /ɪɡˌzɪləˈreɪʃn/ noun [U] ▶ **radosne ożywienie**

exile /ˈeksaɪl/ noun **1** [U] the state of being forced to live outside your own country (especially for political reasons): *He went into exile* (wyemigrował) *after the revolution of 1968.* ◇ *They lived **in exile*** (żyli na uchodźstwie) *in London for many years.* ◇ *the Polish Government-in-Exile* Rząd Polski na Uchodźstwie ▶ **wygnanie 2** [C] a person who is forced to live outside their own country (especially for political reasons) ▶ **uchodźca** ➲ look at **refugee**
■ **exile** verb [T, usually passive]: *After the revolution the king was exiled.* ▶ **skazywać na wygnanie**

exist /ɪɡˈzɪst/ verb [I] **1** [not used in the continuous tenses] to be real; to be found in the real world; to live: *Dreams only exist in our imagination.* ◇ *Fish cannot exist out of water.* ▶ **istnieć 2 exist (on sth)** to manage to live: *I don't know how she exists on the wage she earns.* ▶ **utrzymywać się przy życiu**

existence /ɪɡˈzɪstəns/ noun **1** [U] the state of existing: *This is the oldest human skeleton **in existence**.* To jest najstarszy istniejący ludzki szkielet. ◇ *How did the universe **come into existence**?* Jak powstał wszechświat? ▶ **istnienie 2** [sing.] a way of living, especially when it is difficult: *They lead a miserable existence* (wiodą ciężkie życie) *in a tiny flat in London.* ▶ **byt**

existential /ˌegzɪˈstenʃəl/ adj. [only before a noun] **1** (formal) connected with human existence ▶ **egzystencjalny** **2** connected with the theory of **existentialism** ▶ **egzystencjalny**

existentialism /ˌegzɪˈstenʃəlɪzəm/ noun [U] (in philosophy) the theory that humans are free and responsible for their own actions in a world without meaning ▶ **egzystencjalizm**

existing /ɪgˈzɪstɪŋ/ adj. [only before a noun] that is already there or being used; present: *Under the existing law you are not allowed to work in this country.* ▶ **istniejący**

⚷ **exit**[1] /ˈeksɪt; ˈegzɪt/ noun [C] **1** a door or way out of a public building or vehicle: *The emergency exit is at the back of the bus.* ▶ **wyjście** OPP **entrance** **2** the act of leaving sth: *If I see her coming I'll make a quick exit.* ◇ *an exit visa* wiza wyjazdowa ▶ **wyjście** OPP **entrance** **3** a place where traffic can leave a road or a **motorway** to join another road: *At the roundabout take the third exit.* ▶ **zjazd**

exit[2] /ˈeksɪt; ˈegzɪt/ verb [I,T] (formal) to leave a place: *He exited through the back door.* ◇ *I exited the database and switched off the computer.* ▶ **wychodzić**; **wychodzić z programu komputerowego**

exonerate /ɪgˈzɒnəreɪt/ verb [T, often passive] (formal) to say officially that sb was not responsible for sth bad that happened ▶ **oczyszczać kogoś z zarzutów**, **zwalniać z odpowiedzialności**

exorbitant /ɪgˈzɔːbɪtənt/ adj. (formal) (used about the cost of sth) much more expensive than it should be ▶ **wygórowany**, **nadmierny**

exorcize (also -ise) /ˈeksɔːsaɪz/ verb [T] **1 exorcize sth (from sb/sth)** to make an evil spirit leave a place or sb's body by special prayers or magic ▶ **egzorcyzmować** **2** (formal) to remove sth that is bad or painful from your mind ▶ **odpędzać** (*np. bolesne wspomnienia*)

exotic /ɪgˈzɒtɪk/ adj. unusual or interesting because it comes from a different country or culture: *exotic plants/animals/fruits* ▶ **egzotyczny**

⚷ **expand** /ɪkˈspænd/ verb [I,T] to become or to make sth bigger: *Metals expand when they are heated.* ◇ *We hope to expand our business this year.* ▶ **rozszerzać (się)**, **powiększać (się)** OPP **contract**

PHR V **expand on sth** to give more details of a story, plan, idea, etc. ▶ **rozwijać coś**

expanse /ɪkˈspæns/ noun [C] a large open area (of land, sea, sky, etc.): *I lay on my back and stared up at the vast expanse of blue sky.* ▶ **obszar**, **przestrzeń**

expansion /ɪkˈspænʃn/ noun [U] the act of becoming bigger or the state of being bigger than before: *The rapid expansion of the university has caused a lot of problems.* ▶ **rozwój**, **ekspansja**

expansionism /ɪkˈspænʃənɪzəm/ noun [U] the belief in and process of increasing the size and importance of sth, especially in a country or a business ▶ **ekspansjonizm** ⓘ Czasami wyraża dezprobatę.
■ **expansionist** /-ʃənɪst/ **1** adj.: *expansionist policies* ▶ **ekspansjonistyczny** **2** noun [C] ▶ **ekspansjonist(k)a**

expansive /ɪkˈspænsɪv/ adj. (formal) (used about a person) who talks a lot in an interesting way; friendly ▶ **wylewny**

expatriate /ˌeksˈpætriət; US -ˈpeɪt-/ (also informal **expat** /ˌeksˈpæt/) noun [C] a person who lives outside their own country: *American expatriates in London* ▶ **osoba żyjąca poza własnym krajem**

⚷ **expect** /ɪkˈspekt/ verb [T] **1** to think or believe that sb/sth will come or that sth will happen: *She was expecting a letter from the bank this morning but it didn't come.* ◇ *I expect that it will rain this afternoon.* ◇ *I know the food's not so good, but what did you expect from such a cheap restaurant?* ◇ *She's expecting a baby in the spring.* ▶ **oczekiwać**, **spodziewać się** ⊃ note at **wait**[1] ⓘ Czasownika **expect** nie używa się w czasach *continuous*. Natomiast często spotyka się go w *present participle* (formie -*ing*): *She flung the door open, expecting to see Richard standing there.* **2 expect sth (from sb)**; **expect sb to do sth** to feel confident that you will get sth from sb or that they will do what you want: *He expects a high standard of work from everyone.* ◇ *Factory workers are often expected to work at nights.* ▶ **wymagać**; **oczekiwać po kimś czegoś** **3** [not used in the continuous tenses] (Brit.) to think that sth is true or correct; to suppose: *'Whose is this suitcase?' 'Oh it's Angela's, I expect.'* ◇ *'Will you be able to help me later on?' 'I* ***expect so*** (chyba tak).*'* ▶ **przypuszczać (że)**

expectancy /ɪkˈspektənsi/ noun [U] the state of expecting sth to happen; hope: *a look/feeling of expectancy* ▶ **oczekiwanie**, **nadzieja** ⊃ look at **life expectancy**

expectant /ɪkˈspektənt/ adj. **1** hoping for sth good and exciting: *an expectant audience* ◇ *expectant faces* ▶ **wyczekujący**, **pełen nadziei** **2** having a baby soon: *an expectant mother/father* ▶ **w ciąży**
■ **expectantly** adv. ▶ **z nadzieją**

⚷ **expectation** /ˌekspekˈteɪʃn/ noun (formal) **1** [U] **expectation (of sth)** the belief that sth will happen or come: *The dog was sitting under the table* ***in expectation*** *of food.* ▶ **przewidywanie**, **oczekiwanie** **2** [C, usually pl.] hope for the future: *They had great expectations for their son, but he didn't really live up to them.* ▶ **nadzieja**

IDM **against/contrary to (all) expectation(s)** very different to what was expected: *Contrary to all expectations, Val won first prize.* ▶ **wbrew wszelkim oczekiwaniom**

not come up to (sb's) expectations to not be as good as expected ▶ **zawodzić (czyjeś) oczekiwania**

expected /ɪkˈspektɪd/ adj. that you think will happen: *Double the expected number of people came to the meeting.* ▶ **oczekiwany** OPP **unexpected**

expedient /ɪkˈspiːdiənt/ adj. (formal) (used about an action) convenient or helpful for a purpose, but possibly not completely honest or moral: *The government decided that it was expedient not to increase taxes until after the election.* ▶ **stosowny**, **dogodny**, **oportunistyczny**
■ **expediency** /ɪkˈspiːdiənsi/ noun [U] ▶ **korzyść**, **wygoda**

expedition /ˌekspəˈdɪʃn/ noun [C] **1** a long journey for a special purpose: *a scientific expedition to Antarctica* ▶ **wyprawa** **2** a short journey that you make for pleasure: *a fishing expedition* ▶ **wyprawa**

expel /ɪkˈspel/ verb [T] (**expelling**; **expelled**) **1** to force sb to leave a country, school, club, etc.: *The government has expelled all foreign journalists.* ◇ *The boy was expelled from school for smoking.* ▶ **wydalać** **2** (technical) to send sth out by force: *to expel* (wydychać) *air from the lungs* ▶ **wydalać** ⊃ noun **expulsion**

expend /ɪkˈspend/ verb [T] (formal) **expend sth (on sth)** to spend or use money, time, care, etc. in doing sth: *I have expended a lot of time and energy on that project.* ▶ **poświęcać**, **wydatkować**

expendable /ɪkˈspendəbl/ adj. (formal) not considered important enough to be saved: *In a war human life is expendable.* ▶ **zbyteczny**, **zbędny**

expenditure /ɪkˈspendɪtʃə(r)/ noun [U, sing.] (formal) the act of spending money; the amount of money that is spent: *Government expenditure on education is very low.* ▶ **wydatki**

⚷ **expense** /ɪkˈspens/ noun **1** [C,U] the cost of sth in time or money: *Running a car is a great expense.* ◇ *The movie was filmed in Tahiti* ***at great expense*** (dużym kosztem). ◇ *They* ***spared no expense in*** (nie szczędzili wydatków, aby) *sending their daughter to the best school.* ▶ **wydatek**, **koszt** **2** (**expenses**) [pl.] money that is spent for a particular purpose: *You can claim back your travelling expenses.* ▶ **wydatki, koszty**

IDM **at sb's expense 1** with sb paying; at sb's cost: *My trip is at the company's expense.* ▶ **na (czyjś) rachunek 2** against sb, so that they look silly: *They were always making jokes at Paul's expense.* ▶ **czyimś kosztem**
at the expense of sth harming or damaging sth: *He was a successful businessman, but it was at the expense of his family life.* ▶ **kosztem czegoś**

expensive /ɪk'spensɪv/ adj. costing a lot of money: *Houses are very expensive in this area.* ▶ **drogi, kosztowny** OPP **inexpensive, cheap**
■ **expensively** adv. ▶ **drogo, kosztownie**

experience¹ /ɪk'spɪəriəns/ noun **1** [U] the things that you have done in your life; the knowledge or skill that you get from seeing or doing sth: *We all learn **by experience**.* ◇ *She has five years' teaching experience.* ◇ *I know **from experience** what will happen.* ▶ **doświadczenie, praktyka 2** [C] something that has happened to you (often sth unusual or exciting): *She wrote a book about her experiences in Africa.* ▶ **przygoda, przeżycie**

experience² /ɪk'spɪəriəns/ verb [T] to have sth happen to you; to feel: *It was the first time I'd ever experienced failure.* ◇ *to experience pleasure/pain/difficulty* ▶ **doznawać**

experienced /ɪk'spɪəriənst/ adj. having the knowledge or skill that is necessary for sth: *He's an experienced diver.* ▶ **doświadczony** OPP **inexperienced**

experiment¹ /ɪk'sperɪmənt/ noun [C,U] a scientific test that is done in order to get proof of sth or to get new knowledge: *to carry out/perform/conduct/do an experiment* ◇ *We need to prove this theory **by experiment**.* ▶ **eksperyment, doświadczenie**

experiment² /ɪk'sperɪmənt/ verb [I] **experiment (on/with sth)** to do tests to see if sth works or to try to improve it: *Is it really necessary to experiment on animals?* ◇ *We're experimenting with a new timetable this month.* ▶ **eksperymentować**

experimental /ɪkˌsperɪ'mentl/ adj. connected with experiments or trying new ideas: *We're still at the experimental stage with the new product* (w fazie doświadczeń nad nowym produktem). ◇ *experimental schools* ▶ **eksperymentalny**
■ **experimentally** /-təli/ adv. ▶ **eksperymentalnie**

expert /'ekspɜːt/ noun [C] **an expert (at/in/on sth)** a person who has a lot of special knowledge or skill: *a computer expert* ◇ *Let me try – I'm an expert at parking cars in small spaces.* ◇ *She's a leading expert in the field of genetics.* ▶ **ekspert, specjalist(k)a**
■ **expert** adj.: *He's an expert cook.* Jest doskonałym kucharzem. ◇ *I think we should get expert advice* (zasięgnąć opinii eksperta) *on the problem.* ▶ **mistrzowski, biegły** | **expertly** adv. ▶ **po mistrzowsku, biegle**

expertise /ˌekspɜː'tiːz/ noun [U] a high level of special knowledge or skill: *I was amazed at his expertise on the word processor.* ▶ **biegłość, znawstwo**

expire /ɪk'spaɪə(r)/ verb [I] (used about an official document, agreement, etc.) to come to the end of the time when you can use it or in which it has effect: *My passport's expired. I'll have to renew it.* ▶ **wygasać** ⓘ W języku codziennym używa się w tym znaczeniu zwrotu **run out**.

expiry /ɪk'spaɪəri/ noun [U] the end of a period when you can use sth ▶ **data ważności**

ex'piry date (US **expi'ration date**) noun [C] the date after which an official document, agreement, etc. is no longer valid, or after which sth should not be used ▶ **data ważności; termin przydatności do spożycia**

explain /ɪk'spleɪn/ verb [I,T] **explain (sth) (to sb) 1** to make sth clear or easy to understand: *She explained how I should fill in the form.* ◇ *I don't understand. Can you explain it to me?* ▶ **wyjaśniać** ⓘ Zwróć uwagę, że poprawnie mówi się **Explain it to me** (nigdy ~~*Explain me it*~~). **2** to give a reason for sth: *'This work isn't very good.' 'I wasn't feeling very well.' 'Oh, that explains it then.'* ◇ *The manager explained to the customers why the goods were late.* ▶ **tłumaczyć, wyjaśniać**

IDM **explain yourself 1** to give reasons for your behaviour, especially when it has upset sb ▶ **tłumaczyć się 2** to say what you mean in a clear way ▶ **wyjaśniać, objaśniać**

PHR V **explain sth away** to give reasons why sth is not your fault or is not important ▶ **usprawiedliwiać się, wytłumaczyć**

explanation /ˌeksplə'neɪʃn/ noun **1** [C,U] **an explanation (for sth)** a statement, fact or situation that gives a reason for sth: *He could not **give an explanation** for his behaviour.* ▶ **wytłumaczenie, wyjaśnienie 2** [C] a statement or a piece of writing that makes sth easier to understand: *That idea needs some explanation.* ▶ **wyjaśnienie**

explanatory /ɪk'splænətri; US -tɔːri/ adj. giving an explanation: *There are some explanatory notes at the back of the book.* ◇ *Those instructions are self-explanatory* (zrozumiałe same przez się). ▶ **wyjaśniający**

expletive /ɪk'spliːtɪv; US 'eksplə-/ noun [C] (formal) a word, especially a rude word, that you use when you are angry, or in pain: *He dropped the book on his foot and muttered several expletives under his breath.* ▶ **przekleństwo** SYN **swear word**

explicable /ɪk'splɪkəbl; 'eksplɪkəbl/ adj. that can be explained: *Barry's strange behaviour is only explicable in terms of the stress he is under.* ▶ **wytłumaczalny** OPP **inexplicable**

explicit /ɪk'splɪsɪt/ adj. **1** clear, making sth easy to understand: *I gave you explicit instructions not to touch anything.* ◇ *She was quite explicit about her feelings on the subject.* ▶ **wyraźny, niedwuznaczny** ➲ look at **implicit 2** not hiding anything: *The movie contains explicit* (śmiałe) *sex scenes.* ▶ **wyraźny, niedwuznaczny**
■ **explicitly** adv.: *He was explicitly forbidden to stay out later than midnight.* ▶ **wyraźnie**

explode /ɪk'spləʊd/ verb [I,T] to burst with a loud noise: *The bomb exploded without warning.* ◇ *The army exploded the bomb at a safe distance from the houses.* ◇ (figurative) *My father exploded when I told him how much the car would cost to repair.* ▶ **wybuchać; wysadzać w powietrze** ➲ noun **explosion**

exploit¹ /ɪk'splɔɪt/ verb [T] **1** to use sth or to treat sb unfairly for your own advantage: *Some employers exploit foreign workers, making them work long hours for low pay.* ▶ **wyzyskiwać, eksploatować 2** to develop sth or make the best use of sth: *This region has been exploited for oil for fifty years.* ◇ *Solar energy is a source of power that needs to be exploited more fully.* ▶ **wykorzystywać** (*np. źródła energii*)
■ **exploitation** /ˌeksplɔɪ'teɪʃn/ noun [U]: *They're making you work 80 hours a week? That's exploitation!* ▶ **wyzysk, wykorzystywanie**

exploit² /'eksplɔɪt/ noun [C] something exciting or interesting that sb has done ▶ **wyczyn, czyn (bohaterski)**

exploration /ˌeksplə'reɪʃn/ noun [C,U] the act of travelling around a place in order to learn about it: *space exploration* badania kosmosu ▶ **badanie, poszukiwanie**

exploratory /ɪk'splɒrətri; US -tɔːri/ adj. done in order to find sth out: *The doctors are doing some exploratory tests to try and find out what's wrong.* ◇ *exploratory drillings for oil* ▶ **rozpoznawczy,** (*med.*) **eksploracyjny**

explore /ɪk'splɔː(r)/ verb [I,T] to travel around a place, etc. in order to learn about it: *I've never been to Paris before – I'm going out to explore.* ◇ *They went on an expedition to explore* (wyruszyli na wyprawę badawczą nad) *the River Amazon.* ◇ (figurative) *We need to explore all the possibilities before we decide.* ▶ **podróżować w celach badawczych**, **zwiedzać (gruntownie)**; **zbadać**

explorer /ɪk'splɔːrə(r)/ noun [C] a person who travels round a place in order to learn about it ▶ **badacz/ka**, **odkryw-ca/czyni**

explosion /ɪk'spləʊʒn/ noun [C] **1** a sudden and extremely violent bursting: *Two people were killed in the explosion.* ▶ **wybuch**; **eksplozja** **2** a sudden and often surprising increase in sth: *the population explosion* wyż demograficzny ▶ **gwałtowny wzrost** ➲ verb **explode**

explosive¹ /ɪk'spləʊsɪv/ adj. **1** capable of exploding and therefore dangerous: *Hydrogen is highly explosive.* ▶ **wybuchowy** **2** causing strong feelings or having dangerous effects: *The situation is explosive. We must do all we can to calm people down.* ▶ **wybuchowy**, **drażliwy**

explosive² /ɪk'spləʊsɪv/ noun [C] a substance that is used for causing explosions ▶ **materiał wybuchowy**

exponent /ɪk'spəʊnənt/ noun [C] **1** a person who supports an idea, a belief, etc. and persuades others that it is good: *She was **a leading exponent** of free trade during her political career.* ▶ **propagator/ka** **2** a person who is able to perform a particular activity with skill: *the most famous exponent of the art of mime* ▶ **adept/ka** **3** a raised figure or symbol that shows how many times a quantity must be multiplied by itself, for example the figure 4 in a^4 ▶ (*mat.*) **wykładnik potęgi**

export¹ /ɪk'spɔːt/ verb [I,T] **1** to send goods, etc. to another country, usually for sale: *India exports tea and cotton.* ▶ **eksportować** **2** to move information from one computer program to another ▶ **eksportować** OPP for both meanings **import**

export² /'ekspɔːt/ noun **1** [U] sending goods to another country for sale: *Most of our goods are produced for export.* ◇ *the export trade* ▶ **eksport** **2** [C, usually pl.] a product or service that is sent to another country for sale: *What are Brazil's main exports?* ▶ **artykuły eksportowe** OPP for both meanings **import**
■ **exporter** noun [C]: *the world's largest exporter of cars* ▶ **eksporter** OPP **importer**

expose /ɪk'spəʊz/ verb [T] **1 expose sth (to sb)**; **expose sb/sth (as sth)** to show sth that is usually hidden; to tell sth that has been kept secret: *She didn't want to expose her true feelings to her family.* ◇ *The politician was exposed as a liar on TV.* ▶ **wystawiać** (*np. na pokaz*), **odsłaniać**; **wyjawiać**, **demaskować** **2 expose sb/sth to sth** to put sb/sth or yourself in a situation that could be difficult or dangerous: *to be exposed to danger* ◇ *Thousands of people were exposed to radiation* (zostało napromieniowanych) *when the nuclear reactor exploded.* ▶ **narażać** (*np. na niebezpieczeństwo*) **3 expose sb to sth** to give sb the chance to experience sth: *I like jazz because I was exposed to it* (miałem kontakt z nim) *as a child.* ▶ **sprawiać, że ktoś ma kontakt z czymś** **4** to allow light onto the film inside a camera when taking a photograph ▶ **prześwietlać** (*kliszę*)

exposed /ɪk'spəʊzd/ adj. (used about a place) not protected from the wind and bad weather ▶ **odkryty**, **wystawiony na działanie czynników zewnętrznych**

exposure /ɪk'spəʊʒə(r)/ noun **1** [U] being allowed or forced to experience sth: *TV can give children exposure to other cultures* (pozwala dzieciom na obcowanie z innymi kulturami) *from an early age.* ◇ *Exposure to radiation* (napromieniowanie) *is almost always harmful.* ▶ **wystawianie (na działanie czegoś)**, **narażanie (się)** **2** [U,C] the act of making sth public; the thing that is made public: *The new movie has been given a lot of exposure* (był nagłośniony) *in the media.* ◇ *The politician resigned because of the exposures about his private life.* ▶ **ujawnianie**, **demaskowanie**; **ujawnione fakty** **3** [U] a harmful condition when a person becomes very cold because they have been outside in very bad weather: *The climbers all died of exposure.* ▶ **wyziębienie** **4** [C] the amount of film that is used when you take one photograph: *How many exposures are there on this film?* ▶ **klatka** (*kliszy*)

express¹ /ɪk'spres/ verb [T] **1** to show sth such as a feeling or an opinion by words or actions: *I found it very hard to express what I felt about her.* ◇ *to express fears/concern about something* ▶ **wyrażać** **2 express yourself** to say or write your feelings, opinions, etc.: *I don't think she expresses herself very well in that article.* ▶ **wypowiadać się**

express² /ɪk'spres/ adj. [only before a noun] **1** going or sent quickly: *an express coach* ◇ *an express letter* ekspres ▶ **ekspresowy** **2** (used about a command, wish, etc.) clearly and definitely stated: *It was her express wish that he should have the picture after her death.* ▶ **wyraźny**, **kategoryczny**
■ **express** adv. by a special service that does sth faster than usual: *to send a parcel express* ▶ **ekspresem**

express³ /ɪk'spres/ (also **ex,press 'train**) noun [C] a fast train that does not stop at all stations ▶ **ekspres**

expression /ɪk'spreʃn/ noun **1** [U,C] something that you say that shows your opinions or feelings: *Freedom of expression* (wolność słowa) *is a basic human right.* ◇ *an expression of gratitude/sympathy/anger* ▶ **wyraz**, **ekspresja** **2** [C] the look on sb's face that shows what they are thinking or feeling: *He had a puzzled expression on his face.* ▶ **wyraz** **3** [C] a word or phrase with a particular meaning: *'I'm starving' is an expression meaning 'I'm very hungry'.* ◇ *a slang/an idiomatic expression* ◇ *You haven't quite got the right expression here.* Nie zastosowałeś tutaj odpowiedniego zwrotu. ▶ **zwrot**

expressionism (also **Expressionism**) /ɪk'spreʃənɪzəm/ noun [U] a style and movement in early 20th century art, theatre, cinema and music that tries to express people's feelings and emotions rather than showing events or objects in a realistic way ▶ **ekspresjonizm**
■ **expressionist** (also **Expressionist**) /-ʃənɪst/ **1** noun [C] ▶ **ekspresjonist(k)a** **2** adj. ▶ **ekspresjonistyczny**

expressive /ɪk'spresɪv/ adj. showing feelings or thoughts: *That is a very expressive piece of music.* ◇ *Kate has a very expressive face.* ▶ **wyrazisty**, **ekspresyjny**
■ **expressively** adv. ▶ **wyraziście**, **sugestywnie**

expressly /ɪk'spresli/ adv. **1** clearly; definitely: *I expressly told you not to do that.* ▶ **wyraźnie**, **kategorycznie** **2** for a special purpose; specially: *These scissors are expressly designed for left-handed people.* ▶ **specjalnie**

expressway (US) = MOTORWAY

expropriate /eks'prəʊprieɪt/ verb [T] **1** (formal) (used about a government or an authority) to officially take away private property from its owner for public use ▶ **konfiskować** (*mienie*) **2** (formal) to take sb's property and use it without permission ▶ **przywłaszczać sobie cudzą własność**
■ **expropriation** /,eks,prəʊpri'eɪʃn/ noun [U] ▶ **konfiskata** (*mienia*)

expulsion /ɪk'spʌlʃn/ noun [C,U] the act of making sb leave a place or an institution: *There have been three expulsions from school this year.* ▶ **wydalenie** ➲ verb **expel**

exquisite /'ekskwɪzɪt; ɪk'skwɪzɪt/ adj. extremely beautiful and pleasing: *I think that ring is exquisite.* ▶ **przepiękny**, **wyśmienity**
■ **exquisitely** adv. ▶ **przepięknie**, **wyśmienicie**

ˌex-ˈserviceman, ˌex-ˈservicewoman noun [C] (pl. **-men** /-mən/; **-women** /-wɪmɪn/) (Brit.) a person who used to be in the army, navy, etc. ▶ *(osoba)* **były wojskowy**

ext. = EXTENSION (3): *ext. 3492*

extend /ɪkˈstend/ verb **1** [T] to make sth longer or larger (in space or time): *Could you extend your visit for a few days?* ◇ *We're planning to extend the back of the house to give us more space.* ◇ *Since my injury I can't extend this leg fully.* ▶ **przedłużać, powiększać, wyciągać 2** [I,T] to cover the area or period of time mentioned: *The desert extends over a huge area of the country.* ◇ *The company is planning to extend its operations into Asia.* ◇ *This project will extend* (przeciągnie się) *well into next year.* ▶ **rozciągać się, przedłużać się 3** [T] (formal) to offer sth to sb: *to extend hospitality/an invitation to somebody* ◇ *The town extended a warm welcome* (serdecznie powitało) *to the president.* ▶ **okazywać** *(uprzejmość)*, **wyrażać**

exˌtended ˈfamily noun [C] a family group with a close relationship among the members that includes not only parents and children but also uncles, aunts, grandparents, etc.: *She grew up surrounded by a large extended family.* ▶ **rodzina wielopokoleniowa** ➲ look at **nuclear family**

extension /ɪkˈstenʃn/ noun [C] **1** a part that is added to a building: *They're building an extension on the hospital* (nowe skrzydło szpitala). ▶ **przybudówka 2** an extra period of time that you are allowed for sth: *I've applied for an extension to my work permit.* ▶ **przedłużenie 3** (abbr. **ext.**) a telephone that is connected to a central telephone in a house or to a **switchboard** in a large office building: *What's your extension number?* ◇ *Can I have extension 4266, please?* ▶ **numer wewnętrzny**

exˈtension lead (also **extension**; **exˈtension cable**, US **exˈtension cord**) noun [C] an extra length of electric wire, used when the wire on an electrical device is not long enough ▶ *(elektr.)* **przedłużacz**

extensive /ɪkˈstensɪv/ adj. large in area or amount: *The house has extensive grounds.* ◇ *Most of the buildings suffered extensive damage* (poważnie ucierpiała). ▶ **rozległy, obszerny**
■ **extensively** adv.: *He has travelled extensively.* Dużo podróżował. ▶ **rozlegle, obszernie**

extent /ɪkˈstent/ noun [U] **the extent of sth** the length, area, size or importance of sth: *I was amazed at the extent of his knowledge* (ogromem jego wiedzy). ◇ *The **full extent of** the damage is not yet known.* ▶ **obszar, rozmiary, zakres**
IDM **to a certain/to some extent** (used to show that sth is only partly true): *I agree with you to a certain extent but there are still a lot of points I disagree with.* ▶ **do pewnego stopnia**
to what extent how far; how much: *I'm not sure to what extent I believe her.* ▶ **do jakiego stopnia**

exterior¹ /ɪkˈstɪəriə(r)/ noun [C] the outside of sth; the appearance of sb/sth: *The exterior of the house is fine* (z zewnątrz dom wygląda dobrze) *but inside it isn't in very good condition.* ◇ *Despite his calm exterior, Steve suffers badly from stress.* ▶ **powierzchowność, zewnętrzna strona** OPP **interior**

exterior² /ɪkˈstɪəriə(r)/ adj. on the outside: *the exterior walls of a house* ▶ **zewnętrzny** OPP **interior**

exterminate /ɪkˈstɜːmɪneɪt/ verb [T] to kill a large group of people or animals: *Once cockroaches infest a building, they are very hard to exterminate.* ▶ **unicestwiać, tępić**
■ **extermination** /ɪkˌstɜːmɪˈneɪʃn/ noun [U] ▶ **zagłada, tępienie**

external /ɪkˈstɜːnl/ adj. **1** connected with the outside of sth: *The cream is for external use only.* ▶ **zewnętrzny 2** coming from another place: *You will be tested by an external examiner.* ▶ **z zewnątrz** OPP for both meanings **internal**

■ **externally** /-nəli/ adv.: *The building has been restored externally and internally.* ◇ *The university has many externally funded research projects.* ▶ **z zewnątrz** OPP **internally**

extinct /ɪkˈstɪŋkt/ adj. **1** (used about a type of animal, plant, etc.) no longer existing: *Tigers are nearly extinct in the wild.* ▶ **wymarły 2** (used about a **volcano**) no longer active ▶ **wygasły**
■ **extinction** noun [U]: *The giant panda is in danger of extinction.* ▶ **wymarcie**

extinguish /ɪkˈstɪŋgwɪʃ/ verb [T] (formal) to cause sth to stop burning: *The fire was extinguished very quickly.* ▶ **ugasić, zgasić** ⓘ W języku codziennym używa się zwrotu **put out**.
■ **extinguisher** = FIRE EXTINGUISHER

extort /ɪkˈstɔːt/ verb [T] (formal) **extort sth (from sb)** to get sth by using threats or violence: *The gang were found guilty of extorting money from small businesses.* ▶ **wymuszać (coś na kimś), wydzierać (coś komuś)**
■ **extortion** noun [U] ▶ **wymuszanie**

extortionate /ɪkˈstɔːʃənət/ adj. (used especially about prices) much too high: *Three pounds for a cup of coffee? That's extortionate* (to zdzierstwo)*!* ▶ **wygórowany**

extra¹ /ˈekstrə/ adj. more than is usual, expected, or than exists already: *I'll need some extra money for the holidays.* ◇ *The football match went into extra time* (odbyła się dogrywka). ◇ *Is wine included in the price of the meal or is it extra?* ▶ **dodatkowy** ➲ look at **additional**
■ **extra** adv.: *'What size is this pullover?' 'Extra large (XL).'* ◇ *I tried to be extra* (nadzwyczajnie) *nice to him yesterday because it was his birthday.* ▶ **dodatkowo, więcej**

extra² /ˈekstrə/ noun [C] **1** something that costs more, or that is not normally included: *Optional extras* (dodatkowe urządzenia) *such as colour printer, scanner and modem are available on top of the basic package.* ▶ **odpłatny dodatek, odpłatna dodatkowa usługa 2** a person in a film, etc. who has a small unimportant part, for example in a crowd ▶ **statyst(k)a**

extract¹ /ˈekstrækt/ noun [C] a part of a book, piece of music, etc., that has often been specially chosen to show sth: *The newspaper published extracts from the controversial novel.* ▶ **fragment, wypis**

extract² /ɪkˈstrækt/ verb [T] (formal) to take sth out, especially with difficulty: *I think this tooth will have to be extracted.* ◇ *I wasn't able to extract an apology from her.* ▶ **usuwać; wydobywać, wyrywać**

extraction /ɪkˈstrækʃn/ noun (formal) **1** [U,C] the act of taking sth out: *extraction of salt from the sea* ◇ *Dentists report that children are requiring fewer extractions.* ▶ **wydobywanie, usunięcie 2** [U] family origin: *He's an American but he's of Italian extraction.* ▶ **pochodzenie**

extra-curricular /ˌekstrə kəˈrɪkjələ(r)/ adj. not part of the **curriculum**: *The school offers many extra-curricular activities such as sport, music, drama, etc.* ▶ **pozalekcyjny, pozaszkolny**

extradite /ˈekstrədaɪt/ verb [T] to send a person who may be guilty of a crime from the country in which they are living to the country which wants to put them on trial for the crime: *The suspected terrorists were captured in Spain and extradited to France.* ▶ **ekstradować**
■ **extradition** /ˌekstrəˈdɪʃn/ noun [C,U] ▶ **ekstradycja**

extrajudicial /ˌekstrədʒuˈdɪʃl/ adj. happening outside the normal power of the law: *an extrajudicial execution* ▶ **pozasądowy**

extramarital /ˌekstrəˈmærɪtl/ adj. happening outside marriage: *an extramarital affair* ▶ **pozamałżeński**

extraneous /ɪk'streɪniəs/ adj. **extraneous (to sth)** (formal) not directly connected with the particular situation you are in or the subject you are dealing with: *We do not want any extraneous* (nieistotnych) *information on the page.* ◇ *We shall ignore factors extraneous to* (niezwiązanych z) *the problem.* ◇ *Coughs and extraneous noises* (hałasy zewnętrzne) *can be edited out.* ▶ **uboczny** SYN **irrelevant**

⚷ **extraordinary** /ɪk'strɔ:dnri; US -dəneri/ adj. **1** not what you would expect in a particular situation; very strange: *That was extraordinary behaviour for a teacher!* ▶ **nadzwyczajny 2** very unusual: *She has an extraordinary ability to whistle and sing at the same time.* ▶ **przedziwny**, **zadziwiający** SYN for both meanings **incredible** OPP for both meanings **ordinary**
■ **extraordinarily** /ɪk'strɔ:dnrəli; US -də'ner-/ adv.: *He was an extraordinarily talented musician.* ▶ **niezwykle**, **zadziwiająco**

extrapolate /ɪk'stræpəleɪt/ verb [I,T] (formal) **extrapolate (sth) (from/to sth)** to form an opinion or make a judgement about a new situation by using facts that you know from a different situation: *The figures were obtained by extrapolating from past trends.* ◇ *We have extrapolated these results from research in other countries.* ▶ **ekstrapolować (coś) (na podstawie czegoś)**
■ **extrapolation** /ɪk,stræpə'leɪʃn/ noun [U,C] ▶ **ekstrapolacja**

extraterrestrial /,ekstrətə'restriəl/ noun [C] (in stories) a creature that comes from another planet; a creature that may exist on another planet ▶ **kosmit(k)a**
■ **extraterrestrial** adj.: *extraterrestrial beings/life* ▶ **pozaziemski**

extravagant /ɪk'strævəgənt/ adj. **1** spending or costing too much money: *He's terribly extravagant – he travels everywhere by taxi.* ◇ *an extravagant present* ▶ **rozrzutny**; **drogi 2** exaggerated; more than is usual, true or necessary: *the extravagant claims of advertisers* ▶ **przesadny**, **nadmierny**
■ **extravagance** noun [C,U] ▶ **rozrzutność**; **ekstrawagancja** | **extravagantly** adv. ▶ **rozrzutnie**, **ekstrawagancko**

⚷ **extreme** /ɪk'stri:m/ adj. **1** [only before a noun] the greatest or strongest possible: *extreme heat/difficulty/poverty* ◇ *You must take extreme care* (musisz bardzo uważać) *when driving at night.* ▶ **najwyższy**, **niesłychany 2** not ordinary or usual; serious or severe: *Children will be removed from their parents only* ***in extreme circumstances.*** ◇ *extreme weather conditions* ▶ **ekstremalny**, **skrajny 3** (used about people, political organizations, opinions, etc.) far from what most people consider to be normal, reasonable or acceptable: *Her extreme views on immigration are shocking to most people.* ◇ *extreme right-wing views* ◇ *politicians on the extreme left of the party* ▶ **ekstremalny** ➲ look at **moderate**, **radical 4** [only before a noun] as far away as possible from the centre in the direction mentioned: *Kerry is in the extreme west* (w najdalej na zachód wysuniętej części) *of Ireland.* ▶ **krańcowy**, **skrajny**
■ **extreme** noun [C]: *Alex used to be very shy but now she's gone to the opposite extreme* (popadła z jednej skrajności w drugą). ▶ **skrajność**

⚷ **extremely** /ɪk'stri:mli/ adv. very: *Listen carefully because this is extremely important.* ▶ **niezmiernie**, **szalenie**

ex'treme sport noun [C] a very dangerous sport or activity which some people do for fun: *The first day of the extreme sports championships featured bungee jumping.* ▶ **sport ekstremalny** ➲ picture on **page A8**

extremist /ɪk'stri:mɪst/ noun [C] a person who has extreme political opinions ▶ **ekstremist(k)a** ➲ look at **moderate**, **radical**
■ **extremism** /ɪk'stri:mɪzəm/ noun [U] ▶ **ekstremizm**

extremity /ɪk'streməti/ noun [C] (pl. **extremities**) the part of sth that is furthest from the centre ▶ **koniec**, **koniuszek**; **skrajność**

extricate /'ekstrɪkeɪt/ verb [T] to manage to free sb/sth from a difficult situation or position: *I finally managed to extricate myself* (zdołałem się wyrwać) *from the meeting by saying that I had a train to catch.* ▶ **wywikłać**

extrovert /'ekstrəvɜ:t/ noun [C] a person who is confident and full of life and who prefers being with other people to being alone ▶ **ekstrawerty-k/czka** OPP **introvert**
■ **extroverted** adj. ▶ **ekstrawertyczny** OPP **introverted**

exuberant /ɪg'zju:bərənt; US -'zu:-/ adj. (used about a person or their behaviour) full of energy and excitement ▶ **tryskający radością/energią**, **wylewny**
■ **exuberance** noun [U] ▶ **wylewność**, **entuzjazm**

exude /ɪg'zju:d; US -'zu:d/ verb [I,T] **1** if you **exude** a particular feeling or quality, or it **exudes** from you, people can easily see that you have it: *She exuded confidence.* ▶ **emanować** (*np. pewnością siebie*) **2** if sth **exudes** a liquid or smell, or a liquid or smell **exudes** from somewhere, the liquid, etc. comes out slowly: *The plant exudes a sticky fluid.* ◇ *An awful smell exuded from the creature's body.* ▶ (*zapach itp.*) **wydzielać (się)**, **roztaczać (się)**

⚷ **eye**[1] /aɪ/ noun [C] **1** one of the two organs of your body that you use to see with: *She opened/closed her eyes.* ◇ *He is blind in one eye.* Nie widzi na jedno oko. ◇ *an eye test* badanie wzroku ◇ *He's got blue eyes.* ◇ *to make eye contact with somebody* nawiązać z kimś kontakt wzrokowy ▶ **oko** ➲ look at **black eye** ➲ picture at **body** ➲ look at **blink**, **wink**

> People with poor **eyesight** usually wear **glasses** or use **contact lenses**.

2 the ability to see sth: *He has* ***sharp eyes*** (dobry wzrok). ◇ *She has* ***an eye for detail*** (jest skrupulatna). ▶ **oko**, **wzrok 3** the hole at one end of a needle that the thread goes through ▶ **ucho**

IDM **as far as the eye can see** → FAR[2]

be up to your eyes in sth (informal) to have more of sth than you can easily do or manage: *I can't come out with you tonight – I'm up to my eyes in work.* ▶ **tkwić w czymś po uszy**

before sb's very eyes in front of sb so that they can clearly see what is happening ▶ **na czyichś oczach**

cast an eye/your eye(s) over sb/sth → CAST[1]

catch sb's attention/eye → CATCH[1]

cry your eyes out → CRY[1]

an eye for an eye (used to say that you should punish sb by doing to them what they have done to sb else) ▶ **oko za oko, ząb za ząb**

have (got) your eye on sb to watch sb carefully to make sure that they do nothing wrong ▶ **pilnować/obserwować kogoś**

have (got) your eye on sth to be thinking about buying sth: *I've got my eye on a suit that I saw in the sales.* ▶ **upatrzyć sobie coś do kupienia**

in the eyes of sb/in sb's eyes in the opinion of sb: *She was still a child in her mother's eyes.* ▶ **w czyichś oczach**

in the public eye → PUBLIC[1]

keep an eye on sb/sth to make sure that sb/sth is safe; to look after sb/sth: *Please could you keep an eye on the house while we're away?* ▶ **pilnować**

keep an eye open/out (for sb/sth) to watch or look out for sb/sth: *I've lost my ring – could you keep an eye out*

for it? ▶ **wypatrywać (kogoś/czegoś), szukać (kogoś/czegoś)**
keep your eyes peeled/skinned (for sb/sth) to watch carefully for sb/sth: *Keep your eyes peeled for the turning to the village.* ▶ **wypatrywać oczy**
look sb in the eye → LOOK[1]
the naked eye → NAKED
not bat an eye → BAT[2]
see eye to eye (with sb) → SEE
set eyes on sb/sth to see sb/sth: *He loved the house the moment he set eyes on it.* ▶ **ujrzeć**
there is more to sb/sth than meets the eye → MEET
turn a blind eye → BLIND[1]
with your eyes open knowing what you are doing: *You went into the new job with your eyes open, so you can't complain now.* ▶ **z pełną świadomością**

eye² /aɪ/ verb [T] (**eyeing** or **eying**; pt, pp **eyed**) to look at sb/sth closely: *She eyed the stranger with suspicion.* ▶ **mierzyć (kogoś) wzrokiem**

eyeball /ˈaɪbɔːl/ noun [C] the whole of your eye (including the part which is hidden inside the head) ▶ **gałka oczna**

eyebrow /ˈaɪbraʊ/ (also **brow**) noun [C] the line of hair that is above your eye ▶ **brew** ➲ picture at **body**
IDM **raise your eyebrows** → RAISE

ˈ**eye candy** noun [U] (informal) a person or thing that is attractive but not intelligent or useful ▶ **osoba/rzecz atrakcyjna, ale mało inteligentna lub użyteczna**

ˈ**eye-catching** adj. (used about a thing) attracting your attention immediately because it is interesting, bright or pretty ▶ **przyciągający wzrok**

eyeglasses (US) = GLASSES

eyelash /ˈaɪlæʃ/ (also **lash**) noun [C] one of the hairs that grow on the edges of your **eyelids** ▶ **rzęsa** ➲ picture at **body**

ˈ**eye level** adj. at the same height as sb's eyes when they are standing up: *an eye-level grill* ▶ **na poziomie oczu**

eyelid /ˈaɪlɪd/ (also **lid**) noun [C] the piece of skin that can move to cover your eye ▶ **powieka** ➲ picture at **body**
IDM **not bat an eyelid**; **not bat an eye** → BAT[2]

eyeliner /ˈaɪlaɪnə(r)/ noun [U] a substance that you use to draw a dark line around your eyes to make them look more attractive ▶ **kredka do oczu, tusz do kresek**

ˈ**eye-opener** noun [C] something that makes you realize the truth about sth: *That TV programme about the inner cities was a real eye-opener.* ▶ **rewelacja**

eyepiece /ˈaɪpiːs/ noun [C] the piece of glass at the end of a telescope or microscope that you look through ▶ **okular** ➲ picture at **laboratory**

eyeshadow /ˈaɪʃædəʊ/ noun [U] colour that is put on the skin above the eyes to make them look more attractive ▶ **cień do powiek**

eyesight /ˈaɪsaɪt/ noun [U] the ability to see: *good/poor eyesight* ▶ **wzrok**

eyesore /ˈaɪsɔː(r)/ noun [C] something that is ugly and unpleasant to look at: *All this litter in the streets is a real eyesore.* ▶ **szkaradzieństwo**

eyewitness = WITNESS[1] (1)

ˈ**e-zine** noun [C] a magazine published in electronic form on the Internet ▶ **elektroniczne czasopismo internetowe**

F f

F, f /ef/ noun [C,U] (pl. **Fs**; **fs**; **F's**; **f's** /efs/) **1** the 6th letter of the English alphabet: *'Five' begins with (an) 'F'.* ▶ **litera** *f* **2** (used about music) the fourth note in the series of notes called the scale of C major: *F major* F-dur ◇ *F minor* f-moll ◇ *F sharp* Fis, fis ▶ **F/f**

F = FAHRENHEIT: *Water freezes at 32° F.*

f 1 = FEMALE **2** = FEMININE

FA /ˌef ˈeɪ/ abbr. (Brit.) **the Football Association**: *the FA Cup* ▶ **związek piłki nożnej** (*odpowiednik PZPN w Polsce*)

fable /ˈfeɪbl/ noun [C] a short story that teaches a moral lesson and that often has animals as the main characters: *Aesop's fables* ▶ **bajka** ➲ look at **fairy tale**

fabric /ˈfæbrɪk/ noun **1** [C,U] (a type of) cloth or soft material that is used for making clothes, curtains, etc.: *cotton fabrics* ▶ **tkanina, materiał 2** [sing.] the basic structure of a building or system: *The Industrial Revolution changed the fabric of society.* ▶ **struktura**

fabricate /ˈfæbrɪkeɪt/ verb [T, often passive] **1** to invent false information in order to trick people: *The evidence was totally fabricated.* ▶ **fabrykować, fałszować** SYN **make sth up 2** to make or produce goods, equipment, etc. from various different materials ▶ **wytwarzać** SYN **manufacture**
■ **fabrication** /ˌfæbrɪˈkeɪʃn/ noun [C, U] ▶ **fabrykacja**

fabulous /ˈfæbjələs/ adj. **1** very good; excellent: *It was a fabulous concert.* ▶ **wyśmienity, znakomity 2** very great: *fabulous wealth/riches/beauty* ▶ **ogromny, znakomity**

facade /fəˈsɑːd/ noun [C] **1** the front wall of a large building that you see from the outside ▶ **fasada 2** the way sb/sth appears to be, which is not the way he/she/it really is: *His good humour was just a facade.* ▶ **fasada**

face¹ /feɪs/ noun [C] **1** the front part of your head; the expression that is shown on it: *Go and wash your face.* ◇ *She has a very pretty face.* ◇ *He came in with a smile on his face.* ◇ *Her face lit up when John came into the room.* ▶ **twarz 2** (**-faced**) [in compounds] having the type of face or expression mentioned: *round/sour-faced* ◇ *red-faced* o czerwonej twarzy ◇ *two-faced* dwulicowy ▶ *(określa cechę twarzy)* **3** the front or one side of sth: *the north face* (ściana północna) *of the mountain* ◇ *He put the cards **face up/down** on the table.* ◇ *a clock face* tarcza zegara ▶ **przód; strona**
IDM **face to face (with sb/sth)** close to and looking at sb/sth: *I deal with customers on the phone and rarely meet them face to face.* ◇ *a face-to-face conversation* ◇ (figurative) *She was brought face to face with the horrors of war.* ▶ **twarzą w twarz (z kimś/czymś)**
keep a straight face → STRAIGHT[2]
lose face → LOSE
make/pull faces/a face (at sb/sth) to make an expression that shows that you do not like sb/sth: *When she saw what was for dinner she pulled a face.* ▶ **robić miny**
make/pull faces to make rude expressions with your face: *The children made faces behind the teacher's back.* ▶ **stroić miny**
save face → SAVE[1]
to sb's face if you say sth to sb's face, you do it when that person is with you: *I wanted to say that I was sorry to her face, not on the phone.* ▶ **prosto w oczy**

face² /feɪs/ verb [T] **1** to have your face or front pointing towards sb/sth or in a particular direction: *Can you all face the front, please?* ◇ *The garden faces south.* Ogród wychodzi na wschód. ▶ **wychodzić na coś, znajdować się naprzeciw kogoś/czegoś; zwracać się 2** to need attention or action from sb: *There are several problems facing the government.* Rząd ma przed sobą wiele problemów. ◇ *We are faced with* (stoimy przed) *a difficult decision.* **3** to have to deal with sth unpleasant; to deal with sb in a difficult situation: *I can't face another argument.* Nie mam siły na kolejną awanturę. ◇ *He couldn't face going to work* (nie mógł się zdobyć na pójście do pracy) *yesterday – he felt too ill.* ▶ **stawiać czoło, spojrzeć prosto w twarz**

IDM **let's face it** (informal) we must accept it as true: *Let's face it, we can't afford a holiday this year.* ▶ **spójrzmy prawdzie w oczy**

PHR V **face up to sth** to accept a difficult or unpleasant situation and do sth about it: *She had to face up to the fact that she was wrong.* ▶ **stawić czemuś czoło**

facecloth /ˈfeɪsklɒθ/ (also **flannel** /ˈflænl/; US **washcloth** /ˈwɒʃklɒθ/) noun [C] a small square piece of cloth that is used for washing the face, hands, etc. ▶ **chusteczka kosmetyczna/higieniczna**

ˈface cream noun [U,C] a thick cream that you put on your face to clean the skin or keep it soft ▶ **krem do twarzy**

faceless /ˈfeɪsləs/ adj. without individual character or identity: *faceless civil servants* ▶ **bezimienny, anonimowy**

facelift /ˈfeɪslɪft/ noun [C] a medical operation that makes your face look younger ▶ **liftingująca operacja plastyczna** ➲ look at **plastic surgery**

ˈface-saving adj. done to stop yourself looking silly or losing other people's respect: *a face-saving compromise* ▶ **dla zachowania twarzy**

facet /ˈfæsɪt/ noun [C] **1** one part or particular aspect of sth: *There are many facets to this argument.* ▶ **strona** **2** one side of a **precious** stone ▶ **faseta**

facetious /fəˈsiːʃəs/ adj. trying to be amusing about a subject at a time that is not appropriate so that other people become annoyed: *He kept making facetious remarks during the lecture.* ▶ **żartobliwy**

■ **facetiously** adv. ▶ **żartobliwie**

ˌface ˈvalue noun [U, sing.] the cost or value that is shown on the front of stamps, coins, etc. ▶ **wartość nominalna**

IDM **take sb/sth at (its, his, etc.) face value** to accept sb/sth as it, he, etc. appears to be: *Don't take his story at face value. There's something he hasn't told us yet.* ▶ **brać coś za dobrą monetę, ślepo ufać komuś**

facial[1] /ˈfeɪʃl/ adj. connected with sb's face: *facial hair* ◇ *a facial expression* wyraz twarzy ▶ **twarzowy, na twarzy**

facial[2] noun [C] a beauty treatment in which a person's face is cleaned using creams, steam, etc.: *to have a facial* ▶ **zabieg oczyszczania twarzy**

facile /ˈfæsaɪl; US ˈfæsl/ adj. (used about a comment, argument, etc.) not carefully thought out ▶ **nieprzemyślany, pochopny**

facilitate /fəˈsɪlɪteɪt/ verb [T] (formal) to make sth possible or easier ▶ **umożliwiać, udogadniać**

🔑 **facility** /fəˈsɪləti/ noun (pl. **facilities**) **1** (**facilities**) [pl.] a service, building, piece of equipment, etc. that makes it possible to do sth: *Our town has excellent sports facilities.* ▶ **warunki, udogodnienia** **2** [C] an extra function or ability that a machine, etc. may have: *a facility for checking spelling* ▶ **możliwość, funkcja**

facsimile /fækˈsɪməli/ noun [C,U] an exact copy of a picture, piece of writing, etc. ▶ **wierna kopia** ➲ look at **fax**

🔑 **fact** /fækt/ noun **1** [C] something that you know has happened or is true: *It is a scientific fact that light travels faster than sound.* ◇ *We need to know all the facts before we can decide.* ◇ *I know **for a fact*** (wiem z całą pewnością) *that Peter wasn't ill yesterday.* ◇ ***The fact that** I am older than you makes no difference at all.* ◇ *You must **face facts*** (musisz spojrzeć prawdzie w oczy) *and accept that he has gone.* ▶ **fakt** **2** [U] true things; reality: *The film is based on fact.* ▶ **fakt, rzeczywistość** OPP **fiction**

IDM **as a matter of fact** → MATTER[1]

the fact (of the matter) is (that)... the truth is that...: *I would love a car, but the fact is that I just can't afford one.* ▶ **prawda jest taka, że**

a fact of life something unpleasant that you must accept because you cannot change it: *Most people now see unemployment as just another fact of life.* ▶ **konieczność życiowa**

facts and figures detailed information: *Before we make a decision, we need some more facts and figures.* ▶ **dokładne dane**

the facts of life the details of sexual behaviour and how babies are born ▶ **sprawy seksualne**

hard facts → HARD[1]

in (actual) fact **1** (used for introducing more detailed information): *It was cold. In fact it was freezing.* ▶ **właściwie, tak naprawdę** **2** (used for emphasizing that sth is true) really; actually: *I thought the lecture would be boring but in actual fact it was rather interesting.* ▶ **w rzeczywistości, w istocie**

ˈfact-finding adj. [only before a noun] done in order to find out information about a country, an organization, a situation, etc.: *a **fact-finding mission/visit*** ▶ **w celu uzyskania informacji**

faction /ˈfækʃn/ noun [C] a small group of people within a larger one, whose members have some different aims and beliefs to those of the larger group: *rival factions within the administration* ▶ **frakcja, odłam**

🔑 **factor** /ˈfæktə(r)/ noun [C] **1** one of the things that influences a decision, situation, etc.: *His unhappiness at home was a major factor in his decision to go abroad.* ▶ **czynnik** **2** (technical) (in mathematics) a whole number (except 1) by which a larger number can be divided: *2, 3, 4 and 6 are factors of 12.* ▶ **dzielnik**

🔑 **factory** /ˈfæktri; -təri/ noun [C] (pl. **factories**) a building or group of buildings where goods are made in large quantities by machine ▶ **fabryka**

ˈfact sheet noun [C] a piece of paper giving information about a subject, especially (in Britain) one discussed on a radio or television programme: *For further details, write in for our free fact sheet.* ▶ **broszura informacyjna z zestawieniem danych**

factual /ˈfæktʃuəl/ adj. based on or containing things that are true or real: *a factual account of the events* ▶ **faktyczny, rzeczywisty** ➲ look at **fictional**

faculty /ˈfæklti/ noun [C] (pl. **faculties**) **1** one of the natural abilities of sb's body or mind: *the faculty of hearing/sight/speech* ▶ **zmysł, zdolność** (*np. myślenia, odczuwania*) **2** (also **Faculty**) one department in a university, college, etc.: *the Faculty of Law/Arts* ▶ **wydział, katedra** **3** [with sing. or pl. verb] all the teachers in a **faculty** of a university, college, etc.: *The Faculty has/have been invited to the meeting.* ▶ **zespół wykładowców wydziału na wyższej uczelni**

fad /fæd/ noun [C] (informal) a fashion, interest, etc. that will probably not last long ▶ **chwilowa moda, kaprys**

faddy /ˈfædi/ adj. (Brit., informal) liking some things and not others, especially food, in a way that other people think is unreasonable: *a faddy eater* ▶ **wybredny, karpyśny**

■ **faddiness** noun [U] ▶ **wybredność, kapryśność**

fade /feɪd/ verb **1** [I,T] to become or make sth become lighter in colour or less strong or fresh: *Jeans fade when you wash them.* ◇ *The sun was setting and the light was fading fast.* ◇ *Look how the sunlight has faded these curtains.* ▶ **blaknąć; przygaszać** **2** [I] **fade (away)** to disappear slowly (from sight, hearing, memory, etc.): *The* *cheering of the crowd faded away.* ◇ *The smile faded from his face.* ▶ **zanikać, gasnąć**

faeces (US **feces**) /ˈfiːsiːz/ noun [pl.] (technical) the solid waste material that you get rid of when you go to the toilet ▶ **kał, stolec** ⓘ **Faeces** używa się głównie w kontekście medycznym. ➲ look at **excrement**

faff /fæf/ verb (Brit., informal)

PHR V **faff about/around** to spend time doing things in a way that is not well organized and that does not achieve much: *Stop faffing about and get on with it!* ▶ **obijać się, unikać pracy**

■ **faff** noun [U, sing.] a lot of activity that is not well organized and that may cause problems or be annoying: *There was the usual faff of finding somewhere to park the car.* ▶ **zamieszanie**

fag /fæg/ noun (Brit.) **1** [C] (slang) a cigarette ▶ **fajka** (*papieros*) **2** [sing.] (informal) something that is boring or tiring to do: *I've got to wash the car. What a fag!* ▶ **mordęga, katorga**

fagged /fægd/ (also ˌ**fagged ˈout**) adj. [not before a noun] (Brit., informal) very tired ▶ **wykończony, skonany** SYN **exhausted**

IDM **I can't be fagged (to do sth)** (used to say that you are too tired or bored to do sth) ▶ **nie mam siły i/lub ochoty (tego zrobić)**

Fahrenheit /ˈfærənhaɪt/ adj. (abbr. **F**) of or using a scale of temperature in which water freezes at 32° and boils at 212°: *fifty degrees Fahrenheit* ▶ **Fahrenheita** ➲ look at **Celsius**

■ **Fahrenheit** noun [U] ▶ **skala Fahrenheita**

🔑 **fail¹** /feɪl/ verb **1** [I,T] to not be successful in sth: *She failed her driving test.* ◇ *I feel that I've failed – I'm 25 and I still haven't got a steady job.* ▶ **nie udawać się (komuś), oblać** (*egzamin*) ➲ look at **pass**, **succeed** **2** [I] **fail to do sth** to not do sth: *She never fails to do her homework.* ◇ *Jimmy failed to arrive on time* (nie przybył na czas). ▶ **nie zrobić czegoś, zaniedbywać coś** **3** [T] to decide that sb is not successful in a test, exam, etc. ▶ **oblać kogoś** (*na egzaminie*) OPP **pass** **4** [I] to stop working: *My brakes failed on the hill but I managed to stop the car.* ▶ **zepsuć się** **5** [I] (used about health, etc.) to become weak: *His eyesight is failing.* ▶ **pogarszać się** **6** [I,T] to not be enough or not do what people are expecting or wanting: *I think the government has failed us.* ◇ *Words fail me!* Nie mam słów! ◇ *If the crops fail* (nie obrodzą), *people will starve.* ▶ **zawodzić**

fail² /feɪl/ noun [C] the act of not being successful in an exam ▶ **oblanie egzaminu** OPP **pass**

IDM **without fail** always, even if there are difficulties: *The postman always comes at 8 o'clock without fail.* ▶ **niezawodnie**

failing¹ /ˈfeɪlɪŋ/ noun [C] a weakness or fault: *She's not very patient – that's her only failing.* ▶ **wada, słabość**

failing² /ˈfeɪlɪŋ/ prep. if sth is not possible: *Ask Jackie to go with you, or failing that, try Anne.* ▶ **w przeciwnym razie**

🔑 **failure** /ˈfeɪljə(r)/ noun **1** [U] lack of success: *All my efforts ended **in failure*** (skończyły się niepowodzeniem). ▶ **niepowodzenie, nieudanie się** OPP **success** **2** [C] a person or thing that is not successful: *I was a failure as a mother.* Byłam kiepską matką. ◇ *His first attempt at skating was a miserable failure.* ▶ **niepowodzenie, do niczego** OPP **success** **3** [C,U] **failure to do sth** not doing sth that people expect you to do: *I was very disappointed at his failure to come* (że nie przyszedł) *to the meeting.* ▶ **niezrobienie czegoś** **4** [C,U] an example of sth not working properly: *There's been a failure in the power supply.* ◇ *She died of heart failure* (na niewydolność serca). ▶ **awaria**; (*med.*) **wada**

🔑 **faint¹** /feɪnt/ adj. **1** (used about things that you can see, hear, feel, etc.) not strong or clear: *a faint light/sound* ◇ *There is still a faint hope that they will find more people alive.* ▶ **słaby, nikły** **2** (used about actions, etc.) done without much effort: *He made a faint protest.* Zaprotestował nieśmiało. ▶ **słaby, od niechcenia** **3** [not before a noun] (used about people) likely to become unconscious; very weak: *I **feel faint.*** Zrobiło mi się słabo. ▶ **omdlały, słaby**

■ **faintly** adv.: *She smiled faintly.* ◇ *He looked faintly embarrassed.* ▶ **słabo; lekko**

IDM **not have the faintest/foggiest (idea)** to not know at all ▶ **nie mieć najmniejszego/zielonego (pojęcia)**

faint² /feɪnt/ verb [I] to become unconscious ▶ **mdleć** SYN **pass out** OPP **come round**

ˌ**faint-ˈhearted** adj. lacking confidence and not brave; afraid of failing ▶ **niepewny siebie, bojaźliwy**

🔑 **fair¹** /feə(r)/ adj. **1** appropriate and acceptable in a particular situation: *That's a fair price for that house.* ◇ *I think **it's fair to say that** the number of homeless people is increasing.* ▶ **sprawiedliwy, fair** OPP **unfair** **2** **fair (to/on sb)** treating each person or side equally, according to the law, the rules, etc.: *That's not fair – he got the same number of mistakes as I did and he's got a better mark.* ◇ *It wasn't fair on her to ask her to stay so late.* ◇ *a fair trial* ▶ **sprawiedliwy, słuszny** OPP **unfair** **3** quite good, large, etc.: *They have a fair chance of success.* ▶ **pokaźny, spory** **4** (used about the skin or hair) light in colour: *Chloe has fair hair and blue eyes.* ▶ **jasny** OPP **dark** **5** (used about the weather) good, without rain: *a fair and breezy autumn day* ▶ **pogodny**

IDM **fair enough** (informal) (used to show that you agree with what sb has suggested) ▶ **w porządku, nie ma sprawy**

fair play equal treatment of both/all sides according to the rules ▶ **gra fair**

(more than) your fair share of sth (more than) the usual or expected amount of sth: *We've had more than our fair share of trouble this year.* ▶ **więcej niż/tyle ile się komuś należy**

■ **fair** adv. according to the rules; in a way that is considered to be acceptable and appropriate ▶ **uczciwie, fair**

fair² /feə(r)/ noun [C] **1** (also **funfair** /ˈfʌnfeə(r)/) a type of entertainment in a field or park. At a fair you can ride on machines or try and win prizes at games. Fairs usually travel from town to town. ▶ **lunapark, wesołe miasteczko** **2** a large event where people, businesses, etc. show and sell their goods: *a trade fair* ◇ *the Frankfurt book fair* ▶ **targi**

fairground /ˈfeəgraʊnd/ noun [C] a large outdoor area where **fairs** are held ▶ **plac, na który przyjeżdża wesołe miasteczko**

ˌ**fair-ˈhaired** adj. with light-coloured hair ▶ **o jasnych włosach** SYN **blonde**

🔑 **fairly** /ˈfeəli/ adv. **1** quite, not very: *He is fairly tall.* ▶ **dosyć, dość** ➲ note at **rather** **2** in an acceptable way; in a way that treats people equally or according to the law, rules, etc.: *I felt that the teacher didn't treat us fairly.* ▶ **sprawiedliwie, słusznie** OPP **unfairly**

ˌ**fair-ˈminded** adj. (used about people) looking at and judging things in a fair and open way ▶ **bezstronny, sprawiedliwy**

fairness /ˈfeənəs/ noun [U] treating people equally or according to the law, rules, etc. ▶ **sprawiedliwość**

ˌ**fair-ˈtrade** adj. involving trade which helps to pay fair prices to workers in poor countries: *We buy 10% of our bananas from fair-trade sources.* ▶ **dotyczący firm prowadzących handel między biednymi krajami wytwarzającymi produkty do bogatych krajów i w sposób uczciwy wynagradzających robotników**

F

fairy /ˈfeəri/ noun [C] (pl. **fairies**) (in stories) a small creature with wings and magic powers ▶ **duszek**, **wróżka**

ˌ**fairy ˈgodmother** noun [C] a person who rescues you when you most need help ▶ **dobra wróżka**

ˈ**fairy tale** (also ˈ**fairy story**) noun [C] a story that is about **fairies**, magic, etc. ▶ **baśń** ➲ look at **fable**

faith /feɪθ/ noun **1** [U] **faith (in sb/sth)** strong belief (in sb/sth); trust: *I have **lost faith** in him.* ◇ *I've got **great faith in** your ability to do the job.* Wierzę, że świetnie poradzisz sobie z tym zadaniem. ▶ **wiara**, **zaufanie** **2** [U] strong religious belief: *He's a man of great faith* Jest osobą głęboko wierzącą. ▶ **wiara** **3** [C] a particular religion: *the Jewish faith* ▶ **religia**

IDM **in good faith** with honest reasons for doing sth: *I bought the car in good faith. I didn't know it was stolen.* ▶ **w dobrej wierze**

faithful /ˈfeɪθfl/ adj. **1 faithful (to sb/sth)** always staying with and supporting a person, organization or belief; loyal: *Peter has been a faithful friend.* ◇ *He was always faithful to his wife.* ▶ **wierny** SYN **loyal** OPP **unfaithful** **2** true to the facts; accurate: *a faithful description* ▶ **wierny**

■ **faithfully** /-fəli/ adv. ▶ **wiernie**, **z oddaniem**

> **Yours faithfully** używa się jako formuły kończącej oficjalny list, jeśli rozpoczęło się go od **Dear Sir/Madam** itp., a nie od imienia lub nazwiska adresata.

faithfulness noun [U] ▶ **wierność** ➲ look at **fidelity**

ˈ**faith healing** noun [U] a method of treating a sick person through the power of belief and prayer ▶ **uzdrawianie modlitwą**

■ ˈ**faith healer** noun [C] ▶ **uzdrowiciel/ka**

fake¹ /feɪk/ noun [C] **1** a work of art, etc. that seems to be real or genuine but is not ▶ **falsyfikat**, **podróbka** **2** a person who is not really what they appear to be ▶ **osoba, która kogoś/coś udaje**, **oszust**

■ **fake** adj.: *a fake passport* ▶ **fałszywy**, **podrobiony**

fake² /feɪk/ verb [T] **1** to copy sth and try to make people believe it is the real thing ▶ **fałszować**, **podrabiać** **2** to make people believe that you are feeling sth that you are not: *I faked surprise when he told me the news.* ▶ **udawać**

falcon /ˈfɔːlkən; US ˈfæl-/ noun [C] a bird with long pointed wings that kills and eats other animals. Falcons can be trained to hunt. ▶ **sokół**

fall¹ /fɔːl/ verb [I] (pt **fell** /fel/, pp **fallen** /ˈfɔːlən/) **1** to drop down towards the ground: *He fell off the ladder* (spadł z drabiny) *onto the grass.* ◇ *The rain was falling steadily.* ▶ **padać** **2 fall (down/over)** to suddenly stop standing and drop to the ground: *She slipped on the ice and fell.* ◇ *The little boy fell over and hurt his knee.* ▶ **upadać**; **przewracać się** **3** to hang down: *Her hair fell down over her shoulders.* ▶ **opadać** **4** to decrease in amount, number or strength: *The temperature is falling.* ◇ *The price of coffee has fallen again.* ◇ *When he heard the bad news, his spirits fell* (upadł na duchu). ◇ *Her voice fell to a whisper.* Jej głos zniżył się do szeptu. ▶ **spadać**, **zmniejszać się** OPP **rise** **5** to be defeated or captured: *The Government fell because of the scandal.* ▶ **upadać** **6** (formal) to be killed (in battle): *Millions of soldiers fell in the war.* ▶ **polec**, **zginąć** **7** to change into a different state; to become: *He **fell asleep*** (zasnął) *on the sofa.* ◇ *They **fell in love** with each other* (zakochali się w sobie) *in Spain.* ◇ *I must get some new shoes – these ones are **falling to pieces*** (rozlatują się). ▶ **zapadać w inny stan** **8** (formal) to come or happen: *My birthday falls on a Sunday this year.* ▶ **przypadać**, **wypadać** **9** to belong to a particular group, type, etc.: *Animals fall into two groups, those with backbones and those without.* ▶ **należeć**

IDM **fall flat** (used about a joke, a story, an event, etc.) to fail to produce the effect that you wanted ▶ **okazać się niewypałem**

fall foul of sb/sth to get in trouble with sb/sth because you have done sth wrong: *At sixteen she fell foul of the law for the first time.* ▶ **wchodzić w konflikt z kimś/czymś** (*po zrobieniu czegoś złego*)

fall/get into arrears → ARREARS

fall/slot into place → PLACE¹

fall/land on your feet → FOOT¹

fall short (of sth) to not be enough; to not reach sth: *The pay rise fell short of the workers' demands.* ▶ **zawodzić** (*np. czyjeś zaufanie*), **nie dosięgać** (*np. poziomu, celu*)

PHR V **fall apart** to break (into pieces): *My car is falling apart.* ▶ **rozpadać się**, **rozlatywać się**

fall back on sb/sth to use sb/sth when you are in difficulty: *When the electricity was cut off we fell back on candles.* ▶ **opierać się na kimś**; **uciekać się do czegoś**

fall behind (sb/sth) to fail to keep level with sb/sth ▶ **zostawać w tyle (za kimś/czymś)**

fall behind with sth to not pay or do sth at the right time: *They had fallen behind with their mortgage repayments.* ◇ *He's fallen behind with his school work again.* ▶ **zalegać z czymś**

fall for sb (informal) to be strongly attracted to sb; to fall in love with sb ▶ **zakochiwać się w kimś**

fall for sth (informal) to be tricked into believing sth that is not true: *He makes excuses and she falls for them every time.* ▶ **nabierać się na coś**

fall out to become loose and drop: *His hair is falling out.* ◇ *My tooth fell out.* ▶ **wypadać**

fall out (with sb) (Brit.) to argue and stop being friendly (with sb) ▶ **pokłócić się (z kimś)**

fall through to fail or not happen: *Our trip to Japan has fallen through.* ▶ **nie wyjść**, **nie dojść do skutku**

fall² /fɔːl/ noun **1** [C] an act of falling down or off sth: *She **had a** nasty **fall** from her horse.* ▶ **upadek**, **przewrócenie się** **2** [C] **a fall (of sth)** the amount of sth that has fallen or the distance that sth has fallen: *We have had a heavy fall of snow.* ◇ *a fall of four metres* ▶ **opad**; **spadek** **3** (**falls**) [pl.] water that falls down the side of a mountain, etc.: *Niagara Falls* ▶ **wodospad** SYN **waterfall** **4** [C] (US) = AUTUMN **5** [C] **a fall (in sth)** a decrease (in value, quantity, etc.): *There has been a sharp fall in the price of oil.* ▶ **spadek**, **obniżka** SYN **drop** OPP **rise** **6** [sing.] **the fall of sth** a (political) defeat; a failure: *the fall of the Roman Empire* ▶ **upadek**

IDM **sb's fall from grace** a situation in which sb loses the respect that people had for them by doing sth wrong or immoral ▶ **utrata szacunku**

fallacious /fəˈleɪʃəs/ adj. (formal) wrong; based on a false idea: *a fallacious argument* ▶ **błędny**

fallacy /ˈfæləsi/ noun [C,U] (pl. **fallacies**) (formal) a false belief or a wrong idea: *It's a fallacy that money brings happiness.* ▶ **błędne przekonanie**, **złuda**

fallen past participle of **fall¹**

fallible /ˈfæləbl/ adj. able or likely to make mistakes: *Even our new computerized system is fallible.* ▶ **zawodny**, **omylny** OPP **infallible**

Fallopian tube (also **fallopian tube**) /fəˌləʊpiən ˈtjuːb; US fəˈləʊpiən tuːb/ noun [C] one of the two tubes in the body of a woman or female animal along which eggs pass from the **ovaries** to the **uterus** ▶ **jajowód**

fallout /ˈfɔːlaʊt/ noun [U] dangerous waste that is carried in the air after a nuclear explosion ▶ **deszcz/opad radioaktywny**

fallow /ˈfæləʊ/ adj. (used about farm land) not used for growing crops, especially so that the quality of the land will improve: *Farmers are now paid to let their land **lie fallow*** (leżała odłogiem). ▶ **ugorowy**

⚷ **false** /fɔːls/ adj. **1** not true; not correct: *Bucharest is the capital of Romania – true or false* (tak, czy nie)*?* ◇ *I think the information you have been given is false.* ◇ *I got a completely false impression of him from our first meeting.* ▶ **błędny**, **nieprawdziwy** OPP **true 2** not real; artificial: *false hair/eyelashes* ▶ **sztuczny** OPP **real**, **natural 3** not genuine, but made to look real in order to trick people: *a false name/passport* ◇ *This suitcase has a false bottom* (podwójne dno). ▶ **fałszywy 4** (used about sb's behaviour or expression) not sincere or honest: *a false smile* ◇ *false modesty* ▶ **fałszywy**, **obłudny**

■ **falsely** adv. **1** : *He was falsely accused of theft.* ▶ **bezpodstawnie 2** : *She smiled falsely at his joke.* ▶ **fałszywie**

IDM **a false alarm** a warning about a danger that does not happen ▶ **fałszywy alarm**

a false friend a word in another language that looks similar to a word in your own but has a different meaning ▶ (*przen.*) **fałszywy przyjaciel**

on/under false pretences pretending to be or to have sth in order to trick people: *She got into the club under false pretences – she isn't a member at all!* ▶ **podstępem**

ˌfalse ˈstart noun [C] **1** an attempt to begin sth that is not successful: *After a number of false starts, she finally found a job she liked.* ▶ **nieudana próba 2** a situation when sb taking part in a race starts before the official signal has been given ▶ (*sport*) **falstart**

ˌfalse ˈteeth (also **dentures** /ˈdentʃəz/) noun [pl.] artificial teeth that are worn by sb who has lost their natural teeth ▶ **sztuczna szczęka**

falsify /ˈfɔːlsɪfaɪ/ verb [T] (**falsifying**; **falsifies**; pt, pp **falsified**) (formal) to change a document, information, etc. so that it is no longer true in order to trick sb: *to falsify data/records/accounts* ▶ **fałszować**

falter /ˈfɔːltə(r)/ verb [I] **1** to become weak or move in a way that is not steady: *The engine faltered* (silnik zakrztusił się) *and stopped.* ▶ **załamywać się**, **zachwiać się 2** to lose confidence and determination: *Murray faltered and missed the ball.* ▶ **wahać się**

⚷ **fame** /feɪm/ noun [U] being known or talked about by many people because of what you have achieved: *Pop stars **achieve fame** at a young age.* ◇ *The town's only **claim to fame*** (powodem do dumy) *is that there was a riot there.* ▶ **sława**, **rozgłos**

famed /feɪmd/ adj. **famed (for sth)** very well known (for sth): *Welsh people are famed for their singing.* ▶ **znany (z czegoś)** ℹ Por. **famous**, które jest częściej używane.

⚷ **familiar** /fəˈmɪliə(r)/ adj. **1 familiar (to sb)** known to you; often seen or heard and therefore easy to recognize: *Chinese music isn't very familiar to people in Europe.* ◇ *It was a relief to see a familiar face in the crowd.* ◇ *to look/sound familiar* ▶ **znany**, **znajomy** OPP **unfamiliar 2 familiar with sth** having a good knowledge of sth: *People in Europe aren't very familiar with Chinese music.* ▶ **obeznany**, **wprawny** OPP **unfamiliar 3 familiar (with sb)** (used about sb's behaviour) too friendly and informal: *I was annoyed by the waiter's familiar behaviour.* ▶ **poufały**

familiarity /fəˌmɪliˈærəti/ noun [U] **1 familiarity (with sth)** having a good knowledge of sth: *His familiarity with the area was an advantage.* ▶ **znajomość**, **obeznanie 2** being too friendly and informal ▶ **poufałość**

familiarize (also **-ise**) /fəˈmɪliəraɪz/ verb [T] **familiarize sb/yourself (with sth)** to teach sb about sth or learn about sth until you know it well: *I want to familiarize myself with the plans before the meeting.* ▶ **zaznajamiać się**

⚷ **family** /ˈfæməli/ noun (pl. **families**) **1** [C, with sing. or pl. verb] a group of people who are related to each other: *I have quite a large family.* ▶ **rodzina 2** [C,U] children: *Do you have any family?* ◇ *We are planning to **start a family*** (mieć pierwsze dziecko) *next year.* ◇ *to bring up/raise a family* ▶ **dzieci 3** [C] a group of animals, plants, etc. that are of a similar type: *Lions belong to the cat family.* ▶ **rodzina**

■ **family** adj.: *a family car* ◇ *family entertainment* ▶ **rodzinny**

IDM **run in the family** to be found very often in a family: *Red hair runs in the family.* ▶ **być dziedzicznym**

> Czasami słowo **family** oznacza „rodzice i dzieci", inaczej **nuclear family**. Czasami używa się go w odniesieniu do innych krewnych, np. dziadków, cioć, wujków, czyli **extended family**.
>
> **Family** występuje z czasownikiem w lp, kiedy odnosi się do rodziny jako jednostki: *Almost every family in the village owns a television.* Czasownik w lm stosuje się, mówiąc o pojedynczych członkach rodziny: *My family are all very tall.*

ˈfamily name noun [C] the name that is shared by members of a family ▶ **nazwisko** SYN **surname** ➲ note at **name**

ˌfamily ˈplanning noun [U] controlling the number of children you have by using birth control ▶ **planowanie rodziny**, **zapobieganie ciąży** ➲ look at **contraception**

ˌfamily ˈtree noun [C] a diagram that shows the relationships between different members of a family over a long period of time: *How far back can you trace your family tree?* ▶ **drzewo genealogiczne**

famine /ˈfæmɪn/ noun [C,U] a lack of food over a long period of time in a large area that can cause the death of many people: *There is a severe famine in many parts of Africa.* ▶ **głód**

famished /ˈfæmɪʃt/ adj. [not before a noun] (informal) very hungry: *When's lunch? I'm absolutely famished* (umieram z głodu)*!* ▶ **zgłodniały**, **głodny jak wilk**

⚷ **famous** /ˈfeɪməs/ adj. **famous (for sth)** known about by many people: *a famous singer* ◇ *Sydney is famous for its opera house.* ▶ **sławny** ℹ Por. **infamous** i **notorious**, które oznaczają „cieszący się złą sławą, niesławny".

famously /ˈfeɪməsli/ adv. in a way that is famous: *the words Nelson famously uttered* (te znane słowa, które Nelson wypowiedział) *just before he died* ▶ **w ogólnie znany sposób**

IDM **get on/along famously** to have a very good relationship with sb, especially from the first meeting: *My girlfriend and my grandfather got on famously.* ▶ **znakomicie**

⚷ **fan¹** /fæn/ noun [C] **1** a person who admires and is very enthusiastic about a sport, a film star, a singer, etc.: *football fans* ◇ *I'm not a great fan of* (nie przepadam za) *modern jazz.* ◇ *fan mail* ◇ *a fan club* ▶ **kibic**, **fan 2** a machine with parts that turn around very quickly to create a current of cool or warm air: *an electric fan* ◇ *a fan heater* ▶ **wiatraczek**; **wentylator 3** an object in the shape of half a circle made of paper, feathers, etc. that you wave in your hand to create a current of cool air ▶ **wachlarz**

fan² /fæn/ verb [T] (**fanning**; **fanned**) **1** to make air blow on sb/sth by waving a **fan¹** (3), your hand, etc. in the air: *She used a newspaper to fan her face.* ▶ **wachlować 2** to make a fire burn more strongly by blowing on it: *The strong wind really fanned the flames.* ▶ **podsycać**

PHR V **fan out** to spread out: *The police fanned out across the field.* ▶ **rozstawiać się wachlarzem**

fanatic /fəˈnætɪk/ noun [C] a person who is very enthusiastic about sth and may have extreme or dangerous opinions (especially about religion or politics): *religious fanatics* ▶ **fanaty-k/czka** SYN **fiend**, **freak** ➲ look at **bigot**

■ **fanatical** /-kl/ (also fanatic) adj.: *He's fanatical about keeping things tidy.* ▶ **fanatyczny** | **fanatically** /-kli/ adv. ▶ **fanatycznie** | **fanaticism** /fə'nætɪsɪzəm/ noun [C,U] ▶ **fanatyzm**

'**fan belt** noun [C] the belt that operates the machinery that cools a car engine ▶ **pasek klinowy**

fanciful /'fænsɪfl/ adj. based on imagination and not facts or reason ▶ **fantastyczny, zmyślony** 🛈 Wyraża dezaprobatę.

■ **fancifully** /-fəli/ adv. ▶ **fantastycznie, w nierealny, zmyślony sposób**

⚷ **fancy**¹ /'fænsi/ verb (**fancying**; **fancies**; pt, pp **fancied**) **1** [T] (Brit., informal) to like the idea of having or doing sth; to want sth or to want to do sth: *What do you fancy to eat?* ◇ *I don't fancy going out in this rain.* ▶ **mieć ochotę (na coś) 2** [T] (Brit., informal) to be sexually attracted to sb: *Jack keeps looking at you – I think he fancies you* (chyba mu się podobasz). **3 fancy yourself (as) sth** (Brit.) [T] to think that you would be good at sth; to think that you are sth (although this may not be true): *He fancied himself (as) a poet.* ▶ **uważać się za kogoś 4** [I,T] (Brit., informal) (used for expressing surprise, shock, etc.): *Fancy meeting you here!* Co za spotkanie! ▶ **coś takiego!, ale niespodzianka! 5** [T] **fancy (that)** (literary) to think or imagine sth ▶ **zdawać się, mieć wrażenie**

fancy² /'fænsi/ noun

IDM **take sb's fancy** to attract or please sb: *If you see something that takes your fancy, I'll buy it for you.* ▶ **spodobać się komuś**

take a fancy to sb/sth to start liking sb/sth: *I think that Laura's really taken a fancy to you.* Myślę, że wpadłeś Laurze w oko. ▶ **upodobać sobie kogoś/coś**

⚷ **fancy**³ /'fænsi/ adj. (**fancier**; **fanciest**) not simple or ordinary: *My father doesn't like fancy food.* ◇ *I just want a pair of black shoes – nothing fancy.* ▶ **wymyślny, wyszukany** OPP **plain**

ˌ**fancy 'dress** noun [U] special clothes that you wear to a party at which people dress up to look like a different person (for example from history or a story): *We've been invited to **a fancy dress party** – I'm going as Napoleon.* ◇ *It was a Halloween party and everyone went **in fancy dress**.* ▶ **przebranie** (*na bal maskowy itp.*)

fanfare /'fænfeə(r)/ noun [C] a short loud piece of music that is used for introducing sb important, for example a king or queen ▶ **fanfara**

fang /fæŋ/ noun [C] a long sharp tooth of a dog, snake, etc. ▶ **kieł, ząb jadowy** ➲ picture on **page A10**

fanny pack (US) = BUMBAG

fantasize (also -ise) /'fæntəsaɪz/ verb [I,T] to imagine sth that you would like to happen ▶ **fantazjować, marzyć**

fantastic /fæn'tæstɪk/ adj. **1** (informal) very good; excellent: *She's a fantastic swimmer.* ▶ **fantastyczny, świetny** ➲ note at **good 2** (informal) very large or great: *A Rolls Royce costs a fantastic amount of money.* ▶ **niesamowity, fantastyczny 3** [usually before a noun] strange and showing a lot of imagination: *a story full of fantastic creatures from other worlds* ▶ **fantastyczny**

■ **fantastically** /-kli/ adv. ▶ **fantastycznie; niesamowicie**

fantasy /'fæntəsi/ noun [C,U] (pl. **fantasies**) situations that are not true, that you just imagine: *I have a fantasy about going to live in the Bahamas.* ◇ *They live in a world of fantasy.* ▶ **fantazja, wyobraźnia** ➲ note at **imagination**

fanzine /'fænziːn/ noun [C] a magazine that is written by and for people who like a particular sports team, singer, etc. ▶ **magazyn dla fanów**

fao abbr. (Brit.) (used in writing to mean **for the attention of**; written on a document or letter to say who should deal with it) ▶ **do wiadomości kogoś** (*kiedy należy podjąć jakieś działanie*) ➲ look at **attn**

FAQ /ˌef eɪ 'kjuː/ abbr. **frequently asked questions** ▶ **(dokument internetowy zawierający) najczęściej zadawane pytania i odpowiedzi na jakiś temat**

⚷ **far**¹ /fɑː(r)/ adj. (**farther** /'fɑːðə(r)/ or **further** /'fɜːðə(r)/; **farthest** /'fɑːðɪst/ or **furthest** /'fɜːðɪst/) **1** a long distance away: *Let's walk – it's not far* (daleko). ▶ **daleki, odległy 2** [only before a noun] the longest distance away of two or more things: *the far side of the river* ▶ (*koniec, strona itp.*) **drugi, odległy 3** [only before a noun] a long way from the centre in the direction mentioned: *politicians from the far left* (ze skrajnej lewicy) *of the party* ▶ **skrajny**

IDM **a far cry from sth/from doing sth** an experience that is very different from sth/doing sth ▶ **daleki od czegoś/robienia czegoś**

⚷ **far**² /fɑː(r)/ adv. (**farther** /'fɑːðə(r)/ or **further** /'fɜːðə(r)/; **farthest** /'fɑːðɪst/ or **furthest** /'fɜːðɪst/) **1** (at) a distance: *London's not far from here.* ◇ *How much further is it?* ◇ *How far did we walk yesterday?* ▶ **daleko**

> W tym znaczeniu używa się **far** w zdaniach przeczących i pytających. W zdaniach oznajmujących mówi się **a long way**: *It's a long way from here to the sea.* Zdarza się jednak, że zdania oznajmujące mają znaczenie negatywne. Wówczas stosuje się **far**: *Let's get a bus. It's much too far to walk.*

2 very much: *She's far more intelligent than I thought.* ◇ *There's far too much salt in this soup.* ▶ **o wiele, znacznie 3** (to) a certain degree: *How far have you got with your homework?* Jak dużo lekcji już odrobiłeś? ◇ *The company employs local people **as far as possible*** (w miarę możliwości). ◇ *'You must have been delighted!' 'I wouldn't go that far* (to za dużo powiedziane), *but I was quite pleased.'* **4** a long time: *This story began **far back*** (dawno (temu)), *in 1850.* ◇ *We danced far into the night* (do późna w nocy). ▶ **długo**

IDM **as far as** to the place mentioned but not further: *We walked as far as the river and then turned back.* ▶ **aż do, tak daleko jak**

as/so far as (used for giving your opinion or judgement of a situation): *As far as I know, she's not coming, but I may be wrong.* ▶ **o ile**

as far as I can see (used for introducing your opinion): *As far as I can see, the accident was John's fault, not Ann's.* ▶ **o ile się orientuję**

as/so far as sb/sth is concerned on the subject of sb/sth; as sb/sth is affected or influenced by sth: *As far as school work is concerned, he's hopeless.* ◇ *As far as I'm concerned* (moim zdaniem), *this is the most important point.* ▶ **co do kogoś/czegoś, jeśli chodzi o kogoś/coś**

as far as the eye can see to the furthest place you can see ▶ **jak okiem sięgnąć**

by far (used for emphasizing comparative or superlative words) by a large amount: *Carmen is by far the best student in the class.* ▶ **zdecydowanie**

far afield far away, especially from where you live or from where you are staying: *We decided to hire a car in order to explore further afield* (dalej). ▶ **daleko**

far from sth/doing sth almost the opposite of sth or of what is expected: *He's far from happy.* ◇ *Far from enjoying the film, he fell asleep in the middle.* Film wcale mu się nie podobał; wręcz przeciwnie, w środku filmu zasnął. ▶ **bynajmniej, żadną miarą**

far from it (informal) certainly not; just the opposite: *'Did you enjoy your holiday?' 'No, far from it. It was awful.'* ▶ **wprost/wręcz przeciwnie**

few and far between → FEW

go far 1 to be enough: *This food won't go very far between three of us.* ▶ **być w wystarczającej ilości,**

wystarczać **2** to be successful in life: *Dan is very talented and should go far.* ▶ (*przen.*) **zajść daleko**
go too far to behave in a way that causes trouble or upsets other people: *He's always been naughty but this time he's gone too far.* ▶ **za dużo sobie pozwalać, za daleko się posunąć**
so far until now: *So far the weather has been good but it might change.* ▶ **dotychczas, jak dotąd**
so far so good (informal) everything has gone well until now ▶ **jak dotąd dobrze**

faraway /ˈfɑːrəweɪ/ adj. [only before a noun] **1** (formal) a great distance away: *He told us stories of faraway countries.* ▶ **odległy, daleki 2** (used about a look in sb's eyes) as if you are thinking of sth else: *She stared out of the window with a faraway look in her eyes.* ▶ (*wzrok*) **rozmarzony, nieprzytomny**

farce /fɑːs/ noun [C] **1** something important or serious that is not organized well or treated with respect: *The meeting was a farce – everyone was shouting at the same time.* ▶ **farsa, kpiny 2** a funny play for the theatre full of ridiculous situations ▶ **farsa**
■ **farcical** /ˈfɑːsɪkl/ adj. ▶ **farsowy**

fare[1] /feə(r)/ noun [C] the amount of money you pay to travel by bus, train, taxi, etc.: *Adults pay **full fare**, and children pay **half fare**.* Dorośli kupują bilet normalny, a dzieci – bilet ulgowy. ◇ *What's the fare* (ile kosztuje bilet) *to Leeds?* ▶ **cena biletu, opłata za przejazd**

fare[2] /feə(r)/ verb [I] (formal) to be successful or not successful in a particular situation: *How did you fare in your examination?* ◇ *The party fared* (wypadła) *badly in the last election.* ▶ **pójść komuś**

the ˌFar ˈEast noun [sing.] China, Japan and other countries in East and South East Asia ▶ **Daleki Wschód** ➲ look at **Middle East**

farewell /ˌfeəˈwel/ interj. (old-fashioned) goodbye ▶ **żegnaj(cie)!**
■ **farewell** noun [C]: *a farewell* (pożegnalne) *party* ◇ *He said his farewells* (pożegnał się) *and left.* ▶ **pożegnanie**

ˌfar-ˈfetched adj. not easy to believe: *It's a good book but the story's too far-fetched.* ▶ **naciągany, przesadzony**

farm[1] /fɑːm/ noun [C] an area of land with fields and buildings that is used for growing crops and keeping animals: *to work **on a farm*** pracować na roli ◇ *farm buildings* zabudowania gospodarcze ◇ *farm workers/animals* ◇ *a dairy farm* ferma mleczna ◇ *a sheep farm* farma owcza ▶ **gospodarstwo rolne**

farm[2] /fɑːm/ verb [I,T] to use land for growing crops or keeping animals: *She farms 200 acres.* ▶ **uprawiać** (*ziemię*), **gospodarować**

farmer /ˈfɑːmə(r)/ noun [C] a person who owns or manages a farm ▶ **rolni-k/czka; gospod-arz/yni** ➲ picture on **page A4**

farmhand /ˈfɑːmhænd/ noun [C] a person who works for a farmer ▶ **robotnik rolny**

farmhouse /ˈfɑːmhaʊs/ noun [C] the house on a farm where the **farmer** lives ▶ **dom w gospodarstwie rolnym**

farming /ˈfɑːmɪŋ/ noun [U] managing a farm or working on it: *Farming* (praca na roli) *is extremely hard work.* ◇ *farming areas* obszar rolniczy ◇ *farming methods* ▶ **gospodarowanie, uprawianie roli, hodowla**

farmyard /ˈfɑːmjɑːd/ noun [C] an outside area near a **farmhouse** surrounded by buildings or walls ▶ **podwórze gospodarskie**

ˌfar-ˈreaching adj. having a great influence on a lot of other things: *far-reaching changes* ▶ **dalekosiężny**

Farsi = PERSIAN

ˌfar-ˈsighted adj. **1** being able to see what will be necessary in the future and making plans for it ▶ **dalekowzroczny, dalekowidzący 2** (US) = LONG-SIGHTED

fart /fɑːt/ verb [I] (informal) to suddenly let gas from the stomach escape from your bottom ▶ **pierdzieć**
■ **fart** noun [C] ▶ **pierdnięcie**
PHR V **fart around** (Brit. also ˌ**fart aˈbout**) (taboo, slang) to waste time by behaving in a silly way: *Stop farting around and give me a hand with this!* ▶ **opierdzielać się, zbijać bąki**

farther → FAR ➲ note at **further**

farthest → FAR

fascinate /ˈfæsɪneɪt/ verb [T] to attract or interest sb very much: *Chinese culture has always fascinated me.* ▶ **urzekać, zachwycać**
■ **fascinating** adj. ▶ **urzekający, zachwycający** | **fascination** /ˌfæsɪˈneɪʃn/ noun [C,U] ▶ **urzeczenie, zachwyt**

fascism (also **Fascism**) /ˈfæʃɪzəm/ noun [U] an extreme **right-wing** political system which is in favour of strong central government and does not allow anyone to speak against it ▶ **faszyzm**
■ **fascist** (also **Fascist**) /-ɪst/ noun [C] ▶ **faszyst(k)a** | **fascist** /-ɪst/ adj. ▶ **faszystowski**

fashion /ˈfæʃn/ noun **1** [C,U] the style of dressing or behaving that is the most popular at a particular time: *What is **the latest fashion** in hairstyles?* ◇ *a fashion show* pokaz mody ◇ *a fashion model/magazine* ▶ **moda, styl** ➲ note at **clothes 2** [sing.] the way you do sth: *Watch him. He's been behaving **in a** very strange **fashion**.* ▶ **sposób**
IDM **come into/be in fashion** to become or to be popular as a style: *Jeans are always in fashion* (modne). ◇ *I think hats will **come back into fashion**.* ▶ **wchodzić w modę; być w modzie**
go/be out of fashion to become or to be unpopular as a style: *That colour is out of fashion this year.* ◇ *Jeans will never go out of fashion.* ▶ **nie być modnym; wychodzić z mody**

fashionable /ˈfæʃnəbl/ adj. **1** popular or in a popular style at the time: *fashionable clothes* ◇ *a fashionable area/opinion* ▶ **modny, popularny** OPP **unfashionable** ➲ look at **old-fashioned 2** considering fashion to be important: *fashionable society* ▶ **elegancki, wytworny**
■ **fashionably** /-əbli/ adv. ▶ **modnie, popularnie**

ˈfashion designer noun [C] a person who designs fashionable clothes ▶ **projektant/ka mody**

fast[1] /fɑːst; US fæst/ adj. **1** able to move or act at great speed: *a fast car/worker/runner/reader/train* ▶ **szybki, pośpieszny** ➲ note at **quick** ⓘ Nie ma rzeczownika pochodnego od **fast**. Używa się wówczas **speed**: *The car was travelling very fast./The car was travelling at great speed.* **2** [not before a noun] (**be fast**) (used about a clock or watch) to show a time that is later than the real time: *The clock is five minutes fast.* ▶ **śpieszyć się** OPP **slow 3** (used about camera film) reacting quickly to light, and therefore good for taking photographs in poor light or of things that are moving quickly ▶ (*fot.*) **czuły 4** [only after a noun] firmly fixed: *Peter made the boat fast* (przycumował) *before he got out.* ◇ *Do you think the colour in this T-shirt is fast* (nie spierze się szybko)*?* ▶ **przymocowany; trwały**
IDM **fast and furious** (used about films, etc.) full of rapid action and sudden changes ▶ **szybki**
hard and fast → HARD[1]

fast[2] /fɑːst; US fæst/ adv. **1** quickly: *The dog ran very fast.* ▶ **szybko 2** firmly or deeply: *Sam was **fast asleep*** (spał jak zabity) *by 10 o'clock.* ◇ *Our car **was stuck fast*** (ugrzązł) *in the mud.* ▶ **mocno, pewnie**

fast[3] /fɑːst; US fæst/ verb [I] to eat no food for a certain time, usually for religious reasons: *Muslims fast during Ramadan.* ▶ **pościć**

■ **fast** noun [C] ▶ **post**

fasten /ˈfɑːsn; US ˈfæsn/ verb **1** [I,T] **fasten sth (up)** to close or join the two parts of sth; to become closed or joined: *Please fasten your seat belts.* ◇ *Fasten your coat up – it's cold outside.* ◇ *My dress fastens at the back.* ▶ **zapinać (się)** OPP **unfasten 2** [T] to close or lock sth firmly so that it will not open: *Close the window and fasten it securely.* ▶ **zamykać szczelnie/mocno** OPP **unfasten 3** [T] **fasten sth (on/to sth)**; **fasten A and B (together)** to fix or tie sth to sth, or two things together: *How can I fasten these pieces of wood together?* ◇ *Fasten this badge on your jacket.* ◇ *His eyes were fastened on me all the time I was speaking.* Przez cały czas, kiedy mówiłam, miał utkwiony we mnie wzrok. ▶ **przymocowywać**, **przypinać**

fastener /ˈfɑːsnə(r); US ˈfæs-/ (also **fastening** /ˈfɑːsnɪŋ; US ˈfæs-/) noun [C] something that fastens things together: *a zip fastener* zamek błyskawiczny ▶ **zapięcie**, **klamra**

ˌfast ˈfood noun [U] food that can be served very quickly in special restaurants and is often taken away to be eaten in the street: *a fast-food restaurant* bar szybkiej obsługi ▶ **fast food**

ˌfast ˈforward verb [T] to make a tape or video go forward quickly without playing it ▶ **szybko przewijać (*taśmę*) do przodu**

■ **fast forward** noun [U]: *Press fast forward to advance the tape.* ◇ *the fast-forward button* ▶ **klawisz szybkiego przewijania taśmy do przodu** ➲ look at **rewind**

fastidious /fæˈstɪdiəs/ adj. difficult to please; wanting everything to be perfect ▶ **wybredny**; **drobiazgowy**

ˈfast track noun [sing.] a quick way to achieve sth, for example a high position in a job ▶ **przyspieszona droga do czegoś** (*np. uzyskania awansu, ukończenia kursu*)

■ **ˈfast-track** adj.: *the fast-track route to promotion* ▶ (*awans, kurs itp.*) **uzyskany/ukończony/wykonywany itp. w trybie przyspieszonym**

fat[1] /fæt/ adj. (**fatter**; **fattest**) **1** (used about people's or animal's bodies) weighing too much; covered with too much fat: *You'll **get fat*** (utyjesz) *if you eat too much.* ▶ **gruby** OPP **thin 2** (used about a thing) thick or full: *a fat wallet/book* ▶ **gruby**

> Niezbyt grzecznie jest mówić o kimś, że jest **fat**. Dlatego częściej używa się innych słów, np. **plump**, **stout**, **large** lub **overweight**: *She's a rather large lady.* ◇ *I'm a bit overweight.* Wyraz **chubby** jest głównie używany do określania dzieci, które są pulchne w przyjemny sposób: *a baby with chubby cheeks.* Lekarze używają wyrazu **obese**, by opisać osoby mające nadwagę, która może zagrażać życiu.

fat[2] /fæt/ noun **1** [U] the soft white substance under the skins of animals and people: *I don't like meat with lots of fat on it.* ▶ **tłuszcz** ➲ adjective **fatty 2** [C,U] the substance containing oil that we obtain from animals, plants or seeds and use for cooking: *Cook the onions in a little fat.* ▶ **tłuszcz**

fatal /ˈfeɪtl/ adj. **1** causing or ending in death: *a fatal accident/disease/crash* ▶ **śmiertelny** ➲ look at **mortal 2** causing trouble or a bad result: *She made the fatal mistake of trusting him.* ▶ **zgubny**, **fatalny**

■ **fatally** /-təli/ adv.: *fatally injured* ▶ **śmiertelnie**; **zgubnie**

fatalistic /ˌfeɪtəˈlɪstɪk/ adj. showing a belief in **fate** and feeling that you cannot control events or stop them from happening: *a **fatalistic attitude/outlook*** ▶ **fatalistyczny**

■ **fatalistically** /ˌfeɪtəˈlɪstɪkəli/ adv. ▶ **fatalistycznie**

fatality /fəˈtæləti/ noun [C] (pl. **fatalities**) sb's death caused by an accident, in war, etc.: *There were no fatalities in the fire.* ▶ **ofiara** (*np. wypadku*)

fate /feɪt/ noun **1** [C] your future; something that happens to you: *Both men **suffered the same fate*** (obu mężczyzn spotkał taki sam los) – *they both lost their jobs.* ▶ **los**, **dola 2** [U] the power that some people believe controls everything that happens: *It was fate that brought them together again after twenty years.* ▶ **los**, **przeznaczenie**

fateful /ˈfeɪtfl/ adj. having an important effect on the future: *a fateful decision* ▶ **brzemienny w skutki**

ˌfat-ˈfree adj. not containing any fat: *fat-free yogurt* ▶ **beztłuszczowy**

father[1] /ˈfɑːðə(r)/ noun [C] **1** sb's male parent: *a foster father* przybrany ojciec ▶ **ojciec 2** (**Father**) the title of certain priests: *Father O'Reilly* ▶ **ojciec**, **ksiądz**

father[2] /ˈfɑːðə(r)/ verb [T] to become a father: *to father a child* ▶ **płodzić** (*dziecko*)

ˌFather ˈChristmas (also **ˈSanta Claus** /ˈsæntə klɔːz/, **Santa**) noun [C] an old man with a red coat and a long white beard who, children believe, brings presents at Christmas ▶ **Święty Mikołaj**

> **Father Christmas** przynosi prezenty w Wigilię, kiedy dzieci śpią. Podróżuje przez niebo saniami zaprzężonymi w renifery, wchodzi do domu przez komin i zostawia prezenty, które dzieci znajdują następnego ranka. Prezenty tradycyjnie wkłada do **Christmas stockings** (torby w kształcie skarpet), które dzieci wywieszają wieczorem poprzedniego dnia. Dzień szóstego grudnia nie jest obchodzony jako specjalny dzień.

fatherhood /ˈfɑːðəhʊd/ noun [U] the state of being a father ▶ **ojcostwo**

ˈfather-in-law noun [C] (pl. **fathers-in-law**) the father of your husband or wife ▶ **teść**

fatherland /ˈfɑːðəlænd/ noun [usually sing.] (old-fashioned) (used especially about Germany) the country where a person, or their family, was born, especially when they feel very loyal towards it ▶ **ojczyzna** (*zwł. o Niemczech*)

fatherless /ˈfɑːðələs/ adj. having no father: *fatherless children/families* ▶ **bez ojca**

fatherly /ˈfɑːðəli/ adj. like or typical of a father: *Would you like a piece of fatherly advice?* ▶ **ojcowski**

Father's Day noun [C] a day when fathers receive cards and gifts from their children, usually the third Sunday in June ▶ **Dzień Ojca**

fathom /ˈfæðəm/ verb [T] [usually in the negative] to understand sth: *I can't fathom what he means.* ▶ **pojmować**, **zgłębiać**

fatigue /fəˈtiːg/ noun [U] **1** the feeling of being extremely tired: *He was suffering from mental and physical fatigue.* ▶ **zmęczenie** SYN **exhaustion 2** weakness in metals caused by a lot of use: *The plane crash was caused by metal fatigue in a wing.* ▶ **zmęczenie** (*materiału*)

fatten /ˈfætn/ verb [T] **fatten sb/sth (up)** to make sb/sth fatter ▶ **tuczyć**

fattening /ˈfætnɪŋ/ adj. (used about food) that makes people fat ▶ **tuczący**

fatty /ˈfæti/ adj. (**fattier**; **fattiest**) (used about food) having a lot of fat in or on it ▶ **tłusty**

fatuous /ˈfætʃuəs/ adj. (formal) stupid: *a fatuous comment/grin* ▶ **głupi**

■ **fatuously** adv. ▶ **głupio**

faucet (US) = TAP[2] (1)

fault[1] /fɔːlt/ noun **1** [C] something wrong or not perfect in sb's character or in a thing: *One of my faults is that I'm always late.* ▶ **wada**, **usterka** ➲ note at **mistake 2** [U] responsibility for a mistake: *It will be your **own fault** if you don't pass your exams.* ▶ **wina**

IDM **be at fault** to be wrong or responsible for a mistake: *The other driver was at fault – he didn't stop at the traffic lights.* ▶ **być winnym, ponosić winę za coś** **find fault (with sb/sth)** → FIND[1]

fault[2] /fɔːlt/ verb [T] to find sth wrong with sb/sth: *It was impossible to fault her English.* ▶ **krytykować, ganić**

faultless /ˈfɔːltləs/ adj. without any mistakes: *The pianist gave a faultless performance.* ▶ **bezbłędny, nienaganny** SYN **perfect**

faulty /ˈfɔːlti/ adj. (used especially about electricity or machinery) not working properly: *a faulty switch* ◇ *faulty goods* wybrakowany towar ▶ **wadliwy**

fauna /ˈfɔːnə/ noun [U] all the animals of an area or a period of time ▶ **fauna** ➲ look at **flora**

faux pas /ˌfəʊ ˈpɑː/ noun [C] (pl. **faux pas** /ˌfəʊ ˈpɑːz/) something you say or do that is embarrassing or offends people: *to **make a faux pas*** ▶ **gafa, lapsus**

favorite (US) = FAVOURITE

favoritism (US) = FAVOURITISM

⚷ **favour**[1] (US **favor**) /ˈfeɪvə(r)/ noun **1** [C] something that helps sb: *Would you **do me a favour*** (oddać mi przysługę) *and post this letter for me?* ◇ *Could I **ask** you **a favour*** (poprosić cię o przysługę)*?* ◇ *Are they paying you for the work, or are you doing it **as a favour*** (robisz to przez grzeczność)*?* ▶ **przysługa 2** [U] **favour (with sb)** liking or approval: *The new boss's methods didn't **find favour** with* (nie zyskały poparcia u) *the staff.* ◇ *The programme has **lost favour** with viewers recently.* ◇ *an athlete who **fell from favour*** (popadł w niełaskę) *after a drugs scandal* ◇ (formal) *The government **looks with favour upon*** (patrzy przychylnie na) *the report's recommendations.* ◇ *She's not **in favour with*** (nie cieszy się teraz przychylnością) *the media just now.* ◇ *It seems Tim is **back in favour*** (odzyskał przychylność) *with the boss.* ◇ *I'm afraid I'm **out of favour** with my neighbour* (popadłem w niełaskę u sąsiada) *since our last argument.* ▶ **poparcie, przychylność**

IDM **in favour of sb/sth** in agreement with: *Are you in favour of private education?* ▶ (*być*) **za kimś/czymś**

in sb's favour to the advantage of sb: *The committee decided in their favour.* ▶ **na czyjąś korzyść**

favour[2] (US **favor**) /ˈfeɪvə(r)/ verb [T] **1** to support sb/sth; to prefer: *Which suggestion do you favour?* ▶ **woleć 2** to treat one person very well and so be unfair to others: *Parents must try not to favour one of their children.* ▶ **faworyzować**

favourable (US **favorable**) /ˈfeɪvərəbl/ adj. **1** showing liking or approval: *He made a favourable impression on the interviewers.* ▶ **przychylny, korzystny 2** (often used about the weather) suitable or helpful: *Conditions are favourable for skiing today.* ▶ **sprzyjający** OPP for both meanings **unfavourable, adverse**

■ **favourably** (US **favorably**) /-əbli/ adv. ▶ **przychylnie, korzystnie**

⚷ **favourite**[1] (US **favorite**) /ˈfeɪvərɪt/ adj. liked more than any other ▶ **ulubiony**

⚷ **favourite**[2] (US **favorite**) /ˈfeɪvərɪt/ noun [C] **1** a person or thing that you like more than any others: *The other kids were jealous of Rose because she was the teacher's favourite.* ▶ **ulubie-niec/nica, coś ulubionego 2 favourite (for sth/to do sth)** the horse, team, person, etc. who is expected to win: *Mimms is the hot favourite for the leadership of the party.* ▶ **faworyt/ka** OPP **outsider**

favouritism (US **favoritism**) /ˈfeɪvərɪtɪzəm/ noun [U] giving unfair advantages to the person or people that you like best: *The referee was accused of **showing favouritism** to the home side.* ▶ **faworyzowanie, protekcja**

fawn[1] /fɔːn/ adj. of a light yellowish-brown colour ▶ **płowy**

■ **fawn** noun [U] ▶ **kolor płowy**

fawn[2] /fɔːn/ noun [C] a young **deer** ▶ **jelonek** ➲ note at **deer**

fax[1] /fæks/ noun **1** [C] (also **ˈfax machine**) the machine that you use for sending **faxes**: *Have you got a fax?* ◇ *What's your fax number?* ▶ **faks 2** [C,U] a copy of a letter, etc. that you can send by telephone lines using a special machine: *They need an answer today so I'll **send a fax**.* ◇ *They contacted us **by fax*** (faksem). ▶ **faks**

fax[2] /fæks/ verb [T] **fax sth (to sb)**; **fax sb (sth)** to send sb a **fax**: *We will fax our order to you tomorrow.* ◇ *I've faxed her a copy of the letter.* ▶ **wysyłać faks, przesyłać faksem**

faze /feɪz/ verb [T] (informal) to make sb worried or nervous: *He doesn't get fazed by things going wrong.* ▶ **denerwować, zmieszać kogoś**

FBI /ˌef biː ˈaɪ/ abbr. (US) **Federal Bureau of Investigation**; a section of the US government which deals with crimes that affect more than one state, such as **terrorism** ▶ **FBI**

FC /ˌef ˈsiː/ abbr. (Brit.) **Football Club**: *Everton FC* ▶ **klub piłki nożnej**

FCO = FOREIGN AND COMMONWEALTH OFFICE

FE = FURTHER EDUCATION

⚷ **fear**[1] /fɪə(r)/ noun [C,U] the feeling that you have when sth dangerous, painful or frightening might happen: *He was shaking **with fear**.* Trząsł się ze strachu. ◇ *People in this area live **in constant fear of** crime.* ◇ *This book helped me **overcome** my **fear of** dogs.* ◇ *She showed no fear.* ◇ *My fears for his safety were unnecessary.* ▶ **strach, obawa, lęk**

IDM **no fear** (informal) (used when answering a suggestion) certainly not ▶ **nie ma obawy, nigdy w życiu!**

⚷ **fear**[2] /fɪə(r)/ verb **1** [T] to be afraid of sb/sth or of doing sth: *We all fear illness and death.* ◇ *We'll get there in time – never fear* (bez obaw)*!* ▶ **bać się 2** [T] to feel that sth bad might happen or might have happened: *The government fears that it will lose the next election.* ◇ *Thousands of people are feared dead in the earthquake.* Istnieją obawy, że w wyniku trzęsienia ziemi zginęły tysiące osób. ▶ **obawiać się**

PHR V **fear for sb/sth** to be worried about sb/sth: *Parents often fear for the safety of their children.* ▶ **bać się o kogoś/coś** ➲ note at **afraid**

fearful /ˈfɪəfl/ adj. (formal) **1 fearful (of sth/doing sth)**; **fearful that...** afraid or worried about sth: *Don't be fearful of* (nie bój się) *starting something new.* ◇ *They were fearful that they would miss the plane.* ▶ **bojący się, bojaźliwy** ❶ Znacznie częściej używa się wyrazów **frightened**, **scared** i **afraid 2** [only before a noun] terrible: *the fearful consequences of war* ▶ **straszliwy, przeraźliwy**

■ **fearfully** /-fəli/ adv. ▶ **z obawą; straszliwie** | **fearfulness** noun [U] ▶ **strach, obawa**

fearless /ˈfɪələs/ adj. never afraid ▶ **nieustraszony, dzielny**

■ **fearlessly** adv. ▶ **nieustraszenie, dzielnie** | **fearlessness** noun [U] ▶ **nieustraszoność, odwaga**

fearsome /ˈfɪəsəm/ adj. (formal) making people feel very frightened: *a fearsome tiger* ◇ *He has a fearsome reputation as a fighter.* ▶ **przerażający**

feasible /ˈfiːzəbl/ adj. possible to do: *a feasible plan* ▶ **wykonalny**

■ **feasibility** /ˌfiːzəˈbɪləti/ noun [U] ▶ **wykonalność, możliwość przeprowadzenia (czegoś)**

feast /fiːst/ noun [C] a large, special meal, especially to celebrate sth ▶ **uczta**

■ **feast** verb [I] **feast (on sth)**: *They feasted on exotic dishes.* ▶ **ucztować**

feat /fiːt/ noun [C] something you do that shows great strength, skill or courage: *That new bridge is a remark-*

able feat of engineering. ◇ *Persuading Helen to give you a pay rise was **no mean feat*** (było nie lada wyczynem). ▶ **wyczyn**

feather /ˈfeðə(r)/ noun [C] one of the light, soft things that grow in a bird's skin and cover its body ▶ **pióro, lotka** ➲ picture on **page A11**

feature¹ /ˈfiːtʃə(r)/ noun [C] **1** an important or noticeable part of sth: *Noise is a feature of city life.* ▶ **cecha, właściwość 2** a part of the face: *Her eyes are her best feature.* W jej twarzy najładniejsze są oczy. ▶ **rys 3 a feature (on sth)** a newspaper or magazine article or TV programme about sth ▶ **artykuł; program 4** (old-fashioned) (also ˈ**feature film**) a long film that tells a story ▶ **film fabularny**
■ **featureless** adj.: *dull, featureless landscape* ▶ **nijaki, bez wyrazu**

feature² /ˈfiːtʃə(r)/ verb **1** [T] to include sb/sth as an important part: *The film features* (w filmie występuje) *many well-known actors.* ▶ **przedstawiać 2** [I] **feature in sth** to have a part in sth: *Does marriage feature in your future plans?* ▶ **odgrywać rolę, figurować** (*w planach*) SYN **figure**

Feb. = FEBRUARY

February /ˈfebruəri; US -ueri/ noun [U,C] (abbr. **Feb.**) the 2nd month of the year, coming after January: *18 February 1993* ▶ **luty** ➲ note at **January**

feces (US) = FAECES

fed past tense, past participle of **feed¹**

federal /ˈfedərəl/ adj. **1** organized as a **federation**: *a federal system of rule* ▶ **federalny 2** connected with the central government of a **federation**: *That is a federal not a state law.* ▶ **federalny**

federation /ˌfedəˈreɪʃn/ noun [C] a group of states, etc. that have joined together to form a single group ▶ **federacja**

ˌ**fed ˈup** adj. [not before a noun] (informal) **be/get/look fed up (with/of sb/sth/doing sth)** to be bored or unhappy; to be tired of sth: *What's the matter? You look really fed up.* ◇ *I'm fed up with waiting* (mam dość czekania) *for the phone to ring.* ▶ **mieć czegoś dość**

fee /fiː/ noun [C] **1** [usually plural] the money you pay for professional advice or service from private doctors, lawyers, schools, universities, etc.: *We can't afford private school fees.* ◇ *Most ticket agencies will **charge a** small **fee*** (pobiera drobną opłatę). ▶ **honorarium, czesne 2** the cost of an exam, the cost of becoming a member of a club, the amount you pay to go into certain buildings, etc.: *How much is the entrance fee* (opłata za wstęp)*?* ▶ **opłata, składka członkowska** ➲ note at **pay²**

feeble /ˈfiːbl/ adj. **1** with no energy or power; weak: *a feeble old man* ◇ *a feeble cry* ▶ **słaby 2** not able to make sb believe sth: *a feeble excuse* ◇ *a feeble* (nieprzekonujący) *argument* ▶ **słaby, kiepski**
■ **feebly** /ˈfiːbli/ adv. ▶ **słabo**

feed¹ /fiːd/ verb (pt, pp **fed** /fed/) **1** [T] **feed sb/sth (on) (sth)** to give food to a person or an animal: *Don't forget to feed the cat.* ◇ *I can't come yet. I haven't fed the baby.* ◇ *Some of the snakes in the zoo are fed (on) rats.* ▶ **karmić 2** [I] **feed (on sth)** (used about animals or babies) to eat: *What do horses feed on in the winter?* ◇ *Bats feed at night.* ▶ **żywić się, żerować, jeść 3** [T] **feed A (with B); feed B into/to/through A** to supply sb/sth with sth; to put sth into sth else: *Metal sheets are fed through the machine one at a time.* ◇ *This channel feeds us with news* (dostarcza nam wiadomości) *and information 24 hours a day.* ◇ *Can you feed this information into the computer* (wpisać te informacje do komputera)*?* ▶ **wprowadzać coś do czegoś**

feed² /fiːd/ noun **1** [C] a meal for an animal or a baby: *When's the baby's next feed due?* ▶ **karmienie** (*np. niemowlęcia*) **2** [U] food for animals: *cattle feed* ▶ **pokarm**

feedback /ˈfiːdbæk/ noun [U] information or comments about sth that you have done which tells you how good or bad it is: *The teacher spent five minutes with each of us to **give** us **feedback on** our homework.* ▶ **opinia, informacja**

feel¹ /fiːl/ verb (pt, pp **felt** /felt/) **1** [I] [usually with an adjective] to be in the state that is mentioned: *to feel cold/sick/tired/happy* ◇ *How are you feeling today?* ◇ *You'll feel better in the morning.* ▶ **czuć się**

> Istnieje grupa czasowników, których nie używa się z przysłówkami, lecz tylko z przymiotnikami, np. **feel, look, smell, sound, taste**: *He felt cold* (nie ~~*coldly*~~). ◇ *The soup tasted good.* ◇ *She looked very elegant.*

2 [T] to notice or experience sth physical or emotional: *I damaged nerves and now I can't feel anything in this hand.* ◇ *I felt something crawling up my back.* ◇ *I don't feel any sympathy for Matt at all.* ◇ *You could feel the tension in the courtroom.* ▶ **czuć 3** [I] (used to say how sth seems to you when you touch, see, smell, experience, etc. it): *He felt as if* (wydawało mu się, że) *he had been there before.* ◇ *My new coat feels like leather but it's not.* ◇ *My head feels as though it will burst.* ◇ *I felt (that) it was a mistake not to ask her advice.* ▶ **wydawać się, być w dotyku jak coś** ⓘ W tym znaczeniu jako podmiotu dla **feel** często używa się **it**: *It feels as if it is going to snow soon* (zanosi się na śnieg). **4** [T] to touch sth in order to find out what it is like: *Feel this material. Is it cotton or silk?* ◇ *I felt her forehead to see if she had got a temperature.* ▶ **dotykać** ➲ note at **can 5** [T] to be affected by sth: *Do you feel the cold in winter?* ◇ *She felt it badly when her mother died.* ▶ **odczuwać 6** [I] **feel (about) (for sb/sth)** to try to find sth with your hands instead of your eyes: *She felt about in the dark for the light switch.* ▶ **szukać po omacku**
IDM **be/feel like jelly** → JELLY
be/feel out of it → OUT OF
be/feel sorry for sb → SORRY¹
feel free (to do sth) (informal) (used to tell sb they are allowed to do sth): *Feel free to use the phone.* ▶ **nie krępować się (robić czegoś)**
feel like sth/doing sth to want sth or to want to do sth: *Do you feel like going out?* ▶ **mieć ochotę na coś**
feel your age to realize that you are getting old, especially compared to other younger people around you ▶ **odczuwać swój wiek**
have/feel a lump in your throat → LUMP¹
not feel yourself to not feel healthy or well ▶ **źle się czuć, czuć się nieswojo**
PHR V **feel for sb** to understand sb's feelings and situation and feel sorry for them: *I really felt for him when his wife died.* ▶ **współczuć komuś**
feel up to sth/to doing sth to have the strength and the energy to do or deal with sth: *I really don't feel up to eating a huge meal.* ▶ **czuć się w dobrej formie do czegoś**

feel² /fiːl/ noun [sing.] **1** an act of touching sth in order to learn about it: *Let me **have a feel of*** (dotknąć) *that material.* ▶ **dotyk 2** the impression sth gives you when you touch it; the impression that a place or situation gives you: *You can tell it's wool **by the feel**.* ◇ *The town has a friendly feel* (ma przyjazną atmosferę). ▶ **dotyk, wyczucie**

feeler /ˈfiːlə(r)/ noun [C, usually pl.] either of the two long thin parts on the heads of some insects and of some animals that live in shells that they use to feel and touch things with ▶ **czułek** SYN **antenna**
IDM **put out feelers** (informal) to try to find out what people think about sth before you do it ▶ **zbadać nastawienie**

ˈfeel-good adj. making you feel happy and pleased about life: *a feel-good movie* ▶ **wprowadzający w dobry nastrój**
IDM **the feel-good factor** (Brit.) (used especially in newspapers, etc.) the feeling of confidence in the future that is shared by many people: *After the recession, people were waiting for the return of the feel-good factor before starting to spend money again.* ▶ **powszechne poczucie, że przyszłość przyniesie dużo dobrego**

feeling /ˈfiːlɪŋ/ noun **1** [C] **a feeling (of sth)** something that you feel in your mind or body: *a feeling of hunger/happiness/fear/helplessness* ◇ *I've got a funny feeling in my leg.* ▶ **uczucie, poczucie 2** [sing.] a belief or idea that sth is true or is likely to happen: *I **have a** nasty **feeling** that Jan didn't get our message.* ◇ *I **get the feeling*** (odnoszę wrażenie) *that Ian doesn't like me much.* ▶ **odczucie, przeczucie 3** [C,U] **feeling(s) (about/on sth)** an attitude or opinion about sth: *What are your feelings on this matter?* Co sądzisz na ten temat? ◇ *My own feeling is that* (moim zdaniem) *we should postpone the meeting.* ◇ *Public feeling* (powszechne nastawienie) *seems to be against the new road.* ▶ **opinia 4** [U,C, usually pl.] sb's emotions; strong emotion: *I have to tell Jeff his work's not good enough but I don't want to **hurt** his **feelings**.* ◇ *Let's practise that song again, this time **with feeling**.* ▶ **uczu-cie/cia, emocje 5** [C,U] **(a) feeling/feelings (for sb/sth)** love or understanding for sb/sth: *She doesn't have much (of a) feeling for music* (wrażliwości na muzykę). ◇ *He still has feelings for* (nadal coś czuje do) *his ex-wife.* ▶ **zrozumienie; sympatia 6** [U] the ability to feel in your body: *After the accident he lost all feeling in his legs.* ▶ **czucie**
IDM **bad/ill feeling** unhappy relations between people: *The decision caused a lot of bad feeling at the factory.* ▶ **animozja, uraza**
no hard feelings → HARD[1]

feet plural of **foot**[1]

feign /feɪn/ verb [T] (formal) to pretend that you have a particular feeling or that you are ill, tired, etc.: *He survived the massacre by feigning death.* ◇ *'Who cares?' said Alex, feigning indifference.* ▶ **udawać**

feisty /ˈfaɪsti/ adj. (**feistier**; **feistiest**) (informal) (used about people) strong, determined and not afraid to argue ▶ **przebojowy, zadziorny**

feline /ˈfiːlaɪn/ adj. connected with an animal of the cat family; like a cat ▶ **koci**

fell[1] past tense of **fall**[1]

fell[2] /fel/ verb [T] to cut down a tree ▶ **ścinać** (*np. drzewo*), **wyrąbywać** (*np. las*)

fellow[1] /ˈfeləʊ/ noun [C] **1** (old-fashioned) a man: *What's that fellow over there doing?* ▶ **gość 2** a person who is paid to study a particular thing at a university: *Lisa Jones is a research fellow in the biology department.* ▶ **stypendyst(k)a 3** a member of an academic or professional organization, or of certain universities: *a fellow of New College, Oxford* ▶ **członek, wykładowca**

fellow[2] /ˈfeləʊ/ adj. [only before a noun] another or others like yourself in the same situation: *fellow workers/passengers/citizens* ◇ *Her fellow students* (koleżanki i koledzy ze studiów) *were all older than her.* ▶ **współ-**

fellowship /ˈfeləʊʃɪp/ noun **1** [U] a feeling of friendship between people who share an interest ▶ **koleżeństwo 2** [C] a group or society of people who share the same interest or belief ▶ **towarzystwo 3** [C] the position of a college or university **fellow** ▶ **członkostwo towarzystwa naukowego lub kolegium uniwersytetu 4** [C] an award of money to a **graduate** student to allow them to continue their studies or to do research ▶ **stypendium**

ˌfellow-ˈtraveller noun [C] **1** a person who is travelling to the same place as another person ▶ **towarzysz/ka podróży 2** a person who agrees with the aims of a political party, especially the Communist party, but is not a member of it ▶ **sympaty-k/czka partii politycznej** (*zwł. komunistycznej*)

felon /ˈfelən/ noun [C] (especially US) a person who has committed a **felony** ▶ **zbrodnia-rz/rka**

felony /ˈfeləni/ noun [C,U] (pl. **felonies**) (especially US) the act of committing a serious crime, such as murder; a crime of this type ▶ **zbrodnia** ➲ look at **misdemeanour**

felt[1] past tense, past participle of **feel**[1]

felt[2] /felt/ noun [U] a type of soft cloth made from wool, etc. which has been pressed tightly together: *a felt hat* ▶ **filc, pilśń**

ˌfelt-tip ˈpen (also **felt ˈtip**) noun [C] a type of pen with a point made of felt ▶ **flamaster** ➲ picture at **stationery**

female[1] /ˈfiːmeɪl/ adj. **1** being a woman or a girl: *a female artist* artystka ◇ *a female employer/student* ◇ *Please state sex: male or female.* (na formularzu) Płeć: mężczyzna czy kobieta. ▶ **płci żeńskiej** ➲ look at **feminine 2** being of the sex that produces eggs or gives birth to babies: *a female cat* kotka ▶ **żeński, samiczy** OPP **male**

> Nazwy **female** i **male** stosuje się tylko do określania płci. Mówiąc o cechach typowo żeńskich/kobiecych lub meskich mówi się odpowiednio **feminine** i **masculine**.

3 (used about plants and flowers) that can produce fruit ▶ (*roślina*) **żeński**

female[2] /ˈfiːmeɪl/ noun [C] **1** an animal that can produce eggs or give birth to babies; a plant that can produce fruit ▶ **samica 2** a woman or a girl: *More females than males become teachers.* ▶ **kobieta; dziewczyna** ➲ look at **male**

feminine /ˈfemənɪn/ adj. **1** typical of or looking like a woman; connected with women: *My daughter always dresses like a boy. She hates looking feminine.* ▶ **kobiecy** ➲ note at **masculine** ➲ look at **female 2** (in English) of the forms of words used to describe females: *'Lioness' is the feminine form of 'lion'.* ▶ (*forma*) **żeńska 3** (in the grammar of some languages) belonging to a certain class of nouns, adjectives or pronouns: *The German word for a flower is feminine.* ▶ (*rodzaj*) **żeński** ➲ look at **masculine, neuter**
■ **femininity** /ˌfeməˈnɪnəti/ noun [U] ▶ **kobiecość** ➲ look at **womanhood**

feminism /ˈfemənɪzəm/ noun [U] the belief that women should have the same rights and opportunities as men ▶ **feminizm**
■ **feminist** /-ɪst/ **1** noun [C] ▶ **feminist(k)a 2** adj. ▶ **feministyczny**

femur /ˈfiːmə(r)/ noun [C] the large thick bone in the top part of your leg above the knee ▶ **kość udowa** SYN **thigh bone** ➲ picture at **body**

fence[1] /fens/ noun [C] a line of wooden or metal posts joined by wood, wire, metal, etc. to divide land or to keep in animals ▶ **płot, ogrodzenie**
IDM **sit on the fence** → SIT

fence[2] /fens/ verb **1** [T] to surround land with a fence ▶ **ograďzać 2** [I] to fight with a **foil** as a sport ▶ **uprawiać szermierkę**
PHR V **fence sb/sth in 1** to surround sb/sth with a fence: *They fenced in their garden to make it more private.* ▶ **odgradzać kogoś/coś 2** to limit sb's freedom: *She felt fenced in by so many responsibilities.* ▶ **ograniczać kogoś**
fence sth off to separate one area from another with a fence ▶ **odgradzać coś**

fencing /ˈfensɪŋ/ noun [U] the sport of fighting with **foils** ▶ **szermierka** ➲ picture on **page A9**

fend /fend/ verb
PHR V **fend for yourself** to look after yourself without help from anyone else ▶ **troszczyć się o siebie**, **dawać sobie radę**
fend sb/sth off to defend yourself from sb/sth that is attacking you: *Politicians usually manage to fend off awkward questions.* ▶ **bronić się przed kimś/czymś**, **odpierać** (*np. atak*)

fender /ˈfendə(r)/ noun [C] **1** (US) = WING (4) **2** a low metal frame in front of an open fire that stops coal or wood falling out ▶ **krata przed kominkiem**

feng shui /ˌfeŋ ˈʃuːi; ˌfʌŋ ˈʃweɪ/ noun [U] a Chinese system for deciding the right position for a building and for placing objects inside a building in order to make people feel comfortable and happy ▶ **feng shui**

fennel /ˈfenl/ noun [U] a vegetable that has a thick round part at the base of the leaves with a strong taste. The seeds and leaves are also used in cooking. ▶ **fenkuł**, **koper włoski**

feral /ˈferəl/ adj. (used about animals) living wild, especially after escaping from life as a pet or on a farm: *feral cats* ▶ **zdziczały**, **dziki**

ferment[1] /fəˈment/ verb [I,T] to change or make the chemistry of sth change, especially sugar changing to alcohol: *The wine is starting to ferment.* ▶ **fermentować**; **powodować fermentację**
■ **fermentation** /ˌfɜːmenˈteɪʃn/ noun [U] ▶ **fermentacja**

ferment[2] /ˈfɜːment/ noun [U] a state of political or social excitement and change: *Iraq is **in ferment*** (w Iraku wrze) *and nobody's sure what will happen next.* ▶ **ferment**, **wzburzenie**

fern /fɜːn/ noun [C] a green plant with no flowers and a lot of long thin leaves ▶ **paproć**, **paprotka**

ferocious /fəˈrəʊʃəs/ adj. very aggressive and violent: *a ferocious beast/attack/storm/war* ▶ **brutalny**
■ **ferociously** adv. ▶ **brutalnie**

ferocity /fəˈrɒsəti/ noun [U] violence; cruel and aggressive behaviour ▶ **brutalność**, **bestialstwo** ➲ adjective **fierce**

ferret[1] /ˈferɪt/ noun [C] a small animal with a long thin body, kept as a pet or for hunting other animals ▶ **fretka**

ferret[2] /ˈferɪt/ verb [I] (informal) **ferret (about/around) (for sth)** to search for sth that is lost or hidden among a lot of things: *She opened the drawer and ferreted around for her keys.* ▶ **szperać (po/w czymś) (za czymś)**, **myszkować (po/w czymś) (w poszukiwaniu czegoś)**
PHR V **ferret sb/sth out** (informal) to discover information or to find sb/sth by searching thoroughly, asking a lot of questions, etc. ▶ **wyszperać**, **wywęszyć**

Ferris wheel (especially US) = BIG WHEEL

ferry[1] /ˈferi/ noun [C] (pl. **ferries**) a boat that carries people, vehicles or goods across a river or across a narrow part of the sea: *a car ferry* ▶ **prom** ➲ note at **boat** ➲ picture at **boat**, picture on **page A6**

ferry[2] /ˈferi/ verb [T] (**ferrying**; **ferries**; pt, pp **ferried**) to carry people or goods in a boat or other vehicle from one place to another, usually for a short distance: *Could you ferry us across to the island?* ◇ *We share the job of ferrying* (dzielimy się dowożeniem) *the children to school.* ▶ **przewozić promem**, **przeprawiać**

fertile /ˈfɜːtaɪl; US -tl/ adj. **1** (used about land or soil) that plants grow well in ▶ **urodzajny**, **żyzny** OPP **infertile** **2** (used about people, animals or plants) that can produce babies, fruit or new plants ▶ **płodny** OPP **infertile** ➲ look at **sterile 3** (used about sb's mind) full of ideas: *She has a fertile imagination.* ▶ **płodny**
■ **fertility** /fəˈtɪləti/ noun [U]: *Nowadays women can take drugs to increase their fertility.* ▶ **płodność**; **urodzajność**, **żyzność** OPP **infertility**

fertilize (also -ise) /ˈfɜːtəlaɪz/ verb [T] **1** (technical) to put a male seed into an egg, a plant or a female animal so that a baby, fruit or a young animal starts to develop ▶ **zapładniać**; **zapylać** **2** to put natural or artificial substances on soil in order to make plants grow better ▶ **nawozić**, **użyźniać**
■ **fertilization** (also -isation) /ˌfɜːtəlaɪˈzeɪʃn; US -ləˈz-/ noun [U] ▶ **zapłodnienie**; **zapylenie**; **nawożenie**, **użyźnianie**

fertilizer (also -iser) /ˈfɜːtəlaɪzə(r)/ noun [C,U] a natural or chemical substance that is put on land or soil to make plants grow better ▶ **nawóz** ➲ look at **manure**

fervent /ˈfɜːvənt/ adj. having or showing very strong feelings about sth: *a fervent belief/hope/desire* ◇ *She's a fervent believer* (żarliwą zwolenniczką) *in women's rights.* ▶ **żarliwy**, **gorliwy**
■ **fervently** adv. ▶ **żarliwie**, **gorliwie**

fervid /ˈfɜːvɪd/ adj. (formal) feeling sth too strongly; showing feelings that are too strong ▶ **żarliwy**
■ **fervidly** adv. ▶ **żarliwie**

fervour (US **fervor**) /ˈfɜːvə(r)/ noun [U] very strong feelings about sth ▶ **ferwor**, **zapał** SYN **enthusiasm**

fester /ˈfestə(r)/ verb [I] **1** (used about a cut or an injury) to become infected: *a festering sore/wound* ▶ **jątrzyć się**, **ropieć** **2** (used about an unpleasant situation, feeling or thought) to become more unpleasant because you do not deal with it successfully ▶ **jątrzyć się**, **zaogniać się**

festival /ˈfestɪvl/ noun [C] **1** a series of plays, films, musical performances, etc. often held regularly in one place: *a jazz festival* ▶ **festiwal** **2** a day or time when people celebrate sth (especially a religious event): *Christmas is an important Christian festival.* ▶ **święto**

festive /ˈfestɪv/ adj. happy, because people are enjoying themselves celebrating sth: *the festive season* święta Bożego Narodzenia ▶ **świąteczny**, **wesoły**

festivity /feˈstɪvəti/ noun (pl. **festivities**) **1** [pl.] happy events when people celebrate sth: *The festivities went on until dawn.* ▶ **obchody**, **uroczystości** **2** [U] being happy and celebrating sth: *The wedding was followed by three days of festivity.* ▶ **świętowanie**, **uroczystość**

festoon /feˈstuːn/ verb [T, usually passive] **festoon sb/sth (with sth)** to decorate sb/sth with flowers, coloured paper, etc., often as part of a celebration: *The streets were festooned with banners and lights.* ▶ **przyozdabiać**

fetch /fetʃ/ verb [T] **1** (especially Brit.) to go to a place and bring back sb/sth: *Shall I fetch your coat for you?* ▶ **pójść i przynieść**, **pojechać i przywieźć** ➲ picture at **bring** **2** (used about goods) to be sold for the price mentioned: *'How much will your car fetch?' 'It should fetch about £900.'* „Ile dostaniesz za swój samochód?" „Powinienem za niego dostać około 900 funtów." ▶ **osiągać cenę**

fetching /ˈfetʃɪŋ/ adj. (informal) (especially used about a person or their clothes) attractive: *She looked very fetching in a little red hat.* ◇ *a fetching smile* ▶ **uroczy**, (*ubranie*) **twarzowy**
■ **fetchingly** adv. ▶ **uroczo**, (*ubranie*) **twarzowo**

fête /feɪt/ noun [C] an outdoor event with competitions, entertainment and things to buy, often organized to make money for a particular purpose: *a church fête* odpust ◇ *a school/village fête* ▶ **festyn**, **kiermasz**

fetish /ˈfetɪʃ/ noun **1** the fact that a person spends too much time doing or thinking about a particular thing:

She has a fetish about cleanliness. ◇ *He makes a fetish of his work.* Fetyszyzuje swoją pracę. ▶ **obsesja 2** the fact of getting sexual pleasure from a particular object: ▶ **fetysz** *(seksualny)* **3** an object that some people worship because they believe that it has magic powers ▶ *(relig.)* **fetysz**

■ **fetishism** noun [U]: *the importance of animal fetishism in the history of Egypt* ▶ **fetyszyzm** | **fetishist** noun [C]: ▶ **fetyszyst(k)a** | **fetishistic** /ˌfetɪˈʃɪstɪk/ adj. ▶ **fetyszystyczny**

fetus (US) = FOETUS

feud /fjuːd/ noun [C] **a feud (between A and B)**; **a feud (with sb) (over sb/sth)** an angry and serious argument between two people or groups that continues over a long period of time: *a family feud* ▶ **waśń, spór**

■ **feud** verb [I] ▶ **waśnić się, toczyć spór**

feudal /ˈfjuːdl/ adj. connected with the system of **feudalism**: *the feudal system* ▶ **feudalny**

feudalism /ˈfjuːdəlɪzəm/ noun [U] the social system which existed in the Middle Ages in Europe, in which people worked and fought for a person who owned land and received land and protection from them in return ▶ **feudalizm**

fever /ˈfiːvə(r)/ noun **1** [C,U] a condition of the body when it is too hot because of illness: *He has a high fever* ▶ **gorączka, wysoka temperatura** ➲ note at **ill** ℹ Synonimem zwrotu **have a fever** jest **have a temperature. 2** [sing.] **a fever (of sth)** a state of nervous excitement: *a fever of impatience* ▶ **gorączka, rozgorączkowanie**

feverish /ˈfiːvərɪʃ/ adj. **1** suffering from or caused by a **fever**: *a feverish cold/dream* ◇ *She was quite feverish.* Miała gorączkę. ▶ **gorączkujący, gorączkowy, z gorączką 2** showing great excitement ▶ **rozgorączkowany, gorączkowy**

■ **feverishly** adv. ▶ **gorączkowo**

ˈ**fever pitch** noun [U,C] a very high level of excitement or activity: *Speculation about his future had **reached fever pitch**.* ▶ **stan najwyższej ekscytacji**

few /fjuː/ determiner, pron. [used with a plural countable noun and a plural verb] **1** not many: *Few people live to be 100.* ◇ *There are fewer* (mniej) *cars here today than yesterday.* ◇ *The few people* (tych kilka osób) *I have asked thought the same as I do.* ◇ *I knew few of the people at the party.* ℹ Por. z podobnym zdaniem w znaczeniu dwa poniżej. ▶ **(tylko/bardzo) niewiel-u/e, (tylko/bardzo) nieliczn-i/e, mało 2** (**a few**) a small number of; some: *a few people* ◇ *a few hours/days/years* ◇ *I'll meet you later. I've got a few things to do first.* ◇ *I knew a few of the people there.* ▶ **kilk-u/a, niektóry** ➲ note at **less**

IDM **few and far between** not happening very often; not common: *Pubs are a bit few and far between in this area.* ◇ *Our visits to the theatre are few and far between.* Bardzo rzadko chodzimy do teatru. ▶ **bardzo rzadki, sporadyczny**

a good few; **quite a few** a fairly large amount or number: *It's been a good few years since I saw him last.* ▶ **sporo**

fiancé (fem. **fiancée**) /fiˈɒnseɪ; US ˌfiːɑːnˈseɪ/ noun [C] a person who has promised to marry sb: *This is my fiancée Liz. We got engaged a few weeks ago.* ▶ **narzeczon-y/a**

fiasco /fiˈæskəʊ/ noun [C] (pl. **fiascos**; US also **fiascoes**) an event that does not succeed, often in a way that causes embarrassment: *Our last party was a complete fiasco.* ▶ **fiasko** SYN **disaster**

fib /fɪb/ noun [C] (informal) something you say that is not true: *Please don't tell fibs.* ▶ **bujda, kłamstewko**

■ **fib** verb [I] (**fibbing**; **fibbed**) ▶ **zmyślać, bujać** SYN **lie** ℹ Wyrazu **fib** używamy, gdy kłamstwo nie jest zbyt poważne.

fibre (US **fiber**) /ˈfaɪbə(r)/ noun **1** [U] parts of plants that you eat which are good for you because they help to move food quickly through your body: *Wholemeal bread is **high in fibre**.* ▶ **błonnik 2** [C,U] a material or a substance that is made from natural or artificial threads ▶ **tkanina**

> **Natural** fibres are, for example, cotton and wool. **Man-made** or **synthetic** fibres are nylon, polyester, etc.

3 [C] one of the thin threads which form a natural or artificial substance: *cotton/wood/nerve/muscle fibres* ▶ **włókno**

fibreglass (US **fiberglass**) /ˈfaɪbəɡlɑːs; US -ɡlæs/ (also **glass ˈfibre**) noun [U] a material made from small threads of plastic or glass, used for making small boats, parts of cars, etc. ▶ **włókno szklane**

F

ˌ**fibre ˈoptics** (US ˌ**fiber ˈoptics**) noun [U] the use of thin **fibres** of glass, etc. for sending information in the form of light signals ▶ **technika światłowodowa**

■ ˌ**fibre-ˈoptic** adj.: *fibre-optic cables* ▶ **światłowodowy**

fibula /ˈfɪbjələ/ noun [C] the outer bone of the two bones in the lower part of your leg, between your knee and your foot ▶ **kość strzałkowa** ➲ look at **tibia** ➲ picture at **body**

fickle /ˈfɪkl/ adj. always changing your mind or your feelings so you cannot be trusted: *a fickle friend* ▶ **niestały, zmienny**

fiction /ˈfɪkʃn/ noun [U] stories, novels, etc. which describe events and people that are not real: *I don't read much fiction.* ▶ **beletrystyka** OPP **non-fiction** ➲ note at **literature** ➲ look at **fact**

fictional /ˈfɪkʃənl/ adj. not real or true; only existing in stories, novels, etc.: *fictional characters* ◇ *The book gave a fictional account of a doctor's life.* Powieść opisywała fikcyjne losy lekarza. ▶ **powieściowy, beletrystyczny** ➲ look at **factual**

fictitious /fɪkˈtɪʃəs/ adj. invented; not real: *The novel is set in a fictitious town called Eden.* ▶ **fikcyjny, zmyślony**

fiddle[1] /ˈfɪdl/ verb **1** [I] **fiddle (about/around) (with sth)** to play with sth carelessly, because you are nervous or not thinking: *Tristram sat nervously, fiddling with a pencil.* ▶ **bawić się czymś (bezwiednie) 2** [T] (informal) to change the details or facts of sth (business accounts, etc.) in order to get money dishonestly: *She fiddled her expenses form.* ▶ **fałszować**

fiddle[2] /ˈfɪdl/ noun [C] (informal) **1** = VIOLIN **2** (Brit.) a dishonest action, especially one connected with money: *a tax fiddle* ▶ **oszustwo, kant**

fiddler /ˈfɪdlə(r)/ noun [C] a person who plays the **violin**, especially to play **folk music** ▶ **skrzyp-ek/aczka**

fiddly /ˈfɪdli/ adj. (**fiddlier**; **fiddliest**) (informal) difficult to do or manage with your hands (because small or complicated parts are involved) ▶ **trudny do uchwycenia, wymagający zręcznych palców i precyzji**

fidelity /fɪˈdeləti/ noun [U] **1** (formal) **fidelity (to sb/sth)** the quality of being faithful, especially to a wife or husband by not having a sexual relationship with anyone else ▶ **wierność** OPP **infidelity** ℹ Mniej formalnym słowem jest **faithfulness. 2** the quality of being accurate or close to the original: *the fidelity of the translation to the original text* ▶ **wierność, zgodność** ➲ look at **hi-fi**

fidget /ˈfɪdʒɪt/ verb [I] **fidget (with sth)** to keep moving your body, hands or feet because you are nervous, bored, excited, etc.: *She fidgeted nervously* (bawiła się nerwowo) *with her keys.* ▶ **wiercić się, kręcić się**

■ **fidgety** adj. ▶ **niespokojny, ruchliwy**

field[1] /fiːld/ noun [C] **1** an area of land on a farm, usually surrounded by fences or walls, used for growing crops or keeping animals in ▶ **pole 2** an area of land used for sports, games or some other activity: *a football field* ◇ *an airfield* lotnisko ◇ *a battlefield* pole bitwy ▶ **boisko**, **plac** ➲ look at **pitch 3** an area of land where oil, coal or other minerals are found: *a coalfield* ◇ *a North Sea oilfield* ▶ **pole**, **zagłębie 4** an area of study or knowledge: *He's an expert in the field of economics.* ▶ **dziedzina**, **zakres 5** an area affected by or included in sth: *a magnetic field* ▶ **pole**

field[2] /fiːld/ verb **1** [T] to choose a team for games such as football, **cricket**, etc.: *New Zealand is fielding an excellent team for the next match.* ▶ **wystawiać** (*drużynę*) **2** [I,T] (in sports such as **cricket**, **baseball**, etc.) to (be ready to) catch and throw back the ball after sb has hit it ▶ **czekać na odbicie piłki przez gracza drużyny przeciwnej, łapać ją i odrzucać z powrotem**

> When one team is **fielding**, the other is **batting**.

ˈ**field day** noun
IDM **have a field day** to get the opportunity to do sth you enjoy, especially sth other people do not approve of: *The newspapers always have a field day when there's a political scandal.* ▶ **mieć ruch w interesie**, **mieć szczególnie ekscytujący dzień**

fielder /ˈfiːldə(r)/ noun [C] (in sports such as **cricket** and **baseball**) a player who is trying to catch the ball rather than hit it ▶ (*krykiet itp.*) **łapacz**

ˈ**field event** noun [C] a sport, such as jumping and throwing, that is not a race and does not involve running ▶ **impreza lekkoatletyczna** (*ale bez konkurencji biegowych*) ➲ look at **track event**

ˈ**field hockey** (US) = HOCKEY (1)

ˌ**field of ˈvision** (also ˌ**field of ˈview**; ˌ**visual ˈfield**) noun [C] (pl. **fields of vision/view**; **visual fields**) the total amount of space that you can see from a particular point without moving your head: *Ann turned and left his field of vision.* ▶ **pole widzenia**

ˈ**field trip** noun [C] a journey made to study sth in its natural environment: *We went on a geography field trip.* ▶ **wycieczka naukowa/badawcza w terenie**

fieldwork /ˈfiːldwɜːk/ noun [U] practical research work done outside school, college, etc. ▶ **badania/ćwiczenia w terenie**

fiend /fiːnd/ noun [C] **1** a very cruel person ▶ **diabeł**, **okrutnik 2** (informal) a person who is very interested in one particular thing: *a health fiend* ▶ **pasjonat**, **fanatyk** SYN **fanatic**

fiendish /ˈfiːndɪʃ/ adj. **1** very unpleasant or cruel: *a fiendish act* ◇ *shrieks of fiendish laughter* ▶ **okrutny 2** (informal) clever and complicated: *a fiendish plan* ▶ **szatański**, **przebiegły**
■ **fiendishly** adv. ▶ **okrutnie**; **piekielnie**

fierce /fɪəs/ adj. **1** angry, aggressive and frightening: *The house was guarded by fierce dogs* (srogie brytany). ▶ **zły**, **zawzięty**, **zapalczywy 2** very strong; violent: *fierce competition for jobs* ◇ *a fierce attack* ▶ **ostry**, **zawzięty** ➲ noun **ferocity**
■ **fiercely** adv. ▶ **zawzięcie**; **ostro**, **gwałtownie**

fiery /ˈfaɪəri/ adj. (**fierier**; **fieriest**) **1** looking like fire: *She has fiery red hair.* ▶ **ognisty**, **gorejący 2** quick to become angry: *a fiery temper* ▶ **zapalczywy** SYN **passionate**

fifteen /ˌfɪfˈtiːn/ number 15 ▶ **piętnaście** ➲ note at **six**
■ **fifteenth** /ˌfɪfˈtiːnθ/ **1** ordinal number 15th ▶ **piętnasty** ➲ note at **sixth 2** noun [C] 1/15; one of fifteen equal parts of sth ▶ **(jedna) piętnasta**

fifth /fɪfθ/ ordinal number 5th ▶ **piąty** ➲ note at **sixth** ➲ look at **five**
■ **fifth** noun [C] ⅕; one of five equal parts of sth ▶ **(jedna) piąta**

fifty /ˈfɪfti/ number 50 ▶ **pięćdziesiąt** ➲ note at **sixty**
■ **fiftieth** /ˈfɪftiəθ/ **1** ordinal number 50th ▶ **pięćdziesiąty** ➲ note at **sixth 2** noun [C] 1/50; one of fifty equal parts of sth ▶ **(jedna) pięćdziesiąta**

ˌ**fifty-ˈfifty** adj. equal (between two people, groups, etc.): *You've got **a fifty-fifty chance** of winning.* ▶ **równy**
■ ˌ**fifty-ˈfifty** adv.: *We'll divide the money fifty-fifty.* ▶ **po połowie**, **równo**

fig /fɪɡ/ noun [C] (a type of tree with) a soft sweet fruit full of seeds that grows in warm countries and is often eaten dried ▶ **figowiec**; **figa** ➲ picture on **page A12**

fig. abbr. **1 figure**; a drawing, diagram or picture: *See diagram at fig. 2.* ▶ **rys.**, **ilustr. 2** = FIGURATIVE

fight[1] /faɪt/ verb (pt, pp **fought** /fɔːt/) **1** [I,T] **fight (against sb)** to use physical strength, guns, weapons, etc. against sb/sth: *Did he fight in the Second World War?* ◇ *They gathered soldiers to fight the invading army.* ◇ *My younger brothers were always fighting.* ▶ **walczyć (z kimś)**, **bić się 2** [I,T] **fight (against sth)** to try very hard to stop or prevent sth: *to fight a fire/a decision/prejudice* ◇ *to fight against crime/disease* ▶ **walczyć (z czymś)**, **zwalczać 3** [I] **fight (for sth/to do sth)** to try very hard to get or keep sth: *to fight for your rights* ▶ **walczyć (o coś) 4** [I] **fight (with sb) (about/over sth)** to argue: *It's not worth fighting about money.* ▶ **kłócić się** ➲ look at **argue**, **quarrel**[2]
■ **fighting** noun [U]: *Fighting broke out in the city last night.* ▶ **walki**, **bójki**
PHR V **fight back (against sb/sth)** to protect yourself with actions or words by attacking sb who has attacked you: *If he hits you again, fight back!* ▶ **oddawać (komuś w bójce)**, **stawiać komuś/czemuś opór**
fight sb/sth off to resist sb/sth by fighting against them/it: *The jeweller was stabbed as he tried to fight the robbers off.* ▶ **odpierać kogoś/coś**, **przepędzać kogoś/coś**

fight[2] /faɪt/ noun **1** [C] **a fight (with sb/sth)**; **a fight (between A and B)** the act of using physical force against sb/sth: *Don't **get into a fight*** (tylko nie wdawaj się w bójkę) *at school, will you?* ◇ ***Fights broke out** between rival groups of fans.* ▶ **walka**, **bójka 2** [sing.] **a fight (against/for sth) (to do sth)** the work done trying to destroy, prevent or achieve sth: *Workers won their fight against the management to stop the factory from closing down.* ▶ **walka (z czymś/o coś)** (*w celu osiągnięcia czegoś*) **3** (especially US) **a fight (with sb/sth) (about/over sth)** an argument about sth: *I **had a fight*** (pokłóciłem się) *with my mum over what time I had to be home.* ▶ **kłótnia z kimś (o coś) 4** [U] the desire to continue trying or fighting: *I've had some bad luck but I've still got plenty of fight in me.* ▶ **duch walki/bojowy**, **chęć walki**
IDM **pick a fight** → PICK[1]

fighter /ˈfaɪtə(r)/ noun [C] **1** (also ˈ**fighter plane**) a small fast military aircraft used for attacking enemy aircraft: *a jet fighter* ◇ *a fighter pilot* ▶ **samolot myśliwski 2** a person who fights in a war or a **boxer** ▶ **żołnierz**, **bojownik**; **bokser**

figment /ˈfɪɡmənt/ noun
IDM **a figment of sb's imagination** something that sb has imagined and that does not really exist: *Are you telling me that these symptoms are just a figment of my imagination?* ▶ **wytwór wyobraźni**

figurative /ˈfɪɡərətɪv/ adj. (abbr. **fig.**) (used about a word or an expression) not used with its exact meaning but in a way that is different to give a special effect: *'He exploded with rage' is a figurative use of the verb 'to explode'.* ▶ **przenośny** ➲ look at **literal**, **metaphor**
■ **figuratively** adv. ▶ **w znaczeniu przenośnym**

figure¹ /ˈfɪɡə(r); US -ɡjər/ noun [C] **1** an amount (in numbers) or a price: *The unemployment figures are lower this month.* ◇ *What sort of figure are you thinking of for your house?* ▶ **liczba**; **cena 2** a written sign for a number (0 to 9): *Write the numbers in figures, not words.* ◇ *He has a six-figure income/an income in six figures* (zarabia setki tysięcy). ◇ *double figures* liczby dwucyfrowe ◇ *in single figures* na poziomie jednocyfrowym ▶ **cyfra 3** (**figures**) [pl.] (informal) mathematics: *I don't **have a head for figures.*** Nie jestem dobry w rachunkach ▶ **liczenie 4** an important person: *an important political figure* ▶ **postać**, **osoba 5** the shape of the human body, especially a woman's body that is attractive: *She's got a beautiful slim figure.* ▶ **figura**, **sylwetka** ➲ note at **build² 6** a person that you cannot see very clearly or do not know: *Two figures were coming towards us in the dark.* ▶ **postać**, **sylwetka 7** (abbr. **fig.**) a diagram or picture used in a book to explain sth: *Figure 3 shows the major cities of Italy.* ▶ **diagram**, **ilustracja**
IDM **a ballpark figure/estimate** → BALLPARK
facts and figures → FACT
in round figures/numbers → ROUND¹

figure² /ˈfɪɡə(r); US -ɡjər/ verb **1** [I] **figure (as sth) (in/among sth)** to be included in sth; to be an important part of sth: *Women don't figure much in his novels.* W jego powieściach kobiety nie odgrywają dużej roli. ▶ **pojawiać się**, **figurować** SYN **feature 2** [T] (especially US) **figure (that…)** to work sth out: *I figured he was here because I saw his car outside.* ▶ **odgadywać**, **pomyśleć**
IDM **it/that figures** (informal) that is what I expected ▶ **tak właśnie myślałem**
PHR V **figure on sth/on doing sth** (especially US) to include sth in your plans: *I figure on arriving in New York on Wednesday.* ▶ **planować coś**
figure sb/sth out to find an answer to sth or to understand sb: *I can't figure out why she married him in the first place.* ▶ **zrozumieć kogoś/coś**; **wydedukować coś**

figurehead /ˈfɪɡəhed; US -ɡjərh-/ noun [C] **1** a person who is in a high position in a country or an organization but who has no real power or authority ▶ **figurant/ka 2** a large wooden statue, usually representing a woman, that used to be fixed to the front end of a ship ▶ **aflaston**

ˌfigure of ˈeight (US ˌfigure ˈeight) noun [C] (pl. **figures of eight**) something in the shape of the number 8 ▶ **ósemka**

ˌfigure of ˈspeech noun [C] (pl. **figures of speech**) a word or expression used in a different way from its usual meaning in order to make a special effect ▶ **figura retoryczna** ➲ look at **figurative**

ˈfigure-skating noun [U] a type of **ice skating** in which you cut patterns in the ice and do jumps and spins ▶ **łyżwiarstwo figurowe**

filament /ˈfɪləmənt/ noun [C] **1** a thin wire in a **light bulb** that produces light when electricity is passed through it ▶ (*elektr.*) **włókno 2** (technical) a long thin piece of sth that looks like a thread: *glass/metal filaments* ▶ **włókno** (*np. szklane*)

file¹ /faɪl/ noun [C] **1** a box or a cover that is used for keeping papers together: *a box file* ▶ **segregator**, **teczka** ➲ picture at **stationery 2** a collection of information or material on one subject that is stored together in a computer or on a disk, with a particular name: *to open/close a file* ◇ *to create/delete/save/copy a file* ▶ (*komput.*) **plik 3 a file (on sb/sth)** a collection of papers or information about sb/sth kept inside a file: *The police are now keeping a file on all known football hooligans.* ▶ **akta 4** a metal tool with a rough surface used for shaping hard substances or for making surfaces smooth: *a nail file* ▶ **pilnik** ➲ picture at **tool**
IDM **in single file** → SINGLE¹
on file kept in a file: *We have all the information you need on file.* ▶ **w aktach/kartotece/archiwum**
the rank and file → RANK¹

file² /faɪl/ verb **1** [T] **file sth (away)** to put and keep documents, etc. in a particular place so that you can find them easily; to put sth into a file: *I filed the letters away in a drawer.* ▶ **włączać do akt/kartoteki/archiwum 2** [I] **file in, out, past, etc.** to walk or march in a line: *The children filed out of the classroom at the end of the lesson.* ▶ **przechodzić/maszerować rzędem/gęsiego 3** [T] **file sth (away, down, etc.)** to shape sth hard or make sth smooth with a file: *to file your nails* ▶ **przepiłowywać**; **opiłowywać**

filename /ˈfaɪlneɪm/ noun [C] a name given to a computer file in order to identify it ▶ **nazwa pliku**

ˈfiling cabinet (US ˈfile cabinet) noun [C] a piece of office furniture with deep drawers for storing files ▶ **szafa na dokumenty**

fill /fɪl/ verb **1** [I,T] **fill (sth/sb) (with sth)** to make sth full or to become full: *Can you fill the kettle for me?* ◇ *The news filled him with excitement.* ◇ *The room filled with smoke within minutes.* ▶ **napełniać (się) 2** [T] to appoint sb to a job: *I'm afraid that teaching post has just been filled.* ▶ **obsadzać 3** [T] **fill sth (up)** to use up your time doing sth: *How do you fill your day now that you've retired?* ▶ **wypełniać**
PHR V **fill in (for sb)** to do sb's job for a short time while they are not there ▶ **zastępować (kogoś) w pracy**
fill sb in (on sth) to tell sb about sth that has happened ▶ **wprowadzać kogoś (w jakiś temat)**
fill sth in 1 (US also **fill sth out**) to complete a form, etc. by writing information on it: *Could you fill in the application form, please?* ▶ **wypełniać coś 2** to fill a hole or space completely to make a surface flat: *You had better fill in the cracks in the wall before you paint it.* ▶ **wypełniać coś**
fill out to become larger, rounder or fatter ▶ **zaokrąglać się**, **przybierać na wadze**
fill up (with sth); **fill sth up (with sth)** to become completely full; to make sth completely full: *Fill up the tank* (do pełna), *please.* ◇ *to fill up the tank with oil* ▶ **wypełniać się/coś całkowicie (czymś)**

fillet (US **filet**) /ˈfɪlɪt; US fɪˈleɪ/ noun [C,U] a piece of meat or fish with the bones taken out ▶ **filet**

filling¹ /ˈfɪlɪŋ/ noun **1** [C] the material that a dentist uses to fill a hole in a tooth: *a gold filling* ▶ **plomba** ➲ note at **tooth 2** [C,U] the food inside a **sandwich**, cake, **pie**, etc. ▶ **nadzienie**, **warstwa** (*kremu/bitej śmietany itp.*) ➲ picture on **page A14**

filling² /ˈfɪlɪŋ/ adj. (used about food) that makes you feel full: *Pasta is very filling.* ▶ **sycący**

filly /ˈfɪli/ noun [C] (pl. **fillies**) a young female horse ▶ **klaczka**

film¹ /fɪlm/ noun **1** (US also **movie** /ˈmuːvi/) [C] a story, play, etc. shown in moving pictures at the cinema or on TV: *Let's go to the cinema – there's a good film on this week.* ◇ *to **watch a film** on TV* ◇ *to **see a film** at the cinema* ◇ *a horror/documentary/feature film* ◇ *a film director* reżyser ◇ *a film producer/critic* producent/krytyk filmowy ◇ *The **film was made/shot*** (film został nakręcony) *on location in Scotland.* ▶ **film** ➲ look at **western 2** [U] the art or business of making films: *She's studying film and theatre.* ◇ *the film industry* ▶ **kinematografia**

> **films**
>
> My favourite **film** (US **movie**) is **set** in Rome. It is **based on** a book and it **stars** several famous **actors**. The **script** was written by the **director**, who won an award for (the) best **screenplay**. The **dialogue** is in Italian, but there are English **subtitles**. **Critics** gave the film good **reviews** and there is a **sequel** coming out next year.

I saw the film at the **cinema** but it is also available on **video** and **DVD**. You can buy the **soundtrack** on CD too.

3 [U] moving pictures of real events: *The programme included film of the town one hundred years ago.* ▶ **film** **4** [C,U] a roll of thin plastic that you use in a camera to take photographs: *to have a film developed* ◇ *Fast film is better if there's not much light.* ▶ (*fot.*) **film** ➲ note at **camera**

camera film

You **load** a film into a camera and **rewind** it when it is finished. When the film is **developed**, you can have **prints** made from the **negatives**.

5 [C, usually sing.] a thin layer of a substance or material: *The oil forms a film on the surface of the water.* ▶ **cienka powłoka, warstewka** ➲ look at **cling film**

film² /fɪlm/ verb [I,T] to record moving pictures of an event, story, etc. with a camera: *They're filming in Oxford today.* ◇ *The man was filmed stealing from the shop.* ▶ **filmować**

'film-goer (Brit. also **'cinema-goer**, US usually **moviegoer** /ˈmuːviɡəʊə(r)/) noun [C] a person who goes to the cinema, especially when they do it regularly ▶ **kinoman/ka**

'film-maker noun [C] a person who directs or produces films for the cinema or television ▶ **reżyser lub producent filmowy**
■ **'film-making** noun [U] ▶ **robienie filmów**

'film star noun [C] a person who is a famous actor in films ▶ **gwiazd-or/a filmow-y/a**

filter¹ /ˈfɪltə(r)/ noun [C] **1** a device for holding back solid substances from a liquid or gas that passes through it: *a coffee filter* ◇ *an oil filter* ▶ **filtr 2** a piece of coloured glass used with a camera to hold back some types of light ▶ (*fot.*) **filtr**

filter² /ˈfɪltə(r)/ verb **1** [T] to pass a liquid through a **filter**: *Do you normally filter your water?* ▶ **filtrować, odcedzać 2** [I] **filter in, out, through, etc.** to move slowly and/or in small amounts: *Sunlight filtered into the room through the curtains.* ◇ (figurative) *News of her illness filtered through to her friends.* ▶ **przeciekać, przenikać**
PHR V **filter sb/sth out (of sth)** to remove sth that you do not want from a liquid, light, etc. using a special device or substance: *This chemical filters impurities out of the water.* ◇ (figurative) *This test is designed to filter out weaker candidates before the interview stage.* ▶ **odfiltrować coś z czegoś**; (*przen.*) **odcedzać coś z czegoś, wyeliminować kogoś z czegoś**

filth /fɪlθ/ noun [U] **1** unpleasant dirt: *The room was covered in filth.* ▶ **brud, nieczystości 2** sexual words or pictures that cause offence ▶ **sprośne/nieprzyzwoite słowa/zdjęcia itp.**

filthy /ˈfɪlθi/ adj. (**filthier**; **filthiest**) **1** very dirty ▶ **bardzo brudny 2** (used about language, books, films, etc.) connected with sex, and causing offence ▶ **sprośny, nieprzyzwoity**
■ **filthy** (informal) adv. **1** (**filthy dirty**) extremely dirty ▶ **obrzydliwie brudny 2** (**filthy rich**) if you call sb **filthy rich**, you are saying that you find the large amount of money they have offensive ▶ **obrzydliwie bogaty**

fin /fɪn/ noun [C] **1** one of the parts of a fish that it uses for swimming ▶ **płetwa** ➲ picture on **page A11** ➲ look at **flipper 2** a flat, thin part that sticks out of an aircraft, a vehicle, etc. to improve its balance and movement through the air or water ▶ **statecznik, lotka**

final¹ /ˈfaɪnl/ adj. **1** [only before a noun] last (in a series): *This will be the final lesson of our course.* ◇ *I don't want to miss the final episode of that serial.* ▶ **ostatni, końcowy 2** not to be changed: *The judge's decision is always final.* ◇ *I'm not lending you the money, and that's final!* ▶ **ostateczny, rozstrzygający**
IDM **the last/final straw** → STRAW
the last/final word (on sth) → WORD

final² /ˈfaɪnl/ noun **1** [C] the last game or match in a series of competitions or sports events: *The first two runners in this race go through to the final.* ▶ (*sport*) **finał** ➲ look at **semi-final 2** (**finals**) [pl.] the exams you take in your last year at university: *I'm taking my finals in June.* ▶ **egzaminy końcowe**

finale /fɪˈnɑːli; US -ˈnæli/ noun [C] the last part of a piece of music, a show, etc. ▶ (*muz.; teatr*) *finał*

finalist /ˈfaɪnəlɪst/ noun [C] a person who is in the **final²** (1) of a competition ▶ **finalist(k)a** ➲ look at **semi-finalist**

finality /faɪˈnæləti/ noun [U] the quality of being final and impossible to change: *the finality of death* ◇ *There was a note of finality in his voice.* ▶ **ostateczność, nieodwołalność**

finalize (also **-ise**) /ˈfaɪnəlaɪz/ verb [T] to make firm decisions about plans, dates, etc.: *Have you finalized your holiday arrangements yet?* ▶ **finalizować**

finally /ˈfaɪnəli/ adv. **1** after a long time or delay: *It was getting dark when the plane finally took off.* ▶ **w końcu, ostatecznie, wreszcie** SYN **eventually 2** (used to introduce the last in a list of things): *Finally, I would like to say how much we have all enjoyed this evening.* ▶ **na koniec, kończąc** SYN **lastly 3** in a definite way so that sth will not be changed: *We haven't decided finally who will get the job yet.* ▶ **ostatecznie**

finance¹ /ˈfaɪnæns/ noun **1** [U] the money you need to start or support a business, etc.: *How will you raise the finance to start the project?* ▶ **fundusze 2** [U] the activity of managing money: *Who is the new Minister of Finance?* ◇ *an expert in finance* ekspert finansowy ▶ **finanse 3** (**finances**) [pl.] the money a person, company, country, etc. has to spend: *What are our finances like at the moment?* Jak obecnie przedstawia się nasza sytuacja finansowa? ▶ **fundusze**

finance² /ˈfaɪnæns; fəˈnæns/ verb [T] to provide the money to pay for sth ▶ **finansować**

financial /faɪˈnænʃl; fəˈnæ-/ adj. connected with money: *The business got into financial difficulties.* ▶ **finansowy**
■ **financially** adv. /-ʃəli/ ▶ **finansowo**

fiˌnancial ˈyear (Brit. also **ˈtax year**, US **ˌfiscal ˈyear**) noun [usually sing.] a period of twelve months over which the accounts and taxes of a company or a person are calculated: *the current financial year* ▶ **rok finansowy**

finch /fɪntʃ/ noun [C] a small bird with a short strong beak ▶ **zięba**

find¹ /faɪnd/ verb [T] (pt, pp **found** /faʊnd/) **1** to discover sth by chance: *I've found a piece of glass in this milk.* ◇ *We went into the house and found her lying on the floor.* ◇ *This particular species can be found* (występuje) *all over the world.* ▶ **odkrywać/znajdować przypadkowo 2** to discover sth that you want or that you have lost after searching for it: *Did you find the pen you lost?* ◇ *After six months she finally found a job.* ◇ *Scientists haven't yet found a cure for colds.* ◇ *I hope you find an answer to your problem.* ▶ **odnaleźć, znaleźć** ℹ Zwróć uwagę na zwroty **find the time, find the money**: *I never seem to find the time* (nigdy nie mam czasu) *to write letters these days.* ◇ *We'd like to go on holiday but we can't find the money* (nie mamy dość pieniędzy). **3** to have an opinion about sth because of your own experience: *I find that book very difficult to understand.* Ta książka jest dla mnie zbyt trudna. ◇ *We didn't find the film at all funny.* Naszym zdaniem film wcale nie był śmieszny. ◇ *How are you finding life as a student?* Jak ci się podoba życie studenckie? ◇ *I find that this rice takes longer to cook than most.* Według mnie ten ryż gotuje się dłużej niż inne. ◇ *The jury found the accused not guilty of murder.* Ława przysięgłych uznała oskarżonego za niewinnego. ▶ **oceniać, uważać 4** to suddenly realize or see sth: *I got home to find that I'd left the tap on all day.* ◇ *Ben turned a corner and suddenly found himself in the port.* ▶ **odkryć 5** to arrive somewhere naturally: *These birds **find their way** to Africa every winter.* ◇ *Water will always find its own level.* Woda zawsze będzie utrzymywać się na odpowiednim poziomie. ▶ **trafiać gdzieś, znajdować** (*drogę dokądś*)

IDM **find fault (with sb/sth)** to look for things that are wrong with sb/sth and complain about them: *Monica wouldn't make a good teacher because she's always finding fault with people.* ▶ **szukać dziury w całym**

find your feet to become confident and independent in a new situation: *Don't worry if the job seems difficult at first – you'll soon find your feet.* ▶ **stanąć na nogi**

get/find your bearings → BEARING

PHR V **find out (about sth/sb); find out sth (about sth/sb)** to get some information about sth/sb by asking, reading, etc.: *She'd been seeing the boy for a while, but didn't want her parents to find out.* ◇ *I haven't found anything out about him yet.* ◇ *Can you find out what time the meeting starts?* ◇ *We found out later that we had been at the same school.* ▶ **dowiadywać się (czegoś) (o czymś/kimś)**

find sb out to discover that sb has done sth wrong: *He had used a false name for years before they found him out.* ▶ **przyłapać kogoś (na czymś)**

find² /faɪnd/ noun [C] a thing or a person that has been found, especially one that is valuable or useful: *Archaeologists made some interesting finds when they dug up the field.* ◇ *This new young player is quite a find!* ▶ **skarb, odkrycie**

finder /ˈfaɪndə(r)/ noun [C] a person or thing that finds sth ▶ **znalazca**

finding /ˈfaɪndɪŋ/ noun [C, usually pl.] information that is discovered as a result of research into sth: *the findings of a survey/report/committee* ▶ **wyniki**

⚷ **fine¹** /faɪn/ adj. **1** [only before a noun] of very good quality, with great beauty or detail: *a fine piece of work* ◇ *fine detail/carving/china* ▶ **wspaniały, piękny 2** in good health, or happy and comfortable: *'How are you?' '**Fine thanks.**'* ◇ *'Do you want to change places?' 'No, I'm fine here, thanks.'* ▶ **zdrowy; zadowolony 3** good enough; acceptable: *'Bob wants to know if he can come too.' 'That's fine by me* (nie mam nic przeciwko temu).*'* ◇ *'Do you want some more milk in your coffee?' 'No, **that's fine**, thanks* (nie, dziękuję).*'* ◇ *Don't cook anything special – a sandwich will be fine* (wystarczy mi kanapka). ◇ *The hotel rooms were fine* (pokoje w hotelu były dość dobre) *but the food was awful.* ▶ **wystarczający, zadowalający** ℹ W znaczeniu 2 i 3 **fine** nie stosuje się w pytaniach ani przeczeniach. Nie można więc powiedzieć ~~*Are you fine?*~~ czy ~~*This isn't fine.*~~ **4** bright with sun; not raining: *Let's hope it stays fine for the match tomorrow.* ▶ (*pogoda*) **ładny 5** very thin or narrow: *That hairstyle's no good for me – my hair's too fine.* ◇ *You must use a fine pencil for the diagrams.* ▶ **cienki** OPP **thick 6** difficult to notice or understand: *I couldn't understand **the finer points** of his argument.* ◇ *There's **a fine line between*** (subtelna różnica) *being reserved and being unfriendly.* ▶ **subtelny, szczegółowy 7** made of very small pieces, grains, etc.: *Salt is finer than sugar.* ▶ **drobny, miałki** OPP **coarse**

fine² /faɪn/ noun [C] a sum of money that you have to pay for breaking a law or rule: *a parking fine* ◇ *You'll **get a fine** if you park your car there.* ▶ **grzywna, kara, mandat**

■ **fine** verb [T] **fine sb (for sth/doing sth)**: *He was fined £50 for driving without lights.* ▶ **karać grzywną/mandatem** ➲ note at **court**

fine ˈart noun [U] (also **fine ˈarts** [pl.]) forms of art, especially painting, drawing and **sculpture**, that are created to be beautiful rather than useful ▶ **sztuki piękne**

⚷ **finely** /ˈfaɪnli/ adv. **1** into small pieces: *The onions must be finely chopped for this recipe.* ▶ **drobno 2** very accurately: *a finely tuned instrument* ▶ **precyzyjnie**

the ˌfine ˈprint (US) = SMALL PRINT

finery /ˈfaɪnəri/ noun [U] (formal) brightly coloured and elegant clothes and jewellery, especially those that are worn for a special occasion: *The mayor was dressed in all his finery.* ▶ **odświętny i wytworny strój oraz dodatki do stroju**

⚷ **finger¹** /ˈfɪŋɡə(r)/ noun [C] one of the five parts at the end of each hand: *the little/ring* (serdeczny) *finger* ◇ *the middle finger* ◇ *the forefinger/index finger* palec wskazujący ▶ **palec** (*u ręki*)

> Czasami również kciuk, **thumb**, jest uważany za palec u ręki, a czasami nie: *Hold the pen between your finger and thumb.*
>
> Palce u nóg to **toes**. ➲ picture at **body**

IDM **cross your fingers; keep your fingers crossed** to hope that sb/sth will be successful or lucky: *There's nothing more we can do now – just cross our fingers and hope for the best.* ◇ *I'll keep my fingers crossed for you in your exams.* ▶ **trzymać kciuki**

> Angielski gest odnoszący się do tych wyrażeń różni się od polskiego tym, że palec środkowy zakłada się na palec wskazujący.

have green fingers; have a green thumb → GREEN¹

snap your fingers → SNAP¹

finger² /ˈfɪŋɡə(r)/ verb [T] to touch or feel sth with your fingers ▶ **dotykać palcami, macać**

fingermark /ˈfɪŋɡəmɑːk/ noun [C] a mark on sth made by a dirty finger ▶ **ślad palca**

fingernail /ˈfɪŋɡəneɪl/ (also **nail**) noun [C] the thin hard layer that covers the outer end of each finger ▶ **paznokieć** ➲ picture at **body**

fingerprint /ˈfɪŋɡəprɪnt/ noun [C] the mark made by the skin of a finger, used for identifying people: *The burglar left his fingerprints all over the house.* ◇ *The police **took** the suspect's **fingerprints*** (zdjęła odciski palców podejrzanego). ▶ **odcisk palca**

fingertip /ˈfɪŋɡətɪp/ noun [C] the end of your finger ▶ **koniuszek palca**

IDM **have sth at your fingertips** to have sth ready for quick and easy use: *They asked some difficult questions but luckily I had all the facts at my fingertips.* ▶ **mieć coś w małym palcu**

finicky /ˈfɪnɪki/ adj. **1** too worried about what you eat, wear, etc.; disliking many things: *a finicky eater* ▶ **wybredny** SYN **fussy 2** needing great care and attention to detail: *It's a very finicky job.* ▶ **wymagający zwracania uwagi na detale** SYN **fiddly**

⚷ **finish¹** /ˈfɪnɪʃ/ verb **1** [I,T] **finish (sth/doing sth)** to complete sth or reach the end of sth: *What time does the film finish?* ◇ *Haven't you finished yet? You've taken ages!* ◇ *The Ethiopian runner won and the Kenyans finished second and third.* ◇ *Finish your work quickly!* ◇ *Have you finished typing that letter?* ▶ **kończyć (się) 2** [T] **finish sth (off/up)** to eat, drink or use the last part of sth: *Finish up your milk, Tony!* ◇ *Who finished off all the bread?* ▶ **skończyć, dokończyć 3** [T] **finish sth (off)** to complete the last details of sth or make sth perfect: *He stayed up all night to finish off the article he was writing.* ◇ *He's just **putting the finishing touches to*** (wykańcza) *his painting.* ▶ **dokończyć**

F

PHR V **finish sb/sth off** (informal) to kill sb/sth; to be the thing that makes sb unable to continue: *The cat played with the mouse before finishing it off.* ◇ *I was very tired towards the end of the race, and that last hill finished me off.* ▶ **wykończyć kogoś/coś, zabić kogoś/coś**
finish up... (Brit.) to be in a particular state or at a particular place after a series of events: *If you're not careful, you could finish up seriously ill* (to się możesz poważnie rozchorować). ▶ **skończyć (gdzieś/w jakiejś sytuacji)**
finish (up) with sth to have sth at the end: *We had a five-course lunch and finished up with coffee and mints.* ◇ *To finish with* (na zakończenie), *we'll listen to a few songs.* ▶ **(za)kończyć czymś**
finish with sb/sth 1 to stop needing or using sb/sth: *I'll borrow that book when you've finished with it.* ▶ **skończyć z kimś/czymś 2** (informal) to end a relationship with sb: *Sally's not going out with David any more – she finished with him last week.* ▶ **zerwać z kimś**

finish² /ˈfɪnɪʃ/ noun [C] **1** the last part or end of sth: *There was a dramatic finish to the race when two runners fell.* ◇ *I enjoyed the film* ***from start to finish*** (od początku do końca). ◇ *The last race was a very close finish.* Przybiegli do mety prawie równocześnie. ▶ **meta 2** the last covering of paint, polish, etc. that is put on a surface to make it look good: *a gloss/matt finish* ▶ **wykończenie**

finished /ˈfɪnɪʃt/ adj. **1** [not before a noun] **be finished (with sb/sth)** to have stopped doing sth, using sth or dealing with sb/sth: *'Are you using the computer?' 'Yes, I won't be finished with it for another hour or so* (będę go używał jeszcze przez około godzinę).*'* ▶ **skończyć z kimś/czymś 2** [not before a noun] not able to continue: *The business is finished – there's no more money.* ▶ **skończony 3** made; completed: *the finished product/article* ▶ **skończony, gotowy**

ˈfinishing line (US ˈ**finish line**) noun [C] the line across a sports track, etc. that marks the end of a race: *The two horses crossed the finishing line together.* ▶ **linia mety**

finite /ˈfaɪnaɪt/ adj. having a definite limit or a fixed size: *The world's resources are finite.* ▶ **ograniczony**, (*matematyka*) **skończony**

fiord = FJORD

fir /fɜː(r)/ (also ˈ**fir tree**) noun [C] a tree with needles that do not fall off in winter ▶ **jodła**

ˈfir cone noun [C] the fruit of the **fir** tree ▶ **szyszka jodły**

fire¹ /ˈfaɪə(r)/ noun **1** [C,U] burning and flames, especially when it destroys and is out of control: *Firemen struggled for three hours to* ***put out the fire.*** ◇ *It had been a dry summer so there were many forest fires.* ◇ *In very hot weather, dry grass can* ***catch fire.*** ◇ *The furniture* ***caught fire*** (zapaliły się) *within seconds.* ◇ *Did someone* ***set fire to*** (podpalił) *that pile of wood?* ◇ *Help! The frying pan's* ***on fire*** (pali się)*!* ▶ **pożar 2** [C] burning wood or coal used for warming people or cooking food: *They tried to* ***light a fire*** *to keep warm.* ◇ *It's cold – don't let the fire go out!* ◇ *a camp fire* ognisko ▶ **ogień 3** [C] a machine for heating a room, etc.: *a gas/an electric fire* ◇ *an open fire* kominek ▶ **piecyk, piec 4** [U] shooting from guns: *The soldiers came* ***under fire*** (znaleźli się pod obstrzałem) *from all sides.* ◇ *I heard machine-gun fire in the distance.* ▶ **ogień**
IDM **come/be under fire** be strongly criticized: *The government has come under fire from all sides for its foreign policy.* ▶ **znaleźć się/być pod ostrzałem krytyki**
get on/along like a house on fire → HOUSE¹
open fire → OPEN²

fire² /ˈfaɪə(r)/ verb **1** [I,T] **fire (sth) (at sb/sth); fire (sth) (on/into sb/sth)** to shoot bullets, etc. from a gun or other weapon: *'Fire* (ognia)*!' shouted the officer.* ◇ *Can you hear the guns firing?* ◇ *She fired an arrow at the target.* ◇ *The soldiers fired on the crowd, killing twenty people.* ◇ (figurative) *If you stop firing questions at me* (jeśli przestaniesz zarzucać mnie pytaniami), *I might be able to answer!* ▶ **strzelać 2** [T] (especially US) = SACK²: *He* ***was fired for*** *always being late.* **3** [T] **fire sb with sth** to produce a strong feeling in sb: *Her speech fired me with determination.* ▶ **wzbudzać** (*silne emocje w kimś*)
PHR V **fire sth off 1** to shoot a bullet from a gun: *They fired off a volley of shots.* ▶ **wystrzeliwać coś 2** to write or say sth to sb very quickly, often when you are angry: *He fired off a letter of complaint.* ▶ **bez zastanowienia napisać jakiś tekst lub coś powiedzieć** (*zwł. w złości*)
fire sb up to make sb excited or interested in sth: *She's all fired up about her new job.* ▶ **zapalać kogoś (do czegoś), rozbudzać w kimś** (*np. zapał*)

ˈfire alarm noun [C] a bell or other signal to warn people that there is a fire ▶ **alarm pożarowy**

firearm /ˈfaɪərɑːm/ noun [C] a gun that you can carry ▶ **broń palna**

ˈfire brigade (US ˈ**fire department**) noun [C, with sing. or pl. verb] an organization of people trained to deal with fires ▶ **straż pożarna**

-fired /ˈfaɪəd/ [in compounds] using the fuel mentioned: *gas-fired central heating* centralne ogrzewanie gazowe ▶ *(w złożeniach – oznacza rodzaj paliwa)*

ˈfire department (US) = FIRE BRIGADE

ˈfire engine noun [C] a special vehicle that carries equipment for dealing with large fires ▶ **wóz strażacki**

ˈfire escape noun [C] a special set of stairs on the outside of a building that people can go down if there is a fire ▶ **wyjście ewakuacyjne**

ˈfire extinguisher (also **extinguisher**) noun [C] a metal container with water or chemicals inside that you use for stopping small fires ▶ **gaśnica**

firefighter /ˈfaɪəfaɪtə(r)/ noun [C] a person whose job is to stop fires ▶ **straża-k/czka**

firelight /ˈfaɪəlaɪt/ noun [U] the light that comes from a fire ▶ **blask ognia**

fireman /ˈfaɪəmən/ noun [C] (pl. **-men** /-mən/) a man whose job is to stop fires ▶ **strażak**

fireplace /ˈfaɪəpleɪs/ noun [C] the open place in a room where you light a fire ▶ **kominek** ➲ look at **hearth**

fireside /ˈfaɪəsaɪd/ noun [sing.] the part of a room beside the fire: *Come and sit by the fireside.* ▶ **miejsce przy kominku**

fireplace

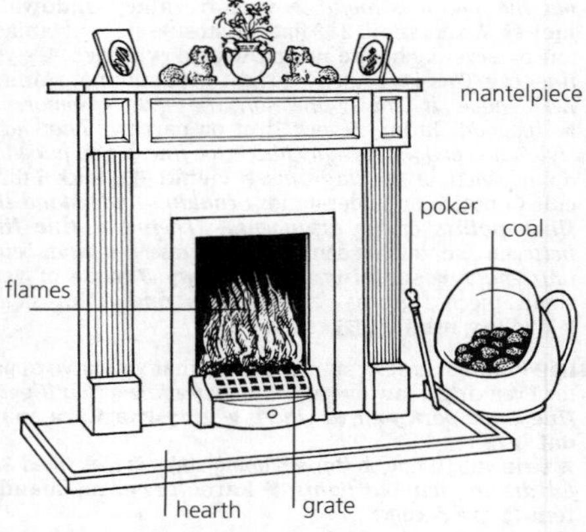

ˈfire station noun [C] a building where **firefighters** wait to be called, and where the vehicles that they use are kept ▶ **remiza strażacka**

firewall /ˈfaɪəwɔːl/ noun [C] part of a computer system that prevents people from looking at or changing information on a computer system without permission, but allows them to receive information that is sent to them ▶ (*komput.*) **zapora sieciowa**

firewood /ˈfaɪəwʊd/ noun [U] wood used for burning on fires ▶ **drewno opałowe**

firework /ˈfaɪəwɜːk/ noun [C] a small object that burns or explodes with coloured lights and loud sounds, used for entertainment ▶ **sztuczny ogień, fajerwerk** ℹ **Firework**, choć poprawne w lp, jest często używane w lm: *We went to watch the fireworks in Hyde Park.*

ˈfiring line noun
IDM **be in the firing line** (US **be on the ˈfiring line**) **1** to be in a position where you can be shot at: *attempts to prevent civilians from being in the firing line* ▶ **być na linii ognia 2** to be in a position where people can criticize or blame you: *The employment secretary found himself in the firing line over recent job cuts.* ▶ **być pod ostrzałem krytyki**

ˈfiring squad noun [C] a group of soldiers who have been ordered to shoot and kill a prisoner ▶ **pluton egzekucyjny**

firm¹ /fɜːm/ noun [C, with sing. or pl. verb] a business company: *The firm is/are opening new stores every year.* ▶ **firma, przedsiębiorstwo**

firm² /fɜːm/ adj. **1** able to stay the same shape when pressed; quite hard: *a firm mattress* ◇ *firm muscles* ▶ **twardy**, (*owoce itp.*) **jędrny** ➲ look at **hard 2** strong and steady or not likely to change: *a firm commitment/decision* ◇ *She kept a firm grip on* (mocno trzymała) *her mother's hand.* ◇ *Have you got a firm date for your holiday yet?* Czy ustaliłeś już datę urlopu? ◇ *I've got a firm offer* (poważną ofertę) *of a job in New York.* ▶ **mocny, niezmienny 3 firm (with sb)** strong and in control: *He's very firm with his children.* ◇ *You have to show the examiner that you have a firm grasp of grammar* (solidną znajomość gramatyki). ▶ **stanowczy (wobec kogoś)**
■ **firmly** adv.: *to hold sth firmly* trzymać coś mocno ◇ *It is now firmly established as one of the leading brands in the country.* Wyrobiła sobie mocną pozycję jednej z wiodących marek w kraju. ◇ *Keep your eyes firmly fixed on the road ahead.* Nie odrywaj wzroku od drogi przed sobą. ▶ **twardo**; **stanowczo** | **firmness** noun [U] ▶ **jędrność**; **stanowczość**
IDM **a firm hand** strong control or discipline: *Those children need a teacher with a firm hand.* ▶ **twarda/żelazna ręka**

first¹ /fɜːst/ determiner, ordinal number coming before all others; that has not happened before: *the first half of the game* ◇ *King Charles I* ◇ *My first choice is blue* (w pierwszej kolejności wezmę niebieski), *but I'll take green if there's no blue left.* ◇ *What were your first impressions of this country when you arrived?* ▶ **pierwszy** ➲ note at **sixth** ➲ look at **one**
IDM **at first glance/sight** when first seen or examined: *The task seemed impossible at first glance, but it turned out to be quite easy.* ◇ *It was* ***love at first sight*** (miłość od pierwszego wejrzenia). ▶ **na pierwszy rzut oka**
first/last thing → THING

first² /fɜːst/ adv. **1** before any others: *Sue arrived first at the party.* ◇ *Mike's very competitive – he always wants to* ***come first*** *when he plays a game.* ◇ *Do you want to* ***go first*** *or second?* ▶ **(jako) pierwszy 2** before doing anything else: *I'll come out later. I've got to finish my homework first.* ▶ **najpierw 3** the time before all the other times; for the first time: *Where did you first meet your husband?* ▶ **po raz pierwszy 4** (used for introducing the first thing in a list): *There are several people I would like to thank: first, my mother.* ▶ **po pierwsze, w pierwszej kolejności** SYN **firstly 5** at the beginning: *When I first started my job I hated it.* ▶ **na początku**
IDM **at first** at the beginning: *At first I thought he was joking, but then I realized he was serious.* ▶ **z początku**
come first to be more important to sb than anything else: *Although she enjoys her job, her family has always come first.* ▶ **być najważniejszym**
first and foremost more than anything else; most importantly: *He worked in TV but he was a stage actor first and foremost.* ▶ **nade wszystko**
first come, first served (informal) people will be dealt with, served, seen, etc. strictly in the order in which they arrive: *Tickets can be bought here on a first come, first served basis.* ▶ **kto pierwszy, ten lepszy**
first of all as the first thing (to be done or said): *In a moment I'll introduce our guest speaker, but first of all, let me thank you all for coming.* ▶ **najpierw**
first off (informal) before anything else: *First off, let's decide who does what.* ▶ **najpierw**
head first → HEAD¹

first³ /fɜːst/ noun **1** (**the first**) [C] (pl. **the first**) the first person or thing, people or things: *Are we the first to arrive?* ◇ *They enjoyed the holiday – their first for ten years.* ▶ **pierwszy 2** (**a first**) [sing.] an important event that is happening for the first time: *This operation is a first in medical history.* ▶ **pierwszy przypadek 3** [C] **a first (in sth)** the highest level of degree given by a British university: *He* ***got a first*** *in History at Liverpool.* ▶ **dyplom ukończenia studiów z wyróżnieniem**
IDM **from the (very) first** from the beginning: *They hated each other from the first.* ▶ **od (samego) początku**

ˌfirst ˈaid noun [U] medical help that you give to sb who is hurt or ill before the doctor arrives: *a first aid kit* apteczka ◇ *a first aid course* ◇ *to give somebody first aid* ▶ **pierwsza pomoc**

ˌfirst ˈclass¹ noun [U] **1** the best and most expensive seats on a train, ship, etc.: *There is more room in first class.* ▶ **pierwsza klasa 2** (Brit.) the way of sending letters, etc. that is faster but more expensive than **second class**: *First class costs more.* ▶ **przesyłka priorytetowa**

W Wlk. Br. są dwa rodzaje znaczków krajowych: **first class** i **second class**. **First-class stamps** są droższe, za to list z takim znaczkiem idzie szybciej.

■ **ˌfirst-ˈclass** adv.: *to travel first-class* podróżować pierwszą klasą ◇ *to send a letter first-class* wysłać list jako priorytetowy

ˌfirst-ˈclass² adj. **1** of the best quality; of the highest standard: *a first-class player* ◇ *This book is really first-class.* ▶ **pierwszorzędny, znakomity** SYN **excellent 2** [only before a noun] (used about the best and most expensive seats on a train, ship, etc.): *a first-class cabin/seat/ticket* ▶ **pierwszej klasy 3** [only before a noun] (Brit.) (used about the way of sending letters, etc. that is faster but more expensive than **second-class**): *first-class mail/letters/stamps* ▶ (*przesyłka itp.*) **priorytetowy 4** [only before a noun] (used about a British university degree) of the highest level: *a first-class honours degree in geography* ▶ (*dyplom wyższej uczelni*) **z wyróżnieniem**

ˌfirst ˈcousin = COUSIN

the ˌfirst ˈfloor noun [C] **1** (Brit.) the floor of a building above the **ground floor**: *I live in a flat* ***on the first floor.*** ◇ *a first-floor flat* ▶ **pierwsze piętro 2** (US) = GROUND FLOOR

ˌfirst ˈgear noun [C] the lowest gear on a car, bicycle, etc.: *To move off,* ***put the car into first gear*** *and slowly release the clutch.* ▶ **pierwszy bieg**

first-hand /ˌfɜːst ˈhænd/ adj. (used about information, experience, a story, etc.) heard, seen or learnt by your-

self, not from other people: *He gave me a first-hand account of the accident.* ▶ **z pierwszej ręki, bezpośredni**
■ **first-hand** adv.: *I've experienced the problem first-hand* (znam ten problem z własnego doświadczenia), *so I know how you feel.* ▶ **z pierwszej ręki, bezpośrednio**

firstly /ˈfɜːstli/ adv. (used to introduce the first point in a list): *They were angry firstly because they had to pay extra, and secondly because no one had told them about it.* ▶ **po pierwsze** SYN **first**[2] (4)

ˈfirst name noun [C] the first of your names that come before your family name: *'What's Mr Kowalski's first name?' 'Jan, I think.'* ▶ **imię** ➲ note at **name**[1]

the ˌfirst ˈperson noun [sing.] **1** the words such as 'I', 'me', 'we', and the verb forms that go with them: *'I am' is the first person singular of the verb 'to be'.* ▶ (*gram.*) **pierwsza osoba 2** the style of telling a story as if it happened to you: *The author writes **in the first person**.* ▶ **pierwsza osoba** (*narracji*)

ˌfirst-ˈrate adj. excellent; of the best quality ▶ **pierwszorzędny**

ˈfir tree = FIR

fiscal /ˈfɪskl/ adj. connected with government or public money, especially taxes: ***fiscal policies/reforms*** ▶ **fiskalny**

ˌfiscal ˈyear (US) = FINANCIAL YEAR

fish[1] /fɪʃ/ noun (pl. **fish** or **fishes**) **1** [C] an animal that lives and breathes in water and swims: *How many fish have you caught?* ▶ **ryba** ➲ picture on **page A11** ➲ note at **salt water** ⓘ W lm najczęściej używa się formy **fish**. **Fishes** stosuje się, gdy mówimy o różnych gatunkach ryb: *I went diving on holiday – it was fantastic to see so many different fishes* (gatunki ryb). **2** [U] fish as food: *We're having fish for dinner.* ▶ **ryba**

fish[2] /fɪʃ/ verb [I] **1 fish (for sth)** to try to catch fish: *He's fishing for trout.* ▶ **łowić ryby** ⓘ Mówiąc o łowieniu ryb dla przyjemności, zwykle używa się zwrotu **go fishing**: *They often go fishing at weekends.* **2 fish (around) (in sth) (for sth)** to search for sth in water or in a deep or hidden place: *She fished (around) for her keys in the bottom of her bag.* ▶ **szukać czegoś w wodzie lub w czymś głębokim** (*np. w torbie*)
PHR V **fish for sth** to try to get sth you want in an indirect way: *to fish for an invitation* ▶ **próbować coś wydębić**
fish sth out (of sth) to take or pull sth out (of sth) especially after searching for it: *After the accident they fished the car out of the canal.* ▶ **wydobyć coś (skądś), wyciągać coś (skądś)**

ˌfish and ˈchips noun [U] fried fish and potato chips often bought already cooked and taken away to eat ▶ **ryba z frytkami**

> You buy fish and chips at a **fish and chip shop**. The fish is covered with **batter** and **deep-fried**. You find a fish and chip shop in most British towns. ➲ picture on **page A14, page A5**

fishcake /ˈfɪʃkeɪk/ noun [C] (especially Brit.) pieces of fish mixed with potato that are made into a flat round shape, covered with **breadcrumbs** and fried ▶ **kotlet rybny**

fisherman /ˈfɪʃəmən/ noun [C] (pl. **-men** /-mən/) a person who catches fish either as a job or as a sport ▶ **rybak, wędkarz** ➲ look at **angler** ➲ picture on **page A4**

fishery /ˈfɪʃəri/ noun [C] (pl. **fisheries**) **1** a part of the sea or a river where fish are caught in large quantities: *a herring fishery* ◇ ***coastal/freshwater fisheries*** ▶ **łowisko** (*na terenach wodnych*) **2** = FISH FARM: *a trout fishery*

ˈfish farm (also **fishery**) noun [C] a place where fish are bred as a business ▶ **gospodarstwo rybne**

ˌfish ˈfinger (US ˌ**fish ˈstick**) noun [C] a long narrow piece of fish covered with **breadcrumbs** or **batter**, usually frozen and sold in packs ▶ **paluszek rybny**

fishing /ˈfɪʃɪŋ/ noun [U] catching fish as a job, sport or hobby: *Fishing is a major industry in Iceland.* ▶ **rybołówstwo; wędkarstwo** ➲ look at **angling**

ˈfishing rod noun [C] a long thin stick with a line and a hook on it for catching fish ▶ **wędka**

fishmonger /ˈfɪʃmʌŋɡə(r)/ noun (Brit.) **1** [C] a person whose job is to sell fish ▶ **sprzedaw-ca/czyni ryb 2** (**the fishmonger's**) [sing.] a shop that sells fish ▶ **sklep rybny**

ˈfish slice (US **spatula**) noun [C] a kitchen utensil that has a broad flat blade with narrow holes in it attached to a long handle, used for turning and lifting food when cooking ▶ **łopatka kuchenna**

ˌfish ˈstick (US) = FISH FINGER

fishy /ˈfɪʃi/ adj. (**fishier**; **fishiest**) **1** (informal) seeming wrong, dishonest or illegal: *The police thought the man's story sounded extremely fishy.* ▶ **podejrzany** SYN **suspicious** **2** tasting or smelling like a fish: *a fishy smell* ▶ **rybi**

fission /ˈfɪʃn/ noun [U] (also ˌ**nuclear ˈfission**) the act or process of splitting the **nucleus** of an atom, when a large amount of energy is produced ▶ (*fiz.*) **rozszczepienie** (*jądra atomu*) ➲ look at **fusion, nuclear**

fissure /ˈfɪʃə(r)/ noun [C] (technical) a long deep crack in sth, especially in rock or in the earth ▶ **szczelina, szpara**

fist /fɪst/ noun [C] a hand with the fingers closed together tightly: *She **clenched** her **fists** in anger.* ▶ **pięść**

fit[1] /fɪt/ verb (**fitting**; **fitted**) **1** [I,T] to be the right size or shape for sb/sth: *These jeans fit very well.* ◇ *This dress doesn't fit me any more.* Ta suknia nie jest już na mnie dobra. ◇ *This key doesn't fit in the lock.* ◇ *How do these two parts fit together* (pasują do siebie)*?* ◇ *The glass fits on top of the jug to form a lid.* Szklanka jest dopasowana do góry dzbanka w taki sposób, by tworzyć pokrywkę. ▶ **być w odpowiednim rozmiarze; pasować 2** [T] **fit (sb/sth) in/into/on/onto sth** to find or have enough space for sb/sth: *I can't fit into these trousers any more.* ◇ *Can you fit one more person in the car?* ◇ *I can't fit all these books onto the shelf.* ▶ **mieścić (się) 3** [T] to put or fix sth in the right place: *They fitted a smoke alarm to the ceiling.* ◇ *The builders are fitting* (wstawiają) *new windows today.* ◇ *I can't fit these pieces of the model together.* Nie mogę złożyć części modelu. ◇ *We fitted together* (ułożyliśmy) *the pieces of the puzzle.* ▶ **montować 4** [T] to be or make sb/sth right or suitable: *The description fits Jo perfectly.* Jo doskonale odpowiada temu opisowi. ◇ *I don't think Tom's fitted* (jest odpowiednią osobą) *for such a demanding job.* ▶ **być/czynić odpowiednim**
PHR V **fit sb/sth in**; **fit sb/sth in/into sth** to find time to see sb or to do sth: *The doctor managed to fit me in this morning.* ◇ *You're tired because you're trying to fit too much into one day.* ▶ **znajdować czas na przyjęcie/spotkanie itp. kogoś, wciskać**
fit in (with sb/sth) to be able to live, work, etc. in an easy and natural way (with sb/sth): *The new girl found it difficult to fit in (with the other children) at school.* ◇ *I will happily change my plans to fit in with yours.* ▶ **dostosowywać się**

fit[2] /fɪt/ adj. (**fitter**; **fittest**) **1 fit (for sth/to do sth)** strong and in good physical health (especially because of exercise): *Swimming is a good way to **keep fit**.* ◇ *My dad's almost recovered from his illness, but he's still not fit enough for work.* ◇ *She goes to keep-fit classes.* ▶ **w (dobrej) formie** OPP **unfit 2 fit (for sb/sth)**; **fit to do sth** good enough; suitable: *Do you think she is fit for the job?* ◇ *These houses are not fit (for people) to live in.* ▶ **odpowiedni, nadający się**

fit³ /fɪt/ noun **1** [C] a sudden attack of an illness, in which sb becomes unconscious and their body may make violent movements: *to have fits* ▶ **atak** (*drgawek*) **2** [C] a sudden short period of coughing, laughing, etc. that you cannot control: *a fit of laughter/anger* ▶ **napad** (*np. złości, śmiechu*), **przypływ** (*np. gniewu*) **3** [sing.] [usually after an adjective] the way in which sth (for example a piece of clothing) fits: *a good/bad/tight/loose fit* ▶ **dopasowanie**, **rozmiar**

fitful /'fɪtfl/ adj. happening only for short periods; not continuous or regular: *a fitful* (niespokojny) *night's sleep* ▶ **krótkotrwały**; **nieciągły**; **nieregularny** ■ **fitfully** /'fɪtfəli/ adv.: *to sleep fitfully* ▶ **krótkotrwale**; **bez ciągłości**; **nieregularnie**

fitness /'fɪtnəs/ noun [U] **1** the condition of being strong and healthy: *Fitness is important in most sports.* ▶ **(dobra) forma**, **kondycja** **2 fitness for sth/to do sth** the quality of being suitable: *The directors were not sure about his fitness for the job.* ▶ **zdatność**

'fitness centre (US **'fitness center**) noun [C] a place where people go to do physical exercise in order to stay or become healthy and fit ▶ **centrum fitnessu**

fitted /'fɪtɪd/ adj. [only before a noun] made or cut to fit a particular space and fixed there: *a fitted carpet* wykładzina dywanowa (położona w pomieszczeniu) ◇ *a fitted kitchen* kuchnia z zamontowanym wyposażeniem ◇ *fitted cupboards* zamontowane szafki ▶ **dopasowany**, **zabudowany**

fitting¹ /'fɪtɪŋ/ adj. **1** (formal) right; suitable: *It was fitting for the Olympics to be held in Greece, as that is where they originated.* ▶ **odpowiedni**, **stosowny** **2** (**-fitting**) (used in compounds to describe how clothes, etc. fit): *a tight-fitting dress* ◇ *loose-fitting trousers* ▶ **dopasowany**

fitting² /'fɪtɪŋ/ noun [C, usually pl.] the things that are fixed in a building or on a piece of furniture but that can be changed or moved if necessary ▶ **wyposażenie ruchome** ➲ look at **fixture**

'fitting room noun [C] a room in a shop where you can put on clothes to see how they look ▶ **przymierzalnia** ➲ look at **changing room**

⚷ **five** /faɪv/ number **1** 5 ▶ **pięć** ➲ note at **six** ➲ look at **fifth** **2** (**five-**) [in compounds] having five of the thing mentioned: *a five-day week* ▶ **pięcio**
IDM **nine to five** → NINE

fiver /'faɪvə(r)/ noun [C] (informal) **1** (Brit.) £5 or a five-pound note: *Can you lend me a fiver?* ▶ **banknot pięciofuntowy**; **pięć funtów** **2** (old-fashioned) $5 or a five dollar note ▶ **banknot pięciodolarowy**; **pięć dolarów**

⚷ **fix¹** /fɪks/ verb [T] **1** to put sth firmly in place so that it will not move: *Can you fix this new handle to the door?* ◇ (figurative) *I found it difficult to keep my mind fixed on my work.* ▶ **zamocować**; **koncentrować** **2 fix sth (up)** to decide or arrange sth: *We need to fix the price.* ◇ *Have you fixed (up) a date for the party?* ▶ **ustalać** **3** (especially US) **fix sth (for sb)** to prepare sth (especially food or drink): *Can I fix you a drink/a drink for you?* ▶ **przygotowywać** **4** to repair sth: *The electrician's coming to fix the cooker.* ▶ **naprawiać** **5** [usually passive] (informal) to arrange the result of sth in a way that is not honest or fair: *Fans of the losing team suspected that the match had been fixed.* ▶ **ustawiać** (*np. wynik meczu*)
PHR V **fix sb up (with sth)** (informal) to arrange for sb to have sth: *I can fix you up with a place to stay.* ▶ **załatwiać coś dla kogoś**
fix sth (up) to get sth ready: *They're fixing up their spare room for the new baby.* ▶ **przygotowywać coś**

fix² /fɪks/ noun [C] **1** a solution to a problem, especially one that is easy or temporary: *There's no* ***quick fix*** *to this problem.* ▶ **rozwiązanie** **2** [usually sing.] (informal) a difficult situation: *I was* ***in a*** *real fix – I'd locked the car keys inside the car.* ▶ **kłopotliwa sytuacja** **3** [usually sing.] (informal) a result that is dishonestly arranged ▶ **wynik sfingowany/sfałszowany** **4** (informal) an amount of something that you need and want frequently, especially an illegal drug ▶ **działka** (*np. narkotyków*), **dawka** (*np. kofeiny*)

fixated /fɪk'seɪtɪd/ adj. [not before a noun] **fixated (on sb/sth)** always thinking and talking about sb/sth in a way that is not normal ▶ **mający obsesję (na punkcie kogoś/czegoś)**

fixation /fɪk'seɪʃn/ noun [C] **a fixation (with sth)** an interest in sth that is too strong and not normal ▶ **mania**, **obsesja**

fixative /'fɪksətɪv/ noun [C, U] **1** a substance that is used to prevent colours or smells from changing or becoming weaker, for example in photography, art or the making of **perfume** ▶ **środek utrwalający** (*zwł. do kolorów i zapachów*) **2** a substance that is used to stick things together or keep things in position ▶ **środek mocujący**

F

⚷ **fixed** /fɪkst/ adj. **1** already decided: *a fixed date/price/rent* ▶ **ustalony** ➲ look at **movable** **2** not changing: *He has such fixed ideas that you can't discuss anything with him.* ◇ *She looked at him with a fixed smile* (z uśmiechem przyklejonym do twarzy). ▶ **niezmienny**, **stały**
IDM **(of) no fixed abode/address** (formal) (with) no permanent place to live: *Daniel Stephens, of no fixed abode, was found guilty of robbery.* ▶ **bez stałego miejsca zamieszkania**

fixture /'fɪkstʃə(r)/ noun [C] **1** a sports event arranged for a particular day: *to arrange/cancel/play a fixture* ▶ **impreza sportowa wyznaczona na dany dzień** **2** [usually pl.] a piece of furniture or equipment that is fixed in a house or building and sold with it: *Does the price of the house include fixtures and fittings?* ▶ **wyposażenie stałe**, **osprzęt** ➲ look at **fitting**

fizz /fɪz/ noun [U] the bubbles in a liquid and the sound they make: *This lemonade's lost its fizz.* ▶ **bąbelki**, **gaz** ■ **fizz** verb [I] ▶ **musować**

fizzle /'fɪzl/ verb
PHR V **fizzle out** to end in a weak or disappointing way: *The game started well but it fizzled out in the second half.* ▶ **kończyć się rozczarowaniem**

fizzy /'fɪzi/ adj. (**fizzier**; **fizziest**) (used about a drink) containing many small bubbles of gas ▶ **gazowany**, **musujący** ➲ look at **still** ℹ Mówiąc o wodzie mineralnej lub winie, zwykle używa się słowa **sparkling**, a nie **fizzy**.

,fizzy 'drink (US **soda**) noun [C] a sweet drink without alcohol that contains many small bubbles ▶ **napój gazowany**

fjord (also **fiord**) /'fjɔːd/ noun [C] a long narrow piece of sea between **cliffs**, especially in Norway ▶ **fiord**

flabbergasted /'flæbəgɑːstɪd; US -gæst-/ adj. (informal) extremely surprised and/or shocked ▶ **oszołomiony**, **wstrząśnięty**

flabby /'flæbi/ adj. (**flabbier**; **flabbiest**) **1** (used about a person) having too much soft fat instead of muscle: *a flabby stomach* ▶ **sflaczały** **2** (used about muscles, arms, legs, etc.) too soft ▶ **zwiotczały**

flack = FLAK

⚷ **flag¹** /flæg/ noun [C] a piece of cloth with a pattern or picture on it, often tied to a **flagpole** or a rope and used as a symbol of a country, club, etc. or as a signal ▶ **flaga**, **chorągiew(ka)**

flag² /flæg/ verb [I] (**flagging**; **flagged**) to become tired or less strong ▶ **tracić siły**, **oklapnąć**
PHR V **flag sb/sth down** to wave to sb in a car to make them stop: *to flag down* (zatrzymać) *a taxi* ▶ **machać na kogoś/coś** (*w celu zatrzymania kogoś/czegoś*)

flagpole /'flægpəʊl/ (also **flagstaff**) noun [C] a tall pole on which a flag is hung ▶ **maszt flagowy**

flagrant /ˈfleɪɡrənt/ adj. [only before a noun] (used about an action) shocking because it is done in a very obvious way and shows no respect for people, laws, etc. ▶ **skandaliczny**, **rażący**

flail /fleɪl/ verb [I,T] to wave or move about without control: *The insect's legs were flailing in the air.* ◇ *Don't flail your arms about like that – you might hurt someone.* ▶ **rzucać się**; **wymachiwać**

flair /fleə(r)/ noun **1** [sing.] **(a) flair for sth** a natural ability to do sth well: *She **has a flair for*** (ma talent do) *languages.* ▶ **talent**, **zdolności 2** [U] the quality of being interesting or having style: *That poster is designed with her usual flair.* ▶ **polot**

flak (also **flack**) /flæk/ noun [U] (informal) criticism: *He'll get some flak for missing that goal.* ◇ *The plans have come in for a lot of flak* (znalazły się pod ostrzałem krytyki). ▶ **krytyka**

flake¹ /fleɪk/ noun [C] a small thin piece of sth: *snowflakes* ◇ *flakes of paint* ▶ **płatek**

flake² /fleɪk/ verb [I] **flake (off)** to come off in **flakes**: *This paint is very old – it's beginning to flake (off).* ▶ **łuszczyć się**, **odpadać płatami**
PHR V **flake out** (informal) to lie down or fall asleep because you are extremely tired: *When I got home he'd already flaked out on the bed.* ▶ **padać ze zmęczenia**

ˈflak jacket noun [C] a heavy jacket without sleeves that has metal inside it to make it stronger, and is worn by soldiers and police officers to protect them from bullets ▶ **kamizelka kuloodporna**

flaky /ˈfleɪki/ adj. **1** tending to break into small, thin pieces: *flaky pastry* ◇ *dry flaky skin* ▶ **odpadający**, **łuszczący się 2** (US, informal) (used about a person) behaving in a strange or unusual way; tending to forget things: *He plays a flaky tourist visiting Europe.* ▶ **dziwaczny**, **roztargniony 3** (informal) (used about a device or software) likely to break down ▶ (*urządzenie, oprogramowanie*) **podatny na zepsucie się/stłuczenie/pęknięcie**
■ **flakiness** noun [U] ▶ **odpadanie**, **łuszczenie się**; **dziwactwo i roztargnienie**; **podatność na zepsucie się/stłuczenie/pęknięcie**

flamboyant /flæmˈbɔɪənt/ adj. **1** (used about a person) acting in a loud, confident way that attracts attention: *a flamboyant gesture/style/personality* ▶ **wyzywający**, **ekstrawagancki 2** bright and easily noticed: *flamboyant colours* ▶ **krzykliwy**
■ **flamboyance** noun [U] ▶ **wyzywający styl**, **ekstrawagancja**; **krzykliwość** | **flamboyantly** adv. ▶ **w sposób wyzywający/ekstrawagancki/krzykliwy**

flame /fleɪm/ noun [C,U] an area of bright burning gas that comes from sth that is on fire: *The flame of the candle flickered by the open window.* ◇ *The house was **in flames*** (płonął) *when the fire engine arrived.* ◇ *The piece of paper **burst into flames*** (stanął w płomieniach) *in the fire.* ▶ **płomień** ➲ picture at **fireplace**

flaming /ˈfleɪmɪŋ/ adj. [only before a noun] **1** (used about anger, an argument, etc.) violent: *We had a flaming argument over the bills.* ▶ **gwałtowny 2** burning brightly ▶ **płonący 3** (slang) (used as a mild swear word): *I can't get in – I've lost the flaming key.* ▶ **przeklęty**, **cholerny 4** (used about colours, especially red) very bright: *flaming red hair* ◇ *a flaming sunset* ▶ **ognisty**, **jaskrawy**

flamingo /fləˈmɪŋɡəʊ/ (pl. **flamingoes** or **flamingos**) noun [C] a large pink and red bird that has long legs and stands in water ▶ **flaming**

flammable /ˈflæməbl/ adj. able to burn easily ▶ **łatwopalny** OPP **non-flammable** ℹ **Inflammable** oznacza to samo co **flammable** i jest słowem częściej używanym.

flan /flæn/ noun [C,U] a round open **pie** that is filled with fruit, cheese, vegetables, etc. ▶ **placek**, **tarta** ➲ note at **pie**

flank¹ /flæŋk/ noun [C] **1** the parts of an army at the sides in a battle ▶ **skrzydło** (*oddziału wojska*) **2** the side of an animal's body ▶ **bok** (*zwierzęcia*)

flank² /flæŋk/ verb [T, usually passive] to be placed at the side or sides of: *The road was flanked by trees.* Droga była wysadzona drzewami. ▶ **znajdować się po obu stronach**

flannel /ˈflænl/ noun **1** [U] a type of soft cloth made of wool ▶ **flanela 2** = FACECLOTH

flap¹ /flæp/ noun [C] a piece of cloth, paper, etc. that is fixed to sth at one side only, often covering an opening: *the flap of an envelope* ▶ **klapka**, **poła**, **skrzydełko**
IDM **be in/get into a flap** (informal) to be in/get into a state of worry or excitement ▶ **być zdenerwowanym**; **zdenerwować się**

flap² /flæp/ verb (**flapping**; **flapped**) **1** [I,T] to move (sth) up and down or from side to side, especially in the wind: *The sails were flapping in the wind.* ◇ *The bird flapped its wings and flew away.* ▶ **trzepotać (się) 2** [I] (informal) to become worried or excited: *Stop flapping – it's all organized!* ▶ **przejmować się**, **denerwować się**

flapjack /ˈflæpdʒæk/ noun **1** [U,C] (Brit.) a thick soft biscuit made from **oats**, butter, sugar and **syrup** ▶ **kruche ciastko z płatkami owsianymi 2** [C] (US) a thick **pancake** ▶ **gruby naleśnik**

flare¹ /fleə(r)/ verb [I] to burn for a short time with a sudden bright flame ▶ **zapłonąć**
PHR V **flare up 1** (used about a fire) to suddenly burn more strongly ▶ **wybuchać płomieniem 2** (used about violence, anger, etc.) to start suddenly or to become suddenly worse ▶ **wybuchać gniewem**

flare² /fleə(r)/ noun **1** [sing.] a sudden bright light or flame ▶ **płomień**, **błysk 2** [C] a thing that produces a bright light or flame, used especially as a signal ▶ **rakieta świetlna**

flared /fleəd/ adj. (used about trousers and skirts) becoming wider towards the bottom edge: *flared jeans/trousers* dzwony ▶ **rozszerzany dołem**

flash¹ /flæʃ/ verb **1** [I,T] to produce or make sth produce a sudden bright light for a short time: *The neon sign above the door flashed on and off all night.* ◇ *That lorry driver's flashing his lights at us.* ▶ **błyskać (się)**, **świecić (się) 2** [T] to show sth quickly: *The detective flashed his card and went straight in.* ▶ **pomachać (czymś)**, **migać (czymś)**; **rzucać** (*np. spojrzenie, uśmiech*) **3** [I] to move very fast: *I saw something flash past the window.* ◇ *Thoughts kept flashing through my mind and I couldn't sleep.* ▶ **migać**, **przemykać 4** [T] to send sth by radio, TV, etc.: *The news of the disaster was flashed across the world.* ▶ **nadawać błyskawicznie**
PHR V **flash back (to sth)** (used about sb's thoughts) to return suddenly to a time in the past: *Something he said made my mind flash back to my childhood.* ▶ **przywołać wspomnienia czegoś**

flash² /flæʃ/ noun **1** [C] a sudden bright light that comes and goes quickly: *a flash of lightning* ▶ **błysk**, **błyskawica 2** [C] **a flash (of sth)** a sudden strong feeling or idea: *a flash of inspiration* ▶ **przypływ** (*np. natchnienia*) **3** [C,U] a bright light that you use with a camera for taking photographs when it is dark; the device for producing this light: *a camera with a built-in flash* ▶ **flesz**
IDM **in/like a flash** very quickly: *The idea came to me in a flash.* ▶ **błyskawicznie**
(as) quick as a flash → QUICK¹

flashback /ˈflæʃbæk/ noun [C,U] a part of a film, play, etc. that shows sth that happened before the main story ▶ (*film; teatr*) **retrospekcja**

flashlight (US) = TORCH (1)

flashy /ˈflæʃi/ adj. (**flashier**; **flashiest**) attracting attention by being very big, bright and expensive: *a flashy sports car* ▶ **efektowny**, **jaskrawy**, **krzykliwy**

flask /flɑːsk; US flæsk/ noun [C] **1** a bottle with a narrow neck that is used for storing and mixing chemicals in scientific work ▶ (*chem.*) **kolba**, **retorta** ➲ picture at **laboratory** **2** (Brit.) = THERMOS

flat¹ /flæt/ adj. (**flatter**; **flattest**) **1** smooth and level, with no parts that are higher than the rest: *I need a flat surface to write this letter on.* ◇ *a flat roof* ◇ *The countryside in Essex is quite flat* (równinny). ▶ **płaski**, **równy** **2** not high or deep: *You need flat shoes for walking.* ◇ *a flat dish* ▶ **płaski**; **płytki** **3** without much interest or energy: *Things have been a bit flat* (nic się nie dzieje) *since Alex left.* ▶ **jednostajny**, **nudny** **4** [only before a noun] (used about sth that you say or decide) that will not change; firm: *He answered our request with a flat 'No!'* Kategorycznie nam odmówił. ▶ **stanowczy**, **kategoryczny** **5** half a note lower than the stated note ▶ **z bemolem** OPP **sharp** **6** lower than the correct note: *That last note was flat. Can you sing it again?* ▶ **za niski** OPP **sharp** **7** not fresh because it has lost its bubbles: *Open a new bottle. That lemonade has* ***gone flat.*** ▶ (*napój gazowany*) **zwietrzały** **8** (Brit.) no longer producing electricity; not working: *We couldn't start the car because the battery was completely flat.* ▶ **wyczerpany** **9** without enough air in it: *This tyre looks flat – has it got a puncture?* ▶ **flakowaty** **10** (used about the cost of sth) that is the same for everyone; that is fixed: *We charge a flat fee of £20, however long you stay.* ▶ **jednolity**

IDM **fall flat** → FALL¹

flat out as fast as possible; without stopping: *He's been working flat out for two weeks and he needs a break.* ▶ **bez przerwy**

■ **flat** adv. **1** in a level position: *She lay flat on her back in the sunshine.* ◇ *He* ***fell flat on his face*** *in the mud.* ▶ **płasko**, (*padać*) **plackiem** **2** lower than the correct note: *You're singing flat.* Fałszujesz. ▶ **za nisko** OPP **sharp** ➲ picture at **music** **3** (used for emphasizing how quickly sth is done) in exactly the time mentioned and no longer: *She can get up and out of the house in ten minutes flat* (dokładnie w dziesięć minut).

flat² /flæt/ noun **1** [C] (especially US **apartment**) a set of rooms that is used as a home (usually in a large building): *Do you rent your flat or have you bought it?* ▶ **mieszkanie** ➲ note at **house**

W Amer. ang. częściej używa się słowa **apartment**. **Flat** zwykle używa się w Br. ang. Jednak **apartment** używa się też w Br. ang., mówiąc o mieszkaniu wynajmowanym tymczasowo, np. na wakacje: *We're renting an apartment in the South of France.*

living in a flat

A tall building that contains many **flats** (US **apartments**) is called a **block of flats** (US an **apartment block**). Blocks of flats are divided into **floors**: *I live in a second-floor flat.* If you **rent** a flat, you are the **tenant** and you pay money to the **landlord**/**landlady**. The money that you pay every month is the **rent**. A **deposit** is money that you pay before you move in but get back when you move out. Your flat may be **furnished** or **unfurnished**. People who share a flat with you but are not your family are called your **flatmates**. If you rent a room in a flat where the owner also lives, you are called a **lodger**.

2 [sing.] **the flat (of sth)** the flat part or side of sth: *the flat of your hand* dłoń ▶ **płaska część czegoś** **3** [C] (symbol ♭) a note which is half a note lower than the note with the same letter ▶ **bemol** ➲ look at **sharp** **4** [C] (especially US) a tyre on a vehicle that has no air in it: *We had to stop to* ***fix a flat.*** ▶ (*opona*) **flak**, **guma**

flatly /ˈflætli/ adv. **1** in a direct way; absolutely: *He flatly denied the allegations.* ▶ **stanowczo**, **kategorycznie** **2** in a way that shows no interest or emotion ▶ **bez zainteresowania**

flatmate /ˈflætmeɪt/ (US ˈ**room-mate**) noun [C] a person who shares a flat with one or more others ▶ **współlokator/ka**

ˈ**flat-pack** noun [C] (Brit.) a piece of furniture that is sold in pieces in a flat box and that you have to build yourself: *You can buy the kitchen as a flat-pack for self-assembly.* ▶ **zakupiony mebel zapakowany w płaską paczkę do samodzielnego złożenia w domu**

flatten /ˈflætn/ verb [I,T] **flatten (sth) (out)** to become or make sth flat: *The countryside flattens out as you get nearer the sea.* ◇ *The storms have flattened crops all over the country.* ▶ **wyrównywać (się)**, **spłaszczać (się)**

flatter /ˈflætə(r)/ verb [T] **1** to say nice things to sb, often in a way that is not sincere, because you want to please them or because you want to get an advantage for yourself ▶ **schlebiać** **2 flatter yourself (that...)** to choose to believe sth good about yourself although other people may not think the same: *He flatters himself that he speaks fluent French.* ▶ **oszukiwać samego siebie**, **schlebiać sobie** **3** [usually passive] to give pleasure or honour to sb: *I felt very flattered when they gave me the job.* ▶ **zaszczycać**

flattering /ˈflætərɪŋ/ adj. making sb look or sound more attractive or important than they really are ▶ (*wygląd itp.*) **korzystny**; (*ubranie*) **twarzowy**

flattery /ˈflætəri/ noun [U] saying good things about sb/sth that you do not really mean ▶ **pochlebstwo**

flaunt /flɔːnt/ verb [T] to show sth that you are proud of so that other people will admire it ▶ **obnosić się z czymś**

flautist /ˈflɔːtɪst; US ˈflaʊt-/ (US **flutist**) noun [C] a person who plays the **flute** ▶ **flecist(k)a**

flavour¹ (US **flavor**) /ˈfleɪvə(r)/ noun **1** [C,U] the taste (of food): *Do you think a little salt would improve the flavour?* ◇ *ten different flavours of yogurt* ◇ *yogurt in ten different flavours* ▶ **smak** **2** [sing.] an idea of the particular quality or character of sth: *This video will give you a flavour of what the city is like.* ▶ **posmak**, **klimat**

flavour² (US **flavor**) /ˈfleɪvə(r)/ verb [T] to give flavour to sth: *Add a little nutmeg to flavour the sauce.* ◇ *strawberry-flavoured* (o smaku truskawkowym) *milkshake* ▶ **przyprawiać**

flavouring (US **flavoring**) /ˈfleɪvərɪŋ/ noun [C,U] something that you add to food or drink to give it a particular taste: *This orange juice contains no* ***artificial flavourings.*** ▶ **dodatek smakowy**, **przyprawa**

flaw /flɔː/ noun [C] **1 a flaw (in sth)** a mistake in sth that makes it not good enough or causes it not to function as it should: *There are some flaws in her argument.* ▶ **błąd**, **słaby punkt** **2** a mark or crack in an object that means that it is not perfect ▶ **skaza**, **pęknięcie** **3 a flaw (in sb/sth)** a bad quality in sb's character: *His only real flaw is impatience.* ▶ **wada**

■ **flawed** adj. with a fault or weakness so that it is not perfect: *I think your plan is flawed.* ▶ **błędny**; **wadliwy**, **ze skazą**

flawless /ˈflɔːləs/ adj. with no faults or mistakes: *a flawless diamond* ▶ **bezbłędny**; **bez skazy** SYN **perfect**

flax /flæks/ noun [U] **1** a small plant with blue flowers, that is grown for its stem and seeds ▶ **len** **2** the thread that is used for making linen. It comes from the flax plant. ▶ **włókno lniane**

flea /fliː/ noun [C] a very small jumping insect without wings that lives on animals, for example cats and dogs.

Fleas bite people and animals and make them scratch. ▶ **pchła** ➔ picture at **insect**

'flea market noun [C] a market, often in a street, that sells old and used goods ▶ **pchli targ**

fleck /flek/ noun [C, usually pl.] a very small mark on sth; a very small piece of sth: *After painting the ceiling, her hair was covered with flecks of blue paint.* ▶ **plamka**; **pyłek**

flee /fliː/ verb [I,T] (pt, pp **fled** /fled/) **flee (to ... /into ...)**; **flee (from) sb/sth** to run away or escape from sth: *The robbers fled the country with £100 000.* ▶ **uciekać (z czegoś)/(przed kimś/czymś)**, **zbiegać**

fleece[1] /fliːs/ noun **1** [C] the wool coat of a sheep ▶ **runo**, **wełna** **2** [U,C] a type of soft warm cloth that feels like sheep's wool; a warm piece of clothing made from this cloth, which you wear on the top half of your body: *a fleece lining* podszewka z polara ◇ *a jacket lined with cotton fleece* (na misiu) ◇ *a bright red fleece* ▶ **polar** ➔ note at **sweater**

fleece[2] /fliːs/ verb [T] (informal) to take a lot of money from sb by charging them too much: *Some local shops have been fleecing tourists.* ▶ **oskubywać kogoś** SYN **rip sb off**

fleet /fliːt/ noun [C, with sing. or pl. verb] **1** a group of ships or boats that sail together: *a fishing fleet* ▶ **flota** **2** **a fleet (of sth)** a group of vehicles (especially taxis, buses or aircraft) that are travelling together or owned by one person ▶ **konwój**, **eskadra** (*samolotów*)

fleeting /'fliːtɪŋ/ adj. [usually before a noun] lasting only a short time: *a **fleeting glimpse/smile*** ◇ *a **fleeting moment** of happiness* ◇ *We paid a **fleeting visit** to Paris.* Wpadliśmy do Paryża na krótko. ▶ **przelotny**, **krótki** SYN **brief**

■ **fleetingly** adv. ▶ **przelotnie**, **krótko**

flesh /fleʃ/ noun [U] **1** the soft part of a human or animal body (between the bones and under the skin): *Tigers are flesh-eating animals.* ▶ **ciało**, **mięso** ⓘ Mięso zwierząt, które się spożywa, to **meat**. **2** the part of a fruit or vegetable that is soft and can be eaten ▶ **miąższ**

IDM **in the flesh** in person, not on TV, in a photograph, etc. ▶ **we własnej osobie**

make your flesh creep to make you feel disgusted and/or nervous: *The way he smiled made her flesh creep.* ▶ **sprawiać, że komuś cierpnie skóra**

your (own) flesh and blood a member of your family ▶ **własna rodzina**

flew past tense of **fly[1]**

flex[1] /fleks/ verb [T] to bend or move a leg, arm, muscle, etc. in order to exercise it ▶ **zginać**, **ćwiczyć**

flex[2] /fleks/ (especially US **cord**) noun [C,U] (a piece of) wire inside a plastic tube, used for carrying electricity to electrical equipment ▶ **przewód elektryczny**, **kabel** ➔ picture at **cable**

> At the end of a flex there is a **plug** which you fit into a socket or a **power point**.

flexible /'fleksəbl/ adj. **1** that can be changed easily: *flexible working hours* ruchomy czas pracy ▶ **elastyczny**, **ustępliwy** **2** able to bend or move easily without breaking ▶ **elastyczny**, **giętki** OPP for both meanings **inflexible**

■ **flexibility** /ˌfleksə'bɪləti/ noun [U] ▶ **elastyczność**, **giętkość**

flexitime /'fleksitaɪm/ (US usually **flextime** /'flekstaɪm/) noun [C] a system in which employees work a particular number of hours each week or month but can choose when they start and finish work each day ▶ **ruchomy czas pracy**

flick /flɪk/ verb **1** [T] **flick sth (away, off, onto, etc.)** to hit sth lightly and quickly with your finger or hand in order to move it: *She flicked the dust off her jacket.* ◇ *Please don't flick ash on the carpet.* ▶ **strzepywać** **2** [I,T] **flick (sth) (away, off, out, etc.)** to move, or to make sth move, with a quick sudden movement: *She flicked the switch and the light came on.* ▶ **przytykać**; **pstryknąć**

■ **flick** noun [C] ▶ **przytyczek**

PHR V **flick/flip through sth** to turn over the pages of a book, magazine, etc. quickly without reading everything ▶ **przerzucać kartki czegoś**

flicker[1] /'flɪkə(r)/ verb [I] **1** (used about a light or a flame) to keep going on and off as it burns or shines: *The candle flickered and went out.* ▶ **drgać**, **migotać** **2** (used about a feeling, thought, etc.) to appear for a short time: *A smile flickered across her face.* ▶ **zabłysnąć**, **przemykać** **3** to move lightly and quickly up and down: *His eyelids flickered for a second and then he lay still.* ▶ **drgać**

flicker[2] /'flɪkə(r)/ noun [C, usually sing.] **1** a light that shines on and off quickly: *the flicker of the TV/flames* ▶ **migotanie**, **miganie** **2** a small, sudden movement of part of the body ▶ **drganie**, **trzepotanie** **3** a feeling of sth that only lasts for a short time: *a flicker of interest/doubt* ◇ *a flicker of hope* iskierka nadziei ▶ **przebłysk** (*uczucia*)

flier = FLYER

flies → FLY

flight /flaɪt/ noun **1** [C] a journey by air: *to book a flight* ◇ *a direct/scheduled/charter flight* ◇ *They met **on a flight** to Australia.* ▶ **lot**, **przelot** ➔ note at **journey**, **plane** **2** [C] an aircraft that takes you on a particular journey: *Flight number 340 from London to New York is boarding now.* ▶ **lot** **3** [U] the act of flying: *It's unusual to see swans **in flight*** (lecące łabędzie). ▶ **lot** **4** [C] a number of stairs or steps going up or down: *a flight of stairs* ▶ **szereg** (*stopni*), **kondygnacja** (*schodów*) **5** [C,U] the act of running away or escaping from a dangerous or difficult situation: *the refugees' flight from the war zone* ▶ **ucieczka**

'flight attendant noun [C] a person whose job is to serve and take care of passengers on an aircraft ▶ **steward/esa**

flighty /'flaɪti/ adj. (informal) a **flighty** woman is one who cannot be relied on because she is always changing activities, ideas and partners without treating them seriously ▶ (*zwł. kobieta*) **zmienny**

flimsy /'flɪmzi/ adj. (**flimsier**; **flimsiest**) **1** not strong; easily broken or torn: *a flimsy bookcase* ◇ *a flimsy blouse* ▶ **kruchy**; **słaby**, **cienki** **2** weak; not making you believe that sth is true: *He gave a **flimsy excuse** for his absence.* ▶ **marny**, **lichy**

flinch /flɪntʃ/ verb [I] **flinch (at sth)**; **flinch (away)** to make a sudden movement backwards because of sth painful or frightening: *She couldn't help flinching away as the dentist came towards her with the drill.* ▶ **cofać się**, **wzdrygać się**

PHR V **flinch from sth/doing sth** to avoid doing sth because it is unpleasant: *She didn't flinch from telling him the whole truth.* ▶ **uchylać się od czegoś**

fling[1] /flɪŋ/ verb [T] (pt, pp **flung** /flʌŋ/) to throw sb/sth suddenly and carelessly or with great force: *He flung his coat on the floor.* ▶ **ciskać**, **rzucać**

fling[2] /flɪŋ/ noun [C] a short period of fun and pleasure ▶ **zabawa**, **uciecha**

flint /flɪnt/ noun **1** [U] very hard grey stone that produces **sparks** when you hit it against steel ▶ **krzemień** **2** [C] a small piece of **flint** or metal that is used to produce **sparks** (for example in a cigarette lighter) ▶ **krzesiwo**, **kamień do zapalniczki**

flip /flɪp/ verb (**flipping**; **flipped**) **1** [I,T] to turn (sth) over with a quick movement: *She flipped the book open and started to read.* ▶ **odwracać (się) szybkim ruchem**

2 [T] to throw sth into the air and make it turn over: *Let's flip a coin to see who starts.* ▶ **podrzucać 3** [I] (informal) **flip (out)** to become very angry or excited: *When his father saw the damage to the car he flipped.* ▶ **wkurzać się; podniecać się**

PHR V **flick/flip through sth** → FLICK

'flip chart noun [C] large sheets of paper fixed at the top to a stand so that they can be turned over, used for presenting information at a talk or meeting ▶ **flipchart**

'flip-flop (US **thong** /θɒŋ/) noun [C, usually pl.] a simple open shoe with a narrow piece of material that goes between your big toe and the toe next to it ▶ **klapek** (*typu japonka*)

flippant /'flɪpənt/ (also informal **flip**) adj. not serious enough about things that are important ▶ **lekceważący**

flipper /'flɪpə(r)/ noun [C] **1** a flat arm that is part of the body of some sea animals which they use for swimming: *Seals have flippers.* ▶ **płetwa** ⇨ look at **fin 2** a rubber shoe shaped like an animal's **flipper** that people wear so that they can swim better, especially underwater: *a pair of flippers* ▶ **płetwa**

'flip phone noun [C] a small mobile phone with a cover that opens upwards ▶ **telefon komórkowy z klapką**

flipping /'flɪpɪŋ/ adj. (Brit., informal) (used as a mild way of swearing): *When's the flipping bus coming?* ▶ **cholerny, przeklęty**

■ **flipping** adv. ▶ **cholernie**

flirt¹ /flɜːt/ verb [I] **flirt (with sb)** to behave in a way that suggests you find sb attractive and are trying to attract them: *Who was that boy Irene was flirting with at the party?* ◇ (figurative) *to flirt with death/danger/disaster* ▶ **flirtować**

PHR V **flirt with sth** to think about doing sth (but not very seriously): *She had flirted with the idea of becoming a teacher for a while.* ▶ **zastanawiać się nad czymś** (*ale nie całkiem poważnie*)

flirt² /flɜːt/ noun [C] a person who often **flirts** with people ▶ **flircia-rz/ra**

flirtatious /flɜː'teɪʃəs/ adj. behaving in a way that shows a sexual attraction to sb that is not serious: *a flirtatious smile* ▶ **flirciarski**

■ **flirtatiously** adv. ▶ **flirciarsko**

flit /flɪt/ verb [I] (**flitting**; **flitted**) **flit (from A to B)**; **flit (between A and B)** to fly or move quickly from one place to another without staying anywhere for long: *She flits from one job to another.* ▶ **przemykać (się), fruwać**

🔑 **float¹** /fləʊt/ verb **1** [I] to move slowly through air or water: *Boats were floating gently down the river.* ◇ *The smell of freshly-baked bread floated in through the window.* ▶ **pływać; szybować 2** [I] **float (in/on sth)** to stay on the surface of a liquid and not sink: *Wood floats in water.* ▶ **unosić się na wodzie 3** [T] to sell shares in a company or business for the first time: *The company was floated on the stock market in 1999.* ▶ **puszczać w obieg 4** [I,T] (used in **economics**) to allow the value of a country's money to change freely according to the value of the money of other countries ▶ (*ekon.*) **upłynniać kurs waluty**

float² /fləʊt/ noun [C] **1** a lorry or other vehicle that is decorated and used in a celebration that travels through the streets: *a carnival float* ▶ **ozdobiony pojazd używany w pochodach 2** a light object used in fishing that moves on the water when a fish has been caught ▶ **pływak** (*u wędki*) **3** a light object used for helping people to learn to swim ▶ **deska do pływania**

floating /'fləʊtɪŋ/ adj. not fixed; not living permanently in one place: *a floating population* ◇ *a floating voter* osoba, która nie zawsze głosuje na tę samą partię ▶ **zmienny, ruchomy**

flock¹ /flɒk/ noun [C] **1** a group of sheep or birds ▶ **stado** ⇨ look at **herd 2** a large number of people: *Flocks of tourists visit Barcelona every summer.* ▶ **gromada, tłum**

flock² /flɒk/ verb [I] (used about people) to go or meet somewhere in large numbers: *People are flocking to her latest exhibition.* ▶ **schodzić się tłumnie, gromadzić się**

flog /flɒg/ verb [T] (**flogging**; **flogged**) **1** [usually passive] to hit sb hard several times with a stick or a **whip** as a punishment ▶ **chłostać 2** (Brit., informal) to sell sth ▶ **sprzedawać, opylać**

flogging /'flɒgɪŋ/ noun [C,U] the act of hitting sb several times with a stick or a **whip** as a punishment ▶ **chłosta**

F

🔑 **flood¹** /flʌd/ verb [I,T] **1** to fill a place with water; to be filled or covered with water: *I left the taps on and flooded the bathroom.* ◇ *The River Trent floods almost every year.* ▶ **wylewać (się), zalewać 2 flood in/into/out of sth** to go somewhere in large numbers: *Since the TV programme was shown, phone calls have been flooding into the studio.* ▶ **napływać masowo 3** (used about a thought, feeling, etc.) to fill sb's mind suddenly: *At the end of the day all his worries came flooding back* (wszystkie jego zmartwienia powróciły dużą falą). ▶ **napływać**

🔑 **flood²** /flʌd/ noun [C] **1** a large amount of water that has spread from a river, the sea, etc. that covers an area which should be dry ▶ **powódź 2 a flood (of sth)** a large number or amount: *She received a flood of letters after the accident.* ◇ *The little boy was in floods of tears* (tonął we łzach). ▶ **lawina**

floodlight /'flʌdlaɪt/ noun [C] a powerful light that is used for lighting places where sports are played, the outside of public buildings, etc. ▶ **reflektor**

floodlit /'flʌdlɪt/ adj. lit by **floodlights**: *a floodlit hockey match* ▶ **oświetlony reflektorami**

🔑 **floor¹** /flɔː(r)/ noun **1** [C, usually sing.] the flat surface that you walk on inside a building: *Don't come in – there's broken glass **on the floor**!* ◇ *ceramic floor tiles* (kafle podłogowe) ▶ **podłoga** ⇨ note at **ground 2** [C] all the rooms that are on the same level of a building: *My office is **on the second floor**.* ▶ **piętro**

> W Wlk. Br. **ground floor** oznacza parter, a **first floor** pierwsze piętro. W Amer. ang. **first floor** oznacza parter.

3 [C, usually sing.] the ground or surface at the bottom of the sea, a forest, etc.: *the ocean/valley/cave/forest floor* ▶ **dno**

floor² /flɔː(r)/ verb [T] (informal) to surprise or confuse sb completely with a question or a problem: *Some of the questions I was asked in the interview completely floored me.* ▶ **zdumiewać, ogłupiać**

floorboard /'flɔːbɔːd/ noun [C] one of the long wooden boards used to make a floor ▶ **deska podłogowa** ⇨ picture at **joist**

flop¹ /flɒp/ verb [I] (**flopping**; **flopped**) **1 flop into/onto sth**; **flop (down/back)** to sit or lie down in a sudden and careless way because you are very tired: *I was so tired that all I could do was flop onto the sofa and watch TV.* ▶ **klapnąć, padać 2 flop around, back, down, etc.** to move, hang or fall in a careless way without control: *I can't bear my hair flopping in my eyes.* ▶ **wpadać** (*np. do oczu*), **zwisać 3** (used about a book, film, record, etc.) to be a complete failure with the public ▶ **zrobić klapę, nie cieszyć się powodzeniem**

flop² /flɒp/ noun [C] **1** (used about a film, play, party, etc.) something that is not a success; a failure: *Her first novel was very successful but her second was a flop.* ◇ *a box-office flop* ▶ **niewypał, klapa 2** [usually sing.] a **floppy** movement ▶ **bezwładny ruch**

floppy /'flɒpi/ adj. (**floppier**; **floppiest**) soft and hanging downwards; not hard and stiff: *a floppy hat* ▶ **miękki**, **sflaczały**

ˌ**floppy 'disk** (also **floppy**, pl. **floppies**; **diskette** /dɪs'ket/) noun [C] a square piece of plastic that can store information from a computer: *Don't forget to back up your files onto a floppy disk.* ▶ **dyskietka** ➲ look at **hard disk**

flora /'flɔːrə/ noun [pl.] all the plants growing in a particular area ▶ **roślinność**, **flora** ➲ look at **fauna**

floral /'flɔːrəl/ adj. decorated with a pattern of flowers, or made with flowers: *wallpaper with a floral design* ▶ **kwiatowy** ➲ picture on **page A1**

florist /'flɒrɪst/ noun **1** [C] a person who has a shop that sells flowers ▶ **kwiacia-rz/rka** **2** (**the florist's**) [sing.] a shop that sells flowers ▶ **kwiaciarnia**

flotation /fləʊ'teɪʃn/ noun **1** [C,U] the process of selling shares in a company to the public for the first time in order to make money: *plans for (a) flotation on the stock exchange* ◇ *a stock-market flotation* ▶ **emisja** (*akcji*) **2** [U] the act of floating on or in water ▶ **pływanie**, **unoszenie się w/na wodzie**

flounder[1] /'flaʊndə(r)/ verb [I] **1** to find it difficult to speak or act (usually in a difficult or embarrassing situation): *The questions they asked her at the interview had her floundering helplessly.* ▶ **plątać się** **2** to have a lot of problems and be in danger of failing completely: *By the late nineties, the business was floundering.* ▶ **być na skraju upadłości**, (*gospodarka*) **kuleć** **3** to move with difficulty, for example when trying to get out of some water, wet earth, etc. ▶ **grzęznąć**, **brnąć**

flounder[2] /'flaʊndə(r)/ noun [C] (pl. **flounder** or **flounders**) a small flat sea fish that you can eat ▶ **flądra**

⚷ **flour** /'flaʊə(r)/ noun [U] a very thin powder made from a type of grain such as **wheat** and used for making bread, cakes, biscuits, etc. ▶ **mąka**

flourish[1] /'flʌrɪʃ; US 'flɜːr-/ verb **1** [I] to be strong and healthy; to develop in a successful way: *a flourishing business* ▶ **dobrze się rozwijać**, **kwitnąć** **2** [T] to wave sth in the air so that people will notice it: *He proudly flourished two tickets for the concert.* ▶ **wymachiwać czymś**

flourish[2] /'flʌrɪʃ; US 'flɜːr-/ noun [C] an exaggerated movement: *He opened the door for her with a flourish.* ▶ **gest teatralny**, **wymachiwanie**

flout /flaʊt/ verb [T] to refuse to obey or accept sth: *to flout the rules of the organization* ◇ *to flout somebody's advice* ▶ **łamać** (*np. zasady*), **lekceważyć**

⚷ **flow**[1] /fləʊ/ noun [sing.] **a flow (of sth/sb)** **1** a steady, continuous movement of sth/sb: *Press hard on the wound to stop the flow of blood* (zatamować upływ krwi). ◇ *There's a steady flow* (odpływ) *of young people from the country to the towns.* ▶ **przepływ**, **dopływ** **2** a supply of sth: *the flow of information between the school and the parents* ▶ **przepływ**, **napływ** **3** the way in which words, ideas, etc. are joined together smoothly: *Once Charlie's* ***in full flow*** (kiedy Charlie się rozgada), *it's hard to stop him talking.* ▶ **potok** (*np. słów*)

IDM **the ebb and flow (of sth)** → EBB

⚷ **flow**[2] /fləʊ/ verb [I] **1** to move in a smooth and continuous way (like water): *This river flows south into the English Channel.* ◇ *a fast-flowing stream* ◇ *Traffic began to flow normally again after the accident.* ▶ **płynąć**, **przepływać** **2** (used about words, ideas, actions, etc.) to be joined together smoothly: *As soon as we sat down at the table, the conversation began to flow.* ▶ **płynąć**, **toczyć się wartko** **3** (used about hair and clothes) to hang down in a loose way: *a long flowing dress* ▶ **spływać miękko**, **powiewać**

'**flow chart** (also '**flow diagram**) noun [C] a diagram that shows the connections between different stages of a process or parts of a system ▶ **schemat (działania)**

⚷ **flower**[1] /'flaʊə(r)/ noun [C] **1** the coloured part of a plant or tree from which seeds or fruit grow: *The roses are* ***in flower*** (kwitną) *early this year.* ▶ **kwiat** **2** a plant that is grown for its flowers: *to grow flowers* ◇ *a bunch of flowers* ▶ **kwiat** ➲ look at **bouquet** ➲ picture at **bar**

flowers

A flower has thin soft coloured **petals**. It grows from a **bud** on the end of a **stem**. We **pick** flowers or buy them at the **florist's**, then **arrange** them in a **vase**. Flowers that are given or carried on a special occasion are called a **bouquet**.

flower[2] /'flaʊə(r)/ verb [I] to produce flowers ▶ **kwitnąć**

'**flower bed** (also **bed**) noun [C] a piece of ground in a garden or park where flowers are grown ▶ **kwietnik**, **klomb**

flowerpot /'flaʊəpɒt/ noun [C] a pot in which a plant can be grown ▶ **doniczka** ➲ picture at **pot**

flowery /'flaʊəri/ adj. **1** covered or decorated with flowers: *a flowery dress/hat/pattern* ▶ **kwiecisty**, **w kwiatki** **2** (used about a style of speaking or writing) using long, difficult words when they are not necessary ▶ **kwiecisty**

flown past participle of **fly**[1]

fl oz = FLUID OUNCE

⚷ **flu** /fluː/ (also formal **influenza** /ˌɪnflu'enzə/) noun [U] an illness that is like a bad cold but more serious. You usually feel very hot and your arms and legs hurt: *There's a lot of flu about.* Dużo ludzi ma grypę. ▶ **grypa**

fluctuate /'flʌktʃueɪt/ verb [I] **fluctuate (between A and B)** (used about prices and numbers, or people's feelings) to change many times from one thing to another: *The number of students fluctuates between 100 and 150.* ▶ **wahać się (między czymś i czymś)**, **zmieniać się**
■ **fluctuation** /ˌflʌktʃu'eɪʃn/ noun [C,U] ▶ **wahanie**, **fluktuacja**

flue /fluː/ noun [C] a pipe or tube that takes smoke, gas or hot air away from a fire, a **heater** or an oven: *a blocked chimney flue* ▶ **rura spalinowa**, **przewód kominowy**

fluent /'fluːənt/ adj. **1** **fluent (in sth)** able to speak or write a foreign language easily and accurately: *After a year in France she was fluent in French* (mówiła biegle po francusku). ▶ **biegły**, **płynny** **2** (used about speaking, reading or writing) expressed in a smooth and accurate way: *He speaks fluent German.* Mówi płynnie po niemiecku. ▶ **biegły**, **płynny**
■ **fluency** /'fluːənsi/ noun [U]: *My knowledge of Japanese grammar is good but I need to work on my fluency.* ▶ **biegła znajomość**, **biegłość** | **fluently** adv. ▶ **biegle**, **płynnie**

fluff /flʌf/ noun [U] **1** very small pieces of wool, cotton, etc. that form into balls and collect on clothes and other surfaces ▶ **kłaczki z materiału na ubraniu** **2** the soft new fur on young animals or birds ▶ **puch**

fluffy /'flʌfi/ adj. (**fluffier**; **fluffiest**) **1** covered in soft fur: *a fluffy kitten* ▶ **puchaty** **2** that looks or feels very soft and light: *fluffy clouds/towels* ▶ **puszysty**

fluid[1] /'fluːɪd/ noun [C,U] a substance that can flow; a liquid: *The doctor told her to drink plenty of fluids.* ◇ *cleaning fluid* ▶ **płyn**, **ciecz**

fluid[2] /'fluːɪd/ adj. **1** able to flow smoothly like a liquid: (figurative) *I like her fluid style of dancing.* ▶ **płynny** **2** (used about plans, etc.) able to change or likely to be changed ▶ **płynny**, **zmienny**

ˌ**fluid 'ounce** noun [C] (abbr. **fl oz**) a measure of liquid; in Britain, 0.0284 of a litre; in the US, 0.0295 of a litre.

▶ **uncja płynu** ⓘ Więcej w dodatku *Wyrażenia liczbowe* na końcu słownika.

fluke /fluːk/ noun [C, usually sing.] (informal) a surprising and lucky result that happens by accident, not because you have been clever or skilful: *The result was no fluke. The better team won.* ▶ **szczęśliwy traf**

flung past tense, past participle of **fling**[1]

fluorescent /ˌflɔːˈresnt; ˌflʊəˈr-/ adj. **1** producing a bright white light: *fluorescent lighting* ▶ **fluoryzujący, jarzeniowy 2** very bright; seeming to shine: *fluorescent pink paint* ▶ **odblaskowy, jaskrawy**

fluoride /ˈflɔːraɪd/ noun [U] a chemical that can be added to water or **toothpaste** to help prevent bad teeth ▶ **fluorek**

flurry /ˈflʌri; US ˈflɜːri/ noun [C] (pl. **flurries**) **1** a short time in which there is suddenly a lot of activity: *a flurry of excitement/activity* ▶ **przypływ** (*emocji*), **burza** (*np. pomysłów*) **2** a sudden short fall of snow or rain ▶ **nagła, krótkotrwała ulewa/śnieżyca**

flush[1] /flʌʃ/ verb **1** [I] (used about a person or their face) to go red: *Susan flushed and could not hide her embarrassment.* ▶ **czerwienić się, rumienić się** ⓘ Częściej używa się słowa **blush**. **2** [T] to clean a toilet by pressing or pulling a handle that sends water into the toilet: *Please remember to flush the toilet after use.* ▶ **spuszczać wodę** (*w toalecie*) **3** [I] (used about a toilet) to be cleaned with a short flow of water: *The toilet won't flush.* ▶ (*toaleta*) **spłukiwać się 4** [T] **flush sth away, down, etc.** to get rid of sth in a flow of water: *You can't flush tea leaves down the sink – they'll block it.* ▶ **spłukiwać, spuszczać coś z wodą**

flush[2] /flʌʃ/ noun [C, usually sing.] **1** a hot feeling or red colour that you have in your face when you are embarrassed, excited, angry, etc.: *The cold wind brought a flush to our cheeks.* ◇ *a flush of anger* ▶ **rumieniec, wypieki 2** the act of cleaning a toilet with a quick flow of water; the system for doing this ▶ **spłukiwanie toalety**

flushed /flʌʃt/ adj. with a hot red face ▶ **zarumieniony, z wypiekami na twarzy**

fluster /ˈflʌstə(r)/ verb [T, usually passive] to make sb feel nervous and confused (because there is too much to do or not enough time): *Don't get flustered* (nie trać głowy) *– there's plenty of time.* ▶ **wzburzać, podniecać**

■ **fluster** noun [C]: *I always get **in a fluster*** (podenerwowany) *before exams.* ▶ **podniecenie**

flute /fluːt/ noun [C] a musical instrument like a pipe that you hold sideways and play by blowing over a hole at one side ▶ **flet** ➲ note at **music**, **piano**

■ **flutist** /-tɪst/ noun (US) = FLAUTIST

flutter[1] /ˈflʌtə(r)/ verb **1** [I,T] to move or make sth move quickly and lightly, especially through the air: *The flags were fluttering in the wind.* ◇ *The bird fluttered its wings and tried to fly.* ▶ **trzepotać, powiewać; opadać łagodnie, szybować 2** [I] your heart or stomach **flutters** when you feel nervous and excited ▶ **kołatać, dygotać**

flutter[2] /ˈflʌtə(r)/ noun [C, usually sing.] **1** a quick, light movement: *the flutter of wings/eyelids* ▶ **trzepotanie, mruganie, dygotanie 2** (Brit., slang) a bet on a race, etc.: *I sometimes **have a flutter** on the horses.* Czasami gram na wyścigach konnych. **3** a state of nervous excitement ▶ **niepokój, podenerwowanie**

flux /flʌks/ noun [U] continuous movement and change: *a country **in a state of flux*** kraj, w którym zachodzą zmiany ▶ **ciągłe zmiany**

⚷ **fly**[1] /flaɪ/ verb (**flying**; **flies**; pt **flew** /fluː/, pp **flown** /fləʊn/) **1** [I,T] to move through the air: *This bird has a broken wing and can't fly.* ◇ *How long does it take to fly the Atlantic?* ▶ **latać, fruwać 2** [I,T] to travel or carry sth in an aircraft, etc.: *My daughter is flying (out) to Singapore next week.* ◇ *Supplies of food were flown (in) to the starving people.* ▶ **lecieć; dostarczać** (*samolotem*) **3** [I,T] (used about a pilot) to control an aircraft: *You have to have special training to fly a jumbo jet.* ▶ **sterować; latać 4** [I] to move quickly or suddenly, especially through the air: *A large stone **came flying*** (wleciał) *through the window.* ◇ *I slipped and my shopping **went flying*** (rozleciały się) *everywhere.* ◇ *Suddenly the door **flew open*** (otworzyły się gwałtownie) *and Mark came running in.* ◇ *to fly the Atlantic* przelecieć przez Atlantyk ◇ (figurative) *The weekend has just **flown by** and now it's Monday again.* ▶ **przelatywać 5** [I,T] to move about or to make sth move about in the air: *The flags are flying.* ◇ *to fly a flag/kite* ▶ **powiewać; puszczać** (*np. latawca*) ➲ noun **flight**

■ **flying** noun [U]: *I'm scared of flying.* Boję się latać. ▶ **latanie**

IDM **as the crow flies** → CROW[1]

fly off the handle (informal) to become very angry in an unreasonable way ▶ **unieść się (gniewem)**

let fly (at sb) 1 to shout angrily at sb: *My parents really let fly at me when I got home late.* ▶ **robić (komuś) awanturę, krzyczeć na kogoś 2** to hit sb in anger: *She let fly at him with her fists.* ▶ **rzucać się na kogoś**

⚷ **fly**[2] /flaɪ/ noun [C] **1** (pl. **flies**) a small insect with two wings: *Flies buzzed round the dead cow.* ▶ **mucha** ➲ picture at **insect 2** (also **flies** [pl.]) an opening down the front of a pair of trousers that fastens with buttons or a **zip** and is covered with a narrow piece of cloth: *Henry, your flies are undone.* ▶ **rozporek** ➲ picture on **page A1**

flyer (also **flier**) /ˈflaɪə(r)/ noun [C] **1** a person who travels in a plane as a pilot or a passenger: *frequent flyers* ◇ *I'm a nervous flyer.* ▶ **lotnik, pilot; osoba często podróżująca samolotem 2** a small sheet of paper that advertises a product or an event and is given to a large number of people ▶ **ulotka**

⚷ **flying** /ˈflaɪɪŋ/ adj. [only before a noun] able to fly: *flying insects* ▶ **latający**

IDM **get off to a flying start** to begin sth well; to make a good start ▶ **świetnie (się) zaczynać**

with flying colours with great success; very well: *Martin passed the exam with flying colours.* ▶ **celująco, zaszczytnie, doskonale**

ˌflying ˈsaucer noun [C] a round **spacecraft** that some people say they have seen and believe comes from another planet ▶ **latający talerz**

ˌflying ˈvisit noun [C] a very quick visit ▶ **krótka wizyta**

flyover /ˈflaɪəʊvə(r)/ (US **overpass** /ˈəʊvəpɑːs; US -pæs/) noun [C] a type of bridge that carries a road over another road ▶ **wiadukt**

FM /ˌef ˈem/ abbr. **frequency modulation**; one of the systems of sending out radio signals ▶ **modulacja częstotliwości**

foal /fəʊl/ noun [C] a young horse ▶ **źrebię** ➲ note at **horse**

foam[1] /fəʊm/ noun [U] **1** (also ˌ**foam ˈrubber**) a light rubber material that is used inside seats, etc. to make them comfortable: *a foam mattress* ▶ **gąbka 2** a mass of small air bubbles that form on the surface of a liquid: *white foam on the tops of the waves* ▶ **piana 3** an artificial substance that is between a solid and a liquid and is made from very small bubbles: *shaving foam* ▶ **pian(k)a**

foam[2] /fəʊm/ verb [I] to produce **foam**: *We watched the foaming river below.* ◇ *The dog **was foaming at the mouth*** (toczył pianę z pyska). ▶ **pienić się**

fob /fɒb/ verb (**fobbing**; **fobbed**)

PHR V **fob sb off (with sth) 1** to try to stop sb asking questions or complaining by telling them sth that is not true: *Don't let them fob you off with any more excuses.*

▶ **zbywać kogoś (czymś) 2** to try to give sb sth that they do not want: *Don't try to fob me off with that old car – I want a new one.* ▶ **wciskać coś komuś** (*np. tandetny towar*), **oszukiwać** ℹ To samo znaczenie ma czasownik złożony **fob sth off on sb**.

focal point /ˈfəʊkl pɔɪnt/ noun [sing.] the centre of interest or activity ▶ **centrum (uwagi)**

focus¹ /ˈfəʊkəs/ verb (**focusing**; **focused** or **focussing**; **focussed**) **focus (sth) (on sth) 1** [I,T] to give all your attention to sth: *to focus on a problem* ▶ **skupiać się**; **skupiać** (*uwagę na czymś*) **2** [I,T] (used about your eyes) to change or be changed so that things can be seen clearly: *Gradually his eyes focused.* ▶ **ześrodkowywać (się)**, **skupiać się 3** [I,T] (used about a camera) to change or be changed so that things can be seen clearly: *I focussed (the camera) on the person in the middle of the group.* ▶ **nastawiać ostrość 4** [T] to direct rays of light onto one particular point ▶ **ogniskować**

focus² /ˈfəʊkəs/ noun [C, usually sing.] **1** the centre of interest or attention; special attention that is given to sb/sth: *Tonight our focus will be on* (dzisiaj skoncentrujemy się na) *modern jazz.* ◇ *The school used to be the focus of village life.* ▶ **centrum** (*np. uwagi*), **ośrodek** (*zainteresowania*) **2** the point at which rays of light meet or from which they appear to come ▶ **ognisko** (*promieni*)
IDM **in focus/out of focus** (used about a photograph or sth in a photograph) clear/not clear ▶ **(nie)wyraźny**

fodder /ˈfɒdə(r)/ noun [U] food that is given to farm animals ▶ **pasza**

foe /fəʊ/ noun [C] (formal) an enemy ▶ **wróg**, **nieprzyjaciel**

foetus (US fetus) /ˈfiːtəs/ noun [C] a young human or animal that is still developing in its mother's body ▶ **płód** ℹ Wcześniejsze stadium rozwoju to **embryo**.

fog /fɒg/ noun [U,C] thick cloud that forms close to or just above the land or sea. Fog makes it difficult for us to see: *Patches of dense fog are making driving dangerous.* ◇ *Bad fogs are common in November.* ◇ (figurative) *His mind was in a fog* (miał zamęt w myślach) *and he couldn't study any more.* ▶ **mgła**

> **Fog** oznacza gęstą mgłę, zaś **mist** to lekka mgła. W gorące dni, pod wpływem wysokiej temperatury, może tworzyć się zamglenie zwane po angielsku **haze**. **Smog** to rodzaj mgły spowodowanej zanieczyszczeniem powietrza. ➲ note at **weather**

foggy /ˈfɒgi/ adj. (**foggier**; **foggiest**) (used to describe the weather when there is **fog**) ▶ **mglisty**
IDM **not have the faintest/foggiest (idea)** → FAINT¹

foil¹ /fɔɪl/ noun **1** (also **tinfoil** /ˈtɪnfɔɪl/) [U] metal that has been made into very thin sheets, used for putting around food: *aluminium foil* ▶ **folia** (*np. aluminiowa*) ➲ look at **cling film 2** [C] a long, thin, pointed weapon used in the sport of **fencing** ▶ **floret** ➲ picture on **page A9**

foil² /fɔɪl/ verb [T] to prevent sb from succeeding, especially with a plan; to prevent a plan from succeeding: *The prisoners were foiled in their attempt to escape.* ▶ **udaremniać** (*wysiłki*), **krzyżować (komuś coś)**

foist /fɔɪst/ verb
PHR V **foist sth on/upon sb** to force sb to accept sth that they do not want: *Jeff had a lot of extra work foisted on him when his boss was away.* ▶ **narzucać (coś komuś)**

fold¹ /fəʊld/ verb **1** [T] **fold sth (up)** to bend one part of sth over another part in order to make it smaller, tidier, etc.: *He **folded** the letter **into three** before putting it into the envelope.* ◇ *Fold up your clothes neatly and put them away please.* ▶ **składać** OPP **unfold 2** [I] **fold (up)** to be able to be made smaller in order to be carried or stored more easily: *This table folds up flat.* ▶ **składać się 3** [T] **fold A in B**; **fold B round/over A** to put sth around sth else:

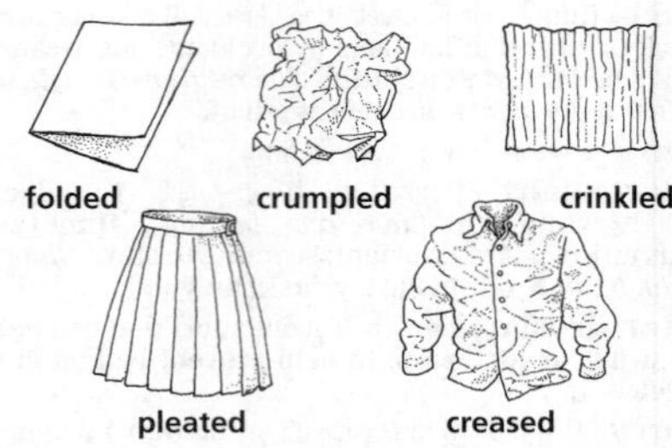

I folded the photos in a sheet of paper and put them away. ▶ **zawijać coś w coś**; **obwijać coś czymś 4** [I] (used about a business, a play in the theatre, etc.) to close because it is a failure ▶ **robić klapę**, **zamykać się**
■ **folding** adj. [only before a noun]: *a folding chair* ◇ *a folding bed* łóżko polowe ▶ **składany**
IDM **cross/fold your arms** → ARM¹

fold² /fəʊld/ noun [C] **1** a curved shape that is made when there is more material, etc. than is necessary to cover sth: *the folds of a curtain/dress* ▶ **fałda 2** the mark or line where sth has been folded ▶ **zagięcie 3** a small area inside a fence where sheep are kept together in a field ▶ **owczarnia**

folder /ˈfəʊldə(r)/ noun [C] **1** a cardboard or plastic cover that is used for holding papers, etc. ▶ **teczka (do akt)**, **skoroszyt** ➲ picture at **stationery 2** a collection of information or files on one subject that is stored in a computer or on a disk ▶ **plik**, **zbiór**

foliage /ˈfəʊliɪdʒ/ noun [U] (formal) all the leaves of a tree or plant ▶ **listowie**

folk¹ /fəʊk/ noun **1** (US **folks** /fəʊks/) [pl.] (informal) people in general: *Some folk are never satisfied.* ▶ **ludzie** ➲ look at **people 2** [pl.] a particular type of people: *Old folk often don't like change.* ◇ *city folk* ◇ *country folk* wieśniacy ▶ **ludzie** (*określona grupa*) **3** (**folks**) [pl.] (informal) (used as a friendly way of addressing more than one person): *What shall we do today, folks?* ▶ (*zwracając się do grupy znajomych*) **moi kochani 4** (**folks**) [pl.] (informal) your parents or close relatives: *How are your folks?* ▶ **rodzice**; **krewni 5** [U] music in the traditional style of a country or community: *Do you like Irish folk?* ▶ **muzyka ludowa/folk**

folk² /fəʊk/ adj. [only before a noun] traditional in a community; of a traditional style: *Robin Hood is an English folk hero.* ◇ *folk music* ◇ *a folk dance/song/singer/tale* ▶ **ludowy**

folklore /ˈfəʊklɔː(r)/ noun [U] traditional stories and beliefs ▶ **folklor**

folklorist /ˈfəʊklɔːrɪst/ noun [C] a person who studies **folklore**, especially as an academic subject ▶ **folklorysт(k)a**

follicle /ˈfɒlɪkl/ noun [C] one of the very small holes in the skin which hair grows from: *a hair follicle* ▶ **mieszek**

follow /ˈfɒləʊ/ verb **1** [I,T] to come, go or happen after sb/sth: *You go first and I'll follow (on) later.* ◇ *The dog followed her (around) wherever she went.* ◇ *We had soup followed by* (a potem) *spaghetti.* ▶ **iść za kimś/czymś**, **następować (po kimś/czymś) 2** to go after somebody in order to catch them ▶ **ścigać**, **gonić 2** [I] **follow (on) (from sth)** to be the logical result of sth; to be the next logical step after sth: *Intermediate Book One follows on from Elementary Book Two.* ◇ *It doesn't follow that* (nigdzie nie jest powiedziane, że) *old people can't lead active lives.* ▶ **następować**, **wynikać 3** [T] to go along a road, etc.; to go in the same direction as sth: *Follow this road* *for a mile and then turn right at the pub.* ◇ *The road follows the river for a few miles.* ▶ **iść/jechać** (*np. drogą*), **iść wzdłuż czegoś, biec równolegle do czegoś 4** [T] to do sth or to happen according to instructions, an example, what is usual, etc.: *When lighting fireworks, it is important to* ***follow the instructions*** *carefully.* ◇ *She always follows the latest fashions.* ◇ *The day's events followed the usual pattern.* ▶ **stosować się do czegoś, nadążać za czymś, odbywać się zgodnie z planem 5** [I,T] to understand the meaning of sth: *The children couldn't follow the plot of that film.* ▶ **rozumieć 6** [T] to keep watching or listening to sb/sth very carefully: *You'll have to follow what he says very carefully if you want to understand it.* ◇ *The film follows the career of a young dancer.* ▶ **słuchać/patrzeć uważnie, śledzić** (*np. czyjeś losy*) **7** [T] to take an active interest in sth: *Have you been following the tennis championships?* ▶ **śledzić z zainteresowaniem**

IDM **a hard act to follow** → HARD[1]

as follows (used for introducing a list): *The names of the successful candidates are as follows* (przedstawiają się następująco)... ▶ **jak następuje, następująco**

follow sb's example/lead to do what sb else has done or decided to do ▶ **iść za czyimś przykładem itp.**

follow in sb's footsteps to do the same job as sb else who did it before you: *He followed in his father's footsteps and joined the army.* ▶ **iść w czyjeś ślady**

follow suit to do the same thing that sb else has just done ▶ **robić to samo, co ktoś inny, naśladować**

follow your nose to go straight forward: *Turn right at the lights and after that just follow your nose until you get to the village.* ▶ **iść prosto przed siebie**

PHR V **follow sth through** to continue doing sth until it is finished ▶ **robić coś od początku do końca**

follow sth up 1 to take further action about sth: *You should follow up your letter with a phone call.* Po wysłaniu listu powinieneś tam zadzwonić. ▶ **uzupełniać, prowadzić dalej 2** to find out more about sth: *We need to follow up the story about the school.* ▶ **zgłębiać, dociekać**

follower /ˈfɒləʊə(r)/ noun [C] a person who follows or supports a person, belief, etc. ▶ **zwolenni-k/czka, wyznaw-ca/czyni**

⚷ **following**[1] /ˈfɒləʊɪŋ/ adj. **1** next (in time): *He became ill on Sunday and died the following day.* ▶ **następny 2** that are going to be mentioned next: *Please could you bring the following items to the next meeting...* ▶ **następujący**

⚷ **following**[2] /ˈfɒləʊɪŋ/ noun **1** [sing.] a group of people who support or admire sth: *The Brazilian team has a large following in all parts of the world.* ▶ **grupa zwolenników, poparcie 2** (**the following**) [pl.] the people or things that are going to be mentioned next: *The following are the winners* (a oto nazwiska zwycięzców) *of the competition...* ▶ **następujące osoby/rzeczy**

⚷ **following**[3] /ˈfɒləʊɪŋ/ prep. after; as a result of: *Following the riots many students have been arrested.* ▶ **po, w następstwie**

ˈfollow-up noun [C] something that is done as a second stage to continue or develop sth: *As a follow-up to the TV series, the BBC is publishing a book.* ▶ **dodatek, kontynuacja**

folly /ˈfɒli/ noun [C,U] (pl. **follies**) (formal) an act that is not sensible and may have a bad result: *It would be folly to ignore their warnings.* ▶ **szaleństwo**

fond /fɒnd/ adj. **1** [not before a noun] **fond of sb/sth; fond of doing sth** liking a person or thing, or liking doing sth: *Elephants are very fond of bananas.* ◇ *I'm not fond of getting up early.* ◇ *Teachers often* ***grow fond*** *of their students.* ◇ *I'm especially fond of* (szczególnie lubię) *his chicken casserole.* ▶ **lubiący, czujący sympatię/przywiązanie do kogoś/czegoś 2** [only before a noun] kind and loving: *I have* ***fond memories*** *of* (mile wspominam) *my aunts.* ▶ **czuły 3** [only before a noun] wished or hoped for but unlikely to come true: *I waited all day* ***in the fond hope that*** (mając złudną nadzieję, że) *she would change her mind.* ▶ **nierealny, łatwowierny**

fondle /ˈfɒndl/ verb [T] to touch sb/sth gently in a loving or sexual way ▶ **pieścić, dotykać czule**

fondly /ˈfɒndli/ adv. in a loving way: *Miss Murphy will be fondly remembered by all her former students.* ▶ **czule**

fondness /ˈfɒndnəs/ noun [U, sing.] **(a) fondness (for sb/sth)** a liking for sb/sth: *I've always had a fondness for cats.* ◇ *My grandmother talks about her schooldays* ***with fondness.*** ▶ **zamiłowanie**

font /fɒnt/ noun [C] **1** a large stone bowl in a church that holds water for a **baptism** ▶ **chrzcielnica 2** the particular size and style of a set of letters that are used in printing, on a computer screen, etc. ▶ **czcionka**

⚷ **food** /fuːd/ noun **1** [U] something that people or animals eat: *Food and drink will be provided after the meeting.* ◇ *There is a shortage of food in some areas.* ▶ **żywność, jedzenie 2** [C,U] a particular type of food that you eat: *My favourite food is pasta.* ◇ *Have you ever had Japanese food?* ◇ *baby food* ◇ *dog food* ◇ *health foods* ▶ **żywność, jedzenie** ➲ note at **restaurant**

ˈfood chain noun [C] (usually **the food chain**) a series of living creatures, each of which feeds on the one below it in the series ▶ **łańcuch pokarmowy**

foodie /ˈfuːdi/ noun [C] (informal) a person who is very interested in cooking and eating different kinds of food ▶ **smakosz/ka**

ˈfood poisoning noun [U] an illness that is caused by eating food that is bad ▶ **zatrucie pokarmowe**

ˈfood processor noun [C] an electric machine that can mix food and also cut food into small pieces ▶ **mikser, robot kuchenny** ➲ picture at **mixer**

foodstuff /ˈfuːdstʌf/ noun [C, usually pl.] a substance that is used as food: *There has been a sharp rise in the cost of basic foodstuffs.* ▶ **artykuł żywnościowy**

fool[1] /fuːl/ noun [C] a person who is silly or who acts in a silly way: *I felt such a fool when I realized my stupid mistake.* ◇ *She was fool enough* (była na tyle naiwna) *to believe it when he said that he loved her.* ▶ **głupiec, dureń** SYN **idiot** ➲ look at **April Fool's Day**

IDM **make a fool of sb/yourself** to make sb/yourself look foolish or silly: *Sheila got drunk and made a complete fool of herself.* ▶ **robić z (siebie/kogoś) głupca**

fool[2] /fuːl/ verb **1** [T] **fool sb (into doing sth)** to trick sb: *Don't be fooled into believing everything that the salesman says.* ▶ **nabierać kogoś, okpiwać 2** [I] to speak without being serious: *You didn't really believe me when I said I was going to America, did you? I was only fooling.* ▶ **żartować**

PHR V **fool about/around** to behave in a silly way: *Stop fooling around with that knife or someone will get hurt!* ▶ **wygłupiać się, błaznować**

foolhardy /ˈfuːlhɑːdi/ adj. taking unnecessary risks ▶ **ryzykancki, szalony**

foolish /ˈfuːlɪʃ/ adj. **1** not sensible: *I was foolish enough to trust him.* ▶ **niemądry, lekkomyślny 2** looking silly or feeling embarrassed: *I felt a bit foolish when I couldn't remember the man's name.* ◇ *He felt rather foolish* (głupio) *when he fell in the street.* ▶ **głupi** SYN for both meanings **silly, stupid**

■ **foolishly** adv.: *I foolishly agreed to lend him money.* ▶ **niemądrze, lekkomyślnie** | **foolishness** noun [U] ▶ **głupota, lekkomyślność**

foolproof /ˈfuːlpruːf/ adj. not capable of going wrong or being wrongly used: *Our security system is absolutely foolproof.* ▶ **nie do zepsucia, niezawodny**

F

foot[1] /fʊt/ noun [C] (pl. **feet** /fiːt/) **1** the lowest part of the body, at the end of the leg, on which a person or an animal stands: *People usually* ***get to their feet*** (powstają) *for the national anthem.* ◇ *She* ***rose*** *to her* ***feet.*** Wstała. ◇ *I usually go to school* ***on foot*** (pieszo). ◇ *I need to sit down – I've been* ***on my feet*** *all day.* ◇ *She sat by the fire and the dog sat at her feet.* ◇ *a foot brake* hamulec nożny ◇ *a foot pump* pompka nożna ◇ *a foot pedal* pedał nożny ▶ **stopa**

Boso to **barefoot** lub **in bare feet**: *There's broken glass on the floor, so don't walk around* ***in bare feet.*** ➲ look at **leg** ➲ picture at **body**

2 [in compounds] having or using the type of foot or number of feet mentioned: *There are no left-footed players in the team.* ◇ *a four-footed creature* czworonożne stworzenie ▶ **-nożny 3** the part of a sock, etc. that covers the foot ▶ **stopa** ℹ Dwojaka lm: **feet** lub **foot**. **4** [sing.] **the foot of sth** the bottom of sth: *There's a note at the foot of the page.* ◇ *the foot of the stairs* ◇ *at the foot of the bed* w nogach łóżka ▶ **dół (czegoś)**, **spód** OPP **top** ℹ Antonimem **the foot of the bed** jest **the head of the bed**. **5** (abbr. **ft**) a measure of length; 30.48 centimetres. There are 3 feet in a yard: *'How tall are you?' 'Five foot six (inches).'* ◇ *a six-foot high wall* ▶ **stopa** ℹ Więcej o miarach w dodatku *Wyrażenia liczbowe* na końcu słownika.

IDM **be rushed/run off your feet** to be extremely busy; to have too many things to do: *Over Christmas we were rushed off our feet at work.* ▶ **mieć pełne ręce roboty**

fall/land on your feet to be lucky in finding yourself in a good situation, or in getting out of a difficult situation: *I really landed on my feet getting such a good job with so little experience.* ▶ **spadać na cztery łapy**, **wychodzić cało z opresji**

find your feet → FIND[1]

get/have cold feet → COLD[1]

get/start off on the right/wrong foot (with sb) (informal) to start a relationship well/badly: *I seem to have got off on the wrong foot with the new boss.* ▶ (*stosunki z kimś*) **zrobić dobry/zły początek**

have one foot in the grave (informal) to be so old or ill that you are not likely to live much longer ▶ **być jedną nogą w grobie**

(back) on your feet completely healthy again after an illness or a time of difficulty ▶ **całkowicie zdrowy** (*po chorobie*), **znów w dobrej formie**

put your feet up to sit down and relax, especially with your feet off the floor and supported: *I'm so tired that I just want to go home and put my feet up.* ▶ **odpoczywać**

put your foot down (informal) to say firmly that sth must (not) happen: *I put my foot down and told Andy he couldn't use our car any more.* ▶ **zawziąć się**, **stawiać na swoim**

put your foot in it (informal) to say or do sth that makes sb embarrassed or upset ▶ **popełniać gafę**, **dawać plamę**

set foot in/on sth to visit, enter or arrive at/in a place: *No woman has ever set foot in the temple.* ▶ **przekraczać próg**

stand on your own (two) feet to take care of yourself without help; to be independent ▶ **stawać na (własne) nogi**, **dawać sobie radę**

under your feet in the way; stopping you from working, etc.: *Would somebody get these children out from under my feet and take them to the park?* ▶ (*przen.*) **pod nogami**

foot[2] /fʊt/ verb

IDM **foot the bill (for sth)** (informal) to pay (for sth) ▶ **płacić rachunek**

footage /ˈfʊtɪdʒ/ noun [U] part of a film showing a particular event: *The documentary included footage of the assassination of Kennedy.* ▶ **materiał filmowy**

football /ˈfʊtbɔːl/ noun **1** (especially US **soccer** /ˈsɒkə(r)/) [U] a game that is played by two teams of eleven players who try to kick a round ball into a goal: *a football pitch/match* ▶ **piłka nożna** ➲ note at **sport**

W USA używa się słowa **soccer**, mówiąc o piłce nożnej, ponieważ tam **football** oznacza **American football**.

2 [C] the large round ball that is used in this game ▶ **piłka futbolowa**

footballer /ˈfʊtbɔːlə(r)/ noun [C] a person who plays football: *a talented footballer* ▶ **piłkarz**

ˈ**football pools** (also **the pools**) noun [pl.] a game in which people bet money on the results of football matches and can win large amounts of money ▶ **zakłady ligi piłkarskiej**

footbridge /ˈfʊtbrɪdʒ/ noun [C] a narrow bridge used only by people who are walking ▶ **kładka**

foothill /ˈfʊthɪl/ noun [usually pl.] a hill or low mountain at the base of a higher mountain or range of mountains: *the foothills of the Himalayas* ▶ **podgórze**

foothold /ˈfʊthəʊld/ noun [C] a place where you can safely put your foot when you are climbing: (figurative) *We need to get a foothold in the European market.* ▶ **oparcie dla nóg**, **punkt zaczepienia**

footing /ˈfʊtɪŋ/ noun [sing.] **1** being able to stand firmly on a surface: *Climbers usually attach themselves to a rope in case they* ***lose their footing.*** ◇ (figurative) *The company is now* ***on a firm footing*** (stoi teraz mocno na nogach) *and should soon show a profit.* ▶ **równowaga**, **oparcie (dla nóg) 2** the level or position of sb/sth (in relation to sb/sth else): *to be* ***on an equal footing*** (na równej stopie) *with sb* ▶ **stosunki** (*np. zażyłe, przyjacielskie*)

footnote /ˈfʊtnəʊt/ noun [C] an extra piece of information that is added at the bottom of a page in a book ▶ **przypis**, **odnośnik**

footpath /ˈfʊtpɑːθ; US -pæθ/ noun [C] a path for people to walk on: *a public footpath* ▶ **ścieżka**

footprint /ˈfʊtprɪnt/ noun [C] a mark that is left on the ground by a foot or a shoe ▶ **ślad** (*stopy*) ➲ look at **track**

footstep /ˈfʊtstep/ noun [C] the sound of sb walking; the mark that a person leaves when walking: *I heard his footsteps in the hall.* ◇ *footsteps in the snow* ▶ **odgłos kroków**; **ślad** (*stopy*)

IDM **follow in sb's footsteps** → FOLLOW

footwear /ˈfʊtweə(r)/ noun [U] boots or shoes ▶ **obuwie**

for[1] /fə(r); strong form fɔː(r)/ prep. **1** showing the person that will use or have sth: *Here is a letter for you.* ◇ *He made lunch for them.* ◇ *It's a book for children.* ▶ **dla 2** in order to help sb/sth: *What can I do for you?* ◇ *You should take some medicine for your cold* (lekarstwo na kaszel). ◇ *Doctors are fighting for his life.* ◇ *Please be friendly to Pete, for my sake* (ze względu na mnie). ◇ *shampoo for dry hair* (do włosów suchych) ▶ **dla**, **na**, **o 3** as a representative (of sb/sth): *She plays hockey for England* (w reprezentacji narodowej Anglii). ▶ **z 4** meaning sth: *What's the 'C' for* (co oznacza „C") *in 'BBC'?* ◇ *What's the Polish for* (jak jest po polsku) *'window'?* **5** in support of (sb/sth): *Are you for or against shops opening on Sundays?* ◇ *Three cheers for the winner!* Na cześć zwycięskiej drużyny trzykrotne: hip hip hurra! ▶ **za 6** in order to do, have or get sth: *What's this gadget for?* Do czego jest ten gadżet? ◇ *Do you learn English for your job or for fun* (do pracy czy dla przyjemności)*?* ◇ *to go for a walk/drink* iść na spacer/drinka ◇ *to go for a swim* iść popływać ◇ *What did you do that for?* Po co to zrobiłeś? ◇ *She asked me for help.* ◇ *Phone now for infor-*

mation (aby uzyskać więcej informacji). ▶ **do (robienia) czegoś, na, o** **7** (showing a reason) as a result of: *Ben didn't want to come for some reason.* ◇ *He was sent to prison for robbery.* ◇ *I couldn't speak for laughing.* Tak się śmiałam, że nie mogłam mówić. ◇ *We'll all feel better for a good night's sleep* (po dobrze przespanej nocy). ◇ *If it weren't/hadn't been for you* (gdyby nie ty), *I would never have got to the airport on time.* ▶ **za, z powodu** **8** (showing the price or value of sth) in exchange for: *I bought this car for £2 000.* ◇ *You get one point for each correct answer.* ◇ *I want to exchange this sweater for a larger one.* ◇ *The officer was accused of giving secret information for cash.* ▶ (*wymiana*) **za; na** **9** [after an adjective] showing how usual, suitable, difficult, etc. sb/sth is in relation to sb/sth else: *She's tall for her age.* ◇ *It's quite warm for January.* ◇ *It's unusual for Alex to be late.* Alexowi rzadko się zdarza spóźnić. ◇ *I think Sandra is perfect for this job* (do tej pracy). ◇ *This game's too hard for me* (jest za trudna dla mnie) – *I give up.* ▶ **jak na** **10** showing the place that sb/sth will go to: *Is this the train for Glasgow?* ◇ *They set off for the shops.* ▶ **do** **11** showing a length of time: *I'm going away for a few days.* ◇ *for a while/a long time/ages* ◇ *They have left the town **for good*** (na zawsze). ◇ *He was in prison for 20 years.* Siedział w więzieniu 20 lat. ◇ *He has been in prison for 20 years.* Siedzi w więzieniu od 20 lat. ▶ **na, przez** ➲ note at **during**, **since** **12** at a particular, fixed time: *What did they give you for your birthday?* ◇ *Shall we have eggs for breakfast?* ◇ *I'm going to my parents' for Christmas.* ◇ *The appointment is for 10.30.* ▶ **na** **13** showing how many times sth has happened: *I'm warning you for the last time.* ◇ *I met him for the second time yesterday.* ▶ **po** (*raz pierwszy/ostatni itp.*) **14** showing a distance: *He walked for ten miles.* ▶ **przez**

IDM **be (in) for it** (Brit., informal) to be going to get into trouble or be punished: *If you arrive late again, you'll be in for it* (dostanie ci się). ▶ **dostawać się komuś (za coś)**

for all in spite of: *For all his money, he's a very lonely man.* ▶ **po/mimo**

for ever → FOREVER

for² /fə(r); strong form fɔː(r)/ conj. (formal) because: *The children soon lost their way, for they had never been in the forest alone before.* ▶ **ponieważ**

forage /ˈfɒrɪdʒ/ verb [I] **forage (for sth)** (used especially about animals) to search for food ▶ **szukać** (*pożywienia*)

forbid /fəˈbɪd/ verb [T] (**forbidding**; pt **forbade** or **forbad** /fəˈbæd/, pp **forbidden** /fəˈbɪdn/) **1 forbid sb to do sth** to order sb not to do sth: *My parents forbade me to see Tim again.* ▶ **zabraniać** OPP **allow** **2** [usually passive] to not allow sth: *Smoking is forbidden inside the building.* ▶ **zabraniać** OPP for both meanings **allow** SYN **prohibit**

forbidding /fəˈbɪdɪŋ/ adj. looking unfriendly or frightening: *The coast near the village is rather grey and forbidding.* ▶ **groźny, odpychający**

⚷ **force¹** /fɔːs/ noun **1** [U] physical strength or power: *The force of the explosion knocked them to the ground.* ◇ *The police **used force** to break up the demonstration.* ▶ **siła** **2** [U] power and influence: *the force of public opinion* ▶ **siła** **3** [C] a person or thing that has power or influence: *Britain is no longer a major force in international affairs.* ◇ *Julia has been **the driving force*** (siłą napędową) *behind the company's success.* ▶ **potęga** **4** [C] a group of people who are trained for a particular purpose: *a highly trained workforce* (siła robocza) ◇ *the police force* policja ◇ *a UN peace-keeping force* (siły pokojowe) ▶ **siły; jednostki** (*np. bojowe*); **siła** **5** [usually plural] the soldiers and weapons that an army, etc. has: *the armed forces* ▶ **siły zbrojne** **6** [C,U] (technical) a power that can cause change or movement: *the force of gravity* (przyciągania) ▶ **siła** (*wiatru*)

IDM **bring sth/come into force** to start using a new law, etc.; to start being used: *The government want to bring new anti-pollution legislation into force next year.* ▶ **wprowadzać (w życie); wchodzić w życie**

force of habit if you do sth from or out of force of habit you do it in a particular way because you have always done it that way in the past ▶ **siła nawyku**

(be) in force **1** (used about people) in large numbers: *The police were present in force at the football match.* ▶ **licznie** **2** (used about a law, rule, etc.) to be used: *The new speed limit is now in force.* ▶ **obowiązywać, być ważnym**

join forces (with sb) → JOIN¹

⚷ **force²** /fɔːs/ verb [T] **1 force sb (to do sth); force sb (into sth/doing sth)** to make sb do sth that they do not want to do: *She forced herself to speak to him.* ◇ *The President was forced into resigning.* ▶ **zmuszać** **2** to use physical strength to do sth or to move sth: *The window had been forced (open).* ◇ *We had to force our way* (przedzierać się) *through the crowd.* ▶ **robić (coś) na siłę, forsować** **3** to make sth happen when it will not happen naturally: *to force a smile/laugh* ◇ *To force the issue, I gave him until midday to decide.* ▶ **wymuszać**

ˌforce-ˈfeed verb [T] to use force to make sb, especially a prisoner, eat or drink, by putting food or drink down their throat ▶ **karmić na siłę**

forceful /ˈfɔːsfl/ adj. having the power to persuade people: *He has a very forceful personality.* ◇ *a forceful speech* ▶ **silny, wpływowy**

forceps /ˈfɔːseps/ noun [pl.] a special instrument that looks like a pair of scissors but is not sharp. **Forceps** are used by doctors for holding things firmly: *a pair of forceps* ▶ **kleszcze**

forcible /ˈfɔːsəbl/ adj. [only before a noun] **1** done using (physical) force: *The police made a forcible entry into the building.* ▶ **dokonany przemocą** **2** (used about ideas, an argument, etc.) strong; convincing: *a forcible reminder* ▶ **dosadny, przekonujący**

■ **forcibly** /-əbli/ adv.: *The squatters were forcibly removed by the police.* ▶ **na siłę, przemocą**

ford /fɔːd/ noun [C] a place in a river where you can walk or drive across because the water is not deep ▶ **bród**

fore /fɔː(r)/ noun

IDM **be/come to the fore** to be in or get into an important position so that you are noticed by people ▶ **być na czele; wysuwać się na pierwszy plan**

forearm /ˈfɔːrɑːm/ noun [C] the part of your arm between your elbow and your wrist ▶ **przedramię**

forebear (also **forbear**) /ˈfɔːbeə(r)/ noun [usually pl.] (formal or literary) a person in your family who lived a long time ago ▶ **przodek** SYN **ancestor**

foreboding /fɔːˈbəʊdɪŋ/ noun [U, sing.] a strong feeling that danger or trouble is coming: *She was filled with **a sense of foreboding**.* ▶ **złe przeczucie**

⚷ **forecast** /ˈfɔːkɑːst; US -kæst/ verb [T] (pt, pp **forecast** or **forecasted**) to say (with the help of information) what will probably happen in the future: *The Chancellor did not forecast the sudden rise in inflation.* ◇ *Rain has been forecast for tomorrow.* ▶ **przewidywać, prognozować**

■ **forecast** noun [C]: *a sales forecast for the coming year* ▶ **prognoza** ➲ look at **weather forecast**

forecourt /ˈfɔːkɔːt/ noun [C] a large open area in front of a building such as a hotel or petrol station ▶ **plac**

forefinger /ˈfɔːfɪŋɡə(r)/ (also **index finger**) noun [C] the finger next to the thumb ▶ **palec wskazujący**

forefront /ˈfɔːfrʌnt/ noun [sing.] the leading position; the position at the front: *Our department is right **at the forefront of*** (zajmuje czołową pozycję) *scientific research.* ▶ **czołowa pozycja**

forego = FORGO

foregone /ˈfɔːɡɒn/ adj.
IDM **a foregone conclusion** a result that is or was certain to happen: *Her promotion was a foregone conclusion.* ▶ **sprawa z góry przesądzona**

foreground /ˈfɔːɡraʊnd/ noun [sing.] **1** the part of a view, picture, photograph, etc. that appears closest to the person looking at it: *Notice the artist's use of colour* ***in the foreground*** *of the picture.* ▶ **przedni plan 2** a position where you will be noticed most: *He likes to be in the foreground at meetings.* ▶ **pierwszy plan** OPP for both meanings **background**

forehand /ˈfɔːhænd/ noun [C] a way of hitting the ball in sports such as **tennis**, that is made with the inside of your hand facing forward ▶ **forhend** OPP **backhand**

forehead /ˈfɔːhed; ˈfɒrɪd; US -red/ (also **brow**) noun [C] the part of sb's face above the eyes and below the hair ▶ **czoło** ➲ picture at **body**

⚷ **foreign** /ˈfɒrən/ adj. **1** belonging to or connected with a country that is not your own: *a foreign country/coin/accent* ◇ *to learn a foreign language* ▶ **obcy, zagraniczny 2** [only before a noun] dealing with or involving other countries: *foreign policy* ◇ *foreign affairs/news/trade* ◇ *the French Foreign Minister* minister spraw zagranicznych Francji ▶ **zagraniczny 3** (used about an object or a substance) not being where it should be: *The X-ray showed up a foreign body in her stomach.* ▶ **obcy**

the ˌ**Foreign and ˈCommonwealth Office** noun [sing., with sing. or pl. verb] (abbr. **FCO** /ˌef siː ˈəʊ/) the British government department that deals with relations with other countries ▶ **brytyjskie Ministerstwo Spraw Zagranicznych** ℹ Wiele osób używa jeszcze dawnej nazwy tego ministerstwa **the Foreign Office**.

foreigner /ˈfɒrənə(r)/ noun [C] a person who belongs to a country that is not your own ▶ **obcokrajowiec**

ˌ**foreign exˈchange** noun [C,U] the system of buying and selling money from a different country; the place where it is bought and sold ▶ **giełda walutowa**

the ˌ**Foreign ˈSecretary** noun [C] the person in the government who is responsible for dealing with foreign countries ▶ **minister spraw zagranicznych** ➲ look at **Home Secretary**

foreleg /ˈfɔːleɡ/ noun [C] either of the two front legs of an animal that has four legs ▶ **przednia łapa** (*zwierząt czworonożnych*) ➲ note at **hind**

foremost /ˈfɔːməʊst/ adj. most famous or important; best: *Laurence Olivier was among the foremost actors of the last century.* ▶ **najsłynniejszy, czołowy**
IDM **first and foremost** → FIRST²

forename /ˈfɔːneɪm/ noun [C] (formal) your first name, that is given to you when you are born ▶ **imię** ➲ note at **name**

forensic /fəˈrensɪk; -ˈrenzɪk/ adj. [only before a noun] using scientific tests to find out about a crime: *The police are carrying out forensic tests to try and find out the cause of death.* ▶ **sądowy, kryminalistyczny**

forerunner /ˈfɔːrʌnə(r)/ noun [C] **a forerunner (of sb/sth)** a person or thing that is an early example or a sign of sth that appears or develops later: *Country music was undoubtedly one of the forerunners of rock and roll.* ▶ **prekursor; zwiastun**

foresee /fɔːˈsiː/ verb [T] (pt **foresaw** /fɔːˈsɔː/, pp **foreseen** /fɔːˈsiːn/) to know or guess that sth is going to happen in the future: *Nobody could have foreseen the result of the election.* ▶ **przewidywać** ➲ look at **unforeseen**

foreseeable /fɔːˈsiːəbl/ adj. that can be expected; that you can guess will happen: *These problems were foreseeable.* ◇ *The weather won't change* ***in the foreseeable future.*** ▶ **możliwy do przewidzenia**

foreseen past participle of **foresee**

foreshadow /fɔːˈʃædəʊ/ verb [T] (formal) to be a sign of sth that will happen in the future ▶ **zapowiadać, zwiastować**

foresight /ˈfɔːsaɪt/ noun [U] the ability to see what will probably happen in the future and to use this knowledge to make careful plans: *My neighbour had the foresight to move house* (mój sąsiad był przewidujący i wyprowadził się) *before the new motorway was built.* ▶ **zdolność przewidywania, przezorność** ➲ look at **hindsight**

foreskin /ˈfɔːskɪn/ noun [C] the piece of skin that covers the end of the male sexual organ ▶ **napletek**

⚷ **forest** /ˈfɒrɪst/ noun [C,U] a large area of land covered with trees: *a forest fire* ◇ *tropical rain forests* tropikalne lasy deszczowe ▶ **las**

> A **forest** is larger than a **wood**. A **jungle** is a forest in a tropical part of the world.

forestall /fɔːˈstɔːl/ verb [T] to take action to prevent sb from doing sth or sth from happening ▶ **ubiegać**

forestry /ˈfɒrɪstri/ noun [U] the science of planting and taking care of trees in forests ▶ **leśnictwo**

foretaste /ˈfɔːteɪst/ noun [sing.] **a foretaste (of sth)** a small amount of a particular experience or situation that shows you what it will be like when the same thing happens on a larger scale in the future ▶ **przedsmak**

foretell /fɔːˈtel/ verb [T] (pt, pp **foretold** /fɔːˈtəʊld/) (formal) to say what will happen in the future ▶ **przepowiadać**

forethought /ˈfɔːθɔːt/ noun [U] careful thought about, or preparation for, the future: *With forethought, anyone can give a good party.* ▶ **przewidywanie, przezorność**

⚷ **forever** /fərˈevə(r)/ adv. **1** (also **for ever**) for all time; permanently: *I wish the holidays would last forever!* ◇ *I realized that our relationship had finished forever.* ◇ *My sister always* ***takes forever*** (zawsze siedzi całą wieczność) *in the bathroom.* ◇ *(literary) I'll regret it for ever more.* Będę tego żałował przez całe życie. ▶ **wiecznie, na zawsze 2** [only used with continuous tenses] very often; in a way which is annoying: *Our neighbours are forever having noisy parties.* ▶ **ciągle**

forewarn /fɔːˈwɔːn/ verb [T, often passive] **forewarn sb (of sth)** (formal) to warn sb about sth bad or unpleasant before it happens ▶ **ostrzegać kogoś zawczasu (o czymś)**
■ **forewarning** noun [U,C] ▶ **ostrzeżenie (zawczasu)**

foreword /ˈfɔːwɜːd/ noun [C] a piece of writing at the beginning of a book that introduces the book and/or its author ▶ **przedmowa**

forfeit /ˈfɔːfɪt; US -fət/ verb [T] to lose sth or have sth taken away from you, usually because you have done sth wrong ▶ **utracić** (*np. prawa, depozyt*)
■ **forfeit** noun [C] ▶ **utrata** (*np. praw*)

forgave past tense of **forgive**

forge¹ /fɔːdʒ/ verb [T] **1** to put a lot of effort into making sth strong and successful: *Our school has forged links with a school in Romania.* ▶ **nawiązywać** (*stosunki*) **2** to make an illegal copy of sth: *to forge a signature/banknote/passport* ▶ **fałszować, podrabiać** ➲ look at **counterfeit**
PHR V **forge ahead** to go forward or make progress quickly: *I think it's now time to forge ahead with our plans to open a new shop.* ▶ **wysuwać się naprzód, wychodzić na prowadzenie**

forge² /fɔːdʒ/ noun [C] a place where objects are made by heating and shaping metal ▶ **kuźnia**

forgery /ˈfɔːdʒəri/ noun (pl. **forgeries**) **1** [U] the crime of illegally copying a document, painting, etc. ▶ **fałszerstwo, podrabianie 2** [C] a document, picture, etc.

that is a copy of the real one ▶ **falsyfikat**; **podrobiony obraz/dokument/podpis**

forget /fə'get/ verb (pt **forgot** /fə'gɒt/, pp **forgotten** /fə'gɒtn/) **1** [T] **forget (doing) sth** to not be able to remember sth: *I've forgotten what I was going to say.* ◇ *I've forgotten her telephone number.* ◇ *He forgot that he had invited her to the party.* ◇ *I'll never forget meeting* (nigdy nie zapomnę, jak spotkałam) *my husband for the first time.* ▶ **zapominać 2** [I,T] **forget (about) sth**; **forget to do sth** to fail to remember to do sth that you ought to have done: *'Why didn't you come to the party?' 'Oh dear! I completely forgot about it!'* ◇ *'Did you feed the cat?' 'Sorry, I forgot.'* ◇ *Don't forget to do your homework!* ▶ **zapominać 3** [T] to fail to bring sth with you: *When my father got to the airport he realized he'd forgotten his passport.* ▶ **zapominać**

> Mówiąc o miejscu, w którym czegoś zapomnieliśmy, należy użyć czasownika **leave.** Uwaga! Nie można powiedzieć ~~*My father forgot his passport at home*~~. Należy powiedzieć: *He left his passport at home.*

4 [I,T] **forget (about) sb/sth**; **forget about doing sth** to make an effort to stop thinking about sb/sth; to stop thinking that sth is possible: *Forget about your work and enjoy yourself!* ◇ *Let's forget about cooking dinner for everyone and just offer them drinks instead.* ◇ *'I'm sorry I shouted at you.' 'Forget it* (nie przejmuj się tym).*'* ▶ **zapominać 5 forget yourself** [T] to behave without proper control; to behave in a way that is not like the way you usually behave: *When he heard the news he completely forgot himself and kissed everybody in the room.* ▶ **zapominać się**

forgetful /fə'getfl/ adj. often forgetting things: *My mother's nearly 80 and she's starting to get a bit forgetful* (zaczyna zapominać o różnych rzeczach). ▶ **zapominalski** SYN **absent-minded**

forget-me-not noun [C,U] a small plant with tiny blue flowers, or a number of these ▶ **niezapominajka**

forgivable /fə'gɪvəbl/ adj. that can be forgiven ▶ **wybaczalny**

forgive /fə'gɪv/ verb [T] (pt **forgave** /fə'geɪv/, pp **forgiven** /fə'gɪvn/) **1 forgive sb/yourself (for sth/for doing sth)** to stop being angry towards sb for sth that they have done wrong: *I can't forgive his behaviour last night.* ◇ *I can't forgive him for his behaviour last night.* ◇ *I will never forgive him for behaving like that last night.* ▶ **przebaczać 2 forgive me (for doing sth)** (used for politely saying sorry): *Forgive me for asking, but where did you get that dress?* ▶ **przepraszać**, **wybaczać**
■ **forgiveness** noun [U]: *He **begged for forgiveness** for what he had done.* ▶ **wybaczenie**; **odpuszczenie (grzechu)**

forgiving /fə'gɪvɪŋ/ adj. **forgiving (of sth)** ready and able to forgive ▶ **wyrozumiały**; **łatwo wybaczający**

forgo (also **forego**) /fɔː'gəʊ/ verb [T] (**forgoes** /-'gəʊz/, pt **forwent** /-'went/, pp **forgone** /-'gɒn/) (formal) to decide not to have or do sth that you want ▶ **wyrzekać się**

forgot past tense of **forget**

forgotten past participle of **forget**

fork¹ /fɔːk/ noun [C] **1** a small metal object with a handle and two or more **prongs** that you use for lifting food to your mouth when eating: *a knife and fork* ▶ **widelec 2** a large tool with a handle and three or more **prongs** that you use for digging the ground: *a garden fork* ▶ **widły** ➲ picture at **garden 3** a place where a road, river, etc. divides into two parts; one of these parts: *After about two miles you'll come to a fork in the road.* ▶ **rozwidlenie**; **odnoga**, **rozdroże**

fork² /fɔːk/ verb [I] **1** (used about a road, river, etc.) to divide into two parts: *Bear right where the road forks.* ▶ **rozwidlać się 2** to go along the left or right fork of a road: *Fork right up the hill.* ▶ **skręcać**

PHR V **fork out (for sth)** (informal) to pay for sth when you do not want to: *I forked out over £20 for that book.* ▶ **bulić**

forked /fɔːkt/ adj. with one end divided into two parts, like the shape of the letter 'Y': *a bird with a forked tail* ◇ *the forked tongue of a snake* ▶ **rozwidlony**

ˌforked 'lightning noun [U] the type of **lightning** that is like a line that divides into smaller lines near the ground ▶ **piorun liniowy** ➲ look at **sheet lightning**

forklift truck /ˌfɔːklɪft 'trʌk/ (also **'forklift**) noun [C] a vehicle with special equipment on the front for moving and lifting heavy objects ▶ **wózek widłowy** ➲ picture at **car**

F

forlorn /fə'lɔːn/ adj. lonely and unhappy; not cared for ▶ **żałosny**, **opuszczony**

form¹ /fɔːm/ noun **1** [C] a particular type or variety of sth or a way of doing sth: *Swimming is a good form of exercise.* ◇ *We never eat meat **in any form.*** ▶ **forma**, **postać 2** [C,U] the shape of sb/sth; the way sth is presented: *He could just make out a shadowy form.* ◇ *The articles were published **in book form.*** ▶ **forma**, **kształt 3** [C] an official document with questions on it and spaces where you give answers and personal information: *an **entry form** for a competition* ◇ *Please fill in an **application form.*** ▶ **formularz** ⓘ W Amer. ang. używa się konstrukcji **fill out a form. 4** [U] the state of being fit and strong for a sports player, team, etc.: *to be **in/out of form*** ◇ *to be **on/off form*** być/nie być w formie ▶ **forma**, **kondycja 5** [U] how well sb/sth is performing at a particular time, for example in sport or business: *On present form* (sądząc z ostatnich wyników) *the Italian team should win easily.* ▶ **wyniki 6** [C] (Brit., old-fashioned) a class in a school: *Who's your form teacher?* ▶ **klasa**

> In Britain, the years at secondary school used to be called **first/second/third**, etc. **form** but now they are called **Year 7** to **Year 11**. However the last two years of school (for pupils aged between 16 and 18) are still referred to as **the sixth form**.

7 [C] a way of spelling or changing a word in a sentence: *the irregular forms of the verbs* ◇ *The plural form of mouse is mice.* ▶ **forma**

IDM **true to form** → TRUE

form² /fɔːm/ verb **1** [I,T] to begin to exist or to make sth exist: *A pattern was beginning to form in the monthly sales figures.* ◇ *These tracks were formed by rabbits.* ▶ **tworzyć (się) 2** [T] to begin to have or think sth: *I haven't formed an opinion about the new boss yet.* ◇ *to form a friendship* zaprzyjaźnić się ▶ **wyrabiać** (*opinię, pogląd*) **3** [T] to make or organize sth: *to form a government* ◇ *In English we usually form the past tense by adding '-ed'.* ▶ **tworzyć 4** [T] to become or make a particular shape: *The police formed a circle around the house.* ◇ *to form a line/queue* ▶ **formować**, **kształtować**; **zmieniać w coś 5** [T] to be the thing mentioned: *Seminars form the main part of the course.* ◇ *The survey **formed part of** a larger programme of market research.* ▶ **tworzyć**, **stanowić część czegoś**

formal /'fɔːml/ adj. **1** (used about language or behaviour) used when you want to appear serious or official and in situations in which you do not know the other people very well: *'Yours faithfully' is a formal way of ending a letter.* ◇ *She has a very formal manner – she doesn't seem to be able to relax.* ◇ *a formal occasion* ▶ **formalny**, **oficjalny** OPP **informal 2** official: *I shall make **a formal complaint** to the hospital about the way I was treated.* ▶ **urzędowy**, **oficjalny**
■ **formally** /-məli/ adv. ▶ **formalnie**, **oficjalnie**

formality /fɔː'mæləti/ noun (pl. **formalities**) **1** [C] an action that is necessary according to custom or law:

There are certain formalities to attend to before we can give you a visa. ▶ **formalność** **2** [C] a thing that you must do as part of an official process, but which has little meaning and will not affect what happens: *Michael already knows he has the job so the interview is* ***just a formality.*** ▶ **formalność** **3** [U] careful attention to rules of language and behaviour ▶ **poprawność** (*np. zachowania*), (*sposób postępowania*) **forma**

formalize (also -ise) /ˈfɔːməlaɪz/ verb [T] **1** to make an arrangement, a plan or a relationship official ▶ **formalizować** **2** to give sth a fixed structure or form by introducing rules ▶ **formalizować**

■ **formalization** (also -isation) /ˌfɔːməlaɪˈzeɪʃn; US -ləˈz-/ noun [U] ▶ **sformalizowanie**

format[1] /ˈfɔːmæt/ noun [C] the shape of sth or the way it is arranged or produced: *It's the same book but in a different format.* ▶ **format**

format[2] /ˈfɔːmæt/ verb [T] (**formatting**; **formatted**) **1** to prepare a computer disk so that data can be recorded on it: *to format a disk* ▶ **formatować** **2** to arrange text on a page or a screen: *to format a document* ▶ **formatować**

formation /fɔːˈmeɪʃn/ noun **1** [U] the act of making or developing sth: *the formation of a new government* ▶ **formowanie**, **budowanie** **2** [C,U] an arrangement or pattern (especially of soldiers, ships, etc.): *A number of planes flew over* ***in formation.*** ▶ **formacja** **3** [C] a thing that is formed; the particular way in which it is formed: *cloud/rock formations* ▶ **formacja**

formative /ˈfɔːmətɪv/ adj. [only before a noun] having an important and lasting influence (on sb's character and opinions): *A child's early years are thought to be the most formative ones.* ▶ **kształtujący**

the **former** /ˈfɔːmə(r)/ noun [sing.] the first (of two people or things just mentioned): *Of the two hospitals in the town – the General and the Royal – the former has the better reputation.* ▶ **poprzedni**, **pierwszy (z dwóch)** ➲ look at **latter**

former /ˈfɔːmə(r)/ adj. [only before a noun] of an earlier time; belonging to the past: *Bill Clinton, the former American President* ◇ *In former times people often had larger families.* ▶ **były**, **dawny**

formerly /ˈfɔːməli/ adv. in the past; before now: *the country of Myanmar (formerly Burma)* ◇ *The hotel was formerly a castle.* ℹ W tym samym znaczeniu częściej używa się wyrażenia **used to**: *The hotel used to be a castle.* ▶ **uprzednio**, **dawniej**

formidable /ˈfɔːmɪdəbl; fəˈmɪd-/ adj. **1** causing you to be quite frightened: *His mother is a rather formidable lady.* ▶ **groźny**, **budzący respekt** **2** difficult to deal with; needing a lot of effort: *Reforming the education system will be a formidable task.* ▶ **ogromny**, **wymagający wiele pracy/wysiłku**

formula /ˈfɔːmjələ/ noun [C] (pl. **formulas** or **formulae** /-liː/) **1** (technical) a group of signs, letters or numbers used in science or mathematics to express a general law or fact: *What is the formula for converting miles to kilometres?* ▶ **wzór** **2** a list of (often chemical) substances used for making sth; the instructions for making sth: *The formula for the new vaccine has not yet been made public.* ▶ **formuła**; **przepis**, **receptura** **3** **a formula for (doing) sth** a plan of how to get or do sth: *What is her formula for success?* ◇ *Unfortunately, there's no* ***magic formula*** *for a perfect marriage.* ▶ **recepta** (*np. na sukces*)

formulate /ˈfɔːmjuleɪt/ verb [T] **1** to prepare and organize a plan or ideas for doing sth: *to formulate a plan* ▶ **formułować** **2** to express sth (clearly and exactly): *She struggled to formulate a simple answer to his question.* ▶ **wyrażać**

forsake /fəˈseɪk/ verb [T] (pt **forsook** /fəˈsʊk/, pp **forsaken** /fəˈseɪkən/) **forsake sb/sth (for sb/sth)** **1** to leave sb/sth, especially when you have a responsibility to stay: *He had made it clear to his wife that he would never forsake her.* ▶ **porzucać** SYN **abandon** **2** to stop doing sth, or leave sth, especially sth that you enjoy: *She forsook the glamour of the city and went to live in the wilds of Scotland.* ▶ **opuszczać** SYN **renounce**

fort /fɔːt/ noun [C] a strong building that is used for military defence ▶ **fort**

forte /ˈfɔːteɪ; US fɔːrt/ noun [sing.] a thing that sb does particularly well: *Languages were never my forte.* ▶ **mocna strona**

forth /fɔːθ/ adv.

IDM **and so forth** and other things like those just mentioned: *The sort of job that you'll be doing is taking messages, making tea and so forth.* ▶ **i tak dalej**, **i tym podobne**

back and forth → BACK[3]

forthcoming /ˌfɔːθˈkʌmɪŋ/ adj. **1** that will happen or appear in the near future: *Look in the local paper for a list of* ***forthcoming events.*** ▶ **nadchodzący** **2** [not before a noun] offered or given: *If no money is forthcoming* (jeżeli nie nadejdą pieniądze) *we shall not be able to continue the project.* ▶ **zaoferowany**; **otrzymany** **3** [not before a noun] (used about a person) ready to be helpful, give information, etc.: *Don't ask the lady at the post office – she's never very forthcoming.* ◇ *Kate isn't very forthcoming about her job* (niechętnie rozmawia o swojej pracy), *so I don't know what she does exactly.* ▶ **rozmowny i pomocny**

forthright /ˈfɔːθraɪt/ adj. saying exactly what you think in a clear and direct way ▶ **otwarty**, **prostolinijny**

forthwith /ˌfɔːθˈwɪθ; -ˈwɪð/ adv. (formal) immediately: *The agreement between us is terminated forthwith.* ▶ **bezzwłocznie**

fortieth /ˈfɔːtiəθ/ ordinal number 40th ▶ **czterdziesty** ➲ note at **sixth**

■ **fortieth** noun [C] 1/40; one of forty equal parts of sth ▶ **(jedna) czterdziesta**

fortification /ˌfɔːtɪfɪˈkeɪʃn/ noun [C, usually pl.] walls, towers, etc., built especially in the past to protect a place against attack ▶ **fortyfikacja**, **umocnienie**

fortify /ˈfɔːtɪfaɪ/ verb [T] (**fortifying**; **fortifies**; pt, pp **fortified**) to make a place stronger and ready for an attack: *to fortify a city* ▶ **fortyfikować**

fortnight /ˈfɔːtnaɪt/ noun [C, usually sing.] (Brit.) two weeks: *We're going on holiday for a fortnight.* ◇ *School finishes in a fortnight/in a fortnight's time* (za dwa tygodnie). ▶ **dwa tygodnie**

fortnightly /ˈfɔːtnaɪtli/ adj., adv. (happening or appearing) once every two weeks: *This magazine is published fortnightly.* ▶ **dwutygodniowy**; **raz na dwa tygodnie**

fortress /ˈfɔːtrəs/ noun [C] a castle or other large strong building that it is not easy to attack ▶ **forteca**

fortuitous /fɔːˈtjuːɪtəs; US -ˈtuː-/ adj. (formal) happening by chance, especially a lucky chance that brings a good result ▶ **szczęśliwym przypadkiem**

■ **fortuitously** adv. ▶ **szczęśliwym przypadkiem**

fortunate /ˈfɔːtʃənət/ adj. lucky: *You were fortunate* (miałeś szczęście) *to have such lovely weather for your holiday.* ◇ *It was fortunate that* (na szczęście) *he was at home when you phoned.* ▶ **szczęśliwy** OPP **unfortunate**

fortunately /ˈfɔːtʃənətli/ adv. by good luck: *Fortunately the traffic wasn't too bad so I managed to get to the meeting on time.* ▶ **na szczęście**, **szczęśliwie (dla kogoś)** SYN **luckily**

fortune /ˈfɔːtʃuːn/ noun **1** [U] chance or the power that affects what happens in sb's life; luck: *Fortune was not on our side that day.* ▶ **fortuna**, **los** SYN **fate** **2** [C,U] a very large amount of money: *I always* ***spend a fortune***

on presents at Christmas. ◇ *She went to Hollywood in search of **fame and fortune**.* ▶ **fortuna**, **majątek** ➲ note at **money 3** [C, usually pl.] the things (both good and bad) that happen to a person, family, country, etc.: *The country's fortunes depend on its industry being successful.* ▶ **losy**, **pomyślność 4** [C] what is going to happen to a person in the future: *Show me your hand and I'll try to **tell your fortune*** (powróżę ci). ▶ **przyszłość** SYN **fate**, **destiny**

IDM **cost the earth/a fortune** → COST[2]

ˈ**fortune-teller** noun [C] a person who tells people what will happen to them in the future ▶ **wróżbita**, **wróżka**

🔑 **forty** /ˈfɔːti/ number 40 ▶ **czterdzieści** ➲ note at **sixty**

IDM **forty winks** (informal) a short sleep, especially during the day ▶ **drzemka (poobiednia)**

forum /ˈfɔːrəm/ noun [C] **a forum (for sth)** a place or meeting where people can exchange and discuss ideas: *TV is now an important forum for political debate.* ▶ **forum**

🔑 **forward**[1] /ˈfɔːwəd/ adv. **1** (also **forwards**) in the direction that is in front of you; towards the front, end or future: *Keep going forward and try not to look back.* ▶ **naprzód**; **w przyszłość** OPP **back**, **backward**, **backwards 2** in the direction of progress: *The discovery of a new form of treatment is a big step forward in the fight against AIDS.* ▶ **naprzód** SYN **ahead** ℹ **Forward** używa się w czasownikach złożonych. Zob. hasła odpowiednich czasowników, np. **bring**, **come**, **look**, **put**.

IDM **backward(s) and forward(s)** → BACKWARDS

🔑 **forward**[2] /ˈfɔːwəd/ adj. **1** [only before a noun] towards the front or future: *forward planning* ▶ **przedni**; **przyszłościowy 2** having developed earlier than is normal or expected; advanced: *Children who read before they are five are considered very forward.* ▶ **nad wiek rozwinięty** OPP **backward 3** behaving towards sb in a way that is too confident or too informal: *I hope you don't think I'm being too forward, asking you so many questions.* ▶ **z tupetem**

forward[3] /ˈfɔːwəd/ verb [T] **1** to send a letter, etc. received at one address to a new address: *The post office is forwarding all our mail.* ▶ **przesyłać dalej** (*na inny/nowy adres*), **przekazywać** ℹ Pisząc do osoby, której nowego adresu nie znasz, możesz wysłać list na stary adres z adnotacją na kopercie **please forward**. **2** to help to improve sth or to make sth progress: *I'm trying to forward my career in publishing.* ▶ **posuwać naprzód**

forward[4] /ˈfɔːwəd/ noun [C] an attacking player in a sport such as football ▶ **napastnik**

ˈ**forwarding address** noun [C] a new address to which letters, etc. should be sent: *The previous owners didn't leave a forwarding address.* ▶ **nowy adres**

ˈ**forward-looking** adj. thinking about or planning for the future; having modern ideas ▶ (*osoba*) **o dalekowzrocznych planach**, **przyszłościowy**

ˈ**forward slash** noun [C] a mark (/) used in computer commands and in Internet addresses ▶ **ukośnik** (*prawy*) ➲ look at **backslash**

forwent past tense of **forgo**

fossil /ˈfɒsl/ noun [C] (part of) an animal or plant that lived thousands of years ago which has turned into rock ▶ **skamielina**

ˈ**fossil fuel** noun [C,U] fuel such as coal or oil, that was formed over millions of years from the remains of animals or plants ▶ **paliwo pochodzenia organicznego**

fossilize (also **-ise**) /ˈfɒsəlaɪz/ verb [I,T] **1** [usually passive] to become or make sth become a **fossil**: *fossilized bones* ▶ **kamienieć**; **tworzyć skamielinę 2** to become or make sb/sth become fixed and unable to change or develop ▶ (*przen.*) **kostnieć**; **powodować kostnienie**

foster /ˈfɒstə(r)/ verb [T] **1** to help or encourage the development of sth (especially feelings or ideas): *to foster somebody's friendship/trust* ▶ **podsycać**, **popierać 2** (especially Brit.) to take a child who needs a home into your family and to take care of them without becoming the legal parent: *to foster a child* ▶ **wychowywać przybrane dziecko** ℹ Przybrani rodzice to **foster parents**, a przybrane dziecko to **foster child**. ➲ note at **child** ➲ look at **adopt**

fought past tense, past participle of **fight**[1]

foul[1] /faʊl/ adj. **1** that smells or tastes disgusting: *a foul-smelling cigar* ◇ *This coffee tastes foul!* ▶ **obrzydliwy**, **cuchnący 2** (especially Brit.) very bad or unpleasant: *Careful what you say – he's got a foul temper* (łatwo wpada w szał). ◇ *The **foul weather** prevented our plane from taking off.* ▶ **podły**, **obrzydliwy 3** (used about language) very rude; full of swearing: *foul language* ◇ *He's got a foul mouth.* Wyraża się wulgarnie. ▶ **ordynarny**, **sprośny**

IDM **fall foul of sb/sth** → FALL[1]

foul[2] /faʊl/ verb **1** [I,T] (used in sports) to attack another player in a way that is not allowed: *Shearer was fouled inside the box and the referee awarded his team a penalty.* ▶ **faulować 2** [T] to make sth dirty (with rubbish, waste, etc.): *Dogs must not foul the pavement.* ▶ **zanieczyszczać**

PHR V **foul sth up** (informal) to spoil sth: *The delay on the train fouled up my plans for the evening.* ▶ **psuć**, **zmarnować**

foul[3] /faʊl/ noun [C] (used in sports) an action that is against the rules: *He was sent off for a foul on the goalkeeper.* ▶ **faul**

ˌ**foul-ˈmouthed** adj. using rude, offensive language: *a foul-mouthed racist* ▶ **wulgarny**

ˌ**foul ˈplay** noun [U] **1** violence or crime that causes sb's death: *The police suspect foul play.* ▶ **przestępstwo** (*zwykle połączone z zabójstwem*) **2** action that is against the rules of a sport ▶ **nieprzepisowe zagranie**

found[1] past tense, past participle of **find**[1]

🔑 **found**[2] /faʊnd/ verb [T] **1** to start an organization, institution, etc.: *This museum was founded in 1683.* ▶ **zakładać**, **fundować 2** to be the first to start building and living in a town or country: *Liberia was founded by freed American slaves.* ▶ **tworzyć**, **budować 3** [usually passive] **found sth (on sth)** to base sth on sth: *The book was founded on real life.* ▶ **opierać**

🔑 **foundation** /faʊnˈdeɪʃn/ noun **1** (**foundations**) [pl.] a layer of bricks, etc. under the surface of the ground that forms the solid base of a building: *The builders have only just started to **lay the foundations** of the new school.* ▶ **fundamenty 2** [C,U] the idea, principle, or fact on which sth is based: *This coursebook aims to give students a solid foundation in grammar.* ◇ *That rumour is completely without foundation* (bez podstaw). ▶ **podstawa 3** [C] an organization that provides money for a special purpose: *The British Heart Foundation* Brytyjska Fundacja Zapobiegania Chorobom Serca ▶ **fundacja 4** [U] the act of starting a new institution or organization: *The organization has grown enormously since its foundation in 1955.* ▶ **założenie**, **ufundowanie 5** a skin-coloured cream that is put on the face underneath make-up ▶ **podkład (kosmetyczny)**

founder /ˈfaʊndə(r)/ noun [C] a person who starts a new institution or organization: *a portrait of the founder of our school* ▶ **założyciel**

ˌ**founder ˈmember** noun [C] one of the original members of a club, organization, etc. ▶ **członek-założyciel**

foundry /ˈfaʊndri/ noun [C] (pl. **foundries**) a place where metal or glass is melted and shaped into objects ▶ **odlewnia**, **huta**

fountain /ˈfaʊntən; US -tn/ noun [C] **1** a decoration (in a garden or in a square in a town) that sends a flow of

F

water into the air; the water that comes out of a **fountain** ▶ **fontanna** **2** a strong flow of liquid or another substance that is forced into the air: *a fountain of blood/sparks* ▶ **fontanna** **3** a person or thing that provides a large amount of sth: *Ed's **a fountain of information** on football.* ▶ **bogate źródło** (*np. wiedzy*)

ˈfountain pen noun [C] a type of pen that you fill with ink ▶ **wieczne pióro** ➲ picture at **stationery**

four /fɔː(r)/ number **1** 4 ▶ **cztery** ➲ note at **six** **2** (**four-**) [in compounds] having four of the thing mentioned: *four-legged animals* ▶ **cztero-, czworo-, czwór-**
IDM **on all fours** bent over with your hands and knees on the ground: *The children went through the tunnel on all fours.* ▶ **na czworakach**

ˌfour-letter ˈword noun [C] a swear word that shocks or offends people (often with four letters) ▶ **nieprzyzwoity wyraz**

fourteen /ˌfɔːˈtiːn/ number 14 ▶ **czternaście** ➲ note at **six**
■ **fourteenth** /ˌfɔːˈtiːnθ/ **1** ordinal number 14th ▶ **czternasty** ➲ note at **sixth** **2** noun [C] 1/14; one of fourteen equal parts of sth ▶ **(jedna) czternasta**

fourth /fɔːθ/ ordinal number 4th ▶ **czwarty** ➲ note at **sixth**
ℹ ¼ nazywa się **quarter**: *a quarter of an hour* kwadrans.
■ **fourth** noun [C] ¼; one of four equal parts of sth ▶ **(jedna) czwarta**

ˌfour-wheel ˈdrive adj. (used about a vehicle) having an engine that turns all four wheels ▶ **napęd na cztery koła**; **samochód z napędem na cztery koła** ➲ picture at **car**

ˌfour-ˈwheeler (US) = QUAD BIKE

fowl /faʊl/ noun [C] (pl. **fowl** or **fowls**) a bird, especially a chicken, that is kept on a farm ▶ **drób**, **ptak**

fox /fɒks/ noun [C] a wild animal like a small dog with reddish-brown fur, a pointed nose and a thick tail ▶ **lis**

> A fox is often described as **sly** or **cunning**. A female fox is a **vixen**, a young fox is a **cub**.

ˈfox-hunting noun [U] a sport in which a **fox** is hunted by people on horses with dogs ▶ **polowanie na lisa**

foyer /ˈfɔɪeɪ/ noun [C] an entrance hall in a cinema, theatre, hotel, etc. where people can meet or wait ▶ **foyer**

fraction /ˈfrækʃn/ noun [C] **1** a small part or amount: *For a fraction of a second I thought the car was going to crash.* ▶ **ułamek**, **cząstka** **2** a division of a number: *½ and ¼ are fractions.* ▶ **ułamek**

fractionally /ˈfrækʃənəli/ adv. to a very small degree; slightly: *fractionally faster/taller/heavier* ▶ **o ułamek sekundy**, **odrobinę**

fracture /ˈfræktʃə(r)/ noun [C,U] a break in a bone or other hard material ▶ **złamanie**, **pęknięcie**
■ **fracture** verb [I,T]: *She fell and fractured her ankle.* ◇ *A water pipe fractured and flooded the bathroom.* ▶ **łamać**, **pękać**

fragile /ˈfrædʒaɪl; US -dʒl/ adj. easily damaged or broken: *This bowl is very fragile. Please handle it carefully.* ▶ **kruchy**, **delikatny**

fragment¹ /ˈfrægmənt/ noun [C] a small piece that has broken off or that comes from sth larger: *The builders found fragments of Roman pottery on the site.* ◇ *I heard only a fragment of their conversation.* ▶ **fragment**, **szczątek**, **okruch**

fragment² /frægˈment/ verb [I,T] (formal) to break (sth) into small pieces: *The country is becoming increasingly fragmented by civil war.* ▶ **rozdrabniać (się)**

fragrance /ˈfreɪgrəns/ noun [C,U] a pleasant smell ▶ **zapach**, **aromat** ➲ note at **smell²**

fragrant /ˈfreɪgrənt/ adj. having a pleasant smell ▶ **pachnący**, **aromatyczny**

frail /freɪl/ adj. weak or not healthy: *My aunt is still very frail after her accident.* ▶ **słaby**, **wątły**

frailty /ˈfreɪlti/ noun [C,U] (pl. **frailties**) weakness of sb's body or character ▶ **słabość**

frame¹ /freɪm/ noun [C] **1** a border of wood or metal that goes around the outside of a door, picture, window, etc.: *a picture frame* ▶ **rama** **2** the basic strong structure of a piece of furniture, building, vehicle, etc. which gives it its shape: *the frame of a bicycle/an aircraft* ▶ **rama**, **szkielet** ➲ picture at **bicycle** **3** [usually pl.] a structure made of plastic or metal that holds the two **lenses** in a pair of glasses: *gold-rimmed frames* ▶ **oprawa** **4** [usually sing.] the basic shape of a human or animal body: *He has a large frame but he's not fat.* ▶ **postura**, **budowa**

frame² /freɪm/ verb [T] **1** to put a border around sth (especially a picture or photograph): *Let's have this photograph framed.* ▶ **oprawiać (w ramę)** **2** [usually passive] to give false evidence against sb in order to make them seem guilty of a crime: *The man claimed that he had been framed by the police.* ▶ **wrabiać (kogoś w coś)** **3** (formal) to express sth in a particular way: *The question was very carefully framed.* ▶ **formułować**

ˌframe of ˈmind noun [sing.] the way you feel or think about sth at a particular time: *We'll discuss this when you're in a better frame of mind.* ▶ **nastrój**, **humor**

ˌframe of ˈreference noun [C] (pl. **frames of reference**) a particular set of beliefs, ideas or experiences that affects how a person understands or judges sth ▶ **układ odniesienia**

framework /ˈfreɪmwɜːk/ noun [C] **1** the basic structure of sth that gives it shape and strength: *A greenhouse is made of glass panels fixed in a metal framework.* ◇ (figurative) *the basic framework of society* ▶ **konstrukcja**, **szkielet** **2** a system of rules or ideas which help you decide what to do: *The plan may be changed but it will provide a framework on which we can build.* ▶ **zrąb**, **podstawa**

franc /fræŋk/ noun [C] the unit of money that is used in Switzerland and several other countries (replaced in 2002 in France, Belgium and Luxembourg by the euro) ▶ **frank**

franchise /ˈfræntʃaɪz/ noun **1** [C,U] official permission to sell a company's goods or services in a particular area: *They have the franchise to sell this product in Cyprus.* ◇ *Most fast-food restaurants are operated **under franchise**.* ▶ **koncesja** **2** [U] (formal) the right to vote in elections ▶ **prawo wyborcze**

frank /fræŋk/ adj. showing your thoughts and feelings clearly; saying what you mean: *To be perfectly frank with you, I don't think you'll pass your driving test.* ▶ **szczery**, **otwarty**
■ **frankly** adv.: *Please tell me frankly what you think about my idea.* ◇ *Quite frankly* (szczerze mówiąc), *I'm not surprised at what has happened.* ▶ **szczerze**, **otwarcie** | **frankness** noun [U] ▶ **szczerość**, **otwartość**

frankfurter /ˈfræŋkfɜːtə(r)/ (US also **wiener** /ˈwiːnə(r)/) noun [C] a type of small smoked **sausage** ▶ **frankfurterka**, **rodzaj parówki**

frantic /ˈfræntɪk/ adj. **1** very busy or done in a hurry: *a frantic search for the keys* ◇ *We're not busy at work now, but things get frantic at Christmas.* ▶ **nerwowy**, **bezładny** SYN **hectic** **2** extremely worried or frightened: *The mother went frantic* (szalała z rozpaczy) *when she couldn't find her child.* ◇ *frantic cries for help* ▶ **oszalały (z czegoś)**, **zrozpaczony**
■ **frantically** /-kli/ adv. ▶ **nerwowo**, **bezładnie**

fraternal /frəˈtɜːnl/ adj. (formal) connected with the relationship that exists between brothers; like a brother: *fraternal love/rivalry* ▶ **braterski**, **bratni**

fra,ternal 'twin noun [C] either of two children or animals born from the same mother at the same time but not from the same egg ▶ **bliźniak dwujajowy** ➲ look at **identical twin**

fraternity /frə'tɜːnəti/ noun (pl. **fraternities**) **1** [C] a group of people who share the same work or interests: *the medical fraternity* ▶ **braterstwo** **2** [U] the feeling of friendship and support between people in the same group ▶ **bractwo**

fraud /frɔːd/ noun **1** [C,U] (an act of) cheating sb in order to get money, etc. illegally: *The accountant was sent to prison for fraud.* ◇ *Massive amounts of money are lost every year in credit card frauds.* ▶ **oszustwo** **2** [C] a person who tricks sb by pretending to be sb else ▶ **oszust/ka**

fraudulent /'frɔːdjələnt; US -dʒə-/ adj. (formal) done in order to cheat sb; dishonest: *the fraudulent use of stolen cheques* ▶ **oszukańczy**, **nieuczciwy**

fraught /frɔːt/ adj. **1 fraught with sth** filled with sth unpleasant: *a situation fraught with danger/difficulty* ▶ **pełny (niebezpieczeństw)**, **brzemienny (w skutki)** **2** (used about people) worried and nervous; (used about a situation) very busy so that people become nervous: *Things are usually fraught at work on Mondays.* ▶ **spięty**, **rozdrażniony**; **napięty**

fray /freɪ/ verb [I,T] **1** if cloth, etc. **frays** or becomes **frayed**, some of the threads at the end start to come apart: *This shirt is beginning to fray at the cuffs.* ◇ *a frayed rope* ◇ *a frayed* (postrzępiony) *cuff* ▶ (*ubranie, materiał*) **strzępić (się)**, **wycierać się** **2** if sb's nerves, etc. **fray** or become **frayed**, they start to get annoyed: *Tempers began to fray* (nerwy zaczęły zawodzić) *towards the end of the match.* ▶ **działać komuś na nerwy**; **zawodzić**

frazzled /'fræzld/ adj. (informal) tired and easily annoyed: *They finally arrived home, hot and frazzled.* ▶ **umęczony i drażliwy**

freak¹ /friːk/ noun [C] **1** (informal) a person who has a very strong interest in sth: *a fitness/computer freak* ▶ **maniak/czka**, **zapaleniec** SYN **fanatic** **2** a very unusual and strange event, person, animal, etc.: *The other kids think Ally's a freak because she doesn't watch TV.* ◇ *a freak storm/result* ◇ *a freak accident* niecodzienny wypadek ▶ **kaprys**; **wybryk (natury)**; **dziwadło**

freak² /friːk/ verb [I,T] (informal) **freak (sb) (out)** if sb **freaks** or if sth **freaks** them, they react very strongly to sth that makes them suddenly feel shocked, surprised, frightened, etc.: *She freaked out when she heard the news.* ◇ *The film 'Psycho' really freaked me out.* ▶ **panikować**; **napędzać komuś strachu**, **szokować**

freakish /'friːkɪʃ/ adj. very strange, unusual or unexpected: *freakish weather/behaviour* ▶ **dziwny**
■ **freakishly** adv. ▶ **dziwnie**

freaky /'friːki/ adj. (informal) very strange or unusual ▶ **dziwaczny**

freckle /'frekl/ noun [C, usually pl.] a small brown spot on your skin: *A lot of people with red hair have got freckles.* ▶ **pieg** ➲ look at **mole**
■ **freckled** adj. ▶ **piegowaty**

⚷ **free¹** /friː/ adj. **1 free (to do sth)** not controlled by the government, rules, etc.: *There is free movement of people across the border.* ◇ *a free press* ▶ **wolny**, **niezależny** **2** not in prison or in a **cage**, etc.; not held or controlled: *The government **set** Mandela **free*** (uwolnił Mandelę) *in 1989.* ◇ *You're free this afternoon to do* (możesz robić) *exactly what you want.* ▶ **wolny**, **swobodny** **3** costing nothing: *Admission to the museum is free/free of charge.* ▶ **bezpłatny** **4 free from/of sth** not having sth dangerous, unpleasant, etc.: *free of worries/responsibility* ◇ *free from pain* ▶ **wolny (od czegoś)** **5** not busy or being used: *I'm afraid Mr Spencer is not free this afternoon.* ◇ *I don't get much **free time**.* ◇ *Is this seat free?* ▶ **wolny**

IDM **feel free** → FEEL¹

free and easy informal or relaxed: *The atmosphere in our office is very free and easy.* ▶ **swobodny**, **zrelaksowany**

get, have, etc. a free hand to get, have, etc. permission to make your own decisions about sth: *I had a free hand in designing the course.* ▶ **mieć wolną rękę**

of your own free will because you want to, not because sb forces you ▶ **z własnej woli**

■ **free** adv. **1** in a free manner: *There is nowhere around here where dogs can run free.* ▶ **wolno**, **swobodnie** **2** without cost or payment: *Children under five usually travel free on trains.* ▶ **bezpłatnie**, **za darmo**

⚷ **free²** /friː/ verb [T] **1 free sb/sth (from sth)** to let sb/sth leave or escape from a place where he/she/it is held: *to free a prisoner* ◇ *The protesters freed the animals from their cages.* ▶ **uwalniać (od czegoś)**, **oswobadzać** SYN **release** **2 free sb/sth of/from sth** to take away sth that is unpleasant from sb: *The medicine freed her from pain for a few hours.* ▶ **uwalniać (od czegoś)** **3 free sb/sth (up) for sth**; **free sb/sth (up) to do sth** to make sth available so that it can be used; to put sb in a position in which they can do sth: *If I cancel my trip, that will free me to see you on Friday.* ▶ **uwalniać (do/dla czegoś)**, **oswobadzać**

,free 'agent noun [C] a person who can do what they want because nobody else has the right to tell them what to do ▶ **osoba niezależna**

freebie /'friːbi/ noun [C] (informal) something that is given to sb without payment, usually by a company ▶ **upominek od firmy** (*rozdawany w ramach promocji itp.*)

⚷ **freedom** /'friːdəm/ noun **1** [C,U] the right or ability to do or say what you want: *You have the freedom to come and go as you please.* ◇ *freedom of speech* ◇ *the rights and freedoms of the individual* ▶ **wolność** ➲ look at **liberty** **2** [U] the state of not being held prisoner or controlled by sb else: *The opposition leader was given his freedom after 25 years.* ▶ **swoboda**, **wolność** **3** [U] **freedom from sth** the state of not being affected by sth unpleasant: *freedom from fear/hunger/pain* ▶ **uwolnienie (od czegoś)**, **oswobodzenie** **4** [U] **the freedom of sth** the right to use sth without restriction: *You can have the freedom of the ground floor* (możesz swobodnie korzystać z parteru), *but please don't go upstairs.* ▶ **swobodny dostęp do czegoś**

'freedom fighter noun [C] a person who belongs to a group that uses violence to try to remove a government from power ▶ **bojowni-k/czka o wolność**

,freedom of as'sembly noun [U] the right to have public meetings which is guaranteed by law in the US ▶ **wolność zgromadzeń**

,freedom of associ'ation noun [U] the right to meet people and to form organizations without needing permission from the government ▶ **wolność zrzeszania się**

,freedom of infor'mation noun [U] the right to see any information that a government has about people and organizations ▶ **wolność informacji**

,free 'enterprise noun [U] the operation of business without government control ▶ **wolna inicjatywa**

Freefone™ = FREEPHONE

freehand /'friːhænd/ adj. [only before a noun] (used about a drawing) done by hand, without the help of any instruments: *a freehand sketch* ▶ **odręczny**
■ **freehand** adv.: *to draw freehand* ▶ **odręcznie**

freehold /'friːhəʊld/ noun [C, U] (especially Brit.) the fact of owning a building or piece of land for a period of time that is not limited: *Private tenants in flats now have the* *right to buy the freehold* (prawo własności) *from their landlord.* ▶ **własność nieruchomości**

■ **freehold 1** adj.: *a freehold property* ▶ (*nieruchomość*) **posiadana na nieograniczoną własność 2** adv.: *to buy a house freehold* ▶ **na nieograniczoną własność** ➲ look at **leasehold**

ˌfree ˈkick noun [C] (in the sports of football or **rugby**) a situation in which a player of one team is allowed to kick the ball because a member of the other team has broken a rule ▶ **rzut wolny**

freelance /ˈfriːlɑːns; US -læns/ adj. earning money by selling your services or work to different organizations rather than being employed by a single company: *a freelance* (niezależny) *journalist* ◇ *freelance work* praca na własną rękę ▶ **(pracujący) na umowę o dzieło/zlecenia itp.**

■ **freelance 1** adv.: *She works freelance.* Pracuje jako wolny strzelec. ▶ **na umowę o dzieło/zlecenia itp. 2** (also **freelancer** /ˈfriːlɑːnsə(r); US -læn-/) noun [C] ▶ **osoba zatrudniona na umowę o dzieło/zlecenia itp. 3** verb [I]: *I left my full-time job because I can earn more by freelancing.* ▶ **pracować na umowę o dzieło/zlecenie**

freeloader /ˈfriːləʊdə(r)/ noun [C] (informal) a person who is always accepting free food and accommodation from other people without giving them anything in exchange ▶ **darmozjad**

■ **freeload** verb [I] ▶ **pasożytować, żyć na cudzy koszt**

⚷ **freely** /ˈfriːli/ adv. **1** in a way that is not controlled or limited: *He is the country's first freely elected* (wybrany w wolnych wyborach) *president for 40 years.* ▶ **swobodnie** ℹ Zwróć uwagę, że **travel free** oznacza podróżować za darmo. **Travel freely** oznacza podróżować bez żadnych ograniczeń. **2** without trying to avoid the truth even though it might be embarrassing; in an honest way: *I freely admit that I made a mistake.* ▶ **dobrowolnie, bez przymusu**

Freemason /ˈfriːmeɪsn/ (also **mason**) noun [C] a man who belongs to an international secret society whose members help each other and who recognize each other by secret signs ▶ **mason**

Freephone (also **Freefone™**) /ˈfriːfəʊn/ noun [U] a system in which the cost of a telephone call is paid for by the organization being called, rather than by the person making the call: *Call now on Freephone 0800 89216 for further details.* ▶ **bezpłatna linia telefoniczna**

Freepost /ˈfriːpəʊst/ noun [U] (in Britain) the system by which the person who sends a letter, etc. does not pay for the cost of sending it ▶ **przesyłka na koszt adresata** ➲ look at **Freephone**

ˌfree-ˈrange adj. (used about farm birds or their eggs) kept or produced in a place where birds can move around freely: *free-range hens/turkeys* ◇ *We always buy free-range eggs.* ▶ (*drób, jajka*) **wiejski** ➲ look at **battery**

freesia /ˈfriːʒə; ˈfriːziə/ noun [C] a plant with sweet-smelling yellow, pink or white flowers ▶ **frezja**

ˌfree ˈspeech noun [U] the right to express any opinion in public ▶ **wolność słowa**

freeway (US) = MOTORWAY

⚷ **freeze¹** /friːz/ verb (pt **froze** /frəʊz/, pp **frozen** /ˈfrəʊzn/) **1** [I,T] to become hard (and often change into ice) because of extreme cold; to make sth do this: *Water freezes at 0° Celsius.* ◇ *The ground was* ***frozen solid*** *for most of the winter.* ◇ *frozen* (mrożony) *peas* ▶ **zamarzać; zamrażać 2** [I] (used with 'it' to describe extremely cold weather when water turns into ice): *I think it's going to freeze* (będzie mróz) *tonight.* ▶ **spadać poniżej zera 3** [I,T] to be very cold or to die from cold: *It was so cold on the mountain that we thought we would* ***freeze to death.*** ▶ **zamarzać, marznąć 4** [I] to stop moving suddenly and completely because you are frightened or in danger: *The terrible scream made her freeze with terror.* ◇ *Suddenly the man pulled out a gun and shouted 'Freeze!'* ▶ **zastygać 5** [T] to keep the money you earn, prices, etc. at a fixed level for a certain period of time: *Spending on defence has been frozen for one year.* ▶ **zamrażać**

PHR V **freeze over** to become completely covered by ice ▶ **zamarzać**

freeze² /friːz/ noun [C] **1** the fixing of the money you earn, prices, etc. at one level for a certain period of time ▶ **zamrożenie 2** a period of weather when the temperature stays below freezing point (0° Celsius) ▶ **mrozy**

freezer /ˈfriːzə(r)/ (also ˌ**deep ˈfreeze**) noun [C] a metal container with a door in which food, etc. is kept frozen so that it stays fresh ▶ **zamrażarka** ➲ look at **fridge**

freezing¹ /ˈfriːzɪŋ/ adj. (informal) very cold: *It's absolutely freezing outside.* ◇ *Can we turn the central heating on? I'm freezing* (strasznie mi zimno). ▶ **mroźny, lodowaty, bardzo zimny** ➲ note at **cold**

freezing² /ˈfriːzɪŋ/ (also ˈ**freezing point**) noun [U] the temperature at which water freezes: *Last night the temperature fell to six degrees below freezing.* ▶ **temperatura zamarzania, zero**

freight /freɪt/ noun [U] goods that are carried from one place to another by ship, lorry, etc.; the system for carrying goods in this way: *a freight train* ◇ *Your order will be sent by air freight* (drogą lotniczą). ▶ **towary; przewóz**

ˈfreight car (US) = WAGON

freighter /ˈfreɪtə(r)/ noun [C] a ship or an aircraft that carries only goods and not passengers ▶ **frachtowiec; transporter** ➲ note at **boat**

ˈfreight train (Brit. also ˈ**goods train**) noun [C] a train that carries only **goods** ▶ **pociąg towarowy**

ˌFrench ˈbread noun [U] white bread in the shape of a long thick stick ▶ **bagietka** ➲ picture at **bread**

ˌFrench ˈfry (especially US) = CHIP¹ (3)

ˌFrench ˈhorn noun [C] a brass musical instrument that consists of a long tube curved around in a circle with a wide opening at the end ▶ **waltornia** ➲ note at **piano**

ˌFrench ˈwindow (US ˌ**French ˈdoor**) noun [C] one of a pair of glass doors that open onto a garden ▶ **drzwi balkonowe**

frenetic /frəˈnetɪk/ adj. involving a lot of energy and activity in a way that is not organized: *a scene of frenetic activity* ▶ **gorączkowy, szalony**

■ **frenetically** /-kli/ adv. ▶ **gorączkowo, szalenie**

frenzied /ˈfrenzid/ adj. that is wild and out of control: *a frenzied attack* ◇ *frenzied activity* ▶ **szalony, dziki**

frenzy /ˈfrenzi/ noun [sing., U] a state of great emotion or activity that is not under control: *There's no need to get* ***in a frenzy*** *– you've got until Friday to finish your essay.* ◇ *I could hear a frenzy of activity in the kitchen.* ▶ **szaleństwo, szał**

frequency /ˈfriːkwənsi/ noun (pl. **frequencies**) **1** [U] the number of times sth happens in a particular period: *Fatal accidents have decreased in frequency* (występują z mniejszą częstotliwością) *in recent years.* ▶ **częstość, częstotliwość 2** [U] the fact that sth happens often: *The frequency of child deaths from cancer near the nuclear power station is being investigated.* ▶ **częstotliwość 3** [C,U] the rate at which a sound wave or radio wave **vibrates**: *a high/low frequency* ▶ **częstotliwość**

⚷ **frequent¹** /ˈfriːkwənt/ adj. happening often: *His visits became less frequent.* ◇ *There is a frequent bus service* (autobusy często jeżdżą) *from the city centre to the airport.* ▶ **częsty** OPP **infrequent**

■ **frequently** adv. ▶ **często**

frequent² /friˈkwent/ verb [T] (formal) to go to a place often: *He spent most of his evenings in Paris frequenting bars and clubs.* ▶ **odwiedzać, uczęszczać**

fresh /freʃ/ adj. **1** (used especially about food) produced or picked very recently; not frozen or in a tin: *fresh bread/fruit/flowers* ▶ **świeży** ➲ look at **stale 2** left somewhere or experienced recently: *fresh blood/footprints* ◇ *Write a few notes while the lecture is still* ***fresh in*** *your* ***mind.*** ▶ **świeży 3** new and different: *They have decided to* ***make a fresh start*** (zacząć od nowa) *in a different town.* ◇ *I'm sure he'll have some fresh ideas on the subject.* ▶ **nowy**, **świeży 4** pleasantly clean or bright: *Open the window and let some* ***fresh air*** *in.* ▶ **świeży 5** (used about water) containing no salt: *a shortage of fresh water* ▶ **słodki** ➲ look at **freshwater**, **saltwater 6** full of energy: *I'll think about the problem again in the morning when I'm fresh.* ▶ **świeży**; **rześki**, **wypoczęty 7 fresh from/out of sth** having just finished sth: *Life isn't easy for a young teacher fresh from university* (tuż po studiach). ▶ **świeżo przybyły skądś 8** (used about the weather) cold and quite windy ▶ **chłodny i wietrzny 9** (used about colours, or a person's skin) bright or clear ▶ **świeży**
■ **freshly** adv.: *freshly baked bread* ▶ **świeżo**; **niedawno**, **dopiero co** | **freshness** noun [U] ▶ **świeżość**
IDM **break fresh/new ground** → GROUND[1]

freshen /ˈfreʃn/ verb [T] **freshen sth (up)** to make sth cleaner or brighter: *Some new curtains and wallpaper would freshen up this room.* ▶ **odświeżać**, **rozjaśniać**
PHR V **freshen up**; **freshen yourself up** to wash and make yourself look clean and tidy: *I'll just go and freshen up before supper.* ▶ **odświeżać się**

fresher /ˈfreʃə(r)/ noun [C] (Brit.) a student who is in their first year at university, college, etc. ▶ **pierwszoroczniak**

freshman /ˈfreʃmən/ noun [C] (pl. **-men** /-mən/) (US) a student who is in their first year at college, high school, university, etc. ▶ **pierwszoroczniak**

freshwater /ˈfreʃwɔːtə(r)/ adj. [only before a noun] **1** living in water that is not the sea and is not salty: *freshwater fish* ▶ **słodkowodny 2** having water that is not salty: *freshwater lakes* ▶ **słodkowodny** ➲ look at **saltwater**

fret[1] /fret/ verb [I] (**fretting**; **fretted**) **fret (about/at/over sth)** to be worried and unhappy about sth: *I was awake for hours fretting about my exams.* ▶ **martwić się**, **niepokoić się**

fret[2] /fret/ noun [C] one of the bars across the long thin part of a **guitar**, etc. that show you where to put your fingers to produce a particular sound ▶ **próg** (*w gitarze*)

Freudian /ˈfrɔɪdiən/ adj. **1** connected with the ideas of Sigmund Freud about the way the human mind works, especially his theories of **subconscious** sexual feelings: *Freudian psychoanalysis* ▶ **freudowski 2** (used about sb's speech or behaviour) showing your secret thoughts or feelings, especially those connected with sex ▶ **freudowski**

Fri. = FRIDAY: *Fri. 27 May*

friction /ˈfrɪkʃn/ noun [U] **1** the rubbing of one surface or thing against another: *You have to put oil in the engine to reduce friction between the moving parts.* ▶ **tarcie 2 friction (between A and B)** disagreement between people or groups: *There is a lot of friction between the older and younger members of staff.* ▶ **tarcia**, **niezgoda**

Friday /ˈfraɪdeɪ; -di/ noun [C,U] (abbr. **Fri.**) the day of the week after Thursday ▶ **piątek** ➲ note at **Monday**

fridge /frɪdʒ/ (also formal **refrigerator** /rɪˈfrɪdʒəreɪtə(r)/; US **icebox** /ˈaɪsbɒks/) noun [C] a metal container with a door in which food, etc. is kept cold (but not frozen) so that it stays fresh ▶ **lodówka**, **chłodziarka** ➲ look at **freezer**

friend /frend/ noun [C] **1** a person that you know and like (not a member of your family), and who likes you: *Dalibor and I are* ***old friends.*** *We were at school together.* ◇ *We're only inviting* ***close friends*** *and relatives to the wedding.* ◇ *Carol's my* ***best friend.*** ◇ *A friend of mine told me about this restaurant.* ◇ *One of my friends told me about this restaurant.* ▶ **przyja-ciel/ciółka**, **kolega/żanka**, **znajom-y/a** ➲ look at **boyfriend**, **girlfriend**, **penfriend**

> **Friend** oznacza zwykle kolegę. **Good/close friend** to odpowiednik polskiego słowa przyjaciel. Kolega z pracy lub uczelni to **colleague**. Osoba znajoma, z którą niewiele nas łączy, to **acquaintance**.

> **friends**
> People often **get to know** each other through work or school, and then **become friends**. A common informal word for friend is **mate**: *I'm going out with my mates.* **Friendly** people **get on well** with lots of people. They usually find it easy to **make friends**. If you and a friend are very **close**, you can **chat** about anything. Even if you don't see each other very often, you can **keep in touch** (for example by phone or email). When you **meet up**/**get together** again, you can **catch up on** each other's news.

2 a friend of/to sth a person who supports an organization, a charity, etc., especially by giving money; a person who supports a particular idea, etc.: *the Friends of the Churchill Hospital* ▶ (*członek stowarzyszenia*) **przyjaciel**
IDM **be/make friends (with sb)** to be/become a friend (of sb): *Tony is rather shy and finds it hard to make friends.* ▶ **przyjaźnić się**; **zaprzyjaźniać się**
a false friend → FALSE

friendless /ˈfrendləs/ adj. without friends ▶ **opuszczony**, **samotny**

friendly[1] /ˈfrendli/ adj. (**friendlier**; **friendliest**) **1 friendly (to/toward(s) sb)** behaving in a kind and open way: *Everyone here has been very friendly towards us.* ▶ **przyjazny**, **troskliwy** OPP **unfriendly** ➲ note at **nice 2** showing kindness; making you feel relaxed and as though you are among friends: *a friendly smile/atmosphere* ◇ *a small friendly hotel* ▶ **przyjemny**, **miły** OPP **unfriendly 3 friendly with sb** treating sb as a friend: *Nick's* ***become*** *quite* ***friendly*** (zaprzyjaźnił się) *with the boy next door.* ◇ *Are you* ***on friendly terms*** *with your neighbours?* ▶ **zaprzyjaźniony z kimś 4** [in compounds] helpful to sb/sth; not harmful to sth: *Our computer is extremely* ***user-friendly.*** ◇ *ozone-friendly sprays* ▶ **łatwy w użyciu**, **przyjazny** (*np. dla środowiska*) **5** in which the people, teams, etc. taking part are not competing seriously: *a friendly argument* ◇ *I've organized a friendly match against my brother's team.* ▶ (*mecz itp.*) **towarzyski**
■ **friendliness** noun [U] ▶ **życzliwość**, **przyjaźń**

friendly[2] /ˈfrendli/ noun [C] (pl. **friendlies**) a sports match that is not part of an important competition ▶ **mecz towarzyski**

friendship /ˈfrendʃɪp/ noun **1** [C] **a friendship (with sb)**; **a friendship (between A and B)** a relationship between people who are friends: *a close/lasting/lifelong friendship* ▶ **przyjaźń**, **koleżeństwo 2** [U] the state of being friends: *Our relationship is based on friendship, not love.* ▶ **przyjaźń**

frigate /ˈfrɪɡət/ noun [C] a small fast ship in the navy that travels with other ships in order to protect them ▶ **fregata**

fright /fraɪt/ noun [C,U] a sudden feeling of fear or shock: *I hope I didn't* ***give you a fright*** (cię nie przestraszyłem) *when I shouted.* ◇ *The child cried out* ***in fright*** *when she saw a dark shadow at the window.* ▶ **strach**, **przerażenie**

frighten /ˈfraɪtn/ verb [T] to make sb/sth afraid or shocked: *That programme about crime really frightened me.* ▶ **przestraszyć**

F

PHR V **frighten sb/sth away/off** to cause a person or an animal to go away by frightening them or it: *Walk quietly so that you don't frighten the birds away.* ▶ **płoszyć/przepłaszać/wystraszyć (kogoś/coś)**

frightened /ˈfraɪtnd/ adj. **1** full of fear or worry: *Frightened children were calling for their mothers.* ◇ *I was frightened* (bałem się) *that they would think that I was rude.* ▶ **przestraszony, przerażony 2 frightened of sb/sth** afraid of a particular person, thing or situation: *When I was young I was frightened of* (bałem się) *cats.* ▶ **bojący się (kogoś/czegoś)** ➲ note at **afraid**

frightening /ˈfraɪtnɪŋ/ adj. making you feel afraid or shocked: *a frightening experience* ◇ *It's frightening how quickly time passes.* ▶ **przerażający**

frightful /ˈfraɪtfl/ adj. (old-fashioned) **1** (used for emphasizing sth) very bad or great: *We're in a frightful rush.* Strasznie nam się śpieszy. ▶ **okropny, straszny 2** very bad or unpleasant: *The weather this summer has been frightful.* ▶ **straszny, okropny** SYN for both meanings **awful, terrible**

frightfully /ˈfraɪtfəli/ adv. (old-fashioned) very: *I'm frightfully sorry.* ▶ **strasznie, okropnie**

frigid /ˈfrɪdʒɪd/ adj. **1** (usually used about a woman) unable to enjoy sex ▶ (*med.*) **oziębły 2** not showing any emotion: *There was a frigid atmosphere in the room.* ▶ (*uczucie itp.*) **chłodny**

frill /frɪl/ noun [C] **1** a decoration for the edge of a dress, shirt, etc. which is made by forming many folds in a narrow piece of cloth ▶ **falbanka 2** [usually pl.] something that is added for decoration that you feel is not necessary: *We just want a plain simple meal – no frills* (bez żadnych wymyślnych potraw). ▶ **upiększenie, ozdoba** ■ **frilly** adj.: *a frilly dress* ▶ **z falbankami**

fringe[1] /frɪndʒ/ noun [C] **1** (US **bangs** /bæŋz/ [pl.]) the part of your hair that is cut so that it hangs over your **forehead**: *Your hair looks better with a fringe.* ▶ **grzywka** ➲ picture at **hair 2** a border for decoration on a piece of clothing, etc. that is made of a lot of hanging threads ▶ **frędzle 3** (Brit.) the outer edge of an area or a group that is a long way from the centre or from what is usual: *Some people **on the fringes of*** (ze skrajnego odłamu) *the socialist party are opposed to the policy on Europe.* ▶ **peryferie, obrzeża**

fringe[2] /frɪndʒ/ verb

IDM **be fringed with sth** to have sth as a border or around the edge: *The lake was fringed with pine trees.* Brzegi jeziora były wysadzane sosnami. ▶ **być obramowanym/okalanym/wysadzanym itp.** (*czymś*)

ˈfringe benefit noun [C, usually pl.] an extra thing that is given to an employee in addition to the money he or she earns: *The fringe benefits of this job include a car and free health insurance.* ▶ **dodatek do pensji** ℹ Bardziej nieformalnym słowem jest **perk**.

ˌfringe ˈtheatre noun [U,C] (Brit.) plays, often by new writers, that are unusual and question the way people think; a theatre where such plays are performed ▶ **teatr awangardowy/niekomercyjny**

frisk /frɪsk/ verb **1** [T] to pass your hands over sb's body in order to search for hidden weapons, drugs, etc. ▶ **rewidować 2** [I] (used about an animal or child) to play and jump about happily and with a lot of energy ▶ **dokazywać, brykać**

frisky /ˈfrɪski/ adj. (**friskier**; **friskiest**) full of life and wanting to play ▶ **rozbrykany, ożywiony**

fritter /ˈfrɪtə(r)/ verb

PHR V **fritter sth away (on sth)** to waste time or money on things that are not important ▶ **trwonić**

frivolity /frɪˈvɒləti/ noun [U] silly behaviour (especially when you should be serious) ▶ **brak powagi, lekkomyślność**

frivolous /ˈfrɪvələs/ adj. not serious; silly ▶ **niepoważny, lekkomyślny**

frizzy /ˈfrɪzi/ adj. (**frizzier**; **frizziest**) (used about hair) very curly ▶ **kędzierzawy**

fro /frəʊ/ adv.

IDM **to and fro** → TO

frock /frɒk/ noun [C] (old-fashioned) (especially Brit.) a dress: *a party frock* ▶ **sukienka**

frog /frɒg/ noun [C] a small animal with smooth skin and long back legs that it uses for jumping. **Frogs** live in or near water: *Our pond is full of frogs in the spring.* ▶ **żaba** ➲ picture on **page A11**

frogman /ˈfrɒgmən/ noun [C] (pl. **-men** /-mən/) a person whose job is to work under the surface of water wearing special rubber clothes and using breathing equipment: *Police frogmen searched the river.* ▶ **płetwonurek**

frogspawn /ˈfrɒgspɔːn/ noun [U] a clear substance that looks like jelly and contains the eggs of a **frog** ▶ **żabi skrzek** ➲ picture on **page A11**

frolic /ˈfrɒlɪk/ verb [I] (**frolicking**; **frolicked**) to play and move around in a lively, happy way: *children frolicking on the beach* ▶ **figlować**

from /frəm; strong form frɒm; US also frʌm/ prep. **1** (showing the place or direction that sb/sth starts or started): *She comes home from work at 7 o'clock.* ◇ *a cold wind from the east* ◇ *Water was dripping from the tap.* ▶ **z 2** (showing the time when sth starts or started): *Peter's on holiday from next Friday.* ◇ *The supermarket is open **from** 8 a.m. **till** 8 p.m. every day.* ▶ **od 3** (showing the person who sent or gave sth): *I borrowed this jacket from my sister.* ◇ *a phone call from my father* ▶ **od 4** (showing the origin of sb/sth): *'Where do you come from* (skąd pochodzisz)*?' 'I'm from Australia.'* ◇ *cheeses from France and Italy* ◇ *quotations from Shakespeare* ▶ **z 5** (showing the material which is used to make sth): *Paper is **made from** wood.* ◇ *This sauce is made from cream and wine.* ▶ **z** ℹ Wyrażenie **made of** wprowadza rodzaj materiału, z jakego wykonano daną rzecz: *a table made of wood* ◇ *a house made of bricks.* **6** (showing the distance between two places): *The house is five miles from the town centre.* ◇ *I work not far from here.* ▶ **od 7** (showing the point at which a series of prices, figures, etc., starts): *Our prices start from £2.50 a bottle.* ◇ *Tickets cost from £3 to £11.* ▶ **od 8** (showing the state of sb/sth before a change): *The time of the meeting has been changed **from** 7 **to** 8 o'clock.* ◇ *The article was translated **from** Polish **into** English.* ◇ *Things have gone **from bad to worse*** Sytuacja znacznie się pogorszyła. ▶ **z 9** (showing that sb/sth is taken away, removed or separated from sb/sth else): *Children don't like being separated from their parents for a long period.* ◇ *(in mathematics) 8 from 12 leaves 4.* ▶ **od, z 10** (showing sth that you want to avoid): *There was no shelter from the wind.* ◇ *This game will stop you from getting bored* (uchroni cię przed nudą). ▶ **przed, od 11** (showing the cause of sth): *People in the camps are suffering from hunger and cold.* ▶ **z 12** (showing the reason for making a judgement or forming an opinion): *You can tell quite a lot from somebody's handwriting.* ▶ **z 13** (showing the difference between two people, places or things): *Can you tell margarine from butter?* ◇ *Is Portuguese very different* (czy portugalski bardzo różni się) *from Spanish?* ▶ **od 14** (showing your position or point of view): *There is a wonderful view from the top of the tower.* ◇ *He always looks at things from his own point of view.* ▶ **z**

IDM **from ... on** starting at a particular time and continuing for ever: *She never spoke to him again **from that day on.*** ◇ ***From now on** you must earn your own living.* ▶ **odtąd, od tego czasu**

🔑 **front**[1] /frʌnt/ noun **1** (**the front**) [C, usually sing.] the side or surface of sth/sb that faces forward: *a dress with buttons down the front* ◇ *the front of a building* ◇ *a card with flowers **on the front*** ▶ **przód**, **front 2** [sing.] (**sb's front**) the part of sb's body that faces forwards; sb's chest: *She slipped on the stairs and spilt coffee all down her front.* ◇ *He was lying on his front* (na brzuchu). ▶ **przód 3** (**the front**) [C, usually sing.] the most forward part of sth; the area that is just outside of or before sb/sth: *Young children should not travel **in the front of** the car.* ◇ *There is a small garden **at the front of** the house.* ▶ **przód**, **przednia część**

> **On the front of** znaczy „na przedniej powierzchni czegoś": *The number is shown on the front of the bus.* **In front of** znaczy „przed kimś/czymś": *A car has stopped in front of the bus.* ◇ *There were three people in front of me in the queue.* ◇ *The teacher usually stands in front of the class.* **At/In the front (of sth)** oznacza „na samym przodzie czegoś": *The driver sits at the front of the bus.*: *The noisy children were asked to sit at the front of the class.*

4 (**the front**) [sing.] the line or area where fighting takes place in a war: *to be sent to the front* ▶ **front** (*wojsk*) **5** [C] a particular area of activity: *Things are difficult **on the** domestic/political/economic **front** at the moment.* ◇ *Progress has been made **on all fronts.*** ▶ **front 6** [sing.] a way of behaving that hides your true feelings: *His brave words were just a front. He was really feeling very nervous.* ▶ **poza**, **maska 7** [C] a line or area where warm air and cold air meet: *A **cold front** is moving in from the north.* ▶ **front atmosferyczny**

IDM **back to front** → BACK[1]

in front further forward than sb/sth: *Some of the children ran on in front.* ◇ *After three laps the Kenyan runner was in front.* ▶ **na przodzie** SYN **ahead**

in front of sb/sth 1 in a position further forward than but close to sb/sth: *The bus stops right in front of our house.* ◇ *Don't stand in front of the TV.* ◇ *The book was open in front of her on the desk.* ▶ **przed 2** if you do sth in front of sb, you do it when that person is there in the same room or place as you: *Don't do that in front of the children.* ▶ **przy**

up front (informal) as payment before sth is done: *I want half the money up front and half when the job is finished.* ▶ **z góry**

🔑 **front**[2] /frʌnt/ adj. [only before a noun] of or at the front [1](1,2): *the front door/garden/room* ◇ *sit in the front row* ◇ *front teeth* ▶ **przedni**, **frontowy**

frontal /ˈfrʌntl/ adj. [only before a noun] from the front: *a frontal attack* ▶ **czołowy**, **frontalny**

frontier /ˈfrʌntɪə(r); US frʌnˈt/ noun **1** [C] **the frontier (between A and B)** the line where one country joins another; border: *the end of frontier controls in Europe* ▶ **granica** ➲ note at **border 2** (**the frontiers**) [pl.] the limit between what we do and do not know: *Scientific research is constantly **pushing back the frontiers of** our knowledge about the world.* ▶ **granice** (*wiedzy ludzkiej*)

ˌ**front-ˈpage** adj. [only before a noun] interesting or important enough to appear on the front page of a newspaper: *front-page news/headlines* ▶ **z pierwszej strony** (*gazety*)

frost[1] /frɒst/ noun **1** [U,C] the weather conditions when the temperature falls below freezing point: *There was a **hard frost*** (silny mróz) *last night.* ◇ *ten degrees of frost* ◇ *a chilly night with some **ground frost*** (z przygruntowymi przymrozkami) ▶ **mróz 2** [U] a very thin layer of little pieces of ice that is formed on surfaces when the temperature is below freezing-point: *The branches of the trees were white with frost.* ▶ **szron**, **oblodzenie**

frost[2] /frɒst/ verb [T] (especially US) = ICE[2]

PHR V **frost over/up** to become covered with a thin layer of ice: *The window has frosted over/up.* ▶ **pokrywać się szronem**, **zamarzać** ➲ look at **defrost**

frostbite /ˈfrɒstbaɪt/ noun [U] a serious medical condition of the fingers, toes, etc. that is caused by very low temperatures: *All the climbers were suffering from frostbite.* ▶ **odmrożenie** ➲ look at **chilblain**

■ **frostbitten** /ˈfrɒstbɪtn/ adj. ▶ (*część ciała*) **odmrożony**

frosted /ˈfrɒstɪd/ adj. [only before a noun] (used about glass or a window) with a special surface so you cannot see through it ▶ **matowy**

frosting (especially US) = ICING

frosty /ˈfrɒsti/ adj. (**frostier**; **frostiest**) **1** very cold, with **frost**: *a cold and frosty morning* ▶ **mroźny**, **oszroniony 2** cold and unfriendly: *a frosty welcome* ▶ **lodowaty**

froth[1] /frɒθ/ noun [U] a mass of small white bubbles on the top of a liquid, etc. ▶ **piana**, **pianka**

■ **frothy** adj.: *frothy beer* ◇ *a frothy cappuccino* ▶ **pienisty**

froth[2] /frɒθ/ verb [I] to have or produce a mass of white bubbles: *The mad dog was frothing at the mouth.* ▶ **pienić się**, **pokrywać się pianą**

frown /fraʊn/ verb [I] to show you are angry, serious, etc. by making lines appear on your **forehead** ▶ **marszczyć brwi**

■ **frown** noun [C]: *She read the letter quickly, a worried frown on her face.* (ze zmartwieniem na twarzy) ▶ **zmarszczenie brwi**

PHR V **frown on/upon sth** to think that sth is not good or suitable: *Smoking is very much frowned upon these days.* ◇ *Her parents frowned on her plans to go backpacking alone.* ▶ **potępiać**, **krzywo patrzeć na coś** SYN **disapprove**

froze past tense of **freeze**[1]

frozen[1] past participle of **freeze**[1]

🔑 **frozen**[2] /ˈfrəʊzn/ adj. **1** (used about food) stored at a low temperature in order to keep it for a long time: *frozen meat/vegetables* ▶ (*żywność*) **mrożony 2** (informal) (used about people and parts of the body) very cold: *My feet are frozen!* ◇ *Turn the heater up – I'm **frozen stiff*** (zmarzłem na kość). ▶ **zmarznięty**, **przemarznięty** SYN **freezing 3** (used about water) with a layer of ice on the surface: *The pond is frozen. Let's go skating.* ▶ **zamarznięty**

frugal /ˈfruːgl/ adj. **1** using only as much money or food as is necessary: *a frugal existence/life* ▶ (*osoba itp.*) **oszczędny** OPP **extravagant 2** (used about meals) small,

simple and not costing very much: *a frugal lunch of bread and cheese* ▶ (*jedzenie itp.*) **skromny** SYN **meagre**
■ **frugality** /fru'gæləti/ noun [U] ▶ **oszczędność**; **skromność** | **frugally** /-gəli/ adv.: *to live/eat frugally* ▶ **oszczędnie**; **skromnie**

fruit /fru:t/ noun **1** [C,U] the part of a plant or tree that contains seeds and that we eat: *Try and eat more* ***fresh fruit*** *and vegetables.* ◇ *Marmalade is made with* ***citrus fruit.*** ◇ *fruit juice* ▶ **owoc**

> **A fruit** oznacza rodzaj owoców: *Most big supermarkets sell all sorts of tropical fruits.* Kiedy chodzi o pojedyncze jabłko, gruszkę itp. mówi się **a piece of fruit**: *What would you like now? Cheese, or a piece of fruit?* Na ogół używa się formy niepoliczalnej: *Would you like some fruit?*

2 [C] the part of any plant in which the seed is formed ▶ **owoc** ➲ picture on **page A12** **3** [pl.] **the fruits (of sth)** a good result or success from work that you have done: *It will be years before we see the fruits of this research.* ▶ **owoce** (*pracy*)
IDM **bear fruit** → BEAR[1]

fruitful /'fru:tfl/ adj. producing good results; useful: *fruitful discussions* ▶ **owocny**

fruition /fru'ɪʃn/ noun [U] (formal) the time when a plan, etc. starts to be successful: *After months of hard work, our efforts were* ***coming to fruition.*** ▶ **urzeczywistnienie**, **spełnienie**

fruitless /'fru:tləs/ adj. producing poor or no results; not successful: *a fruitless search* ◇ *It's fruitless to keep trying – she'll never agree to it.* ▶ **bezowocny**, **nieskuteczny**

frump /frʌmp/ noun [C] a woman who wears clothes that are not fashionable ▶ **niemodnie ubrana kobieta**
■ **frumpy** (also **frumpish**) adj.: *frumpy clothes* ◇ *a frumpy housewife* ▶ **niemodny**; **niemodnie ubrany**

frustrate /frʌ'streɪt; US 'frʌs-/ verb [T] **1** to cause a person to feel annoyed or impatient because they cannot do or achieve what they want: *It's the lack of money that really frustrates him.* ▶ **frustrować** **2** (formal) to prevent sb from doing sth or sth from happening: *The rescue work has been frustrated by bad weather conditions.* ▶ **udaremniać**
■ **frustrated** adj.: *He felt very frustrated at his lack of progress in learning Chinese.* ▶ **sfrustrowany** | **frustrating** adj. ▶ **frustrujący**

frustration /frʌ'streɪʃn/ noun [C,U] a feeling of anger because you cannot get what you want; sth that causes you to feel like this: *He felt anger and frustration at no longer being able to see very well.* ◇ *Every job has its frustrations.* ▶ **frustracja**

fry[1] /fraɪ/ verb [I,T] (**frying**; **fries**; pt, pp **fried** /fraɪd/) to cook sth or to be cooked in hot fat or oil: *to fry an egg* ◇ *a fried egg* ◇ *I could smell bacon frying in the kitchen.* ▶ **smażyć (się)** ➲ note at **cook**, **recipe**

fry[2] (especially US) = CHIP[1] (3)

'**frying pan** (US **frypan** /'fraɪpæn/) noun [C] a flat pan with a long handle that is used for frying food ▶ **patelnia** ➲ picture at **pan**

ft = FOOT[1] (5): *a room 10 ft by 6 ft*

fuchsia /'fju:ʃə/ noun [C, U] a small bush with flowers in two colours of red, purple or white, that hang down ▶ **fuksja**

fudge[1] /fʌdʒ/ noun [U] a type of soft brown sweet made from sugar, butter and milk ▶ **kajmak**, **krówka**

fudge[2] verb [I,T] (informal) to say or do sth in a way that is unclear or unsatisfactory, usually because you intend to mislead sb or because you want to avoid making a definite choice: *Politicians are quite adept at fudging (the issue).* ▶ **kręcić**, **mącić**

fuel[1] /'fju:əl/ noun **1** [U] material that is burned to produce heat or power: *What's the car's fuel consumption?* ▶ **paliwo**, **opał** **2** [C] a type of fuel: *I think gas is the best fuel for central heating.* ▶ **opał**

fuel[2] /'fju:əl/ verb [T] (**fuelling**; **fuelled**; US **fueling**; **fueled**) to make sb feel an emotion more strongly: *Her interest in the Spanish language was fuelled by a visit to Spain.* ▶ **podsycać**

fugitive /'fju:dʒətɪv/ noun [C] a person who is running away or escaping (for example from the police) ▶ **zbieg**, **uciekinier/ka** ➲ look at **refugee**

fulfil (US **fulfill**) /fʊl'fɪl/ verb [T] (**fulfilling**; **fulfilled**) **1** to make sth that you wish for happen; to achieve a goal: *He finally fulfilled his childhood dream of becoming a doctor.* ◇ *to fulfil your ambition/potential* ▶ **spełniać**, **realizować** **2** to do or have everything that you should or that is necessary: *to fulfil a duty/obligation/promise/need* ◇ *The conditions of entry to university in this country are quite difficult to fulfil.* ▶ **spełniać** **3** to have a particular role or purpose: *Italy fulfils a very important role within the European Union.* ▶ **spełniać**, **wypełniać** **4 fulfil sb/yourself** to make sb feel completely happy and satisfied: *I need a job that really fulfils me.* Potrzebuję pracy, w której będę naprawdę mógł się zrealizować. ▶ **(pozwalać komuś) realizować się** **5** to satisfy a need: *The local town can fulfill most of your shopping needs.* ▶ **zaspokajać** (*potrzeby*)
■ **fulfilled** adj.: *When I had my baby I felt totally fulfilled.* ▶ **zadowolony** (*z powodu spełnienia marzeń itp.*), **zaspokojony** | **fulfilling** adj.: *I found working abroad a very fulfilling experience.* ▶ **satysfakcjonujący**

fulfilment (US **fulfillment**) /fʊl'fɪlmənt/ noun [U] **1** the act of fulfilling or state of being fulfilled: *the fulfilment of your dreams/hopes/ambitions* ▶ **spełnienie**, **zrealizowanie** **2** the feeling of satisfaction that you have when you have done sth: *to find personal/emotional fulfilment* ▶ **samorealizacja**, **satysfakcja**

full[1] /fʊl/ adj. **1** holding or containing as much or as many as possible: *The bin needs emptying. It's* ***full up.*** ◇ *a full bottle* ◇ *The bus was full so we had to wait for the next one.* ◇ (figurative) *We need a good night's sleep because we've got a full* (pracowity) *day tomorrow.* ▶ **pełny** **2 full of sb/sth** containing a lot of sb/sth: *The room was full of people.* ◇ *His work was full of mistakes.* ◇ *The children are full of energy.* ◇ *a full house* sala pełna po brzegi ▶ **pełny**, **zapełniony** **3 full (up)** having had enough to eat and drink: *No more, thank you. I'm full (up).* ▶ **syty** **4** [only before a noun] complete; not leaving anything out: *I should like* ***a full report*** *on the accident, please.* ◇ ***Full details*** *of today's TV programmes are on page 20.* ◇ *He took* ***full responsibility*** *for what had happened.* ◇ *Please give your* ***full name and address.*** ▶ **dokładny**, **pełny** **5** [only before a noun] the highest or greatest possible: *She got* ***full marks*** *in her French exam.* ◇ *The train was travelling* ***at full speed.*** ▶ **najwyższy** **6 full of sb/sth/yourself** pleased about or proud of sb/sth/yourself: *When she got back from holiday she was full of everything they had seen.* ◇ *He's* ***full of himself*** *since he got that new job.* ▶ **pochłonięty (kimś/czymś)**; **zadufany** **7** round or rather fat in shape: *She's got quite* ***a full figure.*** ◇ *He's quite* ***full in the face.*** ▶ **okrągły** **8** (used about clothes) made with plenty of cloth: *a full skirt* ▶ **bufiasty**, **luźny**
IDM **at full strength** (used about a group) having all the people it needs or usually has: *Nobody is injured, so the team will be at full strength for the game.* ▶ **w pełnej obsadzie**
at full stretch working as hard as possible: *When the factory is operating at full stretch, it employs 800 people.* ▶ **pełną parą**

full of beans/life with a lot of energy and enthusiasm: *They came back from their holiday full of beans.* ▶ **pełen życia**
have your hands full → HAND[1]
in full with nothing missing; completely: *Your money will be refunded in full.* ◇ *Please write your name in full* (pełne imię i nazwisko). ▶ **w całości**
in full swing at the stage when there is the most activity: *When we arrived the party was already in full swing* (zabawa trwała już na całego). ▶ **na całego**
in full view (of sb/sth) in a place where you can easily be seen: *In full view of the guards* (na oczach strażników), *he tried to escape over the prison wall.* ◇ *in full view of the house* (widoczny z budynku) ▶ **na widoku**
to the full as much as possible: *to enjoy life to the full* używać życia na całego ▶ **na całego**

full[2] /fʊl/ adv. **full in/on (sth)** straight; directly: *John hit him full in the face.* ◇ *The two cars crashed full on.* ▶ **prosto**

ˌfull-ˈblown adj. [only before a noun] fully developed: *to have full-blown AIDS* ▶ **rozwinięty**

ˌfull ˈboard noun [U] (in a hotel, etc.) including all meals ▶ **z pełnym wyżywieniem** ➲ note at **hotel** ➲ look at **half board**, **bed and breakfast**

ˌfull-ˈfledged (US) = FULLY FLEDGED

ˌfull-ˈlength adj. [only before a noun] **1** (used about a picture, mirror, etc.) showing a person from head to foot ▶ **pokazujący osobę od stóp do głów 2** not made shorter: *a full-length film* ▶ **pełnometrażowy**, **normalnej długości 3** (used about a dress, skirt, etc.) reaching the feet ▶ **do ziemi**

ˌfull ˈmoon noun [sing.] the moon when it appears as a complete circle ▶ **pełnia** OPP **new moon**

ˌfull-ˈscale adj. [only before a noun] **1** using every thing or person that is available: *The police have started a full-scale murder investigation.* ▶ **na dużą skalę 2** (used about a plan, drawing, etc.) of the same size as the original object: *a full-scale plan/model* ▶ **wielkości naturalnej**

ˌfull ˈstop (especially US **period**) noun [C] a mark (.) that is used in writing to show the end of a sentence ▶ **kropka**

ˌfull-ˈtime adj. for a whole of the normal period of work: *He has a full-time job.* ◇ *We employ 800 full-time staff.* ▶ **pełnoetatowy**
■ **full-time** adv.: *He works full-time.* ▶ **na pełny etat** ➲ look at **part-time**

fully /ˈfʊli/ adv. completely; to the highest possible degree: *I'm fully aware of the problem.* ◇ *All our engineers are fully trained.* ▶ **całkowicie**, **w pełni**

ˌfully ˈfledged (US also **ˌfull-ˈfledged**) adj. completely trained or completely developed: *Computer science is now a fully fledged academic subject.* ▶ **w pełni rozwinięty**

fumble /ˈfʌmbl/ verb [I] to try to find or take hold of sth with your hands in a nervous or careless way: *'It must be here somewhere', she said, fumbling in her pocket for her key.* ▶ **grzebać**, **mocować się** (*np. z zamkiem błyskawicznym*)

fume /fjuːm/ verb [I] to be very angry about sth ▶ **kipieć ze złości**

fumes /fjuːmz/ noun [pl.] smoke or gases that smell unpleasant and that can be dangerous to breathe in: *diesel/petrol/exhaust fumes* ▶ **spaliny**, **wyziewy**

fumigate /ˈfjuːmɪɡeɪt/ verb [T] to use special chemicals, smoke or gas to destroy the harmful insects or bacteria in a place: *to fumigate a room* ▶ **przeprowadzać dezynsekcję**, **dezynfekować**
■ **fumigation** /ˌfjuːmɪˈɡeɪʃn/ noun [U,C] ▶ **dezynsekcja**, **dezynfekcja**

fun[1] /fʌn/ noun [U] pleasure and enjoyment; an activity or a person that gives you pleasure and enjoyment: *We **had** a lot of **fun** at the party last night.* ◇ ***It's no fun** having to get up at 4 o'clock every day.* ◇ *Have fun!* Baw się dobrze! ◇ *He was extremely clever but he was also great fun* (można się było z nim dobrze bawić). ▶ **zabawa**, **przyjemność**

> Uwaga! **Funny** oznacza, że coś/ktoś jest śmieszny, dziwny, dziwaczny, a **fun** oznacza, że coś/ktoś jest przyjemny, zabawny: *The party was **great fun**.* Bardzo dobrze bawiliśmy się na imprezie. ◇ *The film was funny.* Film był śmieszny. ◇ *There's something funny about her.* Jest trochę dziwna.

IDM **(just) for fun/for the fun of it** (just) for entertainment or pleasure; not seriously: *I don't need English for my work. I'm learning it for fun.* ▶ **dla przyjemności**, **dla zabawy**
in fun as a joke: *It was said in fun. They didn't mean to upset you.* ▶ **na żarty**
make fun of sb/sth to laugh at sb/sth in an unkind way; to make other people do this: *The older children are always making fun of him because of his accent.* ▶ **wyśmiewać się z kogoś/czegoś**
poke fun at sb/sth → POKE

fun[2] /fʌn/ adj. amusing or enjoyable: *to have a fun time/day out* ◇ *Brett's a fun guy.* ◇ *Staying in a cottage over Christmas **sounds fun*** (brzmi nieźle). ▶ **fajny**, **wesoły**

function[1] /ˈfʌŋkʃn/ noun [C] **1** the purpose or special duty of a person or thing: *The function of the heart is to pump blood through the body.* ◇ *to perform/fulfil a function* ▶ **funkcja**, **rola 2** an important social event, ceremony, etc.: *The princess attends hundreds of official functions every year.* ▶ **uroczystość**

function[2] /ˈfʌŋkʃn/ verb [I] to work correctly; to be in action: *Only one engine was still functioning.* ▶ **działać** SYN **operate**

functional /ˈfʌŋkʃənl/ adj. **1** practical and useful rather than attractive: *cheap functional furniture* ▶ **funkcjonalny**, **praktyczny 2** working; being used: *The system is now fully functional.* ▶ **sprawny**, **w użyciu**

functionality /ˌfʌŋkʃəˈnæləti/ noun (pl. **functionalities**) **1** [U] the quality in sth of being very suitable for the purpose it was designed for ▶ **funkcjonalność**, **sprawność** SYN **practicality 2** [U] the purpose that sth is designed for: *Manufacturing processes may be affected by the functionality of the product.* ▶ **funkcjonalność 3** [C,U] the functions that a computer or other electronic system can perform: *new software with additional functionality* ▶ **funkcja**

ˈfunction key noun [C] one of several keys on a computer, each marked with 'F' and a number, that can be used to perform a particular operation ▶ **klawisz funkcyjny**

fund[1] /fʌnd/ noun **1** [C] a sum of money that is collected for a particular purpose: *They contributed £30 to the disaster relief fund.* ▶ **fundusz 2** (**funds**) [pl.] money that is available and can be spent: *The hospital is trying to **raise funds** for a new kidney machine.* ▶ **fundusze**, **środki**

fund[2] /fʌnd/ verb [T] to provide a project, school, charity, etc. with money: *The Channel Tunnel is not funded by government money.* ▶ **fundować**, **dostarczać środki**

fundamental /ˌfʌndəˈmentl/ adj. basic and important; from which everything else develops: *There will be fundamental changes in the way the school is run.* ◇ *There is a fundamental difference between your opinion and mine.* ▶ **zasadniczy** ➲ look at **essential**

■ **fundamentally** /-təli/ adv.: *The government's policy on this issue has changed fundamentally.* ▶ **zasadniczo**

fundamentalism /ˌfʌndəˈmentəlɪzəm/ noun [U] **1** the practice of following very strictly the basic rules and teachings of any religion ▶ **fundamentalizm** **2** (in Christianity) the belief that everything that is written in the Bible is completely true ▶ **fundamentalizm**
■ **fundamentalist** /-ɪst/ noun [C] ▶ **fundamentalist(k)a** | **fundamentalist** /-ɪst/ adj. ▶ **fundamentalistyczny**

fundamentals /ˌfʌndəˈmentlz/ noun [pl.] basic facts or principles ▶ **podstawy**, **zasady**

ˈ**fund-raiser** noun [C] a person whose job is to find ways of collecting money for a charity or an organization ▶ **osoba gromadząca fundusze**, **kwestarz**
■ **fund-raising** noun [U]: *fund-raising events* ▶ **gromadzenie funduszy**, **kwesta**

⚷ **funeral** /ˈfjuːnərəl/ noun [C] a ceremony (usually religious) for burying or burning a dead person: *The funeral will be held next week.* ▶ **pogrzeb**

> The body of the dead person is carried in a **coffin**, on which there are often **wreaths** of flowers. The coffin is buried in a **grave** or is **cremated**.

ˈ**funeral director** = UNDERTAKER

ˈ**funeral parlour** (US ˈ**funeral parlor**, **mortuary**, especially US ˈ**funeral home**) noun [C] a place where dead people are prepared for being buried or **cremated** and where visitors can see the body ▶ **dom/zakład pogrzebowy**

funereal /fjuˈnɪəriəl/ adj. (formal) suitable for a funeral; sad: *a funereal atmosphere* ▶ **pogrzebowy**, **posępny**

funfair = FAIR² (1)

fungicide /ˈfʌŋɡɪsaɪd; ˈfʌndʒɪ-/ noun [C, U] a substance that kills **fungus** ▶ **środek grzybobójczy**

fungus /ˈfʌŋɡəs/ noun [C,U] (pl. **fungi** /ˈfʌŋɡiː; -ɡaɪ/ or **funguses**) a plant without leaves, flowers or green colouring, such as a **mushroom**, or that is like a wet powder and grows on old wood or food, walls, etc. Some **fungi** can be harmful. ▶ **grzyb** ➲ note at **mushroom** ➲ look at **mould**, **toadstool**
■ **fungal** /ˈfʌŋɡl/ adj.: *a fungal disease/infection/growth* ▶ **grzyb(k)owy**

funky /ˈfʌŋki/ adj. (**funkier**; **funkiest**) (informal) **1** (used about pop music) with a strong rhythm that is easy to dance to: *a funky disco beat* ▶ **funkowy** **2** fashionable and unusual: *She wears really funky clothes.* ▶ **odjechany** ℹ Często wyraża dezaprobatę.

ˈ**fun-loving** adj. (used about people) liking to enjoy themselves ▶ **lubiący dobrą zabawę**

funnel /ˈfʌnl/ noun [C] **1** an object that is wide at the top and narrow at the bottom, used for pouring liquid, powder, etc. into a small opening ▶ **lejek** ➲ picture at **laboratory** **2** the metal pipe which takes smoke or steam out of a ship, an engine, etc. ▶ **komin**

funnily /ˈfʌnəli/ adv. in a strange or unusual way: *She's walking very funnily.* ▶ **śmiesznie**
IDM **funnily enough** (used for expressing surprise at sth strange that has happened): *Funnily enough, my parents weren't at all cross about it.* ▶ **dziwne, że**

⚷ **funny** /ˈfʌni/ adj. (**funnier**; **funniest**) **1** that makes you smile or laugh: *a funny story* ◇ *He's an extremely funny person.* ◇ *That's the funniest thing I've heard in ages!* ▶ **śmieszny**, **zabawny** ➲ note at **fun**¹, **humour**¹ **2** strange or unusual; difficult to explain or understand: *Oh dear, the engine is making a funny noise.* ◇ *It's funny that they didn't phone to let us know they couldn't come.* ◇ ***That's funny*** *– he was here a moment ago and now he's gone.* ▶ **dziwny**, **niesamowity** SYN **peculiar** **3** (informal) slightly ill: *Can I sit down for a minute? I **feel** a bit **funny*** (zrobiło mi się słabo). ▶ **słaby**

ˈ**funny bone** noun [usually sing.] (informal) the part of the elbow containing a very sensitive nerve that is painful if you hit it against sth ▶ **czułe miejsce w łokciu**

⚷ **fur** /fɜː(r)/ noun **1** [U] the soft thick hair that covers the bodies of some animals ▶ **futro**, **sierść** ➲ picture on **page A10** **2** [C,U] the skin and hair of an animal that is used for making clothes, etc.; a piece of clothing that is made from this: *a fur coat* ▶ **futro**

furious /ˈfjʊəriəs/ adj. **1 furious (with sb)**; **furious (at sth)** very angry: *He was furious with her for losing the car keys.* ◇ *He was furious at having to catch the train home.* ▶ **wściekły** ➲ noun **fury** **2** very strong; violent: *They had a furious argument.* ▶ **zaciekły**
■ **furiously** adv. ▶ **wściekle**, **zaciekle**
IDM **fast and furious** → FAST¹

furnace /ˈfɜːnɪs/ noun [C] a large, very hot fire surrounded on all sides by walls that is used for melting metal, burning rubbish, etc. ▶ **piec**, **kocioł**

furnish /ˈfɜːnɪʃ/ verb [T] to put furniture in a room, house, etc.: *The room was comfortably furnished.* ▶ **meblować**
■ **furnished** adj.: *She's renting a furnished room in Birmingham.* ▶ **umeblowany**

furnishings /ˈfɜːnɪʃɪŋz/ noun [pl.] the furniture, carpets, curtains, etc. in a room, house, etc. ▶ **wyposażenie wnętrza**

⚷ **furniture** /ˈfɜːnɪtʃə(r)/ noun [U] the things that can be moved, for example tables, chairs, beds, etc. in a room, house or office: *modern/antique/second-hand furniture* ◇ *garden/office furniture* ▶ **meble** ℹ Uwaga! **Furniture** jest rzeczownikiem niepoliczalnym: *They only got married recently and they haven't got much furniture.* Kiedy chodzi o pojedynczy mebel, mówi się **a piece of furniture**: *The only nice piece of furniture in the room was an antique desk.*

ˈ**furniture van** (Brit.) = REMOVAL VAN

furore /fjuˈrɔːri; ˈfjʊərɔː(r); US ˈfjʊər-/ (especially US **furor** /ˈfjʊərɔː(r)/) noun [sing.] **furore (about/over sth)** great anger or excitement shown by a number of people, usually caused by a public event: *His novel about Jesus caused a furore among Christians.* ▶ **wrzawa** SYN **uproar**

furrow /ˈfʌrəʊ; US ˈfɜːr-/ noun [C] **1** a line in a field that is made for planting seeds in by a **plough** ▶ **bruzda** **2** a deep line in the skin on sb's face ▶ **zmarszczka** ➲ look at **wrinkle**

furry /ˈfɜːri/ adj. (**furrier**; **furriest**) having fur: *a small furry animal* ▶ **futrzany**, **puszysty**

further¹ /ˈfɜːðə(r)/ adj. **1** [the comparative of *far*] more distant or far; farther ▶ **dalszy**, **dalej** **2** more; additional: *Are there **any further questions**?* ◇ *I have **nothing further to say** on the subject.* ◇ *Please let us know if you require **any further information**.* ◇ *The museum is closed **until further notice*** (do odwołania). ▶ **dodatkowy**, **dalszy**
IDM **further afield** → FAR²
■ **further** adv. **1** at or to a greater distance in time or space; farther: *It is not safe to go any further.* ◇ *The hospital is further down the road on the left.* ◇ *I can't remember any further back than 1970.* ▶ **dalej**, **więcej** **2** more; to a greater degree: *Can I have time to consider the matter further?* ▶ **w większym stopniu**, **dokładniej**

> Zarówno **further** jak i **farther** mogą być stosowane w odniesieniu do odległości: *Bristol is further/farther from London than Oxford is.* ◇ *I jumped further/farther than you did.* W pozostałych znaczeniach stosuje się jedynie **further**: *We need a further week to finish the job.*

further² /ˈfɜːðə(r)/ verb [T] (formal) to help sth to develop or be successful: *to further the cause of peace* ▶ **posuwać do przodu** (*np. sprawę*), **wspierać**

ˌfurther eduˈcation noun [U] (abbr. **FE** /ˌef ˈiː/) (Brit.) education for people who have left school (but not at a university) ▶ **kursy dla absolwentów szkół średnich** ➲ look at **higher education**

furthermore /ˌfɜːðəˈmɔː(r)/ adv. also; in addition ▶ **ponadto**

furthermost /ˈfɜːðəməʊst/ adj. (formal) located at the greatest distance from sth: *at the furthermost end of the street* ▶ **najdalszy**, **najbardziej oddalony**

ˈfurther to prep. (formal) (used in letters, emails, etc. to refer to a previous letter, email, conversation, etc.): *Further to our conversation of last Friday, I would like to book the conference centre for 26 June.* ▶ (*w korespondencji*) **w nawiązaniu do**

furthest → FAR

furtive /ˈfɜːtɪv/ adj. secret, acting as though you are trying to hide sth because you feel guilty: *a furtive glance at the letter* ▶ **ukradkowy**, **potajemny**
■ **furtively** adv. ▶ **ukradkowo**, **potajemnie**

fury /ˈfjʊəri/ noun [U] very great anger: *She was speechless with fury.* ▶ **wściekłość**, **furia** ➲ adjective **furious**

fuse¹ /fjuːz/ noun [C] **1** a small piece of wire in an electrical system, machine, etc. that melts and breaks if there is too much power. This stops the flow of electricity and prevents fire or damage: *A fuse has blown – that's why the house is in darkness.* ◇ *That plug needs a 15 amp fuse.* ▶ **bezpiecznik** ➲ picture at **plug** **2** a piece of rope, string, etc. or a device that is used to make a bomb, etc. explode at a particular time ▶ **lont** **3** a device that makes a bomb etc.explode at a particular time ▶ **zapalnik**

fuse² /fjuːz/ verb [I,T] **1** (used about two things) to join together to become one; to make two things do this: *As they heal, the bones will fuse together* (zrosną się). ◇ *The two companies have been fused into one large organization.* ▶ **stapiać**, **łączyć się** **2** to stop working because a **fuse¹** (1) has melted; to make a piece of electrical equipment do this: *The lights have fused.* ◇ *I've fused the lights.* ▶ **przepalać (się)**

ˈfuse box noun [C] a small box or cupboard that contains the **fuses** of the electrical system of a building ▶ **skrzynka bezpiecznikowa**

fuselage /ˈfjuːzəlɑːʒ; US ˈfjuːs-/ noun [C] the main part of a plane (not the engines, wings or tail) ▶ **kadłub samolotu** ➲ picture at **plane**

fusion /ˈfjuːʒn/ noun [U, sing.] the process or the result of joining different things together to form one: *the fusion of two political systems* ▶ **fuzja**, **zlewanie się**

fuss¹ /fʌs/ noun **1** [sing., U] unnecessary nervous excitement or activity: *Now get on with your work without making a fuss.* ◇ *What's all the fuss about?* ▶ **zamieszanie** **2** [sing.] anger or complaints about sth, especially sth that is not important: *There will be a dreadful fuss if my parents find out that I borrowed the car.* ▶ **awantura**
IDM **make/kick up a fuss (about/over sth)** to complain strongly: *The waiter didn't* ***make a fuss*** *when I spilt my drink.* ▶ **zrobić awanturę (o coś)**
make a fuss of/over sb/sth to pay a lot of attention to sb/sth: *My grandmother used to make a big fuss of me when she visited.* ▶ **skakać koło kogoś/czegoś**

fuss² /fʌs/ verb [I] **1 fuss (over sb/sth)** to pay too much attention to sb/sth: *Stop fussing over all the details.* ▶ **zbytnio przejmować się** **2** to be worried or excited about small things: *Stop fussing. We're not going to be late.* ▶ **przejmować się drobiazgami**
IDM **not be fussed (about sb/sth)** (Brit., informal) to not care very much: *'Where do you want to go for lunch?' 'I'm not fussed* (wszystko mi jedno).*'* ▶ **nie dbać o coś**

fusspot /ˈfʌspɒt/ (US **fussbudget** /ˈfʌsbʌdʒɪt/) noun [C] (informal) a person who is often worried about unimportant things and is difficult to please ▶ **maruda**, **zrzęda**

fussy /ˈfʌsi/ adj. (**fussier**; **fussiest**) **1 fussy (about sth)** (used about people) giving too much attention to small details and therefore difficult to please: *He is very fussy about food.* ▶ **wybredny** ➲ look at **particular**, **picky** **2** having too much detail or decoration: *I don't like that pattern. It's too fussy.* ▶ **przeładowany**

futile /ˈfjuːtaɪl; US -tl/ adj. (used about an action) having no success; useless: *They made a last futile attempt to make him change his mind.* ▶ **daremny**
■ **futility** /fjuːˈtɪləti/ noun [U] ▶ **daremność**

futon /ˈfuːtɒn/ noun [C] a Japanese **mattress**, often on a wooden frame, that can be used for sitting on or rolled out to make a bed ▶ **rodzaj materaca z ramą do siedzenia lub spania** ➲ note at **bed**

future /ˈfjuːtʃə(r)/ noun **1** (**the future**) [sing.] the time that will come after the present: *Who knows what will happen* ***in the future?*** ◇ *in the near/distant future* ◇ *What are your plans* ***for the*** *immediate* ***future*** (na najbliższą przyszłość)*?* ▶ **przyszłość** **2** [C] what will happen to sb/sth in the time after the present: *Our children's futures depend on a good education.* ◇ *The company's future does not look very hopeful.* ▶ **przyszłość** **3** [U] the possibility of being successful: *I could see no future in this country so I left to work abroad.* ▶ **przyszłość** **4** (**the future (tense)**) [sing.] the form of a verb that expresses what will happen after the present ▶ **czas przyszły**
■ **future** adj. [only before a noun]: *She met her future husband when she was still at school.* ◇ *You can keep that book for future reference* (żeby z niej korzystać w przyszłości). ◇ *What are your future plans* (plany na przyszłość)*?* ▶ **przyszły**
IDM **in future** from now on: *Please try to be more careful in future.* ▶ **w przyszłości**

the ˌfuture ˈperfect noun [sing.] the form of a verb which expresses an action in the future that will be finished before the time mentioned. The future perfect is formed with the future tense of *have* and the past participle of the verb: *'We'll have been married for ten years next month' is in the future perfect.* ▶ **czas przyszły dokonany**

futuristic adj. extremely modern and unusual in appearance, as if belonging to a future time; imagining what the future will be like: *a futuristic novel/movie* ▶ **futurystyczny**

fuzzy /ˈfʌzi/ adj. (**fuzzier**; **fuzziest**) not clear: *The photo was a bit fuzzy but I could just make out my mother in it.* ▶ **niewyraźny**, **zamazany**

ˈF-word noun [sing.] (informal) (used to refer to the offensive swear word *fuck*, to avoid having to say it) ▶ **słowo na k**

FYI /ˌef waɪ ˈaɪ/ abbr. **for your information** ▶ **do wiadomości kogoś** (*bez potrzeby podejmowania działania*) ➲ look at **attn**

Gg

G, g /dʒiː/ noun [C,U] (pl. **Gs**; **gs**; **G's**; **g's** /dʒiːz/) **1** the 7th letter of the English alphabet: *'Gentleman' begins with (a) 'G'.* ▶ **litera** *g* **2** (used about music) the fifth note in the series of notes called the scale of C major: *G major* G-dur ◇ *G minor* g-moll ◇ *G sharp* Gis, gis ◇ *G flat* Ges, ges ▶ **G/g**

g = GRAM ▶ **g**

gabble /ˈɡæbl/ verb [I,T] **gabble (on/away)** (informal) to talk quickly so that people cannot hear you clearly or understand you: *They were gabbling on about the past.* ◇ *He was gabbling nonsense.* Plótł bzdury. ▶ **trajkotać**
■ **gabble** noun [sing.] fast speech that is difficult to understand, especially when a lot of people are talking at the same time ▶ **trajkot**

gable /ˈɡeɪbl/ noun [C] the pointed part at the top of an outside wall of a house between two parts of the roof ▶ **szczyt** (*dachu*)

gad /ɡæd/ verb (**gadding**; **gadded**)
PHR V **gad about/around** (informal) to go around from one place to another in order to enjoy yourself ▶ **włóczyć się**

gadget /ˈɡædʒɪt/ noun [C] (informal) a small device, tool or machine that has a particular but usually unimportant purpose: *This car has all the latest gadgets.* ▶ **gadżet**

Gaelic /ˈɡeɪlɪk; ˈɡælɪk/ noun [U] the Celtic language and the culture of Ireland or Scotland ▶ **język celtycki**
■ **Gaelic** adj. ▶ **celtycki**

gaffe /ɡæf/ noun [C] a mistake that a person makes in public or in a social situation, especially sth embarrassing: *a social gaffe* ▶ **gafa** SYN **faux pas**

gag¹ /ɡæɡ/ noun [C] **1** a piece of cloth, etc. that is put in or over sb's mouth in order to stop them from talking ▶ **knebel 2** a joke ▶ **żart**

gag² /ɡæɡ/ verb [T] (**gagging**; **gagged**) to put a **gag** in or over sb's mouth: (figurative) *The new laws are an attempt to gag the press* (próbą nałożenia prasie kagańca). ▶ **zakneblować**

gage (US) = GAUGE¹

gaiety /ˈɡeɪəti/ noun [U] a feeling of happiness and fun ▶ **wesołość** ➲ adjective **gay**

gaily /ˈɡeɪli/ adv. **1** in a bright and attractive way: *a gaily decorated room* ▶ **barwnie 2** happily: *She waved gaily to the crowd.* ▶ **wesoło 3** without thinking or caring about the effect of your actions on other people: *She gaily announced that she was leaving.* ▶ **beztrosko, radośnie**

🔑 **gain¹** /ɡeɪn/ verb **1** [T] to gradually get more of sth: *to gain confidence* ◇ *The train was gaining speed.* ◇ *I've gained a lot of weight recently.* Ostatnio przybrałem dużo na wadze. ▶ **zyskiwać, nabierać** OPP **lose 2** [T] to obtain or win sth, especially sth that you need or want: *They managed to gain access to secret information.* ◇ *The country gained its independence ten years ago.* ▶ **zdobywać** (*np. dostęp do czegoś, sławę*) **3** [I] **gain (sth) (by/from sth/ doing sth)** to get an advantage: *Many people will gain from the changes in the law.* ◇ *I've got* ***nothing to gain*** (nic nie skorzystam) *by staying in this job.* ▶ **odnosić korzyść** OPP **lose 4** [I,T] (used about a clock or watch) to go too fast and show the incorrect time: *My watch gains five minutes a day.* Mój zegarek śpieszy się pięć minut na dobę. ▶ **śpieszyć się** ℹ Aby powiedzieć, że zegar śpieszy się o pięć minut, używa się też przymiotnika **fast**: *My watch is five minutes fast.*
IDM **gain ground** to make progress; to become stronger or more popular ▶ **robić postępy**
PHR V **gain in sth** to gradually get more of sth: *He's gained in confidence in the past year.* ▶ **zyskiwać na czymś**
gain on sb/sth to get closer to sb/sth that you are trying to catch: *I saw the other runners were gaining on me so I increased my pace.* ▶ **doganiać kogoś/coś, zbliżać się do kogoś/czegoś**

🔑 **gain²** /ɡeɪn/ noun **1** [C,U] an increase in money; (a) profit or advantage: *We hope to make a gain when we sell our house.* ◇ *He will do anything for* ***personal gain***, *even if it means treating people badly.* ▶ **zysk, korzyść 2** an increase in size, amount or power: *a* ***gain in weight*** *of one kilo* ◇ *The Liberal Democrat Party is expected to* ***make gains*** (prawdopodobnie zdobędzie więcej głosów) *at the next election.* ▶ **wzrost** OPP for both meanings **loss**

gait /ɡeɪt/ noun [sing.] the way that sb/sth walks ▶ **chód**

gal. = GALLON

gala /ˈɡɑːlə; US ˈɡeɪlə/ noun [C] a special social occasion or sports event ▶ **gala, uroczystość**

galaxy /ˈɡæləksi/ noun **1** [C] (pl. **galaxies**) a large group of stars and planets in space ▶ **galaktyka 2** (**the Galaxy**; **the ˌMilky ˈWay**) [sing.] the system of stars that contains our sun and its planets, seen as a bright band in the night sky ▶ **Droga Mleczna**

gale /ɡeɪl/ noun [C] a very strong wind: *Several trees blew down in the gale.* ▶ **huragan** ➲ look at **storm**

gallant /ˈɡælənt/ adj. (formal) **1** showing courage in a difficult situation: *gallant men/soldiers/heroes* ◇ *He made a gallant attempt to speak French, but nobody could understand him.* ▶ **dzielny** SYN **brave 2** (used about men) polite to and showing respect for women ▶ **rycerski**

gallantry /ˈɡæləntri/ noun [U] **1** courage, especially in battle ▶ **odwaga 2** polite behaviour towards women by men ▶ **rycerskość**

gall bladder /ˈɡɔːl blædə(r)/ noun [C] an organ that is attached to the liver that stores and releases bile. ▶ **pęcherzyk żółciowy**

gallery /ˈɡæləri/ noun [C] (pl. **galleries**) **1** a building or room where works of art are shown to the public: *an art gallery* ▶ **galeria (sztuki) 2** an upstairs area at the back or sides of a large hall where people can sit ▶ **miejsca dla publiczności 3** the highest level of seating in a theatre ▶ (*teatr*) **galeria, najwyższy balkon**

galley /ˈɡæli/ noun [C] **1** a long flat ship with sails, especially one used by the ancient Greeks or Romans in war ▶ **galera 2** the kitchen on a ship or plane ▶ **kambuz; kuchnia w samolocie**

galling /ˈɡɔːlɪŋ/ adj. [not usually before a noun] (used about a situation or fact) making you angry because it is unfair ▶ **napełniający złością i goryczą**

🔑 **gallon** /ˈɡælən/ noun [C] (abbr. **gal.**) a measure of liquid; 4.5 litres (3.8 litres in the US) ▶ **galon** ℹ Więcej o jednostkach objętości w dodatku *Wyrażenia liczbowe* na końcu słownika.

gallop /ˈɡæləp/ verb [I] (used about a horse or a rider) to go at the fastest speed ▶ **galopować** ➲ look at **canter**, **trot**
■ **gallop** noun [sing.] ▶ **galop**

gallows /ˈɡæləʊz/ noun [C] (pl. **gallows**) a structure on which people, for example criminals, are killed by hanging ▶ **szubienica**

gallstone /ˈɡɔːlstəʊn/ noun [C] a hard painful mass that can form in the **gall bladder** ▶ **kamień żółciowy**

galore /ɡəˈlɔː(r)/ adv. [only after a noun] in large numbers or amounts: *There will be prizes galore at our children's party on Saturday.* ▶ **mnóstwo, w bród**

galvanize (also **-ise**) /ˈɡælvənaɪz/ verb [T] **1 galvanize sb (into sth/into doing sth)** to make sb take action by shocking them or by making them excited: *The urgency of his voice* ***galvanized them into action.*** ▶ **pobudzić kogoś**

(do czegoś) 2 (technical) to cover metal with **zinc** in order to protect it from being damaged by water: *a galvanized bucket ◇ galvanized steel* ▶ **galwanizować, cynkować**

gamble¹ /ˈɡæmbl/ verb [I,T] **gamble (sth) (on sth)** to bet money on the result of a card game, horse race, etc.: *to gamble on horses* ▶ **uprawiać hazard**, (*gra, zakłady*) **stawiać na coś** SYN **bet**

■ **gambler** noun [C]: *He's a compulsive gambler.* ▶ **gracz, hazardzist(k)a, ryzykant/ka** | **gambling** noun [U] ▶ **uprawianie gier hazardowych**

PHR V **gamble on sth/on doing sth** to act in the hope that sth will happen although it may not: *I wouldn't gamble on the weather staying fine.* ▶ **liczyć na coś, spodziewać się czegoś**

gamble² /ˈɡæmbl/ noun [C] something you do that is a risk: *Setting up this business was a bit of a gamble. ◇ I wouldn't like to **take a gamble** on this plan working.* Nie chciałbym podejmować ryzyka sprawdzenia, czy ten plan zadziała. ▶ **ryzyko**

game¹ /ɡeɪm/ noun **1** [C] **a game (of sth)** a form of play or sport with rules; a time when you play it: *Shall we **play a game**? ◇ Let's **have a game** of chess.* Zagrajmy partię szachów. ◇ *a game of football/rugby/tennis ◇ 'Monopoly' is a very popular **board game*** (grą planszową). ◇ *Tonight's game is between Holland and Italy. ◇ The game ended in a draw.* ▶ **sport, gra, mecz 2** (**games**) [pl.] an important sports competition: *Where were the last Olympic Games held?* ▶ **zawody sportowe, rozgrywki 3** [C] (in sports such as **tennis**) a section of a match that forms a unit in scoring: *two games all* ▶ **gem 4** [C] how well sb plays a sport: *My new racket has really improved my game.* ▶ **styl/sposób gry, gra 5** [C] an activity that you do to have fun: *Some children were playing a game of hide-and-seek.* ▶ **zabawa 6** [C] (informal) a secret plan or trick: *Stop **playing games** with me* (żartować sobie ze mnie) *and tell me where you've hidden the bag.* ▶ **gra** (*ukryte motywy postępowania*) **7** [U] wild animals or birds that are killed for sport or food: *big game* gruba zwierzyna ▶ **zwierzyna łowna**

IDM **give the game away** to tell a person sth that you are trying to keep secret: *It was the expression on her face that gave the game away.* ▶ **zdradzać tajemnicę**

game² /ɡeɪm/ adj. (used about a person) ready to try sth new, unusual, difficult, etc.: *I've never been sailing before but I'm game to try.* ▶ **ochoczy, gotowy**

gamekeeper /ˈɡeɪmkiːpə(r)/ noun [C] a person who is responsible for private land where people hunt animals and birds ▶ **leśniczy**

ˈ**game show** noun [C] a television programme in which people play games or answer questions to win prizes ▶ **teleturniej** ➲ look at **quiz**

gammon /ˈɡæmən/ noun [U] (Brit.) meat from the back leg or side of a pig that has been **cured**, usually served in thick slices ▶ **szynka** ➲ look at **bacon, ham, pork**

the **gamut** /ˈɡæmət/ noun [sing.] the complete range of a particular kind of thing: *The network will provide the gamut of computer services to your home. ◇ She felt she had **run the (whole) gamut of** human emotions* (doświadczyła wszystkich (możliwych) ludzkich emocji) *from joy to despair.* ▶ **zakres, skala**

gander /ˈɡændə(r)/ noun [C] a male **goose** ▶ **gąsior**

gang¹ /ɡæŋ/ noun [C, with sing. or pl. verb] **1** an organized group of criminals ▶ **gang, szajka 2** a group of young people who cause trouble, fight other groups, etc.: *The woman was robbed by a gang of youths. ◇ gang warfare/violence* ▶ **banda, szajka 3** (informal) a group of friends who meet regularly ▶ **paczka** (*przyjaciół*)

gang² /ɡæŋ/ verb

PHR V **gang up on sb** (informal) to join together with other people in order to act against sb: *She's upset because she says the other kids are ganging up on her.* ▶ **zmawiać się przeciwko komuś**

gangrene /ˈɡæŋɡriːn/ noun [U] the death of a part of the body because the blood supply to it has been stopped as a result of disease or injury ▶ **zgorzel, gangrena**

■ **gangrenous** /ˈɡæŋɡrɪnəs/ adj. ▶ **zgorzelinowy, gangrenowaty**

gangster /ˈɡæŋstə(r)/ noun [C] a member of a group of criminals ▶ **bandyta, gangster**

gangway /ˈɡæŋweɪ/ noun [C] **1** (Brit.) a passage between rows of seats in a cinema, an aircraft, etc. ▶ **przejście 2** a bridge that people use for getting on or off a ship ▶ **trap**

gaol, gaoler (Brit.) = JAIL, JAILER

gap /ɡæp/ noun [C] **1 a gap (in/between sth)** an empty space in sth or between two things: *The sheep got out through a gap in the fence.* ▶ **dziura, otwór 2** a period of time when sth stops, or between two events: *I returned to teaching after a gap of about five years. ◇ a gap in the conversation* ▶ **przerwa 3** a difference between people or their ideas: *The gap between the rich and the poor is getting wider.* ▶ **przepaść** (*dzieląca poglądy itp.*) **4** a part of sth that is missing: *In this exercise you have to fill (in) the gaps in the sentences. ◇ I think our new product should fill **a gap in the market.*** ▶ **luka**

IDM **bridge a/the gap** → BRIDGE²

gape /ɡeɪp/ verb [I] **1 gape (at sb/sth)** to look at sb/sth for a long time with your mouth open because you are surprised, shocked, etc.: *We gaped in astonishment when we saw what Amy was wearing.* ▶ **gapić się 2 gape (open)** to be or become wide open: *a gaping wound ◇ There was a gaping hole in the wall after the explosion.* Wybuch zrobił w ścianie ziejącą dziurę. ▶ (*otwór*) **ziać**

ˈ**gap year** noun [C] (Brit.) a year that a young person spends working and/or travelling, often between leaving school and starting university: *I'm planning to take a gap year and go backpacking in India.* ▶ **rok przerwy po zakończeniu nauki w liceum, a przed rozpoczęciem studiów**

garage /ˈɡærɑːʒ; -rɪdʒ; US ɡəˈrɑːʒ; -ˈrɑːdʒ/ noun [C] **1** a small building where a car, etc. is kept: *The house has a double garage.* ▶ **garaż 2** a place where vehicles are repaired and/or petrol is sold: *a garage mechanic* ▶ **stacja obsługi/benzynowa** ➲ look at **petrol station**

ˈ**garage sale** noun [C] a sale of used clothes, furniture, etc., held in the garage of sb's house ▶ **wyprzedaż rzeczy używanych we własnym garażu**

garbage (especially US) = RUBBISH

ˈ**garbage can** (US) = DUSTBIN

ˈ**garbage man** (US) = DUSTMAN

ˈ**garbage truck** (US) = DUSTCART

garbled /ˈɡɑːbld/ adj. (used about a message, story, etc.) difficult to understand because it is not clear ▶ **pogmatwany**

garden¹ /ˈɡɑːdn/ noun [C] **1** (US **yard**) a piece of land next to a house where flowers and vegetables can be grown, usually with a **lawn**: *the back/front garden ◇ garden chairs* ▶ **ogród** ➲ note at **yard 2** (**gardens**) [pl.] a public park: *the Botanical Gardens* Ogród Botaniczny ▶ **park**

garden² /ˈɡɑːdn/ verb [I] to work in a garden ▶ **uprawiać ogród**

ˈ**garden centre** noun [C] a place where plants, seeds, garden equipment, etc. are sold ▶ **centrum ogrodnicze** ➲ picture on **page A5**

gardener /ˈɡɑːdnə(r)/ noun [C] a person who works in a garden as a job or for pleasure ▶ **ogrodni-k/czka**

gardening /ˈɡɑːdnɪŋ/ noun [U] looking after a garden: *I'm going to **do some gardening** this afternoon. ◇ gar-*

garden equipment

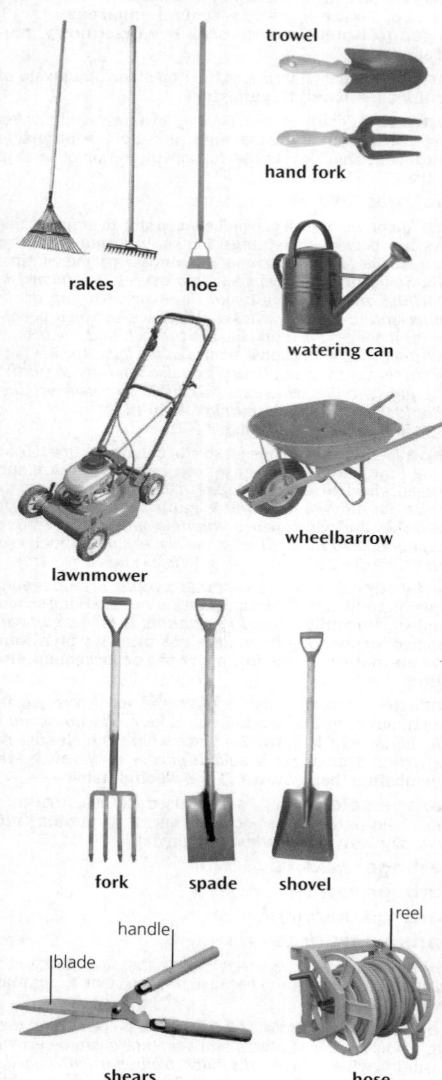

dening tools/gloves narzędzia/rękawice ogrodnicze ▶ **ogrodnictwo**

'garden party noun [C] a formal social event that takes place outside usually in a large garden in summer ▶ **przyjęcie towarzyskie pod gołym niebem**

gargle /'gɑ:gl/ verb [I] to wash your throat with a liquid (which you do not swallow) ▶ **płukać gardło**

gargoyle /'gɑ:gɔɪl/ noun [C] an ugly figure of a person or an animal that is made of stone and through which water is carried away from the roof of a building, especially a church ▶ **rzygacz**

garish /'geərɪʃ/ adj. very bright or decorated and therefore unpleasant ▶ **jaskrawy, krzykliwy** SYN **gaudy**

garlic /'gɑ:lɪk/ noun [U] a plant with a strong taste and smell that looks like a small onion and is used in cooking: *a **clove of garlic*** ząbek czosnku ▶ **czosnek** ➲ picture on **page A13**

garment /'gɑ:mənt/ noun [C] (formal) one piece of clothing ▶ **część garderoby, ubranie** ➲ look at **clothes**

garnish /'gɑ:nɪʃ/ verb [T] to decorate a dish of food with a small amount of another food: *Garnish the soup with a little parsley before serving.* ▶ **dekorować** (*potrawę*)
■ **garnish** noun [U,C] ▶ **przybranie, dekoracja**

garrison /'gærɪsn/ noun [C] a group of soldiers who are living in and guarding a town or building ▶ **garnizon**

gas¹ /gæs/ noun (pl. **gases**; US also **gasses**) **1** [C,U] a substance like air that is not a solid or a liquid: *Hydrogen and oxygen are gases.* ▶ **gaz 2** [U] a particular type of gas or mixture of gases that is used for heating or cooking: *a gas cooker* ▶ **gaz 3** [U] (US) = PETROL **4** [U] a poisonous gas that is used in war ▶ **gaz bojowy**

gas² /gæs/ verb [T] (**gassing**; **gassed**) to poison or kill sb with gas ▶ **zagazowywać**

gasbag /'gæsbæg/ noun [C] (informal, humorous) a person who talks a lot ▶ **gaduła**

'gas chamber noun [C] a room that can be filled with poisonous gas in order to kill animals or people ▶ **komora gazowa**

gash /gæʃ/ noun [C] a long deep cut or wound: *He had a nasty gash in his arm.* ▶ **głębokie cięcie, głęboka rana**
■ **gash** verb [T] ▶ **głęboko rozcinać, rozpłatywać** (*np. materiał, ciało*)

'gas mask noun [C] an piece of equipment that is worn over the face to protect against poisonous gas ▶ **maska przeciwgazowa**

'gas meter noun [C] an instrument that measures the amount of gas that you use in your home ▶ **licznik gazowy**

gasoline (US) = PETROL

gasp /gɑ:sp; US gæ-/ verb **1** [I] **gasp (at sth)** to take a sudden loud breath with your mouth open, usually because you are surprised or in pain: *She gasped in surprise at the news.* ▶ **wstrzymać oddech** (*ze zdumienia*), **głośno oddychać** (*z bólu*) **2** [I] to have difficulty breathing: *I pulled the boy out of the pool and he lay there **gasping for breath**.* ◇ *'I can't go on,' he gasped* (wysapał), *'I've got to sit down.'* ▶ **sapać**
■ **gasp** noun [C]: *to give a gasp of pain/horror* ◇ *Suddenly she gave a gasp of surprise* (dech jej zaparło ze zdumienia). ▶ **sapnięcie** (*ze zdziwienia, bólu*)

'gas station (US) = PETROL STATION

gastric /'gæstrɪk/ adj. [only before a noun] (technical) connected with the stomach: *gastric juices* ◇ *a gastric ulcer* wrzód żołądka ▶ **żołądkowy, gastryczny**

gastronomic /,gæstrə'nɒmɪk/ adj. [only before a noun] connected with good food ▶ **gastronomiczny**

gasworks /'gæswɜ:ks/ noun [C, with sing. or pl. verb] (pl. **gasworks**) a factory where gas for lighting and heating is made from coal ▶ **gazownia**

gate /geɪt/ noun [C] **1** the part of a fence, wall, etc. like a door that can be opened to let people or vehicles through ▶ **brama 2** (also **gateway**) the space in a wall, fence, etc. where the gate is: *Drive through the gates and you'll find the car park on the right.* ▶ **brama wjazdowa 3** the place at an airport where you get on or off a plane: *Lufthansa Flight 139 to Geneva is now boarding at gate 16.* ▶ **wyjście do samolotu**

gateau /ˈgætəʊ/ noun [C] (pl. **gateaux**) a large cake that is usually decorated with cream, fruit, etc.: *a strawberry gateau* ▶ **tort** ➲ picture at **cake**

gatecrash /ˈgeɪtkræʃ/ verb [I,T] to go to a private party without being invited ▶ **iść na przyjęcie bez zaproszenia**
■ **gatecrasher** noun [C] ▶ **intruz** (*na przyjęciu*)

gateway /ˈgeɪtweɪ/ noun [C] **1** = GATE (2) **2** [sing.] **the gateway to sth** the place which you must go through in order to get to somewhere else: *The port of Dover is England's gateway to Europe.* ◇ (figurative) *A good education can be the gateway to success.* ▶ **droga** (*np. do sławy, sukcesu*)

gather /ˈgæðə(r)/ verb **1** [I,T] **gather (round) (sb/sth)**; **gather sb/sth (round) (sb/sth)** (used about people) to come or be brought together in a group: *A crowd soon gathered at the scene of the accident.* ◇ *We all gathered round and listened to what the guide was saying.* ▶ **zbierać (się), gromadzić (się) 2** [T] **gather sth (together/up)** to bring many things together: *He gathered up all his papers and put them away.* ◇ *They have gathered together a lot of information on the subject.* ▶ **zbierać 3** [T] (formal) to pick wild flowers, fruit, etc. from a wide area: *to gather mushrooms* ▶ **zbierać 4** [T] to understand or find out sth (from sb/sth): *I gather from your letter that you have several years' experience of this kind of work.* ◇ *'She's been very ill recently.' 'So I gather.'* ▶ **wnioskować, rozumieć (z czegoś, że) 5** [I,T] to gradually become greater; to increase: *In the gathering darkness* (w zapadającej ciemności) *it was hard to see the ball.* ◇ *The train is gathering speed.* Pociąg nabiera szybkości. ▶ **zwiększać 6** [T] to pull material together into small folds and sew it: *a gathered skirt* ▶ **fałdować** (*materiał*) ➲ look at **pleat**

gathering /ˈgæðərɪŋ/ noun [C] a time when people come together; a meeting: *a social/family gathering* ▶ **zgromadzenie**

gauche /gəʊʃ/ adj. awkward when dealing with people and often saying or doing the wrong thing ▶ **niezręczny** (*w zachowaniu*), **nieporadny**
■ **gaucheness** noun [U] ▶ **niezręczność, nieporadność**

gaudy /ˈgɔːdi/ adj. (**gaudier**; **gaudiest**) very bright or decorated and therefore unpleasant ▶ **jaskrawy, krzykliwy** SYN **garish**

gauge¹ (US also **gage**) /geɪdʒ/ noun [C] **1** an instrument for measuring the amount of sth: *a fuel/temperature/pressure gauge* ▶ **wskaźnik, przyrząd pomiarowy 2** (technical) a measurement of the width of sth or of the distance between two things: *a narrow-gauge railway* kolej wąskotorowa ▶ **rozstaw, szerokość 3 a gauge (of sth)** a fact that you can use to judge a situation, sb's feelings, etc. ▶ **miernik, wyznacznik**

gauge² /geɪdʒ/ verb [T] **1** to make a judgement or to calculate sth by guessing: *It was difficult to gauge the mood of the audience.* ▶ **oceniać 2** to measure sth accurately using a special instrument ▶ **mierzyć, dokonywać pomiaru**

gaunt /gɔːnt/ adj. (used about a person) very thin because of illness, not having enough food, or worry ▶ **wychudzony**

gauze /gɔːz/ noun [U] a thin material like a net, that is used for covering an area of skin that you have hurt or cut ▶ **gaza** ➲ picture at **laboratory**

gave past tense of **give¹**

gawp /gɔːp/ verb [I] (informal) **gawp (at sb/sth)** to look for a long time in a stupid way because you are surprised, shocked, etc.: *Lots of drivers slowed down to gawp at the accident.* ▶ **gapić się**

gay¹ /geɪ/ adj. **1** sexually attracted to people of the same sex: *a gay bar/club* ◇ *the gay community* (środowisko gejów) *of New York* ◇ *He told me he was gay* (że jest gejem). ▶ **gejowski** SYN **homosexual** OPP **straight** ➲ look at **lesbian 2** (old-fashioned) happy and full of fun ▶ **wesoły** ➲ noun **gaiety**

gay² /geɪ/ noun [C] someone, especially a man, who is sexually attracted to people of the same sex ▶ **gej; lesbijka** SYN **homosexual** ➲ look at **lesbian**

gaze /geɪz/ verb [I] to look steadily for a long time: *She sat at the window gazing dreamily into space.* ▶ **przypatrywać się**
■ **gaze** noun [sing.] ▶ **nieruchomy wzrok**

GB 1 = GREAT BRITAIN **2** (also **Gb**) = GIGABYTE

GCSE /ˌdʒiː siː es ˈiː/ abbr. **General Certificate of Secondary Education**; an examination that students in England, Wales and Northern Ireland take when they are about 16. They often take **GCSEs** in five or more subjects. For Scottish examinations, look at SCE. ▶ **egzamin szkolny zdawany dwa lata przed egzaminem A level** ➲ look at **A level**

GDP /ˌdʒiː diː ˈpiː/ abbr. **gross domestic product**; the total value of all goods and services produced by a country in one year ▶ **produkt krajowy brutto** ➲ look at **GNP**

gear¹ /gɪə(r)/ noun **1** [C] the machinery in a vehicle that turns engine power into a movement forwards or backwards: *Most cars have four or five forward gears and a reverse* (cztery lub pięć biegów do jazdy do przodu i jeden bieg wsteczny). ▶ **przekładnia** ➲ picture at **bicycle 2** [U] a particular position of the gears in a vehicle: *first/second/top/reverse gear* ◇ *to change gear* ▶ **bieg** (*auta*)

> A car can be **in** or **out of** gear. You use a **low** gear (**first** gear) when you first start moving and then **change** gear as you go faster. For the fastest speeds you use **top** gear.

3 [U] equipment or clothing that you need for a particular activity, etc.: *camping/fishing/sports gear* ▶ **sprzęt 4** [U] (informal) clothes: *wearing the latest gear* ▶ **ciuchy 5** [sing.] a piece of machinery that is used for a particular purpose: *the landing gear of an aeroplane* ▶ **mechanizm lub część mechanizmu, układ**

gear² /gɪə(r)/ verb
PHR V **gear sth to/towards sb/sth** [often passive] to make sth suitable for a particular purpose or person: *There is a special course geared towards the older learner.* ▶ **przystosowywać coś do kogoś/czegoś**
gear up (for sb/sth); **gear sb/sth up (for sb/sth)** to get ready or to make sb/sth ready ▶ **przygotowywać się/kogoś/coś (do kogoś/czegoś)**

gearbox /ˈgɪəbɒks/ noun [C] the metal case that contains the gears of a car, etc. ▶ **skrzynia biegów**

ˈgear lever (US **ˈgear shift**) noun [C] a stick that is used for changing gear in a car, etc. ▶ **dźwignia zmiany biegów** ➲ picture at **car**

gee /dʒiː/ interj. (US) (used for expressing surprise, pleasure, etc.) ▶ **ojej!, ho, ho!**

geek /giːk/ noun [C] (informal) a person who is boring, wears clothes that are not fashionable, does not know how to behave in social situations, etc.: *a computer geek* maniak komputerowy ▶ **osoba, która jest nudna, niemodna i nie cieszy się popularnością** SYN **nerd**
■ **geeky** adj. ▶ **nudny i niemodny**

geese plural of **goose**

Geiger counter /ˈgaɪgə kaʊntə(r)/ noun [C] a device for detecting and measuring radioactive substances ▶ **licznik Geigera**

gel /dʒel/ noun [C,U] [in compounds] a thick substance that is between a liquid and a solid: *hair gel* ◇ *shower gel* ▶ **żel**

gelatin /ˈdʒelətɪn/ (also **gelatine** /ˈdʒelətiːn/) noun [U] a clear substance that is made by boiling animal bones and is used in many products, especially in cooking to make liquid thick or firm ▶ **żelatyna**

gelignite /ˈdʒelɪɡnaɪt/ noun [U] a substance that is used for making explosions ▶ **nitroglicerynowy materiał wybuchowy**

gem /dʒem/ noun [C] **1** a rare and valuable stone that is used in jewellery ▶ **kamień szlachetny 2** a person or thing that is especially good ▶ *(przedmiot/osoba)* **skarb**

Gemini /ˈdʒemɪnaɪ/ noun [C,U] the 3rd sign of the **zodiac**, the Twins; a person born under this sign: *I'm a Gemini* ▶ **Bliźnięta**; **osoba spod znaku Bliźniąt**

Gen. = GENERAL²

gender /ˈdʒendə(r)/ noun [C,U] **1** (formal) the fact of being male or female ▶ **płeć** SYN **sex 2** (in some languages) the division of nouns, pronouns, etc. into classes (for example **masculine**, **feminine**, **neuter**); one of these classes ▶ *(gram.)* **rodzaj**

gene /dʒiːn/ noun [C] a unit of information inside a cell which controls what a living thing will be like. **Genes** are passed from parents to children. ▶ **gen** ➲ look at **genetics**

genealogy /ˌdʒiːniˈælədʒi/ noun (pl. **-ies**) **1** [U] the study of family history, including the study of who the **ancestors** of a particular person were ▶ **genealogia 2** [C] a particular person's line of **ancestors**; a diagram that shows this ▶ **genealogia**, **rodowód**
■ **genealogical** /ˌdʒiːniəˈlɒdʒɪkl/ adj. [only before a noun]: *a **genealogical chart/table/tree*** ▶ **genealogiczny**

ˈ**gene pool** noun [C] all of the **genes** that are available within breeding populations of a particular **species** of animal or plant ▶ **pula genów**

genera plural of **genus**

⚷ **general¹** /ˈdʒenrəl/ adj. **1** affecting all or most people, places, things, etc.: *Fridges were once a luxury, but now they are in general use.* ◇ *a matter of general interest* ◇ *the general public* (o ludziach) ogół ▶ **ogólny**, **powszechny 2** [only before a noun] referring to or describing the main part of sth, not the details: *Your general health is very good.* ◇ *The introduction gives you a general idea of what the book is about.* ◇ ***As a general rule**, the most common verbs in English tend to be irregular.* ▶ **ogólny 3** not limited to one subject, use or activity: *Children need a good general education.* ▶ **ogólny 4** [in compounds] with responsibility for the whole of an organization: *a general manager* ▶ **naczelny**, **generalny**
IDM **in general 1** in most cases; usually: *In general, standards of hygiene are good.* ▶ **zwykle 2** as a whole: *I'm interested in Spanish history in general, and the civil war in particular.* ▶ **w ogóle**

general² /ˈdʒenrəl/ noun [C] (abbr. **Gen.**) an army officer in a very high position ▶ **generał**

ˌ**general anaesˈthetic** noun [C,U] a substance that is given to a patient in hospital before an operation so that they become unconscious and do not feel any pain ▶ **środek znieczulający stosowany w znieczuleniu ogólnym** ➲ look at **local anaesthetic**

ˌ**general eˈlection** noun [C] an election in which all the people of a country vote to choose a government ▶ **wybory powszechne** ➲ note at **election** ➲ look at **by-election**

generalization (also **-isation**) /ˌdʒenrəlaɪˈzeɪʃn; US -ləˈz-/ noun **1** [U] the act of **generalizing** ▶ **uogólnianie 2** [C] a general statement about sth that does not consider details: *You can't **make sweeping generalizations about** French people if you've only been to France for a day!* ▶ **uogólnienie**

generalize (also **-ise**) /ˈdʒenrəlaɪz/ verb [I] **generalize (about sth)** to form an opinion or make a statement using only a small amount of information instead of looking at the details: *You can't generalize about English food from only two meals.* ▶ **uogólniać**

ˌ**general ˈknowledge** noun [U] knowledge of facts about a lot of different subjects ▶ **wiedza ogólna**

⚷ **generally** /ˈdʒenrəli/ adv. **1** by or to most people: *He is generally considered to be a good doctor.* ▶ **ogólnie 2** usually: *She generally cycles to work.* ▶ **zwykle 3** without discussing the details of sth: *Generally speaking, houses in America are bigger than houses in this country.* ▶ **ogólnie**

ˌ**general ˈstore** noun [C] (Brit. also ˌgeneral ˈstores [pl.]) a shop that sells a wide variety of goods, especially one in a small town or village: *She runs the post office and general store.* ▶ **sklep wielobranżowy**

⚷ **generate** /ˈdʒenəreɪt/ verb [T] **1** to produce power, heat, electricity, etc.: *to generate heat/power/electricity* ▶ **wytwarzać 2** to cause sth to exist ▶ **powodować**, **przynosić** *(np. dochód)*

⚷ **generation** /ˌdʒenəˈreɪʃn/ noun **1** [C, with sing. or pl. verb] all the people in a family, group or country who were born at about the same time: *We should look after the planet for future generations.* ◇ *This photograph shows three generations of my family.* ▶ **pokolenie** ⓘ Rzeczownik **generation** w lp łączy się z czasownikiem w lp lub lm: *The younger generation only seem/seems to be interested in money.* **2** [C] the average time that children take to grow up and have children of their own, usually considered to be about 25-30 years: *A generation ago foreign travel was still only possible for a few people.* ▶ **pokolenie 3** [U] the production of sth, especially heat, power, etc.: *the generation of electricity by water power* ▶ **wytwarzanie**

the ˌ**geneˈration gap** noun [sing.] the difference in behaviour, and the lack of understanding, between young people and older people ▶ **konflikt pokoleń**

generator /ˈdʒenəreɪtə(r)/ noun [C] a machine that produces electricity ▶ **prądnica**, **generator**

generic /dʒəˈnerɪk/ adj. **1** shared by, including or typical of a whole group of things: *'Vine fruit' is the **generic term** for currants and raisins.* ▶ **ogólny 2** (used about a product, especially a drug) not using the name of the company that made it ▶ **generyczny**
■ **generically** /-kli/ adv. ▶ **ogólnie**; **generycznie**

generosity /ˌdʒenəˈrɒsəti/ noun [U] the quality of being generous ▶ **hojność**, **wspaniałomyślność**

⚷ **generous** /ˈdʒenərəs/ adj. **1** happy to give more money, help, etc. than is usual or expected: *It was very generous of your parents to lend us all that money.* ▶ **hojny**, **wspaniałomyślny 2** larger than usual: *a generous helping of pasta* ▶ **obfity**
■ **generously** adv.: *People gave very generously to our appeal for the homeless.* ▶ **hojnie**, **wspaniałomyślnie**; **obficie**

genesis /ˈdʒenəsɪs/ noun [sing.] (formal) the beginning or origin of sth ▶ **geneza**

ˈ**gene therapy** noun [U] a treatment in which normal **genes** are put into cells to replace ones that are missing or not normal ▶ **terapia genowa**

genetic /dʒəˈnetɪk/ adj. connected with **genes**, or with **genetics**: *The disease is caused by a genetic defect.* ▶ **genetyczny**
■ **genetically** /-kli/ adv. ▶ **genetycznie**

geˌ**netically ˈmodified** adj. (abbr. **GM** /ˌdʒiː ˈem/) (used about food, plants, etc.) that has been grown from cells whose **genes** have been changed in an artificial way ▶ **genetycznie modyfikowany**

geˌ**netic ˈcode** noun [C] the arrangement of **genes** that controls how each living thing will develop ▶ **kod genetyczny**

ge,netic engi'neering noun [U] the science of changing the way a human, animal or plant develops by changing the information in its **genes** ▶ **inżynieria genetyczna**

ge,netic 'fingerprinting (also ,**DNA 'fingerprinting**) noun [U] the method of finding the particular pattern of **genes** in an individual person, particularly to identify sb or find out if sb has committed a crime ▶ **identyfikacja osoby za pomocą badań DNA**
■ **ge,netic 'fingerprint** noun [C] ▶ (*przen.*) **genetyczny odcisk palca**

geneticist /dʒə'netɪsɪst/ noun [C] a scientist who studies **genetics** ▶ **genetyk**

genetics /dʒə'netɪks/ noun [U] the scientific study of the way that the development of living things is controlled by qualities that have been passed on from parents to children ▶ **genetyka** ➲ look at **gene**

genial /'dʒiːniəl/ adj. (used about a person) pleasant and friendly ▶ **dobroduszny**, **towarzyski**

genie /'dʒiːni/ noun [C] a spirit with magic powers, especially one that lives in a bottle or a lamp ▶ **dżinn**

genital /'dʒenɪtl/ adj. [only before a noun] connected with the outer sexual organs of a person or an animal: *the genital area* ▶ (*narząd*) **płciowy**, **genitalny**

genitals /'dʒenɪtlz/ (also **genitalia** /,dʒenɪ'teɪliə/) noun [pl.] (formal) the parts of sb's sex organs that are outside the body ▶ **genitalia**

genius /'dʒiːniəs/ noun **1** [U] very great and unusual intelligence or ability: *Her idea was* ***a stroke of genius.*** ▶ **wielki talent** **2** [C] a person who has very great and unusual ability, especially in a particular subject: *Einstein was a mathematical genius.* ▶ **geniusz** ➲ look at **prodigy** **3** [sing.] **a genius for (doing) sth** a very good natural skill or ability ▶ **talent**

genocide /'dʒenəsaɪd/ noun [U] the murder of all the people of a particular race, religion, etc. ▶ **ludobójstwo**

genome /'dʒiːnəʊm/ noun [C] the complete set of **genes** in a cell or living thing: *the human genome* ▶ **genom**

genre /'ʒɒ̃rə; 'ʒɒnrə/ noun [C] (formal) a particular type or style of literature, art, film or music ▶ **gatunek literacki**, **rodzaj sztuki**

gent (informal) = GENTLEMAN

genteel /dʒen'tiːl/ adj. behaving in a very polite and quiet way, often in order to make people think that you are from a high social class ▶ **(przesadnie) wytworny**
ℹ Często używa się w znaczeniu ironicznym.
■ **gentility** /dʒen'tɪləti/ noun [U] ▶ **szlacheckie urodzenie**; **wytworność** (*manier*)

gentile /'dʒentaɪl/ (also **Gentile**) noun [C] a person who is not Jewish ▶ **goj/ka**
■ **gentile** (also **Gentile**) adj. [only before a noun] ▶ **nieżydowski**

⚷ **gentle** /'dʒentl/ adj. **1** (used about people) kind and calm; touching or treating people or things in a careful way so that they are not hurt: *'I'll try and be as gentle as I can,' said the dentist.* ▶ **łagodny**, **delikatny** **2** not strong, violent or extreme: *gentle exercise* ◇ *a gentle slope/curve* ◇ *a gentle breeze* ▶ **łagodny**
■ **gentleness** noun [U] ▶ **łagodność**, **delikatność** | **gently** /'dʒentli/ adv. ▶ **łagodnie**, **delikatnie**

⚷ **gentleman** /'dʒentlmən/ noun [C] (pl. **-men** /-mən/) **1** (also informal **gent** /dʒent/) a man who is polite and who behaves well towards other people ▶ **dżentelmen** **2** (formal) (used when speaking to or about a man or men in a polite way): ***Ladies and gentlemen***... Szanowni Państwo ◇ *Mrs Flinn, there is a gentleman here to see you* (jakiś pan chce się z panią zobaczyć). ▶ **pan**, **mężczyzna** **3** (old-fashioned) a rich man with a high social position: *a country gentleman* ▶ **bogaty mężczyzna o wysokiej pozycji społecznej**

gentry /'dʒentri/ noun [pl.] (usually **the gentry**) (old-fashioned) people belonging to a high social class: *the landed gentry* ziemiaństwo ▶ **szlachta**

the 'gents (also **the 'Gents**) noun [sing.] (Brit., informal) a public toilet for men ▶ **ubikacja dla panów** ➲ look at **ladies** ➲ note at **toilet**

⚷ **genuine** /'dʒenjuɪn/ adj. **1** real; true: *He thought that he had bought a genuine Rolex watch but it was a cheap fake.* ▶ **autentyczny** ➲ look at **imitation** **2** sincere and honest; that can be trusted: *a very genuine person* ▶ **szczery**, **prawdziwy**
■ **genuinely** adv. ▶ **autentycznie**, **szczerze**

genus /'dʒiːnəs/ noun [C] (pl. **genera** /'dʒenərə/) (technical) a group into which animals, plants, etc. that have similar characteristics are divided ▶ (*systematyka roślin i zwierząt*) **rodzaj** ➲ look at **class**, **family**, **species**

geographer /dʒi'ɒgrəfə(r)/ noun [C] an expert in, or a student of, **geography** ▶ **geograf**

⚷ **geography** /dʒi'ɒgrəfi/ noun [U] **1** the study of the world's surface, physical qualities, climate, countries, products, etc.: *human/physical/economic geography* ▶ **geografia** **2** the physical arrangement of a place: *We're studying the geography of Asia.* ▶ **geografia**
■ **geographical** /,dʒiːə'græfɪkl/ adj. ▶ **geograficzny** | **geographically** /-kli/ adv. ▶ **geograficznie**, **terenowo**

geologist /dʒi'ɒlədʒɪst/ noun [C] an expert in, or a student of, **geology** ▶ **geolog**

geology /dʒi'ɒlədʒi/ noun [U] the study of rocks, and of the way they are formed ▶ **geologia**
■ **geological** /,dʒiːə'lɒdʒɪkl/ adj. ▶ **geologiczny**

geometric /,dʒiːə'metrɪk/ (also **geometrical** /-ɪkl/) adj. **1** connected with **geometry** ▶ **geometryczny** **2** consisting of regular shapes and lines: *a geometric design/pattern* ▶ **geometryczny**
■ **geometrically** /-kli/ adv. ▶ **geometrycznie**

geometry /dʒi'ɒmətri/ noun [U] the study in mathematics of lines, shapes, curves, etc. ▶ **geometria**

geopolitics /,dʒiːəʊ'pɒlətɪks/ noun [U, with sing. or pl. verb] the political relations between countries and groups of countries in the world; the study of these relations ▶ **geopolityka**
■ **geopolitical** /,dʒiːəʊpə'lɪtɪkl/ adj. ▶ **geopolityczny**

geothermal /,dʒiːəʊ'θɜːml/ adj. connected with the natural heat of rock deep in the ground: *geothermal energy* ▶ **geotermalny**

geranium /dʒə'reɪniəm/ noun [C] a garden plant with red, pink or white flowers ▶ **geranium**, **pelargonia** ➲ picture on **page A15**

geriatrics /,dʒeri'ætrɪks/ noun [U] the medical care of old people ▶ **geriatria**
■ **geriatric** adj. ▶ **geriatryczny**

germ /dʒɜːm/ noun **1** [C] a very small living thing that causes disease ▶ **zarazek**, **drobnoustrój** ➲ look at **bacteria**, **virus** **2** [sing.] **the germ of sth** the beginning of sth that may develop: *the germ of an idea* ▶ **zawiązek**, **zarodek**

Germanic /dʒɜː'mænɪk/ noun having German characteristics ▶ **germański**

German measles /,dʒɜːmən 'miːzlz/ (also **rubella** /ruː'belə/) noun [U] a mild disease that causes red spots all over the body. If a woman catches it when she is pregnant, it may damage the baby. ▶ **różyczka**

,German 'shepherd (especially US) = ALSATIAN

germinate /'dʒɜːmɪneɪt/ verb [I,T] (used about a seed) to start growing; to cause a seed to do this ▶ **kiełkować**; **doprowadzać do kiełkowania**

■ **germination** /ˌdʒɜːmɪˈneɪʃn/ noun [U] ▶ **kiełkowanie**

ˌ**germ ˈwarfare** = BIOLOGICAL WARFARE

gerund /ˈdʒerənd/ noun [C] a noun, ending in -ing, that has been made from a verb: *In the sentence 'His hobby is collecting stamps', 'collecting' is a gerund.* ▶ **rzeczownik odczasownikowy**

gestation /dʒeˈsteɪʃn/ noun [U, sing.] the period of time that a baby human or animal develops inside its mother's body; the process of developing inside the mother's body: *The **gestation period** of a horse is about eleven months.* ▶ **okres ciąży**; **rozwój** (*płodu*)

gesticulate /dʒeˈstɪkjuleɪt/ verb [I] to make movements with your hands and arms in order to express sth ▶ **gestykulować**

gesture[1] /ˈdʒestʃə(r)/ noun [C] **1** a movement of the hand, head, etc. that expresses sth: *I saw the boy **make a** rude **gesture** at the policeman before running off.* ▶ **gest 2** something that you do that shows other people what you think or feel ▶ **gest**

gesture[2] /ˈdʒestʃə(r)/ verb [I,T] to point at sth, to make a sign to sb: *She asked them to leave and gestured towards the door.* ▶ **wskazywać**, **wykonywać gest**

get /get/ verb (**getting**; pt **got** /gɒt/; pp **got**, US **gotten** /ˈgɒtn/) **1** [T] [no passive] to receive, obtain or buy sth: *I got a letter from my sister.* ◇ *Did you get a present for your mother?* ◇ *Did you get your mother a present?* ◇ *She got a job in a travel agency.* ◇ *Louise got 75% in the maths exam.* ◇ *I'll come if I can get time off work.* ◇ *How much did you get for your old car?* ◇ *to get a shock* doznać szoku ◇ *to get a surprise* zostać zaskoczonym ◇ *You get* (masz) *a wonderful view from that window.* ▶ **dostawać**, **otrzymywać**, **kupować 2** [T] **have/has got sth** to have sth: *I've got a lot to do today.* ◇ *Lee's got blond hair.* ◇ *Have you got a spare pen?* ▶ **mieć 3** [T] [no passive] to go to a place and bring sth back: ***Go and get** me a pen, please.* ◇ *Sam's gone to get his mother from the station.* ◇ *The police have got* (złapała) *the gang who carried out the robbery.* ▶ **przynosić**, **przywozić**, **przyprowadzać** SYN **fetch 4** [T] to catch or have an illness, pain, etc.: *I think I'm getting a cold.* Chyba się przeziębiłem. ◇ *He often gets really bad headaches.* Często cierpi na ból głowy. ▶ **zachorować na coś 5** [I] to become; to reach a particular state or condition: *It's getting dark.* Ściemnia się. ◇ *to get angry* złościć się ◇ *to get bored* nudzić się ◇ *to get hungry* zgłodnieć ◇ *to get fat* utyć ◇ *I can't **get used to*** (przyzwyczaić się do) *my new bed.* ◇ *to **get dressed*** ubierać się ◇ *When did you **get married*** (się pobraliście)? ◇ *to **get divorced*** rozwieść się ◇ *to get pregnant* zajść w ciążę ◇ *Just give me five minutes to **get ready*** (żebym się przygotował). ◇ *He's always **getting into trouble*** (wpada w kłopoty) *with the police.* ◇ *She's shy, but she's great fun once you **get to know*** (poznasz) *her.* ◇ *How did you get to know* (jak dowiedziałeś się) *that the money had gone.* ▶ **robić się**, **stawać się 6** [T] to make sb/sth be in a particular state or condition: *I'm **getting** my clothes **ready*** (przygotowuję ubrania) *for tomorrow.* ◇ *He got his fingers caught in the door.* Przytrzasnął sobie palce drzwiami. ◇ *Don't get your dress dirty!* Nie pobrudź sukienki! **7** [I] to have sth happen to you: *She got bitten by a dog.* Ugryzł ją pies. ◇ *Don't leave your wallet on the table or it'll get stolen* (ktoś go ukradnie). ℹ **Get** używa się jako czasownika posiłkowego w stronie biernej. Zwykle opisuje krótkie, przypadkowe zdarzenia. W tłumaczeniu na polski często używa się wówczas czasownika w stronie czynnej. **8** [T] **get sb/sth to do sth** to make sb/sth do sth or persuade sb to do sth: *I got him to agree to the plan.* ◇ *I can't get the TV to work.* Nie mogę nic zrobić, żeby telewizor zaczął działać. ▶ **nakłaniać kogoś do czegoś**, **przekonać kogoś**, **aby coś zrobił 9** [T] **get sth done** to cause sth to be done: *Let's get this work done – then we can go out.* ◇ *She finally got the book finished.* Skończyła wreszcie pisać książkę. ▶ **zrobić coś albo zlecić komuś wykonanie jakiejś czynności**

> Czasownika **get** używa się również wtedy, gdy na naszą prośbę czy zamówienie ktoś inny ma wykonać daną czynność: *I have to **get my hair cut.*** Muszę obciąć włosy. ◇ *You must get the car serviced every 10 000 miles.* Musisz zrobić przegląd samochodu po każdych dziesięciu tysiącach mil. ◇ *I had to get the car repaired.* Musiałam oddać samochód do naprawy.

10 [I] [used with verbs in the -ing form] to start doing sth: *We don't have much time so we'd better get working* (lepiej weźmy się do pracy). ◇ *I got talking* (zacząłem rozmawiać) *to a woman on the bus.* ◇ *We'd better **get going*** (lepiej pośpieszmy się) *if we don't want to be late.* ▶ **zabierać się do czegoś 11** [I] **get to do sth** to have the chance to do sth: *Did you get to see* (czy udało ci się zobaczyć) *the Rembrandt exhibition?* ◇ *Did you get to try the new computer?* ▶ **mieć okazję**, **udawać się 12** [I] to arrive at or reach a place: *We should get to London at about ten.* ◇ *Can you tell me how to get to the hospital?* ◇ *What time do you usually **get home*** (wracasz do domu)? ◇ *I got half way up the mountain then gave up.* ◇ *How far have you got with your book?* ◇ *I didn't **get to bed** until* (nie poszedłem spać aż do) *three last night.* ▶ **dojechać**, **dojść** ➲ look at **get in 13** [I] to move or go somewhere;: *I can't swim so I couldn't get across* (przejść przez) *the river.* ◇ *My grandmother's 92 and she doesn't get out of* (nie wychodzi z) *the house much.* **14** [T] to move or put sth somewhere: *We couldn't get the piano upstairs* (wnieść pianina na górę). ◇ *My foot was swollen and I couldn't get my shoe off* (zdjąć buta). ▶ **przenosić**, **zanosić**, **kłaść 15** [T] to use a form of transport: *Shall we walk or get the bus?* ▶ **jechać/lecieć czymś 16** [T] **get (sb) sth**; **get sth (for sb)** to prepare food: *Can I get you anything to eat?* ◇ *Joe's in the kitchen getting breakfast for everyone.* ▶ **przygotowywać** (*coś do jedzenia*) **17** [I] to hit, hold or catch sb/sth: *He got me by the throat and threatened to kill me.* ◇ *A boy threw a stone at me but he didn't get me.* ▶ **uderzyć**; **zatrzymać**; **chwycić 18** [T] to hear or understand sth: *I'm sorry, I didn't get that. Could you repeat it?* ◇ *Did you **get** that **joke** that Karen told?* ▶ **słyszeć**; **rozumieć**

IDM **get somewhere/nowhere (with sb/sth)** to make/not make progress: *I'm getting nowhere with my research.* ▶ **posuwać się (do przodu)**; **stać w miejscu**

ℹ **Get** używa się także w innych idiomach, np. **get rid of sb/sth.** Zob. hasła odpowiednich rzeczowników, przymiotników itp.

PHR V **get about/around/round** (used about news, a story, etc.) to become known by many people: *The rumour got around that Freddie wore a wig.* ▶ (*plotki itp.*) **rozchodzić się**

get above yourself (especially Brit.) to have too high an opinion of yourself ▶ **mieć zbyt wysokie mniemanie o sobie**

get sth across (to sb) to succeed in making people understand sth: *Your meaning didn't really get across.* Nie udało ci się wytłumaczyć nam, o co ci chodzi. ◇ *He's not very good at getting his ideas across.* Nie jest zbyt dobry w wyrażaniu swoich poglądów. ◇ *The party failed to get its policies across to the voters.* Partii nie udało się przekonać wyborców do swojej polityki. ▶ **wywoływać oddźwięk**

get ahead to progress and be successful in sth, especially a career ▶ **robić postępy**, **rozwijać się pomyślnie**

get along 1 [usually used in the continuous tenses] (informal) to leave a place: *I'd love to stay, but I should be getting along now.* ▶ **iść**, **zbierać się 2** = GET ON

get around 1 (Brit. also **get about**) to move or travel from place to place: *My grandmother needs a stick to get*

around these days. ▶ **dużo podróżować, nie siedzieć w (jednym) miejscu** **2** = GET ABOUT/AROUND/ROUND
get around sb = GET ROUND/AROUND SB
get around sth = GET ROUND/AROUND STH
get around to sth/doing sth = GET ROUND/AROUND TO STH/DOING STH
get at sb to criticize sb a lot: *The teacher's always getting at me about my spelling.* ▶ **czepiać się kogoś**
get at sb/sth to be able to reach sb/sth; to have sb/sth available for immediate use: *The files are locked away and I can't get at them.* ▶ **dosięgać kogoś/czegoś**
get at sth [only used in the continuous tenses] to try to say sth without saying it in a direct way; to suggest: *I'm not quite sure what you're getting at – am I doing something wrong?* ▶ **zmierzać do czegoś, sugerować coś**
get away (from...) to succeed in leaving or escaping from sb or a place: *He kept talking to me and I couldn't get away from him.* ◇ *The thieves got away in a stolen car.* ◇ *I'm hoping to get away* (wyjechać na urlop) *for a few days in May.* ▶ **uciekać, wyrywać się**
get away with sth/doing sth to do sth bad and not be punished for it: *He lied but he got away with it.* ▶ **uchodzić (komuś) na sucho**
get back to return to the place where you live or work: *When did you get back from Italy?* ▶ **wracać**
get sth back to be given sth that you had lost or lent: *Can I borrow this book? You'll get it back next week, I promise.* ▶ **dostawać coś z powrotem, odzyskiwać coś**
get back (in) (used about a political party) to win an election after having lost the previous one ▶ **wygrać wybory po poprzedniej porażce**
get back at sb (informal) to do sth bad to sb who has done sth bad to you; to get **revenge** on sb ▶ **odgrywać się na kimś, odpłacać komuś**
get back to sb to speak to, write to or telephone sb later, especially in order to give an answer: *I'll get back to you on prices when I've got some more information.* ▶ **kontaktować się z kimś ponownie** (*w tej samej sprawie*)
get back to sth to return to doing sth or talking about sth: *Let's get back to the point you raised earlier.* ◇ *I woke up early and couldn't get back to sleep* (nie mogłem znowu zasnąć). ▶ **wracać ponownie** (*np. do tematu*), **jeszcze raz coś robić**
get behind (with sth) to fail to do, pay sth, etc. on time, and so have more to do, pay, etc. the next time: *to get behind with your work/rent* ▶ **zalegać z czymś**
get by (on/in/with sth) to manage to live or do sth with difficulty: *It's very hard to get by on* (bardzo trudno jest przeżyć na) *such a low income.* ◇ *My Italian is good and I can get by in Spanish* (mogę dogadać się po hiszpańsku). ▶ **egzystować (dzięki czemuś), radzić sobie (z czymś)**
get sb down to make sb unhappy ▶ **przygnębiać kogoś**
get sth down **1** to swallow sth, usually with difficulty ▶ **połykać** (*zwł. z trudem*) **2** to make a note of sth: *He spoke so fast I couldn't get it all down.* ▶ **zapisywać** ➲ look at **write sth down**
get down to sth/doing sth to start working on sth: *We'd better stop chatting and get down to work.* ◇ *I must get down to answering these letters.* ▶ **zabierać się (za coś/do czegoś)**
get in to reach a place: *What time does your train get in?* ▶ **przyjeżdżać, przychodzić**
get in; **get into sth** **1** to climb into a car: *We all got in and Tim drove off.* ▶ **wsiadać** (*do samochodu*) **2** to be elected to a political position: *Who do you think will get in at the next election?* ▶ **być wybranym**
get sb in to call sb to your house to do a job: *We had to get a plumber in to fix the pipes.* ▶ **wzywać** (*fachowca*)
get sth in **1** to collect or bring sth inside; to buy a supply of sth: *It's going to rain – I'd better get the washing in from outside.* ▶ **wnieść coś do domu/środka** **2** to manage to find an opportunity to say or do sth: *He talked all the time and I couldn't get a word in.* ▶ **wtrącać** (*słowo*)

get in on sth to become involved in an activity ▶ **włączać się do czegoś**
get into sb (informal) (used about a feeling or attitude) to start affecting sb strongly, causing them to behave in an unusual way: *I wonder what's got into him – he isn't usually unfriendly.* ▶ **wstępować w kogoś**
get into sth **1** to put on a piece of clothing with difficulty: *I've put on so much weight I can't get into my trousers.* ▶ **wciskać się w ubranie** **2** to start a particular activity; to become involved in sth: *How did you first get into the music business?* ◇ *She has got into the habit* (nabrała przyzwyczajenia) *of turning up late.* ◇ *We got into an argument about politics.* ▶ **zaczynać (coś robić)** **3** to become more interested in or familiar with sth: *I've been getting into yoga recently.* ◇ *It's taking me a while to get into my new job.* ▶ **zainteresować się czymś; zaangażować się w coś**
get into sth; **get yourself/sb into sth** to reach a particular state or condition; to make sb reach a particular state or condition: *He got into trouble with the police while he was still at school.* ◇ *Three people were rescued from a yacht which got into difficulties.* ◇ *She got herself into a real state* (bardzo się denerwowała) *before the interview.* ▶ **wdawać się w coś; wplątywać się/kogoś w coś**
get off (sb/sth) (used especially to tell sb to stop touching you/sb/sth): *Get off (me) or I'll call the police!* ◇ *Get off that money, it's mine!* ▶ (*przen.*) **zejść z kogoś/czegoś**
get off (sth) **1** to leave a bus, train, etc.; to climb down from a bicycle, horse, etc. ▶ **wysiadać/zsiadać z czegoś** **2** to leave work with permission at a particular time: *I might be able to get off early today.* ▶ **wychodzić z pracy**
get (sb) off (with sth) to be lucky to receive no serious injuries or punishment; to help sb to receive little or no punishment: *to get off with just a warning* skończyć się tylko na ostrzeżeniu ◇ *A good lawyer might be able to get you off.* ▶ **wywinąć się z czegoś; pomóc komuś uniknąć kary**
get off on sth (informal) to be excited by sth, especially in a sexual way ▶ **podniecać się czymś**
get off with sb (especially Brit., informal) to start a sexual or romantic relationship with sb ▶ **zacząć z kimś romans**
get sth off (sth) to remove sth from sth ▶ **zdejmować coś (z czegoś)**
get on **1** to progress or become successful in life, in a career, etc.: *After leaving university she was determined to get on.* ▶ **osiągać powodzenie** **2** [only used in the continuous tenses] to be getting old: *He's getting on – he's over 70, I'm sure.* ▶ **starzeć się** **3** [only used in the continuous tenses] to be getting late: *Time's getting on – we don't want to be late.* ▶ **robić się późno**
get on/along **1** (used to talk or ask about how well sb is doing in a particular situation): *He's getting on very well at school.* ◇ *How did you get on* (jak ci poszło) *at your interview?* ▶ **robić postępy; radzić sobie** **2** to be successful in your career, etc.: *Parents are always anxious for their children to get on.* ◇ *I don't know how he's going to* **get on in life** (poradzi sobie w życiu). ▶ **odnosić sukcesy**
get on/onto sth to climb onto a bus, train, bicycle, horse, etc.: *I got on just as the train was about to leave.* ▶ **wsiadać do czegoś/na coś**
get on for sth [only used in the continuous tenses] to be getting near to a certain time or age: *I'm not sure how old he is but he must be getting on for 50.* ▶ **zbliżać się do czegoś**

G

get on to sb (about sth) to speak or write to sb about a particular matter ▶ **skontaktować się z kimś (w sprawie czegoś)**
get on to sth to begin to talk about a new subject: *It's time we got on to the question of costs.* ▶ **przechodzić do czegoś**
get on/along with sb; **get on/along (together)** to have a friendly relationship with sb: *Do you get on well with your colleagues?* ◇ *We're not close friends but we get on together quite well.* ▶ **mieć dobre/przyjazne stosunki z kimś, dobrze z kimś żyć**
get on/along with sth to make progress with sth that you are doing: *How are you getting on* (jak ci idzie) *with that essay?* ▶ **radzić sobie z czymś**
get on with sth to continue doing sth, especially after an interruption: *Stop talking and get on with your work!* Przestań gadać i wracaj do pracy. ▶ **robić coś dalej**
get sth on to put on a piece of clothing ▶ **wkładać, nakładać, ubierać (się)**
get out (used about a piece of information) to become known, after being secret until now ▶ **wydać się, wyjść na jaw**
get out (of sth) to leave or escape from a place: *Get out!/ Get out of here!* Wynoś się stąd! ▶ **wychodzić (skądś); uciekać (skądś)**
get sth out (of sth) to take sth from its container: *I got my keys out of my bag.* ▶ **wyjmować coś (z czegoś)**
get out of sth/doing sth to avoid a duty or doing sth that you have said you will do ▶ **wykręcać się od czegoś**
get sth out of sb to persuade or force sb to give you sth: *His parents finally got the truth out of him.* ▶ **wydobywać coś z kogoś**
get sth out of sb/sth to gain sth from sb/sth: *I get a lot of pleasure out of music.* ▶ **czerpać coś z czegoś; wyciągać coś od kogoś**
get over sth to deal with a problem successfully: *We'll have to get over the problem of finding somewhere to live first.* ▶ **rozwiązywać problem**
get over sth/sb to return to your usual state of health, happiness, etc. after an illness, a shock, the end of a relationship, etc.: *He still hasn't got over his wife's death.* ◇ *I'll never get over him!* Nigdy nie dojdę do siebie, po tym jak ode mnie odszedł! ▶ **przychodzić do siebie po czymś, przeboleć coś, pogodzić się z czymś**
get sth over (with) (informal) to do and complete sth unpleasant that has to be done: *I'll be glad to get my visit to the dentist's over with.* ▶ **mieć coś za sobą**
get round = GET ABOUT/AROUND/ROUND
get round/around sb (informal) to persuade sb to do sth or agree with sth: *My father says he won't lend me the money but I think I can get round him.* ▶ **przekonać kogoś**
get round/around sth to find a way of avoiding or dealing with a problem ▶ **znajdować sposób na coś, omijać** *(np. przepisy)*
get round/around to sth/doing sth to find the time to do sth, after a delay: *I've been meaning to reply to that letter for ages but I haven't got round to it yet.* ▶ **zabierać się do czegoś**
get through sth to use or complete a certain amount or number of sth: *I got through a lot of money at the weekend.* ◇ *I got through an enormous amount of work today.* ▶ **wydawać coś; wykonywać coś**
get (sb) through (sth) to manage to complete sth difficult or unpleasant; to help sb to do this: *She got through her final exams easily.* ▶ **przechodzić przez coś; pomagać komuś przejść przez coś**
get through (to sb) 1 to succeed in making sb understand sth: *They couldn't get through to him* (nie mogli mu uzmysłowić) *that he was completely wrong.* ▶ *(przen.)* **docierać (do kogoś) 2** to succeed in speaking to sb on the telephone: *I couldn't get through to them because their phone was engaged all day.* ▶ **dodzwonić się (do kogoś)**
get through (to sth) (used about a player or team) to reach the next stage of a competition: *Moya has got through to the final.* ▶ **przechodzić (do czegoś)**
get to sb (informal) to affect sb in a bad way: *Public criticism is beginning to get to the team manager.* ▶ **wywierać negatywny wpływ na kimś**
get sb/sth together to collect people or things in one place: *I'll just get my things together and then we'll go.* ▶ **zbierać kogoś/coś**
get together (with sb) to meet socially or in order to discuss or do sth: *Let's get together and talk about it.* ▶ **spotykać się (z kimś)** ➲ look at **meet up (with sb)**
get up to stand up: *He got up to let an elderly woman sit down.* ▶ **wstawać**
get (sb) up to get out of bed or make sb get out of bed: *What time do you have to get up in the morning?* ◇ *Could you get me up at 6 tomorrow?* ▶ **wstawać; budzić (się/kogoś)** ➲ note at **routine**
get up to sth 1 to reach a particular point or stage in sth: *We've got up to the last section of our grammar book.* ▶ **dochodzić do czegoś/dokądś 2** to be busy with sth, especially sth secret or bad: *I wonder what the children are getting up to* (co dzieci wyprawiają)*?* ▶ **kombinować coś**

getaway /ˈgetəweɪ/ noun [C] an escape (after a crime): *I made a quick getaway.* Szybko uciekłem. ◇ *a getaway car* samochód służący do ucieczki ◇ *a getaway driver* kierowca samochodu służącego do ucieczki ▶ **ucieczka**

ˈget-together noun [C] (informal) an informal social meeting or party: *We're going to have a get-together on Saturday evening.* ▶ **spotkanie, prywatka**

geyser /ˈgiːzə(r); US ˈgaɪz-/ noun [C] **1** a place where hot water or steam is sent up naturally into the air from under the ground ▶ **gejzer** ➲ look at **spring 2** (Brit.) a piece of equipment in a kitchen or bathroom that heats water, usually by gas ▶ **piecyk gazowy, terma gazowa**

ghastly /ˈgɑːstli; US ˈgæstli/ adj. (**ghastlier**; **ghastliest**) extremely unpleasant or bad: *a ghastly accident* ◇ *You look ghastly* (okropnie (blado))*. Do you want to lie down?* ▶ **okropny** SYN **terrible**

gherkin /ˈgɜːkɪn/ noun [C] a small green cucumber that is preserved in vinegar before being eaten ▶ **korniszon** ➲ look at **pickle**

ghetto /ˈgetəʊ/ noun [C] (pl. **ghettoes**) a part of a town where many people of the same race, religion, etc. live in poor conditions ▶ **getto**

ghost /gəʊst/ noun [C] the spirit of a dead person that is seen or heard by sb who is still living: *I don't believe in ghosts.* ◇ *a ghost story* historia o duchach ▶ **duch, zjawa** ➲ look at **apparition, spectre**

ghostly /ˈgəʊstli/ adj. (**ghostlier**; **ghostliest**) looking or sounding like a **ghost**; full of **ghosts**: *ghostly noises* hałas wywoływany przez duchy ▶ **widmowy, upiorny**

ˈghost town noun [C] a town that used to be busy and have people living in it, but is now empty ▶ **miasto-widmo**

ghostwriter /ˈgəʊstraɪtə(r)/ noun [C] a person who writes a book, etc. for a famous person (whose name appears as the author) ▶ **osoba pisząca książkę dla kogoś sławnego**

⚷ **giant** /ˈdʒaɪənt/ noun [C] **1** an extremely large, strong person: *a giant of a man* ▶ **olbrzym 2** something that is very large: *the multinational oil giants* ▶ **gigant**
■ **giant** adj.: *a giant new shopping centre* ▶ **olbrzymi, gigantyczny**

gibber /ˈdʒɪbə(r)/ verb [I,T] to speak quickly in a way that is difficult to understand, often because of fear: *By this time I was a **gibbering wreck**.* ▶ **bełkotać**

gibberish /ˈdʒɪbərɪʃ/ noun [U] words that have no meaning or that are impossible to understand ▶ **bełkot, bzdury**

gibbon /ˈɡɪbən/ noun [C] a small **ape** with long arms, that lives in SE Asia ▶ **gibon**

giblets /ˈdʒɪbləts/ noun [pl.] the inside parts of a chicken or other bird, including the heart and stomach, that are usually removed before it is cooked ▶ **podroby**

giddy /ˈɡɪdi/ adj. (**giddier**; **giddiest**) having the feeling that everything is going round and that you are going to fall: *I feel giddy.* Słabo mi. ▶ **mający zawrót głowy** SYN **dizzy**

⚷ **gift** /ɡɪft/ noun [C] **1** something that you give to sb; a present: *This watch was a gift from my mother.* ◇ *This week's magazine contains a **free gift** of some make-up.* ◇ *The company **made a gift of** a computer to a local school.* ▶ **prezent, upominek** SYN **present 2 a gift (for sth/doing sth)** natural ability: *I'd love to **have a gift** for languages like Mike has.* ▶ **talent, wrodzona umiejętność** SYN **talent**

gifted /ˈɡɪftɪd/ adj. having natural ability or great intelligence ▶ **utalentowany**

ˈ**gift shop** noun [C] a shop that sells goods that are suitable for giving as presents ▶ **sklep z upominkami**

gig /ɡɪɡ/ noun [C] (informal) an event where a musician or band is paid to perform: *The band are doing gigs all around the country.* ▶ **koncert muzyków pop lub jazzowych**

gigabyte /ˈɡɪɡəbaɪt/ (abbr. **Gb** /ˌdʒiː ˈbiː/) noun [C] a unit of computer memory, equal to 2^{30} **bytes** ▶ **gigabajt**

gigantic /dʒaɪˈɡæntɪk/ adj. extremely big ▶ **gigantyczny** SYN **enormous, huge**

giggle /ˈɡɪɡl/ verb [I] to laugh in a silly way that you can't control, because you are amused or nervous ▶ **chichotać** ➲ look at **chuckle**

■ **giggle** noun [C]: *I've got the giggles.* Nie mogę się przestać śmiać. ▶ **chichot, chichotanie**

gild /ɡɪld/ verb [T] **1** (literary) to make sth look bright, as if covered with gold: *The golden light gilded the sea.* ▶ **złocić 2** to cover sth with a thin layer of gold or gold paint ▶ **pozłacać**

gill /ɡɪl/ noun [C, usually pl.] one of the parts on the side of a fish's head that it breathes through ▶ **skrzele** ➲ picture on **page A11**

gilt /ɡɪlt/ noun [U] a thin covering of gold ▶ **złocenie**

gimmick /ˈɡɪmɪk/ noun [C] an idea for attracting customers or persuading people to buy sth ▶ **chwyt**

■ **gimmicky** /ˈɡɪmɪki/ adj.: *a gimmicky idea* tani chwyt ▶ **efekciarski** | **gimmickry** /ˈɡɪmɪkri/ noun [U] the use of **gimmicks** in selling, etc. ▶ **używanie tanich chwytów** ℹ Wyraża dezaprobatę.

gin /dʒɪn/ noun [C,U] a strong, alcoholic drink with no colour ▶ **dżin**

ginger /ˈdʒɪndʒə(r)/ noun [U] **1** a root that tastes hot and is used as a spice in cooking: *ground ginger* ▶ **imbir** ➲ picture on **page A12 2** a light brownish-orange colour ▶ **kolor rudy/ryży**

■ **ginger** adj. **1** : *ginger biscuits* ▶ **imbirowy 2** : *ginger hair* ▶ **rudy, ryży**

ˌ**ginger** ˈ**ale** noun [U] a drink that does not contain alcohol and is flavoured with **ginger** ▶ **napój bezalkoholowy przyprawiany imbirem**

> Podobny napój to **ginger beer**, który jednak zawiera trochę alkoholu.

gingerbread /ˈdʒɪndʒəbred/ noun [U] a sweet cake or biscuit flavoured with ginger ▶ **piernik, pierniczek**

gingerly /ˈdʒɪndʒəli/ adv. very slowly and carefully so as not to cause harm, make a noise, etc.: *I removed the bandage very gingerly and looked at the cut.* ▶ **ostrożnie**

Gipsy = GYPSY

giraffe /dʒəˈrɑːf; US -ˈræf/ noun [C] (pl. **giraffe** or **giraffes**) a large African animal with a very long neck and legs and big dark spots on its skin ▶ **żyrafa**

girder /ˈɡɜːdə(r)/ noun [C] a long, heavy piece of iron or steel that is used in the building of bridges, large buildings, etc. ▶ **dźwigar**

girdle /ˈɡɜːdl/ noun [C] a piece of women's underwear that fits closely around the body from the waist to the top of the legs, designed to make a woman look thinner ▶ **pas wyszczuplający**

⚷ **girl** /ɡɜːl/ noun [C] **1** a female child: *Is the baby a boy or a girl?* ◇ *There are more boys than girls in the class.* ▶ **dziewczynka 2** a daughter: *They have two boys and a girl.* ▶ **dziewczynka, córka 3** a young woman: *The girl at the cash desk was very helpful.* ▶ **dziewczyna, panienka 4** (**girls**) [pl.] a woman's female friends of any age: *a night out with the girls* ▶ **dziewczęta, przyjaciółki**

⚷ **girlfriend** /ˈɡɜːlfrend/ noun [C] **1** a girl or woman with whom sb has a romantic and/or sexual relationship: *Has Frank got a girlfriend?* ▶ **dziewczyna, przyjaciółka 2** (especially US) a girl or woman's female friend: *I had lunch with a girlfriend.* ▶ **przyjaciółka**

Girl ˈ**Guide** (old-fashioned) = GUIDE[1] (5)

girlhood /ˈɡɜːlhʊd/ noun [U] the time when sb is a girl (1) ▶ **wiek dziewczęcy**

girlish /ˈɡɜːlɪʃ/ adj. looking, sounding or behaving like a girl: *a girlish figure/giggle* ▶ **dziewczęcy**

giro /ˈdʒaɪrəʊ/ noun (pl. **giros**) (Brit.) **1** [U] a system for moving money from one bank, etc. to another ▶ **system przelewowy** (*bankowy, pocztowy*) **2** [C] a cheque that the government pays to people who are unemployed or cannot work: *Sasha was waiting for her giro.* ▶ **czek z zasiłkiem** (*np. dla bezrobotnych*)

girth /ɡɜːθ/ noun [U,C] the measurement around sth, especially sb's waist: *a man of enormous girth* ◇ *a tree one metre in girth/with a girth of one metre* ▶ **obwód** (*np. osoby w talii/pasie, drzewa*)

gist /dʒɪst/ noun [sing.] **the gist (of sth)** the general meaning of sth rather than all the details: *I know a little Spanish so I was able to **get the gist** of what he said.* ▶ **ogólny sens**

git /ɡɪt/ noun [C] (Brit., slang) a stupid or unpleasant man ▶ **dupek**

⚷ **give**[1] /ɡɪv/ verb (pt **gave** /ɡeɪv/, pp **given** /ˈɡɪvn/) **1** [T] **give sb sth; give sth to sb** to let sb have sth, especially sth that they want or need: *I gave Jackie a book for her birthday.* ◇ *I gave my bag to my friend to look after.* ◇ *The doctor gave me this cream for my skin.* ◇ *He was thirsty so I gave him a drink.* ◇ *Could you give me some help* (czy mógłbyś mi pomóc) *with this essay?* ▶ **dawać, podawać, podarować 2** [T] **give sb sth; give sth to sb** to make sb have sth, especially sth they do not want: *Mr Johns gives us too much homework.* ◇ *Playing chess gives me a headache.* Granie w szachy przyprawia mnie o ból głowy. ◇ *If you go to school with the flu, you'll give it to everyone* (zarazisz wszystkich). ▶ **dawać, sprawiać 3** [T] to make sb have a particular feeling, idea, etc.: *Swimming always gives me a good appetite.* ◇ *to give somebody a surprise/shock/fright* ◇ *What gives you the idea that he was lying?* ◇ *From what her staff told me, I was **given to understand that*** (dano mi do zrozumienia) *Miss Murphy was not popular.* ▶ **powodować, przyprawiać, sprawiać 4** [T] **give (sb) sth; give sth to sb** to let sb have your opinion, decision, judgement, etc.: *Can you give me some advice?* ◇ *My boss has given me permission to leave early.* ◇ *The judge gave him five years in prison.* ▶ **dawać, udzielać**

5 [T] **give sb sth**; **give sth to sb** to speak to people in a formal situation: *to give* (wygłaszać) *a speech/talk/lecture* ◇ *The officer was called to give evidence* (do złożenia zeznań) *in court.* ◇ *Sarah's going to give me* (udzieli mi) *a cooking lesson.* ◇ *The chairman will be giving a press conference later today.* Dziś w godzinach późniejszych odbędzie się konferencja prasowa z udziałem prezesa. **6** [T] **give (sb) sth for sth**; **give (sb) sth (to do sth)** to pay in order to have sth: *How much did you give him for fixing the car?* ◇ (figurative) *I'd give anything to be able to sing like that.* ▶ **płacić**, **dawać** **7** [T] to spend time dealing with sb/sth: *We need to give some thought to this matter urgently.* ▶ **poświęcać** **8** [T] **give (sb/sth) sth** to do sth to sb/sth; to make a particular sound or movement: *to give somebody a kiss/push/hug/bite* ◇ *to give something a clean/wash/polish* ◇ ***Give** me **a call** when you get home.* ◇ *She opened the door and gave a shout of horror.* ◇ *When the child saw the snow, he gave a shout of delight* (krzyknął z radości). ◇ *to give a sigh* westchnąć ◇ *to give a cry of pain* krzyknąć z bólu ◇ *She gave my hand a squeeze.* Ścisnęła moją rękę. ◇ *They gave us a warm welcome.* Ciepło nas powitali. ◇ *I asked a short question and he gave me a very long answer* (udzielił mi bardzo długiej odpowiedzi). ◇ *She gave him a kiss.* Pocałowała go. **9** [T] to perform or organize sth for people: *The company gave a party to celebrate its 50th anniversary.* ▶ **wydawać** (*np. przyjęcie*) **10** [I] to bend or stretch under pressure: *The branch began to give under my weight.* ▶ **wyginać się**, **ustępować pod naciskiem**

IDM **give or take** more or less the number mentioned: *It took us two hours to get here, give or take five minutes.* ▶ **plus minus**, **w tę czy w tamtą stronę**

ℹ **Give** występuje w innych idiomach, np. **give way**. Zob. hasła odpowiednich rzeczowników i przymiotników.

PHR V **give sth away** to give sth to sb without wanting money in return: *When she got older she gave all her toys away.* ◇ *We are giving away a free CD with this month's issue.* W tym miesiącu w każdym egzemplarzu naszego czasopisma znajduje się bezpłatna płyta CD. ▶ **rozdawać coś**

give sth/sb away to show or tell the truth about sth/sb which was secret: *He smiled politely and didn't give away his real feelings.* ▶ **zdradzać coś/kogoś**

give sb away (at a wedding in a church) to go with the bride into the church and officially give her to the bridegroom during the marriage ceremony: *Her father gave her away.* ▶ **prowadzić pannę młodą do ołtarza**

give sth back to return sth to the person that you took or borrowed it from: *I lent him some books months ago and he still hasn't given them back to me.* ▶ **oddawać coś**

give sth in (to sb) to give sth to the person who is collecting it: *I've got to give this essay in to my teacher by Friday.* ▶ **dawać/wręczać coś (komuś)**

give in (to sb/sth) to stop fighting against sb/sth; to accept that you have been defeated ▶ **poddawać się (komuś/czemuś)**

give off sth to send sth (for example smoke, a smell, heat, etc.) out into the air: *Cars give off poisonous fumes.* ▶ **wydzielać coś**

give out (used about a machine, etc.) to stop working: *His heart gave out and he died.* ▶ **stawać**, **przestać pracować**

give out sth **1** to produce sth such as heat, light, etc.: *The radiator gives out a lot of heat.* ▶ **wydzielać coś** **2** [often passive] (especially Brit.) to tell people about sth or broadcast sth ▶ **przekazywać coś**

give sth out to give one of sth to each person: *Please give out these books to the class.* ▶ **rozdawać coś**

give up to stop trying to do sth; to accept that you cannot do sth: *They gave up once the other team had scored their third goal.* ◇ *I give up. What's the answer?* ▶ **poddawać się**, **dawać za wygraną**

give sb up; **give up on sb** to stop expecting sb to arrive, succeed, improve, etc.: *Her work was so poor that all her teachers gave up on her.* ◇ *When he was four hours late, I gave him up* (straciłam nadzieję, że go zobaczę). ▶ **dać sobie z kims spokój**

give sth up; **give up doing sth** to stop doing or having sth that you did or had regularly before: *I've tried many times to give up smoking.* ◇ *Don't give up hope* (nie porzucaj nadziei). ▶ **rzucać** (*np. palenie*), **zaprzestać coś robić**

give yourself/sb up (to sb) to go to the police when they are trying to catch you; to tell the police where sb is ▶ **oddawać (się) w ręce policji**

give sth up (to sb) to give sth to sb who needs or asks for it: *He gave up his seat on the bus to an elderly woman.* ▶ **ustępować (komuś) czegoś** (*np. miejsca*), **oddawać coś (komuś)**

give² /gɪv/ noun [U] the quality of being able to bend or stretch a little ▶ **elastyczność**

IDM **give and take** a situation in which two people, groups, etc., respect each other's rights and needs: *There has to be some give and take for a marriage to succeed.* ▶ **kompromis**, **wzajemne ustępstwa**

giveaway /ˈgɪvəweɪ/ noun [C] (informal) **1** a thing that is included free when you buy sth: *There's usually some giveaway with that magazine.* ▶ **bezpłatny dodatek** **2** something that makes you guess the truth about sb/sth: *She said she didn't know about the money but her face was **a dead giveaway*** (zdradzała ją). ▶ **coś co zdradza prawdę**

given¹ past participle of **give¹**

given² /ˈgɪvn/ adj. [only before a noun] already stated or decided: *At any given time, up to 200 people are using the library.* ▶ **dany**

given³ /ˈgɪvn/ prep. considering sth: *Given that you had very little help, I think you did very well.* ▶ **biorąc pod uwagę**

ˈgiven name (especially US) = FIRST NAME

glacial /ˈgleɪʃl; ˈgleɪsiəl/ adj. **1** (technical) connected with, or caused by **glaciers**: *a glacial landscape* ◇ *glacial deposits/erosion* ▶ **lodowcowy** **2** very cold: *glacial winds/temperatures* ▶ **lodowaty** SYN **icy**

glacier /ˈglæsiə(r); US ˈgleɪʃər/ noun [C] a large mass of ice that moves slowly down a valley ▶ **lodowiec**

glad /glæd/ adj. **1** [not before a noun] **glad (about sth)**; **glad to do sth/that ...** happy; pleased: *I'm glad (that) he's feeling better.* ◇ *I'll be glad when these exams are over.* ◇ *Are you glad about* (czy cieszysz się z) *your new job?* ◇ *We'd be glad* (będzie nam miło) *to see you if you're in the area.* ▶ **zadowolony** ➲ note at **happy** **2** **glad (of sth)**; **glad (if...)** grateful for sth: *If you are free, I'd be glad of some help.* ◇ *I'd be glad if you could help me.* ▶ **wdzięczny (za coś)** **3** [only before a noun] bringing happiness: *I want to be the first to bring you the glad news.* ▶ **radosny**

■ **gladness** noun [U] ▶ **radość**, **szczęście**

glade /gleɪd/ noun [C] a small open area of grass in a wood or forest ▶ **polana** ➲ look at **clearing**

gladiator /ˈglædieɪtə(r)/ noun [C] (in ancient Rome) a man who fought against another man or a wild animal in a public show ▶ **gladiator**

gladly /ˈglædli/ adv. (used for politely agreeing to a request or accepting an invitation): *'Could you help me carry these bags?' 'Gladly.'* ◇ *She gladly accepted the invitation to stay the night.* ▶ **chętnie**, **ochoczo**

glamorize (also -ise) /ˈglæməraɪz/ verb [T] to make sth appear more attractive or exciting than it really is: *TV tends to glamorize violence.* ▶ **dodawać uroku**, **uatrakcyjniać**

glamour (US also **glamor**) /ˈglæmə(r)/ noun [U] the quality of seeming to be more exciting or attractive than ordinary things or people: *Young people are often attracted by the glamour of city life.* ▶ **blask**
■ **glamorous** /ˈglæmərəs/ adj.: *the glamorous world of opera* ▶ **olśniewający, atrakcyjny** | **glamorously** adv. ▶ **olśniewająco, wspaniale**

glance[1] /glɑːns; US glæ-/ verb [I] to look quickly at sb/sth: *She glanced round the room to see if they were there.* ◇ *He glanced at her and smiled.* ◇ *The receptionist glanced down the list of names.* ▶ **spojrzeć, zerknąć**
PHR V **glance off (sth)** to hit sth at an angle and move off again in another direction: *The ball glanced off his knee and into the net.* ▶ **odbić się rykoszetem, ześlizgnąć się**

glance[2] /glɑːns; US glæ-/ noun [C] a quick look: *to take/have a glance at the newspaper headlines* ◇ *She stole a glance* (ukradkiem spojrzała) *at her watch.* ▶ **zerknięcie, rzut oka**
IDM **at a (single) glance** with one look: *I could tell at a glance that something was wrong.* ▶ **na pierwszy rzut oka**
at first glance/sight → FIRST[1]

gland /glænd/ noun [C] any of the organs inside your body that produce chemical substances for your body to use: *sweat glands* ◇ *swollen glands* powiększone węzły chłonne ▶ **gruczoł**
■ **glandular** /ˈglændjʊlə(r); US -dʒə-/ adj. ▶ **gruczołowy**

ˌglandular ˈfever (US or technical **mononucleosis** /ˌmɒnəʊˌnjuːkliˈəʊsɪs; US -ˌnuːk-/) noun [U] an infectious disease that causes swelling of the **lymph glands** and makes the person feel very weak for a long time ▶ **mononukleoza zakaźna**

glare[1] /gleə(r)/ verb [I] **1 glare (at sb/sth)** to look at sb in a very angry way: *They stood glaring at each other* (mierząc się wzrokiem). ▶ **patrzeć ze złością na kogoś 2** to shine with strong light that hurts your eyes ▶ **świecić** (*oślepiającym blaskiem*)

glare[2] /gleə(r)/ noun **1** [U] strong light that hurts your eyes: *the glare of the sun/a car's headlights* ▶ **oślepiający blask 2** [C] a very angry look ▶ **spojrzenie pełne gniewu/nienawiści itp.**

glaring /ˈgleərɪŋ/ adj. **1** very easy to see; shocking: *a glaring mistake/injustice* ▶ **rażący, jaskrawy 2** (used about a light) too strong and bright ▶ **oślepiający 3** angry: *glaring eyes* piorunujący wzrok ▶ **wściekły**
■ **glaringly** adv.: *a **glaringly obvious** mistake* ▶ **rażąco, jaskrawo**

glass /glɑːs; US glæs/ noun **1** [U] a hard substance that you can usually see through that is used for making windows, bottles, etc.: *He cut himself on broken glass.* ◇ *a sheet/pane of glass* szyba ◇ *a glass jar/dish/vase* ▶ **szkło 2** [C] a drinking container made of glass; the amount of liquid it contains: *a wine glass* ◇ *a brandy glass* ◇ *Could I have a glass of water, please?* ▶ **szklanka, kieliszek 3** (also **glassware**) [U] a collection of objects made of glass ▶ **szkło** (*np. stołowe*)

glasses /ˈglɑːsɪz; US ˈglæsɪz/ (also **spectacles** /ˈspektəklz/; informal **specs** /speks/; US also **eyeglasses** /ˈaɪglɑːsɪz/) noun [pl.] two **lenses** in a frame that a person wears in front of their eyes in order to be able to see better: *My sister has to **wear glasses**.* ◇ *I need **a new pair of glasses**./I need some new glasses.* ◇ *reading glasses* okulary do czytania ◇ *dark glasses/sunglasses* okulary przeciwsłoneczne ▶ **okulary**

glass ˈfibre = FIBREGLASS

glassful /ˈglɑːsfʊl/ noun [C] the amount of liquid that one glass(2) holds ▶ **szklanka, kieliszek**

glasshouse /ˈglɑːshaʊs; US ˈglæs-/ noun [C] a building with glass sides and a glass roof, for growing plants in ▶ **szklarnia** ➲ look at **greenhouse**

glassware /ˈglɑːsweə(r); US ˈglæs-/ noun [U] objects made of glass ▶ **szkło**

glassy /ˈglɑːsi; US ˈglæ-/ adj. (**glassier**; **glassiest**) **1** looking like glass ▶ **szklisty, przezroczysty 2** (used about the eyes) showing no interest or expression ▶ **szklany, szklisty**

glaze[1] /gleɪz/ verb [T] **1** to fit a sheet of glass into a window, etc. ▶ **szklić** ➲ look at **double glazing 2 glaze sth (with sth)** to cover a pot, brick, **pie**, etc. with a shiny transparent substance (before it is put into an oven): *Glaze* (posmarować) *the pie with beaten egg.* ▶ **emaliować; lukrować**
PHR V **glaze over** (used about the eyes) to show no interest or expression ▶ **stawać się szklistym**

glaze[2] /gleɪz/ noun [C,U] (a substance that gives) a shiny transparent surface on a pot, brick, **pie**, etc. ▶ **polewa; emalia; lukier**

glazed /gleɪzd/ adj. (used about the eyes, etc.) showing no interest or expression ▶ **szklisty**

glazier /ˈgleɪziə(r); US -ʒər/ noun [C] a person whose job is to fit glass into windows, etc. ▶ **szklarz**

gleam /gliːm/ noun [C, usually sing.] **1** a soft light that shines for a short time: *the gleam of moonlight on the water* ▶ **blask, odblask 2** a small amount of sth: *a faint gleam of hope* ▶ **przebłysk 3** a sudden expression of an emotion in sb's eyes: *I saw a gleam of amusement in his eyes.* ▶ (*przen.*) **iskierka**
■ **gleam** verb [I]: *gleaming white teeth* ◇ *The children's eyes gleamed with enthusiasm.* ▶ **połyskiwać, błyszczeć**

glean /gliːn/ verb [T] **glean sth (from sb/sth)** to obtain information, knowledge etc., sometimes with difficulty and often from various different places: *These figures have been gleaned from a number of studies.* ▶ **zbierać** (*np. dane*)

glee /gliː/ noun [U] a feeling of happiness, usually because sth good has happened to you or sth bad has happened to sb else: *She couldn't hide her glee when her rival came last in the race.* ▶ **radość**
■ **gleeful** /ˈgliːfl/ adj. ▶ **radosny** | **gleefully** /-fəli/ adv. ▶ **radośnie**

glen /glen/ noun [C] a deep, narrow valley, especially in Scotland or Ireland ▶ **dolina górska**

glib /glɪb/ adj. using words in a way that is clever and quick, but not sincere: *a glib salesman/politician* ◇ *a glib answer/excuse* gładka odpowiedź/wymówka ▶ **wygadany**
■ **glibly** adv. ▶ **bez namysłu, gładko** | **glibness** noun [U] ▶ **gładkość** (*mowy*)

glide /glaɪd/ verb [I] **1** to move smoothly without noise or effort: *The dancers glided across the floor.* ▶ **sunąć, ślizgać się 2** to fly in a **glider** ▶ **szybować**
■ **gliding** noun [U]: *I've always wanted to **go gliding**.* ▶ **szybownictwo** ➲ look at **hang-gliding**

glider /ˈglaɪdə(r)/ noun [C] a light aircraft without an engine that flies using air currents ▶ **szybowiec** ➲ look at **hang-glider** ➲ picture on **page A6**

glimmer /ˈglɪmə(r)/ noun [C] **1** a weak light that is not steady: *I could see a faint glimmer of light in one of the windows.* ▶ **migotanie 2** a small sign of sth: *a glimmer of hope* ▶ **przebłysk**
■ **glimmer** verb [I] ▶ **migotać**

glimpse /glɪmps/ noun [C] **1 a glimpse (at/of sth)** a very quick and not complete view of sb/sth: *I just managed to **catch a glimpse** of the fox's tail as it ran down a hole.*

▶ **przelotne spojrzenie, mignięcie 2 a glimpse (into/of sth)** a short experience of sth that helps you understand it: *The programme gives us an interesting glimpse into* (w ciekawy sposób przybliża) *the life of the cheetah.* ▶ **pojęcie (o czymś)**
■ **glimpse** verb [T] ▶ **zobaczyć (przelotnie)**

glint /glɪnt/ verb [I] to shine with small bright flashes of light: *His eyes glinted at the thought of all that money.* ▶ **błyskać, skrzyć się**
■ **glint** noun [C] ▶ **blask; błysk**

glisten /ˈglɪsn/ verb [I] (used about wet surfaces) to shine: *Her eyes glistened with tears.* ◇ *Tears glistened in her eyes.* ▶ **błyszczeć, lśnić**

glitch /glɪtʃ/ noun [C] (informal) a small problem or fault that stops sth working successfully: *A few technical glitches forced us to postpone the demonstration.* ▶ **usterka**

glitter /ˈglɪtə(r)/ noun [U] **1** a shiny appearance consisting of many small flashes of light: *the glitter of jewellery* ▶ **blask, lśnienie 2** the exciting quality that sth appears to have: *the glitter of a career in show business* ▶ (*przen.*) **blask 3** very small, shiny pieces of thin metal or paper, used as a decoration: *The children decorated their pictures with glitter.* ▶ **brokat**
■ **glitter** verb [I] ▶ **skrzyć się, lśnić**

glittering /ˈglɪtərɪŋ/ adj. **1** very impressive or successful: *a glittering event/career/performance* ▶ **błyskotliwy 2** shining brightly with many small flashes of light ▶ **błyszczący, skrzący się**

glitz /glɪts/ noun [U] the quality of appearing very attractive, exciting and impressive, in a way that is not always genuine: *the glitz and glamour of the music scene* ▶ **blichtr**
■ **glitzy** adj. ▶ **efekciarski**

gloat /gləʊt/ verb [I] **gloat (about/over sth)** to feel or express happiness in an unpleasant way because sth good has happened to you or sth bad has happened to sb else ▶ **napawać/rozkoszować się czymś**
■ **gloatingly** adv. ▶ **chełpliwie**

⚷ **global** /ˈgləʊbl/ adj. **1** affecting the whole world: *the global effects of pollution* ▶ **globalny, ogólnoświatowy 2** considering or including all parts: *We must take a global view of the problem.* ▶ **globalny, całościowy**
■ **globally** /-bəli/ adv. ▶ **ogólnie, szeroko** (*np. rozpowszechniony*)

globalization (also **-isation**) /ˌgləʊbəlaɪˈzeɪʃn; US -ləˈz-/ noun [U] the fact that different cultures and economic systems around the world are becoming connected and similar to each other because of the influence of large companies and of improved communication ▶ **globalizacja**

globalize (also **-ise**) /ˈgləʊbəlaɪz/ verb [I,T] if sth, for example a company, **globalizes** or is **globalized**, it operates all around the world ▶ **globalizować**

the ˌ**global ˈvillage** noun [sing.] the world considered as a single community connected by computers, telephones, etc. ▶ **globalna wioska**

ˌ**global ˈwarming** noun [sing.] the increase in the temperature of the earth's atmosphere, caused by the increase of certain gases ▶ **globalne ocieplenie** ➲ note at **environment** ➲ look at **greenhouse effect**

globe /gləʊb/ noun **1** [C] a round object with a map of the world on it ▶ **globus 2 (the globe)** [sing.] the earth: *to travel all over the globe* ▶ **kula ziemska 3** [C] any object shaped like a ball ▶ **kula**

ˌ**globe ˈartichoke** = ARTICHOKE

globetrotter /ˈgləʊbtrɒtə(r)/ noun [C] (informal) a person who travels to many countries ▶ **globtroter, obieżyświat**

globule /ˈglɒbjuːl/ noun [C] a small drop or ball of a liquid: *There were globules of fat in the soup.* ▶ **kropelka, kulka**

gloom /gluːm/ noun [U] **1** a feeling of being sad and without hope: *The news brought deep gloom to the village.* ▶ **przygnębienie 2** the state of being almost totally dark ▶ **mrok, ciemność**

gloomy /ˈgluːmi/ adj. (**gloomier**; **gloomiest**) **1** dark in a way that makes you feel sad: *This dark paint makes the room very gloomy.* ▶ **ponury, przygnębiający 2** sad and without much hope: *Don't be so gloomy – cheer up!* ▶ **ponury, przygnębiony**
■ **gloomily** adv.: *He stared gloomily at the phone.* ▶ **ponuro, przygnębiająco** | **gloominess** noun [U] ▶ **przygnębienie, posępność**

glorified /ˈglɔːrɪfaɪd/ adj. [only before a noun] described in a way that makes sb/sth seem better, bigger, more important, etc. than he/she/it really is ▶ **wyidealizowany, upiększony**

glorify /ˈglɔːrɪfaɪ/ verb [T] (**glorifying**; **glorifies**; pt, pp **glorified**) to make sb/sth appear better or more important than he/she/it really is: *His biography does not attempt to glorify his early career.* ▶ **idealizować, wychwalać**

glorious /ˈglɔːriəs/ adj. **1** having or deserving fame or success: *a glorious victory* ▶ **sławny, chlubny 2** very beautiful or impressive: *a glorious day/view* ▶ **wspaniały, znakomity**
■ **gloriously** adv. ▶ **wspaniale, znakomicie**

glory[1] /ˈglɔːri/ noun [U] **1** fame or honour that you get for achieving sth: *The winning team was welcomed home* ***in a blaze of glory.*** ▶ **sława, chwała 2** great beauty ▶ **blask, wspaniałość**

glory[2] /ˈglɔːri/ verb (**glorying**; **glories**; pt, pp **gloried**)
PHR V **glory in sth** to take (too much) pleasure or pride in sth: *He gloried in his sporting successes.* ▶ **rozkoszować/przechwalać się czymś**

gloss[1] /glɒs/ noun [U, sing.] (a substance that gives sth) a smooth, shiny surface: *gloss paint* ◇ *You can have the photos with either a gloos or a matt finish.* ▶ **połysk** ➲ look at **matt**

gloss[2] /glɒs/ verb
PHR V **gloss over sth** to avoid talking about a problem, mistake, etc. in detail ▶ **przechodzić nad czymś do porządku dziennego; tuszować**

glossary /ˈglɒsəri/ noun [C] (pl. **glossaries**) a list of special or unusual words and their meanings, usually at the end of a text or book ▶ **słowniczek**

glossy /ˈglɒsi/ adj. (**glossier**; **glossiest**) **1** smooth and shiny: *glossy hair* ▶ **błyszczący, połyskliwy 2** (used about a magazine, etc.) printed on good quality paper and having many colour photographs ▶ **na błyszczącym/kredowym papierze**

⚷ **glove** /glʌv/ noun [C] a piece of clothing that covers your hand and has five separate parts for the fingers: *I need a new pair of gloves for the winter.* ◇ *leather/woollen/rubber/suede gloves* ▶ **rękawi-czka/ca** ➲ picture on **page A1** ➲ look at **mitten**

ˈ**glove compartment** (also ˈ**glove box**) noun [C] a small space or shelf facing the front seats of a car, used for keeping small things in ▶ **schowek** (*w samochodzie*)

glow /gləʊ/ verb [I] **1** to produce light and/or heat without smoke or flames: *A cigarette glowed in the dark.* ▶ **żarzyć się, jarzyć się 2 glow (with sth)** to be warm or red because of excitement, exercise, etc.: *to glow with health/enthusiasm/pride/pleasure* ▶ **promieniować (czymś), rumienić się**

■ **glow** noun [sing.] **1** a warm light: *the glow of the sky at sunset* ▶ **blask, żar 2** a feeling or look of warmth or satisfaction ▶ **rumieniec**

glower /'glaʊə(r)/ verb [I] **glower (at sb/sth)** to look angrily (at sb/sth) ▶ **groźnie patrzeć na kogoś/coś**

glowing /'gləʊɪŋ/ adj. saying that sb/sth is very good: *His teacher wrote a glowing report about his work.* ▶ **pochlebny**

■ **glowingly** adv. ▶ **pochlebnie**, (*mówić, pisać*) **w samych superlatywach**

glucose /'glu:kəʊs; -kəʊz/ noun [U] a type of sugar that is found in fruit ▶ **glukoza**

🔑 **glue¹** /glu:/ noun [U] a thick sticky liquid that is used for joining things together: *You can make glue from flour and water.* ◇ *Stick the photo in with glue.* ▶ **klej**

🔑 **glue²** /glu:/ verb [T] (**gluing**) **glue A (to/onto B)**; **glue A and B (together)** to join a thing or things together with **glue**: *Do you think you can glue the handle back onto the teapot?* ▶ **przyklejać, sklejać**

IDM **glued to sth** (informal) giving all your attention to sth and not wanting to leave it: *He just sits there every evening glued to the TV.* ▶ **przyklejony do czegoś**

'glue-sniffing noun [U] breathing in the chemicals that are given off by glue to get the same effect as that produced by alcohol or drugs ▶ **wąchanie kleju**

glum /glʌm/ adj. sad and quiet ▶ **markotny, ponury**

■ **glumly** adv. ▶ **markotnie, z ponurą miną** | **glumness** noun [U] ▶ **przygnębienie, rozgoryczenie**

glut /glʌt/ noun [C, usually sing.] more of sth than is needed: *The glut of coffee has forced down the price.* ▶ **nadmiar, przesyt**

gluten /'glu:tn/ noun [U] a sticky substance that is a mixture of two **proteins** and is left when **starch** is removed from flour, especially **wheat** flour: *We sell a range of **gluten-free*** (bezglutenowych) *products.* ▶ **gluten**

glutton /'glʌtn/ noun [C] **1** a person who eats too much ▶ **żarłok 2** (informal) **a glutton for sth** a person who enjoys having or doing sth difficult, unpleasant, etc.: *She's a glutton for hard work.* Jest tytanem pracy ▶ **człowiek niezmordowany**

gluttony /'glʌtəni/ noun [U] the habit of eating and drinking too much ▶ **obżarstwo**

GM = GENETICALLY MODIFIED

gm = GRAM

GMT /ˌdʒi: em 'ti:/ abbr. **Greenwich Mean Time**; the time system that is used in Britain during the winter and for calculating the time in other parts of the world ▶ **średni czas zachodnioeuropejski**

gnarled /nɑ:ld/ adj. rough and having grown into a strange shape, because of old age or hard work: *The old man had gnarled fingers.* ◇ *a gnarled oak tree* ▶ **wykrzywiony, sękaty**

gnash /næʃ/ verb

IDM **gnash your teeth** to feel very angry and upset about sth ▶ **zgrzytać zębami**

gnat /næt/ noun [C] a type of very small fly that bites ▶ **komar** SYN **midge**

gnaw /nɔ:/ verb **1** [I,T] **gnaw (away) (at/on) sth** to bite a bone, etc. many times with your back teeth ▶ **ogryzać, gryźć 2** [I] **gnaw (away) at sb** to make sb feel worried or frightened over a long period of time: *Fear of the future gnawed away at her all the time.* ▶ **dręczyć kogoś, targać kimś**

gnome /nəʊm/ noun [C] (in children's stories, etc.) a little old man with a beard and a pointed hat who lives under the ground ▶ **krasnal, gnom**

GNP /ˌdʒi: en 'pi:/ abbr. **gross national product**; the total value of all the goods and services produced by a country in one year, including money received from foreign countries ▶ **produkt narodowy brutto** (*całkowita wartość towarów i usług, wraz z wpływami z eksportu*) ⓘ **GNP** = **GDP** + zysk pochodzący z eksportu netto

🔑 **go¹** /gəʊ/ verb [I] (**going**; **goes** /gəʊz/, pt **went** /went/, pp **gone** /gɒn/) **1** to move or travel from one place to another: *She always goes home by bus.* ◇ *We're going to London tomorrow.* ◇ *He went to the cinema yesterday.* ◇ *How fast does this car go?* ◇ *Caroline threw the ball and the dog went running* (pobiegł) *after it.* ▶ **iść, jechać**

> Czasownik **go** ma dwie formy *past participle*: **been** i **gone**. **Been** używa się wtedy, gdy ktoś udał się dokądś i już stamtąd wrócił: *I've just been to Berlin* (byłem w Berlinie). *I got back this morning.* **Gone** również oznacza, że ktoś dokądś się udał, lecz jeszcze nie wrócił: *John's gone to Peru. He'll be back in two weeks.*

2 to travel to a place to take part in an activity or do sth: *Are you going to Dave's party?* ◇ *Shall we go swimming/go for a swim* (pójdziemy popływać) *this afternoon?* ◇ *We went to watch* (poszliśmy obejrzeć) *the match.* ◇ *to go for a drive* wybrać się na przejażdżkę samochodem ◇ *to go for a drink/walk/meal* iść na drinka/spacer/posiłek ◇ *We went on a school trip to a museum.* ◇ *They've gone on holiday.* ◇ *I'll go and make the tea.* Pójdę zrobić nam herbatę. ▶ **iść/jechać** (*dokądś w określonym celu*) **3** to leave a place: *I have to go now. It's nearly 4 o'clock.* ◇ *What time does the train go* (odchodzi pociąg)*?* ▶ **iść, jechać 4** to belong to or stay in an institution: *Which school does Ralph go to?* ◇ *to go to hospital/prison/college/university* ▶ **chodzić (regularnie)** (*np. do szkoły*); **iść** (*np. do szpitala; więzienia*) **5** to lead to or reach a place or time: *Where does this road go to?* ◇ *This cut on my hand goes quite deep* (jest dosyć głęboka). ▶ **prowadzić, ciągnąć się 6** to be put or to fit in a particular place: *Where does this vase go?* Gdzie postawić tę wazę? ◇ *My clothes won't all go in one suitcase.* ▶ **stać** (*na stałym miejscu*), **mieścić się 7** to happen in a particular way; to develop: *How's the new job going?* Jak ci idzie w nowej pracy? ◇ *How's it going?* ▶ (*sprawy*) **iść, mieć się dobrze/źle 8** to become; to reach a particular state: *to go deaf* głuchnąć ◇ *to go bald* łysieć ◇ *to go senile* niedołężnieć ◇ *Her hair is going grey* (siwieją). ◇ *He went blind* (stracił wzrok) *when he was 20.* ◇ *Everybody thought that we had gone mad* (oszaleliśmy). ◇ *The baby has gone to sleep* (zasnęło). ▶ **stawać się 9** to stay in the state mentioned: *Many mistakes go unnoticed.* ▶ **pozostawać 10** to have certain words or a certain tune: *How does that song go?* ▶ **iść, brzmieć 11** to make a sound: *The bell went* (dzwon rozbrzmiał) *early today.* ◇ *Cats go 'miaow'* (miauczą). ▶ **wydawać określony dźwięk 12** (informal) (used in the present tense for saying what a person said): *I said, 'How are you, Jim?' and he goes, 'It's none of your business!'* ▶ **mówić 13** to start an activity: *Everybody ready to sing? Let's go!* ▶ **zaczynać 14** to work correctly: *This clock doesn't go.* ◇ *Is your car going at the moment?* ▶ **działać, chodzić 15** to be removed, lost, used, etc.; to disappear: *Has your headache gone yet?* ◇ *About half my salary goes on rent.* ◇ *I like the furniture, but that carpet will have to go* (ale tego dywanu musimy się pozbyć). ▶ **minąć, iść 16** to become worse or stop working correctly: *The brakes on the car have gone.* ◇ *His sight/voice/mind has gone.* Traci wzrok/głos/pamięć. ▶ **psuć się 17** [only used in the continuous tenses] (informal) to be available: *Are there any jobs going in your department?* ▶ **być wolnym 18** (used about time) to pass: *The last hour went very slowly.* ▶ **mijać 19** (informal) (used for saying that you do not want sb to do sth bad or stupid): *You can use my bike but don't go breaking* (nie zepsuj) *it this time!* ◇ *I hope John doesn't go and tell* (nie rozpowie) *everyone about our* *plan.* **20** to look or taste good with something else: *Does this sweater go with my skirt?* ▶ **pasować**

IDM **as people, things, etc. go** compared to the average person or thing: *As Chinese restaurants go, it wasn't bad.* ▶ **jak na kogoś/coś**

be going to do sth 1 (used for showing what you plan to do in the future): *We're going to sell our car.* ▶ **zamierzać (coś zrobić) 2** (used for saying that you think sth will happen): *It's going to rain soon.* Zaraz będzie padać. ◇ *Oh no! He's going to fall!* Zaraz się przewróci!

go all out for sth; **go all out to do sth** to make a great effort to do sth ▶ **iść na całego**, **bardzo się starać**

go for it (informal) to do sth after not being sure about it: *'Do you think we should buy it?' 'Yeah, let's go for it* (zróbmy to)*!'* ▶ **zrobić coś** (*po wahaniu*)

have a lot going for you to have many advantages ▶ **mieć wszystkie atuty/wszelkie szanse**

Here goes! said just before you start to do sth difficult or exciting ▶ **do dzieła!**, **uwaga! już!**

to go that is/are left before sth ends: *There's only one minute left to go.* Została jeszcze tylko minuta. ◇ *We've still got 50 miles to go.* Zostało nam jeszcze 50 mil. ▶ (*zostaje/ma itd.*) **jeszcze**

🛈 **Go** występuje w innych idiomach, np. **go astray**. Zob. hasła odpowiednich rzeczowników, przymiotników itp.

PHR V **go about** = GO ROUND/AROUND/ABOUT

go about sth to continue to do what you usually do: *We went about our normal routine.* ▶ **zajmować się** (*czymś, co zwykle robimy*)

go about sth/doing sth to start trying to do sth difficult: *I wouldn't have any idea how to go about building a house.* ▶ **zabierać się** (*do czegoś trudnego*)

go about with sb = GO ROUND/AROUND/ABOUT WITH SB

go after sb/sth to try to catch or get sb/sth: *I went after the boy who stole my wallet but he was too fast for me.* ▶ **ruszać w pogoń** (*za osobą*), **próbować coś zdobyć**

go against sb to not be in sb's favour or not be to sb's advantage: *The referee's decision went against him.* ▶ **być niepomyślnym (dla kogoś)**

go against sb/sth to do sth that sb/sth says you should not do: *She went against her parents' wishes and married him.* ▶ **być niezgodnym/sprzecznym z czymś**, **sprzeciwiać się**

go ahead 1 to travel in front of other people in your group and arrive before them: *I'll go ahead and tell them you're coming.* ▶ **iść/jechać przodem 2** to take place after being delayed or in doubt: *Although several members were missing, the meeting went ahead without them.* ▶ **odbywać się (zgodnie z planem)**

go ahead (with sth) to do sth after not being sure that it was possible: *We decided to go ahead with the match in spite of the heavy rain.* ◇ *'Can I take this chair?' 'Sure, go ahead* (oczywiście, proszę bardzo)*.'* ▶ **rozpoczynać**

go along to continue; to progress: *My work's going along nicely at the moment.* Obecnie moja praca dobrze się posuwa. ◇ *The course gets more difficult as you go along* (w miarę upływu czasu). ▶ **posuwać się**

go along with sb/sth to agree with sb/sth; to do what sb else has decided: *I'm happy to go along with whatever you suggest.* ▶ **zgadzać się z kimś/czymś**; **postępować zgodnie z czyjąś decyzją**

go around = GO ROUND/AROUND/ABOUT

go around with sb = GO ROUND/AROUND/ABOUT WITH SB

go away 1 to disappear or leave: *I've got a headache that just won't go away.* ◇ *Just go away and leave me alone!* Idź sobie i zostaw mnie w spokoju! ▶ **znikać 2** to leave home for a period of time, especially for a holiday: *We're going away to the coast this weekend.* ▶ **wyjeżdżać**

go back (to sth) 1 to return to a place: *It's a wonderful city and I'd like to go back there one day.* ▶ **wracać dokądś 2** to return to an earlier matter or situation: *Let's go back to the subject we were discussing a few minutes ago.* ▶ **wracać** (*np. do tematu*) **3** to have its origins in an earlier period of time: *A lot of the buildings in the village go back to the 15th century.* ▶ **sięgać (wstecz)**, **pochodzić** (*z jakiegoś czasu*)

go back on sth to break a promise, an agreement, etc.: *I promised to help them and I can't go back on my word.* ▶ **złamać** (*obietnicę*)

go back to sth/doing sth to start doing again sth that you had stopped doing: *When the children got a bit older she went back to full-time work.* ▶ **wracać do czegoś**

go before to exist or happen in an earlier time: *The present crisis is worse than any that have gone before.* ▶ **poprzedzać**

go beyond sth to be more than sth: *This year's sales figures go beyond all our expectations.* ▶ **przekraczać coś** SYN **exceed**

go by 1 (used about time) to pass: *As time went by* (w miarę upływu czasu), *her confidence grew.* ▶ (*czas*) **upływać 2** to pass a place: *She stood at the window watching people go by.* ▶ **przechodzić** (*np. obok jakiegoś miejsca*)

go by sth to use particular information, rules, etc. to help you decide your actions or opinions: *You can't go by the railway timetables – the trains are very unreliable.* ▶ **kierować się (czymś)**, **opierać się** (*np. na jakimś dowodzie*)

go down 1 (used about a ship, etc.) to sink ▶ **zatonąć 2** (used about the sun) to disappear from the sky ▶ (*słońce*) **zachodzić 3** to become lower in price, level, etc.; to fall: *The number of people out of work went down last month.* ▶ **obniżać się**

go down (with sb) [used with adverbs, especially 'well' or 'badly' or in questions beginning with 'how'] to be received in a particular way by sb: *The film went down well with the critics.* Krytycy dobrze przyjęli ten film. ▶ **zostać (dobrze/źle) odebranym (przez kogoś)**

go down with sth (especially Brit.) to catch an illness; to become ill with sth ▶ **zachorować na coś** SYN **catch**

go for sb to attack sb ▶ **(agresywnie) rzucać się na kogoś**

go for sb/sth 1 to be true for a particular person or thing: *We've got financial problems but I suppose the same goes for a great many people.* ▶ **dotyczyć kogoś/czegoś 2** to choose sb/sth: *I think I'll go for the roast chicken.* ▶ **decydować się na kogoś/coś**, **wybierać kogoś/coś**

go for sth to put a lot of effort into sth, so that you get or achieve sth: ***Go for it**, John! You know you can beat him.* ◇ *It sounds a great idea.* ***Go for it!*** ▶ **starać się coś osiągnąć**

go in 1 to enter a room, house, etc.: *Let's go in – it's getting cold.* ▶ **wchodzić** (*np. do pokoju*) **2** (used about the sun) to disappear behind a cloud ▶ **zachodzić za chmurę**

go in for sth to enter or take part in an exam or competition ▶ **przystępować** (*np. do zawodów, konkurencji*)

go in for sth/doing sth to do or have sth as a hobby or interest ▶ **interesować się czymś** (*jako hobby*)

go into sth 1 to enter a room, house, etc.: *He went into the kitchen to get a spoon.* ▶ **wchodzić do pokoju itp. 2** to hit sth while travelling in/on a vehicle: *I couldn't stop in time and went into the back of the car in front.* ▶ **wjechać na/w coś 3** to start working in a certain type of job: *When she left school she went into nursing.* ▶ **obierać zawód 4** to look at or describe sth in detail: *I haven't got time to go into all the details now.* ▶ **rozwodzić się nad czymś**, **wdawać się w szczegóły**

go off 1 to explode: *A bomb has gone off in the city centre.* ▶ **wybuchać 2** to make a sudden loud noise: *I woke up when my alarm clock went off.* ▶ **zadzwonić 3** (used about lights, heating, etc.) to stop working: *There was a power cut and all the lights went off.* ▶ **gasnąć**, **wyłączać się 4** (used about food and drink) to become too old to eat or drink; to go bad ▶ (*jedzenie*) **psuć się** **5** to become worse in quality: *I used to like that band but they've gone off recently.* ▶ **popsuć się, pogorszyć się** **6** (used about an event) to take place or happen in a certain way: *I think their wedding went off very well.* ▶ **wypadać** (*np. dobrze/źle*)

go off sb/sth to stop liking or being interested in sb/sth: *I went off spicy food after I was ill last year.* ▶ **przestawać lubić**

go off (with sb) to leave with sb: *I don't know where Sid is – he went off with John an hour ago.* ◇ *He went off* (odszedł) *with his best friend's wife.* ▶ **wychodzić (z kimś)**

go off with sth to take sth that belongs to sb else ▶ **zabierać coś komuś, świsnąć coś**

go on **1** (used about lights, heating, etc.) to start working: *I saw the lights go on in the house opposite.* ▶ **zapalać się; włączać się** **2** (used about time) to pass: *As time went on* (w miarę upływu czasu), *she became more and more successful.* ▶ (*czas*) **upływać** **3** [used especially in the continuous tenses] to happen or take place: *Can anybody tell me what's going on here?* ▶ **dziać się** **4** (used about a situation) to continue without changing: *This is a difficult period but it won't go on forever.* ▶ **trwać** **5** to continue speaking after stopping for a moment: *Go on. What happened next?* ▶ **mówić dalej** **6** (used for encouraging sb to do sth): *Oh go on* (bardzo cię proszę), *let me borrow your car. I'll bring it back in an hour.* ▶ **no dalej!, no zgódź się!**

go on sth to use sth as information so that you can understand a situation: *There were no witnesses to the crime, so the police had very little to go on.* ▶ **opierać się** (*np. na dowodzie*) ➲ look at **go by sth**

go on (about sb/sth) to talk about sb/sth for a long time in a boring or annoying way: *She went on and on about the people she works with.* ▶ **ględzić/gadać (o czymś)**

go/be on (at sb) (about sth) to keep complaining about sth: *She's always (going) on at me to mend the roof.* ▶ **gderać (na kogoś) (z jakiegoś powodu), marudzić (z jakiegoś powodu)**

go on (doing sth) to continue doing sth without stopping or changing: *We don't want to go on living here* (ciągle tu mieszkać) *for the rest of our lives.* ▶ **kontynuować (coś)**

go on to sth to pass from one item to the next: *Let's go on to the next item on the agenda.* ▶ **przechodzić do czegoś**

go on (with sth) to continue doing sth, perhaps after a pause or break: *She ignored me and went on with her meal* (i dalej jadła). ▶ **kontynuować (coś), robić coś dalej**

go on to do sth to do sth after completing sth else ▶ **robić coś po zakończeniu innej czynności**

go out **1** to leave the place where you live or work for a short time, especially in order to do sth enjoyable: *Let's go out for a meal tonight.* ◇ *I'm just going out for a walk, I won't be long.* ◇ *He goes out with his friends a lot.* ▶ **wychodzić/wyjeżdżać (do czegoś/na coś)** ➲ look at **socialize** **2** to stop being fashionable or in use: *That kind of music went out in the seventies.* ▶ **wychodzić z mody/użycia** **3** (used about the sea) to move away from the land: *Is the tide coming in or going out?* Jest przypływ czy odpływ? SYN **ebb** **4** to stop shining or burning: *Suddenly all the lights went out.* ▶ **gasnąć**

go out (with sb); go out (together) to spend time with sb and have a romantic and/or sexual relationship with them: *Is Fiona going out with anyone?* ◇ *They went out together for five years before they got married.* ▶ **chodzić ze sobą, spotykać się z kimś**

go over sth to look at, think about or discuss sth carefully from beginning to end: *Go over your work before you hand it in.* ▶ **sprawdzać/omawiać coś**

go over to sth to change to a different side, system, habit, etc. ▶ **przechodzić do czegoś/na coś innego**

go round [used especially after 'enough'] to be shared among all the people: *In this area, there aren't enough jobs to go round.* ▶ **wystarczać (dla wszystkich/na wszystko)**

go round/around/about (used about a story, an illness, etc.) to pass from person to person: *There's a rumour going round that he's going to resign.* ◇ *There's a virus going round at work.* ▶ (*przen.*) **krążyć**

go round (to...) to visit sb's home, usually a short distance away: *I'm going round to Jo's for dinner tonight.* ▶ **zachodzić do kogoś** (*w odwiedziny*)

go round/around/about with sb to spend time and go to places regularly with sb: *Her parents don't like the people she has started going round with.* ▶ **zadawać się/przestawać z kimś**

G

go through to be completed successfully: *The deal went through as agreed.* ▶ **dochodzić do skutku**

go through sth **1** to look in or at sth carefully, especially in order to find sth: *I always start the day by going through my email.* ◇ *I went through all my pockets but I couldn't find my wallet.* ▶ **przeglądać coś** **2** to look at, think about or discuss sth carefully from beginning to end: *Let's go through the arrangements for the trip again.* ◇ *We'll start the lesson by going through your homework.* ▶ **omawiać, przechodzić przez coś** **3** to have an unpleasant experience: *I'd hate to go through such a terrible ordeal again.* ▶ **przechodzić przez coś, przeżywać coś**

go through with sth to do sth unpleasant or difficult that you have decided, agreed or threatened to do: *Do you think she'll go through with her threat to leave him?* ▶ **doprowadzać coś do końca, realizować coś**

go together [used about two or more things] **1** to belong to the same set or group ▶ **należeć** (*do tej samej grupy*), **tworzyć całość** **2** to look or taste good together ▶ **pasować (do czegoś)** ➲ look at **match**[3]

go towards sth to be used as part of the payment for sth: *The money I was given for my birthday went towards my new bike.* ▶ (*fundusze*) **iść** (*na jakiś cel*)

go under **1** to sink below the surface of some water ▶ **iść na dno, zatonąć** **2** (informal) (used about a company) to fail and close: *A lot of firms are going under in the recession.* ▶ **plajtować**

go up **1** to become higher in price, level, amount, etc.: *The birth rate has gone up by 10%.* ▶ **wzrastać** SYN **rise** **2** to start burning suddenly and strongly: *The car crashed into a wall and went up in flames.* ▶ **stawać** (*w płomieniach*) **3** to be built: *New buildings are going up all over town.* ▶ (*przen.*) **wyrastać**

go with sth **1** to be included with sth; to happen as a result of sth: *Pressure goes with the job.* ▶ **towarzyszyć czemuś, być częścią czegoś** **2** to look or taste good with sth else: *What colour carpet would go with the walls?* ▶ **pasować do czegoś** SYN **match**

go without (sth) to choose or be forced to not have sth: *They went without sleep night after night while the baby was ill.* ▶ **obywać się bez czegoś**

go[2] /gəʊ/ noun [C] (pl. **goes** /gəʊz/) **1** a turn to play in a game, etc.: *Whose go is it?* ◇ *Hurry up – it's your go.* ▶ **kolej/ka** SYN **turn** **2** (informal) **a go (at sth/doing sth)** an occasion when you try to do sth: *I'm not sure if I can fix it, but I'll* ***have a go*** (spróbuję). ◇ *I've never played this game before, but I'll* ***give it a go.*** ◇ *Andrew passed his driving test* ***first go*** (przy pierwszej próbie). ▶ **próba, podejście** (*np. do egzaminu*) SYN **attempt**

IDM **be on the go** (informal) to be very active or busy: *I'm exhausted. I've been on the go all day.* ▶ **być w ruchu, być na nogach**

have a go at sb (informal) to criticize sb/sth: *Dad's always having a go at me about my hair.* ▶ **czepiać się kogoś, krytykować kogoś**

make a go of sth (informal) to be successful at sth: *'How's your new job?' 'The work is hard, but I'm determined to make a go of it* (jestem zdeterminowany, żeby mi się powiodło).*'* ◇ *We've had a few problems in our marriage, but we're both determined to make a go of it* (ale oboje staramy się, aby przetrwało).

goad /gəʊd/ verb [T] **goad sb/sth (into sth/doing sth)** to cause sb to do sth by making them angry ▶ **prowokować, pobudzać**

PHR V **goad sb on** to drive or encourage sb to do sth: *The boxers were goaded on by the shrieking crowd.* ▶ **dopingować kogoś**

'go-ahead[1] noun [sing.] **the go-ahead (for sth)** permission to do sth: *It looks like the council will* ***give us the go-ahead*** *for the new building.* ▶ **pozwolenie, żeby coś zacząć**

'go-ahead[2] adj. enthusiastic to try new ways of doing things ▶ **rzutki, przedsiębiorczy**

goal /gəʊl/ noun [C] **1** (in games such as football, **rugby**, **hockey**) the area between two posts into which the ball must be kicked, hit, etc. for a point or points to be scored: *He crossed the ball in front of the goal.* ▶ **bramka** ➲ picture on **page A8** **2** a point that is scored when the ball goes into the goal: *Everton won by three goals to two.* ◇ *to score* (strzelić) *a goal* ◇ *an own goal* bramka samobójcza ▶ **gol** **3** your purpose or aim: *This year I should* ***achieve*** *my* ***goal*** *of visiting all the capital cities of Europe.* ▶ **cel**

goalkeeper /'gəʊlki:pə(r)/ (also informal **goalie** /'gəʊli/ or **keeper**) noun [C] (in games such as football and **hockey**) the player who stands in front of the goal(1) and tries to stop the other team from scoring: *The goalkeeper made a magnificent save* (wspaniałą obronę). ▶ **bramka-rz/rka**

goalless /'gəʊlləs/ adj. with no goals scored: *a goalless draw* ◇ *The match finished goalless.* ▶ **bezbramkowy**

goalpost /'gəʊlpəʊst/ noun [C] (in games such as football, **hockey**, etc.) one of the two posts that form the sides of a goal. They are joined together by a **crossbar**. ▶ **słupek (bramki)**

goat /gəʊt/ noun [C] a small animal with horns which lives in mountain areas or is kept on farms for its milk and meat ▶ **kozioł, koza** ➲ picture on **page A10**

goatee /gəʊ'ti:/ noun [C] a small pointed beard on a man's chin ▶ **kozia bródka** ➲ picture at **hair**

gobble /'gɒbl/ verb [I,T] (informal) **gobble sth (up/down)** to eat quickly and noisily ▶ **jeść łapczywie i głośno**; **zmiatać jedzenie z talerza**

gobbledegook (also **gobbledygook**) /'gɒbldigu:k/ noun [U] (informal) complicated language that is hard to understand ▶ **urzędowa (niezrozumiała) gadanina**, **nowomowa**

'go-between noun [C] a person who takes messages between two people or groups ▶ **posłaniec**, **pośrednik/czka**

goblet /'gɒblət/ noun [C] a cup for wine, usually made of glass or metal, with a **stem** and base but no handle ▶ **kielich**

goblin /'gɒblɪn/ noun [C] (in stories) a small ugly creature who tricks people ▶ **chochlik**

gobsmacked /'gɒbsmækt/ adj. (informal) so surprised that you are unable to speak ▶ **oniemiały**

god /gɒd/ noun **1** (**God**) [sing.] [not used with *the*] the being or spirit in Christianity, Islam and Judaism who people say prayers to and who people believe created the universe: *Do you believe in God?* ◇ *Muslims worship God in a mosque.* ▶ **Bóg** **2** (fem. **goddess** /'gɒdes/) [C] a being or spirit that people believe has power over a particular part of nature or that represents a particular quality: *Mars was the Roman god of war and Venus was the goddess of love.* ▶ **bóg**

Słowo **God** spotyka się w kilku wyrażeniach. Jednak nie należy ich stosować zbyt często, ponieważ niektóre osoby mogą to uznać za niewłaściwe. Wyrażenie **Oh my God!** oznacza czyjeś zaskoczenie lub szok: *Oh my God* (Boże)*! I've won £1 000!* Wyrażenie **thank God** oznacza, że odczuwamy ulgę z jakiegoś powodu: *Thank God you've arrived – I was beginning to think you'd had an accident.* Wyrażenie **for God's sake** stosuje się w celu określenia, że jakaś sprawa jest pilna i należy ją jak najszybciej wykonać lub gdy chcemy wyrazić zniecierpliwienie: *For God's sake* (na miłość boską)*, shut up!* Aby uniknąć nadużywania słowa **God**, stosuje się **heaven** i **goodness**.

godchild /'gɒdtʃaɪld/ (also **'god-daughter**; **godson**) noun [C] a child who has a **godparent** ▶ **chrześnia-k/czka**; **chrześniaczka**

goddess /'gɒdes; -əs/ noun [C] a female god ▶ **bogini**

godforsaken /'gɒdfəseɪkən/ adj. [only before a noun] (used about a place) not interesting or attractive in any way ▶ **zapomniany przez Boga i ludzi**, **zapadły**

godparent /'gɒdpeərənt/ (also **godfather** /'gɒdfɑ:ðə(r)/, **godmother** /'gɒdmʌðə(r)/) noun [C] a person chosen by a child's family who promises to help the child and to make sure they are educated as a Christian ▶ **rodzic chrzestny**; **ojciec chrzestny**; **matka chrzestna**

godsend /'gɒdsend/ noun [C] something unexpected that is very useful because it comes just when it is needed ▶ **dar niebios**

goggles /'gɒglz/ noun [pl.] special glasses that you wear to protect your eyes from water, wind, dust, etc. ▶ **okulary ochronne**, **gogle** ➲ look at **mask**

going[1] /'gəʊɪŋ/ noun **1** [sing.] (formal) the act of leaving a place: *We were all saddened by his going.* ▶ **odejście**, **odjazd** SYN **departure** **2** [U] [used with an adjective] the speed with which sb does sth; how difficult sth is: *Three children in four years? That's* ***not bad going*** (to nieźle im idzie)*!* ◇ *The path up the mountain was* ***rough going.*** Trasa ścieżki prowadzącej na górę była bardzo ciężka. ◇ *The mud made the path very hard going.* Błoto utrudniało przebycie ścieżki. ◇ *It'll be* ***hard going*** (będzie ciężko) *if we need to finish this by Friday!* ◇ *I'm finding this novel very* ***heavy going.*** Ciężko mi się czyta tę powieść.

IDM **get out, go, leave, etc. while the going is good** to leave a place or stop doing sth while it is still easy to do so ▶ **przestawać coś robić w odpowiednim/dobrym czasie**

going[2] /'gəʊɪŋ/ adj.

IDM **a going concern** a successful business ▶ **kwitnący interes**

the going rate (for sth) the usual cost (of sth): *What's the going rate for an office cleaner?* ▶ **zwyczajowa stawka (za coś)**

,going-'over noun [sing.] (informal) **1** a very careful examination of sth: ***Give the car a good going-over*** (dokładny przegląd) *before deciding to buy it.* ▶ **drobiazgowe badanie** **2** a serious physical attack on sb ▶ (*przen.*) **wycisk**

,goings-'on noun [pl.] (informal) unusual things that are happening ▶ **(moralnie podejrzane) wydarzenia**

go-kart /'gəʊ kɑ:t/ (also **kart**) noun [C] a vehicle like a very small car with no roof or doors, used for racing ▶ **gokart**

gold /gəʊld/ noun **1** [U] (symbol **Au**) a rare and valuable yellow metal that is used for making coins, jewellery, etc.: *Is your bracelet made of solid gold?* ◇ *22 carat gold* ◇ *a gold chain/watch* ▶ **złoto** **2** [C] = GOLD MEDAL

■ **gold** adj.: *The invitation was written in gold letters.* ▶ **złoty** ➲ look at **golden**

IDM **(as) good as gold** very well behaved ▶ **grzeczny jak aniołek**

have a heart of gold → HEART

golden /ˈɡəʊldən/ adj. **1** made of gold or having a bright yellow colour like gold: *a golden crown* ◇ *golden hair/sand* ▶ **złoty**, **złocisty 2** best, most important, most liked, etc.: *a golden opportunity* ▶ **złoty**, **doskonały 3** celebrating the 50th anniversary of sth: *The couple celebrated their golden wedding last year.* ▶ **złoty** ➲ look at **silver**, **diamond**

IDM **the golden rule (of sth)** an important principle that should be followed when doing sth in order to be successful: *When you run a marathon, the golden rule is: don't start too fast.* ▶ **złota zasada**

goldfish /ˈɡəʊldfɪʃ/ noun [C] (pl. **goldfish**) a small orange fish, often kept as a pet in a bowl ▶ **złota rybka** ➲ note at **pet**

ˌ**gold ˈmedal** (also **gold**) noun [C] the prize for first place in a sports competition: *How many gold medals did we win in the 2004 Olympics?* ▶ **złoty medal** ➲ look at **silver medal**, **bronze medal**

ˌ**gold ˈmedallist** noun [C] the winner of a **gold medal** ▶ **złot-y/a medalist(k)a**

ˈ**gold mine** noun [C] **1** a place where gold is taken from the ground ▶ **kopalnia złota 2 a gold mine (of sth)** a place, person or thing that provides a lot of sth: *This website is a gold mine of information.* ▶ (*przen.*) **kopalnia**

golf /ɡɒlf; US ɡɔːlf/ noun [U] a game that is played outdoors on a **golf course** and in which you use a **golf club** to hit a small hard ball into a series of holes (usually 18): *to play a round of golf* zagrać rundę golfa ▶ **golf** ➲ picture on **page A9**

ˈ**golf club** a long metal stick that is specially shaped at one end and used for hitting a ball when playing **golf** ▶ **kij golfowy** ➲ look at **bat**, **racket**, **stick** ➲ picture on **page A9**

golfer /ˈɡɒlfə(r)/ noun [C] a person who plays **golf** ▶ **gracz w golfa** ➲ picture on **page A9**

golly /ˈɡɒli/ interj. (informal) (used for expressing surprise) ▶ **o rany!**, **ojej!**

gone[1] past participle of **go**[1]

gone[2] /ɡɒn/ adj. [not before a noun] not present any longer; completely used or finished: *He stood at the door for a moment, and then he was gone* (i już go nie było). ◇ *Can I have some more ice cream please or is it all gone* (czy już nie ma)*?* ▶ **nieobecny**, **zużyty**

> **Gone** w znaczeniu „zniknąwszy" lub „zużyty" stosuje się z czasownikiem **be**, tak jak w powyższych przykładach. Zastanawiając się nad tym, gdzie ktoś się podział, używa się **have**: *Nobody knows where John has gone.*

gone[3] /ɡɒn/ prep. later than: *Hurry up! It's gone six already* (już po szóstej)*!* ▶ **po** ⓘ Tłumacząc **be gone** na polski, często używa się czasownika „mijać/przemijać".

gong /ɡɒŋ/ noun **1** a round piece of metal that hangs in a frame and makes a loud deep sound when it is hit with a stick. **Gongs** are used as musical instruments or to give signals, for example that a meal is ready. ▶ **gong 2** (Brit., informal) an award or **medal** given to sb for the work they have done ▶ **nagroda**, **medal**

gonna /ˈɡənə; ˈɡɒnə/ (informal) a way of writing 'going to' to show that sb is speaking in an informal way: *What's he gonna do now?* ⓘ Nie należy pisać **gonna** (chyba, że naśladuje się czyjś akcent), ponieważ może to być uznane za błąd. Podobnie jest z **wanna** (= want to) i **gotta** (= got to).

goo /ɡuː/ noun [U] (informal) a sticky wet substance ▶ **maź** SYN **slime**

⚷ **good**[1] /ɡʊd/ adj. (**better**; **best**) **1** of a high quality or standard: *a good book/film/actor* ◇ *That's a really good idea!* ◇ *The hotel was quite/pretty good, but not fantastic.* ▶ **dobry 2** pleasant or enjoyable: *It's good to be home again.* Dobrze być znów w domu. ◇ ***Have a good time** at the party!* Baw się dobrze na przyjęciu! ◇ *good news/weather* ▶ **dobry 3** (used about a reason, etc.) acceptable and easy to understand: *a good excuse/explanation* ◇ *She has good reason to be pleased – she's just been promoted.* ▶ **dobry**, **ważny 4 good at sth**; **good with sb/sth** able to do sth or deal with sb/sth well: *Jane's really good at science subjects but she's **no good at** languages.* ◇ *Are you any good at drawing?* ◇ *He's very good with children.* Dobrze sobie radzi z dziećmi. ▶ **dobry (w czymś) 5** morally right or well behaved: *She was a very good person – she spent her whole life trying to help other people.* ◇ *Were the children good while we were out?* ▶ **dobry**, **grzeczny 6 good (to sb)**; **good of sb (to do sth)** kind; helpful: *It was good of you to come.* To ładnie z twojej strony, że przyszedłeś. ◇ *They were good to me* (byli dla mnie dobrzy) *when I was ill.* ▶ **dobry 7 good (for sb/sth)** having a positive effect on sb/sth's health or condition: *Green vegetables are very good for you.* ◇ *This cream is good for burns.* ▶ **dobry**; **zdrowy 8 good (for sb/sth)** suitable or convenient: *I think Paul would be a good person for the job.* Myślę, że Paweł nadawałby się do tej pracy. ◇ *This beach is very good for surfing.* Ta plaża nadaje się do surfingu. ◇ *'When shall we meet?' 'Thursday would be a good day for me.'* ▶ **dobry 9** (used when you are pleased about sth): *'Tom's invited us to dinner next week.' 'Oh, good* (dobrze)*!'* ▶ **dobry 10** (**a good ...**) great in number, amount, etc.: ***a good many/a good few** people* sporo ludzi ◇ *a good distance* ◇ *Give the fruit a good wash before you eat it.* ◇ *Take a good look at this photograph.* Dobrze się przyjrzyj tej fotografii. ◇ *We waited for a good ten minutes* (dobre dziesięć minut). ◇ *It's a good three miles to the station.* Do stacji są dobre trzy mile. ◇ *What you need is a good rest.* Potrzebujesz dobrego odpoczynku. ▶ **dobry 11 good (for sth)** that can be used or can provide sth: *I've only got one good pair of shoes.* ◇ *This ticket's good for* (ważny przez) *another three days.* ◇ *That car is good for* (tym samochodem będzie można jeszcze pojeździć) *a few more years yet.* ◇ *Let's invite Jess – she's always good for a laugh* (z nią zawsze dobrze się bawi). ▶ **dobry (do czegoś)**

IDM **as good as** almost: *The project is as good as finished.* ▶ **prawie**, **niemal(że)** SYN **virtually**

good for you, him, her, etc. (informal) (used to show that you are pleased that sb has done sth clever): *'I passed my driving test!' 'Well done! Good for you!'* ▶ **gratulacje!**, **brawo!**

good morning/afternoon/evening/night → AFTERNOON, EVENING, MORNING, NIGHT

good gracious, good grief, good heavens, etc. (used for expressing surprise) ▶ **coś takiego/podobnego!**

ⓘ **Good** używa się w innych idiomach. Zob. hasła odpowiednich rzeczowników, przymiotników itp.

> **good**
>
> W nieformalnym angielskim zamiast **very good** mówi się **brilliant**, **fantastic**, **great** lub **terrific**. Wyrazy **excellent** i **wonderful** są bardziej formalne: *an excellent example/opportunity*. W niektórych kontekstach używamy specjalnych wyrazów, aby powiedzieć, że coś jest dobre: ***delicious**/**tasty** food* ◇ *a **talented** artist/player/writer* ◇ *an **outstanding** achievement/performance/piece of work.*

⚷ **good**[2] /ɡʊd/ noun [U] **1** behaviour that is morally right or acceptable: *the difference between good and evil* ◇ *I'm*

G

sure there's some good in everybody. ▶ **dobro 2** something that will help sb/sth; advantage: *She did it* ***for the good of*** *her country.* ◇ *I know you don't want to go into hospital, but it's* ***for your own good.*** ◇ ***What's the good of*** *learning French if you have no chance of using it?* ▶ **dobro, pożytek** ➲ look at **goods**

IDM be no good (doing sth) to be of no use or value: *It's no good standing here in the cold. Let's go home.* ◇ *This sweater isn't any good. It's too small.* ▶ **nie warto (czegoś robić), być bezużytecznym**

do you good to help or be useful to you: *It'll do you good to meet some new people.* ▶ **dobrze (coś komuś) robić**

do sb a/the world of good → WORLD

for good for ever: *I hope they've gone for good this time!* ▶ **na dobre**

not much good (informal) bad or not useful: *'How was the party?' 'Not much good.'* ▶ **kiepski, taki sobie**

goodbye /ˌɡʊdˈbaɪ/ interj. said when sb goes or you go: *We said goodbye* (pożegnaliśmy się) *to Steven at the airport.* ▶ **do widzenia** ⓘ **Bye, cheers** i **cheerio** mają identyczne znaczenie.

■ **goodbye** noun [C]: *We said our goodbyes and left.* ◇ *Their goodbye was very sad because they knew they wouldn't see each other again for years.* ▶ **pożegnanie**

ˈgood-for-nothing noun [C] (informal) a person who is lazy and has no skills ▶ **wałkoń**

■ **ˈgood-for-nothing** adj. [usually before a noun]: *Where's that good-for-nothing son of yours?* ▶ **bezużyteczny**

ˌGood ˈFriday noun [C] the Friday before Easter when Christians remember the death of Christ ▶ **Wielki Piątek**

ˌgood-ˈhearted adj. kind; willing to help other people ▶ (*osoba*) **dobry, serdeczny**

ˌgood ˈhumour (US ˌ**good ˈhumor**) noun [U, sing.] a cheerful mood: *Everyone admired her patience and unfailing good humour.* ▶ **dobry nastrój, pogoda ducha** **OPP ill humour**

■ **ˌgood-ˈhumoured** (Brit.) (US ˌ**good-ˈhumored**) adj. pleasant and friendly: *a good-humoured atmosphere* ▶ **pogodny**

goodie (informal) = GOODY

goodies /ˈɡʊdiz/ noun [pl.] (informal) **1** things that are very nice to eat ▶ **smakołyki 2** things that are attractive and that people want to have: *We're giving away lots of free goodies – T-shirts, hats and DVDs!* ▶ **prezenty**

ˌgood-ˈlooking adj. (usually used about a person) attractive ▶ **przystojny** **OPP ugly** ➲ note at **beautiful**

ˌgood ˈlooks noun [pl.] an attractive appearance (of a person) ▶ **uroda**

ˌgood-ˈnatured adj. friendly or kind ▶ **dobroduszny, łagodnego usposobienia**

goodness /ˈɡʊdnəs/ noun [U] **1** the quality of being good ▶ **dobroć** **SYN virtue 2** the part of sth that has a good effect, especially on sb/sth's health: *Wholemeal bread has more goodness in it* (pieczywo pełnoziarniste jest zdrowsze) *than white.* ▶ **wartości zdrowotne/odżywcze**

> **Goodness** używa się w kilku zwrotach zamiast słowa Bóg. **Goodness (me)!** wyraża zdziwienie. **Thank goodness!** wyraża zadowolenie i ulgę: *Thank goodness it's stopped raining!* Mówi się **For goodness' sake** w celu przydania prośbie ponaglenia, lub okazując zniecierpliwienie: *For goodness' sake, hurry up!*

goodnight /ˌɡʊdˈnaɪt/ interj. said late in the evening, before you go home or before you go to sleep ▶ **dobranoc**

goods /ɡʊdz/ noun [pl.] **1** things that are for sale: *a wide range of consumer goods* ◇ *electrical goods* ◇ *stolen goods* ▶ **towary** (*na sprzedaż*) **2** (Brit.) things that are carried by train or lorry: *a goods train* pociąg towarowy ◇ *a heavy goods vehicle (=HGV)* ciężki pojazd ciężarowy ▶ **ładunek** ➲ look at **freight**

IDM come up with/deliver the goods (informal) to do what you have promised to do ▶ **dostarczać towar** (*wypełnić zobowiązanie*)

ˌgood ˈsense noun [U] good judgement or intelligence: *He had the good sense to refuse the offer.* ▶ **zdrowy rozsądek**

ˌgood-ˈtempered adj. not easily made angry ▶ **opanowany, łagodny**

goodwill /ˌɡʊdˈwɪl/ noun [U] friendly, helpful feelings towards other people: *The visit was designed to promote friendship and goodwill.* ▶ **dobra wola, życzliwość**

goody (also **goodie**) /ˈɡʊdi/ noun [C] (pl. **goodies**) (informal) **1** a good person in a film, book, etc. ▶ **bohater pozytywny** **OPP baddy 2** ➲ look at **goodies**

ˈgoody-goody noun [C] (usually used in a critical way) a person who always behaves well so that other people have a good opinion of them ▶ **świętosz-ek/ka** ⓘ Wyraża dezaprobatę.

gooey /ˈɡuːi/ adj. (informal) soft and sticky: *gooey cakes* ▶ **ciągnący się, maziowaty**

goof /ɡuːf/ verb [I] (especially US, informal) to make a silly mistake ▶ **popełniać głupi błąd/pomyłkę, wygłupić się**

PHR V goof around (informal) (especially US) to spend your time doing silly or stupid things ▶ **wygłupiać się** **SYN mess about/around**

goof off (US, informal) to spend your time doing nothing, especially when you should be working ▶ **obijać się**

goofy /ˈɡuːfi/ adj. (informal) (especially US) silly; stupid: *a goofy grin* ▶ **głupkowaty**

google /ˈɡuːɡl/ verb [I,T] to type words into a **search engine** on the Internet, especially the Google™search engine, in order to find information about sb/sth: *You can google someone you've recently met to see what information is available about them on the Internet.* ◇ *I tried googling but couldn't find anything relevant.* ▶ **wyszukiwać** (*przez internet*)

goose /ɡuːs/ noun [C] (pl. **geese** /ɡiːs/) a large bird with a long neck that lives on or near water. **Geese** are kept on farms for their meat and eggs. ▶ **gęś**

> A male goose is called a **gander** and a young goose is a **gosling**.

gooseberry /ˈɡʊzbəri; US ˈɡuːsberi/ noun [C] (pl. **gooseberries**) a small green fruit that is covered in small hairs and has a sour taste ▶ **agrest** ➲ picture on **page A12**

IDM play gooseberry (Brit.) to be with two people who have a romantic relationship and want to be alone together ▶ **być intruzem**

ˈgoose pimples (also **goosebumps** /ˈɡuːsbʌmps/) noun [pl.] small points or lumps which appear on your skin because you are cold or frightened ▶ **gęsia skórka**

gore[1] /ɡɔː(r)/ noun [U] thick blood that comes from a wound: *His new film is full of gore.* W jego nowym filmie jest pełno krwi. ▶ **posoka, rozlana/zakrzepła krew** ➲ adjective **gory**

gore[2] /ɡɔː(r)/ verb [T] (used about an animal) to wound sb with a horn, etc.: *She was gored to death by a bull.* ▶ **ubóść**

gorge[1] /ɡɔːdʒ/ noun [C] a narrow valley with steep sides and a river running through it ▶ **przełom** (*rzeki*)

gorge[2] /ɡɔːdʒ/ verb [I,T] **gorge (yourself) (on/with sth)** to eat a lot of food ▶ **objadać się**

gorgeous /ˈɡɔːdʒəs/ adj. (informal) extremely pleasant or attractive: *What gorgeous weather!* ◇ *You look gorgeous in that dress.* ▶ **wspaniały, przepiękny, pyszny** ➲ note at **beautiful**

■ **gorgeously** adv. ▶ **wspaniale, przepięknie**

gorilla /gəˈrɪlə/ noun [C] a large black African **ape** ▶ **goryl**

gormless /ˈgɔːmləs/ adj. (Brit., informal) stupid ▶ **tępy**

gorse /gɔːs/ noun [U] a bush with yellow flowers and thin thorny leaves that do not fall off in winter. Gorse often grows on land that is not used or cared for. ▶ **janowiec**

gory /ˈgɔːri/ adj. (**gorier**; **goriest**) full of violence and blood: *a gory film* ◇ *He told me all **the gory details*** (drastyczne szczegóły) *about the divorce.* ▶ **krwawy, ociekający krwią** ➲ noun **gore**[1]

gosh /gɒʃ/ interj. (informal) (used for expressing surprise, shock, etc.) ▶ **ojej!, ho ho!**

gosling /ˈgɒzlɪŋ/ noun [C] a young **goose** ▶ **gąsiątko**

gospel /ˈgɒspl/ noun **1** (**Gospel**) [sing.] one of the four books in the Bible that describe the life of Jesus Christ and the ideas which he taught: *St Matthew's/Mark's/Luke's/John's Gospel* ▶ **Ewangelia 2** (also ˌ**gospel ˈtruth**) [U] the truth: *You can't take what he says as gospel.* ▶ **święta prawda 3** (also ˈ**gospel music**) [U] a style of religious music that is especially popular among black American Christians ▶ **chrześcijańska, religijna muzyka Murzynów amerykańskich**

gossip /ˈgɒsɪp/ noun **1** [U] informal talk about other people and their private lives, that is often unkind or not true: *Matt phoned me up to tell me the latest gossip.* ▶ **plotka 2** [C] an informal conversation about other people's private lives: *The two neighbours were having a gossip* (plotkowali) *over the fence.* ▶ **plotkowanie, plotkarstwo 3** [C] a person who enjoys talking about other people's private lives ▶ **plotka-rz/rka**

■ **gossip** verb [I] ▶ **plotkować**

ˈ**gossip column** noun [C] a part of a newspaper or magazine where you can read about the private lives of famous people ▶ **kronika towarzyska** ➲ note at **newspaper**

■ ˈ**gossip columnist** noun [C] ▶ **redaktor kronik towarzyskiej**

got past tense, past participle of **get** ➲ look at **gotten**

Gothic /ˈgɒθɪk/ adj. (used about architecture) connected with a style that was common in Europe from the 12th to the 16th centuries. Typical features of Gothic architecture are pointed arches, tall thin pillars, elaborate decoration, etc. ▶ **gotycki**

gotta /ˈgɒtə/ (US, informal) (a way of writing 'got to' or 'got a' to show that sb is speaking in an informal way): *I gotta go* (= I have got to go). ◇ *Gotta* (= have you got a) *minute?* ❶ Nie należy pisać **gotta** (chyba, że naśladuje się czyjś akcent), ponieważ może to być uznane za błąd ➲ look at **gonna**, **wanna**

gotten (US) past participle of **get** ❶ W większości wypadków w Amer. ang. **gotten** używa się częściej niż **got**: *Has he gotten back yet?* ◇ *I've gotten myself a new job.*

gouge /gaʊdʒ/ verb [T] to make a hole in a surface using a sharp object in a rough way: *We gouged a deep scratch* (zarysowaliśmy) *in the wooden floor when we moved the table.* ▶ **za/drapać**

PHR V **gouge sth out** to remove or form sth by digging into a surface ▶ **wyżłabiać coś, wydłubywać coś**

gourd /gʊəd; Brit. also gɔːd/ noun [C] a type of large fruit, not normally eaten, with hard skin. **Gourds** are often dried and used as containers. ▶ **tykwa**

gourmet /ˈgʊəmeɪ/ noun [C] a person who enjoys food and wine and knows a lot about it: *a gourmet restaurant* restauracja dla smakoszy ▶ **smakosz/ka**

⚷ **govern** /ˈgʌvn; US -vərn/ verb **1** [I,T] to rule or control the public affairs of a country, city, etc.: *Britain is governed by the Prime Minister and the Cabinet.* ▶ **rządzić, kierować 2** [T, often passive] to influence or control sb/sth: *Our decision will be governed* (uzależniona) *by the amount of money we have to spend.* ▶ **wpływać**

governess /ˈgʌvənəs/ noun [C] (especially in the past) a woman employed to teach the children of a rich family in their home and to live with them ▶ **guwernantka**

⚷ **government** /ˈgʌvənmənt/ noun **1** (often **the Government**) [C, with sing. or pl. verb] the group of people who rule or control a country: *He has resigned from the Government.* ◇ *The foreign governments involved are meeting in Geneva.* ◇ *government policy/money/ministers/officials* polityka/fundusze/ministrowie/urzędnicy rządu ▶ **rząd** ➲ note at **politics** ➲ look at **opposition** ❶ Po słowie **government** w lp może następować czasownik w lp lub lm. Czasownika w lp używa się mówiąc o rządzie jako całości: *The Government welcomes the proposal.* Czasownika w lm używa się, mówiąc o rządzie jako grupie poszczególnych osób: *The Government are still discussing the problem.*

> Different types of government are: **communist**, **conservative**, **democratic**, **liberal**, **reactionary**, **socialist**, etc. A country or state may also have a **military**, **provisional**, **central** or **federal**, **coalition**, etc. government.

2 [U] the activity or method of controlling a country, city, etc.: *weak/strong/corrupt government* ◇ *communist/democratic/totalitarian government* ◇ *Which party is **in government*** (u władzy)? ▶ **rządy**

■ **governmental** /ˌgʌvnˈmentl/ adj. ▶ **rządowy**

⚷ **governor** /ˈgʌvənə(r)/ noun [C] **1** a person who rules or controls a region or state (especially in the US): *the Governor of New York State* ▶ **gubernator, wojewoda 2** the leader or member of a group of people who control an organization: *the governor of the Bank of England* ◇ *school governors* ▶ **prezes/ka, przewodnicząc-y/a, członek komitetu administracyjnego** (*np. szkoły*)

ˌ**Governor ˈGeneral** noun [C] (pl. **Governors General** or **Governor Generals**) the official representative in a country of the country that has or had political control over it, especially the representative of the British King or Queen in a Commonwealth country ▶ **gubernator generalny**

gown /gaʊn/ noun [C] **1** a woman's long formal dress for a special occasion: *a ball gown* suknia balowa ▶ **suknia 2** a long loose piece of clothing that is worn by judges, doctors performing operations, etc. ▶ **toga, fartuch**

GP /ˌdʒiː ˈpiː/ abbr. **general practitioner**; a doctor who treats all types of illnesses and works in a practice in a town or village, not in a hospital ▶ **lekarz pierwszego kontaktu**

⚷ **grab** /græb/ verb (**grabbing**; **grabbed**) **1** [I,T] **grab sth (from sb)** to take sth with a sudden movement: *Helen grabbed the toy car from her little brother.* ◇ ***Grab hold of** his arm in case he tries to run!* ◇ *Someone had arrived before us and grabbed all the seats.* ◇ (figurative) *He grabbed the opportunity of a free trip* (skorzystał z okazji i pojechał na darmową wycieczkę) *to America.* ◇ (figurative) *I'll try to grab the waitress's attention.* ▶ **wyrywać, chwytać,** (*i przen.*) **łapać** ➲ look at **snatch 2** [I] **grab at/for sth** to try to get or catch sb/sth: *Jonathan grabbed at the ball but missed.* ▶ **rzucać się na kogoś/coś 3** [T] to do sth quickly because you are in a hurry: *I'll just grab something to eat* (szybko coś przekąszę) *and then we'll go.* ◇ *I grabbed an hour's sleep* (przespałem się godzinę) *on the train so I'm not too tired now.* ▶ **szybko coś zrobić**

■ **grab** /græb/ noun [C]: *She made a grab for the boy but she couldn't stop him falling.* ▶ **szybki ruch mający na celu chwycenie/złapanie kogoś/czegoś**

ˈ**grab bag** (US) = LUCKY DIP

grace /greɪs/ noun [U] **1** the ability to move in a smooth and controlled way ▶ **wdzięk 2** extra time that is allowed for sth ▶ **prolongata terminu płatności,**

G

karencja **3** a short prayer of thanks to God before or after a meal: *to say grace* ▶ **modlitwa przed posiłkiem/po posiłku** **4** (His/Her/Your Grace) (used when speaking about, or to, a duke, duchess or archbishop) ▶ **Wasza Wysokość, Ekselencjo**

IDM **sb's fall from grace** → FALL[2]

have the grace to do sth to be polite enough to do sth ▶ **być na tyle przyzwoitym, żeby**

with good grace in a pleasant and reasonable way, without complaining: *He accepted the refusal with good grace.* ▶ **z uśmiechem na twarzy**

graceful /ˈgreɪsfl/ adj. having a smooth, attractive movement or form: *a graceful dancer* ◇ *graceful curves* ▶ **pełen wdzięku/gracji** ℹ Por. **gracious**. Ma inne znaczenie.

■ **gracefully** /-fəli/ adv.: *The goalkeeper rose gracefully to catch the ball.* ◇ *She accepted the decision gracefully.* ▶ **z uśmiechem na twarzy; wdzięcznie** | **gracefulness** noun [U] ▶ **wdzięk, gracja**

graceless /ˈgreɪsləs/ adj. **1** not knowing how to be polite to people ▶ **szorstki** **2** (used about a movement or a shape) ugly and not elegant ▶ **bez wdzięku/gracji**

■ **gracelessly** adv. ▶ **bez wdzięku/gracji**

gracious /ˈgreɪʃəs/ adj. **1** (used about a person or their behaviour) kind, polite and generous: *a gracious smile* ▶ **łaskawy** **2** [only before a noun] showing the easy comfortable way of life that rich people can have: *gracious living* ▶ **zbytkowny, wykwintny** ➲ look at **graceful** **3** [only before a noun] (formal) (used when speaking about royal people): *by gracious permission of Her Majesty* ▶ **łaskawy**

■ **graciously** adv. ▶ **łaskawie** | **graciousness** noun [U] ▶ **łaskawość**

IDM **good gracious!** (used for expressing surprise): *Good gracious! Is that the time?* ▶ **o rety!, coś takiego!**

gradation /grəˈdeɪʃn/ noun **1** [C, U] (formal) any of the small changes or levels which sth is divided into; the process or result of sth changing gradually: *gradations of colour* ▶ **stopniowanie** **2** [C] a mark showing a division on a scale: *the gradations on a thermometer* ▶ **stopień podziałki**

⚷ **grade**[1] /greɪd/ noun [C] **1** the quality or the level of ability, importance, etc. that sb/sth has: *Which grade of petrol do you need?* ◇ *We need to use high-grade materials for this job.* ▶ **stopień, jakość** **2** a mark that is given for school work, etc. or in an exam: *He got good/poor grades this term.* ◇ *Very few students pass the exam with a grade A* (na najwyższą ocenę). ▶ **ocena, stopień** **3** (US) a class or classes in a school in which all the children are the same age: *My daughter is in the third grade.* ▶ **klasa szkolna**

IDM **make the grade** (informal) to reach the expected standard; to succeed: *She wanted to be a professional tennis player, but she didn't make the grade.* ▶ **osiągać (oczekiwany) poziom; odnosić sukces**

⚷ **grade**[2] /greɪd/ verb [T, often passive] to put things or people into groups according to their quality, ability, size, etc.: *I've graded their work from 1 to 10.* ◇ *Eggs are graded by size.* ▶ **klasyfikować, segregować**

gradient /ˈgreɪdiənt/ noun [C] the degree at which a road, etc. goes up or down: *The hill has a gradient of 1 in 4.* ◇ *a steep gradient* ▶ **stopień nachylenia**

⚷ **gradual** /ˈgrædʒuəl/ adj. happening slowly or over a long period of time; not sudden: *There has been a gradual increase in the number of people without jobs.* ▶ **stopniowy** OPP **sudden**

■ **gradually** /-dʒuəli/ adv.: *After the war life gradually got back to normal.* ▶ **stopniowo**

graduate[1] /ˈgrædʒuət/ noun [C] **1** **a graduate (in sth)** a person who has a first degree from a university, etc.: *a law graduate/a graduate in law* ◇ *a graduate of London University/a London University graduate* ◇ *a graduate student* student/ka podyplomow-y/a (zwłaszcza osoba na studiach magisterskich) ➲ look at **postgraduate, undergraduate, bachelor, student** ▶ **absolwent/ka studiów wyższych (licencjackich)** **2** (US) a person who has completed a course at a school, college, etc.: *a high-school graduate* ▶ **absolwent/ka**

graduate[2] /ˈgrædʒueɪt/ verb [I] **1** **graduate (in sth) (from sth)** to get a (first) degree from a university, etc.: *She graduated in History from Cambridge University.* ▶ **kończyć studia wyższe (licencjackie)** **2** (US) **graduate (from sth)** to complete a course at a school, college, etc. ▶ **kończyć** (*np. szkołę*) **3** **graduate (from sth) to sth** to change (from sth) to sth more difficult, important, expensive, etc.: *She's graduated from being a classroom assistant to teaching.* ▶ **przechodzić na wyższy poziom**

graduation /ˌgrædʒuˈeɪʃn/ noun **1** [U] the act of successfully completing a university degree or (in the US) studies at a high school ▶ **ukończenie studiów wyższych** **2** [sing.] a ceremony in which certificates are given to people who have **graduated** ▶ **uroczystość nadania dyplomów akademickich**

graffiti /grəˈfiːti/ noun [U, pl.] pictures or writing on a wall, etc. in a public place ▶ **graffiti**

graft /grɑːft; US græft/ noun [C] **1** a piece of a living plant that is fixed onto another plant so that it will grow ▶ **szczep** **2** a piece of living skin, bone, etc. that is fixed onto a damaged part of a body in an operation: *a skin graft* ▶ **przeszczep**

■ **graft** verb [T] **graft sth onto sth**: *Skin from his leg was grafted onto the burnt area of his face.* ▶ **szczepić, przeszczepiać** ➲ look at **transplant**

⚷ **grain** /greɪn/ noun **1** [U,C] the seeds of food plants such as rice, etc.: *The US is a major producer of grain.* ◇ *grain exports* ◇ *a few grains of rice* ▶ **zboże, produkty zbożowe; ziarno** **2** [C] **a grain of sth** a very small piece of sth: *a grain of sand/salt/sugar* ◇ (figurative) *There isn't* ***a grain of truth*** (nie ma ziarna prawdy) *in the rumour.* ▶ **ziarenko, szczypta** **3** [U] the natural pattern of lines that can be seen or felt in wood, rock, stone, etc.: *to cut a piece of wood along/across the grain* ▶ **słój** (*w drewnie*), **żyłkowanie** (*w kamieniu*)

IDM **(be/go) against the grain** to be different from what is usual or natural ▶ **przeciwny czyjejś naturze/usposobieniu**

grainy /ˈgreɪni/ adj. **1** (especially used about photographs) not having completely clear images because they look as if they are made of a lot of small dots and marks: *The film is shot in grainy black and white.* ▶ **ziarnisty** **2** having a rough surface or containing small bits, seeds, etc.: *a grainy texture* ▶ **ziarnisty**

⚷ **gram** (also **gramme**) /græm/ noun [C] (abbr. **g, gm**) a measure of weight. There are 1 000 grams in a kilogram. ▶ **gram** ℹ Więcej o wagach w dodatku *Wyrażenia liczbowe* na końcu słownika.

⚷ **grammar** /ˈgræmə(r)/ noun **1** [U] the rules of a language, for example for forming words or joining words together in sentences: *Polish grammar can be difficult for foreign learners.* ▶ **gramatyka, zasady gramatyki** **2** [U] the way in which sb uses the rules of a language: *You have a good vocabulary, but your grammar needs improvement.* ▶ **gramatyka** **3** [C] a book that describes and explains the rules of a language: *a French grammar* ▶ **gramatyka**

ˈ**grammar school** noun [C] (in Britain, especially in the past) a type of secondary school for children from 11-18 who are good at academic subjects ▶ **szkoła średnia ogólnokształcąca**

grammatical /grəˈmætɪkl/ adj. **1** connected with grammar: *the grammatical rules for forming plurals* ▶ **gramatyczny** **2** following the rules of a language: *The sentence is not grammatical.* ▶ **gramatyczny**

■ **grammatically** /-kli/ adv. ▶ **gramatycznie**

gramme = GRAM

gran /græn/ noun [C] (Brit., informal) the mother of your father or mother ▶ **babcia**, **babunia**

granary /ˈgrænəri/ noun [C] (pl. **granaries**) a building where grain is stored ▶ **spichlerz**

⚷ **grand¹** /grænd/ adj. **1** impressive and large or important (also used in names): *Our house isn't very grand, but it has a big garden.* ◇ *She thinks she's very grand because she drives a Porsche.* ◇ *the Grand Canyon* ◇ *the Grand Hotel* ▶ **wielki**, **okazały**; **ważny** ➲ noun **grandeur 2** (informal) very good or pleasant: *You've done a grand job!* ▶ **wspaniały**, **znakomity**

■ **grandly** adv. ▶ **z rozmachem**, **wielkopańsko** | **grandness** noun [U] ▶ **wspaniałość**, **okazałość**

grand² /grænd/ noun [C] (pl. **grand**) (slang) 1 000 pounds or dollars ▶ *(pieniądze)* **patyk**

grandad /ˈgrændæd/ noun [C] (Brit., informal) the father of your father or mother ▶ **dziadzio**

⚷ **grandchild** /ˈgræntʃaɪld/ noun [C] the daughter or son of your child ▶ **wnuk**, **wnuczka**

granddaughter /ˈgrændɔːtə(r)/ noun [C] a daughter of your son or daughter ▶ **wnuczka** ➲ look at **grandson**

grandeur /ˈgrændʒə(r)/ noun [U] (formal) **1** the quality of being large and impressive: *the grandeur of the Swiss Alps* ▶ **majestat**, **okazałość**, **wspaniałość** **2** the feeling of being important: *She seems to be suffering from delusions of grandeur* (cierpi na manię wielkości). ▶ **wielkość**, **znaczenie**

grandfather /ˈgrænfɑːðə(r)/ noun [C] the father of your father or mother ▶ **dziadek** ➲ note at **grandparent** ➲ look at **grandad**

ˈ**grandfather clock** noun [C] a clock that stands on the floor in a tall wooden case ▶ **zegar stojący**

grandiose /ˈgrændiəʊs/ adj. bigger or more complicated than necessary ▶ **wyolbrzymiony** ⓘ Wyraża dezaprobatę.

grandma /ˈgrænmɑː/ noun [C] (informal) the mother of your father or mother ▶ **babcia**, **babunia**

grandmother /ˈgrænmʌðə(r)/ noun [C] the mother of your father or mother ▶ **babka** ➲ note at **grandparent** ➲ look at **granny**, **gran**, **nana**

grandpa /ˈgrænpɑː/ noun [C] (informal) the father of your father or mother ▶ **dziadzio**

⚷ **grandparent** /ˈgrænpeərənt/ noun [C] the mother or father of one of your parents: *This is a picture of two of my grandparents.* ▶ **dziadek**; **babka** ➲ look at **great¹** (5)

> Aby odróżnić dziadków ze strony ojca od dziadków ze strony matki używa się określeń **my paternal/maternal grandfather** lub **my father's/mother's father**.

ˌ**grand piˈano** noun [C] a large flat piano (with horizontal strings) ▶ **fortepian**

ˌ**grand ˈslam** noun [C] winning all the important matches or competitions in a particular sport, for example **tennis** or **rugby** ▶ **wielki szlem**

grandson /ˈgrænsʌn/ noun [C] a son of your son or daughter ▶ **wnuk** ➲ look at **granddaughter**

grandstand /ˈgrænstænd/ noun [C] rows of seats, usually covered by a roof, from which you get a good view of a sports competition, etc. ▶ **kryte trybuny**

ˌ**grand ˈtotal** noun [C] the amount that you get when you add several totals together ▶ **suma ogólna**

granite /ˈgrænɪt/ noun [U] a hard grey rock ▶ **granit**

granny /ˈgræni/ noun [C] (Brit., informal) (pl. **grannies**) the mother of your father or mother ▶ **babcia**, **babunia**]

⚷ **grant¹** /grɑːnt; US grænt/ verb [T] **1** (formal) to (officially) give sb what they have asked for: *He was granted permission to leave early.* Zezwolono mu na wcześniejsze wyjście. ▶ **przyznawać**, **zezwalać**, **udzielać** **2** to agree (that sth is true): *I grant you that New York is an interesting place but I still wouldn't want to live there.* ▶ **przyznawać (rację)**, **zgadzać się**

IDM **take sb/sth for granted** to be so used to sb/sth that you forget their or its true value and are not grateful: *In developed countries we take running water for granted.* ▶ **przyjmować coś za rzecz oczywistą/ naturalną**, **nie doceniać kogoś/czegoś**

take sth for granted to accept sth as being true: *We can take it for granted that the new students will have at least an elementary knowledge of English.* ▶ **zakładać z góry**

⚷ **grant²** /grɑːnt; US grænt/ noun [C] money that is given by the government, etc. for a particular purpose: *a student grant* ◇ *to apply for/be awarded a grant* ▶ **do/finansowanie**, **stypendium**, **subwencja**

granted /ˈgrɑːntɪd; US ˈgræn-/ adv. (used for saying that sth is true, before you make a comment about it): *'We've never had problems before.' 'Granted, but this year a lot more people are here.'* ▶ **zgadza się**, **to prawda**

granulated sugar /ˌgrænjuleɪtɪd ˈʃʊgə(r)/ noun [U] white sugar in the form of small grains ▶ **cukier kryształ**

granule /ˈgrænjuːl/ noun [C] a small hard piece of sth: *instant coffee granules* ▶ **granulka**, **ziarenko**

grape /greɪp/ noun [C] a small soft green or purple fruit that grows in bunches on a **vine** and that is used for making wine: *a bunch of grapes* kiść winogron ▶ **winogrono** ➲ picture on **page A12**, picture at **bar**

> Green grapes are usually called 'white' and purple grapes are usually called 'black' (czerwone). Grapes that have been dried are called **raisins**, **currants** or **sultanas**.

IDM **sour grapes** → SOUR

grapefruit /ˈgreɪpfruːt/ noun [C] (pl. **grapefruit** or **grapefruits**) a large round yellow fruit with a thick skin and a sour taste ▶ **grejpfrut** ➲ picture on **page A12**

the **grapevine** /ˈgreɪpvaɪn/ noun [sing.] the way that news is passed from one person to another: *I heard **on/through the grapevine** that you're moving.* ▶ **poczta pantoflowa**

graph /græf; Brit. also grɑːf/ noun [C] a diagram in which a line or a curve shows the relationship between two quantities, measurements, etc.: *a graph showing/to show the number of cars sold each month* ▶ **wykres**, **diagram**

graphic /ˈgræfɪk/ adj. **1** [only before a noun] connected with drawings, diagrams, etc.: *a graphic artist* ◇ *graphic design* grafika ▶ **graficzny** **2** (used about descriptions) clear and giving a lot of detail, especially about sth unpleasant: *She described the accident in graphic detail.* ▶ **obrazowy**, **malowniczy**

■ **graphically** /-kli/ adv. ▶ **graficznie**; **obrazowo**, **malowniczo**

graphical /ˈgræfɪkl/ adj. **1** [only before a noun] connected with art or computer **graphics**: *The system uses an impressive graphical interface.* ▶ **graficzny** **2** in the form of a diagram or **graph**: *a graphical presentation of results* ▶ **graficzny**

graphics /ˈgræfɪks/ noun [pl.] the production of drawings, diagrams, etc.: *computer graphics* ▶ **grafika**

graphite /ˈgræfaɪt/ noun [U] a soft black mineral that is used in pencils ▶ **grafit**

ˈ**graph paper** noun [U] paper with small squares of equal size printed on it, used for drawing **graphs** and other diagrams ▶ **papier milimetrowy**

G

grapple /ˈgræpl/ verb [I] **grapple (with sb)** to get hold of sb and fight with or try to control them ▶ **siłować się**; **borykać się**

grasp¹ /grɑːsp; US græ-/ verb [T] **1** to take hold of sb/sth suddenly and firmly: *Lisa grasped the child firmly by the hand before crossing the road.* ◇ (figurative) *to grasp an opportunity/a chance* ▶ **chwytać**, **mocno trzymać 2** to understand sth completely: *I don't think you've grasped how serious the situation is.* ▶ **rozumieć**, **pojmować** PHR V **grasp at sth** to try to take hold of sth ▶ **próbować chwycić**, **sięgać**

grasp² /grɑːsp; US græ-/ noun [sing., U] **1** a firm hold of sb/sth: *Get a good grasp on the rope before pulling yourself up.* ◇ *I grabbed the boy, but he slipped from my grasp.* ▶ **uchwyt**; **trzymanie w ręce/garści 2** sb's understanding of a subject or of difficult facts: *He has **a good grasp of** English grammar.* Dobrze rozumie zasady gramatyki angielskiej. ▶ **zrozumienie**, **pojęcie (o czymś) 3** the ability to get or achieve sth: *Finally their dream was **within their grasp*** (w zasięgu ręki).

grasping /ˈgrɑːspɪŋ; US ˈgræs-/ adj. wanting very much to have a lot more money, power, etc. ▶ **chciwy**, **zachłanny**

⚷ **grass** /grɑːs; US græs/ noun **1** [U] the common green plant with thin leaves which covers fields and parts of gardens. Cows, sheep, horses, etc. eat grass: *Don't walk on the grass.* ◇ *I must cut the grass at the weekend.* ◇ *a blade* (źdźbło) *of grass* ▶ **trawa**

An area of grass in a garden is called a **lawn**.

2 [C] one type of grass: *an arrangement of dried flowers and grasses* ▶ **trawa**

grasshopper /ˈgrɑːshɒpə(r); US ˈgræ-/ noun [C] an insect that lives in long grass or trees and that can jump high in the air. **Grasshoppers** make loud noises. ▶ **konik polny** ➲ picture at **insect**

ˌgrass ˈroots noun [pl.] the ordinary people in an organization, not those who make decisions: *the grass roots of the party* ▶ **zwykli członkowie**

grassy /ˈgrɑːsi; US ˈgræ-/ adj. (**grassier**; **grassiest**) covered with grass ▶ **trawiasty**

grate¹ /greɪt/ noun [C] the metal frame that holds the wood, coal, etc. in a **fireplace** ▶ **ruszt**; **palenisko** ➲ picture at **fireplace**

grate² /greɪt/ verb **1** [T] to rub food into small pieces using a **grater**: *grated cheese/carrot* ▶ **trzeć**, **ścierać 2** [I] **grate (on sb)** to annoy ▶ **denerwować**, **drażnić** SYN **irritate 3** [I] **grate (against/on sth)** to make a sharp unpleasant sound (when two metal surfaces rub against each other) ▶ **zgrzytać**

⚷ **grateful** /ˈgreɪtfl/ adj. **grateful (to sb) (for sth)**; **grateful (that ...)** feeling or showing thanks (to sb): *We are very grateful to you for all the help you have given us.* ◇ *He was very grateful that you did as he asked.* ▶ **wdzięczny** OPP **ungrateful** ➲ noun **gratitude**
■ **gratefully** /-fəli/ adv. ▶ **z wdzięcznością**

grater /ˈgreɪtə(r)/ noun [C] a kitchen tool that is used for cutting food (for example cheese) into small pieces by rubbing it across its rough surface ▶ **tarka** ➲ picture at **kitchen**

gratify /ˈgrætɪfaɪ/ verb [T] (**gratifying**; **gratifies**; pt, pp **gratified**) [usually passive] (formal) to give sb pleasure and satisfaction: *I was gratified to hear* (z zadowoleniem dowiedziałem się) *that you enjoyed my book.* ▶ **zadowalać**, **sprawiać przyjemność**
■ **gratifying** adj. ▶ **zadowalający**, **sprawiający przyjemność**

grating /ˈgreɪtɪŋ/ noun [C] a frame made of metal bars that is fixed over a hole in the road, a window, etc. ▶ **krata** (*metalowa*)

gratis /ˈgrætɪs; ˈgreɪtɪs/ adv. done or given without having to be paid for ▶ **bezpłatnie** SYN **free of charge**
■ **gratis** adj.: *a gratis copy of a book* ▶ **bezpłatny**

gratitude /ˈgrætɪtjuːd; US -tuːd/ noun [U] **gratitude (to sb) (for sth)** the feeling of being grateful or of wanting to give your thanks: *We should like to express our gratitude to David for all his help.* ▶ **wdzięczność** OPP **ingratitude** ➲ adjective **grateful**

gratuitous /grəˈtjuːɪtəs; US -ˈtuː-/ adj. done without any good reason or purpose and often having harmful effects: *gratuitous violence on television* ▶ **nieuzasadniony** SYN **unnecessary**
■ **gratuitously** adv.: *The film was gratuitously offensive.* ▶ **niepotrzebnie**

gratuity /grəˈtjuːəti; US -ˈtuː-/ noun [C] (pl. **gratuities**) (formal) money that you give to sb who has provided a service for you ▶ **napiwek** SYN **tip**

⚷ **grave¹** /greɪv/ noun [C] the place where a dead body is buried: *I put some flowers on my grandmother's grave.* ▶ **grób** ➲ note at **funeral** ➲ look at **tomb**
IDM **have one foot in the grave** → FOOT¹

⚷ **grave²** /greɪv/ adj. (formal) **1** bad or serious: *These events could have **grave consequences** for us all.* ◇ *The children were **in grave danger**.* ▶ **poważny**, **groźny 2** (used about people) sad or serious: *He was looking extremely grave.* ▶ **poważny** ❶ W obu znaczeniach częściej używa się przymiotnika **serious**. ➲ noun **gravity**.
■ **gravely** adv.: *gravely ill* ▶ **poważnie**

gravel /ˈgrævl/ noun [U] very small stones that are used for making roads, paths, etc. ▶ **żwir** ➲ look at **grit**

gravestone /ˈgreɪvstəʊn/ noun [C] a stone in the ground that shows the name, dates, etc. of the dead person who is buried there ▶ **kamień nagrobny** ➲ look at **headstone**, **tombstone**

graveyard /ˈgreɪvjɑːd/ noun [C] an area of land next to a church where dead people are buried ▶ **cmentarz** ➲ look at **cemetery**, **churchyard**

gravitate /ˈgrævɪteɪt/ verb (formal)
PHR V **gravitate to/toward(s) sb/sth** to move towards sb/sth that you are attracted to: *Many young people gravitate to the cities in search of work.* ▶ **ciążyć ku komuś/czemuś**

gravity /ˈgrævəti/ noun [U] **1** the natural force that makes things fall to the ground when you drop them: *the force of gravity* ▶ **grawitacja 2** (formal) importance ▶ **powaga** ❶ Częściej używa się rzeczownika **seriousness**. ➲ adjective **grave**

gravy /ˈgreɪvi/ noun [U] a thin sauce that is made from the juices that come out of meat while it is cooking ▶ **sos pieczeniowy** ➲ look at **sauce**

gray (especially US) = GREY

grayish (especially US) = GREYISH

graze¹ /greɪz/ verb **1** [I] (used about cows, sheep, etc.) to eat grass (that is growing in a field): *There were cows grazing by the river.* ▶ **paść się 2** [T] to break the surface of your skin by rubbing it against sth rough: *The child fell and grazed her knee.* ▶ **ocierać 3** [T] to pass sth and touch it lightly: *The bullet grazed his shoulder.* ▶ **ocierać się o coś**

graze² /greɪz/ noun [C] a slight injury where the surface of the skin has been broken by rubbing it against sth rough ▶ **otarcie**, **zadrapanie**

grease¹ /griːs/ noun [U] **1** any thick substance containing oil, especially one that is used to make machines run smoothly: *Her hands were covered with oil and grease.* ▶ **smar 2** the fat that comes from cooking meat: *You'll* *need very hot water to get all the grease off those pans.* ▶ **tłuszcz**

grease² /gri:s/ verb [T] to rub **grease** or fat on or in sth: *Grease the tin thoroughly to stop the cake from sticking.* ▶ **smarować** (*tłuszczem*)

greasy /'gri:si/ adj. (**greasier**; **greasiest**) covered with or containing a lot of **grease**: *greasy skin/hair* ◇ *greasy food* ▶ **tłusty**

great¹ /greɪt/ adj. **1** large in amount, degree, size, etc.; a lot of: *We had great difficulty in solving the problem.* ◇ *The party was a great success.* ▶ **wielki**, **ogromny** ➲ note at **big** **2** (informal) good; wonderful: *We had **a great time** in Paris.* Wspaniale bawiliśmy się w Paryżu. ◇ ***It's great** to see you again.* Świetnie, że znów cię widzę. ▶ **wspaniały** ➲ note at **good**, **nice** ⓘ Czasami używa się słowa **great**, aby wyrazić sarkazm, ironię: *Oh great! I've spilled coffee all over my homework!* **3** particularly important; of unusually high quality: *Einstein was perhaps the greatest scientist of the century.* ▶ **wielki** ➲ note at **big** **4** [only before a noun] (informal) (used to emphasize adjectives of size, quantity, etc.) very; very good: *There was a **great big*** (bardzo duży) *dog in the garden.* ◇ *They were great friends.* ▶ **wielki**, **świetny** **5** (**great-**) (used before a noun to show a family relationship) ▶ **pra-**

> Przedrostek **great-** można dodać do innych słów oznaczających powinowactwo: *great-grandfather* pradziadek ◇ *great-grandmother* prababka ◇ *great-grandson* prawnuk ◇ *great-granddaughter* prawnuczka ◇ *great-grandchildren* prawnuki ◇ *great-grandparents* pradziadkowie ◇ *your great-great-grandfather* prapradziadek ◇ *your great-aunt* stryjeczna/cioteczna babka ◇ *your great-nephew* syn bratanka/bratanicy/siostrzeńca/siostrzenicy.

■ **greatness** noun [U] ▶ **wielkość**

IDM **go to great lengths** to make more effort than usual in order to achieve sth: *I went to great lengths to find this book for you.* ▶ **bardzo się starać**

a good/great deal → DEAL²

a good/great many → MANY

make great strides to make very quick progress ▶ **robić wielkie postępy**

great² /greɪt/ noun [C, usually pl.] (informal) a person or thing of special ability or importance: *That film is one of the all-time greats.* To jeden z największych filmów, jakie kiedykolwiek nakręcono. ▶ **osoba lub rzecz o szczególnym znaczeniu** ⓘ Rzeczownik **great** zwykle tłumaczy się przymiotnikiem „wielki" lub „największy".

,Great 'Britain (also **Britain** /'brɪtn/) noun [sing.] (abbr. **GB** /,dʒi: 'bi:/) England, Wales and Scotland ▶ **Wielka Brytania** ➲ note at **United Kingdom**

,Great 'Dane noun [C] a type of very large dog with short hair ▶ **dog**

greatly /'greɪtli/ adv. very much: *She will be greatly missed by friends and family.* Rodzina i przyjaciele będą za nią bardzo tęsknić. ▶ **ogromnie**

greed /gri:d/ noun [U] **greed (for sth)** a strong desire for more food, money, power, etc. than you really need ▶ **chciwość**, **zachłanność**

greedy /'gri:di/ adj. (**greedier**; **greediest**) **greedy (for sth)** wanting more food, money, power, etc. than you really need: *Don't be so greedy – you've had three pieces of cake already.* ▶ **chciwy**, **zachłanny**

■ **greedily** adv. ▶ **chciwie**, **zachłannie** | **greediness** noun [U] ▶ **chciwość**, **zachłanność**

green¹ /gri:n/ adj. **1** having the colour of grass or leaves: *dark/light/pale green* ▶ **zielony** **2** connected with protecting the environment or the natural world: *the Green Party* Partia Zielonych ◇ *green products* ▶ **zielony**, **ekologiczny** **3** (informal) with little experience of life or a particular job: *I'm not so green as to believe that!* ▶ (*niedoświadczony*) **zielony** **4** a strange, pale colour (because you feel sick): *At the sight of all the blood he **turned green*** (zbladł) *and fainted.* ▶ **blady**

IDM **give sb/get the green light** (informal) to give sb/get permission to do sth ▶ **zapalać/dostać zielone światło**

green with envy wanting to have what sb else has got: *He was **green with envy** when he saw his neighbour's new car.* ▶ **żółty** (*z zazdrości*) SYN **jealous**

have green fingers; US **have a green thumb** (informal) to have the ability to make plants grow well ▶ **mieć dobrą rękę do (uprawy) roślin**

green² /gri:n/ noun **1** [C,U] the colour of grass or leaves: *They were dressed in green* (na zielono). ◇ *The room was decorated in greens and blues.* ▶ **zieleń** **2** (**greens**) [pl.] green vegetables that are usually eaten cooked: *To have a healthy complexion you should eat more greens.* ▶ **warzywa zielone** (*np. kapusta, groszek*) **3** [C] (Brit.) an area of grass in the centre of a village: *the village green* ▶ **błonie wiejskie** **4** [C] a flat area of very short grass used in games such as **golf**: *the green at the 18th hole* ▶ **murawa** **5** (**the Greens**) [pl.] the Green Party ▶ (*polit.*) **Zieloni**

,green 'belt noun [C,U] (Brit.) an area of open land around a city where building is not allowed ▶ **pas/strefa zieleni**

'green card noun [C] a document that allows sb from another country to live and work legally in the US ▶ **zielona karta**

greenery /'gri:nəri/ noun [U] attractive green leaves and plants ▶ **zieleń**

greengage /'gri:ngeɪdʒ/ noun [C] a small round yellowish-green fruit ▶ **renkloda**

greengrocer /'gri:ngrəʊsə(r)/ noun (Brit.) **1** [C] a person who has a shop that sells fruit and vegetables ▶ **sprzedawca w sklepie warzywnym** ➲ look at **grocer** **2** (**the greengrocer's**) [sing.] a shop that sells fruit and vegetables ▶ **sklep warzywny**

greenhouse /'gri:nhaʊs/ noun [C] a small building made of glass in which plants are grown ▶ **szklarnia**, **cieplarnia** ➲ look at **glasshouse**, **hothouse**

the 'greenhouse effect noun [sing.] the warming of the earth's atmosphere as a result of harmful gases, etc. in the air ▶ **efekt cieplarniany** ➲ look at **global warming**

,greenhouse 'gas noun [C] a gas such as carbon dioxide that is thought to contribute to the rise in temperature of the earth's atmosphere ▶ **gaz cieplarniany**

greenish /'gri:nɪʃ/ adj. slightly green ▶ **zielonkawy**

,green 'onion (US) = SPRING ONION

,green 'pepper = PEPPER¹ (2)

greet /gri:t/ verb [T] **1 greet sb (with sth)** to welcome sb when you meet them; to say hello to sb: *He greeted me with a friendly smile.* ◇ (figurative) *As we entered the house we were greeted by the smell of cooking.* ▶ **witać** **2** [usually passive] **greet sb/sth (as/with sth)** to react to sb or receive sth in a particular way: *The news was greeted with a loud cheer.* ▶ **witać**, **przyjmować**

greeting /'gri:tɪŋ/ noun [C] **1** the first words you say when you meet sb or write to them: *'Hello' and 'Hi' are informal greetings.* ▶ **powitanie**, **pozdrowienie** **2** (**greetings**) [pl.] a good wish: *a greetings card* ▶ **życzenia**, **pozdrowienia**

gregarious /grɪ'geəriəs/ adj. liking to be with other people ▶ **towarzyski** SYN **sociable**

grenade /grə'neɪd/ noun [C] a small bomb that is thrown by hand or fired from a gun ▶ **granat**

grew past tense of **grow**

grey¹ (especially US **gray**) /greɪ/ adj. **1** having the colour between black and white: *dark/light/pale grey* ◇ *He was wearing a grey suit.* ▶ **szary** **2** having grey hair: *He's*

G

going grey (siwieje). ▶ **siwy 3** (used about the weather) full of cloud; not bright: *grey skies* ◇ *a grey day* ▶ **ponury 4** boring and sad; without interest or variety: *Life seems very grey and pointless since my wife died.* ▶ **nudny**

⚷ **grey²** (especially US **gray**) /ɡreɪ/ noun [C,U] the colour between black and white: *dressed in grey* ▶ **kolor szary**

greyhound /ˈɡreɪhaʊnd/ noun [C] a large thin dog that can run very fast and that is used for racing: *greyhound racing* ▶ **chart**

> Greyhound racing (at a **stadium** or **track**) is very popular in Britain. People **bet** on which dog is going to win the race.

greyish (especially US **grayish**) /ˈɡreɪɪʃ/ adj. slightly grey ▶ **szarawy**, (*o włosach*) **szpakowaty**

grid /ɡrɪd/ noun [C] **1** a pattern of straight lines that cross each other to form squares: *She drew a grid to show how the students had scored in each part of the test.* ▶ **krata, siatka 2** a frame of parallel metal or wooden bars, usually covering a hole in sth ▶ **krata 3** a system of squares that are drawn on a map so that the position of any place can be described or found: *a grid reference* ▶ **siatka geograficzna 4** the system of electricity wires, etc. taking power to all parts of a country: *the National Grid* ▶ **sieć energetyczna**

gridlock /ˈɡrɪdlɒk/ noun [U,C] a situation in which there are so many cars in the streets of a town that the traffic cannot move at all ▶ **korek/paraliż komunikacyjny**
■ **gridlocked** adj. ▶ **zakorkowany**

grief /ɡriːf/ noun [U] great sadness (especially because of the death of sb you love) ▶ **żałoba, żal**
IDM **good grief** (informal) (used for expressing surprise or shock): *Good grief! Whatever happened to you?* ▶ **o rany!**

grievance /ˈɡriːvəns/ noun [C] **a grievance (against sb)** something that you think is unfair and that you want to complain or protest about ▶ **skarga, zażalenie**

grieve /ɡriːv/ verb **1** [I] **grieve (for sb)** to feel great sadness (especially about the death of sb you love): *He is still grieving for his wife.* Jest jeszcze w żałobie po stracie żony. ▶ **być w żałobie/pogrążonym w żalu 2** [T] (formal) to cause unhappiness ▶ **martwić, zasmucać**

grill¹ /ɡrɪl/ noun [C] **1** a part of a cooker where the food is cooked by heat from above ▶ **ruszt w piecyku 2** a metal frame that you put food on to cook over an open fire ▶ **rożen, grill**

grill² /ɡrɪl/ verb [T] **1** (especially US **broil** /brɔɪl/) to cook under a **grill**: *grilled steak/chicken/fish* ▶ **grillować, piec na grillu** ➲ note at **cook 2** (informal) **grill sb (about sth)** to question sb for a long time ▶ **przepytywać, maglować (kogoś)**

grille (also **grill**) /ɡrɪl/ noun [C] a metal frame that is placed over a window, a piece of machinery, etc. ▶ **krata**

grim /ɡrɪm/ adj. (**grimmer**; **grimmest**) **1** (used about a person) very serious; not smiling ▶ **poważny, ponury 2** (used about a situation, news, etc.) unpleasant or worrying: *The news is grim, I'm afraid.* ▶ **nieprzyjemny, ponury 3** (used about a place) unpleasant to look at; not attractive: *a grim block of flats* ▶ **ponury, brzydki 4** [not before a noun] (Brit., informal) feeling ill: *I was feeling grim yesterday but I managed to get to work.* ▶ **chory**
■ **grimly** adv. ▶ **ponuro**

grimace /ˈɡrɪməs; ɡrɪˈmeɪs/ noun [C] an ugly expression on your face that shows that you are angry, disgusted or that sth is hurting you: *a grimace of pain* ▶ **grymas**
■ **grimace** verb [I]: *She grimaced with pain.* ▶ **robić grymas, wykrzywiać twarz w grymasie** (*np. bólu*)

grime /ɡraɪm/ noun [U] a thick layer of dirt ▶ **brud**

grimy /ˈɡraɪmi/ adj. (**grimier**; **grimiest**) very dirty ▶ **bardzo brudny** ➲ look at **filthy**

grin /ɡrɪn/ verb [I] (**grinning**; **grinned**) **grin (at sb)** to give a wide smile (so that you show your teeth): *She grinned at me as she came into the room.* ▶ **uśmiechać się szeroko**
■ **grin** noun [C] ▶ **szeroki uśmiech**

grind¹ /ɡraɪnd/ verb [T] (pt, pp **ground** /ɡraʊnd/) **1 grind sth (down/up)**; **grind sth (to/into sth)** to press and break sth into very small pieces or into a powder between two hard surfaces or in a special machine: *Wheat is ground into flour.* ◇ *ground pepper* pieprz mielony ▶ **mleć 2** to make sth sharp or smooth by rubbing it on a rough hard surface: *to grind a knife on a stone* ▶ **ostrzyć, szlifować 3 grind sth in/into sth** to press or rub sth into a surface: *He ground his cigarette into the ashtray.* ▶ **wciskać, wcierać 4** to rub sth together or make sth rub together, often producing an unpleasant noise: *Some people **grind** their **teeth*** (zgrzytają zębami) *while they're asleep.* ▶ **zgrzytać**
IDM **grind to a halt/standstill** to stop slowly ▶ **utknąć w martwym punkcie**
PHR V **grind sb down** to treat sb in a cruel unpleasant way over a long period of time, so that they become very unhappy ▶ **gnębić kogoś**
grind sth out to produce sth in large quantities, often sth that is not good or interesting: *She grinds out romantic novels at the rate of five a year.* ▶ **produkować coś** SYN **churn sth out**

grind² /ɡraɪnd/ noun [sing.] (informal) an activity that is tiring and boring and that takes a lot of time: *the **daily grind** of working life* ▶ **harówka**

grinder /ˈɡraɪndə(r)/ noun [C] a machine for **grinding**: *a coffee grinder* ▶ **młynek**

grip¹ /ɡrɪp/ noun **1** [sing.] **a grip (on sb/sth)** a firm hold (on sb/sth): *I relaxed my grip and he ran away.* ◇ *The climber slipped and lost her grip.* ◇ (figurative) *You need tyres that give a good grip* (które dobrze trzymają się szosy). ◇ *The teacher kept a firm grip on the class.* Nauczyciel panował nad klasą. ▶ **uchwyt, uścisk; panowanie 2** [sing.] **a grip (on sth)** an understanding of sth ▶ **opanowanie (czegoś) 3** [C] the person whose job it is to move the cameras while a film is being made ▶ **pomocni-k/ca kamerzysty**
IDM **come/get to grips with sth** to start to understand and deal with a problem ▶ **opanować**
get/keep/take a grip/hold (on yourself) (informal) to try to behave in a calmer or more sensible way; to control yourself ▶ **brać się w garść**
in the grip of sth experiencing sth unpleasant that cannot be stopped: *a country in the grip of recession* ▶ **w kleszczach czegoś**

grip² /ɡrɪp/ verb [I,T] (**gripping**; **gripped**) **1** to hold sb/sth tightly: *She gripped my arm in fear.* ▶ **ściskać, chwytać 2** to interest sb very much; to hold sb's attention: *The book grips you from start to finish.* ▶ **zawładnąć** (*umysłem, wyobraźnią*) ➲ adjective **gripping**

gripe /ɡraɪp/ noun [C] (informal) a statement complaining about sth ▶ **biadolenie** SYN **complaint**
■ **gripe** verb [I] ▶ **biadolić**

gripping /ˈɡrɪpɪŋ/ adj. exciting; holding your attention: *a gripping film/book* ▶ **trzymający w napięciu**

grisly /ˈɡrɪzli/ adj. (**grislier**; **grisliest**) extremely unpleasant and frightening and usually connected with death and violence: *a grisly crime/death/murder* ▶ **przerażający, makabryczny** ➲ look at **gruesome**

gristle /ˈɡrɪsl/ noun [U] a hard substance in a piece of meat that is unpleasant to eat: *a lump of gristle* ▶ **chrząstka**
■ **gristly** adj. ▶ **chrząstkowaty, łykowaty**

grit[1] /grɪt/ noun [U] **1** small pieces of stone or sand: *I've got some grit/a piece of grit in my shoe.* ▶ **kamyki** ➲ look at **gravel 2** (informal) courage; determination that makes it possible for sb to continue doing sth difficult or unpleasant ▶ **odwaga**, **determinacja**

grit[2] /grɪt/ verb [T] (**gritting**; **gritted**) to spread small pieces of stone and sand on a road that is covered with ice ▶ **posypywać żwirem**

IDM **grit your teeth 1** to bite your teeth tightly together: *She gritted her teeth against the pain as the doctor examined her injured foot.* ▶ **zaciskać zęby 2** to use your courage or determination in a difficult situation ▶ (*przen.*) **zaciskać zęby**

gritty adj. **1** containing or like grit: *a layer of gritty dust* ▶ **żwirowaty 2** showing the courage and determination to continue doing sth difficult or unpleasant: *gritty determination* ◇ *a gritty performance from the British player* ▶ **z zacięciem 3** showing sth unpleasant as it really is: *a gritty description of urban violence* ◇ *gritty realism* ▶ **ostry**, **konkretny** ➲ look at **nitty-gritty**

grizzle /ˈgrɪzl/ verb [I] (Brit., informal) (especially used about a baby or child) to cry or complain continuously in a way that is annoying ▶ **marudzić**

groan /grəʊn/ verb [I] **groan (at/with sth)** to make a deep sad sound because you are in pain, or to show that you are unhappy about sth: *He groaned with pain.* ◇ *They were all* ***moaning and groaning*** *about the amount of work they had to do.* ▶ **jęczeć**

■ **groan** noun [C] ▶ **jęk**

grocer /ˈgrəʊsə(r)/ noun **1** [C] a person who has a shop that sells food and other things for the home ▶ **sprzedawca w sklepie spożywczym** ➲ look at **greengrocer 2** (**the grocer's**) [sing.] a shop that sells food and other things for the home ▶ **sklep spożywczy** ➲ picture on **page A14**

grocery /ˈgrəʊsəri/ noun (pl. **groceries**) **1** (US usually ˈ**grocery store**) [C] a shop that sells food and other things used in the home. In American English 'grocery store' is often used to mean 'supermarket'. ▶ **sklep spożywczy 2** (**groceries**) [pl.] food and other goods sold by a **grocer** or at a supermarket: *Can you help me unload the groceries from the car, please?* ▶ **artykuły spożywcze**

groggy /ˈgrɒgi/ adj. (**groggier**; **groggiest**) (informal) weak and unable to walk steadily because you feel ill, have not had enough sleep, etc.: *She felt a bit groggy when she came round from the operation.* ▶ **słaniający się**

groin /grɔɪn/ noun [C] the front part of your body where it joins your legs ▶ **pachwina**

groom[1] /gruːm/ verb [T] **1** to clean or look after an animal by brushing, etc.: *to groom a horse/dog/cat* ▶ **obrządzać** (*konia*), **szczotkować** (*np. psa/kota*) **2** [usually passive] **groom sb (for/as sth)** to choose and prepare sb for a particular career or job ▶ **przygotowywać kogoś do objęcia stanowiska**

groom[2] /gruːm/ noun [C] **1** a person who looks after horses, especially by cleaning and brushing them ▶ **stajenny 2** = BRIDEGROOM

groove /gruːv/ noun [C] a long deep line that is cut in the surface of sth ▶ **rowek**, **wyżłobienie**

groovy /ˈgruːvi/ adj. (old-fashioned, informal) fashionable, attractive and interesting ▶ **kapitalny**

grope /grəʊp/ verb **1** [I] **grope (about/around) (for sth)** to search for sth or find your way using your hands because you cannot see: *He groped around for the light switch.* ▶ **szukać po omacku 2** [T] (informal) to touch sb sexually, especially when they do not want you to ▶ **macać**

gross[1] /grəʊs/ adj. **1** [only before a noun] being the total amount before anything is taken away: *gross income* ▶ **brutto**, **przed potrąceniem** ➲ look at **net 2** [only before a noun] (formal) very great or serious: *gross indecency/negligence/misconduct* ▶ **rażący 3** very rude and unpleasant ▶ **grubiański 4** very fat and ugly ▶ **monstrualny**, **opasły**

gross[2] /grəʊs/ verb

PHR V **gross sb out** (US, informal) to be very unpleasant and make sb feel disgusted ▶ (*i przen.*) **przyprawiać kogoś o mdłości** SYN **disgust**

grossly /ˈgrəʊsli/ adv. very: *grossly unfair* ▶ **rażąco**

grotesque /grəʊˈtesk/ adj. strange or ugly in a way that is not natural ▶ **groteskowy**

grotty /ˈgrɒti/ adj. (**grottier**; **grottiest**) (Brit., informal) unpleasant; of poor quality: *She lives in a grotty flat.* ▶ **marny**, **podły**

grouch /graʊtʃ/ noun [C] (informal) **1** a person who complains a lot ▶ **zrzęda 2** a complaint about sth unimportant ▶ **zrzędzenie**

■ **grouch** verb [I] ▶ **zrzędzić**

G

⚷ **ground**[1] /graʊnd/ noun **1** (**the ground**) [sing.] the solid surface of the earth: *We sat on the ground to eat our picnic.* ◇ *He slipped off the ladder and fell to the ground.* ◇ *waste ground* nieużytki ▶ **grunt**, **ziemia** ➲ look at **earth**, **land**, **soil 2** [U] an area or type of soil: *solid/marshy/stony ground* ▶ **gleba**, **ziemia 3** [C] a piece of land that is used for a particular purpose: *a sports ground* ◇ *a playground* ▶ **podwórko**, **boisko**, **plac** (*np. zabaw*) **4** (**grounds**) [pl.] land or gardens surrounding a large building: *the grounds of the palace* ▶ **teren**, **park 5** [U] an area of interest, study, discussion, etc.: *The lecture went over* ***the same old ground****/covered a lot of* ***new ground.*** ◇ *to be on dangerous ground* ▶ **obszar** (*zagadnień*), **materiał** (*w nauce*) **6** [C, usually pl.] **grounds (for sth/doing sth)** a reason for sth: *She retired* ***on*** *medical* ***grounds*** (z powodu złego stanu zdrowia). ◇ *grounds for divorce* ▶ **przyczyna**, **podstawa (do czegoś) 7** (US) = EARTH[1] (4)

IDM **above/below ground** above/below the surface of the earth ▶ **nad/pod ziemią**

break fresh/new ground to make a discovery or introduce a new method or activity ▶ **dokonywać odkrycia**, **przecierać szlak (w jakiejś dziedzinie)**

gain ground → GAIN[1]

get off the ground (used about a business, project, etc.) to make a successful start ▶ **ruszać z miejsca**

give/lose ground (to sb/sth) to allow sb to have an advantage; to lose an advantage for yourself: *They are not prepared to give ground on tax cuts.* ◇ *The Conservatives lost a lot of ground to the Liberal Democrats at the election.* ▶ **ustępować (komuś pola w jakiejś sprawie)**, **tracić pozycję (w stosunku do kogoś)**

hold/keep/stand your ground to refuse to change your opinion or to be influenced by pressure from other people ▶ **nie godzić się na ustępstwa**

thin on the ground → THIN[1]

ground

Earth to nazwa naszej planety. **Land** to ląd: *The sailors sighted land.* ◇ *The astronauts returned to Earth.* Ziemia, którą się kupuje lub sprzedaje, to również **land**: *The price of land in Tokyo is extremely high.* Ziemia, w której rosną rośliny, to **earth** lub **soil**. Kiedy jest się na dworze, powierzchnia ziemi nazywa się **the ground**. Kiedy jest się wewnątrz budynku, podłoga nazywa się **the floor**: *Don't sit on the ground. You'll get wet.* ◇ *Don't sit on the floor. I'll get another chair.*

ground[2] /graʊnd/ verb [T] **1** [usually passive] to force an aircraft, etc. to stay on the ground: *to be grounded by fog* ▶ **unieruchamiać**, **uziemiać 2** [usually passive] to punish a child by not allowing them to go out with friends for a period of time ▶ **zabronić dziecku wychodzenia z kolegami itp. 3** (US) = EARTH[2]

ground³ past tense, past participle of **grind**¹

ˌ**ground 'beef** (US) = MINCE

groundbreaking /'graʊndbreɪkɪŋ/ adj. [only before a noun] making new discoveries; using new methods: *a groundbreaking piece of research* ▶ **przełomowy**

'**ground crew** (also 'ground staff) noun [C,U] the people in an airport whose job it is to look after an aircraft while it is on the ground ▶ **załoga naziemna**

ˌ**ground 'floor** (US ˌfirst 'floor) noun [C] the floor of a building that is at ground level: *a ground-floor flat* mieszkanie na parterze ▶ **parter** ➲ note at **floor**

grounding /'graʊndɪŋ/ noun [sing.] **a grounding (in sth)** the teaching of the basic facts or principles of a subject: *This book provides a good grounding in grammar.* ▶ **podstawa**

groundless /'graʊndləs/ adj. having no reason or cause: *Our fears were groundless.* ▶ **bezpodstawny** ■ **groundlessly** ▶ **bezpodstawnie**

groundnut = PEANUT

'**ground rule** noun [C] **1** [usually pl.] a basic principle: *The new code of conduct lays down the ground rules for management-union relations.* ▶ **podstawy**, **zasady 2** (US) a rule adapted for a particular playing field ▶ (*baseball*) **zmodyfikowane reguły w zależności od boiska**

'**ground staff** = GROUND CREW

groundwork /'graʊndwɜːk/ noun [U] work that is done in preparation for further work or study ▶ **praca przygotowawcza**

⚷ **group**¹ /gruːp/ noun [C] **1** [with sing. or pl. verb] a number of people or things that are together in the same place or that are connected in some way: *a group of girls/trees/houses* ◇ *Students were standing* ***in groups*** *waiting for their exam results.* ◇ *He is in the 40-50* ***age group.*** ◇ *Many young people start smoking because of pressure from their peer group* (w wyniku presji rówieśników). ◇ *people of many different social groups* ◇ *a pressure group* grupa nacisku ◇ *Which blood group do you belong to?* ▶ **grupa**, **ugrupowanie** ℹ **Group** w lp może występować z czasownikiem w lp albo lm: *Our discussion group* ***is/are*** *meeting this week.* Mając na myśli poszczególnych członków grupy na ogół używa się czasownika w lm: *A group of us* ***are*** *planning to meet for lunch.* **2** (used in business) a number of companies that are owned by the same person or organization: *a newspaper group* ▶ **grupa 3** (old-fashioned) a number of people who play music together: *a pop group* ▶ **zespół muzyczny**, **grupa** SYN **band** ➲ note at **pop**

group² /gruːp/ verb [I,T] **group (sb/sth) (around/round sb/sth); group (sb/sth) (together)** to put sb/sth or to form into one or more groups: *Group these words according to their meaning.* ▶ **grupować**, **segregować**

grouse /graʊs/ noun [C] (pl. **grouse**) a fat brown bird with feathers on its legs that is shot for sport ▶ **cietrzew**

grove /grəʊv/ noun [C] a small group of trees, especially of one particular type: *an olive grove* ▶ **gaj**, **zagajnik**

grovel /'grɒvl/ verb [I] (**grovelling**; **grovelled**; US **groveling**; **groveled**) **1 grovel (to sb) (for sth)** to try too hard to please sb who is more important than you or who can give you sth that you want: *to grovel for forgiveness* ▶ **płaszczyć się (przed kimś) 2 grovel (around/about) (for sth)** to move around on your hands and knees (usually when you are looking for sth) ▶ **czołgać się**
■ **grovelling** adj. ▶ **płaszczący się**

⚷ **grow** /grəʊ/ verb (pt **grew** /gruː/, pp **grown** /grəʊn/) **1** [I] **grow (in sth)** to increase in size or number; to develop into an adult form: *a growing child* ◇ *She's growing in confidence* (nabiera pewności siebie) *all the time.* ◇ *You must invest if you want your business to grow.* ▶ **rosnąć**, **wzrastać 2** [I,T] (used about plants) to exist and develop in a particular place; to make plants grow by giving them water, etc.: *Palm trees don't grow in cold climates.* ◇ *We grow vegetables in our garden.* ▶ **rosnąć**; **uprawiać 3** [T] to allow your hair or nails to grow: *Claire's growing her hair long.* ◇ *to grow a beard/moustache* ▶ **zapuszczać** (*np. włosy*) **4** [I] to gradually change from one state to another; to become: *It began to grow dark.* ◇ *The teacher was growing more and more impatient.* ◇ *to grow older* starzeć się ◇ *to grow wiser* mądrzeć ◇ *to grow taller/bigger* ▶ **stawać się** ℹ Zamiast wyrazu **grow** można użyć mniej formalnego **get.**

PHR V **grow apart (from sb)** to stop having a close relationship with sb over a period of time ▶ **oddalać się (od kogoś)**

grow back to begin growing again after being cut off or damaged: *His eyebrows never grew back after the accident.* ▶ **odrastać**

grow into sth [no passive] **1** to gradually develop into a particular type of person: *She has grown into a very attractive young woman.* ▶ **wyrastać na kogoś/coś**, **zmienić się w coś 2** to become big enough to fit into clothes, etc.: *The coat is too big for him, but he will soon grow into it.* ▶ **dorastać do czegoś 3** to become more confident in a new job, etc. and learn to do it better: *She's still growing into her new role as a mother.* ▶ **dorastać do czegoś**

grow on sb to become more pleasing: *I didn't like ginger at first, but it's a taste that grows on you.* ▶ **dawać się polubić**

grow out of sth to become too big or too old for sth: *She's grown out of that dress I made her last year.* ▶ (*i przen.*) **wyrastać z czegoś**

grow (sth) out (used about the style in which you have your hair cut) to disappear gradually as your hair grows; to allow your hair to grow in order to change the style ▶ (*fryzura itp.*) **zarastać**; **zapuszczać** (*włosy*)

grow up 1 to develop into an adult: *What do you want to be when you grow up?* ◇ *She grew up in Spain.* ◇ *Oh, grow up!* Nie bądź dzieckiem! ▶ **dorastać**, **dojrzewać 2** (used about a feeling, etc.) to develop or become strong: *A close friendship has grown up between them.* ▶ **rosnąć**

growing /'grəʊɪŋ/ adj. [only before a noun] increasing: *A growing number of people are becoming vegetarian these days.* ▶ **narastający**

growl /graʊl/ verb [I] **growl (at sb/sth)** (used about dogs and other animals) to make a low noise in the throat to show anger or to give a warning ▶ **warczeć**, **ryczeć**
■ **growl** noun [C] ▶ **warczenie**, **ryk**

grown¹ past participle of **grow**

grown² /grəʊn/ adj. [only before a noun] physically an adult: *a fully-grown elephant* ▶ **dorosły**, **dojrzały**

ˌ**grown-'up**¹ adj. physically or mentally adult: *She's very grown-up for her age.* ▶ **dorosły**, **dojrzały** SYN **mature**

'**grown-up**² noun [C] (used by children) an adult person ▶ **osoba dorosła** SYN **adult**

⚷ **growth** /grəʊθ/ noun **1** [U] the process of growing and developing: *A good diet is very important for children's growth.* ◇ *a growth industry* (szybko) rozwijający się przemysł ▶ **wzrost**, **rozwój 2** [U, sing.] an increase (in sth): *population growth* ▶ **wzrost**, **przyrost 3** [C] a lump caused by a disease that grows in a person's or an animal's body: *a cancerous growth* ▶ **narośl 4** [U] something that has grown: *several days' growth* (kilkudniowy zarost) *of beard* ▶ **przyrost**

grub /grʌb/ noun **1** [C] the first form that an insect takes when it comes out of the egg. **Grubs** are short, fat and white. ▶ **larwa 2** [U] (informal) food ▶ **żarcie**

grubby /'grʌbi/ adj. (**grubbier**; **grubbiest**) (informal) dirty after being used and not washed ▶ **utytłany**, **umorusany**

grudge[1] /grʌdʒ/ noun [C] **a grudge (against sb)** unfriendly feelings towards sb, because you are angry about what has happened in the past: *to* ***bear a grudge*** *against somebody* mieć komuś coś za złe ▶ **uraza, żal**

grudge[2] /grʌdʒ/ verb [T] **grudge sb sth**; **grudge doing sth** to be unhappy that sb has sth or that you have to do sth: *I don't grudge him his success – he deserves it.* ◇ *I grudge having to pay so much tax.* ▶ **żałować czegoś komuś** ➲ look at **begrudge**

grudging /ˈgrʌdʒɪŋ/ adj. given or done although you do not want to: *grudging thanks* ▶ **niechętny**
■ **grudgingly** adv. ▶ **niechętnie**

gruelling (US **grueling**) /ˈgruːəlɪŋ/ adj. very tiring and long: *a gruelling nine-hour march* ▶ **wyczerpujący, męczący**

gruesome /ˈgruːsəm/ adj. very unpleasant or shocking, and usually connected with death or injury ▶ **makabryczny, potworny** ➲ look at **grisly**

gruff /grʌf/ adj. (used about a person or a voice) rough and unfriendly ▶ **gburowaty, burkliwy**
■ **gruffly** adv. ▶ **gburowato, burkliwie** | **gruffness** noun [U] ▶ **gburowatość, burkliwość**

grumble /ˈgrʌmbl/ verb [I] to complain in a bad-tempered way; to keep saying that you do not like sth: *The students were always grumbling about the standard of the food.* ▶ **narzekać, utyskiwać**

Grumble, moan lub **whinge** używa się, narzekając na coś, co nie spełnia naszych oczekiwań. Natomiast skarżąc się komuś lub wnosząc oficjalną skargę w celu zmiany sytuacji na lepsze, używa się czasownika **complain**.

■ **grumble** noun [C] ▶ **narzekanie, utyskiwanie**

grump /grʌmp/ noun [C] (informal) a bad-tempered person ▶ **złośni-k/ca**

grumpy /ˈgrʌmpi/ adj. (**grumpier**; **grumpiest**) (informal) bad-tempered ▶ **zły, naburmuszony**
■ **grumpily** adv. ▶ **mrukliwie** | **grumpiness** noun [U] ▶ **naburmuszenie**

grungy /ˈgrʌndʒi/ adj. (informal) dirty in an unpleasant way ▶ **brudny i niechlujny**

grunt /grʌnt/ verb [I,T] to make a short low sound in the throat. People **grunt** when they do not like sth or are not interested and do not want to talk: *I tried to find out her opinion but she just grunted.* ▶ **chrząkać, odmruknąć**
■ **grunt** noun [C] ▶ **chrząknięcie, mruknięcie**

⚷ **guarantee**[1] /ˌgærənˈtiː/ noun [C,U] **1** a firm promise that sth will be done or that sth will happen: *The refugees are demanding guarantees about their safety before they return home.* ▶ **poręczenie, gwarancja** **2** a written promise by a company that it will repair or replace a product if it breaks in a certain period of time: *The watch comes with a year's guarantee.* ◇ *Is the computer still* ***under guarantee****?* (na gwarancji) ▶ **gwarancja** ➲ look at **warranty** **3** something that makes sth else certain to happen: *If you don't have a reservation there's no guarantee that you'll get a seat on the train.* ▶ **gwarancja**

⚷ **guarantee**[2] /ˌgærənˈtiː/ verb [T] **1** to promise that sth will be done or will happen: *They have guaranteed delivery within one week.* ▶ **gwarantować, ręczyć** **2** to give a written promise to repair or replace a product if anything is wrong with it: *This washing machine is guaranteed for three years* (ma trzyletnią gwarancję). ▶ **gwarantować** **3** to make sth certain to happen: *Tonight's win guarantees the team a place in the final.* ▶ **gwarantować**

⚷ **guard**[1] /gɑːd/ noun **1** [C] a person who protects a place or people, or who stops prisoners from escaping: *a security guard* ▶ **strażnik** ➲ look at **warder**, **bodyguard** **2** [U] the state of being ready to prevent attack or danger: *Soldiers* ***keep guard*** *at the gate.* ◇ *Who is* ***on guard****?* ◇ *The prisoner arrived* ***under*** *armed* ***guard.*** ▶ **straż, warta** **3** [sing., with sing. or pl. verb] a group of soldiers, police officers, etc. who protect sb/sth: *The president always travels with an armed guard* (z uzbrojoną ochroną). ◇ *a guard of honour* warta honorowa ◇ *the changing of the guard* (zmiana warty) *at Buckingham Palace* ▶ **warta, straż** **4** [C] [in compounds] something that covers sth dangerous or protects sth: *a fireguard* krata ochronna przed kominkiem ◇ *a mudguard* błotnik ▶ **ochraniacz** **5** (US **conductor**) [C] a person who is in charge of a train but does not drive it ▶ **konduktor, kierownik pociągu** **6** [U] a position that you take to defend yourself, especially in sports such as **boxing**: (figurative) *She doesn't trust journalists, and never* ***lets her guard drop*** (zawsze ma się na baczności) *during interviews.* ▶ **czujność**
IDM **off/on (your) guard** not ready/ready for an attack, surprise, mistake, etc.: *The question caught me off (my) guard and I didn't know what to say.* ▶ **(być) zaskoczonym, (mieć się) na baczności**

⚷ **guard**[2] /gɑːd/ verb [T] **1** to keep sb/sth safe from other people; protect: *The building was guarded by men with dogs.* ◇ (figurative) *a closely guarded secret* ▶ **strzec, chronić** **2** to be ready to stop prisoners from escaping: *The prisoner was closely guarded on the way to court.* ▶ **strzec, pilnować**
PHR V **guard against sth** to try to prevent sth or stop sth happening ▶ **strzec przed czymś, zabezpieczać**

ˈ**guard dog** noun [C] a dog that is kept to guard a building ▶ **pies łańcuchowy (podwórzowy)**

guarded /ˈgɑːdɪd/ adj. (used about an answer, statement, etc.) careful; not giving much information or showing what you feel: *a guarded reply* ▶ **ostrożny** OPP **unguarded**
■ **guardedly** adv. ▶ **ostrożnie**

guardian /ˈgɑːdiən/ noun [C] **1** a person or institution that guards or protects sth: *The police are the guardians of law and order.* ▶ **stróż, obrońca** **2** a person who is legally responsible for the care of another person, especially of a child whose parents are dead ▶ **opiekun/ka**

guerrilla (also **guerilla**) /gəˈrɪlə/ noun [C] a member of a small military group who are not part of an official army and who make surprise attacks on the enemy: *guerrilla warfare* partyzantka ▶ **partyzant/ka**

⚷ **guess**[1] /ges/ verb **1** [I,T] **guess (at sth)** to try and give an answer or make a judgement about sth without being sure of all the facts: *I'd guess that he's about 45.* ◇ *If you're not sure of an answer, guess.* ◇ *We can only guess at her reasons for leaving.* ▶ **zgadywać, domyślać się** **2** [I,T] to guess correctly; to give the correct answer when you are not sure about it: *Can you guess my age?* ◇ *You'll never guess what Adam just told me!* ◇ *Did I guess right?* ▶ **zgadywać** **3** [T] (especially US, informal) to imagine that sth is probably true or likely; to suppose: *I guess you're tired after your long journey.* ▶ **przypuszczać** **4** [T] (used to show that you are going to say sth surprising or exciting): *Guess what!* (Nie uwierzysz!) *I'm getting married!*

⚷ **guess**[2] /ges/ noun [C] an effort you make to imagine a possible answer or give an opinion when you cannot be sure if you are right: *If you don't know the answer, then* ***have a guess*** (zgadnij)*!* ◇ *My guess is* (przypuszczam) *that they've been delayed by the traffic.* ◇ *I don't know how far it is, but* ***at a guess*** (na oko) *I'd say about 50 miles.* ◇ *I'd say it'll take about four hours, but that's just* ***a rough guess*** (ale to tylko przypuszczenie). ▶ **domniemanie**
IDM **anybody's/anyone's guess** something that nobody can be certain about: *What's going to happen next is anybody's guess.* ▶ **wielka niewiadoma**

your guess is as good as mine I do not know: *'Where's Ron?' 'Your guess is as good as mine.'* ▶ **wiem tyle, co ty; nie mam pojęcia**

guesstimate (also **guestimate**) /ˈgestɪmət/ noun [C] (informal) an attempt to calculate sth that is based more on guessing than on information ▶ **szacunkowe obliczenie**

guesswork /ˈgeswɜːk/ noun [U] an act of guessing: *I arrived at the answer* ***by pure guesswork.*** ▶ **zgadywanie, domysły**

guest /gest/ noun [C] **1** a person who is invited to a place or to a special event: *wedding guests* ◇ *Who is the guest speaker at the conference?* ▶ **gość 2** a person who is staying at a hotel, etc.: *This hotel has accommodation for 500 guests.* ▶ **gość hotelowy**
IDM **be my guest** (informal) (used to give sb permission to do sth that they have asked to do): *'Do you mind if I have a look at your newspaper?' 'Be my guest!'* ▶ **proszę bardzo**

ˈ**guest house** noun [C] a small hotel, sometimes in a private house ▶ **pensjonat**

guidance /ˈgaɪdns/ noun [U] **guidance (on sth)** help or advice: *The centre offers guidance for unemployed people on how to find work.* ▶ **porada, poradnictwo**

guide[1] /gaɪd/ noun [C] **1** a book, magazine, etc. that gives information or help on a subject: *Your Guide to Using the Internet* ◇ *Have we got a TV guide* (program telewizyjny) *for this week?* ▶ **przewodnik 2** (also **guidebook** /ˈgaɪdbʊk/) a book that gives information about a place to tourists or people who are travelling: *The guide says that it was built 500 years ago.* ▶ **przewodnik 3** a person who shows tourists or people who are travelling where to go: *She works as a* ***tour guide*** *in Venice.* ▶ **przewodnik/czka 4** something that helps you to judge or plan sth: ***As a rough guide,*** *use* (ogólna wskazówka jest taka, aby używać) *twice as much water as rice.* ▶ **wskazówka 5** (**Guide**) a member of an organization called **the Guides** that teaches girls practical skills and organizes activities such as camping ▶ **harcerka** ➲ look at **Scout**

guide[2] /gaɪd/ verb [T] **1** to help a person or a group of people to find the way to a place; to show sb a place that you know well: *He guided us through the busy streets to our hotel.* ▶ **prowadzić, nakierowywać** ➲ note at **lead 2** to have an influence on sb/sth: *I was guided by your advice.* ▶ **kierować 3** to help sb deal with sth difficult or complicated: *The manual will guide you through every step of the procedure.* ▶ **(po)prowadzić 4** to carefully move sb/sth or to help sb/sth to move in a particular direction: *A crane lifted the piano and two men carefully guided it through the window.* ▶ **kierować**

guided /ˈgaɪdɪd/ adj. led by a **guide**: *a guided tour/walk* ▶ **z przewodnikiem**

ˌ**guided ˈmissile** noun [C] a missile that can be guided to its destination by electronic devices while in flight ▶ **pocisk kierowany**

ˈ**guide dog** noun [C] a dog trained to **guide** a person who is unable to see ▶ **pies przewodnik**

guideline /ˈgaɪdlaɪn/ noun [C] **1** [usually pl.] official advice or rules on how to do sth ▶ **wytyczna, zalecenie 2** something that can be used to help you make a decision or form an opinion: *These figures are a useful guideline when buying a house.* ▶ (*przen.*) **wskazówka**

guild /gɪld/ noun [C, with sing. or pl. verb] an organization of people who do the same job or who have the same interests or aims: *the Screen Actors' Guild* ▶ **stowarzyszenie, cech**

guile /gaɪl/ noun [U] (formal) the use of clever but dishonest behaviour in order to trick people: *George was a man completely lacking in guile.* ▶ **przebiegłość** SYN **deceit**

guillotine /ˈgɪlətiːn/ noun [C] **1** a machine that was used in France in the past for cutting people's heads off ▶ **gilotyna 2** a machine used for cutting paper ▶ **gilotyna**
■ **guillotine** verb [T] ▶ **ścinać na gilotynie**

guilt /gɪlt/ noun [U] **1 guilt (about/at sth)** the unpleasant feelings that you have when you know or think that you have done sth bad: *I sometimes feel guilt about not spending more time with my children.* ▶ **wina 2** the fact of having broken a law: *We took his refusal to answer questions as an admission of guilt.* ◇ *His guilt was not proved* (nie udowodniono mu winy) *and so he went free.* ▶ **przekroczenie prawa** OPP **innocence 3** the responsibility for doing sth wrong or for sth bad that has happened: *It's difficult to say whether the guilt lies with the parents or the children.* ▶ **wina** SYN **blame**

guilty /ˈgɪlti/ adj. (**guiltier**; **guiltiest**) **1 guilty (about sth)** having an unpleasant feeling because you have done sth bad: *I* ***feel*** *really* ***guilty*** *about lying to Sam.* ◇ ***a guilty conscience*** nieczyste sumienie ▶ **winny 2 guilty (of sth)** having broken a law; being responsible for doing sth wrong: *She* ***pleaded (not) guilty*** *to the crime.* (Nie) przyznała się do winy. ◇ *to be guilty of murder* ◇ *The jury* ***found*** *him* ***guilty*** *of fraud.* ▶ **winny** OPP **innocent**
■ **guiltily** adv. ▶ **z poczuciem winy**

guinea pig /ˈgɪni pɪg/ noun [C] **1** a small animal with no tail that is often kept as a pet ▶ **świnka morska** ➲ note at **pet 2** a person who is used in an experiment: *I volunteered to act as a guinea pig in their research into dreams.* ▶ **królik doświadczalny**

guise /gaɪz/ noun [C] a way in which sb/sth appears, which is often different from usual or hides the truth: *The President was at the meeting* ***in his guise as*** (jako) *chairman of the charity.* ◇ *His speech presented racist ideas* ***under the guise of*** (pod płaszczykiem) *nationalism.* ▶ **pozór**

guitar /gɪˈtɑː(r)/ noun [C] a type of musical instrument with strings that you play with your fingers or with a **plectrum** ▶ **gitara** ➲ look at **piano** ➲ note at **music**

guitarist /gɪˈtɑːrɪst/ noun [C] a person who plays the **guitar** ▶ **gitarzyst(k)a**

gulf /gʌlf/ noun **1** [C] a part of the sea that is almost surrounded by land: *the Gulf of Mexico* ▶ **zatoka** ➲ look at **bay**[1] **2** (**the Gulf**) [sing.] the Persian Gulf ▶ **Zatoka Perska 3** [C] an important or serious difference between people in the way they live, think or feel: *the gulf between rich and poor* ▶ **przepaść**

gull /gʌl/ (also **seagull** /ˈsiːgʌl/) noun [C] a white or grey bird that makes a loud noise and lives near the sea ▶ **mewa**

gullet /ˈgʌlɪt/ noun [C] the tube through which food pases from your mouth to your stomach ▶ **przełyk** ℹ Bardziej formalnym słowem jest **oesophagus.**

gullible /ˈgʌləbl/ adj. (used about a person) believing and trusting people too easily, and therefore easily tricked ▶ **łatwowierny**

gulp[1] /gʌlp/ verb **1** [I,T] **gulp sth (down)**; **gulp (for) sth** to swallow large amounts of food, drink, etc. quickly: *He gulped down his breakfast and went out.* ◇ *She finally came to the surface, desperately gulping (for) air.* ▶ **połykać w pośpiechu 2** [I] to make a swallowing movement because you are afraid, surprised, etc. ▶ **przełykać (ślinę)** (*z emocji*)

gulp[2] /gʌlp/ noun [C] **1 a gulp (of sth)** the amount that you swallow when you **gulp** ▶ **łyk 2** the act of breathing in or swallowing sth: *I drank my coffee* ***in one gulp*** (jednym haustem) *and ran out of the door.* ▶ **przełknięcie, złapanie powietrza**

gum /gʌm/ noun **1** [C] either of the firm pink parts of your mouth that hold your teeth ▶ **dziąsło** ➲ picture at **body 2** [U] a substance that you use to stick things together (especially pieces of paper) ▶ **klej 3** = CHEWING GUM

'gum tree noun [C] a **eucalyptus** tree ▶ **eukaliptus**

gun[1] /gʌn/ noun [C] **1** a weapon that is used for shooting: *The robber held a gun to the bank manager's head.* ▶ **broń palna**

> Verbs often used with 'gun' are **load**, **unload**, **point**, **aim**, **fire**. Different types of gun include a **machine-gun**, **pistol**, **revolver**, **rifle** and **shotgun**.

2 a tool that uses pressure to send out a substance or an object: *a grease gun* towotnica ◇ *a staple gun* rodzaj zszywacza ▶ **rodzaj narzędzia** (*wyrzucającego pod ciśnieniem płyn/rzecz*)
IDM **jump the gun** → JUMP[1]

gun[2] /gʌn/ verb [T] (**gunning**; **gunned**)
PHR V **gun sb down** (informal) to shoot and kill or seriously injure sb ▶ **zastrzelić, postrzelić**

gunboat /'gʌnbəʊt/ noun [C] a small ship used in war that carries heavy guns ▶ **kanonierka**

gunfire /'gʌnfaɪə(r)/ noun [U] the repeated firing of guns: *We could hear gunfire.* ▶ **wystrzał, strzelanie**

gunge /gʌndʒ/ (especially US **gunk** /gʌŋk/) noun [U] (informal) any unpleasant, sticky or dirty substance ▶ **maź**
■ **gungy** adj. ▶ **mazisty**

gunk (especially US) = GUNGE

gunman /'gʌnmən/ noun [C] (pl. **-men** /-mən/) a man who uses a gun to steal from or kill people ▶ **uzbrojony bandyta**

gunpoint /'gʌnpɔɪnt/ noun
IDM **at gunpoint** threatening to shoot sb: *He held the hostages at gunpoint.* ▶ **na muszce**

gunpowder /'gʌnpaʊdə(r)/ noun [U] a powder that can explode and is used in guns, etc. ▶ **proch strzelniczy**

gunshot /'gʌnʃɒt/ noun [C] the firing of a gun or the sound that it makes ▶ **wystrzał**

gurgle /'gɜːgl/ verb [I] **1** to make a sound like water flowing quickly through a narrow space: *a gurgling stream* ▶ **gulgotać, bulgotać 2** if a baby **gurgles**, it makes a noise in its throat because it is happy ▶ **gaworzyć**
■ **gurgle** noun [C] ▶ **gulgot, bulgot; gaworzenie**

guru /'gʊruː/ noun [C] **1** a spiritual leader or teacher in the Hindu religion ▶ **guru 2** a person whose opinions you admire and respect, and whose ideas you follow: *a management/fashion guru* ▶ **mistrz, guru**

gush /gʌʃ/ verb **1** [I] **gush (out of/from/into sth)**; **gush out/in** (used about a liquid) to flow out suddenly and in great quantities: *Blood gushed from the wound.* ◇ *I turned the tap on and water gushed out.* ▶ **tryskać 2** [T] (used about a container/vehicle, etc.) to produce large amounts of a liquid: *The broken pipe was gushing water all over the road.* ▶ **wyrzucać/wylewać potoki czegoś 3** [I,T] to express pleasure or admiration so much that it does not sound sincere ▶ **rozpływać się nad kimś/czymś**
■ **gush** noun [C]: *a sudden gush of water* ▶ **tryśnięcie**

gust /gʌst/ noun [C] a sudden strong wind ▶ **poryw wiatru**
■ **gust** verb [I] ▶ **wiać porywiście**

gusto /'gʌstəʊ/ noun
IDM **with gusto** with great enthusiasm: *They sang with great gusto.* ▶ **z werwą/zapałem**

gut[1] /gʌt/ noun **1** [C] the tube in the body that food passes through when it leaves the stomach ▶ **kiszka, jelito** ℹ Zob. **intestine**, które jest terminem bardziej naukowym. **2** (**guts**) [pl.] the organs in and around the stomach, especially of an animal ▶ **wnętrzności 3** [C] a person's fat stomach ▶ **kałdun, brzuszysko 4** (**guts**) [pl.] (informal) courage and determination: *It **takes guts** to admit that you are wrong.* ◇ *I don't **have the guts** to tell my boss what he's doing wrong.* ▶ **odwaga**
IDM **work/sweat your guts out** to work extremely hard ▶ **wypruwać z siebie flaki**

gut[2] /gʌt/ verb [T] (**gutting**; **gutted**) **1** to destroy the inside of a building: *The warehouse was gutted by fire.* ▶ **zniszczyć wnętrze budynku 2** to remove the organs from inside an animal, fish, etc. ▶ **patroszyć**

gut[3] /gʌt/ adj. [only before a noun] based on emotion or feeling rather than on reason: *a gut feeling/reaction* ▶ **odruchowy**

gutter /'gʌtə(r)/ noun [C] **1** a long piece of metal or plastic with a curved bottom that is fixed to the edge of a roof to carry away the water when it rains ▶ **rynna 2** a lower part at the edge of a road along which the water flows away when it rains ▶ **ściek, rynsztok 3** the very lowest level of society: *She rose from the gutter to become a great star.* ▶ **rynsztok**

guy /gaɪ/ noun **1** [C] (informal) a man or a boy: *He's a nice guy.* ▶ **facet, chłop/ak 2** (**guys**) [pl.] (informal) (used when speaking to a group of men and women): *What do you guys want to eat?* Co chcecie zjeść? ▶ (*zwracając się do grupy ludzi*) **wy tam! ludzie! 3** [sing.] (Brit.) a model of a man that is burned on 5 November in memory of Guy Fawkes ▶ **słomiana kukła palona 5 listopada dla upamiętnienia spisku Guya Fawkesa** ➲ look at **Bonfire Night**

guzzle /'gʌzl/ verb [I,T] (informal) to eat or drink too fast and too much ▶ **zażerać się**

gym /dʒɪm/ noun **1** (also formal **gymnasium** /dʒɪm'neɪziəm/ (pl. **gymnasiums** or **gymnasia** /-zɪə/) [C] a large room or a building with equipment for doing physical exercise: *I work out at the gym twice a week.* ▶ **sala gimnastyczna, siłownia 2** [U] = GYMNASTICS

gymnasium = GYM (1)

gymnast /'dʒɪmnæst/ noun [C] a person who does **gymnastics** ➲ picture on **page A9** ▶ **gimnasty-k/czka**

gymnastics /dʒɪm'næstɪks/ (also **gym**) noun [U] physical exercises that are done inside a building, often using special equipment such as bars and ropes: *I did gymnastics at school.* ▶ **gimnastyka** ➲ picture on **page A9**

gynaecology (US **gynecology**) /ˌgaɪnə'kɒlədʒi/ noun [U] the study and treatment of the diseases and medical problems of women ▶ **ginekologia**
■ **gynaecological** (US **gynecological**) /ˌgaɪnəkə'lɒdʒɪkl/ adj. ▶ **ginekologiczny** | **gynaecologist** (US **gynecologist**) /ˌgaɪnə'kɒlədʒɪst/ noun [C] ▶ **ginekolog**

Gypsy (also **Gipsy**) /'dʒɪpsi/ noun [C] (pl. **Gypsies**) a member of a race of people who traditionally spend their lives travelling around from place to place, living in **caravans** ▶ **Rom/ka, Cygan/ka** ➲ look at **traveller**

Hh

H, h /eɪtʃ/ noun [C,U] (pl. **Hs**; **hs**; **H's**; **h's** /'eɪtʃɪz/) the 8th letter of the English alphabet: *'Hat' begins with (an) 'H'.* ▶ **litera** *h*

ha[1] /hɑː/ interj. **1** (used for showing that you are surprised or pleased): *Ha! I knew he was hiding something!* ▶ **ha! 2** (**ha! ha!**) (used in written language to show that sb is laughing) ▶ **ha! ha! 3** (**ha! ha!**) (used to show that you do not think that sth is funny) ▶ **cha, cha, cha!**

ha[2] = HECTARE

haberdashery /ˌhæbə'dæʃəri; US 'hæbəd-/ noun (pl. **-ies**) **1** [U] (old-fashioned) (Brit.) small articles for sewing, for example needles, pins, cotton and buttons ▶ **pasmanteria 2** [C] a shop or part of a shop where **haberdashery** is sold ▶ **pasmanteria; stoisko pasmanteryjne**

habit /'hæbɪt/ noun **1** [C] **a/the habit (of doing sth)** something that you do often and almost without thinking, especially sth that is hard to stop doing: *I'm trying to* ***get into the habit*** *of* (przyzwyczaić się do) *hanging up my clothes every night.* ◇ *I don't mind you being late this time, but don't* ***make a habit of it*** (ale nie rób tego więcej). ◇ *Once you start smoking it's hard to* ***break the habit*** (zerwać z nałogiem). ▶ **zwyczaj, nawyk** ➲ adjective **habitual**

> **Habit** oznacza właściwy jednostce sposób postępowania. **Custom** oznacza sposób postępowania charakterystyczny dla grupy ludzi, społeczności lub narodu: *the custom of giving presents at Christmas.*

2 [U] usual behaviour: *I think I only smoke* ***out of habit*** (z przyzwyczajenia) *now – I don't really enjoy it.* ▶ **przyzwyczajenie**
IDM **force of habit** → FORCE[1]
kick the habit → KICK[1]

habitable /ˈhæbɪtəbl/ adj. (used about buildings) suitable to be lived in ▶ **mieszkalny** OPP **uninhabitable**

habitat /ˈhæbɪtæt/ noun [C] the natural home of a plant or an animal: *I've seen wolves in the zoo, but not in their natural habitat.* ▶ **środowisko naturalne** (*roślin i zwierząt*)

habitation /ˌhæbɪˈteɪʃn/ noun [U] the act of living in a place: *These houses are not fit for human habitation* (nie nadają się do zamieszkania). ▶ **zamieszk(iw)anie**

habitual /həˈbɪtʃuəl/ adj. **1** which you always have or do; usual: *He had his habitual cigarette after lunch.* ▶ **zwykły, zwyczajowy 2** [only before a noun] doing sth very often: *a habitual criminal/drinker/liar* ▶ **nałogowy**
■ **habitually** /-tʃuəli/ adv. ▶ **zwykle**; **nałogowo**

hack /hæk/ verb [I,T] **1 hack (away) (at) sth** to cut sth in a rough way with a tool such as a large knife: *He hacked away at the bushes.* ▶ **siekać, rąbać 2** (informal) **hack (into) (sth)** to use a computer to look at and/or change information that is stored on another computer without permission ▶ **uprawiać piractwo komputerowe**

ˌhacked ˈoff adj. [not before a noun] (Brit., informal) extremely annoyed ▶ **wściekły** SYN **fed up**

hacker /ˈhækə(r)/ noun [C] (informal) a person who secretly looks at and/or changes information on sb else's computer system without permission ▶ **pirat komputerowy, haker**

had[1] /hæd; həd/ past tense, past participle of **have**

had[2] /hæd/ adj.
IDM **be had** (informal) to be tricked: *I've been had. This watch I bought doesn't work.* ▶ **okantowany**

hadn't /ˈhædnt/ short for **had not**

haemoglobin (US **hemoglobin**) /ˌhiːməˈɡləʊbɪn/ noun [U] a red substance in the blood that carries **oxygen** and contains iron ▶ **hemoglobina**

haemophilia (US **hemophilia**) /ˌhiːməˈfɪliə/ noun [U] a disease that causes a person to lose a lot of blood even from very small injuries because the blood does not **clot** ▶ **hemofilia**

haemophiliac (US **hemophiliac**) /ˌhiːməˈfɪliæk/ noun [C] a person who suffers from **haemophilia** ▶ **osoba chora na hemofilię**

haemorrhage (US **hemorrhage**) /ˈhemərɪdʒ/ noun [C,U] the loss of a lot of blood inside the body ▶ **krwotok**
■ **haemorrhage** verb [I] ▶ **krwawić**

haemorrhoids (especially US **hemorrhoids**) /ˈhemərɔɪdz/ (also **piles** /paɪlz/) noun [pl.] a medical condition in which the **veins** to the **anus** swell and become painful ▶ **hemoroidy**

hag /hæɡ/ noun [C] an ugly and/or unpleasant old woman ▶ **wiedźma**

haggard /ˈhæɡəd/ adj. (used about a person) looking tired or worried ▶ **wymizerowany, zmizerniały**

haggis /ˈhæɡɪs/ noun [C,U] a Scottish dish that looks like a large round sausage made from the heart, lungs and liver of a sheep that are finely chopped, mixed with oats, herbs, etc. and boiled in a bag that is usually made from part of a sheep's stomach ▶ **szkocka potrawa z baraniny podobna do kaszanki**

haggle /ˈhæɡl/ verb [I] **haggle (with sb) (over/about sth)** to argue with sb until you reach an agreement, especially about the price of sth: *In the market, some tourists were haggling over the price of a carpet.* ▶ **targować się**

hail[1] /heɪl/ verb **1** [T] **hail sb/sth as sth** to say in public that sb/sth is very good or very special: *The book was hailed as a masterpiece.* ◇ *A student who rescued a boy from a river is being hailed as a hero.* ▶ **ogłaszać/okrzykiwać kogoś/coś kimś/czymś 2** [T] to call or wave to sb/sth: *to hail a taxi* ▶ **za/wołać 3** [I] when it **hails**, small balls of ice fall from the sky like rain ▶ (*grad*) **padać** ➲ note at **weather**

hail[2] /heɪl/ noun **1** [U] small balls of ice, called **hailstones**, that fall from the sky like rain ▶ **grad 2** [sing.] **a hail of sth** a large amount of sth that is aimed at sb in order to harm them: *a hail of bullets/stones/abuse* ▶ (*przen.*) **grad, potok** (*np. wyzwisk*)

hailstone /ˈheɪlstəʊn/ noun [usually pl.] a small ball of ice that falls like rain ▶ **ziarnko gradu**

hailstorm /ˈheɪlstɔːm/ noun [C] a storm during which hail falls from the sky ▶ **burza gradowa**

hair /heə(r)/ noun **1** [U,C] the mass of long thin things that grow on the head and body of people and animals; one of these things: *He has got short black hair.* ◇ *Dave's losing his hair.* ◇ *The dog left hairs all over the furniture.* ▶ **włosy**; **włos** ➲ picture at **body 2 (-haired)** adj. [in compounds] having the type of hair mentioned: *a dark-haired woman* ◇ *a long-haired* (długowłosy) *rabbit* ▶ **(określa rodzaj włosów) 3** a thing that looks like a very thin thread that grows on the surface of some plants: *The leaves and stem are covered in fine hairs.* ▶ (*bot.*) **włos(ek)**
IDM **keep your hair on** (informal) (used to tell sb to stop shouting and become less angry) calm down ▶ **nie gorączkować się**
let your hair down (informal) to relax and enjoy yourself after being formal ▶ **rozluźnić się**
make sb's hair stand on end to frighten or shock sb ▶ **sprawiać, że komuś włosy stają dęba**
not turn a hair to not show any reaction to sth that many people would find surprising or shocking ▶ **niczego po sobie nie pokazać, nawet nie mrugnąć okiem** (*w trudnej sytuacji*)
split hairs → SPLIT[1]

> **hair**
> Some special words for the colour of hair are: **blond(e), fair, ginger, auburn** or **red.** As people get older they might **go grey.** In order to make your hair tidy or **style** it you **brush** or **comb** it. You wash it with **shampoo** and use a **hairdryer** to **blow-dry** it. You can **part** it/have a **parting** in the middle or on one side, and you might have a **fringe** (US **bangs**). When you **go to the hairdresser's** you can **have your hair cut** or **trimmed**. You might also **have it permed** or **coloured**. A **barber** is a male hairdresser who only cuts men's hair.

hairband /ˈheəbænd/ noun [C] a strip of cloth or curved plastic worn by women in their hair, that fits closely over the top of the head and behind the ears ▶ **opaska na włosy**

hairbrush /ˈheəbrʌʃ/ noun [C] a brush that you use on your hair ▶ **szczotka do włosów** ➲ picture at **brush**

haircut /ˈheəkʌt/ noun [C] **1** the act of sb cutting your hair: *You need (to have) a haircut.* Musisz się ostrzyc.

▶ **strzyżenie** (*włosów*) **2** the style in which your hair has been cut: *That haircut really suits you.* ▶ **fryzura**

hairdo (informal) = HAIRSTYLE

⚷**hairdresser** /ˈheədresə(r)/ noun **1** [C] a person whose job is to cut, shape, colour, etc. hair ▶ **fryzjer/ka** ➲ look at **barber** ➲ picture on **page A4** **2** (**the hairdresser's**) [sing.] the place where you go to have your hair cut: *I've made an appointment at the hairdresser's for 10 o'clock.* ▶ **salon/zakład fryzjerski**

hairdryer (also **hairdrier**) /ˈheədraɪə(r)/ noun [C] a machine that dries hair by blowing hot air through it ▶ **suszarka do włosów**

hairgrip /ˈheəɡrɪp/ (US ˈ**bobby pin**) noun [C] a piece of wire that is folded in the middle and used for holding hair in place ▶ **spinka do włosów** ➲ look at **hairpin**

hairless /ˈheələs/ adj. without hair ▶ **bezwłosy** ➲ look at **bald**

hairline¹ /ˈheəlaɪn/ noun [C] the edge of sb's hair, especially at the front ▶ **granica włosów**

hairline² /ˈheəlaɪn/ adj. (used about a crack in sth) very thin: *a hairline fracture of the leg* ▶ **bardzo cienki**

hairpin /ˈheəpɪn/ noun [C] a piece of wire, shaped like a U, used for holding hair in place ▶ **spinka do włosów** ➲ look at **hairgrip**

ˌ**hairpin ˈbend** (US ˌ**hairpin ˈcurve**; ˌ**hairpin ˈturn**) noun [C] (Brit.) a very sharp bend in a road, especially a mountain road ▶ **serpentyna** (*drogi*)

ˈ**hair-raising** adj. that makes you very frightened: *a hair-raising experience* ▶ **sprawiający, że włosy jeżą się na głowie**

hairspray /ˈheəspreɪ/ noun [U,C] a substance you spray onto your hair to hold it in place ▶ **lakier do włosów** SYN **lacquer**

hairstyle /ˈheəstaɪl/ (also informal **hairdo** /ˈheəduː/) noun [C] the style in which your hair has been cut or arranged ▶ **fryzura**

hairstylist /ˈheəstaɪlɪst/ (also **stylist**) noun [C] a person whose job it is to cut and shape sb's hair ▶ **stylist(k)a**

hairy /ˈheəri/ adj. (**hairier**; **hairiest**) **1** having a lot of hair ▶ **owłosiony, włochaty** **2** (slang) dangerous or worrying ▶ **przerażający**

hajj (also **haj**) /hædʒ/ noun [sing.] the **pilgrimage** to Mecca that many Muslims make ▶ (*religia muzułmańska*) **hadż**

halal /ˈhælæl/ adj. [only before a noun] (used about meat) from an animal that has been killed according to Muslim law ▶ (*religia muzułmańska, mięso*) **pochodzące z uboju rytualnego**

⚷**half**¹ /hɑːf; US hæf/ determiner, pron., noun [C] (pl. **halves** /hɑːvz; US hævz/) one of two equal parts of sth: *three and a half kilos of potatoes* ◇ *Two halves make a whole.* ◇ *half an hour* ◇ *an hour and a half* półtorej godziny ◇ *The second half of the book is more exciting.* ◇ *Ronaldo scored in the first half.* ◇ *Two halves* (dwa małe) *of bitter, please.* ◇ *Half of this money is yours.* ◇ *Half the people in the office leave at 5.* ▶ **połowa, pół** ➲ verb **halve**

IDM **break, cut, etc. sth in half** to break, etc. sth into two parts ▶ **łamać/ciąć na pół**

go half and half/go halves with sb (Brit.) to share the cost of sth with sb ▶ **dzielić się po połowie (kosztem)**

do nothing/not do anything by halves to do whatever you do completely and properly ▶ **wywiązywać się doskonale** (*z pracy itp.*)

⚷**half**² /hɑːf; US hæf/ adv. not completely: *half full* ◇ *The hotel was only **half finished**.* ◇ *He's half German.* ◇ *I half thought* (prawie myślałem) *he might come, but he didn't.* ▶ **do połowy, w połowie**

IDM **half past ...** (in time) 30 minutes past an hour: *half past six* (= 6.30) wpół do siódmej ❶ W mówionym Br. ang. „wpół do siódmej" może również wystąpić jako **half six**. ▶ **wpół do** (*danej godziny*)

hair

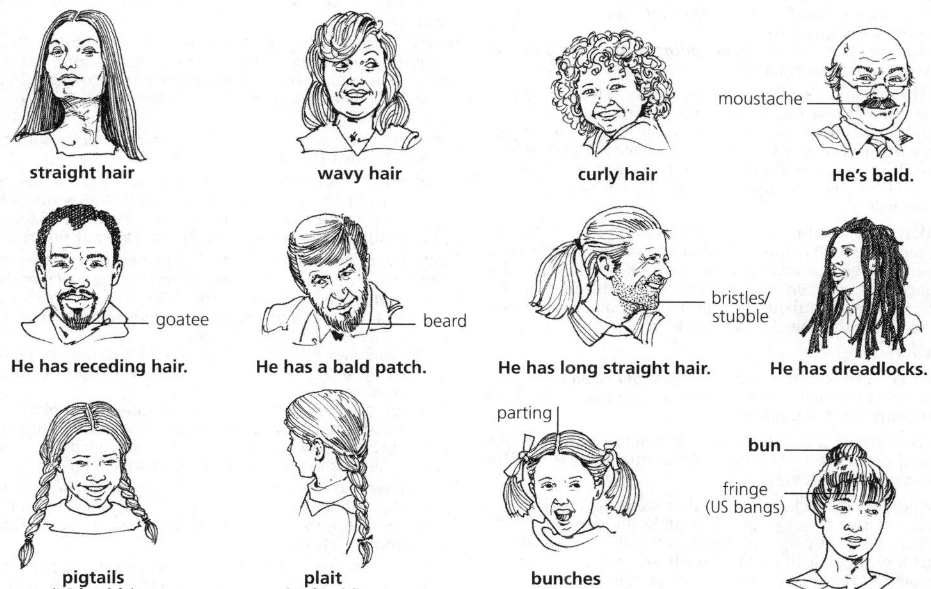

not half as much, many, good, bad, etc. much less: *This episode wasn't half as good* (był o wiele gorszy) *as the last.* ▶ **o wiele mniej/gorszy itp.**

ˌhalf-ˈbaked adj. (informal) not thought about or planned well: *a half-baked idea/scheme* ▶ **niedopracowany, nieprzemyślany do końca**

ˌhalf ˈboard noun [U] (Brit.) a price for a room in a hotel, etc. which includes breakfast and an evening meal ▶ **z częściowym wyżywieniem** ➲ note at **hotel** ➲ look at **full board, bed and breakfast**

ˈhalf-brother noun [C] a brother with whom you share one parent ▶ **brat przyrodni** ➲ look at **stepbrother**

ˌhalf-ˈhearted adj. without interest or enthusiasm ▶ **bez entuzjazmu, wymuszony**
■ **half-heartedly** adv. ▶ **bez entuzjazmu**

ˈhalf-life noun [C] the time taken for the **radioactivity** of a substance to fall to half its original value ▶ **okres połowicznego rozpadu**

ˈhalf note (US) = MINIM

ˌhalf-ˈprice adj. costing half the usual price: *a half-price ticket* ▶ **za połowę ceny, ze zniżką 50 %**
■ **ˌhalf-ˈprice** adv.: *Children aged under four go half-price.* ▶ **za połowę ceny**

ˈhalf-sister noun [C] a sister with whom you share one parent ▶ **siostra przyrodnia** ➲ look at **stepsister**

ˈhalf step (US) = SEMITONE

ˌhalf-ˈterm noun [C] (Brit.) a short holiday in the middle of one of the periods into which a school year is divided ▶ **krótka przerwa w połowie semestru szkolnego**

ˌhalf-ˈtime noun [U] (in sport) the period of time between the two halves of a match ▶ **połowa (meczu)**

ˈhalf-tone (US) = SEMITONE

halfway /ˌhɑːfˈweɪ; US ˌhæf-/ adv. at an equal distance between two places; in the middle of a period of time: *They have a break halfway through the morning.* ▶ **w połowie drogi/czasu**
■ **halfway** adj.: *the* ***halfway point/stage*** ▶ **w połowie drogi/czasu** SYN **midway**

hall /hɔːl/ noun [C] **1** (also **hallway** /ˈhɔːlweɪ/) a room or passage that is just inside the front entrance of a house or public building: *There is a public telephone in the* ***entrance hall*** *of this building.* ▶ **przedpokój, hol 2** a building or large room in which meetings, concerts, dances, etc. can be held: *a concert hall* ▶ **sala** ➲ look at **town hall**

hallmark /ˈhɔːlmɑːk/ noun [C] **1** a characteristic that is typical of sb: *The ability to motivate students is the hallmark of a good teacher.* ▶ **cecha charakterystyczna 2** a mark that is put on objects made of valuable metals, giving information about the quality of the metal and when and where the object was made ▶ **próba** (*np. złota*)

hallo = HELLO

ˌhall of ˈresidence noun [C] (pl. **halls of residence**) (US **dormitory**) (in colleges, universities, etc.) a building where students live ▶ **akademik**

Halloween (also **Hallowe'en**) /ˌhæləʊˈiːn/ noun [sing.] the night of October 31st (before All Saints' Day) ▶ **wigilia Wszystkich Świętych**

> Jak głosi tradycja, w czasie **Halloween** pojawiają się czarownice i duchy. Dzieci przebierają się za czarownice, duchy itp. Chodzą po domach i mówią **trick or treat**. Jeśli odwiedzani ludzie nie dadzą im słodyczy (**treat**), wówczas dzieci płatają im figle (**trick**).

hallucinate /həˈluːsɪneɪt/ verb [I] to see or hear things that are not really there because of illness or drugs ▶ **mieć halucynacje**

hallucination /həˌluːsɪˈneɪʃn/ noun [C,U] seeing or hearing sth that is not really there (because you are ill or have taken a drug) ▶ **halucynacja**

hallucinogenic /həˌluːsɪnəˈdʒenɪk/ adj. (used about a drug) affecting people's minds and making them see and hear things that are not really there: ***hallucinogenic drugs/effects*** ▶ **halucynogenny**

hallway = HALL (1)

halo /ˈheɪləʊ/ noun [C] (pl. **halos** or **haloes**) the circle of light that is drawn around the head of an important religious person in a painting ▶ **aureola**

halt /hɔːlt/ noun [sing.] a stop (that does not last very long): *Work* ***came to a halt*** (praca stanęła) *when the machine broke down.* ◇ *to bring sth to a halt* zatrzymywać coś ▶ **postój, zatrzymanie się**
■ **halt** [I,T] verb (formal): *An accident halted the traffic in the town centre for half an hour.* ▶ **przystawać; zatrzymywać**
IDM **grind to a halt/standstill** → GRIND[1]

halter /ˈhɔːltə(r); Brit. also ˈhɒlt-/ noun [C] **1** a rope or narrow piece of leather put around the head of a horse for leading it with ▶ **postronek 2** [usually used as an adjective] a narrow piece of cloth around the neck that holds a woman's dress or shirt in position, with the back and shoulders not covered: *She was dressed in a halter top* (w zawiązaną na szyi bluzkę bez pleców i rękawów) *and shorts.*

halve /hɑːv; US hæv/ verb **1** [I,T] to reduce by a half; to make sth reduce by a half: *Shares in the company have halved in value.* ◇ *We aim to halve the number of people on our waiting list in the next six months.* ▶ **zmniejszać o połowę 2** [T] to divide sth into two equal parts: *First halve the peach and then remove the stone.* ▶ **dzielić na pół**

halves plural of **half**

ham /hæm/ noun [U] meat from a pig's back leg that has been **cured** ▶ **szynka** ➲ note at **meat** ➲ look at **bacon, gammon, pork**

hamburger /ˈhæmbɜːɡə(r)/ noun **1** (also **burger** /ˈbɜːɡə(r)/) [C] meat that has been cut up small and pressed into a flat round shape. **Hamburgers** are often eaten in a bread roll. ▶ **hamburger** ➲ look at **beefburger 2** [U] (US) = MINCE

hamlet /ˈhæmlət/ noun [C] a very small village ▶ **wioska, osada**

hammer[1] /ˈhæmə(r)/ noun [C] **1** a tool with a heavy metal head that is used for hitting nails, etc. ▶ **młotek** ➲ picture at **tool 2** (**the hammer**) a sports event in which a metal ball attached to a wire is thrown ▶ **rzut młotem**

hammer[2] /ˈhæmə(r)/ verb **1** [I,T] **hammer sth (in/into/onto sth)** to hit with a hammer: *She hammered the nail into the wall.* ▶ **uderzać młotem, stukać 2** [I] to hit sth several times, making a loud noise: *He hammered on the door until somebody opened it.* ▶ **walić**
PHR V **hammer sth into sb** to make sb learn or remember sth by repeating it many times ▶ **wbijać komuś coś do głowy**
hammer sth out 1 to succeed in making a plan or agreement after a lot of discussion ▶ **wypracowywać, osiągnąć (z trudem) 2** to hammer sth back into the shape that it should be ▶ **wyklepywać** (*metal*)

hammering /ˈhæmərɪŋ/ noun **1** [U] the noise that is made by sb using a hammer or by sb hitting sth many times ▶ **stukanie 2** [C] (Brit., informal) a very bad defeat ▶ **sromotna klęska**

hammock /ˈhæmək/ noun [C] a bed, made of rope or strong cloth, which is hung up between two trees or poles ▶ **hamak**

hamper[1] /ˈhæmpə(r)/ verb [T, usually passive] to make sth difficult: *The building work was hampered by bad weather.* ▶ **przeszkadzać**

hamper[2] /ˈhæmpə(r)/ noun [C] a large **basket** with a lid that is used for carrying food ▶ **kosz z pokrywą**

hamster /ˈhæmstə(r)/ noun [C] a small animal that is kept as a pet. **Hamsters** are like mice but are fatter and do not have a tail. They store food in the sides of their mouths. ▶ **chomik** ➲ note at **pet**

hamstring /ˈhæmstrɪŋ/ noun [C] **1** one of the five **tendons** behind the knee that connect the muscles of the upper leg to the bones of the lower leg: *a hamstring injury* ◇ *She's pulled a hamstring.* ▶ **ścięgno podkolanowe 2** a **tendon** behind the middle joint (= **hock**) of the back leg of a horse and some other animals ▶ **ścięgno stawu kolanowego**

hand[1] /hænd/ noun **1** [C] the part of your body at the end of your arm which has five fingers: *He **took** the child **by the hand**.* ◇ *She was on her hands and knees looking for an earring.* ◇ *He held the bird in the palm of his hand* (na dłoni). ▶ **ręka** ➲ look at **arm**[1] ➲ picture at **body**, **kneel 2** (**-handed**) adj. [in compounds] having, using or made for the type of hand(s) mentioned: *right-handed/left-handed* ◇ *heavy-handed* niezręczny ◇ *left-handed scissors* nożyce dla leworęcznych ▶ **(*określa cechy rąk*) 3** (**a hand**) [sing.] (informal) some help: *I'll give you a hand with the washing up.* ◇ *Do you want/need a hand?* ▶ **pomoc 4** [C] the part of a clock or watch that points to the numbers: *the hour/minute/second hand* ▶ **wskazówka 5** [C] a person who does physical work on a farm, in a factory, etc.: *farmhands* ◇ *All hands on deck!* Wszyscy na pokład! ▶ **robotni-k/ca 6** [C] the set of playing cards that sb has been given in a game of cards: *to be dealt a good/bad hand* ▶ **rozdanie kart**

IDM **(close/near) at hand** (formal) near in space or time: *Help is close at hand.* ▶ **blisko**

be an old hand (at sth) → OLD

by hand 1 done by a person and not by machine: *I had to do all the sewing by hand.* ▶ **ręcznie 2** not by post: *The letter was delivered by hand.* ▶ **doręczony osobiście**

catch sb red-handed → CATCH[1]

change hands → CHANGE[1]

a firm hand → FIRM[2]

(at) first hand (used about information that you have received) from sb who was closely involved: *Did you get this information first hand?* ▶ (*informacja*) **z pierwszej ręki** ➲ look at **second-hand**

get, have, etc. a free hand → FREE[1]

get, have, etc. the upper hand → UPPER

get/lay your hands on sb (informal) to catch sb: *Just wait till I get my hands on that boy!* ▶ **dostać kogoś w swoje ręce**

get/lay your hands on sth to find or obtain sth: *I need to get my hands on a good computer.* ▶ **znajdować, dostawać**

give sb a big hand → BIG

hand in hand 1 holding each other's hands: *The couple walked hand in hand along the beach.* ▶ **trzymając się za ręce 2** usually happening together; closely connected: *Drought and famine usually go hand in hand.* ▶ **w parze z czymś, jednocześnie**

your hands are tied to not be in a position to do as you would like because of rules, promises, etc.: *I'd like to help but my hands are tied.* ▶ **mieć związane ręce**

hands off (sb/sth) (informal) (used for ordering sb not to touch sb/sth) ▶ **ręce przy sobie!**

hands up 1 (used in a school, etc. for asking people to lift one hand and give an answer): *Hands up who'd like to go on the trip this afternoon?* ▶ **podnieście ręce 2** (used by a person with a gun to tell other people to put their hands in the air) ▶ **ręce do góry!**

have sb eating out of your hand → EAT

have a hand in sth to take part in or share sth: *Even members of staff had a hand in painting and decorating the new office.* ▶ **mieć w czymś udział**

have your hands full to be very busy so that you cannot do anything else ▶ **być bardzo zajętym/zapracowanym**

a helping hand → HELP[1]

hold sb's hand to give sb support in a difficult situation: *I'll come to the dentist's with you to hold your hand.* ▶ **pomagać, pocieszać**

hold hands (with sb) (used about two people) to hold each other's hands ▶ **trzymać się za ręce**

in hand 1 (used about money, etc.) not yet used: *If you have time in hand at the end of the exam, check what you have written.* ▶ (*pieniądze itp.*) **niewydany 2** being dealt with at the moment; under control: *The situation is in hand.* ▶ **rozpatrywany; pod kontrolą** OPP **(get/be) out of hand**

in your hands; in the hands of sb in your possession, control or care: *The matter is in the hands of a solicitor.* ◇ *She is in capable hands* (w dobrych rękach). ▶ **we władaniu/zarządzaniu, w czyichś rękach**

in safe hands → SAFE[1]

keep your hand in to do an activity from time to time so that you do not forget how to do it or lose the skill: *I play tennis from time to time just to keep my hand in.* ▶ **nie wychodzić z wprawy**

know sth like the back of your hand → KNOW[1]

lend (sb) a hand/lend a hand (to sb) → LEND

off your hands not your responsibility any more ▶ (*mieć*) **z głowy**

on hand available to help or to be used: *There is always an adult on hand to help when the children are playing outside.* ▶ **pod ręką, do pomocy**

on your hands being your responsibility: *We seem to have a problem on our hands.* ▶ (*przen.*) **na głowie**

on the one hand ... on the other (hand) (used for showing opposite points of view): *On the one hand, of course, cars are very useful. On the other hand, they cause a huge amount of pollution.* ▶ **z jednej strony ... z drugiej strony**

(get/be) out of hand not under control: *Violence at football matches is getting out of hand.* ▶ **(wymykać się) z rąk** OPP **in hand**

out of your hands not in your control; not your responsibility: *I can't help you, I'm afraid. The matter is out of my hands.* ▶ **poza czyjąś kontrolą**

shake sb's hand/shake hands (with sb)/shake sb by the hand → SHAKE[1]

to hand near or close to you: *I'm afraid I haven't got my diary to hand.* ▶ **pod ręką, w zasięgu ręki**

try your hand at sth → TRY[1]

turn your hand to sth to have the ability to do sth: *She can turn her hand to all sorts of jobs.* ▶ **mieć umiejętność wykonywania czegoś**

wash your hands of sb/sth → WASH[1]

with your bare hands → BARE

hand[2] /hænd/ verb [T] **hand sb sth; hand sth to sb** to give or pass sth to sb ▶ **podawać, wręczać**

IDM **have (got) to hand it to sb** (used to show admiration and approval of sb's work or efforts): *You've got to hand it to Rita – she's a great cook.* ▶ **to zasługa kogoś, uznawać (wyższość) kogoś**

PHR V **hand sth around/round** to offer to pass sth, especially food and drinks, to all the people in a group ▶ **częstować wszystkich, podawać**

hand sth back (to sb) to give or return sth to the person who owns it or to where it belongs ▶ **zwracać coś komuś**

hand sth down (to sb) 1 to pass customs, etc. from older people to younger ones: *These stories have been handed*

down from generation to generation. ▶ **przekazywać** (*potomności*) **2** to pass clothes, toys, etc. from older children to younger ones in the family ▶ **przekazywać** (*młodszemu rodzeństwu*)
hand sth in (to sb) to give sth to sb in authority, especially a piece of work or sth that is lost: *I found a wallet and handed it in to the police.* ◇ *She handed in her resignation.* Złożyła rezygnację. ▶ **wręczać**, **oddawać**
hand sth on (to sb) to send or give sth to another person: *When you have read the article, please hand it on to another student.* ▶ **przekazywać**
hand sth out (to sb) to give sth to many people in a group: *Food was handed out to the starving people.* ▶ **wydawać** (*komuś*)
hand (sth) over (to sb) to give sb else your position of power or the responsibility for sth: *She resigned as chairperson and handed over to one of her younger colleagues.* ▶ **przekazywać coś komuś**, **przenosić na kogoś** (*np. odpowiedzialność*)
hand (sb) over to sb (used at a meeting or on the TV, radio, telephone, etc.) to let sb speak or listen to another person ▶ **przekazywać (kogoś) komuś**
hand sb/sth over (to sb) to give sb/sth (to sb): *People were tricked into handing over large sums of money.* ▶ **oddawać/wręczać kogoś/coś (komuś)**
hand sth round = HAND STH AROUND/ROUND

handbag /ˈhændbæg/ (US **purse**) noun [C] a small bag in which women carry money, keys, etc. ▶ **torebka damska** SYN **shoulder bag** ➲ picture at **bag**

ˈ**hand baggage** (especially US) = HAND LUGGAGE

handbook /ˈhændbʊk/ noun [C] a small book that gives instructions on how to use sth or advice and information about a particular subject ▶ **podręcznik** ➲ look at **manual**[2]

handbrake /ˈhændbreɪk/ (US eˈ**mergency brake**; ˈ**parking brake**) noun [C] a device that is operated by hand to stop a car from moving when it is parked ▶ **hamulec ręczny** ➲ picture at **car**

ˈ**hand cream** noun [U] cream that you put on your hands to prevent dry skin ▶ **krem do rąk**

handcuffs /ˈhændkʌfs/ (also **cuffs**) noun [pl.] a pair of metal rings that are joined together by a chain and put around the wrists of prisoners ▶ **kajdanki**

handful /ˈhændfʊl/ noun **1** [C] **a handful (of sth)** as much or as many of sth as you can hold in one hand: *a handful of sand* ▶ **garść 2** [sing.] a small number (of sb/sth): *Only a handful of people came to the meeting.* ▶ **garstka 3** (**a handful**) [sing.] (informal) a person or an animal that is difficult to control: *The little girl is quite a handful.* ▶ **nieposłuszny**; **narowisty**

handgun /ˈhændgʌn/ noun [C] a small gun that you can hold and fire with one hand ▶ **broń ręczna**

handicap[1] /ˈhændikæp/ noun **1** [C,U] (old-fashioned) = DISABILITY ℹ Obecnie słowo to często uważa się za obraźliwe. **2** [C] something that makes doing sth more difficult; a disadvantage: *Not speaking French is going to be a bit of a handicap in my new job.* ▶ **przeszkoda**, **zawada 3** [C] a disadvantage that is given to the strongest people competing in a sports event, etc. so that the weaker people have more chance ▶ (*sport*) **wyrównanie szans**

handicap[2] /ˈhændikæp/ verb [T] (**handicapping**; **handicapped**) [usually passive] to give or be a disadvantage to sb: *They were handicapped by their lack of education.* ▶ **utrudniać**, **przeszkadzać**

handicapped (old-fashioned) ℹ Obecnie słowo to często uważa się za obraźliwe. = DISABLED

handicraft /ˈhændikrɑːft; US -kræft/ noun **1** [C] an activity that needs skill with the hands as well as artistic ability, for example sewing ▶ **rękodzieło 2** (**handicrafts**) [pl.] the objects that are produced by this activity ▶ **rękodzieła**

handiwork /ˈhændiwɜːk/ noun [U] **1** a thing that you have made or done, especially using your artistic skill: *We admired her exquisite handiwork.* ▶ **własne/własnoręczne dzieło 2** a thing done by a particular person or group, especially sth bad: *This looks like the handiwork of criminals.* ▶ (*przen., zwł. o czymś złym*) **robota**

handkerchief /ˈhæŋkətʃɪf; Brit. also -tʃiːf/ noun [C] (pl. **handkerchiefs** or **handkerchieves** /-tʃiːvz/) (also **hanky** /ˈhæŋki/, (pl. **hankies**) a square piece of cloth or soft thin paper that you use for clearing your nose ▶ **chusteczka do nosa** ℹ W mowie potocznej używa się słowa **hanky**. Chustka papierowa nazywa się **paper handkerchief** lub **tissue**.

🔑 **handle**[1] /ˈhændl/ verb [T] **1** to deal with or to control sb/sth: *I have a problem at work and I don't really know how to handle it.* ◇ *This port handles* (przeładowuje) *100 million tons of cargo each year.* ▶ **załatwiać**, **uporać się**, **zajmować się 2** to touch or hold sth with your hand(s): *Wash your hands before you handle food.* ◇ *Handle with care!* Ostrożnie! ▶ **dotykać**
■ **handler** noun [C]: *baggage/dog/food handlers* ▶ **zajmujący się czymś**

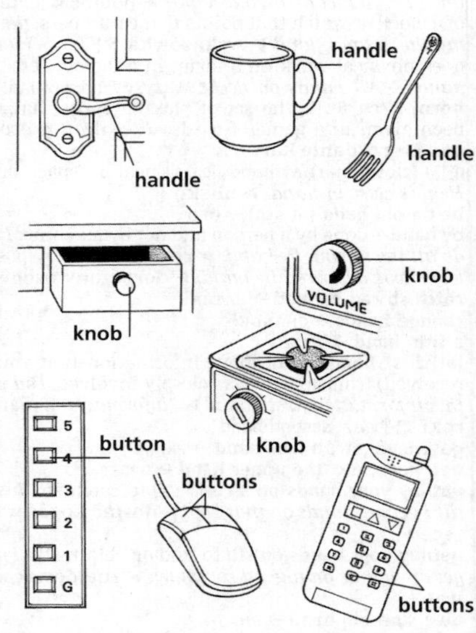

🔑 **handle**[2] /ˈhændl/ noun [C] a part of sth that is used for holding or opening it: *She turned the handle and opened the door.* ◇ *He broke the handle off the cup by accident.* ▶ **rączka**, **klamka**, **uchwyt**, **ucho**, **rękojeść** ➲ picture at **bag**
IDM **fly off the handle** → FLY[1]

handlebar /ˈhændlbɑː(r)/ noun [C, usually pl.] the metal bar at the front of a bicycle that you hold when you are riding it ▶ **kierownica** (*roweru*) ➲ picture at **bicycle**

ˈ**hand luggage** noun [U] a small bag, etc. that you can keep with you on a plane ▶ **bagaż podręczny**

handmade /ˌhændˈmeɪd/ adj. made by hand and of very good quality, not by machine ▶ **ręcznej roboty**

handout /ˈhændaʊt/ noun [C] **1** food, money, etc. given to people who need it badly ▶ **jałmużna 2** a free document that is given to a lot of people, to advertise sth or explain sth, for example in a class ▶ **ulotka**; **informacja na piśmie** (*objaśniająca coś na lekcji lub wykładzie*)

ˌhand-ˈpicked adj. carefully or personally chosen for a special purpose ▶ **wyselekcjonowany**

handrail /ˈhændreɪl/ noun [C] a long narrow wooden or metal bar at the side of some steps, a bath, etc. that you hold for support or balance ▶ **poręcz**, **bariera**

handset = RECEIVER (1)

ˈhands-free adj. if a mobile, etc. is **hands-free**, you can use it without needing to hold it in your hand: *hands-free mobile phones* ▶ **telefon komórkowy ze słuchawkami itp.**

handshake /ˈhændʃeɪk/ noun [C] the act of shaking sb's right hand with your own when you meet them ▶ **uścisk dłoni**

handsome /ˈhænsəm/ adj. **1** (used about a man) attractive ▶ **przystojny** ➲ note at **beautiful 2** (used about money, an offer, etc.) large or generous: *a handsome profit* ▶ (*zysk*) **duży**, **hojny**
■ **handsomely** adv.: *Her efforts were handsomely rewarded.* ▶ **hojnie**

ˌhands-ˈon adj. learnt by doing sth yourself, not watching sb else do it; practical: *She needs some hands-on computer experience.* ▶ **bezpośredni**

handstand /ˈhændstænd/ noun [C] a movement in which you balance on your hands and put your legs straight up in the air: *Can you do handstands?* ▶ **stanie na rękach**

handwriting /ˈhændraɪtɪŋ/ noun [U] sb's style of writing by hand ▶ **charakter pisma**

handwritten /ˌhændˈrɪtn/ adj. written by hand, not typed or printed ▶ **pisany ręcznie**

handy /ˈhændi/ adj. (**handier**; **handiest**) **1** easy to use: *a handy tip* ◇ *a handy gadget* ▶ **poręczny**; **wygodny w użyciu** SYN **useful 2 handy (for sth/doing sth)** within easy reach of sth; in a convenient place: *Always keep a first-aid kit handy for emergencies.* ◇ *The house is very handy for the shops* (blisko sklepów). ▶ **pod ręką**, **bliski 3** skilful in using your hands or tools to make or repair things: *James is very handy around the house.* ▶ **zręczny**
IDM **come in handy** to be useful at some time: *Don't throw that box away. It may come in handy.* ▶ **okazać się przydatnym**, **przydawać się kiedyś**

handyman /ˈhændimæn/ noun [sing.] a person who is clever at making or repairing things, especially around the house ▶ **złota rączka**

hang¹ /hæŋ/ verb (pt, pp **hung** /hʌŋ/) ℹ Czasu przeszłego i imiesłowu biernego **hanged** używa się tylko w znaczeniu 2. **1** [I,T] to fasten sth or be fastened at the top so that the lower part is free or loose: *Hang your coat on the hook.* ◇ *I left the washing hanging on the line all day.* Zostawiłem pranie rozwieszone na zewnątrz na cały dzień. ◇ *A cigarette hung* (zwisał) *from his lips.* ◇ *People were hanging out* (wychylali się) *of windows to see the Queen go past.* ▶ **wieszać 2** [T] (pt, pp **hanged** /hæŋd; US /) to kill sb/yourself by putting a rope around the neck and allowing the body to drop downwards: *He was hanged for murder.* ▶ **wieszać (kogoś) 3** [I] **hang (above/over sb/sth)** to stay in the air in a way that is unpleasant or threatening: *Smog hung in the air over the city.* ▶ **wisieć**
IDM **be/get hung up (about/on sb/sth)** to think about sb/sth all the time in a way that is not healthy or good: *She's really hung up about her parents' divorce.* ▶ **myśleć o czymś obsesyjnie**
hang (on) in there (informal) to have courage and keep trying, even though a situation is difficult: *The worst part is over now. Just hang on in there and be patient.* ▶ **trzymać się**
PHR V **hang about/around** (informal) to stay in or near a place not doing very much ▶ **obijać się**
hang back 1 to not want to do or say sth, often because you are shy or not sure of yourself ▶ **ociągać się 2** to stay in a place after other people have left it ▶ **pozostawać gdzieś na dłużej** (*po wyjściu innych*)
hang on 1 to hold sth tightly: *Hang on, don't let go!* ▶ **kurczowo się trzymać 2** (informal) to wait for a short time: *Hang on a minute. I'm nearly ready.* ▶ **czekać przez chwilę**
hang on sth to depend on sth ▶ **zależeć od czegoś**
hang on to sth 1 to hold sth tightly: *He hung on to the child's hand as they crossed the street.* ▶ **kurczowo się trzymać (czegoś) 2** (informal) to keep sth: *Let's hang on to the car for another year.* ▶ **zatrzymywać (coś)**
hang out (informal) to spend a lot of time in a place: *The local kids hang out at the park.* ▶ **przesiadywać**
hang sth out to put washing, etc. on a clothes line so that it can dry ▶ **wieszać** (*pranie*)
hang over sb to be present or about to happen in a way which is unpleasant or threatening: *This essay has been hanging over me for days.* ▶ **wisieć nad kimś**
hang together to fit together well; to be the same as or **consistent** with each other: *Their accounts of what happened don't hang together.* ▶ **pasować do siebie**
hang up to end a telephone conversation and put the telephone down ▶ **odkładać słuchawkę**, **zakończyć rozmowę telefoniczną** ➲ note at **telephone**
hang sth up to put sth on a nail, hook, etc.: *Hang your coat up over there.* ▶ **wieszać**
hang up on sb (informal) to end a telephone conversation without saying goodbye because you are angry ▶ **rzucić słuchawkę, gdy w złości na kogoś kończy się rozmowę telefoniczną**

hang² /hæŋ/ noun
IDM **get the hang of (doing) sth** (informal) to learn how to use or do sth: *It took me a long time to get the hang of my new computer.* ▶ **połapać się w czymś**

hangar /ˈhæŋə(r)/ noun [C] a big building where planes are kept ▶ **hangar**

hanged past tense, past participle of **hang¹** (2)

hanger /ˈhæŋə(r)/ (also ˈ**coat hanger**; ˈ**clothes hanger**) noun [C] a metal, plastic or wooden object with a hook that is used for hanging up clothes in a cupboard ▶ **wieszak**

ˌhanger-ˈon noun [C] (pl. **hangers-on**) a person who tries to be friendly with sb who is rich or important ▶ **pochlebca** (*w stosunku do kogoś bogatego/ważnego*)

ˈhang-glider noun [C] a type of frame covered with cloth, which a person holds and flies through the air with as a sport ▶ **lotnia** ➲ look at **glider**
■ **hang-gliding** noun [U]: *to go hang-gliding* ▶ **lotniarstwo**

hanging /ˈhæŋɪŋ/ noun [C,U] death as a form of punishment for a crime, caused by putting rope around a person's neck and letting the body drop downwards ▶ **powieszenie** (*kara śmierci*)

hangman /ˈhæŋmən/ noun [sing.] **1** a person whose job is to kill criminals as a form of punishment by hanging them with a rope ▶ **kat 2** a word game where the aim is to guess all the letters of a word before a picture of a person hanging is completed ▶ **gra w wisielca**

hangover /ˈhæŋəʊvə(r)/ noun [C] pain in your head and a sick feeling that you have if you have drunk too much alcohol the night before ▶ **kac**

ˈhang-up noun [C] (informal) **a hang-up (about sb/sth)** an emotional problem about sth that makes you embarrassed or worried: *He has a real hang-up about his height.* ▶ **kompleks** (*np.niższości*)

hanker /ˈhæŋkə(r)/ verb [I] **hanker after/for sth** to want sth very much (often sth that you cannot easily have) ▶ **bardzo chcieć czegoś**

hanky (informal) = HANDKERCHIEF

Hanukkah /ˈhænʊkə/ noun [U] an eight-day Jewish festival and holiday in November or December ▶ **Chanuka**

haphazard /hæpˈhæzəd/ adj. with no particular order or plan; badly organized ▶ **przypadkowy**, **chaotyczny** ■ **haphazardly** adv. ▶ **przypadkowo**, **na chybił trafił**

happen /ˈhæpən/ verb [I] **1** (used about an event or situation) to take place, usually without being planned first: *Can you describe to the police what happened after you left the party?* ◇ *How did the accident happen?* ▶ **zdarzać się**

Happen i **occur** używa się zwykle w odniesieniu do nie planowanych wydarzeń. **Occur** jest bardziej formalne niż **happen**. **Take place** sugeruje, że wydarzenie zostało zaplanowane: *The wedding took place on Saturday June 13th.*

2 happen to sb/sth to be what sb/sth experiences: *What do you think has happened to Julie? She should have been here an hour ago.* ◇ *What will happen to the business when your father retires?* ▶ **stawać się**, **przytrafiać się** **3 happen to do sth** to do sth by chance: *I happened to meet him in London yesterday.* ▶ **przypadkowo coś zrobić**

IDM **as it happens/happened** (used when you are adding to what you have said) actually: *As it happens, I did remember to bring the book you wanted.* ▶ **tak się składa/złożyło, że**

it (just) so happens → SO[1]

happening /ˈhæpənɪŋ/ noun [C, usually pl.] a thing that happens; an event (that is usually strange or difficult to explain): *Strange happenings have been reported in that old hotel.* ▶ **zdarzenie**, **wydarzenie**

Happening zwykle oznacza przypadkowe zdarzenie. **Event** stosuje się, mówiąc o wydarzeniach zaplanowanych. Użycie **event** sugeruje też, że zdarzenie ma charakter ważny lub wyjątkowy.

happily /ˈhæpɪli/ adv. **1** in a happy way: *I would happily give up my job if I didn't need the money.* ▶ **szczęśliwie**; **chętnie** **2** it is lucky that: *The police found my handbag and, happily, nothing had been stolen.* ▶ **na szczęście** SYN **fortunately**

happy /ˈhæpi/ adj. (**happier**; **happiest**) **1 happy (to do sth)**; **happy for sb**; **happy that...** feeling or showing pleasure; pleased: *a happy baby* ◇ *You look very happy today.* ◇ *I was really happy to see Mark again yesterday.* ◇ *Congratulations! I'm very happy for you.* Bardzo się cieszę (np. że coś ci się udało). ▶ **szczęśliwy**, **radosny** OPP **sad** **2** giving or causing pleasure: *a happy marriage/memory/childhood* ◇ *The film is sad but it has* ***a happy ending.*** ▶ **szczęśliwy**, **wesoły** **3** (**Happy**) (used to wish sb an enjoyable time): *Happy Birthday!* Wszystkiego najlepszego z okazji urodzin! ◇ *Happy New Year!* Szczęśliwego Nowego Roku! ◇ *Happy Christmas!* Wesołych Świąt (Bożego Narodzenia)! ◇ *Happy Easter!* Wesołych Świąt (Wielkanocnych)! **4 happy (with/about sb/sth)** satisfied that sth is good and right; not worried: *She doesn't feel happy about the salary she's been offered.* ◇ *I'm not very happy with what you've done.* ▶ **zadowolony** **5** [not before a noun] **happy to do sth** ready to do sth; pleased: *I'll be* ***more than happy*** *to give* (z wielką przyjemnością udzielę) *you extra classes if you think you need them.* ◇ *I'll be happy to* (chętnie) *see you any day next week.* ▶ **chętny do (zrobienia) czegoś** ⓘ **Be happy to do sth** często tłumaczy się zwrotem „robić coś z radością, przyjemnością itp.". **6** [only before a noun] lucky: *He's in the happy position of being able to* (jest w takiej szczęśliwej sytuacji, że może) *retire at 50!* ◇ *a happy coincidence.* ▶ **szczęśliwy**, **udany** SYN **fortunate**

IDM **many happy returns (of the day)** (used as a greeting to sb on his/her birthday) ▶ **Sto lat!** (*w życzeniach urodzinowych*)

happy

Glad i **pleased** odnoszą się do konkretnej sytuacji lub wydarzenia. **Happy** określa nastrój, stan umysłu; może występować przed rzeczownikiem: *This kind of music always makes me feel happy.* ◇ *She's such a happy child – she's always laughing.* **Delighted** oznacza odczuwanie wielkiej przyjemności z powodu jakiegoś wydarzenia itp: *I was delighted to meet her.* Osoba, którą określa się jako **cheerful**, jest radosna i uzewnętrznia to swoim zachowaniem: *a cheerful, hard-working employee.*

■ **happiness** noun [U] ▶ **szczęście**

ˌhappy-go-ˈlucky adj. not caring or worried about life and the future ▶ **beztroski**, **niefrasobliwy**

ˈhappy hour noun [C, usually sing.] a time, usually in the evening, when a pub or bar sells alcoholic drinks at lower prices than usual ▶ **pora, o jakiej tanieją drinki w barach**

harangue /həˈræŋ/ verb [T] to speak loudly and angrily in a way that criticizes sb/sth or tries to persuade people to do sth: *He walked to the front of the stage and began to harangue the audience.* ▶ **ciskać gromy na kogoś**

harass /ˈhærəs; həˈræs/ verb [T] to annoy or worry sb by doing unpleasant things to them, especially over a long time: *The court ordered him to stop harassing his ex-wife.* ▶ **dręczyć**, **nękać**, **prześladować** ■ **harassment** noun [U]: *She accused her boss of sexual harassment* (molestowanie seksualne). ▶ **gnębienie**

harassed /ˈhærəst; həˈræst/ adj. tired and worried because you have too much to do ▶ **umęczony**

harbour[1] (US **harbor**) /ˈhɑːbə(r)/ noun [C,U] a place on the coast where ships can be tied up and protected from the sea and bad weather ▶ **port**, **przystań**

harbour[2] (US **harbor**) /ˈhɑːbə(r)/ verb [T] **1** to hide or protect sb/sth that is bad: *They were accused of harbouring terrorists.* ▶ **dawać schronienie** (*np. przestępcy, zbiegowi*) **2** to keep feelings or thoughts secret in your mind for a long time: *She began to* ***harbour doubts*** *about the decision.* ▶ **skrywać** (*np. uczucia*)

hard[1] /hɑːd/ adj. **1** not soft to touch; not easy to break or bend: *The bed was so hard that I couldn't sleep.* ▶ **twardy** OPP **soft** ➲ look at **firm[2]** **2 hard (for sb) (to do sth)** difficult to do or understand; not easy: *The first question in the exam was very hard.* ◇ *I find his attitude very hard to take.* ◇ *This book is hard to understand./It is a hard book to understand.* Trudno zrozumieć tę książkę. ◇ *It's hard* (trudno) *to know why he made that decision.* ◇ *It's hard* (trudno) *for young people to find good jobs nowadays.* ▶ **trudny** SYN **difficult** OPP **easy** **3** needing or using a lot of physical strength or mental effort: *It's a hard climb to the top of the hill.* ◇ ***Hard work*** *is said to be good for you.* ◇ *We had some long, hard talks* (twarde rozmowy) *before we came to an agreement.* ◇ *He's a hard worker.* Jest sumiennym pracownikiem. ▶ **ciężki**, **trudny** **4** (used about conditions) full of difficulty: *He had a hard time when his parents died.* ◇ *to have a hard day/life/childhood* ▶ **trudny**, **ciężki** **5** not feeling or showing kindness or pity; not gentle: *You have to be hard to succeed in business.* ▶ **surowy**, **twardy** OPP **soft**, **lenient** **6** very cold: *The forecast is for a hard winter/frost.* ▶ **surowy**, **srogi** OPP **mild** **7** containing particular minerals so that soap does not make many bubbles: *a* ***hard water*** *area* ▶ **twardy** OPP **soft** ■ **hardness** noun [U] ▶ **twardość**

IDM a hard act to follow a person or a thing that it is difficult to do better than: *Lynn is leaving the firm after ten years and her successor will certainly find her a hard act to follow.* ▶ **osoba, której trudno dorównać; rzecz, którą trudno wykonać lepiej**
be hard at it to be working very hard doing sth ▶ **harować**
be hard on sb/sth 1 to treat sb/sth in a very strict or unkind way: *Don't be too hard on her – she's only a child.* ◇ *Managing with very little money can be hard on* (może być trudne dla) *students.* ▶ **być surowym dla kogoś/czegoś 2** to be difficult for or unfair to sb/sth ▶ **być niesprawiedliwym dla kogoś/w stosunku do czegoś, być nie fair wobec kogoś**
give sb a hard time (informal) to make a situation unpleasant, embarrassing or difficult for sb ▶ **dokuczać komuś**
hard and fast (used about rules, etc.) that cannot be changed: *There are no hard and fast rules about this.* ▶ (*reguły*) **twardy**
hard facts information that is true, not just people's opinions ▶ **rzeczywistość**
hard of hearing unable to hear well ▶ **o słabym/przytępionym słuchu**
hard luck! → LUCK
have a hard job doing/to do sth; have a hard time doing sth to do sth with great difficulty ▶ **robić coś z wielkim trudem**
learn the hard way → LEARN
no hard feelings (informal) (used to tell sb you do not feel angry after an argument, etc.): *'No hard feelings, I hope,' he said, offering me his hand.* ▶ **bez urazy**
take a hard line (on sth) to deal with sth in a very serious way that you will not allow anyone to change: *The government has taken a hard line on people who drink and drive.* ▶ **rządzić/władać itp. twardą ręką/despotycznie**

hard² /hɑːd/ adv. **1** with great effort, energy or attention: *He worked hard all his life.* ◇ *She looked hard at the man* (bardzo uważnie przyglądała się mężczyźnie) *but she didn't recognize him.* ◇ *You'll have to try a bit harder than that.* Będziesz musiał bardziej się postarać. ▶ **ciężko, z wysiłkiem 2** with great force; heavily: *It was raining/snowing hard.* ◇ *He hit her hard across the face.* ▶ **mocno**

Uwaga! Nie myl **hard** z **hardly**. **Hardly** to przysłówek, który oznacza „prawie/wcale nie": *I hardly ever go to concerts.* ◇ *I can hardly wait for my birthday.*

IDM be hard pressed/pushed/put to do sth to find sth very difficult to do: *He was hard pressed to explain her sudden disappearance.* ▶ **mieć z czymś trudności**
be hard up (for sth) to have too few or too little of sth, especially money ▶ **być spłukanym**
die hard → DIE
hard done by (Brit.) not fairly treated: *He felt very hard done by when he wasn't chosen for the team.* ▶ **niesprawiedliwie potraktowany**

hardback /ˈhɑːdbæk/ noun [C] a book that has a hard cover: *This book is only available **in hardback**.* ▶ **książka w twardej oprawie** ➲ look at **paperback**

ˌhard-ˈboiled adj. (used about an egg) boiled until it is solid inside ▶ **ugotowany na twardo**

ˌhard ˈcopy noun [U] printed material produced by a computer, usually on paper, to be read in the ordinary way ▶ **wydruk z komputera**

ˌhard ˈcore noun [sing., with sing. or pl. verb] the members of a group who are the most active ▶ **aktyw**, (*ludzie w grupie*) **jądro stowarzyszenia**

ˌhard ˈcurrency noun [U] money belonging to a particular country that is easy to exchange and not likely to fall in value ▶ **twarda waluta**

ˌhard ˈdisk noun [C] a piece of hard plastic that is fixed inside a computer and is used for storing data and programs permanently ▶ **twardy dysk** ➲ look at **floppy disk**

ˈhard drive noun [C] a part of a computer that reads data on a **hard disk** ▶ **twardy dysk**

ˌhard ˈdrug noun [C, usually pl.] a powerful and illegal drug that some people take for pleasure and can become **addicted** to: *Heroin and cocaine are hard drugs.* ▶ **(twardy) narkotyk** ➲ look at **soft**

harden /ˈhɑːdn/ verb **1** [I,T] to become or to make sth hard or less likely to change: *The varnish takes a few hours to harden.* ◇ (figurative) *The firm has hardened its attitude on this question.* ▶ **twardnieć; utwardzać;** (*stanowisko*) **usztywniać (się) 2** [I] (used about sb's face, voice, etc.) to become serious and unfriendly ▶ **usztywnić się 3** [T, usually passive] **harden sb (to sth/doing sth)** to make sb less kind or less easily shocked: *a hardened* (zatwardziały) *criminal* ◇ *War reporters get hardened to seeing suffering.* ▶ **znieczulać kogoś (na coś)**

Harden używa się tylko wtedy, gdy **hard** oznacza „twardy" lub „nieżyczliwy": *The concrete will harden* (cement stwardnieje) *in 24 hours.* ◇ *He hardened himself* (znieczulił się na) *to the feelings of other people.* **Get harder** używa się, kiedy **hard** ma inne znaczenie, np. „trudny": *Learning a foreign language gets harder as you get older.* Nauka obcego języka staje się coraz trudniejsza wraz z upływem lat.

ˌhard-ˈheaded adj. determined and not allowing yourself to be influenced by emotions: *a hard-headed businessman* ▶ (*osoba*) **twardy, rzeczowy** SYN **tough-minded**

ˌhard-ˈhearted adj. not kind to other people and not considering their feelings ▶ **nieczuły, bezlitosny** OPP **soft-hearted**

ˌhard-ˈhitting adj. that talks about or criticizes sb/sth in an honest and very direct way: *a hard-hitting campaign/speech/report* ▶ (*krytyka itp.*) **otwarty, odważny**

ˌhard ˈline noun [sing.] a way of thinking or a plan which will not be changed or influenced by anything: *The government has taken a very hard line on people who drink and drive.* ▶ **twarde stanowisko**

hardly /ˈhɑːdli/ adv. **1** almost no; almost not; almost none: *There's **hardly any** coffee left.* Nie ma już prawie wcale kawy. ◇ *We hardly ever go to the theatre nowadays.* Prawie wcale nie chodzimy teraz do teatru. ◇ ***Hardly anybody** I knew was at the party.* Na przyjęciu nie było prawie żadnych moich znajomych. ◇ *It hardly matters whether you are there or not.* Właściwie nie jest ważne, czy będziesz tam, czy nie. ◇ *I hardly spoke any English when I first came here.* ▶ **mało (co/kto), prawie (nie/nigdy/nikt itp.)** ➲ look at **almost 2** (used especially after 'can' and 'could' and before the main verb to emphasize that sth is difficult to do): *Speak up – I can hardly hear you.* ◇ *I can hardly wait for the holidays to begin.* Nie mogę się doczekać wakacji. ◇ *Winning this money could hardly have come at a better time.* Wygrana tych pieniędzy nie mogła przyjść w lepszym czasie. ▶ **ledwie; prawie nie 3** (used to say that sth has just begun, happened, etc.) only just: *She'd **hardly** gone to sleep **than** it was time to get up again.* Ledwie zasnęła, już trzeba było znowu wstawać. ▶ **ledwie** ❶ Zwróć uwagę, że kiedy **hardly** występuje na początku zdania, bezpośrednio po nim następuje czasownik. Ta konstrukcja jest używana przede wszystkim w formalnym języku pisanym: *Hardly had she gone to sleep than it was time to get up again.* **4** (used to suggest that sth is unlikely or unreasonable) not really: *It's hardly surprising* (trudno się dziwić) *that you're tired after all the work you've done.* ◇ *She hasn't written for two years – she's hardly likely to* *write now* (trudno spodziewać się, że napisze teraz). ◇ *He can hardly expect me to do all his washing for him!* Chyba nie oczekuje, że zrobię mu to całe pranie. ▶ **trudno** (*np. spodziewać się, uwierzyć, zrobić*), **chyba (nie)** ➲ note at **hard** ➲ look at **barely**, **scarcely**

ˌhard-ˈnosed adj. not affected by feelings or emotions when trying to get what you want: *hard-nosed journalists/politicians* ▶ **nie ulegający emocjom**

hardship /ˈhɑːdʃɪp/ noun [C,U] the fact of not having enough money, food, etc.: *This new tax is going to cause a lot of hardship.* ▶ **duża niewygoda**, **trudność**

ˌhard ˈshoulder (US **shoulder**) noun [C] a narrow section of road at the side of a **motorway** where cars are allowed to stop in an emergency ▶ **pobocze**

hardware /ˈhɑːdweə(r)/ noun [U] **1** the machinery and electronic parts of a computer system ▶ **sprzęt komputerowy** ➲ look at **software** **2** tools and equipment that are used in the house and garden: *a hardware shop* ▶ **narzędzia**, **towary żelazne** **3** heavy machinery or weapons ▶ **ciężki sprzęt**, **broń**

ˌhard-ˈwearing adj. (Brit.) (used about materials, clothes, etc.) strong and able to last for a long time ▶ **mocny**, **wytrzymały**

ˌhard-ˈworking adj. working with effort and energy: *a hard-working man* ▶ **pracowity**

hardy /ˈhɑːdi/ adj. (**hardier**; **hardiest**) strong and able to survive difficult conditions and bad weather: *a hardy plant* ▶ **odporny**

hare /heə(r)/ noun [C] an animal like a **rabbit** but bigger with longer ears and legs ▶ **zając**

harelip /ˈheəlɪp/ noun [C] an old-fashioned and now offensive word for **cleft lip** ▶ **zajęcza warga**

harem /ˈhɑːriːm; -rəm; US ˈhærəm/ noun [C] a number of women living with one man, especially in Muslim societies. The part of the building the women live in is also called a **harem**. ▶ **harem**

🔑 **harm¹** /hɑːm/ noun [U] damage or injury: *Peter ate some of those berries but they didn't* ***do*** *him* ***any harm.*** ▶ **krzywda**; **szkoda**

IDM **come to harm** [usually with a negative] to be hurt or damaged: *Experienced staff watch over the children to make sure they don't come to any harm.* ▶ **doznawać krzywdy/nieszczęścia**

no harm done (informal) (used to tell sb that they have not caused any damage or injury): *'Sorry about what I said to you last night.' 'That's all right, Jack, no harm done!'* ▶ **nic się nie stało!**

out of harm's way in a safe place: *Put the medicine out of harm's way where the children can't reach it.* ▶ **w bezpieczn-e/ym miejsc-e/u**

there is no harm in doing sth; **it does no harm (for sb) to do sth** there's nothing wrong in doing sth (and sth good may result): *I'm sure he'll say no, but there's no harm in asking.* ▶ **nie zaszkodzi (coś zrobić)**

🔑 **harm²** /hɑːm/ verb [T] to cause injury or damage; hurt: *Too much sun can harm your skin.* ▶ **krzywdzić**; **wyrządzać szkodę**

🔑 **harmful** /ˈhɑːmfl/ adj. **harmful (to sb/sth)** causing harm: *Traffic fumes are harmful to the environment.* ▶ **szkodliwy**

🔑 **harmless** /ˈhɑːmləs/ adj. **1** not able or not likely to cause damage or injury; safe: *You needn't be frightened – these insects are totally harmless.* ▶ **nieszkodliwy** **2** not likely to upset people: *The children can watch that film – it's quite harmless.* ▶ **nieszkodliwy**, **niewinny**

■ **harmlessly** adv. ▶ **nieszkodliwie**

harmonic /hɑːˈmɒnɪk/ adj. [usually before a noun] relating to the way notes are played or sung together to make a pleasing sound: *the harmonic and rhythmic interest of the music* ▶ **harmoniczny**

■ **harmonic** noun [usually pl.] **1** a note that sounds together with the main note being played and is higher and quieter than that note ▶ **harmoniczna** **2** a high quiet note that can be played on some instruments like the **violin** by touching the string very lightly ▶ **harmoniczna**

harmonica /hɑːˈmɒnɪkə/ (also ˈ**mouth organ**) noun [C] a small musical instrument that you play by moving it across your lips while you are blowing ▶ **organki**, **harmonijka ustna**

harmonious /hɑːˈməʊniəs/ adj. **1** friendly, peaceful and without disagreement ▶ **zgodny** **2** (used about musical notes, colours, etc.) producing a pleasant effect when heard or seen together ▶ **harmoniczny**, **melodyjny**

■ **harmoniously** adv. ▶ **harmonijnie**

harmonize (also **-ise**) /ˈhɑːmənaɪz/ verb [I] **1 harmonize (with sth)** (used about two or more things) to produce a pleasant effect when seen, heard, etc. together ▶ **harmonizować** **2 harmonize (with sb/sth)** to sing or play music that sounds good combined with the main tune ▶ **harmonizować**

■ **harmonization** (also **-isation**) /ˌhɑːmənaɪˈzeɪʃn; US -nəˈz-/ noun [U] ▶ **dopasowywanie**; **harmonizowanie**

harmony /ˈhɑːməni/ noun (pl. **harmonies**) **1** [U] a state of agreement or of living together in peace: *We need to live more* ***in harmony with*** *our environment.* ▶ **zgoda** **2** [C,U] a pleasing combination of musical notes, colours, etc.: *There are some beautiful harmonies in that music.* ▶ **harmonia**

harness¹ /ˈhɑːnɪs/ noun [C] **1** a set of narrow pieces of leather that is put around a horse's neck and body so that it can pull sth ▶ **uprząż** **2** a set of narrow pieces of material for fastening sth to sb's body or for stopping sb from moving around, falling, etc.: *a safety harness* ▶ **szelki (zabezpieczające)**

harness² /ˈhɑːnɪs/ verb [T] **1 harness sth (to sth)** to put a **harness** on a horse, etc. or to tie a horse, etc. to sth using a **harness**: *Two ponies were harnessed to the cart.* ▶ **zaprzęgać**, **nakładać uprząż** **2** to control the energy of sth in order to produce power or to achieve sth: *to harness the sun's rays as a source of energy* ▶ **wprzęgać**, **wykorzystywać (do czegoś)**

harp¹ /hɑːp/ noun [C] a large musical instrument which has many strings stretching from the top to the bottom of a frame. You play the **harp** with your fingers. ▶ **harfa**

■ **harpist** /-pɪst/ noun [C] ▶ **harfist(k)a**

harp² /hɑːp/ verb

PHR V **harp on (about) sth** to keep on talking or to talk too much about sth: *He's always harping on about his problems.* ▶ **ględzić o czymś**

harpoon /hɑːˈpuːn/ noun [C] a long thin weapon with a sharp pointed end and a rope tied to it that is used to catch **whales** ▶ **harpun**

■ **harpoon** verb [T] ▶ **łowić na harpun**

harpsichord /ˈhɑːpsɪkɔːd/ noun [C] an early type of musical instrument similar to a piano, but with strings that are **plucked**, not hit ▶ **klawesyn**

■ **harpsichordist** /ˈhɑːpsɪkɔːdɪst/ noun [C] a person who plays the **harpsichord** ▶ **klawesynist(k)a**

harrowing /ˈhærəʊɪŋ/ adj. making people feel very sad or upset: *The programme showed harrowing scenes of the victims of the war.* ▶ **wstrząsający**, **przerażający**

harsh /hɑːʃ/ adj. **1** very strict and unkind: *a harsh punishment/criticism* ◇ *The judge had some* ***harsh words*** *for the journalist's behaviour.* ▶ **surowy** ➲ look at **severe** **2** unpleasant and difficult to live in, look at, listen to, etc.: *She grew up in the harsh environment of New York City.* ◇ *a harsh light/voice* ▶ **trudny**, **ostry**, **niemiły**, surowy (*np. klimat, zima*) **3** too strong or rough and likely to damage sth: *This soap is too harsh for a baby's skin.* ▶ **chropowaty**; **o silnym działaniu**

■ **harshly** adv. ▶ **surowo** | **harshness** noun [U] ▶ **surowość**; **ostrość**

harvest /ˈhɑːvɪst/ noun **1** [C,U] the time of year when the grain, fruit, etc. is collected on a farm; the act of collecting the grain, fruit, etc.: *Farmers always need extra help with the harvest.* ▶ **żniwa 2** [C] the amount of grain, fruit, etc. that is collected: *This year's wheat harvest was very poor.* ▶ **zbiór/zbiory**

■ **harvest** verb [I,T]: *to harvest crops* ▶ **zbierać** (*plony z pól*) ➲ look at **combine harvester**

has /həz; strong form hæz/ → HAVE

ˈ**has-been** noun [C] (informal) a person or thing that is no longer as famous, successful or important as before ▶ **przebrzmiała sława**

hash /hæʃ/ noun **1** [U] a hot dish of meat and potatoes that are cut into small pieces, mixed together and fried ▶ **zapiekanka ze smażonego mięsa i ziemniaków 2** [U] (informal) = HASHISH **3** (also ˈ**hash sign**) (Brit.) [C] the symbol (#), especially one on a telephone ▶ **krzyżyk** (*na tarczy telefonu*)

IDM **make a hash of sth** (informal) to do sth badly ▶ **partaczyć coś**

hashish /ˈhæʃiːʃ/ (also informal **hash**) noun [U] a drug made from **hemp** that some people smoke for pleasure and which is illegal in many countries ▶ **haszysz**

ˈ**hash sign** = HASH (3)

hasn't /ˈhæznt/ short for **has not**

hassle[1] /ˈhæsl/ noun (informal) **1** [C,U] a thing or situation that is annoying because it is complicated or involves a lot of effort: *It's going to be a hassle having to change trains with all this luggage.* ▶ **kłopot 2** [U] disagreeing or arguing: *I've decided what to do – please don't give me any hassle about it* (nie kłóć się ze mną na ten temat). ▶ **spieranie się**, **zawracanie (komuś) głowy**

hassle[2] /ˈhæsl/ verb [T] (informal) to annoy sb, especially by asking them to do sth many times: *I wish he'd stop hassling me about decorating the house.* ▶ **zawracać głowę** SYN **bother**

haste /heɪst/ noun [U] speed in doing sth, especially because you do not have enough time: *The letter had clearly been written **in haste**.* ▶ **pośpiech**

hasten /ˈheɪsn/ verb (formal) **1** [I] **hasten to do sth** to be quick to do or say sth: *She hastened to apologize.* Pośpieszyła z przeprosinami. ▶ **pośpieszać 2** [T] to make sth happen or be done earlier or more quickly ▶ **przyśpieszać**

hasty /ˈheɪsti/ adj. (**hastier**; **hastiest**) **1** said or done too quickly: *He said a hasty 'goodbye' and left.* ▶ **pośpieszny 2 hasty (in doing sth/to do sth)** (used about a person) acting or deciding too quickly or without enough thought: *Maybe I was too hasty in rejecting her for the job.* ▶ **pochopny**

■ **hastily** adv. ▶ **pośpiesznie**; **pochopnie**

hat /hæt/ noun [C] a covering that you wear on your head, usually when you are outside: *to wear a hat* ◇ ***a sun hat*** kapelusz od słońca ▶ **kapelusz**

IDM **at the drop of a hat** → DROP[2]

hatch[1] /hætʃ/ verb **1** [I] **hatch (out)** (used about a baby bird, insect, fish, etc.) to come out of an egg: *Ten chicks hatched out this morning.* ▶ **wykluwać się 2** [T] to make a baby bird, etc. come out of an egg ▶ **wysiadywać** (*jaja*) **3** [I] (used about an egg) to break open and allow the baby bird, etc. inside to get out ▶ (*jajko*) **pękać 4** [T] **hatch sth (up)** to think of a plan (usually to do sth bad): *He hatched a plan to avoid paying any income tax.* ▶ **knuć**

hatch[2] /hætʃ/ noun [C] **1** an opening in the **deck** of a ship or the bottom of an aircraft through which goods are passed ▶ **luk 2** an opening in the wall between a kitchen and another room that is used for passing food through ▶ **okienko**, **otwór w ścianie 3** the door in a plane or **spacecraft** ▶ **drzwi**; **właz**

hatchback /ˈhætʃbæk/ noun [C] a car with a large door at the back that opens upwards ▶ **samochód typu hatchback** ➲ picture at **car**, picture on **page A7**

hatchet /ˈhætʃɪt/ noun [C] a tool with a short handle and a heavy metal head with a sharp edge used for cutting wood ▶ **toporek**

hate[1] /heɪt/ verb [T] **1** to have a very strong feeling of not liking sb/sth at all: *I hate grapefruit.* ◇ *I hate it when it's raining like this.* ◇ *She hated* (znienawidziła) *her stepmother as soon as she saw her.* ◇ *I hate to see the countryside spoilt.* ◇ *He hates driving at night.* ▶ **nienawidzić**, **nie znosić** ➲ note at **dislike** ❶ Por. **detest** i **loathe**. Wyrażają one jeszcze mocniejsze negatywne uczucia. **2** (used as a polite way of saying sorry for sth you would prefer not to have to say): *I hate to bother you* (przepraszam, że przeszkadzam) *but did you pick up my keys by mistake?* ◇ *I hate to say it* (przepraszam bardzo), *but I think that's my drink you're drinking.*

hate[2] /heɪt/ noun **1** [U] a very strong feeling of not liking sb/sth at all: *Do you feel any hate towards the kidnappers?* ▶ **nienawiść** SYN **hatred 2** [C] a thing that you do not like at all ▶ **przedmiot szczególnej awersji** ❶ Często używane z **pet**, wówczas oznacza coś, czego się wyjątkowo nie lubi: *Plastic flowers are one of my pet hates.*

hateful /ˈheɪtfl/ adj. **hateful (to sb)** extremely unpleasant: *It was a hateful thing to say.* ▶ **nienawistny**, **wstrętny**

hatred /ˈheɪtrɪd/ noun [U] **hatred (for/of sb/sth)** a very strong feeling of not liking sb/sth; hate ▶ **nienawiść** SYN **hate**

ˈ**hat-trick** noun [C] three points, goals, etc. scored by one player in the same game; three successes achieved by one person: *to score a hat-trick* ▶ **zwycięstwo odniesione trzy razy pod rząd**

haughty /ˈhɔːti/ adj. (**haughtier**; **haughtiest**) proud, and thinking that you are better than other people: *She gave me a haughty look.* ▶ **wyniosły**

■ **haughtily** adv. ▶ **wyniośle** | **haughtiness** noun [U] ▶ **wyniosłość**

haul[1] /hɔːl/ verb [T] to pull sth with a lot of effort or difficulty: *A lorry hauled the car out of the mud.* ▶ **ciągnąć**, **wlec**

haul[2] /hɔːl/ noun **1** [C, usually sing.] **a haul (of sth)** a large amount of sth that has been stolen, caught, collected, etc.: *The fishermen came back with a good haul of fish.* ▶ **połów**; **łup 2** [sing.] a distance to be travelled: *It seemed **a long haul** back home.* ▶ **(długa) droga do przebycia 3** [sing.] the act of hauling ▶ **ciągnienie**, **wleczenie**

haulage /ˈhɔːlɪdʒ/ noun [U] (Brit.) the transport of goods by road, rail, etc.; the money charged for this ▶ **przewóz**; **koszt przewozu**

haunches /ˈhɔːntʃəz/ noun [pl.] the tops of the legs and **buttocks**; the similar parts at the back of the body of an animal that has four legs: *to crouch/squat **on your haunches*** ▶ **pośladki** (*razem z tylną częścią ud*), **zad**

haunt[1] /hɔːnt/ verb [T] **1** [often passive] if a **ghost haunts** a place, people say that they have seen it there: *The house is said to be haunted.* ▶ **nawiedzać**, (*duchy*) **straszyć 2** (used about sth unpleasant or sad) to be always in your mind: *His unhappy face has haunted me for years.* ▶ **prześladować**

haunt[2] /hɔːnt/ noun [C] a place that you visit regularly: *This cafe has always been a favourite haunt of mine.* ▶ **często odwiedzane miejsce**

haunting /ˈhɔːntɪŋ/ adj. having a quality that stays in your mind: *a haunting song* ▶ **prześladujący, nie dający komuś spokoju**

have[1] /hæv/ verb [T] ℹ Formy czasowników **have** podane są w dodatku *Czasowniki nieregularne* na końcu słownika. **1** (Brit. also **have got**) [not used in the continuous tenses] to own or to hold sth: *I've got a new camera.* ◇ *The flat has two bedrooms.* ◇ *He's got short dark hair.* ◇ *to have patience/enthusiasm/skill* ◇ *Have you got any brothers and sisters?* ◇ *Do you have time to check my work?* ▶ **mieć** SYN **possess** **2** (also **have got**) [not used in the continuous tenses] to have a particular duty or plan: *Do you have any homework tonight?* ◇ *I've got a few things to do this morning, but I'm free later.* ◇ *We've got my parents coming next week* (rodzice przyjeżdżają do nas w przyszłym tygodniu) *so we're quite busy.* ▶ **mieć coś do zrobienia, musieć coś zrobić** **3** (also **have got**) [not used in the continuous tenses] to hold sb/sth; to keep sth in a particular place: *The dog had me by the leg.* ◇ *We've got our TV up on a shelf.* ▶ **mieć, trzymać** **4** (also **have got**) [not used in the continuous tenses] to be ill with sth: *She's got a bad cold.* ◇ *to have flu/a headache/cancer/AIDS* ▶ **chorować na coś, mieć** **5** to experience sth: *to have fun/a good time* dobrze/wesoło spędzić czas ◇ *He's had* (doznał) *a terrible shock.* ◇ *to have problems/difficulties* ◇ *to have an idea/an impression/a feeling* ◇ *to have an accident* ◇ *She had her bag stolen* (ukradziono jej torebkę) *on the underground.* ◇ *Charles I had his head cut off.* Karolowi I obcięto głowę. ◇ *He had his driving licence taken off him for six months.* Odebrano mu prawo jazdy na sześć miesięcy. ▶ **mieć** **6** (used with many nouns to talk about doing sth): *What time do you have breakfast?* O której jesz śniadanie? ◇ *to have a drink* napić się ◇ *to have something to eat* zjeść coś ◇ *to have* (napić się) *a cup of coffee* ◇ *to have* (zjeść) *a sandwich* ◇ *to have a* (zapalić) *cigarette* ◇ *'Where's Jane?' 'She's having a shower* (bierze prysznic).*'* ◇ *to have an argument* pokłócić się ◇ *to have a talk/chat* porozmawiać **7** to cause sb/sth to do sth or to be in a particular state: *The music soon had everyone dancing.* Wkrótce muzyka sprawiła, że wszyscy zaczęli tańczyć. ◇ *I'll have dinner ready when you get home.* Kolacja już będzie gotowa, gdy wrócisz. ◇ *Ian had us worried when he wouldn't open his eyes* (kiedy Ian nie otwierał oczu, bardzo sie zaniepokoiliśmy), *but he was only joking.* ▶ **sprawiać** **8** to arrange for sb to do sth: *I have my hair cut* (chodzę do fryzjera, aby obciąć włosy) *every six weeks.* ◇ *You should have your eyes tested* (zbadać oczy u okulisty). ▶ **doprowadzać do spowodowania czegoś** (*zwykle za zapłatą*) **9** to look after or entertain sb: *We're having some people to dinner tomorrow.* ▶ **mieć** (*gości*); **opiekować się kimś**

IDM **have had it** (informal) (used about things that are completely broken, or dead): *This television has had it.* Telewizor szlag trafił. ▶ **zepsuć się całkowicie**

ℹ **Have** używa się w innych idiomach, np. **not have a clue**. Zob. hasła odpowiednich rzeczowników, przymiotników itp.

PHR V **have (got) sth against sb/sth** [not used in the progressive tenses] to dislike sb/sth for a particular reason: *What have you got against Ruth? She's always been good to you.* ▶ **mieć coś przeciwko komuś**

have sb on to trick sb as a joke: *Don't listen to what Jim says – he's only having you on.* ▶ **nabierać kogoś**

have (got) sth on **1** to be wearing sth: *She's got a green jumper on.* ▶ **mieć na sobie** **2** (informal) to have an arrangement to do sth: *I've got nothing on* (nie mam nic w planie) *on Monday. Are you free then?* ◇ *I've got a lot on* (mam dużo rzeczy do zrobienia) *this week.* ▶ **mieć** (*w programie itp.*)

have sth out to allow part of your body to be removed: *to have a tooth/your appendix out* ▶ **usuwać, wyrywać** (*ząb*)

have[2] /həv; strong form hæv/ auxiliary verb (used for forming the perfect tenses): *I've seen this film before.* Widziałem już ten film. ◇ *She's been in England for six months.* Ona jest w Anglii od 6 miesięcy. ◇ *Ian hasn't written to me yet.* Ian jeszcze do mnie nie napisał. ◇ *Have you been waiting long?* Czy długo czekasz? ◇ *They had already told us the news.* Już nam przekazali wiadomości. ▶ (*czasownik używany do tworzenia czasów* **perfect**)

haven /ˈheɪvn/ noun [C] **a haven (of sth)**; **a haven (for sb/sth)** a place where people or animals can be safe and rest: *a haven of peace* ◇ *The lake is a haven for water birds.* ◇ *a **tax haven*** kraj o niskich podatkach ▶ **schronienie**

haven't /ˈhævnt/ short for **have not**

have to /ˈhæv tə; ˈhæf tə; strong form and before vowels ˈhæv tuː; ˈhæf tuː/ (also **have got to**) modal verb (used for saying that sb must do sth or that sth must happen): *I usually have to work on Saturday mornings.* ◇ *Do you have to have a visa to go to America?* ◇ *We had to do* (mieliśmy do zrobienia) *lots of boring exercises.* ◇ *She's got to go* (ma iść) *to the bank this afternoon.* ◇ *Oh good, I haven't got to get up early tomorrow!* ◇ *We don't have to go to the party if you don't want to* ▶ **musieć** ℹ W Br. ang. częściej używanym i mniej formalnym wyrażeniem jest **have got to**. ➲ note at **must**

havoc /ˈhævək/ noun [U] a situation in which there is a lot of damage or confusion: *The rail strikes will **cause havoc** all over the country.* ◇ *The bad weather will **play havoc with** our plans* (zniweczyła nasze plany). ◇ *These insects can **wreak havoc on*** (mogą zniszczyć) *crops.* ▶ **spustoszenie**

hawk /hɔːk/ noun [C] **1** a type of large bird that catches and eats small animals and birds. **Hawks** can see very well. ▶ **jastrząb**

Hawks are a type of **bird of prey**.

2 (in politics) a person who supports strong action and the use of force rather than peaceful solutions ▶ (*polityk*) **jastrząb**

hawthorn /ˈhɔːθɔːn/ noun [U,C] a bush or small tree with sharp thorns, white, red or pink flowers and small dark red berries ▶ **głóg**

hay /heɪ/ noun [U] grass that has been cut and dried for use as animal food ▶ **siano**

ˈ**hay fever** noun [U] an illness that affects the eyes, nose and throat and is caused by breathing in **pollen** ▶ **katar sienny** ➲ look at **allergy**

haywire /ˈheɪwaɪə(r)/ adj.
IDM **be/go haywire** (informal) to be or become out of control: *I can't do any work because the computer's gone haywire.* ▶ **z/wariować**

hazard[1] /ˈhæzəd/ noun [C] a danger or risk: *Smoking is a serious health hazard.* ▶ **niebezpieczeństwo, ryzyko**

hazard[2] /ˈhæzəd/ verb [T] to make a guess or to suggest sth even though you know it may be wrong: *I don't know what he paid for the house but I could **hazard a guess**.* ▶ **zgadywać, zaryzykować**

hazardous /ˈhæzədəs/ adj. involving risk or danger ▶ **niebezpieczny, ryzykowny**

haze /heɪz/ noun **1** [C,U] air that is difficult to see through because of heat, dust or smoke ▶ **mgiełka** ➲ note at **fog** **2** [sing.] a mental state in which you cannot think clearly ▶ **otumanienie**

hazel[1] /ˈheɪzl/ noun [C] a small tree or bush that produces nuts ▶ **leszczyna**

hazel[2] /ˈheɪzl/ adj. (used especially about eyes) light brown in colour ▶ **piwny**

hazelnut /ˈheɪzlnʌt/ noun [C] a small brown nut that we eat ▶ **orzech laskowy**

hazy /ˈheɪzi/ adj. (**hazier**; **haziest**) **1** not clear, especially because of heat: *The fields were hazy in the early morning sun.* ▶ **mglisty**; **niejasny** **2** difficult to remember or understand clearly: *a hazy memory* ▶ **mglisty** **3** (used about a person) uncertain, not expressing things clearly: *She's a bit hazy about the details of the trip.* ▶ **niepewny (czegoś)**

he¹ /hiː/ pron. (the subject of a verb) the male person mentioned earlier: *I spoke to John before he left.* ◇ *Look at that boy – he's going to fall in!* ▶ **on**

> O osobie, której płeć nie jest znana, można powiedzieć: **he or she**, **him or her** lub **his or her**, a w pisowni **he/she** lub **s/he**: *If you are not sure, ask your doctor. He/she can give you further information.* Obecnie używa się często form **they**, **them**, lub **their**: *Everybody knows what they want.* ◇ *When somebody asks me a question I always try to give them a quick answer.* Można też zbudować zdanie w lm: *A baby cries when he/she is tired.* staje się: *Babies cry when they are tired.* **They**, **them** i **their** są tak właśnie używane w tym słowniku.

he² /hiː/ noun [sing.] a male animal: *Is your cat a he or a she?* ▶ **on**

head¹ /hed/ noun **1** [C] the part of your body above your neck: *She turned her head to look at him.* ▶ **głowa** ➲ picture at **body** **2** [in compounds] having the type of head mentioned: *a bald-headed* (łysy) *man* ▶ **(określa rodzaj głowy)** **3** [C] sb's mind, brain or mental ability: *Use your head!* Rusz głową! ◇ *A horrible thought entered my head.* ◇ *I usually add the prices up in my head* (w pamięci) *as I go round the supermarket.* ▶ (*przen.*) **głowa** **4** [C,U] the person in charge of a group of people: *the head of the family* ◇ *Several* ***heads of state*** *attended the funeral.* ◇ *the head of the Church of England* ◇ *the head waiter* kierownik sali w restauracji ▶ **głowa**, **szef/owa**, **przewodniczący/a** **5** (also **head teacher**) [C] the teacher in charge of a school: *Who is going to be the new head?* ▶ **dyrektor/ka szkoły** **6** (**heads**) [U] the side of a coin with the head of a person on it: *Heads or tails* (orzeł czy reszka)*? Heads I go first, tails you do.* ▶ **reszka** **7** [C, sing.] the top, front or most important part: *to sit at the head* (na szczycie) *of the table* ◇ *Put your name at the head* (w nagłówku) *of the paper.* ◇ *the head of the queue* ▶ **czoło**, **przód** **8** something that is like a head in shape or position: *the head of* (główka) *a hammer* ◇ *the head of* (łebek) *a nail* **9** (**a head**) [sing.] the height or length of one head ▶ **o głowę**

IDM **bite sb's head off** → BITE¹

come to a head; **bring sth to a head** if a situation comes to a head or if you bring it to a head, it suddenly becomes very bad and you have to deal with it immediately ▶ **doprowadzać coś do punktu kulminacyjnego/krytycznego**; **być na ostrzu noża**

do sb's head in (Brit., informal) to make sb upset and confused ▶ **dręczyć kogoś**

get sth into your head; **put sth into sb's head** to start or to make sb start believing or thinking sth: *Barry's got it into his head that glasses would make him more attractive.* ▶ **wbić sobie/komuś coś do głowy**, **ubzdurać coś sobie**

go to sb's head **1** to make sb drunk: *Wine always goes straight to my head.* ▶ **iść do głowy** **2** to make sb too proud: *If you keep telling him how clever he is, it will go to his head!* ▶ **uderzać komuś do głowy**

have a head for sth to be able to deal with sth easily: *You need a good head for heights* (nie możesz cierpieć na lęk wysokości) *if you live on the top floor!* ◇ *to have a head for business/figures* ▶ **mieć głowę do czegoś**

a/per head for each person: *How much will the meal cost a head?* ▶ **na głowę**

head first **1** with your head before the rest of your body: *Don't go down the slide head first.* ▶ **głową naprzód** **2** too quickly or suddenly: *Don't rush head first into a decision.* ▶ **bez namysłu**

head over heels (in love) loving sb very much: *Jane's fallen head over heels in love with her new boss.* ▶ (*zakochać się*) **bez pamięci**

hit the nail on the head → HIT¹

hold your head high; **hold up your head** to be proud of or not feel ashamed about sth that you have done: *She managed to hold her head high and ignore what people were saying.* ▶ **nosić głowę wysoko**

keep your head to stay calm ▶ **nie tracić głowy**

keep your head above water to just manage to survive in a difficult situation, especially one in which you do not have enough money ▶ **(ledwo) wiązać koniec z końcem**

keep your head down to try not to be noticed ▶ (*przen.*) **siedzieć cicho**

laugh, scream, etc. your head off to laugh, shout, etc. very loudly and for a long time ▶ **śmiać się do rozpuku**, **wydzierać się**

lose your head → LOSE

make head or tail of sth to understand sth: *I can't make head or tail of this exercise.* ▶ **zrozumieć coś**

off the top of your head → TOP¹

out of/off your head (informal) crazy, often because of the effects of drugs or alcohol: *He's off his head!* Odbiło mu! ▶ **oszalały** (*np. z powodu narkotyków/alkoholu*)

put/get your heads together to make a plan with sb ▶ **wspólnie się naradzać**

a roof over your head → ROOF

shake your head → SHAKE¹

take it into your head to do sth to suddenly decide to do sth that other people consider strange: *I don't know why Kevin took it into his head to enter that marathon!* ▶ **wpaść na pomysł zrobienia czegoś**

head² /hed/ verb **1** [I] to move in the direction mentioned: *The ship headed towards the harbour.* ◇ *Where are you heading?* ▶ **iść/jechać/płynąć** (*w kierunku opisanym*) **2** [T] to be in charge of or to lead sth: *Do you think that he has the experience necessary to head a government?* ▶ **przewodzić** **3** [T] to be at the front of a line, top of a list, etc.: *to head a procession* ▶ **być na czele** **4** [T, often passive] to give a title at the top of a piece of writing: *The report was headed 'The State of the Market'.* ▶ **zatytułować**, **poprzedzać** **5** [T] to hit the ball with your head: *He headed the ball into the net.* ▶ **zagrać głową**

PHR V **head for sth** to move towards a place: *It's getting late – I think it's time to head for home* (iść do domu). ▶ **iść/jechać** (*w kierunku opisanym*), **zmierzać do czegoś**

headache /ˈhedeɪk/ noun [C] **1** a pain in your head: *I've got a splitting* (rozsadzający) *headache.* ▶ **ból głowy** ➲ note at **ache** **2** a person or thing that causes worry or difficulty: *Paying the bills is a constant headache.* ▶ **utrapienie**

headband /ˈhedbænd/ noun [C] a strip of fabric worn around the head, especially to keep hair or sweat out of your eyes when playing sports ▶ **opaska na głowę**

headdress /ˈheddres/ noun [C] a covering worn on the head on special occasions ▶ **przybranie głowy**

headhunt /ˈhedhʌnt/ verb [T] to find sb who is suitable for a senior job and persuade them to leave their present job: *I was headhunted by a marketing agency.* ▶ **wyszukiwać kandydatów do pracy** (*z innych instytucji*) ■ **headhunting** noun [U] ▶ **wyszukiwanie kandydatów do pracy** (*z innych instytucji*)

heading /ˈhedɪŋ/ noun [C] the words written as a title at the top of a page or a piece of writing: *The company's* *aims can be grouped under three main headings.* ▶ **nagłówek**

headlamp = HEADLIGHT

headland /ˈhedlənd; -lænd/ noun [C] a narrow piece of land that sticks out into the sea ▶ **cypel**, **przylądek**

headlight /ˈhedlaɪt/ (also **headlamp** /ˈhedlæmp/) noun [C] one of the two large bright lights at the front of a vehicle ▶ **reflektor** (*w samochodzie*) ➲ picture at **car**, picture on **page A7**

headline /ˈhedlaɪn/ noun **1** [C] the title of a newspaper article printed in large letters above the story ▶ **nagłówek 2** (**the headlines**) [pl.] the main items of news read on TV or radio ▶ **skrót najważniejszych wiadomości**

headlong /ˈhedlɒŋ/ adv. **1** with your head before the rest of your body: *I tripped and fell headlong into the road.* ▶ **głową naprzód 2** too quickly; without enough thought: *He rushed headlong into buying the business.* ▶ **na łeb na szyję**, **nierozważnie**
■ **headlong** adj. [only before a noun]: *a headlong dive/rush* ▶ **głową naprzód**

headmaster /ˌhedˈmɑːstə(r); US -ˈmæs-/ (fem. **headmistress** /ˌhedˈmɪstrəs/) noun [C] (old-fashioned) (US usually **principal**) a teacher who is in charge of a school, especially a private school ▶ **dyrektor/ka szkoły** ℹ Te słowa powoli wychodzą z użycia. Obecnie częściej używa się **head(teacher)**.

ˌhead ˈoffice noun [C, U, with sing. or pl. verb] the main office of a company; the managers who work there: *I don't know what head office will think about this proposal.* ▶ **centrala**

ˌhead of ˈstate noun [C] (pl. **heads of state**) the official leader of a country who is sometimes also the leader of the government: *The Queen was joined by the US President and other heads of state from around the world.* ▶ **głowa państwa**

ˌhead-ˈon adj. [only before a noun] with the front of one car, etc. hitting the front of another: *a head-on crash* ▶ **czołowy**
■ **ˌhead-ˈon** adv.: *The cars* ***crashed head-on.*** ▶ **czołowo**

headphones /ˈhedfəʊnz/ noun [pl.] a piece of equipment worn over or in the ears that makes it possible to listen to music, the radio, etc. without other people hearing it ▶ **słuchawki** ➲ note at **listen**

headquarters /ˌhedˈkwɔːtəz; US ˈhedkw-/ noun [pl., with sing. or pl. verb] (abbr. **HQ** /ˌeɪtʃ ˈkjuː/) the place from where an organization is controlled; the people who work there: *Where is/are the firm's headquarters?* ▶ **centralny zarząd**

headrest /ˈhedrest/ noun [C] the part of a seat or chair that supports a person's head, especially on the front seat of a car ▶ **zagłówek**

headset /ˈhedset/ noun [C] a pair of **headphones**, especially one with a **microphone** fixed to it: *The pilot was talking into his headset.* ▶ **zestaw słuchawkowy**

ˌhead ˈstart noun [sing.] an advantage that you have from the beginning: *Being able to speak English gave her a head start at school.* ▶ **fory**

headstone /ˈhedstəʊn/ noun [C] a large stone with writing on, used to mark where a dead person is buried ▶ **nagrobek** ➲ look at **gravestone**, **tombstone**

headstrong /ˈhedstrɒŋ/ adj. doing what you want, without listening to advice from other people ▶ **nieustępliwy**, **uparty**

ˌhead ˈteacher = HEAD[1] (5)

headway /ˈhedweɪ/ noun
IDM **make headway** to go forward or make progress in a difficult situation ▶ **posuwać się (z trudem) naprzód**, **robić (z trudem) postępy**

ˈheadword /ˈhedwɜːd/ noun [C] the first word of an entry in a dictionary, which is followed by an explanation of its meaning ▶ (*słownik*) **hasło**

heady /ˈhedi/ adj. **1** having a quick and exciting effect on the senses: *a heady perfume* ◇ *the heady days* (szalone dni) *of her youth* ▶ **mocny**, **odurzający**, **raptowny 2** (used about alcoholic drinks) likely to make people drunk quickly; potent: *a heady wine* ▶ **mocny**, **idący do głowy 3** (used about a person) excited and acting without careful thought: *to be heady with success* ▶ **odurzony**

🔑 **heal** /hiːl/ verb [I,T] **heal (over/up)** to become healthy again; to make sth healthy again: *The cut will heal up in a few days.* ◇ (figurative) *Nothing he said could heal the damage done to their relationship.* ▶ **leczyć**; **goić się**; **naprawiać**

healer /ˈhiːlə(r)/ noun [C] a person who cures people of illnesses and disease using natural powers rather than medicine: *a faith/spiritual healer* ▶ **uzdrowiciel**

🔑 **health** /helθ/ noun [U] **1** the condition of sb's body or mind: *Fresh fruit is good for your health.* ◇ *in good /poor health* ◇ (figurative) *the health of your marriage/finances* ▶ **zdrowie**; **kondycja 2** the state of being well and free from illness: *As long as you have your health, nothing else matters.* ▶ **zdrowie 3** the work of providing medical care: *The government has promised to spend more on health* (na służbę zdrowia). ◇ *health insurance* ubezpieczenie zdrowotne ◇ *health and safety regulations* przepisy bezpieczeństwa i higieny pracy ▶ **zdrowie**

ˈhealth care noun [U] the service of providing medical care: *the costs of health care for the elderly* ◇ ***health care workers/professionals*** ▶ **opieka medyczna**

ˈhealth centre noun [C] a building where a group of doctors see their patients ▶ **przychodnia**

ˈhealth food noun [C,U] natural food that many people think is especially good for your health because it has been made or grown without adding chemicals ▶ **zdrowa żywność**

the ˈhealth service noun [C] the organization of the medical services of a country ▶ **służba zdrowia** ➲ look at **National Health Service**

ˈhealth visitor noun [C] (in Britain) a trained nurse whose job is to visit people in their homes, for example new parents, and give them advice on some areas of medical care ▶ **pielęg-niarka/niarz środowiskow-a/y**

🔑 **healthy** /ˈhelθi/ adj. (**healthier**; **healthiest**) **1** not often ill; strong and well: *a healthy child/animal/plant* ▶ **zdrowy 2** helping to produce good health: *a healthy climate/diet/lifestyle* ▶ **zdrowy 3** showing good health (of body or mind): *healthy skin and hair* ▶ **zdrowy 4** normal and sensible: *There was plenty of healthy competition between the brothers.* ▶ **zdrowy** OPP for all meanings **unhealthy**
■ **healthily** adv. ▶ **zdrowo**, **dobrze**

heap[1] /hiːp/ noun [C] **1 a heap (of sth)** an untidy pile of sth: *a heap of books/papers* ◇ *All his clothes are* ***in a heap*** *on the floor!* ▶ **kupa**, **stos** ➲ note at **pile** ➲ look at **scrap heap 2** (informal) **a heap (of sth)**; **heaps (of sth)** a large number or amount; plenty: *I've got a heap of work to do.* ▶ **mnóstwo**, **masa**
IDM **heaps better, more, older, etc.** (informal) much better, etc. ▶ **znacznie lepiej itp.**

heap[2] /hiːp/ verb [T] **1 heap sth (up)** to put things in a pile: *I'm going to heap all the leaves up over there.* ◇ *Add six heaped* (kopiastych) *tablespoons of flour.* ▶ **układać** (*w stos*), **usypywać** (*w kopiec*) **2 heap A on/onto B**; **heap B with A** to put a large amount of sth on sth/sb: *He heaped food onto his plate.* Nałożył sobie górę jedzenia. ◇ *The* *press heaped the team with praise.* ▶ **nakładać** (*stertę czegoś na coś*); **obsypywać kogoś czymś**

hear /hɪə(r)/ verb (pt, pp **heard** /hɜːd/) **1** [I,T] [not used in the continuous tenses] to receive sounds with your ears: *Can you speak a little louder – I can't hear very well.* ◇ *I didn't hear you go out this morning.* ◇ *Did you hear what I said?* ▶ **słyszeć** ➲ note at **smell**[1] ⓘ Por. **listen**. Czasem **hear** ma podobne znaczenie co **listen to**: *We'd better hear what they have to say.* Czasownika **hear** w znaczeniu 1-2 nie używa się w czasach *continuous*. Natomiast często spotyka się go w *present participle* (formie *-ing*): *Not hearing what he'd said over the roar of the machines, she just nodded in reply.* ➲ note at **can**[1] **2** [T] [not used in the continuous tenses] to be told about sth: *I hear that you've been offered a job in Canada.* ◇ *'I passed my test!' '**So I've heard** – well done!'* ◇ *I was sorry to hear about your mum's illness.* ▶ **dowiadywać się** **3** [T] (used about a judge, a court, etc.) to listen to the evidence in a trial in order to make a decision about it: *Your case will be heard this afternoon.* ▶ **rozpatrywać**

IDM **hear! hear!** (used for showing that you agree with what sb has just said, especially in a meeting) ▶ **brawo!, racja!**

won't/wouldn't hear of sth to refuse to allow sth: *I wanted to go to art school but my parents wouldn't hear of it.* ▶ **nie chcieć słyszeć (o czymś)**

PHR V **hear (sth) from sb** to receive a letter, telephone call, etc. from sb ▶ **otrzymywać wiadomość (od kogoś)**

hear (sth) of sb/sth to know that sb/sth exists because you have heard them or it mentioned: *Have you heard of the Bermuda Triangle?* ▶ **słyszeć (coś) o kimś/czymś**

hearing /ˈhɪərɪŋ/ noun **1** [U] the ability to hear: *Her hearing isn't very good so you need to speak louder.* ▶ **słuch** **2** [sing.] a time when evidence is given to a judge in a court of law: *a court/disciplinary hearing* ▶ **rozprawa sądowa** **3** [sing.] a chance to give your opinion or explain your position: *to get/give somebody a fair hearing* ◇ *If everybody comes to the meeting, it will give all points of view a fair hearing.* Jeżeli wszyscy przyjdą na zebranie, to wysłucha się wszystkich stron. ▶ **wysłuchanie**

IDM **hard of hearing** → HARD[1]

in/within sb's hearing near enough to sb so that they can hear what is being said ▶ **w zasięgu słuchu**

ˈhearing aid noun [C] a small device for people who cannot hear well that fits inside the ear and makes sounds louder ▶ **aparat słuchowy**

hearsay /ˈhɪəseɪ/ noun [U] things you have heard another person or other people say, which may or may not be true ▶ **pogłoska**

hearse /hɜːs/ noun [C] a large, black car used for carrying a dead person to their funeral ▶ **karawan**

heart /hɑːt/ noun **1** [C] the organ inside your chest that sends blood round your body: *When you exercise your heart beats faster.* ◇ *heart disease/failure* ▶ **serce** ➲ picture at **body** **2** [C] the centre of sb's feelings and emotions: *She has a kind heart.* ◇ *They say he died of a broken heart.* ▶ **serce, dusza** **3** [in compounds] having the type of feelings or character mentioned: *kind-hearted* dobrotliwy ◇ *cold-hearted* nieczuły ▶ (*określa uczuciowość lub charakter danej osoby*) **4** [sing.] **the heart (of sth)** the most central or important part of sth; the middle: *Rare plants can be found **in the heart of** the forest.* ◇ *Let's get straight to **the heart of the matter**.* ▶ **środek**; **sedno** **5** [C] a symbol that is shaped like a heart, often red or pink and used to show love: *He sent her a card with a big red heart on it.* ▶ **serduszko, serce** **6** (**hearts**) [pl.] in a pack of playing cards, the **suit** with red shapes like hearts (5) on them: *the queen of hearts* ▶ **kiery** ➲ note at **card** **7** [C] one of the cards from this suit: *Play a heart, if you've got one.* ▶ **kier**

IDM **after your own heart** (used about people) similar to yourself or of the type you like best ▶ **bratnia dusza**

at heart really; in fact: *My father seems strict but he's a very kind man at heart.* ▶ **w głębi serca**

break sb's heart to make sb very sad ▶ **łamać serce (komuś)**

by heart by remembering exactly; from memory: *Learning lists of words off by heart isn't a good way to increase your vocabulary.* ▶ **na pamięć**

a change of heart → CHANGE[2]

close/dear/near to sb's heart having a lot of importance and interest for sb: *a subject that is very dear to my heart* ▶ **bliski sercu**

cross my heart → CROSS[2]

from the (bottom of your) heart in a way that is true and sincere: *I mean what I said from the bottom of my heart.* ▶ **z głębi serca**

have a heart of gold to be a very kind person ▶ **mieć złote serce**

have/with sb's (best) interests at heart → INTEREST[1]

heart and soul with a lot of energy and enthusiasm ▶ **z wielkim zapałem**

your heart is not in sth (used to say that you are not very interested in or enthusiastic about sth): *It's hard to do a job if your heart isn't in it.* ▶ **nie mieć serca do czegoś**

your heart sinks to suddenly feel disappointed or sad: *When I saw the queues of people in front of me my heart sank.* ▶ (*serce*) **zamierać**

in your heart (of hearts) (used to say that you know that sth is true although you do not want to admit or believe it): *She knew in her heart of hearts that she was making the wrong decision.* ▶ **w głębi serca**

lose heart → LOSE

not have the heart (to do sth) to be unable to do sth unkind: *I don't really have the time to help her, but I didn't have the heart to say no.* ▶ **nie mieć serca (do robienia czegoś)**

pour your heart out (to sb) → POUR

set your heart on sth; **have your heart set on sth** to decide you want sth very much; to be determined to do or have sth ▶ **pragnąć czegoś z całej duszy**

take heart (from sth) to begin to feel positive about sth ▶ **nabierać otuchy**

take sth to heart to be deeply affected or upset by sth ▶ **brać sobie coś do serca**

to your heart's content as much as you want ▶ **ile tylko chcesz**

with all your heart; **with your whole heart** completely: *I hope with all my heart that things work out for you.* ▶ **całym sercem**

young at heart → YOUNG[1]

heartache /ˈhɑːteɪk/ noun [U] great sadness or worry ▶ **strapienie**

ˈheart attack noun [C] a sudden serious illness when the heart stops working correctly, sometimes causing death ▶ **atak serca**

heartbeat /ˈhɑːtbiːt/ noun [C] the regular movement or sound of the heart as it sends blood round the body ▶ **uderzenie serca, bicie serca**

heartbreak /ˈhɑːtbreɪk/ noun [U] very great sadness ▶ **bolesne przeżycie**

heartbreaking /ˈhɑːtbreɪkɪŋ/ adj. making you feel very sad ▶ **rozdzierający serce**

heartbroken /ˈhɑːtbrəʊkən/ (also ˌ**broken-ˈhearted**) adj. extremely sad because of sth that has happened: *Mary was heartbroken when John left her.* ▶ **zrozpaczony**

heartburn /ˈhɑːtbɜːn/ noun [U] a pain that feels like sth burning in your chest caused by **indigestion** ▶ **zgaga**

hearten /ˈhɑːtn/ verb [T, usually passive] to encourage sb; to make sb feel happier ▶ **dodawać odwagi/ducha** OPP **dishearten**

heartening /ˈhɑːtnɪŋ/ adj. encouraging; making you believe that sth good will happen ▶ **podnoszący na duchu** OPP **disheartening**

ˈ**heart failure** noun [U] a serious medical condition in which the heart does not work correctly ▶ **niewydolność serca**

heartfelt /ˈhɑːtfelt/ adj. deeply felt; sincere: *a heartfelt apology* ▶ **płynący z głębi serca**

hearth /hɑːθ/ noun [C] the place where you have an open fire in the house or the area in front of it ▶ **palenisko**; **kominek** ➲ picture at **fireplace**

heartily /ˈhɑːtɪli/ adv. **1** with obvious enthusiasm and enjoyment: *He joined in heartily with the singing.* ▶ **z werwą 2** very much; completely ▶ **całkowicie**, **gruntownie**

heartland /ˈhɑːtlænd/ noun [C] the most central or important part of a country, area, etc. ▶ **centrum**

heartless /ˈhɑːtləs/ adj. unkind; cruel ▶ **nieczuły**, **bez serca**
■ **heartlessly** adv. ▶ **nieczule** | **heartlessness** noun [U] ▶ **nieczułość**

ˈ**heart-rending** adj. making you feel very sad: *The mother of the missing boy made a heart-rending appeal on TV.* ▶ **rozdzierający serce**

ˈ**heart-throb** noun [C] (used especially in newspapers) a famous man, usually an actor or a singer, that a lot of women find attractive: *a Hollywood heart-throb* ▶ **gwiazdor**

ˌ**heart-to-ˈheart** noun [C] a conversation in which you say exactly what you really feel or think: *John's teacher had a heart-to-heart with him to find out what was worrying him.* ▶ **szczera rozmowa**

hearty /ˈhɑːti/ adj. (**heartier**; **heartiest**) **1** showing warm and friendly feelings: *a hearty welcome* ▶ **serdeczny 2** loud, happy and full of energy: *a hearty and boisterous fellow* ◇ *hearty voice* ◇ *a hearty laugh* donośny śmiech ▶ **rubaszny**, **jowialny 3** [only before a noun] (used about a meal) large; making you feel full: *a hearty appetite* dobry apetyt ▶ **obfity 4** showing that you feel strongly about sth: *Hearty congratulations to everyone involved.* ◇ *He nodded his head in hearty agreement* (z pełnym zrozumieniem). ▶ **szczery**

⚷ **heat**[1] /hiːt/ noun **1** [U] the feeling of sth hot: *This fire doesn't* ***give out*** *much* ***heat***. ▶ **ciepło**, **gorąco 2** [sing.] [often with *the*] hot weather: *I like the English climate because I can't stand the heat.* ▶ **upał 3** [sing.] a thing that produces heat: *Remove the pan from the heat.* ▶ **ogień 4** [U] a state or time of anger or excitement: ***In the heat of the moment****, she threatened to resign.* ▶ **ogień 5** [C] one of the first parts of a race or competition. The winners of the heats compete against other winners until the final result is decided: *He won his heat and went through to the final.* ▶ **etap eliminacji**
IDM **be on heat** (used about some female animals) to be ready to have sex because it is the right time of the year ▶ **być w okresie rui**

⚷ **heat**[2] /hiːt/ verb [I,T] **heat (sth) (up)** to become or to make sth hot or warm: *Wait for the oven to heat up before you put the pie in.* ◇ *a heated* (ogrzewany) *swimming pool* ◇ *The meal will need heating up* (posiłek trzeba będzie podgrzać). ▶ **grzać (się)**
PHR V **heat up** (especially US) = HOT UP

heated /ˈhiːtɪd/ adj. (used about a person or discussion) angry or excited: *a heated argument/debate* ▶ **rozogniony**; **ożywiony**, **gorący**
■ **heatedly** adv. ▶ **z żarem**

heater /ˈhiːtə(r)/ noun [C] a machine used for making water or the air in a room, car, etc. hotter: *an electric/gas heater* ◇ *a water heater* ▶ **grzejnik**

heath /hiːθ/ noun [C] an area of open land that is not used for farming and that is often covered with rough grass and other wild plants ▶ **wrzosowisko**

heathen /ˈhiːðn/ noun [C] (old-fashioned) (used by religious people to refer to sb who has no religion, or who does not believe in one of the world's main religions) ▶ **poga-n-in/ka**

heather /ˈheðə(r)/ noun [U] a low wild plant that grows especially on hills and land that is not farmed and has small purple, pink or white flowers ▶ **wrzos**

⚷ **heating** /ˈhiːtɪŋ/ noun [U] a system for making rooms and buildings warm: *Our heating goes off at 10 p.m. and comes on again in the morning.* ▶ **ogrzewanie** ➲ look at **central heating**

heatwave /ˈhiːtweɪv/ noun [C] a period of unusually hot weather ▶ **upały**

heave[1] /hiːv/ verb **1** [I,T] to lift, pull or throw sb/sth heavy with one big effort: *Take hold of this rope and heave!* ◇ *We heaved the cupboard up the stairs.* ▶ **dźwigać**; **ciągnąć** (*z trudem*); **rzucać** (*coś ciężkiego*) **2** [I] **heave (with sth)** to move up and down or in and out in a heavy but regular way: *His chest was heaving with the effort of carrying the cooker.* ▶ **ciężko falować 3** [I] to experience the tight feeling you get in your stomach when you are just about to **vomit**: *The sight of all that blood made her stomach heave.* ▶ **mieć mdłości**
IDM **heave a sigh** to breathe out slowly and loudly: *He heaved a sigh of relief when he heard the good news.* ▶ **wzdychać (głęboko)**

heave[2] /hiːv/ noun [C,U] a strong pull, push, throw, etc. ▶ **szarpnięcie**; **dźwignięcie**; **rzut** (*czymś ciężkim*)

⚷ **heaven** /ˈhevn/ noun **1** (also **Heaven**) [sing.] the place where, in some religions, it is believed that God lives and where good people go when they die: *to go to/be in heaven* ▶ **niebo**, **niebiosa** OPP **hell** ➲ note at **god 2** [U,C] a place or a situation in which you are very happy: *It was heaven being away from work for a week.* ▶ **raj 3** (**the heavens**) [pl.] (used in poetry and literature) the sky: *The stars shone brightly in the heavens* (na niebie) *that night.* ▶ **niebo**, **niebiosa**
IDM **(good) heavens!** (used to express surprise) ▶ **wielkie nieba!**

heavenly /ˈhevnli/ adj. **1** [only before a noun] connected with heaven or the sky: *heavenly bodies* ciała niebieskie ▶ **niebiański 2** (informal) very pleasant; wonderful ▶ **boski**

⚷ **heavy** /ˈhevi/ adj. (**heavier**; **heaviest**) **1** weighing a lot; difficult to lift or move: *This box is too heavy for me to carry.* ▶ **ciężki 2** (used when asking or stating how much sb/sth weighs): ***How heavy is your suitcase?*** ▶ **ciężki 3** larger, stronger or more than usual: *a heavy sleeper* ktoś, kto ma mocny sen ◇ *a heavy* (ciężkostrawny) *meal* ◇ *heavy rain* rzęsisty deszcz ◇ *heavy traffic* duży ruch ◇ *He felt a heavy blow* (mocne uderzenie) *on the back of his head.* ◇ *a heavy smoker/drinker* nałogowy palacz/pijak ◇ *The sound of his heavy breathing told her that he was asleep.* ▶ **ciężki**, **duży**, **mocny 4** (used about a material or substance) solid or thick: *heavy soil* ◇ *a heavy coat* ▶ **ciężki**; **gruby** OPP **light 5** full of hard work; (too) busy: *a heavy day/schedule/timetable* ▶ **ciężki**, **obciążony 6** serious, difficult or boring: *His latest novel makes* ***heavy reading***. ◇ *Things got a bit heavy when she started talking about her failed marriage.* ▶ **żmudny**, **trudny 7 heavy on sth** using large quantities of sth: *My car is rather heavy on petrol.* ▶ **zużywający dużo (czegoś)**
■ **heavily** adv. ▶ **ciężko**, **mocno**, **dużo** | **heaviness** noun [U] ▶ **ciężar**

IDM make heavy weather of sth to make sth seem more difficult than it really is ▶ **wyolbrzymiać**
take a heavy toll/take its toll (on sth) → TOLL

ˌheavy-ˈduty adj. [only before a noun] not easily damaged and therefore suitable for regular use or for hard physical work: *a heavy-duty tyre/carpet* ▶ **wytrzymały, trwały**

ˌheavy-ˈhanded adj. **1** not showing much understanding of other people's feelings: *a heavy-handed approach* ▶ **gruboskórny, nietaktowny 2** using unnecessary force: *heavy-handed police methods* ▶ **bezwzględny** (*niepotrzebnie używający przemocy*)

ˌheavy ˈindustry noun [C,U] industry that uses large machinery to produce metal, coal, vehicles, etc. ▶ **przemysł ciężki**

ˌheavy ˈmetal noun [U] a style of very loud rock music that is played on electric instruments ▶ **heavy metal**

heavyweight /ˈheviweɪt/ noun [C] a person who is in the heaviest weight group in certain fighting sports: *the world heavyweight boxing champion* ▶ **waga ciężka**

Hebrew /ˈhiːbruː/ noun **1** [C] a member of a Semitic people in ancient Palestine ▶ **Izraelit(k)a, Żyd/ówka 2** [U] the language of the Hebrews; the modern form of this language, used especially in Israel ▶ **język hebrajski** ➲ look at **Yiddish**
■ **Hebrew** adj. ▶ **hebrajski, żydowski**

heck /hek/ interj., noun [sing.] (used to express or emphasize annoyance or surprise or to emphasize the amount or size of sth): *It's a heck of a long way to drive* (to piekielnie długa droga do przebycia) *in one day.* ▶ **do licha!**
IDM for the heck of it just for pleasure rather than for a reason ▶ **dla zabawy**
what the heck! (used to say that you are going to do sth that you know you should not do) ▶ **ale co mi tam!**

heckle /ˈhekl/ verb [I,T] to interrupt a speaker at a public meeting by shouting out questions or rude remarks ▶ **przerywać mówcy niegrzecznymi pytaniami/uwagami**
■ **heckler** noun [C] ▶ **przerywający mówcy niegrzecznymi pytaniami/uwagami**

hectare /ˈhekteə(r)/ noun [C] (abbr. **ha**) a measure of land; 10 000 square metres ▶ **hektar**

hectic /ˈhektɪk/ adj. very busy with of a lot of things that you have to do quickly ▶ **szalony, gorączkowy**
■ **hectically** /-kli/ adv. ▶ **szalenie, gorączkowo**

hector /ˈhektə(r)/ verb [T] (formal) to try to make sb do sth by talking or behaving in an aggressive way ▶ **napastować** SYN **bully**
■ **hectoring** adj.: *a hectoring tone of voice* ▶ **napastliwy**

he'd /hiːd/ short for **he had; he would**

hedge¹ /hedʒ/ noun [C] a row of bushes or trees planted close together at the edge of a garden or field to separate one piece of land from another ▶ **żywopłot**

hedge² /hedʒ/ verb **1** [I] to avoid giving a direct answer to a question ▶ **kręcić 2** [T] to put a hedge round a field, garden, etc. ▶ **sadzić żywopłot**
IDM hedge your bets to protect yourself against losing or making a mistake by supporting more than one person or opinion ▶ **asekurować się**

hedgehog /ˈhedʒhɒg/ noun [C] a small brown animal covered with **spines** ▶ **jeż**

hedgerow /ˈhedʒrəʊ/ noun [C] a row of bushes, etc. especially at the side of a country road or around a field ▶ **żywopłot**

hedonism /ˈhiːdənɪzəm/ noun [U] the belief that pleasure is the most important thing in life ▶ **hedonizm**
■ **hedonistic** /ˌhiːdəˈnɪstɪk/ adj. ▶ **hedonistyczny**

hedonist /ˈhiːdənɪst/ noun [C] a person who believes that pleasure is the most important thing in life ▶ **hedonist(k)a**

heed¹ /hiːd/ verb [T] (formal) to pay attention to advice, a warning, etc. ▶ **zważać**

heed² /hiːd/ noun
IDM take heed (of sb/sth); pay heed (to sb/sth) (formal) to pay careful attention to what sb says: *You should take heed of your doctor's advice.* ▶ **zwracać uwagę**

heel¹ /hiːl/ noun [C] **1** the back part of your foot below your ankle: *These shoes rub against my heels.* ▶ **pięta** ➲ picture at **body 2** the part of a sock, etc. that covers your **heel** ▶ **pięta 3** the higher part of a shoe under the **heel** of your foot: *High heels are not practical for long walks.* ▶ **obcas** ➲ picture at **shoe 4** (**-heeled**) having the type of **heel** mentioned: *high-heeled/low-heeled shoes* buty na wysokich/niskich obcasach ▶ **(***określa rodzaj obcasów***)**
IDM dig your heels in → DIG¹
head over heels → HEAD¹

heel² /hiːl/ verb [T] to repair the **heel** of a shoe ▶ **naprawiać obcas**

hefty /ˈhefti/ adj. (**heftier; heftiest**) (informal) big and strong or heavy: *a hefty young man* ◇ *She's earning a hefty salary* (wysoką pensję) *in London.* ▶ **mocny, silny, duży**

height /haɪt/ noun **1** [C,U] the measurement from the bottom to the top of a person or thing: *The nurse is going to check your height and weight.* ◇ *We need a fence that's about two metres* ***in height.*** ▶ **wysokość, wzrost** ➲ note at **tall** ➲ picture at **dimension** ➲ adjective **high 2** [U] the fact that sb/sth is tall or high: *He looks older than he is because of his height.* ▶ **wysoki wzrost 3** [C,U] the distance that sth is above the ground: *We are now flying at a height of 10 000 metres.* ◇ *The plane* ***lost/gained height*** *steadily.* ▶ **wysokość** ⓘ Mówiąc o samolotach, wysokość można też określić bardziej formalnym słowem **altitude. 4** [C, usually pl.] a high place or area: *I'm afraid of heights* (mam lęk wysokości). ▶ **wysokość 5** [U] the strongest or most important part of sth: *the height of summer* pełnia lata ◇ *She's always dressed in the height of fashion.* Jej ubrania są zawsze szczytem mody. ▶ **szczyt**

heighten /ˈhaɪtn/ verb [I,T] to become or to make sth greater or stronger: *I'm using yellow paint to heighten* (spotęgować) *the sunny effect of the room.* ▶ **wzmagać (się), uwydatniać (się), powiększać (się)**

heinous /ˈheɪnəs/ adj. [usually before a noun] (formal) morally very bad: *a heinous crime* ▶ **ohydny**

heir /eə(r)/ noun [C] **heir (to sth)** the person with the legal right to **inherit** money, property or a title when the owner dies: *He's the heir to a large fortune.* ◇ *Who is the heir to the throne* (następca tronu)*?* ▶ **spadkobierca, dziedzic** ⓘ Spadkobierczyni, dziedziczka to **heiress.**

heirloom /ˈeəluːm/ noun [C] something valuable that has belonged to the same family for many years ▶ **scheda, pamiątka rodzinna**

held past tense, past participle of **hold¹**

helicopter /ˈhelɪkɒptə(r)/ (also informal **chopper**) noun [C] a small aircraft that can go straight up into the air. **Helicopters** have long thin metal parts on top that go round very fast. ▶ **helikopter** ➲ picture on **page A6**

helium /ˈhiːliəm/ noun [U] (symbol **He**) a gas which is lighter than air and which does not burn ▶ **hel**

helix /ˈhiːlɪks/ noun [C] (pl. **helices** /ˈhiːlɪsiːz/) a shape like a **spiral** or a line curved around a **cylinder** or **cone** ▶ **helisa**

he'll /hiːl/ short for **he will**

hell /hel/ noun **1** [sing.] the place where, in some religions, it is believed that bad people go to when they die: *to go* *to/be in hell* ◇ (figurative) *Go to hell!* Idź do diabła! ▶ **piekło** ➲ look at **heaven 2** [C,U] (informal) a situation or place that is very unpleasant or painful: *He went through hell when his wife left him.* ▶ **piekło 3** [U] (slang) (used as a swear word to show anger): *Oh hell, I've forgotten my money!* ▶ **cholera! 4** (**the hell**) (slang) (used as a swear word in questions to show anger or surprise): *Who the hell is that at the front door?* ◇ *Why the hell didn't you tell me this before?* ▶ (*kto/jak/gdzie/dlaczego itp.*) **u diabła** ℹ Uwaga! Użycie **hell** w znaczeniach 3 i 4 oraz w idiomach poniżej często uważa się za obraźliwe.

IDM **all hell broke loose** (informal) there was suddenly a lot of noise and confusion ▶ **rozpętało się piekło**

(just) for the hell of it (informal) for fun ▶ **dla draki**

give sb hell (informal) to speak to sb very angrily or to be very strict with sb ▶ **robić komuś piekło**

a/one hell of a... (informal) (used to make an expression stronger or to mean 'very'): *He got into a hell of a fight.* ▶ **piekielny**, **cholerny**

like hell → LIKE[1]

hellish /ˈhelɪʃ/ adj. terrible; very unpleasant ▶ **piekielny**

⚷ **hello** (Brit. also **hallo**) /həˈləʊ/ interj., noun (used when you meet sb, for attracting sb's attention or when you are using the telephone) ▶ **cześć!**, **dzień dobry!**; **halo!** ➲ note at **introduce** ℹ Inne nieformalne pozdrowienia stosowane na powitanie to **hi** i **hiya**.

helm /helm/ noun [C] the part of a boat or ship that is used to change direction. The **helm** can be a handle or a wheel. ▶ **ster**

IDM **at the helm** in charge of an organization, group of people, etc. ▶ **u steru**

helmet /ˈhelmɪt/ noun [C] a type of hard hat that you wear to protect your head: *a crash helmet* ▶ **hełm**

⚷ **help[1]** /help/ verb **1** [I,T] **help (sb) (with sth)**; **help (sb) (to) do sth**; **help sb (across, over, out of, into, etc.)** to do sth for sb in order to be useful or to make sth easier for them: *Can I help?* ◇ *Could you help me with the cooking?* ◇ *My son's helping in our shop at the moment.* ◇ *She helped her grandmother up the stairs.* ▶ **pomagać** ℹ **Can I help you?** („Słucham.") to standardowy zwrot używany przez sprzedawców. **2** [I] (informal) (used to get sb's attention when you are in danger or difficulty): *Help! I'm going to fall!* ▶ **ratunku! 3** [I,T] to make sth better or easier: *If you apologize to him, it might help.* ◇ *This medicine should help your headache.* ▶ **pomagać**, **ratować (coś) 4** [T] **help yourself (to sth)** to take sth (especially food and drink) that is offered to you: *'Can I borrow your pen?' 'Yes, help yourself.'* ▶ **częstować się**, **obsługiwać się 5** [T] **help yourself to sth** to take sth without asking permission; to steal: *Don't just help yourself to my money!* ▶ **brać bez pytania**

IDM **can/can't/could(n't) help (doing) sth/yourself** be able/not be able to stop or avoid doing sth: *It was so funny I couldn't help laughing* (nie mogłem się powstrzymać od śmiechu). ◇ *I just couldn't help myself* (nie mogłem nic poradzić) – *I had to laugh.* ◇ *He can't help being so small.* To nie jego wina, że jest taki mały. ◇ *The accident couldn't be helped.* Nie można było uniknąć wypadku. ▶ **móc/nie móc uniknąć czegoś/robienia czegoś**

a helping hand some help: *My neighbour is always ready to give me a helping hand.* ▶ **pomocna dłoń**

PHR V **help (sb) out** to help sb in a difficult situation; to give money to help sb ▶ **pomagać**

⚷ **help[2]** /help/ noun **1** [U] **help (with sth)** the act of helping: *Do you need any help with that?* ◇ *This map isn't much help.* ◇ *She stopped smoking **with the help of** her family and friends.* ◇ *'Run and **get help** – my son's fallen in the river!'* ▶ **pomoc**, **ratunek 2** [sing.] **a help (to sb)** a person or thing that helps: *Your directions were a great help – we found the place easily.* ▶ **pomoc**

helper /ˈhelpə(r)/ noun [C] a person who helps (especially with work) ▶ **pomocni-k/ca**

⚷ **helpful** /ˈhelpfl/ adj. giving help: *helpful advice* ▶ **pomocny**; **użyteczny**

■ **helpfully** /-fəli/ adv. ▶ **pomocnie**, **przydatnie** | **helpfulness** noun [U] ▶ **pomoc**; **użyteczność**

helping /ˈhelpɪŋ/ noun [C] the amount of food that is put on a plate at one time ▶ **porcja** ➲ look at **portion**

helpless /ˈhelpləs/ adj. unable to take care of yourself or do things without the help of other people: *a helpless baby* ▶ **bezradny**

■ **helplessly** adv.: *They watched helplessly as their house went up in flames.* ▶ **bezradnie** | **helplessness** noun [U] ▶ **bezradność**

hem[1] /hem/ noun [C] the edge at the bottom of a piece of cloth (especially on a skirt, dress or trousers) that has been turned up and sewn ▶ **rąbek**

hem[2] /hem/ verb [T] (**hemming**; **hemmed**) to turn up and sew the bottom of a piece of clothing or cloth ▶ **obrębiać**

PHR V **hem sb in** to surround sb and prevent them from moving away: *We were hemmed in by the crowd and could not leave.* ▶ **osaczać kogoś**

hemisphere /ˈhemɪsfɪə(r)/ noun [C] **1** one half of the earth: *the northern/southern/eastern/western hemisphere* ▶ **półkula ziemska 2** the shape of half a ball ▶ **półkula**

hemophilia, hemophiliac (US) = HAEMOPHILIA, HAEMOPHILIAC

hemorrhage (US) = HAEMORRHAGE

hemorrhoids (US) = HAEMORRHOIDS

hemp /hemp/ noun [U] a plant that is used for making rope and rough cloth and for producing **cannabis** ▶ **konopie**

hen /hen/ noun [C] **1** a female bird that is kept for its eggs or its meat ▶ **kura** ➲ note at **chicken 2** the female of any type of bird: *a hen pheasant* ▶ **samica** (*ptaków*) ℹ Samiec różnych ptaków to **cock**.

⚷ **hence** /hens/ adv. (formal) **1** from here or now ▶ **stąd**; **od tej chwili 2** for this reason: *I've got some news to tell you – hence the letter.* ▶ **stąd**, **więc**

henceforth /ˌhensˈfɔːθ/ (also **henceforward** /ˌhensˈfɔːwəd/) adv. (formal) from now on; in future ▶ **odtąd**, **na przyszłość**

henchman /ˈhentʃmən/ noun [C] (pl. **-men** /-mən/) a person who is employed by sb to protect them and who may do things that are illegal or violent ▶ **popleczni-k/czka**

henna /ˈhenə/ noun [U] a natural reddish-brown **dye**, used especially on the hair and skin ▶ **henna**

ˈ**hen party** (also ˈ**hen night**) noun [sing.] a party that a woman who will soon be getting married has with her female friends ▶ **panieński wieczór** ➲ look at **stag night**

henpecked /ˈhenpekt/ adj. (used to describe a husband who always does what his wife tells him to do) ▶ **pod pantoflem**

hepatitis /ˌhepəˈtaɪtɪs/ noun [U] a serious disease of the **liver** ▶ **zapalenie wątroby**

⚷ **her[1]** /hɜː(r)/ pron. (the object of a verb or preposition) the woman or girl that was mentioned earlier: *He told Sue that he loved her.* ◇ *I've got a letter for your mother. Could you give it to her, please?* ◇ *That must be her now.* To na pewno ona. ▶ **ją**, **jej** ➲ note at **he** ➲ look at **she**

⚷ **her[2]** /hɜː(r)/ determiner of or belonging to the woman or girl mentioned earlier: *That's her book.* ◇ *Fiona has broken her leg.* ▶ **jej**, **swój** ➲ look at **hers**

herald /ˈherəld/ verb [T] (formal) to be a sign that sb/sth is going to happen soon: *The minister's speech heralded a change of policy.* ▶ **zwiastować**

■ **herald** noun [C] a person in former times who gave important messages from a ruler to the people ▶ **herold**

heraldry /ˈherəldri/ noun [U] the study of the history of old and important families and their special family symbols (coats of arms) ▶ **heraldyka**

herb /hɜːb; US ɜːb/ noun [C] a plant whose leaves, seeds, etc. are used in medicine or in cooking ▶ **zioło** ➲ look at **spice**

herbal /ˈhɜːbl; US ˈɜːbl/ adj. made of or using **herbs**: *herbal medicine/remedies* ▶ **ziołowy**

herbalism /ˈhɜːblɪzəm; US also ˈɜːbl-/ noun [U] the medical use of plants, especially as a form of **alternative medicine** ▶ **ziołolecznictwo**

herbalist /ˈhɜːbəlɪst; US also ˈɜːb-/ noun [C] a person who grows, sells or uses **herbs** for medical purposes ▶ **zielarz/rka**

ˌ**herbal** ˈ**tea** noun [U,C] a drink made from dried **herbs** and hot water ▶ **herbata ziołowa**

herbicide /ˈhɜːbɪsaɪd; US also ˈɜːb-/ noun [C, U] a chemical that is poisonous to plants, used to kill plants that are growing where they are not wanted ▶ **herbicyd** ➲ look at **insecticide**, **pesticide**

herbivore /ˈhɜːbɪvɔː(r)/ noun [C] an animal that only eats grass and plants ▶ **zwierzę roślinożerne** ➲ look at **carnivore**, **omnivore**
■ **herbivorous** adj. ▶ **roślinożerny**

herd[1] /hɜːd/ noun [C] a large number of animals that live and feed together: *a herd of cattle/deer/elephants* ▶ **stado**, **trzoda** ➲ note at **cow** ➲ look at **flock**

herd[2] /hɜːd/ verb [T] to move people or animals somewhere together in a group: *The prisoners were herded onto the train.* ▶ **pędzić**

⚷ **here**[1] /hɪə(r)/ adv. **1** [after a verb or a preposition] in, at or to the place where you are or which you are pointing to: *Come (over) here.* ◇ *The school is a mile from here* (stąd). ◇ *Please sign here.* ▶ **tutaj**, **tu 2** at this point in a discussion or a piece of writing: *Here the speaker stopped and looked around the room.* ▶ (*moment*) **w tym miejscu 3** (used at the beginning of a sentence to introduce or draw attention to sb/sth): *Here is the 10 o'clock news.* ◇ *Here comes the bus.* ◇ *Here we are.* Już jesteśmy. ▶ **oto** ⓘ Zwróć uwagę na szyk zdania w ostatnim przykładzie. Mówi się **Here are the children**, ale **Here they are**. Zwróć też uwagę na wyrażenie **Here you are**, które stosuje się, podając coś komuś i znaczy „proszę (bardzo)": *Here you are – this is that book I was talking about.* **4** (used for emphasizing a noun): *I think you'll find this book here very useful.* ▶ **tu obecny**
IDM **here and there** in various places ▶ **tu i tam**, **tu i ówdzie**
here goes (informal) (used to say that you are about to do sth exciting, dangerous, etc.): *I've never done a backward dive before, but here goes!* ▶ **no to jazda!**, **raz kozie śmierć!**
here's to sb/sth (used for wishing for the health, success, etc. of sb/sth while holding a drink): *Here's to a great holiday!* ◇ *Here's to your future happiness!* Wypijmy za twoje szczęście. ▶ (*wznosząc toast*) **za**
neither here nor there not important: *My opinion is neither here nor there. If you like the dress then buy it.* ▶ **mniejsza o (to)**

here[2] /hɪə(r)/ interj. (used for attracting sb's attention, when offering help or when giving sth to sb): *Here, let me help!* ▶ **halo!**, **proszę pan-a/i!**

hereabouts /ˌhɪərəˈbaʊts/ (US **hereabout**) adv. near this place ▶ **gdzieś tutaj**

hereafter /ˌhɪərˈɑːftə(r); US -ˈæf-/ adv. (formal) (used in legal documents, etc.) from now on ▶ **od tej chwili**, **w przyszłości**

hereditary /həˈredɪtri; US -teri/ adj. passed on from parent to child: *a hereditary disease* ▶ **dziedziczny** ➲ look at **inherit**

heredity /həˈredəti/ noun [U] the process by which physical or mental qualities pass from parent to child ▶ **dziedziczność** ➲ look at **inherit**

heresy /ˈherəsi/ noun [C,U] (pl. **heresies**) a (religious) opinion or belief that is different from what is generally accepted to be true ▶ **herezja**

heretic /ˈherətɪk/ noun [C] a person whose religious beliefs are believed to be wrong or evil ▶ **herety-k/czka**
■ **heretical** /həˈretɪkl/ adj. ▶ **heretycki**

herewith /ˌhɪəˈwɪð/ adv. (formal) with this letter, etc.: *Please fill in the form enclosed herewith.* ▶ **w załączeniu**, **wraz z tym**

heritage /ˈherɪtɪdʒ/ noun [C, usually sing.] the customs, qualities and culture of a country that have existed for a long time and that have great importance for the country ▶ **dziedzictwo**, **spuścizna**

hermetic /hɜːˈmetɪk/ adj. tightly closed so that no air can escape or enter ▶ **hermetyczny** SYN **airtight**
■ **hermetically** /-kli/ adv.: *a hermetically sealed container* ▶ **hermetycznie**

hermit /ˈhɜːmɪt/ noun [C] a person who prefers to live alone, without contact with other people ▶ **pustelni-k/ca**

hernia /ˈhɜːniə/ (also **rupture**) noun [C,U] the medical condition in which an organ inside the body, for example the stomach, pushes through the wall of muscle which surrounds it ▶ **przepuklina**

⚷ **hero** /ˈhɪərəʊ; US also ˈhiː-/ noun [C] (pl. **heroes**) **1** a person who is admired, especially for having done sth difficult or good: *The team were given a* ***hero's welcome*** *on their return home.* ◇ *an anti-hero* antybohater ▶ **bohater 2** the most important male character in a book, play, film, etc. ▶ **bohater**, **główna postać** ➲ look at **heroine**, **villain**

heroic /həˈrəʊɪk/ adj. (used about people or their actions) having a lot of courage: *a heroic effort* ▶ **bohaterski**
■ **heroically** /-kli/ adv. ▶ **bohatersko**

heroin /ˈherəʊɪn/ noun [U] a powerful illegal drug that some people take for pleasure and then cannot stop taking ▶ **heroina**

heroine /ˈherəʊɪn/ noun [C] **1** a woman who is admired, especially for having done sth difficult or good ▶ **bohaterka 2** the most important female character in a book, play, film, etc. ▶ **bohaterka**, **główna postać** ➲ look at **hero**

heroism /ˈherəʊɪzəm/ noun [U] great courage ▶ **bohaterstwo**

heron /ˈherən/ noun [C] a large bird with a long neck and long legs that lives near water ▶ **czapla**

herpes /ˈhɜːpiːz/ noun [U] one of a group of infectious diseases, caused by a virus, that cause painful spots on the skin, especially on the face and sexual organs ▶ **opryszczka**

herring /ˈherɪŋ/ noun [C,U] (pl. **herring** or **herrings**) a fish that swims in **shoals** in cold seas and is used for food ▶ **śledź** ➲ look at **kipper**
IDM **a red herring** → RED

⚷ **hers** /hɜːz/ pron. of or belonging to her: *I didn't have a pen but Helen lent me hers.* ▶ **jej**, **swój**

⚷ **herself** /hɜːˈself; weak form həˈs-/ pron. **1** (used when the female who does an action is also affected by it): *She hurt herself quite badly when she fell downstairs.* ◇ *Irene*

looked at herself in the mirror. ▶ **się, siebie 2** (used to emphasize the female who does the action): *She told me the news herself.* ◇ *Has Rosy done this herself?* ▶ **sama, osobiście 3** in her normal state; healthy: *She's not feeling herself* (czuje się nieswojo) *today.* ▶ **zdrowa**
IDM **(all) by herself 1** alone: *She lives by herself.* ▶ **sama, samotnie** ➲ note at **alone 2** without help: *I don't think she needs any help – she can change a tyre by herself.* ▶ **samodzielnie**
(all) to herself without having to share: *Julie has the bedroom to herself now her sister's left home.* ▶ **tylko dla siebie (samej)**

he's /hi:z/ short for **he is; he has**

hesitant /ˈhezɪtənt/ adj. **hesitant (to do/about doing sth)** slow to speak or act because you are not sure if you should or not: *I'm very hesitant about criticizing him too much.* ▶ **niezdecydowany, niepewny**
■ **hesitancy** /ˈhezɪtənsi/ noun [U] ▶ **niezdecydowanie, wahanie** | **hesitantly** adv. ▶ **niezdecydowanie, niepewnie**

hesitate /ˈhezɪteɪt/ verb [I] **1 hesitate (about/over sth)** to pause before you do sth or before you take a decision, usually because you are uncertain or worried: *He hesitated before going into her office.* ◇ *Alan replied without hesitating* (bez wahania). ▶ **wahać się 2 hesitate (to do sth)** to not want to do sth because you are not sure that it is right: *Don't hesitate to phone* (dzwoń śmiało) *if you have any problems.* ▶ **wahać się**
■ **hesitation** /ˌhezɪˈteɪʃn/ noun [C,U]: *She agreed without a moment's hesitation.* ▶ **wahanie, niezdecydowanie**

heterogeneous /ˌhetərəˈdʒi:niəs/ adj. (formal) made up of different kinds of people or things: *the heterogeneous population of the USA* ▶ **różnorodny, heterogeniczny** OPP **homogeneous**

heterosexual /ˌhetərəˈsekʃuəl/ adj. sexually attracted to a person of the opposite sex ▶ **heteroseksualny** ➲ look at **bisexual, homosexual**
■ **heterosexual** noun [C] ▶ **heteroseksualist(k)a**

het up /ˌhet ˈʌp/ adj. [not before a noun] (informal) **het up (about/over sth)** worried or excited about sth ▶ **rozdrażniony, spięty**

hew /hju:/ verb [I,T] (formal) to make or shape sth large by cutting: *roughly hewn stone* ▶ **rąbać, ciosać**

hexagon /ˈheksəgən/ noun [C] a shape with six sides ▶ **sześciokąt**
■ **hexagonal** /heksˈægənl/ adj. ▶ **sześciokątny**

hey /heɪ/ interj. (informal) (used to attract sb's attention or to show that you are surprised or interested): *Hey, what are you doing?* ▶ **hej!**
IDM **hey presto** people sometimes say **'hey presto'** when they have done sth so quickly that it seems like magic ▶ **zrobione!**

heyday /ˈheɪdeɪ/ noun [sing.] the period when sb/sth was most powerful, successful, rich, etc. ▶ **szczyt** (*np. kariery*)

HGV /ˌeɪtʃ dʒi: ˈvi:/ abbr. (Brit.) **heavy goods vehicle**; a large vehicle such as a lorry ▶ **ciężki pojazd ciężarowy**

hi /haɪ/ interj. (informal) an informal word used when you meet sb you know well; hello ▶ **cześć!, witaj!**

hibernate /ˈhaɪbəneɪt/ verb [I] (used about animals) to spend the winter in a state like deep sleep ▶ **zapadać w sen zimowy**
■ **hibernation** /ˌhaɪbəˈneɪʃn/ noun [U] ▶ **sen zimowy**

hiccup (also **hiccough**) /ˈhɪkʌp/ noun **1** [C] a sudden, usually repeated sound that is made in the throat and that you cannot control ▶ **czkawka 2 ((the) hiccups)** [pl.] a series of **hiccups**: *Don't eat so fast or you'll* ***get hiccups!*** ◇ *If you* ***have the hiccups****, try holding your breath.* ▶ **czkawka 3** [C] a small problem or difficulty: *There's been a slight hiccup in our holiday arrangements but I've got it sorted out now.* ▶ **drobne potknięcie**
■ **hiccup** (also **hiccough**) verb [I] ▶ **czkać**

hide¹ /haɪd/ verb (pt **hid** /hɪd/, pp **hidden** /ˈhɪdn/) **1** [T] to put or keep sb/sth in a place where they or it cannot be seen; to cover sth so that it cannot be seen: *Where shall I hide the money?* ◇ *You couldn't see Bill in the photo – he was hidden behind John.* ▶ **chować, ukrywać 2** [I] to be or go in a place where you cannot be seen or found: *Quick, run and hide!* ◇ *The child was hiding under the bed.* ▶ **chować się, ukrywać się 3** [T] **hide sth (from sb)** to keep sth secret, especially your feelings: *She tried to hide her disappointment from them.* ▶ **skrywać**

hide² /haɪd/ noun **1** [C] a place from which people can watch wild animals, birds, etc. without being seen ▶ **kryjówka** (*np. dla obserwatorów ptaków*) **2** [C,U] the skin of a large animal, especially when it is used for leather ▶ **skóra** (*zwierzęcia*)

ˌhide-and-ˈseek noun [U] a children's game in which one person hides and the others try to find them ▶ **zabawa w chowanego**

hideous /ˈhɪdiəs/ adj. very ugly or unpleasant: *a hideous sight* ◇ *a hideous crime* ▶ **ohydny, odrażający**
■ **hideously** adv. ▶ **ohydnie, odrażająco**

hideout /ˈhaɪdaʊt/ noun [C] a place where sb goes when they do not want anyone to find them ▶ **kryjówka**

hiding /ˈhaɪdɪŋ/ noun **1** [U] the state of being hidden: *The escaped prisoners are believed to be* ***in hiding*** (uważa się, że zbiegli więźniowie ukrywają się) *somewhere in London.* ◇ *to go into hiding* ukryć się ▶ **ukrycie (się) 2** [C, usually sing.] (informal) a punishment involving being hit hard many times: *You deserve a good hiding for what you've done.* ▶ **lanie, cięgi**

ˈhiding place noun [C] a place where sb/sth is or could be hidden ▶ **kryjówka**

hierarchy /ˈhaɪərɑ:ki/ noun [C] (pl. **hierarchies**) a system or organization that has many levels from the lowest to the highest ▶ **hierarchia**
■ **hierarchical** /ˌhaɪəˈrɑ:kɪkl/ adj. ▶ **hierarchiczny**

hieroglyphics /ˌhaɪərəˈglɪfɪks/ noun [pl.] the system of writing that was used in ancient Egypt in which a small picture represents a word or sound ▶ **hieroglify**

hi-fi /ˈhaɪ faɪ/ noun [C] equipment for playing recorded music that produces high quality sound ▶ **sprzęt hi-fi**
■ **hi-fi** adj.: *a hi-fi system* ▶ (*sprzęt elektroakustyczny*) **hi-fi**

higgledy-piggledy /ˌhɪgldi ˈpɪgldi/ adv., adj. (informal) not in any order; mixed up together: *a higgledy-piggledy collection of houses* chaotyczna zabudowa ▶ **w nieładzie, jak groch z kapustą**

high¹ /haɪ/ adj. **1** (used about things) having a large distance between the bottom and the top: *high cliffs* ◇ *What's the highest mountain in the world?* ◇ *high heels* ◇ *The garden wall was so high that we couldn't see over it.* ▶ **wysoki** OPP **low** ➲ note at **tall** ➲ noun **height 2** having a particular height: *The hedge is one metre high* (ma metr wysokości). ◇ *knee-high boots* buty do kolan ▶ **mający** *x* **wysokości 3** at a level which is a long way from the ground, or from sea level: *a high shelf* ◇ *The castle was built on high ground.* ▶ **wysoko położony, górny** OPP **low 4** above the usual or normal level or amount: *high prices* ◇ *at high speed* ◇ *a high level of unemployment* ◇ *He's got a high temperature.* ◇ *Oranges are high in* (mają dużo) *vitamin C.* ▶ **wysoki, duży** OPP **low 5** better than what is usual: *high-quality goods* ◇ *Her work is of a very high standard.* ◇ *He has a high opinion of you.* ◇ *What was the high point* (główną atrakcją) *of your trip?* ◇ *We have high hopes for* (wiele sobie obiecujemy po) *our new product.* ▶ **wysokiej (jakości), korzystny** OPP **poor 6** having an important position: *We shall have* *to refer the matter to a higher authority.* ◇ *Sam only joined the company three years ago, but she's already quite high up* (ale już zajmuje wysokie stanowisko). ▶ (*władza*) **wysoki, główny** **7** morally good: *high ideals* ▶ **wzniosły** **8** (used about sounds) not deep or low: *Dogs can hear very high sounds.* ◇ *Women usually have higher voices than men.* ▶ (*dźwięk*) **wysoki** OPP **low** **9** [not before a noun] (informal) **high (on sth)** under the influence of drugs, alcohol, etc. ▶ **naćpany, na haju** **10** (used about a gear in a car) that allows a faster speed ▶ **wysoki** OPP **low** **11** [not before a noun] (used about some kinds of food) beginning to go bad: *That cheese smells a bit high.* ▶ **zatęchły**

IDM **be left high and dry** → LEAVE[1]
a high/low profile → PROFILE

high² /haɪ/ noun [C] **1** a high level or point: *Profits reached an all-time high last year.* ▶ **szczyt, wysoki poziom** OPP **low** **2** an area of high air pressure ▶ **wyż** OPP **low** **3** (informal) a feeling of great pleasure or happiness that sb gets from doing sth exciting or being successful: *He was **on a high*** (w euforii) *after passing all his exams.* ◇ *the **highs and lows*** (wzloty i upadki) *of her career* ▶ **stan euforii** OPP **low** **4** (informal) a feeling of great pleasure or happiness that may be caused by a drug, alcohol, etc. ▶ **uniesienie, rausz**

IDM **on high** **1** (formal) (in) a high place, the sky or heaven ▶ **na wysokości, w niebiosach** **2** (humorous) the people in senior positions in an organization: *The order came from on high* (z góry).

⚷ **high³** /haɪ/ adv. **1** at or to a high position or level: *The sun was high in the sky.* ◇ *I can't jump any higher.* ◇ *You should aim high.* ▶ **wysoko** ➲ noun **height** **2** at a high level: *How high can you sing?* ▶ **wysoko** (*np. śpiewać*) OPP for both meanings **low**

IDM **high and low** everywhere: *We've searched high and low for the keys.* ▶ **wszędzie, po całym** (*np. domu*)
it's about/high time → TIME[1]
run high (used about the feelings of a group of people) to be especially strong: *Emotions are running high in the neighbourhood where the murders took place.* ▶ (*uczucia, nastroje itp.*) **wzburzać się**

highbrow /ˈhaɪbraʊ/ adj. interested in or concerned with matters that many people would find too serious to be interesting: *highbrow newspapers/TV programmes* ▶ (*dzieła sztuki*) **intelektualny** ℹ Czasami wyraża dezaprobatę.

ˈ**high chair** noun [C] a special chair with long legs and a little seat and table, for a small child to sit in when eating ▶ **wysokie krzesełko do sadzania małych dzieci przy stole**

ˌ**high-ˈclass** adj. of especially good quality: *a high-class restaurant* ▶ **znakomity, pierwszorzędny**

ˌ**High ˈCourt** noun [C] the most important court of law in some countries ▶ **sąd najwyższy**

ˌ**higher eduˈcation** noun [U] education and training at a college or university, especially to degree level ▶ **studia wyższe** ➲ look at **further education**

ˈ**high jump** noun [sing.] the sport in which people try to jump over a bar in order to find out who can jump the highest ▶ **skok wzwyż** ➲ look at **long jump**

highland /ˈhaɪlənd/ adj. [only before a noun] **1** in or connected with an area of land that has mountains: *highland streams* ▶ **górski** ➲ look at **lowland** **2** (**Highland**) in or connected with the Highlands of Scotland ▶ **dot. gór w Szkocji**

ˌ**high-ˈlevel** adj. involving important people: *high-level talks* ▶ **na szczycie**

⚷ **highlight¹** /ˈhaɪlaɪt/ verb [T] **1** to emphasize sth so that people give it special attention: *The report highlighted the need for improved safety at football grounds.* ▶ **podkreślać** **2** to mark part of a text with a different colour, etc. so that people give it more attention: *I've highlighted the important passages in yellow.* ▶ **zaznaczać markerem**

⚷ **highlight²** /ˈhaɪlaɪt/ noun **1** [C] the best or most interesting part of sth: *The highlights of the match will be shown on TV tonight.* ▶ **najciekawszy fragment** **2** (**highlights**) [pl.] areas of lighter colour that are put in sb's hair ▶ **pasemka**

highlighter /ˈhaɪlaɪtə(r)/ (also ˈ**highlighter pen**) noun [C] a special pen used for marking words in a text in bright colours ▶ **marker** ➲ picture at **stationery**

⚷ **highly** /ˈhaɪli/ adv. **1** to a high degree; very: *highly trained/educated/developed* ◇ *It's highly unlikely that anyone will complain.* ▶ **bardzo, w wysokim stopniu** **2** with admiration: *I think highly of* (wysoko cenię) *your work.* ◇ *a highly-paid job* dobrze płatna praca ▶ **wysoko, korzystnie**

ˌ**highly ˈstrung** adj. nervous and easily upset ▶ **nerwowy, przewrażliwiony**

Highness /ˈhaɪnəs/ noun (**your/his/her Highness**) [C] a title used when speaking about or to a member of a royal family ▶ **(Jego/Jej) Wysokość**

ˌ**high-ˈpowered** adj. **1** (used about people) important and successful: *high-powered executives* ▶ **ważny** **2** (used about things) having great power: *a high-powered engine* ▶ **wysokiej mocy**

ˌ**high-resoˈlution** adj. (used about a photograph or an image on a computer or television screen) showing a lot of clear sharp detail: *a high-resolution scan* ▶ **o wysokiej rozdzielczości** OPP **low-resolution**

ˈ**high-rise** adj. [only before a noun] (used about a building) very tall and having a lot of floors ▶ **wielopiętrowy**

ˈ**high school** noun [C,U] (in the US and some other countries) a school for young people between the ages of 14 and 18; (often used in Britain in the names of schools for young people between the ages of 11 and 18) ▶ **szkoła średnia**

ˈ**high street** noun [C] (Brit.) (often used in names) the main street of a town: *The Post Office is in the High Street.* ▶ **główna ulica**

high-tech (also **hi-tech**) /ˌhaɪ ˈtek/ adj. **1** using the most modern methods and machines, especially electronic ones: *high-tech industries/hospitals* ▶ **zautomatyzowany, skomputeryzowany** OPP **low-tech** **2** using designs or styles taken from industry, etc.; very modern ▶ **supernowoczesny**

ˌ**high ˈtide** noun [U] the time when the sea comes furthest onto the land ▶ **przypływ** OPP **low tide** ➲ look at **ebb**

⚷ **highway** /ˈhaɪweɪ/ noun [C] (especially US) a main road (between towns) ▶ **główna szosa, autostrada** ➲ look at **motorway** ➲ note at **road**

hijack /ˈhaɪdʒæk/ verb [T] **1** to take control of a plane, etc. by force, usually for political reasons ▶ **porywać** (*np. samolot*) ➲ note at **crime** ➲ look at **kidnap** **2** to take control of a meeting, an event, etc. in order to force people to pay attention to sth: *The rally was hijacked by right-wing extremists.* ▶ **zakłócać**

■ **hijack** noun [C]: *The hijack was ended by armed police.* ▶ **porwanie** | **hijacker** noun [C] ▶ **porywacz** (*np. samolotu*) | **hijacking** noun [C,U] ▶ **porwanie** (*np. samolotu*)

hike /haɪk/ noun [C] a long walk in the country: *We went on a ten-mile hike at the weekend.* ▶ **wędrówka, piesza wycieczka**

■ **hike** verb [I] ▶ **wędrować, iść na wycieczkę** ℹ **Go hiking** stosuje się, mówiąc o turystyce pieszej: *They went hiking in Wales for their holiday.* | **hiker** noun [C] ▶ **wędrowiec, turyst(k)a piesz-y/a**

hilarious /hɪˈleəriəs/ adj. extremely funny ▶ **prześmieszny** ➲ note at **humour**

■ **hilariously** adv. ▶ **prześmiesznie**

hilarity /hɪˈlærəti/ noun [U] the state of finding sth very funny, which causes people to laugh loudly ▶ **wesołość, głośny śmiech**

hill /hɪl/ noun [C] a high area of land that is not as high as a mountain: *There was a wonderful view from the top of the hill.* ▶ **wzgórze** ➲ look at **uphill, downhill**

hillside /ˈhɪlsaɪd/ noun [C] the side of a hill ▶ **zbocze, stok**

hilltop /ˈhɪltɒp/ noun [C] the top of a hill ▶ **wzgórze, szczyt**

hilly /ˈhɪli/ adj. (**hillier; hilliest**) having a lot of hills ▶ **górzysty**

hilt /hɪlt/ noun [C] the handle of a knife or a **sword** ▶ **garda, rękojeść**

IDM **to the hilt** to a high degree; completely: *I'll defend you to the hilt.* ▶ **całkowicie, gruntownie**

him /hɪm/ pron. (the object of a verb or preposition) the man or boy who was mentioned earlier: *Helen told Ian that she loved him.* ◇ *I've got a letter for your father – can you give it to him, please?* ◇ *That must be him now.* To na pewno on. ▶ **(je)go, (je)mu, nim** ➲ note at **he**

himself /hɪmˈself/ pron. **1** (used when the male who does an action is also affected by it): *He cut himself when he was shaving.* ◇ *John looked at himself in the mirror.* ▶ **się, siebie 2** (used to emphasize the male who does the action): *He told me the news himself.* ◇ *Did he write this himself?* ▶ **sam, osobiście 3** in his normal state; healthy: *He's not feeling himself* (czuje się nieswojo) *today.* ▶ **zdrowy**

IDM **(all) by himself 1** alone: *He lives by himself.* ▶ **sam, samotnie** ➲ note at **alone 2** without help: *He should be able to cook a meal by himself.* ▶ **samodzielnie**

(all) to himself without having to share: *Charlie has the bedroom to himself now his brother's left home.* ▶ **tylko dla siebie (samego)**

hind /haɪnd/ adj. [only before a noun] (used about an animal's legs, etc.) at the back ▶ **tylny** ℹ Mówi się również **back legs**. Przednie łapy to **front legs** lub **forelegs**. ➲ picture on **page A10**

hinder /ˈhɪndə(r)/ verb [T] to make it more difficult for sb/sth to do sth: *A lot of scientific work is hindered by lack of money.* ▶ **powstrzymywać, przeszkadzać**

hindrance /ˈhɪndrəns/ noun [C] a person or thing that makes it difficult for you to do sth ▶ **przeszkoda, zawada**

hindsight /ˈhaɪndsaɪt/ noun [U] the understanding that you have of a situation only after it has happened: ***With hindsight**, I wouldn't have lent him the money.* ▶ **wiedza po fakcie** ➲ look at **foresight**

Hindu /ˈhɪnduː; ˌhɪnˈduː/ noun [C] a person whose religion is Hinduism ▶ **wyznawca hinduizmu**

■ **Hindu** adj.: *Hindu beliefs* ▶ **hinduski**

Hinduism /ˈhɪnduːɪzəm/ noun [U] the main religion of India. Hindus believe in many gods and that, after death, people will return to life in a different form. ▶ **hinduizm**

hinge¹ /hɪndʒ/ noun [C] a piece of metal that joins two sides of a box, door, etc. together and allows it to be opened or closed ▶ **zawias**

hinge² /hɪndʒ/ verb

PHR V **hinge on sth** to depend on sth: *The future of the project hinges on the meeting today.* ▶ **zależeć od czegoś**

hint¹ /hɪnt/ noun [C] **1** something that you suggest in an indirect way: *If you keep mentioning parties, maybe they'll **take the hint** and invite you.* ▶ **aluzja, napomknięcie 2** sth that suggests what will happen in the future: *The first half of the match **gave no hint** of the excitement to come.* ▶ **wskazówka** SYN **sign 3** a small amount of sth: *There was a hint of sadness in his voice.* ▶ **odrobina** SYN **suggestion 4** a piece of advice or information: *helpful hints* ▶ **porada** SYN **tip**

hint² /hɪnt/ verb [I,T] **hint (at sth); hint that ...** to suggest sth in an indirect way: *They only hinted at their great disappointment.* ◇ *He hinted that he might be moving to Greece.* ▶ **robić aluzję, dawać do zrozumienia**

hip¹ /hɪp/ noun [C] the part of the side of your body above your legs and below your waist: *He stood there angrily with his hands on his hips.* ▶ **biodro** ➲ picture at **body**

hip² /hɪp/ interj.

IDM **hip, hip, hurray/hurrah** (shouted three times when a group wants to show that it is pleased with sb or with sth that has happened) ▶ **hip, hip (hura)!**

hip hop noun [U] a type of dance music with spoken words and a steady beat played on electronic instruments ▶ **hip hop**

ˈhip-huggers (US) = HIPSTERS

hippie (also **hippy**) /ˈhɪpi/ noun [C] (pl. **hippies**) a person who rejects the usual values and way of life of western society. Especially in the 1960s, **hippies** showed that they were different by wearing brightly coloured clothes, having long hair and taking drugs. ▶ **hipis**

hippopotamus /ˌhɪpəˈpɒtəməs/ noun [C] (also informal **hippo** /ˈhɪpəʊ/) a large African animal with a large head and short legs that lives in or near rivers ▶ **hipopotam**

hipsters /ˈhɪpstəz/ (US **ˈhip-huggers**) noun [pl.] trousers that cover the hips but not the waist: *a pair of hipsters* ▶ **spodnie biodrówki**

■ **hipster** adj. [only before a noun]: *hipster jeans* ▶ **typu biodrówki**

hire¹ /ˈhaɪə(r)/ verb [T] **1** (US **rent**) **hire sth (from sb)** to have the use of sth for a short time by paying for it ▶ **wynajmować, wypożyczać**

> W Br. ang. **hire** znaczy wypożyczać coś na krótki czas: *We hired a car for the day.* ◇ *I hired a suit for the wedding*; **rent** znaczy wypożyczać coś na dłużej: *rent a television/video* ◇ *rent a house/flat/holiday cottage.* W Amer. ang. **rent** używa się w obu powyższych sytuacjach.

2 to give sb a job for a short time: *We'll have to hire somebody to mend the roof.* ▶ **najmować** (*do pracy*) ℹ W Amer. ang. **hire** dotyczy również zatrudnienia na stałe: *We just hired a new secretary.*

PHR V **hire sth (out) (to sb)** (US **rent**) to allow sb to use sth for a short fixed period in exchange for money: *We hire (out) our vans by the day.* ▶ **wynajmować coś (komuś)** ℹ W Br. ang. **rent** i **let** używa się, mówiąc o wynajmowaniu na dłuższy czas: *Mrs Higgs rents out rooms to students.* ◇ *We let out our house while we were in France for a year.*

hire² /ˈhaɪə(r)/ noun [U] the act of paying to use sth for a short time: *Car hire is expensive in this country.* ◇ *Do you have bicycles **for hire**?* ▶ **wynajęcie, najem**

ˌhire ˈpurchase noun [U] (Brit.) (abbr. **h.p.**) a way of buying goods. You do not pay the full price immediately but by **instalments** until the full amount is paid: *We're buying the television on hire purchase.* ▶ **kupno na raty**

his¹ /hɪz/ determiner of or belonging to the man or boy who was mentioned earlier: *Peter has sold his car.* ◇ *He hurt his shoulder skiing.* ▶ **jego, swój**

his² /hɪz/ pron. of or belonging to him: *This is my book so that one must be his.* ▶ **jego, swój** ➲ note at **he**

hiss /hɪs/ verb **1** [I,T] to make a sound like a very long 's' to show that you are angry or do not like sth: *The cat hissed at me.* ◇ *The speech was hissed and booed.* ▶ **syczeć, wygwizdywać 2** [T] to say sth in a quiet angry voice: *'Stay away from me!' she hissed.* ▶ **syczeć**

■ **hiss** noun [C] ▶ **syk, syczenie**

historian /hɪˈstɔːriən/ noun [C] a person who studies or who is an expert in history ▶ **historyk**

historic /hɪˈstɒrɪk/ adj. famous or important in history: *The ending of apartheid was a historic event.* ▶ **historyczny, o znaczeniu historycznym** ➲ look at **historical** ➲ note at **important**

⚷**historical** /hɪˈstɒrɪkl/ adj. **1** connected with history or the study of history ▶ **historyczny, dotyczący historii** ➲ look at **historic 2** that really lived or happened; connected with real people or events in the past: *historical events/records/research* ▶ **historyczny, faktyczny**
■ **historically** /-kli/ adv. ▶ **historycznie**

⚷**history** /ˈhɪstri/ noun (pl. **histories**) **1** [U] all the events of the past: *an important moment in history* ▶ **historia** ➲ look at **natural history 2** [C, usually sing.] the series of events or facts that is connected with sb/sth: *He has a history of violence.* ◇ *There is a history of heart disease* (choroba serca często występowała) *in our family.* ▶ **historia 3** [U] the study of past events: *a degree in history* ▶ **historia 4** [C] a written description of past events: *She's writing a new history of Europe.* ▶ **historia**
IDM **go down in/make history** to be or do sth so important that it will be recorded in history: *She made history by becoming the first woman President.* ▶ **tworzyć historię**
the rest is history → REST[2]

histrionic /ˌhɪstriˈɒnɪk/ adj. [usually before a noun] (formal) **histrionic** behaviour is very emotional and is intended to attract attention in a way that does not seem sincere: *histrionic gestures* ▶ **teatralny**
■ **histrionically** /-kli/ adv. ▶ **teatralnie** | **histrionics** noun [pl.]: *She was used to her mother's histrionics.* ▶ **komedianctwo**

⚷**hit**[1] /hɪt/ verb [T] (**hitting**; pt, pp **hit**) **1** to make sudden, violent contact with sb/sth: *The bus left the road and hit a tree.* ◇ *to hit somebody in the eye/across the face/on the nose* ◇ *She hit him on the head with her umbrella.* ◇ (figurative) *The smell of burning hit her as she entered the room.* ▶ **uderzać, stukać; trafiać (na coś)**

> **hit**
> **Strike** jest bardziej formalne niż **hit**. **Beat** oznacza „uderzać wiele razy": *He was badly beaten in the attack.* **Punch** oznacza mocno uderzać kogoś/w coś pięścią, na przykład w czasie bójki: *She punched him in the face.* **Smack** oznacza uderzać kogoś otwartą dłonią, szczególnie jako sposób wymierzenia kary: *I think it's wrong to smack children.*

2 hit sth (on/against sth) to knock a part of your body, etc. against sth: *Peter hit his head on the low beam.* ▶ **uderzać się, stuknąć się 3** to have a bad or unpleasant effect on sb/sth: *Her father's death has hit her very hard.* ◇ *Inner city areas have been badly hit by unemployment* (cierpią z powodu bezrobocia). ▶ **godzić w kogoś/coś, uderzać 4** to reach a place or a level: *If you follow this road, you should hit the motorway in about ten minutes.* ◇ *The price of oil hit a new high yesterday.* ▶ **osiągnąć, dojść 5** to experience sth unpleasant or difficult: *Things were going really well until we hit this problem.* ▶ **natrafiać na coś, natykać się na coś 6** to suddenly come into sb's mind; to make sb realize or understand sth: *I thought I recognized the man's face and then it hit me* (olśniło mnie) *– he was my old maths teacher!* ▶ **uzmysłowić coś sobie/komuś**
IDM **hit it off (with sb)** (informal) to like sb when you first meet them: *When I first met Tony's parents, we didn't really hit it off.* ▶ **przypadać (sobie) do gustu**
hit the nail on the head to say sth that is exactly right ▶ **trafiać w (samo) sedno rzeczy**
hit the jackpot to win a lot of money or have a big success ▶ **wygrać (główny) los na loterii**
hit the roof (informal) to become very angry ▶ **wściec się**
PHR V **hit back (at sb/sth)** to attack (with words) sb who has attacked you: *The Prime Minister hit back at his critics.* ▶ **odgryzać się komuś**
hit on/upon sth to suddenly find sth by chance: *I finally hit on a solution to the problem.* ▶ **wpaść na coś**
hit out (at sb/sth) to attack sb/sth: *The man hit out at the policeman.* ▶ **atakować (kogoś/coś)**

⚷**hit**[2] /hɪt/ noun [C] **1** the act of hitting sth: *The ship took a* ***direct hit*** *and sank.* ◇ *She gave her brother a hard hit on the head.* ◇ *What a brilliant hit!* ▶ **uderzenie** ➲ look at **miss 2** a person or thing that is very popular or successful: *The record was a big hit.* ▶ **przebój, sensacja** ➲ look at **blockbuster 3** a result of a search on a computer, especially on the Internet ▶ **wynik wyszukiwania** (*w komputerze/internecie*)
IDM **make a hit (with sb)** (informal) to make a good impression on sb: *The new teacher seems to have made a hit with the girls.* ▶ (*przen.*) **zawojowywać (kogoś), podbijać czyjeś serce itp.**

ˌhit-and-ˈmiss (also **ˌhit-or-ˈmiss**) adj. (informal) not well organized; careless: *This method is a bit hit-or-miss, but it usually works.* ▶ **chaotyczny**

ˌhit-and-ˈrun adj. [only before a noun] **1** (used about a car driver) causing an accident and not stopping to see if anybody is hurt ▶ **uciekający z miejsca wypadku 2** (used about a road accident) caused by a hit-and-run driver ▶ **taki, którego sprawca zbiegł**

hitch[1] /hɪtʃ/ verb **1** [I,T] (informal) to get a free ride in a person's car; to travel around in this way by waiting by the side of a road and trying to get passing cars to stop: *I managed to hitch to Paris in just six hours.* ◇ *We missed the bus so we had to* ***hitch a lift.*** ▶ **prosić o podwiezienie; podróżować autostopem** ➲ note at **hitchhike 2** [T] to fasten sth to sth else: *to hitch a trailer to the back of a car* ▶ **wiązać, przyczepiać**

hitch[2] /hɪtʃ/ noun [C] a small problem or difficulty: *a technical hitch* (usterka techniczna) ▶ **szkopuł, przeszkoda**

hitchhike /ˈhɪtʃhaɪk/ (also informal **hitch**) verb [I] to travel by waiting by the side of a road and holding out your hand or a sign until a driver stops and takes you in the direction you want to go: *He hitchhiked across Europe.* ▶ **jechać autostopem**

> **Hitchhike** zwykle używa się, mówiąc o dalekiej podróży autostopem dla przyjemności. To samo znaczenie ma **hitch**, którego używa się również, mówiąc o krótkich przejazdach, np. gdy zepsuł się nam samochód lub spóźniliśmy się na autobus. **Hitch** też stosuje się w formie czasownika przechodniego: *I hitched a lift/ride to the nearest petrol station.* To samo znaczy **thumb a lift**.

■ **hitchhiker** noun [C] ▶ **autostopowicz/ka**

hi-tech = HIGH-TECH

hitherto /ˌhɪðəˈtuː/ adv. (formal) until now ▶ **dotychczas, dotąd**

ˈhit man noun [C] (informal) a person who is paid to kill another person ▶ **płatny morderca**

ˌhit-or-ˈmiss = HIT-AND-MISS

ˈhit squad noun [C] a group of criminals who are paid to kill a person ▶ **banda płatnych zabójców**

HIV /ˌeɪtʃ aɪ ˈviː/ abbr. **human immunodeficiency virus**; the virus that is believed to cause **AIDS** ▶ **HIV**

hive = BEEHIVE

hiya /ˈhaɪjə/ interj. (informal) an informal word used when you meet sb you know well; hello ▶ **cześć, siema!**

HM abbr. **His/Her Majesty's** ▶ **Jego/Jej Królewska Mość**

hmm (also **hm**) /m; hm/ interj. (used when you are not sure or when you are thinking about sth) ▶ **hm**

HMS /ˌeɪtʃ em ˈes/ **Her/His Majesty's Ship** (for ships in the British Royal Navy) ▶ **okręt brytyjski**, **okręt Jej Królewskiej Mości**

hoard¹ /hɔːd/ noun [C] a store (often secret) of money, food, etc.: *a hoard of treasure* skarb ▶ **zapas**, **zbiór**

hoard² /hɔːd/ verb [I,T] **hoard (sth) (up)** to collect and store large quantities of sth (often secretly) ▶ **gromadzić**, **chować**, **robić zapasy**

hoarding /ˈhɔːdɪŋ/ (Brit.) (especially US **billboard** /ˈbɪlbɔːd/) noun [C] a large board near a road where advertisements are put ▶ **duża tablica reklamowa**, **billboard**

hoarse /hɔːs/ adj. (used about a person or their voice) sounding rough and quiet, especially because of a sore throat: *a hoarse whisper* ◇ *The spectators shouted themselves hoarse.* Widzowie ochrypli od krzyku. ▶ **chrapliwy**, **ochrypły**
■ **hoarsely** adv. ▶ **chrapliwie**

hoax /həʊks/ noun [C] a trick to make people believe sth that is not true, especially sth unpleasant: *The fire brigade answered the call, but found that it was a hoax.* ▶ **psikus**, **fałszywy alarm**

hob /hɒb/ (US **stovetop** /ˈstəʊvtɒp/) noun [C] the surface on the top of a cooker that is used for boiling, frying, etc. ▶ **płyta kuchenna**, **płytka** (*kuchenki*)

hobble /ˈhɒbl/ verb [I] to walk with difficulty because your feet or legs are hurt: *He hobbled home on his twisted ankle.* ▶ **kuleć**

hobby /ˈhɒbi/ noun [C] (pl. **hobbies**) something that you do regularly for pleasure in your free time: *Danesh's hobbies are flower arranging and mountain biking.* ▶ **konik**, **hobby** SYN **pastime**

ˈ**hobby horse** noun **1** a subject that sb feels strongly about and likes to talk about: *to* ***get on your hobby horse*** ▶ **konik** ℹ Czasami wyraża dezaprobatę. **2** a toy made from a long stick that has a horse's head at one end. Children pretend to ride on it. ▶ **kij zakończony głową konia**

hockey /ˈhɒki/ noun [U] **1** a game that is played on a field by two teams of eleven players who try to hit a small hard ball into a goal with a curved wooden stick ▶ **hokej na trawie** ➲ picture on **page A8** ℹ W USA **hockey** nazywa się zwykle **field hockey** w celu odróżnienia od **ice hockey**. **2** (US) = ICE HOCKEY

hodgepodge (US usually) = HOTCHPOTCH

hoe /həʊ/ noun [C] a garden tool with a long handle that is used for turning the soil and for removing plants that you do not want ▶ **motyka** ➲ picture at **garden**

hog¹ /hɒg/ noun [C] a male pig that is kept for its meat ▶ **wieprz**
IDM **go the whole hog** (informal) to do sth as completely as possible: *Instead of getting a taxi, why not go the whole hog and hire a limousine for the evening?* ▶ **iść na całego**

hog² /hɒg/ verb [T] (**hogging**; **hogged**) (informal) to take or keep too much or all of sth for yourself: *Don't hog the bathroom* (nie okupuj łazienki) *when everyone's getting ready to go out!* ◇ *The red car was hogging the middle of the road* (jechał środkiem drogi) *so no one could overtake.* ▶ **monopolizować**

Hogmanay /ˈhɒgməneɪ; US ˌhɑːgməˈneɪ/ noun [C] the Scottish name for New Year's Eve (31 December) and the celebrations that take place then ▶ **sylwester**; **zabawa sylwestrowa**

hoist /hɔɪst/ verb [T] to lift or pull sth up, often by using ropes, etc.: *to hoist a flag/sail* ▶ **podnosić**, **ciągnąć (w górę)**, **wciągać** (*np. flagę na maszt*)

hold¹ /həʊld/ verb (pt, pp **held** /held/) **1** [T] to take sb/sth and keep them or it in your hand, etc.: *He held a gun in his hand.* ◇ *The woman was holding a baby in her arms.* ◇ *Hold my hand. This is a busy road.* ▶ **trzymać 2** [T] to keep sth in a certain position: *Hold your head up straight.* ◇ *Hold the camera still or you'll spoil the picture.* ◇ *These two screws hold the shelf in place.* ▶ **trzymać 3** [T] to take the weight of sb/sth: *Are you sure that branch will be strong enough to hold you?* ▶ **utrzymywać 4** [T] to contain or have space for a particular amount: *The car holds five people.* ◇ *How much does this bottle hold?* ▶ **zawierać**, **mieścić (w sobie) 5** [T] to keep a person in a position or place by force: *The terrorists are* ***holding*** *three men* ***hostage.*** ▶ **trzymać**, **zatrzymywać 6** [I] to remain the same: *I hope this weather holds till the weekend.* ◇ *What I said still holds – nothing has changed.* ▶ **trwać**, **utrzymywać się**, **być aktualnym 7** [T] to have sth, usually in an official way: *Does she* ***hold a*** *British* ***passport?*** ◇ *She holds the world record* (jest rekordzistką) *in the 100 metres.* ▶ **mieć**, **posiadać 8** [T] to have an opinion, etc.: *They* ***hold the view*** *that* (oni uważają, że) *we shouldn't spend any more money.* ▶ **uważać**, **utrzymywać 9** [T] to believe that sth is true about a person: *I* ***hold*** *the parents* ***responsible*** *for the child's behaviour.* ▶ **uważać, że 10** [T] to organize an event; to have a meeting, an election, a concert, etc.: *They're holding a party for his fortieth birthday.* ◇ *The Olympic Games are held every four years.* ◇ *The elections will be held* (odbędą się) *in the autumn.* ▶ **wydawać**, **organizować** (*np. przyjęcie*) **11** [T] to have a conversation: *It's impossible to* ***hold a conversation*** *with all this noise.* ▶ **prowadzić** (*rozmowę*) **12** [I,T] to wait until the person you are calling is ready: *I'm afraid his phone is engaged. Will you* ***hold the line?*** ▶ **czekać/nie odkładać słuchawki**
IDM **hold it!** (informal) Stop! Do not move! ▶ **stój!**, **czekaj!**
ℹ **Hold** występuje w innych idiomach, np. **hold your own**. Zob. hasła odpowiednich rzeczowników, przymiotników itp.
PHR V **hold sth against sb** to not forgive sb because of sth they have done ▶ **mieć coś komuś za złe**
hold sb/sth back 1 to prevent sb from making progress ▶ **powstrzymywać/zahamowywać kogoś/coś 2** to prevent sb/sth from moving forward: *The police tried to hold the crowd back.* ▶ **powstrzymywać/zatrzymywać kogoś/coś**
hold (sb) back (from doing sth) to hesitate or to make sb hesitate to act or speak: *She held back, not knowing how to break the terrible news.* ◇ *I wanted to tell him the truth, but something held me back.* ▶ **powstrzymywać się/kogoś (od zrobienia czegoś)**
hold sth back 1 to refuse to give some of the information that you have: *The police are sure that she is holding something back.* ▶ **ukrywać** (*np. informację*), **zachowywać coś (dla siebie) 2** to control an emotion and stop yourself from showing what you really feel: *He fought to hold back tears of anger and frustration.* ▶ **powstrzymywać** (*np. łzy*)
hold sth down 1 to keep sth at a low level: *The rate of inflation must be held down.* ▶ **utrzymywać coś 2** [no passive] to keep a job for some time: *He was unable to hold down a job after his breakdown.* ▶ **utrzymywać coś**
hold off (sth/doing sth) to delay sth ▶ **opóźniać coś/robienie czegoś**, **wstrzymywać (się)**
hold on 1 to wait or stop for a moment: *Hold on. I'll be with you in a minute.* ▶ **czekać**, **stać 2** to manage in a difficult or dangerous situation: *They managed to hold on until a rescue party arrived.* ▶ **wytrzymywać**
hold on (to sb/sth); **hold onto sb/sth** to hold sb/sth tightly: *The boy held onto his mother because he didn't want her to go.* ▶ **trzymać się kogoś/czegoś**
hold on to sth; **hold onto sth** to keep sth; to not give or sell sth: *They've offered me a lot of money for this painting, but I'm going to hold onto it.* ▶ **zatrzymywać coś (dla siebie)**, **nie oddawać czegoś**

hold sth on to keep sth in position: *These nuts and bolts hold the wheels on.* ◇ *The knob is only held on by sticky tape.* ▶ **przytrzymywać coś**
hold out to last (in a difficult situation): *How long will our supply of water hold out?* ▶ **wystarczać**
hold sth out to offer sth by moving it towards sb in your hand: *He held out a carrot to the horse.* ▶ **podawać coś (komuś/czemuś)**
hold out for sth (informal) to cause a delay while you continue to ask for sth: *Union members are holding out for a better pay offer.* ▶ **czekać (na coś lepszego)**
hold together (used about an argument, a theory or a story) to be logical or **consistent**: *Their case doesn't hold together when you look at the evidence.* ▶ **trzymać się dobrze** ➲ look at **hang together**
hold (sth) together 1 to remain, or to keep sth, united: *A political party should hold together.* ◇ *It's the mother who usually holds the family together.* ▶ **trzymać się/coś razem 2** if a machine or an object **holds together** or sth **holds it together**, the different parts stay together so that it does not break ▶ **trzymać się/coś dobrze**
hold sb/sth up to make sb/sth late; to cause a delay: *We were held up by the traffic.* ▶ **opóźniać/zatrzymywać kogoś/coś**
hold up sth to steal from a bank, shop, vehicle, etc. using a gun ▶ **napadać na coś zbrojnie**

⚷ **hold²** /həʊld/ noun **1** [C] the act or manner of having sb/sth in your hand(s): *to have a firm hold on the rope* ◇ *judo/wrestling holds* ▶ **chwyt 2** [sing.] **a hold (on/over sb/sth)** influence or control: *The new government has strengthened its hold on the country.* ▶ **władza**, **wpływ**, **silna ręka 3** [C] the part of a ship or an aircraft where goods are stored: *Five men were found hiding in the ship's hold.* ▶ **ładownia** ➲ picture at **plane 4** [C] a place where a climber can put his/her hand or foot when climbing ▶ **punkt oparcia** ➲ look at **foothold**
IDM **catch, get, grab, take, etc. hold (of sb/sth) 1** to take sb/sth in your hands: *I managed to catch hold of the dog before it ran out into the road.* ▶ **złapać**, **schwytać 2** to take control of sb/sth; to start to have an effect on sb/sth: *Mass hysteria seemed to have taken hold of the crowd.* ▶ **zawładnąć**
get/keep/take a grip/hold (on yourself) → GRIP¹
get hold of sb to find sb or make contact with sb: *I've been trying to get hold of the complaints department all morning.* ▶ **nawiązać kontakt z kimś**
get hold of sth to find sth that will be useful: *I must try and get hold of a good second-hand bicycle.* ▶ **zdobyć coś**

holdall /ˈhəʊldɔːl/ noun [C] a large bag that is used for carrying clothes, etc. when you are travelling ▶ **torba podróżna** ➲ picture at **bag**

holder /ˈhəʊldə(r)/ noun [C] [in compounds] **1** a person who has or holds sth: *a season ticket holder* ◇ *the world record holder in the 100 metres* ◇ *holders of European passports* ▶ **posiadacz/ka**, **okaziciel/ka 2** something that contains or holds sth: *a toothbrush holder* ▶ **futerał**, **teczka**, **pojemnik**

ˈ**hold-up** noun [C] **1** a delay: *'What's the hold-up?' 'There's been an accident ahead of us.'* ▶ **opóźnienie 2** the act of stealing from a bank, etc. using a gun: *The gang have carried out three hold-ups of high street banks.* ▶ **zbrojny napad**

⚷ **hole** /həʊl/ noun **1** [C] an opening; an empty space in sth solid: *The pavement is full of holes.* ◇ *There are holes in my socks.* ◇ *I've got a hole in my tooth.* ▶ **dziura 2** [C] the place where an animal lives in the ground or in a tree: *a mouse hole* ▶ **jama**, **nora 3** [C] (in the sport of **golf**) the hole in the ground that you must hit the ball into. Each section of the **golf course** is also called a hole: *an eighteen-hole golf course* ▶ **dołek 4** [sing.] (informal) a small dark and unpleasant room, flat, etc. ▶ **dziura**, **nora**

holey /ˈhəʊli/ adj. a **holey** piece of clothing or material has a lot of holes in it ▶ **dziurawy**

⚷ **holiday** /ˈhɒlədeɪ/ noun **1** (US **vacation**) [C,U] a period of rest from work or school (often when you go and stay away from home): *We're going to Italy **for our** summer **holidays*** (na wakacje) *this year.* ◇ *How much holiday do you get a year in your new job?* ◇ *Mr Phillips isn't here this week. He's away **on holiday*** (jest na urlopie). ◇ *I'm going to **take a** week's **holiday*** (wezmę tygodniowy urlop) *in May and spend it at home.* ◇ *the school/Christmas / Easter / summer holidays* wakacje / ferie / święta ▶ **wakacje**, **urlop**

> W Br. ang. **vacation** oznacza czas, gdy zamknięte są uniwersytety i sądy: *Maria wants to get a job in the long vacation.* **Leave** oznacza okres nieobecności w pracy z jakiegoś specjalnego powodu: *sick leave* zwolnienie chorobowe ◇ *maternity leave* urlop macierzyński ◇ *unpaid leave* urlop bezpłatny.

2 [C] a day of rest when people do not go to work, school, etc. often for religious or national celebrations: *Next Monday is a holiday.* ◇ *New Year's Day is a **bank/public holiday** in Britain.* ▶ **święto**, **dzień wolny** (*od pracy*)

> **Holiday** używa się w tym znaczeniu zarówno w brytyjskiej jak i amerykańskiej angielszczyźnie. Dzień wolny od pracy jest też często nazywany **a day off**: *I'm having two days off next week when we move house.*

> **holidays**
> You can choose your holiday from a **brochure** and book it at a **travel agent's**. Some people do a lot of **sightseeing** when they **go on holiday** (US **vacation**). They **look round** historical buildings and **take photographs**. Others prefer to **sunbathe** on a **beach** and **go swimming** or **snorkelling**. Many people go on a **package holiday** (US **package tour**) which is organized by a company, and they pay a fixed price that includes their travel, accommodation, etc. They might stay in a large hotel in a holiday **resort**. Other people **go backpacking**, **go on safari**, or go on a **cruise**. Most people like to buy some **souvenirs** before they go home.

ˈ**holiday camp** noun [C] (Brit.) a place that provides a place to stay and organized entertainment for people on holiday ▶ **obóz wakacyjny**

holidaymaker /ˈhɒlədeɪmeɪkə(r); -dimeɪ-/ noun [C] (Brit.) a person who is away from home on holiday ▶ **letni-k/czka**, **urlopowicz/ka**

holistic /həʊˈlɪstɪk; hɒˈl-/ adj. **1** (informal) considering a whole thing or being to be more than a collection of parts: *a holistic approach to life* ▶ **holistyczny 2** treating the whole person rather than just the **symptoms** of a disease: *holistic medicine* ▶ **holistyczny**
■ **holistically** /-kli/ adv. ▶ **holistycznie**

⚷ **hollow¹** /ˈhɒləʊ/ adj. **1** with a hole or empty space inside: *a hollow tree* ▶ **pusty**, **wydrążony 2** (used about parts of the face) sinking deep into the face: *hollow cheeks* ◇ *hollow-eyed* ▶ **zapadnięty 3** (used about a sound) seeming to come from a **hollow** place: *hollow footsteps* ▶ (*dźwięk*) **głuchy 4** not sincere: *a hollow laugh/voice* ◇ *hollow promises/threats* ▶ **nieszczery**

hollow² /ˈhɒləʊ/ noun [C] an area that is lower than the land around it ▶ **wklęsłość** (*np. terenu*), **zagłębienie**

hollow³ /ˈhɒləʊ/ verb
PHR V **hollow sth out** to take out the inside part of sth ▶ **wydrążać/wyżłabiać coś**

holly /ˈhɒli/ noun [U] a plant that has shiny dark green leaves with sharp points and red **berries** in the winter.

It is often used as a Christmas decoration. ▶ **ostrokrzew**

holocaust /ˈhɒləkɔːst; US also ˈhəʊlə-/ noun [C] a situation where a great many things are destroyed and a great many people die: *a nuclear holocaust* ▶ **zagłada**, **Holocaust**

hologram /ˈhɒləɡræm; US also ˈhəʊl-/ noun [C] an image or picture which appears to stand out from the flat surface it is on when light falls on it ▶ **hologram**

holograph /ˈhɒləɡrɑːf; US -ɡræf; ˈhəʊl-/ noun [C] a piece of writing that has been written by hand by its author ▶ **holograf**

holster /ˈhəʊlstə(r)/ noun [C] a leather case used for carrying a gun that is fixed to a belt or worn under the arm ▶ **kabura**, **pochwa**

holy /ˈhəʊli/ adj. (**holier**; **holiest**) **1** connected with God or with religion and therefore very special or important: *the Holy Bible* ▶ **święty** **2** (used about a person) good in a moral and religious way: *a holy life/man* ▶ **święty**
■ **holiness** noun [U] ▶ **świętość**

the ˌ**Holy** ˈ**Ghost** = THE HOLY SPIRIT

ˌ**holy** ˈ**orders** noun [pl.] the official position of being a priest: *to take holy orders* ▶ **święcenia kapłańskie**

the ˌ**Holy** ˈ**Spirit** (also **the** ˌ**Holy Ghost**) noun [sing.] Christians believe God consists of three parts: God the Father, God the Son (Jesus Christ) and God the Holy Ghost ▶ **Duch Święty**

ˈ**Holy Week** noun [C] (in the Christian Church) the week before Easter Sunday ▶ **Wielki Tydzień**

homage /ˈhɒmɪdʒ/ noun [U,C, usually sing.] (formal) **homage (to sb/sth)** something that is said or done to show respect publicly for sb: *Thousands came to* ***pay/do homage*** (złożyć hołd) *to the dead leader* ▶ **hołd**, **cześć**

home[1] /həʊm/ noun **1** [C,U] the place where you live or where you feel that you belong: *She* ***left home*** *at the age of 21.* ◇ *Children from* ***broken homes*** (z rozbitych domów) *sometimes have learning difficulties.* ◇ *That old house would make an ideal* ***family home.*** ◇ *Stephen went abroad and* ***made his home*** (zamieszkał) *in Canada.* ◇ *Now we've got this computer, we'd better* ***find a home for it*** (znajdźmy dla niego jakieś miejsce). ▶ **dom**, **mieszkanie** ➲ note at **house** ➲ picture on **page A3**

> Uwaga! Przed **home** nie używa się przyimka **to**: *It's time to* ***go home.*** ◇ *She's usually tired when she gets home.* Mając na myśli czyjś dom, należy powiedzieć **at Jane and Andy's** lub **at Jane and Andy's place/house/flat.**

2 [C] a place that provides care for a particular type of person or for animals: *a children's home* dom dziecka ◇ *an* ***old people's home*** dom spokojnej starości ▶ (*instytucja państwowa, społeczna itp.*) **dom** **3** [sing.] **the home of sth** the place where sth began: *Greece is said to be the home of democracy.* ▶ (*przen.*) **kolebka**
IDM **at home 1** in your house, flat, etc.: *Tomorrow we're staying at home all day.* ◇ *Is anybody at home?* ⓘ W Amer. ang. często używa się **home** bez przyimka **at**: *Is anybody home?* ▶ **w domu** **2** comfortable, as if you were in your own home: *Please make yourself at home.* ◇ *I felt quite at home on the ship.* ▶ **jak (u siebie) w domu** **3** (used in sport) played in the town to which the team belongs: *Liverpool are playing at home on Saturday.* ▶ **u siebie**
romp home/to victory → ROMP

home[2] /həʊm/ adj. [only before a noun] **1** connected with home: *home cooking* ◇ *your home address/town* ◇ *a happy home life* ▶ **domowy**, **rodzinny** **2** (especially Brit.) connected with your own country, not with a foreign country: *The* ***Home Secretary*** *is responsible for home affairs.* ▶ **krajowy**, **wewnętrzny** **3** (used in sport) connected with a team's own sports ground: *The home team has a lot of support.* ◇ *a home game* ▶ **swój**, **miejscowy** OPP **away**

home[3] /həʊm/ adv. at, in or to your home or home country: *She'll be flying home for New Year.* ◇ *We must be getting home soon.* Musimy wkrótce wracać do domu. ▶ **do/w domu**; **do/w kraju**
IDM **bring sth home to sb** to make sb understand sth fully ▶ **przekonywać kogoś**, **uzmysławiać coś komuś/sobie**
drive sth home (to sb) → DRIVE[1]

home[4] /həʊm/ verb
PHR V **home in on sb/sth** to move towards sb/sth: *The police homed in on the house where the thieves were hiding.* ▶ **namierzać kogoś/coś**

homebuyer /ˈhəʊmbaɪə(r)/ noun [C] a person who buys a house, flat, etc. ▶ **nabywca domu/mieszkania**

homecoming /ˈhəʊmkʌmɪŋ/ noun [C,U] the act of returning home, especially when you have been away for a long time ▶ **powrót do domu/ojczyzny**

the ˌ**Home** ˈ**Counties** noun [pl.] the area of Britain around London ▶ **hrabstwa w Wielkiej Brytanii sąsiadujące z Londynem**

ˌ**home eco**ˈ**nomics** noun [U] cooking and other skills needed at home, taught as a subject in school ▶ **zajęcia z gospodarstwa domowego**

ˌ**home-**ˈ**grown** adj. (used about fruit and vegetables) grown in your own garden ▶ **własnej hodowli**

homeland /ˈhəʊmlænd/ noun [C] the country where you were born or that your parents came from, or to which you feel you belong: *Many refugees have been forced to leave their homeland.* ▶ **ojczyzna**

homeless /ˈhəʊmləs/ adj. **1** having no home ▶ **bezdomny** **2** (**the homeless**) noun [pl.] people who have no home ▶ **bezdomni**
■ **homelessness** noun [U] ▶ **bezdomność**

homely /ˈhəʊmli/ adj. (**homelier**; **homeliest**) (Brit.) **1** (used about a place) simple but also pleasant or welcoming ▶ **niewyszukany**, **prosty**, **przytulny** **2** (used about a person) not very attractive ▶ **nieatrakcyjny**, **pospolity**

ˌ**home-**ˈ**made** adj. made at home; not bought in a shop: *home-made cakes* ▶ **domowego/własnego wyrobu**

the ˈ**Home Office** noun [sing.] (Brit.) the department of the British Government that is responsible for the law, the police and prisons within Britain and for decisions about who can enter the country ▶ **Ministerstwo Spraw Wewnętrznych** ➲ look at **internal**

homeopath (Brit. also **homoeopath**) /ˈhəʊmiəpæθ; ˈhɒmi-/ noun [C] a person who treats sick people using **homeopathy** ▶ **homeopat(k)a**

homeopathy (Brit. also **homoeopathy**) /ˌhəʊmiˈɒpəθi; ˌhɒmi-/ noun [U] the treatment of a disease by giving very small amounts of a drug that would cause the disease if given in large amounts ▶ **homeopatia**
■ **homeopathic** (Brit. also **homoeopathic**) /ˌhəʊmiəˈpæθɪk; ˌhɒm-/ adj.: *homeopathic medicine* ▶ **homeopatyczny**

homeowner /ˈhəʊməʊnə(r)/ noun [C] a person who owns their house or flat ▶ **właściciel/ka domu/mieszkania**

ˈ**home page** noun [C] the first of a number of pages of information on the Internet that belongs to a person or an organization. A home page contains connections to other pages of information. ▶ **strona domowa (internetowa)**

the ˌ**Home** ˈ**Secretary** noun [C] (Brit.) the minister who is in charge of the Home Office ▶ **Minister Spraw Wewnętrznych** ➲ look at **Foreign Secretary**

homesick /ˈhəʊmsɪk/ adj. **homesick (for sb/sth)** sad because you are away from home and you miss it: *She was very homesick for* (bardzo tęskniła za) *Canada.* ▶ **stęskniony za domem/ojczyzną**
■ **homesickness** noun [U] ▶ **tęsknota za domem/ojczyzną**

hometown /ˈhəʊmtaʊn/ noun [C] the place where you were born or lived as a child ▶ **miasto rodzinne**

homeward /ˈhəʊmwəd/ adj. going towards home: *the homeward journey* ▶ **wiodący ku domowi/ojczyźnie, powrotny**
■ **homeward** (also **homewards**) /-wədz/ adv. towards home: *We drove homewards in silence.* ▶ **ku domowi, do kraju**

🔑 **homework** /ˈhəʊmwɜːk/ noun [U] work that is given by teachers for students to do at home: *Have we got any homework?* ◇ *We've got a translation to do for homework.* ◇ *The minister had not done his homework* (nie przygotował się) *and there were several questions that he couldn't answer.* ▶ **praca/zadanie domowe** ➲ note at **study** ➲ look at **housework** ℹ Zwróć uwagę, że **homework** to rzeczownik niepoliczalny i dlatego nie można go użyć w lm. Mając na myśli jakiś pojedynczy fragment pracy domowej, trzeba powiedzieć **a piece of homework**, a dużo zadań domowych – **a lot of homework**.

homicidal /ˌhɒmɪˈsaɪdl/ adj. likely to murder sb: *a homicidal maniac* ▶ **morderczy, zabójczy**

homicide /ˈhɒmɪsaɪd/ noun [C,U] (especially US) the illegal killing of one person by another; murder ▶ **zabójstwo**

homoeopath, homoeopathy (Brit.) = HOMEOPATH, HOMEOPATHY

homogeneous /ˌhɒməˈdʒiːniəs/ adj. made up of parts that are all of the same type ▶ **jednolity, jednorodny** OPP **heterogeneous**

homonym /ˈhɒmənɪm; US also ˈhəʊm-/ noun [C] a word that is spelt and pronounced like another word but that has a different meaning ▶ **homonim**

homophobia /ˌhɒməˈfəʊbiə; ˌhəʊm-/ noun [U] a strong dislike and fear of **homosexual** people ▶ **homofobia**
■ **homophobic** adj. ▶ **homofobiczny**

homophone /ˈhɒməfəʊn/ noun [C] a word that is pronounced the same as another word but that has a different spelling and meaning: *'Flower' and 'flour' are homophones.* ▶ **homofon**

homosexual /ˌhəʊməˈsekʃuəl; Brit. also ˌhɒm-/ adj. sexually attracted to people of the same sex ▶ **homoseksualny** ➲ look at **heterosexual, bisexual, gay, lesbian**
■ **homosexual** noun [C] ▶ **homoseksualista** | **homosexuality** /ˌhəʊməˌsekʃuˈæləti; Brit. also ˌhɒm-/ noun [U] ▶ **homoseksualizm**

Hon **1** = HONORARY (2) **2** = HONOURABLE (2): *Hon President*

hone /həʊn/ verb [T] **hone sth (to sth)** **1** to develop and improve sth, especially a skill, over a period of time: *She honed her debating skills at college.* ◇ *It was a finely honed piece of writing.* ◇ *His body was honed* (wyćwiczone) *to perfection.* ▶ **udoskonalać (do czegoś)** **2** to make a blade sharp or sharper: *The knife had been honed to razor sharpness.* ▶ **(na)ostrzyć** SYN **sharpen**

🔑 **honest** /ˈɒnɪst/ adj. **1** (used about a person) telling the truth and never stealing or cheating: *Just be honest – do you like this skirt or not?* ◇ ***To be honest**, I don't think that's a very good idea.* ▶ **uczciwy, szczery, prawy** **2** showing honest qualities: *an honest face* ◇ *I'd like your honest opinion, please.* ▶ **uczciwy, szczery** OPP for both meanings **dishonest**
■ **honesty** noun [U] ▶ **uczciwość** OPP **dishonesty**

🔑 **honestly** /ˈɒnɪstli/ adv. **1** in an honest way: *He tried to answer the lawyer's questions honestly.* ▶ **szczerze, uczciwie** **2** (used for emphasizing that what you are saying is true): *I honestly don't know where she has gone.* ▶ **naprawdę, szczerze** **3** (used for expressing disapproval): *Honestly! What a mess!* ▶ **naprawdę!**

honey /ˈhʌni/ noun **1** [U] the sweet sticky substance that is made by **bees** and that people eat ▶ **miód** ➲ picture on **page A14** **2** [C] (informal) a way of addressing sb that you like or love: *Honey, I'm home.* ▶ **kochanie**

honeycomb /ˈhʌnikəʊm/ noun [C,U] a structure of shapes with six sides, in which bees keep their eggs and **honey** ▶ **plaster miodu**

honeymoon /ˈhʌnimuːn/ noun [C] a holiday that is taken by a man and a woman who have just got married: *We had our first argument while we were **on our honeymoon**.* ▶ **miesiąc miodowy**

honeysuckle /ˈhʌnisʌkl/ noun [U,C] a climbing plant with sweet-smelling yellow or pink flowers ▶ **kapryfolium**

honk /hɒŋk/ verb [I,T] to sound the horn of a car; to make this sound ▶ **trąbić** (*klaksonem*)

honorable (US) = HONOURABLE

honorary /ˈɒnərəri; US -reri/ adj. **1** given as an honour (without the person needing the usual certificates, etc.): *to be awarded an honorary degree* ▶ **honorowy** **2** (often **Honorary**) (abbr. **Hon**) not paid: *He is the Honorary President.* ▶ **honorowy**

🔑 **honour**[1] (US **honor**) /ˈɒnə(r)/ noun **1** [U] the respect from other people that a person, country, etc. gets because of high standards of behaviour and moral character: *the guest of honour* ▶ **honor, cześć** ➲ look at **dishonour** **2** [sing.] (formal) something that gives pride or pleasure: *It was a great honour to be asked to speak at the conference.* ▶ **zaszczyt** **3** [U] the quality of doing what is morally right: *I give you my word of honour.* ▶ **honor** **4** (**Honours**) [pl.] (abbr. **Hons** /ɒnz/) a university course that is of a higher level than a basic course: *a First Class Honours degree* ▶ **końcowa ocena studiów akademickich, wyższa od dostatecznej** **5** [C] something that is given to a person officially to show great repect: *He has been given several honours for his work with disabled children.* ▶ **zaszczyt, honory**
IDM **in honour of sb/sth; in sb/sth's honour** out of respect for sb/sth: *A party was given in honour of the guests from Bonn.* ▶ **na cześć kogoś/czegoś**

honour[2] (US **honor**) /ˈɒnə(r)/ verb [T] **1** **honour sb/sth (with sth)** to show great (public) respect for sb/sth or to give sb pride or pleasure: *I am very honoured by the confidence you have shown in me.* ▶ **zaszczycać, uczcić** **2** to do what you have agreed or promised ▶ **dotrzymywać** (*obietnicy/słowa*)

honourable (US **honorable**) /ˈɒnərəbl/ adj. **1** acting in a way that makes people respect you; having or showing honour ▶ **honorowy, uczciwy** OPP **dishonourable** **2** [only before a noun] (**the Honourable**) (abbr. **the Hon**) a title that is given to some high officials and to Members of Parliament when they are speaking to each other ▶ **czcigodny**
■ **honourably** /-əbli/ adv. ▶ **honorowo, uczciwie**

Hons /ɒnz/ = HONOURS[1] (4): *John North BSc (Hons)*

hood /hʊd/ noun [C] **1** the part of a coat, etc. that you pull up to cover your head and neck in bad weather ▶ **kaptur** **2** (especially Brit.) a folding cover for a car, etc.: *We drove all the way with the hood down.* ▶ **budka, daszek** **3** (US) = BONNET (2)

hoody (also **hoodie**) /ˈhʊdi/ noun [C] (pl. **hoodies**) (Brit., informal) a jacket or **sweatshirt** with a **hood** ▶ **kurtka/bluza z kapturem**

hoof /huːf/ noun [C] (pl. **hoofs** or **hooves** /huːvz/) the hard part of the foot of horses and some other animals ▶ **ko-**

pyto, racica ➲ look at **paw** ➲ picture at **horse**, picture on **page A10**

hook¹ /hʊk/ noun [C] **1** a curved piece of metal, plastic, etc. that is used for hanging sth on or for catching fish: *Put your coat on the hook over there.* ◇ *a fish-hook* ▶ **hak** **2** (used in boxing) a way of hitting sb that is done with the arm bent: *a right hook* ▶ **cios sierpowy**
IDM **off the hook** (used about the top part of a telephone) not in position, so that telephone calls cannot be received ▶ (*słuchawka telefoniczna*) **źle odłożona**
get/let sb off the hook (informal) to free yourself or sb else from a difficult situation or punishment: *My father paid the money I owed and got me off the hook.* ▶ **wyciągać kogoś/wyjść z tarapatów**

hook² /hʊk/ verb **1** [I,T] to fasten or catch sth with a hook or sth in the shape of a hook; to be fastened in this way: *We hooked the trailer to the back of the car.* ◇ *The curtain simply hooks onto the rail.* ▶ **zahaczać (się), zaczepiać (się)** **2** [T] to put sth around sth else so that you can hold on to it or move it: *Hook the rope through your belt.* ▶ **przeciągać/przekładać coś przez coś, łapać na hak**
PHR V **hook up (to sth)**; **hook sb/sth up (to sth)** to connect sb/sth to a piece of electronic equipment, to a power supply or to the Internet: *She was then hooked up to an IV drip.* ◇ *Check that the computer is hooked up to the printer.* ◇ *A large proportion of the nation's households are hooked up to the Internet.* ▶ **podłączać się/kogoś/coś (do czegoś)**

ˌhook and ˈeye noun [C] a thing that is used for fastening clothes ▶ **haftka** ➲ picture at **button**

hooked /hʊkt/ adj. **1** shaped like a hook: *a hooked nose* ▶ **zakrzywiony, haczykowaty** **2** [not before a noun] (informal) **be/get hooked (on sth)** to need sth that is bad for you, especially drugs: *to be hooked on gambling* ▶ **być w szponach (czegoś)** SYN **addicted** **3** [not before a noun] (informal) **be/get hooked (on sth)** to enjoy sth very much, so that you want to do it, see it, etc. as much as possible: *Suzi is hooked on computer games.* ▶ **być napalonym/napalać się na coś**

hooky /ˈhʊki/ (US)
IDM **play hooky** (old-fashioned, informal) = PLAY TRUANT

hooligan /ˈhuːlɪɡən/ noun [C] a person who behaves in a violent and aggressive way in public places: *football hooligans* ▶ **chuligan** ➲ look at **lout**, **yob**
■ **hooliganism** /ˈhuːlɪɡənɪzəm/ noun [U] ▶ **chuliganizm**

hoop /huːp/ noun [C] a large metal or plastic ring ▶ **obręcz, koło**

hooray = HURRAY

hoot¹ /huːt/ verb [I,T] to sound the horn of a car or to make a loud noise: *The driver hooted (his horn) at the dog but it wouldn't move.* ◇ *They hooted with laughter at the suggestion.* ▶ **trąbić** (*klaksonem*); **ryczeć**

hoot² /huːt/ noun **1** [C] (especially Brit.) a short loud laugh or shout: *hoots of laughter* ▶ **parsknięcie** (*śmiechem*); **krzyk** **2** [sing.] (informal) a situation or a person that is very funny: *Bob is a real hoot!* ▶ **ubaw**; **błazen** **3** [C] the loud sound that is made by the horn of a vehicle ▶ **trąbienie** (*klaksonu*), **gwizd** (*pociągu*), **wycie** (*syreny statku*) **4** [C] the cry of an **owl** ▶ **hukanie** (*sowy*)

hoover /ˈhuːvə(r)/ verb [I,T] (Brit.) to clean a carpet, etc. with a machine that sucks up the dirt: *This carpet needs hoovering.* ▶ **odkurzać** SYN **vacuum**
PHR V **hoover sth up** to remove sth from a carpet, floor, etc. with a **vacuum cleaner**: *to hoover up all the dust* ▶ **odkurzać coś**
■ **Hoover™** noun [C] (Brit.) = VACUUM CLEANER

hooves plural of **hoof**

hop¹ /hɒp/ verb [I] (**hopping**; **hopped**) **1** (used about a person) to jump on one leg: *I twisted my ankle so badly I had to hop all the way back to the car.* ▶ **skakać na jednej nodze** **2** (used about an animal or a bird) to jump with both or all feet together ▶ **skakać** **3** **hop (from sth to sth)** to change quickly from one activity or subject to another ▶ **przeskakiwać** **4** to go somewhere quickly or for a short time: *Hop upstairs* (skocz na górę) *and get my glasses, would you?* ▶ **skakać (szybko pójść/pobiec)**
IDM **hop it!** (slang) Go away! ▶ **spadaj!, zjeżdżaj!**
PHR V **hop in/into sth**; **hop out (of sth)** (informal) to get in or out of a car, etc. (quickly) ▶ **wskakiwać/wyskakiwać (do/z czegoś)**
hop on/onto sth; **hop off sth** (informal) to get onto/off a bus, etc. (quickly) ▶ **wskakiwać/wyskakiwać (do/z czegoś)**

hop² /hɒp/ noun **1** [C] a short jump by a person on one leg or by a bird or an animal with its feet together ▶ **podskok (na jednej nodze)** **2** [C] a tall climbing plant with flowers ▶ **chmielina** **3** (**hops**) [pl.] the flowers of this plant that are used in making beer ▶ **chmiel**

hope¹ /həʊp/ verb [I,T] **hope that ...**; **hope to do sth**; **hope (for sth)** to want sth to happen or be true: *I hope that you feel better soon.* ◇ *Hoping to hear from you soon.* (formułka na zakończenie listu) ◇ *'Is it raining?' '**I hope not.** I haven't got a coat with me.'* ◇ *'Are you coming to London with us?' 'I'm not sure yet but **I hope so.**'* ▶ **mieć nadzieję**; **ufać, że**; **oczekiwać czegoś**

hope² /həʊp/ noun **1** [C,U] **(a) hope (of/for sth)**; **(a) hope of doing sth**; **(a) hope that ...** the feeling of wanting sth to happen and thinking that it will: *What hope is there for the future?* ◇ *There is no hope of finding anybody else alive.* ◇ *David has **high hopes*** (wielką nadzieję) *of becoming a jockey.* ◇ *She never **gave up hope*** (nigdy nie traciła nadziei) *that a cure for the disease would be found.* ◇ *I'll do what I can but don't **get your hopes up*** (ale nie rób sobie nadziei). ▶ **nadzieja** **2** [sing.] a person, a thing or a situation that will help you get what you want: *Please can you help me? You're my **last hope.*** ▶ **nadzieja**
IDM **dash sb's hopes (of sth/of doing sth)** → DASH²
in the hope of sth/that ... because you want sth to happen: *I came here in the hope that we could talk privately.* ▶ **w nadziei na coś/że**; **w oczekiwaniu czegoś/że**
pin (all) your hopes on sb/sth → PIN²
a ray of hope → RAY

hopeful /ˈhəʊpfl/ adj. **1** **hopeful (about sth)**; **hopeful that ...** believing that sth that you want will happen: *He's very hopeful about the success of the business.* ▶ **pełen nadziei, ufny** SYN **optimistic** **2** making you think that sth good will happen: *a hopeful sign* ▶ **obiecujący, rokujący nadzieję** SYN **promising**

hopefully /ˈhəʊpfəli/ adv. **1** (informal) (used to say what you hope will happen): *Hopefully, we'll be finished by 6 o'clock.* ▶ **mam/y nadzieję, że; jak dobrze pójdzie, to** **2** showing hope: *She smiled hopefully at me, waiting for my answer.* ▶ **z nadzieją**

hopeless /ˈhəʊpləs/ adj. **1** giving no hope that sth/sb will be successful or get better: *It's hopeless. There is nothing we can do.* ▶ **beznadziejny** **2** (especially Brit., informal) **hopeless (at sth)** (used about a person) often doing things wrong; very bad at doing sth: *I'm absolutely hopeless at tennis.* ▶ **beznadziejny**
■ **hopelessly** adv.: *They were hopelessly lost.* ▶ **beznadziejnie, rozpaczliwie** | **hopelessness** noun [U] ▶ **beznadziejność**

hopscotch /ˈhɒpskɒtʃ/ noun [U] a children's game played on a pattern of squares marked on the ground. Each child throws a stone into a square then **hops** and jumps along the empty squares to pick up the stone again. ▶ **gra w klasy**

horde /hɔːd/ noun [C] a very large number of people ▶ **horda**

horizon /həˈraɪzn/ noun **1** [sing.] the line where the earth and sky appear to meet: *The ship appeared on/disappeared over the horizon.* ▶ **horyzont** **2** (**horizons**) [pl.] the limits of your knowledge or experience: *Foreign travel is a good way of expanding your horizons.* ▶ **horyzonty**
IDM **on the horizon** likely to happen soon: *There are further job cuts on the horizon.* ▶ **w perspektywie**

horizontal /ˌhɒrɪˈzɒntl; US -rəˈz-/ adj. going from side to side, not up and down; flat or level ▶ **poziomy** ➲ look at **vertical**, **perpendicular**
■ **horizontally** /-təli/ adv. ▶ **poziomo**

hormone /ˈhɔːməʊn/ noun [C] a substance in your body that influences how you grow and develop ▶ **hormon**

horn /hɔːn/ noun [C] **1** one of the hard pointed things that some animals have on their heads ▶ **róg** ➲ picture on **page A10** **2** one of the family of metal musical instruments that you play by blowing into them: *the French horn* ▶ **róg** ➲ note at **piano** **3** the thing in a car, etc. that gives a loud warning sound: *Don't sound your horn late at night.* ▶ **klakson** ➲ picture at **car**

hornet /ˈhɔːnɪt/ noun [C] a large wasp that can give you a painful sting ▶ **szerszeń**
IDM **a hornet's nest** angry argument, criticism, etc. involving a lot of people: *His letter to the papers has stirred up/uncovered a real hornet's nest.* ▶ (*wywołać*) **burzę**

horoscope /ˈhɒrəskəʊp/ noun [C] (also **stars** [pl.]) a statement about what is going to happen to a person in the future, based on the position of the stars and planets when they were born: *What does my horoscope for next week say?* ▶ **horoskop** ➲ note at **zodiac** ➲ look at **astrology**

horrendous /hɒˈrendəs/ adj. (informal) very bad or unpleasant: *The queues were absolutely horrendous.* ▶ **straszliwy, horrendalny**
■ **horrendously** adv. ▶ **straszliwie, horrendalnie**

horrible /ˈhɒrəbl/ adj. **1** (informal) bad or unpleasant: *This coffee tastes horrible!* ◇ *Don't be so horrible!* ◇ *I've got a horrible feeling that I've forgotten something.* ▶ **straszny, paskudny, okropny** ➲ note at **bad** **2** shocking and/or frightening: *a horrible murder/death/nightmare* ▶ **straszny, okropny** SYN for both meanings **terrible**
■ **horribly** /-əbli/ adv. ▶ **strasznie, okropnie**

horrid /ˈhɒrɪd/ adj. (informal) very unpleasant or unkind: *horrid weather* ◇ *I'm sorry that I was so horrid last night.* ▶ **straszny; nieznośny, wstrętny** SYN **horrible**

horrific /həˈrɪfɪk/ adj. **1** extremely bad and shocking or frightening: *a horrific murder/accident/attack* ▶ **przerażający, straszny** **2** (informal) very bad or unpleasant ▶ **okropny, paskudny**
■ **horrifically** /-kli/ adv.: *horrifically expensive* ▶ **strasznie, okropnie, przerażająco**

horrify /ˈhɒrɪfaɪ/ verb [T] (**horrifying**; **horrifies**; pt, pp **horrified**) to make sb feel extremely shocked, disgusted or frightened ▶ **przerażać**
■ **horrified** adj.: *He was horrified when he discovered the truth.* ▶ **przerażony** | **horrifying** adj. ▶ **przerażający**

horror /ˈhɒrə(r)/ noun **1** [U, sing.] a feeling of great fear or shock: *They watched **in horror** as the building collapsed.* ▶ **przerażenie, wstręt** **2** [C] something that makes you feel frightened or shocked: *a horror film* horror ◇ *a horror story* ▶ **okropność, makabra**

hors d'oeuvre /ˌɔː ˈdɜːv/ noun [C] (pl. **hors d'oeuvres** /ˌɔː ˈdɜːv/) a small amount of food, usually cold, usually served before the main part of a meal ▶ **przystawka, przekąska** ➲ look at **starter**

H

horse

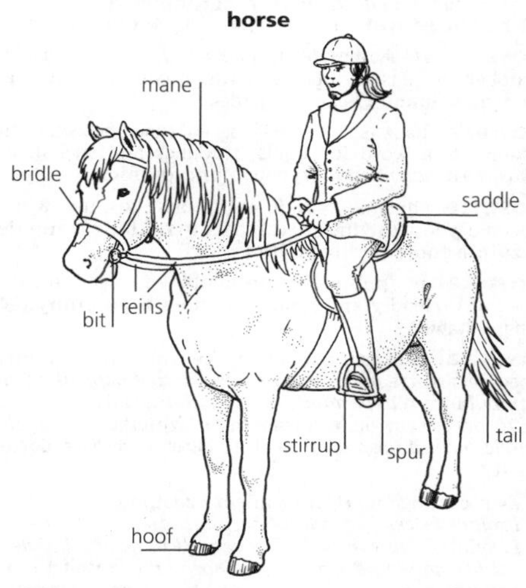

horse /hɔːs/ noun **1** [C] a large animal that is used for riding on or for pulling or carrying heavy loads: *a horse and cart* ◇ *horse riding* jazda konna ▶ **koń**

> A male horse is a **stallion**, a female horse is a **mare** and a young horse is a **foal**. A horse **neighs**.

2 (**the horses**) [pl.] (informal) horse racing: *He won some money on the horses.* ▶ **wyścigi konne**
IDM **on horseback** sitting on a horse: *Policemen on horseback* (na koniach) *were controlling the crowds.* ▶ **konno** ℹ Policja jeżdżąca konno nazywa się także **mounted police**.

ˈhorseback riding (US) = RIDING

ˌhorse ˈchestnut noun [C] **1** a large tall tree with pink or white flowers, and nuts that grow inside cases that are covered with sharp points ▶ **kasztanowiec zwyczajny** **2** (also informal **conker** /ˈkɒŋkə(r)/) the smooth brown nut from this tree ▶ **kasztan** (*owoc*)

horseman /ˈhɔːsmən/ noun [C] (pl. **-men** /-mən/) a man who rides a horse well ▶ **jeździec**

horsepower /ˈhɔːspaʊə(r)/ noun [C] (pl. **horsepower**) (abbr. **h.p.**) a measure of the power of an engine ▶ **koń mechaniczny**

'horse racing (also **racing**) noun [U] the sport in which a **jockey** rides a horse in a race to win money ▶ **wyścigi konne**

> **Horse racing** takes place at a **racecourse**. People often **bet** on the results of **horse races**. ➲ picture on **page A9**

horseradish /'hɔːsrædɪʃ/ noun [U] a plant with a hot-tasting root which is used for making a cold sauce ▶ **chrzan**

horseshoe /'hɔːsʃuː; 'hɔːʃʃuː/ (also **shoe**) noun [C] a piece of metal in the shape of a U that is fixed to the bottom of a horse's foot. Some people believe that horseshoes bring good luck. ▶ **podkowa**

horsewoman /'hɔːswʊmən/ noun [C] (pl. **-women** /-wɪmɪn/) a woman who rides a horse well ▶ **amazonka**

horticulture /'hɔːtɪkʌltʃə(r)/ noun [U] the study or practice of growing flowers, fruit and vegetables: *a college of agriculture and horticulture* ▶ **ogrodnictwo**
■ **horticultural** /ˌhɔːtɪ'kʌltʃərəl/ adj. ▶ **ogrodniczy**

hose /həʊz/ (also **hosepipe** /'həʊzpaɪp/) noun [C,U] a long rubber or plastic tube that water can flow through ▶ **wąż, szlauch** ➲ picture at **garden**

hosiery /'həʊziəri; US -ʒəri/ noun [U] (used especially in shops as a word for **tights**, **stockings** and socks): *the hosiery department* ▶ **wyroby pończosznicze**

hospice /'hɒspɪs/ noun [C] a special hospital where people who are dying are cared for ▶ **zakład dla nieuleczalnie chorych, hospicjum**

hospitable /hɒ'spɪtəbl; 'hɒspɪtəbl/ adj. (used about a person) friendly and kind to visitors ▶ **gościnny** OPP **inhospitable**

⚷ **hospital** /'hɒspɪtl/ noun [C] a place where ill or injured people are treated: *He was rushed* ***to hospital*** *in an ambulance.* ◇ *to be admitted to/discharged from hospital* być przyjętym do/wypisanym ze szpitala ◇ *a psychiatric/mental hospital* ▶ **szpital** ➲ note at **disease**, **doctor**, **hurt**

> Zwróć uwagę na różnicę między zdaniami *My brother works in the local hospital.*, *He went to the hospital to visit Jane.* i *He's very ill in hospital.*, *She cut her hand and had to go to hospital.* **In hospital** i **to hospital** to specjalne wyrażenia, które oznaczają czyjś pobyt w szpitalu z powodu choroby; używa się ich bez przedimka **a** lub **the**.

> **hospitals**
> If sb has an **accident** they may need to go to **hospital** (US **the hospital**) for medical **treatment**. Dial *999* (US *911*) and call an **ambulance**. They will be taken first to the **accident and emergency** department (US **emergency room**). If you **cut** yourself very badly, you might need **stitches**. If your arm, ankle, etc. is **painful** and **swollen**, a doctor might take an **x-ray** to see if it is **broken**. A person who is being treated in a hospital by **doctors** and **nurses** is a **patient**. If people **have an operation/have surgery**, it is performed by a **surgeon** in an **operating theatre**. Patients sleep in a **ward**. The fixed hours during the day when you are allowed to visit sb in hospital are called the **visiting hours**.

hospitality /ˌhɒspɪ'tæləti/ noun [U] looking after guests and being friendly and welcoming towards them ▶ **gościnność**

hospitalize (also **-ise**) /'hɒspɪtəlaɪz/ verb [T, usually passive] to send sb to a hospital for treatment: *Eight people were hospitalized after receiving bullet wounds.* ▶ **hospitalizować**

⚷ **host** /həʊst/ noun [C] **1** a person who invites guests to their house, etc. and provides them with food, drink, etc. ▶ **gospod-arz/yni** ➲ look at **hostess 2** a person who introduces a TV or radio show and talks to the guests: *a game show host* ▶ **gospod-arz/yni programu 3 a host of sth** a large number of people or things: *I've got a whole host of things I want to discuss with him.* ▶ **chmara, mnóstwo**
■ **host** verb [T]: *The city is aiming to host the Olympic Games in ten years' time.* ▶ **gościć, pełnić honory/obowiązki gospodarza/gospodyni**

hostage /'hɒstɪdʒ/ noun [C] a person who is caught and kept prisoner. A **hostage** may be killed or injured if the person or group who is holding them does not get what the person or group is asking for: *The robbers tried to* ***take*** *the staff* ***hostage.*** ◇ *The hijackers say they will* ***hold*** *the passengers* ***hostage*** *until their demands are met.* ▶ **zakładni-k/czka** ➲ look at **ransom**

hostel /'hɒstl/ noun [C] **1** a place like a cheap hotel where people can stay when they are living away from home or on holiday: *a youth hostel* ◇ *a student hostel* ▶ **schronisko** (*np. młodzieżowe*) **2** a building where people who have no home can stay for a short time ▶ **schronisko** (*np. dla bezdomnych*)

hostess /'həʊstəs; Brit. also -es/ noun [C] **1** a woman who invites guests to her house, etc. and provides them with food, drink, etc. ▶ **gospodyni** ➲ look at **host 2** a woman who introduces a TV or radio show and talks to the guests ▶ **gospodyni programu**

hostile /'hɒstaɪl; US also -stl/ adj. **hostile (to/towards sb/sth)** having very strong feelings against sb/sth: *a hostile crowd* ◇ *They are very hostile to any change.* ▶ **wrogi, nieprzyjazny**

hostility /hɒ'stɪləti/ noun **1** [U] **hostility (to/towards sth)** very strong feelings against sb/sth: *She didn't say anything but I could sense her hostility.* ▶ **wrogość 2** (**hostilities**) [pl.] fighting in a war ▶ **działania wojenne**

⚷ **hot¹** /hɒt/ adj. (**hotter**; **hottest**) **1** having a high temperature: *Can I open the window? I'm really hot* (jest mi strasznie gorąco). ◇ *It's hot today* (gorąco dzisiaj), *isn't it?* ◇ *It was* ***boiling hot*** *on the beach.* ◇ *Be careful – the plates are hot.* ◇ *a hot meal* ▶ **gorący** ➲ note at **cold** ➲ look at **humid 2** (used about food) causing a burning feeling in your mouth: *hot curry* ▶ **palący, ostry** SYN **spicy 3** (informal) difficult or dangerous to deal with: *The defenders found the French strikers* ***too hot to handle.*** Francuscy napastnicy byli za dobrzy dla obrońców. ◇ *When things got too hot* (gdy sprawy przybrały zbyt ostry obrót) *most journalists left the area.* ▶ **skomplikowany, niebezpieczny 4** (informal) exciting and popular: *This band is* ***hot stuff!*** ▶ **popularny, modny**
IDM **be hot at/on sth** to know a lot about sth ▶ **być dobrze zorientowanym, dobrze znać się (na czymś)**
be in hot pursuit to follow sb who is moving fast ▶ **tropić (kogoś) niezmordowanie**

hot² /hɒt/ verb (**hotting**; **hotted**)
PHR V **hot up**; especially US ˌ**heat 'up** (informal) to become more exciting or to show an increase in activity: *Things are really hotting up in the election campaign.* ▶ **rozkręcać się**

ˌ**hot-'air balloon** = BALLOON (2)

ˌ**hot-'blooded** adj. (used about a person) having strong emotions and easily becoming very excited or angry: *a hot-blooded lover* ▶ **porywczy** SYN **passionate** ➲ look at **warm-blooded**

hotchpotch /'hɒtʃpɒtʃ/ (US usually **hodgepodge** /'hɒdʒpɒdʒ/) noun [sing.] (informal) a number of things mixed together without any particular order or reason: *a hotchpotch of ideas* ▶ **miszmasz**

ˌ**hot cross 'bun** noun [C] a small sweet bread roll that contains currants and has a pattern of a cross on top, traditionally eaten in Britain around Easter ▶ **ciasto drożdżowe z rodzynkami**

ˌ**hot-ˈdesking** noun [U] the practice in an office of giving desks to workers when they are required, rather than giving each worker their own desk ▶ **praktyka gorących biurek**

ˈ**hot dog** noun [C] a hot **sausage** in a soft bread roll ▶ **hot dog** ➲ picture on **page A14**

⚷**hotel** /həʊˈtel/ noun [C] a place where you pay to stay when you are on holiday or travelling: *to stay in/at a hotel* ◇ *I've booked a double room at the Grand Hotel.* ◇ *a two-star hotel* ▶ **hotel**

> **hotels**
>
> You make a **reservation** for a **double**, **single** or **twin-bedded** room at a hotel. When you arrive you **check in** or **register** at **reception** and when you leave you **check out**. If your accommodation is **full board**, all your meals are included, and **half board** includes breakfast and evening meal. If you stay in a **motel**, you can park your car near your room. A **bed and breakfast (B and B)** is a private house which provides a room for the night and breakfast.

hotelier /həʊˈteliə(r); -lieɪ; US -ˈteljər; ˌoʊtelˈjeɪ/ noun [C] a person who owns or manages a hotel ▶ **właściciel/ka lub dyrektor/ka hotelu**

ˌ**hot-ˈheaded** adj. often acting too quickly without thinking what might happen: *The riots were started by a few hot-headed youths.* ▶ **w gorącej wodzie kąpany**

hothouse /ˈhɒthaʊs/ noun [C] a heated glass building where plants are grown ▶ **cieplarnia** ➲ look at **greenhouse**

hotline /ˈhɒtlaɪn/ noun [C] a direct telephone line to a business or organization ▶ **gorąca linia**

hotlink = HYPERLINK

hotly /ˈhɒtli/ adv. **1** in an angry or excited way: *They have hotly denied the newspaper reports.* ▶ **gniewnie, gorąco, gwałtownie** **2** closely and with determination: *The dog ran off, hotly pursued by its owner.* ▶ **gorączkowo, blisko**

ˈ**hot spot** noun [C] (informal) **1** a place where fighting is common, especially for political reasons: *UN peacekeeping forces have helped ease tensions in world hot spots since 1948.* ▶ **punkt zapalny** **2** a place where there is a lot of activity or entertainment ▶ **lokal rozrywkowy**

ˌ**hot-ˈtempered** adj. (especially Brit.) tending to become very angry easily ▶ **porywczy**

ˌ**hot-ˈwater bottle** noun [C] a rubber container that is filled with hot water and put in a bed to warm it ▶ **termofor**

houmous = HUMMUS

hound¹ /haʊnd/ noun [C] a type of dog that is used for hunting or racing: *a foxhound* ▶ **ogar, pies gończy**

hound² /haʊnd/ verb [T] to follow and disturb sb: *Many famous people complain of being hounded by the press.* ▶ **tropić**

⚷**hour** /ˈaʊə(r)/ noun **1** [C] (abbr. **hr**) a period of 60 minutes: *He studies* ***for*** *three* ***hours*** *most evenings.* ◇ ***In*** *two* ***hours' time*** *I'll be having lunch.* ◇ *a four-hour journey* ◇ *I get paid* ***by the hour.*** ◇ *How much do you get paid* ***per/an hour?*** ▶ **godzina** **2** [C] the distance that you can travel in about 60 minutes: *London is only two hours away.* ▶ **godzina drogi** **3** [C] a period of about an hour when sth particular happens: *I'm going shopping in my* ***lunch hour.*** ◇ *The traffic is very bad in* ***the rush hour*** (w godzinie szczytu). ▶ **godzina** **4** (**hours**) [pl.] the period of time when sb is working or a shop, etc. is open: *Office hours* (godziny pracy/otwarcia) *are usually from 9am to 5pm.* ◇ *Visiting hours* (godziny odwiedzin) *in the hospital are from 2 to 3pm.* ◇ *The men are demanding shorter working hours* (krótszego dnia pracy). ▶ **godziny** **5** (**hours**) [pl.] a long time: *'How long did it last?' 'Oh,* ***hours and hours!'*** ◇ *He went on speaking* ***for hours and hours.*** ▶ **godzin-y/ami** **6** (**the hour**) [sing.] the time when a new hour starts (= 1 o'clock, 2 o'clock, etc.): *Buses are* ***on the hour*** *and at twenty past the hour.* ▶ **(pełna) godzina**

IDM **at/till all hours** at/until any time: *She stays out till all hours.* ▶ **o różnych porach**; **do późnych godzin**

at an unearthly hour → UNEARTHLY

the early hours → EARLY

hourly /ˈaʊəli/ adj. [only before a noun] **1** done, happening, etc. every hour: *an hourly news bulletin* ▶ **cogodzinny** **2** for one hour: *What is your hourly rate of pay?* ▶ **godzinowy**

■ **hourly** adv.: *Trains run hourly.* ▶ **co godzina**

⚷**house¹** /haʊs/ noun [C] (pl. **houses** /ˈhaʊzɪz/) **1** a building that is made for people to live in: *Is yours a four-bedroomed or a three-bedroomed house?* ▶ **dom** ➲ look at **bungalow, cottage, flat** ➲ picture on **page A3**

> **Home** jest miejscem, gdzie mieszkasz, nawet jeżeli nie jest to dom w architektonicznym sensie tego słowa: *Let's go home to my flat.* Słowo **home** oznacza też miejsce, z którym się identyfikujesz. Natomiast **house** oznacza tylko budynek: *We've only just moved into our new house and it doesn't feel like home yet.*

2 [usually sing.] all the people who live in one house: *Don't shout. You'll wake the whole house up* (zbudzisz cały dom). ▶ **wszyscy ludzie w domu** **3** a building that is used for a particular purpose: *a warehouse* magazyn ◇ *a public house* pub ▶ **budynek konkretnego przeznaczenia** **4** a large firm involved in a particular kind of business: *a fashion house* dom mody ◇ *a publishing house* wydawnictwo **5** a restaurant, usually that sells one particular type of food: *a curry/spaghetti house* ◇ *house wine* wino firmowe ▶ **rodzaj restauracji** **6** (**House**) a group of people who meet to make a country's laws: *the House of Commons* Izba Gmin ◇ *the Houses of Parliament* izby parlamentu/parlament ▶ **izba parlamentu** ➲ note at **parliament** **7** [usually sing.] the audience at a theatre or cinema, or the area where they sit: *There was a full house for the play this evening.* ▶ **widownia**

IDM **get on/along like a house on fire** to immediately become good friends with sb ▶ **świetnie się dogadywać**

on the house paid for by the pub, restaurant, etc. that you are visiting; free: *Your first drink is on the house.* ▶ **na rachunek firmy**

> **houses**
>
> If you want to **move house**, you go to an **estate agent** (US **real estate agent**), who is a person whose job is to sell **property**. The money that you borrow in order to buy a house is called a **mortgage**. You may **rent** a house from somebody or **let** it out to somebody else. A party given by sb who has just **moved into** a house is called a **house-warming**.
>
> You can **extend** your house to make it bigger. You **do up/redecorate/renovate** your house, by repairing and decorating it. If you do the work yourself, it is called **DIY** (= do it yourself): *They're spending the weekend doing DIY.* Otherwise you may need a **plumber**, an **electrician** or a **carpenter**.

house² /haʊz/ verb [T] **1** to provide sb with a place to live: *The Council must house homeless families.* ▶ **dawać mieszkanie, zapewniać schronienie** **2** to contain or keep sth: *Her office is housed in a separate building.* ▶ **umieszczać**

ˈ**house arrest** noun [U] the state of being a prisoner in your own house rather than in a prison: *to **be under house arrest** ◇ She was **placed under house arrest*** (zatrzymana w areszcie domowym). ▶ **areszt domowy**

houseboat /ˈhaʊsbəʊt/ noun [C] a boat on a river, etc. where sb lives and which usually stays in one place ▶ **(stacjonarna) łódź mieszkalna**

housebound /ˈhaʊsbaʊnd/ adj. unable to leave your house because you are old or ill ▶ **nie wychodzący z domu (z powodu choroby, starości)**

🔑 **household** /ˈhaʊshəʊld/ noun [C] all the people who live in one house and the work, money, organization, etc. that is needed to look after them: *Almost all households have a TV.* ▶ **gospodarstwo domowe**
■ **household** adj. [only before a noun]: *household expenses* ▶ **związany z gospodarstwem domowym**

householder /ˈhaʊshəʊldə(r)/ noun [C] a person who rents or owns a house ▶ **właściciel lub najemca domu/mieszkania**

ˌ**household ˈname** noun [C] a name that has become very well known ▶ **powszechnie znane nazwisko**

housekeeper /ˈhaʊski:pə(r)/ noun [C] a person who is paid to look after sb else's house and organize the work in it ▶ **osoba prowadząca dom, gosposia**

housekeeping /ˈhaʊski:pɪŋ/ noun [U] **1** the work involved in looking after a house ▶ **gospodarowanie** (*w domu*) **2** the money that you need to manage a house ▶ **pieniądze na życie/prowadzenie domu**

housemate /ˈhaʊsmeɪt/ noun [C] (especially Brit.) a person that you share a house with, but who is not one of your family ▶ **współlokator/ka**

the ˌ**House of ˈCommons** (also **the Commons** /ˈkɒmənz/) noun [sing.] (in Britain and Canada) the part of Parliament whose members are elected by the people of the country ▶ **Izba Gmin** (*niższa, wybieralna izba parlamentu brytyjskiego*) ➲ note at **parliament**

ˈ**house officer** noun [C] (in Britain) a doctor who has finished medical school and who is working at a hospital to get further practical experience ▶ **młody lekarz odbywający staż w szpitalu** ➲ look at **intern**

the ˌ**House of ˈLords** noun [sing.] the group of people (who are not elected) who meet to discuss the laws that have been suggested by the House of Commons ▶ **Izba Lordów** (*wyższa, nie wybieralna izba parlamentu brytyjskiego*) ➲ note at **parliament**

the ˌ**House of ˌRepreˈsentatives** noun [sing.] the group of people who are elected to make new laws in the US ▶ **Izba Reprezentantów** (*niższa izba parlamentu amerykańskiego*) ➲ look at **Congress**, **senate**

ˈ**house-proud** adj. paying great attention to the care, cleaning, etc. of your house ▶ **dbający o wygląd swojego domu**

ˌ**house-to-ˈhouse** adj. [only before a noun] going to each house: *The police are making house-to-house enquiries.* ▶ **od domu do domu**

ˈ**house-warming** noun [C] a party that you have when you have just moved into a new home ▶ **parapetówka**

housewife /ˈhaʊswaɪf/ noun [C] (pl. **housewives**) a woman who does not have a job outside the home and who spends her time cleaning the house, cooking, looking after her family, etc. ▶ **gospodyni domowa** ⓘ Używa się tylko o kobiecie zamężnej. Odpowiednik męski: **house husband**.

housework /ˈhaʊswɜ:k/ noun [U] the work that is needed to take care of a home and family, for example cleaning and cooking: *to do the housework* ▶ **prace domowe** ➲ note at **clean** ⓘ Uwaga! Słowo oznaczające pracę domową zadaną uczniom przez nauczyciela to **homework**.

🔑 **housing** /ˈhaʊzɪŋ/ noun [U] houses, flats, etc. for people to live in: *the Council's housing department* (wydział mieszkaniowy) ▶ **mieszkania, lokale**

ˈ**housing estate** noun [C] an area where there are a large number of similar houses that were built at the same time ▶ **osiedle mieszkaniowe**

hovel /ˈhɒvl; US ˈhʌvl/ noun [C] a house or room that is not suitable to live in because it is dirty or in very bad condition ▶ (*przen.*) **nora**

hover /ˈhɒvə(r); US ˈhʌvər/ verb [I] **1** (used about a bird, etc.) to stay in the air in one place ▶ **wisieć w powietrzu, unosić się** **2** (used about a person) to wait near sb/sth: *He hovered nervously outside the office.* ▶ **kręcić się (koło kogoś/czegoś)**

hovercraft /ˈhɒvəkrɑ:ft; US ˈhʌvərkræft/ noun [C] (pl. **hovercraft**) a type of boat that moves over land or water, held up by air being forced downwards ▶ **poduszkowiec** ➲ picture at **boat**, picture on **page A6**

🔑 **how** /haʊ/ adv., conj. **1** (often used in questions) in what way: *How do you spell your name? ◇ Can you show me how to use this machine? ◇ I can't remember how to get there* (w jaki sposób/jak tam się dostać). ◇ ***How ever*** (jakim cudem) *did you manage to find me here?* ▶ **jak, w jaki sposób** ➲ look at **however 2** (used when you are asking about sb's health or feelings): *'How is your mother?' 'She's much better, thank you.' ◇ How are you feeling today?* ▶ **jak**

> **How** używa się tylko w pytaniach o czyjeś zdrowie. Kiedy pytanie dotyczy czyjegoś charakteru lub wyglądu, stosuje się **what ... like?**: *What is your mother like?* Jaka jest twoja mama?

3 (used when you are asking about sb's opinion of a thing or a situation): *How was the weather? ◇ How is your meal? ◇ **How** did the interview **go**?* ▶ **jak, jaki** **4** (used in questions when you are asking about the degree, amount, age, etc. of sb/sth): *How old are you?* Ile masz lat? ◇ *How much is that?* Ile to kosztuje? ▶ **ile, jak** **5** (used for expressing surprise, pleasure, etc.): *She's gone. How strange! ◇ I can't believe how expensive it is! ◇ How sweet* (jak miło) *of you to remember my birthday.* ▶ **jak**

IDM how/what about ... ? → ABOUT[2]
how come? → COME
how do you do? (formal) (used when meeting sb for the first time) ▶ **miło mi** ➲ note at **introduce**

> Uwaga! Na pytania **How are you?** i **How do you do?** odpowiada się w różny sposób. Na pytanie **How do you do?** odpowiada się tymi samymi słowami **How do you do?** Odpowiedź na **How are you?** zależy od tego, jak się czujesz: *'How are you?' 'I'm fine.'/'Very well.'/'Much better.'*

🔑 **however** /haʊˈevə(r)/ adv. **1** (formal) (used for adding a comment to what you have just said) although sth is true: *Sales are poor this month. There may, however, be an increase before Christmas.* ▶ **jednak, jakkolwiek** **2** in whatever way: *However I sat I couldn't get comfortable. ◇ You can dress however you like.* ▶ **jakkolwiek** **3** [before an adjective or adverb] to whatever degree: *He won't wear a hat however cold it is* (bez względu na to, jak jest zimno). ▶ **bez względu (na coś)** ⓘ Kiedy słowo **ever** używane jest do podkreślenia wyrazu **how**, i oznacza „w jaki sposób", wówczas pisze się je jako dwa osobne wyrazy: ***How ever*** *could he afford a car like that?* Jakim cudem mógł sobie pozwolić na taki samochód?

howl /haʊl/ verb [I] to make a long loud sound: *I couldn't sleep because there was a dog howling all night. ◇ The wind howled around the house.* ▶ **wyć**

■ **howl** noun [C]: *The Prime Minister's statement met with howls of protest.* Oświadczenie premiera zostało przyjęte głośnymi protestami. ▶ **wycie**; **ryk**

h.p. /ˌeɪtʃ ˈpiː/ (also **HP**) abbr. **1** = HORSEPOWER **2** (Brit.) = HIRE PURCHASE

HQ = HEADQUARTERS

HR = HUMAN RESOURCES

hr (pl. **hrs**) = HOUR (1): *3 hrs 15 min.*

HRH /ˌeɪtʃ ɑːr ˈeɪtʃ/ abbr. **His/Her Royal Highness**: *HRH Prince Harry* ▶ **Jego/Jej Królewska Mość**

HRT /ˌeɪtʃ ɑː ˈtiː/ noun [U] **hormone replacement therapy**; medical treatment for women going through the **menopause** in which **hormones** are added to the body ▶ **zastępcza terapia hormonalna**

hub /hʌb/ noun [usually sing.] **1 the hub (of sth)** the central and most important part of a place or an activity: *the commercial hub of the city* ▶ **centrum**, **środek 2** the central part of a wheel ▶ **piasta**

hubbub /ˈhʌbʌb/ noun [sing., U] **1** the noise made by a lot of people talking at the same time: *I couldn't hear the announcement over the hubbub.* ▶ **zgiełk**, **wrzawa 2** a situation in which there is a lot of noise, excitement and activity: *the hubbub of city life* ▶ **zgiełk**

hubcap /ˈhʌbkæp/ noun [C] a round metal cover that fits over the **hub** of a vehicle's wheel ▶ **dekiel** ➲ picture at **car**

hubris /ˈhjuːbrɪs/ noun [U] (literary) the fact of sb being too proud. In literature, a character with this pride ignores warnings and laws and this usually results in their **downfall** and death. ▶ **nieposkromiona duma**

huddle¹ /ˈhʌdl/ verb [I] **huddle (up) (together) 1** to get close to other people because you are cold or frightened: *The campers huddled together around the fire.* ▶ **stłoczyć się**, **zbijać się w grupę/kupę 2** to make your body as small as possible because you are cold or frightened: *She huddled up in her sleeping bag and tried to get some sleep.* ▶ **kulić się**, **zwijać się w kłębek**
■ **huddled** adj.: *We found the children lying huddled together on the ground.* ▶ **skulony**, **zwinięty**

huddle² /ˈhʌdl/ noun [C] a small group of people or things that are close together: *They all stood* ***in a huddle****, laughing and chatting.* ▶ **grupa**; **kupa**

hue /hjuː/ noun [C] (formal) a colour; a particular shade of a colour ▶ **barwa**, **odcień**
IDM **hue and cry** strong public protest about sth: *There was hue and cry about the new taxes.* ▶ **wrzawa**, **krzyki protestu**

huff /hʌf/ noun
IDM **in a huff** (informal) in a bad mood because sb has annoyed or upset you: *Did you see Stan* ***go off in a huff*** *when he wasn't chosen for the team?* ▶ **poirytowany**, **rozdrażniony**

huffy /ˈhʌfi/ adj. (informal) in a bad mood, especially because sb has annoyed or upset you: *She gets all huffy if you mention his name.* ▶ **naburmuszony**
■ **huffily** adv. ▶ **z naburmuszeniem**

hug /hʌg/ verb [T] (**hugging**; **hugged**) **1** to put your arms around sb, especially to show that you love them: *He hugged his mother and sisters and got on the train.* ▶ **obejmować (kogoś)**, **uściskać**, **przytulać 2** to hold sth close to your body: *She hugged the parcel to her chest as she ran.* ▶ **przyciskać 3** (used about a ship, car, road, etc.) to stay close to sth: *to hug the coast* ▶ **(blisko) trzymać się (czegoś)**
■ **hug** noun [C]: *Noel's crying – I'll go and* ***give him a hug.*** ▶ **uścisk**, **objęcie**

⚷ **huge** /hjuːdʒ/ adj. very big: *a huge amount/quantity/sum/number* ◇ *a huge building* ◇ *The film was a huge success.* ◇ *This a huge problem for us.* ▶ **ogromny**, **olbrzymi** SYN **enormous**

■ **hugely** adv.: *hugely successful/popular/expensive* ▶ **ogromnie**

huh /hʌ/ interj. (informal) (used for expressing anger, surprise, etc. or for asking a question): *They've gone away, huh? They didn't tell me.* ▶ **co**

hull /hʌl/ noun [C] the body of a ship ▶ **kadłub**

hullabaloo /ˌhʌləbəˈluː/ noun [sing.] a lot of loud noise, for example made by people shouting ▶ **zgiełk**, **harmider**

hum /hʌm/ verb (**humming**; **hummed**) **1** [I,T] to sing with your lips closed: *You can hum the tune if you don't know the words.* ▶ **śpiewać mormorando**, **nucić 2** [I] to make a continuous low noise: *The machine began to hum as I switched it on.* ◇ *The classroom was humming with activity.* W klasie wrzała praca. ▶ **brzęczeć**, **buczeć**
■ **hum** noun [sing.]: *the hum of machinery/distant traffic* ▶ **szum**, **pomruk**, **buczenie**

⚷ **human¹** /ˈhjuːmən/ adj. connected with people, not with animals, machines or gods; typical of people: *the human body* ◇ *The disaster was caused by* ***human error.*** ◇ *It's* ***only human*** (to ludzkie) *to be upset in a situation like that.* ◇ *I'm not surprised she's crying – she's* ***only human*** (jest tylko człowiekiem)*!* ▶ **ludzki**, **człowieczy**
■ **humanly** adv.: *They did all that was humanly possible* (w ludzkiej mocy) *to rescue him.* ▶ **po ludzku**

⚷ **human²** /ˈhjuːmən/ (also ˌ**human ˈbeing**) noun [C] a person ▶ **człowiek**, **istota ludzka**

humane /hjuːˈmeɪn/ adj. having or showing kindness or understanding, especially to a person or an animal that is suffering: *Animals must be kept in humane conditions.* ▶ **humanitarny**, **ludzki** OPP **inhumane**
■ **humanely** adv. ▶ **humanitarnie**, **po ludzku**

humanism /ˈhjuːmənɪzəm/ noun [U] a system of thought that considers that solving human problems with the help of reason is more important than religious beliefs. It emphasizes the fact that the basic nature of humans is good. ▶ **humanizm**
■ **humanistic** /ˌhjuːməˈnɪstɪk/ adj.: *humanistic ideals* ▶ **humanistyczny**

humanist /ˈhjuːmənɪst/ noun [C] a person who believes in **humanism** ▶ **humanist(k)a**

humanitarian /hjuːˌmænɪˈteəriən/ adj. concerned with trying to make people's lives better and reduce suffering: *Many countries have sent humanitarian aid to the earthquake victims.* ▶ **humanitarny**, **filantropijny**

humanity /hjuːˈmænəti/ noun [U] **1** all the people in the world, thought of as a group: *crimes against humanity* ▶ **ludzkość** SYN **human race 2** the quality of being kind and understanding: *The prisoners were treated with humanity* (po ludzku). ▶ **humanitarność** OPP **inhumanity 3** (**(the) humanities**) noun [pl.] the subjects of study that are concerned with the way people think and behave, for example literature, history, etc. ▶ **nauki humanistyczne** ➲ look at **science**

humankind /ˌhjuːmənˈkaɪnd/ noun [U] people in general ▶ **ludzkość** ➲ look at **mankind**

ˌ**human ˈnature** noun [U] feelings, behaviour, etc. that all people have in common ▶ **natura ludzka**

the ˌ**human ˈrace** noun [sing.] all the people in the world, when thought of as a group ▶ **rasa ludzka** SYN **humanity**

ˌ**human reˈsources** noun [U, with sing. or pl. verb] (abbr. **HR** /ˌeɪtʃ ˈɑː(r)/) the department in a company that deals with employing and training people ▶ (*dział*) **kadry** SYN **personnel**

ˌ**human ˈright** noun [usually pl.] one of the basic rights that everyone has to be treated fairly and not in a cruel way, especially by their government: *The country has a poor* *record on human rights.* ◇ ***human rights abuses/violations*** ▶ **prawo człowieka**

humble¹ /ˈhʌmbl/ adj. **1** not thinking that you are better or more important than other people; not proud: *He became very rich and famous but he always remained a very humble man.* ▶ **skromny, pokorny** ➲ look at **modest** ➲ noun **humility** **2** not special or important: *She comes from a humble background.* Pochodzi z prostej rodziny. ▶ **skromny**

■ **humbly** /ˈhʌmbli/ adv.: *He apologized very humbly for his behaviour.* ▶ **pokornie**

humble² /ˈhʌmbl/ verb [T] to make sb feel that they are not as good or important as they thought ▶ **upokarzać**

humerus /ˈhjuːmərəs/ noun [C] the large bone in the top part of the arm between your shoulder and your elbow ▶ **kość ramienna** ➲ picture at **body**

humid /ˈhjuːmɪd/ adj. (used about the air or climate) warm and feeling slightly wet: *Hong Kong is hot and humid in summer.* ▶ **wilgotny**

■ **humidity** /hjuːˈmɪdəti/ noun [U] ▶ **wilgotność, wilgoć**

humidifier /hjuːˈmɪdɪfaɪə(r)/ noun [C] a machine used for making the air in a room less dry ▶ **nawilżacz powietrza**

humiliate /hjuːˈmɪlieɪt/ verb [T] to make sb feel very embarrassed: *I felt humiliated when the teacher laughed at my work.* ▶ **upokarzać**

■ **humiliating** adj.: *a humiliating defeat* ▶ **upokarzający** | **humiliation** /hjuːˌmɪliˈeɪʃn/ noun [C,U] ▶ **upokorzenie**

humility /hjuːˈmɪləti/ noun [U] the quality of not thinking that you are better than other people ▶ **uniżoność, pokora** ➲ adjective **humble**

hummus (also **houmous**) /ˈhʊməs; ˈhuːməs/ noun [U] a type of food, originally from the Middle East, that is a soft mixture of **chickpeas**, oil and **garlic** ▶ **sos z ciecierzycy**

humorless (US) = HUMOURLESS

⚷ **humorous** /ˈhjuːmərəs/ adj. amusing or funny ▶ **zabawny, śmieszny**

■ **humorously** adv. ▶ **śmiesznie, zabawnie**

⚷ **humour¹** (US **humor**) /ˈhjuːmə(r)/ noun [U] **1** the funny or amusing qualities of sb/sth: *It is sometimes hard to understand the humour* (poczucie humoru) *of another country.* ▶ **humor** **2** being able to see when sth is funny and to laugh at things: *I can't stand people with no **sense of humour**.* ▶ **poczucie humoru** **3** (**-humoured**) (US **-humored**) [in compounds] having or showing a particular mood: *good-humoured* dobroduszny ▶ *(określa nastrój)*

> **humour**
>
> Do you have a **good sense of humour**? What do you find **funny/amusing**? When sth is **hilarious**, do you **burst out laughing**? Some people are **witty**. **Clowns** like **slapstick**. A **practical joke** is sth you do to make a person look silly. **Comedians** tell **jokes** and may use **satire** to **make fun of** people such as politicians.

humour² (US **humor**) /ˈhjuːmə(r)/ verb [T] to keep sb happy by doing what they want ▶ **ustępować** *(komuś dla świętego spokoju)*

humourless (US **humorless**) /ˈhjuːmələs/ adj. having no sense of fun; serious ▶ **bez poczucia humoru**

hump /hʌmp/ noun [C] a large lump that sticks out above the surface of sth, for example on the back of a **camel** ▶ **garb**

hunch¹ /hʌntʃ/ verb [I,T] to bend your back and shoulders forward into a round shape: *They sat there hunched up with the cold* (skuleni z zimna). ▶ **garbić się**

hunch² /hʌntʃ/ noun [C] (informal) a thought or an idea that is based on a feeling rather than on facts or information: *I'm not sure, but I've got a hunch that she's got a new job.* ▶ **przeczucie, podejrzenie**

hunchback /ˈhʌntʃbæk/ noun [C] a person with a back that has a round lump on it ▶ **garbus/ka**

⚷ **hundred** /ˈhʌndrəd/ number **1** (pl. **hundred**) 100: *two hundred* ◇ *There were a/one hundred people in the room.* ◇ *She's a hundred today.* Skończyła dzisiaj sto lat. ▶ **sto**

> Zwróć uwagę, że używając liczb, np. 420, stawia się spójnik **and** po słowie **hundred**: *four hundred and twenty.*

2 (**hundreds**) (informal) a lot; a large amount: *I've got hundreds of things to do today.* ◇ *The boat cost hundreds of pounds* (setki funtów). ▶ **wiele, dużo** ⓘ Więcej o liczebnikach w dodatku *Wyrażenia liczbowe* na końcu słownika.

⚷ **hundredth** /ˈhʌndrədθ/ ordinal number 100th ▶ **setny** ➲ note at **sixth**

■ **hundredth** noun [C] 1⁄100; one of a hundred equal parts of sth ▶ **(jedna) setna**

hundredweight /ˈhʌndrədweɪt/ noun [C] (abbr. **cwt.**) a measure of weight, about 50.8 kilograms ▶ **cetnar** ⓘ Amerykański cetnar odpowiada 100 funtom (45,4 kg). Więcej o wagach w dodatku *Wyrażenia liczbowe* na końcu słownika.

hung past tense, past participle of **hang¹**

hunger¹ /ˈhʌŋɡə(r)/ noun **1** [U] the state of not having enough food to eat, especially when this causes illness or death: *In the Third World many people die of hunger each year.* ▶ **głód** ➲ look at **thirst** **2** [U] the feeling caused by a need to eat: *Hunger is one reason why babies cry.* ▶ **głód** ⓘ Uwaga! Nie można powiedzieć ~~*I have hunger*~~. Mówi się **I am hungry**. **3** [sing.] **hunger (for sth)** a strong desire for sth: *a hunger for knowledge/fame/success* ▶ *(przen.)* **głód (czegoś)**

hunger² /ˈhʌŋɡə(r)/ verb

PHR V **hunger for/after sth** (formal) to have a strong desire for sth ▶ **bardzo czegoś pragnąć**

ˈ**hunger strike** noun [C,U] a time when sb (especially a prisoner) refuses to eat because they are protesting about sth: *to be/go **on hunger strike*** ▶ **strajk głodowy**

⚷ **hungry** /ˈhʌŋɡri/ adj. (**hungrier**; **hungriest**) **1** wanting to eat: *I'm hungry. Let's eat soon.* ◇ *There were hungry children begging for food in the streets.* ▶ **głodny** ➲ look at **thirsty** **2** **hungry for sth** wanting sth very much: *I'm hungry for some excitement tonight.* ▶ **spragniony**

■ **hungrily** adv. ▶ **pożądliwie, chciwie**

IDM **go hungry** to not have any food ▶ **głodować**

hunk /hʌŋk/ noun [C] **1** a large piece of sth: *a hunk of bread/cheese/meat* ▶ **pajda, kawał** **2** (informal) a man who is big, strong and attractive ▶ **(wielkie) chłopisko, przystojniak**

hunky-dory /ˌhʌŋki ˈdɔːri/ adj. [not before a noun] (informal) if you say that **everything is hunky-dory**, you mean that there are no problems and that everyone is happy ▶ **fajny**

⚷ **hunt¹** /hʌnt/ verb [I,T] **1** **hunt (for) (sb/sth)** to try to find sb/sth: *The police are still hunting the murderer.* ▶ **szukać, polować (na kogoś), gonić** **2** to chase wild animals or birds in order to catch or kill them for food, sport or to make money: *Owls hunt at night.* ◇ *Are tigers still being hunted in India?* ▶ **polować** ⓘ Często używa się wyrażenia **go hunting**, które oznacza, że ktoś spędza czas polując.

PHR V **hunt sb down** to search for sb until you catch or find them, especially in order to punish or harm them ▶ **wytropić kogoś**

hunt sth down/out to search for sth until you find it: *We hunted down their phone number and gave them a call.*

◇ *I hunted out my old school photos to show Mary.* ▶ **odszukać coś**

hunt² /hʌnt/ noun [C] **1** the act of hunting wild animals, etc.: *a fox-hunt* polowanie na lisy ▶ **polowanie 2** [usually sing.] **a hunt (for sb/sth)** the act of looking for sb/sth that is difficult to find: *The police have launched a hunt for the missing child.* ▶ **poszukiwania**

hunter /ˈhʌntə(r)/ noun [C] a person that hunts wild animals for food or sport; an animal that hunts its food: *a bargain hunter* łowca okazji (tanich zakupów) ▶ **myśliwy**; (*zwierzę*) **drapieżnik**

⚷ **hunting** /ˈhʌntɪŋ/ noun [U] the act of following and killing wild animals or birds as a sport or for food ▶ **polowanie** ➲ look at **shoot**

hurdle¹ /ˈhɜːdl/ noun **1** [C] a type of light fence that a person or a horse jumps over in a race: *to clear a hurdle* pokonywać przeszkodę ▶ **płotek** (*w sporcie*) **2** (**hurdles**) [pl.] a race in which runners or horses have to jump over **hurdles**: *the 200 metres hurdles* ▶ **bieg przez płotki 3** [C] a problem or difficulty that you must solve or deal with before you can achieve sth ▶ **przeszkoda**

hurdle² /ˈhɜːdl/ verb [I,T] **hurdle (over sth)** to jump over sth while you are running ▶ **skakać przez płotki**

hurl /hɜːl/ verb [T] to throw sth with great force ▶ **ciskać, miotać**

hurray (also **hooray**) /həˈreɪ/ (also **hurrah** /həˈrɑː/) interj. (used for expressing great pleasure, approval, etc.): *Hurray! We've won!* ▶ **hura**

IDM **hip, hip, hurray/hurrah** → HIP²

hurricane /ˈhʌrɪkən; US ˈhɜːrə-; -keɪn/ noun [C] a violent storm with very strong winds ▶ **huragan** ➲ note at **storm**

hurried /ˈhʌrid; US ˈhɜːr-/ adj. done (too) quickly: *a hurried meal* ▶ **pośpieszny**

■ **hurriedly** adv. ▶ **pośpiesznie**

⚷ **hurry¹** /ˈhʌri; US ˈhɜːri/ verb (**hurrying**; **hurries**; pt, pp **hurried**) **1** [I] to move or do sth quickly because there is not much time: *Don't hurry. There's plenty of time.* ◇ *They hurried back home after school.* ◇ *Several people hurried to help.* ▶ **spieszyć się 2** [T] **hurry sb (into sth/doing sth)** to cause sb/sth to do sth, or sth to happen more quickly: *Don't hurry me. I'm going as fast as I can.* ◇ *He was hurried into a decision.* ▶ **przynaglać, popędzać 3** [usually passive] to do sth too quickly: *Good food should never be hurried.* Nigdy nie powinno się spożywać dobrego jedzenia w pośpiechu. ▶ **wykonywać coś w pośpiechu** SYN for all meanings **rush**

PHR V **hurry up (with sth)** (informal) to move or do sth more quickly: *Hurry up or we'll miss the train.* ▶ **pośpieszyć się**

⚷ **hurry²** /ˈhʌri; US ˈhɜːri/ noun [U] the need or wish to do sth quickly: *Take your time. There's **no hurry**.* ◇ *What's the hurry?* Skąd ten pośpiech? ▶ **pośpiech** SYN **rush**

IDM **in a hurry** quickly: *She got up late and left in a hurry.* ▶ **w pośpiechu, pośpiesznie**

be in a hurry (to do sth) to want to do sth soon; to be impatient: *They are in a hurry to get the job done before the winter.* ▶ **spieszyć się**

be in no hurry (to do sth); **not be in any hurry (to do sth) 1** to not need or wish to do sth quickly: *We weren't in any hurry so we stopped to admire the view.* ▶ **nie śpieszyć się 2** to not want to do sth: *I am in no hurry to repeat that experience.* ▶ **nie kwapić się**

⚷ **hurt¹** /hɜːt/ verb (pt, pp **hurt**) **1** [T,I] to cause sb/yourself physical pain or injury: *Did he hurt himself?* ◇ *I fell and hurt my arm.* ◇ *No one was seriously hurt in the accident.* ◇ *These shoes hurt; they're too tight.* ▶ **kaleczyć, ranić; krzywdzić 2** [I] to feel painful: ***It hurts*** (boli mnie) *when I lift my leg.* ◇ *Where exactly does it hurt?* ◇ *My leg hurts.* Boli mnie noga. ▶ **boleć 3** [T] to make sb unhappy; to upset sb: *His unkind remarks hurt her deeply.* ◇ *I didn't want to **hurt** his **feelings**.* ▶ **urażać, obrażać**

IDM **it won't/wouldn't hurt (sb/sth) (to do sth)** (informal) (used to say that sb should do sth): *It wouldn't hurt you to help with the housework occasionally.* ▶ **nie zaszkodzi**

> **hurt**
>
> A person may be **wounded** by a knife, sword, gun, etc., usually as a result of fighting: *a wounded soldier.* People are usually **injured** in an accident: *Five people were killed in the crash and twelve others were injured.* **Hurt** and **injured** are similar in meaning but **hurt** is more often used when the damage is not very great: *I hurt my leg when I fell off my bike.*

hurt² /hɜːt/ adj. **1** injured physically: *None of the passengers were **badly/seriously hurt**.* ▶ **ranny 2** upset and offended by sth that sb has said or done: *She was **deeply hurt** that she had not been invited to the party.* ▶ **urażony, obrażony**

hurt³ /hɜːt/ noun [U] a feeling of unhappiness because sb has been unkind or unfair to you: *There was hurt and real anger in her voice.* ▶ **cierpienie** (*umysłu*), **uraza**

hurtful /ˈhɜːtfl/ adj. **hurtful (to sb)** making sb feel upset and offended ▶ **bolesny, obraźliwy** SYN **unkind**

hurtle /ˈhɜːtl/ verb [I] to move with great speed, perhaps causing danger: *The lorry **came hurtling** towards us.* ▶ **pędzić, lecieć**

⚷ **husband** /ˈhʌzbənd/ noun [C] a man that a woman is married to: *Her ex-husband sees the children once a month.* ▶ **mąż**

hush¹ /hʌʃ/ verb [I] (informal) (used to tell sb to be quiet, to stop talking or crying): *Hush now and try to sleep.* ▶ **sza!**

PHR V **hush sth up** to hide information to stop people knowing about sth; to keep sth secret ▶ **zatuszować**

hush² /hʌʃ/ noun [sing.] no noise or sound at all ▶ **cisza**

ˌhush-ˈhush adj. (informal) very secret ▶ **tajny**

husk /hʌsk/ noun [C] the dry outer covering of nuts, fruits and seeds, especially of grain: *Brown rice has not had the husks removed.* ▶ **łupina, łuska**

husky¹ /ˈhʌski/ adj. (**huskier**; **huskiest**) (used about sb's voice) sounding rough and quiet as if your throat were dry ▶ **ochrypły, matowy**

husky² /ˈhʌski/ noun [C] (pl. **huskies**) a strong dog with thick fur that is used in teams for pulling heavy loads over snow ▶ **husky**

hustle /ˈhʌsl/ verb [T] to push or move sb in a way that is not gentle: *The demonstrators were hustled into* (zostali wepchnięci do) *police vans.* ▶ **popychać, szturchać**

hut /hʌt/ noun [C] a small building with one room, usually made of wood or metal: *a beach hut* ◇ *a wooden/mud hut* ▶ **chata, szałas**

hutch /hʌtʃ/ noun [C] a wooden box with a front made of wire, that is used for keeping **rabbits** or other animals ▶ **klatka** (*dla królików itp.*)

hyacinth /ˈhaɪəsɪnθ/ noun [C] a plant with a mass of small blue, white or pink flowers with a sweet smell that grow closely together around a thick **stem** ▶ **hiacynt**

hybrid /ˈhaɪbrɪd/ noun [C] **1** an animal or a plant that has parents of different types: *A mule is a hybrid of a male donkey and a female horse.* ▶ **mieszaniec, hybryd 2 hybrid (between/of A and B)** something that is the product of mixing two or more different things: *The music was a hybrid of Western pop and traditional folk song.* ▶ **skrzyżowanie** SYN for both meanings **mixture**

■ **hybrid** adj. ▶ **hybrydowy**

hydrangea /haɪˈdreɪndʒə/ noun [C] a bush with white, pink or blue flowers that grow closely together in the shape of a large ball ▶ **hortensja**

hydrant /ˈhaɪdrənt/ noun [C] a pipe in a street from which water can be taken for stopping fires, cleaning the streets, etc.: *a fire hydrant* ▶ **hydrant**

hydraulic /haɪˈdrɔːlɪk/ adj. operated by water or another liquid moving through pipes, etc. under pressure: *hydraulic brakes* ▶ **hydrauliczny**

hydrochloric acid /ˌhaɪdrəˌklɒrɪk ˈæsɪd/ noun [U] (symbol **HCl**) an acid containing **hydrogen** and **chlorine** ▶ **kwas solny**

hydroelectric /ˌhaɪdrəʊɪˈlektrɪk/ adj. using the power of water to produce electricity; produced by the power of water: *a hydroelectric dam/plant* ◇ *hydroelectric power* ▶ **hydroelektryczny** ➲ note at **environment**

hydrogen /ˈhaɪdrədʒən/ noun [U] (symbol **H**) a light gas with no colour. **Hydrogen** and **oxygen** form water (H_2O). ▶ **wodór**

hydrospeeding /ˈhaɪdrəʊsiːdɪŋ/ noun [U] a sport that involves being carried along in fast-flowing water at high speed lying on a floating board similar to a surfboard ▶ **rodzaj sportu wodnego**

hygiene /ˈhaɪdʒiːn/ noun [U] (the rules of) keeping yourself and things around you clean, in order to prevent disease: *High standards of hygiene are essential when you are preparing food.* ◇ *personal hygiene* ▶ **higiena**

hygienic /haɪˈdʒiːnɪk/ adj. clean, without the bacteria that cause disease: *hygienic conditions* ▶ **higieniczny**
■ **hygienically** /-kli/ adv. ▶ **higienicznie**

hymn /hɪm/ noun [C] a religious song that Christians sing together in church, etc. ▶ **hymn**, **pieśń religijna**

hype¹ /haɪp/ noun [U] advertisements that tell you how good and important a new product, film, etc. is: *Don't believe all the hype – the book is rubbish!* ▶ (*przen.*) **krzykliwa reklama**, **szum** (*np.medialny*)

hype² /haɪp/ verb [T] **hype sth (up)** to exaggerate how good or important sth is: *His much-hyped new movie is released next week.* ▶ **robić szum (wokół czegoś)**

hyperactive /ˌhaɪpərˈæktɪv/ adj. (used especially about children and their behaviour) too active and only able to keep quiet and still for short periods ▶ **nadpobudliwy**
■ **hyperactivity** /ˌhaɪpərækˈtɪvəti/ noun [U] ▶ **nadpobudliwość**

hyperinflation /ˌhaɪpərɪnˈfleɪʃn/ noun [U] a situation in which prices rise very fast, causing damage to a country's economy ▶ **hiperinflacja**

hyperlink /ˈhaɪpəlɪŋk/ (also **hotlink** /ˈhɒtlɪŋk/) noun [C] a place in an electronic document on a computer that is connected to another electronic document: *Click on the hyperlink.* ▶ **hiperłącze**

hypermarket /ˈhaɪpəmɑːkɪt; US -pərmɑːrk-/ noun [C] (Brit.) a very large shop outside a town that sells a wide variety of goods ▶ **hipermarket**

hypersensitive /ˌhaɪpəˈsensətɪv/ adj. **hypersensitive (to sth)** **1** very easily offended: *He's hypersensitive to any kind of criticism.* ▶ **przewrażliwiony** **2** extremely physically sensitive to particular substances, medicines, light, etc.: *Her skin is hypersensitive.* ▶ **nadwrażliwy**

hypertension /ˌhaɪpəˈtenʃn/ noun [U] blood pressure that is higher than is normal ▶ **nadciśnienie**

hypertext /ˈhaɪpətekst/ noun [U] text stored in a computer system that contains links that allow the user to move from one piece of text or document to another: *a hypertext link on the Internet* ▶ **hipertekst**

hyperventilate /ˌhaɪpəˈventɪleɪt/ verb [I] to breathe too quickly because you are very frightened or excited ▶ **zbyt szybko oddychać**
■ **hyperventilation** /ˌhaɪpəˌventɪˈleɪʃn/ noun [U] ▶ **hiperwentylacja**

hyphen /ˈhaɪfn/ noun [C] the mark (-) used for joining two words together (for example *left-handed*, *red-hot*) or to show that a word has been divided and continues on the next line ▶ **łącznik** ➲ look at **dash**

hyphenate /ˈhaɪfəneɪt/ verb [T] to join two words together with a **hyphen** ▶ **pisać z łącznikiem**
■ **hyphenation** /ˌhaɪfəˈneɪʃn/ noun [U] ▶ **pisanie z łącznikiem**, **dzielenie/przenoszenie wyrazów**

hypnosis /hɪpˈnəʊsɪs/ noun [U] (the producing of) an unconscious state where sb's mind and actions can be controlled by another person: *She was questioned **under hypnosis**.* ▶ **hipnoza**

hypnotize (also -ise) /ˈhɪpnətaɪz/ verb [T] to put sb into an unconscious state where the person's mind and actions can be controlled ▶ **hipnotyzować**
■ **hypnotic** /hɪpˈnɒtɪk/ adj. ▶ **hipnotyczny** | **hypnotism** /ˈhɪpnətɪzəm/ noun [U] ▶ **hipnotyzm** | **hypnotist** /-tɪst/ noun [C] ▶ **hipnotyzer/ka**

hypochondriac /ˌhaɪpəˈkɒndriæk/ noun [C] a person who is always worried about their health and believes they are ill, even when there is nothing wrong ▶ **hipochondry-k/czka**

hypocrisy /hɪˈpɒkrəsi/ noun [U] behaviour in which sb pretends to have moral standards or opinions that they do not really have ▶ **obłuda**, **hipokryzja**

hypocrite /ˈhɪpəkrɪt/ noun [C] a person who pretends to have moral standards or opinions which they do not really have. **Hypocrites** say one thing and do another: *What a hypocrite! She says she's against the hunting of animals but she's wearing a fur coat.* ▶ **obłudni-k/ca**, **hipokryt(k)a**
■ **hypocritical** /ˌhɪpəˈkrɪtɪkl/ adj. ▶ **obłudny** | **hypocritically** /-kli/ adv. ▶ **obłudnie**

hypodermic /ˌhaɪpəˈdɜːmɪk/ adj. a medical instrument with a long needle that is used for giving sb an **injection**: *a hypodermic needle/syringe* ▶ **podskórny**

hypotenuse /haɪˈpɒtənjuːz; US also -nuːs/ noun [C] the side opposite the **right angle** of a **right-angled** triangle ▶ **przeciwprostokątna**

hypothesis /haɪˈpɒθəsɪs/ noun [C] (pl. **hypotheses** /-siːz/) an idea that is suggested as the possible explanation for sth but has not yet been found to be true or correct ▶ **hipoteza**

hypothetical /ˌhaɪpəˈθetɪkl/ adj. based on situations that have not yet happened, not on facts: *That's a hypothetical question because we don't know what the situation will be next year.* ▶ **hipotetyczny**, **przypuszczalny**
■ **hypothetically** /-kli/ adv. ▶ **hipotetycznie**

hysterectomy /ˌhɪstəˈrektəmi/ noun (pl. **hysterectomies**) [C, U] a medical operation to remove a woman's **womb**: *She had to have a hysterectomy.* ▶ **histerektomia**

hysteria /hɪˈstɪəriə/ noun [U] a state in which a person or a group of people cannot control their emotions, for example cannot stop laughing, crying, shouting, etc.: *mass hysteria* ▶ **histeria**

hysterical /hɪˈsterɪkl/ adj. **1** very excited and unable to control your emotions: *hysterical laughter* ◇ *She was hysterical with grief.* Z żalu dostała ataku histerii. ▶ **histeryczny** **2** (informal) very funny ▶ **bardzo śmieszny**
■ **hysterically** /-kli/ adv. ▶ **histerycznie**

hysterics /hɪˈsterɪks/ noun [pl.] **1** an expression of extreme fear, excitement or anger that makes sb lose control of their emotions: *She **went into hysterics*** (dostała ataku histerii) *when they told her the news.* ◇ (informal) *My father would **have hysterics*** (dostałby histerii) *if he knew I was with you.* ▶ **histeria 2** (informal) a state of being unable to stop laughing: *The audience was **in hysterics*** (zanosiła się od śmiechu). ▶ **histeryczny śmiech**

Hz /hɜːts/ abbr. **hertz**; (used in radio) a measure of **frequency** ▶ **Hz**

I i

I, i /aɪ/ noun [C,U] (pl. **Is**; **is**; **I's**; **i's** /aɪz/) the 9th letter of the English alphabet: *'Ice' begins with (an) 'I'.* ▶ **litera** *i*

I /aɪ/ pron. (the subject of a verb) the person who is speaking or writing: *I phoned and said that I was busy.* ◇ *I'm not going to fall, am I?* ▶ **ja**

ice¹ /aɪs/ noun [U] water that has frozen and become solid: *Do you want ice in your orange juice?* ◇ *I slipped on a patch of ice.* ◇ *black ice* mało widoczne oblodzenie drogi ▶ **lód**
IDM **break the ice** to say or do sth that makes people feel more relaxed, especially at the beginning of a party or meeting: *She smiled to break the ice.* ▶ **przełamywać lody**
cut no ice (with sb) to have no influence or effect on sb: *His excuses cut no ice with me* (przeprosinami nic u mnie nie wskórał).
on ice 1 (used about wine, etc.) kept cold by being surrounded by ice: *The table is set, the candles are lit and the champagne is on ice.* ▶ **w wiaderku itp. z lodem 2** (used about a plan, etc.) waiting to be dealt with later; delayed: *We've had to put our plans to go to Australia on ice for the time being.* ▶ **do rozpatrzenia w późniejszym terminie**

ice² /aɪs/ (especially US **frost**) verb [T] to decorate a cake by covering it with a mixture of sugar, butter, chocolate, etc. ▶ **lukrować** ➲ look at **icing**
PHR V **ice (sth) over/up** to cover sth or become covered with ice: *The windscreen of the car had iced over in the night.* ▶ **oblodzić (się), pokrywać (się) lodem**

iceberg /ˈaɪsbɜːɡ/ noun [C] a very large block of ice that floats in the sea ▶ **góra lodowa**
IDM **the tip of the iceberg** → TIP¹

icebox (US) = FRIDGE

ˌice-ˈcold adj. very cold: *ice-cold beer* ◇ *Your hands are ice-cold.* ▶ **lodowaty**

ˌice ˈcream noun **1** [U] a frozen sweet food that is made from cream: *Desserts are served with cream or ice cream.* ▶ **lody** ➲ picture on **page A14 2** [C] an amount of **ice cream** that is served to sb, often in a **cone**: *a strawberry ice cream* ▶ **lody**

ˈice cube noun [C] a small block of ice that you put in a drink to make it cold ▶ **kostka lodu**

iced /aɪst/ adj. (used about drinks) very cold: *iced tea* ▶ **mrożony**

ˈice hockey (US **hockey**) noun [U] a game that is played on ice by two teams who try to hit a **puck** into a goal with long wooden sticks ▶ **hokej na lodzie** ➲ note at **hockey** ➲ picture on **page A8**

ˌice ˈlolly noun [C] (pl. **ice lollies**) (US **Popsicle** /ˈpɒpsɪkl/) a piece of flavoured ice on a stick ▶ **lody na patyku** ➲ look at **lollipop**

ˈice rink = SKATING RINK

ˈice skate = SKATE² (1)

ˈice-skate = SKATE¹

ˈice skating = SKATING (1)

icicle /ˈaɪsɪkl/ noun [C] a pointed piece of ice that is formed by water freezing as it falls or runs down from sth ▶ **sopel lodu**

icing /ˈaɪsɪŋ/ (US **frosting** /ˈfrɒstɪŋ/) noun [U] a sweet mixture of sugar and water, milk, butter, etc. that is used for decorating cakes ▶ **lukier**

ˈicing sugar noun [U] (US **conˈfectioner's sugar**; **ˈpowdered sugar**) white sugar in fine powder form, used especially to make icing for cakes ▶ **cukier puder** ➲ look at **caster sugar**

icon /ˈaɪkɒn/ noun [C] **1** a small picture or symbol on a computer screen that represents a program: *Click on the printer icon with the mouse.* ▶ **ikona, piktogram 2** a person or thing that is considered to be a symbol of sth: *Madonna and other pop icons of the 1980s* ▶ **symbol 3** (also **ikon**) a picture or figure of an important religious person, used by some types of Christians ▶ **ikona**

iconic /aɪˈkɒnɪk/ adj. acting as a sign or symbol of sth ▶ **symboliczny**

iconoclastic /aɪˌkɒnəˈklæstɪk/ adj. (formal) criticizing popular beliefs or established customs and ideas ▶ **obrazoburczy**
■ **iconoclasm** /aɪˈkɒnəklæzəm/ noun [U]: *the iconoclasm of the early Christians* ▶ **obrazoburstwo**

icy /ˈaɪsi/ adj. (**icier**; **iciest**) **1** very cold: *icy winds/water/weather* ▶ **lodowaty, mroźny** SYN **freezing 2** covered with ice: *icy roads* ▶ **oblodzony**

I'd /aɪd/ short for **I had; I would**

ID (informal) = IDENTIFICATION (2), IDENTITY: *You must carry ID at all times.*

Id = EID

I'D card = IDENTITY CARD

idea /aɪˈdɪə; US -ˈdiːə/ noun **1** [C] **an idea (for sth); an idea (of sth/of doing sth)** a plan, thought or suggestion, especially about what to do in a particular situation: *That's a good idea!* ◇ *He's **got an idea** for a new play.* ◇ *I had the **bright idea** of getting Jane to help me with my homework.* ◇ *Has anyone got any ideas of how to tackle this problem?* ◇ *It was your idea to invite so many people to the party.* ◇ *We're toying with the idea of buying* (rozważamy możliwość kupienia) *a villa in Spain.* ▶ **pomysł, myśl 2** [sing.] **an idea (of sth)** a picture or impression in your mind: *You have no idea how difficult it was to find a time that suited everybody.* ◇ *The programme **gave a good idea** of what life was like before the war.* ◇ *Staying in to watch the football on TV is not my idea of a good time.* ▶ **pojęcie, wyobrażenie 3** [C] **an idea (about sth)** an opinion or belief: *She has her own ideas about how to bring up children.* ◇ *Hiding my handbag? If that's your idea of* (czy tak sobie wyobrażasz) *a joke, I don't think it's funny!* ▶ **wyobrażenie, pojęcie 4** (**the idea**) [sing.] **the idea (of sth/of doing sth)** the aim or purpose of sth: *The idea of the course is to teach the basics of car maintenance.* ▶ **zamysł, idea**
IDM **get the idea** to understand the aim or purpose of sth: *Right! I think I've got the idea.* ▶ **zrozumieć**
get the idea that... to get the feeling or impression that...: *Where did you get the idea that I was paying for this meal?* ▶ **wydawać się**
have an idea that... to have a feeling or think that...: *I'm not sure but I have an idea that they've gone on holiday.* ▶ **wydawać się**
not have the faintest/foggiest (idea) → FAINT¹

ideal¹ /aɪˈdiːəl/ adj. **ideal (for sb/sth)** the best possible; perfect: *She's the ideal candidate for the job.* ◇ ***In an ideal world*** *there would be no poverty.* ◇ *It would be an **ideal opportunity** for you to practise your Spanish.* ▶ **idealny, doskonały**

ideal² /aɪˈdiːəl/ noun [C] **1** an idea or principle that seems perfect to you and that you want to achieve: *She finds it hard to live up to her parents' high ideals.* ◇ *political/moral/social ideals* ▶ **ideał 2** [usually sing.] **an ideal (of sth)**

a perfect example of a person or thing: *It's my ideal of what a family home should be.* ▶ **ideał**

idealism /aɪˈdiːəlɪzəm/ noun [U] the belief that a perfect life, situation, etc. can be achieved, even when this is not very likely: *Young people are usually full of idealism.* ▶ **idealizm** ➲ look at **realism**
■ **idealist** /-ɪst/ noun [C]: *Most people are idealists when they are young.* ▶ **idealist(k)a** | **idealistic** /ˌaɪdiəˈlɪstɪk/ adj. ▶ **idealistyczny**

idealize (also -ise) /aɪˈdiːəlaɪz/ verb [T] to imagine or show sb/sth as being better than he/she/it really is: *Old people often idealize the past.* ▶ **idealizować**

⚷ **ideally** /aɪˈdiːəli/ adv. **1** perfectly: *They are ideally suited to each other.* ▶ **doskonale, idealnie 2** in an **ideal** situation: *Ideally, no class should be larger than 25.* ▶ **idealnie**

identical /aɪˈdentɪkl/ adj. **1 identical (to/with sb/sth)** exactly the same as; similar in every detail: *I can't see any difference between these two pens – they look identical to me.* ◇ *That watch is identical to the one I lost yesterday.* ▶ **taki sam, identyczny 2** (**the identical**) [only before a noun] the same: *This is the identical room we stayed in last year.* ▶ **ten sam**
■ **identically** /-kli/ adv. ▶ **identycznie, tak samo**

iˌdentical ˈtwin noun [C] either of two children or animals born from the same mother at the same time who have developed from a single egg ▶ **bliźniak jednojajowy**

identifiable /aɪˌdentɪˈfaɪəbl/ adj. that can be recognized: *identifiable groups/characteristics* ◇ *The house is easily identifiable by the large tree outside.* ▶ **rozpoznawalny**

identification /aɪˌdentɪfɪˈkeɪʃn/ noun **1** [U,C] the process of showing, recognizing or giving proof of who or what sb/sth is: *The identification of the bodies of those killed in the explosion was very difficult.* ▶ **identyfikacja 2** (abbr. **ID** /ˌaɪ ˈdiː/) [U] an official paper, document, etc. that is proof of who you are: *Do you have any identification?* ▶ **dowód tożsamości, legitymacja 3** [U,C] **identification (with sb/sth)** a strong feeling of understanding or sharing the same feelings as sb/sth: *children's identification with TV heroes* ▶ **utożsamianie się**

iˌdentifiˈcation parade (also informal **iˈdentity parade**, especially US **ˈline-up**) noun [C] a row of people, including one person who is suspected of a crime, who are shown to a witness to see if he or she can recognize the criminal ▶ **konfrontacja** (*w celu rozpoznania przestępcy*)

⚷ **identify** /aɪˈdentɪfaɪ/ verb [T] (**identifying**; **identifies**; pt, pp **identified**) **identify sb/sth (as sb/sth)** to recognize or be able to say who or what sb/sth is: *The police need someone to identify the body.* ◇ *We must identify the cause of the problem before we look for solutions.* ▶ **identyfikować, ustalać** (*tożsamość*)
PHR V **identify sth with sth** to think or say that sth is the same as sth else: *You can't identify nationalism with fascism.* ▶ **utożsamiać**
identify with sb to feel that you understand and share what sb else is feeling: *I found it hard to identify with the woman in the film.* ▶ **utożsamiać się, identyfikować się**
identify sb with sth to consider sb to be sth: *He was not the 'tough guy' the public identified him with.* ▶ **uznawać kogoś za coś**
identify (yourself) with sb/sth to support or be closely connected with sb/sth: *She became identified with the new political party.* ▶ **związywać się**

⚷ **identity** /aɪˈdentəti/ noun [C,U] (pl. **identities**) (abbr. **ID** /ˌaɪ ˈdiː/) who or what a person or a thing is: *There are few clues to the identity of the killer.* ◇ *The region has its own cultural identity.* ◇ *The arrest was a case of mistaken identity.* Zaaresztowano nieodpowiednią osobę. ▶ **tożsamość**

iˈdentity card (also **IˈD card**) noun [C] a card with your name, photograph, etc. that is proof of who you are: *an ID card* ▶ **dowód tożsamości, legitymacja**

ideology /ˌaɪdiˈɒlədʒi/ noun [C,U] (pl. **ideologies**) a set of ideas that a political or economic system is based on: *Marxist ideology* ▶ **ideologia**
■ **ideological** /ˌaɪdiəˈlɒdʒɪkl/ adj. ▶ **ideologiczny**

idiom /ˈɪdiəm/ noun [C] an expression whose meaning is different from the meanings of the individual words in it: *The idiom 'bring something home to somebody' means 'make somebody understand something'.* ▶ **idiom**

idiomatic /ˌɪdiəˈmætɪk/ adj. **1** using language that contains expressions that are natural to sb who has spoken that language from birth: *He speaks good idiomatic English.* ▶ **idiomatyczny 2** containing an **idiom**: *an idiomatic expression* ▶ **idiomatyczny**

idiosyncrasy /ˌɪdiəˈsɪŋkrəsi/ noun [C,U] (pl. **idiosyncrasies**) sb's particular way of behaving, thinking, etc., especially when it is unusual: *Wearing a raincoat, even on a hot day, is one of her idiosyncrasies.* ▶ **specificzna cecha; dziwactwo**
■ **idiosyncratic** /ˌɪdiəsɪŋˈkrætɪk/ adj.: *His teaching methods are idiosyncratic but successful.* ▶ **specyficzny; dziwny**

idiot /ˈɪdiət/ noun [C] (informal) a very stupid person: *I was an idiot to forget my passport.* ▶ **idiot(k)a**
■ **idiotic** /ˌɪdiˈɒtɪk/ adj. ▶ **idiotyczny** | **idiotically** /-kli/ adv. ▶ **idiotycznie**

idle /ˈaɪdl/ adj. **1** not wanting to work hard: *He has the ability to succeed but he is just* ***bone idle*** (bardzo leniwy). ▶ **leniwy** SYN **lazy 2** not doing anything; not being used: *She can't bear to be idle.* ◇ *The factory* ***stood idle*** *while the machines were being repaired.* ▶ **bezczynny 3** [only before a noun] not to be taken seriously because it will not have any result: *an idle promise/threat* ◇ *idle chatter/curiosity* ▶ **próżny, pusty**
■ **idleness** noun [U] ▶ **bezczynność** | **idly** /ˈaɪdli/ adv. ▶ **bezczynnie**

idol /ˈaɪdl/ noun [C] **1** a person (such as a film star) who is admired or loved: *a pop/football/teen/screen idol* ▶ **idol 2** a statue that people treat as a god ▶ **bożek**

idolize (also -ise) /ˈaɪdəlaɪz/ verb [T] to love or admire sb very much or too much: *He is an only child and his parents idolize him.* ▶ **ubóstwiać**

idyllic /ɪˈdɪlɪk; US aɪˈd-/ adj. very pleasant and peaceful; perfect: *an idyllic holiday* ▶ **sielankowy**

⚷ **i.e.** /ˌaɪ ˈiː/ abbr. that is; in other words: *deciduous trees, i.e. those which lose their leaves in autumn* ▶ **tj., tzn.**

⚷ **if** /ɪf/ conj. **1** (used in sentences in which one thing only happens or is true when another thing happens or is true): *If you see him, give him this letter.* ◇ *We won't go to the beach if it rains.* ◇ *If I had more time, I would learn another language.* ◇ *I might see her tomorrow. If not, I'll see her at the weekend.* ▶ **jeżeli, jeśli, gdyby, o ile** ➲ note at **case**, **when 2** when; every time: *If I try to phone her she just hangs up.* ◇ *If metal gets hot it expands.* ▶ **(zawsze) gdy 3** (used after verbs such as 'ask', 'know', 'remember'): *They asked if we would like to go too.* ◇ *I can't remember if I posted the letter or not.* ▶ **czy** (*w pytaniach zależnych*) ➲ note at **whether 4** (used when you are asking sb to do sth or suggesting sth politely): *If you could just come this way, sir.* ◇ *If I might suggest something...* ▶ **jeżeli, gdyby**
IDM **as if; as though** → AS
even if → EVEN[2]
if I were you (used when you are giving sb advice): *If I were you, I'd leave now.* ▶ **na twoim miejscu**

if it wasn't/weren't for sb/sth if a particular person or situation did not exist or was not there; without sb/sth: *If it wasn't for him, I wouldn't stay in this country.* ▶ **gdyby nie ktoś/coś**
if only (used for expressing a strong wish): *If only I could drive.* ◇ *If only he'd write.* ▶ **żeby tylko**

igloo /ˈɪgluː/ noun [C] (pl. **igloos**) a small house that is built from blocks of hard snow ▶ **igloo**

ignite /ɪgˈnaɪt/ verb [I,T] (formal) to start burning or to make sth start burning: *A spark from the engine ignited the petrol.* ▶ **zapalać**

ignition /ɪgˈnɪʃn/ noun **1** [C] the electrical system that starts the engine of a car: *to turn the ignition on/off* ◇ *First of all, put the key in the ignition.* ▶ **zapalanie** ➲ picture at **car** **2** [U] the act of starting to burn or making sth start to burn ▶ **zapłon**

ignoble /ɪgˈnəʊbl/ adj. (formal) not good or honest; that should make you feel shame: *ignoble thoughts* ▶ **nikczemny** SYN **base** OPP **noble**

ignominious /ˌɪgnəˈmɪniəs/ adj. (formal) making you feel embarrassed: *The team suffered an ignominious defeat.* ▶ **haniebny**, **sromotny**
■ **ignominiously** adv. ▶ **haniebnie**, **sromotnie**

ignoramus /ˌɪgnəˈreɪməs/ noun [C] usually (humorous) a person who does not have much knowledge: *When it comes to music, I'm a complete ignoramus.* ▶ **ignorant/ka**

ignorance /ˈɪgnərəns/ noun [U] **ignorance (of/about sth)** a lack of information or knowledge: *The workers were **in** complete **ignorance*** (pozostawali w zupełnej nieświadomości) *of the management's plans.* ▶ **ignorancja**, **nieznajomość**

ignorant /ˈɪgnərənt/ adj. **1 ignorant (of/about sth)** not knowing about sth: *Many people are ignorant of their rights.* ◇ *I'm very ignorant about* (wielkim ignorantem w zakresie) *modern technology, I'm afraid.* ▶ **nieświadomy (czegoś)** **2** (informal) having or showing bad manners: *an ignorant person/remark* ▶ **prostacki** ➲ look at **ignore**

⚷ **ignore** /ɪgˈnɔː(r)/ verb [T] to pay no attention to sb/sth: *I said hello to Debbie but she totally ignored me.* ◇ *Alison ignored her doctor's advice about drinking and smoking less.* ▶ **ignorować**, **nie zważać na kogoś/coś**

> Zwróć uwagę, że **ignore** i **be ignorant** bardzo różnią się znaczeniem.

ikon = ICON (3)

il- → IN-

ilk /ɪlk/ noun [usually sing.] type; kind: *the world of media people **and their ilk*** ▶ **rodzaj** ⓘ Czasami wyraża dezaprobatę.

I'll /aɪl/ short for **I will**; **I shall**

⚷ **ill¹** /ɪl/ adj. **1** [not before a noun] (US **sick**) not in good health; not well: *I can't drink milk because it makes me **feel ill*** (robi mi się od niego niedobrze). ◇ *My mother was **taken ill*** (zachorowała) *suddenly last week.* ◇ *My grandfather is **seriously ill** in hospital.* ▶ **chory** ➲ note at **doctor** ➲ look at **sick** **2** [only before a noun] bad or harmful: *He resigned because of **ill health**.* ◇ *I'm glad to say I suffered no **ill effects** from all that rich food.* ◇ ***ill humour*** ▶ **zły**, **szkodliwy** ➲ noun **illness**

> **feeling ill**
>
> If you are **suffering from** an **illness**, you feel **ill** (US **sick**). If you have a **fever**, for example when you have **flu**, you have a high **temperature**. If you catch a **cold**, you will start **sneezing**. You might also have a **cough** and a **sore throat**. If you **come down with chickenpox** or **measles**, your skin is covered in red **spots**. If you become ill when you eat, touch or breathe sth that does not normally make other people ill, you have an **allergy**, for example **hay fever**. You might come out in a **rash**. A disease that moves easily from one person to another is **contagious** or **infectious**. If your illness is not serious, you will quickly **get better**. When sb is ill we usually wish them **'Get well soon!'**

ill² /ɪl/ adv. **1** [in compounds] badly or wrongly: *You would be **ill-advised*** (byłbyś nierozsądny) *to drive until you have fully recovered.* ▶ **źle**, **nieodpowiednio** **2** only with difficulty; not easily: *They could ill afford* (z trudem mogli sobie pozwolić na) *the extra money for better heating.* ▶ **z trudem**, **ciężko**
IDM **augur well/ill for sb/sth** → AUGUR
bode well/ill (for sb/sth) → BODE
bad/ill feeling → FEELING

ill- prefix /ɪl/ [in adjectives and adverbs] badly: *ill-advised* nierozsądny ◇ *ill-founded* bezpodstawny ◇ *ill-mannered* źle wychowany ▶ **źle**

⚷ **illegal** /ɪˈliːgl/ adj. not allowed by the law: *It is illegal to own a gun without a special licence.* ◇ *illegal drugs/immigrants/activities* ▶ **nielegalny**, **bezprawny** OPP **legal**
■ **illegally** /-gəli/ adv. ▶ **nielegalnie**

illegality /ˌɪliˈgæləti/ noun (pl. **illegalities**) **1** [U] the state of being illegal ▶ **nielegalność** **2** [C] an illegal act ▶ **bezprawie** ➲ look at **legality**

illegible /ɪˈledʒəbl/ adj. difficult or impossible to read: *Your handwriting is quite illegible.* ▶ **nieczytelny** OPP **legible**
■ **illegibly** /-əbli/ adv. ▶ **nieczytelnie**

illegitimate /ˌɪləˈdʒɪtəmət/ adj. **1** (old-fashioned) (used about a child) born to parents who are not married to each other ▶ **nieślubny** **2** not allowed by law; against the rules: *the illegitimate use of company money* ▶ **bezprawny** OPP for both meanings **legitimate**
■ **illegitimacy** /ˌɪləˈdʒɪtəməsi/ noun [U] ▶ **nieślubne pochodzenie**; **nieprawość** | **illegitimately** adv. ▶ **bezprawnie**; **z nieślubnego łoża**

illiberal /ɪˈlɪbərəl/ adj. (formal) not allowing much freedom of opinion or action: *illiberal policies* ▶ **nietolerancyjny** SYN **intolerant**

illicit /ɪˈlɪsɪt/ adj. (used about an activity or substance) not allowed by law or by the rules of society: *the illicit trade in ivory* ◇ *They were having an illicit affair.* ▶ **nielegalny**, **zakazany**

illiterate /ɪˈlɪtərət/ adj. **1** not able to read or write ▶ **niepiśmienny** OPP **literate** **2** (used about a piece of writing) very badly written ▶ **niegramatyczny**, **niepoprawny językowo** **3** not knowing much about a particular subject: *He's computer illiterate.* Jest komputerowym analfabetą. ▶ **niedouczony**
■ **illiteracy** /ɪˈlɪtərəsi/ noun [U]: *adult illiteracy* ▶ **analfabetyzm** OPP **literacy**

⚷ **illness** /ˈɪlnəs/ noun **1** [U] the state of being physically or mentally ill: *He's missed a lot of school through illness.* ◇ *There is a history of mental illness in the family.* ▶ **choroba** **2** [C] a type or period of physical or mental ill health: *a **minor/serious** illness* ◇ *My dad is just getting over his illness.* ▶ **choroba** ➲ note at **disease** ➲ adjective **ill**

illogical /ɪˈlɒdʒɪkl/ adj. not sensible or reasonable: *It seems illogical to me to pay somebody to do work that you could do yourself.* ▶ **nieuzasadniony**, **nielogiczny** OPP **logical**
■ **illogicality** /ɪˌlɒdʒɪˈkæləti/ noun [C,U] (pl. **illogicalities**) ▶ **nielogiczność** | **illogically** /ɪˈlɒdʒɪkli/ adv. ▶ **nielogicznie**

ˌill-ˈtreat verb [T] to treat sb/sth badly or in an unkind way: *This cat has been ill-treated.* ▶ **maltretować**
■ **ˌill-ˈtreatment** noun [U] ▶ **maltretowanie**

illuminate /ɪ'lu:mɪneɪt/ verb [T] (formal) **1** to shine light on sth or to decorate sth with lights: *The palace was illuminated by spotlights.* ▶ **oświetlać, iluminować 2** to explain sth or make sth clear ▶ **wyjaśniać, rzucać światło na coś**

illuminating /ɪ'lu:mɪneɪtɪŋ/ adj. helping to explain sth or make sth clear: *an illuminating discussion* ▶ **wyjaśniający**

illumination /ɪˌlu:mɪ'neɪʃn/ noun **1** [U,C] light or the place where a light comes from: *These big windows give good illumination.* ▶ **oświetlenie, iluminacja 2** (**illuminations**) [pl.] (Brit.) brightly coloured lights that are used for decorating a street, town, etc.: *Christmas illuminations* ▶ **iluminacje, ozdoby świetlne**

illusion /ɪ'lu:ʒn/ noun **1** [C,U] a false idea, belief or impression: *I **have no illusions** about the situation – I know it's serious.* ◇ *I think Peter's **under the illusion*** (łudzi się) *that he'll be the new director.* ▶ **złudzenie, złuda 2** [C] something that your eyes tell you is there or is true but in fact is not: *That line looks longer, but in fact they're the same length. It's an **optical illusion.*** ▶ **złudzenie**

illusory /ɪ'lu:səri/ adj. (formal) not real, although seeming to be: *The profits they had hoped for proved to be illusory.* ▶ **iluzoryczny**

illustrate /'ɪləstreɪt/ verb [T] **1** to add pictures, diagrams, etc. to a book or magazine: *Most cookery books are illustrated.* ▶ **ilustrować 2** to explain or make sth clear by using examples, pictures or diagrams: *These statistics **illustrate the point** that I was making very well.* ▶ **ilustrować**

illustration /ˌɪlə'streɪʃn/ noun **1** [C] a drawing, diagram or picture in a book or magazine: *colour illustrations* ▶ **ilustracja 2** [U] the activity or art of **illustrating** ▶ **ilustracja 3** [C] an example that makes a point or an idea clear: *Can you give me an illustration of what you mean?* ▶ **ilustracja, przykład**

illustrator /'ɪləstreɪtə(r)/ noun [C] a person who draws or paints pictures for books, etc. ▶ **ilustrator/ka**

illustrious /ɪ'lʌstriəs/ adj. (formal) famous and successful ▶ **znakomity, sławny**

I'm /aɪm/ short for **I am**

im- → IN-

image /'ɪmɪdʒ/ noun [C] **1** the general impression that a person or organization gives to the public: *When you meet him, he's very different from his public image.* ▶ **wizerunek, obraz 2** a mental picture or idea of sb/sth: *I have an image of my childhood as always sunny and happy.* ▶ **wizerunek, wyobrażenie 3** a picture or description that appears in a book, film or painting: *horrific images of war* ▶ **obraz 4** a copy or picture of sb/sth seen in a mirror, through a camera, on TV, computer, etc.: *A perfect image of the building was reflected in the lake.* ◇ (figurative) *He's **the (spitting) image of** his father.* ▶ **odbicie**

imagery /'ɪmɪdʒəri/ noun [U] language that produces pictures in the minds of the people reading or listening: *poetic imagery* ▶ **obrazowość**

imaginable /ɪ'mædʒɪnəbl/ adj. that you can imagine: *Sophie made all the excuses imaginable when she was caught stealing.* ◇ *His house was equipped with every imaginable luxury.* ▶ **wyobrażalny**

imaginary /ɪ'mædʒɪnəri; US -neri/ adj. existing only in the mind; not real: *Many children have imaginary friends.* ▶ **zmyślony, urojony**

imagination /ɪˌmædʒɪ'neɪʃn/ noun **1** [U,C] the ability to create mental pictures or new ideas: *He has a lively imagination.* ◇ *She's very clever but she doesn't **have** much **imagination.*** ▶ **wyobraźnia**

> **Imagination** oznacza twórczą umiejętność danej osoby. **Fantasy** oznacza czyjeś mrzonki, które nie mają odniesienia do rzeczywistości.

2 [C] the part of the mind that uses this ability: *If you **use your imagination**, you should be able to guess the answer.* ▶ **wyobraźnia**

imaginative /ɪ'mædʒɪnətɪv/ adj. having or showing imagination: *She's always full of imaginative ideas.* ▶ **obdarzony wyobraźnią, pełen wyobraźni** ■ **imaginatively** adv. ▶ **z wyobraźnią**

imagine /ɪ'mædʒɪn/ verb [T] **1 imagine that ...; imagine sb/sth (doing/as sth)** to form a picture or idea in your mind of what sth/sb might be like: *Imagine that you're lying on a beach.* ◇ *It's not easy to imagine your brother as a doctor.* ◇ *I can't imagine myself cycling 20 miles a day.* ▶ **wyobrażać sobie 2** to see, hear or think sth that is not true or does not exist: *She's always imagining that she's ill but she's fine really.* ◇ *I thought I heard someone downstairs, but I must have been **imagining things.*** ▶ **wyobrażać sobie 3** to think that sth is probably true: *I imagine he'll be coming by car.* ▶ **wydawać się, przypuszczać** SYN **suppose**

imbalance /ɪm'bæləns/ noun [C] **an imbalance (between A and B); an imbalance (in/of sth)** a difference; not being equal: *an imbalance in the numbers of men and women teachers* ▶ **nierównowaga**

imbecile /'ɪmbəsi:l; US -sl/ noun [C] a stupid person ▶ **imbecyl** SYN **idiot**

imbed = EMBED

imbibe /ɪm'baɪb/ verb **1** [I,T] (formal or humorous) to drink sth, especially alcohol ▶ **pić alkohol 2** [T] (formal) to absorb sth, especially information: *He imbibed elements of oriental mysticism from the years he spent in India.* ▶ **chłonąć**

imbue /ɪm'bju:/ verb [T, often passive] **imbue sb/sth (with sth)** (formal) to fill sb/sth with strong feelings, opinions or values: *Her voice was imbued with an unusual seriousness.* ▶ **przepełniać** SYN **infuse**

IMF /ˌaɪ em 'ef/ abbr. the **International Monetary Fund** ▶ **Międzynarodowy Fundusz Walutowy**

imitate /'ɪmɪteɪt/ verb [T] **1** to copy sb/sth: *Small children learn by imitating their parents.* ▶ **naśladować, wzorować się 2** to copy the speech or actions of sb/sth, often in order to make people laugh: *She could imitate her mother perfectly.* ▶ **parodiować**

imitation /ˌɪmɪ'teɪʃn/ noun **1** [C] a copy of sth real: *Some artificial flowers are good imitations of real ones.* ◇ *This suitcase is made of imitation leather* (ze sztucznej skóry). ▶ **imitacja, naśladowanie, podróbka** ➲ look at **genuine 2** [U] the act of copying sb/sth: *Good pronunciation of a language is best learnt **by imitation.*** ▶ **imitacja, naśladowanie 3** [C] the act of copying the way sb talks and behaves, especially in order to make people laugh: *Can you **do** any **imitations** of politicians?* ▶ **naśladowanie**

immaculate /ɪ'mækjələt/ adj. **1** perfectly clean and tidy: *immaculate white shirts* ▶ **nieskazitelny 2** without any mistakes: *an immaculate performance* ▶ **bez skazy, doskonały** SYN **perfect** ■ **immaculately** adv. ▶ **nieskazitelnie, bez skazy, doskonale**

immaterial /ˌɪmə'tɪəriəl/ adj. **immaterial (to sb/sth)** not important: *It's immaterial to me whether we go today or tomorrow.* ▶ **nieistotny, błahy**

immature /ˌɪmə'tjʊə(r); US -'tʃʊər; -'tʊər/ adj. **1** (used about a person) behaving in a way that is not sensible and is typical of people who are much younger: *He's too immature to take his work seriously.* ▶ **niedojrzały, niedorosły 2** not fully grown or developed: *an immature* *body* ▶ **nierozwinięty; niedojrzały** OPP for both meanings **mature**

immeasurable /ɪˈmeʒərəbl/ adj. (formal) too large, great, etc. to be measured: *to cause immeasurable harm* ▶ **niezmierny**
■ **immeasurably** /-əbli/ adv.: *Housing standards improved immeasurably after the war.* ▶ **niezmiernie**

immediacy /ɪˈmiːdiəsi/ noun [U] the quality of being available or seeming to happen close to you and without delay: *Letters do not have the same immediacy as email.* ▶ **natychmiastowość, bliskość**

immediate /ɪˈmiːdiət/ adj. **1** happening or done without delay: *I'd like an immediate answer to my proposal.* ◇ *The government responded with immediate action.* ▶ **natychmiastowy 2** [only before a noun] existing now and needing urgent attention: *Tell me what your immediate needs are.* ▶ **pilny, nagły 3** [only before a noun] nearest in time, position or relationship: *They won't make any changes in **the immediate future**.* ◇ *He has left most of his money to his immediate family.* ▶ **najbliższy, bezpośredni**

immediately /ɪˈmiːdiətli/ adv. **1** at once; without delay: *Can you come home immediately after work?* ◇ *I couldn't immediately see what he meant.* ▶ **natychmiast, bezzwłocznie, zaraz 2** nearest in time or position: *Who's the girl immediately in front of Simon?* ◇ *What did you do immediately after the war?* ▶ **bezpośrednio 3** very closely; directly: *He wasn't immediately involved in the crime.* ▶ **bezpośrednio, tuż**
■ **immediately** conj. (Brit.) as soon as: *I opened the letter immediately I got home.* ▶ **ledwo, jak tylko**

immense /ɪˈmens/ adj. very big or great: *immense difficulties/importance/power* ◇ *She gets immense pleasure from her garden.* ▶ **ogromny, niezmierny**

immensely /ɪˈmensli/ adv. extremely; very much: *immensely enjoyable* ◇ *'Did you enjoy the party?' 'Yes, immensely.'* ▶ **ogromnie, niezmiernie**

immensity /ɪˈmensəti/ noun [U] an extremely large size: *the immensity of the universe* ▶ **ogrom, bezmiar**

immerse /ɪˈmɜːs/ verb [T] **1 immerse sth (in sth)** to put sth into a liquid so that it is covered: *Make sure the spaghetti is fully immersed in the boiling water.* ▶ **zanurzać, zatapiać 2 immerse yourself (in sth)** to involve yourself completely in sth so that you give it all your attention: *Rachel's usually immersed in a book.* ▶ **pogrążać się, zagłębiać się**
■ **immersion** /ɪˈmɜːʃn/ noun [U]: *Immersion in cold water resulted in rapid loss of heat.* ◇ *his long immersion in politics* długi okres, gdy był pochłonięty polityką ◇ *a two-week immersion course in French* intensywny, dwutygodniowy kurs języka francuskiego ▶ **zanurzenie**

immigrant /ˈɪmɪɡrənt/ noun [C] a person who has come into a foreign country to live there permanently: *The government plans to tighten controls to prevent **illegal immigrants**.* ◇ *London has a high immigrant population.* ▶ **imigrant/ka**

> A society with many immigrant communities is a **multicultural society**. Groups of immigrants or children of immigrants who share a common cultural tradition are an **ethnic minority**.

immigration /ˌɪmɪˈɡreɪʃn/ noun [U] **1** the process of coming to live permanently in a country that is not your own; the number of people who do this: *There are greater controls on immigration than there used to be.* ▶ **imigracja 2** (also **immiˈgration control**) the control point at an airport, port, etc. where the official documents of people who want to come into a country are checked: *When you leave the plane you have to go through customs and immigration.* ▶ **kontrola paszportów** ➲ look at **emigrate, emigrant, emigration**

> Istnieje czasownik **immigrate**, zwłaszcza w Amer. ang. W Br. ang. zwykle używa się wyrażenia **be an immigrant** lub czasownika **emigrate**, stosowanego w odniesieniu do miejsca, z którego ktoś przyjechał: *Were you born here in Britain? Yes I was, but my parents emigrated to Britain from Barbados.*

imminent /ˈɪmɪnənt/ adj. (usually used about sth unpleasant) almost certain to happen very soon: *Heavy rainfall in the south of England means that flooding is imminent* (oznacza zagrożenie powodzią). ▶ **nadciągający, niebezpiecznie bliski**
■ **imminently** adv. ▶ **blisko**

immobile /ɪˈməʊbaɪl; US -bl/ adj. not moving or not able to move: *The hunter stood immobile until the lion had passed.* ▶ **nieruchomy, znieruchomiały** OPP **mobile**
■ **immobility** /ˌɪməˈbɪləti/ noun [U] ▶ **bezruch, nieruchomość, znieruchomienie**

immobilize (also -ise) /ɪˈməʊbəlaɪz/ verb [T] to prevent sb/sth from moving or working normally: *The railways have been completely immobilized by the strike.* ◇ *This device immobilizes the car to prevent it being stolen.* ▶ **unieruchamiać, zatrzymywać**

immobilizer (also -iser) /ɪˈməʊbəlaɪzə(r)/ noun [C] a device in a vehicle that prevents thieves from starting the engine when the vehicle is parked ▶ **immobilizer**

immoderate /ɪˈmɒdərət/ adj. [usually before a noun] (formal) extreme; not reasonable: *immoderate drinking* ▶ **nieumiarkowany** SYN **excessive** OPP **moderate**
■ **immoderately** adv. ▶ **nieumiarkowanie**

immodest /ɪˈmɒdɪst/ adj. **1** having or showing a very high opinion of yourself and your abilities: *I am immodest enough to think that I played an important part in her decision.* ▶ **zarozumiały** ⓘ Wyraża dezaprobatę. SYN **conceited 2** not considered to be socially acceptable by most people, especially concerning sexual behaviour: *an immodest dress* ▶ **nieskromny** OPP for both meanings **modest**

immoral /ɪˈmɒrəl/ adj. (used about people or their behaviour) considered wrong or not honest by most people: *It's immoral to steal.* ▶ **niemoralny** OPP **moral** ➲ look at **amoral**
■ **immorality** /ˌɪməˈræləti/ noun [U] ▶ **niemoralność** OPP **morality** | **immorally** /ɪˈmɒrəli/ adv. ▶ **niemoralnie**

immortal /ɪˈmɔːtl/ adj. living or lasting for ever: *Shakespeare's immortal plays* ▶ **nieśmiertelny; wiekopomny** OPP **mortal**
■ **immortality** /ˌɪmɔːˈtæləti/ noun [U] ▶ **nieśmiertelność; wiekopomność**

immortalize (also -ise) /ɪˈmɔːtəlaɪz/ verb [T] to give lasting fame to sb/sth: *He immortalized their relationship in a poem.* ▶ **uwieczniać, unieśmiertelniać**

immune /ɪˈmjuːn/ adj. **1 immune (to sth)** having natural protection against a certain disease or illness: *You should be immune to measles if you've had it already.* ▶ **uodporniony, odporny 2 immune (to sth)** not affected by sth: *You can say what you like – I'm immune to criticism!* ▶ **niepodatny, odporny 3 immune (from sth)** protected from a danger or punishment: *Young children are immune from prosecution.* ▶ **nie podlegający czemuś**

imˈmune system noun [C] the system in your body that produces substances to help it fight against infection and disease ▶ **system odpornościowy**

immunity /ɪˈmjuːnəti/ noun [U] the ability to avoid or not be affected by disease, criticism, punishment by law, etc.: *In many countries people have no immunity to diseases like measles.* ◇ *Ambassadors to other countries receive **diplomatic immunity**.* ▶ **odporność; nietykalność, immunitet**

immunize (also -ise) /ˈɪmjunaɪz/ verb [T] **immunize sb/sth (against sth)** to protect sb from a disease, usually by putting a **vaccine** into their blood ▶ **uodparniać, szczepić** ➲ look at **inoculate, vaccinate**
■ **immunization** (also -isation) /ˌɪmjunaɪˈzeɪʃn; US -nəˈz-/ noun [C,U] ▶ **uodpornienie, szczepienie**

imp /ɪmp/ noun [C] (in stories) a small creature like a little man, who has magic powers and behaves badly ▶ **diabełek, chochlik**

🔑**impact** /ˈɪmpækt/ noun **1** [C, usually sing.] **an impact (on/upon sb/sth)** a powerful effect or impression: *I hope this anti-smoking campaign will **make/have an impact** on young people.* ▶ **wrażenie, wpływ 2** [U] the action or force of one object hitting another: *The impact of the crash threw the passengers out of their seats.* ◇ *The bomb exploded **on impact*** (przy uderzeniu). ▶ **uderzenie, wstrząs**

impair /ɪmˈpeə(r)/ verb [T] to damage sth or make it weaker: *Ear infections can result in impaired hearing.* ▶ **uszkadzać, osłabiać**

impale /ɪmˈpeɪl/ verb [T] **impale sb/sth (on sth)** to push a sharp pointed object through sb/sth: *The boy fell out of the tree and impaled his leg on some railings.* ▶ **nadziewać (się) na coś**

impart /ɪmˈpɑːt/ verb [T] (formal) **1 impart sth (to sb)** to pass information, knowledge, etc. to other people: *He rushed home eager to impart the good news.* ▶ **dzielić się** (*np. wiadomościami*), **przekazywać** (*np. wiedzę*) **2 impart sth (to sth)** to give a certain quality to sth: *The low lighting imparted a romantic atmosphere to the room.* ▶ **dodawać, przydawać**

impartial /ɪmˈpɑːʃl/ adj. not supporting one person or group more than another; fair: *The referee must be impartial.* ▶ **bezstronny**
■ **impartiality** /ˌɪmˌpɑːʃiˈæləti/ noun [U] ▶ **bezstronność** OPP **partiality** | **impartially** /ɪmˈpɑːʃəli/ adv. ▶ **bezstronnie**

impassable /ɪmˈpɑːsəbl; US -ˈpæs-/ adj. (used about a road, etc.) impossible to travel on because it is blocked ▶ **nieprzejezdny, nie do przebycia** OPP **passable**

impasse /ˈæmpɑːs; US ˈɪmpæs/ noun [usually sing.] a difficult situation in which no progress can be made because the people involved cannot agree what to do: *to **break/end the impasse*** ◇ *Negotiations have **reached an impasse**.* ▶ **impas** SYN **deadlock**

impassioned /ɪmˈpæʃnd/ adj. (used especially about a speech) showing strong feelings about sth: *an impassioned plea/speech/defence* ▶ **płomienny, żarliwy**

impassive /ɪmˈpæsɪv/ adj. (used about a person) showing no emotion or reaction ▶ **niewzruszony, obojętny**
■ **impassively** adv. ▶ **niewzruszenie, obojętnie**

🔑**impatient** /ɪmˈpeɪʃnt/ adj. **1 impatient (at sth/with sb)** not able to stay calm and wait for sb/sth; easily annoyed by sb/sth that seems slow: *The passengers are getting impatient at the delay.* ◇ *It's no good being impatient with small children.* ▶ **niecierpliwy, zniecierpliwiony** OPP **patient 2 impatient for/to do sth** wanting sth to happen soon: *By the time they are sixteen many young people are impatient to leave school.* ▶ **nie mogący się doczekać, rwący się (do czegoś)**
■ **impatience** noun [U]: *He began to explain for the third time with growing impatience.* ▶ **niecierpliwość, zniecierpliwienie** | **impatiently** adv. ▶ **niecierpliwie**

impeccable /ɪmˈpekəbl/ adj. without any mistakes or faults; perfect: *impeccable behaviour* ◇ *His accent is impeccable.* ▶ **nieskazitelny, bez zarzutu**
■ **impeccably** /-əbli/ adv. ▶ **nieskazitelnie, bez zarzutu**

impede /ɪmˈpiːd/ verb [T] (formal) to make it difficult for sb/sth to move or go forward: *The completion of the new motorway has been impeded by bad weather conditions.* ▶ **wstrzymywać, utrudniać**

impediment /ɪmˈpedɪmənt/ noun [C] (formal) **1 an impediment (to sth)** something that makes it difficult for a person or thing to move or progress: *The high rate of tax is a major impediment to new businesses.* ▶ **przeszkoda, utrudnienie 2** something that makes speaking difficult: *Jane had a speech impediment.* ▶ **wada wymowy**

impending /ɪmˈpendɪŋ/ adj. [only before a noun] (usually used about sth bad) that will happen soon: *There was a feeling of impending disaster in the air.* ▶ **wiszący w powietrzu**

impenetrable /ɪmˈpenɪtrəbl/ adj. **1** impossible to enter or go through: *The jungle was impenetrable.* ▶ **niedostępny, niezgłębiony 2** impossible to understand: *an impenetrable mystery* ▶ **niezgłębiony**

imperative /ɪmˈperətɪv/ adj. very important or urgent: *It's imperative that* (trzeba koniecznie) *you see a doctor immediately.* ▶ **naglący, konieczny**

the **imperative** /ɪmˈperətɪv/ noun [C] the form of the verb that is used for giving orders: *In 'Shut the door!' the verb is in the imperative.* ▶ **tryb rozkazujący**

imperceptible /ˌɪmpəˈseptəbl/ adj. too small to be seen or noticed: *The difference between the original painting and the copy was almost imperceptible.* ▶ **niedostrzegalny, nieuchwytny** OPP **perceptible** ➲ verb **perceive**
■ **imperceptibly** /-əbli/ adv.: *Almost imperceptibly winter was turning into spring.* ▶ **niedostrzegalnie, nieuchwytnie**

imperfect /ɪmˈpɜːfɪkt/ adj. with mistakes or faults: *an imperfect system* ▶ **wadliwy, niedoskonały** OPP **perfect**
■ **imperfectly** adv. ▶ **wadliwie, niedoskonale**

the **imperfect** /ɪmˈpɜːfɪkt/ noun [U] the form of a verb that expresses an action in the past that is not completed: *In the sentence 'I was having a bath', the verb is in the imperfect.* ▶ **czas przeszły niedokonany** ℹ Czas ten nazywa się częściej *past continuous* lub *past progressive*.

imperfection /ˌɪmpəˈfekʃn/ noun [C,U] a fault or weakness in sb/sth: *They learned to live with each other's imperfections.* ▶ **niedoskonałość, wada**

imperial /ɪmˈpɪəriəl/ adj. [only before a noun] **1** connected with an empire or its ruler: *the imperial palace* ▶ **cesarski, monarszy, imperatorski 2** belonging to a system of weighing and measuring that, in the past, was used for all goods in the United Kingdom and is still used for some ▶ (*system miar i wag*) **angielski** ➲ look at **metric, inch, foot, yard, ounce, pound, pint, gallon** ℹ W tych hasłach podane są odpowiedniki wymienionych jednostek miar i wag w metrach, kilogramach i litrach.

imperialism /ɪmˈpɪəriəlɪzəm/ noun [U] a political system in which a rich and powerful country has **colonies** ▶ **imperializm**
■ **imperialist** /-ɪst/ noun [C] ▶ **imperialist(k)a**

imperious /ɪmˈpɪəriəs/ adj. (formal) expecting people to obey you and treating them as if they are not as important as you: *an **imperious gesture/voice/command*** ▶ **władczy**
■ **imperiously** adv.: *'Get it now,' she demanded imperiously.* ▶ **władczo**

impermeable /ɪmˈpɜːmiəbl/ adj. **impermeable (to sth)** not allowing a liquid or gas to pass through: *impermeable rock* ◇ *The container is impermeable to water vapour.* ▶ **nie przepuszczający** ➲ look at **permeable**

impersonal /ɪmˈpɜːsənl/ adj. **1** not showing friendly human feelings; cold in feeling or atmosphere: *My hotel room was very impersonal.* ▶ **bezosobowy**; (*uczucia, atmosfera*) **zimny 2** not referring to any particular person: *Can we try to keep the discussion as impersonal as possible, please?* ▶ **bezosobowy**

impersonate /ɪmˈpɜːsəneɪt/ verb [T] to copy the behaviour and way of speaking of a person or to pretend to be a different person: *a comedian who impersonates politicians* ◇ *He was arrested for impersonating a policeman* (podawanie się za policjanta). ▶ **odtwarzać**; **podawać się za kogoś innego**, **odgrywać** (*rolę*)
■ **impersonation** /ɪmˌpɜːsəˈneɪʃn/ noun [C,U] ▶ **odtworzenie**, **podawanie się za kogoś innego** | **impersonator** /ɪmˈpɜːsəneɪtə(r)/ noun [C] ▶ **odtwórca**; **podający się za kogoś innego**

impertinent /ɪmˈpɜːtɪnənt; US -tn-/ adj. (formal) not showing respect; rude: *I do apologize. It was impertinent of my son to speak to you like that.* ▶ **bezczelny**, **zuchwały** ⓘ Uwaga! Antonim: **polite** lub **respectful** (nie ~~*pertinent*~~).
■ **impertinence** noun [U]: *He had the impertinence to ask my age.* ▶ **bezczelność**, **zuchwałość** | **impertinently** adv. ▶ **bezczelnie**, **zuchwale**

imperturbable /ˌɪmpəˈtɜːbəbl/ adj. (formal) not easily worried by a difficult situation ▶ **niewzruszony**

impervious /ɪmˈpɜːviəs/ adj. **impervious (to sth) 1** not affected or influenced by sth: *She was impervious to criticism.* ▶ **nieczuły**, **głuchy na coś 2** (technical) not allowing water, etc. to pass through ▶ **nieprzepuszczalny**, **nieprzenikliwy**

impetuous /ɪmˈpetʃuəs/ adj. acting or done quickly and without thinking: *an impetuous decision* ▶ **zapalczywy**, **porywczy** ⓘ Częściej używa się **impulsive**.
■ **impetuously** adv. ▶ **zapalczywie**, **porywczo**

impetus /ˈɪmpɪtəs/ noun [U, sing.] **(an) impetus (for sth)**; **(an) impetus (to do sth)** something that encourages sth else to happen: *This scandal provided the main impetus for changes in the rules.* ◇ *I need fresh impetus to start working on this essay again.* ▶ **rozpęd**

impinge /ɪmˈpɪndʒ/ verb [I] (formal) **impinge on/upon sth** to have a noticeable effect on sth, especially a bad one: *I'm not going to let my job impinge on my home life.* ▶ **kolidować**, **wkraczać**

implacable /ɪmˈplækəbl/ adj. **1** (used about strong negative opinions or feelings) that cannot be changed: *implacable hatred* ▶ **nieprzejednany 2** (used about a person) unwilling to stop opposing sb/sth: *an implacable enemy* ▶ **nieustępliwy**
■ **implacably** /ɪmˈplækəbli/ adv.: *to be implacably opposed to the plan* ▶ **nieustępliwie**

implant /ˈɪmplɑːnt; US -plænt/ noun [C] something that is put into a part of the body in a medical operation, often in order to make it bigger or a different shape ▶ **implant**

implausible /ɪmˈplɔːzəbl/ adj. not easy to believe: *an implausible excuse* ▶ **nieprzekonujący**, **niewiarygodny** OPP **plausible**

implement[1] /ˈɪmplɪment/ verb [T] to start using a plan, system, etc.: *Some teachers are finding it difficult to implement the government's educational reforms.* ▶ **wdrażać**, **wprowadzać w życie**
■ **implementation** /ˌɪmplɪmenˈteɪʃn/ noun [U] ▶ **wdrożenie**, **wprowadzenie w życie**

implement[2] /ˈɪmplɪmənt/ noun [C] a tool or instrument (especially for work outdoors): *farm implements* ▶ **narzędzie**, **instrument** ➲ note at **tool**

implicate /ˈɪmplɪkeɪt/ verb [T] **implicate sb (in sth)** to show that sb is involved in sth unpleasant, especially a crime: *A well-known politician was implicated in the scandal.* ▶ **wplątywać**, **mieszać**

🔑 **implication** /ˌɪmplɪˈkeɪʃn/ noun **1** [C, usually pl.] **implications (for/of sth)** the effect that sth will have on sth else in the future: *The new law will **have serious implications** for our work.* ▶ **implikacja 2** [C,U] something that is suggested or said in a way that is not direct: *The implication of what she said was that* (z tego, co powiedziała, można się było domyślić, że) *we had made a bad mistake.* ▶ **ukryte znaczenie** ➲ verb **imply 3** [U] **implication (in sth)** the fact of being involved, or of involving sb, in sth unpleasant, especially a crime: *The player's implication in this scandal could affect his career.* ▶ **zamieszanie (w coś)** ➲ verb **implicate**

implicit /ɪmˈplɪsɪt/ adj. **1** not expressed in a direct way but understood by the people involved: *We had an implicit agreement that we would support each other.* ▶ **milczący**, **domniemany** ➲ look at **explicit 2** complete; total: *I have implicit faith in your ability to do the job.* ▶ **bezwarunkowy**, **bezwzględny**
■ **implicitly** adv. ▶ **bezwarunkowo**, **bezwzględnie**

implode /ɪmˈpləʊd/ verb [I] **1** to burst or explode and collapse into the centre ▶ **implodować** ➲ note at **explode 2** (used about an organization, a system, etc.) to fail suddenly and completely ▶ **upaść**
■ **implosion** /ɪmˈpləʊʒn/ noun [C, U] ▶ **implozja**; **upadek**

implore /ɪmˈplɔː(r)/ verb [T] (formal) to ask sb with great emotion to do sth, because you are in a very serious situation: *She implored him not to leave her alone.* ▶ **błagać** SYN **beg**

🔑 **imply** /ɪmˈplaɪ/ verb [T] (**implying**; **implies**; pt, pp **implied**) to suggest sth in an indirect way or without actually saying it: *He didn't say so – but he implied that I was lying.* ▶ **dawać do zrozumienia** ➲ noun **implication**

impolite /ˌɪmpəˈlaɪt/ adj. rude: *I think it was impolite of him to ask you to leave.* ▶ **niegrzeczny**, **nieuprzejmy** SYN **rude**, **discourteous** OPP **polite**
■ **impolitely** adv. ▶ **niegrzecznie**, **nieuprzejmie**

🔑 **import**[1] /ˈɪmpɔːt/ noun **1** [C, usually pl.] a product or service that is brought into one country from another ▶ **towar importowany** OPP **export 2** [U] (also **importation** /ˌɪmpɔːˈteɪʃn/) the act of bringing goods or services into a country: *new controls on the import of certain goods from abroad* ▶ **import**, **importowanie**

🔑 **import**[2] /ɪmˈpɔːt/ verb [T] **1 import sth (from ...)** to buy goods, etc. from a foreign country and bring them into your own country: *imported goods* ◇ *Britain imports wine from France.* ◇ (figurative) *We need to import some extra help from somewhere fast.* ▶ **sprowadzać**; **importować** OPP **export 2** to move information onto a computer program from another program ▶ **importować**
■ **importer** noun [C] ▶ **importer** OPP **exporter**

🔑 **importance** /ɪmˈpɔːtns/ noun [U] the quality of being important: *The decision was **of great importance** to the future of the business.* ▶ **znaczenie**, **ważność**, **doniosłość**

🔑 **important** /ɪmˈpɔːtnt/ adj. **1 important (to sb)**; **important (for sb/sth) (to do sth)**; **important that ...** having great value or influence; very necessary: *an important meeting/decision/factor* ◇ *This job is very important to me.* ◇ *It's important not to be late.* ◇ *It's important for people to see the results of what they do.* ◇ *It was important to me that you were there.* ▶ **ważny**, **doniosły 2** (used about a person) having great influence or authority: *Milton was one of the most important writers of his time.* ▶ **ważny**
■ **importantly** adv. ▶ **w znaczący sposób**

important

Zarówno **essential**, jak i **vital** znaczą „bardzo ważny lub absolutnie konieczny": *It is essential/vital that our children get the best possible education.* ◇ *Fresh fruit and vegetables are **an essential/a vital part** of a healthy diet.* Mówimy również **play a vital/key role in ...**: *The police play a key role in our society.* Wydarzenie o znaczeniu historycznym określane jest słowem **historic**: *a historic decision/event/occasion.*

importation = IMPORT[1] (2)

impose /ɪm'pəʊz/ verb **1** [T] **impose sth (on/upon sb/sth)** to make a law, rule, opinion, etc. be accepted by using your power or authority: *A new tax will be imposed on cigarettes.* ◇ *Parents should try not to impose their own ideas on their children.* ▶ **narzucać, nakazywać, nakładać 2** [I] **impose (on/upon sb/sth)** to ask or expect sb to do sth that may cause extra work or trouble: *I hate to impose on you but can you lend me some money?* ▶ **narzucać (coś/ komuś), narzucać się**

■ **imposition** /ˌɪmpə'zɪʃn/ noun **1** [U] the action of imposing: *I'm against the imposition of unnecessary rules and regulations on people.* ◇ *the imposition of military rule* ▶ **nakazywanie, narzucanie 2** [C] an unfair or unpleasant thing that sb has to accept; sth that causes extra work or trouble ▶ **narzucanie się, naciąganie**

imposing /ɪm'pəʊzɪŋ/ adj. big and important; impressive: *They lived in a large, imposing house near the park.* ▶ **imponujący, okazały**

impossible /ɪm'pɒsəbl/ adj. **1** not able to be done or to happen: *It's impossible for me to be there before 12.* ◇ *I find it almost impossible to get up in the morning!* ◇ *That's impossible!* ▶ **niemożliwy, niewykonalny** OPP **possible 2** very difficult to deal with: *This is an impossible situation!* ◇ *He's always been an impossible child.* ▶ **nieznośny, niemożliwy**

■ **the impossible** noun [sing.]: *Don't attempt the impossible!* ▶ **rzecz niewykonalna** | **impossibility** /ɪmˌpɒsə'bɪləti/ noun [C,U] (pl. **impossibilities**): *What you are suggesting is a complete impossibility!* ▶ **niemożliwość, niewykonalność**

impossibly /ɪm'pɒsəbli/ adv. extremely: *impossibly complicated* ▶ **niemożliwie, nieprawdopodobnie**

impostor /ɪm'pɒstə(r)/ noun [C] a person who pretends to be sb else in order to trick other people ▶ **oszust/ka**

impotent /'ɪmpətənt/ adj. **1** without enough power to influence a situation or to change things ▶ **bezsilny** SYN **powerless 2** (used about men) not capable of having sex ▶ **cierpiący na impotencję**

■ **impotence** noun [U] ▶ **bezsilność; impotencja**

impoverish /ɪm'pɒvərɪʃ/ verb [T] (formal) to make sb/sth poor or lower in quality ▶ **zubożać** OPP **enrich**

impracticable /ɪm'præktɪkəbl/ adj. impossible to use or do in practice: *Your plan is completely impracticable.* ▶ **niewykonalny, nie do przeprowadzenia**

impractical /ɪm'præktɪkl/ adj. **1** not sensible or realistic: *It would be impractical to take our bikes on the train.* ▶ **niepraktyczny 2** (used about a person) not good at doing ordinary things that involve using your hands; not good at organizing or planning things: *He's clever but completely impractical.* ▶ **niepraktyczny** OPP for both meanings **practical**

imprecise /ˌɪmprɪ'saɪs/ adj. not clear or exact: *imprecise instructions* ▶ **niedokładny, nieprecyzyjny** OPP **precise**

impregnable /ɪm'pregnəbl/ adj. **1** an **impregnable** building is so strongly built that it cannot be entered by force: *an impregnable fortress* ▶ **nie do zdobycia 2** strong and impossible to defeat or change: *The team built up an impregnable 5-1 lead.* ▶ **niezwyciężony** SYN **invincible**

impregnate /'ɪmpregneɪt; US ɪm'preg-/ verb [T] **1** [usually passive] **impregnate sth (with sth)** to make a substance spread through an area so that the area is full of the substance: *The pad is impregnated with insecticide.* ▶ **nasączać coś (czymś) 2** (formal) to make a woman or female animal pregnant ▶ **zapładniać**

■ **impregnation** /ˌɪmpreg'neɪʃn/ noun [U] ▶ **nasączenie; zapłodnienie**

impress /ɪm'pres/ verb [T] **1 impress sb (with sth); impress sb that...** to make sb feel admiration and respect: *She's always trying to impress people with her new clothes.* ◇ *It impressed me that he understood immediately what I meant.* ▶ **wywierać wrażenie 2** (formal) **impress sth on/ upon sb** to make the importance of sth very clear to sb: *You should impress on John that he must pass these exams.* ▶ **wpajać, zaszczepiać (coś komuś)**

impressed /ɪm'prest/ adj. **impressed (by/with sb/sth)** feeling admiration for sb/sth because you think they are particularly good, interesting, etc. ▶ **pod wrażeniem (kogoś/czegoś)**

impression /ɪm'preʃn/ noun [C] **1** an idea, a feeling or an opinion that you get about sb/sth: *What's your **first impression** of the new director?* ◇ *I'm not sure but I **have/get the impression** that Jane's rather unhappy.* ◇ *I was **under the impression** that you were married.* ▶ **wrażenie 2** the effect that a person or thing produces on sb else: *She **gives the impression** of being older than she really is.* ◇ *Do you think I **made a good impression** on your parents?* ▶ **wrażenie 3** an amusing copy of the way sb acts or speaks: *My brother can do a good impression of the Prime Minister.* ▶ **parodia, parodiowanie** SYN **impersonation 4** a mark that is left when an object has been pressed hard into a surface ▶ **odcisk, odbicie**

impressionable /ɪm'preʃənəbl/ adj. easy to influence: *Sixteen is a very impressionable age.* ▶ **podatny**

Impressionism /ɪm'preʃənɪzəm/ noun [U] a style in painting developed in France in the late 19th century that uses colour to show the effects of light on things and to suggest atmosphere rather than showing exact details ▶ **impresjonizm**

■ **Impressionist** adj. [usually before a noun]: *Impressionist landscapes* ▶ **impresjonistyczny**

impressive /ɪm'presɪv/ adj. causing a feeling of admiration and respect because of the importance, size, quality, etc. of sth: *an impressive building/speech* ◇ *The way he handled the situation was most impressive.* ▶ **imponujący, wywierający wrażenie**

imprint[1] /'ɪmprɪnt/ noun [C] a mark made by pressing an object on a surface: *the imprint of a foot in the sand* ▶ **odbicie, odcisk, ślad**

imprint[2] /ɪm'prɪnt/ verb [T] **imprint A in/on B; imprint B with A 1** to have a great effect on sth so that it cannot be forgotten, changed, etc.: *The terrible scenes were indelibly imprinted on his mind.* ▶ **wryć się** (*w pamięć/serce/ duszę*) **2** to print or press a mark or design onto a surface: *clothes imprinted with the logos of sports teams* ▶ **nadrukować** (*np. wzór, logo*)

imprison /ɪm'prɪzn/ verb [T, often passive] to put or keep in prison: *He was imprisoned for armed robbery.* ▶ **uwięzić, wtrącać do więzienia**

■ **imprisonment** noun [U]: *life imprisonment* dożywocie ◇ *She was sentenced to five years' imprisonment.* Została skazana na karę pięciu lat więzienia. ▶ **uwięzienie**

improbable /ɪm'prɒbəbl/ adj. not likely to be true or to happen: *an improbable explanation* ◇ *It is **highly improbable** that Alexandra will arrive tonight.* ▶ **nieprawdopodobny** SYN **unlikely** OPP **probable**

■ **improbability** /ɪmˌprɒbə'bɪləti/ noun [U] ▶ **nieprawdopodobieństwo** | **improbably** /ɪm'prɒbəbli/ adv. ▶ **nieprawdopodobnie**

impromptu /ɪm'prɒmptjuː; US -tuː/ adj. (done) without being prepared or organized: *an impromptu party* ▶ **zaimprowizowany**

■ **impromptu** adv. ▶ **bez przygotowania**

improper /ɪm'prɒpə(r)/ adj. **1** illegal or dishonest: *It seems that she had been involved in improper business deals.* ▶ **nieodpowiedni, nieprawidłowy** OPP **proper 2** not suitable for the situation: *It would be improper to say anything else at this stage.* ▶ **niewłaściwy, niestosowny** OPP **proper 3** rude in a sexual way: *He lost his* *job for making improper suggestions to several of the women.* ▶ **nieprzyzwoity**

■ **improperly** adv. ▶ **nieodpowiednio, nieprawidłowo, niewłaściwie** OPP **properly**

impropriety /ˌɪmprəˈpraɪəti/ noun [U,C] (pl. **improprieties**) (formal) behaviour or actions that are morally wrong or not appropriate: *She was unaware of the impropriety of her remark.* ▶ **niewłaściwość, nieprawidłowość; nieprzyzwoitość**

improve /ɪmˈpruːv/ verb [I,T] to become or to make sth better: *Your work has greatly improved.* ◇ *I hope the weather will improve later on.* ◇ *Your vocabulary is excellent but you could improve your pronunciation.* ▶ **polepszać (się), poprawiać (się)**

PHR V **improve on/upon sth** to produce sth that is better than sth else: *Nobody will be able to improve on that score.* ▶ **przewyższać/poprawiać coś**

improvement /ɪmˈpruːvmənt/ noun [C,U] **(an) improvement (on/in sth)** (a) change which makes the quality or condition of sb/sth better: *Your written work is in need of some improvement.* ◇ *There's been a considerable **improvement in** your mother's condition.* ◇ *These marks are an **improvement on** your previous ones.* ▶ **postęp, poprawa**

improvise /ˈɪmprəvaɪz/ verb [I,T] **1** to make, do or manage sth without preparation, using what you have: *If you're short of teachers today you'll just have to improvise.* ▶ **improwizować 2** to play music, speak or act using your imagination instead of written or remembered material: *It was obvious that the actor had forgotten his lines and was trying to improvise.* ▶ **improwizować**

■ **improvisation** /ˌɪmprəvaɪˈzeɪʃn; US ɪmˌprɑːvə-/ noun [C,U] ▶ **improwizacja**

imprudent /ɪmˈpruːdnt/ adj. (formal) not wise or sensible: *It would be imprudent to invest all your money in one company.* ▶ **nierozsądny** SYN **unwise** OPP **prudent**

■ **imprudence** /-ns/ noun [U] ▶ **brak rozwagi** | **imprudently** adv. ▶ **nierozsądnie**

impudent /ˈɪmpjədənt/ adj. (formal) very rude; lacking respect and not polite ▶ **bezczelny** ❶ Mniej formalnym słowem jest **cheeky**.

■ **impudently** adv. ▶ **bezczelnie** | **impudence** noun [U] ▶ **bezczelność**

impulse /ˈɪmpʌls/ noun [C] **1** [usually sing.] **an impulse (to do sth)** a sudden desire to do sth without thinking about the results: *Her first impulse was to run away.* ▶ **impuls 2** (technical) a force or movement of energy that causes a reaction: *nerve/electrical impulses* ▶ **bodziec**

IDM **on (an) impulse** without thinking or planning and not considering the results: *When I saw the child fall in the water, I just acted on impulse and jumped in after her.* ▶ **spontanicznie**

impulsive /ɪmˈpʌlsɪv/ adj. likely to act suddenly and without thinking; done without careful thought: *He is an impulsive character.* ▶ **popędliwy**

■ **impulsively** adv. ▶ **popędliwie** | **impulsiveness** noun [U] ▶ **popędliwość**

impunity /ɪmˈpjuːnəti/ noun [U] (formal) if a person does sth bad **with impunity**, they do not get punished for what they have done: *They continue to break the law with impunity.* ▶ **bezkarność** ❶ Wyraża dezaprobatę.

impure /ɪmˈpjʊə(r)/ adj. **1** not pure or clean; consisting of more than one substance mixed together (and therefore not of good quality): *impure metals* ▶ **zanieczyszczony 2** (old-fashioned) (used about thoughts and actions connected with sex) not moral; bad ▶ **nieczysty, brudny** OPP for both meanings **pure**

impurity /ɪmˈpjʊərəti/ noun (pl. **impurities**) **1** [C, usually pl.] a substance that is present in small amounts in another substance, making it dirty or of poor quality: *People are being advised to boil their water because certain impurities have been found in it.* ▶ **zanieczyszczenie 2** [U] (old-fashioned) the state of being morally bad ▶ **nieczystość**
➲ look at **purity**

in¹ /ɪn/ adv., prep. **1** (used to show place) inside or to a position inside a particular area or object: *in a box* ◇ *a country in Africa* ◇ *islands in the Pacific* ◇ *I read about it in the newspaper.* ◇ *He lay **in bed**.* ◇ *His wife's **in hospital**.* ◇ *My suitcase is full. I can't get any more in* (nie mogę nic więcej włożyć). ◇ *When does the train get in* (przyjeżdża)? ◇ *Let's go in.* Wejdźmy. ▶ **w 2** at home or at work: *I phoned him last night but he wasn't in.* ◇ *She won't **be in** till late today.* Będzie dziś późno w domu/pracy. ▶ **w domu/pracy** OPP **out 3** contained in; forming the whole or part of sth: *What's in this casserole?* ◇ *There are 31 days in January.* ▶ **w 4** (showing time) during a period of time: *My birthday is in August.* ◇ *in spring/summer/autumn/winter* ◇ *He was born in 1980.* ◇ *You could walk there in about an hour* (w ciągu około godziny). ▶ **w 5** (showing time) after a period of time: *I'll be finished in ten minutes.* ▶ **za 6** wearing sth: *I've never seen you in a suit before.* ◇ *a woman in a yellow dress* ◇ *They were all dressed in black* (ubrani na czarno) *for the funeral.* ▶ **w; na 7** showing the condition or state of sb/sth: *My parents are in poor health* (są słabego zdrowia). ◇ *This room is **in a mess**!* W tym pokoju jest bałagan. ◇ *Richard's **in love*** (jest zakochany). ◇ *He's in his mid-thirties.* ▶ *(używane do wyrażenia stanu czegoś/kogoś)* **8** (used with feelings): *I watched **in horror** as the plane crashed to the ground.* ◇ *He was **in** such **a rage*** (wpadł w taki szał, że) *I didn't dare to go near him.* ▶ **z** *(np. przerażeniem, rozbawieniem)* **9** showing sb's job or the activity sb is involved in: *He's got a good job in advertising.* ◇ *All her family are in politics.* ◇ *He's in the army.* ▶ **w 10** (used for saying how things are arranged): *We sat in a circle.* ◇ *She had her hair in plaits.* ▶ **w 11** (used for saying how sth is written or expressed): *Please write in pen* (pisać piórem). ◇ *They were talking **in Italian*** (po włosku). ◇ *to work in groups/teams* pracować w grupach/zespołach ▶ *(stosuje się przy określaniu sposobu pisania, np. piórem, atramentem)*; *(mówić)* **po 12** (used for giving the rate of sth and for talking about numbers): *Nowadays, **one** family **in three** owns a dishwasher.* ▶ **w, na 13** received by sb official: *Entries should **be in** by 20 March.* Podania należy nadesłać do 20 marca. ▶ **nadesłany** *(do danej daty do danej instytucji)* **14** (used about the sea) at the highest point, when the water is closest to the land: *The tide's coming in.* Nadchodzi przypływ. ▶ **w porze przypływu** ❶ **In** występuje z rzeczownikami w wielu zwrotach, np. **in time**. Zob. hasła odpowiednich rzeczowników.

IDM **be in for it/sth** to be going to experience sth unpleasant: *He'll be in for a shock* (czeka go szok) *when he gets the bill.* ◇ *You'll be in for it* (dostanie ci się) *when Mum sees what you've done.* ▶ *(dot. tylko przyszłości)* **doświadczyć (czegoś nieprzyjemnego)**

be/get in on sth to be included or involved in sth: *I'd like to be in on the new project.* ▶ **brać udział; zostać dopuszczonym**

have (got) it in for sb (informal) to be unpleasant to sb because they have done sth to upset you: *The boss has had it in for me ever since I asked to be considered for the new post.* ▶ **być ciętym (na kogoś)** ❶ **In** występuje w czasownikach złożonych. Zob. hasła odpowiednich czasowników, np. **give**, **come**.

in² /ɪn/ adj. (informal) fashionable at the moment: *the in place to go* ◇ *The colour grey is very in this season.* ▶ **modny**

in³ /ɪn/ noun

IDM **the ins and outs (of sth)** the details and difficulties (involved in sth): *Will somebody explain the ins and outs of the situation to me?* ▶ **tajniki, szczegóły**

in[4] = INCH[1]

in- prefix /ɪn/ **1** (also il- /ɪl/, im- /ɪm/, ir- /ɪr/) [in adjectives, adverbs and nouns] not; the opposite of: *infinite* ◇ *illogical* ◇ *immorally* ◇ *irrelevance* ▶ **nie 2** (also im- /ɪm/) [in verbs] to put into the condition mentioned: *inflame* rozpalać ◇ *imperil* narażać na niebezpieczeństwo ▶ **za-**

inability /ˌɪnəˈbɪləti/ noun [sing.] **inability (to do sth)** lack of ability, power or skill: *He has a complete inability to listen to other people's opinions.* ▶ **niezdolność**, **niemożność** OPP **ability** ➲ adjective **unable**

inaccessible /ˌɪnækˈsesəbl/ adj. very difficult or impossible to reach or contact: *That beach is inaccessible by car.* ▶ **niedostępny**; **nieprzystępny** OPP **accessible**
■ **inaccessibility** /ˌɪnækˌsesəˈbɪləti/ noun [U] ▶ **niedostępność**; **nieprzystępność**

inaccurate /ɪnˈækjərət/ adj. not correct or accurate; with mistakes: *an inaccurate report/description/statement* OPP **accurate**
■ **inaccuracy** /ɪnˈækjərəsi/ noun [C,U] (pl. **inaccuracies**): *The inaccuracy of the statistics was immediately obvious.* ◇ *There are always some inaccuracies in newspaper reports.* ▶ **nieścisłość** OPP **accuracy** | **inaccurately** adv. ▶ **nieścisły**

inaction /ɪnˈækʃn/ noun [U] doing nothing; lack of action: *The crisis was blamed on the government's earlier inaction.* ▶ **bezczynność**, **inercja** OPP **action**

inactive /ɪnˈæktɪv/ adj. doing nothing; not active: *The virus remains inactive in the body.* ▶ **bezczynny**, **bierny** OPP **active**
■ **inactivity** /ˌɪnækˈtɪvəti/ noun [U] ▶ **bezczynność**, **bierność** OPP **activity**

inadequate /ɪnˈædɪkwət/ adj. **1 inadequate (for sth/to do sth)** not enough; not good enough: *the problem of inadequate housing* ▶ **nieodpowiedni**, **niedostateczny** OPP **adequate 2** (used about a person) not able to deal with a problem or situation; not confident: *There was so much to learn in the new job that for a while I felt totally inadequate.* (czułem, że całkowicie nie umiem sprostać wymaganiom) ▶ **nieodpowiedni**, **nienadający się**
■ **inadequately** adv. ▶ **nieodpowiednio**, **niedostatecznie** | **inadequacy** /ɪnˈædɪkwəsi/ noun [C,U] (pl. **inadequacies**): *his inadequacy as a parent* ▶ **nieodpowiedniość**, **niedostateczność**, **nieudolność**

inadmissible /ˌɪnədˈmɪsəbl/ adj. (formal) that cannot be allowed or accepted, especially in a court of law: *inadmissible evidence* ▶ **niedopuszczalny**, **nie do przyjęcia** OPP **admissible**

inadvertent /ˌɪnədˈvɜːtənt/ adj. (used about actions) done without thinking; not on purpose ▶ **nieumyślny**, **mimowolny** OPP **intentional**, **deliberate**
■ **inadvertently** adv.: *She had inadvertently left the letter where he could find it.* ▶ **nieumyślnie**, **mimowolnie**

inadvisable /ˌɪnədˈvaɪzəbl/ adj. not sensible; not showing good judgement: *It is inadvisable to go swimming after a meal.* ▶ **nierozsądny**, **niewskazany** OPP **advisable**

inane /ɪˈneɪn/ adj. without any meaning; silly: *an inane remark* ▶ **bezmyślny**, **głupi**
■ **inanely** adv. ▶ **głupio**, **bezmyślnie**

inanimate /ɪnˈænɪmət/ adj. not alive: *A rock is an inanimate object.* ▶ **martwy**, **nieożywiony** OPP **animate**

inappropriate /ˌɪnəˈprəʊpriət/ adj. not suitable: *Isn't that dress rather inappropriate for the occasion?* ▶ **nieodpowiedni**, **niewłaściwy** OPP **appropriate**

inarticulate /ˌɪnɑːˈtɪkjələt/ adj. **1** (used about a person) not able to express ideas and feelings clearly ▶ **nieelokwentny 2** (used about speech) not clear or well expressed ▶ **mętny**, **niewyraźny** OPP for both meanings **articulate**
■ **inarticulately** adv. ▶ **nieelokwentnie**, **mętnie**, **niewyraźnie**

inasmuch as /ˌɪnəzˈmʌtʃ əz/ conj. (formal) because of the fact that: *We felt sorry for the boys inasmuch as they had not realized that what they were doing was wrong.* ▶ **ponieważ**, **gdyż**, **o tyle (że)**

inattention /ˌɪnəˈtenʃn/ noun [U] lack of attention: *The tragic accident was the result of a moment's inattention.* ▶ **nieuwaga**, **zaniedbanie** OPP **attention**

inattentive /ˌɪnəˈtentɪv/ adj. not paying attention: *One inattentive student can disturb the whole class.* ▶ **nieuważny** OPP **attentive**

inaudible /ɪnˈɔːdəbl/ adj. not loud enough to be heard ▶ **niesłyszalny** OPP **audible**
■ **inaudibly** /-əbli/ adv. ▶ **niesłyszalnie**, **nieuchwytnie dla ucha**

inaugurate /ɪˈnɔːgjəreɪt/ verb [T] **1** to introduce a new official, leader, etc. at a special formal ceremony: *He will be inaugurated as President next month.* ▶ **inaugurować**, **wprowadzać uroczyście na stanowisko 2** to start, introduce or open sth new, often at a special formal ceremony ▶ **inaugurować**, **zapoczątkować**
■ **inaugural** /ɪˈnɔːgjərəl/ adj. [only before a noun]: *the President's inaugural speech* ▶ **inauguracyjny** | **inauguration** /ɪˌnɔːgjəˈreɪʃn/ noun [C,U] ▶ **inauguracja**

inauspicious /ˌɪnɔːˈspɪʃəs/ adj. (formal) showing signs that the future will not be good or successful: *He made an inauspicious start.* ▶ **nie wróżący sukcesu**, **złowróżbny** OPP **auspicious**

inauthentic /ˌɪnɔːˈθentɪk/ adj. not genuine; that you cannot believe or rely on ▶ **nieautentyczny** OPP **authentic**
■ **inauthenticity** /ˌɪnɔːθenˈtɪsəti/ noun [U] ▶ **brak autentyczności**

inbox /ˈɪnbɒks/ noun [C] the place on a computer where you can see new email messages: *I have a stack of emails in my inbox.* ▶ **skrzynka odbiorcza**

Inc. (also inc) (US) = INCORPORATED: *Manhattan Drugstores Inc.*

incalculable /ɪnˈkælkjələbl/ adj. very great; too great to calculate: *an incalculable risk* ▶ **nieobliczalny**

incapable /ɪnˈkeɪpəbl/ adj. **1 incapable of sth/doing sth** not able to do sth: *She is incapable of hard work/working hard.* ◇ *He's quite incapable of unkindness.* ▶ **niezdolny do czegoś 2** not able to do, manage or organize anything well: *As a doctor, she's totally incapable.* ▶ **nieudolny** OPP for both meanings **capable**

incapacitate /ˌɪnkəˈpæsɪteɪt/ verb [T] to make sb unable to do sth: *They were completely incapacitated by the heat in Spain.* Hiszpański upał całkowicie ich rozłożył. ▶ **uczynić niezdolnym (do czegoś)**

incarcerate /ɪnˈkɑːsəreɪt/ verb [T] (formal) **incarcerate sb (in sth)** to put sb in prison or in another place from which they cannot escape ▶ **więzić** SYN **imprison**
■ **incarceration** /ɪnˌkɑːsəˈreɪʃn/ noun [U] ▶ **uwięzienie**

incarnation /ˌɪnkɑːˈneɪʃn/ noun [C] **1** a period of life in a particular form: *He believed he was a prince in a previous incarnation.* ▶ (*osoba*) **wcielenie** ➲ look at **reincarnation 2 the incarnation of sth** (a person that is) a perfect example of a particular quality: *She is the incarnation of goodness.* ▶ (*forma istnienia*) **wcielenie (czegoś)**

incendiary /ɪnˈsendiəri; US -dieri/ adj. [only before a noun] that causes a fire: *an incendiary bomb/device* ▶ **zapalający**

incense /ˈɪnsens/ noun [U] a substance that produces a sweet smell when burnt, used especially in religious ceremonies ▶ **kadzidło**

incensed /ɪnˈsenst/ adj. **incensed (by/at sth)** very angry ▶ (*przen.*) **wściekły** SYN **furious**

incentive /ɪnˈsentɪv/ noun [C,U] **(an) incentive (for/to sb/sth) (to do sth)** something that encourages you (to do sth): *There's no incentive for young people to do well at school because there aren't any jobs when they leave.* ▶ **zachęta**

inception /ɪnˈsepʃn/ noun [sing.] (formal) the start of an institution, an organization, etc.: *The club has grown rapidly since its inception in 1990.* ▶ **powstanie**

incessant /ɪnˈsesnt/ adj. never stopping (and usually annoying): *incessant rain/noise/chatter* ▶ **bezustanny** SYN **constant** ➲ look at **continual**
■ **incessantly** adv. ▶ **bezustannie, bez przerwy**

incest /ˈɪnsest/ noun [U] illegal sex between members of the same family, for example brother and sister ▶ **kazirodztwo**

incestuous /ɪnˈsestjuəs; US -tʃuəs/ adj. **1** involving illegal sex between members of the same family: *an incestuous relationship* ▶ **kazirodczy 2** (used about a group of people and their relationships with each other) too close; not open to anyone outside the group: *Life in a small community can be very incestuous.* ▶ (*grupa ludzi*) **zamknięty, zbyt zażyły**

⚷ **inch**[1] /ɪntʃ/ noun [C] (abbr. **in**) a measure of length; 2.54 centimetres. There are 12 **inches** in a foot: *He's 5 foot 10 inches tall.* ◇ *Three inches of rain fell last night.* ▶ **cal** ℹ Więcej o wyrażeniach miar w dodatku *Wyrażenia liczbowe* na końcu słownika.

inch[2] /ɪntʃ/ verb [I,T] **inch forward, past, through, etc.** to move slowly and carefully in the direction mentioned: *He inched (his way) forward along the cliff edge.* ▶ **posuwać (się) krok po kroku**

incidence /ˈɪnsɪdəns/ noun [sing.] (formal) **incidence of sth** the number of times sth (usually unpleasant) happens; the rate of sth: *a high incidence of crime / disease / unemployment* ▶ **występowanie, rozmiary**

⚷ **incident** /ˈɪnsɪdənt/ noun [C] (formal) something that happens (especially sth unusual or unpleasant): *There were a number of incidents after the football match.* ◇ *a diplomatic incident* ▶ **incydent, zajście**

incidental /ˌɪnsɪˈdentl/ adj. **incidental (to sth)** happening as part of sth more important: *The book contains various themes that are incidental to the main plot.* ▶ **nieistotny, marginesowy**

incidentally /ˌɪnsɪˈdentli/ adv. (used to introduce extra news, information, etc. that the speaker has just thought of): *Incidentally, that new restaurant you told me about is excellent.* ▶ **nawiasem mówiąc, à propos** ℹ Mniej formalnym zwrotem jest **by the way**.

incinerate /ɪnˈsɪnəreɪt/ verb [T] (formal) to destroy sth completely by burning ▶ **spopielać, spalać**

incinerator /ɪnˈsɪnəreɪtə(r)/ noun [C] a container or machine for burning rubbish, etc. ▶ **piec do spalania nieczystości**

incipient /ɪnˈsɪpiənt/ adj. [usually before a noun] (formal) just beginning: *signs of incipient unrest* ▶ **początkowy**

incision /ɪnˈsɪʒn/ noun [C] (formal) a cut carefully made into sth (especially into a person's body as part of a medical operation) ▶ **nacięcie**

incisive /ɪnˈsaɪsɪv/ adj. **1** showing clear thought and good understanding of what is important, and having the ability to express this: *an incisive mind* ▶ **bystry, przenikliwy 2** showing sb's ability to take decisions and act with force: *an incisive move* ▶ **bystry, prędki**

incite /ɪnˈsaɪt/ verb [T] **incite sb (to sth)** to encourage sb to do sth by making them very angry or excited: *He was accused of inciting the crowd to violence.* ▶ **podburzać**
■ **incitement** noun [C,U]: *He was guilty of incitement to violence.* ▶ **podburzanie**

incl.: *total £59.00 incl. tax* ▶ **wliczając**; **włącznie** = INCLUDING, INCLUSIVE

inclination /ˌɪnklɪˈneɪʃn/ noun [C,U] **inclination (to do sth)**; **inclination (towards/for sth)** a feeling that makes sb want to behave in a particular way: *He did not show **the slightest inclination** to help.* ◇ *She had no inclination for a career in teaching.* ◇ *My inclination is to say* (powiedziałbym) *'no', but what do you think?* ▶ **skłonność**

incline[1] /ɪnˈklaɪn/ verb **1** [I] (formal) **incline to/towards sth** to want to behave in a particular way or make a particular choice: *I don't know what to choose, but I'm inclining towards the fish.* ▶ **skłaniać się ku czemuś 2** [T] (formal) to bend (your head) forward: *They sat round the table, heads inclined, deep in discussion.* ▶ **schylać** (*głowę*) **3** [I] **incline towards sth** to be at an angle in a particular direction: *The land inclines towards the shore.* ▶ **nachylać się**

incline[2] /ˈɪnklaɪn/ noun [C] (formal) a slight hill: *a steep/slight incline* ▶ **pochyłość** SYN **slope**

inclined /ɪnˈklaɪnd/ adj. **1** [not before a noun] **inclined (to do sth)** wanting to do sth: *There'll be time for a swim if you **feel so inclined.*** ◇ *I know Amir well so I'm **inclined to believe** what he says.* ▶ **mający ochotę (coś zrobić), skłonny 2 inclined to do sth** likely to do sth: *She's inclined* (ma skłonność) *to change her mind very easily.* ▶ **mający skłonność 3** having a natural ability in the subject mentioned: *to be musically inclined* ▶ **uzdolniony**

⚷ **include** /ɪnˈkluːd/ verb [T] [not used in the continuous tenses] **1** to have as one part; to contain (among other things): *The price of the holiday includes the flight, the hotel and car hire.* ◇ *The crew included one woman.* ▶ **zawierać, wliczać** ➲ note at **contain 2 include sb/sth (as/in/on sth)** to make sb/sth part (of another group, etc.): *The children immediately included the new girl in their games.* ◇ *Everyone was disappointed, myself included.* ▶ **włączać, wliczać** OPP for both meanings **exclude**
■ **inclusion** /ɪnˈkluːʒn/ noun [U]: *The inclusion of all that violence in the film was unnecessary.* ▶ **włączenie**

⚷ **including** /ɪnˈkluːdɪŋ/ prep. (abbr. **incl.**) having as a part: *It costs $17.99, including postage and packing.* ▶ **wliczając** OPP **excluding**

inclusive /ɪnˈkluːsɪv/ adj. (abbr. **incl.**) **1 inclusive (of sth)** (used about a price, etc.) including or containing everything; including the thing mentioned: *Is that an inclusive price or are there some extras?* ◇ *The rent is inclusive of electricity* (łącznie z opłatą za energię elektryczną). ▶ **obejmujący, zawierający 2** [only after a noun] including the dates, numbers, etc. mentioned: *You are booked at the hotel from Monday to Friday inclusive.* ▶ (od ... do) **włącznie** ℹ W Amer. ang. **through** powszechnie używa się zamiast **inclusive**, mówiąc o czasie: *We'll be away from Friday through Sunday.*

incognito /ˌɪnkɒɡˈniːtəʊ/ adv. hiding your real name and identity (especially if you are famous and do not want to be recognized): *to travel incognito* ▶ **incognito**

incoherent /ˌɪnkəʊˈhɪərənt/ adj. not clear or easy to understand; not saying sth clearly: *incoherent mumbling* ▶ **chaotyczny, bezładny** OPP **coherent**
■ **incoherence** noun [U] ▶ **chaotyczność** | **incoherently** adv. ▶ **chaotycznie, bezładnie**

⚷ **income** /ˈɪnkʌm; -kəm/ noun [C,U] the money you receive regularly as payment for your work or as interest on money you have saved, etc.: *It's often difficult for a fam-*

ily to live on one income. ◇ *a source of income* źródło przychodów ▶ **dochód**, **wpływy** ➲ note at **pay**

> We talk about a **monthly** or an **annual** income. An income may be **high** or **low**. Your **gross** income is the amount you earn before paying tax. Your **net** income is your income after tax.

'income tax noun [U] the amount of money you pay to the government according to how much you earn ▶ **podatek dochodowy**

incoming /ˈɪnkʌmɪŋ/ adj. [only before a noun] **1** arriving or being received: *incoming flights/passengers* ◇ *incoming telephone calls* przychodzące rozmowy telefoniczne ▶ **przybywający 2** new; recently elected: *the incoming government* ▶ **nowo wybrany**

incomparable /ɪnˈkɒmprəbl/ adj. so good or great that it does not have an equal: *incomparable beauty* ▶ **niezrównany** ➲ verb **compare**

incompatible /ˌɪnkəmˈpætəbl/ adj. **incompatible with sb/sth** very different and therefore not able to live or work happily with sb or exist with sth: *Their marriage won't last – they're completely incompatible* (zupełnie do siebie nie pasują). ◇ *The working hours of the job are incompatible with family life.* ▶ **niekompatybilny**, **niezgodny (z kimś/czymś)** OPP **compatible**
■ **incompatibility** /ˌɪnkəmˌpætəˈbɪləti/ noun [C,U] (pl. **incompatibilities**) ▶ **niekompatybilność**, **niezgodność** (*np. pojęć, usposobień*)

incompetent /ɪnˈkɒmpɪtənt/ adj. lacking the necessary skill to do sth well: *He is completely incompetent at his job.* ◇ *an incompetent teacher/manager* ▶ **nieudolny**, **niekompetentny** OPP **competent**
■ **incompetent** noun [C]: *She's a total incompetent at basketball.* ▶ **osoba nieudolna** | **incompetence** noun [U] ▶ **nieudolność**, **niekompetencja** | **incompetently** adv.: *The business was run incompetently.* ▶ **nieudolnie**, **niekompetentnie**

incomplete /ˌɪnkəmˈpliːt/ adj. having a part or parts missing; not total: *Unfortunately the jigsaw puzzle was incomplete.* ▶ **niezupełny**, **niecałkowity** OPP **complete**
■ **incompletely** adv. ▶ **niezupełnie**, **niecałkowicie**

incomprehensible /ɪnˌkɒmprɪˈhensəbl/ adj. impossible to understand: *an incomprehensible explanation* ◇ *Her attitude is totally incomprehensible to the rest of us.* ▶ **niezrozumiały**, **niepojęty** OPP **comprehensible**, **understandable**
■ **incomprehension** /ɪnˌkɒmprɪˈhenʃn/ noun [U] ▶ **niezrozumienie**

inconceivable /ˌɪnkənˈsiːvəbl/ adj. impossible or very difficult to believe or imagine: *It's inconceivable that he would have stolen anything.* ▶ **niepojęty**, **niewyobrażalny** OPP **conceivable**

inconclusive /ˌɪnkənˈkluːsɪv/ adj. not leading to a definite decision or result: *an inconclusive discussion* ◇ *inconclusive evidence* ▶ **nierozstrzygający**, **nieprzekonujący** OPP **conclusive**
■ **inconclusively** adv. ▶ **nie rozstrzygająco**, **nieprzekonująco**

incongruous /ɪnˈkɒŋgruəs/ adj. strange and out of place; not suitable in a particular situation: *That huge table looks rather incongruous in such a small room.* ▶ **niestosowny**, **nie na miejscu**
■ **incongruously** adv. ▶ **nieodpowiednio**, **niestosownie** | **incongruity** /ˌɪnkɒnˈgruːəti/ noun [U] ▶ **niezgodność**, **niestosowność**

inconsequential /ɪnˌkɒnsɪˈkwenʃl/ adj. not important or worth considering SYN **trivial**: *inconsequential details* ◇ *inconsequential chatter* ▶ **błahy**
■ **inconsequentially** /-ʃəli/ adv.: *They chatted inconsequentially about this and that.* ▶ **o błahych sprawach**

inconsiderate /ˌɪnkənˈsɪdərət/ adj. (used about a person) not thinking or caring about the feelings, or needs of other people: *It was inconsiderate of you not to offer her a lift.* ▶ **niezważający** (*np. na czyjeś potrzeby, uczucia*) SYN **thoughtless** OPP **considerate**
■ **inconsiderately** adv. ▶ **nie zważając** (*np. na czyjeś potrzeby, uczucia*) | **inconsiderateness** noun [U] ▶ **nieliczenie się** (*np. z czyimiś potrzebami, uczuciami*)

inconsistent /ˌɪnkənˈsɪstənt/ adj. **1 inconsistent (with sth)** (used about statements, facts, etc.) not the same as sth else; not matching, so that one thing must be wrong or not true: *The witnesses' accounts of the event are inconsistent.* ◇ *These new facts are inconsistent with the earlier information.* ▶ **niezgodny**, **sprzeczny 2** (used about a person) likely to change (in attitude, behaviour, etc.) so that you cannot depend on them: *She's so inconsistent – sometimes her work is good and sometimes it's really awful.* ▶ **niekonsekwentny** OPP for both meanings **consistent**
■ **inconsistency** /ˌɪnkənˈsɪstənsi/ noun [C,U] (pl. **inconsistencies**): *There were far too many inconsistencies in her argument.* ▶ **niekonsekwencja**; **niezgodność** OPP **consistency** | **inconsistently** adv. ▶ **niekonsekwentnie**, **niezgodnie** (*z czymś*)

inconsolable /ˌɪnkənˈsəʊləbl/ (also **unconsolable**) adj. very sad and unable to accept help or comfort: *They were inconsolable when their only child died.* ◇ *inconsolable grief* ▶ **niepocieszony**, **nieukojony**
■ **inconsolably** /-əbli/ adv.: *to weep inconsolably* ▶ **w sposób nieukojony**

inconspicuous /ˌɪnkənˈspɪkjuəs/ adv. not easily noticed: *I tried to* ***make myself*** *as* ***inconspicuous*** *as possible so that no one would ask me a question.* ▶ **nierzucający się w oczy**, **niezwracający na siebie uwagi**, **niepozorny** OPP **conspicuous**
■ **inconspicuously** adv. ▶ **nie rzucając się w oczy**, **nie zwracając na siebie uwagi**

incontestable /ˌɪnkənˈtestəbl/ adj. (formal) that is true and cannot be disagreed with or denied: *an incontestable right/fact* ▶ **niezaprzeczalny** SYN **indisputable**

incontinent /ɪnˈkɒntɪnənt/ adj. unable to control the passing of **urine** and **faeces** from the body ▶ **nie panujący nad utrzymaniem moczu/stolca**
■ **incontinence** noun [U] ▶ **niemożność utrzymania moczu/stolca**

incontrovertible /ˌɪnkɒntrəˈvɜːtəbl/ adj. (formal) that is true and cannot be disagreed with or denied: ***incontrovertible evidence/proof*** ▶ **niepodważalny** SYN **indisputable**
■ **incontrovertibly** /-təbli/ adv.: *Her book shows incontrovertibly that he was innocent.* ▶ **niepodważalnie**

inconvenience /ˌɪnkənˈviːniəns/ noun [U,C] trouble or difficulty, especially when it affects sth that you need to do; a person or thing that causes this: *We apologize for any inconvenience caused by the delays.* ▶ **niewygoda**
■ **inconvenience** verb [T] ▶ **sprawiać kłopot** SYN **put sb out**

inconvenient /ˌɪnkənˈviːniənt/ adj. causing trouble or difficulty, especially when it affects sth that you need to do: *It's a bit inconvenient at the moment – could you phone again later?* ▶ **niewygodny**, **kłopotliwy** OPP **convenient**
■ **inconveniently** adv. ▶ **niewygodnie**, **kłopotliwie**

incorporate /ɪnˈkɔːpəreɪt/ verb [T] **incorporate sth (in/into/within sth)** to make sth a part of sth else; to have sth as a part: *I'd like you to incorporate this information into your report.* ▶ **wcielać**; **zawierać** SYN **include**
■ **incorporation** /ɪnˌkɔːpəˈreɪʃn/ noun [U] ▶ **wcielanie**, **włączanie**

incorporated /ɪnˈkɔːpəreɪtɪd/ adj. (abbr. **Inc.** /ɪŋk/) (following the name of a company) formed into a **corporation** ▶ (*towarzystwo, firma*) **zarejestrowany**

incorrect /ˌɪnkəˈrekt/ adj. not right or true: *Incorrect answers should be marked with a cross.* ▶ **nieprawidłowy, niestosowny** OPP **correct**
■ **incorrectly** adv. ▶ **błędnie**

incorrigible /ɪnˈkɒrɪdʒəbl/ adj. (used about a person or their behaviour) very bad; too bad to be corrected or improved: *an incorrigible liar* ▶ **zatwardziały, niepoprawny**

incorruptible /ˌɪnkəˈrʌptəbl/ adj. **1** (used about people) not able to be persuaded to do sth wrong or dishonest, even if sb offers them money: *Bribery won't work with him. He's incorruptible.* ▶ **nieprzekupny 2** that cannot decay or be destroyed ▶ **niezniszczalny**
■ **incorruptibility** /ˌɪnkəˌrʌptəˈbɪləti/ noun [U] ▶ **nieprzekupność; niezniszczalność**

⚷ **increase¹** /ɪnˈkriːs/ verb [I,T] **increase (sth) (from A) (to B); increase (sth) (by sth)** to become or to make sth larger in number or amount: *She increased her speed* (przyśpieszyła) *to overtake the lorry.* ◇ *My employer would like me to increase my hours of work from 25 to 30.* ◇ *The rate of inflation has increased by 1% to 7%.* ▶ **zwiększać (się), wzrastać** OPP **decrease, reduce**

⚷ **increase²** /ˈɪŋkriːs/ noun [C,U] **(an) increase (in sth)** a rise in the number, amount or level of sth: *There has been a* ***sharp increase*** *of nearly 50% on last year's figures.* ◇ *Doctors expect some further increase in the spread of the disease.* ◇ *They are demanding a large wage increase* (podwyżki) *in line with inflation.* ▶ **przyrost, wzrost** OPP **decrease, reduction**
IDM **be on the increase** to become larger or more common; to increase: *Attacks by dogs on children are on the increase.* ▶ **wzrastać**

⚷ **increasingly** /ɪnˈkriːsɪŋli/ adv. more and more: *It's becoming increasingly difficult/important/dangerous to stay here.* ▶ **coraz (bardziej)**

incredible /ɪnˈkredəbl/ adj. **1** impossible or very difficult to believe: *I found Jacqueline's account of the event incredible.* ▶ **niewiarygodny, nieprawdopodobny** SYN **unbelievable** OPP **credible 2** (informal) extremely good or big: *He earns an incredible salary.* ▶ **niewiarygodny, ogromny**
■ **incredibly** /-əbli/ adv.: *We have had some incredibly strong winds recently.* ▶ **niewiarygodnie**

incredulous /ɪnˈkredjələs; US -dʒəl-/ adj. not willing or not able to believe sth; showing an inability to believe sth: *'Here?' said Kate, incredulous.* ◇ *an incredulous look* ▶ **pełen niedowierzania**
■ **incredulity** /ˌɪnkrəˈdjuːləti; US -ˈduː-/ noun [U]: *a look of surprise and incredulity* ▶ **niedowierzanie** SYN **disbelief** | **incredulously** adv.: *He laughed incredulously.* ▶ **z niedowierzaniem**

increment /ˈɪŋkrəmənt/ noun [C] (formal) an increase in a number or an amount, especially a regular pay increase: *a salary of £25 000 with annual increments* ▶ **(automatyczna) podwyżka, przyrost**
■ **incremental** /ˌɪŋkrəˈmentl/ adj.: *incremental costs* ▶ **przyrostowy, narastający** | **incrementally** /-təli/ adv. ▶ **przyrostowo, narastająco**

incriminate /ɪnˈkrɪmɪneɪt/ verb [T] to provide evidence that sb is guilty of a crime: *The police searched the house but found nothing to incriminate the man.* ▶ **oskarżać**

incubate /ˈɪŋkjubeɪt/ verb **1** [T] to keep an egg at the right temperature so that it can develop and break open ▶ **wysiadywać** (*jaja*), **przechodzić/poddawać proces/owi wylęgu 2** [I,T] (used about a disease) to develop without showing signs; (used about a person or an animal) to carry a disease without showing signs: *Some viruses take weeks to incubate.* Okres inkubacji niektórych wirusów trwa całe tygodnie. ◇ *There was no way of knowing that I was incubating an infectious disease* (rozwijała się we mnie zakaźna choroba). ▶ **rozwijać się**

incubation /ˌɪŋkjuˈbeɪʃn/ noun **1** [U] the process of **incubating** eggs ▶ **wylęganie 2** [C] (also ˌ**incuˈbation period**) the period between catching a disease and the time when signs of it appear ▶ **okres inkubacji/wylęgania**

incubator /ˈɪŋkjubeɪtə(r)/ noun [C] **1** a heated machine used in hospitals for keeping small or weak babies alive ▶ **inkubator 2** a heated machine for keeping eggs warm until the young birds are born ▶ **wylęgarka**

inculcate /ˈɪnkʌlkeɪt; US ɪnˈkʌl-/ verb [T] **inculcate sth (in/into sb); inculcate sb with sth** (formal) to cause sb to learn and remember ideas, moral principles, etc., especially by repeating them often: *to inculcate a sense of responsibility in sb* ◇ *to inculcate sb with a sense of responsibility* ▶ **wpajać coś komuś**
■ **inculcation** /ˌɪnkʌlˈkeɪʃn/ noun [U] ▶ **wpojenie**

incur /ɪnˈkɜː(r)/ verb [T] (**incurred**; **incurring**) (formal) to suffer the unpleasant results of a situation that you have caused: *to incur debts* zaciągać długi ◇ *to incur sb's anger* ściągać na siebie czyjś gniew ▶ **ponosić** (*np. koszty*), **narażać się (na coś)**

incurable /ɪnˈkjʊərəbl/ adj. that cannot be cured or made better: *an incurable disease* ▶ **nieuleczalny** OPP **curable**
■ **incurably** /-əbli/ adv.: *incurably ill/romantic* ▶ **nieuleczalnie**

indebted /ɪnˈdetɪd/ adj. **indebted (to sb) (for sth)** very grateful to sb: *I am deeply indebted* (mam duży dług wdzięczności) *to my family for their help.* ▶ **wdzięczny, zobowiązany**

indecent /ɪnˈdiːsnt/ adj. shocking to many people in society, especially because sth involves sex or the body: *indecent photos/behaviour/language* ◇ *Those tiny swimming trunks are indecent!* ▶ **nieprzyzwoity** OPP **decent**
■ **indecency** /ɪnˈdiːsnsi/ noun [U, sing.] ▶ **nieprzyzwoitość** | **indecently** adv. ▶ **nieprzyzwoicie**

indecipherable /ˌɪndɪˈsaɪfrəbl/ adj. (used about writing or speech) impossible to read or understand ▶ **nie do rozszyfrowania**

indecision /ˌɪndɪˈsɪʒn/ (also **indecisiveness** /ˌɪndɪˈsaɪsɪvnəs/) noun [U] the state of being unable to decide: *This indecision about the future is really worrying.* ▶ **niezdecydowanie**

indecisive /ˌɪndɪˈsaɪsɪv/ adj. not able to make decisions easily ▶ **niezdecydowany** OPP **decisive**
■ **indecisively** adv.: *He stood at the crossroads indecisively, wondering which way to go.* ▶ **niezdecydowanie**

indecisiveness = INDECISION

⚷ **indeed** /ɪnˈdiːd/ adv. **1** (used for emphasizing a positive statement or answer) really; certainly: *'Have you had a good holiday?' 'We have indeed.'* ▶ **rzeczywiście 2** (used after 'very' with an adjective or adverb to emphasize the quality mentioned): *Thank you very much indeed.* ◇ *She's very happy indeed.* ▶ **naprawdę, rzeczywiście 3** (used for adding information to a statement) in fact: *It's important that you come at once. Indeed, it's essential.* ▶ **naprawdę, istotnie 4** (used for showing interest, surprise, anger, etc.): *'They were talking about you last night.' 'Were they indeed!'* ▶ **czyżby?, naprawdę?**

indefensible /ˌɪndɪˈfensəbl/ adj. (used about behaviour, etc.) completely wrong; that cannot be defended or excused ▶ **nie do usprawiedliwienia**

indefinable /ˌɪndɪˈfaɪnəbl/ adj. difficult or impossible to describe: *She has that indefinable quality that makes an actress a star.* ▶ **nieokreślony**
■ **indefinably** /-əbli/ adv. ▶ **w sposób nieokreślony**

indefinite /ɪnˈdefɪnət/ adj. not fixed or clear: *Our plans are still rather indefinite.* ▶ **nieokreślony, niesprecyzowany** OPP **definite**

the **inˌdefinite ˈarticle** noun [C] the name used for the words *a* and *an* ▶ **przedimek nieokreślony** ➲ look at **definite article**

indefinitely /ɪnˈdefɪnətli/ adv. for a period of time that has no fixed end: *The meeting was postponed indefinitely.* ▶ **na czas nieokreślony, bez końca**

indelible /ɪnˈdeləbl/ adj. that cannot be removed or washed out: *indelible ink* ◇ (figurative) *The experience made an indelible impression on me.* ▶ (*atrament itp.*) **nieusuwalny**; (*i przen.*) **niezatarty**
■ **indelibly** /-əbli/ adv. ▶ **w sposób nie dający się usunąć; trwale**

indelicate /ɪnˈdelɪkət/ adj. (formal) likely to be thought rude or embarrassing: *an indelicate question* ▶ **niedelikatny, prostacki**
■ **indelicacy** /-kəsi/ noun [U] ▶ **niedelikatność, prostactwo**

indemnify /ɪnˈdemnɪfaɪ/ verb (**indemnifies**; **indemnifying**; **indemnified**; **indemnified**) [T] **1 indemnify sb (against sth)** to promise to pay sb an amount of money if they suffer any damage or loss: *The contract indemnifies them against loss of earnings.* ▶ **zabezpieczać kogoś (przed czymś) 2 indemnify sb (for sth)** to pay sb an amount of money because of the damage or loss that they have suffered: *The tenant is legally required to indemnify the landlord for any damage caused to the property.* ▶ **wypłacać komuś odszkodowanie (za coś)**
■ **indemnification** /ɪnˌdemnɪfɪˈkeɪʃn/ noun [U] ▶ **zabezpieczenie; odszkodowanie**

indemnity /ɪnˈdemnəti/ noun (pl. **-ies**) (formal or technical) **1** [U] **indemnity (against sth)** protection against damage or loss, especially in the form of a promise to pay for any that happens: *an indemnity clause/fund/policy* ◇ *indemnity insurance* ▶ **ubezpieczenie (od czegoś) 2** [C] a sum of money that is given as payment for damage or loss ▶ **odszkodowanie**

indent /ɪnˈdent/ verb [T] to start a line of writing further away from the edge of the page than the other lines ▶ **wcinać** (*akapit*)

⚷ **independence** /ˌɪndɪˈpendəns/ noun [U] **independence (from sb/sth)** (used about a person, country, etc.) the state of being free and not controlled by another person, country, etc.: *In 1947 India achieved independence from Britain.* ◇ *financial independence* ▶ **niepodległość, niezależność**

> Czwartego lipca Amerykanie obchodzą **Independence Day.** Tego dnia w 1776 roku Ameryka ogłosiła swoją niepodległość.

⚷ **independent** /ˌɪndɪˈpendənt/ adj. **1 independent (of/from sb/sth)** free from and not controlled by another person, country, etc.: *Many former colonies are now independent nations.* ◇ *independent schools/TV* ▶ **niepodległy, niezależny 2** not influenced by or connected with sb/sth: *Complaints against the police should be investigated by an independent body.* ◇ *Two independent opinion polls have obtained similar results.* ▶ **niezależny, osobny 3 independent (of/from sb/sth)** not needing or wanting help: *I got a part-time job because I wanted to be financially independent from my parents.* ▶ **niezależny** OPP **dependent**
■ **independently** adv. **independently (of sb/sth)**: *Scientists working independently of each other have had very similar results.* ▶ **niezależnie, osobno**

indescribable /ˌɪndɪˈskraɪbəbl/ adj. too good or bad to be described: *indescribable poverty/luxury/noise* ▶ **nieopisany**
■ **indescribably** /-əbli/ adv. ▶ **nieopisanie**

indestructible /ˌɪndɪˈstrʌktəbl/ adj. that cannot be easily damaged or destroyed ▶ **niezniszczalny**

indeterminate /ˌɪndɪˈtɜːmɪnət/ adj. that cannot be identified easily or exactly: *She was a tall woman of indeterminate age.* ▶ **nieokreślony**
■ **indeterminacy** /-nəsi/ noun [U] ▶ **nieokreśloność**

⚷ **index** /ˈɪndeks/ noun [C] (pl. **indexes**) **1** a list in order from A to Z, usually at the end of a book, of the names or subjects that are referred to in the book: *If you want to find all the references to London, look it up in the index.* ▶ **indeks, skorowidz 2** = CARD INDEX **3** (pl. **indexes** or **indices** /ˈɪndɪsiːz/) a way of showing how the price, value, rate, etc. of sth has changed: *the cost-of-living index* ▶ **wskaźnik, indeks**
■ **index** verb [T]: *The books in the library are indexed by subject and title.* ▶ **sporządzać indeks/skorowidz**

ˈindex card noun [C] a small card that you can write information on and keep with other cards in a box or file ▶ **fiszka, karta katalogowa** ➲ look at **card index**

ˈindex finger = FOREFINGER

Indian /ˈɪndiən/ adj. from the Republic of India: *Indian food is hot and spicy.* ▶ **indyjski**
■ **Indian** noun [C] **1** a person from the Republic of India ▶ **mieszkaniec Indii 2** (old-fashioned) = NATIVE AMERICAN ➲ look at **West Indian**

⚷ **indicate** /ˈɪndɪkeɪt/ verb **1** [T] to show that sth is probably true or exists: *Recent research indicates that children are getting too little exercise.* ▶ **wskazywać (na coś), sygnalizować 2** [T] to say sth in an indirect way: *The spokesman indicated that an agreement was likely soon.* ▶ **sygnalizować, sugerować 3** [T] to make sb notice sth, especially by pointing to it: *The receptionist indicated where I should sign.* ◇ *The boy seemed to be indicating that I should follow him.* ▶ **wskazywać** (*zwł. ręką*), **pokazywać 4** [I,T] to signal that your car, etc. is going to turn: *The lorry indicated left but turned right.* ▶ **sygnalizować**

⚷ **indication** /ˌɪndɪˈkeɪʃn/ noun [C,U] **an indication (of sth/doing sth)**; **an indication that ...** something that shows sth; a sign: *There was no indication of a struggle.* ◇ *There is every indication that* (wszystko wskazuje na to, że) *he will make a full recovery.* ▶ **oznaka**

indicative /ɪnˈdɪkətɪv/ adj. (formal) **be indicative (of sth)** to be or give a sign of sth: *Is the unusual weather indicative* (czy anomalie pogodowe są oznaką) *of climatic changes?* ▶ **wskazywać (na coś)**

indicator /ˈɪndɪkeɪtə(r)/ noun [C] **1** something that gives information or shows sth; a sign: *The indicator showed that we had plenty of petrol.* ◇ *The unemployment rate is a reliable indicator of economic health.* ▶ **wskaźnik 2** (US **ˈturn signal**) (informal **blinker**) the flashing light on a car, etc. that shows that it is going to turn right or left ▶ **kierunkowskaz** ➲ picture at **car**, picture on **page A7**

indices plural of **index** (3)

indict /ɪnˈdaɪt/ verb [T, usually passive] **indict sb (for sth)**; **indict sb (on charges/on a charge of sth)** (especially US) to officially charge sb with a crime: *The senator was indicted for murder.* ◇ *She was indicted on charges of corruption.* ▶ **postawić kogoś w stan oskarżenia (za coś/pod zarzutem czegoś)**

indictment /ɪnˈdaɪtmənt/ noun [C] **1 an indictment (of sth)** something that shows how bad sth is: *The fact that many children leave school with no qualifications is an indictment of our education system.* ▶ **oskarżenie 2** a written paper that officially accuses sb of a crime ▶ **akt oskarżenia**

indie /ˈɪndi/ adj. [only before a noun] (used about a company, person or product) not part of a large organization; independent: *an indie publisher* ◇ *indie music* ▶ **niezależny**

indifference /ɪnˈdɪfrəns/ noun [U] **indifference (to sb/sth)** a lack of interest or feeling towards sb/sth: *He has always shown indifference to the needs of others.* ▶ **obojętność**

indifferent /ɪnˈdɪfrənt/ adj. **1 indifferent (to sb/sth)** not interested in or caring about sb/sth: *The manager of the shop seemed indifferent to our complaints.* ▶ **obojętny 2** not very good: *The standard of football in the World Cup was rather indifferent.* ▶ **mierny, marny**
■ **indifferently** adv. ▶ **obojętnie; miernie**

indigenous /ɪnˈdɪdʒənəs/ adj. (used about people, animals or plants) living or growing in the place where they are from originally ▶ **macierzysty, miejscowy**

indigestible /ˌɪndɪˈdʒestəbl/ adj. (used about food) difficult or impossible for the stomach to deal with ▶ **niestrawny**

indigestion /ˌɪndɪˈdʒestʃən/ noun [U] pain in the stomach that is caused by difficulty in dealing with food: *Peppers give me indigestion.* Po papryce cierpię na niestrawność. ▶ **niestrawność**

indignant /ɪnˈdɪɡnənt/ adj. **indignant (with sb) (about/at sth); indignant that...** shocked or angry because sb has said or done sth that you do not like and do not agree with: *They were indignant that they had to pay more for worse services.* ▶ **oburzony**
■ **indignantly** adv. ▶ **z oburzeniem**

indignation /ˌɪndɪɡˈneɪʃn/ noun [U] **indignation (at/about sth); indignation that...** shock and anger: *commuters' indignation at the rise in fares* ▶ **oburzenie**

indignity /ɪnˈdɪɡnəti/ noun [U,C] (pl. **indignities**) **indignity (of sth/of doing sth)** a situation that makes you feel embarrassed because you are not treated with respect; an act that causes this feeling: *the daily indignities of imprisonment* ▶ **upokorzenie** SYN **humiliation**

indigo /ˈɪndɪɡəʊ/ adj. very dark blue in colour ▶ **w kolorze indygo**
■ **indigo** noun [U] ▶ **kolor indygo**

⚷ **indirect** /ˌɪndəˈrekt; -daɪˈr-/ adj. **1** not being the direct cause of sth; not having a direct connection with sth: *an indirect result* ▶ **pośredni 2** that avoids saying sth in an obvious way: *an indirect answer to a question* ▶ (*odpowiedź itp.*) **wymijający 3** not going in a straight line or using the shortest route: *We came the indirect route to avoid driving through London.* ▶ **okrężny, z przesiadką** OPP **direct**
■ **indirectly** adv. ▶ **pośrednio; wymijająco; okrężną drogą** OPP **directly** | **indirectness** noun [U] ▶ **pośredniość; brak jasności** (*np. w odpowiedzi*); **brak bezpośredniego dojazdu**

ˌindirect ˈobject noun [C] a person or thing that an action is done to or for: *In the sentence, 'I wrote him a letter', 'him' is the indirect object.* ▶ **dopełnienie dalsze**
⮌ look at **direct object**

ˌindirect ˈspeech = REPORTED SPEECH

indiscreet /ˌɪndɪˈskriːt/ adj. not careful or polite in what you say or do ▶ **niedyskretny, nieroztropny** OPP **discreet**
■ **indiscreetly** adv. ▶ **niedyskretnie, nieroztropnie**

indiscretion /ˌɪndɪˈskreʃn/ noun [C,U] behaviour that is not careful or polite, and that might cause embarrassment or offence ▶ **niedyskrecja, nieostrożność**

indiscriminate /ˌɪndɪˈskrɪmɪnət/ adj. done or acting without making sensible judgement or caring about the possible harmful effects: *the indiscriminate shooting of civilians* ◇ *Martin's indiscriminate in his choice of friends.* ▶ (*dokonany*) **bez rozróżnienia**, (*przeprowadzany*) **na oślep, masowy; niewybredny**
■ **indiscriminately** adv. ▶ **bez rozróżnienia**

indispensable /ˌɪndɪˈspensəbl/ adj. very important, so that it is not possible to be without it: *A car is indispensable nowadays if you live in the country.* ▶ **niezbędny** SYN **essential** OPP **dispensable**

indisputable /ˌɪndɪˈspjuːtəbl/ adj. definitely true; that cannot be shown to be wrong ▶ **bezsporny, niekwestionowany**

indistinct /ˌɪndɪˈstɪŋkt/ adj. not clear: *indistinct figures/sounds/memories* ▶ **niewyraźny, niejasny** OPP **distinct**
■ **indistinctly** adv. ▶ **niewyraźnie, niejasno**

indistinguishable /ˌɪndɪˈstɪŋɡwɪʃəbl/ adj. **indistinguishable (from sth)** appearing to be the same: *From a distance the two colours are indistinguishable.* ▶ **nie do odróżnienia** OPP **distinguishable**

⚷ **individual**[1] /ˌɪndɪˈvɪdʒuəl/ adj. **1** [only before a noun] considered separately rather than as part of a group: *Each individual animal is weighed and measured before being set free.* ▶ **pojedynczy, poszczególny 2** for or from one person: *Children need individual attention when they are learning to read.* ◇ *an individual portion of butter* porcja masła dla jednej osoby ▶ **indywidualny, osobisty 3** typical of one person in a way that is different from other people: *I like her individual style of dressing.* ▶ **indywidualny, specyficzny**

⚷ **individual**[2] /ˌɪndɪˈvɪdʒuəl/ noun [C] **1** one person, considered separately from others or a group: *Are the needs of society more important than the rights of the individual?* ▶ **jednostka, (jedna) osoba 2** (informal) a person of the type that is mentioned: *She's a strange individual.* ▶ **osoba, osobnik**

individualism /ˌɪndɪˈvɪdʒuəlɪzəm/ noun [U] **1** the quality of being different from other people and doing things in your own way ▶ **indywidualizm 2** the belief that individual people in society should have the right to make their own decisions, etc., rather than be controlled by the government ▶ **indywidualizm**
■ **individualist** /-əlɪst/ noun [C]: *She's a complete individualist in her art.* ▶ **indywidualist(k)a** | **individualistic** /ˌɪndɪˌvɪdʒuəˈlɪstɪk/ (also **individualist**) adj.: *an individualistic culture* ◇ *His music is highly individualistic and may not appeal to everyone.* ▶ **swoisty, indywidualistyczny**

individuality /ˌɪndɪˌvɪdʒuˈæləti/ noun [U] the qualities that make sb/sth different from other people or things: *People often try to express their individuality by the way they dress.* ▶ **indywidualność**

individually /ˌɪndɪˈvɪdʒuəli/ adv. separately; one by one: *The teacher talked to each member of the class individually.* ▶ **indywidualnie, pojedynczo**

indivisible /ˌɪndɪˈvɪzəbl/ adj. that cannot be divided or split into smaller pieces ▶ **niepodzielny**

indoctrinate /ɪnˈdɒktrɪneɪt/ verb [T] to force sb to accept particular beliefs without considering others: *For 20 years the people have been indoctrinated by the government.* ▶ **indoktrynować**
■ **indoctrination** /ɪnˌdɒktrɪˈneɪʃn/ noun [U] ▶ **indoktrynacja**

ˌIndo-ˌEuroˈpean adj. of or connected with the family of languages spoken in most of Europe and parts of western Asia (including English, French, Latin, Greek, Swedish, Russian and Hindi) ▶ **indoeuropejski**

indolent /ˈɪndələnt/ adj. (formal) not wanting to work ▶ **gnuśny, leniwy** SYN **lazy**
■ **indolence** /-əns/ noun [U] ▶ **gnuśność, lenistwo**

⚷ **indoor** /ˈɪndɔː(r)/ adj. [only before a noun] done or used inside a building: *indoor games* zawody halowe ◇ *an indoor swimming pool* basen kryty ◇ *indoor shoes* pantofle domowe ▶ **odbywający się/używany wewnątrz budynku** OPP **outdoor**

indoors /ˌɪnˈdɔːz/ adv. in or into a building: *Let's go indoors.* ◇ *Oh dear! I've left my sunglasses indoors.* ▶ **w/do domu** OPP outdoors, out of doors

induce /ɪnˈdjuːs; US -duːs/ verb [T] (formal) **1** to make or persuade sb to do sth: *Nothing could induce him to change his mind.* ▶ **skłaniać** **2** to cause or produce sth: *drugs that induce sleep* ▶ **wywoływać, powodować**

inducement /ɪnˈdjuːsmənt; US ɪnˈduːsmənt/ noun [C,U] something that is offered to sb to make them do sth: *The player was offered a car as an inducement to join the club.* ▶ **zachęta**

induction /ɪnˈdʌkʃn/ noun [U,C] the process of introducing sb to a new job, skill, organization, etc.; an event at which this takes place: *an induction day* (dzień wprowadzający) *for new students* ▶ **wprowadzanie**

inˈduction course noun [C] (Brit.) a training course for new employees, students, etc. that is designed to give them a general introduction to the business, school, etc. ▶ **kurs wprowadzający**

indulge /ɪnˈdʌldʒ/ verb **1** [I,T] **indulge (yourself) (in sth)** to allow yourself to have or do sth for pleasure: *I'm going to indulge myself and go shopping for some new clothes.* ◇ *Maria never indulges in gossip.* ▶ **pozwalać sobie (na coś), folgować sobie (w czymś)** **2** [T] to give sb/sth what he/she/it wants or needs: *You shouldn't indulge that child. It will make him very selfish.* ◇ *At the weekends he indulges his passion for fishing.* ▶ **pobłażać, dogadzać**

indulgence /ɪnˈdʌldʒəns/ noun **1** [U] the state of having or doing whatever you want: *to lead a life of indulgence* ◇ *Over-indulgence in chocolate makes you fat.* ▶ **pobłażanie sobie, oddawanie się (czemuś)** **2** [C] something that you have or do because it gives you pleasure: *A cigar after dinner is my only indulgence.* ▶ **przyjemność, ekstrawagancja**

indulgent /ɪnˈdʌldʒənt/ adj. allowing sb to have or do whatever they want: *indulgent parents* ▶ **pobłażliwy**
■ **indulgently** adv. ▶ **pobłażliwie**

industrial /ɪnˈdʌstriəl/ adj. **1** [only before a noun] connected with industry: *industrial development/workers* ▶ **przemysłowy** **2** having a lot of factories, etc.: *an industrial region/country/town* ▶ **uprzemysłowiony**

inˌdustrial ˈaction noun [U] action that workers take, especially stopping work, in order to protest about sth to their employers: *to threaten (to take) industrial action* ▶ **strajk** ℹ Tego zwrotu używa się w języku formalnym. Ma odcień łagodniejszy niż **strike**, którego używa się w języku codziennym. SYN strike

inˌdustrial eˈstate (US inˌdustrial ˈpark) noun [C] an area especially for factories, on the edge of a town ▶ **teren przemysłowy**

industrialist /ɪnˈdʌstriəlɪst/ noun [C] a person who owns or manages a large **industrial** company ▶ **przemysłowiec**

industrialize (also -ise) /ɪnˈdʌstriəlaɪz/ verb [I,T] to develop industries in a country: *Japan industrialized rapidly at the end of the 19th century.* ▶ **uprzemysławiać (się)**
■ **industrialization** (also -isation) /ɪnˌdʌstriəlaɪˈzeɪʃn; US -ləˈz-/ noun [U] ▶ **uprzemysłowienie**

inˌdustrial reˈlations noun [pl.] relations between employers and employees ▶ **stosunki między pracodawcami i pracownikami**

industrious /ɪnˈdʌstriəs/ adj. always working hard SYN hard-working ▶ **pracowity**

industry /ˈɪndəstri/ noun (pl. **industries**) **1** [U] the production of goods in factories: *Is British industry being threatened by foreign imports?* ◇ *heavy/light industry* ▶ **przemysł** **2** [C] the people and activities involved in producing sth, providing a service, etc.: *the tourist/catering/entertainment industry* ▶ **gałąź przemysłu, branża**

inebriated /ɪˈniːbrieɪtɪd/ adj. (formal or humorous) drunk ▶ **nietrzeźwy**
■ **inebriation** /ɪˌniːbriˈeɪʃn/ noun [U] ▶ **upojenie alkoholowe**

inedible /ɪnˈedəbl/ adj. (formal) not suitable to be eaten: *an inedible plant* ▶ **niejadalny** OPP edible

ineffective /ˌɪnɪˈfektɪv/ adj. not producing the effect or result that you want ▶ **nieefektywny, nieskuteczny** OPP effective

ineffectual /ˌɪnɪˈfektʃuəl/ adj. (formal) without the ability to achieve much; weak; not achieving what you want to: *an ineffectual teacher* ◇ *an ineffectual attempt to reform the law* ▶ **nieskuteczny**
■ **ineffectually** /-tʃuəli/ adv. ▶ **nieskutecznie**

inefficient /ˌɪnɪˈfɪʃnt/ adj. not working or producing results in the best way, so that time or money is wasted: *Our heating system is very old and extremely inefficient.* ◇ *an inefficient secretary* ▶ **niewydajny, nieskuteczny** OPP efficient
■ **inefficiency** /ˌɪnɪˈfɪʃənsi/ noun [U] ▶ **niewydajność, nieskuteczność** | **inefficiently** adv. ▶ **niewydajnie, nieskutecznie**

inelegant /ɪnˈelɪgənt/ adj. not attractive or elegant: *an inelegant fall* ◇ *an inelegant phrase* ▶ **nieelegancki** OPP elegant
■ **inelegantly** adv. ▶ **nieelegancko**

ineligible /ɪnˈelɪdʒəbl/ adj. **ineligible (for/to do sth)** without the necessary certificates, etc. to do or get sth: *ineligible to vote* ▶ **nie mający kwalifikacji/uprawnień/prawa (do czegoś)** OPP eligible
■ **ineligibility** /ɪnˌelɪdʒəˈbɪləti/ noun [U] ▶ **brak kwalifikacji/uprawnień**

inept /ɪˈnept/ adj. **inept (at sth)** not able to do sth well: *She is totally inept at dealing with people.* ▶ **nieudolny** OPP adept

inequality /ˌɪnɪˈkwɒləti/ noun [C,U] (pl. **inequalities**) (a) difference between groups in society because one has more money, advantages, etc. than the other: *There will be problems as long as inequality between the races exists.* ▶ **nierówność** OPP equality

inert /ɪˈnɜːt/ adj. not able to move or act ▶ **bezwładny, bierny**

inertia /ɪˈnɜːʃə/ noun [U] **1** a lack of energy; not being able to move or change ▶ **opieszałość** **2** the physical force that keeps things where they are or keeps them moving in the direction they are travelling ▶ **bezwładność, inercja**

inescapable /ˌɪnɪˈskeɪpəbl/ adj. (formal) that cannot be avoided: *an inescapable conclusion* ▶ **nieunikniony**

inevitable /ɪnˈevɪtəbl/ adj. that cannot be avoided or prevented from happening: *With more cars on the road, traffic jams are inevitable.* ▶ **nieunikniony, nieuchronny**
■ **the inevitable** noun [sing.]: *They fought to save the firm from closure, but eventually had to accept the inevitable.* ▶ **rzecz nieuchronna/nieunikniona** | **inevitability** /ɪnˌevɪtəˈbɪləti/ noun [U] ▶ **nieuchronność** | **inevitably** /ɪnˈevɪtəbli/ adv. ▶ **nieuchronnie**

inexact /ˌɪnɪgˈzækt/ adj. not accurate or exact: *an inexact description* ◇ *Economics is an inexact science.* ▶ **niedokładny**

inexcusable /ˌɪnɪkˈskjuːzəbl/ adj. that cannot be allowed or forgiven: *Their behaviour was quite inexcusable.* ▶ **niewybaczalny** OPP excusable

inexhaustible /ˌɪnɪgˈzɔːstəbl/ adj. that cannot be finished or used up completely: *Our energy supplies are not inexhaustible.* ▶ **niewyczerpany**

inexpensive /ˌɪnɪk'spensɪv/ adj. low in price: *an inexpensive camping holiday* ▶ **niedrogi** SYN **cheap** OPP **expensive**
■ **inexpensively** adv. ▶ **niedrogo**

inexperience /ˌɪnɪk'spɪəriəns/ noun [U] not knowing how to do sth because you have not done it before: *The mistakes were all due to inexperience.* ▶ **brak doświadczenia** OPP **experience**

inexperienced /ˌɪnɪk'spɪəriənst/ adj. having little knowledge or experience of sth: *inexperienced drivers/staff* ◇ *inexperienced in modern methods* ▶ **niedoświadczony** OPP **experienced**

inexpert /ɪn'ekspɜːt/ adj. without much skill: *an inexpert dancer* ▶ **niewprawny, niefachowy** ➲ look at **expert**
■ **inexpertly** adv. ▶ **niewprawnie, niefachowo**

inexplicable /ˌɪnɪk'splɪkəbl/ adj. that cannot be explained: *Her sudden disappearance is quite inexplicable.* ▶ **niewytłumaczalny** OPP **explicable**
■ **inexplicably** /-əbli/ adv. ▶ **nie do wytłumaczenia, w sposób niewytłumaczalny**

infallible /ɪn'fæləbl/ adj. **1** (used about a person) never making mistakes or being wrong: *Even the most careful typist is not infallible.* ▶ **nieomylny 2** always doing what you want it to do; never failing: *No computer is infallible.* ▶ **niezawodny** OPP for both meanings **fallible**
■ **infallibility** /ɪnˌfælə'bɪləti/ noun [U] ▶ **nieomylność; niezawodność**

infamous /'ɪnfəməs/ adj. **infamous (for sth)** famous for being bad: *The area is infamous for crime.* ▶ **niesławny, haniebny** SYN **notorious** ➲ look at **famous**

infamy /'ɪnfəmi/ noun (pl. **-ies**) (formal) **1** [U] the state of being well known for sth bad or evil: *a day that will live in infamy* ▶ **niesława 2** [U,C] evil behaviour; an evil act: *scenes of horror and infamy* ▶ **niegodziwość**

infancy /'ɪnfənsi/ noun [U] the time when you are a baby or young child: (figurative) *Research in this field is still in its infancy* (w powijakach). ▶ **niemowlęctwo**

infant /'ɪnfənt/ noun [C] a baby or very young child: *There is a high rate of infant mortality* (wysoki wskaźnik umieralności noworodków). ◇ *Mrs Davies teaches infants.* ◇ *2 adults, 2 children, 1 infant* ▶ **niemowlę; małe dziecko**
ⓘ W języku codziennym częściej używa się określeń **baby, toddler** lub **child.**

infantile /'ɪnfəntaɪl/ adj. (used about behaviour) typical of, or connected with, a baby or very young child and therefore not appropriate for adults or older children: *infantile jokes* ▶ **infantylny, dziecinny**

infantry /'ɪnfəntri/ noun [U, with sing. or pl. verb] soldiers who fight on foot: *The infantry was/were supported by heavy gunfire.* ▶ **piechota**

'infant school noun [C] a school for children between the ages of 4 and 7 ▶ **niższy oddział szkoły podstawowej**

> Brytyjska szkoła podstawowa ma dwa oddziały: **infants/the infant school** dla dzieci w wieku 4-7 lat i **juniors/the junior school** dla dzieci w wieku 7-11 lat.

infatuated /ɪn'fætʃueɪtɪd/ adj. **infatuated (with sb/sth)** having a very strong feeling of love or attraction for sb/sth that usually does not last long and makes you unable to think about anything else: *The young girl was infatuated with one of her teachers.* ▶ **zadurzony**
■ **infatuation** /ɪnˌfætʃu'eɪʃn/ noun [C,U] ▶ **zadurzenie**

🔑 **infect** /ɪn'fekt/ verb [T] **1** [usually passive] **infect sb/sth (with sth)** to cause sb/sth to have a disease or illness: *We must clean the wound before it becomes infected.* ◇ *Many thousands of people have been infected with the virus.* ▶ **zakażać, zarażać 2** to make people share a particular feeling or emotion: *Paul's happiness infected* (udzieliła się) *the whole family.* ▶ (*przen.*) **zarażać**

infected /ɪn'fektɪd/ adj. containing harmful bacteria ▶ **zakażony**

🔑 **infection** /ɪn'fekʃn/ noun **1** [U] the act of becoming or making sb ill: *A dirty water supply can be a source of infection.* ◇ *There is a danger of infection.* ▶ **infekcja, zakażenie 2** [C] a disease or illness that is caused by harmful bacteria, etc. and affects one part of your body: *She is suffering from a chest infection.* ◇ *an ear infection* ▶ **infekcja**

> Infections can be caused by **bacteria** or **viruses.** An informal word for these is **germs.**

🔑 **infectious** /ɪn'fekʃəs/ adj. (used about a disease, illness, etc.) that can be easily passed on to another person: *Flu is a highly infectious disease.* ◇ (figurative) *infectious laughter* ▶ **zaraźliwy, zakaźny** ➲ look at **contagious**

infer /ɪn'fɜː(r)/ verb [T] (**inferring**; **inferred**) **infer sth (from sth)** to form an opinion or decide that sth is true from the information you have: *I inferred from our conversation that he was unhappy with his job.* ▶ **wnioskować**
■ **inference** /'ɪnfərəns/ noun [C] ▶ **wniosek**

inferior /ɪn'fɪəriə(r)/ adj. **inferior (to sb/sth)** low or lower in social position, importance, quality, etc.: *This material is obviously inferior to that one.* ◇ *Don't let people make you* ***feel inferior.*** ▶ **niższy** (*w hierarchii*), **gorszy** OPP **superior**
■ **inferior** noun [C]: *She always treats me as her intellectual inferior* (jako osobę intelektualnie gorszą). ▶ **podwładn-y/a, osoba o niższej/gorszej pozycji** (*np. społecznej*) | **inferiority** /ɪnˌfɪəri'ɒrəti/ noun [U] ▶ **niższość, gorszy gatunek**

inferi'ority complex noun [C] the state of feeling less important, clever, successful, etc. than other people ▶ **kompleks niższości**

infertile /ɪn'fɜːtaɪl; US -tl/ adj. **1** (used about a person or an animal) not able to have babies or produce young ▶ **bezpłodny 2** (used about land) not able to grow strong healthy plants ▶ **nieurodzajny** OPP for both meanings **fertile**
■ **infertility** /ˌɪnfɜː'tɪləti/ noun [U]: *infertility treatment* ▶ **bezpłodność; nieurodzajność** OPP **fertility**

infest /ɪn'fest/ verb [T, usually passive] (especially of insects or animals such as **rats**) to exist in large numbers in a particular place, often causing damage or disease: *shark-infested waters* wody rojące się od rekinów ◇ *The kitchen was infested with ants.* ▶ (*insekty, inne szkodniki*) **atakować**
■ **infestation** /ˌɪnfe'steɪʃn/ noun [C, U] ▶ **plaga**

infested /ɪn'festɪd/ adj. **infested (with sth)** (used about a place) with large numbers of unpleasant animals or insects in it: *The warehouse was infested with rats.* ▶ **opanowany (przez coś), rojący się (od czegoś)**

infidelity /ˌɪnfɪ'deləti/ noun [U,C] (pl. **infidelities**) the act of not being faithful to your wife, husband or partner, by having a sexual relationship with sb else ▶ **niewierność** ⓘ Słowo mniej formalne to **unfaithfulness.**

infiltrate /'ɪnfɪltreɪt/ verb [T] to enter an organization, etc. secretly so that you can find out what it is doing: *The police managed to infiltrate the gang of terrorists.* ▶ **przenikać, infiltrować**
■ **infiltration** /ˌɪnfɪl'treɪʃn/ noun [C,U] ▶ **przeniknięcie, infiltracja, przenikanie** | **infiltrator** /'ɪnfɪltreɪtə(r)/ noun [C] ▶ **osoba dokonująca infiltracji**

infinite /'ɪnfɪnət/ adj. **1** very great: *You need infinite patience for this job.* ▶ **niewyczerpany, ogromny 2** without limits; that never ends: *Supplies of oil are not infinite.* ▶ **nieograniczony, nieskończony** OPP for both meanings **finite**

infinitely /ˈɪnfɪnətli/ adv. very much: *Compact discs sound infinitely better than audio cassettes.* ▶ **nieskończenie, o wiele**

infinitive /ɪnˈfɪnətɪv/ noun [C] the basic form of a verb ▶ **bezokolicznik** ⓘ Bezokolicznika używa się zarówno z **to**, jak i bez **to** w zależności od poprzedzającego słowa: *He can sing.* ◇ *He wants to sing.*

infinity /ɪnˈfɪnəti/ noun **1** [U] space or time without end: (figurative) *The ocean seemed to stretch over the horizon into infinity.* ▶ **bezkres, wieczność 2** [U,C] (symbol ∞) (in mathematics) the number that is larger than any other ▶ **nieskończoność**

infirm /ɪnˈfɜːm/ adj. ill or weak, e.g. because of old age ▶ **niedołężny**
■ **infirmity** /ɪnˈfɜːməti/ noun [C,U] (pl. **infirmities**) weakness or illness ▶ **niedołężność, niemoc**

infirmary /ɪnˈfɜːməri/ noun [C] (pl. **infirmaries**) (used mainly in names) a hospital: *The Manchester Royal Infirmary* ▶ **szpital**

inflame /ɪnˈfleɪm/ verb [T] (formal) **1** to cause very strong feelings, especially anger or excitement, in a person or in a group of people: *His comments have inflamed teachers all over the country.* ◇ *The latest revelations are set to inflame* (rozjuszą) *public opinion still further.* ▶ **rozpalać** (*uczucia*) **2** to make a situation worse or more difficult to deal with: *The situation was further inflamed by the arrival of the security forces.* ▶ **zaogniać**

inflamed /ɪnˈfleɪmd/ adj. (used about a part of the body) red and swollen or painful because of an infection or injury ▶ **zaogniony, w stanie zapalnym**

inflammable /ɪnˈflæməbl/ adj. that burns easily: *Petrol is highly inflammable.* ▶ **łatwopalny** ⓘ Uwaga! **Flammable** ma to samo znaczenie, ale jest rzadziej używane. OPP **non-flammable**

inflammation /ˌɪnfləˈmeɪʃn/ noun [C,U] a condition in which a part of the body becomes red, sore and swollen because of infection or injury ▶ **zapalenie**

inflatable /ɪnˈfleɪtəbl/ adj. that can or must be filled with air: *an inflatable dinghy/mattress* ▶ **nadmuchiwany, pneumatyczny**

inflate /ɪnˈfleɪt/ verb [I,T] (formal) to fill sth with air; to become filled with air ▶ **napompowywać; nadymać (się)** ⓘ Mniej formalne słowo to **blow up**. OPP **deflate**

inflation /ɪnˈfleɪʃn/ noun [U] a general rise in prices; the rate at which prices rise: *the inflation rate/rate of inflation* ◇ *Inflation now stands at 3%.* ▶ **inflacja**

inflection (also **inflexion**) /ɪnˈflekʃn/ noun **1** [U] the act of changing the ending or form of a word to show its grammatical function ▶ **fleksja, odmiana 2** [C,U] something that is added to a word that changes its grammatical function, e.g. *-ed*, *-est* ▶ **końcówka fleksyjna 3** [C,U] the rise and fall of your voice when you are talking ▶ **modulacja** (*głosu*) SYN **intonation**

inflexible /ɪnˈfleksəbl/ adj. **1** that cannot be changed or made more suitable for a particular situation: *He has a very inflexible attitude to change.* ▶ (*przen.*) **nieelastyczny, sztywny 2** (used about a material) difficult or impossible to bend ▶ **nieelastyczny** SYN for both meanings **rigid** OPP for both meanings **flexible**
■ **inflexibility** /ɪnˌfleksəˈbɪləti/ noun [U] ▶ **nieelastyczność, sztywność** | **inflexibly** /ɪnˈfleksəbli/ adv. ▶ **nieelastycznie, sztywno**

inflict /ɪnˈflɪkt/ verb [T] **inflict sth (on sb)** to force sb to have sth unpleasant or that they do not want: *Don't inflict your problems on me – I've got enough of my own.* ▶ **narzucać** (*np. swoje poglądy*), **zadawać** (*np. ból*)

ˈin-flight adj. [only before a noun] happening or provided during a journey in a plane: *in-flight entertainment* program rozrywek na pokładzie samolotu, np. projekcja filmów ▶ **podczas lotu**

influence¹ /ˈɪnfluəns/ noun **1** [U,C] **(an) influence (on/upon sb/sth)** the power to affect, change or control sb/sth: *TV can have a strong influence on children.* ◇ *Nobody should drive while they are **under the influence of** alcohol.* ▶ **wpływ 2** [C] **an influence (on sb/sth)** a person or thing that affects or changes sb/sth: *cultural/environmental influences* ◇ *His new girlfriend has been a good influence on him* (ma na niego dobry wpływ). ▶ **czynnik/osoba wywierająca-y/a wpływ**

influence² /ˈɪnfluəns/ verb [T] to have an effect on or power over sb/sth so that he/she/it changes: *You must decide for yourself. Don't let anyone else influence you.* ◇ *Her style of painting has been influenced by Japanese art.* ▶ **wpływać, oddziaływać**

> Czasowniki **affect** i **influence** mają podobne znaczenie. Czasownika **affect** zwykle używa się opisując zmiany materialne, podczas gdy **influence** odnosi się najczęściej do zmiany uczuć czy opinii: *Drinking alcohol can affect your ability to drive.* ◇ *The TV advertisements have influenced my attitude towards drinking and driving.*

influential /ˌɪnfluˈenʃl/ adj. **influential (in sth/in doing sth)** having power or influence: *an influential politician* ◇ *He was influential* (miał duży wpływ) *in getting the hostages set free.* ▶ **wpływowy, wywierający wpływ**

influenza (formal) = FLU

influx /ˈɪnflʌks/ noun [C, usually sing.] **an influx (of sb/sth) (into ...)** large numbers of people or things arriving suddenly: *the summer influx of visitors from abroad* ▶ **napływ**

inform /ɪnˈfɔːm/ verb [T] **inform sb (of/about sth)** to give sb information (about sth), especially in an official way: *You should inform the police of the accident.* ◇ *Do **keep** me **informed*** (informuj mnie) *of any changes.* ▶ **informować, powiadamiać**
PHR V **inform on sb** to give information to the police, etc. about what sb has done wrong: *The wife of the killer informed on her husband.* ▶ **donosić na kogoś**

informal /ɪnˈfɔːml/ adj. relaxed and friendly or suitable for a relaxed occasion: *Don't get dressed up for the party – it'll be very informal.* ◇ *The two leaders had informal discussions before the conference began.* ▶ **nieformalny, nieoficjalny**

> Niektóre słowa i wyrażenia w tym słowniku opisane są jako (*informal*). Oznacza to, że można ich używać w rozmowach z przyjaciółmi czy znajomymi, ale nie powinno się ich używać w piśmie lub w sytuacjach oficjalnych. OPP **formal**

■ **informality** /ˌɪnfɔːˈmæləti/ noun [U]: *an atmosphere of informality* atmosfera spotkania towarzyskiego ▶ **nieformalność, nieoficjalność** | **informally** /-məli/ adv.: *I was told informally that our plans had been accepted.* ▶ **nieformalnie, nieoficjalnie**

informant /ɪnˈfɔːmənt/ noun [C] a person who gives secret knowledge or information about sb/sth to the police or a newspaper: *The journalist refused to name his informant.* ▶ **informator/ka** ➲ look at **informer**

information /ˌɪnfəˈmeɪʃn/ noun [U] **information (on/about sb/sth)** knowledge or facts: *For further information please send for our fact sheet.* ◇ *Can you give me some information about evening classes in Italian, please?* ▶ **informacja, wiadomość** ⓘ Uwaga! Rzeczownik **information** jest niepoliczalny. Nie dodaje się do niego końcówki **s**. Nie można powiedzieć ~~*I need an information*~~. Zamiast tego używa się wyrażeń **a bit/a piece of information**.

inforˌmation techˈnology noun [U] (abbr. **IT** /ˌaɪ ˈtiː/) the study or use of electronic equipment, especially computers, for collecting, storing and sending out information ▶ **informatyka**

informative /ɪnˈfɔːmətɪv/ adj. giving useful knowledge or information ▶ **informacyjny, pouczający**

informed /ɪnˈfɔːmd/ adj. having knowledge or information about sth: *Consumers cannot make informed choices* (nie mogą dokonać przemyślanego wyboru) *unless they are told all the facts.* ▶ **poinformowany, oparty na posiadanej wiedzy**

informer /ɪnˈfɔːmə(r)/ noun [C] a criminal who gives the police information about other criminals ▶ **donosiciel/ka** ➲ look at **informant**

infrared /ˌɪnfrəˈred/ adj. (used about light) that produces heat but that you cannot see: *infrared radiation* ◇ *an infrared lamp* ▶ **podczerwony** ➲ look at **ultraviolet**

infrastructure /ˈɪnfrəstrʌktʃə(r)/ noun [C,U] the basic systems and services that are necessary for a country or an organization to run smoothly, for example transport, and water and power supplies ▶ **infrastruktura**

infrequent /ɪnˈfriːkwənt/ adj. not happening often ▶ **rzadki, nieczęsty** OPP **frequent**
■ **infrequently** adv. ▶ **rzadko, nieczęsto**

infringe /ɪnˈfrɪndʒ/ verb (formal) **1** [T] to break a rule, law, agreement, etc.: *The material can be copied without infringing copyright.* ▶ **naruszać** (*np. prawo*) **2** [I] **infringe on/upon sth** to reduce or limit sb's rights, freedom, etc.: *She refused to answer questions that infringed on her private affairs.* ▶ **ograniczać, naruszać** (*np. czyjeś prawa*)
■ **infringement** noun [C,U] ▶ **naruszenie** (*np. prawa*)

infuriate /ɪnˈfjʊərieɪt/ verb [T] to make sb very angry ▶ **rozwścieczyć, wzburzyć**
■ **infuriating** adj.: *an infuriating habit* ▶ **doprowadzający do wściekłości/szału** | **infuriatingly** adv. ▶ **w sposób doprowadzający do wściekłości**

infuse /ɪnˈfjuːz/ verb **1** [T] (formal) **infuse A into B**; **infuse B with A** to make sb/sth have a particular quality: *Her novels are infused with sadness.* ▶ (*przen.*) **przepełniać 2** [T] (formal) to have an effect on all parts of sth: *Politics infuses all aspects of our lives.* ▶ **dotyczyć czegoś, mieć wpływ na coś 3** [I,T] if you **infuse herbs**, etc. or they **infuse**, you put them in hot water until their flavour has passed into the water ▶ (*herbata itp.*) **parzyć; naciągać**

infusion /ɪnˈfjuːʒn/ noun **1** [C,U] (formal) **infusion of sth (into sth)** the act of adding sth to sth else in order to make it stronger or more successful: *a cash infusion into the business* ◇ *an infusion of new talent into science education* ▶ (*przen.*) **zastrzyk 2** [C] a drink or medicine made by leaving **herbs**, etc. in hot water ▶ **napar, wyciąg**

ingenious /ɪnˈdʒiːniəs/ adj. **1** (used about a thing or an idea) made or planned in a clever way: *an ingenious plan for making lots of money* ◇ *an ingenious device/experiment/invention* ▶ **pomysłowy 2** (used about a person) full of new ideas and clever at finding solutions to problems or at inventing things ▶ **pomysłowy**
■ **ingeniously** adv. ▶ **pomysłowo** | **ingenuity** /ˌɪndʒəˈnjuːəti; US -ˈnuː-/ noun [U] ▶ **pomysłowość**

ingenuous /ɪnˈdʒenjuəs/ adj. (formal) honest, innocent and willing to trust people: *You're too ingenuous.* ◇ *an ingenuous smile* ▶ **prostoduszny, naiwny** SYN **naive** ➲ look at **disingenuous** ℹ Czasami wyraża dezaprobatę.
■ **ingenuously** adv. ▶ **prostodusznie, naiwnie**

ingrained /ɪnˈgreɪnd/ adj. **ingrained (in sb/sth)** (used about a habit, an attitude, etc.) that has existed for a long time and is therefore difficult to change: *ingrained prejudices/beliefs* ▶ **zakorzeniony (w kimś/czymś)**

ingratiate /ɪnˈgreɪʃieɪt/ verb [T] (formal) **ingratiate yourself (with sb)** to make yourself liked by doing or saying things that will please people, especially people who might be useful to you: *He was always trying to ingratiate himself with his teachers.* ▶ **wkradać się (w czyjeś łaski)**
■ **ingratiating** adj.: *an ingratiating smile* ▶ **przymilny** | **ingratiatingly** adv. ▶ **przymilnie**

ingratitude /ɪnˈgrætɪtjuːd; US -tuːd/ noun [U] (formal) the state of not showing or feeling thanks for sth that has been done for you; not being grateful ▶ **niewdzięczność** ℹ Mniej formalnym słowem jest **ungratefulness**. OPP **gratitude**

⚷ **ingredient** /ɪnˈgriːdiənt/ noun [C] **1** one of the items of food you need to make sth to eat: *Mix all the ingredients together in a bowl.* ▶ (*kulin.*) **składnik 2** one of the qualities necessary to make sth successful: *The film has all the ingredients of success.* ▶ (*przen.*) **składnik**

inhabit /ɪnˈhæbɪt/ verb [T] to live in a place: *Are the Aran Islands still inhabited?* ▶ **zamieszkiwać**

inhabitant /ɪnˈhæbɪtənt/ noun [C, usually pl.] a person or an animal that lives in a place: *The local inhabitants protested at the plans for a new motorway.* ▶ **mieszkan-iec/ka**

> Pytając o liczbę ludności w danym miejscu, należy powiedzieć: *What is the population of…?*, a nie ~~*How many inhabitants are there in…?*~~ Jednak odpowiadając na to pytanie, można powiedzieć: *The population is 10 000./It has 10 000 inhabitants.*

inhale /ɪnˈheɪl/ verb [I,T] to breathe in: *Be careful not to inhale the fumes from the paint.* ▶ **wdychać** OPP **exhale**

inhaler /ɪnˈheɪlə(r)/ noun [C] a small device containing medicine that you breathe in through your mouth, used by people who have problems with breathing ▶ **inhalator**

inherent /ɪnˈhɪərənt; Brit. also -ˈher-/ adj. **inherent (in sb/sth)** that is a basic or permanent part of sb/sth and that cannot be removed: *The risk of collapse is inherent in any* (jest nieodłącznym elementem każdego) *business.* ▶ **nieodłączny, właściwy (komuś/czemuś)**
■ **inherently** adv.: *No matter how safe we make them, cars are inherently dangerous.* ▶ **nieodłącznie, z natury**

inherit /ɪnˈherɪt/ verb [T] **inherit sth (from sb) 1** to receive property, money, etc. from sb who has died: *I inherited quite a lot of money from my mother. She left me $12 000 when she died.* ▶ **dziedziczyć, dostawać w spadku** ℹ Osoba, która dziedziczy po kimś, to **heir**. **2** to receive a quality, characteristic, etc. from your parents or family: *She has inherited her father's gift for languages.* ▶ **dziedziczyć** (*np. talent*) ➲ look at **hereditary, heredity**

inheritance /ɪnˈherɪtəns/ noun [C,U] the act of **inheriting**; the money, property, etc. that you **inherit**: *inheritance tax* podatek spadkowy ▶ **dziedziczenie; dziedzictwo, spadek**

inhibit /ɪnˈhɪbɪt/ verb [T] **1** to prevent sth or make sth happen more slowly: *a drug to inhibit the growth of tumours* ▶ **hamować, wstrzymywać; 2 inhibit sb (from sth/from doing sth)** to make sb nervous and embarrassed so that they are unable to do sth: *The fact that her boss was there inhibited her from saying what she really felt.* ▶ **powstrzymywać kogoś (przed czymś)**
■ **inhibited** adj.: *The young man felt shy and inhibited in the roomful of women.* ▶ **mający zahamowania, spięty** OPP **uninhibited**

inhibition /ˌɪnhɪˈbɪʃn; ˌɪnɪˈb-/ noun [C,U] a shy or nervous feeling that stops you from saying or doing what you really want: *After the first morning of the course, people started to* ***lose their inhibitions*** (pozbywać się swoich zahamowań). ▶ **zahamowanie**

inhospitable /ˌɪnhɒˈspɪtəbl/ adj. **1** (used about a place) not pleasant to live in, especially because of the weather:

the inhospitable Arctic regions ▶ (*rejon itp.*) **surowy, nieprzyjazny** **2** (used about a person) not friendly or welcoming to guests ▶ **niegościnny** OPP for both meanings **hospitable**

inhuman /ɪnˈhjuːmən/ adj. **1** very cruel and without pity: *inhuman treatment/conditions* ▶ **nieludzki, okrutny** **2** not seeming to be human and therefore frightening: *an inhuman noise* ▶ **nieludzki**

inhumane /ˌɪnhjuːˈmeɪn/ adj. very cruel; not caring if people or animals suffer: *the inhumane conditions in which animals are kept on some large farms* ▶ **niehumanitarny, okrutny** OPP **humane**

inhumanity /ˌɪnhjuːˈmænəti/ noun [U] very cruel behaviour: *The 20th century is full of examples of man's inhumanity to man.* ▶ **okrucieństwo, bestialstwo** OPP **humanity**

inimical /ɪˈnɪmɪkl/ adj. (formal) **1** **inimical to sth** harmful to sth; not helping sth: *These policies are inimical to the interests of society.* ▶ **niesprzyjający czemuś** **2** unfriendly: *an inimical stare* ▶ **nieprzychylny**

inimitable /ɪˈnɪmɪtəbl/ adj. too good or individual for anyone else to copy with the same effect: *John related in his own* ***inimitable way*** *the story of his trip to Tibet.* ▶ **niepowtarzalny, niezrównany**

⚷ **initial¹** /ɪˈnɪʃl/ adj. [only before a noun] happening at the beginning; first: *My initial reaction was to refuse, but I later changed my mind.* ◇ *the initial stages of our survey* ▶ **początkowy, wstępny**

⚷ **initial²** /ɪˈnɪʃl/ noun [C, usually pl.] the first letter of a name: *Alison Elizabeth Waters' initials are A.E.W.* ▶ **inicjał, pierwsza litera**

initial³ /ɪˈnɪʃl/ verb [T] (**initialling; initialled**; US **initialing; initialed**) to mark or sign sth with your **initials**: *Any changes made when writing a cheque should be initialled by you.* ▶ **podpisywać się inicjałami, parafować**

⚷ **initially** /ɪˈnɪʃəli/ adv. at the beginning; at first: *I liked the job initially but it soon got quite boring.* ▶ **początkowo, wstępnie**

initiate /ɪˈnɪʃieɪt/ verb [T] **1** (formal) to start sth: *to initiate peace talks* ▶ **zapoczątkowywać, inicjować** **2** **initiate sb (into sth)** to explain sth to sb or make them experience sth for the first time: *I wasn't initiated into the joys of skiing until I was 30.* ▶ **wprowadzać kogoś** (*w arkana czegoś*) **3** **initiate sb (into sth)** to bring sb into a group by means of a special ceremony: *to initiate somebody into a secret society* ▶ **wprowadzać kogoś (do czegoś), dokonywać czyjejś inicjacji (w coś)**

■ **initiation** /ɪˌnɪʃiˈeɪʃn/ noun [U]: *All the new students had to go through a strange* ***initiation ceremony.*** ▶ **zapoczątkowanie, inicjacja**

⚷ **initiative** /ɪˈnɪʃətɪv/ noun **1** [C] a new plan for solving a problem or improving a situation: *a new government initiative to help people start small businesses* ▶ **inicjatywa** **2** [U] the ability to see and do what is necessary without waiting for sb to tell you: *Don't keep asking me how to do it. Use your initiative.* ▶ **inicjatywa, pomysłowość** **3** (**the initiative**) [sing.] the stronger position because you have done sth first; the advantage: *to take/lose the initiative* ▶ **przewaga, inicjatywa**

IDM **on your own initiative** without being told by sb else what to do ▶ **z własnej inicjatywy**

take the initiative to be first to act to influence a situation: *Let's take the initiative and start organizing things now.* ▶ **występować z inicjatywą**

inject /ɪnˈdʒekt/ verb [T] **1** to put a drug under the skin of a person's or an animal's body with a **syringe** ▶ **dawać zastrzyk** **2** **inject sth (into sth)** to add sth: *They injected a lot of money* (wpompowali mnóstwo pieniędzy) *into the business.* ▶ (*przen.*) **dawać zastrzyk (czegoś)**

injection /ɪnˈdʒekʃn/ noun **1** [C,U] **(an) injection (of sth) (into sb/sth)** the act of **injecting** a drug or other substance: *to give somebody an injection of penicillin* ◇ *a tetanus injection* zastrzyk przeciwtężcowy ◇ *An anaesthetic was administered* ***by injection*** (w formie zastrzyku). ▶ **zastrzyk** SYN **jab** **2** [C] a large amount of sth that is added to sth to help it: *The theatre needs a huge* ***cash injection*** *if it is to stay open.* ▶ (*przen.*) **zastrzyk** **3** [U,C] the act of forcing liquid into sth: *fuel injection* ▶ **wtrysk**

injunction /ɪnˈdʒʌŋkʃn/ noun [C] **an injunction (against sb)** an official order from a court of law to do/not do sth: *An injunction prevented the programme from being shown on TV.* ▶ **nakaz/zakaz sądowy**

⚷ **injure** /ˈɪndʒə(r)/ verb [T] to harm or hurt yourself or sb else physically, especially in an accident: *The goalkeeper seriously injured himself when he hit the goalpost.* ◇ *She fell and injured her back* (zraniła się w plecy). ▶ **ranić, kaleczyć** ➲ note at **hurt**

⚷ **injured** /ˈɪndʒəd/ adj. **1** physically or mentally hurt: *an injured arm/leg* ◇ *injured pride* ▶ **zraniony; urażony** **2** (**the injured**) noun [pl.] people who have been hurt: *The injured were rushed to hospital.* ▶ **ranni**

⚷ **injury** /ˈɪndʒəri/ noun [C,U] (pl. **injuries**) **injury (to sb/sth)** harm done to a person's or an animal's body, especially in an accident: *They escaped from the accident with only* ***minor injuries*** (lekkie obrażenia). ◇ *serious injury/injuries* ◇ *injury to the head* ▶ **rana**

ˈinjury time noun [U] (Brit.) time that is added to the end of a football, etc. match when there has been time lost because of injuries to players ▶ (*sport*) **doliczony czas**

injustice /ɪnˈdʒʌstɪs/ noun [U,C] the fact of a situation being unfair; an unfair act: *racial/social injustice* ◇ *People are protesting about the injustice of the new tax.* ◇ *The report exposed the injustices of the system.* ▶ **niesprawiedliwość; krzywda**

IDM **do sb an injustice** to judge sb unfairly: *I'm afraid I've done you both an injustice.* ▶ **wyrządzać komuś krzywdę**

⚷ **ink** /ɪŋk/ noun [U,C] coloured liquid that is used for writing, drawing, etc.: *Please write* ***in ink*** (atramentem), *not pencil.* ▶ **atrament**

inkling /ˈɪŋklɪŋ/ noun [usually sing.] **an inkling (of sth/that ...)** a slight feeling (about sth): *I had an inkling that something was wrong.* ▶ **przeczucie, przypuszczenie**

inky /ˈɪŋki/ adj. **1** made black with ink: *inky fingers* ▶ **poplamiony atramentem** **2** very dark: *an inky night sky* ▶ **czarny jak atrament**

inland /ˈɪnlænd/ /ˌɪnˈlænd/ adj. away from the coast or borders of a country ▶ **śródlądowy**

■ **inland** adv.: *The village lies twenty miles inland.* ◇ *Goods are carried inland along narrow mountain roads.* ▶ **w głąb/głębi kraju/lądu**

ˌInland ˈRevenue noun [sing.] (Brit.) the government department that collects taxes ▶ **urząd skarbowy**

ˈin-laws noun [pl.] (informal) your husband's or wife's mother and father or other relatives: *My in-laws are coming to lunch on Sunday.* ▶ **teściowie, krewni żony lub męża**

inlet /ˈɪnlet/ noun [C] **1** a narrow area of water that stretches into the land from the sea or a lake, or between islands ▶ **przesmyk, zatoczka** **2** an opening through which liquid, air or gas can enter a machine: *a fuel inlet* ▶ (*techn.*) ▶ **wlot** OPP **outlet**

inmate /ˈɪnmeɪt/ noun [C] one of the people living in an institution such as a prison ▶ **pensjonariusz/ka, więzień/źniarka**

inn /ɪn/ noun [C] (Brit.) a small hotel or old pub usually in the country ▶ **gospoda, zajazd**

innate /ɪ'neɪt/ adj. (used about an ability or a quality) that you have when you are born: *the innate ability to learn* ▶ **wrodzony**

inner /'ɪnə(r)/ adj. [only before a noun] **1** (of the) inside; towards or close to the centre of a place: *an inner courtyard* ◇ *The inner ear* (ucho środkowe) *is very delicate.* ▶ **wewnętrzny** OPP **outer 2** (used about a feeling, etc.) that you do not express or show to other people; private: *Everyone has inner doubts.* ▶ (*przen.*) **wewnętrzny**, (*uczucia itp.*) **skryty**

ˌinner 'city noun [C] the poor parts of a large city, near the centre, that often have a lot of social problems ▶ **podupadłe dzielnice śródmieścia**
■ **inner-city** adj. [only before a noun]: *Inner-city schools often have difficulty in attracting good teachers.* ▶ **dotyczący podupadłych dzielnic śródmieścia**

innermost /'ɪnəməʊst/ adj. [only before a noun] **1** (used about a feeling or thought) most secret or private: *She never told anyone her innermost thoughts.* ▶ **najskrytszy**, **najgłębszy 2** nearest to the centre or inside of sth: *the innermost shrine of the temple* ▶ **najgłębszy**, **znajdujący się najbliżej centrum**

innings /'ɪnɪŋz/ noun [C] (pl. **innings**) a period of time in a game of **cricket** when it is the turn of one player or team to **bat** ▶ **kolej na uderzenie piłki przez danego zawodnika lub drużynę**

innit /'ɪnɪt/ exclamation (Brit.) (a way of saying 'isn't it'): *Cold, innit?* ▶ **nieprawdaż** ℹ To wyrażenie jest bardzo potoczne.

innocence /'ɪnəsns/ noun [U] **1** the fact of not being guilty of a crime, etc.: *The accused man* ***protested*** *his* ***innocence*** (utrzymywał, że jest niewinny) *throughout his trial.* ▶ **niewinność** OPP **guilt 2** lack of knowledge and experience of the world, especially of bad things: *the innocence of childhood* ▶ **niewinność**

innocent /'ɪnəsnt/ adj. **1 innocent (of sth)** not having done wrong: *An innocent man was arrested by mistake.* ◇ *to be innocent of a crime* ▶ **niewinny (czegoś)** SYN **blameless** OPP **guilty 2** [only before a noun] being hurt or killed in a crime, war, etc. although not involved in it in any way: ***innocent victims*** *of a bomb blast* ◇ *He was an innocent bystander.* ▶ **przypadkowy**, **niewinny 3** not wanting to cause harm or upset sb, although it does: *He got very aggressive when I asked an* ***innocent question*** *about his past life.* ▶ **niewinny**, **nieszkodliwy 4** not knowing the bad things in life; believing everything you are told: *She was so innocent as to believe that politicians never lie.* ▶ **niewinny**, **naiwny** SYN **naive**
■ **innocently** adv.: *'What are you doing here?' she asked innocently.* ▶ **naiwnie**, **niewinnie**

innocuous /ɪ'nɒkjuəs/ adj. (formal) not meant to cause harm or upset sb: *I made an* ***innocuous remark*** *about teachers and she got really angry.* ▶ (*substancja itp.*) **nieszkodliwy**; (*uwaga itp.*) **niewinny** SYN **harmless**
■ **innocuously** adv. ▶ **nieszkodliwie**; **niewinnie**

innovate /'ɪnəveɪt/ verb [I] to create new things, ideas or ways of doing sth ▶ **wprowadzać innowacje/zmiany**
■ **innovation** /ˌɪnə'veɪʃn/ noun [C,U] **(an) innovation (in sth)** [C]: *technological innovations in industry* ▶ **innowacja** | **innovative** /'ɪnəveɪtɪv; Brit. also -vətɪv/ (also **innovatory** /ˌɪnə'veɪtəri; US also 'ɪnəvətɔːri/) adj.: *innovative methods/designs/products* ▶ **innowacyjny** | **innovator** /'ɪnəveɪtə(r)/ noun [C] ▶ **innowator/ka**

innuendo /ˌɪnju'endəʊ/ noun [C,U] (pl. **innuendoes** or **innuendos**) an indirect way of talking about sb/sth, usually suggesting sth bad or rude: *His speech was full of sexual innuendo.* ▶ **insynuacja**

innumerable /ɪ'njuːmərəbl; US ɪ'nuː-/ adj. too many to be counted ▶ **niezliczony**

inoculate /ɪ'nɒkjuleɪt/ verb [T] **inoculate sb (against sth)** to protect a person or an animal from a disease by giving them a mild form of the disease with an **injection**: *The children have been inoculated against tetanus.* ▶ **szczepić kogoś** ➲ look at **immunize**, **vaccinate**
■ **inoculation** /ɪˌnɒkju'leɪʃn/ noun [C,U] ▶ **szczepienie**

inoffensive /ˌɪnə'fensɪv/ adj. not likely to offend or upset sb: *a gentle and inoffensive man* ▶ **nieszkodliwy**, **niewinny** SYN **harmless** OPP **offensive**

inopportune /ɪn'ɒpətjuːn; US ɪnˌɑːpə'tuːn/ adj. (formal) happening at a bad time ▶ **niefortunny**, **nieodpowiedni** SYN **inappropriate**, **inconvenient** OPP **opportune**

inordinate /ɪn'ɔːdɪnət/ adj. (formal) much greater than usual or expected: *They spent an* ***inordinate amount*** *of* (nieproporcjonalnie dużo) *time and money on the production.* ▶ **nadmierny**, **wygórowany**
■ **inordinately** adv. ▶ **nadmiernie**

inorganic /ˌɪnɔː'gænɪk/ adj. not made of or coming from living things: *Rocks and metals are inorganic substances.* ▶ **nieorganiczny** OPP **organic**

input[1] /'ɪnpʊt/ noun **1** [C,U] **input (of sth) (into/to sth)** what you put into sth to make it successful: *We need some input from teachers into this book.* ▶ **wkład (w coś)**, **nakład (czegoś) 2** [U] the act of putting information into a computer: *The computer breakdown means we have lost the whole day's input.* ▶ **dane** (*wprowadzane do komputera*) ➲ look at **output**

input[2] /'ɪnpʊt/ verb [T] (**inputting**; pt, pp **input** or **inputted**) to put information into a computer: *to input text/data/figures* ▶ **wprowadzać** (*dane do komputera*)

inquest /'ɪŋkwest/ noun [C] an official process to find out how sb died: *to hold an inquest* ▶ **dochodzenie przyczyny zgonu**

inquire, **inquirer**, **inquiring**, **inquiry** (especially US) = ENQUIRE, ENQUIRER, ENQUIRING, ENQUIRY

inquisition /ˌɪnkwɪ'zɪʃn/ noun [C] (formal) a series of questions that sb asks you, especially when they ask them in an unpleasant way: *She then subjected me to an inquisition about my romantic life.* ▶ **przesłuchanie**, **przepytywanie**

inquisitive /ɪn'kwɪzətɪv/ adj. **1** too interested in finding out about what other people are doing: *Don't be so inquisitive. It's none of your business.* ▶ **wścibski** SYN **nosy 2** interested in finding out about many different things: *You need an inquisitive mind to be a scientist.* ▶ **dociekliwy** SYN **curious**
■ **inquisitively** adv. ▶ **wścibsko**; **dociekliwie** | **inquisitiveness** noun [U] ▶ **wścibstwo**; **dociekliwość**

insane /ɪn'seɪn/ adj. **1** seriously mentally ill ▶ **obłąkany**, **chory umysłowo 2** not showing sensible judgement: *You must be insane to leave such a great job.* ▶ **szalony** ➲ look at **mad**
■ **insanely** adv.: *insanely jealous* ▶ **szaleńczo**, **obłąkańczo** | **insanity** /ɪn'sænəti/ noun [U] ▶ **obłęd**; **szaleństwo**

insanitary /ɪn'sænətri; US -teri/ adj. (formal) dirty and likely to cause disease: *The restaurant was closed because of the insanitary conditions of the kitchen.* ▶ **niehigieniczny** ➲ look at **sanitary**

insatiable /ɪn'seɪʃəbl/ adj. that cannot be satisfied; very great: *an insatiable appetite* ◇ *an insatiable desire for knowledge* ▶ **nienasycony**, **niezaspokojony**

inscribe /ɪn'skraɪb/ verb [T] (formal) **inscribe A (on/in B)**; **inscribe B (with A)** to write on sth or cut words into the surface of sth: *The names of all the previous champions are inscribed on the cup.* ◇ *The book was inscribed with the author's name.* ▶ **wpisywać**, **ryć**

inscription /ɪn'skrɪpʃn/ noun [C] words that are written or cut on sth: *There was a Latin inscription on the tombstone.* ▶ **napis** (*wypisany lub wyryty*)

/ɪnˌsensəˈtɪvəti/ noun [U] ▶ **bezduszność, nieczułość**

inseparable /ɪnˈseprəbl/ adj. that cannot be separated from sb/sth: *inseparable friends* ▶ **nierozłączny, nieodłączny** OPP **separable**

insert /ɪnˈsɜːt/ verb [T] (formal) to put sth into sth or between two things: *I decided to insert a paragraph in the text.* ▶ **wkładać, wstawiać** (*np. dodatkowy tekst*)
■ **insertion** noun [C,U] ▶ **dopisek, wstawka, wkładanie**

inset /ˈɪnset/ noun [C] **1** a small picture, map, etc. inside a larger one: *For the Shetland Islands, see inset.* ▶ **ramka** (*zawierająca dodatkową informację, np. mapkę*) **2** something that is added on to sth else, or put inside sth else: *The windows have beautiful stained glass insets.* ▶ **wstawka**
■ **inset** verb (**insetting**; pt, pp **inset**) [T] **1** [usually passive] **inset A (with B); inset B (into A)** to fix sth into the surface of sth else, especially as a decoration: *The tables were inset with ceramic tiles.* ◇ *Ceramic tiles were inset into the tables.* ▶ **wstawiać 2 inset sth (into sth)** to put a small picture, map, etc. inside the borders of a bigger one ▶ **wstawiać coś (do czegoś)**

inshore /ˈɪnʃɔː(r); ˌɪnˈʃɔː(r)/ adj. in or towards the part of the sea that is close to the land: *inshore fishermen* ▶ **przybrzeżny**
■ **inshore** adv.: *Sharks don't often come inshore.* ▶ **ku brzegowi**

inside¹ /ˌɪnˈsaɪd/ prep., adv. **1** in, on or to the inner part or surface of sth: *Is there anything inside the box?* ◇ *It's safer to be inside the house in a thunderstorm.* ◇ *We'd bet-*

insect /ˈɪnsekt/ noun [C] a small animal with six legs, two pairs of wings and a body which is divided into three parts: *Ants, flies, beetles, butterflies and mosquitoes are all insects.* ◇ *an insect bite/sting* ▶ **owad, insekt** ⓘ Niektóre inne zwierzęta, np. pająki, też często są nazywane **insects**, chociaż jest to niepoprawne.

insecticide /ɪnˈsektɪsaɪd/ noun [C,U] a substance that is used for killing insects ▶ **środek owadobójczy** ➲ look at **pesticide**

insecure /ˌɪnsɪˈkjʊə(r)/ adj. **1 insecure (about sb/sth)** not confident about yourself or your relationships with other people: *Many teenagers are insecure about their appearance.* ▶ **niepewny (czegoś) 2** not safe or protected: *This ladder feels a bit insecure.* ◇ *The future of the company looks very insecure.* ▶ **niepewny, niezabezpieczony** OPP for both meanings **secure**
■ **insecurely** adv. ▶ **niepewnie** | **insecurity** /ˌɪnsɪˈkjʊərəti/ noun [U]: *Their aggressive behaviour is a sign of insecurity.* ▶ **brak pewności siebie** OPP **security**

insensitive /ɪnˈsensətɪv/ adj. **insensitive (to sth) 1** not knowing or caring how another person feels and therefore likely to hurt or upset them: *Some insensitive reporters tried to interview the families of the accident victims.* ◇ *an insensitive remark* ▶ **nietaktowny, nieczuły (na coś) 2** not able to feel or react to sth: *insensitive to pain/cold/criticism* ▶ **niewrażliwy (na coś)** OPP for both meanings **sensitive**
■ **insensitively** adv. ▶ **nietaktownie** | **insensitivity**

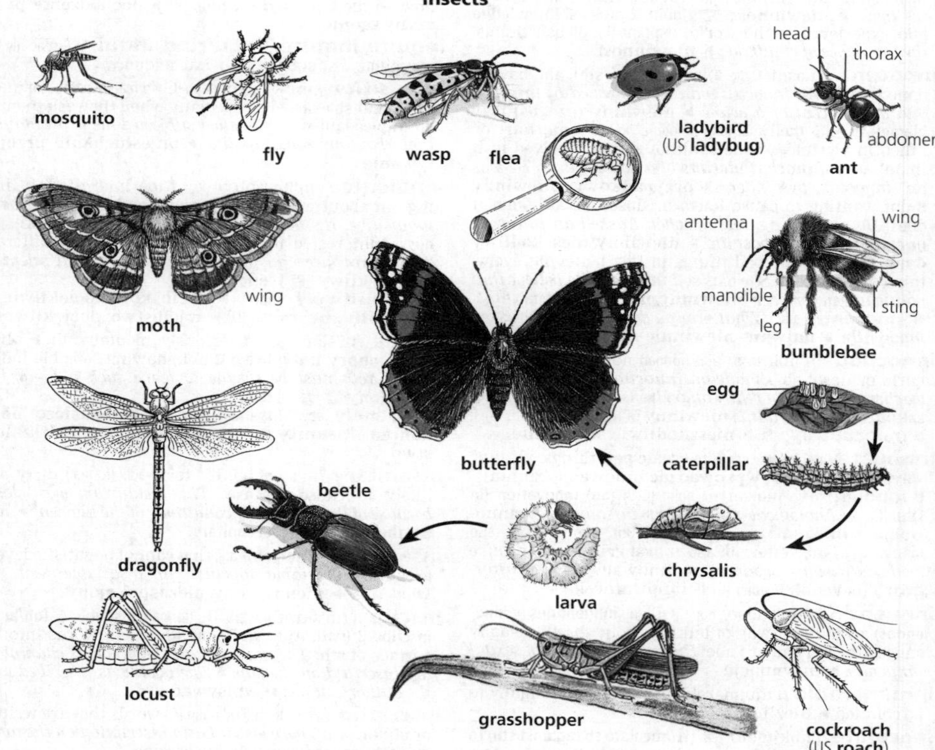

ter stay inside until the rain stops. ◇ *It's getting cold. Let's go inside.* ▶ **(do) wewnątrz**, **w środku**, **do środka** OPP **outside 2** (formal) (used about time) in less than; within: *Your photos will be ready inside an hour.* ▶ **w niespełna 3** (slang) in prison: *He was sentenced to three years inside.* ▶ **w pudle**

■ **inside** adj. **1** in, on or to the inner part or surface of sth: *the inside pages of a newspaper* ▶ **wewnętrzny 2** (used about information, etc.) told secretly by sb who belongs to a group, organization, etc.: *The robbers seemed to have had some inside information about the bank's security system.* ▶ **poufny**, **zakulisowy**

inside² /ˌɪnˈsaɪd/ noun **1** [C] the inner part or surface of sth: *The door was locked from the inside* (od wewnątrz). ◇ *There's a label somewhere **on the inside*** (po wewnętrznej stronie). ▶ **wnętrze**, **wewnętrzna strona** OPP **outside 2** (**insides**) [pl.] (informal) the organs inside the body: *The coffee warmed his insides.* ◇ *I've got a pain in my insides.* Boli mnie brzuch. ▶ **brzuch**, **żołądek**

IDM **inside out** with the inner surface on the outside: *You've got your jumper on inside out.* ▶ **na lewą stronę**, **podszewką na zewnątrz** ⊃ picture at **back**

know sth inside out → KNOW¹

ˌinside ˈlane (US **ˈslow lane**) noun [C] the part of a wide road or motorway where traffic moves more slowly ▶ **pas drogi przeznaczony dla wolniejszego ruchu**

insider /ɪnˈsaɪdə(r)/ noun [C] a person who knows a lot about a group or an organization because they are a part of it: *The book gives us an insider's view of how government works.* ▶ **człon-ek/kini**, **osoba wtajemniczona**

insidious /ɪnˈsɪdiəs/ adj. (formal) spreading gradually or without being noticed, but causing serious harm: *the insidious effects of polluted water supplies* ▶ **podstępny**, **zdradliwy**

■ **insidiously** adv. ▶ **podstępnie**

insight /ˈɪnsaɪt/ noun [C,U] **(an) insight (into sth)** an understanding of what sb/sth is like: *The book gives a good insight into the lives of the poor.* ▶ **wgląd (w coś)**, **rozumienie**

insignia /ɪnˈsɪgniə/ noun [C] (pl. **insignia**) the symbol or sign that shows sb's position, or that they are a member of a group or an organization: *the royal insignia* ▶ **insygnium**

insignificant /ˌɪnsɪgˈnɪfɪkənt/ adj. of little value or importance: *an insignificant detail* ◇ *Working in such a big company made her feel insignificant.* ▶ **nieistotny** OPP **significant**

■ **insignificance** noun [U] ▶ **znikomość** | **insignificantly** adv. ▶ **nieistotnie**

insincere /ˌɪnsɪnˈsɪə(r); US -ˈsɪr/ adj. saying or doing sth that you do not really believe: *His apology sounded insincere.* ◇ *Dan gave an insincere smile.* ▶ **nieszczery** OPP **sincere**

■ **insincerely** adv. ▶ **nieszczerze** | **insincerity** /ˌɪnsɪnˈserəti/ noun [U] ▶ **nieszczerość** OPP **sincerity**

insinuate /ɪnˈsɪnjueɪt/ verb [T] to suggest sth unpleasant in an indirect way: *She seemed to be insinuating that our work was below standard.* ▶ **insynuować**, **sugerować**

■ **insinuation** /ɪnˌsɪnjuˈeɪʃn/ noun [C,U]: *to **make insinuations** about somebody's honesty* ▶ **insynuacja**

insipid /ɪnˈsɪpɪd/ adj. having too little taste, flavour or colour ▶ **mdły**, **bezbarwny**

insist /ɪnˈsɪst/ verb [I] **1 insist (on sth/doing sth)**; **insist that ...** to say strongly that you must have or do sth, or that sb else must do sth: *He always insists on the best.* Zawsze wymaga tego, co najlepsze. ◇ *Dan insisted on coming too.* ◇ *My parents insist that I come home by taxi.* ◇ *'Have another drink.' 'Oh all right, if you insist.'* ▶ **nalegać**, **upierać się 2 insist (on sth)**; **insist that ...** to say firmly that sth is true (when sb does not believe you): *She insisted on her innocence.* ◇ *Benjamin insisted that the accident wasn't his fault.* ▶ **upierać się**, **utrzymywać**

■ **insistence** noun [U] ▶ **naleganie**, **upieranie się**

insistent /ɪnˈsɪstənt/ adj. **1 insistent (on sth/doing sth)**; **insistent that ...** saying strongly that you must have or do sth, or that sb else must do sth: *She was most insistent that we should all be there.* Bardzo nalegała, żebyśmy wszyscy tam byli. ◇ *Doctors are insistent on the need* (usilnie podkreślają potrzebę) *to do more exercise.* ▶ **stanowczy 2** continuing for a long time in a way that cannot be ignored: *the insistent ringing of the telephone* ▶ **natarczywy**, **uporczywy**

■ **insistently** adv. ▶ **stanowczo**; **uporczywie**, **natarczywie**

insolent /ˈɪnsələnt/ adj. (formal) lacking respect; rude: *insolent behaviour* ▶ **bezczelny**

■ **insolence** noun [U] ▶ **bezczelność** | **insolently** adv. ▶ **bezczelnie**

insoluble /ɪnˈsɒljəbl/ adj. **1** that cannot be explained or solved: *We faced almost insoluble problems.* ▶ **nierozwiązalny 2** that cannot be dissolved in a liquid ▶ **nierozpuszczalny** OPP for both meanings **soluble**

insolvent /ɪnˈsɒlvənt/ adj. not having enough money to pay what you owe: *The company has been declared insolvent.* ▶ **niewypłacalny** SYN **bankrupt** OPP **solvent**

■ **insolvency** /-ənsi/ noun [U,C] (pl. **-ies**): *The company is close to insolvency.* ▶ **niewypłacalność**

insomnia /ɪnˈsɒmniə/ noun [U] the condition of being unable to sleep: *Do you ever suffer from insomnia?* ▶ **bezsenność** ⊃ look at **sleepless**

insomniac /ɪnˈsɒmniæk/ noun [C] a person who cannot sleep ▶ **osoba cierpiąca na bezsenność**

inspect /ɪnˈspekt/ verb [T] **1 inspect sb/sth (for sth)** to look at sth closely or in great detail: *The detective inspected the room for fingerprints.* ▶ **badać**, **sprawdzać** SYN **examine 2** to make an official visit to make sure that rules are being obeyed, work is being done properly, etc.: *All food shops should be inspected regularly.* ▶ **kontrolować**

■ **inspection** noun [C,U]: *The fire prevention service will **carry out an inspection** of the building next week.* ◇ *On inspection* (przy bliższym zbadaniu), *the passport turned out to be false.* ▶ **inspekcja**, **kontrola**

inspector /ɪnˈspektə(r)/ noun [C] **1** an official who visits schools, factories, etc. to make sure that rules are being obeyed, work is being done properly, etc.: *a health and safety inspector* ▶ **kontroler**, **inspektor 2** (Brit.) a police officer with quite an important position ▶ **inspektor policji 3** a person whose job is to check passengers' tickets on buses or trains ▶ **kontroler/ka biletów 4** (US) = SURVEYOR (2)

inspiration /ˌɪnspəˈreɪʃn/ noun **1** [C,U] **an inspiration (to/for sb)**; **inspiration (to do/for sth)** a feeling, person or thing that makes you want to do sth or gives you exciting new ideas: *The beauty of the mountains was a great **source of inspiration** to the writer.* ◇ *What gave you the inspiration to become a dancer?* ▶ **natchnienie 2** [C] (informal) a sudden good idea: *I've had an inspiration – why don't we go to that new club?* ▶ **nagły/dobry pomysł**

inspire /ɪnˈspaɪə(r)/ verb [T] **1 inspire sth**; **inspire sb (to do sth)** to make sb want to do or create sth: *Nelson Mandela's autobiography inspired her to go into politics.* ◇ *The attack was inspired by racial hatred.* Powodem ataku była nienawiść rasowa. ▶ **stanowić natchnienie**, **być natchnieniem 2 inspire sb (with sth)**; **inspire sth (in sb)** to make sb feel, think, etc. sth: *The guide's nervous manner did not **inspire** much **confidence** in us.* ◇ *to be inspired with enthusiasm* być zarażonym entuzjazmem ▶ **wzbudzać**

■ **inspiring** adj.: *an inspiring speech.* ▶ **inspirujący, będący źródłem natchnienia**

inspired /ɪn'spaɪəd/ adj. influenced or helped by a particular feeling, thing or person: *The pianist gave an inspired performance.* ◇ *a politically inspired killing* morderstwo o podłożu politycznym ▶ **natchniony**

instability /ˌɪnstə'bɪləti/ noun [U] the state of being likely to change: *There are growing signs of political instability.* ▶ **niestałość, niestabilność** ➲ adjective **unstable** OPP **stability**

install (US also **instal**) /ɪn'stɔːl/ verb [T] **1** to put a piece of equipment, etc. in place so that it is ready to be used: *We are waiting to have our new washing machine installed.* ◇ *to install a computer system* ▶ **podłączać, montować** SYN **put sth in 2 install sb (as sth)** to put sb or yourself in a position or place: *He was installed as President yesterday.* ◇ *She installed herself* (usadowiła się) *in a deckchair for the afternoon.* ▶ **wprowadzać na urząd**

■ **installation** /ˌɪnstə'leɪʃn/ noun [C,U]: *a military/nuclear installation* ◇ *the installation of a new chairman* ▶ **montaż; wprowadzenie na urząd**

instalment (US **installment**) /ɪn'stɔːlmənt/ noun [C] **1** one of the regular payments that you make for sth until you have paid the full amount: *to pay for something* ***in instalments*** ▶ **rata 2** one part of a story that is shown or published as a series: *Don't miss next week's exciting instalment of this new drama.* ▶ **odcinek** (*np.serialu*)

instance /'ɪnstəns/ noun [C] **an instance (of sth)** an example or case (of sth): *There have been several instances of racial attacks in the area.* ◇ *In most instances the drug has no side effects.* ▶ **przypadek, przykład**

IDM **for instance** for example: *There are several interesting places to visit around here – Warwick, for instance.* ▶ **na przykład**

instant[1] /'ɪnstənt/ adj. **1** happening immediately: *The film was an instant success.* ◇ *She took an instant dislike to me.* ◇ *A new government cannot bring about instant change.* ▶ **natychmiastowy, nagły** SYN **immediate 2** [only before a noun] (used about food) that can be prepared quickly and easily, usually by adding hot water: *instant coffee* kawa rozpuszczalna ▶ (*potrawa*) **błyskawiczny**

instant[2] /'ɪnstənt/ noun [usually sing.] **1** a very short period of time: *Alex thought* ***for an instant*** *and then agreed.* ▶ **chwila 2** a particular point in time: *Stop doing that this instant* (natychmiast)*!* ◇ ***At that instant*** (w tym momencie) *I realized I had been tricked.* ◇ *The instant I saw him* (w chwili, gdy go zobaczyłem) *I knew he would say no.* ▶ **chwila** SYN for both meanings **moment**

instantaneous /ˌɪnstən'teɪniəs/ adj. happening immediately or extremely quickly ▶ **natychmiastowy**

■ **instantaneously** adv. ▶ **natychmiastowo**

instantly /'ɪnstəntli/ adv. without delay; immediately: *I asked him a question and he replied instantly.* ▶ **natychmiast**

ˌinstant 'messaging noun [U] a system on the Internet that allows people to exchange written messages with each other very quickly ▶ **system szybkiego powiadamiania w internecie** (*np. gadu-gadu*)

ˌinstant 'replay (US) = ACTION REPLAY

instead /ɪn'sted/ adv. in the place of sb/sth: *I couldn't go so my husband went instead.* ▶ **zamiast tego/kogoś/czegoś**

■ **instead** prep. **instead of sb/sth/doing sth** in the place of sb/sth: *Instead of 7.30 could I come at 8.00?* ◇ *You should play football instead of just watching it on TV.* ▶ **zamiast, w miejsce**

instigate /'ɪnstɪgeɪt/ verb [T] (formal) to make sth start to happen ▶ **wywoływać, podjudzać**

■ **instigation** /ˌɪnstɪ'geɪʃn/ noun [U] ▶ **namowa, podjudzanie**

instil (US **instill**) /ɪn'stɪl/ verb [T] (**instilling; instilled**) **instil sth (in/into sb)** to make sb think or feel sth: *Parents should try to instil a sense of responsibility into their children.* ▶ **wpajać**

instinct /'ɪnstɪŋkt/ noun [C,U] the natural force that causes a person or an animal to behave in a particular way without thinking or learning about it: *Birds learn to fly* ***by instinct.*** ◇ *In a situation like that you don't have time to think – you just* ***act on instinct*** (działa się instynktownie). ▶ **instynkt**

instinctive /ɪn'stɪŋktɪv/ adj. based on **instinct**, not thought or training: *instinctive knowledge* ◇ *She's an instinctive player.* ◇ *My instinctive reaction was to deny everything.* ▶ **instynktowny**

■ **instinctively** adv.: *He knew instinctively that something was wrong.* ▶ **instynktownie**

instinctual /ɪn'stɪŋktʃuəl/ adj. based on natural **instinct**; not learned ▶ **instynktowny**

institute[1] /'ɪnstɪtjuːt; US -tuːt/ noun [C] an organization that has a particular purpose; the building used by this organization: *the Institute of Science and Technology* ◇ *institutes of higher education* ▶ **instytut**

institute[2] /'ɪnstɪtjuːt; US -tuːt/ verb [T] (formal) to introduce a system, policy, etc., or start a process: *The government has instituted a new scheme for youth training.* ▶ **wprowadzać**

institution /ˌɪnstɪ'tjuːʃn; US -'tuːʃn/ noun **1** [C] a large, important organization that has a particular purpose, such as a bank, a university, etc.: *the financial institutions in the City of London* ▶ **instytucja 2** [C] a building where certain people with special needs live and are looked after: *She's been in institutions all her life.* ◇ *a mental institution* zakład dla umysłowo chorych ▶ **zakład 3** [C] a social custom or habit that has existed for a long time: *the institution of marriage* ▶ **instytucja, zwyczaj 4** [U] the act of introducing a system, policy, etc., or of starting a process: *the institution of new safety procedures* ▶ **wprowadzanie**

institutional /ˌɪnstɪ'tjuːʃənl; US -'tuː-/ adj. connected with an institution: *The old lady is in need of institutional care.* ▶ **instytucjonalny, zakładowy**

institutionalize (also **-ise**) /ˌɪnstɪ'tjuːʃənəlaɪz; US -'tuː-/ verb [T] **1** to send sb who is not capable of living independently to live in a special building, especially when it is for a long period of time ▶ **umieszczać kogoś w zakładzie 2** to make sth become part of an organized system, society or culture, so that it is considered normal ▶ **instytucjonalizować**

■ **institutionalization** (also **-isation**) /ˌɪnstɪˌtjuːʃənəlaɪ'zeɪʃn; US -ˌtuːʃənələ'z-/ noun [U] ▶ **umieszczanie kogoś w zakładzie; instytucjonalizacja**

instruct /ɪn'strʌkt/ verb [T] **1 instruct sb (to do sth)** to give an order to sb; to tell sb to do sth: *The soldiers were instructed to shoot above the heads of the crowd.* ▶ **rozkazywać, polecać, zlecać 2** (formal) **instruct sb (in sth)** to teach sb sth: *Children must be instructed in road safety before they are allowed to ride a bike on the road.* ▶ **nauczać**

instruction /ɪn'strʌkʃn/ noun **1 (instructions)** [pl.] detailed information on how you should use sth, do sth, etc.: *Read the instructions on the back of the packet carefully.* ◇ *You should always* ***follow the instructions.*** ▶ **instrukcja** (*obsługi*) **2** [C] **an instruction (to do sth)** an order that tells you what to do or how to do sth: *The guard was* ***under*** *strict* ***instructions*** (strażnik miał surowy rozkaz) *not to let anyone in or out.* ▶ **rozkaz, polecenie 3** [U] (formal) **instruction (in sth)** the act of teaching sth to sb: *The staff need instruction in the use of computers.* ▶ **szkolenie (się)**

instructive /ɪn'strʌktɪv/ adj. giving useful information ▶ **pouczający**
■ **instructively** adv. ▶ **pouczająco**

instructor /ɪn'strʌktə(r)/ noun [C] a person whose job is to teach a practical skill or sport: *a driving/fitness/golf instructor* ▶ **instruktor/ka**

instrument /'ɪnstrəmənt/ noun [C] **1** a tool that is used for doing a particular job or task: *surgical/optical/precision instruments* ▶ **narzędzie, przyrząd** ➲ note at **tool 2** something that is used for playing music: *Do you play an instrument?* ▶ **instrument muzyczny** ➲ note at **music 3** something that is used for measuring speed, distance, temperature, etc. in a car, plane or ship: *the instrument panel* (tablica rozdzielcza) *of a plane* ▶ **przyrząd pomiarowy 4** something that sb uses in order to achieve sth: *The press should be more than an instrument of the government.* ▶ (*przen.*) **narzędzie, środek**

> **musical instruments**
> Musical instruments may be **stringed** (*violins, guitars, etc.*), **brass** (*horns, trumpets, etc.*), **woodwind** (*flutes, clarinets, etc.*) or **keyboard** (*piano, organ, synthesizer, etc.*). **Percussion** instruments include *drums* and *cymbals*.

instrumental /,ɪnstrə'mentl/ adj. **1 instrumental in doing sth** helping to make sth happen: *She was instrumental in getting him the job.* Bez jej pomocy nie dostałby tej pracy. ▶ **przyczyniający się do zrobienia czegoś 2** for musical instruments without voices: *instrumental music* ▶ (*muz.*) **instrumentalny**

insubordinate /,ɪnsə'bɔːdɪnət/ adj. (formal) (used about a person or behaviour) not obeying rules or orders ▶ **nieposłuszny; niesubordynowany**
■ **insubordination** /,ɪnsə,bɔːdɪ'neɪʃn/ noun [U]: *He was dismissed from the army for insubordination.* ▶ **nieposłuszeństwo; niesubordynacja**

insubstantial /,ɪnsəb'stænʃl/ adj. not large, solid or strong: *a hut built of insubstantial materials* ◇ *an insubstantial meal* ▶ **nietrwały, nieobfity** OPP **substantial**

insufferable /ɪn'sʌfrəbl/ adj. (formal) (used about a person or behaviour) extremely unpleasant or annoying ▶ **nieznośny**
■ **insufferably** /-əbli/ adv. ▶ **nieznośnie**

insufficient /,ɪnsə'fɪʃnt/ adj. **insufficient (for sth/to do sth)** not enough: *The students complained that they were given insufficient time for the test.* ▶ **niewystarczający** OPP **sufficient**
■ **insufficiently** adv. ▶ **niewystarczająco**

insular /'ɪnsjələ(r); US -sələr/ adj. only interested in your own country, ideas, etc. and not in those from outside ▶ **ciasny w poglądach, zaściankowy**
■ **insularity** /,ɪnsju'lærəti; US -sə'l-/ noun [U] ▶ **zaściankowość, ciasnota poglądów**

insulate /'ɪnsjuleɪt; US -səl-/ verb [T] **insulate sth (against/from sth)** to protect sth with a material that prevents electricity, heat or sound from passing through: *You can save a lot of money on heating if you insulate your house* (jeżeli twój dom jest dobrze uszczelniony). ◇ *The walls are insulated against noise.* ◇ (figurative) *This industry has been insulated from the effects of competition.* ▶ **izolować, uszczelniać**
■ **insulation** /,ɪnsju'leɪʃn; US -sə'l-/ [U] **1** noun the material used for insulating sth ▶ **izolacja, uszczelnienie 2** the process of insulating or the state of being insulated ▶ **za/izolowanie, uszczelnianie**

insulin /'ɪnsjulɪn; US -səl-/ noun [U] a substance, normally produced by the body itself, which controls the amount of sugar absorbed into the blood: *insulin injections* ▶ **insulina**

insult¹ /ɪn'sʌlt/ verb [T] to speak or act rudely to sb: *I felt very insulted when I didn't even get an answer to my letter.* ◇ *He was thrown out of the hotel for insulting the manager.* ▶ **znieważać, obrażać**

insult² /'ɪnsʌlt/ noun [C] a rude comment or action: *The drivers were standing in the road yelling insults at each other* (obrzucając się obelgami). ▶ **zniewaga, obraza**

insulting /ɪn'sʌltɪŋ/ adj. **insulting (to sb/sth)** making sb feel offended: *insulting behaviour/remarks* ◇ *That poster is insulting to women.* ▶ **obraźliwy, znieważający**

insuperable /ɪn'suːpərəbl/ adj. (formal) (used about a problem, etc.) impossible to solve ▶ **nie do pokonania/zwyciężenia, nierozwiązywalny**

insurance /ɪn'ʃʊərəns; Brit. also -'ʃɔːr-/ noun **1** [U] **insurance (against sth)** an arrangement with a company in which you pay them regular amounts of money and they agree to pay the costs if, for example, you die or are ill, or if you lose or damage sth: *life insurance* ubezpieczenie na życie ◇ *car/household insurance* ◇ *travel insurance* ubezpieczenie na czas podróży ◇ *an insurance policy* polisa ubezpieczeniowa ◇ *to take out insurance against* (ubezpieczyć się od) *fire and theft* ◇ *insurance premiums* składki ubezpieczeniowe ◇ *Our roof was blown off in the storm but we claimed for it on the insurance* (wystąpiliśmy o odszkodowanie w ramach ubezpieczenia). ▶ **ubezpieczenie**

> You **take out** an **insurance policy**. An **insurance premium** is the regular amount you pay to the insurance company. You can take out **life, health, car, travel** and **household insurance**.

2 [U] the business of providing insurance: *He works in insurance* (pracuje w firmie ubezpieczeniowej). ▶ **ubezpieczenie 3** [U, sing.] **(an) insurance (against sth)** something you do to protect yourself (against sth unpleasant): *Many people take vitamin pills as an insurance against illness.* ▶ **zabezpieczenie (się)**

insure /ɪn'ʃʊə(r); Brit. also -'ʃɔː(r)/ verb [T] **1 insure yourself/sth (against/for sth)** to buy or to provide insurance: *They insured the painting for £10 000 against damage or theft.* ▶ **ubezpieczać 2** (US) = ENSURE

insurgent /ɪn'sɜːdʒənt/ noun [C, usually pl.] (formal) a person fighting against the government or armed forces of their own country ▶ **rebeliant/ka** SYN **rebel**
■ **insurgent** adj. ▶ **rebeliancki** SYN **rebellious**

insurmountable /,ɪnsə'maʊntəbl/ adj. (formal) (used about a problem, etc.) impossible to solve ▶ **nie do pokonania/zwyciężenia, nierozwiązywalny**

insurrection /,ɪnsə'rekʃn/ noun [C,U] (formal) violent action against the rulers of a country or the government ▶ **powstanie**

intact /ɪn'tækt/ adj. [not before a noun] complete; not damaged: *Very few of the buildings **remain intact** following the earthquake.* ▶ **nienaruszony, nietknięty**

intake /'ɪnteɪk/ noun [C, usually sing.] **1** the amount of food, drink, etc. that you take into your body: *The doctor told me to cut down my alcohol intake.* ▶ **spożycie 2** the (number of) people who enter an organization or institution during a certain period: *This year's intake of students is down 10%.* ▶ **nabór 3** the act of taking sth into your body, especially breath: *a sharp intake of breath* gwałtowny wdech ▶ **pobór** (*np. powietrza*)

intangible /ɪn'tændʒəbl/ adj. difficult to describe, understand or measure: *The benefits of good customer relations are intangible.* ▶ **niepojęty, nienamacalny** OPP **tangible**

integral /'ɪntɪgrəl/ adj. **1 integral (to sth)** necessary in order to make sth complete: *Spending a year in France is **an integral part of** the university course.* ▶ **zasadniczy, integralny 2** included as part of sth: *The car has an integral CD player.* ▶ **integralny**

integrate /ˈɪntɪɡreɪt/ verb **1** [T] **integrate sth (into sth); integrate A and B/integrate A with B** to join things so that they become one thing or work together: *The two small schools were integrated into one large one.* ◇ *These programs can be integrated with your existing software.* ▶ **łączyć (w jedną całość), scalać 2** [I,T] **integrate (sb) (into/with sth)** to join in and become part of a group or community, or to make sb do this: *It took Amir a while to integrate into his new school.* ▶ **integrować kogoś/się z czymś** ➲ look at **segregate**

■ **integration** /ˌɪntɪˈɡreɪʃn/ noun [U]: *racial integration* ▶ **połączenie, scalanie; integracja** ➲ look at **segregation**

integrity /ɪnˈteɡrəti/ noun [U] the quality of being honest and having strong moral principles: *He's a person* ***of great integrity*** *who will say exactly what he thinks.* ▶ **prawość, uczciwość**

intellect /ˈɪntəlekt/ noun **1** [U] the power of the mind to think and to learn: *a woman of considerable intellect* ▶ **umysł, rozum 2** [C] an extremely intelligent person: *He was one of the most brilliant intellects of his time.* ▶ **umysł**

intellectual[1] /ˌɪntəˈlektʃuəl/ adj. **1** [only before a noun] connected with sb's ability to think, reason and understand things: *The boy's intellectual development was very advanced for his age.* ▶ **umysłowy, intelektualny 2** (used about a person) enjoying activities in which you have to think deeply about sth ▶ **intelektualny**

■ **intellectually** /-tʃuəli/ adv. ▶ **umysłowo, intelektualnie**

intellectual[2] /ˌɪntəˈlektʃuəl/ noun [C] a person who enjoys thinking deeply about things ▶ **intelektualist(k)a, inteligent/ka**

ˌintelˌlectual ˈproperty noun [U] an idea, a design, etc. that sb has created and that the law prevents other people from copying: *intellectual property rights* ▶ **własność intelektualna**

intelligence /ɪnˈtelɪdʒəns/ noun [U] **1** the ability to understand, learn and think: *a person of normal intelligence* ◇ *an intelligence test* ▶ **inteligencja 2** important information about an enemy country: *to receive intelligence about somebody* ▶ **wywiad** (*np. szpiegowski*)

intelligent /ɪnˈtelɪdʒənt/ adj. having or showing the ability to understand, learn and think; clever: *All their children are very intelligent.* ◇ *an intelligent question* ▶ **inteligentny, mądry**

■ **intelligently** adv. ▶ **inteligentnie, mądrze**

intelligent

Wyrazy **bright**, **clever** oraz (zwł. w Amer. ang.) **smart** również oznaczają „mądry". Wyrazu **bright** zwykle używa się w odniesieniu do osób młodych: *She's the brightest girl in the class.* Osoby, które opisuje się jako **clever** lub **smart**, szybko uczą się nowych rzeczy: *She's smarter than her brother.* Wyrazy **clever** i **smart** opisują również działanie lub pomysły, które charakteryzują się inteligencją: *What a clever idea!* ◇ *a smart career move.*

intelligentsia /ɪnˌtelɪˈdʒentsiə/ (usually **the intelligentsia**) noun [sing., with sing. or pl. verb] the people in a country or society who are well educated and are interested in culture, politics, literature, etc. ▶ (*grupa społeczna*) **inteligencja**

intelligible /ɪnˈtelɪdʒəbl/ adj. (used especially about speech or writing) possible or easy to understand ▶ **zrozumiały, czytelny** SYN **understandable** OPP **unintelligible**

intend /ɪnˈtend/ verb [T] **1 intend to do sth/doing sth** to plan or mean to do sth: *I'm afraid I spent more money than I had intended.* ◇ *I certainly don't intend to wait here all day!* ◇ *They had intended staying in Wales for two weeks but the weather was so bad that they left after one.* ▶ **zamierzać, mieć zamiar** ➲ noun **intention 2 intend sth for sb/sth; intend sb to do sth** to plan, mean or make sth for a particular person or purpose: *You shouldn't have read that letter – it wasn't intended for you.* ◇ *I didn't intend you to have all the work.* ▶ **przeznaczać dla kogoś/czegoś; chcieć/zamierzać, żeby ktoś coś zrobił**

intended /ɪnˈtendɪd/ adj. [only before a noun] **1** that you are trying to achieve or reach: *the intended purpose* ◇ *The bullet missed its intended target.* ▶ **zamierzony, planowany 2 intended for sb/sth; intended as sth; intended to be/do sth** planned or designed for sb/sth: *The book is intended for children.* ◇ *The notes are intended as an introduction to the course.* ◇ *The lights are intended to be used in the garden.* ▶ **przeznaczony jako coś dla kogoś/czegoś**

intense /ɪnˈtens/ adj. very great, strong or serious: *intense heat/cold/pressure* ◇ *intense anger/interest/desire* ▶ **wielki, silny, poważny**

■ **intensely** adv.: *They dislike each other intensely.* ▶ **mocno, głęboko, skrajnie** | **intensity** /ɪnˈtensəti/ noun [U]: *I wasn't prepared for the intensity of his reaction to the news.* ▶ **intensywność**

intensify /ɪnˈtensɪfaɪ/ verb [I,T] (**intensifying; intensifies**; pt, pp **intensified**) to become or to make sth greater or stronger: *The government has intensified its anti-smoking campaign.* ◇ *Fighting in the region has intensified.* ▶ **wzmacniać (się), przybierać na sile**

■ **intensification** /ɪnˌtensɪfɪˈkeɪʃn/ noun [U] ▶ **wzmacnianie (się), nasilanie (się)**

intensive /ɪnˈtensɪv/ adj. **1** involving a lot of work or care in a short period of time: *an intensive investigation/course* ◇ *The course only lasted a week but it was very intensive.* ▶ **wzmożony, intensywny 2** (used about methods of farming) aimed at producing as much food as possible from the land or money available: *intensive agriculture* ▶ **intensywny**

■ **intensively** adv. ▶ **intensywnie**

inˌtensive ˈcare noun [U] special care in hospital for patients who are very seriously ill or injured; the department that gives this care: *She was in intensive care for a week after the crash.* ▶ **intensywna opieka medyczna; oddział intensywnej opieki medycznej**

intent[1] /ɪnˈtent/ adj. **1 intent (on/upon sth)** showing great attention ▶ **uważny, baczny 2 intent on/upon sth/doing sth** determined to do sth: *He's always been intent on making a lot of money.* ◇ *She was so intent upon her work* (była tak pochłonięta pracą) *that she didn't hear me come in.* ▶ **zdeterminowany, oddany (czemuś)**

■ **intently** adv. ▶ **uważnie, z przejęciem**

intent[2] /ɪnˈtent/ noun [U] (formal) what sb intends to do; intention: *He was charged with possession of a gun* ***with intent to*** *commit a robbery.* ◇ *to do something with evil/good intent* ▶ **zamiar, cel**

IDM **to/for all intents and purposes** in effect, even if not completely true: *When they scored their fourth goal the match was, to all intents and purposes, over.* ▶ **praktycznie rzecz biorąc**

intention /ɪnˈtenʃn/ noun [C,U] **(an) intention (of doing sth/to do sth)** what sb intends or means to do; a plan or purpose: *Our intention was to leave early in the morning.* ◇ *I* ***have no intention of*** *staying indoors on a nice sunny day like this.* ◇ *I borrowed the money* ***with the intention of*** *paying it back the next day.* ▶ **zamiar, zamierzenie**

intentional /ɪnˈtenʃənl/ adj. done on purpose, not by chance: *I'm sorry I took your jacket – it wasn't intentional!* ▶ **zamierzony, umyślny** SYN **deliberate**

■ **intentionally** /-ʃənəli/ adv.: *I can't believe the boys broke the window intentionally.* ▶ **umyślnie, celowo**

interact /ˌɪntər'ækt/ verb [I] **1 interact (with sb)** (used about people) to communicate or mix with sb, especially while you work, play or spend time together: *He is studying the way children interact with each other at different ages.* ▶ **oddziaływać (wzajemnie na siebie) 2** (used about two things) to have an effect on each other ▶ **wywierać wzajemny wpływ na siebie**
■ **interaction** noun [U,C] **interaction (between/with sb/sth)** [U]: *interaction between the two departments* ▶ **wzajemne oddziaływanie**; **współdziałanie**

interactive /ˌɪntər'æktɪv/ adj. **1** that involves people working together and having an influence on each other: *The college uses interactive language-learning techniques.* ▶ **interakcyjny 2** involving direct communication both ways, between a computer, etc. and the person using it: *interactive computer games* ◇ *interactive TV* ▶ **interaktywny**

interbreed /ˌɪntə'bri:d/ verb [I,T] if animals from different **species interbreed**, or sb **interbreeds** them, they produce young together ▶ **krzyżować (się)**

intercede /ˌɪntə'si:d/ verb [I] **intercede (with sb) (for/on behalf of sb)** (formal) to speak to sb in order to persuade them to show pity on sb else or to help settle an argument: *They interceded with the authorities on behalf of the detainees.* ▶ **interweniować (u kogoś) (w imieniu kogoś)** SYN **intervene**
■ **intercession** /ˌɪntə'seʃn/ noun [U]: *the intercession of a priest* ▶ **interwencja**

intercept /ˌɪntə'sept/ verb [T] to stop or catch sb/sth that is moving from one place to another: *Detectives intercepted him at the airport.* ▶ **przechwytywać**, **przejmować**
■ **interception** noun [U,C] ▶ **przechwytywanie**, **przejmowanie** (*np. wiadomości*), **podsłuch** (*radiowy, telefoniczny*)

interchangeable /ˌɪntə'tʃeɪndʒəbl/ adj. **interchangeable (with sth)** able to be used in place of each other without making any difference to the way sth works: *Are these two words interchangeable?* ▶ **zamienny**, **wymienny**
■ **interchangeably** /-əbli/ adv. ▶ **wymiennie**, **zamiennie**

intercom /'ɪntəkɒm/ noun [C] a system of communication by radio or telephone inside an office, plane, etc.; the device you press or switch on to start using this system ▶ **telefon wewnętrzny**, **interkom**

interconnect /ˌɪntəkə'nekt/ verb [I,T] **interconnect (A) (with B)**; **interconnect A and B** to connect similar things; to be connected to similar things: *electronic networks which interconnect thousands of computers around the world* ▶ **po/łączyć (się)**

intercontinental /ˌɪntəˌkɒntɪ'nentl/ adj. between continents: *intercontinental flights* ▶ **międzykontynentalny**

intercourse (formal) = SEX (3)

interdepartmental /ˌɪntəˌdi:pɑ:t'mentl/ adj. between departments; involving more than one department: *interdepartmental committees/meetings/rivalry* ▶ **międzywydziałowy**

interdependent /ˌɪntədɪ'pendənt/ adj. depending on each other: *Exercise and good health are generally interdependent.* ◇ *interdependent economies/organizations* ▶ **współzależny**
■ **interdependence** /-əns/ (also **interdependency**, pl. **-ies**) noun [U,C] ▶ **współzależność**

🔑 **interest**[1] /'ɪntrəst/ noun **1** [U, sing.] **an interest (in sb/sth)** a desire to learn or hear more about sb/sth or to be involved with sb/sth: *She's begun to* ***show*** *a great* ***interest*** *in politics.* ◇ *I wish he'd* ***take*** *more* ***interest in*** (bardziej zainteresował się) *his children.* ◇ *Don't* ***lose interest*** *now!* ▶ **zainteresowanie 2** [U] the quality that makes sth interesting: *I thought this article might* ***be of interest*** (ciekawy) *to you.* ◇ *Computers* ***hold no interest for*** *me.* ◇ *places of historical interest* ▶ **zainteresowanie 3** [C, usually pl.] something that you enjoy doing or learning about: *What are your interests and hobbies?* ▶ **zainteresowania 4** [U] **interest (on sth)** the money that you pay for borrowing money from a bank, etc. or the money that you earn when you keep money in a bank, etc.: *If you invest your capital wisely, it will* ***earn*** *a lot of* ***interest*** (przyniesie wysokie procenty). ◇ *We pay 6% interest on our mortgage at the moment.* ◇ *Some companies offer* ***interest-free*** (nieoprocentowane) *loans.* ◇ *The* ***interest rate*** (stopa procentowa) *has never been so high/low.* ◇ ***simple/compound interest*** odsetki proste/składane ▶ **odsetki**, **oprocentowanie** ➲ note at **loan 5** [C] a legal right to share in a business, etc., especially in its profits: *When he retired he sold his interests in the company.* ▶ **udział**
IDM **have/with sb's (best) interests at heart** to want sb to be happy and successful, even though your actions may not show it: *Don't be angry with your father – you know he has your best interests at heart.* ▶ **mieć dobre (najlepsze) intencje wobec kogoś**
in sb's interest(s) to sb's advantage: *Using lead-free petrol is in the public interest.* ▶ **w (czyimś) interesie**
in the interest(s) of sth in order to achieve or protect sth: *In the interest(s) of safety, please fasten your seat belts.* ▶ **w imię (czegoś)**; **ze względu** (*np. na bezpieczeństwo*)

🔑 **interest**[2] /'ɪntrəst/ verb [T] to make sb want to learn or hear more about sth or to become involved in sth: *It might interest you to know that I didn't accept the job.* ◇ *The subject of the talk was one that interests me greatly.* ▶ **interesować**, **ciekawić**
PHR V **interest sb in sth** to persuade sb to buy, have or do sth: *Can I interest you in our new brochure?* ▶ **zainteresować kogoś czymś**, **polecać coś komuś**

🔑 **interested** /'ɪntrəstɪd/ adj. **1** [not before a noun] **interested (in sth/sb)**; **interested in doing sth**; **interested to do sth** wanting to know or hear more about sth/sb; enjoying or liking sth/sb: *They weren't interested in my news at all!* ◇ *I was interested to hear that you've got a new job. Where is it?* ◇ *She's too young to be interested* (aby już interesować się) *in boys yet.* ◇ *I'm really not interested in going to university.* ▶ **ciekawy**, **zainteresowany** OPP **uninterested** ➲ note at **like**

> Uwaga! Wyraz **interested** oznacza „zainteresowany", a **interesting** – „interesujący".

2 [only before a noun] involved in or affected by sth; in a position to gain from sth: *I think they should have talked to the interested parties* (ze stronami zainteresowanymi) *before they made that decision.* ▶ **zainteresowany** OPP **disinterested**

🔑 **interesting** /'ɪntrəstɪŋ; -trest-/ adj. **interesting (to do sth)**; **interesting that ...** enjoyable and entertaining; holding your attention: *an interesting person/book/idea/job* ◇ *It's always interesting to hear about the customs of other societies.* ◇ *It's interesting that Luisa chose Peru for a holiday.* ▶ **ciekawy**, **interesujący** ➲ note at **interested**
■ **interestingly** adv. ▶ **ciekawie**; **co ciekawe**

interface /'ɪntəfeɪs/ noun [C] **1** the way a computer program gives information to a user or receives information from a user, in particular the appearance of the screen: *the user interface* ▶ **interfejs 2** a connection or computer program that joins one device or system to another: *the interface between computer and printer* ▶ **interfejs**, **złącze 3 interface (between A and B)** the point where two people, things, systems, etc. meet and affect each other: *the interface between manufacturing and sales* ▶ **złącze**

interfere /ˌɪntəˈfɪə(r)/ verb [I] **1 interfere (in sth)** to get involved in a situation which does not involve you and where you are not wanted: *You shouldn't interfere in your children's lives – let them make their own decisions.* ▶ **wtrącać się, mieszać się 2 interfere (with sb/sth)** to prevent sth from succeeding or to slow down the progress that sb/sth makes: *Every time the telephone rings it interferes with my work.* ◇ *She never lets her private life interfere with her career.* ▶ **przeszkadzać 3 interfere (with sth)** to touch or change sth without permission: *Many people feel that scientists shouldn't interfere with nature.* ▶ **ingerować**
■ **interfering** adj.: *She's a nosy, interfering busybody!* ▶ **wścibski, mieszający się**

interference /ˌɪntəˈfɪərəns/ noun [U] **1 interference (in sth)** the act of getting involved in a situation that does not involve you and where you are not wanted: *I left home because I couldn't stand my parents' interference in my affairs.* ▶ **wtrącanie się, mieszanie się 2** extra noise (because of other signals or bad weather) that prevents you from receiving radio, TV or telephone signals clearly ▶ **zakłócenia** (*np. atmosferyczne*)

interim[1] /ˈɪntərɪm/ adj. [only before a noun] not final or lasting; temporary until sb/sth more permanent is found: *an interim arrangement* ◇ *The deputy head teacher took over in* ***the interim period*** *until a replacement could be found.* ▶ **tymczasowy, przejściowy**

interim[2] /ˈɪntərɪm/ noun
IDM **in the interim** in the time between two things happening; until a particular event happens ▶ **tymczasem**

interior /ɪnˈtɪəriə(r)/ noun **1** [C, usually sing.] the inside part of sth: *I'd love to see the interior of the castle.* ▶ **wnętrze, środek** OPP **exterior**[1] **2 (the interior)** [sing.] the central part of a country or continent that is a long way from the coast: *an expedition into the interior of Australia* ▶ **głąb** (*kraju*) **3 (the Interior)** [sing.] a country's own news and affairs that do not involve other countries: *the Department of the Interior* ▶ **sprawy wewnętrzne** (*kraju*)
■ **interior** adj. [only before a noun]: *interior walls* ▶ **wewnętrzny**

inˌterior ˈdecorator noun [C] a person whose job is to design and/or decorate a room or the inside of a house, etc. with paint, paper, carpets, etc. ▶ **dekorator/ka wnętrz**
■ **inˌterior decoˈration** noun [U] ▶ **wystrój wnętrz**

inˌterior deˈsign noun [U] the art or job of choosing colours, furniture, carpets, etc. to decorate the inside of a house ▶ **projektowanie wnętrz**
■ **interior designer** noun [C] ▶ **projektant/ka wnętrz**

interject /ˌɪntəˈdʒekt/ verb [I,T] (formal) to interrupt what sb is saying with your opinion or a remark: *'You're wrong,' interjected Susan.* ▶ **wtrącać**

interjection /ˌɪntəˈdʒekʃn/ noun [C] **1** a word or phrase that is used to express surprise, pain, pleasure, etc. (for example *Oh!*, *Hurray!* or *Wow!*) ▶ **wykrzyknik, okrzyk** SYN **exclamation 2** (formal) something you say that interrupts sb else ▶ **wtrącenie**

interlude /ˈɪntəluːd/ noun [C] a period of time between two events or activities: *Their stay in Karnak was a pleasant interlude in their busy lives.* ◇ *They finally met again after an interlude of* (po okresie) *several years.* ▶ **przerwa** ➲ note at **interval**

intermarry /ˌɪntəˈmæri/ verb [I] (**intermarrying**; **intermarries**; pt, pp **intermarried**) to marry sb from a different religion, culture, country, etc. ▶ **zawierać małżeństwo mieszane**
■ **intermarriage** /ˌɪntəˈmærɪdʒ/ noun [U] ▶ **małżeństwo mieszane**

intermediary /ˌɪntəˈmiːdiəri/ noun [C] (pl. **intermediaries**) **an intermediary (between A and B)** a person or an organization that helps two people or groups to reach an agreement, by being a means of communication between them ▶ **mediator/ka** (*zwł. w sporach*)

intermediate /ˌɪntəˈmiːdiət/ adj. **1** in between two things in position, level, etc.: *an intermediate step/stage in a process* ▶ **pośredni, środkowy 2** having more than a basic knowledge of sth but not yet advanced; suitable for sb who is at this level: *an intermediate student/book/level* ▶ **średnio zaawansowany**

interminable /ɪnˈtɜːmɪnəbl/ adj. lasting for a very long time and therefore boring or annoying: *an interminable delay/speech* ◇ *The wait seemed interminable.* ▶ **niekończący się** SYN **endless**
■ **interminably** /-əbli/ adv. ▶ **bez końca**

intermission /ˌɪntəˈmɪʃn/ noun [C] (especially US) a short period of time separating the parts of a film, play, etc. ▶ **przerwa** ➲ note at **interval**

intermittent /ˌɪntəˈmɪtənt/ adj. stopping for a short time and then starting again several times: *There will be intermittent showers* (opady przejściowe). ▶ **przerywany, sporadyczny**
■ **intermittently** adv. ▶ **sporadycznie, z przerwami**

intern[1] /ɪnˈtɜːn/ verb [T, usually passive] (formal) **intern sb (in sth)** to keep sb in prison for political reasons, especially during a war ▶ **internować**
■ **internment** noun [U] ▶ **internowanie**

intern[2] /ˈɪntɜːn/ noun [C] (US) (also **interne**) an advanced student of medicine, whose training is nearly finished and who is working in a hospital to get further practical experience ▶ **lekarz pracujący w szpitalu na stażu** ➲ look at **house officer**

internal /ɪnˈtɜːnl/ adj. **1** [only before a noun] of or on the inside (of a place, person or object): *internal injuries/organs* ▶ **wewnętrzny 2** happening or existing inside a particular organization: *an internal exam* ◇ *an internal police inquiry* ▶ **wewnętrzny 3** (used about political or economic affairs) inside a country: *a country's internal affairs/trade/markets* ◇ *an internal flight* ▶ **wewnętrzny, krajowy** OPP **external**

> Brytyjski minister spraw wewnętrznych to **Home Secretary**, a ministerstwo spraw wewnętrznych – **Home Office**.

■ **internally** /-nəli/ adv.: *This medicine is not to be taken internally* (doustnie). ▶ **wewnętrznie** OPP **externally**

international /ˌɪntəˈnæʃnəl/ adj. involving two or more countries: *an international agreement/flight/football match* ▶ **międzynarodowy** ➲ look at **local**, **national**, **regional**
■ **internationally** /-ʃənəli/ adv. ▶ **międzynarodowo, na arenie międzynarodowej**

Internet /ˈɪntənet/ (usually **the Internet**) (also informal **the Net**) noun [sing.] the international system of computers that makes it possible for you to see information from all around the world on your computer and to send information to other computers: *I read about it* ***on the Internet.*** ◇ *Do you have Internet access?* ▶ **internet** ➲ look at **intranet**, **ISP**

> **the Internet**
>
> If you want to **use the Internet**, you need a computer with a **modem**. If you don't have **Internet access** at home, you can go to a **cybercafe** to **surf the Net**. In order to visit a **website**, you need to type in a **URL/web address** (for example, www.oup.com/elt, said 'double-U double-U double-U dot o-u-p dot com slash e-l-t'). If you want to find information about something **on the Internet**, but you don't know where to **look it up**, you can **do a search** using a **search engine**. You can buy things **online**, join a discussion in a **chat room**, **post**

questions on a **message board**, or **download** music (but be careful you don't get a **virus**!).

internship /ˈɪntɜːnʃɪp/ noun (US) **1** a period of time during which a student or new **graduate** gets practical experience in a job, for example during the summer holiday: *an internship at a television station* ▶ **staż** ➲ look at **work experience 2** a job that an advanced student of medicine, whose training is nearly finished, does in a hospital to get further practical experience ▶ **staż** (*w szpitalu*)

interpolate /ɪnˈtɜːpəleɪt/ verb [T] (formal) **1** to make a remark that interrupts a conversation: *'But why?' he interpolated.* ▶ **wtrącać** SYN **interject 2** [T] **interpolate sth (into sth)** to add sth to a piece of writing: *The lines were interpolated into the manuscript at a later date.* ▶ **wstawiać coś (do czegoś)** SYN **insert**
■ **interpolation** /ɪnˌtɜːpəˈleɪʃn/ noun [U,C] ▶ **wtrącanie**; **wstawianie**

interpret /ɪnˈtɜːprɪt/ verb **1** [T] **interpret sth (as sth)** to explain or understand the meaning of sth: *Your silence could be interpreted as arrogance.* ◇ *How would you interpret this part of the poem?* ▶ **objaśniać**, **rozumieć** OPP **misinterpret 2** [I] **interpret (for sb)** to translate what sb is saying into another language as you hear it: *He can't speak English so he'll need somebody to interpret for him.* ▶ **tłumaczyć ustnie** (*z jednego języka na drugi*)

interpretation /ɪnˌtɜːprɪˈteɪʃn/ noun [C,U] **1** an explanation or understanding of sth: *What's your interpretation of these statistics?* ◇ *What he meant by that remark is **open to interpretation*** (można różnie interpretować). ◇ *He's always putting a wrong interpretation on* (przeinacza) *what I say.* ▶ **objaśnienie**, **interpretacja 2** the way an actor or musician chooses to perform or understand a character or piece of music: *a modern interpretation of 'Hamlet'* ▶ **interpretacja**

interpreter /ɪnˈtɜːprɪtə(r)/ noun [C] a person whose job is to translate what sb is saying immediately into another language: *The President spoke to the crowd through an interpreter.* ▶ **tłumacz/ka ustn-y/a** ➲ look at **translator**

interrelate /ˌɪntərɪˈleɪt/ verb [I,T] [usually passive] (formal) (used about two or more things) to connect or be connected very closely so that each has an effect on the other ▶ **wiązać ze sobą** (*np. fakty*); **wiązać się**
■ **interrelated** adj. ▶ **wzajemnie powiązany**

interrogate /ɪnˈterəgeɪt/ verb [T] **interrogate sb (about sth)** to ask sb a lot of questions over a long period of time, especially in an aggressive way: *The prisoner was interrogated for six hours.* ▶ **przesłuchiwać**
■ **interrogator** /ɪnˈterəgeɪtə(r)/ noun [C] ▶ **osoba przesłuchująca** | **interrogation** /ɪnˌterəˈgeɪʃn/ noun [C,U]: *The prisoner broke down **under interrogation*** (podczas przesłuchania) *and confessed.* ▶ **przesłuchanie**

interrogative¹ /ˌɪntəˈrɒgətɪv/ adj. **1** (formal) asking a question; having the form of a question: *an interrogative tone/gesture/remark* ▶ **pytający 2** (used in questions): *an interrogative sentence/pronoun/determiner/adverb* ▶ **pytajny** (*np. przysłówek*)

interrogative² /ˌɪntəˈrɒgətɪv/ noun [C] a question word: *'Who', 'what' and 'where' are interrogatives.* ▶ **zaimek pytajny**

interrupt /ˌɪntəˈrʌpt/ verb **1** [I,T] **interrupt (sb/sth) (with sth)** to say or do sth that makes sb stop what they are saying or doing: *He kept interrupting me with silly questions.* ▶ **przerywać**, **przeszkadzać 2** [T] to stop the progress of sth for a short time: *The programme was interrupted by an important news flash.* ▶ **przerywać**

interruption /ˌɪntəˈrʌpʃn/ noun [U,C] the act of interrupting sb/sth; the person or thing that interrupts sb/sth: *I've had so many interruptions this morning that I've done nothing!* ◇ *I need to work for a few hours without interruption* (bez przerwy). ▶ **przerywanie**, **zakłócanie**

intersect /ˌɪntəˈsekt/ verb [I,T] (used about roads, lines, etc.) to meet or cross each other: *The lines intersect at right angles.* ▶ **przecinać (się)**

intersection /ˌɪntəˈsekʃn/ noun [C] the place where two or more roads, lines, etc. meet or cross each other ▶ **skrzyżowanie**, **punkt przecięcia się**

intersperse /ˌɪntəˈspɜːs/ verb [T, usually passive] to put things at various points in sth: *He interspersed his speech with jokes.* ▶ **przeplatać**, **urozmaicać**

intertwine /ˌɪntəˈtwaɪn/ verb [I,T] if two things **intertwine** or if you **intertwine** them, they become very closely connected and difficult to separate: *His interests in business and politics were closely intertwined.* ▶ **splatać (się)**

interval /ˈɪntəvl/ noun [C] **1** a period of time between two events: *There was a long interval between sending the letter and getting a reply.* ▶ **przerwa**, **odstęp 2** a short break separating the different parts of a play, film, concert, etc.: *There will be two 15-minute intervals when the bar will be open.* ▶ **przerwa**, **antrakt 3** [usually pl.] a short period during which sth different happens from what is happening for the rest of the time: *There will be a few **sunny intervals*** (przejaśnienia) *between showers today.* ▶ **krótki okres**
IDM **at intervals** with time or spaces between: *I write home **at regular intervals**.* ◇ *Plant the trees at two-metre intervals.* ▶ **w odstępach**, **z przerwami**

> **interval**
> Inne słowa o podobnym znaczeniu to **intermission**, **break**, **recess**, **interlude** i **pause**. W Br. ang. rzeczownik **interval** oznacza przerwę w przedstawieniu. Odpowiednik amerykański to **intermission**. Rzeczownika **break** zwykle używa się w odniesieniu do przerw w pracy lub nauce, np. w biurze, fabryce lub szkole: *a lunch/tea break* ◇ *The children play outside in the breaks at school.* ◇ *You've worked so hard you've earned a break.* W Amer. ang. rzeczownik **recess** oznacza przerwę między lekcjami. W Br. ang. oznacza on dłuższą przerwę w pracy, zwłaszcza parlamentu lub sądu: *Parliament is in recess.* ◇ *the summer recess.* Słowo **interlude** oznacza krótki okres pomiędzy dwoma wydarzeniami, w którym dzieje się coś odmiennego: *a peaceful interlude in the fighting*. Rzeczownik **pause** oznacza chwilową przerwę w działaniu lub mówieniu: *After a moment's pause, she answered.*

intervene /ˌɪntəˈviːn/ verb [I] **1 intervene (in sth)** to become involved in a situation in order to improve it: *She would have died if the neighbours hadn't intervened.* ◇ *to intervene in a dispute* ▶ **interweniować**, **mieszać się 2** to interrupt sb who is speaking in order to say sth ▶ **przerywać**, **wtrącać 3** (used about events, etc.) to happen in a way that delays sth or stops it from happening: *If no further problems intervene, we should be able to finish in time.* ▶ **wydarzać się 4** (used about time) to come between ▶ **upływać**
■ **intervention** /ˌɪntəˈvenʃn/ noun [U,C] **intervention (in sth)**: *military intervention in the crisis* ▶ **interwencja**; **wtrącanie się**

intervening /ˌɪntəˈviːnɪŋ/ adj. [only before a noun] coming or existing between two events, dates, objects, etc.: *the intervening years/days/months* ▶ **upływający**, **zachodzący (między czymś)**

interview¹ /ˈɪntəvjuː/ noun [C] **1 an interview (for sth)** a meeting at which sb is asked questions to find out if they are suitable for a job, course of study, etc.: *to attend an interview* ▶ **rozmowa kwalifikacyjna** ➲ note at **job**

2 an interview (with sb) a meeting at which a journalist asks sb questions in order to find out their opinion, etc.: *There was an interview with the Prime Minister on TV last night.* ◇ *The actress refused to **give an interview*** (udzielić wywiadu). ▶ **wywiad (dziennikarski)**

⚷ **interview**[2] /ˈɪntəvjuː/ verb [T] **1 interview sb (for sth)** to ask sb questions to find out if they are suitable for a job, course of study, etc.: *How many applicants did you interview for the job?* ▶ **przeprowadzać rozmowę kwalifikacyjną** **2 interview sb (about sth)** to ask sb questions about their opinions, private life, etc. especially on the radio or TV or for a newspaper, magazine, etc.: *Next week, I will be interviewing Spielberg about his latest movie.* ▶ **przeprowadzać wywiad** **3 interview sb (about sth)** to ask sb questions at a private meeting: *The police are waiting to interview the injured girl.* ▶ **przesłuchiwać**

interviewee /ˌɪntəvjuːˈiː/ noun [C] a person who is questioned in an **interview** ▶ **kandydat/ka odbywając-y/a rozmowę kwalifikacyjną; osoba udzielająca wywiadu; osoba przesłuchiwana**

interviewer /ˈɪntəvjuːə(r)/ noun [C] a person who asks the questions in an **interview** ▶ **osoba przeprowadzająca wywiad/rozmowę kwalifikacyjną/przesłuchanie**

intestine /ɪnˈtestɪn/ noun [C, usually pl.] the tube in your body that carries food away from your stomach to the place where it leaves your body ▶ **jelito** ⓘ Mniej formalnym wyrazem jest **gut**. ➲ picture at **body**
■ **intestinal** /ɪnˈtestɪnl; ˌɪnteˈstaɪnl/ adj. ▶ **jelitowy**

intimacy /ˈɪntɪməsi/ noun [U] the state of having a close personal relationship with sb: *Their intimacy grew over the years.* ◇ *sexual intimacy* intymność ▶ **zażyłość**

intimate /ˈɪntɪmət/ adj. **1** (used about people) having a very close relationship: *They're intimate friends.* ▶ **zażyły, bliski** **2** very private and personal: *They told each other their most intimate secrets.* ▶ **intymny, najskrytszy** **3** (used about a place, an atmosphere, etc.) quiet and friendly: *I know an intimate little restaurant we could go to.* ▶ **przytulny, kameralny** **4** very detailed: *He's lived here all his life and has an **intimate knowledge** of the area.* ▶ **gruntowny, dokładny**
■ **intimately** adv. ▶ **blisko; poufale**

intimidate /ɪnˈtɪmɪdeɪt/ verb [T] **intimidate sb (into sth/doing sth)** to frighten or threaten sb, often in order to make them do sth: *She refused to be intimidated by their threats.* ▶ **zastraszać, onieśmielać**
■ **intimidating** adj.: *The teacher had rather an intimidating manner.* ▶ **zastraszający, onieśmielający** | **intimidation** /ɪnˌtɪmɪˈdeɪʃn/ noun [U]: *The rebel troops controlled the area by intimidation.* ▶ **zastraszenie**

⚷ **into** /ˈɪntə; before vowels ˈɪntu; strong form ˈɪntuː/ prep. **1** moving to a position inside or in sth: *Come into the house.* ◇ *I'm going into town.* ▶ **do** OPP **out of** **2** in the direction of sth: *Please speak into the microphone.* ◇ *At this point we were driving into the sun and had to shade our eyes.* ▶ **do** **3** to a point at which you hit sth: *I backed the car into a wall.* ◇ *She walked into a glass door.* ▶ **w (coś)** **4** showing a change from one thing to another: *We're turning the spare room into a study.* ◇ *She changed into her jeans.* ◇ *The new rules will **come into force*** (wejdą w życie) *next year.* ◇ *Translate the passage into German.* ▶ **na/w (coś)** **5** concerning or involving sth: *an inquiry into safety procedures* ▶ **w sprawie czegoś** **6** (used when you are talking about dividing numbers): *7 into 28 goes 4 times.* ▶ **na, przez**
IDM **be into sth** (informal) to be very interested in sth, for example as a hobby: *I'm really into canoeing.* ▶ **być entuzjast(k)ą czegoś** ➲ note at **like**

intolerable /ɪnˈtɒlərəbl/ adj. too bad, unpleasant or difficult to bear or accept: *The living conditions were intolerable.* ◇ *intolerable pain* ▶ **nieznośny, nie do zniesienia/przyjęcia** SYN **unbearable** OPP **tolerable**
■ **intolerably** /-əbli/ adv. ▶ **nieznośnie**

intolerant /ɪnˈtɒlərənt/ adj. **intolerant (of sb/sth)** not able to accept behaviour or opinions that are different from your own; finding sb/sth too unpleasant to bear: *She's very intolerant of young children.* ▶ **nietolerancyjny** OPP **tolerant**
■ **intolerance** noun [U] ▶ **nietolerancja** OPP **tolerance** | **intolerantly** adv. ▶ **nietolerancyjnie**

intonation /ˌɪntəˈneɪʃn/ noun [C,U] the rise and fall of your voice while you are speaking ▶ **intonacja** SYN **inflection**

intoxicated /ɪnˈtɒksɪkeɪtɪd/ adj. (formal) **1** having had too much alcohol to drink; drunk ▶ **w stanie nietrzeźwym** **2** very excited and happy: *She was intoxicated by her success.* ▶ **odurzony, upojony**
■ **intoxication** /ɪnˌtɒksɪˈkeɪʃn/ noun [U] ▶ **odurzenie alkoholowe, stan nietrzeźwy**

intranet /ˈɪntrənet/ noun [C] a system of computers inside an organization that makes it possible for people who work there to look at the same information and to send information to each other ▶ **wewnętrzna sieć komputerowa** ➲ look at **Internet**

intransigent /ɪnˈtrænsɪdʒənt; US -ˈtrænz-/ adj. (formal) (used about people) unwilling to change their opinions or behaviour in a way that would be helpful to others SYN **stubborn**: *an intransigent attitude* ▶ **nieprzejednany**
■ **intransigence** /-əns/ noun [U] ▶ **nieprzejednanie**

intransitive /ɪnˈtrænsətɪv/ adj. (used about a verb) used without an object. Intransitive verbs are marked '[I]' in this dictionary. ▶ **nieprzechodni** ⓘ W niniejszym słowniku czasowniki nieprzechodnie są oznaczone [I]. OPP **transitive**
■ **intransitively** adv.: *The verb is being used intransitively.* ▶ **w sposób nieprzechodni**

intravenous /ˌɪntrəˈviːnəs/ adj. (abbr. **IV**) (used about drugs or food) going into a **vein**: *intravenous fluids* ◇ *an intravenous drug user* ▶ **dożylny**
■ **intravenously** adv. ▶ **dożylnie**

ˈ**in tray** noun [C] (in an office) a container on your desk for letters that are waiting to be read or answered: *She had a full in tray to deal with when she got back.* ▶ **tacka na korespondencję przychodzącą**

intrepid /ɪnˈtrepɪd/ adj. without any fear of danger: *an intrepid climber* ▶ **nieustraszony**

intricacy /ˈɪntrɪkəsi/ noun **1** (**intricacies**) [pl.] **the intricacies of sth** the complicated parts or details of sth: *It's difficult to understand all the intricacies of the situation.* ▶ **zawiłość, złożoność** **2** [U] the quality of having complicated parts, details or patterns ▶ **kunsztowność, misterność**

intricate /ˈɪntrɪkət/ adj. having many small parts or details put together in a complicated way: *The story has an intricate plot.* ◇ *an intricate pattern* ▶ **złożony, zawiły; kunsztowny**
■ **intricately** adv. ▶ **w sposób złożony; kunsztwonie**

intrigue[1] /ɪnˈtriːg/ verb [T] to make sb very interested and wanting to know more: *I was intrigued by the way he seemed to know all about us already.* ▶ **ciekawić, intrygować**
■ **intriguing** adj.: *an intriguing story* ▶ **intrygujący**

intrigue[2] /ˈɪntriːg/ noun [C,U] secret plans to do sth, especially sth bad: *The film is about political intrigues against the government.* ◇ *His new novel is full of intrigue and suspense.* ▶ **intryga, knowanie**

intrinsic /ɪnˈtrɪnsɪk; -zɪk/ adj. [only before a noun] belonging to sth as part of its nature; basic: *The object is of no*

intrinsic value (bez żadnej wartości). ▶ **istotny, rzeczywisty, faktyczny**
■ **intrinsically** /-kli/ adv. ▶ **istotnie, rzeczywiście, faktycznie**

intro /ˈɪntrəʊ/ noun [C] (pl. **-os**) (informal) an introduction to sth, especially to a piece of music or writing ▶ **wstęp**

introduce /ˌɪntrəˈdjuːs; US ˈduːs/ verb [T] **1 introduce sb (to sb)** to tell two or more people who have not met before what each other's names are: *'Who's that girl over there?' 'Come with me and I'll introduce you to her.'* ▶ **przedstawiać, zapoznawać 2 introduce yourself (to sb)** to tell sb you have met for the first time what your name is: *He came over and introduced himself to me.* ▶ **przedstawiać się 3** to be the first or main speaker on a radio or TV programme telling the audience who is going to speak, perform, etc.: *May I introduce my first guest on the show tonight...* ▶ **przedstawiać, zapowiadać** (*czyjś występ*) **4 introduce sb to sth** to make sb begin to learn about sth or do sth for the first time: *This pamphlet will introduce you to the basic aims of our society.* ▶ **zapoznawać kogoś z czymś, wprowadzać kogoś w coś 5 introduce sth (in/into sth)** to bring in sth new, use sth, or take sth to a place for the first time: *The new law was introduced in 1991.* ◇ *The company is introducing a new range of cars this summer.* ◇ *Rabbits were first introduced* (pierwsze króliki zostały przywiezione) *to Australia in the 18th century.* ▶ **wprowadzać coś (gdzieś)**

introducing people

W Wlk. Br. istnieje kilka sposobów przedstawienia sobie osób, w zależności od sytuacji. W sytuacjach oficjalnych poprzedzamy czyjeś nazwisko odpowiednim tytułem. W sytuacji nieoficjalnej lub kiedy przedstawiamy dzieci zazwyczaj używamy tylko imion. W obu sytuacjach używamy konstrukcji **this is**; nie używamy konsktrucji z ~~he/she is~~ lub ~~here is~~ (formal) *'May I introduce you. Dr Waters, **this is** Mr Jones. Mr Jones, Dr Waters.'* ◇ (informal) *'John, meet Mary.'* ◇ (informal) *'Mrs Smith, **this is** my daughter, Jane.'* Nieformalna odpowiedź na przedstawienie kogoś komuś to **Hello** lub **Nice/Pleased to meet you**. Odpowiedź formalna (i coraz częściej odczuwana jako staromodna) to **How do you do?** Druga osoba także odpowiada **How do you do?** Niektórzy ludzie, zwłaszcza w kręgach biznesu, przy przedstawieniu wymieniają uścisk dłoni, ale młodzi najczęściej tego nie stosują.

introduction /ˌɪntrəˈdʌkʃn/ noun **1** [U] **introduction of sth (into sth)** the act of bringing in sth new; using sth or taking sth to a place for the first time: *the introduction of computers into the classroom* ▶ **wprowadzanie, za/stosowanie 2** [C, usually pl.] the act of telling two or more people each other's names for the first time: *I think I'll get my husband to **make/do the introductions*** (dokonał prezentacji) – *he's better at remembering names!* ▶ **przedstawianie, zaznajamianie (kogoś z kimś) 3** [sing.] **an introduction to sth** first experience of sth: *My first job – in a factory – was not a pleasant introduction to work.* ▶ **wprowadzenie 4** [C] the first part of a book, a piece of written work or a talk which gives a general idea of what is going to follow: *a brief introduction* ▶ **wstęp, przedmowa 5** [C] **an introduction (to sth)** a book for people who are beginning to study a subject: *'An Introduction to English Grammar'* ▶ **wprowadzenie**

introductory /ˌɪntrəˈdʌktəri/ adj. **1** happening or said at the beginning in order to give a general idea of what will follow: *an introductory speech/chapter/remark* ▶ **wstępny, wprowadzający** SYN **opening 2** intended as an introduction to a subject or an activity: *introductory courses* ▶ (*kurs itp.*) **wprowadzający 3** offered for a short time only, when a product is first on sale: *an **introductory price/offer*** ▶ (*cena itp.*) **promocyjny**

introspection /ˌɪntrəˈspekʃn/ noun [U] the careful examination of your own thoughts, feelings and reasons for behaving in a particular way ▶ **introspekcja**

introspective /ˌɪntrəˈspektɪv/ adj. tending to think a lot about your own thoughts, feelings, etc. ▶ **introspektywny**

introvert /ˈɪntrəvɜːt/ noun [C] a quiet, shy person who prefers to be alone than with other people ▶ **introwerty-k/czka** OPP **extrovert**
■ **introverted** adj. ▶ **zamknięty w sobie, introwertyczny** OPP **extroverted**

intrude /ɪnˈtruːd/ verb [I] **intrude on/upon sb/sth** to enter a place or situation without permission or when you are not wanted: *I'm sorry to intrude on your Sunday lunch but...* ▶ **wchodzić gdzieś niespodziewanie i nie będąc zaproszonym**

intruder /ɪnˈtruːdə(r)/ noun [C] a person who enters a place without permission and often secretly ▶ **intruz**

intrusion /ɪnˈtruːʒn/ noun [C,U] **(an) intrusion (on/upon/ into sth)** something that disturbs you or your life when you want to be private: *This was another example of press intrusion into the affairs of the royals.* ▶ **narzucanie się, wtargnięcie, naruszenie czyjejś prywatności**
■ **intrusive** /ɪnˈtruːsɪv/ adj. ▶ **nieproszony**

intuition /ˌɪntjuˈɪʃn; US -tu-/ noun [C,U] the feeling or understanding that makes you believe or know sth is true without being able to explain why: *She knew, by intuition* (intuicyjnie), *about his illness although he never mentioned it.* ▶ **intuicja, przeczucie**

intuitive /ɪnˈtjuːɪtɪv; US -ˈtuː-/ adj. **1** (used about ideas) obtained by using your feelings rather than by considering the facts: *He had an intuitive sense of what the reader wanted.* ▶ **intuicyjny 2** (used about people) able to understand sth by using feelings rather than by considering the facts ▶ **intuicyjny 3** (used about computer software, etc.) easy to understand and to use ▶ (*program komputerowy itp.*) **przyjazny**
■ **intuitively** adv.: *Intuitively, she knew that he was lying.* ▶ **intuicyjnie**

Inuit /ˈɪnuɪt/ noun [pl.] a race of people from northern Canada and parts of Greenland and Alaska ▶ **Inuit/ka, Eskimos/ka** ➲ look at **Eskimo**
■ **Inuit** adj. ▶ **dotyczący Inuitów, eskimoski**

inundate /ˈɪnʌndeɪt/ verb [T, usually passive] **1 inundate sb (with sth)** to give or send sb so many things that they cannot deal with them all: *We were inundated with applications for the job.* ▶ **zasypywać (czymś)** SYN **swamp 2** (formal) to cover an area of land with water: *After the heavy rains the fields were inundated.* ▶ **zalewać** ⓘ Mniej formalne słowo to **flood**.

invade /ɪnˈveɪd/ verb **1** [I,T] to enter a country with an army in order to attack and take control of it: *When did the Romans invade Britain?* ▶ **najeżdżać** ➲ note at **war 2** [T] to enter in large numbers, often where sb/sth is not wanted: *The whole area has been invaded by tourists.* ◇ *The town is invaded with* (opanowany przez) *tourists every summer.* ▶ (*przen.*) **dokonywać inwazji, okupować** ➲ noun **invasion**
■ **invader** noun [C] ▶ **najeźdźca**

invalid[1] /ɪnˈvælɪd/ adj. **1** not legally or officially acceptable: *I'm afraid your passport is invalid.* ▶ **nieprawomocny, nieważny** OPP **valid 2** not correct according to reason; not based on all the facts: *an invalid argument* ▶ **nieważny, bezpodstawny 3** (used about an instruction, etc.) of a type that the computer cannot recognize: *an invalid command* ▶ **nieprawidłowy**

invalid[2] /ˈɪnvəlɪd/ noun [C] a person who has been very ill for a long time and needs to be looked after ▶ **osoba niepełnosprawna**

invalidate /ɪnˈvælɪdeɪt/ verb [T] (formal) **1** to prove that an idea, a story, an argument, etc. is wrong: *This new piece of evidence invalidates his version of events.* ▶ **obalać** (*np. teorię*) **2** to make a document, contract, election, etc. no longer legally or officially valid or acceptable ▶ **unieważniać** (*np. kontrakt*) OPP for both meanings **valid-ate**
■ **invalidation** /ɪnˌvælɪˈdeɪʃn/ noun [U] ▶ **obalenie**; **unieważnienie**

invaluable /ɪnˈvæljuəbl/ adj. **invaluable (to/for sb/sth)** extremely useful: *invaluable help/information/support* ▶ **nieoceniony**, **bezcenny** ℹ Uwaga! **Invaluable** nie jest antonimem **valuable**. Słowem o przeciwnym znaczeniu jest **valueless** lub **worthless**.

invariable /ɪnˈveəriəbl/ adj. not changing ▶ **niezmienny**

invariably /ɪnˈveəriəbli/ adv. almost always: *She invariably arrives late.* ▶ **niezmiennie**, **zawsze**

invasion /ɪnˈveɪʒn/ noun **1** [C,U] the act of entering another country with your army in order to take control of it: *the threat of invasion* ▶ **najazd**; **inwazja** **2** [C] the act of entering a place where you are not wanted and disturbing sb: *Such questions are an* ***invasion of privacy.*** ▶ **naruszenie** (*np. czyjejś prywatności*) ➲ verb **invade**

invasive /ɪnˈveɪsɪv/ adj. (formal) **1** (especially used about diseases within the body) spreading very quickly and difficult to stop: *invasive cancer* ▶ **inwazyjny** **2** (used about medical treatment) involving cutting into the body: *invasive surgery* ▶ **inwazyjny** ➲ look at **invade**

invective /ɪnˈvektɪv/ noun [U] (formal) rude language and unpleasant remarks that sb shouts when they are very angry: *The gesture infuriated him and he let out a stream of invective.* ▶ **inwektywa**

⚷ **invent** /ɪnˈvent/ verb [T] **1** to think of or make sth for the first time: *When was the camera invented?* ▶ **wynaleźć** **2** to say or describe sth that is not true: *I realized that he had invented the whole story.* ▶ **wymyślać**
■ **inventor** noun [C] ▶ **wynalaz-ca/czyni**

⚷ **invention** /ɪnˈvenʃn/ noun **1** [C] a thing that has been made or designed by sb for the first time: *The microwave oven is a very useful invention.* ▶ **wynalazek** **2** [U] the action or process of making or designing sth for the first time: *Books had to be written by hand before the invention of printing.* ▶ **wynalezienie** **3** [C,U] telling a story or giving an excuse that is not true: *It was obvious that his story about being robbed was (an) invention.* ▶ **wymysł**

inventive /ɪnˈventɪv/ adj. having clever and original ideas ▶ **pomysłowy**, **wynalazczy**
■ **inventiveness** noun [U] ▶ **pomysłowość**

inventory /ˈɪnvəntri; US -tɔːri/ noun [C] (pl. **inventories**) a detailed list, for example of all the furniture in a house: *The landlord is coming to* ***make an inventory*** *of the contents of the flat.* ▶ **inwentarz**

inverse /ˌɪnˈvɜːs/ adj. [only before a noun] opposite in amount or position to sth else: *A person's wealth is often* ***in inverse proportion to*** *their happiness.* ◇ *There is often an* ***inverse relationship*** *between the power of the tool and how easy it is to use.* ▶ **odwrotny**
■ **the inverse** noun [sing.] the exact opposite of sth ▶ **odwrotność** | **inversely** /ˌɪnˈvɜːsli/ adv.: *We regard health as inversely related to social class.* ▶ **odwrotnie**

invert /ɪnˈvɜːt/ verb [T] (formal) to put sth in the opposite order or position to the way it usually is: *What you see in a mirror is an inverted image* (odwrócone odbicie) *of yourself.* ▶ **odwracać**

invertebrate /ɪnˈvɜːtɪbrət/ noun [C] an animal with no backbone ▶ (*biol.*) **bezkręgowiec**

inˌverted ˈcommas (Brit.) = QUOTATION MARKS

⚷ **invest** /ɪnˈvest/ verb [I,T] **invest (sth) (in sth)** **1** to put money into a bank, business, property, etc. in the hope that you will make a profit: *Many firms have invested heavily in this project.* ◇ *I've invested all my money in the company.* ▶ **inwestować** ➲ note at **money** **2** to spend money, time or energy on sth that you think is good or useful: *I'm thinking of investing in a computer.* ◇ *You have to invest a lot of time if you really want to learn a language well.* ▶ **kupować**; **inwestować**, **wkładać (w coś)** (*np. kapitał, czas, energię*)
■ **investor** noun [C] ▶ **inwestor/ka**

⚷ **investigate** /ɪnˈvestɪgeɪt/ verb [I,T] to try to find out all the facts about sth: *A murder was reported and the police were sent to investigate.* ◇ *A group of experts are investigating the cause of the crash.* ▶ **prowadzić dochodzenie**, **badać**
■ **investigator** noun [C] ▶ **badacz/ka**, **osoba prowadząca dochodzenie**

⚷ **investigation** /ɪnˌvestɪˈgeɪʃn/ noun [C,U] **(an) investigation (into sth)**: *The airlines are going to* ***carry out an investigation*** *into security procedures at airports.* ◇ *The matter is still* ***under investigation*** (jest nadal przedmiotem dochodzenia) *by the police.* ▶ **dochodzenie**, **badanie**

investigative /ɪnˈvestɪgətɪv; US -geɪtɪv/ adj. trying to find out all the facts about sb/sth: *investigative journalism* dziennikarstwo śledcze ▶ **badawczy**, **dochodzeniowy**

⚷ **investment** /ɪnˈvestmənt/ noun **1** [U,C] **(an) investment (in sth)** the act of putting money in a bank, business, property, etc.; the amount of money that you put in: *investment in local industry* ◇ *The company will have to* ***make an*** *enormous* ***investment*** *to computerize production.* ▶ **inwestycja**, **inwestowanie** **2** [C] (informal) a thing that you have bought: *This coat has been a good investment – I've worn it for three years.* ▶ **inwestycja** (*zakupiony przedmiot*)

inˈvestment bank (US) = MERCHANT BANK

invidious /ɪnˈvɪdiəs/ adj. (formal) unpleasant and unfair; likely to offend sb or make them jealous: *We were* ***in the invidious position*** (w niewdzięcznej sytuacji) *of having to choose whether to break the law or risk lives.* ◇ *It would be invidious to single out any one person to thank.* ▶ **krzywdzący**

invigilate /ɪnˈvɪdʒɪleɪt/ verb [I,T] (Brit.) to watch the people taking an exam to make sure that nobody is cheating ▶ **pilnować podczas egzaminu**
■ **invigilator** noun [C] ▶ **osoba pilnująca podczas egzaminu**

invigorate /ɪnˈvɪgəreɪt/ verb [I,T] to make sb feel healthy, fresh and full of energy: *I felt invigorated after my run.* ▶ **orzeźwiać**, **dodawać energii**
■ **invigorating** adj. ▶ **orzeźwiający**, **dodający energii**

invincible /ɪnˈvɪnsəbl/ adj. too strong or powerful to be defeated ▶ **niezwyciężony**, **niepokonany**, (*wiara itp.*) **niezachwiany**

invisible /ɪnˈvɪzəbl/ adj. **invisible (to sb/sth)** that cannot be seen: *bacteria that are invisible to the naked eye* ▶ **niewidzialny**, **niewidoczny** OPP **visible**
■ **invisibility** /ɪnˌvɪzəˈbɪləti/ noun [U] ▶ **niewidzialność**, **niewidoczność** | **invisibly** /-əbli/ adv. ▶ **niewidzialnie**, **niewidocznie**

⚷ **invitation** /ˌɪnvɪˈteɪʃn/ noun **1** [C] **an invitation to sb/sth (to sth/to do sth)** a written or spoken request to go somewhere or do sth: *Did you get an invitation to the conference?* ◇ *a wedding invitation* ◇ *to* ***accept an invitation*** ◇ *to* ***turn down****/(formal)* ***decline an invitation*** ▶ **zaproszenie** **2** [U] the act of inviting sb or being invited:

Entry is by invitation only. ◇ *a letter of invitation* list zapraszający ▶ **zaproszenie**, **zapraszanie**

invite /ɪn'vaɪt/ verb [T] **1 invite sb (to/for sth)** to ask sb to come somewhere or to do sth: *We invited all the family to the wedding.* ◇ *Successful applicants will be invited for interview next week.* ▶ **zapraszać 2** to make sth unpleasant likely to happen: *You're inviting trouble* (narobisz sobie biedy) *if you carry so much money around.* ▶ **prowokować**; **zachęcać (do czegoś)**

PHR V **invite sb back 1** to ask sb to return with you to your home: *Shall we invite the others back for coffee after the meeting?* ▶ **zapraszać kogoś do swojego domu po wspólnym pobycie gdzieś 2** to ask sb to come to your home a second time, or after you have been a guest at their home ▶ **zapraszać na rewizytę**

invite sb in to ask sb to come into your home ▶ **zapraszać kogoś do środka** (*do siebie do domu*)

invite sb out to ask sb to go out somewhere with you: *We've been invited out to lunch by the neighbours.* ▶ **zapraszać kogoś na wspólne wyjście**

invite sb over/round (informal) to ask sb to come to your home: *I've invited Jacek and his family round for lunch on Sunday.* ▶ **zapraszać kogoś do siebie do domu** ℹ Zwróć uwagę, że we wszystkich podanych znaczeniach można stosować czasownik **ask** wymiennie z czasownikiem **invite**.

inviting /ɪn'vaɪtɪŋ/ adj. attractive and pleasant: *The smell of cooking was very inviting.* ▶ **pociągający**, **zapraszający**

in vitro /ɪn 'viːtrəʊ/ adj. (used about a process or a reaction) taking place in a glass tube or dish, not inside a living body: *in vitro experiments* ◇ *the development of in vitro fertilization* ▶ **in vitro**

■ **in vitro** adv.: *an egg fertilized in vitro* ▶ **in vitro**

invoice /'ɪnvɔɪs/ noun [C] an official paper that lists goods or services that you have received and says how much you have to pay for them ▶ **faktura**

involuntary /ɪn'vɒləntri; US -teri/ adj. done without wanting or meaning to: *She gave an involuntary gasp of pain as the doctor inserted the needle.* ▶ **mimowolny**, **nieumyślny** OPP **voluntary**, **deliberate**

■ **involuntarily** /ɪn'vɒləntrəli; US ɪnˌvɑːlən'terəli/ adv. ▶ **mimowolnie**, **nieumyślnie**

involve /ɪn'vɒlv/ verb [T] **1** [not used in the continuous tenses] to make sth necessary: *The job involves a lot of travelling.* ▶ **wymagać**, **pociągać za sobą 2** [not used in the continuous tenses] if a situation, an event or an activity involves sb/sth, he/she/it takes part in it: *The story involves a woman who went on holiday with her child.* ◇ *More than 100 people were involved in the project.* ▶ **dotyczyć**; **angażować** ℹ Mimo że czasownika **involve** w znaczeniu 1 i 2 nie używa się w czasach *continuous*, często spotyka się go w *present participle* (formie *-ing*): *There was a serious accident involving a stolen car.* **3 involve sb/sth in (doing) sth** to cause sb/sth to take part in or be concerned with sth: *Please don't involve me in your family arguments.* ▶ **wciągać/mieszać (kogoś w coś)**

■ **involvement** noun [C,U]: *They deny any involvement in the robbery.* ▶ **zaangażowanie**

involved /ɪn'vɒlvd/ adj. **1** [not before a noun] **involved (in sth)** closely connected with sth; taking an active part in sth: *I'm very involved in local politics.* ▶ **zaangażowany 2** [not before a noun] **involved (with sb)** having a sexual relationship with sb: *She is involved with an older man.* ▶ **zaangażowany** (*np. uczuciowo*) **3** difficult to understand; complicated: *The book has a very involved plot.* ▶ **pogmatwany**, **zawiły**

inward /'ɪnwəd/ adv. (also **inwards**) towards the inside or centre: *Stand in a circle facing inwards.* ▶ **skierowany do środka/wnętrza** OPP **outward**

■ **inward** adj. [only before a noun] inside your mind, not shown to other people: *my inward feelings* ▶ **myślowy**, **wewnętrzny**, **duchowy** OPP **outward**

inwardly /'ɪnwədli/ adv. in your mind; secretly: *He was inwardly relieved that they could not come to the party.* ▶ **w duchu**, **skrycie**

iodine /'aɪədiːn; US -daɪn/ noun [U] (symbol **I**) a substance that is found in sea water. A purple liquid containing **iodine** is sometimes used to clean cuts in your skin. ▶ **jod**, **jodyna**

IOU /ˌaɪ əʊ 'juː/ abbr. **I owe you**; a piece of paper that you sign showing that you owe sb some money ▶ **jestem dłużny**; **skrypt dłużny**

IPA /ˌaɪ piː 'eɪ/ abbr. the **International Phonetic Alphabet** ▶ **międzynarodowy alfabet fonetyczny**

IQ /ˌaɪ 'kjuː/ abbr. **intelligence quotient**; a measure of how intelligent sb is: *to have a high/low IQ* ◇ *an IQ of 120* ▶ **iloraz inteligencji**

ir- → IN-

IRA /ˌaɪ ɑːr 'eɪ/ abbr. the **Irish Republican Army** ▶ **Irlandzka Armia Republikańska**

irate /aɪ'reɪt/ adj. (formal) very angry ▶ **wściekły**, **rozgniewany**

iridescent /ˌɪrɪ'desnt/ adj. (formal) showing many bright colours that seem to change in different lights ▶ **opalizujący**

■ **iridescence** /-'desns/ noun [U] ▶ **opalizacja**

iris /'aɪrɪs/ noun [C] **1** the coloured part of your eye ▶ **tęczówka** ➲ look at **pupil 2** a tall plant with long pointed leaves and large bright yellow or purple flowers ▶ **kosaciec**, **irys**

Irish /'aɪrɪʃ/ adj. from Ireland ▶ **irlandzki** ℹ Więcej informacji w dodatku *Nazwy geograficzne i mapy* na końcu słownika.

irk /ɜːk/ verb [T] (formal or literary) to annoy or irritate sb: *Her flippant tone irked him.* ▶ **drażnić**

irksome /'ɜːksəm/ adj. (formal) annoying or irritating ▶ **męczący**, **denerwujący** SYN **tiresome**

iron¹ /'aɪən/ noun **1** [U] (symbol **Fe**) a hard strong metal that is used for making steel and is found in small quantities in food and in blood: *an iron bar* ◇ *iron ore* ruda żelaza ◇ *wrought-iron* (z kutego żelaza) *railings* ◇ *a pot made of cast iron* (z lanego żelaza) ◇ *The roof of the hut was made of corrugated iron* (z blachy falistej). ◇ *The doctor gave me iron tablets.* ◇ (figurative) *The general has an iron will* (żelazną wolę). ▶ **żelazo 2** [C] an electrical instrument with a flat bottom that is heated and used to smooth clothes after you have washed and dried them: *a steam iron* ▶ **żelazko**

iron² /'aɪən/ verb [I,T] to use an iron to make clothes, etc. smooth: *That shirt needs ironing.* ▶ **prasować** ℹ Zamiast czasownika **iron** stosuje się często zwrot **do the ironing**: *I usually do the ironing on Sunday.*

PHR V **iron sth out** to get rid of any problems or difficulties that are affecting sth ▶ **rozwiązywać** (*np. problemy*)

the ˌIron 'Curtain noun [sing.] the name that people used for the border that used to exist between Western Europe and the **communist** countries of Eastern Europe ▶ **żelazna kurtyna**

ironic /aɪ'rɒnɪk/ (also **ironical** /aɪ'rɒnɪkl/) adj. **1** meaning the opposite of what you say: *an ironic sense of humour* ▶ **ironiczny** ➲ look at **sarcastic 2** (used about a situation) strange or amusing because it is unusual or unexpected: *It is ironic that* (paradoksalnie) *the busiest people are often the most willing to help.* ▶ **ironiczny**, **paradoksalny**

■ **ironically** /-kli/ adv. ▶ **ironicznie**, **jak na ironię**

ironing /ˈaɪənɪŋ/ noun [U] clothes, etc. that you have just ironed or that you need to iron: *a large pile of ironing* ▶ **prasowanie** (*rzeczy do prasowania lub już wyprasowane*)

ˈ**ironing board** noun [C] a special narrow table covered with cloth that you iron clothes on ▶ **deska do prasowania**

irony /ˈaɪrəni/ noun (pl. **ironies**) **1** [C,U] an unusual or unexpected part of a situation, etc. that seems strange or amusing: *The irony was that* (jak na ironię losu) *he was killed in a car accident soon after the end of the war.* ▶ **ironia**, **paradoks 2** [U] a way of speaking that shows you are joking or that you mean the opposite of what you say: *'The English are such good cooks', he said with heavy irony.* ▶ **ironia**

irradiate /ɪˈreɪdieɪt/ verb [T] to send rays of radioactivity through sth ▶ **napromieniowywać**

irrational /ɪˈræʃənl/ adj. not based on reason or clear thought: *an irrational fear of spiders* ▶ **irracjonalny**, **nieracjonalny**
■ **irrationality** /ɪˌræʃəˈnæləti/ noun [U] ▶ **irracjonalność**, **nieracjonalność** | **irrationally** /ɪˈræʃənəli/ adv. ▶ **irracjonalnie**, **nieracjonalnie**

irreconcilable /ɪˌrekənˈsaɪləbl/ adj. (formal) (used about people or their ideas and beliefs) so different that they cannot be made to agree ▶ **nie do pogodzenia**, **nieprzejednany**
■ **irreconcilably** /-əbli/ adv. ▶ **(w sposób) nie do pogodzenia**, **nieprzejednanie**

irredeemable /ˌɪrɪˈdiːməbl/ adj. (formal) too bad to be corrected, improved or saved ▶ **niereformowalny**, **zatwardziały**, **nieodwracalny** SYN **hopeless**
■ **irredeemably** /-əbli/ adv.: *irredeemably spoilt* ▶ **nieodwracalnie**

irrefutable /ˌɪrɪˈfjuːtəbl; ɪˈrefjətəbl/ adj. (formal) that cannot be proved wrong and that must therefore be accepted: *irrefutable evidence* ▶ **niezbity**
■ **irrefutably** /-əbli/ adv. ▶ **niezbicie**

irregular /ɪˈregjələ(r)/ adj. **1** not having a shape or pattern that we recognize or can predict: *an irregular shape* ▶ **nieregularny**, **nierównomierny**, **nierówny** OPP **regular 2** happening at times that you cannot predict: *His visits became more and more irregular.* ▶ **nieregularny**, **nierównomierny** OPP **regular 3** not allowed according to the rules or social customs: *It is highly irregular for a doctor to give information about patients without their permission.* ▶ **niezgodny z przepisami/zasadami 4** not following the usual rules of grammar: *'Caught' is an irregular past tense form.* ▶ **nieregularny** OPP **regular**
■ **irregularity** /ɪˌregjəˈlærəti/ noun [C,U] (pl. **irregularities**) ▶ **nieregularność**, **nierównomierność**, **nierówność**; **niezgodność z przepisami/zasadami** | **irregularly** adv. ▶ **nieregularnie**, **nierównomiernie**, **nierówno**; **niezgodnie z przepisami**

irrelevant /ɪˈreləvənt/ adj. not connected with sth or important to it: *That evidence is irrelevant to the case.* ▶ **oderwany od tematu/rzeczy itp.** OPP **relevant**
■ **irrelevance** (also **irrelevancy** pl. **irrelevancies**) noun **1** [C] something that is irrelevant ▶ **rzecz nieistotna**, **błahostka 2** [U] the state of being irrelevant ▶ **oderwanie od tematu** | **irrelevantly** adv. ▶ **niestosownie**, **od rzeczy**

irreparable /ɪˈrepərəbl/ adj. that cannot be repaired: *Irreparable damage has been done to the ancient forests of Eastern Europe.* ▶ **nie do naprawienia**, **niepowetowany**
■ **irreparably** /-əbli/ adv. ▶ **w sposób nie do naprawienia**

irreplaceable /ˌɪrɪˈpleɪsəbl/ adj. (used about sth very valuable or special) that cannot be replaced ▶ **niezastąpiony** OPP **replaceable**

irrepressible /ˌɪrɪˈpresəbl/ adj. full of life and energy: *young people full of irrepressible good humour* ▶ **niepohamowany**, **niepowstrzymany**
■ **irrepressibly** /-əbli/ adv. ▶ **w sposób niepohamowany**, **niepowstrzymanie**

irreproachable /ˌɪrɪˈprəʊtʃəbl/ adj. (used about a person or their behaviour) free from fault and impossible to criticize ▶ **nienaganny**; **nieskazitelny** SYN **blameless**

irresistible /ˌɪrɪˈzɪstəbl/ adj. **1** so strong that it cannot be stopped or prevented: *an irresistible urge to laugh* ▶ **nieprzeparty**, **nieodparty 2 irresistible (to sb)** very attractive: *He seems to think he's irresistible to women.* ▶ **taki, że nie można się (czemuś/komuś) oprzeć** ➲ verb **resist**
■ **irresistibly** /-əbli/ adv. ▶ **nieprzeparcie**, **nieodparcie**

irrespective of /ˌɪrɪˈspektɪv əv/ prep. not affected by: *Anybody can take part in the competition, irrespective of age.* ▶ **niezależnie (od czegoś)**, **bez względu (na coś)**

irresponsible /ˌɪrɪˈspɒnsəbl/ adj. not thinking about the effect your actions will have; not sensible ▶ **nieodpowiedzialny**, **lekkomyślny** OPP **responsible**
■ **irresponsibility** /ˌɪrɪˌspɒnsəˈbɪləti/ noun [U] ▶ **nieodpowiedzialność**, **lekkomyślność** | **irresponsibly** /ˌɪrɪˈspɒnsəbli/ adv. ▶ **nieodpowiedzialnie**, **lekkomyślnie**

irretrievable /ˌɪrɪˈtriːvəbl/ adj. (formal) that you can never make right or get back: *the irretrievable breakdown of the marriage* ◇ *The money already paid is irretrievable.* ▶ **bezpowrotnie stracony**, **nieodwracalny**
■ **irretrievably** /-əbli/ adv.: *Some of our old traditions are irretrievably lost.* ▶ **nieodwracalnie**

irreverent /ɪˈrevərənt/ adj. not feeling or showing respect: *This comedy takes an irreverent look at the world of politics.* ▶ **bez szacunku**, **lekceważący**
■ **irreverence** noun [U] ▶ **brak szacunku**, **lekceważenie** | **irreverently** adv. ▶ **bez szacunku**, **lekceważąco**

irreversible /ˌɪrɪˈvɜːsəbl/ adj. that cannot be stopped or changed: *an irreversible decision* ◇ *The disease can do irreversible damage to the body.* ▶ **nieodwołalny**, **nieodwracalny**
■ **irreversibly** /-əbli/ adv. ▶ **nieodwołalnie**, **nieodwracalnie**

irrigate /ˈɪrɪgeɪt/ verb [T] to supply water to an area of land so that crops will grow: *irrigated land/crops* ▶ **nawadniać**
■ **irrigation** /ˌɪrɪˈgeɪʃn/ noun [U] ▶ **nawadnianie**

irritable /ˈɪrɪtəbl/ adj. becoming angry easily: *to be/feel/get irritable* ▶ **drażliwy**, **skory do gniewu** SYN **bad-tempered**
■ **irritability** /ˌɪrɪtəˈbɪləti/ noun [U] ▶ **drażliwość**, **nadpobudliwość** | **irritably** /ˈɪrɪtəbli/ adv. ▶ **z rozdrażnieniem/irytacją**

ˌ**irritable ˈbowel syndrome** noun [U] a condition of the **bowels** that causes pain and **diarrhoea** or **constipation**, often caused by stress or anxiety ▶ **zespół nadwrażliwości jelita grubego**

🔑 **irritate** /ˈɪrɪteɪt/ verb [T] **1** to make sb angry: *It really irritates me the way he keeps repeating himself.* ▶ **denerwować**, **drażnić** SYN **annoy 2** to cause a part of the body to be painful or sore: *I don't use soap because it irritates my skin.* ▶ **podrażniać**
■ **irritated** adj. **irritated (at/by/with sth)** annoyed or angry: *She was getting more and more irritated at his comments.* ▶ **zdenerwowany**, **rozdrażniony/podirytowany (z powodu czegoś)** | **irritating** adj.: *I found her extremely irritating* ▶ **denerwujący**, **drażniący**; **po-**

drażniający | **irritation** /ˌɪrɪˈteɪʃn/ noun [C,U] | ▶ **zdenerwowanie**, **gniew**; **podrażnienie**

is /ɪz/ → BE

ISBN /ˌaɪ es biː ˈen/ noun [C] International Standard Book Number ▶ **ISBN** (*międzynarodowy znormalizowany numer książki*)

-ish [in compounds] **1** from the country mentioned: *Turkish* ▶ **-cki**, **-dzki** **2** having the nature of; like: *childish* dziecinny ◇ *boyish* chłopięcy ◇ *clownish* błazeński **3** fairly; approximately: *reddish* ◇ *thirtyish* około trzydziestki ▶ **-awy**

Islam /ɪzˈlɑːm/ noun [U] the religion of Muslim people. Islam teaches that there is only one God and that Muhammad is His Prophet. ▶ **islam**
■ **Islamic** adj.: *Islamic law* ▶ **muzułmański**, **islamski**

island /ˈaɪlənd/ noun [C] **1** a piece of land that is surrounded by water: *the Greek islands* ▶ **wyspa** **2** (Brit.) = TRAFFIC ISLAND

islander /ˈaɪləndə(r)/ noun [C] a person who lives on a small island ▶ **wyspia-rz/rka**

isle /aɪl/ noun [C] an island: *the Isle of Wight* ◇ *the British Isles* ▶ **wyspa** ℹ **Isle** najczęściej używa się w nazwach geograficznych.

isn't /ˈɪznt/ short for **is not**: *This is enough, isn't it* (prawda)*?*

isolate /ˈaɪsəleɪt/ verb [T] **isolate sb/sth (from sb/sth)** to put or keep sb/sth separate from other people or things: *Some farms were isolated by the heavy snowfalls.* ◇ *We need to isolate all the animals with the disease so that the others don't catch it.* ▶ **izolować**, **odseparowywać**

isolated /ˈaɪsəleɪtɪd/ adj. **1 isolated (from sb/sth)** alone or apart from other people or things: *an isolated village deep in the countryside* ◇ *I was kept isolated from the other patients.* ▶ **odizolowany**, **osamotniony** **2** not connected with others; happening once: *an isolated case of food poisoning* ▶ **odosobniony**, **odizolowany**

isolation /ˌaɪsəˈleɪʃn/ noun [U] **isolation (from sb/sth)**; **in isolation (from sb/sth)** the state of being separate and alone; the act of separating sb/sth: *He lived **in** complete **isolation** from the outside world.* ◇ ***In isolation** each problem* (każdy problem z osobna) *does not seem bad, but together they are quite daunting.* ▶ **odosobnienie**, **izolacja** ➲ look at **loneliness**, **solitude**

isotope /ˈaɪsətəʊp/ noun [C] one of two or more forms of a chemical element which have the same number of **protons** but a different number of **neutrons** in their atoms. They have different physical **properties** but the same chemical ones: *radioactive isotopes* ▶ **izotop**

ISP /ˌaɪ es ˈpiː/ abbr. **Internet Service Provider**; a company that provides you with an Internet connection and services such as email, etc. ▶ **dostawca usług internetowych**

issue¹ /ˈɪʃuː; ˈɪsjuː/ noun **1** [C] a problem or subject for discussion: *I want to **raise the issue** of overtime pay at the meeting.* ◇ *The school cannot avoid the issue of truancy any longer.* ◇ *The government seems to be treating environmental protection as a **side issue**.* ▶ **kwestia**, **sprawa** **2** [C] one in a series of things that are published or produced: *Do you have last week's issue of this magazine?* ▶ **wydanie**, **emisja**, **numer** (*czasopisma*) **3** [U] the act of publishing or giving sth to people: *the issue of blankets to the refugees* ▶ **wydawanie**, **przydział**
IDM **make an issue (out) of sth** to give too much importance to a small problem: *OK, we disagree on this but let's not make an issue of it.* ▶ **robić z czegoś dużą sprawę**

issue² /ˈɪʃuː; ˈɪsjuː/ verb **1** [T] to give or say sth to sb, often officially: *The new employees were issued with uniforms.* ◇ *to issue a visa* ◇ *The police will issue a statement later today.* ▶ **wydawać** **2** [T] to print and supply sth: *to issue a magazine* ▶ **wydawać**, **emitować**
PHR V **issue from sth** (formal) to come or go out: *An angry voice issued from the loudspeaker.* ▶ **wydobywać się**

IT = INFORMATION TECHNOLOGY

it /ɪt/ pron. **1** [(used as the subject or object of a verb, or after a preposition)] the animal or thing mentioned earlier: *Look at that car. It's going much too fast.* ◇ *The children went up to the dog and patted it.* ▶ **on/ona/ono**, **jego/ją itp.** ℹ **It** może też odnosić się do niemowlęcia niewiadomej płci: *Is it a boy or a girl?* **2** (used for identifying a person): *It's your Mum on the phone.* ◇ *'Who's that?' 'It's the postman.'* ◇ *It's me!* To ja! ▶ **to** **3** (used in the position of the subject or object of a verb when the real subject or object is at the end of the sentence): *It's hard for them* (trudno jest im) *to talk about their problems.* ◇ *I think it doesn't really matter* (myślę, że nie jest ważne) *what time they arrive.* ▶ **to** ℹ Często nie tłumaczy się. **4** (used in the position of the subject of a verb when you are talking about time, the date, distance, the weather, etc.): *It's nearly* (już prawie) *half past eight.* ◇ *It's Tuesday today.* Dziś mamy wtorek. ◇ *It's about 100 kilometres from London.* ◇ *It was very cold* (było bardzo zimno) *at the weekend.* ◇ *It's raining.* Pada deszcz. ▶ **to (jest)** ℹ Często nie tłumaczy się. **5** (used when you are talking about a situation): *It gets* (robi się) *very crowded in the summer.* ◇ *I'll come at 7 o'clock if it's convenient* (jeżeli to pasuje). ◇ *It's a pity* (szkoda, że) *they can't come to the party.* ℹ Często nie ma odpowiednika – **it** + czasownik tłumaczy się wtedy czasownikiem. **6** (used for emphasizing a part of a sentence): *It's John who's good at cooking, not me.* To John jest dobry w gotowaniu, nie ja. ◇ *It's your health I'm worried about, not the cost.* O twoje zdrowie się martwię, nie o koszt. ▶ **to (właśnie)**
IDM **that is it** (used for saying that you have had enough of a situation): *That's it! I'm leaving!* ▶ **koniec!**, **dosyć!**
that/this is it that/this is the answer: *That's it! You've solved the puzzle!* ▶ **tak jest!**, **dobrze!**

italics /ɪˈtælɪks/ noun [pl.] a type of writing or printing in which the letters do not stand straight up: *All the example sentences in the dictionary are printed **in italics*** (kursywą). ▶ **kursywa**, **pismo pochyłe**
■ **italic** adj.: *italic handwriting* pismo pochyłe ▶ **pisany/drukowany kursywą**

itch /ɪtʃ/ noun [C] the feeling on your skin that makes you want to rub or scratch it: *I've got an itch on my back.* ▶ **Swędzą mnie plecy.**; **swędzenie**
■ **itch** verb [I]: *My whole body is itching.* ▶ **swędzieć** | **itchy** adj.: *This shirt is itchy.* ◇ *My skin is all itchy.* ▶ **swędzący**; (*ubranie*) **drapiący**

it'd /ˈɪtəd/ short for **it had**; **it would**

item /ˈaɪtəm/ noun [C] **1** one single thing on a list or in a collection: *Some items arrived too late to be included in the catalogue.* ◇ *What is the first item on the agenda?* ▶ **pozycja**, **punkt programu** **2** one single article or object: *Can I pay for each item separately?* ◇ *an item of clothing* sztuka odzieży ▶ **artykuł**, **rzecz** **3** a single piece of news: *There was an interesting item about Spain in yesterday's news.* ▶ **wiadomość**

itemize (also -ise) /ˈaɪtəmaɪz/ verb [T] to make a list of all the separate items in sth: *an itemized telephone bill* ▶ **wyszczególniać**

itinerant /aɪˈtɪnərənt/ adj. [only before a noun] travelling from place to place: *an itinerant circus family* ▶ **wędrowny**

itinerary /aɪˈtɪnərəri; US -reri/ noun [C] (pl. **itineraries**) a plan of a journey, including the route and the places that you will visit ▶ **plan podróży**, **marszruta**

it'll /ˈɪtl/ short for **it will**

it's /ɪts/ short for **it is**; **it has** ℹ Uwaga! **It's** to skrót od **it is** lub **it has**. Zob. **its** w następnym haśle.

its /ɪts/ determiner of or belonging to a thing: *The club held its Annual General Meeting last night.* ▶ **jego, jej, swój** ➲ note at **it's**

itself /ɪt'self/ pron. **1** (used when the animal or thing that does an action is also affected by it): *The cat was washing itself* (mył się). ◇ *The company has got itself* (firma wpakowała się) *into financial difficulties.* ▶ **się, siebie, sam 2** (used to emphasize sth): *The village itself* (sama wioska) *is pretty but the countryside is rather dull.* ▶ **sam, sobie**
IDM **(all) by itself 1** without being controlled by a person; automatically: *The central heating comes on by itself* (włącza się samo). ▶ **sam, samodzielnie, automatycznie 2** alone: *The house stood all by itself* (samotnie) *on the hillside.* ▶ **samotny, sam** ➲ note at **alone**

ITV /ˌaɪ tiː 'viː/ abbr. (Brit.) **Independent Television**; the group of TV companies that are paid for by advertising: *to watch a film on ITV* ▶ **niezależna sieć telewizyjna**

IUD /ˌaɪ juː 'diː/ noun [C] **intrauterine device**; a small metal or plastic object that is placed inside a woman's uterus to stop her becoming pregnant ▶ **wkładka wewnątrzmaciczna**

I've /aɪv/ short for **I have**

ivory /'aɪvəri/ noun [U] the hard white substance that the **tusks** of an elephant are made of ▶ **kość słoniowa**

ivy /'aɪvi/ noun [U] a climbing plant that has dark leaves with three or five points ▶ **bluszcz**

J j

J, j /dʒeɪ/ noun [C,U] (pl. **Js**; **js**; **J's**; **j's** /dʒeɪz/) the 10th letter of the English alphabet: *'Jam' begins with (a) 'J'.* ▶ **litera** *j*

jab¹ /dʒæb/ verb **1** [I,T] **jab (at sb/sth) (with sth)**; **jab sb/sth (with sth)** to push at sb/sth with a sudden, rough movement, usually with sth sharp: *He kept jabbing at his potato with his fork.* Ciągle dziobał kartofel widelcem. ◇ *She jabbed me in the ribs with her elbow.* ▶ **kłuć, dźgać 2** [T] **jab sth into sb/sth** to push sth roughly into sb/sth: *The robber jabbed a gun into my back and ordered me to move.* ▶ **uderzać czymś w kogoś/coś, wpychać coś w kogoś/coś**

jab² /dʒæb/ noun [C] **1** a sudden rough push with sth sharp: *He **gave me a jab*** (dźgnął mnie) *in the ribs with the stick.* ▶ **ukłucie, dźgnięcie 2** (Brit., informal) the act of putting a drug, etc. under sb's skin with a needle: *I'm going to the doctor's to **have a flu jab*** (żeby zaszczepić się przeciwko grypie) *today.* ▶ **zastrzyk** SYN **injection**

jack¹ /dʒæk/ noun [C] **1** a piece of equipment for lifting a car, etc. off the ground, for example in order to change its wheel ▶ **podnośnik, lewarek 2** the card between the ten and the queen in a pack of cards ▶ **walet** ➲ note at **card**

jack² /dʒæk/ verb
PHR V **jack sth in** (slang) to stop doing sth: *Jerry got fed up with his job and jacked it in.* ▶ **rzucać** *(np. pracę)*
jack sth up to lift a car, etc. using a **jack**: *We jacked the car up to change the wheel.* ▶ **podnosić coś lewarkiem**

jacket /'dʒækɪt/ noun [C] **1** a short coat with sleeves: *Do you have to wear a jacket and tie to work?* ◇ *a denim/leather jacket* ▶ **marynarka, kurtka** ➲ picture on **page A1** ➲ look at **life jacket 2** a cover for a hot-water tank, etc. that stops heat from being lost ▶ **osłona, otulina, płaszcz 3** (US) = SLEEVE

ˌjacket po'tato (also **ˌbaked po'tato**) noun [C] a potato that is cooked in the oven in its skin ▶ **ziemniak w mundurku** ➲ picture on **page A14**

jackhammer (US) = PNEUMATIC DRILL

jackknife /'dʒæknaɪf/ verb [I] (used about a lorry that is in two parts) to go out of control and bend suddenly in a dangerous way ▶ **łamać się na złączu, składać się jak scyzoryk**
■ **jackknife** noun [C] a large pocket knife that folds in half when not in use ▶ **duży scyzoryk**

the jackpot /'dʒækpɒt/ noun [C] the largest money prize that you can win in a game ▶ **pula, największa wygrana w grze**
IDM **hit the jackpot** → HIT¹

Jacuzzi™ /dʒə'kuːzi/ noun [C] a special bath in which powerful movements of air make bubbles in the water ▶ **wanna z masażem wodnym**

jade /dʒeɪd/ noun [U] **1** a hard stone that is usually green and is used in making jewellery ▶ **jadeit, nefryt 2** a bright green colour ▶ **kolor jasnozielony**
■ **jade** adj. ▶ **jasnozielony**

jaded /'dʒeɪdɪd/ adj. tired and bored after doing the same thing for a long time without a break ▶ **sterany, znużony**

jagged /'dʒægɪd/ adj. rough with sharp points: *jagged rocks* ▶ **postrzępiony, ząbkowany, wyszczerbiony**

jaguar /'dʒægjuə(r)/ noun [C] a large wild cat with black spots that comes from Central and South America ▶ **jaguar**

jail¹ /dʒeɪl/ noun [C,U] (a) prison: *She was **sent to jail** for ten years.* ▶ **więzienie** ⓘ W Br. ang. stosuje się też pisownię **gaol** i **gaoler**.

jail² /dʒeɪl/ verb [T] to put sb in prison: *She was jailed for ten years.* ▶ **wsadzać do więzienia**

jailer /'dʒeɪlə(r)/ noun [C] (old-fashioned) a person whose job is to guard prisoners ▶ **strażni-k/czka więzienn-y/a**

jam¹ /dʒæm/ noun **1** (especially US **jelly**) [U] a sweet substance that you spread on bread, made by boiling fruit and sugar together: *a jar of raspberry jam* ◇ *a jam jar* słoik do dżemu ▶ **dżem, konfitur-a/y** ➲ picture on **page A14**

> Zwróć uwagę, że dżem z pomarańczy lub cytryn nazywa się **marmalade**.

2 [C] a situation in which you cannot move because there are too many people or vehicles: *a traffic jam* ▶ **korek (w ruchu ulicznym) 3** [C] (informal) a difficult situation: *We're **in a bit of a jam** without our passports or travel documents.* ▶ **kłopotliwa sytuacja**

jam² /dʒæm/ verb (jamming; jammed) **1** [T] **jam sb/sth in, under, between, etc. sth** to push or force sb/sth into a place where there is not much room: *She managed to jam everything into* (udało jej się wszystko upchać w) *her suitcase.* ▶ **wciskać, stłaczać 2** [I,T] **jam (sth) (up)** to become or to make sth unable to move or work: *Something is jamming (up) the machine.* ◇ *The paper keeps jamming in the photocopier.* ◇ *I can't open the door. The lock's jammed* (zamek się zaciął). ▶ **blokować; zacinać się 3** [T, usually passive] **jam sth (up) (with sb/sth)** to fill sth with too many people or things: *The cupboard was **jammed full*** (była wypełniona) *of old newspapers and magazines.* ◇ *The switchboard was jammed with hundreds of calls from unhappy customers.* ▶ **blokować, zapychać 4** [T] to send out signals in order to stop radio programmes, etc. from being received or heard clearly ▶ **zagłuszać** *(np. fale radiowe)* **5** [I,T] to play music with other musicians in an informal way without preparing or practising first ▶ **improwizować, mieć jam session**
PHR V **jam on the brakes/jam the brakes on** to stop a car suddenly by pushing hard on the **brake** with your foot ▶ **gwałtownie zahamować**

ˌjam-'packed adj. [not usually before a noun] **jam-packed (with sb/sth)** (informal) very full or crowded: *The train was jam-packed with commuters.* ◇ *The suitcase was jam-packed* *with designer clothes.* ▶ **wypełniony po brzegi, zapchany**

Jan. = JANUARY: *1 Jan. 1993*

jangle /ˈdʒæŋgl/ verb [I,T] to make a noise like metal hitting against metal; to move sth so that it makes this noise: *The baby smiles if you jangle your keys.* ▶ **pobrzękiwać; podzwaniać**

■ **jangle** noun [U] ▶ **pobrzękiwanie; podzwanianie**

janitor (US) = CARETAKER

January /ˈdʒænjuəri; US -jueri/ noun [U,C] (abbr. **Jan.**) the 1st month of the year, coming after December ▶ **styczeń**

Nazw miesięcy można używać w zdaniach: *We're going skiing **in January**.* ◇ *last/next January* ◇ *We first met **on January 31st**, 2002.* ◇ *Our wedding anniversary is at the end of January.* ◇ *January mornings can be very dark in Britain.* ◇ *Michael's birthday is (on) January 17.* Można powiedzieć **on January the seventeenth** lub **on the seventeenth of January** lub w Amer. ang. **January seventeenth**. Nazwy miesięcy zawsze pisze się dużą literą.

jar[1] /dʒɑː(r)/ noun [C] **1** a container with a lid, usually made of glass and used for keeping food, etc. in: *a jam jar* słoik do dżemu ◇ *a large storage jar for flour* ▶ **słój, słoik** ➲ picture at **container** **2** the food that a **jar** contains: *a jar of honey/jam/coffee* ▶ **słój/słoik (czegoś)**

jar[2] /dʒɑː(r)/ verb (**jarring**; **jarred**) **1** [T] to hurt or damage sth as a result of a sharp knock: *He fell and jarred his back* (obił sobie plecy). ▶ **wstrząsać, (s)tłuc** **2** [I] **jar (on sb/sth)** to have an unpleasant or annoying effect: *The dripping tap jarred on my nerves.* ▶ **drażnić, działać na nerwy**

jargon /ˈdʒɑːgən/ noun [U] special or technical words that are used by a particular group of people in a particular profession and that other people do not understand: *medical/scientific/legal/computer jargon* ▶ **żargon**

jasmine /ˈdʒæzmɪn/ noun [U,C] a plant with white or yellow sweet-smelling flowers ▶ **jaśmin**

jaundice /ˈdʒɔːndɪs/ noun [U] a disease that makes your skin and eyes yellow ▶ **żółtaczka**

jaundiced /ˈdʒɔːndɪst/ adj. **1** not expecting sb/sth to be good or useful, especially because of experiences that you have had in the past: *He had a jaundiced view of life.* Ma pesymistyczne spojrzenie na życie. ◇ *She looked on politicians with a jaundiced eye.* Patrzyła na polityków złym okiem. ▶ **cyniczny, pełen żółci** **2** suffering from **jaundice** ▶ **chory na żółtaczkę**

jaunt /dʒɔːnt/ noun [C] (old-fashioned or humorous) a short journey that you make for pleasure ▶ **przejażdżka** SYN **excursion**

javelin /ˈdʒævlɪn/ noun **1** [C] a long stick with a pointed end that is thrown in sports competitions ▶ **oszczep** **2** (**the javelin**) [sing.] the event or sport of throwing the **javelin** as far as possible ▶ **rzut oszczepem**

jaw /dʒɔː/ noun **1** [C] either of the two bones in your face that contain your teeth: *the lower/upper jaw* ▶ **szczęka** ➲ picture at **body** **2** (**jaws**) [pl.] the mouth (especially of a wild animal): *The lion came towards him with its jaws open.* ▶ **paszcza, szczęki**

jawbone /ˈdʒɔːbəʊn/ noun [C] the bone that forms the lower **jaw** ▶ **kość szczękowa** ➲ picture at **body**

jaywalk /ˈdʒeɪwɔːk/ verb [I] to walk along or across a street illegally or without paying attention to the traffic ▶ **nieprawidłowo przechodzić przez jezdnię**

■ **jaywalker** noun [C] ▶ **pieszy nieprawidłowo przechodzący przez jezdnię** | **jaywalking** noun [U] ▶ **nieprawidłowe przechodzenie przez jezdnię**

jazz[1] /dʒæz/ noun [U] a style of music with a strong rhythm, originally of African American origin: *modern/traditional jazz* ▶ **jazz** ➲ look at **classical**, **pop**, **rock**

jazz[2] /dʒæz/ verb

PHR V **jazz sth up** (informal) to make sth brighter, more interesting or exciting ▶ **ożywiać coś**

jazzy /ˈdʒæzi/ adj. (informal) **1** in the style of **jazz**: *a jazzy melody/tune* ▶ **jazzowy** **2** brightly coloured and likely to attract attention: *That's a jazzy tie you're wearing.* ▶ **jaskrawy i ekscentryczny** ⓘ Czasami wyraża dezaprobatę.

jealous /ˈdʒeləs/ adj. **1** feeling upset or angry because you think that sb you like or love is showing interest in sb else: *Tim gets jealous whenever Sue speaks to another boy!* ▶ **zazdrosny** **2** **jealous (of sb/sth)** feeling angry or sad because you want to be like sb else or because you want what sb else has: *He's always been jealous of his older brother.* ◇ *I'm very jealous of your new car – how much did it cost?* ▶ **zazdrosny, zawistny** SYN **envious**

■ **jealously** adv. ▶ **zazdrośnie, zawistnie** | **jealousy** noun [C,U] (pl. **jealousies**) ▶ **zazdrość, zawiść**

jeans /dʒiːnz/ noun [pl.] trousers made of **denim**: *These jeans are a bit too tight.* ◇ *a pair of jeans* ▶ **dżinsy** ➲ picture on **page A1**

Jeep™ /dʒiːp/ noun [C] a small, strong vehicle suitable for travelling over rough ground ▶ **jeep, łazik**

jeer /dʒɪə(r)/ verb [I,T] **jeer (at) sb/sth** to laugh or shout rude comments at sb/sth to show your lack of respect for them or it: *The spectators booed and jeered at the losing team.* ▶ **wyśmiewać, wyszydzać**

■ **jeer** noun [C, usually pl.]: *The Prime Minister was greeted with jeers in the House of Commons today.* ▶ **drwina, szyderstwo**

jelly /ˈdʒeli/ noun (pl. **jellies**) (US **Jell-O**™ /ˈdʒeləʊ/) **1** [C,U] a soft, solid brightly coloured food that shakes when it is moved. **Jelly** is made from sugar and fruit juice and is eaten cold at the end of a meal, especially by children: *raspberry jelly and ice cream* ▶ **galaretka** **2** [U] a type of jam that does not contain any solid pieces of fruit: *blackcurrant jelly* ▶ **dżem**

IDM **be/feel like jelly** (used especially about the legs or knees) to feel weak because you are nervous, afraid, etc.: *My legs felt like jelly* (miałem nogi jak z waty) *before the exam.* ▶ (*kolana itp.*) **uginać się** (*pod kimś*)

turn to jelly (used about the legs and knees) to suddenly become weak because of fear ▶ (*nogi/kolana*) **ugiąć się (pod kimś)**

jellyfish /ˈdʒelifɪʃ/ noun [C] (pl. **jellyfish**) a sea animal with a soft transparent body and long thin parts that can sting you. ▶ **meduza** ➲ picture on **page A11**

jeopardize (also -ise) /ˈdʒepədaɪz/ verb [T] to do sth that may damage sth or put it at risk: *He would never do anything to jeopardize his career.* ▶ **narażać, wystawiać na niebezpieczeństwo**

jeopardy /ˈdʒepədi/ noun

IDM **in jeopardy** in a dangerous position and likely to be lost or harmed: *The future of the factory and 15 000 jobs are in jeopardy.* ▶ **w niebezpieczeństwie**

jerk[1] /dʒɜːk/ verb [I,T] to move or make sb/sth move with a sudden sharp movement: *She jerked the door open.* Z gwałtownym szarpnięciem otworzyła drzwi. ◇ *His head jerked back* (jego głowa gwałtownie odchyliła się do tyłu) *as the car set off.* ▶ **szarpać** (*nagłym/gwałtownym ruchem*), **trząść się, telepać się**

■ **jerky** adj. ▶ **szarpany, gwałtowny** | **jerkily** /-kɪli/ adv. ▶ **nierówno, spazmatycznie**

jerk[2] /dʒɜːk/ noun [C] **1** a sudden sharp movement ▶ **szarpnięcie, drgnięcie** **2** (especially US, slang) a stupid or annoying person ▶ **palant, dupek**

jersey /ˈdʒɜːzi/ noun **1** [C] a piece of clothing made of wool that you wear over a shirt ▶ **sweter wełniany** SYN **jumper, pullover, sweater** **2** [U] a soft thin cloth made of cotton or wool that is used for making clothes ▶ **materiał wełniany typu jersey**

jester /ˈdʒestə(r)/ noun [C] a man employed in the past at the **court** of a king or queen to amuse people by telling jokes and funny stories: *the court jester* ▶ **błazen**

Jesus = CHRIST

jet[1] /dʒet/ noun [C] **1** a fast modern plane ▶ **odrzutowiec 2** a fast, thin current of water, gas, etc. coming out of a small hole ▶ **strumień**, **wytrysk**

jet[2] /dʒet/ (**jetting**; **jetted**) verb [I] (informal) **jet off** to fly somewhere in a plane ▶ **podróżować/latać odrzutowcem**

ˌjet ˈblack adj. very dark black in colour ▶ **czarny jak smoła**

ˈjet engine noun [C] a powerful engine that makes planes fly by pushing out a current of hot air and gases at the back ▶ **silnik odrzutowy** ➲ picture at **plane**

ˈjet lag noun [U] the tired feeling that people often have after a long journey in a plane to a place where the local time is different ▶ **zmęczenie po długiej podróży samolotem** (*spowodowane zmianą stref czasowych*) ■ **ˈjet-lagged** adj. ▶ **zmęczony po długiej podróży samolotem** (*z powodu zmiany stref czasowych*)

the ˈjet set noun [sing.] the group of rich, successful and fashionable people (especially those who travel around the world a lot) ▶ **bogaci i modni ludzie sukcesu, którzy dużo podróżują po świecie**

ˈJet Ski™ noun [C] a vehicle with an engine, like a motorbike, for riding across water ▶ **skuter wodny** ■ **ˈjet-skiing** noun [U] ▶ **jazda skuterem wodnym**

jetty /ˈdʒeti/ noun [C] (pl. **jetties**) (also **ˈlanding stage**; US **dock**) a stone wall or wooden platform built out into the sea or a river where boats are tied and where people can get on and off them ▶ **molo**, **nabrzeże**

Jew /dʒuː/ noun [C] a person whose family originally came from the ancient Hebrew people of Israel and/or whose religion is Judaism ▶ **Żyd/ówka** ■ **Jewish** adj.: *He's Jewish.* On jest Żydem. ▶ **żydowski**

jewel /ˈdʒuːəl/ noun **1** [C] a valuable stone (for example a diamond) ▶ **kamień szlachetny** SYN **gem 2** [pl.] a piece of jewellery or an object that contains **precious** stones ▶ **klejnot**

jeweller (US **jeweler**) /ˈdʒuːələ(r)/ noun **1** [C] a person whose job is to buy, sell, make or repair jewellery and watches ▶ **jubiler**, **złotnik 2** (**the jeweller's**) [sing.] a shop where jewellery and watches are made, sold and repaired ▶ **sklep jubilerski**

⚷ **jewellery** (US **jewelry**) /ˈdʒuːəlri/ noun [U] objects such as rings, etc. that are worn as personal decoration: *a piece of jewellery* ▶ **biżuteria**, **kosztowności**

jewellery

bracelet

bangle

ˈJiffy bag™ noun [C] (Brit.) a thick soft envelope for sending things that might break or tear easily ▶ **koperta wzmocniona folią bąbelkową**

jig[1] /dʒɪɡ/ noun [C] a type of quick dance with jumping movements; the music for this dance ▶ **giga** (*skoczny taniec*)

jig[2] /dʒɪɡ/ verb [I] (**jigging**; **jigged**) **jig about/around** to move about in an excited or impatient way ▶ **wiercić się**, **podskakiwać**

jiggle /ˈdʒɪɡl/ verb (informal) **1** [I] to move up or down or from side to side with short quick movements: *Stop jiggling around!* ▶ **kołysać się**, **kiwać się 2** [T] to move sth quickly from side to side: *She jiggled her car keys to try to distract the baby.* ▶ **telepać**, **potrząsać**

jigsaw /ˈdʒɪɡsɔː/ (also **ˈjigsaw puzzle**) noun [C] a picture on cardboard or wood that is cut into small pieces and has to be fitted together again ▶ **układanka**, **puzzle**

jingle[1] /ˈdʒɪŋɡl/ noun **1** [sing.] a ringing sound like small bells, made by metal objects gently hitting each other: *the jingle of coins* ▶ **dzwonienie**, **brzęczenie 2** [C] a short simple tune or song that is easy to remember and is used in advertising on TV or radio ▶ **dżingiel**

jingle[2] /ˈdʒɪŋɡl/ verb [I,T] to make or cause sth to make a pleasant gentle sound like small bells ringing: *She jingled the coins in her pocket.* ▶ **podzwaniać**, **pobrzękiwać**

jinx /dʒɪŋks/ noun [C, usually sing.] (informal) bad luck; a person or thing that people believe brings bad luck to sb/sth ▶ **pech**; **rzecz/osoba przynosząca pecha** ■ **jinx** verb [T] ▶ **przynosić pecha** | **jinxed** adj.: *After my third accident in a month, I began to think I was jinxed.* ▶ **pechowy**, **mający pecha**

the jitters /ˈdʒɪtəz/ noun [pl.] (informal) feelings of fear or worry, especially before an important event or before having to do sth difficult: *Just thinking about the exam **gives me the jitters**!* Już na samą myśl o egzaminie jestem cała roztrzęsiona! ▶ **zdenerwowanie**, **trema**

jittery /ˈdʒɪtəri/ adj. (informal) nervous or worried: *She felt jittery and tense.* ▶ **zdenerwowany**, **stremowany**

Jnr (also **Jr**) (especially US) = JUNIOR[1] (3): *Samuel P Carson, Jnr*

⚷ **job** /dʒɒb/ noun [C] **1** the work that you do regularly to earn money: *She **took/got a job** as a waitress* (podjęła/dostała pracę kelnerki). ◊ *A lot of people will **lose** their **jobs** if the factory closes.* ◊ *to look for/apply for* (starać się o)*/find a job* ◊ *a well-paid/highly paid job* ◊ *a badly-paid/low-paid job* ◊ *a full-time/part-time job* ◊ *a permanent/temporary job* ◊ *job-sharing* dzielenie się pracą ▶ **praca** ➲ note at **office**, **pay**, **retire**, **work**

Odpowiedniki **job** w języku formalnym **post** i **position**: *I would like to apply for the post/position of Marketing Manager.*

2 a task or a piece of work: *The garage has **done a good/bad job on** our car.* Warsztat dobrze/źle naprawił nasz samochód. ◊ *I always have a lot of jobs to do in the house at weekends.* ▶ **praca**, **robota 3** [usually sing.] a duty or responsibility: *It's not his job to tell us what we can and can't do.* ▶ **sprawa**, **zadanie**

> **jobs**
>
> When you **apply for a job**, you usually **fill in an application form** or send your **CV** with a **covering letter**. Then you **have an interview**. If it goes well and the employer is satisfied with your **references**, you will **get the job**. You **sign the contract** and become an **employee**. A job can be **well-paid/highly-paid** or **badly-paid/low-paid**. A job can be **full-time** or **part-time**, **permanent** or **temporary**. If your **working conditions** are good and you have the chance to **be promoted**, then you will probably get a lot of **job satisfaction**.

IDM **do the job/trick** (informal) to get the result that is wanted: *This extra strong glue should do the job.* ▶ (*pomysł, przedsięwzięcie itp.*) **(za)działać**

have a hard job to do sth/doing sth → HARD[1]

it's a good job (informal) it is a good or lucky thing: *It's a good job you reminded me – I had completely forgotten!* ▶ **(to) dobrze, że**

just the job/ticket (informal) exactly what is needed in a particular situation: *This dress will be just the job for Helen's party.* ▶ **to, o co właśnie chodzi**; **właśnie to, co trzeba**

make a bad, good, etc. job of sth to do sth badly, well, etc. ▶ **źle/dobrze wywiązywać się z czegoś**

make the best of sth/a bad job → BEST[3]
out of a job without paid work ▶ **bezrobotny** ℹ Bardziej formalne słowo to **unemployed**.

> **leaving a job**
> If you want to **leave your job**, you **resign** or **hand in** your **resignation**. If a company no longer needs an employee, it will **make** him/her **redundant**. If an employee's work is not good enough, the company may **dismiss** him/her. In less formal English we use the verbs **fire** or **sack**, or the noun **the sack**: *Her boss fired/sacked her.* ◇ *Her boss gave her the sack.* ◇ *She got the sack.* When you stop working because you have reached a certain age (usually 60 or 65), you **retire**.

jobcentre /ˈdʒɒbsentə(r)/ noun [C] (Brit.) a government office where people can get advice in finding work and where jobs are advertised ▶ **urząd pracy**, **biuro pośrednictwa pracy**

ˈjob description noun [C] a written description of the exact work and responsibilities of a job ▶ **zakres obowiązków**

jobless /ˈdʒɒbləs/ adj. **1** (usually used about large numbers of people) without paid work ▶ **bezrobotn-y/i** SYN **unemployed** **2** (**the jobless**) noun [pl.] people without paid work ▶ **bezrobotni**
■ **joblessness** noun [U] ▶ **bezrobocie** SYN **unemployment**

jockey /ˈdʒɒki/ noun [C] a person who rides horses in races, especially as a profession ▶ **dżokej** ➲ look at **DJ** ➲ picture on **page A9**

jocular /ˈdʒɒkjələ(r)/ adj. (formal) **1** humorous: *a jocular comment* ▶ **żartobliwy** **2** (used about a person) enjoying making people laugh ▶ **pełen humoru** SYN for both meanings **jolly** ➲ look at **joke**
■ **jocularity** /ˌdʒɒkjəˈlærəti/ noun [U] ▶ **żartobliwość** | **jocularly** adv. ▶ **żartobliwie**

jodhpurs /ˈdʒɒdpəz/ noun [pl.] special trousers that you wear for riding a horse ▶ **bryczesy**

Joe Bloggs /ˌdʒəʊ ˈblɒgz/ (US ˌ**Joe** ˈ**Blow**) noun [sing.] (informal) a way of referring to a typical ordinary person ▶ **Jan Kowalski**

jog[1] /dʒɒg/ verb (**jogging**; **jogged**) **1** [I] to run slowly, especially as a form of exercise ▶ **uprawiać jogging**, **biegać dla zdrowia** **2** [T] to push or knock sb/sth slightly: *He jogged my arm and I spilled the milk.* ▶ **trącać**, **szturchać** SYN **nudge**
IDM **jog sb's memory** to say or do sth that makes sb remember sth ▶ **odświeżać czyjąś pamięć**

jog[2] /dʒɒg/ noun [sing.] **1** a slow run as a form of exercise: *She* ***goes for a jog*** *before breakfast.* ▶ **bieg dla zdrowia** ℹ Kiedy biega się dla przyjemności lub w ramach ćwiczeń, często mówi się **go jogging** zamiast **jog**: *I go jogging most evenings.* **2** a slight push or knock ▶ **trącenie**, **szturchnięcie** SYN **nudge**

jogger /ˈdʒɒgə(r)/ noun [C] a person who goes **jogging** for exercise ▶ **osoba biegająca dla zdrowia**

join[1] /dʒɔɪn/ verb **1** [T] **join A to B**; **join A and B (together)** to fasten or connect one thing to another: *The Channel Tunnel joins Britain to Europe.* ◇ *The two pieces of wood had been carefully joined together.* ◇ *We've knocked down the wall and joined the two rooms into one.* ▶ **łączyć** **2** [I,T] **join (up) (with sb/sth)** to meet or unite (with sb/sth) to form one thing or group: *Do the two rivers join (up) at any point?* ◇ *Where does this road join the motorway?* ◇ *Would you like to join us* (pójść z nami) *for a drink?* ▶ **łączyć (się) (z kimś/czymś)**, **zespalać (się) (z kimś/czymś)** **3** [T] to become a member of a club or organization: *to join a club* ◇ *I've joined an aerobics class.* ◇ *He joined the company* (zaczął pracować w tej firmie) *three months ago.* ▶ **zapisać się do czegoś/na coś**, **przystępować/wstępować do czegoś** **4** [T] to take your place in sth or to take part in sth: *We'd better go and join the queue if we want to see the film.* ◇ *Come downstairs and join the party.* ▶ **przyłączać się/dołączać się do czegoś** **5** [I,T] **join (with) sb in sth/in doing sth/to do sth**; **join together in doing sth/to do sth** to take part with sb (often in doing sth for sb else): *Everybody here joins me in wishing* (każdy przyłączy się do życzeń) *you the best of luck in your new job.* ◇ *The whole school joined together to sing the school song.* ▶ **przyłączać się**, **dołączać się**
IDM **join forces (with sb)** to work together in order to achieve a shared goal: *The two companies joined forces to win the contract.* ▶ **łączyć siły**
PHR V **join in (sth/doing sth)** to take part in an activity: *Everyone started singing but Frank refused to join in.* ▶ **przyłączać się**, **włączać się**
join up to become a member of the army, navy or air force ▶ **wstępować do wojska**

join[2] /dʒɔɪn/ noun [C] a place where two things are fixed or connected: *He glued the handle back on so cleverly that you couldn't see the join.* ▶ **złącze**, **miejsce złączenia**

joiner /ˈdʒɔɪnə(r)/ noun [C] a person whose job is to make the wooden parts of a building ▶ **stolarz budowlany** ➲ look at **carpenter**

joinery /ˈdʒɔɪnəri/ noun [U] the work of a **joiner** or things made by a **joiner** ▶ **stolarka**

joint[1] /dʒɔɪnt/ adj. [only before a noun] shared or owned by two or more people: *Have you and your husband got a* ***joint account****?* ◇ *a joint decision* ▶ **wspólny**
■ **jointly** adv. ▶ **wspólnie**

joint[2] /dʒɔɪnt/ noun [C] **1** a part of the body where two bones fit together and are able to bend: *the knee joint* ▶ **staw** **2** the place where two or more things are fastened or connected together, especially to form a corner ▶ **złącze**, **przegub** **3** a large piece of meat that you cook whole in the oven: *a joint of lamb* ◇ *the Sunday joint* typowy angielski obiad składający się ze sztuki pieczonego mięsa, jedzony w niedzielę ▶ **udziec** **4** (informal) a cigarette containing **marihuana** ▶ (*papieros*) **skręt**

ˌjoint ˈventure noun [C] a business project or activity that is begun by two or more companies, etc., which remain separate organizations ▶ **spółka typu joint venture**, **wspólne przedsięwzięcie**

joist /dʒɔɪst/ noun [C] a long thick piece of wood, metal etc. that is used to support a floor or ceiling in a building ▶ **belka stropowa**; **legar podłogowy** ➲ look at **beam**

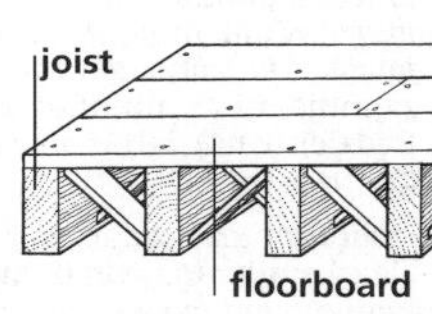

joke[1] /dʒəʊk/ noun **1** [C] something said or done to make you laugh, especially a funny story: *to tell/crack jokes* opowiadać dowcipy/sypać dowcipami ◇ *a dirty joke* świński dowcip ◇ *I'm sorry, I didn't* ***get the joke*** (nie zrozumiałem tego dowcipu). *Can you explain it to me?* ▶ **dowcip**, **żart** ➲ note at **humour** **2** [sing.] a ridiculous person, thing or situation: *The salary he was offered was a joke!* ▶ **żart**, **pośmiewisko**
IDM **play a joke/a trick/tricks on sb** → PLAY
see the joke → SEE
take a joke to be able to laugh at a joke against yourself: *The trouble with Pete is he can't take a joke.* ▶ **pozwalać z siebie żartować**

joke[2] /dʒəʊk/ verb [I] **1 joke (with sb) (about sth)** to say sth to make people laugh; to tell a funny story: *She spent the evening laughing and joking with her old friends.* ▶ **dowcipkować**, **opowiadać kawał** **2** to say sth that is not true because you think it is funny: *I never joke about* *religion.* ◇ *Don't get upset. I was **only joking**!* ▶ **żartować**

IDM **you must be joking; you're joking** (informal) (used to express great surprise) you cannot be serious ▶ **chyba żartujesz!**

joker /ˈdʒəʊkə(r)/ noun [C] **1** a person who likes to tell jokes or play tricks ▶ **żartowniś, dowcipniś 2** an extra card which can be used instead of any other one in some card games ▶ **dżoker**

jolly /ˈdʒɒli/ adj. (**jollier**; **jolliest**) happy ▶ **wesoły, radosny**

■ **jolly** adv. very ▶ **bardzo**

jolt¹ /dʒəʊlt/ verb **1** [T] to make sb/sth move in a sudden rough way: *The crash jolted all the passengers forward* (rzucił pasażerów do przodu). ▶ **wstrząsać, szarpać 2** [I] to move in a sudden rough way: *The lorry jolted* (telepała się) *along the bumpy track.* ▶ **podskoczyć**

jolt² /dʒəʊlt/ noun [usually sing.] **1** a sudden movement: *The train stopped with a jolt.* ▶ **szarpnięcie, wstrząs 2** a sudden surprise or shock: *His sudden anger **gave** her quite **a jolt*** (była dla niej zupełnym szokiem). ▶ **wstrząs, szok**

jostle /ˈdʒɒsl/ verb [I,T] to push hard against sb in a crowd ▶ **przepychać się, rozpychać się; szturchać**

jot /dʒɒt/ verb (**jotting**; **jotted**)

PHR V **jot sth down** to make a quick short note of sth: *Let me jot down your address.* ▶ **zanotować coś**

journal /ˈdʒɜːnl/ noun [C] **1** a newspaper or a magazine, especially one in which all the articles are about a particular subject or profession: *a medical/scientific journal* ▶ **czasopismo** (*zwł. monotematyczne*) **2** a written record of the things you do, see, etc. each day: *Have you read his journal of the years he spent in India?* ▶ **dziennik, pamiętnik** ➲ look at **diary**

journalism /ˈdʒɜːnəlɪzəm/ noun [U] the profession of collecting and writing about news in newspapers and magazines or talking about it on the TV or radio ▶ **dziennikarstwo**

⚷ **journalist** /ˈdʒɜːnəlɪst/ noun [C] a person whose job is to collect and write about news in newspapers and magazines or to talk about it on the TV or radio ▶ **dziennika-rz/rka** ➲ note at **newspaper** ➲ look at **reporter**

⚷ **journey** /ˈdʒɜːni/ noun [C] the act of travelling from one place to another, usually on land: *Did you have a good journey?* Jak minęła podróż? ◇ *a two-hour journey* ◇ *The journey to work takes me 45 minutes.* Dojazd do pracy zajmuje mi 45 minut. ◇ *We'll have to break the journey.* Będziemy musieli zrobić przerwę w podróży. ▶ **podróż** ➲ note at **travel**

> **Journey** może oznaczać zarówno podróż samolotem, jak i statkiem, jednak mówiąc konkretnie o podróży samolotem używa się słowa **flight**, a o podróży morskiej **voyage**. Rejs statkiem dla przyjemności to **cruise**.

jovial /ˈdʒəʊviəl/ adj. (used about a person) happy and friendly ▶ **jowialny**

⚷ **joy** /dʒɔɪ/ noun **1** [U] a feeling of great happiness: *We'd like to wish you joy and success in your life together.* ◇ *to shout/cry with joy* (z radości) ◇ *to dance/jump/shout for joy* (z radości) ▶ **radość 2** [C] a person or thing that gives you great pleasure: *the joys of fatherhood* ◇ *That class is a joy to teach.* Uczenie tej klasy to prawdziwa przyjemność. ▶ **radość, uciecha 3** [U] [used in questions and negative sentences] (Brit., informal) success or satisfaction: *'I asked again if we could have seats with more legroom but **got no joy** from the check-in clerk.'* ▶ **powodzenie**

IDM **jump for joy** → JUMP¹

sb's pride and joy → PRIDE¹

joyful /ˈdʒɔɪfl/ adj. very happy: *a joyful occasion* ▶ **radosny, uradowany**

■ **joyfully** /-fəli/ adv. ▶ **radośnie, z uciechą** | **joyfulness** noun [U] ▶ **radość, uciecha**

joyless /ˈdʒɔɪləs/ adj. unhappy: *The couple had a joyless marriage.* ▶ **nieszczęśliwy**

joyous /ˈdʒɔɪəs/ adj. (literary) very happy; causing people to be happy ▶ **radosny** SYN **joyful**

■ **joyously** adv. ▶ **radośnie**

joyriding /ˈdʒɔɪraɪdɪŋ/ noun [U] the crime of stealing a car and driving it for pleasure, usually in a fast and dangerous way ▶ **jazda** (*zwykle skradzionym samochodem*)

■ **joyride** noun [C] ▶ **przejażdżka** (*zwykle skradzionym samochodem*) | **joyrider** noun [C] ▶ **osoba odbywająca przejażdżkę** (*zwykle skradzionym samochodem*)

joystick /ˈdʒɔɪstɪk/ noun [C] a handle used for controlling movement on a computer, aircraft, machine, etc. ▶ **joystick**

JP = JUSTICE OF THE PEACE

Jr = JUNIOR¹ (3)

jubilant /ˈdʒuːbɪlənt/ adj. (formal) extremely happy, especially because of a success: *The football fans were jubilant at their team's victory in the cup.* ▶ **pełen triumfu, nie posiadający się z radości**

jubilation /ˌdʒuːbɪˈleɪʃn/ noun [U] (formal) great happiness because of a success ▶ **triumfowanie, radowanie się**

jubilee /ˈdʒuːbɪliː/ noun [C] a special anniversary of an event that took place a certain number of years ago, and the celebrations that go with it: *It's the company's **golden jubilee** this year.* ▶ **jubileusz** ℹ Wyróżnia się następujące jubileusze: **silver jubilee** (25 lat), **golden jubilee** (50 lat) i **diamond jubilee** (60 lat).

Judaism /ˈdʒuːdeɪɪzəm; US -dəɪzəm/ noun [U] the religion of the Jewish people ▶ **judaizm**

⚷ **judge¹** /dʒʌdʒ/ noun [C] **1** a person in a court of law whose job is to decide how criminals should be punished and to make legal decisions: *The judge sentenced the man to seventeen years in prison.* ▶ **sę-dzia/dzina** ➲ note at **court 2** a person who decides who has won a competition: *a panel of judges* ◇ *The judges' decision is final.* ▶ **sędzia (sportowy), juror/ka 3** [usually sing.] **a judge of sth** a person who has the ability or knowledge to give an opinion about sth: *You're a good judge of character* (ty dobrze znasz się na ludziach) – *what do you think of him?* ▶ **znawca, sędzia**

⚷ **judge²** /dʒʌdʒ/ verb **1** [I,T] to form or give an opinion about sb/sth based on the information you have: ***Judging by/from** what he said, his work is going well.* ◇ *It's difficult to judge how long the project will take.* ◇ *The party was judged a great success by everybody.* Wszyscy uznali imprezę za wielki sukces. ▶ **sądzić, oceniać 2** [T] to decide the result or winner of a competition: *The head teacher will judge the competition.* ▶ **sędziować 3** [T] to form an opinion about sb/sth, especially when you do not approve of them or it: *Don't judge him too harshly – he's had a difficult time.* ▶ **osądzać, wydawać sąd (o kimś) 4** [T] to decide if sb is guilty or innocent in a court of law: *It was the hardest case he had ever had to judge.* ▶ **sądzić** (*sprawę*)

⚷ **judgement** (also **judgment**) /ˈdʒʌdʒmənt/ noun **1** [U] the ability to form opinions or to make sensible decisions: *He always shows excellent judgement in his choice of staff.* ◇ *to have good/poor/sound judgement* ▶ **rozsądek, rozum 2** [C,U] an opinion that you form after carefully considering the information you have: *What, **in your judgement*** (twoim zdaniem), *would be the best course of action?* ▶ **opinia, zdanie 3** (**judgment**) [C,U] an official decision made by a judge or a court of law: *The man collapsed when the judgment was read out in court.* ▶ **wyrok, orzeczenie**

judgemental (Brit.) (also **judgmental**; especially US) /dʒʌdʒ'mentl/ adj. judging people and criticizing them too quickly: *Stop always being so judgemental!* ▶ **krytyczny**

judicial /dʒu'dɪʃl/ adj. connected with a court of law, a judge or a legal judgement: *the judicial system* ▶ **sądowy**, **sędziowski**

judiciary /dʒu'dɪʃəri; US -ʃieri/ noun (**the judiciary**) [C, with sing. or pl. verb] (pl. **judiciaries**) the judges of a country or a state, when they are considered as a group: *an independent judiciary* ▶ **sędziowie** ➲ look at **executive**, **legislature**

judicious /dʒu'dɪʃəs/ adj. (used about a decision or an action) sensible and carefully considered; showing good judgement ▶ **rozsądny**, **rozumny**
■ **judiciously** adv. ▶ **rozsądnie**, **rozumnie**

judo /'dʒu:dəʊ/ noun [U] a sport from Asia in which two people fight and try to throw each other to the ground ▶ **dżudo** ➲ look at **martial arts** ➲ picture on **page A9**

jug /dʒʌg/ (US **pitcher**) noun [C] a container with a handle used for holding or pouring liquids: *a milk jug* dzbanek do mleka ◇ *a jug of water* dzbanek wody ▶ **dzbanek**

juggle /'dʒʌgl/ verb [I,T] **1 juggle (with sth)** to keep three or more objects such as balls in the air at the same time by throwing them one at a time and catching them quickly ▶ **żonglować 2 juggle sth (with sth)** to try to deal with two or more important jobs or activities at the same time: *Many women have to juggle* (łączyć) *a career with having a family.* ▶ (*przen.*) **żonglować**

juggler /'dʒʌglə(r)/ noun [C] a person who **juggles** to entertain people ▶ **żongler/ka**

⚷**juice** /dʒu:s/ noun [C,U] **1** the liquid that comes from fruit and vegetables: *carrot/grapefruit/lemon juice* ◇ *I'll have an orange juice, please.* ▶ **sok** (*owocowy/warzywny*) **2** the liquid that comes from a piece of meat when it is cooked ▶ **sos własny** (*z mięsa*) **3** the liquid in your stomach that helps you break down the food you eat: *gastric/digestive juices* ▶ **sok trawienny**

juicy /'dʒu:si/ adj. (**juicier**; **juiciest**) **1** containing a lot of juice: *juicy oranges* ▶ **soczysty 2** (informal) (used about information) interesting because it is shocking ▶ (*plotka itp.*) **pikantny**

jukebox /'dʒu:kbɒks/ noun [C] a machine in a bar, etc. that plays music when money is put in ▶ **szafa grająca**

Jul. = JULY: *4 Jul. 1999*

⚷**July** /dʒu'laɪ/ noun [U,C] (abbr. **Jul.**) the 7th month of the year, coming after June ▶ **lipiec** ➲ note at **January**

jumble¹ /'dʒʌmbl/ verb [T, usually passive] **jumble sth (up/together)** to mix things together in a confused and untidy way: *I must sort my clothes out – they're all jumbled up in the drawer.* ▶ **mieszać**, **gmatwać**

jumble² /'dʒʌmbl/ noun **1** [sing.] an untidy group of things: *a jumble of papers/ideas* ▶ **gmatwanina**, **mieszanina** SYN **mess 2** [U] (Brit.) a collection of old things for a **jumble sale**: *Have you got any jumble you don't want?* ▶ **rzeczy używane** (*przeznaczone do wyprzedaży dobroczynnej*)

'jumble sale (US **'rummage sale**) noun [C] a sale of old things that people do not want any more. Clubs, churches, schools and other organizations hold **jumble sales** to get money. ▶ **wenta dobroczynna**, **wyprzedaż rzeczy używanych** ➲ look at **car boot sale**

jumbo¹ /'dʒʌmbəʊ/ noun [C] (pl. **jumbos**) (also ˌ**jumbo 'jet**) a very large aircraft that can carry several hundred passengers ▶ **wielki pasażerski odrzutowiec**, **jumbo jet**

jumbo² /'dʒʌmbəʊ/ adj. [only before a noun] (informal) very large ▶ **ogromny**, **kolosalny**

⚷**jump¹** /dʒʌmp/ verb **1** [I] to move quickly into the air by pushing yourself up with your legs and feet, or by stepping off a high place: *to jump into the air/off a bridge/onto a chair* ◇ *How high can you jump?* ◇ *Jump up and down to keep warm.* ▶ **skakać** ➲ picture at **hop 2** [T] to get over sth by jumping: *The dog jumped the fence and ran off down the road.* ▶ **przeskakiwać 3** [I] to move quickly and suddenly: *The phone rang and she jumped up to answer it* (rzuciła się, żeby go odebrać). ◇ *He jumped out of bed* (wyskoczył z łóżka) *when he realized what time it was.* ◇ *A taxi stopped and we jumped in* (wskoczyliśmy do środka). **4** [I] to make a sudden movement because of surprise or fear: *'Oh, it's only you – you made me jump,' he said.* ▶ **podskoczyć** (*np. z przestrachu*) **5** [I] **jump (from sth) to sth**; **jump (by) (sth)** to increase suddenly by a very large amount: *His salary jumped from £20 000 to £28 000 last year.* ▶ (*ceny, pensja itp.*) **podskoczyć 6** [I] **jump (from sth) to sth** to go suddenly from one point in a series, a story, etc. to another: *The book kept jumping from the present to the past.* ▶ **skakać z (tematu) na (temat)**

IDM **climb/jump on the bandwagon** → BANDWAGON

jump for joy to be extremely happy about sth ▶ **skakać z radości**

jump the gun to do sth too soon, before the proper time ▶ **robić coś przedwcześnie**

jump the queue to go to the front of a line of people without waiting for your turn ▶ **iść bez kolejki**

jump to conclusions to decide that sth is true without thinking about it carefully enough ▶ **pochopnie wysnuwać wnioski**

PHR V **jump at sth** to accept an opportunity, offer, etc. with enthusiasm: *Of course I jumped at the chance to work in New York for a year.* ▶ **skwapliwie skorzystać z czegoś**

⚷**jump²** /dʒʌmp/ noun [C] **1** an act of jumping: *With a huge jump the horse cleared the hedge.* ◇ *to do a parachute jump* ▶ **skok**, **podskok** ➲ look at **high jump**, **long jump 2** a thing to be jumped over: *The third jump consisted of a five-bar gate.* ▶ **przeszkoda do przeskoczenia** ➲ picture on **page A9 3 a jump (in sth)** a sudden increase in amount, price or value: *a 20% jump in profits* ▶ **skok** (*cen/wartości*)

jumper /'dʒʌmpə(r)/ noun [C] **1** (Brit.) a piece of clothing with sleeves, usually made of wool, that you wear on the top part of your body ▶ **sweter** (*wkładany przez głowę*) ➲ note at **sweater 2** a person or an animal that jumps ▶ **skoczek**

jumpy /'dʒʌmpi/ adj. (informal) nervous or worried ▶ **nerwowy**

Jun. = JUNE: *10 Jun. 1999*

junction /'dʒʌŋkʃn/ noun [C] a place where roads, railway lines, etc. meet ▶ **skrzyżowanie**, **węzeł kolejowy**

juncture /'dʒʌŋktʃə(r)/ noun [C] (formal) a particular point or stage in an activity or a series of events: ***At this juncture**, I would like to make an important announcement.* ▶ **punkt**

⚷**June** /dʒu:n/ noun [U,C] (abbr. **Jun.**) the 6th month of the year, coming after May ▶ **czerwiec** ➲ note at **January**

jungle /'dʒʌŋgl/ noun [C,U] a thick forest in a hot tropical country ▶ **dżungla** ➲ note at **forest**

⚷**junior¹** /'dʒu:niə(r)/ adj. **1 junior (to sb)** having a low or lower position (than sb) in an organization, etc.: *a junior doctor/employee* ◇ *a junior officer* podoficer ◇ *A lieutenant is junior to a captain in the army.* ▶ **niższy/młodszy rangą 2** [only before a noun] (Brit.) of or for children below a particular age: *the junior athletics championships* mistrzostwa atletyczne juniorów ◇ *She's moving from the infant school to the junior school* (do ostatnich czterech lat szkoły podstawowej dla dzieci od 7 do 11 lat) *next term.* **3** (**Junior**) (abbr. **Jnr**, **Jr**) (especially US) (used after the name of a son who has the same first name as his father): *Sammy Davis, Junior* ▶ (*po nazwisku*) **Młodszy**, **Junior** ➲ look at **senior**

J

junior² /ˈdʒuːniə(r)/ noun **1** [C] a person who has a low position in an organization, etc.: *office juniors* ▶ **osoba niższa/młodsza (rangą) 2** [sing.] [with *his, her, your*, etc.] a person who is younger than sb else by the number of years mentioned: *She's two years his junior/his junior by two years.* Jest od niego dwa lata młodsza. **3** [C] (Brit.) a child who goes to **junior school**: *The juniors are having an outing to a museum today.* ▶ **dziecko chodzące do szkoły dla dzieci w wieku od 7 do 11 lat** ➲ look at **senior**

ˌjunior ˈhigh school (also ˌ**junior ˈhigh**) noun [C,U] (in the US) a school for young people between the ages of 12 and 14 ▶ **gimnazjum**, **szkoła średnia** ➲ look at **senior high school**

ˈjunior school noun [C,U] (in Britain) a school for children between the ages of 7 and 11 ▶ **szkoła dla dzieci w wieku od 7 do 11 lat**

junk /dʒʌŋk/ noun [U] (informal) things that are old or useless or do not have much value: *There's an awful lot of junk up in the attic.* ▶ **rupiecie**, **graty**

ˈjunk food noun [U] (informal) food that is not very good for you but that is ready to eat or quick to prepare ▶ **niezdrowa żywność** (*produkty gotowe lub łatwe do przyrządzenia*)

junkie /ˈdʒʌŋki/ noun [C] (informal) a person who is unable to stop taking dangerous drugs ▶ **ćpun/ka** SYN **addict**

ˈjunk mail noun [U] advertising material that is sent to people who have not asked for it ▶ **reklamy przysyłane pocztą** ➲ look at **spam**

junta /ˈdʒʌntə; US ˈhʊn-/ noun [C, with sing. or pl. verb] a group, especially of military officers, who rule a country by force ▶ **junta**

Jupiter /ˈdʒuːpɪtə(r)/ noun [sing.] the planet that is fifth in order from the sun ▶ **Jowisz**

jurisdiction /ˌdʒʊərɪsˈdɪkʃn/ noun [U] legal power or authority; the area in which this power can be used: *That question is outside the jurisdiction of this council.* ▶ **jurysdykcja**, **kompetencja władzy**; **obszar kompetencji władzy**

jurisprudence /ˌdʒʊərɪsˈpruːdns/ noun [U] the scientific study of law ▶ **prawoznawstwo**

juror /ˈdʒʊərə(r)/ noun [C] a member of a **jury** ▶ **członek ławy przysięgłych**, **juror/ka** (*konkursu*)

jury /ˈdʒʊəri/ noun [C, with sing. or pl. verb] (pl. **juries**) **1** a group of members of the public in a court of law who listen to the facts about a crime and decide if sb is guilty or not guilty: *Has/have the jury reached a verdict?* ▶ **ława przysięgłych** ➲ note at **court 2** a group of people who decide who is the winner in a competition: *The jury is/are about to announce the winners.* ▶ **jury**, **sąd konkursowy**

just¹ /dʒʌst/ adv. **1** exactly: *It's just 8 o'clock.* ◇ *That's just what I meant.* ◇ *You're **just as** clever **as** he is.* ◇ *The room was too hot before, but now it's just right* (w sam raz). ◇ *He looks **just like** his father.* ▶ **dokładnie 2** almost not: *I could **only just** hear what she was saying.* ◇ *We got to the station **just in time**.* ▶ **ledwo**, **zaledwie 3** a very short time before: *She's just been to the shops.* ◇ *He'd just returned from France when I saw him.* ◇ *They came here just before* (tuż przed) *Easter.* ▶ **właśnie 4** at exactly this/that moment, or immediately after: *He was **just about to** break the window when he noticed a policeman.* ◇ ***Just as** I was beginning to enjoy myself, John said it was time to go.* ◇ ***Just then** the door opened.* ◇ *Wait a minute! I'm just coming* (zaraz idę). ◇ *I was **just about to** phone my mother* (właśnie miałem zadzwonić do mamy) *when she arrived.* ▶ **zaraz**, **właśnie**; **dokładnie** (*wtedy, gdy*) **5** really; absolutely: *The whole day was just fantastic!* ▶ **doprawdy**, **całkowicie**, **naprawdę 6** only: *She's just a child.* ◇ *It was worth it just to see her face* (warto było to zrobić, chociażby dlatego, by zobaczyć jej minę) *as she opened the present.* ◇ *Just a minute* (jeszcze tylko chwileczkę)*! I'm nearly ready.* ▶ **tylko**, **dopiero 7** [often with the imperative] (used for getting attention or to emphasize what you are saying): *Just let me speak for a moment, will you?* ◇ *I just don't want* (po prostu nie chcę) *to go to the party.* ◇ *Just imagine* (proszę sobie tylko wyobrazić) *how awful she must feel.* ▶ **tylko**, **proszę 8** (used with *might, may* or *could* to express a slight possibility): *This might just/just might be* (całkiem możliwe, że to jest) *the most important decision of your life.*

IDM **all/just the same** → SAME

it is just as well (that ...) it is a good thing: *It's just as well you remembered to bring your umbrella!* ▶ **dobrze, że**, **całe szczęście, że** ⓘ Por. też **(just) as well (to do sth)** przy **well**.

just about almost or approximately: *I've just about finished.* ◇ *Karen's plane should be taking off just about now.* ▶ **(już) prawie**, **właśnie**

just now 1 at this exact moment or during this exact period: *I can't come with you just now – can you wait 20 minutes?* ▶ **właśnie teraz 2** a very short time ago: *I saw Tony just now.* ▶ **dopiero co**

just so exactly right ▶ **właśnie/dokładnie tak**

not just yet not now, but probably quite soon ▶ **jeszcze nie teraz**

just² /dʒʌst/ adj. fair and right; reasonable: *a just punishment* ▶ **sprawiedliwy**, **rozsądny**

■ **justly** adv. ▶ **sprawiedliwie**, **rozsądnie**

justice /ˈdʒʌstɪs/ noun **1** [U] the fair treatment of people: *a struggle for justice* ▶ **sprawiedliwość 2** [U] the quality of being fair or reasonable: *Everybody realized the justice of what he was saying.* ▶ **słuszność 3** [U] the law and the way it is used: *the criminal justice system* ▶ **sprawiedliwość 4** (**Justice**) [C] (US) a judge in a court of law ▶ (*tytuły*) **sę-dzia/dzina**

IDM **do justice to sb/sth**; **do sb/sth justice** to treat sb/sth fairly or to show the real quality of sb/sth: *I don't like him, but to do him justice, he's a very clever man.* ◇ *The photograph doesn't do justice to her incredible beauty.* ▶ **oddawać komuś sprawiedliwość**, **ukazywać czyjeś zalety**

a miscarriage of justice → MISCARRIAGE

ˌJustice of the ˈPeace noun [C] (abbr. **JP** /ˌdʒeɪ ˈpiː/) a person who judges less serious cases in a court of law in Britain ▶ **sędzia pokoju** ➲ look at **magistrate**

justifiable /ˈdʒʌstɪfaɪəbl; ˌdʒʌstɪˈfaɪəbl/ adj. that you can accept because there is a good reason for it ▶ **usprawiedliwiony**, **uzasadniony**

■ **justifiably** /-əbli/ adv. ▶ **w usprawiedliwiony/uzasadniony sposób**

justification /ˌdʒʌstɪfɪˈkeɪʃn/ noun [C,U] **(a) justification (for sth/doing sth)** (a) good reason ▶ **usprawiedliwienie**, **uzasadnienie**

justify /ˈdʒʌstɪfaɪ/ verb [T] (**justifying**; **justifies**; pt, pp **justified**) to give or be a good reason for sth: *Can you justify your decision?* ▶ **usprawiedliwiać**, **uzasadniać**

jut /dʒʌt/ verb [I] (**jutting**; **jutted**) **jut (out) (from/into/over sth)** to stick out further than the surrounding surface, objects, etc.: *rocks that jut out into the sea* ▶ **wystawać**, **sterczeć**

juvenile /ˈdʒuːvənaɪl; US -vənl/ adj. **1** [only before a noun] (formal) of, for or involving young people who are not yet adults: *juvenile crime* ▶ **nieletni**, **młodociany 2** silly and more typical of a child than an adult ▶ **dziecinny** SYN **childish**

■ **juvenile** noun [C] ▶ **nieletn-i/a**, **młodocian-y/a**

ˌjuvenile deˈlinquent noun [C] a young person who is guilty of committing a crime ▶ **młodociany przestępca**

juxtapose /ˌdʒʌkstəˈpəʊz/ verb [T] (formal) to put two people, things, etc. very close together, especially in

order to show how they are different: *The artist achieves a special effect by juxtaposing light and dark.* ▶ **zestawiać, umieszczać obok siebie**
■ **juxtaposition** /ˌdʒʌkstəpəˈzɪʃn/ noun [U] ▶ **zestawianie, umieszczanie obok siebie**

K k

K, k /keɪ/ noun [C,U] (pl. **Ks**; **ks**; **K's**; **k's** /keɪz/) the 11th letter of the English alphabet: *'Kate' begins with (a) 'K'.* ▶ **litera** ***k***

K /keɪ/ abbr. **1** (informal) one thousand: *She earns 22K (= £22 000) a year.* ▶ **tys. 2** = KILOMETRE, KILOMETRES

kaleidoscope /kəˈlaɪdəskəʊp/ noun [C] **1** a toy that consists of a tube containing mirrors and small pieces of coloured glass. When you look into one end of the tube and turn it, you see changing patterns of colours. ▶ **kalejdoskop 2** a large number of different things ▶ **kalejdoskop**

kangaroo /ˌkæŋgəˈruː/ noun [C] (pl. **kangaroos**) an Australian animal that moves by jumping on its strong back legs and that carries its young in a **pouch** on its stomach ▶ **kangur**

karaoke /ˌkæriˈəʊki/ noun [U] a type of entertainment in which a machine plays only the music of popular songs so that people can sing the words themselves ▶ **karaoke**

karat (US) = CARAT

karate /kəˈrɑːti/ noun [U] a style of fighting originally from Japan in which the hands and feet are used as weapons ▶ **karate** ➲ look at **martial arts**

kart = GO-KART

kayak /ˈkaɪæk/ noun [C] a light narrow boat for one person, that you move using a **paddle** ▶ **kajak** ➲ look at **canoe** ➲ picture at **boat**

KB (also **Kb**) = KILOBYTE

kebab /kɪˈbæb/ noun [C] small pieces of meat, vegetables, etc. that are cooked on a **skewer** ▶ **kebab, szaszłyk** ➲ picture on **page A14**

keel¹ /kiːl/ noun [C] a long piece of wood or metal on the bottom of a boat that stops it falling over sideways in the water ▶ **stępka, kil**

keel² /kiːl/ verb

PHR V **keel over** to fall over ▶ **przewracać się, upadać**

⚷ **keen** /kiːn/ adj. **1 keen (to do sth/on doing sth/that ...)** very interested in sth; wanting to do sth: *They are both keen gardeners.* ◇ *I failed the first time but I'm keen to try again* (chcę spróbować ponownie). ◇ *I wasn't too keen on going camping.* Nie miałem zbytniej ochoty na wyjazd pod namiot. ◇ *She was keen that we should all be there.* Bardzo chciała, żebyśmy tam wszyscy byli. ▶ **zapalony (do czegoś); chętny** ➲ note at **like 2** (used about one of the senses, a feeling, etc.) good or strong: *Foxes have a keen sense of smell.* ▶ **wrażliwy, czuły**

IDM **keen on sb/sth** very interested in or having a strong desire for sb/sth: *He's very keen on jazz.* Bardzo lubi jazz. ◇ *Tracey seems very keen on a boy* (chyba kocha się w chłopaku) *at college.* ◇ *I'm not very keen on the idea* (nie za bardzo palę się do pomysłu) *of going camping.* ▶ **bardzo zainteresowany kimś/czymś, będący miłośnikiem czegoś**

■ **keenly** adv. ▶ **dotkliwie, przenikliwie** | **keenness** noun [U] ▶ **zapał, gorliwość**

⚷ **keep¹** /kiːp/ verb (pt, pp **kept** /kept/) **1** [I] to continue to be in a particular state or position: *You must keep warm.* Musisz dbać, żeby ci było ciepło. ◇ *That child can't keep still* (nie może usiedzieć w jednym miejscu). ◇ *I still* ***keep in touch with*** (utrzymuję kontakt z) *my old school*

friends. ◇ *Remember to keep left* (trzymać się lewej strony jezdni) *when you're driving in Britain.* ▶ **trzymać się, pozostawać 2** [T] to make sb/sth stay in a particular state, place or condition: *Please keep this door closed.* ◇ *He kept his hands in his pockets.* ◇ *I'm sorry to keep you waiting.* Przepraszam, że kazałem ci czekać. ◇ *It's hard to keep the children amused* (trudno nieustannie zabawiać dzieci) *when they can't go outside.* ▶ **trzymać 3** [T] **keep doing sth** to continue doing sth or to repeat an action many times: *Keep going until you get to the church* (idź dalej, aż dojdziesz do kościoła) *and then turn left.* ◇ *She keeps asking me silly questions.* ▶ **wciąż/ciągle coś robić 4** [T] to delay sb/sth; to prevent sb from leaving: *Where's the doctor? What's keeping him?* ▶ **zatrzymywać 5** [T] to continue to have sth; to save sth for sb: *You can keep that book – I don't need it any more.* ◇ *Can I keep the car until next week?* ◇ *I gave the taxi driver a £10 note and told him to keep the change* (żeby zachował resztę). ◇ *Can you keep my seat for me till I get back?* ▶ **zatrzymywać, mieć 6** [T] to have sth in a particular place: *Where do you keep the matches?* ◇ *Keep your passport in a safe place.* ▶ **przechowywać, trzymać 7** [T] to have and look after animals: *They keep ducks on their farm.* ▶ **hodować, trzymać 8** [I] to stay fresh ▶ (*żywność*) **dobrze przechowywać się, zachowywać świeżość 9** [T] to do what you promised or arranged: *Can you keep a promise?* ◇ *to keep a secret* ◇ *She didn't keep her appointment* (nie przyszła na wizytę) *at the dentist's.* ▶ **dotrzymywać, zachowywać 10** [T] to write down sth that you want to remember: *to keep a diary* ▶ **prowadzić** (*np. zapiski*) **11** [T] to support sb with your money: *You can't keep a family on the money I earn.* ▶ **utrzymywać kogoś, dawać na czyjeś utrzymanie 12** [T] to own and manage a shop or restaurant ▶ **prowadzić**

IDM **keep it up** to continue doing sth as well as you are doing it now ▶ **dobrze robić coś dalej, podtrzymywać** (*np. wysoki poziom*)

ⓘ **Keep** używa się w innych idiomach, np. **keep count**. Zob. hasła odpowiednich rzeczowników i przymiotników itp.

PHR V **keep at it/sth** to continue to work on/at sth: *Keep at it – we should be finished soon.* ▶ **pracować nadal/wytrwale nad czymś, nie przestawać (czegoś robić)**

keep away from sb/sth to not go near sb/sth: *Keep away from the town centre this weekend.* ▶ **trzymać się z dala od kogoś/czegoś, omijać kogoś/coś z daleka**

keep back (from sb/sth) to stay at a distance from sb/sth: *Keep well back from the road.* ▶ **trzymać się z dala (od kogoś/czegoś)**

keep sb/sth back (from sb/sth) to prevent sb/sth from moving forwards: *The police tried to keep the crowd back.* ▶ **powstrzymywać kogoś/coś (od czegoś), nie dopuszczać kogoś/czegoś (do kogoś/czegoś)**

keep sth back (from sb) to refuse to tell sb sth: *I know he's keeping something back; he knows much more than he says.* ▶ **zatajać coś (przed kimś), nie wyjawiać czegoś (komuś)**

keep sth down to make sth stay at a low level; to stop sth increasing: *Keep your voice down.* Nie podnoś głosu! ▶ **utrzymywać na niskim poziomie**

keep sb from sth/from doing sth to prevent sb from doing sth ▶ **powstrzymywać kogoś przed czymś**

keep sth from sb to refuse to tell sb sth ▶ **zatajać coś przed kimś, nie wyjawiać czegoś komuś**

keep off sth to not go near or on sth: *Keep off the grass!* Nie deptać trawy! ▶ **nie zbliżać się do czegoś, trzymać się z dala od czegoś**

keep sth off (sb/sth) to stop sth touching or going on sb/sth: *I'm trying to keep the flies off the food.* ▶ **odpędzać coś (od czegoś), nie pozwalać czemuś się zbliżać (do kogoś/czegoś)**

keep on (doing sth) to continue doing sth or to repeat an action many times, especially in an annoying way: *He keeps on interrupting me.* ▶ **bezustannie coś robić, nie przestawać czegoś robić**
keep on (at sb) (about sb/sth) to continue talking to sb in an annoying or complaining way: *She kept on at me about my homework until I did it.* ▶ **męczyć (kogoś) (czymś), zanudzać (kogoś) (czymś)**
keep (sb/sth) out (of sth) to not enter sth; to stop sb/sth entering sth: *They put up a fence to keep people out of* (żeby ludzie nie wchodzili do) *their garden.* ◇ *The sign said 'Danger – Keep out* (wstęp wzbroniony)*!'* ▶ **trzymać (się) z dala (od czegoś)**
keep out of sth; keep sb out of sth to avoid sth; to prevent sb from being involved in sth or affected by sth: *That child can't keep out of mischief.* ◇ *Keep the baby out of the sun.* ▶ **unikać czegoś, nie narażać kogoś na coś**
keep to sth to not leave sth; to do sth in the usual, agreed or expected way: *Keep to the path!* ◇ *He didn't keep to our agreement.* ▶ **trzymać się czegoś, nie odstępować od czegoś, stosować się do czegoś**
keep sth to/at sth to not allow sth to rise above a particular level: *We're trying to keep costs to a minimum.* ▶ **utrzymywać coś na (niezmienionym) poziomie**
keep up (with sb) to move at the same speed as sb: *Can't you walk a bit slower? I can't keep up with you.* ▶ **dotrzymywać kroku, nadążać (za kimś)**
keep up (with sth) 1 to know about what is happening: *You have to read the latest magazines if you want to keep up.* ◇ *She likes to keep up with the latest fashions.* ▶ **być na bieżąco, nadążać (za czymś) 2** to continue to pay or do sth regularly: *If you do not keep up with the payments, you could lose your home.* ▶ **regularnie dokonywać płatności, regularnie coś robić**
keep sth up 1 to prevent sth from falling down ▶ **podtrzymywać coś, podpierać coś 2** to make sth stay at a high level: *We want to keep up standards of education.* ▶ **utrzymywać coś na wysokim poziomie 3** to continue doing sth: *How long can the baby keep up that crying?* ▶ **bezustannie/wytrwale coś robić, nie przestawać czegoś robić**
keep up with sb to continue to be in contact with sb: *How many of your old school friends do you keep up with?* ▶ **utrzymywać z kimś kontakt**
keep (yourself) to yourself to avoid meeting people socially or becoming involved in their affairs ▶ **trzymać się z dala**
keep sth to yourself to not tell other people about sth: *She keeps her problems to herself.* ▶ **nie mówić o czymś nikomu**

keep² /kiːp/ noun [U] food, clothes and all the other things that you need to live ▶ **utrzymanie**
IDM **for keeps** (informal) for always: *Take it. It's yours for keeps.* ▶ **na zawsze, na własność**

keeper /ˈkiːpə(r)/ noun [C] **1** a person who guards or looks after sth: *a zookeeper* ▶ **dozor-ca/czyni, opiekun/ka 2** (informal) = GOALKEEPER

keeping /ˈkiːpɪŋ/ noun
IDM **in/out of keeping (with sth) 1** that does/does not look good with sth: *That modern table is out of keeping with the style of the room.* ▶ **(nie)harmonizujący (z czymś), (nie)pasujący (do czegoś) 2** in/not in agreement with a rule, belief, etc.: *The Council's decision is in keeping with government policy.* ▶ **(nie)zgodn-y/ie (z czymś)**

keg /keg/ noun [C] a round metal or wooden container, used especially for storing beer ▶ **baryłka, antałek**

kennel /ˈkenl/ noun [C] a small house for a dog ▶ **psia buda**

kept past tense, past participle of **keep¹**

kerb (especially US **curb**) /kɜːb/ noun [C] the edge of the raised path at the side of a road, usually made of long pieces of stone ▶ **krawężnik**

kernel /ˈkɜːnl/ noun [C] **1** the inner part of a nut or seed ▶ **jądro, pestka 2** the most important part of an idea or a subject: *There may be a kernel of truth* (ziarno prawdy) *in what she said.* ▶ **sedno, istota**

kerosene (US) = PARAFFIN

ketchup /ˈketʃəp/ noun [U] a thick cold sauce made from tomatoes that is eaten with hot or cold food ▶ **keczup**

kettle /ˈketl/ noun [C] a container with a lid, used for boiling water: *an electric kettle* ▶ **czajnik**

kettledrum /ˈketldrʌm/ noun [C] a large metal drum with a round bottom and a thin plastic top that can be made looser or tighter to produce different musical notes. A set of kettledrums is usually called **timpani**. ▶ (*muz.*) **kocioł**

key¹ /kiː/ noun [C] **1** a metal object that is used for locking a door, starting a car, etc.: *Have you seen my car keys* (kluczyki do samochodu) *anywhere?* ◇ *We need a spare key to the front door.* ◇ *a bunch of keys* pęk kluczy ▶ **klucz 2** [usually sing.] **the key (to sth)** something that helps you achieve or understand sth: *A good education is the key to success.* ▶ **klucz 3** one of the parts of a piano, computer, etc. that you press with your fingers to make it work: *Press the return key to enter the information.* ▶ **klawisz 4** a set of musical notes that is based on one particular note: *The concerto is in the key of A minor.* ◇ *the key signature* oznaczenie tonacji ▶ **tonacja 5** a set of answers to exercises or problems: *an answer key* ▶ **klucz** (*do ćwiczeń*), **odpowiedzi 6** a list of the symbols and signs used in a map or book, showing what they mean ▶ **legenda, objaśnienie**
IDM **under lock and key** → LOCK²

key² /kiː/ verb [T] **key sth (in)** to put information into a computer or give it an instruction by typing: *First, key in your password.* ▶ **wpisywać** (*do komputera*)

key³ /kiː/ adj. [only before a noun] very important: *Tourism is a key industry in Spain.* ▶ **kluczowy** ➲ note at **important**

keyboard¹ /ˈkiːbɔːd/ noun [C] **1** the set of keys on a piano, computer, etc. ▶ **klawiatura 2** an electrical musical instrument like a small piano ▶ **syntetyzator**
ℹ Zwróć uwagę, że słowo **keyboards**, mimo że ma formę liczby mnogiej, może się odnosić do jednego instrumentu.

■ **keyboardist** noun [C] a person who plays an electronic musical instrument with a keyboard ▶ **osoba grająca na syntetyzatorze**

keyboard² /ˈkiːbɔːd/ verb [I,T] to type information into a computer ▶ **wprowadzać dane do komputera**
■ **keyboarder** noun [C] a person whose job is to type data into a computer ▶ **osoba wprowadzająca dane do komputera** | **keyboarding** noun [U] ▶ **wprowadzanie danych do komputera**

keyhole /ˈkiːhəʊl/ noun [C] the hole in a lock where you put the key ▶ **dziurka od klucza**

ˈ**key ring** noun [C] a ring on which you keep keys ▶ **kółko na klucze**

ˈ**key signature** noun [C] the set of marks at the beginning of a printed piece of music to show what **key** the piece is in ▶ **oznaczenie tonacji** ➲ picture at **music**

keyword /ˈkiːwɜːd/ noun [C] **1** a word that tells you about the main idea or subject of sth: *When you're studying a language, the keyword is patience.* ▶ **słowo kluczowe 2** a word or phrase that is used to give an instruction to a computer ▶ (*komput.*) **polecenie, słowo kluczowe**

kg = KILO: *weight 10kg*

khaki /ˈkɑːki/ adj., noun [U] (of) a pale brownish-yellow or brownish-green colour: *The khaki uniforms of the desert soldiers.* ▶ **kolor khaki; (koloru) khaki**

kHz /ˈkɪləhɜːts/ abbr. **kilohertz**; (used in radio) a measure of **frequency** ▶ **kHz**

kibbutz /kɪˈbʊts/ noun [C] (pl. **kibbutzim** /ˌkɪbʊtˈsiːm/) a farm or village in Israel where many people live and work together, sharing the work and the money that is earned ▶ **kibuc**

⚷**kick¹** /kɪk/ verb **1** [T] to hit or move sb/sth with your foot: *He kicked the ball wide of the net.* ◇ *The police kicked the door down.* ▶ **kopać 2** [I,T] to move your foot or feet: *You must kick harder* (pracować nogami z całych sił) *if you want to swim faster.* ▶ **wierzgać, machać nogami**
IDM **kick the habit** to stop doing sth harmful that you have done for a long time ▶ **zrywać z nałogiem**
kick yourself to be annoyed with yourself because you have done sth stupid, missed an opportunity, etc. ▶ **być złym na siebie**
PHR V **kick sb around** (informal) to treat sb in a rough or unfair way ▶ **pomiatać kimś**
kick off to start a game of football ▶ **rozpoczynać mecz piłki nożnej**
kick sb out (of sth) (informal) to force sb to leave a place: *to be kicked out of university* ▶ **wykopywać/wyrzucać kogoś (skądś)**

⚷**kick²** /kɪk/ noun [C] **1** an act of kicking: *She gave the door a kick* (kopnęła drzwi) *and it closed.* ◇ *The referee gave a **free kick*** (rzut wolny) *for a foul on the goalkeeper.* ▶ **kopnięcie, kopniak 2** (informal) a feeling of great pleasure, excitement, etc.: *He seems to **get a** real **kick out of** driving fast.* Szybka jazda samochodem chyba sprawia mu nie lada frajdę! ▶ **frajda**

ˈ**kick-off** noun [C] the start of a game of football ▶ **początek meczu piłki nożnej**

⚷**kid¹** /kɪd/ noun **1** [C] (informal) a child or young person ▶ **dziecko 2** (**kid brother/sister**) [C] (especially US, informal) younger brother/sister ▶ **młodsz-y/a brat/siostra 3** [C,U] a young **goat** or its skin ▶ **koźlę**

kid² /kɪd/ verb [I,T] (**kidding**; **kidded**) (informal) to trick sb/yourself by saying sth that is not true; to make a joke about sth: *I didn't mean it. I was only kidding.* ▶ **żartować; nabierać (kogoś/się)**

kiddie (also **kiddy**) /ˈkɪdi/ noun [C] (pl. **kiddies**) (informal) a child ▶ **dzieciak**

kidnap /ˈkɪdnæp/ verb [T] (**kidnapping**; **kidnapped**) to take sb away by force and demand money for their safe return: *The child was kidnapped and £50 000 ransom was demanded for her release.* ▶ **porywać, uprowadzać** (*dla okupu*) ➲ look at **hijack**
■ **kidnapper** noun [C] ▶ **porywacz/ka** | **kidnapping** noun [C,U] ▶ **porwanie, uprowadzenie** (*dla okupu*) ➲ note at **crime**

kidney /ˈkɪdni/ noun **1** [C] one of the two parts of your body that separate waste liquid from your blood ▶ **nerka** ➲ picture at **body 2** [U,C] the **kidneys** of an animal when they are cooked and eaten as food: *steak and kidney pie* ▶ **cynaderk-a/i, cynadr-a/y**

ˈ**kidney bean** noun [C] a type of reddish-brown **bean** shaped like a **kidney** that is usually dried before it is sold and then left in water before cooking ▶ **fasola czerwona typu kidney**

⚷**kill¹** /kɪl/ verb **1** [I,T] to make sb/sth die: *Smoking kills.* ◇ *She was killed instantly in the crash.* ▶ **zabijać, uśmiercać 2** [T] (informal) to be very angry with sb: *My mum will kill me when she sees this mess.* ▶ **zabijać 3** [T] to cause sth to end or fail: *The minister's opposition killed the idea stone dead.* ◇ *Jake's tactless comment killed* (ucięła) *the conversation.* ▶ **obalać, niweczyć 4** [T] (informal) to cause sb pain; to hurt: *My feet are killing me.* Nie czuję nóg! ▶ **strasznie boleć 5** [T] (informal) **kill yourself/sb** to make yourself/sb laugh a lot: *We were **killing ourselves laughing.*** Umieraliśmy ze śmiechu. ▶ **zaśmiewać się; rozśmieszać**

> **kill**
>
> **Murder** oznacza umyślne zabicie kogoś: *This was no accident. The old lady was murdered.* **Assassinate** oznacza zabicie kogoś z powodów politycznych: *President Kennedy was assassinated.* **Slaughter** i **massacre** oznaczają zabicie wielu ludzi: *Hundreds of people were massacred when the army opened fire.* **Slaughter** oznacza też bicie zwierząt rzeźnych.

IDM **kill time, an hour, etc.** to spend time doing sth that is not interesting or important while you are waiting for sth else to happen ▶ **robić coś dla zabicia czasu**
kill two birds with one stone to do one thing which will achieve two results ▶ **upiec dwie pieczenie przy jednym ogniu**
PHR V **kill sb/sth off** to make a lot of plants, animals, etc. die: *Some drugs kill off useful bacteria in the user's body.* ▶ **wybijać kogoś/coś**
kill sth off to stop or get rid of sth: *He has effectively killed off any political opposition.* ▶ **niszczyć coś**

kill² /kɪl/ noun [sing.] **1** the act of killing: *Lions often **make a kill** in the evening.* ▶ **polowanie, zabicie 2** an animal or animals that have been killed: *The eagle took the kill back* (orzeł zabrał zdobycz) *to its young.* ▶ **upolowana zwierzyna**

killer /ˈkɪlə(r)/ noun [C] a person, animal or thing that kills: *He's a dangerous killer who may strike again.* ◇ *a killer disease* śmiertelna choroba ▶ **zabój-ca/czyni**

⚷**killing** /ˈkɪlɪŋ/ noun [C] act of killing a person on purpose; a murder: *There have been a number of brutal killings in the area recently.* ▶ **zabójstwo**
IDM **make a killing** to make a large profit quickly ▶ **obłowić się**

kiln /kɪln/ noun [C] a type of large oven for baking pots, bricks, etc. that are made of **clay** to make them hard ▶ **piec** (*do wypalania, suszenia i prażenia*)

kilo = KILOGRAM

kilobyte /ˈkɪləbaɪt/ noun [C] (abbr. **KB**; **Kb**) a unit of computer memory, equal to 1 024 **bytes** ▶ **kilobajt**

⚷**kilogram** /ˈkɪləgræm/ (also **kilogramme**; **kilo** /ˈkiːləʊ/, pl. **kilos**) noun [C] (abbr. **kg**) a measure of weight; 1 000 grams ▶ **kilogram** ℹ Więcej o wagach w dodatku *Wyrażenia liczbowe* na końcu słownika.

K

kilometre (US **kilometer**) /ˈkɪləmiːtə(r); kɪˈlɒmɪtə(r)/ noun [C] (abbr. **k**, **km**) a measure of length; 1 000 metres ▶ **kilometr**

kilowatt /ˈkɪləwɒt/ noun [C] (abbr. **kW**; **kw**) a measure of electric power; 1 000 **watts** ▶ **kilowat**

kilt /kɪlt/ noun [C] a skirt that is worn by men as part of the national dress of Scotland ▶ **część tradycyjnego męskiego stroju w Szkocji** ➲ picture at **bagpipes**

kin → NEXT OF KIN

kind¹ /kaɪnd/ noun [C] a group whose members all have the same qualities: *The concert attracted people **of all kinds**.* ◇ *The concert attracted **all kinds of** people.* ◇ ***What kind of** car have you got?* ◇ *Many kinds of plant and animal are being lost every year.* ◇ *In the evenings I listen to music, write letters, that **kind of thing**.* ▶ **rodzaj** SYN **sort**, **type**

Rzeczownik **kind** jest policzalny i dlatego zdanie ~~*I like all kind of music.*~~ jest niepoprawne. Poprawna forma to: *I like all kinds of music.* Po **kinds of** może następować rzeczownik w lp lub lm: *There are so many kinds of camera/cameras on the market that it's hard to know which is best.*

IDM **a kind of** (informal) (used for describing sth in a way that is not very clear): *I had a kind of feeling that something would go wrong.* ◇ *There's a funny kind of smell in here.* ▶ **jakiś (taki)**, **(coś) w rodzaju**

kind of (informal) slightly; a little: *I'm kind of worried about the interview.* ▶ **trochę**

of a kind **1** of poor quality: *The village has a bus service of a kind – two buses a week!* ▶ **coś w rodzaju**, **niby** **2** the same: *The friends were two of a kind – very similar in so many ways.* ▶ **tego samego rodzaju**

kind² /kaɪnd/ adj. **kind (to sb)**; **kind (of sb) (to do sth)** caring about others; friendly and generous: *Everyone's been so kind to us since we came here!* ◇ *It was kind of you to offer, but I don't need any help.* ▶ **uprzejmy**, **życzliwy**, **sympatyczny** OPP **unkind**

kindergarten /ˈkɪndəgɑːtn/ noun [C] a school for children aged from about 2 to 5 ▶ **przedszkole** SYN **nursery school**

ˌkind-ˈhearted adj. kind and generous ▶ **dobry**, **dobrotliwy**, **o dobrym/wielkim sercu**

kindle /ˈkɪndl/ verb [I,T] **1** to start burning; to make a fire start burning: *We watched as the fire slowly kindled.* ◇ *to **kindle a fire/flame*** ▶ **rozpalać** *(ogień)* **2** to make sth such as an interest, emotion, etc. start to grow in sb; to start to be felt by sb: *It was her teacher who kindled her interest in music.* ◇ *Suspicion kindled within her.* ▶ **rozbudzać**

kindly /ˈkaɪndli/ adv. **1** in a kind way: *The nurse smiled kindly.* ▶ **uprzejmie**, **życzliwie**, **sympatycznie** **2** adv. (old-fashioned, informal) (used for asking sb to do sth) please: *Would you kindly wait a moment?* ▶ **łaskawie**, **uprzejmie**

■ **kindly** adj. [only before a noun] kind and friendly: *a kindly face* ▶ **dobrotliwy**, **dobry**

kindness /ˈkaɪndnəs/ noun [C,U] **1** [U] the quality of being kind: *Thank you very much for all your kindness.* ▶ **życzliwość**, **uprzejmość** **2** [C] a kind act ▶ **przysługa**, **wyświadczona uprzejmość**

kindred /ˈkɪndrəd/ noun (old-fashioned or formal) **1** [pl.] your family and relatives ▶ **krewni** ➲ look at **kin** **2** [U] the fact of being related to another person: *ties of kindred* ▶ **pokrewieństwo**

■ **kindred** adj. [only before a noun] (formal) very similar; related: *I knew I'd found **a kindred spirit**.* ▶ **pokrewny**

king /kɪŋ/ noun [C] **1** (the title of) a man who rules a country. A king is usually the son or close relative of the former ruler: *King Edward VII* (mówi się: (King) Edward the Seventh) ◇ (figurative) *The lion is the king of the jungle.* ▶ **król** ➲ look at **queen**, **prince**, **princess** **2** the most important piece used in the game of **chess**, that can move one square in any direction ▶ **król** **3** one of the four playing cards in a pack with a picture of a king: *the king of spades* ▶ **król** ➲ note at **card**

kingdom /ˈkɪŋdəm/ noun [C] **1** a country that is ruled by a king or queen: *the United Kingdom* ▶ **królestwo** **2** one of the parts of the natural world: *the animal kingdom* ▶ **królestwo**

ˈking-size (also **ˈking-sized**) adj. bigger than usual: *a king-size bed* ▶ **olbrzymi**, **bardzo duży**

kink /kɪŋk/ noun [C] a turn or bend in sth that should be straight ▶ **skręt**, **zagięcie**

kinky /ˈkɪŋki/ adj. (informal) (used to describe sexual behaviour that most people would consider strange or unusual) ▶ **perwersyjny** ℹ Zwykle wyraża dezaprobatę.

kinsfolk /ˈkɪnzfəʊk/ noun [pl.] (formal or old-fashioned) a person's relatives ▶ **krewni**

kiosk /ˈkiːɒsk/ noun [C] a very small building in the street where newspapers, sweets, cigarettes, etc. are sold ▶ **kiosk** ➲ look at **newsagent**

kip /kɪp/ verb [I] (**kipping**; **kipped**) (Brit., informal) to sleep: *You could kip on the sofa if you like.* ▶ **spać**

■ **kip** noun [sing., U]: *I didn't get much kip last night.* ◇ *It's time to have a kip.* Czas uderzyć w kimono. ▶ **sen**

kipper /ˈkɪpə(r)/ noun [C] a type of fish that has been kept for a long time in salt, and then smoked ▶ **śledź wędzony**

kiss /kɪs/ verb [I,T] to touch sb with your lips to show love or friendship, or when saying hello or goodbye: *He kissed her on the cheek.* ◇ *They kissed each other goodbye.* ▶ **całować (się)**

■ **kiss** noun [C]: *Give Daddy a goodnight kiss.* Pocałuj tatę na dobranoc. ◇ *a kiss on the lips/cheek* ▶ **pocałunek**, **całus**

kit¹ /kɪt/ noun **1** [C] a set of parts that you buy and put together in order to make sth: *a kit for a model aeroplane* ▶ **zestaw (modelarski)** **2** [C,U] a set of tools, equipment or clothes that you need for a particular purpose, sport or activity: *a tool kit* ◇ *a drum kit* ◇ *football/gym kit* ◇ *a first-aid kit* apteczka pierwszej pomocy ▶ **sprzęt**, **komplet** **3** the clothes and other things that are needed e.g. by a soldier ▶ **rynsztunek**

kit² /kɪt/ verb (**kitting**; **kitted**)

PHR V **kit sb/yourself out/up (in/with sth)** to give sb all the necessary clothes, equipment, tools, etc. for sth ▶ **wyposażać (się)**

kitchen /ˈkɪtʃɪn/ noun [C] a room where food is prepared and cooked ▶ **kuchnia**

kite /kaɪt/ noun [C] a toy which consists of a light frame covered with paper or cloth. **Kites** are flown in the wind on the end of a long piece of string: *to fly a kite* ▶ **latawiec**

kitsch /ˈkɪtʃ/ noun [U] popular art or design that is lacking in good taste and is too bright or sentimental in style ▶ **kicz**

kitten /ˈkɪtn/ noun [C] a young cat ▶ **kociątko** ➲ note at **cat**

kitty /ˈkɪti/ noun [C] (pl. **kitties**) **1** a sum of money that is collected from a group of people and used for a particular purpose: *All the students in the flat put £5 a week into the kitty.* ▶ **wspólna pula/kasa**, **bank** **2** (informal) (a way of calling or referring to a cat) ▶ **kici**; **kiciuś**

kiwi /'ki:wi:/ noun [C] (pl. **kiwis**) **1** a New Zealand bird with a long beak and short wings that cannot fly ▶ **kiwi 2** = KIWI FRUIT

'**kiwi fruit** noun [C] (pl. **kiwi fruit**) (also **kiwi**) a small fruit with thin brown skin covered with small hairs, soft green flesh and black seeds, originally from New Zealand ▶ (*owoc*) **kiwi** ➲ picture on **page A12**

km = KILOMETRE

knack /næk/ noun [sing.] (informal) **knack (of/for doing sth)** skill or ability to do sth (difficult) that you have naturally or you can learn: *Knitting isn't difficult once you've got the knack of it* (jak już się tego nauczysz). ▶ **wprawa**

knackered /'nækəd/ adj. (Brit., slang) **1** [not usually before a noun] extremely tired: *I was knackered after the game.* ▶ **wykończony** SYN **exhausted**, **worn out 2** too old or broken to use: *The car's knackered.* ▶ **zarżnięty**

knead /ni:d/ verb [T] to press and squeeze **dough** with your hands in order to make bread, etc. ▶ **gnieść, ugniatać**

⚷ **knee** /ni:/ noun [C] **1** the place where your leg bends in the middle: *Angie fell and grazed her knee.* ◇ *She was* ***on her hands and knees*** *on the floor looking for her earrings.* ◇ *Come and sit on my knee.* ▶ **kolano** ➲ picture at **body 2** the part of a pair of trousers, etc. that covers the knee: *There's a hole in the knee of those jeans.* ▶ **kolano**
IDM **on your knees 1** in a kneeling position ▶ **na klęczkach 2** in a very difficult or weak state: *When they took over, the company was on its knees.* ▶ **u kresu sił**

kneecap /'ni:kæp/ (also technical **patella** /pə'telə/) noun [C] the bone that covers the front of the knee ▶ (*anat.*) **rzepka** SYN **patella** ➲ picture at **body**

ˌ**knee-'deep** adj. up to your knees: *The water was knee-deep in places.* ▶ **po kolana**
■ ˌ**knee-'deep** adv.: *I waded in knee-deep but the water was too cold to swim in.* ▶ **po kolana**

'**knee-jerk** adj. [only before a noun] produced automatically, without any serious thought: *It was* ***a knee-jerk reaction*** *on her part.* ▶ **odruchowy** ⓘ Wyraża dezaprobatę.

kneel /ni:l/ verb [I] (pt, pp **knelt** /nelt/ or **kneeled**) **kneel (down)** to rest on one or both knees ▶ **klękać**

knew past tense of **know**[1]

knickers /'nɪkəz/ (especially US **panties** /'pæntiz/) noun [pl.] a piece of underwear for women that covers the area between the waist and the top of the legs: *a pair of knickers* ▶ **majtki damskie**

⚷ **knife**[1] /naɪf/ noun [C] (pl. **knives** /naɪvz/) a sharp blade with a handle. A knife is used for cutting things or as a weapon: *a knife and fork* ◇ *The carving knife* (nóż do krajania mięsa) *is very blunt/sharp.* ◇ *a flick knife* nóż sprężynowy ◇ *a pocket knife/penknife* scyzoryk ▶ **nóż**

kneel

knife[2] /naɪf/ verb [T] to deliberately injure sb with a knife ▶ **dźgać, pchnąć nożem** SYN **stab**

knight /naɪt/ noun [C] **1** a soldier of a high level who fought on a horse in the Middle Ages ▶ **rycerz 2** a man who has been given a title of honour by a king or queen for good work he has done and who can use *Sir* in front of his name ▶ **nobilitowany mężczyzna mający prawo tytułowania się Sir przy imieniu** ➲ note at **sir 3** a piece used in the game of **chess** that is shaped like a horse's head ▶ **skoczek**
■ **knighthood** /'naɪthʊd/ noun [C,U] ▶ **tytuł/stan szlachecki**

⚷ **knit** /nɪt/ verb [I,T] (**knitting**; pt, pp **knitted** or (US) **knit**) **1** to make sth (for example an article of clothing) with wool using two long needles or a special machine: *I'm knitting a sweater for my nephew.* ▶ **robić na drutach** ➲ look at **crochet 2** (**knit**) [only used in this form] joined closely together: *a* ***close(ly)-knit/tightly knit*** (bardzo zżyta) *village community* ▶ **zażyły, zjednoczony**

kitchen utensils

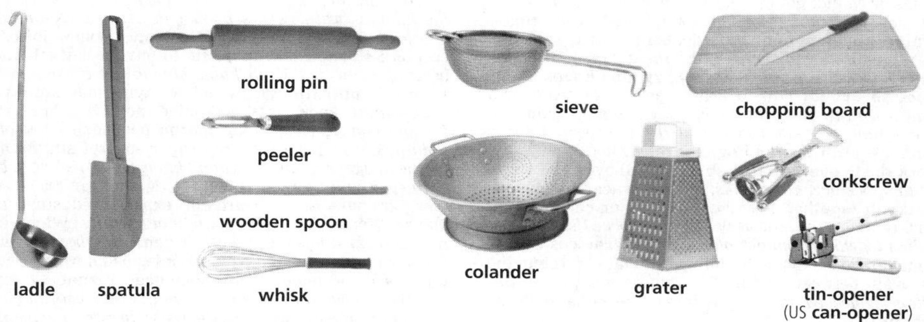

■ **knitting** noun [U]: *I usually do some knitting while I'm watching TV.* ▶ **robienie/robótka na drutach**

'**knitting needle** = NEEDLE (2)

knitwear /'nɪtweə(r)/ noun [U] articles of clothing that have been knitted: *the knitwear department* ▶ **dziewiarstwo**

knives plural of **knife**

knob /nɒb/ noun [C] **1** a round switch on a machine (e.g. a TV) that you press or turn: *the volume control knob* ▶ **pokrętło**, **guzik 2** a round handle on a door, drawer, etc. ▶ **gałka** ➲ picture at **handle**

knobbly /'nɒbli/ (also **knobby** /'nɒbi/) adj. having small hard lumps: *knobbly* (kościste) *knees* ▶ **guzowaty**

⚷ **knock¹** /nɒk/ verb **1** [I] **knock (at/on sth)** to make a noise by hitting sth firmly with your hand: *Is that someone knocking at the door?* Czy to ktoś puka do drzwi? ◇ *I knocked on the window but she didn't hear me.* ▶ **pukać**, **stukać 2** [T] **knock sth (on/against sth)** to hit sb/sth hard, often by accident: *Be careful not to knock your head on the shelf when you get up.* ◇ *He knocked* (strącił) *the vase onto the floor.* ◇ *to knock sb unconscious* nokautować kogoś ▶ **uderzać (się) (w/o coś) 3** [T] (informal) to say bad things about sb/sth; to criticize sb/sth: *'I hate this town.' 'Don't knock it – there are far worse places to live.'* ▶ **obgadywać**, **krytykować**

IDM **knock on wood** → WOOD

PHR V **knock about/around** (informal) to be in a place; to travel and live in various places: *Is last week's newspaper still knocking about?* ▶ **plątać się** (*np. pod nogami, po podłodze*), **bujać** (*np. po świecie*)

knock sb/sth around (Brit. also ˌ**knock sb/sth a'bout**) (informal) to hit sb/sth repeatedly; to treat sb/sth roughly ▶ **maltretować kogoś/coś fizycznie**

knock sb back 1 (Brit.) to prevent sb from achieving sth or making progress, especially by rejecting them or sth that they suggest or ask ▶ **odrzucać kogoś 2** (Brit.) to surprise or shock sb: *Hearing the news really knocked me back.* ▶ **zaskakiwać kogoś**

knock sb down to hit sb causing them to fall to the ground: *The old lady was knocked down by a cyclist.* ▶ **potrącać/przewracać kogoś**

knock sth down/over to destroy a building, etc.: *They knocked down the old factory because it was unsafe.* ▶ **wyburzać coś**

knock off (sth) (informal) to stop working: *Do you want to knock off early today?* ◇ *What time do you knock off work?* ◇ *Let's knock off for lunch.* ▶ **skończyć pracę**

knock sth off 1 (informal) to reduce a price by a certain amount: *He agreed to knock £10 off the price.* ▶ **obniżać cenę (o pewną wartość) 2** (slang) to steal sth ▶ **zwędzić coś**

knock sb out 1 to hit sb so that they become unconscious or cannot get up again for a while: *The punch on the nose knocked him out.* ▶ **nokautować kogoś**, **zwalać kogoś z nóg 2** (used about a drug, alcohol, etc.) to cause sb to sleep: *Those three glasses of vodka really knocked her out.* ▶ (*przen.*) **zwalać kogoś z nóg**

knock sb out (of sth) to beat a person or team in a competition so that they do not play any more games in it: *Belgium was knocked out of the European Cup by France.* ▶ **eliminować kogoś** (*z zawodów*)

knock sb/sth over to cause sb/sth to fall over: *Be careful not to knock over the drinks.* ▶ **przewracać kogoś/coś**

knock sth together 1 (informal) to make or complete sth quickly and often not very well: *I knocked some bookshelves together from old planks.* ▶ **sklecać coś 2** (Brit.) to make two rooms or buildings into one by removing the wall between them: *The house consists of two cottages knocked together.* ▶ **łączyć ze sobą pokoje/budynki**

knock sth up to prepare or make sth quickly and without much effort: *She knocked up a meal in ten minutes.* Upichciła posiłek w dziesięć minut. ▶ **szybko coś przygotować**

⚷ **knock²** /nɒk/ noun [C] a sharp hit from sth hard or the sound it makes: *a nasty knock on the head* ◇ *I thought I heard a knock at the door* (pukanie do drzwi). ◇ (figurative) *She has suffered some hard knocks in her life.* Dostała od życia parę razy w kość. ▶ **uderzenie**, **cios**

knocker /'nɒkə(r)/ noun [C] a piece of metal fixed to the outside of a door that you hit against the door to attract attention ▶ **kołatka**

'**knock-on** adj. (especially Brit.) causing other events to happen one after the other: *An increase in the price of oil has a **knock-on effect** on other fuels.* ▶ **następujący po czymś**

knockout /'nɒkaʊt/ noun [C] **1** a hard hit that causes sb to become unconscious or to be unable to get up again for a while ▶ **nokaut 2** (especially Brit.) a competition in which the winner of each game goes on to the next part but the person who loses plays no more games ▶ **zawody eliminacyjne**

⚷ **knot¹** /nɒt/ noun [C] **1** a place where two ends or pieces of rope, string, etc. have been tied together: *to tie/untie a knot* ▶ **węzeł**, **supeł 2** a measure of the speed of a ship; approximately 1.8 kilometres per hour ▶ (*żegl.*) **węzeł**

knot² /nɒt/ verb [T] (**kno<u>tt</u>ing**; **kno<u>tt</u>ed**) to fasten sth together with a knot ▶ **z(a)wiązywać**

⚷ **know¹** /nəʊ/ verb (pt **knew** /nju:; US nu:/, pp **known** /nəʊn/) [not used in the continuous tenses] **1** [I,T] **know (about sth)**; **know (that)...** to have knowledge or information in your mind: *I don't know much about sport.* ◇ *Did you know that she was coming?* ◇ *Do you know where this bus stops?* ◇ *Do you know their telephone number?* ◇ *'You've got a flat tyre.' 'I know.'* ◇ *Do you **know the way** to the restaurant?* ▶ **wiedzieć**, **znać 2** [T,I] to feel certain; to be sure of sth: *I just know you'll pass the exam!* ◇ ***As far as I know*** (o ile wiem), *the meeting is next Monday afternoon.* ▶ **wiedzieć 3** [T] to be familiar with a person or a place; to have met sb or been somewhere before: *We've known each other for years.* ◇ *I don't know this part of London well.* ◇ *I **know** Frank **by sight*** (znam Franka z widzenia), *but not to talk to.* ▶ **znać (kogoś/coś)**, **znać się (z kimś)**

> Mówiąc o poznaniu kogoś, tzn. o spotkaniu kogoś po raz pierwszy, używa się czasownika **meet**: *We met at university in 2001.* Mówiąc o pogłębianiu znajomości, używa się zwrotu **get to know sb**: *Kevin's wife seems very interesting. I'd like to get to know her better* (chciałbym ją bliżej poznać). Natomiast mówiąc o poznawaniu nowych miejsc, używa się **see** lub **visit**: *I'd like to go to the States and see/visit New York.*

4 [T, often passive] **know sb/sth as sth**; **know sb/sth for sth**; **know sb/sth to be sth** to give sth a particular name; to recognize sb/sth as sth: *Istanbul was previously known as Constantinople.* ◇ *She's best known for her work on the human brain.* ◇ *He's known to be an outstanding physicist.* ▶ **być znanym jako**, **znać kogoś jako/z czegoś 5** [T] **know how to do sth** to have learnt sth and be able to do it: *Do you know how to use a computer?* ▶ **umieć**, **potrafić** ℹ Uwaga! W tym znaczeniu po czasowniku **know** trzeba koniecznie użyć **how to**: *I know how to swim.* (Nie można powiedzieć ~~*I know swim*~~.) **6** [T] to have personal experience of sth: *Many people in western countries don't know what it's like to be hungry.* ▶ **znać**, **zaznawać 7** [T] [only in the past and perfect tenses] to have seen, heard, or experienced sth: *I've known him go a whole day without eating.* Wiem, że niejeden raz nie jadł przez cały dzień. ◇ *It's been known to snow in June.* Zdarzało się, że śnieg padał w czerwcu. **8** to speak or understand a language ▶ **znać** ℹ Czasownika **know** nie używa się w czasach *continuous*. Natomiast często spotyka się go w *present participle*

(formie *-ing*): *Knowing how he'd react if he ever found out about it, she kept quiet.*
IDM **God, goodness, Heaven, etc. knows 1** I do not know: *They've ordered a new car but goodness knows how they're going to pay for it.* ▶ **kto wie, nie wiadomo 2** (used for emphasizing sth): *I hope I get an answer soon. Goodness knows, I've waited long enough.* ▶ **z całą pewnością**
I might have known → MIGHT[1]
know better (than that/than to do sth) to have enough sense to realize that you should not do sth: *I thought you knew better than to go out in the rain with no coat on.* ▶ **mieć więcej rozumu w głowie**
know sth inside out/like the back of your hand (informal) to be very familiar with sth ▶ **znać jak własną kieszeń**
know what's what (informal) to have all the important information about sth; to fully understand sth ▶ **wiedzieć, co i jak**; **dobrze orientować się**
know what you are talking about (informal) to have knowledge of sth from your own experience: *I've lived in London so I know what I'm talking about.* ▶ **wiedzieć o czym się mówi**; **znać się na czymś**
let sb know to tell sb about sth: *Could you let me know what time you're arriving?* ▶ **dawać komuś znać**
show sb/know/learn the ropes → ROPE[1]
you know (used when the speaker is thinking of what to say next, or to remind sb of sth): *Well, you know, it's rather difficult to explain.* ◇ *I've just met Marta. You know – Jim's ex-wife.* ▶ **no wiesz**
you never know (informal) you cannot be certain: *Keep those empty boxes. You never know, they might come in handy one day.* ▶ **nigdy nie wiadomo**
PHR V **know of sb/sth** to have information about or experience of sb/sth: *Do you know of any pubs around here that serve food?* ▶ **znać kogoś/coś**, **wiedzieć o kimś/czymś**

know[2] /nəʊ/ noun
IDM **in the know** (informal) having information that other people do not ▶ **wtajemniczony**

'know-all (also **'know-it-all**) noun [C] an annoying person who behaves as if they know everything ▶ **mądrala**

'know-how noun [U] (informal) practical knowledge of or skill in sth ▶ **know-how**, **znajomość rzeczy**

knowing /'nəʊɪŋ/ adj. showing that you know about sth that is thought to be secret: *a knowing look* ▶ (*spojrzenie itp.*) **pełny zrozumienia**

knowingly /'nəʊɪŋli/ adv. **1** on purpose; deliberately: *I've never knowingly lied to you.* ▶ **świadomie**, **umyślnie 2** in a way that shows that you know about sth that is thought to be secret: *He smiled knowingly at her.* ▶ **ze zrozumieniem**

'know-it-all = KNOW-ALL

knowledge /'nɒlɪdʒ/ noun **1** [U, sing.] **knowledge (of/about sth)** information, understanding and skills that you have gained through learning or experience: *I have **a working knowledge** (praktyczną znajomość) of French.* ▶ **wiedza**, **znajomość** (*np. przedmiotu*) **2** [U] the state of knowing about a particular fact or situation: ***To my knowledge** (o ile wiem) they are still living there.* ◇ *She did it **without my knowledge**.* ▶ **wiedza**
IDM **be common/public knowledge** to be sth that everyone knows ▶ **być rzeczą powszechnie znaną**

knowledgeable /'nɒlɪdʒəbl/ adj. having a lot of knowledge: *She's very knowledgeable about history.* ▶ **znający się na rzeczy**, **mądry**
■ **knowledgeably** /-əbli/ adv. ▶ **ze znawstwem**

known past participle of **know**[1]

knuckle[1] /'nʌkl/ noun [C] the bones where your fingers join the rest of your hand ▶ **knykieć**, **staw** (*palca*) ➲ picture at **body**

knuckle[2] /'nʌkl/ verb
PHR V **knuckle down (to sth)** (informal) to begin to work hard at sth: *I'm going to have to knuckle down to some serious study.* ▶ **zabierać się poważnie (do czegoś)** SYN **get down to sth/doing sth**
knuckle under (to sb/sth) (informal) to accept sb else's authority ▶ **poddawać się (komuś/czemuś)**

koala /kəʊ'ɑːlə/ noun [C] an Australian animal with thick grey fur that lives in trees and looks like a small bear ▶ **(miś) koala**

the Koran (also **Qur'an**) /kə'rɑːn/ noun [sing.] the most important book in the Islamic religion ▶ **Koran**

kosher /'kəʊʃə(r)/ adj. (used about food) prepared according to the rules of Jewish law ▶ **koszerny**

kph /ˌkeɪ piː 'eɪtʃ/ abbr. **kilometres per hour** ▶ **km/godz.**

kung fu /ˌkʌŋ 'fuː/ noun [U] a Chinese style of fighting using the feet and hands as weapons ▶ **kung fu** ➲ look at **martial arts**

kW (also **kw**) = KILOWATT: *a 2 kW electric heater*

Ll

L, l /el/ noun [C,U] (pl. **Ls**; **ls**; **L's**; **l's** /elz/) the 12th letter of the English alphabet: *'Language' begins with (an) 'L'.* ▶ **litera** *l*

l abbr. **1** (**l**) = LITRE, LITRES **2** (**L**) (Brit.) (used on a sign on a car to show that the driver is learning to drive) ▶ **nauka jazdy** (*początkujący kierowca*) **3** (**L**) large (size): *S, M and L* ▶ **duży** (*rozmiar*) **4** (**l**) left ▶ **lewy 5** (**l**) line ▶ **linia**

Lab abbr. (in British politics) **Labour** ▶ (*brytyjska polityka*) **Partia Pracy**

lab (informal) = LABORATORY

label[1] /'leɪbl/ noun [C] **1** a piece of paper, etc. that is fixed to sth and which gives information about it: *There is a list of all the ingredients on the label.* ◇ *He'll only wear clothes with a **designer label**.* On nosi wyłącznie ubrania znanych projektantów. ◇ (figurative) *She hated the label of 'housewife'.* ▶ **metka**, **etykieta**; **określenie 2** (also **'record label**) a company that produces and sells records, CDs, etc.: *It's his first release for a major label.* ▶ **wytwórnia płyt**

label[2] /'leɪbl/ verb [T] (**labelling**; **labelled**; US **labeling**; **labeled**) **1** [usually passive] to fix a label or write information on sth ▶ **oznaczać** (*np. naszywką, etykietką*) **2 label sb/sth (as) sth** to describe sb/sth in a particular way, especially unfairly ▶ **określać kogoś mianem**

laboratory /lə'bɒrətri; US 'læbrətɔːri/ noun [C] (pl. **laboratories**) (also informal **lab** /læb/) a room or building that is used for scientific research, testing, experiments, etc. or for teaching about science: *a physics laboratory* ▶ **laboratorium** ➲ look at **language laboratory** ➲ picture on page 430

laborious /lə'bɔːriəs/ adj. needing a lot of time and effort: *a laborious task/process/job* ▶ **żmudny**, **mozolny**
■ **laboriously** adv. ▶ **żmudnie**, **mozolnie**

labour¹ (US labor) /ˈleɪbə(r)/ noun **1** [U] work, usually of a hard, physical kind: *manual labour* praca fizyczna ▶ **praca**, **robota 2** [U] workers, when thought of as a group: *There is a shortage of skilled labour.* Brakuje wykwalifikowanych robotników. ◇ *Labour relations* (stosunki między kadrą kierowniczą a robotnikami) *have improved in recent years.* ▶ **siła robocza 3** [U,C, usually sing.] the process of giving birth to a baby: *She **went into labour*** (zaczęła rodzić) *in the early hours of this morning.* ◇ *She **was in labour*** (rodziła) *for ten hours.* ▶ **poród 4** = LABOUR PARTY

labour² (US labor) /ˈleɪbə(r)/ verb [I] **1 labour (away)** to work hard at sth: *She laboured on her book for two years.* ▶ **pracować (ciężko)**, **mozolić się 2** to move or do sth with difficulty and effort ▶ **posuwać się (z trudem)**; **mozolnie coś robić**

laboured (US labored) /ˈleɪbəd/ adj. done slowly or with difficulty: *laboured breathing* ▶ **z wysiłkiem**, **ciężki**

labourer (US laborer) /ˈleɪbərə(r)/ noun [C] a person whose job involves hard physical work: *Unskilled labourers are not usually well paid.* ▶ **robotni-k/ca**

ˈlabour force (US ˈlabor force) noun [C] all the people who work for a company or in a country: *a skilled/an unskilled labour force* ▶ **siła robocza** SYN **workforce**

the ˈLabour Party (also **Labour**) noun [sing., with sing. or pl. verb] one of the main political parties in Britain. The **Labour Party** supports the interests of working people: *He has always voted Labour.* ▶ **Partia Pracy** ➲ note at **party** ➲ look at **Conservative Party**, **Liberal Democrats**

ˈlabour-saving adj. reducing the amount of work needed to do sth: *labour-saving devices such as washing machines and dishwashers* ▶ **usprawniający pracę**

Labrador /ˈlæbrədɔː(r)/ noun [C] a type of large yellow or black dog, often used by blind people as a guide ▶ **labrador**

labyrinth /ˈlæbərɪnθ/ noun [C] a complicated set of paths and passages, through which it is difficult to find your way ▶ **labirynt** SYN **maze**

lace¹ /leɪs/ noun **1** [U] cloth that is made of very thin threads sewn in patterns with small holes in between: *a collar made of lace* ◇ *lace curtains* ▶ **koronka** ➲ adjective **lacy 2** [C] a string that is used for tying a shoe: *Your shoelace is undone.* ◇ *Do up your laces* (zawiąż sznurówki) *or you'll trip over them.* ▶ **sznurówka**

lace² /leɪs/ verb [I,T] **lace (sth) (up)** to tie or fasten sth with a **lace¹** (2): *She was sitting on the end of the bed lacing up her boots.* ▶ **sznurować (się)**

■ **lace-up 1** adj.: *lace-up shoes* ▶ **sznurowany 2** noun [C]: *a pair of lace-ups* para sznurowanych butów

lack¹ /læk/ noun [U, sing.] **a lack (of sth)** the state of not having sth or not having enough of sth: *The trip was cancelled through lack of interest.* ▶ **brak**, **niedostatek**

lack² /læk/ verb [T] to have none or not enough of sth: *She seems to lack* (wydaje się, że brak jej) *the will to succeed.* ▶ **nie mieć**, **mieć za mało**

lacking /ˈlækɪŋ/ adj. [not before a noun] **1 be lacking in sth** to not have enough of sth: *He's certainly not lacking in intelligence.* Z pewnością nie brakuje mu inteligencji. ▶ **brakować komuś czegoś 2** not present or available: *I feel there is something lacking in my life.* ▶ **brakować**

lacklustre /ˈlæklʌstə(r)/ adj. not interesting or exciting: *a lacklustre performance* ◇ *lacklustre* (matowe) *hair* ▶ **bezbarwny**, **nijaki**, **bez życia** SYN **dull**

laconic /ləˈkɒnɪk/ adj. (formal) using only a few words to say sth ▶ **lakoniczny**, **lapidarny**

■ **laconically** /-kli/ adv. ▶ **lakonicznie**, **lapidarnie**

lacquer /ˈlækə(r)/ noun [U] **1** a type of transparent paint that is put on wood, metal, etc. to give it a hard, shiny

laboratory apparatus

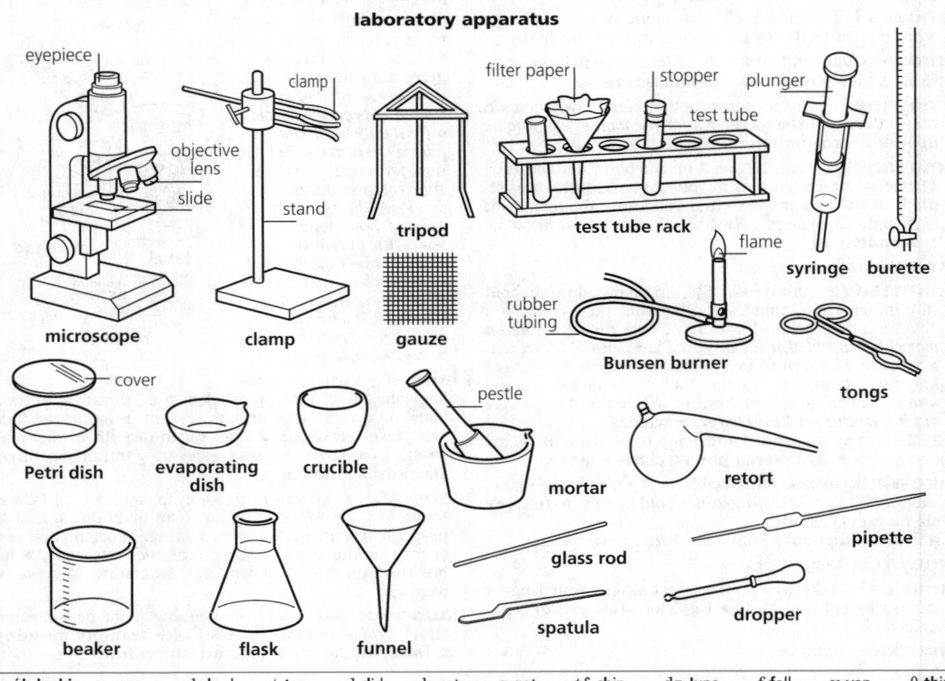

surface ▶ **lakier 2** (old-fashioned) a liquid that you put on your hair to keep it in place ▶ **lakier do włosów** SYN **hairspray**

lacy /ˈleɪsi/ adj. made of or looking like **lace** ▶ **koronkowy**

lad /læd/ noun [C] (informal) a boy or young man ▶ **chłopiec; chłopak**

ladder /ˈlædə(r)/ noun [C] **1** a piece of equipment that is used for climbing up sth. A **ladder** consists of two long pieces of metal, wood or rope with steps fixed between them: (figurative) *to climb the ladder of success* ▶ **drabina** ➲ look at **stepladder 2** (US **run**) a long hole in **tights** or **stockings**, where the threads have broken: *Oh no! I've got a ladder in my tights.* ▶ **oczko** (*np. w rajstopach*)
■ **ladder** verb [T]: *Oh no, I've laddered my tights* (poleciało mi oczko w rajstopach).

laden /ˈleɪdn/ adj. [not before a noun] **laden (with sth)** having or carrying a lot of sth: *The travellers were laden down with luggage.* ◇ *The orange trees were laden with fruit.* ◇ (figurative) *to be laden with guilt* ▶ **obładowany; uginający się pod ciężarem** (*np. winy, trosk*)

the ˈLadies noun [sing.] (Brit., informal) a public toilet for women ▶ **toaleta damska** ➲ look at **gents** ➲ note at **toilet**

ladle[1] /ˈleɪdl/ noun [C] a large deep spoon with a long handle, used especially for serving soup ▶ **łyżka wazowa** ➲ picture at **kitchen**

ladle[2] /ˈleɪdl/ verb [T] to serve food with a **ladle** ▶ **nalewać łyżką wazową**

lady /ˈleɪdi/ noun (pl. **ladies**) **1** [C] (a word used to mean 'woman' that some people, especially older people, consider is more polite): *The old lady next door lives alone.* ◇ *There's a lady waiting to see you.* ▶ **pani 2** [C] a woman who is polite and well educated, has excellent manners and always behaves well: *A real lady does not scream and shout.* ▶ **dama 3** [C, usually pl.] (formal) (used when speaking to or about a girl or a woman, especially one you do not know: *Can I have your attention, **ladies and gentlemen*** (Panie i Panowie)*?* ▶ **pani 4** [C] (old-fashioned) (in Britain) a woman belonging to a high social class: *the lords and ladies of the court* ▶ **dama 5** (**Lady**) [C] (in Britain, a title used by a woman who is a member of the **nobility**, or by sb who has been given the title 'lady' as an honour): *Lady Elizabeth Groves* ▶ **dama** ➲ look at **Lord**

ladybird /ˈleɪdibɜːd/ (US **ladybug** /ˈleɪdibʌɡ/) noun [C] a small insect that is red or yellow with black spots ▶ **biedronka** ➲ picture at **insect**

ˈladylike adj. (old-fashioned) polite and quiet; typical of what is supposed to be socially acceptable for a woman ▶ **wytworny, dystyngowany**

lag[1] /læɡ/ verb [I] (**lagging**; **lagged**) **lag (behind) (sb/sth)** to move or develop more slowly than sb/sth: *James has missed a lot of classes and is lagging behind the others at school.* ▶ **zostawać w tyle; być opóźnionym** (*w stosunku do czegoś*)

lag[2] /læɡ/ (also ˈ**time lag**) noun [C] a period of time between two events; a delay ▶ **zwłoka, opóźnienie** ➲ look at **jet lag**

lager /ˈlɑːɡə(r)/ noun [C,U] (Brit.) a type of light beer that is a gold colour ▶ **piwo jasne** (*leżakowane*) ➲ note at **beer**

lagoon /ləˈɡuːn/ noun [C] a lake of salt water that is separated from the sea by sand or rock ▶ **laguna**

laid past tense, past participle of **lay**[1]

laid-back /ˌleɪd ˈbæk/ adj. (informal) calm and relaxed; seeming not to worry about anything ▶ **na luzie, nie przejmujący się niczym** SYN **easy-going**

lain past participle of **lie**[2]

lair /leə(r)/ noun [usually sing.] **1** a place where a wild animal sleeps or hides ▶ **matecznik, legowisko 2** a place where sb goes to hide or to be alone: *Grandad retreated to his lair in the basement.* ▶ **kryjówka** SYN **den, hideout**

lake /leɪk/ noun [C] a large area of water that is surrounded by land: *They've gone sailing **on the lake**.* ◇ *We all swam **in the lake**.* ◇ *Lake Constance* ▶ **jezioro**

> **lake**
> A **lake** is usually big enough to sail on: *Lake Como*. A **pond** may be big enough for animals to drink from or may be a very small area of water in a garden: *We have a fish pond in our garden.* A **pool** is a much smaller area of water: *When the tide went out, pools of water were left among the rocks.* An artificial pool, however, can be larger: *a swimming pool*. A **puddle** is a small pool of water made by the rain.

lamb /læm/ noun **1** [C] a young sheep ▶ **jagnię, baranek** ➲ note at **sheep 2** [U] the meat of a young sheep: *lamb chops* ▶ **jagnięcina, mięso jagnięce** ➲ note at **meat**

lame /leɪm/ adj. **1** (used mainly about animals) not able to walk properly because of an injury to the leg or foot: *The horse is lame and cannot work.* ▶ **kulawy, kulejący**

> W odniesieniu do ludzi zwykle nie używa się **lame**. Częściej stosowane jest **limp**, jako czasownik i rzeczownik: *You're limping. Have you hurt your leg?* ◇ *He's got a limp.* Kuleje.

2 (used about an excuse, argument, etc.) not easily believed; weak ▶ (*argument itp.*) **słaby, nieprzekonujący**

lament /ləˈment/ noun [C] (formal) a song, poem or other expression of sadness for sb who has died or for sth that has ended ▶ **lament, pieśń żałobna**
■ **lament** verb [T] ▶ **opłakiwać, lamentować**

laminated /ˈlæmɪneɪtɪd/ adj. **1** (used about wood, plastic, etc.) made by sticking several thin layers together: *laminated glass* ▶ **wielowarstwowy 2** covered with thin transparent plastic for protection ▶ **laminowany**

lamp /læmp/ noun [C] a device that uses electricity, gas or oil to produce light: *a table/desk/bicycle lamp* ◇ *an oil lamp* lampa naftowa ◇ *a sunlamp* lampa kwarcowa ◇ *a street lamp* latarnia uliczna ▶ **lampa, latarnia** ➲ picture at **light**

ˈlamp post noun [C] a tall pole at the side of the road with a light on the top ▶ **słup latarni**

lampshade /ˈlæmpʃeɪd/ noun [C] a cover for a lamp that makes it look more attractive and makes the light softer ▶ **abażur** ➲ picture at **light**

LAN /læn/ abbr. **local area network**; a system that connects computers inside a single building or buildings in the same area ▶ **lokalna sieć komputerowa** ➲ look at **WAN**

land[1] /lænd/ noun **1** [U] the solid part of the surface of the earth (= not sea): *After three months at sea she was glad to reach **dry land*** (stałego lądu). ◇ *Penguins can't move very fast **on land**.* ▶ **ląd** OPP **sea** ➲ note at **ground 2** [U] an area of ground: *The land rose to the east.* ◇ *She owns 500 acres of land in Scotland.* ▶ **ziemia, teren 3** [U] ground, soil or earth of a particular kind: *The land is rich and fertile.* ◇ *arid/barren land* ◇ *arable/agricultural/industrial land* ▶ **ziemia, grunt 4** [C] (formal) a country or region: *to travel to distant lands* ◇ *She died far from her native land* (z dala od ziemi ojczystej). ▶ **kraj** ➲ note at **country**

land[2] /lænd/ verb **1** [I,T] to come down from the air or to bring sth down to the ground: *His flight is due to land at 3 o'clock.* ◇ *The pilot landed the aeroplane safely.* Pilot bezpiecznie sprowadził samolot na ziemię. ◇ *The bird landed* (usiadł) *on the roof.* ◇ *He fell off the ladder and landed on his back* (upadł na plecy). ▶ **lądować 2** [I,T] to go onto land or put sth onto land from a ship: *to land cargo* ▶ **lądować; wyładowywać** (*np. towar*) **3** [T] to succeed in getting sth, especially sth that a lot of people want: *The company has just landed a million-dollar contract.* ▶ **zdobyć**

IDM **fall/land on your feet** → FOOT[1]

PHR V **land up (in ...)** (Brit., informal) to finish in a certain position or situation: *He landed up in a prison cell for the night.* ▶ **wylądować (gdzieś), trafić (gdzieś)**

land sb with sb/sth (informal) to give sb sth unpleasant to do, especially because nobody else wants to do it ▶ **zwalić coś na kogoś**

landfill /ˈlændfɪl/ noun **1** [C,U] an area of land where large amounts of waste material are buried ▶ **wysypisko** (*śmieci*) **2** [U] waste material that will be buried; the burying of waste material ▶ **śmieci**; **zwałka**

landing /ˈlændɪŋ/ noun [C] **1** the area at the top of a set of stairs in a house, or between one set of stairs and another in a large building ▶ **podest**, **półpiętro 2** the act of coming down onto the ground (in an aircraft): *The plane made an **emergency landing*** (wylądował awaryjnie) *in a field.* ◇ *a crash landing* lądowanie awaryjne ▶ **lądowanie** OPP **take-off**

ˈ**landing card** noun [C] a form on which you have to write details about yourself when flying to a foreign country ▶ **karta lądowania**

ˈ**landing gear** = UNDERCARRIAGE

ˈ**landing stage** = JETTY

ˈ**landing strip** = AIRSTRIP

landline /ˈlændlaɪn/ noun [C] a telephone connection that uses wires carried on poles or under the ground ▶ (*telekom.*) **linia naziemna** ➲ look at **mobile phone**

landlord /ˈlændlɔːd/ (fem. **landlady** /ˈlændleɪdi/) noun [C] (pl. **landladies**) **1** a person who rents a house or room to people for money ▶ **gospod-arz/yni**, **właściciel/ka** (*domu czynszowego*) **2** (Brit.) a person who owns or manages a pub, small hotel, etc. ▶ **właściciel/ka**, **menedżer/ka** (*np. pubu, hotelu*)

landmark /ˈlændmɑːk/ noun [C] **1** an object (often a building) that can be seen easily from a distance and will help you to recognize where you are: *Big Ben is one of the landmarks on London's skyline.* ▶ **punkt charakterystyczny/orientacyjny** (*w terenie*) **2 a landmark (in sth)** an important stage or change in the development of sth ▶ **punkt zwrotny** (*np. w historii*)

landmine /ˈlændmaɪn/ noun [C] a bomb placed on or under the ground, which explodes when sb moves or drives over it ▶ **mina lądowa**

landowner /ˈlændəʊnə(r)/ noun [C] a person who owns land, especially a large area of land ▶ **właściciel/ka ziemsk-i/a**

■ **landownership** (also **landowning**) noun [U]: *private landownership* ▶ **własność ziemi** | **landowning** adj. [only before a noun]: *the great landowning families* ▶ **ziemiański**

⚷ **landscape**[1] /ˈlændskeɪp/ noun **1** [C, usually sing.] everything you can see when you look across a large area of land: *an urban/industrial landscape* ▶ **krajobraz** ➲ note at **country**, **scenery 2** [C,U] a picture or a painting that shows a view of the countryside; this style of painting: *one of Constable's landscapes* ▶ **pejzaż 3** [U] (technical) the way of printing a document in which the top of the page is one of the longer sides: *Select the landscape option when printing the file.* ▶ **orientacja pozioma** (*w opcji ustawienia strony pliku*) ➲ look at **portrait**

landscape[2] /ˈlændskeɪp/ verb [T] to improve the appearance of an area of land by changing its design and planting trees, flowers, etc. ▶ **projektować** (*krajobraz*)

ˌ**landscape ˈarchitect** noun [C] a person whose job is planning and designing the environment, especially so that roads, buildings, etc. combine with the landscape in an attractive way ▶ **architekt krajobrazu**

■ ˌ**landscape ˈarchitecture** noun [U] ▶ **architektura krajobrazu**

landslide /ˈlændslaɪd/ noun [C] **1** the sudden fall of a mass of earth, rocks, etc. down the side of a mountain: *Part of the railway line was buried beneath a landslide.* ▶ **obsunięcie się ziemi 2** a great victory for one person or one political party in an election: *a landslide victory at the election* ▶ (*zwycięstwo*) **przytłaczający**

⚷ **lane** /leɪn/ noun [C] **1** a narrow road in the country: *We found a route through country lanes to avoid the traffic jam on the main road.* ▶ **boczna droga 2** (used in the names of roads): *Crossley Lane* ▶ **ulica 3** a section of a wide road that is marked by painted white lines to keep lines of traffic separate: *a four-lane motorway* ◇ *the inside/middle/fast/outside lane* ▶ **pas ruchu 4** a section of a sports track, swimming pool, etc. for one person to go along: *The British athlete is in lane two.* ▶ **tor 5** a route or path that is regularly used by ships or aircraft: *the busy **shipping lanes** of the English Channel* ▶ **szlak** (*wodny*), **korytarz** (*powietrzny*)

⚷ **language** /ˈlæŋgwɪdʒ/ noun **1** [C] the system of communication in speech and writing that is used by people of a particular country: *How many languages can you speak?* ◇ *What is your first language?* ◇ *They fell in love in spite of **the language barrier**.* ▶ **język 2** [U] the system of sounds and writing that people use to express their thoughts, ideas and feelings: *written/spoken language* ▶ **język 3** [U] words of a particular type or words that are used by a particular person or group: *bad* (wulgarny) *language* ◇ *legal language* ◇ *the language of Shakespeare* ▶ **język**, **mowa 4** [U] any system of signs, symbols, movements, etc. that is used to express sth: *sign language* język migowy ▶ **język** ➲ look at **body language 5** [C,U] a system of symbols and rules that is used to operate a computer ▶ **język**

ˈ**language laboratory** noun [C] a room in a school or college that contains special equipment to help students to learn foreign languages by listening to tapes, watching videos, recording themselves, etc. ▶ **laboratorium językowe**

languid /ˈlæŋgwɪd/ adj. moving slowly in an elegant manner, not needing energy or effort: *a languid wave of the hand* ◇ *a languid* (ospałe) *afternoon in the sun* ▶ **powolny i elegancki**

■ **languidly** adv. ▶ **z wolna**

languish /ˈlæŋgwɪʃ/ verb [I] (formal) **1 languish (in sth)** to be forced to stay somewhere or suffer sth unpleasant for a long time: *She continues to languish in a foreign prison.* ▶ **marnieć 2** to become weaker or fail to make progress: *Share prices languished* (stanęły w miejscu) *at 89p.* ▶ **podupadać**

languor /ˈlæŋgə(r)/ noun [U, sing.] (literary) the pleasant state of feeling lazy and without energy ▶ **rozleniwienie**

■ **languorous** /ˈlæŋgərəs/ adj.: *a languorous* (senny) *pace of life* ▶ **rozleniwiony**

lanky /ˈlæŋki/ adj. (**lankier**; **lankiest**) (used about a person) very tall and thin ▶ **tyczkowaty**, **kościsty i wysoki**

lantern /ˈlæntən/ noun [C] a type of light that can be carried, with a metal frame, glass sides and a light or **candle** inside ▶ **latarnia**, **lampion**

lap[1] /læp/ noun [C] **1** the flat area that is formed by the upper part of your legs when you are sitting down: *The child sat on his mother's lap* (u mamy na kolanach) *and listened to the story.* ▶ **podołek**, **kolana 2** one journey around a running track, etc.: *There are three more laps to go in the race.* ▶ **okrążenie** (*bieżni*) **3** one part of a long journey ▶ **etap** (*np. podróży*)

lap[2] /læp/ verb (**lapping**; **lapped**) **1** [I] (used about water) to make gentle sounds as it moves against sth: *The waves* *lapped against the side of the boat.* ▶ **chlupotać, pluskać 2** [T] **lap sth (up)** (usually used about an animal) to drink sth using the tongue: *The cat lapped up the cream.* ▶ **chłeptać 3** [T] to pass another person in a race who has been round the track fewer times than you ▶ **wyprzedzać przeciwnika o całe okrążenie toru**

PHR V **lap sth up** (informal) to accept sth with great enjoyment without stopping to think if it is good, true, etc. ▶ **pochłaniać coś**

lapel /lə'pel/ noun [C] one of the two parts of the front of a coat or jacket that are folded back ▶ **klapa** (*np. u marynarki*)

lapse¹ /læps/ noun [C] **1** a short time when you cannot remember sth or you are not thinking about what you are doing: *The crash was the result of a temporary lapse in concentration* (chwilowej nieuwagi). ◇ *a lapse of memory* chwilowe zapomnienie ▶ **chwilowa utrata, luka 2** a period of time between two things that happen: *She returned to work after a lapse of ten years bringing up her family.* ▶ **upływ, okres** ➲ look at **elapse 3** a piece of bad behaviour from sb who usually behaves well ▶ **(chwilowe) zapomnienie się, chwila słabości**

lapse² /læps/ verb [I] **1** (used about a contract, an agreement, etc.) to finish or stop, often by accident: *My membership has lapsed because I forgot to renew it.* ▶ **wygasać 2** to become weaker or stop for a short time: *My concentration lapsed during the last part of the exam.* ▶ (*pamięć itp.*) **zawodzić**

PHR V **lapse into sth** to gradually pass into a worse or less active state or condition; to start speaking or behaving in a less acceptable way: *to lapse into silence/a coma* ▶ **zapadać w coś; popadać** (*w złe nawyki*)

laptop /'læptɒp/ noun [C] a small computer that is easy to carry and that can use batteries for power ▶ **laptop** ➲ note at **computer** ➲ look at **desktop**

larch /lɑːtʃ/ noun [C] a tree that has cones and sharp pointed leaves that fall in the winter ▶ **modrzew**

lard /lɑːd/ noun [U] hard white fat that is used in cooking ▶ **smalec**

larder /'lɑːdə(r)/ noun [C] a large cupboard or small room that is used for storing food ▶ **spiżarnia** SYN **pantry**

🔑 **large** /lɑːdʒ/ adj. greater in size, amount, etc. than usual; big: *a large area/house/family/appetite* ◇ *a large number of people* ◇ *I'd like a large coffee, please.* ◇ *We have this shirt in small, medium or large.* ▶ **duży** ➲ note at **big, fat**

IDM **at large 1** as a whole; in general: *He is well known to scientists but not to the public at large.* ◇ *Society at large* (ogół społeczeństwa) *is becoming more concerned about the environment.* ▶ **w całości 2** (used about a criminal, animal, etc.) not caught; free: *One of the escaped prisoners is still at large.* ▶ **na wolności**

by and large mostly; in general: *By and large the school is very efficient.* ▶ **ogólnie mówiąc**

🔑 **largely** /'lɑːdʒli/ adv. mostly: *His success was largely due to hard work.* ▶ **głównie, w dużej mierze**

'large-scale adj. happening over a large area or affecting a lot of people: *large-scale production/unemployment* ▶ **na wielką skalę, dużych rozmiarów**

lark /lɑːk/ noun [C] a small brown bird with a pleasant song ▶ **skowronek**

larva /'lɑːvə/ noun [C] (pl. **larvae** /'lɑːviː/) an insect that has just come out of its egg and has a short fat soft body with no legs ▶ **larwa** ➲ picture at **insect**

laryngitis /ˌlærɪn'dʒaɪtɪs/ noun [U] a mild illness of the throat that makes it difficult to speak ▶ **zapalenie krtani**

larynx /'lærɪŋks/ noun [C] (**larynges** /lə'rɪndʒiːz; -nʒiːz/) the area at the top of the throat that contains the **vocal cords** ▶ **krtań** SYN **voice box** ➲ picture at **body**

laser /'leɪzə(r)/ noun [C] a device that produces a controlled line of very powerful light ▶ **laser**

lash¹ /læʃ/ verb **1** [I,T] (used especially about wind, rain and storms) to hit sth with great force: *The rain lashed against the windows.* ▶ (*deszcz itp.*) **smagać, zacinać 2** [T] to hit sb with a piece of rope, leather, etc.; to move sth like a piece of rope, leather, etc. violently ▶ **uderzać** (*np. batem, rzemieniem*), **wywijać 3** [T] **lash A to B; lash A and B together** to tie two things together firmly with rope, etc.: *The two boats were lashed together.* ▶ **uwiązywać, przycumowywać**

PHR V **lash out (at/against sb/sth)** to suddenly attack sb/sth (with words or by hitting them or it): *The actor lashed out at a photographer outside his house.* ▶ **ostro napadać (na kogoś/coś)**

lash² /læʃ/ noun [C] **1** = EYELASH **2** a hit with a **whip** ▶ **uderzenie** (*batem/biczem*)

lass /læs/ (also **lassie** /'læsi/) noun [C] (informal) a girl or young woman ▶ **dziewczyna** ℹ **Lass** jest słowem typowym dla Szkocji i północnej Anglii.

lasso /'læsəʊ; Brit. also læ'suː/ noun [C] (pl. **lassos** or **lassoes**) a long rope that is tied in a circle at one end and is used for catching cows and horses ▶ **lasso**

■ **lasso** verb [T] ▶ **chwytać na lasso**

🔑 **last¹** /lɑːst; US læst/ determiner **1** at the end; after all the others: *December is the last month of the year.* ◇ *Would the last person to leave please turn off the lights?* ◇ *Our house is the last one on the left.* ◇ *She lived alone for the last years of her life.* ▶ **ostatni 2** (used about a time, period, event, etc. in the past that is nearest to the present): *last night/week/Saturday/summer* ◇ *We have been working on the book for the last six months.* ◇ ***The last time*** *I saw her was in London.* ◇ *We'll win this time, because they beat us* ***last time.*** ▶ **ubiegły, ostatni** ℹ **The latest** znaczy „najnowszy" lub „nowy". **The last** to „poprzedni": *His last novel was a huge success, but the latest one is much less popular.* **3** final: *This is my last chance to take the exam.* ◇ *Alison's retiring – tomorrow is her last day at work.* ▶ **ostatni 4** [only before a noun] not expected or not suitable: *He's the last person I thought would get the job.* ▶ **ostatni, najmniej pożądany**

IDM **first/last thing** → THING

have the last laugh to be the person, team, etc. who is successful in the end ▶ **śmiać się ostatni** ℹ Odpowiednikiem angielskim bardzo bliskiego znaczeniowo polskiego przysłowia „ten się śmieje, kto się śmieje ostatni" jest **he who laughs last laughs longest.**

in the last resort; (as) a last resort when everything else has failed; the person or thing that helps when everything else has failed: *In the last resort my grandad could play in the match.* ▶ **w najgorszym razie, w ostateczności**

last but not least (used before the final item in a list) just as important as all the other items ▶ **ostatni, ale nie mniej ważny**

last/next but one, two, etc. one, two, etc. away from the last/next: *X is the last letter but two* (trzecia litera od końca) *of the alphabet.* ▶ **przedostatni, drugi/trzeci itd. od końca**

a last-ditch attempt a final effort to avoid sth unpleasant or dangerous ▶ **ostatnia szansa**

the last minute/moment the final minute/moment before sth happens: *We arrived at the last minute to catch the train.* ◇ *a last-minute change of plan* ▶ **ostatnia chwila**

the last/final straw → STRAW

the last/final word (on sth) → WORD

last² adv. **1** at the end; after all the others: *The British athlete came in last.* ◇ *Her name is last on the list.* ▶ **na końcu 2** on the occasion in the past that is nearest to the present: *When did you last have your eyes checked?* ◇ *When I saw her last she seemed very happy.* ▶ **ostatnio**

IDM at (long) last in the end; finally: *After months of separation they were together at last.* ▶ **nareszcie**
■ **lastly** adv.: *Lastly, I would like to thank the band who played this evening.* ▶ **na samym końcu, na zakończenie** SYN **finally**

last[3] /lɑːst; US læst/ noun [C] (pl. **the last**) **1** a person or thing that is last: *Alex was the last to arrive.* Alex przyszedł ostatni. ▶ **(ten) ostatni 2** the only remaining part of sth: *We finished **the last of the** bread at breakfast so we'd better get some more.* ▶ **resztka**

last[4] /lɑːst; US læst/ verb [not used in the continuous tenses] **1** [T] to continue for a period of time: *The exam lasts three hours.* ◇ *How long does a cricket match last?* ◇ *The flight seemed to last forever.* ▶ **trwać 2** [I,T] to continue to be good or to function: *Do you think this weather will last* (utrzyma się) *till the weekend?* ◇ *It's only a cheap radio but it'll probably last a year or so.* ▶ **przetrwać, starczyć (komuś) na coś 3** [I,T] to be enough for what sb needs: *This money won't last me till the end of the month.* ▶ **starczyć** ℹ Czasownika **last** nie używa się w czasach *continuous*. Natomiast często spotyka się go w *present participle* (formie *-ing*): *An earthquake lasting approximately 20 seconds struck the city yesterday.*

lasting /ˈlɑːstɪŋ; US ˈlæstɪŋ/ adj. continuing for a long time: *The book left a lasting impression on me.* ▶ **trwały**

ˈ**last name** = SURNAME

latch[1] /lætʃ/ noun [C] **1** a small metal bar that is used for fastening a door or a gate. You have to lift the **latch** in order to open the door. ▶ **zasuwka 2** (especially Brit.) a type of lock for a door that you open with a key from the outside ▶ **zatrzask**
IDM on the latch (used about a door) closed but not locked ▶ (*drzwi*) **zatrzaśnięty** (*a nie zamknięty na klucz*)

latch[2] /lætʃ/ verb
PHR V latch on (to sth) (informal) to understand sth: *It took them a while to latch on to what she was talking about.* ▶ **skapować, kojarzyć**

late[1] /leɪt/ adj. **1** near the end of a period of time: *in the late morning/afternoon/summer* ◇ *His mother's in her late fifties* (zbliża się do sześćdziesiątki). ◇ *in late May* ◇ *The late nineteenth century* (koniec dziewiętnastego wieku) *was a time of great change.* ▶ **pod koniec, późno** OPP **early 2** after the usual or expected time: *I'm sorry I'm late.* Przepraszam za spóźnienie. ◇ *She was ten minutes late* (spóźniła się o dziesięć minut) *for school.* ▶ **spóźniony** OPP **early 3** near the end of the day: *It's late.* Późno już. ▶ **późny** OPP **early 4** [only before a noun] no longer alive; dead: *his late wife* ▶ **zmarły, świętej pamięci**
IDM an early/a late night → NIGHT

late[2] /leɪt; US / adv. **1** near the end of a period of time: *late in May* ◇ *We got back home late in the evening.* ▶ **pod koniec, późno** OPP **early 2** after the usual or expected time: *The ambulance arrived too late to save him.* ◇ *The buses are running late* (z opóźnieniem) *today.* ◇ *to be late with the rent* spóźniać się z czynszem ◇ *to stay up late* siedzieć do późna w nocy ▶ **późno, do późna** OPP **early 3** near the end of the day: *It's getting late – let's go home.* ▶ **późno** OPP **early**
IDM later on at a later time: *Later on you'll probably wish that you'd worked harder at school.* ◇ *Bye – I'll see you a bit later on.* ▶ **później, potem**
sooner or later → SOON

latecomer /ˈleɪtkʌmə(r)/ noun [C] a person who arrives or starts sth late ▶ **spóźnialsk-i/a, spóźnion-y/a**

lately /ˈleɪtli/ adv. in the period of time up until now; recently: *What have you been doing lately?* ◇ *Hasn't the weather been dreadful lately?* ▶ **ostatnio, niedawno** ➲ note at **recently**

latent /ˈleɪtnt/ adj. existing, but not yet very noticeable, active or well developed: *latent defects/disease* ◇ *latent talent* ▶ **ukryty, utajony**

lateral /ˈlætərəl/ adj. connected with the side of sth or with movement to the side: *the lateral branches of a tree* ◇ *lateral eye movements* ▶ **boczny**
■ **laterally** /-rəli/ adv. ▶ **bocznie**

ˌ**lateral ˈthinking** noun [U] (especially Brit.) a way of solving problems by using your imagination to find new ways of looking at the problem ▶ **myślenie lateralne**

latest /ˈleɪtɪst/ adj. [only before a noun] very recent or new: *the latest fashion/news* ◇ *the terrorists' latest attack on the town* ▶ **ostatni, najnowszy** ➲ note at **last**[1]

the latest noun [sing.] (informal) the most recent or the newest thing or piece of news: *This is the very latest in computer technology.* ◇ *This is the latest in a series of attacks by this terrorist group.* ◇ *Have you heard the latest* (nowiny)? *Jan's getting married.* ▶ **nowość, najnowszy**
IDM at the latest no later than the time or the date mentioned: *You need to hand your projects in by Friday at the latest.* ▶ **najpóźniej**

lathe /leɪð/ noun [C] a machine that shapes pieces of wood or metal by holding and turning them against a cutting tool ▶ **tokarka**

lather /ˈlɑːðə(r); US ˈlæð-/ noun [U] a white mass of bubbles that are produced when you mix soap with water ▶ **piana** (*z mydła*), **mydliny**

Latin /ˈlætɪn; US ˈlætn/ noun [U] the language that was used in ancient Rome ▶ **łacina**
■ **Latin** adj. **1** of or in Latin: *Latin poetry* ▶ **łaciński 2** of the countries or people that use languages that developed from Latin, such as French, Italian, Spanish or Portuguese: *Spanish, Italian and other Latin languages* ▶ **romański**

ˌ**Latin Aˈmerican** adj. from Latin America (the parts of Central and South America where Spanish or Portuguese is spoken): *Latin American music* ▶ **latynoamerykański**
■ ˌ**Latin Aˈmerican** noun [C] a person who comes from Latin America ▶ **Latynos/ka**

latish adj. /ˈleɪtɪʃ/ rather late ▶ **dość późny**
■ **latish** adv. ▶ **dość późno**

latitude /ˈlætɪtjuːd; US -tuːd/ noun [U] the distance of a place north or south of the **equator** ▶ **szerokość geograficzna** ➲ look at **longitude**

Latitude is measured in **degrees**.

latter /ˈlætə(r)/ adj. [only before a noun] (formal) nearer to the end of a period of time; later: *Interest rates should fall in the latter half* (w drugiej połowie) *of the year.* ▶ **późniejszy, końcowy**
■ **latterly** adv. ▶ **ostatnio**

the latter noun [sing.], pron. the second (of two people or things that are mentioned): *The options were History and Geography. I chose the latter.* ▶ **drugi** (*z dwu wymienionych*) ℹ Pierwsza z dwu wymienionych osób lub rzeczy to **former**.

lattice /ˈlætɪs/ noun [C,U] a structure that is made of long narrow pieces of wood or metal that cross over each other with spaces shaped like a diamond between them; any structure or pattern like this: *a lattice fence* ▶ **kratownica, kratka** (*do kwiatów itp.*)
■ **latticed** adj. ▶ **w formie kratownicy**

laud /lɔːd/ verb [T] (formal) to praise sb/sth: *He was lauded for his courage.* ▶ **chwalić**

laudable /ˈlɔːdəbl/ adj. (formal) deserving to be praised or admired, even if not really successful: *a laudable aim/attempt* ▶ **godny pochwały** SYN **commendable**

■ **laudably** /-əbli/ adv. ▶ **w sposób godny pochwały**

laugh¹ /lɑːf; US læf/ verb [I] to make the sounds that show you are happy or amused: *to laugh out loud* ◇ *His jokes always make me laugh.* Jego dowcipy zawsze mnie rozśmieszają. ▶ **śmiać się, roześmiać się** ➲ note at **humour**
IDM **die laughing** → DIE
PHR V **laugh at sb/sth 1** to show, by laughing, that you think sb/sth is funny: *The children laughed at the clown.* ▶ **śmiać się z kogoś/czegoś 2** to show that you think sb is ridiculous: *Don't laugh at him. He can't help the way he speaks.* ▶ **wyśmiewać kogoś/coś, wyśmiewać się z kogoś/czegoś**
laugh sth off (informal) to try to make people think that sth is not serious or important, especially by making a joke about it: *He laughed off suggestions that he was going to resign.* ▶ **zbywać coś śmiechem**

laugh² /lɑːf; US læf/ noun [C] **1** the sound or act of laughing: *Her jokes got a lot of laughs.* ◇ *We all **had a good laugh*** (dobrze się uśmialiśmy) *at what he'd written.* ▶ **śmiech 2** (**a laugh**) [sing.] (informal) an occasion or a person that is very funny: *The party was a good laugh.* ▶ **wesołek, zabawna osoba/rzecz**
IDM **for a laugh** as a joke ▶ **dla śmiechu/zabawy**
have the last laugh → LAST¹

laughable /ˈlɑːfəbl; US ˈlæf-/ adj. deserving to be laughed at; of very poor quality; ridiculous ▶ **śmieszny, śmiechu wart**

ˈ**laughing stock** noun [C] a person or thing that other people laugh at (in an unpleasant way) ▶ **pośmiewisko**

laughter /ˈlɑːftə(r); US ˈlæf-/ noun [U] the sound or act of laughing: *Everyone roared with laughter.* ▶ **śmiech**

launch¹ /lɔːntʃ/ verb [T] **1** to start sth new or to show sth for the first time: *to launch a new product onto the market* ▶ **rozpoczynać; lansować 2** to send a ship into the water or a **spacecraft** into the sky ▶ **wodować** (*statek*), **wystrzelić** (*rakietę*)
PHR V **launch into sth**; **launch yourself into sth** to begin sth in an enthusiastic way, especially sth that will take a long time: *He launched into a lengthy account of his career.* ▶ **zabierać się do czegoś z entuzjazmem**
launch out to do sth new in your career, especially sth more exciting: *It's time I launched out on my own.* ▶ **zabierać się do czegoś (nowego)**

launch² /lɔːntʃ/ noun [C] **1** [usually sing.] the act of **launching** a ship, **spacecraft**, new product, etc. ▶ **wodowanie** (*statku*); **wystrzelenie** (*rakiety*); **wylansowanie 2** a large motorboat ▶ **łódź motorowa**

ˈ**launch pad** (also ˈ**launching pad**) noun [C] a platform from which a **spacecraft**, etc. is sent into the sky: (figurative) *She regards the job as a launch pad for her career in the media.* ▶ **wyrzutnia rakietowa; odskocznia**

launder /ˈlɔːndə(r)/ verb [T] **1** (formal) to wash, dry and iron clothes, etc.: *freshly laundered sheets* ▶ **prać 2** to move money that has been obtained illegally into foreign bank accounts or legal businesses so that it is difficult for other people to know where the money came from ▶ **prać** (*brudne pieniądze*)

launderette /lɔːnˈdret/ (US **Laundromat** /ˈlɔːndrəmæt/) noun [C] a type of shop where you pay to wash and dry your clothes in machines ▶ **pralnia samoobsługowa**

laundry /ˈlɔːndri/ noun (pl. **laundries**) **1** [U] clothes, etc. that need washing or that are being washed: *dirty laundry* rzeczy do prania ▶ **pranie** ⓘ W codziennej Br. ang. częściej używa się zwrotu **the washing**. **2** [C] a business where you send sheets, clothes, etc. to be washed and dried ▶ **pralnia**

laurel /ˈlɒrəl/ noun **1** [C,U] an evergreen bush with dark smooth shiny leaves ▶ **wawrzyn, laur 2** (**laurels**) [pl.] honour and distinction following a great achievement ▶ **laury**

lava /ˈlɑːvə/ noun [U] hot liquid rock that comes out of a **volcano** ▶ **lawa**

lavatory /ˈlævətri; US -tɔːri/ noun [C] (pl. **lavatories**) (formal) **1** a toilet ▶ **klozet, sedes 2** a room that contains a toilet, a place to wash your hands, etc.: *Where's the ladies' lavatory, please?* ▶ **ubikacja, toaleta** ➲ note at **toilet**

lavender /ˈlævəndə(r)/ noun [U] a garden plant with purple flowers that smells very pleasant ▶ **lawenda**

lavish¹ /ˈlævɪʃ/ adj. **1** large in amount or number: *a lavish meal* ▶ **suty, obfity 2** giving or spending a large amount of money: *She was always very lavish with her presents.* ▶ **hojny, rozrzutny**

lavish² /ˈlævɪʃ/ verb
PHR V **lavish sth on sb/sth** to give a lot of sth, often too much, to sb/sth ▶ **hojnie obdarzać**

law /lɔː/ noun **1** (**the law**) [U] all the laws in a country or state: *Stealing is **against the law.*** ◇ *to break the law* ◇ *to obey the law* ▶ **prawo** ➲ look at **legal 2** [C] an official rule of a country or state that says what people may or may not do: *There's a new law about wearing seat belts in the back of cars.* ▶ **prawo, ustawa** ➲ note at **rule 3** [U] the law as a subject of study or as a profession: *She is studying law.* ◇ *My brother works for **a law firm*** (w firmie prawniczej) *in Brighton.* ▶ **prawo** ➲ look at **legal 4** [C] (in science) a statement of what always happens in certain situations or conditions: *the laws of mathematics/gravity* ▶ **zasada, prawo**
IDM **law and order** a situation in which the law is obeyed ▶ **praworządność** ➲ note at **court, crime**

ˈ**law-abiding** adj. (used about a person) obeying the law: *law-abiding citizens* ▶ **praworządny; prawomyślny**

lawbreaker /ˈlɔːbreɪkə(r)/ noun [C] a person who does not obey the law; a criminal ▶ **przestęp-ca/czyni**

ˈ**law court** (Brit.) = COURT¹ (1)

lawful /ˈlɔːfl/ adj. allowed or recognized by law: *We shall use all lawful means to obtain our demands.* ◇ *his lawful wife* jego ślubna żona ▶ **legalny, prawowity** ➲ look at **legal, legitimate**

lawless /ˈlɔːləs/ adj. (used about a person or their actions) breaking the law ▶ **łamiący prawo**
■ **lawlessness** noun [U] ▶ **bezprawie**

lawn /lɔːn/ noun [C,U] an area of grass in a garden or park that is regularly cut: *I'm going to **mow the lawn** this afternoon.* ▶ **trawnik** ➲ picture on **page A3**

lawnmower /ˈlɔːnməʊə(r)/ noun [C] a machine that is used for cutting the grass in a garden ▶ **kosiarka** ➲ picture at **garden**

lawsuit /ˈlɔːsuːt/ noun [C] a legal argument in a court of law that is between two people or groups and not between the police and a criminal: *to file a lawsuit* wnosić sprawę do sądu ▶ **proces** (*sądowy*)

lawyer /ˈlɔːjə(r)/ noun [C] a person who has a certificate in law: *to consult a lawyer* ▶ **adwokat, prawni-k/czka**

> **Solicitor** to notariusz. **Barrister** to adwokat. Odpowiednik amerykański – **attorney** /əˈtɜːni/.

lax /læks/ adj. not having high standards; not strict: *Their security checks are rather lax.* ▶ **rozluźniony, luźny** SYN **careless**

laxative /ˈlæksətɪv/ noun [C] a medicine, food or drink that makes the body get rid of solid waste material easily ▶ **środek przeczyszczający**
■ **laxative** adj. ▶ (*lek itp.*) **przeczyszczający**

lay¹ /leɪ/ verb [T] (pt, pp **laid** /leɪd/) **1** to put sb/sth carefully in a particular position or on a surface: *Before they started they laid newspaper on the floor.* ◇ *He laid the child gently down on her bed.* ◇ *'Don't worry,' she said, laying* *her hand on my shoulder.* ▶ **kłaść, położyć, układać** ➲ note at **lie²** **2** to put sth in the correct position for a particular purpose: *They're laying new electricity cables in our street.* ▶ **zakładać** **3** to produce eggs: *Hens lay eggs.* ▶ **znosić** (*jajka*) **4** to prepare sth for use: *The police have laid a trap for him and I think they'll catch him this time.* ◇ *Can you **lay the table** please?* Czy możesz nakryć do stołu? ▶ **zastawiać** (*np. pułapkę*), **przygotowywać** **5** (used with some nouns to give a similar meaning to a verb) to put: *They laid all the blame on him* (przypisali mu winę). ◇ *to lay emphasis* (kłaść nacisk) *on sth*

IDM **get/lay your hands on sb/sth** → HAND¹

PHR V **lay sth down** to give sth as a rule: *It's all laid down in the rules of the club.* ▶ **ustanawiać** (*przepis*)

lay off (sb) (informal) to stop annoying sb: *Can't you lay off me for a bit?* ▶ **odczepiać się (od kogoś)**

lay sb off to stop employing sb because there is not enough work for them to do: *200 workers at the factory have been laid off.* ▶ **zwalniać kogoś z pracy** SYN **make sb redundant**

lay sth on (informal) to provide sth: *They're laying on a trip to London for everybody.* ▶ **organizować coś, fundować coś**

lay sth out **1** to spread out a number of things so that you can see them easily or so that they look nice: *All the food was laid out on a table in the garden.* ▶ **rozstawiać coś, rozkładać coś** **2** to arrange sth in a planned way: *The new shopping centre is very attractively laid out.* ▶ **rozplanowywać coś, projektować coś**

lay over (at/in ...) (US) to stay somewhere for a short time during a long journey ▶ **zatrzymać się gdzieś/w czymś** ➲ look at **layover**, **stop over at/in**

lay² /leɪ/ adj. [only before a noun] **1** without special training in or knowledge of a particular subject ▶ **laicki** **2** (used about a religious teacher) who has not been officially trained as a priest: *a lay preacher* ▶ **świecki**

lay³ past tense of **lie²**

layabout /ˈleɪəbaʊt/ noun [C] (Brit., informal) a person who is lazy and does not do much work ▶ **nierób, leniuch**

ˈlay-by (US ˈ**rest stop**) noun [C] (pl. **lay-bys**) an area at the side of a road where vehicles can stop for a short time ▶ **zato(cz)ka** (*na szosie*)

⚷ **layer** /ˈleə(r); Brit. also ˈleɪə(r)/ noun [C] a piece or quantity of sth that is on sth else or between other things: *A thin layer of dust covered everything in the room.* ◇ *It's very cold. You'll need several layers of clothing.* ◇ *the top/bottom layer* ◇ *the inner/outer layer* ▶ **warstwa**

layman /ˈleɪmən/ noun [C] (pl. **laymen** /-mən/) (also ˈ**lay person**) **1** a person who does not have expert knowledge of a particular subject: *a book written for professionals and laymen alike* ◇ *to explain sth **in layman's terms*** ▶ **laik** **2** a person who is a member of a Church but is not a priest or member of the **clergy** ▶ **osoba świecka** ➲ look at **laywoman**

layout /ˈleɪaʊt/ noun [C, usually sing.] the way in which the parts of sth are arranged: *the magazine has a new page layout* (układ graficzny) ▶ **rozplanowanie, rozkład**

layover (US) = STOPOVER

layperson /ˈleɪpɜːsn/ noun [C] (also ˈ**lay person**) (pl. **lay people** or **laypersons**) a **layman** or **laywoman**: *The layperson cannot really understand mental illness.* ▶ **laik**

laywoman /ˈleɪwʊmən/ noun [C] (pl. **laywomen** /-wɪmɪn/) a woman who is a member of a Church but is not a priest or member of the **clergy** ▶ **kobieta świecka** ➲ look at **layman**, **layperson**

laze /leɪz/ verb [I] **laze (about/around)** to do very little; to rest or relax ▶ **leniuchować, zbijać bąki**

⚷ **lazy** /ˈleɪzi/ adj. (**lazier**; **laziest**) **1** (used about a person) not wanting to work: *Don't be lazy. Come and give me a hand.* ▶ **leniwy, próżniaczy** **2** making you feel that you do not want to do very much: *a lazy summer's afternoon* ▶ **senny, leniwy** **3** moving slowly or without much energy: *a lazy smile* ▶ **powolny**

■ **lazily** adv. ▶ **leniwie, powolnie** | **laziness** noun [U] ▶ **lenistwo, próżniactwo**

lb abbr. **pound(s)**; a measure of weight ▶ (*miara wagi*) **funt**

⚷ **lead¹** /liːd/ verb (pt, pp **led** /led/) **1** [T] to go with or in front of a person or an animal to show the way or to make them or it go in the right direction: *She led the horse into its stable.* ◇ *The receptionist **led the way** to the boardroom.* ◇ *to lead somebody by the hand* ▶ **prowadzić, wieść**

> Mówiąc o oprowadzaniu turystów lub doprowadzeniu do jakiegoś miejsca osoby potrzebującej pomocy, używa się czasownika **guide**: *to guide visitors around Oxford* ◇ *He guided the blind woman to her seat.* Pytając o drogę lub udzielając szczegółowych wskazówek w odpowiedzi na takie pytanie, używa się czasownika **direct**: *Could you direct me to the nearest post office, please?*

2 [I] to go to a place: *I don't think this path leads anywhere.* ▶ **doprowadzać** **3** [I] **lead to sth** to have sth as a result: *Eating too much sugar can lead to all sorts of health problems.* ▶ **prowadzić** **4** [T] **lead sb to do sth** to influence what sb does or thinks: *He led me to believe* (przekonał mnie) *he really meant what he said.* ◇ *He's too easily led.* Łatwo ulega wpływom. ▶ **skłaniać kogoś do zrobienia czegoś** **5** [T] to have a particular type of life: *They lead a very busy life.* ◇ *to lead a life of crime* prowadzić przestępczy tryb życia ▶ **prowadzić, wieść** **6** [I,T] to be winning or in first place in front of sb: *Williams is leading by two games to love.* ◇ *Williams is leading Davenport by two games to love.* ▶ **wyprzedzać, prowadzić** **7** [I,T] to be in control or the leader of sth: *to lead a discussion* ▶ **przewodzić, kierować**

IDM **lead sb astray** to make sb start behaving or thinking in the wrong way ▶ **zwieść kogoś na manowce**

PHR V **lead up to sth** to be an introduction to or cause of sth ▶ **doprowadzać do czegoś**

⚷ **lead²** /liːd/ noun **1** (**the lead**) [sing.] the first place or position in front of other people or organizations: *The French athlete has gone **into the lead*** (objął prowadzenie). ◇ *Who is **in the lead?*** ▶ **czoło, prowadzenie** **2** [sing.] the distance or amount by which sb/sth is in front of another person or thing: *Britain has **taken the lead** in developing computer software for that market.* ◇ *The company has a lead of several years in the development of the new technology.* ▶ **prym; przewaga** **3** [C] a piece of information that may help to give the answer to a problem: *The police are **following** all possible **leads** to track down the killer.* ▶ **ślad, trop** **4** [C] the main part in a play, show or other situation: *Who's playing the lead in the new film?* ◇ *Jill played **a lead role** in getting the company back into profit.* ▶ **główna rola** **5** (especially US **leash** /liːʃ/) [C] a long piece of leather, chain or rope that is used for controlling a dog. The **lead** is connected to a **collar**: *All dogs must be **kept on a lead.*** ▶ **smycz** **6** [C] a piece of wire that carries electricity to a piece of equipment: *The lead on this stereo isn't long enough.* ▶ **przewód elektryczny** ➲ picture at **cable**

IDM **follow sb's example/lead** → FOLLOW

⚷ **lead³** /led; US / noun **1** [U] (symbol **Pb**) a soft heavy grey metal. Lead is used in pipes, roofs, etc. ▶ **ołów** **2** [C,U] the black substance inside a pencil that makes a mark when you write ▶ **grafit** ➲ picture at **stationery**

⚷ **leader** /ˈliːdə(r)/ noun [C] **1** a person who is a manager or in charge of sth: *a strong leader* ◇ *She is a natural leader.* ▶ **przywód-ca/czyni, przewodnicząc-y/a** **2** the person or thing that is best or in first place: *The leader has* *just finished the third lap. ◇ The new shampoo soon became a market leader.* ▶ **lider**

leadership /ˈliːdəʃɪp/ noun **1** [U] the state or position of being a manager or the person in charge: *Who will take over the leadership of the party?* ▶ **przywództwo**, **przewodnictwo** **2** [U] the qualities that a leader should have: *She's got good leadership skills.* ▶ **umiejętność przewodzenia** **3** [C, with sing. or pl. verb] the people who are in charge of a country, organization, etc. ▶ **kierownictwo**, **władza**

leading /ˈliːdɪŋ/ adj. [only before a noun] **1** best or most important: *He's one of the leading experts in this field. ◇ She played a leading role in getting the business started.* ▶ **wybitny**, **czołowy** **2** that tries to make sb give a particular answer: *The lawyer was warned not to ask the witness* ***leading questions.*** ▶ (*pytanie*) **naprowadzający**

lead story /ˈliːd stɔːri/ noun [C] the most important piece of news in a newspaper or on a news programme ▶ **najważniejsza wiadomość**, **temat dnia**

leaf¹ /liːf/ noun [C] (pl. **leaves** /liːvz/) one of the thin, flat, usually green parts of a plant or tree: *The trees lose their leaves in autumn.* ▶ **liść**

leaf² /liːf/ verb

PHR V **leaf through sth** to turn the pages of a book, etc. quickly and without looking at them carefully ▶ **kartkować**

leaflet /ˈliːflət/ noun [C] a printed piece of paper that gives information about sth. **Leaflets** are usually given free of charge: *I picked up a leaflet advertising a new club.* ▶ **ulotka**

leafy /ˈliːfi/ adj. (**leafier**; **leafiest**) **1** having many leaves: *a leafy bush* ▶ **bogato ulistniony** **2** (used about a place) with many trees ▶ **pełen zieleni**, **zielony**

league /liːg/ noun [C] **1** a group of sports clubs that compete with each other for a prize: *the football league ◇ Which team is top of the league at the moment?* ▶ **liga** ➲ look at **rugby** **2** a level of quality, ability, etc.: *He is so much better than the others. They're just not in the same league.* ▶ **ranga**, **klasa** **3** a group of people, countries, etc. that join together for a particular purpose: *the League of Nations* ▶ **liga**, **przymierze**

IDM **in league (with sb)** having a secret agreement (with sb) ▶ **w zmowie/sprzysiężeniu z kimś**

ˈ**league table** noun [C] (Brit.) **1** a table that shows the position of sports teams and how successfully they are performing in a competition ▶ **tabela ligi** **2** a table that shows how well institutions such as schools or hospitals are performing in comparison with each other ▶ **ranking**

leak¹ /liːk/ verb **1** [I,T] to allow liquid or gas to get through a hole or crack: *The boat was leaking badly.* ▶ **przeciekać**, **przepuszczać** **2** [I] (used about liquid or gas) to get out through a hole or crack: *Water is leaking in through the roof.* ▶ **wyciekać**, **ulatniać się** **3** [T] **leak sth (to sb)** to give secret information to sb: *The committee's findings were leaked to the press before the report was published.* ▶ **powodować przeciek** (*informacji*), **ujawniać tajemnicę**

PHR V **leak out** (used about secret information) to become known ▶ (*tajne informacje*) **przeciekać**, **wydawać się**

leak² /liːk/ noun [C] **1** a small hole or crack which liquid or gas can get through: *There's a leak in the pipe. ◇ The roof has sprung a leak.* ▶ **nieszczelność**, **szczelina** **2** the liquid or gas that gets through a hole: *a gas leak* ▶ **wyciek**, **ulatniający się gaz** **3** the act of giving away information that should be kept secret ▶ **przeciek** (*informacji*)

■ **leaky** adj. ▶ **nieszczelny**, **przeciekający**

leakage /ˈliːkɪdʒ/ noun [C,U] the act of coming out of a hole or crack; the liquid or gas that comes out: *a leakage of dangerous chemicals* ▶ **wyciek**

lean¹ /liːn/ verb (pt, pp **leant** /lent/ or **leaned** /liːnd/) **1** [I] to move the top part of your body and head forwards, backwards or to the side: *She leaned out of the window and waved. ◇ Just lean back and relax.* ▶ **pochylać się**, **wychylać się** **2** [I] to be in a position that is not straight or vertical: *That wardrobe leans to the right.* ▶ **opierać się**, **wspierać się** **3** [I,T] **lean (sth) against/on sth** to rest against sth so that it gives support; to put sth in this position: *She stopped and leant on the gate. ◇ Please don't lean bicycles against this window. ◇ You can rely on me. I'll always be there for you to lean on.* ▶ **opierać (się) o coś**

lean² /liːn/ adj. **1** (used about a person or an animal) thin and in good health ▶ **szczupły** **2** (used about meat) having little or no fat ▶ **chudy**, **bez tłuszczu** **3** not producing much: *a lean harvest* ▶ **nieurodzajny**, **niewydajny**

leap¹ /liːp/ verb [I] (pt, pp **leapt** /lept/ or **leaped** /liːpt/) **1** to jump high or a long way: *The horse leapt over the wall. ◇ A fish suddenly leapt out of* (wyskoczyła z) *the water. ◇ We all leapt into the air when they scored the goal. ◇ The children leapt up and down* (podskakiwały) *with excitement.* ◇ (figurative) *Share prices leapt to a record high yesterday.* ▶ **skakać**, **przeskakiwać** **2** to move quickly: *I looked at the clock and leapt out of bed* (wyskoczyłem z łóżka). ◇ *She leapt back* (odskoczyła) *when the pan caught fire.* ▶ **skakać**

PHR V **leap at sth** to accept a chance or offer with enthusiasm: *She leapt at the chance to work in TV.* ▶ **skwapliwie przyjąć coś**

leap² /liːp/ noun [C] **1** a big jump: *He took* ***a flying leap*** *at the wall but didn't get over it.* ◇ (figurative) *My heart* ***gave a leap*** (podskoczyło) *when I heard the news.* ▶ **skok**, **podskok**, **sus** **2** a sudden large change or increase in sth: *The development of penicillin was a great* ***leap forward*** *in the field of medicine.* ▶ **skok (naprzód/w górę)**, **wzrost**

leapfrog /ˈliːpfrɒg/ noun [U] a children's game in which one person bends over and another person jumps over their back ▶ **zabawa polegająca na skakaniu przez kogoś jak przez kozła**

leapfrog

leapt past tense, past participle of **leap¹**

ˈ**leap year** noun [C] one year in every four, in which February has 29 days instead of 28 ▶ **rok przestępny**

learn /lɜːn/ verb (pt, pp **learnt** /lɜːnt/ or **learned** /ˈlɜːnd/) **1** [I,T] **learn (sth) (from sb/sth)** to get knowledge, a skill, etc. (from sb/sth): *I'm not very good at driving yet – I'm still learning. ◇ We're learning about China at school. ◇ Debbie is learning to play the piano. ◇ to learn a foreign language/a musical instrument ◇ Where did you learn how to swim?* Gdzie się nauczyłaś pływać? ▶ **uczyć się** ➲ note at **study** **2** [I] **learn (of/about) sth** to get some information about sth; to find out: *I was sorry to learn about your father's death.* ▶ **dowiadywać się** **3** [T] to study sth so that you can repeat it from memory: *The teacher said we have to learn the poem for tomorrow.* ▶ **nauczyć się** (*na pamięć*) **4** [I] to understand or realize: *We should have learned by now that we can't rely on her. ◇ It's important* *to learn from your mistakes* (uczyć się na własnych błędach). ▶ **zrozumieć**

IDM **learn the hard way** to understand or realize sth by having an unpleasant experience rather than by being told ▶ **zrozumieć coś na podstawie (przykrego) doświadczenia**

learn your lesson to understand what you must do/not do in the future because you have had an unpleasant experience ▶ **zrozumieć coś dopiero po przykrym doświadczeniu**

show sb/know/learn the ropes → ROPE[1]

learned /ˈlɜːnɪd/ adj. having a lot of knowledge from studying; for people who have a lot of knowledge ▶ **o dużej wiedzy**, **uczony**; **naukowy**

learner /ˈlɜːnə(r)/ noun [C] a person who is learning: *a learner driver* ◇ *textbooks for young learners* ◇ *The 'L' plate on a car means the driver is a learner* (że kierowca dopiero się uczy prowadzić) *and hasn't passed the test yet.* ▶ **ucząc-y/a się**

learning /ˈlɜːnɪŋ/ noun [U] **1** the process of learning sth: *new methods of language learning* ▶ **uczenie się**, **poznawanie** **2** knowledge that you get from studying: *men and women of learning* (wielkiej wiedzy) ▶ **wiedza**, **nauka**

learnt past tense, past participle of **learn**

lease /liːs/ noun [C] a legal agreement that allows you to use a building or land for a fixed period of time in return for rent: *The lease on the flat runs out/expires next year.* ▶ **dzierżawa**

■ **lease** verb [T]: *They lease the land from a local farmer.* ◇ *Part of the building is leased out to tenants.* ▶ **dzierżawić**

leasehold /ˈliːshəʊld/ adj. (especially Brit.) (used about property or land) that can be used for a limited period of time, according to the arrangements in a **lease**: *a leasehold property* ▶ (*budynek, ziemia*) **dzierżawiony**

■ **leasehold** **1** adv.: *to purchase land leasehold* ▶ (*kupno budynku/ziemi*) **na zasadach dzierżawy lub najmu** **2** noun [C, U] the right to use a building or a piece of land according to the arrangements in a **lease**: *to obtain/own the leasehold of a house* ▶ **dzierżawa** (*nieruchomości*)

leash (especially US) = LEAD[2] (5): *All dogs must be kept* ***on a leash*** *in public places.*

least /liːst/ determiner, pron. [used as the superlative of *little*] smallest in size, amount, degree, etc.: *He's got the least experience of all of us.* ◇ *You've done the most work, and I'm afraid John has done the least.* ▶ **najmniej**; **najmniejszy**

■ **least** adv. less than anyone/anything else; less than at any other time: *He's the person who needs help least.* ◇ *I bought the least expensive tickets.* ◇ *My uncle always appears when we're least expecting him.* ▶ **najmniej** OPP **most**

IDM **at least** **1** not less than, and probably more: *It'll take us at least two hours to get there.* ▶ **(co) najmniej** **2** even if nothing else is true or you do nothing else: *It may not be beautiful but at least it's cheap.* ◇ *You could at least say you're sorry!* ▶ **przynajmniej** **3** (used for correcting sth that you have just said): *I saw him – at least I think I saw him.* ▶ **przynajmniej**

at the (very) least not less and probably much more: *It'll take six months to build at the very least.* ▶ **co najmniej**

last but not least → LAST[1]

least of all especially not: *Nobody should be worried, least of all you.* ▶ **zwłaszcza nie** (*np. ty*)

not in the least (bit) not at all: *I'm not in the least bit worried.* ◇ *It doesn't matter in the least.* To nie ma najmniejszego znaczenia. ▶ **bynajmniej**, **w najmniejszym stopniu**

to say the least → SAY[1]

leather /ˈleðə(r)/ noun [U] the skin of animals which has been specially treated. Leather is used to make shoes, bags, coats, etc.: *a leather jacket* ▶ **skóra**

leave[1] /liːv/ verb (pt, pp **left** /left/) **1** [I,T] to go away from sb/sth: *We should leave now if we're going to get there by 8 o'clock.* ◇ *I felt sick in class so I left the room.* ◇ *At what age do most people leave school in your country?* ◇ *He left* (zostawił) *his mother in tears.* ◇ *Barry left* (porzucił) *his wife for another woman.* ◇ *He leaves home* (wychodzi z domu) *at 8.00 every morning.* ◇ *He left home* (wyprowadził się z domu) *and went to live with his girlfriend.* ▶ **wyjeżdżać**, **odchodzić**

> Por. **leave** i **depart**. Czasownika **leave** używa się, kiedy opuszcza się kogoś/coś na stałe lub na krótko: *He leaves the house at 8.00 every morning.* ◇ *He left New York and went to live in Canada.* **Depart** to słowo bardziej formalne, używane wówczas, gdy mówi się o odjeździe statków, pociągów, samolotów itp: *The 6.15 train for Southampton departs from Platform 3.*

2 [T] to cause or allow sb/sth to stay in a particular place or condition; to not deal with sth: *Leave the door open, please.* ◇ *Don't leave the iron on when you are not using it.* ◇ *Why do you always leave your homework till the last minute?* ▶ **zostawiać** **3** [T] to put sth somewhere: *Val left a message on her answerphone.* ◇ *I left him a note.* ▶ **zostawiać** **4** [T] to make sth happen or stay as a result: *Don't put that cup on the table. It'll leave a mark.* ▶ **zostawiać** **5** [T] to not use sth: *Leave some milk for me, please.* ▶ **zostawiać** **6** [T] **leave sth (behind)** to forget to bring sth with you: *I'm afraid I've left my homework at home. Can I give it to you tomorrow?* ◇ *I can't find my glasses. Maybe I left them behind at work.* ▶ **zostawiać**, **zapominać** ➲ note at **forget** **7** [T] to give sth to sb when you die: *In his will he left everything to his three sons.* ▶ **zostawiać** **8** [T] to give the care of or responsibility for sb/sth to another person: *I'll* ***leave it to*** *you to organize all the food.* ▶ **zostawiać (komuś coś do zrobienia)**

IDM **be left high and dry** to be left without help in a difficult situation ▶ **być pozostawionym bez pomocy/środków do życia**

leave sb/sth alone to not touch, annoy or speak to sb/sth ▶ **zostawiać kogoś/coś (w spokoju)**

leave go (of sth) to stop touching or holding sth: *Will you please leave go of my arm.* ▶ **puszczać (coś)**

leave sb in the lurch to leave sb without help in a difficult situation ▶ **zostawić kogoś na pastwę losu**

leave sth on one side → SIDE[1]

PHR V **leave sb/sth behind** **1** [usually passive] to make much better progress than sb: *Britain is being left behind in the race for new markets.* ▶ **zostawiać kogoś/coś w tyle** **2** to leave a person, place or state permanently: *She knew that she had left childhood behind.* ▶ **porzucać kogoś/coś** ➲ look at **leave** (6)

leave sb/sth off (sth) to not include sb/sth on a list, etc.: *You've left off a zero.* ◇ *We left him off the list.* ▶ **pomijać kogoś/coś (na czymś)**

leave sb/sth out (of sth) to not include sb/sth: *This doesn't make sense. I think the typist has left out a line.* ▶ **opuszczać kogoś/coś** (*np. na liście, w tekście*), **pomijać kogoś/coś** (*np. w spisie*)

leave[2] /liːv/ noun [U] a period of time when you do not go to work: *Diplomats working abroad usually get a month's home leave each year.* ◇ *annual leave* ◇ *sick leave* zwolnienie chorobowe ◇ *Molly's not working – she's* ***on maternity leave*** (na urlopie macierzyńskim). ▶ **urlop**, **zwolnienie** ➲ note at **holiday**

leaves plural of **leaf[1]**

lecherous /ˈletʃərəs/ adj. having too much interest in sexual pleasure ▶ **lubieżny** SYN **lustful**

lecture /ˈlektʃə(r)/ noun [C] **1** **a lecture (on/about sth)** a talk that is given to a group of people to teach them about a particular subject, especially as part of a university course: *The college has asked a journalist to come and **give a lecture** on the media.* ◇ *a course* (cykl) *of lectures* ▶ **wykład** ➲ note at **university 2** a serious talk to sb that explains what they have done wrong or how they should behave: *We got a lecture from a policeman about playing near the railway.* ▶ **nagana**, **upomnienie**

■ **lecture** verb **1** [I] to give a lecture or lectures (on a particular subject): *Alex lectures in European Studies at London University.* ▶ **wykładać 2** [T] to talk seriously to sb about what they have done wrong or how they should behave: *The policeman lectured the boys about playing ball games in the road.* ▶ **udzielać nagany**, **upominać**

lecturer /ˈlektʃərə(r)/ noun [C] a person who gives talks to teach people about a subject, especially as a job in a university ▶ **wykładowca**

ˈ**lecture theatre** (US ˈlecture theater) noun [C] a large room with rows of seats on a slope, where lectures are given ▶ **sala wykładowa**

led past tense, past participle of **lead**[1]

ledge /ledʒ/ noun [C] a narrow shelf underneath a window, or a narrow piece of rock that sticks out on the side of a **cliff** or mountain ▶ **parapet**, **występ**

leech /liːtʃ/ noun [C] a small creature with a soft body and no legs that usually lives in water and that fastens itself to other creatures and sucks their blood ▶ **pijawka**

leek /liːk/ noun [C] a long thin vegetable that is white at one end with thin green leaves ▶ **por** ➲ picture on **page A13**

leer /lɪə(r)/ verb [I] **leer (at sb)** to look or smile at sb in an unpleasant way that shows an evil or sexual interest in them ▶ **patrzeć złośliwie/lubieżnie (na kogoś)**, **uśmiechać się złośliwie/lubieżnie (do kogoś)**

■ **leer** noun [C] an unpleasant look or smile that shows sb is interested in a person in an evil or sexual way: *He looked at her with an evil leer.* ▶ **złe spojrzenie**; **lubieżny uśmiech**

left[1] past tense, past participle of **leave**[1]

⚷ **left**[2] /left/ adj. **1** [only before a noun] on the side where your heart is in the body: *I've broken my left arm.* ▶ **lewy** OPP **right 2** (**be left**) still available after everything else has been taken or used: ***Is there any bread left?*** ◇ *How much time do we **have left**?* ◇ *If there's any money **left over**, we'll have a cup of coffee.* ▶ **zostawać**

⚷ **left**[3] /left/ adv. to or towards the left: *Turn left just past the Post Office.* ▶ **na/w lewo** OPP **right**

⚷ **left**[4] /left/ noun [sing.] **1** the left side: *In Britain we drive **on the left*** (po lewej stronie). ◇ *Our house is just **to/on the left of** that tall building.* ◇ *If you look **to your left** you'll see one of the city's most famous landmarks.* ◇ *Take the first turning on the left* (na lewo). ▶ **lewa strona** OPP **right 2** (**the Left**) [with sing. or pl. verb] political parties or groups that support **socialism**: *The Left is/are losing popularity.* ▶ **lewica** ➲ look at **left wing**

ˈ**left-hand** adj. [only before a noun] of or on the left: *the left-hand side of the road* ◇ *a left-hand drive car* ▶ **lewy**; **po lewej stronie**, **z lewej strony** OPP **right-hand**

ˌ**left-ˈhanded** adj. **1** using the left hand rather than the right hand: *Are you left-handed?* ▶ **leworęczny 2** made for **left-handed** people to use: *left-handed scissors* ▶ **dla leworęcznych** OPP **right-handed**

■ ˌ**left-ˈhanded** adv.: *I write left-handed.* ▶ **leworęcznie**

leftist /ˈleftɪst/ noun [C] a person who supports **left-wing** political parties and their ideas ▶ **osoba o lewicowych poglądach**

■ **leftism** noun [U] ▶ **lewicowość** | **leftist** adj.: *leftist groups* ▶ **lewicowy**

ˌ**left-ˈluggage office** (US ˈbaggage room) noun [C] the place at a railway station, etc. where you can leave your luggage for a short time ▶ **przechowalnia**

leftovers /ˈleftəʊvəz/ noun [pl.] food that has not been eaten when a meal has finished ▶ **resztki** (*jedzenia*)

ˌ**left ˈwing** noun [sing.] **1** [with sing. or pl. verb] the members of a political party, group, etc. that want more social change than the others in their party: *the left wing of the Labour Party* ▶ **lewica 2** the left side of the field in some team sports: *He plays on the left wing for Manchester United.* ▶ **lewe skrzydło** (*boiska*)

■ **left-wing** adj. strongly supporting the ideas of **socialism**: *left-wing groups* ▶ **lewicowy** OPP **right wing**

ˌ**left-ˈwinger** noun [C] **1** a person on the **left wing** of a political party: *a Labour left-winger* ▶ **lewicowiec 2** a person who plays on the left side of the field in a sports game ▶ **lewoskrzydłowy** OPP for both meanings **right-winger**

⚷ **leg** /leg/ noun [C] **1** one of the parts of the body on which a person or an animal stands or walks: *A spider has eight legs.* ◇ *She sat down and crossed her legs.* ▶ **noga** ➲ look at **foot** ➲ picture at **body 2** the part of a pair of trousers, etc. that covers the leg: *There's a hole in the leg of my trousers/my trouser leg.* ▶ **nogawka 3** one of the parts of a chair, table etc. on which it stands: *the leg of a chair/table* ◇ *a chair/table leg* ▶ **noga** (*np. stołu*) **4** one part or section of a journey, competition, etc.: *The band are in Germany on the first leg of their world tour.* ▶ **etap**, **odcinek**

IDM **pull sb's leg** → PULL[1]

stretch your legs → STRETCH[1]

legacy /ˈlegəsi/ noun [C] (pl. **legacies**) money or property that is given to you after sb dies, because they wanted you to have it: *He received a large legacy from his grandmother.* ▶ **legat**, **dziedzictwo**

⚷ **legal** /ˈliːgl/ adj. **1** [only before a noun] using or connected with the law: *legal advice* ◇ *to take legal action against somebody* ◇ *the legal profession* ▶ **legalny 2** allowed by law: *It is not legal to own a gun without a licence.* ▶ **prawny**, **prawniczy** OPP **illegal** ➲ look at **lawful**, **legitimate**

■ **legally** /ˈliːgəli/ adv.: *Schools are legally* (według prawa) *responsible for the safety of their pupils.* ▶ **prawnie**, **legalnie**

legality /liːˈgæləti/ noun [U] the state of being legal ▶ **legalność** OPP **illegality**

legalize (also -ise) /ˈliːgəlaɪz/ verb [T] to make sth legal ▶ **legalizować**

legend /ˈledʒənd/ noun **1** [C,U] an old story or group of stories that may or may not be true; this type of story: *the legend of Robin Hood* ◇ *According to legend, Robin Hood lived in Sherwood Forest.* ▶ **legenda**, **zbiór legend** SYN **myth 2** [C] a famous person or event: *a movie/jazz/baseball legend* ▶ **legenda** ➲ look at **star**

legendary /ˈledʒəndri; US -deri/ adj. **1** very famous and talked about by a lot of people, especially in a way that shows admiration: *Michael Jordan, the legendary basketball star* ▶ **legendarny 2** mentioned in stories from ancient times: *the legendary heroes of Greek myths* ▶ **legendarny**

leggings /ˈlegɪŋz/ noun [pl.] a piece of women's clothing that fits tightly over both legs from the waist to the feet, like a very thin pair of trousers ▶ **leginsy**

legible /ˈledʒəbl/ adj. that is clear enough to be read easily: *His writing is so small that it's barely legible.* ◇ *legible handwriting* ▶ **czytelny** OPP **illegible** ➲ look at **readable**

■ **legibility** /ˌledʒəˈbɪləti/ noun [U] ▶ **czytelność** | **legibly** /ˈledʒəbli/ adv. ▶ **czytelnie**

L

legion /ˈliːdʒən/ noun [C] **1** a special military unit, often made up of volunteers serving with the army of another country: *the French Foreign Legion* ▶ **legia 2** a large number of people who have something in common: *legions of admirers/photographers* ▶ **legion**

legislate /ˈledʒɪsleɪt/ verb [I] **legislate (for/against sth)** to make a law or laws ▶ **ustanawiać prawo**

legislation /ˌledʒɪsˈleɪʃn/ noun [U] **1** a group of laws: *The government is introducing new legislation to help small businesses.* ▶ **ustawy 2** the process of making laws ▶ **ustawodawstwo**

legislative /ˈledʒɪslətɪv; US -leɪtɪv/ adj. [only before a noun] (formal) connected with the act of making and passing laws: *a legislative assembly/body/council* ▶ **ustawodawczy**

legislature /ˈledʒɪsleɪtʃə(r)/ noun [C] (formal) a group of people who have the power to make and change laws: *the national/state legislature* ▶ **władza ustawodawcza** ➲ look at **executive**, **judiciary**

legitimate /lɪˈdʒɪtɪmət/ adj. **1** reasonable or acceptable: *a legitimate excuse/question/concern* ▶ **prawnie dozwolony 2** allowed by law: *Could he earn so much from legitimate business activities?* ▶ **właściwy, słuszny** OPP **illegitimate** ➲ look at **lawful**, **legal 3** (old-fashioned) (used about a child) having parents who are married to each other ▶ *(dziecko)* **ślubny** OPP **illegitimate**
■ **legitimacy** /lɪˈdʒɪtɪməsi/ noun [U] ▶ **legalność, zasadność** *(prawa)* | **legitimately** adv. ▶ **w granicach prawa, słusznie**

legitimize (also -ise) /lɪˈdʒɪtəmaɪz/ verb [T] (formal) **1** to make sth that is wrong or unfair seem acceptable: *The movie has been criticized for apparently legitimizing violence.* ▶ **sankcjonować 2** to make sth legal ▶ **legalizować** SYN for both meanings **legalize 3** to give a child whose parents are not married to each other the same rights as those whose parents are ▶ **uznawać prawnie**

leisure /ˈleʒə(r); US ˈliːʒər/ noun [U] the time when you do not have to work; free time: *Shorter working hours mean that people have more leisure.* ◇ *leisure activities* ▶ **czas wolny**
IDM **at your leisure** (formal) when you have free time: *Look through the catalogue at your leisure and then order by telephone.* ▶ **w dogodnej chwili, w wolnej chwili**

ˈ**leisure centre** noun [C] a public building where you can do sports and other activities in your free time ▶ **ośrodek rekreacyjny**

leisurely /ˈleʒəli/ adj. without hurry: *a leisurely Sunday breakfast* ◇ *I always cycle at a leisurely pace.* ▶ **niespieszny, powolny**

⚷ **lemon** /ˈlemən/ noun [C,U] a yellow fruit with sour juice that is used for giving flavour to food and drink: *a slice of lemon* ◇ *Add the juice of 2 lemons.* ▶ **cytryna** ➲ note at **rind** ➲ picture at **bar**, picture on **page A12**

lemonade /ˌleməˈneɪd/ noun [C,U] **1** (Brit.) a sweet lemon drink with a lot of bubbles in it ▶ **lemoniada 2** a drink that is made from fresh lemon juice, sugar and water ▶ **napój cytrynowy**

ˈ**lemon squeezer** noun [C] an instrument that is used for pressing the juice out of a lemon ▶ **wyciskacz do cytryn**

⚷ **lend** /lend/ verb [T] (pt, pp **lent** /lent/) **1 lend sb sth; lend sth to sb** to allow sb to use sth for a short time or to give sb money that must be paid back after a certain period of time: *Could you lend me £10 until Friday?* ◇ *He lent me his bicycle.* ◇ *He lent his bicycle to me.* ▶ **pożyczać (komuś)**

Uwaga! **Lend** znaczy pożyczać komuś a **borrow** pożyczać od kogoś.

If a bank, etc. lends you money, you must **pay it back/repay** it over a fixed period of time with **interest**. ➲ picture at **borrow**

2 (formal) **lend sth (to sth)** to give or add sth: *to lend advice/support* ◇ *This evidence lends weight to our theory.* ▶ **udzielać, dodawać**
IDM **lend (sb) a hand/lend a hand (to sb)** to help sb ▶ **pomagać komuś**
PHR V **lend itself to sth** to be suitable for sth ▶ **nadawać się (do czegoś)**

lender /ˈlendə(r)/ noun [C] a person or organization that lends sth, especially money ▶ **pożyczkodawca, pożyczający**

⚷ **length** /leŋθ/ noun **1** [U,C] how long sth is; the size of sth from one end to the other: *to measure the length of a room* ◇ *It took an hour to walk the length of Oxford Street.* ◇ *The tiny insect is only one millimetre **in length**.* ◇ *This snake can grow to a length of two metres.* ▶ **długość, odległość** ➲ look at **width**, **breadth** ➲ picture at **dimension 2** [U] the amount of time that sth lasts: *Many people complained about the **length of time** they had to wait* (skarżyło się na długi czas oczekiwania). ◇ *the length of a class/speech/film* ▶ **czas trwania 3** [U] the number of pages in a book, a letter, etc.: *Her novels vary in length.* ▶ **objętość** *(np. książki)* **4** [C] the distance from one end of a swimming pool to the other: *I can swim a length in thirty seconds.* ▶ **długość, dystans 5** [C] a piece of sth long and thin: *a length of material/rope/string* ▶ **kawałek, długość**
IDM **at length** for a long time or in great detail: *We discussed the matter at great length.* ▶ **długo; szczegółowo**
go to great lengths → GREAT[1]
the length and breadth of sth to or in all parts of sth: *They travelled the length and breadth of India.* ▶ **wzdłuż i wszerz**

lengthen /ˈleŋθən/ verb [I,T] to become longer or to make sth longer ▶ **wydłużać (się)**

lengthways /ˈleŋθweɪz/ (also **lengthwise** /ˈleŋθwaɪz/) adv. in a direction from one end to the other of sth: *Fold the paper lengthwise.* ▶ **wzdłuż, na długość**

lengthy /ˈleŋθi/ adj. (**lengthier**; **lengthiest**) very long ▶ **długi, rozwlekły**

lenient /ˈliːniənt/ adj. (used about a punishment or person who punishes) not as strict as expected ▶ **łagodny**
■ **lenience** (also **leniency** /ˈliːniənsi/) noun [U] ▶ **łagodność** | **leniently** adv. ▶ **łagodnie**

lens /lenz/ noun [C] **1** a curved piece of glass that makes things look bigger, clearer, etc. when you look through it ▶ **soczewka; obiektyw**

You may use a **zoom** or **telephoto lens** on your camera.

2 = CONTACT LENS

Lent /lent/ noun [U] a period of 40 days starting in February or March, when some Christians stop doing or eating certain things for religious reasons: *I'm giving up smoking for Lent.* ▶ **Wielki Post**

lent past tense, past participle of **lend**

lentil /ˈlentl/ noun [C] a small brown, orange or green seed that can be dried and used in cooking: *lentil soup/stew* ▶ **soczewica**

Leo /ˈliːəʊ/ noun [C,U] (pl. **Leos**) the 5th sign of the **zodiac**, the Lion; a person born under this sign: *I'm a Leo* ▶ **Lew; zodiakalny Lew**

leopard /ˈlepəd/ noun [C] a large wild animal of the cat family that has yellow fur with dark spots. **Leopards** live in Africa and Southern Asia. ▶ **lampart**

A female leopard is called a **leopardess** and a baby is called a **cub**.

leotard /ˈliːətɑːd/ noun [C] a piece of clothing that fits the body tightly from the neck down to the tops of the legs. **Leotards** are worn by dancers or women doing certain sports. ▶ **trykot**

leper /ˈlepə(r)/ noun [C] a person who suffers from **leprosy** ▶ **trędowat-y/a**

leprosy /ˈleprəsi/ noun [U] a serious infectious disease that affects the skin, nerves, etc. and can cause parts of the body to fall off ▶ **trąd**

lesbian /ˈlezbiən/ noun [C] a woman who is sexually attracted to other women ▶ **lesbijka**
■ **lesbian** adj.: *a lesbian relationship* ◇ *the lesbian and gay community* ▶ **lesbijski** | **lesbianism** /ˈlezbiənɪzəm/ noun [U] ▶ **miłość lesbijska** ➲ look at **gay**, **homosexual**

less¹ /les/ determiner, pron. [used with uncountable nouns] a smaller amount (of sth): *It took less time than I thought.* ◇ *I'm too fat – I must try to eat less.* ◇ *It's not far – it'll take less* (krócej) *than an hour to get there.* ▶ **mniej** OPP **more**

Chociaż wiele osób używa słowa **less** także z rzeczownikami w lm (np. **less cars**), to jednak za poprawną formę gramatyczną uważa się w takim wypadku **fewer**: *fewer cars*.

less² /les/ adv. not so much (as): *He's less intelligent than his brother.* ◇ *It rains less in London than in Manchester.* ◇ *People work less well* (gorzej) *when they're tired.* ▶ **mniej**
IDM **I, etc. couldn't care less** → CARE²
less and less becoming smaller and smaller in amount or degree: *She found the job less and less attractive.* ▶ **coraz mniej**
more or less → MORE²

less³ /les/ prep. taking a certain number or amount away: *You'll earn £10 an hour, less tax.* ▶ **bez**, **minus** SYN **minus**

lessen /ˈlesn/ verb [I,T] to become less; to make sth less: *The noise began to lessen.* ◇ *to lessen the risk/impact/effect of sth* ▶ **zmniejszać (się)**, **skracać**

lesser /ˈlesə(r)/ adj. [only before a noun] not as great/much as: *He is guilty and so, **to a lesser extent**, is his wife.* ▶ **mniejszy**, **pomniejszy**
■ **lesser** adv.: *a lesser-known artist* ▶ **mniej**
IDM **the lesser of two evils** the better of two bad things ▶ **mniejsze zło**

lesson /ˈlesn/ noun [C] **1** a period of time when you learn or teach sth: *She gives piano lessons.* ◇ *I want to have/take extra lessons in English conversation.* ◇ *a driving lesson* ▶ **lekcja**, **zajęcia** **2** something that is intended to be or should be learnt: *I'm sure we can all learn some lessons from this disaster.* To nieszczęście będzie dla nas wszystkich nauczką na przyszłość. ▶ **lekcja**, **nauczka**
IDM **learn your lesson** → LEARN
teach sb a lesson → TEACH

let /let/ verb [T] (**letting**; pt, pp **let**) **1** to allow sth to happen: *He's let the dinner burn again!* ◇ *Don't let the fire go out.* ◇ *Why did you let the dog get so dirty?* Jak mogłeś dopuścić do tego, żeby pies się tak pobrudził! ▶ **pozwalać, żeby coś się stało** **2 let sb/sth do sth** to allow sb/sth to do sth; to make sb/sth able to do sth: *Don't let the dog jump on the sofa.* ◇ *My parents let me stay out till 11 o'clock.* ◇ *I wanted to borrow Dave's bike but he wouldn't let me.* ◇ *This ticket lets you travel* (ten bilet daje możliwość podróżowania) *anywhere in the city for a day.* ▶ **pozwalać** ➲ note at **allow**

W tym znaczeniu **let** nie występuje w stronie biernej. Używa się wówczas czasownika **allow** lub **permit** z **to**: *They let him take the exam again.* ◇ *He was allowed/permitted to take the exam again.*

3 to allow sb/sth to go somewhere: *Open the windows and let some fresh air in.* ◇ *She was let out of prison yesterday.* ▶ **wpuszczać**, **wypuszczać** **4** (used for making suggestions about what you and other people can do): *'Let's go* (chodźmy) *to the cinema tonight.' 'Yes, let's.'* ▶ **(*tworzy 1 os. lm trybu rozkazującego*)** ⓘ Forma przecząca to **let's not** lub (tylko w Br. ang.) **don't let's**: *Let's not/Don't let's go* (nie idźmy) *to that awful restaurant again.* **5** (used for offering help to sb): *Let me help you carry your bags.* ▶ **pozwalać** **6 let sth (out) (to sb)** to allow sb to use a building, room, etc. in return for rent: *They let out two rooms to students.* ◇ *There's a flat to let in our block.* ▶ **wynajmować** ➲ note at **hire** **7** (used for making requests or giving instructions): *Don't help him. Let him do it himself.* ◇ *If she refuses to come home with us now, let her walk home.* ◇ *Let me have your report by Friday.* Proszę złożyć u mnie swój raport do piątku. ▶ **niech**
IDM **let sb/sth go**; **let go of sb/sth** to stop holding sb/sth: *Let me go. You're hurting me!* ◇ *Hold the rope and don't let go of it.* ▶ **(wy)puszczać coś**
let us; **let's say** for example: *You could work two mornings a week, let's say Tuesday and Friday.* ▶ **powiedzmy**
let yourself go 1 to relax without worrying what other people think: *After work I like to go out with friends and let myself go.* ▶ **dać się ponieść** (*np. chwili, uczuciom*), **czuć się nieskrępowanym** **2** to allow yourself to become untidy, dirty, etc.: *She used to be so smart but after her husband died she just let herself go* (przestało jej zależeć na wyglądzie). ▶ **zaniedbać (się)**
ⓘ **Let** używa się w innych idiomach, np. **let sth slip**. Zob. hasła odpowiednich czasowników, rzeczowników itp.
PHR V **let sb down** to not do sth that you promised to do for sb; to disappoint sb: *Rob really let me down when he didn't finish the work on time.* ▶ **zawodzić kogoś**
let sb/sth down to make sb/sth less successful than they/it should be: *She speaks French very fluently, but her pronunciation lets her down.* ▶ **zawodzić kogoś/coś**
let sth down 1 to let or make sth go down: *We let the bucket down by a rope.* ▶ **spuszczać coś** **2** to make a dress, skirt, coat, etc. longer, by reducing the amount of material that is folded over at the bottom: *This skirt needs letting down.* ▶ **podłużać coś** OPP **take sth up** **3** (Brit.) to allow the air to escape from sth deliberately: *Some kids had let my tyres down.* ▶ **spuszczać powietrze z czegoś**
let on (about sth) (to sb) to tell sb a secret: *He didn't let on how much he'd paid for the vase.* ▶ **zdradzać (komuś)** (*tajemnicę*)
let sb off (with sth) to not punish sb, or to give sb less of a punishment than expected: *He expected to go to prison but they let him off with a fine* (zwolnili go, poprzestając na grzywnie). ▶ **darować komuś winę**, **wypuszczać kogoś** (*zwł. z lekką karą*)
let sth off to fire a gun or make a bomb, etc. explode: *The boys were letting off fireworks.* ▶ **odpalać/detonować coś**
let sth out 1 to make a sound with your voice: *to **let out** a scream/sigh/groan/yell* ◇ *to **let out** a gasp of delight* ▶ **wydawać** (*np. okrzyk*) **2** to tell people sth that was secret: *Who let the story about Michael Jones out?* ▶ **ujawniać** (*tajemnicę*) **3** to make a shirt, coat, etc. looser or larger ▶ **poszerzać** (*np. ubranie*) OPP **take sth in**

ˈlet-down noun [C, usually sing., U] something that is disappointing because it is not as good as you expected it to be ▶ **rozczarowanie** SYN **disappointment**, **anticlimax**

lethal /ˈliːθl/ adj. that can cause death or great damage: *a lethal weapon/drug* ▶ **śmiertelny**, **morderczy**
■ **lethally** /ˈliːθəli/ adv. ▶ **śmiertelnie**, **morderczo**

lethargy /'leθədʒi/ noun [U] the feeling of being very tired and not having any energy ▶ **ospałość**
■ **lethargic** /lə'θɑːdʒɪk/ adj. ▶ **ospały**

letter /'letə(r)/ noun [C] **1** a written or printed message that you send to sb: *I got a letter from Matthew this morning.* ◇ *I'm writing* ***a thank-you letter*** *to my uncle for the flowers he sent.* ▶ **list** ➲ note at **post**

When you have written a letter you put it in an **envelope**, **address** it, **put/stick** a **stamp** on it and then **post** (US **mail**) it. You may **forward** a letter to a person who has moved away.

2 a written or printed sign that represents a sound in a language: *'Z' is the last letter of the English alphabet.* ▶ **litera**

Letters may be written or printed as **capitals** or **small** letters: *Is 'east' written with a capital or a small 'e'?*

'letter box noun [C] **1** a hole in a door or wall for putting letters, etc. through ▶ **skrzynka pocztowa**

W wielu brytyjskich domach nie ma skrzynki pocztowej na zewnątrz budynku, a listy i inne przesyłki wrzucane są do środka przez specjalny otwór w drzwiach.

2 (US **mailbox**) a small box near the main door of a building or by the road in which letters are left for the owner to collect ▶ **skrzynka pocztowa 3** = POSTBOX

letterhead /'letəhed/ noun [C] the name and address of a person, a company or an organization printed at the top of their writing paper ▶ **nagłowek listu** (*na papierze firmowym*)

lettuce /'letɪs/ noun [C,U] a plant with large green leaves which are eaten cold in salads: *a lettuce leaf* ▶ **sałata** ➲ look at **salad** ➲ picture on **page A13**, picture at **salad**

leukaemia (US **leukemia**) /luː'kiːmiə/ noun [U] a serious disease of the blood which often results in death ▶ **białaczka**

level[1] /'levl/ noun [C] **1** the amount, size or number of sth (compared to sth else): *a low level of unemployment* ◇ *high stress/pollution levels* ▶ **poziom 2** the height, position, standard, etc. of sth: *He used to play tennis at a high level.* ◇ *intermediate-level students* ◇ *top-level discussions* dyskusje na najwyższym szczeblu ▶ **poziom 3** a way of considering sth: ***on a*** *spiritual/personal/professional* ***level*** ▶ **poziom 4** a flat surface or layer: *a multi-level* (wielopoziomowy) *shopping centre* ▶ **poziom**

level[2] /'levl/ adj. **1** with no part higher than any other; flat: *Put the tent up on level ground.* ◇ *a level teaspoon of sugar* ◇ *Make sure the shelves are level* (są ustawione poziomo) *before you fix them in position.* ▶ **płaski, poziomy 2 level (with sb/sth)** at the same height, standard or position: *The boy's head was level with his father's shoulder.* ◇ *A red car drew level with mine at the traffic lights* (zrównał się z moim). ◇ *The teams are level on 34 points.* ▶ **równy, na tym samym poziomie**
IDM **a level playing field** a situation in which everyone has an equal chance of success ▶ **wyrównane szanse**

level[3] /'levl/ verb [T] (**levelling**; **levelled**; US **leveling**; **leveled**) to make sth flat, equal or level: *The ground needs levelling before we lay the patio.* ◇ *Juventus levelled the score with a late goal.* ◇ *Many buildings were levelled* (zostało zrównanych z ziemią) *in the earthquake.* ▶ **wyrównywać, niwelować**
PHR V **level sth at sb/sth** to aim sth at sb/sth: *They levelled serious criticisms at the standard of teaching.* ▶ **kierować w kogoś/coś** (*np. krytykę*)
level off/out to become flat, equal or level: *Share prices rose sharply yesterday but today they have levelled out.* (pozostawały na stałym poziomie) ▶ **wyrównywać się, zrównywać się**

,level 'crossing (US **'railroad crossing**) noun [C] a place where a railway crosses the surface of a road ▶ **przejazd kolejowy**

,level-'headed adj. calm and sensible; able to make good decisions in a difficult situation ▶ **zrównoważony**

lever /'liːvə(r); US 'levər/ noun [C] **1** a handle that you pull or push in order to make a machine, etc. work: *Pull the lever towards you.* ◇ *the gear lever in a car* ▶ **dźwignia, drążek 2** a bar or tool that is used to lift or open sth when you put pressure or force on one end: *You need to get the tyre off with a lever.* ▶ **dźwignia**
■ **lever** verb [T]: *The police had to lever the door open.* ▶ **podważać, przesuwać coś za pomocą dźwigni**

leverage /'liːvərɪdʒ; US 'lev-/ noun [U] the act of using a lever to lift or open sth; the force needed to do this ▶ **siła dźwigni**

levy /'levi/ verb [T] (**levying**; **levies**; pt, pp **levied**) (formal) **levy sth (on sb)** to officially demand and collect money, etc.: *to levy a tax* ▶ **ściągać, pobierać**

lewd /luːd; Brit. also ljuːd/ adj. referring to sex in a rude and offensive way: *lewd behaviour/jokes/suggestions* ▶ **sprośny** SYN **obscene**
■ **lewdly** adv. ▶ **sprośnie** | **lewdness** noun [U] ▶ **sprośność**

lexical /'leksɪkl/ adj. [usually before a noun] connected with the words of a language: ***lexical items*** ▶ **leksykalny**

liability /ˌlaɪə'bɪləti/ noun (pl. **liabilities**) **1** [U] **liability (for sth)** the state of being responsible for sth: *The company cannot accept liability for damage to cars in this car park.* ▶ **odpowiedzialność 2** [C] (informal) a person or thing that can cause a lot of problems, cost a lot of money, etc. ▶ **problem, ciężar**

liable /'laɪəbl/ adj. [not before a noun] **1 liable (for sth)** (in law) responsible for sth ▶ **odpowiedzialny (za coś) 2 liable to do sth** likely to do sth: *We're all liable to have accidents* (każdemu może przydarzyć się wypadek) *when we are very tired.* ◇ *The bridge is liable to collapse* (może łatwo się zawalić) *at any moment.* ▶ **podatny na coś, łatwo (o coś/coś się dzieje) 3 liable to sth** likely to have or suffer from sth: *The area is liable to floods.* ▶ **narażony na coś; mający skłonność do czegoś**

liaise /li'eɪz/ verb [I] **liaise (with sb/sth)** to work closely with a person, group, etc. and give them or it regular information about what you are doing ▶ **pozostawać w ścisłym kontakcie, informować na bieżąco**

liaison /li'eɪzn; US li'eɪzɑːn; 'liəzɑːn/ noun **1** [U, sing.] **liaison (between A and B)** communication between two or more people or groups that work together ▶ **łączność, kontakt 2** [C] a secret sexual relationship ▶ **romans, związek**

liar /'laɪə(r)/ noun [C] a person who does not tell the truth: *She called me a liar.* ▶ **kłam-ca/czucha** ➲ look at **lie**[1]

Lib Dem = LIBERAL DEMOCRATS

libel /'laɪbl/ noun [C,U] the act of printing a statement about sb that is not true and would give people a bad opinion of them: *The singer is suing the newspaper for libel.* ▶ **zniesławienie** (*na piśmie*)
■ **libel** verb [T] (**libelling**; **libelled**; US **libeling**; **libeled**): *He claims he was libelled in the magazine article.* ▶ **zniesławiać**

liberal /'lɪbərəl/ adj. **1** accepting different opinions or kinds of behaviour: *He has very liberal parents.* ▶ **liberalny** SYN **tolerant 2** (in politics) believing in or based on principles of commercial freedom, freedom of choice, and avoiding extreme social and political change: *liberal policies/politicians* ▶ **liberalny 3** not strictly limited in amount or variety ▶ **hojny, obfity**

■ **liberal** noun [C]: *Charles has always considered himself a liberal.* ▶ **liberał** | **liberalism** /ˈlɪbərəlɪzəm/ noun [U] ▶ **liberalizm**

the ˌ**Liberal** ˈ**Democrats** noun [pl.] (abbr. **Lib Dems** /ˌlɪb ˈdemz/) a political party in Britain that represents views that are not extreme ▶ (*partia w Wlk. Br.*) **Liberalni Demokraci**

liberalize (also -ise) /ˈlɪbrəlaɪz/ verb [T] to make sth such as a law or a political or religious system less strict ▶ **liberalizować**

■ **liberalization** (also -isation) /ˌlɪbrəlaɪˈzeɪʃn; US -ləˈz-/ noun [U] ▶ **liberalizacja**

liberally /ˈlɪbərəli/ adv. freely or in large amounts ▶ **hojnie, obficie**

liberate /ˈlɪbəreɪt/ verb [T] **liberate sb/sth (from sth)** to allow sb/sth to be free: *France was liberated in 1945.* ▶ **wyzwalać, uwalniać**

■ **liberated** adj. free from the restrictions of traditional opinions or ways of behaving ▶ **wyzwolony** | **liberation** /ˌlɪbəˈreɪʃn/ noun [U] ▶ **wyzwolenie, uwolnienie**

liberator /ˈlɪbəreɪtə(r)/ noun [C] a person who liberates ▶ **wyzwoliciel/ka**

liberty /ˈlɪbəti/ noun [C,U] (pl. **liberties**) the freedom to go where you want, do what you want, etc.: *We must defend our civil liberties at all costs.* ▶ **wolność, swoboda** ➲ look at **freedom**

IDM **at liberty (to do sth)** free or allowed to do sth: *You are at liberty* (możesz) *to leave when you wish.* ▶ **wolno (ci/mi itp.)**

libido /lɪˈbiːdəʊ; ˈlɪbɪdəʊ/ noun (pl. **-os**) [U,C, usually sing.] sexual desire: *loss of libido* ▶ **libido**

Libra /ˈliːbrə/ noun [C,U] the 7th sign of the **zodiac**, the Scales; a person born under this sign: *I'm a Libra* ▶ **Waga**; **zodiakalna Waga**

librarian /laɪˈbreəriən/ noun [C] a person who works in or is in charge of a library ▶ **biblioteka-rz/rka**

⚷ **library** /ˈlaɪbrəri; Brit. also ˈlaɪbri/ noun [C] (pl. **libraries**) **1** a room or building that contains a collection of books, etc. that can be looked at or borrowed: *My library books are due back tomorrow.* ▶ **biblioteka 2** a private collection of books, etc.: *a new edition to add to your library* ▶ **księgozbiór, biblioteka**

lice plural of **louse**

⚷ **licence** (US license) /ˈlaɪsns/ noun **1** [C] **a licence (for sth/to do sth)** an official paper that shows you are allowed to do or have sth: *Do you have a licence for this gun?* ◇ *The shop has applied for a licence to sell alcoholic drinks.* ▶ **licencja, pozwolenie** ➲ look at **driving licence 2** [U] (formal) **licence (to do sth)** permission or freedom to do sth: *The soldiers were given licence to kill if they were attacked.* ▶ **zezwolenie**

⚷ **license**[1] /ˈlaɪsns/ verb [T] to give official permission for sth: *Is that gun licensed?* ▶ **wydawać zezwolenie/licencję/koncesję/pozwolenie**

license[2] (US) = LICENCE

licensee /ˌlaɪsənˈsiː/ noun [C] a person who is officially allowed to sell alcoholic drinks ▶ **posiadacz zezwolenia/licencji/koncesji** (*na sprzedawanie alkoholu*)

ˈ**license plate** (US) = NUMBER PLATE

ˈ**licensing laws** noun [pl.] (Brit.) the laws that control when and where alcoholic drinks can be sold ▶ **ustawy o sprzedaży napojów alkoholowych**

licentious /laɪˈsenʃəs/ adj. (formal) behaving in a way that is considered sexually immoral ▶ **rozwiązły**

■ **licentiousness** noun [U] ▶ **rozwiązłość**

lichen /ˈlaɪkən; ˈlɪtʃən/ noun [U,C] a very small grey or yellow plant that spreads over the surface of rocks, walls and trees and does not have any flowers ▶ (*bot.*) **porost** ➲ look at **moss**

lick /lɪk/ verb [T] to move your tongue across sth: *The child licked the spoon clean.* ◇ *I licked the envelope and stuck it down.* ▶ **lizać**

■ **lick** noun [C]: *Let me have a lick of* (pozwól mi polizać) *your ice cream.* ▶ **liźnięcie**

licorice = LIQUORICE

⚷ **lid** /lɪd/ noun [C] **1** the top part of a box, pot, etc. that can be lifted up or taken off: *I can't get the lid off this jar.* ▶ **pokrywka, wieko** ➲ look at **cap**, **top** ➲ picture at **container 2** = EYELID

⚷ **lie**[1] /laɪ/ verb [I] (**lying**; pt, pp **lied**) **lie (to sb) (about sth)** to say or write sth that you know is not true: *He lied about his age in order to join the army.* ◇ *How could you lie to me?!* ▶ **kłamać**

■ **lie** noun [C]: *to tell a lie* ◇ *That story about his mother being ill was just* ***a pack of lies.*** ◇ *a white lie* niewinne kłamstwo ▶ **kłamstwo** ➲ look at **fib**, **liar**

⚷ **lie**[2] /laɪ/ verb [I] (**lying**; pt **lay** /leɪ/, pp **lain** /leɪn/) **1** to be in or move into a flat or horizontal position (so that you are not standing or sitting): *He lay on the sofa and went to sleep.* ◇ *to lie on your back/side/front* ◇ *The book lay open in front of her.* ▶ **leżeć**; **kłaść się**

> Uwaga! Por. **lie** i **lay**. Czasownik **lay** (kłaść, położyć) wymaga dopełnienia, a **lie** (leżeć) nie: *He is lying on the beach.* ◇ *He is laying a carpet in our new house.* Forma czasu przeszłego czasownika **lie** to **lay**, a imiesłów *past participle* to **lain**: *He lay quietly for a few minutes.* ◇ *She had lain there all night.* Forma czasu przeszłego oraz imiesłowu *past participle* czasownika **lay** to **laid**: *She laid her child on the bed.*

2 to be or stay in a certain state or position: *Snow lay thick on the ground.* ◇ *The hills lie to the north of the town.* ◇ *They are young and their whole lives* ***lie ahead*** (mają przed sobą całe życie) *of them.* ▶ **leżeć, być 3 lie (in sth)** to exist or to be found somewhere: *The problem lies in deciding when to stop.* ▶ **tkwić (w czymś)**

IDM **lie in wait (for sb)** to hide somewhere waiting to attack, surprise or catch sb ▶ **(przy)czaić się (na kogoś)**

lie low (informal) to try not to attract attention to yourself: *At the time of the murder he was lying low in a Scottish village.* ▶ **starać się nie rzucać w oczy**; **przebywać w miejscu, które nie przyciąga uwagi**

PHR V **lie about/around** to relax and do nothing ▶ **nic nie robić, odpoczywać**

lie back to relax and do nothing while sb else works, etc. ▶ **próżnować**

lie behind sth to be the real hidden reason for sth: *We may never know what lay behind his decision to resign.* ▶ **kryć się za czymś**

lie down (used about a person) to be in or move into a flat or horizontal position so that you can rest ▶ **kłaść się** ⓘ Inny zwrot o tym samym znaczeniu to **have a lie-down**.

lie in (informal) to stay in bed later than usual because you do not have to get up ▶ **dłużej poleżeć w łóżku** ➲ look at **oversleep** ⓘ Inny zwrot o tym samym znaczeniu to **have a lie-in**.

lie with sb (to do sth) (formal) to be sb's responsibility to do sth ▶ **należeć do czyichś obowiązków**

ˈ**lie detector** noun [C] a piece of equipment that can show if a person is telling the truth or not ▶ **wykrywacz kłamstw**

lieu /luː; Brit. also ljuː/ noun (formal)

IDM **in lieu (of sth)** instead of: *They took cash in lieu of the prize they had won.* ◇ *We work on Saturdays and have a day off in lieu during the week.* ▶ **zamiast czegoś**

Lieut. = LIEUTENANT

L

lieutenant /lefˈtenənt; US luːˈt-/ noun [C] (abbr. **Lieut.**; **Lt**) an officer at a middle level in the army, navy or air force ▶ **porucznik**

life /laɪf/ noun (pl. **lives** /laɪvz/) **1** [U] the quality that people, animals or plants have when they are not dead: *Do you believe in life after death?* ◇ *to bring somebody/come back to life* ▶ **życie 2** [C,U] the state of being alive as a human being: *The hostages were rescued without loss of life* (bez ofiar w ludziach). ◇ *Would you **risk** your **life** to protect your property?* ◇ *Doctors fought all night to **save** her **life**.* ▶ **życie 3** [U] living things: *Life on earth began in a very simple form.* ◇ *No life was found on the moon.* ◇ *There was no sign of life in the deserted house.* ◇ *plant life* ◇ *Three lives were lost* (trzy osoby zginęły) *in the fire.* ▶ **życie 4** [C,U] the period during which sb/sth is alive or exists: *I've lived in this town **all my life**.* ◇ *I spent my early life in London.* ◇ *to have a short/long/exciting life* ◇ *She was sent to prison **for life**./She was sentenced to life in prison.* Skazano ją na dożywocie. ◇ *life* (dożywotnie) *membership of a club* ▶ **życie 5** [U] the things that you may experience while you are alive: *Life can be hard for a single parent.* ◇ *I'm not happy with the situation, but I suppose **that's life**.* ▶ **życie 6** [C,U] a way of living: *They went to America to **start a new life**.* ◇ *They **lead a** busy **life**.* Są bardzo zajęci. ◇ *married life* ▶ **życie 7** [U] energy; activity: *Young children are **full of life**.* ◇ *This town **comes to life*** (ożywia się) *in the evenings.* ▶ **życie 8** [U] something that really exists and is not just a story, a picture, etc.: *I wonder what that actor's like **in real life**.* ◇ *Do you draw people **from life** or from photographs?* ▶ **życie 9** [C] the story of sb's life: *He's writing a life of John Lennon.* ▶ **biografia**

IDM **a fact of life** → FACT

the facts of life → FACT

full of beans/life → FULL[1]

get a life (informal) (used to tell sb to stop being boring and do sth more interesting) ▶ **wymyśl coś innego!, zmień temat!**

have the time of your life → TIME[1]

lose your life → LOSE

a matter of life and/or death → MATTER[1]

take your (own) life to kill yourself ▶ **odbierać sobie życie**

this is the life (used to say that you are very happy with your present circumstances) ▶ **to dopiero jest życie!**

a walk of life → WALK[2]

a/sb's way of life → WAY[1]

ˌlife-and-ˈdeath (also ˌ**life-or-ˈdeath**) adj. [only before a noun] very serious or dangerous: *a life-and-death struggle/matter/decision* ▶ **na śmierć i życie**, (*kwestia*) **życia i śmierci**

lifebelt /ˈlaɪfbelt/ (also **lifebuoy** /ˈlaɪfbɔɪ/) noun [C] (Brit.) a ring that is made from light material which will float. A **lifebelt** is thrown to a person who has fallen into water to stop them from sinking. ▶ **koło ratunkowe**

lifeboat /ˈlaɪfbəʊt/ noun [C] **1** a special boat that is used for rescuing people who are in danger at sea ▶ **łódź ratownicza** ➲ picture on **page A6 2** a small boat that is carried on a large ship and that is used to escape from the ship if it is in danger of sinking ▶ **łódź ratunkowa** ➲ note at **boat**

lifebuoy = LIFEBELT

ˈlife coach noun [C] a person who is employed by sb to give them advice about how to achieve the things they want in their life and work ▶ **trener rozwoju osobistego**

ˈlife cycle noun [C] the series of forms into which a living thing changes as it develops ▶ **cykl życia**

ˈlife expectancy noun [C,U] (pl. **life expectancies**) the number of years that a person is likely to live ▶ **średnia długość życia**

lifeguard /ˈlaɪfɡɑːd/ noun [C] a person at a beach or swimming pool whose job is to rescue people who are in difficulty in the water ▶ **ratowni-k/czka**

ˈlife jacket (especially US ˈ**life vest**) noun [C] a plastic or rubber jacket without sleeves that can be filled with air. A life jacket is used to make sb float if they fall into water. ▶ **kamizelka ratunkowa**

lifeless /ˈlaɪfləs/ adj. **1** dead or appearing to be dead ▶ **nieżywy, martwy 2** without energy or interest ▶ **bez życia/energii** SYN **dull**

lifelike /ˈlaɪflaɪk/ adj. looking like a real person or thing: *The flowers are made of silk but they are very lifelike.* ▶ **jak żywy**

lifeline /ˈlaɪflaɪn/ noun [C] something that is very important for sb and that they depend on: *For many old people the radio is a lifeline* (jedynym oknem na świat). ▶ **zbawienie**

lifelong /ˈlaɪflɒŋ/ adj. [only before a noun] for all of your life: *a lifelong friend* dozgonny przyjaciel ▶ **na całe życie**

ˌlife-or-ˈdeath = LIFE-AND-DEATH

lifesaver /ˈlaɪfseɪvə(r)/ noun [C] a thing that helps sb in a difficult situation; sth that saves sb's life: *The new drug is a potential lifesaver.* ▶ (*przen.*) **wybawienie, środek itp. ratujący życie**

ˈlife-saving adj. [usually before a noun] that is going to save sb's life: *a life-saving heart operation* ▶ **ratujący życie** ■ ˈ**life-saving** noun [U] the skills needed to save sb who is in water and is **drowning**: *a life-saving qualification* ▶ **ratownictwo**

ˈlife sentence noun [C] the punishment by which sb spends the rest of their life in prison ▶ **dożywocie**

ˈlife-size (also ˈ**life-sized**) adj. of the same size as the real person or thing: *a life-sized statue* ▶ **wielkości naturalnej**

lifespan /ˈlaɪfspæn/ noun [C] the length of time that sth is likely to live, work, last, etc.: *A mosquito has a lifespan of only a few days.* ▶ **życie, okres** (*np. pracy, trwania*)

ˈlife story noun [C] (pl. **life stories**) the story of sb's life ▶ **historia życia**

lifestyle /ˈlaɪfstaɪl/ noun [C] the way that you live ▶ **styl/tryb życia**

ˌlife supˈport noun [U] the fact of sb being on a **life-support machine**: *Families want the right to refuse life support.* ◇ *She's critically ill, **on life support**.* ▶ **utrzymywanie kogoś przy życiu za pomocą respiratora**

ˌlife-supˈport machine (also ˌ**life-supˈport system**) noun [C] a piece of equipment that keeps sb alive when they are extremely ill and cannot breathe without help: *He was put on a life-support machine in intensive care.* ▶ **respirator**

ˈlife-threatening adj. that is likely to kill sb ▶ **zagrażający życiu**

lifetime /ˈlaɪftaɪm/ noun [C] the period of time that sb is alive: *It's **a chance of a lifetime*** (życiowa okazja). *Don't miss it!* ▶ **życie**

ˈlife vest (especially US) = LIFE JACKET

lift[1] /lɪft/ verb **1** [T] **lift sb/sth (up)** to move sb/sth to a higher level or position: *He lifted the child up onto his shoulders.* ◇ *Lift your arm very gently and see if it hurts.* ◇ *It took two men to lift the piano.* ▶ **podnosić 2** [T] to move sb/sth from one place or position to another: *She lifted the suitcase down* (zdjęła walizkę) *from the rack.* ▶ **podnosić 3** [T] to end or remove a rule, law, etc.: *The ban on public meetings has been lifted.* ▶ **znosić 4** [I,T] to become or make sb happier: *The news lifted our spirits.* ◇ *Our* *spirits lifted.* Nabraliśmy otuchy. ▶ **podnosić kogoś** (*na duchu*) **5** [I] to rise up and disappear: *The mist lifted towards the end of the morning.* ▶ **podnosić się, rozwiewać się 6** [T] (informal) **lift sth (from sb/sth)** to steal or copy sth: *Most of his essay was lifted straight from the textbook.* ▶ **zwędzić, kopiować** ➲ look at **shoplifting**

PHR V **lift off** (used about a **spacecraft**) to rise straight up from the ground ▶ **startować**

lift² /lɪft/ noun **1** (US **elevator** /ˈelɪveɪtə(r)/) [C] a machine in a large building that is used for carrying people or goods from one floor to another: *It's on the third floor so we'd better **take the lift**.* ▶ **winda 2** [C] a free ride in a car, etc.: *Can you give me **a lift*** (czy możesz mnie podwieźć) *to the station, please?* ◇ *I got a lift* (podwiózł mnie) *from a passing car.* ▶ **podwiezienie 3** [sing.] (informal) a feeling of being happier or more confident than before: *Passing the exam gave him a real lift.* ▶ **podniesienie na duchu, ożywienie 4** [sing.] the act of moving or being moved to a higher position: *Her only reaction was a slight lift of one eyebrow.* ▶ **podniesienie**

IDM **thumb a lift** → THUMB²

ˈlift-off noun [C] the start of the flight of a **spacecraft** when it leaves the ground ▶ **start**

ligament /ˈlɪɡəmənt/ noun [C] a short, strong part inside the body that joins a bone to another bone ▶ **wiązadło** ➲ look at **tendon**

lights

light¹ /laɪt/ noun **1** [U,C] the energy from the sun, a lamp, etc. that allows you to see things: *a beam/ray of light* ◇ *The light was too dim for us to read by.* ◇ *Strong light is bad for the eyes.* ◇ *We could see strange lights in the sky.* ▶ **światło, oświetlenie**

> You may see things by **sunlight**, **moonlight**, **firelight**, **candlelight** or **lamplight**.

2 [C] something that produces light, for example an electric lamp: *Suddenly all the lights went out/came on.* ◇ *the lights of the city in the distance* ◇ *If the lights are red, stop!* ◇ *That car hasn't got its lights on.* ◇ *a neon light* lampa jarzeniowa ▶ **światło**

> A light may be **on** or **off**. You **put**, **switch** or **turn** a **light on** or **off** and **put** or **turn a light out**: *Shall I put the light on? It's getting dark in here.* ◇ *Please turn the lights out before you leave.*

3 [C] something, for example a match, that can be used to light a cigarette, start a fire, etc.: *Have you got a light?* ▶ **ogień**

IDM **bring sth to light** to make sth known ▶ **wyciągać coś na światło dzienne**

cast light on sth → CAST¹

come to light to become known ▶ **wychodzić na jaw**

give sb/get the green light → GREEN¹

in a good, bad, etc. light (used about the way that sth is seen or described by other people) well, badly, etc.: *The newspapers often portray his behaviour in a bad light.* ▶ **w dobrym/złym świetle**

in the light of sth because of; considering ▶ **w świetle czegoś**

set light to sth to cause sth to start burning ▶ **podpalać**

shed light on sth → SHED²

light² /laɪt/ adj. **1** having a lot of light: *In summer it's still light* (jest jeszcze widno) *at 10 o' clock.* ◇ *a light room* ▶ **jasny, dobrze oświetlony** OPP **dark 2** pale: *a light-blue* (jasnoniebieski) *sweater* ▶ **jasny** OPP **dark 3** not of great weight: *Carry this bag – it's the lightest.* ◇ *light clothes* ◇ *I've lost weight – I'm five kilos lighter* (ważę o pięć kilo mniej) *than I used to be.* ▶ **lekki** OPP **heavy 4** not using much force: *a light touch on the shoulder* ▶ **lekki 5** not tiring or difficult: *light exercise* ◇ *light entertainment/reading* ◇ *After his accident he was moved to lighter work.* ▶ **lekki, łatwy 6** not great in amount, degree, etc.: *Traffic in London is light on a Sunday.* ◇ *a light prison sentence* ◇ *a light wind* ◇ *a light breakfast* ▶ **niewielki, lekki 7** [only before a noun] (used about sleep) not deep: *I'm a light sleeper, so the slightest noise wakes me.* ▶ **lekki**

■ **lightness** noun [U] ▶ **lekkość**

light³ /laɪt/ verb (pt, pp **lit**) **1** [I,T] to begin or to make sth begin to burn: *The gas cooker won't light.* ◇ *to light a fire* ▶ **zapalać (się)**

> Słowo **lighted** występuje w znaczeniu przymiotnikowym przed rzeczownikiem, natomiast **lit** jako forma *past participle* czasownika: *Candles were lit in memory of the dead.* ◇ *The church was full of lighted candles.*

2 [T] to give light to sth: *The street is well/badly lit at night.* ◇ *We only had a small torch to light our way through the forest.* ▶ **oświetlać**

PHR V **light up** (used about sb's face, eyes, etc.) to become bright with happiness or excitement ▶ (*twarz itp.*) **rozjaśniać się,** (*oczy*) **zapalać się**

light (sth) up to start smoking a cigarette: *Several people got off the train and lit up immediately.* ▶ **zapalać** (*papierosa*)

light sth up to make sth bright with light: *The fireworks lit up the whole sky.* ▶ **oświetlać**

light⁴ /laɪt/ adv. without much luggage: *I always travel light.* ▶ **bez ciężkiego/dużego bagażu**

ˈlight bulb = BULB (1)

lighted past tense, past participle of **light³**

lighten /ˈlaɪtn/ verb [I,T] **1** to become or to make sth brighter ▶ **rozjaśniać (się) 2** to become lighter in weight or to make sth lighter ▶ **stawać się lżejszym; zmniejszać ciężar**

lighter = CIGARETTE LIGHTER

ˌlight-ˈheaded adj. not in complete control of your thoughts and movements ▶ **cierpiący na zawroty głowy**

L

ˌ**light-ˈhearted** adj. **1** intended to be funny and enjoyable ▶ **zabawny**, **rozrywkowy** **2** happy and without problems ▶ **niefrasobliwy**, **wesoły**

lighthouse /ˈlaɪthaʊs/ noun [C] a tall building with a light at the top to warn ships of danger near the coast ▶ **latarnia morska** ➲ picture on **page A2**

lighting /ˈlaɪtɪŋ/ noun [U] the quality or type of lights used in a room, building, etc. ▶ **oświetlenie**

🔑**lightly** /ˈlaɪtli/ adv. **1** gently; with very little force: *He touched her lightly on the arm.* ▶ **lekko** **2** only a little; not much: *lightly cooked/spiced/whisked* ▶ **lekko**, **słabo** **3** not seriously; without serious thought: *We do not take our customers' complaints lightly.* ▶ **niefrasobliwie**

IDM **get off/be let off lightly** to avoid serious punishment or trouble ▶ **uniknąć surowej kary/poważnych kłopotów**; **otrzymać łagodny wyrok**

lightning¹ /ˈlaɪtnɪŋ/ noun [U] a bright flash of light that appears in the sky during a storm: *The tree was **struck by lightning** and burst into flames.* ◇ *a flash of lightning* błyskawica ◇ *a lightning conductor* piorunochron ◇ *forked/sheet lightning* błyskawica zygzakowata/płaska ▶ **piorun** ➲ note at **storm** ➲ look at **thunder** ➲ picture on **page A16**

lightning² /ˈlaɪtnɪŋ/ adj. [only before a noun] very quick or sudden: *a lightning attack* ▶ **błyskawiczny**

lightweight /ˈlaɪtweɪt/ adj. **1** (used about a boxer, etc.) in one of the lightest weight groups: *a lightweight boxing champion* ▶ (*bokser itp.*) **wagi lekkiej** **2** weighing less than usual: *a lightweight suit for the summer* ▶ **lekki**, **lżejszy**

■ **lightweight** noun [C] **1** a boxer, etc. in one of the lightest weight groups ▶ **bokser wagi lekkiej** **2** (informal) a person or thing of little importance or influence: *a political lightweight* ◇ *He's an intellectual lightweight.* ▶ **osoba/rzecz przeciętna**

ˈ**light year** noun [C] the distance that light travels in one year, 9.4607×10^{12} kilometres: *The nearest star to earth is about 4 light years away.* ▶ **rok świetlny**

likable = LIKEABLE

🔑**like¹** /laɪk/ prep. **1** similar to sb/sth: *You **look** very/just/exactly **like** your father.* ◇ *Those two singers **sound like** cats!* ◇ *Your house is **nothing like** how I imagined it.* ▶ **jak**, **podobny do kogoś/czegoś** ➲ note at **how**

> Kiedy prosimy o opis kogoś/czegoś, mówimy **What is he/she/it like?**: *Tell me about your town. What's it like?* ◇ *What was it like being interviewed on TV?* W odpowiedzi nie używa się **like**: *'What's your brother like?' 'He's tall and fair, and quite serious.'* Kiedy pytamy tylko o wygląd danej osoby lub rzeczy, mówimy **What does he/she/it look like?** W odpowiedzi nie używa się **look like**: *'What does your brother look like?' 'He's tall and fair, with blue eyes.'*

2 [in compounds] in the manner of; similar to: *childlike innocence/simplicity* ◇ *a very lifelike* (jak żywy) *statue* ◇ *ladylike* ◇ *soldier-like* ▶ **jak**, **po** (*np. żołniersku*) **3** typical of a particular person: *It was just like Maria to be late.* ▶ **typowy**

> Zwróć uwagę na różnicę w znaczeniu między **as** i **like**, kiedy mówimy o czyimś zawodzie, zajęciu itp: *Geoff acted as* (był) *our leader.* ◇ *Geoff acted like* (zachowywał się jak) *our leader.*

4 in the same way as sb/sth: *Stop behaving like children.* ◇ *That's not right. Do it like this* (zrób to tak). ▶ **tak samo, jak** ➲ note at **as** **5** for example; such as: *They enjoy most team games, like football and rugby.* ▶ **taki jak** ➲ note at **as** **6** (slang) (used before saying what sb said, how sb felt, etc.): *When I saw the colour of my hair I was like 'Wow, I can't believe it!'* ▶ (*stosuje się przed podaniem, co ktoś powiedział/odczuwał itp.*)

IDM **like anything** (informal) very much, fast, hard, etc.: *We had to pedal like anything to get up the hill.* ▶ **bardzo mocno/ciężko/szybko itp.**

like hell (informal) very much; with a lot of effort: *I'm working like hell at the moment.* ▶ **jak diabli**

nothing like → NOTHING

something like → SOMETHING

that's more like it (used to say that sth is better than before): *The sun's coming out now – that's more like it!* ▶ **tak jest o wiele lepiej!**

like² /laɪk/ conj. (informal) **1** in the same way as: *She can't draw like her sister can.* ▶ **tak, jak** **2** as if: *She acts like she owns the place.* ▶ **jak gdyby** ➲ note at **as**

🔑**like³** /laɪk/ verb [T] **1 like sb/sth; like doing sth; like to do sth; like sth about sb/sth** to find sb/sth pleasant; to enjoy sth: *He's nice. I like him a lot.* ◇ *Do you like their new flat?* ◇ *How do you like John's new girlfriend?* ◇ *I like my coffee strong.* ◇ *I like playing tennis.* ◇ *I like to go to the cinema on Thursdays.* ◇ *What is it you like about Sarah so much?* ◇ *She didn't like it when I shouted at her.* ◇ *I don't like him borrowing my things without asking.* ◇ *The job seems strange at first, but you'll **get to like** it.* ◇ *I don't **like the look/sound/idea/thought of** that.* ▶ **lubić**, **podobać się** OPP **dislike** ➲ note at **dislike**

> Jeżeli czasownik **like** występuje w znaczeniu „mieć coś w zwyczaju" lub „uważać, że dobrze jest coś robić", wtedy następujący po nim czasownik ma formę bezokolicznika: *I like to get up early so that I can go for a run before breakfast.* Por. **like doing sth** oraz **like to do sth**. Wyrażenia **like doing sth** używamy, kiedy mówimy o robieniu rzeczy, które sprawiają nam przyjemność: *I like listening to music.* Kiedy chcemy zrobić coś, za czym niekoniecznie przepadamy, ale należy to do naszej rutyny lub jest dla nas niezbędne, wówczas używamy wyrażenia **like to do sth**: *I like to go to the dentist every six months.*

2 to want: *Do what you like. I don't care.* ◇ *We can go whenever you like.* ◇ *I didn't like to disturb you while you were eating.* ▶ **chcieć**

> Użycie wyrażenia **would like** jest bardziej uprzejme niż zastosowanie czasownika **want**: *I would like* (chciałbym) *some more cake, please.* ◇ *Would you like something to eat?* ◇ *How would you like to come to Scotland with us?* ◇ *I'd like to speak to the manager.* Po **would like** zawsze występuje bezokolicznik, nigdy forma *-ing* czasownika.

> **like**
>
> Synonimami **like** są wyrażenia **enjoy sth**, **spend a lot of time doing sth**, **love (doing) sth**, **be keen on (doing) sth** lub **be really into sth**. Kiedy chcemy się więcej dowiedzieć na jakiś temat, wtedy możemy powiedzieć **be interested in sth**: *She enjoys playing tennis.* ◇ *He loves (playing) football.* ◇ *I'm keen on gardening.* ◇ *I'm really into jazz.* ◇ *He's very interested in the history of tennis.*

IDM **I like that!** (Brit., old-fashioned, informal) (used for saying that sth is not true or not fair) ▶ **a to dobre!**, **bardzo mądrze!**

if you like (used for agreeing with sb or suggesting sth in a polite way): *'Shall we stop for a rest?' 'Yes, if you like.'* ▶ **jeśli masz na to ochotę**

like the look/sound of sb/sth to have a good impression of sb/sth after seeing or hearing about them or it: *I like the sound of John's new school.* Na podstawie tego, co o niej słyszę, szkoła Johna bardzo mi się podoba. ▶ (*to co zobaczono/usłyszano*) **podobać się**

like⁴ /laɪk/ noun **1** (**likes**) [pl.] things that you like: *Tell me about some of your **likes and dislikes**.* Powiedz mi, co lubisz, a czego nie lubisz. ▶ **upodobania 2** [sing.] a person or thing that is similar to sb/sth else: *I enjoy going round castles, old churches **and the like.*** ◇ *She was a great singer, and we may never see her like/the like of her again.* ▶ **osoba lub rzecz podobna**

like[5] /laɪk/ adj. (formal) ▶ **taki sam**, **podobny**

likeable (also **likable**) /ˈlaɪkəbl/ adj. (used about a person) easy to like; pleasant ▶ **sympatyczny**

likelihood /ˈlaɪklihʊd/ noun [U] the chance of sth happening; how likely sth is to happen: *There seems very little likelihood of* (są małe szanse na) *success.* ▶ **prawdopodobieństwo** SYN **probability**

⚷ **likely** /ˈlaɪkli/ adv. **1 likely (to do sth)** probable or expected: *Do you think it's likely to rain?* ◇ *The boss is not likely to agree.* ◇ *It's not likely that the boss will agree.* ▶ **prawdopodobnie**

IDM **as likely as not**; **most/very likely** very probably ▶ **prawdopodobnie**

not likely! (informal) certainly not ▶ **niemożliwe!**, **na pewno nie!**

■ **likely** adj. (**likelier**; **likeliest**) probably suitable: *a likely candidate for the job* ▶ **możliwy** ➲ note at **probable**

ˌlike-ˈminded adj. having similar ideas and interests: *The club offers an opportunity for like-minded people to get together.* ▶ **o podobnych zapatrywaniach/zainteresowaniach**

liken /ˈlaɪkən/ verb [T] (formal) **liken sb/sth to sb/sth** to compare one person or thing with another: *This young artist has been likened to Picasso.* ▶ **porównywać**

likeness /ˈlaɪknəs/ noun [C,U] the fact of being similar in appearance; an example of this: *The witness's drawing turned out to be **a good likeness of** the attacker.* ▶ **podobieństwo**, **podobizna**

likewise /ˈlaɪkwaɪz/ adv. (formal) the same; in a similar way: *I intend to send a letter of apology and suggest that you do likewise.* ▶ **podobnie**

liking /ˈlaɪkɪŋ/ noun [sing.] **a liking (for sb/sth)** the feeling that you like sb/sth: *I have a liking for spicy food.* Lubię pikantne jedzenie. ◇ *I hope the kids **take a liking to*** (polubią) *their new teacher.* ▶ **upodobanie**

IDM **be to your liking** (formal) to be the way that you like sth: *I trust that everything is to your liking.* Mam nadzieję, że wszystko państwu odpowiada. ▶ **odpowiadać (komuś)**, (*potrawy*) **smakować**

too ... for your liking that you do not like because he/she/it has too much of a particular quality: *The music was a bit too loud for my liking.* ▶ **zbyt ... jak na czyjś gust**

lilac /ˈlaɪlək/ noun [C,U] **1** a tree or large bush that has large purple or white flowers in spring ▶ (*bot.*) **bez 2** a pale purple colour ▶ **kolor liliowy**

■ **lilac** adj. ▶ **liliowy**

lilo (also **Li-lo**™) /ˈlaɪləʊ/ noun [C] (pl. **lilos**) (Brit.) a plastic or rubber bed that you fill with air when you want to use it. A **Lilo** is used on the beach or for camping. ▶ **materac nadmuchiwany**

lilt /lɪlt/ noun [sing.] **1** the pleasant way in which a person's voice rises and falls: *Her voice had a soft Welsh lilt to it.* ▶ **śpiewna intonacja 2** a regular rising and falling pattern in music, with a strong rhythm: *Many of his patriotic songs have a stirring lilt.* ▶ **rytmiczna i śpiewna linia melodyczna**

■ **lilting** adj. ▶ **melodyjny**, **śpiewny**

lily /ˈlɪli/ noun [C] (pl. **lilies**) a type of plant that has large white or coloured flowers in the shape of a bell ▶ **lilia** ➲ picture on **page A15**

ˌlily of the ˈvalley noun [C,U] (pl. **lilies of the valley**) a plant with small sweet-smelling white flowers shaped like bells ▶ **konwalia**

limb /lɪm/ noun [C] **1** a leg or an arm of a person ▶ **kończyna 2** one of the main branches of a tree ▶ **konar**

IDM **out on a limb** without the support of other people: *I'm willing to go out on a limb* (jestem skłonny narazić się) *and say I disagree with the decision.* ▶ **bez niczyjej pomocy**

limbo /ˈlɪmbəʊ/ noun **1** [C] a West Indian dance in which you lean backwards and go under a bar which is made lower each time you go under it ▶ **rodzaj tańca 2** [U, sing.] a situation in which you are not certain what to do next, cannot take action, etc., especially because you are waiting for sb else to make a decision ▶ **stan zawieszenia**

lime /laɪm/ noun **1** [U] a white substance that is used in traditional building methods and also to help plants grow ▶ **wapno 2** [C] a fruit that looks like a small green lemon ▶ **limon(k)a** ➲ picture on **page A12 3** [U] (also ˌ**lime ˈgreen**) a yellowish-green colour ▶ **kolor żółtozielony 4** (also **ˈlime tree**) [C] a large tree with smooth pale green leaves and yellow flowers ▶ **lipa**

the **limelight** /ˈlaɪmlaɪt/ noun [U] the centre of public attention: *to be in/out of the limelight* ▶ **centrum zainteresowania**

limerick /ˈlɪmərɪk/ noun [C] a type of humorous poem with five lines. The first two rhyme with the last. ▶ **limeryk**

limescale /ˈlaɪmskeɪl/ noun [U] (Brit.) the hard white substance that is left by water on the inside of pipes, etc. ▶ (*osad wapienny*) **kamień**

limestone /ˈlaɪmstəʊn/ noun [U] a type of white rock that is used as a building material and in making cement ▶ **wapień**

⚷ **limit**[1] /ˈlɪmɪt/ noun [C] **1** the greatest or smallest amount of sth that is allowed or possible: *a speed/age/time limit* ◇ *He was fined for exceeding the speed limit.* ◇ *There's a limit to the amount of time I'm prepared to spend on this.* ◇ *I had to stretch myself **to the limit*** (musiałem dać z siebie wszystko) *to finish the race.* ▶ **ograniczenie**, **granica 2** the outside edge of a place or area: *the city limits* ◇ *Lorries are not allowed within a two-mile limit of the town centre.* Ciężarówki mają zakaz wjazdu do dwukilometrowej strefy w centrum miasta. ▶ **granica**

IDM **off limits** (used about a place) where people are not allowed to go ▶ **z zakazem wstępu**

within limits only up to a reasonable point or amount ▶ **w granicach (rozsądku)**

⚷ **limit**[2] /ˈlɪmɪt/ verb [T] **limit sb/sth (to sth)** to keep sb/sth within or below a certain amount, size, degree or area: *I'm limiting myself to one cup of coffee a day.* ◇ *Red squirrels are limited* (obszar występowania rudych wiewiórek ograniczony jest) *to a few areas in Britain.* ▶ **ograniczać**

limitation /ˌlɪmɪˈteɪʃn/ noun **1** [C,U] **(a) limitation (on sth)** the act of limiting or controlling sth; a condition that puts a limit on sth: *There are no limitations on what we can do.* ▶ **ograniczenie**, **zastrzeżenie 2** (**limitations**) [pl.] things that you cannot do: *It is important to know your own limitations.* ▶ **granica możliwości**

⚷ **limited** /ˈlɪmɪtɪd/ adj. small in number, amount, etc.: *Book early for the show because there are only a limited number of seats available.* ▶ **ograniczony** OPP **unlimited**

ˌlimited ˈcompany noun [C] (abbr. **Ltd** /ˈlɪmətɪd/) a company whose owners only have to pay a limited amount of the money that they owe if the company fails ▶ **spółka z ograniczoną odpowiedzialnością**

limousine /ˈlɪməziːn; ˌlɪməˈziːn/ (also informal **limo** /ˈlɪməʊ/) noun [C] a large expensive car that usually has a sheet of glass between the driver and the passengers in the back ▶ **limuzyna**

limp[1] /lɪmp/ adj. not firm or strong: *You should put those flowers in water before they go limp.* ▶ **miękki**; **słaby**, **omdlały**

limp[2] /lɪmp/ verb [I] to walk with difficulty because you have hurt your leg or foot: *The goalkeeper limped off the field with a twisted ankle.* ◇ *After the accident the ship limped back* (wolno popłynął) *to the harbour.* ▶ **kuśtykać**

■ **limp** noun [sing.]: *to walk with a bad limp* mocno utykać ▶ **kuśtykanie**

linchpin (also **lynchpin**) /ˈlɪntʃpɪn/ noun [C] a person or thing that is the most important part of an organization, a plan, etc., because everything else depends on them or it ▶ (*przen.*) **filar**

line[1] /laɪn/ noun **1** [C] a long thin mark on the surface of sth or on the ground: *to draw a line* ◇ *a straight/wiggly/dotted line* ◇ *The old lady had lines* (zmarszczki) *on her forehead.* ◇ *The ball was definitely over the line.* ◇ *the finishing line* (meta) *of a race* ▶ **linia 2** [C] a border or limit between one place or thing and another: *to cross state lines* ◇ *There's a thin line between showing interest and being nosy.* ▶ **granica 3** [C] a row of people, things, words on a page, etc.: *There was a long line of people waiting at the Post Office.* ◇ *a five-line poem* ◇ *Start each paragraph on a new line.* ▶ **kolejka** (*np. w sklepie*); **linia, szereg; wiersz 4** [C] a series of people in a family, or of things or events that follow each other in time: *He comes from* ***a long line of*** *musicians* (pochodzi z rodziny o tradycjach muzycznych). ▶ **linia, ród 5** (**lines**) [pl.] the words that are spoken by an actor in a play, etc.: *to learn your lines* ▶ **rola** (*aktora*) **6** [C] a piece of rope or string: *Hang out the clothes on the (washing) line, please.* ◇ *a fishing line* żyłka wędkarska ▶ **sznurek, lina 7** [C] a telephone or electricity wire or connection: *I'm sorry – the line is engaged. Can you try again later?* ◇ *I'll just check for you. Can you* ***hold the line*** (proszę się nie rozłączać)? ▶ **linia; przewód 8** [C] a section of railway track: *The accident was caused by a cow on the line.* ▶ **linia, tor 9** [C, usually sing.] a direction or course of movement, thought or action: *He was so drunk he couldn't walk* ***in a straight line.*** ◇ *Could you move, please? You're in my line of vision* (w moim polu widzenia). ◇ *The answer's not quite correct, but you're* ***on the right lines.*** ◇ *The two countries' economies are developing* ***along*** *similar* ***lines.*** ◇ *a line of argument* teza, na której oparto dowód/wywód ▶ **kurs/kierunek** (*działania*) **10** [C] something that you do as a job, do well, or enjoy doing: *What* ***line of business/work*** *are you in?* ▶ **dziedzina, branża 11** [sing.] one type of goods in a shop, etc.: *a new line in environment-friendly detergents* ▶ **linia** (*produktów/towarów*), **gama** (*artykułów handlowych*) **12** [C] a company that provides transport by air, ship, etc.: *an airline* ▶ **linia** (*np. lotnicza, morska*) **13** [C] the place where an army is fighting: *There's renewed fighting on* ***the front line.*** ▶ **linia 14** [C] a route that people send messages, etc. along ▶ **linia**

IDM **draw the line at sth/doing sth** → DRAW[1]

drop sb a line → DROP[1]

in line for sth likely to get sth: *You could be in line for promotion if you keep working like this.* ▶ **w kolejce (do czegoś)**

be in line with sth to be similar to sth; to be in agreement with sth: *These changes will bring the industry in line with the new laws.* ▶ **pasować (do czegoś), być zgodnym z czymś**

on line connected to or available on a computer system ▶ **online**

overstep the mark/line → OVERSTEP

somewhere along/down the line → SOMEWHERE

stand in/on line (US) to wait in a queue ▶ **stać w kolejce**

take a hard line (on sth) → HARD[1]

toe the (party) line → TOE[2]

line[2] /laɪn/ verb [T] **1** [often passive] to cover the inside surface of sth with a different material ▶ **podszywać, wykładać (coś czymś) 2 line sth (with sth)** [usually passive] to form lines or rows along sth: *The walls were lined with books.* Ściany były wyłożone książkami. ◇ *Crowds lined the streets* (wzdłuż ulic ustawiły się tłumy ludzi) *to watch the race.*

PHR V **line up (for sth)** to form a line of people ▶ **ustawiać się w kolejce** SYN **queue**

line sth up to arrange or organize sth: *She lined the bottles up on the shelf.* ▶ **zaplanować; ustawiać**

linear /ˈlɪniə(r)/ adj. **1** of or in lines: *In his art he broke the laws of scientific linear perspective.* ▶ **liniowy 2** going from one thing to another in a single series of stages: *Students do not always progress in a linear fashion.* ▶ **linearny 3** of length: *linear measurement* ▶ **liniowy**

lined /laɪnd/ adj. **1** covered in lines: *a face lined with age* ◇ *lined paper* ▶ (*papier itp.*) **w linie;** (*twarz itp.*) **pomarszczony, pokryty zmarszczkami 2** (**-lined**) [in compounds] having the object mentioned all along the side(s); having the inside surface covered with the material mentioned: *a tree-lined avenue* ulica obsadzona szpalerem drzew ◇ *fur-lined boots* botki wykładane futrem

ˈ**line dancing** noun [U] a type of dancing originally from the US, in which people dance in lines, all doing a complicated series of steps at the same time ▶ **rodzaj tańca country** (*tancerze ustawiają się w kilku rzędach*)

linen /ˈlɪnɪn/ noun [U] **1** a type of strong cloth that is made from a natural substance from a plant ▶ **płótno lniane 2** sheets and other types of cloth used in the house to cover beds, tables, etc.: *bedlinen* ▶ **bielizna** (*np. pościelowa, stołowa*)

liner /ˈlaɪnə(r)/ noun [C] **1** a large ship that carries people, etc. long distances ▶ **statek dalekomorski** ➲ look at **ship** ➲ note at **boat**, picture at **boat** ➲ picture on **page A6 2** something that is put inside sth else to keep it clean or protect it. A **liner** is usually thrown away after it has been used: *a dustbin liner* worek do pojemnika na śmieci ▶ **wymienny wkład** (*chroniący pojemnik, wnętrze czegoś*)

linesman /ˈlaɪnzmən/ noun [C] an official person in some games such as football or tennis. The linesman watches to see if a player breaks a rule or if the ball goes over the line. ▶ **sędzia liniowy**

linger /ˈlɪŋgə(r)/ verb [I] **1 linger (on)** to continue to exist for longer than expected: *The smell of her perfume lingered on long after she had left.* ▶ (*zapach*) **długo się unosić 2** to stay somewhere longer because you do not want to leave; to spend a long time doing sth: *She lingered for a few minutes to talk to Nick.* ◇ *to linger over a meal* przeciągać posiłek ▶ **przewlekać pobyt; robić coś bez pośpiechu 3 linger (on sb/sth)** to continue to look at sb/sth or think about sb/sth for longer than usual: *His eyes lingered on the money in her bag.* ▶ **zatrzymywać dłużej wzrok/myśli na kimś/czymś**

lingerie /ˈlænʒəri; US ˌlɑːndʒəˈreɪ/ noun [U] (used in shops, etc.) women's underwear ▶ **bielizna damska**

linguist /ˈlɪŋgwɪst/ noun [C] a person who is good at learning foreign languages; a person who studies or teaches language(s) ▶ **językoznawca, lingwista**

linguistic /lɪŋˈgwɪstɪk/ adj. connected with language or the study of language ▶ **językoznawczy, językowy**

linguistics /lɪŋˈgwɪstɪks/ noun [U] the scientific study of language ▶ **językoznawstwo, lingwistyka**

lining /ˈlaɪnɪŋ/ noun [C,U] material that covers the inside surface of sth: *I've torn the lining of my coat.* ▶ **podszewka, okładzina**

IDM **every cloud has a silver lining** → CLOUD[1]

link[1] /lɪŋk/ noun [C] **1 a link (between A and B); a link (with sb/sth)** a connection or relationship between two or more people or things: *There is a strong link between smoking and heart disease.* ▶ **powiązanie; łącznik 2** a means of travelling or communicating between two places: *To visit similar websites to this one, click on the links at the bottom of the page.* ▶ **połączenie**, **link 3** one ring of a chain ▶ **ogniwo**

link² /lɪŋk/ verb [T] **link A to/with B**; **link A and B (together)** to make a connection between two or more people or things: *The new bridge will link the island to the mainland.* ◇ *The computers are linked together in a network.* ◇ *to link arms* brać (się/kogoś) za ręce ▶ **łączyć**
PHR V **link (sth) up (with sb/sth)** to join (sth) together (with sb/sth): *All our branches are linked up by computer.* Wszystkie nasze oddziały połączone są siecią komputerową. ▶ **łączyć coś/się (z kimś/czymś)**

'link-up noun [C] the joining together or connection of two or more things ▶ **połączenie**

linoleum /lɪ'nəʊliəm/ (also informal **lino** /'laɪnəʊ/) noun [U] a type of plastic covering for floors ▶ **linoleum**

linseed oil /ˌlɪnsiːd 'ɔɪl/ noun [U] an oil made from flax seeds, used in paint, to protect wood, etc. ▶ **olej lniany**

lion /'laɪən/ noun [C] a large animal of the cat family that lives in Africa and parts of southern Asia ▶ **lew**

> A female lion is called a **lioness** and a young lion is called a **cub**. A male lion has a **mane**. A lion **roars**. ➲ picture on **page A10**

IDM **the lion's share (of sth)** (Brit.) the largest or best part of sth when it is divided ▶ **lwia część (czegoś)**

lip /lɪp/ noun [C] **1** either of the two soft edges at the opening of your mouth: *to kiss somebody on the lips* (w usta) ▶ **warga** ➲ picture at **body**

> You have a **top**/**upper** lip and a **bottom**/**lower** lip.

2 (**-lipped**) [in compounds] having the type of lips mentioned: *thin-lipped* o wąskich wargach ▶ **(***określa rodzaj warg***) 3** the edge of a cup or sth that is shaped like a cup ▶ **brzeg**
IDM **purse your lips** → PURSE²

'lip-read verb [I,T] (pt, pp **lip-read** /-red/) to understand what sb is saying by looking at the movements of their lips ▶ **czytać z ruchu warg**

lipstick /'lɪpstɪk/ noun [C,U] a substance that is used for giving colour to your lips: *to put on some lipstick* ◇ *a new lipstick* ▶ **szminka do ust**

liqueur /lɪ'kjʊə(r); US -'kɜːr/ noun [C,U] a strong sweet alcoholic drink that is often drunk in small quantities after a meal ▶ **likier**

liquid /'lɪkwɪd/ noun [C,U] a substance, for example water, that is not solid or a gas and that can flow or be poured ▶ **płyn**
■ **liquid** adj. ▶ **ciekły**

liquidate /'lɪkwɪdeɪt/ verb [T] **1** to close a business because it has no money left ▶ **likwidować**, **rozwiązywać** (*np. firmę*) **2** to destroy or remove sb/sth that causes problems ▶ **likwidować** (*źródło problemów*)
■ **liquidation** /ˌlɪkwɪ'deɪʃn/ noun [U]: *If the company doesn't receive a big order soon, it will have to **go into liquidation*** (zostanie postawiona w stan likwidacji). ▶ **likwidacja**

liquidize (also **-ise**) /'lɪkwɪdaɪz/ verb [T] to cause sth to become liquid ▶ **miksować**
■ **liquidizer** (also **-iser**) (Brit.) = BLENDER

liquor /'lɪkə(r)/ noun [U] (US) strong alcoholic drinks; spirits ▶ **napój alkoholowy**

liquorice (US **licorice**) /'lɪkərɪʃ/ noun [U] a black substance, made from a plant, that is used in some sweets ▶ **lukrecja**

'liquor store (US) = OFF-LICENCE

lisp /lɪsp/ noun [C] a speech fault in which 's' is pronounced as 'th': *He speaks with a slight lisp.* Lekko sepleni. ▶ **seplenienie**
■ **lisp** verb [I,T] ▶ **seplenić**

list /lɪst/ noun [C] a series of names, figures, items, etc. that are written, printed or said one after another: *a checklist of everything that needs to be done* ◇ *a waiting list* lista oczekujących ◇ *Your name is third **on the list**.* ▶ **lista**, **spis**
■ **list** verb [T]: *to list items in alphabetical order* ▶ **tworzyć listę/spis**; **umieszczać na liście/w spisie**

listen /'lɪsn/ verb [I] **1** **listen (to sb/sth)** to pay attention to sb/sth in order to hear them or it: *Now please listen carefully to what I have to say.* ◇ *to listen to music/the radio* ▶ **słuchać** ➲ note at **hear 2** **listen to sb/sth** to take notice of or believe what sb says: *You should listen to your parents' advice.* ▶ **słuchać**
■ **listen** noun (informal) ***Have a listen*** (posłuchaj) *and see if you can hear anything.* ▶ **słuchanie**
PHR V **listen (out) for sth** to wait to hear sth: *to listen (out) for a knock on the door* ▶ **nadsłuchiwać czegoś**
listen in (on/to sth) to listen to sb else's private conversation: *Have you been listening in on my phone calls?* ▶ **podsłuchiwać** (*czyjąś rozmowę*)

> **listening to music**
>
> A **stereo** is a machine used for listening to CDs, tapes, etc. A small CD or tape player that you carry around with you is called a **personal stereo**. You listen to a personal stereo with **headphones**. When you want to listen to music, etc. you **put** a CD or tape **on**. An **MP3 player** allows you to listen to music files that you have downloaded from your computer. If you want to make the music louder, you **turn** the volume **up**. If you want to make it quieter, you **turn** it **down**.

listener /'lɪsənə(r)/ noun [C] a person who listens: *When I'm unhappy I always phone Charlie – he's a good listener* (potrafi słuchać). ◇ *The new radio show has attracted a record number of listeners.* ▶ **słuchacz/ka**

listless /'lɪstləs/ adj. tired and without energy ▶ **apatyczny**
■ **listlessly** adv. ▶ **apatycznie**

lit past tense, past participle of **light³**

liter (US) = LITRE

literacy /'lɪtərəsi/ noun [U] the ability to read and write ▶ **umiejętność czytania i pisania** OPP **illiteracy** ➲ look at **numeracy**

literal /'lɪtərəl/ adj. **1** (used about the meaning of a word or phrase) original or basic: *The adjective 'big-headed' is hardly ever used in its literal sense.* ▶ **dosłowny**, **podstawowy** ➲ look at **figurative**, **metaphor 2** (used when translating, etc.) dealing with each word separately without looking at the general meaning: *A literal translation is not always accurate.* ▶ **dosłowny**

literally /'lɪtərəli/ adv. **1** according to the basic or original meaning of the word, etc.: *You can't translate these idioms literally.* ▶ **dosłownie 2** (informal) (used for emphasizing sth): *We were literally frozen to death.* ▶ **dosłownie**

literary /'lɪtərəri; US -reri/ adj. of or concerned with literature: *literary criticism* ◇ *a literary journal* ▶ **literacki**

literate /'lɪtərət/ adj. **1** able to read and write ▶ **piśmienny**, **umiejący czytać i pisać** OPP **illiterate** ➲ look at **numerate** ➲ noun **literacy 2** having education or knowledge in a particular area: *computer-literate* znający się na komputerach ▶ **wykształcony**, **obeznany z czymś**

literature /'lɪtrətʃə(r)/ noun [U] **1** writing that is considered to be a work of art: *French literature* ◇ *a great work of literature* ▶ **literatura 2 literature (on sth)** printed material about a particular subject: *promotional literature* ▶ **materiały, literatura** (*np. fachowa*)

> **literature**
> If you study **literature** at school or university, you study **poetry**, **drama** and **fiction**. A person who writes plays is a **playwright** and one who writes poetry is a **poet**. A great work of literature is called a **classic**: *'Alice in Wonderland' is a childhood classic.* The study of Greek and Latin literature is called **classics**.

lithe /laɪð/ adj. (used about a person or their body) moving or bending easily, in a way that is elegant ▶ **gibki, sprężysty**
■ **lithely** adv.: *She moved lithely to the music.* ▶ **sprężyście**

litigate /ˈlɪtɪɡeɪt/ verb [I,T] to take a claim or disagreement to court ▶ **procesować się**; **zaskarżać do sądu**
■ **litigator** noun [C] ▶ **osoba zaskarżająca sprawę do sądu**

litigation /ˌlɪtɪˈɡeɪʃn/ noun [U] the process of taking legal action in a court of law: *The company has been in litigation with its previous auditors for a year.* ◇ *to run the risk of litigation* ryzykować, że zostawnie się pozwanym do sądu ▶ **spór sądowy**

litigious /lɪˈtɪdʒəs/ adj. (formal) too ready to take disagreements to court ▶ **skłonny do pieniactwa**

litre (US **liter**) /ˈliːtə(r)/ noun [C] (abbr. **l**) a measure of liquid: *ten litres of petrol* ◇ *a litre bottle of wine* ▶ **litr** ⓘ Więcej o wyrażeniach miar w dodatku *Wyrażenia liczbowe* na końcu słownika.

litter /ˈlɪtə(r)/ noun **1** [U] pieces of paper, rubbish, etc. that are left in a public place ▶ **śmieci** **2** [C] all the young animals that are born to one mother at the same time: *a litter of six puppies* ▶ **miot**
■ **litter** verb [T]: *The streets were littered with rubbish.* ▶ **śmiecić**

ˈlitter bin noun [C] a container to put rubbish in, in the street or a public building ▶ **kosz na śmieci** ➲ picture at **bin**

little¹ /ˈlɪtl/ adj. **1** not big; small: *a little bag of sweets* ◇ *Do you want the big one or the little one?* ◇ *a little mistake/problem* ▶ **mały** ➲ note at **small**

> Przymiotnik **little** często występuje z innymi przymiotnikami: *a little old lady* ◇ *a cute little kitten* ◇ *What a funny little shop!* Rzeczownik, przed którym występuje przymiotnik **little**, często tłumaczy się jako zdrobnienie: *a little shop* sklepik ◇ *a little cat* kotek.

2 young: *a little girl/boy* ◇ *my little brother* ◇ *I was very naughty when I was little.* ▶ **mały, młodszy** **3** (used about distance or time) short: *Do you mind waiting **a little while*** (chwileczkę)? ◇ *We only live **a little way*** (niedaleko) *from here.* ◇ *We have only **a little way*** (kawałek) *to go.* ▶ (*dystans*) **krótki**

little² /ˈlɪtl/ adv. not much or not enough: *I slept very little last night.* ◇ *a little-known author* ▶ **mało** ➲ look at **less**, **least**
IDM **little by little** slowly: *After the accident her strength returned little by little.* ▶ **stopniowo**

little³ /ˈlɪtl/ determiner, pron. [also as a noun after *the*] not much or not enough: *They have very little money.* ◇ *There is little hope that she will recover.* ◇ *The little I know of him has given me a good impression.* Chociaż znam go mało, to, co o nim wiem, zrobiło na mnie dobre wrażenie. ◇ *We studied Latin at school but I remember very little.* ▶ **mało, niewiele**

a little /ə ˈlɪtl/ adv. rather; to a small degree: *This skirt is a little too tight.* ◇ *It's only a little further.* ▶ **trochę, odrobinę** ⓘ Często zamiast **a little** używa się wyrażeń **a little bit** albo **a bit**: *I was feeling a little bit tired so I decided not to go out.*
■ **a little** determiner, pron. a small amount (of sth): *I like a little sugar in my tea.* ◇ *Could I have a little help, please?* ◇ *'Is there any butter left?' 'Yes, just a little.'* ▶ **trochę**
IDM **after/for a little** after/for a short distance or time: *You must rest for a little.* ▶ **po chwili**; **przez chwilę**

liturgy /ˈlɪtədʒi/ noun [C] a fixed form of public worship used in churches ▶ **liturgia**

live¹ /lɪv/ verb **1** [I] to have your home in a particular place: *Where do you live?* ◇ *He still lives with his parents.* ▶ **mieszkać** ➲ look at **stay** **2** [I] to be or stay alive: *to live to a great age* ◇ *She hasn't got long to live.* Pozostaje jej niedużo życia. ▶ **żyć**, **dożywać** **3** [I,T] to pass or spend your life in a certain way: *to live a quiet life* ◇ *to live in comfort/poverty* ▶ **prowadzić** (*np. spokojne*) **życie** **4** [I] to enjoy all the opportunities of life fully: *I want to live a bit before settling down.* ▶ **żyć pełnią życia**
IDM **live/sleep rough** → ROUGH⁴
PHR V **live by sth** to follow a particular belief or set of principles ▶ **żyć zgodnie z czymś**
live by doing sth to get the money, food, etc. you need by doing a particular activity: *They live by hunting and fishing.* ▶ **żyć z czegoś**
live for sb/sth to consider sb/sth to be the most important thing in your life: *He felt he had nothing to live for after his wife died.* ▶ **żyć dla kogoś/czegoś**
not live sth down to be unable to make people forget sth bad or embarrassing that you have done ▶ **wymazywać z pamięci** (*np. winę, ośmieszenie*)
live off sb/sth to depend on sb/sth in order to live: *Barry lives off tinned food.* ◇ *She could easily get a job but she still lives off her parents.* ▶ **żyć** (*np. o chlebie*), **żyć** (*np. z ziemi*), **żyć cudzym kosztem**
live on to continue to live or exist: *Mozart is dead but his music lives on.* ◇ *After his retirement he lived on* (przeżył jeszcze) *for another 25 years.* ▶ **żyć dalej**; **przetrwać**
live on sth **1** to have sth as your only food: *to live on bread and water* ▶ **żyć** (*np. o chlebie*) **2** to manage to buy what you need to live: *I don't know how they live on so little money!* ▶ **wy/żyć (z czegoś)**
live out sth **1** to actually do sth that you only imagined doing before: *to live out your dreams/fantasies* ▶ **realizować, urzeczywistniać** (*np. marzenia*) **2** to spend the rest of your life in a particular way: *They lived out their last few years in Peru.* ▶ **przeżywać**
live through sth to survive an unpleasant experience: *She lived through two wars.* ▶ **przeżywać**
live together to live in the same house, etc. as sb and have a sexual relationship with them ▶ **żyć ze sobą**
live it up to enjoy yourself in an exciting way, usually spending a lot of money ▶ **używać sobie**
live up to sth to be as good as expected: *Children sometimes find it hard to live up to their parents' expectations.* ▶ **spełniać czyjeś oczekiwania**
live with sb = LIVE TOGETHER
live with sth to accept sth unpleasant that you cannot change: *It can be hard to live with the fact that you are getting older.* ▶ **pogodzić się (z czymś)**

live² /laɪv/ adj. **1** having life; not dead: *Have you ever touched a **real live** snake?* ▶ **żywy** ➲ look at **alive**, **living** **2** seen or heard as it is happening: *live coverage of the Olympic Games* ▶ **na żywo** **3** given or made when people are watching or listening; not recorded: *That pub has live music on Saturdays.* ▶ (*koncert, transmisja itp.*) **na żywo**, (*płyta, nagranie*) **koncertowy** **4** (used about a wire, etc.) carrying electricity: *That cable is live.* ▶ **pod napięciem** ➲ picture at **plug** **5** (used about a bomb, bullet, etc.) that has not yet exploded: *live* (ostra) *ammunition* ◇ *a live bomb* niewypał ▶ (*mina itp.*) **uzbrojony, zawierający ładunek wybuchowy**

■ **live** adv. broadcast at the time of an actual event; played or recorded at an actual performance: *to go out live on TV* ◇ *This programme is coming live* (transmitowany jest bezpośrednio) *from Wembley Stadium.* ◇ *He's funny on video, but he's even funnier live.* ▶ **na żywo**

livelihood /ˈlaɪvlihʊd/ noun [C, usually sing.] the way that you earn money: *When the factory closed he lost his livelihood.* ▶ **środki utrzymania**

lively /ˈlaɪvli/ adj. (**livelier**; **liveliest**) full of energy, interest, excitement, etc.: *lively children* ◇ *The town is quite lively at night.* ▶ **żywy**

liven /ˈlaɪvn/ verb

PHR V **liven (sb/sth) up** to become or make sb/sth become more interesting and exciting: *Once the band began to play the party livened up.* ▶ **ożywiać (się)**

liver /ˈlɪvə(r)/ noun **1** [C] the part of your body that cleans your blood ▶ **wątroba** ➲ picture at **body** **2** [U] the **liver** of an animal when it is cooked and eaten as food: *fried liver and onions* ▶ **wątróbka**

lives plural of **life**

livestock /ˈlaɪvstɒk/ noun [U] animals that are kept on a farm, such as cows, pigs, sheep, etc. ▶ **żywy inwentarz**

livid /ˈlɪvɪd/ adj. **1** extremely angry ▶ **wściekły** SYN **furious** **2** dark bluish-grey in colour: *a livid bruise* ▶ **siny**

living[1] /ˈlɪvɪŋ/ adj. **1** alive now: *He has no living relatives.* ▶ **żyjący**, **żywy** ➲ note at **alive** **2** [only before a noun] still used or practised now: *living languages/traditions* ▶ **żywy** OPP **dead**

living[2] /ˈlɪvɪŋ/ noun **1** [C, usually sing.] money to buy things that you need in life: *What do you do **for a living**?* ▶ **utrzymanie**, **życie** **2** [U] your way or quality of life: *The **standard of living** is very high in that country.* ◇ *The **cost of living*** (koszty utrzymania) *has risen in recent years.* ▶ **życie**

ˈ**living room** (Brit. also ˈ**sitting room**) noun [C] the room in a house where people sit, relax, watch TV, etc. together ▶ **pokój dzienny**, **salon**

lizard /ˈlɪzəd/ noun [C] a small animal with four legs, dry skin and a long tail ▶ **jaszczurka** ➲ picture on **page A11**

load[1] /ləʊd/ noun [C] **1** something (heavy) that is being or is waiting to be carried: *a truck carrying a load of sand* ▶ **ładunek**; **ciężar** **2** [in compounds] the quantity of sth that can be carried: *bus loads of tourists* ▶ **cały** (*np. autobus*) **3** (**loads (of sth)**) [pl.] (informal) a lot (of sth): *There are loads of things to do in London in the evenings.* ▶ **mnóstwo**, **masa**

IDM **a load of rubbish, etc.** (informal) nonsense ▶ **bzdury**

load[2] /ləʊd/ verb **1** [I,T] **load (sth/sb) (up) (with sth)**; **load (sth/sb) (into/onto sth)** to put a large quantity of sth into or onto sb/sth: *Have you finished loading yet?* ◇ *They loaded the plane (up) with supplies.* ◇ *Load the washing into the machine.* ◇ *Uncle Tim arrived loaded down* (obładowany) *with presents.* ▶ **ładować**, **obciążać** **2** [I] to receive a load: *The ship is still loading.* ▶ **brać ładunek** **3** [T] to put sth into a machine, a weapon, etc. so that it can be used: *to load film into a camera* ◇ *to load a gun* ▶ **ładować**, **wkładać** (*film, nabój*) **4** [T] to put a program or disk into a computer: *First, switch on the machine and load the disk.* ▶ **wkładać**; **wgrywać program komputerowy** OPP for all meanings **unload**

PHR V **load sb/sth down (with sth)** [usually passive] to give sb/sth a lot of heavy things to carry: *She was loaded down with bags of groceries.* ▶ **obładowywać kogoś/coś (czymś)** SYN **weigh sb/sth down**

loaded /ˈləʊdɪd/ adj. **1 loaded (with sth)** carrying a load; full and heavy ▶ **załadowany**, **obciążony** **2** [not before a noun] (informal) having a lot of money; rich ▶ **nadziany** **3 be loaded in favour of sb/sth; be loaded against sb/sth** giving an advantage: *The system is loaded in their favour.* ▶ **działać na czyjąś korzyść/niekorzyść** **4** (used especially about a gun or a camera) containing a bullet, a film, etc. ▶ **naładowany** **5** having more meaning than you realize at first and intended to make you think in a particular way: *a loaded question* ▶ **podchwytliwy**

loaf /ləʊf/ noun [C] (pl. **loaves** /ləʊvz/) bread baked in one piece: *a loaf of bread* ▶ **bochenek** ➲ picture at **bread**

loan /ləʊn/ noun **1** [C] money, etc. that sb/sth lends you: ***to take out a** bank **loan*** ◇ *to pay off a loan* ▶ **pożyczka**, **kredyt** ➲ note at **money** ➲ look at **borrow** **2** [U] the act of lending sth or the state of being lent: *The books are **on loan*** (wypożyczone) *from the library.*

■ **loan** verb [T] (formal) **loan sth (to sb)** ▶ **pożyczać**, **wypożyczać** ⓘ W Amer. ang. czasownik **loan** występuje częściej i brzmi mniej formalnie.

> **loans**
>
> If you **can't afford** sth, you can **take out** a **loan**, for example from a bank. You can say: *I'm going to **borrow** some money **from** the bank* or: *The bank is going to **lend** me some money.* You will then **owe** the money and you will have to **pay** it **back**: *I'm paying back the £1000 that I owe in instalments – £50 every month.* The money you owe is called a **debt** (/det/): *I've got lots of debts.* When you borrow from a bank you also have to pay extra money called **interest**. The money that you borrow in order to buy a house, etc. is a **mortgage** (/ˈmɔːɡɪdʒ/).

loath (also **loth**) /ləʊθ/ adj. (formal) **loath to do sth** not willing to do sth: *He was loath to admit his mistake.* Niechętnie przyznał się do błędu. ▶ **niechętny**

loathe /ləʊð/ verb [T] [not used in the continuous tenses] to hate sb/sth ▶ **nienawidzić**, **czuć odrazę/wstręt** SYN **detest** ⓘ Czasownika **loathe** nie używa się w czasach *continuous*. Natomiast często spotyka się go w *present participle* (formie *-ing*): *Loathing the thought of having to apologize, she knocked on his door.*

■ **loathing** noun [U] ▶ **nienawiść**, **wstręt** | **loathsome** /ˈləʊðsəm/ adj.: *a loathsome place* ▶ **wstrętny**, **obrzydliwy**

loaves plural of **loaf**

lob /lɒb/ verb [I,T] (**lobbing**; **lobbed**) (in sport) to hit, kick or throw a ball high into the air, so that it lands behind your opponent ▶ **lobować**

■ **lob** noun [C] ▶ **lob**

lobby[1] /ˈlɒbi/ noun [C] (pl. **lobbies**) **1** the area that is just inside a large building, where people can meet and wait: *a hotel lobby* ▶ **hall** **2** [with sing. or pl. verb] a group of people who try to influence politicians to do or not do sth: *the anti-smoking lobby* ▶ **lobby**

lobby[2] /ˈlɒbi/ verb [I,T] (**lobbying**; **lobbies**; pt, pp **lobbied**) to try to influence a politician or the government to do or not do sth ▶ **wywierać nacisk na rząd w jakiejś sprawie**

lobe /ləʊb/ noun [C] **1** = EAR LOBE **2** one part of an organ of the body, especially the brain or lungs ▶ (*anat.*) **płat**

lobster /ˈlɒbstə(r)/ noun **1** [C] a sea creature with a hard shell, a long body divided into sections, eight legs and two large **claws**. Its shell is black but turns red when it is cooked. ▶ **homar** ➲ picture on **page A11** **2** [U] meat from a **lobster** eaten as food ▶ **homar**

local[1] /ˈləʊkl/ adj. of a particular place (near you): *local newspapers/radio* ◇ *the local doctor/policeman/butcher* ◇ *a local call* ▶ **miejscowy**, **lokalny** ➲ look at **international**, **national**, **regional**

■ **locally** /-kəli/ adv.: *I do most of my shopping locally.* ▶ **lokalnie**, **w najbliższej okolicy**

local[2] /ˈləʊkl/ noun [C] **1** [usually pl.] a person who lives in a particular place: *The locals seem very friendly.*

▶ **miejscowy**, **mieszkan-iec/ka** **2** (Brit., informal) a pub that is near your home where you often go to drink ▶ **lokalny pub**

ˌlocal anaesˈthetic noun [C,U] medicine that is injected into one part of your body so that you do not feel pain there ▶ **środek znieczulający miejscowo** ➲ look at **general anaesthetic**

ˌlocal auˌthority noun [C] (Brit.) the organization which is responsible for the government of an area of Britain ▶ **władze samorządowe**

ˌlocal ˈgovernment noun **1** [U] (especially Brit.) the system of government of a town or an area by elected representatives of the people who live there ▶ **samorząd lokalny** **2** [C] (US) the organization that is responsible for the government of a local area and for providing services, etc. ▶ **samorząd lokalny**

localize (also -ise) /ˈləʊkəlaɪz/ verb [T] to limit sth to a particular place or area ▶ **umiejscawiać**, **lokalizować**

ˈlocal time noun [U] the time at a particular place in the world: *We arrive in Singapore at 2 o'clock in the afternoon, local time.* ▶ **czas miejscowy**

locate /ləʊˈkeɪt; US ˈloʊkeɪt/ verb [T] **1** to find the exact position of sb/sth: *The damaged ship has been located two miles off the coast.* ▶ **umiejscawiać** **2** to put or build sth in a particular place: *They located their headquarters in Swindon.* ▶ **umiejscawiać**, **umieszczać**
■ **located** adj. **be located**: *Where exactly is your office located?* ▶ **znajdować się**

location /ləʊˈkeɪʃn/ noun **1** [C] a place or position: *Several locations have been suggested for the new office block.* ▶ **lokalizacja**, **położenie** **2** [U] the act of finding where sb/sth is: *Police enquiries led to the location of the terrorists' hideout.* ▶ **zlokalizowanie**
IDM **on location** (used about a film, TV programme, etc.) made in a suitable place away from the building where films, etc. are usually made: *The series was filmed on location in Thailand.* ▶ **w plenerze**

loch /lɒk; lɒx/ noun [C] the Scottish word for a lake: *the Loch Ness monster* ▶ (*nazwa szkocka*) **jezioro**

lock¹ /lɒk/ verb **1** [I,T] to close or fasten (sth) so that it can only be opened with a key: *Have you locked the car?* ◇ *The door won't lock.* ▶ **zamykać (się) na klucz/zatrzask** OPP **unlock** **2** [T] to put sb/sth in a safe place and lock it: *Lock your passport in a safe place.* ▶ **chować/trzymać pod kluczem** **3** [T] **be locked in/into sth** to be involved in an angry argument, etc. with sth: *The two sides were locked in a bitter dispute.* ▶ **być zaplątanym** (*np. w kłótnię*) **4** [T] **be locked together; be locked in sth** to be holding sb very tightly: *They were locked in a passionate embrace.* ▶ **być splecionym** (*np. w uścisku*) **5** [I,T] to fix sth or be fixed in one position: *The wheels locked and the car crashed into the wall.* ▶ **blokować (się)**
PHR V **lock sth away** to keep sth in a safe or secret place that is locked ▶ **chować/trzymać pod kluczem**
lock sb in/out to lock a door so that a person cannot get in/out: *I locked myself out of the house and had to climb in through the window.* ▶ **zamykać kogoś (w pomieszczeniu) na klucz**; **zamykać pomieszczenie tak, że nie można wejść do środka**
lock (sth) up to lock all the doors, windows, etc. of a building: *Make sure that you lock up before you leave.* ▶ **(po)zamykać wszystkie drzwi i okna**
lock sb up to put sb in prison ▶ **wtrącać kogoś do więzienia**

lock² /lɒk/ noun [C] **1** something that is used for fastening a door, lid, etc. so that you need a key to open it again: *to turn the key in the lock* ▶ **zamek** ➲ look at **padlock** **2** a part of a river or a **canal** where the level of water changes. Locks have gates at each end and are used to allow boats to move to a higher or lower level. ▶ **śluza**
IDM **pick a lock** → PICK¹
under lock and key in a locked place ▶ **pod kluczem**

locker /ˈlɒkə(r)/ noun [C] a small cupboard that can be locked in a school or sports centre, where you can leave your clothes, books, etc. ▶ **szafka**, **schowek**

locket /ˈlɒkɪt/ noun [C] a piece of jewellery that you wear on a chain around your neck and which opens so that you can put a picture, etc. inside ▶ **medalion**

locksmith /ˈlɒksmɪθ/ noun [C] a person who makes and repairs locks ▶ **ślusarz**

locomotive = ENGINE (2)

locust /ˈləʊkəst/ noun [C] a flying insect from Africa and Asia that moves in very large groups, eating and destroying large quantities of plants ▶ **szarańcza** ➲ picture at **insect**

lodge¹ /lɒdʒ/ noun [C] **1** a small house in the country where people stay when they want to take part in some types of outdoor sport: *a hunting lodge* ▶ **domek** (*np. myśliwski*) **2** a room at the entrance to a large building such as a college or factory ▶ **portiernia** **3** a small house at the gates of a park or in the land belonging to a large house ▶ **stróżówka**

lodge² /lɒdʒ/ verb **1** [T] (formal) **lodge sth (with sb) (against sb/sth)** to make a statement complaining about sth to a public organization or authority: *They lodged a compensation claim against the factory.* ▶ **wnosić** **2** [I] to pay to live in sb's house with them: *He lodged with a family for his first term at university.* ▶ **mieszkać w wynajętym pokoju** **3** [I,T] to become firmly fixed or to make sth do this ▶ **utkwić** ➲ look at **dislodge**

lodger /ˈlɒdʒə(r)/ noun [C] a person who pays rent to live in a house as a member of the family ▶ **lokator/ka** ➲ look at **boarder**

lodging /ˈlɒdʒɪŋ/ noun **1** [C,U] a place where you can stay: *The family offered full board and lodging in exchange for English lessons.* ▶ **zakwaterowanie**, **mieszkanie** **2** (**lodgings**) [pl.] (old-fashioned) a room or rooms in sb's house where you can pay to stay ▶ **pok-ój/oje do wynajęcia**

loft /lɒft/ noun [C] the room or space under the roof of a house or other building ▶ **strych** ➲ look at **attic**

lofty /ˈlɒfti/ adj. (**loftier**; **loftiest**) (formal) **1** (used about buildings, mountains, etc.) very high and impressive: *lofty ceilings/rooms/towers* ▶ **strzelisty** **2** [usually before a noun] (used about a thought, an aim, etc.) deserving praise because of its high moral quality: ***lofty ambitions/ideals/principles*** ▶ **wzniosły** **3** showing a belief that you are worth more than other people: *her lofty disdain for other people* ▶ **wyniosły** SYN **haughty**
■ **loftily** /-ɪli/ adv. ▶ **wyniośle** | **loftiness** noun [U] ▶ **wzniosłość**; **wyniosłość**

log¹ /lɒg/ noun [C] **1** a thick piece of wood that has fallen or been cut from a tree: *logs for the fire* drewno na ognisko ▶ **kłoda**, **kloc** **2** (also **logbook** /ˈlɒgbʊk/) the official written record of a ship's or an aircraft's journey: *to keep a log* ▶ **dziennik okrętowy/pokładowy**

log² /lɒg/ verb [T] (**logging**; **logged**) **1** to keep an official written record of sth ▶ **odnotowywać**, **rejestrować** **2** to write sth in the log of a ship or aeroplane ▶ **zapisywać coś w dzienniku okrętowym/pokładowym**
PHR V **log in/on** to perform the actions that allow you to start using a computer system: *You need to key in your password to log on.* ▶ **(za)logować się do sieci komputerowej** ➲ note at **computer**
log sb in/on to allow sb to begin using a computer system: *The system is unable to log you on.* ▶ **logować kogoś (do czegoś)**
log off/out to perform the actions that allow you to finish using a computer system ▶ **wylogować się z sieci komputerowej**

log sb off/out to cause sb to finish using a computer system: *The system will automatically log you off after 30 minutes.* ▶ **wylogowywać kogoś (z czegoś)**

logarithm /ˈlɒɡərɪðəm/ (also informal **log**) noun [C] one of a series of numbers arranged in lists that allow you to solve problems in mathematics by adding or taking away numbers instead of multiplying or dividing ▶ **logarytm**

logbook = LOG[1] (2)

loggerheads /ˈlɒɡəhedz/ noun
IDM **at loggerheads (with sb)** strongly disagreeing (with sb) ▶ **w niezgodzie (z kimś)**

logic /ˈlɒdʒɪk/ noun [U] **1** a sensible reason or way of thinking: *There is no logic in your argument.* ▶ **logika** **2** the science of using reason: *the rules of logic* ▶ **logika**

logical /ˈlɒdʒɪkl/ adj. **1** seeming natural, reasonable or sensible: *There is only one logical conclusion.* ▶ **logiczny, rozsądny** OPP **illogical** **2** thinking in a sensible way: *a logical mind* ▶ **logiczny**
■ **logically** /-kli/ adv. ▶ **logicznie, sensownie**

login /ˈlɒɡɪn/ (also **logon** /ˈlɒɡɒn/) noun **1** [U] the act of starting to use a computer system, usually by typing a name or word that you choose to use: *If you've forgotten your login ID, click this link.* ▶ **logowanie się** **2** [C] the name that you use to enter a computer system: *Enter your login and password and press 'go'.* ▶ **login**

logistics /ləˈdʒɪstɪks/ noun [U, with sing. or pl. verb] **logistics (of sth)** the practical organization that is needed to make a complicated plan successful when a lot of people and equipment is involved: *the logistics of moving the company to a new building* ▶ **logistyka**
■ **logistic** (also **logistical** /ləˈdʒɪstɪkl/) adj.: *logistic support* ◇ *Organizing famine relief presents huge logistical problems.* ▶ **logistyczny** | **logistically** /-kli/ adv. ▶ **logistycznie**

logo /ˈləʊɡəʊ/ noun [C] (pl. **logos**) a printed symbol or design that a company or an organization uses as its special sign: *the company/brand logo* ▶ **znak firmowy, logo**

logoff /ˈlɒɡɒf/ (also **logout** /ˈlɒɡaʊt/) noun [U] the act of finishing using a computer system ▶ **wylogowanie się**

logon = LOGIN

logout = LOGOFF

loiter /ˈlɔɪtə(r)/ verb [I] to stand or walk around somewhere for no obvious reason ▶ **wałęsać się; tkwić gdzieś bez celu**

lollipop /ˈlɒlipɒp/ (also **lolly** /ˈlɒli/) noun [C] a sweet on a stick ▶ **lizak** ➲ look at **ice lolly**

lone /ləʊn/ adj. [only before a noun] **1** without any other people; alone: *a lone swimmer* ▶ **samotny, jedyny** SYN **solitary** **2** (used about a parent) single; without a partner ▶ **samotny** ➲ look at **lonely**

lonely /ˈləʊnli/ adj. (**lonelier**; **loneliest**) **1** unhappy because you are not with other people: *to feel sad and lonely* ▶ **samotny** **2** (used about a situation or a period of time) sad and spent alone: *lonely nights in front of the TV* ▶ **samotny** **3** [only before a noun] far from other people and places where people live: *a lonely house in the hills* ▶ **samotny; odludny** ➲ note at **alone** ➲ look at **lone**
■ **loneliness** noun [U] ▶ **samotność** ➲ look at **solitude**, **isolation**

loner /ˈləʊnə(r)/ noun [C] (informal) a person who prefers being alone to being with other people ▶ **samotnik**

lonesome /ˈləʊnsəm/ adj. (US) lonely or making you feel lonely ▶ **samotny; powodujący uczucie osamotnienia** ➲ note at **alone**

long[1] /lɒŋ/ adj. (**longer** /ˈlɒŋɡə(r)/; **longest** /ˈlɒŋɡɪst/) measuring a large amount in distance or time: *long hair* ◇ *We had to wait a long time.* ◇ *a very long journey/book/corridor* ◇ *Nurses work very long hours.* ◇ *I walked a long way today.* ▶ **długi** OPP **short** ➲ note at **far** ➲ noun **length**

> Przymiotnika **long** używa się także w twierdzeniach i pytaniach o długość, odległość lub czas trwania: *How long is the film?* ◇ *The insect was only 2 millimetres long* (miał dwa milimetry długości). ◇ *a five-mile-long traffic jam.*

IDM **a long shot** a person or thing that probably will not succeed, win, etc. ▶ **osoba/próba prawdopodobnie z góry skazana na niepowodzenie**
at the longest not longer than the stated time: *It will take a week at the longest.* ▶ **najdalej, najwyżej**
go a long way (used about money, food, etc.) to be used for buying a lot of things, feeding a lot of people, etc. ▶ **wystarczać na długo**
have a long way to go to need to make a lot more progress before sth can be achieved ▶ (*przen.*) **mieć długą drogę przed sobą**
in the long run after a long time; in the end ▶ **na dłuższą metę; w końcu**
in the long/short term → TERM[1]
(pull, wear, etc.) a long face (to have) an unhappy or a disappointed expression ▶ **smutna/kwaśna mina**

long[2] /lɒŋ/ adv. (**longer** /ˈlɒŋɡə(r)/; **longest** /ˈlɒŋɡɪst/) **1** for a long time: *She didn't stay long.* ◇ *You shouldn't have to wait long.* ◇ *I hope we don't have to wait much longer.* ◇ *They won't be gone **for long**.* Nie będzie ich przez krótki czas. ◇ *Just wait here – I won't be long.* ◇ *'How long will it take to get there?' 'Not long.'* ▶ **długo**

> Zarówno **long**, jak i **a long time** określają czas trwania czegoś. W zdaniach twierdzących zwykle używa się **a long time**: *They stood there for a long time.* W zdaniach twierdzących **long** występuje tylko z innym przysłówkiem, np. **too**, **enough**, **ago**: *We lived here long ago.* ◇ *I've put up with this noise long enough. I'm going to make a complaint.* W pytaniach występuje zarówno **long**, jak i **a long time**: *Were you away long/a long time?* W zdaniach przeczących występuje czasem różnica znaczeniowa pomiędzy **long** a **a long time**: *I haven't been here long.* Jestem tu od niedawna. ◇ *I haven't been here for a long time.* Dawno tu nie byłem.

2 a long time before or after a particular time or event: *We got married **long before** we moved here.* ◇ *Don't worry – they'll be here **before long**.* ◇ *All that happened long ago.* ▶ **dawno, na długo** **3** for the whole of the time that is mentioned: *The baby cried **all night long**.* ▶ **przez cały** (*np. dzień*)
IDM **as/so long as** on condition that: *As long as no problems arise we should get the job finished by Friday.* ▶ **pod warunkiem, o ile** SYN **provided**
for (so) long for (such) a long time: *I'm sorry I haven't written to you for so long.* Przepraszam, że dawno nie pisałem. ▶ **dużo czasu, długo**
no/not any longer not any more: *They no longer live here.* ◇ *They don't live here any longer.* ▶ **już nie**

long[3] /lɒŋ/ verb [I] **long for sth**; **long (for sb) to do sth** to want sth very much, especially sth that is not likely: *She longed to return to Greece.* ▶ **pragnąć, tęsknić** SYN **yearn**
■ **longing** noun [C,U]: *a longing for peace* ▶ **pragnienie, tęsknota** | **longingly** adv. ▶ **tęsknie, z upragnieniem**

ˌlong-ˈdistance adj. [only before a noun] (used about travel or communication) between places that are far from each other: *a long-distance lorry driver* kierowca ciężarówki jeżdżący na długich trasach ▶ **międzymiastowy, międzynarodowy, długodystansowy** ➲ look at **local**

L

▪ **long distance** adv.: *to phone long distance* dzwonić do innego miasta/kraju

ˌ**long-drawn-ˈout** adj. lasting longer than necessary: *long drawn-out negotiations* ▶ **przeciągający się, długotrwały**

longevity /lɒnˈdʒevəti/ noun [U] (formal) long life; the fact of lasting a long time: *We wish you both health and longevity.* ▶ **długowieczność**

longhand /ˈlɒŋhænd/ noun [U] ordinary writing, not typed or written in **shorthand**: *I prefer to write my work down in longhand first.* ▶ **pismo odręczne**

ˈ**long-haul** adj. [only before a noun] connected with the transport of people or goods over long distances: *a long-haul flight* ▶ (*przewozy ludzi/towarów*) **daleki, dalekiego zasięgu**

longitude /ˈlɒŋgɪtjuːd; ˈlɒndʒɪ-; US ˈlɑːndʒətuːd/ noun [U] the distance of a place east or west of a line from the North Pole to the South Pole that passes through Greenwich in London. **Longitude** is measured in degrees. ▶ **długość geograficzna** ➲ look at **latitude**

ˈ**long jump** noun [sing.] the sport in which people try to jump as far as possible ▶ **skok w dal** ➲ look at **high jump**

ˌ**long-ˈlife** adj. made to last for a long time: *a long-life battery* ◇ *long-life milk* ▶ **o długim terminie przydatności do użycia/spożycia**

ˌ**long-ˈlived** adj. that has lived or lasted for a long time: *a long-lived dispute* ▶ **długowieczny**; **długotrwały**

ˈ**long-range** adj. [only before a noun] **1** that can go or be sent over long distances: *long-range nuclear missiles* ▶ **dalekiego zasięgu 2** of or for a long period of time starting from the present: *the long-range weather forecast* ▶ **długoterminowy**

ˌ**long-ˈsighted** (US ˌfar-ˈsighted) adj. able to see things clearly only when they are quite far away ▶ **dalekowzroczny** OPP **short-sighted, near-sighted**

ˌ**long-ˈstanding** adj. that has lasted for a long time: *a long-standing arrangement* ▶ **długotrwały**

ˌ**long-ˈsuffering** adj. (used about a person) having a lot of troubles but not complaining ▶ **wytrwale znoszący coś, cierpliwy**

ˌ**long-ˈterm** adj. of or for a long period of time: *long-term planning* ▶ **długoterminowy**

ˈ**long wave** noun [U] (abbr. **LW**) the system of broadcasting radio using sound waves of 1 000 metres or more ▶ **fale długie**

ˌ**long-ˈwinded** adj. (used about sth that is written or spoken) boring because it is too long ▶ **rozwlekły, przydługi**

loo /luː/ noun [C] (pl. **loos**) (Brit., informal) toilet ▶ **kibel** ➲ note at **toilet**

🔑 **look**[1] /lʊk/ verb **1** [I,T] **look (at sth)** to turn your eyes in a particular direction (in order to pay attention to sb/sth): *Sorry, I wasn't looking. Can you show me again?* ◇ *Look carefully at this picture.* ◇ *to look out of* (wyglądać przez) *the window* ◇ *She blushed and looked away* (odwróciła wzrok). ◇ *Look who's come to see us.* ◇ *Look where you're going!* ▶ **patrzeć**

> **Look, watch** czy **see**? Czasownika **look** używamy wówczas, gdy patrzymy na coś: *Look carefully. Can you see anything strange?* Kiedy przyglądamy się czemuś przez dłuższy czas, wówczas stosujemy czasownik **watch**: *Watch what I do, then you try.* ◇ *to watch television/a football match.* **See** używamy wówczas, gdy patrzymy na coś świadomie, zwracamy uwagę na to, co widzimy: *I saw a girl riding past on a bicycle.* Czasownik **see** stosuje się też w znaczeniu „oglądać" film, przedstawienie, telewizję itp: *We went to see a movie last night.* ◇ *Have you seen Tom Stoppard's latest play?*

2 [I] **look (for sb/sth)** to try to find (sb/sth): *We've been looking for you everywhere. Where have you been?* ◇ *to look for work* ◇ *'I can't find my shoes.' 'Have you looked under the bed?'* ▶ **szukać 3** [I] **look (like sb/sth) (to sb)**; **look (to sb) as if.../as though...** to seem or appear: *You look very smart in that shirt.* ◇ *to look tired/ill/sad/well/happy* ◇ *The boy looks like his father.* ◇ *That film looks good – I might go and see it.* ◇ *You look (to me) as if/as though* (wygląda (mi) na to, że) *you need some sleep.* ◇ *It looks like rain.* Zanosi się na deszcz. ▶ **wyglądać (na to, że) 4** [I] to face a particular direction: *This room looks south so it gets the sun all day.* ▶ **wychodzić na coś 5** [I] **look to do sth** to aim to do sth: *We are looking to double our profits over the next five years.* ▶ **mieć na celu**

▪ **look** interj. (used for asking sb to listen to what you are saying): *Look, William, I know you are busy but could you give me a hand?* ▶ **posłuchaj/cie**

IDM **look bad**; **not look good** to be considered bad manners: *It'll look bad if we get there an hour late.* ▶ (*zachowanie*) **źle wyglądać**

look your best to look as beautiful or attractive as possible ▶ **wyglądać jak najlepiej**

look down your nose at sb/sth (especially Brit., informal) to think that you are better than sb else; to think that sth is not good enough for you ▶ **patrzeć na kogoś/coś z góry**

look good to seem to be encouraging: *This year's sales figures are looking good.* ▶ **być zachęcającym, wyglądać dobrze**

look here (old-fashioned) (used for protesting about sth): *Now look here! That's not fair!* ▶ **ale posłuchaj!**

look sb in the eye to look straight at sb without feeling embarrassed or afraid ▶ **patrzeć komuś prosto w oczy**

look on the bright side (of sth) to be positive about a bad situation, thinking of the advantages and not the disadvantages ▶ **dostrzegać jasny punkt w złej sytuacji**

(not) look yourself to (not) look as well or healthy as usual: *What's the matter? You're not looking yourself today.* ▶ **wyglądać nieswojo**; **wyglądać normalnie**

never/not look back to become and continue being successful ▶ **osiągać coraz większe sukcesy**

PHR V **look after sb/sth/yourself** to be responsible for or take care of sb/sth/yourself: *I want to go back to work if I can find somebody to look after the children.* ◇ *The old lady's son looked after all her financial affairs.* ▶ **opiekować się kimś/czymś, dbać o kogoś/coś, pilnować** (*interesów*) ➲ note at **care**[2]

look ahead (to sth) to think about or plan for the future ▶ **patrzeć/spoglądać w przyszłość**

look around/round to turn your head so that you can see sth ▶ **rozglądać się**

look around/round (sth) to visit a place or building, walking around it to see what is there: *Let's look round the town this afternoon.* ▶ **zwiedzać (coś)**

look around/round for sth to search for sth in a number of different places: *We're looking around for a house in this area.* ▶ **rozglądać się za czymś**

look at sth 1 to examine sth (closely): *My tooth aches. I think a dentist should look at it.* ▶ **przyglądać się, zobaczyć 2** to think about or study sth: *The government is looking at ways of reducing unemployment.* ▶ **zastanawiać się 3** to read sth: *Could I look at the newspaper when you've finished with it?* ▶ **czytać, zobaczyć 4** to consider sth: *Different races and nationalities look at life differently.* ▶ **patrzeć (na coś)**

look back (on sth) to think about sth in your past ▶ **spoglądać/patrzeć w przeszłość, powracać wspomnieniami do czegoś**

look down on sb/sth to think that you are better than sb/sth ▶ **patrzeć z góry na kogoś/coś**
look forward to sth/doing sth to wait with pleasure for sth to happen: *I'm really looking forward to the weekend.* ◇ *I look forward to hearing from you.* (zwrot często używany na końcu oficjalnego listu) ▶ **oczekiwać czegoś z radością, cieszyć się na coś**
look into sth to study or try to find out sth: *A committee was set up to look into the causes of the accident.* ▶ **badać coś**
look on to watch sth happening without taking any action: *All we could do was look on as the house burned.* ▶ **przypatrywać się (biernie)**
look on sb/sth as sth to consider sb/sth to be sth: *They seem to look on me as someone who can advise them.* ▶ **postrzegać kogoś/coś jako kogoś/coś**
look on sb/sth with sth to think of sb/sth in a particular way ▶ **patrzeć na kogoś/coś** (*np. ze złością, z radością*)
look out to be careful or to pay attention to sth dangerous: *Look out* (uwaga)*! There's a bike coming.* ▶ **uważać**
look out (for sb/sth) to pay attention in order to see, find or avoid sb/sth: *Look out for thieves!* ▶ **uważać** (*np. na zagrożenie, niebezpieczeństwo*) SYN **watch out**
look out for sb/sth to keep trying to find sth or meet sb: *I'll look out for you at the conference.* ▶ **rozglądać się za kimś/czymś** ➲ look at **lookout**
look round 1 to turn your head in order to see sb/sth: *She looked round when she heard the noise.* ▶ **rozglądać się, oglądać się dokoła 2** to look at many things (before buying sth): *She looked round but couldn't find anything she liked.* ▶ **rozglądać się, oglądać dużo rzeczy**
look round sth to walk around a place looking at things: *to look round a town/shop/museum* ▶ **zwiedzać/oglądać coś**
look through sth to read sth quickly ▶ **przeglądać coś**
look to sb for sth; look to sb to do sth to expect sb to do or to provide sth: *He always looked to his father for advice.* ▶ **oczekiwać, że ktoś coś zrobi, oczekiwać czegoś od kogoś**
look up 1 to move your eyes upwards to look at sb/sth: *She looked up and smiled.* ▶ **spoglądać/patrzeć w górę 2** (informal) to improve: *Business is looking up.* ▶ **polepszać się, poprawiać się**
look sth up to search for information in a book: *to look up a word in a dictionary* ▶ **sprawdzać coś**
look up to sb to respect and admire sb ▶ **szanować/podziwiać kogoś**

⚷ **look²** /lʊk/ noun **1** [C] the act of looking: ***Have a look*** (popatrz) *at this article.* ◇ ***Take a** close **look** at the contract before you sign it.* ▶ **spojrzenie 2** [C, usually sing.] a **look (for sb/sth)** a search: *I'll **have a** good **look** for* (poszukam) *that book later.* ◇ *I've had a look* (rozejrzałem się) *but I can't find it.* **3** [C] the expression on sb's face: *He had a worried look* (wyglądał na zmartwionego) *on his face.* ◇ *I knew something was wrong – everybody was giving me funny looks* (wszyscy dziwnie się mi przyglądali). ▶ **wyraz twarzy 4** (**looks**) [pl.] sb's appearance: *He's lucky – he's got good looks* (jest przystojny) *and intelligence.* ▶ **uroda, wygląd 5** [C] a fashion or style: *The shop has a new look to appeal to younger customers.* ▶ **wygląd, styl**
IDM **by/from the look of sb/sth** judging by the appearance of sb/sth: *It's going to be a fine day by the look of it.* ▶ **sądząc z wyglądu**
like the look/sound of sb/sth → LIKE²

lookalike /ˈlʊkəlaɪk/ noun [C] [often used after a person's name] a person who looks very similar to the person mentioned: *an Elvis lookalike* ▶ **sobowtór**

ˈlook-in noun
IDM **(not) give sb a look-in; (not) get/have a look-in** (informal) to (not) give sb, or to (not) have a chance to do sth ▶ **(nie) dopuszczać (kogoś do czegoś); mieć wgląd/dostęp do czegoś, nie mieć wglądu/dostępu do czegoś**

-looking /ˈlʊkɪŋ/ [in compounds] having the appearance mentioned: *an odd-looking* (dziwaczny) *building* ◇ *He's very good-looking* (przystojny). ▶ (*określa wygląd*)

lookout /ˈlʊkaʊt/ noun [C] (a person who has) the responsibility of watching to see if danger is coming; the place this person watches from: *One of the gang acted as lookout.* ▶ **czujka, obserwator; punkt obserwacyjny**
IDM **be on the lookout for sb/sth; keep a lookout for sb/sth** to pay attention in order to see, find or avoid sb/sth ▶ **wypatrywać kogoś/czegoś; uważać na kogoś/coś**

loom¹ /luːm/ verb [I] **loom (up)** to appear as a shape that is not clear and in a way that seems frightening: *The mountain loomed (up) in the distance.* ▶ **majaczyć; wisieć**

loom² /luːm/ noun [C] a piece of equipment that is used for **weaving** ▶ **krosno**

loony /ˈluːni/ noun [C] (pl. **loonies**) (also **loon**) (informal) a person who has strange ideas or behaves in a strange way ▶ **pomyleniec, wariat**
■ **loony** adj. (**loonier; looniest**): *I'm tired of listening to his loony plans.* ▶ **wariacki**

loop /luːp/ noun [C] a curved or round shape made by a line curving round and joining or crossing itself: *a loop in a rope* ◇ *The road goes around the lake in a loop.* ▶ **pętla**
■ **loop** verb **1** [T] to form or bend sth into a loop: *He was trying to loop a rope over the horse's head.* ▶ **zawiązywać pętlę, zapętlać 2** [I] to move in a way that makes the shape of a loop: *The river loops around the valley.* ▶ **tworzyć zakole/pętlę,** (*rzeka itp.*) **zawracać**
IDM **in the loop/out of the loop** (informal) part of a group of people that is dealing with sth important/not part of this group ▶ **(nie)będący w grupie osób podejmujących ważne decyzje**

loophole /ˈluːphəʊl/ noun [C] a way of avoiding sth because the words of a rule or law are badly chosen ▶ **luka**

⚷ **loose¹** /luːs/ adj. **1** not tied up or shut in sth; free: *The dog broke loose* (zerwał się z uwięzi) *and ran away.* ◇ *The horse managed to **get loose** and escape.* ◇ *I take the dog to the woods and **let** him **loose*** (spuszczam go ze smyczy). ◇ *She wore her long hair loose.* ▶ **swobodny, nieuwiązany, rozpuszczony 2** not firmly fixed: *The saucepan handle is a bit loose so be careful.* ◇ *a loose tooth* ruszający się ząb ▶ **luźny, rozchwiany 3** not contained in sth or joined together: *loose change* ◇ *some loose sheets of paper* ▶ **luźny 4** not fitting closely; not tight: *These trousers don't fit. They're much too loose round the waist.* ▶ **luźny, obszerny** OPP **tight 5** not completely accurate or the same as sth: *a loose interpretation of the rules* ◇ *a loose translation* wolny przekład ▶ **luźny, nieprecyzyjny**
■ **loosely** adv.: *The film is loosely based on the life of Beethoven.* ▶ **luźno, nieprecyzyjnie**
IDM **all hell broke loose** → HELL
at a loose end having nothing to do and feeling bored ▶ **znudzony brakiem zajęcia**

loose² /luːs/ noun
IDM **on the loose** escaped and dangerous: *a lion on the loose from a zoo* ▶ **zbiegły i niebezpieczny**

ˌloose ˈcannon noun [C] a person, usually a public figure, who often behaves in a way that nobody can predict ▶ **osoba publiczna, która często zachowuje się w sposób nieprzewidywalny**

ˌ**loose-ˈleaf** adj. (used about a book, file, etc.) with pages that can be removed or added separately: *a loose-leaf binder* ▶ **z kartkami do wyjmowania**

loosen /ˈluːsn/ verb [I,T] to become or make sth less tight: *to loosen your tie/belt* ◇ *Don't loosen your grip on the rope or you'll fall.* ▶ **luzować, rozluźniać (się)**
PHR V **loosen (sb/sth) up** to relax or move more easily: *These exercises will help you to loosen up.* ▶ **rozluźniać (się), odprężać (się)**

loot /luːt/ verb [I,T] to steal things during a war or period of fighting: *Many shops were looted during the riot.* ▶ **plądrować**
■ **loot** noun [U] money and valuable objects taken by soldiers from the enemy after winning a battle ▶ **łup** SYN **booty**

lop /lɒp/ verb [T] (**lopping**; **lopped**) to cut branches off a tree ▶ **obcinać gałęzie**
PHR V **lop sth off (sth)** to cut sth off/away ▶ **obcinać, odcinać**

lopsided /ˌlɒpˈsaɪdɪd/ adj. with one side lower or smaller than the other: *a lopsided smile* ▶ **skrzywiony, koślawy**

lord /lɔːd/ noun [C] **1** a man with a very high position in society: *the Lord Mayor* (burmistrz) *of London* ◇ *Lord and Lady Derby* ▶ **lord, (wielki) pan 2** (**the Lord**) [sing.] God; Christ ▶ **Pan Bóg 3** (**the Lords**) [with sing. or pl. verb] (Brit.) (members of) the House of Lords: *The Lords has/have voted against the bill.* ▶ **członkowie Izby Lordów; Izba Lordów 4** (**My Lord**) (in Britain) (used for addressing a judge, bishop, nobleman, etc.) ▶ **milordzie, ekscelencjo**
IDM **(Good) Lord!** (used for expressing surprise, worry, etc.): *Good Lord, what have you done to your hair?* ▶ **wielki Boże!**

ˌ**Lord ˈChancellor** (also ˌ**Lord High ˈChancellor**) noun [usually sing.] the government minister who is head of all the judges in England and Wales and in charge of the **House of Lords** ▶ **minister sprawiedliwości oraz marszałek Izby Lordów**

> The **Lord Chancellor** is the head of the **judiciary** in England and Wales and the **Speaker of the House of Lords**.

lordship /ˈlɔːdʃɪp/ noun [C] (**His/Your Lordship**) (used when speaking to or about a judge, bishop, nobleman, etc.) ▶ **wasza ekselencjo; (jego/wasza) lordowska mość; (jego/wasza) ekscelencja; (jego/wasza) wysokość**

the ˌ**Lord's ˈPrayer** noun [sing.] the prayer that Jesus Christ taught the people who followed him, that begins 'Our Father ...' ▶ (*modlitwa*) **Ojcze nasz**

lorry /ˈlɒri/ (Brit.) noun [C] (pl. **lorries**) (especially US **truck**) a large strong motor vehicle that is used for carrying goods by road ▶ **ciężarówka** ➲ note at **van** ➲ picture at **truck**, picture on **page A7**

lose /luːz/ verb (pt, pp **lost** /lɒst/) **1** [T] to become unable to find sth: *I've lost my purse. I can't find it anywhere.* ▶ **gubić 2** [T] to no longer have sb/sth: *She lost a leg in the accident.* ◇ *He lost his wife last year.* ◇ *to lose your job* ▶ **stracić 3** [T] to have less of sth: *to lose weight* (tracić na wadze)*/interest/patience* ◇ *The company is losing money all the time.* ▶ **tracić, ponosić straty** OPP **gain 4** [T] (informal) to cause sb not to understand sth: *You've totally lost me* (całkowicie się zgubiłem)*! Please explain again.* ▶ **tłumaczyć coś w tak zawiły sposób, że trudno to zrozumieć 5** [I,T] to not win; to be defeated: *We played well but we lost 2-1.* ◇ *to lose a court case/an argument* ◇ *Parma lost to Milan in the final.* ▶ **przegrywać 6** [I,T] to become poorer (as a result of sth): *The company lost on the deal.* ▶ **ponosić straty 7** [T] to waste

lorry

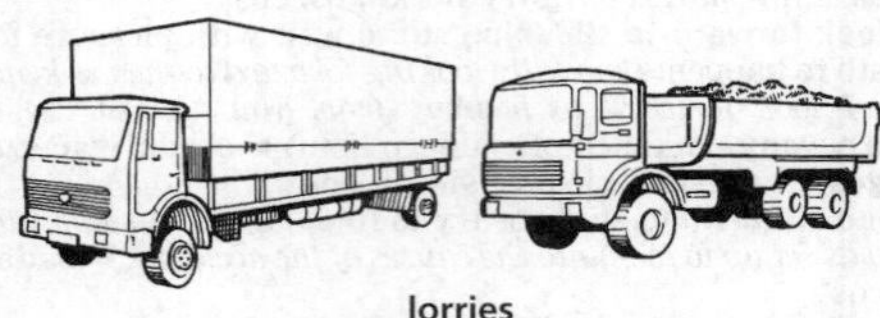

lorries
(especially US **trucks**)

vans

time, a chance, etc.: *Hurry up! There's **no time to lose.*** ▶ **tracić; przepuszczać, marnować** (*okazję*) **8** [I,T] (used about a clock, watch, etc.) to go too slowly: *My watch loses two minutes a day.* ▶ **późnić się** OPP **gain**
IDM **give/lose ground (to sb/sth)** → GROUND[1]
keep/lose your cool → COOL[3]
keep/lose count (of sth) → COUNT[2]
keep/lose your temper → TEMPER
keep/lose track of sb/sth → TRACK[1]
lose your bearings to become confused about where you are ▶ **tracić orientację, gubić się**
lose face to lose the respect of other people ▶ **tracić twarz**
lose your head to become confused or very excited ▶ **tracić głowę**
lose heart to stop believing that you will be successful in sth you are trying to do ▶ **tracić serce (do czegoś)**
lose it (informal) to go crazy or suddenly become unable to control your emotions ▶ **zwariować**
lose your life to be killed ▶ **tracić życie**
lose your place to be unable to find the place in a book, etc. where you stopped reading ▶ **gubić miejsce** (*np. w książce*)
lose sight of sb/sth 1 to no longer be able to see sb/sth ▶ **tracić kogoś/coś z pola widzenia 2** to forget sb/sth: *We mustn't lose sight of our original aim.* ▶ **tracić kogoś/coś z oczu, zapominać o kimś/czymś**
lose your touch to lose a special skill or ability ▶ **tracić (specjalną) umiejętność**
lose touch (with sb/sth) to no longer have contact (with sb/sth): *I've lost touch with a lot of my old school friends.* ▶ **tracić kontakt (z kimś, z czymś)**
a losing battle a competition, fight, etc. in which it seems that you will fail to be successful ▶ **przegrana bitwa**
win/lose the toss → TOSS
PHR V **lose out (on sth/to sb)** (informal) to be at a disadvantage: *If a teacher pays too much attention to the brightest students in the class, the others lose out.* ▶ **tracić (na czymś)**

loser /ˈluːzə(r)/ noun [C] **1** a person who is defeated: *He is a bad loser.* Nie umie przegrywać. ▶ **przegrywający-y/a, zwyciężon-y/a 2** a person who is never successful ▶ **ofiara** (*życiowa*) **3** a person who suffers because of a particular situation, decision, etc. ▶ **przegran-y/a, poszkodowan-y/a**

loss /lɒs/ noun **1** [C,U] **(a) loss (of sth)** the state of no longer having sth or not having as much as before; the act of losing sth: *loss of sleep* ◇ *loss of blood* (upływ krwi)*/money* ◇ *weight/hair loss* ◇ *Have you reported the loss of your wallet?* ◇ *The plane crashed with great **loss of life.*** ▶ **strata, zguba 2** [C] **a loss (of sth)** the amount of money which is lost by a business: *The firm **made a loss** of £5 million.* ▶ **strata, ubytek** ➲ look at **profit 3** [C] **a loss (to**

sb) the disadvantage that is caused when sb/sth leaves or is taken away; the person or thing that causes this disadvantage: *If she leaves, it/she will be a big loss to the school.* ▶ **strata**

IDM **at a loss** not knowing what to do or say ▶ **nie wiedząc, co zrobić/powiedzieć**

cut your losses to stop wasting time or money on sth that is not successful ▶ **zapobiegać dalszym stratom**

lost¹ past tense, past participle of **lose**

lost² /lɒst/ adj. **1** unable to find your way; not knowing where you are: *This isn't the right road – we're completely lost!* ◇ *If you* ***get lost****, stop and ask someone the way.* ◇ *Don't get lost!* Nie zgub się! ▶ **zgubiony, zagubiony** **2** that cannot be found or that no longer exists: *The letter must have* ***got lost*** *in the post.* ▶ **zaginiony, zgubiony** **3** unable to deal with a situation or to understand sth: *Sorry, I'm lost* (zgubiłem się). *Could you explain the last part again?* ▶ **zgubiony (bez czegoś)** **4** **lost on sb** not noticed or understood by sb: *The humour of the situation was completely lost on John* (komizm tej sytuacji w ogóle nie dotarł do Johna) *and he got quite angry.* ▶ **niezauważony, niezrozumiały**

IDM **get lost** (slang) (used to rudely tell sb to go away) ▶ **spływaj!, zjeżdżaj!**

a lost cause a goal or an aim that cannot be achieved ▶ **przegrana sprawa**

be lost for words to not know what to say ▶ **nie znajdować słów**

ˌlost and ˈfound (US) = LOST PROPERTY (2)

ˌlost ˈproperty noun [U] (Brit.) **1** things that people have lost or left in a public place and that are kept in a special office for the owners to collect: *a lost property office* ▶ **rzeczy zagubione** **2** (US **lost and found**) the place where items that have been found are kept until they are collected ▶ **biuro rzeczy znalezionych**

lot¹ /lɒt/ pron., determiner (**a lot (of)**; **lots (of)**) a large amount or number (of things or people): *'How many do you need?' 'A lot.'* ◇ *I've got* ***a lot to do*** *today.* ◇ *Have some more cake. There's lots left.* ◇ ***An awful lot*** *of people will be disappointed if the concert is cancelled.* ◇ *There seem to be* ***quite a lot*** *of new shops opening.* ◇ *Sit here – there's lots of room.* ▶ **dużo, wiele** ➲ note at **many**

lot² /lɒt/ adv. (informal) **1** (**a lot**; **lots**) [before an adjective or adverb] very much: *a lot bigger/better/faster* ◇ *They see lots more of each other than before.* ▶ **znacznie, o wiele** **2** (**a lot**) very much or often: ***Thanks a lot*** (bardzo) *– that's very kind.* ◇ *It generally rains a lot at this time of year.* ▶ **dużo; często**

lot³ /lɒt/ noun **1** [sing., with sing. or pl. verb] (informal) all of sth; the whole of a group of things or people: *When we opened the bag of potatoes* ***the whole lot*** *was/were bad.* ◇ *The manager has just sacked* ***the lot of them!*** ◇ *Just one more suitcase and* ***that's the lot!*** ◇ *'How many of these books shall we take?' '****The lot.****'* ▶ **wszystko/wszyscy (razem), całość** **2** [C, with sing. or pl. verb] a group or set of people or things: *You count those kids and I'll count* ***this lot.*** ◇ *This lot of clothes needs/need ironing.* ▶ **grupa** (*ludzi*); **partia** (*rzeczy*) **3** [sing.] the quality or state of a person's life; your fate: *Although things have not been easy for him, he's always been perfectly happy with his lot.* ▶ **los, dola** **4** [C] an object or group of objects that are for sale at an auction ▶ **pozycja** **5** [C] an area of land used for a particular purpose: *a parking lot* ▶ **działka, parcela**

IDM **draw lots** → DRAW¹

a lot of /ə ˈlɒt əv/ (also informal **lots of** /ˈlɒts əv/) determiner a large amount or number of (sb/sth): *There's been a lot of rain this year.* ◇ *There were a lot of people at the meeting.* ◇ *Lots of love* (uściski), *Billy.* ◇ *What a lot of books!* Ile książek! ▶ **dużo, mnóstwo** ➲ look at **many**

ˌlo-ˈtech = LOW-TECH

loth = LOATH

lotion /ˈləʊʃn/ noun [C,U] liquid that you use on your hair or skin: *suntan lotion* ▶ **emulsja** (*kosmetyczna*), **krem** (*np. do rąk*), **mleczko** (*do twarzy*)

lotta /ˈlɒtə/ (also **lotsa** /ˈlɒtsə/) (informal) (a written form of 'lot of' or 'lots of' that shows how it sounds in informal speech): *We're gonna have a lotta fun.* Będziemy mieli kupę zabawy. ▶ **dużo** ℹ To wyrażenie jest bardzo potoczne.

lottery /ˈlɒtəri/ noun [C] (pl. **lotteries**) a way of making money for the government, for charity, etc. by selling tickets with numbers on them and giving prizes to the people who have bought certain numbers which are chosen by chance ▶ **loteria**

loud /laʊd/ adj. **1** making a lot of noise; not quiet: *Can you turn the TV down – it's too loud.* ▶ **głośny, hałaśliwy** OPP **quiet, soft**

> Przymiotnika **loud** zwykle używa się do opisania samego dźwięku lub przedmiotu wydającego dźwięk: *a loud noise/bang* ◇ *loud music.* **Noisy** oznacza osobę, zwierzę, miejsce, wydarzenie itp., które jest bardzo głośne lub zbyt głośne: *a noisy road/party/engine/child/neighbours.*

2 (used about clothes or colours) too bright: *a loud shirt* ▶ **krzykliwy**

■ **loud** adv. making a lot of noise: *Could you speak a bit louder – the people at the back can't hear.* ▶ **głośno** | **loudly** adv. ▶ **głośno** | **loudness** noun [U] ▶ **głośność; krzykliwość**

IDM **out loud** so that people can hear it: *Shall I read this bit out loud to you?* ▶ **głośno, na głos**

loudspeaker /ˌlaʊdˈspiːkə(r)/ noun [C] **1** a piece of electrical equipment for speaking, playing music, etc. to a lot of people ▶ **głośnik** **2** = SPEAKER (3)

lounge¹ /laʊndʒ/ noun [C] **1** the part of an airport where passengers wait: *the departure lounge* ▶ **hala odlotów** **2** (Brit.) a comfortable room in a house or hotel where you can sit and relax ▶ **salon, hol** SYN **living room**

lounge² /laʊndʒ/ verb [I] **lounge (about/around)** to sit, stand or in a lazy way: *Stop lounging about* (przestań się wałkonić) *and do something useful!* ▶ **stać/siedzieć/leżeć w niedbałej pozie**

ˈlounge bar (also **saloon**) noun [C] (Brit.) a smart, comfortable bar in a pub or hotel (where the drinks may be more expensive) ▶ **sala klubowa, bar hotelowy** ➲ note at **pub, bar**

louse /laʊs/ noun [C] (pl. **lice** /laɪs/) a small insect that lives on the bodies of animals and people ▶ **wesz**

lousy /ˈlaʊzi/ adj. (**lousier**; **lousiest**) (informal) very bad: *We had lousy weather on holiday.* ▶ **parszywy, wstrętny**

lout /laʊt/ noun [C] a young man who behaves in a rude, rough or stupid way ▶ **gbur** ➲ look at **hooligan, yob**

■ **loutish** adj. ▶ **gburowaty**

lovable (also **loveable**) /ˈlʌvəbl/ adj. having a character or appearance that is easy to love: *a lovable little boy* ▶ **kochany; sympatyczny**

love¹ /lʌv/ noun **1** [U] a strong feeling that you have when you like sb/sth very much: *a mother's love for her children* ◇ *to* ***fall in love*** *with somebody* zakochać się w kimś ◇ *It was* ***love at first sight.*** *They got married two months after they met!* ◇ *He's* ***madly in love*** (szalenie zakochany) *with her.* ◇ *a love song/story* ◇ *How's your love life* (życie intymne)*?* ▶ **miłość** OPP **hate, hatred** **2** [U, sing.] a strong feeling of interest in or enjoyment of sth: *a love of adventure/nature/sport* ▶ **zamiłowanie** **3** [C] a person, a thing or an activity that you like very much: *His great love was always music.* ◇ *Who was your first love?* ◇ *Of course, my love* (kochanie). ▶ **miłość (do kogoś/czegoś)** **4** [C] (Brit., informal) (used as a friendly way of speaking to sb, often

sb you do not know): *'Hello, love. What can I do for you?'* ▶ **kochanie** ➲ look at **darling** ℹ Spotyka się również pisownię **luv**. **5** [U] (in tennis) a score of zero: *'15-love* (piętnaście do zera), *' called the umpire.* ▶ (*w tenisie*) **zero**
IDM **give/send sb your love** to give/send sb a friendly message: *Give Maria my love when you next see her.* ▶ **pozdrawiać, przesyłać pozdrowienia**
(lots of) love (from) (used at the end of a letter to a friend or a member of your family): *See you soon. Love, Jim* ▶ **pozdrowienia, serdeczne uściski** ℹ Spotyka się również pisownię **luv**.
make love (to sb) to have sex ▶ **kochać się (z kimś)**

⚷ **love²** /lʌv/ verb [T] **1** [not used in the continuous tenses] to like sb/sth in the strongest possible way: *I split up from my girlfriend last year, but I still love her.* ◇ *She loves her children.* ▶ **kochać 2** to like or enjoy sth very much: *I love the summer!* ◇ *I really love swimming in the sea.* ◇ *'What do you think of this music?' 'I love it!'* ▶ **lubić, uwielbiać 3 would love sth/to do sth** (used to say that you would very much like sth/to do sth): *'Would you like to come?' 'I'd love to* (z przyjemnością)*.'* ◇ *'What about a drink?' 'I'd love one* (chętnie)*.'* ◇ *We'd love you to come and stay with us.* ▶ **(bardzo) chcieć**

ˈ**love affair** noun [C] **1** a romantic and/or sexual relationship between two people who are in love and not married to each other: *She had a love affair with her tennis coach.* ▶ **romans 2** a great enthusiasm for sth ▶ **zamiłowanie**

ˈ**love life** noun [C] the part of your life that involves your romantic and sexual relationships ▶ **życie intymne**

⚷ **lovely** /ˈlʌvli/ adj. (**lovelier**; **loveliest**) **1** beautiful or attractive: *a lovely room/voice/expression* ◇ *You look lovely with your hair short.* ▶ **uroczy, śliczny 2** enjoyable or pleasant; very nice: *We had a lovely holiday.* ▶ **wspaniały, świetny** ➲ note at **nice**
■ **loveliness** noun [U] ▶ **urok**
IDM **lovely and warm, peaceful, fresh, etc.** (used for emphasizing how good sth is because of the quality mentioned): *These blankets are lovely and soft.* ▶ **rozkosznie** (*np. ciepły*), **doskonale** (*np. spokojny*)

⚷ **lover** /ˈlʌvə(r)/ noun [C] **1** a partner in a sexual relationship with sb who they are not married to: *He discovered that his wife had a lover.* ◇ *The park was full of young lovers holding hands.* ▶ **kochan-ek/ka** ➲ look at **mistress 2** a person who likes or enjoys the thing mentioned: *a music lover* ◇ *an animal lover* ◇ *a music lover* meloman/ka ▶ **miłośni-k/czka**

ˈ**love story** noun [C] (pl. **love stories**) a story or novel that is mainly about love ▶ **romans** (*powieść*), **historia miłosna**

loving /ˈlʌvɪŋ/ adj. **1** feeling or showing love or care: *She's very loving towards her brother.* ◇ *a loving family* ▶ **kochający, oddany** SYN **affectionate 2** [in compounds] (**-loving**) loving the thing or activity mentioned: *a fun-loving girl* ▶ **kochający**
■ **lovingly** adv. ▶ **z miłością, z oddaniem**

⚷ **low¹** /ləʊ/ adj. **1** close to the ground or to the bottom of sth: *Hang that picture a bit higher – it's much too low* (jest za nisko)*!* ▶ **niski 2** below the usual or normal level or amount: *Temperatures were very low last winter.* ◇ *The price of fruit is lower in the summer.* ◇ *low wages* ◇ *low-fat* (chudy) *yogurt* ▶ **niski, o niskiej zawartości** (*np. soli, alkoholu*) **3** below what is normal or acceptable in quality, importance or development: *a low standard of living* ◇ *low status* ▶ **niski 4** deep or quiet: *His voice is already lower than his father's.* ◇ *A group of people in the library were speaking in low voices* (ściszonym głosem). ▶ (*głos/dźwięk*) **niski 5** not happy and lacking energy: *He's been **feeling** a bit **low** since his illness.* ◇ *The team are **in low spirits*** (jest przygnębiona) *after their defeat.* ▶ **kiepski, przygnębiony 6** (used about a light, an oven, etc.) made to produce only a little light or heat: *Cook the rice on a low heat* (na słabym ogniu) *for 25 minutes.* ◇ *The low lighting adds to the restaurant's atmosphere.* ▶ **(o) niskiej/słabej mocy 7** (used about a gear in a car) that allows a slower speed ▶ **niski** OPP **high 8** (used about behaviour, etc.) unpleasant, not respectable and honest: *That was rather a low trick to play on you.* ▶ **podły, niski**
IDM **high and low** → HIGH³
a high/low profile → PROFILE
lie low → LIE²
run low (on sth) to start to have less of sth than you need; to start to be less than is needed: *We're running low on coffee – shall I go and buy some?* ▶ (*zapasy, produkty itp.*) **kończyć się**

low² adv. /ləʊ/ **1** in or to a low position, level, etc.; near the ground or bottom; not high: *That plane is flying very low.* ▶ **nisko 2** (in music) with deep notes: *I can't sing that low.* ▶ **nisko**

low³ /ləʊ/ noun [C] a low point, level, figure, etc.: *Unemployment has fallen to a new low.* ▶ **niski poziom** OPP **high**

ˈ**low-down** noun
IDM **give sb/get the low-down (on sb/sth)** (informal) to tell sb/be told the true facts or secret information (about sb/sth) ▶ **poufna wiadomość**

lower¹ /ˈləʊə(r)/ adj. [only before a noun] below sth or at the bottom of sth: *She bit her lower lip.* ◇ *the lower deck of a ship* ▶ **niższy, dolny** OPP **upper**

lower² /ˈləʊə(r)/ verb [T] **1** to make or let sb/sth go down: *They lowered the boat into the water.* ◇ *to lower your head/eyes* ▶ **zniżać, spuszczać 2** to make sth less in amount, quality, etc.: *The virus lowers resistance to other diseases.* ◇ *Could you **lower your voice*** (zciszyć głos) *slightly? I'm trying to sleep.* ▶ **obniżać, zmniejszać, osłabiać** OPP for both meanings **raise**

ˌ**lower ˈcase** noun [U] letters that are written or printed in their small form; not in capital letters: *The text is all in lower case.* ◇ *lower-case letters* ▶ **pisany małą literą; małe litery** OPP **upper case**

ˌ**lower-ˈclass** adj. belonging to a low social class ▶ **niższej warstwy społecznej**

ˌ**low-ˈkey** adj. quiet and not wanting to attract a lot of attention: *The wedding will be very low-key. We're only inviting ten people.* ▶ **dyskretny, cichy**

lowland /ˈləʊlənd/ noun [C, usually pl.] a flat area of land at about sea level: *the lowlands near the coast* ◇ *lowland areas* ▶ **nizina** ➲ look at **highland**

lowly /ˈləʊli/ adj. (**lowlier**; **lowliest**) (often humorous) low in status or importance: *a lowly government clerk* ▶ **podrzędny** SYN **humble, obscure**

ˌ**low-ˈlying** adj. (used about land) near to sea level; not high ▶ **nizinny**

ˌ**low-ˈpaid** adj. not paying or earning much money ▶ **nisko płatny**

ˌ**low-ˈprofile** adj. [only before a noun] receiving or involving very little attention: *a low-profile* (dyskretna) *campaign* ▶ **nieprzyciągający uwagi**

ˌ**low-resoˈlution** adj. (used about a photograph or an image on a computer or television screen) not showing a lot of clear detail: *a low-resolution scan* ▶ **o niskiej rozdzielczości** OPP **high-resolution**

low-tech (also **lo-tech**) /ˌləʊ ˈtek/ adj. (informal) not using the most modern technology or methods ▶ **wykorzystujący technikę tradycyjną** OPP **high-tech**

ˌ**low ˈtide** noun [U] the time when the sea is at its lowest level: *At low tide you can walk out to the island.* ▶ **odpływ** OPP **high tide**

loyal /ˈlɔɪəl/ adj. (used about a person) not changing in your friendship or beliefs: *a loyal friend/supporter* ▶ **lojalny** SYN **faithful** OPP **disloyal**
■ **loyally** adv. ▶ **lojalnie** | **loyalty** /ˈlɔɪəlti/ noun [C,U] (pl. **loyalties**) ▶ **lojalność**

lozenge /ˈlɒzɪndʒ/ noun [C] a sweet that you suck if you have a cough or a sore throat ▶ **pastylka do ssania**

L-plate /ˈel pleɪt/ noun [C] a sign with a large red letter L (for 'learner') on it, that you fix to a car to show that the driver is learning to drive ▶ **tablica oznaczająca, że kierujący pojazdem uczy się jeździć, nauka jazdy**

Lt = LIEUTENANT

Ltd (Brit.) = LIMITED COMPANY: *Pierce and Co Ltd*

lubricant /ˈluːbrɪkənt/ noun [C,U] a substance, for example oil, that makes the parts of a machine work easily and smoothly ▶ **smar, oliwa**

lubricate /ˈluːbrɪkeɪt/ verb [T] to put oil, etc. onto or into sth so that it works smoothly ▶ **smarować, oliwić**
■ **lubrication** /ˌluːbrɪˈkeɪʃn/ noun [U] ▶ **smarowanie, oliwienie**

lucid /ˈluːsɪd/ adj. (formal) **1** (used about sth that is said or written) clear and easy to understand: *a lucid style/description* ▶ **klarowny, jasny** **2** (used about sb's mind) not confused; clear and normal ▶ **trzeźwy, jasny**
■ **lucidly** adv. ▶ **klarownie, jasno** | **lucidity** /luːˈsɪdəti/ noun [U] ▶ **klarowność, jasność**

luck /lʌk/ noun [U] **1** success or good things that happen by chance: *We'd like to **wish** you lots of **luck** in your new career.* ◇ *He says this necklace will **bring** you **luck**.* ◇ *I could hardly believe my luck when they offered me the job.* ◇ ***With a bit of luck**, we'll finish this job today.* ▶ **powodzenie, szczęście** **2** chance; the force that people believe makes things happen: *There's no skill in this game – it's all luck.* ◇ *to have good/bad luck* mieć szczęście/nieszczęście ▶ **traf, los** ➲ look at **fortune**
IDM **bad luck!; hard luck!** (used to show pity for sb): *'Bad luck. Maybe you'll win next time.'* ▶ **a to pech!**
be in/out of luck to be lucky/to not be lucky: *I was in luck – they had one ticket left!* ▶ **(nie) mieć szczęści-e/a**
good luck (to sb) (used to wish that sb is successful): *Good luck* (powodzenia)*! I'm sure you'll get the job.* ▶ **powodzenie, szczęście**
push your luck → PUSH[1]
worse luck → WORSE

lucky /ˈlʌki/ adj. (**luckier**; **luckiest**) **1** (used about a person) having good luck: *He's lucky to be alive after an accident like that.* ◇ *With so much unemployment, I **count myself lucky** that I've got a job.* ◇ *'I'm off on holiday next week.' 'Lucky you!'* ◇ *I'm very lucky* (jestem szczęściarzem) *to have such good friends.* ▶ **mający szczęście** **2** (used about a situation, event, etc.) having a good result: *It's lucky* (na szczęście) *you reminded me.* ▶ **szczęśliwy** **3** (used about a thing) bringing success or good luck: *a lucky number* ◇ *It was not my lucky day.* ▶ **szczęśliwy** OPP **unlucky**
■ **luckily** adv.: *Luckily, I remembered to bring some money.* ▶ **szczęśliwie, na szczęście**
IDM **you'll be lucky** (used to tell sb that sth they are expecting will probably not happen): *You're looking for a good English restaurant? You'll be lucky!* ▶ **nie licz na to!**

ˌlucky ˈdip (US ˈgrab bag) noun [usually sing.] a game in which people choose a present from a container of presents without being able to see what it is going to be ▶ **kosz szczęścia**

lucrative /ˈluːkrətɪv/ adj. (formal) allowing sb to earn a lot of money: *a lucrative contract/business/market* ▶ **zyskowny**

ludicrous /ˈluːdɪkrəs/ adj. very silly: *What a ludicrous idea!* ▶ **śmieszny, niedorzeczny** SYN **ridiculous**
■ **ludicrously** adv.: *a ludicrously expensive project* ▶ **śmiesznie, niedorzecznie**

lug /lʌg/ verb [T] (**lugging**; **lugged**) (informal) to carry or pull sth very heavy with great difficulty ▶ **wlec, taszczyć**

luggage /ˈlʌgɪdʒ/ noun [U] bags, suitcases, etc. used for carrying sb's clothes and things on a journey: *'How much luggage are you taking with you?' 'Only one suitcase.'* ▶ **bagaż** SYN **baggage**

> When flying, you will be asked to pay for **excess luggage** if your suitcases weigh more than is allowed. You are only allowed one piece of **hand luggage**.

ˈluggage rack noun [C] a shelf above the seats in a train or bus for putting your bags, etc. on ▶ **półka na bagaż** ➲ picture at **rack**

lukewarm /ˌluːkˈwɔːm/ adj. **1** (used about liquids) only slightly warm ▶ **letni** **2 lukewarm (about sb/sth)** not showing much interest or desire ▶ **bez zapału**

lull[1] /lʌl/ noun [C, usually sing.] **a lull (in sth)** a short period of quiet between times of activity ▶ **chwilowa cisza**

lull[2] /lʌl/ verb [T] **1** to make sb relaxed and calm: *She sang a song to **lull** the children **to sleep**.* ▶ **lulać, ukołysać** **2 lull sb into sth** to make sb feel safe, and not expecting anything bad to happen: *Our first success **lulled** us **into a false sense of security*** (uśpił naszą czujność). ▶ **usypiać** (*np. czujność*)

lullaby /ˈlʌləbaɪ/ noun [C] (pl. **lullabies**) a gentle song that you sing to help a child to go to sleep ▶ **kołysanka**

lumber[1] (especially US) = TIMBER (1)

lumber[2] /ˈlʌmbə(r)/ verb **1** [I] to move in a slow, heavy way: *A family of elephants lumbered past.* ▶ **chodzić ociężale** **2** [T, usually passive] (informal) **lumber sb (with sb/sth)** to give sb a responsibility or job that they do not want ▶ **zwalać na kogoś** (*np. pracę*)

luminous /ˈluːmɪnəs/ adj. that shines in the dark: *a luminous watch* ▶ **świecący (się), jarzący**

lump[1] /lʌmp/ noun [C] **1** a piece of sth solid of any size or shape: *The sauce was full of lumps.* ◇ *a lump of coal/cheese/wood* ▶ **kawałek, grudka, bryła** ➲ picture at **bar** **2** a swelling under the skin: *You'll have a bit of a lump on your head where you banged it.* ▶ **guz**
IDM **have/feel a lump in your throat** to feel pressure in your throat because you are about to cry ▶ **mieć ściśnięte gardło**

lump[2] /lʌmp/ verb [T] **lump A and B together**; **lump A (in) with B** to put or consider different people or things together in the same group ▶ **wrzucać do jednego worka**
IDM **lump it** (informal) to accept sth unpleasant because you have no choice: *That's the deal – like it or lump it.* ▶ **pogodzić się z czymś**

ˈlump sum noun [C] an amount of money paid all at once rather than in several smaller amounts ▶ **jednorazowa wypłata**

lumpy /ˈlʌmpi/ adj. full of or covered with lumps: *This bed is very lumpy.* ▶ **bryłowaty, guzowaty, grudkowaty** OPP **smooth**

lunacy /ˈluːnəsi/ noun [U] behaviour that is very stupid: *It was lunacy to drive so fast in that terrible weather.* ▶ **obłęd, szaleństwo** SYN **madness**

lunar /ˈluːnə(r)/ adj. connected with the moon: *a lunar spacecraft/eclipse/landscape* ▶ **księżycowy**

lunatic[1] /ˈluːnətɪk/ noun [C] (informal) **1** a person who behaves in a stupid way doing crazy and often dangerous things ▶ **wariat/ka, szaleniec** SYN **madman, maniac** **2** (old-fashioned) a person who is mad ▶ **człowiek umysłowo chory**

L

Uwaga! „Lunaty-k/czka" to **sleepwalker**.

lunatic² /ˈluːnətɪk/ adj. stupid; crazy: *a lunatic idea* ▶ **wariacki, szaleńczy**

lunch /lʌntʃ/ noun [C,U] a meal that you have in the middle of the day: *Hot and cold lunches are served between 12 and 2.* ◇ *What would you like for lunch?* ◇ *to have lunch* jeść lunch ◇ *a* ***packed lunch*** kanapki itp. przygotowane jako drugie śniadanie poza domem ◇ *a picnic lunch* piknik ◇ *a business/working lunch* lunch roboczy ▶ **lunch, obiad** ➲ note at **meal**, **dinner**
■ **lunch** verb [I] (formal) ▶ **jeść lunch/obiad, iść na lunch/obiad**

ˈ**lunch box** noun [C] a container to hold a meal that you take away from home to eat ▶ **pojemnik na drugie śniadanie/lunch**

luncheon /ˈlʌntʃən/ noun [C,U] (formal) **lunch**

ˈ**lunch hour** noun [C, usually sing.] the time around the middle of the day when you stop work or school to have **lunch**: *I went to the shops in my lunch hour.* ▶ **przerwa obiadowa**

lunchtime /ˈlʌntʃtaɪm/ noun [C,U] the time around the middle of the day when **lunch** is eaten: *I'll meet you at lunchtime.* ▶ **pora lunchu/obiadu**

lung /lʌŋ/ noun [C] one of the two organs of your body that are inside your chest and are used for breathing ▶ **płuco** ➲ picture at **body**

lunge /lʌndʒ/ noun [C, usually sing.] **a lunge (at sb)**; **a lunge (for sb/sth)** a sudden powerful forward movement of the body, especially when trying to attack sb/sth: *She made a lunge for the ball.* ▶ **gwałtowny ruch do przodu**
■ **lunge** verb [I]: *He lunged towards me with a knife.* ▶ **rzucać się do przodu**

lurch /lɜːtʃ/ noun [C, usually sing.] a sudden movement forward or to one side ▶ **przechył**
■ **lurch** verb [I] ▶ **przechylać się**
IDM **leave sb in the lurch** → LEAVE¹

lure¹ /lʊə(r)/ verb [T] to persuade or trick sb to go somewhere or do sth, usually by offering them sth nice: *Young people are lured to the city by the prospect of a job and money.* ▶ **kusić, wabić**

lure² /lʊə(r)/ noun [C] the attractive qualities of sth: *the lure of money/fame/adventure* ▶ **przynęta, pokusa**

lurid /ˈlʊərɪd; Brit. also ˈljʊər-/ adj. **1** having colours that are too bright, in a way that is not attractive: *a lurid purple and orange dress* ▶ **jaskrawy, krzyczący 2** (used about a story or a piece of writing) deliberately shocking, especially because of violent or unpleasant detail ▶ **krzykliwy**
■ **luridly** adv. ▶ **przerażająco; krzykliwie**

lurk /lɜːk/ verb [I] to wait somewhere secretly especially in order to do sth bad or illegal: *I thought I saw somebody lurking among the trees.* ▶ **czaić się, kryć się**

luscious /ˈlʌʃəs/ adj. (used about food) tasting very good: *luscious fruit* ▶ **smakowity, wyśmienity**

lush /lʌʃ/ adj. (used about plants or gardens) growing well, with a lot of healthy grass and plants close together ▶ **bujny**

lust¹ /lʌst/ noun **1** [U] **lust (for sb)** strong sexual desire ▶ **żądza, namiętność 2** [C,U] **(a) lust (for sth)** (a) very strong desire to have or get sth: *a lust for power* ◇ *(a) lust for life* ▶ **żądza, pożądanie**

lust² /lʌst/ verb [I] **lust (after sb)** ; **lust (after/for sth)** to feel a very strong desire for sb/sth: *to lust for power/success/fame* ▶ **pożądać, pragnąć**

lustful /ˈlʌstfl/ adj. full of sexual desire: *lustful thoughts* ▶ **pożądliwy, lubieżny**
■ **lustfully** /-fəli/ adv. ▶ **pożądliwie, lubieżnie**

lute /luːt/ noun [C] a musical instrument with strings, played like a guitar. Lutes were used especially in the 14th-17th centuries. ▶ **lutnia**

luv /lʌv/ noun **1** (Brit.) (a way of spelling 'love', when used as an informal way of addressing sb): *Never mind, luv.* ▶ **kochanie 2** (an informal way of spelling 'love', for example when ending a letter): *See you soon, lots of luv, Sue.* ▶ **całusy**

luxuriant /lʌgˈʒʊəriənt/ adj. (used about plants or hair) growing thickly and strongly in a way that is attractive: *luxuriant vegetation* ◇ *thick, luxuriant hair* ▶ **bujny**
■ **luxuriance** /-əns/ noun [U] ▶ **bujność; bogactwo**

luxurious /lʌgˈʒʊəriəs/ adj. very comfortable; full of expensive and beautiful things: *a luxurious hotel* ▶ **luksusowy**
■ **luxuriously** adv. ▶ **luksusowo; rozkosznie**

luxury /ˈlʌkʃəri/ noun (pl. **luxuries**) **1** [U] the enjoyment of expensive and beautiful things; great comfort and pleasure: *They are said to be* ***living in luxury*** *in Barbados.* ◇ *to lead* ***a life of luxury*** ◇ *a luxury hotel/car/yacht* ▶ **luksus, zbytek 2** [C] something that is enjoyable and expensive that you do not really need: *luxury goods, such as wine and chocolates* ▶ **luksus 3** [U, sing.] a pleasure which you do not often have: *It was (an) absolute luxury to do nothing all weekend.* ▶ **luksus**

LW abbr. (especially Brit.) **long wave**; a band of radio waves with a length of more than 1000 metres: *1 500m LW* ▶ *(radio)* **fale długie**

lynch /lɪntʃ/ verb [T] (used about a crowd of people) to kill, usually by hanging, sb who is thought to be guilty of a crime without a legal trial in a court of law ▶ **linczować, dokonywać samosądu**

lynchpin = LINCHPIN

lyric /ˈlɪrɪk/ adj. (used about poetry) expressing personal feelings and thoughts: *lyric poems* ▶ **liryczny**

lyrical /ˈlɪrɪkl/ adj. like a song or a poem, expressing strong personal feelings ▶ **liryczny**

lyricist /ˈlɪrɪsɪst/ noun [C] a person who writes the words of songs ▶ **autor tekstów piosenek**

lyrics /ˈlɪrɪks/ noun [pl.] the words of a song ▶ **słowa** *(piosenki)*

Mm

M, m /em/ noun [C,U] (pl. **Ms**; **ms**; **M's**; **m's** /emz/) the 13th letter of the English alphabet: *'Mark' begins with (an) 'M'.* ▶ **litera** *m*

M abbr. **1** (also **med**) = MEDIUM¹ **2** (Brit.) = MOTORWAY: *heavy traffic on the M25*

m abbr. **1** (**m**) = METRE: *a 500m race* **2** (**m**) = MILLION: *population 10m*

MA /ˌem ˈeɪ/ abbr. **Master of Arts**; a second degree that you receive when you complete a more advanced course or piece of research in an arts subject at university or college ▶ **mgr** ➲ look at **BA**, **MSc**

mac (also **mack**) /mæk/ (also **mackintosh** /ˈmækɪntɒʃ/) noun [C] (especially Brit.) a coat that is made to keep out the rain ▶ **płaszcz nieprzemakalny**

macabre /məˈkɑːbrə/ adj. unpleasant and frightening because it is connected with death: *a macabre tale/joke/ritual* ▶ **makabryczny**

macaroni /ˌmækəˈrəʊni/ noun [U] a type of **pasta** in the shape of short tubes ▶ **makaron** *(typu rurki)* ➲ look at **noodle**

machete /məˈʃeti/ noun [C] a wide heavy knife used as a cutting tool and as a weapon ▶ **maczeta**

🔑 **machine** /mə'ʃi:n/ noun [C] [often in compounds] a piece of equipment with moving parts that is designed to do a particular job. A machine usually needs electricity, gas, steam, etc. in order to work: *a machine for making pasta* ◇ *a sewing/knitting machine* ◇ *a washing machine* pralka automatyczna ➲ note at **tool** ▶ **maszyna**

ma'chine gun noun [C] a gun that fires bullets very quickly and continuously ▶ **karabin maszynowy** ➲ note at **gun**

ma,chine-'readable adj. (used about data) in a form that a computer can understand ▶ **nadający się do przetwarzania automatycznego/komputerowego**

🔑 **machinery** /mə'ʃi:nəri/ noun [U] machines in general, especially large ones; the moving parts of a machine: *farm/agricultural/industrial machinery* ▶ **maszyneria**, **mechanizm**

machinist /mə'ʃi:nɪst/ noun [C] **1** a person whose job is operating a machine, especially machines used in industry for cutting and shaping things, or a sewing machine ▶ **operator/ka maszyny** **2** a person whose job is to make or repair machines ▶ **mechanik**; **konstruktor/ka maszyn**

macho /'mætʃəʊ; US 'mɑ:-/ adj. (informal) (used about a man or his behaviour) having qualities typical of men, like strength and courage, but using them in an aggressive way: *He's too macho to ever admit he was wrong and apologize.* ▶ **macho**

mack = MAC

mackerel /'mækrəl/ noun [C] (pl. **mackerel**) a sea fish that you can eat, that has greenish-blue bands on its body ▶ **makrela**

mackintosh (Brit., old-fashioned) = MAC

macro /,mækrəʊ/ noun [C] (pl. **-os**) a single instruction in a computer program that automatically causes a complete series of instructions to be put into effect, in order to perform a particular task ▶ **makro**

macroeconomics /,mækrəʊi:kə'nɒmɪks; US -,ekə'n-/ noun [U] the study of large economic systems, such as those of whole countries or areas of the world ▶ **makroekonomia**

■ **macroeconomic** adj.: *macroeconomic policy* ▶ **makroekonomiczny**

🔑 **mad** /mæd/ adj. **1** having a mind that does not work normally; mentally ill: *They realized that he had* ***gone mad.*** ▶ **obłąkany**

> Zwykle nie używa się obecnie **mad** ani **insane** do określenia osoby umysłowo chorej. Odpowiednim zwrotem jest **mentally ill**.

2 (Brit.) not at all sensible; stupid: *You must be mad to drive in this weather.* ◇ *Have a good shopping trip, but* ***don't go mad*** (tylko nie szalej za bardzo) *and spend too much!* ▶ **szalony**, **zwariowany** **3** [not before a noun] **mad (at/with sb) (about sth)** very angry: *His laziness* ***drives*** *me* ***mad*** (doprowadza mnie do szału)*!* ◇ (especially US) *Don't* ***get/go mad*** *at him. He didn't mean to do it.* ▶ **wściekły** **4** (informal) **mad about/on sb/sth** liking sb/sth very much: *He's mad on computer games at the moment.* ◇ *Steve's mad about Jane.* ▶ **zwariowany (na punkcie kogoś/czegoś)** **5** not controlled; wild or very excited: *The audience was cheering and clapping like mad.* ◇ *When Brad Pitt appeared on the hotel balcony his fans* ***went mad.*** ▶ **dziki**, **oszalały**

madam /'mædəm/ noun [sing.] **1** (formal) (used as a polite way of speaking to a woman, especially to a customer in a shop or restaurant): *Can I help you, madam?* ▶ **proszę pani** ➲ look at **sir** **2** (**Madam**) (used for beginning a formal letter to a woman when you do not know her name): *Dear Madam* (Szanowna Pani), *I am writing in reply...* ▶ **pani** (*w nagłówku listu do nieznajomej kobiety*)

,mad 'cow disease (informal) = BSE

maddening /'mædnɪŋ/ adj. that makes you very angry or annoyed: *She has some really maddening habits.* ▶ **irytujący**

■ **maddeningly** adv. ▶ **irytująco**

made past tense, past participle of **make**[1]

,made to 'order adj. (especially US) (used about clothes, furniture, etc.) made specially for a particular customer ▶ **robiony na zamówienie**

'made-up adj. **1** wearing make-up: *a heavily* ***made-up face/woman*** ▶ **umalowany** **2** not true or real; invented: *a* ***made-up story/word/name*** ▶ **wymyślony**

madly /'mædli/ adv. **1** in a wild or crazy way: *They were rushing about madly.* ▶ **wściekle** **2** (informal) very; extremely: *They're madly in love.* ▶ **szalenie**

madman /'mædmən/, **madwoman** /'mædwʊmən/ noun [C] (pl. **-men** /-mən/) (pl. **-women** /-wɪmɪn/) a person who behaves in a wild or crazy way ▶ **obłąkaniec**; **wariat/ka** SYN **lunatic**

madness /'mædnəs/ noun [U] **1** crazy or stupid behaviour that could be dangerous: *It would be madness to take a boat out on the sea in such rough weather.* ▶ **szaleństwo** **2** (old-fashioned) the state of having a serious mental illness ▶ **obłęd**, **obłąkanie** ➲ **insanity**

🔑 **magazine** /,mægə'zi:n; US 'mægəzi:n/ (also informal **mag** /mæg/) noun [C] a type of large thin book with a paper cover that you can buy every week or month containing articles, photographs, etc. often on a particular topic: *a woman's/computer/gardening magazine* ▶ **czasopismo** ➲ note at **newspaper**

magenta /mə'dʒentə/ adj. reddish-purple in colour ▶ **o kolorze między czerwienią i fioletem**

■ **magenta** noun [U] ▶ **kolor fioletowo-czerwony**

maggot /'mægət/ noun [C] a young insect before it grows wings and legs and becomes a fly ▶ **larwa**

🔑 **magic**[1] /'mædʒɪk/ noun [U] **1** a secret power that some people believe can make strange or impossible things happen by saying special words or doing special things: *The witch had used her magic to turn the children into frogs.* ▶ **czary**, **magia** ➲ look at **black magic** **2** the art of doing tricks that seem impossible in order to entertain people ▶ **sztuczki magiczne** **3** a special quality that makes sth seem wonderful: *I'll never forget the magic of that moment.* ▶ **czar**, **magia**

🔑 **magic**[2] /'mædʒɪk/ adj. **1** (used in or using magic): *a magic spell/potion/charm/trick* ▶ **magiczny**, **czarodziejski** **2** having a special quality that makes sth seem wonderful: *Respect is the magic ingredient in our relationship.* ▶ **magiczny**

magical /'mædʒɪkl/ adj. **1** that seems to use magic: *a herb with magical powers to heal* ▶ **magiczny**, **czarodziejski** **2** wonderful and exciting: *Our holiday was absolutely magical.* ▶ **magiczny**

■ **magically** /-kli/ adv. ▶ **magicznie**; **cudownie**

magician /mə'dʒɪʃn/ noun [C] **1** a person who performs magic tricks to entertain people ▶ **magik** ➲ look at **conjuror** **2** (in stories) a man who has magic powers ▶ **czarodziej/ka** ➲ look at **wizard**

magistrate /'mædʒɪstreɪt/ noun [C] an official who acts as a judge in cases involving less serious crimes ▶ **urzędnik z uprawnieniami sędziowskimi, zajmujący się lżejszymi przestępstwami** ➲ look at **Justice of the Peace**

magnanimous /mæg'nænɪməs/ adj. kind, generous and forgiving (especially towards an enemy or opponent) ▶ **wielkoduszny**, **wspaniałomyślny**

M

magnate /ˈmæɡneɪt/ noun [C] a person who is rich, powerful and successful, especially in business: *a media/property/shipping magnate* ▶ **magnat**

magnesium /mæɡˈniːziəm/ noun [U] (symbol **Mg**) a light, silver-white metal that burns with a bright white flame ▶ (*chem.*) **magnez**

magnet /ˈmæɡnət/ noun [C] a piece of iron, steel, etc. that can attract and pick up other metal objects ▶ **magnes**

magnetic /mæɡˈnetɪk/ adj. **1** having the ability to attract metal objects: *magnetic fields* ◇ *a magnetic tape/disk* ▶ **magnetyczny 2** having a quality that strongly attracts people: *a magnetic personality* ▶ **porywający, przyciągający**
■ **magnetism** /ˈmæɡnətɪzəm/ noun [U]: *iron's magnetism* ◇ *Nobody could resist his magnetism.* ▶ **magnetyzm**

magnetize /ˈmæɡnətaɪz/ verb [T] **1** (technical) to make sth **magnetic** ▶ **magnetyzować 2** to strongly attract sb: *Cities have a powerful magnetizing effect on young people.* ▶ **pociągać, fascynować**

magnificent /mæɡˈnɪfɪsnt/ adj. extremely impressive and attractive: *What a magnificent castle!* ▶ **wspaniały, świetny** SYN **splendid**
■ **magnificence** noun [U] ▶ **wspaniałość, świetność** | **magnificently** adv. ▶ **wspaniale, świetnie**

magnify /ˈmæɡnɪfaɪ/ verb [T] (**magnifying**; **magnifies**; pt, pp **magnified**) **1** to make sth look bigger than it is, usually using a special piece of equipment: *to magnify something under a microscope* ▶ **powiększać** SYN **enlarge 2** to make sth seem more important than it really is: *to magnify a problem* ▶ **wyolbrzymiać, przesadzać** SYN **exaggerate**
■ **magnification** /ˌmæɡnɪfɪˈkeɪʃn/ noun [U] ▶ **powiększenie; wyolbrzymienie**

ˈ**magnifying glass** noun [C] a round piece of glass, usually with a handle, that is used for making things look bigger than they are ▶ **szkło powiększające**

magnitude /ˈmæɡnɪtjuːd; US -tuːd/ noun [U] the great size or importance of sth ▶ **ogrom, ważność**

magpie /ˈmæɡpaɪ/ noun [C] a noisy black and white bird that is attracted by, and often takes away, small bright objects ▶ **sroka**

mahogany /məˈhɒɡəni/ noun [U] the hard dark reddish-brown wood from a tropical tree that is used especially for making furniture ▶ **mahoń**

maid /meɪd/ noun [C] a woman whose job is to clean in a hotel or large house ▶ **pokojówka, służąca** ➲ look at **chambermaid**

maiden /ˈmeɪdn/ noun [C] (literary) a girl or an unmarried woman ▶ **panna, kobieta niezamężna**

ˈ**maiden name** noun [C] a woman's family name before marriage ▶ **nazwisko panieńskie** ➲ note at **name** ➲ look at **née**

ˌ**maiden ˈvoyage** noun [C] the first journey of a new ship ▶ **dziewiczy rejs**

⚷ **mail** /meɪl/ (Brit. also **post**) noun [U] **1** the system for collecting and sending letters and packages: *to send a parcel by airmail/surface mail* (pocztą lotniczą/lądową) ◇ *a mail van* furgonetka pocztowa ▶ **poczta, usługi pocztowe** ➲ note at **post 2** the letters, etc. that you receive: *There isn't much mail today.* ◇ *junk mail* niezamawiana korespondencja (zwykle reklamowa) ▶ **poczta, korespondencja 3** = EMAIL
■ **mail** verb [T] (especially US) ▶ **wysyłać** (*pocztą*)

mailbox /ˈmeɪlbɒks/ noun [C] **1** (US) = LETTER BOX (2) **2** (US) = POSTBOX **3** a computer program that receives and stores email ▶ **skrzynka pocztowa**

ˈ**mailing list** noun [C] a list of the names and addresses of people to whom advertising material or information is regularly sent by a business or an organization ▶ **lista adresowa**

mailman (US) = POSTMAN

ˌ**mail ˈorder** noun [U] a method of shopping. You choose what you want from a **catalogue** and the goods are sent to you by post. ▶ **sprzedaż wysyłkowa**

maim /meɪm/ verb [T] to hurt sb so badly that part of their body can no longer be used ▶ **okaleczyć**

⚷ **main**[1] /meɪn/ adj. [only before a noun] most important: *My main reason for wanting to learn English is to get a better job.* ◇ *a busy main road* ◇ *He doesn't earn very much but he's happy, and that's* ***the main thing.*** ▶ **główny, najważniejszy** SYN **chief**
IDM **in the main** (formal) generally; mostly: *We found English people very friendly in the main.* ▶ **przeważnie, głównie, na ogół**

main[2] /meɪn/ noun **1** [C] a large pipe or wire that carries water, gas or electricity between buildings: *The water main has burst.* ▶ **główna rura wodociągowa/kanalizacyjna/gazowa, główny przewód elektryczny 2** (**the mains**) [pl.] (Brit.) the place where the supply of gas, water or electricity to a building starts; the system of providing these services to a building: *Turn the water off at the mains.* ◇ *Plug the radio into the mains* (do sieci elektrycznej). ◇ *mains gas/water/electricity* ▶ **główny zawór; sieć** (*np. kanalizacyjna, elektryczna*)

mainframe /ˈmeɪnfreɪm/ (also ˌ**mainframe comˈputer**) noun [C] a large powerful computer, usually the centre of a system that is shared by many users ▶ **mainframe** ➲ look at **PC**

mainland /ˈmeɪnlænd/ noun [sing.] the main part of a country or continent, not including the islands around it: *mainland Greece* ▶ **ląd stały, kontynent**

⚷ **mainly** /ˈmeɪnli/ adv. mostly: *The students here are mainly from Japan.* ▶ **w większości, przeważnie, głównie**

mainstay /ˈmeɪnsteɪ/ noun [C] a person or thing that is the most important part of sth, which makes it possible for it to exist or to be successful: *Cocoa is the mainstay of the country's economy.* ▶ **ostoja, oparcie**

mainstream /ˈmeɪnstriːm/ noun [sing.] the ideas and opinions that are considered normal because they are shared by most people; the people who hold these opinions and beliefs: *The Green Party is not* ***in the mainstream*** *of British politics.* ▶ **główny nurt**

⚷ **maintain** /meɪnˈteɪn/ verb [T] **1** to make sth continue at the same level, standard, etc.: *We need to maintain the quality of our goods but not increase the price.* ◇ *to maintain law and order* ▶ **utrzymywać, zachowywać, podtrzymywać 2** to keep sth in good condition by checking and repairing it regularly: *to maintain a road/building/machine* ◇ *The house is large and expensive to maintain.* ▶ **konserwować, utrzymywać w dobrym stanie 3** to keep saying that sth is true even when others disagree or do not believe it: *I still maintain that I was right to sack him.* ◇ *She has always maintained her innocence.* ▶ **utrzymywać, twierdzić 4** to support sb with your own money: *He has to maintain a child from his previous marriage.* ▶ **utrzymywać, mieć na utrzymaniu**

maintenance /ˈmeɪntənəns/ noun [U] **1** keeping sth in good condition: *This house needs a lot of maintenance.* ◇ *car maintenance* ▶ **konserwacja, utrzymywanie w dobrym stanie 2** (Brit.) money that sb must pay regularly to a former wife, husband or partner especially when they have had children together: *He has to pay maintenance to his ex-wife.* ▶ **alimenty**

maisonette /ˌmeɪzəˈnet/ noun [C] (Brit.) a flat on two floors that is part of a larger building ▶ **mieszkanie dwupoziomowe**

maize /meɪz/ (US **corn**) noun [U] a tall plant which produces yellow grains in a large mass that are cooked and eaten ▶ **kukurydza** ➲ look at **sweetcorn**

maj. = MAJOR[2] (1)

majestic /mə'dʒestɪk/ adj. impressive because of its size or beauty: *a majestic mountain landscape* ▶ **majestatyczny, królewski**
■ **majestically** /-kli/ adv. ▶ **majestatycznie, po królewsku**

majesty /'mædʒəsti/ noun (pl. **majesties**) **1** [U] the impressive and attractive quality that sth has: *the splendour and majesty of the palace and its gardens* ▶ **majestat 2** (**His/Her/Your Majesty**) [C] (formal) (used when speaking to or about a royal person): *Her Majesty the Queen* ▶ **(Wasza/Jego/Jej) Królewska Mość**

major[1] /'meɪdʒə(r)/ adj. **1** [only before a noun] very large, important or serious: *The patient needs major heart surgery.* ◇ *There haven't been any major problems.* ▶ **główny, poważny, większy** OPP **minor 2** of one of the two types of **key**[1] (4) in which music is usually written: *the key of D major* ▶ **dur** ➲ look at **minor**

major[2] /'meɪdʒə(r)/ noun **1** (abbr. **maj.**) [C] an officer of a middle level in the army or the US air force ▶ **major 2** [C] (US) the main subject or course of a student at college or university; the student who studies it: *Her major is French.* ▶ **przedmiot kierunkowy, specjalizacja; student odbywający studia z przedmiotu kierunkowego 3** [U] (used in music) a type of key or scale ▶ **dur**

major[3] /'meɪdʒə(r)/ verb
PHR V **major in sth** (US) to study sth as your main subject at college or university ▶ **specjalizować się**

ˌmajor 'general noun [C] an officer of a high level in the army ▶ (*w armii brytyjskiej*) **generał brygady**, (*w armii amerykańskiej*) **generał dywizji**

majority /mə'dʒɒrəti/ noun (pl. **majorities**) **1** [sing., with sing. or pl. verb] **majority (of sb/sth)** the largest number or part of a group of people or things: *The majority of students in the class come/comes from Japan.* ◇ *This treatment is not available in* ***the vast majority*** *of hospitals.* ▶ **większość** OPP **minority 2** [C, usually sing.] **majority (over sb)** (in an election) the difference in the number of votes for the person/party who came first and the person/party who came second: *He was elected by/with a majority of almost 5 000 votes.* ◇ *The government does not have an* ***overall majority*** (bezwzględnej większości). ▶ (*w głosowaniu/wyborach*) **przewaga (nad kimś)**
IDM **be in the/a majority** to form the largest number or part of sth: *Women are in the majority in the teaching profession.* ▶ **być w większości, stanowić większość**

make[1] /meɪk/ verb [T] (pt, pp **made** /meɪd/) **1** to produce or create sth: *to make bread* ◇ *This model is* ***made of*** *steel, and that one is* ***made out of*** *used matches.* ◇ *Cheese is* ***made from*** *milk.* ◇ *Those cars are* ***made in*** *Slovakia.* ◇ *Shall I make you a sandwich/make a sandwich for you?* ◇ *to make a hole in something* ◇ *to make* (ustanawiać) *a law/rule* ◇ *to make a movie* ▶ **robić, wytwarzać, produkować 2** [used with nouns] to perform a certain action: *to make progress* ◇ *to make a mistake/a noise* ◇ *to make trouble/a mess* ◇ *I've made an appointment to see the doctor.* Umówiłem się na wizytę do lekarza. ◇ *to make a guess* zgadnąć ◇ *to make a comment* wygłosić komentarz ◇ *to make a suggestion* przedstawić propozycję ◇ *to make a statement* wydać oświadczenie ▶ **robić**

> **Make** często łączy się z rzeczownikami, tworząc konstrukcje, które znaczą to samo, co odpowiadający im czasownik np. **make a decision** = **decide**. W takich wyrażeniach można też użyć przymiotnika: *He made the right decision.* Podjął dobrą decyzję. ◇ *They made a generous offer.* Przedstawili szczodrą ofertę.

3 to cause a particular effect, feeling, situation, etc.: *The film made me cry.* Ten film wzruszył mnie do łez. ◇ *That dress makes you look thin.* Ta sukienka cię wyszczupla. ◇ *Flying makes him nervous.* Latanie samolotem bardzo go denerwuje. ◇ *Her remarks made the situation worse.* Jej uwagi pogorszyły sytuację. ◇ *We can make this room into a bedroom.* Możemy przerobić ten pokój na sypialnię. ◇ *I'll* ***make it clear*** *to him* (dam mu wyraźnie do zrozumienia) *that we won't pay.* ◇ ***Make sure*** (upewnij się, że) *you lock the car.* ◇ *We left early to* ***make certain*** *of arriving in time* (aby mieć pewność, że przyjedziemy na czas). ◇ *You don't need to know much of a language to* ***make yourself understood.*** ▶ **wywoływać, powodować (że) 4** to make sb/sth become sth; to have the right qualities to become sth: *She was made President.* Wybrano ją na prezydenta. ◇ *She'll make* (będzie) *a good teacher.* ◇ *You can borrow some money this time, but don't* ***make a habit of*** *it* (ale żeby to ci nie weszło w zwyczaj). ◇ *I'll* ***make it*** *my* ***business*** *to find out* (postanowiłem, że dowiem się) *what they're planning.* ◇ *The beautiful weather really made our holiday.* Piękna pogoda sprawiła, że mieliśmy doskonałe wakacje. ▶ **wyznaczać, wybierać; mieć zadatki na coś, sprawdzać się 5** to become sth; to achieve sth: *I'm hoping to make head of the department by the time I'm thirty.* ▶ **zostawać 6** to force sb/sth to do sth: *You can't make her come with us if she doesn't want to.* ◇ *They made me repeat the whole story.* ▶ **zmuszać, kazać** ⓘ W stronie biernej należy używać **to**: *He was made to wait at the police station.* **7** (used with money, numbers and time): *How much do you think he makes a month?* ◇ *He makes* (zarabia) *£20 000 a year.* ◇ *to make a lot of money* ◇ *5 and 7 make* (równa się) *12.* ◇ *'What's the time?' 'I make it 6.45.'* „Która godzina?" „U mnie jest 6:45." ◇ *'What do you make the answer?' '28'* „Jaka jest twoja odpowiedź?" „28." ◇ *'What time shall we meet?' 'Let's make it eight o'clock* (powiedzmy, o ósmej).*'* ▶ **uzyskiwać, wynosić, być 8** to manage to reach a place or go somewhere: *We should make Bristol by about 10.* ◇ *I can't make the meeting* (nie mogę iść na zebranie) *next week.* ▶ **docierać dokądś; (móc) się udać (gdzieś)**
IDM **make do with sth** to use sth that is not good enough because nothing better is available: *If we can't get limes, we'll have to make do with lemons.* ▶ **zadowalać się (czymś)**
make it 1 to get to a place (in time); to go to a place you have been invited to ▶ **zdążyć (gdzieś na czas); przybywać 2** to be successful: *She'll never make it as an actress.* ◇ *The doctors think he's going to make it* (przeżyje). ▶ **odnosić sukces**
ⓘ **Make** używa się w innych idiomach, np. **make love.** Zob. hasła odpowiednich rzeczowników i przymiotników.
PHR V **be made for sb/each other** to be well matched to sb/each other: *Jim and Alice seem made for each other.* ▶ **być stworzonym dla kogoś/siebie**
make for sb/sth to move towards sb/sth ▶ **poruszać się w kierunku kogoś/czegoś, kierować się do kogoś/czegoś**
make for sth to help or allow sth to happen: *Arguing all the time doesn't make for a happy marriage.* ▶ **przyczyniać się do czegoś, pomagać w osiągnięciu czegoś**
make sb/sth into sb/sth to change sb/sth into sb/sth: *She made her spare room into an office.* ▶ **zrobić z kogoś/czegoś coś**
make sth of sb/sth to understand the meaning or nature of sb/sth: *What do you make of Colin's letter?* ▶ **sądzić/myśleć o kimś/czymś; przerabiać coś na coś**
make off (informal) to leave or escape in a hurry ▶ **uciekać, wychodzić pośpiesznie**
make off (with sth) to steal sth and leave quickly with it: *Someone's made off with my wallet!* ▶ **porywać (coś)**
make sth out to write or complete sth: *She made out a cheque for £100.* ▶ **wypisywać coś, sporządzać coś**

M

make sb/sth out 1 to understand sb/sth: *I just can't make him out.* ▶ **rozumieć kogoś/coś**, **odczytać coś 2** to be able to see or hear sb/sth; to manage to read sth: *I could just make out her signature.* ▶ **rozpoznawać kogoś/coś**; **odcyfrowywać coś**

make out that ...; **make yourself out to be sth** to say that sth is true and try to make people believe it: *He made out that he was a millionaire.* ◇ *She's not as clever as she makes herself out to be.* ▶ **udawać, że**; **podawać się za coś**

make (yourself/sb) up to put powder, colour, etc. on your/sb's face to make it look attractive ▶ **malować (się)**

make sth up 1 to form sth: *the different groups that make up our society* ▶ **tworzyć 2** to invent sth, often sth that is not true: *to make up an excuse* ▶ **zmyślać 3** to make a number or an amount complete; to replace sth that has been lost: *We need one more person to make up our team.* ▶ **uzupełniać**

make up for sth to do sth that corrects a bad situation: *Her enthusiasm makes up for her lack of experience.* ▶ **kompensować coś**

make it up to sb (informal) to do sth that shows that you are sorry for what you have done to sb or that you are grateful for what they have done for you: *You've done me a big favour. How can I make it up to you?* ▶ **wynagradzać komuś**, **odwdzięczać się komuś**

make (it) up (with sb) to become friends again after an argument: *Has she made it up with him yet?* ▶ **pogodzić się (z kimś)**

make² /meɪk/ noun [C] the name of the company that produces sth: *'What make is your TV?' 'It's a Sony.'* ▶ **marka**

IDM **on the make** always trying to make money for yourself, especially in a dishonest way: *The country is being ruined by politicians on the make.* ▶ **w pogoni za zyskiem**

'make-believe noun [U] things that sb imagines or invents that are not real ▶ **udawanie**, **pozory**, **wymysł**

makeover /'meɪkəʊvə(r)/ noun [C,U] the process of improving the appearance of a person or a place, or of changing the impression that sth gives ▶ **zmiana wizerunku/wyglądu**

maker /'meɪkə(r)/ noun [C] a person, company or machine that makes sth: *a film-maker* ◇ *If it doesn't work, send it back to the maker.* ◇ *an ice cream maker* ◇ *a dressmaker* krawcowa ▶ **producent/ka**, **wytwór-ca/czyni**

makeshift /'meɪkʃɪft/ adj. made to be used for only a short time until there is sth better: *makeshift shelters out of old cardboard boxes* ▶ **prowizoryczny**

'make-up noun **1** [U] powder, cream, etc. that you put on your face to make yourself more attractive. Actors use **make-up** to change their appearance when they are acting: *to put on/take off make-up* ▶ **makijaż**, **charakteryzacja** ➲ look at **cosmetic** ➲ verb **make (yourself/sb) up 2** [sing.] sb's character: *He can't help his temper. It's part of his make-up.* ▶ **charakter**

making /'meɪkɪŋ/ noun [sing.] the act of doing or producing sth; the process of being made: *breadmaking* ◇ *This movie has been three years in the making.* ▶ **robienie**, **tworzenie**, **produkowanie**

IDM **be the making of sb** to be the reason that sb is successful: *University was the making of Gina.* ▶ **być podstawą czyjegoś powodzenia**

have the makings of sth to have the necessary qualities for sth: *The book has the makings of a good film.* ▶ **mieć zadatki na coś**

mal- /mæl/ prefix [in nouns, verbs and adjectives] bad or badly; not correct or correctly: *malpractice* nadużycia ◇ *malodorous* cuchnący ◇ *malfunction* źle działać ▶ **źle**

maladjusted /ˌmælə'dʒʌstɪd/ adj. (used about a person) not able to behave well with other people ▶ **nieprzystosowany** (*społecznie*)

■ **maladjustment** /ˌmælə'dʒʌstmənt/ noun [U] ▶ **nieprzystosowanie**

malaria /mə'leəriə/ noun [U] a serious disease in hot countries that you get from the bite of a **mosquito** ▶ **malaria**

male¹ /meɪl/ adj. belonging to the sex that does not give birth to babies or produce eggs: *a male goat* ◇ *a male model/nurse* ▶ **płci męskiej**, **męski** ➲ look at **masculine**, **female**

male² /meɪl/ noun [C] a male person or animal ▶ **mężczyzna**; **samiec** ➲ look at **female**

male 'chauvinism = CHAUVINISM (2)

malevolent /mə'levələnt/ adj. [usually before a noun] having or showing a desire to harm other people: ***malevolent intentions/thoughts*** ◇ *his dark malevolent eyes* ▶ **(zło)wrogi** SYN **malicious**, **wicked** OPP **benevolent**

■ **malevolence** /-əns/ noun [U]: *an act of pure malevolence* ▶ **wrogość** | **malevolently** adv. ▶ **(zło)wrogo**

malfunction /ˌmæl'fʌŋkʃn/ verb [I] (used about a machine, etc.) to fail to work correctly: *He was killed when his parachute malfunctioned.* Zginął z powodu awarii technicznej spadochronu. ▶ **źle działać**

■ **malfunction** noun [C, U]: *The drug caused a malfunction in the brain.* ▶ **niewydolność**, **awaria**

malice /'mælɪs/ noun [U] a wish to hurt other people ▶ **złośliwość**

malicious /mə'lɪʃəs/ adj. having or showing hatred and a desire to harm sb or hurt their feelings: ***malicious gossip/lies/rumours*** ▶ **złośliwy** SYN **malevolent**, **spiteful**

■ **maliciously** adv. ▶ **złośliwie**

malign /mə'laɪn/ verb [T] (formal) to say bad things about sb/sth publicly: *She feels she has been* ***much maligned*** *by the press.* ▶ **szkalować** SYN **slander**

■ **malign** adj. [usually before a noun] (formal) causing harm: *a* ***malign force/influence/effect*** ▶ **zgubny** ➲ look at **benign**

malignant /mə'lɪgnənt/ adj. (used about a disease, or a **tumour**) likely to cause death if not controlled: *He has a malignant brain tumour.* ▶ (*nowotwór itp.*) **złośliwy** OPP **benign**

mall = SHOPPING MALL

malleable /'mæliəbl/ adj. **1** (used about metal or plastic) that can be hit or pressed into different shapes easily without breaking ▶ **kowalny 2** (used about people or ideas) easily influenced or changed ▶ **podatny na czyjś wpływ**

■ **malleability** /ˌmæliə'bɪləti/ noun [U] ▶ **kowalność**; **podatność na czyjś wpływ**

mallet /'mælɪt/ noun [C] a heavy wooden hammer ▶ **drewniany młotek** ➲ picture at **tool**

malnourished /ˌmæl'nʌrɪʃt; US -'nɜːr-/ adj. in bad health because of a lack of food or a lack of the right type of food: *The children were badly malnourished.* ▶ **niedożywiony**; **źle odżywiany**

malnutrition /ˌmælnju:'trɪʃn; US -nu:-/ noun [U] bad health that is the result of not having enough food or enough of the right kind of food ▶ **niedożywienie**; **złe odżywianie**

malpractice /ˌmæl'præktɪs/ noun [U,C] careless, wrong or illegal behaviour while in a professional job: *medical malpractice* błąd w sztuce medycznej ▶ **nadużycia**, **postępowanie niezgodne z etyką zawodową**

malt /mɔːlt/ noun [U] grain that is used for making beer and whisky ▶ **słód**

maltreat /ˌmælˈtriːt/ verb [T] (formal) to treat a person or an animal in a cruel or unkind way ▶ **maltretować, poniewierać**
■ **maltreatment** noun [U] ▶ **maltretowanie, poniewieranie**

mammal /ˈmæml/ noun [C] an animal of the type that gives birth to live babies, not eggs, and feeds its young on milk from its own body ▶ **ssak** ➲ picture on **page A10**

mammoth /ˈmæməθ/ adj. very big ▶ **olbrzymi**

man[1] /mæn/ noun (pl. **men** /men/) **1** [C] an adult male person: *men, women and children* ▶ **mężczyzna 2** [U] humans as a group; the human race: *Early man lived by hunting.* ◇ *the damage man has caused to the environment* ▶ **rodzaj ludzki; człowiek 3** [C] a person of either sex, male or female: *All men are equal.* ◇ *No man could survive long in such conditions.* ▶ **człowiek, istota ludzka**

Niektórzy nie akceptują użycia rzeczownika **man** w znaczeniach 2 i 3 (oraz rzeczownika **mankind** w znaczeniu „wszyscy mężczyźni i wszystkie kobiety"), ponieważ można odnieść wrażenie, że słowa te nie obejmują kobiet. Zamiast **man** i **mankind** osoby te używają rzeczowników **humanity, the human race** lub **people**.

4 [C] [in compounds] a man who comes from a particular place; a man who has a particular job or interest: *a Frenchman* Francuz ◇ *a businessman* ◇ *sportsmen and women* ◇ *I'm not a betting/drinking man.* Nie jestem osobą, która lubi się zakładać/pić. ◇ *a countryman* mieszkaniec wsi ◇ *a fireman* strażak ▶ **osoba wykonująca daną pracę/pochodząca z danego miejsca 5** [C] a husband or sexual partner: *to become man and wife* stać się mężem i żoną ▶ **partner 6** [C, usually pl.] a man of low rank in the army, etc. who takes orders from an officer: *officers and men* ▶ **szeregowy, żołnierz** (*poniżej stopnia oficerskiego*) **7** [sing.] (informal) (especially US) (used for addressing a male person): *Nice shirt, man!* ◇ *Hey man. Back off!* Słuchaj, człowieku, cofnij się! ▶ **człowieku!**
IDM **the man in the street** (Brit.) an ordinary man or woman ▶ **szary człowiek**
the odd man/one out → ODD

man[2] /mæn/ verb [T] (**manning**; **manned**) to operate sth or to provide people to operate sth: *The telephones are manned 24 hours a day.* ◇ *When was the first manned space flight?* Kiedy pierwszy człowiek poleciał w kosmos? ▶ **obsługiwać; obsadzać ludźmi**

manage /ˈmænɪdʒ/ verb **1** [I,T] [often with *can* or *could*] to succeed in doing or dealing with sth difficult; to be able to do sth: *However did you manage to find us here?* ◇ *I can't manage this suitcase. It's too heavy.* ◇ *Paula can't manage next Tuesday* (nie może przyjść w przyszły wtorek) *so we'll meet another day.* ▶ **potrafić, umieć sobie radzić** ➲ note at **could 2** [I] **manage (without/with sb/sth)**; **manage (on sth)** to deal with a difficult situation; to continue in spite of difficulties: *My grandmother couldn't manage without her neighbours.* ◇ *Can you manage with just one assistant?* ◇ *It's hard for a family to manage on just one income.* ▶ **dawać sobie radę, radzić sobie 3** [T] to be in charge or control of sth: *She manages a small advertising business.* ◇ *You need to manage your time more efficiently.* ▶ **kierować, zarządzać, prowadzić** (*np. firmę*)

manageable /ˈmænɪdʒəbl/ adj. not too big or too difficult to deal with: *The debt has been reduced to a more manageable level.* Dług został zmniejszony do poziomu, przy którym łatwiej jest nim zarządzać. ◇ *Use conditioner regularly to make your hair soft and manageable.* ▶ **taki, z którym można sobie poradzić, możliwy do zarządzania/utrzymania, wykonalny**

management /ˈmænɪdʒmənt/ noun **1** [U] the control or organization of sth: *Good classroom management is vital with large groups of children.* ▶ **zarządzanie, kierownictwo, gospodarowanie 2** [C,U, with sing. or pl. verb] the people who control a business or company: *The hotel is now **under new management**.* ▶ **zarząd, dyrekcja, kierownictwo** ⓘ W lp **management** można użyć z czasownikiem występującym w lp lub lm: *The management is/are considering making some workers redundant.*

manager /ˈmænɪdʒə(r)/ noun [C] **1** a man or woman who controls an organization or part of an organization: *a bank manager* ◇ *a sales manager* kierownik sprzedaży ◇ *an assistant manager* zastępca dyrektora ▶ **dyrektor/ka, kierowni-k/czka 2** a person who looks after the business affairs of a singer, actor, etc.; a person who is in charge of a sports team: *the England manager* ▶ **menedżer**

manageress /ˌmænɪdʒəˈres/ noun [C] a woman who is in charge of a shop or restaurant ▶ **dyrektorka, kierowniczka**

managerial /ˌmænəˈdʒɪəriəl/ adj. connected with the work of a manager: *Do you have any managerial experience?* ▶ **kierowniczy, menedżerski**

ˌmanaging diˈrector noun [C] a person who controls a business or company ▶ **dyrektor naczelny**

mandarin /ˈmændərɪn/ noun [C] a type of small orange ▶ **mandarynka**

mandate /ˈmændeɪt/ noun [usually sing.] the power that is officially given to a group of people to do sth, especially after they have won an election: *The union leaders had a clear mandate from their members to call a strike.* ▶ **mandat** (*np. poselski*) ⓘ Uwaga! Por. **ticket** (3).

mandatory /ˈmændətəri; US -tɔːri; Brit. also mænˈdeɪtəri/ adj. (formal) that you must do, have, obey, etc.: *a mandatory life sentence* ▶ **obowiązkowy** SYN **obligatory** OPP **optional**

mandible /ˈmændɪbl/ noun [C] **1** the lower of the two bones in your face that contain your teeth ▶ **żuchwa** ➲ picture at **body 2** either of the two parts that are at the front and on either side of an insect's mouth, used especially for biting and crushing food ▶ **żuwaczka** ➲ picture at **insect**

mane /meɪn/ noun [C] the long hair on the neck of some animals ▶ **grzywa** ➲ picture at **horse** ➲ picture on **page A10**

maneuver (US) = MANOEUVRE

mange /meɪndʒ/ noun [U] a skin disease which affects **mammals**, caused by a **parasite** ▶ **świerzb**

manger /ˈmeɪndʒə(r)/ noun [C] a long open box that horses and cows can eat from ▶ **żłób**

mangetout /ˌmɑːnʒ ˈtuː/ (US ˈ**snow pea**) noun [usually pl.] a type of very small **pea** that grows in long, flat green **pods** that are cooked and eaten whole ▶ **groszek śnieżny**

mangle /ˈmæŋgl/ verb [T, usually passive] to damage sth so badly that it is difficult to see what it looked like originally: *The motorway was covered with the mangled wreckage* (powyginanymi wrakami) *of cars.* ▶ **wyginać, (po) szarpać**

mango /ˈmæŋgəʊ/ noun [C] (pl. **mangoes** or **mangos**) a tropical fruit that has a yellow and red skin and is yellow inside ▶ **mango** ➲ picture on **page A12**

mangy /ˈmeɪndʒi/ adj. [usually before a noun] **1** (used about an animal) suffering from **mange**: *a mangy dog* ▶ **dotknięty parchem 2** (informal) dirty and in bad condition: *a mangy old coat* ▶ **wyliniały**

manhole /ˈmænhəʊl/ noun [C] a hole in the street with a lid over it through which sb can go to look at the pipes, wires, etc. that are underground ▶ **studzienka, właz kanalizacyjny**

M

manhood /ˈmænhʊd/ noun [U] the state of being a man rather than a boy ▶ **męskość, wiek męski**

mania /ˈmeɪniə/ noun **1** [C] (informal) a great enthusiasm for sth: *World Cup mania is sweeping the country.* ▶ **szał 2** [U] a serious mental illness that may cause sb to be very excited or violent ▶ (*psych.*) **mania**

maniac /ˈmeɪniæk/ noun [C] **1** a person who behaves in a wild and stupid way: *to drive like a maniac* (jak wariat) ▶ **obłąkan-y/a** SYN **lunatic, madman 2** a person who has a stronger love of sth than is normal: *a football/sex maniac* ▶ **fanaty-k/czka (czegoś), miłośni-k/czka (czegoś)**

manic /ˈmænɪk/ adj. **1** full of nervous energy or excited activity: *His behaviour became more manic as he began to feel stressed.* ◇ *Things are manic at work at the moment.* W tej chwili w pracy mamy istne szaleństwo. ▶ **szaleńczy 2** connected with **mania** (2) ▶ **maniakalny**

ˌmanic deˈpression = BIPOLAR DISORDER

ˌmanic-deˈpressive = BIPOLAR

manicure /ˈmænɪkjʊə(r)/ noun [C,U] treatment to make your hands and nails look attractive: *to have a manicure* ▶ **manicure**

manifest /ˈmænɪfest/ verb [I,T] (formal) **manifest (sth/itself) (in/as sth)** to show sth or to be shown clearly: *Mental illness can manifest itself in many forms.* ▶ **przejawiać (coś/się) (czymś); (p)okazywać (coś/się)**
■ **manifest** adj.: *manifest failure/anger* ▶ **wyraźny, oczywisty** | **manifestly** adv.: *manifestly unfair* ▶ **wyraźnie, w oczywisty sposób**

manifestation /ˌmænɪfeˈsteɪʃn/ noun [C,U] (formal) a sign that sth is happening ▶ **dowód (czegoś/na coś), przejawianie (się)**

manifesto /ˌmænɪˈfestəʊ/ noun [C] (pl. **manifestos**) a written statement by a political party that explains what it hopes to do if it becomes the government in the future ▶ **manifest**

manioc = CASSAVA

manipulate /məˈnɪpjuleɪt/ verb [T] **1** to influence sb so that they do or think what you want: *Clever politicians know how to manipulate public opinion.* ▶ (*przen.*) **manipulować 2** to use, move or control sth with skill ▶ **manipulować** (*np. przyciskami*)
■ **manipulation** /məˌnɪpjuˈleɪʃn/ noun [C,U] ▶ **manipulacja; manipulowanie**

manipulative /məˈnɪpjələtɪv; US -leɪt-/ adj. **1** able to influence sb or force sb to do what you want, often in an unfair way: *manipulative behaviour* ▶ **manipulacyjny, intrygancki 2** (formal) connected with the ability to handle objects with skill: *manipulative skills* (zdolności manualne) *such as typing and knitting* ▶ **manipulacyjny**

mankind /mænˈkaɪnd/ noun [U] all the people in the world: *A nuclear war would be a threat to all mankind.* ▶ **ludzkość, rodzaj ludzki** ➲ note at **man**

manky /ˈmæŋki/ adj. (Brit., informal) dirty and unpleasant ▶ **zapyziały**

manly /ˈmænli/ adj. (**manlier**; **manliest**) typical of or suitable for a man: *a deep manly voice* ▶ **męski**
■ **manliness** noun [U] ▶ **męskość**

ˌman-ˈmade adj. made by people, not formed in a natural way; artificial: *man-made fabrics such as nylon and polyester* ▶ **sztuczny, syntetyczny** OPP **natural**

mannequin /ˈmænəkɪn/ noun [C] (old-fashioned) **1** a person whose job is to wear and display new styles of clothes ▶ **model/ka** ➲ look at **model 2** a model of a human body, used for displaying clothes in shops ▶ **manekin**

manner /ˈmænə(r)/ noun **1** [sing.] the way that you do sth or that sth happens: *Stop arguing! Let's try to act **in a civilized manner**.* ▶ **sposób 2** [sing.] the way that sb behaves towards other people: *to have an aggressive/a relaxed/a professional manner* ▶ **sposób zachowania 3** (**manners**) [pl.] a way of behaving that is considered acceptable in your country or culture: *In some countries it is bad manners to show the soles of your feet* (pokazywanie podeszwy swoich stóp jest oznaką złego wychowania). ◇ *Their children have no manners* (nie potrafią się zachować). ◇ *table manners* odpowiednie zachowanie się przy stole ▶ **zasady zachowania się**
IDM **all manner of...** every kind of...: *You meet all manner of people in my job.* ▶ **wszelkiego rodzaju**

mannerism /ˈmænərɪzəm/ noun [C] sb's particular way of speaking or a particular movement they often do ▶ **maniera, manieryzm**

manoeuvre[1] (US **maneuver**) /məˈnuːvə(r)/ noun **1** [C] a movement that needs care or skill: *Parking the car in such a small space would be a tricky manoeuvre.* ▶ **manewr 2** [C,U] something clever that you do in order to win sth, trick sb, etc.: *political manoeuvre(s)* ▶ **fortel, podstęp** SYN **move 3** (**manoeuvres**) [pl.] a way of training soldiers when large numbers of them practise fighting in battles ▶ **manewry**

manoeuvre[2] (US **maneuver**) /məˈnuːvə(r)/ verb [I,T] to move (sth) to a different position using skill: *The driver was manoeuvring his lorry into a narrow gateway.* ▶ **manewrować**

manor /ˈmænə(r)/ (also **ˈmanor house**) noun [C] a large house in the country that has land around it ▶ **dwór, majątek ziemski**

> W średniowieczu, do rodziny mieszkającej w **manor house** należały też otaczające go ziemie wraz z wioskami. ➲ look at **feudalism**

manpower /ˈmænpaʊə(r)/ noun [U] the people that you need to do a particular job: *There is a shortage of skilled manpower in the computer industry.* ▶ **siła robocza**

mansion /ˈmænʃn/ noun [C] a very large house ▶ **rezydencja, dwór, pałac**

manslaughter /ˈmænslɔːtə(r)/ noun [U] the crime of killing sb without intending to do so ▶ (*prawn.*) **nieumyślne spowodowanie śmierci** ➲ look at **murder**

mantelpiece /ˈmæntlpiːs/ noun [C] a narrow shelf above the space in a room where a fire goes ▶ **półka nad kominkiem** ➲ picture at **fireplace**

manual[1] /ˈmænjuəl/ adj. using your hands; operated by hand: *Office work can sometimes be more tiring than **manual work**.* ◇ *a skilled **manual worker*** ◇ *Does your car have a manual or an automatic gearbox?* ▶ **ręczny, fizyczny**
■ **manually** /-juəli/ adv. ▶ **ręcznie, fizycznie**

manual[2] /ˈmænjuəl/ noun [C] a book that explains how to do or operate sth: *a training manual* ◇ *a car manual* ▶ **podręcznik, instrukcja obsługi**

manufacture /ˌmænjuˈfæktʃə(r)/ verb [T] to make sth in large quantities using machines: *a local factory that manufactures furniture* ▶ **produkować/wytwarzać (maszynowo)** SYN **produce**
■ **manufacture** noun [U]: *The manufacture of chemical weapons should be illegal.* ▶ **produkcja, wytwarzanie**

manufacturer /ˌmænjuˈfæktʃərə(r)/ noun [C] a person or company that makes sth: *a car manufacturer* ▶ **producent/ka, wytwórca**

manufacturing /ˌmænjuˈfæktʃərɪŋ/ noun [U] the business or industry of producing goods in large quantities in factories, etc.: *Many jobs in manufacturing were lost during the recession.* ▶ **produkcja** (*przemysłowa*)

manure /məˈnjʊə(r); US -ˈnʊər/ noun [U] the waste matter from animals that is put on the ground in order to make plants grow better: *horse manure* ▶ **nawóz naturalny**, **gnój** ➲ look at **fertilizer**

manuscript /ˈmænjuskrɪpt/ noun [C] **1** a copy of a book, piece of music, etc. before it has been printed ▶ **maszynopis**, **rękopis** **2** a very old book or document that was written by hand ▶ **rękopis**, **manuskrypt**

Manx /mænks/ adj. of the Isle of Man, its people or language ▶ **dotyczący wyspy Man/jej mieszkańców i ich języka**

⚷ **many** /ˈmeni/ determiner, pron. [used with plural nouns or verbs] **1** a large number of people or things: *Have you made many friends at school yet?* ◇ *Not many of my friends smoke.* ◇ *Many of the mistakes were just careless.* ◇ *There are **too many** mistakes in this essay.* ▶ **wiel-e/u**, **dużo**, **sporo**

> **Many** czy **a lot of**? **Many** w zdaniach oznajmujących brzmi bardzo formalnie: *Many schools teach computing nowadays.* W języku mówionym, a także w nieformalnym języku pisanym, używa się **a lot of**: *A lot of schools teach computing nowadays.* Jednak w zdaniach pytających i przeczących **many** nie brzmi już formalnie: *I don't know many cheap places to eat.* ◇ *Are there many hotels in this town?*

2 (used to ask about the number of people or things, or to refer to a known number): ***How many** children have you got?* ◇ *How many came to the meeting?* ◇ *I don't work **as many** hours **as** you.* ◇ *There are **half/twice as many*** (o połowę/dwa razy więcej) *boys as girls in the class.* ▶ **il-e/u**, (*jak/tak itp.*) **wiele/wielu/dużo** **3** [in compounds] having a lot of the thing mentioned: *a many-sided shape* wielościan ▶ **wielo-** **4** (**many a**) [used with a singular noun and verb] a large number of: *I've heard him say that many a time* (nieraz). ▶ **niejeden**, **wiele**

IDM **a good/great many** very many ▶ **bardzo dużo**, **mnóstwo**

Maori /ˈmaʊri/ noun [C] (pl. **Maori** or **Maoris**) a member of the race of people who were the original people to live in New Zealand ▶ **Maorys/ka**

■ **Maori** adj. ▶ **maoryski**

⚷ **map¹** /mæp/ noun [C] a drawing or plan of (part of) the surface of the earth that shows countries, rivers, mountains, roads, etc.: *a map of the world* ◇ *a road map* mapa samochodowa/drogowa ◇ *a street map* (plan miasta) *of Oxford* ◇ *a relief map* mapa plastyczna (często dwuwymiarowa) ◇ *I can't find Cambridge **on the map**.* ◇ *to read a map* ▶ **mapa**, **plan** ➲ look at **atlas**

map² verb [T] (**mapping**; **mapped**): *The region is so remote it has not yet been mapped.* ▶ **sporządzać mapę/plan**

PHR V **map sth out** to plan or arrange sth in a careful or detailed way: *He has his career path clearly mapped out.* ▶ **opracowywać coś**

maple /ˈmeɪpl/ noun [C] a tree that has leaves with five points and that produces a very sweet liquid that you can eat: *maple syrup* ▶ **klon**

Mar. = MARCH: *17 Mar. 1956*

mar /mɑː(r)/ verb (**marring**; **marred**) [T] to damage or spoil sth good: *The game was marred by the behaviour of drunken fans.* ▶ **psuć** SYN **blight**, **ruin**

marathon /ˈmærəθən; US -θɑːn/ noun [C] **1** a long running race, in which people run about 42 kilometres: *Have you ever run a marathon?* ▶ **maraton** **2** an activity that lasts much longer than expected: *The interview was a real marathon.* ▶ (*przen.*) **maraton**

marble /ˈmɑːbl/ noun **1** [U] a hard attractive stone that is used to make statues and parts of buildings: *a marble statue* ▶ **marmur** **2** [C] a small ball of coloured glass that children play with ▶ **kolorowa kula ze szkła marmurkowego używana do gier dziecięcych** **3** (**marbles**) [pl.] the children's game that you play by rolling **marbles** along the ground trying to hit other **marbles** ▶ **gra w kulki**

⚷ **March** /mɑːtʃ/ noun [U,C] (abbr. **Mar.**) the 3rd month of the year, coming after February ▶ **marzec** ➲ note at **January**

⚷ **march¹** /mɑːtʃ/ verb **1** [I] to walk with regular steps (like a soldier): *The President saluted as the troops marched past* (wojska defilowały). ▶ **maszerować** **2** [I] to walk in a determined way: *He marched in* (wkroczył) *and demanded an explanation.* ▶ **kroczyć** **3** [T] to make sb walk or march somewhere: *The prisoner was marched away.* ▶ **prowadzić kogoś krokiem marszowym** **4** [I] to walk in a large group to protest about sth: *The demonstrators marched through the centre of town.* ▶ **iść w pochodzie**

⚷ **march²** /mɑːtʃ/ noun [C] **1** an organized walk by a large group of people who are protesting about sth: *a peace march* ▶ **pochód** ➲ look at **demonstration** **2** a journey made by marching: *The soldiers were tired after their long march.* ▶ **marsz**

mare /meə(r)/ noun [C] a female horse ▶ **klacz** ➲ note at **horse**

margarine /ˌmɑːdʒəˈriːn; US ˈmɑːrdʒərən/ noun [U] a food that is similar to butter, made of animal or vegetable fats ▶ **margaryna**

margin /ˈmɑːdʒɪn; US -dʒən/ noun [C] **1** the empty space at the side of a page in a book, etc. ▶ **margines**, **brzeg strony** **2** [usually sing.] the amount of space, time, votes, etc. by which you win sth: *He won by **a wide/narrow/comfortable margin**.* ▶ **przewaga**, **różnica** **3** the amount of profit that a company makes on sth ▶ **marża** **4** [usually sing.] an amount of space, time, etc. that is more than you need: *It is a complex operation with little **margin for error*** (z małym marginesem błędu). ▶ **margines** (*np. bezpieczeństwa*) **5** the area around the edge of sth: *the margins of the Pacific Ocean* ◇ *We need to give more help to people **on the margins of society*** (na marginesie społeczeństwa). ▶ **(s)kraj**, **krawędź**

marginal /ˈmɑːdʒɪnl/ adj. small in size or importance: *The differences are marginal.* ▶ **marginesowy**, **nieznaczny**

■ **marginally** /-nəli/ adv.: *In most cases costs will increase only marginally.* ▶ **marginesowo**, **nieznacznie**

marginalize (also -ise) /ˈmɑːdʒɪnəlaɪz/ verb [T] to make sb feel as if they are not important and cannot influence decisions or events; to put sb in a position in which they have no power ▶ **usuwać na dalszy plan**, **marginalizować**

■ **marginalization** (also -isation) noun [U]: *the marginalization of the elderly* ▶ **usuwanie na dalszy plan**, **marginalizacja**

ˌmargin of ˈerror noun [usually sing.] an amount that you allow when you calculate sth, for the possibility that a number is not completely accurate: *The survey has a margin of error of 2.5%.* ▶ **margines błędu**

marigold /ˈmærigəʊld/ noun [C] an orange or yellow garden flower. There are several types of **marigold**. ▶ **nagietek**

marijuana /ˌmærəˈwɑːnə/ noun [U] a drug that is smoked and is illegal in many countries ▶ **marihuana**

marina /məˈriːnə/ noun [C] a place where pleasure boats can be tied up and protected from the sea and bad weather ▶ **przystań jachtowa**

marinade /ˌmærɪˈneɪd/ noun [C,U] a mixture of oil, wine, spices, etc. in which meat or fish is left before it is cooked in order to make it softer or to give it a particular flavour ▶ **marynata**

M

marinate /ˈmærɪneɪt/ (also **marinade**) verb [I,T] if you **marinate** food or it **marinates**, you leave it in a **marinade** before cooking it ▶ **marynować (się)**

marine[1] /məˈriːn/ adj. [only before a noun] **1** connected with the sea: *marine life* ▶ **morski 2** connected with ships or sailing: *marine insurance* ▶ **morski**

marine[2] /məˈriːn/ noun [C] a soldier who has been trained to fight on land or at sea ▶ **żołnierz piechoty morskiej**

marionette /ˌmæriəˈnet/ noun [C] a **puppet** whose arms, legs and head are moved by strings ▶ **marionetka**

marital /ˈmærɪtl/ adj. [only before a noun] connected with marriage: *marital problems* ▶ **małżeński**

ˌmarital ˈstatus noun [U] (formal) (used on official documents) if you are married, single, divorced, etc. ▶ **stan cywilny**

maritime /ˈmærɪtaɪm/ adj. connected with the sea or ships ▶ **morski**

marjoram /ˈmɑːdʒərəm/ noun [U] a plant whose sweet-smelling leaves are used in cooking ▶ **majeranek**

mark[1] /mɑːk/ verb [T] **1** to put a sign on sth: *We marked the price on all items in the sale.* ◇ *I'll mark all the boxes I want you to move.* ◇ *The route is marked in red.* ▶ **oznaczać, oznakowywać 2** to spoil the appearance of sth by making a mark on it: *The white walls were dirty and marked.* ▶ **plamić 3** to show where sth is or where sth happened: *Flowers mark the spot where he died.* ▶ **oznaczać, określać 4** to celebrate or officially remember an important event: *The ceremony marked the fiftieth anniversary of the opening of the school.* ▶ **obchodzić 5** to be a sign that sth new is going to happen: *This decision marks a change in government policy.* ▶ **oznaczać 6** to look at sb's schoolwork, etc., show where there are mistakes and give it a number or letter to show how good it is: *Why did you mark that answer wrong?* ◇ *He has 100 exam papers to mark.* ▶ **oceniać, wystawiać stopień/ocenę 7** to stay close to a player of the opposite team so that they cannot play easily: *Hughes was marking Taylor.* ▶ **kryć** (*przeciwnika*)

PHR V **mark sth down/up** to increase/decrease the price of sth that you are selling: *All goods have been marked down by 15%.* ▶ **podnosić/obniżać (cenę) czegoś**

mark sb down as sth to decide that sb is of a particular type or suitable: *From the first day of school, the teachers marked Fred down as a troublemaker.* ▶ **przesądzać, że ktoś jest ...**

mark sth down for sth to decide that sth is suitable for a particular use ▶ **przeznaczać coś do czegoś**

mark sth out to draw lines to show the position of sth: *Spaces for each car were marked out in the car park.* ▶ **wytyczać/oznaczać coś**

mark[2] /mɑːk/ noun [C] **1** a spot or line that spoils the appearance of sth: *There's a dirty mark on the front of your shirt.* ◇ *If you put a hot cup down on the table, it will **leave a mark**.* ▶ **plama, znak, ślad** ➲ look at **birthmark 2** something that shows who or what sb/sth is, especially by making them or it different from others: *My horse is the one with the white mark on its face.* ▶ **znak, kreska, plamka 3** a written or printed symbol that is a sign of sth: *a question/punctuation/exclamation mark* ▶ **znak 4** a sign of a quality or feeling: *They stood in silence for two minutes as **a mark of respect**.* ▶ **dowód, oznaka 5** a number or letter you get for school work that tells you how good your work was: *She got very good marks in the exam.* ◇ *The **pass mark** is 60 out of 100.* Ocena dostateczna zaczyna się od 60 punktów. ◇ *to get full* (najlepsze) *marks* ▶ **stopień, ocena 6** the level or point that sth/sb has reached: *The race is almost at the half-way mark.* ▶ **poziom, pułap 7** an effect that people notice and will remember: *The time he spent in prison **left** its **mark on** him.* ◇ *He was only eighteen when he first **made** his **mark** in politics.* ▶ **ślad, piętno 8** a particular model or type of sth: *the new SL 53 Mark III* ▶ **model**

> Uwaga! Słowa **mark** nie wolno stosować, mówiąc o samym produkcie lub o jego producencie. Używa się wówczas **brand** lub **make**: *What make is your car?* ◇ *What brand of coffee do you buy?*

9 (formal) a person or an object towards which sth is directed: *The arrow hit/missed its mark.* ◇ *His judgement of the situation is **wide of the mark**.* Jego ocena sytuacji jest całkowicie chybiona. ▶ **cel** SYN **target 10** the former unit of money in Germany (replaced in 2002 by the euro) ▶ **marka niemiecka**

IDM **on your marks, get set, go!** (used at the start of a sports race) ▶ **do startu, gotowi, hop!**

overstep the mark/line → OVERSTEP

quick, slow, etc. off the mark quick, slow, etc. in reacting to a situation ▶ **nie zwlekać/zwlekać ze zrobieniem czegoś**

marked /mɑːkt/ adj. clear; noticeable: *There has been a marked increase in vandalism in recent years.* ▶ **wyraźny, znaczny**

■ **markedly** /ˈmɑːkɪdli/ adv.: *Her background is markedly different from mine.* ▶ **wyraźnie, znacznie**

marker /ˈmɑːkə(r)/ noun [C] **1** something that shows the position of sth: *A marker flag shows* (flaga oznacza) *where the water is dangerous.* ▶ **znacznik, znak 2** (Brit. also **ˈmarker pen**) a pen with a thick **felt** tip: *You can write on the whiteboard with these marker pens.* ▶ **flamaster** ➲ picture at **stationery**

market[1] /ˈmɑːkɪt/ noun **1** [C] a place where people go to buy and sell things: *a market stall/trader/town* ◇ *a cattle/fish/meat market* ▶ **rynek, targ, jarmark** ➲ note at **shop** ➲ look at **flea market, hypermarket, supermarket** ➲ picture on **page A5 2** [C] business or commercial activity; the amount of buying and selling of a particular type of goods: *The company currently has a 10% share of the market.* ◇ *the property/job market* ▶ (*fin.*) **rynek, zbyt 3** [C,U] a country, an area or a group of people that buys sth; the number of people who buy sth: *The company is hoping to expand into the European Market.* ◇ *There's no market for very large cars when petrol is so expensive.* ◇ *the home/overseas market* rynek wewnętrzny/zagraniczny ▶ **rynek (zbytu)** ➲ look at **black market, stock market**

IDM **on the market** available to buy: *This is one of the best cameras on the market.* ▶ **na rynku, w sprzedaży**

market[2] /ˈmɑːkɪt/ verb [T] to sell sth with the help of advertising ▶ **wprowadzać na rynek** (*za pomocą reklamy*)

marketable /ˈmɑːkɪtəbl/ adj. that can be sold easily because people want it ▶ **możliwy do zbycia/sprzedaży**

ˌmarket ˈforces noun [pl.] a free system of trade in which prices and wages rise and fall without being controlled by the government ▶ **tendencje rynkowe**

ˌmarket ˈgarden noun [C] a farm where vegetables and fruit are grown in large quantities ▶ **gospodarstwo warzywno-owocowe**

marketing /ˈmɑːkɪtɪŋ/ noun [U] the activity of showing and advertising a company's products in the best possible way: *Effective marketing will lead to increased sales.* ◇ *the international marketing department* ▶ **marketing**

ˌmarket ˈleader noun [C] **1** the company that sells the largest quantity of a particular kind of product: *We are the market leader in hi-fi.* ▶ **lider na rynku 2** a product that is the most successful of its kind ▶ **produkt wiodący**

marketplace /ˈmɑːkɪtpleɪs/ noun **1** (**the marketplace**) [sing.] the activity of competing with other companies to buy and sell goods, services, etc. ▶ (*fin.*) **rynek 2** [C] the place in a town where a market is held ▶ **plac targowy**

ˌmarket reˈsearch noun [U] the study of what people want to buy and why: *to carry out/do market research* ▶ **badanie rynku**

marking /ˈmɑːkɪŋ/ noun [C, usually pl.] shapes, lines and patterns of colour on an animal or a bird, or painted on a road, vehicle, etc. ▶ **plamy**, **cętka**, **oznaczenie**, **znak** (*drogowy*)

marksman /ˈmɑːksmən/ noun [C] (pl. **-men** /-mən/) a person who can shoot very well with a gun ▶ **strzelec wyborowy**, **dobry strzelec**

markup /ˈmɑːkʌp/ noun **1** [usually sing.] an increase in the price of sth based on the difference between the cost of producing it and the price it is sold at: *an average markup of 10%* ▶ **marża 2** [U] the symbols used in computer documents which give information about the structure of the document and tell the computer how it is to appear on the computer screen, or how it is to appear when printed: *a markup language* ▶ **znaczniki**

marmalade /ˈmɑːməleɪd/ noun [U] a type of jam that is made from oranges or lemons ▶ **dżem pomarańczowy/cytrynowy**

maroon /məˈruːn/ adj. of a dark brownish-red colour ▶ **rudawobrązowy** ➲ look at **auburn**, **chestnut**, **crimson**, **scarlet**
■ **maroon** noun [U] ▶ **kolor rudawobrązowy**

marooned /məˈruːnd/ adj. in a place that you cannot leave: *The sailors were marooned* (zostali osadzeni) *on a desert island.* ▶ **znajdujący się w miejscu, którego nie można opuścić**

marquee /mɑːˈkiː/ noun [C] a very large tent that is used for parties, shows, etc. ▶ **duży namiot** (*np. na festyny, wesela*)

⚷ **marriage** /ˈmærɪdʒ/ noun **1** [C,U] the state of being husband and wife: *They are getting divorced after five years of marriage.* ◇ *a happy marriage* ◇ *a mixed marriage* ▶ **małżeństwo**, **stan małżeński 2** [C] a wedding ceremony: *The marriage took place at a registry office in Birmingham.* ▶ **ślub** ➲ note at **wedding** ➲ verb **get married (to sb)** or **marry (sb)**

ˌmarriage of conˈvenience noun [C] a marriage that is made for practical, financial or political reasons and not because the two people love each other ▶ **małżeństwo z rozsądku**

⚷ **married** /ˈmærid/ adj. **1 married (to sb)** having a husband or wife: *a married man/woman/couple* ◇ *They're planning to* ***get married*** (planują się pobrać) *in summer.* ◇ *They've been married* (są małżeństwem) *for nearly 50 years.* ◇ *Ewa's married to Mark.* Ewa jest żoną Marka. ▶ **żonaty**; **zamężna** OPP **unmarried**, **single 2** [only before a noun] connected with marriage: *How do you like married life?* ▶ **małżeński**

marrow /ˈmærəʊ/ noun **1** = BONE MARROW **2** [C,U] (Brit.) a large vegetable with green skin that is white inside ▶ **kabaczek** ➲ picture on **page A13**

⚷ **marry** /ˈmæri/ verb (**marrying**; **marries**; pt, pp **married**) **1** [I,T] to take sb as your husband or wife: *They married when they were very young.* ◇ *When did he ask you to marry him?* ▶ **pobierać się**; **wychodzić za mąż**, **żenić się** ➲ note at **wedding** ➲ look at **divorce**

> Częściej używa się zwrotu **get married**: *When are Jo and Mark getting married?* ◇ *Many people live together without getting married.* ◇ *Are you getting married in church or at the registry office?* Uwaga! Mówi się **get married TO sb**, a nie ~~*with sb*~~.

2 [T] to join two people together as husband and wife: *We asked the local vicar to marry us.* ▶ **udzielać ślubu** ➲ noun **marriage**

Mars /mɑːz/ noun [sing.] the red planet, that is fourth in order from the sun ▶ **Mars** ➲ look at **Martian**

marsh /mɑːʃ/ noun [C,U] an area of soft wet land ▶ **bagno**, **błota**, **moczary**
■ **marshy** adj. ▶ **błotnisty**, **bagnisty**

marshal /ˈmɑːʃl/ noun [C] **1** a person who helps to organize or control a large public event: *Marshals are directing traffic in the car park.* ▶ **członek służb porządkowych** (*w czasie dużej imprezy publicznej, meczu itp.*) **2** (US) an officer of a high level in the police or fire department or in a court of law ▶ **marszałek**

marshmallow /ˌmɑːʃˈmæləʊ; US -ˈmel-/ noun [C,U] a soft pink or white sweet ▶ **rodzaj miękkiego cukierka** (*podobny do ptasiego mleczka, bez czekolady*)

marsupial /mɑːˈsuːpiəl/ noun [C] any animal that carries its young in a **pouch** on the mother's stomach: *Kangaroos and koalas are marsupials.* ▶ **torbacz**

martial /ˈmɑːʃl/ adj. [only before a noun] (formal) connected with war: *to declare/impose/lift martial law* (stan wojenny) ▶ **wojenny**

ˌmartial ˈarts noun [pl.] fighting sports such as **karate** or **judo**, in which you use your hands and feet as weapons ▶ **wschodnie sztuki walki**

ˌmartial ˈlaw noun [U] a situation where the army of a country controls an area instead of the police during a time of trouble: *to* ***declare/impose/lift martial law*** ◇ *The city remains firmly* ***under martial law.*** ▶ **stan wojenny**

Martian /ˈmɑːʃn/ noun [C] (in stories) a creature that comes from the planet Mars ▶ **Marsjan-nin/ka**

martyr /ˈmɑːtə(r)/ noun [C] **1** a person who is killed because of what they believe ▶ **męczenni-k/ca 2** a person who tries to make people feel sorry for them: *Don't be such a martyr! You don't have to do all the housework.* ▶ (*przen.*) **męczenni-k/ca**
■ **martyrdom** /ˈmɑːtədəm/ noun [U] ▶ **męczeństwo**

marvel /ˈmɑːvl/ noun [C] a person or thing that is wonderful or that surprises you: *The new building is a marvel of modern technology.* ▶ **cud**, **fenomen**, **rzecz niepojęta**
■ **marvel** verb [I] (**marvelling**; **marvelled**; US **marveling**; **marveled**) (formal) **marvel (at sth)**: *We marvelled at how much they had managed to do.* ▶ **podziwiać**, **zdumiewać się**

marvellous (US **marvelous**) /ˈmɑːvələs/ adj. very good; wonderful: *a marvellous opportunity* ▶ **cudowny**, **zdumiewający** SYN **fantastic**
■ **marvellously** (US **marvelously**) adv. ▶ **cudownie**, **zdumiewająco**

Marxism /ˈmɑːksɪzəm/ noun [U] the political and economic thought of Karl Marx ▶ **marksizm**
■ **Marxist** /-ɪst/ **1** noun [C] ▶ **marksist(k)a 2** adj.: *Marxist ideology* ▶ **marksistowski**

marzipan /ˈmɑːzɪpæn; ˌmɑːzɪˈpæn; US ˈmɑːrtsəpæn; ˈmɑːrz-/ noun [U] a food that is made of sugar, egg and **almonds**. Marzipan is used to make sweets or to put on cakes. ▶ **marcepan**

masc = MASCULINE

mascara /mæˈskɑːrə; US -ˈskærə/ noun [U] a beauty product that is used to make your **eyelashes** dark and attractive ▶ **tusz do rzęs**

mascot /ˈmæskət; US -skɑːt/ noun [C] a person, animal or thing that is thought to bring good luck ▶ **maskotka**

masculine /ˈmæskjəlɪn/ adj. with the qualities that people think are typical of men: *a deep, masculine voice*

M

◇ *Her short hair makes her look quite masculine.* ▶ **męski, płci męskiej** ➲ look at **feminine**, **male**, **manly** ➲ note at **female** ℹ W języku angielskim rzeczowniki rodzaju **masculine** odnoszą się zazwyczaj tylko do ludzi lub zwierząt rodzaju męskiego, a **feminine** tylko do ludzi lub zwierząt rodzaju żeńskiego: *'He' is a masculine pronoun.*

■ **masculinity** /ˌmæskjuˈlɪnəti/ noun [U] ▶ **męskość, cechy męskie**

mash /mæʃ/ verb [T] to mix or crush sth until it is soft: *mashed potatoes* ▶ **tłuc, ubijać**

mask¹ /mɑːsk; US mæsk/ noun [C] something that you wear that covers your face or part of your face. People wear **masks** in order to hide or protect their faces or to make themselves look different: *a surgical/Halloween mask* ▶ **maska** ➲ look at **gas mask**, **goggles**

mask² /mɑːsk; US mæsk/ verb [T] to hide a feeling, smell, fact, etc.: *He masked his anger with a smile.* ▶ **maskować**

masked /mɑːskt; US mæskt/ adj. wearing a **mask**: *a masked gunman* ▶ **zamaskowany, w masce**

masochism /ˈmæsəkɪzəm/ noun [U] the enjoyment of pain, or of what most people would find unpleasant: *He swims in the sea even in winter – that's sheer masochism!* ▶ **masochizm** ➲ look at **sadism**

■ **masochist** /-ɪst/ noun [C] ▶ **masochist-a/ka** | **masochistic** /ˌmæsəˈkɪstɪk/ adj. ▶ **masochistyczny**

mason /ˈmeɪsn/ noun [C] **1** a person who makes things from stone ▶ **kamieniarz 2** = FREEMASON

masonry /ˈmeɪsənri/ noun [U] the parts of a building that are made of stone ▶ **kamieniarka**

masquerade /ˌmæskəˈreɪd; ˌmɑːsk-/ noun [C] a way of behaving that hides the truth or sb's true feelings ▶ **maskarada**

■ **masquerade** verb [I] **masquerade as sth**: *Two people, masquerading as doctors, knocked at the door and asked to see the child.* ▶ **podawać się za kogoś/coś**

⚷ **mass¹** /mæs/ noun **1** [C] **a mass (of sth)** a large amount or number of sth: *a dense mass of smoke* ◇ (informal) *There were masses of people at the market today.* ▶ **masa; mnóstwo 2** (**the masses**) [pl.] ordinary people when considered as a political group: *a TV programme that brings science to the masses* ▶ **masy, rzesze 3** [U] (in physics) the quantity of material that sth contains: *the mass of a planet* ▶ **masa 4** (**Mass**) [C,U] the ceremony in some Christian churches when people eat bread and drink wine in order to remember the last meal that Christ had before he died: *to go to Mass* ▶ **msza**

⚷ **mass²** /mæs/ adj. [only before a noun] involving a large number of people or things: *mass unemployment* ◇ *a mass meeting* wiec ◇ *a mass* (seryjny) *murderer* ▶ **masowy**

mass³ /mæs/ verb [I,T] to come together or bring people or things together in large numbers: *The students massed in the square.* ▶ **gromadzić (się)**

massacre /ˈmæsəkə(r)/ noun [C] the killing of a large number of people or animals ▶ **masakra, rzeź**

■ **massacre** verb [T] ▶ **masakrować, urządzać rzeź/jatkę** ➲ note at **kill**

massage /ˈmæsɑːʒ; US məˈsɑːʒ/ noun [C,U] the act of rubbing and pressing sb's body in order to reduce pain or to help them relax: *to give sb a massage* ▶ **masaż**

■ **massage** verb [T] ▶ **masować, robić komuś masaż**

masseur /mæˈsɜː(r)/ noun [C,U] a person whose job is giving people massage ▶ **masażyst(k)a**

masseuse /mæˈsɜːz/ noun [C,U] a woman whose job is giving people massage ▶ **masażystka**

⚷ **massive** /ˈmæsɪv/ adj. very big: *a massive increase in prices* ▶ **ogromny, wielki** SYN **huge**

■ **massively** adv. ▶ **ogromnie**

ˌ**mass ˈmedia** noun [pl.] newspapers, TV and radio that reach a large number of people ▶ **środki masowego przekazu**

ˌ**mass-proˈduce** verb [T] to make large numbers of similar things by machine in a factory: *mass-produced goods* ▶ **produkować masowo/seryjnie**

■ **mass production** noun [U] ▶ **produkcja masowa/seryjna**

mast /mɑːst; US mæst/ noun [C] **1** a tall wooden or metal pole for holding a ship's sails or a flag ▶ **maszt** ➲ picture on **page A6 2** a tall pole that is used for sending out radio or TV signals ▶ **maszt**

mastectomy /mæˈstektəmi/ noun [C] (pl. **-ies**) a medical operation to remove a person's breast ▶ **mastektomia**

⚷ **master¹** /ˈmɑːstə(r); US ˈmæs-/ noun [C] **1** a person who has great skill at doing sth: *a master builder* mistrz murarski ◇ *an exhibition of work by French masters* ▶ **mistrz 2** (Brit., old-fashioned) a male teacher (usually in a private school): *the chemistry master* ▶ **nauczyciel** ➲ look at **headmaster**, **mistress 3** a film or tape from which copies can be made: *the master copy* ▶ **negatyw główny, taśma-matka 4** (**Master**) (old-fashioned) (sometimes used when speaking or writing to a boy who is too young to be called Mr): *Master James Wilson* ▶ **panicz 5** a man who has people or animals in his control: *The dog ran to his master.* ◇ (figurative) *to be master of a difficult situation* ▶ **pan, właściciel** ➲ look at **mistress**

master² /ˈmɑːstə(r); US ˈmæs-/ verb [T] **1** to learn how to do sth well: *It takes years of study to master a foreign language.* ▶ **opanowywać, nabierać biegłości/wprawy w czymś 2** to control sth: *to master a situation* ▶ **panować nad czymś**

masterclass /ˈmɑːstəklɑːs; US ˈmæstəklæs/ noun [C] a lesson, especially in music, given by a famous expert to very skilled students ▶ **lekcja mistrzowska**

mastermind /ˈmɑːstəmaɪnd; US ˈmæs-/ noun [C] a very clever person who has planned or organized sth: *The mastermind behind the robbery was never caught.* ▶ **mózg** (*np. akcji*)

■ **mastermind** verb [T]: *The police failed to catch the man who masterminded the robbery.* ▶ **być mózgiem czegoś**

ˌ**master of ˈceremonies** noun [C] (abbr. **MC**) a person who introduces guests or entertainers at a formal occasion ▶ **mistrz ceremonii**

masterpiece /ˈmɑːstəpiːs; US ˈmæs-/ noun [C] a work of art, music, literature, etc. that is of the highest quality ▶ **arcydzieło**

ˈ**master's degree** (also **master's**) noun [C] a second or higher university degree. You usually get a **master's degree** by studying for one or two years after your first degree: *Master of Arts (MA)* ◇ *Master of Science (MSc)* ▶ **stopień magistra** ➲ look at **bachelor** ➲ note at **degree**

mastery /ˈmɑːstəri; US ˈmæs-/ noun [U] **1 mastery (of sth)** great skill at doing sth: *His mastery of the violin was quite exceptional for a child.* ▶ **biegłość (w czymś), wprawa (w czymś) 2 mastery (of/over sb/sth)** control over sb/sth: *The battle was fought for mastery of the seas.* ▶ **panowanie/władza (nad kimś/czymś)**

masturbate /ˈmæstəbeɪt/ verb [I,T] to make yourself or sb else feel sexually excited by touching and rubbing the sex organs ▶ **masturbować (się)**

■ **masturbation** /ˌmæstəˈbeɪʃn/ noun [U] ▶ **masturbacja**

mat /mæt/ noun [C] **1** a piece of carpet or other thick material that you put on the floor: *a doormat* wycieraczka (przed drzwiami) ▶ **dywanik, mata** ➲ look at **rug 2** a small piece of material that you put under sth on a table: *a table mat* ◇ *a beer mat* ◇ *a mouse mat* ▶ **podstawka, podkładka**

match[1] /mætʃ/ noun **1** [C] a small stick of wood, cardboard, etc. that you use for starting a fire, lighting a cigarette, etc.: *a box of matches* ◇ *to light/strike a match* zapalać/pocierać zapałkę ▶ **zapałka 2** [C] an organized game or sports event: *a tennis/football match* ◇ *They beat us last time but we hope to win the return match* (mecz rewanżowy). ▶ **mecz 3** [sing.] **a match for sb; sb's match** a person or thing that is as good as or better than sb/sth else: *Charo is no match for her mother when it comes to cooking.* Charo nie dorównuje swojej matce w gotowaniu. ◇ *I think you've* **met** *your* **match** *in Dave – you won't beat him.* ▶ **osoba/rzecz dorównująca drugiej (w czymś) 4** [sing.] **a match (for sb/sth)** something that looks good with sth else: *Those shoes aren't a very good match with your dress.* ◇ *Bill and Sam are a good match* (dobrze pasują do siebie). *They should be very happy together.* ▶ **osoba/rzecz dopasowana (do kogoś innego/czegoś innego), osoba/rzecz harmonizująca (z kimś/czymś innym)**

match[2] /mætʃ/ verb **1** [I,T] to have the same colour or pattern as sth else; to look good with sth else: *That shirt doesn't match your jacket.* ◇ *Your shirt and jacket don't match.* ▶ **harmonizować (z czymś), być dobrze dobranym (do czegoś), pasować (do czegoś)**

> **Match, go with sth** i **go (together)** używa się, kiedy rzeczy harmonizują ze sobą kolorem lub kształtem: *a scarf with gloves to match* ◇ *Does this jacket go with this skirt?* ◇ *Those colours go well together.* **Suit** używa się, kiedy coś na kimś ładnie wygląda: *That dress really suits you.*

2 [T] to find sb/sth that is like or suitable for sb/sth else: *The agency tries to match single people with suitable partners.* ◇ *I don't think Mike and Emma are very well matched as a couple.* ▶ **kojarzyć** (*np. ludzi*), **dopasowywać 3** [T] to be as good as or better than sb/sth else: *Taiwan produces the goods at a price that Europe cannot match.* ◇ *The two teams are evenly matched* (są na tym samym poziomie). ▶ **dorównywać**

PHR V **match sth against sth** to compare sth with sth else in order to find things that are the same or similar: *New information is matched against existing data in the computer.* ▶ **dopasowywać coś do czegoś**

match sb/sth against/with sb/sth to arrange for sb to compete in a game or competition against sb else: *We are matched against last year's champions in the first round.* ▶ **zmierzyć kogoś/coś z kimś/czymś**

match up (to sb/sth) to be as good as sb/sth: *The film didn't match up to my expectations.* ▶ **dorównywać komuś/czemuś, dorastać do czegoś**

match up (with sth) to be the same: *The statements of the two witnesses don't match up.* ▶ **pasować (do siebie)**

match sth up (with sth) to fit or put sth together (with sth else): *What you have to do is match up each star with his or her pet.* ▶ **dopasowywać coś (do czegoś)**

matchbox /ˈmætʃbɒks/ noun [C] a small box for matches ▶ **pudełko (od) zapałek** ➲ picture at **container**

matching /ˈmætʃɪŋ/ adj. [only before a noun] (used about clothes, objects, etc.) having the same colour, pattern, style, etc. and therefore looking attractive together: *a pine table with four matching chairs* ▶ **pasujący (do siebie), dopasowany**

matchstick /ˈmætʃstɪk/ noun [C] the thin wooden part of a match ▶ **zapałka**

mate[1] /meɪt/ noun [C] **1** (informal) a friend or sb you live, work or do an activity with: *He's an old mate of mine.* ◇ *a classmate/team-mate/playmate* ◇ *a flatmate* współlokator/ka ▶ **kole-ga/żanka; kumpel/ka** ➲ note at **friend 2** (Brit., slang) (used when speaking to a man): *Can you give me a hand, mate?* ▶ **stary 3** one of a male and female pair of animals, birds, etc.: *The female sits on the eggs while her mate hunts for food.* ▶ **sami-ec/ca 4** an officer on a ship ▶ **oficer okrętowy, zastępca kapitana**

mate[2] /meɪt/ verb **1** [I] (used about animals and birds) to have sex and produce young: *Pandas rarely mate in zoos.* ▶ **parzyć się 2** [T] to bring two animals together so that they can **mate** ▶ **parzyć** SYN for both meanings **breed**

material[1] /məˈtɪəriəl/ noun **1** [C,U] cloth (for making clothes, etc.): *Is there enough material for a dress?* ▶ **materiał, tkanina 2** [C,U] a substance that can be used for making or doing sth: *raw materials* ◇ *teaching/building materials* ◇ *writing materials* artykuły piśmienne ◇ *This new material is strong but it is also very light.* ▶ **materiał, surowiec 3** [U] facts or information that you collect before you write a book, article, etc.: *She's collecting material for her latest novel.* ▶ **materiał, źródła**

material[2] /məˈtɪəriəl/ adj. **1** [only before a noun] connected with real or physical things rather than the spirit or emotions: *We should not value material comforts too highly.* ▶ **materialny, cielesny** ➲ look at **spiritual 2** important and needing to be considered: *material evidence* ▶ **istotny, ważny** ⓘ To słowo nie jest często spotykane. ➲ look at **immaterial**

■ **materially** /-riəli/ adv. ▶ **materialnie; istotnie**

materialism /məˈtɪəriəlɪzəm/ noun [U] the belief that money and possessions are the most important things in life ▶ **materializm**

■ **materialist** /-ɪst/ noun [C] ▶ **materialist(k)a** | **materialistic** /məˌtɪəriəˈlɪstɪk/ adj. ▶ **materialistyczny**

materialize (also **-ise**) /məˈtɪəriəlaɪz/ verb [I] to become real; to happen: *The pay rise that they had promised never materialized.* ▶ **materializować się, dochodzić do skutku**

maternal /məˈtɜːnl/ adj. **1** behaving as a mother would behave; connected with being a mother: *maternal love/instincts* ▶ **matczyny, macierzyński 2** [only before a noun] related through your mother's side of the family: *your maternal grandfather* ▶ **ze strony matki** ➲ look at **paternal**

maternity /məˈtɜːnəti/ adj. connected with women who are going to have or have just had a baby: *maternity clothes* ubranie ciążowe ◇ *maternity leave* urlop macierzyński ◇ *the hospital's maternity ward* oddział położniczy ▶ **macierzyński, położniczy** ➲ look at **paternity**

mathematician /ˌmæθəməˈtɪʃn/ noun [C] a person who studies or is an expert in mathematics ▶ **matematyk**

mathematics /ˌmæθəˈmætɪks/ noun [U] the science or study of numbers, quantities or shapes ▶ **matematyka** ➲ look at **algebra, arithmetic, geometry** ⓘ Brytyjski skrót tego słowa to **maths**, zaś amerykański to **math**: *Maths is my favourite subject.*

■ **mathematical** /ˌmæθəˈmætɪkl/ adj.: *mathematical calculations/problems* ▶ **matematyczny** | **mathematically** /-kli/ adv. ▶ **matematycznie**

matinee (also **matinée**) /ˈmætɪneɪ; US ˌmætnˈeɪ/ noun [C] an afternoon performance of a play, film, etc. ▶ (*seans, przedstawienie*) **popołudniówka**

matrices plural of **matrix**

matrimony /ˈmætrɪməni; US -məʊni/ noun [U] (formal) the state of being married ▶ **stan małżeński, małżeństwo**

■ **matrimonial** /ˌmætrɪˈməʊniəl/ adj. ▶ **małżeński, matrymonialny**

matrix /ˈmeɪtrɪks/ noun [C] (pl. **matrices** /ˈmeɪtrɪsiːz/) **1** an arrangement of numbers, symbols, etc. in rows and columns, treated as a single quantity ▶ **macierz 2** (formal) the formal social, political, etc. situation from which a society or person grows and develops: *the European cultural matrix* ▶ **kontekst 3** (formal or literary) a system of lines, roads, etc. that cross each other, forming a series

M

of squares or shapes in between: *a matrix of paths* ▶ **sieć** SYN **network**

matron /ˈmeɪtrən/ noun [C] **1** a woman who works as a nurse in a school ▶ **pielęgniarka szkolna 2** (old-fashioned) a nurse who is in charge of the other nurses in a hospital (now usually called a **senior nursing officer**) ▶ **przełożona** (*pielęgniarek*) **3** (old-fashioned) an older married woman ▶ **matrona**

matt (US also **matte**) /mæt/ adj. not shiny: *This paint gives a matt finish.* ▶ **matowy** ➲ look at **gloss**

matted /ˈmætɪd/ adj. (used especially about hair) forming a thick mass, especially because it is wet and/or dirty ▶ **skudłacony** (*zwł. z wilgoci, brudu itp.*)

⚷ **matter**[1] /ˈmætə(r)/ noun **1** [C] a subject or situation that you must think about and give your attention to: *It's a personal matter and I don't want to discuss it with you.* ◇ *Finding a job will be* ***no easy matter.*** ◇ *to simplify/complicate matters* ◇ *They should try to settle matters* (wyrównać rachunki) *between themselves before going to court.* ▶ **sprawa**, **kwestia 2** [sing.] **the matter (with sb/sth)** the reason sb/sth has a problem or is not good: *She looks sad.* ***What's the matter*** *with her* (co jej się stało)*?* ◇ *There seems to be* ***something the matter*** (wygląda na to, że coś się dzieje) *with the car.* ◇ *Eat that food! There's* ***nothing the matter*** *with it* (niczego mu nie brakuje). ▶ **problem 3** [U] all physical substances; a substance of a particular kind: *waste matter* odpadki/odpady ◇ *reading matter* lektura ▶ **materia**, **substancja 4** [U] the contents of a book, film, etc.: *unsuitable subject matter for children* ▶ **treść**

IDM **another/a different matter** something much more serious, difficult, etc.: *I can speak a little Japanese, but reading it is quite another matter.* ▶ **to inna sprawa**

as a matter of fact to tell the truth; in reality: *I like him very much, as a matter of fact.* ▶ **prawdę mówiąc**, **w rzeczywistości**

for that matter in addition; now that I think about it: *Mick is really fed up with his course. I am too, for that matter.* ▶ **jeśli o to idzie**

(be) a matter of sth/doing sth a situation in which sth is needed: *Learning a language is largely a matter of practice.* ▶ **kwestia (robienia) czegoś**

a matter of course something that you always do; the usual thing to do: *Goods leaving the factory are checked as a matter of course* (są rutynowo sprawdzane). ▶ **rzecz naturalna**, **normalny tok postępowania**

a matter of hours, miles, etc. (used to say that sth is not very long, far, expensive, etc.): *The fight lasted a matter of seconds.* ▶ **(jakieś) parę godzin, mil itp.**

a matter of life and/or death extremely urgent and important ▶ **sprawa życia lub śmierci**

a matter of opinion a subject on which people do not agree: *'I think the government is doing a good job.' 'That's a matter of opinion.'* ▶ **sprawa dyskusyjna**

no matter who, what, where, etc. it is not important who, what, where, etc.: *They never listen no matter what you say.* ▶ **bez względu na kogoś/coś**, **wszystko jedno gdzie itp.**

to make matters/things worse → WORSE

⚷ **matter**[2] /ˈmætə(r)/ verb [I] [not used in the continuous tenses] **matter (to sb)** to be important: ***It doesn't*** *really* ***matter*** (to naprawdę nieważne) *how much it costs.* ◇ *Does it matter* (czy coś się stanie) *if we are a little bit late?* ◇ *If you can't eat it all, it doesn't matter* (nic nie szkodzi). ◇ *Nobody's hurt, and* ***that's all that matters.*** ◇ *Some things matter more than others.* ◇ *It doesn't matter to me what he does in his free time.* ▶ **znaczyć**, **mieć znaczenie** ❶ Por. **it doesn't matter** i **I don't mind**: *'I've broken a cup!' 'It was an old one. It doesn't matter* (nic się nie stało)*.'* ◇ *'What shall we have for dinner?' 'I don't mind* (cokolwiek)*.'*

ˌ**matter-of-ˈfact** adj. said or done without showing any emotion, especially when it would seem more normal to express your feelings: *He was very matter-of-fact about his illness.* ▶ **rzeczowy**, **obojętny**

mattress /ˈmætrəs/ noun [C] a large soft thing that you lie on to sleep, usually put on a bed ▶ **materac** ➲ picture at **bed**

mature /məˈtʃʊə(r); Brit. also -ˈtjʊə(r); US also -ˈtʊr/ adj. **1** behaving in a sensible adult way: *Is she mature enough for such responsibility?* ▶ **dojrzały**, **dorosły 2** fully grown or fully developed: *a mature tree/bird/animal* ▶ **dojrzały**, **dorosły** OPP for both meanings **immature**

■ **mature** verb [I]: *He matured a lot during his two years at college.* ▶ **dojrzewać**, **dorośleć** | **maturity** /məˈtʃʊərəti; Brit. also -ˈtjʊə-; US also -ˈtʊr-/ noun [U] ▶ **dojrzałość**, **dorosłość**

maul /mɔːl/ verb [T] (usually used about a wild animal) to attack and injure sb ▶ **kaleczyć**, **szarpać**

Maundy Thursday /ˌmɔːndi ˈθɜːzdeɪ; -di/ noun [U,C] (in the Christian Church) the Thursday before Easter ▶ **Wielki Czwartek**

mauve /məʊv/ adj. of a pale purple colour ▶ **fiołkoworóżowy**

■ **mauve** noun [U] ▶ **kolor fiołkoworóżowy**

maverick /ˈmævərɪk/ noun [C] a person who does not behave or think like everyone else, but who has independent, unusual opinions: *a political maverick* ▶ **indywidualist(k)a**

■ **maverick** adj. [only before a noun]: *a maverick film director* ▶ **nieszablonowy**

mawkish /ˈmɔːkɪʃ/ adj. expressing or sharing emotion in a way that is exaggerated or embarrassing: *a mawkish poem* ▶ **ckliwy** SYN **sentimental**

max = MAXIMUM: *max temp 21° C*

maxim /ˈmæksɪm/ noun [C] a few words that express a rule for good or sensible behaviour: *Our maxim is: 'If a job's worth doing, it's worth doing well.'* ▶ **sentencja**, **maksyma**

maximize (also **-ise**) /ˈmæksɪmaɪz/ verb [T] to increase sth as much as possible: *to maximize profits* ▶ **maksymalizować** OPP **minimize**

⚷ **maximum** /ˈmæksɪməm/ noun [sing.] (abbr. **max** /mæks/) the greatest amount or level of sth that is possible, allowed, etc.: *The bus can carry a maximum of 40 people.* ◇ *That is the maximum we can afford.* ◇ *to set the dial to maximum* ▶ **maksimum** OPP **minimum**

■ **maximum** adj. [only before a noun]: *a maximum speed of 120 miles per hour* ▶ **maksymalny**

⚷ **May** /meɪ/ noun [U,C] the 5th month of the year, coming after April ▶ **maj** ➲ note at **January**

⚷ **may** /meɪ/ modal verb (negative **may not**; pt **might** /maɪt/, negative **might not**) **1** (used for saying that sth is possible): *You may be right.* Być może masz rację. ◇ *I may be going* (możliwe, że pojadę) *to China next year.* ◇ *'Where's Sue?' 'She may be* ((być) może jest) *in the garden.'* ◇ *They may have forgotten the meeting.* Być może zapomnieli o spotkaniu. ◇ *He may have been driving too fast.* Być może jechał zbyt szybko. **2** (used for contrasting two facts): *He may be very clever* (może i jest bardzo mądry) *but he can't do anything practical.* **3** (used as a polite way of asking for and giving permission): *May I use your phone?* Czy mógłbym skorzystać z telefonu? ◇ *You may only borrow books for a week.* Możesz wypożyczać książki tylko na tydzień. ◇ *You may not take photographs* (nie wolno fotografować) *in the museum.* ▶ **móc 4** (formal) (used for expressing wishes and hopes): *May you both be very happy.* ▶ **oby**, **niech**

IDM **may/might as well (do sth)** → WELL[1]

⚷ **maybe** /ˈmeɪbi/ adv. perhaps; possibly: *'Are you going to come?' 'Maybe.'* ◇ *There were three, maybe four armed* men. ◇ *Maybe I'll accept the invitation and maybe I won't.* ▶ **może, być może, że** ➲ note at **perhaps**

'May Day noun [C] 1st May ▶ **Święto 1 Maja**

> **May Day** jest tradycyjnie obchodzony jako święto wiosny, a w niektórych krajach także jako święto pracy.

mayhem /'meɪhem/ noun [U] confusion and fear, usually caused by violent behaviour or by some sudden shocking event: *There was absolute mayhem when everyone tried to get out at once.* ▶ **chaos, zamęt**

mayonnaise /ˌmeɪə'neɪz; US 'meɪəneɪz/ noun [U] a cold thick pale yellow sauce made with eggs and oil ▶ **majonez**

⚷ **mayor** /meə(r); US 'meɪər/ noun [C] a person who is elected to be the leader of a group of people who manage the affairs of a town or city ▶ **burmistrz**

mayoress /meə'res; US 'meɪərəs/ noun [C] **1** (also ˌlady 'mayor) a woman **mayor** ▶ **kobieta-burmistrz 2** (in England, Wales and Northern Ireland) a woman who is married to or helps a **mayor** ▶ **burmistrzowa, kobieta pomagająca burmistrzowi w oficjalnych obowiązkach**

maze /meɪz/ noun [C] a system of paths which is designed to confuse you so that it is difficult to find your way out: (figurative) *a maze of winding streets* ▶ **labirynt** SYN **labyrinth**

Mb = MEGABYTE

MBA /ˌem biː 'eɪ/ abbr. **Master of Business Administration**; an advanced university degree in business ▶ **mgr zarządzania**

MC /ˌem 'siː/ noun **1 master of ceremonies** ▶ **mistrz ceremonii 2** (**M.C.**) **Member of Congress** ▶ **członek Kongresu 3** a person who speaks the words of a **rap** song ▶ **raper**

MD /ˌem 'diː/ abbr. **Doctor of Medicine** ▶ **lek. med.**

ME /ˌem 'iː/ (especially US **chronic fatigue syndrome**) noun [U] **myalgic encephalomyelitis**; an illness that makes people feel extremely weak and tired and that can last a long time ▶ **zapalenie mózgu i rdzenia z mialgią**

⚷ **me** /miː/ pron. (used as an object) the person who is speaking or writing: *He telephoned me yesterday.* ◇ *She wrote to me last week.* ◇ *Hello, is that Frank? It's me, Sadiq.* ◇ *'Who's this photograph of?' 'Me.'* ◇ *'Somebody's spilt the wine.' 'I'm afraid it was me* (obawiam się, że to ja).*'* ℹ **It is/was me** używa się znacznie częściej niż **it is/was I**, chociaż ta druga forma może być stosowana w języku formalnym w mowie i piśmie. ▶ **mnie, mi, (to) ja**

meadow /'medəʊ/ noun [C] a field of grass ▶ **łąka**

meagre (US **meager**) /'miːgə(r)/ adj. too small in amount: *a meagre salary* ▶ **skromny, niewielki**

⚷ **meal** /miːl/ noun [C] the time when you eat or the food that is eaten at that time: *Shall we **go out for a meal** on Friday?* ◇ *a heavy/light meal* ▶ **posiłek** ➲ note at **lunch, restaurant**

IDM **a square meal** → SQUARE[1]

> **meals**
>
> The main **meals** of the day are **breakfast**, **lunch** and **dinner. Tea** and **supper** are usually smaller meals, but some people use these words to talk about the main evening meal. The midday meal can be called **dinner**. Before a meal you **lay the table** by putting a **tablecloth**, **cutlery**, etc. on it. After the meal you **clear the table** and **wash up/wash the dishes**. If you don't want to cook, you can **go out for a meal/eat out** or you can get a **takeaway**. A **picnic** is a meal you prepare at home and take to eat outdoors. Something small that you eat between meals is a **snack**.

mealtime /'miːltaɪm/ noun [C] the time at which a meal is usually eaten ▶ **pora posiłku**

⚷ **mean[1]** /miːn/ verb [T] (pt, pp **meant** /ment/) **1** [not used in the continuous tenses] to express, show or have as a meaning: ***What does** this word **mean?*** ◇ *The bell means that the lesson has ended.* ◇ *Does the name 'Kate Wright' mean anything to you?* ▶ **znaczyć, mówić** ℹ Czasownik **mean** nie występuje w czasach *continuous*. Natomiast często spotyka się go w *present participle* (formie *-ing*): *The weather during filming was terrible, meaning that several scenes had to be shot again later.* **2** to want or intend to say sth; to refer to sb/sth: *Well, she said 'yes' but I think she really meant 'no'.* ◇ *What do you mean by 'a lot of money'?* ◇ *I only meant that I couldn't come tomorrow – any other day would be fine.* ◇ ***I see what you mean**, but I'm afraid it's not possible.* ▶ **mieć na myśli, chcieć powiedzieć** ➲ note at **think**

> Zwróć uwagę, że **mean** nie można używać w znaczeniu „być zdania, że". Stosuje się wówczas zwroty **I think that...** lub **in my opinion...**: *I think that she'd be silly to buy that car.* Zwrot **I mean** często stosuje się w rozmowie w celu wyjaśnienia czegoś, o czym mówiło się przed chwilą lub podania dodatkowej informacji: *What a terrible summer – I mean it's rained almost all the time.* ◇ *I think the film will have started – I mean it's past 8 o'clock.*
> **I mean** używa się też w celu skorygowania czegoś, co zostało dopiero co powiedziane: *We went there on Tuesday, I mean Thursday.*

3 [often passive] **mean (sb) to do sth; mean sth (as/for sth/sb); mean sb/sth to be sth** to intend sth; to be supposed to be/do sth: *I'm sure she didn't mean to offend you* (nie chciała cię obrazić). ◇ *She meant the present to be for both of us.* Prezent, który nam dała, jest dla nas obojga. ◇ *I didn't mean you to cook the whole meal!* Nie chciałem, żebyś gotował cały obiad! ◇ *It was only meant as a joke.* To miał być tylko żart. ◇ *What's this picture meant to be?* Co ten obraz ma przedstawiać? ◇ *You're meant to get to work at 9 o'clock.* Do pracy masz przychodzić na dziewiątą. ▶ **mieć zamiar, zamierzać 4** to be serious or sincere about sth: *He said he loved me but I don't think he meant it!* ▶ **mówić poważnie 5** to make sth likely; to cause: *The shortage of teachers means that classes are larger.* ▶ **oznaczać 6 mean sth (to sb)** to be important to sb: *This job means a lot to me.* ◇ *Money means nothing to her.* ▶ **znaczyć (coś ważnego), mieć (duże) znaczenie**

IDM **be meant to be sth** to be considered or said to be sth: *That restaurant is meant to be excellent.* Ta restauracja ma być wspaniała. ▶ **być czymś z założenia**

mean well to want to be kind and helpful but usually without success: *My mother means well but I wish she'd stop treating me like a child.* ▶ **chcieć jak najlepiej**

mean[2] /miːn/ adj. **1 mean (with sth)** wanting to keep money, etc. for yourself rather than let other people have it: *It's no good asking him for any money – he's much too mean.* ◇ *They're mean with the food in the canteen.* ▶ **skąpy, małostkowy** OPP **generous 2 mean (to sb)** (used about people or their behaviour) unkind: *It was mean of him not to invite you too.* ▶ **nieprzyjemny, złośliwy 3** [only before a noun] average: *the mean temperature* ▶ **średni**

■ **meanness** noun [U] ▶ **skąpstwo, nieuprzejmość**

meander /mi'ændə(r)/ verb [I] **1** (used about a river, road, etc.) to have a lot of curves and bends ▶ **wić się 2** to walk or travel slowly or without any definite direction ▶ **błąkać się 3** (used about a conversation, discussion, etc.) to develop slowly and change subject often, in a way that makes it boring or difficult to understand) ▶ (*rozmowa itp.*) **toczyć się długo i z wieloma dygresjami**

M

meaning /'mi:nɪŋ/ noun **1** [C,U] the thing or idea that sth represents; what sb is trying to communicate: *This word has two different meanings in English.* ◇ *What do you think the meaning is of the last line of the poem?* ▶ **znaczenie 2** [U] the purpose or importance of an experience: *With his child dead there seemed to be no meaning in life.* ▶ **treść, znaczenie**

meaningful /'mi:nɪŋfl/ adj. **1** useful, important or interesting: *Most people need a meaningful relationship with another person.* ▶ **znaczący, treściwy 2** (used about a look, expression, etc.) trying to express a certain feeling or idea: *They kept giving each other meaningful glances across the table.* ▶ **porozumiewawczy**
■ **meaningfully** /-fəli/ adv. ▶ **znacząco, treściwie**

meaningless /'mi:nɪŋləs/ adj. without meaning, reason or sense: *The figures are meaningless if we have nothing to compare them with.* ▶ **bez znaczenia**

means /mi:nz/ noun **1** [C] (pl. **means**) **a means (of doing sth)** a method of doing sth: *Is there any means of contacting your husband?* ◇ *Do you have any means of transport?* Czy masz czym dojechać? ▶ **sposób, środek 2** [pl.] (formal) all the money that sb has: *This car is* ***beyond the means of*** *most people.* ▶ **środki** (*do życia*), **zasoby finansowe**
IDM **by all means** (used to say that you are happy for sb to have or do sth): *'Can I borrow your newspaper?' 'By all means.'* ▶ **jak najbardziej!**
by means of by using: *We got out of the hotel by means of the fire escape.* ▶ **za pomocą/pośrednictwem, drogą**
by no means; not by any means (used to emphasize sth) not at all: *I'm by no means sure that this is the right thing to do.* ▶ **w żaden sposób, stanowczo nie**
a means to an end an action or thing that is not important in itself but is a way of achieving sth else: *I don't enjoy my job, but it's a means to an end.* ▶ **środek do osiągnięcia celu**

'means test noun [C] an official enquiry to find out how much money sb has in order to decide whether they should get financial help from the state ▶ **ocena dochodów/sytuacji majątkowej**

meant past tense, past participle of **mean[1]**

meantime /'mi:ntaɪm/ noun
IDM **in the meantime** in the time between two things happening: *Our house isn't finished so in the meantime we're living with my mother.* ▶ **tymczasem**

meanwhile /'mi:nwaɪl/ adv. during the same time or during the time between two things happening: *Peter was at home studying. Omar, meanwhile, was out with his friends.* ▶ **tymczasem, na razie**

measles /'mi:zlz/ noun [U] a common infectious disease, especially among children, in which your body feels hot and your skin is covered in small red spots ▶ **odra**
ⓘ **Measles**pozornie wygląda jak rzeczownik w lm, ale jest to rzeczownik niepoliczalny i używa się go z czasownikami w lp: *In many countries measles is a very dangerous disease.*

measly /'mi:zli/ adj. (informal) much too small in size, amount or value: *All that work for this measly amount of money!* ▶ **nędzny, mizerny**

measure[1] /'meʒə(r)/ verb **1** [I,T] to find the size, weight, quantity, etc. of sb/sth in standard units by using an instrument: *to measure the height/width/length/depth of something* ◇ *Could you measure how wide the table is to see if it will fit into our room?* ▶ **mierzyć 2** [T] to be a certain height, width, length, etc.: *The room measures five metres across.* ▶ **mierzyć, mieć rozmiar 3** [T] **measure sth (against sth)** to judge the value or effect of sth: *Our sales do not look good when measured against those of our competitors.* ▶ **mierzyć; oceniać**
PHR V **measure sth out** to take the amount of sth that you need from a larger amount: *He measured out a cup of milk and added it to the mixture.* ▶ **odmierzać coś**
measure up (to sth) to be as good as you need to be or as sb expects you to be: *Did the holiday measure up to your expectations?* ▶ **dorastać (do czegoś)**

measure[2] /'meʒə(r)/ noun **1** [C, usually pl.] an official action that is done for a special reason: *As a temporary measure, the road will have to be closed.* ◇ *emergency measures* ◇ *The government is to* ***take*** *new* ***measures*** (podjąć nowe środki) *to reduce inflation.* ▶ **środki, kroki 2** [sing.] (formal) **a/some measure of sth** a certain amount of sth; some: *The play achieved a measure of success.* ▶ **stopień, miara 3** [sing.] a way of understanding or judging sth: *The school's popularity is a measure of the teachers' success.* ▶ **miara, wyznacznik 4** [C] a way of describing the size, amount, etc. of sth: *A metre is a measure of length.* ▶ **miara** ➲ look at **tape measure**
IDM **for good measure** in addition to sth, especially to make sure that there is enough: *He made a few extra sandwiches for good measure.* ▶ **na zapas**
made to measure specially made or perfectly suitable for a particular person, use, etc.: *I'm getting a suit made to measure for the wedding.* ▶ **zrobiony/uszyty na miarę**

measurement /'meʒəmənt/ noun **1** [U] the act or process of measuring sth: *the metric system of measurement* ▶ **pomiar/y, mierzenie 2** [C] a size, amount, etc. that is found by measuring: *What are the exact measurements of the room?* ◇ *Shall I* ***take*** *your* ***measurements*** (wziąć pani miarę)*?* ▶ **rozmiar, miara**

'measuring cup noun [C] a metal or plastic container used in the US for measuring quantities when cooking ▶ **pojemnik z miarką do mierzenia produktów**

'measuring jug noun [C] (Brit.) a glass or plastic container for measuring liquids when cooking ▶ **pojemnik z miarką do mierzenia płynów**

'measuring tape = TAPE MEASURE

meat /mi:t/ noun [U] the parts of animals or birds that people eat: *meat and two vegetables* ◇ *meat-eating animals* ▶ **mięso**

> **meat**
> We get **pork, ham** or **bacon** from a pig, **beef** from a cow and **veal** from a calf. **Mutton** comes from a sheep, but we get **lamb** from a lamb. We often call beef, mutton and lamb **red meat**. The meat from birds is called **white meat**. We can **fry, grill, roast** or **stew** meat. We **carve** a **joint** of meat. Meat can be described as **tough** or **tender, lean** or **fatty**. Uncooked meat is **raw**. You buy meat at **the butcher's**. A person who does not eat meat is a **vegetarian**.

meatball /'mi:tbɔ:l/ noun [C] a small ball of minced meat ▶ **pulpet**

meaty /'mi:ti/ adj. (**meatier; meatiest**) **1** like meat, or containing a lot of meat: *meaty sausages* ▶ **mięsny 2** containing a lot of important or good ideas: *a meaty topic for discussion* ▶ **treściwy 3** large and fat: *meaty tomatoes* ▶ **mięsisty**

Mecca /'mekə/ noun **1** [sing.] the city in Saudi Arabia where Muhammad was born, which is the centre of Islam ▶ **Mekka 2** (**mecca**) [C, usually sing.] a place that many people wish to visit because of a particular interest: *Italy is a mecca for art lovers.* ▶ **mekka**

mechanic /mə'kænɪk/ noun **1** [C] a person whose job is to repair and work with machines: *a car mechanic* ▶ **mechanik 2** (**mechanics**) [U] the science of how machines work ▶ **mechanika 3** (**the mechanics**) [pl.] the way in which sth works or is done: *Don't ask me – I don't understand the mechanics of the legal system.* ▶ **działanie**

mechanical /mə'kænɪkl/ adj. **1** connected with or produced by machines: *a mechanical pump* ◇ *mechanical engineering* inżynieria mechaniczna ◇ *a mechanical mind* zmysł techniczny ▶ **mechaniczny 2** (used about sb's behaviour) done like a machine as if you are not thinking about what you are doing: *He played the piano in a dull and mechanical way.* ▶ **mechaniczny**, **machinalny**

■ **mechanically** /-kli/ adv. ▶ **mechanicznie**, **machinalnie**

mechanism /'mekənɪzəm/ noun [C] **1** a set of moving parts in a machine that does a certain task: *Our car has an automatic locking mechanism.* ▶ **mechanizm**, **maszyneria 2** the way in which sth works or is done: *I'm afraid there is no mechanism for dealing with your complaint.* ▶ **mechanizm**

mechanize (also -ise) /'mekənaɪz/ verb [T] to use machines instead of people to do work: *We have mechanized the entire production process.* ▶ **mechanizować**

■ **mechanization** (also -isation) /ˌmekənaɪ'zeɪʃn; US -nə'z-/ noun [U] ▶ **mechanizacja**

the **Med** (informal) = MEDITERRANEAN

med = MEDIUM² (2)

medal

medals shield trophy rosette cup

medal /'medl/ noun [C] a small flat piece of metal, usually with a design and words on it, which is given to sb who has shown courage or as a prize in a sport: *to win a gold/silver/bronze medal in the Olympics* ▶ **medal**

medallion /mə'dæliən/ noun [C] a small round piece of metal on a chain which is worn as jewellery around the neck ▶ **medalion**

medallist (US **medalist**) /'medəlɪst/ noun [C] a person who has won a **medal**, especially in sport: *an Olympic gold medallist* ▶ **medalist(k)a**

meddle /'medl/ verb [I] **meddle (in/with sth)** to take too much interest in sb's private affairs or to touch sth that does not belong to you: *She hated her mother meddling in her private life.* ▶ **wtrącać się**, **grzebać (w czymś)**

media /'miːdiə/ noun [U, with sing. or pl. verb] TV, radio and newspapers used as a means of communication: *The reports **in the media** have been greatly exaggerated.* ◇ *There has been full **media coverage** of the trial.* Cały proces cieszył się zainteresowaniem mediów. ▶ **środki masowego przekazu** ➲ note at **newspaper** ➲ look at **mass media**, **press** ⓘ Rzeczownika **media** używa się z czasownikiem w lp lub lm: *The media always take/takes a great interest in the royal family.*

mediaeval = MEDIEVAL

median /'miːdiən/ adj. [only before a noun] **1** having a value in the middle of a series of values: *the **median age/price*** ▶ **średni 2** located in or passing through the middle: *a **median point/line*** ▶ **środkowy**

■ **median** noun **1** the middle value of a series of numbers arranged in order of size ▶ **mediana**

'**media studies** noun [U, with sing. or pl. verb] the study of newspapers, television, radio, etc. as a subject at school, etc. ▶ **studia dot. mediów i kultury medialnej**

mediate /'miːdieɪt/ verb [I,T] **mediate (in sth) (between A and B)** to try to end a disagreement between two or more people or groups: *As a supervisor she had to mediate between her colleagues and the management.* ▶ **pośredniczyć** (*w rozwiązywaniu sporu*)

■ **mediation** /ˌmiːdi'eɪʃn/ noun [U] ▶ **pośrednictwo** (*w rozwiązywaniu sporu*), **mediacja** | **mediator** /'miːdieɪtə(r)/ noun [C] ▶ **pośrednik** (*w rozwiązywaniu sporu*), **mediator**

M

medical¹ /'medɪkl/ adj. connected with medicine and the treatment of illness: *medical treatment/care* opieka medyczna ◇ *the medical profession* ◇ *a medical student* ◇ *a medical school* akademia medyczna ▶ **medyczny**

■ **medically** /-kli/ adv. ▶ **medycznie**

medical² /'medɪkl/ noun [C] an examination of your body by a doctor to check your state of health: *to have a medical* ▶ **badanie lekarskie**

medicated /'medɪkeɪtɪd/ adj. containing a substance like a medicine: *medicated shampoo* ▶ **leczniczy**

medication /ˌmedɪ'keɪʃn/ noun [C,U] (especially US) medicine that a doctor has given to you: *Are you **on any medication**?* ▶ **lekarstwo**

medicinal /mə'dɪsɪnl/ adj. useful for curing illness or infection: *medicinal plants* ▶ **leczniczy**

medicine /'medsn; 'medɪsn/ noun **1** [U] the science of preventing and treating illness: *to study medicine* ▶ **medycyna 2** [C,U] a substance, especially a liquid, that you take in order to cure an illness: ***Take this medicine** three times a day.* ◇ *cough medicine* ▶ **lekarstwo** ➲ note at **doctor**

medieval (also **mediaeval**) /ˌmedi'iːvl/ adj. connected with **the Middle Ages** ▶ **średniowieczny**

mediocre /ˌmiːdi'əʊkə(r)/ adj. of not very high quality: *He gave a mediocre performance* ▶ **średni**, **mierny**

■ **mediocrity** /ˌmiːdi'ɒkrəti/ noun [U] ▶ **mierność**, **lichość**

meditate /'medɪteɪt/ verb [I] **1 meditate (on/upon sth)** to think carefully and deeply (about sth): *I've been meditating on what you said last week.* ▶ **rozmyślać 2** to spend time thinking deeply in a special way so that you become calm and peaceful, often as part of religious training ▶ **medytować**

■ **meditation** /ˌmedɪ'teɪʃn/ noun [U] ▶ **rozmyślanie**; **medytacja**

the **Mediterranean** /ˌmedɪtə'reɪniən/ (also informal **the Med** /med/) noun [sing.] the Mediterranean Sea or the countries around it ▶ **Morze Śródziemne**; **kraje śródziemnomorskie**

■ **Mediterranean** adj. [only before a noun]: *Mediterranean cookery* ▶ **śródziemnomorski**

medium¹ /'miːdiəm/ adj. **1** in the middle between two sizes, lengths, temperatures, etc.; average: *She was of medium height.* ◇ *Would you like the small, medium or* *large packet?* ◇ *a medium-sized car/town/dog* ▶ **średni** **2** (used about meat) cooked until it is brown all the way through ▶ (*kulin.*) **średnio wypieczony/wysmażony** ➲ look at **rare**, **well done**

medium² /'mi:diəm/ noun **1** [C] (pl. **media** or **mediums**) a means you can use to express or communicate sth: *English is the medium of instruction in the school.* ▶ **środek** (*np. komunikacji*), **środek przekazu** ➲ look at **media**, **mass media** **2** [C,U] (abbr. **med**) **medium** size: *Have you got this shirt in (a) medium?* ▶ **średni rozmiar** **3** [C] (pl. **mediums**) a person who says that they can speak to the spirits of dead people ▶ **medium**

'medium-sized adj. of average size: *a medium-sized saucepan* ▶ **średniej wielkości**

'medium wave noun [U] the system of broadcasting radio using sound waves between 100 and 1000 metres ▶ **fale średnie**

medley /'medli/ noun [C] **1** a piece of music consisting of several tunes or songs played one after the other without a break ▶ (*muz.*) **składanka** **2** a mixture of different things: *a medley of styles/flavours* ▶ **mieszanka**, **mieszanina**

meek /mi:k/ adj. (used about people) quiet, and doing what other people say without asking questions ▶ **potulny**, **łagodny**
■ **meekly** adv. ▶ **potulnie**, **łagodnie** | **meekness** noun [U] ▶ **potulność**, **łagodność**

meet /mi:t/ verb (pt, pp **met** /met/) **1** [I,T] to come together by chance or because you have arranged it: *I just met Kareem on the train.* ◇ *What time shall we meet for lunch?* ▶ **spotykać (się)**, **zbierać się** **2** [T] to go to a place and wait for sb/sth to arrive: *I'll come and meet you at the station.* ▶ **wychodzić na spotkanie**, **oczekiwać** **3** [I,T] to see and know sb for the first time: *Where did you first meet your husband?* ◇ *Have you two met before?* ▶ **zapoznawać się z kimś** ➲ note at **know** **4** [I,T] to play, fight, etc. together as opponents in a sports competition: *These two teams met in last year's final.* ◇ *Yamada will meet Suzuki in the second round.* ▶ **spotykać się** **5** [T] to experience sth, often sth unpleasant: *We will never know how he met his death.* ▶ **doświadczać czegoś** **6** [I,T] to touch, join or make contact with: *His eyes met hers.* ◇ *The two roads meet not far from here.* ◇ *The rivers meet* (rzeki zlewają się) *in Oxford.* ▶ **spotykać (się)**, **schodzić (się)** **7** [T] to be enough for sth; to be able to deal with sth: *The money that I earn is enough to meet* (wystarczają na zaspokojenie) *our basic needs.* ◇ *to meet a challenge* ▶ **sprostać czemuś**, **odpowiadać czemuś**, **zadośćuczynić czemuś**
IDM **make ends meet** → END¹
there is more to sb/sth than meets the eye sb/sth is more interesting or complicated than he/she/it seems: *Do you think there's more to their relationship than meets the eye?* ▶ **jest więcej, niż się wydaje**; **nie tylko to, co widać**
PHR V **meet up (with sb)** to meet sb, especially after a period of being apart: *I have a few things I need to do now, but let's meet up later.* ▶ **spotykać się** ➲ look at **get together (with sb)**
meet with sb (especially US) to meet sb, especially for discussion: *The President met with his advisers early this morning.* ▶ **spotykać się**
meet with sth to get a particular answer, reaction or result: *to meet with success/failure/opposition* ▶ **spotykać się (z czymś)**

meeting /'mi:tɪŋ/ noun **1** [C] an organized occasion when a number of people come together in order to discuss or decide sth: *The group **hold** regular **meetings** all year.* ◇ *We need to **have a meeting** to discuss these matters.* ▶ **zebranie**, **posiedzenie**

We **call**, **arrange** or **organize** a meeting. We can also **cancel** or **postpone** a meeting.

2 [sing.] the people at a meeting: *The meeting was in favour of the new proposals.* ▶ **zebrani** **3** [C] the coming together of two or more people: *Christmas is a time of family meetings and reunions.* ▶ **spotkanie**, **zebranie**

'meeting place noun [C] a place where people often meet ▶ **miejsce spotkań**

mega /'megə/ adj. (informal) [usually before a noun] very large or impressive: *Their song was a mega hit last year* ▶ **mega**
■ **mega** adv.: *They're mega rich.* ▶ **strasznie**

mega- /'megə-/ prefix [in nouns] **1** very large or great: *a megastore* hipermarket ◇ *a megastar* megagwiazd-a/or ▶ **mega-** **2** [in units of measurement] one million: *a megawatt* megawat ▶ **mega-** **3** 1 048 576 (= 2^{20}): *a megabyte* megabajt ▶ **mega-**

megabyte /'megəbaɪt/ noun [C] (abbr. **MB**) a unit of computer memory, equal to 2^{20} **bytes**: *a 40-megabyte hard disk* ▶ **megabajt**

megalomania /,megələ'meɪniə/ noun [U] **1** a mental illness or condition in which sb has an exaggerated belief in their own importance or power ▶ **megalomania** **2** a strong feeling that you want to have more and more power ▶ **megalomania**

megalomaniac /,megələ'meɪniæk/ noun a person suffering from or showing **megalomania** ▶ **megaloman/ka**
■ **megalomaniac** adj. ▶ **megalomański**

megaphone /'megəfəʊn/ noun [C] a piece of equipment that you speak through to make your voice sound louder when speaking to a crowd ▶ **megafon**

melancholy /'melənkəli; -kɒli/ noun [U] (formal) a feeling of sadness which lasts for a long time ▶ **melancholia**, **smutek**
■ **melancholy** adj. ▶ **melancholijny**, **smutny**

mellow /'meləʊ/ adj. **1** (used about colours or sounds) soft and pleasant ▶ **miękki**, **aksamitny**; **ciepły**, **spokojny** **2** (used about people) calm and relaxed: *My dad's grown mellower as he's got older.* ▶ **filozoficzny**, **łagodny**, **jowialny** (*w rezultacie wieku lub doświadczenia*)
■ **mellow** verb [I,T]: *Experience had mellowed her views about many things.* ▶ **łagodzić**; **stawać się łagodnym**

melodic /mə'lɒdɪk/ adj. **1** [only before a noun] connected with the main tune in a piece of music: *The melodic line is carried by the clarinets.* ▶ **melodyczny** **2** = MELODIOUS

melodious /mə'ləʊdiəs/ (also **melodic**) adj. pleasant to listen to, like music: *a rich melodious voice* ▶ **melodyjny**
■ **melodiously** adv. ▶ **melodyjnie**

melodrama /'melədrɑ:mə/ noun [C,U] a story, play or film in which a lot of exciting things happen and in which people's emotions are stronger than in real life ▶ **melodramat**

melodramatic /,melədrə'mætɪk/ adj. (used about sb's behaviour) making things seem more exciting or serious than they really are: *Don't be so melodramatic, Simon – of course you're not going to die!* ▶ **melodramatyczny**

melody /'melədi/ noun [C] (pl. **melodies**) a song or tune; the main tune of a piece of music ▶ **melodia**

melon /'melən/ noun [C,U] a large round fruit with a thick yellow or green skin and a lot of seeds ▶ **melon** ➲ picture on **page A12**

melt /melt/ verb **1** [I,T] to change or make sth change from a solid to a liquid by means of heat: *When we got up in the morning the snow had melted.* ◇ *First melt the butter in a saucepan.* ▶ **topić (się)**, **topnieć** ➲ look at **thaw** **2** [I] (used about sb's feelings, etc.) to become softer or less strong:

My heart melted when I saw the baby. ▶ **mięknąć, rozczulać się**

PHR V **melt away** to disappear: *The crowd slowly melted away when the speaker had finished.* ▶ **ulatniać się, znikać**

melt sth down to heat a metal or glass object until it becomes liquid ▶ **przetapiać**

meltdown /ˈmeltdaʊn/ noun [U,C] a serious accident in which the central part of a nuclear **reactor** melts, causing harmful **radiation** to escape: (figurative) *meltdown on the New York Stock Exchange* ▶ **topnienie rdzenia reaktora nuklearnego**; (*fin.*) **krach**

ˈ**melting point** noun [U,C] the temperature at which a solid melts ▶ **temperatura topnienia**

ˈ**melting pot** noun [C] a place where a lot of different cultures, ideas, etc. come together: *New York is a melting pot of different cultures.* ▶ **tygiel**

member /ˈmembə(r)/ noun [C] a person, animal or thing that belongs to a group, club, organization, etc.: *All the members of the family were there.* ◇ *to become a member of a club* ◇ *a member of staff* ▶ **człon-ek/kini**

ˌ**Member of ˈParliament** noun [C] (abbr. **MP** /ˌem ˈpiː/) a person who has been elected to represent people from a particular area in Parliament: *the MP for Oxford East* ▶ **pos-eł/łanka**

membership /ˈmembəʃɪp/ noun **1** [U] the state of being a member of a group, organization, etc.: *To* ***apply for membership****, please fill in the enclosed form.* ◇ *a membership card/fee* ▶ **członkostwo 2** [C,U] the people who belong to a group, organization, etc.: *Membership has fallen in the past year.* ▶ **członkostwo, liczba członków** ❶ W lp słowa **membership** można używać z czasownikiem w lp lub lm.

membrane /ˈmembreɪn/ noun [C] a thin skin which covers certain parts of a person's or an animal's body ▶ **błona**

memento /məˈmentəʊ/ noun [C] (pl. **mementoes**; **mementos**) something that you keep to remind you of sb/sth ▶ **pamiątka** SYN **souvenir**

memo /ˈmeməʊ/ noun [C] (pl. **memos**) (also formal **memorandum** /ˌmeməˈrændəm/ (pl. **memoranda** /-də/) a note sent from one person or office to another within an organization ▶ **notatka** (*służbowa*), **memorandum**

memoirs /ˈmemwɑːz/ noun [pl.] sb's written account of their own life and experiences ▶ **pamiętniki** SYN **autobiography**

memorabilia /ˌmemərəˈbɪliə/ noun [U] things that people buy because they are connected with a famous person, event, etc.: *Beatles/Titanic/war memorabilia* ▶ **pamiątki**

memorable /ˈmemərəbl/ adj. worth remembering or easy to remember: *The concert was a memorable experience.* ▶ **niezapomniany, łatwy do zapamiętania** SYN **unforgettable**

■ **memorably** /-əbli/ adv. ▶ **pamiętnie, w sposób niezapomniany**

memorandum (formal) = MEMO

memorial /məˈmɔːriəl/ noun [C] **a memorial (to sb/sth)** something that is built or done to remind people of an event or a person: *a memorial to the victims of the bombing* ◇ *a war memorial* ◇ *a memorial service* nabożeństwo w intencji upamiętniającej ▶ **pomnik, memoriał**

memorize (also -ise) /ˈmeməraɪz/ verb [T] to learn sth so that you can remember it exactly: *Actors have to memorize their lines.* ▶ **uczyć się na pamięć**

memory /ˈmeməri/ noun (pl. **memories**) **1** [C] sb's ability to remember things: *to have a good/bad memory* ◇ *The drug can affect your short-term memory.* ▶ **pamięć 2** [C,U] the part of your mind in which you store things that you remember: *That day remained firmly* ***in my memory*** *for the rest of my life.* ◇ *Are you going to do your speech* ***from memory****, or are you going to use notes?* ◇ *The appointment completely slipped my memory* (wyleciało mi z głowy). ▶ **pamięć 3** [C] something that you remember: *That is one of my happiest memories.* ◇ *childhood memories* ▶ **wspomnienie 4** [C,U] the part of a computer where information is stored: *This computer has a 640k memory/640k of memory.* ▶ **pamięć (komputerowa)**

IDM **in memory of sb** in order to remind people of sb who has died: *A service was held in memory of the dead.* ▶ **ku pamięci (kogoś)**

jog sb's memory → JOG[1]

refresh your memory → REFRESH

ˈ**Memory Stick™** = USB STICK

men plural of **man[1]**

menace /ˈmenəs/ noun **1** [C] **a menace (to sb/sth)** a danger or threat: *The new road is a menace to everyone's safety.* ▶ **zagrożenie, niebezpieczeństwo 2** [U] a quality, feeling, etc. that is threatening or frightening: *He spoke with menace in his voice.* ▶ **groźba 3** [C] a person or thing that causes trouble ▶ **utrapienie, zmora**

■ **menace** verb [T]: *This species is menaced by hunting.* Polowanie jest zagrożeniem dla tego gatunku. ▶ **grozić (komuś)** | **menacing** adj. ▶ **groźny**

mend[1] /mend/ verb [T] to repair sth that is damaged or broken: *Can you mend the hole* (czy możesz zaszyć/zacerować dziurę) *in this jumper for me?* ▶ **naprawiać, reperować** SYN **repair**

mend[2] /mend/ noun

IDM **be on the mend** (informal) to be getting better after an illness or injury: *She's been in bed for a week but she's on the mend now.* ▶ (*zdrowie*) **polepszać się, zdrowieć**

menial /ˈmiːniəl/ adj. (used about work) not skilled or important: *a menial job* ▶ (*praca*) **nie wymagający kwalifikacji**

meningitis /ˌmenɪnˈdʒaɪtɪs/ noun [U] a dangerous illness which affects the brain and the **spinal cord** ▶ **zapalenie opon mózgowych**

the **menopause** /ˈmenəpɔːz/ noun [sing.] the time when a woman stops **menstruating** and can no longer have children. This usually happens around the age of 50. ▶ **menopauza**

menstrual /ˈmenstruəl/ adj. connected with the time when a woman **menstruates** each month: *The average length of a woman's* ***menstrual cycle*** *is 28 days.* ▶ **miesiączkowy**

menstruate /ˈmenstrueɪt/ verb [I] (formal) (used about women) to lose blood once a month from the **womb** ▶ **miesiączkować** ❶ W języku codziennym używa się zwrotu **have a period**.

■ **menstruation** /ˌmenstruˈeɪʃn/ noun [U] ▶ **miesiączkowanie, menstruacja**

mental /ˈmentl/ adj. [only before a noun] **1** of or in the mind; involving the process of thinking: *It's fascinating to watch a child's mental development.* ◇ *mental arithmetic* rachunek pamięciowy ◇ *I've got a mental picture* (portret pamięciowy) *of the man but I can't remember his name.* ▶ **umysłowy 2** connected with illness of the mind: *a mental illness/hospital* ◇ *a mental hospital* szpital dla psychicznie/umysłowo chorych ▶ **umysłowy, psychiczny**

■ **mentally** /-təli/ adv.: *She's mentally ill.* ▶ **umysłowo, psychicznie**

mentality /menˈtæləti/ noun [C] (pl. **mentalities**) a type of mind or way of thinking: *I just can't understand his mentality!* ◇ *the criminal mentality* ▶ **mentalność, sposób myślenia**

mention /ˈmenʃn/ verb [T] to say or write sth about sb/sth without giving much information: *He mentioned (to*

M

me) that he might be late. ◇ *Did she mention what time the film starts?* ▶ **wspominać o kimś/czymś, nadmieniać**
■ **mention** noun [C,U]: *It was odd that there wasn't even a mention of the riots in the newspaper.* ▶ **wzmianka**
IDM **don't mention it** (used as a polite reply when sb thanks you for sth): *'Thank you for all your help.' 'Don't mention it.'* ▶ **proszę bardzo, nie ma o czym mówić**
not to mention (used to emphasize sth) and also; as well as: *This is a great habitat for birds, not to mention other wildlife.* ▶ **nie mówiąc o czymś**

mentor /ˈmentɔː(r)/ noun [C] an experienced person who advises and helps sb with less experience over a period of time: *She was a friend and mentor to many young actors.* ▶ **mentor/ka**
■ **mentoring** noun [U] ▶ **(fachowe) poradnictwo**

🔑 **menu** /ˈmenjuː/ noun [C] **1** a list of the food that you can choose at a restaurant: *I hope there's soup on the menu.* ◇ *They do a special lunchtime menu here.* ▶ **jadłospis, karta** *(dań)* ➲ note at **restaurant** **2** a list of choices in a computer program which is shown on the screen: *a pull-down menu* ▶ **menu** *(komputerowe)*

ˈ**menu bar** noun [C] a horizontal bar at the top of a computer screen that contains **pull-down** menus such as 'File', 'Edit' and 'Help': *Click on 'Tools' in the menu bar.* ▶ **pasek menu**

MEP /ˌem iː ˈpiː/ abbr. **Member of the European Parliament** ▶ **poseł do Parlamentu Europejskiego**

mercenary¹ /ˈmɜːsənəri; US -neri/ noun [C] (pl. **mercenaries**) a soldier who fights for any group or country that will pay them ▶ **najemnik**

mercenary² /ˈmɜːsənəri; US -neri/ adj. interested only in making money: *I know his motives are entirely mercenary.* ▶ **interesowny**

merchandise /ˈmɜːtʃəndaɪs; -daɪz/ noun [U] (formal) goods that are for sale ▶ **towar**

merchant /ˈmɜːtʃənt/ noun [C] a person whose job is to buy and sell goods, usually of one particular type, in large amounts ▶ **kupiec, handlowiec**

ˌ**merchant** ˈ**bank** noun [C] (US **inˈvestment bank**) a bank that specializes in large commercial loans and financial support for industry ▶ **bank specjalizujący się w inwestycjach przemysłowych**

the ˌ**merchant** ˈ**navy** noun [C, with sing. or pl. verb] a country's commercial ships and the people who work on them ▶ **marynarka handlowa**

merciful /ˈmɜːsɪfl/ adj. feeling or showing **mercy**: *His death was a merciful release from pain.* ▶ **litościwy**
■ **mercifully** /-fəli/ adv. **1** in a merciful way ▶ **litościwie** **2** luckily: *It was bitterly cold but mercifully it was not raining.* ▶ **na szczęście**

merciless /ˈmɜːsɪləs/ adj. showing no **mercy** ▶ **bezlitosny**
■ **mercilessly** adv. ▶ **bezlitośnie**

Mercury /ˈmɜːkjəri/ noun [sing.] the planet that is nearest to the sun ▶ **Merkury**

mercury /ˈmɜːkjəri/ noun [U] (symbol **Hg**) a heavy silver-coloured metal that is usually in liquid form. **Mercury** is used in **thermometers.** ▶ **rtęć**

mercy /ˈmɜːsi/ noun [U] kindness shown by sb/sth who has the power to make sb suffer: *The rebels were shown no mercy. They were taken out and shot.* ▶ **litość, łaska**
IDM **at the mercy of sb/sth** having no power against sb/sth that is strong: *The climbers spent the night on the mountain at the mercy of the wind and rain.* ▶ **na łasce**

🔑 **mere** /mɪə(r)/ adj. [only before a noun] **1** (used for emphasizing how small or unimportant sth is) nothing more than: *You've got the job. The interview is a mere formality.* ◇ *90% of the country's land is owned by a mere 2% of the population.* ▶ **tylko, jedynie, zaledwie** **2** (used to say that just the fact that sb/sth is present in a situation is enough to have an influence): *The mere thought* (sama myśl) *of speaking in public makes me feel sick.* ▶ **(już) sam**
IDM **the merest** even a very small amount of sth: *The merest smell of the fish market made her feel ill.* ▶ **(nawet) najmniejszy, (już) sam**

🔑 **merely** /ˈmɪəli/ adv. (formal) only; just: *I don't want to place an order. I am merely making an enquiry.* ▶ **tylko**

merge /mɜːdʒ/ verb **1** [I] **merge (with/into sth)**; **merge (together)** to become part of sth larger: *This stream merges with the Thames* (zlewa się z Tamizą) *a few miles downstream.* ◇ *Three small companies merged into one large one.* ◇ *Fact and fiction merge together in his latest book.* ▶ **łączyć się, mieszać się (w coś)** **2** [T] to join things together so that they become one: *We have merged the two classes into one.* ▶ **scalać**

merger /ˈmɜːdʒə(r)/ noun [C,U] **a merger (with sb/sth)**; **a merger (between/of A and B)** the act of joining two or more companies together ▶ **fuzja** *(przedsiębiorstw)*

meridian /məˈrɪdiən/ noun [C] a line that we imagine on the surface of the earth that joins the North Pole to the South Pole and passes through a particular place: *the Greenwich meridian* ▶ **południk** ➲ look at **longitude**

meringue /məˈræŋ/ noun **1** [U] a mixture of sugar and egg white that is cooked in the oven: *a lemon meringue pie* ▶ **merenga** **2** [C] a small cake made from this mixture ▶ **beza**

merit¹ /ˈmerɪt/ noun **1** [U] the quality of being good: *There is a lot of merit in her ideas.* ◇ *He got the job* **on merit**, *not because he's the manager's son.* ▶ **zasługa, zaleta** **2** [C, usually pl.] an advantage or a good quality of sb/sth: *Each case must be judged separately on its own merits.* ▶ **zaleta**

merit² /ˈmerɪt/ verb [T] (formal) to be good enough for sth; to deserve: *This suggestion merits further discussion.* ▶ **zasługiwać**

mermaid /ˈmɜːmeɪd/ noun [C] (in stories) a woman who has the tail of a fish instead of legs and who lives in the sea ▶ **syrena**

merriment /ˈmerimənt/ noun [U] happiness, fun and the sound of people laughing ▶ **uciecha** SYN **mirth**

merry /ˈmeri/ adj. (**merrier**; **merriest**) **1** happy: *merry laughter* ◇ ***Merry Christmas*** ▶ **wesoły** **2** (especially Brit., informal) slightly drunk ▶ **podchmielony**
■ **merrily** adv.: *She was singing merrily.* ▶ **wesoło**

ˈ**merry-go-round** (Brit. also **roundabout**; US also **carousel**) noun [C] a big round platform that turns round and round and has model animals, etc. on it for children to ride on ▶ **karuzela** ➲ picture at **roundabout**

mesh /meʃ/ noun [C,U] material that is like a net (= made of plastic, wire or rope threads with holes in between): *a fence made of wire mesh* (z drucianej siatki) ▶ **siatka**

mesmerize (also **-ise**) /ˈmezməraɪz/ verb [T] to hold sb's attention completely: *The audience seemed to be mesmerized by the speaker's voice.* ▶ **hipnotyzować**

🔑 **mess¹** /mes/ noun **1** [C, usually sing.] a dirty or untidy state: *The kitchen's **in a** terrible **mess**!* ◇ *You can paint the door, but don't **make a mess**!* ◇ *My hair is a mess.* Mam włosy jak stóg siana. ▶ **nieporządek** **2** [usually sing.] a situation that is full of problems, usually because of a lack of organization or because of mistakes that sb has made: *The company is **in a** financial **mess*** (jest w finansowych tarapatach). ◇ *to **make a mess of** your life* pogmatwać sobie życie ◇ *Let's try and sort out this mess.* ▶ **kłopotliwe położenie** **3** [sing.] a person who is dirty or whose clothes and hair are not tidy: *You look a mess!* Jak ty wyglądasz! ▶ **brudny i/albo wymiętoszony, i/albo rozczochrany** **4** [sing.] (informal) a person who has serious problems and is in a bad mental condition ▶ **osoba,**

która ma poważne problemy i jest w złym stanie psychicznym **5** [C] a room or building where soldiers eat together: *the officers' mess* ▶ **mesa, stołówka wojskowa**

mess² /mes/ verb [T] (US, informal) to make sth dirty or untidy: *Don't mess your hands.* ▶ **brudzić; bałaganić**

PHR V **mess about/around** **1** to behave in a silly and annoying way ▶ **robić głupstwa** **2** to spend your time in a relaxed way without any real purpose: *We spent Sunday just messing around at home.* ▶ **obijać się, kręcić się bez celu**

mess sb about/around to treat sb in a way that is not fair or reasonable, for example by changing your plans without telling them ▶ **omamiać kogoś, robić kogoś w konia**

mess about/around with sth to touch or use sth in a careless way: *It is dangerous to mess about with fireworks.* ▶ **dłubać przy czymś**

mess sb up (informal) to cause sb to have serious emotional or mental problems ▶ (*psychicznie*) **załamać kogoś**

mess sth up **1** to make sth dirty or untidy ▶ **brudzić; bałaganić** **2** to do sth badly or spoil sth: *I really messed up the last question in the exam.* ▶ **partaczyć**

mess with sb/sth to deal or behave with sb/sth in a way that you should not: *I wouldn't mess with him if I were you!* Na twoim miejscu nie zaczynałbym z nim! ◇ *You shouldn't mess* (bawić się) *with people's feelings.* ◇ *You should read the label before you start messing with dangerous products.* ▶ **wtrącać się do czegoś/w czyjeś sprawy, nie traktować kogoś/czegoś odpowiednio,** (*przen.*) **bawić się czymś, eksperymentować z czymś**

message /'mesɪdʒ/ noun **1** [C] a written or spoken piece of information that you send to or leave for a person when you cannot speak to them: *Mr Vos is not here at the moment. Can I* ***take a message****?* ◇ *Could you* ***give a message*** *to Kate, please?* ◇ *If he's not in I'll* ***leave a message*** *on his answering machine.* ◇ *an email message* ▶ **wiadomość** **2** [sing.] an important idea that a book, speech, etc. is trying to communicate: *It was a funny film but it also had a serious message.* ◇ *The advertising campaign is trying to* ***get the message across*** *that smoking kills.* ▶ **morał**

IDM **get the message** (informal) to understand what sb means even if it is not clearly stated: *He finally got the message and went home.* ▶ **załapywać (coś)**

'message board noun [C] a place on a website where a user can write or read messages: *I posted a question on the message board.* ▶ **internetowa tablica ogłoszeń** ➲ note at **Internet**

messenger /'mesɪndʒə(r)/ noun [C] a person who carries a message ▶ **posłaniec**

Messiah (also **messiah**) /mə'saɪə/ noun [C] a person, for example Jesus Christ, who is expected to come and save the world ▶ **mesjasz**

Messrs /'mesəz/ abbr. (used as the plural of *Mr* before a list of men's names and before names of business firms): *Messrs Smith, Brown and Jones* ▶ **panowie**

messy /'mesi/ adj. (**messier**; **messiest**) **1** dirty or untidy: *a messy room* ▶ **brudny; nieporządny** **2** that makes sb/sth dirty: *Painting the ceiling is a messy job* (to brudna robota). ▶ **brudny** **3** having or causing problems or trouble: *a messy divorce* ▶ **przykry, kłopotliwy**

met past tense of **meet**

metabolism /mə'tæbəlɪzəm/ noun [U, sing.] the chemical processes in the body that change food, etc. into energy: *The body's metabolism is slowed down by extreme cold.* ▶ **metabolizm, przemiana materii**

■ **metabolic** /ˌmetə'bɒlɪk/ adj.: *a high/low metabolic rate* ◇ *a metabolic process/disorder* ▶ **metaboliczny**

metal /'metl/ noun [C,U] a type of solid substance that is usually hard and shiny and that heat and electricity can travel through: *metals such as tin, iron, gold and steel* ◇ *to recycle scrap metal* ◇ *a metal bar/pipe* ▶ **metal**

metalanguage /'metəlæŋgwɪdʒ/ noun [C, U] the words and phrases that people use to talk about or describe language or a particular language ▶ **metajęzyk**

metallic /mə'tælɪk/ adj. looking like metal or making a noise like one piece of metal hitting another: *a metallic blue car* ◇ *harsh metallic sounds* ▶ (*dźwięk*) **metaliczny;** (*lakier*) **metalik**

metallurgy /mə'tælədʒi; US 'metlɜ:rdʒi/ noun [U] the scientific study of metals and their uses ▶ **metaloznawstwo**

■ **metallurgical** /ˌmetə'lɜ:dʒɪkl; US ˌmetl'ɜ:rdʒ-/ adj. ▶ **metalurgiczny, dot. metaloznawstwa**

metamorphosis /ˌmetə'mɔ:fəsɪs/ noun [C] (pl. **metamorphoses** /-əsi:z/) (formal) a complete change of form (as part of natural development): *the metamorphosis of a tadpole into a frog* ▶ **przemiana**

metaphor /'metəfə(r); -fɔ:(r)/ noun [C,U] a word or phrase that is used to show that one thing has the same qualities as another; a way of making a comparison: *'Her words were a knife in his heart' is a metaphor.* ▶ **przenośnia** ➲ look at **simile, figurative, literal**

■ **metaphorical** /ˌmetə'fɒrɪkl/ adj. ▶ **metaforyczny** | **metaphorically** /-kli/ adv. ▶ **w przenośni**

metaphysics /ˌmetə'fɪzɪks/ noun [U] the branch of philosophy that deals with the nature of existence, truth and knowledge ▶ **metafizyka**

■ **metaphysical** /-'fɪzɪkl/ adj.: *metaphysical problems/speculation* ▶ **metafizyczny**

mete /mi:t/ verb

PHR V **mete sth out (to sb)** (formal) to give sb a punishment; to make sb suffer bad treatment: *Severe penalties were meted out by the court.* ▶ **wymierzać** (*np. karę*)

meteor /'mi:tiə(r); -iɔ:(r)/ noun [C] a small piece of rock, etc. in space. When a **meteor** enters the earth's atmosphere it makes a bright line in the night sky. ▶ **meteor**

meteoric /ˌmi:ti'ɒrɪk/ adj. very fast or successful: *a meteoric rise to fame* ▶ **błyskawiczny**

meteorite /'mi:tiəraɪt/ noun [C] a piece of rock from space that hits the earth's surface ▶ **meteoryt**

meteorologist /ˌmi:tiə'rɒlədʒɪst/ noun [C] a person who studies the weather ▶ **meteorolog**

meteorology /ˌmi:tiə'rɒlədʒi/ noun [U] the study of the weather and climate ▶ **meteorologia**

■ **meteorological** /ˌmi:tiərə'lɒdʒɪkl/ adj. ▶ **meteorologiczny**

meter /'mi:tə(r)/ noun [C] **1** a piece of equipment that measures the amount of gas, water, electricity, etc. you have used: *a parking meter* parkometr ▶ **licznik** **2** (US) = METRE

■ **meter** verb [T]: *Is your water metered?* ▶ **mierzyć za pomocą licznika**

method /'meθəd/ noun [C] a way of doing sth: *What method of payment do you prefer? Cash, cheque or credit card?* ◇ *modern teaching methods* ▶ **metoda, sposób**

methodical /mə'θɒdɪkl/ adj. having or using a well organized and careful way of doing sth: *Paul is a very methodical worker.* ▶ **systematyczny**

■ **methodically** /-kli/ adv. ▶ **systematycznie**

Methodist /'meθədɪst/ noun [C] a member of a Protestant Church that was started by John Wesley in the 18th century ▶ **metodyst(k)a**

■ **Methodist** adj. ▶ **metodystyczny**

methodology /ˌmeθə'dɒlədʒi/ noun [C,U] (pl. **methodologies**) a way of doing sth based on particular principles and methods: *language teaching methodologies* ▶ **metodologia**

■ **methodological** /ˌmeθədəˈlɒdʒɪkl/ adj. ▶ **metodologiczny**

methylated spirit /ˌmeθəleɪtɪd ˈspɪrɪt/ (also methylated spirits) noun [U] a type of alcohol that is not fit for drinking, used as a fuel for lighting and heating and for cleaning off dirty marks ▶ **spirytus metylowy**

meticulous /məˈtɪkjələs/ adj. giving or showing great attention to detail; very careful: *meticulous checking* ▶ **drobiazgowy**

■ **meticulously** adv. ▶ **drobiazgowo**

metre (US meter) /ˈmiːtə(r)/ noun [C] (abbr. **m**) a measure of length; 100 centimetres: *a two-metre high wall* ◇ *Who won the 100 metres?* ▶ **metr**

metric /ˈmetrɪk/ adj. using the system of measurement that is based on metres, grams, litres, etc.: *the metric system* ▶ **metryczny** ➲ look at **imperial**

metropolis /məˈtrɒpəlɪs/ noun [C] a very large city ▶ **metropolia**

■ **metropolitan** /ˌmetrəˈpɒlɪtən/ adj. ▶ **wielkomiejski, miejski**

mg = MILLIGRAM

MHz /ˈmegəhɜːts/ abbr. **megahertz**; (used in radio) a measure of **frequency** ▶ **MHz**

MI5 /ˌem aɪ ˈfaɪv/ noun [U] the British government organization that deals with national security within Britain. Its official name is 'the Security Service'. ▶ **brytyjska agencja bezpieczeństwa wewnętrznego**

MI6 /ˌem aɪ ˈsɪks/ noun [U] the British government organization that deals with national security from outside Britain. Its official name is 'the Secret Intelligence Service'. ▶ **brytyjska agencja wywiadu**

miaow /miˈaʊ/ noun [C] the sound that a cat makes ▶ **miauczenie**

■ **miaow** verb [I] ▶ **miauczeć** ➲ look at **purr**

mice plural of **mouse**

mickey /ˈmɪki/ noun

IDM **take the mickey (out of sb)** to make sb look silly by laughing at them ▶ **robić (sobie) żarty/jaja z kogoś** ➲ look at **tease**

microbe /ˈmaɪkrəʊb/ noun [C] an extremely small living thing that you can only see under a **microscope** and that may cause disease ▶ **mikrob**

microchip /ˈmaɪkrəʊtʃɪp/ (also **chip**) noun [C] a very small piece of **silicon** that is used inside a computer, etc. to make it work ▶ **mikroukład, układ scalony**

microcomputer /ˈmaɪkrəʊkəmpjuːtə(r)/ (also informal micro) noun [C] a small computer ▶ **mikrokomputer**

microcosm /ˈmaɪkrəʊkɒzəm/ noun [C] **a microcosm (of sth)** something that is a small example of sth larger: *Our little village is a microcosm of society as a whole.* ▶ **mikrokosmos**

microfiche /ˈmaɪkrəʊfiːʃ/ noun [U] a piece of film on which information is stored in very small print: *The directory is available **on microfiche**.* ▶ **mikrofilm**

microphone /ˈmaɪkrəfəʊn/ (also informal **mike** /maɪk/) noun [C] a piece of electrical equipment that is used for making sounds louder or for recording them ▶ **mikrofon**

microprocessor /ˌmaɪkrəʊˈprəʊsesə(r)/ noun [C] a small unit of a computer that controls all the other parts of the system ▶ **mikroprocesor**

microscope /ˈmaɪkrəskəʊp/ noun [C] a piece of equipment that makes very small objects look big enough for you to be able to see them: *to examine something **under a microscope*** ▶ **mikroskop** ➲ picture at **laboratory**

microscopic /ˌmaɪkrəˈskɒpɪk/ adj. too small to be seen without a **microscope** ▶ **mikroskopijny**

microwave /ˈmaɪkrəweɪv/ noun [C] **1** (also ˌmicrowave ˈoven) a type of oven that cooks or heats food very quickly using **microwaves** ▶ **kuchenka mikrofalowa 2** a short electric wave that is used for sending radio messages and for cooking food ▶ **mikrofala**

■ **microwave** verb [T] ▶ **podgrzewać/gotować w kuchence mikrofalowej** ➲ note at **cook**

mid /mɪd/ adj. [only before a noun] **1** the middle of: *I'm away from mid June* (od połowy czerwca). ◇ *the mid 1990s* ▶ **średni, środkowy 2** (**mid-**) [in compounds] in the middle of: *a mid-air collision* zderzenie w powietrzu ▶ **w połowie**

midday /ˌmɪdˈdeɪ/ noun [U] at or around 12 o'clock in the middle of the day: *We arranged to meet **at midday**.* ◇ *the heat of the midday sun* ▶ **południe** SYN **noon** ➲ look at **midnight**

middle¹ /ˈmɪdl/ noun **1** [sing.] **the middle (of sth)** the part, point or position that is at about the same distance from the two ends or sides of sth: *the white line **in the middle of** the road* ◇ *Here's a photo of me with my two brothers. I'm the one **in the middle**.* ▶ **środek, połowa**

> **Centre** i **middle** często mają podobne znaczenie, ale **centre** używa się w celu określenia dokładnego środka czegoś: *How do you find the centre of a circle?* ◇ *There was a large table in the middle of the room.* Mówiąc o odcinku czasu, należy stosować tylko **middle**: *The baby woke up in the middle of the night.* ◇ *the middle of July.*

2 [C] (informal) your waist: *I want to lose weight around my middle.* ▶ **pas**

IDM **be in the middle of sth/doing sth** to be busy doing sth: *Can you call back in five minutes – I'm in the middle of feeding the baby.* ▶ **być w trakcie czegoś/robienia czegoś**

in the middle of nowhere a long way from any town ▶ **gdzie diabeł mówi dobranoc**

middle² /ˈmɪdl/ adj. [only before a noun] in the middle: *I wear my ring on my middle finger.* ▶ **środkowy**

ˌ**middle ˈage** noun [U] the time when you are about 40 to 60 years old: *in late middle age* ▶ **średni wiek**

■ ˌ**middle-ˈaged** adj.: *a middle-aged man* ▶ **w średnim wieku**

the ˌMiddle ˈAges noun [pl.] the period of European history from about 1100 to 1450 AD ▶ **Średniowiecze**

the ˌmiddle ˈclass noun [sing., with sing. or pl. verb] (also **the** ˌmiddle ˈclasses [pl.]) the group of people in society whose members are neither very rich nor very poor and that includes professional and business people: *the upper/lower middle class* ◇ *the growth of the middle classes* ▶ **klasa średnia** ➲ look at **upper class, working class**

■ ˌ**middle-ˈclass** adj.: *a middle-class background* ◇ *a middle-class attitude* ▶ **klasy średniej**

the ˌMiddle ˈEast noun [sing.] the part of the world between Egypt and Pakistan ▶ **Środkowy Wschód**

ˌ**middle ˈfinger** noun [C] the longest finger in the middle of each hand ▶ **palec środkowy**

middleman /ˈmɪdlmæn/ noun [C] (pl. **-men** /-men/) **1** a person or company who buys goods from the company that makes them and then sells them to sb else ▶ **pośredni-k/czka 2** a person who helps to arrange things between two people who do not want to meet each other ▶ **mediator/ka**

ˌ**middle ˈname** noun [C] a name that comes after your first name and before your family name ▶ **drugie imię**

ˌ**middle-of-the-ˈroad** adj. (used about people, policies, etc.) not extreme; acceptable to most people: *a middle-of-the-road newspaper* ◇ *Their music is very middle-of-the-road* (dla przeciętnego słuchacza). ▶ **umiarkowany** SYN **moderate**

'middle school noun [C] (in Britain) a school for children aged between 9 and 13 ▶ **szkoła podstawowa** (*dla dzieci w wieku od 9 do 13 lat*)

midge /mɪdʒ/ noun [C] a very small flying insect that can bite people ▶ **meszka** SYN **gnat**

midget /ˈmɪdʒɪt/ noun [C] a very small person ▶ **karzeł, karlica** ℹ Uwaga! To słowo często uważa się za obraźliwe.

the **Midlands** /ˈmɪdləndz/ noun [sing., with sing. or pl. verb] the central part of England around Birmingham and Nottingham ▶ **środkowa część Anglii**

midnight /ˈmɪdnaɪt/ noun [U] 12 o'clock at night: *They left the party **at midnight**.* ◇ *The clock struck midnight.* ▶ **północ** ➲ look at **midday**

midriff /ˈmɪdrɪf/ noun [C] the part of your body between your chest and your waist ▶ **przepona brzuszna, talia**

midst /mɪdst/ noun [U] the middle of sth; among a group of people or things: *The country is **in the midst of*** (w trakcie) *a recession.* ◇ *Such beauty was unexpected **in the midst of*** (w środku) *the city.* ◇ *They realized with a shock that there was an enemy **in their midst*** (wśród nich).

midsummer /ˌmɪdˈsʌmə(r)/ noun [U] the time around the middle of summer: *a beautiful midsummer's evening* ▶ **środek lata**

midway /ˌmɪdˈweɪ/ adv. in the middle of a period of time or between two places: *I began to feel ill midway through the exam.* ◇ *The village lies midway* (w połowie drogi) *between two large towns.* ▶ **w połowie** SYN **halfway**
■ **midway** adj.: *to reach the midway point* ▶ **środkowy, znajdujący się w połowie drogi**

midweek /ˌmɪdˈwiːk/ noun [U] the middle of the week (= Tuesday, Wednesday and Thursday) ▶ **połowa tygodnia**
■ **midweek** adv.: *If you travel midweek it will be less crowded.* ▶ **w połowie tygodnia**

the **Midwest** /ˌmɪdˈwest/ noun [sing.] the northern central part of the US ▶ **Środkowy Zachód**

midwife /ˈmɪdwaɪf/ noun [C] (pl. **midwives** /-waɪvz/) a person who has been trained to help women give birth to babies ▶ **akuszerka**

midwifery /ˌmɪdˈwɪfəri/ noun [U] the profession and work of a **midwife** ▶ **akuszerstwo**

midwinter /ˌmɪdˈwɪntə(r)/ noun [U] the time around the middle of winter ▶ **środek zimy**

might¹ /maɪt/ modal verb (negative **might not**; short form **mightn't** /ˈmaɪtnt/) **1** (used as the form of 'may' when you report what sb has said): *He said he might be late* (może się spóźnić). ▶ *(czas przeszły od)* **may 2** (used for saying that sth is possible): *'Where's Vinay?' 'He might be upstairs.'* ◇ *I think I might have forgotten the tickets.* ◇ *She might not come if she's very busy.* ◇ *If I'd have known the film was about Wales, I might have gone to see it.* Gdybym wiedział, że ten film jest o Walii, pewnie bym na niego poszedł. ▶ **(być) może, możliwe 3** (Brit., formal) (used to ask for sth or suggest sth very politely): *I wonder if I might go home half an hour early today?* ▶ **czy mógłbym ...?; czy mógłby pan/mogłaby pani/mogliby państwo ...?**
IDM **I might have known** (used for saying that you are not surprised that sth has happened): *I might have known he wouldn't help.* ▶ **powin-ienem/nam wiedzieć, że**
may/might as well (do sth) → WELL[1]
you, etc. might do sth (used when you are angry to say what sb could or should have done): *You might tell me if you're going to be late.* Możesz mi powiedzieć, że masz zamiar się spóźnić! ◇ *They might at least have phoned if they're not coming.* ▶ **móc**

might² /maɪt/ noun [U] (formal) great strength or power: *I pushed **with all my might**, but the rock did not move.* ▶ **potęga**

mighty¹ /ˈmaɪti/ adj. (**mightier**; **mightiest**) very strong or powerful ▶ **potężny, mocny**

mighty² /ˈmaɪti/ adv. (US, informal) very: *That's mighty kind of you.* ▶ **bardzo**

migraine /ˈmiːɡreɪn; US ˈmaɪɡ-/ noun [C,U] a terrible pain in your head that makes you feel sick ▶ **migrena**

migrant /ˈmaɪɡrənt/ noun [C] a person who goes from place to place looking for work ▶ **osoba, która przenosi się z miejsca na miejsce w poszukiwaniu pracy**

migrate /maɪˈɡreɪt; US ˈmaɪɡreɪt/ verb [I] **1** (used about animals and birds) to travel from one part of the world to another at the same time every year ▶ **migrować 2** (used about a large number of people) to go and live and work in another place: *Country people were forced to migrate to the cities to find work.* ▶ **migrować** ➲ look at **emigrate**
■ **migration** /maɪˈɡreɪʃn/ noun [C,U] ▶ **migracja** | **migratory** /ˈmaɪɡrətri; maɪˈɡreɪtəri; US ˈmaɪɡrətɔːri/ adj.: *migratory flights/birds* ▶ **migracyjny, wędrowny**

mike (informal) = MICROPHONE

milage = MILEAGE

mild /maɪld/ adj. **1** not strong; not very bad: *a mild soap* ◇ *a mild winter* ◇ *a mild punishment* ▶ **łagodny, umiarkowany 2** kind and gentle: *He's a very mild man – you never see him get angry.* ▶ **łagodny 3** (used about food) not having a strong taste: *mild cheese* ▶ **łagodny, nieostry**
■ **mildness** noun [U] ▶ **łagodność, umiarkowanie**

mildew /ˈmɪldjuː; US -duː/ noun [U] a living white substance like fur that grows on walls, plants, food, etc. in warm wet conditions ▶ **rodzaj pleśni** ➲ look at **mould**

mildly /ˈmaɪldli/ adv. **1** not very; slightly: *mildly surprised* ▶ **w miarę 2** in a gentle way ▶ **łagodnie, umiarkowanie**

mile /maɪl/ noun **1** [C] a measure of length; 1.6 kilometres. There are 1 760 yards in a **mile**: *The nearest beach is seven miles away.* ◇ *It's a seven-mile drive* (siedmiomilowa jazda) *to the sea.* ◇ *My car does 7 miles to the litre.* Mój samochód spala jeden litr benzyny na 7 mil. ▶ **mila** ℹ Więcej o wyrażeniach miar w dodatku *Wyrażenia liczbowe* na końcu słownika. **2** (**miles**) [pl.] a long way: *How much further is it? We've walked miles already.* ◇ *From the top of the hill you can see **for miles*** (masz rozległy widok na wiele kilometrów). ▶ **długa droga 3** [C] a lot: *I'm feeling miles* (znacznie) *better this morning.* ◇ *to miss the target by a mile* strzelić daleko od celu
IDM **see, hear, tell, spot, etc. sb/sth a mile off** (informal) (used to say that sb/sth is very obvious): *He's lying – you can tell that a mile off.* ▶ **widzieć, czuć itp. coś na kilometr**

mileage (also **milage**) /ˈmaɪlɪdʒ/ noun **1** [C,U] the distance that has been travelled, measured in **miles**: *The car is five years old but it has a low mileage* (ma mały przebieg). ▶ **odległość w milach 2** [U] (informal) the amount of use that you get from sth: *The newspapers got a lot of mileage out of the scandal.* ▶ **pożytek, korzyść**

mileometer = MILOMETER

milestone /ˈmaɪlstəʊn/ noun [C] **1** a very important event: *The concert was a milestone in the band's history.* ▶ **kamień milowy 2** a stone at the side of the road that shows how far it is to the next town ▶ **słupek milowy**

militant /ˈmɪlɪtənt/ adj. ready to use force or strong pressure to get what you want: *The workers were in a very militant mood.* ▶ **wojowniczy**

■ **militant** noun [C] ▶ **bojowni-k/czka** | **militancy** /-ənsi/ noun [U] ▶ **wojowniczość**

militarism /ˈmɪlɪtərɪzəm/ noun [U] the belief that a country should have great military strength in order to be powerful ▶ **militaryzm** ℹ Zwykle wyraża dezaprobatę. ■ **militarist** noun [C] ▶ **militaryst(k)a** | **militaristic** /ˌmɪlɪtəˈrɪstɪk/ adj. ▶ **militarystyczny**

militarize (also -ise) /ˈmɪlɪtəraɪz/ verb [T, usually passive] **1** to send armed forces to an area: *a militarized zone* ▶ **militaryzować** OPP **demilitarize** **2** to make sth similar to an army: *a militarized police force* ▶ **militaryzować** ■ **militarization** (also -isation) /ˌmɪlɪtəraɪˈzeɪʃn; US -rəˈz-/ noun [U] ▶ **militaryzacja**

⚷ **military** /ˈmɪlətri; US -teri/ adj. [only before a noun] connected with soldiers or the army, navy, etc.: *to take military action* ◇ *All men in that country have to do two years' **military service*** (służby wojskowej). ▶ **wojskowy**

militia /məˈlɪʃə/ noun [C, with sing. or pl. verb] a group of people who are not professional soldiers but who have had military training ▶ **milicja, bojówka**

⚷ **milk¹** /mɪlk/ noun [U] **1** a white liquid that is produced by women and female animals to feed their babies. People drink the milk of some animals and use it to make butter and cheese: *skimmed/long-life/low-fat milk* ◇ *a bottle of milk* butelka mleka ◇ *a milk bottle* butelka na mleko ◇ *a carton of milk* ▶ **mleko** **2** the juice of some plants or trees that looks like milk: *coconut milk* ▶ **mleczko** ➲ picture on **page A12**

milk² /mɪlk/ verb [T] **1** to take milk from an animal such as a cow ▶ **doić** **2** to get as much money, advantage, etc. for yourself from sb/sth as you can, without caring about others ▶ (*przen.*) **doić**

ˌmilk ˈchocolate noun [U] chocolate that is made with milk ▶ **czekolada mleczna**

milkman /ˈmɪlkmən/ noun [C] (pl. **-men** /-mən/) a person who takes milk to people's houses every day ▶ **mlecza-rz/rka**

ˈmilkshake /ˈmɪlkʃeɪk/ noun [C,U] a drink made of milk with an added flavour of fruit or chocolate ▶ **napój mleczny** ➲ picture on **page A14**

milky /ˈmɪlki/ adj. **1** like milk, or made with milk: *milky coffee* ▶ **mleczny** **2** of a pale white colour: *milky white skin* ▶ **mleczny**

the **ˌMilky ˈWay** = THE GALAXY (2)

mill¹ /mɪl/ noun [C] **1** a building that contains a large machine that was used in the past for making grain into flour: *a watermill* młyn wodny ◇ *a windmill* wiatrak ▶ **młyn** **2** a factory that is used for making certain kinds of material: *a paper mill* papiernia ◇ *a steel mill* huta stali ◇ *a cotton mill* przędzalnia bawełny ▶ **fabryka**, **zakład** **3** a kitchen tool that is used for making sth into powder: *a pepper mill* młynek do pieprzu ▶ **młynek**

mill² /mɪl/ verb [T] to produce sth in a **mill** ▶ **mleć**
PHR V **mill about/around** (informal) (used about a large number of people or animals) to move around in a place with no real purpose ▶ **kręcić się bez celu**

millennium /mɪˈleniəm/ noun [C] (pl. **millennia** /-niə/ or **millenniums**) a period of 1 000 years: *How did you celebrate the millennium?* ▶ **tysiąclecie**

millepede = MILLIPEDE

miller /ˈmɪlə(r)/ noun [C] a person who owns or works in a **mill** for making flour ▶ **młyna-rz/rka**

millet /ˈmɪlɪt/ noun [U] a plant with a lot of small seeds that are used as food for people and birds ▶ **proso**

milli- /ˈmɪli/ [in compounds] (used in units of measurement) one thousandth: *millisecond* ▶ **mili-**

⚷ **milligram** (also **milligramme**) /ˈmɪligræm/ noun [C] (abbr. **mg**) a measure of weight. There are 1 000 **milligrams** in a gram. ▶ **miligram**

millilitre (US **milliliter**) /ˈmɪlili:tə(r)/ noun [C] (abbr. **ml**) a measure of liquid. There are 1 000 **millilitres** in a litre. ▶ **mililitr**

⚷ **millimetre** (US **millimeter**) /ˈmɪlimi:tə(r)/ noun [C] (abbr. **mm**) a measure of length. There are 1 000 **millimetres** in a metre. ▶ **milimetr**

millinery /ˈmɪlɪnəri; US -neri/ noun [U] the business of making or selling women's hats ▶ **kapelusznictwo**

⚷ **million** /ˈmɪljən/ number (abbr. **m**) **1** 1 000 000: *Millions of people are at risk from the disease.* ▶ **milion** ℹ Zwróć uwagę, że przy liczeniu nie używa się liczebnika **million** w lm: *six million pounds* ◇ *Nearly 60 million people live in Britain.* **2** (**a million**; **millions (of)**) (informal) a very large amount: *I still have a million things to do.* ▶ **mnóstwo** ℹ Więcej informacji w dodatku *Wyrażenia liczbowe* na końcu słownika.

millionaire /ˌmɪljəˈneə(r)/ noun [C] a person who has a million pounds, dollars, etc.; a very rich person ▶ **milioner**

⚷ **millionth** /ˈmɪljənθ/ ordinal number 1 000 000th ▶ **milionowy**
■ **millionth** noun [C] one of a million equal parts of sth: *a millionth of a second* ▶ **(jedna) milionowa**

millipede (also **millepede**) /ˈmɪlɪpi:d/ noun [C] a small creature like an insect, with a long thin body divided into many sections, each with two pairs of legs ▶ **krocionóg**

milometer (also **mileometer**) /maɪˈlɒmɪtə(r)/ (US **odometer** /əʊˈdɒmɪtə(r)/) noun [C] an instrument in a vehicle that measures the distance it has travelled ▶ **drogomierz**, **licznik do pomiaru przebytej drogi**, **hodometr**

mime /maɪm/ (also **pantomime**) noun [U,C] the use of movements of your hands and body and the expression on your face to tell a story or to act sth without speaking; a performance using this method of acting: *The performance consisted of dance, music and mime.* ▶ **pantomima**, **mimika**
■ **mime** verb [I,T] ▶ **grać/wyrażać (coś) mimicznie/mimiką**

mimic¹ /ˈmɪmɪk/ verb [T] (**mimicking**; **mimicked**) to copy sb's behaviour, movements, voice, etc. in an amusing way: *She's always mimicking the teachers.* ▶ **naśladować**

mimic² /ˈmɪmɪk/ noun [C] a person who can copy sb's behaviour, movements, voice, etc. in an amusing way: *He is a gifted mimic.* ▶ **naśladowca**, **imitator**
■ **mimicry** /ˈmɪmɪkri/ noun [U] ▶ **parodiowanie**, **mimika**

min. abbr. **1** = MINUTE¹ (1): *fastest time: 6 min.* **2** = MINIMUM²: *min. temp tomorrow 2°*

minaret /ˌmɪnəˈret/ noun [C] a tall thin tower, usually part of a **mosque**, from which Muslims are called to come and say prayers ▶ **minaret**

mince /mɪns/ (US **ground ˈbeef**; **hamburger**) noun [U] meat that has been cut into very small pieces with a special machine ▶ **mięso mielone**
■ **mince** verb [T] ▶ **siekać/przepuszczać przez maszynkę** (*mięso*)

mincemeat /ˈmɪnsmi:t/ noun [U] a mixture of dried fruit, nuts, sugar, etc. (but no meat) that is used as a filling for sweet dishes ▶ **rodzaj farszu bakaliowego**

ˌmince ˈpie noun [C] a small round **pastry** case with **mincemeat** inside, traditionally eaten in Britain at Christmas time ▶ **babeczka z kruchego ciasta z nadzieniem bakaliowym**

⚷ **mind¹** /maɪnd/ noun [C,U] the part of your brain that thinks and remembers; your thoughts, feelings and

intelligence: *He has a brilliant mind.* ◇ *Not everybody has the right sort of mind for this work.* ▶ **umysł, głowa**
IDM **at/in the back of your mind** → BACK[1]
be in two minds (about sth/about doing sth) → TWO
be/go out of your mind (informal) to be or become crazy or very worried: *I was going out of my mind when Tina didn't come home on time.* ▶ **postradać zmysły, zwariować**
bear in mind (that); bear/keep sb/sth in mind to remember or consider (that); to remember sb/sth: *Have a snack now if you want, but bear in mind that we'll be eating a big meal later.* ◇ *We'll bear/keep your suggestion in mind for the future.* ▶ **pamiętać, że/o czymś**
bring/call sb/sth to mind to be reminded of sb/sth; to remember sb/sth ▶ **przywodzić kogoś/coś na myśl, przypominać sobie kogoś/coś**
cast your mind back → CAST[1]
change your mind → CHANGE[1]
come/spring to mind if sth comes/springs to mind, you suddenly remember or think of it ▶ **(nagle) przychodzić do głowy**
cross your mind → CROSS[2]
ease sb's mind → EASE[2]
frame of mind → FRAME[1]
give sb a piece of your mind → PIECE[1]
go clean out of your mind → CLEAN[3]
have/keep an open mind → OPEN[1]
have sb/sth in mind (for sth) to be considering sb/sth as suitable for sth; to have a plan: *Who do you have in mind for the job?* ▶ **brać kogoś pod uwagę** (*np. przy wyborze na stanowisko*), **mieć plan**
keep your mind on sth to continue to pay attention to sth: *Keep your mind on the road while you're driving!* ▶ **skupiać się na czymś**
make up your mind to decide: *I can't make up my mind which sweater to buy.* ▶ **zdecydować się**
on your mind worrying you: *Don't bother her with that. She's got enough on her mind already.* ▶ **na głowie**
prey on sb's mind → PREY[2]
put/set your/sb's mind at rest to make sb stop worrying: *The results of the blood test set his mind at rest.* ▶ **uspokajać (się)**
slip your mind → SLIP[1]
speak your mind → SPEAK
state of mind → STATE[1]
take sb's mind off sth to help sb not to think or worry about sth ▶ **odwracać czyjąś uwagę od czegoś**
to my mind in my opinion: *To my mind, this is a complete waste of time!* ▶ **moim zdaniem**

mind[2] /maɪnd/ verb **1** [I,T] [usually in questions, answers, and negative sentences] to feel annoyed, upset or uncomfortable about sth/sb: *I'm sure Simon won't mind* (nie będzie miał ci tego za złe) *if you don't invite him.* ◇ *Do you mind having to travel* (czy nie przeszkadza ci, że musisz dojeżdżać) *so far to work every day?* ◇ *Are you sure your parents won't mind me coming* (nie będą mieli nic przeciwko temu, że przyjdę)*?* ◇ *'Would you like tea or coffee?' 'I don't mind* (wszystko mi jedno).*'* ◇ *I don't mind what you do.* Wszystko mi jedno, co robisz. ◇ *'Do you mind if I smoke* (czy pozwolisz, że zapalę)*?' 'No, not at all* (tak, proszę bardzo).*'* ◇ *We've got four children so I hope you won't mind about* (nie będzie ci przeszkadzał) *the mess!* ◇ *I wouldn't mind a holiday* (nie miałbym nic przeciwko wakacjom) *in the sun this year!* ▶ **mieć coś przeciwko** ➲ note at **matter**[2] **2** [T] (used in a question as a polite way of asking sb to do sth or for permission to do sth) could you ...?; may I ...?: *Would you mind closing the window?* Czy mógłbyś zamknąć okno? ◇ *Would you mind if I used your phone?* Czy mogę skorzystać z twojego telefonu? ▶ **czy mógłbyś, czy byłbyś łaskaw 3** [T] (used to tell sb to be careful of sth or to pay attention to sb/sth): *It's a very low doorway so mind your head.* ◇ *Mind that step!* Uwaga! Stopień! ◇ *Don't mind me! I won't disturb you.* ▶ **uważać na coś 4** [T] (especially Brit.) to look after or watch sb/sth for a short time: *Could you mind my bag while I go and get us some drinks?* ▶ **pilnować**
IDM **mind you** (used for attracting attention to a point you are making or for giving more information): *Paul seems very tired. Mind you, he has been working very hard recently.* ▶ **przecież, no ale**
mind your own business to pay attention to your own affairs, not other people's: *Stop asking me personal questions and mind your own business!* ▶ **nie wtrącać się, zajmować się swoimi sprawami**
never mind do not worry; it does not matter: *'I forgot to post your letter.' 'Never mind, I'll do it later.'* ◇ *Never mind about the cost* (nie przejmuj się kosztami) – *just enjoy yourself!* ▶ **nieważne, nie szkodzi**
PHR V **mind out** (informal) Get out of the way!: *Mind out! There's a car coming.* ▶ **z drogi!**

ˈ**mind-blowing** adj. (informal) very exciting, impressive or surprising: *Watching your baby being born is a mind-blowing experience.* ▶ **niesamowity, zaskakujący**

ˈ**mind-boggling** adj. (informal) difficult to imagine, understand or believe: *Mind-boggling amounts of money were being discussed.* ▶ **niewyobrażalny**

minded /ˈmaɪndɪd/ adj. [in compounds] **1** having the type of mind mentioned: *a strong-minded/an open-minded/a narrow-minded person* człowiek o silnej osobowości/otwartym umyśle/wąskich horyzontach ▶ **(***określa nastawienie, typ osobowości***) 2** interested in the thing mentioned: *He is very money-minded.* Myśli tylko o pieniądzach. ▶ **nastawiony na coś, mający coś na uwadze**

minder /ˈmaɪndə(r)/ noun [C] a person whose job is to look after and protect sb/sth: *a star surrounded by her minders* ▶ **opiekun/ka**

mindful /ˈmaɪndfl/ adj. (formal) **mindful of sb/sth; mindful that...** remembering sb/sth and considering them or it when you do sth: *Mindful of the danger of tropical storms, I decided not to go out.* ▶ **mający kogoś/coś na uwadze/względzie, świadomy czegoś**

mindless /ˈmaɪndləs/ adj. **1** done or acting without thought and for no particular reason: *mindless violence* ▶ **bezmyślny 2** not needing thought or intelligence: *a mindless and repetitive task* ▶ **bezmyślny, automatyczny**

ˈ**mind-numbing** adj. very boring: *mind-numbing conversation* ▶ **otępiający**
■ **mind-numbingly** adv.: *The lecture was mind-numbingly tedious.* ▶ **otępiająco**

mindset /ˈmaɪndset/ noun [C] a set of attitudes or fixed ideas that sb has and that are often difficult to change: *a conservative mindset* ◇ *the mindset of the computer generation* ▶ **sposób myślenia** SYN **mentality**

mine[1] /maɪn/ pron. of or belonging to me: *'Whose is this jacket?' 'It's mine.'* ◇ *She wanted one like mine.* ◇ *May I introduce a friend of mine* (jednego z moich przyjaciół)*?* ▶ **mój, moja itp.** ➲ look at **my**

mine[2] /maɪn/ noun [C] **1** a deep hole, or a system of passages under the ground where minerals such as coal, tin, gold, etc. are dug: *a coal/salt/gold mine* ▶ **kopalnia** ➲ look at **colliery, quarry 2** a bomb that is hidden under the ground or underwater and explodes when sb/sth touches it: *The car went over a mine and blew up.* ▶ **mina**

mine[3] /maɪn/ verb **1** [I,T] to dig in the ground for minerals such as coal, tin, gold, etc.: *Diamonds are mined in South Africa.* ▶ **wydobywać** ➲ look at **mining 2** [T] to put **mines**[2] (2) in an area of land or sea ▶ **minować**

minefield /ˈmaɪnfiːld/ noun [C] **1** an area of land or sea where **mines**[2] (2) have been hidden ▶ **pole minowe 2** a situation that is full of hidden dangers or difficulties: *a political minefield* ▶ **trudna/niebezpieczna sytuacja**

miner /ˈmaɪnə(r)/ noun [C] a person whose job is to work in a **mine²** (1) to get coal, salt, tin, etc. ▶ **górnik**

mineral /ˈmɪnərəl/ noun [C] a natural substance such as coal, salt, oil, etc., especially one that is found in the ground. Some minerals are also present in food and drink and are very important for good health: *a country rich in minerals* ◇ *the recommended daily intake of vitamins and minerals* ▶ **minerał**

ˈmineral water noun [U] water from a spring in the ground that contains minerals or gases and is thought to be good for your health ▶ **woda mineralna**

mingle /ˈmɪŋɡl/ verb [I,T] **mingle A and B (together)**; **mingle (A) (with B)** to mix with other things or people: *The colours slowly mingled together to make a muddy brown.* ◇ *His excitement was mingled with fear.* ◇ *to mingle with the rich and famous* ▶ **mieszać (się)**, **wmieszać się** (*np. w tłum*)

mini- /ˈmɪni/ [in compounds] very small: *a miniskirt* ◇ *minigolf* ▶ **mały**, **mini**

miniature /ˈmɪnətʃə(r)/ noun [C] a small copy of sth which is much larger: *a miniature camera* ▶ **miniatura**
IDM **in miniature** exactly the same as sb/sth else but in a very small form ▶ **w miniaturze**

minibus /ˈmɪnibʌs/ noun [C] (especially Brit.) a small bus, usually for no more than twelve people ▶ **mikrobus** ➲ picture at **bus**

minicam /ˈmɪnikæm/ noun [C] a video camera that is small enough to hold in one hand ▶ **minikamera**

minicomputer /ˈmɪnikəmpjuːtə(r)/ noun [C] a computer that is smaller and slower than a **mainframe** but larger and faster than a **microcomputer** ▶ **minikomputer**

minidisc /ˈmɪnɪdɪsk/ noun [C] a disc like a small CD that can record and play sound or data ▶ **minidysk**

minim /ˈmɪnɪm/ (US **ˈhalf note**) noun [C] (used about music) a note that lasts twice as long as a crotchet ▶ **półnuta** ➲ picture at **music**

minimal /ˈmɪnɪməl/ adj. very small in amount, size or level; as little as possible: *The project must be carried out at minimal cost.* ▶ **minimalny**

minimalist /ˈmɪnɪməlɪst/ noun [C] an artist, a musician, etc. who uses very simple ideas or a very small number of simple things in their work ▶ **artyst(k)a minimalist(k)a**
■ **minimalism** noun [U] ▶ **minimalizm** | **minimalist** adj. ▶ **minimalistyczny**

minimize (also **-ise**) /ˈmɪnɪmaɪz/ verb [T] **1** to make sth as small as possible (in amount or level): *We shall try to minimize the risks to the public.* ▶ **zmniejszać**, **minimalizować 2** to try to make sth seem less important than it really is ▶ **umniejszać 3** to make sth small on a computer screen ▶ **zmniejszać** OPP **maximize**

minimum¹ /ˈmɪnɪməm/ adj. [only before a noun] the smallest possible or allowed; extremely small: *to introduce a national* ***minimum wage*** ▶ **minimalny** OPP **maximum**
■ **minimum** adv.: *We'll need £200 minimum for expenses.* ▶ **minimum**

minimum² /ˈmɪnɪməm/ noun [sing.] (abbr. **min.**) the smallest amount or level that is possible or allowed: *I need a minimum of seven hours' sleep.* ◇ *We will try and* ***keep*** *the cost of the tickets* ***to a minimum.*** ▶ **minimum** OPP **maximum**

ˌminimum ˈwage noun [sing.] the lowest wage that an employer is allowed to pay by law: *to introduce a national minimum wage* ▶ **najniższa płaca**

mining /ˈmaɪnɪŋ/ noun [U] [in compounds] the process or industry of getting minerals, metals, etc. out of the ground by digging: *coal/tin/gold mining* ▶ **wydobycie**; **górnictwo**

minister /ˈmɪnɪstə(r)/ noun [C] **1** (Brit.) (**Minister**) a member of the government, often the head of a government department: *the Minister for Trade and Industry* ▶ **minister** ➲ look at **prime minister**, **cabinet**, **secretary 2** a priest in some Protestant churches ▶ **pastor** ➲ look at **vicar**

ministerial /ˌmɪnɪˈstɪəriəl/ adj. connected with a government minister or department ▶ **ministerialny**

ministry /ˈmɪnɪstri/ noun [C] (pl. **ministries**) (Brit.) (also **department**) **1** a government department that has a particular area of responsibility: *the Ministry of Defence* ▶ **ministerstwo** ℹ W Amer. ang. używa się tylko słowa **department**. **2** (**the ministry**) [sing.] the profession of being a priest (in Protestant churches): *to enter the ministry* zostać duchownym ▶ **kapłaństwo**, **stan duchowny**

minivan (US) = PEOPLE CARRIER

mink /mɪŋk/ noun [C] a small wild animal that is kept for its thick brown fur which is used to make expensive coats ▶ **norka**

minor¹ /ˈmaɪnə(r)/ adj. **1** not very big, serious or important (when compared with others): *It's only a minor problem. Don't worry.* ◇ *She's gone into hospital for a minor operation.* ▶ **drugorzędny**, **drobny** OPP **major 2** of one of the two types of **key¹** (4) in which music is usually written: *a symphony in F minor* ▶ **minorowy**, **moll** ➲ look at **major**

minor² /ˈmaɪnə(r)/ noun [C] (used in law) a person who is not legally an adult ▶ **nieletni/a**

> In Britain you are a minor until you are eighteen when you **come of age**.

minority /maɪˈnɒrəti/ noun [C] (pl. **minorities**) **1** [usually sing., with sing. or pl. verb] the smaller number or part of a group; less than half: *Only a minority of teenagers become/becomes involved in crime.* ◇ *minority interests* potrzeby mniejszości ▶ **mniejszość** OPP **majority 2** a small group of people who are of a different race or religion to most of the people in the community or country where they live: *Schools in Britain need to do more to help children of* ***ethnic minorities.*** ▶ **mniejszość narodowa/etniczna**
IDM **be in a/the minority** to be the smaller of two groups: *Men are in the minority in the teaching profession.* ▶ **być w mniejszości** ➲ look at **be in the/a majority**

mint /mɪnt/ noun **1** [U] a **herb** whose leaves are used to give flavour to food, drinks, etc.: *lamb with mint sauce* ▶ **mięta** ➲ picture on **page A12 2** [C] a type of sweet with a strong fresh flavour ▶ **cukierek miętowy 3** [sing.] the place where money in the form of coins and notes is made by the government ▶ **mennica**
■ **mint** verb [T]: *freshly minted coins* ▶ **bić** (*monetę*)

minus¹ /ˈmaɪnəs/ prep. **1** (used in sums) less; take away: *Six minus two is four (6 - 2 = 4).* ▶ **minus**, **mniej** OPP **plus** ➲ look at **subtract 2** (used about a number) below zero: *The temperature will fall to minus 10.* ▶ **minus**, **poniżej zera 3** (informal) without sth that was there before: *We're going to be minus a car for a while.* ▶ **bez**

minus² /ˈmaɪnəs/ noun [C] **1** (also **ˈminus sign**) the symbol (-) used in mathematics ▶ **znak odejmowania 2** (also **ˈminus point**) (informal) a negative quality; a disadvantage: *Let's consider the pluses and minuses of moving out of the city.* ▶ **minus** OPP for both meanings **plus**

minus³ /ˈmaɪnəs/ adj. **1** (used in mathematics) lower than zero: *a minus figure* ▶ **ujemny 2** [not before a noun] (used in a system of grades given for school work) slightly lower than: *I got A minus (A-) for my essay.* ▶ **minus** OPP for both meanings **plus**

minuscule /ˈmɪnəskjuːl/ adj. extremely small ▶ **maleńki**

ˈ**minus point** = MINUS[2] (2)

ˈ**minus sign** = MINUS[2] (1)

minute[1] /ˈmɪnɪt/ noun **1** [C] (abbr. **min.**) one of the 60 parts that make up one hour; 60 seconds: *It's twelve minutes to nine.* ◇ *He telephoned ten minutes ago.* ◇ *The programme lasts for about fifty minutes.* ▶ **minuta 2** [sing.] (informal) a very short time; a moment: ***Just/Wait a minute!** You've forgotten your notes.* ◇ *Have you got a minute? – I'd like to talk to you.* ▶ **chwila 3** (**the minutes**) [pl.] a written record of what is said and decided at a meeting: *to take the minutes* spisywać protokół ▶ **protokół**
IDM **(at) any minute/moment (now)** (informal) very soon: *The plane should be landing any minute now.* ▶ **w każdej chwili**
in a minute very soon: *I'll be with you in a minute.* ▶ **za chwilę**
just a minute (informal) (used for stopping a person, pausing to think, etc.) to wait for a short time: *Just a minute. Is that your book or mine?* ▶ **chwileczkę**
the last minute/moment → LAST[1] (1)
the minute/moment (that) as soon as: *I'll tell him you rang the minute (that) he gets here* (jak tylko przyjdzie). ▶ **jak tylko**
this minute immediately; now: *Come down this minute!* ◇ *I don't know what I'm going to do yet – I've **just this minute** found out.* ▶ **natychmiast**; **w tej chwili**
up to the minute (informal) having the most recent information: *For up to the minute information on flight times, phone this number...* ▶ **ostatni**, **aktualny**

minute[2] /maɪˈnjuːt; US -ˈnuːt/ adj. (**minutest**) [no comparative] **1** very small: *I couldn't read his writing. It was minute!* ▶ **mikroskopijny**, **drobniutki** SYN **tiny 2** very exact or accurate: *She was able to describe the man **in minute/the minutest detail**.* ▶ **szczegółowy**, **drobiazgowy**

ˈ**minute hand** noun [usually sing.] the hand on a watch or clock that points to the minutes ▶ **wskazówka minutowa**

miracle /ˈmɪrəkl/ noun **1** [C] a wonderful event that seems impossible and that is believed to be caused by God or a god ▶ **cud 2** [sing.] a lucky thing that happens that you did not expect or think was possible: *It's a miracle (that) nobody was killed in the crash.* ▶ (*przen.*) **cud**
IDM **work/perform miracles** to achieve very good results: *The new diet and exercise programme have worked miracles for her.* ▶ **czynić/działać cuda**

miraculous /mɪˈrækjələs/ adj. completely unexpected and very lucky: *She's made a miraculous recovery.* ▶ **cudowny**, **nadprzyrodzony**
■ **miraculously** adv. ▶ **cudownie**

mirage /ˈmɪrɑːʒ; mɪˈrɑːʒ; US məˈrɑːʒ/ noun [C] something that you think you see in very hot weather, for example water in a desert, but which does not really exist ▶ **fatamorgana**, **złudzenie**

mirror /ˈmɪrə(r)/ noun [C] a piece of special flat glass that you can look into in order to see yourself or what is behind you: *to look **in the mirror*** ◇ *a **rear-view mirror*** ▶ **lustro** ➲ picture at **car**

> A mirror **reflects** images. What you see in a mirror is a **reflection**.

■ **mirror** verb [T]: *The trees were mirrored in the lake.* ▶ **odzwierciedlać**

mirth /mɜːθ/ noun [U] (formal) happiness, fun and the sound of people laughing: *There was much mirth in the audience.* ▶ **wesołość** SYN **merriment**

mis- /mɪs/ prefix [in verbs and nouns] bad or wrong; badly or wrongly: *misbehaviour* niewłaściwe zachowanie ◇ *misinterpret* błędnie interpretować ▶ **zły**; **źle**

misanthrope /ˈmɪsənθrəʊp/ noun [C] (formal) a person who hates and avoids other people ▶ **mizantrop**

misanthropic /ˌmɪsənˈθrɒpɪk/ adj. (formal) hating and avoiding other people ▶ **mizantropijny**
■ **misanthropy** /mɪˈsænθrəpi/ noun [U] ▶ **mizantropia**

misapprehension /ˌmɪsæprɪˈhenʃn/ noun [U,C] (formal) to have the wrong idea about sth or to believe sth is true when it is not: *I was **under the misapprehension*** (w błędnym przekonaniu) *that this course was for beginners.* ▶ **błędne przekonanie**

misappropriate /ˌmɪsəˈprəʊprieɪt/ verb [T] (formal) to take sb else's money or property for yourself, especially when they have trusted you to take care of it ▶ **sprzeniewierzać** SYN **embezzle** ➲ look at **appropriate**
■ **misappropriation** /ˌmɪsəˌprəʊpriˈeɪʃn/ noun [U]: *the misappropriation of funds* ▶ **sprzeniewierzenie**

misbehave /ˌmɪsbɪˈheɪv/ verb [I] to behave badly ▶ **źle się zachowywać** OPP **behave**
■ **misbehaviour** (US **misbehavior**) /ˌmɪsbɪˈheɪvjə(r)/ noun [U] ▶ **złe zachowanie**

misc = MISCELLANEOUS

miscalculate /ˌmɪsˈkælkjuleɪt/ verb [I,T] to make a mistake in calculating or judging a situation, an amount, etc.: *The driver totally miscalculated the speed at which the other car was travelling.* ▶ **źle obliczyć**, **przeliczyć się**
■ **miscalculation** /ˌmɪskælkjuˈleɪʃn/ noun [C,U] ▶ **błąd w obliczeniach**, **przeliczenie się**

miscarriage /ˈmɪskærɪdʒ/ noun [C,U] giving birth to a baby a long time before it is ready to be born, with the result that it cannot live ▶ **poronienie** ➲ look at **abortion**
IDM **a miscarriage of justice** an occasion when sb is punished for a crime that they did not do ▶ **pomyłka sądowa**

miscarry /ˌmɪsˈkæri/ verb [I] (**miscarrying**; **miscarries**; pt, pp **miscarried**) **1** to give birth to a baby before it is ready to be born, with the result that it cannot live ▶ **poronić 2** (used about a plan, idea, etc.) to fail ▶ **nie udać się**

miscellaneous /ˌmɪsəˈleɪniəs/ adj. (abbr. **misc**) consisting of many different types or things: *a box of miscellaneous items for sale* ▶ **różny**, **rozmaity**

mischief /ˈmɪstʃɪf/ noun [U] bad behaviour (usually of children) that is not very serious: *The children are always **getting into mischief**.* ◇ *You can go and see your friends but keep out of mischief* (bądź grzeczny) *this time.* ▶ **psota**, **złe zachowanie**

mischievous /ˈmɪstʃɪvəs/ adj. (usually used about children) liking to behave badly and embarrassing or annoying people ▶ **psotny** ➲ note at **evil**
■ **mischievously** adv. ▶ **psotnie**, **figlarnie**

misconception /ˌmɪskənˈsepʃn/ noun [C] a wrong idea or understanding of sth: *It is a popular misconception that people need meat to be healthy.* ▶ **błędne pojęcie/zrozumienie**

misconduct /ˌmɪsˈkɒndʌkt/ noun [U] (formal) unacceptable behaviour, especially by a professional person: *The doctor was dismissed for **gross misconduct**.* ▶ **złe/nieprofesjonalne postępowanie**

misconstrue /ˌmɪskənˈstruː/ verb [T] (formal) **misconstrue sth (as sth)** to understand sb's words or actions wrongly ▶ **błędnie/źle rozumieć/interpretować** ➲ look at **construe**

misdemeanour (US **misdemeanor**) /ˌmɪsdɪˈmiːnə(r)/ noun [C] something slightly bad or wrong that a person does; a crime that is not very serious ▶ **złe sprawowanie**; **drobne wykroczenie** ➲ look at **felony**

miser /ˈmaɪzə(r)/ noun [C] a person who loves having a lot of money but hates spending it ▶ **skąpiec**

M

■ **miserly** adj. ▶ **skąpy**

miserable /ˈmɪzrəbl/ adj. **1** very unhappy: *Oh dear, you look miserable. What's wrong?* ▶ **nieszczęśliwy, przygnębiony** **2** unpleasant; making you feel unhappy: *What miserable weather!* ▶ **przykry** SYN **dismal** **3** too small or of bad quality: *I was offered a miserable salary so I didn't take the job.* ▶ **marny, nędzny**

■ **miserably** /-əbli/ adv.: *I stared miserably out of the window.* ◇ *He* ***failed miserably*** *as an actor.* Jako aktor poniósł sromotną klęskę. ▶ **nieszczęśliwie; żałośnie; marnie**

misery /ˈmɪzəri/ noun [U,C] (pl. **miseries**) great unhappiness or suffering: *I couldn't bear to see him in such misery.* ◇ *the miseries of war* ▶ **cierpienia, nieszczęście**

IDM **put sb out of his/her misery** (informal) to stop sb worrying about sth by telling the person what they want to know: *Put me out of my misery – did I pass or not?* ▶ **skrócić czyjeś cierpienie, rozwiać czyjś niepokój**

put sth out of its misery to kill an animal because it has an illness or injury that cannot be treated ▶ **uśpić** (*zwierzę*)

misfire /ˌmɪsˈfaɪə(r)/ verb [I] to fail to have the intended result or effect: *The plan misfired.* ▶ **spełznąć na niczym**

misfit /ˈmɪsfɪt/ noun [C] a person who is not accepted by other people, especially because their behaviour or ideas are very different ▶ **osoba nie umiejąca dostosować się do otoczenia, osoba nie przystosowana**

misfortune /ˌmɪsˈfɔːtʃuːn/ noun [C,U] (formal) (an event, accident, etc. that brings) bad luck or disaster: *I hope I don't ever* ***have the misfortune to*** *meet him again.* ▶ **nieszczęście, pech**

misgiving /ˌmɪsˈɡɪvɪŋ/ noun [C,U] a feeling of doubt or worry: *I* ***had serious misgivings*** *about leaving him on his own.* ▶ **obawa**

misguided /ˌmɪsˈɡaɪdɪd/ adj. wrong because you have understood or judged a situation badly: *She only moved the victim in a misguided effort to help.* ▶ **mylny, błędny**

mishap /ˈmɪshæp/ noun [C,U] a small accident or piece of bad luck that does not have serious results: *to have a slight mishap* ▶ **niefortunny wypadek**

misinform /ˌmɪsɪnˈfɔːm/ verb [T] (formal) to give sb the wrong information: *I think you've been misinformed – no one is going to lose their job in the near future.* ▶ **źle informować, udzielać fałszywych informacji**

misinterpret /ˌmɪsɪnˈtɜːprɪt/ verb [T] **misinterpret sth (as sth)** to understand sth wrongly: *His comments were misinterpreted as a criticism of the project.* ▶ **źle interpretować/rozumieć** OPP **interpret**

■ **misinterpretation** /ˌmɪsɪntɜːprɪˈteɪʃn/ noun [C,U]: *Parts of the speech were* ***open to misinterpretation*** (można było źle zrozumieć). ▶ **zła interpretacja, złe rozumienie**

misjudge /ˌmɪsˈdʒʌdʒ/ verb [T] **1** to form a wrong opinion of sb/sth, usually in a way which is unfair to them or it ▶ **źle osądzać, nie doceniać** **2** to guess time, distance, etc. wrongly: *He misjudged the speed of the other car and almost crashed.* ▶ **błędnie oceniać**

■ **misjudgement** (also **misjudgment**) noun [C,U] ▶ **zła ocena, fałszywe mniemanie**

mislay /ˌmɪsˈleɪ/ verb [T] (**mislaying**; **mislays**; pt, pp **mislaid** /-ˈleɪd/) to lose sth, usually for a short time, because you cannot remember where you put it ▶ **zapodziewać, gubić**

mislead /ˌmɪsˈliːd/ verb [T] (pt, pp **misled** /-ˈled/) to make sb have the wrong idea or opinion about sb/sth ▶ **wprowadzać w błąd, zwodzić**

■ **misleading** adj.: *a misleading advertisement* ▶ **wprowadzający w błąd, zwodniczy**

mismanage /ˌmɪsˈmænɪdʒ/ verb [T] to manage or organize sth badly ▶ **źle kierować/nadzorować**

■ **mismanagement** noun [U] ▶ **złe kierownictwo**

misogynist /mɪˈsɒdʒɪnɪst/ noun [C] (formal) a man who hates women ▶ **mizogin**

■ **misogynistic** /mɪˌsɒdʒɪˈnɪstɪk/ (also **misogynist**) adj.: *misogynistic attitudes* ▶ **mizoginistyczny** | **misogyny** noun [U] ▶ **mizoginia**

misplaced /ˌmɪsˈpleɪst/ adj. given to sb/sth that is not suitable or good enough to have it: *misplaced loyalty* ▶ **źle ulokowany**

misprint /ˈmɪsprɪnt/ noun [C] a mistake in printing or typing ▶ **błąd drukarski**

mispronounce /ˌmɪsprəˈnaʊns/ verb [T] to say a word or letter wrongly ▶ **niepoprawnie wymawiać**

■ **mispronunciation** /ˌmɪsprəˌnʌnsiˈeɪʃn/ noun [C,U] ▶ **zła wymowa**

misread /ˌmɪsˈriːd/ verb [T] (pt, pp **misread** /-ˈred/) **misread sth (as sth)** to read or understand sth wrongly: *He misread my silence as a refusal.* ▶ **źle przeczytać/interpretować**

misrepresent /ˌmɪsˌreprɪˈzent/ verb [T, usually passive] to give a wrong description of sb/sth: *In the newspaper article they were misrepresented as uncaring parents.* ▶ **fałszywie przedstawiać, dawać fałszywy obraz**

■ **misrepresentation** /ˌmɪsˌreprɪzenˈteɪʃn/ noun [C,U] ▶ **złe przedstawienie, fałszywy obraz**

Miss /mɪs/ (used as a title before the family name of a young woman or a woman who is not married) ▶ **panna**

> **Miss, Mrs, Ms i Mr** używa się przed nazwiskiem osoby, a nie przed imieniem, chyba że imię występuje razem z nazwiskiem. Można powiedzieć: *Is there a Miss (Tamsin) Hudson here?* (ale nie ~~*Miss Tamsin*~~).

miss[1] /mɪs/ verb **1** [I,T] to fail to hit, catch, etc. sth: *She tried to catch the ball but she missed.* ◇ *The bullet narrowly missed his heart.* ▶ **chybić** **2** [T] to not see, hear, understand, etc. sb/sth: *The house is on the corner so* ***you can't miss it.*** ◇ *They completely* ***missed the point*** *of what I was saying.* ◇ *My Mum will know there's something wrong. She* ***doesn't miss much.*** ▶ **nie dostrzegać; nie słyszeć; nie rozumieć** **3** [T] to fail to go to or do sth: *Of course I'm coming to your wedding. I* ***wouldn't miss it for the world.*** ◇ *You can't afford to miss meals now you're pregnant.* ▶ **przegapić** **4** [T] to arrive too late for sth/sb: *Hurry up or you'll miss the plane!* ▶ **spóźnić się na coś; rozminąć się z kimś** **5** [T] to feel sad because sb is not with you any more, or because you have not got or cannot do sth that you once had or did: *I'll miss you terribly when you go away.* ◇ *What did you miss most when you lived abroad?* ▶ **tęsknić za kimś/czymś** **6** [T] to notice that sb/sth is not where they or it should be: *When did you first miss your handbag?* ▶ **zauważyć brak** **7** [T] to avoid sth unpleasant: *If we leave now, we'll miss the rush-hour traffic.* ▶ **unikać**

PHR V **miss sb/sth out** to not include sb/sth: *You've missed out several important points in your report.* ▶ **opuszczać kogoś/coś**

miss out (on sth) to not have a chance to have or do sth: *You'll miss out on all the fun if you stay at home.* ▶ **tracić** (*sposobność, okazję*)

miss[2] /mɪs/ noun [C] a failure to hit, catch or reach sth: *After several misses he finally managed to hit the target.* ▶ **chybienie; nie złapanie**

IDM **give sth a miss** (especially Brit., informal) to decide not to do or have sth: *I think I'll give aerobics a miss tonight.* ▶ **odpuszczać sobie, nie zrobić czegoś**

a near miss → NEAR[1]

missile /ˈmɪsaɪl; US ˈmɪsl/ noun [C] **1** a powerful exploding weapon that can be sent long distances through the air: *nuclear missiles* ▶ **pocisk 2** an object that is thrown at sb in order to hurt them: *The rioters threw missiles such as bottles and stones.* ▶ **przedmiot wystrzelony/rzucony**

⚷ **missing** /ˈmɪsɪŋ/ adj. **1** lost, or not in the right or usual place: *Two files have **gone missing** from my office.* ◇ *a missing person* zaginiony ▶ **zgubiony, brakujący 2** (used about a person) not present after a battle, an accident, etc. but not known to have been killed: *Many soldiers were listed as **missing in action.*** ▶ **zaginiony** (*np. w toku działań*) **3** not included, often when it should have been: *Fill in the missing words in the text.* ▶ **brakujący**

mission /ˈmɪʃn/ noun [C] **1** an important official job that sb is sent somewhere to do, especially to another country: *Your mission is to send back information about the enemy's movements.* ▶ **misja, zadanie specjalne 2** a group of people who are sent to a foreign country to perform a special task: *a British trade mission to China* ▶ **misja 3** a place where people are taught about the Christian religion, given medical help, etc. by **missionaries** ▶ **misja 4** a particular task which you feel it is your duty to do: *Her work with the poor was more than just a job – it was her **mission in life.*** ▶ **posłannictwo, misja 5** a special journey made by a **spacecraft** or military aircraft: *a mission to the moon* ▶ **misja**

missionary /ˈmɪʃənri; US -neri/ noun [C] (pl. **missionaries**) a person who is sent to a foreign country to teach about the Christian religion ▶ **misjona-rz/rka**

misspell /ˌmɪsˈspel/ verb [T] (pt, pp **misspelled** or **misspelt** /ˌmɪsˈspelt/) to spell sth wrongly ▶ **pisać z błędem ortograficznym**

misspent /ˌmɪsˈspent/ adj. (used about time or money) used in a foolish way; wasted ▶ **roztrwoniony**

mist¹ /mɪst/ noun [C,U] a cloud made of very small drops of water in the air just above the ground, that makes it difficult to see: *The fields were covered in mist.* ▶ **mgła, mgiełka** ➲ note at **fog**, **weather**

■ **misty** /ˈmɪsti/ adj.: *a misty morning* ▶ **mglisty** ➲ look at **foggy**

mist² /mɪst/ verb

PHR V **mist (sth) up/over** to cover or be covered with very small drops of water that make it difficult to see: *My glasses misted up when I came in from the cold.* ▶ **pokrywać (się) mgłą, zaparować**

⚷ **mistake¹** /mɪˈsteɪk/ noun [C] something that you think or do that is wrong: *Try not to **make** any **mistakes** in your essays.* ◇ *a spelling mistake* ◇ *It was a big mistake to trust her.* ◇ *I made the mistake of giving him my address.* ▶ **błąd, pomyłka**

IDM **by mistake** as a result of being careless: *The terrorists shot the wrong man by mistake.* ▶ **przez pomyłkę, błędnie**

> **mistake**
>
> **Error** jest bardziej formalne niż **mistake**: (formal) *Please accept my apologies. I opened your letter in error.* ◇ (informal) *I'm sorry. I opened your letter by mistake.* ◇ *a computing error.* **Fault** wskazuje na winną osobę: *The accident wasn't my fault. The other driver pulled out in front of me.* **Fault** używa się także, mówiąc o istnieniu lub braku jakiejś usterki przedmiotu lub wady człowieka: *a technical fault* ◇ *Laziness is not one of her faults.* Synonimem wyrażenia **make a mistake** jest **do sth wrong**: *This man has **done nothing wrong.*** Zwróć uwagę na następujące przykłady z wyrazem **wrong**: *I got the answer wrong.* ◇ *You must have the wrong number.*

⚷ **mistake²** /mɪˈsteɪk/ verb [T] (pt **mistook** /mɪˈstʊk/, pp **mistaken** /mɪˈsteɪkən/) **1 mistake A for B** to think wrongly that sb/sth is sb/sth else: *I'm sorry, I mistook you for a friend of mine.* ▶ **brać za kogoś/coś 2** to be wrong about sth: *I think you've mistaken my meaning.* ▶ **źle rozumieć**

⚷ **mistaken** /mɪˈsteɪkən/ adj. wrong; not correct: *a case of mistaken identity* ◇ *a mistaken belief/idea* ◇ *I thought the film was a comedy but I must have been mistaken* (musiałam się pomylić). ▶ **błędny, źle zrozumiany**

■ **mistakenly** adv. ▶ **błędnie, przez pomyłkę**

mistletoe /ˈmɪsltəʊ; ˈmɪzl-/ noun [U] a plant with white **berries** and green leaves. **Mistletoe** grows on trees. ▶ **jemioła**

> W Wlk. Br. używa się jemioły do dekoracji domów w czasie Bożego Narodzenia. Istnieje tradycja całowania się pod jemiołą.

mistook past tense of **mistake²**

mistreat /ˌmɪsˈtriːt/ verb [T] to be cruel to a person or an animal: *The owner of the zoo was accused of mistreating the animals.* ▶ **źle się obchodzić, maltretować**

■ **mistreatment** noun [U] ▶ **złe obchodzenie się, maltretowanie**

mistress /ˈmɪstrəs/ noun [C] (old-fashioned) **1** a man's mistress is a woman who is having a (secret) sexual relationship with him ▶ **kochanka** ➲ look at **lover 2** a female teacher (usually in a private school) ▶ **nauczycielka** ➲ look at **master 3** a woman who has people or animals in her control ▶ **pani; właścicielka** ➲ look at **master**

M

mistrust /ˌmɪsˈtrʌst/ verb [T] to have no confidence in sb/sth because you think they or it may be harmful: *I always mistrust politicians who smile too much.* ▶ **nie ufać** ➲ look at **distrust**

■ **mistrust** noun [U, sing.]: *She has a deep mistrust of strangers.* ▶ **brak zaufania**

misty → MIST¹

misunderstand /ˌmɪsʌndəˈstænd/ verb [I,T] (pt, pp **misunderstood** /-ˈstʊd/) to understand sb/sth wrongly: *I misunderstood the instructions and answered too many questions.* ▶ **źle rozumieć/tłumaczyć sobie**

misunderstanding /ˌmɪsʌndəˈstændɪŋ/ noun **1** [C,U] a situation in which sb/sth is not understood correctly: *The contract is written in both languages to avoid any misunderstanding.* ▶ **nieporozumienie 2** [C] a disagreement or an argument ▶ **nieporozumienie**

misuse /ˌmɪsˈjuːz/ verb [T] to use sth in the wrong way or for the wrong purpose: *These chemicals can be dangerous if misused.* ▶ **niewłaściwie używać, źle się obchodzić z czymś**

■ **misuse** /ˌmɪsˈjuːs/ noun [C,U] ▶ **niewłaściwe używanie, złe obchodzenie się (z czymś)**

mitigate /ˈmɪtɪɡeɪt/ verb [T] (formal) to make sth less serious, painful, unpleasant, etc. ▶ **łagodzić**

■ **mitigating** adj.: *Because of the **mitigating circumstances** the judge gave her a lighter sentence.* ▶ **łagodzący**

mitten /ˈmɪtn/ (also **mitt** /mɪt/) noun [C] a type of glove that has one part for the thumb and another part for all four fingers ▶ **rękawica z jednym palcem** ➲ look at **glove**

⚷ **mix¹** /mɪks/ verb **1** [I,T] **mix (A) (with B)**; **mix (A and B) (together)** if two or more substances mix or if you mix them, they combine to form a new substance: *Oil and water don't mix.* ◇ *Mix all the ingredients together in a bowl.* ◇ *to mix a cocktail* ▶ **mieszać (się), łączyć (się) 2** [I] **mix (with sb)** to be with and talk to other people: *He mixes with all types of people at work.* ▶ **obcować** (*towarzysko*) **3** [T] to combine different recordings of voices and/or instruments to produce a single piece of music ▶ **miksować** (*dźwięk*)

IDM **be/get mixed up in sth** (informal) to be/become involved in sth bad or unpleasant ▶ **być w coś wplątanym, wplątać się w coś**

PHR V **mix sth in (with sth)** to add one substance to others, especially in cooking: *Mix the remaining cream in with the sauce.* ▶ **dodawać coś (do czegoś), mieszając**

mix sth into sth to combine one substance with others, especially in cooking: *Mix the fruit into the rest of the mixture.* ▶ **łączyć coś z czymś, mieszając**

mix sth into/to sth to produce sth by combining two or more substances, especially in cooking: *Add the milk and mix to a smooth dough.* ▶ **(wy)mieszać dwa lub więcej składników, aż powstanie coś nowego** SYN **blend**

mix sth up to put sth in the wrong order: *He was so nervous that he dropped his speech and got the pages all mixed up.* ▶ **plątać coś (z czymś)**

mix sb/sth up (with sb/sth) to confuse sb/sth with sb/sth else: *I always get him mixed up with his brother.* ▶ **mylić kogoś/coś (z kimś/czymś), brać kogoś/coś (za kogoś/coś innego)**

mix[2] /mɪks/ noun **1** [C, usually sing.] a group of different types of people or things: *We need a good racial mix in the police force.* ▶ **mieszanka, mieszanina 2** [C,U] a special powder that contains all the substances needed to make sth. You add water or another liquid to this powder: *a packet of cake mix* ciasto w proszku ▶ **proszek**

mixed /mɪkst/ adj. **1** being both good and bad: *The weather has been very mixed recently.* ◇ *The play was given a **mixed reception** by the critics.* ▶ **mieszany 2** made or consisting of different types of person or thing: *a mixed salad* ◇ *Was your school mixed* (koedukacyjna) *or single-sex?* ▶ **mieszany** ➲ look at **unisex**

IDM **have mixed feelings (about sb/sth)** to have some good and some bad feelings about sb/sth; to not be sure about what you think ▶ **mieć mieszane uczucia**

ˌmixed ˈdoubles noun [U] a game of tennis, etc. in which there is a man and a woman on each side ▶ **mieszany debel**

ˌmixed ˈmarriage noun [C] a marriage between people of different races or religions ▶ **mieszane małżeństwo**

ˌmixed-ˈup adj. (informal) confused because of emotional problems: *He has been very mixed-up since his parents' divorce.* ▶ **niepewny (czegoś/siebie), zmieszany**

mixer /ˈmɪksə(r)/ noun [C] a machine that is used for mixing sth: *a food/cement mixer* ▶ **mikser, mieszarka**

mixture /ˈmɪkstʃə(r)/ noun **1** [sing.] a combination of different things: *Monkeys eat a mixture of leaves and fruit.* ▶ **mieszanina 2** [C,U] a substance that is made by mixing other substances together: *a mixture of eggs, flour and milk* ◇ *cake mixture* ◇ *Put the mixture into a baking dish* (włóż ciasto do formy). ◇ *cough mixture* syrop na kaszel ▶ **mieszanka**

ˈmix-up noun [C] (informal) a mistake in the planning or organization of sth: *Because of a mix-up at the travel agent's* (ponieważ w biurze podróży coś poplątali) *we didn't get our tickets on time.* ▶ **plątanina, gmatwanina**

ml = MILLILITRE: *contents 75ml*

mm = MILLIMETRE: *a 35mm camera*

mo (US) (pl. **mos**) = MONTH

moan /məʊn/ verb [I] **1** to make a low sound because you are in pain, very sad, etc.: *to moan with pain* ▶ **jęczeć 2** (informal) to keep saying what is wrong about sth; to complain: *The English are always moaning about the weather.* ▶ **jęczeć** (*na jakiś temat*), **lamentować** ➲ note at **grumble**

■ **moan** noun [C] ▶ **jęczenie**

mixers

moat /məʊt/ noun [C] a hole that was dug around a castle and filled with water to make it difficult for enemies to attack ▶ **fosa** ➲ picture on **page A3**

mob[1] /mɒb/ noun [C, with sing. or pl. verb] a large crowd of people that may become violent or cause trouble ▶ **motłoch**

mob[2] /mɒb/ verb [T] (**mobbing**; **mobbed**) to form a large crowd around sb, for example in order to see or touch them: *The band was mobbed by fans as they left the hotel.* ▶ **gromadzić się (wokół kogoś), rzucić się (tłumnie na kogoś)**

mobile[1] /ˈməʊbaɪl; US -bl/ adj. **1** [usually before a noun] that is not fixed in one place and can be moved easily and quickly: *mobile* (przenośny) *equipment* ◇ *a **mobile library*** biblioteka objazdowa ◇ *a **mobile shop*** sklep na kółkach ▶ **ruchomy** OPP **stationary 2** [not usually before a noun] (used about a person) able to move or travel around easily: *My daughter is much more mobile now she has her own car.* ◇ *a kitchen specially designed for the elderly or people who are less mobile* ▶ **mogący łatwo przemieszczać się/podróżować** OPP **immobile**

■ **mobility** /məʊˈbɪləti/ noun [U] ▶ **ruchliwość, mobilność**

mobile[2] /ˈməʊbaɪl; US -bl/ noun [C] **1** = MOBILE PHONE **2** a decoration that you hang from the ceiling and that moves when the air around it moves ▶ **mobil**

ˌmobile ˈhome noun [C] **1** (especially US) (US also **trailer**) a small building for people to live in that is made in a factory and moved to a permanent place ▶ **dom(ek) przenośny 2** (Brit.) (US **trailer**) a large caravan that sb lives in permanently (not just for holidays) ▶ **duża przyczepa kempingowa** (*używana jako miejsce zamieszkania na stałe*)

ˈmobile phone (Brit. **mobile**; US **cellphone** /ˈselfəʊn/) noun [C] a small telephone that you can carry around with you ▶ **telefon komórkowy** ➲ note at **telephone**

mobile phones

Calling from a **mobile phone/cellphone** can be more convenient than from a **landline** because **mobiles** can be used anywhere where there is a **signal**. You can also use a mobile to **text** sb/ **send** sb a **text (message)**. If you call sb, but you cannot **get through**, you can **leave a message** on his/her **voicemail**. To use a **pay-as-you-go** phone you first have to buy **credit**, and then **top up** your phone when the credit **runs out**. You also need to **recharge** your phone when its **battery** is **flat**.

mobilize (also -ise) /ˈməʊbəlaɪz/ verb **1** [T] to organize people or things to do sth: *They mobilized the local residents to oppose the new development.* ▶ **mobilizować** **2** [I,T] if a country **mobilizes** its army, or if a country or army **mobilizes**, it makes itself ready to fight in a war ▶ **mobilizować (się) na wojnę**

mock¹ /mɒk/ verb [I,T] (formal) to laugh at sb/sth in an unkind way or to make other people laugh at them or it ▶ **kpić/wyśmiewać się (z kogoś/czegoś)** ⓘ Zwroty **laugh at** i **make fun of** są mniej formalne i częściej ich się używa.

mock² /mɒk/ adj. [only before a noun] not real or genuine: *He held up his hands in mock surprise.* ◇ *a mock exam* próbny egzamin ◇ *The houses are built in a mock Georgian style* (w stylu udającym styl georgiański). ▶ **sztuczny, udawany**

mock³ /mɒk/ noun [usually pl.] (in Britain) a practice exam that you do before the official one ▶ **próbny egzamin**

mockery /ˈmɒkəri/ noun [U] comments or actions that make sb/sth look silly or stupid: *She couldn't stand any more of their mockery.* ▶ **kpiny** SYN **ridicule**

IDM **make a mockery of sth** to make sth seem silly or useless: *The trial made a mockery of justice.* Ten proces ośmieszył wymiar sprawiedliwości. ▶ **wystawiać coś na pośmiewisko**

ˈ**mock-up** noun [C] a model of sth that shows what it will look like or how it will work ▶ **makieta**

modal /ˈməʊdl/ (also ˈ**modal verb**) noun [C] a verb, for example 'might', 'can' or 'must' that is used with another verb for expressing possibility, permission, intention, etc. ▶ **czasownik modalny**

mode /məʊd/ noun [C] **1** a type of sth or way of doing sth: *a mode of transport/life* ▶ **środek, tryb** **2** one of the ways in which a machine can work: *Switch the camera to automatic mode.* ▶ **tryb**

🔑 **model¹** /ˈmɒdl/ noun [C] **1** a copy of sth that is usually smaller than the real thing: *a model aeroplane* ▶ **model, wzór** **2** one of the machines, vehicles, etc. that is made by a particular company: *The latest models are on display at the show.* ▶ **model** **3** a person or thing that is a good example to copy: *a model student* ◇ *Children often use older brothers or sisters as* ***role models.*** ▶ **wzór** **4** a person who is employed to wear clothes at a fashion show or for magazine photographs: *a fashion/male model* ▶ **model/ka** **5** a person who is painted, drawn or photographed by an artist ▶ **model/ka**

model² /ˈmɒdl/ verb (**modelling**; **modelled**; US **modeling**; **modeled**) **1** [I,T] to wear and show clothes at a fashion show or for photographs: *to model swimsuits* ▶ **prezentować** *(strój na pokazie mody)* **2** [I,T] to make a model of sth: *This clay is difficult to model.* ▶ **modelować**

PHR V **model sth/yourself on sb/sth** to make sth/yourself similar to sth/sb else: *The house is modelled on a Roman villa.* ▶ **wzorować coś/kogoś na kimś/czymś, naśladować coś/kogoś**

modelling (US **modeling**) /ˈmɒdəlɪŋ/ noun [U] the work of a fashion model ▶ **praca model-a/ki**

modem /ˈməʊdem/ noun [C] a piece of equipment that connects two or more computers together by means of a telephone line so that information can go from one to the other ▶ **modem** ➲ note at **Internet**

moderate¹ /ˈmɒdərət/ adj. **1** being, having, using, etc. neither too much nor too little of sth: *a moderate speed* ◇ *We've had a moderate amount of success.* ▶ **umiarkowany, średni** **2** having or showing opinions, especially about politics, that are not extreme: *moderate policies/views* ▶ **umiarkowany** ➲ look at **extreme**, **radical**

■ **moderately** adv.: *His career has been moderately successful.* ▶ **średnio, umiarkowanie**

moderate² /ˈmɒdəreɪt/ verb [I,T] to become or to make sth less strong or extreme: *The union moderated its original demands.* ▶ **uspokajać (się), tracić na gwałtowności/sile**

moderate³ /ˈmɒdərət/ noun [C] a person whose opinions, especially about politics, are not extreme ▶ **osoba o umiarkowanych poglądach** ➲ look at **extremist**

moderation /ˌmɒdəˈreɪʃn/ noun [U] the quality of being reasonable and not being extreme: *Alcohol can harm unborn babies even if it's taken* ***in moderation*** (z umiarem). ▶ **powściągliwość, umiar**

🔑 **modern** /ˈmɒdn/ adj. **1** of the present or recent times: *Pollution is one of the major problems in the modern world.* ▶ **nowoczesny, nowożytny** **2** [only before a noun] (used about styles of art, music, etc.) new and different from traditional styles: *modern jazz/architecture/art* ▶ **współczesny** **3** having all the newest methods, equipment, designs, etc.: *It is one of the most modern hospitals in the country.* ▶ **nowoczesny** SYN **up to date** ➲ look at **old-fashioned**

modernism /ˈmɒdənɪzəm/ noun [U] **1** modern ideas or methods ▶ **modernizm** **2** a style and movement in art, **architecture** and literature popular in the middle of the 20th century in which modern ideas, methods and materials were used rather than traditional ones ▶ **modernizm** ➲ look at **postmodernism**

■ **modernist** /ˈmɒdənɪst/ adj. [only before a noun]: *modernist art* ▶ **modernistyczny** | **modernist** noun [C] ▶ **modernist(k)a**

modernistic /ˌmɒdəˈnɪstɪk/ adj. (used about a painting, building, piece of furniture, etc.) painted, designed, etc. in a very modern style ▶ **modernistyczny**

modernity /məˈdɜːnəti/ noun [U] the condition of being new and modern: *a style of architecture that combines tradition and modernity* ▶ **nowoczesność**

modernize (also -ise) /ˈmɒdənaɪz/ verb [T] to make sth suitable for use today using new methods, styles, etc. ▶ **unowocześniać (się)**

■ **modernization** (also -isation) /ˌmɒdənaɪˈzeɪʃn; US -nəˈz-/ noun [U]: *The house is large but is in need of modernization.* ▶ **unowocześnienie**

ˌ**modern** ˈ**languages** noun [pl.] languages that are spoken now ▶ **języki nowożytne**

modest /ˈmɒdɪst/ adj. **1** not very large: *a modest pay increase* ▶ **skromny, nieznaczny** **2** not talking too much about your own abilities, good qualities, etc.: *She got the best results in the exam but she was too modest to tell anyone.* ▶ **skromny** ➲ look at **humble**, **proud** **3** (used about a woman's clothes) not showing much of the body ▶ **skromny**

■ **modesty** noun [U] ▶ **skromność** | **modestly** adv. ▶ **skromnie**

modify /ˈmɒdɪfaɪ/ verb [T] (**modifying**; **modifies**; pt, pp **modified**) to change sth slightly: *We shall need to modify the existing plan.* ▶ **modyfikować**

■ **modification** /ˌmɒdɪfɪˈkeɪʃn/ noun [C,U] ▶ **modyfikacja**

modular /ˈmɒdjələ(r); US -dʒə-/ adj. **1** (used about a course of study, especially at a British university or college) consisting of separate units from which students may choose several: *a modular course* ▶ (*kurs itp.*) **podzielony na moduły 2** (used about machines, buildings, etc.) consisting of separate parts or units that can be joined together ▶ **modułowy**

module /ˈmɒdjuːl; US -dʒuːl/ noun [C] a unit that forms part of sth bigger: *You must complete three modules in your first year.* ▶ **moduł, blok** (*nauczania*)

mohair /ˈməʊheə(r)/ noun [U] very soft wool that comes from a **goat** ▶ **moher**

Mohammed = MUHAMMAD

moist /mɔɪst/ adj. slightly wet: *Her eyes were moist with tears.* ◇ *Keep the soil moist or the plant will die.* ◇ *a rich moist cake* ▶ **wilgotny, zwilżony** ➲ note at **wet**
■ **moisten** /ˈmɔɪsn/ verb [I,T] ▶ **zwilżać (się)**

moisture /ˈmɔɪstʃə(r)/ noun [U] water in small drops on a surface, in the air, etc. ▶ **wilgoć**

moisturize (also -ise) /ˈmɔɪstʃəraɪz/ verb [I,T] to put a special cream on your skin to make it less dry: *a **moisturizing cream/lotion*** ▶ **nawilżać**

moisturizer (Brit. also -iser) /ˈmɔɪstʃəraizə(r)/ noun [C,U] a special cream that you put on your skin to make it less dry ▶ **krem nawilżający**

molar /ˈməʊlə(r)/ noun [C] one of the large teeth at the back of your mouth ▶ **ząb trzonowy**

molasses (US) = TREACLE

mold, moldy (US) = MOULD, MOULDY

mole /məʊl/ noun [C] **1** a small animal with dark fur that lives underground and is almost unable to see ▶ **kret 2** a small dark spot on sb's skin that never goes away ▶ **pieprzyk** ➲ look at **freckle 3** (informal) a person who works in one organization and gives secret information to another organization ▶ (*przen.*) **kret** ➲ look at **spy**

molecule /ˈmɒlɪkjuːl/ noun [C] the smallest unit into which a substance can be divided without changing its chemical nature ▶ **cząsteczka, molekuła** ➲ look at **atom**

ˈmolehill /ˈməʊlhɪl/ noun [C] a small pile of earth that is made by a mole while it is digging underground ▶ **kretowisko**

molest /məˈlest/ verb [T] to attack sb, especially a child, in a sexual way ▶ **molestować seksualnie**

molt (US) = MOULT

molten /ˈməʊltən/ adj. (used about metal or rock) made liquid by very great heat ▶ **ciekły, płynny**

🔑**mom** (US) = MUM

🔑**moment** /ˈməʊmənt/ noun **1** [C] a very short period of time: *One moment, please.* ◇ *Joe left just a few moments ago.* ▶ **chwila, moment 2** [sing.] a particular point in time: *Just at that moment my mother arrived.* ◇ *the moment of birth/death* ▶ **chwila, moment**
IDM **(at) any minute/moment (now)** → MINUTE[1]
at the moment now: *I'm afraid she's busy at the moment. Can I take a message?* ▶ **w tej chwili** ➲ note at **actually**
for the moment/present for a short time; for now: *I'm not very happy at work but I'll stay there for the moment.* ▶ **chwilowo, na razie**
in a moment very soon: *Just wait here. I'll be back in a moment.* ▶ **za chwilę**
the last minute/moment → LAST[1]
the minute/moment (that) → MINUTE[1]
on the spur of the moment → SPUR[1]

momentary /ˈməʊməntri; US -teri/ adj. lasting for a very short time: *a momentary lack of concentration* ▶ **chwilowy**
■ **momentarily** /ˈməʊməntrəli; US ˌməʊmənˈterəli/ adv. ▶ **chwilowo**

momentous /məˈmentəs; US məʊˈm-/ adj. very important: *a momentous decision/event/change* ▶ **ważny, doniosły**

momentum /məˈmentəm; US məʊˈm-/ noun [U] the ability to keep increasing or developing; the force that makes sth move faster and faster: *The environmental movement is **gathering momentum**.* ▶ **rozpęd, impet**

mommy (US) = MUMMY (1)

Mon. = MONDAY: *Mon. 6 June*

monarch /ˈmɒnək; US also -ɑːrk/ noun [C] a king or queen ▶ **monarch-a/ini**

monarchy /ˈmɒnəki/ noun (pl. **monarchies**) **1** [sing., U] the system of government or rule by a king or queen ▶ **monarchia 2** [C] a country that is governed by a king or queen ▶ **monarchia** ➲ look at **republic**

monastery /ˈmɒnəstri; US -teri/ noun [C] (pl. **monasteries**) a place where **monks** live together in a religious community ▶ **klasztor** ➲ look at **convent**

🔑**Monday** /ˈmʌndeɪ; -di/ noun [C,U] (abbr. **Mon.**) the day of the week after Sunday: *'What day is it today?' 'It's Monday.'* ◇ *I'm going to see her **on Monday**.* ◇ (informal) *I'll see her Monday.* ◇ *They go to the youth club every Monday.* ◇ *I finish work a bit later **on Mondays/on a Monday*** (w poniedziałki). ◇ *Monday morning/afternoon/evening/night* ◇ *last/next Monday* ◇ *the Monday before last* zeszły poniedziałek (tj. w zeszłym tygodniu, jeżeli dziś nie jest poniedziałek; jeżeli jest, to zwrot oznacza poniedziałek dwa tygodnie temu) ◇ *the Monday after next* poniedziałek za dwa tygodnie ◇ *a week on Monday/Monday week* poniedziałek za tydzień ◇ *The museum is open Monday to Friday, 10 till 4.30.* ◇ *Did you see that article about Italy in Monday's paper?* ▶ **poniedziałek**

Uwaga! Dni tygodnia po angielsku zawsze pisze się dużą literą.

monetary /ˈmʌnɪtri; US -teri/ adj. [only before a noun] connected with money: *the government's monetary policy* ▶ **pieniężny, monetarny**

🔑**money** /ˈmʌni/ noun [U] the means of paying for sth or buying sth (= coins or notes): *Will you **earn** more **money** in your new job?* ◇ *The new road will **cost** a lot of **money**.* ◇ *If we do the work ourselves, we will **save money**.* ◇ *The government **make** a huge amount of **money** out of tobacco tax.* ▶ **pieniądze** ⓘ Uwaga! **Money** jest rzeczownikiem niepoliczalnym i występuje z czasownikiem w lp: *The money is on the table.* ➲ note at **pay** ➲ look at **pocket money**
IDM **be rolling in money/in it** → ROLL[2]
get your money's worth to get full value for the money you have spent ▶ **ponosić w pełni opłacalny wydatek**
make money to earn money or to make a profit on a business ▶ **zarabiać; osiągać zysk**
put money on sth to bet money on sth: *He put all his money on a horse.* ▶ **stawiać pieniądze na coś** SYN **bet** ➲ note at **loan**

money

You can **save** money in a bank **account**, and this money is called your **savings**. You can spend **cash** to buy things, or you can write a **cheque**. If you use a **debit card**, the money comes straight out of your bank account. If you use a **credit card**, you pay later. If you have a **cash card** (US **ATM card**), you can **withdraw** money from your bank account at a **cash machine**. If you spend more money than is in your account, you are **overdrawn**.

Some people **invest** money, for example in the **stock market**, and make a **fortune**. People who have a lot of money are **rich/wealthy**, and someone who often **gives** money **away**, for example to **charity**, is **generous**.

ˈmoney box noun [C] a box into which you put money that you want to save ▶ **skarbonka**

mongrel /ˈmʌŋɡrəl/ noun [C] a dog that has parents of different breeds ▶ **kundel** ➲ look at **pedigree**

monitor[1] /ˈmɒnɪtə(r)/ noun [C] **1** a machine that shows information or pictures on a screen like a TV: *a PC with a 17-inch colour monitor* ▶ **monitor 2** a machine that records or checks sth: *A monitor checks the baby's heartbeat.* ▶ **urządzenie kontrolne 3** a pupil who has a special job to do in the classroom ▶ **ucze-ń/nnica do specjalnych poruczeń w klasie**, **dyżurn-y/a** (*odpowiedzialn-y/a za porządek w klasie*)

monitor[2] /ˈmɒnɪtə(r)/ verb [T] **1** to check, record or test sth regularly for a period of time: *Pollution levels in the lake are closely monitored.* ▶ **kontrolować (regularnie) 2** to listen to and record foreign radio or television broadcasts ▶ **prowadzić nasłuch** (*zagranicznego radia i TV*)

monk /mʌŋk/ noun [C] a member of a religious group of men who live in a **monastery** and do not get married or have possessions ▶ **mnich** ➲ look at **nun**

monkey /ˈmʌŋki/ noun [C] an animal with a long tail that lives in hot countries and can climb trees ▶ **małpa** ➲ look at **ape**

> **Chimpanzees** and **gorillas** are **apes**, although people sometimes call them monkeys.

IDM **monkey business** silly or dishonest behaviour ▶ **machlojki**

mono /ˈmɒnəʊ/ adj. (used about recorded music or a system for playing it) having the sound coming from one direction only ▶ **monofoniczny** ➲ look at **stereo**
■ **mono** noun [U]: *The concert was recorded in mono.* ▶ **monofonia**

monochrome /ˈmɒnəkrəʊm/ adj. (used about a photograph or picture) using only black, white and shades of grey ▶ **czarno-biały**

monogamy /məˈnɒɡəmi/ noun [U] the fact or custom of being married to, or having a sexual relationship with, only one person at a particular time ▶ **monogamia** ➲ look at **bigamy**, **polygamy**
■ **monogamous** /məˈnɒɡəməs/ adj. ▶ **monogamiczny**

monolingual /ˌmɒnəˈlɪŋɡwəl/ adj. using only one language: *a monolingual dictionary* ▶ **jednojęzyczny** ➲ look at **bilingual**

monolith /ˈmɒnəlɪθ/ noun [C] **1** a large single vertical block of stone, especially one that was shaped into a column by people living in ancient times, and that may have had some religious meaning ▶ **monolit 2** a single, very large organization, etc. that is very slow to change and not interested in individual people ▶ (*przen.: partia itp.*) **beton**
■ **monolithic** /ˌmɒnəˈlɪθɪk/ adj.: *the monolithic structure of the state* ▶ **monolitowy**, **monolityczny**

monologue (US also **monolog**) /ˈmɒnəlɒɡ/ noun [C] a long speech by one person, for example in a play ▶ **monolog**

mononucleosis (US) or (technical) = GLANDULAR FEVER

monopolize (also -ise) /məˈnɒpəlaɪz/ verb [T] to control sth so that other people cannot share it: *She completely monopolized the conversation. I couldn't get a word in.* ▶ **monopolizować**

monopoly /məˈnɒpəli/ noun [C] (pl. **monopolies**) **a monopoly (on/in sth) 1** the control of an industry or service by only one company; a type of goods or a service that is controlled in this way: *The company has a monopoly on broadcasting international football.* ▶ **monopol 2** the complete control, possession or use of sth; something that belongs to only one person or group and is not shared ▶ **monopol**

monorail /ˈmɒnəʊreɪl/ noun [C] a railway in which the train runs on a single track, usually high above the ground ▶ **kolej jednoszynowa**

monosyllabic /ˌmɒnəsɪˈlæbɪk/ adj. **1** having only one syllable: *a monosyllabic word* ▶ **jednozgłoskowy 2** saying very little, in a way that seems rude to other people ▶ **mrukliwy**

monosyllable /ˈmɒnəsɪləbl/ noun [C] a short word, such as 'leg', that has only one syllable ▶ **monosylaba**

monotonous /məˈnɒtənəs/ adj. never changing and therefore boring: *monotonous work* ◇ *a monotonous voice* ▶ **monotonny**
■ **monotonously** adv. ▶ **monotonnie**

monotony /məˈnɒtəni/ noun [U] the state of being always the same and therefore boring: *the monotony of working on a production line* ▶ **jednostajność**, **monotonia**

monsoon /ˌmɒnˈsuːn/ noun [C] the season when it rains a lot in Southern Asia; the rain that falls during this period ▶ **monsun**; **deszcz monsunowy**

monster /ˈmɒnstə(r)/ noun [C] (in stories) a creature that is large, ugly and frightening: (figurative) *The murderer was described as a dangerous monster.* ▶ **potwór**, **poczwara**

monstrosity /mɒnˈstrɒsəti/ noun [C] (pl. **monstrosities**) something that is very large and ugly, especially a building: *That new office block on the High Street is a monstrosity.* ▶ **potworność**, **monstrualność**

monstrous /ˈmɒnstrəs/ adj. **1** that people think is shocking and unacceptable because it is morally wrong or unfair: *It's monstrous that she earns less than he does for the same job!* ▶ **potworny**, **ohydny 2** very large (and often ugly or frightening): *a monstrous spider/wave* ▶ **olbrzymi**, **potworny**

month /mʌnθ/ noun [C] (abbr. **mth**) **1** one of the twelve periods of time into which the year is divided: *They are starting work next month.* ◇ *Have you seen this month's 'Vogue'?* ◇ *The rent is £300 a month* (na miesiąc). ▶ **miesiąc 2** the period of about 30 days from a certain date in one month to the same date in the next, for example 13 May to 13 June: *'How long will you be away?' 'For about a month.'* ◇ *a six-month course* ◇ *The window cleaner will come again in a month/in a month's time* (za miesiąc). ▶ **miesiąc kalendarzowy**

monthly[1] /ˈmʌnθli/ adj. (happening or produced) once every month: *a monthly meeting/magazine/visit* ▶ **miesięczny**, **comiesięczny**
■ **monthly** adv.: *Are you paid weekly or monthly?* ▶ **miesięcznie**, **co miesiąc**

monthly[2] /ˈmʌnθli/ noun [C] (pl. **monthlies**) a magazine that is published once a month ▶ **miesięcznik**

monument /ˈmɒnjumənt/ noun [C] **1 a monument (to sb/sth)** a building or statue that is built to remind people of a famous person or event ▶ **pomnik**, **monument 2** an old building or other place that is of historical importance: *Stonehenge is a famous ancient monument.* ▶ **monument**, **pomnik** ➲ picture on **page A2**

monumental /ˌmɒnjuˈmentl/ adj. [only before a noun] **1** (used about a building) very large and impressive ▶ **monumentalny 2** very great: *a monumental success/task/achievement* ▶ **olbrzymi**, **ogromny**

moo /muː/ noun [C] the sound that a cow makes ▶ **muu!** ➲ note at **cow**
■ **moo** verb [I] ▶ (*krowa*) **ryczeć**

mooch /muːtʃ/ verb [I] (Brit., informal) to walk slowly with no particular purpose; to be somewhere not doing very much: *He's happy to mooch around the house all day.* ▶ **wałęsać się** SYN **potter**

M

mood /mu:d/ noun **1** [C,U] the way that you are feeling at a particular time: *to be in a bad/good mood* ◇ *Turn that music down a bit – I'm not* ***in the mood for it.*** ▶ **nastrój, usposobienie 2** [C] a time when you are angry or bad-tempered: *Debby's in one of her moods again.* ▶ **kiepski nastrój** SYN **temper 3** [sing.] the way that a group of people feel about sth: *The mood of the crowd suddenly changed and violence broke out.* ▶ **nastrój**

moody /'mu:di/ adj. (**moodier**; **moodiest**) **1** often changing moods in a way that people cannot predict: *You never know where you are with Andy because he's so moody.* ▶ **zmiennego usposobienia, humorzasty 2** bad-tempered or unhappy, often for no particular reason ▶ **humorzasty, markotny, w złym humorze**
■ **moodily** adv. ▶ **markotnie** | **moodiness** noun [U] ▶ **zmienne usposobienie; zły humor, markotność**

moon /mu:n/ noun **1** (**the moon**) [sing.] the object that shines in the sky at night and that moves round the earth once every 28 days: *The moon's very bright tonight.* ▶ **Księżyc** ➲ adjective **lunar**

> The moon as it appears at its different stages, can be called a **new moon**, a **full moon**, a **half-moon** or a **crescent moon**.

2 [C] an object like the moon that moves around another planet: *How many moons does Neptune have?* ▶ **księżyc**
IDM **once in a blue moon** → ONCE
over the moon (especially Brit., informal) extremely happy and excited about sth ▶ **nie posiadający się z radości**

moonlight /'mu:nlaɪt/ noun [U] light that comes from the moon: *The lake looked beautiful in the moonlight.* ▶ **światło księżyca**

moonlit /'mu:nlɪt/ adj. lit by the moon: *a moonlit evening* księżycowy wieczór ▶ **oświetlony światłem księżyca**

moor[1] /mʊə(r); Brit. also mɔ:(r)/ (also **moorland** /'mʊələnd; Brit. also 'mɔ:l-/) noun [C,U] a wild open area of high land that is covered with grass and **heather**: *We walked across the* ***moors.*** ▶ **wrzosowisko** ➲ look at **heath**

moor[2] /mʊə(r); Brit. also mɔ:(r)/ verb [I,T] **moor (sth to sth)** to fasten a boat to the land or to an object in the water with a rope or chain ▶ **cumować**

mooring /'mʊərɪŋ; Brit. also 'mɔ:r-/ noun [C, usually pl.] a place where a boat is tied; the ropes, chains, etc. used to fasten a boat ▶ **miejsce do cumowania**

moorland = MOOR[1]

moose (US) = ELK

moot /mu:t/ adj. (US) unlikely to happen and therefore not worth considering: *He argued that the issue had become moot since the board had changed its policy.* ▶ **bezprzedmiotowy**
IDM **a moot point/question** a matter about which there may be disagreement or confusion: *Whether this should be enforced by law or not is a moot point.* ▶ **kwestia dyskusyjna**
■ **moot** verb [T, usually passive] (formal) to suggest an idea for people to discuss: *The plan was first mooted at last week's meeting.* ▶ **poddawać pod dyskusję** SYN **propose, put sth forward** (2)

mop[1] /mɒp/ noun [C] a tool for washing floors that has a long handle with a bunch of thick strings or soft material at the end ▶ **szczotka do zmywania podłogi**

mop[2] /mɒp/ verb [T] (**mopping**; **mopped**) **1** to clean a floor with water and a **mop** ▶ **myć** (*podłogę*) **mopem 2** to remove liquid from sth using a dry cloth: *to mop your forehead with a handkerchief* ▶ **wycierać**
PHR V **mop sth up** to get rid of liquid from a surface with a **mop** or dry cloth: *Mop up that tea you've spilt or it'll leave a stain!* ▶ **wycierać coś**

mope /məʊp/ verb [I] **mope (about/around)** to spend your time doing nothing and feeling sorry for yourself because you are unhappy: *Moping around the house all day won't make the situation any better.* ▶ **pogrążać się w czarnych myślach, poddawać się chandrze/przygnębieniu**

moped /'məʊped/ noun [C] a type of small, not very powerful motorbike ▶ **moped**

moral[1] /'mɒrəl/ adj. **1** [only before a noun] concerned with what is right and wrong: *Some people refuse to eat meat* ***on moral grounds.*** ◇ *a moral dilemma/issue/question* ▶ **moralny 2** having a high standard of behaviour that is considered good and right by most people: *She has always led a very moral life.* ▶ **moralny** OPP **immoral** ➲ look at **amoral**
IDM **moral support** help or confidence that you give to sb who is nervous or worried: *I went to the dentist's with him just to give him some moral support.* ▶ **wsparcie duchowe**

moral[2] /'mɒrəl/ noun **1** (**morals**) [pl.] standards of good behaviour: *These people appear to have no morals.* ▶ **moralność 2** [C] a lesson in the right way to behave that can be learnt from a story or an experience: *The moral of the play is that friendship is more important than money.* ▶ **morał**

morale /mə'rɑ:l; US -'ræl/ noun [U] how happy, sad, confident, etc. a group of people feels at a particular time: *The team's morale was low/high before the match.* ◇ *to boost/raise/improve morale* ▶ **duch** (*np. armii, zespołu*), **morale**

moralistic /ˌmɒrə'lɪstɪk/ adj. having or showing very fixed ideas about what is right and wrong, especially when this causes you to judge other people's behaviour ▶ **moralizatorski**

morality /mə'ræləti/ noun [U] principles concerning what is good and bad or right and wrong behaviour: *a debate about the morality of abortion* ▶ **moralność** SYN **ethics** OPP **immorality**

moralize (also **-ise**) /'mɒrəlaɪz/ verb [I] **moralize (about/on sth)** to tell other people what the right or wrong way to behave is ▶ **moralizować, umoralniać**

morally /'mɒrəli/ adv. **1** connected with standards of what is right or wrong: *Parents should be morally responsible for their children.* ▶ **moralnie 2** in a way that is good or right: *to behave morally* ▶ **moralnie**

moratorium /ˌmɒrə'tɔ:riəm/ noun [C] (pl. **-riums** or **-toria** /-riə/) **moratorium (on sth)** a temporary stopping of an activity, especially by official agreement ▶ **moratorium**

morbid /'mɔ:bɪd/ adj. showing interest in unpleasant things, for example disease and death ▶ **chorobliwy**

more[1] /mɔ:(r)/ determiner, pron. a larger number or amount of people or things; sth extra as well as what you have: *There were* ***more*** *people* ***than*** *I expected.* ◇ *I couldn't eat any more.* ◇ *I can't stand much more of this.* ◇ *Tell me more about your job.* ◇ *There's room for three more people* (jeszcze dla trzech osób). ▶ **więcej** OPP **less, fewer**
IDM **more and more** an increasing amount or number: *There are more and more cars on the road.* ▶ **coraz więcej/bardziej**

more[2] /mɔ:(r)/ adv. **1** (used to form the comparative of many adjectives and adverbs): *a course for more advanced students* ◇ *Please write more carefully.* ▶ **bardziej** OPP **less 2** to a greater degree than usual or than sth else: *I like him* ***far/much more*** *than his wife.* ◇ *She was* ***far/much more*** *intelligent* ***than*** *her sister.* ▶ **bardziej, więcej** OPP for both meanings **less**
IDM **more or less** approximately; almost: *We are more or less the same age.* ▶ **mniej więcej**
not any more not any longer: *She doesn't live here any more.* ▶ **już nie**

what's more (used for adding another fact) also; in addition: *The hotel was awful and what's more it was miles from the beach.* ▶ **co więcej, w dodatku**

moreover /mɔːr'əʊvə(r)/ adv. (formal) (used for adding another fact) also; in addition: *This firm did the work very well. Moreover, the cost was not too high.* ▶ **ponadto, poza tym**

morgue /mɔːg/ noun [C] a building where dead bodies are kept until they are buried or burned ▶ **kostnica** ➲ look at **mortuary**

morning /'mɔːnɪŋ/ noun [C,U] **1** the early part of the day between the time when the sun rises and midday: *Pat's going to London* ***tomorrow morning.*** ◇ *Bye, see you* ***in the morning*** (jutro rano). ◇ *The time of death was about 10.30* ***in the morning*** (około 10.30 rano). ◇ *I've been studying hard* ***all morning.*** ◇ *Dave makes breakfast* ***every morning.*** ◇ *the morning paper* ▶ **rano, przedpołudnie 2** the part of the night that is after midnight: *I was woken by a noise in* ***the early hours of the morning.*** ◇ *He didn't come home until three* ***in the morning.*** ▶ **(wcześnie) rano**

Zwróć uwagę, że kiedy wypowiadamy się na temat konkretnego poranka, wówczas mówimy **on Monday, Tuesday, Wednesday**, etc. **morning**: *We're meeting on Tuesday morning.* Kiedy jednak wypowiadamy się ogólnie o zrobieniu czegoś o tej porze dnia, wówczas mówimy **in the morning/in the mornings/mornings**: *She only works* ***in the mornings.*** W ten sam sposób stosuje się **afternoon** i **evening**. Kiedy używa się przymiotników **early** lub **late** przed **morning**, **afternoon** lub **evening**, należy przed nimi stawiać przyimek **in**: *The accident happened in the early morning.* ◇ *We arrived in the late afternoon.* Przed innymi przymiotnikami stawia się przyimek **on**: *School starts on Monday morning.* ◇ *They set out on a cold, windy afternoon.* ◇ *The accident happened on the following evening.* Nie stawia się żadnego przyimka przed **this, tomorrow** i **yesterday**: *Let's go swimming this morning.* ◇ *I'll phone Liz tomorrow evening.* ◇ *We went to the zoo yesterday afternoon.*

IDM **Good morning** (formal) (used when you see sb for the first time in the morning) ▶ **dzień dobry** ❶ Często mówi się tylko **Morning**: *Morning Kay, how are you today?*

moron /'mɔːrɒn/ noun [C] (informal) a rude way of referring to sb who you think is very stupid: *Stop treating me like a moron!* ▶ **kretyn, głupol**
■ **moronic** /mə'rɒnɪk/ adj. ▶ **kretyński, głupi**

morose /mə'rəʊs/ adj. bad-tempered, and not saying much to other people ▶ **posępny, markotny**
■ **morosely** adv. ▶ **posępnie, markotnie**

morphine /'mɔːfiːn/ noun [U] a powerful drug that is used for reducing pain ▶ **morfina**

morphology /mɔː'fɒlədʒi/ noun [U] **1** the form and structure of animals and plants, studied as a science ▶ **morfologia 2** the forms of words, studied as a branch of **linguistics** ▶ **morfologia** ➲ look at **grammar**, **syntax**
■ **morphological** /ˌmɔːfə'lɒdʒɪkl/ adj. ▶ **morfologiczny**

morsel /'mɔːsl/ noun [C] a very small piece of sth, usually food ▶ **kęs, kąsek, odrobina** (*pokarmu*)

mortal[1] /'mɔːtl/ adj. **1** that cannot live for ever and must die: *We are all mortal.* ▶ **śmiertelny** OPP **immortal 2** (formal) that will result in death: *a mortal wound/blow* ◇ *to be in mortal danger* ▶ **śmiertelny** ➲ look at **fatal 3** very great or extreme: *They were in mortal fear of the enemy.* ▶ **śmiertelny**
■ **mortally** /-təli/ adv. **1** in a way that will result in death ▶ **śmiertelnie 2** very; extremely ▶ **na śmierć** (*np. obrazić się*), **śmiertelnie**

mortal[2] /'mɔːtl/ noun [C] (formal) a human being ▶ **śmiertelni-k/czka**

mortality /mɔː'tæləti/ noun [U] **1** the fact that you will die: *He didn't like to think about his own mortality.* ▶ **śmiertelność 2** the number of deaths in one period of time or in one place: *Infant mortality is high in the region.* ▶ **współczynnik umieralności, śmiertelność**

mortar /'mɔːtə(r)/ noun **1** [U] a mixture of **cement**, sand and water used in building for holding bricks and stones together ▶ **zaprawa murarska 2** [C] a type of heavy gun that fires a type of bomb high into the air ▶ **moździerz 3** [C] a small hard bowl in which you can crush some foods or substances into powder with a **pestle** ▶ **moździerz** ➲ picture at **laboratory**

mortgage /'mɔːgɪdʒ/ noun [C] money that you borrow in order to buy a house or flat: *We took out a £40 000 mortgage.* Mamy hipotekę w wysokości £40 000. ▶ **kredyt hipoteczny**

You usually borrow money from a **bank** or a **building society**, who decide what **rate** of **interest** you must pay on the **loan**. ➲ note at **loan**

mortician (US) = UNDERTAKER

mortify /'mɔːtɪfaɪ/ verb [I,T] (**mortifying**; **mortifies**; pt, pp **mortified**) [usually passive] to feel or to make sb feel very embarrassed: *She was mortified to realize he had heard every word she said.* ▶ **zawstydzać, żenować**
■ **mortification** /ˌmɔːtɪfɪ'keɪʃn/ noun [U] ▶ **wstyd, zażenowanie** | **mortifying** adj.: *How mortifying to have to apologize to him!* ▶ **zawstydzający, żenujący**

mortuary /'mɔːtʃəri; US -ʃueri/ noun [C] (pl. **mortuaries**) a room, usually in a hospital, where dead bodies are kept before they are buried or burned ▶ **kostnica** ➲ look at **morgue**

mosaic /məʊ'zeɪɪk/ noun [C,U] a picture or pattern that is made by placing together small coloured stones, pieces of glass, etc. ▶ **mozaika**

Moslem = MUSLIM

mosque /mɒsk/ noun [C] a building where Muslims meet and worship ▶ **meczet**

mosquito /mə'skiːtəʊ; mɒs-/ noun [C] (pl. **mosquitoes**) a small flying insect that lives in hot countries and bites people or animals to drink their blood. Some types of **mosquito** spread **malaria**. ▶ **moskit, komar** ➲ picture at **insect**

moss /mɒs/ noun [C,U] a small soft green plant, with no flowers, that grows in wet places, especially on rocks or trees ▶ **mech**
■ **mossy** adj. ▶ **omszały, porosły mchem**

most[1] /məʊst/ determiner, pron. **1** [used as the superlative of *many* and *much*] greatest in number or amount: *Who got the most points?* ◇ *The children had the most fun.* ◇ *We all worked hard but I did the most.* ▶ **najwięcej** OPP **least, fewest 2** nearly all of a group of people or things: *Most people in this country have a TV.* ◇ *I like most Italian food.* ▶ **większość, przeważająca część** ❶ Zwróć uwagę, że przed rzeczownikiem poprzedzonym **the** (także **this, my** itp.) używa się **most of**: *Most of the people I invited were able to come.* ◇ *It rained most of the time we were in Ireland.*

IDM **at (the) most** not more than a certain number, and probably less: *There were 20 people there, at the most.* ▶ **najwyżej, w najlepszym razie/wypadku**
for the most part usually or mostly ▶ **przeważnie**
make the most of sth to get as much pleasure, profit, etc. as possible from sth: *You won't get another chance – make the most of it!* ▶ **wykorzystywać, jak się tylko da; wyciągać z czegoś jak najwięcej**

M

most² /məʊst/ adv. **1** (used to form the superlative of many adjectives and adverbs): *I think this machine works the most efficiently.* ◇ *I work most comfortably in the attic.* ◇ *It's the most beautiful house I've ever seen.* ▶ **najbardziej** OPP **least 2** more than anyone/anything else: *What do you miss most when you're abroad?* ▶ **najwięcej, najbardziej** OPP **least 3** (formal) very: *We heard a most interesting talk about Japan.* ▶ **bardzo**

mostly /ˈməʊstli/ adv. **1** almost all: *Our students come mostly from Japan.* ▶ **przeważnie, w większości 2** usually: *I play football mostly at the weekend but sometimes on Wednesday too.* ▶ **najczęściej, zazwyczaj**

MOT /ˌem əʊ ˈtiː/ noun [C] (also **MOT test**) a test to make sure that vehicles over a certain age are safe to drive: *My car failed its MOT.* ▶ **diagnostyka pojazdu**

motel /məʊˈtel/ noun [C] a hotel near a main road for people who are travelling by car ▶ **motel** ➲ note at **hotel**

moth /mɒθ/ noun [C] an insect with wings that usually flies at night. Some **moths** eat cloth and leave small holes in your clothes. ▶ **ćma, mól** ➲ picture at **insect**

mothball /ˈmɒθbɔːl/ noun [C] a small ball made of a chemical substance that protects clothes in cupboards from **moths** ▶ **kulka naftalinowa (przeciw molom)**

mother¹ /ˈmʌðə(r)/ noun [C] the female parent of a person or an animal: *an expectant mother/a mother-to-be* kobieta spodziewająca się dziecka ◇ *a single mother* samotna matka ◇ *a foster mother* przybrana matka ▶ **matka** ➲ look at **mum, mummy, stepmother**

mother² /ˈmʌðə(r)/ verb [T] to look after sb as a mother does: *Stop mothering me – I can look after myself!* ▶ **matkować**

ˈ**mother country** noun [sing.] the country where a person was born or grew up ▶ **ojczyzna**

motherhood /ˈmʌðəhʊd/ noun [U] the state of being a mother ▶ **macierzyństwo**

ˈ**mother-in-law** noun [C] (pl. **mothers-in-law**) the mother of your husband or wife ▶ **teściowa**

motherland /ˈmʌðəlænd/ noun [C] (formal) the country where you or your family were born and which you feel a strong emotional connection with ▶ **ojczyzna**

motherless /ˈmʌðələs/ adj. having no mother ▶ **bez matki**

motherly /ˈmʌðəli/ adj. having the qualities of a good mother: *motherly love/instincts/advice* ▶ **macierzyński**

ˈ**Mother's Day** noun [C] a day when mothers receive cards and gifts from their children, celebrated in Britain on the fourth Sunday in Lent and in the US on the 2nd Sunday in May ▶ **Dzień Matki**

ˈ**mother tongue** noun [C] the first language that you learnt to speak as a child ▶ **język ojczysty**

motif /məʊˈtiːf/ noun [C] a picture or pattern on sth: *a flower motif* ▶ **motyw, wzór**

motion¹ /ˈməʊʃn/ noun **1** [U] movement or a way of moving: *The motion of the ship made us all feel sick.* ◇ *Pull the lever to* ***set*** *the machine* ***in motion*** (żeby wprawić maszynę w ruch). ▶ **ruch, poruszanie się** ➲ look at **slow motion 2** [C] a formal suggestion at a meeting that you discuss and vote on: *The* ***motion*** *was* ***carried/rejected*** (wniosek podtrzymano/odrzucono) *by a majority of eight votes.* ▶ **inicjatywa, wniosek**

motion² /ˈməʊʃn/ verb [I,T] **motion to sb (to do sth); motion (for) sb (to do sth)** to make a movement, usually with your hand, that tells sb what to do: *I motioned to the waiter.* ◇ *The manager motioned for me to sit down.* ▶ **dawać znak, kiwać (na kogoś)**

motionless /ˈməʊʃnləs/ adj. not moving ▶ **nieruchomy, bez ruchu**

motivate /ˈməʊtɪveɪt/ verb [T] **1** [usually passive] to cause sb to act in a particular way: *Her reaction was motivated by fear.* ▶ **motywować, być pobudką/bodźcem (do czegoś), powodować 2** to make sb want to do sth, especially sth that involves hard work and effort: *Our new teacher certainly knows how to motivate his classes.* ◇ *I just can't motivate myself to do anything this morning.* ▶ **dostarczać pobudek/motywacji**

■ **motivated** adj.: *highly motivated students* ▶ **mający (silną) motywację** | **motivation** /ˌməʊtɪˈveɪʃn/ noun [C,U]: *He's clever enough, but he lacks motivation.* ▶ **motywacja**

motive /ˈməʊtɪv/ noun [C,U] **(a) motive (for sth/doing sth)** a reason for doing sth, often sth bad: *The police couldn't discover a motive for the murder.* ▶ **motyw, pobudka**

motley /ˈmɒtli/ adj. consisting of many different types of people or things that do not seem to belong together: *She had a motley group of friends at college.* ▶ **stanowiący zbieraninę**

motor¹ /ˈməʊtə(r)/ noun [C] a device that uses petrol, gas, electricity, etc. to produce movement and makes a machine, etc. work: *The washing machine doesn't work. I think something is wrong with the motor.* ▶ **motor, silnik**

> W odniesieniu do samochodów i motocykli zwykle używa się rzeczownika **engine**, chociaż słowo **motor** jest też niekiedy stosowane. Pojawia się ono nawet w samej nazwie samochodu – **motor car. Engine** oznacza zazwyczaj silnik benzynowy, zaś **motor** – silnik napędzany prądem elektrycznym.

motor² /ˈməʊtə(r)/ adj. [only before a noun] **1** having or using the power of an engine or a motor: *a motor vehicle* ▶ **motorowy 2** (especially Brit.) connected with vehicles that have engines, especially cars: *motor racing* wyścigi samochodowe ◇ *a motor mechanic* mechanik samochodowy ◇ *the motor industry* ▶ **samochodowy**

motorbike /ˈməʊtəbaɪk/ (also formal **motorcycle** /ˈməʊtəsaɪkl/) noun [C] a vehicle that has two wheels and an engine ▶ **motocykl** ➲ picture on **page A7**

motorboat /ˈməʊtəbəʊt/ noun [C] a small fast boat that has a motor ▶ **motorówka** ➲ picture at **boat**

ˈ**motor car** (Brit., formal) = CAR (1)

motorcycle (formal) = MOTORBIKE

motorcyclist /ˈməʊtəsaɪklɪst/ noun [C] a person who rides a motorbike ▶ **motocyklist(k)a**

motoring /ˈməʊtərɪŋ/ adj. [only before a noun] connected with driving a car: *a motoring holiday* ◇ *to commit a motoring offence* popełniać wykroczenie drogowe ▶ **samochodowy**

motorist /ˈməʊtərɪst/ noun [C] a person who drives a car ▶ **kierowca** ➲ note at **driving** ➲ look at **pedestrian**

motorized (also **-ised**) /ˈməʊtəraɪzd/ adj. [only before a noun] that has an engine: *a motorized wheelchair* ▶ **motorowy, zmotoryzowany**

motorway /ˈməʊtəweɪ/ (US **expressway** /ɪkˈspresweɪ/, **freeway** /ˈfriːweɪ/) noun [C] (abbr. **M**) a wide road where traffic can travel fast for long distances between large towns: *a motorway service station* stacja obsługi przy autostradzie ▶ **autostrada** ➲ note at **road**

> A motorway has two or three **lanes** on each **carriageway**. On the left of each carriageway there is a **hard shoulder**.

mottled /ˈmɒtld/ adj. marked with shapes of different colours without a regular pattern: *the mottled skin of a snake* ▶ **cętkowany**

motto /ˈmɒtəʊ/ noun [C] (pl. **mottoes** or **mottos**) a short sentence or phrase that expresses the aims and beliefs of a person, a group, an organization, etc.: *'Live and let live' that's my motto.* ▶ **dewiza, motto**

mould[1] (US **mold**) /məʊld/ noun **1** [C] a container that you pour a liquid or substance into. The liquid then becomes solid in the same shape as the container, for example after it has cooled or cooked. ▶ **forma odlewnicza, matryca 2** [C, usually sing.] a particular type: *She doesn't fit into the usual mould of sales directors.* ▶ (*osoba*) **typ, pokrój 3** [U] a soft green or black substance like fur that grows in wet places or on old food ▶ **pleśń** ➲ look at **fungus**, **mildew**
■ **mouldy** (US **moldy**) adj.: *The cheese had gone mouldy.* ▶ **zapleśniały, stęchły**

mould[2] (US **mold**) /məʊld/ verb [T] **mould A (into B)**; **mould B (from/out of A)** to make sth into a particular shape or form by pressing it or by putting it into a **mould**[1] (1): *First mould the dough into a ball.* ◇ *a bowl moulded from clay* ▶ **kształtować, modelować, odlewać**

moult (US **molt**) /məʊlt/ verb [I] (used about an animal or a bird) to lose hairs or feathers before growing new ones ▶ **linieć, pierzyć się**

mound /maʊnd/ noun [C] **1** a large pile of earth or stones; a small hill ▶ **kopiec, hałda 2** (informal) **a mound (of sth)** a pile or a large amount of sth: *I've got a mound of work to do.* ▶ **sterta** SYN for both meanings **heap**

⚷ **mount**[1] /maʊnt/ verb **1** [T] to organize sth: *to mount a protest/a campaign/an exhibition/an attack* ▶ **organizować, montować 2** [I] to increase gradually in level or amount: *The tension mounted as the end of the match approached.* ▶ **podnosić się, zwiększać się 3** [T] (formal) to go up sth or up on to sth: *He mounted the platform and began to speak.* ▶ **wchodzić/wspinać się (na coś) 4** [I,T] to get on a horse or bicycle: *He mounted his horse and rode away.* ▶ **dosiadać** (*np. konia*), **siadać** (*np. na rower*) OPP **dismount 5** [T] **mount sth (on/onto/in sth)** to fix sth firmly on sth else: *The gas boiler was mounted on the wall.* ▶ **montować**
PHR V **mount up** to increase (often more than you want): *When you're buying food for six people the cost soon mounts up.* ▶ **narastać**

⚷ **mount**[2] /maʊnt/ noun [C] (**Mount**) (abbr. **Mt**) (used in names) a mountain: *Mt Everest/Vesuvius/Fuji* ▶ **góra** (*w nazwach*), **szczyt**

⚷ **mountain** /ˈmaʊntən; US -tn/ noun [C] **1** a very high hill: *Which is the highest mountain in the world?* ◇ *Have you ever climbed a mountain?* ◇ *mountain roads/scenery/villages* ◇ *a mountain range* ▶ **góra 2 a mountain (of sth)** a large amount of sth: *I've got a mountain of work to do.* ▶ **góra (czegoś)**

ˈ**mountain bike** noun [C] a bicycle with a strong frame, wide tyres and many different gears designed for riding on rough ground ▶ **rower górski**

ˈ**mountain biking** noun [U] the activity of riding a mountain bike ▶ **jazda rowerem górskim** ℹ Wyrażenia **go mountain biking** zwykle używa się, mówiąc o jeździe rowerem w górach dla przyjemności.

mountaineering /ˌmaʊntəˈnɪərɪŋ; US -tnˈɪrɪŋ/ noun [U] the sport of climbing mountains ▶ **wspinaczka górska**
■ **mountaineer** noun [C] ▶ **alpinist(k)a**

mountainous /ˈmaʊntənəs/ adj. **1** having many mountains: *a mountainous region* ▶ **górzysty 2** very large in size or amount: *The mountainous waves made sailing impossible.* ▶ **ogromny, olbrzymi, zawrotny** SYN **huge**

mountainside /ˈmaʊntənsaɪd/ noun [C] the land on the side of a mountain ▶ **stok górski**

mounted /ˈmaʊntɪd/ adj. [only before a noun] riding a horse: *mounted police* ▶ **konny**

mounting /ˈmaʊntɪŋ/ adj. [only before a noun] increasing: *mounting unemployment/tension/concern* ▶ **narastający**

mourn /mɔːn/ verb [I,T] **mourn (for/over) sb/sth** to feel and show great sadness, especially because sb has died: *She is still mourning (for) her child.* ▶ **opłakiwać**
■ **mourning** noun [U]: *He wore a black armband to show he was **in mourning**.* ▶ **żałoba**

mourner /ˈmɔːnə(r)/ noun [C] a person who goes to a funeral as a friend or relative of the person who has died ▶ **żałobnik**

mournful /ˈmɔːnfl/ adj. (formal) very sad: *a mournful song* ▶ **pełen smutku, ponury**
■ **mournfully** /-fəli/ adv. ▶ **z wielkim smutkiem, ponuro**

⚷ **mouse** /maʊs/ noun [C] (pl. **mice** /maɪs/) **1** a very small animal with fur and a long thin tail ▶ **mysz** ➲ Mice are members of the **rodent** family.
2 a piece of equipment, connected to a computer, for moving around the screen and entering commands without touching the keys: *Use the mouse to drag the icon to a new position.* ▶ **mysz komputerowa**

ˈ**mouse mat** (US ˈ**mouse pad**) noun [C] a small piece of material that is the best kind of surface on which to use a computer mouse ▶ **podkładka pod mysz komputerową**

mousse /muːs/ noun [C,U] **1** a cold **dessert** made with cream and egg whites and flavoured with fruit, chocolate, etc.; a similar dish flavoured with fish, vegetables, etc.: *a chocolate/strawberry mousse* ◇ *salmon mousse* ▶ **pianka, mus 2** a substance that is used on hair to make it stay in a particular style ▶ **pianka do włosów**

moustache (US **mustache**) /məˈstɑːʃ/ noun [C] hair that grows on a man's top lip, between the mouth and nose ▶ **wąs/y** ➲ picture at **hair**

mousy (also **mousey**) /ˈmaʊsi/ adj. **1** (used about hair) of a dull brown colour ▶ **mysi 2** (used about people) shy and quiet; without a strong personality: *He was accompanied by his mousy little wife.* ▶ **nieśmiały**

⚷ **mouth**[1] /maʊθ/ noun [C] (pl. **mouths** /maʊðz/) **1** the part of your face that you use for eating and speaking: *to open/close your mouth* ◇ *They have a low income and five mouths to feed* (i pięć gąb do wykarmienia). ▶ **usta** ➲ picture at **body 2** the place where a river enters the sea ▶ **ujście** (*rzeki*) **3** (**-mouthed**) /-maʊðd/ [in compounds] having a particular type of mouth or a particular way of speaking: *We stared open-mouthed.* Gapiliśmy się z otwartymi ustami. ◇ *loud-mouthed* o niewyparzonej gębie ▶ (*określa usta*); (*określa sposób mówienia*)
IDM **keep your mouth shut** (informal) to not say sth to sb because it is a secret or because it will upset or annoy them ▶ **trzymać język za zębami**

mouth[2] /maʊð/ verb [I,T] to move your mouth as if you were speaking but without making any sound: *Vinay was outside the window, mouthing something to us.* ▶ **mówić bez słów** (*ruszać bezgłośnie ustami*)

mouthful /ˈmaʊθfʊl/ noun **1** [C] the amount of food or drink that you can put in your mouth at one time ▶ **kęs, łyk 2** [sing.] a word or phrase that is long or difficult to say: *Her name is a bit of a mouthful.* ▶ **długie/trudne słowo; długi/trudny zwrot**

ˈ**mouth organ** = HARMONICA

mouthpiece /ˈmaʊθpiːs/ noun [C] **1** the part of a telephone, musical instrument, etc. that you put in or near your mouth ▶ **ustnik, mikrofon 2** a person, newspaper, etc. that a particular group uses to express its opinions: *Pravda was the mouthpiece of the Soviet government.* ▶ **rzeczni-k/czka, wyraziciel/ka**

mouthwash /ˈmaʊθwɒʃ/ noun [C,U] liquid that you use for cleaning your mouth and making it smell nice ▶ **płyn do płukania ust**

ˈ**mouth-watering** adj. (used about food) that looks or smells very good ▶ **powodujący, że ślinka komuś cieknie,** (*wygląd/zapach jedzenia*) **smakowity**

M

movable /ˈmuːvəbl/ adj. that can be moved ▶ **ruchomy** OPP **fixed** ➲ look at **portable**, **mobile**

move¹ /muːv/ verb **1** [I,T] to change position or to put sth in a different position: *Please move your car – it's blocking the road.* ◇ *The station is so crowded you* ***can hardly move.*** ◇ *The meeting has been moved to Thursday.* ▶ **ruszać (się)**, **przemieszczać (się)**, **przenosić (się) 2** [I,T] **move along, down, over, up, etc.** to move (sth) further in a particular direction in order to make space for sb/sth else: *If we move up a bit, Rob can sit here too.* ◇ *Move your head down – I can't see the screen.* ▶ **przesuwać (się)** (*np. dalej*) **3** [I] **move (on/ahead)** to make progress: *When the new team of builders arrived things started moving very quickly.* ▶ **ruszać się (z miejsca)**, **posuwać się (naprzód) 4** [I] to take action: *Unless we move quickly lives will be lost.* ▶ **działać**, **przystępować do czynu 5** [I,T] to change the place where you live, work, study, etc.: *Our neighbours are moving to Exeter next week.* ◇ *to* ***move house*** ◇ *Yuka's moved down to the beginners' class.* ▶ **przeprowadzać się**, **przenosić się 6** [T] to cause sb to have strong feelings, especially of sadness: *Many people were* ***moved to tears*** *by reports of the massacre.* ▶ **wzruszać kogoś 7** [I,T] to change the position of a piece in a game like chess ▶ **wykonywać ruch**

IDM **get moving** to go, leave or do sth quickly ▶ **ruszać się**

get sth moving to cause sth to make progress ▶ **posuwać coś (naprzód)**

PHR V **move in**; **move into sth** to start to live in your new home: *Our new neighbours moved in yesterday.* ▶ **wprowadzać się (do czegoś)** OPP **move out**

move in with sb to start living in a new house with sb ▶ **rozpocząć z kimś nowe życie** (*w nowym domu*)

move on (to sth) to start doing or discussing sth new ▶ **posuwać się dalej/naprzód**; **przechodzić** (*do nowego tematu*)

move off (used about a vehicle) to start a journey; to leave ▶ **odjeżdżać**

move out to leave your old home ▶ **wyprowadzać się**

move² /muːv/ noun [C] **1** a change of place or position: *She was watching every move I made.* ▶ **ruch 2** a change in the place where you live or work: *a move to a bigger house* ▶ **przeprowadzka**; **zmiana pracy 3** action that you take because you want to achieve a particular result: *Both sides want to negotiate but neither is prepared to* ***make the first move.*** ◇ *Asking him to help me was* ***a good move.*** ▶ **ruch**, **krok**, **posunięcie 4** (in chess and other games) a change in the position of a piece: *It's your move.* ▶ **ruch**

IDM **be on the move** to be going somewhere: *We've been on the move for four hours so we should stop for a rest.* ▶ **być w rozjazdach**

get a move on (informal) to hurry: *I'm late. I'll have to get a move on.* ▶ **szybciej się ruszać**, **pośpieszyć się**

make a move to start to go somewhere: *It's time to go home. Let's make a move.* ▶ **ruszać się** (*z miejsca*)

movement /ˈmuːvmənt/ noun **1** [C,U] an act of moving: *The dancer's movements were smooth and controlled.* ◇ *The seat belt doesn't allow much freedom of movement.* ◇ *I could see some movement in the trees.* ▶ **ruch 2** [C,U] an act of moving or being moved from one place to another: *the slow movement of the clouds across the sky* ▶ **przemieszczanie (się) 3** [C] a group of people who have the same aims or ideas: *the Animal Rights movement* Ruch na Rzecz Praw Zwierząt ◇ *I support the peace movement.* ▶ **ruch 4** (**movements**) [pl.] sb's actions or plans during a period of time: *Detectives have been watching the man's movements for several weeks.* ▶ **posunięcia**, **ruchy 5** [C, usually sing.] **a movement (away from/towards sth)** a general change in the way people think or behave: *There's been a movement away from the materialism of the 1980s.* ▶ **odchodzenie**; **zbliżanie się 6** [C] one of the main parts of a long piece of music: *a symphony in four movements* ▶ **część**

movie (especially US) **1** = FILM¹ (1): *Shall we go and* ***see a movie?*** ◇ *a science fiction/horror movie* ◇ *a movie director/star* ◇ *a movie theater* **2** (**the movies**) [pl.] = CINEMA (1): *Let's* ***go to the movies.*** Chodźmy do kina.

moviegoer (especially US) = FILM-GOER

moving /ˈmuːvɪŋ/ adj. **1** causing strong feelings, especially of sadness: *a deeply moving speech/story* ▶ **wzruszający**, **poruszający 2** [only before a noun] that moves: *It's a computerized machine with few moving parts.* ▶ **ruchomy**, **poruszający się**

ˈmoving van (US) = REMOVAL VAN

mow /məʊ/ verb [I,T] (pt **mowed**; pp **mown** /məʊn/ or **mowed**) to cut grass using a **mower**: *to mow the lawn* ▶ **kosić**

PHR V **mow sb down** to kill sb with a gun or a car ▶ **wykosić kogoś**

mower /ˈməʊə(r)/ noun [C] a machine for cutting grass: *a lawnmower* ◇ *an electric mower* ▶ **kosiarka** (*do trawy*)

mown past participle of **mow**

MP (especially Brit.) = MEMBER OF PARLIAMENT

MP3 /ˌem piː ˈθriː/ noun [C,U] a method of reducing the size of a computer file containing sound, or a file that is reduced in size in this way ▶ **kompresja stratna do MP3**; **plik dźwiękowy w formacie MP3**

MPˈ3 player noun [C] a piece of computer equipment that can open and play **MP3** files ▶ **odtwarzacz MP3** ➲ note at **listen**

mpg /ˌem piː ˈdʒiː/ abbr. **miles per gallon**: *This car does 40 mpg.* ▶ **mile na galon**

mph /ˌem piː ˈeɪtʃ/ abbr. **miles per hour**: *a 70 mph speed limit* ▶ **mile na godzinę**

MPV /ˌem piː ˈviː/ noun [C] **multi-purpose vehicle**; a large car that can carry a number of people ▶ **pojazd wielozadaniowy**

Mr /ˈmɪstə(r)/ abbr. (used as a title before the name of a man): *Mr (Matthew) Botham* ▶ **Pan** ➲ note at **Miss**

Mrs /ˈmɪsɪz/ abbr. (used as a title before the name of a married woman): *Mrs (Sylvia) Allen* ▶ **Pani** ➲ note at **Miss**, **Ms**

MS = MULTIPLE SCLEROSIS

Ms /mɪz; məz/ (used as a title before the family name of a woman who may or may not be married): *Ms (Keiko) Harada* ▶ **pani** ℹ Niektóre kobiety wolą być tytułowane **Ms** zamiast **Mrs** lub **Miss**. Tytuł ten można też stosować, kiedy nie wie się, czy kobieta jest zamężna, czy też nie. ➲ note at **Miss**

MSc /ˌem es ˈsiː/ abbr. **Master of Science**; a second degree that you receive when you complete a more advanced course or piece of research in a science subject at university or college ▶ **mgr nauk ścisłych** ➲ look at **BSc**, **MA**

Mt = MOUNT²: *Mt Everest*

mth (US **mo**) abbr. (pl. **mths**) = MONTH

much¹ /mʌtʃ/ determiner, pron. **1** [used with uncountable nouns, mainly in negative sentences and questions, or after *as, how, so, too*] a large amount of sth: *I haven't got much money.* ◇ *Did she say much?* ◇ *You've given me* ***too much*** *food.* ◇ *I can't carry* ***that much!*** ◇ *'Is there any post?' 'Not much.'* ◇ *Eat* ***as much as*** (tyle, ile) *you can.* ▶ **dużo**, **wiele** ℹ W zdaniach twierdzących używa się zwykle **a lot of**, a nie **much**: *I've got a lot of experience.* **How much** tłumaczy się „ile": ***How much*** *time have you got?* ◇ *How much is it?*

IDM **much the same** very similar: *Softball is much the same as baseball.* ▶ **bardzo podobny**

not much good (at sth) not skilled (at sth): *I'm not much good at singing.* ▶ **niezbyt (bardzo) dobry (w czymś)**

not much of a ... not a good ...: *She's not much of a cook.* ▶ **niezbyt dobry**

not up to much → UP
nothing much → NOTHING

much² /mʌtʃ/ adv. **1** to a great degree: *I don't like her very much.* Niezbyt ją lubię. ◇ *Do you see Sashi much?* ◇ *Do you see much of Sashi?* ◇ *much taller/prettier/harder* ◇ *much more interesting/unusual* ◇ *much more quickly/happily* ◇ *You ate* ***much more*** *than me.* ◇ *We are very much looking forward to meeting you.* Bardzo się cieszymy na wspólne spotkanie. ◇ *Do you go to the cinema much?* Czy często chodzisz do kina? ▶ **bardzo, znacznie, (o) wiele 2** [with past participles used as adjectives] very: *a much-needed* (bardzo potrzebny) *rest* ▶ **bardzo**

muck¹ /mʌk/ noun [U] **1** the waste from farm animals, used to make plants grow better ▶ **gnój, nawóz** ℹ Częściej stosuje się słowo **manure. 2** (Brit., informal) dirt or mud ▶ **brud, błoto**

muck² /mʌk/ verb (informal)
PHR V **muck about/around** to behave in a silly way or to waste time: *Stop mucking around and come and help me!* ▶ **wygłupiać/wałkonić się**
muck about/around with sth (Brit., informal) to do sth, especially to a machine, so that it does not work correctly: *Who's mucking around with my radio?* ▶ **(z)majstrować przy czymś** SYN **mess about/around**
muck sb about/around (Brit., informal) to treat sb badly, especially by changing your mind a lot, or by not being honest: *They've really mucked us about over our car insurance.* ▶ **omamiać kogoś, robić kogoś w konia** SYN **mess sb about/around**
muck sth up to do sth badly; to spoil sth: *I was so nervous that I completely mucked up my interview.* ▶ **partaczyć/zaprzepaszczać coś**

mucky /ˈmʌki/ adj. (especially Brit., informal) dirty: *mucky hands* ▶ **umorusany**

mucus /ˈmjuːkəs/ noun [U] (formal) a sticky substance that is produced in some parts of the body, especially the nose ▶ **śluz**
■ **mucous** /ˈmjuːkəs/ adj.: *mucous glands* ▶ **śluzowy**

🔑 **mud** /mʌd/ noun [U] soft, wet earth: *He came home from the football match* ***covered in mud.*** ▶ **błoto**

muddle /ˈmʌdl/ verb [T] **1 muddle sth (up)** to put things in the wrong place or order or to make them untidy: *Try not to* ***get*** *those papers* ***muddled up.*** ▶ **mieszać, plątać 2 muddle sb (up)** to confuse sb: *I do my homework and schoolwork in separate books so that I don't* ***get muddled up.*** ▶ **mieszać komuś w głowie**
PHR V **muddle along** (especially Brit.) to continue doing sth without any clear plan or purpose: *We can't just keep muddling along like this.* ▶ **kontynuować bezsensownie**
muddle through to achieve your aims even though you do not know exactly what you are doing and do not have the correct equipment, knowledge, etc.: *We'll muddle through somehow.* ▶ **jakoś dawać sobie radę**
■ **muddle** noun [C,U]: *If you* ***get in a muddle,*** *I'll help you.* ◇ *Your room's in a terrible muddle.* W twoim pokoju jest okropny bałagan. ▶ **zamęt, plątanina, gmatwanina** | **muddled** adj. ▶ **poplątany, pogmatwany**

ˌmuddle-ˈheaded adj. confused or with confused ideas: *muddle-headed thinkers* ▶ **rozkojarzony**

muddy /ˈmʌdi/ adj. (**muddier**; **muddiest**) full of or covered in mud: *muddy boots* ◇ *It's very muddy down by the river.* ▶ **błotnisty, zabłocony**

mudguard /ˈmʌdgɑːd/ noun [C] a curved cover over the wheel of a bicycle or motorbike ▶ **błotnik**

muesli /ˈmjuːzli/ noun [U] food made of grains, nuts, dried fruit, etc. that you eat with milk for breakfast ▶ **muesli**

muffin /ˈmʌfɪn/ noun [C] **1** (US ˌ**English** ˈ**muffin**) a type of bread roll often eaten hot with butter ▶ **rodzaj pieczywa** (*okrągła, płaska bułka*) **2** a type of small cake ▶ **rodzaj ciasteczka** ➲ picture at **cake**

muffle /ˈmʌfl/ verb [T] to make a sound quieter and more difficult to hear: *He put his hand over his mouth to muffle his laughter.* ▶ **tłumić**
■ **muffled** adj.: *I heard muffled voices outside.* ▶ **przytłumiony, stłumiony**

muffler (US) = SILENCER

mug¹ /mʌg/ noun [C] **1** a large cup with straight sides and a handle: *a coffee mug* ◇ *a mug of tea* ▶ **kubek 2** (informal) a person who seems stupid ▶ **naiwniak, frajer**

mug² /mʌg/ verb [T] (**mugging**; **mugged**) to attack and steal from sb in the street: *Keep your wallet out of sight or you'll* ***get mugged.*** ▶ **napaść i obrabować**
■ **mugger** noun [C] ▶ **napastnik (uliczny), rabuś (uliczny)** ➲ note at **thief** | **mugging** noun [C,U]: *The mugging took place around midnight.* ▶ **rabunek uliczny, napaść uliczna**

muggy /ˈmʌgi/ adj. (used about the weather) warm and slightly wet in an unpleasant way ▶ (*powietrze*) **duszny, parny**

Muhammad (also **Mohammed**) /məˈhæmɪd/ noun [sing.] the **prophet** who started the religion of Islam ▶ **Mahomet**

mule /mjuːl/ noun [C] an animal that is used for carrying heavy loads and whose parents are a horse and a **donkey** ▶ **muł**

mull /mʌl/ verb
PHR V **mull sth over** to think about sth carefully and for a long time: *Don't ask me for a decision right now. I'll have to mull it over.* ▶ **przemyśliwać coś**

mulled /mʌld/ adj. [only before a noun] **mulled** wine has been mixed with sugar and spices and heated ▶ (*wino*) **grzany**

multi- /ˈmʌlti/ [in compounds] more than one; many: *multi-coloured* ◇ *a multi-ethnic society* ◇ *a multimillionaire* multimilioner ▶ **wielo-, różno-**

multicultural /ˌmʌltiˈkʌltʃərəl/ adj. for or including people of many different races, languages, religions and customs: *a multicultural society* ▶ **wielokulturowy**

multilateral /ˌmʌltiˈlætərəl/ adj. involving more than two groups of people, countries, etc.: *They signed a multilateral agreement.* ▶ **wielostronny** ➲ look at **unilateral**

multimedia /ˌmʌltiˈmiːdiə/ adj. [only before a noun] using sound, pictures and film on a computer in addition to text on the screen: *multimedia systems/products* ▶ **multimedialny**

multinational¹ /ˌmʌltiˈnæʃnəl/ adj. existing in or involving many countries: *multinational companies* ▶ **wielonarodowy, wielopaństwowy**

multinational² /ˌmʌltiˈnæʃnəl/ noun [C] a large and powerful company that operates in several different countries: *The company is owned by Ford, the US multinational.* ▶ **firma międzynarodowa**

multiple¹ /ˈmʌltɪpl/ adj. [only before a noun] involving many people or things or having many parts: *a multiple pile-up on the motorway* karambol na autostradzie ◇ *to receive multiple injuries* odnieść liczne obrażenia ▶ **złożony, wielokrotny**

multiple² /ˈmʌltɪpl/ noun [C] a number that contains another number an exact number of times: *12, 18 and 24 are multiples of 6.* ▶ **wielokrotność**

ˌmultiple-ˈchoice adj. (used about exam questions) showing several different answers from which you have to choose the right one: *a multiple-choice test* ▶ (*test*) **wielokrotnego wyboru**

multiple sclerosis /ˌmʌltɪpl skləˈrəʊsɪs/ noun [U] (abbr. **MS** /ˌem ˈes/) a serious disease which causes you to slow-

M

ly lose control of your body and become less able to move ▶ **stwardnienie rozsiane**

multiplex /ˈmʌltɪpleks/ noun [C] a large cinema with several separate rooms with screens ▶ **multipleks**

multiplication /ˌmʌltɪplɪˈkeɪʃn/ noun [U] the act or process of multiplying ▶ **mnożenie** ➲ look at **division**, **addition**, **subtraction**

ˌmultipliˈcation table (also **table**) noun [C] a list showing the results when a number is multiplied by a set of other numbers, especially 1 to 12, in turn ▶ **tabliczka mnożenia**

multiply /ˈmʌltɪplaɪ/ verb (**multiplying**; **multiplies**; pt, pp **multiplied**) **1** [I,T] **multiply A by B** to increase a number by the number of times mentioned: *2 multiplied by 4 makes 8* ▶ **mnożyć** OPP **divide** **2** [I,T] to increase or make sth increase by a very large amount: *We've multiplied our profits over the last two years.* ▶ **pomnażać (się)**, **zwielokrotniać (się)** **3** [I] (used especially about animals) to increase in number by producing large numbers of young ▶ **rozmnażać się**

multi-purpose /ˌmʌlti ˈpɜːpəs/ adj. that can be used for several different purposes: *a multi-purpose tool/machine* ▶ **wielofunkcyjny**

multiracial /ˌmʌltiˈreɪʃl/ adj. including or involving several different races of people: *a multiracial society* ▶ **wielorasowy**

ˌmulti-storey ˈcar park (also **ˌmulti-ˈstorey**; US **ˈparking garage**) noun [C] a large building with several floors for parking cars in ▶ **parking wielopoziomowy**

multitasking /ˌmʌltiˈtɑːskɪŋ; US -ˈtæsk-/ noun [U] **1** the ability of a computer to operate several programs at the same time ▶ **wielozadaniowość** **2** the activity of doing several things at the same time: *Are women better at multitasking than men?* ▶ **wykonywanie kilku czynności jednocześnie**

multitude /ˈmʌltɪtjuːd; US -tuːd/ noun [C] (formal) a very large number of people or things ▶ **mnóstwo**, **mnogość**

mum /mʌm/ (US **mom** /mɒm/) noun [C] (informal) mother: *Is that your mum?* ◇ *Can I have a drink, Mum?* ▶ **mama** ➲ look at **mummy**

mumble /ˈmʌmbl/ verb [I,T] to speak quietly without opening your mouth properly, so that people cannot hear the words: *I can't hear if you mumble.* ▶ **mamrotać** ➲ look at **mutter**

mummy /ˈmʌmi/ noun [C] (pl. **mummies**) **1** (US **mommy** /ˈmɒmi/) (informal) (used by or to children) mother: *Here comes your mummy now.* ▶ **mamusia** ➲ look at **mum** **2** the dead body of a person or an animal which has been kept by rubbing it with special oils and covering it in cloth ▶ **mumia**

mumps /mʌmps/ noun [U] an infectious disease, especially of children, that causes the neck to swell: *to have/catch (the) mumps* ▶ (*choroba*) **świnka**

munch /mʌntʃ/ verb [I,T] **munch (on sth)** to bite and eat sth noisily: *He sat there munching (on) an apple.* ▶ **chrupać**

mundane /mʌnˈdeɪn/ adj. ordinary; not interesting or exciting: *a mundane job* ▶ **prozaiczny**, **przyziemny**, **pospolity**

municipal /mjuːˈnɪsɪpl/ adj. connected with a town or city that has its own local government: *municipal buildings* ▶ **miejski**, **komunalny**

munitions /mjuːˈnɪʃnz/ noun [pl.] military supplies, especially bombs and guns ▶ **amunicja**, **uzbrojenie**

mural /ˈmjʊərəl/ noun [C] a large picture painted on a wall ▶ **malowidło ścienne**

murder /ˈmɜːdə(r)/ noun **1** [C,U] the crime of killing a person illegally and on purpose: *to commit murder* ◇ *a vicious murder* ◇ *the murder victim* ◇ *the murder weapon* narzędzie zbrodni ▶ **morderstwo** ➲ note at **crime** ➲ look at **manslaughter** **2** [U] (informal) a very difficult or unpleasant experience: *It's murder trying to work when it's as hot as this.* Zmuszać się do pracy w tak upalny dzień – to morderstwo. ▶ **morderstwo**

■ **murder** verb [I,T] ▶ **mordować** ➲ note at **kill** | **murderer** noun [C] ▶ **morder-ca/czyni**

IDM **get away with murder** to do whatever you want without being stopped or punished: *He lets his students get away with murder.* ▶ **robić co tylko chcesz** (*bez skrępowania/bezkarnie*)

murderous /ˈmɜːdərəs/ adj. intending or likely to murder ▶ **morderczy**

murky /ˈmɜːki/ adj. (**murkier**; **murkiest**) dark and unpleasant or dirty: *The water in the river looked very murky.* ◇ (figurative) *According to rumours, the new boss had a murky past.* ▶ **mroczny**, **ciemny**, **brudny**

murmur /ˈmɜːmə(r)/ verb [I,T] to say sth in a low quiet voice: *He murmured a name in his sleep.* ▶ **mruczeć**, **pomrukiwać**, **mówić półgłosem**

■ **murmur** noun [C] **1** the sound of words that are spoken quietly ▶ **mruczenie**, **pomrukiwanie**, **mówienie półgłosem** **2** a low, gentle, continuous sound that is often not very clear ▶ **szemranie**, **pomruk**

muscle /ˈmʌsl/ noun [C,U] one of the parts inside your body that you can make tight or relax in order to produce movement: *Riding a bicycle is good for developing the leg muscles.* ◇ *Lifting weights builds muscle.* ◇ *Don't carry such heavy weights or you'll pull a muscle* (bo naciągniesz sobie mięsień). ▶ **mięsień**

muscular /ˈmʌskjələ(r)/ adj. **1** connected with the muscles: *muscular pain/tissue* ▶ **mięśniowy** **2** having large strong muscles: *a muscular body* ▶ **muskularny**, **umięśniony**

muse /mjuːz/ noun [C] **1** a person or spirit that gives a writer, painter, etc. ideas and the desire to create things ▶ **muza** SYN **inspiration** **2** (**Muse**) (in ancient Greek and Roman stories) one of the nine **goddesses** who encouraged poetry, music and other branches of art and literature ▶ **muza**

■ **muse** verb (formal) **1** [I] **muse (about/on/over/upon sth)** to think carefully about sth for a time, ignoring what is happening around you: *I sat quietly, musing on the events of the day.* ▶ **rozmyślać nad czymś** SYN **ponder** **2** [T] to say sth to yourself in a way that shows you are thinking carefully about it: *'I wonder why?' she mused.* ▶ **zastanawiać się nad czymś**

museum /mjuˈziːəm/ noun [C] a building where collections of valuable and interesting objects are kept and shown to the public: *Have you been to the Science Museum in London?* ▶ **muzeum** ➲ look at **gallery**

mush /mʌʃ/ noun [U, sing.] a soft thick mass or mixture ▶ **papka**, **breja** ⓘ Zwykle wyraża dezaprobatę.

mushroom[1] /ˈmʌʃrʊm; -ruːm/ noun [C] a type of plant which grows very quickly, has a flat or round top and can be eaten as a vegetable: *A mushroom is a type of fungus.* ◇ *mushroom soup* ◇ *to go mushroom picking* iść na grzyby ▶ **grzyb jadalny**, **pieczarka** ➲ picture on **page A13**

> Zbieranie grzybów nie jest popularną formą spędzania czasu w krajach anglojęzycznych. Słowo **mushroom** prawie zawsze oznacza pieczarkę. **Toadstool** to muchomor.

mushroom[2] /ˈmʌʃrʊm; -ruːm/ verb [I] **1** to rapidly grow or increase in number: *We expect the market to mushroom in the next two years.* ▶ **wyrastać jak grzyby po deszczu** **2** (usually **go mushrooming**) to gather mushrooms in a field or wood ▶ **iść na grzyby**

mushy /ˈmʌʃi/ adj. (**mushier**; **mushiest**) **1** soft and thick, like **mush**: *Cook until the fruit is soft but not mushy.* ▶ **brejowaty** **2** (informal) too emotional in a way that is embarrassing: *mushy romantic novels* ▶ **ckliwy** SYN **sentimental**

music /ˈmjuːzɪk/ noun [U] **1** an arrangement of sounds in patterns to be sung or played on instruments: *What sort of music do you like?* ◇ *classical/pop/rock music* ◇ *to write/compose music* ◇ *a music lesson/teacher* ◇ *That poem has been set to music.* Do tego wiersza napisano muzykę. ▶ **muzyka** ➲ note at **instrument**, **pop 2** the written signs that represent the sounds of music: *Can you read music?* ▶ **nuty** ➲ note at **piano**

> **music**
>
> A large group of **musicians** playing **classical music** together on different **instruments** is a **orchestra**. Smaller **ensembles** include a **chamber orchestra**, a **quartet**, a **trio**, a **quintet**, and so on: *She plays (the) cello in a string quartet.* They are directed by a **conductor**. A group of musicians playing pop or jazz is called a **band**/**group**. Music is **composed** by a **composer** and musicians learn to **read music** in order to play it. There are different types of musical **composition**, for example a **symphony** or an **opera**.

musical¹ /ˈmjuːzɪkl/ adj. **1** [only before a noun] connected with music: *Can you play a musical instrument?* ▶ **muzyczny 2** interested in or good at music: *He's very musical.* ▶ **muzykalny 3** having a pleasant sound like music: *a musical voice* ▶ **melodyjny**
■ **musically** /-kli/ adv.: *She is musically gifted.* ▶ **muzycznie**, **muzykalnie**

musical² /ˈmjuːzɪkl/ noun [C] a play or film which has singing and dancing in it ▶ (*spektakl, przedstawienie*) **musical** ➲ look at **opera**

musician /mjuˈzɪʃn/ noun [C] a person who plays a musical instrument or writes music, especially as a job ▶ **muzyk**, **muzykant** ➲ note at **music**

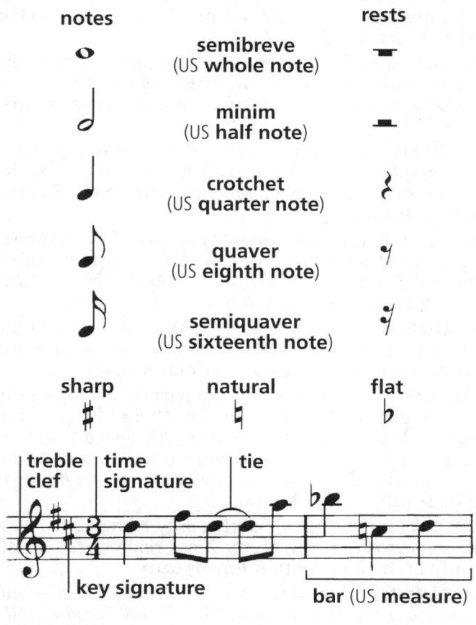

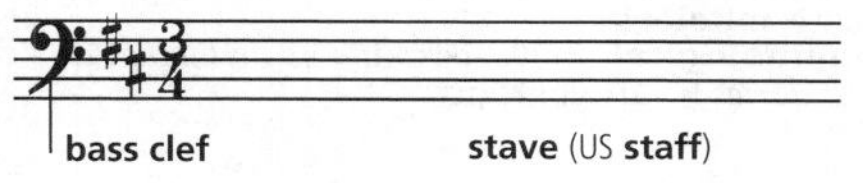

musicology /ˌmjuːzɪˈkɒlədʒi/ noun [U] the study of the history and theory of music ▶ **muzykologia**
■ **musicologist** /ˌmjuːzɪˈkɒlədʒɪst/ noun [C] ▶ **muzykolog**

ˈ**music stand** noun [C] a frame, especially one that you can fold, that is used for holding sheets of music while you play a musical instrument ▶ **pulpit**

musk /mʌsk/ noun [U] a substance with a strong smell that is used in making some **perfumes**. It is produced naturally by a type of male **deer**. ▶ **piżmo**
■ **musky** adj. smelling of or like musk: *a musky perfume* ▶ **piżmowy**

Muslim /ˈmʊzlɪm/ noun [C] a person whose religion is Islam ▶ **muzułman-in/ka**
■ **Muslim** (also **Moslem** /ˈmɒzləm/) adj.: *Muslim traditions/beliefs* ▶ **muzułmański**

muslin /ˈmʌzlɪn/ noun [U] a type of thin cotton cloth ▶ **muślin**

mussel /ˈmʌsl/ noun [C] a **shellfish** that you can eat, with a black shell in two parts ▶ **małż jadalny**

must¹ /məst; strong form mʌst/ modal verb (negative **must not**; short form **mustn't** /ˈmʌsnt/) **1** (used for saying that it is necessary that sth happens): *I must remember to go to the bank today.* ◇ *You mustn't* (nie wolno) *take photographs in here. It's forbidden.* ▶ **musieć**, **potrzebować**

> **Must** czy **have to**? **Must** wyraża osobiste odczucia osoby mówiącej: *I must wash my hair tonight.* Natomiast **have to** używane jest w kontekście prawa, reguł lub opinii wyrażanej przez osobę reprezentującą władzę: *Children have to go to school.* ◇ *My doctor says I have to give up smoking.* **Must** stosuje się też w pisanym języku formalnym w celu formułowania praw lub reguł: *Mobile phones must be switched off in the library.* Uważaj na formę **mustn't**, która znaczy „nie wolno": *You mustn't use a dictionary in the exam.* Konstrukcja **don't have to** znaczy „nie musisz": *This book is easy to understand, so you don't have to use a dictionary.*

2 (used for saying that you feel sure that sth is true): *Have something to eat. You must be hungry* (z pewnością jesteś głodny). ◇ *I can't find my watch. I must have left it at home.* ◇ *There's a lot of noise from next door. They must be having a party.* Musi się tam odbywać jakieś przyjęcie. ▶ **musieć**, **(być) pewnie**

> Kiedy, według nas, coś jest prawdziwe w danej chwili, używamy **must** z bezokolicznikiem: *I can smell smoke. There must be a fire somewhere.* Kiedy, według nas, coś było prawdziwe w przeszłości, używamy **must have** z imiesłowem przeszłym (*past participle*): *It's wet outside. It must have rained last night.* W takich zdaniach **must have** wymawia się /mʌstəv/.

3 (used for giving sb advice): *You really must see that film. It's wonderful.* ▶ **musieć**

must² /mʌst/ noun [C] a thing that you strongly recommend: *This book is a must for all science fiction fans.* ▶ **konieczność**

mustache (US) = MOUSTACHE

mustard /ˈmʌstəd/ noun [U] a cold yellow or brown sauce that tastes hot and is eaten in small amounts with meat ▶ **musztarda**

muster /ˈmʌstə(r)/ verb **1** [T] **muster sth (up)** to find as much support, courage, etc. as you can: *We mustered what support we could for the plan.* ◇ *She left the room **with all the dignity she could muster*** (jaką zdołała z siebie wykrzesać). ▶ **zbierać**, **zdobywać** SYN **summon** **2** [I,T] to come together, or bring people, especially soldiers, together for example for military action: *The*

M

troops mustered. ◇ *The force mustered 1000 strong.* ◇ *to muster an army* ▶ **zbierać (się)** SYN **gather**

musty /ˈmʌsti/ adj. (**mustier**; **mustiest**) having an unpleasant old or wet smell because of a lack of fresh air: *The rooms in the old house were dark and musty.* ▶ **stęchły**, **spleśniały**, **zbutwiały**

mutant /ˈmjuːtənt/ noun [C] a living thing that is different from other living things of the same type because of a change in its **genetic** structure ▶ **mutant**

mutate /mjuːˈteɪt; US ˈmjuːt-/ verb **mutate (into sth) 1** [I,T] to develop or make sth develop a new form or structure, because of a **genetic** change: *the ability of the virus to mutate into new forms* ◇ *mutated genes* ▶ **mutować (się)**, **przekształcać się (w coś) 2** [I] to change into a new form: *Rhythm and blues mutated into rock and roll.* ▶ **przekształcać się (w coś)** ➲ look at **mutation**

mutation /mjuːˈteɪʃn/ noun [C,U] a change in the **genetic** structure of a living or developing thing; an example of such a change: *mutations caused by radiation* ▶ **mutacja**

mute /mjuːt/ adj. **1** not speaking: *a look of mute appeal* ◇ *The child sat mute in the corner of the room.* ▶ **niemy**, **oniemiały** SYN **silent 2** (old-fashioned) (used about a person) unable to speak ▶ **niemy** SYN **dumb**

muted /ˈmjuːtɪd/ adj. **1** (used about colours or sounds) not bright or loud; soft ▶ **pastelowy**, **łagodny**; **przytłumiony 2** (used about a feeling or reaction) not strongly expressed: *muted criticism* ◇ *a muted response* ▶ **stłumiony**, **powściągliwy**

mutilate /ˈmjuːtɪleɪt/ verb [T, usually passive] to damage sb's body very badly, often by cutting off parts ▶ **okaleczać**, **masakrować**

■ **mutilation** /ˌmjuːtɪˈleɪʃn/ noun [C,U] ▶ **okaleczenie**, **masakrowanie**

mutiny /ˈmjuːtəni/ noun [C,U] (pl. **mutinies**) an act of a group of people, especially sailors or soldiers, refusing to obey the person who is in command: *There'll be a mutiny if conditions don't improve.* ▶ **bunt**, **rewolta**

■ **mutiny** verb [I] ▶ **buntować się**, **wszczynać rewoltę**

mutter /ˈmʌtə(r)/ verb [I,T] to speak in a low, quiet and often angry voice that is difficult to hear: *He muttered something about being late and left the room.* ▶ **mamrotać**, **mruczeć** ➲ look at **mumble**

mutton /ˈmʌtn/ noun [U] the meat from an adult sheep: *a leg/shoulder of mutton* udo/łopatka barani-e/a ▶ **baranina** ➲ note at **meat**, **sheep**

mutual /ˈmjuːtʃuəl/ adj. **1** (used about a feeling or an action) felt or done equally by both people involved: *We have **a mutual agreement** to help each other out when necessary.* ◇ *I just can't stand her and I'm sure **the feeling is mutual.*** ▶ **wzajemny**, **obustronny 2** [only before a noun] shared by two or more people: *mutual interests* ◇ *It seems that Jane is **a mutual friend** of ours.* ▶ **wspólny**

■ **mutually** /-tʃuəli/ adv.: *The two views are not mutually exclusive* (nie są ze sobą sprzeczne). ▶ **wzajemnie**, **obustronnie**

muzzle /ˈmʌzl/ noun [C] **1** the nose and mouth of an animal, especially a dog or a horse ▶ **pysk**, **morda**, **ryj** ➲ picture on **page A10 2** a cover made of leather or wire that is put over an animal's nose and mouth so that it cannot bite ▶ **kaganiec 3** the open end of a gun where the bullets come out ▶ **wylot lufy**

■ **muzzle** verb [T, usually passive]: *Dogs must be kept muzzled.* ▶ **nakładać kaganiec**

MW abbr. **1 medium wave**; a band of radio waves with a length of between 100 and 1000 metres ▶ **fale średnie 2** (pl. **MW**) **megawatt(s)** ▶ **megawat**

my /maɪ/ determiner **1** of or belonging to me: *This is my husband, Jim.* ◇ *My favourite colour is blue.* ▶ **mój** ➲ look at **mine[1] 2** (used before a noun or an adjective as a way of talking to sb): *My dear Anne, ...* ◇ *Goodbye, my darling.* ▶ **mój 3** (used in exclamations): *My goodness* (mój Boże)*! Look at the time.* ▶ **mój**

myriad /ˈmɪriəd/ noun [C] (literary) an extremely large number of sth: *Designs are available in a myriad of colours.* ▶ **miriady**

■ **myriad** adj.: *the myriad problems of modern life* ▶ **liczny**

myself /maɪˈself/ pron. **1** (used when the person who does an action is also affected by it): *I looked at myself in the mirror.* ◇ *I felt rather pleased with myself.* ▶ **się**, **siebie 2** (used to emphasize the person who does the action): *I'll speak to her myself.* ◇ *I'll do it myself.* ▶ **(ja) sam/a**, **osobiście**

IDM **(all) by myself 1** alone: *I live by myself.* ▶ **sam/a** ➲ note at **alone 2** without help: *I painted the house all by myself.* ▶ **sam/a**

mysterious /mɪˈstɪəriəs/ adj. **1** that you do not understand or cannot explain; strange: *Several people reported seeing mysterious lights in the sky.* ▶ **tajemniczy 2** (used about a person) keeping sth secret or refusing to explain sth: *They're being very mysterious about where they're going this evening.* ▶ **skryty**, **tajemniczy**

■ **mysteriously** adv. ▶ **tajemniczo**

mystery /ˈmɪstri/ noun (pl. **mysteries**) **1** [C] a thing that you cannot understand or explain: *The cause of the accident is a complete mystery.* ◇ ***It's a mystery to me** what my daughter sees in her boyfriend.* ▶ **tajemnica 2** [U] the quality of being strange and secret and full of things that are difficult to explain: *There's a lot of mystery surrounding this case.* ▶ **tajemniczość 3** [C] a story, film or play in which crimes or strange events are only explained at the end: *Agatha Christie was a prolific writer of (murder) mysteries.* ▶ **opowiadanie, film itp., w którym niezwykłe wydarzenia są wyjaśnione dopiero na końcu**

mystic /ˈmɪstɪk/ noun [C] a person who spends their life developing their spirit and communicating with God or a god ▶ **misty-k/czka**

mystical /ˈmɪstɪkl/ (also **mystic**) adj. connected with the spirit; strange and wonderful: *Watching the sun set over the island was an almost mystical experience.* ▶ **mistyczny**

mysticism /ˈmɪstɪsɪzəm/ noun [U] the belief that you can reach complete truth and knowledge of God or gods by prayer, thought and development of the spirit: *Eastern mysticism* ▶ **mistycyzm**

mystify /ˈmɪstɪfaɪ/ verb [T] (**mystifying**; **mystifies**; pt, pp **mystified**) to make sb confused because they cannot understand sth: *I was mystified by the strange note he'd left behind.* ▶ **zmieszać**, **zbić z tropu**

mystique /mɪˈstiːk/ noun [U, sing.] the quality of being mysterious or secret that makes sb/sth seem interesting or attractive ▶ **mistyka**, **aura tajemniczości**

myth /mɪθ/ noun [C] **1** a story from past times, especially one about gods and men of courage. **Myths** often explain natural or historical events. ▶ **mit** SYN **legend 2** an idea or story which many people believe but that does not exist or is false: *The idea that money makes you happy is a myth.* ▶ **mit**, **mistyfikacja**

mythical /ˈmɪθɪkl/ adj. **1** existing only in **myths** (1): *mythical beasts/heroes* ▶ **mityczny 2** not real or true; existing only in the imagination ▶ **mityczny**

mythology /mɪˈθɒlədʒi/ noun [U] very old stories and the beliefs contained in them: *Greek and Roman mythology* ▶ **mitologia**

■ **mythological** /ˌmɪθəˈlɒdʒɪkl/ adj.: *mythological figures/stories* ▶ **mitologiczny**

Nn

N, n /en/ noun [C,U] (pl. **Ns**; **ns**; **N's**; **n's** /enz/) the 14th letter of the English alphabet: *'Nicholas' begins with (an) 'N'.* ▶ **litera** *n*

N (US **No.**) = NORTH[1,2], NORTHERN: *N Yorkshire*

naff /næf/ adj. (Brit., informal) lacking style, taste or quality: *There was a naff band playing.* ▶ **w złym guście**, **niemodny**, **do kitu**

nag /næg/ verb (**nagging**; **nagged**) **1** [I,T] **nag (at) sb** to continuously complain to sb about their behaviour or to ask them to do sth many times: *My parents are always nagging (at) me to work harder.* ▶ **zrzędzić**; **łajać**, **nie dawać komuś spokoju** **2** [T] to worry or trouble sb continuously: *a nagging doubt/headache* ▶ **nękać**

nail /neɪl/ noun [C] **1** the thin hard layer that covers the ends of your fingers and toes: *fingernails/toenails* ▶ **paznokieć** **2** a small thin piece of metal that is used for holding pieces of wood together, hanging pictures on, etc.: *to hammer in a nail* ▶ **gwóźdź** ➲ picture at **bolt**
■ **nail** verb [T] ▶ **przybijać gwoździem**
IDM **hit the nail on the head** → HIT[1]
PHR V **nail sb down (to sth)** to make a person say clearly what they want or intend to do: *She says she'll visit us in the summer but I can't nail her down to a definite date.* ▶ **wyciągać od kogoś** (*np. fakty*)

'nail brush noun [C] a small brush for cleaning your nails ▶ **szczoteczka do paznokci** ➲ picture at **brush**

'nail clippers noun [pl.] a small tool for cutting the nails on your fingers and toes ▶ **cążki do obcinania paznokci**

'nail file noun [C] a small metal tool with a rough surface that you use for shaping your nails ▶ **pilnik do paznokci**

'nail polish (Brit. also **'nail varnish**) noun [U] a liquid that people paint on their nails to give them colour ▶ **lakier do paznokci**

'nail scissors noun [pl.] small scissors for cutting your nails: *a pair of nail scissors* ◇ *Have you got any nail scissors?* ▶ **nożyczki do paznokci**

naive (also **naïve**) /naɪ'iːv/ adj. without enough experience of life and too ready to believe or trust other people: *I was too naive to realize what was happening.* ◇ *a naive remark/question/view* ▶ **naiwny** SYN **innocent**
■ **naively** (also **naïvely**) adv.: *She naively accepted the first price he offered.* ▶ **naiwnie** | **naivety** (also **naïvety** /naɪ'iːvəti/) noun [U] ▶ **naiwność**

naked /'neɪkɪd/ adj. **1** not wearing any clothes: *He came to the door naked except for a towel.* ◇ *naked shoulders/arms* ▶ **nagi**, **goły** ➲ look at **bare**, **nude** **2** [only before a noun] (used about sth that is usually covered) not covered: *a naked flame/bulb/light* ▶ **odkryty**, **goły** **3** [only before a noun] (used about emotions, etc.) clearly shown or expressed in a way that is often shocking: *naked aggression/ambition/fear* ▶ **nagi**, **obnażony**
IDM **the naked eye** the normal power of your eyes without the help of glasses, a machine, etc.: *Bacteria are too small to be seen with the naked eye.* ▶ (*przen.*) **gołe oko**

name[1] /neɪm/ noun **1** [C] a word or words by which sb/sth is known: *What's your name, please?* ◇ *Do you know the name of this flower?* ▶ **imię (i nazwisko)**, **nazwa** **2** [sing.] an opinion that people have of a person or thing: *That area of London has rather a bad name.* ▶ (*dobre/złe*) **imię**, **reputacja** SYN **reputation** **3** [C] a famous person: *All the big names in show business were invited to the party.* ▶ (*znana osoba*) **sława**, **osobistość**
IDM **by name** using the name of sb/sth: *It's a big school but the head teacher knows all the children by name.* ▶ **z imienia/nazwiska**
call sb names → CALL[1]
in the name of sb; **in sb's name** **1** for sb/sth; officially belonging to sb: *The contract is in my name.* ◇ *The table is reserved in the name of Shea.* ▶ **na czyjeś nazwisko** **2** representing a certain group of people ▶ **w imieniu kogoś**
in the name of sth (used to give a reason or excuse for an action, even when what you are doing might be wrong): *They acted in the name of democracy.* ▶ **w imię czegoś**
make a name for yourself; **make your name** to become well known and respected: *She made a name for herself as a journalist.* ▶ **wyrabiać sobie (dobre) imię**, **stawać się sławnym**

names

First name (w USA często **given name**) oznacza imię nadane dziecku przez rodziców po urodzeniu. W krajach chrześcijańskich czasami nazywa się je **Christian name**. Rodzice mogą dziecku również nadać drugie, a nawet trzecie imię, **middle name(s)**, które jest/są używane tylko w dokumentach urzędowych, wówczas nazywa(ją) się **forenames**. Słowo **surname** to „nazwisko". Rzadziej używane synonimy to **last name** i **family name**. Po zamążpójściu kobieta może zmienić nazwisko na nazwisko męża; jej nazwisko panieńskie to **maiden name**.

name[2] /neɪm/ verb [T] **1** **name sb/sth (after sb)** to give sb/sth a name: *Columbia was named after Christopher Columbus.* ▶ **nazywać (po kimś)**

Uwaga! Mówiąc o tym, jak ktoś się nazywa, używa się zwrotu **be called**: *The baby is called Dan and his brother is Joe.*

2 to say what the name of sb/sth is: *The journalist refused to name the person who had given her the information.* ◇ *Can you name all the planets?* ▶ **nazywać**, **wymieniać imię/nazwisko/nazwę** **3** to state sth exactly: *Name your price – we'll pay it!* ▶ **wyznaczać**

nameless /'neɪmləs/ adj. **1** without a name or with a name that you do not know ▶ **bezimienny**, **nieznany** **2** whose name is kept a secret: *a well-known public figure who shall* ***remain nameless*** (której nazwisko nie zostanie wymienione) ▶ **anonimowy** SYN **anonymous** **3** not easily described or explained, e.g. because it is so terrible: *the nameless horrors of war* ▶ **niesłychany**

namely /'neɪmli/ adv. (used for giving more detail about what you are saying) that is to say: *There is only one person who can overrule the death sentence, namely the President.* ▶ **mianowicie**

namesake /'neɪmseɪk/ noun [C] a person who has the same name as another ▶ **imienni-k/czka**

nana /'nɑːnə/ noun [C] **1** (Brit. also **nan**, **nanna**) (used by children, especially as a form of address) a grandmother ▶ **babcia**, **babunia** ➲ look at **granny** **2** (old-fashioned, Brit., informal) a silly person: *I felt a right nana.* ▶ **kretyn/ka**

nanny /'næni/ noun [C] (pl. **nannies**) a woman whose job is to look after a family's children and who usually lives in the family home ▶ **niania**

'nanny goat noun [C] a female **goat** ▶ **koza** ➲ look at **billy goat**

nanometre (US **nanometer**) /'nænəʊmiːtə(r)/ noun [C] (abbr. **nm**) one thousand millionth of a metre ▶ **nanometr**

nanotechnology /ˌnænəʊtek'nɒlədʒi/ noun [U] the branch of technology that deals with structures that are less than 100 **nanometres** long. Scientists often build these structures using individual **molecules** of substances. ▶ **nanotechnologia**

nap /næp/ noun [C] a short sleep that you have during the day ▶ **drzemka** ➲ look at **snooze**
■ **nap** verb [I] (**napping**; **napped**) ▶ **drzemać**

nape /neɪp/ noun [sing.] the back part of your neck ▶ **kark**

napkin /ˈnæpkɪn/ noun [C] a piece of cloth or paper that you use when you are eating to protect your clothes or for cleaning your hands and mouth: *a paper napkin* ▶ **serwetka** SYN **serviette**

nappy /ˈnæpi/ noun [C] (pl. **nappies**) (US **diaper** /ˈdaɪəpə(r)/) a piece of soft thick cloth or paper that a baby or very young child wears around its bottom and between its legs: *Does his nappy need changing?* ◇ *disposable* (jednorazowe) *nappies* ▶ **pieluszka**

narcissism /ˈnɑːsɪsɪzəm/ noun [U] (formal) the habit of admiring yourself too much, especially your appearance ▶ **narcyzm**
■ **narcissistic** /ˌnɑːsɪˈsɪstɪk/ adj. ▶ **narcystyczny**

narcotic /nɑːˈkɒtɪk/ noun [C] **1** a powerful illegal drug that affects your mind in a harmful way ▶ **narkotyk 2** a substance or drug that relaxes you, stops pain, or makes you sleep ▶ **narkotyk**; **środek nasenny**
■ **narcotic** adj. ▶ **narkotyczny**

narrate /nəˈreɪt/ verb [T] (formal) to tell a story ▶ **opowiadać**
■ **narration** /nəˈreɪʃn/ noun [C,U] ▶ **opowiadanie**

narrative /ˈnærətɪv/ noun (formal) **1** [C] the description of events in a story ▶ **opowiadanie 2** [U] the process or skill of telling a story ▶ **narracja**

narrator /nəˈreɪtə(r)/ noun [C] the person who tells a story or explains what is happening in a play, film, etc. ▶ **narrator**

narrow¹ /ˈnærəʊ/ adj. **1** having only a short distance from side to side: *The bridge is too narrow for two cars to pass.* ▶ **wąski** OPP **wide**, **broad 2** by a small amount: *That was a very narrow escape* (to było uniknięcie nieszczęścia o włos). *You were lucky.* ◇ *a narrow defeat/victory* nieznaczna porażka/ledwo zdobyte zwycięstwo ▶ **nieznaczny 3** not large: *a narrow circle of friends* ▶ **wąski**
■ **narrowness** noun [U] ▶ **wąskość**; **ograniczoność**

narrow² /ˈnærəʊ/ verb [I,T] to become or make sth narrower: *The road narrows in 50 metres.* ◇ *He narrowed his eyes at her.* ▶ **zwężać (się)**
PHR V **narrow sth down** to make a list of things smaller: *The police have narrowed down their list of suspects to three.* ▶ **zawężać**

narrowly /ˈnærəʊli/ adv. only by a small amount ▶ **ledwo ledwo**

ˌnarrow-ˈminded adj. not willing to listen to new ideas or to the opinions of other people ▶ **ograniczony**, **o ciasnym umyśle** OPP **broad-minded**, **open-minded**

nasal /ˈneɪzl/ adj. **1** connected with the nose: *a nasal spray* ▶ **nosowy 2** (used about sb's voice) produced partly through the nose ▶ **nosowy**

nasty /ˈnɑːsti; US ˈnæsti/ adj. (**nastier**; **nastiest**) **1** very bad or unpleasant: *a nasty accident* ◇ *I had a nasty feeling he would follow me.* ◇ *a nasty bend in the road* ▶ **groźny**, **poważny**, **nieprzyjemny 2** ugly or unpleasant: *What's that nasty smell in this cupboard?* ▶ **niemiły**, **paskudny 3** angry or aggressive: *When she was asked to leave she* ***got/turned nasty.*** ▶ **niebezpieczny**, **groźny**, **złośliwy 4** unkind ▶ **paskudny**, **złośliwy**
■ **nastily** adv. ▶ **paskudnie**; **złośliwie** | **nastiness** noun [U] ▶ **złośliwość**

nation /ˈneɪʃn/ noun [C] a country or all the people in a country: *a summit of the leaders of seven nations* ▶ **państwo**, **naród** ➲ note at **country**

national¹ /ˈnæʃnəl/ adj. connected with all of a country; typical of a particular country: *Here is today's national and international news.* ◇ *a national newspaper* ◇ *national costume* ▶ **narodowy**, **państwowy** ➲ look at **international**, **regional**, **local**
■ **nationally** /-nəli/ adv. ▶ **po całym kraju**

national² /ˈnæʃnəl/ noun [C, usually pl.] (formal) a citizen of a particular country ▶ **obywatel/ka**

ˌnational ˈanthem noun [C] the official song of a country that is played at public events ▶ **hymn narodowy**

the **ˌNational ˈHealth Service** noun [sing.] (abbr. **NHS** /ˌen eɪtʃ ˈes/) (Brit.) the system that provides free or cheap medical care for everyone in Britain and that is paid for by taxes ▶ (*w Wlk. Br.*) **państwowa służba zdrowia** ➲ look at **health service**

ˌNational Inˈsurance noun [U] (abbr. **NI**) (Brit.) the system of payments that have to be made by employers and employees to the government to help people who are ill, unemployed, old, etc.: *to pay National Insurance contributions* ▶ **system ubezpieczeń społecznych**

nationalise = NATIONALIZE

nationalism /ˈnæʃnəlɪzəm/ noun [U] **1** the desire of a group of people who share the same race, culture, language, etc. to form an independent country ▶ **nacjonalizm 2** a feeling of love or pride for your own country; a feeling that your country is better than any other ▶ **nacjonalizm**

nationalist /ˈnæʃnəlɪst/ noun [C] a person who wants their country or region to become independent: *a Welsh nationalist* ▶ **nacjonalist(k)a**

nationalistic /ˌnæʃnəˈlɪstɪk/ adj. having strong feelings of love for or pride in your own country so that you think it is better than any other ▶ **nacjonalistyczny** ⓘ **Nationalistic** zwykle ma wydźwięk krytyczny, oznaczający, że czyjeś uczucia lub duma narodowa są zbyt silne.

nationality /ˌnæʃəˈnæləti/ noun [C,U] (pl. **nationalities**) the state of being legally a citizen of a particular country: *to have French nationality* ◇ *students of many nationalities* ◇ *to have* ***dual nationality*** (podwójne obywatelstwo) ◇ *Am I eligible to take out British nationality?* Czy spełniłem warunki, żeby otrzymać obywatelstwo brytyjskie? ▶ **narodowość**, **obywatelstwo**

nationalize (also **-ise**) /ˈnæʃnəlaɪz/ verb [T] to put a company or organization under the control of the government ▶ **upaństwawiać**, **nacjonalizować** OPP **privatize**
■ **nationalization** (also **-isation**) /ˌnæʃnəlaɪˈzeɪʃn; US -ləˈz-/ noun [U] ▶ **upaństwowienie**, **nacjonalizacja**

ˌnational ˈpark noun [C] a large area of beautiful land that is protected by the government so that the public can enjoy it ▶ **park narodowy**

ˌnational ˈservice noun [U] the period of time that a young person must spend in the army, navy, etc. of their country: *to do national service* ▶ **zasadnicza służba wojskowa**

nationwide /ˌneɪʃnˈwaɪd/ adj. over the whole of a country: *The police launched a nationwide hunt for the killer.* ▶ **ogólnokrajowy**
■ **nationwide** adv. ▶ **w całym kraju**

native¹ /ˈneɪtɪv/ adj. **1** [only before a noun] connected with the place where you were born or where you have always lived: *your native language/country/city* ◇ *native Londoners* ▶ **rodzinny**, **ojczysty 2** [only before a noun] connected with the people who originally lived in a country before other people, especially white people, came to live there: *native art/dance* ▶ **tubylczy** ⓘ Uwaga! Słowo **native** w tym znaczeniu jest czasem uważane za obraźliwe. **3 native (to ...)** (used about an animal or plant) living or growing naturally in a particular place: *This plant is native to South America.* ◇ *a native species/habitat* ▶ **rodzimy**, **pochodzący skądś**

native² /ˈneɪtɪv/ noun [C] **1** a person who was born in a particular place: *a native of New York* ▶ **człowiek miejscowy**, **tubylec 2** [usually pl.] (old-fashioned) the people who were living in Africa, America, etc. originally, before the Europeans arrived there ▶ **krajowiec**, **tubylec** ℹ Uwaga! Słowo **native** w tym znaczeniu obecnie uważa się za obraźliwe. **3** an animal or plant that lives or grows naturally in a particular place: *The koala is a native of Australia* (pochodzi z Australii). ▶ **rodzimy mieszkaniec itp.**

ˌNative Aˈmerican (also **American Indian**) adj. of a member of the race of people who were the original people to live in America ▶ **indiański**
■ **ˌNative Aˈmerican** noun [C] ▶ **(rdzenn-y/a) Indianin/ka**

ˌnative ˈspeaker noun [C] a person who speaks a language as their first language and has not learnt it as a foreign language: *All our Spanish teachers are native speakers.* ▶ **osoba mówiąca jakimś językiem od urodzenia**

nativity /nəˈtɪvəti/ noun **1** (**the Nativity**) [sing.] the birth of Jesus Christ, celebrated by Christians at Christmas ▶ **narodzenie Chrystusa 2** [C] a picture or a model of the baby Jesus Christ and the place where he was born ▶ **narodzenie Chrystusa**, **szopka**

NATO (also **Nato**) /ˈneɪtəʊ/ abbr. **North Atlantic Treaty Organization**; a group of European countries, Canada and the US, who agree to give each other military help if necessary ▶ **NATO**

natter /ˈnætə(r)/ verb [I] (Brit., informal) to talk a lot about things that are not very important ▶ **paplać**, **gadać** ➲ look at **chat**
■ **natter** noun [sing.]: *to have a natter* ▶ **paplanina**, **gadanina**

🔑 **natural¹** /ˈnætʃrəl/ adj. **1** [only before a noun] existing in nature; not made or caused by humans: *I prefer to see animals in their **natural habitat** rather than in zoos.* ◇ *Britain's **natural resources** include coal, oil and gas.* ◇ *She died of **natural causes.*** ◇ ***natural disasters*** (klęski żywiołowe) *such as earthquakes and floods* ▶ **naturalny 2** usual or normal: *It's natural to feel nervous before an interview.* ▶ **normalny**, **naturalny** OPP **unnatural 3** that you had from birth or that was easy for you to learn: *a natural gift for languages* ▶ **wrodzony**, **rodzimy 4** [only before a noun] (used about parents or their children) related by blood: *She's his stepmother, not his natural mother.* ▶ **naturalny 5** (used after the name of a note to show that the note is neither sharp nor flat. The written symbol is ♮.): *B natural* ▶ **niealterowany** ➲ picture at **music**

natural² /ˈnætʃrəl/ noun [C] a normal musical note, not its sharp or flat form. The written symbol is ♮. ▶ **nuta niealterowana**

ˌnatural ˈhistory noun [U] the study of plants and animals ▶ **przyrodoznawstwo**

naturalist /ˈnætʃrəlɪst/ noun [C] a person who studies plants and animals ▶ **przyrodni-k/czka**

naturalize (also **-ise**) /ˈnætʃrəlaɪz/ verb [T, usually passive] to make sb a citizen of a country where they were not born ▶ **naturalizować**, **nadawać prawa obywatelstwa**
■ **naturalization** (also **-isation**) /ˌnætʃrəlaɪˈzeɪʃn; US -ləˈz-/ noun [U] ▶ **naturalizacja**

🔑 **naturally** /ˈnætʃrəli/ adv. **1** of course; as you would expect: *The team was naturally upset about its defeat.* ▶ **naturalnie**, **oczywiście 2** in a natural way; not forced or artificial: *naturally wavy hair* ◇ *He is naturally a very cheerful person.* ◇ *Working with computers comes naturally to Nick* (leży w jego naturze). ▶ **naturalnie**, **z natury 3** in a way that is relaxed and normal: *Don't try and impress people. Just **act naturally.*** ▶ **swobodnie**, **niewymuszenie**, **naturalnie**

🔑 **nature** /ˈneɪtʃə(r)/ noun **1** [U] all the plants, animals, etc. in the universe and all the things that happen in it that are not made or caused by people: *the forces of nature* ◇ *the wonders/beauties of nature* ▶ **natura**, **przyroda** ➲ note at **scenery**

> Słowo **nature** w języku angielskim nie ma tak szerokiego znaczenia jak „przyroda" w języku polskim. Nie można powiedzieć ~~*I love walking in the nature*~~. W takich wypadkach trzeba użyć innych wyrazów: *I love walking in **the countryside.*** Lubię spacerować w otoczeniu przyrody. ◇ *We have to protect **the environment.***

2 [C,U] the qualities or character of a person or thing: *He's basically honest **by nature.*** ◇ *The nature of my work is secret* (moja praca ma tajny charakter) *and I cannot discuss it.* ◇ *It's **not in his nature** to be unkind.* ◇ *It's **human nature** never to be completely satisfied.* ▶ **natura**, **usposobienie 3** [sing.] a type of sth: *I'm not very interested in things of that nature.* ◇ *books of a scientific nature* ▶ **rodzaj 4** (**-natured**) [in compounds] having a particular quality or type of character: *a kind-natured man* ◇ *good-natured* dobrego usposobienia ▶ (*określa usposobienie*)
IDM **second nature** → SECOND¹

naughty /ˈnɔːti/ adj. (**naughtier**; **naughtiest**) (especially Brit.) (used when you are talking to or about a child) not obeying: *It was very naughty of you to wander off on your own.* ▶ **niegrzeczny**, **nieposłuszny** ➲ note at **evil**
■ **naughtily** adv. ▶ **niegrzecznie**, **nieposłusznie** | **naughtiness** noun [U] ▶ **niegrzeczne/brzydkie zachowanie**

nausea /ˈnɔːziə/ noun [U] the feeling that you are going to **vomit** ▶ **nudności** ➲ look at **sick**

nauseate /ˈnɔːzieɪt/ verb [T] to cause sb to feel sick or disgusted ▶ **przyprawiać o mdłości**, **zbierać na wymioty**
■ **nauseating** adj. ▶ **obrzydliwy**, **przyprawiający o mdłości**

nauseous /ˈnɔːziəs; ˈnɔːsiəs; US ˈnɔːʃəs/ adj. **1** feeling as if you want to **vomit** ▶ **mający mdłości 2** making you feel as if you want to **vomit**: *a nauseous smell* ▶ **przyprawiający o mdłości**

nautical /ˈnɔːtɪkl/ adj. connected with ships, sailors or sailing ▶ **morski**, **żeglarski**

naval /ˈneɪvl/ adj. connected with the navy: *a naval base/officer/battle* ▶ **morski**, **okrętowy**, **Marynarki Wojennej**

navel /ˈneɪvl/ (also informal **ˈbelly button**) noun [C] the small hole or lump in the middle of your stomach ▶ **pępek** ➲ look at **umbilical cord**

navigable /ˈnævɪgəbl/ adj. (used about a river or narrow area of sea) that boats can sail along ▶ **spławny**, **żeglowny**

navigate /ˈnævɪgeɪt/ verb **1** [I] to use a map, etc. to find your way to somewhere: *If you drive, I'll navigate.* ▶ **pilotować 2** [T] to sail a boat along a river or across a sea ▶ **nawigować**, **żeglować**, **pilotować 3** [I,T] to find your way around on the Internet or on a website ▶
■ **navigator** /-geɪtə(r)/ noun [C] ▶ **nawigator**, **żeglarz** | **navigation** /ˌnævɪˈgeɪʃn/ noun [U] ▶ **nawigacja**, **żegluga**, **pilotowanie**

🔑 **navy** /ˈneɪvi/ noun [C, with sing. or pl. verb] (pl. **navies**) the part of a country's armed forces that fights at sea in times of war: *to join the navy/the Navy* ◇ *Their son is in **the navy/the Navy.*** ▶ **Marynarka Wojenna**, **flota wojenna** ℹ Rzeczownik **navy** w lp może być używany z czasownikami występującymi w lp lub lm: *The Navy is/are intro-*

N

ducing a new warship this year. ➲ note at **war** ➲ look at **air force**, **army**, **merchant navy** ➲ adjective **naval**

ˌnavy ˈblue (also navy) adj. of a very dark blue colour ▶ **granatowy**
■ **ˌnavy ˈblue** noun [U] ▶ **kolor granatowy**

NB (also nb) /ˌen ˈbiː/ abbr. (from Latin) **nota bene**; (used before a written note) take special notice of: *NB There is a charge for reservations.* ▶ **notabene**

NE = NORTH-EAST[1]: *NE Scotland*

near[1] /nɪə(r)/ adj. **1** not far away in time or distance; close: *Let's walk to the library. It's quite near.* ◇ *We're hoping to move to Wales* ***in the near future.*** ◇ *Where's the nearest Post Office?* ◇ *The day of the interview was getting nearer.* ◇ *She was* ***near to tears.*** Była bliska płaczu. ▶ **bliski**, **niedaleki** ➲ note at **nearby**, **next**

> **Close** i **near** często znaczą to samo, ale w niektórych zwrotach nie mogą występować wymiennie: *a close friend/relative* ◇ *the near future* ◇ *a close contest.*

2 (**near-**) [in compounds] almost: *a near-perfect performance* ▶ **prawie**
IDM **close/dear/near to sb's heart** → HEART
a near miss a situation where sth nearly hits you or where sth bad nearly happens: *The bullet flew past his ear. It was a very near miss.* ▶ **uniknięcie czegoś o włos**
or near(est) offer; **ono** (used when you are selling sth) or an amount that is less than but near the amount that you have asked for: *Motorbike for sale. £750 ono.* ▶ (*cena w ofercie*) **do negocjacji**

near[2] /nɪə(r)/ adv., prep. not far away in time or distance; close (to sb/sth): *They live quite near.* ◇ *It's a little village near Cardiff.* ◇ *I wasn't sitting near enough to see.* ▶ **blisko**, **niedaleko**
IDM **nowhere near** → NOWHERE

near[3] /nɪə(r)/ verb [T,I] to get closer to sth in time or distance: *At last we were nearing the end of the project.* ▶ **zbliżać się**

nearby /ˌnɪəˈbaɪ/ adj. not far away in distance: *We went out to a nearby restaurant.* ▶ **(po)bliski**, **sąsiedni**
ⓘ Zwróć uwagę, że **nearby** używa się tylko przed rzeczownikiem. **Near** nie można użyć przed rzeczownikiem w ten sam sposób: *We went out to a restaurant near our house.* ◇ *The restaurant we went to is quite near.*
■ **nearby** adv.: *A new restaurant has opened nearby.* ▶ **blisko**, **niedaleko**

nearly /ˈnɪəli/ adv. almost; not completely or exactly: *It's nearly five years since I've seen him.* ◇ *Linda was so badly hurt she very nearly died.* ◇ *It's not far now. We're nearly there.* ▶ **prawie**
IDM **not nearly** much less than; not at all: *It's not nearly as warm as it was yesterday.* ▶ **bynajmniej (nie)**, **wcale nie**

nearsighted (especially US) = SHORT-SIGHTED (1)

neat /niːt/ adj. **1** arranged or done carefully; tidy and in order: *Please keep your room* ***neat and tidy.*** ◇ *neat rows of figures* ▶ **porządny**, **staranny**, **schludny** **2** (used about a person) liking to keep things tidy and in order: *The new secretary was very neat and efficient.* ▶ **porządny**, **systematyczny** **3** simple but clever: *a neat solution/explanation/idea/trick* ▶ **trafny**, **zgrabny** **4** (US, informal) good; nice: *That's a really neat car!* ▶ **fajny**, **dobry** **5** (US **straight**) (used about an alcoholic drink) on its own, without ice, water or any other liquid: *a neat whisky* ▶ (*alkohol*) **czysty**
■ **neatly** adv.: *neatly folded clothes* ▶ **porządnie**; **systematycznie**; **trafnie** | **neatness** noun [U] ▶ **porządek**; **systematyczność**

neaten /ˈniːtn/ verb [T] to make sth tidy ▶ **porządkować**

necessarily /ˈnesəsərəli; ˌnesəˈserəli/ adv. (used to say that sth cannot be avoided or has to happen): *The number of tickets available is necessarily limited.* ▶ **koniecznie**, **nieodzownie**
IDM **not necessarily** (used to say that sth might be true but is not definitely or always true) ▶ **niekoniecznie**

necessary /ˈnesəsəri; US -seri/ adj. **necessary (for sb/sth) (to do sth)** that is needed for a purpose or a reason: *A good diet is necessary for a healthy life.* ◇ *It's not necessary for you all to come.* ◇ *If necessary I can pick you up after work that day.* ▶ **konieczny**, **potrzebny**, **nieodzowny** SYN **essential** OPP **unnecessary**

necessitate /nəˈsesɪteɪt/ verb [T] (formal) to make sth necessary ▶ **wymagać**

necessity /nəˈsesəti/ noun (pl. **necessities**) **1** [U] **necessity (for sth/to do sth)** the need for sth; the fact that sth must be done or must happen: *Is there any necessity for change?* ◇ *There's no necessity to write every single name down.* ◇ *They sold the car* ***out of necessity.*** ▶ **potrzeba**, **konieczność**, **nieodzowność** **2** [C] something that you must have: *Clean water is an absolute necessity.* ▶ **artykuł pierwszej potrzeby**

neck /nek/ noun **1** [C] the part of your body that joins your head to your shoulders: *She wrapped a scarf around her neck.* ◇ *Giraffes have long necks.* ▶ **szyja** ➲ picture at **body** **2** [C] the part of a piece of clothing that goes round your neck: *The neck on this shirt is too tight.* ◇ *a polo-neck sweater* golf ◇ *a V-neck sweater* sweter z wycięciem w szpic ▶ **kołnierz(yk)** **3** (**-necked**) [in compounds] having the type of neck mentioned: *a round-necked sweater* ▶ **(***określa rodzaj szyi lub kołnierz(yk)a***)** **4** [C] the long narrow part of sth: *the neck of a bottle* ▶ **szyjka** (*np. butelki*)
IDM **by the scruff (of the/your neck)** → SCRUFF
neck and neck (with sb/sth) equal or level with sb/sth in a race or competition ▶ **łeb w łeb**
up to your neck in sth having a lot of sth to deal with: *We're up to our necks in work at the moment.* ▶ **po szyję w czymś**

necklace /ˈnekləs/ noun [C] a piece of jewellery that you wear around your neck ▶ **naszyjnik**

necktie (US) = TIE[2] (1)

nectar /ˈnektə(r)/ noun [U] **1** a sweet liquid that is produced by flowers and collected by **bees** to make **honey** ▶ **nektar** **2** the thick juice of some fruit, used as a drink: *apricot nectar* ▶ **nektar**

nectarine /ˈnektəriːn/ noun [C] a type of peach with a smooth skin ▶ **nektarynka**

née /neɪ/ adj. (used in front of the family name that a woman had before she got married): *Louise Mitchell, née Greenan* ▶ **z domu** ➲ look at **maiden name**

need[1] /niːd/ verb [T] [not usually used in the continuous tenses]
ⓘ Czasownika **need** zwykle nie używa się w czasach *continuous*. Natomiast często spotyka się go w *present participle* (formie *-ing*): *Patients needing emergency treatment will go to the top of the waiting list.* **1 need sb/sth (for sth/to do sth)** if you need sb/sth, you want or must have them or it: *All living things need water.* ◇ *I need a new film for my camera.* ◇ *Does Roshni need any help?* ◇ *I need to find a doctor.* Potrzebuję lekarza. ◇ *I need you to go to the shop for me.* Chcę, żebyś poszedł do sklepu. ▶ **potrzebować**, **wymagać** **2** to have to: *Do we need to buy the tickets in advance?* ◇ *I need to ask some advice.* ◇ *You didn't need to bring any food but it was very kind of you.* ▶ **potrzebować**, **musieć**

> Zwróć uwagę, że pytania z czasownikiem **need** tworzy się za pomocą **do** lub **does** (**do I need?** itp.), a forma czasu przeszłego to **needed** (w pytaniach **did you need?** itp.; w przeczeniach **didn't need**). Por. formy czasownika **need**[2].

3 need (sth) doing if sth needs doing, it is necessary or must be done: *This jumper needs washing/to be washed.* Trzeba uprać ten sweter. ◇ *He needed his eyes testing.* Musiał zrobić badanie wzroku. ◇ *She needs her head examined.* Ona jest szalona.

need² /niːd/ modal verb ⓘ W czasie teraźniejszym we wszystkich osobach stosuje się **need**; w przeczeniach **need not (needn't)**; w pytaniach **need I?** itp. [not used in the continuous tenses; used mainly in questions or negative sentences after *if* and *whether*, or with words like *hardly, only, never*] to have to: *Need we pay the whole amount now?* ◇ *You needn't come to the meeting if you're too busy.* ◇ *I **hardly need** remind you that this is very serious.* ▶ **musieć, potrzebować**

Forma **needn't have done** oznacza, że coś zostało niepotrzebnie zrobione: *We needn't have packed* (niepotrzebnie zapakowaliśmy) *our thick clothes. The weather was really warm* ◇ *He needn't have gone to the bank* (niepotrzebnie poszedł do banku) – *I have plenty of money with me.* Por. **didn't need to**, po którym występuje bezokolicznik, i który oznacza, że coś nie zostało zrobione, ponieważ wcześniej, tj. przed podjęciem działania, było wiadomo, że nie jest ono konieczne: *He didn't need to go to the bank* (nie musiał iść do banku) – *he had plenty of money.*

need³ /niːd/ noun **1** [U, sing.] **need (for sth)**; **need (for sb/sth) to do sth** a situation in which you must have or do sth: *We are all **in need of** a rest.* ◇ *There is a growing need for new books in schools.* ◇ *There's **no need for** you to come if you don't want to.* ◇ *Do phone me if you **feel the need** to talk to someone.* ▶ **potrzeba, wymóg 2** [C, usually pl.] the things that you must have: *He doesn't earn enough to pay for his basic needs.* ◇ *Parents must consider their children's emotional as well as their physical needs.* ▶ **potrzeby, wymagania 3** [U] the state of not having enough food, money or support: *a campaign to help families **in need*** ▶ **niedostatek, trudne położenie**

needle /ˈniːdl/ noun [C] **1** a small thin piece of metal with a point at one end and an **eye** at the other that is used for sewing: *to thread a needle with cotton* ▶ **igła** (*do szycia*) ➲ look at **pins and needles 2** (also ˈ**knitting needle**) one of two long thin pieces of metal or plastic with a point at one end that are used for knitting ▶ **drut 3** the sharp metal part of a **syringe**: *a hypodermic needle* ▶ **igła 4** a thin metal part on a scientific instrument that moves to point to the correct measurement or direction: *The needle on the petrol gauge showed 'empty'.* ▶ **igła 5** the thin, hard pointed leaf of certain trees that stay green all year: *pine needles* ▶ **igła**

needless /ˈniːdləs/ adj. that is not necessary and that you can easily avoid ▶ **niepotrzebny, zbyteczny** ⓘ Uwaga! Wyraz **unnecessary** ma inne znaczenie.
■ **needlessly** adv. ▶ **niepotrzebnie, zbytecznie**

needlework /ˈniːdlwɜːk/ noun [U] sth that you sew by hand, especially for decoration ▶ **szycie, haftowanie**

needy /ˈniːdi/ adj. (**needier**; **neediest**) **1** not having enough money, food, clothes, etc. ▶ **potrzebujący, w biedzie 2** (**the needy**) noun [pl.] people who do not have enough money, food, clothes, etc. ▶ **potrzebujący**

neg. = NEGATIVE¹

negate /nɪˈɡeɪt/ verb [T] (formal) **1** to stop sth from having any effect: *Alcohol negates the effects of the drug.* ▶ **niweczyć 2** to state that sth does not exist ▶ **zaprzeczać**

negative¹ /ˈneɡətɪv/ adj. **1** bad or harmful: *The effects of the new rule have been rather negative.* ▶ **negatywny** OPP **positive 2** only thinking about the bad qualities of sb/sth: *I'm feeling very negative about my job – in fact I'm thinking about leaving.* ◇ *If you go into the match with a negative attitude, you'll never win.* ▶ **negatywny, ujemny** OPP **positive 3** (used about a word, phrase or sentence) meaning 'no' or 'not': *a negative sentence* ◇ *His reply was negative/He gave a negative reply.* ▶ **przeczący** OPP **affirmative 4** (used about a medical or scientific test) showing that sth has not happened or has not been found: *The results of the pregnancy test were negative.* ▶ **negatywny, ujemny** OPP **positive 5** (used about a number) less than zero ▶ **ujemny** OPP **positive**
■ **negatively** adv. ▶ **negatywnie; ujemnie**

negative² /ˈneɡətɪv/ noun [C] **1** a word, phrase or sentence that says or means 'no' or 'not': *Roger answered **in the negative*** (odmownie). ◇ *'Never', 'neither' and 'nobody' are all negatives* (to słowa przeczące). ▶ **przeczenie** OPP **affirmative 2** a piece of film from which we can make a photograph. The light areas of a negative are dark on the final photograph and the dark areas are light. ▶ **negatyw**

neglect /nɪˈɡlekt/ verb [T] **1** to give too little or no attention or care to sb/sth: *Don't neglect your health.* ◇ *The old house had stood neglected for years.* ▶ **zaniedbywać, lekceważyć 2 neglect to do sth** to fail or forget to do sth: *He neglected to mention that he had spent time in prison.* Zataił fakt, że był w więzieniu. ▶ **nie zrobić czegoś umyślnie lub przez przeoczenie**
■ **neglect** noun [U]: *The garden was like a jungle after years of neglect.* ▶ **zaniedbanie, opuszczenie** | **neglected** adj.: *neglected children* ▶ **zaniedbany**

negligence /ˈneɡlɪdʒəns/ noun [U] not being careful enough; lack of care: *The accident was a result of negligence.* ▶ **zaniedbanie, niedbalstwo**
■ **negligent** /-dʒənt/ adj. ▶ **niedbały, opieszały, lekceważący (coś)** | **negligently** adv. ▶ **niedbale, lekceważąco**

negligible /ˈneɡlɪdʒəbl/ adj. very small and therefore not important ▶ **nieistotny, bez znaczenia, mało znaczący**

negotiable /nɪˈɡəʊʃiəbl/ adj. that can be decided or changed by discussion: *The price is not negotiable/non-negotiable.* ▶ **(możliwy) do wynegocjowania**

negotiate /nɪˈɡəʊʃieɪt/ verb **1** [I] **negotiate (with sb) (for/about sth)** to talk to sb in order to decide or agree about sth: *The unions are still negotiating with management about this year's pay claim.* ▶ **negocjować, pertraktować, układać się 2** [T] to decide or agree sth by talking about it: *to negotiate an agreement/a deal/a settlement* ▶ **negocjować 3** [T] to get over, past or through sth difficult: *To escape, prisoners would have to negotiate a five-metre wall.* ▶ **pokonywać**
■ **negotiator** noun [C] ▶ **negocjator/ka**

negotiation /nɪˌɡəʊʃiˈeɪʃn/ noun [pl., U] discussions at which people try to decide or agree sth: *to enter into/break off negotiations* rozpocząć/przerywać negocjacje ◇ *The pay rise is still **under negotiation**.* ▶ **negocjacje, pertraktacj-a/e**

Negro /ˈniːɡrəʊ/ noun [C] (pl. **Negroes**) (old-fashioned) a black person ▶ **Murzyn/ka** ⓘ Obecnie to określenie uważa się za obraźliwe. ➲ look at **African American, Afro-Caribbean, black**

ˌ**Negro** ˈ**spiritual** = SPIRITUAL

neigh /neɪ/ noun [C] the long high sound that a horse makes ▶ **rżenie**
■ **neigh** verb [I] ▶ **rżeć**

neighbour (US **neighbor**) /ˈneɪbə(r)/ noun [C] **1** a person who lives near you: *My neighbours are very friendly.* ◇ *our **next-door neighbours*** ▶ **sąsiad/ka 2** a person or thing that is near or next to another: *Britain's nearest neighbour is France.* ◇ *Discuss the answers with your neighbour.* ▶ **sąsiad/ka**

neighbourhood (US **neighborhood**) /ˈneɪbəhʊd/ noun [C] a particular part of a town and the people who live there: *a friendly neighbourhood* ▶ **sąsiedztwo**

neighbouring (US **neighboring**) /ˈneɪbərɪŋ/ adj. [only before a noun] near or next to: *Farmers from neighbouring villages come into town each week for the market.* ▶ **sąsiedni, ościenny**

neighbourly (US **neighborly**) /ˈneɪbəli/ adj. friendly and helpful ▶ **dobrosąsiedzki**

neither /ˈnaɪðə(r); ˈniːðə(r)/ determiner, pron., adv. **1** (used about two people or things) not one and not the other: *Neither team played very well.* ◇ *Neither of the teams played very well.* ◇ *'Would you like tea or juice?' 'Neither, thank you. I'm not thirsty.'* ▶ **żaden** (*z dwóch*), **ani ten, ani tamten**; **ani jeden, ani drugi**

Uwaga! Po **neither** stawia się rzeczownik lub czasownik w lp: *Neither day was suitable.* Rzeczownik lub zaimek następujący po **neither of** występuje w lm, ale czasownik może być w lp: (zwł. w języku formalnym): *Neither of the days is suitable.* lub w lm (zwł. w języku codziennym): *Neither of the days are suitable.*

2 also not; not either: *I don't eat meat and neither does Tom.* Nie jem mięsa i Tom też (go) nie je. ◇ *'I don't like fish.' 'Neither do I.'* ◇ (informal) *'I don't like fish.' 'Me neither.'* ◇ *'I haven't seen that film.' 'Neither have I* (ja też nie).*'* ▶ **też nie**, **ani**

W tym samym znaczeniu i w taki sam sposób można stosować **nor**: *'I haven't seen that film.' 'Nor have I.'* Uwaga! Kiedy stosuje się zwrot **not ... either** wyrazy w zdaniu występują w innej kolejności: *I don't eat meat and Tom doesn't either.* ◇ *'I haven't seen that film.' 'I haven't either.'*

3 (**neither ... nor**) not ... and not: *Neither Carlos nor I eat meat.* ▶ **ani ..., ani (też) ...** ➲ look at **either**

Zwrot **neither ... nor** może być stosowany z czasownikiem występującym w lp: (zwł. w języku formalnym): *Neither Stella nor Jane was at the meeting.* lub lm (zwł. w języku codziennym): *Neither Stella nor Jane were at the meeting.*

neon /ˈniːɒn/ noun [U] (symbol **Ne**) a type of gas that is used for making bright lights and signs ▶ **neon**

nephew /ˈnefjuː; ˈnevjuː/ noun [C] the son of your brother or sister; the son of your husband's or wife's brother or sister ▶ **siostrzeniec**, **bratanek** ➲ look at **niece**

nepotism /ˈnepətɪzəm/ noun [U] giving unfair advantages to your own family if you are in a position of power, especially by giving them jobs ▶ **nepotyzm**

Neptune /ˈneptjuːn/ noun [sing.] the planet that is 8th in order from the sun ▶ **Neptun**

nerd /nɜːd/ noun [C] a person who spends a lot of time on a particular interest and who is not always popular or fashionable: *a computer nerd* ▶ **osoba nieciekawa, o niemodnych poglądach/zainteresowaniach itp.** SYN **geek**
■ **nerdy** adj. ▶ **niemodny i nudny**

nerve /nɜːv/ noun **1** [C] one of the long thin threads in your body that carry feelings or other messages to and from your brain: *nerve endings* ▶ **nerw 2** (**nerves**) [pl.] worried, nervous feelings: *Breathing deeply should help to **calm/steady your nerves**.* ◇ *I was **a bag of nerves** before my interview.* ▶ **nerwy 3** [U] the courage that you need to do sth difficult or dangerous: *Racing drivers need a lot of nerve.* ◇ *He didn't **have the nerve** to ask Maria to go out with him.* ◇ *Some pilots **lose their nerve** and can't fly any more.* ▶ **odwaga**, **zimna krew 4** [sing.] a way of behaving that people think is not acceptable: *You've got a nerve, calling me lazy!* ▶ **tupet**
IDM **get on sb's nerves** (informal) to annoy sb or make sb angry ▶ **działać (komuś) na nerwy**

ˈ**nerve-racking** adj. making you very nervous or worried ▶ **szarpiący nerwy**

nervous /ˈnɜːvəs/ adj. **1 nervous (about/of sth/doing sth)** worried or afraid: *I'm a bit nervous about travelling on my own.* ◇ *I always **get nervous** just before a match.* ◇ *She was a nervous wreck* (kłębkiem nerwów). ◇ *a nervous laugh/smile/voice* ◇ *She was nervous of giving the wrong answer.* ▶ **nerwowy**, **stremowany** OPP **confident 2** connected with the nerves of the body: *a nervous disorder* ▶ **nerwowy**
■ **nervously** adv. ▶ **nerwowo** | **nervousness** noun [U] ▶ **nerwowość**, **zdenerwowanie**

ˌ**nervous ˈbreakdown** (also **breakdown**) noun [C] a time when sb suddenly becomes so unhappy that they cannot continue living and working normally: *to have a nervous breakdown* ▶ **załamanie nerwowe**

the ˈnervous system noun [C] your brain and all the nerves in your body ▶ **układ nerwowy**

nest /nest/ noun [C] **1** a structure that a bird builds to keep its eggs and babies in ▶ **gniazdo** ➲ picture on **page A11 2** the home of certain animals or insects: *a wasps' nest* ▶ **gniazdo**, **nora**
■ **nest** verb [I] ▶ **gnieździć się**

ˈ**nest egg** noun [C] (informal) an amount of money that you save to use in the future ▶

nestle /ˈnesl/ verb [I,T] to be or go into a position where you are comfortable, protected or hidden: *The baby nestled her head on her mother's shoulder.* ◇ *Ulfa is a typical German village nestling* (wtulona) *in a beautiful river valley.* ▶ **tulić się (do kogoś/czegoś)**

net[1] /net/ noun **1** [U] material that has large, often square, spaces between the threads: *net curtains* firanki ▶ **sieć**, **siatka 2** [C] a piece of net that is used for a particular purpose: *a tennis/fishing/mosquito net* ▶ **siatka**, **sieć** ➲ look at **safety net 3** (**the Net**) (informal) = INTERNET
IDM **surf the Net** → SURF[2]

net[2] (also **nett**) /net/ adj. **net (of sth)** (used about a number or amount) from which nothing more needs to be taken away: *I earn about £15 000 net* ◇ *The net weight of the biscuits is 350g.* ◇ *a net profit* ◇ *What is your net income?* ▶ **czysty**, **netto** ➲ look at **gross**

net[3] /net/ verb [T] (**netting**; **netted**) **1** to gain sth as a profit ▶ **zarabiać/przynosić na czysto 2** to catch sth with a net; to kick a ball into a net ▶ **łowić w sieć**, **trafiać w siatkę** (*np. piłką*)

netball /ˈnetbɔːl/ noun [U] a game that is played by two teams of seven players, usually women. Players score by throwing the ball through a high net hanging from a ring. ▶ **rodzaj koszykówki**

ˈ**Net surfer** = SURFER (2)

netting /ˈnetɪŋ/ noun [U] material that is made of long pieces of string, thread, wire, etc. that are tied together with spaces between them: *a fence made of wire netting* (z drucianej siatki) ▶ **siatka**, **sieć**

nettle /ˈnetl/ noun [C] a wild plant with large leaves. Some **nettles** make your skin red and painful if you touch them. ▶ **pokrzywa**

network /ˈnetwɜːk/ noun [C] **1** a system of roads, railway lines, nerves, etc. that are connected to each other: *an underground railway network* ▶ **sieć** (*np. kolejowa*) **2** a group of people or companies that work closely together: *We have a network of agents who sell our goods all over the country.* ▶ **sieć** (*np. przedsiębiorstw*) **3** a number of computers that are connected together so that information can be shared: *The network allows users to share files.* ▶ **sieć komputerowa 4** a group of TV or radio companies that are connected and that send out the same programmes at the same time in different parts of a country: *The four big US television networks.* ▶ **sieć telewizyjna/radiowa**

neurologist /njʊəˈrɒlədʒɪst; US nʊə-/ noun [C] a doctor who studies and treats diseases of the nerves ▶ **neurolog**

neurology /njʊəˈrɒlədʒi; US nʊə-/ noun [U] the scientific study of nerves and their diseases ▶ **neurologia** ■ **neurological** /ˌnjʊərəˈlɒdʒɪkl; US ˌnʊə-/ adj.: *He suffered severe neurological damage.* ▶ **neurologiczny**

neuron /ˈnjʊərɒn; US ˈnʊr-/ (especially Brit. **neurone** /ˈnjʊərəʊn; US ˈnʊər-/) noun [C] a cell that carries information within the brain and between the brain and other parts of the body; a nerve cell ▶ **neuron**

neurosis /njʊəˈrəʊsɪs; US nʊə-/ noun [C] (pl. **neuroses** /-əʊsiːz/) a mental illness that causes strong feelings of fear and worry ▶ **nerwica**

neurotic /njʊəˈrɒtɪk; US nʊə-/ adj. **1** suffering from a **neurosis** ▶ **cierpiący na nerwicę 2** worried about things in a way that is not normal ▶ **neurotyczny**, **nerwicowy**

neuter[1] /ˈnjuːtə(r); US ˈnuː-/ adj. (used about a word in some languages) not **masculine** or **feminine** according to the rules of grammar ▶ **rodzaju nijakiego** ➲ note at **masculine**

neuter[2] /ˈnjuːtə(r); US ˈnuː-/ verb [T] to remove the sexual parts of an animal ▶ **kastrować** (*zwierzę*) ➲ look at **castrate**

neutral[1] /ˈnjuːtrəl; US ˈnuː-/ adj. **1** not supporting or belonging to either side in an argument, war, etc.: *I don't take sides when my brothers argue – I **remain neutral**.* ◇ *The two sides agreed to meet on neutral ground.* ▶ **neutralny**, **bezstronny 2** having or showing no strong qualities, emotions or colour: *neutral colours* ◇ *a neutral tone of voice* ▶ **neutralny**, **nijaki 3** having neither a positive nor a negative charge ▶ (*elektr.*) **zerowy**; (*chem.*) **obojętny** ➲ picture at **plug**

neutral[2] /ˈnjuːtrəl; US ˈnuː-/ noun [U] the position of the gears when no power is sent from the engine to the wheels: *Make sure the car is **in neutral*** (na luzie) *before you turn on the engine.* ▶ **bieg jałowy**

neutrality /njuːˈtræləti; US nuː-/ noun [U] the state of not supporting either side in an argument, war, etc. ▶ **neutralność**, **bezstronność**

neutralize (also -ise) /ˈnjuːtrəlaɪz; US ˈnuː-/ verb [T] to take away the effect of sth: *to neutralize a threat* ▶ **oddalać** (*np. obawy*), **unieszkodliwiać**

neutron /ˈnjuːtrɒn; US ˈnuː-/ noun [C] part of the **nucleus** of an atom that carries no electric charge ▶ **neutron** ➲ look at **electron**, **proton**

never /ˈnevə(r)/ adv. **1** at no time; not ever: *I've never been to Portugal.* ◇ *He never ever* (przenigdy) *eats meat.* ◇ (formal) *Never before has such a high standard been achieved.* ▶ **nigdy 2** (used for emphasizing a negative statement): *I never realized she was so unhappy.* ◇ *Roy never so much as looked at us.* Roy nawet na nas nie spojrzał. ◇ *'I got the job!' 'Never* (niemożliwe)*!'* ▶ **nigdy**
IDM **never mind** → MIND[2]
you never know → KNOW[1]

nevertheless /ˌnevəðəˈles/ adv., conj. (formal) in spite of that: *It was a cold, rainy day. Nevertheless, more people came than we had expected.* ▶ **(tym) niemniej (jednak)**, **mimo to** SYN **nonetheless**

new /njuː; US nuː/ adj. **1** that has recently been built, made, discovered, etc.: *a new design/film/hospital* ◇ *a new method of treating mental illness* ◇ *new evidence* ▶ **nowy** OPP **old 2** different or changed from what was before: *I've just started reading a new book.* ◇ *to make new friends* ▶ **nowy** OPP **old 3 new (to sb)** that you have not seen, learnt, etc. before: *This type of machine is new to me.* ◇ *to learn a new language* ▶ **nowy (dla kogoś) 4 new (to sth)** having just started being or doing sth: *a new parent* ◇ *She's new to the job and needs a lot of help.* ◇ *a new member of the club* ▶ **nowy**, **świeżo/niedawno przybyły**
■ **newness** noun [U] ▶ **nowość**, **brak doświadczenia**
IDM **a (whole) new/different ball game** → BALL GAME
break fresh/new ground → GROUND

ˈ**New Age** adj. connected with a way of life that rejects modern Western values and is based on spiritual ideas and beliefs: *a New Age festival* ◇ ***New Age travellers*** grupa ludzi w Wlk. Brytanii, którzy odrzucają wartości nowoczesnego społeczeństwa, wędrują z miejsca na miejsce i śpią w swoich pojazdach ▶ **New Age**

newborn /ˈnjuːbɔːn; US ˈnuː-/ adj. [only before a noun] (used about a baby) that has been born very recently ▶ **nowo narodzony**

newcomer /ˈnjuːkʌmə(r); US ˈnuː-/ noun [C] a person who has just arrived in a place ▶ **nowo przybył-y/a**

newfangled /ˌnjuːˈfæŋgld; US ˌnuː-/ adj. new or modern in a way that the speaker does not like ▶ **nowomodny**

newly /ˈnjuːli; US ˈnuː-/ adv. [usually before a past participle] recently: *the newly appointed* (nowo mianowany) *Minister of Health* ▶ **niedawno**, **nowo**

ˈ**newly-wed** noun [C, usually pl.] a person who has recently got married ▶ **świeżo poślubiony**

ˌ**new** ˈ**man** noun [C] (Brit.) a man who shares the work in the home that is traditionally done by women, such as cleaning, cooking and taking care of children. **New men** are considered sensitive and not aggressive. ▶ **mężczyzna przejmujący część tradycyjnych obowiązków kobiety w rodzinie**

ˌ**new** ˈ**moon** noun [C] the moon when it appears as a thin line ▶ **nów** ➲ look at **full moon**

news /njuːz; US nuːz/ noun **1** [U] information about sth that has happened recently: *Write and tell me all your news.* ◇ *Have you had any news from Susie recently?* ◇ *That's news to me.* Pierwszy raz słyszę. ◇ *I've got some good news: you've passed the exam!* ◇ *News is coming in* (napływają wiadomości) *of a plane crash in Thailand.* ◇ *There will be a further news bulletin* (wydanie wiadomości) *at 1 o'clock.* ◇ *Our town has been **in the news** a lot recently.* Ostatnio w mediach sporo się mówi o naszym mieście. ◇ *a newsflash* wiadomość z ostatniej chwili ▶ **wiadomości** ⓘ **News** jest rzeczownikiem niepoliczalnym. Mówiąc o jednej wiadomości, należy użyć zwrotu **a piece of news**, a nie ~~a news~~: *We had a piece of good news yesterday.* Po rzeczowniku **news** czasownik występuje w lp: *The news is very depressing.* **2** (**the news**) [sing.] a regular programme giving the most recent news on the radio or TV: *We always watch the 10 o'clock news on TV.* ◇ *I heard about the accident **on the news*** (usłyszałem w wiadomościach). ▶ **wiadomości** (*radiowe/telewizyjne*)
IDM **break the news (to sb)** to be the first to tell sb about sth important that has happened ▶ **zawiadamiać** (*zwł. o czymś przykrym*)

newsagent /ˈnjuːzeɪdʒənt; US ˈnuːz-/ (US **newsdealer** /ˈnjuːzdiːlə(r); US ˈnuːz-/) noun **1** [C] a person who owns or works in a shop that sells newspapers, magazines, etc. ▶ **sprzedaw-ca/czyni w sklepie z gazetami, papierosami itp. 2** (**the newsagent's**) [sing.] a shop that sells newspapers, magazines, etc. ▶ **sklep z prasą**

> **Newsagent's** oznacza sklep. W centrum dużych miast, na dworcach kolejowych itp. znajdują się czasami budki, gdzie można kupić gazety. Określa się je mianem **kiosk**, a nie **newsagent's**.

newscaster = NEWSREADER

newsgroup /ˈnjuːzgruːp; US ˈnuːz-/ noun [C] a place in a computer network, especially the Internet, where people can discuss a particular subject and exchange information about it ▶ (*komput.*) **grupa dyskusyjna**

newsletter /ˈnjuːzletə(r); US ˈnuːz-/ noun [C] a printed report about a club or organization that is sent regularly to members and other people who may be interested ▶ **biuletyn informacyjny**

newspaper /ˈnjuːzpeɪpə(r); US ˈnuːz-/ noun **1** (also **paper**) [C] large folded pieces of paper printed with news, advertisements and articles on various subjects. Newspapers are printed and sold either every day or every week: *a daily/weekly/Sunday paper* dziennik/tygodnik/wydanie niedzielne gazety ◇ *a newspaper article* ◇ *I read about it* ***in the newspaper.*** ▶ **gazeta 2** [U] the paper on which newspapers are printed: *We wrapped the plates in newspaper so they would not get damaged.* ▶ **gazeta** ➲ look at **media 3** (also **paper**) [C] an organisation that produces a newspaper: *She works for the local newspaper.* ◇ *Which paper is he from?* ▶ **gazeta**

newspapers
Newspapers and the **journalists/reporters** who write **articles** for them are called **the press**. The **editor** decides what is printed. **Quality** newspapers deal with the news in a serious way. **Tabloids** are smaller in size and some of them have **sensational** stories and **gossip columns**. Photographers who follow famous people in order to take photographs of them are called **paparazzi**. You can buy **newspapers** and **magazines** at **the newsagent's** or you might have them delivered to your house by a **paper boy** or **paper girl**.

newsreader /ˈnjuːzriːdə(r); US ˈnuːz-/ (also **newscaster** /ˈnjuːzkɑːstə(r); US ˈnuːzkæs-/) noun [C] a person who reads the news on the radio or TV ▶ **prezenter/ka wiadomości radiowych/telewizyjnych**

ˈnews-stand (US) = BOOKSTALL

the ˌ**New ˈTestament** noun [sing.] the second part of the Bible that describes the life and teachings of Jesus ▶ **Nowy Testament**

new ˈyear (also **New Year**) noun [sing.] the first few days of January: *Happy New Year!* ◇ *We will get in touch in the new year.* ◇ *New Year's Eve* Sylwester ◇ *New Year's Day* Nowy Rok ▶ **nowy rok**

next[1] /nekst/ adj. **1** [usually with *the*] coming immediately after sth in order, space or time; closest: *The next bus leaves in twenty minutes.* ◇ *The next name on the list is Paulo.* ◇ *Who is next?* ▶ **następny, najbliższy, następujący (tuż po/za czymś), sąsiedni**

Por. **nearest** z **next. The next** oznacza „następny" w ciągu zdarzeń lub miejsc: *When is your next appointment?* ◇ *Turn left at the next traffic lights.* **(The) nearest** oznacza „najbliższy" w czasie lub przestrzeni: *Where's the nearest supermarket?*

2 [used without *the* before days of the week, months, seasons, years, etc.] the one immediately following the present one: *See you again next Monday.* ◇ *Let's go camping next weekend.* ◇ *next summer/next year/next Christmas* ◇ *Rachel hopes to get a job abroad next year* (w przyszłym roku). ▶ **następny, przyszły**
■ **the next** noun [sing.] the person or thing that is next: *If we miss this train, we'll have to wait two hours for the next.* ▶ **następny**
IDM **last/next but one, two etc.** → LAST[1]

next[2] /nekst/ adv. **1** after this or after that; then: *I know Joe arrived first, but who came next?* ◇ *I wonder what will happen next* (co teraz będzie). ◇ *It was ten years until I next saw her.* Dopiero po dziesięciu latach znowu ją zobaczyłem. ▶ **w następnej kolejności, potem 2** (**next best, biggest, most important, etc. ... (after/to sb/sth)**) following in the order mentioned: *Jo was the next oldest after Martin.* ◇ *The* ***next best thing*** *to flying is gliding.* ▶ (*po kimś/czymś*) **drugi najlepszy/największy/najważniejszy itp.**

ˌ**next ˈdoor** adv. in or into the next house or building: *The school is* ***next door to*** (w budynku obok) *an old people's home.* ◇ *Who lives next door?* Kto mieszka obok ciebie? ◇ *I'm going next door* (do najbliższych sąsiadów) *to borrow some eggs.* ▶ **obok** (*zza ściany/płotu itp.*)
■ ˌ**next ˈdoor** adj. [only before a noun]: *our next-door neighbours* najbliżsi sąsiedzi ◇ *the next-door house* dom obok ▶ **po sąsiedzku**

next of kin /ˌnekst əv ˈkɪn/ noun [C] (pl. **next of kin**) your closest living relative or relatives: *My husband is my next of kin.* ◇ *Her next of kin have been informed of her death.* ▶ **najbliż-szy/si krewn-y/i**

next to prep. **1** at the side of sb/sth; beside: *He sat down next to Gita.* ◇ *There's a public telephone next to the bus stop.* ▶ **obok, koło 2** in a position after sth: *Next to Paris* (po Paryżu) *I think my favourite city is Madrid.* ◇ *Next to English my favourite subject is Maths.* ▶ **po**
IDM **next to nothing** almost nothing: *We took plenty of money but we've got next to nothing left.* ▶ **prawie (tyle co) nic**

NGO /ˌen dʒiː ˈəʊ/ abbr. **non-governmental organization**; a charity, association, etc. that is independent of government and business ▶ **organizacja pozarządowa**

NHS (Brit.) = NATIONAL HEALTH SERVICE

NI = NATIONAL INSURANCE

nib /nɪb/ noun [C] the metal point of a pen, where the ink comes out ▶ **stalówka** ➲ picture at **stationery**

nibble /ˈnɪbl/ verb [I,T] to eat sth by taking small bites: *The bread had been nibbled by mice.* ▶ **ogryzać, skubać**
■ **nibble** noun [C] ▶ **ogryzanie, skubanie**

nice /naɪs/ adj. **1** pleasant, enjoyable or attractive: *a nice place/feeling/smile* ◇ *I'm not eating this – it doesn't taste very nice.* ◇ *Did you* ***have a nice time?*** ◇ *You look very nice today.* Bardzo ładnie dziś wyglądasz. ◇ *It would be nice to spend more time at home.* ◇ *'Hi, I'm Kate.' 'I'm Fergus –* ***nice to meet you*** (bardzo mi miło).*'* ▶ **przyjemny, miły,** (*potrawa*) **dobry,** (*pogoda, wygląd, widok*) **ładny 2** (informal) (used before adjectives and adverbs to emphasize how pleasant or suitable sth is): *a nice long chat* ▶ **(*używany z innym przymiotnikiem; oznacza, że coś jest bardzo przyjemne, miłe, sympatyczne itp.*) 3 nice (to sb); nice (of sb) (to do sth); nice (about sth)** kind; friendly: *What a nice girl!* ◇ *Everyone was very nice to me when I felt ill.* ◇ *It was really nice of Donna to help us.* ◇ *The neighbours were very nice about it when I hit their car.* ▶ **sympatyczny, uprzejmy** OPP **nasty**

nice
W nieformalnym angielskim zamiast **(very) nice** można powiedzieć **great, lovely** lub **wonderful**: *The party was great.* ◇ *We had a lovely weekend.* Kiedy rozmawia się o osobie, można powiedzieć: *He/She is* ***lovely.*** lub: *He/She is very* ***friendly.*** Mówi się również: *a* ***cosy****/an* ***attractive*** *room* ◇ ***beautiful/lovely*** *weather* ◇ ***expensive/fashionable/smart*** *clothes.*

IDM **nice and ...** (used for saying that you like sth): *It's nice and warm by the fire.* Przy kominku jest cieplutko. ▶ **(*używany z innym przymiotnikiem; oznacza, że coś jest bardzo przyjemne, miłe, sympatyczne itp.*)**
Nice one! (Brit., informal) (used to show you are pleased when sth good has happened or sb has said sth amusing) ▶ **świetnie!**
■ **nicely** adv. **1** in a pleasant way: *I might help you if you ask nicely.* ▶ **grzecznie 2** very well: *This flat will suit us nicely.* To mieszkanie bardzo nam odpowiada. ▶ **bardzo** | **niceness** noun [U] ▶ **uprzejmość**

niche /niːʃ; nɪtʃ/ noun [C] **1** a job, position, etc. that is suitable for you: *to find your niche in life* ▶ **odpowiednie**

miejsce **2** (in business) an opportunity to sell a particular product to a particular group of people ▶ **nisza 3** a place in a wall that is further back, where a statue, etc. can be put ▶ **nisza**, **wnęka** *(zwykle z półką)*

nick[1] /nɪk/ noun **1** [C] a small cut in sth ▶ **nacięcie 2** (**the nick**) [sing.] (Brit., slang) ▶ **pudło** *(więzienie)*
IDM **in good/bad nick** (Brit., slang) in a good/bad state or condition ▶ **w dobrym/złym stanie**
in the nick of time only just in time ▶ **w samą porę**

nick[2] /nɪk/ verb [T] **1** to make a very small cut in sb/sth ▶ **nacinać 2** (Brit., slang) to steal sth ▶ **gwizdnąć (komuś/skądś) 3** (Brit., slang) to arrest sb ▶ **aresztować**

nickel /ˈnɪkl/ noun **1** [U] (symbol **Ni**) a hard silver-white metal that is often mixed with other metals ▶ **nikiel 2** [C] an American or Canadian coin that is worth five cents ▶ **pięciocentówka**

nickname /ˈnɪkneɪm/ noun [C] an informal name that is used instead of your real name, usually by your family or friends ▶ **przydomek**, **przezwisko**
■ **nickname** verb [T] ▶ **nadawać przydomek/przezwisko**

nicotine /ˈnɪkətiːn/ noun [U] the poisonous chemical substance in **tobacco** ▶ **nikotyna**

niece /niːs/ noun [C] the daughter of your brother or sister; the daughter of your husband's or wife's brother or sister ▶ **siostrzenica**, **bratanica** ➲ look at **nephew**

nifty /ˈnɪfti/ adj. (informal) **1** skilful and accurate: *There's some nifty guitar work on his latest CD.* ▶ **zręczny 2** practical; working well: *a nifty little gadget for slicing cucumbers* ▶ **praktyczny** SYN **handy**

niggle /ˈnɪɡl/ verb **1** [I,T] **niggle (at) sb** to annoy or worry sb: *His untidy habits really niggled her.* ▶ **drażnić 2** [I] **niggle (about/over sth)** to complain or argue about things that are not important ▶ **tracić czas na drobiazgi**

niggling /ˈnɪɡlɪŋ/ adj. not very serious (but that does not go away): *a niggling injury* ◇ *niggling* (dręczące) *doubts* ▶ **(nic poważnego, ale) dokuczliwy**, **uporczywy**

night /naɪt/ noun [C,U] **1** the part of the day when it is dark and when most people sleep: *I had a strange dream last night.* ◇ *The baby cried **all night**.* ◇ *It's a long way home. Why don't you **stay the night**?* Może zostaniesz na noc? ◇ *We will be away for a few nights.* ▶ **noc 2** the time between late afternoon and when you go to bed: *Let's go out on Saturday night.* ◇ *I went out with Kate **the other night**.* ▶ **wieczór**

> Z rzeczownikiem **night** stosuje się różne przyimki. Najczęściej spotykany to **at**: *I'm not allowed out after 11 o'clock at night* (wieczorem). **By** jest słowem bardziej literackim niż **at**. Wyrażenie **by night** często stosuje się, aby uwypuklić kontrast z wyrażeniem **by day**: *They slept by day and travelled by night.* **In/during the night** stosuje się zwykle w odniesieniu do minionej nocy: *I woke up twice in the night.* **On** używa się, mówiąc o konkretnej nocy: *On the night of Saturday 30 June.* **Tonight** oznacza nadchodzącą właśnie noc lub wieczór: *Where are you staying tonight?*

IDM **an early/a late night** an evening when you go to bed earlier/later than usual ▶ **wczesne/późne pójście spać**
in the/at dead of night → DEAD[2]
a night out an evening that you spend out of the house enjoying yourself ▶ **wieczór spędzony (miło) poza domem**

nightclub = CLUB[1] (2)

nightdress /ˈnaɪtdres/ (also informal **nightie** /ˈnaɪti/) noun [C] a loose dress that a girl or woman wears in bed ▶ **koszula nocna**

nightfall /ˈnaɪtfɔːl/ noun [U] (formal or literary) the time in the evening when it becomes dark: *He wanted to be home before nightfall.* ▶ **zmrok** SYN **dusk**

nightingale /ˈnaɪtɪŋɡeɪl/ noun [C] a small brown bird that has a beautiful song ▶ **słowik**

nightlife /ˈnaɪtlaɪf/ noun [U] the entertainment that is available in the evenings in a particular place: *It's a small town with very little nightlife.* ▶ **nocne życie**

nightly /ˈnaɪtli/ adj., adv. happening every night: *a nightly news bulletin* ▶ **(powtarzający się) co wieczór/noc**

nightmare /ˈnaɪtmeə(r)/ noun [C] **1** a frightening or unpleasant dream: *I had a terrible nightmare about being stuck in a lift last night.* ▶ **koszmar 2** (informal) an experience that is very unpleasant or frightening: *Travelling in the rush hour can be a real nightmare.* ▶ **koszmar**

nightstick (US usually) = TRUNCHEON

ˈ**night-time** noun [U] the time when it is dark ▶ **nocna pora**

nightwatchman /naɪtˈwɒtʃmən/ noun [C] (pl. **-men** /-mən/) a person who guards a building at night ▶ **stróż/ka nocn-y/a**

nil /nɪl/ noun [U] the number 0 (especially as the score in some games): *We won two-nil/by two goals to nil.* ▶ **nic**, **zero** ➲ note at **zero**

nimble /ˈnɪmbl/ adj. able to move quickly and lightly ▶ **zwinny**
■ **nimbly** /ˈnɪmbli/ adv. ▶ **zwinnie**

nine /naɪn/ number 9 ▶ **dziewięć** ➲ note at **six**
IDM **nine to five** the hours that you work in most offices: *a nine-to-five job* praca od ósmej do czwartej ▶ **całodzienny**

nineteen /ˌnaɪnˈtiːn/ number 19 ▶ **dziewiętnaście** ➲ note at **six**
■ **nineteenth** /ˌnaɪnˈtiːnθ/ **1** ordinal number ▶ **dziewiętnasty** ➲ note at **sixth 2** noun [C] 1/19th; one of nineteen equal parts of sth ▶ **(jedna) dziewiętnasta**

ninety /ˈnaɪnti/ number 90 ▶ **dziewięćdziesiąt** ➲ note at **sixty**
■ **ninetieth** /ˈnaɪntiəθ/ **1** ordinal number 90th ▶ **dziewięćdziesiąty** ➲ note at **sixth 2** noun [C] 1/90; one of ninety equal parts of sth ▶ **(jedna) dziewięćdziesiąta**

ninth /naɪnθ/ ordinal number 9th ▶ **dziewiąty** ➲ note at **sixth**
■ **ninth** noun [C] ⅑; one of nine equal parts of sth ▶ **(jedna) dziewiąta**

nip /nɪp/ verb (**nipping**; **nipped**) **1** [I,T] to give sb/sth a quick bite or to quickly squeeze a piece of sb's skin between your thumb and finger: *She nipped him on the arm.* ▶ **lekko ugryźć**, **uszczypnąć 2** [I] (Brit., informal) to go somewhere quickly and/or for a short time ▶ **skakać (dokądś)**, **latać (dokądś)**
■ **nip** noun [C] ▶ **gryz**, **uszczypnięcie**
IDM **nip sth in the bud** to stop sth bad before it develops or gets worse ▶ **zdusić coś złego w zarodku**

nipple /ˈnɪpl/ noun [C] **1** either of the two small dark circles on either side of your chest. A baby can suck milk from his or her mother's breast through the **nipples**. ▶ **sutek 2** (US) = TEAT (1)

nippy /ˈnɪpi/ adj. **1** (Brit.) able to move quickly and easily: *a nippy little sports car* ▶ **zrywny 2** (informal) (used about the weather) cold ▶ **rześki**

nit /nɪt/ noun [C] **1** the egg of a small insect that lives in the hair of people or animals ▶ **gnida 2** (Brit., informal) a silly person ▶ **głup-ek/ia**

N

ˈnit-picking noun [U] the habit of finding small mistakes in sb's work or paying too much attention to small, unimportant details ▶ **szukanie dziury w całym**
■ **ˈnit-picker** noun [C] ▶ **osoba małostkowa** | **ˈnit-picking** adj. ▶ **małostkowy**, **drobiazgowy**

nitrogen /ˈnaɪtrədʒən/ noun [U] (symbol **N**) a gas that has no colour, taste or smell. **Nitrogen** forms about 80% of the air around the earth. ▶ **azot**

the **nitty-gritty** /ˌnɪtiˈɡrɪti/ noun [sing.] (informal) the most important facts, not the small or unimportant details ▶ **konkrety**, **sprawy zasadnicze**

No. (also **no.**) abbr. **1** (pl. **Nos**; **nos**) (US #) = NUMBER[1] (2), (3): *No. 10 Downing Street* ◇ *tel no. 512364* **2** (US) = NORTH, NORTHERN

⚷ **no[1]** /nəʊ/ interj. **1** (used for giving a negative reply): *'Are you ready?' 'No, I'm not.'* ◇ *'Would you like something to eat?' '**No, thank you.**'* ◇ *'Can I borrow the car?' 'No, you can't.'* ▶ **nie** OPP **yes** ℹ **No** używa się również w sytuacjach, gdy rozmówca zgadza się ze stwierdzeniem przeczącym: *'This programme's not very good.' 'No, you're right. It isn't.'.* **2** (used for expressing surprise or shock): *'Mike's had an accident.' 'Oh, no!'* ▶ **nie!**

⚷ **no[2]** /nəʊ/ determiner **1** not any; not a: *I have no time to talk now.* ◇ *No visitors may enter without a ticket.* ◇ *He's no friend of mine.* On nie jest żadnym moim przyjacielem. ◇ *No news is good news.* Brak wiadomości jest dobrą wiadomością. ▶ **nie**, **żaden** **2** (used for saying that sth is not allowed): *No smoking.* Nie palić. ◇ *No flash photography.* ◇ *No parking.* ▶ **nie (wolno)**, **zakaz/wzbronione** (*w zakazach*)
■ **no** adv. not any: *Alice is feeling no better this morning.* ▶ **nie**, **ani trochę**

nobility /nəʊˈbɪləti/ noun **1** (**the nobility**) [sing., with sing. or pl. verb] people of high social position who have titles such as that of Duke or Duchess ▶ **szlachta**, **arystokracja** SYN **aristocracy** **2** [U] (formal) the quality of having courage and honour ▶ **szlachetność**

noble[1] /ˈnəʊbl/ adj. **1** honest; full of courage and care for others: *a noble leader* ◇ *noble ideas/actions* ▶ **szlachetny**, **uczciwy** **2** belonging to the highest social class: *a man of noble birth* ▶ **szlachecki**, **arystokratyczny**
■ **nobly** /ˈnəʊbli/ adv.: *He nobly sacrificed his own happiness for that of his family.* ▶ **szlachetnie**

noble[2] /ˈnəʊbl/ noun [C] (in past times) a person who belonged to the highest social class and had a special title ▶ **szlachcic**, **arystokrata** ℹ Obecnie częściej używa się wyrazu **peer**.

⚷ **nobody[1]** /ˈnəʊbədi/ (also ˈ**no one**) pron. no person; not anyone: *He screamed but nobody came to help him.* ◇ *No one else was around.* ◇ *There was nobody at home.* ▶ **nikt**

> Przed zaimkami oraz przed takimi wyrazami jak **the**, **his**, **her**, **those** itp. należy stosować **none of**, a nie **nobody**: *Nobody remembered my birthday.* ◇ *None of my friends remembered my birthday.* ◇ *I've asked all my classmates but nobody is free.* ◇ *None of them are free.*

nobody[2] /ˈnəʊbədi/ noun [C] (pl. **nobodies**) a person who is not important or famous: *She rose from being a nobody to a superstar.* ▶ **zero**, **nikt**

nocturnal /nɒkˈtɜːnl/ adj. **1** (used about animals and birds) awake and active at night and asleep during the day: *Owls are nocturnal birds.* ▶ **nocny** **2** (formal) happening in the night: *a nocturnal adventure* ▶ **nocny**

nod /nɒd/ verb [I,T] (**nodding**; **nodded**) to move your head up and down as a way of saying 'yes' or as a sign to sb to do sth: *Everybody at the meeting nodded in agreement.* ◇ *Nod your head if you understand what I'm saying and shake it if you don't.* ▶ **skinąć** (*głową*), **kłaniać się**
■ **nod** noun [C] ▶ **kiwnięcie** (*głową*), **ukłon**
PHR V **nod off** (informal) to go to sleep for a short time ▶ **przysypiać**

node /nəʊd/ noun [C] **1** a place on the **stem** of a plant from which a branch or leaf grows ▶ **węzeł** **2** a small swelling on a root or branch ▶ **zgrubienie** **3** a point at which two lines or systems meet or cross: *a network node* ▶ **węzeł** **4** a small hard mass of **tissue**, especially near a joint in the human body: *a lymph node* ▶ **guzek**

ˌno-ˈgo area noun [sing.] a place, especially part of a city, where it is very dangerous to go because there is a lot of violence or crime ▶ **niebezpieczna dzielnica**

⚷ **noise** /nɔɪz/ noun [C,U] a sound, especially one that is loud or unpleasant: *Did you hear a noise downstairs?* ◇ *Try not to **make a noise*** (nie hałasować) *if you come home late.* ◇ *What an awful noise!* ◇ *Why is the engine making so much noise?* ▶ **hałas**

noiseless /ˈnɔɪzləs/ adj. making no sound ▶ **bezszelestny**
■ **noiselessly** adv. ▶ **bezszelestnie**

⚷ **noisy** /ˈnɔɪzi/ adj. (**noisier**; **noisiest**) making a lot of or too much noise; full of noise: *The clock was so noisy that it kept me awake.* ◇ *noisy children/traffic/crowds* ◇ *The classroom was very noisy.* ▶ **hałaśliwy**, **głośny** ➲ note at **loud**
■ **noisily** adv. ▶ **hałaśliwie**, **głośno**

nomad /ˈnəʊmæd/ noun [C] a member of a community that moves with its animals from place to place ▶ **koczowni-k/czka**
■ **nomadic** /nəʊˈmædɪk/ adj. ▶ **koczowniczy**

ˈno-man's-land noun [U, sing.] an area of land between the borders of two countries or between two armies during a war and which is not controlled by either ▶ **ziemia niczyja**

nominal /ˈnɒmɪnl/ adj. **1** being sth in name only but not in reality: *the nominal* (tytularny) *leader of the country* ▶ **nominalny** **2** (used about a price, sum of money, etc.) very small; much less than normal: *Because we are friends he only charges me **a nominal rent**.* ▶ **symboliczny**
■ **nominally** /-nəli/ adj.: *He was nominally in charge of the company.* ▶ **nominalnie**, **tytularnie**

nominate /ˈnɒmɪneɪt/ verb [T] **nominate sb/sth (for/as sth)**; **nominate sb (to/as sth) (to do sth)** to formally suggest that sb/sth should be given a job, role, prize, etc.: *I would like to nominate Bob Fry as chairman.* ◇ *The novel has been nominated for the Booker prize.* ◇ *You may nominate a representative to speak for you.* ▶ **nominować**; **wyznaczać**
■ **nomination** /ˌnɒmɪˈneɪʃn/ noun [C,U] ▶ **nominacja**; **mianowanie**

nominee /ˌnɒmɪˈniː/ noun [C] a person who is suggested for an important job, role, prize, etc. ▶ **kandydat/ka (na coś/do czegoś)**

⚷ **non-** /nɒn/ [in compounds] not: *non-biodegradable* ◇ *non-flammable* ▶ **nie-**, **bez-**

ˌnon-acaˈdemic adj. connected with technical or practical subjects rather than subjects of interest to the mind ▶ (*przedmioty*) **techniczny**, **praktyczny**

ˌnon-alcoˈholic adj. (used about drinks) not containing any alcohol: *non-alcoholic drinks* ▶ **bezalkoholowy**

ˌnon-aˈligned adj. (used about a country) not supporting any major country or group of countries ▶ **niezaangażowany**

nonchalant /ˈnɒnʃələnt; US ˌnɒnʃəˈlɑːnt/ adj. not feeling or showing interest or excitement about sth ▶ **nonszalancki**, **obojętny**
■ **nonchalance** noun [U] ▶ **nonszalancja**, **obojętność** | **nonchalantly** adv. ▶ **nonszalancko**, **obojętnie**

non-committal /ˌnɒn-kəˈmɪtl/ adj. not saying or showing exactly what your opinion is or which side of an argument you agree with ▶ **wymijający, unikający wyraźnej odpowiedzi**

nonconformist /ˌnɒnkənˈfɔːmɪst/ noun [C] a person who behaves or thinks differently from most other people in society ▶ **nonkonformist(k)a** OPP **conformist**
■ **nonconformist** adj. ▶ **nonkonformistyczny**

ˌnon-ˈcontact sport noun [C] a sport in which players do not have physical contact with each other ▶ **sport niekontaktowy** OPP **contact sport**

nondescript /ˈnɒndɪskrɪpt/ adj. not having any interesting or unusual qualities ▶ **nieokreślony, bezbarwny**

none[1] /nʌn/ pron. **none (of sb/sth)** not any, not one (of a group of three or more): *They gave me a lot of information but none of it was very helpful.* ◇ *I've got four brothers but none of them live/lives nearby.* ◇ *'Have you brought any books to read?' 'No, none.'* ◇ *I went to several shops but none had what I was looking for.* ◇ *'Could you pass me the wine, please?' 'I'm afraid there's none left* (nic nie zostało)*.'* ▶ **nic, nikt, żaden**

Jeżeli używamy **none of** z rzeczownikiem niepoliczalnym, wówczas czasownik występuje w lp: *None of the work was done.* Jeśli natomiast **none of** używamy z rzeczownikiem w lm lub z zaimkiem, lub z rzeczownikiem w lp odnoszącym się do grupy osób lub rzeczy, wówczas czasownik występuje w lp lub lm. Formę czasownika w lp stosuje się w Br. ang. w języku formalnym: *None of the trains is/are going to Birmingham.* ◇ *None of her family has/have been to university.* Mówiąc o dwóch osobach lub rzeczach, używamy **neither**, a nie **none**. Zwróć uwagę na różnicę między **none** i **no**. **No** zawsze poprzedza rzeczownik, podczas gdy **none** go zastępuje: *I told him that I had **no money** left.* ◇ *When he asked me how much money I had left, I told him that I had **none**.*

none[2] /nʌn/ adv.
IDM **none the wiser** knowing no more than before: *We talked for a long time but I'm still **none the wiser**.* ▶ **wcale/bynajmniej nie mądrzejszy**
none too happy, clean, pleased, etc. (informal) not very happy, clean, pleased, etc. ▶ **niezbyt szczęśliwy, czysty, zadowolony itp.**
be none the worse (for sth) to be unhurt or undamaged by sth ▶ **nie ucierpieć (w wyniku czegoś)**

nonentity /nɒˈnentəti/ noun [C] (pl. **-ies**) a person without any special qualities, who has not achieved anything important ▶ **miernota** SYN **nobody** ℹ Wyraża dezaprobatę.

ˌnon-esˈsential adj. [usually before a noun] not completely necessary ▶ **nieistotny** ➲ look at **essential** ℹ To słowo nie jest tak mocne jak **inessential** i jest częściej stosowane. **Inessential** czasem oznacza dezaprobatę.
■ **ˌnon-esˈsential** noun [usually pl.]: *I've got no money for non-essentials.* ▶ **nieistotne sprawy/rzeczy, drobiazgi**

nonetheless /ˌnʌnðəˈles/ adv. (formal) in spite of this fact: *It won't be easy but they're going to try nonetheless.* ▶ **niemniej jednak** SYN **nevertheless**

ˌnon-eˈvent noun [C] (informal) an event that was expected to be interesting, exciting and popular but is in fact very disappointing: *The party turned out to be a non-event – hardly anyone came!* ▶ **niewypał** SYN **anticlimax**

ˌnon-eˈxistent adj. not existing or not available: *In some areas public transport is completely non-existent.* (zupełnie nie istnieje) ▶ **nieistniejący**

ˌnon-ˈfiction noun [U] writing that is about real people, events and facts: *You'll find biographies in the non-fiction section of the library.* ▶ **literatura faktu** OPP **fiction**

ˌnon-ˈflammable adj. not likely to burn easily: *non-flammable nightwear* ▶ **niepalny** OPP **flammable**

ˌnon-neˈgotiable adj. **1** that cannot be discussed or changed: *non-negotiable demands* ▶ **niepodlegający negocjacjom 2** (used about a cheque, etc.) that cannot be changed for money by anyone except the person whose name is on it ▶ (*czek itp.*) **niezbywalny** OPP for both meanings **negotiable**

ˌno-ˈnonsense adj. [only before a noun] simple and direct; only paying attention to important and necessary things: *a **no-nonsense approach/style*** ▶ **zasadniczy**

nonplussed /ˌnɒnˈplʌst/ adj. confused; not able to understand ▶ **zakłopotany**

ˌnon-reˈnewable adj. (used about natural sources of energy such as gas or oil) that cannot be replaced after use ▶ **nieodnawialny**

nonsense /ˈnɒnsns; US also -sens/ noun [U] **1** ideas, statements or beliefs that you think are ridiculous or not true: *Don't **talk nonsense**!* ◇ *It's nonsense to say you aren't good enough to go to university!* ▶ **bzdur-a/y** SYN **rubbish 2** silly or unacceptable behaviour: *The head teacher won't stand for any nonsense.* ▶ **szaleństwo**

nonsensical /nɒnˈsensɪkl/ adj. ridiculous; without meaning ▶ **niedorzeczny**

ˌnon-ˈsmoker noun [C] a person who does not smoke cigarettes, etc. ▶ **niepaląc-y/a** OPP **smoker**

ˌnon-ˈsmoking (also **ˌno-ˈsmoking**) adj. [usually before a noun] **1** (used about a place) where people are not allowed to smoke: *a non-smoking area in a restaurant* ▶ **dla niepalących 2** (used about a person) who does not smoke: *She's a non-smoking, non-drinking fitness fanatic.* ▶ **niepalący**
■ **ˌnon-ˈsmoking** (also **ˌno-ˈsmoking**) noun [U]: *Non-smoking is now the norm in most workplaces.* ▶ **niepalenie**

ˌnon-ˈstarter noun [C] a person, plan or idea that has no chance of success ▶ **coś/ktoś bez szans (na powodzenie)**

ˌnon-ˈstick adj. (used about a pan, etc.) covered with a substance that prevents food from sticking to it ▶ **teflonowy**

ˌnon-ˈstop adj. without a stop or a rest: *a non-stop flight to Mumbai* ▶ **bezpośredni, nieprzerwany**
■ **ˌnon-ˈstop** adv.: *He talked non-stop for two hours about his holiday.* ▶ **bezpośrednio, nieprzerwanie**

ˌnon-ˈviolence noun [U] fighting for political or social change without using force, for example by not obeying laws ▶ **powstrzymywanie się od użycia przemocy z powodów ideologicznych**

ˌnon-ˈviolent adj. **1** using peaceful methods, not force, to bring about political or social change: *non-violent resistance* ▶ **pokojowy 2** not involving force, or injury to sb: *non-violent crimes* ▶ **niestosujący przemocy**

noodle /ˈnuːdl/ noun [C, usually pl.] long thin pieces of food made of flour, egg and water that are cooked in boiling water or used in soups ▶ **makaron** (*typu nitki*) ➲ look at **macaroni**

nook /nʊk/ noun [C] a small quiet place or corner (in a house, garden, etc.) ▶ **kącik, zakamarek**
IDM **every nook and cranny** (informal) every part of a place ▶ **każdy zakamarek**

noon /nuːn/ noun [U] 12 o'clock in the middle of the day; midday: ***At noon*** (w południe) *the sun is at its highest point in the sky.* ▶ **południe** SYN **midday** ➲ look at **midnight**

ˈno one = NOBODY[1]

N

noose /nuːs/ noun [C] **1** a circle that is tied in the end of a rope and that gets smaller as one end of the rope is pulled ▶ **pętla 2** a circle like this in a rope that is used for hanging a person ▶ **stryczek**

nope /nəʊp/ exclamation (informal) (used to say 'no'): *'Have you seen my pen?' 'Nope.'* ▶ **nie**

nor /nɔː(r)/ conj., adv. **1 neither... nor...** and not: *I have neither the time nor the inclination to listen to his complaints again.* ▶ **ani 2** [used before a positive verb to agree with sth negative that has just been said] also not; neither: *'I don't like golf.' 'Nor do I.'* (ja też nie) ◇ *'We haven't been to America.' 'Nor have we.'* ▶ **też nie** ❶ W tym samym znaczeniu można też użyć **neither**: *'I won't be here tomorrow.' 'Nor/Neither will I.'* **3** [used after a negative statement to add some more information] also not: *Michael never forgot her birthday. Nor their wedding anniversary for that matter.* ▶ **ani też**

norm /nɔːm/ noun [C] [often with *the*] a situation or way of behaving that is usual or expected: *social/cultural norms* ▶ **norma, reguła**

normal[1] /ˈnɔːml/ adj. typical, usual or ordinary; what you expect: *I'll meet you at the normal time.* ◇ *It's quite normal* (to zupełnie naturalne) *to feel angry in a situation like this.* ◇ *In/Under normal circumstances* (w normalnych okolicznościach) *the meeting would only have lasted an hour.* ▶ **zwykły, normalny, typowy** OPP **abnormal**

normal[2] /ˈnɔːml/ noun [U] the usual or average state, level or standard: *temperatures above/below normal* ◇ *Things are* ***back to normal*** (rzeczy wróciły do normy) *at work now.* ▶ **norma**

normality /nɔːˈmæləti/ (US **normalcy** /ˈnɔːmlsi/) noun [U] the state of being normal ▶ **normalność**

normalize (also **-ise**) /ˈnɔːməlaɪz/ verb [I,T] (formal) to become or make sth become normal again or return to how it was before: *The two countries agreed to normalize relations.* ▶ **normalizować (się)**

normally /ˈnɔːməli/ adv. **1** usually: *I normally leave the house at 8 o'clock.* ◇ *Normally he takes the bus.* ▶ **zazwyczaj 2** in the usual or ordinary way: *The man wasn't behaving normally.* ▶ **normalnie**

Norse /nɔːs/ noun [U] the Norwegian language, especially in an ancient form, or the Scandinavian language group ▶ **język nordyjski**

north[1] /nɔːθ/ noun [sing.] (abbr. **N**) **1** (also **the north**) the direction that is on your left when you watch the sun rise; one of the **points of the compass**: *cold winds from the north* ◇ *Which way is north?* ◇ *I live* ***to the north of*** (na północ od) *Belfast.* ▶ **północ 2** (**the north**; **the North**) the northern part of a country, a city, a region or the world: *Houses are less expensive in the North of England than in the South.* ◇ *I live in the north of Athens.* ▶ **północ** ➲ look at **south**, **east**, **west**

north[2] /nɔːθ/ adj. **1** (also **North**) [only before a noun] in the north: *The new offices will be in North London.* ◇ *The north wing of the hospital was destroyed in a fire.* ▶ **północny 2** (used about a wind) coming from the north ▶ **północny, z północy**

■ **north** adv. to or towards the north: *We got onto the motorway going north instead of south.* ◇ *The house faces north.* ◇ *Is Leeds north of Manchester?* ▶ **na północ/y**

northbound /ˈnɔːθbaʊnd/ adj. travelling or leading towards the north: *northbound traffic* ▶ (*jadący/idący itp.*) **w kierunku północnym, na północ**

ˌnorth-ˈeast[1] (also **the North-East**) noun [sing.] (abbr. **NE**) the direction or a region that is an equal distance between north and east ▶ **północny wschód**

ˌnorth-ˈeast[2] adj. in, from or to the **north-east** of a place or country: *the north-east coast of Australia* ▶ **północno-wschodni**

■ **ˌnorth-ˈeast** adv.: *If you look north-east, you can see the mountains.* ▶ **w kierunku północno-wschodnim**

ˌnorth-ˈeasterly adj. **1** [only before a noun] towards the north-east: *in a north-easterly direction* ▶ **północno-wschodni 2** (used about a wind) coming from the north-east ▶ **północno-wschodni**

ˌnorth-ˈeastern adj. (abbr. **NE**) [only before a noun] connected with the north-east of a place or country ▶ **północno-wschodni**

ˌnorth-ˈeastwards (also **ˌnorth-ˈeastward**) adv. towards the north-east: *Follow the A619 north-eastward.* ▶ **w kierunku północno-wschodnim**

northerly /ˈnɔːðəli/ adj. **1** [only before a noun] to, towards or in the north: *Keep going in a northerly direction.* ▶ **północny 2** (used about a wind) coming from the north ▶ **północny, z północy**

northern (also **Northern**) /ˈnɔːðən/ adj. (abbr. **N**) of, in or from the north of a place: *She has a northern accent.* ◇ *in northern Australia* ▶ **północny**

northerner (also **Northerner**) /ˈnɔːðənə(r)/ noun [C] a person who was born in or who lives in the northern part of a country ▶ **mieszkan-iec/ka północnej części kraju** OPP **southerner**

northernmost /ˈnɔːðənməʊst/ adj. furthest north: *the northernmost island of Japan* ▶ **najdalej położony na północ**

the **ˌNorth ˈPole** noun [sing.] the point on the Earth's surface which is furthest north ▶ **biegun północny**

northwards /ˈnɔːθwədz/ (also **northward**) adv. towards the north: *Continue northwards out of the city for about five miles.* ▶ **na północ**

■ **northward** adj.: *in a northward direction* ▶ **północny**

ˌnorth-ˈwest[1] (also **the North-West**) noun [sing.] (abbr. **NW**) the direction or a region that is an equal distance between north and west ▶ **północny zachód**

ˌnorth-ˈwest[2] adj. in, from or to the **north-west** of a place or country: *the north-west coast of Scotland* ▶ **północno-zachodni**

■ **ˌnorth-ˈwest** adv.: *Our house faces north-west.* ▶ **w kierunku północno-zachodnim**

ˌnorth-ˈwesterly adj. **1** [only before a noun] towards the north-west: *in a north-westerly direction* ▶ **północno-zachodni 2** (used about a wind) coming from the north-west ▶ **północno-zachodni**

ˌnorth-ˈwestern adj. (abbr. **NW**) [only before a noun] connected with the north-west of a place or country ▶ **północno-zachodni**

ˌnorth-ˈwestwards (also **ˌnorth-ˈwestward**) adv. towards the north-west: *Follow the A40 north-westward for ten miles.* ▶ **w kierunku północno-zachodnim**

nose[1] /nəʊz/ noun [C] **1** the part of your face, above your mouth, that is used for breathing and smelling: *Breathe in through your nose and out through your mouth.* ◇ *This medicine should stop your nose running* (powinno wyleczyć katar). ◇ *Picking your nose* (dłubanie w nosie) *is not a nice habit.* ◇ *a nose stud* kolczyk (wkrętka) w nosie ▶ **nos** ➲ look at **nasal** ➲ picture at **body 2** (**-nosed**) [in compounds] having the type of nose mentioned: *red-nosed* ◇ *big-nosed* ◇ *runny-nosed* zakatarzony ▶ (*określa cechę nosa*) **3** the front part of a plane, etc.: *The nose of the plane was badly damaged.* ▶ **dziób** (*np. samolotu*) ➲ picture at **plane**

IDM **blow your nose** → BLOW[1]

follow your nose → FOLLOW

look down your nose at sb/sth → LOOK[1]

poke/stick your nose into sth (informal) to be interested in or try to become involved in sth which does not concern you ▶ **wtykać nos w nie swoje sprawy**
turn your nose up at sth (informal) to refuse sth because you do not think it is good enough for you ▶ **kręcić na coś nosem**

nose² /nəʊz/ verb [I] (used about a vehicle) to move forward slowly and carefully ▶ **(powoli) posuwać się naprzód**
PHR V **nose about/around** (informal) to look for sth, especially private information about sb ▶ **węszyć**

nosebleed /ˈnəʊzbliːd/ noun [C] a sudden flow of blood that comes from your nose ▶ **krwawienie z nosa**

nosedive /ˈnəʊzdaɪv/ noun [C] **1** a sudden steep fall or drop; a situation where sth suddenly becomes worse or begins to fail: *Oil prices* ***took a nosedive*** (gwałtownie spadły) *in the crisis.* ▶ **gwałtowny spadek**; **gwałtowne pogorszenie (się) 2** the sudden sharp fall of an aircraft towards the ground with its front part pointing down ▶ **pikowanie**
■ **nosedive** verb [I]: *Building costs have nosedived.* ▶ **gwałtownie spadać**; **pikować**

nosh /nɒʃ/ noun [U, sing.] (old-fashioned, Brit., slang) food; a meal: *She likes her nosh.* ◇ *Did you have a good nosh?* ▶ **żarcie**

ˌno-ˈsmoking = NON-SMOKING

nostalgia /nɒˈstældʒə; US also nəˈs-/ noun [U] a feeling of pleasure, mixed with sadness, when you think of happy times in the past: *She was suddenly filled with* ***nostalgia for*** *her university days.* ▶ **nostalgia**
■ **nostalgic** /nɒˈstældʒɪk; US also nəˈs-/ adj. ▶ **nostalgiczny** | **nostalgically** /-kli/ adv. ▶ **tęsknie**, **nostalgicznie**

nostril /ˈnɒstrəl/ noun [C] one of the two openings at the end of your nose that you breathe through ▶ **nozdrze** ➲ picture at **body**

nosy (also **nosey**) /ˈnəʊzi/ adj. too interested in other people's personal affairs: *a nosy neighbour* ▶ **wścibski**

⚷ **not** /nɒt/ adv. **1** (used to form the negative with **auxiliary verbs** and with **modal verbs**. *Not* is often pronounced or written *n't* in informal situations): *It's not/it isn't raining now.* ◇ *I cannot/can't see from here.* ◇ *He didn't invite me.* ◇ *Don't you like spaghetti?* ◇ *I hope she will not/won't be late.* ◇ *You're German, aren't you* (czyż nie)*?* ◇ *You shouldn't have said that.* ▶ **nie 2** (used to give the following word or phrase a negative meaning): *He told me not to telephone.* ◇ *She accused me of not telling the truth.* ◇ *Not one person replied to my advertisement.* ◇ *It's not easy.* ◇ *He's not very tall.* ▶ **nie 3** (used to give a short negative reply): *'Whose turn is it to do the shopping?' 'Not mine.'* ◇ *'Do you think they'll get divorced?' 'I hope not* (mam nadzieję, że nie)*.'* ◇ *'You can't drive all that way alone.' 'I suppose not* (chyba nie)*.'* ◇ *'Can I borrow £20?'* ***'Certainly not*** (wykluczone)*!'* ◇ *'Are you coming to the theatre with us?' 'I'd rather not* (wolałbym nie)*, if you don't mind.'* ◇ *'Did you see her?' 'I'm afraid not* (niestety nie)*.'* ▶ **nie 4** (used with *or* to give a negative possibility): *Shall we tell her* ***or not*** (czy nie)*?* ◇ *I don't know if/whether he's telling the truth or not.* ▶ **nie**
IDM **not at all 1** (used to politely accept thanks): *'Thanks a lot.' 'Not at all.'* ▶ **proszę (bardzo)**, **nie ma za co 2** (used to agree to sth): *'Do you mind if I come too?' 'Not at all.'* Ależ skąd? ▶ **wcale nie 3** (used as a way of saying 'definitely not'): *The instructions are not at all clear.* ▶ **wcale nie**
not only... (but) also (used for emphasizing the fact that there is sth more to add): *They not only have two houses in London, they also have one in France.* ▶ **nie tylko ... ale także**

notable /ˈnəʊtəbl/ adj. **notable (for sth)** interesting or important enough to receive attention: *The area is notable for* (słynie z) *its wildlife.* ▶ **godny uwagi**, **sławny**

notably /ˈnəʊtəbli/ adv. (used for giving an especially important example of what you are talking about): *Several politicians, most notably the Prime Minister and the Home Secretary, have given the proposal their full support.* ▶ **zwłaszcza**

notation /nəʊˈteɪʃn/ noun [U,C] a system of signs or symbols used to represent information, especially in mathematics, science and music ▶ **notacja**

notch¹ /nɒtʃ/ noun [C] **1** a level on a scale of quality: *This meal is certainly* ***a notch above*** (trochę lepszy niż) *the last one we had here.* ▶ **stopień 2** a cut in an edge or surface in the shape of a V or a circle, sometimes used to help you count sth ▶ **karb**

notch² /nɒtʃ/ verb
PHR V **notch sth up** to score or achieve sth: *Lewis notched up his best ever time in the 100 metres.* ▶ **osiągać**, **zdobywać**

⚷ **note¹** /nəʊt/ noun **1** [C] some words that you write down quickly to help you remember sth: *I'd better* ***make a note of*** *your name and address.* ◇ ***Keep a note of*** (zapisuj) *who has paid and who hasn't.* ◇ *The lecturer advised the students to* ***take notes*** (robić notatki) *while he was speaking.* ▶ **notatka 2** [C] a short letter: *This is just a note to thank you for having us to dinner.* ◇ *If Mark's not at home, we'll leave a note for him.* ◇ *a sick note* (zwolnienie lekarskie) *from your doctor* ▶ **parę słów**, **liścik 3** [C] a short explanation or extra piece of information that is given at the back of a book, etc. or at the bottom or side of a page: *See note 5, page 340.* ▶ **przypis/ek** ➲ look at **footnote 4** [C] (also **banknote** /ˈbæŋknəʊt/; US **bill** /bɪl/) a piece of paper money: *I'd like the money in £10 notes, please.* ▶ **banknot 5** [C] a single musical sound made by a voice or an instrument; a written sign that represents a musical sound: *I can only remember the first few notes of the song.* ▶ **nuta 6** [sing.] something that shows a certain quality or feeling: *The meeting ended on a rather unpleasant note* (zakończyło się dość nieprzyjemnie). ▶ **ton**; **nut(k)a**
IDM **compare notes (with sb)** → COMPARE
take note (of sth) to pay attention to sth and be sure to remember it ▶ **brać coś pod uwagę**

⚷ **note²** /nəʊt/ verb [T] **1** to notice or pay careful attention to sth: *He noted a slight change in her attitude towards him.* ◇ *Please note that this office is closed on Tuesdays.* ▶ **zauważać 2** to mention sth: *I'd like to note that the project has so far been extremely successful.* ▶ **zauważać**
PHR V **note sth down** to write sth down so that you remember it ▶ **notować**, **zapisywać**

notebook /ˈnəʊtbʊk/ noun [C] **1** a small book in which you write down things that you want to remember ▶ **notes 2** (also **ˌnotebook comˈputer**) a very small computer that you can carry with you and use anywhere ▶ **notebook** ➲ look at **desktop computer**, **laptop**

noted /ˈnəʊtɪd/ adj. (formal) **noted (for/as sth)** well known; famous: *The hotel is noted for* (słynie z) *its food.* ▶ **słynny (z czegoś)**

notepad /ˈnəʊtpæd/ noun [C] sheets of paper in a block that are used for writing things on ▶ **notatnik**

notepaper /ˈnəʊtpeɪpə(r)/ noun [U] paper that you write letters on ▶ **papier listowy**

noteworthy /ˈnəʊtwɜːði/ adj. interesting or important; that is worth noticing ▶ **godny uwagi**, **znaczący**

⚷ **nothing** /ˈnʌθɪŋ/ pron. not anything; no thing: *There's nothing* (nic nie ma) *in this suitcase.* ◇ *I'm bored – there's* ***nothing to do*** (nie ma co robić) *here.* ◇ *There was* ***nothing else*** (nic więcej) *to say.* ◇ *'What's the matter?' 'Oh, nothing.'* ◇ *'Thank you so much for all your help.' 'It was nothing* (drobiazg)*.'* ◇ *The doctor said there's nothing*

N

wrong with me. ◇ *Don't leave the baby there with nothing on* (nieubranego) *– he'll get cold.* ▶ **nic** ➲ note at **zero**

IDM **be/have nothing to do with sb/sth** to have no connection with sb/sth: *That question has nothing to do with what we're discussing.* ◇ *Keep out of this – it's nothing to do with you.* ◇ *Put my diary down – it's nothing to do with you* (to nie twoja sprawa). ▶ **nie mieć nic wspólnego z kimś/czymś**

come to nothing; not come to anything → COME

do nothing/not do anything by halves → HALF[1]

for nothing 1 for no payment; free: *Children under four are allowed in for nothing.* ▶ **za darmo 2** for no good reason or with no good result: *His hard work was all for nothing.* ▶ **na nic**

next to nothing → NEXT TO

nothing but only: *He does nothing but sit around watching TV all day.* ▶ **wyłącznie, nic tylko**

nothing like 1 not at all like: *She looks nothing like* (w niczym nie przypomina) *either of her parents.* ▶ **całkiem inny (niż) 2** not at all; not nearly: *There's nothing like enough food for all of us.* ▶ **wcale nie**

nothing much not a lot of sth; nothing of importance: *It's a nice town but there's nothing much to do in the evenings.* ◇ *'What did you do at the weekend?' 'Nothing much.'* ▶ **nic wielkiego/specjalnego**

(there's) nothing to it (it's) very easy: *You'll soon learn – there's nothing to it really.* ▶ **nie ma nic łatwiejszego**

stop at nothing → STOP[1] ▶ **nie cofać się przed niczym**

there is/was nothing (else) for it (but to do sth) there is/was no other action possible: *There was nothing for it but to resign.* ▶ **nie pozostaje nic innego, jak**

⚷ **notice**[1] /ˈnəʊtɪs/ noun **1** [U] the act of paying attention to sth or knowing about sth: *The protests are finally making the government **take notice**.* Protesty w końcu sprawiły, że rząd zwrócił uwagę na problemy. ◇ ***Take no notice of** what he said – he was just being silly.* ◇ *It has **come to my notice*** (zauważyłem) *that you have missed a lot of classes.* ▶ **uwaga 2** [C] a piece of paper or a sign giving information, a warning, etc. that is put where everyone can read it: *There's a notice on the board saying that the meeting has been cancelled.* ◇ *The notice said 'No dogs allowed'.* ▶ **zawiadomienie 3** [U] a warning that sth is going to happen: *I can't produce a meal **at such short notice*** (w tak krótkim terminie)*!* ◇ *I wish you'd **give** me more **notice*** (szkoda, że nie powiedziałeś mi wcześniej) *when you're going to be off work.* ◇ *The swimming pool is closed **until further notice*** (do odwołania). ▶ **ostrzeżenie, wymówienie**

⚷ **notice**[2] /ˈnəʊtɪs/ verb [I,T] [not usually used in the continuous tenses] to see and become conscious of sth: *'What kind of car was the man driving?' 'I'm afraid I didn't notice.'* ◇ *I noticed (that) he was carrying a black briefcase.* ◇ *Did you notice which direction she went in?* ◇ *We didn't notice him leave/him leaving.* ▶ **zauważać, zwracać uwagę (na kogoś/coś)**

⚷ **noticeable** /ˈnəʊtɪsəbl/ adj. easy to see or notice: *The scar from the accident was hardly noticeable.* ▶ **widoczny, zauważalny**

■ **noticeably** /-əbli/ adv. ▶ **widocznie, zauważalnie**

noticeboard /ˈnəʊtɪsbɔːd/ (US **ˈbulletin board**) noun [C] a board on a wall for putting written information where everyone can read it ▶ **tablica ogłoszeń**

notify /ˈnəʊtɪfaɪ/ verb [T] (**notifying**; **notifies**; pt, pp **notified**) **notify sb (of sth)** to tell sb about sth officially ▶ **zawiadamiać**

■ **notification** /ˌnəʊtɪfɪˈkeɪʃn/ noun [C,U] ▶ **zawiadomienie**

notion /ˈnəʊʃn/ noun [C] **a notion (that .../of sth)** something that you have in your mind; an idea: *I had a vague notion that I had seen her before.* ◇ *You seem to have no notion* (wydaje się, że zupełnie nie masz pojęcia) *of how difficult it is going to be.* ▶ **pojęcie**

notional /ˈnəʊʃənl/ adj. existing only in the mind; not based on facts or reality ▶ **hipotetyczny**

notoriety /ˌnəʊtəˈraɪəti/ noun [U] the state of being well known for sth bad ▶ **zła sława**

notorious /nəʊˈtɔːriəs/ adj. **notorious (for/as sth)** well known for sth bad: *a notorious criminal* ◇ *This road is notorious for* (słynie z) *the number of accidents on it.* ▶ **notoryczny** SYN **infamous**

■ **notoriously** adv. ▶ **notorycznie**

notwithstanding /ˌnɒtwɪθˈstændɪŋ; -wɪð-/ prep. (formal) without being affected by sth; in spite of sth ▶ **pomimo**

■ **notwithstanding** adv. (formal) anyway; in spite of this ▶ **jednakże**

nougat /ˈnuːɡɑː; US -ɡət/ noun [U] a hard pink or white sweet that contains nuts and fruit ▶ **nugat**

nought /nɔːt/ (especially US **zero**) noun [C] the figure 0: *A million is written with six noughts.* ◇ *We say 0.1 'nought point one'.* ▶ **zero** ➲ note at **decimal**[2]

IDM **noughts and crosses** a game for two players in which each person tries to win by writing three 0s or three Xs in a line. ▶ **kółko i krzyżyk**

noun /naʊn/ noun [C] a word that is the name of a thing, an idea, a place or a person: *'Water', 'happiness', 'James' and 'France' are all nouns.* ◇ *an abstract noun* (rzeczownik abstrakcyjny) *e.g. 'happiness'* ◇ *a common noun* (rzeczownik pospolity) *e.g. 'table', 'cat', 'sea'* ◇ *a collective noun* (rzeczownik zbiorowy) *e.g. 'committee', 'team'* ◇ *a proper noun* (rzeczownik własny) *e.g. 'Africa', 'Jane'* ▶ **rzeczownik** ➲ look at **countable**, **uncountable**

nourish /ˈnʌrɪʃ; US ˈnɜːrɪʃ/ verb [T] **1** to give sb/sth the right kind of food so that they or it can grow and be healthy ▶ **odżywiać 2** (formal) to allow a feeling, an idea, etc. to grow stronger ▶ **kultywować, żywić**

■ **nourishment** noun [U] ▶ **pożywienie**

Nov. = NOVEMBER: *17 Nov. 2001*

⚷ **novel**[1] /ˈnɒvl/ noun [C] a book that tells a story about people and events that are not real: *a romantic/historical/detective novel* ▶ **powieść** ➲ note at **book**

novel[2] /ˈnɒvl/ adj. new and different: *That's a novel idea! Let's try it.* ▶ **nowatorski**

novelist /ˈnɒvəlɪst/ noun [C] a person who writes novels ▶ **powieściopisa-rz/rka**

novelty /ˈnɒvlti/ noun (pl. **novelties**) **1** [U] the quality of being new and different: *The novelty of her new job soon wore off.* Wkrótce nowa posada przestała być dla niej nowością. ▶ **nowość 2** [C] something new and unusual: *It was quite a novelty not to have to get up early.* ▶ **coś nowego, innowacja 3** [C] a small, cheap object that is sold as a toy or decoration ▶ **drobiazg, pamiątka**

⚷ **November** /nəʊˈvembə(r)/ noun [U,C] (abbr. **Nov.**) the 11th month of the year, coming after October ▶ **listopad** ➲ note at **January**

novice /ˈnɒvɪs/ noun [C] a person who is new and without experience in a certain job, situation, etc. ▶ **nowicjusz/ka** SYN **beginner**

⚷ **now** /naʊ/ adv. **1** (at) the present time: *We can't go for a walk now – it's raining.* ◇ *Where are you living now?* ◇ ***From now on*** (odtąd) *I'm going to work harder.* ◇ ***Up till now*** (dotychczas) *we haven't been able to afford a house of our own.* ◇ *He will be on his way home **by now**.* ◇ *I can manage **for now** but I might need some help later.* ◇ *I've been living with my parents until now* (dotychczas). ▶ **teraz, obecnie 2** immediately: *Go now before anyone sees you.* ◇ *You must go to the doctor **right now*** (natychmiast). ▶ **zaraz 3** (used to introduce or to emphasize what you are saying, or while pausing to think): *Now listen to what he's saying.* ◇ *What does he want now?*

◇ *Now, let me think.* ◇ *Be quiet, now!* No bądźże cicho! ▶ **no; zaraz, zaraz** ℹ Można też użyć **now then**: *Now then, are there any questions?* ◇ *Now then, what was I saying?* **4** because of what has happened: *I've lost my pen. Now I'll have to buy a new one.* ▶ **teraz**

IDM **any moment/second/minute/day (now)** → ANY

just now → JUST[1]

(every) now and again/then from time to time: *We see each other now and then, but not very often.* ▶ **co jakiś czas** SYN **occasionally**

right now → RIGHT[2]

■ **now** (**now (that)**) conj. because of the fact that: *Now (that) the children have left home we can move to a smaller house.* ▶ **teraz, gdy**

nowadays /ˈnaʊədeɪz/ adv. at the present time (when compared with the past): *I don't go to London much nowadays.* ▶ **obecnie** SYN **today**

nowhere /ˈnəʊweə(r)/ adv. not in or to any place; not anywhere: *I'm afraid there's nowhere to stay* (nie ma gdzie się zatrzymać) *in this village.* ◇ *I don't like it here, but there's **nowhere else** for us to sit.* ◇ *We got to the meeting place on time, but our group was **nowhere to be seen/nowhere in sight*** (nigdzie nie było widać naszej grupy). ◇ *There's nowhere interesting to go* (nie ma interesujących miejsc) *round here.* ◇ *It's so hot I'm getting nowhere* (nie robię żadnych postępów) *with this work.* ◇ *'Don't leave the car there!' 'There's nowhere else* (nie ma innego miejsca) *to park it.'* ▶ **nigdzie**

IDM **get somewhere/nowhere (with sb/sth)** → GET

in the middle of nowhere → MIDDLE[1]

nowhere near far from: *We've sold nowhere near enough tickets to make a profit.* ▶ **(nawet) nie zbliżając się do (uzyskania/osiągnięcia) czegoś, daleko od (uzyskania/osiągnięcia) czegoś**

ˌno-ˈwin adj. [only before a noun] (used about a situation, policy, etc.) that will end badly whatever you decide to do ▶ **bez wyjścia**

noxious /ˈnɒkʃəs/ adj. (formal) harmful or poisonous: *noxious gases* ▶ **szkodliwy; trujący**

nozzle /ˈnɒzl/ noun [C] a narrow tube that is put on the end of a pipe to control the liquid or gas coming out ▶ **dysza**

nr abbr. = NEAR[1] (1): *Masham, nr Ripon*

nuance /ˈnjuːɑːns; US ˈnuː-/ noun [C] a very small difference in meaning, feeling, sound, etc. ▶ **niuans**

nuclear /ˈnjuːkliə(r); US ˈnuː-/ adj. **1** using, producing or resulting from the energy that is produced when the **nucleus** of an atom is split: *nuclear energy* ◇ *a nuclear power station* ◇ *nuclear war/weapons* ◇ *nuclear disarmament* ◇ *nuclear fission* rozszczepienie jądra atomu ◇ *nuclear fusion* synteza jądrowa ◇ *nuclear waste* ▶ **jądrowy** ➲ look at **atomic** **2** connected with the **nucleus** of an atom: *nuclear physics* ▶ **jądrowy** ➲ look at **atomic**

ˌnuclear ˈfamily noun [C] (technical) a family that consists of father, mother and children, when it is thought of as a unit in society ▶ **rodzina** *(jako podstawowa komórka społeczna)*

ˌnuclear reˈactor (also **reactor** /riˈæktə(r)/) noun [C] a very large machine that produces nuclear energy ▶ **reaktor jądrowy**

nucleus /ˈnjuːkliəs; US ˈnuː-/ noun [C] (pl. **nuclei** /-kliaɪ/) **1** the central part of an atom or of certain cells ▶ **jądro** **2** the central or most important part of sth ▶ **jądro; zaczątek**

nude[1] /njuːd; US nuːd/ adj. not wearing any clothes ▶ **nagi** ➲ look at **bare**, **naked**

■ **nudity** /ˈnjuːdəti; US ˈnuː-/ noun [U]: *This film contains scenes of nudity.* ▶ **nagość**

nude[2] /njuːd; US nuːd/ noun [C] a picture or photograph of a person who is not wearing any clothes ▶ **akt**

IDM **in the nude** not wearing any clothes ▶ **nagi; nago**

nudge /nʌdʒ/ verb [T] to touch or push sb/sth gently, especially with your elbow ▶ **trącać łokciem**

■ **nudge** noun [C]: *to give sb a nudge* trącić kogoś łokciem ▶ **trącenie łokciem**

nudist /ˈnjuːdɪst; US ˈnuː-/ noun [C] a person who does not wear any clothes because they believe this is more natural and healthy: *a nudist beach/camp* ▶ **naturyst(k)a**

■ **nudism** /ˈnjuːdɪzəm; US ˈnuː-/ noun [U] ▶ **naturyzm**

nugget /ˈnʌɡɪt/ noun [C] **1** a small lump of a valuable metal or mineral, especially gold, that is found in the earth ▶ **bryłka** **2** a small round piece of some types of food: *chicken nuggets* ▶ **kawałek** **3** a small thing such as an idea or a fact that people think of as valuable: *a useful nugget of information* ▶ **urywek** SYN **snippet**

nuisance /ˈnjuːsns; US ˈnuː-/ noun [C] a person, thing or situation that annoys you or causes you trouble: *It's a nuisance having to queue for everything.* ◇ *Your sister's doing her homework, so don't **make a nuisance of** yourself* (nie naprzykrzaj się). ◇ *I'm sorry to be a nuisance* (przepraszam za kłopot), *but could you change my appointment?* ▶ **rzecz/osoba dokuczliwa/uciążliwa**

nuke /njuːk/ verb [T] (informal) to attack a place with nuclear weapons ▶ **zrzucać bombę atomową**

■ **nuke** noun [C] a nuclear weapon ▶ **broń jądrowa**

null /nʌl/ adj.

IDM **null and void** (formal) not valid in law: *The contract was declared null and void.* ▶ **nieważny, nie mający mocy prawnej**

numb /nʌm/ adj. not able to feel anything; not able to move: *My fingers were numb with cold.* ◇ *I'll give you an injection and the tooth will **go numb**.* ◇ *He was numb with fear.* Zdrętwiał ze strachu. ▶ **zdrętwiały, bez czucia**

■ **numb** verb [T]: *We were numbed by the dreadful news.* ▶ **wprowadzać w stan odrętwienia, paraliżować** | **numbness** noun [U] ▶ **odrętwienie, brak czucia**

number[1] /ˈnʌmbə(r)/ noun **1** [C] a word or symbol that indicates a quantity: *Choose a number between ten and twenty.* ◇ *2, 4, 6, etc. are **even numbers*** (liczby parzyste) *and 1, 3, 5, etc. are **odd numbers*** (liczby nieparzyste). ◇ *a three-figure* (trzycyfrowa) *number* ▶ **liczba** **2** [C] (abbr. **No.**; **no.**) (used before a number to show the position of sth in a series): *We live in Croft Road, at number* (pod numerem) *25.* ◇ *room No. 347* ▶ **numer** **3** [C] a group of numbers that is used to identify sb/sth: *a telephone number* ◇ *a code number* ▶ **numer** **4** [C,U] **a number (of sth)** a quantity of people or things: *a large number of visitors* ◇ *We must reduce the number of accidents on the roads.* ◇ *Pupils in the school have doubled **in number** in recent years.* ◇ *There are **a number of*** (kilka) *things I don't understand.* ▶ **liczba, ilość** ℹ Gdy słowo **number** poprzedzone jest przymiotnikiem, to następujący po nim czasownik występuje zawsze w lm: *A small number of pupils study Latin.* **5** [C] a copy of a magazine, newspaper, etc.: *Back numbers of 'New Scientist' are available from the publishers.* ▶ **numer, egzemplarz** **6** [C] (informal) a song or dance: *They sang a slow romantic number.* ▶ **kawałek** *(np. piosenka)*

IDM **any number of** very many: *There could be any number of reasons why she isn't here.* ▶ **mnóstwo, bardzo dużo**

in round figures/numbers → ROUND[1]

your opposite number → OPPOSITE

number one (informal) **1** the most important or best person or thing: *We're number one in the used car business.* ▶ **najważniejsza/najlepsza osoba/rzecz** **2** yourself: ***Looking after number one*** (dbanie o siebie) *is all she thinks about.*

number[2] /ˈnʌmbə(r)/ verb [T] **1** to give a number to sth: *The houses are numbered from 1 to 52.* ▶ **numerować**

N

2 (used for saying how many people or things there are): *Our forces number 40 000.* ▶ **liczyć**

'number plate (US 'license plate) noun [C] the sign on the front and back of a vehicle that shows the **registration number** ▶ **tablica rejestracyjna** ➲ picture at **car**

numeracy /'nju:mərəsi; US 'nu:-/ noun [U] a good basic knowledge of mathematics; the ability to understand and work with numbers: *standards of numeracy and literacy* ▶ **umiejętność liczenia** ➲ look at **literacy**

numeral /'nju:mərəl; US 'nu:-/ noun [C] a sign or symbol that represents a quantity: *Roman numerals* ▶ **cyfra**

numerate /'nju:mərət; US 'nu:-/ adj. having a good basic knowledge of mathematics ▶ **umiejący liczyć** ➲ look at **literate**

numerical /nju:'merɪkl; US nu:-/ adj. of or shown by numbers: *to put something* ***in numerical order*** ▶ **liczbowy; cyfrowy**

numerous /'nju:mərəs; US 'nu:-/ adj. (formal) existing in large numbers; many ▶ **liczny**

nun /nʌn/ noun [C] a member of a religious group of women who live together in a **convent** and do not marry or have possessions ▶ **zakonnica** ➲ look at **monk**

🔑 **nurse**[1] /nɜ:s/ noun [C] a person who is trained to look after sick or injured people: *a male nurse ◇ a psychiatric nurse ◇ a community/district nurse* pielęgniarka środowiskowa/rejonowa ▶ **pielęgnia-rz/rka** ➲ note at **hospital** ➲ picture on **page A4**

nurse[2] /nɜ:s/ verb **1** [T] to take care of sb who is sick or injured; to take care of an injury: *Ahmed is still nursing a back injury. ◇ She nursed her mother back to health.* Pielęgnowała matkę dopóki nie wróciła do zdrowia. ▶ **pielęgnować**, **opiekować się** **2** [T] (formal) to have a strong feeling or idea in your mind for a long time: *Tim had long nursed the hope that Sharon would marry him.* ▶ **żywić** (*np. nadzieję*) **3** [T] to hold sb/sth in a loving way: *He nursed the child in his arms.* ▶ **tulić** **4** [I] to feed a baby or young animal with milk from the breast; to drink milk from the mother's breast ▶ **karmić/być karmionym piersią**

nursery /'nɜ:səri/ noun [C] (pl. **nurseries**) **1** a place where small children and babies are looked after so that their parents can go to work ▶ **żłobek** ➲ look at **crèche** **2** a place where young plants are grown and sold ▶ **szkółka (ogrodnicza)**

'nursery rhyme noun [C] a traditional poem or song for young children ▶ **wierszyk dla dzieci**

'nursery school (also **playgroup** /'pleɪgru:p/, **playschool** /'pleɪsku:l/) noun [C] a school for children aged from about 2 to 5 ▶ **przedszkole** SYN **kindergarten**

nursing /'nɜ:sɪŋ/ noun [U] the job of being a nurse ▶ **pielęgniarstwo**

'nursing home noun [C] a small private hospital, often for old people ▶ **prywatna klinika dla rekonwalescentów lub ludzi w starszym wieku**

nurture /'nɜ:tʃə(r)/ verb [T] (formal) **1** to take special care of sth/sb that is growing and developing: *These delicate plants need careful nurturing. ◇ children nurtured by loving parents* ▶ **wychowywać**, **pielęgnować**, **żywić** **2** to help sb/sth to develop and be successful: *It's important to nurture a good working relationship. ◇ My father nurtured a love of art in me.* ▶ **pielęgnować** (*np. związki, talent*)

■ **nurture** noun [U] (formal) ▶ **wychowanie**; **pielęgnowanie**

🔑 **nut** /nʌt/ noun [C] **1** a dry fruit that consists of a hard shell with a seed inside. Many types of nut can be eaten: *to crack a nut* ▶ **orzech** **2** a small piece of metal with a round hole in the middle through which you put a **bolt** to fasten things together: *to tighten a nut* ▶ **nakrętka** ➲ picture at **bolt** **3** (Brit., slang) a person's head or brain ▶ **głowa**, **pała** **4** (informal) (Brit. also **nutter** /'nʌtə(r)/) a mad or foolish person: *He's a complete nut, if you ask me.* ▶ **pomyleniec**

IDM **do your nut** (Brit., informal) to be very angry ▶ **wpadać w szał**

nutcase /'nʌtkeɪs/ noun [C] (informal) a crazy person: *She's a complete nutcase.* ▶ **wariat/ka**

nutcracker /'nʌtkrækə(r)/ noun [C] (Brit. also **nutcrackers** [pl.]) a tool for cracking open the shells of nuts ▶ **dziadek do orzechów**

nutmeg /'nʌtmeg/ noun [C,U] a type of hard seed that is often made into powder and used as a spice in cooking ▶ **gałka muszkatołowa**

nutrient /'nju:triənt; US 'nu:-/ noun [C] a substance that is needed to keep sb/sth alive and healthy: *Plants take minerals and other nutrients from the soil.* ▶ **składnik pokarmowy**

nutrition /nju'trɪʃn; US nu-/ noun [U] the food that you eat and the way that it affects your health: *Good nutrition is essential for children's growth.* ▶ **odżywianie**

■ **nutritional** /-ʃənl/ adj. ▶ **odżywczy**

nutritious /nju'trɪʃəs; US nu-/ adj. (used about a food) very good for you ▶ **odżywczy**, **pożywny**

nuts /nʌts/ adj. [not before a noun] (informal) **1** crazy: *I'll go nuts if that phone doesn't stop ringing. ◇ She's* ***driving me nuts*** (doprowadza mnie do szału) *with all her stupid questions.* ▶ **zwariowany** **2 nuts about sb/sth** very much in love with sb; very enthusiastic about sth: *He's absolutely nuts about her.* ▶ **zakochany do szaleństwa**; **zwariowany na punkcie czegoś**

nutshell /'nʌtʃel/ noun

IDM **in a nutshell** using few words ▶ **(mówiąc) krótko i węzłowato**

nutter (Brit., informal) = NUT (4): *His friends are a bunch of nutters.*

nutty /'nʌti/ adj. (**nuttier**; **nuttiest**) **1** containing or tasting of nuts ▶ **z orzechami**; **orzechowy** **2** (informal) mad or foolish: *He's* ***as nutty as a fruitcake*** (zupełnie stuknięty). ▶ **zbzikowany**

nuzzle /'nʌzl/ verb [I,T] to press or rub sb/sth gently with the nose ▶ (*zwłaszcza o zwierzętach*) **dotykać/trącać nosem**

NVQ /,en vi: 'kju:/ noun [C] **National Vocational Qualification**; a British qualification that shows that you have reached a particular standard in the work that you do: *NVQ Level 3 in Catering* ▶ **kwalifikacje zawodowe**

NW = NORTH-WEST[1], NORTH-WESTERN: *NW Australia*

nylon /'naɪlɒn/ noun [U] a very strong artificial material that is used for making clothes, rope, brushes, etc. ▶ **nylon**

nymph /nɪmf/ noun [C] (in ancient Greek and Roman stories) a spirit of nature in the form of a young woman that lives in rivers, woods, etc. ▶ **nimfa**

O o

O, o /əʊ/ noun [C,U] (pl. **Os**; **os**; **O's**; **o's** /əʊz/) **1** the 15th letter of the English alphabet: *'Orange' begins with (an) 'O'.* ▶ **litera** *o* **2** (used when you are speaking) zero: *My number is five O nine double four.* ▶ **zero** ➲ note at **zero**

O = OH

oak /əʊk/ noun **1** (also **'oak tree**) [C] a type of large tree with hard wood that is common in many northern parts of the world ▶ **dąb**

The fruit of the oak is an **acorn**.

2 [U] the wood from the **oak** tree: *a solid oak table* ▶ **dębina**, **dąb**

OAP (Brit.) = OLD-AGE PENSIONER

oar /ɔː(r)/ noun [C] a long pole that is flat and wide at one end and that you use for **rowing** ▶ **wiosło** ➲ look at **paddle**

oasis /əʊ'eɪsɪs/ noun [C] (pl. **oases** /-siːz/) a place in the desert where there is water and where plants grow ▶ **oaza**

oath /əʊθ/ noun [C] **1** a formal promise: *They have to **swear/take an oath** of loyalty.* ▶ **przysięga** **2** (old-fashioned) = SWEAR WORD

IDM **be on/under oath** to have made a formal promise to tell the truth in a court of law ▶ **zeznawać pod przysięgą**

oats /əʊts/ noun [pl.] a type of grain that is used as food for animals and for making flour, etc.: *porridge oats* owsianka ▶ **owies**

obedient /ə'biːdiənt/ adj. **obedient (to sb/sth)** doing what you are told to do: *As a child he was always obedient to his parents.* ▶ **posłuszny** **OPP** **disobedient**

■ **obedience** noun [U] ▶ **posłuszeństwo** | **obediently** adv. ▶ **posłusznie**

obese /əʊ'biːs/ adj. (used about people) very fat, in a way that is not healthy ▶ **otyły** ➲ note at **fat**

■ **obesity** /əʊ'biːsəti/ noun [U] ▶ **otyłość**

obey /ə'beɪ/ verb [I,T] to do what you are told to do: *Soldiers are trained to obey* (wykonywać) *orders.* ▶ **słuchać**, **być posłusznym** **OPP** **disobey**

obituary /ə'bɪtʃuəri; US əʊ'bɪtʃueri/ noun [C] (pl. **obituaries**) a piece of writing about sb's life that is printed in a newspaper soon after they have died ▶ **nekrolog**

object¹ /'ɒbdʒɪkt; US also -dʒekt/ noun [C] **1** a thing that can be seen and touched, but is not alive: *The shelves were filled with objects of all shapes and sizes.* ◇ *everyday/household objects* ▶ **przedmiot** **2** **the object of sth** a person or thing that causes a feeling, interest, thought, etc.: *the object of his desire/affections* ▶ **przedmiot** **3** the noun or phrase describing the person or thing that is affected by the act of a verb ▶ **dopełnienie** ➲ look at **subject**

> W zdaniach: *I sent a letter to Ewa.* ◇ *I sent Ewa a letter.* rzeczownik **letter** to dopełnienie bliższe, czyli **direct object**, a *Ewa* to dopełnienie dalsze, czyli **indirect object**.

4 an aim or purpose: *Making money is his sole object in life.* ▶ **cel**

IDM **money, etc. is no object** money, etc. is not important or is no problem: *They always want the best. Expense is no object.* ▶ **nie odgrywać roli**, **nie stanowić problemu**

object² /əb'dʒekt/ verb **1** [I] **object (to sb/sth)**; **object (to doing sth/to sb doing sth)** to not like or to be against sb/sth: *Many people object to the new tax.* ◇ *I object to companies trying to sell me things over the phone.* ▶ **być przeciwnym komuś/czemuś**, **protestować przeciw czemuś** **2** [T] to say a reason why you think sth is wrong: *'I think that's unfair,' he objected.* ▶ **sprzeciwiać się**, **protestować** **SYN** for both meanings **protest**

■ **objector** noun [C] ▶ **osoba sprzeciwiająca się**, **osoba protestująca**

objection /əb'dʒekʃn/ noun [C] **an objection (to sb/sth)**; **an objection (to doing sth/to sb doing sth)** a reason why you do not like or are against sb/sth: *We listed our objections to the proposed new road.* ◇ *I **have no objection** to you using my desk while I'm away.* ▶ **obiekcja**; **sprzeciw**

objectionable /əb'dʒekʃənəbl/ adj. very unpleasant ▶ **nieprzyjemny**, **okropny**

objective¹ /əb'dʒektɪv/ noun [C] something that you are trying to achieve; an aim: *Our objective is to finish by the end of the year.* ◇ *to achieve your objective* ▶ **cel** **SYN** **goal**

objective² /əb'dʒektɪv/ adj. not influenced by your own personal feelings; considering only facts: *Please try and give an objective report of what happened.* ◇ *It's hard to be objective about your own family.* ▶ **obiektywny** **OPP** **subjective**

■ **objectively** adv.: *He is too upset to see things objectively.* ▶ **obiektywnie** | **objectivity** /ˌɒbdʒek'tɪvəti/ noun [U] ▶ **bezstronność**, **obiektywność**

obligation /ˌɒblɪ'geɪʃn/ noun **1** [C] **an obligation (to sb) (to do sth)** something which you must do because you have promised, because of a law, etc.: *We **have a moral obligation** to help people who are in need.* ◇ *to fulfil your **legal/professional/financial obligations*** ▶ **obowiązek**; **zobowiązanie** **2** [U] the state of being forced to do sth because it is your duty, or because of a law, etc.: *Unfortunately the shop is **under** no **obligation*** (nie ma obowiązku) *to give you your money back.* ◇ *I don't want people coming to see me out of **a sense of obligation**.* ▶ **obowiązek**

obligatory /ə'blɪgətri; US -tɔːri/ adj. (formal) that you must do: *It is obligatory to get insurance before you drive a car.* ▶ **obowiązkowy**, **obowiązujący** **OPP** **optional**

oblige /ə'blaɪdʒ/ verb **1** [T, usually passive] to force sb to do sth: *Parents are obliged by law to send their children to school.* ◇ *Although I wasn't hungry, I felt obliged to eat something.* ◇ *You are not obliged* (nie musisz) *to answer these questions but it would be a great help if you did.* ▶ **zmuszać**, **zobowiązywać** **2** [I,T] (formal) to do what sb asks; to be helpful: *If you ever need any help, I'd be happy to oblige.* ▶ **służyć**, **robić komuś grzeczność**

■ **obliged** adj.: *Thanks for your help. I'm **much obliged** to you.* ▶ **zobowiązany** | **obliging** adj.: *I asked my neighbour for advice and he was very obliging.* ▶ **uprzejmy**; **usłużny**

oblique /ə'bliːk/ adj. **1** not expressed or done in a direct way: *an oblique reference/approach/comment* ▶ (*o komentarzu, aluzji itp.*) **pokrętny** **SYN** **indirect** **2** (used about a line) at an angle ▶ **skośny** **SYN** **sloping**

■ **obliquely** adv.: *He referred only obliquely to their recent problems.* ◇ *Always cut stems obliquely to enable flowers to absorb more water.* ▶ (*wypowiedzieć się itp.*) **pokrętnie**; **skośnie**

obliterate /ə'blɪtəreɪt/ verb [T, often passive] (formal) to remove all signs of sth by destroying or covering it completely ▶ **niszczyć doszczętnie**, **zacierać** (*np. ślady*)

oblivion /ə'blɪviən/ noun [U] **1** a state in which you do not realize what is happening around you, usually because you are unconscious or asleep: *I was in a state of complete oblivion.* ▶ **nieświadomość** **2** the state in which sb/sth has been forgotten and is no longer famous or important: *His work **faded into oblivion*** (odeszła w zapomnienie) *after his death.* ▶ **zapomnienie**

oblivious /ə'blɪviəs/ adj. **oblivious (to/of sb/sth)** not noticing or realizing what is happening around you:

She was completely oblivious of all the trouble she had caused. ▶ **niepomny (czegoś), niezwracający uwagi**

oblong /ˈɒblɒŋ/ noun [C] a shape with two long sides and two short sides and four **right angles** ▶ **prostokąt** SYN **rectangle**
■ **oblong** adj. ▶ **podłużny** SYN **rectangle**

obnoxious /əbˈnɒkʃəs/ adj. extremely unpleasant, especially in a way that offends people ▶ **wstrętny, ohydny**

oboe /ˈəʊbəʊ/ noun [C] a musical instrument made of wood that you play by blowing through it ▶ **obój** ➲ note at **music**, **piano**

obscene /əbˈsiːn/ adj. **1** connected with sex in a way that most people find disgusting and which causes offence: *obscene books/gestures/language* ▶ **sprośny, nieprzyzwoity 2** very large in size or amount in a way that some people find unacceptable: *He earns an obscene amount of money.* ▶ **obrzydliwie duży**

obscenity /əbˈsenəti/ noun (pl. **obscenities**) **1** [U] sexual language or behaviour, especially in books, plays, etc. which shocks people and causes offence ▶ **sprośność, nieprzyzwoitość 2** [C] sexual words or acts that shock people and cause offence: *He shouted a string of obscenities out of the car window.* ▶ **nieprzyzwoit-e/y słowo/czyn**

obscure[1] /əbˈskjʊə(r)/ adj. **1** not well known: *an obscure Spanish poet* ▶ **nieznany 2** not easy to see or understand: ***For some obscure reason**, he decided to give up his well-paid job, to become a writer.* ▶ **niejasny, niezrozumiały**
■ **obscurity** /əbˈskjʊərəti/ noun [U] ▶ **zapomnienie**

obscure[2] /əbˈskjʊə(r)/ verb [T] to make sth difficult to see or understand: *A high fence obscured our view.* ▶ **przysłaniać; zaciemniać**

obsequious /əbˈsiːkwiəs/ adj. (formal) trying too hard to please sb, especially sb who is important: *an obsequious manner* ▶ **służalczy** SYN **servile**
■ **obsequiously** adv.: *smiling obsequiously* ▶ **służalczo**

observance /əbˈzɜːvəns/ noun [U, sing.] **observance (of sth)** the practice of obeying or following a law, custom, etc. ▶ **przestrzeganie, poszanowanie**

observant /əbˈzɜːvənt/ adj. good at noticing things around you: *An observant passer-by gave the police a full description of the men.* ▶ **spostrzegawczy, uważny**

🔑 **observation** /ˌɒbzəˈveɪʃn/ noun **1** [U] the act of watching sb/sth carefully, especially to learn sth: *My research involves the observation of animals in their natural surroundings.* ◇ *The patient is being kept **under observation*** (być pod obserwacją). ▶ **obserwacja 2** [U] the ability to notice things: *Scientists need good **powers of observation**.* ▶ **spostrzegawczość 3** [C] **an observation (about/on sth)** something that you say or write about sth: *He began by making a few general observations about the sales figures.* ▶ **spostrzeżenie, uwaga** ℹ Por. **remark** i **comment**, które są częściej używane.

observatory /əbˈzɜːvətri; US -tɔːri/ noun [C] (pl. **observatories**) a building from which scientists can watch the stars, the weather, etc. ▶ **obserwatorium**

🔑 **observe** /əbˈzɜːv/ verb [T] **1** (formal) to see or notice sb/sth: *A man and a woman were observed leaving by the back door.* ▶ **zauważać 2** to watch sb/sth carefully, especially to learn more about them or it: *We observed the birds throughout the breeding season.* ▶ **obserwować 3** (formal) to make a comment: *'We're late,' she observed.* ▶ **zrobić uwagę, zauważać 4** (formal) to obey a law, rule, etc.: *to observe the speed limit* ▶ **przestrzegać** (*np. prawa*)

observer /əbˈzɜːvə(r)/ noun [C] **1** a person who watches sb/sth: *According to observers, the plane exploded shortly after take-off.* ▶ **obserwator/ka 2** a person who attends a meeting, lesson, etc. to watch and listen but who does not take part ▶ **obserwator/ka**

obsess /əbˈses/ verb [T, usually passive] **be obsessed (about/with sb/sth)** to completely fill your mind with sb/sth so that you cannot think of anything else: *He became obsessed with getting his revenge.* ▶ **mieć obsesję (na punkcie czegoś/kogoś), być opętanym (przez kogoś/czymś)**

obsession /əbˈseʃn/ noun **obsession (with sb/sth) 1** [U] the state in which you can only think about one person or thing so that you cannot think of anything else: *the tabloid press's obsession with the sordid details of the affair* ▶ **obsesja, opętanie 2** [C] a person or thing that you think about too much ▶ **obsesja**

obsessive /əbˈsesɪv/ adj. thinking too much about one particular person or thing; behaving in a way that shows this: *obsessive cleanliness* ◇ *He's obsessive about not being late.* Ma obsesję na punkcie punktualności. ▶ **obsesyjny**

obsolescent /ˌɒbsəˈlesnt/ adj. becoming old-fashioned and no longer useful ▶ **zanikający**

obsolete /ˈɒbsəliːt; US -səˈliːt/ adj. no longer useful because sth better has been invented ▶ **przestarzały**

obstacle /ˈɒbstəkl/ noun [C] **an obstacle (to sth/doing sth)** something that makes it difficult for you to do sth or go somewhere: *Not speaking a foreign language was a major obstacle to her career.* ▶ **przeszkoda**

obstetrician /ˌɒbstəˈtrɪʃn/ noun [C] a hospital doctor who looks after women who are pregnant ▶ **ginekolog-położnik**

obstetrics /əbˈstetrɪks/ noun [U] the area of medicine connected with the birth of children ▶ **położnictwo**

obstinate /ˈɒbstɪnət/ adj. refusing to change your opinions, way of behaving, etc. when other people try to persuade you to: *an obstinate refusal to apologize* ▶ **uparty, uporczywy** SYN **stubborn**
■ **obstinacy** /ˈɒbstɪnəsi/ noun [U] ▶ **upór, zatwardziałość** | **obstinately** adv. ▶ **uparcie, uporczywie**

obstruct /əbˈstrʌkt/ verb [T] to stop sb/sth from happening or moving either by accident or deliberately: *Could you move on, please? You're obstructing the traffic if you park there.* ▶ **tamować, tarasować**

obstruction /əbˈstrʌkʃn/ noun **1** [U] the act of stopping sth from happening or moving ▶ **tamowanie, tarasowanie 2** [C] a thing that stops sb/sth from moving or doing sth: *This car is **causing an obstruction**.* ▶ **zator, zawada**

obstructive /əbˈstrʌktɪv/ adj. trying to stop sb/sth from moving or doing sth ▶ **tamujący, zawadzający**

🔑 **obtain** /əbˈteɪn/ verb [T] (formal) to get sth: *to obtain advice/information/permission* ▶ **dostawać, uzyskiwać**

obtainable /əbˈteɪnəbl/ adj. that you can get: *Full details are obtainable from our website.* ▶ **(możliwy) do nabycia/uzyskania**

obtuse /əbˈtjuːs; US -ˈtuːs/ adj. (formal) slow to understand sth: *Are you being deliberately obtuse?* ▶ (*o osobie*) **tępy**
■ **obtuseness** noun [U] ▶ **tępota**

obˌtuse ˈangle noun [C] an angle between 90° and 180° ▶ **kąt rozwarty** ➲ look at **acute angle**, **right angle**

🔑 **obvious** /ˈɒbviəs/ adj. **obvious (to sb)** easily seen or understood: ***For obvious reasons**, I'd prefer not to give my name.* ◇ *His disappointment was obvious to everyone.* ▶ **oczywisty, jasny** SYN **clear**
■ **obviously** adv.: *There has obviously been a mistake.* ▶ **oczywiście**

🔑 **occasion** /əˈkeɪʒn/ noun **1** [C] a particular time when sth happens: *I have met Bill on two occasions.* ▶ **okazja 2** [C] a special event, ceremony, etc.: *Their wedding was a memorable occasion.* ▶ **okazja**, **wydarzenie** **3** [sing.] the suitable or right time (for sth): *I shall tell her what I think if the occasion arises* (jeśli nadarzy się okazja). ▶ **sposobność**, **okazja**

Occasion oznacza dogodną porę, aby coś zrobić: *I saw them at the funeral, but it was not a suitable occasion for discussing holiday plans.* **Opportunity** lub **chance** oznaczają faktyczną możliwość wykonania czegoś: *I was only in Paris for one day and I didn't get the opportunity/chance to visit the Louvre.*

IDM **on occasion(s)** sometimes but not often ▶ **czasami**

occasional /ə'keɪʒənl/ adj. [only before a noun] done or happening from time to time but not very often: *We have the occasional argument but most of the time we get on.* ▶ **sporadyczny**
■ **occasionally** /ə'keɪʒnəli/ adv.: *We see each other occasionally.* ▶ **od czasu do czasu**

occult /ə'kʌlt; 'ɒkʌlt/ adj. [only before a noun] connected with magic powers and things that cannot be explained by reason or science ▶ **tajemny**, **nadprzyrodzony**
■ **the occult** noun [sing.] magic powers, ceremonies, etc. ▶ **okultyzm**, **wiedza tajemna**

occupant /'ɒkjəpənt/ noun [C] a person who is in a building, car, etc. at a particular time ▶ **lokator/ka**, **mieszkan-iec/ka**

occupation /ˌɒkju'peɪʃn/ noun **1** [C] (formal) a job or profession; the way in which you spend your time: *Please state your occupation on the form.* ▶ **zajęcie**; **zawód** ➲ note at **work**[2] **2** [U] the act of the army of one country taking control of another country; the period of time that this situation lasts: *the Roman occupation of Britain* ▶ **okupacja** **3** [U] the act of living in or using a room, building, etc. ▶ **zamieszkiwanie**

occupational /ˌɒkju'peɪʃənl/ adj. [only before a noun] connected with your work: *Accidents are an* ***occupational hazard*** *on building sites.* ▶ **zawodowy**

ˌoccuˌpational 'therapist noun [C] a person whose job is to help people get better after illness or injury by giving them special activities to do ▶ **terapeuta zajęciowy**

ˌoccuˌpational 'therapy noun [U] the work of an **occupational therapist** ▶ **terapia zajęciowa**

⚷ **occupied** /'ɒkjupaɪd/ adj. **1** [not before a noun] being used by sb: *Is this seat occupied?* ▶ **zajęty** **2** busy doing sth: *Looking after the children keeps me fully occupied.* (zajmuje mi cały czas) ▶ **zajęty** ➲ look at **preoccupied** **3** (used about a country or a piece of land) under the control of another country: *He spent his childhood in occupied Europe.* ▶ **okupowany**

occupier /'ɒkjupaɪə(r)/ noun [C] (formal) a person who owns, lives in or uses a house, piece of land, etc. ▶ **lokator/ka**; **dzierżawca**

⚷ **occupy** /'ɒkjupaɪ/ verb [T] (**occupying**; **occupies**; pt, pp **occupied**) **1** to fill a space or period of time: *The large table occupied most of the room.* ▶ **okupować**; **zajmować** SYN **take up sth** **2** (formal) to live in or use a house, piece of land, etc.: *The house next door has not been occupied for some months.* ▶ **zamieszkiwać**, **zajmować** **3** to take control of a building, country, etc. by force: *The rebel forces have occupied the TV station.* ▶ **zajmować** **4 occupy sb/yourself** to keep sb/yourself busy: *How does he occupy himself* (czym się teraz zajmuje) *now that he's retired?* ▶ **zajmować (się)**

⚷ **occur** /ə'kɜː(r)/ verb [I] (**occurring**; **occurred**) **1** (formal) to happen, especially in a way that has not been planned: *The accident occurred late last night.* ▶ **wydarzać się** ➲ note at **happen** **2** to exist or be found somewhere: *The virus occurs more frequently in children.* ▶ **występować**

PHR V **occur to sb** (used about an idea or a thought) to come into your mind: *It never occurred to John that his wife might be unhappy.* ▶ **przychodzić do głowy**

occurrence /ə'kʌrəns; US ə'kɜːr-/ noun [C] something that happens or exists ▶ **wydarzenie**, **zjawisko**

⚷ **ocean** /'əʊʃn/ noun **1** [U] (especially US) the mass of salt water that covers most of the surface of the earth: *Two thirds of the earth's surface is covered by ocean.* ◇ *the ocean floor* dno oceanu ◇ *an ocean-going* (oceaniczny) *yacht* ▶ **ocean** **2** (**Ocean**) [C] one of the five main areas into which the water is divided: *the Atlantic/Indian/Pacific Ocean* ▶ **ocean** ➲ look at **sea**
■ **oceanic** /ˌəʊʃi'ænɪk/ adj.: *oceanic fish* ▶ **oceaniczny**
IDM **a drop in the ocean** → DROP[2]

ochre (US also **ocher**) /'əʊkə(r)/ noun [U] a pale brownish-yellow colour ▶ **kolor ochry**
■ **ochre** adj. ▶ **koloru ochry**

⚷ **o'clock** /ə'klɒk/ adv. (used after the numbers one to twelve for saying what the time is): *Lunch is at 12 o'clock.* ▶ **godzina** ❶ Uwaga! Wyrażenia **o'clock** używa się wyłącznie podając pełne godziny: *We arranged to meet at 5 o'clock* (o godzinie piątej). *It's 5.30 already and he's still not here.*

Oct. = OCTOBER: *13 Oct. 1999*

octagon /'ɒktəgən/ noun [C] a shape that has eight straight and equal sides ▶ **ośmiobok**
■ **octagonal** /ɒk'tægənl/ adj. ▶ **ośmioboczny**

octane /'ɒkteɪn/ noun [C] a chemical substance in petrol, used as a way of measuring its quality: *high-octane fuel* ▶ **oktan**

octave /'ɒktɪv/ noun [C] the set of eight musical notes that western music is based on ▶ **oktawa**

⚷ **October** /ɒk'təʊbə(r)/ noun [U,C] (abbr. **Oct.**) the 10th month of the year, coming after September ▶ **październik** ➲ note at **January**

octopus /'ɒktəpəs/ noun [C] a sea animal with a soft body and eight **tentacles** ▶ **ośmiornica**

⚷ **odd** /ɒd/ adj. **1** strange; unusual: *There's something odd about him.* ◇ *It's a bit odd that she didn't phone to say she couldn't come.* ▶ **dziwny**, **osobliwy** SYN **peculiar** **2** (**odd-**) [in compounds] strange or unusual in the way mentioned: *an odd-sounding name* ▶ *(określa, w jaki sposób ktoś/coś jest dziwaczny/niezwykły)* **3** [only before a noun] not regular or fixed; happening sometimes: *I do my exercises at odd moments* (w wolnych chwilach) *during the day.* ◇ *He makes the odd mistake* (od czasu do czasu robi błąd), *but nothing very serious.* **4** [only before a noun] that is left after other similar things have been used: *He made the bookshelves out of a few odd bits of wood.* ▶ **pozostały**, **przypadkowy**, **zbywający** **5** not with the pair or set it belongs to; not matching: *You're wearing odd socks.* ▶ **nie do pary**, **pojedynczy** **6** a number that cannot be divided by two: *One, three, five and seven are all odd numbers.* ▶ **nieparzysty** OPP **even** **7** (usually used after a number) a little more than: *'How old do you think he is?' 'Well, he must be thirty-odd, I suppose.'* ▶ **ponad**, **z okładem**
■ **oddly** adv.: ***Oddly enough****, the most expensive tickets sold fastest.* ▶ **dziwnie**, **osobliwie** | **oddness** noun [U] ▶ **osobliwość**, **niezwykłość**
IDM **the odd man/one out** one that is different from all the others in a group: *Her brothers and sisters were much older than she was. She was always the odd one out.* ▶ **niepasujący**, **inny**

oddball /'ɒdbɔːl/ noun [C] (informal) a person who behaves in a strange or unusual way ▶ **dziwa-k/czka**
■ **oddball** adj.: *oddball characters* ▶ **dziwaczny**

oddity /'ɒdəti/ noun **1** [C] (pl. **oddities**) a person or thing that is unusual ▶ **dziwak**; **osobliwość** **2** [U] the quality

O

of being strange or unusual: *She suddenly realized the oddity of her remark and blushed.* ▶ **osobliwość; dziwaczność**

ˌodd-ˈjob man noun [C] (especially Brit.) a person paid to do **odd jobs** ▶ **osoba wykonująca prace dorywcze**

ˌodd ˈjobs noun [pl.] small jobs or tasks of various types ▶ **dorywcze zajęcia/prace**

oddment /ˈɒdmənt/ noun [C, usually pl.] (especially Brit.) a small piece of cloth, wood, etc. that is left after the rest has been used ▶ **resztki**

odds /ɒdz/ noun [pl.] **the odds (on/against sth/sb)** (used for saying how probable sth is) the degree to which sth is likely to happen: *The odds on him surviving are very slim.* ◇ *The odds are against you.* Masz małe szanse na powodzenie. ◇ *The odds are in your favour.* ◇ *The odds on that horse winning are seven to one.* Prawdopodobieństwo, że ten koń wygra, wynosi siedem do jednego. ▶ **szansa, prawdopodobieństwo**

IDM **against (all) the odds** happening although it seemed impossible ▶ **(po)mimo wszystkich przeciwności**

be at odds (with sb) (over sth) to disagree with sb about sth ▶ **nie zgadzać się z kimś (co do czegoś)**

be at odds (with sth) to be different from sth, when the two things should be the same ▶ **nie pasować (do czegoś)**

odds and ends (Brit., informal) small things of little value or importance ▶ **drobiazgi, rupiecie**

ode /əʊd/ noun [C] a poem that is written to or about a person or thing or to celebrate a special event: *Keats's 'Ode to a Nightingale'* ▶ **oda**

odious /ˈəʊdiəs/ adj. (formal) extremely unpleasant: *What an odious man!* ▶ **wstrętny** SYN **horrible**

odometer (US) = MILOMETER

odour (US **odor**) /ˈəʊdə(r)/ noun [C] (formal) a smell (often an unpleasant one) ▶ **woń, zapach** ➲ note at **smell**[2]

odourless (US **odorless**) /ˈəʊdələs/ adj. without a smell ▶ **bezwonny**

OECD /ˌəʊ iː siː ˈdiː/ abbr. **Organization for Economic Cooperation and Development**; an organization of industrial countries that encourages trade and economic growth ▶ **Organizacja Współpracy Gospodarczej i Rozwoju**

oesophagus (US **esophagus**) /iˈsɒfəgəs/ noun [C] (pl. **-phaguses** or **-phagi** /-gaɪ/) the tube through which food passes from the mouth to the stomach ▶ **przełyk** ➲ look at **gullet** ➲ picture at **body**

oestrogen /ˈiːstrədʒən/ (US **estrogen** /ˈes-/) noun [U] a **hormone** produced in women's **ovaries** that causes them to develop the physical and sexual features that are characteristic of females and that causes them to prepare their body to have babies ▶ **estrogen** ➲ look at **progesterone, testosterone**

🔑 **of** /əv; strong form ɒv; US ʌv/ prep. ℹ Najczęściej **of** nie tłumaczy się odrębnie. Zwykle **of** + rzeczownik odpowiada rzeczownikowi w dopełniaczu. Czasami **of** tłumaczy się przyimkiem, zwłaszcza **z**. **1** belonging to, connected with, or part of sth/sb: *the roof of the house* dach domu ◇ *the result of the exam* wynik egzaminu ◇ *the back of the book* grzbiet książki ◇ *the leader of the party* przywódca partii ◇ *a friend of mine* jeden z moich przyjaciół **2** made, done or produced by sb: *the poems of Milton* wiersze Miltona **3** (used after a noun describing an action to show either who did the action or who it happened to): *the arrival of the president* przyjazd prezydenta ◇ *the murder of the president* morderstwo prezydenta ◇ *That was nice of her.* Ładnie się zachowała. **4** showing sb/sth: *a map of York* plan miasta York ◇ *a photograph of my parents* zdjęcie moich rodziców **5** (used for saying what sb/sth is or what a thing contains or is made of): *a woman of intelligence* inteligentna kobieta ◇ *the city of Paris* miasto Paryż ◇ *a glass of milk* szklanka mleka ◇ *a crowd of people* tłum ludzi ◇ *It's made of silver* (ze srebra). ◇ *a feeling of anger* uczucie złości **6** with measurements, directions and expressions of time and age: *a litre of milk* litr mleka ◇ *the fourth of July* czwarty lipca ◇ *a girl of 12* dwunastoletnia dziewczynka ◇ *five miles north of Leeds* (na północ od Leeds) ◇ *an increase of 2.5%* 2,5% wzrostu **7** showing that sb/sth is part of a larger group: *some of the people* ◇ *three of the houses* ▶ **z (większej liczby)** **8** indicating the reason for or cause of sth: *He died of pneumonia.* ▶ **na** (*jakąś chorobę*), **z powodu czegoś** **9** with some verbs: *This perfume smells of roses.* Te perfumy mają zapach róż. ◇ *It reminds me of you.* Przypomina mi to ciebie. ◇ *Think of a number.* Pomyśl o jakiejś liczbie. **10** with some adjectives: *I'm proud of you.* Jestem z ciebie dumny. ◇ *She's jealous of her.* Jest o nią zazdrosna.

🔑 **off**[1] /ɒf/ adv., prep. **1** down or away from a place or a position on sth: *He fell off the ladder.* ◇ *We got off* (wysiedliśmy z) *the bus.* ◇ *I shouted to him but he just walked off* (odszedł). ◇ ***I must be off*** (muszę iść). *It's getting late.* ◇ *When are you off* (wyjeżdżacie) *to Spain?* ◇ (figurative) *We've got off* (zeszliśmy z) *the subject.* ▶ **z** **2** (used with verbs that mean 'remove' or 'separate'): *She took her coat off* (zdjęła płaszcz). ◇ *Don't leave the top off the toothpaste.* Zawsze zamykaj tubkę po użyciu. ◇ *He shook the rain off* (strząsnął krople deszczu z) *his umbrella.* OPP **on** **3** joined to and leading away from: *The bathroom is off the main bedroom.* ◇ *My street is off* (to boczna od ulicy) *the Cowley Road.* ▶ **tuż przy** **4** at some distance from sth: *The Isle of Wight is just off* (niedaleko) *the south coast of England.* ◇ *Christmas is still a long way off.* Jeszcze daleko do Bożego Narodzenia. ▶ **w pewnej odległości** **5** (used about a plan or arrangement) not going to happen; cancelled: *The meeting/wedding/trip is off.* ▶ **odwołany** OPP **on** **6** (used about a machine, a light, etc.) not connected, working or being used: *Please make sure the TV/light/heating is off.* ▶ **wyłączony** **7** not present at work, school, etc.: *She's **off work/off sick** with a cold.* ◇ *I'm having **a day off** next week.* ▶ **nieobecny; wolny** **8** cheaper; less by a certain amount: *cars with £400 off* ◇ *£400 off the price of a car* ▶ **z bonifikatą** **9** not eating or using sth: *The baby's off* (nie je) *his food.*

IDM **off and on; on and off** sometimes; starting and stopping: *It has been raining on and off all day.* ▶ **od czasu do czasu, dorywczo**

well/badly off having/not having a lot of money: *They don't seem too badly off – they have smart clothes and a nice house.* ▶ **w dobrej/złej sytuacji materialnej**

ℹ **Off** występuje w czasownikach złożonych, np. **go off**. Zob. hasła odpowiednich czasowników.

off[2] /ɒf/ adj. [not before a noun] **1** (used about food or drink) no longer fresh enough to eat or drink: *The milk's off.* ▶ **nieświeży, zepsuty** **2** (informal) unfriendly: *My neighbour was rather off with me today.* ▶ **nieprzyjazny**

offal /ˈɒfl/ noun [U] the heart and other organs of an animal, used as food ▶ **podroby**

ˈoff chance noun [sing.] a slight possibility: *She popped round **on the off chance*** (w nadziei, że go zastanie) *of finding him at home.* ▶ **znikoma szansa**

ˈoff day noun [C] (informal) a day when things go badly or you do not work well: *Even the best players have off days occasionally.* ▶ **zły dzień**

ˌoff-ˈduty adj. not at work: *an off-duty police officer* ▶ (*policjant itp.*) **nie na służbie**

🔑 **offence** (US **offense**) /əˈfens/ noun **1** [C] (formal) **an offence (against sth)** a crime; an illegal action: *to commit an offence* ◇ *a criminal/minor/serious/sexual offence* ▶ **przestępstwo, wykroczenie** **2** [U] **offence (to sb/sth)** the act of upsetting or insulting sb: *I didn't mean to **cause** you any **offence**.* Nie chciałem cię obrazić. ▶ **obraza, przykrość**

IDM **take offence (at sth)** to feel upset or hurt by sb/sth ▶ **obrażać się**

offend /ə'fend/ verb **1** [T, often passive] to hurt sb's feelings; to upset sb: *I hope they won't be offended* (że się nie obrażą) *if I don't come.* ◇ *He felt offended that she hadn't written for so long.* ▶ **obrażać 2** [I] (formal) to do sth illegal; to commit a crime: *The prisoner had offended again within days of his release from jail.* ▶ **naruszać/łamać prawo/zwyczaj**; **popełniać przestępstwo**

offender /ə'fendə(r)/ noun [C] **1** (formal) a person who breaks the law or commits a crime: ***Young offenders*** (nieletni przestępcy) *should not be sent to adult prisons.* ◇ *a first offender* osoba, która popełniła przestępstwo/wykroczenie po raz pierwszy ▶ **przestęp-ca/czyni**, **osoba popełniająca wykroczenie 2** a person or thing that does sth wrong ▶ **winowaj-ca/czyni**

offensive[1] /ə'fensɪv/ adj. **1 offensive (to sb)** unpleasant; insulting: *offensive behaviour / language / remarks* ▶ **obraźliwy**, **nieprzyzwoity** OPP **inoffensive 2** [only before a noun] (formal) (used for or connected with attacking): *offensive weapons* ▶ **ofensywny**, **zaczepny** OPP **defensive**

■ **offensively** adv. ▶ **obraźliwie**; **nieprzyzwoicie**

offensive[2] /ə'fensɪv/ noun [C] a military attack ▶ **ofensywa**

IDM **be on the offensive** to be the first to attack sb/sth, rather than waiting for them to attack you ▶ **być w ofensywie**

take the offensive to be the first to attack ▶ **przechodzić do ofensywy**

offer[1] /'ɒfə(r)/ verb **1** [T] **offer sth (to sb) (for sth)**; **offer (sb) sth** to ask if sb would like sth or to give sb the chance to have sth: *He offered his seat on the bus to an old lady.* ◇ *I've been offered a job in London.* ◇ *He offered (me) £2 000 for the car and I accepted.* ▶ **proponować**, **oferować 2** [I] **offer (to do sth)** to say or show that you will do sth for sb if they want: *I don't want to do it but I suppose I'll have to offer.* ◇ *My brother's offered to help me paint the house.* ▶ **proponować**, **okazywać gotowość 3** [T] to make sth available or to provide the opportunity for sth: *The job offers plenty of opportunity for travel.* ▶ **dostarczać**, **dawać**

offer[2] /'ɒfə(r)/ noun [C] **1 an offer (of sth)**; **an offer (to do sth)** a statement offering to do sth or give sth to sb: *She accepted my offer of help.* ◇ *Thank you for your kind offer to help.* ▶ **oferta**, **propozycja**

> We can **make**, **accept**, **refuse**, **turn down** or **withdraw** an offer.

2 an offer (of sth) (for sth) an amount of money that you say you will give for sth: *They've made an offer for the house.* ◇ *We've turned down an offer of £90 000.* ▶ **oferta**, **propozycja** (*ceny*) **3** a low price for sth in a shop, usually for a short time: *See below for details of our special holiday offer.* ▶ **oferta** (*oferowana cena*), **okazja**

IDM **on offer 1** for sale or available: *The college has a wide range of courses on offer.* ▶ **do zaoferowania**, **do nabycia 2** (especially Brit.) for sale at a lower price than usual for a certain time: *This cheese is on offer until next week.* ▶ **do nabycia w promocyjnej cenie**

or nearest offer; **ono** → NEAR[1]

offering /'ɒfərɪŋ/ noun [C] something that is given or produced for other people to watch, enjoy, etc.: *He gave me a bottle of wine as **a peace offering*** (na zgodę). ◇ *The latest offering* (najnowszą produkcją) *from the Youth Theatre is 'Macbeth'.* ▶ **propozycja**, **oferta**

offhand[1] /ˌɒf'hænd/ adj. (used about behaviour) not showing any interest in sb/sth in a way that seems rude: *an offhand manner/voice* ▶ **bezceremonialny**, **niegrzeczny**

offhand[2] /ˌɒf'hænd/ adv. without having time to think; immediately: *I can't tell you what it's worth offhand.* ▶ **od razu**, **bez zastanowienia**

■ **offhandedly** adv. in an unfriendly way or in a way that shows that you are not interested: *'Oh really?' she said offhandedly, looking at her watch.* ▶ **bez zainteresowania**, **na odczepnego**

office /'ɒfɪs/ noun **1** [C] a room, set of rooms or a building where people work, usually sitting at desks: *I usually get to the office at about 9 o'clock.* ◇ *The firm's **head office*** (centrala firmy) *is in Glasgow.* ◇ *Please phone again during **office hours*** (w czasie godzin urzędowania). ▶ **biuro**, **urząd**

> W USA gabinety lekarskie i dentystyczne nazywają się **offices**, a w Wielkiej Brytanii **surgeries**.

2 [C] [in compounds] a room or building that is used for a particular purpose, especially for providing a service: *the tax/ticket/tourist office* ▶ **urząd**, **biuro** ➲ look at **booking office**, **box office**, **post office 3** (**Office**) [sing.] a government department, including the people who work there and the work they do: *the Home Office* (w Wlk. Br.) Ministerstwo Spraw Wewnętrznych ◇ *the Foreign Office* Ministerstwo Spraw Zagranicznych ▶ **ministerstwo**, **departament 4** [U] an official position, often as part of a government or other organization: *The Labour party has been **in office*** (u władzy) *since 1997.* ▶ **stanowisko**, **urząd**

> **office work**
> I work as a **secretary** for a large **firm** of accountants. The **company** employs over 50 **members of staff**. I work in an **open-plan office** so I share a large room with my **colleagues**. On my desk I have a **PC**, **printer** and a **fax machine**. My **duties** include **typing** letters and emails for my boss, **filing**, answering the phone and doing the **photocopying**. I go to **meetings** and take the **minutes**. I am also **responsible for** ordering stationery. I work **nine to five** and have twenty days' holiday a year.

'**office block** (especially US '**office building**) noun [C] a large building that contains offices, usually belonging to more than one company ▶ **biurowiec** ➲ picture on **page A2**

officer /'ɒfɪsə(r)/ noun [C] **1** a person who is in a position of authority in the armed forces: *an army/air-force officer* ▶ **oficer 2** a person who is in a position of authority in the government or a large organization: *a prison/customs/welfare officer* ▶ **funkcjonariusz/ka**, **(wyższy) urzędnik 3** = POLICE OFFICER

'**office worker** noun [C] a person who works in the offices of a business or company ▶ **urzędni-k/czka**

official[1] /ə'fɪʃl/ adj. **1** [only before a noun] connected with the position of sb in authority: *official duties/responsibilities* ▶ **oficjalny**, **urzędowy 2** accepted and approved by the government or some other authority: *The scheme has not yet received official approval.* ◇ *The country's official language is Spanish.* ▶ **oficjalny**, **urzędowy 3** that is told to the public, but which may or may not be true: *The official reason for his resignation was that he wanted to spend more time with his family.* ▶ **oficjalny** OPP **unofficial**

official[2] /ə'fɪʃl/ noun [C] a person who has a position of authority: *The reception was attended by MPs and high-ranking officials.* ▶ **(wyższy) urzędnik** (*np. państwowy, kościelny*)

> **Office worker** to pracownik biurowy. **Official** to osoba zajmująca odpowiedzialne stanowisko w firmie lub organizacji, zwł. w administracji rządowej: *senior government officials.* Osoba uprawniona do

O

wydawania rozkazów w wojsku, marynarce i policji to **officer**, choć słowa tego używa się też w znaczeniu podobnym do **official**: *She's an executive officer in the Civil Service.*

officialdom /əˈfɪʃldəm/ noun [U] groups of people in positions of authority in large organizations who seem more interested in following the rules than in being helpful ▶ **oficjele, sfery urzędowe**

officially /əˈfɪʃəli/ adv. **1** publicly and by sb in a position of authority: *The new school was officially opened last week.* ▶ **oficjalnie, formalnie 2** according to a particular set of laws, rules, etc.: *Officially we don't accept children under six, but we'll make an exception in this case.* ▶ **oficjalnie, urzędowo**

officious /əˈfɪʃəs/ adj. too ready to tell other people what to do and use the power you have to give orders ▶ **nadgorliwy**

offing /ˈɒfɪŋ/ noun
IDM **in the offing** (informal) likely to appear or happen soon: *Do you think there's a romance in the offing* (wisi w powietrzu)*? Jane and Trevor seem to be getting on very well.* ▶ **spodziewany**

ˈoff-licence noun [C] (US **ˈliquor store**) a shop which sells alcoholic drinks in bottles and cans ▶ **sklep monopolowy**

offline /ˌɒfˈlaɪn/ adj., adv. not directly controlled by or connected to a computer or the Internet: *For offline orders, call this number.* ◇ *Could you tell me how to write an email offline?* ▶ **odłączony od komputera/sieci** ➲ look at **online**

offload /ˌɒfˈləʊd/ verb [T] (informal) **offload sth (on/onto sb)** to give away sth that you do not want to sb else: *It's nice to have someone you can offload your problems onto.* ▶ **pozbywać się, uszczęśliwiać kogoś** (*np. prezentem, który nam nie odpowiada*)

ˌoff-ˈpeak adj., adv. [only before a noun] available, used or done at a less popular or busy time: *an off-peak train ticket/bus pass/phone call* ◇ *It's cheaper to travel off-peak.* ▶ **poza godzinami szczytu** ➲ look at **peak**

ˌoff-ˈputting adj. (especially Brit.) unpleasant in a way that stops you from liking sb/sth ▶ **niepociągający**

offset /ˈɒfset/ verb [T] (**offsetting**; pt, pp **offset**) to make the effect of sth less strong or noticeable: *The disadvantages of the scheme are more than offset by the advantages.* ▶ **równoważyć, rekompensować**

offshoot /ˈɒfʃuːt/ noun [C] a thing that develops from sth else, especially a small organization that develops from a larger one ▶ (*przen.*) **gałąź**

offshore /ˌɒfˈʃɔː(r)/ adj. in the sea but not very far from the land: *an offshore oil rig* ▶ **przybrzeżny** (*tylko o brzegu morza*), **niedaleko lądu**

offside adj. **1** /ˌɒfˈsaɪd/ (used about a player in football) in a position that is not allowed by the rules of the game: *the offside rule* zasada spalonego ▶ **na spalonym 2** /ˈɒfsaɪd/ (Brit.) (used about a part of a vehicle) on the side that is furthest away from the edge of the road ▶ (*część samochodu*) **po stronie kierowcy**

offspring /ˈɒfsprɪŋ/ noun [C] (pl. **offspring**) (formal) a child or children; the young of an animal: *to produce/raise offspring* ▶ **potomek; potomstwo, młode**

ˌoff-ˈwhite adj. not pure white ▶ **białawy**

often /ˈɒfn; ˈɒftən/ adv. **1** many times: *We often go swimming at the weekend.* ◇ *I'm sorry I didn't write very often.* ◇ ***How often** should you go to the dentist?* ▶ **często** SYN **frequently 2** in many cases: *Old houses are often damp.* ▶ **często, w wielu wypadkach** SYN **commonly**
IDM **every so often** sometimes; from time to time ▶ **od czasu do czasu**
more often than not usually ▶ **zazwyczaj, bardzo często**

ogre /ˈəʊɡə(r)/ noun [C] **1** (in children's stories) a very large, cruel and frightening creature that eats people ▶ **zły olbrzym 2** a person who is unpleasant and frightening ▶ **potwór, poczwara**

oh (also **O**) /əʊ/ interj. **1** (used for reacting to sth that sb has said, for emphasizing what you are saying, or when you are thinking of what to say next): *'What time should we leave?' 'Oh, early, I think.'* ◇ *'I'm a teacher.' 'Oh? Where?'* ▶ **och!; aha! 2** (used for expressing surprise, fear, pain, sudden pleasure, etc.): *'Oh no!' she cried as she began to read the letter.* ▶ **och!, ojej!**

OHP /ˌəʊ eɪtʃ ˈpiː/ noun [C] **overhead projector** ▶ **rzutnik**

ˈoh well = WELL[3] (2)

oil /ɔɪl/ noun [U] **1** a thick dark liquid that comes from under the ground and is used as a fuel or to make machines work smoothly: *Britain obtains oil from the North Sea.* ◇ *Crude oil* (ropa naftowa) *is transported by tanker to the refinery.* ▶ **ropa naftowa, olej 2** a thick liquid that comes from animals or plants and is used in cooking: *cooking/vegetable/sunflower oil* ◇ *olive oil* oliwa ▶ **olej, oliwa**
■ **oil** verb [T] ▶ **oliwić, oleić**

oilfield /ˈɔɪlfiːld/ noun [C] an area where there is oil under the ground or under the sea ▶ **pole naftowe**

ˈoil painting noun [C] a picture that has been painted using paint made with oil ▶ **obraz olejny**

ˈoil rig (also **rig**) noun [C] a large platform in the sea with equipment for getting oil out from under the sea ▶ **platforma wiertnicza**

ˈoil slick (also **slick**) noun [C] an area of oil that floats on the sea, usually after a ship carrying oil has crashed ▶ **plama ropy**

ˈoil well (also **well**) noun [C] a hole that is made deep in the ground or under the sea in order to obtain oil ▶ **szyb naftowy**

oily /ˈɔɪli/ adj. (**oilier**; **oiliest**) covered with oil or like oil: *oily food* ◇ *Mechanics always have oily hands.* ▶ **natłuszczony; oleisty, olejowy**

ointment /ˈɔɪntmənt/ noun [C,U] a smooth substance that you put on sore skin or on an injury to help it get better ▶ **maść**

OK[1] (also **okay**) /əʊˈkeɪ/ adj., adv. (informal) all right; good or well enough: *'Did you have a nice day?' 'Well, it was OK, I suppose.'* ◇ *If it's okay with you,* (jeżeli ci to odpowiada) *I'll come at about 7.* ◇ *I did OK in the test.* Na egzaminie poszło mi dobrze. ▶ **w porządku, dobrze**
■ **OK** interj. **1** yes; all right: *'Do you want to come with us?' 'OK.'* ▶ **tak, zgoda 2** (used to attract sb's attention or to introduce a comment): *Okay, let's go.* ▶ **dobrze, okej 3** (used to check that sb agrees with you or understands you): *The meeting's at 2, OK?* ▶ **zgadza się?, tak? 4** (used to stop people arguing with you or criticizing you): *OK, so I was wrong. I'm sorry.* ▶ **dobra**

OK[2] (also **okay**) /əʊˈkeɪ/ noun [sing.] (informal) agreement or permission: *As soon as my parents **give me the OK**, I'll come and stay with you.* ▶ **zgoda; pozwolenie**
■ **OK** (also **okay**) verb [T] (**OK'ing**; **OK's**; pt, pp **OK'd**) **OK sth (with sb)**: *If you need time off, you have to OK it with your boss.* ▶ **uzyskać (czyjąś) zgodę**

okey-doke /ˌəʊki ˈdəʊk/ (also **okey-dokey** /ˌəʊki ˈdəʊki/) exclamation (Brit., informal) (used to express agreement) ▶ **zgoda, okej** SYN **OK**

old /əʊld/ adj. **1** [used with a period of time or with *how*] of a particular age: *That building is 500 years old.* ◇ *The book is aimed at eight- to ten-year-olds.* ◇ *How old are you?* Ile masz lat? ◇ *They have a two-year-old* (dwulatka). ▶ **stary**

ⓘ **Old** nie tłumaczy się przy podawaniu wieku lub pytaniu o wiek. ➲ note at **age 2** having lived a long time: *My mother wasn't very old when she died.* ◇ *He's only 50 but he looks older.* ◇ *to **get/grow** old* ▶ **stary** OPP **young 3** (**the old**) noun [pl.] old people: *The old feel the cold more than the young.* ▶ **ludzie starsi** ➲ look at **the elderly**, **the aged 4** that has existed for a long time; connected with past times: *This house is quite old.* ◇ *old ideas/traditions* ◇ *In the old days, people generally had larger families than nowadays.* ▶ **stary**, **(staro)dawny** OPP **new**, **modern 5** having been used a lot: *I got rid of all my old clothes.* ▶ **stary** OPP **new** ➲ look at **second-hand 6** [only before a noun] former: *I earn more now than I did in my old job.* ▶ **poprzedni** SYN **previous 7** [only before a noun] known for a long time: *She's a very old friend of mine. We knew each other at school.* ▶ **stary**, **dawny** ➲ note at **age**

Zwyczajny stopień wyższy i najwyższy przymiotnika **old** to **older** i **oldest**: *My father's older than my mother.* Formy **elder** i **eldest** stosuje się przy porównywaniu wieku różnych osób, szczególnie członków rodziny. Nie można ich jednak używać ze słowem **than**. Przymiotniki te występują wyłącznie przed rzeczownikami.

8 [only before a noun] (informal) (used for expressing friendship and affection): *Good old Tom has solved the problem.* ▶ **stary**, **drogi**

IDM **be an old hand (at sth)** to be good at sth because you have done it often before: *She's an old hand at dealing with the press.* ▶ **być doświadczonym**, **być starym wyjadaczem**

any old ... (informal) any item of the type mentioned (used when it is not important which particular item is chosen): *'What time shall I come?' 'Oh, any old time* (kiedykolwiek) – *it doesn't matter.'* ◇ *I write any old* (jakąkolwiek) *rubbish in my diary.* ▶ **byle**

old hat (informal) not new; old-fashioned ▶ **staromodny**, **staroświecki**

ˌold ˈage noun [U] the part of your life when you are old: *He's enjoying life **in his old age*** (na starość). ▶ **starość** ➲ look at **youth**

ˌold-age ˈpension noun [U] money paid by the state to people above a certain age ▶ **emerytura**

■ **ˌold-age ˈpensioner** (also **pensioner**) noun [C] (abbr. **OAP** /ˌəʊ eɪ ˈpiː/) ▶ **emeryt** ⓘ Obecnie bardziej przyjęte jest określenie **senior citizen.** ➲ look at **pension**

ˌOld ˈEnglish = ANGLO-SAXON (3)

⚷ **ˌold-ˈfashioned** adj. **1** usual in the past but not now: *old-fashioned clothes/ideas* ◇ *That word sounds a bit old-fashioned.* ▶ **staromodny**, **staroświecki 2** (used about people) believing in old ideas, customs, etc.: *My parents are quite old-fashioned about some things.* ▶ **staroświecki**, **starej daty** ➲ look at **modern**, **unfashionable**

ˌold ˈpeople's home noun [C] (Brit.) (especially US **reˈtirement home**) a place where old people live and are cared for ▶ **dom spokojnej starości**

the ˌOld ˈTestament noun [sing.] the first part of the Bible that tells the history of the Jewish people ▶ **Stary Testament**

olive /ˈɒlɪv/ noun **1** [C] a small green or black fruit with a bitter taste, used for food and oil ▶ **oliwka 2** (also **ˌolive ˈgreen**) [U] a colour between yellow and green ▶ **kolor oliwkowy**

■ **olive** adj. ▶ **oliwkowy**

ˈolive oil noun [U] oil produced from **olives**, used in cooking and on salad ▶ **oliwa z oliwek**

the Olympic Games /əˌlɪmpɪk ˈɡeɪmz/ (also **the Oˈlympics**) noun [pl.] an international sports competition which is organized every four years in a different country: *to win a medal at/in the Olympics* ▶ **olimpiada**

■ **Olympic** adj. [only before a noun]: *Who holds the Olympic record for the 1500 metres?* ▶ **olimpijski**

ombudsman /ˈɒmbʊdzmən; -mæn/ noun [sing.] a government official who ordinary people can contact to complain officially about public organizations ▶ **rzecznik praw obywatelskich**

omelette (also **omelet**) /ˈɒmlət/ noun [C] a dish made of eggs that have been beaten and fried: *a plain* (naturalny) *cheese/mushroom omelette* ▶ **omlet**

omen /ˈəʊmən/ noun [C] a sign of sth that will happen in the future: *a good/bad omen for the future* ◇ *an **omen of death/disaster*** ▶ **znak**, **zapowiedź**

ominous /ˈɒmɪnəs/ adj. suggesting that sth bad is going to happen: *Her expression was rather ominous* (wróżył nic dobrego). ◇ *Those black clouds look ominous.* ▶ **złowróżbny**

omission /əˈmɪʃn/ noun [C,U] something that has not been included; the act of not including sb/sth: *There were several omissions on the list of names.* Na liście pominięto kilka nazwisk. ◇ *The film was criticized for its omission of certain important details.* ▶ **przeoczenie**, **pominięcie**

omit /əˈmɪt/ verb [T] (**omitting**; **omitted**) **1** to not include sth; to leave sth out: *Several verses of the song can be omitted.* ▶ **opuszczać**, **pomijać 2** (formal) **omit to do sth** to forget or choose not to do sth ▶ (*celowo lub nie*) **zapominać**

omni- /ˈɒmnɪ-/ prefix [in nouns, adjectives and adverbs] of all things; in all ways or places: *omnivore* zwierzę wszystkożerne ◇ *omnipresent* wszechobecny ▶ **wielo-**, **wszech-**, **wszystko-**

omnivore /ˈɒmnɪvɔː(r)/ noun [C] an animal or a person that eats all types of food, especially both plants and meat ▶ **zwierzę wszystkożerne** ➲ look at **carnivore**, **herbivore**

■ **omnivorous** /ɒmˈnɪvərəs/ adj.: *an omnivorous* (wieloskładnikowa) *diet* ▶ **wszystkożerny**

⚷ **on** /ɒn/ adv., prep. ⓘ **On** używa się w czasownikach złożonych i w zwrotach z rzeczownikami, np. **get on, on holiday.** Zob. hasła odpowiednich czasowników i rzeczowników. **1** (also formal **upon** /əˈpɒn/) supported by, fixed to or touching sth, especially a surface: *on the table/ceiling/wall* ◇ *We sat on the beach/grass/floor.* ◇ *She was carrying the baby on her back.* ◇ *Write it down on a piece of paper.* ◇ *The ball hit me on the head* (w głowę). ▶ **na 2** in a place or position: *on a farm/housing estate/campsite* ◇ *a café on the border* ◇ *I live on the other side* (po drugiej stronie) *of town.* ◇ *a house on the river/seafront* (nad rzeką/morzem) ▶ **na 3** (used with ways of travelling and types of travel): *on the bus/train/plane* ◇ *Eddie went past on his bike.* ◇ *We came **on foot*** (piechotą). ◇ *to go on a trip/journey/excursion* ▶ **w**, **na** ⓘ Uwaga! – **on the bus/train/plane**, ale **in the car. 4** (with expressions of time): *on August 19th* dziewiętnastego sierpnia ◇ *on Monday* ◇ *on Christmas Day* ◇ *on your birthday* ▶ **w 5** (showing that sth continues): *The man shouted at us but we walked on.* ◇ *The war went on* (ciągnęła się) *for five years.* ◇ *The speeches went **on and on*** (mówili bez końca) *until everyone was bored.* ▶ **dalej (coś robić) 6** wearing sth; carrying sth in your pocket or bag: *What did she **have on?*** W co była ubrana? ◇ *to **put** your shoes/coat/hat **on*** załóż buty/płaszcz/kapelusz ◇ *to **put** make-up **on*** pomalować się ◇ *I've got no money on me.* ◇ *You should carry ID on you at all times.* ▶ **(mieć) na sobie**; **przy (sobie) 7** working: *Is Nurse Peters on* (czy siostra Peters pracuje) *today, or is it her day off?* **8** being used: *All the lights were on.* Paliły się wszystkie światła. ◇ ***Switch** the TV **on.*** Włącz telewizor. ▶ **włączony 9** immediately; soon after: *He telephoned her on his return from New York.* ◇ *She began to weep on hearing*

O

(usłyszawszy) *the news.* ▶ **po 10** about sth: *We've got a test on irregular verbs tomorrow.* ◇ *a talk/a book/an article on Japan* ▶ **z (zakresu/tematu), o 11** happening or arranged to happen: *What's on* (co grają) *at the cinema?* ◇ *We haven't got anything on* (nie mamy nic zaplanowanego) *this weekend.* ◇ *There are loads of people in the park – there must be something on* (coś się musi tam dziać). ◇ *Is the meeting still on* (czy spotkanie jest nadal aktualne), *or has it been cancelled?* **12** using a particular kind of food or fuel; using drugs or medicine: *Does this car run on petrol or diesel?* ◇ *to be on* (brać) *medication/antibiotics/heroin* ◇ *Gorillas live on leaves* (żywią się liśćmi) *and fruit.* ▶ **na 13** (showing direction): *on the right/left* ◇ *on the way* (po drodze) *to school* ▶ **na 14** (showing the reason for or starting point of sth): *She doesn't drink* ***on principle*** (z zasady). ◇ *The film is* ***based on*** (oparty na) *a true story.* ◇ *On their advice* (za ich radą) *I applied for the job.* **15** receiving a certain amount of money: *He's been (living) on unemployment benefit since he lost his job.* ◇ *What will you be on* (ile będziesz zarabiać) *in your new job?* ▶ **na 16** paid for by sb: *The drinks are on me!* Ja stawiam! ◇ *on the house* na koszt firmy **17** using sth; by means of sth: *I was (talking)* ***on the phone*** (przez telefon) *to Laura.* ◇ *I saw it* ***on TV.*** ◇ *I heard it* ***on the radio.*** ◇ *Dave spends most evenings* ***on the Internet.*** ◇ *I cut my hand on some glass.* Skaleczyłem rękę odłamkiem szkła. ▶ **w** ⓘ Uwaga! **on TV/the radio/the Internet**, ale **in the paper. 18** (showing the thing or person that is affected by an action or is the object of an action): *Divorce can have a bad effect on children.* ◇ *He spends a lot on clothes.* ◇ *Don't waste your time on that.* ▶ **na 19** compared to: *Sales are up 10% on last year.* ▶ **w stosunku do czegoś**

IDM **be/go on at sb** → GO[1]

be on about sth to talk about sth; to mean sth ▶ **mówić o czymś, mieć coś na myśli**

from now/then on starting from this/that time and continuing: *From then on she never smoked another cigarette.* ▶ **od tego czasu**

not on not acceptable: *No, you can't stay out that late. It's just not on.* Nie ma mowy. ▶ **nie do przyjęcia**

off and on; on and off → OFF[1]

once /wʌns/ adv. **1** one time only; on one occasion: *I've only been to France once.* ◇ *once a* (raz na) *week/month/year* ◇ *I visit them about once every six months* (raz na pół roku). ▶ **raz 2** at some time in the past: *This house was once the village school.* ▶ **kiedyś** SYN **formerly**

■ **once** conj. as soon as; when: *Once you've practised a bit you'll find that it's quite easy.* ▶ **kiedy (tylko)**

IDM **all at once 1** all at the same time: *People began talking all at once.* ▶ **naraz, równocześnie 2** suddenly: *All at once she got up and left the room.* ▶ **nagle, naraz**

at once 1 immediately; now: *Come here at once!* ▶ **natychmiast 2** at the same time: *I can't understand if you all speak at once.* ▶ **naraz, równocześnie**

just this once; (just) for once on this occasion only: *Just this once, I'll help you with your homework.* ▶ **tylko ten (jeden) raz**

once again/more again, as before: *Spring will soon be here once again.* ▶ **znowu, jeszcze raz**

once and for all now and for the last time: *You've got to make a decision once and for all.* ▶ **raz na zawsze**

once in a blue moon (informal) almost never ▶ **od wielkiego dzwonu**

once in a while sometimes but not often ▶ **z rzadka, od czasu do czasu**

once more one more time: *Let's listen to that cassette once more, shall we?* ▶ **jeszcze raz**

once upon a time (used at the beginning of a children's story) a long time ago; in the past: *Once upon a time there was a princess ...* ▶ **dawno, dawno temu**

oncoming /ˈɒnkʌmɪŋ/ adj. [only before a noun] coming towards you: *oncoming traffic* ▶ **nadchodzący, nadjeżdżający**

one[1] /wʌn/ number, determiner [C] **1** the number 1: *There's only one biscuit left.* ◇ *The journey takes one hour.* ◇ *If you take one from ten, it leaves nine.* ▶ **jeden** ➲ note at **six** ➲ look at **first 2** (used with *the other*, *another* or *other(s)* to make a contrast): *The twins are so alike that it's hard to tell one from the other.* ▶ **jeden 3** (**the one**) (used for emphasizing that there is only one of sth) only: *She's the one person I trust.* ▶ **jedyny, właśnie ten 4** (**the one**) the same: *We can't all get in the one car.* ▶ **ten sam 5** (used when you are talking about a time in the past or future without actually saying when) a certain: *He came to see me one evening last week.* ◇ *We must go and visit them one day.* ▶ **pewien, jakiś**

IDM **(all) in one** all together or combined: *It's a phone and fax machine all in one.* ▶ **razem**

the odd man/one out → ODD

one after another/the other first one, then the next, etc.: *One after another the winners went up to get their prizes.* ▶ **jeden za drugim**

one at a time separately: *I'll deal with the problems one at a time.* ▶ **pojedynczo** SYN **individually**

one by one separately: *One by one, people began to arrive at the meeting.* ▶ **pojedynczo, każdy oddzielnie**

one or two a few: *I've borrowed one or two new books from the library.* ▶ **jeden czy dwa**

one[2] /wʌn/ pron. [C] **1** (used instead of repeating a noun): *I think I'll have an apple. Would you like one?* ▶ ***(tłumaczy się, powtarzając rzeczownik, do którego odnosi się to słowo)*** **2** (used after *this, that, which* or after an adjective instead of a noun): *'Which dress do you like?' 'This one.* (tę)*'* ◇ *'Can I borrow some books of yours?' 'Yes. Which ones* (które)*?'* ◇ *'This coat's a bit small. You need a bigger one* (potrzebujesz większego).*'* ◇ *That idea is a very good one.* Ten pomysł jest bardzo dobry. **3** (**the one/the ones**) (used before a group of words that show which person or thing you are talking about): *My house is the one after the post office.* ◇ *If you find some questions difficult, leave out the ones you don't understand.* ▶ **ten 4 one of** a member (of a certain group): *He's staying with one of his friends.* ▶ **jeden** *(z kilku/wielu)* ⓘ Po wyrażeniu **one of** zawsze występuje rzeczownik w lm. Czasownik natomiast jest w lp, ponieważ podmiot zdania to **one**: *One of our assistants is ill.* ◇ *One of the buses was late.* **5** (formal) (used for referring to people in general, including the speaker or writer): *One must be sure* (trzeba być pewnym) *of one's facts before criticizing other people.* ◇ *Plenty of exercise makes one fit.* Dużo ruchu sprawia, że jest się w formie.

> Takie użycie **one** jest bardzo formalne i staromodne. W codziennym użyciu częściej występuje słowo **you**. Zwróć uwagę, że **one's** to forma zaimka dzierżawczego: *One must be sure of one's facts/You must be sure of your facts before criticizing other people.*

6 someone: *She's not one to get upset easily.* ▶ **ktoś**

ˌone aˈnother pron. each other: *We exchanged news with one another.* ▶ **się, siebie (wzajemnie)** ⓘ Często nie tłumaczy się.

ˌone-ˈoff noun [C] (informal) something that is made or that happens only once ▶ **jedyna okazja, jedyny (w swoim rodzaju)**

■ **ˌone-ˈoff** adj. [only before a noun]: *a one-off payment/opportunity* ▶ **jednorazowy, unikatowy**

ˌone-on-ˈone (US) = ONE-TO-ONE

ˌone-parent ˈfamily noun [C] a family in which the children live with only one parent rather than two ▶ **rodzina niepełna**

onerous /'əʊnərəs; US also 'ɑːn-/ adj. (formal) needing great effort; causing trouble or worry: *an onerous duty/task/responsibility* ▶ **uciążliwy** SYN **taxing**

one's /wʌnz/ determiner the possessive form of *one*: *One tries one's best.* ▶ **czyjś**

oneself /wʌn'self/ pron. **1** (used when the person who does an action is also affected by it): *One can teach oneself to play the piano but it is easier to have lessons.* ▶ **się, siebie 2** (used to emphasize the person who does the action): *One could easily arrange it all oneself.* ▶ **sam**
IDM **(all) by oneself 1** alone ▶ **sam, samotnie** ➲ note at **alone 2** without help ▶ **bez pomocy**

,one-'sided adj. **1** (used about an opinion, an argument, etc.) showing only one point of view; not balanced: *Some newspapers give a very one-sided view of politics.* ▶ **stronniczy 2** (used about a relationship or a competition) not equal: *The match was very one-sided* (nierówny) *– we lost 12-1.* ▶ **jednostronny**

'one-time adj. [only before a noun] **1** former: *a one-time mayor of New York* ▶ **były 2** not to be repeated: *a one-time fee of $500* ▶ **jednorazowy** SYN **one-off**

,one-to-'one (US usually **,one-on-'one**) adj. between only two people: *one-to-one English lessons* ▶ **indywidualny**
■ **,one-to-'one** adv.: *He teaches one-to-one.* Uczy w systemie indywidualnym. ▶ **indywidualnie**

,one-'way adj. **1** (used about roads) that you can only drive along in one direction: *a one-way street* ▶ **jednokierunkowy 2** (especially US) (used about a ticket) that you can use to travel somewhere but not back again: *a one-way ticket* ▶ **w jedną stronę** SYN **single**

ongoing /'ɒngəʊɪŋ/ adj. [only before a noun] continuing to exist now: *It's an ongoing problem.* ▶ **trwający**

⚷ **onion** /'ʌnjən/ noun [C,U] a white or red vegetable with many layers. Onions are often used in cooking and have a strong smell that makes some people cry ▶ **cebula** ➲ picture on **page A13**

online /,ɒn'laɪn/ adj. controlled by or connected to a computer or to the Internet: *an online ticket booking system* ▶ **komputerowy** ➲ note at **Internet** ➲ look at **offline**
■ **online** adv.: *I'm studying French online.* ▶ **przez komputer/Internet**

onlooker /'ɒnlʊkə(r)/ noun [C] a person who watches sth happening without taking part in it ▶ **gap, obserwator/ka**

⚷ **only** /'əʊnli/ adj. [only before a noun] **1** with no others existing or present: *I was the only woman in the room.* ▶ **jedyny 2** the most suitable or the best: *She's the only person for the job.* ▶ **jedyny, najlepszy**
■ **only** adv. and nobody or nothing else; no more than: *She only likes pop music.* ◇ *I've only asked a few friends to the party.* ◇ *It's only* (dopiero) *1 o'clock.* ▶ **tylko**

> W angielszczyźnie pisanej **only** występuje zwykle przed wyrazem, do którego się odnosi. W języku mówionym odniesienie takie można ustalić za pomocą odmiennego akcentowania, przez co **only** występuje w różnych miejscach w zdaniu: *I only kissed 'Jane.* Pocałowałem tylko Jane i nikogo więcej. ◇ *I only 'kissed Jane.* Pocałowałem Jane, ale nie zrobiłem niczego więcej.

only conj. (informal) except that; but: *The film was very good, only it was a bit too long.* ▶ **tylko**
IDM **if only** → IF
not only... but also → NOT
only just 1 not long ago: *I've only just started this job.* ▶ **dopiero co, niedawno 2** almost not: *We only just had enough money to pay for the meal.* ▶ **ledwie** SYN **hardly**

,only 'child noun [C] a child who has no brothers or sisters ▶ **jedyna-k/czka**

onset /'ɒnset/ noun [sing.] **the onset (of sth)** the beginning (often of sth unpleasant): *the onset of winter/a headache* ▶ **początek** (*np. choroby*), **nadejście** (*np. zimy*)

onslaught /'ɒnslɔːt/ noun [C] **an onslaught (on/against sb/sth)** a violent or strong attack: *an onslaught on government policy* ▶ **napaść**

⚷ **onto** (also **on to**) /'ɒntə; before vowels 'ɒntu/ prep. to a position on sth: *The cat jumped onto the sofa.* ◇ *The bottle fell off the table onto the floor.* ◇ *The crowd ran onto the pitch.* ▶ **na**
IDM **be onto sb 1** (informal) to know about what sb has done wrong: *The police were onto the car thieves.* ▶ **być na czyimś tropie 2** to be talking to sb, usually in order to tell them sth: *They've been onto me for ages to get a job.* ▶ **naprzykrzać się komuś**
be onto sth to have some information, etc. that could lead to an important discovery ▶ **być na tropie czegoś**

onus /'əʊnəs/ noun (usually **the onus**) [sing.] (formal) the responsibility for sth: *The* ***onus is on*** *employers to follow health and safety laws.* ◇ *The* ***onus of proof*** *lies with the prosecution.* ▶ **obowiązek**

onward /'ɒnwəd/ adj. [only before a noun] (formal) continuing or moving forward: *Ticket prices include your flight and onward rail journey.* ◇ *the onward march of time* ▶ **dalszy**

onwards /'ɒnwədz/ (also **onward** /'ɒnwəd/) adv. **1 from... onwards** continuing from a particular time: *From September onwards* (począwszy od września) *it usually begins to get colder.* ▶ **dalej 2** (formal) forward: *The road stretched onwards into the distance.* ▶ **naprzód, dalej**

oodles /'uːdlz/ noun [pl.] **oodles (of sth)** (old-fashioned, informal) a large amount of sth: *Bob makes oodles of money, you know.* ▶ **mnóstwo** SYN **loads (of sth)**

ooze /uːz/ verb [I,T] **ooze from/out of sth; ooze (with) sth** to flow slowly out or to allow sth to flow slowly out: *Blood was oozing from a cut on his head.* ◇ *The fruit was oozing juice.* ◇ *She was oozing confidence.* Biła od niej pewność siebie. ▶ **sączyć się, wyciekać**

op (informal) = OPERATION (1)

opaque /əʊ'peɪk/ adj. **1** that you cannot see through: *opaque glass in the door* ▶ **matowy, nieprzezroczysty 2** (formal) difficult to understand; not clear ▶ **nieprzejrzysty, niejasny** OPP for both meanings **transparent**

OPEC /'əʊpek/ abbr. **Organization of Petroleum Exporting Countries** ▶ **Organizacja Państw Eksportujących Ropę Naftową**

the **open** /'əʊpən/ noun [sing.] the outside or the countryside: *After working in an office I like to be* ***out in the open*** (na świeżym powietrzu) *at weekends.* ▶ **świeże powietrze**
IDM **bring sth out into the open** to make sth known publicly ▶ **ujawniać**
come out into the open to be known publicly: *I'm glad our secret has come out into the open at last.* ▶ **ujawniać się**

⚷ **open¹** /'əʊpən/ adj. **1** not closed or covered: *Don't leave the door open.* ◇ *an open window* ◇ *I can't get this bottle of wine open.* Nie mogę otworzyć tej butelki wina. ◇ *She stared at me with her eyes wide open.* ◇ *The diary was lying open on her desk.* ◇ *The curtains were open* (rozsunięte) *so that we could see into the room.* ◇ *Families used to have an open* (odkryty) *fire to keep them warm.* ▶ **otwarty 2** (used about clothes) with the buttons not fastened: *His shirt was open at the neck.* ▶ **rozpięty 3** [only before a noun] away from towns and buildings; at a distance from the land: *open country* wolna przestrzeń ◇ *Once we were out in the open sea* (na pełnym morzu), *the wind got stronger.* ▶ **wolny 4 open (to sb/sth); open (for sth)** available for people to enter, visit, use, etc.; not

O

closed to the public: *The bank isn't open till 9.30.* ◇ *The new shopping centre will soon be open.* ◇ *The competition is open to everyone.* ◇ *The gardens are **open to the public** in the summer.* ◇ *The hotel damaged by the bomb is now **open for business** again.* ◇ *After the heavy snow many minor roads were not open* (przejezdne) *to traffic.* ▶ **otwarty** OPP **closed**, **shut** **5** not keeping feelings and thoughts hidden: *Elena doesn't mind talking about her feelings – she's a very open person.* ◇ *He looked at him with open dislike* (jawną niechęcią). ▶ **otwarty** **6** [not before a noun] not finally decided; still being considered: *Let's leave the details open.* ▶ **otwarty**

IDM **have/keep an open mind (about/on sth)** to be ready to listen to or consider new ideas and suggestions ▶ **chętnie/bez uprzedzeń podchodzić do nowości**

in the open air outside: *Somehow, food eaten in the open air tastes much better.* ▶ **na świeżym powietrzu**

keep an eye open/out (for sb/sth) → EYE[1]

open to sth willing to receive sth: *I'm always open to suggestions.* ▶ **otwarty na coś**

with your eyes open → EYE[1]

with open arms in a friendly way that shows that you are pleased to see sb or have sth: *The unions welcomed the government's decision with open arms.* ▶ **z otwartymi ramionami**

🔑 **open²** /ˈəʊpən/ verb **1** [I,T] to move sth or part of sth so that it is no longer closed; to move so as to be no longer closed: *This window won't open* (nie chce się otworzyć) *– it's stuck.* ◇ *The parachute failed to open and he was killed.* ◇ *The book opened at the very page I needed.* ◇ *Open* (rozsuń) *the curtains, will you?* ◇ *to open your eyes/hand/mouth* ◇ *to open a bag/letter/box* ▶ **otwierać (się)** OPP **close**, **shut** **2** [I,T] to make it possible for people to enter a place: *Does that shop open on Sundays?* ◇ *The museum opens at 10.* ◇ *The company is opening two new branches soon.* ◇ *Police finally opened the road* (otworzyła przejazd dla samochodów) *six hours after the accident.* ▶ **otwierać (się)** OPP **close**, **shut** **3** [I,T] to start (sth): *The chairman opened the meeting by welcoming everybody.* ◇ *I'd like to open a bank account.* ◇ *The play opens* (premiera sztuki odbędzie się) *in London next month.* ▶ **otwierać (się)**, **rozpoczynać (się)** OPP **close** **4** [T] to start a computer program or file so that you can use it on the screen ▶ **otwierać**

IDM **open fire (at/on sb/sth)** to start shooting: *He ordered his men to open fire.* ▶ **otwierać ogień**

PHR V **open into/onto sth** to lead to another room, area or place: *This door opens onto the garden.* ▶ **wychodzić na coś**

open out to become wider ▶ **poszerzać się**

open up **1** to talk about what you feel and think ▶ **rozmawiać szczerze** **2** to open a door: *'Open up,' shouted the police to the man inside.* ▶ **otwierać drzwi**

open (sth) up **1** to become available or to make sth available: *When I left school all sorts of opportunities opened up for me.* ◇ *Parts of the desert may soon be opened up* (mogą być wkrótce dostępne) *for farming.* ▶ **otwierać się**; **uczynić coś dostępnym** **2** to start business: *The restaurant opened up last year.* ▶ **otwierać** (*np. interes, sklep*)

ˌopen-ˈair adj. [only before a noun] not inside a building: *an open-air* (odkryty) *swimming pool* ▶ **odkryty**, **na dworze**

ˈopen day noun [C] a day when the public can visit a place that they cannot usually go into: *The hospital is having an open day next month.* ▶ **dzień otwartych drzwi**

ˌopen-ˈended adj. without any limits, aims or dates fixed in advance: *an open-ended* (otwarta) *discussion* ◇ *The contract is open-ended* (na czas nieokreślony). ▶ **nieograniczony**, **elastyczny**

opener /ˈəʊpnə(r)/ noun [C] [in compounds] a thing that takes the lid, etc. off sth: *a tin-opener* ◇ *a bottle-opener* ▶ **otwieracz**

🔑 **opening** /ˈəʊpnɪŋ/ noun [C] **1** a space or hole that sb/sth can go through: *We were able to get through an opening in the hedge.* ▶ **otwór**, **dziura** **2** the beginning or first part of sth: *The film is famous for its dramatic opening.* ▶ **początek**, **otwarcie** **3** a ceremony to celebrate the first time a public building, road, etc. is used: *the opening of the new hospital* ▶ **otwarcie**, **inauguracja**, (*przedstawienie itp.*) **premiera** **4** a job which is available: *We have an opening for a sales manager at the moment.* ▶ **wakat** **5** a good opportunity: *I'm sure she'll be a great journalist – all she needs is an opening.* ▶ **okazja**, **sposobność**

■ **opening** adj. [only before a noun]: *the opening chapter of a book* ◇ *the opening ceremony of the Olympic Games* ▶ **początkowy**, **wstępny**

ˈopening hours noun [pl.] the time during which a shop, bank, etc. is open for business: *The museum has extended its opening hours.* ▶ **godziny otwarcia**

ˌopening ˈnight noun [usually sing.] the first night that, for example, a play is performed or a film is shown to the public ▶ **premiera**

🔑 **openly** /ˈəʊpənli/ adv. honestly; not keeping anything secret: *I think you should discuss your feelings openly with each other.* ▶ **otwarcie**

ˌopen-ˈminded adj. ready to consider new ideas and opinions ▶ **bez uprzedzeń** OPP **narrow-minded**

openness /ˈəʊpənnəs/ noun [U] the quality of being honest and ready to talk about your feelings ▶ **otwartość**

ˌopen-ˈplan adj. (used about a large area inside a building) not divided into separate rooms: *an open-plan office* ▶ **otwarta przestrzeń** (*np. biurowa*)

the ˌOpen Uniˈversity noun [sing.] (Brit.) a university whose students study mainly at home. Their work is sent to them by post or email and there are special television and radio programmes for them. ▶ **uniwersytet otwarty**

opera /ˈɒprə/ noun [C,U] a play in which most of the words are sung to music; works of this kind performed as entertainment: *Do you like opera?* ◇ *grand opera* opera poważna ◇ *a comic opera* opera komiczna ▶ **opera** ➲ look at **musical**, **soap opera**

ˈopera house noun [C] a theatre where **operas** are performed ▶ (*budynek*) **opera**

🔑 **operate** /ˈɒpəreɪt/ verb **1** [I,T] to work, or to make sth work: *I don't understand how this machine operates.* ◇ *These switches here operate the central heating.* ▶ **działać**; **obsługiwać** SYN for all meanings **function** **2** [I] to act or to have an effect: *Several factors were operating to our advantage* (przemawiało na naszą korzyść). ▶ **działać**, **znajdować zastosowanie** **3** [I,T] to do business; to manage sth: *The firm operates from its central office in Bristol.* ▶ **prowadzić** (*np. interesy, usługi*), **działać** **4** [I] **operate (on sb/sth) (for sth)** to cut open sb's body in hospital in order to deal with a part that is damaged, infected, etc.: *The surgeon is going to operate on her in the morning.* ◇ *He was operated on for appendicitis.* ▶ **operować**

operatic /ˌɒpəˈrætɪk/ adj. connected with **opera** ▶ **operowy**

ˈoperating system noun [C] a computer program that organizes a number of other programs at the same time ▶ **system operacyjny**

ˈoperating table noun [C] a special table that you lie on to have a medical operation in a hospital ▶ **stół operacyjny**

ˈoperating theatre (also **theatre**) noun [C] a room in a hospital where medical operations are performed ▶ **sala operacyjna**

operation /ˌɒpəˈreɪʃn/ noun **1** [C] (also informal **op** /ɒp/) the process of cutting open a patient's body in order to deal with a part inside: *He **had an operation** to remove his appendix.* ▶ **operacja** ➲ note at **hospital** **2** [C] an organized activity that involves many people doing different things: *A rescue operation was mounted to find the missing children.* ▶ **działanie, akcja** **3** [C] a business or company involving many parts: *a huge international operation* ▶ **firma** **4** [C] an act performed by a machine, especially a computer: *The computer can perform millions of operations per second.* ▶ **operacja, praca** (*komputera, maszyny*) **5** [U] the way in which you make sth work: *The operation of these machines is extremely simple.* ▶ **działanie**

IDM **be in operation**; **come into operation** to be/start working or having an effect: *The new tax system will come into operation in the spring.* ▶ **działać; rozpocząć działanie, wchodzić w życie**

operational /ˌɒpəˈreɪʃənl/ adj. **1** connected with the way a business, machine, system, etc. works: *operational activities/costs/difficulties* ▶ **operacyjny** **2** ready for use: *The new factory is now fully operational.* ▶ **gotowy do działania, sprawny** **3** [only before a noun] connected with military operations: *operational headquarters* ◇ *an operational* (w gotowości bojowej) *squadron* ▶ **operacyjny, bojowy**

operative /ˈɒpərətɪv; US also -reɪt-/ adj. (formal) **1** working; able to be used; in use: *The new law will be operative from 1 May.* ▶ **obowiązujący, działający** **2** [only before a noun] connected with a medical operation ▶ **operacyjny**

operator /ˈɒpəreɪtə(r)/ noun [C] **1** a person whose job is to work a particular machine or piece of equipment: *a computer operator* ▶ **operator/ka** **2** (Brit. also **telephonist** /təˈlefənɪst/) a person whose job is to connect telephone calls, for the public or in a particular building: *Dial 100 for the operator.* ◇ *a switchboard operator* ▶ **telefonist(k)a** **3** a person or company that does certain types of business: *a tour operator* biuro podróży ▶ **firma; osoba prowadząca firmę**

opinion /əˈpɪnjən/ noun **1** [C] **an opinion (of sb/sth)**; **an opinion (on/about sth)** what you think about sb/sth: *She asked me for my opinion of her new hairstyle and I told her.* ◇ *He has very strong opinions on almost everything.* ◇ ***In my opinion*** (moim zdaniem), *you're making a terrible mistake.* ▶ **zdanie, opinia** ➲ note at **point of view**, **think** **2** [U] what people in general think about sth: *Public opinion is in favour of a change in the law.* ▶ **opinia**

IDM **be of the opinion that ...** (formal) to think or believe that ... ▶ **uważać, że**

have a good, high, etc. opinion of sb/sth; **have a bad, low, poor, etc. opinion of sb/sth** to think that sb/sth is good/bad ▶ **mieć o kimś/czymś dobre/złe itp. zdanie**

a matter of opinion → MATTER[1]

opinionated /əˈpɪnjəneɪtɪd/ adj. having very strong opinions that you are not willing to change: *I've never met anyone so arrogant and opinionated.* ▶ **zadufany w sobie**

oˈpinion poll = POLL[1] (1)

opium /ˈəʊpiəm/ noun [U] a powerful drug that is made from the juice of a type of **poppy** ▶ **opium**

opp abbr. = OPPOSITE

opponent /əˈpəʊnənt/ noun [C] **1** (in sport or competitions) a person who plays against sb: *They are the toughest opponents we've played against.* ▶ **przeciwni-k/czka** **2 an opponent (of sth)** a person who disagrees with sb's actions, plans or beliefs and tries to stop or change them: *He is an outspoken opponent of nuclear power.* ▶ **oponent/ka**

opportune /ˈɒpətjuːn; US ˌɒpərˈtuːn/ adj. (formal) **1** (used about a time) suitable for doing a particular thing, so that it is likely to be successful: *The offer could not have come at a more opportune moment.* ▶ **dogodny, pomyślny** SYN **favourable** **2** (used about an action or event) done or happening at the right time to be successful: *an opportune* (trafna) *remark* ▶ **w porę** OPP for both meanings **inopportune**

opportunism /ˌɒpəˈtjuːnɪzəm; US -ˈtuː-/ noun [U] making use of a situation for your own good and not caring about other people ▶ **oportunizm**

opportunist /ˌɒpəˈtjuːnɪst; US -ˈtuː-/ (also **opportunistic** /ˌɒpətjuːˈnɪstɪk; US -tuː-/) adj. not done in a planned way; making use of an opportunity: *an opportunist crime* ▶ **oportunistyczny**

■ **opportunist** noun [C]: *80% of burglaries are committed by casual opportunists.* ▶ **oportunist(k)a**

opportunistic /ˌɒpətjuːˈnɪstɪk; US -tuː-/ adj. **1** = OPPORTUNIST **2** [only before a noun] harmful to people whose **immune system** has been made weak by disease or drugs: *an opportunistic infection* ▶ **oportunistyczny**

opportunity /ˌɒpəˈtjuːnəti; US ˈtuː-/ noun [C,U] (pl. **opportunities**) **an opportunity (for sth/to do sth)** a chance to do sth that you would like to do; a situation or a time in which it is possible to do sth that you would like to do: *There will be **plenty of opportunity** for asking questions later.* ◇ *I have a **golden opportunity** to go to America now that my sister lives there.* ◇ *When we're finally alone, I'll **take the opportunity*** (skorzystam ze sposobności) *to ask him a few personal questions.* ◇ *I'll give Steve your message if I **get the opportunity*** (jeśli nadarzy się okazja). ◇ *an equal opportunity employer* pracodawca realizujący zasady równouprawnienia (bez względu na płeć, kolor skóry itp.) ▶ **okazja, sposobność** SYN **chance** ➲ note at **occasion**

oppose /əˈpəʊz/ verb [T] to disagree with sb's beliefs, actions or plans and to try to change or stop them: *They opposed the plan to build a new road.* ▶ **sprzeciwiać się**

opposed /əˈpəʊzd/ adj. **opposed to sth** disagreeing with a plan, action, etc.; believing that sth is wrong: *She has always been strongly opposed to experiments on animals.* ▶ **przeciwny**

IDM **as opposed to** (used to emphasize the difference between two things) rather than; and not: *Your work will be judged by quality, as opposed to quantity.* ▶ **w przeciwieństwie do czegoś**

opposing /əˈpəʊzɪŋ/ adj. [only before a noun] **1** (used about teams, armies, etc.) playing, fighting, working, etc. against each other: *a player from the opposing side* ▶ **przeciwny** **2** (used about opinions, attitudes, etc.) very different from each other: *They have opposing views.* ▶ **przeciwstawny, odmienny**

opposite /ˈɒpəzɪt; -sɪt; US -zət/ adj. **1** in a position on the other side of sb/sth; facing: *The old town and the new town are on opposite sides of the river.* ▶ **przeciwny, przeciwległy** ℹ Czasami **opposite** używa się po rzeczowniku: *Write your answer in the space opposite.* **2** completely different: *I can't walk with you because I'm going in the opposite direction.* ◇ *the opposite sex* ▶ **przeciwny, odmienny**

■ **opposite** **1** adv., prep. on the other side of a particular area from sb/sth; facing sb/sth: *You sit there and I'll sit opposite.* ◇ *See opposite* (po drugiej stronie) *for further details.* ▶ **naprzeciwko** **2** noun [C]: *'Hot' is **the opposite of** 'cold'.* ▶ **antonim, przeciwieństwo**

IDM **your opposite number** a person who does the same job or has the same position as you in a different company, organization, team, etc.: *The Prime Minister met his Italian opposite number.* ▶ **odpowiedni-k/czka**

opposition /ˌɒpəˈzɪʃn/ noun [U] **1 opposition (to sb/sth)** the feeling of disagreeing with sth and the act of trying to change it: *He expressed strong opposition to the plan.* ▶ **sprzeciw, opór** **2** (**the opposition**) [sing., with sing. or pl.

O

verb] the person or team who you compete against in sport, business, etc.: *We need to find out what the opposition is doing.* ▶ **rywal/ka, konkurent/ka, drużyna przeciwna 3** (**the Opposition**) [sing., with sing. or pl. verb] the politicians or the political parties that are in Parliament but not in the government: *the leader of the Opposition* ◇ *Opposition MPs* ▶ **opozycja** ℹ W znaczeniach 2 i 3 **opposition** można użyć zarówno z czasownikiem w lp, jak i lm.

oppress /ə'pres/ verb [T, usually passive] to treat a group of people in a cruel and unfair way by not allowing them the same freedom and rights as others ▶ **uciskać, gnębić**

■ **oppressed** adj.: *an oppressed minority* ▶ **uciskany, gnębiony** | **oppression** /ə'preʃn/ noun [U]: *a struggle against oppression* ▶ **ucisk**

oppressive /ə'presɪv/ adj. **1** allowing no freedom; controlling by force: *The military government announced oppressive new laws.* ▶ **surowy, uciskający 2** (used about the weather) extremely hot and unpleasant and lacking fresh air ▶ **ciężki, duszny 3** making you feel unhappy and anxious: *an oppressive relationship* ▶ **przytłaczający**

oppressor /ə'presə(r)/ noun [C] a person or group of people that treats sb in a cruel and unfair way, especially by not giving them the same rights, etc. as other people ▶ **gnębiciel/ka**

opt /ɒpt/ verb [I] **opt to do sth/for sth** to choose to do or have sth after thinking about it: *She opted for a career in music.* ▶ **decydować się na coś, opowiadać się za czymś**

PHR V **opt out (of sth)** to choose not to take part in sth: *Employees may opt out of the company's pension plan.* ▶ **rezygnować z czegoś**

optic /'ɒptɪk/ adj. [usually before a noun] connected with the eye or the sense of sight: *the optic nerve* ▶ **wzrokowy**

optical /'ɒptɪkl/ adj. connected with the sense of sight: *optical instruments* ▶ **optyczny**

ˌoptical 'fibre (US ˌ**optical 'fiber**) noun [C, U] a thin glass thread through which light can be **transmitted** ▶ **światłowód**

ˌoptical il'lusion noun [C] an image that tricks the eye and makes you think you can see sth that you cannot ▶ **złudzenie optyczne**

optician /ɒp'tɪʃn/ (also **optometrist** /ɒp'tɒmətrɪst/) noun [C] a person whose job is to test eyes, sell glasses, etc.: *to go to the optician's* (do zakładu optycznego) ▶ **optyk** ➲ picture on **page A5**

optimal = OPTIMUM

optimism /'ɒptɪmɪzəm/ noun [U] the feeling that the future will be good or successful: *There is considerable optimism that the economy will improve.* ▶ **optymizm** OPP **pessimism**

■ **optimist** /-ɪst/ noun [C] ▶ **optymist(k)a**

optimistic /ˌɒptɪ'mɪstɪk/ adj. **optimistic (about sth/that ...)** expecting good things to happen or sth to be successful; showing this feeling: *I've applied for the job but I'm not very optimistic that I'll get it* (ale nie za bardzo wierzę, że ją dostanę). ▶ **optymistyczny** SYN **positive** OPP **pessimistic**

■ **optimistically** /-kli/ adv. ▶ **optymistycznie**

optimize (also **-ise**) /'ɒptɪmaɪz/ verb [T] to make sth as good as it can be; to use sth in the best possible way: *to optimize the use of resources* ▶ **optymalizować**

optimum /'ɒptɪməm/ (also **optimal** /'ɒptɪməl/) adj. [only before a noun] the best possible; producing the best possible results: *optimum growth* ◇ *the optimum conditions for effective learning* ▶ **optymalny**

⚷ **option** /'ɒpʃn/ noun **1** [U] the freedom to choose; choice: *If you're late again, you will give us* ***no option but to*** *dismiss you* (nie będziemy mieli innego wyjścia, jak tylko cię zwolnić). ▶ **wybór 2** [C] a thing that you choose or can choose: *She looked carefully at all the options before deciding on a career.* ◇ *Students* ***have the option*** (mają możliwość) *of studying part-time or full-time.* ▶ **ewentualność** SYN for both meanings **choice**

optional /'ɒpʃənl/ adj. that you can choose or not choose: *an optional subject at school* ◇ *The CD player is an optional extra* (możesz mieć odtwarzacz za dodatkową opłatą) *with this car.* ▶ **dodatkowy, nadobowiązkowy** OPP **compulsory, obligatory**

optometrist = OPTICIAN

opulent /'ɒpjələnt/ adj. (formal) **1** made or decorated using expensive materials: *opulent fabrics/surroundings* ▶ **wykwintny** SYN **luxurious 2** (used about people) extremely rich ▶ **bardzo bogaty** SYN **wealthy**

■ **opulence** /-ləns/ noun [U] ▶ **wykwintność; wielkie bogactwo** | **opulently** adv. ▶ **wykwintnie; bogato**

⚷ **or** /ɔː(r)/ conj. **1** (used in a list of possibilities or choices): *Would you like to sit here or next to the window?* ◇ *Are you interested or not?* ◇ *For the main course, you can have lamb, beef or fish.* ▶ **czy, albo** ➲ look at **either 2** [after a negative] and neither; and not: *She hasn't phoned or written to me for weeks.* ◇ *I've never been either to Italy or Spain.* ▶ **ani** ➲ look at **neither 3** if not; otherwise: *Don't drive so fast or you'll have an accident!* ▶ **(bo) w przeciwnym razie** SYN **or else, otherwise 4** (used between two numbers to show approximately how many): *I've been there five or six times.* ▶ **czy/albo/lub (też) 5** (used before a word or phrase that explains or comments on what has been said before): *20% of the population, or one in five* ▶ **czy/albo/lub (też)**

IDM **or something/somewhere** (informal) (used for showing that you are not sure, cannot remember or do not know which thing or place): *She's a computer programmer or something.* ▶ **czy coś takiego, czy gdzieś tam** ℹ Innym zwrotem używanym przy braku pewności jest **something or other**: *He muttered something or other about having no time and disappeared.*

oracle /'ɒrəkl/ noun [C] **1** (in ancient Greece) a place where people could go to ask the gods for advice or information about the future; the priest or **priestess** through whom the gods were thought to give their message: *They consulted the oracle at Delphi.* ▶ **wyrocznia 2** (in ancient Greece) the advice or information that the gods gave, which often had a hidden meaning ▶ **wyrocznia 3** [usually sing.] a person or book that gives valuable advice or information: *My sister's the oracle on investment matters.* ▶ **wyrocznia**

oral[1] /'ɔːrəl/ adj. **1** spoken, not written: *an oral test* ▶ **ustny 2** [only before a noun] concerning or using the mouth: *oral hygiene* higiena jamy ustnej ▶ **ustny** ➲ look at **aural**

■ **orally** /'ɔːrəli/ adv. using speech, not writing; through the mouth and swallowed: *You can ask the questions orally or in writing.* ◇ *This medicine is taken orally* (doustnie). ▶ **ustnie**

oral[2] /'ɔːrəl/ noun [C] a spoken exam: *I've got my German oral next week.* ▶ **egzamin ustny**

⚷ **orange**[1] /'ɒrɪndʒ/ noun **1** [C,U] (Brit.) a round fruit with a thick skin that is divided into sections inside and is a colour between red and yellow: *orange juice/peel* ◇ *an orange tree* ▶ **pomarańcza** ➲ picture on **page A12 2** [U,C] a drink made from oranges or with the taste of oranges; a glass of this drink: *freshly squeezed orange* ▶ **sok/napój pomarańczowy 3** [U,C] the colour of this fruit, between red and yellow ▶ **kolor pomarańczowy**

⚷ **orange**[2] /'ɒrɪndʒ/ adj. having the colour orange: *orange paint* ▶ **pomarańczowy**

ˌ**orange ˈsquash** noun [C,U] (Brit.) a drink made by adding water to a liquid that tastes of orange ▶ **napój pomarańczowy**

orang-utan /ɔːˌræŋ uːˈtæn; əˈræŋ uːtæn; US əˈræŋ ətæn/ noun [C] a large animal that has long arms and reddish hair, like a **monkey** with no tail and that lives in South East Asia ▶ **orangutan**

orator /ˈɒrətə(r)/ noun [C] (formal) a person who is good at making public speeches ▶ **(kraso)mów-ca/czyni**

orb /ɔːb/ noun [C] **1** (literary) an object shaped like a ball, especially the sun or moon: *The red orb of the sun sank beneath the horizon.* ▶ **kula 2** a gold ball with a cross on top, carried by a king or queen at formal ceremonies as a symbol of power ▶ **jabłko** (*królewskie*) ➲ look at **sceptre**

orbit /ˈɔːbɪt/ noun [C,U] a curved path taken by a planet or another object as it moves around another planet, star, moon, etc.: *the earth's orbit around the sun* ◇ *to* ***put*** *a satellite* ***into orbit*** (umieścić satelitę na orbicie) *around the moon* ▶ **orbita**
■ **orbit** verb [I,T] ▶ **krążyć po orbicie**

orbital /ˈɔːbɪtl/ adj. [only before a noun] **1** connected with the **orbit** of a planet or another object in space ▶ **orbitalny 2** (used about a road) built around the outside of a city or town to reduce the amount of traffic travelling through the centre ▶ **dotyczący obwodnicy**
■ **orbital** noun [C, usually sing.] ▶ **obwodnica**

orchard /ˈɔːtʃəd/ noun [C] a piece of land on which fruit trees are grown: *a cherry orchard* ▶ **sad**

orchestra /ˈɔːkɪstrə/ noun [C] a large group of musicians who play various musical instruments together, led by a **conductor**: *a symphony orchestra* ▶ **orkiestra** ❶ **Orchestra** zazwyczaj gra muzykę poważną. Muzykę typu pop, jazzową itp. wykonuje **group** lub **band.** ➲ note at **music**
■ **orchestral** /ɔːˈkestrəl/ adj. ▶ **orkiestrowy**

ˈ**orchestra pit** (also **pit**) noun [C] the place in a theatre just in front of the stage where the **orchestra** sits and plays for an **opera**, a **ballet**, etc. ▶ **fosa orkiestrowa**

orchestrate /ˈɔːkɪstreɪt/ verb [T] **1** to arrange a piece of music in parts so that it can be played by an **orchestra** ▶ **aranżować** (*dla orkiestry*) **2** to organize a complicated plan or event very carefully or secretly: *a carefully orchestrated publicity campaign* ▶ **organizować**
■ **orchestration** /ˌɔːkɪˈstreɪʃn/ noun [C, U] ▶ **aranżacja**; **organizowanie**

orchid /ˈɔːkɪd/ noun [C] a beautiful and sometimes rare type of plant that has flowers of unusual shapes and bright colours ▶ **storczyk**, **orchidea**

ordain /ɔːˈdeɪn/ verb [T, usually passive] **ordain sb (as) (sth)** to make sb a priest or minister: *He was ordained (as) a priest last year.* ▶ **wyświęcać**

ordeal /ɔːˈdiːl; Brit. also ˈɔːdiːl/ noun [C, usually sing.] a very unpleasant or difficult experience ▶ **ciężkie przejścia**, **przeprawa**

🔑 **order¹** /ˈɔːdə(r)/ noun **1** [U, sing.] the way in which people or things are arranged in relation to each other: *a list of names in* ***alphabetical order*** ◇ *Try to put the things you have to do* ***in order of importance*** (ułożyć rzeczy, które masz do zrobienia, według ich ważności). ◇ *What's the order of events today?* ▶ **porządek**, **układ 2** [U] an organized state, where everything is in its right place: *I really must* ***put*** *my notes* ***in order*** (uporządkować swoje notatki), *because I can never find what I'm looking for.* ▶ **porządek** OPP **disorder 3** [U] the situation in which laws, rules, authority, etc. are obeyed: *Following last week's riots, order has now been restored.* ▶ **ład** ➲ look at **disorder 4** [C] **an order (for sb) (to do sth)** sth that you are told to do by sb in a position of authority: *In the army, you have to* ***obey orders*** *at all times.* ◇ *She* ***gave the order*** (wydała rozkaz) *for the work to be started.* ▶ **rozkaz 5** [C,U] **an order (for sth)** a request asking for sth to be made, supplied or sent: *The company has just received a major export order.* ◇ *The book I need is* ***on order*** (jest zamówiona). ◇ *an order form* ▶ **zamówienie (handlowe) 6** [C] a request for food or drinks in a hotel, restaurant, etc.; the food or drinks you asked for: *Can I* ***take your order*** (przyjąć zamówienie) *now, sir?* ▶ **zamówienie** (*np. w restauracji*)
IDM **in order to do sth** with the purpose or intention of doing sth; so that sth can be done: *We left early in order to avoid the traffic.* ▶ **żeby**
in/into reverse order → REVERSE³
in working order → WORKING
law and order → LAW
out of order 1 (used about a machine, etc.) not working properly or not working at all: *I had to walk up to the tenth floor because the lift was out of order.* ▶ **zepsuty 2** (informal) (used about sb's behaviour) unacceptable, because it is rude, etc.: *That comment was completely out of order!* ▶ **nie na miejscu**

🔑 **order²** /ˈɔːdə(r)/ verb **1** [T] **order sb (to do sth)** to use your position of authority to tell sb to do sth or to say that sth must happen: *I'm not asking you to do your homework – I'm ordering you!* ◇ *The company was ordered to pay compensation to its former employees.* ▶ **kazać 2** [T] to ask for sth to be made, supplied or sent somewhere: *The shop didn't have the book I wanted so I ordered it.* ▶ **zamawiać 3** [I,T] **order (sb) (sth)**; **order (sth) (for sb)** to ask for food or drinks in a restaurant, hotel, etc.: *Are you ready to order yet, madam?* ◇ *Can you order me a sandwich while I make a phone call?* ◇ *Could you order a sandwich for me?* ▶ **zamawiać**
PHR V **order sb about/around** to keep telling sb what to do and how to do it: *Stop ordering me about! You're not my father.* ▶ **rozkazywać (komuś)**, **rządzić (kimś)**

orderly¹ /ˈɔːdəli/ adj. **1** arranged or organized in a tidy way: *an orderly office/desk* ▶ **uporządkowany**, **systematyczny 2** peaceful; behaving well: *The teacher told the pupils to form an orderly queue* (ustawić się grzecznie w kolejce). ▶ **spokojny**, **uporządkowany** OPP for both meanings **disorderly**

orderly² /ˈɔːdəli/ noun [C] (pl. **orderlies**) a worker in a hospital, usually doing jobs that do not need special training ▶ **sanitariusz/ka**

ordinal /ˈɔːdɪnl; US -dənl/ (also ˌ**ordinal ˈnumber**) noun [C] a number that shows the order or position of sth in a series: *'First', 'second', and 'third' are ordinals.* ▶ **liczebnik porządkowy** ➲ look at **cardinal**

ordinarily /ˈɔːdnrəli; US -dnˈerə-/ adv. usually; generally: *Ordinarily, I don't work as late as this.* ▶ **zazwyczaj**, **zwykle** SYN **normally**

🔑 **ordinary** /ˈɔːdnri; US -dneri/ adj. normal; not unusual or different from others: *It's interesting to see how ordinary people live in other countries.* ▶ **zwykły**, **normalny** OPP **extraordinary**
IDM **out of the ordinary** unusual; different from normal ▶ **niezwykły**, **niecodzienny**

ordination /ˌɔːdɪˈneɪʃn; US -dnˈeɪ-/ noun [U,C] the act or ceremony of making sb a priest, etc. ▶ **święcenia** (*kapłańskie*) ➲ look at **ordain**

ore /ɔː(r)/ noun [C,U] rock or earth from which metal can be taken: *iron ore* ▶ **ruda**

🔑 **organ** /ˈɔːgən/ noun [C] **1** one of the parts inside your body that have a particular function: ***vital organs*** narząd istotny dla życia ◇ *sexual/reproductive organs* ▶ **narząd 2** a large musical instrument like a piano with pipes through which air is forced. Organs are often found in churches: *organ music* ▶ **organy** ➲ note at **piano**
■ **organist** /-nɪst/ noun [C]: *the church organist* ▶ **organist(k)a**

O

organic /ɔːˈɡænɪk/ adj. **1** (used about food or farming methods) produced by or using natural materials, without artificial chemicals: *organic vegetables ◇ organic farming* ▶ **naturalny**, **ekologiczny** **2** produced by or from living things: *organic compounds/molecules* ▶ **organiczny** OPP **inorganic**

■ **organically** /-kli/ adv.: *organically grown/produced* ▶ **ekologicznie**; **organicznie**

organism /ˈɔːɡənɪzəm/ noun [C] a living thing, especially one that is so small that you can only see it with a **microscope** ▶ **organizm**

organization (also -isation) /ˌɔːɡənaɪˈzeɪʃn; US -nəˈz-/ noun **1** [C] a group of people who form a business, club, etc. together in order to achieve a particular aim: *She works for a voluntary organization* (dla organizacji charytatywnej) *helping homeless people.* ▶ **organizacja** **2** [U] the activity of making preparations or arrangements for sth: *An enormous amount of organization went into the festival.* ▶ **planowanie**, **organizacja** **3** [U] the way in which sth is organized, arranged or prepared: *Your written work lacks organization.* ▶ **organizacja** OPP **disorganization**

■ **organizational** (also -isational) /-ʃənl/ adj.: *The job requires a high level of organizational ability.* ▶ **organizacyjny**

organize (also -ise) /ˈɔːɡənaɪz/ verb **1** [T] to plan or arrange an event, activity, etc. ▶ **organizować** **2** [I,T] to put or arrange things into a system or logical order: *Can you decide what needs doing? I'm hopeless at organizing. ◇ You need to organize your work more carefully.* ▶ **organizować**

■ **organizer** (also -iser) noun [C] ▶ **organizator/ka**

organized (also -ised) /ˈɔːɡənaɪzd/ adj. **1** [only before a noun] involving a large number of people working together to do sth in a way that has been carefully planned: *an organized campaign against cruelty to animals ◇ organized crime* ▶ **zorganizowany** **2** arranged or planned in the way mentioned: *a carefully/badly/well-organized trip* ▶ **zorganizowany** OPP **disorganized** **3** (used about a person) able to plan your work, life, etc. well: *I wish I were as organized as you!* ▶ **zorganizowany** OPP **disorganized**

orgasm /ˈɔːɡæzəm/ noun [U,C] the point of greatest sexual pleasure: *to have an orgasm* ▶ **orgazm**

orgy /ˈɔːdʒi/ noun [C] (pl. **orgies**) **1** a party, involving a lot of eating, drinking and sexual activity ▶ **orgia** **2 an orgy (of sth)** a period of doing sth in a wild way, without control: *The gang went on an orgy of destruction.* ▶ **orgia**

the **Orient** /ˈɔːriənt/ noun [sing.] (formal) the eastern part of the world, especially China and Japan ▶ **Daleki Wschód**

orient /ˈɔːrient/ (Brit. also **orientate** /ˈɔːriənteɪt/) verb [T] **orient yourself** to find out where you are; to become familiar with a place ▶ **orientować się** (*w terenie*) ➲ look at **disorientate**

oriental /ˌɔːriˈentl/ adj. (**Oriental**) (old-fashioned) coming from or belonging to the East or Far East: *oriental languages* ▶ **orientalny** ⓘ Uwaga! W odniesieniu do osoby, słowo to uważa się za obraźliwe. Lepiej używać **Asian**.

orientate (Brit.) = ORIENT

oriented /ˈɔːrientɪd/ (also **orientated** /ˈɔːriənteɪtɪd/) adj. for or interested in a particular type of person or thing: *Our products are male-oriented. ◇ She's very career orientated.* ▶ **skierowany do kogoś/czegoś**

orienteering /ˌɔːriənˈtɪərɪŋ/ noun [U] a sport in which you find your way across country on foot, as quickly as possible, using a map and a **compass** ▶ **bieg na orientację**

origin /ˈɒrɪdʒɪn/ noun [C,U] **1** [often plural] the point from which sth starts; the cause of sth: *This particular tradition **has its origins in** Wales. ◇ Many English words are of Latin **origin**.* ▶ **geneza**, **pochodzenie** **2** [often plural] the country, race, culture, etc. that a person comes from: *people of African origin* ▶ **pochodzenie**

original[1] /əˈrɪdʒənl/ adj. **1** [only before a noun] first; earliest (before any changes or developments): *The original meaning of this word is different from the meaning it has nowadays.* ▶ **pierwotny** **2** new and interesting; different from others of its type: *There are no original ideas in his work.* ▶ **oryginalny**, **niezwykły** **3** made or created first, before copies: *'Is that the original painting* (oryginał)*?' 'No, it's a copy.'* ▶ **autentyczny**, **oryginalny**

original[2] /əˈrɪdʒənl/ noun [C] the first document, painting, etc. that was made; not a copy ▶ **oryginał**

originality /əˌrɪdʒəˈnæləti/ noun [U] the quality of being new and interesting ▶ **oryginalność**, **niezwykłość**

originally /əˈrɪdʒənəli/ adv. **1** in the beginning; in the first form (before changes or developments) ▶ **pierwotnie** **2** in a way or style that is unlike others ▶ **oryginalnie**

originate /əˈrɪdʒɪneɪt/ verb [I] (formal) to happen or appear for the first time in a particular place or situation ▶ **powstawać**, **pojawiać się**

ornament /ˈɔːnəmənt/ noun [C] an object that you have because it is attractive, not because it is useful. **Ornaments** are used to decorate rooms, etc. ▶ **ozdoba**, **bibelot**

ornamental /ˌɔːnəˈmentl/ adj. made or put somewhere in order to look attractive, not for any practical use ▶ **ozdobny**

ornate /ɔːˈneɪt/ adj. covered with a lot of small complicated designs as decoration ▶ **ozdobny**, **kwiecisty**

ornithology /ˌɔːnɪˈθɒlədʒi/ noun [U] the study of birds ▶ **ornitologia**

■ **ornithologist** /-dʒɪst/ noun [C] ▶ **ornitolog**

orphan /ˈɔːfn/ noun [C] a child whose parents are dead ▶ **sierota**

■ **orphan** verb [T, usually passive]: *She was orphaned when she was three.* ▶ **osierocać** ➲ note at **child**

orphanage /ˈɔːfənɪdʒ/ noun [C] a home for children whose parents are dead ▶ **sierociniec** ⓘ Częściej używa się wyrażenia **children's home**.

orthodox /ˈɔːθədɒks/ adj. **1** that most people believe, do or accept; usual: *orthodox opinions/methods* ▶ **ortodoksyjny**, **konwencjonalny** OPP **unorthodox** **2** (in certain religions) closely following the old, traditional beliefs, ceremonies, etc.: *an orthodox Jew ◇ the (Eastern) Orthodox Church* kościół prawosławny ▶ **ortodoksyjny**

orthography /ɔːˈθɒɡrəfi/ noun [U] (formal) the system of spelling in a language ▶ **ortografia**

■ **orthographic** /ˌɔːθəˈɡræfɪk/ adj. ▶ **ortograficzny**

orthopaedics (US **orthopedics**) /ˌɔːθəˈpiːdɪks/ noun [U] the area of medicine connected with injuries and diseases of the bones or muscles ▶ **ortopedia**

■ **orthopaedic** (US **orthopedic**) adj.: *an orthopaedic surgeon/hospital* ▶ **ortopedyczny**

oscillate /ˈɒsɪleɪt/ verb [I] (formal) **oscillate (between A and B)** **1** to keep changing from one extreme of feeling or behaviour to another, and back again: *Her moods oscillated between joy and depression.* ▶ **oscylować** **2** to keep moving from one position to another and back again: *Watch how the needle oscillates as the current changes.* ▶ **odchylać się** **3** (used about electric current, radio waves, etc.) to change in strength or direction at regular times ▶ **wahać się**

■ **oscillation** /ˌɒsɪˈleɪʃn/ noun [U] ▶ **oscylacja**; **wahanie**

osmosis /ɒzˈməʊsɪs/ noun [U] **1** (*biol.* or *chem.*) the gradual passing of a liquid through a **membrane** as a result of there being different amounts of dissolved substances on either side of the **membrane**: *Water passes into the roots of a plant by osmosis.* ▶ **osmoza 2** the gradual process of learning or being influenced by sth, as a result of being in close contact with it: *As if by osmosis, the facts became clear over a period of time.* ▶ **asymilacja**

ossify /ˈɒsɪfaɪ/ verb [I,T] [usually passive] (**ossifies**; **ossifying**; **ossified**; **ossified**) (formal) **1** to become or make sth fixed and unable to change: *an ossified political system* ▶ **(s)kostnieć; powodować kostnienie czegoś 2** to become or make sth hard like bone ▶ **(s)kostnieć; powodować kostnienie czegoś**
■ **ossification** noun [U] (formal) ▶ **(s)kostnienie**

ostensible /ɒˈstensəbl/ adj. [only before a noun] seeming or stated to be real or true, when this is perhaps not the case: *The ostensible reason for his absence was illness.* ▶ **rzekomy** SYN **apparent**
■ **ostensibly** /-əbli/ adv.: *Troops were sent in, ostensibly to protect the civilian population.* ▶ **rzekomo**

ostentatious /ˌɒstenˈteɪʃəs/ adj. **1** expensive or noticeable in a way that is intended to impress other people: *ostentatious gold jewellery* ▶ **ostentacyjny 2** behaving in a way that is intended to impress people with how rich or important you are ▶ **ostentacyjny**
■ **ostentatiously** adv. ▶ **ostentacyjnie**

osteopath /ˈɒstiəpæθ/ noun [C] a person whose job is treating some diseases and physical problems by pressing and moving the bones and muscles ▶ **kręgarz**

osteopathy /ˌɒstiˈɒpəθi/ noun [U] the treatment of some diseases and physical problems by pressing and moving the bones and muscles ▶ **kręgarstwo**
■ **osteopathic** /ˌɒstiəˈpæθɪk/ adj. ▶ **kręgarski**

osteoporosis /ˌɒstiəʊpəˈrəʊsɪs/ noun [U] a condition in which the bones become weak and are easily broken, usually when people get older or because they do not eat enough of certain substances ▶ **osteoporoza**

ostracize (also **-ise**) /ˈɒstrəsaɪz/ verb [T] (formal) to refuse to allow sb to be a member of a social group; to refuse to meet or talk to sb ▶ **bojkotować** (*towarzysko*)

ostrich /ˈɒstrɪtʃ/ noun [C] a very large African bird with a long neck and long legs, which can run very fast but which cannot fly ▶ **struś**

⚷ **other** /ˈʌðə(r)/ adj., pron. **1** in addition to or different from the one or ones that have already been mentioned: *I hadn't got any other plans that evening so I accepted their invitation.* ◇ *If you're busy now, I'll come back some other time.* ◇ *I like this jumper but not the colour. Have you got any others?* ◇ *Some people care about the environment – others don't.* ◇ *She doesn't care what other people think.* ▶ **inny** ℹ **Other** nie używa się po **an**. ➲ look at **another 2** [after *the, my, your, his, her*, etc. with a singular noun] the second of two people or things, when the first has already been mentioned: *I can only find one sock. Have you seen the other one?* ▶ **drugi (od pary) 3** [after *the, my, your, his, her*, etc. with a plural noun] the rest of a group or number of people or things: *Their youngest son still lives with them but their other children have left home.* ◇ *I'll have to wear this shirt because all my others are dirty.* ◇ *Mick and I got a taxi there – the others walked.* ▶ **inny, pozostały**
IDM **in other words** (used for saying sth in a different way): *My boss said she would have to let me go. In other words, she sacked me.* ▶ **innymi słowy**
one after another/the other → ONE[1]
the other day, morning, week, etc. recently, not long ago: *An old friend rang me the other day.* ▶ **niedawno, kilka dni temu**
other than [usually after a negative] **1** apart from; except (for): *The plane was a little late, but other than that the journey was fine.* ▶ **poza tym 2** (formal) different or in a different way from; not ▶ **inaczej niż; inny niż**
the other way round/around in the opposite way or order: *My appointment's at 3 and Lella's is at 3.15 – or was it the other way round?* ▶ **odwrotnie, w odwrotnej kolejności**
sb/sth/somewhere or other → OR

⚷ **otherwise** /ˈʌðəwaɪz/ adv. **1** apart from that: *I'm a bit tired but otherwise I feel fine.* ▶ **poza tym 2** in a different way to the way mentioned; differently: *I'm afraid I can't see you next weekend, I'm **otherwise engaged*** (mam inne plany). ▶ **inaczej, w inny sposób 3** of a different type ▶ **innego rodzaju**
■ **otherwise** conj. (used for stating what would happen if you do not do sth or if sth does not happen) if not: *You have to press the red button, otherwise it won't work.* ▶ **w przeciwnym razie**

otter /ˈɒtə(r)/ noun [C] a river animal that has brown fur and eats fish ▶ **wydra**

ouch /aʊtʃ/ (also **ow** /aʊ/) interj. (used when reacting to a sudden feeling of pain) ▶ **oj!**

⚷ **ought to** /ˈɔːt tə; before vowels and in final position ˈɔːt tu/ modal verb (negative **ought not to**; short form **oughtn't to** /ˈɔːtnt tə/ before vowels and in final position /ˈɔːtnt tu/) **1** (used for asking for and giving advice about what to do): *You ought to visit your parents more often.* ◇ *She oughtn't to make private phone calls in work time.* ◇ *He oughtn't to have been driving so fast.* ▶ **powinien (coś zrobić) 2** (used to say what should happen or what you expect): *She ought to pass her test.* ◇ *They ought to be here by now. They left at six.* ▶ **powinien**

ounce /aʊns/ noun **1** [C] (abbr. **oz**) a measure of weight; 28.35 grams. There are 16 **ounces** in a pound: *For this recipe you need four ounces of flour.* ▶ **uncja** ℹ Więcej na temat wag w dodatku *Wyrażenia liczbowe* na końcu słownika. **2** [sing.] [usually in negative statements] **an ounce of sth** a very small amount of sth: *That boy hasn't got an ounce of imagination.* ▶ **krzt(yn)a** O

⚷ **our** /ɑː(r); ˈaʊə(r)/ determiner of or belonging to us ▶ **nasz**

⚷ **ours** /ɑːz; ˈaʊəz/ pron. the one or ones belonging to us: *Their garden is quite nice but I prefer ours.* ▶ **nasz**

⚷ **ourselves** /ɑːˈselvz; ˌaʊəˈs-/ pron. **1** (used when the people who do an action are also affected by it): *Let's forget all about work and just enjoy ourselves.* ◇ *They asked us to wait so we sat down and made ourselves comfortable* (rozgościliśmy się). ◇ *We should be angry with ourselves* (powinniśmy być źli na siebie samych) *for making such a stupid mistake.* ▶ **się/siebie 2** (used to emphasize the people who do the action): *Do you think we should paint the flat ourselves?* ▶ **sami, osobiście**
IDM **(all) by ourselves 1** alone: *Now that we're by ourselves, could I ask you a personal question?* ▶ **sami** (*bez towarzystwa*) ➲ note at **alone 2** without help: *We managed to move all our furniture into the new flat by ourselves.* ▶ **sami** (*bez niczyjej pomocy*)

oust /aʊst/ verb [T] **oust sb (from sth/as sth)** to force sb out of a job or position of power, especially in order to take their place: *The rebels finally managed to oust the government from power.* ◇ *He was ousted as chairman.* ▶ **usuwać kogoś** (*np. ze stanowiska*)

⚷ **out**[1] /aʊt/ adv. ℹ **Out** występuje w czasownikach złożonych, np. **look out**. Zob. hasła odpowiednich czasowników. **1** away from the inside of a place: *He opened the drawer and took a fork out* (wyjął widelec). ◇ *She opened the window and put her head out* (wystawiła głowę). ◇ *Can you show me the way out?* Czy może mi pan pokazać wyjście? ◇ *I threw out* (wyrzuciłem) *that old shirt of yours.* ◇ *Her ears stick out.* Ona ma odstające uszy. **2** not at home or in your place of work: *I'd love a night out – I'm bored with staying at home.* ▶ **poza domem/pracą 3** a long distance away from a place, for example from land or your country: *The current is quite strong so don't swim too far out.* ▶ **daleko 4** (used about the sea) when the water is furthest away from the land: *Don't swim when the tide is going out* (kiedy jest odpływ). **5** made available to the public; published: *There'll be a lot of controversy when her book comes out* (kiedy jej książka ukaże się) *next year.* **6** in a loud voice; clearly: *She cried out* (krzyknęła) *in pain.* ◇ *Read it* ***out loud.*** Przeczytaj to na głos. ◇ *Nobody* ***spoke out*** *in his defence.* Nikt nie wystąpił w jego obronie. **7** (**go out**) (used about a player in a game or sport) not allowed to continue playing ▶ **wypadać z gry 8** (used about a ball, etc. in a game or sport) not inside the playing area and therefore not allowed: *She hit the ball too hard and it went out.* ▶ **aut 9** not in fashion: *That style went out* (wyszedł z mody) *years ago!* ▶ **niemodny 10** (used about a light or a fire) not on; not burning: *Don't let the fire go out* (żeby ogień zgasł).

■ **out** adj. **1** away from the inside of a place: *You should be out in the fresh air.* ▶ **na dworze**; **na zewnątrz 2** not at home or in your place of work: *My manager was out when she called.* ▶ **poza domem/pracą 3** (used about the sea) when the water is furthest away from the land: *The tide is out.* Jest odpływ. **4** (**be out**) (used for showing that sth is no longer hidden): *Oh look! The sun's out!* ◇ *I love the spring when all the flowers are out.* ◇ *The secret's out now. There's no point pretending any more.* ▶ **ukazywać się**, **wychodzić na jaw**, (*kwiat*) **rozkwitać 5** made available to the public; published: *Is it out on DVD yet?* Czy to wyszło już na DVD? ▶ **wydany 6** (**be out**) (used about a player in a game or sport) to not be allowed to continue playing: *If you get three answers wrong, you're out.* ▶ **wypadać z gry 7** (used about a ball, etc. in a game or sport) not inside the playing area and therefore not allowed: *Although the player argued with the umpire, the ball was clearly out.* ▶ **aut 8** (**be out**) (used when you are calculating sth) to make or contain a mistake; to be wrong: *My guess was only out by a few centimetres.* ▶ (*rachunek*) **zawierać błąd**; **mylić się** (*w rachunkach*) **9** (**be out**) (informal) to not be possible or acceptable: *I'm afraid Friday is out. I've got a meeting that day.* ▶ **nie wchodzić w rachubę 10** not in fashion: *Short skirts are out* (całkiem wyszły z mody) *this season.* ▶ **niemodny 11** (used about a light or a fire) not on; not burning: *The lights are out. They must be in bed.* ▶ **zgaszony 12** (informal) having told other people that you are **homosexual**: *I've been out since I was 17.* ◇ *an out gay man* ▶ **otwarcie przyznający się do homoseksualizmu** ➲ look at **come out**

IDM **be out for sth**; **be out to do sth** to try hard to get or do sth: *I'm not out for revenge.* ▶ **być w pogoni** (*np. za sukcesem*)

down and out → DOWN[1]

out-and-out complete: *It was out-and-out war between us.* ▶ **totalny**

out loud = ALOUD

out² /aʊt/ verb [T] to say publicly that sb is **homosexual**, especially when they would rather keep it a secret: *The politician was eventually outed by a tabloid newspaper.* ▶ **ujawniać, że ktoś jest homoseksualistą**

the **outback** /ˈaʊtbæk/ noun [sing.] the part of a country (especially Australia) which is a long way from the coast and towns, where few people live: *in the Australian outback* w głębi Australii ▶ **odludzie**

outboard motor /ˌaʊtbɔːd ˈməʊtə(r)/ noun [C] an engine that can be fixed to a boat ▶ **silnik zewnętrzny/(znajdujący się) za burtą**

outbreak /ˈaʊtbreɪk/ noun [C] the sudden start of sth unpleasant (especially a disease or violence): *an outbreak of cholera/fighting* ▶ **wybuch**

outburst /ˈaʊtbɜːst/ noun [C] a sudden expression of a strong feeling, especially anger: *Afterwards, she apologized for her outburst.* ▶ **wybuch**

outcast /ˈaʊtkɑːst; US -kæst/ noun [C] a person who is no longer accepted by society or by a group of people: *a social outcast* ▶ **wyrzutek**

outclass /ˌaʊtˈklɑːs; US -ˈklæs/ verb [T, often passive] to be much better than sb/sth, especially in a game or competition ▶ **przewyższać o klasę, być (o wiele) lepszym**

outcome /ˈaʊtkʌm/ noun [C] the result or effect of an action or an event ▶ **rezultat**, **wynik**

outcrop /ˈaʊtkrɒp/ noun [C] a large mass of rock that stands above the surface of the ground ▶ (*geol.*) **wychodnia**

outcry /ˈaʊtkraɪ/ noun [C, usually sing.] (pl. **outcries**) a strong protest by a large number of people because they disagree with sth: *The public outcry forced the government to change its mind about the new tax.* ▶ **głośny sprzeciw**, **krzyk** (*np. oburzenia*)

outdated /ˌaʊtˈdeɪtɪd/ adj. not useful or common any more; old-fashioned: *A lot of the computer equipment is getting outdated.* ▶ **przestarzały**

outdo /ˌaʊtˈduː/ verb [T] (**outdoing**; **outdoes** /-ˈdʌz/, pt **outdid** /-ˈdɪd/, pp **outdone** /-ˈdʌn/) to do sth better than another person; to be more successful than sb else: ***Not to be outdone*** (aby nie dać się prześcignąć), *she tried again.* ▶ **prześcigać/przewyższać kogoś**

⚷ **outdoor** /ˈaʊtdɔː(r)/ adj. [only before a noun] happening, done, or used outside, not in a building: *an outdoor swimming pool* ◇ *outdoor clothing/activities* ◇ *outdoor furniture* meble ogrodowe ▶ **na dworze, na świeżym powietrzu** OPP **indoor**

⚷ **outdoors** /ˌaʊtˈdɔːz/ adv. outside a building: *It's a very warm evening so why don't we eat outdoors?* ▶ **na dworze**, **na zewnątrz** SYN **out of doors** OPP **indoors** ➲ look at **outside**

⚷ **outer** /ˈaʊtə(r)/ adj. [only before a noun] **1** on the outside of sth: *the outer layer of skin on an onion* ▶ **zewnętrzny 2** far from the inside or the centre of sth: *the outer suburbs of a city* ▶ **peryferyjny** OPP for both meanings **inner**

outermost /ˈaʊtəməʊst/ adj. [only before a noun] furthest from the inside or centre ▶ **najdalszy (od centrum)** OPP **innermost**

ˌouter ˈspace = SPACE¹ (2)

outfit /ˈaʊtfɪt/ noun [C] **1** a set of clothes that are worn together for a particular occasion or purpose: *I'm going to buy a whole new outfit for the party.* ▶ **kostium**, **ubranie 2** (informal) an organization, a company, etc. ▶ **organizacja**, **firma**

outgoing /ˈaʊtɡəʊɪŋ/ adj. **1** friendly and interested in other people and new experiences ▶ **towarzyski**, **bezpośredni** SYN **sociable 2** [only before a noun] leaving a job or a place: *the outgoing president/government* ◇ *Put all the outgoing mail* (pocztę do wysłania) *in a pile on that table.* ▶ **ustępujący** OPP **incoming**

outgoings /ˈaʊtɡəʊɪŋz/ noun [pl.] (Brit.) an amount of money that you spend regularly, for example every week or month ▶ **rozchód** OPP **income**

outgrow /ˌaʊtˈɡrəʊ/ verb [T] (pt **outgrew** /-ˈɡruː/, pp **outgrown** /-ˈɡrəʊn/) to become too old or too big for sth ▶ **wyrastać (z czegoś)**

outing /ˈaʊtɪŋ/ noun [C] a short trip for pleasure: ***to go on an outing*** *to the zoo* ▶ **wycieczka**

outlandish /aʊtˈlændɪʃ/ adj. very strange or unusual: *outlandish clothes* ▶ **dziwaczny**

outlast /ˌaʊtˈlɑːst; US -ˈlæst/ verb [T] to continue to exist or to do sth for a longer time than sb/sth ▶ **przeżyć**, **przetrwać**

outlaw[1] /ˈaʊtlɔː/ verb [T] to make sth illegal ▶ **zakazywać**

outlaw[2] /ˈaʊtlɔː/ noun [C] (used in past times) a person who has done sth illegal and is hiding to avoid being caught ▶ **osoba wyjęta spod prawa**, **banita**

outlay /ˈaʊtleɪ/ noun [C, usually sing.] **outlay (on sth)** money that is spent, especially in order to start a business or project ▶ **nakład** (*pieniędzy*), **wydatek**

outlet /ˈaʊtlet/ noun [C] **1 an outlet (for sth)** a way of expressing and making good use of strong feelings, ideas or energy: *Gary found an outlet for his aggression in boxing.* ▶ **ujście (dla czegoś) 2** a shop, business, etc. that sells goods made by a particular company or of a particular type: *fast food/retail outlets* ▶ **punkt** (*sprzedaży detalicznej*) **3** a pipe through which a gas or liquid can escape ▶ **wylot**, **odpływ**, **ujście** OPP **inlet**

outline[1] /ˈaʊtlaɪn/ verb [T] **outline sth (to sb)** to tell sb or give the most important facts or ideas about sth ▶ **nakreślać w ogólnym zarysie**

outline[2] /ˈaʊtlaɪn/ noun [C] **1** a description of the most important facts or ideas about sth: *a brief outline of Indian history* ▶ **zarys 2** a line that shows the shape or outside edge of sb/sth: *She could see the outline of a person through the mist.* ▶ **zarys**, **kontur**

outlive /ˌaʊtˈlɪv/ verb [T] to live or exist longer than sb/sth ▶ **przeżyć**

outlook /ˈaʊtlʊk/ noun [C] **1 an outlook (on sth)** your attitude to or feeling about life and the world: *an optimistic outlook on life* ▶ **pogląd na świat 2 outlook (for sth)** what will probably happen: *The outlook for the economy is not good.* Nie ma dobrych perspektyw dla ekonomii. ▶ **perspektywy**

outlying /ˈaʊtlaɪɪŋ/ adj. [only before a noun] far from the centre of a town or city: *The bus service to the outlying villages is very poor.* ▶ **oddalony**, **odosobniony**

outmoded /ˌaʊtˈməʊdɪd/ adj. [only before a noun] no longer common or fashionable ▶ **niemodny**

outnumber /ˌaʊtˈnʌmbə(r)/ verb [T, often passive] to be greater in number than an enemy, another team, etc.: *The enemy troops outnumbered us by three to one.* ▶ **przewyższać liczebnie**

ˈout of prep. **1** (used with verbs expressing movement) away from the inside of sth: *She took her purse out of her bag.* ◇ *to get out of bed* wstawać z łóżka ▶ **z** OPP **into 2** away from or no longer in a place or situation: *He's out of the country on business.* ◇ *The doctors say she's* ***out of danger*** (najgorsze już ma za sobą). ▶ **poza 3** at a distance from a place: *We live a long way out of London.* ▶ **od 4** (used for saying which feeling causes you to do sth): *We were only asking out of curiosity.* ▶ **z 5** (used for saying what you use to make sth else): *What is this knife* ***made out of****?* ◇ *to be made out of wood/metal/plastic/gold* ▶ **z 6** from among a number or set: *Nine out of ten people prefer this model.* ▶ **z/spośród 7** from; having sth as its source: *I copied the recipe out of a book.* ◇ *I paid for it out of the money I won on the lottery.* ▶ **z 8** (used for saying that you no longer have sth): *We're out of milk* (mleko się skończyło). ◇ *He's been* ***out of work*** *for months.* Od miesięcy jest bez pracy. ◇ *I'm out of breath.* Mam zadyszkę. ▶ **bez 9** (used for saying that sth is not as it should be): *The photocopier's* ***out of action*** (nie działa) *today.* ◇ *My notes are all* ***out of order*** (nie po kolei) *and I can't find the right page.*
IDM **be/feel out of it** to be/feel lonely and unhappy because you are not included in sth: *I don't speak French so I felt rather out of it at the meeting.* ▶ **być/czuć się poza nawiasem**

ˌout-of-ˈwork adj. [only before a noun] unable to find a job; unemployed: *an out-of-work actor* ▶ **bezrobotny**

outpatient /ˈaʊtpeɪʃnt/ noun [C] a person who goes to a hospital for treatment but who does not stay there during the night ▶ **pacjent/ka ambulatoryjn-y/a**

outpost /ˈaʊtpəʊst/ noun [C] a small town or camp that is away from other places: *a remote outpost* ◇ *the last outpost* (bastion) *of civilization* ▶ **placówka**

output /ˈaʊtpʊt/ noun [U,C] **1** the amount that a person or machine produces: *Output has increased in the past year.* ▶ **produkcja**, **wytwórczość 2** the information that a computer produces: *data output* ▶ **dane z komputera** ➲ look at **input**

outrage /ˈaʊtreɪdʒ/ noun **1** [U] great anger: *a feeling of outrage* ▶ **oburzenie**, **zniewaga 2** [C] something that is very bad or wrong and that causes you to feel great anger: *It's an outrage that such poverty should exist in the 21st century.* ▶ **rzecz oburzająca**, **zniewaga**
■ **outrage** verb [T] ▶ **oburzać**

outrageous /aʊtˈreɪdʒəs/ adj. that makes you very angry or shocked: *outrageous behaviour/prices* ▶ **oburzający**; **skandaliczny**
■ **outrageously** adv. ▶ **oburzająco**; **skandalicznie**

outright /ˈaʊtraɪt/ adv. **1** open and direct; in an open and direct way: *She told them outright what she thought about it.* ▶ **szczerze**, **otwarcie 2** complete and clear; completely and clearly: *to win outright* ▶ **całkowicie 3** not gradually; immediately: *to be killed outright* ◇ *They were able to buy the house outright.* ▶ **na miejscu**, **od razu**
■ **outright** adj. [only before a noun] complete and clear, without any doubt: *an outright victory* ▶ **całkowity**, **niekwestionowany**

outset /ˈaʊtset/ noun
IDM **at/from the outset (of sth)** at/from the beginning (of sth) ▶ **od (samego) początku**; **na (samym) początku**

outside[1] /ˌaʊtˈsaɪd/ noun **1** [C, usually sing.] the outer side or surface of sth: *There is a list of all the ingredients on the outside of the packet.* ▶ **zewnętrzna strona 2** [sing.] the area that is near or round a building, etc.: *We've only seen the church from the outside.* ▶ (*na/z*) **zewnątrz 3** [sing.] the part of a road, a track, etc. that is away from the side that you usually drive on, run on, etc.: *The other runners all overtook him on the outside.* ▶ **zewnętrzny pas/tor** OPP for all meanings **inside**
IDM **at the outside** at the most: *It will take us 3 days at the outside.* ▶ **maksymalnie**

outside[2] /ˈaʊtsaɪd/ adj. [only before a noun] **1** of or on the outer side or surface of sth: *the outside walls of a building* ▶ **zewnętrzny** SYN **external 2** not part of the main building: *an outside toilet* ▶ **zewnętrzny** SYN **external 3** not connected with or belonging to a particular group or organization: *We can't do all the work by ourselves. We'll need outside help.* ▶ **zewnętrzny 4** (used about a chance or possibility) very small: *an* ***outside chance*** *of winning* ▶ **znikomy**
IDM **the outside world** people, places, activities, etc. that are away from the area where you live and your own experience of life ▶ **świat zewnętrzny**

outside[3] /ˌaʊtˈsaɪd/ prep. **1** in, at or to a place that is not in a room or not in a building: *Leave your muddy boots outside the door.* ▶ **na zewnątrz**, **przed**, **poza 2** (US also **outside of**) not in: *You may do as you wish outside office hours.* ◇ *a small village just outside Stratford* ▶ **poza**, **pod**
■ **outside** adv. **1** in or to a place that is not in a room: *Please wait outside for a few minutes.* ▶ **na zewnątrz 2** in or to a place that is not in a building: *Let's eat outside.* ◇ *Go outside and see if it's raining.* ▶ **na zewnątrz**, **na dworze/dwór** ➲ look at **outdoors**, **out of doors**

O

ˌ**outside ˈlane** noun [C] the part of a wide road or motorway that is for the fastest cars ▶ **lewy (szybki) pas ruchu**

W Wlk. Br., gdzie jeździ się lewą stroną, **outside lane** to prawy pas.

outsider /ˌaʊtˈsaɪdə(r)/ noun [C] **1** a person who is not accepted as a member of a particular group ▶ **osoba z zewnątrz, obcy 2** a person or an animal in a race or competition that is not expected to win ▶ **zawodnik/koń nie mający szans zwycięstwa** OPP **favourite**

outsize /ˈaʊtsaɪz/ adj. (often used about clothes) larger than usual ▶ **ponadwymiarowy**

outskirts /ˈaʊtskɜːts/ noun [pl.] the parts of a town or city that are furthest from the centre: *They live **on the outskirts** of Athens.* ▶ **peryferie** (*miasta*)

outspoken /aʊtˈspəʊkən/ adj. saying exactly what you think or feel although you may shock or upset other people: *Linda is very outspoken in her criticism.* ▶ **mówiący bez ogródek**

■ **outspokenness** noun ▶ **otwartość, szczerość**

⚷ **outstanding** /aʊtˈstændɪŋ/ adj. **1** extremely good; excellent: *The results in the exams were outstanding.* ▶ **doskonały, znakomity 2** not yet paid, done or dealt with: *A large amount of the work is still outstanding.* ◇ *outstanding debts/issues* ▶ **(o zapłacie itp.) zaległy**

outstandingly /aʊtˈstændɪŋli/ adv. very well; extremely: *outstandingly good/successful* ▶ **doskonale, znakomicie**

outstretched /ˌaʊtˈstretʃt/ adj. reaching as far as possible: *He came towards her with his arms outstretched.* ▶ **rozpostarty, wyciągnięty**

outward /ˈaʊtwəd/ adj. [only before a noun] **1** connected with the way things seem to be rather than what is actually true: *Despite her cheerful outward appearance, she was in fact very unhappy.* ▶ **widoczny, zewnętrzny 2** (used about a journey) going away from the place that you will return to later ▶ **odjeżdżający** OPP **return 3** away from the centre or from a particular point: *outward movement/pressure* ▶ **odśrodkowy** OPP **inward**

■ **outwardly** adv.: *He remained outwardly calm so as not to frighten the children.* ▶ **widocznie, zewnętrznie**

outwards /ˈaʊtwədz/ (especially US **outward**) adv. towards the outside or away from the place where you are: *This door opens outwards.* ▶ **na zewnątrz**

outweigh /ˌaʊtˈweɪ/ verb [T] to be more in amount or importance than sth: *The advantages outweigh the disadvantages.* ▶ **przeważać, mieć większe znaczenie**

outwit /ˌaʊtˈwɪt/ verb [T] (**outwitting**; **outwitted**) to gain an advantage over sb by doing sth clever ▶ **przechytrzyć, wywodzić kogoś w pole**

oval /ˈəʊvl/ adj., noun [C] shaped like an egg; a shape like that of an egg ▶ **owalny**; **owal**

ovary /ˈəʊvəri/ noun [C] (pl. **ovaries**) one of the two parts of the female body that produce eggs ▶ **jajnik**

ovation /əʊˈveɪʃn/ noun [C] an enthusiastic reaction given by an audience when they like sb/sth very much: *The dancers got **a standing ovation** at the end of the performance.* ▶ **owacja**

⚷ **oven** /ˈʌvn/ noun [C] the part of a cooker shaped like a box with a door on the front. You put food in the oven to cook or heat it: *Cook in a hot oven for 50 minutes.* ◇ *a microwave oven* kuchenka mikrofalowa ▶ **piekarnik, kuchenka** ➲ note at **cook**

⚷ **over** /ˈəʊvə(r)/ adv., prep. ℹ **Over** używa się w czasownikach złożonych, np. **get over sth**. Zob. hasła odpowiednich czasowników. **1** covering sth: *He hung his coat over the back of the chair.* ◇ *She put her hand over her mouth to stop herself from screaming.* ▶ **na 2** straight above sth, but not touching it: *There's a painting over the bookcase.* ◇ *We watched the plane fly over.* ▶ **nad**; **ponad** ➲ look at **above 3** across to the other side of sth: *The horse jumped over the fence.* ◇ *a bridge over the river* ▶ **przez, w poprzek** ➲ note at **across 4** on or to the other side: *She lives over the road.* ◇ *The student turned the paper over* (odwrócił kartkę) *and read the first question.* ▶ **po drugiej stronie 5** down or sideways from a vertical position: *He leaned over* (wychylił się) *to speak to the woman next to him.* ◇ *I fell over* (przewróciłem się) *in the street this morning.* **6** above or more than a number, price, etc.: *She lived in Athens for over ten years.* ◇ *suitable for children aged 10 and over* ▶ **ponad, więcej 7** (used for expressing distance): *He's over in America at the moment.* ◇ *Sit down **over there*** (tam). ◇ *Come **over here*** (podejdź tu), *please.* ◇ *The book is **over here*** (tu). ▶ **tam 8** not used: *There are a lot of cakes **left over*** (zostało dużo ciastek) *from the party.* **9** [used with *all*] everywhere: *There was blood **all over the place.*** ◇ *I can't find my glasses. I've looked all over for them.* ▶ **wszędzie 10** (used for saying that sth is repeated): *You'll have to start **all over again*** (znowu od początku). ◇ *She kept saying the same thing **over and over again.*** Ciągle powtarzała to samo. **11** about; on the subject of: *We quarrelled over money.* ▶ **o, na temat 12** during: *We met several times over the Christmas holiday.* ▶ **podczas, przez**

■ **over** adj. finished: *The exams are all over now.* ▶ **skończony**

over- /ˈəʊvə(r)/ [in compounds] **1** more than usual; too much: *oversleep* zaspać ◇ *over-optimistic* ◇ *overact* ◇ *overeat* przejadać się ◇ *I'm overworked* (przepracowany). ▶ **prze-, nadmiernie 2** completely: *overjoyed* niezmiernie uradowany ▶ **całkowicie 3** upper; outer: *overcoat* płaszcz ▶ **zewnętrzny 4** extra: *overtime* nadgodziny ▶ **dodatkowy 5** over; above: *His fat belly overhung his belt.* Miał obwisły brzuch. ◇ *a path with overhanging trees* ścieżka wysadzana nisko zwieszającymi się drzewami ▶ **powyżej**

overall

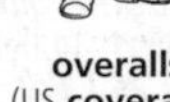

aprons **overalls** (US **coveralls**) **dungarees** (US **overalls**)

⚷ **overall¹** /ˌəʊvərˈɔːl/ adv. **1** including everything: *What does the garden measure overall?* ▶ **w całości 2** generally; when you consider everything: *Overall, I can say that we are pleased with the year's work.* ▶ **ogólnie mówiąc**

■ **overall** adj. [only before a noun] including everything; total: *What will the overall cost of the work be?* ▶ **całkowity**

overall² /ˈəʊvərɔːl/ noun **1** [C] a piece of clothing like a coat that you wear over your clothes to keep them clean when you are working ▶ **kitel, fartuch** (*z rękawami*) **2** (**overalls**) (US **coveralls** /ˈkʌvərɔːlz/) [pl.] a piece of clothing that covers your legs and body (and sometimes your arms) that you wear over your clothes to keep them clean when you are working ▶ **kombinezon 3** (**overalls**) (US) = DUNGAREES

overawe /ˌəʊvər'ɔː/ verb [T, usually passive] to impress sb so much that they feel nervous or frightened ▶ **onieśmielać, peszyć**

overbalance /ˌəʊvə'bæləns/ verb [I] to lose your balance and fall ▶ **przeważać, tracić równowagę**

overbearing /ˌəʊvə'beərɪŋ/ adj. trying to control other people in an unpleasant way: *an overbearing manner* ▶ **władczy, apodyktyczny** SYN **domineering**

overboard /'əʊvəbɔːd/ adv. over the side of a boat or ship into the water ▶ **za burt-ą/ę**
IDM **go overboard (on/about/for sb/sth)** to be too excited or enthusiastic about sb/sth ▶ **zbytnio się podniecać**

overcame past tense of **overcome**

overcast /ˌəʊvə'kɑːst; US -'kæst/ adj. (used about the sky) covered with cloud ▶ **zachmurzony**

overcharge /ˌəʊvə'tʃɑːdʒ/ verb [I,T] to ask sb to pay too much money for sth: *The taxi driver overcharged me.* ▶ **doliczać pewną sumę do ceny artykułu, oszukiwać na cenie** ➲ look at **charge**

overcoat /'əʊvəkəʊt/ noun [C] a long thick coat that you wear in cold weather ▶ **palto**

⚷ **overcome** /ˌəʊvə'kʌm/ verb [T] (pt **overcame** /-'keɪm/, pp **overcome**) **1** to manage to control or defeat sb/sth: *She tried hard to overcome her fear of flying.* ▶ **przezwyciężać; pokonywać 2** [usually passive] to be extremely strongly affected by sth: *He was overcome with emotion* (wzruszył się) *and had to leave the room.* ◇ *to be overcome by smoke* dusić się od dymu ▶ (*zwł. coś negatywnego*) **ogarniać, przytłaczać**

overcrowded /ˌəʊvə'kraʊdɪd/ adj. (used about a place) with too many people inside: *The trains are overcrowded on Friday evenings.* ▶ **zatłoczony, przepełniony**

overdo /ˌəʊvə'duː/ verb [T] (**overdoing**; **overdoes** /-'dʌz/, pt **overdid** /-'dɪd/, pp **overdone** /-'dʌn/) **1** to use or do too much of sth: *If you overdo the praise, it won't seem sincere.* ◇ *He overdid the pepper in the stew.* ▶ **przesadzać (z czymś) 2** to cook sth too long: *The meat was overdone.* ▶ **przegotowywać**
IDM **overdo it/things** to work, etc. too hard: *Exercise is fine but don't overdo it.* ▶ **przesadzać** (*np. z pracą*)

overdose /'əʊvədəʊs/ noun [C] an amount of a drug or medicine that is too large and so is not safe: *to take an overdose* przedawkować ▶ **za duża dawka** ➲ look at **dose**

overdraft /'əʊvədrɑːft; US -dræft/ noun [C] an amount of money that you have spent that is greater than the amount you have in your bank account; an arrangement that allows you to do this ▶ **przekraczanie stanu konta bankowego, debet**

overdrawn /ˌəʊvə'drɔːn/ adj. having spent more money than you have in your bank account: *I checked my balance and discovered I was overdrawn.* ▶ **mający przekroczone konto bankowe, z debetem na koncie**

overdue /ˌəʊvə'djuː; US -'duː/ adj. late in arriving, happening, being paid, returned, etc.: *an overdue library book* ◇ *Her baby is a week overdue.* Dziecko miało się urodzić tydzień temu. ◇ *Change is long overdue* (jest od dawna potrzebna). ▶ **spóźniony**

overestimate /ˌəʊvər'estɪmeɪt/ verb [T] to guess that sb/sth is bigger, better, more important, etc. than he/she/it really is: *I overestimated how much we could manage to do in a weekend.* ▶ **przeceniać** OPP **underestimate**

overflow /ˌəʊvə'fləʊ/ verb **1** [I,T] **overflow (with sth)** to be so full that there is no more space: *The tap was left on and the bath overflowed.* ◇ *The roads are overflowing with cars.* ◇ *After the heavy rains the river overflowed its banks* (wystąpiła z brzegów). ▶ **przelewać się 2** [I] **overflow (into sth)** to be forced out of a place or a container that is too full: *The crowd overflowed into the street.* ▶ **wylewać się**

overgrown /ˌəʊvə'grəʊn/ adj. covered with plants that have grown too big and untidy ▶ (*trawnik itp.*) **zarośnięty**

overhang /ˌəʊvə'hæŋ/ verb [I,T] (pt, pp **overhung**) to stick out above sth else: *The overhanging trees kept the sun off us.* ▶ **zwisać; sterczeć**

overhaul /ˌəʊvə'hɔːl/ verb [T] to look at sth carefully and change or repair it if necessary: *to overhaul an engine* ▶ **gruntownie zbadać, przeprowadzać kapitalny remont**
■ **overhaul** /'əʊvəhɔːl/ noun [C] ▶ **gruntowna reforma, kapitalny remont**

overhead /'əʊvəhed/ adj. above your head: *overhead electricity cables* ▶ **napowietrzny, w górze**
■ **overhead** /ˌəʊvə'hed/ adv.: *A helicopter flew overhead.* ▶ **na górze**

ˌ**overhead pro'jector** noun [C] (abbr. **OHP**) a device that projects images onto a wall or screen above and behind the person who is using it ▶ **rzutnik**

overheads /'əʊvəhedz/ noun [pl.] money that a company must spend on things like heat, light, rent, etc. ▶ **koszty stałe**

overhear /ˌəʊvə'hɪə(r)/ verb [T] (pt, pp **overheard** /-'hɜːd/) to hear what sb is saying by accident, when they are speaking to sb else and not to you ▶ **przypadkowo usłyszeć**

overhung past tense, past participle of **overhang**

overjoyed /ˌəʊvə'dʒɔɪd/ adj. [not before a noun] **overjoyed (at sth/to do sth)** very happy ▶ **rozradowany**

overland /'əʊvəlænd/ adj. not by sea or by air: *an overland journey* ▶ **lądowy**
■ **overland** adv. ▶ **lądem**

overlap /ˌəʊvə'læp/ verb [I,T] (**overlapping**; **overlapped**) **1** when two things **overlap**, part of one covers part of the other: *Make sure that the two pieces of material overlap.* ▶ **zachodzić (za/na coś), pokrywać się (częściowo) 2** to be partly the same as sth: *Our jobs overlap to some extent.* ▶ **pokrywać się (częściowo)**
■ **overlap** /'əʊvəlæp/ noun [C,U] ▶ **zachodzenie (jednej rzeczy/czynności na drugą), pokrywanie się (częściowe)**

overleaf /ˌəʊvə'liːf/ adv. on the other side of the page: *Full details are given overleaf.* ▶ **na odwrocie (strony)**

overload /ˌəʊvə'ləʊd/ verb [T] **1** [often passive] to put too many people or things into or onto sth: *an overloaded vehicle* ▶ **przeładowywać 2 overload sb (with sth)** to give sb too much of sth: *to be overloaded with work/information* ▶ (*przen.*) **przeciążać 3** to put too much electricity through sth: *If you use too many electrical appliances at one time you may overload the system.* ▶ **przeciążać** (*linię elektryczną*)

overlook /ˌəʊvə'lʊk/ verb [T] **1** to fail to see or notice sth: *to overlook a spelling mistake* ◇ *She felt that her opinion had been completely overlooked* (jej zdanie nie zostało zupełnie wzięte pod uwagę). ▶ **przeoczyć, nie zauważać 2** to see sth wrong but decide to forget it: *I will overlook your behaviour this time but don't let it happen again.* ▶ **nie zwracać uwagi, patrzeć przez palce 3** to have a view over sth: *My room overlooks the sea.* ▶ (*okno itp.*) **wychodzić na coś**

overnight /ˌəʊvə'naɪt/ adj. [only before a noun] **1** for one night: *an overnight bag* torba podręczna z przyborami kosmetycznymi, piżamą itp., zabierana na nocleg poza domem ▶ **nocny 2** happening very suddenly: *The play was an overnight success.* ▶ **nagły**
■ **overnight** adv. **1** for one night: *We stayed overnight in Hamburg.* ▶ **w ciągu nocy, przez noc, na noc 2** very

suddenly: *She became a star overnight.* ▶ **z dnia na dzień, nagle**

overpass (US) = FLYOVER

overpay /ˌəʊvəˈpeɪ/ verb [T] (pt, pp **overpaid**) [usually passive] to pay sb too much; to pay sb more than their job is worth ▶ **przepłacać** OPP **underpay**

overpower /ˌəʊvəˈpaʊə(r)/ verb [T] to be too strong for sb: *The fireman was overpowered by the heat and smoke.* ▶ **opanowywać, pokonywać**
■ **overpowering** adj.: *an overpowering smell* ▶ **przemożny, obezwładniający, przytłaczający**

overpriced adj. too expensive; costing more than it is worth ▶ **za drogi**

overran past tense of **overrun**

overrate /ˌəʊvəˈreɪt/ verb [T, often passive] to think that sth/sb is better than he/she/it really is ▶ **przeceniać** OPP **underrate**

overreact /ˌəʊvəriˈækt/ verb [I] **overreact (to sth)** to react too strongly, especially to sth unpleasant ▶ **reagować za mocno/emocjonalnie (na coś)**
■ **overreaction** noun [sing., U] ▶ **za mocna reakcja**

override /ˌəʊvəˈraɪd/ verb [T] (pt **overrode** /-ˈrəʊd/, pp **overridden** /-ˈrɪdn/) **1** to use your authority to reject sb's decision, order, etc.: *They overrode my protest and continued with the meeting.* ▶ **lekceważyć, nie zważać** (*np. na protest*) **2** to be more important than sth ▶ **mieć pierwszeństwo**

overriding /ˌəʊvəˈraɪdɪŋ/ adj. [only before a noun] more important than anything else: *Our overriding concern is safety.* ▶ **nadrzędny**

overrode past tense of **override**

overrule /ˌəʊvəˈruːl/ verb [T] to use your authority to change what sb else has already decided or done: *The Appeal Court overruled the judge's decision.* ▶ **uchylać, odrzucać** (*np. wniosek*)

overrun /ˌəʊvəˈrʌn/ verb (pt **overran** /-ˈræn/, pp **overrun**) **1** [T, often passive] to spread all over an area in great numbers: *The city was overrun by rats* (zaroiło się od szczurów). ▶ **opanowywać, pokrywać 2** [I,T] to use more time or money than expected: *The meeting overran by 30 minutes.* ▶ **przekraczać (wyznaczony czas)**

oversaw past tense of **oversee**

overseas /ˌəʊvəˈsiːz/ adj. [only before a noun] in, to or from another country that you have to cross the sea to get to: *overseas students studying in Britain* ▶ **zagraniczny, zamorski**
■ **overseas** adv.: *Frank has gone to live overseas.* ◇ *People overseas will be able to vote in the election.* ▶ **za granic-ę/ą**

oversee /ˌəʊvəˈsiː/ verb [T] (pt **oversaw** /-ˈsɔː/, pp **overseen** /-ˈsiːn/) to watch sth to make sure that it is done properly ▶ **nadzorować**

overshadow /ˌəʊvəˈʃædəʊ/ verb [T] **1** to cause sb/sth to seem less important or successful: *Connor always seemed to be overshadowed by his sister.* ▶ **zaćmiewać, usuwać kogoś w cień 2** to cause sth to be less enjoyable ▶ **przyćmiewać**

oversight /ˈəʊvəsaɪt/ noun [C,U] something that you do not notice or do (that you should have noticed or done) ▶ **przeoczenie**

oversimplify /ˌəʊvəˈsɪmplɪfaɪ/ verb [I,T] (**oversimplifying**; **oversimplifies**; pt, pp **oversimplified**) to explain sth in such a simple way that its real meaning is lost ▶ **nadmiernie upraszczać, spłycać** (*np. zagadnienie*)

oversleep /ˌəʊvəˈsliːp/ verb [I] (pt, pp **overslept** /-ˈslept/) to sleep longer than you should have done: *I overslept and was late for school.* ▶ **zaspać, przespać** (*właściwy moment*) ➲ look at **lie in**, **sleep in**

overstate /ˌəʊvəˈsteɪt/ verb [T] to say sth in a way that makes it seem more important than it really is ▶ **wyolbrzymiać** OPP **understate**

overstep /ˌəʊvəˈstep/ verb [T] (**overstepping**; **overstepped**) to go further than what is normal or allowed: *to overstep your authority* ◇ *He tends to **overstep the boundaries** of good taste.* ▶ **przekraczać** (*np. uprawnienia, granice*)
IDM **overstep the mark/line** to behave in a way that people think is not acceptable ▶ **posuwać się za daleko**

overt /əʊˈvɜːt; ˈəʊvɜːt/ adj. (formal) done in an open way and not secretly: *There was little overt support for the project.* ▶ **otwarty, jawny** OPP **covert**
■ **overtly** adv.: *overtly political activities* ▶ **otwarcie, jawnie**

overtake /ˌəʊvəˈteɪk/ verb [I,T] (pt **overtook** /-ˈtʊk/, pp **overtaken** /-ˈteɪkən/) to go past another person, car, etc. because you are moving faster: *The lorry overtook me on the bend.* ▶ **wyprzedzać**

overthrow /ˌəʊvəˈθrəʊ/ verb [T] (pt **overthrew** /-ˈθruː/, pp **overthrown** /-ˈθrəʊn/) to remove a leader or government from power, by using force ▶ **obalać**
■ **overthrow** /ˈəʊvəθrəʊ/ noun [sing.] ▶ **obalenie**

overtime /ˈəʊvətaɪm/ noun [U] time that you spend at work after your usual working hours; the money that you are paid for this: *Betty did ten hours' overtime last week.* ▶ **nadgodziny; godziny nadliczbowe**
■ **overtime** adv.: *I have been working overtime for weeks.* ▶ **w godzinach nadliczbowych, nadprogramowo**

overtone /ˈəʊvətəʊn/ noun [C, usually pl.] something that is suggested but not expressed in an obvious way: *Some people claimed there were racist overtones in the advertisement.* ▶ **podtekst**

overtook past tense of **overtake**

overture /ˈəʊvətʃʊə(r); Brit. also -tjʊə(r); US also -tʃər/ noun **1** [C] a piece of music that is the introduction to a musical play such as an **opera** or a **ballet** ▶ **uwertura 2** [C, usually pl.] (formal) an act of being friendly towards sb, especially because you want to be friends, to start a business relationship, etc.: *It's time to **make** some peace **overtures to*** (podjąć pokojowe kroki w stosunku do szefa) *the boss.* ▶ **zabieganie o czyjeś względy**

overturn /ˌəʊvəˈtɜːn/ verb **1** [I,T] to turn over so that the top is at the bottom: *The car overturned but the driver escaped unhurt.* **2** [T] to officially decide that a decision is wrong and change it ▶ **przewracać (się)** (*do góry nogami*), **obalać** (*decyzję*)

overview /ˈəʊvəvjuː/ noun [C] a general description that gives the most important facts about sth ▶ **przegląd, zarys**

overweight /ˌəʊvəˈweɪt/ adj. too heavy or fat: *I'm a bit overweight – I think I might go on a diet.* ▶ **z nadwagą** OPP **underweight** ➲ note at **fat**

overwhelm /ˌəʊvəˈwelm/ verb [T, usually passive] **1** to cause sb to feel such a strong emotion that they do not know how to react: *The new world champion was overwhelmed by all the publicity.* ▶ **przytłaczać, druzgotać** (*np. wiadomością*) **2** to be so powerful, big, etc., that sb cannot deal with it: *He overwhelmed his opponent with his superb technique.* ◇ *The TV company were overwhelmed by complaints.* ◇ *The army was overwhelmed by the rebels.* ▶ **zasypywać, obezwładniać**

overwhelming /ˌəʊvəˈwelmɪŋ/ adj. extremely great or strong: *Anne-Marie had an overwhelming desire to return home.* ▶ **nieprzeparty, przytłaczający**
■ **overwhelmingly** adv. ▶ **przytłaczająco**

overwork /ˌəʊvəˈwɜːk/ verb [T] to make sb work too hard: *They are overworked* (przepracowani) *and underpaid.* ▶ **przeładowywać**
■ **overwork** noun [U] ▶ **przepracowanie**

ovulate /ˈɒvjuleɪt/ verb [I] (of a woman or female animal) to produce an egg from the **ovary** ▶ **jajeczkować**
■ **ovulation** /ˌɒvjuˈleɪʃn/ noun [U]: *methods of predicting ovulation* ▶ **jajeczkowanie**

ow = OUCH

owe /əʊ/ verb [T] **1 owe sth (to sb)**; **owe sb for sth** to have to pay money to sb for sth that they have done or given: *I owe Katrina a lot of money.* ◇ *I owe a lot of money to Katrina.* ◇ *I still owe you for that bread you bought yesterday.* ▶ **być winnym/dłużnym** ➲ note at **loan** ➲ look at **debt 2 owe sth to sb**; **owe sb sth** to feel that you should do sth for sb or give sth to sb, especially because they have done sth for you: *Claudia owes me an explanation.* ◇ *I owe you an apology.* ◇ *I owe* (zawdzięczam) *you a lot for all you did for me when I was young.* ▶ **być komuś coś winnym 3 owe sth (to sb/sth)** to have sth (for the reason given): *She said she owes her success to hard work and determination.* ▶ **zawdzięczać**

owing /ˈəʊɪŋ/ adj. [not before a noun] **owing (to sb)** not yet paid: *How much is still owing to you?* Ile ci się jeszcze należy? ▶ **należny**

ˈ**owing to** prep. because of: *The match was cancelled owing to bad weather.* ▶ **z powodu, wskutek (czegoś)** ➲ note at **due**[1]

owl /aʊl/ noun [C] a bird with large eyes that hunts small animals at night ▶ **sowa**

own[1] /əʊn/ adj., pron. **1** (used to emphasize that sth belongs to a particular person): *I saw him do it with **my own** eyes.* ◇ *This is **his own** house.* ◇ *This house is his own.* ◇ *Virginia would like her own room/a room **of her own*** (swój własny pokój). ▶ **własny, swój** ⓘ Nie można stawiać **own** po **a** lub **the**. Nie można powiedzieć ~~I would like an own car~~. Poprawnie mówi się **I would like my own car** lub **I would like a car of my own. 2** (used to show that sth is done or made without help from another person): *The children are old enough to get their own breakfast.* ▶ **własny, swój**
IDM **come into your own** to have the opportunity to show your special qualities: *When the traffic is this bad, a bicycle really comes into its own.* ▶ **przydawać się, sprawdzać się**
get/have your own back (on sb) (informal) to hurt sb who has hurt you ▶ **odpłacać pięknym za nadobne**
hold your own (against sb/sth) to be as strong, good, etc. as sb/sth else: *Business isn't good but we're managing to hold our own.* ▶ **utrzymywać swoją pozycję (wobec kogoś/czegoś), nie poddawać się (czemuś)**
(all) on your, etc. own 1 alone: *John lives all on his own.* ▶ **(całkiem) sam, samotnie** ➲ note at **alone 2** without help: *I managed to repair the car all on my own.* ▶ **sam, bez pomocy**

own[2] /əʊn/ verb [T] to have sth belonging to you: *We don't own the house. We just rent it.* ◇ *a privately owned company* ▶ **mieć na własność, być właścicielem (czegoś)**
PHR V **own up (to sth)** (informal) to tell sb that you have done sth wrong: *None of the children owned up to breaking the window.* ▶ **przyznawać się (do czegoś), wyznawać** (*winę*) ⓘ Por. **confess**, który jest czasownikiem bardziej formalnym.

owner /ˈəʊnə(r)/ noun [C] a person who owns sth: *a house/dog owner* ▶ **właściciel/ka**

ownership /ˈəʊnəʃɪp/ noun [U] the state of owning sth: *in private/public **ownership*** ▶ **własność, posiadanie**

ox /ɒks/ noun [C] (pl. **oxen** /ˈɒksn/) a male cow that cannot produce young, which is used for pulling or carrying heavy loads ▶ **wół** ➲ note at **cow** ➲ look at **bull**

oxidize (also **-ise**) /ˈɒksɪdaɪz/ verb [T,I] to remove one or more **electrons** from a substance, or to combine or to make sth combine with **oxygen**, especially when this causes metal to become covered with **rust** ▶ **utleniać**
■ **oxidation** /ˌɒksɪˈdeɪʃn/ noun [U] ▶ **utlenianie**

oxygen /ˈɒksɪdʒən/ noun [U] (symbol **O**) a gas that you cannot see, taste or smell. Plants and animals cannot live without **oxygen.** ▶ **tlen**

oyster /ˈɔɪstə(r)/ noun [C] a type of **shellfish** that you can eat. Some **oysters** produce **pearls.** ▶ **ostryga**

oz = OUNCE (1): *Add 4oz flour.*

ozone /ˈəʊzəʊn/ noun [U] a poisonous gas which is a form of **oxygen** ▶ **ozon**

ˌ**ozone-ˈfriendly** adj. (used about cleaning products, etc.) not containing chemicals that could harm the **ozone layer** ▶ **nie niszczący warstwy ozonowej**

the ˈ**ozone layer** noun [sing.] the layer of **ozone** high up in the atmosphere that helps to protect the earth from the harmful effects of the sun: *a hole in the ozone layer* ▶ **warstwa ozonowa** ➲ note at **environment** ➲ look at **CFC**

Ozzie = AUSSIE

Pp

P, p /piː/ noun [C,U] (pl. **Ps**; **ps**; **P's**; **p's** /piːz/) the 16th letter of the English alphabet: *'Pencil' begins with (a) 'P'.* ▶ **litera** *p*

p abbr. **1** (pl. **pp**): *See p 94.* ◇ *pp 63-96* = PAGE[1] **2** (Brit., informal): *a 27p stamp* = PENNY (1), PENCE **3** (**P**) (on a road sign) parking ▶ **P**

PA /ˌpiː ˈeɪ/ abbr., noun [C] (especially Brit.) **personal assistant**; a person who types letters, answers the telephone, arranges meetings, etc. for just one manager ▶ **sekreta-rz/rka**

p.a. abbr. (from Latin) **per annum**; in or for a year: *salary £15 000 p.a.* ▶ **rocznie, na rok**

pace[1] /peɪs/ noun **1** [U, sing.] **pace (of sth)** the speed at which you walk, run, etc. or at which sth happens: *to run at a steady/gentle pace* ◇ *I can't stand the pace of life in London.* ◇ *Students are encouraged to work **at their own pace** .* ▶ **tempo, szybkość 2** [C] the distance that you move when you take one step: *Take two paces forward* (zrób dwa kroki w przód) *and then stop.* ▶ **krok** (*odległość*) SYN **step**
IDM **keep pace (with sb/sth)** to move or do sth at the same speed as sb/sth else; to change as quickly as sth else is changing: *Wages are not keeping pace with inflation.* ▶ **dotrzymywać kroku**
set the pace to move or do sth at the speed that others must follow: *Pinto set the pace for the first three miles.* ▶ **nadawać tempo**

pace[2] /peɪs/ verb [I,T] to walk up and down in the same area many times, especially because you are nervous or angry: *Fran paced nervously up and down the room* (nerwowo przemierzała pokój), *waiting for news.* ▶ **kroczyć, stąpać**

pacemaker /ˈpeɪsmeɪkə(r)/ noun [C] **1** a machine that helps to make sb's heart beat regularly or more strongly ▶ **stymulator serca 2** (especially US **pacesetter** /ˈpeɪssetə(r)/) a person in a race who sets the speed that the others try to follow ▶ **osoba nadająca tempo**

pacifier (US) = DUMMY (4)

pacifism /ˈpæsɪfɪzəm/ noun [U] the belief that all wars are wrong and that you should not fight in them ▶ **pacyfizm**
■ **pacifist** /-ɪst/ noun [C] ▶ **pacyfist(k)a**

pacify /ˈpæsɪfaɪ/ verb [T] (**pacifying**; **pacifies**; pt, pp **pacified**) to make sb who is angry or upset be calm or quiet ▶ **uspokajać**

pack¹ /pæk/ verb **1** [I,T] to put your things into a suitcase, etc. before you go away or go on holiday: *I'll have to pack my suitcase in the morning.* ◇ *Have you packed your toothbrush?* ▶ **pakować (się)** ℹ Zwróć uwagę na wyrażenie **do your packing**: *I'll do my packing in the morning.* **2** [I,T] to put things into containers so they can be stored, transported or sold: *I packed all my books into boxes.* ▶ **pakować** (*np. w pudła*) OPP **unpack** **3** [T, often passive] (informal) to fill with people or things until crowded or full: *The train was absolutely packed.* ◇ *The book is* ***packed with*** *useful information.* ◇ *People packed the pavements, waiting for the president to arrive.* ▶ **(na)pakować, wypełniać**

PHR V **pack sth away** to put sth in a box, etc. when you have finished using it: *We packed away the summer clothes.* ▶ **odkładać coś na miejsce**

pack sth in (informal) to stop doing sth: *I've packed in my job.* ◇ *I've had enough of you boys arguing – just pack it in, will you!* ▶ **rzucać coś**

pack sth in/into sth to do a lot in a short time: *They packed a lot into their three days in Rome.* ▶ **napychać coś czymś, wtłaczać coś do czegoś**

pack sth out [usually passive] to fill sth with people: *The bars* ***are packed out*** *every night.* ▶ **napychać/wypełniać coś ludźmi**

pack up (informal) **1** (used about a machine, engine, etc.) to stop working: *My old car packed up last week so now I cycle to work.* ▶ (*silnik itp.*) **zacinać się** **2** to finish working or doing sth: *There was nothing else to do so we packed up and went home.* ▶ **zbierać manatki**

pack up; pack sth up to put your possessions into a bag, etc. before leaving a place: *Are you packing up already? It's only 4 o'clock.* ▶ **pakować się/coś przed odjazdem**

pack² /pæk/ noun [C] **1** (especially US) a small box, bag, etc. in which things are packed to be sold in a shop ▶ **pudełko, torebka** **2** a set of things that are supplied together for a particular purpose: *an information pack* pakiet informacyjny ◇ *These batteries are sold in packs of four* (w opakowaniach po cztery sztuki). ◇ (figurative) *Everything she told me was* ***a pack of lies*** (to stek bzdur). ▶ **paczka** ➲ look at **package**, **packet**, **parcel** **3** a bag that you carry on your back: *It was hard to walk fast with the heavy pack on my back.* ▶ **plecak** SYN **rucksack**, **backpack** **4** [with sing. or pl. verb] a group of wild animals that hunt together: *a pack of dogs/wolves* ▶ **stado** (*np. wilków*) **5** a large group of similar people or things, especially one that you do not like or approve of: *a pack of journalists* ▶ **banda** **6** (US **deck**) a complete set of playing cards: *a pack of cards* ▶ **talia** (*kart*) ➲ note at **card**

package /ˈpækɪdʒ/ noun [C] **1** (US) = PARCEL, PACKET (1) **2** (Brit.) something, or a number of things, covered in paper or in a box: *There's a large package on the table for you.* ▶ **pakunek, paczka** ➲ look at **pack**, **packet**, **parcel** **3** a number of things that must be bought or accepted together: *a word-processing package* ◇ *a financial aid package* ▶ **pakiet, zestaw**

■ **package** verb [T]: *Goods that are attractively packaged sell more quickly.* ▶ **pakować**

ˈpackage holiday (US ˈ**package tour**) noun [C] a holiday that is organized by a company for a fixed price that includes the cost of travel, hotels, etc. ▶ **zorganizowany wyjazd wakacyjny przez biuro podróży** ➲ note at **holiday**

packaging /ˈpækɪdʒɪŋ/ noun [U] all the materials (boxes, bags, paper, etc.) that are used to cover or protect goods before they are sold ▶ **opakowanie** ➲ note at **parcel**

ˌpacked ˈlunch noun [C] a meal of **sandwiches**, fruit, etc. that is prepared at home and eaten at school, work, etc. ▶ **kanapki itp. przygotowane jako drugie śniadanie do zjedzenia poza domem** ➲ look at **bag lunch**, **box lunch**

packer /ˈpækə(r)/ noun [C] a person, company or machine that puts goods, especially food, into boxes, plastic, paper, etc. to be sold ▶ **pakowacz/ka**

packet /ˈpækɪt/ noun **1** (abbr. **pkt**) (US **pack**; **package**) [C] a small box, bag, etc. in which things are packed to be sold in a shop: ***a packet of*** *sweets/biscuits/crisps* ◇ *a cigarette packet* ▶ **pudełko, torebka** ➲ look at **pack**, **package**, **parcel** ➲ picture at **container** **2** [sing.] (informal) a large amount of money: *That new kitchen must have cost them a packet.* ▶ (*przen.*) **majątek**

packing /ˈpækɪŋ/ noun [U] **1** the act of putting your clothes, possessions, etc. into boxes or cases in order to take or send them somewhere: *We're going on holiday tomorrow so I'll* ***do my packing*** *tonight.* ▶ **pakowanie (się)** **2** (Brit.) soft material that you use to stop things from being damaged or broken when you are sending them somewhere: *The price includes* ***postage and packing.*** ▶ **opakowanie**

pact /pækt/ noun [C] **(a) pact between A and B** a formal agreement between two or more people, groups or countries ▶ **pakt**

pad¹ /pæd/ noun [C] **1** a thick piece of soft material, used for cleaning or protecting sth or to make sth a different shape: *Press the cotton wool pad* (gazik) *onto the wound to stop the bleeding.* ◇ *a jacket with shoulder pads* ◇ *Footballers wear shin pads* (ochraniacze na golenie) *to protect their legs.* ▶ **poduszka** (*np. usztywniająca ramiona marynarki*), **tampon, wyściółka** **2** a number of pieces of paper that are fastened together at one end: *a notepad* ▶ **blok papieru** **3** the soft part on the bottom of the feet of some animals, for example dogs and cats ▶ **poduszka** (*np. łapy kota*) **4** the place where a **spacecraft** takes off: *a launch pad* ▶ **lądowisko helikopterów, baza wyrzutni rakietowej**

pad² /pæd/ verb (pa**dd**ing; pa**dd**ed) **1** [T, usually passive] **pad sth (with sth)** to fill or cover sth with soft material in order to protect it, make it larger or more comfortable, etc.: *I sent the photograph frame in a padded envelope.* ▶ **wyściełać, watować** **2** [I] **pad about, along, around, etc.** to walk quietly, especially because you are not wearing shoes: *He got up and padded into the bathroom.* ▶ **iść szybko i cicho**

PHR V **pad sth out** to make a book, speech, etc. longer by adding things that are not necessary ▶ **rozwlekać** (*tekst*); (*przen.*) **lać wodę**

padding /ˈpædɪŋ/ noun [U] soft material that is put inside sth to protect it or to make it larger, more comfortable, etc. ▶ **wyściółka, podbicie/podszycie** (*np. palta*), **obicie** (*np. drzwi*)

paddle¹ /ˈpædl/ noun [C] a short pole that is flat and wide at one or both ends and that you use for moving a small boat through water ▶ **krótkie wiosło o szerokim piórze** ➲ look at **oar**

paddle² /ˈpædl/ verb **1** [I,T] to move a small boat through water using a short pole that is flat and wide at one or both ends: *We paddled down the river.* ▶ **wiosłować** (*krótkim wiosłem*) ➲ look at **row** **2** [I] to walk in water that is not very deep: *We paddled in the stream.* ▶ **brodzić**

paddock /ˈpædək/ noun [C] a small field where horses are kept ▶ **wybieg dla koni**

paddy /ˈpædi/ (also ˈ**paddy field**) noun [C] (pl. **paddies**) a field in which rice is grown: *a rice paddy* ▶ **pole ryżowe**

padlock /ˈpædlɒk/ noun [C] a type of lock that you can use for fastening gates, bicycles, etc. ▶ **kłódka**

■ **padlock** verb [T] **padlock sth (to sth)**: *I padlocked my bicycle to a lamp post.* ▶ **zamykać na kłódkę**

paediatrician (US **pediatrician**) /ˌpiːdiəˈtrɪʃn/ noun [C] a doctor who deals with the diseases of children ▶ **pediatra**

paediatrics (US **pediatrics**) /ˌpi:di'ætrɪks/ noun [U] the area of medicine connected with the diseases of children ▶ **pediatria**
■ **paediatric** (US **pediatric**) adj. ▶ **pediatryczny**

paedophile /'pi:dəfaɪl/ noun [C] a person who is sexually attracted to children ▶ **pedofil**

pagan /'peɪgən/ adj. having religious beliefs that do not belong to any of the main religions ▶ **pogański**
■ **pagan** noun [C] ▶ **pogan-in/ka**

page¹ /peɪdʒ/ noun [C] (abbr. **p**) **1** one side of a piece of paper: *The letter was three pages long.* ◇ *Start each answer **on a new/blank page.*** ◇ *Look at the picture **on page 63.*** ◇ *Turn to page 12 of your book.* ◇ ***the front page** of a newspaper* ▶ **stronica**, **strona 2** one piece of paper in a book, etc.: *One page had been torn from her diary.* ▶ **kartka**

page² /peɪdʒ/ verb [T] to call sb by sending a message to a **pager**, or by calling their name through a **loudspeaker** ▶ **przywoływać kogoś przez głośnik**

pageant /'pædʒənt/ noun [C] **1** a type of public entertainment at which people dress in clothes from past times and give outdoor performances of scenes from history ▶ **widowisko w plenerze 2** (US) a beauty competition for young women ▶ **konkurs piękności 3** any colourful ceremony ▶ **(kolorowy) pochód**

pageantry /'pædʒəntri/ noun [U] impressive public events or ceremonies with many people wearing special clothes: *the pageantry of royal occasions* ▶ **gala**, **parada**

pager /'peɪdʒə(r)/ noun [C] a small machine that you carry, that makes a sound when sb sends you a message ▶ **pager** SYN **bleeper**

paid past tense, past participle of **pay¹**

ˈ**paid-up** adj. [only before a noun] having paid all the money that you owe, for example to become a member of a club: *He's a fully paid-up member of Friends of the Earth.* ▶ **bez zaległych składek/pełnoprawny**

pail (old-fashioned) = BUCKET

pain¹ /peɪn/ noun **1** [C,U] the unpleasant feeling that you have when a part of your body has been hurt or when you are ill: *to **be in pain*** cierpieć ból ◇ *I've got a terrible pain in my back.* Strasznie bolą mnie plecy. ◇ *He screamed with pain.* Krzyczał z bólu. ◇ *chest pains* ból w piersiach ◇ *After I took the tablets **the pain wore off.*** ▶ **ból**

> Por. **pain** i **ache**. Słowa **ache** używa się, opisując długotrwały, ciągły ból, natomiast **pain** oznacza nagły, krótkotrwały ból. Dlatego zazwyczaj mówimy: *I've got earache/backache/toothache/a headache.* ale: *He was admitted to hospital with pains in his chest.* Więcej o użyciu przedimka **a(n)** z wyrazem **ache** przy haśle **ache**.

2 [U] sadness that you feel because sth bad has happened: *the pain of losing a parent* ▶ **cierpienie**, **ból (psychiczny)**
IDM **a pain (in the neck)**; Brit. also **a pain in the arse**; US also **a pain in the ass** (informal) a person, thing or situation that makes you angry or annoyed ▶ **utrapienie**, **udręka**

pain² /peɪn/ verb [T] (formal) to make sb feel sad or upset: ***It pains me** to think how much money we've wasted.* ▶ **zasmucać (kogoś)**, **sprawiać (komuś) przykrość** SYN **hurt**

pained /peɪnd/ adj. showing that you are sad or upset: *a pained expression* ▶ **zasmucony**, **bolesny**

painful /'peɪnfl/ adj. **painful (for sb) (to do sth) 1** that causes pain: *A wasp sting can be very painful.* ◇ *painful joints* ▶ **bolący 2** making you feel upset or embarrassed: *a painful experience/memory* ▶ **bolesny**
■ **painfully** /-fəli/ adv. ▶ **boleśnie**, **dotkliwie**

painkiller /'peɪnkɪlə(r)/ noun [C] a drug that is used for reducing pain ▶ **środek przeciwbólowy**

painless /'peɪnləs/ adj. that does not cause pain: *The animals' death is quick and painless.* ▶ **bezbolesny**
■ **painlessly** adv. ▶ **bezboleśnie**

pains /peɪnz/ noun
IDM **be at/take (great) pains to do sth**; **take (great) pains (with/over sth)** to make a special effort to do sth well: *He was at pains to hide his true feelings.* ▶ **dokładać (wszelkich) starań, żeby**

painstaking /'peɪnzteɪkɪŋ/ adj. very careful and taking a long time: *The painstaking search of the wreckage gave us clues as to the cause of the crash.* ▶ **staranny**, **dokładny** SYN **thorough**
■ **painstakingly** adv. ▶ **starannie**, **dokładnie**

paint¹ /peɪnt/ noun **1** [U] coloured liquid that you put onto a surface to decorate or protect it: *green/orange/yellow paint* ◇ *The door will need another **coat of paint.*** ◇ *The paint was peeling off* (łuszczyła się) *the walls.* ◇ *Wet paint!* Świeżo malowane! ▶ **farba 2** [U] coloured liquid that you can use to make a picture: *oil paint* ◇ *watercolour paint* ▶ **farba 3** (**paints**) [pl.] a collection of tubes or blocks of paint that an artist uses for painting pictures: *oil paints* ▶ **farby (artysty malarza)**

paint² /peɪnt/ verb [I,T] **1** to put paint onto a surface or an object: *We painted the fence.* ◇ *The walls were painted pink* (pomalowane na różowo). ▶ **malować 2** to make a picture of sb/sth using paints: *We painted some animals on the wall.* ▶ **namalować**

paintbox /'peɪntbɒks/ noun [C] a box that contains blocks or tubes of paint of many colours ▶ **pudełko z farbami**

paintbrush /'peɪntbrʌʃ/ noun [C] a brush that you use for painting with ▶ **pędzel** ➲ picture at **brush**

painter /'peɪntə(r)/ noun [C] **1** a person whose job is to paint buildings, walls, etc.: *a painter and decorator* ▶ **malarz pokojowy** ➲ picture on **page A4 2** a person who paints pictures: *a famous painter* ▶ **mala-rz/rka** ➲ note at **art** ➲ look at **artist**

painting /'peɪntɪŋ/ noun **1** [C] a picture that sb has painted: *a famous painting by Van Gogh* ▶ **obraz**, **płótno 2** [U] the act of painting pictures or buildings: *She studies Indian painting.* ▶ **malowanie**, **malarstwo** ➲ note at **art** ➲ look at **drawing**

paintwork /'peɪntwɜ:k/ noun [U] a painted surface, especially on a vehicle ▶ **malowanie** (*pomalowana powierzchnia*)

pair¹ /peə(r)/ noun **1** [C] two things of the same type that are used or worn together: *a pair of shoes/gloves/earrings* ▶ **para 2** [C] a thing that consists of two parts that are joined together: *a pair of scissors/glasses/trousers* ▶ **para 3** [C, with sing. or pl. verb] two people or animals that are doing sth together: *These boxers have fought several times, and tonight the pair meet again.* ▶ **para** ℹ Para małżonków, narzeczonych lub partnerów żyjących w wolnym związku to **couple**.
IDM **in pairs** two at a time: *These earrings are only sold in pairs.* ◇ *The students were working in pairs.* ▶ **parami**, **w parach**

pair² /peə(r)/ verb
PHR V **pair (sb) off (with sb)** to come together, especially to form a romantic relationship; to bring two people together for this purpose: *She's always trying to pair me off with her brother.* ▶ **dobierać do pary**
pair up (with sb) to join together with another person or group to work, play a game, etc.: *I paired up with another student and we did the project together.* ▶ **dołączać** (*do kogoś lub do grupy osób*)

pajamas (US) = PYJAMAS

P

pal /pæl/ noun [C] (informal, becoming old-fashioned) a friend ▶ **kumpel/ka**

palace /ˈpæləs/ noun [C] a large house that is or was the home of a king or queen ▶ **pałac**

palatable /ˈpælətəbl/ adj. **1** (used about food or drink) having a pleasant or acceptable taste: *a very palatable local wine* ▶ **smaczny 2 palatable (to sb)** pleasant or acceptable to sb: *Some of the dialogue has been changed to make it more palatable to an American audience.* ▶ **do przyjęcia (dla kogoś)**

palate /ˈpælət/ noun [C] the top part of the inside of your mouth ▶ **podniebienie**

pale /peɪl/ adj. **1** (used about a person or their face) having skin that is light in colour, often because of fear or illness: *She has a pale complexion.* ◇ *I felt myself **go/turn pale** with fear.* Zbladłem ze strachu. ▶ **blady** ➲ look at **pallid** ➲ noun **pallor 2** not bright or strong in colour: *pale yellow* bladożółty ▶ **blady** OPP **dark**
■ **pale** verb [I] ▶ **blednąć**

palette /ˈpælət/ noun [C] a thin board on which an artist mixes colours when painting, with a hole for the thumb to hold it by ▶ **paleta**

pall /pɔːl/ verb [I] **pall (on sb)** to become less interesting or important: *Even the impressive scenery began to pall on me after a few hundred miles.* ▶ **znudzić się, sprzykrzyć się**

pallid /ˈpælɪd/ adj. (used about a person or their face) light in colour, especially because of illness: *His pallid complexion made him look unhealthy.* ▶ **blady** ➲ look at **pale**

pallor /ˈpælə(r)/ noun [U] pale colouring of the face, especially because of illness or fear ▶ **bladość**

palm¹ /pɑːm/ noun [C] **1** the flat, inner surface of your hand: *She held the coins tightly in the palm of her hand.* ▶ **dłoń** ➲ picture at **body 2** (also ˈ**palm tree**) a tall straight type of tree that grows in hot countries. **Palms** have a lot of large leaves at the top but no branches. ▶ **palma**

palm² /pɑːm/ verb
PHR V **palm sb off (with sth)** (informal) to persuade sb to believe sth that is not true in order to stop them asking questions or complaining ▶ **wciskać/wmawiać (coś) komuś**
palm sth off (on sb) to persuade sb to accept sth that they do not want: *She's always palming off the worst jobs on her assistant.* ▶ **wciskać coś (komuś)**

Palmcorder™ /ˈpɑːmkɔːdə(r)/ noun [C] a small **camcorder** that can be held in the **palm** of one hand ▶ **minikamera**

Palm ˈSunday noun [U,C] (in the Christian Church) the Sunday before Easter ▶ **Niedziela Palmowa**

palmtop /ˈpɑːmtɒp/ noun [C] a very small computer that can be held in one hand ▶ **palmtop**

palpable /ˈpælpəbl/ adj. that is easily noticed by the mind or the senses: *a **palpable sense** of relief* ◇ *His statement is palpable nonsense.* ▶ **wyraźny**
■ **palpably** /-əbli/ adv.: *It was palpably clear what she really meant.* ▶ **wyraźnie**

palpitate /ˈpælpɪteɪt/ verb [I] (used about the heart) to beat rapidly and/or in an **irregular** way especially because of fear or excitement ▶ **kołatać**

paltry /ˈpɔːltri/ adj. too small to be considered important or useful: *a paltry sum of money* ▶ **lichy, nędzny**

pamper /ˈpæmpə(r)/ verb [T] to take care of sb very well and make them feel as comfortable as possible ▶ **rozpieszczać, hołubić**

pamphlet /ˈpæmflət/ noun [C] a very thin book with a paper cover containing information about a particular subject ▶ **broszura, prospekt**

pans

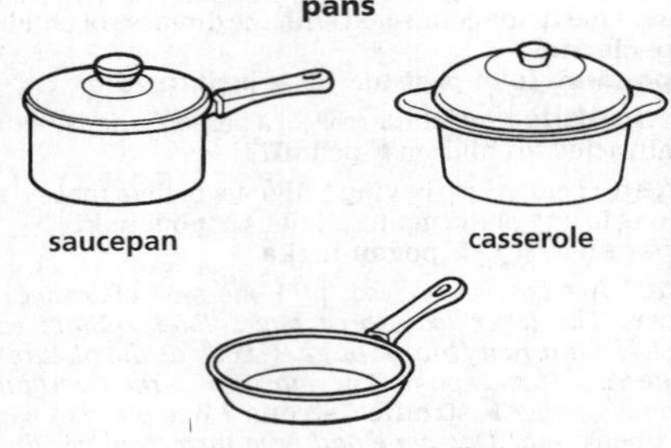

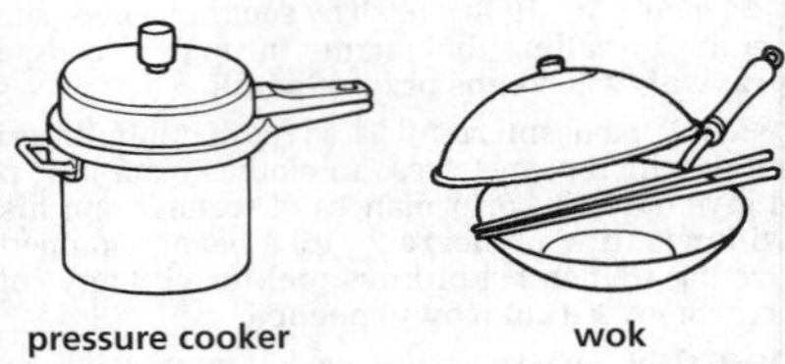

pan¹ /pæn/ noun [C] a metal container with a handle or handles that is used for cooking food in; the contents of a pan: *Cook the spaghetti in a pan of boiling water.* ◇ *All the pots and pans* (gary) *are kept in that cupboard.* ◇ *a frying pan* patelnia ▶ **rondel**

pan² /pæn/ verb
PHR V **pan out** (informal) (used about events or a situation) to develop in a particular way: *I'm happy with the way things have panned out.* ▶ **układać się**

panacea /ˌpænəˈsiːə/ noun [C] **panacea (for sth)** something that will solve all the problems of a particular situation: *There is no single panacea for the problem of unemployment.* ▶ **panaceum**

panache /pəˈnæʃ; pæˈn-; US also -ˈnɑːʃ/ noun [U] the quality of being able to do things in a confident and elegant way that other people find attractive: *She carried off the performance with panache.* ▶ **polot** SYN **flair, style**

pancake /ˈpænkeɪk/ noun [C] a type of very thin round cake that is made by frying a mixture of flour, milk and eggs ▶ **naleśnik** ➲ picture on **page A14**

ˈ**Pancake Day** noun [U,C] (informal) a Tuesday in February when people in Britain traditionally eat **pancakes**. Pancake Day is the day before the period of Lent begins. ▶ **ostatki** (*wtorek przed Środą Popielcową*) ➲ look at **Shrove Tuesday**

pancreas /ˈpæŋkriəs/ noun [C] an organ near the stomach that produces **insulin** and a liquid that helps the body to **digest** food ▶ **trzustka**

panda /ˈpændə/ noun [C] a large black and white bear that comes from China ▶ **panda**

pandemonium /ˌpændəˈməʊniəm/ noun [U] a state of great noise and confusion ▶ **harmider, rozgardiasz** SYN **chaos**

pander /ˈpændə(r)/ verb
PHR V **pander to sb/sth** to do or say exactly what sb wants especially when this is not reasonable: *He refuses to pander to his boss's demands.* ▶ **(fałszywie) schlebiać komuś, ulegać komuś/czemuś**

p. and p. (also **p. & p.**) abbr. (Brit.) **postage and packing**: *price: £29 incl. p. and p.* ▶ **opłata za przesyłkę i opakowanie**

pane /peɪn/ noun [C] a piece of glass in a window, etc.: *a windowpane* ▶ **szyba**

panel /'pænl/ noun [C] **1** a square or long thin piece of wood, metal or glass that forms part of a door or wall: *They smashed one of the glass panels in the front door.* ▶ **filunek**, **płycina**, **kaseton** **2** [with sing. or pl. verb] a group of people who give their advice or opinions about sth; a group of people who discuss topics of interest on TV or radio: *a panel of judges* ◇ *a panel game* quiz telewizyjny ▶ **zespół** (*np. specjalistów*), **panel** **3** a flat surface that contains the equipment for controlling a vehicle, machine, etc.: *a control/display panel* ▶ **tablica rozdzielcza**

panelling (US **paneling**) /'pænəlɪŋ/ noun [U] large flat pieces of wood used to cover and decorate walls, ceilings, etc. ▶ **boazeria**

panellist (US **panelist**) /'pænəlɪst/ noun [C] a member of a **panel (2)** ▶ **uczestni-k/czka dyskusji panelowej**

pang /pæŋ/ noun [C, usually pl.] a sudden strong feeling of emotional or physical pain: *a pang of* (ukłucie) *jealousy* ◇ *hunger pangs* ssanie w żołądku ▶ **(ostre, nagłe) uczucie** (*np. bólu, głodu, winy*)

panic /'pænɪk/ noun [C,U] a sudden feeling of fear that cannot be controlled and stops you from thinking clearly: *People fled* ***in panic*** *as the fire spread.* ◇ *There was a mad panic when the alarm went off.* ▶ **popłoch**
■ **panic** verb [I] (**panicking**; **panicked**): *Stay calm and don't panic.* ▶ **panikować**, **wpadać w popłoch**

'**panic-stricken** adj. very frightened in a way that stops you from thinking clearly ▶ **owładnięty panicznym lękiem**

panorama /ˌpænə'rɑːmə; US -'ræmə/ noun [C] a view over a wide area of land ▶ **panorama**
■ **panoramic** /ˌpænə'ræmɪk/ adj. ▶ **panoramiczny**

pansy /'pænzi/ noun [C] (pl. **pansies**) a garden plant with a short stem and broad flat flowers of various bright colours ▶ **bratek** ➲ picture on **page A15**

pant /pænt/ verb [I] to breathe quickly, for example after running or because it is very hot ▶ **sapać**, **dyszeć**
■ **pant** noun [C] ▶ **zadyszka**

panther /'pænθə(r)/ noun [C] a large wild animal of the cat family with black fur ▶ **pantera**

panties (especially US) = KNICKERS

pantomime /'pæntəmaɪm/ noun [C,U] **1** (also informal **panto** /'pæntəʊ/) (Brit.) a type of play for children, with music, dancing and jokes ▶ **przedstawienie dla dzieci urządzane po Bożym Narodzeniu**

> **Pantomimes** to spektakle muzyczne tworzone na podstawie znanych bajek jak np. **Aladdin** (Cudowna lampa Alladyna), **Jack and the Beanstalk** (Jaś i magiczna fasola), **Dick Whittington** czy **Cinderella** (Kopciuszek).

2 = MIME

pantry /'pæntri/ noun [C] (pl. **pantries**) a small room where food is kept ▶ **spiżarnia** SYN **larder**

pants **1** (Brit.) = UNDERPANTS **2** (US) = TROUSERS

pantyhose (US) = TIGHTS

papaya /pə'paɪə/ (also **pawpaw** /'pɔːpɔː/) noun [C] a large tropical fruit which is sweet and orange inside and has small black seeds ▶ **papaja** ➲ picture on **page A12**

paper /'peɪpə(r)/ noun **1** [U] a material made in thin sheets that you use for writing or drawing on, covering things, etc.: *a piece/sheet of paper* ◇ *a paper* (z ligniny) *handkerchief* ◇ *wallpaper* tapeta ◇ *Scrap paper* (makulatura) *can be recycled.* ◇ *filter/tissue/toilet/writing paper* filtr papierowy/bibuła/papier toaletowy/papier listowy ◇ *graph paper* papier milimetrowy ◇ *greaseproof/wax paper* papier woskowany ▶ **papier** **2** [C] a newspaper: *Where's today's paper?* ▶ **gazeta** ➲ note at **newspaper** **3** (**papers**) [pl.] important letters or pieces of paper that have information written on them: *The document you want is somewhere in the pile of papers on her desk.* ▶ **dokumenty**, **papiery** **4** [C] the written questions or the written answers in an exam: *The teacher gave out the* ***question papers*** (arkusze z pytaniami egzaminacyjnymi), *and we began the exam.* ◇ *The history exam is divided into three papers* (podzielony jest na trzy komponenty). ▶ **egzamin pisemny** **5** [C] a piece of writing on a particular subject that is written for people who know a lot about the subject: *At the conference, the Professor presented a paper on Sri Lankan poetry.* ▶ **rozprawa**, **referat**
IDM **on paper** **1** in writing: *I've had nothing on paper to say that I've been accepted.* ▶ **na piśmie** **2** as an idea, but not in a real situation: *The scheme seems fine on paper, but would it work in practice?* ▶ **na papierze** SYN **in theory**

paperback /'peɪpəbæk/ noun [C,U] a book that has a paper cover: *The novel is available* ***in paperback.*** ▶ (*książka*) **w miękkiej/broszurowej okładce** ➲ look at **hardback**

'**paper boy**, '**paper girl** noun [C] a child who takes newspapers to people's houses ▶ **gazecia-rz/rka**, **roznosiciel/ka**

'**paper clip** noun [C] a small piece of bent wire that is used for holding pieces of paper together ▶ **spinacz** ➲ picture at **stationery**

'**paper round** (US '**paper route**) noun [C] the job of delivering newspapers to houses; the route taken when doing this ▶ **roznoszenie gazet**; **trasa pokonywana przez roznosiciela gazet**

paperwork /'peɪpəwɜːk/ noun [U] **1** the written work that is part of a job, such as writing letters and reports and filling in forms, etc.: *I hate doing paperwork.* ▶ **papierkowa robota** **2** documents that need to be prepared, collected, etc. in order for a piece of business to be completed: *Some of the paperwork is missing from this file.* ▶ **papiery**

paprika /'pæprɪkə/ noun [U] a red powder that you can use in cooking as a mild spice ▶ **papryka** (*przyprawa*)

> Uwaga! Owoc papryki to **pepper**.

'**Pap smear** (US) = SMEAR TEST

par[1] /pɑː(r)/ noun [U] (in the sport of **golf**) the standard number of times a player should hit the ball in order to complete a particular hole or series of holes ▶ (*golf*) **norma**
IDM **below par** (informal) not as good or as well as usual ▶ **poniżej przeciętnej**
on a par with sb/sth of an equal level, standard, etc. to sb/sth else: *Is a teacher's salary on a par with a doctor's?* ▶ **na równi z kimś/czymś**

par[2] (also **para**) abbr. = PARAGRAPH

parable /'pærəbl/ noun [C] a short story that teaches a lesson, especially one told by Jesus in the Bible ▶ **przypowieść**

parabola /pə'ræbələ/ noun [C] a curve like the path of an object that is thrown through the air and falls back to earth ▶ **parabola**

parachute /'pærəʃuːt/ noun [C] a piece of equipment made of thin cloth, that opens and lets the person fall to the ground slowly when they jump from a plane ▶ **spadochron**
■ **parachute** verb [I] ▶ **skakać z samolotu ze spadochronem**

parade /pə'reɪd/ noun [C] an occasion when a group of people stand or walk in a line so that people can look at them: *a military parade* ◇ *a fashion parade* pokaz mody ▶ **defilada**, **parada**

P

paradigm /ˈpærədaɪm/ noun [C] **1** (formal or technical) a typical example or pattern of sth: *a paradigm for students to copy* ▶ **paradygmat**, **model** **2** a set of all the different forms of a word: *verb paradigms* ▶ **paradygmat**
■ **paradigmatic** /ˌpærədɪɡˈmætɪk/ adj. ▶ **paradygmatyczny**

paradise /ˈpærədaɪs/ noun **1** (**Paradise**) [sing.] [without *a* or *the*] the place where some people think that good people go after they die ▶ **raj** SYN **heaven** **2** [C] a perfect place: *This beach is a paradise for windsurfers.* ▶ **raj**

paradox /ˈpærədɒks/ noun [C] a situation or statement with two or more parts that seem strange or impossible together: *It's a paradox that some countries produce too much food while in many other countries people are starving.* ▶ **paradoks**
■ **paradoxical** /ˌpærəˈdɒksɪkl/ adj. ▶ **paradoksalny** | **paradoxically** /-kli/ adv. ▶ **paradoksalnie**

paraffin /ˈpærəfɪn/ (US **kerosene** /ˈkerəsiːn/) noun [U] a type of oil that is burned to produce heat or light ▶ **nafta**

paragliding /ˈpærəɡlaɪdɪŋ/ noun [U] a sport in which you wear a special structure like a parachute, jump from a plane or a high place and are carried along by the wind before coming down to earth ▶ **paralotniarstwo** ⮕ look at **hang-gliding**

paragraph /ˈpærəɡrɑːf; US -ɡræf/ noun [C] (abbr. **para**) a part of a piece of writing that consists of one or more sentences. A **paragraph** always starts on a new line. ▶ **akapit**

🔑 **parallel**[1] /ˈpærəlel/ adj. **1** **parallel (to sth)** (used about two lines, etc.) with the same distance between them for all their length: *parallel lines* ▶ **równoległy** **2** similar and happening at the same time: *The two brothers followed parallel careers in different companies.* ▶ **analogiczny**
■ **parallel** adv. **parallel (to sth)**: *The railway runs parallel to the road.* ▶ **równolegle**

parallel[2] /ˈpærəlel/ noun **1** [C,U] a person, thing or situation that is similar to another one in a different situation, place or time: *The government's huge election victory is* ***without parallel*** *this century* (to rzecz niebywała). ◇ *He* ***drew a parallel*** (przeprowadził paralelę) *between Margaret Thatcher and Winston Churchill.* ▶ **porównanie** **2** (also ˌ**parallel ˈline**) [C] a line, etc. that is parallel to another ▶ **równoległa linia**

parallelogram /ˌpærəˈleləɡræm/ noun [C] a flat shape with four straight sides, the opposite sides being parallel and equal to each other ▶ **równoległobok**

paralyse (US **paralyze**) /ˈpærəlaɪz/ verb [T] **1** to make a person unable to move their body or a part of it: *She is paralysed from the waist down.* ▶ **paraliżować** **2** to make sb/sth unable to work in a normal way ▶ **paraliżować**, **porażać**
■ **paralysis** /pəˈræləsɪs/ noun [U]: *The disease can cause paralysis or even death.* ◇ *There has been complete paralysis of the country's railway system.* ▶ **paraliż**

paramedic /ˌpærəˈmedɪk/ noun [C] a person who has had special training in treating people who are hurt or ill, but who is not a doctor or nurse ▶ **ratownik medyczny**

paramilitary /ˌpærəˈmɪlətri; US -teri/ adj. organized in the same way as, but not belonging to, an official army: *a paramilitary group* ▶ **paramilitarny**

paramount /ˈpærəmaʊnt/ adj. (formal) most important: *Safety is paramount in car design.* ▶ **najważniejszy**

paranoia /ˌpærəˈnɔɪə/ noun [U] **1** a type of mental illness in which you wrongly believe that other people want to harm you ▶ **paranoja** **2** (informal) a feeling that other people want to harm you or are saying bad things about you, when you have no evidence for this ▶ **paranoiczny lęk/podejrzliwość** ℹ Zwróć uwagę, że **paranoia** nie znaczy „zwariowana sytuacja, wariackie zachowanie".

paranoid /ˈpærənɔɪd/ adj. wrongly believing that other people are trying to harm you or are saying bad things about you ▶ **paranoidalny**, **paranoiczny**

paraphernalia /ˌpærəfəˈneɪliə/ noun [U] a large number of different objects that you need for a particular purpose ▶ **sprzęt**, **przybory**

paraphrase /ˈpærəfreɪz/ verb [T] to express sth again using different words so that it is easier to understand ▶ **parafrazować**
■ **paraphrase** noun [C] ▶ **parafraza**

parasite /ˈpærəsaɪt/ noun [C] a plant or an animal that lives in or on another plant or animal and gets its food from it ▶ **pasożyt**

parasol /ˈpærəsɒl/ noun [C] an object that you open and hold over your head to create shade and protect you from the sun ▶ **parasolka** (*od słońca*) ⮕ look at **umbrella**

paratroops /ˈpærətruːps/ noun [pl.] soldiers who are trained to jump from a plane with a **parachute** ▶ **wojska spadochronowe**

parcel /ˈpɑːsl/ (US also **package**) noun [C] something that is covered in paper or put into a thick envelope and sent or given to sb ▶ **paczka**, **pakunek** ⮕ look at **pack**, **package**, **packet**

> **Parcel** (w USA **package**) oznacza paczkę wysyłaną pocztą. **Package** ma podobne znaczenie, ale jest to zwykle paczka doręczana osobiście. **Packet** (w USA **pack**) oznacza jedną lub kilka rzeczy, w specjalnym opakowaniu, przeznaczonych do sprzedaży. **Pack** oznacza rozmaite rzeczy sprzedawane razem: *The pack contains needles and a pair of scissors.* **Packaging** oznacza wszelki materiał (np. pudełko, torba) używany do zapakowania sprzedawanego towaru.

PHR V **parcel sth out** to divide sth into parts or between several people: *The land was parcelled out into small lots.* ▶ **rozdzielać coś**
parcel sth up to wrap sth up into a parcel ▶ **paczkować** (*towar*)

parched /pɑːtʃt/ adj. very hot and dry, or very thirsty: *Can I have a drink? I'm parched!* ▶ **spieczony**; **wysuszony (na pieprz)**; **bardzo spragniony**

parchment /ˈpɑːtʃmənt/ noun **1** [U] material made from the skin of a sheep or **goat**, used in the past for writing on: *parchment scrolls* ▶ **pergamin** **2** [U] a thick yellowish type of paper: *a sheet of non-stick baking parchment* ▶ **pergamin** **3** [C] a document written on a piece of **parchment** ▶ **pergamin**

pardon[1] /ˈpɑːdn/ (also ˌ**pardon ˈme**) interj. **1** (used for asking sb to repeat what they have just said because you did not hear or understand it) ▶ **słucham?**

> **I beg your pardon** to formalny zwrot oznaczający „przepraszam": *Oh, I do beg your pardon. I had no idea this was your seat.*

2 (used by some people to mean *sorry* or *excuse me*) ▶ **przepraszam!**

pardon[2] /ˈpɑːdn/ noun [C,U] an official decision not to punish sb for a crime ▶ **akt łaski**
■ **pardon** verb [T] **pardon sb (for sth/doing sth)** ▶ **darować** (*winę*), **wybaczać** | **pardonable** /ˈpɑːdnəbl/ adj. that can be forgiven or excused ▶ **wybaczalny**

pare /peə(r)/ verb [T] **1** **pare sth (off/away)** to remove the thin outer layer of a piece of fruit: *First, pare the skin away.* ◇ *She pared the apple.* ▶ **obierać ze skórki** **2** **pare sth (back/down)** to gradually reduce the size or amount: *The training budget has been pared back to a minimum.* ◇ *The workforce has been* ***pared to the bone*** (została zredukowana do absolutnego minimum). ▶ **redukować**

parent /ˈpeərənt/ noun [C] **1** sb's mother or father: *He's still living with his parents.* ◇ *a single parent* samotna matka/samotny ojciec ◇ *a foster parent* przybrana matka/przybrany ojciec ▶ **matka lub ojciec 2** a company that owns smaller companies of the same type: *a parent company* ▶ **firma macierzysta**

parental /pəˈrentl/ adj. [only before a noun] of a parent or parents: *parental support/advice* ▶ **rodzicielski**

parenthesis /pəˈrenθəsɪs/ (pl. **parentheses** /-siːz/) (especially US) = BRACKET[1] (1)

IDM **in parenthesis** as an extra comment or piece of information ▶ **w nawiasie**

parenthetical /ˌpærənˈθetɪkl/ (also **parenthetic** /-ɪk/) adj. [usually before a noun] (formal) given as extra information in a speech or piece of writing: *parenthetical remarks* ▶ **wtrącony mimochodem**

■ **parenthetically** /-kli/ adv. ▶ **mimochodem**

parenthood /ˈpeərənthʊd/ noun [U] the state of being a parent ▶ **stan rodzicielski**

pariah /pəˈraɪə/ noun [C] a person who is not acceptable to society and is avoided by everyone ▶ **parias** SYN **outcast**

parish /ˈpærɪʃ/ noun [C] **1** an area or district which has its own church; the people who live in this area: *the parish church* ▶ **parafia**; **parafianie 2** (in England) a small area which has its own local government ▶ **obszar administracyjny**

■ **parishioner** /pəˈrɪʃənə(r)/ noun [C] ▶ **parafian-in/ka**

ˌparish ˈcouncil noun [C, with sing. or pl. verb] a division of local government which looks after the interests of a very small area, especially a village ▶ **rada parafialna** ➲ look at **local government**, **local authority**

parity /ˈpærəti/ noun (pl. **-ies**) **1** [U] **parity (with sb/sth)**; **parity (between A and B)** (formal) the state of being equal, especially the state of having equal pay or status: *Prison officers are demanding pay parity with the police force.* ▶ **równość (z kimś/czymś, między A i B) 2** [U,C] the fact of the units of money of two different countries being equal: *to achieve parity with the dollar* ▶ **parytet**

park[1] /pɑːk/ noun [C] **1** an open area in a town, often with grass or trees, where people can go to walk, play, etc.: *Let's go for a walk in the park.* ▶ **park 2** [in compounds] a large area of land that is used for a special purpose: *a national park* ◇ *a business park* ◇ *a theme park* ▶ **park 3** (in Britain) the land that surrounds and belongs to a large country house ▶ **park** (*pałacowy*) **4** (US) a sports ground or field ▶ **kompleks sportowy**

park[2] /pɑːk/ verb [I,T] to leave the vehicle that you are driving somewhere for period a time: *It's very expensive to park in the centre of town.* ◇ *Somebody's parked their car in front of the exit.* ▶ **parkować**

parka /ˈpɑːkə/ noun [C] a warm jacket or coat with a **hood** ▶ **kurtka z kapturem**

parking /ˈpɑːkɪŋ/ noun [U] the act of leaving a car, lorry, etc. somewhere for a time: *The sign said 'No Parking'* (parkowanie zabronione). ▶ **parkowanie**

> A place where many cars can be parked and left is called a **car park**. A place where one car can be parked is called a **parking space**. If you **park** where you are not allowed to, a **traffic warden** might give you a **parking ticket**.

ˈparking brake (US) = HANDBRAKE

ˈparking garage (US) = MULTI-STOREY CAR PARK

ˈparking lot (US) = CAR PARK

ˈparking meter noun [C] a metal post that you put coins into to pay for parking a car in the space beside it for a period of time ▶ **parkometr**

ˈparking ticket noun [C] a piece of paper that orders you to pay money as a punishment for parking your car where it is not allowed ▶ **mandat za parkowanie w miejscu niedozwolonym**

parliament /ˈpɑːləmənt/ noun **1** [C, with sing. or pl. verb] the group of people who are elected to make and change the laws of a country: *the German parliament* ▶ **parlament 2** (**Parliament**) [sing., with sing. or pl. verb] the parliament of the United Kingdom: *a Member of Parliament (MP)* ◇ *the Houses of Parliament* Izby Parlamentu ▶ **Parlament (brytyjski)**

> Parlament brytyjski składa się z **the House of Commons** i **the House of Lords. House of Commons** składa się z posłów i posłanek do parlamentu, wybranych w celu reprezentowania różnych okręgów kraju (zwanych **constituencies**). **House of Lords** składa się z osób pochodzenia arystokratycznego, biskupów kościoła anglikańskiego i innych mianowanych, nieobieralnych osób.

parliamentarian /ˌpɑːləmənˈteəriən/ noun [C] a member of a parliament, especially one with a lot of skill and experience ▶ **parlamentarzyst(k)a**

parliamentary /ˌpɑːləˈmentri/ adj. [only before a noun] connected with parliament ▶ **parlamentarny**

parochial /pəˈrəʊkiəl/ adj. **1** [usually before a noun] (formal) connected with a church **parish**: *parochial schools* ▶ **parafialny 2** only concerned with small issues that happen in your local area and not interested in more important things: *They need to be better informed and less parochial in their thinking.* ▶ **prowincjonalny**

■ **parochialism** /-ɪzəm/ noun [U]: *the parochialism of a small community* ▶ **prowincjonalizm**

parody /ˈpærədi/ noun [C,U] (pl. **parodies**) **1** a piece of writing, speech or music that copies the style of sb/sth in a funny way: *a parody of a spy novel* ▶ **parodia 2** a very bad example or copy (of sth) ▶ **parodia**

■ **parody** verb [T] (**parodying**; **parodies**; pt, pp **parodied**) ▶ **parodiować**

parole /pəˈrəʊl/ noun [U] permission that is given to a prisoner to leave prison early on the condition that he or she behaves well: *He's going to be released **on parole**.* ▶ **zwolnienie warunkowe** (*z więzienia*)

parquet /ˈpɑːkeɪ; US pɑːrˈkeɪ/ noun [U] a floor covering made of flat pieces of wood fixed together in a pattern: *a parquet floor* ◇ *parquet flooring* ▶ **parkiet**

parrot /ˈpærət/ noun [C] a type of tropical bird with a curved beak and usually with very bright feathers. **Parrots** that are kept as pets can be trained to copy what people say. ▶ **papuga**

ˈparrot-fashion adv. without understanding the meaning of something: *to learn something parrot-fashion* ▶ **jak papuga**

parsley /ˈpɑːsli/ noun [U] a **herb** with small curly leaves that is used in cooking or for decorating food ▶ **pietruszka**, **natka** ➲ picture on **page A12**

parsnip /ˈpɑːsnɪp/ noun [C] a long thin white vegetable, that grows under the ground ▶ **pasternak** ➲ picture on **page A13**

part[1] /pɑːt/ noun **1** [U] **part of sth** some, but not all of sth: *Part of the problem is lack of information.* ◇ *Part of the building was destroyed in the fire.* ▶ **część** ➲ note at **area 2** [C] one of the pieces, areas, periods, things, etc. that together with others forms the whole of sth: *Which part of Spain do you come from?* ◇ *The film is good **in parts**.* ◇ *a part of the body* ◇ *I enjoy being part of a team.* ▶ **część 3** (**parts**) [pl.] (old-fashioned, informal) a region or area: *Are you from these parts?* ▶ **strona**, **okolica** ➲ note at **area 4** [C] a section of a book, TV series, etc.: *You can see part two of this series at the same time next week.* ▶ **część**; **odcinek 5** [C] a role or character in a play, film, etc.: *He played the*

P

part of Macbeth. ◇ *I had a small part in the school play.* ▶ **rola** **6** [C] an amount or quantity (of a liquid or substance): *Use one part cleaning fluid to ten parts water.* Zmieszać płyn do czyszczenia z wodą w proporcji jeden do dziesięciu. ▶ **część** **7** [C,U] **part (in sth)** a person's share in an activity, event, etc.: *Did you have any part in the decision?* ▶ **udział** **8** one of the essential pieces that make up a machine: ***spare parts*** (części zamienne) *for a car* ▶ **część składowa**

IDM **the best/better part of sth** most of sth; more than half of sth, especially a period of time: *They've lived here for the best part of* (prawie od) *forty years.* ▶ **przeważająca część**

for the most part → MOST[1]

for my, his, their, etc. part in my, his, their, etc. opinion; personally ▶ **co do mnie/ciebie itp.**

have/play a part (in sth) to be involved in sth ▶ **odgrywać rolę (w czymś)**

in part not completely: *The accident was, in part, the fault of the driver.* ▶ **częściowo**

on the part of sb/on sb's part made, done or felt by sb: *There is concern on the part of the teachers that class sizes will increase.* ◇ *I'm sorry. It was a mistake on my part.* ▶ **z czyjejś strony**

take part (in sth) to join with other people in an activity: *We all took part in the discussion.* ▶ **uczestniczyć**

part[2] /pɑːt/ verb **1** [I,T] (formal) **part (sb) (from sb)** to leave or go away from sb; to separate people or things: *We exchanged telephone numbers when we parted.* ◇ *He hates being parted from his children for long.* ▶ **rozstawać się (z kimś)**; **rozłączać kogoś (z kimś)** **2** [I,T] to move apart; to make things or people move apart: *Her lips were slightly parted.* ▶ **rozdzielać (się)**, **rozsuwać (się)** **3** [T] to separate the hair on your head so as to make a clear line that goes from the back of your head to the front: *She parts her hair in the middle.* ▶ **czesać się z przedziałkiem** ➲ look at **parting**

IDM **part company (with sb/sth)** to go different ways or to separate after being together ▶ **rozstawać się**

PHR V **part with sth** to give or sell sth to sb: *When we went to live in Italy, we had to part with our horses.* ▶ **rozstawać się z czymś**

part[3] /pɑːt/ adv. not completely one thing and not completely another: *She's part Russian and part Chinese.* ▶ **częściowo**

ˌpart exˈchange noun [U] a way of buying sth, such as a car, in which you give your old one as some of the payment for a more expensive one ▶ **system sprzedaży, w którym w rozliczeniu przyjmuje się używany sprzęt** (*np.samochód*)

partial /ˈpɑːʃl/ adj. **1** not complete: *The project was only a partial success.* ▶ **częściowy** **2** **partial to sb/sth** (old-fashioned) liking sb/sth very much: *He's very partial to ice cream.* ▶ **mający słabość do czegoś**, **mający sentyment do kogoś/czegoś**

■ **partially** /-ʃəli/ adv. ▶ **częściowo**

partiality /ˌpɑːʃiˈæləti/ noun [U] (formal) the unfair support of one person, team, etc. above another: *The referee was accused of partiality towards the home team.* ▶ **stronniczość** OPP **impartiality** ➲ look at **impartial**

participant /pɑːˈtɪsɪpənt/ noun [C] a person who takes part in sth ▶ **uczestni-k/czka**

participate /pɑːˈtɪsɪpeɪt/ verb [I] **participate (in sth)** to take part or become involved in sth: *Students are encouraged to participate in the running of the college.* ▶ **uczestniczyć**

■ **participation** /pɑːˌtɪsɪˈpeɪʃn/ noun [U] ▶ **uczestnictwo**

participle /pɑːˈtɪsɪpl/ noun [C] a word that is formed from a verb and that ends in *-ing* (present participle) or *-ed*, *-en*, etc. (past participle). Participles are used to form tenses of the verb, or as adjectives: *'Hurrying' and 'hurried' are the present and past participles* (to imiesłowy czasu teraźniejszego i przeszłego) *of 'hurry'.* ▶ **imiesłów**

particle /ˈpɑːtɪkl/ noun [C] **1** a very small piece: *dust particles* ▶ **cząstka**, **odrobina** **2** a small word that is not as important as a noun, verb or adjective: *In the phrasal verb 'break down', 'down' is an adverbial particle.* ▶ **partykuła**

⚷ **particular** /pəˈtɪkjələ(r)/ adj. **1** [only before a noun] (used to emphasize that you are talking about one person, thing, time, etc. and not about others): *Is there any particular dish you enjoy making?* ◇ *At that particular time* (w tym właśnie czasie) *I was working in London.* ▶ **szczególny**, **konkretny** **2** connected with one person or thing and not with others: *Everybody has their own particular* (swoje własne) *problems.* ▶ **indywidualny**, **osobisty** **3** [only before a noun] greater than usual; special: *Are you going to Dublin for any particular reason* (z jakiegoś specjalnego powodu)*?* ◇ *This article is of particular interest to me.* ▶ **szczególny** **4** [not before a noun] **particular (about/over sth)** difficult to please: *Some people are extremely particular about what they eat.* ▶ **wybredny**, **wymagający** ➲ look at **fussy**

IDM **in particular** **1** especially: *Is there **anything in particular** you'd like to do tomorrow?* ▶ **w szczególności** **2** (used for giving more detail about sth that you have said): *You must be careful about what you eat. In particular, avoid anything fatty.* ▶ **szczególnie**

⚷ **particularly** /pəˈtɪkjələli/ adv. especially; more than usual or more than others: *I'm particularly interested in Indian history.* ◇ *The match was excellent, particularly the second half.* ▶ **szczególnie**, **zwłaszcza**

particulars /pəˈtɪkjələz/ noun [pl.] (formal) facts or details about sb/sth: *The police took down all the particulars about the missing child.* ▶ **szczegóły**, **dokładne dane**

parting /ˈpɑːtɪŋ/ noun **1** [C,U] saying goodbye to, or being separated from, another person (usually for quite a long time) ▶ **rozstanie** **2** [C] the line in sb's hair where it is divided in two with a **comb**: *a side/centre parting* ▶ **przedziałek** ➲ look at **part**

partisan[1] /ˌpɑːtɪˈzæn; ˈpɑːtɪzæn; US ˈpɑːrtəzn/ adj. showing too much support for one person, group or idea, especially without considering it carefully: *Most newspapers are politically partisan.* ▶ **stronniczy** SYN **one-sided**

partisan[2] /ˈpɑːtɪzæn; US -təzn/ noun [C] **1** a person who strongly supports a particular leader, group or idea ▶ **zwolenni-k/czka** SYN **follower** **2** a member of an armed group that is fighting secretly against enemy soldiers who have taken control of its country ▶ **partyzant/ka**

partition /pɑːˈtɪʃn/ noun **1** [C] something that divides a room, office, etc. into two or more parts, especially a thin or temporary wall ▶ **przepierzenie** **2** [U] the division of a country into two or more countries: *the three partitions of Poland* ▶ **podział**, **rozbiór** (*państwa*)

■ **partition** verb [T] ▶ **dzielić**, **parcelować**

PHR V **partition sth off** to separate one area, one part of a room, etc. from another with a wall or screen ▶ **przedzielać coś**

⚷ **partly** /ˈpɑːtli/ adv. not completely: *She was only partly responsible for the mistake.* ▶ **częściowo**

⚷ **partner** /ˈpɑːtnə(r)/ noun [C] **1** the person that you are married to or live with as if you are married: *a marriage partner* ▶ **małżon-ek/ka**, **towarzysz/ka życia** **2** one of the people who owns a business: *business partners* ▶ **wspólni-k/czka** **3** a person that you are doing an activity with as a team, for example dancing or playing a game: *a tennis partner* ▶ **partner/ka** **4** a country or organization that has an agreement with another: *Britain's EU partners* ▶ **partner** (*kraj/organizacja*)

■ **partner** verb [T]: *Hales partnered his brother in the doubles, and they won the gold medal.* ▶ **być partnerem/ką**

partnership /ˈpɑːtnəʃɪp/ noun **1** [U] the state of being a partner in business: *Simona went into partnership* (zawiązała spółkę) *with her sister and opened a shop in Rome.* ▶ **współudział 2** [C] a relationship between two people, organizations, etc.: *Marriage is a partnership for life.* ▶ **partnerstwo 3** [C] a business owned by two or more people: *a junior member of the partnership* ▶ **spółka**

ˌ**part of ˈspeech** noun [C] one of the groups that words are divided into, for example noun, verb, adjective, etc. ▶ **część mowy**

partridge /ˈpɑːtrɪdʒ/ noun [C] (pl. **partridges** or **partridge**) a wild bird hunted for food or sport. Partridges have brown feathers, round bodies and short tails. ▶ **kuropatwa**

ˌ**part-ˈtime** adj., adv. for only a part of the working day or week: *She's got a part-time job.* ◇ *I work part-time, about 20 hours a week.* ▶ (*praca*) **w niepełnym wymiarze godzin** ➲ look at **full-time**

party /ˈpɑːti/ noun [C] (pl. **parties**) **1** (also **Party**) a group of people who have the same political aims and ideas and who are trying to win elections to parliament, etc.: *Which party are you going to vote for in the next election?* ▶ **partia** (*polityczna*) ➲ note at **politics**

> The two main political parties in Great Britain are **the Labour Party** (traditionally left-wing) and **the Conservative** (or **Tory**) **Party** (right-wing). Other parties that have had some success in local politics are **the Liberal Democrats** and **the Green Party**. In the United States the main political parties are the **Republicans** and the **Democrats**.

2 a social occasion to which people are invited in order to eat, drink and enjoy themselves: *When we've moved into our new house we're going to* ***have a party.*** ◇ *I'm going to a* ***birthday party*** *tonight.* ◇ *I've been invited to a* ***dinner party*** (na proszoną kolację). ◇ *As Julia's leaving, we're arranging a* ***farewell party*** (przyjęcie pożegnalne). ◇ *a house-warming party* parapetówka ◇ *a garden party* przyjęcie w ogrodzie ▶ **przyjęcie**, **prywatka 3** a group of people who are working, travelling, etc. together: *a party of tourists* ▶ **grupa**, **zespół 4** (formal) one of the people or groups of people involved in a legal case: *the guilty/innocent party* ▶ **strona** (*np. umowy, sporu*) ➲ look at **third party**

pass[1] /pɑːs; US pæs/ verb **1** [I,T] to move past or to the other side of sb/sth: *The street was crowded and the two buses couldn't pass.* ◇ *I passed him in the street but he didn't say hello.* ◇ (figurative) *The number of children at the school has passed 50.* ▶ **mijać (się)**, **przechodzić (przez coś/obok czegoś)**; **przekraczać** (*np. liczbę*)

> Czas przeszły **passed** brzmi identycznie jak słowo **past**, które może być przymiotnikiem lub przyimkiem: *The summer months passed slowly.* ◇ *The past week was very hot.* ◇ *Our house is just past the church.*

2 [I,T] **pass (sth) along, down, through, etc. (sth)** to go or move, or make sth move, in the direction mentioned: *A plane passed overhead.* ◇ *We'll have to pass the wire through the window.* ▶ **przemieszczać się (w jakimś kierunku)**; **przesuwać (przez coś)**, **prowadzić 3** [T] **pass sth (to sb)** to give sth to sb: *Could you pass (me) the salt, please?* ▶ **podawać 4** [I,T] **pass (sth) (to sb)** to kick, hit or throw the ball to sb on your own team: *He passed (the ball) to Owen.* ▶ **podawać piłkę 5** [I] to go by: *At least a year has passed since I last saw them.* ◇ *It was a long journey but the time passed very quickly.* ▶ (*czas*) **mijać 6** [T] to spend time, especially when you are bored or waiting for sth: *I'll have to think of something to do to pass the time in hospital.* ▶ **zabijać czas 7** [I,T] to achieve the necessary standard in an exam, test, etc.: *Good luck in the exam! I'm sure you'll pass.* ▶ **zdać** (*egzamin*) OPP **fail** ⓘ Zwróć uwagę, że **do/sit/take an exam** znaczy „zdawać egzamin". **8** [T] to test sb/sth and say that he/she/it is good enough: *The examiner passed most of the students.* ▶ **przepuszczać**, **zatwierdzać (kogoś) 9** [T] to officially approve a law, etc. by voting: *One of the functions of Parliament is to* ***pass*** *new* ***laws.*** ▶ **uchwalać** (*np. ustawę*) **10** [I] to be allowed or accepted: *I didn't like what he was saying but I* ***let it pass.*** ▶ **być dozwolonym/dopuszczonym 11** [T] **pass sth (on sb/sth)** to give an opinion, judgement, etc.: *The judge* ***passed sentence*** *on the young man.* ▶ **wydawać**

IDM **pass the buck (to sb)** to make sb else responsible for a difficult situation ▶ **zrzucać odpowiedzialność (na kogoś)**

pass water (formal) to get rid of waste liquid from your body ▶ **oddawać mocz**

PHR V **pass sth around/round** (Brit.) to give sth to another person, who gives it to sb else, etc. until everyone has seen it: *Can you pass these pictures around for everyone to look at, please?* ▶ **puszczać coś obiegiem**

pass as sb/sth = PASS FOR/AS SB/STH

pass away (used as a polite way of saying 'die') ▶ **umierać**, **odchodzić**

pass by (sb/sth) to go past: *I pass by your house on the way to work.* ▶ **przechodzić/przejeżdżać (przez coś/obok czegoś)**

pass sth down to give or teach sth to people who will live after you have died ▶ **przekazywać (w spadku)**

pass for/as sb/sth to be accepted as sb/sth that he/she/it is not: *His mother looks so young she'd pass for his sister.* ▶ **uchodzić za kogoś**; **być postrzeganym jako coś**

pass sb/yourself/sth off (as sb/sth) to say that a person or a thing is sth that he/she/it is not: *He tried to pass the work off as his own.* ▶ **podawać kogoś/się/coś (za kogoś/coś)**

pass sth on (to sb) to give sth to sb else, especially after you have been given it or used it yourself: *Could you pass the message on to Mr Roberts?* ▶ **przekazać dalej (komuś)**

pass out to become unconscious ▶ **zemdleć** SYN **faint** OPP **come round**

pass[2] /pɑːs; US pæs/ noun [C] **1** a successful result in an exam: *The pass mark is 50%.* ◇ *Grades A, B and C are passes.* ▶ **pozytywny wynik egzaminu** OPP **fail 2** an official piece of paper that gives you permission to enter or leave a building, travel on a bus or train, etc.: *Show your student pass when you buy a ticket.* ◇ *Which towns do we pass through* (przez jakie miasta przejeżdżamy) *on the way to Bath?* ◇ *You pass over a bridge* (przechodzisz przez most) *and then the pub is on the right.* ▶ **przepustka**; **bilet okresowy 3** the act of kicking, hitting or throwing the ball to sb on your own team in some sports ▶ **podanie piłki 4** a road or way over or through mountains: *a mountain pass* ▶ **przełęcz**

passable /ˈpɑːsəbl; US ˈpæs-/ adj. **1** good enough but not very good: *My French is not brilliant but it's passable.* ▶ **dostateczny 2** [not before a noun] (used about roads, rivers, etc.) possible to use or cross; not blocked ▶ **jezdny**, **(możliwy) do przebycia** OPP **impassable**

passage /ˈpæsɪdʒ/ noun **1** [C] (also **passageway** /ˈpæsɪdʒweɪ/) a long, narrow way with walls on either side that connects one place with another: *a secret underground passage* ▶ **korytarz**, **przejście 2** [C] a tube in your body which air, liquid, etc. can pass through: *the nasal passages* kanał nosowy ▶ **przewód 3** [C] a short part of a book, a speech or a piece of music: *The students were given a passage from the novel to study.* ▶ **ustęp 4** [sing.] the process of passing: *We watched the ants slow passage*

P

across the road. ◇ *The team have had an easy passage* (łatwo przeszła) *to the final.* ◇ *His painful memories faded with **the passage of time*** (z upływem czasu). ▶ **przemieszczanie się 5** [C] a route by sea or a journey by ship ▶ **podróż**

passenger /ˈpæsɪndʒə(r)/ noun [C] a person who is travelling in a car, bus, train, plane, etc. but who is not driving it or working on it ▶ **pasażer/ka**

ˌpasser-ˈby noun [C] (pl. **passers-by**) a person who is walking past sb/sth ▶ **przechodzień**

passing¹ /ˈpɑːsɪŋ; US ˈpæs-/ noun [U] the process of going by: *the passing of time* ▶ **upływ**; **mijanie**

IDM **in passing** done or said quickly, while you are thinking or talking about sth else: *He mentioned the house in passing but he didn't give any details.* ▶ **mimochodem**, **przy okazji**

passing² /ˈpɑːsɪŋ; US ˈpæs-/ adj. [only before a noun] **1** lasting for only a short time: *a passing phase/thought/interest* ▶ **przemijający**, **przejściowy** SYN **brief 2** going past: *I stopped a passing car and asked for help.* ▶ **przejeżdżający**, **przechodzący**, **przepływający**

passion /ˈpæʃn/ noun **1** [C,U] (a) very strong feeling, especially of love, hate or anger: *He was a very violent man, controlled by his passions.* ▶ **namiętność 2** [sing.] **a passion (for sb)** very strong sexual love or attraction: *He longed to tell Sashi of his passion for her.* ▶ **pasja 3** [sing.] **a passion for sth** a very strong liking for or interest in sth: *He has a passion for history.* ▶ **pasja**

passionate /ˈpæʃənət/ adj. **1** showing or feeling very strong love or sexual attraction: *a passionate kiss* ▶ **namiętny 2** showing or caused by very strong feelings: *The President gave a passionate speech about crime.* ▶ **żarliwy**

■ **passionately** adv.: *He believes passionately in democracy.* ▶ **namiętnie**; **żarliwie**

passive /ˈpæsɪv/ adj. **1** showing no reaction, feeling or interest; not active: *Some people prefer to play a passive role in meetings.* ▶ **bierny 2** (used about the form of a verb or a sentence when the subject of the sentence is affected by the act of the verb): *In the sentence 'He was bitten by a dog', the verb is passive.* ℹ Można też powiedzieć **the verb is in the passive.** ▶ **w stronie biernej** ➲ look at **active**

■ **passively** adv. ▶ **biernie**

ˌpassive ˈsmoking noun [U] the act of breathing in smoke from other people's cigarettes ▶ **bierne palenie**

Passover /ˈpɑːsəʊvə(r); US ˈpæs-/ noun [sing.] the most important Jewish festival, which takes place in spring and lasts seven or eight days ▶ (*w religii żydowskiej*) **święto Paschy**

passport /ˈpɑːspɔːt; US ˈpæs-/ noun [C] **1** an official document that identifies you as a citizen of a particular country and that you have to show when you enter or leave a country: *You have to go through passport control at the airport.* ▶ **paszport**

> You **apply for** or **renew** your passport at the **passport office**. This office **issues** new passports.

2 a passport to sth a thing that makes it possible to achieve sth: *a passport to success* ▶ **paszport**, **przepustka** (*np. do sławy*)

password /ˈpɑːswɜːd/ noun [C] **1** a secret word or phrase that you need to know in order to be allowed into a place ▶ **tajne hasło 2** a series of letters or numbers that you must type into a computer or computer system in order to be able to use it: *Please enter your password.* ▶ **hasło do komputera**

past¹ /pɑːst; US pæst/ adj. **1** [only before a noun] just finished; last: *He's had to work very hard during the past year.* ▶ **ubiegły**, **ostatni 2** already gone; belonging to a time before the present: *in past centuries/times* ◇ *I'd rather forget some of my past mistakes.* ▶ **miniony**, **przeszły**

past² /pɑːst; US pæst/ noun **1** (**the past**) [sing.] the time that has gone by; things that happened in an earlier time: *the **recent/distant past*** ◇ *Writing letters seems to be **a thing of the past**.* ▶ **przeszłość 2** [C] sb's life or career before now: *We don't know anything about his past.* ▶ **przeszłość 3** (**the past**; **the ˌpast ˈtense**) [sing.] the form of a verb used to describe actions in the past: *The past tense of 'take' is 'took'.* ▶ **czas przeszły**

past³ /pɑːst; US pæst/ prep. **1** (used when telling the time) after; later than: *It's ten (minutes) past three.* ◇ *It was past midnight when we got home.* ◇ *It's a quarter past seven.* Jest kwadrans po siódmej. ▶ **po** (*danej godzinie*) **2** from one side to the other of sb/sth; further than or on the other side of sb/sth: *He walked straight past me.* ◇ *She looked right past me without realizing who I was.* ▶ **obok**, **przed**; **za 3** above or further than a certain point, limit or age: *Unemployment is now past the 2 million mark.* ◇ *I'm so tired that I'm **past caring** what we eat* (jest mi wszystko jedno, co będziemy jeść). ◇ *She was past the age* (przekroczyła już wiek) *when she could have children.* ▶ **poza (czasem/wiekiem na robienie czegoś)**; (*wiek*) **po**

IDM **not put it past sb (to do sth)** [used with *would*] to think sb is capable of doing sth bad: *I wouldn't put it past him to do a thing like that.* ▶ **uważać, że ktoś jest zdolny do zrobienia czegoś złego**

past it (informal) too old: *I don't think I'll go skiing this year. I'm afraid I'm past it.* Obawiam się, że to już nie dla mnie. ▶ **za stary** (*na coś*)

■ **past** adv. **1** by; from one side of sb/sth to another: *He waved as he drove past.* ▶ **obok**, **mimo 2** (used to describe time passing): *A week went past* (minął) *and nothing had changed.*

pasta /ˈpæstə; US ˈpɑːstə/ noun [U] an Italian food made from flour, water and sometimes eggs, formed into different shapes, cooked, and usually served with a sauce ▶ **makaron** ℹ Rzeczownik **pasta** jest niepoliczalny. Do wyrażenia lp używamy konstrukcji **a bit of pasta** (a nie ~~a pasta~~). ➲ picture on **page A14**

ˌpast ˈcontinuous noun [sing.] the tense of a verb that describes an action that was happening when sth else happened ▶ **czas przeszły ciągły**

paste¹ /peɪst/ noun **1** [C,U] a soft, wet mixture, usually made of a powder and a liquid and sometimes used for sticking things: *wallpaper paste* ◇ *Mix the flour and milk into a paste.* ▶ **masa klejąca** (*np. do tapet*) **2** [U] [in compounds] a soft mixture of food that you can spread onto bread, etc.: *fish/chicken paste* ▶ **pasta (spożywcza)**

paste² /peɪst/ verb [T] **1** to stick sth to sth else using **paste**: *He pasted the picture into his book.* ▶ **wklejać**, **przyklejać 2** (in computing) to copy or move text into a document from somewhere else: *This function allows you to **cut and paste** text.* ▶ **wklejać**

pastel /ˈpæstl; US pæˈstel/ adj. (used about colours) pale; not strong ▶ **pastelowy**

pasteurized (also **-ised**) /ˈpɑːstʃəraɪzd/ adj. (used about milk or cream) free from bacteria because it has been heated and then cooled ▶ **pasteryzowany**

pastime /ˈpɑːstaɪm; US ˈpæs-/ noun [C] something that you enjoy doing when you are not working ▶ **rozrywka** SYN **hobby**

pastoral /ˈpɑːstərəl; US ˈpæs-/ adj. **1** (connected with the work of a priest or a teacher) giving help and advice on personal matters rather than on matters of religion or education ▶ **duszpasterski**, **pastoralny 2** connected with pleasant country life ▶ **sielski**, **wiejski**

ˌpast ˈparticiple noun [C] the form of the verb that ends in *-ed*, *-en*, etc. ▶ **imiesłów czasu przeszłego**

ˌ**past ˈperfect** (also **pluperfect** /ˌpluːˈpɜːfɪkt/) noun [sing.] the tense of a verb that describes an action that was finished before another event happened ▶ **czas przeszły dokonany**

ˌ**past ˌperfect conˈtinuous** noun [sing.] the tense of a verb that describes an action in the past that continued up until another action happened ▶ **czas przeszły dokonany ciągły**

pastry /ˈpeɪstri/ noun (pl. **pastries**) **1** [U] a mixture of flour, fat and water that is rolled out flat and cooked as a base or covering for **pies**, etc. ▶ **ciasto 2** [C] a small cake made with **pastry** ▶ **ciastko**, **pasztecik**

pasture /ˈpɑːstʃə(r); US ˈpæs-/ noun [C,U] a field or land covered with grass, where cows, etc. can feed ▶ **pastwisko**

pasty /ˈpæsti/ noun [C] (pl. **pasties**) (Brit.) a small **pie** containing meat and/or vegetables ▶ **pasztecik**

pat[1] /pæt/ verb [T] (**patting**; **patted**) to touch sb/sth gently with a flat hand, especially as a sign of friendship, care, etc. ▶ **poklepywać** ➲ picture at **stroke**

pat[2] /pæt/ noun [C] a gentle friendly touch with a flat hand: *He gave her knee an affectionate pat.* ▶ **głaskanie**, **klepnięcie**

IDM **a pat on the back (for sth/doing sth)** approval for sth good that a person has done: *She deserves a pat on the back for all her hard work.* ▶ **pochwała**

pat[3] /pæt/ adj. [only before a noun] (used about an answer, comment, etc.) said in a quick or simple way that does not sound natural or realistic ▶ **błyskawiczny**, **bez namysłu**

■ **pat** adv. at once; without hesitation: *The answer came back pat.* ▶ **z miejsca**, **od razu**

patch[1] /pætʃ/ noun [C] **1 a patch (of sth)** a part of a surface that is different in some way from the area around it: *Drive carefully. There are patches of ice on the roads.* ◇ *a bald patch* ▶ **płat**, **plama 2** a piece of material that you use to cover a hole in clothes, etc.: *I sewed patches on the knees of my jeans.* ▶ **łata 3** a small piece of cloth that you wear over one eye, usually because the eye is damaged ▶ **przepaska 4** a small piece of land, especially for growing vegetables or fruit: *a vegetable patch* ▶ **zagon**, **grządka**

IDM **go through a bad patch** (especially Brit., informal) to experience a difficult or unhappy period of time ▶ **mieć złą passę**

not be a patch on sb/sth (especially Brit., informal) to not be nearly as good as sb/sth: *Her new book isn't a patch on her others.* ▶ **nie umywać się do kogoś/czegoś**

patch[2] /pætʃ/ verb [T] to cover a hole in clothes, etc. with a piece of cloth in order to repair it: *patched jeans* ▶ **łatać**

PHR V **patch sth up 1** to repair sth, especially in a temporary way by adding a new piece of material ▶ **klecić**, **składać do kupy**, **łatać** (*np. dach*) **2** to stop arguing with sb and to be friends again: *Have you tried to **patch things up** with her?* ▶ **załagodzić** (*np. spór*)

patchwork /ˈpætʃwɜːk/ noun [U] a type of sewing in which small pieces of cloth of different colours and patterns are sewn together ▶ **zszywanka** (*z różnych materiałów*), **patchwork**

patchy /ˈpætʃi/ adj. **1** existing or happening in some places but not others: *patchy* (lokaln-y/a) *clouds/rain/fog* ◇ *The grass was dry and patchy* (i rosła nierówno). ▶ **nierównomierny 2** (used about your knowledge of sth) not complete; (used about a performance, etc.) good in some parts but not in others: *My knowledge of German is rather patchy.* ▶ **niejednolity**, **fragmentaryczny**

pâté /ˈpæteɪ; US pɑːˈteɪ/ noun [U] food that is made by making meat, fish or vegetables into a smooth, thick mixture that is served cold and spread on bread, etc.: *liver pâté* ▶ **pasztet**

patella = KNEECAP

patent[1] /ˈpætnt; ˈpeɪtnt/ noun [C,U] the official right to be the only person to make, use or sell a new product; the document that proves this ▶ **patent**

■ **patent** verb [T] ▶ **patentować**

patent[2] /ˈpeɪtnt/ adj. [only before a noun] (formal) clear; obvious: *a patent lie* ▶ **jawny**, **bezsporny**

■ **patently** adv. ▶ **bezspornie**, **najwyraźniej**

ˌ**patent ˈleather** noun [U] a type of leather with a hard, shiny surface, used especially for making shoes and bags ▶ **skóra lakierowana**

paternal /pəˈtɜːnl/ adj. **1** behaving as a father would behave; connected with being a father ▶ **ojcowski 2** [only before a noun] related through the father's side of the family: *my paternal grandparents* ▶ **po ojcu** ➲ look at **maternal**

paternity /pəˈtɜːnəti/ noun [U] the fact of being the father of a child: *paternity leave* ▶ **ojcostwo** ➲ look at **maternity**

🔑 **path** /pɑːθ; US pæθ/ noun [C] **1** a way across a piece of land that is made by or used by people walking: *the garden path* ◇ (figurative) *We're on the path to victory!* Jesteśmy na drodze do zwycięstwa! ▶ **ścieżka** ➲ look at **footpath**

ⓘ **Pathway** ma podobne znaczenie: *There was a narrow pathway leading down the cliff.* **2** the line along which sb/sth moves; the space in front of sb/sth as he/she/it moves: *the **flight path** of an aeroplane* ▶ **droga**, **tor**

pathetic /pəˈθetɪk/ adj. **1** causing you to feel pity or sadness: *the pathetic cries of the hungry children* ▶ **żałosny**, **rozrzewniający 2** (informal) very bad, weak or useless: *What a pathetic performance! The team deserved to lose.* ▶ **żenująco kiepski**

■ **pathetically** /-kli/ adv. ▶ **kiepsko**, **żenująco**

pathological /ˌpæθəˈlɒdʒɪkl/ adj. **1** caused by feelings that you cannot control; not reasonable or sensible: *He's a pathological liar.* ◇ *pathological fear/hatred/violence* ▶ **chorobliwy 2** caused by or connected with disease or illness: *pathological depression* ▶ **patologiczny**; **chorobliwy 3** connected with **pathology** ▶ (*med.*) **patologiczny**

■ **pathologically** /-kli/ adv. ▶ **chorobliwie**; **patologicznie**

pathologist /pəˈθɒlədʒɪst/ noun [C] a doctor who is an expert in **pathology**, and examines dead bodies to find out why a person has died ▶ **patolog**

pathology /pəˈθɒlədʒi/ noun [U] the scientific study of diseases of the body ▶ **patologia**

pathos /ˈpeɪθɒs/ noun [U] (in writing, speech and plays) a quality that produces feelings of sadness and pity: *The scene was full of pathos.* To była bardzo wzruszająca scena. ▶ **smutek**, **tragizm**

🔑 **patience** /ˈpeɪʃns/ noun [U] **1 patience (with sb/sth)** the quality of being able to stay calm and not get angry, especially when there is a difficulty or you have to wait a long time: *I've got no patience with people who don't even try.* ◇ *to **lose patience** with somebody* ▶ **cierpliwość** OPP **impatience 2** (US **solitaire**) a card game for only one player ▶ **pasjans**

🔑 **patient**[1] /ˈpeɪʃnt/ noun [C] a person who is receiving medical treatment: *a hospital patient* ▶ **pacjent/ka** ➲ note at **hospital**

🔑 **patient**[2] /ˈpeɪʃnt/ adj. **patient (with sb/sth)** able to stay calm and not get angry, especially when there is a difficulty or you have to wait a long time: *She's very patient with young children.* ▶ **cierpliwy** OPP **impatient**

■ **patiently** adv.: *She sat patiently waiting for her turn.* ▶ **cierpliwie**

patio /ˈpætiəʊ/ noun [C] (pl. **patios** /-əʊz/) a flat, hard area, usually behind a house, where people can sit, eat, etc. outside ▶ **patio** ➲ look at **balcony**, **terrace**, **veranda**

patriot /ˈpeɪtriət; ˈpæt-/ noun [C] a person who loves their country and is ready to defend it against an enemy ▶ **patriot(k)a**
■ **patriotism** /ˈpeɪtriətɪzəm; ˈpæt-/ noun [U] ▶ **patriotyzm**

patriotic /ˌpeɪtriˈɒtɪk; ˌpæt-/ adj. having or showing great love for your country ▶ **patriotyczny**
■ **patriotically** /-kli/ adv. ▶ **patriotycznie**

patrol[1] /pəˈtrəʊl/ verb [I,T] (**patrolling**; **patrolled**) to go round an area, building, etc. at regular times to make sure that it is safe and that nothing is wrong ▶ **patrolować**

patrol[2] /pəˈtrəʊl/ noun **1** [C,U] the act of going round an area, building, etc. at regular times to make sure that it is safe and that nothing is wrong: *a police car **on patrol** in the area* ▶ **patrol 2** [C] a group of soldiers, vehicles, etc. that **patrol** sth: *a naval/police patrol* ◇ *a patrol car/boat* ▶ **patrol**

patron /ˈpeɪtrən/ noun [C] **1** a person who gives money and support to artists, writers and musicians: *a patron of the arts* ▶ **mecenas/ka sztuki 2** a famous person who supports an organization such as a charity and whose name is used in advertising it ▶ **patron/ka honorow-y/a** ➲ look at **sponsor 3** (formal) a person who uses a particular shop, theatre, restaurant, etc.: *This car park is for patrons only.* ▶ **gość**, **klient/ka**

patronage /ˈpætrənɪdʒ; ˈpeɪt-/ noun [U] the support, especially financial, that is given to a person or an organization by a **patron**: *Patronage of the arts comes from businesses and private individuals.* ▶ **patronat**

patronize (also **-ise**) /ˈpætrənaɪz; US ˈpeɪt-/ verb [T] **1** to treat sb in a way that shows that you think you are better, more intelligent, experienced, etc. than they are ▶ **traktować (kogoś) protekcjonalnie 2** (formal) to be a regular customer of a shop, restaurant, etc. ▶ **(często) chodzić** (*np. do pewnego teatru*)
■ **patronizing** (also **-ising**) adj.: *I hate that patronizing smile of hers.* ▶ **protekcjonalny** | **patronizingly** (also **-isingly**) adv. ▶ **protekcjonalnie**

ˌpatron ˈsaint noun [C] a religious being who is believed by Christians to protect a particular place or people doing a particular activity ▶ **święt-y/a patron/ka**

patter /ˈpætə(r)/ noun [sing.] the sound of many quick light steps or knocks on a surface: *the patter of the children's feet on the stairs* ▶ **tupot**, **stukot**
■ **patter** verb [I] ▶ **stukać**

⚷ **pattern** /ˈpætn; US -tərn/ noun [C] **1** the regular way in which sth happens, develops, or is done: *Her days all seemed to follow the same pattern.* ◇ *changing patterns of behaviour / work / weather* ▶ **schemat 2** a regular arrangement of lines, shapes, colours, etc. as a design: *a shirt with a floral pattern on it* ◇ *Her periods of mental illness all followed the same pattern* (następowały według tego samego schematu). ▶ **wzór**, **deseń** SYN **design 3** a design, a set of instructions or a shape to cut around that you use in order to make sth: *a dress/sewing pattern* ▶ **szablon**, **wykrój**

patterned /ˈpætənd/ adj. decorated with a pattern(2) ▶ **wzorzysty** ➲ picture on **page A1**

⚷ **pause**[1] /pɔːz/ verb [I] **pause (for sth)** to stop talking or doing sth for a short time before continuing ▶ **przerywać**, **robić (krótką) przerwę**

⚷ **pause**[2] /pɔːz/ noun **1** [C] **a pause (in sth)** a short period of time during which sb stops talking or stops what they are doing: *He continued playing for twenty minutes without a pause.* ▶ **przerwa**, **pauza** ➲ note at **interval 2** (also ˈ**pause button**) [U] a control that allows you to stop a CD or tape player, etc. for a short time: *Can you press pause to stop the tape while I go and make a cup of tea?* ▶ **pauza** (*przycisk*)

pave /peɪv/ verb [T, often passive] **pave sth (with sth)** to cover an area of ground with **paving stones** or bricks ▶ **brukować**, **wykładać (czymś)**

pavement /ˈpeɪvmənt/ (US **sidewalk** /ˈsaɪdwɔːk/) noun [C] a hard flat area at the side of a road for people to walk on ▶ **chodnik**

pavilion /pəˈvɪliən/ noun [C] (Brit.) a building at a sports ground where players can change their clothes ▶ **budynek koło placu gry, gdzie zawodnicy przebierają się**

ˈ**paving stone** noun [C] a flat piece of stone that is used for covering the ground ▶ **kamień brukowy**

paw[1] /pɔː/ noun [C] the foot of animals such as dogs, cats, bears, etc. ▶ **łapa** ➲ picture on **page A10**

Paws have sharp **claws** and soft **pads** underneath.

paw[2] /pɔː/ verb [I,T] **paw (at) sth** (used about an animal) to touch or scratch sb/sth several times with a **paw**: *The dog pawed at my sleeve.* ▶ **trącać łapą**

pawn[1] /pɔːn/ noun [C] **1** (in the game of **chess**) one of the eight pieces that are of least value and importance ▶ **pionek 2** a person who is used or controlled by other more powerful people ▶ **pionek (w czyichś rękach)**

pawn[2] /pɔːn/ verb [T] to leave a valuable object with a **pawnbroker**, in return for money. If you cannot pay back the money after a certain period, the object can be sold or kept. ▶ **zastawiać (w lombardzie)**

pawnbroker /ˈpɔːnbrəʊkə(r)/ noun [C] a person who lends money to people when they leave sth of value with them ▶ **osoba pożyczająca pieniądze pod zastaw**, **lichwia-rz/rka**

pawpaw = PAPAYA

⚷ **pay**[1] /peɪ/ verb (pt, pp **paid**) **1** [I,T] **pay (sb) (for sth)**; **pay (sb) sth (for sth)** to give sb money for work, goods, services, etc.: *She is very **well paid**.* Ma bardzo dobrą płacę. ◇ *Do you want to **pay by cheque**, **by credit card** or **in cash*** (czekiem, kartą kredytową czy gotówką)*?* ◇ *The work's finished but we haven't paid for it yet.* ◇ *We paid the dealer £3 000 for the car.* ◇ *to be paid by the hour* otrzymywać zapłatę za godziny ▶ **płacić**, **wypłacać** (*np. pensję*) **2** [T] **pay sth (to sb)** to give the money that you owe for sth: *Have you paid her the rent yet?* ◇ *to pay a bill/fine* ▶ **płacić** (*za coś*), **opłacać** (*rachunki*) **3** [I,T] to make a profit; to be worth doing: *It would pay you to get professional advice before making a decision.* ▶ **opłacać się 4** [I] **pay (for sth)** to suffer or be punished because of your beliefs or actions: *You'll pay for that remark!* ▶ **płacić** (*np. za wyrządzoną krzywdę*)

IDM **charge/pay the earth** → EARTH[1]

pay attention (to sb/sth) to listen carefully to or to take notice of sb/sth ▶ **uważać na kogoś/coś**

pay sb a compliment; **pay a compliment to sb** to say that you like sth about sb ▶ **prawić komuś komplementy**

pay your respects (to sb) (formal) to visit sb as a sign of respect: *Hundreds came to pay their last respects to her* (oddać jej ostatnią posługę). ▶ **składać (komuś) kurtuazyjną wizytę**

pay tribute to sb/sth to say good things about sb/sth and show your respect for sb/sth ▶ **wyrażać komuś uznanie**, **oddawać komuś/czemuś hołd**

put paid to sth to destroy or finish sth: *The bad weather put paid to our picnic.* ▶ **niweczyć/wykańczać coś**

PHR V **pay sb back (for sth)** to punish sb for making you or sb else suffer: *What a mean trick! I'll pay you back one day.* ▶ **odpłacać (się) komuś (za coś)**

pay sth back (to sb) to give money back to sb that you borrowed from them: *Can you lend me £5? I'll pay you back/I'll pay it back to you on Friday.* ▶ **spłacać (komuś)** (*dług*)

pay sth in; pay sth into sth to put money into a bank account: *I paid in a cheque this morning.* ▶ **wpłacać coś**
pay off (informal) to be successful: *All her hard work has paid off! She passed her exam.* ▶ (*coś*) **opłacać się**
pay sb off 1 to pay sb what they have earned and tell them to leave their job ▶ **dać komuś odprawę i zwolnić z pracy 2** (informal) to give sb money to prevent them from doing sth or talking about sth illegal or dishonest that you have done: *All the witnesses had been paid off.* ▶ **płacić komuś za milczenie**
pay sth off to pay all the money that you owe for sth: *to pay off a debt/mortgage* ▶ **spłacać** (*dług, ratę*)
pay up (informal) to pay the money that you owe: *If you don't pay up, we'll take you to court.* ▶ **spłacać, wyrównywać**

pay² /peɪ/ noun [U] money that you get regularly for work that you have done ▶ **płaca, wynagrodzenie, wypłata**

> **pay**
> **Pay** oznacza pieniądze regularnie otrzymywane za pracę. **Wages** wypłaca się cotygodniowo lub codziennie w gotówce. **Salary** wypłaca się co miesiąc na konto bankowe. **Pay rise** to podwyżka płacy. **Income** to dochód otrzymywany z różnych źródeł. **Payment** oznacza zapłatę za pracę jednorazową lub wykonywaną dorywczo. Za usługę profesjonalną, np. wizytę lekarską lub poradę u prawnika, płaci się **fee**. **Tax** to podatek.

payable /ˈpeɪəbl/ adj. [not before a noun] that should or must be paid: *A 10% deposit is payable in advance.* ◇ ***Please make the cheque payable to** Diane Weller.* Proszę wypisać czek na Dianę Weller. ▶ **płatny, do zapłacenia**

ˌpay-as-you-ˈgo adj. connected with a system of paying for a service just before you use it, rather than paying for it later: *pay-as-you-go mobile phones* ▶ **na kartę** ➲ note at **mobile phone**

payday /ˈpeɪdeɪ/ noun [U,C] the day on which you get your wages or salary ▶ **dzień wypłaty**

PAYE /ˌpiː eɪ waɪ ˈiː/ abbr. **pay as you earn**; a British system of paying income tax in which money is taken from your wages by your employer and paid to the government ▶ **system odliczania podatku dochodowego od wynagrodzenia** (*przez pracodawcę*)

payee /ˌpeɪˈiː/ noun [C] (formal) a person that money, especially a cheque, is paid to ▶ **odbior-ca/czyni** (*jakiejś kwoty*)

payment /ˈpeɪmənt/ noun **payment (for sth) 1** [U] the act of paying sb or of being paid: *I did the work last month but I haven't had any payment for it yet.* ▶ **spłata** ➲ note at **pay² 2** [C] an amount of money that you must pay: *They asked for a payment of £100 as a deposit.* ▶ **opłata**

ˌpay-per-ˈview noun [U] a system of receiving television programmes in which you pay an extra sum of money to watch a particular programme, such as a film or a sports event ▶ **system opłaty za możliwość oglądania wybranych, zakodowanych programów telewizyjnych**

payphone /ˈpeɪfəʊn/ noun [C] a telephone, usually in a public place, that is operated using coins or a card ▶ **automat telefoniczny**

payroll /ˈpeɪrəʊl/ noun **1** [C] a list of people employed by a company showing the amount of money to be paid to each of them: *We have 500 people **on the payroll**.* ▶ **lista płac 2** [usually sing.] the total amount paid in wages by a company: *The firm is growing fast with a monthly payroll of $1 million.* ▶ **wypłaty z tytułu zatrudnienia**

PC /ˌpiː ˈsiː/ abbr. **1 personal computer**; a computer that is designed for one person to use at work or at home ▶ **komputer osobisty** ➲ note at **computer** ➲ look at **mainframe 2** = POLICE CONSTABLE **3** = POLITICALLY CORRECT

PE /ˌpiː ˈiː/ abbr. **physical education**: *a PE lesson* ▶ **wychowanie fizyczne, WF**

pea /piː/ noun [C] a small round green seed that is eaten as a vegetable. A number of **peas** grow together in a **pod**. ▶ **groszek** ➲ picture on **page A13** ⓘ Zwróć uwagę, że **pea** jest rzeczownikiem policzalnym: *She left three peas on her plate.*

peace /piːs/ noun [U] **1** a situation or a period of time in which there is no war or violence in a country or area: *The two communities now manage to live **in peace** together.* ◇ *A UN force has been sent in to **keep the peace**.* ▶ **pokój 2** the state of being calm or quiet: *He longed to escape from the city to the **peace and quiet** of the countryside.* ▶ **spokój**

peaceful /ˈpiːsfl/ adj. **1** not wanting or involving war, violence or argument: *a peaceful protest/demonstration* ▶ **pokojowy 2** calm and quiet: *a peaceful village* ▶ **spokojny**
■ **peacefully** /-fəli/ adv.: *The siege ended peacefully and nobody was hurt.* ▶ **spokojnie, pokojowo** | **peacefulness** noun [U] ▶ **spokój, pokojowość**

peacekeeping /ˈpiːskiːpɪŋ/ adj. [only before a noun] intended to help stop people fighting and prevent war or violence in a place where this is likely: *a United Nations peacekeeping force* siły pokojowe Narodów Zjednoczonych ▶ **utrzymujący pokój**

peacetime /ˈpiːstaɪm/ noun [U] a period when a country is not at war ▶ **okres pokoju**

peach /piːtʃ/ noun **1** [C] a soft round fruit with reddish-orange skin and a large stone in its centre ▶ **brzoskwinia** ➲ picture on **page A12 2** [U] a pinkish-orange colour ▶ **kolor brzoskwiniowy**
■ **peach** adj. ▶ **brzoskwiniowy**

peacock /ˈpiːkɒk/ noun [C] a large bird with beautiful long blue and green tail feathers that it can lift up and spread out ▶ **paw**

peak¹ /piːk/ noun [C] **1** the point at which sth is the highest, best, strongest, etc.: *a man **at the peak of** his career* ▶ **szczyt** ➲ look at **rush hour 2** the pointed top of a mountain: *snow-covered peaks* ▶ **szczyt, wierzchołek 3** the stiff front part of a cap which sticks out above your eyes ▶ **daszek**

peak² /piːk/ verb [I] to reach the highest point or value: *Sales peak just before Christmas.* ▶ **osiągać szczyt**

peak³ /piːk/ adj. [only before a noun] (used to describe the highest level of sth, or a time when the greatest number of people are doing or using sth): *The athletes are all in peak condition.* ◇ *Summer is the peak period for most hotels.* ◇ *peak hours* godziny szczytu (dot. zużycia prądu itp.) ➲ look at **rush hour** ▶ **szczytowy** ➲ look at **off-peak**

peal /piːl/ noun [C] the loud ringing of a bell or bells: (figurative) *peals of laughter* ▶ **bicie** (*dzwonów*); **salwa** (*śmiechu*)
■ **peal** verb [I] ▶ (*dzwony*) **bić; zanosić się** (*śmiechem*)

peanut /ˈpiːnʌt/ (Brit. also **groundnut** /ˈɡraʊndnʌt/) noun **1** [C] a nut that grows underground in a thin shell ▶ **orzeszek ziemny 2** (**peanuts**) [pl.] (informal) a very small amount of money: *We get paid peanuts for doing this job.* ▶ **grosze**

ˌpeanut ˈbutter noun [U] a thick soft substance made from very finely chopped **peanuts**, usually eaten spread on bread ▶ **masło orzechowe** (*z orzeszków ziemnych*)

pear /peə(r)/ noun [C] a fruit that has a yellow or green skin and is white inside. **Pears** are thinner at the top than at the bottom. ▶ **gruszka** ➲ picture on **page A12**

pearl /pɜːl/ noun [C] a small hard round white object that grows inside the shell of an **oyster**. Pearls are used to make jewellery: *pearl earrings* ▶ **perła**

P

peasant /ˈpeznt/ noun [C] **1** (used especially when talking about the past or poorer countries) a person who owns or rents a small piece of land on which they grow food and keep animals in order to feed their family ▶ **chłop/ka, wieśnia -k/czka** ℹ Słowa **peasant** obecnie nie używa się w odniesieniu do rolników w krajach angielskiego obszaru językowego. ➲ look at **farmer 2** (informal) a person who is rude, behaves badly, or has little education ▶ (*osoba*) **burak, cham** ➲ **lout**

peat /piːt/ noun [U] a soft black or brown natural substance that is formed from dead plants just under the surface of the ground in cool, wet places. It can be burned as a fuel or put on the garden to make plants grow better. ▶ **torf**

pebble /ˈpebl/ noun [C] a smooth round stone that is found in or near water ▶ **kamyk, otoczak**

pecan /ˈpiːkən; pɪˈkæn; US pɪˈkɑːn/ noun [C] a type of nut that we eat, with a smooth pinkish-brown shell ▶ (*orzech*) **pekan**

pecan

peck /pek/ verb [I,T] **1 peck (at) sth** (used about a bird) to eat or bite sth with its beak ▶ **dziobać 2** (informal) to kiss sb quickly and lightly: *She pecked him on the cheek and then left.* ▶ **cmoknąć**

■ **peck** noun [C] **1** an act of pecking sb/sth ▶ **dziobnięcie 2** a quick kiss: *She gave him a quick peck on the cheek and then left.* ▶ **cmoknięcie**

peckish /ˈpekɪʃ/ adj. (informal) hungry ▶ **głodny**

peculiar /pɪˈkjuːliə(r)/ adj. **1** unusual or strange: *There's a very peculiar smell in here.* ▶ **dziwny, dziwaczny** SYN **odd 2 peculiar to sb/sth** only belonging to one person or found in one place: *a species of bird peculiar to South East Asia* ▶ **specyficzny (dla kogoś/jakiegoś miejsca)**

peculiarity /pɪˌkjuːliˈærəti/ noun (pl. **peculiarities**) **1** [C] a strange or unusual characteristic, quality or habit: *There are some peculiarities in her behaviour.* ▶ **dziwaczność, specyficzność 2** [C] a characteristic or a quality that only belongs to one particular person, thing or place: *the cultural peculiarities of the English* ▶ **specyficzność, właściwość 3** [U] the quality of being strange or unusual ▶ **dziwactwo**

peculiarly /pɪˈkjuːliəli/ adv. **1** especially; very: *Lilian's laugh can be peculiarly annoying.* ▶ **szczególnie 2** in a way that is especially typical of one person, thing or place: *a peculiarly Italian custom* ▶ **typowo, specyficznie 3** in a strange and unusual way: *Luke is behaving very peculiarly.* ▶ **dziwacznie**

pedagogic /ˌpedəˈɡɒdʒɪk/ (also **pedagogical** /-ɪkl/) adj. connected with ways of teaching ▶ **pedagogiczny**

pedal /ˈpedl/ noun [C] the part of a bicycle or other machine that you push with your foot in order to make it move or work ▶ **pedał** ➲ picture at **bicycle**

■ **pedal** verb [I,T] (**pedalling; pedalled**; US **pedaling; pedaled**): *She had to pedal hard to get up the hill.* ▶ **pedałować**

pedant /ˈpednt/ noun [C] a person who is too concerned with small details or rules especially when learning or teaching ▶ **pedant/ka**

pedantic /pɪˈdæntɪk/ adj. too worried about rules or details ▶ **pedantyczny**

■ **pedantically** /-kli/ adv. ▶ **pedantycznie**

peddle /ˈpedl/ verb [T] **1** to try to sell goods by going from house to house or from place to place: *to peddle illegal drugs* ▶ **handlować (jako domokrążca) 2** to spread an idea or story in order to get people to accept it: *to peddle malicious gossip* ◇ *This line is being peddled by all the government spokesmen.* ▶ **rozpowszechniać**

pedestal /ˈpedɪstl/ noun [C] the base on which a column, statue, etc. stands ▶ **cokół**

pedestrian[1] /pəˈdestriən/ noun [C] a person who is walking in the street (not travelling in a vehicle) ▶ **pieszy** ➲ look at **motorist**

pedestrian[2] /pəˈdestriən/ adj. **1** of or for pedestrians: *a pedestrian bridge* ▶ **dla pieszych 2** ordinary; not interesting; dull ▶ **przyziemny**

peˌdestrian ˈcrossing (US **crosswalk** /ˈkrɒswɔːk/) noun [C] a place for **pedestrians** to cross the road ▶ **przejście dla pieszych** ➲ look at **zebra crossing**

peˌdestrian ˈprecinct (US **peˌdestrian ˈmall**) noun [C] a part of a town where there are many shops and where cars are not allowed ▶ **deptak**

pediatrician, pediatrics (US) = PAEDIATRICIAN, PAEDIACTRICS

pedicure /ˈpedɪkjʊə(r)/ noun [C, U] care and treatment of the feet and **toenails** ▶ **pedikiur** ➲ look at **manicure**

pedigree[1] /ˈpedɪɡriː/ noun [C] **1** an official record of the parents, etc. from which an animal has been bred ▶ **rodowód** ➲ look at **mongrel 2** sb's family history, especially when this is impressive ▶ **rodowód**

pedigree[2] /ˈpedɪɡriː/ adj. [only before a noun] (used about an animal) of high quality because the parents, etc. are all of the same breed and specially chosen ▶ **rasowy**

pedophile (US) = PAEDOPHILE

pee /piː/ verb [I] (informal) to get rid of waste water from your body ▶ **siusiać** SYN **urinate**

■ **pee** noun [sing.]: *to have a pee* zrobić siusiu ▶ **siusianie**

peek /piːk/ verb [I] (informal) **peek (at sth)** to look at sth quickly and secretly because you should not be looking at it: *No peeking at your presents before your birthday!* ▶ **zerkać**

■ **peek** noun [sing.]: *to have a quick peek* ▶ **zerknięcie**

peel[1] /piːl/ verb **1** [T] to take the skin off a fruit or vegetable: *Could you peel the potatoes, please?* ▶ **obierać** (*ze skórki*) **2** [I,T] **peel (sth) (off/away/back)** to come off or to take sth off a surface in one piece or in small pieces: *I peeled off the price label before handing her the book.* ▶ **odklejać (się), łuszczyć się**

IDM **keep your eyes peeled/skinned (for sb/sth)** → EYE[1]

peel[2] /piːl/ noun [U] the skin of a fruit or vegetable: *apple/potato peel* ➲ look at **rind, skin** ▶ **skórka** ➲ picture on **page A12**

peeler /ˈpiːlə(r)/ noun [C] a special knife for taking the skin off fruit and vegetables: *a potato peeler* ▶ **obieraczka** (*do warzyw, ziemniaków*) ➲ picture at **kitchen**

peep[1] /piːp/ verb [I] **1 peep (at sth)** to look at sth quickly and secretly, especially through a small opening ▶ **zerkać 2** to be in a position where a small part of sb/sth can be seen: *The moon is peeping out from behind the clouds.* ▶ **wyglądać/wyzierać (skądś/zza czegoś) 3** [I,T] to make a short high sound; to make sth make this sound ▶ **piszczeć; zatrąbić klaksonem**

peep[2] /piːp/ noun [sing.] (informal) **1** a quick look: *Have a peep in the bedroom and see if the baby is asleep.* ◇ *Have a peep* (zajrzyj) *at the baby.* ▶ **rzut oka 2** a short high sound like the one made by a young bird or by a whistle: *There hasn't been a peep out of the children for hours.* ▶ **piszczenie; pi-pip!**

peer[1] /pɪə(r)/ noun [C] **1** a person who is of the same age or position in society as you: *Children hate to look stupid in front of their peers.* ▶ **rówieśnik; osoba równa (komuś) rangą 2** (Brit.) (in Britain) a member of the **nobility** ▶ **par**

peer[2] /pɪə(r)/ verb [I] **peer (at sb/sth)** to look closely or carefully at sb/sth, for example because you cannot see very well: *He peered at the photo, but it was blurred.* ▶ **baczne/badawczo przyglądać się (komuś/czemuś)**

peerage /ˈpɪərɪdʒ/ noun **1** [sing.] all the **peers**[1] (2) as a group ▶ **parowie, zgromadzenie parów 2** [C] the position of a **peer**[1] (2) ▶ **godność para**

ˈ**peer group** noun [C] a group of people who are all of the same age and social position ▶ **grupa osób równych wiekiem i rangą**

peeved /piːvd/ adj. (informal) quite angry or annoyed ▶ **rozdrażniony, zirytowany**

peg[1] /peg/ noun [C] **1** a piece of wood, metal, etc. on a wall or door that you hang your coat on ▶ **kołek, wieszak 2** (also ˈ**tent peg**) a piece of metal that you push into the ground to keep one of the ropes of a tent in place ▶ **śledź** (*do namiotu*) **3** (also ˈ**clothes peg**; US ˈ**clothes pin**) a type of small wooden or plastic object used for fastening wet clothes to a clothes line ▶ **klamerka do bielizny**

peg[2] /peg/ verb [T] (**pegging**; **pegged**) **1 peg sth (out)** to fix sth with a **peg** ▶ **przyczepiać klamerkami** (*np. pranie*) **2 peg sth (at/to sth)** to fix or keep sth at a certain level: *Wage increases were pegged at 5%.* ▶ **ustalać/utrzymywać na pewnym poziomie** (*np. cenę*)

pejorative /pɪˈdʒɒrətɪv/ adj. (formal) a word or remark that is **pejorative** expresses disapproval or criticism ▶ **pejoratywny**
■ **pejoratively** adv. ▶ **pejoratywnie** SYN **derogatory**

pelican /ˈpelɪkən/ noun [C] a large bird that lives near water in warm countries. A **pelican** has a large beak that it uses for catching and holding fish. ▶ **pelikan**

pellet /ˈpelɪt/ noun [C] **1** a small hard ball of any substance, often of soft material that has become hard ▶ **kulka 2** a very small metal ball that is fired from a gun: *shotgun pellets* ▶ **śrut**

pelt /pelt/ verb **1** [T] to attack sb/sth by throwing things ▶ **obrzucać 2** [I] **pelt (down)** (used about rain) to fall very heavily: *It's absolutely pelting down.* ▶ **lunąć 3** [I] (informal) to run very fast: *Some kids pelted past us.* ▶ **pędzić, gnać**

pelvis /ˈpelvɪs/ noun [C] the set of wide bones at the bottom of your back, to which your leg bones are joined ▶ **miednica** ➲ picture at **body**
■ **pelvic** /ˈpelvɪk/ adj. ▶ **miednicowy**

⚷ **pen** /pen/ noun [C] **1** an object that you use for writing in ink: *a ballpoint pen* długopis ◇ *a fountain pen* wieczne pióro ◇ *a felt-tip/marker pen* flamaster ▶ **pióro** ➲ picture at **stationery 2** a small piece of ground with a fence around it that is used for keeping animals in: *a sheep pen* ▶ **zagroda, wybieg**

penal /ˈpiːnl/ adj. [only before a noun] connected with punishment by law: *the penal system* ◇ *a penal code* ▶ **karny**

penalize (also -**ise**) /ˈpiːnəlaɪz/ verb [T] **1** to punish sb for breaking a law or rule ▶ **karać 2** to cause sb to have a disadvantage: *Children should not be penalized because their parents cannot afford to pay.* ▶ (*przen.*) **karać**

penalty /ˈpenəlti/ noun [C] (pl. **penalties**) **1** a punishment for breaking a law, rule or contract: *the death penalty* ◇ *What's the maximum penalty for smuggling drugs?* ▶ **kara, grzywna 2** a disadvantage or sth unpleasant that happens as the result of sth: *I didn't work hard enough and I* ***paid the penalty*** (i zapłaciłem za to). *I failed all my exams.* ▶ (*przen.*) **cena 3** (in sport) a punishment for one team and an advantage for the other team because a rule has been broken: *The referee awarded a penalty to the home team.* ▶ (*sport*) **kara**

the ˈ**penalty area** noun [C] the marked area in front of the goal in football ▶ **pole karne**

ˌ**penalty** ˈ**shoot-out** noun [C] (in football) a way of deciding the winner when both teams have the same score at the end of a game. Each team takes a certain number of penalty kicks and the team that scores more wins. ▶ **rzuty karne**

penance /ˈpenəns/ noun [C,U] a punishment that you give yourself to show you are sorry for doing sth wrong ▶ **pokuta**

pence plural of **penny**

⚷ **pencil**[1] /ˈpensl/ noun [C,U] an object that you use for writing or drawing. Pencils are usually made of wood and contain a thin stick of a black or coloured substance: *Bring a pencil and paper with you.* ◇ *Write* ***in pencil****, not ink* (ołówkiem, nie piórem). ▶ **ołówek, kredka** ➲ picture at **stationery**

pencil[2] /ˈpensl/ verb [T] (**pencilling**; **pencilled**; US **penciling**; **penciled**) to write or draw with a pencil ▶ **pisać/rysować ołówkiem/kredką**
PHR V **pencil sth/sb in** to write down the details of an arrangement that might have to be changed later: *Shall we pencil the next meeting in for the fourteenth?* ▶ **wpisywać kogoś/coś wstępnie**

ˈ**pencil case** noun [C] a small bag or box that you keep pens, pencils, etc. in ▶ **piórnik**

ˈ**pencil sharpener** noun [C] an instrument that you use for making pencils sharp ▶ **temperówka** ➲ picture at **stationery**

pendant /ˈpendənt/ noun [C] a small attractive object that you wear on a chain around your neck ▶ **wisiorek, wisior**

pending /ˈpendɪŋ/ prep. (formal) until sth happens: *He took over the leadership pending the elections.* ▶ **do czasu**
■ **pending** adj. waiting to be done or decided: *The judge's decision is still pending.* ▶ **w toku, nierozstrzygnięty**

pendulum /ˈpendjələm; US -dʒə-/ noun [C] **1** a chain or stick with a heavy weight at the bottom that moves regularly from side to side to work a clock ▶ **wahadło 2** a way of describing a situation that changes from one thing to its opposite: *Since last year's election, the pendulum of public opinion has swung against* (opinia publiczna odwróciła się od) *the government.*

penetrate /ˈpenətreɪt/ verb [I,T] **1** to go through or into sth, especially when this is difficult: *The knife penetrated ten centimetres into his chest.* ◇ *We've penetrated* (weszliśmy na) *the Spanish market.* ▶ **przebijać (się), przenikać (przez coś), wciskać się (gdzieś) 2** to manage to understand sth difficult: *Scientists have still not penetrated the workings of the brain.* ▶ **zgłębić** (*np. tajniki czegoś*) **3** to be understood or realized: *I was back at home when the meaning of her words finally penetrated.* ▶ (*myśl, wyjaśnienie*) **dotrzeć (do kogoś)**
■ **penetration** /ˌpenəˈtreɪʃn/ noun [U] **1** the act of penetrating ▶ **przebijanie się/przenikanie (przez coś) 2** the ability to think and understand quickly and well ▶ **przenikliwość, wnikliwość**

penetrating /ˈpenətreɪtɪŋ/ adj. **1** (used about sb's eyes or of a way of looking) making you feel uncomfortable because it seems sb knows what you are thinking: *a penetrating look/stare/gaze* ◇ *penetrating blue eyes* ▶ **przenikliwy 2** showing that you have understood sth completely and quickly: *a penetrating question/comment* ▶ **wnikliwy 3** that can be heard, felt, smelt, etc. a long way away ▶ **przeszywający**

penfriend /ˈpenfrend/ (especially US ˈ**pen pal**) noun [C] a person that you become friendly with by exchanging letters, often a person who you have never met ▶ **przyjaci-el/ółka korespondencyjn-y/a**

penguin /ˈpeŋgwɪn/ noun [C] a black and white bird that cannot fly and that lives in the Antarctic ▶ **pingwin**

penicillin /ˌpenɪˈsɪlɪn/ noun [U] a substance that is used as a drug for preventing and treating infections caused by bacteria ▶ **penicylina**

peninsula /pəˈnɪnsjələ; US -sələ/ noun [C] an area of land that is almost surrounded by water: *the Iberian peninsula* (tj. Hiszpania i Portugalia) ▶ **półwysep**

penis /ˈpiːnɪs/ noun [C] the male sex organ that is used for getting rid of waste liquid and for having sex ▶ **penis, prącie**

penitent /ˈpenɪtənt/ adj. (formal) sorry for having done sth wrong ▶ **skruszony**

penitentiary /ˌpenɪˈtenʃəri/ noun [C] (pl. **penitentiaries**) (US) a prison ▶ **więzienie**

penknife /ˈpennaɪf/ (especially US **pocketknife** /ˈpɒkɪtnaɪf/ (pl. **pocketknives**) noun [C] (pl. **penknives**) a small knife with one or more blades that fold away when not being used ▶ **scyzoryk**

penniless /ˈpeniləs/ adj. having no money; poor ▶ **bez grosza**

⚷ **penny** /ˈpeni/ noun [C] (pl. **pence** /pens/ or **pennies**) **1** (abbr. **p**) a small brown British coin. There are a hundred pence in a pound: *a fifty-pence piece/coin* ▶ **pens** ℹ Można używać w lm **pennies**, mówiąc o monetach jednopensowych: *She put five pennies in the slot.* Mówi się **pence** lub używa skrótu **p**, mówiąc o jakiejś ilości pieniędzy. Skrót **p** jest mniej formalny. **2** (US) a cent ▶ **cent**

ˈ**pen pal** (especially US) = PENFRIEND

⚷ **pension** /ˈpenʃn/ noun [C] money that is paid regularly by a government or company to sb who has stopped working because of old age or who cannot work because they are ill ▶ **emerytura, renta** ➲ note at **retire**
■ **pensioner** = OLD-AGE PENSIONER

pentagon /ˈpentəgən; US -gɑːn/ noun **1** [C] a shape that has five straight and equal sides ▶ **pięciokąt 2** (**the Pentagon**) [sing.] a large government building near Washington DC in the US that contains the main offices of the US military forces; the military officials who work there ▶ **Pentagon**

pentathlon /penˈtæθlən/ noun [C] a sports competition in which you have to take part in five different events ▶ **pięciobój**

penthouse /ˈpenthaʊs/ noun [C] an expensive flat at the top of a tall building ▶ **drogie mieszkanie na ostatniej kondygnacji wysokościowca**

pent-up /ˈpent ʌp/ adj. [only before a noun] (used about feelings) that you hold inside and do not express: *pent-up anger* ▶ **tłumiony**

penultimate /penˈʌltɪmət/ adj. [only before a noun] (in a series) the one before the last one: *'Y' is the penultimate letter of the alphabet.* ▶ **przedostatni**

peony /ˈpiːəni/ noun [C] (pl. **peonies**) a garden plant with large round pink, red or white flowers ▶ **piwonia, peonia**

⚷ **people** /ˈpiːpl/ noun **1** [pl.] more than one person: *How many people are coming to the party?* ◇ *Young people* (młodzież) *often rebel against their parents.* ▶ **ludzie**

> Uwaga! **People** prawie zawsze używa się zamiast formy lm słowa **person**. **Persons** jest bardzo oficjalnym słowem, używanym zwykle w języku prawniczym itp: *Persons under the age of sixteen are not permitted to buy cigarettes.* Rzeczownik **folk** to nieformalne słowo oznaczające ludzi. Powszechnie używa się go, mówiąc o ludziach starszych lub mieszkających na wsi: *The old folk have seen many changes in the village over the years.*

2 [C] (pl. **peoples**) (formal) all the men, women and children who belong to a particular place or race: *The President addressed the American people.* ◇ *the French-speaking peoples of the world* ▶ **naród, nacja 3** [pl.] the inhabitants of a particular place: *the people of London* ▶ **mieszkańcy 4** (**the people**) [pl.] the ordinary citizens of a country: *The President is popular because he listens to the people.* ▶ **lud 5** [pl.] men and women who work in a particular activity: *business people* biznesmeni ◇ *sports people* sportowcy ▶ **ludzie** (*zajmujący się jakąś działalnością*)

ˈ**people carrier** (also ˈ**people mover**, US **minivan**) noun [C] a large car, like a van, designed to carry up to eight people ▶ **samochód rodzinny typu minivan** ➲ picture on **page A7**

pep /pep/ verb [T] (**pepping**; **pepped**)
PHR V **pep sb/sth up** (informal) to make sb/sth more interesting or full of energy: *A walk in the fresh air will pep you up.* ▶ **ożywiać kogoś/coś** SYN **liven (sb/sth) up**
■ **pep** noun [U] energy and enthusiasm ▶ **wigor**

⚷ **pepper**[1] /ˈpepə(r)/ noun **1** [U] a black or white powder with a hot taste that is used for flavouring food: *salt and pepper* ▶ **pieprz 2** (US ˈ**bell pepper**) [C] a green, red or yellow vegetable that is almost empty inside: *stuffed green peppers* ▶ **papryka** (*warzywo*) ➲ picture on **page A13** ➲ look at **paprika**

pepper[2] /ˈpepə(r)/ **1** verb [T, usually passive] **pepper sb/sth with sth** to hit sb/sth with a series of small objects, especially bullets: *The wall had been peppered with bullets.* ▶ **obsypywać/obrzucać** (*gradem czegoś*) **2** to put pepper on sth ▶ **pieprzyć**

peppermint /ˈpepəmɪnt/ noun **1** [U] a natural substance with a strong fresh flavour that is used in sweets and medicines ▶ **mięta 2** [C] (also **mint**) a sweet with a peppermint flavour ▶ **cukierek miętowy** ➲ look at **spearmint**

pep talk /ˈpep tɔːk/ noun [C] (informal) a speech that is given to encourage people or to make them work harder ▶ **przemówienie zagrzewające do wysiłku lub dodające odwagi/optymizmu**

⚷ **per** /pə(r); strong form pɜː(r)/ prep. for each: *The speed limit is 110 kilometres per hour.* ◇ *Rooms cost 60 dollars per person per night.* ▶ **na, od** (*np. osoby*)

perceive /pəˈsiːv/ verb [T] (formal) **1** to notice or realize sth: *Scientists failed to perceive how dangerous the level of pollution had become.* ▶ **uświadamiać sobie, dostrzegać 2** to understand or think of sth in a particular way: *I perceived his comments as a criticism.* ▶ **odbierać, odczuwać** SYN **see** ➲ noun **perception**

⚷ **per ˈcent** (US **percent**) adj. (symbol **%**) in or of each hundred; one part in every hundred ▶ **procentowy**
■ **per ˈcent 1** adv.: *House prices rose five per cent last year.* ▶ **procentowo 2** noun [C, with sing. or pl. verb] (pl. **per cent**) one part in every hundred: *You get 10% off if you pay cash.* ◇ *90% of the population owns a TV.* ◇ *The price of bread has gone up* ***by*** *50* ***per cent*** *in two years.* ▶ **procent**

percentage /pəˈsentɪdʒ/ noun [C, with sing. or pl. verb] the number, amount, rate, etc. of sth, expressed as if it is part of a total which is a hundred; a part or share of a whole: *What percentage of people voted in the last election?* ◇ *Please express your answer as a percentage* (stosunek procentowy). ▶ **procent**

perceptible /pəˈseptəbl/ adj. (formal) that can be seen or felt: *a barely perceptible change in colour* ▶ **dostrzegalny, odczuwalny** OPP **imperceptible**
■ **perceptibly** /-əbli/ adv. ▶ **dostrzegalnie, odczuwalnie**

perception /pəˈsepʃn/ noun **1** [U] the ability to notice or understand sth ▶ **postrzeganie, percepcja 2** [C] a particular way of looking at or understanding sth; an opinion: *What is your perception of the situation?* ▶ **percepcja**, **zrozumienie** ➲ verb **perceive**

perceptive /pəˈseptɪv/ adj. (formal) quick to notice or understand things: *She is very perceptive.* ▶ **spostrzegawczy**, **bystry**

■ **perceptively** adv. ▶ **spostrzegawczo**

perch¹ /pɜːtʃ/ verb **1** [I] (used about a bird) to sit on a branch, etc. ▶ **usiąść**, **przycupnąć** **2** [I,T] to sit or be put on the edge of sth: *The house was perched on the edge of a cliff.* ▶ **sadowić się/umieszczać (na skraju czegoś)**

perch² /pɜːtʃ/ **1** noun [C] a place where a bird sits, especially a branch or a bar for this purpose ▶ **grzęda**, **żerdź** **2** (pl. **perch**) a common fish that you can eat that lives in rivers or lakes ▶ **okoń**

percolate /ˈpɜːkəleɪt/ verb **1** [I] (used about a liquid, gas, etc.) to move gradually through a surface that has very small holes or spaces in it: *Water had percolated down through the rocks.* ▶ (*woda itp.*) **sączyć się** **2** [I] to gradually become known or spread through a group or society: *Changes percolate through gradually.* ▶ **rozprzestrzeniać się** **3** [I,T] to make coffee in a percolator; to be made in this way ▶ **zaparzać (*kawę*) w ekspresie**; **być zaparzonym**

percussion /pəˈkʌʃn/ noun [U] drums and other instruments that you play by hitting them ▶ **perkusja** ➲ note at **instrument**

peremptory /pəˈremptəri/ adj. (formal) (especially used about sb's manner or behaviour) expecting to be obeyed immediately and without question or refusal: *a peremptory summons* ▶ **nieznoszący sprzeciwu** ⓘ Wyraża dezaprobatę.

perennial /pəˈreniəl/ adj. that happens often or that lasts for a long time: *a perennial problem* ▶ **odwieczny**, **częsty**

⚷ **perfect¹** /ˈpɜːfɪkt/ adj. **1** completely good; without faults or weaknesses: *The car is two years old but it is still in perfect condition.* ▶ **doskonały** OPP **imperfect** **2 perfect (for sb/sth)** exactly suitable or right: *Ken would be perfect for the job.* ▶ **doskonały** **3** [only before a noun] complete; total: *What he was saying made perfect sense to me.* ◇ *a perfect stranger* ▶ **zupełny**, **całkowity** **4** (used to describe the tense of a verb that is formed with *has/have/had* and the past participle): *the present perfect tense* ▶ (*gram.*) **dokonany**

■ **perfectly** adv. **1** in a perfect way: *He played the piece of music perfectly.* ▶ **doskonale** **2** very; completely: *Laura understood perfectly what I meant.* ▶ **zupełnie**, **całkowicie**

perfect² /pəˈfekt/ verb [T] to make sth perfect: *Vinay is spending a year in France to perfect his French.* ▶ **doskonalić**

the ˈ**perfect** = PERFECT TENSE

perfection /pəˈfekʃn/ noun [U] the state of being perfect or without fault: *The steak was cooked **to perfection**.* ▶ **doskonałość**, **perfekcja**

perfectionist /pəˈfekʃənɪst/ noun [C] a person who always does things as well as they possibly can and who expects others to do the same ▶ **perfekcjonist(k)a**

the ˈ**perfect tense** (also the ˈperfect) noun [sing.] the tense of a verb that is formed with *has/have/had* and the past participle: *'I have finished' is in the present perfect tense.* ▶ **czas dokonany**

perforate /ˈpɜːfəreɪt/ verb [T] to make a hole or holes in sth ▶ **dziurkować**

perforation /ˌpɜːfəˈreɪʃn/ noun **1** [C] a series of small holes in paper, etc. that make it easy for you to tear ▶ **perforacja** **2** [U] the act of making a hole or holes in sth ▶ **dziurawienie**; **dziurkowanie**

⚷ **perform** /pəˈfɔːm/ verb **1** [T] (formal) to do a piece of work or sth that you have been ordered to do: *to perform an operation/an experiment/a task* ▶ **wykonywać**, **spełniać** **2** [I,T] to take part in a play or to sing, dance, etc. in front of an audience: *She is currently performing at the National Theatre.* ▶ **przedstawiać**, **wykonywać** (*np. piosenkę*), **grać** **3** [I] **perform (well/badly/poorly)** to work or function well or badly: *The company has not been performing well recently.* ▶ **działać**

IDM **work/perform miracles** → MIRACLE

⚷ **performance** /pəˈfɔːməns/ noun **1** [C] the act of performing sth in front of an audience; something that you perform: *What time does the performance start?* ▶ **przedstawienie** **2** [C] the way a person performs in a play, concert, etc.: *His moving performance in the film won him an Oscar.* ▶ **występ**, **gra** (*np. sztuki*) **3** [C] the way in which you do sth, especially how successful you are: *The company's performance was disappointing last year.* ▶ **wyniki** (*np. pracy*), **osiągnięcia** **4** [U] (used about a machine, etc.) the ability to work well: *This car has a high performance engine.* ▶ **działanie**, **wydajność** **5** [U, sing.] (formal) the act or process of doing a task, an action, etc.: *the performance of your duties* ▶ **wykonywanie**, **spełnienie**

⚷ **performer** /pəˈfɔːmə(r)/ noun [C] **1** a person who performs for an audience: *a brilliant performer* ▶ **wykonaw-ca/czyni**, **artyst(k)a** (*np. estradow-y/a*) **2** a person or thing that behaves or works in the way mentioned: *Diana is a poor performer in exams* (kiepsko wypada na egzaminach). ◇ *This car is the star performer of the motor industry this year.* Ten samochód został w tym roku uznany za gwiazdę przemysłu motoryzacyjnego.

perfume /ˈpɜːfjuːm; US pəˈf-/ noun [C,U] **1** (Brit. also **scent**) a liquid with a sweet smell that you put on your body to make yourself smell nice: *Are you wearing perfume?* ▶ **perfumy** **2** a pleasant, often sweet, smell ▶ **zapach**, **woń** ➲ note at **smell²**

perfunctory /pəˈfʌŋktəri/ adj. (formal) (used about an action) done as a duty or habit, without real interest, attention or feeling: *a perfunctory nod/smile* ◇ *They only made a perfunctory effort.* ▶ **zdawkowy**, **powierzchowny**

■ **perfunctorily** /-trəli/ adv.: *to nod/smile perfunctorily* ▶ **zdawkowo**, **powierzchownie**

⚷ **perhaps** /pəˈhæps; Brit. also præps/ adv. (used when you are not sure about sth) possibly: *Perhaps he's forgotten.* ◇ *She was, perhaps, one of the most famous writers of the time.* ▶ **(być) może**, **możliwe** SYN **maybe**

> **Perhaps** i **maybe** mają podobne znaczenie. Używa się ich często w celu uczynienia wypowiedzi bardziej uprzejmą: *Perhaps I could borrow your book, if you're not using it?* ◇ *Maybe I'd better explain ...* ◇ *Perhaps/Maybe it would be better if you came back tomorrow.*

peril /ˈperəl/ noun (formal) **1** [U] great danger: *A lack of trained nurses is putting patients' lives **in peril*** (zagraża życiu pacjentów). ▶ **wielkie niebezpieczeństwo** **2** [C] something that is very dangerous: *the perils of drug abuse* ▶ **wielkie niebezpieczeństwo**

perilous /ˈperələs/ adj. (formal or literary) very dangerous: *a perilous adventure/journey* ▶ **bardzo niebezpieczny**, **ryzykowny** SYN **hazardous** ⓘ Częściej używa się **danger** i **dangerous**.

■ **perilously** adv.: *We came **perilously close** to disaster.* ▶ **bardzo niebezpiecznie**

perimeter /pəˈrɪmɪtə(r)/ noun [C] the outside edge or limit of an area of land: *the perimeter fence of the army camp* ▶ **obwód**

⚷ **period** /ˈpɪəriəd/ noun [C] **1** a length of time: *Her son is going through a difficult period at the moment.* ◇ *What period of history are you most interested in?* ◇ *The scheme will be introduced for a six-month trial period* (okres

P

próbny). ◇ *period costume* kostium historyczny ▶ **okres** **2** a lesson in school: *We have five periods of English a week.* ▶ **godzina lekcyjna** **3** the time every month when a woman loses blood from her body: *I've got my period and don't feel too great.* ◇ *period pains* ▶ **okres**, **miesiączka** **4** (especially US) = FULL STOP

periodic /ˌpɪəriˈɒdɪk/ (also **periodical**) adj. happening fairly regularly: *We have periodic meetings to check on progress.* ▶ **okresowy**, **periodyczny**
■ **periodically** /-kli/ adv.: *All machines need to be checked periodically.* ▶ **okresowo**, **periodycznie**

periodical /ˌpɪəriˈɒdɪkl/ noun [C] (formal) a magazine that is produced regularly ▶ **czasopismo**

the ˌperiodic ˈtable noun [sing.] a list of all the chemical elements, arranged according to their **atomic number** ▶ **układ okresowy pierwiastków**

peripheral[1] /pəˈrɪfərəl/ adj. **1** (formal) **peripheral (to sth)** not as important as the main aim, part, etc. of sth: *peripheral information* ◇ *Fund-raising is peripheral to their main activities.* ▶ **marginalny** **2** (technical) connected with the edge of a particular area: *the peripheral nervous system* ◇ *peripheral vision* ▶ **peryferyjny**, **obwodowy**

peripheral[2] /pəˈrɪfərəl/ noun [C] a piece of equipment that is connected to a computer: *monitors, printers and other peripherals* ▶ (*komput.*) **urządzenie peryferyjne**

periphery /pəˈrɪfəri/ noun [C, usually sing.] (pl. **peripheries**) (formal) **1** the outer edge of a particular area: *industrial development **on the periphery of** the town* ▶ **peryferie** **2** the less important part of sth, for example of a particular activity or of a social or political group: *minor parties **on the periphery of** American politics* ▶ **margines** (*np. życia politycznego*)

perish /ˈperɪʃ/ verb [I] (formal) to die or be destroyed: *Thousands perished in the war.* ▶ **ginąć**

perishable /ˈperɪʃəbl/ adj. (used about food) that will go bad quickly ▶ **łatwo psujący się**

perjury /ˈpɜːdʒəri/ noun [U] (formal) the act of telling a lie in a court of law ▶ **krzywoprzysięstwo**
■ **perjure** /ˈpɜːdʒə(r)/ verb [T] **perjure yourself**: *She admitted that she had perjured herself while giving evidence.* ▶ **krzywoprzysięgać**

perk[1] /pɜːk/ noun [C] (informal) something extra that you get from your employer in addition to money: *Travelling abroad is one of the perks of the job.* ▶ **dodatek** (*do podstawowego uposażenia*)

perk[2] /pɜːk/ verb
PHR V **perk (sb/sth) up** to become happier; to make sb become happier and have more energy ▶ **ożywiać się**; **dodawać animuszu**

perm /pɜːm/ noun [C] the treatment of hair with special chemicals in order to make it curly ▶ **trwała (ondulacja)** ➲ look at **wave**
■ **perm** verb [T]: *She has had her hair permed.* ▶ **robić trwałą (ondulację)**

permanent /ˈpɜːmənənt/ adj. lasting for a long time or for ever; that will not change: *The accident left him with a permanent scar.* ◇ *Are you looking for a permanent or a temporary job?* ▶ **stały**, **trwały**, **niezmienny**
■ **permanence** noun [U] ▶ **stałość**, **trwałość** | **permanently** adv.: *Has she left permanently* (na stałe)*?* ▶ **stale**, **trwale**

permeate /ˈpɜːmieɪt/ verb [T] (formal) **1** (used about a liquid, gas, etc.) to spread to every part of an object or a place: *The smell of cooking permeated the house.* ▶ **przenikać** **2** (used about an idea, a feeling, etc.) to affect every part of sth: *a belief that permeates all levels of society* ▶ **przenikać**

■ **permeable** /ˈpɜːmiəbl/ adj. (technical) **permeable (to sth)** allowing a liquid or gas to pass through: *A frog's skin is permeable to water.* ▶ **przepuszczalny** OPP **impermeable**

permissible /pəˈmɪsəbl/ adj. (formal) **permissible (for sb) (to do sth)** that is allowed by law or by a set of rules: *It is not permissible for banks to release their customers' personal details.* ▶ **dopuszczalny**, **dozwolony**

permission /pəˈmɪʃn/ noun [U] **permission (for sth)**; **permission (for sb) (to do sth)** the act of allowing sb to do sth, especially when this is done by sb in a position of authority: *I'm afraid you can't leave **without permission**.* ◇ *to **ask/give permission** for something* ▶ **pozwolenie**, **zezwolenie** ℹ Uwaga! **Permission** jest rzeczownikiem niepoliczalnym. Dokument zezwalający na coś to **permit**.

permissive /pəˈmɪsɪv/ adj. having, allowing or showing a lot of freedom that many people do not approve of, especially in sexual matters ▶ **pobłażliwy**, **liberalny**

permit[1] /pəˈmɪt/ verb (**permitting**; **permitted**) **1** [T] (formal) to allow sb to do sth or to allow sth to happen: *You are not permitted to smoke in the hospital.* ◇ *His visa does not permit him to work.* ▶ **pozwalać**, **zezwalać** ➲ look at **let** ➲ note at **allow** **2** [I,T] to make sth possible: *Let's have a picnic at the weekend, **weather permitting*** (jeżeli będzie dobra pogoda). ▶ **umożliwiać**, **pozwalać (na coś)**

permit[2] /ˈpɜːmɪt/ noun [C] an official document that says you are allowed to do sth, especially for a limited period of time: *Next month I'll have to apply for a new **work permit**.* ▶ **pozwolenie**, **zezwolenie**, **przepustka**

perpendicular /ˌpɜːpənˈdɪkjələ(r)/ adj. **1** at an angle of 90° to sth: *Are the lines perpendicular to each other?* ▶ **prostopadły** ➲ look at **horizontal**, **vertical** **2** pointing straight up: *The path was almost perpendicular.* ▶ **pionowy**

perpetrate /ˈpɜːpətreɪt/ verb [T] (formal) **perpetrate sth (against/upon/on sb)** to commit a crime or do sth wrong or evil: *to perpetrate a crime/fraud/massacre* ◇ *violence perpetrated against women and children* ▶ **popełniać** (*np. zbrodnię*)

perpetual /pəˈpetʃuəl/ adj. **1** continuing for a long period of time without stopping: *They lived in perpetual fear of losing their jobs.* ▶ **wieczny**, **bezustanny** **2** repeated many times in a way which is annoying: *How can I work with these perpetual interruptions?* ▶ **ciągły**
■ **perpetually** /-tʃuəli/ adv. ▶ **ciągle**, **bezustannie**

perpetuate /pəˈpetʃueɪt/ verb [T] (formal) to cause sth to continue for a long time: *to perpetuate an argument* ▶ **utrwalać**, **powodować dalsze trwanie czegoś**

perplex /pəˈpleks/ verb [T, usually passive] if sth **perplexes** you, it makes you confused or worried because you do not understand it: *They were perplexed by her response.* ▶ **wprawiać w zakłopotanie**, **konsternować** SYN **puzzle**
■ **perplexing** adj. ▶ **wprawiający w zakłopotanie**

perplexed /pəˈplekst/ adj. not understanding sth; confused ▶ **zakłopotany**, **zmieszany**

per se /ˌpɜː ˈseɪ/ adv. (used meaning 'by itself' to show that you are referring to sth on its own, rather than in connection with other things): *The drug is not harmful per se, but is dangerous when taken with alcohol.* ▶ **jako taki**

persecute /ˈpɜːsɪkjuːt/ verb [T] **1** [often passive] **persecute sb (for sth)** to treat sb in a cruel and unfair way, especially because of race, religion or political beliefs: *persecuted minorities* ▶ **prześladować** (*np. politycznie, religijnie*) **2** to deliberately annoy sb and make their life unpleasant ▶ **nie dawać komuś spokoju**
■ **persecution** /ˌpɜːsɪˈkjuːʃn/ noun [C,U]: *the persecution of minorities* ▶ **prześladowanie**, **szykanowanie**

persecutor /ˈpɜːsɪkjuːtə(r)/ noun [C] ▶ **prześladow-ca/czyni**

persevere /ˌpɜːsɪˈvɪə(r)/ verb [I] **persevere (at/in/with sth)** to continue trying to do or achieve sth that is difficult: *The treatment is painful but I'm going to persevere with it.* ▶ **wytrwać, nie ustawać**

■ **perseverance** noun [U] ▶ **wytrwałość**

Persian /ˈpɜːʃn; -ʒn/ noun **1** [C] a person from ancient Persia, or modern Persia, now called Iran ▶ **Pers/janka 2** (also **Farsi** /ˈfɑːsiː/) [U] the official language of Iran ▶ **język perski 3** (also **Persian cat**) [C] a breed of cat with long hair, short legs and a round flat face ▶ **kot perski**

■ **Persian** adj. ▶ **perski**

persist /pəˈsɪst/ verb [I] **1 persist (in sth/doing sth)** to continue doing sth even though other people say that you are wrong or that you cannot do it: *If you persist in making so much noise, I shall call the police.* ▶ **obstawać (przy czymś), upierać się (przy czymś), utrzymywać się (w czymś) 2** to continue to exist: *If your symptoms persist, you should consult your doctor.* ▶ **utrzymywać się, trwać**

■ **persistence** noun [U] ▶ **wytrwałość, uporczywość; trwałość, stałość**

persistent /pəˈsɪstənt/ adj. **1** determined to continue doing sth even though people say that you are wrong or that you cannot do it: *Some salesmen can be very persistent.* ▶ **uporczywy, wytrwały 2** lasting for a long time or happening often: *a persistent cough* ▶ **trwały, uporczywy, ciągły**

■ **persistently** adv. ▶ **uporczywie, wytrwale**

⚷ **person** /ˈpɜːsn/ noun [C] (pl. **people**) **1** a man or woman; a human being: *I would like to speak to the person in charge.* ▶ **osoba, człowiek** ⓘ W bardzo formalnym języku lm słowa **person** to **persons.** ➲ note at **people 2** (**-person**) [in compounds] a person doing the job mentioned: *a spokesperson* rzeczni-k/czka ◇ *a salesperson* sprzedawca/czyni ▶ **osoba wykonująca jakąś pracę 3** one of the three types of pronoun in grammar. *I/we* are the first person, *you* is the second person and *he/she/it/they* are the third person. ▶ **osoba**

IDM **in person** seeing or speaking to sb face to face (not speaking on the telephone or writing a letter, etc.) ▶ **osobiście**

⚷ **personal** /ˈpɜːsənl/ adj. **1** [only before a noun] of or belonging to one particular person: *personal belongings* ◇ *Judges should not let their **personal feelings** influence their decisions.* ▶ **osobisty, prywatny 2** connected with your feelings, health or relationships with other people: *I should like to speak to you in private. I have something personal to discuss.* ◇ *Do you mind if I ask you a **personal question**?* ◇ *The letter was marked 'personal* (do rąk własnych)*'.* ▶ **osobisty, prywatny 3** not connected with sb's job or official position: *Please keep personal phone calls to a minimum.* ◇ *I try not to let work interfere with my **personal life**.* ▶ **prywatny, osobisty 4** [only before a noun] done by a particular person rather than by sb who is acting for them: *The Prime Minister made a personal visit to the victims in hospital.* ▶ **osobisty 5** [only before a noun] made or done for one particular person rather than for a large group of people or people in general: *We offer a personal service to all our customers.* ▶ **indywidualny 6** speaking about sb's appearance or character in an unpleasant or unfriendly way: *It started as a general discussion but then people started to **get personal*** (robić osobiste wycieczki) *and an argument began.* ▶ **osobisty 7** [only before a noun] connected with the body: *personal hygiene* ◇ *She's always worrying about her personal appearance.* ▶ **osobisty**

ˌpersonal asˈsistant = PA

ˌpersonal comˈputer = PC (1)

⚷ **personality** /ˌpɜːsəˈnæləti/ noun (pl. **personalities**) **1** [C,U] the different qualities of sb's character that make them different from other people: *Joe has a kind personality.* ▶ **osobowość 2** [U] the quality of having a strong, interesting and attractive character: *A good entertainer needs a lot of personality.* ▶ **indywidualność, osobowość 3** [C] a famous person (especially in sport, on TV, etc.): *a TV personality* ▶ **osobistość, indywidualność** SYN **celebrity**

personalize (also **-ise**) /ˈpɜːsənəlaɪz/ verb [T] to mark sth, for example with the first letters of your name, to show that it belongs to you: *a car with a personalized number plate* ▶ **podpisywać, oznaczać** (*np. własnym inicjałem/imieniem/znakiem*)

⚷ **personally** /ˈpɜːsənəli/ adv. **1** (used to show that you are expressing your own opinion): *Personally, I think that nurses deserve more money.* ▶ **osobiście; co do mnie, to 2** done by you yourself, not by sb else acting for you: *I will deal with this matter personally.* ▶ **osobiście 3** in a way that is connected with one particular person rather than a group of people: *I wasn't talking about you personally – I meant all teachers.* ▶ **osobiście 4** in a way that is intended to offend: *Please don't **take it personally*** (nie bierz tego do siebie), *but I would just rather be alone this evening.* ◇ *I didn't mean it personally.* Nie chciałem cię obrazić. **5** in a way that is connected with sb's private life, rather than their job: *Have you had any dealings with any of the suspects, either personally or professionally?* ▶ **prywatnie**

ˌpersonal ˈpronoun noun [C] any of the pronouns *I, me, she, her, he, him, we, us, you, they, them* ▶ **zaimek osobowy**

ˌpersonal ˈstereo noun [C] a small CD or tape player that you can carry with you and listen to using **headphones** ▶ **walkman**

ˌpersonal ˈtrainer noun [C] a person who is paid by sb to help them exercise, especially by deciding what types of exercise are best for them ▶ **trener/ka osobist-y/a**

personify /pəˈsɒnɪfaɪ/ verb [T] (**personifying**; **personifies**; pt, pp **personified**) **1** to be an example in human form of a particular quality: *She is kindness personified.* ▶ **uosabiać, ucieleśniać 2** to describe an object or a feeling as if it were a person: *The river was personified as a goddess.* ▶ **uosabiać, personifikować**

■ **personification** /pəˌsɒnɪfɪˈkeɪʃn/ noun [C,U] ▶ **uosobienie, personifikacja**

personnel /ˌpɜːsəˈnel/ noun **1** [pl.] the people who work for a large organization or one of the armed forces: *sales/medical/technical personnel* ▶ **personel 2** (also **perˈsonnel department**) [U, with sing. or pl. verb] the department of a large company or organization that deals with employing and training people: *Personnel is/are currently reviewing pay scales.* ▶ **kadry, dział personalny** SYN **human resources**

perspective /pəˈspektɪv/ noun **1** [C] your opinion or attitude towards sth: *Try and look at this from my perspective.* ▶ **punkt widzenia 2** [U] the ability to think about problems and decisions in a reasonable way without exaggerating them: *Hearing about others' experiences often helps to **put** your own problems **into perspective*** (patrzeć na własne problemy z dystansu). ◇ *Try to **keep** these issues **in perspective**.* Spróbuj widzieć te sprawy we właściwych proporcjach. ◇ *If you go away for a few days, you will see everything in a new perspective* (w nowym świetle). ▶ (*przen.*) **dystans, punkt widzenia 3** [U] the art of drawing on a flat surface so that some objects appear to be further away than others ▶ (*malarstwo itp.*) **perspektywa**

perspire /pəˈspaɪə(r)/ verb [I] (formal) to lose liquid through your skin when you are hot ▶ **pocić się**

■ **perspiration** /ˌpɜːspəˈreɪʃn/ noun [U] **1** the act of perspiring ▶ **pocenie się 2** the liquid that you lose through your skin ▶ **pot** ℹ W języku codziennym częściej używa się **sweat** (zarówno jako czasownika jak i rzeczownika).

persuade /pə'sweɪd/ verb [T] **1 persuade sb (to do sth); persuade sb (into sth/doing sth)** to make sb do sth by giving them good reasons: *It was difficult to persuade Louise to change her mind.* ◇ *We eventually persuaded Sanjay into coming with us.* ◇ *to persuade sb not to do sth* wyperswadować coś komuś ▶ **przekonać**, **namówić** OPP **dissuade** **2** (formal) **persuade sb that ...; persuade sb (of sth)** to make sb believe sth: *She had persuaded herself that she was going to fail.* ◇ *The jury was not persuaded of her innocence.* ▶ **przekonać (o czymś)** ➲ look at **convince**

persuasion /pə'sweɪʒn/ noun **1** [U] the act of persuading sb to do sth or to believe sth: *It took a lot of persuasion to get Alan to agree.* ▶ **przekonywanie**, **perswazja** **2** [C] (formal) a religious or political belief: *politicians of all persuasions* ▶ **wyznanie**, **przekonanie**

persuasive /pə'sweɪsɪv/ adj. able to persuade sb to do or believe sth: *the persuasive power of advertising* ▶ **przekonujący**
■ **persuasively** adv. ▶ **w sposób przekonujący** | **persuasiveness** noun [U] ▶ **dar perswazji**

pertain /pə'teɪn/ verb [I] (formal) to exist or to apply in a particular situation or at a particular time: *Those laws no longer pertain.* ▶ **mieć zastosowanie**
PHR V **pertain to sth/sb** (formal) to be connected with sth/sb: *the laws pertaining to adoption* ▶ **dotyczyć czegoś/kogoś**

pertinent /'pɜːtɪnənt; US -tnənt/ adj. (formal) closely connected with the subject being discussed: *to ask a pertinent question* ▶ **trafny**, **związany (z czymś)**

perturb /pə'tɜːb/ verb [T] (formal) to make sb worried or upset ▶ **niepokoić**, **trwożyć**
■ **perturbed** adj. ▶ **zaniepokojony**

peruse /pə'ruːz/ verb [T] (formal or humorous) to read sth, especially in a careful way: *A copy of the report is available for you to peruse at your leisure.* ▶ **przeglądać**
■ **perusal** /pə'ruːzl/ noun [U, sing.] ▶ **przejrzenie**

pervade /pə'veɪd/ verb [T] (formal) to spread through and be noticeable in every part of sth: *A sadness pervades most of her novels.* ▶ **szerzyć się**, **przenikać**

pervasive /pə'veɪsɪv/ adj. that is present in all parts of sth: *a pervasive mood of pessimism* ▶ **wszechobecny**, **rozpowszechniony**

perverse /pə'vɜːs/ adj. (formal) liking to behave in a way that is not acceptable or reasonable or that most people think is wrong: *Derek gets perverse pleasure from shocking his parents.* ▶ **przewrotny**, **perwersyjny**
■ **perversely** adv. ▶ **przewrotnie**, **perwersyjnie** | **perversity** /pə'vɜːsəti/ noun [U] ▶ **przewrotność**, **perwersyjność**

perversion /pə'vɜːʃn; US -vɜːʒn/ noun [U,C] **1** sexual behaviour that is not considered normal or acceptable by most people ▶ **zboczenie**, **perwersja** **2** the act of changing sth from right to wrong or from good to bad: *That statement is a perversion of the truth.* ▶ **wypaczenie**, **przekręcenie**

pervert¹ /pə'vɜːt/ verb [T] **1** to change a system, process, etc. in a bad way: *to pervert the course of justice* ▶ **wypaczać** **2** to cause sb to think or behave in a way that is not moral or acceptable ▶ **wypaczać**, **psuć** (*charakter*)

pervert² /'pɜːvɜːt/ noun [C] a person whose sexual behaviour is not thought to be natural or normal by most people ▶ **zboczeniec**

pessimism /'pesɪmɪzəm/ noun [U] **pessimism (about/over sth)** the state of expecting or believing that bad things will happen and that sth will not be successful ▶ **pesymizm** OPP **optimism**
■ **pessimistic** /ˌpesɪ'mɪstɪk/ adj. ▶ **pesymistyczny** | **pessimistically** /-kli/ adv. ▶ **pesymistycznie**

pessimist /'pesɪmɪst/ noun [C] a person who always thinks that bad things will happen or that sth will not be successful ▶ **pesymist(k)a** OPP **optimist**

pest /pest/ noun [C] **1** an insect or an animal that destroys plants, food, etc. ▶ **szkodnik**, **plaga** **2** (informal) a person or thing that annoys you: *That child is such a pest!* ▶ (*przen.*) **utrapienie**

pester /'pestə(r)/ verb [T] **pester sb (for sth); pester sb (to do sth)** to annoy sb, for example by asking them sth many times: *to pester somebody for money* ◇ *The kids kept pestering me to take them to the park.* ▶ **nagabywać**, **niepokoić**

pesticide /'pestɪsaɪd/ noun [C,U] a chemical substance that is used for killing animals, especially insects, that eat food crops ▶ **środek przeciw szkodnikom** ➲ look at **insecticide**

pestle /'pesl/ noun [C] a small heavy tool with a round end used for crushing some foods or substances in a **mortar** ▶ **tłuczek** (*do moździerza*)

pet¹ /pet/ noun [C] **1** an animal or bird that you keep in your home for pleasure rather than for food or work: *a pet dog/cat/hamster* ◇ *a pet shop* sklep zoologiczny ▶ **zwierzę domowe**, **zwierzak** **2** a person who is treated better because they are liked more than any others: *teacher's pet* ▶ **ulubieni-ec/ca**, **pieszczoch**

> **pets**
> **Dogs**, **cats**, **rabbits**, **hamsters** and **guinea pigs** are all popular pets. **Goldfish** are kept in **tanks**, and **budgerigars** in **cages**. Some people keep **exotic** pets, such as **snakes**. Some pets love being **stroked**, but they might **scratch** or **bite** if they are frightened. If you **have a pet**, you need to **look after** it. You should **feed** it, **groom** it and take it to the **vet**. If an animal is very ill, the vet might have to **put** it **down** to stop it suffering.

pet² /pet/ verb (**petting**; **petted**) **1** [T] to treat an animal with affection, e.g. by stroking it ▶ **pieścić** **2** [I] (informal) (used about two people) to kiss and touch in a sexual way ▶ **pieścić się**

petal /'petl/ noun [C] one of the thin soft coloured parts of a flower ▶ **płatek**

peter /'piːtə(r)/ verb
PHR V **peter out** to slowly become smaller, quieter, etc. and then stop ▶ **wyczerpywać się**, (*silnik*) **zgasnąć**

ˌpet 'hate noun [C] sth that you particularly do not like: *Filling in forms is one of my pet hates* (to coś, czego nie znoszę). ▶ **rzecz/czynność szczególnie nielubiana**

petite /pə'tiːt/ adj. (used about a girl, woman or her figure) small and thin: *a petite blonde* ▶ **drobna** ℹ Wyraża aprobatę.

petition /pə'tɪʃn/ noun [C] a written document, signed by many people, that asks a government, etc. to do or change sth: *More than 50 000 people signed the petition protesting about the new road.* ▶ **petycja**
■ **petition** verb [I,T] ▶ **wnosić petycję**

Petri dish /'petri dɪʃ/ noun [C] a covered dish that is not very deep, used for growing bacteria, etc. in ▶ **płytka Petriego** ➲ picture at **laboratory**

petrified /'petrɪfaɪd/ adj. very frightened ▶ **przerażony**, **skamieniały (ze strachu)**, **sparaliżowany strachem**

petrol /'petrəl/ (US **gas**; **gasoline** /'gæsəliːn/) noun [U] the liquid that is used as fuel for vehicles such as cars and motorbikes ▶ **paliwo** (*płynne*), **benzyna** ➲ note at **car** ➲ look at **diesel**

petroleum /pə'trəʊliəm/ noun [U] mineral oil that is found under the ground or sea and is used to make petrol, plastic and other types of chemical substances ▶ **ropa naftowa**

'**petrol station** (also 'service station; US gas station) noun [C] a place where you can buy petrol and other things for your car ▶ **stacja benzynowa** ➲ look at **garage**

pet 'subject noun [C] a subject that you are very interested in or that you feel very strongly about ▶ **ulubiony temat**

petticoat (Brit., old-fashioned) = SLIP² (4)

petty /'peti/ adj. **1** small and unimportant: *He didn't want to get involved with the petty details.* ◇ *petty crime/theft* ▶ **drobny**, **pomniejszy** SYN **minor** **2** unkind or unpleasant to other people (for a reason that does not seem very important): *petty jealousy/revenge* ▶ **małostkowy**

petunia /pə'tju:niə; US -'tu:-/ noun [C] a garden plant with white, pink, purple or red flowers ▶ **petunia**

pew /pju:/ noun [C] a long wooden seat in a church ▶ **ławka kościelna**

pewter /'pju:tə(r)/ noun [U] a grey metal made by mixing tin with **lead**, used especially in the past for making cups, dishes, etc.; objects made from this metal ▶ **stop cyny z ołowiem**

PG /ˌpi: 'dʒi:/ abbr. (Brit.) **parental guidance**. A film that has the label 'PG' is not suitable for children to watch without an adult. ▶ **kategoria filmu, który dzieci mogą oglądać tylko w towarzystwie dorosłych.**

Jest to jedna z pięciu kategorii klasyfikacyjnych, ustanowionych w Wlk. Bryt. dla filmów i kaset wideo przez British Board of Film Classification. U to skrót od **universal** i oznacza, że każdy może oglądać dany film. Pozostałe kategorie to 12, 15 i 18, które oznaczają odpowiednio wiek, od którego dzieci i młodzież mogą dany film oglądać.

PGCE /ˌpi: dʒi: si: 'i:/ abbr. (in Britain) Postgraduate Certificate of Education ▶ **świadectwo ukończenia nauczycielskich studiów podyplomowych**

pH /ˌpi: 'eɪtʃ/ noun [sing.] a measurement of the level of acid or **alkali** in a substance. In the pH range of 0 to 14 a reading of below 7 shows an acid and of above 7 shows an **alkali**. ▶ **pH**

phantom /'fæntəm/ noun [C] **1** (formal) the spirit of a dead person that is seen or heard by sb who is still living ▶ **widmo**, **upiór** ⓘ Częściej używa się słowa **ghost**. **2** something that you think exists, but that is not real ▶ **złudzenie**

pharmaceutical /ˌfɑ:mə'su:tɪkl; Brit. also -'sju:-/ adj. [only before a noun] connected with the production of medicines and drugs: *pharmaceutical companies* ▶ **farmaceutyczny**

pharmacist = CHEMIST (1)

pharmacology /ˌfɑ:mə'kɒlədʒi/ noun [U] the scientific study of drugs and their use in medicine ▶ **farmakologia**
■ **pharmacological** /ˌfɑ:məkə'lɒdʒɪkl/ adj. ▶ **farmakologiczny**

pharmacy /'fɑ:məsi/ noun (pl. **pharmacies**) **1** [C] a shop or part of a shop where medicines and drugs are prepared and sold ▶ **apteka** ⓘ Sklep, w którym można kupić lekarstwa nazywa się też **chemist's (shop)** (Br. ang.) lub **drugstore** (Amer. ang.). **2** [U] the preparation of medicines and drugs ▶ **farmacja**

pharynx /'færɪŋks/ noun [C] (pl. **pharynges** /fə'rɪndʒi:z/) the soft area at the top of the throat where the passages to the nose and mouth connect with the throat ▶ **gardło**

🔑 **phase¹** /feɪz/ noun [C] a stage in the development of sb/sth: *Julie went through a difficult phase when she started school.* ▶ **faza**, **etap**

phase² /feɪz/ verb
PHR V **phase sth in** to introduce or start using sth gradually in stages over a period of time: *The metric system was phased in over several years.* ▶ **wprowadzać stopniowo**
phase sth out to stop using sth gradually in stages over a period of time: *The older machines are gradually being phased out and replaced by new ones.* ▶ **usuwać stopniowo**

PhD /ˌpi: eɪtʃ 'di:/ abbr. **Doctor of Philosophy**; an advanced university degree that you receive when you complete a piece of research into a special subject: *She has a PhD in History.* ▶ (*stopień naukowy*) **dr**

pheasant /'feznt/ noun [C] (pl. **pheasants** or **pheasant**) a type of bird with a long tail. The males have brightly coloured feathers. **Pheasants** are often shot for sport and eaten. ▶ **bażant**

phenomenal /fə'nɒmɪnl/ adj. very great or impressive: *phenomenal success* ▶ **niezwykły**
■ **phenomenally** /-nəli/ adv. ▶ **niezwykle**

phenomenon /fə'nɒmɪnən/ noun [C] (pl. **phenomena** /-ɪnə/) a fact or an event in nature or society, especially one that is not fully understood: *Acid rain is not a natural phenomenon. It is caused by pollution.* ▶ **zjawisko**

phew /fju:/ interj. a sound which you make to show that you are hot, tired or happy that sth bad did not happen or has finished: *Phew, it's hot!* ◇ *Phew, I'm glad that interview's over!* ▶ **uf!**, **phi!**

philanthropist /fɪ'lænθrəpɪst/ noun [C] a rich person who helps the poor and those in need, especially by giving money ▶ **filantrop/ka**

philanthropy /fɪ'lænθrəpi/ noun [U] the practice of helping the poor and those in need, especially by giving money ▶ **filantropia**
■ **philanthropic** /ˌfɪlən'θrɒpɪk/ adj.: *philanthropic work* ▶ **filantropijny**

philatelist /fɪ'lætəlɪst/ noun [C] a person who collects or studies stamps ▶ **filatelist(k)a**

philology /fɪ'lɒlədʒi/ noun [U] the scientific study of the development of language or of a particular language ▶ **filologia** ⓘ Słowo **philology** jest rzadko stosowane w jęz. ang. Zob. przykłady poniżej, gdzie zamiast niego używa się innych wyrażeń: *a French language course* ◇ *a student of English.*
■ **philological** /ˌfɪlə'lɒdʒɪkl/ adj. ▶ **filologiczny**

philosopher /fə'lɒsəfə(r)/ noun [C] a person who has developed a set of ideas and beliefs about the meaning of life: *the Greek philosopher Aristotle* ▶ **filozof/ka**

philosophical /ˌfɪlə'sɒfɪkl/ (also **philosophic**) adj. **1** connected with **philosophy**: *a philosophical debate* ▶ **filozoficzny** **2 philosophical (about sth)** staying calm and not getting upset or worried about sth bad that happens: *He is quite philosophical about failing the exam and says he will try again next year.* ▶ **filozoficzny**
■ **philosophically** /-kli/ adv. ▶ **filozoficznie**

philosophize (also -ise) /fə'lɒsəfaɪz/ verb [I] **philosophize (about/on sth)** to talk about sth in a serious way, especially when other people think this is boring ▶ **filozofować**

🔑 **philosophy** /fə'lɒsəfi/ noun (pl. **philosophies**) **1** [U] the study of ideas and beliefs about the meaning of life: *a degree in philosophy* ▶ **filozofia** **2** [C] a set of beliefs that tries to explain the meaning of life or give rules about how to behave: *Her philosophy is 'If a job's worth doing, it's worth doing well'.* ▶ **filozofia**

phlegm /flem/ noun [U] the thick substance that is produced in your nose and throat when you have a cold ▶ **flegma**

phlegmatic /fleg'mætɪk/ adj. (formal) not easily made angry or upset; calm ▶ **flegmatyczny**, **spokojny**

phobia /'fəʊbiə/ noun [C] a very strong fear or hatred that you cannot explain: *She **has a phobia about** flying.* ▶ **fobia**

phone /fəʊn/ noun (informal) **1** [U] = TELEPHONE (1): *a phone conversation* ◇ *You can book the tickets **by phone/over the phone.*** **2** [C] = TELEPHONE (2): *The phone is ringing – could you answer it?* ➲ note at **telephone**
■ **phone** verb [I,T]: *Did anybody phone while I was out?* ◇ *Could you phone the restaurant and book a table?* ▶ **telefonować** SYN **ring**, **call**
IDM **be on the phone/telephone** **1** to use the telephone ▶ **rozmawiać przez telefon** **2** to have a telephone in your home: *I'll have to write to her because she's not on the phone.* ▶ **mieć telefon w domu**
PHR V **phone in** (especially Brit.) **1** to make a telephone call to the place where you work: *Three people have **phoned in sick** already this morning.* ▶ **dzwonić do swojego miejsca pracy** **2** to make a telephone call to a radio or television station: *Listeners are invited to phone in with their comments.* ▶ **dzwonić do radia/telewizji** ➲ look at **phone-in**

'phone book = TELEPHONE DIRECTORY

'phone booth (also **'telephone booth**) noun [C] a place that is partly separated from the surrounding area, containing a public telephone, in a hotel, restaurant, in the street, etc. ▶ **budka telefoniczna**

'phone box = TELEPHONE BOX

'phone call = CALL[2] (1)

phonecard /'fəʊnkɑːd/ noun [C] a small plastic card that you can use to pay for calls in a public telephone box ▶ **karta telefoniczna**

'phone-in noun [C] a radio or TV programme during which you can ask a question or give your opinion by telephone ▶ **audycja radiowa/telewizyjna, podczas której można zadzwonić do studia, aby zadać pytanie lub wyrazić swoją opinię**

phoneme /'fəʊniːm/ noun [C] any one of the set of smallest units of speech in a language that distinguish one word from another. In English, the /s/ in *sip* and the /z/ in *zip* represent two different **phonemes**. ▶ **fonem**
■ **phonemic** /fə'niːmɪk/ adj. ▶ **fonematyczny**

phonetic /fə'netɪk/ adj. **1** (used about spelling) having a close relationship with the sounds represented: *Spanish spelling is phonetic, unlike English spelling.* ▶ **fonetyczny** **2** connected with the sounds of human speech; using special symbols to represent these sounds: *the phonetic alphabet* ▶ **fonetyczny**
■ **phonetically** /-kli/ adv. ▶ **fonetycznie**

phonetics /fə'netɪks/ noun [U] the study of the sounds of human speech ▶ **fonetyka**

phoney (US **phony**) /'fəʊni/ adj. (**phonier**; **phoniest**) not real: *She spoke with a phoney Russian accent.* ▶ **fałszywy**, **udawany** SYN **fake**
■ **phoney** (US **phony**) noun [C] ▶ **osoba udająca kogoś innego** | **phoniness** noun [U] ▶ **fałsz**, **udawanie**

phonology /fə'nɒlədʒi/ noun [U] the speech sounds of a particular language; the study of these sounds ▶ **fonologia**
■ **phonological** /ˌfəʊnə'lɒdʒɪkl; ˌfɒn-/ adj. ▶ **fonologiczny** | **phonologist** /fə'nɒlədʒɪst/ noun [C] ▶ **fonolog**

photo (informal) = PHOTOGRAPH

photocopier /'fəʊtəʊkɒpiə(r)/ (especially US **copier** /'kɒpiə(r)/) noun [C] a machine that makes copies of documents by photographing them ▶ **kserograf**

photocopy /'fəʊtəʊkɒpi/ noun [C] (pl. **photocopies**) a copy of a document, a page in a book, etc. that is made by a **photocopier** ▶ **odbitka kserograficzna** SYN **Xerox** ➲ look at **copy**
■ **photocopy** verb (also **copy**) [I,T] (**photocopying**; **photocopies**; pt, pp **photocopied**) ▶ **kserować**

photogenic /ˌfəʊtəʊ'dʒenɪk/ adj. looking attractive in photographs ▶ **fotogeniczny**

photograph /'fəʊtəgrɑːf; US -græf/ (also informal **photo** /'fəʊtəʊ/; pl. **photos** /-təʊz/) noun [C] a picture that is taken with a camera: *She looks younger in real life than she did **in the photograph**.* ◇ *to take a photo(graph)* robić zdjęcie ◇ *This photo is a bit out of focus* (trochę nieostre). ◇ *to have a photograph enlarged* dać zdjęcie do powiększenia ▶ **zdjęcie** ➲ note at **camera** ➲ look at **negative**, **slide**
■ **photograph** verb [T] ▶ **fotografować**

photographer /fə'tɒgrəfə(r)/ noun [C] a person who takes photographs: *a fashion/wildlife photographer* ▶ **fotograf** ➲ look at **cameraman**

photographic /ˌfəʊtə'græfɪk/ adj. connected with photographs or **photography** ▶ **fotograficzny**

photography /fə'tɒgrəfi/ noun [U] the skill or process of taking photographs ▶ **fotografia**

photosynthesis /ˌfəʊtəʊ'sɪnθəsɪs/ noun [U] the process by which green plants turn **carbon dioxide** and water into food using energy obtained from light from the sun ▶ **fotosynteza**

photosynthesize (also **-ise**) /ˌfəʊtəʊ'sɪnθəsaɪz/ verb [I,T] (used about plants) to make food by means of **photosynthesis** ▶ **fotosyntetyzować**

phrasal verb /ˌfreɪzl 'vɜːb/ noun [C] a verb that is combined with an adverb or a preposition to give a new meaning, such as 'look after' or 'put sb off' ▶ **czasownik złożony** ➲ look at **verb**

phrase[1] /freɪz/ noun [C] a group of words that are used together. A phrase does not contain a full verb: *'First of all' and 'a bar of chocolate' are phrases.* ▶ **wyrażenie**, **zwrot** ➲ look at **sentence**

phrase[2] /freɪz/ verb [T] to express sth in a particular way: *The statement was phrased so that it would offend no one.* ▶ **formułować**

'phrase book noun [C] a book that gives common words and useful phrases in a foreign language. People often use phrase books when they travel to another country whose language they do not know. ▶ **rozmówki obcojęzyczne**

phraseology /ˌfreɪzi'ɒlədʒi/ noun [U] (formal) the particular way in which words and phrases are arranged when saying or writing sth: *legal phraseology* ▶ **frazeologia**

physical /'fɪzɪkl/ adj. **1** connected with your body rather than your mind: *physical fitness/strength/disabilities* ▶ **cielesny**, **fizyczny** **2** [only before a noun] connected with real things that you can touch, or with the laws of nature: *physical geography* ▶ **fizyczny** **3** [only before a noun] connected with physics: *physical chemistry/laws* ▶ **fizyczny**
■ **physically** /-kli/ adv.: *to be physically fit* ◇ *It will be physically impossible to get to London before ten.* ▶ **fizycznie**, **cieleśnie**

ˌphysical 'therapy (US) = PHYSIOTHERAPY

physician (US, formal) = DOCTOR[1] (1)

physicist /'fɪzɪsɪst/ noun [C] a person who studies or is an expert in physics ▶ **fizyk**

physics /'fɪzɪks/ noun [U] the scientific study of natural forces such as light, sound, heat, electricity, pressure, etc. ▶ **fizyka** ➲ note at **science**

physiology /ˌfɪzi'ɒlədʒi/ noun **1** [U] the scientific study of the normal functions of living things: *the department of anatomy and physiology* ▶ **fizjologia** **2** [U, sing.] the way in which a particular living thing functions: *the physiology of the horse* ◇ *plant physiology* ▶ **fizjologia**
■ **physiological** /ˌfɪziə'lɒdʒɪkl/ adj.: *the physiological effect of space travel* ▶ **fizjologiczny** | **physiologically** /-kli/ adv. ▶ **fizjologicznie**

physiotherapist /ˌfɪziəʊ'θerəpɪst/ noun [C] a person who is trained to use **physiotherapy** ▶ **fizjoterapeuta**

physiotherapy /ˌfɪziəʊ'θerəpi/ (US ˌ**physical 'therapy**) noun [U] the treatment of disease or injury by exercise, light, heat, **massage**, etc. ▶ **fizjoterapia**

physique /fɪ'ziːk/ noun [C] the size and shape of sb's body: *a strong muscular physique* ▶ **budowa ciała** SYN **build**

pianist /'pɪənɪst/ noun [C] a person who plays the piano ▶ **pianist(k)a**

piano /pi'ænəʊ/ noun [C] (pl. **pianos** /-nəʊz/) a large musical instrument that you play by pressing down black and white keys: *an upright piano* pianino ◇ *a grand piano* fortepian ▶ **fortepian, pianino**

Zwróć uwagę, że mówiąc o grze na instrumentach muzycznych zwykle używa się przedimka określonego **the**: *I play the piano.* Jednak mówiąc o grze w zespołach, możemy opuścić przedimek: *She plays (the) cello in string quartet.*, zwłaszcza gdy mówimy o muzyce nowoczesnej (np. o jazzie lub rocku): *I play lead guitar.* ◇ *He plays bass in a band.* ◇ *This recording features Miles Davis on trumpet.*

piccolo /'pɪkələʊ/ noun [C] (pl. **piccolos**) a small **flute** that plays high notes ▶ (*muz.*) **pikolo** ➲ note at **music**, **piano**

pick[1] /pɪk/ verb [T] **1** to choose sb/sth from a group of people or things: *They picked Giles as their captain.* ◇ *Have I picked a bad time to visit?* ▶ **wybierać, sortować** ➲ look at **select** **2** to take a flower, fruit or vegetable from the place where it is growing: *to pick flowers/grapes/cotton* ▶ **zrywać, zbierać** **3** to remove a small piece or pieces of sth from sth else, especially with your fingers: *She picked a hair off her jacket.* ◇ *He picked the nuts off the top of the cake.* ◇ *Don't **pick your nose/teeth**!* Nie dłub w nosie/zębach! ◇ *The dog picked the bones clean* (obgryzł kości z mięsa). ▶ **zdejmować (coś z czegoś)**

IDM **have a bone to pick with sb** → BONE[1]

pick and choose to choose only the things that you like or want very much ▶ **przebierać, wybredzać**

pick a fight (with sb) to start a fight with sb deliberately ▶ **prowokować bijatykę/kłótnię (z kimś)**

pick a lock to open a lock without using a key ▶ **otwierać zamek wytrychem**

pick sb's pocket to steal money, etc. from sb's pocket or bag ▶ **kraść komuś z kieszeni**

pick your way across, over, through, etc. sth to walk carefully, choosing the best places to put your feet: *She picked her way over the rough ground.* ▶ **iść powoli i ostrożnie przez coś/wśród czegoś**

PHR V **pick at sth** **1** to eat only small amounts of food because you are not hungry ▶ (*przen.*) **dziobać** (*jedzenie*) **2** to touch sth many times with your fingers ▶ **ciągnąć za coś/dotykać czegoś wielokrotnie**

pick sth off to remove sth from sth such as a tree, a plant, etc.: *Pick off all the dead leaves.* ▶ **zrywać coś**

pick on sb to behave unfairly or in a cruel way towards sb ▶ **uwziąć się (na kogoś), przyczepiać się (do kogoś)**

pick sb/sth out to choose or recognize sb/sth from a number of people or things; identify: *I immediately picked Jean out in the photo.* ▶ **wyławiać kogoś/coś (skądś/spośród kogoś/czegoś)**

pick up to become better; to improve ▶ **odzyskiwać zdrowie, poprawiać się**

pick sb up **1** to collect sb, in a car, etc.: *We've ordered a taxi to pick us up at ten.* ▶ **podjeżdżać po kogoś** **2** (informal) to start talking to sb you do not know and try to start a sexual relationship with them ▶ **podrywać kogoś** **3** (informal) (used about the police) to stop sb and question them: *The drug dealers were picked up in Dover.* ▶ **zatrzymywać kogoś**

pick sb/sth up **1** to take hold of and lift sb/sth: *Lucy picked up the child and gave him a cuddle.* ▶ **podnosić kogoś/coś** **2** to receive an electronic signal, sound or picture: *In the north of France you can pick up English TV programmes.* ▶ **odbierać** (*np. program telewizyjny*)

pick sth up **1** to learn sth without formal lessons: *Joe picked up a few words of Spanish on holiday.* ▶ **nauczyć się czegoś** **2** to go and get sth; to collect sth: *I have to pick up my jacket from the cleaner's.* ▶ **odbierać/pobierać coś**, **3** to get or find sth: *I picked up this book at the market.* ◇ *You can pick up a lot of information* (wiele się dowiedzieć) *by talking to the residents.* ▶ **uzyskiwać** (*np. informacje*), **znaleźć coś**

pick up on sth **1** to notice sth and perhaps react to it: *She failed to pick up on the humour in his remark.* ▶ **wychwytywać coś** **2** to return to a point that has already been mentioned or discussed: *If I could just pick up on a question you raised earlier.* ▶ **wracać do czegoś** (*w rozmowie/dyskusji*)

pick[2] /pɪk/ noun **1** [sing.] the one that you choose; your choice: *You can have whichever cake you like.* ***Take your pick.*** ▶ **wybór** **2** [sing.] the best of a group: *You can see **the pick of** the new films at this year's festival.* ▶ **wybór** **3** (also **pickaxe**; US **pickax** /'pɪkæks/) [C] a tool that consists of a curved iron bar with sharp points at both ends, fixed onto a wooden handle. **Picks** are used for breaking stones or hard ground. ▶ **kilof, oskard**

picket /'pɪkɪt/ noun [C] a worker or group of workers who stand outside the entrance to a building to protest about sth, especially in order to stop people entering a factory, etc. during a strike: *Fire crews refused to cross the **picket line*** (przejść przez kordon pikietujących). ▶ **pikieta**
■ **picket** verb [I,T] ▶ **pikietować**

pickle /'pɪkl/ noun **1** [C, usually pl.] a vegetable that is cooked and put in salt water or **vinegar**, served cold with meat, salads, etc.: *dill pickles* ogórki kiszone ▶ **marynata** ➲ look at **gherkin** **2** [U] (Brit.) a cold thick sauce with a strong taste made from fruit and vegetables that have been boiled, that is served with meat, cheese, etc. ▶ **pikle**
■ **pickle** verb [T]: *pickled onions* ▶ **marynować, kisić**

pickpocket /'pɪkpɒkɪt/ noun [C] a person who steals things from other people's pockets or bags in public places ▶ **kieszonkowiec**

pickup /'pɪkʌp/ (also **'pickup truck**) noun [C] a type of vehicle that has an open part with low sides at the back ▶ **samochód typu pickup** ➲ picture at **truck**

picky /'pɪki/ adj. (informal) (used about a person) liking only certain things and difficult to please ▶ **wybredny** ➲ look at **fussy**

picnic /'pɪknɪk/ noun [C] a meal that you take with you to eat outdoors; a trip that you make for pleasure during which you eat a picnic: *We had a picnic on the beach.* ◇ *a picnic lunch* ◇ *Let's go for a picnic.* ▶ **piknik** ➲ note at **meal**
■ **picnic** verb [I] (**picnicking**; **picnicked**) ▶ **urządzać piknik**

pictorial /pɪk'tɔːriəl/ adj. expressed in pictures: *pictorial representations of objects* ▶ **obrazowy**

picture[1] /'pɪktʃə(r)/ noun [C] **1** a painting, drawing or photograph: *Who painted the picture in the hall?* ◇ *The teacher asked us to **draw a picture** of our families.* ◇ *Come and have your picture taken* (daj sobie zrobić zdjęcie). ▶ **obraz**, **zdjęcie**, **rysunek** **2** an image on a TV screen: *They showed pictures of the crash on the news.* ▶ **obraz** **3** a description of sth that gives you a good idea of what it is like: *The police are trying to build up a picture of exactly what happened.* ▶ **wyobrażenie**, **obraz** **4** [C] a film (in a cinema) ▶ **film** **5** (**the pictures**) [pl.] (old-fashioned, informal) the cinema: *We are going to the pictures tonight.* ▶ **kino**

picture² /ˈpɪktʃə(r)/ verb [T] **1 picture sb/sth (as sth)** to imagine sth in your mind: *I can't picture Ivan as a father.* ▶ **wyobrażać sobie** **2** [usually passive] to show sb/sth in a photograph or picture: *She is pictured here with her parents.* ▶ **przedstawiać** (*na rysunku/fotografii*)

ˈpicture book noun [C] a book with a lot of pictures, especially one for children ▶ **książeczka z obrazkami**

picturesque /ˌpɪktʃəˈresk/ adj. (usually used about an old building or place) attractive: *a picturesque fishing village* ▶ **malowniczy**

piddle /ˈpɪdl/ verb [I] (old-fashioned, informal) to **urinate** ▶ **siusiać**

piddling /ˈpɪdlɪŋ/ adj. [only before a noun] (informal) small and unimportant: *I spent all day doing piddling little jobs.* ▶ **śmiesznie mały/nieważny** SYN **trivial**

pie /paɪ/ noun [C,U] a type of food consisting of fruit, meat or vegetables inside a **pastry** case: *apple pie* ◇ *meat pie* ▶ **nadziewany placek**, **pasztecik**

> W Wlk. Br. **pie** to ciasto z farszem w środku. W USA **pie** może mieć tylko spód z ciasta, zaś farsz na wierzchu. **Tart** lub **flan** to słodkie ciasto z ułożonymi na wierzchu owocami lub innymi dodatkami. **Quiche** to słone ciasto z ułożoną na wierzchu masą z jaj, sera itp. ➲ look at **mince pie** ➲ picture on **page A14**

piece¹ /piːs/ noun [C] **1** an amount or example of sth ℹ Słowo **piece** stosuje się przy rzeczownikach niepoliczalnych (abstrakcyjnych i zbiorowych) w celu oznaczenia ich ilości jednostkowej. Często nie tłumaczy się odrębnie.: *a piece of news* wiadomość ◇ *an interesting piece of information* ciekawa informacja ◇ *a piece of advice* rada ◇ *a piece of paper* kartka ◇ *a lovely piece of furniture* piękny mebel ◇ *a very good piece of work* bardzo dobra robota ▶ **kawałek**, **część** **2** one of the parts that sth is made of: *We'll have to **take** the engine **to pieces** to find the problem.* ◇ *a three-piece suite* trzyczęściowy komplet wypoczynkowy ▶ **część**, **kawałek** **3** one of the parts into which sth breaks: *The plate fell to the floor and smashed **to pieces**.* ◇ *The vase lay **in pieces** on the floor.* ▶ **część**, **kawałek** ℹ **Bit** i **piece** mają bardzo podobne znaczenie, ale **bit** częściej stosuje się w języku codziennym. **4** a single work of art, music, etc.: *He played a piece by Chopin.* ▶ **utwór**, **sztuka (teatralna)** **5 a piece (on/about sb/sth)** an article in a newspaper or magazine: *There's a good piece on China in today's paper.* ▶ **artykuł** **6** a coin of the value mentioned: *a fifty-pence piece* ▶ **moneta** **7** one of the small objects that you use when you are playing games such as **chess** ▶ **figura (szachowa)**, **pionek** (*np. w warcabach*)

IDM **bits and pieces** → BIT¹

give sb a piece of your mind to speak to sb angrily because of sth they have done ▶ **wygarnąć komuś prawdę w oczy**

go to pieces to be no longer able to work or behave normally because of a difficult situation: *When his wife died he seemed to go to pieces.* ▶ **załamywać się**, **tracić panowanie nad sobą**

in one piece not broken or injured: *I've only been on a motorbike once, and I was just glad to get home in one piece.* ▶ **cały i zdrowy**

a piece of cake (informal) a thing that is very easy to do ▶ **nic trudnego**, (*przen.*) **pestka**

piece² /piːs/ verb

PHR V **piece sth together** **1** to discover the truth about sth from different pieces of information: *Detectives are trying to piece together the last few days of the man's life.* ▶ **kojarzyć** (*np. fakty*), **wnioskować** **2** to put sth together from several pieces ▶ **łączyć**

piecemeal /ˈpiːsmiːl/ adj. done or happening a little at a time ▶ **fragmentaryczny**, **cząstkowy** ■ **piecemeal** adv. ▶ **po kawałku**

ˈpie chart noun [C] a diagram consisting of a circle divided into parts to show the size of particular parts in relation to the whole ▶ **diagram kołowy**

pier /pɪə(r)/ noun [C] **1** (in Britain) a large wooden or metal structure that is built out into the sea in holiday towns, where people can walk ▶ **molo spacerowe**

> W Wlk. Bryt. **pier** jest to molo zabudowane, na którym często można znaleźć teatry, wesołe miasteczko i sklepy.

2 a large wooden or metal structure that is built out into the sea from the land. Boats can stop at **piers** so that people or goods can be taken on or off ▶ **molo**

pierce /pɪəs/ verb **1** [T] to make a hole in sth with a sharp point: *I'm going to **have my ears pierced**.* ▶ **przekłuwać**, **przedziurawiać** **2** [I,T] **pierce (through/into) sth** to manage to go through or into sth: *A scream pierced the air.* ▶ **przeszywać**

piercing¹ /ˈpɪəsɪŋ/ adj. **1** (used about sb's eyes or a look) seeming to know what you are thinking ▶ **przeszywający**, **przenikliwy** **2** (used about the wind, pain, a loud noise, etc.) strong and unpleasant ▶ **przeszywający**, **przenikliwy**

piercing² /ˈpɪəsɪŋ/ noun [U,C] the act of making holes in parts of the body as a decoration; a hole that is made: *body piercing* ◇ *Her face is covered in piercings.* ▶ **piercing**

piety /ˈpaɪəti/ noun [U] a way of behaving that shows a deep respect for God and religion ▶ **pobożność** ➲ adjective **pious**

piffling /ˈpɪflɪŋ/ adj. (informal) small and unimportant: *piffling amounts* ▶ **śmiesznie mały/nieważny**

pig¹ /pɪg/ noun [C] **1** an animal with pink, black or brown skin, short legs, a wide nose and a curly tail, and that is kept on farms for **pork**: *a pig farmer* ▶ **świnia** ➲ note at **meat**

> A male pig is a **boar**, a female pig is a **sow** and a young pig is a **piglet**. When they make a noise, piglets **squeal** and pigs **grunt**.

2 (informal) an unpleasant person or a person who eats too much: *She **made a pig of herself** with the ice cream.* ▶ (*osoba*) **świnia**, **obżartuch**

pig² /pɪg/ verb [T] (**pigging**; **pigged**) (slang) **pig yourself** to eat too much ▶ **obżerać się**

PHR V **pig out (on sth)** (slang) to eat too much of sth ▶ **obżerać się (czymś)**

pigeon /ˈpɪdʒɪn/ noun [C] a fat grey bird that often lives in towns ▶ **gołąb**

pigeonhole /ˈpɪdʒɪnhəʊl/ noun [C] one of a set of small open boxes that are used for putting papers or letters in ▶ **przegródka**

piggyback /ˈpɪgibæk/ noun [C] the way of carrying sb, especially a child, on your back: *to give somebody a piggyback* ▶ (*nosić*) **na barana**

ˈpiggy bank noun [C] a small box, often shaped like a pig, that children save money in ▶ **skarbonka**

ˌpig-ˈheaded adj. (informal) not prepared to change your mind or say that you are wrong ▶ **uparty** ℹ Por. **stubborn** (stosowane w języku codziennym) i **obstinate** (używane w języku formalnym).

piglet /ˈpɪglət/ noun [C] a young pig ▶ **prosiak**

pigment /ˈpɪɡmənt/ noun [C,U] a substance that gives colour to things: *The colour of your skin depends on the amount of pigment in it.* ▶ **pigment**

pigsty /ˈpɪɡstaɪ/ (also sty; US ˈpigpen /ˈpɪɡpen/) noun [C] (pl. **pigsties**) a small building where pigs are kept ▶ **chlew**

pigtail /ˈpɪɡteɪl/ (US **braid**) noun [C] hair that is tied together in one or two lengths made by **plaiting** ▶ **mysi ogonek**, **warkoczyk** ➲ look at **plait** ➲ picture at **hair**

pike /paɪk/ noun [C] (pl. **pike**) a large fish that lives in rivers, lakes, etc. and has very sharp teeth ▶ **szczupak**

pilchard /ˈpɪltʃəd/ noun [C] a small sea fish similar to a herring, that you can eat ▶ **sardela**

⚷ **pile**[1] /paɪl/ noun [C] **1** a number of things lying on top of each other, or an amount of sth lying in a mass: *a pile of books/sand* ◇ *He put the coins **in** neat **piles**.* ◇ *She threw the clothes **in a pile** on the floor.* ▶ **stos**, **kupa** ℹ **Pile** może składać się z elementów ułożonych równo lub nierówno. **Heap** natomiast składa się z elementów ułożonych nierówno. **2** [usually plural] (informal) **piles of sth** a lot of sth: *I've got piles of work to do this evening.* ▶ **kupa**, **góra** ℹ Inne często używane wyrażenie o tym samym znaczeniu to **loads of sth**.

⚷ **pile**[2] /paɪl/ verb [T] **1 pile sth (up)** to put things one on top of the other to form a pile: *We piled the boxes in the corner.* ▶ **usypywać**, **układać w stos 2 pile A on(to) B**; **pile B with A** to put a lot of sth on top of sth: *She piled the papers on the desk.* ◇ *The desk was piled with papers.* ▶ **układać w stos**

PHR V **pile into, out of, off, etc. sth** (informal) to go into, out of, off, etc. sth quickly and all at the same time: *The children piled onto the train.* ▶ **wtłaczać się**; **wysypywać się**

pile up (used about sth bad) to increase in quantity: *Our problems are really piling up.* ▶ **gromadzić się**, **rosnąć**

piles = HAEMORRHOIDS

ˈ**pile-up** noun [C] a crash that involves several cars, etc. ▶ **karambol**

pilfer /ˈpɪlfə(r)/ verb [I,T] **pilfer (sth) (from sb/sth)** to steal things of little value or in small quantities, especially from the place where you work: *She regularly pilfered stamps from work.* ▶ **podkradać (coś) (komuś/z czegoś)**

pilgrim /ˈpɪlɡrɪm/ noun [C] a person who travels a long way to visit a religious place ▶ **pielgrzym**

pilgrimage /ˈpɪlɡrɪmɪdʒ/ noun [C,U] a long journey that a person makes to visit a religious place ▶ **pielgrzymka**

⚷ **pill** /pɪl/ noun **1** [C] a small round piece of medicine that you swallow: *Take one pill, three times a day after meals.* ◇ *a sleeping pill* pigułka nasenna ▶ **pigułka** ➲ look at **tablet 2 (the pill**; **the Pill)** [sing.] a **pill** that some women take regularly so that they do not become pregnant: *She is **on the pill**.* ▶ **pigułka antykoncepcyjna**

pillage /ˈpɪlɪdʒ/ verb [I,T] to steal things from a place or region, especially in a war, using violence: *The rebels went looting and pillaging.* ◇ *Works of art were pillaged from churches and museums.* ▶ **plądrować** SYN **plunder**

■ **pillage** noun [U]: *They brought back horrific accounts of murder and pillage.* ▶ **grabież** ➲ look at **loot**, **plunder**

pillar /ˈpɪlə(r)/ noun [C] **1** a column of stone, wood or metal that is used for supporting part of a building ▶ **kolumna**, **filar 2** a person who has a strong character and is important to sb/sth: *Dave was a **pillar of strength** to his sister when she was ill.* ▶ **podpora**, **filar**

ˈ**pillar box** noun [C] (in Britain) a tall round red box in a public place into which you can post letters, which are then collected by sb from the post office ▶ **skrzynka pocztowa** ➲ look at **postbox**, **letter box**

pillion /ˈpɪliən/ noun [C] a seat for a passenger behind the driver on a motorbike ▶ **tylne siodełko motocykla**

■ **pillion** adv.: *to ride pillion on a motorbike* jechać na tylnym siodełku motocykla

pillow /ˈpɪləʊ/ noun [C] a large cloth bag filled with soft material that you put under your head when you are in bed ▶ **poduszka** ➲ picture at **bed**

Poduszka do spania nazywa się **pillow**. Poduszka ozdobna to **cushion**.

pillowcase /ˈpɪləʊkeɪs/ noun [C] a thin soft cover for a pillow ▶ **poszewka**

⚷ **pilot**[1] /ˈpaɪlət/ noun [C] **1** a person who flies an aircraft: *an airline pilot* ▶ **pilot/ka** ➲ picture on **page A4 2** a person with special knowledge of a difficult area of water, who guides ships through it ▶ **pilot/ka**

pilot[2] /ˈpaɪlət/ verb [T] **1** to operate the controls of a vehicle, especially an aircraft or a boat: *to pilot a ship* ▶ **pilotować 2** to lead sb/sth through a difficult situation: *The booklet pilots you through the process of starting your own business.* ▶ **pilotować**, **służyć za przewodnika 3** to test a new product, idea, etc. that will be used by everyone: *The new exam is being piloted in schools in Italy.* ▶ **wprowadzać pilotażowo**

pilot[3] /ˈpaɪlət/ adj. [only before a noun] done as an experiment or to test sth that will be used by everyone: *The pilot scheme will run for six months.* ▶ **próbny**, **pilotażowy**

pimp /pɪmp/ noun [C] a man who controls prostitutes, finds customers for them and takes part of the money they earn ▶ **alfons**, **rajfur**

pimple /ˈpɪmpl/ noun [C] a small spot on your skin ▶ **pryszcz** ➲ look at **goose pimples**

PIN /pɪn/ (also ˈ**PIN number**) noun [C, usually sing.] **personal identification number**; a number given to you by your bank so that you can use a plastic card to take out money from a **cash machine**: *I've forgotten my PIN.* ▶ **osobisty numer identyfikacyjny**

⚷ **pin**[1] /pɪn/ noun [C] **1** a short thin piece of metal with a round head at one end and a sharp point at the other. Pins are used for fastening together pieces of cloth, paper, etc. ▶ **szpilka** ➲ look at **drawing pin**, **safety pin 2** a thin piece of wood or metal that is used for a particular purpose: *a two-pin plug* wtyczka z dwoma bolcami ◇ *a hairpin* spinka/wsuwka do włosów ▶ **trzpień**, **kołek** ➲ picture at **plug**

⚷ **pin**[2] /pɪn/ verb [T] (**pinning**; **pinned**) **1 pin sth to/on sth**; **pin sth together** to fasten sth with a pin or pins: *Could you pin this notice on the board, please?* ◇ *The dress is just pinned together.* (spięta szpilkami) *I've not sewn it yet.* ◇ *The policeman held him with his arms pinned to his sides* (przyciśniętymi do boków). ▶ **przypinać**, **spinać (szpilką)**, **przyczepiać 2 pin sb/sth against, to, under, etc. sth** to make sb/sth unable to move by holding or pressing down on them or it: *They pinned him against a wall and stole his wallet.* ◇ *He was pinned under* (został przygnieciony) *the fallen tree.* ▶ **przygważdżać/przypierać kogoś do czegoś**

IDM **pin (all) your hopes on sb/sth** to believe completely that sb/sth will help you or will succeed: *All our hopes are pinned on him.* ▶ **pokładać (całą) nadzieję w kimś/czymś**

PHR V **pin sb down 1** to hold sb so they cannot move ▶ **przygważdżać/przypierać kogoś do muru 2** to force sb to decide sth or to say exactly what they are going to do: *Can you pin her down to what time she'll be coming?* ▶ **zmuszać kogoś do podania/sprecyzowania czegoś** (*np. do podjęcia decyzji*)

pin sth down to describe or explain exactly what sth is ▶ **precyzować coś**

P

pinafore /ˈpɪnəfɔː(r)/ noun [C] (especially Brit.) a loose dress with no sleeves, usually worn over other clothes ▶ **fartuch** ➲ look at **apron**

pincer /ˈpɪnsə(r)/ noun **1** (**pincers**) [pl.] a tool made of two crossed pieces of metal that is used for holding things, pulling nails out of wood, etc. ▶ **obcęgi**, **szczypce** **2** [C] one of the two sharp, curved front legs of some **shellfish** that are used for holding things ▶ **kleszcze** (*skorupiaka*) ➲ picture on **page A11**

pinch¹ /pɪntʃ/ verb **1** [T] to hold a piece of sb's skin tightly between your thumb and first finger, especially in order to hurt them: *Paul pinched his brother and made him cry.* ▶ **szczypać** **2** [I,T] to hold sth too tight, often causing pain: *I've got a pinched nerve* (przygnieciony nerw) *in my neck.* ▶ **cisnąć**, **uwierać** **3** [T] (informal) to steal: *Who's pinched my pen?* ▶ **gwizdnąć** (*ukraść*)

pinch² /pɪntʃ/ noun [C] **1** the holding of sb's skin tightly between your finger and thumb: *She gave him a little pinch on the arm.* ▶ **uszczypnięcie** **2** the amount of sth that you can pick up with your thumb and first finger: *a pinch of salt* ▶ **szczypta**

IDM **at a pinch** (used to say that sth can be done if it is really necessary): *We really need three cars but we could manage with two at a pinch.* ▶ **w razie potrzeby**, (*przen.*) **na siłę**

take sth with a pinch of salt to think that sth is probably not true or accurate ▶ **traktować coś z przymrużeniem oka**

pinched /pɪntʃt/ adj. (used about sb's face) thin and pale because of illness or cold ▶ **ściągnięty**, **wynędzniały**

pine¹ /paɪn/ noun **1** [C] (also ˈ**pine tree**) a tall tree that has needles ▶ **sosna**

> Trees, such as the **pine**, that do not lose their leaves in winter are called **evergreen**.

2 [U] the wood from **pine** trees, often used for making furniture: *a pine table* ▶ **drewno sosny**

pine² /paɪn/ verb [I] **pine (for sb/sth)** to be very unhappy because sb has died or gone away: *She pined for months after he'd gone.* ▶ **usychać z tęsknoty**

pineapple /ˈpaɪnæpl/ noun [C,U] a large sweet fruit that is yellow inside and has a thick brown skin with sharp points. **Pineapples** grow in hot countries. ▶ **ananas** ➲ picture on **page A12**

ˈ**pine tree** = PINE¹ (1)

ping /pɪŋ/ noun [C] a short high noise that is made by a small bell or by a metal object hitting against sth: *The lift went ping and the doors opened.* ▶ **brzdęk**, **brzęk**
■ **ping** verb [I] ▶ **brzęczeć**; **sprawiać, żeby coś zabrzęczało**

ˈ**ping-pong** (informal) = TABLE TENNIS

pink /pɪŋk/ adj. of a pale red colour ▶ **różowy**
■ **pink** noun [U] ▶ **kolor różowy**

pinkish /ˈpɪŋkɪʃ/ adj. rather pink ▶ **różowawy**

pinnacle /ˈpɪnəkl/ noun [C] **1** the most important or successful part of sth: *Celia is at the pinnacle of her career.* ▶ **szczyt** **2** a high pointed rock on a mountain ▶ **szczyt** **3** a pointed stone ornament on the top of a church or castle ▶ **wieżyczka**, **sterczyna**

pinpoint /ˈpɪnpɔɪnt/ verb [T] **1** to find the exact position of sth: *to pinpoint a place on the map* ▶ **określać dokładną pozycję czegoś** **2** to describe or explain exactly what sth is: *First we have to pinpoint the cause of the failure.* ▶ **precyzować**

ˌ**pins and** ˈ**needles** noun [U] a strange, sometimes painful feeling that you get in a part of your body after it has been in one position for too long and when the blood is returning to it ▶ **mrowienie**

pinstriped /ˈpɪnstraɪpt/ adj. [only before a noun] (used about dark material) having white vertical lines printed on it: *a pinstriped suit* ▶ **w jasne prążki** (*na ciemnym materiale*)

pint /paɪnt/ noun [C] **1** (abbr. **pt**) a measure of liquid; 0.57 of a litre: *a pint of milk* ▶ **pół kwarty**

> There are 8 **pints** in a gallon. An American pint is 0.47 of a litre.

ℹ Więcej o wyrażeniach miar w dodatku *Wyrażenia liczbowe* na końcu słownika. **2** (Brit., informal) a pint of beer: *We had a pint and a sandwich at the local pub.* ▶ **pół kwarty piwa**

ˈ**pin-up** noun [C] (informal) a picture of an attractive person, made to be put on a wall; a person who appears in these pictures ▶ **zdjęcie atrakcyjnej osoby** (*w magazynie lub przyczepione do ściany*)

pioneer /ˌpaɪəˈnɪə(r)/ noun [C] **1 a pioneer (in/of sth)** a person who is one of the first to develop an area of human knowledge, culture, etc.: *Yuri Gagarin was one of the pioneers of space exploration.* ▶ **pionier/ka** **2** a person who is one of the first to go and live in a particular area: *the pioneers of the American West* ▶ **pionier/ka**
■ **pioneer** verb [T]: *a technique pioneered in the US* ▶ **zapoczątkować**; **torować drogę** | **pioneering** adj. [usually before a noun] introducing ideas and methods that have never been used before: *pioneering work on infant mortality* ▶ **pionierski**

pious /ˈpaɪəs/ adj. having or showing a deep belief in religion ▶ **pobożny** ➲ noun **piety**
■ **piously** adv. ▶ **pobożnie**

pip¹ /pɪp/ noun [C] (Brit.) the small seed of an apple, a lemon, an orange, etc. ▶ **pestka** ➲ picture on **page A12**

pip² /pɪp/ verb

IDM **pip sb at the post** to defeat sb at the last moment or by a small amount ▶ **wygrywać w ostatniej chwili/o włos**

pipe¹ /paɪp/ noun [C] **1** a tube that carries gas or liquid: *a drainpipe* rynna ▶ **rura**, **przewód** **2** a tube with a small bowl at one end that is used for smoking **tobacco**: *to smoke a pipe* ▶ **fajka** **3** a simple musical instrument that consists of a tube with holes in it. You blow into it to play it. ▶ **piszczałka**, **fujarka**

pipe² /paɪp/ **1** verb [T] to carry liquid or gas in pipes: *Water is piped to all the houses in the town.* ◇ *Many supermarkets have piped music playing* (puszczają muzykę przez głośniki). ▶ **doprowadzać**, **dostarczać** **2** to play music on a pipe ▶ **grać na piszczałce/fujarce**

PHR V **pipe up (with sth)** to suddenly say sth: *Suddenly Shirin piped up* (wyskoczył z) *with a question.* ▶ **nagle coś powiedzieć**

ˌ**piped** ˈ**music** noun [U] (Brit.) recorded music that is played continuously in shops, restaurants, etc. ▶ **muzyka z głośników** (*np. w supermarkecie*)

pipeline /ˈpaɪplaɪn/ noun [C] a line of pipes that are used for carrying liquid or gas over a long distance ▶ **rurociąg**

IDM **in the pipeline** being planned or prepared ▶ **w trakcie przygotowań**

piper /ˈpaɪpə(r)/ noun [C] a person who plays music on a pipe, or who plays the **bagpipes** ▶ **osoba grająca na piszczałce lub fujarce**, **kobziarz**

pipette /pɪˈpet/ noun [C] a narrow tube used in a laboratory for measuring or moving small amounts of liquids ▶ **pipet(k)a** ➲ picture at **laboratory**

piracy /ˈpaɪrəsi/ noun [U] **1** the crime of attacking ships in order to steal from them ▶ **piractwo**, **korsarstwo** **2** the illegal copying of books, video tapes, etc. ▶ **piractwo**

pirate¹ /ˈpaɪrət/ noun [C] **1** (usually in the past or in stories) a criminal who attacks ships in order to steal from them ▶ **pirat**, **korsarz** **2** a person who copies books, video tapes, computer programs, etc. in order to sell them illegally ▶ **pirat**

pirate² /ˈpaɪrət/ verb [T] to make an illegal copy of a book, video tape, etc. in order to sell it ▶ **nielegalnie kopiować**

Pisces /ˈpaɪsiːz/ noun [C,U] the 12th sign of the **zodiac**, the Fishes; a person born under this sign: *I'm a Pisces.* ▶ **Ryby**; **osoba spod znaku Ryb**

piss¹ /pɪs/ verb [I] (taboo, slang) to **urinate** ▶ **sikać** ⓘ Grzeczny odpowiednik tego wyrażenia: **go to the toilet/loo** (Brit.), **go to the bathroom** (US) lub **to go**.
PHR V **piss off** (especially Brit.) [usually used in orders] to go away: *Why don't you just piss off and leave me alone?* ▶ **spieprzać**
piss sb off to make sb annoyed or bored: *Her attitude really pisses me off.* ▶ **wkurzać kogoś**

piss² /pɪs/ noun (taboo, slang) **1** [U] = URINE **2** [sing.] an act of **urinating**: *to go for a piss* iść się odlać ▶ **sikanie**
IDM **take the piss (out of sb/sth)** (Brit.) to make fun of sb, especially by copying them or laughing at them for reasons they do not understand ▶ **robić sobie jaja (z kogoś/czegoś)**

pissed /pɪst/ adj. (Brit., taboo, slang) drunk ▶ **nawalony**

pistachio /pɪˈstæʃiəʊ; -ˈstɑːʃ-/ noun [C] (pl. **pistachios**) (also **piˈstachio nut**) the small green nut of an Asian tree ▶ **orzech pistacjowy**

pistol /ˈpɪstl/ noun [C] a small gun that you hold in one hand ▶ **pistolet** ➲ note at **gun**

piston /ˈpɪstən/ noun [C] a piece of metal in an engine, etc. that fits tightly inside a metal tube. The piston is moved up and down inside the tube and causes other parts of the engine to move. ▶ **tłok**

pit¹ /pɪt/ noun **1** [C] a large hole that is made in the ground: *They dug a large pit to bury the dead animals.* ▶ **dół** **2** = COAL MINE **3** (**the pits**) [pl.] the place on a motor racing track where cars stop for fuel, new tyres, etc. during a race ▶ **punkt obsługi na wyścigach samochodowych** **4** [C] = ORCHESTRA PIT
IDM **be the pits** (slang) to be very bad: *The food in that restaurant is the pits!* ▶ **być okropnym**

pit² /pɪt/ verb [T] (**pitting**; **pitted**) to make small holes in the surface of sth: *The front of the building was pitted with bullet marks.* ▶ **pokryć dołkami/dziobami**
PHR V **pit A against B** to test one person or thing against another in a fight or competition: *The two strongest teams were pitted against each other in the final.* ▶ **przeciwstawiać kogoś/coś komuś/czemuś**

🔑 **pitch¹** /pɪtʃ/ noun **1** [C] (Brit.) a special area of ground where you play certain sports: *a football/hockey/cricket pitch* ▶ **boisko** ➲ look at **court**, **field** **2** [sing.] the strength or level of feelings, activity, etc.: *The children's excitement almost reached fever pitch.* ▶ **pułap** **3** [U] how high or low a sound is, especially a musical note: *I think somebody's singing **off pitch*** (fałszuje). ▶ **wysokość tonu** **4** [C] talk or arguments used by sb who is trying to sell sth or persuade sb to do sth: *a sales pitch* ◇ *to make a pitch for something* ▶ **przekonywanie kogoś, aby coś kupił lub zrobił** **5** [U] the movement of a ship or an aeroplane up or down or from side to side ▶ **kołysanie się** (*statku, samolotu*)

pitch² /pɪtʃ/ verb **1** [I,T] to throw: *Doug pitched his empty can into the bushes.* ▶ **rzucać** **2** [I,T] to be thrown: *Her bike hit a stone and she pitched forwards over the handlebars* (przeleciała przez kierownicę). ▶ **upadać** (*głową naprzód*) **3** [T] to set sth at a particular level: *The talk was pitched at* (odczyt był na poziomie) *people with more experience than me.* ◇ *a high-pitched voice* wysoki głos ▶ **ustawiać** (*na jakimś poziomie*) **4** [T] **pitch sth (at sb)** to try to sell a product to a particular group of people or in a particular way: *This new breakfast cereal is being pitched at kids.* ▶ (*reklama itp.*) **kierować do określonej grupy odbiorców** **5** [T] to put up a tent or tents: *We could pitch our tents in that field.* ▶ **rozbijać namiot** **6** [I] (used about a ship or an airplane) to move up and down or from side to side ▶ (*statek, samolot*) **kołysać się**
PHR V **pitch in** (informal) to join in and work together with other people: *Everybody pitched in to clear up the flood damage.* ▶ **brać się wspólnie do roboty**

ˌpitch-ˈblack adj. completely dark; with no light at all ▶ **czarny jak smoła**

pitcher /ˈpɪtʃə(r)/ noun [C] **1** a large container for holding and pouring liquids ▶ **dzban** **2** (in the sport of **baseball**) the player who throws the ball to a player from the other team, who tries to hit it ▶ (*baseball*) **zawodnik rzucający piłkę**

pitchfork /ˈpɪtʃfɔːk/ noun [C] a fork with a long handle and two sharp metal points, that is often used on a farm for lifting and moving cut grass, etc. ▶ **widły**

piteous /ˈpɪtiəs/ adj. (formal) that makes you feel pity or sadness ▶ **żałosny**
■ **piteously** adv. ▶ **żałośnie**

pitfall /ˈpɪtfɔːl/ noun [C] a danger or difficulty, especially one that is hidden or not obvious ▶ **pułapka**

pith /pɪθ/ noun [U] the white substance inside the skin of an orange, lemon, etc. ▶ **biała część skórki niektórych owoców**

pithy /ˈpɪθi/ adj. (**pithier**; **pithiest**) (used about a comment, piece of writing, etc.) short but expressed in a clear, direct way: *a pithy comment* ▶ **zwięzły**, **treściwy**

pitiful /ˈpɪtɪfl/ adj. causing you to feel pity or sadness: *the pitiful groans of the wounded soldiers* ▶ **żałosny** ➲ look at **pathetic**
■ **pitifully** /-fəli/ adv. ▶ **żałośnie**

pitiless /ˈpɪtiləs/ adj. having or showing no pity for other people's suffering ▶ **bezlitosny**, **niemiłosierny**
■ **pitilessly** adv. ▶ **bezlitośnie**, **niemiłosiernie**

pittance /ˈpɪtns/ noun [usually sing.] a very small amount of money that sb receives, for example as a wage, and that is hardly enough to live on: *to pay sb a pittance* ▶ **nędzne grosze**

pituitary /pɪˈtjuːɪtəri; US -ˈtuːəteri/ (also **piˈtuitary gland**) noun [C] a small organ at the base of the brain that produces **hormones** that influence growth and sexual development ▶ **przysadka mózgowa**

🔑 **pity¹** /ˈpɪti/ noun **1** [U] a feeling of sadness that you have for sb/sth that is suffering or in trouble: *The situation is his fault so I don't feel any pity for him.* ▶ **litość**, **współczucie** **2** [sing.] something that makes you feel a little sad or disappointed: *'You're too late. Emily left five minutes ago.' 'Oh, **what a pity**!'* ◇ *It's a pity that Bina couldn't come.* ▶ **szkoda (że)**
IDM **take pity on sb** to help sb who is suffering or in trouble because you feel sorry for them ▶ **wspierać kogoś/pomagać komuś z litości**

pity² /ˈpɪti/ verb [T] (**pitying**; **pities**; pt, pp **pitied**) to feel pity or sadness for sb who is suffering or in trouble: *We shouldn't just pity these people; we must help them.* ▶ **współczuć**
■ **pitying** adj. showing pity: *a pitying look* ▶ **litościwy**, **współczujący**

pivot¹ /ˈpɪvət/ noun [C] **1** the central point on which sth turns or balances ▶ **trzpień**, **oś** **2** the central or most important person or thing: *West Africa was the pivot of the cocoa trade.* ▶ **główna postać/rzecz**

pivot² /ˈpɪvət/ verb [I] to turn or balance on a central point ▶ **obracać się** (*wokół osi/dookoła czegoś*)

P

pivotal /ˈpɪvətl/ adj. of great importance because other things depend on it: *a pivotal role in European affairs* ▶ **zasadniczy**

pixel /ˈpɪksl/ noun [C] any of the very small individual areas on a computer screen, which together form the whole image ▶ **piksel**

pixelate (also **pixellate**) /ˈpɪksəleɪt/ verb [T] **1** to divide an image into **pixels** ▶ **dzielić obraz na piksele 2** to show an image on television as a small number of large **pixels**, especially in order to hide sb's identity ▶ **pokazać obraz w formie pikseli**

pixie /ˈpɪksi/ noun [C] (in children's stories) a creature like a small person with pointed ears that has magic powers ▶ **chochlik**

pizza /ˈpiːtsə/ noun [C,U] an Italian dish consisting of a flat round bread base with vegetables, cheese, meat, etc. on top, which is cooked in an oven ▶ **pizza** ➲ picture on **page A14**

pkt = PACKET (1)

pl. = PLURAL

placard /ˈplækɑːd/ noun [C] a large written or printed notice that is put in a public place or carried on a stick in a protest march ▶ **afisz**, **plakat**

placate /pləˈkeɪt; US ˈpleɪkeɪt/ verb [T] to make sb feel less angry about sth ▶ **łagodzić**, **udobruchać**

🔑 **place¹** /pleɪs/ noun [C] **1** a particular position or area: *Show me the exact place where it happened.* ◇ *This would be a good place to sit down and have a rest.* ◇ *The wall was damaged in several places.* ▶ **miejsce 2** a particular village, town, country, etc.: *Which places did you go to in Italy?* ◇ *Vienna is a very beautiful place.* ▶ **miejsce 3** a building or area that is used for a particular purpose: *The square is a popular* ***meeting place*** *for young people.* ◇ *The town is full of inexpensive eating places.* ▶ **miejsce 4** a seat or position that can be used by sb/sth: *They went into the classroom and sat down in their places.* ◇ *Go on ahead and* ***save me a place*** *in the queue.* ◇ *to lay six places for dinner* nakryć stół na sześć osób ▶ **miejsce**, **krzesło**

> **Place** to miejsce lub pozycja, w jakiej ktoś/coś ma się znaleźć: *If you arrive first, can you keep a place for me?* O miejscu do parkowania samochodu mówi się też **space**. Mówiąc o jakiejś ogólnej przestrzeni używa się słowa **space** lub **room**: *This piano* ***takes up*** *a lot of* ***space/room.*** ◇ *There is enough* ***space/room for*** *three people in the back of the car.*

5 your position in society; your role: *I feel* ***it is not my place*** (nie na miejscu) *to criticize my boss.* ▶ **pozycja 6** an opportunity to study at a college, play for a team, etc.: *Abina has got a place to study law at Oxford University.* ◇ *Laila is now sure of a place on the team.* ▶ **miejsce 7** the usual or correct position or occasion for sth: *The room was tidy. Everything had been put away* ***in its place.*** ◇ *A funeral is not the place to discuss business.* ▶ **miejsce**, **sposobność 8** [sing.] (informal) sb's home: *Her parents have got a place on the coast.* ◇ *Why not stay the night at our place* (u nas)*?* ▶ **mieszkanie**, **dom 9** the position that you have at the end of a race, competition, etc.: *Cara finished* ***in second place.*** ▶ **miejsce 10** the position of a number after the **decimal point**: *Your answer should be correct to three decimal places.* ▶ **miejsce**

IDM **all over the place** everywhere ▶ **wszędzie**

change/swap places (with sb) to take sb's seat, position, etc. and let them have yours: *Let's change places so that you can look out of the window.* ▶ **zamieniać się miejscami**

fall/slot into place (used about sth that is complicated or difficult to understand) to become organized or clear in your mind: *After two weeks in my new job, everything suddenly started to fall into place.* ▶ **ułożyć się** (*w głowie*), **wyjaśnić się**

in the first, second, etc. place (informal) (used when you are giving a list of reasons for sth or explaining sth) ▶ **po pierwsze/drugie itp.** SYN **firstly**, **secondly**, etc.

in my, your, etc. place/shoes in my, your, etc. situation or position: *If I were in your place I would wait a year before getting married.* ▶ **na moim/twoim itp. miejscu**

in place 1 in the correct or usual position: *Use tape to hold the picture in place.* ▶ **na (swoim) miejscu 2** (used about plans or preparations) finished and ready to be used: *All the preparations for the trip are now in place.* ▶ **gotowy**

in place of sb/sth; **in sb/sth's place** instead of sb/sth ▶ **na czyjeś miejsce**, **zamiast**

out of place 1 not in the correct or usual place ▶ **nie na miejscu**, **niestosowny 2** not suitable for a particular situation: *I felt very out of place among all those clever people.* ▶ **nie na (swoim) miejscu**

put sb in his/her place to show that sb is not as clever, important, etc. as they believe: *It really put her in her place when she failed to qualify for the race.* ▶ **pokazać komuś, gdzie jest jego miejsce**

put yourself in sb's place to imagine that you are in the same situation as sb else: *Put yourself in Steve's place and you will realize how worried he must be.* ▶ **postawić się na czyimś miejscu**

take place (used about a meeting, an event, etc.) to happen: *The ceremony took place in glorious sunshine.* ▶ **odbywać się**, **mieć miejsce** ➲ note at **happen**

take sb's/sth's place; **take the place of sb/sth** to replace sb/sth ▶ **zastępować**, **zajmować czyjeś miejsce**

🔑 **place²** /pleɪs/ verb [T] **1** (formal) to put sth carefully or deliberately in a particular position: *The chairs had all been placed in neat rows.* ◇ *The poster was placed where everyone could see it.* ▶ **umieszczać 2** to put sb in a particular position or situation: *His behaviour placed me in a difficult situation.* ◇ *Rhoda was placed third in the competition.* ◇ *to place sb in charge* powierzać komuś kierownictwo ▶ **stawiać**, **umieszczać 3** (used to express the attitude that sb has to sb/sth): *We placed our trust in you* (ufaliśmy ci) *and you failed us.* ◇ *The blame for the disaster was placed firmly on the company.* Całą winą za to nieszczęście obarczono firmę. ▶ **obdarzać kogoś** (*zaufaniem*), **pokładać w kimś/czymś** (*nadzieję*), **obarczać kogoś** (*winą, odpowiedzialnością*) **4** [usually in negative statements] to recognize sb/sth and be able to identify them or it: *Her face is familiar but I just can't quite place her.* ▶ **rozpoznawać**, **określać 5** to give instructions about sth or to ask for sth to happen: *to place a bet on something* ◇ *to place an order for something* ▶ **składać** (*zamówienie*)

placebo /pləˈsiːbəʊ/ noun [C] (pl. **-os**) a substance that has no physical effects, given to patients who do not need medicine but think that they do, or used when testing new drugs: *the* ***placebo effect*** ▶ **placebo**

ˈplace name noun [C] the name of a city, town, etc. ▶ **nazwa** (*np. miasta*)

placenta /pləˈsentə/ (usually **the placenta**) noun [C] the material that comes out of a woman or female animal's body after a baby has been born, and which was necessary to feed and protect the baby ▶ **łożysko**

placid /ˈplæsɪd/ adj. (used about a person or an animal) calm and not easily excited: *a placid baby/horse* ▶ **łagodny**, **spokojny**

■ **placidly** adv. ▶ **spokojnie**

plagiarize (also **-ise**) /ˈpleɪdʒəraɪz/ verb [T,I] to copy another person's ideas, words or work and pretend that they are your own: *He was accused of plagiarizing his colleague's results.* ▶ **dokonywać plagiatu**

■ **plagiarism** /ˈpleɪdʒərɪzəm/ noun [U,C]: *accusations of plagiarism* ◇ *The text was full of plagiarisms.* ▶ **plagiatorstwo**; **plagiat**

plague¹ /pleɪɡ/ noun **1** (**the plague**) [U] an infectious disease spread by **rats** that makes large spots form on the body, causes a very high temperature and often results in death ▶ **dżuma 2** [C,U] any infectious disease that spreads quickly and kills many people ▶ **zaraza**, **dżuma 3** [C] **a plague of sth** a large number of unpleasant animals or insects that come into an area at one time: *a plague of ants/locusts* ▶ **plaga**

plague² /pleɪɡ/ verb [T] to cause sb/sth a lot of trouble: *The project was plagued by a series of disasters.* ▶ **sprowadzać na kogoś nieszczęście**, **dotykać plagą**

plaice /pleɪs/ noun [C,U] (pl. **plaice**) a type of flat sea fish that we eat ▶ **płastuga**

⚷ **plain¹** /pleɪn/ adj. **1** easy to see, hear or understand; clear: *It was plain that he didn't want to talk about it.* ◇ *She **made it plain that** she didn't want to see me again.* ▶ **jasny**, **zrozumiały 2** (used about people, thoughts, actions, etc.) saying what you think; direct and honest: *I'll be plain with you. I don't like the idea.* ▶ **szczery**, **bezpośredni 3** simple in style; not decorated or complicated: *My father likes plain English cooking.* ▶ **zwykły**, **prosty 4** [only before a noun] all one colour; without a pattern on it: *a plain blue jumper* ▶ (*tkanina*) **gładki**, **jednolity** (*w kolorze*) ➲ picture on **page A1** **5** (used especially about a woman or girl) not beautiful or attractive: *She's a rather plain child.* ▶ **nieładny**

plain² /pleɪn/ noun [C] **1** a large area of flat land with few trees ▶ **równina 2** a simple stitch used in knitting ▶ **zwykły ścieg**

plain³ /pleɪn/ adv. (informal) completely: *That's plain silly.* ▶ **zupełnie**

ˌplain ˈchocolate (Brit.) = DARK CHOCOLATE

ˌplain ˈclothes noun [pl.] ordinary clothes, not uniform, when worn by police officers on duty: *officers **in plain clothes*** (ubrani po cywilnemu). ▶ **cywilne ubranie**

■ **ˌplain-ˈclothes** adj. [only before a noun]: *a plain-clothes detective* ▶ **po cywilnemu**

ˌplain ˈflour noun [U] flour that does not contain **baking powder** ▶ **mąka bez dodatku proszku do pieczenia** ➲ look at **self-raising flour**

plainly /ˈpleɪnli/ adv. **1** clearly: *He was plainly very upset.* ▶ **wyraźnie**, **dokładnie 2** using simple words to say sth in a direct and honest way: *She told him plainly that he was not doing his job properly.* ▶ **otwarcie**, **szczerze 3** in a simple way, without decoration: *She was plainly dressed and wore no make-up.* ▶ **prosto**, **zwyczajnie**

plaintiff /ˈpleɪntɪf/ noun [C] a person who starts a legal action against sb in a court of law ▶ **powód/ka** ➲ look at **defendant**

plaintive /ˈpleɪntɪv/ adj. sounding sad, especially in a weak complaining way: *a plaintive cry/voice* ▶ **żałosny**, **płaczliwy**

■ **plaintively** adv. ▶ **żałośnie**, **płaczliwie**

plait /plæt/ (US **braid**) verb [T] to cross three or more long pieces of hair, rope, etc. over and under each other to make one thick piece ▶ **zaplatać**, **splatać**

■ **plait** noun [C] ▶ **warkocz**, **plecionka** ➲ look at **pigtail** ➲ picture at **hair**

⚷ **plan¹** /plæn/ noun **1** [C] **a plan (for sth/to do sth)** an idea or arrangement for doing or achieving sth in the future: *We usually **make** our holiday **plans** in January.* ◇ *The firm has no plans to employ more people.* ◇ *There has been **a change of plan** – we're meeting at the restaurant.* ◇ *If everything **goes according to plan*** (pójdzie zgodnie z planem), *we should be home by midnight.* ▶ **plan**, **sposób 2** [C] a detailed map of a building, town, etc.: ***a street plan** of Lublin* ▶ **plan**, **mapa 3** (**plans**) [pl.] detailed drawings of a building, machine, road, etc. that show its size, shape and measurements: *We're getting an architect to **draw up** some **plans** for a new kitchen.* ▶ **plan**, **projekt 4** [C] a diagram that shows how sth is to be organized or arranged: *Before you start writing an essay, you should make a brief plan.* ▶ **plan**

⚷ **plan²** /plæn/ verb (**planning**; **planned**) **1** [I,T] **plan (sth) (for sth)** to decide, organize or prepare for sth you want to do in the future: *to plan for the future* ◇ *You need to plan your work more carefully.* ▶ **planować 2** [I] **plan (on sth/doing sth)**; **plan (to do sth)** to intend or expect to do sth: *I'm planning on having a holiday in July.* ◇ *We plan to arrive at about 4 o'clock.* ▶ **zamierzać**, **zamyślać 3** [T] to make a diagram or a design of sth: *You need an expert to help you plan the garden.* ▶ **planować**, **projektować**

■ **planning** noun [U]: *The project requires careful planning.* ◇ *Family planning* (planowanie rodziny) *enables people to control the number of children they have.* ▶ **planowanie**

⚷ **plane¹** /pleɪn/ noun [C] **1** = AEROPLANE: *Has her plane landed yet?* ◇ *a plane crash* katastrofa lotnicza ➲ picture on **page 566 2** (technical) a flat surface: *the horizontal/vertical plane* ▶ **płasz-czyzna 3** a tool used for making the surface of wood smooth by taking very thin pieces off it ▶ **hebel** ➲ picture at **tool**

> **travelling by plane**
>
> A large **airport** may have more than one **terminal**. You go to the **check-in desk** and **check in**. You might be able to choose an **aisle** seat or a **window** seat. You **check in** the **baggage** that will go into the **hold** but you carry your **hand luggage** (US **carry-on bags**) with you onto the plane. You wait in the **departure lounge** and when your flight is called you go to the correct **gate**. You need to show your **boarding card** in order to get on the plane. The plane **takes off** from the **runway**. The **flight attendants/cabin crew** look after you during the flight. If you are taking an international flight, you will have to show your **passport** at **immigration** when you land. Then you collect your luggage from **baggage reclaim** and exit through **customs**.

plane² /pleɪn/ verb [T] to make the surface of a piece of wood flat and smooth using a **plane¹** (3) ▶ **heblować**

⚷ **planet** /ˈplænɪt/ noun **1** [C] a very large round object in space that moves around the sun or another star: *the planets of our solar system* ▶ **planeta** ➲ note at **space** **2** (**the planet**) [sing.] the world we live in; the Earth, especially when talking about the environment: *the battle to save the planet* ▶ **ziemia**

planetarium /ˌplænɪˈteəriəm/ noun [C] a building with a curved ceiling that represents the sky at night. It is used for showing the positions and movements of the planets and stars for education and entertainment. ▶ **planetarium**

plank /plæŋk/ noun [C] a long flat thin piece of wood that is used for building or making things ▶ **deska**

plankton /ˈplæŋktən/ noun [U, with sing. or pl. verb] very small forms of plant and animal life that live in water ▶ **plankton**

planner /ˈplænə(r)/ noun [C] **1** (also **ˌtown ˈplanner**) a person whose job is to plan the growth and development of a town ▶ **urbanist(k)a 2** a person who makes plans for a particular area of activity: *curriculum/economic planners* ▶ **planist(k)a 3** a book, computer program, etc. that contains dates and is used for recording information, arranging meetings, etc.: *a year planner* ▶ **terminarz**, **organizator**

⚷ **plant¹** /plɑːnt; US plænt/ noun **1** [C] a living thing that grows in the ground and usually has leaves, a **stem** and

P

roots: *a plant pot* ◇ *a tomato plant* krzak pomidora ▶ **roślina** **2** [C] a very large factory: *a car plant* ◇ *a nuclear reprocessing plant* ▶ **zakład przemysłowy**

plant² /plɑːnt; US plænt/ verb [T] **1** to put plants, seeds, etc. in the ground to grow: *Bulbs should be planted in the autumn.* ▶ **sadzić**; **siać** **2 plant sth (with sth)** to cover or supply a garden, area of land, etc. with plants: *The field's been planted with wheat this year.* ▶ **obsadzać/obsiewać coś** (*roślinami*) **3** to put yourself/sth firmly in a particular place or position: *He planted himself in the best seat.* ▶ **usadawiać** **4 plant sth (on sb)** to hide sth, especially sth illegal, in sb's clothing, property, etc. in order to make them seem guilty of a crime: *The police think that terrorists may have* ***planted the bomb.*** ◇ *The women claimed that the drugs had been planted on them.* ▶ **podkładać** (*np. bombę*)

plantation /plɑːnˈteɪʃn; US plæn-/ noun [C] **1** a large area of land, especially in a hot country, where **tobacco**, tea, cotton, etc. are grown: *a coffee plantation* ▶ **plantacja** **2** an area of land where trees are grown to produce wood ▶ **plantacja leśna**

plaque /plɑːk/ noun **1** [C] a flat piece of stone or metal, usually with names and dates on it, that is fixed on a wall in memory of a famous person or event ▶ **płyta pamiątkowa** **2** [U] a harmful substance that forms on your teeth ▶ **kamień nazębny**

plasma /ˈplæzmə/ (also **plasm** /ˈplæzəm/) noun [U] the clear liquid part of blood, in which the blood cells, etc., float ▶ **osocze**

ˌplasma ˈscreen noun [C] a type of television or computer screen that is larger and thinner than most screens and produces a very clear image ▶ **ekran plazmowy**

ˌplasma TˈV noun [C] a television set with a **plasma screen** ▶ **telewizor plazmowy**

plaster¹ /ˈplɑːstə(r); US ˈplæs-/ noun **1** [U] a mixture of a special powder and water that becomes hard when it is dry. **Plaster** is put on walls and ceilings to form a smooth surface. ▶ **gips**, **tynk** **2** (also ˌ**plaster of ˈParis**) [U] a white powder that is mixed with water and becomes hard when dry. It is then used especially for making copies of statues or for putting round broken bones until they get better: *a plaster bust of Julius Caesar* ◇ *When Alan broke his leg it was* ***in plaster*** *for six weeks.* ▶ **gips** **3** (also ˈ**sticking plaster**, US **Band-Aid™**) [C] a small piece of sticky material that is used to cover a cut, etc. on the body ▶ **plaster**

plaster² /ˈplɑːstə(r); US ˈplæs-/ verb [T] **1** to cover a wall, etc. with **plaster¹** (1) to make the surface smooth ▶ **gipsować**, **tynkować** **2 plaster sb/sth (in/with sth)** to cover sb/sth with a large amount of sth: *He plastered his walls with posters.* ▶ **oblepiać**, **pokrywać coś (grubą) warstwą**

plasterboard /ˈplɑːstəbɔːd; US ˈplæs-/ noun [U] a building material made of sheets of cardboard with **plaster** between them, used for inside walls and ceilings ▶ **płyta gipsowa**

plastered /ˈplɑːstəd; US ˈplæs-/ adj. [not before a noun] (informal) drunk: *to be/get plastered* ▶ **spity**

plasterer /ˈplɑːstərə(r); US ˈplæs-/ noun [C] a person whose job is to put **plaster** on walls and ceilings ▶ **tynkarz**, **sztukator**

plasterwork /ˈplɑːstəwɜːk; US ˈplæs-/ noun [U] the dry **plaster** on ceilings when it has been formed into shapes and patterns for decoration ▶ **sztukatorstwo**

plastic¹ /ˈplæstɪk/ noun [C,U] a light, strong material that is made with chemicals and is used for making many different kinds of objects ▶ **plastyk**

plastic² /ˈplæstɪk/ adj. made of plastic: *plastic cups* ◇ *a plastic bag* ▶ **plastykowy**, **ze sztucznego tworzywa**

ˌplastic ˈsurgeon noun [C] a doctor who is qualified to perform **plastic surgery** ▶ **chirurg plastyczny**

ˌplastic ˈsurgery noun [U] a medical operation to repair or replace damaged skin or to improve the appearance of sb's face or body ▶ **operacja plastyczna**; **chirurgia plastyczna** ➲ look at **facelift**, **surgery**

plate /pleɪt/ noun **1** [C] a flat, usually round, dish for eating or serving food from: *a plastic/paper/china plate* ◇ *a plate of food* ▶ **talerz**

> You eat your main course from a **dinner plate.** You may put bread, etc. on a **side plate**. You eat cereal or a pudding from a **bowl**.

2 [C] a thin flat piece of metal or glass: *a steel/metal plate* ▶ **płyta** **3** [C] a flat piece of metal with sth written on it: *The brass plate beside the door said 'Dr Dawson'.*

plane

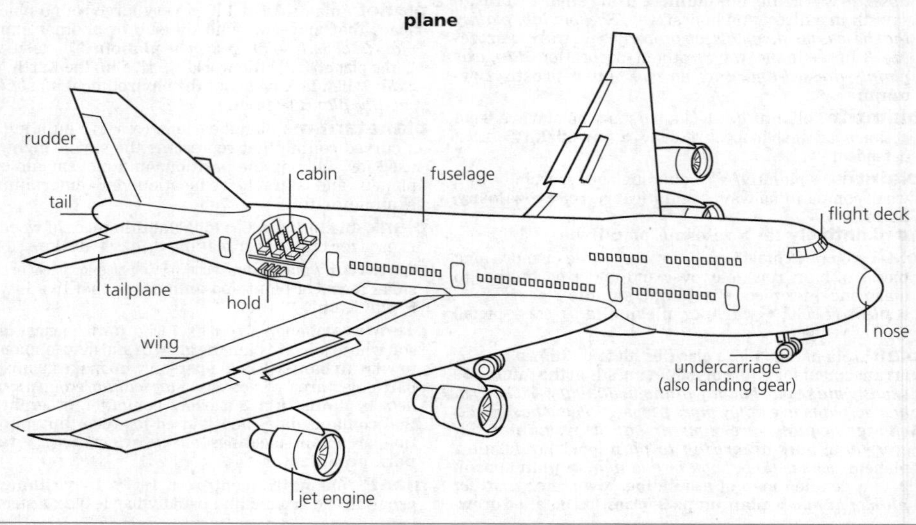

▶ **tablica** **4** [U] metal that has a thin covering of gold or silver: *gold/silver plate* ▶ **płyta** (*powlekana złotem/srebrem*) **5** [C] a picture or photograph in a book that takes up a whole page: *colour plates* ▶ **plansza** **6** [C] a piece of plastic with false teeth fixed to it that fits inside a person's mouth ▶ **sztuczna szczęka**

plateau /'plætəʊ; US plæ'təʊ/ noun [C] (pl. **plateaus** /-təʊz; US -'təʊz/ or **plateaux** /-təʊ; US -'təʊ/) **1** a large high area of flat land ▶ **płaskowyż** **2** a state where there is little development or change: *House prices seem to have* ***reached a plateau.*** ▶ **zastój**

plateful /'pleɪtfʊl/ noun [C] the amount of food that a plate(1) can hold ▶ **pełny talerz (czegoś)**

platform /'plætfɔːm/ noun [C] **1** the place where you get on or off trains at a railway station: *Which platform does the train to York leave from?* ▶ **peron** **2** a flat surface, higher than the level of the floor or ground, on which people stand when they are speaking or performing, so that the audience can see them: *Coming onto the platform now is tonight's conductor, Jane Glover.* ▶ **podium, estrada** **3** [usually sing.] the ideas and aims of a political party who want to be elected: *They fought the election on a platform of low taxes.* ▶ **platforma (wyborcza)** **4** a shoe with a very thick sole: *I wore platforms when I was a teenager.* ◇ *platform shoes* ▶ **buty na platformach**

platinum /'plætɪnəm/ noun [U] (symbol **Pt**) a silver metal that is often used for making expensive jewellery: *a platinum wedding ring* ▶ **platyna**

platitude /'plætɪtjuːd; US -tuːd/ noun [C] a comment or statement that has been made very often before and is therefore not interesting: *a political speech full of platitudes and empty promises* ▶ **frazes**
■ **platitudinous** /ˌplætɪ'tjuːdɪnəs; US -'tuːdənəs/ adj. (formal) ▶ **frazesowy**

platonic /plə'tɒnɪk/ adj. (used about a relationship between two people) friendly but not sexual ▶ **platoniczny**

platoon /plə'tuːn/ noun [C] a small group of soldiers ▶ **pluton**

platypus /'plætɪpəs/ noun [C] an Australian animal that is covered in fur and has a beak like a duck, webbed feet (= with skin between the toes) and a flat tail. Platypuses lay eggs but give milk to their young. ▶ **dziobak**

plausible /'plɔːzəbl/ adj. that you can believe; reasonable: *a plausible excuse* ▶ **prawdopodobny, możliwy do przyjęcia** OPP **implausible**

play¹ /pleɪ/ verb **1** [I] **play (with sb/sth)** to do sth to enjoy yourself; to have fun: *The children have been playing on the beach all day.* ◇ *Emma's found a new friend to play with.* ▶ **bawić się** **2** [I,T] **play (sth) (with/against) sb**; **play sb (at sth)** to take part in a game or sport: *to play football/tennis/hockey* ◇ *Do you know how to play chess?* ◇ *I usually play against Bill.* ◇ *She played him at cards* (grała z nim w karty) *and won!* ◇ *Who's Brazil playing next in the World Cup?* ▶ **grać (w coś) (z kimś/przeciwko komuś)** **3** [I,T] **play (sth) (on sth)** to make music with a musical instrument: *to play the piano/guitar/trumpet* ◇ *My son's learning the piano. He plays very well.* ◇ *She played a few notes on the violin.* ▶ **grać** ➲ note at **music**, **piano** **4** [T] to turn on a video, CD, etc. so that it produces sound: *Shall I play the DVD for you again?* ▶ **puszczać** **5** [I,T] to act in a play, film, TV programme, etc.; to act the role of sb: *Richard is going to play Romeo.* ▶ **odgrywać** (*rolę*) ℹ Zwrot **play a part/role** itp. stosuje się często w przenośni: *Britain has played an active part in the recent discussions.* ◇ *John played a key role in organizing the protest.* **6** [I] (formal) to move quickly and lightly: *Sunlight played on the surface of the sea.* ▶ (*światło itp.*) **migotać, mienić się**, (*uśmiech*) **igrać, błąkać się**

IDM **play a joke/a trick/tricks on sb** to do something which may surprise or annoy sb for your own amusement: *Children often play tricks on their teachers.* ◇ *to play a practical joke* zrobić komuś kawał ▶ **płatać komuś psikusa**

ℹ **Play** występuje w innych idiomach, np. **play it by ear.** Zob. hasła odpowiednich rzeczowników, przymiotników itp.

PHR V **play about/around (with sb)** (informal) to have a sexual relationship with sb, usually with sb who is not your usual partner: *Her husband is always playing around.* ▶ **zabawiać się (z kimś)**

play about/around (with sth) to behave or treat sth in a careless way: *Don't play around with my tools!* ▶ **bawić się (czymś)**

play along (with sb/sth) to pretend to agree with sb/sth: *I decided to play along with her idea.* ▶ **pozornie się zgadzać (na coś) (z kimś)**

play at sth/being sth to do sth with little interest or effort: *He's only playing at studying. He'd prefer to get a job now.* ◇ *Whatever is that driver playing at?* Co ten kierowca kombinuje? ▶ **robić sobie zabawę z czegoś, robić coś od niechcenia**

play away (from home) (Brit.) (used about a sports team) to play a match at the opponent's ground or **stadium** ▶ **grać na wyjeździe**

play sth back (to sb) to turn on and watch or listen to a film, tape, etc. that you have recorded: *Play that last scene back to me again.* ▶ **puszczać, odtwarzać**

play sth down to make sth seem less important than it really is: *to play down a crisis* ▶ **minimalizować**

play A off against B to make people compete or argue with each other, especially for your own advantage: *I think she enjoys playing one friend off against another.* ▶ **napuszczać kogoś przeciw komuś, skłócać kogoś z kimś, szczególnie gdy samemu z tego wynosi się korzyść**

play on/upon sth to use and take advantage of sb's fears or weaknesses: *This advertising campaign plays on people's fears of illness.* ▶ **grać** (*na czyichś uczuciach itp.*) SYN **exploit**

play (sb) up (informal) to cause sb trouble or pain: *The car always plays up in wet weather.* ▶ **dawać się we znaki**

play² /pleɪ/ noun **1** [U] activity done for enjoyment only, especially by children: *Young children learn through play.* ◇ *the happy sound of children* ***at play*** ▶ **zabawa, rozrywka** **2** [C] a piece of writing performed by actors in the theatre, or on TV or radio: *Would you like to see a play while you're in London?* ◇ *a radio/TV play* ◇ *The children always put on a school play* (wystawiają jakąś sztukę) *at Christmas.* ▶ **sztuka** ➲ note at **theatre** **3** [U] the playing of a game or sport: *Bad weather stopped play yesterday.* ▶ **gra** ➲ look at **match²** ℹ Mówi się **play tennis/football** itp., lecz nie można powiedzieć ~~a play of tennis, football, etc.~~. W takim wypadku używa się zwrotu **a game of tennis/football** itp. **4** [U] a control on a video or tape player, etc. that you press to start the tape, etc. running: *Put the DVD into the machine then* ***press play.*** ▶ **przycisk play**

IDM **fair play** → FAIR¹

a play on words the humorous use of a word or phrase that can have two different meanings ▶ **gra słów** SYN **pun**

playback /'pleɪbæk/ noun [U,C, usually sing.] the act of playing music, showing a film or listening to a telephone message that has been recorded before; a recording that you listen to or watch again ▶ **odtwarzanie, playback**

playboy /'pleɪbɔɪ/ noun [C] a rich man who spends his time enjoying himself ▶ **playboy**

player /'pleɪə(r)/ noun [C] **1** a person who plays a game or sport: *a game for four players* ◇ *She's an excellent tennis player.* ▶ **gracz, zawodni-k/czka** **2** [in compounds] a machine on which you can listen to sound that has been recorded on CD, tape, etc.: *a CD/cassette player* ▶ **odtwarzacz 3** a person who plays a musical instrument: *a piano player* pianista ▶ **muzy-k/czka 4** (old-fashioned) an actor ▶ **aktor/ka**

playful /ˈpleɪfl/ adj. **1** full of fun; wanting to play: *a playful puppy* ▶ **figlarny 2** done or said in fun; not serious: *a playful remark* ▶ **żartobliwy, wesoły**

playground /ˈpleɪɡraʊnd/ noun [C] an area of land where children can play: *the school playground* ▶ **plac zabaw, boisko**

playgroup (Brit.) = NURSERY SCHOOL

playhouse /ˈpleɪhaʊs/ noun **1** [sing.] (used in the name of some theatres): *the Liverpool Playhouse* ▶ **teatr 2** [C] (Brit. also **Wendy house** /ˈwendi haʊs/) a model of a house for children to play in ▶ **domek dla dzieci**

ˈ**playing card** = CARD (4)

ˈ**playing field** noun [C] (in football, **cricket**, etc.) a large field used for sports ▶ **boisko**

IDM **a level playing field** → LEVEL[2]

playmate /ˈpleɪmeɪt/ noun [C] a friend with whom a child plays ▶ **towarzysz/ka zabaw**

ˈ**play-off** noun [C] a match between two teams or players who have equal scores to decide the winner: *They lost to Chicago in the play-offs.* ▶ **dogrywka** (*w grze*)

playschool (Brit.) = NURSERY SCHOOL

plaything /ˈpleɪθɪŋ/ noun [C] (formal) a toy ▶ **zabawka**

playtime /ˈpleɪtaɪm/ noun [C,U] a period of time between lessons when children at school can go outside to play ▶ **przerwa** (*w szkole*)

playwright /ˈpleɪraɪt/ noun [C] a person who writes plays for the theatre, TV or radio ▶ **dramaturg** SYN **dramatist** ➲ note at **literature**

plc (also **PLC**) /ˌpiː el ˈsiː/ abbr. (Brit.) **Public Limited Company** ▶ **firma notowana na giełdzie papierów wartościowych**

plea /pliː/ noun [C] **1** (formal) **a plea (for sth)** an important and emotional request: *a plea for help* ▶ **usilna prośba 2 a plea of sth** a statement made by or for sb in a court of law: *a plea of guilty/not guilty* ▶ **w procesie sądowym formalne przyznanie/nie przyznanie się do winy**

plead /pliːd/ verb **1** [I] **plead (with sb) (to do/for sth)** to ask sb for sth in a very strong and serious way: *She pleaded with him not to leave her.* ◇ *He pleaded for mercy.* ▶ **błagać** ➲ look at **beg 2** [T] to state in a court of law that you did or did not do a crime: *The defendant* ***pleaded not guilty*** *to the charge of theft.* ▶ **formalnie (nie) przyznawać się do winy 3** [T] **plead (sth) (for sth)** to give sth as an excuse or explanation for sth: *He pleaded family problems for his lack of concentration.* ▶ **przytaczać coś na usprawiedliwienie 4** [I,T] **plead (sth) (for sb/sth)** (used especially about a lawyer in a court of law) to support sb's case: *He needs the very best lawyer to plead (his case) for him.* ▶ **prowadzić czyjąś sprawę**

⚷**pleasant** /ˈpleznt/ adj. nice, enjoyable or friendly: *a pleasant evening/climate/place/view* ◇ *a pleasant smile/voice/manner* ▶ **przyjemny, miły** OPP **unpleasant**

■ **pleasantly** adv. ▶ **przyjemnie**

pleasantry /ˈplezntri/ noun [C, usually pl.] (pl. **-ies**) (formal) a friendly remark made in order to be polite: *After exchanging the usual pleasantries, they got down to serious discussion.* Po wymianie zwykłych uprzejmości, przeszli do poważnej dyskusji. ▶ **grzecznościowa uwaga**

⚷**please**[1] /pliːz/ interj. (used as a polite way of asking for sth or telling sb to do sth): *Come in, please.* ◇ *Please don't spend too much money.* ◇ *Sit down, please.* ◇ *Two cups of coffee, please.* ▶ **proszę**

Zwróć uwagę, że w odpowiedzi na **thank you** nie używa się **please**. Można wówczas nie odpowiedzieć nic. Można też (zwłaszcza gdy wyświadczyłeś komuś przysługę) użyć jednego z następujących zwrotów: **that's all right/OK, it's/it was a pleasure, my pleasure, don't mention it**, (zwł. w Amer. ang.) **you're welcome** lub (formalnie) **not at all**.

Podając coś komuś, zapraszając kogoś do stołu lub częstując kogoś, również nie używa się **please**. Przy podawaniu można powiedzieć **Here/There you are**, ale nie jest to konieczne.

IDM **yes, please** (used when you are accepting an offer of sth politely): *'Sugar?' 'Yes, please.'* ▶ **tak, proszę** OPP **no, thank you**

⚷**please**[2] /pliːz/ verb **1** [I,T] to make sb happy: *There's just no pleasing some people.* ▶ **zadowalać, sprawiać przyjemność** SYN **satisfy 2** [I] [not used as the main verb in a sentence; used after words like *as, what, whatever, anything*, etc.] to want; to choose: *You can't always* ***do as you please.*** ◇ *She has so much money she can buy anything she pleases.* ▶ **chcieć**

IDM **please yourself** to be able to do whatever you want: *Without anyone else to cook for, I can please myself what I eat.* ▶ **robić, co się chce**

⚷**pleased** /pliːzd/ adj. [not before a noun] **pleased (with sb/sth)**; **pleased to do sth**; **pleased that ...** happy or satisfied about sth: *John seems very pleased with his new car.* ◇ *Aren't you pleased to see me?* ◇ *We're* ***only too pleased*** *to help.* Bardzo się cieszymy, że możemy pomóc. ◇ *I'm so pleased that you've decided to stay another week.* ◇ *Pleased to meet you.* Miło cię/pana/panią/państwa poznać. ▶ **zadowolony, ucieszony** ➲ note at **happy**

⚷**pleasing** /ˈpliːzɪŋ/ adj. giving you pleasure and satisfaction: *The exam results are very pleasing this year.* ▶ **przyjemny, zadowalający**

pleasurable /ˈpleʒərəbl/ adj. (formal) enjoyable: *a pleasurable experience* ▶ **przyjemny**

⚷**pleasure** /ˈpleʒə(r)/ noun **1** [U] the feeling of being happy or satisfied: *Parents* ***get a lot of pleasure out of*** *watching their children grow up.* ◇ ***It gives me great pleasure*** *to introduce our next speaker.* ▶ **przyjemność; zadowolenie 2** [U] enjoyment (rather than work): *What brings you to Paris – business or pleasure?* ▶ **przyjemność 3** [C] an event or activity that you enjoy or that makes you happy: *It's been a pleasure to work with you.* ◇ *'Thanks for your help.'* ***'It's a pleasure.'*** ▶ **przyjemność**

IDM **take (no) pleasure in sth/doing sth** to enjoy/not enjoy (doing) sth ▶ **(nie) znajdować przyjemnoś-ć/ci w czymś**

with pleasure (used as a polite way of saying that you are happy to do sth): *'Could you give me a lift into town?' 'Yes, with pleasure.'* ▶ **z przyjemnością**

pleat /pliːt/ noun [C] a permanent fold that is sewn or pressed into a piece of cloth: *a skirt with pleats at the front* ▶ **fałda, plisa**

■ **pleat** verb [T]: *a pleated skirt* ▶ **plisować** ➲ picture at **fold**

pleb /pleb/ noun [C] an ordinary person, especially one who is poor or not well educated ▶ **prosta-k/czka** ℹ Wyraża dezaprobatę.

plectrum /ˈplektrəm/ noun [C] (pl. **plectrums** or **plectra** /-trə/) a small piece of metal, plastic, etc. used for **plucking** the strings of a musical instrument such as a **guitar** ▶ **plektron**

pledge /pledʒ/ noun [C] **a pledge (to do sth)** a formal promise or agreement ▶ **zobowiązanie, przyrzeczenie**

■ **pledge** verb [T] **pledge sth (to sb/sth)**: *The Government has pledged £250 000 to help the victims of the crash.* ▶ **zobowiązywać się, ręczyć**

plenary /ˈpliːnəri/ adj. [only before a noun] (formal) (used about meetings) to be attended by everyone who has the right to attend: *The new committee holds its first **plenary session** this week.* ▶ **plenarny**
■ **plenary** noun [C] (pl. **plenaries**): *the opening plenary of the conference* ▶ **sesja plenarna**

plenipotentiary /ˌplenɪpəˈtenʃəri; US also -ʃieri/ noun [C] (pl. **-ies**) a person who has full powers to take action, make decisions, etc. on behalf of their government, especially in a foreign country ▶ **pełnomocni-k/czka**
■ **plenipotentiary** adj.: *plenipotentiary powers* pełnomocnictwa ▶ **pełnomocny**

plentiful /ˈplentɪfl/ adj. available in large amounts or numbers: *Fruit is plentiful at this time of year.* ▶ **obfity; liczny** OPP **scarce**

⚷ **plenty** /ˈplenti/ pron. **1 plenty (of sb/sth)** a large amount; as much or as many as you need: *'Shall I get some more coffee?' 'No, we've still got plenty.'* ◇ *There's still plenty of time to get there.* ◇ *Have you brought plenty to drink?* ▶ **pod dostatkiem, dużo**
■ **plenty** adv. **1 plenty more (of) (sth)** a lot: *There's plenty more ice cream.* ▶ **pod dostatkiem, dużo 2** [with *big, long, tall,* etc. followed by *enough*] (informal) more than big, long, etc. enough: *'This shirt's too small.' 'Well, it looks plenty big enough to me.'* ▶ **wystarczająco** (*np. duży*)

plethora /ˈpleθərə/ noun [sing.] (formal) an amount that is greater than is needed or can be used: *The report contained a plethora of detail.* ▶ **nadmiar** SYN **excess**

pliable /ˈplaɪəbl/ (also **pliant** /ˈplaɪənt/) adj. **1** easy to bend or shape ▶ **giętki 2** (used about a person) easy to influence ▶ **podatny** (*na wpływy*)

pliers /ˈplaɪəz/ noun [pl.] a tool made of two crossed pieces of metal with handles, that is used for holding things firmly and for cutting wire: *a pair of pliers* ▶ **obcęgi, szczypce** ➲ picture at **tool**

plight /plaɪt/ noun [sing.] (formal) a bad or difficult state or situation ▶ **trudne położenie, ciężki stan**

plimsoll /ˈplɪmsəl/ (also **pump**) noun [C] (Brit.) a light shoe made of **canvas** that is especially used for sports, etc.: *a pair of plimsolls* ▶ **tenisówka** ➲ look at **trainer**

plod /plɒd/ verb [I] (**plodding**; **plodded**) **plod (along/on)** to walk slowly and in a heavy or tired way: *We plodded on through the rain for nearly an hour.* ▶ **wlec się, ciężko stąpać**
PHR V **plod along/on** to make slow progress, especially with difficult or boring work: *I just plod on with my work and never seem to get anywhere.* ▶ **mozolić się**

plonk¹ /plɒŋk/ verb [T] (informal) **1 plonk sth (down)** to put sth down on sth, especially noisily or carelessly: *Just plonk your bag down anywhere.* ▶ **stawiać/upuszczać coś ciężkiego, rzucać coś niedbale 2 plonk (yourself) (down)** to sit down heavily and carelessly: *He just plonked himself down in front of the TV.* ▶ **uwalić się** (*np. na kanapie*)

plonk² /plɒŋk/ noun [U] (Brit., informal) cheap wine: *Let's open a bottle of plonk!* ▶ **sikacz**

plop¹ /plɒp/ noun [C, usually sing.] a sound like that of a small object dropping into water ▶ **plusk**

plop² /plɒp/ verb [I] (**plopping**; **plopped**) to fall making a plop: *The frog plopped back into the water.* ▶ **plusnąć**

⚷ **plot¹** /plɒt/ noun [C] **1** the series of events which form the story of a novel, film, etc.: *The play had a very weak plot.* ◇ *I can't follow the plot of this novel.* ▶ **wątek, akcja 2 a plot (to do sth)** a secret plan made by several people to do sth wrong or illegal: *a plot to kill the president* ▶ **spisek 3** a small piece of land, used for a special purpose: *a plot of land* ▶ **działka**

⚷ **plot²** /plɒt/ verb (**plotting**; **plotted**) **1** [I,T] **plot (with sb) (against sb)** to make a secret plan to do sth wrong or illegal: *They were accused of plotting against the government.* ◇ *The terrorists had been plotting this campaign for years.* ▶ **spiskować 2** [T] to mark sth on a map, diagram, etc.: *to plot the figures on a graph* ▶ **nanosić**

plough /plaʊ/ (US **plow**) noun [C] a large farm tool which is pulled by a **tractor** or by an animal. A plough turns the soil over ready for seeds to be planted. ▶ **pług, socha** ➲ look at **snowplough**
■ **plough** verb [I,T] to break up and turn over the soil, with a plough: *to plough the fields* ◇ (figurative): *The book was long and boring but I managed to plough through it* (przez nią przebrnąć). ▶ **orać**

ploy /plɔɪ/ noun [C] **a ploy (to do sth)** something that you say or do in order to get what you want or to persuade sb to do sth ▶ **sztuczka** (*w celu osiągnięcia czegoś*), **fortel**

pluck¹ /plʌk/ verb [T] **1 pluck sth/sb (from sth/out)** to remove or take sth/sb from a place: *He plucked the letter from my hands.* ▶ **wyrywać, skubać 2** to pull the feathers out of a bird in order to prepare it for cooking ▶ **skubać** (*drób*) **3** to make the strings of a musical instrument play notes by moving your fingers across them ▶ **szarpać** (*struny*)
IDM **pluck up courage** to try to get enough courage to do sth ▶ **zbierać się na odwagę**
PHR V **pluck at sth** to pull sth gently several times: *The little girl plucked at her mother's skirt.* ▶ **szarpać za coś**

pluck² /plʌk/ noun [U] (informal) courage and determination ▶ **odwaga, śmiałość**
■ **plucky** adj. ▶ **odważny, śmiały**

⚷ **plug¹** /plʌg/ noun [C] **1** a plastic or rubber object with two or three metal pins, which connects a piece of electrical equipment to the electricity supply: *I'll have to change the plug on the kettle.* ▶ **wtyczka 2** a round piece of rubber or plastic that you use to block the hole in a sink, bath, etc.: *She **pulled out the plug** and let the water drain away.* ▶ **zatyczka, korek 3** (informal) a mention that sb makes of a new book, film, etc. in order to encourage people to buy or see it: *He managed to get in a plug for his new book.* ▶ **publiczna promocja czegoś 4** (informal) (especially Brit.) = SOCKET

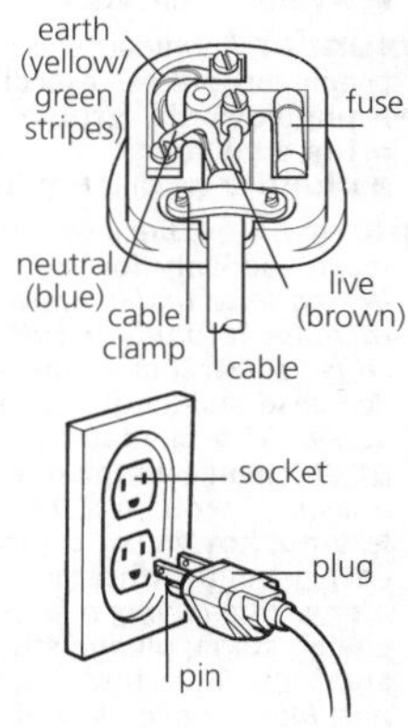

plug² /plʌg/ verb [T] (**plugging**; **plugged**) **1** to fill or block a hole with sth that fits tightly into it: *He managed to plug the leak in the pipe.* ▶ **zatykać, tamować 2** (informal) to say good things about a new book, film, etc. in order to make people buy or see it: *They're really plugging that song on the radio at the moment.* ▶ **publicznie promować, reklamować**
PHR V **plug sth in** to connect a piece of electrical equipment to the electricity supply or to another piece of equipment: *Is the microphone plugged in?* ▶ **wkładać wtyczkę do kontaktu** OPP **unplug**

plughole /ˈplʌghəʊl/ noun [C] (Brit.) a hole in a bath, etc. where the water flows away ▶ **odpływ**

plum /plʌm/ noun [C] a soft, round fruit with red or yellow skin and a stone in the middle: *wild plums* mirabelki ▶ **śliwka** ➲ picture on **page A12**

plumage /ˈpluːmɪdʒ/ noun [U] a bird's feathers ▶ **upierzenie**

plumber /ˈplʌmə(r)/ noun [C] a person whose job is to put in or repair water pipes, baths, toilets, etc. ▶ **hydrauli-k/czka** ➲ note at **house**

plumbing /ˈplʌmɪŋ/ noun [U] **1** all the pipes, taps, etc. in a building ▶ **instalacja wodnokanalizacyjna** **2** the work of a person who puts in and repairs water pipes, taps, etc. ▶ **zakładanie instalacji wodno-kanalizacyjnej**

plume /pluːm/ noun [C] **1** a quantity of smoke that rises in the air ▶ **smuga** **2** a large feather or group of feathers, often worn as a decoration ▶ (*duże i często kolorowe*) **pióro** **3** something worn in the hair or on a hat, made from feathers or long, thin pieces of material ▶ **kita z piór/materiału**

plummet /ˈplʌmɪt/ verb [I] to fall suddenly and quickly from a high level or position: *Share prices have plummeted to an all-time low.* ◇ *Her spirits plummeted* (jej nastrój gwałtownie się pogorszył) *at the thought of meeting him again.* ▶ **gwałtownie spadać/obniżać się** SYN **plunge**

plump¹ /plʌmp/ adj. (used about a person or an animal) pleasantly fat: *the baby's plump cheeks* ▶ **tłuściutki**, **pulchny**

plump² /plʌmp/ verb

PHR V **plump (yourself/sb/sth) down** to sit down or to put sb/sth down heavily: *She plumped herself down by the fire.* ▶ **klapnąć**; **zrzucać**

plump for sb/sth (Brit., informal) to choose or decide to have sb/sth: *I think I'll plump for the roast chicken, after all.* ▶ **wybierać**, **decydować się na kogoś/coś**

plunder /ˈplʌndə(r)/ noun [U] **1** the act of stealing from people or places, especially during war or fighting ▶ **plądrowanie**, **grabież** **2** the goods that are stolen ▶ **łup**, **zdobycz**

■ **plunder** verb [I,T] ▶ **plądrować**, **grabić**

plunge¹ /plʌndʒ/ verb **1** [I,T] to move or make sb/sth move suddenly forwards and/or downwards: *She lost her balance and plunged 100 feet to her death.* ◇ *The earthquake plunged entire towns over the edge of the cliffs.* ▶ **(z)rzucać (się/kogoś) do/z czegoś** **2** [I] to decrease suddenly and quickly: *Share prices plunged overnight.* ▶ **spadać**

PHR V **plunge in**; **plunge into sth** **1** to jump into sth, especially with force: *He ran to the river and plunged in.* ▶ **zanurkować w czymś** **2** to start doing sth with energy and enthusiasm: *Think carefully before you plunge into buying a house.* ▶ **rzucać się w wir czegoś**

plunge sth in; **plunge sth into sth** to push sth suddenly and with force into sth: *He plunged the knife* (zatopił nóż) *into her arm.* ▶ **wbić coś w coś**

plunge sb/sth into sth to cause sb/sth to suddenly be in the state mentioned: *The country has been plunged into chaos by the floods.* ▶ **pogrążać kogoś/coś w czymś**

plunge² /plʌndʒ/ noun [C] a sudden jump, drop or fall: *I slipped and took a plunge in the river.* ◇ *the plunge in house prices* ▶ **skok**, **nurkowanie**, **spadek**

IDM **take the plunge** to decide to do sth difficult after thinking about it for quite a long time: *After going out together for five years, they took the plunge and got married.* ▶ **podejmować stanowczy krok** (*po długim namyśle*)

plunger /ˈplʌndʒə(r)/ noun [C] **1** a piece of equipment used for clearing kitchen and bathroom pipes ▶ **przepychacz** (*np. do zlewu*) **2** a part of a piece of equipment that can be pushed down, for example in a syringe ▶ **tłok** (*np. w skrzykawce*) ➲ picture at **laboratory**

pluperfect = PAST PERFECT

plural /ˈplʊərəl/ noun [C] (abbr. **pl.**) the form of a noun, verb, etc. which refers to more than one person or thing: *The plural of 'boat' is 'boats'.* ◇ *The verb should be **in the plural**.* ▶ **liczba mnoga**

■ **plural** adj. ▶ **w liczbie mnogiej** ➲ look at **singular**

pluralist /ˈplʊərəlɪst/ adj. (also **pluralistic** /ˌplʊərəˈlɪstɪk/) **1** (used about a society) having many different groups of people and different political parties in it: *a pluralist democracy* ▶ **pluralistyczny** **2** not based on a single set of principles or beliefs: *a pluralist approach to politics* ▶ **pluralistyczny**

plus¹ /plʌs/ prep. **1** and; added to: *Two plus two is four (2 + 2 = 4).* ▶ **plus**, **dodać** OPP **minus** **2** in addition to; and also: *You have to work five days a week plus every other weekend.* ▶ **plus**, **oraz**

plus² /plʌs/ noun [C] **1** an advantage of a situation: *My work is five minutes from my house, which is a definite plus.* ▶ **plus** **2** the symbol (+) used in mathematics: *He put a plus instead of a minus.* ▶ **plus**, **znak dodawania** OPP **minus**

plus³ /plʌs/ adj. [only after a noun] **1** or more: *I'd say there were 30 000 plus at the match.* ▶ **ponad** **2** [not before a noun] (used for marking work done by students) slightly above: *I got a B plus for my homework.* ▶ **z plusem** OPP **minus**

plush /plʌʃ/ adj. comfortable and expensive: *a plush hotel* ▶ **wykwintny**, **szykowny**

Pluto /ˈpluːtəʊ/ noun [sing.] the name of a large round object in space which **orbits** the sun ▶ **Pluton**

> In 2006, the International Astronomical Union declared that **Pluto** was to be called a **dwarf planet**, rather than a proper planet, because it has different characteristics from other planets (**Mercury**, **Mars**, **Venus**, etc.) in our **solar system**. From 1930, when it was first discovered, until 2006, Pluto was known as the ninth planet in the solar system because of its position furthest from the sun.

plutonium /pluːˈtəʊniəm/ noun [U] (symbol **Pu**) a chemical element that is used in nuclear weapons and in producing nuclear energy ▶ **pluton**

ply /plaɪ/ verb [I,T] (**plying**; **plies**; pt, pp **plied**) **1** to try to sell services or goods to people, especially on the street: *Boat owners were **plying** their **trade** to passing tourists.* ◇ *to ply for business* ▶ **próbować sprzedawać towar lub usługi** (*zwł. na ulicy*) **2** (used about ships, boats and buses etc.) to travel regularly on a certain route ▶ **kursować**

PHR V **ply sb with sth** to keep giving sb food and drink, or asking sb questions: *They plied us with food from the moment we arrived.* ▶ **natarczywie częstować kogoś czymś**; **zasypywać kogoś pytaniami**

plywood /ˈplaɪwʊd/ noun [U] board made by sticking several thin layers of wood together ▶ **sklejka**

PM = PRIME MINISTER

p.m. (US also **P.M.**) /ˌpiː ˈem/ abbr. (from Latin) **post meridiem**; after midday: *The appointment is at 3 p.m.* ▶ **po południu** ➲ look at **a.m.**

PMS /ˌpiː em ˈes/ (Brit.) (US also **PMT**) /ˌpiː em ˈtiː/ noun [U] **premenstrual syndrome/tension**; physical and emotional problems such as pain and feeling depressed that many women experience before their period each month. ▶ **zespół napięcia przedmiesiączkowego**

pneumatic /njuːˈmætɪk; US nuː-/ adj. **1** filled with air: *a pneumatic tyre* ▶ **pneumatyczny** **2** worked by air under pressure ▶ **pneumatyczny**

pneuˌmatic ˈdrill (US **jackhammer** /ˈdʒækhæmə(r)/) noun [C] a large powerful tool, worked by air pressure, used especially for breaking up road surfaces ▶ **młot pneumatyczny**

pneumonia /nju:ˈməʊniə; US nu:-/ noun [U] a serious illness of the lungs which makes breathing difficult ▶ **zapalenie płuc**

PO abbr. [in compounds] = POST OFFICE: *a PO box*

poach /pəʊtʃ/ verb **1** [T] to cook food gently in a small amount of liquid: *poached eggs* jajka w koszulkach ◇ *poached fish* ryba z wody ▶ **gotować w małej ilości wody/mleka** ➲ note at **cook 2** [I,T] to hunt animals illegally on sb else's land: *The men were caught poaching elephants.* ▶ **kłusować 3** [T] to take an idea from sb else and use it as though it is your own ▶ **kraść** (*cudze myśli*) **4** [T] to take workers from another company in an unfair way ▶ **werbować do pracy** (*ludzi z innej firmy*)

poacher /ˈpəʊtʃə(r)/ noun [C] a person who hunts animals illegally on sb else's land ▶ **kłusowni-k/czka**

PO box /pi: ˈəʊ bɒks/ noun [C] a place in a post office where letters, packages, etc. are kept until they are collected by the person they were sent to: *The address is PO Box 4287, Nairobi, Kenya.* ▶ **skrytka pocztowa**

pocket[1] /ˈpɒkɪt/ noun [C] **1** a piece of cloth like a small bag that is sewn inside or on a piece of clothing and is used for carrying things in: *He always walks with his hands in his trouser pockets.* ◇ *a pocket* (kieszonkowy) *calculator/dictionary* ▶ **kieszeń** ➲ picture on **page A1 2** a small bag or container that is fixed to the inside of a car door, suitcase, etc. and used for putting things in: *There are safety instructions in the pocket of the seat in front of you.* ▶ **kieszeń 3** (used to talk about the amount of money that you have to spend): *He had no intention of paying for the meal **out of** his **own pocket**.* ◇ *They sell cars to suit every pocket.* ▶ **kieszeń 4** a small area or group that is different from its surroundings: *a pocket of warm air* ▶ **mały obszar**, **enklawa**, **dziura** (*powietrza*)

IDM **pick sb's pocket** → PICK[1]

pocket[2] /ˈpɒkɪt/ verb [T] **1** to put sth in your pocket: *He took the letter and pocketed it quickly.* ▶ **wkładać do kieszeni 2** to steal or win money ▶ **przywłaszczać sobie** (*pieniądze*); **zgarniać** (*np. wygraną*)

pocketbook /ˈpɒkɪtbʊk/ noun [C] **1** a small book ▶ **notes**, **notatnik 2** (US) = WALLET

pocketful /ˈpɒkɪtfʊl/ noun [C] the amount that a pocket holds: *I took a pocketful of coins for the phone.* ▶ **pełna kieszeń**

pocketknife (especially US) = PENKNIFE

ˈpocket money noun [U] (especially US **allowance**) an amount of money that parents give a child to spend, usually every week ▶ **kieszonkowe**

pod /pɒd/ noun [C] the long, green part of some plants, such as **peas** and **beans**, that contains the seeds ▶ **strąk** ➲ picture on **page A13**

podgy /ˈpɒdʒi/ (especially US **pudgy** /ˈpʌdʒi/) adj. (informal) slightly fat: *podgy arms* ▶ (*osoba*) **tłusty** ℹ Zwykle wyraża dezaprobatę.

podiatrist (US) = CHIROPODIST

podiatry (US) = CHIROPODY

podium /ˈpəʊdiəm/ noun [C] a small platform for people to stand on when they are speaking, performing, etc. ▶ **podium**

poem /ˈpəʊɪm; US -əm/ noun [C] a piece of writing arranged in short lines. Poems try to express thoughts and feelings with the help of sound and rhythm. ▶ **wiersz**, **poemat**

poet /ˈpəʊɪt; US -ət/ noun [C] a person who writes poems ▶ **poet(k)a** ℹ **Poet** stosuje się, mówiąc zarówno o poecie, jak i poetce. Istnieje słowo **poetess**, oznaczające poetkę, lecz obecnie rzadko się go używa.

poetic /pəʊˈetɪk/ (also **poetical** /-ɪkl/) adj. **1** connected with poetry or like a poem ▶ **poetycki 2** beautiful and full of imagination ▶ **poetyczny**, **pełen poezji**

■ **poetically** /-kli/ adv. ▶ **poetycznie**

poetry /ˈpəʊətri/ noun [U] a collection of poems; poems in general: *Shakespeare's poetry and plays* ◇ *Do you like poetry?* ▶ **poezja** SYN **verse** ➲ note at **literature** ➲ look at **prose**

poignant /ˈpɔɪnjənt/ adj. causing sadness or pity: *a poignant memory* ▶ **wzruszający**, **przejmujący**
■ **poignancy** /-jənsi/ noun [U] ▶ **wzruszenie**, **siła** | **poignantly** adv. ▶ **boleśnie**, **przejmująco**

point[1] /pɔɪnt/ noun **1** [C] a particular fact, idea or opinion that sb expresses: *You **make** some interesting **points** in your essay.* ◇ *I see your point* (rozumiem, o co ci chodzi) *but I don't agree with you.* ▶ **argument**, **punkt widzenia**

> We can **bring up**, **raise**, **make**, **argue**, **emphasize** and **illustrate** a point.

2 (**the point**) [sing.] the most important part of what is being said; the main piece of information: *It makes no difference how much it costs – **the point is** we don't have any money!* ◇ *She always talks and talks and takes ages to **get to the point**.* ▶ **sedno/istota (sprawy/rzeczy) 3** [C] an important idea or thought that needs to be considered: *'Have you checked what time the last bus back is?' 'That's a point – no I haven't.'* ▶ **racja**, **dobra uwaga 4** [sing.] **the point (of/in sth/doing sth)** the meaning, reason or purpose of sth: *She's said no, so **what's the point** of telephoning her again?* ◇ ***There's no point** in talking to my parents – they never listen.* ▶ **sens 5** [C] a detail, characteristic or quality of sb/sth: *Make a list of your **strong points** and your **weak points**.* ▶ **punkt**, **strona 6** [C] [often in compounds] a particular place, position or moment: *The library is a good **starting point** for that sort of information.* ◇ *He has reached the **high point*** (wyżyny swojej kariery) *of his career.* ◇ *He waved to the crowd and it was **at that point** that the shot was fired.* ◇ ***At one point** I thought I was going to laugh.* ◇ *the boiling/freezing point of water* temperatura wrzenia/zamarzania wody ◇ *melting point* temperatura topnienia ▶ **punkt**, **miejsce**; **moment 7** [C] one of the marks of direction around a **compass**: *the points of the compass* ▶ **rumb 8** [C] (abbr. **pt**) a single mark in some games, sports, etc. that you add to others to get the score: *to score a point* ◇ *Rios needs two more points to win the match.* ▶ **punkt 9** [C] a unit of measurement for certain things: *The value of the dollar has fallen by a few points.* ▶ **jednostka miary minimalnej zmiany**, **punkt 10** [C] a small round mark used when writing parts of numbers: *She ran the race in 11.2 (eleven point two) seconds.* ▶ **przecinek** (*jako znak dziesiętny*) **11** [C] the thin sharp end of sth: *the point of a pin/needle/pencil* ▶ **czubek**, **szpic 12** (**points**) (Brit.) (US **switch**) [pl.] a set of rails where a railway line divides into two tracks. Points can be moved to allow a train to use either track. ▶ **zwrotnica**

IDM **be on the point of doing sth** just going to do sth: *I was on the point of going out when the phone rang.* ▶ **zabierać się do czegoś**

beside the point → BESIDE

have your, etc. (good) points to have some good qualities: *Bill has his good points, but he's very unreliable.* ▶ **mieć dobre strony**, **mieć zalety**

make a point of doing sth to make sure you do sth because it is important or necessary: *He made a point of locking all the doors and windows before leaving the house.* ▶ **dbać (szczególnie) o to, żeby**

point of view a way of looking at a situation; an opinion: *From my point of view it would be better to wait a little longer.* ▶ **punkt widzenia** SYN **viewpoint**, **standpoint** ➲ note at **think**

Nie mylić **from my point of view** z **in my opinion**. Pierwszy zwrot oznacza „z mojej perspektywy", tzn. jako kobieta, dziecko, nauczyciel itp. Drugi zwrot oznacza „myslę/sądzę/uważam, że": *From an advertiser's point of view, television is a wonderful medium.* ◇ *In my opinion, people watch too much television.*

a sore point → SORE[1]
sb's strong point → STRONG
take sb's point to understand and accept what sb is saying ▶ **pojąć, zrozumieć**
to the point connected with what is being discussed: *His speech was short and to the point.* ▶ **trafny, do rzeczy** SYN **relevant**
up to a point partly: *I agree with you up to a point.* ▶ **częściowo, do pewnego stopnia**

point[2] /pɔɪnt/ verb **1** [I] **point (at/to sb/sth)** to show where sth is or to draw attention to sth using your finger, a stick, etc.: *'I'll have that one,' she said, pointing to a chocolate cake.* ▶ **wskazywać 2** [I,T] **point (sth) (at/towards sb/sth)** to aim (sth) in the direction of sb/sth: *She pointed the gun at the target and fired.* ▶ **nakierowywać (na kogoś/coś), celować 3** [I] to face in a particular direction or to show that sth is in a particular direction: *The sign pointed towards the motorway.* ◇ *Turn round until you're pointing north.* ▶ **wskazywać, zwracać się (w jakimś kierunku) 4** [I] **point to sth** to show that sth is likely to exist, happen or be true: *Research points to a connection between diet and cancer.* ▶ **wskazywać (na coś)**
PHR V **point sth out (to sb)** to make sb look at sth; to make sth clear to sb: *The guide pointed out all the places of interest to us on the way.* ◇ *I'd like to point out that we haven't got much time left.* ▶ **wskazywać (coś komuś/na to)** SYN **highlight**

ˌpoint-ˈblank adj. [only before a noun] **1** (used about a shot) from a very close position: *He was shot in the leg **at point-blank range.*** ▶ (*wystrzał*) **z bliskiej odległości 2** (used about sth that is said) very direct and not polite; not allowing any discussion: *a point-blank refusal* ▶ **bez ogródek**
■ **ˌpoint-ˈblank** adv.: *She fired point-blank at his chest.* ◇ *He told her point-blank to get out of the house and never come back.* ▶ **z bliska; bezceremonialnie**

pointed /ˈpɔɪntɪd/ adj. **1** having a sharp end: *a pointed stick/nose* ▶ **spiczasty, ostry 2** (used about sth that is said) critical of sb in an indirect way: *She made a pointed comment about people who are always late.* ▶ **uszczypliwy, sarkastyczny**
■ **pointedly** adv. ▶ **niedwuznacznie, uszczypliwie**

pointer /ˈpɔɪntə(r)/ noun [C] **1** a piece of helpful advice or information: *Could you **give** me some **pointers** on how best to tackle the problem?* ▶ **wskazówka 2** a stick that is used to point to things on a map, etc. ▶ **wskaźnik 3** a small arrow on a computer screen that you move by moving the mouse ▶ **kursor**

pointless /ˈpɔɪntləs/ adj. without any use or purpose: *It's pointless to try and make him agree.* ▶ **bezsensowny, bezcelowy**
■ **pointlessly** adv. ▶ **bezsensownie, bezcelowo** | **pointlessness** noun [U] ▶ **bezsensowność, bezcelowość**

poise /pɔɪz/ noun [U] a calm, confident way of behaving ▶ **opanowanie**

poised /pɔɪzd/ adj. [not before a noun] **1** not moving but ready to move: *'Shall I call the doctor or not?' he asked, his hand poised* (zawieszona) *above the telephone.* ▶ **zatrzymany** (*w powietrzu*), **gotowy do wykonania jakiegoś ruchu 2 poised (to do sth)** ready to act; about to do sth: *The government is poised to take action if the crisis continues.* ▶ **nastawiony (na coś), przygotowany 3** calm and confident ▶ **opanowany, zrównoważony**

poison[1] /ˈpɔɪzn/ noun [C,U] a substance that kills or harms you if you eat or drink it: *rat poison* trutka na szczury ◇ *poison gas* gaz trujący ▶ **trucizna**

poison[2] /ˈpɔɪzn/ verb [T] **1** to kill, harm or damage sb/sth with poison: *The police confirmed that the murder victim had been poisoned.* ▶ **(o)truć 2** to put poison in sth: *The cup of coffee had been poisoned.* ▶ **dodawać do czegoś truciznę, skażać** (*np. środowisko*) **3** to spoil or ruin sth: *The quarrel had poisoned their relationship.* ▶ **zatruwać**
■ **poisoned** adj. **1** containing poison: *a poisoned drink* ▶ **zaprawiony trucizną, zatruty 2** damaged by dangerous substances: *poisoned water* ▶ **zatruty, zanieczyszczony**

poisoning /ˈpɔɪzənɪŋ/ noun [U] the giving or taking of poison or a dangerous substance: *His death was the result of poisoning.* ◇ *He got **food poisoning*** (dostał zatrucia pokarmowego) *from eating fish that wasn't fresh.* ▶ **otrucie, zatrucie**

poisonous /ˈpɔɪzənəs/ adj. **1** causing death or illness if you eat or drink it: *a poisonous plant* ▶ **trujący, toksyczny 2** (used about animals, etc.) producing and using poison to attack its enemies: *He was bitten by a poisonous snake.* ▶ **jadowity 3** very unpleasant and intended to upset sb: *She wrote him a poisonous letter criticizing his behaviour.* ▶ **jadowity**

poke /pəʊk/ verb **1** [T] to push sb/sth with a finger, stick or other long, thin object: *Be careful you don't poke yourself in the eye* (nie uderz się w oko) *with that stick!* ▶ **szturchać, popychać 2** [I,T] **poke (sth) into, through, out of, down, etc. sth** to push sth quickly into sth or in a certain direction: *He poked the stick down the hole to see how deep it was.* ◇ *A child's head poked up from behind the wall.* ◇ *She poked her head out of the window* (wystawiła głowę przez okno) *and shouted to us.* ▶ **wtykać, wsuwać**
■ **poke** noun [C] ▶ **szturchaniec, kuksaniec**
IDM **poke fun at sb/sth** to make jokes about sb/sth, often in an unkind way ▶ **kpić, żartować z kogoś/czegoś**
poke/stick your nose into sth → NOSE[1]
PHR V **poke about/around** (informal) to try to find sth by looking behind, under, etc. things: *Someone had been poking about in my desk.* ▶ **myszkować, szperać**
poke out of/through sth; poke out/through/up to appear in a certain place in a sudden or surprising way ▶ **pojawiać się (skądś) znienacka, wyskakiwać** (*jak diabeł z pudełka*)

poker /ˈpəʊkə(r)/ noun **1** [U] a type of card game usually played to win money ▶ **poker 2** [C] a metal stick for moving the coal or wood in a fire ▶ **pogrzebacz** ➲ picture at **fireplace**

poky /ˈpəʊki/ adj. (**pokier**; **pokiest**) (Brit., informal) (used about a house, room, etc.) too small: *a poky little office* ▶ **ciasny**

polar /ˈpəʊlə(r)/ adj. [only before a noun] of or near the North or South Pole: *the polar regions* ▶ **polarny, podbiegunowy**

ˈpolar bear noun [C] a large white bear that lives in the area near the North Pole ▶ **niedźwiedź polarny**

polarize (also **-ise**) /ˈpəʊləraɪz/ verb [I,T] (formal) to separate or make people separate into two groups with completely opposite opinions: *Public opinion has polarized on this issue.* ◇ *The issue has polarized public opinion.* ▶ **polaryzować**

pole /pəʊl/ noun [C] **1** a long, thin piece of wood or metal, used especially to hold sth up: *a tent pole* ◇ *a flagpole* maszt flagowy ▶ **słup/ek, pal 2** either of the two points at the exact top and bottom of the earth: *the North/South Pole* ▶ **biegun**

polemical /pəˈlemɪkl/ (also **polemic**) adj. (formal) involving strong arguments for or against sth, often in opposition to the opinion of others: *a polemical attack* ▶ **polemiczny**

the 'pole vault noun [C] the sport of jumping over a high bar with the help of a long pole ▶ **skok o tyczce**

police[1] /pə'li:s/ noun [pl.] the official organization whose job is to make sure that people obey the law, and to prevent and solve crime: *Dial 999 if you need to* ***call the police.*** ◇ *Kamal wants to join* ***the police force*** (wstąpić do policji) *when he finishes school.* ◇ *a police car* ◇ *the secret police* tajna policja ▶ **policja** ⓘ **Police** jest rzeczownikiem występującym zawsze w lm i zawsze używa się go z czasownikiem w lm. Nie można powiedzieć ~~*a police*~~ na określenie jednego policjanta lub policjantki, wtedy użwa się wyrazu **a policeman** lub **a policewoman.** Mówiąc o policji jako organizacji, zawsze używa się **the**: *There were over 100 police on duty.* ◇ *The police are investigating the murder.*

police[2] /pə'li:s/ verb [T] to keep control in a place by using the police or a similar official group: *The cost of policing football games is extremely high.* ▶ **patrolować**

po,lice 'constable (also **constable** /'kʌnstəbl/) noun [C] (Brit.) (abbr. **PC**) a police officer of the lowest level ▶ **posterunkowy**

po'liceman /pə'li:smən/ noun [C] (pl. **-men** /-mən/) a man who is a member of the police ▶ **policjant** ➲ look at **police officer**

po'lice officer (also **officer**) noun [C] a member of the police ▶ **policjant/ka** ➲ note at **official**[2]

po'lice state noun [C] a country where people's freedom, especially to travel and to express political opinions, is controlled by the government, with the help of the police ▶ **państwo policyjne**

po'lice station noun [C] an office of a local police force ▶ **komisariat, posterunek policji**

po'licewoman /pə'li:swʊmən/ noun [C] (pl. **-women** /-wɪmɪn/) a woman who is a member of the police ▶ **policjantka** ➲ look at **police officer**

policy /'pɒləsi/ noun [C,U] (pl. **policies**) **1 policy (on sth)** a plan of action agreed or chosen by a government, a company, etc.: *Labour has a new set of policies on health.* ◇ *It is company policy not to allow smoking in meetings.* ▶ **polityka, zasady postępowania** ➲ note at **politics 2** a way of behaving that you think is best in a particular situation: *It's my policy only to do business with people I like.* ▶ **strategia postępowania 3** a document that shows an agreement that you have made with an insurance company: *an insurance policy* ▶ **polisa ubezpieczeniowa**

polio /'pəʊliəʊ/ noun [U] a serious disease which can cause you to lose the power in certain muscles ▶ **choroba Heinego-Medina**

polish[1] /'pɒlɪʃ/ noun **1** [U] a cream, liquid, etc. that you put on sth to clean it and make it shine: *a tin of shoe polish* ▶ **pasta/płyn/wosk do polerowania 2** [sing.] the act of polishing sth: *I'll give the glasses* ***a polish*** *before the guests arrive.* ▶ **polerowanie, nadawanie połysku**

polish[2] /'pɒlɪʃ/ verb [T] to make sth shine by rubbing it and often by putting a special cream or liquid on it: *to polish your shoes/a table* ▶ **polerować, nadawać połysk**

PHR V **polish sth off** (informal) to finish sth quickly: *The two of them polished off a whole chicken for dinner!* ▶ **szybko kończyć**

polished /'pɒlɪʃt/ adj. **1** shiny because of polishing: *polished wood floors* ▶ **wypolerowany, wyfroterowany 2** (used about a performance, etc.) of a high standard: *Most of the actors gave* ***a polished performance.*** ▶ **na wysokim poziomie**

polite /pə'laɪt/ adj. having good manners and showing respect for others: *The assistants in that shop are always very helpful and polite.* ◇ *He gave me a polite smile.* ▶ **uprzejmy, grzeczny** OPP **impolite**

■ **politely** adv. ▶ **uprzejmie, grzecznie** | **politeness** noun [U] ▶ **uprzejmość, grzeczność**

political /pə'lɪtɪkl/ adj. **1** connected with politics and government: *a political leader/debate/party* ◇ *She has very strong political opinions.* ▶ **polityczny 2** (used about people) interested in politics: *She became very political at university.* ▶ **interesujący się polityką, zaangażowany politycznie 3** concerned with the competition for power inside an organization: *I suspect he was dismissed for political reasons.* ▶ **związany z polityką firmy**

■ **politically** /-kli/ adv.: *Politically he's fairly right wing.* ▶ **politycznie, z politycznego punktu widzenia**

po,litical a'sylum noun [U] protection given by a state to a person who has left their own country for political reasons ▶ **azyl polityczny**

po,litically cor'rect adj. (abbr. **PC**) (used to describe language or behaviour that carefully avoids offending particular groups of people) ▶ **politycznie poprawny**

■ **po,litical cor'rectness** noun [U] ▶ **polityczna poprawność** ⓘ Może być używane w znaczeniu krytycznym.

po,litical 'science (US) = POLITICS (4)

politician /,pɒlə'tɪʃn/ noun [C] a person whose job is in politics, especially one who is a member of parliament or of the government: *Politicians of all parties supported the war.* ▶ **polityk** ➲ look at **politics**

politicize (also **-ise**) /pə'lɪtɪsaɪz/ verb [T, often passive] **1** to make sth a political issue: *the highly politicized issue of unemployment* ▶ **upolityczniać 2** to make sb/sth become more involved in politics: *The rural population has become increasingly politicized in recent years.* ▶ **upolityczniać**

■ **politicization** (also **-isation**) /pə,lɪtɪsaɪ'zeɪʃn/ noun [U] ▶ **upolitycznianie**

politics /'pɒlətɪks/ noun **1** [U, with sing. or pl. verb] the work and ideas that are connected with governing a country, a town, etc.: *to go into politics.* ◇ *Politics has/have never been of great interest to me.* ▶ **polityka 2** [pl.] sb's political opinions and beliefs: *His politics are extreme.* ◇ *A government's policy* (polityka) *will depend on its politics* (zapatrywań politycznych). ▶ **poglądy polityczne, zapatrywania polityczne 3** [U, with sing. or pl. verb] matters concerned with competition for power between people in an organization: *office politics* ▶ **polityka** (*firmy*) **4** (US **Po,litical 'Science**) [U] the scientific study of government: *a degree in Politics* ▶ **politologia** ➲ note at **congress, election, parliament, party**

politics

In **democratic** countries, **the government** are chosen in **elections.** People **vote for** a **candidate.** Most **politicians** belong to a **political party. Left-wing** parties support social change and equality and believe that the government should own the main industries. **Right-wing** parties are against social change and support the system in which industries are owned by individual people and not the state. In the United Kingdom the person who leads the government is called the **Prime Minister** and the people who make and change laws are called **Parliament.** In the United States these people are called **Congress** and the head of the government is the **President.**

poll[1] /pəʊl/ noun [C] **1** (also **opinion poll**) a way of finding out public opinion by asking a number of people their views on sth: *This was voted best drama series in a viewers' poll.* ▶ **badanie opinii publicznej 2** the process of voting in a political election; the number of votes given: *The country will **go to the polls** in June.* ▶ **głosowanie**

poll² /pəʊl/ verb [T] **1** to receive a certain number of votes in an election: *The Liberal Democrat candidate polled over 3 000 votes.* ▶ **zdobywać głosy w wyborach 2** to ask members of the public their opinion on a subject: *Of those polled, only 20 per cent were in favour of changing the law.* ▶ **badać opinię publiczną**

pollen /ˈpɒlən/ noun [U] a fine, usually yellow, powder which is formed in flowers. It makes other flowers of the same type produce seeds when it is carried to them by the wind or by insects, etc. ▶ **pyłek**

pollinate /ˈpɒləneɪt/ verb [T] to put **pollen** into a flower or plant so that it produces seeds: *flowers pollinated by bees/the wind* ▶ **zapylać**
■ **pollination** /ˌpɒləˈneɪʃn/ noun [U] ▶ **zapylanie**

polling /ˈpəʊlɪŋ/ noun [U] the process of voting in an election ▶ **głosowanie** (*w wyborach*)

pollutant /pəˈluːtənt/ noun [C] a substance that **pollutes** air, rivers, etc. ▶ **substancja zanieczyszczająca**

pollute /pəˈluːt/ verb [T] to make air, rivers, etc. dirty and dangerous: *Traffic fumes are polluting our cities.* ◇ *The beach has been polluted with oil.* ▶ **zanieczyszczać**

⚷ **pollution** /pəˈluːʃn/ noun [U] **1** the act of making the air, water, etc. dirty and dangerous: *Major steps are being taken to control the pollution of beaches.* ▶ **zanieczyszczenie 2** substances that **pollute**: *The rivers are full of pollution.* ▶ **zanieczyszczenie** ➲ note at **environment**

polo /ˈpəʊləʊ/ noun [U] a game for two teams of horses and riders. The players try to score goals by hitting a ball with long wooden hammers. ▶ **polo**

ˈpolo neck noun [C] a high round **collar** on a piece of clothing that is rolled over and that covers most of your neck; a piece of clothing with a **polo neck** ▶ **golf**; **sweter itp. z golfem**

polyester /ˌpɒliˈestə(r); US also ˈpɒli-/ noun [U] an artificial cloth that is used for making clothes, etc. ▶ **poliester**

polygamy /pəˈlɪɡəmi/ noun [U] the custom of having more than one wife or husband at the same time ▶ **poligamia**; **poliandria** ➲ look at **bigamy**, **monogamy**
■ **polygamist** /-mɪst/ noun [C] ▶ **poligamist(k)a** | **polygamous** /pəˈlɪɡəməs/ adj. ▶ **poligamiczny**

polygon /ˈpɒlɪɡən; US -ɡɑːn/ noun [C] a flat shape with at least three angles and straight sides, and usually five or more ▶ **wielokąt**

polystyrene /ˌpɒliˈstaɪriːn/ noun [U] a light firm plastic substance that is used for packing things so that they do not get broken ▶ **polistyren**

polythene /ˈpɒlɪθiːn/ (US **polyethylene** /ˌpɒliˈeθəliːn/) noun [U] a type of very thin plastic material often used to make bags for food, etc. or to keep things dry ▶ **polietylen**

polyunsaturated /ˌpɒliʌnˈsætʃəreɪtɪd/ adj. (used about fats and oils) having the type of chemical structure that is thought to not be harmful to your health: *foods that are high in polyunsaturated fats* ◇ *polyunsaturated margarine* ▶ **wielonienasycony**

pomegranate /ˈpɒmɪɡrænɪt/ noun [C] a round fruit which has thick smooth skin and is red inside and full of large seeds ▶ (*biol.*) **granat** ➲ picture on **page A12**

pomp /pɒmp/ noun [U] the impressive nature of a large official occasion or ceremony ▶ **pompa**, **parada**

pompom /ˈpɒmpɒm/ (also **pompon** /ˈpɒmpɒn/) noun [C] **1** a small ball made of wool, used for decoration, especially on a hat ▶ **pompon** SYN **bobble 2** (especially in the US) a large round bunch of strips of plastic, tied to a handle, used by **cheerleaders** ▶ **pompon czirliderki**

pompous /ˈpɒmpəs/ adj. showing that you think you are more important than other people, for example by using long words that sound impressive ▶ **pompatyczny**, **napuszony**

ponce¹ /pɒns/ noun (Brit., informal) **1** a man who controls one or several **prostitutes** and the money that they earn ▶ **alfons** SYN **pimp 2** an offensive word for a man whose appearance and behaviour seem similar to a woman's, or who is thought to be **homosexual** ▶ **ciota**, **pedał**

ponce² /pɒns/ verb
PHR V **ponce about/around** (Brit., informal) [usually used in the progressive tenses] to waste time when you are doing sth so that you achieve nothing; to do silly things in a way that looks ridiculous ▶ **obijać się**; **wdzięczyć się**

pond /pɒnd/ noun [C] an area of water that is smaller than a lake ▶ **staw** ➲ note at **lake**

ponder /ˈpɒndə(r)/ verb [I,T] (formal) **ponder (on/over) sth** to think about sth carefully or for a long time: *The teacher gave us a question to ponder over before the next class.* ▶ **rozmyślać**, **rozważać**

ponderous /ˈpɒndərəs/ adj. (formal) **1** (used about speech and writing) too slow and careful; serious and boring ▶ (*mowa, styl pisania*) **ciężki** SYN **tedious 2** moving slowly and heavily; able to move only slowly: *She watched the cow's ponderous progress.* ▶ **ociężały** SYN **laboured**
■ **ponderously** adv. ▶ **ciężko**; **ociężale**

pong /pɒŋ/ noun [C] (Brit., slang) a strong unpleasant smell: *a terrible pong* ▶ **smród**, **fetor** ➲ note at **smell²**
■ **pong** verb [I] ▶ **śmierdzieć**

pontificate verb [I] /pɒnˈtɪfɪkeɪt/ [I] **pontificate (about/on sth)** to give your opinions about sth in a way that shows that you think you are right ▶ **perorować** ❶ Wyraża dezaprobatę.

pony /ˈpəʊni/ noun [C] (pl. **ponies**) a small horse ▶ **kucyk**

ponytail /ˈpəʊniteɪl/ noun [C] long hair that is tied at the back of the head and that hangs down in one piece ▶ **koński ogon**

ˈpony-trekking (US **ˈtrail riding**) noun [U] the activity of riding horses for pleasure in the country ▶ **rajd konny**; **wakacje w siodle**

poo (also **pooh**) /puː/ noun [U,C] a child's word for the solid waste that is passed through the **bowels**: *dog poo* ◇ *I want to do a poo!* ▶ **kupa** SYN **faeces**
■ **poo** (also **pooh**) verb [I] ▶ **robić kupę**

poodle /ˈpuːdl/ noun [C] a type of dog with thick curly fur that is sometimes cut into a special pattern ▶ **pudel**

pooh /puː/ interj. (Brit., informal) said when you smell sth unpleasant ▶ **fuj**

⚷ **pool¹** /puːl/ noun **1** : *She swims ten lengths of the pool every morning.* = SWIMMING POOL **2** a small area of still water, especially one that has formed naturally: *a rock pool* ▶ **sadzawka** ➲ note at **lake 3** [C] **a pool (of sth)** a small amount of liquid lying on a surface: *There's a huge pool of water on the kitchen floor.* ▶ **kałuża** (*np. krwi*) ➲ look at **puddle 3** [C] a small area of light: *a pool of light* ▶ **plama** (*światła*) **4** [C] a quantity of money, goods, etc. that is shared between a group of people: *There is a pool of cars that anyone in the company can use.* ▶ **pula 5** [U] a game that is played on a table with 16 coloured balls with numbers on them. Two players try to hit these balls into pockets at the corners and sides of the table with **cues**: *a pool table* ▶ **rodzaj gry bilardowej** ➲ look at **billiards**, **snooker 6** (**the pools**) [pl.] = FOOTBALL POOLS

pool² /puːl/ verb [T] to collect money, ideas, etc. together from a number of people: *If we pool our ideas we should come up with a good plan.* ▶ **sumować**, **składać**

pooped /pu:pt/ (also ˌ**pooped** ˈ**out**) adj. (especially US, informal) [not before a noun] very tired ▶ **wykończony**

poor /pɔ:(r); pʊə(r)/ adj. **1** not having enough money to have a comfortable life: *The family was too poor to buy new clothes.* ◇ *Richer countries could do more to help poorer countries.* ▶ **biedny** OPP **rich 2** (**the poor**) noun [pl.] people who do not have enough money to have a comfortable life: *They provided food and shelter for the poor.* ▶ **biedni 3** [only before a noun] (used when you are showing that you feel sorry for sb): *Poor Dan! He's very upset!* ▶ **biedny 4** of low quality or in a bad condition: *Paul is in very poor health.* ◇ *The industry has a poor safety record.* ▶ **słaby**

poorly[1] /ˈpɔ:li; ˈpʊəli/ adv. not well; badly: *a poorly paid job* ▶ **kiepsko, słabo**

poorly[2] /ˈpɔ:li; ˈpʊəli; US / adj. (Brit., informal) not well; ill: *I'm feeling a bit poorly.* ▶ (*czuć się*) **słabo/kiepsko**

pop[1] /pɒp/ noun **1** [U] (also ˈ**pop music**) modern music that is most popular among young people: *a pop group* ▶ **pop** ➲ look at **jazz**, **rock**, **classical 2** [C] a short sudden sound like a small explosion: *There was a loud pop as the champagne cork came out of the bottle.* ▶ **wystrzał**, **trzask 3** [U] (informal) a sweet drink with bubbles in it that does not contain alcohol ▶ **napój gazowany 4** [C] (US, informal) father ▶ **papcio**
■ **pop** adv.: *The balloon went pop.* Balon strzelił.

> **pop music**
> I like most kinds of music, including **pop**, **rock**, **hip hop** and **reggae**. My favourite **band**/**group** is 'Virgin'. I'm one of their biggest **fans**. I love the **singer** because he has such a great **voice**! The **drummer** and **guitarist** play well too. All their **songs** have good **lyrics** and the **tunes**/**melodies** are very **catchy**. Last year they released an **album** which became a big **hit**. They don't often **play live**, but next year they are going **on tour**. I already have tickets to **go to a concert**.

pop[2] /pɒp/ verb (**popping**; **popped**) **1** [I,T] to make a short sudden sound like a small explosion; to cause sth to do this: *The balloon popped.* ◇ *He popped the balloon.* ▶ **pękać z trzaskiem**; **przebijać 2** [I] **pop across, down, out, etc.** to come or go somewhere quickly or suddenly: *I'm just popping out to the shops.* ▶ **skakać/wpadać (dokądś) 3** [T] **pop sth in, into, etc. sth** to put or take sth somewhere quickly or suddenly: *She popped the note into her bag.* ◇ *He popped his head round the door* (wyjrzał zza drzwi) *and said goodbye.* ▶ **wsuwać/wetknąć coś dokądś**, **podrzucać coś**
PHR V **pop in** to make a quick visit: *Why don't you pop in for a cup of tea?* ▶ **wpadać**
pop sth on (Brit., informal) **1** to put on a piece of clothing: *I'll just pop on a sweater and meet you outside.* ▶ **wrzucać coś na siebie 2** to turn on a piece of electrical equipment ▶ **włączać coś**
pop out to come out (of sth) suddenly or quickly: *Her eyes nearly popped out of her head in surprise.* ▶ **wyskakiwać (jak diabeł z pudełka)**, (*oczy*) **wytrzeszczać**
pop up (informal) to appear or happen when you are not expecting it ▶ **pojawiać się znienacka**, **wypadać**

pop[3] abbr. = POPULATION: *pop 12m*

popcorn /ˈpɒpkɔ:n/ noun [U] a type of food made from **maize** that is heated until it bursts and forms light white balls that are eaten with salt or sugar on them ▶ **prażona kukurydza**

pope /pəʊp/ noun [C] the head of the Roman Catholic Church ▶ **papież**

ˈ**pop-eyed** adj. (informal) having eyes that are wide open, especially because you are very surprised, excited or frightened: *She was pop-eyed with excitement.* ▶ **o wyłupiastych/wytrzeszczonych oczach**

poplar /ˈpɒplə(r)/ noun [C] a tall thin straight tree with soft wood ▶ **topola**

ˈ**pop music** = POP[1] (1)

popper /ˈpɒpə(r)/ (also ˈ**press stud**; US **snap**) noun [C] two round pieces of metal or plastic that you press together in order to fasten a piece of clothing ▶ **zatrzask** ➲ picture at **button**

poppy /ˈpɒpi/ noun [C] (pl. **poppies**) a bright red wild flower that has small black seeds ▶ **mak** ➲ picture on **page A15**

Popsicle™ (US) = ICE LOLLY

populace /ˈpɒpjələs/ (usually **the populace**) noun [sing., with sing. or pl. verb] (formal) all the ordinary people of a particular country or area: *He had the support of large sections of the local populace.* ◇ *The populace at large is/are opposed to sudden change.* ▶ **ludność**

popular /ˈpɒpjələ(r)/ adj. **1 popular (with sb)** liked by many people or by most people in a group: *a popular holiday resort* ◇ *That teacher has always been very popular with his pupils.* ▶ **popularny** OPP **unpopular 2** made for the tastes and knowledge of ordinary people: *The popular newspapers seem more interested in scandal than news.* ▶ **popularny**, **przystępny** (*np. dla laików*) **3** [only before a noun] of or for a lot of people: *The programme is being repeated* ***by popular demand*** (na powszechne żądanie widzów). ▶ **powszechny**

popularity /ˌpɒpjuˈlærəti/ noun [U] the quality or state of being liked by many people: *The band's popularity is growing.* ▶ **popularność**

popularize (also -ise) /ˈpɒpjələraɪz/ verb [T] to make a lot of or most people like sth: *The film did a lot to popularize her novels.* ▶ **popularyzować**, **propagować**

popularly /ˈpɒpjələli/ adv. by many people; generally: *The Conservatives are popularly known as the Tories.* ▶ **powszechnie**, **ogólnie**

populate /ˈpɒpjuleɪt/ verb [T, usually passive] to fill a particular area with people: *Parts of the country are very thinly populated.* ▶ **zaludniać**

population /ˌpɒpjuˈleɪʃn/ noun (abbr. **pop**) **1** [C,U] the number of people who live in a particular area, city or country: *What is the population of your country?* ◇ *an increase/a fall in population* ▶ **liczba ludności 2** [C] all the people who live in a particular place or all the people or animals of a particular type that live somewhere: *the male/female population* ◇ *The prison population has increased* (liczba więźniów wzrosła) *in recent years.* ◇ *The local population* (społeczność miejscowa) *is/are against the changes.* ▶ **ludność**, **populacja**

porcelain /ˈpɔ:səlɪn/ noun [U] a hard white substance that is used for making expensive cups, plates, etc. ▶ **porcelana**

porch /pɔ:tʃ/ noun [C] **1** (Brit.) a small covered area at the entrance to a house or church ▶ **przedsionek**; **kruchta 2** (US) = VERANDA

pore[1] /pɔ:(r)/ noun [C] one of the small holes in your skin through which sweat can pass ▶ **por**

pore[2] /pɔ:(r)/ verb
PHR V **pore over sth** to study or read sth very carefully ▶ **ślęczeć (nad czymś)**, **zagłębiać się (w czymś)**

pork /pɔ:k/ noun [U] meat from a pig ▶ **wieprzowina** ➲ note at **meat** ➲ look at **bacon**, **gammon**, **ham**

pornography /pɔ:ˈnɒgrəfi/ (also informal **porn** /pɔ:n/) noun [U] books, magazines, films, etc. that describe or show sexual acts in order to cause sexual excitement ▶ **pornografia**
■ **pornographic** /ˌpɔ:nəˈgræfɪk/ adj. ▶ **pornograficzny**

P

porous /ˈpɔːrəs/ adj. having many small holes that allow water or air to pass through slowly: *porous material/rocks/surfaces* ▶ **porowaty, gąbczasty**

porpoise /ˈpɔːpəs/ noun [C] a sea animal that looks like a large fish with a pointed nose and that lives in groups ▶ **morświn** ➲ look at **dolphin**

porridge /ˈpɒrɪdʒ/ noun [U] a soft, thick, white food that is made from **oats** boiled with milk or water and eaten hot, especially for breakfast ▶ **owsianka**

port /pɔːt/ noun **1** [C] a town or city that has a large area of water where ships load goods, etc.: *Hamburg is a major port.* ▶ **miasto portowe 2** [C,U] an area where ships stop to let goods and passengers on and off: *a fishing port* ◇ *The damaged ship reached port safely.* ▶ **port 3** [U] a strong sweet red wine ▶ **porto, portwajn 4** [U] the side of a ship that is on your left when you are facing towards the front of the ship: *the port side* ▶ **lewa burta** (*statku*) OPP **starboard** ➲ note at **boat**

portable /ˈpɔːtəbl/ adj. that can be moved or carried easily: *a portable TV* ▶ **przenośny** ➲ look at **movable, mobile**

portal /ˈpɔːtl/ noun [C] a website which is used as a point to enter the Internet, where information has been collected that will be useful to a person interested in particular kinds of things: *a business/news/shopping portal* ▶ **portal internetowy**

porter /ˈpɔːtə(r)/ noun [C] **1** a person whose job is to carry suitcases, etc. at a railway station, airport, etc. ▶ **bagażowy, tragarz 2** a person whose job is to be in charge of the entrance of a hotel or other large building ▶ **portier, odźwierny**

portfolio /pɔːtˈfəʊliəʊ/ noun (pl. **-os**) **1** a thin flat case used for carrying documents, drawings, etc. ▶ **aktówka, teczka 2** a collection of photographs, drawings, etc. that you use as an example of your work, especially when applying for a job: *She spent most of last year getting her portfolio together.* ▶ **teczka 3** a set of shares owned by a particular person or organization: *an **investment/share portfolio*** ▶ **portfel 4** (formal) (especially Brit.) the particular area of responsibility of a government minister: *the defence portfolio* ◇ *He was asked to join as a **minister without portfolio*** ▶ **teka**

porthole /ˈpɔːthəʊl/ noun [C] a small round window in a ship ▶ **luk**

portion /ˈpɔːʃn/ noun [C] **a portion (of sth) 1** a part or share of sth: *What portion of your salary goes on tax?* ◇ *We must both accept a portion of the blame.* ▶ **udział, część 2** an amount of food for one person (especially in a restaurant): *Could we have two extra portions of chips, please?* ▶ **porcja** ➲ look at **helping**

portrait /ˈpɔːtreɪt; -trət/ noun **1** [C] a picture, painting or photograph of a person: *to paint somebody's portrait* ▶ **portret 2** [C] a description of sb/sth in words ▶ **portret 3** [U] (technical) the way of printing a document in which the top of the page is one of the shorter sides ▶ **orientacja pionowa** (*ustawienia strony dokumentu do wydruku*) ➲ look at **landscape**

portray /pɔːˈtreɪ/ verb [T] **1** to show sb/sth in a picture; to describe sb/sth in a piece of writing: *Zola portrayed life in 19th-century France.* ▶ **portretować 2 portray sb/sth as sth** to describe sb/sth in a particular way: *In many of his novels life is portrayed as being hard.* ▶ **opisywać, portretować 3** to act the part of sb in a play or film: *In this film she portrays a very old woman.* ▶ **odtwarzać**
■ **portrayal** /pɔːˈtreɪəl/ noun [C] ▶ **przedstawienie, portretowanie**

pose¹ /pəʊz/ verb **1** [T] to create or give sb sth that they have to deal with: *to pose a problem/threat/challenge/risk* ◇ *to pose a question* ▶ **stwarzać, stawiać** (*pytanie*) **2** [I] to sit or stand in a particular position for a painting, photograph, etc.: *After the wedding we all posed for photographs.* ▶ **pozować 3** [I] **pose as sb/sth** to pretend to be sb/sth: *The robbers got into the house by posing as telephone engineers.* ▶ **udawać (kogoś) 4** [I] to behave in a way that is intended to impress people who see you: *They hardly swam at all. They just sat posing at the side of the pool.* ▶ **pozować, szpanować**

pose² /pəʊz/ noun [C] **1** a position in which sb stands, sits, etc. especially in order to be painted or photographed: *He adopted a relaxed pose for the camera.* ▶ **poza 2** a way of behaving that is intended to impress people who see you ▶ **poza**

posh /pɒʃ/ adj. (informal) **1** fashionable and expensive: *We went for a meal in a really posh hotel.* ▶ **szpanerski** SYN **stylish 2** (Brit.) (used about people) belonging to or typical of a high social class ▶ **dystyngowany, wykwintny**

position¹ /pəˈzɪʃn/ noun **1** [C,U] the place where sb/sth is or should be: *Are you happy with the position of the chairs?* ◇ *All the dancers were **in position*** (na swoich miejscach) *waiting for the music to begin.* ▶ **pozycja, miejsce 2** [C,U] the way in which sb/sth sits, sleeps or stands, or the direction that sth is pointing in: *My leg hurts when I **change position.*** ◇ *Turn the switch to the off position.* ▶ **pozycja 3** [C, usually sing.] the state or situation that sb/sth is in: *I'm in a very **difficult position.*** ◇ *I'm sorry, I'm not **in a position*** (nie jestem w stanie) *to help you financially.* ▶ **sytuacja 4** [C] **a position (on sth)** what you think about sth; your opinion: *What is your position on smoking?* ▶ **stanowisko (w jakiejś sprawie) 5** [C,U] the place or level of a person, company, team, etc. compared to others: *the position of women in society* ◇ *Max finished the race in second position.* ◇ *Wealth and position are very important to some people.* ▶ **pozycja, miejsce 6** [C] a job: *There have been over a hundred applications for the position of Sales Manager.* ▶ **stanowisko, posada** SYN **post 7** [C] the part you play in a team game: *Danny can play any position except goalkeeper.* ▶ **pozycja gry** (*w drużynie sportowej*)

position² /pəˈzɪʃn/ verb [T] to put sb/sth in a particular place or position: *Mary positioned herself* (Mary zajęła pozycję) *near the door.* ▶ **umieszczać**

positive /ˈpɒzətɪv/ adj. **1** thinking or talking mainly about the good things in a situation; feeling confident and sure that sth good will happen: *Their reaction to my idea was generally positive.* ◇ *I **feel** very **positive** about our team's chances this season.* ◇ ***Positive thinking** will help you to succeed.* ◇ *The teacher tried to make positive suggestions.* ▶ **pozytywny, konstruktywny** OPP **negative 2 positive (about sth/that ...)** certain; sure: *Are you positive that this is the woman you saw?* ▶ **pewny, przekonany 3** clear; definite: *There is no positive evidence that he is guilty.* ◇ *to take positive action* ▶ **pewny, stanowczy 4** showing that sth has happened or is present: *The result of the pregnancy test was positive.* ◇ *Two athletes tested positive for steroids.* ▶ **dodatni** OPP **negative 5** more than zero ▶ **dodatni** OPP **negative**

positively /ˈpɒzətɪvli/ adv. **1** (informal) (used for emphasizing sth) really; extremely: *He wasn't just annoyed – he was positively furious!* ▶ **strasznie, bardzo 2** in a way that shows you are thinking about the good things in a situation, not the bad: *Thinking positively helps many people deal with stress.* ▶ **pozytywnie 3** with no doubt; firmly: *I was positively convinced that I was doing the right thing.* ▶ **stanowczo, kategorycznie, całkowicie**

possess /pəˈzes/ verb [T] [not used in the continuous tenses] **1** (formal) to have or own sth: *They lost everything they possessed in the fire.* ◇ *Paola possesses a natural ability to make people laugh.* ▶ **posiadać, mieć 2** to influence sb or to make sb do sth: *What possessed you to say a thing like that!* ▶ **opętywać kogoś (czymś)** ⓘ Czasownika **possess** nie używa się w czasach *continuous*. Natomiast często spotyka się go w *present participle* (formie *-ing*):

Any student possessing the necessary qualifications will be considered for the course.

possession /pəˈzeʃn/ noun **1** [U] the state of having or owning sth: *The gang were caught* ***in possession of*** *stolen goods.* ◇ *Enemy forces* ***took possession of*** (siły nieprzyjaciela zdobyły) *the town.* ▶ **posiadanie 2** [C, usually pl.] something that you have or own: *Bud packed all his possessions and left.* ▶ **dobytek**

possessive /pəˈzesɪv/ adj. **1 possessive (of/about sb/sth)** not wanting to share sb/sth: *Dan is so possessive with his toys – he won't let other children play with them.* ▶ **zaborczy 2** (used to describe words that show who or what a person or thing belongs to): *'My', 'your' and 'his' are possessive adjectives.* ◇ *'Mine', 'yours' and 'his' are possessive pronouns.* ▶ **dzierżawczy**

possessor /pəˈzesə(r)/ noun [C] a person who has or owns sth ▶ **właściciel/ka, posiadacz/ka**

possibility /ˌpɒsəˈbɪləti/ noun (pl. **possibilities**) **1** [U,C] **(a) possibility (of sth/doing sth); (a) possibility that ...** the fact that sth might exist or happen, but is not likely to: *There's not much possibility of the letter reaching you before Saturday.* ◇ *There is* ***a strong possibility*** *that the fire was started deliberately.* ▶ **możliwość, ewentualność 2** [C] one of the different things that you can do in a particular situation or in order to achieve sth: *There is a wide range of possibilities open to us.* ▶ **możliwość**

possible /ˈpɒsəbl/ adj. **1** that can happen or be done: *I'll phone you back* ***as soon as possible.*** ◇ *Could you give me your answer today,* ***if possible?*** ◇ *The doctors did* ***everything possible*** *to save his life.* ◇ *You were warned of all the possible dangers.* ▶ **możliwy** OPP **impossible 2** that may be suitable or acceptable: *There are four possible candidates for the job.* ▶ **prawdopodobny, możliwy** ➲ look at **probable 3** (used after adjectives to emphasize that sth is the best, worst, etc. of its type): *Alone and with no job or money, I was in the worst possible situation.* ▶ **z możliwych**

possibly /ˈpɒsəbli/ adv. **1** perhaps: *'Will you be free on Sunday?' 'Possibly.'* ▶ **możliwie, być może** SYN for all meanings **maybe 2** (used for emphasizing sth) according to what is possible: *I will leave as soon as I possibly can* (jak tylko będę mógł). ▶ **jak tylko możliwe**

post¹ /pəʊst/ noun **1** (especially US **mail**) [U] the system or organization for collecting and dealing with letters, packages, etc.: *The document is too valuable to send* ***by post.*** ▶ **poczta 2** (US **mail**) [U] letters, packages, etc. that are collected or brought to your house: *Has the post come yet this morning?* ◇ *There wasn't any post for you.* ◇ *I'll stop now or I'll miss the post* (nie zdążę przed opróżnieniem skrzynki). ▶ **poczta, korespondencja 3** [C] a job: *The post was advertised in the local newspaper.* ▶ **posada, stanowisko** SYN **position 4** [C] a place where sb is on duty or is guarding sth: *The soldiers had to remain at their posts all night.* ▶ **posterunek, stanowisko 5** [C] a vertical piece of metal or wood that is put in the ground to mark a position or to support sth: *a goalpost* słupek bramki ◇ *Can you see a signpost* (drogowskaz) *anywhere?* ▶ **słup/ek**
IDM **by return (of post)** → RETURN²

post² /pəʊst/ verb [T] **1** (especially US **mail**) to send a letter, package, etc. by post: *This letter was posted in Edinburgh yesterday.* ▶ **wysyłać** (*pocztą*) **2** to send sb to go and work somewhere: *After two years in London, Angela was posted to the Tokyo office.* ▶ **delegować 3** to put sb on guard or on duty in a particular place: *Policemen were posted outside the building.* ▶ **stawiać** (*na posterunku/straży*) **4** [often passive] (formal) to put a notice where everyone can see it: *The exam results will be posted on the main noticeboard.* ◇ *The winners' names will be posted on our website.* ▶ **ogłaszać, wywieszać** (*np. wyniki egzaminów*)

Post (rzeczownika i czasownika) częściej używa się w Br. ang., natomiast **mail** w Amer. ang. Jednakże **mail** występuje dosyć często także w Br. ang. Oficjalna nazwa urzędu poczty brytyjskiej to **the Royal Mail**. Zwróć też uwagę na wyrażenia **airmail** i **surface mail**. Kiedy zamawia się towary wysyłkowo, używa się usługi **mail order**.

When you have written a **letter** you put it in an **envelope**, **address** it, **put/stick** a **stamp** on it and put it in a **postbox** (US **mailbox**). The address should include the **postcode** (US **zip code**). You can choose to send **parcels** and letters by **airmail** or **surface mail**. If it is urgent you might send it by **courier**.

postage /ˈpəʊstɪdʒ/ noun [U] the amount that you must pay to send a letter, package etc. ▶ **opłata pocztowa**

ˈpostage stamp = STAMP¹ (1)

postal /ˈpəʊstl/ adj. [only before a noun] connected with the sending and collecting of letters, packages, etc. ▶ **pocztowy**

ˈpostal order noun [C] a piece of paper that you can buy at a post office that represents a certain amount of money. A **postal order** is a safe way of sending money by post. ▶ **przekaz pocztowy**

ˈpostal vote (US **ˌabsentee ˈballot**) noun [C] a vote in an election that you can send when you cannot be present ▶ **głosowanie korespondencyjne**

postbox /ˈpəʊstbɒks/ (also **ˈletter box**; US **mailbox**) noun [C] a box in a public place where you put letters, etc. that you want to send ▶ **skrzynka pocztowa** ➲ look at **pillar box**

postcard /ˈpəʊstkɑːd/ noun [C] a card that you write a message on and send to sb. **Postcards** have a picture on one side and are usually sent without an envelope. ▶ **kartka pocztowa, pocztówka**

postcode /ˈpəʊstkəʊd/ (US **zip code**) noun [C] a group of letters and/or numbers that you put at the end of an address ▶ **kod pocztowy**

poster /ˈpəʊstə(r)/ noun [C] **1** a large printed picture or a notice in a public place, often used to advertise sth ▶ **plakat, afisz 2** a large picture printed on paper that is put on a wall for decoration ▶ **plakat**

posterity /pɒˈsterəti/ noun [U] the future and the people who will be alive then: *We should all look after our environment for the sake of posterity.* ▶ **potomność**

postgraduate /ˌpəʊstˈɡrædʒuət/ noun [C] a person who is doing further studies at a university after taking their first degree ▶ **doktorant/ka, magistrant/ka** ➲ look at **graduate, undergraduate**

posthumous /ˈpɒstjʊməs; US -tʃəm-/ adj. given or happening after sb has died: *a posthumous medal for bravery* ▶ **pośmiertny**
■ **posthumously** adv. ▶ **pośmiertnie**

posting /ˈpəʊstɪŋ/ noun [C] a job in another country that you are sent to do by your employer: *an overseas posting* ▶ **oddelegowanie** (*do pracy w innym kraju*), **delegacja**

ˈPost-it™ (also **ˈPost-it note**) noun [C] a small piece of coloured, sticky paper that you use for writing a note on, and that can be easily removed ▶ **kartka samoprzylepna** (*do robienia notatek*)

postman /ˈpəʊstmən/ (US **mailman** /ˈmeɪlmæn/), **postwoman** /ˈpəʊstwʊmən/ noun [C] (pl. **-men** /-mən/; **-women** /-wɪmɪn/) a person whose job is to collect letters, packages, etc. and take them to people's houses ▶ **listonosz/ka**

postmark /ˈpəʊstmɑːk/ noun [C] an official mark over a stamp on a letter, package, etc. that says when and where it was posted ▶ **stempel pocztowy**

P

postmodern /ˌpəʊstˈmɒdn; US -dən/ adj. connected with or influenced by **postmodernism**: *postmodern architecture* ▶ **postmodernistyczny**

postmodernism /ˌpəʊstˈmɒdənɪzəm/ noun [U] a style and movement in art, **architecture**, literature, etc. in the late 20th century that reacts against modern styles, for example by mixing features from traditional and modern styles ▶ **postmodernizm** ➲ look at **modernism**
■ **postmodernist 1** noun ▶ **postmodernist(k)a 2** adj. [usually before a noun] ▶ **postmodernistyczny**

post-mortem /ˌpəʊst ˈmɔːtəm/ noun [C] a medical examination of a dead body to find out how the person died ▶ **sekcja zwłok**

post-natal /ˌpəʊst ˈneɪtl/ adj. [only before a noun] connected with the period after the birth of a baby ▶ **poporodowy** OPP **antenatal**

ˈpost office noun [C] (abbr. **PO** /ˌpiː ˈəʊ/) **1** a place where you can buy stamps, post packages, etc.: *Where's the main post office?* ▶ **poczta, urząd pocztowy 2** (**the Post Office**) [sing.] the national organization that is responsible for collecting and dealing with letters, packages, etc.: *He works for the Post Office.* ▶ **Urząd Pocztowy**

ˈpost office box = PO BOX

postpone /pəˈspəʊn; US pəʊˈs-/ verb [T] to arrange that sth will happen at a later time than the time you had planned; to delay: *The match was postponed because of water on the pitch.* ▶ **odraczać, przesuwać** (*w czasie*) ➲ look at **cancel**
■ **postponement** noun [C,U] ▶ **odroczenie, przesunięcie (w czasie)**

postscript = PS

posture /ˈpɒstʃə(r)/ noun [C,U] the way that a person sits, stands, walks, etc.: *Poor posture can lead to backache.* ▶ **postawa, postura**

ˌpost-ˈwar adj. existing or happening in the period after the end of a war, especially the Second World War ▶ **powojenny**

postwoman → POSTMAN

pot¹ /pɒt/ noun [C] **1** a round container that is used for cooking food in: *pots and pans* ▶ **garnek 2** a container that you use for a particular purpose: *a flowerpot* ◇ *a pot of paint* ▶ **doniczka, dzbanek, puszka 3** the amount that a pot contains: *We drank two pots of tea.* ▶ **dzbanek, garnek, puszka** (*zawartość*)

pot² /pɒt/ verb [T] (**potting; potted**) **1** to put a plant into a pot filled with soil ▶ **sadzić w doniczce 2** to hit a ball into one of the pockets in the table in the game of **pool**, **billiards** or **snooker**: *He potted the black ball into the corner pocket.* ▶ (*bilard*) **wbijać** (*kulę do łuzy*)

potassium /pəˈtæsiəm/ noun [U] (symbol **K**) a chemical element that exists as a soft, silver-white metal and is used combined with other elements in industry and farming ▶ **potas**

potato /pəˈteɪtəʊ/ noun [C,U] (pl. **potatoes**) a round vegetable that grows under the ground with a brown, yellow or red skin. Potatoes are white or yellow inside: *mashed potato* ziemniaki tłuczone ◇ *Linda peeled the potatoes* (obrała ziemniaki) *for supper.* ◇ *potatoes baked in their jackets* (pieczone w mundurkach) ▶ **ziemniak, kartofel** ➲ note at **recipe** ➲ picture on **page A13**

poˌtato ˈcrisp (US **poˈtato chip**) = CRISP²

potent /ˈpəʊtnt/ adj. strong or powerful: *a potent drug* ▶ **mocny, silny**
■ **potency** /ˈpəʊtnsi/ noun [U] ▶ **siła, moc, potencja**

potential¹ /pəˈtenʃl/ adj. [only before a noun] that may possibly become sth, happen, be used, etc.: *Wind power is a potential source of energy.* ◇ *potential customers* ▶ **potencjalny** SYN **possible**
■ **potentially** /-ʃəli/ adv. ▶ **potencjalnie**

potential² /pəˈtenʃl/ noun [U] the qualities or abilities that sb/sth has but that may not be fully developed yet: *That boy **has great potential** as an athlete.* ▶ **potencjał**

pothole /ˈpɒthəʊl/ noun [C] **1** a hole in the surface of a road that is formed by traffic and bad weather ▶ **wybój 2** a deep hole in rock that is formed by water over thousands of years ▶ **kocioł erozyjny**

potholing /ˈpɒthəʊlɪŋ/ noun [U] the sport of climbing down inside **potholes** (2) and walking through underground tunnels: *to go potholing* ▶ **speleologia**

ˈpot plant noun [C] (Brit.) a plant that you grow in a pot and keep inside a building ▶ **roślina doniczkowa**

potter¹ /ˈpɒtə(r)/ (US **putter** /ˈpʌtə(r)/) verb [I] **potter (about/around)** to spend your time doing small jobs or things that you enjoy without hurrying: *Grandpa spends most of the day pottering in the garden.* ▶ **dłubać, majsterkować**

potter² /ˈpɒtə(r)/ noun [C] a person who makes **pottery** from baked **clay** ▶ **garncarz**

pottery /ˈpɒtəri/ noun (pl. **potteries**) **1** [U] pots, dishes, etc. that are made from baked **clay** ▶ **wyroby garncarskie 2** [U] the activity or skill of making dishes, etc. from **clay**: *a pottery class* ▶ **garncarstwo 3** [C] a place where **clay** pots and dishes are made ▶ **warsztat garncarski**

potty¹ /ˈpɒti/ adj. (**pottier; pottiest**) (Brit., informal) **1** crazy or silly ▶ **stuknięty, postrzelony 2 potty about sb/sth** liking sb/sth very much: *Penny's potty about Mark.* ▶ **zwariowany** (*na czyimś/jakimś punkcie*)

potty² /ˈpɒti/ noun [C] (pl. **potties**) a plastic bowl that young children use when they are too small to use a toilet ▶ **nocnik**

ˈpotty-train verb [T] to teach a small child to use a **potty** or toilet ▶ **uczyć dziecko siadania na nocnik/korzystania z toalety**

pouch /paʊtʃ/ noun [C] **1** a small leather bag ▶ **worek, sakiewka 2** a pocket of skin on the stomach of some female animals, for example **kangaroos**, in which they carry their babies ▶ **torba** (*np. kangura*)

poultry /ˈpəʊltri/ noun **1** [pl.] birds, for example chickens, **ducks**, etc. that are kept for their eggs or their meat ▶ **drób 2** [U] the meat from these birds: *Eat plenty of fish and poultry.* ▶ **drób, mięso drobiowe** ➲ note at **meat**

pounce /paʊns/ verb [I] **pounce (on sb/sth)** to attack sb/sth by jumping suddenly on them or it: (figurative) *He was quick to pounce on any mistakes I made.* ▶ **rzucać się/skakać (na kogoś/coś)**

pound[1] /paʊnd/ noun **1** [C] (also ˌpound ˈsterling) (symbol £) the unit of money in Britain; one hundred pence (100p): *Melissa earns £16 000 a year.* ◇ *Can you change a ten-pound note?* ◇ *a pound coin* ▶ **funt (szterling) 2** (**the pound**) [sing.] the value of the British pound on international money markets: *How many yen are there **to the pound**?* ◇ *The pound has fallen against the dollar.* Wartość funta spadła w stosunku do dolara. ▶ **funt 3** [C] (abbr. **lb**) a measure of weight; equal to 0.454 of a kilogram: *The carrots cost 30p a pound.* ◇ *Half a pound of mushrooms, please.* ▶ **funt** ℹ Więcej o wagach w dodatku *Wyrażenia liczbowe* na końcu słownika.

pound[2] /paʊnd/ verb **1** [I] **pound (at/against/on sth)** to hit sth hard many times making a lot of noise: *She pounded on the door with her fists.* ▶ **walić, tłuc, łomotać 2** [I] **pound along, down, up, etc.** to walk with heavy, noisy steps in a particular direction: *Jason went pounding up the stairs three at a time.* ▶ **ciężko biec 3** [I] (used about your heart, blood, etc.) to beat quickly and loudly: *Her heart was pounding with fear.* ◇ *I've got a pounding headache.* Głowa pęka mi z bólu. ▶ (*serce itp.*) **walić 4** [T] to hit sth many times to break it into smaller pieces ▶ **tłuc, kuć**

pour /pɔː(r)/ verb **1** [T] to make a liquid or other substance flow steadily out of or into a container: *Pour the sugar into a bowl.* ◇ *People were pouring out of the station.* Ludzie tłumnie wychodzili ze stacji. ▶ **lać (się), wlewać, wylewać 2** [I] (used about a liquid, smoke, light, etc.) to flow out of or into sth quickly and steadily, and in large quantities: *Tears were pouring down her cheeks.* Łzy spływały jej po policzkach. ◇ *She opened the curtains and sunlight poured into the room.* ▶ **wlewać, wylewać 3** [T] **pour sth (out)** to serve a drink to sb by letting it flow from a container into a cup or glass: *Have you poured out the tea?* ▶ **nalewać, rozlewać 4** [I] **pour (down) (with rain)** to rain heavily: *The rain poured down all day long.* ◇ *I'm not going out. It's pouring with rain.* ▶ **lać 5** [I] to come or go somewhere continuously in large numbers: *People were pouring out of the station.* ▶ (*przen.*) **spływać,** (*przen.*) **wpływać,** (*przen.*) **napływać**

IDM **pour your heart out (to sb)** to tell sb all your personal problems, feelings, etc. ▶ **otworzyć serce (przed kimś)**

PHR V **pour sth out** to speak freely about what you think or feel about sth that has happened to you: *to pour out all your troubles* ▶ **wylewać (przed kimś)** (*np. żale*)

pout /paʊt/ verb [I] to push your lips, or your bottom lip, forward to show that you are annoyed about sth or to look sexually attractive ▶ **wydymać usta**

■ **pout** noun [C] ▶ **wydęcie ust**

poverty /ˈpɒvəti/ noun [U] the state of being poor: *There are millions of people in this country who are living **in poverty**.* ▶ **ubóstwo, bieda**

poverty-stricken /ˈpɒvəti strɪkən/ adj. very poor ▶ **ubogi, biedny**

powder /ˈpaʊdə(r)/ noun **1** [U,C] a dry substance that is in the form of very small grains: *washing powder* ◇ *Grind the spices into a fine powder.* ▶ **proszek 2** [U] powder that you use on your skin ▶ **puder**

■ **powder** verb [T] ▶ **pudrować**

powdered /ˈpaʊdəd/ adj. (used about a substance that is usually liquid) dried and made into powder: *powdered milk/soup* ▶ **sproszkowany, w proszku**

power[1] /ˈpaʊə(r)/ noun **1** [U] **power (over sb/sth)**; **power (to do sth)** the ability to control people or things or to do sth: *The aim is to give people more power over their own lives.* ◇ *to have somebody **in your power*** ◇ ***It's not in my power*** (nie mam możliwości) *to help you.* ▶ **moc, możliwość 2** [U] political control of a country or area: *When did this government **come to power**?* ◇ *to take/seize power* ▶ **władza, siła 3** (**powers**) [pl.] a particular ability of the body or mind: *He has great powers of observation.* ◇ *She had to use all her powers of persuasion on him.* ▶ **zdolność, umiejętność 4** [C] **the power (to do sth)** the right or authority to do sth: *Do the police have the power to stop cars without good reason?* ▶ **prawo, upoważnienie 5** [C] a country with a lot of influence in world affairs or that has great military strength: *Britain is no longer **a world power**.* ◇ *a military/economic power* ▶ **mocarstwo, potęga 6** [U] the energy or strength that sb/sth has: *The ship was helpless against the power of the storm.* ◇ *I've lost all power in my right arm.* ▶ **potęga, siła 7** [U] energy that can be collected and used for operating machines, making electricity, etc.: *nuclear/wind/solar power* ◇ *This car has power steering* (wspomaganie kierownicy). ▶ **energia** (*np. elektryczna*)

power[2] /ˈpaʊə(r)/ verb [T] to supply energy to sth to make it work: *What powers the motor in this machine?* ▶ **zasilać**

■ **-powered** adj.: *a solar-powered calculator* ◇ *a high-powered engine* ▶ **zasilany**

ˈ**power cut** noun [C] a time when the supply of electricity stops, for example during a storm ▶ **przerwa w dopływie prądu**

powerful /ˈpaʊəfl/ adj. **1** having a lot of control or influence over other people: *a powerful nation* ◇ *a rich and powerful businessman* ▶ **potężny, wpływowy 2** having great strength or force: *a powerful car/engine/telescope* ◇ *a powerful swimmer* ▶ **potężny 3** having a strong effect on your mind or body: *The Prime Minister made a powerful speech* (mocne przemówienie). ◇ *a powerful drug* ▶ **silny, bardzo skuteczny**

■ **powerfully** /-fəli/ adv. ▶ **potężnie; silnie**

powerless /ˈpaʊələs/ adj. **1** without strength, influence or control ▶ **bezsilny 2 powerless to do sth** completely unable to do sth: *I stood and watched him struggle, powerless to help* (nie mogąc mu pomóc). ▶ **niezdolny** (*do zrobienia czegoś*)

ˈ**power plant** (US) = POWER STATION

ˈ**power point** (Brit.) = SOCKET (1)

ˈ**power station** (US ˈpower plant) noun [C] a place where electricity is produced ▶ **elektrownia, siłownia**

pp abbr. **1** plural of **p** (1) **2** (before the name at the end of a letter) instead of: *pp Mark Dilks* ▶ **z up., wz**

PR 1 = PUBLIC RELATIONS **2** = PROPORTIONAL REPRESENTATION

practicable /ˈpræktɪkəbl/ adj. (used about an idea, a plan or a suggestion) able to be done successfully: *The scheme is just not practicable.* ▶ **wykonalny**

practical[1] /ˈpræktɪkl/ adj. **1** concerned with actually doing sth rather than with ideas or thought: *Have you got any **practical experience** of working on a farm?* ▶ **praktyczny** ➲ look at **theoretical 2** that is likely to succeed; right or sensible: *Your plan just isn't practical.* ◇ *We need to find a practical solution to the problem.* ▶ **wykonalny** OPP **impractical 3** very suitable for a particular purpose; useful: *a practical little car, ideal for the city* ▶ **praktyczny** OPP **impractical 4** (used about people) making sensible decisions and good at dealing with problems: *We must be practical. It's no good buying a house we cannot afford.* ▶ **praktyczny, realnie/trzeźwo myślący** OPP **impractical 5** (used about a person) good at making and repairing things: *Brett's very practical and has made a lot of improvements to their new house.* ▶ **zręczny, sprawny manualnie**

practical[2] /ˈpræktɪkl/ noun [C] (Brit., informal) a lesson or exam where you do or make sth rather than just writing: *He passed the theory paper but failed the practical.* ▶ **egzamin praktyczny**

practicality /ˌpræktɪˈkæləti/ noun (pl. **practicalities**) **1** [U] the quality of being suitable and realistic, or likely to

P

succeed: *I am not convinced of the practicality of the scheme.* ▶ **wykonalność** **2** (**practicalities**) [pl.] the real facts rather than ideas or thoughts: *Let's look at the practicalities of the situation.* ▶ **strona praktyczna**

ˌpractical ˈjoke noun [C] a trick that you play on sb that makes them look silly and makes other people laugh ▶ **psikus**, **figiel** ➲ note at **humour**

practically /ˈpræktɪkli/ adv. **1** (informal) almost; very nearly: *My essay is practically finished now.* ▶ **niemal**, **prawie (że)** **2** in a realistic or sensible way: *Practically speaking, we can't afford it.* ▶ **praktycznie**

practice /ˈpræktɪs/ noun **1** [U] action rather than ideas or thought: *Your suggestion sounds fine in theory, but would it work* ***in practice?*** ◇ *I can't wait to* ***put*** *what I've learnt* ***into practice.*** ▶ **praktyka**, **zastosowanie** **2** [C,U] (formal) the usual or expected way of doing sth in a particular organization or situation; a habit or custom: *It is standard practice not to pay bills until the end of the month.* ▶ **zwyczaj**, **praktyka** **3** [C,U] (a period of) doing an activity many times or training regularly so that you become good at it: *piano/football practice* ◇ *His accent should improve* ***with practice.*** ▶ **wprawa**, **ćwiczenie** **4** [U] the work of a doctor or lawyer: *Dr Roberts doesn't work in a hospital. He's in* ***general practice*** (praktykuje w przychodni). ▶ **praktyka** (*np. praca lekarza, adwokata*) **5** [C] the business of a doctor, dentist or lawyer: *a successful medical/dental practice* ▶ **przychodnia lekarska**; **kancelaria adwokacka**

IDM **be/get out of practice** to find it difficult to do sth because you have not done it for a long time: *I'm not playing very well at the moment. I'm really out of practice.* ▶ **wyjść z wprawy**

practise (US **practice**) /ˈpræktɪs/ verb [I,T] **1 practise for sth; practise (sth) (on sb/sth)** to do an activity or train regularly so that you become very good at sth: *If you want to play a musical instrument well, you must practise every day.* ◇ *He likes to* ***practise*** *his English* ***on me.*** ▶ **ćwiczyć** **2** to do sth or take part in sth regularly or publicly: *a practising Catholic/Jew/Muslim* ▶ **praktykować**, **uprawiać** (*np. sport*) **3 practise (sth/as sth)** to work as a doctor or lawyer: *She's practising as a barrister in Leeds.* ◇ *He was banned from practising medicine.* ▶ **praktykować**

practised (US **practiced**) /ˈpræktɪst/ adj. **practised (in sth)** very good at sth, because you have done it a lot or often: *He was practised in the art of inventing excuses.* ▶ **doświadczony**, **wprawny**, **wytrawny** (*np. specjalista*)

practitioner /prækˈtɪʃənə(r)/ noun [C] (formal) a person who works as a doctor, dentist or lawyer ▶ **praktykujący lekarz/dentysta/adwokat** ➲ look at **GP**

pragmatic /prægˈmætɪk/ adj. dealing with problems in a practical way rather than by following ideas or principles ▶ **pragmatyczny**

prairie /ˈpreəri/ noun [C] a very large area of flat land covered in grass with few trees (especially in North America) ▶ **preria**

praise¹ /preɪz/ noun [U] what you say when you are expressing admiration for sb/sth: *The survivors were full of praise for the paramedics.* ▶ **pochwała**, **chwała**

praise² /preɪz/ verb [T] **praise sb/sth (for sth)** to say that sb/sth is good and should be admired: *The firefighters were praised for their courage.* ▶ **chwalić**, **sławić**

praiseworthy /ˈpreɪzwɜːði/ adj. that should be admired and recognized as good ▶ **chwalebny**, **godny pochwały**

pram /præm/ (US ˈ**baby carriage**) noun [C] a small vehicle on four wheels for a young baby, pushed by a person on foot ▶ **wózek dziecinny**

pram

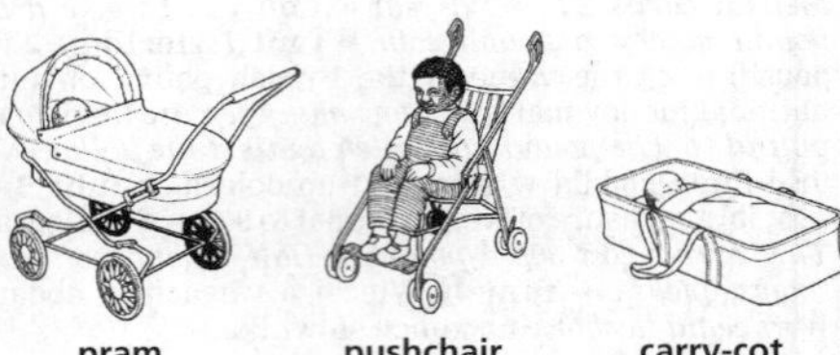

prance /prɑːns; US præns/ verb [I] to move about with quick, high steps, often because you feel proud or pleased with yourself ▶ **podskakiwać**

prank /præŋk/ noun [C] a trick that is played on sb as a joke: *a childish prank* ▶ **psikus**

prat /præt/ noun [C] (Brit., slang) a stupid person: *What a prat!* ▶ **głupek**, **cymbał**

prattle /ˈprætl/ verb [I] **prattle (on/away) (about sb/sth)** (old-fashioned) to talk a lot about unimportant things: *She prattled on about her children all evening.* ▶ **paplać**
■ **prattle** noun [U] ▶ **paplanina**

prawn /prɔːn/ (US **shrimp**) noun [C] a small **shellfish** that you can eat, which becomes pink when cooked ▶ **krewetka** ➲ look at **scampi**, **shrimp** ➲ picture on **page A11**

pray /preɪ/ verb [I,T] **pray (to sb) (for sb/sth)** to speak to God or a god in order to give thanks or to ask for help: *They knelt down and prayed for peace.* ▶ **modlić się**

prayer /preə(r)/ noun **1** [C] **a prayer (for sb/sth)** the words that you use when you speak to God or a god: *Let's* ***say a prayer*** *for all the people who are ill.* ◇ *a prayer book* modlitewnik/książeczka do nabożeństwa ▶ **modlitwa**, **pacierz** **2** [U] the act of speaking to God or a god: *to kneel in prayer* ▶ **modlitwa**

preach /priːtʃ/ verb **1** [I,T] to give a **sermon**, especially in a church ▶ **wygłaszać kazanie** **2** [T] to say that sth is good and persuade other people to accept it: *I always preach caution in situations like this.* ▶ **zalecać**, **radzić** **3** [I] to give sb advice on moral behaviour, in a way which they find boring or annoying: *I'm sorry, I didn't mean to preach.* ▶ **prawić (komuś) kazania/morały**

preacher /ˈpriːtʃə(r)/ noun [C] a person who gives **sermons**, for example in a church ▶ **kaznodzieja**

preamble /priˈæmbl; ˈpriːæmbl/ noun [C, U] (formal) an introduction to a book or a written document; an introduction to sth you say: *The aims of the treaty are stated in its preamble.* ◇ *She gave him the bad news* ***without preamble*** (bez zbędnych wstępów). ▶ **preambuła**

prearranged /ˌpriːəˈreɪndʒd/ adj. planned or arranged in advance: *a prearranged signal* ▶ **umówiony**

ˌpre-ˈbook verb [I,T] (Brit.) to arrange to have sth such as a room, table, seat or ticket in advance ▶ **rezerwować z wyprzedzeniem**

precarious /prɪˈkeəriəs/ adj. not safe or certain; dangerous: *That ladder looks very precarious.* ▶ **niebezpieczny**, **ryzykowny**
■ **precariously** adv. ▶ **niebezpiecznie**, **ryzykownie**

precaution /prɪˈkɔːʃn/ noun [C] **a precaution (against sth)** something that you do now in order to avoid danger or problems in the future: *You should always* ***take the precaution of*** *locking your valuables in the hotel safe.* ◇ *precautions against fire/theft* ▶ **środek ostrożności**, **ostrożność**
■ **precautionary** /prɪˈkɔːʃənəri; US -neri/ adj.: *I'm going to photocopy all these documents as a precautionary measure* (środek ostrożności).

precede /prɪ'si:d/ verb [I,T] (formal) to happen, come or go before sb/sth: *Look at the table on the preceding page.* ▶ **poprzedzać**

precedence /'presɪdəns/ noun [U] **precedence (over sb/sth)** the right that sb/sth has to come before sb/sth else because he/she/it is more important: *In business, making a profit seems to* ***take precedence*** *over everything else.* ▶ **pierwszeństwo (przed kimś/czymś)**

precedent /'presɪdənt/ noun [C,U] an official action or decision that has happened in the past and that is considered as an example or rule to follow in the same situation later: *We don't want to* ***set a precedent*** (stwarzać precedensu) *by allowing one person to come in late or they'll all want to do it.* ◇ *Such protests are* ***without precedent*** *in recent history.* ▶ **precedens** ➲ look at **unprecedented**

precinct /'pri:sɪŋkt/ noun **1** [C] (Brit.) a special area of shops in a town where cars are not allowed: *a shopping precinct* ▶ **obszar wydzielony tylko dla ruchu pieszego 2** [C] (US) a part of a town that has its own police station ▶ **dzielnica miasta posiadająca własną policję i straż pożarną 3** (**precincts**) [pl.] (formal) the area near or around a building: *the hospital and its precincts* ▶ **obrzeże/najbliższe otoczenie budynku**

precious /'preʃəs/ adj. **1** of great value (usually because it is rare or difficult to find): *In overcrowded Hong Kong, every small piece of land is precious.* ▶ **cenny, wartościowy 2** loved very much: *The painting was very precious to her.* ▶ **bardzo drogi, umiłowany**

ˌprecious 'metal noun [C] a metal which is very rare and valuable and often used in jewellery: *Gold and silver are precious metals.* ▶ **metal szlachetny**

ˌprecious 'stone (also **stone**) noun [C] a stone which is very rare and valuable and often used in jewellery: *diamonds and other precious stones* ▶ **kamień szlachetny**

precipice /'presəpɪs/ noun [C] a very steep side of a high mountain or rock ▶ **przepaść**

precis /'preɪsi:; US preɪ'si:/ noun [C,U] (pl. **precis** /-si:z/) a short version of a speech or a piece of writing that gives the main points or ideas: *to* ***write/give/make a precis*** *of a report* ▶ **streszczenie** SYN **summary**

⚷ **precise** /prɪ'saɪs/ adj. **1** clear and accurate: *precise details/instructions/measurements* ◇ *He's in his forties – well, forty-four,* ***to be precise*** (ściśle mówiąc). ◇ *She couldn't be very precise about what her attacker was wearing.* ▶ **dokładny, ścisły, ściśle określony** OPP **imprecise 2** [only before a noun] exact; particular: *I'm sorry. I can't come just* ***at this precise moment.*** ▶ **dokładny 3** (used about a person) taking care to get small details right: *He's very precise about his work.* ▶ **precyzyjny, skrupulatny**

⚷ **precisely** /prɪ'saɪsli/ adv. **1** exactly: *The time is 10.03 precisely.* ▶ **dokładnie 2** (used to emphasize that sth is very true or obvious): *It's precisely because I care about you that I got so angry when you stayed out late.* ▶ **właśnie 3** (informal) (used for agreeing with a statement) yes, that is right: *'So, if we don't book now, we probably won't get a flight?' 'Precisely.'* ▶ **właśnie tak**

precision /prɪ'sɪʒn/ noun [U] the quality of being clear or exact: *The plans were drawn with great precision.* ▶ **precyzja, dokładność**

preclude /prɪ'klu:d/ verb [T] (formal) **preclude sth**; **preclude sb from doing sth** to prevent sth from happening or sb from doing sth; to make sth impossible: *Lack of time precludes any further discussion.* ▶ **uniemożliwiać, wykluczać** (*np. możliwość*)

precocious /prɪ'kəʊʃəs/ adj. **1** (used about children, often in a critical way) having developed certain abilities and ways of behaving at a much younger age than usual ▶ **rozwinięty nad wiek 2** (used about a talent etc.) developed very early ▶ (*talent itp.*) **wcześnie/przedwcześnie rozwinięty**

preconceived /ˌpri:kən'si:vd/ adj. [only before a noun] (used about an idea or opinion) formed before you have enough information or experience ▶ **z góry wyrobiony**

preconception /ˌpri:kən'sepʃn/ noun [C] an idea or opinion that you have formed about sb/sth before you have enough information or experience ▶ **uprzedzenie, z góry wyrobiony sąd/wyobrażenie**

precondition /ˌpri:kən'dɪʃn/ noun [C] **precondition (for/of sth)** something that must happen or exist before sth else can exist or be done: *A ceasefire is an essential precondition for negotiation.* ▶ **warunek wstępny** SYN **prerequisite**

predator /'predətə(r)/ noun [C] an animal that kills and eats other animals ▶ **drapieżnik**

predatory /'predətri; US -tɔ:ri/ adj. **1** (used about animals) living by killing and eating other animals ▶ **drapieżny 2** (used about people) using weaker people for their own financial or sexual advantage: *a predatory insurance salesman* ◇ *a predatory look* ▶ (*przen.*) **drapieżny**

predecessor /'pri:dɪsesə(r); US 'predəs-/ noun [C] **1** the person who was in the job or position before the person who is in it now: *The new head teacher is much better than her predecessor.* ▶ **poprzedni-k/czka 2** a thing such as a machine, that has been followed or replaced by sth else: *This computer is faster than its predecessors.* ▶ **poprzedni-k/czka** ➲ look at **successor**

predestined /ˌpri:'destɪnd/ adj. **predestined (to do sth)** (formal) already decided or planned by God or by **fate**: *It seems she was predestined to be famous.* ▶ **przeznaczony**

predetermine /ˌpri:dɪ'tɜ:mɪn/ verb [T] (formal) to decide sth in advance so that it does not happen by chance: *The sex of the embryo is predetermined at fertilization.* ▶ **określać z góry**

predicament /prɪ'dɪkəmənt/ noun [C] an unpleasant and difficult situation that is hard to get out of ▶ **kłopot, kłopotliwe położenie**

predicate[1] /'predɪkət/ noun [C] a part of a sentence containing a verb that makes a statement about the subject of the verb, such as *went home* in *John went home.* ▶ (*gram.*) **orzeczenie** ➲ look at **object** (5)

predicate[2] /'predɪkeɪt/ verb [T] (formal) [usually passive] **predicate sth on/upon sth** to base sth on a particular belief, idea or principle: *Democracy is predicated upon the rule of law.* ▶ **opierać coś na czymś**

predicative /prɪ'dɪkətɪv; US 'predɪkeɪtɪv/ adj. (used about an adjective) not used before a noun: *You cannot say 'an asleep child' because 'asleep' is a predicative adjective.* ▶ **orzecznikowy** ➲ look at **attributive**
■ **predicatively** adv. ▶ **orzecznikowo**

⚷ **predict** /prɪ'dɪkt/ verb [T] to say that sth will happen in the future: *Scientists still cannot predict exactly when earthquakes will happen.* ▶ **przewidywać, prorokować**

predictable /prɪ'dɪktəbl/ adj. **1** that was or could be expected to happen: *a predictable result* ▶ **przewidywalny 2** (used about a person) always behaving in a way that you would expect and therefore rather boring: *I knew you were going to say that – you're so predictable.* ▶ **przewidywalny** OPP for both meanings **unpredictable**
■ **predictably** /-əbli/ adv. ▶ **przewidywalnie**

prediction /prɪ'dɪkʃn/ noun [C,U] saying what will happen; what sb thinks will happen: *The exam results confirmed my predictions.* ▶ **przewidywanie**

predilection /ˌpri:dɪ'lekʃn; US ˌpredl'ek-/ noun [usually sing.] **predilection (for sth)** (formal) if you **have a predilection for sth**, you like it very much: *an artist with a predilec-*

P

tion for bright colours ▶ **upodobanie** SYN **liking**, **preference**

predispose /ˌpriːdɪˈspəʊz/ verb [T] (formal) **1 predispose sb to sth/to do sth** to influence sb so that they are likely to think or behave in a particular way: *He believes that some people are predisposed to criminal behaviour.* ▶ **predysponować kogoś do czegoś 2 predispose sb to sth** to make it likely that you will suffer from a particular illness: *Stress can predispose people to heart attacks.* ▶ **uczynić podatnym kogoś na coś**

predominance /prɪˈdɒmɪnəns/ noun [sing.] the state of being more important or greater in number than other people or things: *There is a predominance of Japanese tourists in Hawaii.* ▶ **przewaga**, **wyższość**

predominant /prɪˈdɒmɪnənt/ adj. most noticeable, powerful or important: *The predominant colour was blue.* ▶ **przeważający**, **dominujący**

predominantly /prɪˈdɒmɪnəntli/ adv. mostly; mainly: *The population of the island is predominantly Spanish.* ▶ **przeważnie**, **głównie**

predominate /prɪˈdɒmɪneɪt/ verb [I] (formal) **predominate (over sb/sth)** to be most important or greatest in number: *Private interest was not allowed to predominate over public good.* ▶ **przeważać**, **dominować**

ˌpre-ˈeminent adj. (formal) more important, more successful or of a higher standard than others: *a pre-eminent example of the artist's work* ◇ *Dickens was pre-eminent among English writers of his day.* ▶ **wybitny** SYN **outstanding**

■ **ˌpre-ˈeminence** noun [U]: *to achieve pre-eminence in public life* ▶ **prymat**

pre-empt /priˈempt/ verb [T] **1** to prevent sth from happening by taking action to stop it: *Her departure pre-empted any further questions.* ▶ **udaremniać 2** to do or say sth before sb else does: *She was just about to apologize when he pre-empted her.* ▶ **uprzedzać** (*np. czyjeś pytanie*)

pre-emptive /priˈemptɪv/ adj. done to stop sb taking action, especially action that will be harmful to yourself: *a* ***pre-emptive attack/strike*** *on the military base* ▶ **wyprzedzający**

ˌpre-eˈxist verb [I] to exist from an earlier time: *a pre-existing medical condition* ▶ **istnieć wcześniej**, **występować wcześniej/uprzednio**

prefab /ˈpriːfæb/ noun [C] (informal) a **prefabricated** building: *prefabs built after the war* ▶ **budynek z prefabrykatów**

prefabricated /ˌpriːˈfæbrɪkeɪtɪd/ adj. (especially used about a building) made in sections that can be put together later ▶ **budowany z prefabrykatów**

preface /ˈprefəs/ noun [C] a written introduction to a book that explains what it is about or why it was written ▶ **przedmowa**, **wstęp**

prefect /ˈpriːfekt/ noun [C] (Brit.) an older girl or boy in a school who has special duties and responsibilities. **Prefects** often help to make sure that the younger students behave properly. ▶ **starszy uczeń** (*często odpowiedzialny za zachowanie młodszych*)

🔑 **prefer** /prɪˈfɜː(r)/ verb [T] (**preferring**; **preferred**) [not used in the continuous tenses] **prefer sth (to sth)**; **prefer to do sth**; **prefer doing sth** to choose sth rather than sth else; to like sth better: *Would you prefer tea or coffee?* ◇ *Marianne prefers not to walk home on her own at night.* ◇ *My parents would prefer me to study law at university.* ▶ **woleć**

ⓘ Czasownika **prefer** nie używa się w czasach *continuous*. Natomiast często spotyka się go w *present participle* (formie *-ing*): *Their elder son had gone to work in London, preferring not to join the family firm.*

Zwróć uwagę, że **prefer** można użyć następująco: *Helen prefers going by train to flying.* ◇ *Helen prefers to go by train rather than to fly.* ◇ *My parents would prefer me to study law at university.* ◇ *My parents would prefer it if I studied law at university.* ◇ *My parents would prefer that I studied law at university.* Dwa ostatnie przykłady stosowane są w języku formalnym. Zwróć też uwagę, że **prefer** w ogóle zalicza się do czasowników dość formalnych. Zamiast *Would you prefer tea or coffee?* można powiedzieć *Would you rather have tea or coffee?* Zamiast *I prefer skating to skiing* można powiedzieć *I like skating better than skiing.*

preferable /ˈprefrəbl/ adj. **preferable (to sth/doing sth)** better or more suitable: *Going anywhere is preferable to staying at home for the weekend.* ▶ **lepszy**, **bardziej odpowiedni**

preferably /ˈprefrəbli/ adv. (used to show which person or thing would be better or preferred, if you are given a choice): *Give me a ring tonight – preferably after 7 o'clock.* ▶ **raczej**, **chętniej**, **lepiej**

🔑 **preference** /ˈprefrəns/ noun [C, U] **(a) preference (for sth)** an interest in or desire for one thing more than another: *What you wear is entirely a matter of* ***personal preference.*** ◇ *Please list your choices* ***in order of preference*** (w porządku preferencyjnym). ◇ *We have both red and white wine. Do you have a preference for* (wolisz) *one or the other?* ▶ **upodobanie**, **przedkładanie (czegoś nad coś)**

IDM **give (a) preference to sb/sth** to give special treatment to one person or group rather than to others: *When allocating accommodation, we will give preference to families with young children.* ▶ **dawać pierwszeństwo komuś/czemuś**

preferential /ˌprefəˈrenʃl/ adj. [only before a noun] giving or showing special treatment to one person or group rather than to others: *I don't see why he should get* ***preferential treatment*** *– I've worked here just as long as he has!* ▶ **uprzywilejowany**, **preferencyjny**

prefix /ˈpriːfɪks/ noun [C] a letter or group of letters that you put at the beginning of a word to change its meaning ▶ **przedrostek** ➲ look at **suffix**

pregnancy /ˈpregnənsi/ noun [U,C] (pl. **pregnancies**) the state of being pregnant; the period of time when a woman or female animal is pregnant ▶ **ciąża**; **okres ciąży**

🔑 **pregnant** /ˈpregnənt/ adj. (used about a woman or female animal) having a baby developing in her body: *to get pregnant* ◇ *Liz is five months pregnant.* ⓘ Mówi się też: *Liz is expecting a baby.* ◇ *Liz is going to have a baby.* ▶ **w ciąży** ➲ note at **baby**

prehistoric /ˌpriːhɪˈstɒrɪk/ adj. from the time in history before events were written down ▶ **prehistoryczny**

prejudice¹ /ˈpredʒudɪs/ noun [C,U] **prejudice (against sb/sth)** a strong unreasonable feeling of not liking or trusting sb, especially when it is based on their race, religion or sex: *a victim of* ***racial prejudice*** ▶ **uprzedzenie**

prejudice² /ˈpredʒudɪs/ verb [T] **1 prejudice sb (against sb/sth)** to influence sb so that they have an unreasonable or unfair opinion about sb/sth: *The newspaper stories had prejudiced the jury against him.* ▶ **nastawiać (kogoś) uprzedzająco/przychylnie (do kogoś/czegoś)**, **zrażać (kogoś do kogoś/czegoś) 2** to have a harmful effect on sb/sth: *Continuing to live with her violent father may prejudice the child's welfare.* ▶ **przynosić uszczerbek**, **szkodzić**

prejudiced /ˈpredʒədɪst/ adj. not liking or trusting sb/sth for no other reason than their race, religion or sex ▶ **uprzedzony**

preliminary¹ /prɪˈlɪmɪnəri; US -neri/ adj. coming or happening before sth else that is more important: *After* *a few preliminary remarks the discussions began.* ▶ **wstępny**

preliminary² /prɪˈlɪmɪnəri; US -neri/ noun [C, usually pl.] (pl. **preliminaries**) an action or event that is done before and in preparation for another event: *Once the preliminaries are over, we can get down to business.* ▶ **wstęp**

prelude /ˈprelju:d/ noun [C] **1** a short piece of music, especially an introduction to a longer piece ▶ **preludium 2** (formal) **prelude (to sth)** an action or event that happens before sth else or that forms an introduction to sth ▶ **wstęp**

premature /ˈpremətʃə(r); US ˌpri:məˈtʃʊr; -ˈtʊr/ adj. **1** happening before the normal or expected time: *Premature babies* (wcześniaki) *need special care.* ▶ **przedwczesny 2** acting or happening too soon: *I think our decision was premature. We should have thought about it for longer.* ▶ **pochopny, przedwczesny**
■ **prematurely** adv. ▶ **przedwcześnie**

premeditated /pri:ˈmedɪteɪtɪd/ adj. (used about a crime) planned in advance ▶ **(dokonany) z premedytacją**

premier¹ /ˈpremiə(r); US prɪˈmɪr; -ˈmjɪr/ adj. [only before a noun] most important; best: *a premier chef* ◇ *the Premier Division* ▶ **pierwszy, najlepszy**

premier² /ˈpremiə(r); US prɪˈmɪr; -ˈmjɪr/ noun [C] (used especially in newspapers) the leader of the government of a country ▶ **premier** SYN **prime minister**

premiere /ˈpremieə(r); US prɪˈmɪr; -ˈmjɪr/ noun [C] the first public performance of a film or play: *the **world premiere** of his new play* ◇ *The film will have its premiere in July.* ▶ **premiera**
■ **premiere** verb [I,T]: *His new movie premieres* (premiera jego nowego filmu odbędzie się) *in New York this week.* ▶ **mieć premierę** (*filmu/sztuki*)

premises /ˈpremɪsɪz/ noun [pl.] the building and the land around it that a business owns or uses: *Smoking is not allowed **on the premises**.* ▶ **budynek z przylegającym terenem**

premium /ˈpri:miəm/ noun [C] **1** an amount of money that you pay regularly to a company for insurance against accidents, damage, etc.: *a monthly premium of £25* ▶ **składka ubezpieczeniowa 2** an extra payment: *You must pay a premium for express delivery.* ▶ **dopłata**

premonition /ˌpri:məˈnɪʃn; ˌprem-/ noun [C] **a premonition (of sth)** a feeling that sth unpleasant is going to happen in the future: *a premonition of disaster* ▶ **złe przeczucie**

preoccupation /priˌɒkjuˈpeɪʃn/ noun **1** [U] **preoccupation (with sth)** the state of thinking and/or worrying continuously about sth: *She was irritated by his preoccupation with money.* ▶ **troska, zaabsorbowanie, pochłonięcie umysłu 2** [C] a thing that you think or worry about all the time ▶ **nieustająca troska**

preoccupied /priˈɒkjupaɪd/ adj. **preoccupied (with sth)** not paying attention to sb/sth because you are thinking or worrying about sb/sth else: *Sarah is very preoccupied with her work at present.* ▶ **zaabsorbowany, pochłonięty** ➲ look at **occupied**

preoccupy /priˈɒkjupaɪ/ verb [T] (**preoccupying**; **preoccupies**; pt, pp **preoccupied**) to fill sb's mind so that they do not think about anything else; to worry ▶ **absorbować, pochłaniać umysł**

preparation /ˌprepəˈreɪʃn/ noun **1** [U] getting sb/sth ready: *The team has been training hard **in preparation for** the big game.* ◇ *exam preparation* ▶ **przygotowanie 2** [C, usually pl.] **preparation (for sth/to do sth)** something that you do to get ready for sth: *We started to **make preparations** for the wedding six months ago.* ▶ **przygotowania**

preparatory /prɪˈpærətri; US -tɔ:ri/ adj. done in order to get ready for sth ▶ **przygotowawczy**

preˈparatory school (also **ˈprep school**) noun [C] **1** (Brit.) a private school for children aged between 7 and 13 ▶ **prywatna szkoła podstawowa 2** (US) a private school that prepares students for college or university ▶ **prywatna szkoła przygotowująca uczniów do dalszej nauki w koledżu lub na uniwersytecie**

prepare /prɪˈpeə(r)/ verb [I,T] **prepare (sb/sth) (for sb/sth)** to get ready or to make sb/sth ready: *Bo helped me prepare for the exam.* ◇ *The course prepares foreign students for studying at university.* ◇ *to prepare a meal* ▶ **przygotowywać (się)**
IDM **be prepared for sth** to be ready for sth difficult or unpleasant ▶ **być przygotowanym (na coś trudnego/niemiłego), być gotowym (na coś trudnego/niemiłego)**
be prepared to do sth to be ready and happy to do sth: *I am not prepared to stay here and be insulted.* ▶ **być chętnym**

preponderant /prɪˈpɒndərənt/ adj. [usually before a noun] (formal) larger in number or more important than other people or things in a group ▶ **przeważający**
■ **preponderantly** adv. ▶ **w przeważającej mierze**

preposition /ˌprepəˈzɪʃn/ noun [C] a word or phrase that is used before a noun or pronoun to show place, time, direction, etc.: *'In', 'for', 'to' and 'out of' are all prepositions.* ▶ **przyimek**

preposterous /prɪˈpɒstərəs/ adj. silly; ridiculous; not to be taken seriously ▶ **niedorzeczny, bzdurny, śmieszny**

ˈprep school = PREPARATORY SCHOOL

prerequisite /ˌpri:ˈrekwəzɪt/ noun [C] **a prerequisite (for/of sth)** something that is necessary for sth to happen or exist: *Is a good education a prerequisite of success?* ▶ **warunek wstępny** ➲ look at **requisite**

prerogative /prɪˈrɒgətɪv/ noun [C] a special right that sb/sth has: *It is the Prime Minister's prerogative to fix the date of the election.* ▶ **przywilej, prerogatywa**

prescribe /prɪˈskraɪb/ verb [T] **1** to say what medicine or treatment sb should have: *Can you prescribe something for my cough please, doctor?* ▶ **przepisywać** (*receptę, lekarstwo, kurację*) **2** (formal) (used about a person or an organization with authority) to say that sth must be done: *The law prescribes that the document must be signed in the presence of two witnesses.* ▶ **nakazywać, określać**

prescription /prɪˈskrɪpʃn/ noun [C,U] **1** an official piece of paper on which a doctor has written the name of the medicine that you need; the medicine itself: *a prescription for sleeping pills* ◇ *Some medicines are only available from the chemist **on prescription**.* ▶ **recepta** ➲ note at **doctor 2** the act of prescribing sth ▶ **przepisywanie** (*recepty, lekarstwa, kuracji*)

presence /ˈprezns/ noun **1** [U] the fact of being in a particular place: *He apologized to her **in the presence of** the whole family.* ◇ *an experiment to test for the presence of oxygen* ▶ **obecność** OPP **absence 2** [sing.] a number of soldiers or police officers who are in a place for a special reason: *There was a huge police presence at the demonstration.* ▶ **obecność**

present¹ /ˈpreznt/ adj. **1** [only before a noun] existing or happening now: *We hope to overcome our present difficulties very soon.* ▶ **obecny, bieżący, niniejszy** OPP **absent 2** [not before a noun] being in a particular place: *There were 200 people present at the meeting.* ▶ **obecny**

present² /ˈpreznt/ noun **1** [C] something that you give to sb or receive from sb: *a birthday/wedding/leaving/Christmas present* ▶ **prezent** SYN **gift 2** (usually **the present**) [sing.] the time now: *We live **in the present** but we must learn from the past.* ◇ *I'm rather busy **at present***

(teraz). *Can I call you back later?* ▶ **teraźniejszość** ➲ note at **actually 3** (**the present**) [sing.] = PRESENT TENSE
IDM **for the moment/present** → MOMENT

present[3] /prɪˈzent/ verb [T] **1 present sb with sth; present sth (to sb)** to give sth to sb, especially at a formal ceremony: *All the dancers were presented with flowers.* ◇ *Flowers were presented to all the dancers.* ▶ **darować, ofiarowywać 2 present sth (to sb)** to show sth that you have prepared to people: *Good teachers try to present their material in an interesting way.* ▶ **przedstawiać (kogoś komuś) 3 present sb with sth; present sth (to sb)** to give sb sth that has to be dealt with: *The manager presented us with a bill for the broken chair.* ◇ *Learning English presented no problem to him.* ▶ **przedstawiać, prezentować, wręczać 4** to introduce a TV or radio programme: *She used to present a gardening programme on TV.* ▶ **przedstawiać, stwarzać 5** to show a play, etc. to the public: *The Theatre Royal is presenting a new production of 'Ghosts'.* ▶ **wystawiać 6 present sb (to sb)** to introduce sb to a person in a formal ceremony: *The teams were presented to the President before the game.* ▶ **prezentować; przedstawiać**

presentable /prɪˈzentəbl/ adj. good enough to be seen by people you do not know well ▶ **dobrze wyglądający, mający dobrą prezencję**

presentation /ˌpreznˈteɪʃn; US ˌpriːzen-/ noun **1** [C,U] the act of giving or showing sth to sb: *The head will now **make a presentation** to the winners of the competition.* ▶ **przedstawianie 2** [U] the way in which sth is shown, explained, offered, etc. to people: *Untidy presentation of your work may lose you marks.* ▶ **prezentacja, sposób prezentacji/podania/przedstawienia itp. czegoś 3** [C] a meeting at which sth is shown or explained to a group of people: *Each student has to **give a** short **presentation** on a subject of his/her choice.* ▶ **wystąpienie 4** [C] a formal ceremony at which a prize, etc. is given to sb ▶ **ceremonia wręczania** (*np. nagród*)

the ˌ**present ˈday** noun [sing.] the situation that exists in the world now, rather than in the past or the future: *a study of European drama, from Ibsen **to the present day*** ▶ **czasy współczesne**
■ ˌ**present-ˈday** adj. [only before a noun]: *present-day fashions* ◇ *present-day America* ▶ **współczesny**

presenter /prɪˈzentə(r)/ noun [C] a person who introduces a TV or radio programme ▶ **prezenter/ka**

presentiment /prɪˈzentɪmənt/ noun [C] (formal) a feeling that sth is going to happen, especially sth unpleasant: *a presentiment of disaster* ▶ **przeczucie** SYN **foreboding**

presently /ˈprezntli/ adv. **1** (especially US) now: *The management are presently discussing the matter.* ▶ **teraz, obecnie** SYN **currently 2** (formal) after a short time: *Presently I heard the car door shut.* ▶ **wkrótce, niebawem 3** soon: *I'll be finished presently.* ▶ **zaraz** SYN **shortly**

> Zwróć uwagę, że gdy **presently** oznacza „zaraz", występuje zwykle na końcu zdania, gdy oznacza „wkrótce", występuje zwykle na początku zdania, kiedy zaś oznacza „teraz", stoi przy czasowniku.

ˌ**present ˈparticiple** noun [C] the form of the verb that ends in *-ing* ▶ **imiesłów czasu teraźniejszego**

the ˌ**present ˈperfect** noun [sing.] the form of a verb that expresses an action done in a time period from the past to the present, formed with the present tense of *have* and the past participle of the verb: *'I've finished' and 'She hasn't arrived' are both **in the present perfect.*** ▶ **czas teraźniejszy dokonany**

the ˌ**present ˈsimple** noun [sing.] the tense that is used to describe sth that happens regularly, such as 'I eat there every day.' ▶ **czas teraźniejszy prosty**

the ˌ**present ˈtense** (also **the present**) noun [C] the tense of the verb that you use when you are talking about what is happening or what exists now ▶ **czas teraźniejszy**

preservative /prɪˈzɜːvətɪv/ noun [C,U] a substance that is used for keeping food, etc. in good condition ▶ **środek konserwujący**

preserve /prɪˈzɜːv/ verb [T] to keep sth safe or in good condition: *They've managed to preserve most of the wall paintings in the caves.* ▶ **chronić, zachowywać, wekować**
■ **preservation** /ˌprezəˈveɪʃn/ noun [U] ▶ **ochrona, utrzymywanie**

preside /prɪˈzaɪd/ verb [I] to be in charge of a discussion, meeting, etc. ▶ **przewodniczyć**
PHR V **preside over sth** to be in control of or responsible for sth ▶ **przewodniczyć czemuś, sprawować nadzór nad czymś**

presidency /ˈprezɪdənsi/ noun (pl. **presidencies**) **1** (**the presidency**) [sing.] the position of being president ▶ **prezydentura 2** [C] the period of time that sb is president ▶ **kadencja prezydenta**

president /ˈprezɪdənt/ noun [C] **1** (**President**) the leader of a **republic**: *the President of France* ◇ *the US President* ▶ **prezydent 2** the person with the highest position in some organizations ▶ **prezes, dyrektor, rektor**
■ **presidential** /ˌprezɪˈdenʃl/ adj.: *presidential elections* ▶ **prezydencki**

press[1] /pres/ noun **1** (usually **the press**) [sing., with sing. or pl. verb] newspapers and the journalists who work for them: *The story has been reported on TV and **in the press.*** ◇ *the local/national press* ◇ *The press support/supports government policy.* ▶ **prasa** ➲ note at **newspaper 2** [sing., U] what or the amount that is written about sb/sth in newspapers: *This company has had **a bad press*** (ostatnio ma złe notowania w prasie) *recently.* ◇ *The strike got very little press* (nie cieszył się wielkim zainteresowaniem ze strony prasy). **3** [U] the process of printing books, newspapers, etc.: *All details were correct at the time of **going to press*** (w momencie/chwili oddania do druku). **4** [C] = PRINTING PRESS **5** [C] a business that prints books, etc.: *Oxford University Press* ▶ **wydawnictwo 6** [C] an act of pushing sth firmly: ***Give that button a press** and see what happens.* ◇ *This shirt needs a press.* (wymaga wyprasowania) ▶ **przyciskanie, prasowanie**

press[2] /pres/ verb **1** [I,T] to push sth firmly: *Just press that button and the door will open.* ◇ *He pressed the lid firmly shut.* ▶ **przyciskać, cisnąć 2** [T] to put weight onto sth, for example in order to get juice out of it: *to press grapes* ◇ *to press wild flowers between the pages of a book* wkładać między kartki książki polne kwiaty do zasuszenia ▶ **tłoczyć, wyciskać, ściskać 3** [T] to hold sb/sth firmly in a loving way: *She pressed the photo to her chest.* ▶ **przyciskać 4** [I] **press across, against, around, etc. (sth)** to move in a particular direction by pushing: *The crowd pressed against the wall of policemen.* ▶ **napierać na kogoś/coś, tłoczyć się do czegoś/w czymś 5** [I,T] **press (sb) (for sth/to do sth)** to try to persuade or force sb to do sth: *to press somebody for an answer* ◇ *I pressed them to stay for dinner.* ▶ **nalegać (na kogoś, żeby), domagać się 6** [T] to express or repeat sth in an urgent way: *I don't want to press the point, but you still owe me money.* ▶ **naciskać, nalegać 7** [T] to make a piece of clothing smooth by using an iron: *This shirt needs pressing.* ▶ **prasować**
IDM **be hard pressed/pushed/put to do sth** → HARD[2]
be pressed for sth to not have enough of sth: *I must hurry. I'm really pressed for time* (naprawdę czas mnie nagli). ▶ **być pod presją** (*np. terminów*)
bring/press charges (against sb) → CHARGE[1]
PHR V **press ahead/forward/on (with sth)** to continue doing sth even though it is difficult or hard work: *They*

pressed on with the building work in spite of the bad weather. ▶ **uparcie kontynuować coś**
press for sth to keep asking for sth: *They continued to press for a change in the law.* ▶ **domagać się czegoś** SYN **demand**, **push for sth**

ˈ**press conference** noun [C] a meeting when a famous or important person answers questions from newspaper and TV journalists: *to hold a press conference* ▶ **konferencja prasowa**

pressing /ˈpresɪŋ/ adj. that must be dealt with immediately ▶ **pilny** SYN **urgent**

ˈ**press release** noun [C] an official announcement or account of sth that is given to journalists, by a government department, political party or company ▶ **nota prasowa**, **oświadczenie dla prasy**

ˈ**press stud** = POPPER

ˈ**press-up** (US ˈ**push-up**) noun [C] a type of exercise in which you lie on your front on the floor and push your body up with your arms: *I do 50 press-ups every morning.* ▶ **pompka**

pressure /ˈpreʃə(r)/ noun **1** [U] the force that is produced when you press on or against sth: *The pressure of the water caused the dam to crack.* ◇ *Apply pressure* (uciśnij) *to the cut and it will stop bleeding.* ▶ **parcie**, **napór**; **nawał 2** [C,U] the force that a gas or liquid has when it is contained inside sth: *high/low blood pressure* ◇ *You should check your tyre pressure regularly.* ▶ **ciśnienie 3** [C,U] worries or difficulties that you have because you have too much to deal with: *financial pressures* ◇ *I find it difficult to cope with pressure at work.* ◇ *They moved to the country to escape the pressures of city life* (żeby uciec przed stresami miejskiego życia). ▶ **presja**, **trudności** SYN **stress**
■ **pressure** verb = PRESSURIZE
IDM **put pressure on sb (to do sth)** to force sb to do sth: *The press is putting pressure on him to resign.* ▶ **wywierać na kogoś presję**
under pressure 1 (used about liquid or gas) contained inside sth or sent somewhere using force: *Water is forced out through the hose under pressure.* ▶ **pod ciśnieniem 2** being forced to do sth: *Anna was under pressure from her parents to leave school and get a job.* ▶ **pod presją 3** worried or in difficulty because you have too much to deal with: *I perform poorly under pressure, so I hate exams.* ▶ **w nawale** (*trudności itp.*)

ˈ**pressure cooker** noun [C] a large pan with a lid in which you can cook things quickly using steam under high pressure ▶ **szybkowar** ➲ picture at **pan**

ˈ**pressure group** noun [C, with sing. or pl. verb] a group of people who are trying to influence what a government or other organization does ▶ **grupa nacisku**

pressurize (also **-ise**) /ˈpreʃəraɪz/ (also **pressure**) verb [T] **pressurize sb (into sth/doing sth)** to use force or influence to make sb do sth: *Some workers were pressurized into taking early retirement.* ▶ **wywierać presję**

pressurized (also **-ised**) /ˈpreʃəraɪzd/ adj. (used about air in an aircraft) kept at the pressure at which people can breathe ▶ **utrzymujący odpowiednie dla ludzi ciśnienie atmosferyczne**

prestige /preˈstiːʒ/ noun [U] the respect and admiration that people feel for a person because they have a high social position or have been very successful: *Nursing isn't a high prestige job.* ▶ **prestiż**
■ **prestigious** /preˈstɪdʒəs/ adj.: *a prestigious prize/school/job* ▶ **prestiżowy**

presumably /prɪˈzjuːməbli; US -ˈzuː-/ adv. I imagine; I suppose: *Presumably this rain means the match will be cancelled?* ▶ **przypuszczalnie**

presume /prɪˈzjuːm; US -ˈzuːm/ verb [T] to think that sth is true even if you do not know for sure; to suppose: *The house looks empty so I presume they are away on holiday.* ◇ *The soldiers were missing, presumed dead.* Zaginieni żołnierze zostali uznani za zmarłych. ▶ **przypuszczać**, **domniemywać** SYN **assume**
■ **presumption** /prɪˈzʌmpʃn/ noun [C] ▶ **przypuszczenie**, **domniemanie**

presumptuous /prɪˈzʌmptʃuəs/ adj. confident that sth will happen or that sb will do sth without making sure first, in a way that annoys people: *It was very presumptuous* (bezczelnie) *of him to say that I would help without asking me first.* ▶ **bezczelny**

presuppose /ˌpriːsəˈpəʊz/ verb [T] (formal) to accept sth as true or existing and act on that belief, before it has been proved to be true: *Teachers sometimes presuppose a fairly high level of knowledge by the students.* ▶ **zakładać z góry istnienie czegoś** SYN **presume**

pretence /prɪˈtens/ (US **pretense**) noun [U, sing.] an action that makes people believe sth that is not true: *She was unable to keep up the pretence that she loved him.* ▶ **pozór**
IDM **on/under false pretences** → FALSE

pretend /prɪˈtend/ verb [I,T] **1** to behave in a particular way in order to make other people believe sth that is not true: *You can't just pretend that the problem doesn't exist.* ◇ *Paul's not really asleep. He's just pretending.* ▶ **udawać 2** (used especially about children) to imagine that sth is true as part of a game: *The kids were under the bed pretending to be snakes.* ◇ *The children pretended to be* (bawiły się w) *doctors.* ▶ **udawać**

pretension /prɪˈtenʃn/ noun [C, usually pl., U] **1** the act of trying to appear more important, intelligent, etc. than you are in order to impress other people: *intellectual pretensions* ◇ *He spoke without pretension.* ▶ **pretensja 2 pretension (to sth/to doing sth)**; **pretension (to do sth)** a claim to be or to do sth: *a building with no pretensions to architectural merit* ▶ **pretendowanie**

pretentious /prɪˈtenʃəs/ adj. trying to appear more serious or important than you really are: *I think it sounds pretentious to use a lot of foreign words.* ▶ **pretensjonalny**

pretext /ˈpriːtekst/ noun [C] a reason that you give for doing sth that is not the real reason: *Tariq left **on the pretext of** having an appointment at the dentist's.* ▶ **pretekst**

pretty[1] /ˈprɪti/ adv. (informal) quite; fairly: *The film was pretty good but not fantastic.* ◇ *I'm pretty certain that Alex will agree.* ▶ **dosyć**, **raczej** ➲ note at **rather**
IDM **pretty much/nearly/well** almost; very nearly: *I won't be long. I've pretty well finished.* ▶ **prawie**

pretty[2] /ˈprɪti/ adj. (**prettier**; **prettiest**) attractive and pleasant to look at or hear: *a pretty girl/smile/dress/garden/name* ▶ **ładny** ➲ note at **beautiful**
■ **prettily** adv.: *The room is prettily decorated.* ▶ **ładnie** | **prettiness** noun [U] ▶ **uroda**

prevail /prɪˈveɪl/ verb [I] **1** to exist or be common in a particular place or at a particular time: *In some areas traditional methods of farming still prevail.* ▶ **istnieć**, **przeważać 2** (formal) **prevail (against/over sb/sth)** to win or be accepted, especially after a fight or discussion: *In the end justice prevailed and the men were set free.* ▶ **triumfować**, **zwyciężać**

prevailing /prɪˈveɪlɪŋ/ adj. [only before a noun] **1** existing or most common at a particular time: *the prevailing climate of opinion* ▶ **przeważający**, **powszechny 2** (used about the wind) most common in a particular area: *The prevailing wind is from the south-west.* ▶ **przeważający**

prevalent /ˈprevələnt/ adj. (formal) most common in a particular place at a particular time: *The prevalent atmosphere was one of fear.* ▶ **panujący**, **przeważający**

■ **prevalence** noun [U]: *an increase in the prevalence of smoking* (coraz większa liczba palących) *among young people* ▶ **(powszechne) występowanie, panowanie**

⚷ **prevent** /prɪˈvent/ verb [T] **prevent sb/sth (from) (doing sth)** to stop sth happening or to stop sb doing sth: *This accident could have been prevented.* ◇ *Her parents tried to prevent her from going to live with her boyfriend.* ▶ **zapobiegać, przeszkadzać, uniemożliwiać** ⓘ **Prevent** jest bardziej formalne niż **stop**.

■ **prevention** noun [U]: *accident/crime prevention* ▶ **zapobieganie, profilaktyka**

preventable /prɪˈventəbl/ adj. that can be prevented: *Many accidents are preventable.* ▶ **możliwy do uniknięcia**

preventive /prɪˈventɪv/ (also **preventative** /prɪˈventətɪv/) adj. [only before a noun] intended to stop or prevent sth from happening: *preventative medicine* ▶ **zapobiegawczy, prewencyjny, profilaktyczny**

preview /ˈpriːvjuː/ noun [C] a chance to see a play, film, etc. before it is shown to the general public ▶ **prapremiera**

⚷ **previous** /ˈpriːviəs/ adj. [only before a noun] coming or happening before or earlier: *Do you have previous experience of this type of work?* ▶ **poprzedni, wcześniejszy**

■ **previously** adv.: *Before I moved to Spain I had previously worked in Italy.* ▶ **poprzednio, wcześniej**

prey¹ /preɪ/ noun [U] an animal or bird that is killed and eaten by another animal or bird: *The eagle is a bird of prey* (jest ptakiem drapieżnym). ▶ **żer, zdobycz**

prey² /preɪ/ verb

IDM **prey on sb's mind** to cause sb to worry or think about sth: *The thought that he was responsible for the accident preyed on the train driver's mind.* ▶ **dręczyć/trawić (kogoś)**

PHR V **prey on sth** (used about an animal or bird) to kill and eat other animals or birds: *Owls prey on mice and other small animals.* ▶ **polować na coś**

prey on/upon sb to harm sb who is weaker than you, or make use of them in a dishonest way to get what you want: *Bogus social workers have been preying on old people living alone.* ▶ **żerować na kimś**

⚷ **price¹** /praɪs/ noun **1** [C] the amount of money that you must pay in order to buy sth: *What's the price of petrol now?* ◇ *We can't afford to buy the car at that price.* ◇ *There's no price on this jar of coffee.* ◇ *Copies of the CD can be purchased at cost price* (po cenie produkcyjnej). ◇ *the retail/selling price* cena detaliczna ▶ **cena**; **koszt**

> **Charge** oznacza ilość pieniędzy, jaką trzeba zapłacić za używanie czegoś: *Is there a charge for parking here?* ◇ *admission charges.* **Cost** używa się, mówiąc o płaceniu za usługi, lub ogólnie o cenach, bez wymieniania sumy: *The cost of electricity is going up.* ◇ *the cost of living.* **Price** oznacza ilość pieniędzy, jaką należy zapłacić, aby coś kupić.

> A shop may **raise/increase**, **reduce/bring down** or **freeze** its prices. The prices **rise/go up** or **fall/go down**.

2 [sing.] unpleasant things that you have to experience in order to achieve sth or as a result of sth: *Sleepless nights are a small price to pay for having a baby.* ▶ (*przen.*) **cena**

IDM **at any price** even if the cost is very high or if it will have unpleasant results: *Richard was determined to succeed at any price.* ▶ **za wszelką cenę**

at a price costing a lot of money or involving sth unpleasant: *He'll help you get a job – at a price* (ale będzie cię to drogo kosztować). ▶ **za (wysoką) cenę**

not at any price never; not for any reason ▶ **za żadną cenę**

price² /praɪs/ verb [T] to fix the price of sth or to write the price on sth: *The books were all priced at between £5 and £10.* ▶ **określać cenę; metkować**

priceless /ˈpraɪsləs/ adj. of very great value: *priceless jewels and antiques* ▶ **bezcenny** ➲ look at **worthless**, **valuable**, **invaluable**

ˈ**price list** noun [C] a list of the prices of the goods that are on sale ▶ **cennik**

ˈ**price tag** noun [C] **1** a label showing the price of sth ▶ **metka** ➲ note at **label 2 a price tag (on sth)** the cost of sth: *The government regard the price tag on the new fighter plane as too high.* ▶ **cena**

pricey /ˈpraɪsi/ adj. (**pricier**; **priciest**) (informal) expensive ▶ **kosztowny**

prick¹ /prɪk/ verb [T] to make a small hole in sth or to cause sb pain with a sharp point: *She pricked her finger on a needle.* ▶ **dziurawić; kłuć**

IDM **prick up your ears** (used about an animal) to hold up the ears in order to listen carefully to sth: (figurative) *Mike pricked up his ears when he heard Emma's name mentioned.* ▶ **nadstawiać usz-y/u**

prick² /prɪk/ noun [C] the sudden pain that you feel when sth sharp goes into your skin ▶ **ukłucie, nakłucie**

prickle¹ /ˈprɪkl/ verb **1** [I,T] to give sb an unpleasant feeling on their skin, as if a lot of small sharp points are pushing into it: *I don't like that shirt – it prickles (my skin).* ▶ (*ubranie itp.*) **drapać 2** [I] (used about skin, eyes, etc.) to sting or feel strange and unpleasant because you are frightened, angry, excited, etc.: *His skin prickled with fear.* Ze strachu ciarki przeszły mu po skórze. ▶ (*skóra, oczy itp.*) **kłuć, szczypać**

prickle² /ˈprɪkl/ noun [C] one of the sharp points on some plants and animals: *Hedgehogs are covered in prickles.* ▶ **kolec** ➲ look at **spine**

prickly /ˈprɪkli/ adj. (**pricklier**; **prickliest**) **1** covered with sharp points: *a prickly bush* ▶ **kolczasty 2** causing an uncomfortable feeling on the skin: *That T-shirt makes my skin go all prickly.* ▶ (*o ubraniu itp.*) **gryzący 3** (informal) (used about a person) easily made angry: *Don't mention his accident – he's a bit prickly about it.* ▶ **nerwowy, przewrażliwiony**

⚷ **pride¹** /praɪd/ noun **1** [U, sing.] **pride (in sth/doing sth)** the feeling of pleasure that you have when you or people who are close to you do sth good or own sth good: *I take a great **pride in*** (jestem bardzo dumny z) *my work.* ◇ *We take great pride in offering* (szczycimy się tym, że oferujemy) *the best service in town.* ◇ *Jane's parents watched with pride as she went up to collect her prize.* ◇ *You should **feel pride** in your achievement.* ▶ **duma** ➲ adjective **proud 2** [sing.] **the pride of sth/sb** a person or thing that is very important or of great value to sth/sb: *The new stadium was the pride of the whole town.* ▶ **duma 3** [U] the respect that you have for yourself: *You'll hurt his pride if you refuse to accept the present.* ▶ **godność osobista 4** [U] the feeling that you are better than other people: *Male pride forced him to suffer in silence.* ▶ **pycha**

IDM **sb's pride and joy** a thing or person that gives sb great pleasure or satisfaction ▶ **powód do dumy**

pride² /praɪd/ verb

PHR V **pride yourself on sth/doing sth** to feel pleased about sth good or clever that you can do: *Fabio prides himself on his ability to cook.* ▶ **szczycić się czymś**

⚷ **priest** /priːst/ noun [C] **1** a person who performs religious ceremonies in the Christian Church ▶ **ksiądz**

> **Priest** jest ogólnym określeniem duchownego, używanym w Kościele Anglikańskim, w Kościele Prawosławnym i w Kościele Rzymskokatolickim. Ksiądz w Kościele Anglikańskim jest też nazywany **vicar**, **rector** lub **clergyman**. W innych kościołach protestanckich księdza nazywa się też **minister**.

2 a person who performs religious ceremonies in some other religions ▶ **kapłan/ka** ℹ Dla znaczenia podanego w tym punkcie istnieje też forma żeńska **priestess**.

prig /prɪg/ noun [C] a person who behaves in a morally correct way and who shows that they disapprove of what other people do ▶ *(osoba)* **świętoszek** *(potępiający innych)*
■ **priggish** adj. ▶ **bardzo moralny i potępiający innych**

prim /prɪm/ adj. (used about a person) always behaving in a careful or formal way and easily shocked by anything that is rude ▶ **bardzo poprawny**
■ **primly** adv. ▶ **wyjątkowo poprawnie**, **sztywno**

primaeval = PRIMEVAL

⚷ **primarily** /ˈpraɪmərəli; praɪˈmerəli/ adv. more than anything else; mainly: *The course is aimed primarily at beginners.* ▶ **zwłaszcza**

⚷ **primary**[1] /ˈpraɪməri; US -meri/ adj. [only before a noun] **1** most important; main: *Smoking is one of the primary causes of lung cancer.* ▶ **główny**, **zasadniczy 2** connected with the education of children between about 5 and 11 years old ▶ *(o wykształceniu itp.)* **podstawowy**

primary[2] /ˈpraɪməri; US -meri/ (also ˌprimary eˈlection) noun [C] (pl. **primaries**) (US) an election in which a political party chooses the person who will represent the party for a later important election, such as for president ▶ **wybory głównego kandydat-a/ki partii politycznej** *(np. na prezydenta)*

ˌprimary ˈcolour noun [C] any of the colours red, yellow or blue. You can make any other colour by mixing **primary colours** in different ways. ▶ **kolor podstawowy**

ˌprimary eˈlection = PRIMARY[2]

ˈprimary industry noun [U,C] the section of industry that provides **raw materials** to be made into goods, for example farming and **mining** ▶ **przemysł surowcowy**

ˈprimary school noun [C] (Brit.) a school for children aged five to eleven ▶ **szkoła podstawowa**

primate /ˈpraɪmeɪt/ noun [C] any animal that belongs to the group that includes humans, and animals such as **monkeys** and **apes** ▶ **ssak naczelny**

prime[1] /praɪm/ adj. [only before a noun] **1** main; the first example of sth that sb would think of or choose: *She is a prime candidate as the next team captain.* ▶ **najważniejszy 2** of very good quality; best: *prime pieces of beef* ▶ **pierwszorzędny 3** having all the typical qualities: *That's **a prime example** of what I was talking about.* ▶ **typowy**

prime[2] /praɪm/ noun [sing.] the time when sb is strongest, most beautiful, most successful, etc.: *Several of the team are **past their prime**.* ◇ ***In his prime**, he was a fine actor.* ◇ *to be **in the prime of life*** ▶ **kwiat (wieku)**, **pełnia** *(np. życia)*

prime[3] /praɪm/ verb [T] **prime sb (for/with sth)** to give sb information in order to prepare them for sth: *The politician had been well primed with all the facts before the interview.* ▶ **udzielać wyczerpujących informacji**

⚷ **ˌprime ˈminister** noun [C] (abbr. **PM**) the leader of the government in some countries, for example Britain ▶ **premier** ➲ look at **minister**

primeval (also **primaeval**) /praɪˈmiːvl/ adj. from the earliest period of the history of the world, very ancient: *primeval forests* ▶ **pierwotny**, **pradawny**

primitive /ˈprɪmətɪv/ adj. **1** very simple and not developed: *The washing facilities in the camp were very primitive.* ▶ **prymitywny 2** [only before a noun] connected with a very early stage in the development of humans or animals: *Primitive man lived in caves and hunted wild animals.* ▶ **pierwotny**

primrose /ˈprɪmrəʊz/ noun [C] a yellow spring flower ▶ **pierwiosnek** *(Primula vulgaris)* ➲ look at **cowslip** ➲ picture on **page A15**

⚷ **prince** /prɪns/ noun [C] **1** a son or other close male relative of a king or queen ▶ **książę**

> W Wlk. Br. najstarszy syn króla lub królowej nosi tytuł **the Prince of Wales**.

2 the male ruler of a small country ▶ **książę**

⚷ **princess** /ˌprɪnˈses/ noun [C] **1** a daughter or other close female relative of a king or queen: *Princess Anne* ▶ **księżniczka 2** the wife of a **prince** ▶ **księżniczka**

principal[1] /ˈprɪnsəpl/ adj. [only before a noun] most important; main: *the principal characters in a play* ▶ **najważniejszy**, **główny**
■ **principally** /-pli/ adv.: *Our products are designed principally for the European market.* ▶ **głównie**

principal[2] /ˈprɪnsəpl/ noun [C] the head of some schools, colleges, etc. ▶ **kierowni-k/czka** ➲ look at **headmaster**

⚷ **principle** /ˈprɪnsəpl/ noun **1** [C,U] a rule for good behaviour, based on what a person believes is right: *He doesn't eat meat **on principle**.* ◇ *She refuses to wear fur. It's **a matter of principle** with her.* ▶ **zasada 2** [C] a basic general law, rule or idea: *The system works **on the principle that** heat rises.* ◇ *The course teaches the basic principles of car maintenance.* ▶ **zasada 3** [sing.] a law of science ▶ **prawo**
IDM **in principle** in general, but possibly not in detail: *His proposal sounds fine in principle, but there are a few points I'm not happy about.* ▶ **zasadniczo**

⚷ **print**[1] /prɪnt/ verb **1** [T] to put words, pictures, etc. onto paper by using a special machine: *How much did it cost to print the posters?* ▶ **drukować 2** [I,T] to produce books, newspapers, etc. in this way: *50 000 copies of the textbook were printed.* ▶ **drukować 3** [T] to include sth in a book, newspaper, etc.: *The newspaper should not have printed the photographs of the crash.* ▶ **drukować 4** [T] to make a photograph from a piece of negative film: *I'm having the pictures developed and printed.* ▶ **robić odbitkę fotograficzną 5** [I,T] to write with letters that are not joined together: *Please print your name clearly at the top of the paper.* ▶ **pisać** *(wyraźnie, każdą literę osobno)* **6** [T] to put a pattern onto cloth, paper, etc.: *printed cotton/wallpaper* ▶ **drukować**
■ **printing** noun [U] ▶ **druk**, **drukowanie**
PHR V **print sth off/out** to produce a document or information from a computer in **printed** form ▶ **drukować z komputera**

⚷ **print**[2] /prɪnt/ noun **1** [U] the letters, words, etc. in a book, newspaper, etc.: *The print is too small for me to read without my glasses.* ▶ **druk 2** [U] (used to refer to the business of producing newspapers, books, etc.): *the print unions/workers* ◇ *a print run* nakład ▶ **wydawanie** *(gazet, książek itp.)* **3** [C] a mark that is made by sth pressing onto sth else: *The police are searching the room for fingerprints.* ◇ *footprints in the snow* ▶ **ślad 4** [C] a picture that was made by printing: *a framed set of prints* ▶ **rycina 5** [C] a photograph (when it has been printed from a negative): *I ordered an extra set of prints for my friends.* ▶ **odbitka**
IDM **in print 1** (used about a book) still available from the company that published it ▶ **jeszcze dostępny w sprzedaży bezpośrednio od wydawcy 2** (used about sb's work) published in a book, newspaper, etc. ▶ **opublikowany**
out of print (used about a book) no longer available from the company that published it; not being printed any more ▶ *(nakład książki)* **wyczerpany**

⚷ **printer** /ˈprɪntə(r)/ noun [C] **1** a machine that prints out information from a computer onto paper: *a laser printer*

P

▶ **drukarka komputerowa 2** a person or company that prints books, newspapers, etc. ▶ **drukarz**; **drukarnia**

ˈ**printing press** (also press) noun [C] a machine that is used for printing books, newspapers, etc. ▶ **prasa drukarska**

printout /ˈprɪntaʊt/ noun [C,U] information from a computer that is printed onto paper ▶ **wydruk komputerowy**

ˈ**print run** noun [C] the number of copies of a book, magazine, etc. printed at one time ▶ **nakład**

⚷ **prior** /ˈpraɪə(r)/ adj. [only before a noun] coming before or earlier ▶ **poprzedni**

prioritize (also -ise) /praɪˈɒrətaɪz/ verb **1** [I,T] to put tasks, problems, etc. in order of importance, so that you can deal with the most important first: *You should make a list of all the jobs you have to do and prioritize them.* ▶ **ustawiać pod względem ważności 2** [T] (formal) to treat sth as being more important than other things: *The organization was formed to prioritize the needs of older people.* ▶ **traktować priorytetowo**
■ **prioritization** (also -isation) /praɪˌɒrətaɪˈzeɪʃn; US -təˈz-/ noun [U] ▶ **ustawianie według ważności**; **traktowanie priorytetowe**

⚷ **priority** /praɪˈɒrəti/ noun (pl. **priorities**) **1** [C] something that is most important or that you must do before anything else: *Our **top priority** is to get food and water to the refugee camps.* ◇ *I'll **make it** my **priority** to sort out your problem.* ▶ **pierwszeństwo 2** [U] **priority (over sb/sth)** the state of being more important than sb/sth or of coming before sb/sth else: *We **give priority** to families with small children.* ◇ *Emergency cases **take priority** over other patients in hospital.* ▶ **priorytet**

ˈ**prior to** prep. (formal) before: *Prepare the surface prior to applying the first coat of paint.* ▶ **przed**

prise /praɪz/ (especially US **prize**, **pry**) verb [T] **prise sth off, apart, open, etc.** to use force to open sth, remove a lid, etc.: *He prised the door open with an iron bar.* ▶ **podważać**, **wyważać**

prism /ˈprɪzəm/ noun [C] **1** a solid figure with ends that are parallel and of the same size and shape, and with sides whose opposite edges are equal and parallel ▶ **graniastosłup 2** a piece of glass or plastic in the shape of a triangle, which separates light that passes through it into seven colours ▶ **pryzmat**

⚷ **prison** /ˈprɪzn/ (also **jail**) noun [C,U] a building where criminals are kept as a punishment: *The terrorists were **sent to prison** for twenty-five years.* ◇ *He will be **released from prison** next month.* ◇ *a prison warder/officer* strażnik więzienny ▶ **więzienie** SYN **jail** ➲ note at **court** ➲ look at **imprison**

> Słowa **prison** używa się bez rodzajnika określonego **the**, mówiąc o kimś osadzonym w więzieniu: *He's in prison – he's serving a three-year sentence for robbery.* Natomiast **the prison** stosuje się, mówiąc o ludziach udających się do więzienia w innym celu: *The minister visited the prison and said that conditions were poor.* Rodzajników **a** i **the** używa się też przy określaniu rodzaju więzienia: *a high-security prison.*

⚷ **prisoner** /ˈprɪznə(r)/ noun [C] a person who is being kept in prison: *a political prisoner* ▶ **więzień/źniarka**
IDM **hold/take sb captive/prisoner** → CAPTIVE[1]

ˌ**prisoner of ˈconscience** noun [C] (pl. **prisoners of conscience**) a person who is kept in prison because of his or her political or religious beliefs ▶ **więzień sumienia**, **więzień polityczny**

ˌ**prisoner of ˈwar** noun [C] a soldier, etc. who is caught by the enemy during a war and who is kept in prison until the end of the war ▶ **jeniec wojenny**

prissy /ˈprɪsi/ adj. (informal) too careful to always behave correctly and appearing easily shocked by rude behaviour, etc.: *She was a prissy* (przesadnie grzeczna i pruderyjna) *little girl.* ◇ *Children's clothes that are attractive without being prissy* (zbyt strojne). ▶ **pruderyjny** SYN **prudish**

pristine /ˈprɪstiːn/ adj. **1** fresh and clean, as if new: *The car is **in pristine condition**.* ◇ *a pristine white tablecloth* ▶ **nieskazitelnie czysty** SYN **immaculate 2** not developed or changed in any way; left in its original condition: *pristine, pollution-free beaches* ▶ **w nienaruszonym stanie**

privacy /ˈprɪvəsi; US ˈpraɪv-/ noun [U] **1** the state of being alone and not watched or disturbed by other people: *There is not much privacy in large hospital wards.* ▶ **prywatność 2** the state of being free from the attention of the public: *The star claimed that the photographs were an **invasion of privacy*** (naruszeniem prywatności). ▶ **prywatność**

⚷ **private**[1] /ˈpraɪvət/ adj. **1** belonging to or intended for one particular person or group and not to be shared by others: *This is private property. You may not park here.* ◇ *a private* (poufn-y/a) *letter/conversation* ▶ **prywatny 2** with nobody else present: *I would like a private interview with the personnel manager.* ▶ **osobisty 3** not wanting to share thoughts and feelings with other people: *He's a very private person.* ▶ **skryty 4** owned, done or organized by a person or company, and not by the government: *a private hospital/school* ◇ *a private detective* ▶ **prywatny** OPP **public 5** not connected with work or business: *He never discusses his **private life** with his colleagues at work.* ▶ **osobisty 6** (used about classes, lessons, etc.) given by a teacher to one student or a small group for payment: *Claire gives private English lessons at her house.* ▶ **prywatny**
■ **privately** adv. ▶ **prywatnie**

private[2] /ˈpraɪvət/ noun [C] a soldier of the lowest level ▶ **szeregowy**
IDM **in private** with nobody else present: *May I speak to you in private?* ▶ **prywatnie**

ˌ**private ˈenterprise** noun [U] the economic system in which industry or business is owned by independent companies or private people and is not controlled by the government ▶ **przedsiębiorczość prywatna** ➲ look at **free enterprise**

ˌ**private ˈview** (also ˌ**private ˈviewing**) noun [C] an occasion when a few people are invited to look at an exhibition of paintings before it is open to the public ▶ **wernisaż**

privatize (also -ise) /ˈpraɪvətaɪz/ verb [T] to sell a business or an industry that was owned by the government to a private company: *The electricity industry has been privatized.* ▶ **prywatyzować** OPP **nationalize**
■ **privatization** (also -isation) /ˌpraɪvətaɪˈzeɪʃn; US -təˈz-/ noun [U] ▶ **prywatyzacja**

privilege /ˈprɪvəlɪdʒ/ noun **1** [C,U] a special right or advantage that only one person or group has: *Prisoners who behave well **enjoy** special **privileges**.* ▶ **przywilej 2** [sing.] a special advantage or opportunity that gives you great pleasure: *It was a great privilege to hear her sing.* ▶ **zaszczyt**

privileged /ˈprɪvəlɪdʒd/ adj. having an advantage or opportunity that most people do not have: *Only **a privileged few** are allowed to enter this room.* ◇ *I feel very privileged to be playing for the national team.* ▶ **wyróżniony** ➲ look at **underprivileged**

⚷ **prize**[1] /praɪz/ noun [C] something of value that is given to sb who is successful in a race, competition, game, etc.: *She won **first prize** in the competition.* ◇ *a prize-winning novel* nagrodzona powieść ▶ **nagroda**

prize² /praɪz/ adj. [only before a noun] winning, or good enough to win, a prize: *a prize flower display* ▶ **nagrodzony; mający szansę na wygraną**

prize³ /praɪz/ verb [T] **1** to consider sth to be very valuable: *This picture is one of my most prized* (najcenniejszych) *possessions.* ▶ **cenić 2** (especially US) = PRISE

pro /prəʊ/ (pl. **pros**) (informal) **1** = PROFESSIONAL²(2): *a golf pro* **2** = PROFESSIONAL²(3)

IDM **the pros and cons** the reasons for and against doing sth: *We should consider all the pros and cons before reaching a decision.* ▶ **za i przeciw** ➲ look at **advantage**

pro- /prəʊ/ [in compounds] in favour of; supporting: *pro-democracy* ▶ **opowiadający się za czymś, popierający coś** ➲ look at **anti-**

proactive /ˌprəʊ'æktɪv/ adj. controlling a situation by making things happen rather than waiting for things to happen and then reacting to them ▶ **proaktywny**

probability /ˌprɒbə'bɪləti/ noun (pl. **probabilities**) **1** [U, sing.] how likely sth is to happen: *At that time there seemed little probability of success.* ▶ **prawdopodobieństwo 2** [C] something that is likely to happen: *Closure of the factory now seems a probability.* ▶ **prawdopodobieństwo**

🔑 **probable** /'prɒbəbl/ adj. that you expect to happen or to be true; likely ▶ **prawdopodobny** OPP **improbable** ➲ look at **possible**

> Zwróć uwagę, że **probable** i **likely** mają to samo znaczenie, ale inaczej się ich używa: ***It's probable that** he will be late.* ◇ *He **is likely to** to be late.*

🔑 **probably** /'prɒbəbli/ adv. almost certainly: *I will phone next week, probably on Wednesday.* ▶ **prawdopodobnie**

probation /prə'beɪʃn; US prəʊ-/ noun [U] **1** a system that allows sb who has committed a crime not to go to prison if they go to see a **probation officer** regularly for a fixed period of time: *Jamie is **on probation** for two years.* ▶ **wyrok w zawieszeniu, zwolnienie warunkowe z więzienia 2** a period of time at the start of a new job when you are tested to see if you are suitable: *a three-month probation period* ▶ **okres próbny**

pro'bation officer noun [C] a person who keeps an official check on people who are on probation ▶ **kurator/opiekun sądowy osób, które otrzymały wyrok w zawieszeniu lub zostały zwolnione warunkowo z więzienia**

probe¹ /prəʊb/ verb [I,T] **1 probe (into sth)** to ask questions in order to find out secret or hidden information: *The newspapers are now probing into the President's past.* ▶ **badać 2** to examine or look for sth, especially with a long thin instrument: *The doctor probed the cut for pieces of broken glass.* ▶ **badać sondą**

■ **probing** adj.: *to ask probing questions* ▶ **gruntowny, badawczy**

probe² /prəʊb/ noun [C] **1** the process of asking questions, collecting facts, etc. in order to find out hidden information about sth: *a police probe into illegal financial dealing* ▶ **sonda 2** a long thin tool that you use for examining sth that is difficult to reach, especially a part of the body ▶ **sonda** (*instrument medyczny*)

🔑 **problem** /'prɒbləm/ noun [C] **1** a thing that is difficult to deal with or to understand: *social/family/financial/technical problems* ◇ *You won't **solve the problem** if you ignore it.* ◇ *The company will **face problems** from unions if it sacks workers.* ◇ *It's going to **cause problems** if Donna brings her husband.* ◇ *I can't play because I've got **a problem with** my knee.* ◇ *'Can you fix this for me?' '**No problem**'* (nie ma sprawy)*.'* ◇ *It's a great painting – **the problem is** I've got nowhere to put it.* ▶ **problem, kłopot 2** a question that you have to solve by thinking about it: *a maths/logic problem* ▶ **zagadka, zadanie**

problematic /ˌprɒblə'mætɪk/ (also **problematical** /-ɪkl/) adj. difficult to deal with; full of problems ▶ **problematyczny**

🔑 **procedure** /prə'siːdʒə(r)/ noun [C,U] the usual or correct way for doing sth: *What's the procedure for making a complaint?* ▶ **sposób postępowania, procedura** (*np. sądowa*)

🔑 **proceed** /prə'siːd; US prəʊ-/ verb [I] **1 proceed (with sth)** to continue doing sth; to continue being done: *The building work was proceeding according to schedule.* ◇ *We're not sure whether we still want to proceed with the sale* (czy nadal jesteśmy zainteresowani sprzedażą)*.* ▶ **kontynuować, przebiegać 2 proceed to do sth** to do sth next, after having done sth else first: *Once he had calmed down he proceeded to tell us what had happened.* ▶ **przystępować do (zrobienia) czegoś**

proceedings /prə'siːdɪŋz/ noun [pl.] (formal) **1 proceedings (against sb/for sth)** legal action: *to start divorce proceedings* ▶ **postępowanie prawne 2** events that happen, especially at a formal meeting, ceremony, etc.: *The proceedings were interrupted by demonstrators.* ▶ **obrady, prace**

proceeds /'prəʊsiːdz/ noun [pl.] **proceeds (of/from sth)** money that you get when you sell sth: *The proceeds from the sale will go to charity.* ▶ **dochód**

🔑 **process¹** /'prəʊses; US 'prɑː-/ noun [C] **1** a series of actions that you do for a particular purpose: *We've just begun the complicated process of selling the house.* ▶ **proces 2** a series of changes that happen naturally: *Mistakes are a normal part of the learning process.* ▶ **proces**

IDM **in the process** while you are doing sth else: *We washed the dog yesterday – and we all got very wet in the process.* ▶ **w trakcie (czegoś)**

in the process of sth/doing sth in the middle of doing sth: *They are in the process of moving house.* ▶ **w trakcie (czegoś/robienia czegoś)**

🔑 **process²** /'prəʊses; US 'prɑː-/ verb [T] **1** to treat sth, for example with chemicals, in order to keep it, change it, etc.: *Cheese is processed so that it lasts longer.* ◇ *I sent two rolls of film away to be processed* (do wywołania)*.* ▶ **przetwarzać 2** to deal with information, for example on a computer: *It will take about ten days to process your application.* ▶ **przetwarzać** (*dane*)

procession /prə'seʃn/ noun [C,U] a number of people, vehicles, etc. that move slowly in a line, especially as part of a ceremony: *to walk **in procession*** ◇ *a funeral procession* ▶ **procesja, pochód**

processor /'prəʊsesə(r); US 'prɑː-/ noun [C] a machine or person that **processes** sth ▶ **przetwarzacz** ➲ look at **food processor, word processor**

proclaim /prə'kleɪm/ verb [T] (formal) to make sth known officially or publicly: *The day has been proclaimed a national holiday.* ▶ **obwieszczać**

■ **proclamation** /ˌprɒklə'meɪʃn/ noun [C,U]: *to make a proclamation of war* ▶ **obwieszczenie**

procrastinate /prəʊ'kræstɪneɪt/ verb [I] (formal) to delay doing sth that you should do, usually because you do not want to do it: *People were dying of starvation while governments procrastinated.* ▶ **zwlekać**

■ **procrastination** /prəʊˌkræstɪ'neɪʃn/ noun [U] ▶ **zwlekanie**

procreate /'prəʊkrieɪt/ verb [I,T] (formal) to produce children or baby animals ▶ **płodzić; rozmnażać się** SYN **reproduce**

■ **procreation** /ˌprəʊkri'eɪʃn/ noun [U] ▶ **prokreacja**

procure /prə'kjʊə(r)/ verb [T] (formal) **procure sth (for sb)** to obtain sth, especially with difficulty: *I managed to procure two tickets for the match.* ▶ **nabywać**

P

prod /prɒd/ verb [I,T] (**prodding**; **prodded**) to push or press sb/sth with your finger or a pointed object: (figurative) *Ruth works quite hard but she does need prodding occasionally.* ▶ **szturchać**; **dopingować**
■ **prod** noun [C]: *to give the fire a prod with a stick* ▶ **szturchnięcie**, **popchnięcie** | **prodding** noun [U] ▶ **dopingowanie**

prodigious /prəˈdɪdʒəs/ adj. very large or powerful and surprising: *He seemed to have a prodigious amount of energy.* ▶ **ogromny**

prodigy /ˈprɒdədʒi/ noun [C] (pl. **prodigies**) a child who is unusually good at sth: *Mozart was a* ***child prodigy*** (cudowne dziecko). ▶ **cud**, **geniusz** ➲ look at **genius**

produce[1] /prəˈdjuːs; US -ˈduːs/ verb [T] **1** to make sth to be sold, especially in large quantities: *The factory produces 20 000 cars a year.* ▶ **wytwarzać**, **produkować** SYN **manufacture** **2** to grow or make sth by a natural process: *This region produces most of the country's wheat.* ◇ (figurative) *He's the greatest athlete this country has produced.* ▶ **wydawać**; **rodzić** **3** to create sth using skill: *The children have produced some beautiful pictures for the exhibition.* ▶ **tworzyć**, **robić** **4** to cause a particular effect or result: *Her remarks produced roars of laughter.* ▶ **wywoływać** **5** to show sth so that sb else can look at or examine it: *to produce evidence in court* ▶ **okazywać** **6** to be in charge of preparing a film, play, etc. so that it can be shown to the public: *She is producing 'Romeo and Juliet' at the local theatre.* ▶ **wystawiać**, **produkować** **7** to give birth to a young animal ▶ **wydawać na świat** (*zwierzęta*)

produce[2] /ˈprɒdjuːs; US -duːs; ˈproʊ-/ noun [U] food, etc. that is grown on a farm and sold: *fresh farm produce* ▶ **płody rolne** ➲ note at **production**

producer /prəˈdjuːsə(r); US -ˈduː-/ noun [C] **1** a person, company or country that makes or grows sth: *Brazil is a major producer of coffee.* ▶ **producent/ka** **2** a person who deals with the business side of organizing a play, film, etc.; a person who arranges for sb to make a programme for TV or radio, or a record: *Hollywood screenwriters, actors and producers* ◇ *an independent television producer* ▶ **producent/ka**, **realizator/ka**

product /ˈprɒdʌkt/ noun [C] **1** something that is made in a factory or that is formed naturally: *dairy/meat/pharmaceutical/software products* ◇ *Carbon dioxide is one of the waste products of this process.* ▶ **produkt**, **wytwór** ➲ note at **production** **2** **product of sth** the result of sth: *The industry's problems are the product of government policy.* ▶ **wynik** **3** the amount that you get if you multiply one number by another ▶ **iloczyn**

production /prəˈdʌkʃn/ noun **1** [U] the making or growing of sth, especially in large quantities: *The latest model will be* ***in production*** *from April.* ◇ *This farm specializes in the production of organic vegetables.* ◇ *mass production* ▶ **produkcja** **2** [U] the amount of sth that is made or grown: *a rise/fall in production* ◇ *a high level of production* ▶ **wydobycie**, **uprawa** **3** [C] a play, film or programme that has been made for the public ▶ **produkcja** (*np. filmu*)

> Zwróć uwagę, że rzeczownik **produce** oznacza jedzenie itp. pochodzenia naturalnego, natomiast **product** to wyrób pochodzenia fabrycznego. **Production** oznacza sztukę teatralną, film itp: *The label on the bottle says 'Produce of Italy'.* ◇ *The company's main products are plastic toys.* ◇ *the Bolshoi Ballet's production of Swan Lake.*

IDM **on production of sth** when you show sth: *You can get a ten per cent discount on production of your membership card.* ▶ **za okazaniem**

pro'duction line (also **as'sembly line**) noun [C] a line of workers and machines in a factory, along which a product passes, having parts made, put together or checked at each stage until the product is finished: *Cars are checked as they come off the production line.* ▶ **linia produkcyjna**

productive /prəˈdʌktɪv/ adj. **1** that makes or grows sth, especially in large quantities: *The company wants to sell off its less productive factories.* ▶ **wydajny** **2** useful (because results come from it): *a productive discussion* ▶ **płodny**
■ **productivity** /ˌprɒdʌkˈtɪvəti; US ˌproʊd-/ noun [U] ▶ **wydajność**

Prof. = PROFESSOR

profane /prəˈfeɪn/ adj. **1** (formal) having or showing a lack of respect for God or holy things: *profane language* ▶ **bluźnierczy** **2** not connected with religion or holy things: *songs of sacred and profane love* ▶ **świecki** SYN **secular**

profess /prəˈfes/ verb [T] (formal) **1** to say that sth is true or correct, even when it is not: *Marianne professed to know nothing at all about it, but I did not believe her.* ▶ **twierdzić** **2** to state honestly that you have a particular belief, feeling, etc.: *He professed his hatred of war.* ▶ **głosić**

profession /prəˈfeʃn/ noun [C] **1** a job that needs a high level of training and/or education: *the medical/legal/teaching profession* ◇ *She's thinking of entering the nursing profession.* ▶ **zawód** ➲ note at **work**[2] **2** (**the ... profession**) [with sing. or pl. verb] all the people who work in a particular profession: *The legal profession* (prawnicy) *is/are trying to resist the reforms.* ▶ **ludzie pracujący w (danym) zawodzie**
IDM **by profession** as your job: *George is an accountant by profession.* ▶ **z zawodu**

professional[1] /prəˈfeʃənl/ adj. **1** [only before a noun] connected with a job that needs a high level of training and/or education: *Get professional advice from your lawyer before you take any action.* ◇ *The flat would be ideal for a professional* (pracującej zawodowo) *couple.* ▶ **fachowy**, **profesjonalny** **2** doing sth in a way that shows skill, training or care: *The police are trained to deal with every situation in a calm and professional manner.* ◇ *Her application was neatly typed and looked very professional.* ▶ **profesjonalny** **3** doing a sport, etc. as a job or for money; (used about a sport, etc.) done by people who are paid: *After his success at the Olympic Games he* ***turned professional*** (został zawodowcem). ◇ *professional football* ▶ **zawodowy** OPP **amateur**

professional[2] /prəˈfeʃənl/ noun [C] **1** a person who works in a job that needs a high level of training and/or education: *doctors and other health professionals* ▶ **profesjonalist(k)a** **2** (also informal **pro**) a person who plays or teaches a sport, etc. for money: *a top golf professional* ▶ **zawodowiec** **3** (also informal **pro**) a person who has a lot of skill and experience: *This was clearly a job for a professional.* ▶ **fachowiec**

professionalism /prəˈfeʃənəlɪzəm/ noun [U] a way of doing a job that shows great skill and experience: *We were impressed by the professionalism of the staff.* ▶ **fachowość**

professionally /prəˈfeʃənəli/ adv. **1** in a way that shows great skill and experience ▶ **fachowo** **2** for money; by a professional person: *Rob plays the saxophone professionally.* ▶ **zawodowo**, **profesjonalnie**

professor /prəˈfesə(r)/ noun [C] (abbr. **Prof.** /prɒf/) **1** a university teacher of the highest level: *She's professor of English at Bristol University.* ▶ **profesor** **2** (US) a teacher at a college or university: *a chemistry professor* ▶ **wykładow-ca/czyni**

proficient /prəˈfɪʃnt/ adj. **proficient (in/at sth/doing sth)** able to do a particular thing well; skilled: *We are looking* *for someone who is proficient in French.* ▶ **biegły, sprawny**

■ **proficiency** /prəˈfɪʃnsi/ noun [U] **proficiency (in sth/ doing sth)**: *a certificate of proficiency in English* ▶ **biegłość, sprawność**

profile /ˈprəʊfaɪl/ noun [C] **1** sb's face or head seen from the side, not the front: *I did a sketch of him **in profile**.* ▶ **profil 2** a short description of sb/sth that gives useful information: *We're building up a profile of our average customer.* ▶ **profil** (*np. klientów*)

IDM **adopt/keep/maintain a high/low profile** to behave in a way that does/does not attract other people's attention: *I don't know much about the subject – I'm going to keep a low profile at the meeting tomorrow.* ▶ **zwracać na siebie uwagę; nie zwracać na siebie uwagi**

profit¹ /ˈprɒfɪt/ noun [C,U] the money that you make when you sell sth for more than it cost you: *Did you **make a profit on** your house when you sold it?* ◇ *I'm hoping to sell my shares **at a profit**.* ▶ **zysk** OPP **loss**

profit² /ˈprɒfɪt/ verb [I,T] (formal) **profit (from/by sth)** to get an advantage from sth; to give sb an advantage: *Who will profit most from the tax reforms?* ▶ **odnosić/przynosić korzyści (z czegoś); zyskiwać (na czymś)**

profitable /ˈprɒfɪtəbl/ adj. **1** that makes money: *a profitable business* ▶ **zyskowny 2** helpful or useful: *We had a profitable discussion yesterday.* ▶ **korzystny**

■ **profitably** /-əbli/ adv.: *to spend your time profitably* ▶ **zyskownie** | **profitability** /ˌprɒfɪtəˈbɪləti/ noun [U] ▶ **zyskowność**

profligate /ˈprɒflɪgət/ adj. (formal) using money, time, materials, etc. in a careless way: *profligate spending* ◇ *the profligate use of resources* ▶ **rozrzutny** SYN **wasteful**

■ **profligacy** /ˈprɒflɪgəsi/ noun [U] ▶ **rozrzutność**

profound /prəˈfaʊnd/ adj. **1** very great; that you feel very strongly: *The experience had a profound influence on her.* ▶ **wielki, głęboki 2** needing or showing a lot of knowledge or thought: *He's always making profound statements about the meaning of life.* ▶ **wyczerpujący**

■ **profoundly** adv.: *I was profoundly relieved to hear the news.* ▶ **ogromnie, głęboko**

profuse /prəˈfjuːs/ adj. (formal) given or produced in great quantity: *profuse apologies* wielkie przeprosiny ▶ **hojny**

■ **profusely** adv.: *She apologized profusely for being late.* Gęsto się tłumaczyła za spóźnienie. ▶ **hojnie**

profusion /prəˈfjuːʒn/ noun [sing., with sing. or pl. verb, U] (formal) a very large quantity of sth: *a profusion of colours* ◇ *Roses grew **in profusion*** (bardzo wiele róż rosło) *against the old wall.* ▶ **obfitość** SYN **abundance**

progesterone /prəˈdʒestərəʊn/ noun [U] a **hormone** produced in the bodies of women and female animals which prepares the body to become pregnant and is also used in **contraception** ▶ **progesteron** ➲ look at **oestrogen, testosterone**

prognosis /prɒgˈnəʊsɪs/ noun [C] (pl. **prognoses** /-siːz/) **1** an opinion, based on medical experience, of the likely development of a disease or an illness: *to make a prognosis* prognozować ▶ **rokowanie 2** (formal) a judgement about how sth is likely to develop in the future: *The prognosis is for more people to work part-time in the future.* ▶ **prognoza** SYN **forecast**

program¹ /ˈprəʊgræm/ noun [C] **1** a set of instructions that you give to a computer so that it will do a particular task: *to write a program* ▶ **program komputerowy**

> Mówiąc o komputerach, zarówno Amer. ang., jak i Br. ang. używa pisowni **program**. Każde inne znaczenie tego słowa w Br. ang. ma pisownię **programme**, natomiast w Amer. ang. **program**.

2 (US) = PROGRAMME¹

program² /ˈprəʊgræm/ verb [T] (**programming**; **programmed**) to give a set of instructions to a computer ▶ **programować komputer**

programme¹ (US **program**) /ˈprəʊgræm/ noun [C] **1** a plan of things to do: *The leaflet outlines the government's programme of educational reforms.* ◇ *What's (on) your programme today?* Co masz dzisiaj w programie? ▶ **program 2** a show or other item that is sent out on the radio or TV: *a TV/radio programme* ◇ *We've just missed an interesting programme on elephants.* ▶ **program, audycja** ➲ note at **television 3** a little book or piece of paper which you get at a concert, a sports event, etc. that gives you information about what you are going to see: *a theatre programme* ▶ **program** ➲ note at **program¹**

programme² (US **program**) /ˈprəʊgræm/ verb [T] (**programming**; **programmed**; US also **programing**; **programed**) **1** to plan for sth to happen at a particular time: *The road is programmed for completion next May.* ▶ **planować 2** to make sb/sth work or act automatically in a particular way: *The lights are programmed to come on as soon as it gets dark.* ▶ **programować**

programmer /ˈprəʊgræmə(r)/ noun [C] a person whose job is to write programs for a computer ▶ **programist(k)a**

progress¹ /ˈprəʊgres; US ˈprɒg-; -grəs/ noun [U] **1** movement forwards or towards achieving sth: *Anna's **making progress** at school.* ◇ *to make slow/steady/rapid/good progress* ◇ *a progress report* sprawozdanie z postępów prac (w nauce) ▶ **posuwanie się (do przodu), postęp/y 2** change or improvement in society: *scientific progress* ▶ **postęp**

IDM **in progress** happening now: *Silence! Examination in progress.* ▶ **w trakcie trwania, w toku**

progress² /prəˈgres/ verb [I] **1** to become better; to develop (well): *Medical knowledge has progressed rapidly in the last twenty years.* ▶ **robić postępy** SYN **advance 2** to move forward; to continue: *I got more and more tired as the evening progressed.* ▶ **posuwać się (do przodu)** SYN **go on**

progression /prəˈgreʃn/ noun [C,U] **(a) progression (from sth) (to sth)** movement forward or a development from one stage to another: *You've made the progression from beginner to intermediate level.* ◇ *There seems to be no logical progression in your thoughts* (brak logicznego rozwoju myśli) *in this essay.* ▶ **postęp**

progressive /prəˈgresɪv/ adj. **1** using modern methods and ideas: *a progressive school* ▶ **postępowy 2** happening or developing steadily: *a progressive reduction in the number of staff* ▶ **stopniowy**

progressively /prəˈgresɪvli/ adv. steadily; a little at a time: *The situation became progressively worse.* ▶ **stopniowo**

the **proˌgressive ˈtense** = CONTINUOUS TENSE

prohibit /prəˈhɪbɪt/ verb [T] (formal) **prohibit sb/sth (from doing sth)** to say that sth is not allowed by law: *English law prohibits children under 16 from buying cigarettes.* ▶ **zabraniać** SYN **forbid, prevent**

prohibition /ˌprəʊɪˈbɪʃn; US -əˈb-/ noun **1** [U] the act of stopping sth being done or used, especially by law: *the prohibition of alcohol in the 1920s* ▶ **zakaz 2** [C] (formal) **a prohibition (on/against sth)** a law or rule that stops sth being done or used: *There is a prohibition on the carrying of knives.* ▶ **zakaz**

prohibitive /prəˈhɪbətɪv/ adj. (used about a price or cost) so high that it prevents people from buying sth or doing sth: *The price of houses in the centre of town is prohibitive.* ▶ **wygórowany**

■ **prohibitively** adv. ▶ **wygórowanie**

project[1] /'prɒdʒekt/ noun [C] **1** a piece of work, often involving many people, that is planned and organized carefully: *a major project to reduce pollution in our rivers* ▶ **projekt**; **plan 2** a piece of school work in which the student has to collect information about a certain subject and then write about it: *Our group chose to do a project on rainforests.* ▶ **zadanie**, **praca pisemna**

project[2] /prə'dʒekt/ verb **1** [T, usually passive] to plan sth that will happen in the future: *the band's projected world tour* ▶ **planować 2** [T, usually passive] to guess or calculate the size, cost or amount of sth: *a projected increase of 10%* ▶ **obliczać** SYN **forecast 3** [T] **project sth (on/onto sth)** to make light, a picture from a film, etc. appear on a flat surface or screen: *Images are projected onto the retina of the eye.* ▶ **rzucać** (*np. światło*), **wyświetlać** (*np. slajdy*) **4** [I] (formal) to stick out: *The balcony projects one metre out from the wall.* ▶ **wystawać 5** [T] to show or represent sb/sth/yourself in a certain way: *The government is trying to project a more caring image.* ▶ **stawiać (kogoś/coś) w złym/dobrym świetle 6** [T] to send or throw sth upwards or away from you: *Actors have to learn to project their voice* (operować głosem). ▶ **wyrzucać coś z siebie**

projection /prə'dʒekʃn/ noun **1** [C] a guess about a future amount, situation, etc. based on the present situation: *sales projections for the next five years* ▶ **prognoza 2** [U] the act of making light, a picture from a film, etc. appear on a surface ▶ **wyświetlanie**

projector /prə'dʒektə(r)/ noun [C] a piece of equipment that **projects** pictures or films onto a screen or wall: *a film/slide projector* ◇ *an overhead projector* rzutnik pisma ▶ **projektor**

proliferate /prə'lɪfəreɪt/ verb [I] (formal) to increase quickly in number ▶ **rozmnażać się**
■ **proliferation** /prəˌlɪfə'reɪʃn/ noun [U] ▶ **rozmnażanie się**, **rozprzestrzenianie się**

prolific /prə'lɪfɪk/ adj. (used especially about a writer, artist, etc.) producing a lot: *a prolific goal scorer* ▶ **płodny**

prologue /'prəʊlɒg/ noun [C] a piece of writing or a speech that introduces a play, poem, etc. ▶ **prolog** ➲ look at **epilogue**

prolong /prə'lɒŋ/ verb [T] to make sth last longer ▶ **przedłużać**

prolonged /prə'lɒŋd/ adj. continuing for a long time: *There was a prolonged silence before anybody spoke.* ▶ **przedłużający się**

prom /prɒm/ noun [C] **1** = PROMENADE **2** (US) a formal dance that is held by a high school class at the end of a school year ▶ **zabawa organizowana na koniec roku szkolnego 3** (Brit.) (also informal ˌ**promenade 'concert**) a concert at which part of the audience stands or sits on the floor: *the last night of the proms* koncert finałowy letniego festiwalu muzycznego w Londynie ▶ **koncert promenadowy**

The proms to festiwal muzyki poważnej, istniejący od 1895 r., który odbywa się latem w londyńskim Royal Albert Hall. Na koncercie finałowym słuchacze oddają się błazeństwom i współuczestniczą w wykonaniu utworów brytyjskich kompozytorów, które tradycyjnie wieńczą festiwal, a popiersie inicjatora festiwalu, Henry'ego Wooda, zostaje udekorowane laurem.

promenade /ˌprɒmə'nɑːd; US -'neɪd/ (also **prom**) noun [C] a wide path where people walk beside the sea in a town on the coast ▶ **promenada nadmorska**

prominent /'prɒmɪnənt/ adj. **1** important or famous: *a prominent political figure* ▶ **wybitny**, **głośny 2** noticeable; easy to see: *The church is the most prominent feature of the village.* ▶ **widoczny**, **wystający**
■ **prominence** noun [U]: *The newspaper gave the affair great prominence.* ▶ **rozgłos**; **widoczność** | **prominently** adv. ▶ **widocznie**

promiscuous /prə'mɪskjuəs/ adj. having sexual relations with many people ▶ **utrzymujący stosunki seksualne z wieloma osobami**
■ **promiscuity**/ˌprɒmɪs'kjuːəti;US-məs-/noun[U]▶ **utrzymywanie stosunków seksualnych z wieloma osobami**

promise[1] /'prɒmɪs/ verb **1** [I,T] **promise (to do sth)**; **promise (sb) that ...** to say definitely that you will do or not do sth or that sth will happen: *She promised to write every week.* ◇ *She promised (me) that she would write.* ▶ **obiecywać**, **przyrzekać 2** [T] **promise sth (to sb)**; **promise sb sth** to say definitely that you will give sth to sb: *Can you promise your support?* ◇ *You have to give him the money if you promised it to him.* ◇ *My dad has promised me a bicycle.* ▶ **przyrzekać 3** [T] to show signs of sth, so that you expect it to happen: *It promises to be an exciting occasion.* ▶ **zapowiadać się**

promise[2] /'prɒmɪs/ noun **1** [C] **a promise (to do sth/that ...)** a written or spoken statement or agreement that you will or will not do sth: *Make sure you **keep** your **promise** to always do your homework.* ◇ *I want you to **make a promise** that you won't do that again.* ◇ *I **give** you my **promise** that I won't tell anyone.* ◇ *You should never **break a promise*** (łamać obietnicy). ▶ **obietnica 2** [U] signs that you will be able to do sth well or be successful: *He **showed** great **promise** as a musician.* Był obiecującym muzykiem. ▶ **nadzieja**

promising /'prɒmɪsɪŋ/ adj. showing signs of being very good or successful: *a promising young writer* ▶ **obiecujący**

promote /prə'məʊt/ verb [T] **1** to encourage sth; to help sth to happen or develop: *to promote good relations between countries* ▶ **zachęcać**; **sprzyjać 2 promote sth (as sth)** to advertise sth in order to increase its sales or make it popular: *The new face cream is being promoted as a miracle cure for wrinkles.* ▶ **promować**, **lansować 3** [often passive] **promote sb (from sth) (to sth)** to give sb a higher position or more important job: *He's been promoted from assistant manager to manager.* ▶ **awansować** OPP **demote** ➲ note at **job**

promoter /prə'məʊtə(r)/ noun [C] a person who organizes or provides the money for an event ▶ **sponsor/ka**

promotion /prə'məʊʃn/ noun **1** [C,U] **promotion (to sth)** a move to a higher position or more important job: *The new job is a promotion for her.* ▶ **awans** OPP **demotion 2** [U,C] things that you do in order to advertise a product and increase its sales: *It's all part of a special promotion of the new book.* ▶ **promocja 3** [U] (formal) **promotion (of sth)** the activity of trying to make sth develop or become accepted by people: *We need to work on the promotion of health, not the treatment of disease.* ▶ **krzewienie**

prompt[1] /prɒmpt/ adj. **1** immediate; done without delay: *We need a prompt decision on this matter.* ▶ **bezzwłoczny 2** [not before a noun] **prompt (in doing sth/to do sth)** (used about a person) quick; acting without delay: *We are always prompt in paying our bills.* ◇ *She was prompt to point out* (szybko zwróciła uwagę na) *my mistake.* ▶ **szybki**

prompt[2] /prɒmpt/ verb **1** [T] to cause sth to happen; to make sb decide to do sth: *What prompted you to give up your job?* ▶ **skłaniać**, **pobudzać 2** [I,T] to encourage sb to speak by asking questions or to remind an actor of his or her words in a play: *The speaker had to be prompted several times.* ▶ **podpowiadać**; **suflerować**
■ **prompting** noun [U]: *He apologized without any prompting.* ▶ **namowa**

prompt³ /prɒmpt/ noun [C] **1** a word or words said to an actor to remind them of what to say next: *When she forgot her lines I had to give her a prompt.* ▶ **podpowiedź** **2** a sign on a computer screen that shows that the computer has finished what it was doing and is ready for more instructions: *Wait for the prompt to come up then type in your password.* ▶ **znak zgłoszenia systemu komputerowego**

promptly /ˈprɒmptli/ adv. **1** immediately; without delay: *I invited her to dinner and she promptly accepted.* ▶ **bezzwłocznie** **2** (also **prompt**) at exactly the time that you have arranged: *We arrived promptly at 12 o'clock.* ◇ *I'll pick you up at 7 o'clock prompt.* ▶ **dokładnie** SYN **punctually**

promulgate /ˈprɒmlgeɪt/ verb [T] (formal) **1** [usually passive] to spread an idea, a belief, etc. among many people ▶ **rozpowszechniać** **2** to announce a new law or system officially or publicly: *The new constitution was promulgated in 1990.* ▶ **ogłaszać**
■ **promulgation** /ˌprɒmlˈgeɪʃn/ noun [U] ▶ **rozpowszechnianie**; **ogłoszenie**

prone /prəʊn/ adj. **prone to sth/to do sth** likely to suffer from sth or to do sth bad: *prone to infection/injury/heart attacks* ◇ *Working without a break makes you more prone to error.* ◇ *to be* ***accident-prone*** mieć skłonność do wypadków ▶ **skłonny**, **mający skłonność**

prong /prɒŋ/ noun [C] **1** each of the two or more long pointed parts of a fork ▶ **ząb** (*widelca, wideł*) **2** each of the separate parts of an attack, argument, etc. that sb uses to achieve sth ▶ (*przen.*) **ostrze** **3** (**-pronged**) [in compounds] having the number or type of **prongs** mentioned: *a three-pronged attack* ▶ **o (kilku) zębach/odnogach/odgałęzieniach**

pronoun /ˈprəʊnaʊn/ noun [C] a word that is used in place of a noun or a phrase that contains a noun: *'He', 'it', 'hers', 'me', 'them', etc. are all pronouns.* ▶ **zaimek** ➲ look at **personal pronoun**

pronounce /prəˈnaʊns/ verb **1** [T] to make the sound of a word or letter in a particular way: *You don't pronounce the 'b' at the end of 'comb'.* ◇ *How do you pronounce your surname?* ▶ **wymawiać** ➲ noun **pronunciation** **2** [T] (formal) to say or give sth formally, officially or publicly: *The judge will pronounce sentence today.* ▶ **wypowiadać się**; **uznawać za kogoś/coś** **3** [I,T] (formal) **pronounce (on sth)** to give your opinion on sth, especially formally: *The play was pronounced 'brilliant' by all the critics.* ▶ **oświadczać**

pronounced /prəˈnaʊnst/ adj. very noticeable; obvious: *His English is excellent although he speaks with a pronounced French accent.* ▶ **wyraźny**

pronunciation /prəˌnʌnsiˈeɪʃn/ noun **1** [U,C] the way in which a language or a particular word or sound is said: *American pronunciation* ▶ **wymowa** ➲ verb **pronounce** **2** [U] sb's way of speaking a language: *His grammar is good but his pronunciation is awful!* ▶ **wymowa**

proof /pruːf/ noun **1** [U] **proof (of sth)**; **proof that...** information, documents, etc. which show that sth is true: *'We need some* ***proof of identity****,' the shop assistant said.* ◇ *You've got no proof that John took the money.* ▶ **dowód** ➲ verb **prove** ➲ look at **evidence** **2** [C, usually pl.] (technical) a first copy of printed material that is produced so that mistakes can be corrected: *She was checking the proofs of her latest novel.* ▶ **korekta**

-proof /pruːf/ adj. [in compounds] able to protect against the thing mentioned: *a soundproof room* pokój dźwiękoszczelny ◇ *a waterproof/windproof jacket* kurtka wodoodporna/przeciwwiatrowa ◇ *bulletproof glass* szkło kuloodporne ◇ *a fireproof door* drzwi ogniotrwałe ◇ *rainproof* nieprzemakalny ◇ *rustproof* nierdzewny ▶ **szczelny**, **odporny**

proofread /ˈpruːfriːd/ verb [I,T] (**proofread**; **proofread** /-red/) to read and correct a piece of written or printed work ▶ **robić korektę**
■ **proofreader** noun [C] ▶ **korektor/ka**

prop¹ /prɒp/ noun [C] **1** a stick or other object that you use to support sth or to keep sth in position: *Rescuers used props to stop the roof of the tunnel collapsing.* ▶ **podpórka**, **stojak** **2** [usually pl.] an object that is used in a play, film, etc.: *He's responsible for all the stage props, machinery and lighting.* ▶ **rekwizyt**

prop² /prɒp/ verb [T] (**propping**; **propped**) to support sb/sth or keep sb/sth in position by putting them or it against or on sth: *I'll use this book to prop the window open.* ◇ *He propped his bicycle against the wall.* ▶ **podpierać**; **opierać**
PHR V **prop sth up** to support sth that would otherwise fall ▶ **podpierać/wspierać coś**

propaganda /ˌprɒpəˈgændə/ noun [U] information and ideas that may be exaggerated or false, which are used to gain support for a political leader, party, etc.: *political propaganda* ▶ **propaganda**

propagate /ˈprɒpəgeɪt/ verb **1** [T] (formal) to spread an idea, a belief or a piece of information among many people: *TV advertising propagates a false image of the ideal family.* ▶ **propagować** **2** [I,T] to produce new plants from a parent plant: *Plants won't propagate in these conditions.* ▶ (*rośliny*) **rozmnażać (się)**
■ **propagation** /ˌprɒpəˈgeɪʃn/ noun [U] ▶ **propagowanie**; **rozmnażanie (się)**

propel /prəˈpel/ verb [T] (**propelling**; **propelled**) to move, drive or push sb/sth forward or in a particular direction ▶ **napędzać**, **pchać do przodu**

propeller /prəˈpelə(r)/ noun [C] a device with several blades that turn round very fast in order to make a ship or a plane move ▶ **śruba**, (*okrętowa*) **śmigło**

propensity /prəˈpensəti/ noun [C] (pl. **propensities**) (formal) **propensity (for sth)**; **propensity (for doing sth)**; **propensity (to do sth)** a habit of or a liking for behaving in a particular way: *He showed a propensity for violence.* ◇ *She has a propensity to exaggerate.* ▶ **skłonność (do czegoś)** SYN **inclination**

proper /ˈprɒpə(r)/ adj. **1** [only before a noun] (especially Brit.) right, suitable or correct: *If you're going skiing you must have the proper clothes.* ◇ *I've got to get these pieces of paper in the proper order.* ▶ **właściwy**, **odpowiedni** **2** [only before a noun] that you consider to be real or good enough: *I didn't see much of the flat yesterday. I'm going to go today and have a proper look.* ▶ **prawdziwy**, **porządny** **3** (formal) socially and morally acceptable: *I think it would be only proper for you to apologize.* ▶ **przyzwoity** OPP **improper** **4** [only after a noun] real or main: *We travelled through miles of suburbs before we got to the city proper.* ▶ **właściwy**

properly /ˈprɒpəli/ adv. **1** (especially Brit.) correctly; in an acceptable way: *The teacher said I hadn't done my homework properly.* ◇ *These shoes don't fit properly.* ▶ **właściwie**, **prawidłowo** **2** in a way that is socially and morally acceptable; politely: *If you two children can't behave properly then we'll have to go home.* ▶ **przyzwoicie** OPP **improperly**

ˌproper ˈnoun (also **ˌproper ˈname**) noun [C] a word that is the name of a person, place, an institution, etc. and is written with a capital letter, for example *Tom, Mrs Jones, Rome, the White House* ▶ **nazwa własna** ➲ look at **abstract noun**, **common noun**

property /ˈprɒpəti/ noun (pl. **properties**) **1** [U] a thing or things that belong to sb: *The sack contained* ***stolen property****.* ◇ *Is this bag your property?* ◇ *This file is government property.* ▶ **własność**, **ruchomości** ➲ look at **lost**

property 2 [U] land and buildings: *Property prices vary enormously from area to area.* ▶ **nieruchomość 3** [C] one building and the land around it: *There are a lot of empty properties in the area.* ▶ **nieruchomość 4** [C, usually pl.] (formal) a special quality or characteristic that a substance, etc. has: *Some plants have healing properties.* ▶ **właściwość**

'property developer = DEVELOPER

prophecy /'prɒfəsi/ noun [C] (pl. **prophecies**) a statement about what is going to happen in the future: *to fulfil a prophecy* ▶ **proroctwo**

prophesy /'prɒfəsaɪ/ verb [T] (**prophesying**; **prophesies**; pt, pp **prophesied**) to say what you think will happen in the future: *to prophesy disaster/war* ▶ **prorokować**

prophet /'prɒfɪt/ noun [C] **1** (also **Prophet**) (in the Christian, Jewish and Muslim religions) a person who is sent by God to teach the people and give them messages from God ▶ **prorok/ini 2** a person who tells what is going to happen in the future ▶ **prorok/ini**
■ **prophetic** /prə'fetɪk/ adj. ▶ **proroczy**

prophylactic /,prɒfɪ'læktɪk/ adj. done or used in order to prevent a disease: *prophylactic treatment* ▶ **zapobiegawczy**
■ **prophylactically** /-kli/ adv. ▶ **zapobiegawczo** | **prophylactic** noun [C] a medicine, device or course of action that prevents disease ▶ **środek zapobiegawczy**, **leczenie zapobiegawcze**

propitious /prə'pɪʃəs/ adj. **propitious (for sth/sb)** (formal) likely to produce a successful result: *It was not a propitious time to start a new business.* ▶ **sprzyjający (czemuś/komuś)**

⚷ **proportion** /prə'pɔːʃn/ noun **1** [C] a part or share of a whole: *A large proportion of the earth's surface is covered by sea.* ▶ **proporcja 2** [U] **proportion (of sth to sth)** the relationship between the size or amount of two things: *The proportion of men to women in the college has changed dramatically over the years.* ▶ **stosunek 3** (**proportions**) [pl.] the size or shape of sth: *a room of fairly generous proportions* ◇ *Political unrest is reaching alarming proportions.* ▶ **proporcje**, **rozmiary**
IDM **in proportion** the right size in relation to other things: *to draw sth in proportion* ◇ *She's so upset that she can't see the problem in proportion any more* (wyolbrzymia problem). ▶ **w(e) właściwej proporcji**
in proportion to sth by the same amount or number as sth else; relative to sth: *Salaries have not risen in proportion to inflation.* ◇ *The room is very long in proportion to its width.* ▶ **w stosunku do czegoś**
out of proportion (to sth) 1 too big, small, etc. in relation to other things ▶ **niewspółmierny 2** too great, serious, important, etc. in relation to sth: *His reaction was completely out of proportion to the situation.* ◇ *Haven't you got this matter rather out of proportion?* Chyba wyolbrzymiasz tę sprawę? ▶ **niewspółmierny**

proportional /prə'pɔːʃənl/ adj. **proportional (to sth)** of the right size, amount or degree compared with sth else: *Salary is proportional to years of experience.* ▶ **proporcjonalny**

pro,portional ,represen'tation noun [U] (abbr. **PR** /,piː 'ɑː(r)/) a system that gives each political party in an election a number of seats in parliament in direct relation to the number of votes it receives ▶ (*polit.*) **system proporcjonalny** ➲ look at **representation**

proportionate /prə'pɔːʃənət/ adj. **proportionate (to sth)** (formal) increasing or decreasing in size, amount or degree according to changes in sth else: *The number of accidents is proportionate to the increased volume of traffic.* ▶ **proporcjonalny (do czegoś)** SYN **proportional** ➲ look at **disproportionate**
■ **proportionately** adv. ▶ **proporcjonalnie**

⚷ **proposal** /prə'pəʊzl/ noun [C] **1 a proposal (for/to do sth)**; **a proposal that ...** a plan that is formally suggested: *a new proposal for raising money* ◇ *a proposal to build more student accommodation* ◇ *May I* ***make a proposal*** *that we all give an equal amount?* ▶ **projekt**, **propozycja 2** an act of formally asking sb to marry you ▶ **oświadczyny**

⚷ **propose** /prə'pəʊz/ verb **1** [T] to formally suggest sth as a possible plan or action: *At the meeting a new advertising campaign was proposed.* ▶ **proponować**, **wysuwać wniosek 2** [T] to intend to do sth; to have sth as a plan: *What do you propose to do now?* ▶ **zamierzać 3** [I,T] **propose (to sb)** to ask sb to marry you: *to propose marriage* ▶ **oświadczać się 4** [T] **propose sb for/as sth** to suggest sb for an official position: *I'd like to propose Anna Marsland as Chairperson.* ▶ **wysuwać kandydaturę**

proposition /,prɒpə'zɪʃn/ noun [C] **1** an idea, a plan or an offer, especially in business; a suggestion: *A month's holiday in Spain is an* ***attractive proposition.*** ▶ **propozycja 2** an idea or opinion that sb expresses about sth: *That's a very interesting proposition. But can you prove it?* ▶ **propozycja 3** a problem or task that you must deal with: *Getting the work finished on time is going to be quite a difficult proposition.* ▶ **sprawa**

proprietary /prə'praɪətri; US -teri/ adj. [usually before a noun] **1** (used about goods) made and sold by a particular company and protected by a **registered trademark**: *a proprietary medicine* ◇ *proprietary brands* ◇ *a proprietary name* ▶ **firmowy**, **patentowy 2** relating to an owner or to the fact of owning sth: *The company has a proprietary right to the property.* ▶ **wynikający z tytułu własności**

proprietor /prə'praɪətə(r)/ (fem. **proprietress** /prə'praɪətres/) noun [C] (formal) the owner of a business, a hotel, etc. ▶ **właściciel/ka**

proprietorial /prə,praɪə'tɔːriəl/ adj. (formal) relating to an owner or to the fact of owning sth: *proprietorial rights* ▶ **własnościowy**, **władczy**

pro rata /,prəʊ 'rɑːtə/ adj. (formal) (used about a payment or share of sth) calculated according to how much of sth has been used, the amount of work done, etc.: *If costs go up, there will be a pro rata increase in prices.* ◇ *Leave entitlement is calculated on a pro rata basis, according to length of service.* ▶ **proporcjonalny** SYN **proportionate**
■ **pro rata** adv.: *Prices will increase pro rata.* ▶ **proporcjonalnie**

prosaic /prə'zeɪɪk/ adj. **1** ordinary and not showing any imagination: *a prosaic style* ▶ **prozaiczny 2** dull; not romantic: *the prosaic side of life* ▶ **prozaiczny** SYN **mundane**
■ **prosaically** /-kli/ adv. ▶ **prozaicznie**

prose /prəʊz/ noun [U] written language that is not poetry: *to write* ***in prose*** ◇ *a prose writer* prozai-k/czka ▶ **proza** ➲ look at **poetry**

prosecute /'prɒsɪkjuːt/ verb [I,T] **prosecute sb (for sth)** to officially charge sb with a crime and try to show that they are guilty, in a court of law: *the prosecuting counsel/lawyer/attorney* ◇ *He was prosecuted for theft.* ▶ **prowadzić sprawę sądową**; **ścigać (sądownie)** ➲ look at **defend**

prosecution /,prɒsɪ'kjuːʃn/ noun **1** [U,C] the process of officially charging sb with a crime and of trying to show that they are guilty, in a court of law: *to bring a prosecution against somebody* ◇ *Failure to pay your parking fine will result in prosecution.* ◇ *the Director of Public Prosecutions* Prokurator Generalny ▶ **sprawa sądowa 2** (**the prosecution**) [sing., with sing. or pl. verb] a person or group of people who try to show that sb is guilty of a crime in a court of law: *The prosecution claim/claims that Lloyd was driving at 100 miles per hour.* ◇ *a witness* *for the prosecution* świadek oskarżenia ▶ **oskarżyciel** ➲ note at **court** ➲ look at **defence**

prosecutor /'prɒsɪkjuːtə(r)/ noun [C] **1** a public official who charges sb officially with a crime and **prosecutes** them in court: *the public/state prosecutor* ▶ **oskarżyciel/ka publiczn-y/a**, **prokurator** **2** a lawyer who leads the case against the person who is accused of a crime ▶ **oskarżyciel**

prospect /'prɒspekt/ noun **1** [U, sing.] **prospect (of sth/of doing sth)** the possibility that sth will happen: *There's little prospect of better weather before next week.* ▶ **szansa** **2** [sing.] **prospect (of sth/of doing sth)** a thought about what may or will happen in the future: *The prospect of becoming a father filled James with horror.* ▶ **perspektywa (na coś)** **3** (**prospects**) [pl.] chances of being successful in the future: *good job/career/promotion prospects* ▶ **widoki**

prospective /prə'spektɪv/ adj. likely to be or to happen; possible: *They are worried about prospective changes in the law.* ▶ **spodziewany**

prospectus /prə'spektəs/ noun [C] a small book which gives information about a school or college in order to advertise it ▶ **prospekt**

prosper /'prɒspə(r)/ verb [I] to develop in a successful way; to be successful, especially with money ▶ **dobrze się powodzić**

prosperity /prɒ'sperəti/ noun [U] the state of being successful, especially with money: *Tourism has brought prosperity to many parts of Spain.* ▶ **dobrobyt**

prosperous /'prɒspərəs/ adj. rich and successful ▶ **zasobny**

prostitute /'prɒstɪtjuːt; US -tuːt/ noun [C] a person, especially a woman, who earns money by having sex with people ▶ **prostytutka**

prostitution /ˌprɒstɪ'tjuːʃn; US -tə'tuː-/ noun [U] working as a **prostitute** ▶ **prostytucja**

prostrate /'prɒstreɪt/ adj. lying flat on the ground, facing downwards ▶ **leżący plackiem** (*twarzą ku ziemi*)

protagonist /prə'tægənɪst/ noun [C] (formal) **1** the main character in a play, film or book ▶ **protagonista**, **główna postać** (*np. w filmie/książce*) ➲ look at **hero** **2** a leader of a movement in a course of action, etc. ▶ **zwolenni- k/czka**, **przywód-ca/czyni**

protect /prə'tekt/ verb [T] **protect sb/sth (against/from sth)** to keep sb/sth safe; to defend sb/sth: *Parents try to protect their children from danger as far as possible.* ◇ *Bats are a **protected species.*** Nietoperze to chroniony gatunek. ▶ **bronić**, **chronić**

protection /prə'tekʃn/ noun [U] **protection (against/from sth)** the act of keeping sb/sth safe so that he/she/it is not harmed or damaged: *Vaccination gives protection against diseases.* ◇ *After the attack the man was put **under police protection.*** ▶ **obrona**, **ochrona**

protective /prə'tektɪv/ adj. **1** [only before a noun] that prevents sb/sth from being damaged or harmed: *In certain jobs workers need to wear protective clothing.* ▶ **ochronny** **2** **protective (of/towards sb/sth)** wanting to keep sb/sth safe: *Female animals are very protective of their young.* ▶ **opiekuńczy**

protector /prə'tektə(r)/ noun [C] a person who protects sb/sth ▶ **obroń-ca/czyni**, **opiekun/ka**

protein /'prəʊtiːn/ noun [C,U] a substance found in food such as meat, fish and eggs. It is important for helping people and animals to grow and be healthy. ▶ **białko**

protest[1] /'prəʊtest/ noun [U,C] **protest (against sth)** a statement or action that shows that you do not like or approve of sth: *He resigned **in protest** against the decision.* ◇ *The trade union organized a protest against the redundancies.* ▶ **protest**, **sprzeciw**

IDM **under protest** not happily and after expressing disagreement: *Fiona agreed to pay in the end but only under protest.* ▶ **protestując**

protest[2] /prə'test/ verb **1** [I] **protest (about/against/at sth)** to say or show that you do not approve of or agree with sth, especially publicly: *Students have been protesting against the government's decision.* ▶ **protestować**, **sprzeciwiać się** ❶ W Amer. ang. **protest** używa się bez przyimka: *They protested the government's handling of the situation.* **2** [T] to say sth firmly, especially when others do not believe you: *She has always **protested** her **innocence.*** ▶ **twierdzić/mówić (coś) kategorycznie**

> **Protest** ma mocniejsze znaczenie niż **complain.** Używa się go, mówiąc o sprawach poważnych, np. gdy w naszym odczuciu coś jest zdecydowanie złe, nieprawidłowe lub nieuczciwe. **Complain** używa się, mówiąc np. o kiepskiej jakości produktów lub o innej mało ważnej sprawie: *to protest about a new tax* ◇ *to complain about the poor weather.*

■ **protester** noun [C]: *Protesters blocked the road outside the factory.* ▶ **protestując-y/a**

Protestant /'prɒtɪstənt/ noun [C] a member of the Christian church that separated from the Catholic church in the 1500s ▶ **protestant/ka**
■ **Protestant** adj.: *a Protestant church* ▶ **protestancki** ➲ look at **Roman Catholic**

protocol /'prəʊtəkɒl/ noun [U] a system of fixed rules and formal behaviour used in official meetings or other very formal situations: *a breach of protocol* ◇ *the protocol of diplomatic visits* ▶ **protokół** (*np. dyplomatyczny*)

proton /'prəʊtɒn/ noun [C] part of the **nucleus** of an atom that carries a positive electric charge ▶ **proton** ➲ look at **electron**, **neutron**

prototype /'prəʊtətaɪp/ noun [C] the first model or design of sth from which other forms will be developed ▶ **prototyp**

protrude /prə'truːd/ verb [I] **protrude (from sth)** to stick out from a place or surface: *protruding eyes/teeth* ▶ **wystawać**, **odstawać**

protrusion /prə'truːʒn; US prəʊ't-/ noun [C,U] (formal) a thing that sticks out from a place or surface; the fact of doing this: *a protrusion on the rock face* ▶ **występ**, **wypukłość**; **wystawanie**, **odstawanie**

proud /praʊd/ adj. **1** **proud (of sb/sth)**; **proud to do sth/that...** feeling pleased and satisfied about sth that you own or have done: *They are very proud of their new house.* ◇ *I feel very proud to be part of such a successful organization.* ◇ *You should feel very proud that you have been chosen.* ▶ **dumny** **2** feeling that you are better and more important than other people: *Now she's at university she'll be much too proud to talk to us!* ▶ **wyniosły** **3** having respect for yourself and not wanting to lose the respect of others: *He was too proud to ask for help.* ▶ **dumny** ➲ noun **pride**
■ **proudly** adv.: *'I did all the work myself,' he said proudly.* ▶ **dumnie**

prove /pruːv/ verb (pp **proved**; US **proven**) **1** [T] **prove sth (to sb)** to use facts and evidence to show that sth is true: *It will be difficult to prove that she was lying.* ◇ *She tried to prove her innocence to the court.* ◇ *He felt he needed **to prove a point.*** ▶ **udowadniać** ➲ noun **proof** **2** [I] to show a particular quality over a period of time: *The job proved more difficult than we'd expected.* ▶ **okazywać się** **3** [T] **prove yourself (to sb)** to show other people how good you are at doing sth and/or that you are capable of doing sth: *He constantly feels that he has to prove himself to others.* ▶ **sprawdzać się**

proven /ˈprəʊvn; Brit. also ˈpruːvn/ adj. [only before a noun] that has been shown to be true: *a proven fact* ▶ **udowodniony**

proverb /ˈprɒvɜːb/ noun [C] a short well-known sentence or phrase that gives advice or says that sth is generally true in life: *'Waste not, want not' is a proverb.* ▶ **przysłowie** ➲ look at **saying**

proverbial /prəˈvɜːbiəl/ adj. [only before a noun] (used to show that you are referring to a particular **proverb** or well-known phrase): *Let's not count our proverbial chickens.* ▶ **przysłowiowy**
■ **proverbially** /-biəli/ adv. ▶ **według przysłowia**

provide /prəˈvaɪd/ verb [T] **provide sb (with sth)**; **provide sth (for sb)** to give sth to sb or make sth available for sb to use: *This book will provide you with all the information you need.* ◇ *We are able to provide accommodation for two students.* ▶ **dostarczać** SYN **supply** ➲ noun **provision**
PHR V **provide for sb** to give sb all that they need to live, for example food and clothing: *Robin has four children to provide for.* ▶ **utrzymywać**
provide for sth to make preparations to deal with sth that might happen in the future: *We did not provide for such a large increase in prices.* ▶ **zabezpieczać się**

provided /prəˈvaɪdɪd/ (also **providing**) conj. **provided/providing (that)** only if; on condition that: *She agreed to go and work abroad provided (that) her family could go with her.* ▶ **pod warunkiem, że**

province /ˈprɒvɪns/ noun **1** [C] one of the main parts into which some countries are divided with its own local government: *Canada has ten provinces.* ▶ **prowincja** ➲ look at **county**, **state** **2** (**the provinces**) [pl.] (Brit.) all the parts of a country except the capital city ▶ **prowincja**

provincial /prəˈvɪnʃl/ adj. **1** [only before a noun] connected with one of the large areas that some countries are divided into: *provincial governments/elections* ▶ (*jednostka administracyjna*) **prowincjonalny** **2** connected with the parts of a country that do not include its most important city: *a provincial town/newspaper* ▶ **prowincjonalny**, **lokalny** **3** (used about a person or their ideas) not wanting to consider new or different ideas or fashions: *provincial attitudes* ▶ **prowincjonalny**, **zaściankowy**

provision /prəˈvɪʒn/ noun **1** [U] the giving or supplying of sth to sb or making sth available for sb to use: *The council is responsible for the provision of education and social services.* ▶ **zaopatrzenie** **2** [U] **provision for sb/sth** preparations that you make to deal with sth that might happen in the future: *She **made provision for*** (zabezpieczyła finansowo) *the children in the event of her death.* ▶ **zabezpieczanie (się)** **3** (**provisions**) [pl.] (formal) supplies of food and drink, especially for a long journey ▶ **aprowizacja** ➲ verb **provide**

provisional /prəˈvɪʒənl/ adj. only for the present time; that is likely to be changed in the future: *The provisional date for the next meeting is 18 November.* ◇ *a **provisional driving licence*** ▶ **tymczasowy** SYN **temporary**

> **Provisional driving licence** to dokument zezwalający prowadzić samochód osobie, która jeszcze uczy się jeździć, pod warunkiem, że ma skończone 17 lat, towarzyszy jej osoba mająca ważne prawo jazdy, a samochód jest opatrzony plakietką „L".

■ **provisionally** /-nəli/ adv.: *I've only repaired the bike provisionally – we'll have to do it properly later.* ▶ **tymczasowo**

provocation /ˌprɒvəˈkeɪʃn/ noun [U,C] doing or saying sth deliberately to try to make sb angry or upset; sth that is said or done to cause this: *You should never hit children, even **under** extreme **provocation.*** ▶ **prowokacja** ➲ verb **provoke**

provocative /prəˈvɒkətɪv/ adj. **1** intended to make sb angry or upset or to cause an argument: *He made a provocative remark about a woman's place being in the home.* ▶ **prowokacyjny** **2** intended to cause sexual excitement: *a provocative look* ▶ **wyzywający**
■ **provocatively** adv. ▶ **prowokacyjnie**; **wyzywająco**

provoke /prəˈvəʊk/ verb [T] **1** to cause a particular feeling or reaction: *an article intended to provoke discussion* ▶ **wywoływać** **2** **provoke sb (into sth/into doing sth)** to say or do sth that you know will make a person angry or upset: *The lawyer claimed his client was provoked into acts of violence.* ▶ **prowokować** ➲ noun **provocation**

prow /praʊ/ noun [C] (formal) the pointed front part of a ship or boat ▶ **dziób** (*łodzi, statku*) OPP **stern**

prowess /ˈpraʊəs/ noun [U] (formal) great skill at doing sth: *academic/sporting prowess* ▶ **wybitna zdolność** (*do robienia czegoś*)

prowl /praʊl/ verb [I,T] **prowl (about/around)** (used about an animal that is hunting or a person who is waiting for a chance to steal sth or do sth bad) to move around an area quietly so that you are not seen or heard: *I could hear someone prowling around outside so I called the police.* ▶ **czaić się**, **skradać się**
■ **prowl** noun [sing.]: *an intruder **on the prowl*** (grasujący) ▶ **grasowanie**, **czajenie się** | **prowler** noun [C]: *The police have arrested a prowler outside the hospital.* ▶ **osoba kręcąca się podejrzanie/skradająca się**

proximity /prɒkˈsɪməti/ noun [U] (formal) **proximity (of sb/sth) (to sb/sth)** the state of being near to sb/sth in distance or time: *An advantage is the proximity of the new offices to the airport.* ▶ **bliskość**

proxy /ˈprɒksi/ noun [U] the authority that you give to sb to act for you if you cannot do sth yourself: *to vote **by proxy*** ▶ **pełnomocnictwo**

prude /pruːd/ noun [C] a person who is easily shocked by anything connected with sex ▶ **świętosz-ek/ka**
■ **prudish** adj. ▶ **pruderyjny**

prudent /ˈpruːdnt/ adj. (formal) sensible and careful when making judgements and decisions; avoiding unnecessary risks: *It would be prudent to get some more advice before you invest your money.* ▶ **roztropny**, **rozważny** OPP **imprudent**
■ **prudence** noun [U] ▶ **roztropność** | **prudently** adv. ▶ **roztropnie**

prudish /ˈpruːdɪʃ/ adj. very easily shocked by things connected with sex ▶ **pruderyjny** SYN **strait-laced** ❶ Wyraża dezaprobatę.
■ **prudishness** noun [U] ▶ **pruderyjność**

prune[1] /pruːn/ noun [C] a dried **plum** ▶ **suszona śliwka**

prune[2] /pruːn/ verb [T] to cut branches or parts of branches off a tree or bush in order to make it a better shape ▶ **przycinać**

pry /praɪ/ verb (**prying**; **pries**; pt, pp **pried**) **1** [I] **pry (into sth)** to try to find out about other people's private affairs: *I'm sick of you prying into my personal life.* ▶ **wtrącać się** **2** [T] (especially US) = PRISE

PS (also **ps**) /ˌpiː ˈes/ abbr. (also **postscript** /ˈpəʊstskrɪpt/) noun [C] an extra message or extra information that is added at the end of a letter, note, etc.: *Love Tessa. PS I'll bring the car.* ▶ **P.S.**

pseudonym /ˈsuːdənɪm; ˈsjuː-/ noun [C] a name used by sb, especially a writer, instead of their real name ▶ **pseudonim**

psoriasis /səˈraɪəsɪs/ noun [U] a skin disease that causes rough red areas where the skin comes off in small pieces ▶ **łuszczyca**

psych /saɪk/ verb
PHR V **psych sb/yourself up (for sth)** (informal) to prepare yourself in your mind for sth difficult: *I've got to psych myself up for this interview.* ▶ **nastawiać się**

psyche /ˈsaɪki/ noun [C] (formal) the mind; your deepest feelings and attitudes: *the human/female/national psyche* ▶ **psychika**

psychedelic /ˌsaɪkəˈdelɪk/ adj. (used about art, music, clothes, etc.) having bright colours or patterns or strange sounds ▶ **psychodeliczny**

psychiatrist /saɪˈkaɪətrɪst/ noun [C] a doctor who is trained to treat people with mental illness ▶ **psychiatra**

psychiatry /saɪˈkaɪətri/ noun [U] the study and treatment of mental illness ▶ **psychiatria** ➲ look at **psychology**

■ **psychiatric** /ˌsaɪkiˈætrɪk/ adj.: *a psychiatric hospital/unit/nurse* ▶ **psychiatryczny**

psychic /ˈsaɪkɪk/ adj. (used about a person or their mind) having unusual powers that cannot be explained, for example knowing what sb else is thinking or being able to see into the future ▶ **medium**

psycho (informal) = PSYCHOPATH

psychoanalysis /ˌsaɪkəʊəˈnæləsɪs/ (also **analysis**) noun [U] a method of treating sb with a mental illness by asking about their past experiences, feelings, dreams, etc. in order to find out what is making them ill ▶ **psychoanaliza**

■ **psychoanalyse** (US **psychoanalyze**) /ˌsaɪkəʊˈænəlaɪz/ verb [T] ▶ **przeprowadzać psychoanalizę**

psychoanalyst /ˌsaɪkəʊˈænəlɪst/ (also **analyst**) noun [C] a person who treats sb with a mental illness by using **psychoanalysis** ▶ **psychoanality-k/czka**

psychological /ˌsaɪkəˈlɒdʒɪkl/ adj. **1** connected with the mind or the way that it works: *Has her ordeal caused her long-term psychological damage?* ▶ **psychologiczny** **2** [only before a noun] connected with **psychology** ▶ **psychologiczny**

■ **psychologically** /-kli/ adv.: *Psychologically, it was a bad time to be starting a new job.* ▶ **psychologicznie**

psychologist /saɪˈkɒlədʒɪst/ noun [C] a scientist who studies the mind and the way that people behave ▶ **psycholog**

psychology /saɪˈkɒlədʒi/ noun **1** [U] the scientific study of the mind and the way that people behave: *child psychology* ▶ **psychologia** ➲ look at **psychiatry** **2** [sing.] the type of mind that a person or group of people has: *If we understood the psychology of the killer we would have a better chance of catching him.* ▶ **umysłowość**

psychometric /ˌsaɪkəˈmetrɪk/ adj. [only before a noun] (used for measuring mental abilities and processes): *psychometric testing* ▶ **psychometryczny**

psychopath /ˈsaɪkəpæθ/ (also informal **psycho** /ˈsaɪkəʊ/) noun [C] a person who has a serious mental illness that may cause them to hurt or kill other people ▶ **psychopat(k)a**

psychosis /saɪˈkəʊsɪs/ noun [C,U] (pl. **psychoses**) a very serious mental illness that affects your whole character ▶ **psychoza**

■ **psychotic** /saɪˈkɒtɪk/ adj., noun [C]: *a psychotic patient/individual* ▶ **psychotyczny**

psychotherapy /ˌsaɪkəʊˈθerəpi/ noun [U] the treatment of mental illness by discussing sb's problems rather than by giving them drugs ▶ **psychoterapia**

■ **psychotherapist** /-pɪst/ (also **therapist**) noun [C] ▶ **psychoterapeut(k)a**

pt abbr. (pl. **pts**) **1** = PINT (1): *2 pts milk* **2** = POINT[1] (7): *Laura 5 pts, Arthur 4 pts*

PTO (also **pto**) /ˌpiː tiː ˈəʊ/ abbr. (at the bottom of a page) **please turn over** ▶ **verte**

⚷ **pub** /pʌb/ (also formal **public house**) noun [C] (Brit.) a place where people go to buy and drink alcohol and that also often serves food ▶ **bar**, **pub**

> In a pub you order your own drinks at the **bar**. There are often two parts of a pub: the **public bar** and the **lounge bar** or **saloon**. ➲ picture on **page A2**

puberty /ˈpjuːbəti/ noun [U] the time when a child's body is changing and becoming physically like that of an adult: *to reach puberty* ▶ **pokwitanie** SYN **adolescence** ▶ **okres dojrzewania płciowego**

pubic /ˈpjuːbɪk/ adj. [only before a noun] of the area around the sexual organs: *pubic hair* ▶ **łonowy**

⚷ **public**[1] /ˈpʌblɪk/ adj. **1** [only before a noun] connected with ordinary people in general, not those who have an important position in society: ***Public opinion** was in favour of the war.* ◇ *How much public support is there for the government's policy?* ▶ **publiczny**, **powszechny** **2** provided for the use of people in general: *a public library/telephone* ◇ *public spending* ▶ **publiczny** OPP **private** **3** known by many people: *We're going to **make** the news **public** soon.* ▶ **jawny** OPP **private**

■ **publicly** /-kli/ adv.: *The company refused to admit publicly that it had acted wrongly.* ▶ **publicznie**

IDM **be common/public knowledge** → KNOWLEDGE

go public 1 to tell people about sth that is a secret: *The sacked employee went public with his stories of corruption inside the company.* ▶ **podać do publicznej wiadomości** **2** (used about a company) to start selling shares to the public ▶ **wystawiać akcje na sprzedaż**

in the public eye often appearing on TV, in magazines, etc. ▶ **być osobą znaną publicznie**

⚷ **public**[2] /ˈpʌblɪk/ noun [sing., with sing. or pl. verb] **1** (**the public**) people in general: *The university swimming pool is **open to the public** in the evenings.* ◇ *The police have asked for help from **members of the public**.* ◇ *The public is/are generally in favour of the new law.* ▶ **ludność**, **ludzie** **2** a group of people who are all interested in sth or who have sth in common: *the travelling public* podróżni ▶ **ludzie**

IDM **in public** when other people are present: *This is the first time that Miss Potter has spoken about her experience in public.* ▶ **publicznie**

publican /ˈpʌblɪkən/ noun [C] a person who owns or manages a pub ▶ **właściciel/ka lub ajent/ka pubu**

⚷ **publication** /ˌpʌblɪˈkeɪʃn/ noun **1** [U] the act of printing a book, magazine, etc. and making it available to the public: *His latest book has just been accepted for publication.* ▶ **publikacja** **2** [C] a book, magazine, etc. that has been published: *specialist publications* ▶ **publikacja** **3** [U] the act of making sth known to the public: *the publication of exam results* ▶ **ogłoszenie**

ˌpublic ˈcompany (also **ˌpublic ˌlimited ˈcompany**) noun [C] (Brit.) (abbr. **plc**) a large company that sells shares in itself to the public ▶ **spółka akcyjna**

ˌpublic conˈvenience noun [C] (Brit.) a toilet in a public place that anyone can use ▶ **toaleta publiczna** ➲ note at **toilet**

ˌpublic ˈholiday noun [C] a day on which most of the shops, businesses and schools in a country are closed, often to celebrate a particular event ▶ **dzień ustawowo wolny od pracy** (*poza niedzielą*) ➲ look at **bank holiday**

ˌpublic ˈhouse (formal) = PUB

⚷ **publicity** /pʌbˈlɪsəti/ noun [U] **1** notice or attention from the newspapers, TV, etc.: *to seek/avoid publicity* ▶ **rozgłos** **2** the business of attracting people's attention to sth/sb; advertising: *There has been a lot of publicity for this film.* ▶ **reklama**

publicize (also **-ise**) /ˈpʌblɪsaɪz/ verb [T] to attract people's attention to sth: *The event has been well publicized and should attract a lot of people.* ▶ **nadawać rozgłos**

ˌpublic ˌlimited ˈcompany = PUBLIC COMPANY

ˌpublic ˈprosecutor noun [C] (Brit.) a lawyer who works for the government and tries to prove people guilty in court ▶ **oskarżyciel publiczny**, **prokurator**

ˌpublic reˈlations noun (abbr. **PR** /ˌpiː ˈɑː(r)/) **1** [U] the job of making a company, an organization, etc. popular with the public: *a Public Relations Officer* ▶ **utrzymywanie kontaktów z klientami 2** [pl.] the state of the relationship between an organization and the public: *Giving money to local charities is good for public relations.* ▶ **stosunki między daną organizacją a ludnością**

ˌpublic ˈschool noun [C] **1** (in Britain, especially in England) a private school for children aged between 13 and 18 ▶ **szkoła prywatna** (*dla dzieci w wieku od 13 do 18 lat, często z internatem*) ℹ Znane angielskie szkoły prywatne to **Eton** i **Rugby**. **2** (in the US, Australia, Scotland and other countries) a local school that any child can go to that provides free education ▶ **szkoła publiczna**

ˌpublic-ˈspirited adj. always ready to help other people and the public in general ▶ **natchnięty duchem obywatelskim**

ˌpublic ˈtransport noun [U] (the system of) buses, trains, etc. that run according to a series of planned times and that anyone can use: *to travel by/on public transport* ▶ **komunikacja miejska**

🔑 **publish** /ˈpʌblɪʃ/ verb **1** [I,T] to prepare and print a book, magazine, etc. and make it available to the public: *This dictionary was published by Oxford University Press.* ▶ **publikować 2** [T] (used about a writer, etc.) to have your work put in a book, magazine, etc.: *Dr Wreth has published several articles on the subject.* ▶ **publikować 3** [T] to make sth known to the public: *Large companies must publish their accounts every year.* ▶ **ogłaszać**

publisher /ˈpʌblɪʃə(r)/ noun [C] a person or company that publishes books, magazines, etc. ▶ **wydawca**; **wydawnictwo**

🔑 **publishing** /ˈpʌblɪʃɪŋ/ noun [U] the business of preparing books, magazines, etc. to be printed and sold: *a career in publishing* ▶ **publikowanie**

puck /pʌk/ noun [C] a small flat rubber object that is used as a ball in **ice hockey** ➲ note at **hockey** ▶ **krążek hokejowy**

pudding /ˈpʊdɪŋ/ noun [C,U] (Brit.) **1** any sweet food that is eaten at the end of a meal: *What's for pudding today?* ▶ **deser** ➲ look at **dessert**, **sweet 2** a type of sweet food that is made from bread, flour or rice with eggs, milk, etc.: *rice pudding* ▶ **pudding** ℹ Uwaga! **Pudding** nie oznacza „budyń". Por. **custard i mousse**.

puddle /ˈpʌdl/ noun [C] a small pool of water or other liquid, especially rain, that has formed on the ground ▶ **kałuża** ➲ look at **pool** ➲ note at **lake**

pudgy = PODGY

puerile /ˈpjʊəraɪl; US -rəl/ adj. silly; suitable for a child rather than an adult ▶ **infantylny** SYN **childish**

puff¹ /pʌf/ verb **1** [I,T] to smoke a cigarette, pipe, etc.: *to puff on a cigarette* ▶ **palić**, **pykać 2** [I,T] (used about air, smoke, wind, etc.) to blow or come out in clouds: *Smoke was puffing out of the chimney.* ▶ **puszczać kłęby** (*dymu*); (*wiatr*) **dmuchać 3** [I] to breathe loudly or quickly, for example when you are running: *He was puffing hard as he ran up the hill.* ▶ **sapać 4** [I] **puff along, in, out, up, etc.** to move in a particular direction with loud breaths or small clouds of smoke: *The train puffed into the station.* ▶ **poruszać się, głośno sapiąc lub puszczając kłęby dymu**

PHR V **puff sth out/up** to cause sth to become larger by filling it with air: *The trumpet player was puffing out his cheeks.* ▶ **nadmuchiwać**

puff up (used about part of the body) to become swollen: *Her arm puffed up when she was stung by a wasp.* ▶ **spuchnąć**

puff² /pʌf/ noun [C] **1** one breath that you take when you are smoking a cigarette or pipe: *to take/have a puff on a cigarette* ▶ **pyknięcie 2** a small amount of air, smoke, wind, etc. that is blown or sent out: *a puff of smoke* ▶ **kłąb**

puffed /pʌft/ (also ˌ**puffed ˈout**) adj. [not before a noun] finding it difficult to breathe, for example because you have been running ▶ **bez tchu**

puffin /ˈpʌfɪn/ noun [C] a black and white bird with a large, brightly coloured beak that lives near the sea, common in the North Atlantic ▶ **maskonur**

puffy /ˈpʌfi/ adj. (**puffier**; **puffiest**) (used about a part of sb's body) looking soft and swollen: *Your eyes look a bit puffy. Have you been crying?* ▶ **nalany**, **podpuchnięty**

puke /pjuːk/ verb [I,T] (slang) to be sick ▶ **rzygać** SYN **vomit** ■ **puke** noun [U] ▶ **rzygowiny**

🔑 **pull¹** /pʊl/ verb **1** [I,T] to use force to move sb/sth towards yourself: *I pulled on the rope to make sure that it was secure.* ◇ *to pull the trigger of a gun* ◇ *I felt someone pull at my sleeve and turned round.* ◇ *They managed to pull the child out of the water just in time.* ◇ *Pull* (przysuń) *your chair a bit nearer to the table.* ▶ **ciągnąć**, **szarpać 2** [T] **pull sth on, out, up, down, etc.** to move sth in the direction that is described: *She pulled her sweater on/She pulled on her sweater.* Wciągnęła na siebie sweter. ◇ *He pulled up his trousers/He pulled his trousers up.* Wciągnął spodnie. ◇ *I switched off the TV and pulled out the plug* (wyciągnąłem wtyczkę). ▶ **ciągnąć 3** [T] to hold or be fastened to sth and move it along behind you in the direction that you are going: *That cart is too heavy for one horse to pull.* ▶ **ciągnąć 4** [I,T] to move your body or a part of your body away with force: *She pulled away as he tried to kiss her.* ◇ *I pulled back my fingers just as the door slammed.* ▶ **cofać (się)** (*gwałtownie*) **5** [T] to damage a muscle, etc. by using too much force: *I've **pulled a muscle** in my thigh.* ▶ **naciągnąć**

IDM **make/pull faces/a face (at sb)** → FACE¹

pull sb's leg (informal) to play a joke on sb by trying to make them believe sth that is not true ▶ **robić kogoś w konia**

pull out all the stops (informal) to make the greatest possible effort to achieve sth ▶ **wysilać się**

pull (your) punches [usually used in negative sentences] (informal) to be careful what you say or do in order not to shock or upset anyone: *The film pulls no punches in its portrayal of* (film z całą siłą przedstawia) *urban violence.* ▶ **powstrzymywać się od zrobienia czegoś** (*zwł. aby kogoś nie zaszokować lub zmartwić*)

pull your socks up (Brit.) to start working harder or better than before ▶ **(za)brać się do roboty**, **przysiąść fałdów**

pull strings to use your influence to gain an advantage ▶ **pociągać za sznurki** (*używać wpływów/protekcji*)

pull your weight to do your fair share of the work ▶ **nie szczędzić wysiłku**

PHR V **pull sth apart** to separate sth into pieces by pulling different parts of it in different directions ▶ **rozkładać coś na części**

pull away (from sb/sth) to start moving forward, leaving sb/sth behind: *We waved as the bus pulled away.* ▶ **odjeżdżać (od kogoś/skądś)**

pull sth down to destroy a building ▶ **zburzyć**

pull in (to sth) 1 (used about a train) to enter a station ▶ **wjeżdżać na stację 2** (used about a car, etc.) to move to the side of the road and stop ▶ **zjechać na pobocze**

pull off (sth) (used about a vehicle or its driver) to leave the road in order to stop for a short time ▶ **zjeżdżać** (*np. z drogi na parking*)

pull sth off (informal) to succeed in sth: *to pull off a business deal* zrobić dobry interes ▶ **dokonać czegoś**

pull out (used about a car, etc.) to move away from the side of the road: *I braked as a car suddenly pulled out in front of me.* ▶ **włączać się do ruchu**
pull out (of sth) (used about a train) to leave a station ▶ **odjeżdżać (ze stacji)**
pull (sb/sth) out (of sth) (to cause sb/sth) to leave sth: *The Americans have pulled their forces out of the area.* ◇ *We've pulled out of the deal.* ▶ **wycofywać (kogoś/się/coś) (skądś)**
pull sth out to take sth out of a place suddenly or with force: *She walked into the bank and pulled out a gun.* ▶ **wyciągać/wyszarpywać coś**
pull over (used about a vehicle or its driver) to slow down and move to the side of the road: *I pulled over to let the ambulance past.* ▶ **zmniejszyć prędkość i zjechać na bok**
pull through (sth) to survive a dangerous illness or a difficult time ▶ **wyzdrowieć** (*z choroby*); **przetrwać** (*trudny okres*)
pull together to do sth or work together with other people in an organized way and without fighting ▶ **współdziałać**
pull yourself together to control your feelings and behave in a calm way: *Pull yourself together and stop crying.* ▶ **opanowywać się**
pull up (to cause a car, etc.) to stop ▶ **zatrzymać pojazd, zahamować**

pull² /pʊl/ noun **1** [C] **a pull (at/on sth)** the act of moving sb/sth towards you using force: *I gave a pull on the rope to check it was secure.* ▶ **pociągnięcie, szarpnięcie 2** [sing.] a physical force or an attraction that makes sb/sth move in a particular direction: *the earth's gravitational pull* ◇ *He couldn't resist the pull of the city.* ▶ **przyciąganie, siła przyciągania 3** [sing.] the act of taking a breath of smoke from a cigarette: *He took a long pull on his cigarette.* Mocno zaciągnął się papierosem. ▶ **zaciąganie się**

'pull-down adj. **1** designed to be used by being pulled down ▶ **opuszczany 2** (**pull-down menu**) a list of possible choices that appears on a computer screen below a menu title ▶ (*komput.*) **menu rozwijane**

pulley /'pʊli/ noun [C] a piece of equipment, consisting of a wheel and a rope, that is used for lifting heavy things ▶ **blok**

pullover /'pʊləʊvə(r)/ noun [C] a knitted piece of clothing for the upper part of the body, made of wool, with long sleeves and no buttons ▶ **pulower** ➲ note at **sweater**

'pull tab (US) = RING PULL

pulmonary /'pʌlmənəri; US -neri/ adj. [only before a noun] connected with the lungs: *pulmonary disease* ◇ *the pulmonary artery* ▶ **płucny**

pulp /pʌlp/ noun **1** [sing., U] a soft substance that is made especially by crushing sth: *Mash the beans to a pulp.* ▶ **papka 2** [U] the soft inner part of some fruits or vegetables ▶ **miąższ 3** [U] a soft substance made from wood that is used for making paper ▶ **masa celulozowa**

pulpit /'pʊlpɪt/ noun [C] a raised platform in a church where the priest stands when they are speaking ▶ **ambona**

pulsate /pʌl'seɪt; US 'pʌlseɪt/ verb [I] to move or shake with strong regular movements: *a pulsating rhythm* ▶ **pulsować**

pulse¹ /pʌls/ noun **1** [C, usually sing.] the regular beating in your body as blood is pushed around it by your heart. You can feel your **pulse** at your wrist, neck, etc.: *Your pulse rate increases after exercise.* ◇ *to feel/take sb's pulse* mierzyć komuś puls ▶ **puls 2** (**pulses**) [pl.] The seeds of some plants such as **beans** and **peas** that are cooked and eaten as food ▶ **nasiona jadalne niektórych roślin strączkowych**

pulse² /pʌls/ verb [I] to move with strong regular movements ▶ **posuwać się miarowo**

pulverize (also -ise) /'pʌlvəraɪz/ verb [T] **1** (formal) to crush sth into a fine powder ▶ **proszkować 2** (especially Brit., informal) to defeat or destroy sb/sth completely: *We pulverized the opposition.* ▶ (*przen.*) **zcierać na proch** SYN **crush**

pump¹ /pʌmp/ noun [C] **1** a machine that is used for forcing a gas or liquid in a particular direction: *Have you got a bicycle pump?* ◇ *a petrol pump* dystrybutor paliwa ▶ **pomp(k)a 2** [usually pl.] a flat woman's shoe with no fastening: *ballet pumps* baletki ▶ **czółenko 3** [C] (Brit.) = PLIMSOLL

pump² /pʌmp/ verb **1** [T] to force a gas or liquid to go in a particular direction: *Your heart pumps blood around your body.* ▶ **pompować 2** [I] (used about a liquid) to flow in a particular direction as if forced by a **pump**: *Blood was pumping out of the wound.* ▶ (*krew itp.*) **tryskać 3** [I,T] to be moved or to move sth very quickly up and down or in and out: *He pumped his arms up and down to keep warm.* ▶ **energicznie machać**
PHR V **pump sth into sth/sb** to put a lot of sth into sth/sb: *He pumped all his savings into the business.* ▶ (*przen.*) **władować**
pump sth up to fill sth with air, for example by using a **pump**: *to pump up a car tyre* ▶ **napompowywać**

'pump-action adj. (used about a machine or device) that you operate using a pumping action of your hand or arm: *a pump-action spray/shotgun* ▶ **na pomp(k)ę**

pumpkin /'pʌmpkɪn/ noun [C,U] a very large round fruit with thick orange skin that is cooked and eaten as a vegetable ▶ **dynia** ➲ picture on **page A13**

pun /pʌn/ noun [C] an amusing use of a word that can have two meanings or of different words that sound the same ▶ **kalambur**

P

punch¹ /pʌntʃ/ verb [T] **1 punch sb (in/on sth)** to hit sb/sth hard with your **fist**: *He punched Mike hard in the stomach and ran away.* ◇ *to punch somebody on the nose* ◇ *He punched the air when he heard the good news.* ▶ **uderzać pięścią** ➲ note at **hit 2** to make a hole in sth with a **punch²** (2): *He punched a hole in the ticket.* ▶ **dziurkować**

punch² /pʌntʃ/ noun **1** [C] a hard hit with your **fist**: *She gave him a hard punch on the arm.* ▶ **uderzenie pięścią 2** [C] a machine or tool that you use for making holes in sth: *a ticket punch* ◇ *a hole punch* ▶ **dziurkacz** ➲ picture at **stationery 3** [U] a drink made from wine, fruit juice and sugar ▶ **poncz**
IDM **pull (your) punches** → PULL¹

punchline /'pʌntʃlaɪn/ noun [C] the last and most important words of a joke or story ▶ **pointa**

'punch-up noun [C] (Brit., informal) a fight in which people hit each other ▶ **bijatyka**

punctual /'pʌŋktʃuəl/ adj. doing sth or happening at the right time; not late: *It is important to be punctual for your classes.* ▶ **punktualny** ⓘ Mówiąc np. o pociągu, zamiast słowa **punctual** używa się wyrażenia **on time**.
■ **punctuality** /ˌpʌŋktʃu'æləti/ noun [U]: *Japanese trains are famous for their punctuality.* ▶ **punktualność** | **punctually** /'pʌŋktʃuəli/ adv. ▶ **punktualnie**

punctuate /'pʌŋktʃueɪt/ verb **1** [T] **punctuate sth (with sth)** to interrupt sth many times: *Her speech was punctuated with bursts of applause.* ▶ **przerywać 2** [I,T] to divide writing into sentences and phrases by adding full stops, question marks, etc. ▶ **stawiać znaki przestankowe**

punctuation /ˌpʌŋktʃu'eɪʃn/ noun [U] the marks used for dividing writing into sentences and phrases: ***Punctuation marks** include full stops, commas and question marks.* ▶ **stawianie znaków przestankowych**

puncture /'pʌŋktʃə(r)/ noun [C] **1** a small hole made by a sharp point, especially in a bicycle or car tyre ▶ **przebi-**

cie (*np. opony/dętki*) **2** a bicycle or car tyre that has a hole in it ▶ **przebita opona/dętka**
■ **puncture** verb [I,T] ▶ **dziurawić, przebijać; pękać**

pungent /ˈpʌndʒənt/ adj. (used about a smell) very strong ▶ **ostry, gryzący**

punish /ˈpʌnɪʃ/ verb [T] **punish sb (for sth/for doing sth)** to make sb suffer because they have done sth bad or wrong: *The children were severely punished for telling lies.* ▶ **karać**

punishable /ˈpʌnɪʃəbl/ adj. **punishable (by sth)** (used about a crime, etc.) that you can be punished for doing: *a punishable offence* ◇ *In some countries drug smuggling is punishable by death.* ▶ **karalny**

punishing /ˈpʌnɪʃɪŋ/ adj. that makes you very tired or weak: *The Prime Minister had a punishing schedule, visiting five countries in five days.* ▶ **wyczerpujący**

punishment /ˈpʌnɪʃmənt/ noun [C,U] the action or way of punishing sb: *He was excluded from school for a week as a punishment.* ◇ *Do you have* ***capital punishment*** (karę śmierci) *in your country?* ▶ **ukaranie, kara**

punitive /ˈpjuːnətɪv/ adj. (formal) **1** intended as a punishment: *to take punitive measures against somebody* ▶ **karny 2** (used about taxes, etc.) very strict and unkind, and that people find difficult to pay: *punitive taxation* ▶ **karzący**

punk /pʌŋk/ noun **1** [U] a type of loud music that was popular in Britain in the late 1970s and early 1980s. **Punk** deliberately tried to offend people with traditional views and behaviour. ▶ **punk 2** [C] a person who likes **punk** music and often has brightly coloured hair and unusual clothes ▶ **punk**

punt /pʌnt/ noun [C] a long boat with a flat bottom and square ends which is moved by pushing the end of a long pole against the bottom of a river ▶ **łódka płaskodenna**
■ **punt** verb [I]: *We spent the day punting on the river.* ◇ *to go punting* ▶ **płynąć łódką płaskodenną**

puny /ˈpjuːni/ adj. (**punier**; **puniest**) very small and weak ▶ **słabowity, drobny**

pup /pʌp/ noun [C] **1** = PUPPY **2** the young of some animals: *a seal pup* ▶ **szczenię, małe** (*np. foki*)

pupil /ˈpjuːpl/ noun [C] **1** a child in school: *There are 28 pupils in my class.* ▶ **ucze-ń/nnica, wychowan-ek/ka** ➲ note at **school** ℹ Słowo **pupil** powoli wychodzi z użycia; coraz częściej używa się wyrazu **student**, szczególnie mówiąc o uczniach starszych klas. **2** a person who is taught artistic, musical, etc. skills by an expert: *He was a pupil of Liszt.* ▶ **ucze-ń/nnica 3** the round black hole in the middle of your eye ▶ **źrenica**

puppet /ˈpʌpɪt/ noun [C] **1** a model of a person or an animal that you can move by pulling the strings which are tied to it or by putting your hand inside it and moving your fingers ▶ **marionetka, kukiełka 2** a person or organization that is controlled by sb else: *The occupying forces set up a puppet government.* ▶ **marionetka**

puppy /ˈpʌpi/ (also **pup**) noun [C] (pl. **puppies**) a young dog ▶ **szczenię** ➲ note at **dog**

purchase /ˈpɜːtʃəs/ noun (formal) **1** [U] the act of buying sth: *to take out a loan for the purchase of a car* ▶ **zakup, nabywanie 2** [C] something that you buy: *These shoes were a poor purchase – they're falling apart already.* ◇ *to make a purchase* ▶ **zakup, nabytek**
■ **purchase** verb [T]: *Many employees have the opportunity to purchase shares in the company they work for.* ▶ **nabywać**

purchaser /ˈpɜːtʃəsə(r)/ noun [C] (formal) a person who buys sth: *The purchaser of the house agrees to pay a deposit of 10%.* ▶ **nabyw-ca/czyni** ➲ look at **vendor**

pure /pjʊə(r)/ adj. **1** not mixed with anything else: *pure orange juice/silk/alcohol* ▶ **czysty, bez domieszki 2** clean and not containing any harmful substances: *pure air/water* ▶ **czysty** OPP **impure 3** [only before a noun] complete and total: *We met by pure chance* (przez czysty przypadek). ▶ **całkowity, zupełny 4** not doing or knowing anything evil or anything that is connected with sex: *a young girl still pure in mind and body* ▶ **czysty, niewinny** OPP **impure 5** very clear; perfect: *She was dressed in pure white.* ▶ **czysty 6** [only before a noun] (used about an area of learning) concerned only with increasing your knowledge rather than having practical uses: *pure mathematics* ▶ **czysty** (*teoretyczny*) OPP **applied**

purée /ˈpjʊəreɪ; US pjʊəˈreɪ/ noun [C,U] a food that you make by cooking a fruit or vegetable and then pressing and mixing it until it is smooth and liquid: *apple/tomato purée* ▶ **purée** (*np. ziemniaczane*), **przecier**

purely /ˈpjʊəli/ adv. only or completely: *It's not purely a question of money.* ▶ **wyłącznie; całkowicie**

purgatory /ˈpɜːgətri; US -tɔːri/ noun [U] (usually **Purgatory**) (in Roman Catholic teaching) a place or state in which the souls of dead people suffer for the bad things they did when they were living, so that they can become pure enough to go to heaven ▶ **czyściec**

purge /pɜːdʒ/ verb [T] **purge sth (of sb)**; **purge sb (from sth)** to remove people that you do not want from a political party or other organization ▶ **przeprowadzać czystkę**
■ **purge** noun [C]: *The General carried out a purge of his political enemies.* ▶ **czystka**

purify /ˈpjʊərɪfaɪ/ verb [T] (**purifying**; **purifies**; pt, pp **purified**) to remove dirty or harmful substances from sth: *purified water* ▶ **oczyszczać**

purist /ˈpjʊərɪst/ noun [C] a person who thinks things should be done in the traditional way and who has strong opinions on what is correct in language, art, etc. ▶ **puryst(k)a**
■ **purism** /ˈpjʊərɪzəm/ noun [U] ▶ **puryzm**

puritan /ˈpjʊərɪtən/ noun [C] a person who thinks that it is wrong to enjoy yourself ▶ **purytan-in/ka**
■ **puritan** (also **puritanical** /ˌpjʊərɪˈtænɪkl/) adj.: *a puritan attitude to life* ▶ **purytański**

purity /ˈpjʊərəti/ noun [U] the state of being pure: *the purity of the water* ▶ **czystość** ➲ look at **impurity**

purl /pɜːl/ noun [U] a simple stitch used in knitting ▶ **oczko lewe**

purple /ˈpɜːpl/ adj. having the colour of blue and red mixed together: *His face was purple with rage.* ▶ **fioletowy, purpurowy**
■ **purple** noun [U] a reddish-blue colour ▶ **kolor fioletowy/purpurowy**

purport verb /pəˈpɔːt/ [T] (formal) to claim to be sth or to have done sth, when this may not be true: *The book does not purport to be a complete history of the period.* ▶ **utrzymywać; podawać się za kogoś** SYN **profess**

purpose /ˈpɜːpəs/ noun **1** [C] the aim or intention of sth: *The main purpose of this meeting is to decide what we should do next.* ◇ *You may only use the telephone for business purposes.* ▶ **cel, zamiar 2** (**purposes**) [pl.] what is needed in a particular situation: ***For the purposes of*** *this demonstration, I will use model cars.* ▶ **potrzeby, wymagania 3** [U] a meaning or reason that is important to you: *A good leader inspires people with a* ***sense of purpose*** (wzbudza w ludziach poczucie celu.) ▶ **cel 4** [U] the ability to plan sth and work hard to achieve it: *I was impressed by his* ***strength of purpose.*** ▶ **umiejętność dążenia do (wytkniętego) celu** ➲ look at **cross purposes**
IDM **on purpose** not by accident; with a particular intention: *'You've torn a page out of my book!' 'I'm sorry, I didn't do it on purpose.'* ▶ **celowo, umyślnie** SYN **deliberately**
to/for all intents and purposes → INTENT[2]

ˌ**purpose-ˈbuilt** adj. (Brit.) designed and built for a particular purpose ▶ **specjalnie przystosowany/wybudowany**

purposeful /ˈpɜːpəsfl/ adj. having a definite aim or plan: *Greg strode off down the street looking purposeful.* ▶ **zdecydowany, dążący do celu**
■ **purposefully** /-fəli/ adv. ▶ **zdecydowanie**

purposely /ˈpɜːpəsli/ adv. with a particular intention: *I purposely waited till everyone had gone so that I could speak to you in private.* ▶ **celowo, umyślnie** SYN **deliberately**

purr /pɜː(r)/ verb [I] (used about a cat) to make a continuous low sound that shows pleasure ▶ **mruczeć** ➲ look at **miaow**

purse¹ /pɜːs/ noun [C] **1** a small bag made of leather, etc., for carrying coins and often also paper money, used especially by women ▶ **portmonetka** ➲ look at **wallet** **2** (US) = HANDBAG

purse² /pɜːs/ verb
IDM **purse your lips** to press your lips together to show that you do not like sth: *He frowned and pursed his lips.* ▶ **zaciskać usta**

purser /ˈpɜːsə(r)/ noun [C] the person on a ship who looks after the accounts and who deals with passengers' problems ▶ **ochmistrz** (*na statku*)

⚷ **pursue** /pəˈsjuː; US -ˈsuː/ verb [T] (formal) **1** to try to achieve sth or to continue to do sth over a period of time: *to pursue a career in banking* mieć pracę w bankowości ◇ *She didn't seem to want to pursue the discussion so I changed the subject.* ◇ *The government is pursuing* (realizuje) *a policy of high taxes.* ▶ **dążyć do osiągnięcia czegoś; dalej prowadzić** **2** to follow sb/sth in order to catch them or it: *The robber ran off pursued by two policemen.* ▶ **ścigać** ⓘ **Pursue** jest słowem bardziej formalnym niż **chase**.

pursuer /pəˈsjuːə(r); US -ˈsuː-/ noun [C] a person who is following and trying to catch sb/sth ▶ **prześladow-ca/czyni**

pursuit /pəˈsjuːt; US -ˈsuːt/ noun **1** [U] the act of trying to achieve or get sth: *the pursuit of pleasure* ▶ **dążenie do osiągnięcia (czegoś), pogoń za kimś/czymś** **2** [C] an activity that you do either for work or for pleasure: *outdoor/leisure pursuits* ▶ **zajęcie, rozrywka**
IDM **in hot pursuit** → HOT¹
in pursuit (of sb/sth) trying to catch or get sb/sth: *He neglected his family in pursuit of his own personal ambitions.* ▶ **w pogoni (za kimś/czymś), na tropie (kogoś/czegoś)**

pus /pʌs/ noun [U] a thick yellowish liquid that may form in a part of your body that has been hurt ▶ **ropa**

⚷ **push¹** /pʊʃ/ verb **1** [I,T] to use force to move sb/sth forward or away from you: *She pushed him into the water.* ◇ *to push a pram* ◇ *She pushed the door shut with her foot.* Zamknęła drzwi, pchnąwszy je nogą. ▶ **pchać** **2** [I,T] to move forward by pushing sb/sth: *John pushed his way through the crowd.* ◇ *to push past somebody* ◇ *People were* ***pushing and shoving*** *to try to get to the front.* ▶ **przepychać się** **3** [I,T] to press a switch, button, etc., for example in order to start a machine: *Push the red button if you want the bus to stop.* ▶ **naciskać, przyciskać** **4** [T] **push sb (to do sth /into doing sth)**; **push sb (for sth)** to try to make sb do sth that they do not want to do: *My friend pushed me into entering the competition.* ◇ *Ella will not work hard unless you push her.* ▶ **przyciskać, wywierać nacisk** **5** [T] (informal) to try to make sth seem attractive, for example so that people will buy it: *They are launching a major publicity campaign to push their new product.* ▶ **forsować**
IDM **be hard pressed/pushed/put to do sth** → HARD²
be pushed for sth (informal) to not have enough of sth: *Hurry up. We're really* ***pushed for time*** (naprawdę nie mamy czasu). ▶ **dotkliwie odczuwać brak** (*np. czasu, pieniędzy*)
push your luck; **push it/things** (informal) to take a risk because you have successfully avoided problems in the past: *You didn't get caught last time, but don't push your luck!* ▶ **kusić los**
PHR V **push sb about/around** to give orders to sb in a rude and unpleasant way: *Don't let your boss push you around.* ▶ **pomiatać kimś**
push ahead/forward (with sth) to continue with sth ▶ **posuwać się, kontynuować**
push for sth to try hard to get sth: *Jim is pushing for a pay rise.* ▶ **usilnie zabiegać o coś**
push in to join a line of people waiting for sth by standing in front of others who were there before you ▶ **wpychać się bez kolejki**
push on to continue a journey: *Although it was getting dark, we decided to push on.* ▶ **jechać dalej**
push sb/sth over to make sb/sth fall down by pushing them or it ▶ **przewracać kogoś/coś**

⚷ **push²** /pʊʃ/ noun [C] an act of pushing: *Can you help me give the car* ***a push*** *to get it started* (popchnąć samochód, żeby zapalił)*?* ◇ *Paul gave the door a push* (popchnął drzwi). ◇ *The car windows opened at the push of a button* (za naciśnięciem guzika). ▶ **pchnięcie, nacisk**
IDM **at a push** (informal) if it is really necessary (but only with difficulty): *We can get ten people round the table at a push.* ▶ **na siłę**
give sb the push (Brit., informal) to tell sb you no longer want them in a relationship, or in a job ▶ **rozstawać się z kimś; wywalać kogoś z posady**

ˈ**push-button** adj. [only before a noun] (used about a machine, etc.) that you work by pressing a button: *a radio with push-button controls* radio ze strojeniem na przyciski ▶ **działający przez naciśnięcie przycisku/klawisza**

pushchair /ˈpʊʃtʃeə(r)/ (Brit. also **buggy** /ˈbʌɡi/, pl. **buggies**; US **stroller** /ˈstrəʊlə(r)/) noun [C] a chair on wheels that you use for pushing a young child in ▶ **składany wózek dziecinny** ➲ picture at **pram**

pusher /ˈpʊʃə(r)/ noun [C] a person who sells illegal drugs ▶ **handla-rz/rka narkotykami**

pushover /ˈpʊʃəʊvə(r)/ noun [C] (informal) **1** something that is easy to do or win ▶ **łatwizna** **2** a person who is easy to persuade to do sth ▶ **mięczak**

ˈ**push-up** (US) = PRESS-UP

pushy /ˈpʊʃi/ adj. (**pushier**; **pushiest**) (informal) (used about a person) trying hard to get what you want, in a way that seems rude: *You need to be pushy to be successful in show business.* ▶ **rozpychający się łokciami, przebojowy**

puss /pʊs/ noun [C] (used when you are speaking to or calling a cat) ▶ **kici** (*wołanie kota*)

⚷ **put** /pʊt/ verb [T] (**putting**; pt, pp **put**) **1** to move sb/sth into a particular place or position: *She put the book on the table.* ◇ *Did you put sugar in my tea?* ◇ *When do you put the children to bed?* ▶ **kłaść, stawiać, umieszczać** **2** to fix sth to or in sth else: *We're going to put a picture on this wall.* ◇ *Can you put* (przyszyć) *a button on this shirt?* ▶ **przymocowywać, przytwierdzać** **3** to write sth: *12.30 on Friday? I'll put it in my diary.* ◇ *What did you put for question 2?* ▶ **notować, zapisywać** **4** **put sb/sth in/into sth** to bring sb/sth into the state or condition mentioned: *This sort of weather always puts me in a bad mood.* ◇ *I was* ***put in charge*** *of the project.* Powierzono mi odpowiedzialność za projekt. ◇ *It was time to* ***put*** *our ideas* ***into practice*** (sprawdzić nasze pomysły w praktyce). ◇ *I've tried to* ***put the matter into perspective*** (spojrzeć na tę kwestię w szerszym kontekście). ▶ **wprowadzać kogoś/coś w coś, stawiać kogoś w jakimś położeniu** **5** to make sb/sth feel sth or be affected by sth: *This will* ***put pressure on*** *them* (wywrze na nich presję) *to finish the job quickly.* ◇ *Don't* ***put the blame***

P

on** me!* Nie obwiniaj mnie! ◇ *The new teacher soon **put a stop (położył kres) ***to** cheating in tests.* **6** to give or fix a particular value or importance to sb/sth: *We'll have to **put a limit on** how much we spend.* ◇ *I'd put him in my* (zaliczyłbym go do moich) *top five favourite writers.* ▶ **ustanawiać 7** to say or express sth: *I don't know exactly how to put this, but...* ◇ ***Put simply**, he just wasn't good enough.* ◇ ***To put it another way*** (innymi słowy)*, you're sacked.* ◇ *I'd like to **put a question*** (zadać pytanie) ***to** the minister.* ◇ *Can I **put a suggestion to** you?* Czy mogę ci przedstawić swoją sugestię? ◇ *She had never tried to **put** this feeling **into words**.* ▶ **wyrażać, formułować**

IDM **put it to sb that...** (formal) to suggest to sb that sth is true: *I put it to you that this man is innocent.* ▶ **poddawać komuś myśl**

ℹ **Put** używa się w innych idiomach, np. **put an end to sth**. Zob. hasła odpowiednich rzeczow-ników, przymiotników itp.

PHR V **put sth/yourself across/over (to sb)** to say what you want to say clearly, so that people can understand it: *He didn't put his ideas across very well at the meeting.* ▶ **wyrażać (się) jasno**

put sth aside 1 to save sth, especially money, to use later ▶ **odkładać coś 2** to ignore or forget sth: *We agreed to put aside our differences and work together.* ▶ **odkładać/pomijać coś**

put sb away (informal) to send sb to prison ▶ **wsadzać kogoś do paki**

put sth away 1 to put sth where you usually keep it because you have finished using it: *Put the tools away if you've finished with them.* ▶ **schować coś** (*na miejsce*), **uprzątać 2** to save money to spend later: *She puts part of her wages away in the bank every week.* ▶ **odkładać** (*pieniądze*)

put sth back 1 to return sth to its place: *to put books back on the shelf* ▶ **kłaść coś z powrotem 2** to move sth to a later time: *The meeting's been put back until next week.* ▶ **odkładać coś** OPP **bring sth forward 3** to change the time shown on a clock to an earlier time: *We have to put the clocks back tonight.* ▶ **cofać** (*wskazówki zegara*) OPP **put sth forward**

put sb/sth before/above sb/sth to treat sb/sth as more important than sb/sth else: *He puts his children before anything else.* ▶ **przedkładać kogoś/coś nad kogoś/coś, stawiać kogoś/coś ponad kogoś/coś**

put sth behind you to try to forget about an unpleasant experience and think about the future ▶ **zapominać o czymś przykrym**

put sth by to save money to use later: *Her grandparents had put some money by for her wedding.* ▶ **odkładać** (*pieniądze*)

put sb down (informal) to say things to make sb seem stupid or silly: *He's always putting his wife down.* ▶ **ośmieszać/upokarzać kogoś**

put sth down 1 to stop holding sth and put it on the floor, a table, etc.: *The policeman persuaded him to put the gun down.* ▶ **kłaść coś 2** to write sth: *I'll put that down in my diary.* ▶ **zapisywać coś 3** to pay part of the cost of sth: *We put down a 10% deposit on a car.* ▶ **wpłacać** (*część należnej kwoty*) **4** (used about a government, an army or the police) to stop sth by force: *to put down a rebellion* ▶ **tłumić coś 5** to kill an animal because it is old, sick or dangerous: *The dog was put down after it attacked a child.* ▶ **usypiać** (*zwierzę*) **6** to put a baby to bed ▶ **kłaść** (*dziecko*) **spać**

put sth down to sth to believe that sth is caused by sth: *I put his bad exam results down to laziness rather than a lack of ability.* ▶ **przypisywać coś czemuś**

put yourself/sb forward to suggest that you or another person should be considered for a job, etc.: *His name was put forward for the position of chairman.* ▶ **wysuwać** (*np. czyjąś kandydaturę*)

put sth forward 1 to change the time shown on a clock to a later time: *We put the clocks forward in spring.* ▶ **posuwać naprzód** (*wskazówki zegara*) OPP **put sth back 2** to suggest sth: *She put forward a plan to help the homeless.* ▶ **wysuwać coś**

put sth in 1 to fix equipment or furniture in position so that it can be used: *We're having a shower put in.* ▶ **wstawiać coś, instalować** (*np. mebel*) SYN **install 2** to include a piece of information, etc. in sth that you write: *In your letter, you forgot to put in* (wpisać) *the time your plane would arrive.* ▶ **dołączać, wtrącać 3** to ask for sth officially: *to put in a request* ◇ *to put in an invoice* wystawić fakturę ▶ **zwracać się z (oficjalną) prośbą**

put sth in; put sth into sth/into doing sth to spend time, etc. on sth: *She puts all her time and energy into her business.* ▶ **wkładać w coś czas/energię**

put sb off (sb/sth/doing sth) 1 to say to a person that you can no longer do what you had agreed: *They were coming to stay last weekend but I had to put them off at the last moment.* ▶ **odwołać** (*np. czyjąś wizytę*), **zbywać kogoś 2** to make sb not like sb/sth or not want to do sth: *The accident put me off driving for a long time.* ▶ **zniechęcać kogoś (do kogoś) 3** to make sb unable to give their attention to sth: *Don't stare at me – you're putting me off!* ▶ **rozpraszać kogoś**

put sth off to turn or switch a light off: *She put off the light and went to sleep.* ▶ **gasić coś**

put sth off; put off doing sth to move sth to a later time: *She put off writing her essay until the last minute.* ▶ **przesuwać coś** (*na inny termin*), **odkładać coś** SYN **delay**

put sth on 1 to dress yourself in sth: *Put on your coat!* ◇ *I'll have to put my glasses on.* ▶ **wkładać/nakładać** *ubranie* **(na siebie)** OPP **take sth off 2** to cover an area of your skin with sth: *You'd better put some sun cream on.* ▶ **nakładać coś 3** to switch on a piece of electrical equipment: *It's too early to put the lights on yet.* ▶ **włączać coś 4** to make a tape, a CD, etc. begin to play: *Let's put some music on.* ▶ **puszczać** (*np. kasetę, płytę*) **5** to become fatter or heavier: *I **put on weight** very easily.* ▶ **przybierać na wadze** OPP **lose 6** to organize or prepare sth for people to see or use: *The school is putting on* (wystawia) *'Macbeth'.* ◇ *They put on extra trains* (wprowadzono do rozkładu dodatkowe pociągi) *in the summer.* ▶ **organizować coś 7** to pretend to be feeling sth; to pretend to have sth: *He's not angry with you really: he's just putting it on.* ▶ **udawać coś**

put sth on sth 1 to add an amount of money, etc. to the cost or value of sth: *The government want to put more tax on the price of a packet of cigarettes.* ▶ **nakładać** (*np. dodatkowe opłaty*) **2** to bet money on sth: *He put £10 on a horse.* ▶ **stawiać coś na coś** SYN **bet**

put sb out 1 to give sb trouble or extra work: *He put his hosts out by arriving very late.* ▶ **przysparzać komuś kłopotu** SYN **inconvenience 2** to make sb upset or angry: *I was quite put out by their selfish behaviour.* ▶ **irytować kogoś, wyprowadzać kogoś z równowagi**

put sth out 1 to take sth out of your house and leave it: *to put the rubbish out* ▶ **wynosić/wystawiać coś 2** to make sth stop burning: *to put out a fire* ▶ **gasić** (*ogień*) SYN **extinguish 3** to switch off a piece of electrical equipment: *They put out the lights and locked the door.* ▶ **gasić** (*np. światło*) **4** to give or tell the public sth, often on the TV or radio or in newspapers: *The police put out a warning about the escaped prisoner.* ▶ **ogłaszać coś**

put yourself out (for sb) (informal) to do sth for sb, even though it brings you trouble or extra work: *'I'll give you a lift home.' 'I don't want you to put yourself out* (nie chcę ci sprawiać kłopotu)*. I'll take a taxi.'* ▶ **zadawać sobie trud (dla kogoś)**

put sth/yourself over (to sb) = PUT STH/YOURSELF ACROSS/OVER (TO SB)
put sb through sth to make sb experience sth unpleasant ▶ **zgotować coś komuś**
put sb/sth through (to sb/...) to make a telephone connection that allows sb to speak to sb: *Could you put me through to Jeanne, please?* ▶ **łączyć kogoś/coś (telefonicznie) (z kimś)**
put sth to sb to suggest sth to sb; to ask sb sth: *I put the question to her.* ▶ **zadawać komuś** (*np. pytanie*), **sugerować komuś coś**
put sth together to make or prepare sth by fitting or collecting parts together: *to put together a model plane/an essay/a meal* ◇ *I think we can put together a very strong case* (zebrać mocne argumenty) *for the defence.* ▶ **składać coś**, **komponować** (*zestaw potraw*) ➲ note at **build**
put sth towards sth to give money to pay part of the cost of sth: *We all put a pound towards a leaving present for Joe.* ▶ **dawać pieniądze na jakiś cel**
put sb up to give sb food and a place to stay: *She had missed the last train home, so I offered to put her up for the night.* ▶ **przyjąć kogoś na nocleg**
put sth up 1 to lift or hold sth up: *Put your hand up if you know the answer.* ▶ **podnosić coś 2** to build sth: *to put up a fence/tent* ▶ **stawiać coś 3** to fix sth to a wall, etc. so that everyone can see it: *to put up a notice* ▶ **wieszać** (*np. ogłoszenie*) **4** to increase sth: *Some shops put up their prices just before Christmas.* ▶ **podnosić coś**
put up sth to try to stop sb attacking you: *The old lady put up a struggle against her attacker.* ▶ **stawiać** (*opór*)
put up with sb/sth to suffer sb/sth unpleasant and not complain about it: *I don't know how they put up with this noise.* ▶ **znosić kogoś/coś**

putrid /ˈpjuːtrɪd/ adj. (used about dead animals or plants) smelling very bad: *the putrid smell of rotten meat* ▶ **cuchnący** (*zwł. ze zgnilizny*) SYN **foul**

putt /pʌt/ verb [I,T] (in the sport of **golf**) to hit the ball gently when it is near the hole ▶ **lekko uderzać piłkę golfową, kiedy znajduje się blisko dołka**

putter (US) = POTTER[1]

putty /ˈpʌti/ noun [U] a soft substance that is used for fixing glass into windows that becomes hard when dry ▶ **kit** (*szklarski*)

puzzle¹ /ˈpʌzl/ noun [C] **1** a game or toy that makes you think a lot: *I like to* ***do puzzles.*** ◇ *to do a crossword puzzle* (krzyżówkę) ◇ *a jigsaw puzzle* układanka ▶ **łamigłówka**, **zagadka 2** [usually sing.] something that is difficult to understand or explain: *The reasons for his actions have remained a puzzle to historians.* ▶ **zagadka** SYN **mystery**

puzzle² /ˈpʌzl/ verb [T] to make sb feel confused because they do not understand sth: *Her strange illness puzzled all the experts.* ▶ **intrygować**, **wprawiać w zakłopotanie**
PHR V **puzzle over/about sth** to think hard about sth in order to understand or explain it: *to puzzle over a mathematical problem* ▶ **głowić się nad czymś**
puzzle sth out to find the answer to sth by thinking hard: *The letter was in Italian and it took us an hour to puzzle out what it said.* ▶ **rozwiązywać** (*np. zagadkę*), **odcyfrowywać** (*np. pismo, list*)

puzzled /ˈpʌzld/ adj. not able to understand or explain sth: *a puzzled expression* ▶ **zakłopotany**

PVC /ˌpiː viː ˈsiː/ noun [U] a strong plastic material used to make a wide variety of products, such as clothing, pipes, floor coverings, etc. ▶ **PCW**

pyjamas (US **pajamas**) /pəˈdʒɑːməz; US -ˈdʒæm-/ noun [pl.] loose trousers and a loose shirt that you wear in bed ▶ **piżama** ⓘ Zwróć uwagę, że przed innym rzeczownikiem słowa **pyjama** używa się bez **s**: *pyjama trousers.* ➲ picture on **page A1**

pylon /ˈpaɪlən/ noun [C] a tall metal tower that supports heavy electrical wires ▶ **słup** (*sieci elektrycznej*)

pyramid /ˈpɪrəmɪd/ noun [C] a shape with a flat base and three or four sides in the shape of triangles ▶ **piramida**, **ostrosłup**

python /ˈpaɪθən; US -θɑːn/ noun [C] a large snake that kills animals by squeezing them very hard ▶ **pyton**

Q q

Q, q /kjuː/ noun [C,U] (pl. **Qs**; **qs**; **Q's**; **q's** /kjuːz/) the 17th letter of the English alphabet: *'Queen' begins with (a) 'Q'.* ▶ **litera** *q*

Q = QUESTION¹ (1): *Qs 1-5 are compulsory.*

qt = QUART

quack /kwæk/ noun [C] the sound made by a **duck** ▶ **kwakanie**
■ **quack** verb [I] ▶ **kwakać** ➲ note at **duck**

quad bike /ˈkwɒd baɪk/ (US ˌ**four-ˈwheeler**) noun [C] a motorbike with four large wheels, used for riding over rough ground, often for fun ▶ **czterokołowiec**

quadrangle /ˈkwɒdræŋgl/ (also **quad**) noun [C] a square open area with buildings round it in a school, college, etc. ▶ **dziedziniec**

quadruple /kwɒˈdruːpl/ verb [I,T] to multiply or be multiplied by four ▶ **powiększać (się) czterokrotnie**; **mnożyć przez cztery**

quail /kweɪl/ noun [C] (pl. **quail** or **quails**) a small brown bird whose flesh and eggs are eaten as food ▶ **przepiórka**

quaint /kweɪnt/ adj. attractive or unusual because it seems to belong to the past ▶ **osobliwy**, **staroświecki**

quake /kweɪk/ verb [I] (used about a person) to shake: *to quake with fear* ▶ **trząść się**, **drżeć**
■ **quake** noun [C] (informal) = EARTHQUAKE

qualification /ˌkwɒlɪfɪˈkeɪʃn/ noun **1** [C] an exam that you have passed or a course of study that you have completed: *to* ***have a*** *teaching/nursing* ***qualification*** ◇ *She left school at 16 with no formal qualifications.* ▶ **kwalifikacje** ➲ note at **degree 2** [C] a skill or quality that you need to do a particular job: *Is there a height qualification for the police force?* ▶ **wymóg 3** [C,U] something that limits the meaning of a general statement or makes it weaker: *I can recommend him for the job* ***without qualification.*** ◇ *She accepted the proposal with only a few qualifications.* ▶ **zastrzeżenie 4** [U] the fact of doing what is necessary in order to be able to do a job, play in a competition, etc.: *A victory in this game will earn them qualification* (pozwoli im zakwalifikować się) *for the World Cup.* ▶ **kwalifikacja**

qualified /ˈkwɒlɪfaɪd/ adj. **1 qualified (for sth/to do sth)** having passed an exam or having the knowledge, experience, etc. in order to be able to do sth: *Duncan is well qualified for this job.* ◇ *a fully qualified doctor* ◇ *I don't feel qualified* (nie czuję się kompetentny) *to comment – I know nothing about the subject.* ▶ **wykwalifikowany**, **dyplomowany** OPP **unqualified 2** not complete; limited: *My boss gave only qualified approval to the plan.* ▶ **ograniczony**, **częściowy**

qualify /ˈkwɒlɪfaɪ/ verb (**qualifying**; **qualifies**; pt, pp **qualified**) **1** [I] **qualify (as sth)** to pass the examination that is necessary to do a particular job; to have the qualities that are necessary for sth: *It takes five years to qualify as a vet.* ◇ *A cup of coffee and a sandwich doesn't really* *qualify as a meal.* ▶ **zdobywać kwalifikacje**; **stanowić** **2** [I,T] **qualify (sb) (for sth/to do sth)** to have or give sb the right to have or do sth; to give sb the right to do a particular job: *This exam will qualify me* (da mi uprawnienia) *to teach music.* ◇ *How many years must you work to qualify for a pension?* Ile lat trzeba przepracować, aby móc ubiegać się o emeryturę? ◇ *Residence in this country does not qualify you to vote.* ▶ **otrzymywać prawa**; **nadawać prawa**, **dawać kwalifikacje** **3** [I] **qualify (for sth)** to win the right to enter a competition or continue to the next part: *Our team has qualified for the final.* ▶ **zakwalifikować się** (*np. do finału*) **4** [T] to limit the meaning of a general statement or make it weaker: *I must qualify what I said earlier – it wasn't quite true.* ▶ **łagodzić**, **osłabiać** (*np. twierdzenie*)

qualitative /ˈkwɒlɪtətɪv; US -teɪt-/ adj. connected with how good sth is, rather than with how much of it there is: *qualitative analysis/research* ▶ **jakościowy** ➲ look at **quantitative**

⚷ **quality** /ˈkwɒləti/ noun (pl. **qualities**) **1** [U, sing.] how good or bad sth is: *This paper isn't very good quality.* ◇ *to be of good/poor/top quality* ◇ *goods of a high quality* ◇ *high-quality goods* ◇ *the* ***quality of life*** *in our cities* ▶ **jakość**, **gatunek** **2** [U] a high standard or level: *Aim for quality rather than quantity in your writing.* ▶ **wysoka jakość**, **wysoki poziom** **3** [C] something that is typical of a person or thing: *Vicky has all the qualities of a good manager.* ▶ **cecha**, **przymiot**

qualm /kwɑːm/ noun [C, usually pl.] a feeling of doubt or worry that what you are doing may not be morally right: *I don't* ***have*** *any* ***qualms about*** *asking them to lend us some money.* ▶ **skrupuły**, **wyrzuty sumienia**

quandary /ˈkwɒndəri/ noun [C, usually sing.] a state of not being able to decide what to do; a difficult situation: *I'm* ***in a quandary*** *– should I ask her or not?* ◇ *to be in a quandary* być w kropce ▶ **dylemat**

quantify /ˈkwɒntɪfaɪ/ verb [T] (**quantifying**; **quantifies**; pt, pp **quantified**) to describe or express sth as an amount or a number: *The risks to health are impossible to quantify.* ▶ **mierzyć**, **obliczać**

quantitative /ˈkwɒntɪtətɪv; US -teɪt-/ adj. connected with the amount or number of sth rather than with how good it is: *quantitative research* ▶ **ilościowy** ➲ look at **qualitative**

⚷ **quantity** /ˈkwɒntəti/ noun [C,U] (pl. **quantities**) **1** a number or an amount of sth: *Add a small quantity of salt.* ◇ *It's cheaper to buy goods* ***in large quantities.*** ▶ **ilość** **2** a large number or amount of sth: *It's usually cheaper to buy goods* ***in quantity*** (w dużej ilości). ▶ **ilość**
IDM **an unknown quantity** → UNKNOWN[1]

quarantine /ˈkwɒrəntiːn/ noun [U] a period of time when a person or an animal that has or may have an infectious disease must be kept away from other people or animals ▶ **kwarantanna**

quarrel¹ /ˈkwɒrəl/ noun [C] **1 a quarrel (about/over sth)** an angry argument or disagreement: *We sometimes* ***have a quarrel*** *about who should do the washing-up.* ▶ **kłótnia**, **sprzeczka** ➲ note at **argument** ➲ look at **fight** **2 a quarrel with sb/sth** a reason for complaining about or disagreeing with sb/sth: *I have no quarrel with what has just been said.* ▶ **coś do zarzucenia**

quarrel² /ˈkwɒrəl/ verb [I] (**quarrelling**; **quarrelled**; US **quarreling**; **quarreled**) **1 quarrel (with sb) (about/over sth)** to have an angry argument or disagreement: *The children are always quarrelling!* ◇ *I don't want to quarrel with you about it.* ▶ **kłócić się** ➲ look at **argue**, **fight¹** **2 quarrel with sth** to disagree with sth ▶ **zaprzeczać czemuś**, **nie zgadzać się (z czymś)**

quarrelsome /ˈkwɒrəlsəm/ adj. (used about a person) liking to argue with other people ▶ **kłótliwy** **SYN** **argumentative**

quarry¹ /ˈkwɒri/ noun (pl. **quarries**) **1** [C] a place where sand, stone, etc. is dug out of the ground ▶ **kamieniołom**, **kopalnia odkrywkowa** ➲ look at **mine** **2** [sing.] a person or an animal that is being hunted ▶ **ofiara nagonki**, **zwierzyna łowna**

quarry² /ˈkwɒri/ verb [I,T] (**quarrying**; **quarries**; pt, pp **quarried**) to dig, stone, sand, etc. out of the ground: *to quarry for marble* ▶ **eksploatować kamieniołom**, **wydobywać z kopalni odkrywkowej**

quart /kwɔːt/ noun [C] (abbr. **qt**) a measure of liquid; 1.14 litres ▶ **kwarta**

> There are 2 **pints** in a quart. An American quart is 0.94 of a litre.

⚷ **quarter** /ˈkwɔːtə(r)/ noun **1** [C] one of four equal parts of sth: *The programme lasts for three quarters of an hour.* ◇ *a mile and a quarter* ◇ *to cut an apple into quarters* ▶ **ćwiartka**, **ćwierć** **2** [sing.] 15 minutes before or after every hour: *I'll meet you at* ***(a) quarter past*** *six.* ◇ *It's* ***(a) quarter to*** *three.* ▶ **kwadrans** ⓘ W Amer. ang. mówi się **(a) quarter after** i **(a) quarter of**: *I'll meet you at (a) quarter after six.* ◇ *It's (a) quarter of three.* **3** [C] a period of three months: *You get a gas bill every quarter.* ▶ **kwartał** **4** [C] a part of a town, especially a part where a particular group of people live: *the Chinese quarter of the city* ▶ **dzielnica** **5** [C] a person or group of people who may give help or information or who have certain opinions: *Jim's parents haven't got much money so he can't expect any help from that quarter.* ▶ **strona**, **sfera** **6** [C] (in the US or Canada) a coin that is worth 25 cents (¼ dollar) ▶ **moneta 25-centowa** **7** (**quarters**) [pl.] a place that is provided for people, especially soldiers, to live in: *married quarters* kwatery dla żonatych ▶ **kwatery** **8** [C] four **ounces** of sth; ¼ of a pound: *a quarter of mushrooms* ▶ **ćwierć funta**
IDM **at close quarters** → CLOSE[3]

ˌquarter-ˈfinal noun [C] one of the four matches between the eight players or teams left in a competition ▶ **ćwierćfinał** ➲ look at **semi-final**

quarterly /ˈkwɔːtəli/ adj. (produced or happening) once every three months: *a quarterly magazine* ▶ **kwartalny** ■ **quarterly** adv.: *The committee meets quarterly.* ▶ **kwartalnie**

ˈquarter note (US) = CROTCHET

quartet /kwɔːˈtet/ noun [C] **1** four people who sing or play music together ▶ **kwartet** **2** a piece of music for four people to sing or play together ▶ **kwartet**

quartz /kwɔːts/ noun [U] a type of hard rock that is used in making very accurate clocks or watches ▶ **kwarc**

quash /kwɒʃ/ verb [T] (formal) **1** to say that an official decision is no longer true or legal ▶ **unieważniać** **2** to stop or defeat sth by force: *to quash a rebellion* ▶ **tłumić**, **dławić**

quaver¹ /ˈkweɪvə(r)/ verb [I] if sb's voice **quavers**, it shakes, usually because the person is nervous or afraid: *'I'm not safe here, am I?' she asked in a quavering voice.* ▶ (*o głosie*) **drżeć**

quaver² /ˈkweɪvə(r)/ (US ˈ**eighth note**) noun [C] (used in music) a note that lasts half as long as a crotchet ▶ **ósemka** ➲ picture at **music**

quay /kiː/ noun [C] a platform where goods and passengers are loaded on and off boats ▶ **nabrzeże**, **molo**

quayside /ˈkiːsaɪd/ noun [sing.] the area of land that is near a **quay** ▶ **teren koło nabrzeża**

queasy /ˈkwiːzi/ adj. feeling sick; wanting to **vomit** ▶ **przyprawiający o mdłości**

queen /kwiːn/ noun [C] **1** (also **Queen**) the female ruler of a country: *the queen mother* królowa matka ▶ **królowa** ℹ **Queen Elizabeth II** wymawia się **Queen Elizabeth the Second.** ➲ look at **king**, **prince**, **princess** **2** (also **Queen**) the wife of a king ▶ **królowa** **3** (in the game of **chess**) the most powerful piece, that can move any distance and in all directions ▶ **hetman**, **królowa** **4** one of the four playing cards in a pack with a picture of a queen: *the queen of hearts* ▶ **dama** ➲ note at **card** **5** the largest and most important female in a group of insects: *the queen bee* ▶ **królowa** (*np. pszczół*)

queer /kwɪə(r)/ adj. **1** (old-fashioned) strange or unusual: *She had a queer feeling that she was being watched.* ▶ **dziwaczny**, **dziwny** SYN **odd** **2** (taboo, slang) homosexual ▶ **homoseksualny** ➲ look at **gay**

■ **queer** noun [C] (taboo, slang) a homosexual man ▶ **ciota**, **pedał** ℹ **Queer** (przymiotnik i rzeczownik) używa się często w obraźliwy sposób, ale niektórzy homoseksualiści sami nazywają się tak.

quell /kwel/ verb [T] (formal) to end sth ▶ **tłumić**, **dławić**

quench /kwentʃ/ verb [T] **quench your thirst** to drink so that you no longer feel thirsty ▶ **gasić pragnienie**

query /ˈkwɪəri/ noun [C] (pl. **queries**) a question, especially one asking for information or expressing a doubt about sth: *Does anyone have any queries?* ▶ **pytanie**

■ **query** verb [T] (**querying**; **queries**; pt, pp **queried**): *We queried the bill but were told it was correct.* ▶ **zadać pytanie**

quest /kwest/ noun [C] (formal) a long search for sth that is difficult to find: *the quest for happiness/knowledge/truth* ▶ **poszukiwanie**

question[1] /ˈkwestʃən/ noun **1** [C] (abbr. **q**) **a question (about/on sth)** a sentence or phrase that asks for an answer: *Put up your hand if you want to* ***ask a question.*** ◇ *In the examination, you must* ***answer*** *five* ***questions*** *in one hour.* ◇ *What's the answer to Question 5?* ▶ **pytanie** **2** [C] a problem or difficulty that needs to be discussed or dealt with: *The resignations* ***raise the question*** *of who will take over.* ◇ ***The question is,*** *how are we going to raise the money?* ▶ **kwestia**, **sprawa** **3** [U] doubt or confusion about sth: *There is no question about Brenda's enthusiasm for the job.* ◇ *His honesty is* ***beyond question.*** ◇ *The results of the report were accepted* ***without question.*** ▶ **wątpliwość**, **zastrzeżenie**

IDM **in question** that is being considered or talked about: *The lawyer asked where she was on the night in question.* ▶ **rozpatrywany**, **dyskutowany**

no question of no possibility of: *There is no question of him leaving hospital yet.* ▶ **nie ma możliwości**

out of the question impossible: *A new car is out of the question. It's just too expensive.* ▶ **wykluczony**, **nie wchodzący w rachubę**

(be) a question of sth/of doing sth a situation in which sth is needed: *It's not difficult – it's just a question of finding the time to do it.* ▶ **kwestia (zrobienia) czegoś**

question[2] /ˈkwestʃən/ verb [T] **1 question sb (about/on sth)** to ask sb a question or questions: *The police questioned him for several hours.* ▶ **pytać**, **indagować** **2** to express or feel doubt about sth: *She told me she was from the council so I didn't question her right to be there.* ◇ *to question somebody's sincerity/honesty* ▶ **kwestionować**

questionable /ˈkwestʃənəbl/ adj. **1** that you have doubts about; not certain: *It's questionable whether we'll finish in time.* ▶ **niejasny**, **wątpliwy** **2** likely to be dishonest or morally wrong: *questionable motives* ▶ **wątpliwy** OPP for both meanings **unquestionable**

ˈquestion mark noun [C] the sign (?) that you use when you write a question ▶ **pytajnik**

questionnaire /ˌkwestʃəˈneə(r)/ noun [C] a list of questions that are answered by many people. A **questionnaire** is used to collect information about a particular subject: *to complete/fill in a questionnaire* ▶ **kwestionariusz**

ˈquestion tag (also **tag**) noun [C] a short phrase such as 'isn't it?' or 'did you?' at the end of a sentence that changes it into a question and is often used to ask sb to agree with you ▶ **krótka fraza pytajna**

queue /kjuː/ (US **line**) noun [C] a line of people, cars, etc. that are waiting for sth or to do sth: *We had to* ***wait in a queue*** *for hours to get tickets.* ◇ *to* ***join the end of a queue*** ◇ *We were told to* ***form a queue*** *outside the doors.* ▶ **kolejka**

■ **queue** verb [I] **queue (up) (for sth)**: *to queue for a bus* ▶ **stać w kolejce**, **ustawiać się w kolejce**

IDM **jump the queue** → JUMP[1]

quibble /ˈkwɪbl/ verb [I] **quibble (about/over sth)** to argue or complain about a small matter or an unimportant detail: *It isn't worth quibbling over such a small amount.* ▶ **spierać się** (*o szczegóły/coś nieważnego*)

■ **quibble** noun [C] a small complaint or criticism, especially one that is not important: *The only quibble about this book is the lack of colour illustrations.* ▶ **drobne zastrzeżenie**, **mały zarzut**

quiche /kiːʃ/ noun [C,U] a type of food made of **pastry** filled with egg and milk with cheese, onion, etc. and cooked in the oven. You can eat **quiche** hot or cold. ▶ **słona tarta z serem itp.** ➲ picture on **page A14**

quick[1] /kwɪk/ adj. **1** done with speed; taking or lasting a short time: *May I make a quick telephone call?* ◇ *This dish is quick and easy to make.* ◇ *His quick thinking saved her life.* ◇ *We need to make a quick decision.* ▶ **szybki** **2 quick (to do sth)** doing sth at speed or in a short time: *It's quicker to travel by train.* ◇ *She is a quick worker.* ◇ *She was quick to point out* (szybko wskazała) *all the mistakes I had made.* ◇ *Run and get your coat and be quick about it* (i zrób to szybko). ▶ **szybki**, **prędki**, **rychły**

> **Fast** używa się częściej do opisania osoby lub rzeczy, która porusza się lub może się poruszać z dużą szybkością: *a fast horse/car/runner.* **Quick** używa się częściej do opisania czynności wykonywanej w krótkim czasie: *a quick decision/breakfast/visit.*

3 (used to form adjectives): *quick-thinking* o bystrym umyśle ◇ *quick-drying paint* farba szybkoschnąca

IDM **(as) quick as a flash** very quickly: *Quick as a flash, he grabbed my money and ran.* ▶ **(szybko) jak błyskawica**

quick/slow on the uptake → UPTAKE

quick[2] /kwɪk/ adv. (informal) quickly: *Come over here quick!* ▶ **szybko**, **prędko**

quicken /ˈkwɪkən/ verb [I,T] (formal) to become quicker or make sth quicker: *She felt her heartbeat quicken* (serce zaczęło jej żywiej bić) *as he approached.* ◇ *He quickened his pace to catch up with them.* ▶ **przyśpieszać**

quickly /ˈkwɪkli/ adv. fast; in a short time: *He quickly undressed and got into bed.* ◇ *I'd like you to get here as quickly as possible.* ▶ **szybko**, **prędko**

quicksand /ˈkwɪksænd/ noun [U] deep wet sand that you sink into if you walk on it ▶ **ruchome piaski**

ˌquick-ˈtempered adj. likely to become angry very quickly ▶ **porywczy**

ˌquick-ˈwitted adj. able to think quickly; intelligent: *a quick-witted student/response* ▶ **błyskotliwy** OPP **slow-witted**

quid /kwɪd/ noun [C] (pl. **quid**) (Brit., informal) a pound (in money); £1: *Can you lend me a couple of quid until tomorrow?* ▶ **funciak**

quiet¹ /ˈkwaɪət/ adj. **1** with very little or no noise: *His voice was quiet but firm.* ◇ *Please keep the children quiet* (dopilnuj, żeby dzieci zachowywały się cicho) *when I'm on the phone.* ◇ *Go into the library if you want to work. It's much quieter in there.* ◇ *Be quiet!* Cicho! ▶ **cichy** OPP **loud 2** without much activity or many people: *The streets are very quiet on Sundays.* ◇ *Business is quiet at this time of year.* ◇ *a quiet country village* ◇ *We lead a quiet life.* ▶ **spokojny**, **cichy 3** (used about a person) not talking very much: *You're very quiet today. Is anything wrong?* ◇ *He's very quiet and shy.* ▶ **spokojny**, **cichy**

■ **quietly** adv.: *Try and shut the door quietly!* ▶ **cicho** | **quietness** noun [U] ▶ **spokój**, **cisza**

IDM **keep quiet about sth**; **keep sth quiet** to say nothing about sth: *Would you keep quiet about me leaving until I've told the boss?* ▶ **trzymać coś w tajemnicy**

quiet² /ˈkwaɪət/ noun [U] the state of being calm and without much noise or activity: *the **peace and quiet** of the countryside* ▶ **cisza**, **spokój**

IDM **on the quiet** secretly: *She's given up smoking but she still has an occasional cigarette on the quiet.* ▶ **w tajemnicy**, **potajemnie**

quieten /ˈkwaɪətn/ verb [T] to make sb/sth quiet ▶ **uciszać**, **uspokajać**

PHR V **quieten (sb/sth) down** to become quiet or to make sb/sth quiet: *When you've quietened down, I'll tell you what happened.* ▶ **uciszać (się)**, **uspokajać (się)**

quill /kwɪl/ noun [C] **1** (also ˈ**quill feather**) a large feather from the wing or tail of a bird ▶ **pióro 2** (also ˌ**quill** ˈ**pen**) a pen made from a **quill feather** ▶ **gęsie pióro** (*do pisania*)

quilt /kwɪlt/ noun [C] a cover for a bed that has a thick warm material, for example feathers, inside it ▶ **kołdra** ➲ look at **duvet**

quilted /ˈkwɪltɪd/ adj. (used about clothes, etc.) made of two layers of cloth with soft material between them, held in place by lines of **stitches**: *a quilted jacket* ▶ **pikowany**

quintessential /ˌkwɪntɪˈsenʃl/ adj. being the most perfect or typical example of sth ▶ **w pełnym znaczeniu tego słowa**, **typowy**

quintet /kwɪnˈtet/ noun [C] **1** a group of five people who sing or play music together ▶ **kwintet 2** a piece of music for five people to sing or play together ▶ **kwintet**

quirk /kwɜːk/ noun [C] **1** an aspect of sb's character or behaviour that is strange: *You'll soon get used to the boss's little quirks.* ▶ **dziwactwo 2** a strange thing that happens by chance: *By **a** strange **quirk of fate** they met again several years later.* ▶ **kaprys** (*np. losu*)

■ **quirky** adj.: *a quirky sense of humour* ▶ **dziwaczny**, **cudaczny**

quit /kwɪt/ verb (**quitting**; pt, pp **quit**) **1** [I,T] **quit (as sth)** to leave a job, etc. or to go away from a place: *She quit as manager of the volleyball team.* ▶ **porzucać coś**, **wyjeżdżać skądś 2** [T] (especially US, informal) to stop doing sth: *to quit smoking* rzucić palenie ▶ **przestawać coś robić 3** [I,T] to close a computer program ▶ **zamykać program komputerowy**

quite /kwaɪt/ adv. **1** not very; to a certain degree; rather: *The film's quite good.* ◇ *It's quite a good film.* ◇ *I quite enjoy cooking.* ◇ *They had to wait quite a long time.* ◇ *It's quite cold today.* ◇ *We still meet up quite often.* ▶ **dosyć**, **dość** ➲ note at **rather 2** (used for emphasizing sth) completely; very: *Are you quite sure you don't mind?* ◇ *I quite agree – you're quite right.* ◇ *To my surprise, the room was quite empty.* ▶ **zupełnie**, **całkowicie** SYN **absolutely 3** (used for showing that you agree with or understand sth): *'We didn't win, but at least we tried.' 'Yes, quite.'* ▶ **racja**, **no**, **właśnie**, **faktycznie**

IDM **not quite** (used for showing that there is almost enough of sth, or that it is almost suitable): *There's not quite enough bread for breakfast.* ◇ *These shoes don't quite fit.* ▶ **nie całkiem**, **niewystarczająco**, **niezupełnie**

quite a (used for showing that sth is unusual): *That's quite a problem.* ▶ **prawdziwy**

quite enough (used for emphasizing that no more of sth is wanted or needed): *I've had quite enough of listening to you two arguing!* ◇ *That's quite enough wine, thanks.* ▶ **dosyć**

quite a few; **quite a lot (of)** a fairly large amount or number: *We've received quite a few enquiries.* ▶ **sporo**, **niemało**

quits /kwɪts/ adj.

IDM **be quits (with sb)** (informal) if two people are **quits**, it means that neither of them owes the other anything: *You buy me a drink and then we're quits.* ▶ **być kwita**

quiver /ˈkwɪvə(r)/ verb [I] to shake slightly: *to quiver with rage/excitement/fear* ▶ **drżeć**, **trząść się** SYN **tremble**

quiz¹ /kwɪz/ noun [C] (pl. **quizzes**) a game or competition in which you have to answer questions: *a general knowledge quiz* ◇ *a television quiz show* ◇ *a quiz programme on TV* teleturniej ▶ **turniej**, **kwiz**

quiz² /kwɪz/ verb [T] (**quizzing**; **quizzes**; pt, pp **quizzed**) to ask sb a lot of questions in order to get information ▶ **przepytywać**

quizzical /ˈkwɪzɪkl/ adj. (used about a look, smile, etc.) seeming to ask a question ▶ **pytający**

■ **quizzically** /-kli/ adv. ▶ **pytająco**

quorum /ˈkwɔːrəm/ noun [sing.] the smallest number of people that must be at a meeting before it can make official decisions ▶ **kworum**, **komplet**

quota /ˈkwəʊtə/ noun [C] the number or amount of sth that is allowed or that you must do: *We have a fixed quota of work to get through each day.* ▶ **kontyngent**, **norma**

quotation /kwəʊˈteɪʃn/ (also **quote**) noun [C] **1** a phrase from a book, speech, play, etc., that sb repeats because it is interesting or useful: *a quotation from Shakespeare* ▶ **cytat 2** a statement that says how much a piece of work will probably cost: *You should get quotations from three different builders.* ▶ **kosztorys** ➲ look at **estimate**

quoˈtation marks (also informal **quotes** /kwəʊts/; Brit. also **inverted commas**) noun [pl.] the signs ('...') or ("...") that you put around a word, a sentence, etc. to show that it is what sb said or wrote, that it is a title or that you are using it in a special way: *to put something **in quotation marks*** ▶ **cudzysłowy**

quote /kwəʊt/ verb **1** [I,T] **quote (sth) (from sb/sth)** to repeat exactly sth that sb else has said or written before: *The minister asked the newspaper not to quote him.* ▶ **cytować**, **przytaczać 2** [T] to give sth as an example to support what you are saying: *She quoted several reasons why she was unhappy about the decision.* ▶ **przytaczać 3** [T] to say what the cost of a piece of work, etc. will probably be: *How much did they quote you for repairing the roof?* ▶ **przedstawiać kosztorys**

quotes (informal) = QUOTATION MARKS

the **Qur'an** = KORAN

Rr

R, r /ɑː(r)/ noun [C,U] (pl. **Rs**; **rs**; **R's**; **r's** /ɑː(r)z/) the 18th letter of the English alphabet: *'Rabbit' begins with an 'R'.* ▶ **litera** *r*

R. = RIVER: *R. Thames*

R & B /ˌɑːr ən 'biː/ noun [U] **rhythm and blues**; a type of music that is a mixture of **blues** and **jazz** ▶ **rhythm and blues**

rabbi /'ræbaɪ/ noun [C] (pl. **rabbis**) a Jewish religious leader and teacher of Jewish law ▶ **rabin**

rabbit /'ræbɪt/ noun [C] a small animal with long ears: *a wild rabbit* ◇ *a rabbit hutch* klatka na króliki ▶ **królik** ℹ Dzieci mówią o króliku **bunny**. ➲ note at **pet**

'rabbit warren (also **warren** /'wɒrən/) noun [C] **1** a system of holes and underground tunnels where wild **rabbits** live ▶ **siedlisko królików 2** a building or part of a city with many narrow passages or streets: *The council offices were a real rabbit warren.* ▶ **labirynt**, **skomplikowany układ przejść**

rabble /'ræbl/ noun [C] a noisy crowd of people who are or may become violent ▶ **motłoch**, **hałastra**

rabid /'ræbɪd; 'reɪb-/ adj. **1** [usually before a noun] (used about a type of person) having very strong feelings about sth and acting in an unacceptable way: *rabid right-wing fanatics* ▶ **zaciekły 2** [usually before a noun] (used about feelings or opinions) violent or extreme: *rabid speculation* ▶ (*przen.*) **wściekły 3** suffering from **rabies**: *a rabid dog* ▶ **wściekły**
■ **rabidly** adv. ▶ **zaciekle**; **wściekle**

rabies /'reɪbiːz/ noun [U] a very dangerous disease that a person can get if they are bitten by an animal that has the disease ▶ **wścieklizna**

RAC /ˌɑːr eɪ 'siː/ abbr. (Brit.) the **Royal Automobile Club**; an organization for people who drive cars. If you are a member of the **RAC** and your car breaks down, you can telephone them and they will send sb to help you. ▶ **brytyjski związek motorowy (odpowiednik PZMot-u i Automobilklubu w Polsce)**

🔑 **race¹** /reɪs/ noun **1** [C] **a race (against/with sb/sth); a race for sth/to do sth** a competition between people, animals, cars, etc. to see which is the fastest or to see which can achieve sth first: *to run/win/lose a race* ◇ *to come first/second/last* ***in a race*** ◇ *Rescuing victims of the earthquake is now* ***a race against time.*** ◇ *the race for the presidency* ◇ *the race to find a cure for AIDS* ▶ **wyścig**, **bieg**; **gonitwa 2** (**the races**) [pl.] (Brit.) an occasion when a number of horse races are held in one place: *We're going to the races for the day.* ▶ **wyścigi konne 3** [C,U] one of the groups into which people can be divided according to the colour of their skin, their hair type, the shape of their face, etc.: *a child of mixed race* ▶ **rasa** ➲ look at **human race 4** [C] a group of people who have the same language, customs, history, etc.: *the Spanish race* ▶ **rasa**
IDM **the rat race** → RAT

> In Britain going to horse races and greyhound races is very popular. People often **bet** with a **bookie** on the result of a race.

🔑 **race²** /reɪs/ verb **1** [I,T] **race (against/with) (sb/sth)** to have a competition with sb/sth to find out who is the fastest or to see who can do sth first: *I'll race you home.* ▶ **ścigać się**, **współzawodniczyć 2** [T] to make an animal or a vehicle take part in a race: *He races pigeons as a hobby.* ▶ **stawiać/zgłaszać do wyścigu/gonitwy 3** [I,T] to go very fast or to move sb/sth very fast: *We raced up the stairs.* ◇ *The child had to be raced to hospital.* Trzeba było szybko odwieźć dziecko do szpitala. ▶ **pędzić**, **gnać**

racecourse /'reɪskɔːs/ (US **racetrack** /'reɪstræk/) noun [C] a place where horse races take place ▶ **tor wyścigów konnych**

racehorse /'reɪshɔːs/ noun [C] a horse that is trained to run in races ▶ **koń wyścigowy**

ˌrace re'lations noun [pl.] the relations between people of different races who live in the same town, area, etc. ▶ **stosunki rasowe**

racetrack = RACECOURSE

racial /'reɪʃl/ adj. connected with people's race; happening between people of different races: *racial tension/discrimination* ▶ **rasowy**
■ **racially** /-ʃəli/ adv.: *a racially mixed school* ▶ **rasowo**

🔑 **racing** /'reɪsɪŋ/ noun [U] **1** = HORSE RACING **2** the sport of taking part in races: *motor racing* ◇ *a racing driver/car* ▶ **wyścigi**

racism /'reɪsɪzəm/ noun [U] the belief that some races of people are better than others; unfair ways of treating people that show this belief: *to take measures to combat racism* ▶ **rasizm**
■ **racist** /-ɪst/ **1** noun [C]: *He's a racist.* ▶ **rasist(k)a 2** adj.: *racist beliefs/views/remarks* ▶ **rasistowski**

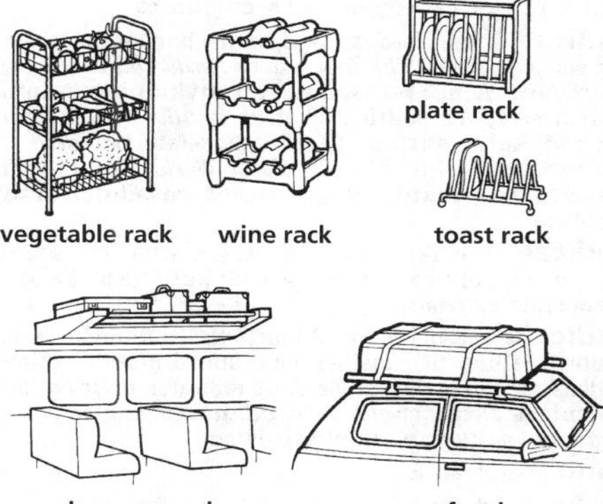

rack¹ /ræk/ noun [C] [in compounds] a piece of equipment, usually made of bars, that you can put things in or on: *I got on the train and put my bags up in the luggage rack.* ◇ *a roof rack* bagażnik dachowy ▶ **półka**
IDM **go to rack and ruin** to be in or get into a bad state because of a lack of care ▶ **podupadać**, **marnieć**

rack² /ræk/ verb
IDM **rack your brains** to try hard to think of sth or remember sth ▶ **głowić się**, **łamać sobie głowę**

racket /'rækɪt/ noun **1** [sing.] (informal) a loud noise: *Stop making that terrible racket!* ▶ **harmider 2** [C] an illegal way of making money: *a drugs racket* ▶ **machinacje**, **kanty 3** (also **racquet**) [C] a piece of sports equipment that you use to hit the ball with in sports such as **tennis** and **badminton** ▶ **rakieta**

> Rackets have **strings**, but **bats** do not. ➲ look at **bat²**, **club²**, **stick¹** ➲ picture on **page A8**

racy /'reɪsi/ adj. (**racier**; **raciest**) (used especially about writing) having a style that is exciting and amusing, sometimes in a way that is connected with sex: *a racy novel* ▶ (*o powieści itp.*) **pikantny**

radar /ˈreɪdɑː(r)/ noun [U] a system that uses radio waves for finding the position of moving objects, for example ships and planes: *This plane is hard to detect by radar.* ▶ **radar, system radiolokacyjny**

radiant /ˈreɪdiənt/ adj. **1** showing great happiness: *a radiant smile* ▶ **promieniejący 2** sending out light or heat: *the radiant heat/energy of the sun* ▶ **promienny, rozpromieniony**

radiate /ˈreɪdieɪt/ verb **1** [T] (used about people) to clearly show a particular quality or emotion in your appearance or behaviour: *She radiated self-confidence in the interview.* ▶ **promieniować 2** [T] to send out light or heat ▶ **emanować 3** [I] to go out in all directions from a central point: *Narrow streets radiate from the village square.* ▶ **rozchodzić się promieniście**

radiation /ˌreɪdiˈeɪʃn/ noun [U] **1** powerful and very dangerous energy that is sent out from certain substances. You cannot see or feel **radiation** but it can cause serious illness or death. ▶ **promieniowanie, radiacja** ➲ look at **radioactive 2** heat, light or energy that is sent out from sth: *ultraviolet radiation* ▶ **promieniowanie**

radiator /ˈreɪdieɪtə(r)/ noun [C] **1** a piece of equipment that is usually fixed to the wall and is used for heating a room. **Radiators** are made of metal and filled with hot water. ▶ **kaloryfer 2** a piece of equipment that is used for keeping a car engine cool ▶ **chłodnica**

radical[1] /ˈrædɪkl/ adj. **1** (used about changes in sth) very great; complete: *The tax system needs radical reform.* ◇ *radical change* ▶ **zasadniczy, radykalny 2** wanting great social or political change: *to have radical views* ▶ **radykalny, skrajny** ➲ look at **moderate, extreme**
■ **radically** /-kli/ adv.: *The First World War radically altered the political map of Europe.* ▶ **zasadniczo, radykalnie**

radical[2] /ˈrædɪkl/ noun [C] a person who wants great social or political change ▶ **radykalist(k)a** ➲ look at **moderate, extremist**

radicalize (also **-ise**) /ˈrædɪkəlaɪz/ verb [T] to make people more willing to consider new and different policies, ideas, etc.; to make people more **radical** in their political opinions: *Recent events have radicalized opinion on educational matters.* ▶ **radykalizować**

radii plural of **radius**

🔑 **radio** /ˈreɪdiəʊ/ noun (pl. **radios**) **1** (often **the radio**) [U, sing.] the activity of sending out programmes for people to listen to; the programmes that are sent out: *I always **listen to the radio** in the car.* ◇ *I heard an interesting report **on the radio** this morning.* ◇ *a radio station/programme* ◇ *national/local radio* ▶ **radio** ➲ look at **media 2** [C] a piece of equipment that is used for receiving and/or sending radio messages or programmes (on a ship, plane, etc. or in your house): *a car radio* ▶ **radio, radioodbiornik** ➲ picture at **car**

> You may **put, switch** or **turn** a radio **on** or **off**. You may also **turn** it **up** or **down** to make it louder or quieter. To choose a particular **station** you **tune** it **in**.

3 [U] the sending or receiving of messages through the air by electrical signals: *to keep in radio contact* ◇ *radio signals/waves* ▶ **radio**
■ **radio** verb [I,T] (pt, pp **radioed**) ▶ **nadawać przez radio**

radioactive /ˌreɪdiəʊˈæktɪv/ adj. sending out powerful and very dangerous energy that is produced when atoms are broken up. This energy cannot be seen or felt but can cause serious illness or death: *the problem of the disposal of **radioactive waste** from power stations* ▶ **radioaktywny** ➲ look at **radiation**
■ **radioactivity** /ˌreɪdiəʊækˈtɪvəti/ noun [U] ▶ **radioaktywność, promieniowanie**

ˌradiocarbon ˈdating (formal) = CARBON DATING

radiographer /ˌreɪdiˈɒɡrəfə(r)/ noun [C] a person in a hospital who is trained to take **X-rays** or to use **X-rays** for the treatment of certain illnesses ▶ **radiolog**

radiologist /ˌreɪdiˈɒlədʒɪst/ noun [C] a doctor who is trained in **radiology** ▶ **radiolog**

radiology /ˌreɪdiˈɒlədʒi/ noun [U] the study and use of different types of **radiation** in medicine, for example to treat diseases ▶ **radiologia**

radish /ˈrædɪʃ/ noun [C] a small red vegetable that is white inside with a strong taste. You eat **radishes** in salads. ▶ **rzodkiewka** ➲ picture on **page A13**

radius /ˈreɪdiəs/ noun [C] (pl. **radii** /-diaɪ/) **1** the distance from the centre of a circle to the outside edge ▶ **promień** ➲ look at **diameter, circumference 2** a round area that is measured from a point in its centre: *The wreckage of the plane was scattered over a radius of several miles.* ▶ **promień, zasięg 3** the shorter bone of the two bones in the lower part of your arm between your wrist and your elbow ▶ **kość promieniowa** ➲ look at **ulna** ➲ picture at **body**

RAF /ˌɑːr eɪ ˈef; informal ræf/ abbr. (Brit.) the **Royal Air Force** ▶ **RAF**

raffle /ˈræfl/ noun [C] a way of making money for a charity or a project by selling tickets with numbers on them. Later some numbers are chosen and the tickets with these numbers on them win prizes. ▶ **loteria fantowa**

raft /rɑːft; US ræft/ noun [C] **1** a flat structure made of pieces of wood tied together and used as a boat or a floating platform ▶ **tratwa 2** a small boat made of rubber or plastic that is filled with air ▶ **ponton** ➲ picture at **boat**

rafter /ˈrɑːftə(r); US ˈræf-/ noun [C] one of the long pieces of wood that support a roof ▶ **krokiew**

rag /ræɡ/ noun **1** [C,U] a small piece of old cloth that you use for cleaning ▶ **szmata, gałgan 2** (**rags**) [pl.] clothes that are very old and torn ▶ **łachmany**

rage[1] /reɪdʒ/ noun [C,U] a feeling of violent anger that is difficult to control: *He was trembling with rage.* ◇ *to fly into a rage* wpadać w furię ▶ **wściekłość**

rage[2] /reɪdʒ/ verb [I] **1 rage (at/against/about sb/sth)** to show great anger about sth, especially by shouting: *He raged against the injustice of it all.* ▶ **wściekać się, wpadać w furię 2** (used about a battle, disease, storm, etc.) to continue with great force: *The battle raged for several days.* ▶ **szaleć**
■ **raging** adj. [only before a noun]: *a raging headache* ▶ **piekielny, cholerny**

ragged /ˈræɡɪd/ adj. **1** (used about clothes) old and torn ▶ **obszarpany, obdarty 2** not straight; untidy: *a ragged edge/coastline* ▶ **poszarpany, nierówny**

raid /reɪd/ noun [C] **a raid (on sth) 1** a short surprise attack on an enemy by soldiers, ships or aircraft: *an air raid* nalot ▶ **najazd, napad 2** a surprise visit by the police looking for criminals or illegal goods ▶ **obława 3** a surprise attack on a building in order to steal sth: *a bank raid* ▶ **napad**
■ **raid** verb [T]: *Police raided the club at dawn this morning.* ▶ **robić obławę**

🔑 **rail** /reɪl/ noun **1** [C] a wooden or metal bar fixed to a wall, which you can hang things on: *a curtain/picture rail* ◇ *a towel rail* poziomy wieszak na ręczniki ▶ **poziomy wieszak, karnisz 2** [C] a bar which you can hold to stop you from falling (on stairs, from a building, etc.): *Hold on to the handrail – these steps are very slippery.* ▶ **poręcz, balustrada 3** [C, usually pl.] each of the two metal bars that form the track that trains run on ▶ **szyna kolejowa 4** [U] the railway system; trains as a means of transport: *rail travel/services/fares* ▶ **kolej**

railcard /ˈreɪlkɑːd/ noun [C] (Brit.) a special card that allows you to buy train tickets at a lower price if you are an old person, a young person, student, etc. ▶ **karta uprawniająca do ulgowych przejazdów kolejowych**

railing /ˈreɪlɪŋ/ noun [C, usually pl.] a fence (around a park, garden, etc.) that is made of metal bars ▶ **ogrodzenie**

railroad /ˈreɪlrəʊd/ noun [C] (US) = RAILWAY: *railroad tracks*

■ **railroad** verb [T] **1 railroad sb (into sth/into doing sth)** to force sb to do sth before they have had enough time to decide whether or not they want to do it: *I will not be railroaded into signing something I don't agree with.* ▶ **zmuszać kogoś (do czegoś) 2 railroad sth (through/through sth)** to make a group of people accept a decision, law, etc. quickly by putting pressure on them: *The bill was railroaded through the House.* ▶ **przepychać** *np. decyzję, ustawę* **(przez coś)**

ˈ**railroad crossing** (US) = LEVEL CROSSING

railway /ˈreɪlweɪ/ (US **railroad** /ˈreɪlrəʊd/) noun [C] **1** (Brit. ˈrailway line) the metal lines on which trains travel between one place and another: *In Canada there is a railway which goes right across the Rocky Mountains.* ▶ **kolej 2** the whole system of tracks, the trains and the organization and people needed to operate them: *He works on the railways.* ◇ *a railway company* ◇ *a railway engine* lokomotywa ▶ **kolej**

ˈ**railway station** = STATION[1] (1)

rain[1] /reɪn/ noun **1** [U] the water that falls from the sky: *Take your umbrella, **it looks like rain.*** ◇ *It's **pouring with rain.*** Leje deszcz. ▶ **deszcz** ➲ note at **weather** ➲ look at **shower**, **acid rain 2 (rains)** [pl.] (in tropical countries) the time of the year when there is a lot of rain: *When the rains come in July, the people move to higher ground.* ▶ **pora deszczowa**

IDM **(as) right as rain** → RIGHT[1]

rain[2] /reɪn/ verb **1** [I] [used with *it*] to fall as rain: *Oh no! **It's raining** again!* ◇ *Is it **raining hard**?* ◇ *We'll go out when it stops raining.* ▶ **padać** ➲ picture on **page A16 2** [I,T] **rain (sth) (down) (on sb/sth)** to fall or make sth fall on sb/sth in large quantities: *Bombs rained down on the city.* ▶ **sypać się na kogoś/coś; obsypywać czymś**

PHR V **be rained off** to be cancelled or to have to stop because it is raining: *The tennis was rained off.* ▶ **przerywać coś z powodu deszczu**

rainbow /ˈreɪnbəʊ/ noun [C] a curved band of many colours that sometimes appears in the sky when the sun shines through rain ▶ **tęcza** ➲ picture on **page A16**

ˈ**rain check** noun

IDM **take a rain check on sth** (especially US, informal) to refuse an invitation or offer but say that you might accept it later ▶ **odrzucać propozycję z możliwością przyjęcia jej w późniejszym terminie**

raincoat /ˈreɪnkəʊt/ noun [C] a long light coat which keeps you dry in the rain ▶ **płaszcz przeciwdeszczowy**

raindrop /ˈreɪndrɒp/ noun [C] a single drop of rain ▶ **kropla deszczu**

rainfall /ˈreɪnfɔːl/ noun [U, sing.] the total amount of rain that falls in a particular place during a month, year, etc. ▶ **wysokość opadów deszczu**

rainforest /ˈreɪnfɒrɪst/ noun [C] a thick forest in tropical parts of the world that have a lot of rain: *the Amazon rainforest* ▶ **las deszczowy**

rainy /ˈreɪni/ adj. (**rainier**; **rainiest**) having or bringing a lot of rain: *a rainy day* ◇ *floods during the rainy season* ▶ **deszczowy**

IDM **keep/save sth for a rainy day** to save sth, especially money, for a time when you really need it ▶ **odkładać coś na czarną godzinę**

raise[1] /reɪz/ verb [T] **1** to lift sth up: *If you want to leave the room, raise your hand.* ◇ *He raised himself up on one elbow.* ▶ **podnosić** OPP **lower** ➲ note at **rise[2] 2 raise sth (to sth)** to increase the level of sth or to make sth better or stronger: *to raise taxes/salaries/prices* ◇ *The hotel needs to **raise** its **standards**.* ◇ *There's no need to **raise your voice**.* ▶ **podnosić, zwiększać, polepszać** OPP **lower** ➲ note at **rise[2] 3** to get money from people for a particular purpose: *We are doing a sponsored walk to **raise money** for charity.* ◇ *a **fund-raising** event* ◇ *We managed to raise* (zebrać) *nearly £1 000 for the school at the Christmas bazaar.* ▶ **uzyskiwać 4** to introduce a subject that needs to be talked about or dealt with: *I would like to **raise the subject** of money.* ◇ *This **raises the question** of why nothing was done before.* ▶ **podnosić 5** to cause a particular reaction or emotion: *The neighbours **raised the alarm** when they saw smoke coming out of the window.* ◇ *to **raise hopes/fears/suspicions** in people's minds* ▶ **podnosić** *(np. alarm)*, **wzbudzać** *(np. nadzieję)* **6** to look after a child or an animal until they are an adult: *You can't **raise a family** on what I earn.* ▶ **utrzymywać, wychowywać** ➲ look at **bring sb up 7** to breed animals or grow a type of plant for a particular purpose: *Sheep are raised for meat and wool.* ▶ **hodować**

IDM **raise your eyebrows** to show that you are surprised or that you do not approve of sth ▶ **unosić brwi**

raise[2] (US) = RISE[1] (2)

raisin /ˈreɪzn/ noun [C] a dried **grape**, used in cakes, etc. ▶ **rodzynek** ➲ look at **sultana**

rake /reɪk/ noun [C] a garden tool with a long handle and a row of metal teeth, used for collecting leaves or making the earth smooth ▶ **grabie** ➲ picture at **garden**

■ **rake** verb [T]: *to rake up the leaves* ▶ **grabić**

PHR V **rake sth in** (informal) to earn a lot of money, especially when it is done easily: *She's been **raking it in** since she got promoted.* ▶ **zarabiać mnóstwo szmalu**

rake sth up to start talking about sth that it would be better to forget: *Don't rake up all those old stories again.* ▶ **odgrzebywać**

rally[1] /ˈræli/ noun [C] (pl. **rallies**) **1** a large public meeting, especially one held to support a political idea: *a peace rally* ▶ **manifestacja 2** (Brit.) a race for cars or motorbikes on public roads ▶ **rajd 3** (in **tennis** and similar sports) a series of hits of the ball before a point is won ▶ **wymiana uderzeń piłki w tenisie**

rally[2] /ˈræli/ verb (**rallying**; **rallies**; pt, pp **rallied**) **1** [I,T] **rally (sb/sth) (around/behind/to sb)** to come together or to bring people together in order to help or support sb/sth: *The cabinet rallied behind the Prime Minister.* ▶ **jednoczyć (się) 2** [I] to get stronger, healthier, etc. after an illness or a period of weakness: *He never really rallied after the operation.* ▶ **wzmacniać się, rosnąć w siłę** SYN **recover**

PHR V **rally round/around (sb)** to come together to help sb: *When I was in trouble my family all rallied round.* ▶ **jednoczyć się (wokół kogoś)**

RAM /ræm/ noun [U] **random-access memory**; computer memory in which data can be changed or removed and can be looked at in any order: *32 megabytes of RAM* ▶ *(komputer)* **pamięć RAM** ➲ look at **ROM**

ram[1] /ræm/ verb [T] (**ramming**; **rammed**) to crash into sth or push sth with great force ▶ **taranować**

ram[2] /ræm/ noun [C] a male sheep ▶ **baran** ➲ note at **sheep**

Ramadan /ˈræmədæn; ˌræməˈdæn/ noun [C,U] the period of a month when, for religious reasons, Muslims do not eat anything from early morning until the sun goes down in the evening ▶ *(religia muzułmańska)* **ramadan** ➲ look at **Eid**

ramble[1] /ˈræmbl/ verb [I] **1** (especially Brit.) to walk in the countryside for pleasure, especially as part of an organized group: *to **go rambling*** ▶ **wędrować 2 ramble (on) (about sth)** to talk for a long time in a confused way: *Halfway through his speech he began to ramble.* ▶ **ględzić**

ramble² /ˈræmbl/ noun [C] (especially Brit.) a long, organized walk in the country for pleasure ▶ **wycieczka krajoznawcza, wędrówka**
■ **rambler** noun [C] ▶ **wędrowiec, turyst(k)a piesz-y/a**

rambling /ˈræmblɪŋ/ adj. **1** (used about a building) spreading in many directions: *a rambling old house in the country* ▶ *(dom)* **budynek z kilkoma skrzydłami 2** (used about speech or writing) very long and confused ▶ *(tekst)* **pogmatwany**

ramp /ræmp/ noun [C] **1** a path going up or down which you can use instead of steps or stairs to get from one place to a higher or lower place: *There are ramps at both entrances for wheelchair access.* ▶ **rampa 2** (US) = SLIP ROAD

rampage¹ /ˈræmpeɪdʒ/ noun
IDM **be/go on the rampage** to move through a place in a violent group, usually breaking things and attacking people ▶ **miotać się**

rampage² /ræmˈpeɪdʒ/ verb [I] to move through a place in a violent group, usually breaking things and attacking people: *The football fans rampaged through the town.* ▶ **robić burdy**

rampant /ˈræmpənt/ adj. (used about sth bad) existing or spreading everywhere in a way that is very difficult to control: *Car theft is rampant in this town.* W mieście szerzą się kradzieże samochodów. ▶ **rozpasany**

rampart /ˈræmpɑːt/ noun [usually pl.] a high wide wall of stone or earth with a path on top, built around a castle, town, etc. to defend it ▶ **wał obronny**

ramshackle /ˈræmʃækl/ adj. (usually used about a building) old and needing repair ▶ **zrujnowany, zdezelowany**

ran past tense of **run¹**

ranch /rɑːntʃ; US ræntʃ/ noun [C] a large farm, especially in the US or Australia, where cows, horses, sheep, etc. are kept ▶ **ranczo**

rancid /ˈrænsɪd/ adj. if food containing fat is **rancid**, it tastes or smells unpleasant because it is no longer fresh: *rancid butter* ◇ *There was a rancid smell coming from the kitchen.* ◇ *Butter soon* ***goes/turns rancid*** (szybko zjełczeje) *in this heat.* ▶ **zjełczały**

random /ˈrændəm/ adj. chosen by chance: *For the survey they interviewed* ***a random selection*** *of people in the street.* ▶ **wyrywkowy**
■ **randomly** adv. ▶ **bez ładu, przypadkowo**
IDM **at random** without thinking or deciding in advance what is going to happen: *The competitors were chosen at random from the audience.* ▶ **wyrywkowo, na chybił trafił**

ˌrandom-ˌaccess ˈmemory = RAM

randy /ˈrændi/ adj. (**randier**; **randiest**) (Brit., informal) sexually excited ▶ **pożądliwy**

rang past tense of **ring²**

range¹ /reɪndʒ/ noun **1** [C, usually sing.] **a range (of sth)** a variety of things that belong to the same group: *The course will cover a* ***whole range*** *of topics.* ◇ *This shop has a very* ***wide range*** *of clothes.* ▶ **zakres 2** [C] the limits between which sth can vary: *That car is outside my* ***price range.*** ◇ *I don't think this game is suitable for all* ***age ranges.*** ▶ **zakres, zasięg, rozpiętość 3** [C,U] the distance that it is possible for sb/sth to travel, see, hear, etc.: *Keep* ***out of range of*** *the guns.* ◇ *The gunman shot the policeman* ***at close range.*** ◇ *They can pick up signals* ***at a range of*** *400 metres.* ▶ **zasięg, rozpiętość 4** [C] a line of mountains or hills: *the great mountain range of the Alps* ▶ **łańcuch (górski)**

range² /reɪndʒ/ verb **1** [I] **range between A and B; range from A to B** to vary between two amounts, sizes, etc., including all those between them: *The ages of the students range from 15 to 50.* ▶ **rozciągać się, obejmować 2** [I] **range (from A to B)** to include a variety of things in addition to those mentioned: *She's had a number of different jobs, ranging from chef to swimming instructor.* ◇ *The conversation ranged widely.* Rozmowa obejmowała wiele tematów. ▶ **poczynać od A, a kończyć na B 3** [T] (usually passive) to arrange things or people in a line ▶ **ustawiać w szeregu**

rank¹ /ræŋk/ noun **1** [C,U] the position, especially a high position, that sb has in an organization such as the army, or in society: *General is one of the highest ranks in the army.* ◇ *She's much higher in rank than I am.* ◇ *As a writer, he's first rank* (pierwszorzędny). ▶ **stopień, ranga, klasa 2** (**the ranks**) [pl.] the ordinary soldiers in the army; the members of any large group: *At the age of 43, he was forced to* ***join the ranks of*** *the unemployed* (zasilić szeregi bezrobotnych). ▶ **szeregowi** *(żołnierze, członkowie)* **3** [C] a group or line of things or people: *a taxi rank* postój taksówek ▶ **rząd, szereg**

rank² /ræŋk/ verb [I,T] [not used in the continuous tenses] **rank (sb/sth) (as sth)** to give sb/sth a particular position on a scale according to importance, quality, success, etc.; to have a position of this kind: *She's ranked as* (uważa się ją za) *one of the world's top players.* ◇ *a high-ranking* (wysokiej rangi) *police officer* ▶ **ustawiać w kolejności; zajmować pozycję**

the ˌrank and ˈfile noun [sing., with sing. or pl. verb] **1** the ordinary soldiers who are not officers ▶ **szeregowi 2** the ordinary members of an organization: *the rank and file of the workforce* ▶ **szeregowi członkowie**

rankle /ˈræŋkl/ verb [I,T] **rankle (with sb)** if sth such as an event or a remark **rankles**, it makes you feel angry or upset for a long time: *Her comments still rankled.* ▶ **boleć**

ransack /ˈrænsæk/ verb [T] **ransack sth (for sth)** to make a place untidy, causing damage, because you are looking for sth: *The house had been ransacked by burglars.* ▶ **plądrować coś (w poszukiwaniu czegoś)**

ransom /ˈrænsəm/ noun [C,U] the money that you must pay to free sb who has been captured illegally and who is being kept as a prisoner: *The kidnappers demanded a ransom of $500 000 for the boy's release.* ▶ **okup**
IDM **hold sb to ransom** to keep sb as a prisoner and say that you will not free them until you have received a certain amount of money ▶ **porywać kogoś dla okupu**
➲ look at **hostage**

rant /rænt/ verb [I,T] **rant (on) (about sth)**; **rant (at sb)** to speak or complain about sth in a loud and/or angry way ▶ **głośno narzekać (na coś), wymyślać (komuś)**
IDM **rant and rave** to show that you are angry by shouting or complaining loudly for a long time ▶ **wykrzykiwać**
■ **rant** noun [C] ▶ **wymyślanie, głośne narzekanie**

rap¹ /ræp/ noun **1** [C] a quick, sharp hit or knock on a door, window, etc.: *There was a sharp rap on the door.* ▶ **szybkie i głośne pukanie 2** [C,U] a style or a piece of music with a fast strong rhythm, in which the words are spoken fast, not sung ▶ **muzyka/utwór w stylu rap**

rap² /ræp/ verb (**rapping**; **rapped**) **1** [I,T] to hit a hard object or surface several times quickly and lightly, making a noise: *She rapped angrily on/at the door.* ▶ **pukać, trzaskać 2** [T] (informal) (used mainly in newspapers) to criticize sb strongly: *Minister raps police over rise in crime.* ▶ **besztać 3** [I] to speak the words of a **rap** (2) ▶ **wokalizować w stylu muzyki rap**

rape¹ /reɪp/ verb [T] to force a person to have sex when they do not want to, using threats or violence ▶ **gwałcić**

rape² /reɪp/ noun **1** [U,C] the crime of forcing sb to have sex when they do not want to: *to commit rape* ▶ **gwałt 2** [sing.] (formal) **the rape (of sth)** the act of destroying sth beautiful ▶ **gwałt**

rapid /ˈræpɪd/ adj. happening very quickly or moving with great speed: *She made rapid progress* (osiągnęła znaczny postęp) *and was soon the best in the class.* ◇ *After leaving hospital he made a rapid recovery* (szybko wyzdrowiał) *and was soon back at work.* ▶ **szybki**
■ **rapidity** /rəˈpɪdəti/ noun (formal): *The rapidity of economic growth has astonished most people.* ▶ **szybkość** | **rapidly** adv. ▶ **szybko**

rapids /ˈræpɪdz/ noun [pl.] a part of a river where the water flows very fast over rocks ▶ **progi** (*na rzece*), **bystrzyna**

rapist /ˈreɪpɪst/ noun [C] a person who forces sb to have sex when they do not want to ▶ **gwałciciel/ka**

rappel (US) = ABSEIL

rapper /ˈræpə(r)/ noun [C] a person who speaks the words of a **rap** song ▶ **raper/ka**

rapport /ræˈpɔː(r)/ noun [sing., U] **rapport (with sb)**; **rapport (between A and B)** a friendly relationship in which people understand each other very well: *She has established a close rapport with clients.* ▶ **porozumienie**, **wzajemne zrozumienie**

rapprochement /ræˈprɒʃmɒ̃; ræˈprəʊʃmɒ̃; US ˌræprəʊʃˈmɑːn; -prɒʃ-/ noun [sing., U] **rapprochement (with sb)**; **rapprochement (between A and B)** (French, formal) a situation in which the relationship between two countries or groups of people becomes more friendly after a period during which they were enemies: *policies aimed at bringing about a rapprochement with China* ▶ **zbliżenie (z kimś/między A i B)**

rapt /ræpt/ adj. so interested in one particular thing that you are not conscious of anything else: *a rapt audience* ◇ *She listened with rapt attention.* ▶ **zaabsorbowany**, **wytężony**

rapture /ˈræptʃə(r)/ noun [U] a feeling of extreme happiness ▶ **zachwyt**, **upojenie**
IDM **go into raptures (about/over sb/sth)** to feel and show that you think that sb/sth is very good: *I didn't like the film much but my boyfriend went into raptures about it.* ▶ **zachwycać się**, **upajać się**

rapturous /ˈræptʃərəs/ adj. [usually before a noun] expressing extreme pleasure or enthusiasm for sb/sth: *rapturous applause* ▶ **entuzjastyczny** SYN **ecstatic**
■ **rapturously** adv. ▶ **entuzjastycznie**

rare /reə(r)/ adj. **1 rare (for sb/sth to do sth)**; **rare (to do sth)** not done, seen, happening, etc. very often: *a rare bird/flower/plant* ▶ **rzadki 2** (used about meat) not cooked for very long so that the inside is still red: *a rare steak* krwisty befsztyk ▶ **niedosmażony** ⊃ look at **medium**, **well done**
■ **rarely** adv.: *Human beings rarely live to be over 100 years old.* ▶ **rzadko**

raring /ˈreərɪŋ/ adj. **raring to do sth** wanting to start doing sth very much: *They were raring to try out the new computer.* ▶ **rwący się do czegoś**

rarity /ˈreərəti/ noun (pl. **rarities**) **1** [C] a thing or a person that is unusual and is therefore often valuable or interesting: *Women lorry drivers are still quite a rarity.* ▶ **rzadkość**, **osobliwość 2** [U] the quality of being rare: *The rarity of this stamp increases its value a lot.* ▶ **rzadkość**, **niezwykłość**

rascal /ˈrɑːskl; US ˈræskl/ noun [C] (informal) a person, especially a child or man, who shows little respect for other people and enjoys playing jokes on them: *Come here, you little rascal!* ▶ **urwis**

rash[1] /ræʃ/ noun **1** [C, usually sing.] an area of small red spots that appear on your skin when you are ill or have a reaction to sth: *He **came out in a rash*** (dostał wysypki) *where the plant had touched him.* ▶ **wysypka 2** [sing.] a **rash (of sth)** a series of unpleasant events of the same kind happening close together ▶ **seria** (*przykrych zdarzeń*)

rash[2] /ræʃ/ adj. **1** (used about people) doing things that might be dangerous or bad without thinking about the possible results first: *You were very rash to give up your job before you had found another one.* Twoja decyzja porzucenia pracy, zanim znalazłeś nową, była bardzo pochopna. ▶ **brawurowy 2** done without much thought: *a rash decision/promise* ▶ **nierozważny**, **nieroztropny**, **pochopny**
■ **rashly** adv. ▶ **brawurowo**, **nieroztropnie**

rasher /ˈræʃə(r)/ noun [C] (Brit.) a slice of **bacon** ▶ **plasterek bekonu**

raspberry /ˈrɑːzbəri; US ˈræzberi/ noun [C] (pl. **raspberries**) **1** a small, soft, red fruit which grows on bushes: *raspberry jam* ▶ **malina** ⊃ picture on **page A12 2** a rude sound that you make with your mouth to show sb that you think they are stupid: *to blow a raspberry at sb* pogardliwie prychać

Rastafarian /ˌræstəˈfeəriən/ (also informal **Rasta**) noun [C] a member of a Jamaican religious group which worships the former Emperor of Ethiopia, Haile Selassie, and which believes that black people will one day return to Africa. Rastafarians often wear dreadlocks and have other distinguishing patterns of behaviour and dress. ▶ **wyznawca rastafarianizmu**
■ **Rastafarian** (also informal **Rasta**) adj. ▶ **rastafariański**

rat /ræt/ noun [C] an animal like a large mouse ▶ **szczur**

> Rats belong to the family of animals that are called **rodents**.

ℹ Jako obelżywe określenie **rat** znaczy „nędzna kreatura".
IDM **the rat race** the way of life in which everyone is only interested in being better or more successful than everyone else ▶ **wyścig szczurów**; **wyścig o karierę**

rate[1] /reɪt/ noun [C] **1** a measurement of the speed at which sth happens or the number of times sth happens or exists during a particular period: *The **birth rate** is falling.* ◇ *the inflation rate/rate of inflation* stopa inflacji ◇ *an **exchange rate*** (kurs wymiany) *of sixty pence to one euro* ◇ *The population is increasing **at the rate of** less than 0.5% a year.* ▶ **wskaźnik**, **tempo 2** a fixed amount of money that sth costs or that sb is paid: *The higher rate of income tax* (wyższą stopą podatku dochodowego) *is 40%.* ◇ *The basic **rate of pay** is £10 an hour.* ◇ *We offer special reduced rates for students.* ▶ **stawka** ⊃ look at **first-rate**, **second-rate**
IDM **at any rate** (informal) **1** whatever else might happen: *Well, that's one good piece of news at any rate.* ▶ **w każdym razie 2** (used when you are giving more exact information about sth): *He said that they would be here by ten. At any rate, I think that's what he said.* ▶ **przynajmniej**, **bądź co bądź**
the going rate (for sth) → GOING[2]

rate[2] /reɪt/ verb [not used in the continuous tenses] **1** [I,T] **rate sb/sth (as) sth**; **rate as sth** to have or think that sb/sth has a particular level of quality, value, etc.: *She's rated among the best tennis players of all time.* ◇ *The match rated as one of their worst defeats.* ▶ **zaliczać do czegoś**, **szacować**; **być uznanym za kogoś/coś 2** [T] to be good, important, etc. enough to be treated in a particular way: *The accident wasn't very serious – it didn't **rate a mention** in the local newspaper.* ▶ **zasługiwać**

ratepayer /ˈreɪtpeɪə(r)/ noun [C] (in Britain in the past) a person who paid taxes to the local authority on the buildings and land they owned ▶ **płatnik podatku od nieruchomości**

rather /ˈrɑːðə(r); US ˈræðər/ adv. quite: *It was a rather nice present./It was rather a nice present.* To był dość miły prezent. ◇ *No, I didn't fail the exam, in fact I did rather* (dość) *well.* ◇ *I'm afraid I owe her rather* (dosyć) *a* *lot of money.* ◇ *He spoke rather too* (zbyt) *quickly for me to understand.* ◇ *It's rather a pity* (wielka szkoda) *that you can't come tomorrow.* ◇ *I was rather* (raczej) *hoping that you'd be free on Friday.* ▶ **raczej**, **dość**

Fairly, **quite**, **rather** i **pretty** mogą wszystkie oznaczać „niezbyt" lub „średnio". **Fairly** ma najsłabszy wydźwięk znaczeniowy, a **rather** i **pretty** (stosowane w języku potocznym) najmocniejszy. **Fairly** przeważnie określa słowa o pozytywnym znaczeniu: *This room was fairly tidy.* **Rather** ma wydźwięk krytyczny: *This room's rather untidy.* Używanie **rather** ze słowem o pozytywnym znaczeniu, nadaje temu słowu znamiona zdziwienia lub zadowolenia: *The new teacher is rather nice. I'm surprised – he didn't look very friendly.*

IDM **or rather** (used as a way of correcting sth you have said, or making it more exact): *She lives in London, or rather she lives in a suburb of London.* ▶ **a raczej**
rather than instead of; in place of: *I think I'll just have a sandwich rather than a full meal.* ▶ **zamiast**
would rather... (than) would prefer to: *I'd rather go to the cinema than watch TV.* ▶ **woleć**

ratify /ˈrætɪfaɪ/ verb [T] (**ratifying**; **ratifies**; pt, pp **ratified**) to make an agreement officially valid by voting for or signing it: *The treaty was ratified by all the member states.* ▶ **ratyfikować**
■ **ratification** /ˌrætɪfɪˈkeɪʃn/ noun [U] ▶ **ratyfikacja**

rating /ˈreɪtɪŋ/ noun [C] **1** a measurement of how popular, important, good, etc. sth is: *Education has been given a high-priority rating by the new government.* Nowy rząd uznał edukację za jeden z najważniejszych priorytetów. ▶ **wskaźnik**, **ocena** **2** (usually **the ratings**) [pl.] a set of figures showing the number of people who watch a particular TV programme, etc., used to show how popular the programme is ▶ **wskaźnik oglądalności**

ratio /ˈreɪʃiəʊ/ noun [C] (pl. **ratios**) **ratio (of A to B)** the relation between two numbers which shows how much bigger one quantity is than another: *The ratio of boys to girls in this class is three to one.* ▶ **stosunek**, **współczynnik**

ration /ˈræʃn/ noun [C] a limited amount of food, petrol, etc. that you are allowed to have when there is not enough for everyone to have as much as they want ▶ **racja** (*żywnościowa*), **przydział**
■ **ration** verb [T]: *In the desert water is strictly rationed.* ▶ **racjonować** | **rationing** noun [U] ▶ **racjonowanie**

rational /ˈræʃnəl/ adj. **1** based on reason; sensible or logical: *There must be a rational explanation for why he's behaving like this.* ▶ **racjonalny** **2** (used about a person) able to use logical thought to make decisions rather than emotions ▶ **rozumny** SYN **reasonable** OPP **irrational**
■ **rationally** /-nəli/ adv. ▶ **sensownie**, **racjonalnie**

rationale /ˌræʃəˈnɑːl; US -ˈnæl/ noun [C] (formal) **rationale (behind/for/of sth)** the principles or reasons which explain a particular decision, plan, belief, etc.: *What is the rationale behind these new exams?* ▶ **racjonalne powody** SYN **reasoning**

rationalize (also **-ise**) /ˈræʃnəlaɪz/ verb **1** [I,T] to find reasons that explain why you have done sth (perhaps because you do not like the real reason) ▶ **uzasadniać**, **usprawiedliwiać** **2** [T] to make a business or a system better organized ▶ **racjonalizować**, **usprawniać**
■ **rationalization** (also **-isation**) /ˌræʃnəlaɪˈzeɪʃn; US -ləˈz-/ noun [C,U] ▶ **racjonalizacja**, **usprawnienie**

rattle¹ /ˈrætl/ verb **1** [I,T] to make a noise like hard things hitting each other or to shake sth so that it makes this noise: *The windows were rattling all night in the wind.* ◇ *He rattled the money in the tin.* ▶ **grzechotać**, **klekotać** **2** [T] (informal) to make sb suddenly become worried: *The news of his arrival really rattled her.* ▶ **wstrząsać (kimś)**, **konsternować**
PHR V **rattle sth off** to say a list of things you have learnt very quickly: *She rattled off the names of every player in the team.* ▶ **wytrajkotać**

rattle² /ˈrætl/ noun [C] **1** a noise made by hard things hitting each other ▶ **grzechot/anie**, **klekot/anie** **2** a toy that a baby can shake to make a noise ▶ **grzechotka**

ratty /ˈræti/ adj. **1** (Brit., informal) becoming angry very easily: *He gets ratty if he doesn't get enough sleep.* ▶ **drażliwy** SYN **grumpy**, **irritable** **2** (US, informal) in bad condition: *long ratty* (skołtuniony) *hair* ◇ *a ratty old pair of jeans* ▶ **złachany** SYN **shabby**

raucous /ˈrɔːkəs/ adj. (used about people's voices) loud and unpleasant: *raucous laughter* ▶ **wrzaskliwy**, **ochrypły**

ravage /ˈrævɪdʒ/ verb [T] to damage sth very badly; to destroy sth: *The forests were ravaged by the winter storms.* ▶ **pustoszyć**

rave¹ /reɪv/ verb [I] **1** (informal) **rave (about sb/sth)** to say very good things about sb/sth: *Everyone's raving about her latest record!* ▶ **szaleć na czyimś punkcie/na punkcie czegoś** **2** to speak angrily or in a wild way ▶ **pieklić się**

rave² /reɪv/ noun [C] (Brit.) a large party held outside or in an empty building, at which people dance to electronic music ▶ **rodzaj dyskoteki** (*przy muzyce elektronicznej*)

raven /ˈreɪvn/ noun [C] a large black bird that has an unpleasant voice ▶ **kruk**

ravenous /ˈrævənəs/ adj. very hungry: *After spending the whole day walking we were ravenous* (umieraliśmy z głodu). ▶ **wygłodniały**
■ **ravenously** adv. ▶ **żarłocznie**

ˌrave reˈview noun [C] an article in a newspaper, etc. that says very good things about a new book, film, play, etc. ▶ **entuzjastyczna recenzja**

ravine /rəˈviːn/ noun [C] a narrow deep valley with steep sides ▶ **wąwóz**

raving /ˈreɪvɪŋ/ adj. [only before a noun] (informal) (used to emphasize a particular state or quality): *His latest novel is a raving success* (szalony sukces). ◇ *She's no raving beauty* (nie jest żadną specjalną pięknością). ▶ **szalony**, **kompletny**
■ **raving** adv.: *Have you gone raving mad* (całkiem oszalałeś)*?* ▶ **szalenie**, **kompletnie**

ravishing /ˈrævɪʃɪŋ/ adj. extremely beautiful: *a ravishing blonde* ▶ **przepiękny**, **zachwycający** SYN **gorgeous**
■ **ravishingly** adv.: *ravishingly beautiful* ▶ **zachwycająco**

raw /rɔː/ adj. **1** not cooked: *Raw vegetables are good for your teeth.* ▶ **surowy** **2** in the natural state; not yet made into anything: *raw sugar* cukier nierafinowany ◇ *raw materials* surowce ▶ **surowy**, **nieobrobiony** **3** (used about an injury where the skin has come off from being rubbed): *There's a nasty raw place on my heel where my shoes have rubbed.* ▶ **obtarty**

ray /reɪ/ noun [C] a line of light, heat or energy: *the sun's rays* ◇ *ultraviolet rays* ▶ **promień** ➲ look at **X-ray**
IDM **a ray of hope** a small chance that things will get better ▶ **promyk nadziei**

razor /ˈreɪzə(r)/ noun [C] a sharp instrument which people use to shave: *an electric razor* golarka ◇ *a disposable razor* ▶ **brzytwa**

ˈrazor blade noun [C] the thin sharp piece of metal that you put in a **razor** ▶ **żyletka**

Rd = ROAD (2): *21 Hazel Rd*

re /riː/ prep. about or concerning sth; used at the beginning of a business letter or an email to introduce the subject: *Re your letter of 1 September... ◇ Re: travel expenses* ▶ **dot.**

re- /riː/ [in compounds] again: *reapply* ponownie składać podanie ◇ *reappearance* ponowne pojawienie się ◇ *renew* odnawiać (np. umowę) ▶ **ponownie**

reach¹ /riːtʃ/ verb **1** [T] to arrive at a place or condition that you have been going towards: *We won't reach Dover before 12. ◇ The two sides hope to* ***reach an agreement*** *sometime today. ◇ Sometimes the temperature reaches 45° C. ◇ The team reached the semi-final last year. ◇ to reach a conclusion/compromise ◇ Have you reached a decision yet?* Czy podjąłeś już decyzję? ▶ **docierać/dojeżdżać/dochodzić do czegoś; osiągać coś 2** [I,T] **reach (out) (for sb/sth); reach (sth) (down)** to stretch out your arm to try and touch or get sth: *The child reached out for her mother. ◇ She reached into her bag for her purse.* ▶ **wyciągać rękę, sięgać po coś 3** [I,T] to be able to touch sth: *Can you get me that book off the top shelf? I can't reach. ◇ He couldn't reach the light switch. ◇ I need a longer ladder – this one won't reach.* ▶ **sięgać 4** [T] to communicate with sb, especially by telephone; contact: *You can reach me at this number.* ▶ **kontaktować się z kimś**

reach² /riːtʃ/ noun [U] the distance that you can stretch your arm ▶ **zasięg**

IDM **beyond/out of (sb's) reach 1** outside the distance that you can stretch your arm: *Keep this medicine out of the reach of children.* ▶ **poza zasięgiem 2** not able to be got or done by sb: *A job like that is completely beyond his reach.* ▶ **nieosiągalny, niedostępny**

within (sb's) reach 1 inside the distance that you can stretch your arm ▶ **w zasięgu, w pobliżu 2** able to be achieved by sb: *We were one goal ahead with ten minutes left and so could sense that victory was within our reach.* ▶ **w zasięgu**

within (easy) reach of sth not far from sth ▶ **(łatwo) dostępny**

react /riˈækt/ verb [I] **1 react (to sth) (by doing sth)** to do or say sth because of sth that has happened or been said: *He reacted to the news by jumping up and down and shouting. ◇ The players reacted angrily to the decision.* ▶ **reagować 2 react (to sth)** to become ill after eating, breathing, etc. a particular substance: *He reacted badly to the drug and had to go to hospital.* ▶ **(za)reagować 3 react (with sth/together)** (used about a chemical substance) to change after coming into contact with another substance: *Iron reacts with water and air to produce rust.* ▶ **reagować**

PHR V **react against sb/sth** to behave or talk in a way that shows that you do not like the influence of sb/sth (for example authority, your family, etc.) ▶ **opierać/sprzeciwiać się komuś/czemuś**

reaction /riˈækʃn/ noun **1** [C,U] **(a) reaction (to sb/sth)** something that you do or say because of sth that has happened: *Could we have your reaction to the latest news, Prime Minister? ◇ I shook him to try and wake him up but there was no reaction.* ▶ **reakcja 2** [C,U] **(a) reaction (against sb/sth)** behaviour that shows that you do not like the influence of sb/sth (for example authority, your family, etc.): *Her strange clothes are a reaction against the conservative way she was brought up.* ▶ **opór, sprzeciw 3** [C] **a reaction (to sth)** a bad effect that your body experiences because of sth that you have eaten, touched or breathed: *She had an* ***allergic reaction*** *to something in the food.* ▶ **reakcja 4** [C, usually pl.] the physical ability to act quickly when sth happens: *If the other driver's reactions hadn't been so good, there would have been an accident.* ▶ **odruch, reakcja 5** [C,U] (technical) a chemical change produced by two or more substances coming into contact with each other: *a nuclear reaction* ▶ **reakcja**

reactionary /riˈækʃənri; US -neri/ noun [C] (pl. **reactionaries**) a person who tries to prevent political or social change ▶ **reakcjonist(k)a**

■ **reactionary** adj.: *reactionary views/politics/groups* ▶ **reakcyjny**

reactivate /riˈæktɪveɪt/ verb [T] to make sth start working or happening again after a period of time ▶ **ponownie uruchamiać**

reactor = NUCLEAR REACTOR

read¹ /riːd/ verb (pt, pp **read** /red/) **1** [I,T] to look at words or symbols and understand them: *He never learnt to read and write. ◇ Have you read any good books lately? ◇ Can you read music?* ▶ **czytać 2** [I,T] **read (sb) (sth); read sth (to sb)** to say written words to sb: *My father used to read me stories when I was a child. ◇ I hate reading out loud* (głośno czytać). ▶ **czytać 3** [T] to be able to understand sth from what you can see: *A man came to read the gas meter. ◇ Profoundly deaf people often learn to* ***read lips.*** *◇ I've no idea what he'll say – I can't* ***read*** *his* ***mind!*** *◇ I can't read the clock* (nie mogę odczytać godziny na zegarze) *– I haven't got my glasses on.* ▶ **odczytywać; czytać** (*np. w myślach, oczach*) **4** [T] to show words or a sign of sth: *The sign read 'Keep Left'.* ▶ (*znak itp.*) **wskazywać 5** [T] (formal) to study a subject at university: *She read Modern Languages at Cambridge.* ▶ **studiować**

PHR V **read sth into sth** to think that there is a meaning in sth that may not really be there ▶ **dorozumiewać się czegoś w czymś, dopatrywać się czegoś w czymś**

read on to continue reading; to read the next part of sth ▶ **czytać dalej**

read sth out to read sth to other people ▶ **czytać coś na głos**

read sth through to read sth to check details or to look for mistakes: *I read my essay through a few times before handing it in.* ▶ **przeczytać coś**

read up on sth to find out everything you can about a subject ▶ **poczytać** (*na jakiś temat*)

read² /riːd/ noun [sing.] (informal) a period or the act of reading: *I generally* ***have a*** *quick* ***read*** *of the newspaper* (szybko przeglądam gazetę) *over breakfast. ◇ a good read* zajmująca książka ▶ **czytanie**

readable /ˈriːdəbl/ adj. **1** easy or interesting to read ▶ **dający się miło/łatwo czytać 2** able to be read: *machine-readable data* dane nadające się do automatycznego odczytu ▶ **czytelny** ➲ look at **legible**

reader /ˈriːdə(r)/ noun [C] **1** a person who reads sth (a particular newspaper, magazine, type of book, etc.): *She's an avid reader of science fiction.* ▶ **czytelni-k/czka 2** [with an adjective] a person who reads in a particular way: *a fast/slow reader* osoba szybko/wolno czytająca ▶ **czytelni-k/czka 3** a book for practising reading: *a series of English graded readers* ▶ **czytanka,** (*książka*) **wypisy**

readership /ˈriːdəʃɪp/ noun [sing.] the number of people who regularly read a particular newspaper, magazine, etc.: *The newspaper has a readership of 200 000.* ▶ **liczba czytelników**

readily /ˈredɪli/ adv. **1** easily, without difficulty: *Most vegetables are* ***readily available*** *at this time of year.* ▶ **łatwo 2** without pausing; without being forced: *He readily admitted that he was wrong.* ▶ **bez wahania**

readiness /ˈredinəs/ noun [U] **1 readiness (for sth)** the state of being ready or prepared ▶ **gotowość, przygotowanie 2 readiness (to do sth)** the state of being prepared to do sth without arguing or complaining: *The bank have indicated their readiness to lend him the money.* ▶ **chęć, gotowość**

reading /ˈriːdɪŋ/ noun **1** [U] what you do when you read: *I haven't had time to do much reading* (dużo czytać) *lately. ◇ Her hobbies include painting and reading.* ▶ **czytanie 2** [U] books, articles, etc. that are intended to be read: *The information office gave me a pile of* ***reading matter***

(materiałów do czytania) *to take away.* ▶ **lektura 3** [C] the particular way in which sb understands sth: *What's your reading of the situation?* ▶ **rozumienie 4** [C] the number or measurement that is shown on an instrument: *a reading of 20°* ▶ **wskazania** (*np. przyrządu pomiarowego*), **odczyt**

'reading group = BOOK GROUP

readjust /ˌriːə'dʒʌst/ verb **1** [I] **readjust (to sth)** to get used to a different or new situation: *After her divorce, it took her a long time to readjust to being single again.* ▶ **ponownie przystosowywać się 2** [T] to change or move sth slightly ▶ **ponownie dopasowywać/regulować**
■ **readjustment** noun [C,U] ▶ **ponowne przystosowanie/dopasowanie**

ˌread-only 'memory = ROM

ready /'redi/ adj. (**readier**; **readiest**) **1 ready to do sth**; **ready (with/for sth)** prepared and happy to do sth: *You know me – I'm always ready to help.* ◇ *Charlie's always ready with advice.* ◇ *The men were angry and ready for a fight.* ◇ *I know it's early, but I'm* ***ready for bed.*** ▶ **chętny, gotowy 2 ready (for sb/sth)**; **ready (to do sth)** prepared and able to do sth or to be used: *The car will be ready for you to collect* (gotowy do odbioru) *on Friday.* ◇ *I can't talk now – I'm getting ready to go out* (przygotowuję się do wyjścia). ◇ *He isn't ready to take his driving test – he hasn't had enough lessons.* ◇ *I'm meeting him at 7, so I don't have long to* ***get ready*** (aby się przygotować). ◇ *I'll go and* ***get*** *the dinner* ***ready*** (przygotuję obiad). ◇ ***Have*** *your money* ***ready*** (pod ręką) *before you get on the bus.* ▶ **gotowy**
■ **ready** adv. [in compounds] already made or done; not done especially for you: *ready-cooked food* jedzenie gotowe do spożycia (często po odgrzaniu) ◇ *There are no* ***ready-made*** *answers* (nie ma gotowych rozwiązań) *to this problem – we'll have to find our own solution.* ▶ **już, uprzednio**

real[1] /'riːəl; rɪəl/ adj. **1** actually existing, not imagined: *The film is based on real life.* ◇ *This isn't a real word, I made it up.* ◇ *We have a real chance of winning.* ◇ *Closure of the factory is a very real danger.* ▶ **prawdziwy 2** natural, not artificial: *This shirt is real silk.* ▶ **prawdziwy 3** actually true; not only what people think is true: *The name he gave to the police wasn't his real name.* ▶ **prawdziwy 4** [only before a noun] having all, not just some, of the qualities necessary to really be sth: *She was my first real girlfriend.* ▶ **prawdziwy 5** [only before a noun] (used to emphasize a state, feeling or quality) strong or big: *Money is a real problem for us at the moment.* ◇ *He made a real effort to be polite.* ▶ **prawdziwy**
IDM **for real** genuine or serious: *Her tears weren't for real.* ◇ *Was he for real* (czy mówił serio) *when he offered you the job?* ▶ **prawdziwy, (na) serio**
the real thing 1 something genuine, not a copy: *This painting is just a copy. The real thing is in a gallery.* ▶ **autentyk 2** the truest and best example of sth: *She's had boyfriends before but this time she says it's the real thing* (prawdziwa miłość). ▶ **(to jest właśnie) to**

real[2] /'riːəl; rɪəl/ adv. (US, informal) very; really ▶ **bardzo**

'real estate noun [U] property in the form of land and buildings ▶ **nieruchomości**

'real estate agent (US) = ESTATE AGENT

realise = REALIZE

realism /'riːəlɪzəm/ noun [U] **1** behaviour that shows that you accept the facts of a situation and are not influenced by your feelings ▶ **realizm** ➲ look at **idealism 2** (in art, literature, etc.) showing things as they really are ▶ **realizm**

realist /'riːəlɪst/ noun [C] **1** a person who accepts the facts of a situation, and does not try to pretend that it is different: *I'm a realist – I don't expect the impossible.* ▶ **realist(k)a 2** an artist or writer who shows things as they really are ▶ **przedstawiciel/ka realizmu** (*w sztuce itp.*)

realistic /ˌriːə'lɪstɪk/ adj. **1** sensible and understanding what it is possible to achieve in a particular situation: *We have to be realistic* (bądźmy realistami) *about our chances of winning.* ▶ **realistyczny 2** showing things as they really are: *a realistic drawing/description* ▶ **realistyczny 3** not real but appearing to be real: *The monsters in the film were very realistic.* ▶ **realistyczny** OPP **unrealistic**
■ **realistically** /-kli/ adv. ▶ **realistycznie, z poczuciem rzeczywistości**

reality /ri'æləti/ noun (pl. **realities**) **1** [U] the way life really is, not the way it may appear to be or how you would like it to be: *I enjoyed my holiday, but now it's back to reality.* ◇ *We have to* ***face reality*** *and accept that we've failed.* ▶ **rzeczywistość 2** [C] a thing that is actually experienced, not just imagined: *Films portray war as heroic and exciting, but the reality is very different.* ◇ *The realities of living in a foreign country* (realność życia w obcym kraju) *were too much for her and she went home.* ◇ *Death is a reality that everyone has to face eventually.* ▶ **rzeczywistość**
IDM **in reality** in fact, really (not the way sth appears or has been described): *People say this is an exciting city but in reality it's rather boring.* ▶ **w rzeczywistości**

reˌality T'V noun [U] television shows that are based on real people (not actors) in real situations, presented as entertainment ▶ **reality TV**

realize (also **-ise**) /'riːəlaɪz/ verb [T] **1** to know and understand that sth is true or that sth has happened: *I'm sorry I mentioned it, I didn't realize how much it upset you.* ◇ *Didn't you realize (that) you needed to bring money?* ▶ **zdawać sobie sprawę 2** to become conscious of sth or that sth has happened, usually some time later: *When I got home, I realized that I had left my keys at the office.* ▶ **uświadamiać/uprzytamniać sobie 3** to make sth that you imagined become reality: *His worst fears were realized when he saw the damage caused by the fire.* ▶ **realizować, urzeczywistniać**
■ **realization** (also **-isation**) /ˌriːəlaɪ'zeɪʃn; ˌrɪəl-; US ˌriːələ'z-/ noun [U] ▶ **uprzytomnienie sobie, spełnienie**

really /'rɪəli/ adv. **1** actually; in fact: *I couldn't believe it was really happening.* ◇ *He said he was sorry but I don't think he really meant it.* ◇ *She wasn't really angry, she was only pretending.* ◇ *Is it really true?* ▶ **naprawdę, rzeczywiście 2** very; very much: *I'm really tired.* ◇ *I really hope you enjoy yourself.* ◇ *I really tried but I couldn't do it.* ▶ **bardzo, usilnie, naprawdę 3** (used in negative sentences to make what you are saying less strong): *I don't really agree with that.* Nie całkiem się z tym zgadzam. ▶ **tak naprawdę 4** (used in questions when you are expecting sb to answer 'No'): *You don't really expect me to believe that, do you?* ▶ **doprawdy?, czyżby? 5** (used as a question for expressing surprise, interest, doubt, etc.): *'She's left her husband.' 'Really? When did that happen?'* ▶ **doprawdy**

realm /relm/ noun [C] (formal) a country that has a king or queen ▶ **królestwo**

Realtor™ (US) = ESTATE AGENT

reap /riːp/ verb [T] to cut and collect a crop, especially **corn**, **wheat**, etc., from a field: (figurative) *If you work hard now you'll* ***reap the benefits*** *later on.* ▶ **zbierać** (*np. plony, korzyści*)

reappear /ˌriːə'pɪə(r)/ verb [I] to appear again or be seen again ▶ **ponownie się ukazywać/pojawiać**
■ **reappearance** noun [C,U] ▶ **ponowne ukazywanie/pojawianie się**

reappraisal /ˌriːəˈpreɪzl/ noun [C,U] the new examination of a situation, way of doing sth, etc. in order to decide if any changes are necessary ▶ **ponowna ocena**

rear¹ /rɪə(r)/ noun [sing.] **1** (**the rear**) the back part: *There are toilets at the rear of the plane.* ▶ **tył** **2** the part of your body that you sit on; your bottom ▶ **tyłek**
■ **rear** adj. [only before a noun]: *the rear window/lights of a car* ▶ **tylny**
IDM **bring up the rear** to be the last one in a race, a line of people, etc. ▶ **zamykać pochód**

rear² /rɪə(r)/ verb **1** [T] to care for young children or animals until they are fully grown: *She reared a family of five on her own.* ▶ **wychowywać** **2** [T] to breed and look after animals on a farm, etc.: *to rear cattle/poultry* ▶ **hodować** **3** [I] **rear (up)** (used about horses) to stand only on the back legs ▶ **stawać dęba**

rearrange /ˌriːəˈreɪndʒ/ verb [T] **1** to change the position or order of things: *We've rearranged the living room* (inaczej urządziliśmy salon) *to make more space.* ▶ **poprzestawiać, pozmieniać** **2** to change a plan, meeting, etc. that has been fixed: *The match has been rearranged for next Wednesday.* Mecz został przesunięty na następną środę. ▶ **zmieniać**

ˌrear-view ˈmirror noun [C] a mirror in which a driver can see the traffic behind ▶ **lusterko wsteczne**

reason¹ /ˈriːzn/ noun **1** [C] **a reason (for sth/for doing sth); a reason why.../that...** a cause or an explanation for sth that has happened or for sth that sb has done: *What's your reason for being so late?* ◇ *Is there any reason why you couldn't tell me this before?* ◇ *He said he couldn't come but he didn't* ***give a reason.*** ◇ *The reason (that) I'm phoning you is to ask a favour.* ◇ *She left the job for personal reasons.* ◇ ***For some reason*** *or another* (z niewiadomych przyczyn) *they can't give us an answer until next week.* ▶ **powód, przyczyna** **2** [C,U] **(a) reason (to do sth); (a) reason (for sth/for doing sth)** something that shows that it is right or fair to do sth: *I* ***have reason*** (mam powody do przypuszczenia) *to believe that you've been lying.* ◇ *You* ***have every reason*** (masz wszelkie powody) *to be angry, considering how badly you've been treated.* ◇ *I think we have reason for complaint.* ◇ *I chose this colour for a reason* (nie bez powodu). ▶ **powód, przesłanka** **3** [U] the ability to think and to make sensible decisions: *Only human beings are capable of reason.* ▶ **rozsądek** **4** [U] what is right or acceptable: *They were determined to have a fight and nobody could make them* ***see reason*** (przemówić im do rozsądku). ◇ *I tried to persuade him not to drive but he just wouldn't* ***listen to reason*** (był głuchy na głos rozsądku). ◇ *I'll pay anything* ***within reason*** (w granicach rozsądku) *for a ticket.* ▶ **rozsądek**
IDM **it stands to reason** (informal) it is obvious if you think about it ▶ **to się rozumie samo przez się**

reason² /ˈriːzn/ verb [I,T] to form a judgement or opinion about sth, after thinking about it in a logical way ▶ **rozumować, wyciągać wnioski**
PHR V **reason with sb** to talk to sb in order to persuade them to behave or think in a more reasonable way ▶ **przemawiać komuś do rozsądku**

reasonable /ˈriːznəbl/ adj. **1** fair, practical and sensible: *I think it's reasonable to expect people to keep their promises.* ◇ *I tried to be reasonable even though I was very angry.* ▶ **rozsądny, sensowny** **2** acceptable and appropriate in a particular situation: *I waited a reasonable time for Sashi then I gave up and went home.* ▶ **sensowny** **3** (used about a price) not too high; not higher than it should be: *It was a lovely meal and the bill was very reasonable!* ▶ **umiarkowany** **3** quite good, high, big, etc. but not very: *They've got a reasonable amount of money but they certainly aren't rich.* ◇ *His work is of a reasonable standard* (na zadowalającym poziomie). ▶ **dostateczny**

reasonably /ˈriːznəbli/ adv. **1** fairly or quite (but not very): *The weather was reasonably good but not brilliant.* ▶ **dość, wystarczająco** **2** in a sensible and fair way: *If you think about my suggestion reasonably, you'll realize that I'm right.* ▶ **racjonalnie, rozsądnie**

reasoning /ˈriːzənɪŋ/ noun [U] the process of thinking about sth and making a judgement or decision: *What's the reasoning behind his sudden decision to leave?* ▶ **rozumowanie**

reassurance /ˌriːəˈʃʊərəns; Brit. also -ˈʃɔːr-/ noun [U,C] advice or help that you give to sb to stop them worrying or being afraid: *I need some reassurance that I'm doing things the right way.* ▶ **zapewnienie**

reassure /ˌriːəˈʃʊə(r); Brit. also -ˈʃɔː(r)/ verb [T] to say or do sth in order to stop sb worrying or being afraid: *The mechanic reassured her that the engine was fine.* ▶ **zapewniać**
■ **reassuring** adj. ▶ **uspokajający** | **reassuringly** adv. ▶ **uspokajająco, zapewniająco**

rebate /ˈriːbeɪt/ noun [C] a sum of money that is given back to you because you have paid too much: *to get a tax rebate* ▶ **zwrot nadpłaty**

rebel¹ /ˈrebl/ noun [C] **1** a person who fights against their country's government because they want things to change SYN **insurgent** **2** a person who refuses to obey people in authority or to accept rules: *At school he had a reputation as a rebel.* ▶ **buntowni-k/czka**

rebel² /rɪˈbel/ verb [I] (**rebelling**; **rebelled**) **rebel (against sb/sth)** to fight against authority, society, a law, etc.: *She rebelled against her parents by marrying a man she knew they didn't approve of.* ▶ **buntować się, wszczynać bunt**

rebellion /rɪˈbeljən/ noun [C,U] **1** an occasion when some of the people in a country try to change the government, using violence ▶ **bunt** **2** the act of fighting against authority or refusing to accept rules: *Voting against the leader of the party was an act of open rebellion.* ▶ **bunt**

rebellious /rɪˈbeljəs/ adj. not doing what authority, society, etc. wants you to do: *rebellious teenagers* ▶ **buntowniczy, zbuntowany**

reboot /ˌriːˈbuːt/ verb [I,T] if you **reboot** a computer or if it **reboots**, you turn it off and then turn it on again immediately ▶ **uruchamiać ponownie** (*komputer*)

rebound /rɪˈbaʊnd/ verb [I] **rebound (from/off sth)** to hit sth/sb and then go in a different direction: *The ball rebounded off Cole and went into the goal.* ▶ **odbijać się, odskakiwać**
■ **rebound** /ˈriːbaʊnd/ noun [C] ▶ **odbicie** (*np. piłki*)

rebuff /rɪˈbʌf/ noun [C] an unkind refusal of an offer or suggestion ▶ **odprawa**
■ **rebuff** verb [T] ▶ **odprawić kogoś z niczym**

rebuild /ˌriːˈbɪld/ verb [T] (pt, pp **rebuilt** /ˌriːˈbɪlt/) to build sth again: *Following the storm, a great many houses will have to be rebuilt.* ▶ **odbudowywać**

rebuke /rɪˈbjuːk/ verb [T] (formal) to speak angrily to sb because they have done sth wrong ▶ **karcić, ganić**
■ **rebuke** noun [C] ▶ **nagana**

rebut /rɪˈbʌt/ verb [T] (**rebutting**; **rebutted**) (formal) to say or prove that a statement or criticism is false ▶ **obalać** SYN **refute**

recall /rɪˈkɔːl/ verb [T] **1** to remember sth (a fact, event, action, etc.) from the past: *I don't recall exactly when I first met her.* ◇ *She couldn't recall meeting him before.* ▶ **przypominać sobie** **2** to order sb to return; to ask for sth to be returned: *The company has recalled all the fridges that have this fault.* ▶ **odwoływać; wycofywać** (*ze sprzedaży itp.*)

recap /ˈriːkæp/ (**recapping**; **recapped**) (informal) (also formal **recapitulate** /ˌriːkəˈpɪtʃuleɪt/) verb [I,T] to repeat or look again at the main points of sth to make sure that they have been understood: *Let's quickly recap what we've done in today's lesson, before we finish.* ▶ **podsumowywać**

recapture /ˌriːˈkæptʃə(r)/ verb [T] **1** to win back sth that was taken from you by an enemy: *Government troops have recaptured the city.* ▶ **odbijać 2** to catch a person or an animal that has escaped ▶ **ponownie łapać**, **odzyskiwać 3** to create or experience again sth from the past: *The film brilliantly recaptures life in the 1930s.* ▶ **oddawać** (*np. nastrój*)

recede /rɪˈsiːd/ verb [I] **1** to move away and begin to disappear: *The coast began to recede into the distance.* ▶ **oddalać się**, **cofać się 2** (used about a hope, fear, chance, etc.) to become smaller or less strong ▶ **słabnąć**, **oddalać się 3** (used about a man's hair) to fall out and stop growing at the front of the head: *He's got a **receding hairline**.* ▶ **rzednąć** ➲ picture at **hair**

receipt /rɪˈsiːt/ noun **1** [C] **a receipt (for sth)** a piece of paper that is given to show that you have paid for sth: *Keep the receipt in case you want to exchange the shirt.* ▶ **pokwitowanie**, **paragon 2** [U] (formal) **receipt (of sth)** the receiving of sth: *Payment must be made within seven days of receipt of the goods.* ▶ **odbiór**

receive /rɪˈsiːv/ verb [T] **1 receive sth (from sb/sth)** to get or accept sth that sb sends or gives to you: *I received a letter from an old friend last week.* ◇ *to receive a phone call/a prize* ▶ **otrzymywać 2** to experience a particular kind of treatment or injury: *We received a warm welcome* (spotkaliśmy się z ciepłym przyjęciem) *from our hosts.* ◇ *He received several cuts and bruises* (odniósł lekkie obrażenia) *in the accident.* **3** [often passive] to react to sth new in a particular way: *The film has been well received by the critics.* ▶ **odbierać**, **przyjmować**

receiver /rɪˈsiːvə(r)/ noun [C] **1** (also **handset** /ˈhændset/) the part of a telephone that is used for listening and speaking ▶ **słuchawka** ➲ note at **telephone**

> To answer or make a telephone call you **pick up** or **lift** the receiver. To end a telephone call you **put down** or **replace** the receiver or you **hang up**.

2 a piece of TV or radio equipment that changes electronic signals into sounds or pictures ▶ **odbiornik**

recent /ˈriːsnt/ adj. that happened or began only a short time ago: ***In recent years** there have been many changes.* ◇ *This is a recent photograph of my daughter.* ▶ **ostatni**, **świeży**, **niedawny**

recently /ˈriːsntli/ adv. **1** a short time ago: *I don't know her very well – I only met her recently.* ◇ *She worked here until quite recently.* ▶ **niedawno**, **ostatnio 2** during a period between not long ago and now: *Have you seen Paul recently?* ▶ **ostatnio**, **niedawno**

> Przysłówek **recently** może odnosić się zarówno do jakiegoś momentu w niedalekiej przeszłości, jak i do pewnego okresu (odcinka czasu). Jeżeli odnosi się do momentu w przeszłości, należy użyć czasu *simple past*: *He died recently.* Jeżeli odnosi się do okresu, należy użyć czasu *present perfect continuous*: *I haven't done anything interesting recently.* ◇ *She's been working hard recently.* **Lately** odnosi się tylko do odcinka czasu. Należy z tym przysłówkiem używać wyłącznie czasu *present perfect* lub *present perfect continuous*: *I've seen a lot of films lately.* ◇ *I've been spending too much money lately.*

receptacle /rɪˈseptəkl/ noun [C] (formal) a container ▶ **naczynie**, **zbiornik**

reception /rɪˈsepʃn/ noun **1** [U] the place inside the entrance of a hotel or office building where guests or visitors go when they first arrive: *Leave your key **at/in reception** if you go out, please.* ◇ *the reception desk* recepcja ▶ **recepcja 2** [C] a formal party to celebrate sth or to welcome an important person: *Their **wedding reception** was held at a local hotel.* ◇ *There will be an official reception at the embassy for the visiting ambassador.* ▶ **przyjęcie 3** [sing.] the way people react to sth: *The play got a mixed reception.* ▶ **przyjęcie** (*np. sztuki, wystawy*), **odbiór 4** [U] the quality of radio or TV signals: *TV reception is very poor where we live.* ▶ **odbiór**

receptionist /rɪˈsepʃənɪst/ noun [C] a person who works in a hotel, an office, etc. answering the telephone and dealing with visitors and guests when they arrive: *a hotel receptionist* ▶ **recepcjonist(k)a**

receptive /rɪˈseptɪv/ adj. **receptive (to sth)** ready to listen to new ideas, suggestions, etc. ▶ **podatny**, **chłonny**

recess /rɪˈses; ˈriːses/ noun **1** [C,U] a period of time when Parliament or other groups that meet for official discussions do not meet ▶ **ferie 2** [U] (US) a short break during a trial in a court of law ▶ **przerwa** (*w trakcie procesu sądowego*) **3** [U] (US) a short period of free time between classes at school ▶ **pauza** ➲ note at **interval 4** [C] part of a wall that is further back than the rest, forming a space ▶ **wnęka 5** [C] a part of a room that receives very little light ▶ **zakamarek**

recession /rɪˈseʃn/ noun [C,U] a period when the business and industry of a country is not successful: *The country is now **in recession**.* ◇ *How long will the recession last?* ▶ **recesja**

recharge /ˌriːˈtʃɑːdʒ/ verb [I,T] to fill a battery with electrical power; to fill up with electrical power: *He plugged the drill in to recharge it.* ▶ **ponownie ładować** (*baterię*) ➲ look at **charge**

■ **rechargeable** adj.: *rechargeable batteries* ▶ **do ponownego ładowania**

recipe /ˈresəpi/ noun [C] **1 a recipe (for sth)** the instructions for cooking or preparing sth to eat: *a recipe for chocolate cake* ▶ **przepis (kulinarny) 2 a recipe for sth** the way to get or produce sth: *Putting Dave in charge of the project is **a recipe for disaster**.* ▶ **recepta**

> **a recipe for shepherd's pie**
>
> **Peel** 4 potatoes, then **cut** them in pieces and **boil** them in a **saucepan** of water. When they are cooked, **strain** them in a **colander** to remove the water, then **mash** them with some butter and milk. Next **slice** an onion thinly, and **fry** it in a **frying pan**. Add some **minced** meat, some **chopped** tomatoes and herbs, and put the mixture in a **casserole** dish, with the **mashed potato** on top. **Grate** some cheese on the potato, and then **bake** it in the **oven** for half an hour.

recipient /rɪˈsɪpiənt/ noun [C] (formal) a person who receives sth ▶ **odbior-ca/czyni**

reciprocal /rɪˈsɪprəkl/ adj. involving two or more people or groups who agree to help each other or to behave in the same way towards each other: *The arrangement is reciprocal. They help us and we help them.* ▶ **obopólny**, **wzajemny**

reciprocate /rɪˈsɪprəkeɪt/ verb [I,T] **reciprocate (sth) (with sth)** to behave or feel towards sb in the same way as they behave or feel towards you: *Her love for him was not reciprocated.* ◇ *I wasn't sure whether to laugh or to reciprocate with a remark of my own.* ▶ **odwzajemniać (się)**

■ **reciprocation** /rɪˌsɪprəˈkeɪʃn/ noun [U] ▶ **odwzajemnienie**

recital /rɪˈsaɪtl/ noun [C] a formal public performance of music or poetry: *a piano recital* ▶ **recital** ➲ look at **concert**

recite /rɪˈsaɪt/ verb [I,T] to say a piece of writing, especially a poem or a list, in a normal speaking voice and from memory ▶ **recytować, deklamować**

reckless /ˈrekləs/ adj. not thinking about possible bad or dangerous results that could come from your actions: *reckless driving* ◇ *a reckless disregard for safety* ▶ **brawurowy, lekkomyślny**
■ **recklessly** adv. ▶ **nierozważnie, brawurowo**

⚷ **reckon** /ˈrekən/ verb [T] (informal) **1** to think; to have an opinion about sth: *She's very late now. I reckon (that) she isn't coming.* ◇ *I think she's forgotten. What do you reckon?* ▶ **sądzić, myśleć 2** to calculate sth approximately: *I reckon the journey will take about half an hour.* ▶ **liczyć, że 3** (Brit.) to expect to do sth: *We reckon to sell about twenty of these suits a week.* ▶ **oczekiwać**
PHR V **reckon on sth** to expect sth to happen and therefore to base a plan or action on it: *I didn't book in advance because I wasn't reckoning on tickets being so scarce.* ▶ **liczyć na coś, oczekiwać**
reckon (sth) up to calculate the total amount or number of sth ▶ **zliczyć, zsumować**
reckon with sb/sth to think about sb/sth as a possible problem ▶ **liczyć się z kimś/czymś**

reckoning /ˈrekənɪŋ/ noun [U,C] the act of calculating sth, especially in a way that is not very exact: ***By my reckoning*** (według moich obliczeń) *you still owe me £5.* ▶ **obliczenie**

reclaim /rɪˈkleɪm/ verb [T] **1 reclaim sth (from sb/sth)** to get back sth that has been lost or taken away: *Reclaim your luggage after you have been through passport control.* ▶ **odzyskiwać, odbierać 2** to make wet land suitable for use ▶ **odzyskiwać** (*teren poprzez osuszanie*) **3** to get back useful materials from waste products ▶ **odzyskiwać, regenerować** (*surowce*)
■ **reclamation** /ˌrekləˈmeɪʃn/ noun [U]: *land reclamation* ▶ **odbiór** (*np. bagażu*); **osuszanie** (*terenów podmokłych*); **odzyskiwanie** (*surowców*)

recline /rɪˈklaɪn/ verb [I] to sit or lie back in a relaxed and comfortable way ▶ **układać (się) w pozycji półleżącej**
■ **reclining** adj.: *The car has **reclining seats** at the front.* ▶ (*siedzenie, fotel*) **rozkładany**

recluse /rɪˈkluːs; US ˈrekluːs/ noun [C] a person who lives alone and likes to avoid other people ▶ **odludek**
■ **reclusive** /rɪˈkluːsɪv/ adj.: *a reclusive millionaire* ▶ **samotniczy**

⚷ **recognition** /ˌrekəgˈnɪʃn/ noun **1** [U] the fact that you can identify sb/sth that you see: *He showed no sign of recognition* (nic nie wskazywało, że mnie rozpoznał) *when he passed me.* ▶ **rozpoznawanie 2** [U, sing.] the act of accepting that sth exists, is true or is official: *There is a growing recognition that older people are important in the workplace.* ▶ **uznanie 3** [U] a public show of respect for sb's work or actions: *She has **received** public **recognition** for her services to charity.* ◇ *Please accept this gift **in recognition of** the work you have done.* ▶ **uznanie**

recognizable (also -isable) /ˈrekəgnaɪzəbl; ˌrekəgˈnaɪzəbl/ adj. **recognizable (as sb/sth)** that can be identified as sb/sth: *He was barely recognizable with his new short haircut.* ▶ **rozpoznawalny**
■ **recognizably** (also -isably) /-əbli/ adv. ▶ **rozpoznawalnie**

⚷ **recognize** (also -ise) /ˈrekəgnaɪz/ verb [T] **1** to know again sb/sth that you have seen or heard before: *I recognized him but I couldn't remember his name.* ▶ **rozpoznawać, poznawać 2** to accept that sth is true: *I recognize that some of my ideas are unrealistic.* ▶ **przyznawać, że 3** to accept sth officially: *My qualifications are not recognized in other countries.* ▶ **uznawać, honorować 4** to show officially that you think sth that sb has done is good: *The company gave her a special present to recognize her long years of service.* ▶ **uznawać**

recoil /rɪˈkɔɪl/ verb [I] to quickly move away from sb/sth unpleasant: *She recoiled in horror* (cofnęła się z przerażeniem) *at the sight of the corpse.* ▶ **cofnąć się** (*szybko, gwałtownie*)

recollect /ˌrekəˈlekt/ verb [I,T] to remember sth, especially by making an effort: *I don't recollect exactly when it happened.* ▶ **przypominać sobie**

recollection /ˌrekəˈlekʃn/ noun **1** [U] **recollection (of sth/doing sth)** the ability to remember: ***I have no recollection*** (nie przypominam sobie) *of promising to lend you money.* ▶ **pamięć o czymś 2** [C, usually pl.] something that you remember: *I have only vague recollections of the town where I spent my early years.* ▶ **wspomnienie** SYN for both meanings **memory**

⚷ **recommend** /ˌrekəˈmend/ verb [T] **1 recommend sb/sth (to sb) (for/as sth)** to say that sb/sth is good and that sb should try or use them or it: *Which film would you recommend?* ◇ *Could you recommend me a good hotel?* ◇ *We hope that you'll recommend this restaurant to all your friends.* ◇ *Doctors don't always recommend drugs as the best treatment for every illness.* ▶ **polecać, zalecać 2** to tell sb what you strongly believe they should do: *I recommend that you get some legal advice.* ◇ *I wouldn't recommend (your) travelling on your own. It could be dangerous.* ▶ **zalecać, radzić** ⓘ Uwaga! Nie można powiedzieć ~~recommend sb to do sth~~.

recommendation /ˌrekəmenˈdeɪʃn/ noun **1** [C] a statement about what should be done in a particular situation: *In their report on the crash, the committee **make** several **recommendations** on how* (przedstawiła zalecenia odnośnie tego, jak) *safety could be improved.* ▶ **zalecenie 2** [C,U] saying that sth is good and should be tried or used: *I visited Seville **on** a friend's **recommendation** and I really enjoyed it.* ▶ **rekomendacja, polecenie**

recompense /ˈrekəmpens/ verb [T] (formal) **recompense sb (for sth)** to give money, etc. to sb for special efforts or work or because you are responsible for a loss they have suffered: *The airline has agreed to recompense us for the damage to our luggage.* ▶ **wynagradzać, kompensować**
■ **recompense** noun [sing., U]: *Please accept this cheque **in recompense for** our poor service.* ▶ **rekompensata, odszkodowanie**

reconcile /ˈrekənsaɪl/ verb [T] **1 reconcile sth (with sth)** to find a way of dealing with two ideas, situations, statements, etc. that seem to be opposite to each other: *She finds it difficult to reconcile her career ambitions with her responsibilities to her children.* ▶ **godzić 2** [often passive] **reconcile sb (with sb)** to make people become friends again after an argument: *After years of not speaking to each other, she and her parents were eventually reconciled.* ▶ **godzić kogoś (z kimś) 3 reconcile yourself to sth** to accept an unpleasant situation because there is nothing you can do to change it ▶ **godzić się z czymś**
■ **reconciliation** /ˌrekənsɪliˈeɪʃn/ noun [sing., U]: *The negotiators are hoping to bring about a reconciliation between the two sides.* ▶ **pojednanie, zgoda**

reconnaissance /rɪˈkɒnɪsns/ noun [C,U] the study of a place or area for military reasons: *The plane was shot down while on a reconnaissance mission over enemy territory.* ▶ **zwiad, rozpoznanie**

reconsider /ˌriːkənˈsɪdə(r)/ verb [I,T] to think again about sth, especially because you may want to change your mind: *Public protests have forced the government to reconsider their policy.* ▶ **rewidować**

reconstruct /ˌriːkənˈstrʌkt/ verb [T] **1** to build again sth that has been destroyed or damaged ▶ **odbudowywać 2** to get a full description or picture of sth using the facts that are known: *The police are trying to reconstruct*

R

the victim's movements on the day of the murder. ▶ **odtwarzać**

■ **reconstruction** noun [C,U]: *a reconstruction of the crime using actors* ▶ **odbudowa**, **odtwarzanie**

⚷ **record**[1] /ˈrekɔːd; US -kərd/ noun **1** [C] **a record (of sth)** a written account of what has happened, been done, etc.: *The teachers* ***keep records*** (prowadzą dziennik) *of the children's progress.* ◇ *It's* ***on record*** *that he was out of the country at the time of the murder.* ◇ *medical records* kartoteki medyczne ▶ **notatka**, **rejestr**, **protokół** **2** [C] a thin, round piece of plastic which can store music so that you can play it when you want: *a record collection* ▶ **płyta gramofonowa** **3** [C] the best performance or the highest or lowest level, etc. ever reached in sth, especially in sport: *Who* ***holds the world record for*** *high jump?* ◇ *She's hoping to* ***break the record*** *for the 100 metres.* ◇ *He did it* ***in record time.*** ▶ **rekord** **4** [sing.] the facts, events, etc. that are known (and sometimes written down) about sb/sth: *The police said that the man had* ***a criminal record*** (był notowany). ◇ *This airline has a bad safety record* (ma złą opinię w sprawach bezpieczeństwa).

IDM **off the record** (used about sth sb says) not to be treated as official; not intended to be made public: *She told me off the record that she was going to resign.* ▶ **nieoficjalnie**; **nieoficjalny**

put/set the record straight to correct a mistake by telling sb the true facts ▶ **wyjaśniać nieporozumienie**, **prostować fakty**

⚷ **record**[2] /rɪˈkɔːd/ verb **1** [T] to write down or film facts or events so that they can be referred to later and will not be forgotten: *He recorded everything in his diary.* ◇ *At the inquest the coroner* ***recorded a verdict*** *of accidental death.* ▶ **utrwalać**, **zapisywać** **2** [I,T] to put music, a film, a programme, etc. onto a CD or tape so that it can be listened to or watched again later: *Quiet, please! We're recording.* ◇ *The band has recently recorded a new album.* ◇ *There's a concert I would like to record from the radio this evening.* ▶ **nagrywać**

ˈ**record-breaking** adj. [only before a noun] the best, fastest, highest, etc. ever: *We did the journey in record-breaking time.* ▶ **rekordowy**

recorder /rɪˈkɔːdə(r)/ noun [C] **1** a machine for recording sound and/or pictures: *a tape/cassette recorder* magnetofon szpulowy/kasetowy ◇ *a video cassette recorder* ◇ *a video recorder* magnetowid ▶ **urządzenie do nagrywania dźwięku i/lub obrazu** **2** a type of musical instrument that is often played by children. You play it by blowing through it and covering the holes in it with your fingers. ▶ **flet prosty**

⚷ **recording** /rɪˈkɔːdɪŋ/ noun **1** [C] sound or pictures that have been put onto a CD, video, etc.: *the Berlin Philharmonic's recording of Mahler's Sixth symphony* ▶ **nagranie** **2** [U] the process of making a CD, film, etc.: *a recording session/studio* ▶ **nagrywanie**

ˈ**record label** = LABEL[1] (2)

ˈ**record player** noun [C] a machine that you use for playing records ▶ **adapter**

recount /rɪˈkaʊnt/ verb [T] (formal) to tell a story or describe an event ▶ **opowiadać**

recourse /rɪˈkɔːs; US ˈriːk-/ noun [C] (formal) having to use sth or ask sb for help in a difficult situation: *She made a complete recovery* ***without recourse to*** *surgery* (bez konieczności operacji). ◇ *The government, when necessary,* ***has recourse to*** *the armed forces* (zwraca się o pomoc do wojska). ▶ **zwracanie się do kogoś/jakiejś instytucji** (*o pomoc*)

⚷ **recover** /rɪˈkʌvə(r)/ verb **1** [I] **recover (from sth)** to become well again after you have been ill: *It took him two months to recover from the operation.* ▶ **zdrowieć** **2** [I] **recover (from sth)** to get back to normal again after a bad experience, etc.: *The old lady never really recovered from the shock of being mugged.* ▶ **przychodzić do siebie**, **wracać do równowagi** **3** [T] **recover sth (from sb/sth)** to find or get back sth that was lost or stolen: *Police recovered the stolen goods from a warehouse in South London.* ▶ **odzyskiwać** **4** [T] to get back the use of your senses, control of your emotions, etc.: *He needs daily exercise if he's going to recover the use of his legs.* ▶ **odzyskiwać**

recovery /rɪˈkʌvəri/ noun **1** [usually sing., U] **recovery (from sth)** a return to good health after an illness or to a normal state after a difficult period of time: *to* ***make a*** *good/quick/speedy/slow* ***recovery*** ◇ *She's* ***on the road to recovery*** *now.* ◇ *the prospects of* ***economic recovery*** (ożywienia gospodarczego) ▶ **wyzdrowienie**; **poprawa** **2** [U] **recovery (of sth/sb)** getting back sth that was lost, stolen or missing ▶ **odzyskanie**, **zwrot**

recreation /ˌrekriˈeɪʃn/ noun [U, sing.] enjoying yourself and relaxing when you are not working; a way of doing this: *recreation activities such as swimming or reading* ▶ **rozrywka**, **rekreacja**

recrimination /rɪˌkrɪmɪˈneɪʃn/ noun [C, usually pl., U] an angry statement accusing sb of sth, especially in answer to a similar statement from them: *bitter recriminations* ▶ **wzajemne oskarżenia**

recruit[1] /rɪˈkruːt/ verb [I,T] to find new people to join a company, an organization, the armed forces, etc.: *to recruit young people to the teaching profession* ▶ **werbować**

■ **recruitment** noun [U] ▶ **werbunek**, **rekrutacja**

recruit[2] /rɪˈkruːt/ noun [C] a person who has just joined the army or another organization ▶ **rekrut/ka**, **nowicjusz/ka**

rectangle /ˈrektæŋgl/ noun [C] a shape with four straight sides and four **right angles**. Two of the sides are longer than the other two. ▶ **prostokąt** SYN **oblong**

■ **rectangular** /rekˈtæŋgjələ(r)/ adj. ▶ **prostokątny**

rectify /ˈrektɪfaɪ/ verb [T] (**rectifying**; **rectifies**; pt, pp **rectified**) (formal) to correct sth that is wrong ▶ **poprawiać**

rector /ˈrektə(r)/ noun [C] (in the Church of England) a priest in charge of a **parish** ▶ **proboszcz** ➲ look at **vicar** ➲ note at **priest**

rectum /ˈrektəm/ noun [C] the end section of the tube where solid food waste collects before leaving the body ▶ **odbytnica**

recuperate /rɪˈkuːpəreɪt/ verb [I] (formal) **recuperate (from sth)** to get well again after an illness or injury ▶ **wracać do zdrowia**

■ **recuperation** /rɪˌkuːpəˈreɪʃn/ noun [U] ▶ **powrót do zdrowia**

recur /rɪˈkɜː(r)/ verb [I] (**recu<u>r</u>ring**; **recu<u>r</u>red**) to happen again or many times: *a recurring problem/nightmare* ▶ **powracać**, **powtarzać się**

■ **recurrence** noun [C,U] ▶ **nawrót** | **recurrent** /rɪˈkʌrənt; US -ˈkɜːr-/ adj. ▶ **powracający**, **powtarzający się**

recycle /ˌriːˈsaɪkl/ verb [T] **1** to put used objects and materials through a process so that they can be used again: *recycled paper* papier makulaturowy ◇ *Aluminium cans can be recycled.* ◇ *We take our empty bottles to the bottle bank for recycling* (do odzysku). ▶ **odzyskiwać**, **regenerować** (*surowce*) ➲ note at **environment** **2** to keep used objects and materials and use them again: *Don't throw away your plastic carrier bags – recycle them!* ▶ **ponownie wykorzystywać**

■ **recyclable** adj.: *Most plastics are recyclable.* ▶ **odzyskiwalny**, **nadający się do odzysku/recyklingu** | **recycling** noun [U] ▶ **utylizacja**, **recykling**

⚷ **red** /red/ adj. (**re<u>d</u>der**; **re<u>d</u>dest**) **1** of the colour of blood: *red wine* ▶ **czerwony** ➲ look at **crimson**, **maroon**, **scarlet** **2** a colour that some people's faces become when they are embarrassed, angry, shy, etc.: *He went bright red when she spoke to him.* ◇ *to turn/be/go red in the face* ▶ **czerwony, zaczerwieniony** **3** (used about sb's hair or an animal's fur) of a colour between red, orange and brown: *She's got red hair and freckles.* ▶ **rudy**

■ **red** noun [C,U] **1** the colour of blood: *She was dressed in red.* ▶ **czerwień** **2** a colour between red, orange and brown ▶ **kolor rudy**

IDM **be in the red** (informal) to have spent more money than you have in the bank, etc.: *I'm £500 in the red at the moment.* ▶ **mieć debet** (*w banku*) OPP **be in the black**

catch sb red-handed → CATCH[1]

a red herring an idea or subject which takes people's attention away from what is really important ▶ **odwrócenie uwagi od sedna sprawy**

see red → SEE

ˌred ˈblood cell noun [C] any of the red-coloured cells in the blood, that carry **oxygen** ▶ **krwinka czerwona**

ˈred-brick adj. (Brit.) (used about British universities) built in the late 19th or early 20th century ▶ (*uniwersytet*) **założony na przełomie XIX i XX wieku**

ˌred ˈcard noun [C] (in football) a card that is shown to a player who is being sent off the field for doing sth wrong ▶ **czerwona kartka** ➲ look at **yellow card**

the ˌred ˈcarpet noun [sing.] a piece of red carpet that is put outside to receive an important visitor; a special welcome for an important visitor: *I didn't expect to be given the red carpet treatment* (że będę przyjęty z takimi honorami)*!* ▶ **czerwony dywan**

redcurrant /ˌredˈkʌrənt; ˈredkʌrənt; US ˌredˈkɜːr-; ˈredkɜːr-/ noun [C] a small round red fruit that you can eat: *redcurrant jelly* ▶ **czerwona porzeczka**

redden /ˈredn/ verb [I,T] to become red or to make sth red ▶ **czerwienić (się)** ℹ Częściej mówi się **go red**, a w wypadku zaczerwienienia się osoby – **blush**.

reddish /ˈredɪʃ/ adj. fairly red in colour ▶ **czerwonawy**

redeem /rɪˈdiːm/ verb [T] **1** to prevent sth from being completely bad: *The **redeeming feature** of the job is the good salary.* ▶ **łagodzić** (*np. niedostatki*), **kompensować** **2 redeem yourself** to do sth to improve people's opinion of you, especially after you have done sth bad ▶ **odkupić, odpokutować** (*winę*) **3** to get sth back by paying the amount needed ▶ **wykupywać, spłacać**

redemption /rɪˈdempʃn/ noun [U] (according to the Christian religion) the act of being saved from evil ▶ **zbawienie, odkupienie**

IDM **beyond redemption** too bad to be saved or improved ▶ **nie do odkupienia/odpokutowania**

redevelop /ˌriːdɪˈveləp/ verb [T] to build or arrange an area, a town, a building, etc. in a different and more modern way: *They're redeveloping the city centre.* ▶ **przebudowywać**

■ **redevelopment** noun [U] ▶ **przebudowa**

redhead /ˈredhed/ noun [C] a person, usually a woman, who has red hair ▶ **rudzielec**

ˌred-ˈhot adj. (used about a metal) so hot that it turns red ▶ **rozpalony do czerwoności**

redial /ˌriːˈdaɪəl/ verb [I,T] to call the same number on a telephone that you have just called ▶ **ponownie wybrać numer telefonu**

redistribute /ˌriːdɪˈstrɪbjuːt; ˌriːˈdɪs-/ verb [T] to share sth out among people in a different way from before ▶ **rozdzielać ponownie**

■ **redistribution** /ˌriːdɪstrɪˈbjuːʃn/ noun [U] ▶ **ponowny rozdział, redystrybucja**

ˌred-ˈlight district noun [C] a part of a town where there are a lot of people, especially women, who earn money by having sex with people ▶ **dzielnica domów publicznych**

ˌred ˈpepper = PEPPER[1] (2)

ˌred ˈtape noun [U] official rules that must be followed and papers that must be filled in, which seem unnecessary and often cause delay and difficulty in achieving sth ▶ **biurokracja**

reduce /rɪˈdjuːs; US -ˈduːs/ verb [T] **reduce sth (from sth) (to sth)**; **reduce sth (by sth)** to make sth less or smaller in quantity, price, size, etc.: *The sign said 'Reduce speed now'.* ▶ **zmniejszać, obniżać** OPP **increase**

PHR V **reduce sb/sth (from sth) to sth** [often passive] to force sb/sth into a particular state or condition, usually a bad one: *One of the older boys **reduced** the small child **to** tears.* ▶ **doprowadzać (do czegoś)**

reduction /rɪˈdʌkʃn/ noun **1** [C,U] **reduction (in sth)** that action of becoming or making sth less or smaller: *a sharp reduction in the number of students* ▶ **zmniejszenie, obniżenie** **2** [C] the amount by which sth is made smaller, especially in price: *There were massive reductions in the June sales.* ▶ **obniżka**

redundant /rɪˈdʌndənt/ adj. **1** (used about employees) no longer needed for a job and therefore out of work: *When the factory closed 800 people were **made redundant**.* ▶ **zwolniony** (*z pracy w wyniku redukcji*) ➲ note at **job** **2** not necessary or wanted ▶ **zbyteczny, niepotrzebny**

■ **redundancy** /rɪˈdʌndənsi/ noun [C,U] (pl. **redundancies**): *redundancy pay* odprawa przy zwolnieniu z pracy ▶ **zwolnienie z pracy** (*w wyniku redukcji*)

reed /riːd/ noun [C] **1** a tall plant, like grass, that grows in or near water ▶ **trzcina** **2** a thin piece of wood at the end of some musical instruments which produces a sound when you blow through it ▶ **stroik**

reef /riːf/ noun [C] a long line of rocks, plants, etc. just below or above the surface of the sea: *a coral reef* ▶ **rafa**

reek /riːk/ verb [I] **reek (of sth)** to smell strongly of sth unpleasant: *His breath reeked of tobacco.* ▶ **cuchnąć**

■ **reek** noun [sing.] ▶ **smród**

reel[1] /riːl/ noun [C] a round object that thread, wire, film for cameras, etc. is put around: *a cotton reel* ◇ *a reel of film* ▶ **szpula, rolka, bęben** (*do nawijania*), **cewka** ➲ look at **spool** ➲ picture at **garden**

reel[2] /riːl/ verb [I] **1** to walk without being able to control your legs, for example because you are drunk or you have been hit ▶ **zataczać się** **2** to feel very shocked or upset about sth: *His mind was still reeling from the shock of seeing her again.* ▶ **kręcić się w głowie** (*np. z nadmiaru wrażeń*)

PHR V **reel sth in/out** to wind sth on/off a **reel**: *to reel in a fish* wyciągnąć rybę z wody za pomocą kołowrotka ▶ **nawijać/rozwijać coś**

reel sth off to say or repeat sth from memory quickly and without having to think about it: *She reeled off a long list of names.* ▶ **wyrecytować, wyklepać**

ref (informal) = REFEREE (1)

ref. = REFERENCE (3): *ref. no. 3456*

refectory /rɪˈfektri/ noun [C] (pl. **refectories**) a large dining room in a college, school, etc. ▶ **refektarz**

refer /rɪˈfɜː(r)/ verb (**referring**; **referred**)

PHR V **refer to sb/sth (as sth)** to mention or talk about sb/sth: *When he said 'some students', do you think he was referring to us?* ◇ *She always referred to Ben as 'that nice man'.* ▶ **mówić o kimś/czymś, mieć coś na myśli**

refer to sb/sth **1** to describe or be connected with sb/sth: *The term 'adolescent' refers to young people between the ages of 12 and 17.* ▶ **odnosić się** **2** to find out information by asking sb or by looking in a book, etc.: *If you don't understand a word, you may refer* (zajrzeć) *to your dictionaries.* ▶ **radzić się, powoływać się**

refer sb/sth to sb/sth to send sb/sth to sb/sth else for help or to be dealt with: *The doctor has referred me to a specialist.* ▶ **kierować do kogoś/jakiejś instytucji, odsyłać**

referee /ˌrefəˈriː/ noun [C] **1** (also informal **ref** /ref/) the official person in sports such as football who controls the match and prevents players from breaking the rules ▶ **sędzia** ➲ look at **umpire 2** (Brit.) a person who gives information about your character and ability, usually in a letter, for example when you are hoping to be chosen for a job: *Her teacher agreed to* ***act as*** *her* ***referee.*** ▶ **osoba udzielająca referencji**

■ **referee** verb [I,T] ▶ **sędziować**

reference /ˈrefrəns/ noun **1** [C,U] **(a) reference (to sb/sth)** a written or spoken comment that mentions sb/sth: *The article* ***made a*** *direct* ***reference*** *to a certain member of the royal family.* ▶ **wzmianka, napomknienie 2** [U] looking at sth for information: *The guidebook might be useful* ***for future reference.*** ▶ **odniesienie 3** [C] (abbr. **ref.** /ref/) a special number that identifies a letter, etc.: *Please quote our reference when replying.* ▶ **numer sprawy 4** [C] a statement or letter describing sb's character and ability that is given to a possible future employer: *My boss gave me a good reference.* ◇ *May I give your name as a reference* (opiniodawca)*?* ▶ **opinia, referencje** ➲ note at **job 5** [C] a note, especially in a book, that tells you where certain information came from or can be found: *There is a list of references at the end of each chapter.* ▶ **odnośnik**

IDM **with reference to sb/sth** (formal) about or concerning sb/sth: *I am writing with reference to your letter of 10 April ...* ▶ **w nawiązaniu do kogoś/czegoś**

ˈreference book noun [C] a book that you use to find a piece of information: *dictionaries, encyclopedias and other reference books* ▶ **książka informacyjna** (*np. słownik, encyklopedia*)

referendum /ˌrefəˈrendəm/ noun [C,U] (pl. **referendums** or **referenda** /-də/) an occasion when all the people of a country can vote on a particular political question: *The government will hold a referendum on the issue.* ▶ **referendum**

refill /ˌriːˈfɪl/ verb [T] to fill sth again: *Can I refill your glass?* ▶ **napełniać ponownie**

■ **refill** /ˈriːfɪl/ noun [C]: *I'd like to buy a refill* (wkład) *for my pen.* ◇ *Would you like a refill* (dolewkę)*?* ▶ **nabój**

refine /rɪˈfaɪn/ verb [T] **1** to make a substance pure and free from other substances: *to refine sugar/oil* ▶ **rafinować, oczyszczać 2** to improve sth by changing little details: *to refine a theory* ▶ **udoskonalać, wysubtelniać**

refined /rɪˈfaɪnd/ adj. **1** (used about a substance) that has been made pure by having other substances taken out of it: *refined sugar/oil/flour* ▶ **rafinowany, oczyszczony 2** (used about a person) polite; having very good manners ▶ **wytworny, dystyngowany 3** improved and therefore producing a better result ▶ **udoskonalony**

refinement /rɪˈfaɪnmənt/ noun **1** [C] a small change that improves sth: *The new model has electric windows and other refinements.* ▶ **udoskonalenie 2** [U] good manners and polite behaviour ▶ **wytworność, dystynkcja**

refinery /rɪˈfaɪnəri/ noun [C] (pl. **refineries**) a factory where a substance is made pure by having other substances taken out of it: *an oil/sugar refinery* ▶ **rafineria**

reflect /rɪˈflekt/ verb **1** [T, usually passive] **reflect sb/sth (in sth)** to show an image of sb/sth on the surface of sth such as a mirror, water or glass: *She caught sight of herself reflected in the shop window.* ▶ **odbijać 2** [T] to send back light, heat or sound from a surface: *The windows reflected the bright morning sunlight.* ▶ **odbijać 3** [T] to show or express sth: *His music reflects his interest in African culture.* ▶ **odzwierciedlać 4** [I] **reflect (on/upon sth)** to think, especially deeply and carefully, about sth: *I really need some time to reflect on what you've said.* ▶ **zastanawiać się, namyślać się**

PHR V **reflect (well, badly, etc.) on sb/sth** to give a particular impression of sb/sth: *It reflects badly on the whole school if some of its pupils misbehave in public.* ▶ **(dobrze/źle itp.) o kimś/czymś świadczyć**

reflection (Brit. also **reflexion**) /rɪˈflekʃn/ noun **1** [C] an image that you see in a mirror, in water or on a shiny surface: *He admired his reflection in the mirror.* ▶ **odbicie 2** [U] the sending back of light, heat or sound from a surface ▶ **odbijanie 3** [C] a thing that shows what sb/sth is like: *Your clothes are a reflection of your personality.* ▶ **odzwierciedlenie 4** [sing.] **a reflection on/upon sb/sth** something that causes people to form a good or bad opinion about sb/sth: *Parents often feel that their children's behaviour is a reflection on themselves* (zachowanie ich dzieci świadczy o nich samych). ▶ (*przen.*) **odzwierciedlenie 5** [U,C] careful thought about sth: *a book of his* ***reflections on*** *fatherhood* ▶ **namysł, zastanowienie się**

IDM **on reflection** after thinking again: *I think, on reflection, that we were wrong.* ▶ **po namyśle**

reflective /rɪˈflektɪv/ adj. **1** (formal) (used about a person, mood, etc.) thinking deeply about things: *a reflective expression* ▶ **refleksyjny 2** (used about a surface) sending back light or heat: *Wear reflective strips when you're cycling at night.* ▶ **odblaskowy 3 reflective (of sth)** showing what sth is like ▶ **będący odzwierciedleniem/odbiciem czegoś**

reflector /rɪˈflektə(r)/ noun [C] **1** a surface that **reflects** light, heat or sound that hits it ▶ **powierzchnia, która odbija padające na nią światło, wysoką temperaturę lub dźwięk 2** a small piece of glass or plastic on a bicycle or on clothing that can be seen at night when light shines on it ▶ **reflektor, światło odblaskowe**

reflex /ˈriːfleks/ noun **1** [C] (also **ˈreflex action**) a sudden movement or action that you make without thinking: *She put her hands out as a reflex to stop her fall.* ▶ **odruch warunkowy, refleks 2** (**reflexes**) [pl.] the ability to act quickly when necessary: *A good tennis player needs to have excellent reflexes.* ▶ **refleks**

reflexion (Brit.) = REFLECTION

reflexive /rɪˈfleksɪv/ adj. (used about a word or verb form) showing that the person who performs an action is also affected by it: *In 'He cut himself', 'cut' is a* ***reflexive verb*** *and 'himself' is a* ***reflexive pronoun.*** ▶ (*zaimek itp.*) **zwrotny**

■ **reflexive** noun [C] ▶ **zaimek itp. zwrotny**

reform /rɪˈfɔːm/ verb **1** [T] to change a system, the law, etc. in order to make it better: *to reform the examination system* ▶ **reformować, usprawniać 2** [I,T] to improve your behaviour; to make sb do this: *Our prisons aim to reform criminals, not simply to punish them.* ▶ **poprawiać się; reedukować społecznie**

■ **reform** noun [C,U] ▶ **reforma**

reformation /ˌrefəˈmeɪʃn/ noun **1** [U] (formal) the act of improving or changing sb/sth ▶ **reforma, ulepszenie 2** (**the Reformation**) [sing.] new ideas in religion in 16th-century Europe that led to the forming of the Protestant Church; the period of time when these changes were taking place ▶ **reformacja**

reformer /rɪˈfɔːmə(r)/ noun [C] a person who tries to change society and make it better ▶ **reformator/ka**

refrain[1] /rɪˈfreɪn/ verb [I] (formal) **refrain (from sth/doing sth)** to stop yourself doing sth; to not do sth: *Please refrain from smoking in the hospital.* ▶ **powstrzymywać się**

refrain[2] /rɪˈfreɪn/ noun [C] (formal) the part of a song that is repeated, usually at the end of each **verse** ▶ **refren** SYN **chorus**

refresh /rɪˈfreʃ/ verb [T] to make sb/sth feel less tired or less hot and full of energy again: *He looked refreshed after a good night's sleep.* ▶ **odświeżać**

IDM **refresh your memory (about sb/sth)** to remind yourself about sb/sth: *Could you refresh my memory about what we said on this point last week?* ▶ **odświeżać pamięć**

refreshing /rɪˈfreʃɪŋ/ adj. **1** pleasantly new or different: *It makes* ***a refreshing change*** *to meet somebody who is so enthusiastic.* ▶ **ożywiający, pokrzepiający 2** making you feel less tired or hot: *a refreshing swim/shower/drink* ▶ **odświeżający, wzmacniający**

refreshment /rɪˈfreʃmənt/ noun **1** (**refreshments**) [pl.] light food and drinks that are available at a cinema, theatre or other public place ▶ **zakąski i napoje 2** [U] (formal) the fact of making sb feel stronger and less tired or hot; food or drink that helps to do this ▶ **orzeźwienie, odpoczynek; zakąski i napoje orzeźwiające**

refrigerate /rɪˈfrɪdʒəreɪt/ verb [T] to make food, etc. cold in order to keep it fresh ▶ **mrozić**

■ **refrigeration** /rɪˌfrɪdʒəˈreɪʃn/ noun [U]: *Keep all meat products* ***under refrigeration*** (w lodówce). ▶ **przechowywanie w lodówce**

refrigerator (formal) = FRIDGE

refuge /ˈrefjuːdʒ/ noun [C,U] **refuge (from sb/sth)** protection from danger, trouble, etc.; a place that is safe: *We had to* ***take refuge*** *from the rain under a tree.* ◇ *a refuge for the homeless* ▶ **schronienie, azyl** SYN **shelter**

refugee /ˌrefjuˈdʒiː/ noun [C] a person who has been forced to leave their country for political or religious reasons, or because there is a war, not enough food, etc.: *a refugee camp* ▶ **uchodźca** ➲ look at **fugitive, exile**

refund /ˈriːfʌnd/ noun [C] a sum of money that is paid back to you, especially because you have paid too much or you are not happy with sth you have bought: *to claim/demand/get a refund* ▶ **zwrot pieniędzy** ➲ note at **shopping**

■ **refund** /rɪˈfʌnd; ˈriːfʌnd/ verb [T] ▶ **zwracać pieniądze** | **refundable** adj.: *The deposit is not refundable.* ▶ (*zadatek itp.*) **zwrotny**

refurbish /ˌriːˈfɜːbɪʃ/ verb [T] to clean and decorate a room, building, etc. in order to make it more attractive, more useful, etc. ▶ **odnawiać, remontować**

■ **refurbishment** noun [U,C]: *The hotel is now closed for refurbishment.* ▶ **odnowa, remont**

refusal /rɪˈfjuːzl/ noun [U,C] **(a) refusal (of sth); (a) refusal (to do sth)** saying or showing that you will not do, give or accept sth: *I can't understand her refusal to see me.* ◇ *We've had a few refusals, but most people have said they can come tonight.* ▶ **odmowa, odrzucenie**

refuse¹ /rɪˈfjuːz/ verb [I,T] to say or show that you do not want to do, give, or accept sth: *He refused to listen to what I was saying.* ◇ *My application for a grant has been refused.* ▶ **odmawiać; odrzucać**

refuse² /ˈrefjuːs/ noun [U] (formal) things that you throw away; rubbish: *the refuse collection* wywożenie śmieci ▶ **odpadki, śmieci**

refute /rɪˈfjuːt/ verb [T] (formal) **1** to prove that sth is wrong: *to* ***refute an argument/a theory*** ▶ **obalać** SYN **rebut 2** to say that sth is not true or fair: *She refutes any suggestion that she behaved unprofessionally.* ▶ **odrzucać** SYN **deny**

regain /rɪˈɡeɪn/ verb [T] to get sth back that you had lost: *to regain consciousness* ▶ **odzyskiwać**

regal /ˈriːɡl/ adj. very impressive; typical of or suitable for a king or queen ▶ **królewski**

regard¹ /rɪˈɡɑːd/ verb [T] **1 regard sb/sth as sth; regard sb/sth (with sth)** to think of sb/sth (in the way mentioned): *Do you regard this issue as important?* ◇ *In some villages newcomers are regarded with suspicion.* ◇ *Her work is highly regarded* (wysoko oceniana). ▶ **uważać (za coś), traktować 2** (formal) to look at sb/sth for a while: *She regarded us suspiciously.* ▶ **przypatrywać się, obserwować**

IDM **as regards sb/sth** (formal) in connection with sb/sth: *What are your views as regards this proposal?* ▶ **w odniesieniu/stosunku do kogoś/czegoś**

regard² /rɪˈɡɑːd/ noun **1** [U] **regard to/for sb/sth** attention to or care for sb/sth: *He shows little regard for other people's feelings.* ▶ **troska, wzgląd 2** [U, sing.] **(a) regard (for sb/sth)** a feeling of admiration for sb/sth: respect: *She obviously* ***has great regard*** *for your ability.* ▶ **szacunek 3** (**regards**) [pl.] (used especially to end a letter politely) kind thoughts; best wishes: *Please* ***give my regards to*** *your parents.* ▶ **wyrazy szacunku, pozdrowienia**

IDM **in/with regard to sb/sth; in this/that/one regard** (formal) about sb/sth; connected with sb/sth: *With regard to the details – these will be finalized later.* ▶ **w odniesieniu do kogoś/czegoś; pod (tym) względem**

regarding /rɪˈɡɑːdɪŋ/ prep. (formal) about or in connection with: *Please write if you require further information regarding this matter.* ▶ **dotyczący, odnoszący się do czegoś**

regardless /rɪˈɡɑːdləs/ adv. paying no attention to sb/sth; treating problems and difficulties as unimportant: *I suggested she should stop but she* ***carried on regardless*** (mimo wszystko). ▶ **mimo to**

■ **regardless** prep. **regardless of sb/sth**: *Everybody will receive the same, regardless of how long they've worked here.* ▶ **bez względu na kogoś/coś**

regatta /rɪˈɡætə/ noun [C] an event at which there are boat races ▶ **regaty**

reggae /ˈreɡeɪ/ noun [U] a type of West Indian music with a strong rhythm ▶ **muzyka reggae**

regime /reɪˈʒiːm/ noun [C] a method or system of government, especially one that has not been elected in a fair way: *a military/fascist regime* ▶ **rządy, reżim**

regiment /ˈredʒɪmənt/ noun [C, with sing. or pl. verb] a group of soldiers in the army who are commanded by a **colonel** ▶ **pułk**

■ **regimental** /ˌredʒɪˈmentl/ adj. ▶ **pułkowy**

regimented /ˈredʒɪmentɪd/ adj. (formal) (too) strictly controlled ▶ **poddany surowej dyscyplinie**

region /ˈriːdʒən/ noun [C] **1** a part of the country or the world; a large area of land: *desert/tropical/polar regions* ◇ *This region of France is very mountainous.* ▶ **region, obszar** ➲ note at **area 2** an area of your body: *He's been having pains in the region of his heart.* ▶ **okolica**

IDM **in the region of sth** about or approximately: *There were somewhere in the region of 30 000 people at the rally.* ▶ **około, mniej więcej**

regional /ˈriːdʒənl/ adj. connected with a particular region: *regional accents* ▶ **regionalny** ➲ look at **local, international, national**

register¹ /ˈredʒɪstə(r)/ verb **1** [I,T] to put a name on an official list: *You should register with a doctor nearby.* ◇ *All births, deaths and marriages must be registered.* ▶ **zapisywać (się) 2** [I,T] to show sth or to be shown on a measuring instrument: *The thermometer registered 32° C.* ◇ *The earthquake registered* (trzęsienie ziemi osiągnęło siłę) *6.4 on the Richter scale.* ▶ (*przyrząd pomiarowy*) **pokazywać 3** [T] to show feelings, opinions, etc.: *Her face registered intense dislike.* ▶ **wyrażać 4** [I,T] [often used in negative sentences] to notice sth and remember it; to be noticed and remembered: *He told me his name but it didn't register* (wypadło mi z głowy). ▶ **(za)notować coś w pamięci; być zauważonym/(za)pamiętanym 5** [T] to send a letter or package by registered mail: *Parcels*

R

containing valuable goods should be registered. ▶ **nadawać (na poczcie) jako przesyłkę poleconą**

register² /ˈredʒɪstə(r)/ noun **1** [C] an official list of names, etc. or a book that contains this kind of list: *The teacher calls the register* (sprawdza listę obecności) *first thing in the morning.* ◇ *the electoral register* spis wyborców ▶ **lista**, **spis 2** [C,U] the type of language (formal or informal) that is used in a piece of writing: *The essay suddenly switches from a formal to an informal register.* ▶ **styl**

ˌregistered ˈmail (Brit. also **ˌregistered ˈpost**) noun [U] a method of sending a letter or package in which the person sending it can claim money if it arrives late or if it is lost or damaged ▶ **przesyłka polecona**

ˈregister office = REGISTRY OFFICE

registrar /ˌredʒɪˈstrɑː(r); ˈredʒɪstrɑː(r)/ noun [C] **1** a person whose job is to keep official lists, especially of births, marriages and deaths ▶ **urzędni-k/czka stanu cywilnego 2** a person who is responsible for keeping information about the students at a college or university ▶ **osoba w administracji uniwersyteckiej zajmująca się przyjmowaniem na studia, egzaminami itp.**

registration /ˌredʒɪˈstreɪʃn/ noun [U] putting sb/sth's name on an official list: *Registration for evening classes will take place on 8 September.* ▶ **zapisy**, **rejestracja**

ˌregiˈstration number noun [C] the numbers and letters on the front and back of a vehicle that are used to identify it ▶ **numer rejestracyjny samochodu** ➲ picture at **car**

registry /ˈredʒɪstri/ noun [C] (pl. **registries**) a place where official lists are kept ▶ **urząd zajmujący się sporządzaniem rejestrów**

ˈregistry office (also **register office**) noun [C] an office where a marriage can take place and where births, marriages and deaths are officially written down ▶ **urząd stanu cywilnego** ➲ note at **wedding**

regress /rɪˈgres/ verb [I] **regress (to sth)** (formal) to return to an earlier or less advanced form or way of behaving ▶ **powracać**, **ulegać regresowi** ℹ Zwykle wyraża dezaprobatę.

regret¹ /rɪˈgret/ verb [T] (**regretting**; **regretted**) **1** to feel sorry that you did sth or that you did not do sth: *I hope you won't regret your decision later.* ◇ *Do you regret not taking the job?* ▶ **żałować**, **ubolewać 2** (formal) (used as a way of saying that you are sorry for sth): *I regret to inform you that your application has been unsuccessful.* ▶ **z przykrością coś zrobić**

regret² /rɪˈgret/ noun [C,U] a feeling of sadness about sth that cannot now be changed: *Do you* ***have any regrets*** *about not going to university?* ▶ **żal**, **przykrość**

regretful /rɪˈgretfl/ adj. feeling or showing sadness or disappointment because of sth that has happened or sth that you have done or not done: *a regretful look/smile* ▶ **pełen żalu/smutku** SYN **rueful**

■ **regretfully** /-fəli/ adv. ▶ **z żalem**, **ze smutkiem**

regrettable /rɪˈgretəbl/ adj. that you should feel sorry or sad about: *It is deeply regrettable that we were not informed sooner.* ▶ **godny pożałowania**

■ **regrettably** /-əbli/ adv. ▶ **niestety**

regular¹ /ˈregjələ(r)/ adj. **1** having the same amount of space or time between each thing or part: *Nurses checked her blood pressure* ***at regular intervals.*** ◇ *The fire alarms are tested* ***on a regular basis.*** ◇ *We have regular meetings every Thursday.* ◇ *a regular heartbeat* ◇ *regular breathing* miarowy oddech ▶ **regularny** OPP **irregular 2** done or happening often: *The doctor advised me to take regular exercise.* ◇ *Accidents are* ***a regular occurrence*** *on this road.* ▶ **regularny 3** [only before a noun] going somewhere or doing sth often: *a regular customer* ◇ *We're regular visitors to Britain.* ▶ **stały 4** [only before a noun] normal or usual: *Who is your regular dentist?* ▶ **stały 5** not having any individual part that is different from the rest: *regular teeth/features* ◇ *a regular pattern* ▶ **równy**, **regularny** OPP **irregular 6** fixed or permanent: *a regular income/job* ◇ *a regular soldier/army* żołnierz zawodowy/armia zawodowa ▶ **stały 7** (especially US) standard, average or normal: *Regular or large fries?* ▶ **normalny 8** (used about a noun, verb, etc.) having the usual or expected plural, verb form, etc.: *'Walk' is a regular verb.* ▶ **regularny** OPP **irregular**

■ **regularly** adv. **1** at regular times or in a regular way: *to have a car serviced regularly* ▶ **regularnie**, **systematycznie 2** often: *Ravi regularly takes part in competitions but this is the first one that he has won.* ▶ **często**, **regularnie** | **regularity** /ˌregjuˈlærəti/ noun [U,C]: *My car breaks down with increasing regularity.* ▶ **regularność**

regular² /ˈregjələ(r)/ noun [C] **1** (informal) a person who goes to a particular shop, bar, restaurant, etc. very often ▶ **stał-y/a klient/ka itp. 2** a person who usually does a particular activity or sport ▶ **stał-y/a zawodni-k/czka 3** a permanent member of the army, navy, etc. ▶ **żołnierz zawodowy**

regulate /ˈregjuleɪt/ verb [T] **1** to control sth by using laws or rules ▶ **regulować**, **kontrolować 2** to control a machine, piece of equipment, etc.: *You can regulate the temperature in the car with this dial.* ▶ **regulować**, **nastawiać**

regulation /ˌregjuˈleɪʃn/ noun **1** [C, usually pl.] an official rule that controls how sth is done: *to observe/obey the safety regulations* ◇ *The plans must comply with EU regulations.* ▶ **przepis**, **regulamin 2** [U] the control of sth by using rules: *state regulation of imports and exports* ▶ **kontrolowanie**, **kierowanie**

regurgitate /rɪˈgɜːdʒɪteɪt/ verb [T] **1** (formal) to bring food that has been swallowed back up into the mouth again ▶ **zwracać** (*jedzenie*) **2** to repeat sth you have heard or read without really thinking about it or understanding it ▶ **bezmyślnie powtarzać**

■ **regurgitation** /rɪˌgɜːdʒɪˈteɪʃn/ noun [U] ▶ **zwracanie**; **bezmyślne powtarzanie**

rehabilitate /ˌriːəˈbɪlɪteɪt/ verb [T] to help sb to live a normal life again after an illness, being in prison, etc. ▶ **rehabilitować**

■ **rehabilitation** /ˌriːəˌbɪlɪˈteɪʃn/ noun [U]: *a rehabilitation centre for drug addicts* ▶ **rehabilitacja**, **odbudowa**

rehash /ˌriːˈhæʃ/ verb [T] to arrange ideas, pieces of writing or pieces of film into a new form but without any great change or improvement: *He just rehashes songs from the 60s.* ▶ **przerabiać** (*utwory literackie/filmowe/muzyczne*)

■ **rehash** /ˈriːhæʃ/ noun [sing.] ▶ **przeróbka**

rehearsal /rɪˈhɜːsl/ noun [C,U] the time when you practise a play, dance, piece of music, etc. before you perform it to other people: *a dress rehearsal* próba generalna ▶ **próba**

■ **rehearse** /rɪˈhɜːs/ verb [I,T] ▶ **robić próbę**, **ćwiczyć**

reign /reɪn/ verb [I] **1 reign (over sb/sth)** (used about a king or queen) to rule a country ▶ **panować 2 reign (over sb/sth)** to be the best or most important in a particular situation: *the reigning world champion* aktualny mistrz świata ◇ *George reigned as chairman* (sprawował funkcję prezesa) *over the company for 10 years.* ◇ *In the field of classical music, he still* ***reigns supreme*** (panuje niepodzielnie). **3** to be present as the most important quality of a particular situation: *Chaos reigned after the first snow of winter.* ▶ **panować**

■ **reign** noun [C] ▶ **panowanie**, **władanie**

reimburse /ˌriːɪmˈbɜːs/ verb [T] (formal) to pay money back to sb: *The company will reimburse you in full for your travelling expenses.* ▶ **zwracać koszty/wydatki**

rein /reɪn/ noun [C, usually pl.] a long thin piece of leather that is held by the rider and used to control a horse's movements ▶ **lejce** ➲ picture at **horse**

reincarnation /ˌriːɪnkɑːˈneɪʃn/ noun **1** [U] the belief that people who have died can live again in a different body: *Do you believe in reincarnation?* ▶ **reinkarnacja** **2** [C] a person or an animal whose body is believed to contain the spirit of a dead person: *She believes she is the reincarnation of an Egyptian princess.* ▶ **ponowne wcielenie** ➲ look at **incarnation**

reindeer /ˈreɪndɪə(r); US -dɪr/ noun [C] (pl. **reindeer**) a type of large brownish wild animal that eats grass and lives in Arctic regions ▶ **renifer**

Według tradycji, renifery ciągną sanie Świętego Mikołaja, kiedy przywozi dzieciom prezenty na Gwiazdkę.

reinforce /ˌriːɪnˈfɔːs/ verb [T] to make sth stronger: *Concrete can be reinforced with steel bars.* ▶ **wzmacniać, wspierać**

ˌreinforced ˈconcrete noun [U] concrete with metal bars or wires inside to make it stronger ▶ **żelazobeton**

reinforcement /ˌriːɪnˈfɔːsmənt/ noun **1** (**reinforcements**) [pl.] extra people who are sent to make an army, navy, etc. stronger ▶ (*wojsk.*) **posiłki** **2** [U] making sth stronger: *The sea wall is weak in places and needs reinforcement.* ▶ **wzmocnienie, podparcie**

reinstate /ˌriːɪnˈsteɪt/ verb [T] **1 reinstate sb (in/as sth)** to give back a job or position that was taken from sb: *He was cleared of the charge of theft and reinstated as Head of Security.* ▶ **przywracać** (*do pracy/na stanowisko*) **2** to return sth to its former position or role ▶ **przywracać** (*np. przepisy*)
■ **reinstatement** noun [U] ▶ **przywrócenie**

reiterate /riˈɪtəreɪt/ verb [T] (formal) to repeat sth that you have already said, especially to emphasize it: *to reiterate an argument/a demand/an offer* ▶ **powtarzać** (*zwł. z naciskiem*)
■ **reiteration** /riˌɪtəˈreɪʃn/ noun [sing.] ▶ **powtórzenie** (*zwł. z naciskiem*)

⚷ **reject**[1] /rɪˈdʒekt/ verb [T] to refuse to accept sb/sth: *The plan was rejected as being impractical.* ▶ **odrzucać, odmawiać przyjęcia**
■ **rejection** noun [C,U]: *Gargi got a rejection from Leeds University.* ◇ *There has been total rejection of the new policy.* ▶ **odmowa, odrzucenie**

reject[2] /ˈriːdʒekt/ noun [C] a person or thing that is not accepted because he/she/it is not good enough: *Rejects are sold at half price.* ▶ **odrzut, wybrakowany towar, odrzucon-y/a kandydat/ka**

rejoice /rɪˈdʒɔɪs/ verb [I] (formal) **rejoice (at/over sth)** to feel or show great happiness ▶ **radować się**
■ **rejoicing** noun [U]: *There were scenes of rejoicing when the war ended.* ▶ **radość, uciecha**

rejuvenate /rɪˈdʒuːvəneɪt/ verb [T, often passive] to make sb/sth feel or look younger ▶ **odmładzać, odżywać**
■ **rejuvenation** /rɪˌdʒuːvəˈneɪʃn/ noun [U] ▶ **odmładzanie, odżywanie**

relapse /rɪˈlæps/ verb [I] to become worse again after an improvement: *to relapse into bad habits* ▶ **powracać do poprzedniego stanu po okresie poprawy, mieć nawrót** (*np. choroby*)
■ **relapse** /ˈriːlæps/ noun [C]: *The patient had a relapse and then died.* ▶ **nawrót choroby**

⚷ **relate** /rɪˈleɪt/ verb [T] **1 relate A to/with B** to show or make a connection between two or more things: *The report relates heart disease to high levels of stress.* ▶ **powiązać, ustalać związek** **2** (formal) **relate sth (to sb)** to tell a story to sb: *He related his side of the story to a journalist.* ▶ **opowiadać**
PHR V **relate to sb/sth** **1** to be concerned or involved with sth: *That question is very interesting but it doesn't really relate to the subject that we're discussing.* ▶ **odnosić się do kogoś/czegoś** **2** to be able to understand how sb feels: *Some teenagers find it hard to relate to their parents.* ▶ **mieć/znajdować wspólny język**

⚷ **related** /rɪˈleɪtɪd/ adj. **related (to sb/sth)** **1** connected with sb/sth: *The rise in the cost of living is directly related to the price of oil.* ▶ **powiązany** **2** of the same family: *We are related* (spowinowaceni) *by marriage.* ▶ **spokrewniony**

⚷ **relation** /rɪˈleɪʃn/ noun **1** (**relations**) [pl.] **relations (with sb)**; **relations (between A and B)** the way that people, groups, countries, etc. feel about or behave towards each other: *The police officer stressed that good relations with the community were essential.* ▶ **stosunki** **2** [U] **relation (between sth and sth)**; **relation (to sth)** the connection between two or more things: *There seems to be little relation between the cost of the houses and their size.* ◇ *Their salaries* ***bear no relation*** *to the number of hours they work.* ▶ **powiązanie, związek** **3** [C] a member of your family: *a near/close/distant relation* ▶ **krewn-y/a, powinowat-y/a** SYN **relative** ⓘ Zwróć uwagę na następujące wyrażenia: *What relation are you to each other?* ◇ *Are you any relation to each other?*
IDM **in/with relation to sb/sth** **1** concerning sb/sth: *Many questions were asked, particularly in relation to the cost of the new buildings.* ▶ **w odniesieniu do kogoś/czegoś** **2** compared with: *Prices are low in relation to those in other parts of Europe.* ▶ **w porównaniu z kimś/czymś, w stosunku do kogoś/czegoś**

⚷ **relationship** /rɪˈleɪʃnʃɪp/ noun [C] **1 a relationship (with sb/sth)**; **a relationship (between A and B)** the way that people, groups, countries, etc. feel about or behave towards each other: *The relationship between the parents and the school has improved greatly.* ▶ **stosunki, kontakty** **2 a relationship (with sb)**; **a relationship (between A and B)** a friendly or loving connection between people: *to* ***have a relationship*** *with somebody* ◇ *He'd never been* ***in a*** *serious* ***relationship*** *before he got married.* ◇ *The film describes the relationship between a young man and an older woman.* ◇ *Do you have a close relationship with your brother?* ▶ **związek, romans** **3 a relationship (to sth)**; **a relationship (between A and B)** the way in which two or more things are connected: *Is there a relationship between violence on TV and the increase in crime?* ▶ **związek** **4 a relationship (to sb)**; **a relationship (between A and B)** a family connection: *'What is your relationship to Bruce?' 'He's married to my cousin.'* ▶ **pokrewieństwo**

R

⚷ **relative**[1] /ˈrelətɪv/ adj. **1 relative (to sth)** when compared to sb/sth else: *the position of the earth relative to the sun* ◇ *They live in relative luxury.* ▶ **względny, stosunkowy** **2** referring to an earlier noun, phrase or sentence: *In the phrase 'the lady who lives next door', 'who' is a relative pronoun.* ▶ **względny**

⚷ **relative**[2] /ˈrelətɪv/ noun [C] a member of your family: *a close/distant relative* ▶ **krewn-y/a, powinowat-y/a** SYN **relation**

⚷ **relatively** /ˈrelətɪvli/ adv. to quite a large degree, especially when compared to others: *Spanish is a relatively easy language to learn.* ▶ **stosunkowo, względnie**

relativity /ˌreləˈtɪvəti/ noun [U] **1** Einstein's theory of the universe, which states that all motion is relative and treats time as a fourth dimension related to space ▶ **teoria względności** **2** the state of being relative: *the relativity of progress* ▶ **względność**

relax /rɪˈlæks/ verb **1** [I] to rest while you are doing sth enjoyable, especially after work or effort: *This holiday will give you a chance to relax.* ◇ *They spent the evening relaxing in front of the TV.* ▶ **odprężać się**, **odpoczywać** SYN **unwind** **2** [I] to become calmer and less worried: *Relax* (spokojnie) *– everything's going to be OK!* ▶ **uspokajać się** ℹ W języku nieformalnym zamiast **relax** można powiedzieć **chill out** lub **take it easy**. **3** [I,T] to become or make sb/sth become less hard or tight: *A hot bath will relax you after a hard day's work.* ◇ *Don't relax your grip on the rope!* ▶ **rozluźniać (się)** **4** [T] to make rules or laws less strict: *The regulations on importing animals have been relaxed.* ▶ **złagadzać**

relaxation /ˌriːlækˈseɪʃn/ noun **1** [C,U] something that you do in order to rest, especially after work or effort: *Everyone needs time for rest and relaxation.* ▶ **odprężanie się**, **odpoczynek** **2** [U] making sth less strict, tight or strong ▶ **rozluźnianie (się)**, **łagodzenie** (*np.wyroku, przepisów*)

relaxed /rɪˈlækst/ adj. not worried or tense: *I felt surprisingly relaxed before my interview.* ◇ *The relaxed atmosphere made everyone feel at ease.* ▶ **odprężony** SYN **calm** ➲ look at **stressed**

relaxing /rɪˈlæksɪŋ/ adj. pleasant, helping you to rest and become less worried: *a quiet relaxing holiday* ▶ **odprężający**

relay¹ /rɪˈleɪ; ˈriːleɪ/ verb [T] (pt, pp **relayed**) **1** to receive and then pass on a signal or message: *Instructions were relayed to us by phone.* ▶ **przekazywać** **2** (Brit.) to put a programme on the radio or TV ▶ **przekazywać**

relay² /ˈriːleɪ/ (also ˈ**relay race**) noun [C] **1** a race in which each member of a team runs, swims, etc. one part of the race ▶ **sztafeta** **2** a fresh set of people or animals that take the place of others that are tired or have finished a period of work: *Rescuers worked **in relays*** (na zmiany) *to save the trapped miners.* ▶ **zmiana**

release¹ /rɪˈliːs/ verb [T] **1 release sb/sth (from sth)** to allow sb/sth to be free: *He's been released from prison.* ◇ (figurative) *His firm released him for two days a week to go on a training course.* ▶ **zwalniać**, **uwalniać** **2** to stop holding sth so that it can move, fly, fall, etc. freely: *1 000 balloons were released at the ceremony.* ◇ (figurative) *Crying is a good way to release pent-up emotions.* ▶ **puszczać** **3** to move sth from a fixed position: *He released the handbrake and drove off.* ▶ **zwalniać** (*np. hamulec*) **4** to allow sth to be known by the public: *The identity of the victim has not been released.* ▶ **ujawniać** **5** to make a film, record, etc. available so the public can see or hear it: *Their new single is due to be released next week.* ▶ **wypuszczać** **6** to let substances escape into the air, sea, etc.: *carbon dioxide released into the atmosphere* ▶ **emitować**, **wypuszczać**

release² /rɪˈliːs/ noun [C,U] **1 (a) release (of sth) (from sth)** the freeing of sth or the state of being freed: *The release of the hostages took place this morning.* ◇ *The release* (wydalanie) *of carbon dioxide into the atmosphere.* ▶ **zwolnienie** **2** the feeling that you are free from pain, anxiety or some other unpleasant feeling: *I had a great feeling of release* (poczułem wielką ulgę) *when my exams were finished.* ▶ **ulga** **2** a book, film, record, piece of news, etc. that has been made available to the public; the act of making sth available to the public: *a press release* oświadczenie prasowe ◇ *The band played their latest release* (swoją ostatnią płytę). ◇ *The film won't **be/go on release*** (nie wejdzie na ekrany) *until March.* ▶ **nowy towar/film/utwór itp. wypuszczony na rynek**; **wypuszczenie na rynek**

relegate /ˈrelɪɡeɪt/ verb [T] to put sb/sth into a lower level or position: *The football team finished bottom and were relegated to the second division.* ◇ *West Ham were relegated* (spadł) *to the Second Division.* ▶ **przenosić (na niższe miejsce/stanowisko)**
■ **relegation** /ˌrelɪˈɡeɪʃn/ noun [U] ▶ **przenoszenie na niższe miejsce/stanowisko**

relent /rɪˈlent/ verb [I] **1** to finally agree to sth that you had refused: *Her parents finally relented and allowed her to go to the concert.* ▶ **ulegać**, **ustępować** **2** to become less determined, strong, etc.: *The heavy rain finally relented and we went out.* ▶ **(z)łagodnieć**

relentless /rɪˈlentləs/ adj. not stopping or changing: *the relentless fight against crime* ▶ **nieugięty**, **nieustępliwy**
■ **relentlessly** adv.: *The sun beat down relentlessly.* ▶ **nieustępliwie**, **nieugięcie**

relevant /ˈreləvənt/ adj. **relevant (to sb/sth)** **1** connected with what is happening or being talked about: *Much of what was said was not directly relevant to my case.* ▶ **odpowiedni**, **związany (z kimś/czymś)** **2** important and useful: *Many people feel that poetry is no longer relevant in today's world.* ▶ **istotny** OPP for both meanings **irrelevant**
■ **relevance** noun [U]: *I honestly can't see the relevance of what he said.* ▶ **związek z kimś/czymś**, **trafność**

reliable /rɪˈlaɪəbl/ adj. that you can trust: *Japanese cars are usually very reliable.* ◇ *Is he a reliable witness?* ◇ *reliable* (wiarygodna) *information* ▶ **solidny**, **pewny** OPP **unreliable** ➲ verb **rely**
■ **reliability** /rɪˌlaɪəˈbɪləti/ noun [U] ▶ **niezawodność**, **wiarygodność** | **reliably** /rɪˈlaɪəbli/ adv.: *I have been reliably informed that there will be no trains tomorrow.* ▶ **rzetelnie**, **wiarygodnie**

reliance /rɪˈlaɪəns/ noun [U] **reliance on sb/sth** **1** being able to trust sb/sth: *Don't **place** too much **reliance*** (nie polegaj za bardzo) *on her promises.* ▶ **zaufanie**, **poleganie na czymś** **2** not being able to live or work without sb/sth: *the country's reliance on imported oil* ▶ **uzależnienie**, **oparcie** SYN for both meanings **dependence** ➲ verb **rely**

reliant /rɪˈlaɪənt/ adj. **reliant on sb/sth** not being able to live or work without sb/sth: *They are totally reliant on the state for financial support.* ▶ **uzależniony** SYN **dependent** ➲ look at **self-reliant** ➲ verb **rely**

relic /ˈrelɪk/ noun [C] an object, custom, etc. from the past that still survives today ▶ **zabytek**, **relikt**

relief /rɪˈliːf/ noun **1** [U, sing.] **relief (from sth)** the feeling that you have when sth unpleasant stops or becomes less strong: *The drugs brought him some relief from the pain.* ◇ ***What a relief!** That awful noise has stopped.* ◇ *It was a great relief to know they were safe.* ◇ *to breathe **a sigh of relief*** ◇ ***To my relief*** (ku mej uldze), *he didn't argue with my suggestion at all.* ▶ **ulga** **2** [U] the act of removing or reducing pain, worry, etc.: *These tablets provide pain relief for up to four hours.* ▶ **uśmierzenie** **3** [U] money or food that is given to help people who are in trouble or difficulty: *disaster relief for the flood victims* ▶ **pomoc** SYN **aid** **4** [U] a reduction in the amount of tax you have to pay ▶ **ulga podatkowa**

relieve /rɪˈliːv/ verb [T] to make an unpleasant feeling or situation stop or get better: *This injection should **relieve the pain.*** ◇ *Four new prisons are being built to relieve overcrowding* (dla zmniejszenia przeludnienia). ◇ *We played cards to relieve the boredom.* ▶ **ulżyć**, **łagodzić**
PHR V **relieve sb of sth** (formal) to take sth away from sb: *General Scott was relieved of his command.* ▶ **zwalniać kogoś** (*np. z obowiązku*)

relieved /rɪˈliːvd/ adj. pleased because your fear or worry has been taken away: *I was very relieved* (doznałem ulgi) *to hear that you weren't seriously hurt.* ▶ **odczuwający ulgę**, **uspokojony**

religion /rɪˈlɪdʒən/ noun **1** [U] the belief in a god or gods and the activities connected with this: *I never discuss politics or religion.* ▶ **religia** **2** [C] one of the systems of beliefs that is based on a belief in a god or gods: *the*

Christian/Hindu/Muslim/Sikh religion ▶ **religia**, **wyznanie**

religious /rɪˈlɪdʒəs/ adj. **1** [only before a noun] connected with religion: *religious faith* ▶ **religijny 2** having a strong belief in a religion: *a deeply religious person* ▶ **pobożny**, **religijny**

religiously /rɪˈlɪdʒəsli/ adv. **1** very carefully or regularly: *She stuck to the diet religiously.* ▶ **skrupulatnie**, **regularnie 2** in a religious way ▶ **religijnie**, **pobożnie**

relinquish /rɪˈlɪŋkwɪʃ/ verb [T] (formal) to stop having or doing sth ▶ **zaniechać**, **zaprzestawać** ⓘ Częściej używa się **give up**.

relish[1] /ˈrelɪʃ/ verb [T] to enjoy sth very much or wait with pleasure for sth to happen: *I don't* ***relish the prospect*** *of getting up early tomorrow.* ▶ **cieszyć się czymś**; **cieszyć się na coś**

relish[2] /ˈrelɪʃ/ noun **1** [U] (formal) great enjoyment: *She accepted the award with obvious relish.* ▶ **(wielka) radość**, **rozkosz 2** [U,C] a thick, cold sauce made from fruit and vegetables ▶ **rodzaj sosu**

relive /ˌriːˈlɪv/ verb [T] to remember sth and imagine that it is happening again ▶ **przeżywać na nowo**

reload /ˌriːˈləʊd/ verb [I,T] to put sth into a machine again: *to reload a gun* ◇ *to reload a disk into a computer* ▶ **załadowywać ponownie**

reluctant /rɪˈlʌktənt/ adj. **reluctant (to do sth)** not wanting to do sth because you are not sure it is the right thing to do ▶ **niechętny**, **ociągający się**

■ **reluctance** noun [U]: *Tony left* ***with obvious reluctance.*** ▶ **niechęć**, **ociąganie się** | **reluctantly** adv. ▶ **niechętnie**, **ociągając się**

rely /rɪˈlaɪ/ verb [I] (**relying**; **relies**; pt, pp **relied**) **rely on/upon sb/sth (to do sth) 1** to need sb/sth and not be able to live or work properly without them or it: *The old lady had to rely on other people to do her shopping for her.* ◇ *Many students do not like having to rely* (być zależnymi) *on their parents for money.* ▶ **polegać na kimś/czymś**, **liczyć na kogoś/coś 2** to trust sb/sth to work or behave well: *Can I rely on you to keep a secret?* ▶ **polegać na kimś/czymś**, **mieć zaufanie do kogoś/czegoś** ➲ look at **reliable**, **reliant** ➲ noun **reliance**

remain /rɪˈmeɪn/ verb [I] **1** to stay or continue in the same place or condition: *to remain standing/seated* ◇ *They remained silent* (zachowywali milczenie) *throughout the trial.* ◇ *Marek went to live in America but his family remained behind in Europe.* ▶ **pozostawać**, **zostawać** ➲ note at **stay 2** to be left after other people or things have gone: *Today only a few stones remain of the castle.* ▶ **pozostawać**, **zostawać 3** to still need to be done, said or dealt with: *It* ***remains to be seen*** *whether* (jeszcze się okaże czy) *we've made the right decision.* ◇ *Although he seems very pleasant,* ***the fact remains*** (faktem jest, że) *that I don't trust him.* ▶ **pozostawać** (*np. do zrobienia/zobaczenia/załatwienia*)

remainder /rɪˈmeɪndə(r)/ noun (usually **the remainder**) [sing., with sing. or pl. verb] the people, things, etc. that are left after the others have gone away or been dealt with; the rest ▶ **reszta**, **pozostali**

remaining /rɪˈmeɪnɪŋ/ adj. [only before a noun] still needing to be done or dealt with: *The remaining twenty patients were transferred to another hospital.* ◇ *Any remaining tickets for the concert will be sold on the door.* ▶ **pozostały**

remains /rɪˈmeɪnz/ noun [pl.] **1** what is left behind after other parts have been used or taken away: *The builders found the remains of a Roman mosaic floor.* ▶ **pozostałości**, **resztki 2** (formal) a dead body (sometimes one that has been found somewhere a long time after death): *Human remains were discovered in the wood.* ▶ **szczątki**

remand /rɪˈmɑːnd; US -ˈmænd/ noun [U] (Brit.) the time before a prisoner's trial takes place: *a remand prisoner* aresztant/ka ▶ **areszt**, **zatrzymanie w areszcie**

■ **remand** verb [T, usually passive] to send sb away from a court to wait for their trial which will take place at a later date: *The man was* ***remanded in custody*** (zatrzymany i osadzony w areszcie). ◇ *to remand sb on bail* zwalniać kogoś tymczasowo z aresztu za kaucją

IDM **on remand** (used about a prisoner) waiting for the trial to take place ▶ **w areszcie**

remark /rɪˈmɑːk/ verb [I,T] **remark (on/upon sb/sth)** to say or write sth: *A lot of people have remarked on the similarity between them.* ▶ **zauważać** SYN **comment** ➲ look at **observation**

■ **remark** noun [C] ▶ **uwaga**, **spostrzeżenie**

remarkable /rɪˈmɑːkəbl/ adj. unusual and surprising in a way that people notice: *That is a remarkable achievement for someone so young.* ▶ **niezwykły**, **znakomity** SYN **astonishing**

■ **remarkably** /-əbli/ adv. ▶ **nadzwyczajnie**, **wielce**

remedial /rɪˈmiːdiəl/ adj. [only before a noun] **1** aimed at improving or correcting a situation ▶ **zaradczy 2** helping people who are slow at learning sth: *remedial English classes* ▶ (*lekcje*) **wyrównawczy**

remedy[1] /ˈremədi/ noun [C] (pl. **remedies**) **a remedy (for sth) 1** a way of solving a problem: *There is no easy remedy for unemployment.* ▶ **remedium**, **lekarstwo** SYN **solution 2** something that makes you better when you are ill or in pain: *Hot lemon with honey is a good remedy for colds.* ▶ **środek** (*zaradczy*)

remedy[2] /ˈremədi/ verb [T] (**remedying**; **remedies**; pt, pp **remedied**) to change or improve sth that is wrong or bad: *to remedy an injustice* ▶ **wynagradzać**, **naprawiać** (*np. straty*)

remember /rɪˈmembə(r)/ verb [I,T] **1 remember (sb/sth)**; **remember (doing sth)**; **remember that...** to have sb/sth in your mind or to bring sb/sth back into your mind: *We arranged to go out tonight – remember?* ◇ ***As far as I can remember****, I haven't seen him before.* ◇ *I'm sorry. I don't remember your name.* ◇ *Do you remember the night we first met?* ◇ *Remember that we're having visitors tonight.* ◇ *Can you remember when we bought the stereo?* ◇ *I vaguely remember grandad reading to me as a little boy.* ▶ **pamiętać**, **przypominać sobie 2 remember (sth/to do sth)** to not forget to do what you have to do: *I remembered to buy the coffee.* ◇ *Remember to turn the lights off before you leave.* ▶ **pamiętać**

> **Remember to do sth** znaczy „pamiętać, żeby coś zrobić": *It's my mother's birthday. I must remember to phone her.* **Remember doing sth** znaczy „przypominać sobie coś z przeszłości": *Do you remember going to the cinema for the first time?*

3 [T] to give money etc. to sb/sth: *to remember someone in your will* ▶ **wymieniać kogoś** (*w testamencie*)

IDM **remember me to sb** (used when you want to send good wishes to a person you have not seen for a long time): *Please remember me to your wife.* ▶ **kłaniać się (komuś od kogoś)** ➲ note at **remind**

remembrance /rɪˈmembrəns/ noun [U] (formal) thinking about and showing respect for sb who is dead: *a service* ***in remembrance of*** *those killed* (ku pamięci poległych) *in the war* ▶ **uczczenie pamięci**

remind /rɪˈmaɪnd/ verb [T] **1 remind sb (about/of sth)**; **remind sb (to do sth/that...)** to help sb to remember sth, especially sth important that they have to do: *Can you remind me of your address?* ◇ *He reminded the children to wash their hands.* ◇ *Remind me what we're supposed to be doing tomorrow.* ▶ **przypominać 2 remind sb of sb/sth** to cause sb to remember sb/sth: *That smell reminds*

R

me of school. ◇ *You remind me of your father.* ▶ **przypominać**

Por. **remember** i **remind**: *Lucy remembered to say thank you after the party.* ◇ *Mother reminded Lucy to say thank you after the party.*

reminder /rɪˈmaɪndə(r)/ noun [C] something that makes you remember sth: *We received a reminder that we hadn't paid the electricity bill.* ▶ **upomnienie**, **pamiątka**

reminisce /ˌremɪˈnɪs/ verb [I] **reminisce (about sb/sth)** to talk about pleasant things that happened in the past ▶ **wspominać**

reminiscent /ˌremɪˈnɪsnt/ adj. [not before a noun] that makes you remember sb/sth; similar to: *His suit was strongly reminiscent of an old army uniform.* ◇ *I think that painting is very reminiscent of* (bardzo przypomina) *one by Monet.* ▶ **przypominający**

remiss /rɪˈmɪs/ adj. [not before a noun] **remiss (of sb) (to do sth); remiss (in sth/in doing sth)** (formal) not giving sth enough care and attention: *It was remiss of them not to inform us of these changes sooner.* To było niedbalstwo z ich strony, że nie poinformowali nas wcześniej o tych zmianach. ◇ *She had clearly been remiss in her duty.* To było wyraźne zaniedbanie jej obowiązków ▶ **niedbały** SYN **negligent**

remission /rɪˈmɪʃn/ noun [U,C] a period during which a serious illness improves for a time and the patient seems to get better: *The patient has been **in remission** for the past six months.* ▶ **remisja**

remit /ˈriːmɪt; rɪˈmɪt/ noun [C, usually sing.] **remit (of sb/sth); remit (to do sth)** (Brit.) the area of activity over which a particular person or group has authority, control or influence: *Such decisions are **outside the remit** of this committee.* ◇ *In future, staff recruitment will **fall within the remit*** (będzie w gestii) *of the division manager.* ▶ **kompetencje**

remnant /ˈremnənt/ noun [C] a piece of sth that is left after the rest has gone: *These few trees are the remnants of a huge forest.* ▶ **pozostałość**, **reszta**

remorse /rɪˈmɔːs/ noun [U] **remorse (for sth/doing sth)** a feeling of sadness because you have done sth wrong: *She was filled with remorse for what she had done.* ▶ **skrucha**, **wyrzut sumienia** ➲ look at **guilt**
■ **remorseful** /-fl/ adj. ▶ **pełen skruchy** | **remorsefully** /-fəli/ adv. ▶ **ze skruchą**

remorseless /rɪˈmɔːsləs/ adj. **1** not stopping or becoming less strong: *a remorseless attack on somebody* ▶ **nieustanny**, **niesłabnący** **2** showing no pity: *a remorseless killer* ▶ **bezlitosny**
■ **remorselessly** adv. ▶ **bezlitośnie**; **nieustannie**

⚷ **remote** /rɪˈməʊt/ adj. **1 remote (from sth)** far away from where other people live: *a remote island in the Pacific* ▶ **odległy**, **daleki** **2** [only before a noun] far away in time: *the remote past/future* ▶ **odległy** **3** not very friendly or interested in other people: *He seemed rather remote.* ▶ **nieprzystępny** **4** not very great: *I haven't **the remotest*** (nie mam najmniejszego pojęcia) *idea who could have done such a thing.* ◇ *a remote possibility* ▶ **mały**
■ **remoteness** noun [U] ▶ **oddalenie**; **nieprzystępność**

reˌmote conˈtrol noun **1** [U] a system for controlling sth from a distance: *The doors can be opened by remote control.* ▶ **zdalne sterowanie** **2** (also **remote**) [C] a piece of equipment for controlling sth from a distance ▶ **pilot** (*do telewizora itp.*)

remotely /rɪˈməʊtli/ adv. (used in negative sentences) to a very small degree; at all: *I'm not remotely interested in your problems.* ▶ **w najmniejszym stopniu**, **ani trochę**

⚷ **removal** /rɪˈmuːvl/ noun **1** [U] the act of taking sb/sth away: *the removal of restrictions/regulations/rights* ▶ **usunięcie** **2** [C,U] the activity of moving from one house to live in another ▶ **przeprowadzka**

reˈmoval van (Brit. also **ˈfurniture van**, US **ˈmoving van**) noun [C] a large van used for moving furniture from one house to another ▶ **samochód do przeprowadzek**

⚷ **remove** /rɪˈmuːv/ verb [T] (formal) **1 remove sb/sth (from sth)** to take sb/sth off or away: *Remove the saucepan from the heat.* ◇ *This washing powder will remove most stains.* ◇ *to remove doubts/fears/problems* ◇ *I would like you to remove my name from your mailing list.* ◇ *He had an operation to remove the tumour.* ▶ **usuwać**, **zdejmować**, **rozpraszać** ⓘ **Take off**, **take out** itp. są mniej formalne. **2 remove sb (from sth)** to make sb leave their job or position: *The person responsible for the error has been removed from his post.* ▶ **odwoływać** (*z posady*)

removed /rɪˈmuːvd/ adj. [not before a noun] far or different from sth: *Hospitals today are **far removed from*** (bardzo się różnią) *what they were fifty years ago.* ▶ **oddalony**, **odmienny**

remover /rɪˈmuːvə(r)/ noun [C,U] a substance that cleans off paint, dirty marks, etc.: *make-up remover* ▶ **odplamiacz**

remuneration /rɪˌmjuːnəˈreɪʃn/ noun [U,C] (formal) an amount of money that is paid to sb for the work they have done: *Generous **remuneration packages** are often attached to overseas postings.* ▶ **wynagrodzenie**

the **Renaissance** /rɪˈneɪsns; US ˈrenəsɑːns/ noun [sing.] the period in Europe during the 14th, 15th and 16th centuries when people became interested in the ideas and culture of ancient Greece and Rome, and used these influences in their own art, literature, etc.: *Renaissance* (renesansowa) *art* ▶ **odrodzenie**

render /ˈrendə(r)/ verb [T] (formal) **1** to cause sb/sth to be in a certain condition: *She was rendered speechless* (zaniemówiła) *by the attack.* ▶ **wprawiać kogoś w jakiś stan** **2** to give help, etc. to sb: *to render somebody a service/render a service to somebody* ▶ **okazywać** (*pomoc*), **wyświadczać** (*przysługę*)

rendezvous /ˈrɒndɪvuː; -deɪ-/ noun [C] (pl. **rendezvous** /-vuːz/) **1 a rendezvous (with sb)** a meeting that you have arranged with sb: *He had a secret rendezvous with Daniela.* ▶ **umówione spotkanie** **2** a place where people often meet: *The cafe is a popular rendezvous for students.* ▶ **miejsce spotkania**

rendition /renˈdɪʃn/ noun [C] the performance of sth, especially a song or piece of music; the particular way in which it is performed ▶ **wykonanie**, **interpretacja**

renegade /ˈrenɪɡeɪd/ noun [C] [often used as an adjective] (formal) (usually used in a critical way) a person who leaves one political, religious, etc. group to join another that has very different views or beliefs ▶ **renegat**, **zdrajca/czyni**

renew /rɪˈnjuː; US -ˈnuː/ verb [T] **1** to start sth again: *renewed outbreaks of violence* ◇ *to renew a friendship* ▶ **wznawiać**, **odświeżać** **2** to give sb new strength or energy: *After a break he set to work with renewed enthusiasm.* ▶ **odnawiać** **3** to make sth valid for a further period of time: *to renew a contract/passport/library book* ▶ **przedłużać**
■ **renewal** /rɪˈnjuːəl; US -ˈnuːəl/ noun [C,U]: *When is your passport due for renewal?* ▶ **przedłużenie** (*np. umowy*), **wznowienie**, **odnowa**

renewable /rɪˈnjuːəbl; US -ˈnuː/ adj. **1** (used about sources of energy) that will always exist: *renewable resources such as wind and solar power* ▶ **odnawialny** OPP **non-renewable** ➲ note at **environment** **2** that can be continued or replaced with a new one for another period of time ▶ **odnawialny**, **do przedłużenia**

renounce /rɪˈnaʊns/ verb [T] (formal) to say formally that you no longer want to have sth or to be connected with sth ▶ **zrzekać się, rezygnować** ➲ noun **renunciation**

renovate /ˈrenəveɪt/ verb [T] to repair an old building and put it back into good condition ▶ **odnawiać, remontować** ➲ note at **house**

■ **renovation** /ˌrenəˈveɪʃn/ noun [C,U]: *The house is in need of renovation.* ▶ **remont, renowacja**

renown /rɪˈnaʊn/ noun [U] (formal) fame and respect that you get for doing sth especially well ▶ **sława**

■ **renowned** adj. **renowned (for/as sth)**: *The region is renowned for its food.* ▶ **sławny**

rent[1] /rent/ noun [U,C] money that you pay regularly for the use of land, a house or a building: *a high/low rent* ◇ *She was allowed to live there* ***rent-free*** *until she found a job.* ◇ *Is this house* ***for rent?*** ▶ **czynsz, komorne**

rent[2] /rent/ verb [T] **1 rent sth (from sb)** to pay money for the use of land, a building, a machine, etc.: *Do you own or rent your TV?* ◇ *to rent a flat* ▶ **wynajmować, wypożyczać, dzierżawić** ➲ note at **flat**, **hire** **2 rent sth (out) (to sb)** to allow sb to use land, a building, a machine, etc. for money: *We could rent out the small bedroom to a student.* ▶ **wynajmować (komuś)** ➲ look at **hire** **3** (US) = HIRE[1] (1) **4** (US) = HIRE[1] (2)

■ **rented** adj.: *a rented house* ▶ **wynajęty**

rental /ˈrentl/ noun [C,U] money that you pay when you rent a telephone, TV, etc. ▶ **opłata za wypożyczenie, abonament telefoniczny/telewizyjny**

renunciation /rɪˌnʌnsiˈeɪʃn/ noun [U] (formal) saying that you no longer want sth or believe in sth ▶ **wyrzekanie się, zrzekanie się** ➲ verb **renounce**

reorganize (also **-ise**) /riˈɔːɡənaɪz/ verb [I,T] to organize sth again or in a new way ▶ **reorganizować**

■ **reorganization** (also **-isation**) /riˌɔːɡənaɪˈzeɪʃn; US -nəˈz-/ noun [C,U]: *reorganization of the school system* ▶ **reorganizacja**

Rep. = REPUBLICAN

rep /rep/ (also formal **representative**) noun [C] a person whose job is to travel round a particular area and visit companies, etc., to sell the products of the firm for which they work: *a sales rep for a drinks company* ▶ **przedstawiciel/ka, komiwojażer/ka**

repair[1] /rɪˈpeə(r)/ verb [T] to put sth old or damaged back into good condition: *These cars can be expensive to repair.* ◇ *How much will it cost to have the TV repaired?* ◇ *It's difficult to see how their marriage can be repaired.* ▶ (*i przen.*) **naprawiać, reperować** SYN **fix, mend** ➲ look at **irreparable**

repair[2] /rɪˈpeə(r)/ noun [C,U] something that you do to fix sth that is damaged: *The school is closed for repairs to the roof.* ◇ *The road is* ***in need of repair.*** ◇ *The bridge is* ***under repair*** (jest w remoncie). ◇ *The bike was damaged* ***beyond repair*** (nie do naprawy) *so I threw it away.* ▶ **naprawa, remont**

IDM **in good, bad, etc. repair** in a good, bad, etc. condition ▶ **w dobrym/złym itp. stanie**

repatriate /ˌriːˈpætrieɪt; US -ˈpeɪt-/ verb [T] to send or bring sb back to their own country ▶ **przesiedlać do kraju**

■ **repatriation** /ˌriːˌpætriˈeɪʃn; US -ˌpeɪt-/ noun [C,U] ▶ **repatriacja**

repay /rɪˈpeɪ/ verb [T] (pt, pp **repaid** /rɪˈpeɪd/) **1 repay sth (to sb); repay (sb) sth** to pay back money that you owe to sb: *to repay a debt/loan* ◇ *When will you repay the money to them?* ◇ *When will you repay them the money?* ▶ **spłacać, zwracać** **2 repay sb (for sth)** to give sth to sb in return for help, kindness, etc.: *How can I ever repay you for all you have done for me?* ▶ **odwzajemniać się, odpłacać (się)**

repayable /rɪˈpeɪəbl/ adj. that you can or must pay back: *The loan is repayable over three years.* ▶ **zwrotny**

repayment /rɪˈpeɪmənt/ noun **1** [U] paying sth back: *the repayment of a loan* ▶ **spłata, zwrot** **2** [C] money that you must pay back to sb/sth regularly: *I make monthly repayments on my loan.* ▶ **spłata**

repeal /rɪˈpiːl/ verb [T] (formal) to officially make a law no longer valid ▶ **uchylać**

repeat[1] /rɪˈpiːt/ verb **1** [I,T] **repeat (sth/yourself)** to say, write or do sth again or more than once: *Don't repeat the same mistake again.* ◇ *Could you repeat what you just said?* ◇ *The essay is quite good, but you repeat yourself several times.* ◇ *Raise your left leg ten times, then repeat with the right.* ▶ **powtarzać** **2** [T] **repeat sth (to sb)** to say or write sth that sb else has said or written or that you have learnt: *Please don't repeat what you've heard here to anyone.* ◇ *Repeat each sentence after me.* ▶ **powtarzać** ➲ noun **repetition**

repeat[2] /rɪˈpiːt/ noun [C] something that is done, shown, given, etc. again: *I think I've seen this programme before – it must be a repeat.* ▶ **powtórka**

repeated /rɪˈpiːtɪd/ adj. [only before a noun] done or happening many times: *There have been repeated accidents on this stretch of road.* ▶ **powtarzający się, wielokrotny**

■ **repeatedly** adv.: *I've asked him repeatedly not to leave his bicycle there.* ▶ **wielokrotnie, nieraz**

repel /rɪˈpel/ verb [T] (**repelling**; **repelled**) **1** to send or push sb/sth back or away ▶ **odpierać, odrzucać** **2** to make sb feel disgusted: *The dirt and smell repelled her.* ▶ **budzić wstręt** ➲ adjective **repulsive**

repellent[1] /rɪˈpelənt/ adj. causing a strong feeling of disgust: *a repellent smell* ▶ **odrażający, odpychający**

repellent[2] /rɪˈpelənt/ noun [C,U] a chemical substance that is used to keep insects, etc. away: *a mosquito repellent* ▶ **środek odstraszający**

repent /rɪˈpent/ verb [I,T] (formal) **repent (of sth)** to feel and show that you are sorry about sth bad that you have done: *to repent of your sins* ◇ *He later repented his hasty decision.* ▶ **okazywać skruchę, żałować (czegoś)**

■ **repentance** noun [U] ▶ **skrucha** | **repentant** adj. ▶ **skruszony**

repercussion /ˌriːpəˈkʌʃn/ noun [C, usually pl.] an unpleasant effect or result of sth you do: *His resignation will* ***have serious repercussions.*** ▶ **przykre/niekorzystne następstwa**

repertoire /ˈrepətwɑː(r)/ noun [C] **1** all the plays or music that an actor or a musician knows and can perform: *He must have sung every song in his repertoire last night.* ▶ **repertuar** **2** all the things that a person is able to do ▶ **repertuar**

repertory /ˈrepətri; US -tɔːri/ noun **1** [U] the type of work of a theatre company in which different plays are performed for short periods of time: *an actor in repertory* ◇ *a repertory company* zespół aktorów w teatrze stałym ▶ **teatr stały** **2** [C] (formal) = REPERTOIRE (1)

repetition /ˌrepəˈtɪʃn/ noun [U,C] doing sth again; sth that you do or that happens again: *to learn by repetition* ◇ *Let's try to avoid a repetition of what happened last Friday.* ▶ **powtarzanie (się), powtórka** ➲ verb **repeat**

repetitious /ˌrepəˈtɪʃəs/ adj. involving sth that is often repeated: *a long and repetitious speech* ▶ **pełen powtórzeń** ℹ Często wyraża dezaprobatę.

repetitive /rɪˈpetətɪv/ (also **repetitious** /ˌrepəˈtɪʃəs/) adj. not interesting because the same thing is repeated many times ▶ **powtarzający się, monotonny**

rephrase /ˌriːˈfreɪz/ verb [T] to say or write sth using different words in order to make the meaning clearer ▶ **ujmować coś innymi słowami**

replace /rɪˈpleɪs/ verb [T] **1** to take the place of sb/sth; to use sb/sth in place of another person or thing: *Teachers*

R

will never be replaced by computers in the classroom. ▶ **zastępować** (*np. na stanowisku*) **2 replace sb/sth (with/by sb/sth)** to exchange sb/sth for sb/sth that is better or newer: *We will replace any goods that are damaged.* ▶ **wymieniać (coś na coś) 3** to put sth back in the place where it was before: *Please replace the books on the shelves when you have finished with them.* ▶ **odkładać, stawiać/kłaść** (*na miejsce*) ℹ Częściej używa się mniej formalnego wyrażenia **put back**.

replaceable /rɪˈpleɪsəbl/ adj. that can be replaced ▶ **możliwy do zastąpienia** OPP **irreplaceable**

replacement /rɪˈpleɪsmənt/ noun **1** [U] exchanging sb/sth for sb/sth that is better or newer: *The carpets are in need of replacement.* ▶ **wymiana 2** [C] a person or thing that will take the place of sb/sth: *Mary left so we advertised for a replacement for her* (kogoś na jej miejsce). ▶ **osoba/rzecz zastępująca kogoś/coś innego**

replay[1] /ˈriːpleɪ/ noun [C] **1** (Brit.) a sports match that is played again because neither team won the first time ▶ **powtórne rozgrywanie meczu 2** something on the TV, on a video or a tape that you watch or listen to again: *Now let's see **an action replay*** (powtórkę) *of that tremendous goal!* ▶ **powtórne odtwarzanie nagrania**

replay[2] /ˌriːˈpleɪ/ verb [T] **1** to play a sports match, etc. again because neither team won the first time ▶ **powtórnie rozgrywać mecz itp. 2** to play again sth that you have recorded: *They kept replaying the goal over and over again.* ▶ **powtórnie odtwarzać nagrany materiał**

replenish /rɪˈplenɪʃ/ verb [T] **replenish sth (with sth)** (formal) to make sth full again by replacing what has been used: *to replenish food and water supplies* ▶ **uzupełniać** (*np. zapasy*)

replica /ˈreplɪkə/ noun [C] **a replica (of sth)** an exact copy of sth ▶ **kopia, duplikat**

replicate /ˈreplɪkeɪt/ verb [T] (formal) to copy sth exactly ▶ **powtarzać, powielać** SYN **duplicate**

■ **replication** /ˌreplɪˈkeɪʃn/ noun [U] ▶ **powtarzanie, powielanie**

⚷ **reply** /rɪˈplaɪ/ verb [I,T] (**replying**; **replies**; pt, pp **replied**) **reply (to sb/sth) (with sth)** to say, write or do sth as an answer to sb/sth: *I wrote to Sue but she hasn't replied* (nie odpisała). ◇ *'Yes, I will,' she replied.* ◇ *to reply to a question* ▶ **odpowiadać** ➲ note at **answer**[2]

■ **reply** noun [C,U] (pl. **replies**): *Al nodded **in reply to** my question.* ▶ **odpowiedź**

⚷ **report**[1] /rɪˈpɔːt/ verb **1** [I,T] **report (on sb/sth) (to sb/sth)**; **report sth (to sb)** to give people information about what you have seen, heard, done, etc.: *The research team will report (on) their findings next month.* ◇ *The company reported huge profits last year.* ◇ *Several people reported seeing/having seen the boy.* ◇ *Several people reported that they had seen the boy.* ◇ *Call me if you have anything new to report.* ▶ **zgłaszać, zawiadamiać 2** [I,T] **report (on) sth** (in a newspaper or on the TV or radio) to write or speak about sth that has happened: *The paper sent a journalist to report on the events.* ▶ **informować, relacjonować 3** [T] (formal) **be reported to be/as sth** (used to say that you have heard sth said, but you are not sure if it is true): *The 70-year-old actor is reported to be/as being comfortable in hospital.* Mówi się, że siedemdziesięcioletni aktor czuje się dobrze w szpitalu. **4** [T] **report sb (to sb) (for sth)** to tell a person in authority about an accident, a crime, etc. or about sth wrong that sb has done: *All accidents must be reported to the police.* ◇ *The boy was reported missing early this morning.* ▶ **donosić (na kogoś), składać skargę 5** [I] **report (to sb/sth) for sth** to tell sb that you have arrived: *On your arrival, please report to the reception desk.* ▶ **zgłaszać się, meldować się**

PHR V **report back (on sth) (to sb)** to give information to sb about sth they have asked you to find out about: *One person in each group will then report back on what you've decided to the class.* ▶ **składać raport, zdawać sprawozdanie**

report to sb [not used in the continuous tenses] if you **report to** a particular manager in an organization that you work for, they are officially responsible for your work and tell you what to do: *Who does he report to?* ▶ **podlegać bezpośrednio komuś** (*w pracy*)

⚷ **report**[2] /rɪˈpɔːt/ noun [C] **1 a report (on/of sth)** a written or spoken description of what you have seen, heard, done, studied, etc.: *newspaper reports* ◇ *a report on the company's finances* ◇ *a first-hand report* ▶ **relacja, sprawozdanie 2** a written statement about the work of a student at school, college, etc.: *to get a good/bad report* ▶ **opinia o postępach w nauce**

reportedly /rɪˈpɔːtɪdli/ adv. according to what some people say: *The band have reportedly decided to split up.* ▶ **podobno**

reˌported ˈspeech (also ˌ**indirect ˈspeech**) noun [U] reporting what sb has said, not using the actual words. If sb says '*I'll phone again later.*', in reported speech this becomes *She said that she would phone again later.* ▶ **mowa zależna** ➲ look at **direct speech**

reporter /rɪˈpɔːtə(r)/ noun [C] a person who writes about the news in a newspaper or speaks about it on the TV or radio ▶ **reporter/ka** ➲ note at **newspaper** ➲ look at **journalist**

reprehensible /ˌreprɪˈhensəbl/ adj. (formal) morally wrong and deserving criticism ▶ **naganny** SYN **deplorable**

⚷ **represent** /ˌreprɪˈzent/ verb [T] **1** to act or speak in the place of sb else; to be the **representative** of a group or country: *You will need a lawyer to represent you in court.* ◇ *It's an honour for an athlete to represent his or her country.* ▶ **reprezentować, być przedstawicielem 2** to be equal to sth; to be sth: *These results represent a major breakthrough in our understanding of cancer.* ▶ **równać się, odpowiadać (czemuś) 3** to be a picture, sign, example, etc. of sb/sth: *The yellow lines on the map represent minor roads.* ▶ **przedstawiać, oznaczać 4** to describe sb/sth in a particular way: *In the book Billy is represented as a very cruel person.* ▶ **przedstawiać**

representation /ˌreprɪzenˈteɪʃn/ noun **1** [U,C] the way that sb/sth is shown or described; something that shows or describes sth: *The article complains about the representation of women in advertising.* ▶ **przedstawienie, wyobrażenie 2** [U] (formal) having sb to speak for you ▶ **przedstawicielstwo, reprezentacja** ➲ look at **proportional representation**

⚷ **representative**[1] /ˌreprɪˈzentətɪv/ noun [C] **1** a person who has been chosen to act or speak for sb else or for a group: *a union representative* ▶ **przedstawiciel/ka 2** (formal) = REP

⚷ **representative**[2] /ˌreprɪˈzentətɪv/ adj. **representative (of sb/sth)** typical of a larger group to which sb/sth belongs: *Tonight's audience is not representative of national opinion.* ▶ **typowy**

repress /rɪˈpres/ verb [T] **1** to control an emotion or to try to prevent it from being shown or felt: *She tried to repress her anger.* ▶ **tłumić** (*np. uczucia*) **2** to limit the freedom of a group of people ▶ **tłumić** (*np. bunt*)

■ **repression** /rɪˈpreʃn/ noun [U]: *protests against government repression* ▶ **represja**

repressed /rɪˈprest/ adj. **1** (used about a person) having emotions and desires that they do not show or express ▶ **zamknięty w sobie, tłumiący/ukrywający** (*np. namiętności*) **2** (used about an emotion) that you do not show: *repressed anger/desire* ▶ **tłumiony, ukryty**

repressive /rɪ'presɪv/ adj. that limits people's freedom: *a repressive government* ▶ **represyjny**

reprieve /rɪ'pri:v/ verb [T] to stop or delay the punishment of a prisoner who was going to be punished by death ▶ **odraczać/zawieszać wykonanie kary śmierci**
■ **reprieve** noun [C]: *The judge granted him a last-minute reprieve.* ▶ **odroczenie/zawieszenie wykonania kary śmierci**

reprimand /'reprɪmɑ:nd; US -mænd/ verb [T] **reprimand sb (for sth)** to tell sb officially that they have done sth wrong ▶ **udzielać nagany**
■ **reprimand** noun [C]: *a severe reprimand* ▶ **nagana**

reprisal /rɪ'praɪzl/ noun [C,U] punishment, especially by military force, for harm that one group of people does to another ▶ **akcja odwetowa, odwet**

reproach /rɪ'prəʊtʃ/ verb [T] **reproach sb (for/with sth)** to tell sb that they are responsible for sth bad that has happened: *You've nothing to reproach yourself for. It wasn't your fault.* ▶ **zarzucać, winić** SYN **blame**
■ **reproach** noun [C,U]: *His behaviour is* ***beyond reproach*** (bez zarzutu). ◇ *Alison felt her manager's reproaches were unfair.* ▶ **zarzut, wymówka** | **reproachful** /-fl/ adj.: *a reproachful look* ▶ **pełen wyrzutu** | **reproachfully** /-fəli/ adv. ▶ **z wyrzutem**

reproduce /ˌri:prə'dju:s; US -'du:s/ verb **1** [T] to produce a copy of sth: *It is very hard to reproduce a natural environment in the laboratory.* ▶ **odtwarzać 2** [I] (used about people, animals and plants) to produce young: *Fish reproduce by laying eggs.* ▶ **rozmnażać się**

reproduction /ˌri:prə'dʌkʃn/ noun **1** [U] the process of producing babies or young: *sexual reproduction* ▶ **rozmnażanie się 2** [U] the production of copies of sth: *Digital recording gives excellent sound reproduction.* ▶ **powielenie; odtwarzanie 3** [C] a copy of a painting, etc. ▶ **reprodukcja**

reproductive /ˌri:prə'dʌktɪv/ adj. [only before a noun] connected with the production of young animals, plants, etc.: *the male reproductive organs* ▶ **rozrodczy**

reproof /rɪ'pru:f/ noun [C,U] (formal) something that you say to sb when you do not approve of what they have done ▶ **wyrzut, wymówka**

reptile /'reptaɪl/ noun [C] an animal that has cold blood and a skin covered in scales, and whose young come out of eggs: *Crocodiles, turtles and snakes are all reptiles.* ▶ **gad** ➲ look at **amphibian** ➲ picture on **page A11**

republic /rɪ'pʌblɪk/ noun [C] a country that has an elected government and a president: *the Republic of Ireland* ▶ **republika** ➲ look at **monarchy**

republican /rɪ'pʌblɪkən/ noun [C] **1** a person who supports the system of an elected government with no king or queen ▶ **republikan-in/ka 2** (**Republican**) (abbr. **Rep.**) a member of the Republican Party ▶ **Republikan-in/ka** ➲ look at **Democrat**
■ **republican** adj. ▶ **republikański**

the **Re'publican Party** noun [sing.] one of the two main political parties of the US ▶ **Partia Republikańska** ➲ look at **Democratic Party**

repudiate /rɪ'pju:dieɪt/ verb [T] to say that you refuse to accept or believe sth: *to repudiate a suggestion/an accusation/responsibility* ▶ **odrzucać, odmawiać**

repugnant /rɪ'pʌgnənt/ adj. (formal) **repugnant (to sb)** making you feel disgust: *We found his suggestion absolutely repugnant.* ◇ *The idea of eating meat was totally repugnant to her.* SYN **repulsive**

repulsive /rɪ'pʌlsɪv/ adj. that causes a strong feeling of disgust ▶ **odrażający, wstrętny** ➲ verb **repel**
■ **repulsion** /rɪ'pʌlʃn/ noun [U] ▶ **odraza, wstręt**

reputable /'repjətəbl/ adj. that is known to be good ▶ **cieszący się dobrą opinią** OPP **disreputable**

reputation /ˌrepju'teɪʃn/ noun [C] **a reputation (for/as sth)** the opinion that people in general have about what sb/sth is like: *to* ***have a good/bad reputation*** ◇ *Adam has a reputation for being late.* ▶ **opinia, reputacja** SYN **name**

repute /rɪ'pju:t/ noun [U] (formal) the opinion that people in general have of sb/sth: *My parents were artists* ***of (some) repute*** (cieszącymi się dobrą sławą). ▶ **reputacja, sława**

reputed /rɪ'pju:tɪd/ adj. generally said to be sth, although it is not certain: *She's reputed to be the highest-paid sportswoman in the world.* ◇ *He's reputed to earn* (on podobno zarabia) *more than £100 000 a year.* ▶ **rzekomy**
■ **reputedly** adv. ▶ **rzekomo**

request¹ /rɪ'kwest/ noun [C,U] **request (for sth/that...)** an act of asking for sth: *a request for help* ◇ *I'm going to* ***make a request*** *for a larger desk.* ◇ *to grant/turn down a request* ◇ *Aid was sent to the earthquake victims* ***at the request of*** (na prośbę) *the Iranian government.* ◇ *Single rooms are available* ***on request.*** ▶ **prośba, życzenie**

request² /rɪ'kwest/ verb [T] (formal) **request sth (from/of sb)** to ask for sth: *Passengers are requested not to smoke on this bus.* ◇ *to request a loan* (składać wniosek o pożyczkę) *from the bank* ▶ **upraszać, prosić o coś** ℹ **Request** jest słowem bardziej formalnym niż **ask**.

require /rɪ'kwaɪə(r)/ verb [T] **1** to need sth: *a situation that requires tact and diplomacy* ▶ **potrzebować, wymagać** ℹ **Require** jest słowem bardziej formalnym niż **need**. **2** [often passive] to officially demand or order sth: *Passengers are required by law to wear seat belts.* ▶ **wymagać, żądać**

requirement /rɪ'kwaɪəmənt/ noun [C] something that you need or that you must do or have: *university entrance requirements* ▶ **potrzeba, wymóg**

requisite /'rekwɪzɪt/ adj. [only before a noun] (formal) necessary for a particular purpose: *She lacks the requisite experience for this job.* ▶ **wymagany**
■ **requisite** noun [C]: *A university degree has become a requisite for entry into most professions.* ▶ **wymóg, wymaganie** ➲ look at **prerequisite**

rescind /rɪ'sɪnd/ verb [T] (formal) to officially state that a law, contract, decision, etc. is no longer valid ▶ **uchylać** (*np. umowę*) SYN **revoke**

rescue /'reskju:/ verb [T] **rescue sb/sth (from sb/sth)** to save sb/sth from a situation that is dangerous or unpleasant: *He rescued a child from drowning.* ▶ **ratować, wybawiać**
■ **rescue** noun [C,U]: *Ten fishermen were saved in a daring sea rescue.* ◇ *Blow the whistle if you're in danger, and someone should* ***come to your rescue*** (pośpieszy ci na ratunek). ◇ *rescue workers/boats/helicopters* ▶ **ratunek, wybawianie** | **rescuer** noun [C] ▶ **ratowni-k/czka, wybaw-ca/czyni**

research /rɪ'sɜ:tʃ; 'ri:sɜ:tʃ/ noun [U] **research (into/on sth)** a detailed and careful study of sth to find out more information about it: *to do research into something* ◇ *scientific/medical/historical research* ◇ *We are carrying out* ***market research*** *to find out who our typical customer is.* ▶ **badania, praca badawcza/naukowa**
■ **research** verb [I,T] **research (into/in/on) (sth)**: *Scientists are researching into the possible causes of childhood diseases.* ◇ *They're researching ways of reducing traffic in the city centre.* ▶ **prowadzić prace badawcze/naukowe**

researcher /rɪ'sɜ:tʃə(r)/ noun [C] a person who does research ▶ **badacz/ka**

resemble /rɪ'zembl/ verb [T] to be or look like sb/sth else: *Laura closely resembles her brother.* ▶ **być podobnym, przypominać**

■ **resemblance** /rɪˈzembləns/ noun [C,U] **(a) resemblance (between A and B)**; **(a) resemblance (to sb/sth)**: *a family resemblance* ◇ *The boys* ***bear*** *no* ***resemblance*** (nie są podobni) *to their father.* ▶ **podobieństwo**

resent /rɪˈzent/ verb [T] to feel angry about sth because you think it is unfair: *I resent his criticism.* ◇ *Louise bitterly resented being treated differently from the men.* ▶ **mieć za złe, czuć się dotkniętym/urażonym**

■ **resentful** /-fl/ adj. ▶ **urażony, rozżalony** | **resentfully** /-fəli/ adv. ▶ **z urazą** | **resentment** noun [sing., U]: *to feel resentment towards somebody/something* ▶ **uraza**

reservation /ˌrezəˈveɪʃn/ noun **1** [C] a seat, table, room, etc. that you have **reserved**: *We have reservations in the name of Dvorak.* ◇ *I'll phone the restaurant to* ***make a reservation.*** ▶ **rezerwacja 2** [C,U] a feeling of doubt about sth (such as a plan or an idea): *I* ***have*** *some* ***reservations*** *about letting Julie go out alone.* ▶ **zastrzeżenie 3** (also **reserve**) [C] an area of land in the US that is kept separate for Native Americans to live in ▶ **rezerwat** (*dla Indian amerykańskich*)

reserve¹ /rɪˈzɜːv/ verb [T] **reserve sth (for sb/sth) 1** to keep sth for a special reason or to use at a later time: *The car park is reserved for hotel guests only.* ▶ **rezerwować 2** to ask for a seat, table, room, etc. to be available at a future time: *to reserve theatre tickets* ▶ **rezerwować** SYN **book**

reserve² /rɪˈzɜːv/ noun **1** [C, usually pl.] something that you keep for a special reason or to use at a later date: *oil reserves* ▶ **zapas, rezerwa 2** [C] an area of land where the plants, animals, etc. are protected by law: *a nature reserve* ◇ *He works as a warden on a* ***game reserve*** *in Kenya.* ▶ **rezerwat 3** [U] the quality of being shy or keeping your feelings hidden: *It took a long time to break down her reserve and get her to relax.* ▶ **powściągliwość, rezerwa 4** [C] (in sport) a person who will play in a game if one of the usual members of the team cannot play ▶ **rezerwa** (*w zespole sportowym*) **5** [C] = RESERVATION (3)

IDM **in reserve** that you keep and use only if you need to: *Keep some money in reserve for emergencies.* ▶ **w zapasie**

reserved /rɪˈzɜːvd/ adj. shy and keeping your feelings hidden ▶ **powściągliwy, skryty** OPP **unreserved**

reservoir /ˈrezəvwɑː(r)/ noun [C] a large lake where water is stored to be used by a particular area, city, etc. ▶ **zbiornik**

reside /rɪˈzaɪd/ verb [I] (formal) **reside (in/at ...)** to have your home in or at a particular place ▶ **rezydować, przebywać**

residence /ˈrezɪdəns/ noun **1** [C] (formal) a house, especially an impressive or important one ▶ **rezydencja, siedziba 2** [U] the state of having your home in a particular place: *The family applied for permanent residence in the United States.* ◇ *a* ***hall of residence*** (akademik) *for college students* ◇ *Some birds have taken up residence* (zamieszkały) *in our roof.* ▶ **pobyt, miejsce zamieszkania**

residency /ˈrezɪdənsi/ noun (pl. **-ies**) (formal) **1** : *She has been granted permanent residency in Britain.* = RESIDENCE (3) **2** [U,C] the period of time that an artist, a writer or a musician spends working for a particular institution ▶ **angaż** (*artysty/pisarza/muzyka*) **3** [U] the state of living in a particular place: *a residency requirement for students* ▶ **prawo stałego pobytu 4** [U,C] (especially US) the period of time when a doctor working in a hospital receives special advanced training ▶ **staż 5** (also **residence**) [C] the official house of sb such as an **ambassador** ▶ **rezydencja**

resident /ˈrezɪdənt/ noun [C] **1** a person who lives in a place: *local residents* ▶ **(stał-y/a) mieszkan-iec/ka 2** a person who is staying in a hotel: *The hotel bar is open only to residents.* ▶ **gość**

■ **resident** adj. ▶ **zamieszkujący**

residential /ˌrezɪˈdenʃl/ adj. **1** (used about a place or an area) that has houses rather than offices, large shops or factories: *They live in a quiet residential area.* ▶ **mieszkaniowy 2** that provides a place for sb to live: *This home provides residential care for the elderly.* ▶ **w miejscu zamieszkania, dla mieszkańców**

residual /rɪˈzɪdjuəl; US -dʒu-/ adj. [only before a noun] (formal) still present at the end of a process: *There are still a few residual problems* (pozostało jeszcze kilka problemów) *with the computer program.* ▶ **pozostały**

residue /ˈrezɪdjuː; US -duː/ noun [C, usually sing.] (formal) what is left after the main part of sth is taken or used: *The washing powder left a white residue on the clothes.* ▶ **pozostałość**

resign /rɪˈzaɪn/ verb [I,T] **resign (from/as) (sth)** to leave your job or position: *He's resigned as chairman of the committee.* ▶ **podawać się do dymisji, rezygnować (z czegoś)** ➲ note at **job**

PHR V **resign yourself to sth/doing sth** to accept sth that is unpleasant but that you cannot change: *Jamie resigned himself to the fact that she was not coming back to him.* ▶ **godzić się z czymś**

resignation /ˌrezɪɡˈneɪʃn/ noun **1** [C,U] **resignation (from sth)** a letter or statement that says you want to leave your job or position: *to hand in your resignation* ◇ *a letter of resignation* ▶ **dymisja, rezygnacja** ➲ note at **job 2** [U] the state of accepting sth unpleasant that you cannot change: *They accepted their defeat with resignation.* ▶ **pogodzenie się (z czymś), rezygnacja**

resigned /rɪˈzaɪnd/ adj. **resigned (to sth/doing sth)** accepting sth that is unpleasant but that you cannot change: *Ben was resigned to the fact* (pogodził się z faktem) *that he would never be an athlete.* ▶ **zrezygnowany**

resilient /rɪˈzɪliənt/ adj. strong enough to deal with illness, a shock, change, etc. ▶ **prężny, zdolny do (szybkiego) powrotu do zdrowia, odporny, silny**

■ **resilience** noun [U] ▶ **prężność, zdolność do (szybkiego) powrotu do zdrowia, odporność**

resin /ˈrezɪn; US -zn/ noun [C,U] **1** a sticky substance that is produced by some trees and plants ▶ **żywica 2** an artificial substance used in making plastics ▶ **żywica**

resist /rɪˈzɪst/ verb **1** [I,T] to try to stop sth happening or to stop sb from doing sth; to fight back against sth/sb: *The government are resisting pressure to change the law.* ◇ *to resist arrest* ▶ **opierać się, stawiać opór** SYN **oppose 2** [T] to stop yourself from having or doing sth that you want to have or do: *I couldn't resist telling Nadia what we'd bought for her.* ▶ **opierać się, powstrzymywać się**

resistance /rɪˈzɪstəns/ noun [U] **1 resistance (to sb/sth)** trying to stop sth from happening or to stop sb from doing sth; fighting back against sb/sth: *The government troops overcame the resistance of the rebel army.* ◇ *passive resistance* bierny opór ▶ **opór, sprzeciw 2 resistance (to sth)** the power in sb's body not to be affected by disease: *People with AIDS have very little resistance to infection.* ▶ **odporność** (*organizmu*)

resistant /rɪˈzɪstənt/ adj. **resistant (to sth) 1** not harmed or affected by sth: *This watch is water-resistant.* ▶ **odporny 2** not wanting sth and trying to prevent sth happening: *resistant to change* ▶ **oporny, sprzeciwiający się**

resolute /ˈrezəluːt/ adj. having or showing great determination: *resolute leadership* ◇ *a resolute refusal to change* ▶ **stanowczy** ⓘ Częściej używa się słowa **determined.**

■ **resolutely** adv. ▶ **stanowczo**

resolution /ˌrezəˈluːʃn/ noun **1** [C] a formal decision that is taken after a vote by a group of people: *The UN reso-*

lution condemned the invasion. ▶ **uchwała 2** [U] solving or settling a problem, disagreement, etc. ▶ **rozwiązanie 3** [U] the quality of being firm and determined ▶ **stanowczość 4** [C] a firm decision to do or not to do sth ▶ **postanowienie**

resolve /rɪˈzɒlv/ verb (formal) **1** [T] to find an answer to a problem: *Most of the difficulties have been resolved.* ▶ **rozwiązać** SYN **settle 2** [I,T] to decide sth and be determined not to change your mind: *He resolved never to repeat the experience.* ▶ **postanowić**

resonant /ˈrezənənt/ adj. (formal) deep, clear and continuing for a long time: *a deep resonant voice* ▶ **donośny, dźwięczny**

■ **resonance** noun **1** [U] (formal) the quality of being deep, clear and continuing for a long time: *Her voice had a strange and thrilling resonance.* ▶ **donośność, dźwięczność 2** [C,U] (technical) the sound produced in an object by sound waves from another object ▶ **rezonans**

resonate /ˈrezəneɪt/ verb [I] (formal) **1** (used about a voice, an instrument, etc.) to make a deep, clear sound that continues for a long time: *Her voice resonated through the theatre.* ▶ (*głos*) **rozbrzmiewać**; (*instrument*) **rezonować 2 resonate (with sth)** (used about a place) to be filled with sound; to make a sound continue longer: *The room resonated with the chatter of 100 people.* ▶ **rozbrzmiewać (czymś)** SYN **resound 3 resonate (with sb/sth)** to remind sb of sth; to be similar to what sb thinks or believes: *These issues resonated with the voters.* ▶ **być zgodnym z czymś**; **przypominać (komuś coś)**

resort[1] /rɪˈzɔːt/ noun [C] a place where a lot of people go to on holiday: *a seaside/ski resort* ▶ **miejscowość wypoczynkowa, kurort** ➲ note at **holiday**

IDM **in the last resort**; **(as) a last resort** → LAST[1]

resort[2] /rɪˈzɔːt/ verb [I] **resort to sth/doing sth** to do or use sth bad or unpleasant because you feel you have no choice: *After not sleeping for three nights I finally resorted to sleeping pills.* ▶ **uciekać się**

resound /rɪˈzaʊnd/ verb [I] (formal) **1 resound (through sth)** (used about a sound, voice, etc.) to fill a place with sound: *Laughter resounded through the house.* ◇ (figurative) *The tragedy resounded* (obiegła) *around the world.* ▶ (*i przen.*) **rozbrzmiewać 2 resound (with/to sth)** (used about a place) to be filled with sound: *The street resounded to the thud of marching feet.* ▶ **rozbrzmiewać (czymś)**

resounding /rɪˈzaʊndɪŋ/ adj. [only before a noun] **1** very great: *a resounding victory / win / defeat / success* ▶ **ogromny 2** very loud: *resounding cheers* ▶ **rozbrzmiewający**

resource /rɪˈsɔːs; -ˈzɔːs; US ˈriːsɔːs; rɪˈsɔːs/ noun [C, usually pl.] a supply of sth, a piece of equipment, etc. that is available for sb to use: *Russia is rich in* ***natural resources*** *such as oil and minerals.* ▶ **zasoby, środek**

resourceful /rɪˈsɔːsfl; Brit. also -ˈzɔːs-/ adj. good at finding ways of doing things ▶ **zaradny, pomysłowy**

respect[1] /rɪˈspekt/ noun **1** [U] **respect (for sb/sth)** the feeling that you have when you admire or have a high opinion of sb/sth: *I* ***have little respect*** *for people who are arrogant.* ◇ *to win/lose somebody's respect* ▶ **szacunek, poważanie** ➲ look at **self-respect 2** [U] **respect (for sb/sth)** polite behaviour or care towards sb/sth that you think is important: *We should all* ***treat*** *older people* ***with respect.*** ◇ *He has no respect for her feelings.* ◇ *The secret police show little respect for human rights.* ▶ **szacunek, poszanowanie** OPP **disrespect 3** [C] a detail or point: ***In what respects*** *do you think things have changed in the last ten years?* ◇ *Her performance was brilliant* ***in every respect.*** ◇ *Electricity is dangerous and should be treated with respect* (z rozwagą). ▶ **wzgląd**

IDM **pay your respects** → PAY[1]

with respect to sth (formal) about or concerning: *The groups differ with respect to age.* ▶ **w nawiązaniu do czegoś**

respect[2] /rɪˈspekt/ verb [T] **1 respect sb/sth (for sth)** to admire or have a high opinion of sb/sth: *I respect him for his honesty.* ▶ **poważać, szanować 2** to show care for or pay attention to sb/sth: *We should respect other people's cultures and values.* ▶ **szanować**

■ **respectful** /-fl/ adj. **respectful (to/towards sb)**: *They are not always respectful towards their teacher.* ▶ **pełen szacunku** OPP **disrespectful** | **respectfully** /-fəli/ adv. ▶ **z szacunkiem**

respectable /rɪˈspektəbl/ adj. **1** considered by society to be good, proper or correct: *a respectable family* ◇ *He combed his hair and tried to look respectable for the interview.* ▶ **zacny, odpowiedni 2** quite good or large: *a respectable salary* ▶ **pokaźny, niemały**

■ **respectability** /rɪˌspektəˈbɪləti/ noun [U] ▶ **powszechny szacunek, poczucie przyzwoitości**

respective /rɪˈspektɪv/ adj. [only before a noun] belonging separately to each of the people who have been mentioned: *After lunch we all got on with our respective jobs* (każdy kontynuował swoją pracę). ▶ **poszczególny**

respectively /rɪˈspektɪvli/ adv. in the same order as sb/sth that was mentioned ▶ **odpowiednio**

respiration /ˌrespəˈreɪʃn/ noun [U] (formal) breathing ▶ **oddychanie**

respiratory /rəˈspɪrətri; ˈrespərətri/ adj. connected with breathing: *the respiratory system* ◇ *respiratory diseases* choroby układu oddechowego ▶ **oddechowy**

respite /ˈrespaɪt; US ˈrespɪt/ noun [sing., U] **respite (from sth)** a short period of rest from sth that is difficult or unpleasant: *There was a brief respite from the fighting.* ▶ **wytchnienie**

respond /rɪˈspɒnd/ verb [I] **1** (formal) **respond (to sb/sth) (with/by sth)** to say or do sth as an answer or reaction to sth: *He responded to my question with a nod.* ◇ *Owen responded to the manager's criticism by scoring two goals.* ▶ **udzielać odpowiedzi, odpowiadać, reagować** ➲ note at **answer** ℹ W języku codziennym częściej używa się **answer** lub **reply. 2 respond (to sb/sth)** to have or show a good or quick reaction to sb/sth: *The patient did not respond very well to the new treatment.* ▶ **reagować**

response /rɪˈspɒns/ noun [C,U] **(a) response (to sb/sth)** an answer or reaction to sb/sth: *I've sent out 20 letters of enquiry but I've had no responses yet.* ◇ *The government acted* ***in response to*** *economic pressure.* ▶ **odpowiedź, oddźwięk**

responsibility /rɪˌspɒnsəˈbɪləti/ noun (pl. **responsibilities**) **1** [U,C] **responsibility (for sb/sth)**; **responsibility (to do sth)** a duty to deal with sth so that it is your fault if sth goes wrong: *I refuse to* ***take responsibility*** *if anything goes wrong.* ◇ *Who* ***has responsibility*** *for the new students?* ◇ *It is John's responsibility to make sure the orders are sent out on time.* ◇ *I feel that I* ***have a responsibility*** (uważam, że jest moim obowiązkiem) *to help them – after all, they did help me.* ◇ *a minister with special responsibility* (odpowiedzialny) *for women's affairs* ◇ *The children are my responsibility.* Ponoszę odpowiedzialność za losy dzieci. ▶ **odpowiedzialność 2** [U] the fact of sth being your fault: *No group has yet admitted responsibility for planting the bomb.* ▶ **odpowiedzialność** SYN **blame**

IDM **shift the blame/responsibility (for sth) (onto sb)** → SHIFT[1]

responsible /rɪˈspɒnsəbl/ adj. **1** [not before a noun] **responsible (for sb/sth)**; **responsible (for doing sth)** having the job or duty of dealing with sb/sth, so that it is your fault if sth goes wrong: *The school is responsible for the safety of*

R

the children in school hours. ◇ *The manager is responsible for making sure the shop is run properly.* ▶ **odpowiedzialny 2** [not before a noun] **be responsible (for sth)** to be the person whose fault sth is: *Who was responsible for the accident?* ▶ **spowodować**, **ponosić winę 3** [not before a noun] **responsible (to sb/sth)** having to report to sb/sth with authority, or to sb who you are working for, about what you are doing: *Members of Parliament are responsible to the electors.* ▶ **odpowiedzialny (przed kimś/czymś) 4** sb who you can trust to behave well and in a sensible way: *Marisa is responsible enough to take her little sister to school.* ▶ **odpowiedzialny** OPP **irresponsible 5** (used about a job) that is important and that should be done by a person who can be trusted ▶ **odpowiedzialny**

responsibly /rɪˈspɒnsəbli/ adv. in a sensible way that shows you can be trusted ▶ **odpowiedzialnie**, **z poczuciem odpowiedzialności**

responsive /rɪˈspɒnsɪv/ adj. paying attention to sb/sth and reacting in a suitable or positive way: *By being responsive to changes in the market, the company has had great success.* ▶ **czuły na coś**, **żywo reagujący na kogoś/coś**

⚷ **rest¹** /rest/ verb **1** [I] to relax, sleep or stop after a period of activity or because of illness: *We've been walking for hours. Let's rest here for a while.* ▶ **odpoczywać 2** [T] to not use a part of your body for a period of time because it is tired or painful: *Your knee will get better as long as you rest it as much as you can.* ▶ **dawać odpocząć 3** [I,T] **rest (sth) on/against sth** to place sth in a position where it is supported by sth else; to be in such a position: *She rested her head on his shoulder and went to sleep.* ▶ **opierać (się) o coś/na czymś**

IDM **let sth rest** to not talk about sth any longer: *He didn't want to answer any more questions so I let the subject rest* (przestałem o tym mówić). ▶ **nie poruszać (dalej)** (*np. tematu*)

PHR V **rest on sb/sth** to depend on sb/sth or be based on sth: *The whole theory rests on a very simple idea.* ▶ **opierać się na kimś/czymś**

⚷ **rest²** /rest/ noun **1** [sing., with sing. or pl. verb] **the rest (of sb/sth)** the part that is left; the ones that are left: *We had lunch and spent the rest of the day on the beach.* ◇ *They were the first people to arrive. The rest came later.* ◇ *The rest of our bags are still in the car.* ◇ *She takes no interest in what happens in the rest of the world* (w innych częściach świata). ▶ **reszta 2** [C,U] a period of relaxing, sleeping or doing nothing: *I need a rest* (muszę odpocząć). ◇ *I'm going upstairs to **have a rest*** (odpocząć) *before we go out.* ◇ ***Get some rest*** (odpocznij trochę) *and think about it again tomorrow.* ◇ *I sat down to **give** my bad leg **a rest*** (aby dać odpocząć bolącej nodze). ◇ *Yes, okay, you're right and I'm wrong. Now **give it a rest!*** (nie mów już o tym) ▶ **odpoczynek 3** [C,U] a period of silence between musical notes; a sign for this ▶ (*muz.*) **pauza** ➲ picture at **music**

IDM **at rest** not moving: *Do not open the door until the vehicle is at rest* (dopóki pojazd się nie zatrzyma). ▶ **nieruchomy**

come to rest to stop moving: *The car crashed through a wall and came to rest in a field.* ▶ **zatrzymywać się**

put/set your/sb's mind at rest → MIND¹

the rest is history (used when you are telling a story to say that you are not going to tell the end of the story, because everyone knows it already) ▶ **co było dalej, każdy wie**

⚷ **restaurant** /ˈrestrɒnt; US also -tər-/ noun [C] a place where you can buy and eat a meal: *a fast food/hamburger restaurant* ◇ *a Chinese restaurant* ▶ **restauracja** ➲ look at **cafe**, **takeaway**

> **restaurants**
>
> A **cafe**, a **sandwich bar**, a **takeaway** or a **fast-food restaurant** is often a good place to **have a snack** or eat cheaply, but for a special occasion you can go to a **restaurant**. If it is popular, you should **reserve/book a table** in advance. You choose from the **menu** and a **waiter** or **waitress** takes your **order**. A **set menu** gives a limited choice of **courses** or **dishes** at a **fixed price**. An **à la carte** menu lists all the separate dishes available. You can **order** a **starter**, a **main course** and a **pudding/dessert**. If you want alcoholic drinks, you can ask to see the **wine list**. At the end of the meal you must pay the **bill**. Friends often **split the bill**. If **service** is not included in the bill, people usually leave a **tip**.

restful /ˈrestfl/ adj. giving a relaxed, peaceful feeling: *I find this piece of music very restful.* ▶ **kojący**

restless /ˈrestləs/ adj. **1** unable to relax or be still because you are bored, nervous or impatient: *The children always get restless on long journeys.* ▶ **niespokojny 2** (used about a period of time) without sleep or rest ▶ **bezsenny**; **niespokojny**

■ **restlessly** adv. ▶ **nerwowo**, **niespokojnie**

restoration /ˌrestəˈreɪʃn/ noun **1** [C,U] the return of sth to its original condition; the things that are done to achieve this: *The house is in need of restoration.* ◇ *Restorations* (prace remontowe) *are being carried out at the castle.* ◇ *the restoration of peace to the country* ▶ **odbudowa**; **przywracanie 2** [U] the return of sth to its original owner: *the restoration of stolen property to its owner* ▶ **zwrot**

⚷ **restore** /rɪˈstɔː(r)/ verb [T] **1 restore sb/sth (to sb/sth)** to put sb/sth back into their or its former condition or position: *She restores old furniture as a hobby.* ◇ *In the recent elections, the former president was restored to power.* ▶ **odnawiać**; **przywracać 2** (formal) **restore sth to sb** to give sth that was lost or stolen back to sb: *The police have now restored the painting to its rightful owner.* ▶ **zwracać (coś komuś)**

restrain /rɪˈstreɪn/ verb [T] **restrain sb/sth (from sth/doing sth)** to keep sb or sth under control; to prevent sb or sth from doing sth: *I had to restrain myself from saying something rude.* ▶ **powstrzymywać (kogoś/coś)/(od czegoś)**

restrained /rɪˈstreɪnd/ adj. not showing strong feelings ▶ **powściągliwy**

restraint /rɪˈstreɪnt/ noun **1** [C] **a restraint (on sb/sth)** a limit or control on sth: *Are there any restraints on what the newspapers are allowed to publish?* ▶ **ograniczenie 2** [U] the quality of behaving in a calm or controlled way: *It took a lot of restraint on my part not to hit him.* ◇ *Soldiers have to exercise **self-restraint*** (panować nad sobą) *even when provoked.* ▶ **powściągliwość**, **opanowanie** SYN **self-control**

⚷ **restrict** /rɪˈstrɪkt/ verb [T] **restrict sb/sth (to sth/doing sth)** to put a limit on sb/sth: *There is a plan to restrict the use of cars in the city centre.* ▶ **ograniczać**

⚷ **restricted** /rɪˈstrɪktɪd/ adj. controlled or limited: *There is only restricted parking available.* ▶ **ograniczony**

⚷ **restriction** /rɪˈstrɪkʃn/ noun **restriction (on sth) 1** [C] something (sometimes a rule or law) that limits the number, amount, size, freedom, etc. of sb/sth: *parking restrictions in the city centre* ◇ *The government is to **impose** tighter **restrictions** on the number of immigrants permitted to settle in this country.* ▶ **ograniczenie**, **restrykcja 2** [U] the act of limiting the freedom of sb/sth: *This ticket permits you to travel anywhere, without restriction.* ▶ **ograniczenie**

restrictive /rɪˈstrɪktɪv/ adj. limiting; preventing people from doing what they want ▶ **ograniczający**

restroom /'restru:m; -rʊm/ noun [C] (US) a public toilet in a hotel, shop, restaurant, etc. ▶ **toaleta** *(publiczna)* ➲ note at **toilet**

'rest stop (US) = LAY-BY

result¹ /rɪ'zʌlt/ noun **1** [C] something that happens because of sth else; the final situation at the end of a series of actions: *The traffic was very heavy and* ***as a result*** (skutkiem tego) *I arrived late.* ◇ *This wasn't really the result that I was expecting.* ▶ **skutek, rezultat 2** [C] the score at the end of a game, competition or election: *Do you know today's football results?* ◇ *The results of this week's competition will be published next week.* ◇ *The result of the by-election was a win for the Liberal Democrats.* ▶ **rezultat 3** [C, usually pl.] the mark given for an exam or test: *When do you* ***get*** *your exam* ***results****?* ▶ **ocena 4** [C] something that is discovered by a medical test: *I'm still waiting for the result of my X-ray.* ◇ *The result of the test was negative.* ▶ **wynik 5** [C,U] a good effect of an action: *He has tried very hard to find a job, until now without result.* ◇ *The treatment is beginning to show results.* ▶ **rezultat, efekt**

result² /rɪ'zʌlt/ verb [I] **result (from sth)** to happen or exist because of sth: *Ninety per cent of the deaths resulted from injuries to the head.* ▶ **być wynikiem czegoś**

PHR V **result in sth** to cause sth to happen; to produce as an effect: *There has been an accident on the motorway, resulting in long delays.* ▶ **przynosić w rezultacie**

resume /rɪ'zu:m; -'zju:-/ verb [I,T] to begin again or continue after a pause or interruption: *Normal service will resume as soon as possible.* ◇ *After the birth of the baby, she resumed her career* (wróciła do pracy). ▶ **wznawiać, podejmować (na nowo)**

résumé (US) = CV

resumption /rɪ'zʌmpʃn/ noun [sing., U] (formal) beginning again or continuing after a pause or interruption ▶ **wznowienie**

resurgence /rɪ'sɜ:dʒəns/ noun [sing., U] the return and growth of an activity that had stopped: *a resurgence of interest in the artist's work* ▶ **odrodzenie (się)**

resurrect /ˌrezə'rekt/ verb [T] to bring back sth that has not been used or has not existed for a long time: *From time to time they resurrect old programmes and show them again on TV.* ▶ **wznawiać**

resurrection /ˌrezə'rekʃn/ noun **1** (**the Resurrection**) [sing.] (in the Christian religion) the return to life of Jesus Christ ▶ **Zmartwychwstanie 2** [U] bringing back sth that has not existed or not been used for a long time ▶ **wznawianie**

resuscitate /rɪ'sʌsɪteɪt/ verb [T] to bring sb who has stopped breathing back to life: *Unfortunately, all efforts to resuscitate the patient failed.* ▶ **reanimować**

■ **resuscitation** /rɪˌsʌsɪ'teɪʃn/ noun [U]: *mouth-to-mouth resuscitation* ▶ **sztuczne oddychanie, reanimacja**

retail /'ri:teɪl/ noun [U] the selling of goods to the public in shops, etc. ▶ **handel detaliczny** ➲ look at **wholesale**

retailer /'ri:teɪlə(r)/ noun [C] a person or company who sells goods to the public in a shop ▶ **sprzedawca (detaliczny); przedsiębiorstwo handlu detalicznego**

retain /rɪ'teɪn/ verb [T] (formal) to keep or continue to have sth; not to lose: *Despite all her problems, she has managed to retain a sense of humour.* ▶ **zachowywać, zatrzymywać** *(np. ciepło)* ➲ noun **retention**

retaliate /rɪ'tælieɪt/ verb [I] **retaliate (against sb/sth)** to react to sth unpleasant that sb does to you by doing sth unpleasant in return: *They have announced that they will retaliate against anyone who attacks their country.* ▶ **oddawać wet za wet**

■ **retaliation** /rɪˌtæli'eɪʃn/ noun [U] **retaliation (against sb/sth) (for sth)**: *The terrorist group said that the shooting was* ***in retaliation*** *for the murder of one of its members.* ▶ **odwet**

retarded /rɪ'tɑ:dɪd/ adj. slower to develop than normal ▶ **opóźniony** *(w rozwoju)* ⓘ To słowo obecnie uważa się za obraźliwe. Zamiast niego należy używać **disabled**.

retch /retʃ/ verb [I] to make sounds and movements as if you are **vomiting** although you do not actually do so: *The smell made her retch.* ▶ **mieć odruch wymiotny**

retention /rɪ'tenʃn/ noun [U] the act of keeping sth or of being kept ▶ **utrzymywanie** ➲ verb **retain**

rethink /'ri:θɪŋk; ˌri:'θɪŋk/ verb [I,T] (pt, pp **rethought** /-'θɔ:t/) to think about sth again because you probably need to change it: *The government has been forced to rethink its economic policy.* ▶ **przemyśleć ponownie**

reticent /'retɪsnt/ adj. **reticent (about sth)** not willing to tell people about things: *She was shy and reticent.* ◇ *He was extremely reticent about his personal life.* ▶ **małomówny, powściągliwy**

■ **reticence** noun [U] (formal) ▶ **małomówność, powściągliwość**

retina /'retɪnə; US 'retənə/ noun [C] the area at the back of your eye that is sensitive to light and sends signals to the brain about what is seen ▶ **siatkówka** *(oka)*

retire /rɪ'taɪə(r)/ verb [I] **1 retire (from sth)** to leave your job and stop working usually because you have reached a certain age: *She retired from the company at the age of 60.* ▶ **odchodzić na emeryturę, wycofywać się z czegoś** ➲ note at **job** ➲ look at **old-age pension**

> After someone **retires**, we say that he/she **is retired.** A **pension** is the money that retired people receive regularly from their former employer and/or the government.

2 (formal) to leave and go to a quiet or private place: *to retire to bed* ▶ **udawać się na spoczynek**

retired /rɪ'taɪəd/ adj. having stopped work permanently: *a retired teacher* ▶ **emerytowany**

retirement /rɪ'taɪəmənt/ noun **1** [C,U] the act of stopping working permanently: *There have been a number of retirements* (wielu ludzi odeszło na emeryturę) *in our department this year.* ◇ *She has decided to* ***take early retirement*** (odejść na wcześniejszą emeryturę). ◇ *The former world champion has announced his retirement* (wycofanie się). ▶ **przejście na emeryturę 2** [sing., U] the situation or period after **retiring** from work: *We all wish you a long and happy retirement.* ▶ **emerytura** ➲ look at **old-age pensioner, senior citizen**

retiring /rɪ'taɪərɪŋ/ adj. (used about a person) shy and quiet ▶ **nieśmiały; małomówny**

retort¹ /rɪ'tɔ:t/ verb [T] to reply quickly to what sb says, in an angry or amusing way: *'Who asked you for your opinion?' she retorted.* ▶ **ripostować**

retort² /rɪ'tɔ:t/ noun [C] **1** a quick, angry or humorous reply: *an angry retort* ▶ **riposta, cięta odpowiedź 2** a closed bottle with a long narrow bent that is used in a laboratory for heating chemicals ▶ **retorta** ➲ picture at **laboratory**

retrace /rɪ'treɪs/ verb [T] to repeat a past journey, series of events, etc.: *I* ***retraced my steps*** (wróciłem tą samą drogą) *in an attempt to find my wallet.* ▶ **odtwarzać, cofać się do czegoś**

retract /rɪ'trækt/ verb [I,T] (formal) to say that sth you have said is not true: *When he appeared in court, he retracted the confession he had made to the police.* ▶ **wycofywać** *(np. skargę)*

retreat¹ /rɪ'tri:t/ verb [I] **1** (used about an army, etc.) to move backwards in order to leave a battle or in order not to become involved in a battle: *The order was given to retreat.* ▶ **cofać się, dokonywać odwrotu** OPP **advance 2** to move backwards; to go to a safe or private

R

place: *A neighbour tried to get into the burning house but he was forced to retreat* (zmuszony do odwrotu) *by the intense heat.* ◇ (figurative) *She seems to retreat into a world of her own sometimes.* ▶ **wycofywać się**

retreat² /rɪˈtriːt/ noun **1** [C,U] the act of moving backwards, away from a difficult or dangerous situation: *The invading forces are now in retreat.* ▶ **odwrót, wycofywanie się, powrót** OPP **advance 2** [C] a private place where you can go when you want to be quiet or to rest: *a religious retreat* rekolekcje ▶ **zacisze**

retribution /ˌretrɪˈbjuːʃn/ noun [U] (formal) **retribution (for sth)** punishment for a crime ▶ **zadośćuczynienie**

retrieve /rɪˈtriːv/ verb [T] **1 retrieve sth (from sb/sth)** to get sth back from the place where it was left or lost: *Police divers retrieved* (wyłowili) *the body from the canal.* ▶ **odnajdować 2** to find information that has been stored on a computer: *The computer can retrieve all the data about a particular customer.* ▶ **odzyskiwać** (*dane z komputera*) **3** to make a bad situation or a mistake better; to put sth right: *The team was losing two-nil at half-time but they managed to* ***retrieve the situation*** *in the second half.* ▶ **ratować**

■ **retrieval** /rɪˈtriːvl/ noun [U]: *retrieval* (wydobywanie) *of the bodies from the wreckage* ▶ **odzyskiwanie, wyszukiwanie**

retrospect /ˈretrəspekt/ noun

IDM **in retrospect** thinking about sth that happened in the past, often seeing it differently from the way you saw it at the time: *In retrospect, I can see what a stupid mistake it was.* ▶ **z perspektywy czasu**

retrospective /ˌretrəˈspektɪv/ adj. **1** looking again at the past: *a retrospective analysis of historical events* ▶ **retrospektywny 2** (used about laws, decisions, payments, etc.) intended to take effect from a date in the past: *Is this new tax law retrospective?* ▶ **działający wstecz**

■ **retrospectively** adv. ▶ **retrospektywnie**

⚷ **return¹** /rɪˈtɜːn/ verb **1** [I] **return (to/from ...)** to come or go back to a place: *I leave on the 10th July and return on the 25th.* ◇ *I shall be returning to this country in six months.* ◇ *When did you return from Italy?* ◇ *He left his home town when he was 18 and never returned.* ▶ **wracać do/z czegoś 2** [I] **return (to sth/doing sth)** to go back to the former or usual activity, situation, condition, etc.: *The strike is over and they will* ***return to work*** *on Monday.* ◇ *It is hoped that train services will* ***return to normal*** *soon.* ▶ **powracać do czegoś 3** [I] to come back; to happen again: *If the pain returns, make another appointment to see me.* ▶ **powracać 4** [T] **return sth (to sb/sth)** to give, send, put or take sth back: *I've stopped lending him things because he never returns them.* ◇ *Application forms must be returned by 14 March.* ▶ **oddawać, odsyłać 5** [T] to react to sth that sb does, says or feels by doing, saying, or feeling sth similar: *I've phoned them several times and left messages but they haven't returned my calls* (nie oddzwonili). ◇ *We'll be happy to return your hospitality if you ever come to our country.* ▶ **odwzajemniać coś 6** [T] to hit or throw the ball back: *to return a service/shot* ▶ **odbijać** (*piłkę do przeciwnika*)

⚷ **return²** /rɪˈtɜːn/ noun **1** [sing.] **a return (to/from ...)** coming or going back to a place or to a former activity, situation or condition: *I'll contact you* ***on my return*** (po powrocie) *from holiday.* ◇ *to make a return to form* wrócić do formy ▶ **powrót 2** [U] giving, sending, putting or taking sth back: *I demand the immediate return of my passport.* ▶ **zwrot 3** [C,U] **(a) return (on sth)** the profit from a business, etc.: *This account offers high returns on all investments.* ▶ **zysk, dochody 4** [C] (Brit. also **reˌturn ˈticket**; US **ˌround ˈtrip**; **ˌround-trip ˈticket**) a ticket to travel to a place and back again: *A* ***day return*** *to Oxford, please.* ◇ *Is the* ***return fare*** *cheaper than two singles?* ▶ **bilet powrotny** OPP **single, one-way 5** (also **the reˈturn key**) [sing.] the button on a computer that you press when you reach the end of a line or of an instruction: *To exit this option, press return.* ▶ (*niektóre komputery*) **klawisz Enter/Return 6** [C] the act of hitting or throwing the ball back: *She hit a brilliant return.* ▶ **odbicie** (*piłki*)

IDM **by return (of post)** (Brit.) immediately; by the next post ▶ **pocztą odwrotną**

in return (for sth) as payment or in exchange (for sth); as a reaction to sth: *Please accept this present in return for all your help.* ▶ **jako zadośćuczynienie, w zamian za coś**

returnable /rɪˈtɜːnəbl/ adj. that can or must be given or taken back: *a non-returnable deposit* ▶ **zwrotny**

the reˈturn key = RETURN² (5)

reˌturn ˈticket = RETURN² (4)

reunion /riːˈjuːniən/ noun **1** [C] a party or occasion when friends or people who worked together meet again after they have not seen each other for a long time: *The college holds an annual reunion for former students.* ▶ **zjazd 2** [C,U] **a reunion (with sb/between A and B)** coming together again after being apart: *The released hostages had an emotional reunion with their families at the airport.* ▶ **ponowne połączenie**

reunite /ˌriːjuːˈnaɪt/ verb [I,T] **reunite (A with/and B)** to come together again; to join two or more people, groups, etc. together again: *The missing child was found by the police and reunited with his parents.* ▶ **łączyć (się) ponownie, jednoczyć (się)**

Rev. = REVEREND: *Rev. Jesse Jackson*

rev¹ /rev/ verb [I,T] (**revving**; **revved**) **rev (sth) (up)** when an engine **revs** or when you **rev** it, it turns quickly and noisily ▶ **rozruszać silnik; przyśpieszać obroty silnika**

rev² /rev/ noun [C] (informal) (used when talking about an engine's speed) one complete turn: *4 000 revs per minute* ▶ **obrót** (*silnika*) ➲ look at **revolution**

revamp /ˌriːˈvæmp/ verb [T] to make changes to the form of sth, usually to improve its appearance ▶ **przerabiać**

■ **revamp** /ˈriːvæmp/ noun [sing.]: *Could your kitchen do with a revamp?* ▶ **przeróbka**

⚷ **reveal** /rɪˈviːl/ verb [T] **1 reveal sth (to sb)** to make sth known that was secret or unknown before: *He refused to reveal any names to the police.* ▶ **wyjawiać 2** to show sth that was hidden before: *The X-ray revealed a tiny fracture in her right hand.* ▶ **ujawniać, odsłaniać**

revealing /rɪˈviːlɪŋ/ adj. **1** allowing sth to be known that was secret or unknown before: *This book provides a revealing insight into the world of politics.* ▶ **ujawniający, odkrywczy 2** allowing sth to be seen that is usually hidden, especially sb's body: *a very revealing swimsuit* ▶ **głęboko wycięty, wydekoltowany**

revel /ˈrevl/ verb (**revelling**; **revelled**; US **reveling**; **reveled**)

PHR V **revel in sth/doing sth** to enjoy sth very much: *He likes being famous and revels in the attention he gets.* ▶ **upajać się czymś**

revelation /ˌrevəˈleɪʃn/ noun **1** [C] something that is made known, that was secret or unknown before, especially sth surprising: *This magazine is full of revelations about the private lives of the stars.* ▶ **odkrycie, rewelacja 2** [sing.] a thing or a person that surprises you and makes you change your opinion about sb/sth ▶ **objawienie**

revenge /rɪˈvendʒ/ noun [U] **revenge (on sb) (for sth)** something that you do to punish sb who has hurt you, made you suffer, etc.: *He made a fool of me and now I want to* ***get my revenge*** (chcę się zemścić). ◇ *He wants to* ***take revenge*** (chce się zemścić) *on the judge who sent him to prison.* ◇ *The shooting was* ***in revenge*** *for* (z zemsty za) *an attack by the nationalists.* ▶ **zemsta** ➲ look at **vengeance**

■ **revenge** verb [T] **revenge yourself on sb**: *She revenged herself on her enemy.* ▶ **mścić się** ➲ look at **avenge**

revenue /ˈrevənjuː; US -nuː/ noun [U, pl.] money regularly received by a government, company, etc.: *Revenue from income tax rose last year.* ▶ **dochody** (*np. państwa*)

reverberate /rɪˈvɜːbəreɪt/ verb [I] (used about a sound) to be repeated several times as it hits and is sent back from different surfaces: *Her voice reverberated around the hall.* ▶ **odbijać się** (*echem*), **rozbrzmiewać**
■ **reverberation** /rɪˌvɜːbəˈreɪʃn/ noun [C,U] ▶ **pogłos**, **odbijanie się** (*np. echa*)

revere /rɪˈvɪə(r)/ verb [T, usually passive] **revere sb (as sth)** (formal) to feel great respect or admiration for sb/sth: *Her name is revered in Spain.* ▶ **czcić kogoś (jako coś)** SYN **idolize**

reverence /ˈrevərəns/ noun [U] (formal) **reverence (for sb/sth)** a feeling of great respect ▶ **cześć**

reverend /ˈrevərənd/ adj. (**Reverend**) [only before a noun] (abbr. **Rev.**) the title of a Christian priest: *the Reverend Charles Dodgson* ▶ **wielebny**

reverent /ˈrevərənt/ adj. (formal) showing respect ▶ **pełen czci**

reversal /rɪˈvɜːsl/ noun [U,C] the act of changing sth to the opposite of what it was before; an occasion when this happens: *The government insists that there will be no reversal of policy.* ◇ *The decision taken yesterday was a complete reversal of last week's decision.* ◇ *a reversal of roles* zamiana ról ▶ **zmiana kierunku**, **odwrotność**

⚷ **reverse**[1] /rɪˈvɜːs/ verb **1** [T] to put sth in the opposite position to normal or to how it was before: *Today's results have reversed the order of the top two teams.* ▶ **odwracać**; **zmieniać 2** [T] to exchange the positions or functions of two things or people: *Jane and her husband have reversed roles – he stays at home now and she goes to work.* ▶ **zmieniać**, **zamieniać się czymś 3** [I,T] to go backwards in a car, etc.; to make a car go backwards: *It will probably be easier to reverse into that parking space.* ◇ *He reversed his brand new car into a wall.* ▶ **cofać**
IDM **reverse (the) charges** (Brit.) to make a telephone call that will be paid for by the person who receives it: *a reverse charge call* ▶ **dzwonić do kogoś na jego koszt**
ℹ Idiom o tym samym znaczeniu w Amer. ang. to **to call collect**.

⚷ **reverse**[2] /rɪˈvɜːs/ noun **1** [sing.] **the reverse (of sth)** the complete opposite of what was said just before, or of what is expected: *Of course I don't dislike you – quite the reverse* (wręcz przeciwnie). ◇ *This course is the exact reverse of what I was expecting.* ▶ **przeciwny 2** (also reˌverse ˈgear) [U] the control in a car, etc. that allows it to move backwards: *Leave the car **in reverse** while it's parked on this hill.* ◇ *Where's reverse in this car?* ◇ *Put the car into reverse.* Włącz wsteczny bieg. ▶ **bieg wsteczny**
IDM **in reverse** in the opposite order, starting at the end and going back to the beginning ▶ **w odwrotnej kolejności** SYN **backwards**

reverse[3] /rɪˈvɜːs/ adj. [only before a noun] opposite to what is expected or has just been described ▶ **odwrotny**
IDM **in/into reverse order** starting with the last one and going backwards to the first one: *The results will be announced in reverse order.* ▶ **w odwrotnej kolejności**

reversible /rɪˈvɜːsəbl/ adj. (used about clothes) that can be worn with either side on the outside: *a reversible coat* ▶ **dwustronny**

revert /rɪˈvɜːt/ verb [I] **revert (to sth)** to return to a former state or activity: *The land will soon revert to jungle if it is not farmed.* ◇ *If this is unsuccessful we will revert to the old system.* ▶ **powracać do czegoś**

⚷ **review**[1] /rɪˈvjuː/ noun **1** [C,U] the examining or considering again of sth in order to decide if changes are necessary: *There will be a review of your contract after the first six months.* ◇ *The system is in need of review.* ▶ **rewizja 2** [C] a newspaper or magazine article, or an item on TV or radio, in which sb gives an opinion on a new book, film, play, etc.: *The film got bad reviews.* ▶ **przegląd 3** [C] a look back at sth in order to check, remember, or be clear about sth: *a review of the major events of the year* ▶ **przegląd**

⚷ **review**[2] /rɪˈvjuː/ verb [T] **1** to examine or consider sth again in order to decide if changes are necessary: *Your salary will be reviewed after one year.* ▶ **poddawać rewizji 2** to look at or think about sth again to make sure that you understand it: *Let's review what we've done in class this week.* ▶ **robić przegląd 3** to write an article or to talk on TV or radio, giving an opinion on a new book, film, play, etc.: *In this week's edition our film critic reviews the latest films.* ▶ **recenzować**

reviewer /rɪˈvjuːə(r)/ noun [C] a person who writes about new books, films, etc. ▶ **krytyk**

⚷ **revise** /rɪˈvaɪz/ verb **1** [T] to make changes to sth in order to correct or improve it: *The book has been revised for this new edition.* ◇ *I revised my opinion of him when I found out that he had lied.* ▶ **poprawiać**, **rewidować 2** [I,T] (Brit.) **revise (for sth)** to read or study again sth that you have learnt, especially when preparing for an exam: *I can't come out tonight. I'm revising for my exam.* ◇ *None of the things I had revised came up in the exam.* ▶ **powtarzać** (*materiał do egzaminu*)

⚷ **revision** /rɪˈvɪʒn/ noun **1** [C,U] the changing of sth in order to correct or improve it: *It has been suggested that the whole system is in need of revision.* ▶ **korekta 2** [U] (Brit.) the work of reading or studying again sth you have learnt, especially when preparing for an exam: *I'm going to have to **do** a lot of **revision** for History.* ▶ **powtórka** (*materiału*)

revival /rɪˈvaɪvl/ noun **1** [C,U] the act of becoming or making sth strong or popular again: *economic revival* ◇ *a revival of interest in traditional farming methods* ▶ **ożywienie 2** [C] a new performance of a play that has not been performed for some time: *a revival of the musical 'The Sound of Music'* ▶ **wznowienie**

revive /rɪˈvaɪv/ verb [I,T] **1** to become, or to make sb/sth become, conscious or strong and healthy again: *Hopes have revived for an early end to the fighting.* ◇ *I'm very tired but I'm sure a cup of coffee will revive me.* ◇ *Attempts were made to revive him but he was already dead.* ▶ **rozbudzać (na nowo)**, **ożywiać**, **cucić 2** to become or to make sth popular again; to begin to do or use sth again: *Public interest in athletics has revived now that the national team is doing well.* ◇ *to revive an old custom* ▶ **budzić (się) na nowo**, **wskrzeszać**

revoke /rɪˈvəʊk/ verb [T] (formal) to officially cancel sth so that it is no longer valid ▶ **unieważniać**, **uchylać**

revolt /rɪˈvəʊlt/ verb **1** [I] **revolt (against sb/sth)** to protest in a group, often violently, against the person or people in power: *A group of generals revolted against the government.* ▶ **buntować się 2** [T] to make sb feel disgusted or ill: *The sight and smell of the meat revolted him.* ▶ **budzić odrazę/wstręt** ➲ noun **revulsion**
■ **revolt** noun [C,U]: *The people rose **in revolt*** (w proteście) *against the corrupt government.* ▶ **bunt**

revolting /rɪˈvəʊltɪŋ/ adj. extremely unpleasant; disgusting: *What a revolting colour/smell.* ▶ **odrażający**

⚷ **revolution** /ˌrevəˈluːʃn/ noun **1** [C,U] action taken by a large group of people to try to change the government of a country, especially by violent action: *the French Revolution of 1789* ◇ *a country on the brink of revolution* ▶ **rewolucja 2** [C] **a revolution (in sth)** a complete change in methods, opinions, etc., often as a result of progress: *the Industrial Revolution* ▶ **rewolucja 3** [C,U] a movement around sth; one complete turn around a central

R

point (for example in a car engine): *400 revolutions per minute* ▶ **obrót** (*dookoła osi*) ➲ look at **rev**

revolutionary[1] /ˌrevəˈluːʃənəri; US -neri/ adj. **1** connected with or supporting political **revolution**: *the revolutionary leaders* ▶ **rewolucyjny 2** producing great changes; very new and different: *a revolutionary new scheme to ban cars from the city centre* ▶ **rewolucyjny**

revolutionary[2] /ˌrevəˈluːʃənəri; US -neri/ noun [C] (pl. **revolutionaries**) a person who starts or supports action to try to change the government of a country, especially by using violent action ▶ **rewolucjonist(k)a**

revolutionize (also -ise) /ˌrevəˈluːʃənaɪz/ verb [T] to change sth completely, usually improving it: *a discovery that could revolutionize the treatment of mental illness* ▶ **rewolucjonizować**

revolve /rɪˈvɒlv/ verb [I] to move in a circle around a central point: *The earth revolves around the sun.* ▶ **obracać się (wokół osi)**
PHR V **revolve around/round sb/sth** to have sb/sth as the most important part: *Her life revolves around the family.* ▶ **obracać się (wokół kogoś/czegoś)**

revolver /rɪˈvɒlvə(r)/ noun [C] a type of small gun with a container for bullets that turns round ▶ **rewolwer** ➲ note at **gun**

revolving /rɪˈvɒlvɪŋ/ adj. that goes round in a circle: *revolving doors* ▶ **obrotowy**

revulsion /rɪˈvʌlʃn/ noun [U] a feeling of disgust (because sth is extremely unpleasant) ▶ **wstręt** ➲ verb **revolt**

⚷ **reward**[1] /rɪˈwɔːd/ noun **reward (for sth/for doing sth) 1** [C,U] something that you are given because you have done sth good, worked hard, etc.: *Winning the match was* ***just reward*** *for all the effort.* ▶ **wynagrodzenie, satysfakcja 2** [C] an amount of money that is given in exchange for helping the police, returning sth that was lost, etc.: *Police are offering a reward for information leading to a conviction.* ▶ **nagroda**

⚷ **reward**[2] /rɪˈwɔːd/ verb [T, often passive] **reward sb (for sth/for doing sth)** to give sth to sb because they have done sth good, worked hard, etc.: *Eventually her efforts were rewarded and she got a job.* ▶ **(wy)nagradzać**

rewarding /rɪˈwɔːdɪŋ/ adj. (used about an activity, a job, etc.) giving satisfaction; making you happy because you think it is important, useful, etc. ▶ **satysfakcjonujący**

rewind /ˌriːˈwaɪnd/ verb [T] (pt, pp **rewound**) to make a video or tape go backwards: *Please rewind the tape at the end of the film.* ▶ **szybko przewijać (***taśmę***) do tyłu**
■ **rewind** noun [U] ▶ **klawisz szybkiego przewijania taśmy do tyłu** ➲ look at **fast forward**

rewrite /ˌriːˈraɪt/ verb [T] (pt **rewrote** /-ˈrəʊt/, pp **rewritten** /-ˈrɪtn/) to write sth again in a different or better way ▶ **przepisywać, przerabiać**

rhetoric /ˈretərɪk/ noun [U] (formal) a way of speaking or writing that is intended to impress or influence people but is not always sincere ▶ **retoryka**
■ **rhetorical** /rɪˈtɒrɪkl/ adj. ▶ **retoryczny** | **rhetorically** /-kli/ adv. ▶ **retorycznie**

rheˌtorical ˈquestion noun [C] a question that does not expect an answer ▶ **pytanie retoryczne**

rheumatism /ˈruːmətɪzəm/ noun [U] an illness that causes pain in your muscles and where your bones are connected ▶ **reumatyzm**

rhino (informal) = RHINOCEROS

rhinoceros /raɪˈnɒsərəs/ (also informal **rhino** /ˈraɪnəʊ/, pl. **rhinos**) noun [C] (pl. **rhinoceros** or **rhinoceroses**) a large animal from Africa or Asia, with thick skin and with one or two horns on its nose ▶ **nosorożec**

rhubarb /ˈruːbɑːb/ noun [U] a plant with red **stalks** that can be cooked and eaten as fruit ▶ **rabarbar**

rhyme[1] /raɪm/ noun **1** [C] a word that has the same sound as another: *Can you think of a rhyme for* (co się rymuje z) *'peace'?* ▶ **rym 2** [C] a short piece of writing, or sth spoken, in which the word at the end of each line sounds the same as the word at the end of the line before it ▶ **wierszyk** ➲ look at **nursery rhyme 3** [U] the use of words in a poem or song that have the same sound, especially at the ends of lines: *All of his poetry was written* ***in rhyme*** (wierszem). ▶ **rym**

rhyme[2] /raɪm/ verb **1** [I] **rhyme (with sth)** to have the same sound as another word; to contain lines that end with words that sound the same: *'Tough' rhymes with 'stuff'.* ▶ **rymować się 2** [T] **rhyme sth (with sth)** to put together words that have the same sound ▶ **rymować (coś z czymś)**

ˈrhyming slang noun [U] a way of talking in which you use words or phrases that rhyme with the word you mean, instead of using that word. For example in cockney rhyming slang 'apples and pears' means 'stairs'. ▶ **rodzaj slangu**

⚷ **rhythm** /ˈrɪðəm/ noun [C,U] a regular repeated pattern of sound or movement: *I'm not keen on the tune but I love the rhythm.* ◇ *He's a terrible dancer because he has no* ***sense of rhythm.*** ◇ *He tapped his foot* ***in rhythm*** *with the music.* ▶ **rytm**
■ **rhythmic** /ˈrɪðmɪk/ (also **rhythmical** /ˈrɪðmɪkl/) adj.: *the rhythmic qualities of African music* ▶ **rytmiczny** | **rhythmically** /-kli/ adv. ▶ **rytmicznie**

rib /rɪb/ noun [C] one of the curved bones that go round your chest: *He's so thin that you can see his ribs.* ◇ *a rib-cage* żebra ▶ **żebro** ➲ picture at **body**

ribbon /ˈrɪbən/ noun [C,U] a long, thin piece of cloth that is used for tying or decorating sth: *a present wrapped in a blue ribbon* ▶ **wstążka**

ribcage /ˈrɪbkeɪdʒ/ noun [C] the structure of curved bones, (called **ribs**), that surrounds and protects the chest ▶ **klatka piersiowa**

⚷ **rice** /raɪs/ noun [U] short, thin, white or brown grain from a plant that grows on wet land in hot countries. We cook and eat rice: *boiled/fried/steamed rice* ◇ *rice pudding* deser z ryżu ▶ **ryż**

⚷ **rich** /rɪtʃ/ adj. **1** having a lot of money or property; not poor: *a rich family/country* ◇ *one of the richest women in the world* ▶ **bogaty** SYN **wealthy, well-to-do** OPP **poor 2** (**the rich**) noun [pl.] people with a lot of money or property: *the rich and famous* ▶ **bogaci 3 rich in sth** containing a lot of sth: *Oranges are rich in vitamin C.* ▶ **bogaty w coś 4** containing a lot of fat, oil, sugar or cream and making you feel full quickly: *a rich chocolate cake* (z dużą ilością jajek, czekolady, tłuszczu itp.) ▶ **tłusty, ciężki 5** containing the substances that make it good for growing plants in: *a rich well-drained soil* ▶ **żyzny, bogaty 6** (used about a colour, a sound or a smell) strong and deep: *a rich purple* ▶ **soczysty, mocny, przyjemny, głęboki**
■ **richness** noun [U] ▶ **bogactwo**

riches /ˈrɪtʃɪz/ noun [pl.] (formal) a lot of money or property ▶ **bogactw-o/a** SYN **wealth**

richly /ˈrɪtʃli/ adv. **1** in a generous way: *She was richly* (suto) *rewarded for her hard work.* ▶ **bogato, wspaniale 2** in a way that people think is right: *His promotion was* ***richly deserved.*** ▶ **w pełni**

rickety /ˈrɪkəti/ adj. likely to break; not strongly made: *a rickety old fence* ◇ *rickety furniture* ▶ **chwiejny, rozklekotany**

ricochet /ˈrɪkəʃeɪ/ verb [I] (**ricocheting** /ˈrɪkəʃeɪɪŋ/, pt, pp **ricocheted** /ˈrɪkəʃeɪd/ (Brit. also) **ricochetting** /ˈrɪkəʃetɪŋ/; **ricochetted** /ˈrɪkəʃetɪd/) **ricochet (off sth)** (used about a moving object) to hit a surface and come off it fast at a different angle: *The bullet ricocheted off the wall and grazed his shoulder.* ▶ **odbić się rykoszetem**

rid /rɪd/ verb [T] (**ridding**; pt, pp **rid**) (formal) **rid yourself/sb/sth of sb/sth** to make yourself/sb/sth free from sb/sth that is unpleasant or not wanted: (Brit.) *He was a nuisance and we're **well rid** of him.* ◇ *He was unable to rid himself* (pozbyć się) *of his fears and suspicions.* ▶ **uwalniać**
IDM **get rid of sb/sth** to make yourself free of sb/sth that is annoying you or that you do not want; to throw sth away: *Let's get rid of that old chair and buy a new one.* ▶ **pozbywać się kogoś/czegoś**

riddance /ˈrɪdns/ noun
IDM **good riddance (to sb/sth)** (informal) (used for expressing pleasure or satisfaction that sb/sth that you do not like has gone) ▶ **nareszcie!**

ridden¹ past participle of **ride¹**

ridden² /ˈrɪdn/ adj. [often in compounds] (formal) full of: *She was guilt-ridden.* ◇ *She was ridden with guilt.* ▶ **pełen**

riddle /ˈrɪdl/ noun [C] **1** a difficult question that you ask people for fun that has a clever or amusing answer ▶ **zagadka 2** a person, a thing or an event that you cannot understand or explain ▶ **zagadkowa osoba/sprawa**

riddled /ˈrɪdld/ adj. **riddled with sth** full of sth, especially sth unpleasant: *This essay is riddled with mistakes.* ▶ **pełny czegoś**

ride¹ /raɪd/ verb (pt **rode** /rəʊd/, pp **ridden** /ˈrɪdn/) **1** [I,T] to sit on a horse and control it as it moves: *We rode through the woods and over the moor.* ◇ *Which horse is Dettori riding in the next race?* ▶ **jeździć konno** ℹ Mówiąc o jeździe konno dla przyjemności, w codziennym Br. ang. używa się wyrażenia **go riding**: *She goes riding every weekend.* W Amer. ang. mówi się wówczas **go horseback riding**. **2** [I,T] to sit on a bicycle, motorbike, etc. and control it as it moves: *She jumped onto her motorbike and rode off.* ◇ *Can John ride a bicycle yet?* ▶ **jeździć na rowerze/motorze 3** [I,T] (especially US) to travel as a passenger in a bus, car, etc.: *She rode the bus to school every day.* ▶ **jeździć**
■ **rider** noun [C] ▶ **jeździec**; **rowerzyst(k)a**; **motocyklist(k)a** ➲ picture on **page A9**

ride² /raɪd/ noun [C] **1** a short journey on a horse or bicycle, or in a car, bus, etc.: *We went for a bike ride on Saturday.* ◇ *It's only a short bus ride into Oxford.* Autobusem jest niedaleko do Oksfordu. ◇ *Would you like to have a ride* (przejechać się) *in my new car?* ▶ **przejażdżka 2** (used to describe what a journey or trip is like): *a smooth/bumpy/comfortable ride* ▶ **jazda 3** a large moving machine which you pay to go on for fun or excitement; an occasion when you go on one of these: *My favourite **fairground ride** is the roller coaster.* ▶ **kolejka górska itp.** (*w wesołym miasteczku*)
IDM **take sb for a ride** (informal) to cheat or trick sb ▶ **nabrać**

ridge /rɪdʒ/ noun [C] **1** a long, narrow piece of high land along the top of hills or mountains ▶ **grzbiet górski 2** a line where two surfaces meet at an angle ▶ **krawędź**, **grzbiet**

ridicule /ˈrɪdɪkjuːl/ noun [U] unkind behaviour or comments that make sb/sth look silly: *He had become an object of ridicule.* ▶ **kpiny**
■ **ridicule** verb [T]: *The idea was ridiculed by everybody.* ▶ **wyśmiewać**

ridiculous /rɪˈdɪkjələs/ adj. very silly or unreasonable: *They're asking a ridiculous price for that house.* ▶ **śmieszny**, **absurdalny** SYN **absurd**
■ **ridiculously** adv. ▶ **śmiesznie**, **absurdalnie**

riding /ˈraɪdɪŋ/ (US ˈ**horseback riding**) noun [U] the sport or hobby of riding a horse: *She **goes riding** every weekend.* ◇ *riding boots* ◇ *a riding school* ▶ **jeździectwo**

rife /raɪf/ adj. [not before a noun] (formal) (used especially about bad things) very common: *Rumours are rife that his wife has left him.* ▶ **rozpowszechniony**

rifle¹ /ˈraɪfl/ noun [C] a long gun that you hold against your shoulder to shoot with: *She fired the rifle.* ▶ **karabin** ➲ note at **gun**

rifle² /ˈraɪfl/ verb [I,T] **rifle (through) sth** to search sth, usually in order to steal sth from it: *I caught him rifling through the papers on my desk.* ▶ **przetrząsać**

rift /rɪft/ noun [C] **1** a serious disagreement between friends, groups, etc. that stops their relationship from continuing: *a growing rift between the brothers* ▶ **przepaść 2** a very large crack or opening in the ground, a rock, etc. ▶ **szczelina**

rig¹ /rɪɡ/ verb [T] (**rigging**; **rigged**) to arrange or control an event, etc. in an unfair way, in order to get the result you want: *a rigged competition* konkurs, w którym wynik był z góry przesądzony ▶ **ukartowywać**, **fałszować**
PHR V **rig sth up** to make sth quickly, using any materials you can find: *We tried to rig up a shelter using our coats.* ▶ **montować**, **sklecić**

rig² = OIL RIG

rigging /ˈrɪɡɪŋ/ noun [U] the ropes, etc. that support a ship's sails ▶ **takielunek**

right¹ /raɪt/ adj. **1** (used about behaviour, actions, etc.) fair; morally and socially correct: *It's not right to pay people so badly.* ◇ *What do you think is **the right thing** to do?* ▶ **słuszny**, **odpowiedni** OPP **wrong 2** correct; true: *I'm afraid that's not the right answer.* ◇ *Have you got **the right time*** (dokładną godzinę)*?* ◇ *'You're Chinese, aren't you?' 'Yes, **that's right.**'* ◇ *You're quite right* (masz całkowitą rację) *– the film does start at 7 o'clock.* ▶ **właściwy**, **poprawny** OPP **wrong 3 right (for sb/sth)** best; most suitable: *I hope I've made **the right decision**.* ◇ *I'm sure we've chosen **the right person** for the job.* ◇ *I would help you to wash the car, but I'm not wearing the right clothes.* ▶ **słuszny**, **odpowiedni** OPP **wrong 4** healthy or normal; as it should be: *The car exhaust doesn't sound right – it's making a funny noise.* ◇ *I don't know what it is, but something's just not right.* ▶ **normalny**, **dobry 5** [only before a noun] on or of the side of the body that faces east when a person is facing north: *Most people write with their right hand.* ◇ *He's blind in his right eye.* ▶ **prawy** OPP **left 6** [only before a noun] (Brit., informal) (used for emphasizing sth bad) real or complete: *I'll look a right idiot in that hat!* ▶ **prawdziwy**, **kompletny 7** (**Right**) (used in some titles): *the Right Honourable James Smith, Foreign Secretary* ◇ *the Right Reverend Richard Pearson, Bishop of Gloucester* ▶ **(*używane w niektórych tytułach*)**
■ **rightness** noun [U] ▶ **prawość**, **słuszność**
IDM **get/start off on the right/wrong foot (with sb)** → FOOT¹
get on the right/wrong side of sb → SIDE¹
on the right/wrong track → TRACK¹
put/set sth right to correct sth or deal with a problem: *There's something wrong with the lawnmower. Do you think you'll be able to put it right?* ▶ **naprawić coś**
right (you are)! (informal) 'yes, I will' or 'yes, I agree': *'See you later.' 'Right you are!'* ▶ **zgoda!**, **dobrze!** SYN **OK**
(as) right as rain completely healthy and normal ▶ **zdrowy**; **dobrze działający**

right² /raɪt/ adv. **1** directly: *The train was right on time* (punktualnie). ◇ *He was sitting right beside me.* ▶ **dokładnie 2** all the way: *Did you watch the film right to the end* (do samego końca)*?* ◇ *There's a high wall that goes right round* (wokół całego) *the house.* **3** immediately: *Wait here a minute – I'll **be right back**.* ▶ **zaraz**, **natychmiast 4** in the way that it should happen or should be done: *Have I spelt your name right?* ◇ *Nothing*

R

seems to be going right for me at the moment. ▶ **poprawnie, dobrze** OPP **wrong** **5** to the right side: *Turn right at the traffic lights.* ▶ **w prawo** OPP **left** **6** (informal) (used for preparing sb for sth that is about to happen) get ready; listen: *Have you got your seat belts on? Right, off we go.* ▶ **dobrze!**

IDM **right/straight away** → AWAY

right now at this moment; exactly now: *We can't discuss this right now.* ▶ **w tej chwili**

serve sb right → SERVE

right³ /raɪt/ noun **1** [U] what is morally good and fair: *Does a child of ten really understand the difference between right and wrong?* ◇ *You* ***did right*** *to tell me what happened.* ▶ **dobro** OPP **wrong** **2** [U,C] **the right (to sth/to do sth)** a thing that you are allowed to do according to the law; a moral authority to do sth: *In Britain everybody* ***has the right*** *to vote at 18.* ◇ *Freedom of speech is one of the basic* ***human rights.*** ◇ ***civil rights*** prawa obywatelskie ◇ *animal rights campaigners* ◇ *You* ***have no right*** *to tell me what to do.* ▶ **prawo** **3** [sing.] the right side or direction: *We live in the first house* ***on the right.*** ◇ *Take the first right and then the second left.* ◇ *If you look slightly to your right* (w kierunku na prawo), *you will see Windsor Castle in the distance.* ▶ **prawa strona** OPP **left** **4** (**the Right**) [sing., with sing. or pl. verb] the people or political parties who are against social change: *The Right in British politics is represented by the Conservative Party.* ▶ **prawica** ➲ look at **right wing**

IDM **be in the right** to be doing what is correct and fair: *You don't need to apologize. You were in the right and he was in the wrong.* ▶ **mieć rację/słuszność**

by rights according to what is fair or correct: *By rights, half the profit should be mine.* ▶ **po sprawiedliwości**

in your own right because of what you are yourself and not because of other people ▶ **sam/a**

be within your rights (to do sth) to act in a reasonable or legal way: *You are quite within your rights* (masz pełne prawo) *to demand to see your lawyer.* ▶ **mieć prawo**

right⁴ /raɪt/ verb [T] to put sb/sth/yourself back into a normal position: *The boat tipped over and then righted itself again.* ▶ **wyprostowywać (się)**

IDM **right a wrong** to do sth to correct an unfair situation or sth bad that you have done ▶ **naprawić krzywdę**

'right angle noun [C] an angle of 90°: *A square has four right angles.* ▶ **kąt prosty** ➲ look at **acute angle**, **obtuse angle**

'right-angled adj. having or consisting of a **right angle**: *a right-angled triangle* ▶ **pod kątem prostym**

righteous /'raɪtʃəs/ adj. (formal) that you think is morally good or fair: *righteous anger/indignation* ▶ **prawy; sprawiedliwy** ➲ look at **self-righteous**

rightful /'raɪtfl/ adj. [only before a noun] (formal) legally or morally correct; fair ▶ **słuszny; prawowity**

■ **rightfully** /-fəli/ adv. ▶ **słusznie; prawnie**

'right-hand adj. [only before a noun] of or on the right of sb/sth: *in the top right-hand corner of the screen* ◇ *The postbox is on the right-hand side* (po prawej stronie) *of the road.* ▶ **prawostronny** OPP **left-hand**

,right-'handed adj. using the right hand for writing, etc. and not the left ▶ **praworęczny** OPP **left-handed**

,right-hand 'man noun [sing.] the person you depend on most to help and support you in your work: *the President's right-hand man* ▶ (*przen.*) **prawa ręka**

rightist /'raɪtɪst/ noun [C] a person who supports **right-wing** political parties and their ideas ▶ **osoba o prawicowych poglądach**

■ **rightist** adj.: *rightist groups* ▶ **prawicowy**

rightly /'raɪtli/ adv. correctly or fairly: *He's been sacked and* ***quite rightly****, I believe.* ▶ **słusznie**

,right of 'way noun (pl. **rights of way**) **1** [C,U] (especially Brit.) a path across private land that the public may use; legal permission to go into or through another person's land: *Walkers have right of way through the farmer's field.* ▶ **dostępna dla wszystkich droga wiodąca przez teren prywatny; prawo przejścia po prywatnej ziemi** **2** [U] (used in road traffic) the fact that a vehicle in a particular position is allowed to drive into or across a road before another vehicle in a different position: *He should have stopped – I had the right of way.* ▶ **prawo pierwszeństwa**

,right-'on adj. (Brit., informal) having political opinions or being aware of social issues that are fashionable and **left-wing**: *right-on middle-class intellectuals* ▶ **lewicowy** (*i politycznie poprawny*) ℹ Czasami wyraża dezaprobatę.

,right 'wing noun [sing., with sing. or pl. verb] the people in a political party who are against social change ▶ **prawe skrzydło** (*partii politycznej*)

■ **,right-'wing** adj. strongly supporting the **capitalist** system: *a right-wing government* ▶ **prawicowy** OPP **left-wing**

,right-'winger noun [C] **1** a person on the **right wing** of a political party ▶ **prawicowiec** **2** a person who plays on the right side of the field in a sports game ▶ **prawoskrzydłowy** OPP for both meanings **left-winger**

rigid /'rɪdʒɪd/ adj. **1** not able or not wanting to change or be changed ▶ **surowy** SYN **inflexible** **2** difficult to bend; stiff: *a rucksack with a rigid frame* ◇ *She was rigid with fear.* ▶ **sztywny**

■ **rigidity** /rɪ'dʒɪdəti/ noun [U] ▶ **surowość; sztywność** | **rigidly** adv.: *The speed limit must be rigidly enforced.* ▶ **sztywno**

rigorous /'rɪɡərəs/ adj. done very carefully and with great attention to detail: *Rigorous tests are carried out on drinking water.* ▶ **dokładny, szczegółowy**

■ **rigorously** adv.: *The country's press is rigorously controlled.* ▶ **rygorystycznie, dokładnie** | **rigorousness** noun [U] ▶ **rygor, dokładność**

rigour (US **rigor**) /'rɪɡə(r)/ noun (formal) **1** [U] doing sth carefully with great attention to detail: *The tests were carried out with rigour.* ▶ **dokładność, skrupulatność** **2** [U] the quality of being strict: *the full rigour of the law* ▶ **surowość, rygor** **3** [C, usually pl.] difficult conditions ▶ **surowość, trudy**

rile /raɪl/ verb [T] to annoy sb or make them angry ▶ **drażnić, rozgniewać** SYN **anger**, **2**

rim /rɪm/ noun [C] an edge at the top or outside of sth that is round: *the rim of a cup* ◇ *spectacles with silver rims* (ze srebrną oprawką) ▶ **brzeg, obrzeże**

rind /raɪnd/ noun [C,U] the thick hard skin on the outside of some fruits, especially citrus fruit; the hard outer edge of some types of cheese or **bacon** ▶ **skór(k)a** ➲ look at **peel**, **skin**

ring¹ /rɪŋ/ noun **1** [C] a piece of jewellery that you wear on your finger: *a gold/wedding ring* ◇ *an engagement ring* ◇ *A diamond ring glittered on her finger.* ▶ **pierścionek, obrączka** **2** [C] [in compounds] a round object of any material with a hole in the middle: *curtain rings* ◇ *a key ring* kółko do kluczy ▶ **kółko** **3** [C] a round mark or shape: *The coffee cup left a ring on the table top.* ◇ *Stand in a ring and hold hands.* ▶ **krąg** **4** [C] the space with seats all around it where a performance, etc. takes place: *a boxing ring* ▶ **arena, ring** **5** (US **burner** /'bɜːnə(r)/) [C] one of the round parts on the top of an electric or gas cooker on which you can put pans: *an electric cooker with an oven, a grill and four rings* ▶ **palnik; płytka** **6** [C] a number of people who are involved in sth that is secret or not legal: *a spy/drugs ring* ▶ **szajka** **7** [C] the sound made by a bell; the act of ringing a bell:

There was a ring at the door. ▶ **dzwonek 8** [sing.] **a ring of sth** a particular quality that words or sounds have: *What the man said* ***had a ring of truth*** *about it* (brzmiało prawdopodobnie). ▶ **brzmienie**
IDM **give sb a ring** (Brit., informal) to telephone sb: *I'll give you a ring in the morning.* ▶ **zadzwonić, zatelefonować**

ring² /rɪŋ/ verb (pt **rang** /ræŋ/, pp **rung** /rʌŋ/) **1** [I,T] (especially US **call**) **ring (sb/sth) (up)** to telephone sb/sth: *What time will you ring tomorrow?* ◇ *I rang up yesterday and booked the hotel.* ◇ *Ring the station and ask what time the next train leaves.* ▶ **dzwonić, telefonować** SYN **phone** ➲ note at **telephone 2** [I,T] to make a sound like a bell or to cause sth to make this sound: *Is that the phone ringing?* ◇ *We rang the door bell but nobody answered.* ▶ **dzwonić 3** [I] **ring (for sb/sth)** to ring a bell in order to call sb, ask for sth, etc.: *'Did you ring, sir?' asked the stewardess.* ◇ *Could you ring for a taxi, please?* ▶ **dzwonić 4** [I] **ring (with sth)** to be filled with loud sounds: *The music was so loud it made my ears ring.* ▶ **rozbrzmiewać, tętnić 5** [I] (used about words or sounds) to have a certain effect when you hear them: *Her words didn't* ***ring true*** (nie brzmiały wiarygodnie/szczerze). ▶ **brzmieć 6** [T] (pt, pp **ringed**) [often passive] to surround sb/sth: *The whole area was ringed with police.* ▶ **otaczać 7** [T] (pt, pp **ringed**) (especially Brit.) to draw a circle around sth: *Ring the correct answer in pencil.* ▶ **okółkowywać, zakreślać** (*kółkiem*) SYN **circle**
IDM **ring a bell** to sound familiar or to remind you, not very clearly, of sb/sth: *'Do you know Jan Kos?' 'Well, the name rings a bell.'* ▶ **mówić (komuś) coś**
PHR V **ring (sb) back** (Brit.) to telephone sb again or to telephone sb who has telephoned you: *I can't talk now – can I ring you back?* ▶ **dzwonić ponownie**
ring in (Brit.) to telephone a TV or radio show, or the place where you work: *Mandy rang in sick this morning.* ▶ **zadzwonić** (*do telewizji, radia, miejsca (swojej) pracy*)
ring out to sound loudly and clearly ▶ **rozbrzmiewać, rozlegać się**
ring off (Brit.) to end a telephone conversation: *I'd better ring off – supper's ready.* ▶ **kończyć rozmowę telefoniczną**

'ring binder noun [C] a file for holding papers, in which metal rings go through holes in the edges of the paper, holding them in place ▶ **segregator** ➲ picture at **stationery**

ringleader /'rɪŋliːdə(r)/ noun [C] a person who leads others in crime or in causing trouble: *The ringleaders were jailed for 15 years.* ▶ **przywódca**

'ring pull (US **'pull tab**) noun [C] a small piece of metal with a ring which you pull to open cans of food, drink, etc. ▶ **uchwyt/uszko do otwierania puszek/konserw**

'ring road noun [C] (Brit.) a road that is built all around a town so that traffic does not have to go into the town centre ▶ **obwodnica** ➲ look at **bypass**

ringtone /'rɪŋtəʊn/ noun [C] the sound that your telephone (especially a mobile phone) makes when sb is calling you. **Ringtones** are often short tunes. ▶ **dzwonek do telefonu**

rink = SKATING RINK

rinse /rɪns/ verb [T] to wash sth in water in order to remove soap or dirt: *Rinse your hair thoroughly after each shampoo.* ▶ **płukać**
PHR V **rinse sth out** to make sth clean, especially a container, by washing it with water: *Rinse the cup out before use.* ▶ **opłukiwać coś**
■ **rinse** noun **1** [C] an act of rinsing ▶ **płukanie 2** [C,U] a liquid used for colouring the hair: *a blue rinse* ▶ **płukanka do włosów**

riot /'raɪət/ noun [C] a situation in which a group of people behave in a violent way in a public place, often as a protest: *Further riots have broken out in Manchester.* ▶ **rozruchy**
■ **riot** verb [I]: *There is a danger that the prisoners will riot if conditions do not improve.* ▶ **wszczynać bunt/zamieszki** | **rioter** noun [C] ▶ **buntownik, uczestnik zamieszek**
IDM **run riot 1** to behave in a wild way without any control: *At the end of the match, the crowd ran riot.* ▶ **rozszaleć się 2** (used about your imagination, feelings, etc.) to allow sth to develop and continue without trying to control it ▶ **szaleć; dawać się ponieść fantazji**

riotous /'raɪətəs/ adj. **1** wild or violent; lacking in control ▶ **buntowniczy 2** wild and full of fun: *a riotous party* ◇ *riotous laughter* ▶ **dziki**

'riot police noun [pl.] police who are trained to deal with people **rioting** ▶ **policyjne siły prewencji**

'riot shield = SHIELD¹ (2)

RIP /ˌɑːr aɪ 'piː/ abbr. (used on the stones where dead people are buried) **rest in peace** ▶ **R.I.P.** (*niech spoczywa w pokoju*)

rip¹ /rɪp/ verb (**ripping**; **ripped**) **1** [I,T] to tear or be torn quickly and suddenly: *Oh no! My dress has ripped!* ◇ *He* ***ripped*** *the letter* ***in half/two*** *and threw it in the bin.* ◇ *The blast of the bomb ripped the house apart.* ▶ **rozdzierać (się), rozrywać (się) 2** [T] to remove sth quickly and violently, often by pulling it: *He ripped the poster from the wall.* ▶ **zrywać**
PHR V **rip sb off** (informal) to cheat sb by charging too much money for sth ▶ **oskubać kogoś**
rip through sth to move very quickly and violently through sth: *The house was badly damaged when fire ripped through the first floor.* ▶ **przemieszczać się szybko, pruć**
rip sth up to tear sth into small pieces ▶ **rwać na strzępy**

rip² /rɪp/ noun [C] a long tear (in cloth, etc.) ▶ **rozdarcie**

ripe /raɪp/ adj. **1** (used about fruit, grain, etc.) ready to be picked and eaten ▶ **dojrzały 2 ripe (for sth)** ready for sth or in a suitable state for sth ▶ **dojrzały**
■ **ripen** /'raɪpən/ verb [I,T] ▶ **dojrzewać**

'rip-off noun [C] (informal) something that costs a lot more than it should: *The food in that restaurant is a complete rip-off!* ▶ **złodziejstwo, oszustwo**

ripple /'rɪpl/ noun [C] **1** a very small wave or movement on the surface of water ▶ **drobna fala 2** [usually sing.] **a ripple (of sth)** a sound that gradually becomes louder and then quieter again; a feeling that gradually spreads through a person or a group of people: *a ripple of laughter* ▶ **fala**
■ **ripple** verb [I,T] ▶ **falować; marszczyć powierzchnię**

rise¹ /raɪz/ noun **1** [C] **a rise (in sth)** an increase in an amount, a number or a level: *There has been a* ***sharp rise*** *in the number of people out of work.* ▶ **wzrost** OPP **drop, fall 2** [C] (US **raise** /reɪz/) an increase in the money you are paid for the work you do: *I'm hoping to* ***get a rise*** *next April.* ◇ *a 10%* ***pay rise*** ▶ **podwyżka 3** [sing.] **the rise (of sth)** the process of becoming more powerful or important: *the rise of fascism in Europe* ◇ *her meteoric* ***rise to fame/power*** ▶ **awans**
IDM **give rise to sth** (formal) to cause sth to happen or exist ▶ **wywoływać, wzniecać**

rise² /raɪz/ verb [I] (pt **rose** /rəʊz/, pp **risen** /'rɪzn/) **1** to move upwards; to become higher, stronger or to increase: *Smoke was rising from the chimney.* ◇ *Her voice rose* (podniosła głos) *in anger.* ◇ *The temperature has risen to nearly forty degrees.* ▶ **podnosić się** OPP **fall**

Czasownik **rise** nie wymaga dopełnienia w zdaniu i oznacza „podnosić się do góry”: *The river has risen*

R

(by) *several metres.* ◇ *The helicopter rose into the air* (uniósł się w powietrze). Czasownik **rise** oznacza również „zwiększać się", „rosnąć": *Prices are always rising.* Czasownik **raise** wymaga dopełnienia w zdaniu i oznacza „podnosić": *He raised his head from the pillow.* ◇ *Shops are always raising prices.*

2 (formal) to get up from a chair, bed, etc.: *The audience rose and applauded the singers.* ▶ **wstawać** ⓘ W tym znaczeniu częściej używa się **get up**. **3** to appear above the **horizon**: *The sun rises in the east and sets in the west.* ▶ **wschodzić** OPP **set** **4** to become more successful, powerful, important, etc.: *She* ***rose to power*** (doszła do władzy) *in the 90s.* ◇ *He* ***rose through the ranks*** (piął się po szczeblach kariery) *to become the company director.* ▶ **awansować** **5** to come from: *Shouts of protest rose from the crowd.* ▶ **podnosić się** **6** **rise (up) (against sb/sth)** to start fighting against your ruler, government, etc.: *The people were afraid to rise up against the dictator.* ▶ **buntować się** **7** to be seen above or higher than sth else: *A range of mountains rose in the distance.* ▶ **wznosić się, wyrastać**

IDM **an early riser** → EARLY

rise to the occasion, challenge, task, etc. to show that you are able to deal with a problem, etc. successfully ▶ **stawać na wysokości zadania**

rising[1] /ˈraɪzɪŋ/ adj. **1** sloping upwards ▶ **wznoszący się** **2** increasing: *the rising cost of living* ▶ **wzrastający** **3** becoming well known or popular: *a rising young rock star* ▶ **nabierający rozgłosu**, (*gwiazda rocka itp.*) **wschodzący**

rising[2] /ˈraɪzɪŋ/ noun [C] fighting by a number of people (against people in authority) ▶ **powstanie** ➲ look at **uprising**

⚷ **risk**[1] /rɪsk/ noun **1** [C,U] **(a) risk (of sth/that ...); (a) risk (to sb/sth)** a possibility of sth dangerous or unpleasant happening; a situation that could be dangerous or have a bad result: *Don't* ***take*** *any* ***risks*** (nie ryzykuj) *when you're driving.* ◇ *You could drive a car without insurance, but it's* ***not worth the risk.*** ◇ *Scientists say these pesticides* ***pose a risk*** *to wildlife* (stanowią ryzyko dla przyrody). ◇ *If we don't leave early enough, we* ***run the risk*** *of missing the plane* (ryzykujemy, że spóźnimy się na samolot). ◇ *Small children are most* ***at risk*** (zagrożone) *from the disease.* ▶ **niebezpieczeństwo, ryzyko** **2** [sing.] a person or thing that might cause danger: *If he knows your real name he's a security risk.* ▶ **zagrożenie**

IDM **at your own risk** having the responsibility for whatever may happen: *This building is in a dangerous condition – enter at your own risk.* ▶ **na własne ryzyko**

at the risk of sth/doing sth even though there could be a bad effect: *He rescued the girl at the risk of his own life.* ◇ *At the risk of interfering* (nie chcę być wścibski), *may I offer you some advice?* ▶ **narażając (się) na coś**

⚷ **risk**[2] /rɪsk/ verb [T] **1** to put sth or yourself in a dangerous position: *The man* ***risked*** *his* ***life*** *to save the little boy.* ▶ **narażać, ryzykować** **2** to take the chance of sth unpleasant happening: *If you don't work hard now you risk failing your exams.* ▶ **ryzykować**

risky /ˈrɪski/ adj. (**riskier; riskiest**) involving the possibility of sth bad happening: *a risky investment* ▶ **ryzykowny, niebezpieczny** SYN **dangerous**

rissole /ˈrɪsəʊl/ noun [C] a small flat mass of chopped meat and spices that is cooked by frying ▶ **kotlet mielony** ➲ look at **cutlet**

rite /raɪt/ noun [C] a ceremony performed by a particular group of people, often for religious purposes: *funeral rites* ▶ **rytuał, obrzęd**

ritual /ˈrɪtʃuəl/ noun [C,U] an action, ceremony or process which is always done the same way: *(a) religious ritual* ▶ **rytuał, zwyczaj**

■ **ritual** adj. [only before a noun] ▶ **rytualny** | **ritually** /-tʃuəli/ adv. ▶ **rytualnie**

⚷ **rival**[1] /ˈraɪvl/ noun [C] a person or thing that is competing with you: *It seems that we're rivals for the sales manager's job.* ▶ **rywal/ka, konkurent/ka; konkurencja**

rival[2] /ˈraɪvl/ verb [T] (**rivalling; rivalled**; US **rivaling; rivaled**) **rival sb/sth (for/in sth)** to be as good as sb/sth: *Nothing rivals skiing for sheer excitement.* ▶ **dorównywać**

rivalry /ˈraɪvlri/ noun [C,U] (pl. **rivalries**) **rivalry (with sb); rivalry (between A and B)** competition between people, groups, etc.: *There was a lot of rivalry between the sisters.* ▶ **rywalizacja, współzawodnictwo**

⚷ **river** /ˈrɪvə(r)/ noun [C] (abbr. **R.**) a large, natural flow of water that goes across land and into the sea: *the River Nile* ◇ *He sat down on the bank of the river to fish.* ▶ **rzeka**

A river **flows** into the sea. The place where it joins the sea is the river **mouth**. A boat sails **on** the river. We sail **up** or **down river** and walk **along** the river. The ground by the side of a river is the **bank**.

riverside /ˈrɪvəsaɪd/ noun [sing.] the land next to a river: *a riverside hotel* hotel położony nad rzeką ▶ **brzeg rzeki**

rivet[1] /ˈrɪvɪt/ noun [C] a metal pin for fastening two pieces of metal together ▶ **nit**

rivet[2] /ˈrɪvɪt/ verb [T, usually passive] to keep sb very interested: *I was absolutely riveted by her story.* ▶ **porywać, przykuwać**

■ **riveting** adj. ▶ **porywający**

rm = ROOM

roach (US) = COCKROACH

⚷ **road** /rəʊd/ noun **1** [C] a hard surface built for vehicles to travel on: *Turn left off the* ***main road.*** ◇ *road signs* ◇ *a road junction* skrzyżowanie ▶ **droga, szosa**

road

Drogi łączące miasta i wsie to **roads**: *a road map of England.* Droga w mieście lub na wsi, wzdłuż której stoją domy, nazywa się **street**: *a street map* (plan miasta) *of York.* Słowo **road** może pojawiać się w nazwach ulic miejskich: *Abbey Road.* Autostrady to **motorways** (US **freeways/expressways**). **A-roads** to drogi główne łączące duże miasta. **B-roads** to boczne drogi o mniejszym znaczeniu. **M** to skrót od **motorway. Lane** to wąska droga zwł. na wsi, a także pas ruchu np. na autostradzie: *He passed me in the fast lane.*

2 (**Road**) (abbr. **Rd**) [sing.] (used in names of roads, especially in towns): *60 Marylebone Road, London* ▶ **ulica**

IDM **by road** in a car, bus, etc.: *It's going to be a terrible journey by road – let's take the train.* ▶ **samochodem/autobusem itp., drogą lądową**

on the road travelling: *We were on the road for 14 hours.* ▶ **w podróży**

roadblock /ˈrəʊdblɒk/ noun [C] a barrier put across a road by the police or army to stop traffic ▶ **zapora drogowa**

roadside /ˈrəʊdsaɪd/ noun [C, usually sing.] the edge of a road: *a roadside* (przydrożna) *café* ▶ **pobocze**

ˈ**road tax** noun [C,U] (Brit.) a tax which the owner of a vehicle has to pay to be allowed to drive it on public roads ▶ **podatek drogowy**

ˈ**road test** noun [C] **1** a test to see how a car functions or what condition it is in ▶ **przegląd samochodu** **2** (US) = DRIVING TEST

the **roadway** /ˈrəʊdweɪ/ noun [sing.] the part of the road used by cars, etc.; not the side of the road ▶ **jezdnia**

roadworks /ˈrəʊdwɜːks/ noun [pl.] work that involves repairing or building roads ▶ **roboty drogowe**

roadworthy /ˈrəʊdwɜːði/ adj. in good enough condition to be driven on the road ▶ (*pojazd*) **sprawny technicznie**

roam /rəʊm/ verb [I,T] to walk or travel with no particular plan or aim: *Gangs of youths were roaming the streets looking for trouble.* ▶ **włóczyć się**

roar /rɔː(r)/ verb **1** [I] to make a loud, deep sound: *The lion opened its huge mouth and roared.* ◇ *She **roared with laughter** at the joke.* ◇ *The engine roared to life* (zastartował z rykiem). ▶ **ryczeć, huczeć 2** [I,T] **roar sth (out)**; **roar (at sb)** to shout sth very loudly: *The audience roared (out) its approval.* Publiczność zawyła, wyrażając swoją aprobatę. ▶ **(wy)wrzeszczeć 3** [I] **roar along, down, past, etc.** to move in the direction mentioned, making a loud, deep sound: *A motorbike roared past us.* ▶ **jechać z łoskotem**
■ **roar** noun [C]: *the roar of heavy traffic on the motorway* ◇ *roars of laughter* ▶ **ryk, huk**

roaring /ˈrɔːrɪŋ/ adj. [only before a noun] **1** making a very loud noise ▶ **huczący, ryczący 2** (used about a fire) burning very well ▶ **buzujący 3** very great: *a roaring success* ▶ **ogromny**

roast¹ /rəʊst/ verb **1** [I,T] to cook or be cooked in an oven or over a fire: *a smell of roasting meat* ◇ *to roast a chicken* ▶ **piec** (*z dodatkiem tłuszczu*) ➲ look at **bake** ➲ note at **cook**, **meat 2** [T] to heat and dry sth: *roasted peanuts* ▶ **prażyć**
■ **roast** adj. [only before a noun]: *roast beef/potatoes/chestnuts* ▶ **pieczony, prażony**

roast² /rəʊst/ noun **1** [C,U] a piece of meat that has been cooked in an oven ▶ **pieczeń 2** [C] (especially US) an outdoor meal at which food is cooked over a fire ▶ **przyjęcie na świeżym powietrzu, na którym podaje się potrawy z rożna** ➲ look at **barbecue**

⚷ **rob** /rɒb/ verb [T] (**robbing**; **robbed**) **rob sb/sth (of sth)** to take money, property, etc. from a person or place illegally: *to rob a bank* ▶ **kraść, okradać** ➲ note at **steal**
PHR V **rob sb/sth (of sth)** to take sth away from sb/sth that they or it should have: *His illness robbed him of the chance to play for his country.* ▶ **pozbawić kogoś/czegoś (czegoś)**

robber /ˈrɒbə(r)/ noun [C] a person who steals from a place or a person, especially using violence or threats ▶ **złodziej** ➲ note at **thief**

robbery /ˈrɒbəri/ noun [C,U] (pl. **robberies**) the crime of stealing from a place or a person, especially using violence or threats: *They were found guilty of **armed robbery**.* ▶ **napad**

robe /rəʊb/ noun [C] **1** a long, loose piece of clothing, especially one that is worn at ceremonies ▶ **szata, toga 2** (US) = DRESSING GOWN

robin /ˈrɒbɪn/ noun [C] a small brown bird with a bright red chest ▶ **rudzik**

robot /ˈrəʊbɒt/ noun [C] **1** a machine that works automatically and can do some tasks that a human can do: *These cars are built by robots.* ▶ **robot 2** a person who behaves like a machine, without thinking or feeling anything ▶ (*osoba*) **automat** SYN **automaton**

robust /rəʊˈbʌst/ adj. strong and healthy ▶ **krzepki**

⚷ **rock¹** /rɒk/ noun **1** [U] the hard, solid material that forms part of the surface of the earth: *layers of rock formed over millions of years* ▶ **skała 2** [C, usually pl.] a large mass of rock that sticks out of the sea or the ground: *The ship hit the rocks and started to sink.* ▶ **skała 3** [C] a single large piece of rock: *The beach was covered with rocks that had broken away from the cliffs.* ▶ **kamień 4** [C] (US) a small piece of rock that can be picked up: *The boy threw a rock at the dog.* ▶ **kamień 5** (also **ˈrock music**) [U] a type of music with a very strong beat, played on musical instruments such as electric **guitars**, drums, etc.: *I prefer jazz to rock.* ◇ *a rock singer/band* ▶ **rock** ➲ look at **classical**, **jazz**, **pop 6** [U] (Brit.) a type of hard sweet made in long, round sticks: *a stick of rock* ▶ **rodzaj cukierka**
IDM **on the rocks 1** (used about a marriage, business, etc.) having problems and likely to fail ▶ **rozbity, na skraju przepaści 2** (used about drinks) served with ice but no water: *whisky on the rocks* ▶ (*napoje alkoholowe*) **z lodem bez wody**

rock² /rɒk/ verb **1** [I,T] to move backwards and forwards or from side to side; to make sb/sth do this: *boats rocking gently on the waves* ◇ *He rocked the baby in his arms to get her to sleep.* ▶ **kołysać (się) 2** [T] to shake sth violently: *The city was rocked by a bomb blast.* ▶ **wstrząsać 3** [T] to shock sb ▶ **wstrząsać**
IDM **rock the boat** to do sth that causes problems or upsets people: *They employ mainly quiet people who won't complain and rock the boat.* ▶ **stwarzać problemy**

ˌrock and ˈroll (also **rock 'n' roll**) noun [U] a type of music with a strong beat that was most popular in the 1950s ▶ **rock and roll**

ˌrock ˈbottom noun [U] the lowest point: *rock-bottom prices* ◇ *He **hit rock bottom*** (stoczył się na samo dno) *when he lost his job and his wife left him.* ▶ **dno, najniższy poziom**

ˈrock climbing noun [U] the sport of climbing rocks and mountains with ropes, etc. ▶ **wspinaczka wysokogórska**

rocket¹ /ˈrɒkɪt/ noun [C] **1** a vehicle that is used for travel into space: *a space rocket* ◇ *to launch a rocket* ▶ **rakieta 2** a weapon that travels through the air and that carries a bomb ▶ **rakieta** SYN **missile 3** an object that shoots high into the air and explodes in a beautiful way when you light it with a flame ▶ **rodzaj fajerwerku**

rocket² /ˈrɒkɪt/ verb [I] to increase or rise very quickly: *Prices have rocketed recently.* ▶ **wzrastać gwałtownie**

ˈrock music = ROCK¹ (5)

ˌrock 'n' ˈroll = ROCK AND ROLL

rocky /ˈrɒki/ adj. (**rockier**; **rockiest**) covered with or made of rocks: *a rocky road/coastline* ▶ **kamienisty**

rod /rɒd/ noun [C] [in compounds] a thin straight piece of wood, metal, etc.: *a fishing rod* wędka ▶ **pręt, drążek**

rode past tense of **ride¹**

rodent /ˈrəʊdnt/ noun [C] a type of small animal, such as a **rat**, a mouse, etc. which has strong sharp front teeth ▶ **gryzoń**

rodeo /ˈrəʊdiəʊ; rəʊˈdeɪəʊ/ noun [C] (pl. **rodeos**) a competition or performance in which people show their skill in riding wild horses, catching cows, etc. ▶ **rodeo**

roe /rəʊ/ noun [U] the eggs of a fish that we eat ▶ **ikra, mlecz**

rogue¹ /rəʊɡ/ adj. [only before a noun] behaving differently from other similar people or things, often causing damage: *a rogue gene* gen uszkodzony ◇ *a rogue police officer* policjant działający w pojedynkę (czasem wbrew centrali) ◇ *a rogue program* program potencjalnie wirusogenny powodujący uszkodzenia systemu

rogue² /rəʊɡ/ noun [C] **1** (humorous) a person who behaves badly, but in a harmless way ▶ (*żartobliwie*) **łobuz 2** (old-fashioned) a man who is dishonest and immoral ▶ **oszust**

⚷ **role** /rəʊl/ noun [C] **1** the position or function of sb/sth in a particular situation: *Parents **play a vital role** in their children's education.* ▶ **rola 2** sb's part in a play, film, etc.: *She was chosen to **play the role** of Cleopatra.* ◇ *a **leading role** in the film* ▶ **rola**

R

ˈ**role-play** noun [C,U] an activity used especially in teaching in which a person acts a part ▶ **odgrywanie scenki**

roll[1] /rəʊl/ noun [C] **1** something made into the shape of a tube by turning it round and round itself: *a roll of film/ wallpaper* ▶ **rolka 2** bread baked in a round shape for one person to eat: *a cheese roll* ▶ **bułka** ➲ picture at **bread 3** an act of moving or making sth move by turning over and over: *The dog was having a roll* (tarzał się) *in the sand.* ◇ *Everything depended on one roll of the dice* (rzutu kostką). ▶ **(po)toczenie (się) 4** a movement from side to side: *the roll of a ship* ▶ **kołysanie (się) 5** an official list of names: *the electoral roll* ▶ **lista 6** a long, low sound: *a roll of drums* ▶ **werbel**, **grzmot 7** = TRILL

roll[2] /rəʊl/ verb **1** [I,T] to move by turning over and over; to make sth move in this way: *The apples fell out of the bag and rolled everywhere.* ◇ *He tried to roll the rock up the hill.* ▶ **toczyć (się) 2** [I,T] **roll (sth) (over)** to turn over and over; to make sth do this: *The car rolled over in the crash.* ◇ *We rolled the log over to see what was underneath.* ◇ *The horse was rolling* (tarzał się) *in the dirt.* ▶ **przekręcać (się) 3** [I] to move smoothly, often on wheels: *The car began to roll back down the hill.* ◇ *Tears were rolling down her cheeks.* ▶ **toczyć się 4** [I,T] **roll (sth) (up)** to make sth into the shape of a ball or tube: *He was rolling himself a cigarette.* ◇ *The insect rolled up when I touched it.* ▶ **zwijać (się)** OPP **unroll 5** [T] **roll sth (out)** to make sth become flat by moving sth heavy over it: *Roll out the pastry thinly.* ▶ **rozwałkować**, **rozwalcować 6** [I] to move from side to side: *The ship began to roll in the storm.* ▶ **kołysać się**, **tarzać się 7** [T] = TRILL

IDM **be rolling in money/in it** (slang) to have a lot of money ▶ **leżeć na pieniądzach**

PHR V **roll sth down 1** to open sth by turning a handle: *He rolled down his car window and started shouting at them.* ▶ **opuszczać** (*np. rolety*) ▶ **otwierać coś** (*przez opuszczenie*) **2** to make a rolled piece of clothing, etc. hang or lie flat: *to roll down your sleeves* ▶ **odwijać coś**

roll in (informal) to arrive in large numbers or amounts: *Offers of help have been rolling in.* ▶ **napływać (masowo)**

roll up (informal) (used about a person or a vehicle) to arrive, especially late ▶ **zjawiać się**

roller /ˈrəʊlə(r)/ noun [C] **1** a piece of equipment or part of a machine that is shaped like a tube and used, for example, to make sth flat or to help sth move: *a roller blind* roleta ▶ **wałek**, **walec 2** [usually pl.] a small plastic tube that is used to make sb's hair curly ▶ **wałki**

Rollerblade™ /ˈrəʊləbleɪd/ noun [C] a boot with one row of narrow wheels on the bottom: *a pair of Rollerblades* ▶ **łyżworolka**

■ **rollerblade** verb [I] ▶ **jeździć na łyżworolkach** ℹ O jeździe na łyżworolkach dla przyjemności zwykle mówi się **go rollerblading**: *We go rollerblading every weekend.*

ˈ**roller coaster** noun [C] a narrow metal track that goes up and down and round tight bends, and that people ride on in a small train for fun and excitement ▶ **kolejka górska** (*w parku rozrywki*)

ˈ**roller skate** (also **skate**) noun [C] a type of shoe with small wheels on the bottom: *a pair of roller skates* ▶ **jeździć na wrotkach**

■ ˈ**roller skate** verb [I] ▶ **jeździć na wrotkach** | ˈ**roller skating** noun [U] ▶ **jazda na wrotkach**

ˈ**rolling pin** noun [C] a piece of wood, etc. in the shape of a tube, that you use for making **pastry** flat and thin before cooking it ▶ **wałek do ciasta** ➲ picture at **kitchen**

ROM /rɒm/ abbr. **read-only memory**; computer memory that contains instructions or data that cannot be changed or removed ▶ **pamięć ROM** ➲ look at **CD-ROM**, **RAM**

Roman /ˈrəʊmən/ adj. **1** connected with ancient Rome or the Roman Empire: *Roman coins* ◇ *the Roman invasion of Britain* ▶ **rzymski 2** connected with the modern city of Rome ▶ **rzymski**

■ **Roman** noun [C] ▶ **Rzymian-in/ka**

the ˌ**Roman** ˈ**alphabet** noun [sing.] the letters A to Z, used especially in Western European languages ▶ **alfabet łaciński**

ˌ**Roman** ˈ**Catholic** (also **Catholic**) noun [C] a member of the Christian Church which has the Pope as its head ▶ **osoba wyznania rzymskokatolickiego**

■ ˌ**Roman** ˈ**Catholic** adj. ▶ **(rzymsko)katolicki** ➲ look at **Protestant**

ˌ**Roman Caˈtholicism** (also **Catholicism**) noun [U] the beliefs of the Roman Catholic Church ▶ **wyznanie rzymskokatolickie**

Romance /ˈrəʊmæns/ adj. [only before a noun] of those languages which are descended from Latin ▶ **romański**

romance /rəʊˈmæns; ˈrəʊmæns/ noun **1** [C] a love affair: *The film was about a teenage romance.* ▶ **romans 2** [U] a feeling or atmosphere of love or of sth new, special and exciting ▶ **romantyczność 3** [C] a novel about a love affair: *historical romances* ▶ **romans**

Romanesque (used to describe a style of **architecture** used in Europe between the 10th and 13th centuries, with round arches, thick walls and tall pillars) ▶ **romański** ℹ W Wlk. Br. w XI i XII w. ze stylu romańskiego rozwinął się styl zwany **Norman.**

ˌ**Roman** ˈ**numerals** noun [pl.] the letters used by the ancient Romans as numbers ▶ **cyfry rzymskie** ℹ W jęz. ang. cyfr rzymskich nie używa się do oznaczenia wieków. Używa się wówczas cyfr arabskich: *Poland in the 11th century.*

romantic[1] /rəʊˈmæntɪk/ adj. **1** having a quality that strongly affects your emotions or makes you think about love; showing feelings of love: *a romantic candlelit dinner* ◇ *He isn't very romantic – he never says he loves me.* ▶ **romantyczny 2** involving a love affair: *Reports of a romantic relationship between the two film stars have been strongly denied.* ▶ **romantyczny 3** having or showing ideas about life that are emotional rather than real or practical: *He has a romantic idea that he'd like to live on a farm in Scotland.* ▶ **romantyczny**

■ **romantically** /-kli/ adv. ▶ **romantycznie**

romantic[2] /rəʊˈmæntɪk/ noun [C] a person who has ideas that are not based on real life or that are not very practical ▶ **romanty-k/czka**

romanticize (also **-ise**) /rəʊˈmæntɪsaɪz/ verb [I,T] to make sth seem more interesting, exciting, etc. than it really is ▶ **koloryzować**; **fantazjować**

Romany /ˈrɒməni; ˈrəʊm-/ noun (pl. **-ies**) **1** [C] a member of a race of people, originally from Asia, who travel around and traditionally live in **caravans** ▶ **Rom/ka** SYN **Gypsy 2** [U] the language of **Romany** people ▶ **język romani**

■ **Romany** adj. [usually before a noun] ▶ **romski**

romp /rɒmp/ verb [I] (used about children and animals) to play in a happy and noisy way ▶ **dokazywać**

■ **romp** noun [C] ▶ **dokazywanie**

IDM **romp home/to victory** to win easily: *United romped to a 4-0 victory over Juventus.* ▶ **wygrać z łatwością**

roof /ruːf/ noun [C] (pl. **roofs**) **1** the part of a building, vehicle, etc. which covers the top of it: *a flat/sloping/ tiled roof* ◇ *the roof of a car* ◇ *The library and the sports hall are* ***under one roof*** (w tym samym budynku). ◇ *We can store a lot of things in the roof* (na strychu). ▶ **dach** ➲ picture on **page A3**, picture at **car 2** the highest part of the inside of sth: *The roof of the cave had collapsed.* ◇ *The soup burned the roof of my mouth.* ▶ **strop**

IDM **hit the roof** → HIT[1]

a roof over your head somewhere to live: *I might not have any money, but at least I've got a roof over my head.* ▶ **dach nad głową**

'roof rack noun [C] a structure that you fix to the roof of a car and use for carrying luggage or other large objects ▶ **bagażnik na dachu samochodu** ➲ picture at **rack**

rooftop /'ru:ftɒp/ noun [C, usually pl.] the outside of the roof of a building: *From the tower we looked down over the rooftops of the city.* ▶ **dach**

rook /rʊk/ noun [C] a large black bird. Rooks build their nests in groups. ▶ **gawron**

⚷ **room** /ru:m; rʊm/ noun **1** [C] a part of a house or building that has its own walls, floor and ceiling: *a sitting/dining/living room* ◇ *I sat down in the waiting room until the doctor called me.* ◇ *I'd like to book a double room for two nights next month.* ◇ *rooms to let* pokoje do wynajęcia ◇ *a spare room* pokój gościnny ◇ *a changing room* szatnia (na basenie itp.) lub przymierzalnia ◇ *a fitting room* przymierzalnia ◇ *a dressing room* garderoba (w teatrze itp.) ▶ **pokój 2** [U] **room (for sb/sth)**; **room (to do sth)** space; enough space: *These chairs **take up** too much **room**.* ◇ *I threw away my old clothes to **make room** in the wardrobe for some new ones.* ◇ *There were so many people that there wasn't any room to move.* ▶ **miejsce** ➲ note at **place**[1] ➲ look at **space 3** [U] **room for sth** the opportunity or need for sth: *It is important to give children room to think for themselves.* ◇ *There's **room for improvement** in your work.* Twoja praca mogłaby być lepsza. ◇ *There could be no **room for doubt**.* Nie mogło być żadnych wątpliwości. ◇ *The lack of time gives us very little **room for manoeuvre*** (pola manewru). ▶ **możliwość**

roomful /'ru:mfʊl; 'rʊm-/ noun [C] a large number of people or things in a room ▶ **pełen pokój, pełna sala**

'room-mate noun [C] a person that you share a room with in a flat, etc. ▶ **współlokator/ka**

'room service noun [U] a service provided in a hotel, by which guests can order food and drink to be brought to their rooms: *He ordered coffee from room service.* ▶ **obsługa kelnerska do pokojów**

roomy /'ru:mi/ adj. (**roomier**; **roomiest**) having plenty of space: *a roomy house/car* ▶ **przestronny** SYN **spacious**

roost /ru:st/ noun [C] a place where birds sleep ▶ **grzęda**
■ **roost** verb [I]: *We've got blackbirds roosting in our roof* (zadomowiły się na naszym dachu). ▶ (*ptaki*) **mieszkać**

rooster (US) = COCK[1] (1)

⚷ **root**[1] /ru:t/ noun **1** [C] the part of a plant that grows under the ground and takes in water and food from the soil: *The deep roots of these trees can cause damage to buildings.* ◇ ***root vegetables** such as carrots and parsnips* ▶ **korzeń 2** [C] the part of a hair or tooth that is under the skin and that fixes it to the rest of the body ▶ **korzeń, cebulka 3** (**roots**) [pl.] the place where you feel that you belong, because you grew up there, live there or your relatives once lived there ▶ **korzenie 4** [C] the basic cause or origin of sth: *Let's try and get to the **root of the problem**.* ▶ **sedno, źródło** ➲ look at **square root**

root[2] /ru:t/ verb
PHR V **root about/around (for sth)** to search for sth by moving things: *What are you rooting around in my desk for?* ▶ **grzebać**
root for sb to give support to sb who is in a competition, etc. ▶ **dopingować**
root sth out to find and destroy sth bad completely ▶ **wykorzeniać**

⚷ **rope**[1] /rəʊp/ noun [C,U] very thick, strong string that is used for tying or lifting heavy things, climbing up, etc.: *We need some rope to tie up the boat with.* ➲ picture at **cable**: *a skipping rope* skakanka ◇ *a rope ladder* drabinka sznurowa ▶ **lina, sznur**

IDM **show sb/know/learn the ropes** to show sb/know/learn how a job should be done ▶ **pouczać/wtajemniczać kogoś; zaznajamiać się, zapoznawać się**

rope[2] /rəʊp; US roʊp/ verb [T] **rope A to B/A and B together** to tie sb/sth with a rope ▶ **wiązać**
PHR V **rope sb in (to do sth)** (informal) to persuade sb to help in an activity, especially when they do not want to: *I've been roped in to help with the school play.* ▶ **wciągać**
rope sth off to put ropes round or across an area in order to keep people out of it ▶ **odgradzać**

ropy (also **ropey**) /'rəʊpi/ adj. (Brit., informal) **1** not in good condition; of bad quality: *We spent the night in a ropy old tent.* ▶ **kiepski 2** feeling slightly ill: *I felt a bit ropy earlier this week, but I'm better now.* ▶ **kiepski, marny**

rosary /'rəʊzəri/ noun [C] (pl. **rosaries**) a string of small round pieces of wood, etc. used for counting prayers ▶ **różaniec**

rose[1] past tense of **rise**[2]

rose[2] /rəʊz/ noun [C] a flower with a sweet smell, that grows on a bush that usually has **thorns** growing on it ▶ **róża** ➲ picture on **page A15**

rosé /'rəʊzeɪ; US rəʊ'zeɪ/ noun [U] pink wine ▶ **wino różowe**

rosemary /'rəʊzməri; US -meri/ noun [U] a **herb** with small narrow leaves that smell sweet and are used in cooking ▶ **rozmaryn**

rosette /rəʊ'zet/ noun [C] a round decoration made from **ribbons** that you wear on your clothes. Rosettes are given as prizes or worn to show that sb supports a particular political party. ▶ **rozetka, wstążeczka orderowa** ➲ picture at **medal**

roster (US) = ROTA

rostrum /'rɒstrəm/ noun [C] a platform that sb stands on to make a public speech, etc. ▶ **mównica**

rosy /'rəʊzi/ adj. (**rosier**; **rosiest**) **1** pink and pleasant in appearance: *rosy cheeks* ▶ **różowy; zaróżowiony** ➲ look at **pink 2** full of good possibilities: *The future was looking rosy.* ▶ **różowy**

rot /rɒt/ verb (**rotting**; **rotted**) **1** [I] to go bad as part of a natural process ▶ **gnić** SYN **decay 2** [T] to make sth go bad: *Too many sweets will rot your teeth!* ▶ **psuć**
■ **rot** noun [U] **1** the condition of being bad or rotten: *The floorboards have got rot in them* (są spróchniałe). ▶ **gnicie, rozkład 2** (Brit., old-fashioned) nonsense ▶ **bzdura** ➲ **rubbish**

rota /'rəʊtə/ (US also **roster** /'rɒstə(r)/) noun [C] a list of people who share a certain job or task and the times that they are each going to do it: *We organize the cleaning **on a rota*** (według rozkładu). ▶ **rozkład** (*zajęć*)

rotary /'rəʊtəri/ adj. [only before a noun] moving in circles round a central point ▶ **obrotowy**

rotate /rəʊ'teɪt/ verb [I,T] **1** to turn in circles round a central point; to make sth do this: *The earth rotates on its axis.* ▶ **obracać (się) 2** to happen in turn or in a particular order; to make sth do this: *The position of president is rotated* (zajmowane jest kolejno) *among all the member countries.* ◇ *We rotate the duties so that nobody is stuck with a job they don't like.* ▶ **zmieniać (się) kolejno**

rotation /rəʊ'teɪʃn/ noun [C,U] **1** movement in circles round a central point: *one rotation every 24 hours* ▶ **ruch obrotowy, obrót 2** happening or making things happen in a particular order: *The company is chaired by all the members **in rotation*** (po kolei przez wszystkich członków). ▶ **kolej**

rote /rəʊt/ noun [U] [often used as an adjective] the process of learning sth by repeating it until you remember it

R

rather than by understanding the meaning of it: *to learn by rote* ◇ *rote learning* ▶ **uczenie się na pamięć**

rotor /ˈrəʊtə(r)/ noun [C] a part of a machine that turns round, for example the blades that go round on top of a helicopter ▶ **wirnik**

rotten /ˈrɒtn/ adj. **1** (used about food and other substances) old and not fresh enough or good enough to use: *rotten vegetables* ▶ **zgniły, spróchniały** **2** (informal) very unpleasant: *We had rotten weather all week.* ◇ *That was a rotten thing to say!* ▶ **paskudny, wstrętny** **3** [only before a noun] (informal) (used to emphasize that you are angry): *You can keep your rotten job!* ▶ **cholerny, przeklęty**

Rottweiler /ˈrɒtvaɪlə(r)/ noun [C] a large, often fierce, black and brown dog ▶ **pies rasy rottweiler**

rouge /ruːʒ/ noun [U] (old-fashioned) a red powder or cream used for giving more colour to the cheeks ▶ **róż**

⚷**rough**[1] /rʌf/ adj. **1** not smooth or level: *rough ground* ▶ **nierówny, szorstki** OPP **smooth** **2** made or done quickly or without much care: *a rough estimate* ◇ *Can you give me a rough idea of what time you'll be arriving?* ▶ **przybliżony** SYN **approximate** **3** violent; not calm or gentle: *You can hold the baby, but don't be rough with him.* ◇ *The sea was rough* (wzburzone) *and half the people on the boat were seasick.* ◇ *This is a rough* (niebezpieczna) *neighbourhood, so be careful at night.* ▶ **brutalny** **4** (informal) looking or feeling ill: *You look a bit rough – are you feeling all right?* ▶ **zły, marny** **5** difficult and unpleasant: *He's had a really rough time* (przeżywa ciężkie chwile) *recently.* ▶ **ciężki**

■ **roughness** noun [U] ▶ **szorstkość, brutalność**

IDM **be rough (on sb)** be unpleasant or bad luck for sb ▶ **układać się (dla kogoś) niekorzystnie/pechowo**

rough[2] /rʌf/ noun

IDM **in rough** done quickly without worrying about mistakes, as a preparation for the finished piece of work or drawing ▶ **na brudno**

take the rough with the smooth to accept difficult or unpleasant things in addition to pleasant things ▶ **pogodzić się z przeciwnościami losu**

rough[3] /rʌf/ verb

IDM **rough it** to live without all the comfortable things that you usually have: *You have to rough it a bit when you go camping.* ▶ **żyć w warunkach spartańskich**

rough[4] /rʌf/ **1** adv. in a rough way: *One of the boys was told off for playing rough.* ▶ **brutalnie** **2** (informal) in a difficult or unpleasant way: *He's had it rough* (przeżywał ciężkie chwile) *since she left.* ▶ **ciężko**

IDM **live/sleep rough** to live or sleep outdoors, usually because you have no home or money ▶ (*zwykle bezdomni*) **mieszkać/spać byle gdzie**

roughage /ˈrʌfɪdʒ/ noun [U] the types of food which help food and waste products to pass through the body ▶ **otręby** SYN **fibre**

roughen /ˈrʌfn/ verb [T] to make sth less smooth or soft ▶ **stracić gładkość, stać się szorstkim**

⚷**roughly** /ˈrʌfli/ adv. **1** not exactly; approximately: *It took roughly three hours, I suppose.* ▶ **w przybliżeniu** **2** in a violent way; not gently: *He grabbed her roughly by her arm.* ▶ **brutalnie**

roulette /ruːˈlet/ noun [U] a game in which a ball is dropped onto a moving wheel that has holes with numbers on them. The players bet on which number hole the ball will be in when the wheel stops. ▶ **ruletka**

⚷**round**[1] /raʊnd/ adj. having the shape of a circle or a ball: *a round table* ▶ **okrągły**

IDM **in round figures/numbers** given to the nearest 10, 100, 1 000, etc.; not given in exact numbers ▶ **w zaokrągleniu**

⚷**round**[2] /raʊnd/ adv. ℹ **Round** używa się w czasownikach złożonych. Zob. hasła przy odpowiednich czasownikach, np. **come, get, go. Around** znaczy to samo co **round** i jest częściej spotykane w Amer. ang. **1** in a full circle: *The wheels spun **round and round** but the car wouldn't move.* ▶ **w kółko** **2** in a circle or curve; on all sides of sth: *You can't get in because there's a fence all round.* ▶ **naokoło, dookoła, wkoło** **3** from one place, person, etc. to another: ***Pass** the photographs **round*** (puść zdjęcia obiegiem) *for everyone to see.* ◇ *I've been rushing round all day.* ▶ **z miejsca na miejsce** **4** in or to a particular area or place: *I'll come round to see you* (wpadnę do ciebie) *at about 8 o'clock.* ▶ **dokądś, do kogoś** **5** turning to look or go in the opposite direction: *Don't **look round*** (nie odwracaj się) *but the teacher's just come in.* ◇ *She **turned** the car **round*** (zawróciła samochód) *and drove off.* ◇ *She moved her chair round* (odwróciła krzesło) *so that she could see out of the window.* ▶ **dookoła**

IDM **the other way round** → OTHER

round about in the area near a place: *We hope to arrive round about 6.* ▶ **w okolicy**

round[3] /raʊnd/ prep. ℹ **Around** znaczy to samo co **round** i jest częściej spotykane w Amer. ang. **1** (used about movement) in a circe round a fixed point: *How long would it take to walk round the world?* ▶ **dookoła** **2** to or on the other side of sth: *There's a postbox just **round the corner.*** ◇ (figurative) *It wasn't easy to see a way round the problem* (sposób rozwiązania). ▶ **za, po drugiej stronie** **3** on all sides of sth; surrounding sth: *He had a bandage right round his head.* ◇ *We sat round the table, talking late into the night.* ▶ **dookoła, wokół** **4** in the area near a place: *Do you live round here?* ▶ **w okolicy** **5** in or to many parts of sth: *He spent six months travelling round Europe.* ◇ *Let me **show** you **round*** (pokazać) *the house.* ◇ *We drove round France* (objechaliśmy), *stopping here and there.* ▶ **po**

IDM **round about sth** approximately: *We hope to arrive round about 6.* ▶ **około**

round the bend (informal) crazy: *His behaviour is **driving me round the bend*** (doprowadza mnie do szaleństwa). ▶ **zwariowany** SYN **mad**

⚷**round**[4] /raʊnd/ noun [C] **1** a number or series of events, etc.: *a further round of talks with other European countries* ▶ **runda, seria** **2** one part of a game or competition: *Parma will play Real Madrid in the next round.* ▶ **runda** **3** (in the sport of **golf**) one game, usually of 18 holes: *to play a round of golf* ▶ **partia** **4** a regular series of visits, etc., often as part of a job: *The postman's round takes him about three hours.* ◇ *Dr Adamou is on his daily round of the wards.* ▶ **obchód, objazd** **5** a number of drinks (one for all the people in a group): *It's my round.* ▶ **kolejka** **6** a short, sudden period of loud noise: *The last speaker got the biggest **round of applause*** (oklaski). **7** a bullet or a number of bullets, fired from a gun: *He fired several rounds at us.* ▶ **nabój, seria**

round[5] /raʊnd/ verb [T] to go round sth: *The police car rounded the corner* (wziął zakręt) *at high speed.* ▶ **okrążać**

PHR V **round sth off (with sth)** to do sth that completes a job or an activity: *We rounded off the meal with coffee and chocolates.* ▶ **zakończyć**

round sb/sth up to bring sb/sth together in one place: *The teacher rounded up the children.* ▶ **zbierać, spędzać**

round sth up/down to increase/decrease a number, price, etc. to the next highest/lowest whole number ▶ **zaokrąglać** (*w górę/w dół*)

roundabout[1] /ˈraʊndəbaʊt/ noun [C] **1** a circle where several roads meet, that all the traffic has to go round in the same direction ▶ **rondo 2** a round platform made for children to play on. They sit or stand on it and sb pushes it round. ▶ **karuzela 3** (Brit.) = MERRY-GO-ROUND

merry-go-round/ roundabout (US carousel)

roundabout

roundabout² /ˈraʊndəbaʊt/ adj. longer than is necessary or usual; not direct: *We got lost and came by rather a roundabout route.* ▶ **okrężny**

rounded /ˈraʊndɪd/ adj. **1** having a round shape: *a surface with rounded edges* ◇ *rounded shoulders* ▶ **zaokrąglony 2** having a wide variety of qualities that combine to produce sth pleasant, complete and balanced: *a fully rounded education* ▶ **wszechstronny**

rounders /ˈraʊndəz/ noun [U] a British game that is similar to **baseball** ▶ **rodzaj palanta**

ˌround-the-ˈclock (also **ˌaround-the-ˈclock**) adj. [only before a noun] lasting or happening all day and night: *round-the-clock nursing care* ▶ **całodobowy**

ˌround ˈtrip noun [C] **1** a journey to a place and back again: *It's a four-mile round trip to the centre of town.* ▶ **podróż w obie strony 2** (also **ˌround-trip ˈticket**) (US) : *a round-trip ticket* bilet powrotny = RETURN² (4)

rouse /raʊz/ verb [T] **1** (formal) to make sb wake up: *She was sleeping so soundly that I couldn't rouse her.* ▶ **budzić 2** to make sb/sth very angry, excited, interested, etc. ▶ **podniecać, pobudzać**

rousing /ˈraʊzɪŋ/ adj. exciting and powerful: *a rousing speech* ▶ **porywający, podniecający**

rout /raʊt/ verb [T] to defeat sb completely ▶ **rozgromić**
■ **rout** noun [C] ▶ **pogrom, klęska**

route /ru:t/ noun [C] **1 a route (from A) (to B)** a way from one place to another: *What is the most direct route from Bordeaux to Lyon?* ◇ *I got a leaflet about the bus routes from the information office.* ▶ **droga, trasa 2 a route to sth** a way of achieving sth: *Hard work is the only route to success.* ▶ **droga, sposób**

routine¹ /ru:ˈti:n/ noun **1** [C,U] the usual order and way in which you regularly do things: *Make exercise part of your daily routine.* ▶ **ustalony porządek 2** [U] tasks that have to be done again and again and so are boring: *I gave up the job because I couldn't stand the routine.* ▶ **rutyna 3** [C] a series of movements, jokes, etc. that are part of a performance: *a dance/comedy routine* ▶ **układ**

my daily routine

On **weekdays** (= Monday to Friday) I **wake up** when the alarm goes off and **get up** at 7.30. If I **oversleep**, I know that I will be late for work. I **have a shower** and wash my hair. I **blow-dry** my hair with a hairdryer and **get dressed**. I have breakfast at about 8.00, while listening to the radio. I **brush my teeth** and then at 8.30 I leave the house to walk to the station. The train is very crowded with other commuters because it is rush hour. I work from **nine to five**, with a **lunch hour** from one until two. After work I like spending time with friends. We go to the cinema, or to a bar or cafe for a drink. **Twice a week** I go to the gym because I like to keep fit. I **get home** some time after 7.00 and have dinner. In the evening I **relax** and watch TV or read the paper. I **go to bed** at 11.00 and **fall asleep** straight away.

routine² /ru:ˈti:n/ adj. **1** normal and regular; not unusual or special: *The police would like to ask you some routine questions.* ▶ **zwyczajowy, rutynowy 2** boring; not exciting: *It's a very routine job, really.* ▶ **rutynowy**

routinely /ru:ˈti:nli/ adv. regularly; as part of a **routine**: *The machines are routinely checked every two months.* ▶ **rutynowo**

ˈrouting number (US) = SORT CODE

rove /rəʊv/ verb **1** [I,T] (formal) to travel from one place to another, often with no particular purpose: *A quarter of a million refugees roved around the country.* ◇ *bands of thieves who roved the countryside* ▶ **włóczyć się** SYN **roam 2** [I] if sb's eyes **rove**, the person keeps looking in different directions ▶ **wodzić wzrokiem**

row¹ /rəʊ/ noun [C] **1** a line of people or things: *a row of books* ◇ *The children were all standing* ***in a row*** *at the front of the class.* ▶ **rząd, szereg 2** a line of seats in a theatre, cinema, etc.: *Our seats were in the back row.* ◇ *a front-row seat* ▶ **rząd**
IDM **in a row** one after another; without a break: *It rained solidly for four days in a row.* ▶ **z rzędu**

row² /rəʊ/ verb **1** [I,T] to move a boat through the water using **oars**: *We often go rowing* (często pływamy łódką) *on the Thames.* ▶ **wiosłować 2** [T] to carry sb/sth in a boat that you row: *Could you row us over to the island?* ▶ **przeprawiać kogoś (łódką)** ➲ look at **paddle**
■ **row** noun [sing.] ▶ **przejażdżka łódką**

row³ /raʊ/ noun **1** [C] **a row (about/over sth)** a noisy argument between two or more people, groups, etc.; a public argument especially among politicians: *A row has broken out between the main parties over education.* ◇ *When I* ***have a row*** (kiedy się pokłócę) *with my girlfriend, I always try to make up as soon as possible.* ▶ **kłótnia; awantura** ➲ note at **argument 2** [sing.] a loud noise: *What a row! Could you be a bit quieter?* ▶ **hałas**
■ **row** verb [I] **row (with sb) (about/over sth)**: *Pete and I are always rowing about money.* ▶ **kłócić się**

rowan /ˈrəʊən; ˈraʊən/ (also **ˈrowan tree**) noun [C] a type of tree that has red berries in the autumn ▶ **jarzębina**

rowboat (US) = ROWING BOAT

rowdy /ˈraʊdi/ adj. (**rowdier; rowdiest**) noisy and likely to cause trouble: *The football fans soon got rowdy.* ▶ **hałaśliwy, awanturniczy**
■ **rowdily** adv. ▶ **hałaśliwie, awanturniczo** | **rowdiness** noun [U] ▶ **awanturowanie się, hałaśliwość**

ˈrowing boat (US **rowboat** /ˈrəʊbəʊt/) noun [C] a small boat that you move through the water using **oars** ▶ **łódź wiosłowa** ➲ note at **boat** ➲ picture at **boat**

royal /ˈrɔɪəl/ adj. [only before a noun] **1** connected with a king or queen or a member of their family: *the royal family* ▶ **królewski 2** (used in the names of organizations) supported by a member of the royal family: *the Royal Society for the Protection of Birds* ▶ **królewski**
■ **royal** noun (informal): *the Queen, the Princes and other royals* ▶ **członek rodziny królewskiej**

ˌroyal ˈblue adj. of deep bright blue ▶ (*kolor*) **ciemnoniebieski**
■ **ˌroyal ˈblue** noun [U] ▶ (*kolor*) **błękit królewski**

ˌRoyal ˈHighness noun [C] (used when you are speaking to or about a member of the royal family) ▶ **Królewska Mość**

royalty /ˈrɔɪəlti/ noun (pl. **royalties**) **1** [U] members of the royal family ▶ **człon-ek/kowie rodziny królewskiej 2** [C] an amount of money that is paid to the person who wrote a book, piece of music, etc. every time their work is sold or performed: *The author earns a 2% royalty on each copy sold.* ▶ **tantiema**

R

rpm /ˌɑː piː ˈem/ abbr. **revolutions per minute**: *engine speed 2500 rpm* ▶ **obr/min**

RSI /ˌɑːr es ˈaɪ/ noun [U] **repetitive strain injury**; pain and swelling, especially in the wrists and hands, caused by doing the same movement many times in a job or an activity ▶ **uszkodzenie przeciążeniowe**

RSVP /ˌɑːr es viː ˈpiː/ abbr. (from French) **répondez s'il vous plaît**; (used on invitations) please reply ▶ **uprasza się o odpowiedź**

Rt Hon abbr. **Right Honourable**; a title used about people of high social rank and the most important ministers in the government ▶ **Wasza Wysokość**

rub /rʌb/ verb (**rubbing**; **rubbed**) **1** [I,T] to move your hand, a cloth, etc. backwards and forwards on the surface of sth while pressing firmly: *The cat rubbed against my leg.* ◇ *Ralph rubbed his hands together* (zacierał ręce) *to keep them warm.* ◇ *He rubbed his hand across his face.* Przeciągnął ręką po twarzy. ▶ **pocierać, ocierać (się)** **2** [T] **rub sth in (to sth)** to put a cream, liquid, etc. onto a surface by rubbing: *Apply a little of the lotion and rub it into the skin.* ▶ **wcierać** **3** [I,T] **rub (on/against sth)** to press on/against sth, often causing pain or damage: *These new shoes are rubbing against my heels.* ▶ **obcierać**

■ **rub** noun [C]: *Give your shoes a rub* (wyczyść buty) *before you go out.* ▶ **polerowanie, nacieranie**

IDM **rub salt into the wound/sb's wounds** to make a situation that makes sb feel bad even worse ▶ **jątrzyć czyjeś rany**

rub shoulders with sb to meet and spend time with famous people: *As a journalist you rub shoulders with the rich and famous.* ▶ **przebywać w towarzystwie znanych ludzi, ocierać się o kogoś**

PHR V **rub it/sth in** to keep reminding sb of sth embarrassing that they want to forget: *I know it was a stupid mistake, but there's no need to rub it in!* ▶ **wypominać coś komuś**

rub off (on/onto sb) (used about a good quality) to be passed from one person to another: *Let's hope some of her enthusiasm rubs off onto her brother.* ▶ **udzielać się komuś**

rub sth off (sth) to remove sth from a surface by rubbing: *He rubbed the dirt off his boots.* ▶ **ścierać coś (z czegoś)**

rub sth out (Brit.) to remove the marks made by a pencil, etc. using a rubber, etc.: *That answer is wrong. Rub it out.* ▶ **ścierać/wymazywać coś** (*zwł. gumką*)

rubber /ˈrʌbə(r)/ noun **1** [U] a strong substance that can be stretched and does not allow water to pass through it, used for making tyres, boots, etc. Rubber is made from the juice of a tropical tree or is produced using chemicals: *a rubber ball* ◇ *rubber gloves* ◇ *foam rubber* ▶ **guma** **2** [C] (especially US **eraser**) a small piece of rubber that you use for removing pencil marks from paper; soft material used for removing pen marks or **chalk** marks from a board ▶ **gumka** ➲ picture at **stationery** **3** (old-fashioned, informal) (especially US) = CONDOM

ˌrubber ˈband (also eˌlastic ˈband) noun [C] a thin round piece of rubber that is used for holding things together: *Her hair was tied back with a rubber band.* ▶ **gumka** ➲ picture at **stationery**

ˌrubber ˈstamp noun [C] **1** a small tool that you use for printing a name, date, etc. on a document ▶ **pieczątka** ➲ picture at **stationery** **2** a person or group who gives official approval to sth without thinking about it first ▶ **urzędnik/instytucja zatwierdzając-y/a coś mechanicznie, bez głębszego zastanowienia się nad tym**

■ **ˌrubber-ˈstamp** verb [T] (usually used about sb with authority) to agree to sth without thinking about it carefully: *The committee have no real power – they just rubber-stamp* (mechanicznie zatwierdzają) *the chairman's ideas.* ▶ **zatwierdzać coś bez zastanowienia się nad tym**

rubbery /ˈrʌbəri/ adj. like rubber: *This meat is rubbery.* ▶ **gumowaty**

rubbish /ˈrʌbɪʃ/ (especially US **garbage** /ˈɡɑːbɪdʒ/, US **trash** /træʃ/) noun [U] **1** things that you do not want any more; waste material: *The dustmen collect the rubbish every Monday.* ◇ *a rubbish bin* ◇ *It's only rubbish – throw it away.* ▶ **śmieci** ➲ look at **waste** **2** something that you think is bad, silly or wrong: *I thought that film was absolute rubbish.* ◇ *Don't talk such rubbish.* ▶ **bzdura, głupstwo** SYN **nonsense**

ˈrubbish tip = TIP[1] (4)

rubble /ˈrʌbl/ noun [U] pieces of broken brick, stone, etc., especially from a damaged building ▶ **gruz**

rubella = GERMAN MEASLES

rubric /ˈruːbrɪk/ noun [C] (formal) a title or set of instructions written in a book, an exam paper, etc. ▶ **tytuł; objaśnienie**

ruby /ˈruːbi/ noun [C] (pl. **rubies**) a red **precious** stone ▶ **rubin**

rucksack /ˈrʌksæk/ noun [C] (Brit.) a bag that you use for carrying things on your back ▶ **plecak** SYN **backpack, pack** ➲ picture at **bag**, picture on **page A1**

rudder /ˈrʌdə(r)/ noun [C] a piece of wood or metal that is used for controlling the direction of a boat or plane ▶ **ster** ➲ picture at **plane**

rude /ruːd/ adj. **1 rude (to sb) (about sb/sth)** not polite: *She was very rude to me about my new jacket.* ◇ *I think it was rude of them* (niegrzecznie z ich strony) *not to phone and say that they weren't coming.* ◇ *It's rude* (to niegrzecznie) *to interrupt when people are speaking.* ▶ **niegrzeczny, nieuprzejmy** SYN **impolite** **2** connected with sex, using the toilet, etc. in a way that might offend people: *a rude joke/word/gesture* ▶ **sprośny, wulgarny** SYN **offensive** **3** [only before a noun] sudden and unpleasant: *If you're expecting any help from him, you're in for a rude shock* (to czeka cię gorzkie rozczarowanie). ▶ **gwałtowny**

■ **rudely** adv. ▶ **niegrzecznie; wulgarnie** | **rudeness** noun [U] ▶ **niegrzeczność; grubiaństwo**

rudimentary /ˌruːdɪˈmentri/ adj. very basic or simple ▶ **podstawowy, elementarny**

rudiments /ˈruːdɪmənts/ noun [pl.] (formal) **the rudiments (of sth)** the most basic facts of a particular subject, skill, etc. ▶ **rudymenty czegoś**

rueful /ˈruːfl/ adj. feeling or showing that you are sad or sorry: *a rueful smile* ▶ **smutny**

■ **ruefully** /ˈruːfəli/ adv.: *He laughed ruefully.* ▶ **ze smutkiem**

ruffle /ˈrʌfl/ verb [T] **1 ruffle sth (up)** to make sth untidy or no longer smooth: *to ruffle somebody's hair* ▶ **stroszyć** **2** [often passive] to make sb annoyed or confused ▶ **irytować**

rug /rʌɡ/ noun [C] **1** a piece of thick material that covers a small part of a floor ▶ **dywanik, kilim** ➲ look at **carpet, mat** **2** a large piece of thick cloth that you put over your legs or around your shoulders to keep warm, especially when travelling ▶ **pled**

rugby /ˈrʌɡbi/ noun [U] a form of football that is played by two teams of 13 or 15 players with a ball shaped like an egg that can be carried, kicked or thrown ▶ **rugby** ➲ look at **league** ➲ picture on **page A8**

> W Wlk. Br. **Rugby League** to gra w drużynach 13-osobowych, natomiast **Rugby Union** – w drużynach 15-osobowych.

rugged /ˈrʌɡɪd/ adj. **1** (used about land) rough, with a lot of rocks and not many plants ▶ **skalisty, dziki, poszarpany** **2** (used about a man) strong and attractive

▶ **krzepki** **3** strong and made for difficult conditions ▶ **twardy**

ruin¹ /ˈruːɪn/ verb [T] **1** to damage sth so badly that it loses all its value, pleasure, etc.: *The bad news ruined my week.* ◇ *That one mistake ruined my chances of getting the job.* ▶ **niszczyć (doszczętnie)**, **rujnować** **2** to cause sb to lose all their money, hope of being successful, etc.: *The cost of the court case nearly ruined them.* ▶ **doprowadzać do ruiny**
■ **ruined** adj. [only before a noun]: *a ruined building* ▶ **zrujnowany**

ruin² /ˈruːɪn/ noun **1** [U] the state of being destroyed or very badly damaged: *The city was in a state of ruin* (w ruinie). ▶ **ruina** **2** [U] the cause or state of having lost all your money, hope of being successful, etc.: *Many small companies are facing **financial ruin**.* ▶ **ruina**, **upadek** **3** [C] the parts of a building that are left standing after it has been destroyed or badly damaged: *the ruins of the ancient city of Pompeii* ▶ **rudera**, **ruina**
➲ picture on **page A2**
IDM **go to rack and ruin** → RACK¹
in ruin(s) badly damaged or destroyed: *After the accident her life seemed to be in ruins.* ▶ **w gruzach**

ruinous /ˈruːɪnəs/ adj. causing serious problems, especially with money ▶ **rujnujący**, **zgubny**

rule¹ /ruːl/ noun **1** [C] an official statement that tells you what you must or must not do in a particular situation or when playing a game: *to **obey/break a rule*** ◇ *Do you know the rules of chess?* ◇ *It's **against the rules*** (niezgodne z regulaminem) *to smoke in this area.* ◇ *The company have strict **rules and regulations*** (regulamin) *governing employees' dress.* ▶ **przepis**, **reguła** **2** [C] a piece of advice about what you should do in a particular situation: *There are no **hard and fast rules** for planning healthy meals.* ▶ **zasada** **3** [sing.] what is usual: *Large families are the exception rather than the rule nowadays.* ◇ ***As a general rule*** (z reguły), *women live longer than men.* ◇ *I don't read much **as a rule**.* ▶ **reguła** **4** [C] a description of what is usual or correct: *What is the rule for forming the past tense?* ▶ **reguła**, **zasada** **5** [U] government; control: *The country is **under** military **rule**.* ◇ *the rule of law* rządy prawa ▶ **panowanie**
IDM **bend the rules** → BEND¹
the golden rule (of sth) → GOLDEN
a rule of thumb a simple piece of practical advice, not involving exact details or figures ▶ **praktyczna zasada**
work to rule → WORK¹

rule² /ruːl/ verb [I,T] **1 rule (over sb/sth)** to have power over a country, group of people, etc.: *Julius Caesar ruled over a vast empire.* ◇ (figurative) *His whole life was ruled by his ambition to become President.* ▶ **panować**; **dominować** **2 rule (on sth)**; **rule (in favour of/against sb/sth)** to make an official decision: *The judge will rule on whether or not the case can go ahead.* ▶ **orzekać**, **postanawiać**
PHR V **rule sb/sth out** to say that sb/sth is not possible, cannot do sth, etc.; to prevent sth: *The government has ruled out further increases in train fares next year.* ▶ **wykluczać**

ruler /ˈruːlə(r)/ noun [C] **1** a person who rules a country, etc. ▶ **wład-ca/czyni** **2** a straight piece of wood, plastic, etc. marked with centimetres, that you use for measuring sth or for drawing straight lines ▶ **linijka**

ruling¹ /ˈruːlɪŋ/ adj. [only before a noun] with the most power in an organization, a country, etc.: *the ruling political party* ▶ **rządzący**, **panujący**

ruling² /ˈruːlɪŋ/ noun [C] an official decision ▶ **orzeczenie**, **postanowienie**

rum /rʌm/ noun [U,C] a strong alcoholic drink that is made from the juice of **sugar cane** ▶ **rum**

rumble /ˈrʌmbl/ verb [I] to make a deep heavy sound: *I was so hungry that my stomach was rumbling.* ▶ **dudnić**, **grzmieć**, **burczeć** (*w brzuchu*)
■ **rumble** noun [sing.]: *a rumble of thunder* ▶ **dudnienie**, **grzmot**, **burczenie** (*w brzuchu*)

rummage /ˈrʌmɪdʒ/ verb [I] to move things and make them untidy while you are looking for sth: *Nina rummaged through the drawer looking for the tin-opener.* ▶ **szperać**, **przetrząsać**

ˈ**rummage sale** = JUMBLE SALE

rumour (US **rumor**) /ˈruːmə(r)/ noun [C,U] **(a) rumour (about/of sb/sth)** (a piece of) news or information that many people are talking about but that is possibly not true: *I didn't start the rumour about Barry's operation.* ◇ ***Rumour has it** that* (podobno) *Kasia has resigned.* ◇ *to confirm/deny a rumour* ▶ **pogłoska**, **plotka**

rumoured (US **rumored**) /ˈruːməd/ adj. reported or said, but perhaps not true: *It is rumoured that* (krąży pogłoska, że) *they are getting divorced.* ◇ *They are rumoured to be getting divorced* (mówią, że oni mają zamiar się rozwieść). ▶ **będący przedmiotem pogłoski**

rump /rʌmp/ noun [C] the back end of an animal: *rump steak* krzyżowa ▶ **zad**, **krzyż**, **comber**

run¹ /rʌn/ verb [I,T] (ru**nn**ing; pt **ran** /ræn/, pp **run**) **1** [I,T] to move using your legs, going faster than a walk: *I had to run to catch the bus.* ◇ *She's running in the 100 metres* (w wyścigu na setkę). ◇ *I often **go running** in the evenings.* ◇ *I ran nearly ten kilometres this morning.* ◇ *The children came running* (przybiegły) *to meet us.* ▶ **biegać**, **biec** **2** [T] to organize or be in charge of sth; to provide a service: *She runs a restaurant.* ◇ *They run English courses all the year round.* ▶ **prowadzić**, **kierować** **3** [T] to use and pay for a vehicle: *It costs a lot to run a car.* Utrzymanie samochodu dużo kosztuje. ▶ **utrzymywać**, **eksploatować** **4** [I,T] to operate or function; to make sth do this: *The engine is running very smoothly now.* ◇ *We're running a new computer program today.* ▶ **funkcjonować**, **działać**; **uruchamiać** **5** [I,T] to move, or move sth, quickly in a particular direction: *I've been running around after the kids all day.* ◇ *The car ran off the road and hit a tree.* ◇ *She ran her finger* (przebiegła palcem) *down the list of passengers.* ▶ **jechać**, **toczyć się**; **przesuwać** **6** [I] to lead from one place to another; to be in a particular position: *The road runs along the side of a lake.* ▶ **biec** **7** [I] to continue for a time: *My contract has two months left to run.* Moja umowa jest jeszcze ważna przez dwa miesiące. ◇ *The play ran* (była grana) *for nearly two years in a London theatre.* **8** [I] to operate at a particular time: *Buses to Oxford run every half hour.* ◇ *All the trains are **running late*** (są opóźnione) *this morning.* ◇ *We'd better hurry up – we're running behind schedule* (mamy opóźnienie). ▶ **kursować** **9** [I,T] to flow; to make water flow: *When it's really cold, my nose runs.* ◇ *I can hear a tap running somewhere* (cieknie z kranu). ◇ *to run a bath* nalewać wody do wanny ◇ *to run a tap* odkręcać kurek z wodą ▶ **cieknąć**, **rozlewać się**; **nalewać** **10** [I] to spread, for example when clothes are washed: *Don't put that red shirt in the washing machine. It might run.* ▶ **farbować** **11** [T] to publish sth in a newspaper or magazine: *'The Independent' is running a series of articles on pollution.* ▶ **publikować** **12** [T] **run a test/check (on sth)** to do a test or check on sth: *They're running checks on the power supply to see what the problem is.* ▶ **przeprowadzać test/kontrolę** **13** [I] **run (for sth)** to be one of the people who hopes to be chosen in an election: *He's running for president.* ▶ **kandydować**
IDM **be running at** to be at a certain level ▶ **być na określonym poziomie**

R

run for it to run in order to escape ▶ **szybko uciekać**
ⓘ **Run** występuje w innych idiomach, np. **run in the family**. Zob. hasła odpowiednich rzeczownikach, przymiotnikach itp.
PHR V **run across sb/sth** to meet or find sb/sth by chance ▶ **wpadać na kogoś/coś (przypadkiem)**
run after sb/sth to try to catch sb/sth ▶ **biec za kimś/czymś**
run away to escape from somewhere: *He's run away from home.* ▶ **uciekać**
run sb/sth down 1 to hit a person or an animal with your vehicle: *She was run down by a bus.* ▶ **przejechać 2** to criticize sb/sth: *He's always running her down in front of other people.* ▶ **ostro krytykować**
run (sth) down to stop functioning gradually; to make sth do this: *Turn the lights off or you'll run the battery down.* ▶ **przestawać działać/funkcjonować; sprawiać, że coś przestaje działać**
run into sb to meet sb by chance ▶ **natknąć się na kogoś (przypadkiem)**
run into sth to have difficulties or a problem: *If you run into any problems, just let me know.* ▶ **natrafiać na coś**
run (sth) into sb/sth to hit sb/sth with a car, etc.: *He ran his car into a brick wall.* ▶ **wjeżdżać na/w kogoś/coś**
run sth off to copy sth, using a machine ▶ **odbijać, kopiować**
run off with sth to take or steal sth ▶ **uciekać z czymś**
run on to continue without stopping; to continue longer than is necessary or expected: *The meeting will finish promptly – I don't want it to run on.* ▶ **ciągnąć się, wlec się w nieskończoność**
run out (of sth) to finish your supply of sth; to come to an end: *Time is running out.* Czas się kończy. ◇ *My passport runs out* (traci ważność) *next month.* ◇ *We've run out of coffee.* Skończyła nam się kawa. ◇ *I'm running out of ideas.* Brakuje mi pomysłów
run sb/sth over to hit a person or an animal with your vehicle: *The child was run over as he was crossing the road.* ▶ **przejechać**
run through sth to discuss or read sth quickly: *She ran through the names on the list.* ▶ **przebiegać przez coś, omawiać**
run sth up 1 to allow a bill, debt, etc. to reach a large total: *How had he managed to run up so many debts?* ▶ **zaciągać** (*znaczne długi*) SYN **accumulate 2** to make a piece of clothing quickly, especially by sewing: *to run up a blouse* ▶ **(u)szyć coś**
run with sth to be covered with flowing water: *My face was running with sweat.* ▶ **być oblanym czymś**

🔑 **run²** /rʌn/ noun **1** [C] an act of running on foot: *I **go for a** three-mile **run** every morning.* Codziennie rano przebiegam trzy mile. ◇ *The prisoner tried to **make a run for it*** (rzucił się do ucieczki). ◇ *a cross-country run* bieg przełajowy ▶ **bieg, wyścig 2** [C] a journey by car, train, etc.: *The bus was picking up kids on the school run.* ▶ **przejażdżka, mała wycieczka 3** [sing.] a series of similar events or sth that continues for a very long time: *We've had a run of bad luck* (mieliśmy złą passę) *recently.* ▶ **seria 4** [sing.] **a run on sth** a sudden great demand for sth: *There's always a run on sunglasses in hot weather.* ▶ **(nagły i masowy) popyt 5** [C] a point in the sports of **baseball** and **cricket**: *Our team won by two runs.* ▶ **punkt zdobyty po przebiegnięciu określonej odległości 6** (US) = LADDER (2) **7** a continous series of performances of a play, film etc.: *Agatha Christie's 'Mousetrap' has had a run of* (nie schodzi z afisza od) *more than twenty years.* ▶ **okres wystawiania (*sztuki*)/wyświetlania (*filmu*)**
IDM **in the long run** → LONG¹
on the run hiding or trying to escape from sb/sth: *The escaped prisoner is still on the run* (jest nadal na wolności). ▶ **uciekający, zbiegły**
the ordinary, average, etc. run of sth the ordinary, average, etc. type of sth ▶ **przeciętny człowiek, przeciętna rzecz, norma**

runaway¹ /ˈrʌnəweɪ/ adj. [only before a noun] **1** having left without telling anyone ▶ **uciekający, zbiegły 2** out of control: *a runaway car/train* ◇ *a runaway horse* koń, który poniósł ▶ **wymykający się spod kontroli 3** happening very easily: *a runaway victory* ▶ **spektakularny**

runaway² /ˈrʌnəweɪ/ noun [C] a person, especially a child, who has left or escaped from somewhere ▶ **zbieg, uciekinier**

ˌ**run-ˈdown** adj. **1** (used about a building or place) in bad condition: *a run-down block of flats* ▶ **zaniedbany, zapuszczony 2** [not before a noun] very tired and not healthy: *You're looking very run-down* (ledwo żywy). ▶ **wyczerpany, osłabiony**

rung¹ /rʌŋ/ noun [C] one of the bars that form the steps of a **ladder** ▶ **szczebel** (*drabiny*), **stopień**

rung² past participle of **ring²**

🔑 **runner** /ˈrʌnə(r)/ noun [C] **1** a person or an animal that runs, especially in a race: *a cross-country/long-distance runner* ▶ **biegacz/ka 2** a person who takes guns, drugs, etc. illegally from one country to another: *a drug runner* ▶ **przemytni-k/czka**

ˌ**runner-ˈup** noun [C] (pl. **runners-up**) the person or team that finished second in a race or competition ▶ **zdobyw-ca/czyni drugiego miejsca**

🔑 **running¹** /ˈrʌnɪŋ/ noun [U] **1** the action or sport of running: *How often do you **go running*** (biegasz)? ◇ *running shoes* buty do biegania ▶ **bieganie 2** the process of managing a business or other organization: *She's not involved in the day-to-day running of the office.* ◇ *the **running costs*** (koszty eksploatacji) *of a car* ▶ **prowadzenie, kierowanie**
IDM **be in/out of the running (for sth)** (informal) to have/not have a good chance of getting or winning sth ▶ **mieć widoki/szanse (na coś); nie mieć widoków/szans (na coś)**

running² /ˈrʌnɪŋ/ adj. **1** (used after a number and a noun to say that sth has happened a number of times in the same way without a change): *Our school has won the competition for four years running.* ▶ **z rzędu 2** [only before a noun] (used about water) flowing or available from a tap: *There is no running water in the cottage.* ▶ **bieżący 3** [only before a noun] not stopping; continuous: *a running battle between two rival gangs* ▶ **nieustający, ciągły**

ˌ**running ˈcommentary** noun [C] a spoken description of sth while it is happening ▶ **komentarz na żywo**

ˈ**running time** noun [usually sing.] the amount of time that a film/movie, a journey, etc. lasts: *The new service will cut 14 minutes off the running time of the journey.* ▶ **czas trwania**

runny /ˈrʌni/ adj. (**runnier**; **runniest**) (informal) **1** (used about your eyes or nose) producing too much liquid: *Their children always seem to have runny noses.* ▶ **cieknący, łzawiący 2** containing more liquid than is usual or than you expected: *runny jam* ▶ **(zbyt) rzadki**

ˌ**run-of-the-ˈmill** adj. ordinary, with no special or interesting features: *a run-of-the-mill job* ▶ **zwyczajny**

ˈ**run-up** noun [sing.] **1** the period of time before a certain event: *the run-up to the election* okres przedwyborczy ▶ **okres ostatnich przygotowań 2** (in sport) a run that people do in order to be going fast enough to do an action ▶ **bieg** (*typu rozgrzewka*)

runway /ˈrʌnweɪ/ noun [C] a long piece of ground with a hard surface where aircraft take off and land at an airport ▶ **pas startowy**

rupture /ˈrʌptʃə(r)/ noun [C,U] **1** a sudden bursting or breaking ▶ **zerwanie, pęknięcie 2** (formal) the sudden ending of good relations between two people or groups ▶ **zerwanie stosunków**, **rozłam** (*np. w partii*) **3** = HERNIA

■ **rupture** verb [I,T]: *Her appendix ruptured and she had to have emergency surgery.* ▶ **zrywać**, **pękać**; **przerywać się**

⚷ **rural** /ˈrʊərəl/ adj. connected with the country, not the town: *We spent our holiday exploring rural France* (zwiedzając francuską wieś). ◇ *a museum of rural life* skansen ▶ **wiejski** ➲ look at **urban**, **rustic**

ruse /ruːz/ noun [C] a trick or clever plan ▶ **fortel**, **podstęp**

⚷ **rush¹** /rʌʃ/ verb **1** [I,T] to move or do sth with great speed, often too fast: *I rushed back home when I got the news.* ◇ *Don't rush off* - (nie uciekaj) *I want to talk to you.* ◇ *The public rushed to buy* (rzucili się kupować) *shares in the company.* ◇ *I always take a long break for my lunch – I hate to rush it* (nie znoszę się śpieszyć (kiedy jem)). ◇ *The children rushed out* (wybiegły) *of school.* ▶ **śpieszyć się**, **pędzić (dokądś)** **2** [T] to take sb/sth to a place very quickly: *He suffered a heart attack and* ***was rushed to hospital*** (został natychmiast zabrany do szpitala). ▶ **zabierać (kogoś/coś) pośpiesznie dokądś** **3** [I,T] **rush (sb) (into sth/into doing sth)** to do sth or make sb do sth without thinking about it first: *Don't let yourself be rushed into marriage.* ◇ *Please don't rush me – I'm thinking!* ◇ *Don't rush your food* (nie jedz tak szybko) – *there's plenty of time.* ▶ **pochopnie decydować się na coś**, **pośpiesznie coś robić**; **ponaglać**

IDM **be rushed/run off your feet** → FOOT¹

PHR V **rush sth out** to produce sth very quickly ▶ **wydawać szybko** (*np. książkę, płytę*)

⚷ **rush²** /rʌʃ/ noun **1** [sing.] a sudden quick movement: *At the end of the match there was a rush for the exits* (wszyscy rzucili się do wyjścia). ◇ *I was so nervous, all my words came out* ***in a rush.*** ▶ **pośpiech**, **pęd** **2** [sing., U] a situation in which you are in a hurry and need to do things quickly: *I can't stop now. I'm* ***in a*** *terrible* ***rush*** (strasznie się śpieszę). ◇ *Don't hurry your meal. There's no rush.* ▶ **pośpiech** **3** [sing.] a time when there is a lot of activity and people are very busy: *We'll leave early to avoid the rush.* ▶ **tłok**, **pośpiech** **4** [sing.] **a rush (on sth)** a time when many people try to get sth: *There's always a rush on umbrellas when it rains.* ▶ **nagły popyt**, **masowy wykup** (*towarów*) **5** [C] a type of tall grass that grows near water ▶ **sitowie**

ˈ**rush hour** noun [C] the time each day when there is a lot of traffic because people are travelling to or from work: *rush-hour traffic* ▶ **godzina szczytu**

rust /rʌst/ noun [U] a reddish-brown substance that forms on the surface of iron, etc., caused by the action of air and water ▶ **rdza**

■ **rust** verb [I,T]: *Some parts of the car had rusted.* ▶ **rdzewieć**; **poddawać (coś) działaniu rdzy**

rustic /ˈrʌstɪk/ adj. typical of the country or of country people; simple: *The whole area is full of rustic charm.* ▶ **wiejski**, **rustykalny** ➲ look at **rural**, **urban**

rustle /ˈrʌsl/ verb [I,T] to make a sound like dry leaves or paper moving: *There was a rustling noise in the bushes.* ▶ **szeleścić (czymś)**

■ **rustle** noun [sing.] ▶ **szelest**

PHR V **rustle sth up (for sb)** (informal) to make or find sth quickly for sb and without planning it: *to rustle up a quick snack* ▶ **przygotowywać (coś) naprędce (dla kogoś)**

rusty /ˈrʌsti/ adj. (**rustier**; **rustiest**) **1** (used about metal objects) covered with **rust** as a result of being in contact with water and air: *rusty tins* ▶ **zardzewiały** **2** (used about a skill) not as good as it was because you have not used it for a long time: *My French is rather rusty.* ◇ *You'll have to remind me of the rules – I'm a bit rusty* (nie pamiętam ich dobrze). ▶ (*przen.*) **zardzewiały**

rut /rʌt/ noun [C] a deep track that a wheel makes in soft ground ▶ **koleina**, **bruzda**

IDM **be in a rut** to have a boring way of life that is difficult to change ▶ **popaść w rutynę**

ruthless /ˈruːθləs/ adj. (used about people and their behaviour) hard and cruel; determined to get what you want and showing no pity to others: *a ruthless dictator* ▶ **bezlitosny**, **bezwzględny**

■ **ruthlessly** adv. ▶ **bezlitośnie**, **bezwzględnie** | **ruthlessness** noun [U] ▶ **bezlitosne postępowanie**, **bezwzględność**

rye /raɪ/ noun [U] a plant that is grown in colder countries for its grain, which is used to make flour and also **whisky** ▶ **żyto**

Ss

S, s /es/ noun [C,U] (pl. **Ss**; **ss**; **S's**; **s's** /ˈesɪz/) the 19th letter of the English alphabet: *'School' begins with (an) 'S'.* ▶ **litera s**

S **1** = SMALL (1) **2** = SOUTH¹, SOUTHERN: *S Yorkshire*

sabbath /ˈsæbəθ/ (often **the Sabbath**) noun [sing.] the day of the week for rest and prayer in certain religions (Sunday for Christians, Saturday for Jews) ▶ **szabas**

sable /ˈseɪbl/ noun [U] the fur of a small Arctic animal, used for making coats or artist's brushes ▶ **soból**

sabotage /ˈsæbətɑːʒ/ noun [U] damage that is done on purpose and secretly in order to prevent an enemy being successful, for example by destroying machinery, roads, bridges, etc.: *industrial/economic/military sabotage* ▶ **sabotaż**

■ **sabotage** verb [T] ▶ **sabotować**

saccharin /ˈsækərɪn/ noun [U] a very sweet substance that can be used instead of sugar ▶ **sacharyna**

sachet /ˈsæʃeɪ; US sæˈʃeɪ/ noun [C] a closed plastic or paper package that contains a very small amount of liquid or powder: *a sachet of shampoo/sugar/coffee* ▶ **saszetka** ➲ picture at **container**

⚷ **sack¹** /sæk/ noun [C] a large bag made from a rough heavy material, paper or plastic, used for carrying or storing things: *sacks of flour/potatoes* ▶ **worek**

IDM **get the sack** (Brit.) to be told by your employer that you can no longer continue working for them (usually because you have done sth wrong): *Tony got the sack for poor work.* ▶ **zostać wyrzuconym z pracy**

give sb the sack (Brit.) to tell an employee that they can no longer continue working for you (because of bad work, behaviour, etc.): *Tony's work wasn't good enough and he was given the sack.* ▶ **wyrzucać kogoś z pracy** ➲ note at **job**

⚷ **sack²** /sæk/ (especially US **fire**) verb [T] to tell an employee that they can no longer work for you (because of bad work, bad behaviour, etc.): *Her boss has threatened to sack her if she's late again.* ▶ **wyrzucać z pracy**

sacrament /ˈsækrəment/ noun **1** [C] a ceremony in the Roman Catholic, Anglican and other Christian Churches, through which Christians believe they are specially blessed by God ▶ **sakrament** **2** (**the sacrament**; **the Holy Sacrament**) [sing.] (in Christianity) the bread and wine of the Eucharist: *to receive the sacrament* ▶ **Najświętszy Sakrament**

■ **sacramental** adj. connected with the sacraments: *sacramental wine* wino mszalne ▶ **sakramentalny**

sacred /ˈseɪkrɪd/ adj. **1** connected with God, a god or religion: *The Koran is the sacred book of Muslims.* ◇ *sacred* (sakralna) *music* ▶ **święty** **2** too important and special to be changed or harmed: *a sacred tradition* ▶ **nienaruszalny**

sacrifice[1] /ˈsækrɪfaɪs/ noun [U,C] **1** giving up sth that is important or valuable to you in order to get or do sth that seems more important; sth that you give up in this way: *If we're going to have a holiday this year, we'll have to **make** some **sacrifices**.* ▶ **wyrzeczenie 2 sacrifice (to sb)** the act of offering sth to a god, especially an animal that has been killed in a special way; an animal, etc. that is offered in this way ▶ **ofiara**

sacrifice[2] /ˈsækrɪfaɪs/ verb **1** [T] **sacrifice sth (for sb/sth)** to give up sth that is important or valuable to you in order to get or do sth that seems more important: *She is not willing to sacrifice her career in order to have children.* ▶ **składać w ofierze**, **poświęcać 2** [I,T] to kill an animal and offer it to a god, in order to please the god ▶ **składać w ofierze**

sacrilege /ˈsækrəlɪdʒ/ noun [U, sing.] treating a religious object or place without the respect that it deserves ▶ **świętokradztwo**
■ **sacrilegious** /ˌsækrəˈlɪdʒəs/ adj. ▶ **świętokradczy**

sad /sæd/ adj. (**sadder**; **saddest**) **1 sad (to do sth)**; **sad (that ...)** unhappy or causing sb to feel unhappy: *We are very sad to hear that you are leaving.* ◇ *I'm very sad* (bardzo mi przykro) *that you don't trust me.* ◇ *That's one of the saddest stories I've ever heard!* ◇ *a sad poem/song/film* ▶ **smutny 2** bad or unacceptable: *It's a sad state of affairs when your best friend doesn't trust you.* ▶ **smutny**

> **sad**
> If something **upsets** you, you feel **unhappy** about it: *This will upset a lot of people.* **Upset** is also an adjective: *I felt upset about what they had said.* If you feel **miserable**, you are very sad. If you feel **depressed**, you feel very sad and without hope. This feeling often lasts for a long period of time: *He's been very depressed since he lost his job.* You can describe sad things that happen as **depressing**: *depressing news.*

■ **sadden** /ˈsædn/ verb [T] (formal): *The news of your father's death saddened me greatly.* ▶ **zasmucać** | **sadness** noun [C,U] ▶ **smutek**

saddle[1] /ˈsædl/ noun [C] **1** a seat, usually made of leather, that you put on a horse so that you can ride it ▶ **siodło** ➲ picture at **saddle 2** a seat on a bicycle or motorbike ▶ **siodełko** ➲ picture at **bicycle**

saddle[2] /ˈsædl/ verb [T] to put a **saddle** on a horse: *Their horses were saddled and waiting.* ▶ **siodłać**
PHR V **saddle sb with sth** to give sb a responsibility or task that they do not want ▶ **obarczać kogoś czymś**

sadism /ˈseɪdɪzəm/ noun [U] getting pleasure, especially sexual pleasure, from hurting other people ▶ **sadyzm** ➲ look at **masochism**

sadist /ˈseɪdɪst/ noun [C] a person who gets pleasure, especially sexual pleasure, from hurting other people ▶ **sadyst(k)a**
■ **sadistic** /səˈdɪstɪk/ adj. ▶ **sadystyczny** | **sadistically** /-kli/ adv. ▶ **sadystycznie**

sadly /ˈsædli/ adv. **1** unfortunately: *Sadly, after eight years of marriage they had grown apart.* ▶ **niestety 2** in a way that shows unhappiness: *She shook her head sadly.* ▶ **ze smutkiem 3** in a way that is wrong: *If you think that I've forgotten what you did, you're **sadly mistaken**.* ▶ **wielce**

sadomasochism /ˌseɪdəʊˈmæsəkɪzəm/ noun [U] enjoyment from hurting sb and being hurt, especially during sexual activity ▶ **sadomasochizm**
■ **sadomasochist** /ˌseɪdəʊˈmæsəkɪst/ noun [C] ▶ **sadomasochist(k)a** | **sadomasochistic** /ˌseɪdəʊˌmæsəˈkɪstɪk/ adj. ▶ **sadomasochistyczny**

sae = STAMPED ADDRESSED ENVELOPE: *Please enclose an sae.*

safari /səˈfɑːri/ noun [C,U] (pl. **safaris**) a trip to see or hunt wild animals, especially in East Africa: *to be/go **on safari*** ▶ **safari** ➲ note at **holiday**

safe[1] /seɪf/ adj. **1** [not before a noun] **safe (from sb/sth)** free from danger; not able to be hurt: *She didn't **feel safe** in the house on her own.* ◇ *Do you think my car will be safe in this street?* ◇ *Keep the papers where they will be safe from fire.* ▶ **bezpieczny**, **zabezpieczony 2 safe (to do sth)**; **safe (for sb)** not likely to cause danger, harm or risk: *Don't sit on that chair, it isn't safe.* ◇ *I left my suitcase in a **safe place** and went for a cup of coffee.* ◇ *Is this drug safe for children?* ◇ *She's a very safe* (ostrożnym) *driver.* ◇ *It's not safe to walk alone in the streets at night here.* ◇ *Is it safe to drink the water here?* Czy ta woda nadaje się do picia? ◇ *I think **it's safe to say*** (można powiedzieć) *that the situation is unlikely to change for some time.* ▶ **bezpieczny 3** [not before a noun] not hurt, damaged or lost: *After five days the child was found, **safe and sound*** (całe i zdrowe). ◇ *After the accident he checked that all the passengers were safe* (sprawdził, czy nikomu nic się nie stało). ▶ **cały**, **zdrowy**
■ **safely** adv.: *I rang my parents to tell them I had arrived safely.* ▶ **bezpiecznie**
IDM **in safe hands** with sb who will take good care of you ▶ **w dobrych rękach**
on the safe side not taking risks; being very careful ▶ **na wszelki wypadek**

safe[2] /seɪf/ noun [C] a strong metal box or cupboard with a special lock that is used for keeping money, jewellery, documents, etc. in ▶ **sejf**

safeguard /ˈseɪfɡɑːd/ noun [C] **a safeguard (against sb/sth)** something that protects against possible dangers ▶ **zabezpieczenie**
■ **safeguard** verb [T]: *to safeguard somebody's interests/rights/privacy* ▶ **zabezpieczać**, **chronić**

safety /ˈseɪfti/ noun [U] the state of being safe; not being dangerous or in danger: *In the interests of safety, smoking is forbidden.* ◇ *She has been missing for several days and police now fear for her safety* (obawia się o jej życie). ◇ *New **safety measures** have been introduced on trains.* ◇ ***road safety*** bezpieczeństwo na drogach ▶ **bezpieczeństwo**

ˈsafety belt = SEAT BELT

ˈsafety net noun [C] **1** a net that is placed to catch sb who is performing high above the ground if they fall ▶ **siatka zabezpieczająca przed upadkiem na ziemię 2** an arrangement that helps to prevent disaster (usually with money) if sth goes wrong ▶ **zabezpieczenie**

ˈsafety pin noun [C] a metal pin with a point that is bent back towards the head, which is covered so that it cannot be dangerous ▶ **agrafka**

ˈsafety valve noun [C] a device in a machine that allows steam, gas, etc. to escape if the pressure becomes too great ▶ **zawór bezpieczeństwa**

saffron /ˈsæfrən/ noun [U] a bright orange powder that comes from certain crocus flowers, and is used in cooking to give colour and flavour to food ▶ **szafran**

sag /sæɡ/ verb [I] (**sagging**; **sagged**) to hang or to bend down, especially in the middle ▶ **obwisać**, **zapadać się**

saga /ˈsɑːɡə/ noun [C] a very long story; a long series of events ▶ **saga**

sage /seɪdʒ/ noun [U] a **herb** with flat, light green leaves that have a strong smell and are used in cooking ▶ **szałwia**

Sagittarius /ˌsædʒɪˈteəriəs/ noun [C,U] the 9th sign of the **zodiac**, the Archer; a person born under this sign: *I'm a Sagittarius.* ▶ **Strzelec**; **zodiakalny Strzelec**

said past tense, past participle of **say**[1]

sail[1] /seɪl/ verb **1** [I] (used about a boat or ship and the people on it) to travel on water in a ship or boat of any type: *I stood at the window and watched the ships sailing by.* ◇ *to sail round the world* ▶ **pływać 2** [I,T] to travel in and control a boat with sails, especially as a sport: *My father is teaching me to sail.* ◇ *I've never sailed this kind of yacht before.* ▶ **żeglować** ℹ Mówiąc o żeglowaniu jako formie spędzania czasu wolnego, często używa się formy **go sailing**: *We often go sailing at weekends.* **3** [I] to begin a journey on water: *When does the ship sail?* ◇ *We sail for Santander at 6 o'clock tomorrow morning.* ▶ **odpłynąć, wyruszyć (w drogę) 4** [I] to move somewhere quickly in a smooth or proud way: *The ball sailed* (poszybowała) *over the fence and into the neighbour's garden.* ◇ *Mary sailed into the room* (dumnie weszła do pokoju), *completely ignoring all of us.*
IDM **sail through (sth)** to pass a test or exam easily ▶ **łatwo sobie (z czymś) radzić**

sail[2] /seɪl/ noun **1** [C] a large piece of strong cloth that is fixed onto a ship or boat. The wind blows against the sail and moves the ship along. ▶ **żagiel** ➲ picture on **page A6 2** [sing.] a trip on water in a ship or boat with a sail: *Would you like to **go for a sail*** (popływać) *in my boat?* ▶ **przejażdżka łodzią 3** [C] any of the long parts that the wind moves round that are fixed to a **windmill** ▶ **śmiga**
IDM **set sail** to begin a journey by sea: *Columbus set sail for India.* ▶ **wyruszać w rejs**

sailboard = WINDSURFER (1)

sailboat (US) = SAILING BOAT

sailing /ˈseɪlɪŋ/ noun **1** [U] the sport of being in, and controlling, small boats with sails ▶ **żeglowanie, żeglarstwo 2** [C] a journey made by a ship or boat carrying passengers from one place to another ▶ **rejs**

ˈ**sailing boat** (US **sailboat** /ˈseɪlbəʊt/) noun [C] a boat with a sail or sails ▶ **żaglówka**

sailor /ˈseɪlə(r)/ noun [C] a person who works on a ship or a person who sails a boat ▶ **marynarz**

saint /seɪnt; snt/ noun [C] **1** (abbr. **St**) a very good or religious person who is given special respect after death by the Christian church ▶ **święt-y/a** ➲ look at **patron saint** ℹ Jako tytuł **saint** pisane jest dużą literą: *Saint Patrick.* W nazwach placów, kościołów itp. używa się zwykle formy skróconej **St**: *St Andrew's Church.* Przed imionami **saint** wymawia się /snt/. **2** a very good, kind person ▶ **święt-y/a**

saintly /ˈseɪntli/ adj. like a **saint**; very holy and good: *to lead a saintly life* ▶ **świątobliwy**

sake /seɪk/ noun [C]
IDM **for Christ's/God's/goodness'/Heaven's/pity's sake** (informal) (used to emphasize that it is important to do sth, or to show that you are annoyed): *For goodness' sake, hurry up!* ◇ *Why have you taken so long, for God's sake?* ▶ **na litość/miłość boską!** ℹ **For Christ's sake** oraz **For God's sake** to wyrażenia dosadne i mogą niektórych razić.
for the sake of sb/sth; for sb's/sth's sake in order to help sb/sth: *Don't go to any trouble for my sake.* ◇ *They only stayed together for the sake of their children/for their children's sake.* ▶ **ze względu na kogoś/coś**
for the sake of sth/of doing sth in order to get or keep sth; for the purpose of sth: *She gave up her job for the sake of her health.* ◇ *You're just arguing **for the sake of it*** (tylko po to, żeby się kłócić). ◇ *It's not worth complaining for the sake of a few pence* (dla paru groszy). ▶ **dla**

salad /ˈsæləd/ noun [C,U] a mixture of vegetables, usually not cooked, that you often eat together with other foods: *All main courses are served with salad.* ◇ *I had chicken salad* (sałatka z kurczakiem) *for lunch.* ◇ *a salad bar* bar sałatkowy ▶ **sałatka** ➲ picture on **page A14** ➲ look at **lettuce**

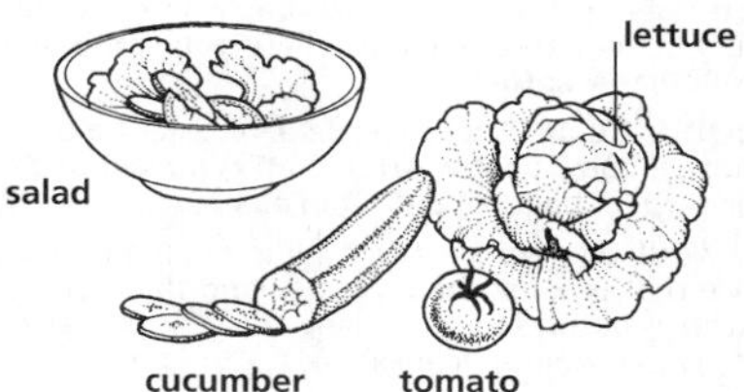

salami /səˈlɑːmi/ noun [U,C] (pl. **salamis**) a type of large spicy sausage served cold in thin slices ▶ **salami**

salary /ˈsæləri/ noun [C,U] (pl. **salaries**) the money that a person receives (usually every month) for the work they have done: *My salary is paid directly into my bank account.* ◇ *a high/low salary* ▶ **pensja** ➲ note at **pay**[2]

sale /seɪl/ noun **1** [C,U] the act of selling or being sold; the occasion when sth is sold: *The sale of alcohol to anyone under the age of 18 is forbidden.* ◇ *a sale of used toys* ◇ *Business is bad. I haven't made a sale* (nic nie sprzedałem) *all week.* ▶ **sprzedaż; wyprzedaż 2** (**sales**) [pl.] the number of items sold: *Sales of personal computers have increased rapidly.* ◇ *The company reported excellent sales figures.* ▶ **sprzedaż, ogół transakcji 3** (**sales**) [U] (also ˈ**sales department**) the part of a company that deals with selling its products: *Jodie works in sales/in the sales department.* ◇ *a sales representative/sales rep* ▶ **dział sprzedaży 4** [C] a time when shops sell things at prices that are lower than usual: *The sale starts on December 28th.* ◇ *I got several bargains in the sales* (na wyprzedaży). ▶ **przecena, wyprzedaż** ➲ look at **car boot sale, jumble sale**
IDM **for sale** offered for sb to buy: *This painting is not for sale.* ◇ *I see our neighbours have **put** their house **up for sale*** (wystawili swój dom na sprzedaż). ▶ **na sprzedaż**
on sale 1 available for sb to buy, especially in shops: *This week's edition is on sale now at your local newsagents.* ▶ **w sprzedaży 2** (US) offered at a lower price than usual ▶ **przeceniony**

ˈ**sales clerk** (US) = SHOP ASSISTANT

ˈ**sales department** = SALE (3)

salesman /ˈseɪlzmən/, ˈ**saleswoman** /ˈseɪlzwʊmən/, ˈ**salesperson** /ˈseɪlzpɜːsn/ noun [C] (pl. **-men** /-mən/; **-women** /-wɪmɪn/; **-persons** or **-people** /-ˈpiːpl/) a person whose job is selling things to people ▶ **sprzedaw-ca/czyni**

ˈ**sales representative** (also informal ˈ**sales rep; rep**) noun [C] an employee of a company who travels around a particular area selling the company's goods to shops, etc. ▶ **przedstawiciel/ka handlow-y/a**

salient /ˈseɪliənt/ adj. [only before a noun] most important or noticeable ▶ **wydatny, główny**

saliva /səˈlaɪvə/ noun [U] the liquid that is produced in the mouth ▶ **ślina** ➲ look at **spit**

salivate /ˈsælɪveɪt/ verb [I] (formal) to produce more **saliva** in your mouth than usual, especially when you see or smell food: (figurative) *He was salivating over the thought of the million dollars.* Ślinka mu ciekła na myśl o milionie dolarów. ▶ **ślinić się**

salmon /ˈsæmən/ noun [C,U] (pl. **salmon**) a large fish with silver skin and pink meat that we eat: *smoked salmon* ▶ **łosoś**

S

salmonella /ˌsælməˈnelə/ noun [U] a type of bacteria that causes food poisoning ▶ **salmonella**

salon /ˈsælɒn; US səˈl-/ noun [C] a shop where you can have beauty or hair treatment or where you can buy expensive clothes ▶ **salon**

saloon /səˈluːn/ (US **sedan** /sɪˈdæn/) noun [C] **1** a car with a fixed roof and a **boot** ▶ **samochód typu sedan** ➲ picture at **car**, picture on **page A7** **2** (Brit.) = LOUNGE BAR

salt¹ /sɔːlt; Brit. also sɒlt/ noun [U] a common white substance that is found in sea water and the earth. Salt is used in cooking for flavouring food: *Season with **salt and pepper*** (doprawić do smaku). ◇ *Add a pinch of salt.* ▶ **sól**
■ **salt** adj. [only before a noun]: *salt water* ▶ **słony**
IDM **rub salt into the wound/sb's wounds** → RUB
take sth with a pinch of salt → PINCH²

salt² /sɔːlt/ verb [T, usually passive] to put salt on or in sth: *salted* (solone) *peanuts* ▶ **solić**

ˈsalt water noun [U] sea water; water containing salt ▶ **wody słone**
■ **ˈsaltwater** adj. [only before a noun] living in the sea: *saltwater fish* ▶ **morski** ➲ look at **freshwater**

salty /ˈsɒlti/ adj. (**saltier**; **saltiest**) having the taste of or containing salt: *I didn't like the meat, it was too salty* (przesolone). ▶ **słony**

salute /səˈluːt/ noun [C] **1** an action that a soldier, etc. does to show respect, by touching the side of his or her head with the right hand: *to give a salute* salutować ▶ **honory wojskowe** **2** something that shows respect for sb: *The next programme is **a salute to** a great film star.* ▶ **hołd**
■ **salute** verb [I,T]: *The soldiers saluted as they marched past the general.* ▶ **salutować**; **oddawać honory wojskowe**

salvage¹ /ˈsælvɪdʒ/ noun [U] saving things that have been or are likely to be lost or damaged, especially in an accident or a disaster; the things that are saved: *an exhibition of the salvage from the shipwreck* ◇ *a salvage operation* operacja ratunkowa ◇ *a salvage company/team* ▶ **ratowanie** (*np. dobra, mienia*), **ocalałe dobro/mienie**

salvage² /ˈsælvɪdʒ/ verb [T] **salvage sth (from sth)** to manage to rescue sth from being lost or damaged; to rescue sth or a situation from disaster: *They salvaged as much as they could from the house after the fire.* ▶ **ratować**

salvation /sælˈveɪʃn/ noun **1** [U] (in the Christian religion) being saved from the power of evil ▶ **ratunek** **2** [U, sing.] a thing or person that rescues sb/sth from danger, disaster, etc. ▶ **zbawienie**

same /seɪm/ adj. **1 the same ... (as sb/sth)**; **the same ... that ...** not different, not another or other; exactly the one or ones that you have mentioned before: *My brother and I had the same teacher at school.* ◇ *They both said the same thing.* ◇ *I'm going to wear the same clothes as/that I wore yesterday.* ◇ *This one looks **exactly the same** as that one.* ▶ **ten sam** **2 the same... (as sb/sth)**; **the same ... that ...** exactly like the one already mentioned: *I wouldn't buy the same* (takiego samego (modelu)) *car again.* ◇ *I had the same experience as you some time ago.* ◇ *All small babies look the same.* ▶ **taki sam** ℹ Nie można powiedzieć ~~a same~~. W tym znaczeniu używa się **the same sort of**: *I'd like the same sort of job as my father.*
■ **the same** adv. in the same way; not differently: *We treat all the children in the class the same.* ▶ **tak samo** | **same** pron. **the same ... (as sb/sth)**: *Is there another word that means the same as this?* ◇ *Things will never be the same again* (nic nie będzie już takie, jak dawniej) *now that my father has died.* ▶ **to samo**
IDM **all/just the same** (used when saying or writing sth which contrasts in some way with what has gone before): *I understand what you're saying. All the same, I don't agree with you.* ◇ *I don't need to borrow any money, but thanks all the same for offering.* ▶ **mimo wszystko**, **w każdym razie**
at the same time 1 together; at one time: *I can't think about more than one thing at the same time.* ▶ **jednocześnie** **2** on the other hand; however: *It's a very good idea but at the same time it's rather risky.* ▶ **zarazem**
much the same → MUCH
on the same wavelength able to understand sb because you have similar ideas and opinions ▶ **podobny**, **identycznie myślący**
(the) same again (informal) a request to be served or given the same drink as before ▶ **to samo**
same here (informal) the same thing is also true for me: *'I'm bored.' 'Same here.'* ▶ **i ja też**
(the) same to you (informal) (used as an answer when sb says sth rude to you or wishes you sth): *'You idiot!' 'Same to you!'* ◇ *'Have a good weekend.' 'The same to you.'* ▶ **nawzajem!**

sample /ˈsɑːmpl; US ˈsæm-/ noun [C] **1** a small number or amount of sth that is looked at, tested, examined, etc. to find out what the rest is like: *to take a blood sample* ◇ *a free sample of shampoo* ▶ **próbka** ➲ look at **specimen** **2** a small number of people who are asked questions in order to find out information about a larger group: *The interviews were given to a **random sample** of shoppers.* ▶ **reprezentatywna grupa** (*do badań*) **2** a piece of recorded music or sound that is used in a new piece of music: *'Candy' includes a sample from a Walker Brothers song.* ▶ (*muz.*) **sample**
■ **sample** verb [T]: *You are welcome to sample any of our wines before making a purchase.* ▶ **próbować**

sanatorium /ˌsænəˈtɔːriəm/ (US **sanitarium** /ˌsænəˈteəriəm/) noun [C] a type of hospital where patients who need a long period of treatment for an illness can stay ▶ **sanatorium**

sanctify /ˈsæŋktɪfaɪ/ verb [T] (**sanctifies**; **sanctified**; **sanctifying**; **sanctified**) [usually passive] (formal) to make sth holy ▶ **uświęcać**

sanctimonious /ˌsæŋktɪˈməʊniəs/ adj. giving the impression that you feel you are better and more moral than other people ▶ **świętoszkowaty** SYN **self-righteous**
■ **sanctimoniously** adv. ▶ **w sposób świętoszkowaty**

sanction¹ /ˈsæŋkʃn/ noun **1** [C, usually pl.] **sanctions (against sb)** an official order that limits business, contact, etc. with a particular country, in order to make it do sth, such as obeying international law: *The sanctions against those countries have now been lifted.* ▶ **sankcja** **2** [U] (formal) official permission to do or change sth ▶ **zezwolenie** **3** [C] a punishment for breaking a rule or law ▶ **kara**

sanction² /ˈsæŋkʃn/ verb [T] to give official permission for sth ▶ **zezwalać**

sanctity /ˈsæŋktəti/ noun [U] **1 sanctity (of sth)** the state of being very important and worth protecting: *the **sanctity of marriage*** ▶ **nienaruszalność**, **świętość** **2** the state of being holy: *a life of sanctity, like that of St Francis* ▶ **świętość**

sanctuary /ˈsæŋktʃuəri; US -tʃueri/ noun (pl. **sanctuaries**) **1** [C] a place where birds or animals are protected from being hunted ▶ **rezerwat** (*przyrody*) **2** [C,U] a place where sb can be safe from enemies, the police, etc. ▶ **sanktuarium**, **azyl**

sand /sænd/ noun **1** [U] a powder consisting of very small grains of rock, found in deserts and on beaches: *a grain of sand* ▶ **piasek** **2** [U,C, usually pl.] a large area of sand: *miles of golden sands* ▶ **piaski**

sandal /ˈsændl/ noun [C] a type of light, open shoe that people wear when the weather is warm ▶ **sandałek** ➲ picture at **shoe**

sandcastle /ˈsændkɑːsl; US -kæsl/ noun [C] a pile of sand that looks like a castle, made by children playing on a beach ▶ **zamek z piasku**

ˈ**sand dune** = DUNE

sandpaper /ˈsændpeɪpə(r)/ noun [U] strong paper with sand on it that is used for rubbing surfaces in order to make them smooth ▶ **papier ścierny**

sandwich[1] /ˈsænwɪtʃ; -wɪdʒ/ noun [C] two slices of bread with food between them: *a ham/cheese sandwich* ▶ **kanapka** ➲ picture on **page A14**

sandwich[2] /ˈsænwɪtʃ; -wɪdʒ/ verb
PHR V **sandwich sb/sth (between sb/sth)** to place sb/sth in a very narrow space between two other things or people ▶ **wciskać kogoś/coś (pomiędzy kogoś/coś)**

sandy /ˈsændi/ adj. (**sandier**; **sandiest**) covered with or full of sand ▶ **piaszczysty**

sane /seɪn/ adj. **1** (used about a person) mentally normal; not crazy: *No sane person would do anything like that.* ▶ **przy zdrowych zmysłach 2** (used about a person or an idea, a decision, etc.) sensible; showing good judgement ▶ **rozsądny** OPP for both meanings **insane** ➲ noun **sanity**

sang past tense of **sing**

sanguine /ˈsæŋɡwɪn/ adj. **sanguine (about sth)** (formal) cheerful and confident about the future: *He tends to* ***take a sanguine view*** *of the problems involved.* ▶ **optymistyczny** SYN **optimistic**
■ **sanguinely** adv. ▶ **optymistycznie**

sanitarium (US) = SANATORIUM

sanitary /ˈsænətri; US -teri/ adj. [only before a noun] connected with the protection of health, for example how human waste is removed: *Sanitary conditions in the refugee camps were terrible.* ▶ **sanitarny**, **higieniczny** ➲ look at **insanitary**

ˈ**sanitary towel** (US ˈsanitary napkin) noun [C] a thick piece of soft material that women use to absorb blood lost during their period ▶ **podpaska** ➲ look at **tampon**

sanitation /ˌsænɪˈteɪʃn/ noun [U] the equipment and systems that keep places clean, especially by removing human waste ▶ **kanalizacja**

sanity /ˈsænəti/ noun [U] **1** the state of having a normal healthy mind ▶ **zdrowie psychiczne 2** the state of being sensible and reasonable ▶ **(zdrowy) rozsądek** OPP for both meanings **insanity** ➲ adjective **sane**

sank past tense of **sink[1]**

Santa Claus = FATHER CHRISTMAS

sap[1] /sæp/ noun [U] the liquid in a plant or tree ▶ **sok**

sap[2] /sæp/ verb [T] (**sapping**; **sapped**) **sap (sb of) sth** to make sb/sth weaker; to destroy sth gradually: *Years of failure have sapped (him of) his confidence.* ▶ **nadwątlać**; **niszczyć**

sapling /ˈsæplɪŋ/ noun [C] a young tree ▶ **drzewko**

sapphire /ˈsæfaɪə(r)/ noun [C,U] a bright blue **precious** stone ▶ **szafir**

sarcasm /ˈsɑːkæzəm/ noun [U] the use of words or expressions to mean the opposite of what they actually say. People use **sarcasm** in order to criticize other people or to make them look silly. ▶ **sarkazm** ➲ look at **irony**
■ **sarcastic** /sɑːˈkæstɪk/ adj.: *He's always making sarcastic comments.* ▶ **sarkastyczny** ➲ look at **ironic** | **sarcastically** /-kli/ adv. ▶ **sarkastycznie**

sardine /ˌsɑːˈdiːn/ noun [C] a type of very small silver fish that we cook and eat: *a tin of sardines* ▶ **sardynka**

sardonic /sɑːˈdɒnɪk/ adj. showing that you think that you are better than other people and do not take them seriously: *a sardonic smile* ▶ **sardoniczny**
■ **sardonically** /-kli/ adv. ▶ **sardonicznie**

sari /ˈsɑːri/ noun [C] a dress that consists of a long piece of silk or cotton that women, particularly Indian women, wear around their bodies ▶ **sari**

sash /sæʃ/ noun [C] a long piece of cloth that is worn round the waist or over the shoulder, often as part of a uniform ▶ **szarfa**

Sat. = SATURDAY: *Sat 2 May*

sat past tense, past participle of **sit**

Satan /ˈseɪtn/ noun [sing.] a name for the Devil ▶ **szatan** ➲ look at **devil**

satchel /ˈsætʃəl/ noun [C] a bag, often carried over the shoulder, used by children for taking books to and from school ▶ **teczka (szkolna)**

satellite /ˈsætəlaɪt/ noun [C] **1** an electronic device that is sent into space and moves round the earth or another planet for a particular purpose: *a weather/communications satellite* ▶ **satelita 2** a natural object that moves round a bigger object in space ▶ **satelita**

ˈ**satellite dish** (also **dish**) noun [C] a large round piece of equipment on the outside of houses that receives signals from a **satellite** (1), so that people can watch **satellite TV** ▶ **antena satelitarna**

ˈ**satellite television** (also ˈsatellite TV) noun [U] TV programmes that are sent out using a **satellite** (1) ▶ **telewizja satelitarna**

satin /ˈsætɪn; US ˈsætn/ noun [U] a type of cloth that is smooth and shiny: *a satin dress/ribbon* ▶ **satyna**, **atłas**

satire /ˈsætaɪə(r)/ noun **1** [U] the use of humour to attack a person, an organization, an idea, etc. that you think is bad or silly ▶ **satyra** ➲ note at **humour 2** [C] **a satire (on sb/sth)** a piece of writing or a play, film, etc. that uses **satire**: *a satire on political life* ▶ **satyra (na kogoś/coś)**
■ **satirical** /səˈtɪrɪkl/ adj.: *a satirical magazine* ▶ **satyryczny** | **satirically** /-kli/ adv. ▶ **satyrycznie**

satirist /ˈsætərɪst/ noun [C] a person who writes or uses **satire** ▶ **satyryk**

satirize (also **-ise**) /ˈsætəraɪz/ verb [T] to use **satire** to show the faults in a person, an organization, an idea, etc. ▶ **ośmieszać**, **wyśmiewać**, **napisać (na coś) satyrę**

satisfaction /ˌsætɪsˈfækʃn/ noun [U,C] the feeling of pleasure that you have when you have done, got or achieved what you wanted; sth that gives you this feeling: *Roshni stood back and looked at her work with a sense of satisfaction.* ◇ *We finally found a solution that was* ***to*** *everyone's* ***satisfaction*** (która wszystkich zadowoliła). ◇ *She was about to* ***have the satisfaction of*** *seeing her book in print.* ▶ **zadowolenie**, **satysfakcja** OPP **dissatisfaction**

satisfactory /ˌsætɪsˈfæktəri/ adj. good enough for a particular purpose; acceptable: *This piece of work is not satisfactory. Please do it again.* ▶ **dostateczny**, **zadowalający**
■ **satisfactorily** /ˌsætɪsˈfæktərəli/ adv.: *Work is progressing satisfactorily.* ▶ **zadowalająco**

satisfied /ˈsætɪsfaɪd/ adj. **satisfied (with sb/sth)** pleased because you have had or done what you wanted: *a satisfied customer* ◇ *a satisfied smile* uśmiech zadowolenia ▶ **zadowolony**, **usatysfakcjonowany** OPP **dissatisfied**

satisfy /ˈsætɪsfaɪ/ verb [T] (**satisfying**; **satisfies**; pt, pp **satisfied**) **1** to make sb pleased by doing or giving them what they want: *No matter how hard I try, my piano teacher is never satisfied.* ▶ **zadowalać**, **satysfakcjonować 2** to have or do what is necessary for sth: *Make sure you satisfy the entry* ***requirements*** *before you apply to the university.* ◇ *I had a quick look inside the parcel just to* ***satisfy my curiosity.*** ▶ **spełniać**; **zaspokajać 3 satisfy sb (that...)** to show or give proof to sb that sth is true or has been done: *Once the police were satisfied that they were telling the truth, they were allowed to go.* ▶ **przekonywać (że)**

satisfying /ˈsætɪsfaɪɪŋ/ adj. pleasing, giving satisfaction: *I find it satisfying to see people enjoying something I've cooked.* ▶ **zadowalający, satysfakcjonujący**

satsuma /sætˈsuːmə/ noun [C] a type of small orange ▶ **satsuma, rodzaj mandarynki**

saturate /ˈsætʃəreɪt/ verb [T] **1** to make sth extremely wet: *The continuous rain had saturated the soil.* ▶ **przemaczać 2** [often passive] to fill sth so completely that it is impossible to add any more: *The market is saturated* (rynek jest zarzucony) *with cheap imports.* ▶ **nasycać, przesiąkać**
■ **saturated** adj.: *Her clothes were saturated.* ▶ **przemoczony; nasycony** | **saturation** /ˌsætʃəˈreɪʃn/ noun [U]: *The market for cars has reached **saturation point*** (punkt nasycenia). ▶ **nasycenie, przepełnienie**

ˌsaturated ˈfat noun [C, U] a type of fat found, for example, in butter, fried food and many types of meat, which encourages the harmful development of **cholesterol**: *I was advised to lower my saturated fat intake.* ▶ **tłuszcz nasycony** ➲ look at **polyunsaturated**

Saturday /ˈsætədeɪ; -di/ noun [C,U] (abbr. **Sat.**) the day of the week after Friday ▶ **sobota** ➲ note at **Monday**

Saturn /ˈsætɜːn; Brit. also -tən/ noun [sing.] the planet that is 6th in order from the sun and that has rings around it ▶ **Saturn**

sauce /sɔːs/ noun [C,U] a thick hot or cold liquid that you eat on or with food: *The chicken was served in a delicious sauce.* ◇ *spaghetti with tomato sauce* ▶ **sos** ➲ look at **gravy** ➲ picture on **page A14**

saucepan /ˈsɔːspən; US -pæn/ noun [C] a round metal pot with a handle that is used for cooking things on top of a cooker ▶ **rondel** ➲ picture at **kettle, pan**

saucer /ˈsɔːsə(r)/ noun [C] a small round plate that you put under a cup ▶ **spodek**

sauerkraut /ˈsaʊəkraʊt/ noun [U] cabbage that has been cut into small pieces and pickled ▶ **kapusta kiszona** ➲ look at **coleslaw**

sauna /ˈsɔːnə/ noun [C] **1** a period of time in which you sit or lie in a small room (also called a **sauna**) which has been heated to a very high temperature by burning coal or wood. Some saunas involve the use of steam: *to have/take a sauna* ▶ **sauna 2** the room that you sit in to have a **sauna** ▶ **sauna**

saunter /ˈsɔːntə(r)/ verb [I] to walk without hurrying ▶ **przechadzać się, iść powolnym krokiem**

sausage /ˈsɒsɪdʒ; US ˈsɔːs-/ noun [C,U] a mixture of meat cut into very small pieces and spices, etc. that is made into a long thin shape. Some **sausage** is eaten cold in slices; other types are cooked and then served whole: *liver sausage* pasztetowa/wątrobianka ◇ *We had sausages and chips for lunch.* ▶ **kiełbas(k)a, parówka, serdelek**

ˌsausage ˈroll noun [C] a piece of sausage meat that is covered in pastry ▶ **parówka/kiełbasa zapiekana w cieście, pasztecik**

savage /ˈsævɪdʒ/ adj. very cruel or violent: *He was the victim of a savage attack.* ◇ *The book received savage criticism.* ▶ **bestialski, okrutny, druzgocący**
■ **savage** verb [T]: *The boy died after being savaged by a dog.* ▶ **rzucać się/napadać z furią na kogoś/coś** | **savagely** adv. ▶ **bestialsko, okrutnie** | **savagery** /ˈsævɪdʒri/ noun [U] ▶ **bestialstwo, okrucieństwo**

save¹ /seɪv/ verb **1** [T] **save sb/sth (from sth/from doing sth)** to keep sb/sth safe from death, harm, loss, etc.: *to **save** somebody's **life*** ◇ *to save somebody from drowning* ◇ *We are trying to save the school from closure.* ▶ **ratować, ocalać 2** [I,T] **save (sth) (up) (for sth)** to keep or not spend money so that you can use it later: *I'm saving up for a new bike.* ◇ *Do you manage to save any of your wages?* ▶ **oszczędzać (na coś); odkładać** (*pieniądze*) **na coś** ➲ note at **money 3** [T] to keep sth for future use: *I'll be home late so please save me some dinner.* ◇ *Save that box. It might come in useful.* ◇ *If you get there first, please save me a seat.* ▶ **zachowywać 4** [I,T] **save (sb) (sth) (on) sth** to avoid wasting time, money, etc.: *It will save you twenty minutes on the journey if you take the express train.* ◇ *You can save on petrol by getting a smaller car.* ◇ *This car will save you a lot on petrol.* ▶ **oszczędzać 5** [T] **save (sb) sth/doing sth** to avoid, or make sb able to avoid, doing sth unpleasant or difficult: *If you make an appointment it will save you waiting.* ▶ **zaoszczędzić 6** [T] (in games such as football, **hockey**, etc.) to stop a goal being scored: *to save a penalty* ▶ **bronić 7** [T] to store information in a computer by giving it a special instruction: *Don't forget to save the file before you close it.* ▶ **zachowywać**
IDM keep/save sth for a rainy day → RAINY
save face to prevent yourself losing the respect of other people ▶ **zachować twarz**

save² /seɪv/ noun [C] (in football, etc.) the act of preventing a goal from being scored: *The goalkeeper made a great save* (wspaniale obronił). ▶ **obrona**

saver /ˈseɪvə(r)/ noun [C] **1** a person who saves money for future use: *The rise in interest rates is good news for savers.* ▶ **osoba oszczędzająca 2** [in compounds] a thing that helps you save time, money, or the thing mentioned ▶ **urządzenie itp. oszczędzające czas**

saving /ˈseɪvɪŋ/ noun **1** [C] **a saving (of sth) (on sth)** an amount of time, money, etc. that you do not have to use or spend: *The sale price represents a saving of 25% on the usual price.* ▶ **oszczędność 2** (**savings**) [pl.] money that you have saved for future use: *All our savings are in the bank.* ◇ *I opened a **savings account*** (rachunek oszczędnościowy) *at my local bank.* ▶ **oszczędności**

saviour (US **savior**) /ˈseɪvjə(r)/ noun [C] a person who rescues or saves sb/sth from danger, loss, death, etc. ▶ **zbawca, wybawiciel**

savour (Brit.) (US **savor**) /ˈseɪvə(r)/ verb [T] **1** to enjoy the full taste or flavour of sth, especially by eating or drinking it slowly: *He ate his meal slowly, savouring every mouthful.* ▶ **delektować się** (*smakiem potrawy/napoju*) **SYN relish 2** to enjoy a feeling or an experience thoroughly: *I wanted to savour every moment.* ▶ **rozkoszować się** (*przeżyciem*) **SYN relish**
■ **savour** noun [usually sing.] (formal or literary) a taste or smell, especially a pleasant one: (figurative): *For Emma, life had lost its savour.* ▶ **zapach**; (*i przen.*) **smak**

savoury (US **savory**) /ˈseɪvəri/ adj. (used about food) having a taste that is not sweet ▶ **pikantny** ➲ look at **sweet**

saw¹ past tense of **see**

saw² /sɔː/ noun [C] a tool that is used for cutting wood, etc. A saw has a blade with sharp teeth on it, and a handle at one or both ends: *an electric chainsaw* piła łańcuchowa ▶ **piła** ➲ picture at **tool**
■ **saw** verb [I,T] (pt **sawed**; pp **sawn** /sɔːn/ (US) **sawed**): *to saw through the trunk of a tree* ◇ *He sawed the log up into small pieces.* ▶ **piłować, rżnąć**

sawdust /ˈsɔːdʌst/ noun [U] very small pieces of wood that fall like powder when you are cutting a large piece of wood ▶ **trociny**

sawn past participle of **saw**

saxophone /ˈsæksəfəʊn/ (also informal **sax** /sæks/) noun [C] a metal musical instrument that you play by blowing into it. **Saxophones** are especially used for playing modern music, for example **jazz**: *This track features Dexter Gordon on sax.* ▶ **saksofon**

saxophonist /sæk'sɒfənɪst; US 'sæksəfəʊn-/ noun [C] a person who plays the **saxophone** ▶ **saksofonist(k)a**

say¹ /seɪ/ verb [T] (**says** /sez/, pt, pp **said** /sed/) **1 say sth (to sb); say that ...; say sth (about sb)** to speak or tell sb sth, using words: *'Please come back,' she said.* ◇ *The teacher said we should hand in our essays on Friday.* ◇ *I said goodbye to her at the station.* ◇ *We can ask him, but I'm sure he'll say no.* ◇ *He said to his mother that he would phone back later.* ◇ *They just sat there without saying anything* (w milczeniu). ◇ *'This isn't going to be easy,' she said to herself* (pomyślała). ◇ *'What time is she coming?' 'I don't know – she didn't say.'* ◇ *He* ***is said to*** (mówią, że on jest) *be very rich.* ◇ ***It is said that*** *cats can sense the presence of ghosts.* ◇ *to say goodbye* żegnać się ◇ *to say your prayers* mówić pacierz ▶ **mówić, powiedzieć**

> **Say** czy **tell**? **Say** zwykle używa się, gdy przytaczając czyjąś wypowiedź, albo w mowie zależnej przed **that**: *'I'll catch the 9 o'clock train,' he said.* ◇ *He said that he would catch the 9 o'clock train.* Zwróć uwagę, że używa się przyimka **to**, żeby określić, do kogo się mówi: *He said to me that he would catch the 9 o'clock train.* **Tell** zawsze łączy się z rzeczownikiem lub zaimkiem oznaczającym osobę, z którą się rozmawia: *He told me that he would catch the 9 o'clock train.* Przytaczając polecenia lub porady, używa się **tell**: *I told them to hurry up.* ◇ *She's always telling me what I ought to do.*

2 to express an opinion on sth: *I wouldn't say she's unfriendly – just shy.* ◇ *What is the artist trying to say in this painting?* ◇ *Well,* ***what do you say****? Do you think it's a good idea?* ◇ *It's* ***hard to say*** *what I like about the book.* ◇ *'When will it be finished?'* ***'I couldn't say'****.* ▶ **mówić, wyrażać 3** to imagine or guess sth about a situation; to suppose: *We will need, say, £5 000 for a new car.* ◇ *Say you don't get a place at university, what will you do then?* ◇ *Well, what do you say* (co ty na to)*? Do you think it's a good idea?* ▶ **przypuśćmy/powiedzmy (że) 4 say sth (to sb)** to show a feeling, a situation, etc. without using words: *His angry look said everything about the way he felt.* ▶ **mówić 5** to give written information: *What time does it say on that clock?* ◇ *The map says the hotel is just past the railway bridge.* ◇ *The sign clearly says 'No dogs'.* ▶ **pokazywać, być napisanym**

IDM **easier said than done** → EASY

go without saying to be clear, so that you do not need to say it: *It goes without saying that the children will be well looked after at all times.* ▶ **to się rozumie (samo przez się)**

have a lot, nothing, etc. to say for yourself to have a lot, nothing, etc. to say in a particular situation: *Late again! What have you got to say for yourself?* ▶ **mieć dużo/nie mieć nic do powiedzenia** (*np. na swoją obronę*)

I dare say → DARE¹

I must say (informal) (used to emphasize your opinion): *I must say, I didn't believe him at first.* ▶ **muszę stwierdzić**

I wouldn't say no (informal) (used to say that you would like sth): *'Coffee?' 'I wouldn't say no.'* ▶ **chętnie**

let's say for example: *You could work two mornings a week, let's say Tuesday and Friday.* ▶ **powiedzmy**

Say when (informal) (used to tell sb to say when you have poured enough drink in their glass or put enough food on their plate) ▶ **powiedz, ile** (*nalać, nałożyć na talerz*)

that is to say... which means ...: *We're leaving on Friday, that's to say in a week's time.* ▶ **czyli**

to say the least (used to say that sth is in fact much worse, more serious, etc. than you are saying): *Adam's going to be annoyed, to say the least, when he sees his car.* ▶ **delikatnie/skromnie mówiąc**

say² /seɪ/ noun [sing., U] **(a) say (in sth)** the authority or right to decide sth: *I'd like to have some say in the arrangements for the party.* ▶ **głos** (*w decyzji*); (*mieć*) **coś do powiedzenia**

IDM **have your say** to express your opinion: *Thank you for your comments. Now let somebody else have their say.* ▶ **wypowiadać swoje zdanie/opinię**

saying /'seɪɪŋ/ noun [C] a well-known phrase that gives advice about sth or says sth that many people believe is true: *'Love is blind' is an old saying.* ▶ **powiedzenie, przysłowie** ➲ look at **proverb**

scab /skæb/ noun [C,U] a mass of dried blood that forms over a part of the body where the skin has been cut or broken ▶ **strup** ➲ look at **scar**

scaffold /'skæfəʊld/ noun [C] a platform on which criminals were killed in past times by hanging ▶ **szafot**

scaffolding /'skæfəldɪŋ/ noun [U] long metal poles and wooden boards that form a structure which is put next to a building so that people who are building, painting, etc. can stand and work on it ▶ **rusztowanie**

scald /skɔːld/ verb [T] to burn sb/sth with very hot liquid: *I scalded my arm badly when I was cooking.* ▶ **(o)parzyć** ■ **scald** noun [C] ▶ **oparzenie** | **scalding** adj.: *scalding hot water* ▶ **wrzący**

scale¹ /skeɪl/ noun **1** [C,U] the size of sth, especially when compared to other things: *We shall be making the product* ***on a large scale*** *next year.* ◇ *At this stage it is impossible to estimate* ***the full scale of*** *the disaster.* ▶ **skala, rozmiar 2** [C] a series of numbers, amounts, etc. that are used for measuring or fixing the level of sth: *The earthquake measured 6.5 on the Richter scale.* ◇ *the new pay scale for nurses* ▶ **skala; tabela 3** [C] a series of marks on a tool or piece of equipment that you use for measuring sth: *The ruler has one scale in centimetres and one scale in inches.* ▶ **podziałka, skala 4** [C] the relationship between the actual size of sth and its size on a map or plan: *The map has a scale* (jest w skali) *of one centimetre to the kilometre.* ◇ *The plan of the building is not drawn* ***to scale*** (nie jest narysowany według skali). ◇ *a scale of 1:50 000* ◇ *We need a map with a larger scale.* ◇ *a scale model* model (w skali) ▶ **skala 5** (**scales**) [pl.] a piece of equipment that is used for weighing sb/sth: *I weighed it on the kitchen scales.* ▶ **waga 6** [C] a series of musical notes which go up or down in a fixed order. People play or sing scales to improve their technical ability: *the scale of C major* ▶ **gama 7** [C] one of the small flat pieces of hard material that cover the body of fish and some animals: *the scales of a snake* ▶ **łuska**

scale² /skeɪl/ verb [T] to climb to the top of sth very high and steep ▶ **wspinać się/wchodzić na coś**

PHR V **scale sth up/down** to increase/decrease the size, number, importance, etc. of sth: *Police have scaled up their search for the missing boy.* ▶ **(proporcjonalnie) zwiększać/zmniejszać**

scallion (US) = SPRING ONION

scallop /'skɒləp; US 'skæləp/ noun [C] a **shellfish** that you can eat, with two flat round shells that fit together ▶ **małż jadalny**

scalp /skælp/ noun [C] the skin on the top of your head that is under your hair ▶ **skóra głowy, skalp**

scalpel /'skælpəl/ noun [C] a small knife that is used by **surgeons** when they are doing operations ▶ **skalpel**

scam /skæm/ noun [C] (informal) a dishonest scheme ▶ **oszustwo**

scamper /'skæmpə(r)/ verb [I] (used especially about a child or small animal) to run quickly ▶ **pędzić, pierzchnąć**

scampi /'skæmpi/ noun [pl.] large prawns that have been fried in a mixture of flour and milk (batter) ▶ **panierowane krewetki**

S

scan /skæn/ verb [T] (**scanning**; **scanned**) **1** to look at or read every part of sth quickly until you find what you are looking for: *Vic scanned the list until he found his own name.* ▶ **badać** (*wzrokiem*), **przebiegać wzrokiem po czymś** **2** to pass light over a picture or document using a **scanner** in order to copy it and put it in the memory of a computer ▶ **skanować** **3** (used about a machine) to examine what is inside sb's body or inside an object such as a suitcase: *Machines scan all the luggage for bombs and guns.* ▶ **prześwietlać**

PHR V **scan sth into sth**; **scan sth in** to pass light over a picture or document using a **scanner** in order to copy it and put it in the memory of a computer: *Text and pictures can be scanned into the computer.* ▶ **wskanować coś do czegoś**

■ **scan** noun [C]: *The scan showed the baby was in the normal position.* ▶ **badanie ultrasonograficzne**, **prześwietlenie**

scandal /ˈskændl/ noun **1** [C,U] an action, a situation or behaviour that shocks people; the public feeling that is caused by such behaviour: *The chairman resigned after being involved in a financial scandal.* ◇ *There was no suggestion of scandal in his private life.* ◇ *The poor state of school buildings is a real scandal.* ▶ **skandal** **2** [U] talk about sth bad or wrong that sb has or may have done: *to spread scandal* (rozgłaszać plotki) *about somebody* ▶ **plotki**, **oszczerstwo**

scandalize (also -ise) /ˈskændəlaɪz/ verb [T] to cause sb to feel shocked by doing sth that they think is bad or wrong ▶ **gorszyć (kogoś)**, **oburzać**

scandalous /ˈskændələs/ adj. very shocking or wrong: *It is scandalous that so much money is wasted.* ▶ **skandaliczny**, **oburzający**

Scandinavia /ˌskændɪˈneɪviə/ noun [sing.] the group of countries in northern Europe that consists of Denmark, Norway and Sweden. Sometimes Finland and Iceland are also said to be part of Scandinavia. ▶ **Skandynawia**

■ **Scandinavian** adj. ▶ **skandynawski**

scanner /ˈskænə(r)/ noun [C] an electronic machine that can look at, record or send images or electronic information: *The scanner can detect cancer at an early stage.* ◇ *I used the scanner to send the document by email.* ▶ **ultrasonograf**, **skaner**

scant /skænt/ adj. [only before a noun] not very much; not as much as necessary: *They paid scant attention* (prawie nie zwracali uwagi) *to my advice.* ▶ **skąpy**, **niewystarczający**

scanty /ˈskænti/ adj. (**scantier**; **scantiest**) too small in size or amount: *We didn't learn much from the scanty information they gave us.* ▶ **skąpy**, **niewystarczający**

■ **scantily** adv.: *I realized I was too scantily dressed for the cold weather.* ▶ **kuso**, **niewystarczająco**

scapegoat /ˈskeɪpɡəʊt/ noun [C] a person who is punished for things that are not their fault: *When Alison was sacked she felt she had been* ***made a scapegoat*** *for all of the company's problems.* ▶ **kozioł ofiarny**

scapula = SHOULDER BLADE

scar /skɑː(r)/ noun [C] a mark on the skin that is caused by a cut that skin has grown over: *The operation didn't leave a very big scar.* ▶ **blizna**, **szrama**; **ślad** ➲ look at **scab**

■ **scar** verb [I,T] (**scarring**; **scarred**): *William's face was* ***scarred for life*** *in the accident.* ▶ **zostawiać bliznę**, **pokiereszować**

scarce /skeəs/ adj. not existing in large quantities; hard to find: *Food for birds and animals is scarce in the winter.* Zimą brakuje pożywienia zwierzętom i ptakom. ▶ **niewystarczający** OPP **plentiful**

■ **scarcity** /ˈskeəsəti/ noun [C,U] (pl. **scarcities**): *(a) scarcity of food/jobs/resources* ▶ **brak**, **niedostatek**

scarcely /ˈskeəsli/ adv. **1** only just; almost not: *She's not a friend of mine. I scarcely know her.* ◇ *I had scarcely sat down/Scarcely had I sat down* (ledwie usiadłem), *when the phone rang.* ◇ *There was scarcely a car in sight.* Prawie nie było samochodów w zasięgu wzroku. ▶ **zaledwie**, **prawie (wcale) nie** ➲ look at **hardly** **2** (used to suggest that sth is not reasonable or likely): *You can scarcely expect* (nie możesz oczekiwać) *me to believe that after all you said before.* ▶ **zaledwie**, **prawie wcale**

scare¹ /skeə(r)/ verb **1** [T] to make a person or an animal frightened: *The sudden noise scared us all.* ◇ *It scares me to think what might happen.* ▶ **przestraszyć** **2** [I] to become frightened: *I don't scare easily, but when I saw the gun I was terrified.* ▶ **przestraszyć się**

PHR V **scare sb/sth away/off** to make a person or an animal leave or stay away by frightening them or it: *Don't make any noise or you'll scare the birds away.* ◇ *Rising prices are scaring customers off.* ▶ **płoszyć/odstraszać kogoś/coś**

scare² /skeə(r)/ noun [C] **1** a situation where many people are afraid or worried about sth: *Last night there was a* ***bomb scare*** (alarm o podłożonej bombie) *in the city centre.* ▶ **panika** **2** a feeling of being frightened: *It wasn't a serious heart attack but it gave him a scare* (przestraszył). ▶ **strach**

scarecrow /ˈskeəkrəʊ/ noun [C] a very simple model of a person that is put in a field in order to frighten away the birds ▶ **strach na wróble**

scared /skeəd/ adj. **scared (of sb/sth)**; **scared (of doing sth/to do sth)** frightened: *She's scared of walking home alone.* ◇ *Everyone was too scared to move.* ◇ *Are you scared of* (czy boisz się) *the dark?* ▶ **przestraszony**

scaremonger /ˈskeəmʌŋɡə(r)/ noun [C] a person who spreads stories deliberately to make people frightened or nervous ▶ **panika-rz/ra**

■ **scaremongering** noun [U]: *journalists accused of scaremongering* ▶ **sianie paniki**

scarf /skɑːf/ noun [C] (pl. **scarves** /skɑːvz/ or **scarfs** /skɑːfs/) **1** a long thin piece of cloth, usually made of wool, that you wear around your neck to keep warm ▶ **szalik** **2** a square piece of cloth that women wear around their neck or over their head or shoulders to keep warm or for decoration ▶ **chust(k)a**, **apaszka**

scarlet /ˈskɑːlət/ adj. of a bright red colour ▶ **szkarłatny** ➲ look at **crimson**, **maroon**

■ **scarlet** noun [U] ▶ **szkarłat**

scary /ˈskeəri/ adj. (**scarier**; **scariest**) (informal) frightening: *a scary ghost story* ◇ *It was a bit scary driving in the mountains at night.* ▶ **straszny**, **przerażający**

scathing /ˈskeɪðɪŋ/ adj. **scathing (about sb/sth)** expressing a very strong negative opinion about sb/sth; very critical: *a scathing attack on the new leader* ◇ *scathing criticism* ▶ **ostry**, **zjadliwy**

scatter /ˈskætə(r)/ verb **1** [T] to drop or throw things in different directions over a wide area: *The wind scattered the papers all over the room.* ▶ **rozrzucać**, **rozsypywać** **2** [I] (used about a group of people or animals) to move away quickly in different directions ▶ **rozbiegać się**, **rozpraszać się**

scatterbrain /ˈskætəbreɪn/ noun [C] (informal) a person who is always losing or forgetting things and cannot think in an organized way ▶ **roztrzepaniec**

■ **scatterbrained** adj. ▶ **roztrzepany**

scattered /ˈskætəd/ adj. spread over a large area or happening several times during a period of time: *There will be sunny intervals with scattered showers* (przejaśnienia i przelotne opady) *today.* ▶ **rozproszony**, **rozrzucony**

scatty /ˈskæti/ adj. (**scattier**; **scattiest**) (Brit., informal) tending to forget things and behave in a slightly silly way ▶ **roztrzepany**

scavenge /ˈskævɪndʒ/ verb [I,T] to look for food, etc. among waste and rubbish ▶ **wygrzebywać ze śmieci** (*np. żywność*)

■ **scavenger** noun [C]: *Scavengers steal the food that the lion has killed.* ▶ **żebra-k/czka**; **padlinożerca**

SCE /ˌes siː ˈiː/ abbr. **Scottish Certificate of Education**. Students in Scotland take the **SCE** at Standard grade at the age of about 16 and at Higher grade at about 17. ▶ **egzamin szkolny zdawany dwa lata przed egzaminem A level**

scenario /səˈnɑːriəʊ; US -ˈnær-/ noun [C] (pl. **scenarios**) **1** one way that things may happen in the future: *A likely scenario is that the company will get rid of some staff.* ▶ **scenariusz** **2** a description of what happens in a play or film ▶ **scenariusz**

scene /siːn/ noun **1** [C] the place where sth happened: *the scene of a crime/an accident* ◇ *An ambulance was* ***on the scene*** *in minutes.* ▶ **miejsce** (*np. zbrodni*) **2** [C] one part of a book, play, film, etc. in which the events happen in one place: *The first scene of 'Hamlet' takes place on the castle walls.* ▶ **scena** **3** (**the scene**) [sing.] the way of life or the present situation in a particular area of activity: *The political scene in that part of the world is very confused.* ◇ *the fashion scene* świat mody ▶ **scena**, **arena** **4** [C,U] what you see around you in a particular place: *Her new job was no better, but at least it would be* ***a change of scene.*** ▶ **scena**, **otoczenie** **5** [C] an occasion when sb expresses great anger or another strong emotion in public: *There was quite a scene when she refused to pay the bill.* ▶ **scena**, **awantura**

IDM **set the scene (for sth)** **1** to create a situation in which sth can easily happen or develop: *His arrival set the scene for another argument.* ▶ **doprowadzać (do czegoś)** **2** to give sb the information and details they need in order to understand what comes next: *The first part of the programme was just setting the scene.* ▶ (*przen.*) **przygotowywać grunt (pod coś)**

scenery /ˈsiːnəri/ noun [U] **1** the natural beauty that you see around you in the country: *The scenery is superb in the mountains.* ▶ **krajobraz**, **sceneria**

> **scenery**
> Jeśli pewien teren jest malowniczo położony i miły dla oka, stosuje się rzeczownik **scenery**. Mówiąc o naturalnych cechach pewnego obszaru, używa się słowa **landscape**: *Trees and hedges are a typical feature of the British landscape.* ➲ note at **country**, **nature**

2 the furniture, painted cloth, boards, etc. that are used on the stage in a theatre: *The scenery is changed during the interval.* ▶ **dekoracje**

scenic /ˈsiːnɪk/ adj. having beautiful **scenery** ▶ **malowniczy**

scent /sent/ noun **1** [C,U] a pleasant smell: *This flower has no scent.* ▶ **zapach**, **aromat** ➲ note at **smell²** **2** [C,U] the smell that an animal leaves behind and that some other animals can follow ▶ **trop** (*zwierzęcia*) **3** [U] (Brit.) = PERFUME (1) **4** [sing.] the feeling that sth is going to happen: *The scent of victory was in the air.* ▶ **powiew**

■ **scent** verb [T] **1** to find sth by using the sense of smell: *The dog scented a rabbit and ran off.* ▶ **wietrzyć**, **węszyć** **2** to begin to feel that sth exists or is about to happen ▶ **wyczuwać** **3** **scent sth (with sth)** [usually passive] to give sth a particular, pleasant smell: *Roses scented the night air.* ▶ **perfumować**, **nadawać zapach** | **scented** adj. ▶ **pachnący**, **perfumowany**

sceptic (US **skeptic**) /ˈskeptɪk/ noun [C] a person who doubts that sth is true, right, etc. ▶ **scepty-k/czka**

■ **sceptical** (US **skeptical**) /-kl/ adj. **sceptical (of/about sth)**: *Many doctors are sceptical about the value of alternative medicine.* ▶ **sceptyczny**, **sceptycznie nastawiony**

scepticism (US **skepticism**) /ˈskeptɪsɪzəm/ noun [U] a general feeling of doubt about sth; a feeling that you are not likely to believe sth ▶ **sceptycyzm**

sceptre /ˈseptə(r)/ noun [C] a decorated **rod** carried by a king or queen at ceremonies as a symbol of their power ▶ **berło**

schedule¹ /ˈʃedjuːl; US ˈskedʒ-/ noun **1** [C,U] a plan of things that will happen or of work that must be done: *Max has a busy schedule for the next few days.* ◇ *to be ahead of/behind schedule* (przed czasem/po czasie) ◇ *to be on schedule* być zgodnie z harmonogramem ▶ **harmonogram**, **plan** **2** (US) = TIMETABLE

schedule² /ˈʃedjuːl; US ˈskedʒ-/ verb [T] **schedule sth (for sth)** to arrange for sth to happen or be done at a particular time: *We've scheduled the meeting for Monday morning.* ◇ *Is it a scheduled flight* (lot planowy/według rozkładu)*?* ◇ *The train was scheduled to arrive* (według rozkładu powinien przyjechać) *at 10.07.* ▶ **planować**, **sporządzać rozkład**

schematic /skiːˈmætɪk/ adj. **1** in the form of a diagram that shows the main features or relationships but not the details: *a schematic diagram* ▶ **schematyczny** **2** according to a fixed plan or pattern: *The play has a very schematic plot.* ▶ **schematyczny**

■ **schematically** /-kli/ adv. ▶ **schematycznie**

scheme¹ /skiːm/ noun [C] **1** **a scheme (to do sth/for doing sth)** an official plan or system for doing or organizing sth: *a new scheme to provide houses in the area* ◇ *a local scheme for recycling newspapers* ▶ **plan**, **program** **2** a clever plan to do sth: *He's thought of a new scheme for making money fast.* ▶ **projekt**, **plan** ➲ look at **colour scheme**

scheme² /skiːm/ verb [I,T] to make a secret or dishonest plan: *She felt that everyone was scheming to get rid of her.* ▶ **knuć**, **spiskować**

schism /ˈskɪzəm; ˈsɪzəm/ noun [C, U] (formal) strong disagreement within an organization, especially a religious one, that makes its members divide into separate groups: *the threat of a schism within the Church* ▶ **schizma**

schizophrenia /ˌskɪtsəˈfriːniə/ noun [U] a serious mental illness in which a person confuses the real world and the world of the imagination and often behaves in strange and unexpected ways ▶ **schizofrenia**

■ **schizophrenic** /ˌskɪtsəˈfrenɪk/ adj., noun [C] ▶ **schizofreniczny**; **schizofreni-k/czka**

schmaltz /ʃmɔːlts/ noun [U] (informal) the quality of being too **sentimental** ▶ **ckliwość** ⓘ Wyraża dezaprobatę.

■ **schmaltzy** adj. (**schmaltzier**; **schmaltziest**) ▶ **ckliwy**

scholar /ˈskɒlə(r)/ noun [C] **1** a person who studies and has a lot of knowledge about a particular subject: *a leading Shakespeare scholar* (szekspirolog) ▶ **uczony**; **ekspert** **2** a person who has passed an exam or won a competition and has been given a **scholarship** (1) to help pay for their studies: *He has come here as a British Council scholar.* ▶ **stypendyst(k)a** ➲ look at **student**

scholarly /ˈskɒləli/ adj. **1** (used about a person) spending a lot of time studying and having a lot of knowledge about an academic subject ▶ **uczony** ➲ look at **studious** **2** connected with academic study: *a scholarly journal* ▶ **naukowy** SYN **academic**

scholarship /ˈskɒləʃɪp/ noun **1** [C] an amount of money that is given to a person who has passed an exam or won a competition, in order to help pay for their studies: *to win a scholarship to Yale* ▶ **stypendium (naukowe)**

2 [U] serious study of an academic subject ▶ **nauka**, **uczoność**

school /sku:l/ noun 1 [C] the place where children go to be educated: *Where did you* **go to school**? ◇ *They're building a new school in our area.* ◇ *Do you have to wear a school uniform?* ◇ *Was your school co-educational or single-sex?* ◇ *a summer school* kurs wakacyjny ▶ **szkoła** 2 [U] the time you spend at a school; the process of being educated in a school: *Their children are still* **at school**. ◇ *Children* **start school** *at 5 years old in Britain and can* **leave school** *at 16.* ◇ *School starts at 9 o'clock and finishes at about 3.30.* ◇ *After school we usually have homework to do.* ▶ **szkoła**, **lekcje**

Mówiąc o szkole jako miejscu nauki dla uczniów lub pracy dla nauczycieli, używa się **school** bez **the**: *Where do your children go to school?* ◇ *I enjoyed being at school.* ◇ *Do you walk to school?* Natomiast **the school** używa się w każdej innej sytuacji, np. gdy rodzice idą do szkoły na zebranie: *I have to go to the school on Thursday to talk to John's teacher.* Kiedy dodaje się więcej informacji o szkole, wtedy należy użyć **a** lub **the**: *Pat goes to the local school.* ◇ *She teaches at a special school for children with learning difficulties.*

3 [sing., with sing. or pl. verb] all the students and teachers in a school: *The whole school is/are going on a trip tomorrow.* ▶ **szkoła** 4 [in compounds] connected with school: *children* **of school age** (w wieku szkolnym) ◇ *The bus was full of* **schoolchildren** (uczniów). ◇ *It is getting increasingly difficult for* **school-leavers** (absolwentów) *to find jobs.* ◇ **Schoolteachers** (nauczyciele) *have been awarded a 2% pay rise.* ◇ *I don't have many good memories of my* **schooldays** (z lat szkolnych). 5 [C] a place where you go to learn a particular subject: *a language/driving/drama/business school* ▶ **szkoła** 6 [C] (US) a college or university: *famous schools like Yale and Harvard* ▶ **szkoła wyższa**, **(wyższa) uczelnia** 7 [C] a department of a university that teaches a particular subject: *the school of geography at Leeds University* ▶ **instytut**, **wydział** 8 [C] a group of writers, artists, etc. who have the same ideas or style: *the Flemish school of painting* ▶ **szkoła** 9 [C] a large group of fish, etc., swimming together: *a school of dolphins* ▶ **ławica**, **stado**

IDM **a school of thought** the ideas or opinions that one group of people share: *There are various schools of thought on this matter.* ▶ **szkoła naukowa**

schools

Children go to **primary** and **secondary** schools. These can be **private** or **state** schools, and sometimes they are also **boarding** schools. A school for very young children is a **nursery school**.

Schools have **classrooms** and every **pupil**/**student** is a member of a **class**. During **lessons** pupils study **subjects**, and after school they can do **extra-curricular** activities, such as sport or drama. Some **teachers** are **strict**, or give pupils a lot of **homework**. It is important to get good **marks**, especially in **exams** at the end of **term**. Students who **bully** their **classmates** or **skip school** usually **get into trouble** with the **head teacher**.

schooling /ˈsku:lɪŋ/ noun [U] the time that you spend at school; your education ▶ **nauka**

science /ˈsaɪəns/ noun 1 [U] the study of and knowledge about the physical world and natural laws: *Modern science has discovered a lot about the origin of life.* ◇ *Fewer young people are studying science at university.* ◇ *a science teacher* nauczyciel przedmiotów ścisłych ▶ **nauki przyrodnicze/ścisłe** 2 [C] one of the subjects into which science can be divided ▶ **nauka ścisła**, **przedmiot ścisły** ➲ look at **art**

Chemistry, **physics** and **biology** are all sciences. **Scientists** do **research** and **experiments** in a **laboratory** to see what happens and to try to discover new information. The study of people and society is called **social science**.

ˌscience ˈfiction (also informal sci-fi) (abbr. **SF**) noun [U] books, films, etc. about events that take place in the future, often involving travel in space ▶ **fantastyka naukowa**

scientific /ˌsaɪənˈtɪfɪk/ adj. 1 connected with or involving science: *We need more funding for scientific research.* ◇ *scientific instruments* ▶ **naukowy** 2 (used about a way of thinking or of doing sth) careful and logical: *a scientific study of the way people use language* ▶ **naukowy**
■ **scientifically** /-kli/ adv.: *Sorting out the files won't take long if we do it scientifically.* ▶ **naukowo**

scientist /ˈsaɪəntɪst/ noun [C] a person who studies or teaches science, especially biology, chemistry or physics ▶ **naukowiec** (*specjalista od nauk ścisłych*), **uczony**

scintillating /ˈsɪntɪleɪtɪŋ/ adj. very clever, amusing and interesting: *The lead actor gave a scintillating performance.* ▶ **błystkotliwy**

scissors /ˈsɪzəz/ noun [pl.] a tool for cutting paper or cloth, which has two flat sharp pieces of metal with handles that are joined together in the middle ▶ **nożyce**, **nożyczki** ⓘ **Scissors** to rzeczownik występujący tylko w lm: *These scissors are blunt.* Nie można powiedzieć **a scissors**. Używa się zamiast tego **a pair**: *I need a new pair of scissors.*

scoff /skɒf/ verb 1 [I] **scoff (at sb/sth)** to speak about sb/sth in a way that shows you think that he/she/it is stupid or ridiculous ▶ **szydzić**, **kpić** 2 [T] (Brit., informal) to eat a lot of sth quickly ▶ **wsuwać**

scold /skəʊld/ verb [I,T] **scold sb (for sth/for doing sth)** to speak angrily to sb because they have done sth bad or wrong ▶ **skrzyczeć**, **skarcić** ⓘ Częściej używa się **tell off**.

scone /skɒn; skəʊn/ noun [C] a small, simple cake, usually eaten with butter on ▶ **rodzaj bułeczki**

scoop¹ /sku:p/ noun [C] 1 a tool like a spoon used for picking up flour, grain, etc., or for serving food like ice cream ▶ **szufelka**; **łyżka do lodów** 2 the amount that one **scoop** contains: *a scoop of* (kulka) *ice cream* ▶ **łyżka czegoś**, **szufelka czegoś** 3 an exciting piece of news that is reported by one newspaper, TV or radio station before it is reported anywhere else ▶ **sensacyjna wiadomość** (*podana wcześniej niż w konkurencyjnych gazetach*)

scoop² /sku:p/ verb [T] 1 **scoop sth (out/up)** to make a hole in sth or to take sth out by using a **scoop** or sth similar: *Scoop out the middle of the pineapple.* ▶ **wydłubywać**, **wygrzebywać**, **wydrążać** 2 **scoop sb/sth (up)** to move or lift sb/sth using a continuous action: *He scooped up the child and ran.* ▶ **nabierać**, **zagarniać**, **podnosić** 3 to get a story before all other newspapers, TV stations, etc. ▶ **wyprzedzać** (*inne dzienniki w podaniu jakiejś wiadomości*) 4 to win a big or important prize: *The film has scooped all the awards this year.* ▶ **zgarniać**

scooter /ˈsku:tə(r)/ noun [C] 1 a light motorbike with a small engine ▶ **skuter** ➲ picture on **page A7** 2 a child's toy with two wheels that you stand on and move by pushing one foot against the ground ▶ **hulajnoga**

scope /skəʊp/ noun 1 [U] **scope (for sth/to do sth)** the chance or opportunity to do sth: *The job offers plenty of scope for creativity.* ▶ **możliwość**, **sposobność** 2 [sing.] the variety of subjects that are being discussed or considered: *The government was unwilling to extend the scope of the inquiry.* ◇ *It is not within the scope of this* *book to discuss these matters in detail.* Szczegółowe omówienie tych spraw wykracza poza zakres tej książki. ▶ **zakres**

scorch /skɔːtʃ/ verb [T] to burn sth so that its colour changes but it is not destroyed: *I scorched my blouse when I was ironing it.* ◇ *the scorched landscape of the Arizona desert* spalona słońcem pustynia Arizony ▶ **przypalać, przypiekać**

scorching /ˈskɔːtʃɪŋ/ adj. very hot: *It was absolutely scorching on Tuesday.* ▶ **skwarny**

score¹ /skɔː(r)/ noun **1** [C] the number of points, goals, etc. that sb/sth gets in a game, a competition, an exam, etc.: *What was the final score?* ◇ *The score is 3-2 to Liverpool.* ◇ *The top score in the test was 80%.* ▶ **wynik 2** [C] the written form of a piece of music: *an orchestral score* ▶ **nuty, partytura 3** (**scores**) [pl.] very many: *Scores of people have written to offer their support.* ▶ **mnóstwo**
IDM **on that score** as far as that is concerned: *Lan will be well looked after. Don't worry on that score.* ▶ **pod tym względem**

score² /skɔː(r)/ verb [I,T] to get points, goals, etc. in a game, a competition, an exam, etc.: *The team still hadn't scored by half-time.* ◇ *Louise scored the highest marks in the exam.* ▶ **zdobywać punkty, osiągać sukces, strzelać bramkę**

scoreboard /ˈskɔːbɔːd/ noun [C] a large board that shows the score during a game, competition, etc. ▶ **tablica wyników**

scorn¹ /skɔːn/ noun [U] **scorn (for sb/sth)** the strong feeling that you have when you do not respect sb/sth ▶ **pogarda**

scorn² /skɔːn/ verb [T] **1** to feel or show a complete lack of respect for sb/sth: *The President scorned his critics.* ▶ **gardzić 2** to refuse to accept help or advice, especially because you are too proud: *The old lady scorned all offers of help.* ▶ **wzgardzić**
■ **scornful** /ˈskɔːnfl/ adj.: *a scornful look/smile/remark* ▶ **pogardliwy** | **scornfully** /-fəli/ adv. ▶ **pogardliwie**

Scorpio /ˈskɔːpiəʊ/ noun [C,U] (pl. **Scorpios**) the 8th sign of the **zodiac**, the **Scorpion**; a person born under this sign: *I'm a Scorpio.* ▶ **Skorpion; zodiakalny Skorpion**

scorpion /ˈskɔːpiən/ noun [C] a creature which looks like a large insect and lives in hot countries. A **scorpion** has a long curved tail with a poisonous sting in it. ▶ **skorpion**

Scot /skɒt/ noun [C] a person who comes from Scotland ▶ **Szkot/ka**

Scotch /skɒtʃ/ noun [U,C] a type of **whisky** that is made in Scotland; a glass of this ▶ **szkocka whisky; whisky** ➲ note at **Scottish**

Scots /skɒts/ adj. of or connected with people from Scotland ▶ **szkocki** ➲ note at **Scottish**

Scottish /ˈskɒtɪʃ/ adj. of or connected with Scotland, its people, culture, etc. ▶ **szkocki**

> **Scots** używa się tylko w odniesieniu do osób: *a Scots piper*. **Scottish** używa się zarówno w odniesieniu do osób, jak i rzeczy pochodzących ze Szkocji: *Scottish law/dancing/lochs* ◇ *She speaks with a Scottish accent.* ◇ *The Scottish Highlands.* **Scotch** używa się tylko w odniesieniu do **whisky** i niektórych szkockich potraw; nigdy w odniesieniu do osób.

scoundrel /ˈskaʊndrəl/ noun [C] (old-fashioned) a man who behaves very badly towards other people, especially by being dishonest ▶ **łotr**

scour /ˈskaʊə(r)/ verb [T] **1** to search a place very carefully because you are looking for sb/sth ▶ **przeszukiwać, przetrząsać 2** to clean sth by rubbing it hard with sth rough: *to scour a dirty pan* ▶ **szorować**

scourge /skɜːdʒ/ noun [C] a person or thing that causes a lot of trouble or suffering: *Raul was the scourge of the United defence.* ▶ **plaga, dopust, utrapienie**

scout /skaʊt/ noun [C] **1** (**Scout**) a member of the **Scouts**. Scouts do sport, learn useful skills, go camping, etc. ▶ **skaut 2** a soldier who is sent on in front of the rest of the group to find out where the enemy is or which is the best route to take ▶ **zwiadowca** ➲ look at **Guide**

scowl /skaʊl/ noun [C] a look on your face that shows you are angry or in a bad mood ▶ **gniewne spojrzenie** ➲ look at **frown**
■ **scowl** verb [I] ▶ **patrzeć wilkiem**

scrabble /ˈskræbl/ verb [I] to move your fingers or feet around quickly, trying to find sth or get hold of sth: *She scrabbled about in her purse for some coins.* ▶ **grzebać**

scraggly /ˈskrægli/ adj. (US, informal) thin and growing in a way that is not even: *a scraggly beard* ▶ **postrzępiony**

scramble /ˈskræmbl/ verb [I] **1** to climb quickly up or over sth using your hands to help you; to move somewhere quickly: *He scrambled up the hill and over the wall.* ◇ *He* ***scrambled to his feet*** (zerwał się na nogi) *and ran off into the trees.* ◇ *The children scrambled into the car.* ▶ **wdrapywać się, przedzierać się** (*w pośpiechu*) **2 scramble (for sth/to do sth)** to fight or move quickly to get sth which a lot of people want: *People stood up and began scrambling for the exits.* ◇ *Everyone was scrambling to get the best bargains.* ▶ **walczyć o coś 3** to move or do something quickly because you are in a hurry: *She scrambled into some clean clothes.* Włożyła na siebie w pośpiechu czyste ubranie. ▶ **robić coś w pośpiechu**
■ **scramble** noun [sing.] ▶ **szarpanina**

ˌscrambled ˈegg noun [U,C] eggs mixed together with milk and then cooked in a pan ▶ **jajecznica**

scrap¹ /skræp/ noun **1** [C] a small piece of sth: *a scrap of paper/cloth* ◇ *scraps of food* ◇ *There is not a scrap of truth* (nie ma odrobiny prawdy) *in what she told me.* ▶ **kawałek, resztka; krzta** SYN **bit 2** [U] something that you do not want any more but that is made of material that can be used again: *The car was sold* ***for scrap.*** ◇ *scrap paper* makulatura ▶ **złom, odpady 3** [C] (informal) a short fight or argument ▶ **utarczka**

scrap² /skræp/ verb [T] (**scrapping**; **scrapped**) to get rid of sth that you do not want any more: *I think we should scrap that idea.* ▶ **wyrzucać**

scrapbook /ˈskræpbʊk/ noun [C] a large book with empty pages that you can stick pictures, newspaper articles, etc. in ▶ **album** (*np. na wycinki prasowe*)

scrape¹ /skreɪp/ verb **1** [T] **scrape sth (down/out/off)** to remove sth from a surface by moving a sharp edge across it firmly: *Scrape all the mud off your boots before you come in.* ◇ *to scrape a pan clean* wyszorować patelnię do czysta ▶ **zeskrobywać 2** [T] **scrape sth (against/along/on sth)** to damage or hurt sth by rubbing it against sth rough or hard: *Mark fell and scraped his knee.* ◇ *Sunita scraped the car against the wall.* ▶ **zadrapać, zarysowywać 3** [I,T] **scrape (sth) against/along/on sth** to rub (sth) against sth and make a sharp unpleasant noise: *The branches scraped against the window.* ▶ **zgrzytać; chrobotać, szurać 4** [T] to manage to get or win sth with difficulty: *I just scraped a pass in the maths exam.* ▶ **zrobić coś z trudem/wysiłkiem**
PHR V **scrape by** to manage to live on the money you have, but with difficulty: *We can just scrape by on my salary.* ▶ **ledwo wiązać koniec z końcem**
scrape through (sth) to succeed in doing sth with difficulty: *to scrape through an exam* ▶ **przebrnąć (przez coś)**

scrape sth together/up to get or collect sth together with difficulty ▶ (*przen.*) **wyskrobać**, **skrobać**

scrape² /skreɪp/ noun [C] **1** the action or unpleasant sound of one thing rubbing hard against another ▶ **zgrzyt** **2** damage or an injury caused by rubbing against sth rough: *I got a nasty scrape on my knee.* ▶ **zadrapanie** **3** (informal) a difficult situation that was caused by your own stupid behaviour ▶ **tarapaty**

'scrap heap noun [C] a large pile of objects, especially metal, that are no longer wanted ▶ **złomowisko**

IDM **on the scrap heap** not wanted any more: *Many of the unemployed feel that they are on the scrap heap.* ▶ **niepotrzebny**

scrappy /'skræpi/ adj. (**scrappier**; **scrappiest**) not organized or tidy and so not pleasant to see: *a scrappy essay/ football match* ▶ **fragmentaryczny**, **niejednolity**

scratch¹ /skrætʃ/ verb **1** [I,T] **scratch (at sth)** to rub your skin with your nails: *Don't scratch at your insect bites or they'll get worse.* ◇ *Could you scratch my back for me?* ◇ *She sat and scratched her head as she thought about the problem.* ▶ **drapać (się)** **2** [I,T] to make a mark on a surface or a slight cut on sb's skin with sth sharp: *The cat will scratch if you annoy it.* ◇ *The table was badly scratched.* ▶ **zadrapać**, **podrapać** **3** [T] to use sth sharp to make or remove a mark: *He scratched his name on the top of his desk.* ◇ *I tried to scratch the paint off the table.* ▶ **wydrapać**; **zdrapywać** **4** [I] to make a sound by rubbing a surface with sth sharp: *The dog was scratching at the door to go outside.* ▶ **drapać**

scratch² /skrætʃ/ noun **1** [C] a cut, mark or sound that was made by sth sharp rubbing a surface: *There's a scratch on the car door.* ▶ **zadrapanie**, **rysa** **2** [sing.] an act of scratching part of the body: *The dog had a good scratch* (porządnie się podrapał). ▶ **drapanie**

IDM **from scratch** from the very beginning: *I'm learning Spanish from scratch.* ▶ **od zera**

(be/come) up to scratch (informal) (to be/become) good enough: *Karen's singing isn't really up to scratch.* Prawdę mówiąc, śpiew Karen nie jest na (wysokim) poziomie. ▶ **być na poziomie**; **spełniać wymogi**

'scratch card noun [C] a card that you buy that has an area that you scratch off to find out if you have won some money or a prize ▶ **zdrapka**

scratchy /'skrætʃi/ adj. (**scratchier**; **scratchiest**) **1** (used about clothes or cloth) rough and unpleasant to the touch: *This sweater is too scratchy.* Ten sweter za bardzo gryzie. ▶ **szorstki** SYN **itchy** **2** (used about a record, voice, etc.) making a rough, unpleasant sound like sth being scratched across a surface: *a scratchy recording of Mario Lanza* ◇ *a scratchy pen* ▶ **trzeszczący**

scrawl /skrɔːl/ verb [I,T] to write sth quickly in an untidy and careless way: *He scrawled his name across the top of the paper.* ▶ **bazgrać**, **gryzmolić**

■ **scrawl** noun [sing.]: *Her signature was just a scrawl.* ▶ **bazgranina**, **gryzmoły** ➲ look at **scribble**

scrawny /'skrɔːni/ adj. (**scrawnier**; **scrawniest**) very thin in a way that is not attractive ▶ **wychudzony**

scream¹ /skriːm/ verb [I,T] **scream (sth) (out) (at sb)** to cry out loudly in a high voice because you are afraid, excited, angry, in pain, etc.: *She saw a rat and screamed out.* ◇ *'Don't touch that,' he screamed.* ◇ *She screamed at the children to stop.* ◇ *He screamed with pain.* ◇ *He clung to the edge of the cliff, screaming for help.* ▶ **krzyczeć**, **wrzeszczeć** ➲ look at **shout**

scream² /skriːm/ noun **1** [C] a loud cry in a high voice: *a scream of pain* ▶ **krzyk**, **wrzask** **2** [sing.] (informal) a person or thing that is very funny: *Sharon's a real scream.* ▶ **śmieszna osoba**; **coś śmiesznego**

screech /skriːtʃ/ verb [I,T] to make an unpleasant loud, high sound: *'Get out of here,' she screeched at him.* ▶ **piszczeć**, **skrzeczeć** ➲ look at **shriek**

■ **screech** noun [sing.]: *the screech of brakes* ▶ **pisk**, **skrzek**

screen¹ /skriːn/ noun **1** [C] the glass surface of a TV or computer where the picture or information appears ▶ **ekran** **2** [C] the large flat surface on which films are shown ▶ **ekran** **3** [sing., U] films and TV: *Some actors look better in real life than on screen.* ▶ **kino**, **film** **4** [C] a flat vertical surface that is used for dividing a room or keeping sb/sth out of sight: *The nurse pulled the screen round the bed.* ▶ **parawan**, **zasłona**

screen² /skriːn/ verb [T] **1 screen sb/sth (off) (from sb/sth)** to hide or protect sb/sth from sb/sth else: *The bed was screened off while the doctor examined him.* ◇ *to screen your eyes from the sun* ▶ **zasłaniać** **2 screen sb (for sth)** to examine or test sb to find out if they have a particular disease or if they are suitable for a particular job: *All women over 50 should be screened for breast cancer.* ◇ *The Ministry of Defence screens all job applicants.* ▶ **monitorować**, **sprawdzać** **3** to show sth on TV or in a cinema ▶ **pokazywać** (*np. w telewizji*), **wyświetlać**

screenplay /'skriːnpleɪ/ noun [C] the words that are written for a film, together with instructions for how it is to be acted and made into a film ▶ **scenariusz** ➲ note at **film**

'screen saver noun [C] a computer program that replaces what is on the screen with a moving image if the computer is not used for a certain amount of time ▶ **wygaszacz ekranu**

screenwriter /'skriːnraɪtə(r)/ noun [C] a person who writes **screenplays** ▶ **scenarzyst(k)a** ➲ look at **playwright**, **scriptwriter**

screw¹ /skruː/ noun [C] a thin pointed piece of metal used for fixing two things, for example pieces of wood, together. You turn a screw with a **screwdriver**. ▶ **śruba** ➲ picture at **bolt**

screw² /skruː/ verb **1** [T] **screw sth (on, down, etc.)** to fasten sth with a screw or screws: *The bookcase is screwed to the wall.* ◇ *The lid is screwed down so you can't remove it.* ▶ **przykręcać**, **przyśrubowywać** **2** [I,T] to fasten sth, or to be fastened, by turning: *The legs screw into holes in the underside of the seat.* ◇ *Make sure that you screw the top of the jar on tightly.* ▶ **zakręcać (się)**, **nakręcać (się)** **3 screw sth (up) (into sth)** to squeeze sth, especially a piece of paper, into a tight ball: *He screwed the letter up into a ball and threw it away.* ▶ **zgniatać w kulkę**

PHR V **screw sb up** (slang) to upset or confuse sb so much that they are not able to deal with problems in their life: *Her father's death really screwed her up.* ▶ **okaleczyć kogoś psychicznie**

screw (sth) up (slang) to make a mistake and cause sth to fail: *You'd better not screw up this deal.* ▶ **zawalić sprawę**

screw your eyes, face, etc. up to change the expression on your face by nearly closing your eyes, in pain or because the light is strong ▶ **mrużyć oczy**, **wykrzywiać twarz**

screwdriver /'skruːdraɪvə(r)/ noun [C] a tool that you use for turning **screws** ▶ **śrubokręt** ➲ picture at **tool**

scribble /'skrɪbl/ verb [I,T] **1** to write sth quickly and carelessly: *to scribble a note down on a pad* ▶ **pisać w pośpiechu i niestarannie** ➲ look at **scrawl** **2** to make marks with a pen or pencil that are not letters or pictures: *The children had scribbled all over the walls.* ▶ **bazgrać**

■ **scribble** noun [C,U] ▶ **bazgranina**

script /skrɪpt/ noun **1** [C] the written form of a play, film, speech, etc.: *Who wrote the script for the movie?* ▶ **scenariusz**, **tekst** **2** [C,U] a system of writing: *Arabic/Cyrillic/Roman script* ▶ **pismo**

scripture /ˈskrɪptʃə(r)/ noun [U] (**the scriptures**) [pl.] the books of a religion, such as the Bible ▶ **Biblia, Pismo Święte**

scriptwriter /ˈskrɪptraɪtə(r)/ noun [C] a person who writes the words for films, television and radio plays ▶ **autor/ka scenariuszy** (*filmowych, telewizyjnych, radiowych*), **scenarzyst(k)a** ➲ look at **playwright**, **screenwriter**

scroll[1] /skrəʊl/ noun [C] a long roll of paper with writing on it ▶ **zwój pergaminu/papieru**

scroll[2] /skrəʊl/ verb [I] **scroll (up/down)** to move text up and down or left and right on a computer screen ▶ **przewijać**

ˈ**scroll bar** noun [C] a tool on a computer screen that you use to move the text up and down or left and right ▶ (*ekran monitora*) **pasek do przewijania**

scrounge /skraʊndʒ/ verb [I,T] (informal) **scrounge (sth) (from/off sb)** to get sth by asking another person to give it to you instead of making an effort to get it for yourself: *Lucy is always scrounging money off her friends.* ▶ **naciągać kogoś na coś**

scrub[1] /skrʌb/ verb [I,T] (**scrubbing**; **scrubbed**) **1 scrub (sth) (down/out)** to clean sth with soap and water by rubbing it hard, often with a brush: *to scrub (down) the floor/walls* ▶ **szorować 2 scrub (sth) (off/out)**; **scrub (sth) (off sth/out of sth)** to remove sth or be removed by **scrubbing**: *to scrub the dirt off the walls* ◇ *I hope these coffee stains will scrub out.* ▶ **ścierać** (*zwł. szczotką*), **szorować**

scrub[2] /skrʌb/ noun **1** [sing.] an act of cleaning sth by rubbing it hard, often with a brush: *This floor needs a good scrub.* Trzeba mocno wyszorować podłogę. ▶ **szorowanie 2** [U] small trees and bushes that grow in an area that has very little rain ▶ **zarośla**

scruff /skrʌf/ noun
IDM **by the scruff (of the/your neck)** by the back of the/your neck ▶ (*brać*) **za kark**

scruffy /ˈskrʌfi/ adj. (**scruffier**; **scruffiest**) dirty and untidy: *He always looks so scruffy.* ◇ *scruffy jeans* ▶ **niechlujny**

scrum /skrʌm/ noun [C] (in the sport of **rugby**) when several players put their heads down in a circle and push against each other to try to get the ball ▶ **młyn**

scrumptious /ˈskrʌmpʃəs/ adj. (informal) tasting very good ▶ **pyszny** SYN **delicious**

scrunchy (also **scrunchie**) /ˈskrʌntʃi/ noun [C] (pl. **scrunchies**) a circular band of elastic covered with cloth used to fasten hair away from the face ▶ **frotka** (do *włosów*)

scruples /ˈskru:plz/ noun [pl.] a feeling that stops you from doing sth that you think is morally wrong: *I've got no scruples about asking them for money.* ▶ **skrupuły**

scrupulous /ˈskru:pjələs/ adj. **1** very careful or paying great attention to detail: *a scrupulous investigation into the causes* (szczegółowe badanie przyczyn) *of the disaster* ▶ **skrupulatny 2** careful to be honest and do what is right ▶ **sumienny** OPP **unscrupulous**
■ **scrupulously** adv.: *scrupulously clean / honest / tidy* ▶ **skrupulatnie**; **sumiennie**

scrutinize (also -ise) /ˈskru:tənaɪz/ verb [T] to look at or examine sth carefully: *The customs official scrutinized every page of my passport.* ▶ **badać szczegółowo**
■ **scrutiny** /ˈskru:təni/ noun [U]: *The police kept all the suspects **under close scrutiny*** (pod dokładną kontrolą). ▶ **badanie szczegółowe**

scuba-diving /ˈsku:bə daɪvɪŋ/ noun [U] swimming underwater using special equipment for breathing: *to go scuba-diving* ▶ **nurkowanie**

scuff /skʌf/ verb [T] to make a mark on your shoes or with your shoes, for example by kicking sth or by rubbing your feet along the ground ▶ **zdzierać** (*buty*); **kaleczyć** (*np. podłogę*)

scuffle /ˈskʌfl/ noun [C] a short, not very violent fight ▶ **utarczka**

sculptor /ˈskʌlptə(r)/ noun [C] a person who makes **sculptures** from stone, wood, etc. ▶ **rzeźbia-rz/rka** ➲ note at **art**

sculpture /ˈskʌlptʃə(r)/ noun **1** [U] the art of making **sculptures** ▶ **rzeźbiarstwo 2** [C,U] a work of art that is a figure or an object made from stone, wood, metal, etc. ▶ **rzeźba** ➲ note at **art**

scum /skʌm/ noun [U] **1** a dirty or unpleasant substance on the surface of a liquid ▶ **kożuch** (*z brudu*) **2** (slang) an insulting word for people that you have no respect for: *Drug dealers are scum.* ▶ **szumowiny**
■ **scummy** /ˈskʌmi/ adj.: *scummy water* ◇ *scummy people dropping litter* szumowiny, które śmiecą ▶ **pokryty szumowiną, brudny**

scumbag /ˈskʌmbæg/ noun [C] (slang) an unpleasant person ▶ **kanalia**

scurrilous /ˈskʌrələs; US ˈskɜ:r-/ adj. (formal) very rude and insulting, and intended to damage sb's reputation: *scurrilous rumours* ▶ **obelżywy, zniesławiający**

scurry /ˈskʌri; US ˈskɜ:-/ verb [I] (**scurrying**; **scurries**; pt, pp **scurried**) to run quickly with short steps; to hurry ▶ **biec drobnymi krokami, pędzić**

scuttle /ˈskʌtl/ verb [I] to run quickly with short steps or with the body close to the ground: *The spider scuttled away when I tried to catch it.* ▶ **biec drobnymi krokami, pędzić**

scythe /saɪð/ noun [C] a tool with a long handle and a long, curved blade. You use a **scythe** to cut long grass, etc. ▶ **kosa**

SE = SOUTH-EAST[1], SOUTH-EASTERN: *SE Asia*

sea /si:/ noun **1** (often **the sea**) [U] the salt water that covers large parts of the surface of the earth: *The sea is quite calm/rough today.* ◇ *Do you live **by the sea*** (nad morzem)? ◇ *to travel **by sea*** podróżować drogą morską ◇ *There were several people swimming **in the sea.*** ▶ **morze 2** (often **Sea**) [C] a particular large area of salt water. A sea may be part of a larger area of water or may be surrounded by land: *the Mediterranean Sea* ◇ *the Black Sea* ▶ **morze** ➲ look at **ocean 3** [C] (also **seas** [pl.]) the state or movement of the waves of the sea: *The boat sank in heavy seas* (na wzburzonym morzu) *off the Scottish coast.* ▶ **morze, wody morskie 4** [sing.] a large amount of sb/sth close together: *The pavement was just a sea of people.* ▶ **morze**
IDM **at sea 1** sailing in a ship: *They spent about three weeks at sea.* ▶ **na morzu 2** not understanding or not knowing what to do: *When I first started this job I was completely at sea.* ▶ **zagubiony**

the ˈ**seabed** noun [sing.] the floor of the sea ▶ **dno morskie**

seafood /ˈsi:fu:d/ noun [U] fish and sea creatures that we eat, especially **shellfish** ▶ **owoce morza**

the **seafront** /ˈsi:frʌnt/ noun [sing.] the part of a town facing the sea: *The hotel is right **on the seafront.*** ◇ *to walk **along the seafront*** ▶ **zabudowania/ulica i miejsce spacerów wzdłuż plaży**

seagull = GULL

ˈ**sea horse** noun [C] a small sea fish that swims in a vertical position and has a head that looks like the head of a horse ▶ **konik morski**

seal[1] /si:l/ verb [T] **1 seal sth (up/down)** to close or fasten a package, an envelope, etc.: *The parcel was sealed with tape.* ◇ *to seal (down) an envelope* ▶ **zamykać, zaklejać 2 seal sth (up)** to fill a hole or cover sth so that air or liquid does not get in or out: *The food is packed in sealed bags to keep it fresh.* ▶ **uszczelniać 3** (formal) to make sth sure, so that it cannot be changed or argued about: *to seal an agreement* ▶ **przypieczętować**

PHR V **seal sth off** to stop any person or thing from entering or leaving an area or building: *The building was sealed off by the police.* ▶ **odcinać** (*dostęp*)

seal² /siːl/ noun [C] **1** an official design or mark that is put on a document, an envelope, etc. to show that it is genuine or that it has not been opened: *The letter bore the President's seal.* ▶ **pieczęć 2** something that stops air or liquid from getting in or out of sth: *The seal has worn and oil is escaping.* ▶ **uszczelnienie**, **uszczelka 3** a small piece of paper, metal, plastic, etc. on a bottle, box, etc. that you must break before you can open it: *Check the seal isn't broken.* ▶ **plomba**, **szczelne zamknięcie 4** a grey animal with short fur that lives in and near the sea and that eats fish. Seals have no legs and swim with the help of **flippers**: *a colony of seals* ▶ **foka** ➲ picture on **page A10**

'sea level noun [U] the average level of the sea, used for measuring the height of places on land: *The town is 500 metres above sea level.* ▶ **poziom morza**

'sea lion noun [C] a type of large animal that lives in the sea and on land and uses two **flippers** to move through the water ▶ **lew morski**

seam /siːm/ noun [C] **1** the line where two pieces of cloth are sewn together ▶ **szew 2** a layer of coal under the ground ▶ **pokład**

seaman /ˈsiːmən/ noun [C] (pl. **-men** /-mən/) a sailor ▶ **marynarz**

seamless /ˈsiːmləs/ adj. with no spaces or pauses between one part and the next: *a seamless flow of talk* ▶ **gładki**, **nieprzerwany**

■ **seamlessly** adv. ▶ **gładko**, **nieprzerwanie**

seance (also séance) /ˈseɪɒs; US -ɒns/ noun [C] a meeting at which people try to talk to the spirits of dead people ▶ **seans spirytystyczny**

search /sɜːtʃ/ verb [I,T] **search (sb/sth) (for sb/sth)**; **search (through sth) (for sth)** to examine sb/sth carefully because you are looking for sth; to look for sth that is missing: *The men were arrested and searched for drugs.* ◇ *Were your bags searched at the airport?* ◇ *They are still searching for the missing child.* ◇ *She searched through the papers* (przerzuciła papiery) *on the desk, looking for the letter.* ▶ **rewidować**, **przeszukiwać**

■ **search** noun [C,U]: *the search for the missing boy* ◇ *She walked round for hours* ***in search of*** *her missing dog.* ▶ **poszukiwanie**, **przeszukiwanie**

searchable /ˈsɜːtʃəbl/ adj. (used about a computer **database** or network) having information organized in such a way that it can be searched for using a computer: *a searchable database* ◇ *The CD contains 200 fully searchable film clips.* ▶ (*komput.*) **oparty na wyszukiwaniu**

'search engine noun [C] a computer program that searches the Internet for information ▶ **wyszukiwarka** ➲ note at **Internet**

searcher /ˈsɜːtʃə(r)/ noun [C] **1** a person who is looking for sb/sth ▶ **poszukiwacz/ka 2** a program that allows you to look for particular information on a computer ▶ **wyszukiwarka**

searching /ˈsɜːtʃɪŋ/ adj. (used about a look, question, etc.) trying to find out the truth: *The customs officers asked a lot of searching questions about our trip.* ▶ **drobiazgowy**, **przenikliwy**

searchlight /ˈsɜːtʃlaɪt/ noun [C] a powerful lamp whose beam can be turned in any direction, for example to look for enemy aircraft at night ▶ **reflektor**, **szperacz**

'search party noun [C] a group of people who look for sb/sth that is lost or missing ▶ **wyprawa poszukiwawcza**

'search warrant noun [C] an official piece of paper that gives the police the right to search a building, etc. ▶ **nakaz rewizji**

seashell /ˈsiːʃel/ noun [C] the empty shell of a small animal that lives in the sea ▶ **muszla**

seashore /ˈsiːʃɔː(r)/ noun (usually **the seashore**) [U] the part of the land that is next to the sea: *We were looking for shells* ***on the seashore.*** ▶ **brzeg morski**, **wybrzeże**

seasick /ˈsiːsɪk/ adj. feeling sick or **vomiting** because of the movement of a boat or ship: *to feel/get/be seasick* ▶ **cierpiący na chorobę morską** ➲ look at **airsick**, **carsick**, **travel-sick**

seaside /ˈsiːsaɪd/ noun (often **the seaside**) [sing.] an area on the coast, especially one where people go on holiday: *Let's go to the seaside* (nad morze). ◇ *a seaside town* ◇ *a seaside hotel* hotel nad morzem ▶ **wybrzeże**

season¹ /ˈsiːzn/ noun [C] **1** one of the periods of different weather into which the year is divided: *In cool countries, the four seasons are spring, summer, autumn and winter.* ◇ *the dry/rainy season* ▶ **pora roku 2** the period of the year when sth is common or popular or when sth usually happens or is done: *the holiday/football season* ◇ *the high season* szczyt sezonu ◇ *the low season* sezon ogórkowy ▶ **sezon**, **pora**

IDM **in season 1** (used about fresh foods) available in large quantities: *Tomatoes are cheapest when they are in season* (kiedy jest na nie sezon). **2** (used about a female animal) ready to have sex ▶ **w rui**

out of season 1 (used about fresh foods) not available in large quantities ▶ **po sezonie 2** (used about a place where people go on holiday) at the time of year when it is least popular with tourists: *This hotel is much cheaper out of season.* ▶ **poza sezonem**

season² /ˈsiːzn/ verb [T] to add salt, spices, etc. to food in order to make it taste better ▶ **doprawiać do smaku**

■ **seasoning** noun [C,U]: *Add seasoning to the soup and serve with bread.* ▶ **przyprawa**

seasonal /ˈsiːzənl/ adj. happening or existing at a particular time of the year: *There are a lot of seasonal jobs in the summer.* ▶ **sezonowy**

seasoned /ˈsiːznd/ adj. having a lot of experience of sth: *a seasoned traveller* ▶ **doświadczony**

'season ticket noun [C] a ticket that allows you to make a particular journey by bus, train, etc. or to go to a theatre or watch a sports team as often as you like for a fixed period of time ▶ **bilet okresowy**

seat¹ /siːt/ noun [C] **1** something that you sit on: *Please* ***take a seat*** (proszę usiąść). ◇ *the back/driving/passenger seat of a car* ▶ **siedzenie** ➲ picture at **bicycle**, **car 2** the part of a chair, etc. that you sit on: *a steel chair with a plastic seat* ▶ **siedzenie 3** a place in a theatre, on a plane, etc. where you pay to sit: *There are no seats left on that flight.* ◇ *The seats for the ballet* (bilety na balet) *cost £30 each.* **4** an official position as a member of a parliament, etc.: *to win/lose a seat* ▶ **mandat 5** the part of the piece of clothing that covers your bottom ▶ **siedzenie**

IDM **be in the driving seat** → DRIVING¹

take a back seat → BACK²

seat² /siːt/ verb [T] **1** [often passive] (formal) to sit down: *Please be seated.* Proszę usiąść. ▶ **sadzać 2** to have seats or chairs for a particular number of people ▶ **mieścić**

'seat belt (also 'safety belt) noun [C] a long narrow piece of cloth that is fixed to the seat in a car or plane and that you wear around your body, so that you are not thrown forward if there is an accident: *to fasten/unfasten your seat belt* ▶ **pas bezpieczeństwa** ➲ look at **belt** ➲ picture at **car**

seating /ˈsiːtɪŋ/ noun [U] the seats or chairs in a place or the way that they are arranged: *The conference hall has seating for 500 people.* ◇ *a seating plan* plan rozmieszczenia gości przy stole ▶ **krzesła** (*ustawione w pewien sposób*)

seaweed /ˈsiːwiːd/ noun [U] a plant that grows in the sea. There are many different types of **seaweed.** ▶ **wodorosty**

sec (informal) = SECOND² (2)

secateurs /ˌsekəˈtɜːz/ noun [pl.] (Brit.) a garden tool like a pair of strong scissors, used for cutting plants and small branches: *a pair of secateurs* ▶ **sekator**

secede /sɪˈsiːd/ verb [I] (formal) **secede (from sth)** to officially leave an organization of states, countries, etc. and become independent: *The Republic of Panama seceded from Colombia in 1903.* ▶ **odłączać się** (*od innego kraju/organizacji itp.*)

secession /sɪˈseʃn/ noun [U,C] **secession (from sth)** the fact of an area or group becoming independent from the country or larger group that it belongs to ▶ **secesja**

secluded /sɪˈkluːdɪd/ adj. far away from other people, roads, etc.; very quiet: *a secluded beach/garden* ▶ **zaciszny**, **ustronny**
■ **seclusion** /sɪˈkluːʒn/ noun [U] ▶ **zacisze**, **ustronie**

⚷ **second¹** /ˈsekənd/ determiner, ordinal number, adv. 2nd: *We are going on holiday in the second week in July.* ◇ *Birmingham is the second largest* (drugie co do wielkości) *city in Britain after London.* ◇ *She poured herself a second cup of coffee.* ◇ *Our team finished second* (na drugim miejscu). ◇ ***I came second*** (byłem drugi) *in the competition.* ◇ *Queen Elizabeth the Second* ◇ ***the second of** January* ◇ *January **the second*** ▶ **drugi** ➲ note at **sixth**
IDM **second nature (to sb)** something that has become a habit or that you can do easily because you have done it so many times: *With practice, typing becomes second nature.* ▶ **druga natura**
second thoughts a change of mind or opinion about sth; doubts that you have when you are not sure if you have made the right decision: *On second thoughts* (po namyśle), *let's go today, not tomorrow.* ◇ *I'm having second thoughts* (chyba zmienię zdanie) *about accepting their offer.* ▶ **namysł**

⚷ **second²** /ˈsekənd/ noun **1** [C] one of the 60 parts into which a minute is divided: *She can run 100 metres in just over 11 seconds.* ▶ **sekunda 2** (also informal **sec** /sek/) [C] a short time: *Wait a second, please.* ▶ **sekunda** SYN **moment 3** [C, usually pl.] something that has a small fault and that is sold at a lower price: *The clothes are all seconds.* ▶ **odrzut 4** [U] the second of the four or five **gears** that a car can move forward in: *Once the car's moving, put it **in second.*** ▶ **drugi bieg 5** [C] (formal) **a second (in sth)** the second highest level of degree given by a British university: *to get an upper/a lower second in physics* ▶ **dyplom ukończenia szkoły wyższej z oceną dobrą**

second³ /ˈsekənd/ verb [T] to support sb's suggestion or idea at a meeting so that it can then be discussed and voted on ▶ **popierać** (*np. wniosek*)

second⁴ /sɪˈkɒnd/ verb [T, usually passive] (especially Brit.) **second sb (from sth) (to sth)** to send an employee to another department, office, etc. in order to do a different job for a short period of time ▶ **przenosić** (*na inne stanowisko, do innego działu*)
■ **secondment** noun [U,C]: *They met while she was **on secondment** from the Foreign Office.* ▶ **przeniesienie tymczasowe**

⚷ **secondary** /ˈsekəndri; US -deri/ adj. **1** less important than sth else: *Other people's opinions are secondary – it's my opinion that counts.* ▶ **drugorzędny 2** caused by or developing from sth else: *She developed a secondary infection following a bad cold.* ▶ **wtórny**

ˈsecondary school noun [C] (Brit.) a school for children aged from 11 to 18 ▶ **szkoła średnia**

ˌsecond ˈbest¹ adj. not quite the best but the next one after the best: *the second-best time in the 100 metres race* ▶ **drugi**, **zajmujący drugie miejsce** ➲ look at **best**

ˌsecond ˈbest² noun [U] something that is not as good as the best, or not as good as you would like: *I'm not prepared to accept second best.* ▶ **coś gorszego (z dwóch)**, **coś podrzędnego**

ˌsecond ˈclass noun [U] **1** (also **ˈstandard class**) the ordinary, less expensive seats on a train, ship, etc.: *You can never get a seat in second class.* ▶ **druga klasa 2** (Brit.) the way of sending letters, etc. that is cheaper but that takes longer than **first class** ▶ **druga klasa**
■ **ˌsecond-ˈclass** adv. ▶ **drugą klasą**

ˌsecond-ˈclass adj. **1** of little importance: *Old people should not be treated as **second-class citizens.*** ▶ **drugiej kategorii 2** [only before a noun] (used about the ordinary, less expensive seats on a train, ship, etc.) ▶ **drugiej klasy 3** [only before a noun] (Brit.) (used about the way of sending letters, etc. that is cheaper but that takes longer than **first class**) ▶ **drugiej klasy 4** [only before a noun] (used about a British university degree) of the level that is next after **first-class** ▶ (*dyplom*) **drugiej klasy**

ˌsecond ˈcousin noun [C] the child of your mother's or father's cousin ▶ **kuzyn/ka w drugiej linii**

ˌsecond ˈfloor noun [C] the floor in a building that is two floors above the lowest floor: *I live on the second floor.* ◇ *a second-floor flat* ▶ **drugie piętro** ⓘ W Amer. ang. **the second floor** to pierwsze piętro.

the ˈsecond hand noun [C] the hand on some clocks and watches that shows seconds ▶ **sekundnik**

ˌsecond-ˈhand adj., adv. **1** already used or owned by sb else: *a second-hand car* ◇ *I bought this camera second-hand.* ◇ *a second-hand shop* sklep z używanymi artykułami ▶ **używany**, **z drugiej ręki** ➲ look at **old 2** (used about news or information) that you heard from sb else, and did not see or experience yourself ▶ **z drugiej ręki** ➲ look at **first-hand**

ˌsecond ˈlanguage noun [C] a language that sb learns to speak well and that they use for work or at school, but that is not the language they learned first: *ESL is short for English as a Second Language.* ▶ **drugi język**

secondly /ˈsekəndli/ adv. (used when you are giving your second reason or opinion) also: *Firstly, I think it's too expensive and secondly, we don't really need it.* ▶ **po drugie**

ˈsecond name noun [C] (especially Brit.) **1** = SURNAME **2** a second personal name ▶ **drugie imię**

ˌsecond-ˈrate adj. of poor quality: *a second-rate poet* ▶ **drugorzędny**

secrecy /ˈsiːkrəsi/ noun [U] being secret or keeping sth secret: *I must stress the importance of secrecy in this matter.* ▶ **tajemnica**, **dyskrecja**

⚷ **secret¹** /ˈsiːkrət/ adj. **1 secret (from sb)** that is not or must not be known by other people: *We have to **keep** the party **secret** from Carmen.* ◇ *a secret address* ◇ *a secret love affair* ◇ *The file was marked 'Top Secret'* (ściśle tajne). ▶ **tajny 2** [only before a noun] (used to describe actions that you do not tell anyone about): *a secret drinker* ◇ *She's got a secret admirer.* ▶ **cichy**, **robiący coś po cichu/ukradkiem**
■ **secretly** adv.: *The government secretly agreed to pay the kidnappers.* ▶ **w tajemnicy**

⚷ **secret²** /ˈsiːkrət/ noun **1** [C] something that is not or must not be known by other people: *to **keep a secret*** ◇ *to let somebody in on/tell somebody a secret* ◇ *I can't tell you where we're going – it's a secret.* ◇ ***It's no secret that*** (to

S

nie tajemnica) *they don't like each other.* ▶ **tajemnica** **2** [sing.] **the secret (of/to sth/doing sth)** the only way or the best way of doing or achieving sth: *What is the secret of your success?* ▶ **tajemnica**
IDM **in secret** without other people knowing: *to meet in secret* ▶ **w tajemnicy**

ˌsecret ˈagent (also **agent**) noun [C] a person who tries to find out secret information, especially about the government of another country ▶ **tajny agent** ➲ look at **spy**

secretarial /ˌsekrəˈteəriəl/ adj. involving or connected with the work that a **secretary** does: *secretarial skills/work* ▶ (*czynności itp.*) **sekreta-rki/rza**

secretariat /ˌsekrəˈteəriət; -iæt/ noun [C] the department of a large international or political organization which is responsible for managing it ▶ **sekretariat**

🔑 **secretary** /ˈsekrətri; US -teri/ noun [C] (pl. **secretaries**) **1** a person who works in an office. A **secretary** types letters, answers the telephone, keeps records, etc.: *the director's personal secretary* ▶ **sekreta-rz/rka** ➲ note at **office** **2** an official of a club or society who is responsible for keeping records, writing letters, etc.: *the membership secretary* ▶ **sekreta-rz/rka** **3** (US) the head of a government department, chosen by the President: *Secretary of the Treasury* ▶ **minister** ➲ look at **minister** **4** (**Secretary**) (Brit.) = SECRETARY OF STATE (1)

ˌSecretary of ˈState noun [C] **1** (also **Secretary**) (in Britain) the head of one of the main government departments: *the Secretary of State for Defence* ▶ **minister** **2** (in the US) the head of the government department that deals with foreign affairs ▶ **sekretarz stanu**

secrete /sɪˈkriːt/ verb [T] **1** (used about a part of a plant, animal or person) to produce a liquid ▶ **wydzielać** **2** (formal) to hide sth in a secret place ▶ **chować**

secretion /sɪˈkriːʃn/ noun (formal) **1** [C] a liquid that is produced by a plant or an animal; the process by which the liquid is produced: *The frog covers its skin in a poisonous secretion for protection.* ▶ **wydzielina** **2** [U] the process by which the liquid is produced ▶ **wydzielanie**

secretive /ˈsiːkrətɪv/ adj. liking to keep things secret from other people: *Wendy is very secretive about her private life.* ▶ **tajemniczy**, **skryty**
■ **secretively** adv. ▶ **w tajemnicy**, **skrycie** | **secretiveness** noun [U] ▶ **tajemniczość**, **skrytość**

ˌsecret poˈlice noun [sing., with sing. or pl. verb] a police force that works secretly to make sure that citizens behave as their government wants ▶ **tajna policja**

the **ˌsecret ˈservice** noun [sing.] the government department that tries to find out secret information about other countries and governments ▶ **tajne służby**

sect /sekt/ noun [C] a group of people who have a particular set of religious or political beliefs. A **sect** has often broken away from a larger group. ▶ **sekta**

sectarian /sekˈteəriən/ adj. connected with the differences that exist between groups of people who have different religious views: *sectarian attacks/violence* ▶ **sekciarski**

🔑 **section** /ˈsekʃn/ noun [C] **1** one of the parts into which sth is divided: *The final section of the road will be opened in June.* ◇ *the string section of an orchestra* ◇ *the financial section of a newspaper* ◇ *The library has an excellent reference section* (dział podręczny). ▶ **odcinek** (*drogi*), **sekcja**, **dział** **2** a view or drawing of sth as if it was cut from the top to the bottom so that you can see the inside: *The illustration shows a section through a leaf.* ▶ **przekrój**

🔑 **sector** /ˈsektə(r)/ noun [C] **1** a part of the business activity of a country: *The manufacturing sector has declined in recent years.* ◇ *the public/private sector* ▶ **sektor** **2** a part of an area or of a large group of people: *the Christian sector of the city* ▶ **dzielnica**, **sektor**

secular /ˈsekjələ(r)/ adj. not concerned with religion or the church ▶ **świecki**

🔑 **secure¹** /sɪˈkjʊə(r); US səˈk-/ adj. **1** free from worry or doubt; confident: *Children need to **feel secure**.* ◇ *to be financially secure* ▶ **bezpieczny**, **zabezpieczony** OPP **insecure** **2** not likely to be lost: *Business is good so his job is secure.* ◇ *a secure investment* ▶ **bezpieczny**, **pewny** SYN **safe** **3** not likely to fall or be broken; firmly fixed: *That ladder doesn't look very secure.* ▶ **dobrze umocowany**, **stabilny** SYN **stable** **4** **secure (against/from sth)** well locked or protected: *Make sure the house is secure before you go to bed.* ▶ **zabezpieczony**, **bezpieczny**
■ **securely** adv.: *All doors and windows must be securely fastened.* ▶ **solidnie**

🔑 **secure²** /sɪˈkjʊə(r); US səˈk-/ verb [T] **1** **secure sth (to sth)** to fix or lock sth firmly: *The load was secured with ropes.* ◇ *Secure the rope to a tree or a rock.* ▶ **przymocowywać** **2** **secure sth (against/from sth)** to make sth safe: *The sea wall needs strengthening to secure the town against flooding.* ▶ **zabezpieczać (przed czymś/przeciw czemuś)** **3** to obtain or achieve sth, especially by having to make a big effort: *The company has secured a contract to build ten planes.* ▶ **uzyskiwać**

🔑 **security** /sɪˈkjʊərəti; US səˈk-/ noun (pl. **securities**) **1** [U] things that you do to protect sb/sth from attack, danger, thieves, etc.: *Security* (Ochrona) *was tightened at the airport before the President arrived.* ◇ *a maximum security prison* więzienie pod specjalnym nadzorem ◇ *the security forces* siły bezpieczeństwa ◇ *The robbers were caught on the bank's **security cameras**.* ▶ **środki bezpieczeństwa** OPP **insecurity** **2** [U] the section of a large company or organization that deals with the protection of buildings, equipment and workers: *If you see a suspicious bag, contact airport security immediately.* ▶ **ochrona** **3** [U] the state of feeling safe and being free from worry; protection against the difficulties of life: *Children need the security of a stable home environment.* ◇ *job security* ◇ *financial security* dobrobyt ▶ **poczucie bezpieczeństwa** OPP **insecurity** **4** [C,U] something of value that you use when you borrow money. If you cannot pay the money back then you lose the thing you gave as **security**: *You may need to use your house **as security for** the loan.* ▶ **zabezpieczenie**

Seˈcurity Service noun [C] a government organization that protects a country and its secrets from enemies ▶ **służby specjalne**

sedan (US) = SALOON

sedate¹ /sɪˈdeɪt/ adj. quiet, calm and well behaved ▶ **spokojny**, **stateczny**

sedate² /sɪˈdeɪt/ verb [T] to give sb a drug or medicine to make them feel calm or want to sleep: *The lion was sedated and treated by a vet.* ▶ **podawać komuś środek uspokajający/usypiający**
■ **sedation** /sɪˈdeɪʃn/ noun [U]: *The doctor put her under sedation* (podał jej środki usypiające). ▶ **działanie środków usypiających/uspokajających**

sedative /ˈsedətɪv/ noun [C] a drug or medicine that makes you feel calm or want to sleep ▶ **środek uspokajający/usypiający** ➲ look at **tranquillizer**

sedentary /ˈsedntri; US -teri/ adj. involving a lot of sitting down; not active: *a sedentary lifestyle/job* ▶ **siedzący**

sediment /ˈsedɪmənt/ noun [C,U] a thick substance that forms at the bottom of a liquid ▶ **osad**

seduce /sɪˈdjuːs; US -ˈduːs/ verb [T] **1** to persuade sb to have sex with you ▶ **uwodzić** **2** **seduce sb (into sth/doing sth)** to persuade sb to do sth they would not usually agree to do: *Special offers seduce customers into spending their money.* ▶ **kusić**

■ **seducer** noun [C] a person who seduces sb ▶ **uwodziciel/ka** | **seduction** /sɪˈdʌkʃn/ noun [C,U] ▶ **uwiedzenie, uwodzenie; pokusa**

seductive /sɪˈdʌktɪv/ adj. **1** sexually attractive: *a seductive smile* ▶ **uwodzicielski 2** attractive in a way that makes you want to have or do sth: *The idea of swimming in this weather is not very seductive.* ▶ **nęcący, kuszący**

⚷ **see** /siː/ verb (pt **saw** /sɔː/, pp **seen** /siːn/) **1** [I,T] to become conscious of sth, using your eyes; to use the power of sight: *It was so dark that we couldn't see.* ◇ *On a clear day you can see for miles.* ◇ *Have you seen my wallet anywhere?* ◇ *I've just seen a mouse run under the cooker.* ◇ *He looked for her but couldn't see her in the crowd.* ▶ **widzieć** ➲ note at **can**, **look**[1], **smell**[1] **2** [T] to look at or watch a film, play, TV programme, etc.: *Did you see that programme on sharks last night?* ◇ *Have you seen Spielberg's latest film?* ▶ **widzieć, oglądać 3** [T] to spend time with sb; to visit sb: *I saw Alan at the weekend; we had dinner together.* ◇ *You should see a doctor* (pójść do lekarza) *about that cough.* ◇ *I'm seeing a lot* (często widuję się z) *of Paul these days.* ▶ **widzieć się z kimś 4** [I,T] to understand sth; to realize sth: *Do you* ***see what I mean?*** ◇ *She doesn't* ***see the point in*** *spending so much money on a car.* ◇ *'You have to key in your password first.' 'Oh,* ***I see*** (aha!).*'* ▶ **rozumieć 5** [T] to have an opinion about sth: *How do you see the situation developing?* Jak, twoim zdaniem, rozwinie się sytuacja? ▶ **widzieć, postrzegać 6** [T] to imagine sth as a future possibility: *I can't see her changing her mind.* ▶ **wyobrażać sobie 7** [T] to find out sth by looking, asking or waiting: ***Go and see*** *if the postman has been yet.* ◇ *We'll* ***wait and see*** *what happens before making any decisions.* ◇ *'Can we go swimming today, Dad?' 'I'll see.'* ◇ *I saw in the paper* (przeczytałem w gazecie) *that they're building a new theatre.* ▶ **zobaczyć 8** [T] to do what is necessary in a situation; to make sure that sb does sth: *I'll see that he gets the letter.* ▶ **dopilnować 9** [T] to be the time when an event happens: *Last year saw huge changes* (w ubiegłym roku zaszły olbrzymie zmiany) *in the education system.* ▶ **być świadkiem czegoś 10** [T] to go with sb, for example to help or protect them: *He asked me if he could see me home, but I said no.* ◇ *I saw* (przeprowadziłem) *the old lady safely across the road.* ◇ *I'll see you to the door.* ▶ **odprowadzać**

IDM **as far as the eye can see** → FAR[2]

let me see; let's see (used when you are thinking or trying to remember sth): *Where did I put the car keys? Let's see. I think I left them by the telephone.* ▶ **zaraz, zaraz, niech pomyślę**

see eye to eye (with sb) to agree with sb; to have the same opinion as sb: *We don't always see eye to eye on political matters.* ▶ **zgadzać się z kimś**

see for yourself to find out or look at sth yourself in order to be sure that what sb is saying is true ▶ **zobaczyć samemu/samej**

see if... to try to do sth: *I'll see if I can find time to do it.* ◇ *See if you can undo this knot.* ▶ **zobaczyć, czy**

see the joke to understand what is funny about a joke or trick ▶ **zrozumieć dowcip/kawał**

see red (informal) to become very angry: *I saw red* (krew mnie zalała) *when I saw him looking in my bag.* ▶ **wściec się**

see you (later) (used for saying goodbye to sb you expect to see soon or later that day) ▶ **na razie**

see you around (informal) (used for saying goodbye to sb you have made no arrangement to see again) ▶ **do zobaczenia**

you see (used for giving a reason): *She's very unhappy. He was her first real boyfriend, you see.* ▶ **rozumie-sz/cie**

PHR V **see about sth/doing sth** to deal with sth: *I've got to go to the bank to see about my traveller's cheques.* ▶ **zajmować się czymś, załatwiać coś**

see sb off to go with sb to the railway station, the airport, etc. in order to say goodbye to them ▶ **odprowadzać kogoś**

see sb out (Brit.) [not used in the progressive tenses] to last longer than the rest of sb's life: *I've had this coat for years, and I'm sure it will see me out.* ▶ **przetrwać kogoś**

see through sb/sth to be able to see that sb/sth is not what he/she/it appears: *The police immediately saw through his story.* ▶ **przejrzeć**

see to sb/sth to do what is necessary in a situation; to deal with sb/sth: *I'll see to the travel arrangements and you book the hotel.* ▶ **zajmować się czymś, dopilnować kogoś/czegoś**

⚷ **seed** /siːd/ noun **1** [C,U] the small hard part of a plant from which a new plant of the same kind can grow: *a packet of sunflower seeds* ▶ **nasienie, ziarno** ➲ picture on **page A12 2** [C] the start of a feeling or an event that continues to grow: *Her answer* ***planted the seeds of*** *doubt* (zasiała ziarno wątpliwości) *in my mind.* ▶ *(przen.)* **zalążek 3** [C] a player in a sports competition, especially **tennis**, who is expected to finish in a high position: *the number one seed* ▶ **zawodnik rozstawiony na korzystnej pozycji**

seeded /ˈsiːdɪd/ adj. (used about a player or a team in a sports competition) expected to finish in a high position ▶ **umieszczony w rankingu** *(na określonej pozycji)*

seedless /ˈsiːdləs/ adj. having no seeds: *seedless grapes* ▶ **bezpestkowy**

seedling /ˈsiːdlɪŋ/ noun [C] a very young plant or tree that has grown from a seed ▶ **sadzonka**

seedy /ˈsiːdi/ adj. (**seedier**; **seediest**) dirty and unpleasant; possibly connected with illegal or immoral activities: *a seedy hotel/neighbourhood* ◇ *a seedy nightclub* spelunka ▶ **podrzędny; podejrzany**

seeing /ˈsiːɪŋ/ (also **seeing that**; **seeing as**) conj. (informal) because; as: *Seeing as we're going the same way, I'll give you a lift.* ▶ **skoro**

⚷ **seek** /siːk/ verb [T] (pt, pp **sought** /sɔːt/) (formal) **1** to try to find or get sth: *Politicians are still seeking a peaceful solution.* ◇ *Dick went to London to seek his fortune* (szukać szczęścia). ▶ **szukać 2 seek sth (from sb)** to ask sb for sth: *You should seek advice from a solicitor about what to do next.* ▶ **szukać** *(np. pomocy, porady)* **u kogoś 3 seek (to do sth)** to try to do sth: *They are still seeking to find a peaceful solution to the conflict.* ▶ **próbować** SYN **attempt 4 (-seeking)** [in compounds] looking for or trying to get the thing mentioned: *attention-seeking behaviour* zachowanie osoby lubiącej być w centrum uwagi ◇ *a heat-seeking missile* pocisk termolokacyjny ▶ **poszukujący**

seeker /ˈsiːkə(r)/ noun [C] [often in compounds] a person who is trying to find or get sth: *an attention seeker* osoba chcąca być w centrum uwagi ◇ *asylum seekers* osoba ubiegająca się o azyl ▶ **poszukiwacz/ka, szukając-y/a czegoś**

⚷ **seem** /siːm/ verb [I] [not used in the continuous tenses] **seem (to sb) (to be) sth; seem (like) sth** to give the impression of being or doing sth: *Emma seems (like) a very nice girl./Emma seems to be a very nice girl.* ◇ *It seems to me that we have no choice.* ◇ *You seem happy today.* ◇ *This machine doesn't seem to work.* ◇ *It doesn't seem as if/though they will find a solution to the problem.* ▶ **wydawać się (komuś)** SYN **appear**

seeming /ˈsiːmɪŋ/ adj. [only before a noun] appearing to be sth: *Despite her seeming enthusiasm, Sandra didn't really help very much.* ▶ **widoczny; pozorny** SYN **apparent**

S

■ **seemingly** adv.: *a seemingly endless list of complaints* ▶ **pozornie**

seen past participle of **see**

seep /siːp/ verb [I] (used about a liquid) to flow very slowly through sth: *Water started seeping in through small cracks.* ▶ **przeciekać**

'see-saw noun [C] an outdoor toy for children that consists of a long piece of wood that is balanced in the middle. One child sits on each end of the **see-saw** and one goes up while the other is down. ▶ **huśtawka (na desce)**

seethe /siːð/ verb [I] **1** to be very angry: *I was absolutely seething.* ▶ **kipieć z gniewu 2 seethe (with sth)** to be very crowded: *The streets were seething with people.* ▶ **roić się, kłębić się**

'see-through adj. (used about cloth) very thin so that you can see through it ▶ **prześwitujący**

segment /'segmənt/ noun [C] **1** a section or part of sth: *I've divided the sheet of paper into three segments.* ◇ *a segment of the population* ▶ **segment, wycinek, odcinek 2** one of the parts into which an orange can be divided ▶ **cząstka** ➲ picture on **page A12**

segregate /'segrɪgeɪt/ verb [T] **segregate sb/sth (from sb/sth)** to separate one group of people or things from the rest: *The two groups of football fans were segregated to avoid trouble.* ▶ **rozdzielać, oddzielać** ➲ look at **integrate**
■ **segregation** /ˌsegrɪ'geɪʃn/ noun [U]: *racial segregation* ▶ **segregacja, podział** ➲ look at **integration**

seismic /'saɪzmɪk/ adj. [only before a noun] connected with or caused by **earthquakes** ▶ **sejsmiczny**

seize /siːz/ verb [T] **1** to take hold of sth suddenly and firmly: *The thief seized her handbag and ran off with it.* ◇ (figurative) *to seize a chance/an opportunity* wykorzystać szansę/okazję ▶ **chwycić** SYN **grab 2** to take control or possession of sb/sth: *The police seized 50 kilos of illegal drugs.* ▶ **przechwycić; objąć coś siłą 3** [usually passive] (used about an emotion) to affect sb suddenly and very strongly: *I felt myself seized by panic.* ▶ **zawładnąć (czymś)**

PHR V **seize (on/upon) sth** to make use of a good and unexpected chance: *He seized on a mistake by the goalkeeper and scored.* ▶ **skorzystać (skwapliwie) z czegoś**

seize up (used about a machine) to stop working because it is too hot, does not have enough oil, etc. ▶ **zaciąć się**

seizure /'siːʒə(r)/ noun **1** [U] using force or legal authority to take control or possession of sth: *the seizure of 30 kilos of heroin by police* ▶ **przechwycenie, przejęcie 2** [C] a sudden strong attack of an illness, especially one affecting the brain ▶ **napad, atak**

seldom /'seldəm/ adv. not often: *There is seldom snow in Athens.* ◇ *I very seldom go to the theatre.* ▶ **rzadko** SYN **rarely**

🔑 **select**[1] /sɪ'lekt/ verb [T] to choose sb/sth from a number of similar things: *The best candidates will be selected for interview.* ▶ **wybierać** ⓘ **Select** jest słowem bardziej formalnym niż **choose** i sugeruje, że decyzja o wyborze została dokładnie przemyślana.

select[2] /sɪ'lekt/ adj. (formal) **1** [only before a noun] carefully chosen as the best of a group: *A university education is no longer the privilege of **a select few**.* ▶ **wybrany, ekskluzywny 2** (used or owned by rich people) ▶ **doborowy, ekskluzywny**

🔑 **selection** /sɪ'lekʃn/ noun **1** [U] choosing or being chosen: *The manager is responsible for team selection.* ▶ **selekcja, wybór 2** [C] a number of people or things that have been chosen: *a selection of hits from the fifties and sixties* ▶ **wybór 3** [C] a number of things from which you can choose: *This shop has a very good selection of toys.* ▶ **wybór** SYN **choice, range**

selective /sɪ'lektɪv/ adj. **1** concerning only some people or things; not general: *selective schools/education* ▶ **selektywny, wybiórczy 2** careful when choosing: *She's very selective about who she invites to her parties.* ▶ **wymagający**
■ **selectively** adv. ▶ **wybiórczo**

🔑 **self** /self/ noun [C] (pl. **selves** /selvz/) sb's own nature or qualities: *It's good to see you back to **your old self*** (w dobrej formie) *again.* ◇ *Her spiteful remark revealed her **true self**.* ▶ **osobowość, natura**

self- /self/ [in compounds] of, to or by yourself or itself: *self-assessment* ◇ *self-aware* ◇ *He's self-taught* Jest samoukiem. ◇ *self-absorbed* pochłonięty sobą ◇ *self-doubt* zwątpienie w siebie ◇ *self-expression* ▶ **samo-**

ˌself-addressed 'envelope = STAMPED ADDRESSED ENVELOPE

ˌself-as'surance = ASSURANCE (2)

ˌself-as'sured = ASSURED

ˌself-'catering adj. (Brit.) (used about a holiday or a place to stay) where meals are not provided for you so you cook them yourself ▶ **bez wyżywienia**

ˌself-'centred (US ˌself-'centered) adj. thinking only about yourself and not about other people ▶ **egocentryczny** ➲ look at **selfish**

ˌself-con'fessed adj. [only before a noun] admitting that you are sth or do sth that most people consider to be bad ▶ **otwarcie przyznający się do czegoś**

ˌself-'confident adj. feeling sure about your own value and abilities ▶ **pewien siebie** ➲ look at **confident**
■ **ˌself-'confidence** noun [U]: *Many women lack the self-confidence to apply for senior jobs.* ▶ **pewność siebie**

ˌself-'conscious adj. too worried about what other people think about you: *He's self-conscious about being short.* ▶ **przewrażliwiony, skrępowany**
■ **ˌself-'consciously** adv. ▶ **z zażenowaniem** | **ˌself-'consciousness** noun [U] ▶ **zakłopotanie; nieśmiałość**

ˌself-con'tained adj. (Brit.) (used about a flat, etc.) having its own private entrance, kitchen and bathroom: *a self-contained apartment* ▶ **z osobnym wejściem**

ˌself-con'trol noun [U] the ability to control your emotions and appear calm even when you are angry, afraid, excited, etc.: *to lose/keep your self-control* ▶ **samokontrola**

ˌself-de'fence (US ˌself-de'fense) noun [U] the use of force to protect yourself or your property: *Lee is learning karate for self-defence.* ◇ *to shoot somebody **in self-defence*** (w obronie własnej) ▶ **samoobrona**

ˌself-de'struct verb [I] (used about a machine, etc.) to destroy itself ▶ **ulegać samozniszczeniu**
■ **ˌself-de'structive** adj. ▶ **samoniszczący się** | **ˌself-de'struction** noun [U] ▶ (*przen.*) **samozniszczenie**

ˌself-deˌtermi'nation noun [U] **1** the right of a nation, country, etc. to decide what form of government it will have or whether it will be independent of another country or not ▶ **samostanowienie 2** the right or opportunity of individuals to control their own lives ▶ **wolna wola**

ˌself-'discipline noun [U] the ability to make yourself do sth difficult or unpleasant: *It takes a lot of self-discipline to give up smoking.* ▶ **dyscyplina wewnętrzna**

ˌself-em'ployed adj. working for yourself and earning money from your own business ▶ **pracujący na własne konto, posiadający własną firmę**

ˌself-es'teem noun [U] a good opinion of your own character and abilities: *a man with high/low self-esteem* ▶ **poczucie własnej wartości/godności**

ˌself-ˈevident adj. that does not need any proof or explanation; clear ▶ **oczywisty, widoczny gołym okiem**

ˌself-exˈplanatory adj. clear and easy to understand; not needing to be explained: *The book's title is self-explanatory.* ▶ **zrozumiały sam przez się**

ˌself-imˈportant adj. thinking that you are more important than other people ▶ **zarozumiały** SYN **arrogant**
■ **ˌself-imˈportance** noun [U] ▶ **zarozumiałość** | **ˌself-imˈportantly** adv. ▶ **zarozumiale**

ˌself-inˈdulgent adj. allowing yourself to have or do things you enjoy (sometimes when it would be better to stop yourself): *a self-indulgent morning* (leniwy poranek) *spent relaxing in the bath* ▶ **pobłażający sobie**
■ **ˌself-inˈdulgence** noun [C,U] ▶ **pobłażanie sobie**

ˌself-ˈinterest noun [U] thinking about what is best for yourself rather than for other people ▶ **interesowność**

selfish /ˈselfɪʃ/ adj. thinking only about your own needs or wishes and not about other people's: *a selfish attitude* ◇ *I'm sick of your selfish behaviour!* ▶ **samolubny** OPP **unselfish, selfless** ➲ look at **self-centred**
■ **selfishly** adv. ▶ **samolubnie** | **selfishness** noun [U] ▶ **samolubstwo**

selfless /ˈselfləs/ adj. thinking more about other people's needs or wishes than your own ▶ **bezinteresowny** OPP **selfish** ➲ look at **unselfish**

ˌself-ˈmade adj. having become rich or successful by your own efforts: *a self-made millionaire* ▶ **zawdzięczający wszystko samemu sobie**

ˌself-ˈpity noun [U] the state of thinking too much about your own problems or troubles and feeling sorry for yourself ▶ **rozczulanie się nad sobą**

ˌself-ˈportrait noun [C] a picture that you draw or paint of yourself ▶ **autoportret**

ˌself-raising ˈflour (US **ˌself-rising ˈflour**) noun [U] flour that contains **baking powder** ▶ **mąka zawierająca środek spulchniający** ➲ look at **plain flour**

ˌself-reˈliant adj. not depending on help from anyone else ▶ **polegający na sobie samym** ➲ look at **reliant**

ˌself-reˈspect noun [U] a feeling of confidence and pride in yourself: *Old people need to keep their dignity and self-respect.* ▶ **poczucie własnej godności** ➲ look at **respect**
■ **ˌself-reˈspecting** adj. [often in negative sentences]: *No self-respecting language student should be without this book.* ▶ **szanujący się**

ˌself-ˈrighteous adj. believing that you are always right and other people are wrong, so that you are better than other people ▶ **zarozumiały** ➲ look at **righteous**
■ **ˌself-ˈrighteously** adv. ▶ **z wyższością** | **ˌself-ˈrighteousness** noun [U] ▶ **poczucie wyższości, zarozumialstwo**

ˌself-rising ˈflour (US) = SELF-RAISING FLOUR

ˌself-ˈsacrifice noun [U] giving up what you need or want in order to help others ▶ **wyrzeczenie**

ˌself-ˈservice adj. (used about a shop, petrol station, restaurant, etc.) where you serve yourself and then pay for the goods ▶ **samoobsługowy**

ˌself-sufˈficient adj. able to produce or provide everything that you need without help from or having to buy from others ▶ **samowystarczalny**

🔑 **sell** /sel/ verb (pt, pp **sold** /səʊld/) **1** [I,T] **sell (sb) (sth) (at/for sth); sell (sth) (to sb) (at/for sth)** to give sth to sb who pays for it and is then the owner of it: *We are going to sell our car.* ◇ *I sold my guitar to my neighbour for £200.* ◇ *Would you sell me your ticket?* ◇ *I offered them a lot of money but they wouldn't sell* (nie chcieli sprzedać). ▶ **sprzedawać, odsprzedawać 2** [T] to offer sth for people to buy: *Excuse me, do you sell stamps?* ◇ *to sell insurance/advertising space* ▶ **sprzedawać 3** [I,T] to be bought by people in the way or in the numbers mentioned; to be offered at the price mentioned: *These watches sell at £1 000 each in the shops but you can have this one for £500.* ◇ *Her books sell well abroad.* ◇ *This paper sells over a million copies a day.* ▶ **sprzedawać się, mieć (duży/mały) zbyt 4** [T] to make people want to buy sth: *They rely on advertising to sell their products.* ▶ **sprzedawać 5** [T] **sell sth/yourself to sb** to persuade sb to accept sth; to persuade sb that you are the right person for a job, position, etc.: *Now we have to try and sell the idea to the management.* ▶ **sprzedawać (się/coś komuś)** ➲ noun for senses **1** to **4** is **sale**

IDM **be sold on sth** (informal) to be very enthusiastic about sth: *She's completely sold on the idea* (kupiła pomysł) *of moving to France.*

PHR V **sell sth off** to sell sth in order to get rid of it, often at a low price: *The shops sell their remaining winter clothes off in the spring sales.* ▶ **wyprzedawać**

sell out; be sold out (used about tickets for a concert, football game, etc.) to be all sold: *All the tickets sold out within two hours.* ◇ *The concert was sold out weeks ago.* ▶ **zostać wyprzedanym**

sell out (of sth); be sold out (of sth) to sell all of sth so that no more is/are available to be bought: *I'm afraid we've sold out of bread.* ▶ **wyprzedawać** (*cały zapas czegoś*)

sell up to sell everything you own, especially your house, your business, etc. (in order to start a new life, move to another country, etc.) ▶ **wyprzedawać się, sprzedawać cały dobytek**

ˈsell-by date noun [C] (Brit.) the date printed on food packages after which the food should not be sold: *This milk is past its sell-by date.* ▶ **termin, do kiedy towar może być wystawiony do sprzedaży**

seller /ˈselə(r)/ noun [C] **1** [in compounds] a person or business that sells: *a bookseller* ◇ *a flower seller* ▶ **sprzedaw-ca/czyni** OPP **buyer 2** something that is sold, especially in the amount or way mentioned: *This magazine is a big seller in the 25-40 age group.* ▶ **coś, co dobrze się sprzedaje** ➲ look at **best-seller**

Sellotape™ /ˈseləteɪp/ noun [U] (Brit.) a type of clear tape that is sold in rolls and used for sticking things ▶ **(przezroczysta) taśma klejąca** ➲ look at **tape** ➲ picture at **stationery**
■ **sellotape** verb [T] ▶ **kleić/przyklejać coś taśmą klejącą**

ˈsell-out noun [C, usually sing.] a play, concert, etc. for which all the tickets have been sold: *Next week's final is likely to be a sell-out.* ▶ **koncert/sztuka itp., na które wysprzedano wszystkie bilety**

selves plural of **self**

semantic /sɪˈmæntɪk/ adj. connected with the meaning of words and sentences ▶ **semantyczny**
■ **semantically** /-kli/ adv. ▶ **semantycznie**

semblance /ˈsembləns/ noun [sing., U] (formal) **(a) semblance of sth** the appearance of being sth or of having a certain quality ▶ **pozór**

semen /ˈsiːmen/ noun [U] the liquid that is produced by the male sex organs containing **sperm** ▶ **sperma, nasienie**

semester /sɪˈmestə(r)/ noun [C] one of the two periods of time that the school or college year is divided into: *the spring/fall semester* ▶ **semestr** ➲ look at **term**

semi /ˈsemi/ noun [C] (pl. **semis** /ˈsemiz/) (Brit., informal) a house that is joined to another one with a shared wall between them, forming a pair of houses ▶ (*dom typu*) **bliźniak**

semi- /ˈsemi/ [in compounds] half; partly: *semicircular* ◇ *semi-final* ▶ **pół-**

S

semibreve /'semibri:v/ noun [C] (US 'whole note) (used in music) a note that lasts four times as long as a crotchet ▶ **cała nuta** ➲ picture at **music**

semicircle /'semisɜ:kl/ noun [C] one half of a circle; something that is arranged in this shape: *Please sit* ***in a semicircle.*** ▶ **półkole**

semicolon /ˌsemi'kəʊlən/ noun [C] a mark (;) used in writing for separating parts of a sentence or items in a list ▶ **średnik**

ˌsemi-de'tached adj. (used about a house) joined to another house with a shared wall on one side forming a pair of houses ▶ **dotyczący domu typu bliźniak** ➲ picture on **page A3**

ˌsemi-'final noun [C] one of the two games in a sports competition that decide which players or teams will play each other in the final: *He's through to the semi-finals.* ▶ **półfinał** ➲ look at **quarter-final**, **final**
■ **ˌsemi-'finalist** noun [C] ▶ **półfinalist(k)a**

seminar /'semɪnɑ:(r)/ noun [C] **1** a class at a university, college, etc. in which a small group of students discuss or study a subject with a teacher: *I've got a seminar on Goethe this morning.* ▶ **seminarium 2** a meeting for business people in which working methods, etc. are taught or discussed: *a one-day management seminar* ▶ **seminarium**

seminary /'semɪnəri/ noun [C] (pl. **seminaries**) a college for training priests or rabbis ▶ **seminarium duchowne**

semiquaver /'semikweɪvə(r)/ noun [C] (US 'sixteenth note) (used in music) a note that lasts half as long as a quaver ▶ **szesnastka** ➲ picture at **music**

semitone /'semitəʊn/ (also 'half step; 'half-tone) noun [C] the shortest step between notes in a musical scale, for example between C♯ and D, or B♭ and B ▶ **półton**

Sen. = SENATOR

senate /'senət/ noun (often **the Senate**) [C, with sing. or pl. verb] one of the two groups of elected politicians who make laws in the government in some countries, for example the US ▶ **senat** ➲ look at **Congress**, **House of Representatives**

senator /'senətə(r)/ noun (often **Senator**) (abbr. **Sen.**) [C] a member of **the Senate**: *Senator McCarthy* ▶ **senator**

send /send/ verb [T] (pt, pp **sent** /sent/) **1 send sth (to sb/sth); send (sb) sth** to make sth go or be taken somewhere, especially by post, radio, etc.: *to send a letter/parcel/message/fax to somebody ◇ Don't forget to send me a postcard.* ▶ **wysyłać**, **odsyłać 2** to tell sb to go somewhere or to do sth; to arrange for sb to go somewhere: *My company is sending me on a training course next month. ◇ She* ***sent*** *the children* ***to bed*** (kazała dzieciom iść do łóżka) *early. ◇ to* ***send somebody to prison*** wsadzać kogoś do więzienia *◇ I'll send someone round* (poślę kogoś) *to collect you at 10.00.* ▶ **wysyłać**, **posyłać 3** to cause sb/sth to move in a particular direction, often quickly or as a reaction that cannot be prevented: *I accidentally pushed the table and* ***sent*** *all the drinks* ***flying*** (spowodowałem, że wszystkie szklanki i kieliszki znalazły się w powietrzu). *◇ This year's poor harvest has sent food prices up* (wywołały podwyżkę cen żywności). ▶ **powodować**, **wywoływać 4 send sb (to/into sth)** to make sb have a particular feeling or enter a particular state: *The movement of the train* ***sent*** *me* ***to sleep*** (uśpił mnie). ▶ **wprawiać kogoś** (*w jakiś stan*)

IDM **give/send sb your love** → LOVE[1]

PHR V **send for sb/sth** to ask for sb to come to you; to ask for sth to be brought or sent to you: *Quick! Send for an ambulance!* ▶ **posyłać po kogoś/coś**, **wzywać kogoś**

send sth in to send sth to a place where it will be officially dealt with: *I sent my application in three weeks ago but I still haven't had a reply.* ▶ **przesyłać/wysyłać coś**

send off (for sth); **send away (to sb) (for sth)** to write to sb and ask for sth to be sent to you: *Let's send off for some holiday brochures.* ▶ **pisać do kogoś z prośbą o coś**

send sb off (used in a sports match) to order a player who has broken a rule to leave the field and not to return: *Beckham was sent off for a foul in the first half.* ▶ **odsyłać z boiska**

send sth off to post sth: *I'll send the information off today.* ▶ **wysyłać pocztą**

send sth out 1 to send sth to a lot of different people or places: *We sent out the invitations two months before the wedding.* ▶ **rozsyłać coś 2** to produce sth, for example light, heat, sound, etc.: *The sun sends out light and heat.* ▶ **wysyłać/emitować/wydzielać coś** SYN **emit**

send sb/sth up (Brit., informal) to make sb/sth look ridiculous or silly, especially by copying them or it in a way that is intended to be amusing ▶ **parodiować kogoś/coś**

sender /'sendə(r)/ noun [C] a person who sends sth: *If undelivered, please return to sender.* ▶ **nadawca**

senile /'si:naɪl/ adj. behaving in a confused and strange way, and unable to remember things because of old age: *I think she's* ***going senile.*** ▶ **zdziecinniały**, **starczy**
■ **senility** /sə'nɪləti/ noun [U] ▶ **zdziecinnienie**

senior[1] /'si:niə(r)/ adj. **1 senior (to sb)** having a high or higher position in a company, an organization, etc.: *a senior lecturer/officer/manager ◇ He's senior to me. ◇ a senior managerial position* kierownicze stanowisko ▶ **starszy** OPP **junior 2** (often **Senior**) (abbr. **Snr**; **Sr**) (especially US) (used after the name of a man who has the same name as his son, to avoid confusion) ▶ (*po nazwisku*) **senior** OPP **junior 3** (Brit.) (used in schools) older: *This common room is for the use of senior pupils only.* ▶ **starszy 4** (US) connected with the final year at high school or college: *the senior prom* ▶ **dotyczący ostatniego roku szkoły średniej**

senior[2] /'si:niə(r)/ noun [C] **1** a person who is older or of a higher position (than one or more other people): *My oldest sister is* ***ten years my senior.*** *◇ She felt undervalued, both by her colleagues and her seniors.* ▶ **osoba starsza o kilka lat**; **osoba wyższa rangą** OPP **junior 2** (Brit.) one of the older students at a school ▶ **uczeń z wyższej klasy 3** (US) a student in the final year of school, college or university: *high school seniors* ▶ **student/ka ostatniego roku studiów**

ˌsenior 'citizen = OLD-AGE PENSIONER

ˌsenior 'high school (also ˌsenior 'high) noun [C,U] (in the US) a school for young people between the ages of 14 and 18 ▶ **liceum**, **szkoła średnia** ➲ look at **junior high school**

seniority /ˌsi:ni'ɒrəti/ noun [U] the position or importance that a person has in a company, an organization, etc. in relation to others: *The names are listed below* ***in order of seniority.*** ▶ **starszeństwo**

sensation /sen'seɪʃn/ noun **1** [C] a feeling that is caused by sth affecting your body or part of your body: *a pleasant/an unpleasant/a tingling sensation* ▶ **uczucie** SYN **feeling 2** [U] the ability to feel when touching or being touched: *For some time after the accident he had no sensation in his legs.* ▶ **czucie** SYN **feeling 3** [C, usually sing.] a general feeling or impression that is difficult to explain: *I had the peculiar sensation that I was floating in the air.* ▶ **uczucie**, **wrażenie** SYN **feeling 4** [C, usually sing.] great excitement, surprise or interest among a group of people; sb/sth that causes this excitement: *The young American* ***caused a sensation*** *by beating the top player. ◇ The show was* ***an overnight sensation*** (stał się sensacją z dnia na dzień). ▶ **sensacja**

sensational /sen'seɪʃənl/ adj. **1** causing, or trying to cause, a feeling of great excitement, surprise or interest

among people: *This magazine specializes in sensational stories about the rich and famous.* ▶ **rewelacyjny, sensacyjny** ➲ note at **newspaper** **2** (informal) extremely good or beautiful; very exciting ▶ **rewelacyjny** SYN **fantastic**
■ **sensationalism** /-ʃənəlɪzəm/ noun [U] a way of getting people's interest by using shocking words or by presenting facts and events as worse or more shocking than they really are ▶ **pogoń za sensacją** | **sensationalist** /-ʃənəlɪst/ adj.: *sensationalist headlines/newspapers* ▶ **goniący za sensacją** | **sensationally** /-ʃənəli/ adv. ▶ **strasznie; nadając czemuś nadmierny rozgłos**

sense[1] /sens/ noun **1** [C] one of the five natural physical powers of sight, hearing, smell, taste and touch, that people and animals have: *I've got a cold and I've lost my **sense of smell**.* ◇ *Dogs have an acute **sense of hearing**.* ▶ **poczucie, zmysł** **2** [sing.] a feeling of sth: *I felt a tremendous **sense of relief** when the exams were finally over.* ◇ *She only visits her family out of a **sense of duty**.* ▶ **uczucie, poczucie** **3** [U, sing.] the ability to understand sth; the ability to recognize what sth is or what its value is: *She seems to have lost all **sense of reality**.* ◇ *I like him – he's got a great **sense of humour**.* ◇ *I'm always getting lost. I've got absolutely no **sense of direction**.* ▶ **poczucie, zmysł** **4** [U, sing.] a natural ability to do or produce sth well: *Good **business sense*** (smykałka do interesów) *made her a millionaire.* ◇ *He's got absolutely no **dress sense*** (nie ma gustu). ▶ **wyczucie** **5** [U] the ability to think or act in a reasonable or sensible way; good judgement: *At least he **had the sense** to stop when he realized he was making a mistake.* ◇ *I think there's a lot of sense in what you're saying.* ▶ **zdrowy rozsądek, rozum** ➲ look at **common sense** **6** [U] **sense (in doing sth)** the reason for doing sth; purpose: *There's no sense in going any further – we're obviously lost.* ◇ ***What's the sense** in making the situation more difficult for yourself?* ▶ **sens** **7** [C] (used about a word, phrase, etc.) a meaning: *This word has two senses.* ▶ **znaczenie**
IDM **come to your senses** to finally realize that you should do sth because it is the most sensible thing to do ▶ **opamiętać się**
in a sense in one particular way but not in other ways; partly: *In a sense you're right, but there's more to the matter than that.* ▶ **w pewnym sensie**
make sense **1** to be possible to understand; to have a clear meaning: *What does this sentence mean? It doesn't make sense to me.* ▶ **mieć sens** **2** (used about an action) to be sensible or logical: *I think it would make sense to wait for a while before making a decision.* ▶ **być sensownym/logicznym**
make sense of sth to manage to understand sth that is not clear or is difficult to understand: *I can't make sense of these instructions.* ▶ **rozumieć**
talk sense → TALK[1]

sense[2] /sens/ verb [T] [not used in the continuous tenses] to realize or become conscious of sth; to get a feeling about sth even though you cannot see it, hear it, etc.: *I sensed that something was wrong as soon as I went in.* ▶ **czuć instynktownie** ℹ Czasownika **sense** nie używa się w czasach *continuous*. Natomiast często spotyka się go w *present participle* (formie *-ing*): *Sensing a scandal, the tabloid photographers rushed to the star's hotel.*

senseless /ˈsensləs/ adj. **1** having no meaning or purpose ▶ **bezsensowny, bezcelowy** **2** [not before a noun] unconscious: *He was beaten senseless.* ▶ **nieprzytomny**

sensibility /ˌsensəˈbɪləti/ noun (pl. **sensibilities**) **1** [U,C] the ability to understand and experience deep feelings, for example in art, literature, etc. ▶ **wrażliwość** **2** (**sensibilities**) [pl.] sb's feelings, especially when they are easily offended: *The article offended her religious sensibilities* (zranił jej uczucia religijne). ▶ **wrażliwość uczuć** ➲ look at **sensitivity**

sensible /ˈsensəbl/ adj. (used about people and their behaviour) able to make good judgements based on reason and experience; practical: *a sensible person/decision/precaution* ◇ *Stop joking and give me a sensible answer.* ◇ *I think it would be sensible* (byłoby rozsądnie) *to leave early.* ▶ **rozsądny** OPP **silly, foolish**
■ **sensibly** /-əbli/ adv.: *Let's sit down and discuss the matter sensibly.* ▶ **rozsądnie**

Por. **sensible** z **sensitive**. **Sensible** odnosi się do zdrowego rozsądku, racjonalnego podejścia i dobrego osądu. **Sensitive** łączy się z uczuciami i emocjami, a także z odczuciami zmysłowymi.

sensitive /ˈsensətɪv/ adj. **1** **sensitive (to sth)** showing that you are conscious of and able to understand people's feelings, problems, etc.: *It wasn't very sensitive of you to mention her boyfriend. You know they've just split up.* ◇ *She always tries to be sensitive to other people's feelings.* ▶ **wrażliwy** OPP **insensitive** ➲ note at **sensible** **2** **sensitive (about/to sth)** easily upset, offended or annoyed, especially about a particular subject: *She's still a bit sensitive about her divorce.* ◇ *He's very sensitive to criticism.* ▶ **wrażliwy (na coś/na punkcie czegoś)** OPP **insensitive** **3** needing to be dealt with carefully because it is likely to cause anger or trouble: *This is a sensitive period in the negotiations between the two countries.* ▶ (*temat itp.*) **delikatny** **4** **sensitive (to sth)** easily hurt or damaged; painful, especially if touched: *a new cream for sensitive skin* ◇ *My teeth are very sensitive to hot or cold food.* ▶ **wrażliwy (na coś)** **5** able to measure very small changes: *a sensitive instrument* ▶ **precyzyjny, czuły**
■ **sensitively** adv.: *The investigation will need to be handled sensitively.* ▶ **delikatnie, z wyczuciem** | **sensitivity** /ˌsensəˈtɪvəti/ noun [U]: *I think your comments showed a complete lack of sensitivity.* ▶ **wrażliwość, wyczucie** ➲ look at **sensibility**

sensitize (also **-ise**) /ˈsensətaɪz/ verb [T, usually passive] **1** **sensitize sb/sth (to sth)** to make sb/sth more aware of sth, especially a problem or sth bad: *People are becoming more sensitized to the dangers threatening the environment.* ▶ **uwrażliwiać** **2** to make sb/sth sensitive to physical or chemical changes, or to a particular substance ▶ **uczulać**
■ **sensitization** (also **-isation**) /ˌsensətaɪˈzeɪʃn; US -təˈz-/ noun [U] ▶ **uwrażliwienie; uczulenie**

sensual /ˈsenʃuəl/ adj. connected with physical or sexual pleasure: *the sensual rhythms of Latin music* ▶ **zmysłowy** ➲ look at **sensuous**
■ **sensuality** /ˌsenʃuˈæləti/ noun [U] ▶ **zmysłowość**

sensuous /ˈsenʃuəs/ adj. giving pleasure to the mind or body through the senses: *the sensuous feel of pure silk* ▶ **zmysłowy** ➲ look at **sensual**
■ **sensuously** adv. ▶ **zmysłowo** | **sensuousness** noun [U] ▶ **zmysłowość**

sent past tense, past participle of **send**

sentence[1] /ˈsentəns/ noun [C] **1** a group of words containing a subject and a verb, that expresses a statement, a question, etc. When a sentence is written it begins with a capital letter and ends with a full stop: *You don't need to write a long letter. A couple of sentences will be enough.* ▶ (*gram.*) **zdanie** ➲ look at **phrase** **2** the punishment given by a judge to sb who has been found guilty of a crime: *20 years in prison was a very harsh sentence.* ▶ **wyrok** ➲ note at **court**

sentence[2] /ˈsentəns/ verb [T] **sentence sb (to sth)** (used about a judge) to tell sb who has been found guilty of a crime what the punishment will be: *The judge sentenced her to three months in prison for shoplifting.* ▶ **skazywać (na coś)**

S

sentiment /ˈsentɪmənt/ noun **1** [C,U] (formal) an attitude or opinion that is often caused or influenced by emotion: *His comments expressed my sentiments exactly.* ▶ **uczucie, opinia 2** [U] feelings such as pity, romantic love, sadness, etc. that influence sb's actions or behaviour (sometimes in situations where this is not appropriate): *There's no room for sentiment in business.* ▶ **sentyment**

sentimental /ˌsentɪˈmentl/ adj. **1** producing or connected with emotions such as romantic love, pity, sadness, etc. which may be too strong or not appropriate: *How can you be sentimental about an old car!* ◇ *a sentimental love song* ▶ **sentymentalny 2** connected with happy memories or feelings of love rather than having any financial value: *The jewellery wasn't worth much but it had great* ***sentimental value*** *to me.* ▶ **sentymentalny**

■ **sentimentality** /ˌsentɪmenˈtæləti/ noun [U] ▶ **sentymentalność, sentymentalizm** | **sentimentally** /ˌsentɪˈmentəli/ adv. ▶ **z sentymentem**

sentry /ˈsentri/ noun [C] (pl. **sentries**) a soldier who stands outside a building and guards it ▶ **wartowni-k/czka**

separable /ˈsepərəbl/ adj. able to be separated ▶ **rozłączny, dający się rozdzielić, odłączny** OPP **inseparable**

⚷ **separate**[1] /ˈseprət/ adj. **1** different; not connected: *We stayed in separate rooms in the same hotel.* ▶ **oddzielny 2 separate (from sth/sb)** apart; not together: *You should always keep your cash and credit cards separate* (oddzielnie). ▶ **osobny**

⚷ **separate**[2] /ˈsepəreɪt/ verb **1** [T] **separate sb/sth (from sb/sth)** to keep people or things apart; to be between people or things with the result that they are apart: *The two sides of the city are separated by the river.* ▶ **oddzielać, rozdzielać 2** [I,T] **separate (sb/sth) (from sb/sth)** to stop being together; to cause people or things to stop being together: *I think we should separate into two groups.* ◇ *The friends separated at the airport.* ◇ *I got separated from my friends in the crowd.* ▶ **rozdzielać (się), oddzielać (się)** SYN **divide 3** [I] to stop living together as a couple with your wife, husband or partner: *His parents separated when he was still a baby.* ▶ **rozchodzić się**

PHR V **separate out**; **separate sth out** to divide into different parts; to divide sth into different parts: *to separate out different meanings* ▶ **dzielić się; podzielić/oddzielać coś**

⚷ **separated** /ˈsepəreɪtɪd/ adj. not living together as a couple any more: *My wife and I are separated.* ▶ *(być)* **w separacji**

⚷ **separately** /ˈseprətli/ adv. apart; not together: *Shall we pay separately or all together?* ▶ **oddzielnie, osobno**

⚷ **separation** /ˌsepəˈreɪʃn/ noun **1** [C,U] the act of separating or being separated; a situation or period of being apart: *Separation from family and friends made me very lonely.* ▶ **rozłąka 2** [C] an agreement where a couple decide not to live together any more: *a trial separation* ▶ **separacja**

Sept. = SEPTEMBER: *2 Sept. 1920*

⚷ **September** /sepˈtembə(r)/ noun [U,C] (abbr. **Sept.**) the 9th month of the year, coming after August ▶ **wrzesień**
➲ note at **January**

septic /ˈseptɪk/ adj. infected with poisonous bacteria: *The wound* ***went septic.*** ▶ **septyczny**

sequel /ˈsiːkwəl/ noun [C] **a sequel (to sth) 1** a book, film, etc. that continues the story of the one before ▶ **dalszy ciąg 2** something that happens after, or is the result of, an earlier event ▶ **następstwo**

sequence /ˈsiːkwəns/ noun [C] **1** a number of things (actions, events, etc.) that happen or come one after another: *Complete the following sequence: 1, 4, 8, 13, ...* ▶ **ciąg 2** [U] the order in which a number of things happen or are arranged: *The photographs are* ***in sequence.*** ▶ **kolejność**

sequin /ˈsiːkwɪn/ noun [C] a small flat shiny circle that is sewn onto clothing as decoration ▶ **cekin**

■ **sequinned** adj. ▶ **wyszywany cekinami**

serene /səˈriːn/ adj. calm and peaceful: *Her smile was serene.* ▶ **pogodny**

■ **serenely** adv. ▶ **pogodnie** | **serenity** /səˈrenəti/ noun [U] ▶ **pogoda ducha**

sergeant /ˈsɑːdʒənt/ noun [C] (abbr. **Sgt**) **1** an officer with a low position in the army or air force ▶ **sierżant 2** an officer with a middle position in the police force ▶ **sierżant**

serial /ˈsɪəriəl/ noun [C] a story in a magazine or on TV or radio that is told in a number of parts over a period of time: *the first part of a sixteen-part drama serial* ▶ **serial**
➲ note at **series**

■ **serialize** (also -ise) /ˈsɪəriəlaɪz/ verb [T] ▶ **wydawać w odcinkach**

ˌ**serial ˈkiller** noun [C] a person who murders several people one after another ▶ **seryjn-y/a morder-ca/czyni**

ˈ**serial number** noun [C] the number put on sth in order to identify it ▶ **numer seryjny**

⚷ **series** /ˈsɪəriːz/ noun [C] (pl. **series**) **1** a number of things that happen one after another and are of the same type or connected: *a series of events* ◇ *There has been a series of burglaries in this district recently.* ▶ **szereg**

> Por. **series** z **serial**. **Series** to film w odcinkach, w którym występują ci sami bohaterowie, lecz każdy odcinek ma inną fabułę i stanowi odrębną całość. **Serial** to film, w którym ta sama fabuła ciągnie się przez wiele odcinków.

⚷ **serious** /ˈsɪəriəs/ adj. **1** bad or dangerous: *a serious accident/illness/offence* ◇ *Pollution is a very serious problem.* ◇ *Her condition is serious and she's likely to be in hospital for some time.* ▶ **poważny 2** needing to be treated as important, not just for fun: *Don't laugh, it's a serious matter.* ◇ *a serious discussion* ▶ **poważny, (na) serio 3 serious (about sth/about doing sth)** (used about a person) not joking; thinking deeply: *Are you serious* (czy mówisz poważnie) *about starting your own business?* ◇ *He's terribly serious. I don't think I've ever seen him laugh.* ◇ *You're looking very serious. Was it bad news?* ▶ **poważny**

■ **seriousness** noun [U] ▶ **powaga**

⚷ **seriously** /ˈsɪəriəsli/ adv. **1** in a serious way: *Three people were seriously injured in the accident.* ◇ *My mother is seriously ill.* ◇ *It's time you started to think seriously about the future.* ▶ **poważnie 2** (used at the beginning of a sentence for showing that you are not joking or that you really mean what you are saying): *Seriously, I do appreciate all your help.* ◇ *Seriously, you've got nothing to worry about.* ▶ **poważnie, naprawdę 3** (used for expressing surprise at what sb has said and asking if it is really true): *'I'm 40 today.' 'Seriously? You look a lot younger.'* ▶ **poważnie**

IDM **take sb/sth seriously** to treat sb or sth as important: *You take everything too seriously! Relax and enjoy yourself.* ▶ **traktować poważnie**

sermon /ˈsɜːmən/ noun [C] a speech on a religious or moral subject that is given as part of a service in church ▶ **kazanie**

serpent /ˈsɜːpənt/ noun [C] (in literature) a snake, especially a large one ▶ **wąż**

serrated /səˈreɪtɪd/ adj. having a row of points in V-shapes along the edge: *a knife with a serrated edge* ▶ **ząbkowany, zębaty**

servant /'sɜːvənt/ noun [C] a person who is paid to work in sb's house, doing work such as cooking, cleaning, etc. ▶ **służąc-y/a** ➲ look at **civil servant**

serve /sɜːv/ verb **1** [T] to give food or drink to sb during a meal; to take an order and then bring food or drink to sb in a restaurant, bar, etc.: *Breakfast is served from 7.30 to 9.00 a.m.* ▶ **podawać** (*do stołu*), **obsługiwać** **2** [T] (used about an amount) to be enough for a certain number of people: *According to the recipe, this dish serves four* (to porcja dla czworga). ▶ **wystarczać** (*dla określonej liczby osób*) **3** [I,T] to take a customer's order; to give help, sell goods, etc.: *There was a long queue of people waiting to be served.* ◇ *Excuse me madam. Are you being served?* Czym mogę służyć? ▶ **obsługiwać** **4** [I,T] to be useful or suitable for a particular purpose: *The judge said the punishment would serve as a warning to others.* ◇ *His pathetic excuses only served to make me even angrier* (tylko coraz bardziej mnie denerwowały). ◇ *It's an old car but it will **serve our purpose*** (ale nam wystarczy) *for a few months.* ▶ **służyć (za/jako coś)** **5** [I,T] to perform a duty or provide a service for the public or for an organization: *During the war, he served in the army.* ◇ *She has served on* (zasiadała w) *a number of committees.* ◇ *She became a nurse because she wanted to serve the community.* ◇ *The town is served* (jest obsługiwane) *by two hospitals.* ▶ **służyć** **6** [T] to spend a period of time in prison as a punishment: *He is currently **serving a** ten-year **sentence** for fraud.* ▶ **odsiadywać** (*wyrok*) **7** [I,T] to start play by hitting the ball: *She served an ace.* ▶ **serwować**

IDM **first come, first served** → FIRST[2]

serve sb right (used when sth unpleasant happens to sb and you do not feel sorry for them because you think it is their own fault): *'I feel sick.' 'It serves you right for eating so much.'* ▶ **dobrze mu, ci itp. tak!**

PHR V **serve sth out** **1** to continue doing sth, especially working or staying in prison, for a fixed period of time that has been set: *He has three more years in prison before he's served out his sentence.* ◇ (Brit.) *They didn't want me to serve out my notice.* ▶ **odsiedzieć** (*np. wyrok*) **2** (Brit.) to share food or drink between a number of people: *I went around the guests serving out drinks.* ▶ **serwować** (*posiłki/napoje*)

serve sth up **1** to put food onto plates and give it to people: *He served up a delicious meal.* ▶ **podawać do stołu**, **serwować** (*posiłki/napoje*) **2** to give, offer or provide sth: *She served up the usual excuse.* ▶ **dostarczać czegoś**, **oferować coś**

server /'sɜːvə(r)/ noun [C] a computer that stores information that a number of computers can share ▶ **serwer** ➲ look at **client**

service¹ /'sɜːvɪs/ noun **1** [C] a system or an organization that provides the public with sth that it needs; the job that an organization does: *the postal service* ◇ *There is a regular bus service* (regularne połączenie autobusowe) *to the airport.* ◇ *The airline is starting a new international service* (nowe połączenie międzynarodowe). ◇ *We offer a number of financial services.* ◇ *room service* obsługa kelnerska do pokoju hotelowego ▶ **służba**; **usługi** ➲ look at **civil service**, **National Health Service** **2** [U] the work or the quality of work done by sb when serving a customer: *I enjoyed the meal but the service was terrible.* ◇ *Is service included in the bill?* ▶ **obsługa**, **serwis (gwarancyjny)** **3** [U,C] work done for sb; help given to sb: *He left the police force after thirty years' service.* ◇ *Do you have to do **military service** in your country?* ◇ *He offered his services* (zaoferował swoje usługi) *as a driver.* ▶ **służba**; **zasługi** **4** [C] the checks, repairs, etc. that are necessary to make sure that a machine is working properly: *We take our car for a service every six months.* ▶ **przegląd (techniczny)** **5** [C, usually pl.] the armed forces; the army, navy or air force: *They both joined **the services** when they left school.* ▶ **siły zbrojne** **6** [C] a religious ceremony, usually including prayers, singing, etc.: *a funeral service* ▶ **nabożeństwo**, **msza** **7** (**services**) [pl.] (also **'service station**) a place at the side of a **motorway** where there is a petrol station, a shop, toilets, a restaurant, etc.: *It's five miles to the next services.* ▶ **kompleks stacji obsługowych przy autostradzie** **8** [C] the first hit of the ball at the start of play; a player's turn to serve (7): *She's not a bad player but her service is weak.* ▶ **serwis**

service² /'sɜːvɪs/ verb [T] to examine and, if necessary, repair a car, machine, etc.: *All cars should be serviced at regular intervals.* ▶ **robić przegląd**

serviceable /'sɜːvɪsəbl/ adj. suitable to be used ▶ **zdatny do użycia**

'service charge noun [C] the amount of money that is added to a restaurant bill for the service given by the waiters and waitresses ▶ **opłata za obsługę**

serviceman /'sɜːvɪsmən/, **servicewoman** /'sɜːvɪswʊmən/ noun [C] (pl. **-men** /-mən/; **-women** /-wɪmɪn/) a person who is a member of the armed forces ▶ **żołnierz**, **kobieta żołnierz**

'service station **1** = PETROL STATION **2** = SERVICE¹ (7)

serviette /ˌsɜːvi'et/ noun [C] a square of cloth or paper that you use when you are eating to keep your clothes clean and to clean your mouth or hands on ▶ **serwetka** **SYN** **napkin**

servile /'sɜːvaɪl; US also -vl/ adj. wanting too much to please sb and obey them ▶ **służalczy**

session /'seʃn/ noun **1** [C] a period of doing a particular activity: *The whole tape was recorded in one session.* ◇ *She has a session at the gym every week.* ▶ **posiedzenie**, **seans** **2** [C,U] a formal meeting or series of meetings of a court of law, parliament, etc.: *This court is now **in session*** (obraduje). ▶ **sesja**, **posiedzenie**

set¹ /set/ verb (**setting**; pt, pp **set**) **1** [T] to put sb/sth or to be in a particular place or position: *I set the box down carefully on the floor.* ◇ *The hotel is set* (jest położony) *in beautiful grounds.* ▶ **umieszczać** **2** [T] to cause a particular state or event; to start sth happening: *The new government **set** the prisoners **free*** (uwolnił więźniów). ◇ *The rioters **set** a number of cars **on fire*** (podpalili kilka samochodów). ◇ *Her comment set him thinking* (zmusiła go do myślenia). ▶ **zapoczątkować jakieś działania** **3** [T, often passive] to make the action of a book, play, film, etc. take place in a particular time, situation, etc.: *The film is set in 16th-century Spain.* ▶ **osadzać**, **rozgrywać się** **4** [T] to prepare or arrange sth for a particular purpose: *I set my alarm for 6.30.* ◇ *to set the table* nakrywać do stołu ▶ **nastawiać** **5** [T] to decide or arrange sth: *Can we **set a limit** of two hours for the meeting?* ◇ *They haven't **set the date** for their wedding yet.* ▶ **ustalać**, **wyznaczać** **6** [T] to fix a **precious** stone, etc. in a piece of jewellery: *The brooch had three diamonds set in gold.* ▶ **osadzać** **7** [T] to do sth good that people have to try to copy or achieve: *Try to **set a good example*** (dawać dobry przykład) *to the younger children.* ◇ *He has **set a** new world **record**.* ◇ *They set high standards of customer service.* ▶ **ustanawiać**, **wyznaczać** **8** [T] to give sb a piece of work or a task: *We've been **set** a lot of **homework** this weekend.* ◇ *I've **set** myself **a target** of four hours' study every evening.* ▶ **zadawać** (*pracę*), **wyznaczać** (*np. zadanie/cel*) **9** [I] to become firm or hard: *The concrete will **set solid/hard** in just a few hours.* ▶ **zsiadać się**, **krzepnąć** **10** [T] to fix a broken bone in the correct position so that it can get better: *The doctor set her broken leg.* ▶ **nastawiać** (*złamaną kość*) **11** [I] to go down below the **horizon** in the evening: *We sat and watched the sun setting.* ▶ **zachodzić** **OPP** **rise** **12** [T] to write music to go with words: *She writes the words of the song and Sam sets them to music.* ▶ **komponować muzykę do tekstu** **13** [T] to arrange sb's hair while it is wet so that it becomes

S

curly, wavy, etc.: *She went to the hairdresser's to have her hair set* (uczesać się). ▶ **układać** (*włosy*)

ⓘ **Set** używa się w idiomach, np. **set sail**. Zob. hasła odpowiednich rzeczowników, przymiotników itp.

PHR V **set about sth** to start doing sth, especially dealing with a problem or task: *How would you set about tackling this problem?* ▶ **zabierać się do czegoś**

set sth aside to keep sth to use later: *I try to set aside part of my wages every week.* ▶ **odkładać**, **rezerwować**

set sb/sth back to delay sb/sth: *The bad weather has set our plans back six weeks.* ▶ **opóźniać**

set forth (formal) to start a journey ▶ **wyruszać**

set sth forth (formal) to show or tell sth to sb or to make sth known ▶ **przedstawiać** (*np. opinię*)

set in to arrive and remain for a period of time: *I'm afraid that the bad weather has set in.* ▶ **ustalać się**, **nastawać**

set off to leave on a journey: *We set off at 3 o'clock this morning.* ▶ **wyruszać** (*w podróż*)

set sb off (doing sth) to make sb start doing sth such as laughing, crying or talking: *The smallest thing can set her off laughing* (potrafi ją rozśmieszyć). ▶ **powodować** (*np. płacz*)

set sth off **1** to make a bomb, etc. explode: *A gang of boys were setting off fireworks in the street.* ▶ **detonować coś** **2** to make an alarm start ringing: *Opening this door will set off the alarm.* ▶ **włączać** (*alarm*) **3** to start a process or series of events: *Panic on the stock market set off a wave of selling.* ▶ **wywoływać coś** **4** to make sth more noticeable or attractive by being placed near it: *That blouse sets off the blue of her eyes.* ▶ **podkreślać coś**

set on/upon sb [usually passive] to attack sb suddenly: *I opened the gate, and was immediately set on by a large dog.* ▶ **atakować kogoś**

set out to leave on a journey ▶ **wyruszać** (*w podróż*)

set out to do sth to decide to achieve sth: *He set out to prove that his theory was right.* ▶ **stawiać sobie jakiś cel**

set sb up **1** to provide sb with the money that they need in order to do sth: *A bank loan helped to set him up in business.* ▶ **ustawiać kogoś** **2** (informal) to make sb healthier, stronger, more lively, etc.: *The break from work really set me up for the new year.* ▶ **stawiać kogoś na nogi** **3** (informal) to trick sb, especially by making them appear guilty of sth: *He denied the charges, saying the police had set him up.* ▶ **wrabiać kogoś**

set (sth) up to start a business, an organization, a system, etc.: *The company has set up a new branch in Wales.* ◇ *After she qualified as a doctor, she set up in practice* (rozpoczęła praktykę) *in Yorkshire.* ▶ **organizować**, **zakładać**

set² /set/ noun [C] **1** a number of things that belong together: *a set of kitchen knives* ◇ *In the first set of questions, you have to fill in the gaps.* ◇ *a set of instructions* ◇ *a spare set of keys* ◇ *a chess set* ▶ **komplet**, **zestaw** **2** a piece of equipment for receiving TV or radio signals: *a TV set* ▶ **odbiornik** **3** the furniture, painted cloth, boards, etc. that are made to be used in a play or film: *a musical with spectacular sets* ▶ **dekoracje** **4** (in sports such as **tennis**) a group of games forming part of a match: *She won in* ***straight sets*** (bez straty seta). ▶ **set**

set³ /set/ adj. **1** placed in a particular position: *deep-set eyes* ◇ *Our house is quite set back from the road.* ▶ **ustawiony**, **położony**, **osadzony** **2** fixed and not changing; firm: *There are no set hours in my job.* ◇ *I'll have the set menu* (zestaw dnia). ◇ *He's getting more and more* ***set in his ways*** (coraz trudniej przystosowuje się do nowych warunków) *as he gets older.* ▶ **ustalony**, **sztywny** **3** that everyone must study for an exam: *We have to study three set texts for French.* ▶ (*lektura itp.*) **obowiązkowy** **4 set (for sth)**; **set (to do sth)** ready, prepared or likely to do sth: *Okay, I'm set – let's go!* ◇ *I was all set to leave when the phone rang.* ◇ *The Swiss team look set for victory.* ▶ **gotowy**, **zdecydowany**

IDM **be set against sth/doing sth** to be determined that sth will not happen or that you will not do sth ▶ **być przeciwnym**

be set on sth/doing sth to be determined to do sth: *She's set on a career in acting.* ◇ *My heart was set on that house* (bardzo mi na tym domu zależało). ▶ **upierać się przy czymś**

setback /ˈsetbæk/ noun [C] a difficulty or problem that stops you progressing as fast as you would like: *She suffered a major setback when she missed the exams through illness.* ▶ **przeszkoda**, **trudność**

ˈ**set square** (US **triangle**) noun [C] an instrument for drawing straight lines and angles, made from a flat piece of plastic or metal in the shape of a triangle with one angle of 90° ▶ **ekierka**

settee /seˈtiː/ noun [C] a long soft seat with a back and arms that more than one person can sit on ▶ **kanapa** SYN **sofa**

setter /ˈsetə(r)/ noun [C] a breed of dog with long hair that can be trained to find animals or birds in a hunt: *an Irish/red setter* ▶ **seter**

setting /ˈsetɪŋ/ noun [C] **1** the position sth is in; the place and time in which sth happens: *The hotel is in a beautiful setting, close to the sea.* ◇ *They decided that the village church would be the perfect setting* (będzie idealnym miejscem) *for their wedding.* ◇ *The child learns to deal with various social settings* (z różnorodnym otoczeniem społecznym). ▶ **sceneria**, **tło** **2** one of the positions of the controls of a machine: *Cook it in the oven on a moderate setting* (w średnio gorącym piekarniku). ▶ **nastawienie**

settle /ˈsetl/ verb **1** [I,T] to put an end to an argument or a disagreement: *They settled the dispute* (doszli do porozumienia) *without going to court.* ◇ *They settled out of court.* ◇ *We didn't speak to each other for years, but we've* ***settled our differences*** (pogodziliśmy się) *now.* ▶ **rozstrzygnąć**, **rozwiązać** **2** [T] to decide or arrange sth finally: *Everything's settled. We leave on the 9 o'clock flight on Friday.* ▶ **załatwić** **3** [I] to go and live permanently in a new country, area, town, etc.: *A great many immigrants have settled in this country.* ▶ **osiedlać się** **4** [I,T] to put yourself or sb else into a comfortable position: *I settled in front of the TV for the evening.* ◇ *She settled herself beside him on the sofa.* ▶ **sadowić (się)** **5** [I,T] to become or to make sb/sth calm or relaxed: *The baby wouldn't settle.* ▶ **uspokajać (się)** **6** [I] to land on a surface and stop moving: *A flock of birds settled on the roof.* ◇ *The snow didn't settle* (nie poleżał długo) *for long.* ▶ **(o)siadać**, **osadzać się** **7** [T] to pay money that you owe: *to settle a bill/a debt* ◇ *The insurance company settled the claim very quickly.* ▶ **wyrównać** (*np. straty*), **regulować** (*rachunek*), **płacić** (*odszkodowanie*) **8** [I] (used about a liquid) to become clear or still ▶ **ustawać się**

PHR V **settle down** **1** to get into a comfortable position, sitting or lying: *I made a cup of tea and settled down with the newspapers.* ▶ **siadać wygodnie**, **rozłożyć się** **2** to start having a quieter way of life, especially by staying in the same place or getting married: *She had a number of jobs abroad before she eventually settled down.* ▶ **ustatkować się** **3** to become calm and quiet: *Settle down* (spokój)*! It's time to start the lesson.* ▶ **uspokajać się**

settle (down) to sth to start doing sth which involves all your attention: *Before you settle down to your work, could I ask you something?* ▶ **brać się do czegoś**

settle for sth to accept sth that is not as good as what you wanted: *We're going to have to settle for the second prize.* ▶ **zadowalać się czymś**

settle in/into sth to start feeling comfortable in a new home, job, etc.: *How are the children settling in at their new school?* ▶ **przystosowywać się** (*np. do nowych warunków*)
settle on sth to choose or decide sth after considering many different things ▶ **zdecydować się na coś**
settle up (with sb) to pay money that you owe to sb ▶ **zapłacić komuś** (*należne mu pieniądze*)

settled /'setld/ adj. **1** not changing or not likely to change: *More settled weather is forecast* (przewiduje się mniej zmienną pogodę) *for the next few days.* ▶ **ustabilizowany 2** comfortable; feeling that you belong (in a home, a job, a way of life, etc.): *We feel very settled here.* Jest nam tu bardzo dobrze. ▶ **zakorzeniony**

settlement /'setlmənt/ noun [C,U] **1** an official agreement that ends an argument; the act of reaching an agreement: *a divorce settlement* ◇ *the settlement of a dispute* ▶ **porozumienie 2** a place that a group of people have built and live in, where few or no people lived before; the process of people starting to live in a place: *There is believed to have been a prehistoric settlement on this site.* ◇ *the settlement of the American West* ▶ **osada**

settler /'setlə(r)/ noun [C] a person who goes to live permanently in a place where not many people live: *the first white settlers in Australia* ▶ **osadni-k/czka**

⚷ **seven** /'sevn/ number **1** 7 ▶ **siedem** ➲ note at **six 2** [in compounds] having seven of the thing mentioned: *a seven-sided coin* ▶ **siedmio-**

⚷ **seventeen** /ˌsevn'tiːn/ number 17 ▶ **siedemnaście** ➲ note at **six**
■ **seventeenth** /ˌsevn'tiːnθ/ **1** ordinal number 17th ▶ **siedemnasty** ➲ note at **sixth 2** noun [C] 1/17; one of seventeen equal parts of sth ▶ **(jedna) siedemnasta**

⚷ **seventh** /'sevnθ/ ordinal number 7th ▶ **siódmy** ➲ note at **sixth**
■ **seventh** noun [C] 1/7; one of seven equal parts of sth ▶ **(jedna) siódma**

⚷ **seventy** /'sevnti/ number 70 ▶ **siedemdziesiąt** ➲ note at **sixty**
■ **seventieth** /'sevntiəθ/ **1** ordinal number 70th ▶ **siedemdziesiąty** ➲ note at **sixth 2** noun [C] 1/70; one of seventy equal parts of sth ▶ **(jedna) siedemdziesiąta**

sever /'sevə(r)/ verb [T] **1** to cut sth into two pieces; to cut sth off: *His hand was almost severed in the accident.* ◇ *The builders accidentally severed* (uszkodzili) *a water pipe.* ▶ **przerywać**, **odłączać 2** to end a relationship or communication with sb: *He has severed all links with his former friends.* ▶ **zrywać**

⚷ **several** /'sevrəl/ pron., determiner more than two but not very many; a few: *It took her several days to recover from the shock.* ◇ *There were lots of applications for the job – several of them from very well-qualified people.* ◇ *I don't think it's a good idea for several reasons.* ▶ **kilka**

⚷ **severe** /sɪ'vɪə(r)/ adj. **1** extremely bad or serious: *The company is in severe financial difficulty.* ◇ *He suffered severe injuries in the fall.* ◇ *severe weather conditions* ◇ *a severe winter* sroga zima ▶ **surowy 2** causing sb to suffer, be upset or have difficulties: *Such terrible crimes deserve the severest punishment.* ◇ *I think your criticism of her work was too severe.* ▶ **poważny**, **ciężki** ➲ look at **harsh**
■ **severely** adv.: *The roof was severely damaged in the storm.* ◇ *The report severely criticizes the Health Service.* ▶ **poważnie**, **surowo** | **severity** /sɪ'verəti/ noun [U]: *I don't think you realize the severity of the problem.* ▶ **powaga**

⚷ **sew** /səʊ/ verb [I,T] (pt **sewed**; pp **sewn** /səʊn/ or **sewed**) **sew (sth) (on)** to join pieces of cloth, or to join sth to cloth, using a needle and thread and forming **stitches**: *I can't sew.* ◇ *A button's come off my shirt – I'll have to sew it back on.* ▶ **szyć**, **przyszywać**
PHR V **sew sth up 1** to join two things by sewing; to repair sth by sewing two things together: *to sew up a hole* ▶ **z(a)szywać 2** to arrange sth so that it is certain to happen or be successful: *I think we've got the deal sewn up.* ▶ **zapinać na ostatni guzik**

sewage /'suːɪdʒ/ noun [U] the waste material from people's bodies that is carried away from their homes in water in **sewers** ▶ **ścieki**

sewed past tense of **sew**

sewer /'suːə(r)/ noun [C] an underground pipe that carries human waste to a place where it can be treated ▶ **ściek**, **kanał (ściekowy)**

⚷ **sewing** /'səʊɪŋ/ noun [U] **1** using a needle and thread to make or repair things: *I always take a sewing kit when I travel.* ◇ *Do you like sewing?* Czy lubisz szyć? ▶ **szycie 2** something that is being sewn: *Have you seen my sewing?* ▶ **szycie**

'sewing machine noun [C] a machine that is used for sewing ▶ **maszyna do szycia**

sewn past participle of **sew**

⚷ **sex** /seks/ noun **1** [U] the state of being either male or female: *Applications are welcome from anyone, regardless of sex or race.* ◇ *Do you mind what sex your baby is?* ▶ **płeć** SYN **gender 2** [C] one of the two groups consisting of all male people or all female people: *the male/female sex* ◇ *He's always found it difficult to get on with **the opposite sex**.* ▶ **płeć 3** (also formal **intercourse**; ˌ**sexual 'intercourse** /'ɪntəkɔːs/) [U] the physical act in which the sexual organs of two people touch and which can result in a woman having a baby: *to **have sex** with somebody* ◇ *sex education in schools* ▶ **stosunek (płciowy)**, **seks**

'sex appeal noun [U] the quality of being attractive in a sexual way: *He exudes sex appeal.* ▶ **seksapil**

'sex change noun [usually sing.] a medical operation in which parts of a person's body are changed so that they become like a person of the opposite sex ▶ **operacja zmiany płci**

sexism /'seksɪzəm/ noun [U] the unfair treatment of people, especially women, because of their sex; the attitude that causes this ▶ **dyskryminacja człowieka ze względu na jego płeć**
■ **sexist** /-ɪst/ adj.: *a sexist attitude to women* ◇ *sexist jokes* ▶ **dyskryminujący** (*ze względu na płeć*)

'sex symbol noun [C] a famous person who is thought by many people to be sexually attractive ▶ **symbol seksu**

⚷ **sexual** /'sekʃuəl/ adj. connected with sex: *sexual problems* ◇ *the sexual organs* ◇ *a campaign for sexual equality* (o równouprawnienie pod względem płci) ▶ **seksualny**, **płciowy**
■ **sexually** /'sekʃəli/ adv.: *to be sexually attracted to somebody* ▶ **seksualnie**, **płciowo**

ˌ**sexual 'intercourse** (formal) = SEX (3)

sexuality /ˌsekʃu'æləti/ noun [U] the nature of sb's sexual activities or desires ▶ **seksualność**, **orientacja seksualna**

sexy /'seksi/ adj. (**sexier**; **sexiest**) (informal) sexually attractive or exciting: *Do you find the lead singer sexy?* ◇ *a sexy dress* ▶ **seksowny**

Sgt = SERGEANT

sh /ʃ/ interj. (used to tell sb to stop making noise): *Sh! People are trying to sleep in here.* ▶ **sza!**

shabby /'ʃæbi/ adj. (**shabbier**; **shabbiest**) **1** in bad condition because of having been used or worn too much: *a shabby suit* ▶ **wyświechtany**, **sfatygowany 2** (used about people) dressed in an untidy way; wearing clothes that are in bad condition ▶ **obdarty 3** (used about the way that sb is treated) unfair; not generous ▶ **podły**

■ **shabbily** adv.: *a shabbily-dressed man* ◇ *She felt she'd been treated shabbily by her employers.* ▶ **nędznie**; **podle**

shack /ʃæk/ noun [C] a small building, usually made of wood or metal, that has not been built well ▶ **szałas**, **chałupa**

shade/shadow

shade¹ /ʃeɪd/ noun **1** [U] an area that is not in direct light from the sun and is darker and cooler than areas in the sun: *It was so hot that I had to go and sit* ***in the shade***. ▶ **cień**

> **Shade** to zacienione miejsce lub obszar, gdzie można schować się przed słońcem. **A shadow** (rzeczownik policzalny) to cień przedmiotu lub osoby utworzony przez odbite światło. **Shadow** (rzeczownik niepoliczalny) oznacza półmrok lub ciemność, w których trudno odróżnić kształty i przedmioty.

2 [C] something that keeps out light or makes it less bright: *a lampshade* ▶ **abażur**, **zasłona 3** [C] **a shade (of sth)** a type of a particular colour: *a shade of green* ▶ **odcień 4** [C] a small difference in the form or nature of sth: *a word with various shades of meaning* ▶ **odcień 5** [sing.] **a shade** a little; slightly: *I feel a shade more optimistic now.* ▶ **odrobinę 6** (**shades**) [pl.] (informal) = SUNGLASSES

shade² /ʃeɪd/ verb [T] **1** to protect sth from direct light; to give shade to sth: *The sun was so bright that I had to shade my eyes.* ▶ **zasłaniać**, **osłaniać 2 shade sth (in)** to make an area of a drawing darker, for example with a pencil: *The trees will look more realistic once you've shaded them in.* ▶ **cieniować**

shadow¹ /ˈʃædəʊ/ noun **1** [C] a dark shape on a surface that is caused by sth being between the light and that surface: *The dog was chasing its own shadow.* ◇ *The shadows lengthened as the sun went down.* ▶ **cień** ➲ picture at **shade 2** [U] an area that is dark because sth prevents direct light from reaching it: *His face was* ***in shadow***. ▶ **cień** ➲ note at **shade 3** [sing.] a very small amount of sth: *I know without* ***a shadow of doubt*** *that he's lying.* ▶ **cień**

IDM **cast a shadow (across/over sth)** → CAST¹

shadow² /ˈʃædəʊ/ verb [T] to follow and watch sb's actions: *The police shadowed the suspect for three days.* ▶ **śledzić**

shadow³ /ˈʃædəʊ/ adj. [only before a noun] (in British politics) belonging to the biggest political party that is not in power, with special responsibility for a particular subject, for example education or defence. **Shadow** ministers would probably become government ministers if their party won the next election: *the shadow Cabinet* ▶ **gabinet cieni**

shadowy /ˈʃædəʊi/ adj. **1** dark and full of **shadows**: *a shadowy forest* ▶ **cienisty 2** difficult to see because there is not much light: *A shadowy figure was coming towards me.* ▶ **niewyraźny 3** that not much is known about ▶ **tajemniczy** SYN **mysterious**

shady /ˈʃeɪdi/ adj. (**shadier**; **shadiest**) **1** giving shade; giving protection from the sun: *I found a shady spot under the trees and sat down.* ▶ **zacieniony 2** (informal) not completely honest or legal ▶ **podejrzany**, **mętny**

shaft /ʃɑːft; US ʃæft/ noun [C] **1** a long, narrow hole in which sth can go up and down or enter or leave: *a lift shaft* ◇ *a mine shaft* ▶ **szyb** (*np. kopalni, windy*) **2** a bar that connects parts of a machine so that power can pass between them ▶ **wał/ek 3** a long thin line of light: *a shaft of light* ▶ **promień**, **snop** (*światła*)

shag /ʃæg/ adj. [only before a noun] (used to describe a carpet, etc., usually made of wool, that has long threads) ▶ **włochaty**

shaggy /ˈʃægi/ adj. (**shaggier**; **shaggiest**) **1** (used about hair, material, etc.) long, thick and untidy ▶ **kosmaty**, **zmierzwiony 2** covered with long, thick, untidy hair: *a shaggy dog* ▶ **kudłaty**

shake¹ /ʃeɪk/ verb (pt **shook** /ʃʊk/, pp **shaken** /ˈʃeɪkən/) **1** [I,T] to move from side to side or up and down with short, quick movements: *I was so nervous that I was shaking.* ◇ *The whole building shakes when big trucks go past.* ◇ (figurative) *His voice shook with emotion as he described the accident.* ◇ *Shake the bottle before taking the medicine.* ◇ *She shook him to wake him up.* ▶ **trząść (się)**, **potrząsać**; **drżeć** (*np. z wrażenia, emocji*) **2** [T] to disturb or upset sb/sth: *The scandal has shaken the whole country.* ▶ **wstrząsać 3** [T] to cause sth to be less certain; to cause doubt about sth: *Nothing seems to shake her belief that she was right.* ▶ **osłabiać**

IDM **shake sb's hand/shake hands (with sb)/shake sb by the hand** to take sb's hand and move it up and down (when you meet sb, to show that you have agreed on sth, etc.) ▶ **podawać komuś rękę**, **ściskać komuś dłoń** ➲ note at **introduce**

shake your head to move your head from side to side, as a way of saying no ▶ **potrząsać/kręcić głową**

PHR V **shake sb/sth off** to get rid of sb/sth; to remove sth by shaking: *I don't seem to be able to shake off this cold.* ◇ *Shake the crumbs off the tablecloth.* ▶ **pozbywać się kogoś/czegoś**; **strząsać coś**

shake² /ʃeɪk/ noun [C] the act of shaking sth or being shaken ▶ **potrząśnięcie**, **wstrząśnięcie**

ˈshake-up noun [C] a complete change in the structure or organization of sth ▶ **przetasowanie**

shaky /ˈʃeɪki/ adj. (**shakier**; **shakiest**) **1** shaking or feeling weak because you are frightened or ill ▶ **trzęsący się**, **słaby 2** not firm; weak or not very good: *The table's a bit shaky so don't put anything heavy on it.* ◇ *They've had a* ***shaky start*** *to the season, losing most of their games.* ▶ **chwiejny**, **niepewny**

■ **shakily** adv. ▶ **drżąco**; **niepewnie**

shall /ʃəl; strong form ʃæl/ modal verb (negative **shall not**; short form **shan't** /ʃɑːnt; US ʃænt/, pt **should** /ʃʊd/, negative **should not**; short form **shouldn't** /ˈʃʊdnt/) **1** (formal) (used with 'I' and 'we' in future tenses, instead of 'will'): *I shall be* (będę) *very happy to see him again.* ◇ *We shan't be arriving* (nie przyjedziemy) *until ten o'clock.* ◇ *At the end of this year, I shall have been working here for five years* (upłynie pięć lat, odkąd tutaj pracuję). **2** (used for asking for information or advice): *What time shall I come?* O której godzinie mam przyjść? ◇ *Where shall we go* (dokąd pojedziemy) *for our holiday?* **3** (used for offering to do sth): *Shall I help you carry that box?* ◇ *Shall we drive you home?* ▶ **czy 4** (**shall we**) (used for suggesting that you do sth with the person or people that you are talking to): *Shall we go out for a meal this evening?* ▶ **czy 5** (formal) (used for saying that sth must happen or will definitely happen): *In the rules it says that a player shall be sent off for using bad language.* ◇ *If you really want a pony, you shall have one* (to będziesz go miał). ▶ **musieć**

shallot /ʃəˈlɒt/ noun [C] a vegetable like a small onion ▶ **szalotka**

shallow /ˈʃæləʊ/ adj. **1** not deep; with not much distance between top and bottom: *The sea is very shallow here.* ◇ *a shallow dish* ▶ **płytki 2** not having or showing serious or deep thought: *a shallow person/book* ▶ **płytki** OPP **deep**

■ **shallowness** noun [U] ▶ **płytkość**; **powierzchowność**

shame[1] /ʃeɪm/ noun **1** [U] the unpleasant feelings such as embarrassment and sadness that you get when you have done sth stupid or wrong; the ability to have these feelings: *She was **filled with shame** at the thought of how she had lied to her mother.* ◇ *His actions have **brought shame on** his whole family.* ◇ *He doesn't care how he behaves in public. He's got no shame!* ▶ **wstyd** ➲ adjective **ashamed 2 (a shame)** [sing.] a fact or situation that makes you feel disappointed: ***It's a shame** about Adam failing his exams, isn't it?* ◇ ***What a shame** you have to leave so soon.* ◇ *It would be a shame to miss an opportunity like this.* ▶ **szkoda**

shame[2] /ʃeɪm/ verb [T] to make sb feel **shame** for sth bad that they have done ▶ **zawstydzać**

PHR V **shame sb into doing sth** to persuade sb to do sth by making them feel ashamed not to do it ▶ **skłonić kogoś do zrobienia czegoś poprzez zawstydzenie**

shameful /ˈʃeɪmfl/ adj. that sb should feel bad about; shocking: *a shameful waste of public money* ▶ **haniebny**
■ **shamefully** /-fəli/ adv. ▶ **haniebnie**

shameless /ˈʃeɪmləs/ adj. not feeling embarrassed about doing sth bad; having no **shame**: *a shameless display of greed and bad manners* ▶ **bezwstydny**
■ **shamelessly** adv. ▶ **bezwstydnie**

shampoo /ʃæmˈpuː/ noun (pl. **shampoos**) **1** [C,U] a liquid that you use for washing your hair; a similar liquid for cleaning carpets, cars, etc.: *shampoo for greasy/dry/normal hair* ▶ **szampon 2** [C] the act of washing sth with **shampoo** ▶ **mycie szamponem**
■ **shampoo** verb [T] (**shampooing**; **shampoos**; pt, pp **shampooed**) ▶ **myć szamponem**

shamrock /ˈʃæmrɒk/ noun [C,U] a plant with three leaves, which is the national symbol of Ireland ▶ **koniczyna biała**

Shamrock to godło Irlandii.

shandy /ˈʃændi/ noun [C,U] (pl. **shandies**) a drink that is a mixture of beer and **lemonade** ▶ **piwo z lemoniadą** ➲ note at **beer**

shan't /ʃɑːnt; US ʃænt/ short for **shall not**

shanty town /ˈʃænti taʊn/ noun [C] an area, usually on the edge of a big city, where poor people live in bad conditions in buildings that they have made themselves ▶ **slumsy**

shape[1] /ʃeɪp/ noun **1** [C,U] the form of the outer edges or surfaces of sth; an example of sth that has a particular form: *a round/square/rectangular shape* ◇ *a cake **in the shape of** a heart* ◇ *clothes to fit people of **all shapes and sizes*** ◇ *Squares, circles and triangles are all different shapes.* ◇ *I could just make out a dark shape in the distance.* ◇ *The country is roughly square **in shape.*** ▶ **kształt**, **figura 2** [U] the physical condition of sb/sth; the good or bad state of sb/sth: *I go swimming regularly to keep **in shape*** (w dobrej kondycji). ▶ **stan**; **kondycja 3** [sing.] **the shape (of sth)** the organization, form or structure of sth: *Recent developments have changed the shape of the company.* ▶ **kształt 4** the organization, form or structure of sth

IDM **out of shape 1** not in the usual or correct shape: *My sweater's gone out of shape* (powyciągał się) *now that I've washed it.* ▶ **zniekształcony 2** not physically fit: *You're out of shape. You should get more exercise.* ▶ **w złej kondycji**

take shape to start to develop well: *Plans to expand the company are beginning to take shape.* ▶ **przybierać kształt**

shape[2] /ʃeɪp/ verb [T] **1 shape sth (into sth)** to make sth into a particular form: *Shape the mixture into small balls.* ▶ **kształtować 2** to influence the way in which sth develops; to cause sth to have a particular form or nature: *His political ideas were shaped by his upbringing.* ▶ **kształtować**

PHR V **shape up 1** to develop in a particular way, especially in a good way: *Our plans are shaping up nicely.* ▶ **rozwijać się**, **robić postępy 2** (informal) to improve your behaviour, work harder, etc.: *If he doesn't shape up, he'll soon be out of a job.* ▶ **poprawiać się**

shaped /ʃeɪpt/ adj. [in compounds] having the shape mentioned: *an L-shaped room* ▶ **w kształcie czegoś**

shapeless /ˈʃeɪpləs/ adj. not having a clear shape: *a shapeless dress* ▶ **bezkształtny**

share[1] /ʃeə(r)/ verb **1** [T] **share sth (out)** to divide sth between two or more people: *We shared the pizza out between the four of us.* ▶ **dzielić 2** [I,T] **share (sth) (with sb)** to have, use, do or pay sth together with another person or other people: *I share a flat with four other people.* ◇ *I shared my sandwiches with Jim.* ◇ *We share the same interests.* Mamy te same zainteresowania. ▶ **dzielić (się) 3** [T] **share sth (with sb)** to tell sb about sth; to allow sb to know sth: *Sometimes it helps to share your problems.* ▶ **dzielić się**

share[2] /ʃeə(r)/ noun **1** [sing.] **share (of sth)** a part or an amount of sth that has been divided between several people: *We each pay a share of the household bills.* ◇ *I'm willing to **take** my **share** of the blame.* ▶ **część 2** [C, usually pl.] **shares (in sth)** one of many equal parts into which the value of a company is divided, that can be sold to people who want to own part of the company: *a fall in share prices* ▶ **akcje**, **udziały**

IDM **(more than) your fair share of sth** → FAIR[1]

the lion's share (of sth) → LION

shareholder /ˈʃeəhəʊldə(r)/ noun [C] an owner of shares in a company ▶ **akcjonariusz/ka**

shark /ʃɑːk/ noun [C] (pl. **sharks** or **shark**) a large, often dangerous, sea fish that has a lot of sharp teeth ▶ **rekin**

sharp[1] /ʃɑːp/ adj. **1** having a very thin but strong edge or point; that can cut or make a hole in sth easily: *a sharp knife* ◇ *sharp teeth* ▶ **ostry** OPP **blunt 2** (used about a change of direction or level) very great and sudden: *a sharp rise/fall in inflation* ◇ *This is a sharp bend so slow down.* ▶ **gwałtowny**, **ostry 3** clear and definite: *the sharp outline of the hills* ◇ *a sharp contrast between the lives of the rich and the poor* ▶ **ostry**, **wyraźny 4** able to think, act, understand, see or hear quickly: *a sharp mind* ◇ *You must have sharp eyes if you can read that sign from here.* ▶ **inteligentny**, **bystry 5** said in an angry way; intended to upset sb or be critical: *During the debate there was a sharp exchange of views between the two parties.* ▶ **ostry 6** quick and sudden: *One short sharp blow was enough to end the fight.* ▶ **ostry**, **mocny 7** very strong and sudden: *a sharp pain in the chest* ▶ **ostry** OPP **dull 8** (used about sth that affects the senses) strong; not mild or gentle, often causing an unpleasant feeling: *a sharp taste* ◇ *a sharp wind* ▶ **ostry**, **pikantny 9** (symbol ♯) half a note higher than the stated note: *F sharp minor* fis-moll ▶ **podwyższony o pół tonu**, **-is** OPP **flat 10** slightly higher than the correct note: *That last note was sharp. Can you sing it again?* ▶ **podwyższony** OPP **flat** ➲ picture at **music**
■ **sharply** adv.: *The road bends sharply to the left.* ◇ *Share prices fell sharply this morning.* ▶ **ostro**, **gwałtownie** | **sharpness** noun [U] ▶ **ostrość**; **bystrość (umysłu)**; **złośliwość**; **ostry/pikantny smak**

sharp[2] /ʃɑːp/ adv. **1** exactly on time: *Be here at 3 o'clock sharp.* ▶ **punktualnie 2** turning suddenly: *Go to the traffic lights and turn sharp right.* ▶ **ostro** (*np. skręcać*) **3** slightly higher than the correct note ▶ **powyżej tonacji** ➲ look at **flat**

sharp[3] /ʃɑːp/ noun [C] (symbol ♯) (in music) a note that is half a note higher than the note with the same letter ▶ **nuta z krzyżykiem** ➲ look at **flat**

S

sharpen /ˈʃɑːpən/ verb [I,T] to become or to make sth sharp or sharper: *to sharpen a knife* ◇ *This knife won't sharpen.* ▶ **ostrzyć, zaostrzać**

sharpener /ˈʃɑːpnə(r)/ noun [C] an object or a tool that is used for making sth sharp: *a pencil/knife sharpener* ▶ **temperówka**

shatter /ˈʃætə(r)/ verb **1** [I,T] (used about glass, etc.) to break into very small pieces: *I dropped the glass and it shattered on the floor.* ◇ *The force of the explosion shattered the windows.* ▶ **roztrzaskiwać (się) 2** [T] to destroy sth completely: *Her hopes were shattered by the news.* ▶ **niweczyć**

shattered /ˈʃætəd/ adj. **1** very shocked and upset ▶ **przygnębiony**, **przybity 2** (informal) very tired: *I'm absolutely shattered.* ▶ **wykończony**

shave¹ /ʃeɪv/ verb [I,T] **shave (sth) (off)** to remove hair from the face or another part of the body with a **razor**: *I cut myself shaving* (przy goleniu) *this morning.* ◇ *When did you shave off your moustache?* ◇ *to shave your legs* ▶ **golić (się)**

PHR V **shave sth off (sth)** to cut a very small amount from sth: *We'll have to shave a bit off the door to make it close properly.* ▶ **strugać**, **wiórkować**

shave² /ʃeɪv/ noun [C, usually sing.] the act of shaving: *I need a shave.* ◇ *to have a shave* golić się ▶ **golenie (się)**

IDM **a close shave/thing** → CLOSE³

shaven /ˈʃeɪvn/ adj. having been shaved: *clean-shaven* gładko wygolony ▶ **ogolony**

shaver /ˈʃeɪvə(r)/ (also **eˌlectric ˈrazor**) noun [C] an electric tool that is used for removing hair from the face or another part of the body ▶ **elektryczna maszynka do golenia**

ˈshaving cream, **ˈshaving foam** noun [U] special cream or **foam** for spreading over the face with a **shaving brush** before shaving ▶ **krem/pianka do golenia**

shawl /ʃɔːl/ noun [C] a large piece of cloth that is worn by a woman round her shoulders or head, or that is put round a baby ▶ **szal**, **chusta**

she /ʃiː/ pron. (the subject of a verb) the female person who has already been mentioned: *'What does your sister do?' 'She's a dentist.'* ◇ *I asked her a question but she didn't answer.* ▶ **ona** ➲ note at **he**

sheaf /ʃiːf/ noun [C] (pl. **sheaves** /ʃiːvz/) **1** a number of papers, etc. lying one on top of the other and often tied together: *a sheaf of notes* ▶ **plik** (*np. papierów*) **2** a bunch of stalks of corn, wheat, etc. tied together after being cut, and left standing up so that they dry ▶ **snop**

shear /ʃɪə(r)/ verb [T] (pt **sheared**; pp **sheared** or **shorn**) to cut the wool off a sheep ▶ **strzyc**

shears /ʃɪəz/ noun [pl.] a tool that is like a very large pair of scissors and that is used for cutting things in the garden: *a pair of shears* ▶ **nożyce (ogrodnicze)** ➲ picture at **garden**

sheath /ʃiːθ/ noun [C] (pl. **sheaths** /ʃiːðz/) a cover for a knife or other sharp weapon ▶ **pochwa** (*np. na miecz, nóż*)

she'd /ʃiːd/ short for **she had; she would**

shed¹ /ʃed/ noun [C] a small building that is used for keeping things or animals in: *a garden shed* ◇ *a bicycle shed* ◇ *a cattle shed* ▶ **szopa**

shed² /ʃed/ verb [T] (**shedding**; pt, pp **shed**) **1** to get rid of or remove sth that is not wanted ▶ **pozbywać się**, **redukować 2** to lose sth because it falls off: *This snake sheds its skin every year.* ◇ *Autumn is coming and the trees are beginning to shed their leaves.* ▶ **zrzucać**, **tracić**

IDM **shed blood** (formal) to kill or injure people ▶ **przelewać krew**

shed light on sth to make sth clear and easy to understand ▶ **rzucać światło na coś**

shed tears to cry ▶ **lać łzy**

sheen /ʃiːn/ noun [sing., U] a soft smooth shiny quality: *hair with a healthy sheen* ▶ **połysk** SYN **shine**

sheep /ʃiːp/ noun [C] (pl. **sheep**) an animal that is kept on farms and used for its wool or meat ▶ **owca** ➲ note at **meat**

> A male sheep is a **ram**, a female sheep is a **ewe** and a young sheep is a **lamb**. Sheep **bleat**. This is written as **baa**. The meat from sheep is called **lamb** or **mutton**.

sheepdog /ˈʃiːpdɒɡ/ noun [C] a dog that has been trained to control sheep ▶ **owczarek**

sheepish /ˈʃiːpɪʃ/ adj. feeling or showing embarrassment because you have done sth silly: *a sheepish grin* ▶ **zawstydzony**, **zażenowany**

■ **sheepishly** adv. ▶ **z zażenowaniem**

sheepskin /ˈʃiːpskɪn/ noun [U] the skin of a sheep, including the wool, from which coats, etc. are made: *a sheepskin rug/jacket* ◇ *a sheepskin coat* kożuch ▶ **owcza skóra**

sheer /ʃɪə(r)/ adj. **1** [only before a noun] (used to emphasize the size, degree or amount of sth): *It's sheer stupidity to drink and drive.* ◇ *It was **sheer luck** that I happened to be in the right place at the right time.* ◇ *Her success is due to sheer hard work* (jedynie dzięki ciężkiej pracy). ◇ *I only agreed out of sheer desperation* (po prostu z desperacji). ▶ **czysty 2** very steep; almost vertical: *Don't walk near the edge. It's **a sheer drop** to the sea.* ▶ **stromy**

sheet /ʃiːt/ noun [C] **1** a large piece of cloth used on a bed: *I've just changed the sheets on the bed.* ▶ **prześcieradło** ➲ picture at **bed 2** a piece of paper that is used for writing, printing, etc. on: *a sheet of notepaper* ◇ *Write each answer on a separate sheet.* ▶ **kartka** (*papieru*) ➲ look at **balance sheet 3** a flat, thin piece of any material: *a sheet of metal/glass* ▶ **arkusz** (*np. blachy*), **płyta** (*np. szklana*) **4** a wide, flat area of sth: *The road was covered with **a sheet of ice**.* ▶ **tafla**

ˌsheet ˈlightning noun [U] **lightning** that appears as a broad area of light in the sky ▶ **błyskawica rozświetlająca dużą część nieba** ➲ look at **forked lightning**

sheikh (also **shaikh**) /ʃeɪk/ noun [C] an Arab ruler ▶ **szejk**

shelf /ʃelf/ noun [C] (pl. **shelves** /ʃelvz/) a long flat piece of wood, glass, etc. that is fixed to a wall or in a cupboard, used for putting things on: *I put up a shelf in the kitchen.* ◇ *I reached up and took down the book from the top shelf.* ◇ *a bookshelf* ▶ **półka**

she'll /ʃiːl/ short for **she will**

shell¹ /ʃel/ noun **1** [C,U] a hard covering that protects eggs, nuts and some animals: *Some children were collecting shells on the beach.* ◇ *a piece of eggshell* ◇ *Tortoises have a hard shell.* ▶ **skorupa**, **muszla**, **pancerz** (*żółwia*) ➲ picture on **page A12**, **page A11 2** [C] a metal container that explodes when it is fired from a large gun ▶ **pocisk artyleryjski 3** [C] the walls or hard outer structure of sth: *The body shell* (karoseria) *of the car is made in another factory.* ▶ **szkielet**, **zrąb** (*budynku*)

IDM **come out of your shell** to become less shy and more confident when talking to other people ▶ **nabierać pewności siebie**

go, retreat, etc. into your shell to suddenly become shy and stop talking ▶ **zamykać się w sobie**

shell² /ʃel/ verb [T] **1** to fire **shells¹** (2) from a large gun ▶ **ostrzeliwać** (*pociskami*) **2** to take the **shell¹** (1) off a nut or another kind of food: *to shell peas* ▶ **łuskać**

shellfish /ˈʃelfɪʃ/ noun (pl. **shellfish**) **1** [C] a type of animal that lives in water and has a shell ▶ **skorupiak**, **mięczak** ➲ picture on **page A11 2** [U] these animals eaten as food ▶ **skorupiak**

shelter¹ /ˈʃeltə(r)/ noun **1** [U] **shelter (from sth)** protection from danger or bad weather: *to give somebody food and shelter* ◇ *We looked around for somewhere to **take shelter***

from (schronić się przed) *the storm.* ▶ **schronienie 2** [C] a small building that gives protection, for example from bad weather or attack: *a bus shelter* wiata na przystanku autobusowym ◇ *an air-raid shelter* schron przeciwlotniczy ▶ **miejsce schronienia 3** [C] a building, usually owned by a charity, where people or animals can stay if they do not have a home, or have been badly treated: *an animal shelter* ▶ **schronisko** (*np. dla bezdomnych*) SYN **refuge**

⚷ **shelter²** /ˈʃeltə(r)/ verb **1** [T] **shelter sb/sth (from sb/sth)** to protect sb/sth; to provide a safe place away from harm or danger: *The trees shelter the house from the wind.* ▶ **osłaniać, chronić 2** [I] **shelter (from sth)** to find protection or a safe place: *Let's shelter from the rain under that tree.* ▶ **chronić się**

sheltered /ˈʃeltəd/ adj. **1** (used about a place) protected from bad weather ▶ **osłonięty 2** protected from unpleasant things in your life: *We had a sheltered childhood, living in the country.* ▶ **bezpieczny**

shelve /ʃelv/ verb **1** [T] to decide not to continue with a plan, etc., either for a short time or permanently: *Plans for a new motorway have been shelved.* ▶ **odkładać coś na półkę** (*nie nadawać sprawie dalszego biegu*) **2** [I] (used about land) to slope in one direction: *The beaches shelve down to the sea.* ▶ (*teren*) **opadać**

shelves plural of **shelf**

shelving /ˈʃelvɪŋ/ noun [U] a set of shelves ▶ **regał** (*np. na książki*)

shepherd¹ /ˈʃepəd/ noun [C] a person whose job is to look after sheep ▶ **paste-rz/rka**

shepherd² /ˈʃepəd/ verb [T] to lead and look after people so that they do not get lost ▶ **pilotować, prowadzić**

sheriff /ˈʃerɪf/ noun [C] an officer of the law who is responsible for a particular town or part of a state in the US ▶ **szeryf**

sherry /ˈʃeri/ noun [C,U] (pl. **sherries**) a type of strong Spanish wine; a glass of this wine ▶ **rodzaj hiszpańskiego wina białego, sherry**

she's /ʃiːz; ʃiz/ short for **she is; she has**

shield¹ /ʃiːld/ noun [C] **1** (in past times) a large piece of metal or wood that soldiers carried to protect themselves ▶ **tarcza** (*np. rycerska*) **2** (also ˈ**riot shield**) a piece of equipment made of strong plastic that the police use to protect themselves from angry crowds ▶ **policyjna tarcza obronna 3** a person or thing that is used to protect sb/sth, especially by forming a barrier: *The metal door acted as a shield against the explosion.* ▶ **osłona 4** an object or a drawing in the shape of a **shield**, sometimes used as a prize in a sports competition ▶ **tarcza, odznaka** ➲ picture at **medal**

shield² /ʃiːld/ verb [T] **shield sb/sth (against/from sb/sth)** to protect sb/sth from danger or damage: *I shielded my eyes from the bright light with my hand.* ▶ **osłaniać, chronić**

⚷ **shift¹** /ʃɪft/ verb **1** [I,T] to move or be moved from one position or place to another: *She shifted uncomfortably in her chair.* ◇ *He shifted his desk closer to the window.* ▶ **przesuwać; zmieniać położenie/kierunek 2** [I] (used about a situation, an opinion, a policy, etc.) to change from one state, position, etc. to another: *Public attitudes towards marriage have shifted over the years.* ▶ **zmieniać się**

IDM **shift the blame/responsibility (for sth) (onto sb)** to make sb else responsible for sth you should do or for sth bad you have done ▶ **przerzucać na kogoś odpowiedzialność; zrzucać winę na kogoś**

⚷ **shift²** /ʃɪft/ noun **1** [C] **a shift (in sth)** a change in your opinion of or attitude towards sth: *There has been a shift in public opinion away from war.* ▶ **zmiana** (*np. kierunku, położenia*) **2** [C, with sing. or pl. verb] (in a factory, etc.) one of the periods that the working day is divided into; the group who work during this period: *The night shift has/have just gone off duty.* ◇ *to work **in shifts*** pracować w systemie zmianowym ◇ *shift work/workers* ◇ *to be on the day/night shift* ◇ *Firemen do shift work* (pracują na zmiany). ▶ **zmiana, szychta 3** [sing.] one of the keys that you use for writing on a computer, etc., that allows you to write a capital letter: *the shift key* ▶ **klawisz „shift"** (*na klawiaturze komputera*), **klawisz zmiany małych liter na wielkie** (*na maszynie do pisania*)

shifty /ˈʃɪfti/ adj. (**shiftier**; **shiftiest**) (used about a person or their appearance) giving the impression that you cannot trust them: *shifty eyes* ▶ **chytry, cwany**

shilling /ˈʃɪlɪŋ/ noun [C] **1** a British coin worth five pence that was used in past times ▶ **szyling 2** the basic unit of money in some countries, for example Kenya ▶ **szyling**

shimmer /ˈʃɪmə(r)/ verb [I] to shine with a soft light that seems to be moving: *Moonlight shimmered on the sea.* ▶ **migotać, lśnić**

shin /ʃɪn/ noun [C] the bone down the front part of your leg from your knee to your ankle ▶ **goleń** SYN **tibia** ➲ picture at **body**

⚷ **shine¹** /ʃaɪn/ verb (pt, pp **shone** /ʃɒn; US ʃoʊn/) **1** [I] to produce or reflect light; to be bright: *I could see a light shining in the distance.* ◇ *The sea shone in the light of the moon.* ▶ **jaśnieć, świecić (się) 2** [T] to direct a light at sb/sth: *The policeman shone a torch on the stranger's face.* ▶ **oświetlać 3** [I] **shine (at/in sth)** to do a school subject, a sport, etc. very well: *She has always shone at languages.* ▶ **błyszczeć** (*np. w nauce*)

shine² /ʃaɪn/ noun [sing.] **1** a bright effect caused by light hitting a polished surface ▶ **połysk 2** the act of polishing sth so that it shines: *He gave his shoes a shine.* Wypucował buty. ▶ **pucowanie, polerowanie**

shingle /ˈʃɪŋgl/ noun [U] small pieces of stone lying in a mass on a beach ▶ **żwirek (na plaży)**

ˈ**shin guard** (Brit. also ˈ**shin pad**) noun [C] a thick piece of material used to protect the **shin** when playing some sports ▶ **nagolennik**

⚷ **shiny** /ˈʃaɪni/ adj. (**shinier**; **shiniest**) causing a bright effect when in the sun or in light: *The shampoo leaves your hair soft and shiny.* ◇ *a shiny new car* ▶ **błyszczący**

⚷ **ship¹** /ʃɪp/ noun [C] a large boat used for carrying passengers or goods by sea: *to travel **by ship*** ◇ *to launch a ship* wodować okręt ▶ **statek, okręt** ➲ note at **boat**

ship² /ʃɪp/ verb [T] (**shipping**; **shipped**) to send or carry sth by ship or by another type of transport ▶ **posyłać** (*towary*) **morzem**

shipbuilder /ˈʃɪpbɪldə(r)/ noun [C] a person or company who makes or builds ships ▶ **stoczniowiec; stocznia**
■ **shipbuilding** noun [U] ▶ **okrętownictwo**

shipment /ˈʃɪpmənt/ noun **1** [U] the carrying of goods from one place to another ▶ **wysyłka** (*towarów*) **drogą morską 2** [C] a quantity of goods that are sent from one place to another ▶ **fracht morski**

shipping /ˈʃɪpɪŋ/ noun [U] **1** ships in general or considered as a group ▶ **jednostki pływające 2** the carrying of goods from one place to another: *a shipping company* ▶ **transport wodny**

shipwreck /ˈʃɪprek/ noun [C,U] an accident at sea in which a ship is destroyed by a storm, rocks, etc. and sinks ▶ **rozbicie statku**
■ **shipwrecked** adj.: *a shipwrecked sailor* rozbitek ◇ *a shipwrecked vessel* wrak

shipyard /ˈʃɪpjɑːd/ noun [C] a place where ships are repaired or built ▶ **stocznia**

shirk /ʃɜːk/ verb [I,T] to avoid doing sth that is difficult or unpleasant, especially because you are too lazy: *to shirk your responsibilities* ▶ **wymigiwać się**

S

shirt /ʃɜːt/ noun [C] a piece of clothing made of cotton, etc. worn on the upper part of the body ▶ **koszula** ➲ picture on **page A1**

> A shirt usually has a **collar** at the neck, long or short **sleeves**, and **buttons** down the front.

shit /ʃɪt/ noun (taboo, slang) **1** [U] solid waste matter from the **bowels** SYN **excrement**: *a pile of dog shit on the path* ℹ Grzeczniejsze wyrażenie tego przykładu to **a pile of dog dirt.** ▶ **gówno 2** [sing.] an act of emptying solid waste matter from the **bowels**: *to have a shit* wysrać się ▶ **sranie 3** [U] stupid remarks or writing; nonsense: *Don't give me that shit!* ▶ **pieprzenie** ➲ look at **bullshit 4** [C] an unpleasant person who treats other people badly: *He's an arrogant little shit.* ▶ **dupek 5** [U] criticism or unfair treatment: *I'm not going to take any shit from them.* ▶ **pieprzenie**

IDM **in the shit**; **in deep shit** in trouble: *I'll be in the shit if I don't get this work finished today.* ◇ *You're in deep shit now.* ▶ **po same uszy w gównie**

like shit really bad, ill, etc.; really badly: *I woke up feeling like shit.* ◇ *We get treated like shit in this job.* ▶ **do dupy**

not give a shit (about sb/sth) to not care at all about sb/sth: *He doesn't give a shit about anybody else.* ▶ **mieć kogoś/coś w dupie**

shit happens (used to express the idea that we must accept that bad things often happen without reason) ▶ **zawsze się przyplącze jakieś gówno**

when the shit hits the fan when sb in authority finds out about sth bad or wrong that sb has done: *When the shit hits the fan, I don't want to be here.* ▶ **kiedy zrobi się chryja**

■ **shit** exclamation (taboo, slang) (a swear word that many people find offensive, used to show that you are angry or annoyed): *Shit* (jasna cholera)*! I've lost my keys!* ℹ Mniej obraźliwe wyrażenia to **blast**, **darn it** (zwł. US), **damn** lub (Brit.) **bother.** | **shit** verb (**shitting**; **shit**; **shit**) (taboo, slang) ℹ Form **shat** /ʃæt/ i w Br. ang. **shitted** używa się w czasie przeszłym i w formie *past participle.* **1** [I,T] to empty solid waste matter from the **bowels** ▶ **srać** ℹ Grzeczniej jest powiedzieć **go to the toilet/lavatory** (Brit.), **go to the bathroom** (US) lub **go.** Bardziej formalne wyrażenie to **empty the bowels. 2** [T] **shit yourself** to empty solid waste matter from the **bowels** by accident ▶ **zesrać się 3** [T] **shit yourself** to be very frightened ▶ **zesrać się ze strachu** | **shit** adj. (taboo, slang) (especially Brit.) very bad: *They're a shit team.* ▶ **do dupy**

shitty /ˈʃɪti/ adj. (taboo, slang) **1** unpleasant; very bad: *a shitty week at work* ▶ **gówniany 2** unfair or unkind: *What a shitty way to treat a friend!* ▶ **zasrany**

shiver /ˈʃɪvə(r)/ verb [I] to shake slightly, especially because you are cold or frightened: *shivering with cold/fright* ▶ **drżeć**

■ **shiver** noun [C]: *The thought sent a shiver down my spine.* Na samą myśl o tym ciarki mi przeszły po plecach. ▶ **drżenie**

shoal /ʃəʊl/ noun [C] a large group of fish that feed and swim together ▶ **ławica**

shock[1] /ʃɒk/ noun **1** [C,U] the feeling that you get when sth unpleasant happens suddenly; the situation that causes this feeling: *The sudden noise **gave** him **a shock*** (wstrząsnął nim). ◇ *I got a shock* (doznałem szoku) *the other day.* ◇ *The bad news **came as a shock** to her.* ◇ *I'm still suffering from shock at the news.* ◇ *His mother is **in a state of shock**.* ▶ **wstrząs 2** [U] a serious medical condition of extreme weakness caused by damage to the body: *He **was in/went into shock** after the accident.* ▶ **porażenie prądem 3** [C] a violent shaking movement (caused by a crash, an explosion, etc.): *the shock of the earthquake* ▶ **cios**, **wstrząs 4** [C] = ELECTRIC SHOCK

shock[2] /ʃɒk/ verb **1** [T] to cause an unpleasant feeling of surprise in sb: *We were shocked by his death.* ◇ *I'm sorry, I didn't mean to shock you* (nie chciałem cię wystraszyć) *when I came in.* ▶ **wstrząsać 2** [I,T] to make sb feel disgusted or offended: *These films deliberately set out to shock.* ▶ **oburzać**

■ **shocked** adj.: *a shocked expression/look* ▶ **zszokowany**

shocking /ˈʃɒkɪŋ/ adj. **1** that offends or upsets people; that is morally wrong: *a shocking accident* ◇ *shocking behaviour/news* ▶ **wstrząsający**, **skandaliczny 2** (especially Brit., informal) very bad: *The weather has been absolutely shocking.* ▶ **okropny**

shod past tense, past participle of **shoe[2]**

shoddy /ˈʃɒdi/ adj. (**shoddier**; **shoddiest**) **1** made carelessly or with poor quality materials: *shoddy goods* ▶ **tandetny 2** dishonest or unfair: *He received shoddy treatment.* Podle go potraktowali. ▶ **nikczemny**, **podły**

■ **shoddily** adv. ▶ **tandetnie**; **podle**

shoe[1] /ʃuː/ noun [C] **1** a type of covering for the foot, usually made of leather or plastic: *a pair of shoes* ◇ *running shoes* buty do biegania ◇ *What size are your shoes/What is your shoe size?* ▶ **but** ➲ picture on **page A1 2** = HORSESHOE

IDM **in my, your, etc. place/shoes** → PLACE[1]

shoe[2] /ʃuː/ verb [T] (pt, pp **shod** /ʃɒd/) to fit a shoe on a horse ▶ **podkuwać**

shoelace /ˈʃuːleɪs/ (especially US **shoestring** /ˈʃuːstrɪŋ/) noun [C] a long thin piece of material like string used to fasten a shoe: *to tie/untie a shoelace* ▶ **sznurowadło** ➲ picture at **shoe**, **button**

shoestring /ˈʃuːstrɪŋ/ noun [C] (especially US) = SHOELACE

IDM **on a shoestring** using very little money: *to live on a shoestring* ▶ **cienko przędąc**

shone past tense, past participle of **shine[1]**

shoo[1] /ʃuː/ interj. (usually said to animals or small children) Go away! ▶ **a sio!**

shoo[2] /ʃuː/ verb [T] (pt, pp **shooed**) **shoo sb/sth away, off, out, etc.** to make sb/sth go away by saying '**shoo**' and waving your hands ▶ **płoszyć**

shook past tense of **shake[1]**

shoot[1] /ʃuːt/ verb (pt, pp **shot** /ʃɒt/) **1** [I,T] **shoot (sth) (at sb/sth)** to fire a gun or another weapon: *Don't shoot!* ◇ *She shot an arrow at the target, but missed it.* ▶ **strzelać 2** [T] to injure or kill sb/sth with a gun: *The policeman was shot* (był postrzelony) *in the arm.* ◇ *The soldier was **shot dead*** (został zastrzelony). ▶ **postrzelić**, **zastrzelić 3** [I,T] to hunt and kill birds and animals with a gun as a sport: *He **goes shooting** at the weekends.* ▶ **polować (na coś)** ➲ look at **hunting 4** [I,T] to move somewhere quickly and suddenly; to make sth move in this way: *The car shot past me at 100 miles per hour.* ▶ **przemykać**; **rzucać** (*np. spojrzenie*) **5** [I] to go very suddenly along part of your body: *The pain shot up my leg.* ◇ *shooting pains in the chest* ▶ **przeszywać 6** [I,T] to make a film or photograph of sth: *They shot the scene ten times.* ▶ **filmować**; **fotografować 7** [I] **shoot (at sth)** (in football, etc.) to try to kick, hit or throw the ball into the goal: *He should have shot instead of passing.* ▶ **strzelać** (*np. gola*) ➲ noun **shot**

PHR V **shoot sb/sth down** to make sb/sth fall to the ground by shooting them or it: *The helicopter was shot down by a missile.* ▶ **zastrzelić**; **zestrzelić**

shoot up to increase by a large amount; to grow very quickly: *Prices have shot up in the past year.* ▶ (*ceny*) **podskoczyć**

shoot[2] /ʃuːt/ noun [C] a new part of a plant or tree ▶ **pęd**

shooting noun **1** [C] a situation in which a person is shot with a gun: *Terrorist groups claimed responsibility for the shootings.* ▶ **strzelanina 2** [U] the sport of shooting animals and birds with guns: *pheasant shooting* ▶ **polo-**

shoes

shoes

sandal

trainers (US **sneakers**)

slippers

boot

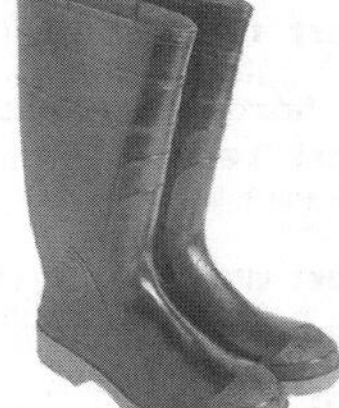

wellingtons (US **rubber boots**)

wanie **3** [U] the process of filming a film: *Shooting began early this year.* ▶ **kręcenie** (*filmu*)

ˌ**shooting ˈstar** noun [C] a piece of rock that burns with a bright light as it travels through space ▶ **spadająca gwiazda** ➲ look at **comet**

shop¹ /ʃɒp/ (US **store**) noun [C] a building or part of a building where things are bought and sold: *a cake/shoe shop* ◇ *When do the shops open?* ◇ *a corner shop* sklep na rogu ▶ **sklep**

Zwykle mówi się **the butcher's**, **the baker's** itp. zamiast **the butcher's shop**, **the baker's shop** itp.

IDM **talk shop** → TALK¹

shops

Before I **go shopping** I make a **shopping list**. I buy bread and cakes **at the baker's**, where a **shop assistant serves** me. I buy meat at the **butcher's**, fish at the **fishmonger's**, fruit and vegetables at the **greengrocer's** and flowers at the **florist's**. If I want to buy everything in one shop, I go to the **supermarket**. There's a **market** in town on Fridays, and once a month there's a **farmer's market**, where you can buy local and **organic** produce.

shop² /ʃɒp/ verb [I] (**shopping**; **shopped**) **shop (for sth)** to go to a shop or shops in order to buy things: *He's shopping for some new clothes.* ◇ *We go shopping* (chodzimy na zakupy) *every Saturday.* ▶ **robić zakupy** ℹ Częściej niż **to shop** używa się wyrażenia **to go shopping**.

■ **shopper** noun [C] ▶ **klient/ka**

PHR V **shop around (for sth)** to look at the price and quality of an item in different shops before you decide where to buy it ▶ **porównywać ceny w kilku sklepach przed dokonaniem zakupu**

shopaholic /ˌʃɒpəˈhɒlɪk/ noun [C] (informal) a person who enjoys shopping very much and spends too much time or money doing it ▶ **zakupoholi-k/czka**

ˈ**shop assistant** (US ˈ**sales clerk**; **clerk**) noun [C] a person who works in a shop ▶ **sprzedaw-ca/czyni**

ˌ**shop ˈfloor** noun [sing.] (Brit.) an area of a factory where things are made; the people who make things in a factory ▶ **załoga** (*fabryki*); **hala produkcyjna**

shopkeeper /ˈʃɒpkiːpə(r)/ (US **storekeeper** /ˈstɔːkiːpə(r)/) noun [C] a person who owns or manages a small shop ▶ **sklepika-rz/rka**

shoplifter /ˈʃɒplɪftə(r)/ noun [C] a person who steals sth from a shop while pretending to be a customer ▶ **osoba kradnąca towary ze sklepu** ➲ note at **thief**

shoplifting /ˈʃɒplɪftɪŋ/ noun [U] the crime of stealing goods from a shop while pretending to be a customer: *He was arrested for shoplifting.* ▶ **kradzież towarów ze sklepu**

shopping /ˈʃɒpɪŋ/ noun [U] **1** the activity of going to the shops and buying things: *We always **do the shopping** on a Friday night.* ◇ *a shopping basket/bag/trolley* ▶ **zakupy** ➲ note at **supermarket** **2** (especially Brit.) the things that you have bought in a shop: *Can you help me to put the shopping in the car?* ▶ **zakupy**

shopping

If you **go shopping** in the **sales**, you can often get good **bargains** (things at a cheaper **price** than usual). You might spend time **browsing**, or **window-shopping** (looking in shop windows without intending to **buy** anything). If you are buying clothes, you **try** them **on** in the **fitting room**. You pay at the **cash desk**, where the **shop assistant** will give you a **receipt**. If you are not satisfied with a **product** you have bought, **take it back** to the shop. There you can **exchange** it or ask for a **refund**.

S

ˈ**shopping centre** (US ˈ**shopping center**) noun [C] a place where there are many shops, either outside or in a covered building ▶ **centrum handlowe** ➲ picture on **page A5**

ˈ**shopping mall** (also **mall** /mæl; mɔːl/) noun [C] (especially US) a covered area or building where there are many shops ▶ **zadaszone centrum handlowe**

shore¹ /ʃɔː(r)/ noun [C,U] the land at the edge of a sea or lake: *The sailors **went on shore*** (zeszli na ląd). ▶ **brzeg, wybrzeże** ➲ look at **ashore**

shore² /ʃɔː(r)/ verb

PHR V **shore sth up 1** to support part of a building or other large structure by placing large pieces of wood or metal against or under it so that it does not fall down ▶ **podpierać coś 2** to help to support sth that is weak or going to fail: *The measures were aimed at shoring up the economy.* ▶ **podtrzymywać coś**

shorn past participle of **shear**

short¹ /ʃɔːt/ adj. **1** not measuring much from one end to the other: *a short line/distance/dress* ◇ *This essay is rather short.* ◇ *short hair* ▶ **krótki** OPP **long** ➲ verb **shorten 2** less than the average height: *a short, fat man*

▶ **niski, niewysoki** OPP **tall 3** not lasting a long time: *a short visit/film* ◇ *to have a short memory* ◇ *She left a short time ago.* Niedawno wyszła. ▶ **krótki** SYN **brief** OPP **long** ➲ verb **shorten 4 short (of/on sth)** not having enough of what is needed: *Because of illness, the team is two players short* (o dwóch zawodników za mało). ◇ *Good secretaries are **in short supply**.* Trudno znaleźć dobrą sekretarkę. ◇ *We're a bit short of money* (brakuje nam pieniędzy) *at the moment.* ◇ *Your essay is a bit short on detail* (zawiera niewiele szczegółów). ▶ **niewystarczający** ➲ noun **shortage 5 short for sth** (used as a shorter way of saying sth): *'Bill' is short for 'William'.* ▶ **skrót (od czegoś) 6 short (with sb)** (used about a person) speaking in an impatient and angry way to sb: *What's the matter with Michael? He was really short with me just now.* ▶ **nieuprzejmy i szorstki** ➲ adverb **shortly**

■ **short** adv. suddenly: *She **stopped short*** (zatrzymała się) *when she saw the accident.* ◇ *a career tragically **cut short*** (przerwana) *by illness* ▶ **nagle**

IDM **cut sb short** to not allow sb to finish speaking; to interrupt sb ▶ **przerywać komuś; skracać, ucinać**

fall short (of sth) → FALL[1]

for short as a short form: *She's called 'Diana', or 'Di' for short.* ▶ **w zdrobnieniu**

go short (of sth) to be without enough (of sth): *He made sure his family never went short of food.* ▶ **zabraknąć**

in the long/short term → TERM[1]

in short in a few words ▶ **krótko mówiąc**

run short (of sth) to have used up most of sth so there is not much left: *We're running short of coffee.* ▶ **brakować**

short of sth/doing sth apart from; except for: *Nothing short of a miracle will save us now.* ▶ **z wyjątkiem**

stop short of sth/doing sth → STOP[1]

the short answer is... (used just before you give sb a short, often blunt, answer, usually to a question involving sth difficult or complicated) ▶ **krótko mówiąc**

short² /ʃɔːt/ noun [C] **1** (especially Brit.) a small strong alcoholic drink: *I prefer wine to shorts.* ▶ **maluch** (*kieliszek mocnego alkoholu*) **2** (informal) = SHORT CIRCUIT

shortage /ˈʃɔːtɪdʒ/ noun [C] a situation where there is not enough of sth: *a food/housing/water shortage* ◇ *a shortage of trained teachers* ▶ **brak**

shortbread /ˈʃɔːtbred/ noun [U] a sweet biscuit made with sugar, flour and butter ▶ **kruche ciastko**

ˌshort ˈcircuit (also informal **short**) noun [C] a bad electrical connection that causes a machine to stop working ▶ **zwarcie elektryczne**

■ **ˌshort-ˈcircuit** verb [I,T]: *The lights short-circuited.* ▶ **zwierać** (*np. obwód*)

shortcoming /ˈʃɔːtkʌmɪŋ/ noun [C, usually pl.] a fault or weakness ▶ **wada**

ˌshort ˈcut noun [C] a quicker, easier or more direct way to get somewhere or to do sth: *He **took a short cut*** (poszedł na skróty) *to school through the park.* ▶ **skrót**

shorten /ˈʃɔːtn/ verb [I,T] to become shorter or to make sth shorter ▶ **skracać (się)** OPP **lengthen**

shortfall /ˈʃɔːtfɔːl/ noun [C] **shortfall (in sth)** the amount by which sth is less than you need or expect ▶ **ubytek, brak**

shorthand /ˈʃɔːthænd/ noun [U] a method of writing quickly that uses signs or short forms of words: *to write **in shorthand*** stenografować ◇ *a shorthand typist* stenotypist(k)a ▶ **stenografia**

shortlist /ˈʃɔːtlɪst/ noun [C, usually sing.] a list of the best people for a job, etc. who have been chosen from all the people who want the job: *She's one of the four people on the shortlist.* ▶ **lista najlepszych kandydatów do rozmowy o pracę/nagrody itp.**

■ **shortlist** verb [T]: *Six candidates were shortlisted for the post.* ▶ **umieszczać kogoś na liście najlepszych kandydatów**

ˌshort-ˈlived adj. lasting only for a short time ▶ **krótkotrwały**

🔑 **shortly** /ˈʃɔːtli/ adv. **1** soon; not long: *The manager will see you shortly.* ▶ **wkrótce 2** in an impatient, angry way: *She spoke rather shortly to the customer.* ▶ (*sposób mówienia*) **sucho**

shorts /ʃɔːts/ noun [pl.] **1** a type of short trousers ending above the knee that you wear in hot weather, while playing sports, etc. ▶ **szorty** ℹ Zwróć uwagę, że **shorts** występuje tylko w lm. Dlatego nie można powiedzieć, np. ~~a new short~~. Można natomiast powiedzieć: *I need some new shorts.* ◇ *I need a pair of shorts.* ◇ *These shorts are too small.* **2** (US) a piece of loose clothing that men wear under their trousers: *boxer shorts* ▶ **bokserki**

ˌshort-ˈsighted adj. **1** (especially US **nearsighted** /ˌnɪəˈsaɪtɪd/) able to see things clearly only when they are very close to you: *I have to wear glasses because I'm short-sighted.* ▶ **krótkowzroczny** OPP **long-sighted 2** not considering what will probably happen in the future: *a short-sighted attitude/policy* ▶ **krótkowzroczny**

ˌshort-ˈstaffed adj. (used about an office, a shop, etc.) not having enough people to do the work ▶ **cierpiący na braki personelu**

ˌshort ˈstory noun [C] a piece of writing that is shorter than a novel ▶ **nowela, opowiadanie**

ˌshort ˈtemper noun [sing.] a tendency to become angry very quickly and easily ▶ **porywczość**

■ **ˌshort-ˈtempered** adj. ▶ **porywczy**

ˌshort-ˈterm adj. lasting for a short period of time from the present: *short-term plans/memory* ▶ **krótkoterminowy**

ˈshort wave noun [U] (abbr. **SW**) the system of broadcasting radio using sound waves of less than 100 metres ▶ **fale krótkie**

🔑 **shot¹** /ʃɒt/ noun [C] **1 a shot (at sb/sth)** an act of firing a gun, etc., or the noise that this makes: *to **take a shot** at the target* strzelić do tarczy ◇ *The policeman fired **a warning shot** into the air.* ▶ **strzał 2** [usually sing.] (informal) **a shot (at sth/at doing sth)** a try at doing sth: *Just **give it your best shot**.* Zrób to najlepiej, jak potrafisz. ◇ *Let me **have a shot*** (spróbować) *at it.* ▶ **próba** SYN **attempt 3** the act of kicking, throwing or hitting a ball in order to score a point or a goal: *Owen scored with a low shot into the corner of the net.* ◇ *Good shot!* ▶ **strzał** (*do bramki*) **4** (often **the shot**) the heavy ball that is used in the sports competition called the **shot-put**: *to put the shot* pchać kulą ▶ **kula** (*sprzęt sportowy*) **5** a photograph or a picture in a film: *I got some good shots of the runners as they crossed the line.* ▶ **zdjęcie; ujęcie 6** a small amount of a drug that is put into your body using a needle: *a shot of penicillin/morphine* ▶ **zastrzyk**

IDM **call the shots/tune** → CALL[1]

like a shot (informal) very quickly; without stopping to think about it: *If someone invited me on a free holiday, I'd go like a shot.* ▶ **migiem**

a long shot → LONG[1]

shot² past tense, past participle of **shoot¹**

shotgun /ˈʃɒtɡʌn/ noun [C] a long gun that is used for shooting small animals and birds ▶ **dubeltówka** ➲ note at **gun**

the ˈshot-put noun [sing.] the event or sport of throwing a heavy metal ball as far as possible ▶ (*sport*) **pchnięcie kulą**

🔑 **should** /ʃəd; strong form ʃʊd/ modal verb (negative **should not**; short form **shouldn't** /ˈʃʊdnt/) **1** (used for saying that it is right or appropriate for sb to do sth, or for sth to happen) ought to: *The police should do something about street crime in this area.* ◇ *Children shouldn't be left on their own.* ◇ *I'm tired. I shouldn't have gone to bed so late/I should have gone to bed earlier.* ▶ **powinien 2** (used for giving or for asking for advice): *Should I try again?* ◇ *You should try that new restaurant.* ◇ *Do you think I should phone him?* ◇ *What should I do?* ◇ *I should get to bed early if I were you.* Na twoim miejscu poszedłbym wcześnie spać. ▶ **powinien, mieć 3** (used for saying that you expect sth is true or will happen): *He should have arrived by now.* Chyba już dojechał. ◇ *It should stop raining soon.* Wkrótce chyba przestanie padać. **4** (Brit., formal) (used with 'I/we' instead of 'would' in 'if' sentences): *I should be most grateful* (byłbym ogromnie zobowiązany) *if you could send me…* **5** (formal) (used to refer to a possible event or situation): *If you should decide to accept/Should you decide to accept…* (jeżeli zaakceptuje pan (naszą propozycję)), *please phone us.* ▶ **jeżeli, gdyby 6** (used as the past tense of 'shall' when we report what sb says): *He asked me if he should come today.* ▶ **powinien (w mowie zależnej) 7 I should imagine, say, think, etc.** (used to give opinions that you are not certain about): *This picture is worth a lot of money, I should think.* ▶ **moim zdaniem 8** (used after certain adjectives): *It's shocking that something like this should happen* (mogło się wydarzyć). ◇ *It's strange that you should mention that* (że o tym wspomniałeś)*…* ◇ *Is it important that we should all go* (żebyśmy wszyscy poszli)*?* **9** (used after 'so that' and 'in order that'): *In order that there should be no delay* (aby uniknąć zwłoki), *we took action immediately.* **10** (used after certain verbs, e.g. when sth is arranged or suggested): *We arranged that they should book the hotel.* ◇ *I suggested that he should cancel the meeting.* ▶ **powinien**

⚷ **shoulder¹** /ˈʃəʊldə(r)/ noun **1** [C] the part of your body between your neck and the top of your arm: *She fell asleep with her head on his shoulder.* ◇ *a shoulder blade* łopatka ◇ *I asked him why he'd done it but he just* ***shrugged his shoulders.*** ▶ **ramię** ➲ picture at **body 2** (**-shouldered**) [in compounds] having the type of shoulders mentioned: *a broad-shouldered* (barczysty) *man* ▶ **(określa cechy ramion) 3** [C] a part of a dress, coat, etc. that covers the shoulders: *a jacket with padded shoulders* ▶ **ramię** (*np. płaszcza*) **4** (**shoulders**) [pl.] the part of your body between your two shoulders: *He carried his little girl on his shoulders.* ▶ **barki 5** (US) = HARD SHOULDER

IDM **have a chip on your shoulder** → CHIP¹

rub shoulders with sb → RUB

a shoulder to cry on (used to describe a person who listens to your problems and understands how you feel) ▶ **osoba, której można się wypłakać**

shoulder² /ˈʃəʊldə(r)/ verb [T] **1** to accept the responsibility for sth: *to* ***shoulder the blame/responsibility*** *for something* ▶ **brać na swe barki** (*np. odpowiedzialność*) **2** to push sb/sth with your shoulder ▶ **rozpychać się**

ˈ**shoulder bag** noun [C] a type of bag that you carry over one shoulder with a long narrow piece of cloth, leather, etc. ▶ **torba na ramię** SYN **handbag** ➲ picture on **page A1**

ˈ**shoulder blade** (also **scapula** /ˈskæpjʊlə/) noun [C] either of the two large flat bones on each side of your back, below your shoulders ▶ **łopatka** ➲ picture at **body**

ˈ**shoulder-length** adj. (especially used about hair) long enough to reach your shoulders ▶ **do ramion**

⚷ **shout** /ʃaʊt/ verb **1** [T] **shout sth (at/to sb)** to say sth in a loud voice: *'Careful,' she shouted.* ◇ *The captain shouted instructions to his team.* ▶ **krzyczeć 2** [I] **shout (at/to sb)** to speak or cry out in a very loud voice: *There's no need to shout – I can hear you.* ◇ *The teacher shouted angrily at the boys.* ▶ **krzyczeć** ➲ look at **scream**

■ **shout** noun [C] ▶ **okrzyk**

PHR V **shout sb down** to shout so that sb who is speaking cannot be heard: *The speaker was shouted down by a group of protesters.* ▶ **zakrzyczeć**

shout (sth) out to say sth in a loud voice; to cry out in a very loud voice: *to shout out in pain/excitement* ▶ **wykrzyczeć (coś)**

shove /ʃʌv/ verb [I,T] (informal) to push with a sudden, rough movement: *Everybody in the crowd was* ***pushing and shoving*** (przepchali się). ◇ *The policeman shoved the thief into the back of the police car.* ◇ *'What should I do with this box?' 'Oh, just shove it over there* (wsadź to tam)*.'* ▶ **pchać (się), wpychać (się)**

■ **shove** noun [C, usually sing.]: *to give somebody/something a shove* ▶ **pchnięcie**

shovel /ˈʃʌvl/ noun [C] a tool used for picking up and moving earth, snow, sand, etc. ▶ **szufla** ➲ look at **spade** ➲ picture at **garden**

■ **shovel** verb [I,T] (**shovelling**; **shovelled**; US **shoveling**; **shoveled**): *to shovel snow* ▶ **szuflować**

⚷ **show¹** /ʃəʊ/ verb (pt **showed**; pp **shown** /ʃəʊn/ or **showed**) **1** [T] to make sth clear; to give information about sth: *Research shows that most people get too little exercise.* ◇ *This graph shows how prices have gone up in the last few years.* ▶ **wykazywać, przedstawiać 2** [T] **show sb/sth (to sb)**; **show sb (sth)** to let sb see sb/sth; to allow sth to be seen: *I showed the letter to him.* ◇ *I showed him the letter.* ◇ *These brown trousers don't show the dirt.* Na tych brązowych spodniach nie widać brudu. ◇ *The picture showed him arguing with a photographer.* Zdjęcie przedstawiało go w trakcie kłótni z fotografem. ◇ *They're showing his latest film at our local cinema.* ◇ *She was showing* (było po niej widać) *signs of stress.* ◇ *She was the first person ever to show* (która okazała) *him any kindness and love.* ▶ **pokazywać 3** [T] to help sb to do sth by doing it yourself; to explain sth: *Can you show me how to put the disk in the computer?* ▶ **demonstrować 4** [T] to lead sb to or round a place; to explain how to go to a place: *I'll come with you and show you the way.* ◇ *Shall I show you to your room?* ◇ *A guide showed us round the museum.* ▶ **prowadzić 5** [I] to be able to be seen; to appear: *I tried not to let my disappointment show.* ◇ *She had a woollen hat on that left only her nose showing.* Miała na sobie wełnianą czapkę, spod której wystawał jej jedynie nos. ◇ *I've got a hole in my sock but it doesn't show* (ale jej nie widać). ◇ *His latest film is showing* (jest grany) *at the local cinema.* ▶ **ukazywać się**

IDM **show sb/know/learn the ropes** → ROPE¹

PHR V **show (sth) off** (informal) to try to impress people by showing them how clever you are or by showing them sth that you are proud of: *John was showing off by driving his new car very fast.* ▶ **popisywać się**

show up (informal) to arrive, especially when sb is expecting you: *Where have you been? I thought you'd never show up.* ▶ **pojawiać się**

show (sth) up to allow sth to be seen: *The sunlight shows up those dirty marks on the window.* ▶ **uwidaczniać**

show sb up (informal) to make sb embarrassed about your behaviour or appearance: *He showed her up by shouting at the waiter.* ▶ **zawstydzać kogoś**

⚷ **show²** /ʃəʊ/ noun **1** [C] a type of entertainment performed for an audience: *a TV comedy show* ◇ *a quiz show* ▶ **widowisko 2** [C,U] an occasion when a collection of things are brought together for people to look at: *a dog show* ◇ *a fashion show* ◇ *Paintings by local children will be* ***on show*** *at the town hall next week.* ◇ *the motor show* pokaz samochodowy ▶ **pokaz, wystawa 3** [sing.] an occasion when you let sb see sth: *a show of* (okazywanie) *emotion/gratitude/temper* ▶ **pokaz, demonstracja 4** [C,U] something that a person does or has in order to make people believe sth that is not true: *Although she hated him, she* ***put on a show of*** *politeness* (była uprzedzająco

S

grzeczna). ◇ *His bravery is **all show*** (jest na pokaz). ▶ **pokaz**

IDM **show your face** to appear among your friends or in public: *She stayed at home, afraid to show her face.* ▶ **pokazać się publicznie**

PHR V **show sb around/round (sth)** to be a guide for sb when they visit sth for the first time and to show them what is interesting ▶ **oprowadzać kogoś (po czymś)**

'show business (also informal **showbiz** /ˈʃəʊbɪz/) noun [U] the business of entertaining people in the theatre, in films, on TV, etc.: *He's been **in show business** since he was five years old.* ▶ **przemysł rozrywkowy**

showdown /ˈʃəʊdaʊn/ noun [C] a final argument, meeting or fight at the end of a long disagreement: *The management are preparing for a showdown with the union.* ▶ **ostateczna rozgrywka** (*w długim sporze*)

shower¹ /ˈʃaʊə(r)/ noun [C] **1** a piece of equipment that produces a spray of water that you stand under to wash; the small room or part of a room that contains a shower: *The shower doesn't work.* ◇ *She's in the shower.* ◇ *I'd like a room with a shower, please.* ▶ **prysznic 2** an act of washing yourself by standing under a shower: *I'll just **have a quick shower*** (wezmę szybki przysznic) *then we can go out.* ▶ **prysznic 3** a short period of rain: *a heavy shower* ▶ **opady przelotne** ➲ look at **rain**, **acid rain 4** a lot of very small objects that fall or fly through the air together: *a shower of sparks/broken glass* ▶ **chmura** (*np. pyłu*), **grad** (*np. kamieni*)

shower² /ˈʃaʊə(r)/ verb **1** [I] to wash yourself under a shower: *I came back from my run, showered and got changed.* ▶ **brać prysznic 2** [I,T] **shower (down) on sb/sth**; **shower sb with sth** to cover sb/sth with a lot of small falling objects: *Ash from the volcano showered down on the town.* ◇ *People suffered cuts after being showered with broken glass.* ▶ **zasypywać czymś**

showing /ˈʃəʊɪŋ/ noun **1** [C] an act of showing a film, etc.: *The second showing of the film begins at 8 o'clock.* ▶ **pokaz 2** [sing.] how sb/sth behaves; how successful sb/sth is: *On its present showing* (według obecnych notowań), *the party should win the election.* ▶ **notowania**, **stan rzeczy**

showjumping /ˈʃəʊdʒʌmpɪŋ/ noun [U] a competition in which a person rides a horse over a series of jumps ▶ **konkurs jazdy konnej z przeszkodami** ➲ picture on page A9

showman /ˈʃəʊmən/ noun [C] (pl. **-men** /-mən/) **1** a person who does things in an entertaining way and is good at getting people's attention ▶ **showman 2** a person who organizes public entertainments, especially at **fairgrounds**: *travelling showmen* ▶ (*osoba*) **organizator widowiska** (*zwł. w wesołym miasteczku*)

shown past participle of **show¹**

'show-off noun [C] a person who tries to impress others by showing them how clever he/she is, or by showing them sth he/she is proud of: *She's such a show-off, always boasting about how good she is at this and that.* ▶ **pozer/ka**

showroom /ˈʃəʊruːm; -rʊm/ noun [C] a type of large shop where customers can look at goods such as cars, furniture and electrical items that are on sale ▶ **salon** (*np. samochodowy, sprzętu grającego*)

showy /ˈʃəʊi/ adj. so brightly coloured, large or exaggerated that it attracts a lot of attention: *showy flowers* ▶ **pretensjonalny** SYN **ostentatious**

shrank past tense of **shrink**

shrapnel /ˈʃræpnəl/ noun [U] small pieces of metal that fly around when a bomb explodes ▶ **odłamki**

shred¹ /ʃred/ verb [T] (**shredding**; **shredded**) to tear or cut sth into **shreds**: *shredded cabbage* ▶ **szatkować**, **targać/ciąć na strzępy**

shred² /ʃred/ noun **1** [C] a small thin piece of material that has been cut or torn off: *His clothes were torn to shreds by the rose bushes.* ▶ **strzęp 2** [sing.] [in negative sentences] **a shred of sth** a very small amount of sth: *There wasn't a shred of truth in her story.* ▶ **krzta**

shrewd /ʃruːd/ adj. able to make good decisions because you understand a situation well: *a shrewd thinker/decision* ▶ **przenikliwy**, **trafny**

■ **shrewdly** adv. ▶ **przenikliwie**, **trafnie**

shriek /ʃriːk/ verb **1** [I] to make a short, loud, noise in a high voice: *She shrieked in fright.* ◇ *The children were shrieking with laughter.* ▶ **piszczeć 2** [T] to say sth loudly in a high voice: *'Stop it!' she shrieked.* ▶ **wrzeszczeć** ➲ look at **screech**

■ **shriek** noun [C] ▶ **pisk**, **wrzask**

shrill /ʃrɪl/ adj. (used about a sound) high and unpleasant: *a shrill cry* ▶ **piskliwy**

shrimp /ʃrɪmp/ noun [C] **1** a small sea creature with a shell and a lot of legs that turns pink when you cook it. **Shrimps** are smaller than **prawns**. ▶ **krewetka 2** (US) = PRAWN

shrine /ʃraɪn/ noun [C] a place that is important to a particular person or group of people for religious reasons or because it is connected with a special person ▶ **sanktuarium**

shrink /ʃrɪŋk/ verb (pt **shrank** /ʃræŋk/ or **shrunk** /ʃrʌŋk/, pp **shrunk**) **1** [I,T] to become smaller or make sth smaller: *My T-shirt shrank in the wash./I've shrunk my T-shirt.* Skurczyła mi się koszulka (w praniu). ◇ *TV has shrunk the world.* ◇ *The rate of inflation has shrunk to 4%.* ▶ **kurczyć się**, **zmniejszać (się) 2** [I] to move back because you are frightened or shocked: *We shrank back against the wall when the dog appeared.* ▶ **cofnąć się** (*z przerażenia*)

PHR V **shrink from sth/doing sth** to not want to do sth because you find it unpleasant ▶ **wzdragać się**

'shrink-wrapped adj. wrapped tightly in a thin plastic covering: *shrink-wrapped software* ▶ **ofoliowany**

shrivel /ˈʃrɪvl/ verb [I,T] (**shrivelling**; **shrivelled**; US **shriveling**; **shriveled**) **shrivel (sth) (up)** to become smaller, especially because of dry conditions: *The plants shrivelled up and died in the hot weather.* ▶ **wysuszać (się)**

shroud¹ /ʃraʊd/ noun [C] a cloth or sheet that is put round a dead body before it is buried ▶ **całun**

shroud² /ʃraʊd/ verb [T, usually passive] **shroud sth (in sth)** to cover or hide sth ▶ **okrywać**, **zasłaniać**

Shrove Tuesday /ˌʃrəʊv ˈtjuːzdeɪ; -di; US ˈtuːz-/ noun [C] the day before **Lent** ▶ **wtorek przed Popielcem**, **ostatki**

Kulturowo dzień ten jest odpowiednikiem tłustego czwartku w Polsce. ➲ look at **Pancake Day**

shrub /ʃrʌb/ noun [C] a small bush ▶ **krzew**

shrubbery /ˈʃrʌbəri/ noun [C] (pl. **shrubberies**) an area where a lot of small bushes have been planted ▶ **zarośla**

shrug /ʃrʌg/ verb [I,T] (**shrugging**; **shrugged**) to lift your shoulders as a way of showing that you do not know sth or are not interested: *'Who knows?' he said and shrugged.* ◇ *'It doesn't matter to me,' he said, **shrugging his***

shrug

'How should I know?' he shrugged.

shoulders. ▶ **wzruszać** (*ramionami*)

■ **shrug** noun [C, usually sing.]: *I asked him if he was sorry and he just answered with a shrug.* ▶ **wzruszenie** (*ramion*)

PHR V **shrug sth off** to not allow sth to affect you in a bad way: *An actor has to learn to shrug off criticism.* ▶ **machać na coś ręką**

shrunk past tense, past participle of **shrink**

shudder /ˈʃʌdə(r)/ verb [I] to suddenly shake hard, especially because of an unpleasant feeling or thought: *The engine shuddered violently and then stopped.* ◇ *Just to think about the accident makes me shudder* (przyprawia mnie o dreszcze). ◇ *I shudder to think* (ciarki mnie przechodzą na myśl) *how much this meal is going to cost.* ▶ **wzdrygać się**

■ **shudder** noun [C] ▶ **dreszcz**, **ciarki**

shuffle[1] /ˈʃʌfl/ verb **1** [I] to walk by sliding your feet along instead of lifting them off the ground: *The child shuffled past, wearing her mother's shoes.* ▶ **szurać/powłóczyć nogami 2** [I,T] to move your body or feet around because you are uncomfortable or nervous: *The audience were so bored that they began to shuffle in their seats.* ▶ **wiercić się 3** [I,T] to mix a pack of playing cards before a game: *It's your turn to shuffle.* ◇ *She shuffled the cards carefully.* ▶ **tasować**

shuffle[2] /ˈʃʌfl/ noun [C, usually sing.] **1** a way of walking without lifting your feet off the ground ▶ **szuranie/powłóczenie nogami 2** an act of **shuffling** cards ▶ **tasowanie**

shun /ʃʌn/ verb [T] (**shunning**; **shunned**) (formal) to avoid sb/sth; to keep away from sb/sth: *She was shunned by her family when she married him.* ▶ **unikać**

shunt /ʃʌnt/ verb [T] **1** to push a train from one track to another ▶ **przetaczać** (*wagony*) **2** to move sb/sth to a different place, especially a less important one: *John was shunted sideways to a job in sales.* ▶ **przemieszczać** (*kogoś z miejsca na miejsce*)

shush /ʃʊʃ/ exclamation (used to tell sb to be quiet): *Shush! Do you want to wake everyone?* ▶ **cii!**

■ **shush** verb [T] to tell sb to be quiet, especially by saying 'shush', or by putting your finger against your lips: *Lyn shushed the children.* ▶ **uciszać**

shut[1] /ʃʌt/ verb (**shutting**; pt, pp **shut**) **1** [I,T] to make sth close; to become closed: *Could you shut the door, please?* ◇ *I can't shut my suitcase.* ◇ *Shut your books, please.* ◇ *He shut his eyes and tried to go to sleep.* ◇ *This window won't shut properly.* ◇ *The doors open and shut automatically.* ▶ **zamykać (się) 2** [I,T] (used about a shop, restaurant, etc.) to stop doing business for the day; to close: *What time do the shops shut on Saturday?* ▶ **zamykać (się)**

PHR V **shut sb/sth away** to keep sb/sth in a place where people cannot find or see them or it ▶ **chować kogoś/coś**

shut (sth) down (used about a factory, etc.) to close for a long time or for ever: *Financial problems forced the business to shut down.* ▶ **zamykać (coś/się)**

shut sb/yourself in (sth) to put sb in a room and keep them there; to go to a room and stay there: *She shut herself in her room and refused to come out.* ▶ **zamykać kogoś/się (gdzieś)**

shut sth in sth to trap sth by closing a door, lid, etc. on it: *Tony shut his fingers in the door of the car.* ▶ **przytrzaskiwać coś czymś**

shut sb/sth off (from sth) to keep sb/sth apart from sth: *He shuts himself off from the rest of the world.* ▶ **odcinać/odizolowywać się/kogoś/coś (od czegoś)**

shut sb/sth out to keep sb/sth out: *Mum, Ben keeps shutting me out of the bedroom!* ◇ (figurative) *He tried to shut out all thoughts of the accident.* ◇ *I wanted to shut John out of my life forever.* Chciałam wyrzucić Johna z mojego życia na zawsze. ▶ **nie puszczać kogoś/czegoś (gdzieś/do siebie)**, **odsuwać kogoś/coś od siebie**

shut (sb) up (informal) **1** to stop talking; to be quiet: *I wish you'd shut up!* ▶ **zamykać gębę 2** to make sb stop talking: *Nothing can shut him up once he's started.* ▶ **zamykać gębę komuś**

shut sb/sth up (in sth) to put sb/sth somewhere and stop them leaving: *He was shut up in prison for nearly ten years.* ▶ **zamykać kogoś/coś (gdzieś)**

shut[2] /ʃʌt/ adj. [not before a noun] **1** in a closed position: *Make sure the door is shut properly before you leave.* ▶ **zamknięty** ℹ Pamiętaj, że **close** można użyć przed rzeczownikiem: *a closed door*, natomiast **shut** nie można. **2** not open to the public: *The restaurant was shut so we went to one round the corner.* ▶ **zamknięty**

IDM **keep your mouth shut** → MOUTH[1]

shutter /ˈʃʌtə(r)/ noun [C] **1** a wooden or metal cover that is fixed outside a window and that can be opened or shut. A shop's **shutter** usually slides down from the top of the shop window. ▶ **żaluzja** (*zewnętrzna*), **roleta** (*zewnętrzna*) **2** the part at the front of a camera that opens for a very short time to let light in so that a photograph can be taken ▶ **migawka**

shuttle /ˈʃʌtl/ noun [C] a plane, bus or train that travels regularly between two places ▶ **wahadłowiec**

shuttlecock /ˈʃʌtlkɒk/ noun [C] (in the sport of **badminton**) the small, light object that is hit over the net ▶ **lotka**

ˈ**shuttle service** noun [C] a regular air, bus or train service between two places ▶ **stała komunikacja między dwoma miejscami**

shy[1] /ʃaɪ/ adj. **1** nervous and uncomfortable about meeting and speaking to people; showing that sb feels like this: *She's very shy with strangers.* ◇ *a shy smile* ▶ **nieśmiały 2** [not before a noun] **be shy (of/about sth/doing sth)** to be frightened to do sth or to become involved in sth: *She's not shy of telling people what she thinks.* ▶ **unikać czegoś**

■ **shyly** adv. ▶ **nieśmiało** | **shyness** noun [U]: *He didn't overcome his shyness till he had left school.* ▶ **nieśmiałość**

shy[2] /ʃaɪ/ verb [I] (**shying**; **shies**; pt, pp **shied**) (used about a horse) to suddenly move back or sideways in fear ▶ **płoszyć się**

PHR V **shy away from sth/from doing sth** to avoid doing sth because you are afraid ▶ **obawiać się czegoś**

Siamese twin /ˌsaɪəmiːz ˈtwɪn/ (also **conˌjoined ˈtwin** /kənˌdʒɔɪnd ˈtwɪn/) noun [C] one of two people who are born with their bodies joined together in some way, sometimes sharing the same organs ▶ **bliźnia-k/czka syjamsk-i/a**

sibling /ˈsɪblɪŋ/ noun [C] (formal) a brother or a sister: *Jealousy between siblings* (zazdrość między rodzeństwem) *is very common.* ▶ **brat/siostra** ℹ W języku codziennym używa się raczej **brother(s) and sister(s)**: *Have you got any brothers and sisters?*

sick[1] /sɪk/ adj. **1** not well: *a sick child* ◇ *Do you get paid for days when you're* ***off sick****?* ◇ *You're too ill to work today – you should* ***phone in sick****.* ▶ **chory 2** (especially Brit.) feeling ill in your stomach so that you may **vomit**: *I feel sick – I think it was that fish I ate.* ◇ *Don't eat any more or you'll make yourself sick.* ▶ **mający nudności** ➲ look at **nausea**, **travel-sick**, **seasick**, **airsick**, **carsick 3 be sick of sb/sth** to feel bored or annoyed because you have had too much of sb/sth: *I'm sick of my job.* ◇ *I'm sick of tidying up your mess!* ▶ **znudzić się czymś**, **mieć dosyć czegoś 4 sick (at/about sth)** very annoyed or disgusted by sth: *He felt sick at the sight of so much waste.* ▶ **wściekły**, **zdegustowany 5** (informal) mentioning disease, suffering, death, etc. in a cruel or disgusting way: *He offended everyone*

S

with a sick joke about blind people. ▶ **okrutny, niezdrowy** (*np. pogląd, upodobanie*)

IDM **be sick** to bring up food from the stomach: *It's common for women to be sick in the first months of pregnancy.* ▶ **wymiotować** SYN **vomit**

make sb sick to make sb very angry: *Oh, stop complaining. You make me sick!* ▶ **rozwścieczać kogoś**

sick to death of sb/sth feeling tired of or annoyed by sb/sth: *I'm sick to death of* (mam po dziurki w nosie) *his grumbling.* ▶ **zanudzony na śmierć**

sick² /sɪk/ noun **1** [U] food that sb has brought up from their stomach: *There was sick all over the car seat.* ▶ **rzygowiny** SYN **vomit 2** (**the sick**) noun [pl.] people who are ill: *All the sick and wounded were evacuated.* ▶ **chorzy**

sicken /ˈsɪkən/ verb [T] to make sb feel disgusted: *The level of violence in the film sickens me.* ▶ **wywoływać obrzydzenie**

■ **sickening** adj.: *His head made a sickening sound as it hit the road.* ▶ **obrzydliwy**

sickle /ˈsɪkl/ noun [C] a tool with a curved blade and a short handle, used for cutting grass, etc. ▶ **sierp**

ˈ**sick leave** noun [U] a period spent away from work, etc. because of illness: *Mike's been off* ***on sick leave*** *since March.* ▶ **zwolnienie lekarskie**

sickly /ˈsɪkli/ adj. (**sicklier**; **sickliest**) **1** (used about a person) weak and often ill: *a sickly child* ▶ **chorowity, słabowity 2** unpleasant; causing you to feel ill: *the sickly smell of rotten fruit* ▶ **wstrętny**; **przyprawiający o mdłości**

sickness /ˈsɪknəs/ noun **1** [U] the state of being ill: *A lot of workers are absent because of sickness.* ▶ **choroba 2** [C,U] a particular type of illness: *Sleeping sickness is carried by the tsetse fly.* ◇ *seasickness pills* tabletki na chorobę morską ▶ **(określony) rodzaj choroby 3** [U] a feeling in your stomach that may make you bring up food through your mouth: *Symptoms of the disease include sickness and diarrhoea.* ▶ **nudności**

side¹ /saɪd/ noun [C] **1** the area to the left or right of sth; the area in front of or behind sth: *We live (on)* ***the other side*** *of the main road.* ◇ *It's more expensive to live on the north side of town.* ◇ *In Japan they drive on* ***the left-hand side*** *of the road.* ◇ *She sat at the side of his bed/at his bedside* (przy łóżku). ◇ *this side up* tą stroną do góry ▶ **strona 2** one of the surfaces of sth except the top, bottom, front or back: *I went round to the side of the building.* ◇ *The side of the car was damaged.* ▶ **strona**, **bok 3** the edge of sth, away from the middle: *Make sure you stay* ***at the side*** *of the road when you're cycling.* ◇ *We moved* ***to one side*** *to let the doctor get past.* ▶ **bok**, **pobocze 4** the right or the left part of your body, especially from under your arm to the top of your leg: *She lay on her side.* ◇ *The soldier stood with his hands by his sides.* ▶ **bok 5** either of the two flat surfaces of sth thin: *Write on both sides of the paper.* ▶ **strona 6** one of the flat outer surfaces of sth: *A cube has six sides.* ▶ **bok 7** (**-sided**) [in compounds] having the number of sides mentioned: *a six-sided coin* ◇ *He was sitting at the far side of the room* (w głębi pokoju). ▶ **-boczny**, **-stronny 8** either of two or more people or groups who are fighting, playing, arguing, etc. against each other: *The two sides agreed to stop fighting.* ◇ *the winning/losing side* ◇ *Whose side are you on?* ▶ **strona 9** what is said by one person or group that is different from what is said by another: *I don't know whose* ***side of the story*** *to believe.* ▶ **wersja 10** your mother's or your father's family: *There is no history of illness* ***on*** *his* ***mother's side.*** ▶ **strona 11** a particular aspect of sth, especially a situation or a person's character: *She has a generous side to her nature.* Ma w sobie pewną wielkoduszność. ▶ **strona**

IDM **err on the side of sth** → ERR

get on the right/wrong side of sb to please/annoy sb: *He tried to get on the right side of his new boss.* ▶ **schlebiać komuś, denerwować kogoś**

look on the bright side → LOOK¹

on/from all sides; **on/from every side** in/from all directions ▶ **ze wszystkich stron**, **ogólnie**

on the big, small, high, etc. side (informal) slightly too big, small, high, etc. ▶ **nieco** (*np. za mały/duży*)

on the safe side → SAFE¹

put sth on/to one side; **leave sth on one side** to leave or keep sth so that you can use it or deal with it later: *You should put some money to one side for the future.* ▶ **odkładać/odsuwać coś na bok**

side by side next to each other; close together: *They walked side by side along the road.* ▶ **obok siebie**

take sides (with sb) to show that you support one person rather than another in an argument: *Parents should never take sides when their children are quarrelling.* ▶ **stawać po czyjejś stronie**

side² /saɪd/ verb

PHR V **side with sb (against sb)** to support sb in an argument ▶ **stawać po czyjejś stronie (przeciw komuś)**

sideboard /ˈsaɪdbɔːd/ noun [C] **1** a type of low cupboard about as high as a table, that is used for storing plates, etc. in a **dining room** ▶ **kredens 2** (Brit.) = SIDEBURN

sideburn /ˈsaɪdbɜːn/ (Brit. also **sideboard**) noun [usually pl.] hair that grows down the sides of a man's face in front of his ears ▶ **baki**

ˈ**side effect** noun [C] **1** an unpleasant effect that a drug may have in addition to its useful effects: *Side effects of the drug include nausea and dizziness.* ▶ **skutek uboczny 2** an unexpected effect of sth that happens in addition to the intended effect: *One of the side effects when the chemical factory closed was that fish returned to the river.* ▶ **skutek uboczny**

sideline /ˈsaɪdlaɪn/ noun **1** [C] something that you do in addition to your regular job, especially to earn extra money: *He's an engineer, but he repairs cars as a sideline* (dodatkowo). ▶ **praca dodatkowa 2** (**sidelines**) [pl.] the lines that mark the two long sides of the area used for playing sports such as football, **tennis**, etc.; the area behind this ▶ **linia autowa/boczna**

IDM **on the sidelines** not involved in an activity; not taking part in sth ▶ (*stać, obserwować itp.*) **z boku**

sidelong /ˈsaɪdlɒŋ/ adj. [only before a noun] directed from the side; sideways: *a sidelong glance* ▶ **z boku**, **na bok**, **boczny**

ˈ**side road** noun [C] a small road which joins a bigger main road ▶ **boczna droga**

ˈ**side show** noun [C] **1** a separate small show or attraction at a fair or a circus where you pay to see a performance or take part in a game ▶ **dodatkowy występ lub inna atrakcja** (*np. w cyrku*) **2** an activity or event that is much less important than the main activity or event ▶ **działalność uboczna**; **wydarzenie mniejszej rangi**

ˈ**side street** noun [C] a narrow or less important street near a main street ▶ **boczna ulica**

sidetrack /ˈsaɪdtræk/ verb [T, usually passive] to make sb forget what they are doing or talking about and start doing or talking about sth less important ▶ **kierować uwagę/sprawę na boczny tor**

sidewalk (US) = PAVEMENT

sideways /ˈsaɪdweɪz/ adv. **1** to, towards or from one side: *He jumped sideways to avoid being hit.* ▶ **na bok 2** with one of the sides at the top: *We'll have to turn the sofa sideways to get it through the door.* ▶ **na bok**

■ **sideways** adj.: *a sideways move* ◇ *She gave him a sideways look.* Popatrzyła na niego z ukosa. ▶ **boczny**

siding /ˈsaɪdɪŋ/ noun [C] **1** a short track beside a main railway line, where trains can stand when they are not being used ▶ **bocznica** 2 (US) material used to cover and protect the outside walls of buildings ▶ **materiał użyty do zewnętrznej ochrony budynków**

sidle /'saɪdl/ verb [I] **sidle up/over (to sb/sth)** to move towards sb/sth in a nervous way, as if you do not want anyone to notice you ▶ **iść bokiem**

siege /si:dʒ/ noun [C,U] a situation in which an army surrounds a town for a long time or the police surround a building so that nobody can get in or out: *The house was* ***under siege*** (był oblężony) *for several hours, until the man released his hostages.* ▶ **oblężenie** (*np. przestępcy przez policję w jakimś budynku*)

siesta /si'estə/ noun [C] a short sleep or rest that people take in the afternoon, especially in hot countries: *to have/take a siesta* ▶ **sjesta**

sieve /sɪv/ noun [C] a type of kitchen tool that has a metal or plastic net, used for separating solids from liquids or very small pieces of food from large pieces: *Pour the soup through a sieve to get rid of any lumps.* ▶ **sito** ➲ picture at **kitchen**

■ **sieve** verb [T]: *to sieve flour* ▶ **przesiewać**

sift /sɪft/ verb **1** [T] to pass flour, sugar or a similar substance through a **sieve** in order to remove any lumps: *to sift flour/sugar* ▶ **przesiewać** **2** [I,T] **sift (through) sth** to examine sth very carefully: *It took weeks to sift through all the evidence.* ▶ **przesiewać** (*np. fakty*)

sigh /saɪ/ verb **1** [I] to let out a long, deep breath that shows you are tired, sad, disappointed, etc.: *She sighed with disappointment at the news.* ▶ **wzdychać** **2** [T] to say sth with a **sigh**: *'I'm so tired,' he sighed.* ▶ **westchnąć** **3** [I] to make a long sound like a **sigh** ▶ **szeptać**

■ **sigh** noun [C] ▶ **westchnienie**

IDM **heave a sigh** → HEAVE[1]

⚷ **sight**[1] /saɪt/ noun **1** [U] the ability to see: *He lost his sight in the war.* ◇ *My grandmother has very poor sight.* ▶ **wzrok** **2** [sing.] **the sight of sb/sth** the act of seeing sb/sth: *I feel ill* ***at the sight of*** *blood.* ◇ *We flew over Paris and had our first sight of the Eiffel Tower* (i po raz pierwszy zobaczyliśmy Wieżę Eiffla). ▶ **widok** **3** [U] a position where sb/sth can be seen: *They waited until the plane was* ***in/within sight*** *and then fired.* ◇ *When we get over this hill the town should* ***come into sight.*** ◇ *She didn't let the child* ***out of*** *her* ***sight.*** ◇ *'Get out of my sight* (zejdź mi z oczu)*!' he shouted, angrily.* ▶ **zasięg wzroku** **4** [C] something that you see: *The burned-out building was a terrible sight.* ▶ **widok** **5** (**sights**) [pl.] places of interest that are often visited by tourists: *When you come to New York I'll show you the sights.* ▶ **ciekawe miejsca** **6** (**a sight**) [sing.] (informal) a person or thing that looks strange or amusing: *You should have seen Anna in my jacket – she did look a sight* (wyglądała przedziwnie)*!* ▶ **widok** **7** [C, usually pl.] the part of a gun that you look through in order to aim it: *He had the deer in his sights now.* ▶ **celownik** **8** (**-sighted**) [in compounds] having eyes that are weak in a particular way: *I'm short-sighted/long-sighted.* Jestem krótkowidzem/dalekowidzem. ▶ **-wzroczny**

IDM **at first glance/sight** → FIRST[1]

catch sight of sb/sth → CATCH[1]

in sight likely to happen or come soon: *A peace settlement is in sight.* ▶ **na widoku**

lose sight of sb/sth → LOSE

on sight as soon as you see sb/sth: *The soldiers were ordered to shoot the enemy on sight.* ▶ **na widok**

sight[2] /saɪt/ verb [T] to see sb/sth, especially after looking out for them or it ▶ **dostrzec**, **zobaczyć**

sighting /'saɪtɪŋ/ noun [C] an occasion when sb/sth is seen: *the first sighting of a new star* ▶ **zaobserwowanie**, **dostrzeżenie**

sightseeing /'saɪtsi:ɪŋ/ noun [U] visiting the sights of a city, etc. as a tourist: *We did some sightseeing in Rome.* ▶ **zwiedzanie** ➲ note at **holiday**

sightseer /'saɪtsi:ə(r)/ noun [C] a person who visits the sights of a city, etc. as a tourist ▶ **zwiedzając-y/a** ➲ look at **tourist**

⚷ **sign**[1] /saɪn/ noun [C] **1 sign (of sth)** something that shows that sb/sth is present, exists or may happen: *The patient was* ***showing*** *some* ***signs*** *of improvement.* ◇ *As we drove into the village there wasn't a sign of life anywhere.* ▶ **znak**, **oznaka**, **ślad** **2** a piece of wood, paper, etc. that has writing or a picture on it that gives you a piece of information, an instruction or a warning: *What does that sign say?* ◇ *a road sign* ◇ *Follow the signs to Banbury.* ▶ **napis**, **znak**, **szyld** **3** a movement that you make with your head, hands or arms that has a particular meaning: *I* ***made a sign*** *for him to follow me.* ◇ *I'll* ***give*** *you* ***a sign*** *when it's time for you to speak.* ▶ **znak** **4** a type of shape, mark or symbol that has a particular meaning: *In mathematics, a cross is a plus sign.* ▶ **znak** **5** = STAR SIGN

⚷ **sign**[2] /saɪn/ verb **1** [I,T] to write your name on a letter, document, etc. to show that you have written it or that you agree with what it says: *'Could you sign here, please?'* ◇ *I forgot to sign the cheque.* ◇ *The two presidents signed the treaty.* ▶ **podpisywać (się)** ➲ noun **signature** **2** [T] **sign sb (up)** to get sb to sign a contract to work for you: *Real Madrid have signed two new players.* ▶ **zawierać kontrakt z kimś** **3** [I] to communicate using sign language: *Dave's deaf friend taught him to sign.* ▶ **posługiwać się językiem migowym**

PHR V **sign in/out** to write your name to show you have arrived at or left a hotel, club, etc. ▶ **wpisywać/wypisywać się**

sign off **1** (Brit.) to end a letter: *She signed off with 'Yours, Janet'.* ▶ **kończyć list** SYN **finish** **2** to end a broadcast by saying goodbye or playing a piece of music ▶ **kończyć program**

sign up (for sth) to arrange to do a course of study by adding your name to the list of people doing it ▶ **zapisywać się (na coś)**

⚷ **signal** /'sɪgnəl/ noun [C] **1** a sign, an action or a sound that sends a particular message: *When I give (you) the signal, run!* ▶ **sygnał**, **znak** **2** an event, an action or a fact that shows that sth exists or is likely to happen: *The fall in unemployment is a clear signal that the economy is improving.* ▶ **sygnał** **3** a set of lights used to give information to train drivers: *a stop signal* ▶ **kolejowe znaki świetlne** **4** a series of radio waves, etc. that are sent out or received: *a signal from a satellite* ▶ **sygnał (radiowy)**

■ **signal** verb [I,T] (**signalling**; **signalled**; US **signaling**; **signaled**): *She was signalling wildly that something was wrong.* ◇ *He signalled his disapproval* (okazał dezaprobatę) *by leaving the room.* ▶ **sygnalizować**, **dawać znak/sygnał**

signatory /'sɪgnətri; US -tɔ:ri/ noun [C] (pl. **signatories**) **signatory (to sth)** one of the people or countries that sign an agreement, etc. ▶ **sygnatariusz/ka**

⚷ **signature** /'sɪgnətʃə(r)/ noun [C] sb's name, written by that person and always written in the same way: *I couldn't read his signature.* ▶ **podpis** ➲ verb **sign**

'signature tune noun [C] (Brit.) a short tune played at the beginning and end of a particular television or radio programme, or one that is connected with a particular performer ▶ **sygnał programu**

significance /sɪg'nɪfɪkəns/ noun [U] the importance or meaning of sth: *Few people realized the significance of the discovery.* ▶ **znaczenie**, **ważność**

⚷ **significant** /sɪg'nɪfɪkənt/ adj. **1** important or large enough to be noticed: *Police said that the time of the murder was extremely significant.* ◇ *There has been a significant improvement in your work.* ▶ **znaczny**, **ważny**

S

2 having a particular meaning: *It could be significant that he took out life insurance shortly before he died.* ▶ **znaczący**

■ **significantly** adv.: *Attitudes have changed significantly since the 1960s.* ▶ **znacznie**; **znacząco**

signify /ˈsɪɡnɪfaɪ/ verb [T] (**signifying**; **signifies**; pt, pp **signified**) (formal) **1** to be a sign of sth: *What do those lights signify?* ▶ **oznaczać**, **znaczyć** SYN **mean** **2** to express or indicate sth: *They signified their agreement by raising their hands.* ▶ **wyrażać**

ˈ**sign language** noun [U] a language used especially by people who cannot hear or speak, using their hands to make signs instead of spoken words ▶ **język migowy**

signpost /ˈsaɪnpəʊst/ noun [C] a sign at the side of a road that gives information about directions and distances to towns ▶ **drogowskaz**

Sikh /siːk/ noun [C] a member of **Sikhism** ▶ **Sikh**

■ **Sikhism** /ˈsiːkɪzəm/ noun [U] ▶ **Sikhizm**

silence /ˈsaɪləns/ noun **1** [U] no noise or sound at all: *There must be silence during examinations.* ▶ **cisza** SYN **quiet** **2** [C,U] a period when nobody speaks or makes a noise: *My question was met with an awkward silence.* ◇ *We ate **in silence**.* ▶ **milczenie** **3** [U] not making any comments about sth: *I can't understand his silence on the matter.* ▶ **milczenie**

■ **silence** verb [T] ▶ **uciszać**

silencer /ˈsaɪlənsə(r)/ (US **muffler** /ˈmʌflə(r)/) noun [C] **1** a device which is fixed to the **exhaust pipe** to reduce the noise made by the engine ▶ **tłumik** **2** the part of a gun that reduces the noise when it is fired ▶ **tłumik**

silent /ˈsaɪlənt/ adj. **1** where there is no noise; making no noise: *The house was empty and silent.* ▶ **cichy** SYN **quiet** **2** [only before a noun] not using spoken words: *a silent prayer/protest* ▶ **niemy** **3** **silent (on/about sth)** refusing to speak about sth: *The policeman told her she had the right to **remain silent*** (prawo do milczenia). ◇ *So far he has remained silent on* (nie wspomina) *his future plans.* ▶ **cichy** **4** (used about a letter) not pronounced: *The 'b' in 'comb' is silent.* ▶ **niemy**

■ **silently** adv.: *She crept silently away.* ▶ **cicho**, **milcząco**

silhouette /ˌsɪluˈet/ noun [C] the dark solid shape of sb/sth seen against a light background ▶ **sylwetka**

■ **silhouetted** adj. ▶ **rysujący się**

silicon /ˈsɪlɪkən/ noun [U] (symbol **Si**) a chemical element that exists as a grey solid or a brown powder, and is found in rocks and sand. It is used in making glass and electronic equipment. ▶ **krzem**

ˌ**silicon** ˈ**chip** noun [C] a piece of **silicon** that is used in computers, etc. ▶ **krzemowy układ scalony**

silk /sɪlk/ noun [U] the soft smooth cloth that is made from threads produced by a **silkworm**: *a silk shirt/dress* ▶ **jedwab**

silky /ˈsɪlki/ adj. (**silkier**; **silkiest**) smooth, soft and shiny; like silk: *silky hair* ▶ **jedwabisty**

sill /sɪl/ noun [C] a shelf that is at the bottom of a window, either inside or outside: *a windowsill* ▶ **parapet**

silly /ˈsɪli/ adj. (**sillier**; **silliest**) **1** not showing thought or understanding; stupid: *a silly mistake* ◇ *Don't be so silly!* ▶ **głupi**, **niemądry** SYN **foolish** OPP **sensible** **2** appearing ridiculous, so that people will laugh: *I'm not wearing that hat – I'd look silly in it.* ▶ **głupi**

■ **silliness** noun [U]: *Stop this silliness and get back to work!* ▶ **brak rozsądku**

silt /sɪlt/ noun [U] sand, soil or mud that collects at the sides or on the bottom of a river ▶ **muł**

silver[1] /ˈsɪlvə(r)/ noun [U] **1** (symbol **Ag**) a valuable greyish-white metal that is used for making jewellery, coins, etc.: *a silver spoon/necklace* ◇ *That's a nice ring. Is it silver?* ▶ **srebro** **2** coins made from silver or sth that looks like silver: *I need £2 in silver for the parking meter.* ▶ **srebrna moneta** **3** objects that are made of silver, for example knives, forks, spoons and dishes: *The thieves stole some jewellery and some valuable silver.* ▶ **srebra** **4** = SILVER MEDAL

IDM **every cloud has a silver lining** → CLOUD[1]

silver[2] /ˈsɪlvə(r)/ adj. **1** having the colour of silver: *a silver sports car* ▶ **srebrny** **2** celebrating the 25th anniversary of sth: *the silver jubilee of the Queen's coronation* ▶ (*dwudziestopięciolecie*) **srebrny** ➲ look at **diamond**, **golden**

silverfish /ˈsɪlvəfɪʃ/ noun [C] (pl. **silverfish**) a small silver insect without wings that lives in houses and that can cause damage to materials such as cloth and paper ▶ **rybik**

ˌ**silver** ˈ**medal** (also **silver**) noun [C] a small flat round piece of silver that is given to the person or team that comes second in a sports competition: *to win a silver medal at the Olympic Games* ▶ **srebrny medal** ➲ look at **bronze medal**, **gold medal**

■ ˌ**silver** ˈ**medallist** noun [C] ▶ **srebrn-y/a medalist(k)a**

silverware /ˈsɪlvəweə(r)/ noun [U] **1** objects that are made of or covered with silver, especially knives, forks, dishes, etc. that are used for eating and serving food: *a piece of silverware* ▶ **srebro stołowe** **2** (US) = CUTLERY

silvery /ˈsɪlvəri/ adj. having the appearance or colour of silver: *an old lady with silvery hair* ▶ **srebrzysty**, **srebrny**

SIM card /ˈsɪm kɑːd/ noun [C] a plastic card inside a mobile phone that stores personal information about the person using the phone ▶ **karta SIM**

similar /ˈsɪmələ(r)/ adj. **similar (to sb/sth)**; **similar (in sth)** like sb/sth but not exactly the same: *Our houses are very similar in size.* ◇ *My teaching style is similar to that of many other teachers.* ▶ **podobny** OPP **different**, **dissimilar** ➲ look at **alike**

■ **similarly** adv.: *The plural of 'shelf' is 'shelves'. Similarly, the plural of 'wolf' is 'wolves'.* ▶ **podobnie**

similarity /ˌsɪməˈlærəti/ noun (pl. **similarities**) **1** [U, sing.] **similarity (to sb/sth)**; **similarity (in sth)** the state of being like sb/sth but not exactly the same: *She **bears a** remarkable/striking **similarity** to her mother.* ▶ **podobieństwo** **2** [C] **a similarity (between A and B)**; **a similarity (in/of sth)** a characteristic that people or things have which makes them similar: *Although there are some similarities between the two towns, there are a lot of differences too.* ◇ *similarities in/of style* ▶ **podobieństwo** OPP **difference**

simile /ˈsɪməli/ noun [C,U] a word or phrase that compares sth to sth else, using the words 'like' or 'as'; the use of such words and phrases. For example, 'a face like a mask' and 'as white as snow' are similes. ▶ **porównanie (literackie)** ➲ look at **metaphor**

simmer /ˈsɪmə(r)/ verb [I,T] to cook gently in a liquid that is almost boiling ▶ **gotować (się) na wolnym ogniu**

simple /ˈsɪmpl/ adj. **1** easy to understand, do or use; not difficult or complicated: *This dictionary is written in simple English.* ◇ *a simple task/method/solution* ◇ *I can't just leave the job. It's not as simple as that.* ▶ **prosty**, **nieskomplikowany** SYN **easy** **2** without decoration or unnecessary extra things: *a simple black dress* ◇ *The food is simple but perfectly cooked.* ▶ **prosty** SYN **basic** OPP **fancy** **3** (used for saying that the thing you are talking about is the only thing that is important or true): *I'm not going to buy it **for the simple reason that** I haven't got enough money.* ▶ **prosty** **4** (used about a person or a way of life) natural and not complicated: *a simple life in the country* ▶ **zwyczajny**, **prosty** **5** not intelligent; slow to understand: *He's not mad – just a little simple.* ▶ **prosty**

ˌ**simple-ˈminded** adj. not intelligent; not able to understand how complicated things are: *a simple-minded approach* ▶ **ograniczony**

simplicity /sɪmˈplɪsəti/ noun [U] **1** the quality of being easy to understand, do or use: *We all admired the simplicity of the plan.* ▶ **prostota, łatwość 2** the quality of having no decoration or unnecessary extra things; being natural and not complicated: *I like the simplicity of her paintings.* ▶ **prostota, naturalność**

simplify /ˈsɪmplɪfaɪ/ verb [T] (**simplifying**; **simplifies**; pt, pp **simplified**) to make sth easier to do or understand; to make sth less complicated: *The process of applying for visas has been simplified.* ▶ **upraszczać, ułatwiać**
■ **simplification** /ˌsɪmplɪfɪˈkeɪʃn/ noun [C,U] ▶ **uproszczenie, ułatwienie**

simplistic /sɪmˈplɪstɪk/ adj. making a problem, situation, etc. seem less difficult and complicated than it really is ▶ **uproszczony**

🔑**simply** /ˈsɪmpli/ adv. **1** (used to emphasize how easy or basic sth is): *Simply add hot water and stir.* ▶ **po prostu 2** (used to emphasize an adjective) completely: *That meal was simply excellent.* ▶ **po prostu** SYN **absolutely 3** in a way that makes sth easy to understand: *Could you explain it more simply?* ▶ **prosto 4** in a simple, basic way; without decoration or unnecessary extra things: *They live simply, with very few luxuries.* ▶ **prosto 5** only: *There's no need to get angry. The whole problem is simply a misunderstanding.* ▶ **po prostu** SYN **just**

simulate /ˈsɪmjuleɪt/ verb [T] to create certain conditions that exist in real life using computers, models, etc., usually for study or training purposes: *The astronauts trained in a machine that simulates conditions in space.* ▶ **symulować**
■ **simulation** /ˌsɪmjuˈleɪʃn/ noun [C,U]: *a computer simulation of a nuclear attack* ▶ **symulacja**

simultaneous /ˌsɪmlˈteɪniəs; US ˌsaɪml-/ adj. happening or done at exactly the same time as sth else ▶ **równoczesny, jednoczesny**
■ **simultaneously** adv. ▶ **równocześnie, jednocześnie**

sin /sɪn/ noun [C,U] an action or way of behaving that is not allowed by a religion: *He believes it is a sin for two people to live together without being married.* ▶ **grzech**
■ **sin** verb [I] (**sinning**; **sinned**) ▶ **grzeszyć** | **sinner** noun [C] ▶ **grzeszni-k/ca**

🔑**since** /sɪns/ prep., adv. **1** from a particular time in the past until a later time in the past or until now: *It was the first time they'd won since 1974.* ◇ *She has had a number of jobs since leaving university.* ◇ *My parents bought this house in 1975 and we've been living here ever since.* ◇ *He had come to see us a few weeks earlier but he hadn't been back since* (ale od tamtego czasu więcej się już nie pokazał). ▶ **od (czasu, kiedy); odtąd, od tamtego/tego czasu 2** at a time after a particular time in the past: *We were divorced two years ago and she has since married someone else.* ▶ **od tamtego/tego czasu, po czym**
➲ note at **ago**, **during**

> **Since** używane jest w czasie *present perfect*, aby podkreślić, że coś ma miejsce od pewnego określonego momentu w przeszłości do chwili obecnej: *He has been in prison since 1970.* **Ago** jest także używane, żeby wskazać kiedy coś się wydarzyło lub rozpoczęło, ale tylko w czasie *past simple*: *He went to prison 20 years ago.*
>
> Zarówno **since**, jak i **for** używa się w celu określenia, jak długo coś trwa. **Since** stosuje się, kiedy mówimy o początku odcinka czasu (roku, tygodnia, godziny itp.), a **for**, gdy mówimy o długości odcinka czasu: *I've known her since 2001.* ◇ *I've known her for six years.* Uwaga! „Od ... (do)" tłumaczy się **from ... (to)**, gdy okres opisanego działania już się skończył: *He lived in London from 1980 to 1995.* ◇ *Mozart played the piano from an early age.* Gdy okres jeszcze trwa, używa się **since**: *He has been living here since 1980.* Zwróć uwagę na użycie czasu *present perfect* lub *present perfect continuous* w zdaniach zawierających słowo **since**.

■ **since** conj. **1** because; as: *Since they've obviously forgotten to phone me, I'll have to phone them.* ▶ **ponieważ, skoro 2** from a particular time in the past until a later time in the past or until now: *I've been working in a bank ever since I left school.* Pracuję w banku od ukończenia szkoły ▶ **od (czasu, kiedy), odkąd**

🔑**sincere** /sɪnˈsɪə(r)/ adj. **1** (used about sb's feelings, beliefs or behaviour) true; showing what you really mean or feel: *Please accept our sincere thanks/apologies.* ▶ **szczery** SYN **genuine 2** (used about a person) really meaning or believing what you say; not pretending: *Do you think she was being sincere when she said she admired me?* ▶ **szczery** SYN **honest** OPP for both meanings **insincere**
■ **sincerely** adv.: *I am sincerely grateful to you for all your help.* ◇ *Yours sincerely,* Z wyrazami szacunku (zwrot grzecznościowy stosowany na zakończenie listu) ▶ **szczerze** | **sincerity** /sɪnˈserəti/ noun [U] ▶ **szczerość** OPP **insincerity**

sinew /ˈsɪnjuː/ noun [C,U] a strong, thin part inside the body that joins a muscle to a bone ▶ **ścięgno**

sinful /ˈsɪnfl/ adj. breaking a religious law; immoral ▶ **grzeszny**

🔑**sing** /sɪŋ/ verb [I,T] (pt **sang** /sæŋ/, pp **sung** /sʌŋ/) to make musical sounds with your voice: *He always sings when he's in the bath.* ◇ *The birds were singing outside my window.* ◇ *She sang all her most popular songs at the concert.* ▶ **śpiewać**
PHR V **sing along (with sb/sth)**; **sing along (to sth)** to sing together with sb who is already singing or while a record, radio, or musical instrument is playing: *Do sing along if you know the words.* ▶ **śpiewać razem (z kimś/czymś)**
■ **singing** noun [U]: *singing lessons* ▶ **śpiew**

singe /sɪndʒ/ verb [I,T] (**singeing**) to burn the surface of sth slightly, usually by accident; to be burned in this way ▶ **osmalać, opalać**

🔑**singer** /ˈsɪŋə(r)/ noun [C] a person who sings, or whose job is singing, especially in public: *an opera singer* ▶ **śpiewa-k/czka, piosenka-rz/rka**

🔑**single**[1] /ˈsɪŋgl/ adj. **1** [only before a noun] only one: *He gave her a single red rose.* ◇ *I managed to finish the whole job in a single afternoon.* ◇ *I went to a* ***single-sex*** *school.* ▶ **pojedynczy, jeden 2** [only before a noun] (used to emphasize that you are talking about each individual item in a group or series): *You answered* ***every single*** (na każde pytanie) *question correctly. Well done!* ◇ *He couldn't see a single person* (ani jednej osoby) *that he knew.* ◇ *I couldn't understand a single word she said* (ani słowa z tego, co mówiła)*!* ▶ **każdy** (*bez wyjątku*) **3** not married: *Are you married or single?* ◇ *a single man/woman* ▶ **nieżonaty, niezamężna 4** [only before a noun] for the use of only one person: *I'd like to book a single room, please.* ▶ **pojedynczy, jednoosobowy** ➲ note at **bed**[1] ➲ look at **double 5** (US ˌ**one-ˈway**) [only before a noun] (used about a ticket or the price of a ticket) for a journey to a particular place, but not back again: *How much is the single fare to York?* ▶ **w jedną stronę** ➲ look at **return**
IDM **in single file** in a line, one behind the other ▶ **(iść) gęsiego**

S

single² /ˈsɪŋɡl/ noun **1** [C] a ticket for a journey to a particular place, but not back again: *Two singles to Hull, please.* ▶ **bilet w jedną stronę** ➲ look at **return 2** [C] a CD, tape, etc. that has only one song on each side; the main song on this tape or CD: *Joss Stone's new single* ▶ **syngiel** ➲ look at **album 3** [C] a bedroom for one person in a hotel, etc. ▶ **pokój jednoosobowy** ➲ look at **double 4** (**singles**) [pl.] people who are not married and do not have a romantic relationship with sb else ▶ **samotni 5** (**singles**) [pl.] (in sports such as **tennis**) a game in which one player plays against one other player ▶ **gra pojedyncza** ➲ look at **doubles**

single³ /ˈsɪŋɡl/ verb

PHR V **single sb/sth out (for sth)** to give special attention or treatment to one person or thing from a group: *She was singled out for criticism.* Jako jedyna stała się obiektem krytyki. ▶ **wyróżniać kogoś/coś (za coś)**

ˌsingle-ˈdecker noun [C] a bus with only one level ▶ **autobus jednopiętrowy** ➲ picture at **bus**

ˌsingle-ˈhanded adj., adv. on your own with nobody helping you: *a single-handed yacht race* regaty samotników ▶ **w pojedynkę**

ˌsingle-ˈminded adj. having one clear aim or goal which you are determined to achieve ▶ **mający jeden (wytyczony) cel**

■ **ˌsingle-ˈmindedness** noun [U] ▶ **determinacja**

ˌsingle ˈparent noun [C] a person who looks after their child or children without a husband, wife or partner: *a single-parent family* ▶ **samotny rodzic**

singlet /ˈsɪŋlət/ noun [C] (Brit.) **1** a piece of clothing for a man, without sleeves, worn under or instead of a shirt ▶ **podkoszulek 2** a similar piece of clothing worn by runners, etc. ▶ **koszulka, podkoszulek**

singly /ˈsɪŋɡli/ adv. one at a time; alone: *You can buy the tapes either singly or in packs of three.* ▶ **pojedynczo** SYN **individually**

singular /ˈsɪŋɡjələ(r)/ adj. **1** in the form that is used for talking about one person or thing only: *'Table' is a singular noun; 'tables' is a plural noun.* ▶ **pojedynczy** ➲ look at **plural 2** (formal) unusual ▶ **niezwykły, osobliwy**

■ **singular** noun [sing.]: *The word 'clothes' has no singular.* ◇ *What's the singular of 'people'?* ▶ **liczba pojedyncza**

singularly /ˈsɪŋɡjələli/ adv. (formal) very; in an unusual way: *He chose a singularly inappropriate moment to make his request.* ◇ *singularly beautiful* ▶ **niezwykle, szczególnie**

sinister /ˈsɪnɪstə(r)/ adj. seeming evil or dangerous; making you feel that sth bad will happen: *There's something sinister about him. He frightens me.* ▶ **złowieszczy, złowrogi**

sink¹ /sɪŋk/ verb (pt **sank** /sæŋk/, pp **sunk** /sʌŋk/) **1** [I,T] to go down or make sth go down under the surface of liquid or a soft substance: *If you throw a stone into water, it sinks.* ◇ *My feet sank into the mud.* ▶ **tonąć, zapadać się, pogrążać się; zatapiać, zanurzać 2** [I] (used about a person) to move downwards, usually by falling or sitting down: *I came home and sank into a chair, exhausted.* ▶ **opadać, upadać 3** [I] to get lower; to fall to a lower position or level: *We watched the sun sink slowly below the horizon.* ▶ **opadać, obniżać się 4** [I] to decrease in value, number, amount, strength, etc. ▶ **spadać**

IDM **your heart sinks** → HEART

PHR V **sink in** (used about information, an event, an experience, etc.) to be completely understood or realized: *It took a long time for the terrible news to sink in.* ▶ **docierać do świadomości**

sink in; sink into sth (used about a liquid) to go into sth solid; to be absorbed ▶ **wsiąkać (w coś)**

sink² /sɪŋk/ noun [C] a large open container in a kitchen, with taps to supply water, where you wash things ▶ **zlewozmywak, zlew** ➲ look at **washbasin**

sinuous /ˈsɪnjuəs/ adj. (literary) turning while moving, in an elegant way; having many curves: *a sinuous movement* ◇ *the sinuous grace of a cat* ◇ *the sinuous* (kręty) *course of the river* ▶ **wijący się**

■ **sinuously** adv. ▶ **w sposób wijący się**

sinus /ˈsaɪnəs/ noun [C, often plural] one of the spaces in the bones of your face that are connected to your nose: *I've got a terrible cold and my sinuses are blocked.* ◇ *a sinus infection* ▶ **zatoka** (*czołowa, szczękowa*)

sip /sɪp/ verb [I,T] (**sipping**; **sipped**) to drink, taking only a very small amount of liquid into your mouth at a time: *We sat in the sun, sipping lemonade.* ▶ **popijać** (*małymi łykami*)

■ **sip** noun [C] ▶ **łyczek**

siphon (also **syphon**) /ˈsaɪfn/ verb [T] **1 siphon sth into/out of sth; siphon sth off/out** to remove a liquid from a container, often into another container, through a tube ▶ **przelewać syfonem/rurką 2 siphon sth off; siphon sth (from/out of sb/sth)** to take money from a company illegally over a period of time ▶ **odprowadzać** (*pieniądze, niezgodnie z przeznaczeniem*), **podkradać**

sir /sɜː(r)/ noun **1** [sing.] (used as a polite way of speaking to a man whose name you do not know, for example in a shop or restaurant, or to show respect): *I'm afraid we haven't got your size, sir.* ▶ **proszę pana** ➲ look at **madam 2** (**Sir**) [C] (used at the beginning of a formal letter to a male person or male people): *Dear Sir...* Szanowny panie ◇ *Dear Sirs ...* Szanowni panowie ▶ **pan/panowie** (*zwrot grzecznościowy w liście do mężczyzny lub mężczyzn*) ➲ look at **madam 3** /sə(r)/ [sing.] the title that is used in front of the name of a man who has received one of the highest British honours ▶ **sir** ⓘ **Sir** stawia się przed imieniem i nazwiskiem w całości lub przed samym imieniem. Nie można go stawiać przed nazwiskiem nie poprzedzonym imieniem.

siren /ˈsaɪrən/ noun [C] a device that makes a long, loud sound as a warning or signal: *an air-raid siren* ◇ *Three fire engines raced past, sirens wailing.* ▶ **syrena (alarmowa)**

sirloin /ˈsɜːlɔɪn/ (also **ˌsirloin ˈsteak**) noun [U,C] good quality meat that is cut from a cow's back ▶ **polędwica wołowa**

sis /sɪs/ noun [C] (informal) sister (used when you are speaking to her) ▶ **siostra**

sister /ˈsɪstə(r)/ noun [C] **1** a girl or woman who has the same parents as another person: *I've got one brother and two sisters.* ◇ *We're sisters.* ▶ **siostra** ➲ look at **half-sister, stepsister** ⓘ W jęz. ang. nie ma powszechnie używanego słowa na zbiorowe określenie braci i sióstr (odpowiednika polskiego „rodzeństwo"): *Have you got any brothers and sisters?* Słowo **sibling** jest bardzo formalne. **2** (informal) a woman who you feel close to because she is a member of the same society, group, etc. as you ▶ **siostra 3** (often **Sister**) (Brit.) a female nurse who has responsibility for part of a hospital ▶ **siostra (przełożona) 4** (**Sister**) a nun: *Sister Mary-Theresa* ▶ **siostra (zakonna) 5** [usually used as an adjective] a thing that belongs to the same type or group as sth else: *We have a sister company in Japan.* ▶ **bliźniaczy**

ˈsister-in-law noun [C] (pl. **sisters-in-law**) **1** the sister of your husband or wife ▶ **szwagierka 2** the wife of your brother ▶ **bratowa**

sisterly /ˈsɪstəli/ adj. of or like a sister: *sisterly love* ▶ **siostrzany**

sit /sɪt/ verb (**sitting**; pt, pp **sat** /sæt/) **1** [I] to rest your weight on your bottom, for example in a chair: *We sat in the garden all afternoon.* ◇ *She was sitting on the sofa, talking to her mother.* ▶ **siedzieć 2** [T] **sit sb (down)** to put sb into a sitting position; to make sb sit down: *He picked up his daughter and sat her down on a chair.* ◇ *She sat me down and offered me a cup of tea.* ▶ **sadzać 3** [I] to be in a particular place or position: *The letter sat* (leżał) *on the table for several days before anybody opened it.* ▶ **przebywać (w jakimś miejscu) 4** [I] (formal) (used about an official group of people) to have a meeting or series of meetings: *Parliament was still sitting at 3 o'clock in the morning.* ▶ **obradować 5** [T] (Brit.) to take an exam: *If I fail, will I be able to **sit the exam** again?* ▶ **zdawać** (*egzamin*), **przystępować** (*do egzaminu*)

IDM **sit on the fence** to avoid saying which side of an argument you support ▶ **nie mieć ochoty podjąć dezycji**

PHR V **sit about/around** (informal) to spend time doing nothing active or useful: *We just sat around chatting all afternoon.* ▶ **przesiadywać, siedzieć sobie**

sit back to relax and not take an active part in what other people are doing: *Sit back and take it easy while I make dinner.* ▶ **relaksować się, odprężać się**

sit down to lower your body into a sitting position: *He sat down in an armchair.* ▶ **siadać, usiąść**

sit sth out 1 to stay in a place and wait for sth unpleasant or boring to finish: *We sat out the storm in a cafe.* ▶ **odsiedzieć, wysiedzieć 2** to not take part in a dance, game, etc.: *I think I'll sit this one out.* ▶ **nie brać w czymś udziału**

sit through sth to stay in your seat until sth boring or long has finished ▶ **wysiedzieć**

sit up 1 to move into a sitting position when you have been lying down, or to make your back straight: *Sit up straight and concentrate!* ◇ *The news made them all sit up and take notice.* Ta wiadomość pobudziła ich do zwrócenia większej uwagi na problem. ▶ **podnosić się 2** to not go to bed although it is very late: *We sat up all night talking.* ▶ **siedzieć do późna w nocy**

sitcom /ˈsɪtkɒm/ (also formal ˌsituation ˈcomedy) noun [C,U] a funny programme on TV that shows the same characters in different amusing situations each week ▶ **serial komediowy** (*oparty na dowcipie sytuacyjnym*)

🔑 **site** /saɪt/ noun [C] **1** a piece of land where a building was, is or will be: *The company is looking for a site for its new offices.* ◇ *a building/construction site* plac budowy ▶ **teren, miejsce 2** a place where sth has happened or that is used for sth: *the site of a famous battle* ▶ **miejsce 3** = WEBSITE

■ **site** verb [T] (formal) ▶ **umiejscawiać**

sitting /ˈsɪtɪŋ/ noun [C] **1** a period of time during which a court of law or a parliament meets and does its work ▶ **sesja, posiedzenie 2** a time when a meal is served in a school, hotel, etc. to a number of people at the same time: *Dinner will be in two sittings.* ▶ **zmiana**

ˈ**sitting room** (Brit.) = LIVING ROOM

situated /ˈsɪtʃueɪtɪd/ adj. [not before a noun] in a particular place or position: *The hotel is conveniently situated close to the beach.* ◇ *Sydney is situated* (znajduje się) *on the coast.* ▶ **usytuowany, umiejscowiony**

🔑 **situation** /ˌsɪtʃuˈeɪʃn/ noun [C] **1** the things that are happening in a particular place or at a particular time: *The situation in the north of the country is extremely serious.* ◇ *Tim is **in a** difficult **situation** at the moment.* ◇ *the economic/financial/political situation* ▶ **sytuacja, położenie 2** (formal) the position of a building, town, etc. in relation to the area around it: *The house is in a beautiful situation on the edge of a lake.* ▶ **położenie 3** (formal, old-fashioned) a job: *Situations Vacant* (rubryka ogłoszeń w gazecie) Praca/Dam pracę. ▶ **stanowisko, posada**

ˌ**situation ˈcomedy** (formal) = SITCOM

ˈ**sit-up** noun [C] an exercise for the stomach muscles in which you lie on your back with your legs bent, then lift the top half of your body from the floor: *to **do sit-ups*** ▶ **rodzaj ćwiczenia na mięśnie brzucha**

🔑 **six** /sɪks/ number **1** 6 ▶ **sześć**

> Zwróć uwagę na sposób użycia liczb w różnych zdaniach: *The answers are on page six.* ◇ *There are six of us for dinner tonight.* ◇ *They have six cats.* ◇ *My son is six (years old)* (skończy sześć lat) *next month.* ◇ *She lives at 6 Elm Drive.* ◇ *a birthday card with a big six on it.*

2 (**six-**) [in compounds] having six of the thing mentioned: *She works a six-day week.* ▶ **sześcio-** ℹ Więcej o liczbach w dodatku *Wyrażenia liczbowe* na końcu słownika.

🔑 **sixteen** /ˌsɪksˈtiːn/ number 16 ▶ **szesnaście** ➲ note at **six**

■ **sixteenth** /ˌsɪksˈtiːnθ/ **1** ordinal number 16th ▶ **szesnasty** ➲ note at **sixth 2** noun [C] 1/16; one of sixteen equal parts of sth ▶ **(jedna) szesnasta**

ˌ**sixˈteenth note** (US) = SEMIQUAVER

🔑 **sixth** /sɪksθ/ ordinal number 6th ▶ **szósty**

> Zwróć uwagę na sposób użycia liczb porządkowych w różnych zdaniach: *Today is the sixth of March.* ◇ *Today is March the sixth.* ◇ *My office is on the sixth floor.* ◇ *This is the sixth time I've tried to phone him.*

ℹ Więcej o liczbach w dodatku *Wyrażenia liczbowe* na końcu słownika.

■ **sixth** noun [C] ⅙; one of six equal parts of sth ▶ **(jedna) szósta**

ˈ**sixth form** noun [C, with sing. or pl. verb] (Brit.) the final two years at secondary school for students from the age of 16 to 18 who are studying for A level exams ▶ **ostatnia i przedostatnia klasa szkoły średniej kończąca się maturą**

■ ˈ**sixth-former** noun [C] ▶ **uczeń/uczennica ostatniej i przedostatnia klasy szkoły średniej kończącej się maturą**

ˌ**sixth-form ˈcollege** noun [C] (in Britain) a school for students over the age of 16 ▶ **dwuletnia szkoła średnia**

ˌ**sixth ˈsense** noun [sing.] a special ability to know sth without using any of the five senses that include sight, touch, etc.: *My sixth sense told me to stay here and wait.* ▶ **szósty zmysł**

🔑 **sixty** /ˈsɪksti/ number **1** 60 ▶ **sześćdziesiąt** ➲ note at **six**

> Zwróć uwagę na sposób użycia liczb w różnych zdaniach: *Sixty people went to the meeting.* ◇ *There are sixty pages in the book.* ◇ *He retired **at sixty**.*

2 (**the sixties**) [pl.] the numbers, years or temperatures between 60 and 69; the 60s: *I don't know the exact number of members, but it's in the sixties.* ◇ *The most famous pop group of the sixties was The Beatles.* ◇ *The temperature tomorrow will be in the high sixties.* ▶ **lata sześćdziesiąte, zakres liczb/temperatury od 60 do 69**

IDM **in your sixties** between the age of 60 and 69: *I'm not sure how old she is but I should think she's in her sixties.* ◇ *in your **early/mid/late sixties*** po sześćdziesiątce/około 65 lat/pod siedemdziesiątkę ▶ **w wieku między 60 i 69 lat**

■ **sixtieth** /ˈsɪkstiəθ/ **1** ordinal number 60th ▶ **sześćdziesiąty** ➲ note at **sixth 2** noun [C] 1/60; one of sixty equal parts of sth ▶ **(jedna) sześćdziesiąta**

🔑 **size**[1] /saɪz/ noun **1** [U] how big or small sth is: *I was surprised at the size of the hotel. It was enormous!* ◇ *The planet Uranus is about four times the size of Earth.* ▶ **rozmiar, wielkość**

> W pytaniach o wielkość czegoś, zwykle mówi się **How big ... ?**: *How big is your house?*. Zwrot **What size ... ?** stosuje się, kiedy pytanie dotyczy rozmiaru czegoś, co jest produkowane w wielu ustalonych

S

rozmiarach: ***What size** shoes **do you take?*** ◇ *What size are you?* Jaki masz rozmiar (ubrania)?

2 [C] one of a number of fixed measurements in which sth is made: *Have you got this dress **in a** bigger **size**?* ◇ *I'm a size 12.* ◇ *What size pizza would you like? Medium or large?* ▶ **rozmiar**, **format** **3** (**-sized**; **-size**) [in compounds] of the size mentioned: *a king-size bed* ◇ *a medium-sized flat* mieszkanie o średnim metrażu ▶ **rozmiaru**

size² /saɪz/ verb
PHR V **size sb/sth up** to form an opinion or a judgement about sb/sth ▶ **oceniać**

sizeable (also **sizable**) /ˈsaɪzəbl/ adj. quite large: *a sizeable sum of money* ▶ **sporych rozmiarów**

sizzle /ˈsɪzl/ verb [I] to make the sound of food frying in hot fat ▶ **skwierczeć**

skate¹ /skeɪt/ verb [I] **1** (also ˈ**ice-skate**) to move on ice wearing **skates**: *Can you skate?* ◇ *They skated across the frozen lake.* ▶ **jeździć na łyżwach** ⓘ **Go skating** to często używany zwrot oznaczający jazdę na łyżwach w celu rekreacyjnym: *We go skating every weekend.* ➲ picture on **page A9** **2** = ROLLER SKATE
■ **skater** noun [C]: *an ice skater* ▶ **łyżwia-rz/rka**; **wrotka-rz/rka**

skate² /skeɪt/ noun [C] **1** (also ˈ**ice skate**) a boot with a thin sharp metal part on the bottom that is used for moving on ice ▶ **łyżwa** **2** = ROLLER SKATE **3** a large flat sea fish that you can eat ▶ **płaszczka**

skateboard /ˈskeɪtbɔːd/ noun [C] a short narrow board with small wheels at each end that you can stand on and ride as a sport ▶ **deskorolka**
■ **skateboarder** noun [C] ▶ **deskorolkarz** | **skateboarding** noun [U]: *When we were children we used to **go skateboarding** in the park.* ▶ **jazda na deskorolce**

skating /ˈskeɪtɪŋ/ noun [U] **1** (also ˈ**ice skating**) the activity or sport of moving on ice wearing special boots: *Would you like to **go skating** this weekend?* ▶ **jazda na łyżwach** **2** = ROLLER SKATING

ˈ**skating rink** (also ˈ**ice rink**; **rink**) noun [C] a large area of ice, or a building containing a large area of ice, which is used for **skating** on ▶ **lodowisko**

skeleton¹ /ˈskelɪtn/ noun [C] the structure formed by all the bones in a human or animal body: *the human skeleton* ◇ *a dinosaur skeleton* ▶ **szkielet**

skeleton² /ˈskelɪtn/ adj. (used about an organization, a service, etc.) having the smallest number of people that is necessary for it to operate ▶ **dyżurny**, **niezbędny**

skeptic, skepticism (US) = SCEPTIC, SCEPTICISM

sketch /sketʃ/ noun [C] **1** a simple, quick drawing without many details: *He drew a **rough sketch** of the new building on the back of an envelope.* ▶ **szkic** **2** a short funny scene on TV, in the theatre, etc.: *The drama group did a sketch about a couple buying a new house.* ▶ **skecz** **3** a short description without any details ▶ **zarys**, **szkic**
■ **sketch** verb [I,T]: *I sat on the grass and sketched the castle.* ▶ **szkicować**

sketchy /ˈsketʃi/ adj. (**sketchier**; **sketchiest**) not having many or enough details ▶ **szkicowy**, **fragmentaryczny**

skewed /skjuːd/ adj. **1** (used about information) not accurate or correct: *skewed statistics* ▶ **wypaczony** **2** **skewed (towards sb/sth)** directed towards a particular group, place, etc. in a way that may not be accurate or fair: *The book is heavily skewed towards American readers.* ◇ *The curriculum is skewed towards the arts.* ◇ *a skewed* (tendencyjny) *account of what happened* ▶ **(przesadnie) ukierunkowany (na kogoś/coś)**

skewer /ˈskjuːə(r)/ noun [C] a long thin pointed piece of metal or wood that is pushed through pieces of meat, vegetables, etc. to hold them together while they are cooking or to check that they are completely cooked ▶ **szpikulec** (*np. do szaszłyków*)
■ **skewer** verb [T] ▶ **nabijać (***np. szaszłyk***) na szpikulec**

ski¹ /skiː/ verb [I] (**skiing**; pt, pp **skied**) to move over snow on **skis**: *When did you learn to ski?* ▶ **jeździć na nartach** ⓘ **Go skiing** to często używany zwrot oznaczający jazdę na nartach w celach rekreacyjnych: *They go skiing in France every year.*
■ **ski** adj. [only before a noun]: *a ski resort/instructor/slope/suit* ▶ **narciarski** | **skiing** noun [U]: *alpine/downhill/cross-country skiing* ▶ **narciarstwo** ➲ picture on **page A9**

ski² /skiː/ noun [C] one of a pair of long, flat, narrow pieces of wood or plastic that are fastened to boots and used for sliding over snow: *a pair of skis* ▶ **narta**

skid /skɪd/ verb [I] (**skidding**; **skidded**) (usually used about a vehicle) to suddenly slide forwards or sideways without any control: *I skidded on a patch of ice and hit a tree.* ▶ **wpadać w poślizg**
■ **skid** noun [C]: *The car went into a skid and came off the road.* ▶ **poślizg**

skier /ˈskiːə(r)/ noun [C] a person who **skis**: *Dita's a good skier.* ▶ **skoczek narciarski** ➲ picture on **page A9**

ˈ**ski jump** noun [C] a very steep artificial slope that ends suddenly and that is covered with snow. People **ski** down the slope, jump off the end and see how far they can travel through the air before landing. ▶ **skocznia narciarska**
■ ˈ**ski jumper** noun [C] ▶ **narcia-rz/rka** | ˈ**ski jumping** noun [U] ▶ **skoki narciarskie**

⚷ **skilful** (US **skillful**) /ˈskɪlfl/ adj. **1** (used about a person) very good at doing sth: *a skilful painter/politician* ◇ *He's very skilful with his hands.* ▶ **wprawny**, **zręczny** **2** done very well: *skilful guitar playing* ▶ **zręczny**, **umiejętny**
■ **skilfully** /-fəli/ adv. ▶ **wprawnie**, **umiejętnie**

ˈ**ski lift** noun [C] a machine for taking skiers up a slope so that they can then ski down ▶ **wyciąg narciarski**

⚷ **skill** /skɪl/ noun **1** [U] the ability to do sth well, especially because of training, practice, etc.: *It takes great skill to make such beautiful jewellery.* ◇ *This is an easy game to play. No skill is required.* ▶ **wprawa**, **zręczność** **2** [C] an ability that you need in order to do a job, an activity, etc. well: *The course will help you to develop your reading and listening skills.* ◇ *management skills* ◇ *Typing is a skill I have never mastered.* ▶ **umiejętność**

⚷ **skilled** /skɪld/ adj. **1** (used about a person) having skill; skilful: *a skilled worker* ▶ **wykwalifikowany**, **fachowy** **2** (used about work, a job, etc.) needing skill or skills; done by people who have been trained: *a highly skilled job* ◇ *Skilled work is difficult to find in this area.* ▶ **wymagający umiejętności/kwalifikacji** OPP for both meanings **unskilled**

skim /skɪm/ verb (**skimming**; **skimmed**) **1** [T] **skim sth (off/from sth)** to remove sth from the surface of a liquid: *to skim the cream off the milk* ▶ **zbierać (z powierzchni)**, **szumować** **2** [I,T] to move quickly over or past sth, almost touching it or touching it slightly: *The plane flew very low, skimming the tops of the buildings.* ▶ **muskać**; **ślizgać się** (*np. po wodzie*) **3** [I,T] **skim (through/over) sth** to read sth quickly in order to get the main idea, without paying attention to the details and without reading every word: *I usually just skim through the newspaper in the morning.* ▶ **przerzucać** (*strony*)

ˌ**skimmed** ˈ**milk** noun [U] milk from which the cream has been removed ▶ **mleko odtłuszczone**

skimp /skɪmp/ verb [I] **skimp (on sth)** to use or provide less of sth than is necessary ▶ **skąpić**, **żałować (komuś czegoś)**

skimpy /ˈskɪmpi/ adj. (**skimpier**; **skimpiest**) using or having less than is necessary; too small or few ▶ **skąpy**, **kusy**

skin¹ /skɪn/ noun [C,U] **1** the natural outer covering of a human or animal body: *to have (a) fair/dark/sensitive skin ◇ skin cancer* ▶ **skóra** **2** (**-skinned**) [in compounds] having the type of skin mentioned: *dark/fair-skinned* ciemnej/jasnej karnacji ▶ *(określa cechę skóry)* **3** [in compounds] the skin of a dead animal, with or without its fur, used for making things: *a bag made of crocodile skin ◇ a sheepskin jacket* kożuch ▶ **z (określonej) skóry** **4** the natural outer covering of some fruits or vegetables; the outer covering of a **sausage**: *(a) banana/tomato skin* ▶ **skórka**, **łupina** (*np. ziemniaka, ale nie orzechów*) ➲ look at **peel**, **rind** **5** the thin solid surface that can form on a liquid: *A skin had formed on top of the milk.* ▶ **kożuszek**
IDM **by the skin of your teeth** (informal) (used to show that sb almost failed to do sth) only just: *I ran into the airport and caught the plane by the skin of my teeth.* ▶ **ledwie**
have a thick skin → THICK¹

skin² /skɪn/ verb [T] (**skinning**; **skinned**) to remove the skin from sth ▶ **obdzierać ze skóry**
IDM **keep your eyes peeled/skinned (for sb/sth)** → EYE¹

ˌ**skin-ˈdeep** adj. (used about a feeling or an attitude) not as important or as strongly felt as it appears to be; only on the surface: *His concern for me was only skin-deep.* ▶ **powierzchowny** SYN **superficial**

ˈ**skin-diving** noun [U] the sport or activity of swimming underwater with simple breathing equipment but without a special suit for protection: *to go skin-diving* ▶ **nurkowanie bez kombinezonu**, **płetwonurkowanie**
■ ˈ**skin-diver** noun [C] ▶ **płetwonurek**

skinhead /ˈskɪnhed/ noun [C] a young person with shaved or extremely short hair. Skinheads are often associated with violent behaviour. ▶ **skin**

skinny /ˈskɪni/ adj. (**skinnier**; **skinniest**) (used about a person) too thin ▶ **wychudzony** ➲ note at **thin**

skint /skɪnt/ adj. (Brit., informal) having no money: *I can't go out tonight – I'm skint.* ▶ **spłukany**, **bez grosza**

skintight /skɪnˈtaɪt/ adj. (used about a piece of clothing) fitting very tightly and showing the shape of the body ▶ **obcisły**

skip¹ /skɪp/ verb (**skipping**; **skipped**) **1** [I] to move along quickly and lightly in a way that is similar to dancing, with little jumps and steps, from one foot to the other: *A little girl came skipping along the road. ◇ Lambs were skipping about in the field.* ▶ **podskakiwać** **2** [I] to jump over a rope that you or two other people hold at each end, turning it round and round over your head and under your feet: *Some girls were skipping in the playground.* ▶ **skakać przez skakankę** **3** [T] to not do sth that you usually do or should do: *I got up rather late, so I skipped breakfast.* ▶ **opuszczać**, **pomijać** **4** [T] to miss the next thing that you would normally read, do, etc.: *I accidentally skipped one of the questions in the test.* ▶ **opuszczać**

skip² /skɪp/ noun [C] **1** a small jumping movement ▶ **podskok** **2** a large, open metal container for rubbish, often used during building work ▶ **kontener na śmieci**

skipper /ˈskɪpə(r)/ noun [C] (informal) the captain of a boat or ship, or of a sports team ▶ **kapitan**

ˈ**skipping rope** noun [C] a rope, often with handles at each end, that you turn over your head and then jump over, for fun or for exercise ▶ **skakanka**

skirmish /ˈskɜːmɪʃ/ noun [C] a short fight between groups of people ▶ **potyczka**, **utarczka**

skirt¹ /skɜːt/ noun [C] a piece of clothing that is worn by women and girls and that hangs down from the waist ▶ **spódnica** ➲ picture on **page A1**

skirt² /skɜːt/ verb [I,T] to go around the edge of sth: *The road skirts the lake.* ▶ **przemieszczać się wzdłuż brzegu**
PHR V **skirt round sth** to avoid talking about sth in a direct way: *The manager skirted round the subject of our pay increase.* ▶ **omijać** (*np. temat*)

ˈ**ski run** noun [C] a track that is marked on a slope that you ski down ▶ **nartostrada**

skittle /ˈskɪtl/ noun **1** (**skittles**) [U] a game in which players try to knock down as many **skittles** as possible by throwing or rolling a ball at them ▶ **kręgle** ➲ look at **bowling**, **tenpin bowling** **2** [C] a wooden object in the shape of a bottle that is used as one of the targets in the game of skittles ▶ **kręgiel**

skive /skaɪv/ verb [I] (Brit., informal) **skive (off)** to not work when you should ▶ **bumelować**

skulk /skʌlk/ verb [I] to stay somewhere quietly and secretly, hoping that nobody will notice you, especially because you are planning to do sth bad: *He was skulking in the bushes.* ▶ **czaić się**, **czyhać**

skull /skʌl/ noun [C] the bone structure of a human or animal head: *She suffered a fractured skull in the fall.* ▶ **czaszka** ➲ picture at **body**

sky /skaɪ/ noun [C, usually sing., U] (pl. **skies**) the space that you can see when you look up from the earth, and where you can see the sun, moon and stars: *I saw a bit of blue sky between the clouds.* ▶ **niebo**

> **Sky** zwykle używa się z przedimkiem **the**: *I saw a plane high up **in the sky**. ◇ The sky's gone very dark. I think it's going to rain.* Kiedy jednak **sky** jest poprzedzone przymiotnikiem, wówczas stosuje się przedimek **a**/**an** lub czasami formę lm bez przedimka: *a cloudless/clear blue sky ◇ cloudless skies.*

skydiving /ˈskaɪdaɪvɪŋ/ noun [U] a sport in which you jump from a plane and fall for as long as you safely can before opening your **parachute**: *to go skydiving* ▶ **akrobatyczne skoki spadochronowe**
■ **skydiver** noun [C] ▶ **spadochronia-rz/rka** (*wykonując-y/a akrobatyczne skoki*)

ˌ**sky-ˈhigh** adj., adv. very high: *He started feeling dizzy and his temperature went sky-high* (poszła szybko w górę). ▶ **do samego nieba**, **bardzo wysoki/wysoko**

skylight /ˈskaɪlaɪt/ noun [C] a small window in a roof ▶ (*okienko w dachu*) **świetlik**

skyline /ˈskaɪlaɪn/ noun [C] the shape that is made by tall buildings, etc. against the sky: *the Manhattan skyline* ▶ **panorama** (*np. miasta*)

skyscraper /ˈskaɪskreɪpə(r)/ noun [C] an extremely tall building ▶ **drapacz chmur**

slab /slæb/ noun [C] a thick, flat piece of sth: *huge concrete slabs* ▶ **płyta**, **pajda**

slack /slæk/ adj. **1** loose; not tightly stretched: *Leave the rope slack.* ▶ **luźny**, **obwisły** **2** (used about a period of business) not busy; not having many customers: *Trade is very slack* (jest zastój w handlu) *here in winter.* ▶ **słaby** **3** not carefully or properly done: *Slack security made terrorist attacks possible.* ▶ **słaby**, **rozluźniony** **4** (used about a person) not doing your work carefully or properly: *You've been rather slack about your homework lately.* ▶ **niedbały**

slacken /ˈslækən/ verb [I,T] **1** to become or make sth less tight: *The rope slackened and he pulled his hand free.* ▶ **rozluźniać (się)**, **obluzowywać (się)** **2** **slacken (sth) (off)** to become or make sth slower or less active: *He slackened off his pace towards the end of the race.* ▶ **zwalniać**, **zmniejszać (się)**

S

slacks /slæks/ noun [pl.] (old-fashioned) trousers (especially not very formal ones): *a pair of slacks* ▶ **spodnie**

slag¹ /slæg/ **1** noun [U] the waste material that is left after metal has been removed from rock ▶ **żużel**

slag² /slæg/ verb
PHR V **slag sb off** (informal) to say cruel or critical things about sb ▶ **obgadywać kogoś**

'slag heap noun [C] a hill made of **slag** ▶ **hałda żużlowa**

slain past participle of **slay**

slalom /'slɑːləm/ noun [C] (in sports such as **skiing**, **canoeing**, etc.) a race along a course on which you have to move from side to side between poles ▶ **slalom**

slam /slæm/ verb (**slamming**; **slammed**) **1** [I,T] to shut or make sth shut very loudly and with great force: *I heard the front door slam.* ◇ *She slammed her book shut and rushed out of the room.* ▶ **zatrzaskiwać (się)**, **zamknąć z trzaskiem 2** [T] to put sth somewhere very quickly and with great force: *He slammed the book down on the table and stormed out.* ▶ **rzucić** (*z trzaskiem*) ➲ look at **grand slam**

slander /'slɑːndə(r); US 'slæn-/ noun [C,U] a spoken statement about sb that is not true and that is intended to damage the good opinion that other people have of them; the legal offence of making this kind of statement ▶ **zniesławienie**, **oszczerstwo**
■ **slander** verb [T] ▶ **zniesławiać** | **slanderous** /'slɑːndərəs/ adj. ▶ **oszczerczy**

slang /slæŋ/ noun [U] very informal words and expressions that are more common in spoken than written language. Slang is sometimes used only by a particular group of people (for example students, young people or criminals) and often stays in fashion for a short time. Some slang is not polite: *'Dough' is slang for 'money'.* ▶ **slang**, **gwara**

slant¹ /slɑːnt; US slænt/ verb **1** [I] to be at an angle, not vertical or horizontal: *My handwriting slants backwards.* ◇ *That picture isn't straight – it's slanting to the right.* ▶ **nachylać (się)**, **być pochyłym 2** [T, usually passive] to describe information, events, etc. in a way that supports a particular group or opinion: *All the political articles in that newspaper are slanted towards the government* (mają prorządowe nastawienie). ▶ **naginać**
■ **slanting** adj.: *She has beautiful slanting eyes.* ▶ **ukośny**, **pochyły**

slant² /slɑːnt; US slænt/ noun **1** [sing.] a position at an angle, not horizontal or vertical: *The sunlight fell on the table **at a slant**.* ▶ **nachylenie 2** [C] a way of thinking, writing, etc. about sth, that sees things from a particular point of view ▶ **zapatrywanie**, **nastawienie**

slap¹ /slæp/ verb [T] (**slapping**; **slapped**) **1** to hit sb/sth with the inside of your hand when it is flat: *She **slapped** her really hard **across the face**.* ◇ *People slapped him on the back and congratulated him on winning.* ◇ *She slapped him across the face.* Spoliczkowała go. ▶ **klepać 2** to put sth onto a surface quickly and carelessly: *to slap some paint* (chlapnąć trochę farby) *onto a wall* ▶ **rzucić**, **ciskać**
■ **slap** noun [C]: *I gave him a slap across the face.* Wymierzyłem mu policzek. ◇ *She deserves **a slap on the back*** (zasługuje na pochwałę) *for all the hard work she's done.* ▶ **klaps**, **klepnięcie**

slap² /slæp/ (also ˌ**slap 'bang**) adv. (informal) **1** straight, and with great force: *I hurried round the corner and walked slap into* (wpadłem na) *someone coming the other way.* ▶ **prosto 2** exactly; right: *The phone rang **slap bang in the middle*** (w samym środku) *of my favourite programme.* ▶ **dokładnie**

slapdash /'slæpdæʃ/ adj. careless, or done quickly and carelessly: *slapdash building methods* ◇ *He's a bit slapdash about doing his homework on time.* ▶ **niedbały**

slapstick /'slæpstɪk/ noun [U] a type of humour that is based on simple physical jokes, for example people falling over or hitting each other ▶ **rodzaj komedii** ➲ note at **humour**

'slap-up adj. (Brit.) [only before a noun] (informal) (used about a meal) very large and very good: *a slap-up meal* wyżerka ▶ **obfity i bardzo smaczny**

slash¹ /slæʃ/ verb **1** [I,T] **slash (at) sb/sth** to make or try to make a long cut in sth with a violent movement ▶ **pociąć**, **ciachać 2** [T] to reduce an amount of money, etc. very much: *The price of coffee has been slashed by 20%.* ▶ **znacznie obniżać**

slash² /slæʃ/ noun [C] **1** a sharp movement made with a knife, etc. in order to cut sb/sth ▶ **cięcie**, **ciachnięcie 2** a long narrow wound or cut: *a slash across his right cheek* ▶ **cięcie**, **rozcięcie 3** the symbol (/) used to show alternatives, as in *lunch and/or dinner*, and in Internet addresses to separate the different parts of the address ▶ **ukośnik** ➲ look at **forward slash**, **backslash**

slat /slæt/ noun [C] one of a series of long, narrow pieces of wood, metal or plastic, used in furniture, fences, etc. ▶ **listewka**

slate /sleɪt/ noun **1** [U] a type of dark grey rock that can easily be split into thin flat pieces ▶ **łupek 2** [C] one of the thin flat pieces of **slate** that are used for covering roofs ▶ **dachówka łupkowa**

slaughter /'slɔːtə(r)/ verb [T] **1** to kill an animal, usually for food ▶ **zarzynać** (*zwierzęta*) **2** to kill a large number of people at one time, especially in a cruel way: *Men, women and children were slaughtered and whole villages destroyed.* ▶ **masakrować** ➲ note at **kill**
■ **slaughter** noun [U] ▶ **rzeź**

slaughterhouse /'slɔːtəhaʊs/ (Brit. also **abattoir** /'æbətwɑː(r)/) noun [C] a place where animals are killed for food ▶ **rzeźnia**

Slav /slɑːv/ noun [C] a member of any of the peoples of Central and Eastern Europe who speak Slavonic languages ▶ **Słowian-in/ka**

slave¹ /sleɪv/ noun [C] (in past times) a person who was owned by another person and had to work for them ▶ **niewolni-k/ca**
■ **slavery** /'sleɪvəri/ noun [U]: *the abolition of slavery in America* ▶ **niewolnictwo**, **niewola**

slave² /sleɪv/ verb [I] **slave (away)** to work very hard ▶ **harować**, **tyrać**

Slavic /'slɑːvɪk/ (also **Slavonic** /slə'vɒnɪk/) adj. of or connected with Slavs or their languages, which include Russian, Polish and Croatian: *the School of Slavonic and East European Studies in London* ▶ **słowiański**

slay /sleɪ/ verb [T] (pt **slew** /sluː/, pp **slain** /sleɪn/) (old-fashioned or literary) to kill violently sb/sth; to murder sb/sth
ⓘ Słowa **slay** nie używa się w codziennym Br. ang., ale występuje ono w Amer. ang., szczególnie w gazetach: *Two passangers were slain by the hijackers.*

sleaze /sliːz/ noun **1** [U] dishonest or illegal behaviour, especially by politicians or business people: *allegations of sleaze* ▶ **zachowanie nieuczciwe/niezgodne z prawem 2** [U] behaviour or conditions that are unpleasant and not socially acceptable, especially because sex is involved: *the sleaze of a town that was once a naval base* ▶ **brud moralny 3** (also **sleazebag** /'sliːzbæg/, **sleazeball** /'sliːzbɔːl/ (especially US)) [C] a dishonest or immoral person ▶ **kanalia**

sleazy /'sliːzi/ adj. (**sleazier**; **sleaziest**) (used about a place or a person) unpleasant and probably connected with criminal activities: *a sleazy nightclub* ▶ **podejrzany**, **obskurny**, **podły**

sledge /sledʒ/ (US also **sled** /sled/) noun [C] a vehicle without wheels that is used for travelling on snow. Large **sledges** are often pulled by dogs, and smaller ones are used for going down hills, for fun or as a sport ▶ **sanie, sanki** ➲ look at **bobsleigh, toboggan**
■ **sledge** verb [I] ▶ **zjeżdżać na sankach**

sledgehammer /ˈsledʒhæmə(r)/ noun [C] a large heavy hammer with a long handle ▶ **młot kowalski**

sleek /sliːk/ adj. **1** (used about hair or fur) smooth and shiny because it is healthy ▶ **lśniący 2** (used about a vehicle) having an elegant, smooth shape: *a sleek new sports car* ▶ **opływowy, zgrabny**

⚷ **sleep**[1] /sliːp/ verb (pt, pp **slept** /slept/) **1** [I] to rest with your eyes closed and your mind and body not active: *Did you sleep well?* ◇ *I only slept for a couple of hours last night.* ◇ *I slept solidly from 10 last night till 11 this morning.* ▶ **spać** ➲ note at **asleep, routine**

Czasownika **sleep** używa się, mówiąc ogólnie o spaniu. W sytuacji, gdy podczas snu wydarza się coś innego, używa się **be asleep**: *I was asleep when the telephone rang.*

2 [T] (used about a place) to have enough beds for a particular number of people: *an apartment that sleeps four people* (w którym mogą przenocować cztery osoby) ▶ **pomieścić**

IDM **live/sleep rough** → ROUGH[4]

PHR V **sleep in** to sleep until later than usual in the morning because you do not have to get up ▶ **późno wstać** ➲ look at **oversleep**

sleep together; **sleep with sb** to have sex with sb (usually when you are not married to or living with that person) ▶ **sypiać z kimś**

sleep over to stay the night at sb else's home ▶ **(prze)-nocować (u kogoś)**

sleep

When we feel **tired** or **sleepy** we usually **yawn. Go to sleep** is the expression we use to mean 'start to sleep': *I was reading in bed last night, and I didn't go to sleep until about 1 o'clock.* Some people **snore** when they are **asleep**. Most people **dream.** Frightening dreams are called **nightmares.** Some people **sleepwalk.** If you **wake up** later than you had planned to, you **oversleep**: *I'm sorry I'm late. I overslept.* Sometimes we don't have to **get up**, so we **have a lie-in**. A short sleep that you have in the day is called a **nap**.

⚷ **sleep**[2] /sliːp/ noun **1** [U] the natural condition of rest when your eyes are closed and your mind and body are not active or conscious: *Most people need at least seven hours' sleep every night.* ◇ *I didn't get much sleep last night.* ◇ *Do you ever talk in your sleep?* ◇ *I couldn't* ***get to sleep*** (zasnąć) *last night.* ◇ *I've just* ***got*** *Tom* ***off to sleep.*** Właśnie uśpiłam Toma. ▶ **sen 2** [sing.] a period of sleep: *You'll feel better after a good night's sleep.* ◇ *I sometimes have a short sleep in the afternoon.* ▶ **sen**

IDM **go to sleep 1** to start sleeping: *He got into bed and went to sleep.* ◇ *Go to sleep* (idź spać). *Everything will seem better in the morning.* ▶ **zasnąć 2** (used about an arm, a leg, etc.) to lose the sense of feeling in it ▶ **cierpnąć, drętwieć**

put (an animal) to sleep to kill an animal that is ill or injured because you want to stop it suffering ▶ **usypiać**

sleeper /ˈsliːpə(r)/ noun [C] **1** [with an adjective] a person who sleeps in a particular way, for example if you are a **light sleeper** you wake up easily: *a light/heavy sleeper* osoba, która ma lekki/twardy sen ▶ **osoba śpiąca** (*w określony sposób*) **2** a bed on a train; a train with beds ▶ **miejsce sypialne w pociągu**; **pociąg z wagonami sypialnymi**

ˈ**sleeping bag** noun [C] a large soft bag that you use for sleeping in when you go camping, etc. ▶ **śpiwór**

ˈ**sleeping pill** noun [C] a medicine in solid form that you swallow to help you sleep: *to take a sleeping pill* ▶ **tabletka nasenna**

sleepless /ˈsliːpləs/ adj. [only before a noun] (used about a period, usually the night) without sleep ▶ **bezsenny**
■ **sleeplessness** noun [U] ▶ **bezsenność** ➲ look at **insomnia**

sleepwalk /ˈsliːpwɔːk/ verb [I] to walk around while you are asleep ▶ **chodzić we śnie**

sleepy /ˈsliːpi/ adj. (**sleepier**; **sleepiest**) **1** tired and ready to go to sleep: *These pills might make you feel a bit sleepy.* ▶ **senny, śpiący 2** (used about a place) very quiet and not having much activity ▶ **senny**
■ **sleepily** adv.: *She yawned sleepily.* ▶ **sennie**

sleet /sliːt/ noun [U] a mixture of rain and snow ▶ **deszcz ze śniegiem** ➲ note at **weather**

⚷ **sleeve** /sliːv/ noun [C] **1** one of the two parts of a piece of clothing that cover the arms or part of the arms: *a blouse with long sleeves* ▶ **rękaw** ➲ picture on **page A1 2** (**-sleeved**) [in compounds] with sleeves of a particular kind: *a short-sleeved shirt* koszula z krótkimi rękawami ▶ **(***określa rodzaj rękawa***) 3** (US **jacket**) a record cover ▶ **okładka** (*na płytę gramofonową*)

sleeveless /ˈsliːvləs/ adj. without sleeves: *a sleeveless sweater* ▶ **bez rękawów**

sleigh /sleɪ/ noun [C] a vehicle without wheels that is used for travelling on snow and that is usually pulled by horses ▶ **sanie** ➲ look at **bobsleigh, sledge**

sleight of hand /ˌslaɪt əv ˈhænd/ noun [U] skilful movements of your hand that other people cannot see: *The trick is done simply by sleight of hand.* ▶ **sztuczki**

slender /ˈslendə(r)/ adj. **1** (used about a person or part of sb's body) thin in an attractive way: *long slender fingers* ▶ **smukły 2** smaller in amount or size than you would like: *My chances of winning are very slender.* ▶ **znikomy, mały**

slept past tense, past participle of **sleep**[1]

slew past tense of **slay**

⚷ **slice**[1] /slaɪs/ noun [C] **1** a flat piece of food that is cut from a larger piece: *a thick/thin slice of bread* ◇ *Cut the meat into thin slices.* ▶ **kromka, plaster** ➲ picture at **bread, bar 2** a part of sth: *The directors have taken a large slice of the profits.* ▶ **udział**

⚷ **slice**[2] /slaɪs/ verb **1** [T] to cut into thin flat pieces: *Peel and slice the apples.* ◇ *a loaf of sliced bread* ▶ **kroić, ciąć na plasterki 2** [I,T] to cut sth easily with sth sharp: *He sliced through the rope with a knife.* ◇ *The glass sliced into her hand.* ▶ **przecinać 3** [T] (in ball sports) to hit the ball on the bottom or side so that it does not travel in a straight line ▶ **podcinać**

slick[1] /slɪk/ adj. **1** done smoothly and well, and seeming to be done without any effort ▶ **zręczny, zgrabny 2** clever at persuading people but perhaps not completely honest ▶ **zręczny, przebiegły**

slick[2] = OIL SLICK

⚷ **slide**[1] /slaɪd/ verb (pt, pp **slid** /slɪd/) **1** [I,T] to move or make sth move smoothly along a surface: *She fell over and slid along the ice.* ◇ *The doors slide open automatically.* ◇ *a sliding door* drzwi rozsuwane ▶ **poślizgnąć się, ślizgać się; sunąć 2** [I,T] to move or make sth move quietly without being noticed: *I slid out of the room* (wyślizgnąłem się z pokoju) *when nobody was looking.* ◇ *She slid her hand into* (wsunęła) *her pocket and took out a gun.* ▶ **(ukradkiem) posuwać (się) 3** [I] (used about prices, values, etc.) to go down slowly and continuously: *The Euro is sliding against the dollar.* ◇ *The pound is sliding against* (traci na wartości względem) *the dollar.* ▶ **zniżkować, spadać powoli 4** [I] to move gradually towards a worse situation: *The company slid into debt and eventually closed.* ▶ **popadać** (*np. w długi*)

slide² /slaɪd/ noun [C] **1** a continuous slow fall, for example of prices, values, levels, etc. ▶ **stopniowe spadanie** (*np. na wartości*) **2** a large toy consisting of steps and a long piece of metal, plastic, etc. Children climb up the steps then slide down the other part. ▶ **zjeżdżalnia** **3** a small photograph on a piece of film in a frame that can be shown on a screen when you shine a light through it ▶ **przeźrocze** ➲ look at **transparency**

You show slides using a **projector** and **screen**.

4 a small piece of glass that you put sth on when you want to examine it under a **microscope** ▶ **szkiełko mikroskopowe** ➲ picture at **laboratory**

slight /slaɪt/ adj. **1** very small; not important or serious: *I've got a slight problem, but it's nothing to get worried about.* ◇ *a slight change/difference/increase/improvement* ◇ *I haven't the slightest idea* (nie mam najmniejszego pojęcia) *what you're talking about.* ▶ **drobny, mały** **2** (used about sb's body) thin and light: *His slight frame is perfect for a long-distance runner.* ▶ **drobny, filigranowy**

IDM **not in the slightest** not at all: *'Are you angry with me?' 'Not in the slightest.'* ▶ **ani trochę**

slightly /ˈslaɪtli/ adv. **1** a little: *I'm slightly older than her.* ▶ **trochę, nieco** **2** a **slightly built** person is small and thin: *She is slightly built* (ma drobną budowę).

slim¹ /slɪm/ adj. (**slimmer**; **slimmest**) **1** thin in an attractive way: *a tall, slim woman* ▶ **szczupły** ➲ note at **thin** **2** not as big as you would like: *Her chances of success are very slim.* ▶ **słaby, mały**

slim² /slɪm/ verb [I] (**slimming**; **slimmed**) to become or try to become thinner and lighter by eating less food, taking exercise, etc. ▶ **odchudzać się** ➲ look at **diet**

slime /slaɪm/ noun [U] a thick unpleasant liquid: *The pond was covered with slime and had a horrible smell.* ▶ **szlam, muł, śluz** SYN **goo** ➲ look at **sludge**

slimy /ˈslaɪmi/ adj. (**slimier**; **slimiest**) **1** covered with **slime** ▶ **mulisty, śluzowaty** **2** (used about a person) pretending to be friendly, in a way that you do not trust or like ▶ **podlizujący się**

sling¹ /slɪŋ/ verb [T] (pt, pp **slung**) **1** to put or throw sth somewhere in a rough or careless way ▶ **rzucać, ciskać** **2** to put sth into a position where it hangs in a loose way ▶ **przewiesić**

sling² /slɪŋ/ noun [C] a piece of cloth that you put under your arm and tie around your neck to support a broken arm, wrist, etc. ▶ **temblak**

slingshot (US) = CATAPULT¹

slink /slɪŋk/ verb [I] (pt, pp **slunk**) to move somewhere slowly and quietly because you do not want anyone to see you, often when you feel guilty or embarrassed ▶ **skradać się, przemieszczać się chyłkiem**

slinky /ˈslɪŋki/ adj. (**slinkier**; **slinkiest**) **1** (used about a woman's clothes) fitting closely to the body in a sexually attractive way: *a slinky black dress* ▶ **seksowny** **2** (used about a movement or sound) smooth and slow, often in a way that is sexually attractive: *a slinky voice* ▶ **zmysłowy, seksowny**

slip¹ /slɪp/ verb (**slipping**; **slipped**) **1** [I] **slip (over)**; **slip (on sth)** to slide accidentally and fall or nearly fall: *She slipped over on the wet floor.* ◇ *His foot slipped on the top step and he fell down the stairs.* ▶ **pośliznąć się** **2** [I] to slide accidentally out of the correct position or out of your hand: *The glass slipped out of my hand and smashed on the floor.* ◇ *This hat's too big. It keeps slipping down over my eyes.* Opada mi na oczy. ▶ **wyślizgiwać się** **3** [I] to move or go somewhere quietly, quickly and often without being noticed: *While everyone was dancing we slipped away and went home.* ▶ **wyśliznąć się** **4** [T] **slip sth (to sb)**; **slip (sb) sth** to put sth somewhere or give sth to sb quietly and often without being noticed: *She picked up the money and slipped it into her pocket.* ▶ **wsuwać** **5** [I,T] **slip into/out of sth**; **slip sth on/off** to put on or take off a piece of clothing quickly and easily: *I slipped off my shoes.* ▶ **narzucać (coś na siebie)**; **zrzucać** (*np. buty*) **6** [I] to fall a little in value, level, etc.: *Sales have been slipping slightly over the last few months.* ▶ **nieco opadać, nieco zmniejszać się**

IDM **let sth slip** to accidentally say sth that you should keep secret ▶ **wypsnąć się, wygadać się**

slip your mind to be forgotten: *I'm sorry, the meeting completely slipped my mind.* ▶ **wypaść z głowy**

PHR V **slip away** to stop existing; to disappear or die: *Their support gradually slipped away.* ▶ **odchodzić; znikać**

slip out to accidentally say sth or tell sb sth: *I didn't intend to tell them. It just slipped out.* ▶ (*uwaga itp.*) **wymknąć się**

slip up (informal) to make a mistake ▶ **pomylić się**

slip² /slɪp/ noun [C] **1** a small mistake, usually made by being careless or not paying attention: *to make a slip* ▶ **pomyłka** **2** a small piece of paper: *I made a note of her name on* ***a slip of paper.*** ◇ (Brit.) *a* ***payslip*** odcinek wypłaty, który otrzymuje każdy pracownik i na którym wymieniona jest zarobiona miesięczna/tygodniowa kwota wypłaty netto, odprowadzone podatki itd. ▶ **kartka, świstek** **3** an act of sliding accidentally and falling or nearly falling ▶ **pośliznięcie się** **4** (also old-fashioned **petticoat** /ˈpetɪkəʊt/) a thin piece of clothing that is worn by a woman under a dress or skirt ▶ **halka**

IDM **give sb the slip** (informal) to escape from sb who is following or trying to catch you ▶ **zwiewać/wymykać się komuś**

a slip of the tongue something that you say that you did not mean to say ▶ **przejęzyczenie się**

ˌslipped ˈdisc noun [C] a painful injury caused when one of the **discs** moves out of its correct position ▶ **obsunięty dysk kręgosłupa**

slipper /ˈslɪpə(r)/ noun [C] a light soft shoe that is worn inside the house: *a pair of slippers* ▶ **kapeć** ➲ picture at **shoe**

slippery /ˈslɪpəri/ (also informal **slippy** /ˈslɪpi/) adj. (used about a surface or an object) difficult to walk on or hold because it is smooth, wet, etc.: *a slippery floor* ▶ **śliski**

ˈslip road (US **ramp**) noun [C] a road that leads onto or off a large road such as a **motorway** ▶ **wjazd; zjazd**

slit¹ /slɪt/ noun [C] a long narrow cut or opening: *a long skirt with a slit up the back* ▶ **szpara, szczelina, rowek**

slit² /slɪt/ verb [T] (**slitting**; pt, pp **slit**) to make a long narrow cut in sth: *She slit the envelope open with a knife.* ◇ *He slit his wrists* (podciął sobie żyły) *in a suicide attempt.* ▶ **rozcinać, nacinać**

slither /ˈslɪðə(r)/ verb [I] to move by sliding from side to side along the ground like a snake: *I saw a snake slithering* (pełznącego) *down a rock.* ▶ **ślizgać się**

sliver /ˈslɪvə(r)/ noun [C] a small, thin or narrow piece of sth cut or broken off from a larger piece ▶ **plasterek**

slob /slɒb/ noun [C] (informal) (used as an insult) a very lazy or untidy person ▶ **wałkoń, flejtuch**

slog¹ /slɒg/ verb [I] (**slogging**; **slogged**) **1** (informal) **slog (away) (at sth)**; **slog (through sth)** to work hard for a long period at sth difficult or boring: *I've been slogging away at this homework for hours.* ▶ **ślęczeć/mozolić się nad czymś** **2** **slog down, up, along, etc.** to walk or move in a certain direction with a lot of effort ▶ **brnąć, wlec się**

slog² /slɒg/ noun [sing.] a period of long, hard, boring work or a long, tiring journey ▶ **mozolna praca/wędrówka, ślęczenie**

slogan /ˈsləʊɡən/ noun [C] a short phrase that is easy to remember and that is used in politics or advertising: *Anti-government slogans had been painted all over the walls.* ◇ *an advertising slogan* ▶ **hasło**

slop /slɒp/ verb [I,T] (**slopping**; **slopped**) (used about a liquid) to pour over the edge of its container; to make a liquid do this: *He filled his glass too full and beer slopped onto the table.* ▶ **rozlewać (się), przelewać się**

slope /sləʊp/ noun **1** [C] a surface or piece of land that goes up or down: *The village is built* ***on a slope.*** ◇ *a steep/gentle slope* ◇ *The best* ***ski slopes*** *are in the Alps.* ▶ **zbocze, pochyłość, wzniesienie 2** [sing.] the amount that a surface is not level; the fact of not being level: *The slope of the football pitch makes it quite difficult to play on.* ▶ **pochyłość, spadek**

■ **slope** verb [I]: *The road slopes down to the river.* ◇ *a sloping roof* spadzisty dach ▶ **nachylać się, pochylać się**

sloppy /ˈslɒpi/ adj. (**sloppier**; **sloppiest**) **1** that shows a lack of care, thought or effort; untidy: *a sloppy worker/writer/dresser* ◇ *a sloppy piece of work* ▶ **niedbały 2** (used about clothes) not tight and without much shape ▶ **niedbały, rozmamłany 3** (Brit., informal) showing emotions in a silly and embarrassing way: *I can't stand sloppy love songs.* ▶ **ckliwy, rzewny** ⓘ Bardziej formalne słowo to **sentimental**.

slosh /slɒʃ/ verb (informal) **1** [I] (used about a liquid) to move around noisily inside a container ▶ **chlupotać 2** [T] to pour or drop liquid somewhere in a careless way ▶ **rozchlapywać, rozpryskiwać**

sloshed /slɒʃt/ adj. (slang) drunk ▶ **zalany**

slot¹ /slɒt/ noun [C] **1** a straight narrow opening in a machine, etc.: *Put your money into the slot and take the ticket.* ▶ **szczelina, otwór 2** a place in a list, a system, an organization, etc.: *He has a regular slot on the late-night programme.* ◇ *The single has occupied the Number One slot for the past two weeks.* ◇ *the airport's take-off and landing slots* ▶ **przedział czasu, okienko** (*np. w harmonogramie*), **miejsce** (*np. w spisie*)

slot² /slɒt/ verb [I,T] (**slotting**; **slotted**) to put sth into a particular space that is designed for it; to fit into such a space: *He slotted a tape into the VCR.* ◇ *The tape slotted in easily.* ▶ **pasować, wpasowywać** (*np. w wolne miejsce*)

IDM **fall/slot into place** → PLACE¹

PHR V **slot sb/sth in** to manage to find a position, a time or an opportunity for sb/sth: *I can slot you in between 3 and 4.* ▶ **wciskać kogoś/coś**

ˈslot machine noun [C] a machine with an opening for coins that sells drinks, cigarettes, etc., or on which you can play games ▶ **automat na monety** (*np. do gry, sprzedający napoje*)

slouch /slaʊtʃ/ verb [I] to sit, stand or walk in a lazy way, with your head and shoulders hanging down ▶ **trzymać się niedbale, garbić się**

slovenly /ˈslʌvnli/ adj. (old-fashioned) lazy, careless and untidy ▶ **niechlujny**

slow¹ /sləʊ/ adj. **1** moving, doing sth or happening without much speed; not fast: *The traffic is always very slow in the city centre.* ◇ *Haven't you finished your homework yet? You're being very slow!* ◇ *Progress was slower than expected.* ◇ *a slow driver/walker/reader* ▶ **powolny, wolny** OPP **fast 2 slow to do sth; slow (in/about) doing sth** not doing sth immediately: *She was rather slow to realize what was going on.* ◇ *They've been rather slow in replying* (zwlekali z odpowiedzią) *to my letter!* ▶ **powolny 3** not quick to learn or understand: *He's the slowest student in the class.* ▶ **niepojętny, tępy 4** not very busy; with little action: *Business is very slow at the moment.* ▶ **ślamazarny, niemrawy 5** [not before a noun] showing a time that is earlier than the real time: *That clock is five minutes slow.* Ten zegar spóźnia się pięć minut. ▶ **chodzący za wolno** OPP **fast**

■ **slow** adv. ▶ **powoli, wolno**

W języku codziennym częściej używa się przysłówka **slowly**. **Slow** jednak często występuje w wyrazach złożonych: *slow-moving traffic*. Przysłówki w stopniu wyższym **slower** i **more slowly** można stosować wymiennie: *Could you drive a bit slower/more slowly please?*

■ **slowness** noun [U] ▶ **powolność, niemrawość**

IDM **quick/slow on the uptake** → UPTAKE

slow² /sləʊ/ verb [I,T] to start to move, do sth or happen at a slower speed; to cause sth to do this: *He slowed his pace a little.* ▶ **zwalniać**

PHR V **slow (sb/sth) down/up** to start to move, do sth or happen at a slower speed; to cause sb/sth to do this: *Can't you slow down a bit? You're driving much too fast.* ◇ *These problems have slowed up the whole process.* ▶ **spowalniać kogoś/coś; zwalniać**

ˈslow lane (US) = INSIDE LANE

slowly /ˈsləʊli/ adv. at a slow speed; not quickly: *He walked slowly along the street.* ▶ **wolno, powoli**

ˌslow ˈmotion noun [U] (in a film or on TV) a method of making action appear much slower than in real life: *They showed the winning goal again, this time* ***in slow motion.*** ▶ **zwolnione tempo**

ˈslow-witted adj. not able to think quickly; slow to learn or understand things ▶ **nierozgarnięty** OPP **quick-witted**

sludge /slʌdʒ/ noun [U] thick, soft, wet mud or a substance that looks like it ▶ **muł, szlam** ➲ look at **slime**

slug /slʌɡ/ noun [C] a small black or brown animal with a soft body and no legs, that moves slowly along the ground and eats garden plants ▶ **ślimak nagi**

sluggish /ˈslʌɡɪʃ/ adj. moving or working more slowly than normal in a way that seems lazy ▶ **niemrawy, powolny, zwolniony**

slum /slʌm/ noun [C] an area of a city where living conditions are extremely bad, and where the buildings are dirty and have not been repaired for a long time ▶ **slumsy**

slumber /ˈslʌmbə(r)/ noun [U,C] (formal) sleep; a time when sb is asleep: *She fell into a deep and peaceful slumber.* ▶ **spokojny sen, drzemka**

■ **slumber** verb [I] ▶ **drzemać**

slump¹ /slʌmp/ verb [I] **1** (used about economic activity, prices, etc.) to fall suddenly and by a large amount: *Shares in BP* ***slumped*** *33p* ***to*** *181p yesterday.* ◇ *The newspaper's circulation has* ***slumped by*** *30%.* ▶ **gwałtownie spadać, załamywać się** SYN **drop 2** to fall or sit down suddenly when your body feels heavy and weak, usually because you are tired or ill ▶ **opadać**

slump² /slʌmp/ noun [C] **1 a slump (in sth)** a sudden large fall in sales, prices, the value of sth, etc.: *a slump in house prices* ▶ **krach, gwałtowny spadek** SYN **decline 2** a period when a country's economy is doing very badly and a lot of people do not have jobs: *The car industry is* ***in a slump.*** ▶ **zastój** (*gospodarczy*) ➲ look at **boom**

slung past tense, past participle of **sling¹**

slunk past tense, past participle of **slink**

slur¹ /slɜː(r)/ verb [T] (**slurring**; **slurred**) to pronounce words in a way that is not clear, often because you are drunk ▶ **bełkotać**

slur² /slɜː(r)/ noun [C] **a slur (on sb/sth)** an unfair comment or an insult that could damage people's opinion of sb/sth ▶ **zniewaga** SYN **insult**

S

slurp /slɜːp/ verb [I,T] (informal) to drink noisily ▶ **siorbać, chlipać**

slush /slʌʃ/ noun [U] **1** snow that has been on the ground for a time and that is now a dirty mixture of ice and water ▶ **breja** **2** (informal) films, books, feelings, etc. that are considered to be silly because they are too romantic and emotional ▶ (*filmy itp.*) **sentymentalne bzdury**
■ **slushy** adj. **1** covered in melting snow: *slushy roads* roztopy ▶ **grząski** **2** romantic or sentimental in a silly way ▶ **ckliwy, płaczliwy**

slut /slʌt/ noun [C] (informal) ℹ To słowo jest bardzo obraźliwe. **1** a woman who has a lot of sexual partners ▶ **kurwa, zdzira** **2** a very lazy or untidy woman ▶ **flejtuch**

sly /slaɪ/ adj. **1** acting or done in a secret or dishonest way, often intending to trick people ▶ **cwany, chytry** SYN **cunning** **2** suggesting that you know sth secret: *a sly smile/look* ▶ **cwany, chytry**
■ **slyly** adv. ▶ **przebiegle, chytrze**

smack /smæk/ verb [T] to hit sb with the inside of your hand when it is flat, especially as a punishment: *I never smack my children.* ▶ **dawać klapsa** ➲ note at **hit**
PHR V **smack of sth** to make you think that sb/sth has an unpleasant attitude or quality ▶ **mieć posmak czegoś,** (*przen.*) **pachnieć** (*czymś nieprzyjemnym*)
■ **smack** noun [C]: *You're going to get a smack if you don't do as I say!* ▶ **klaps**

⚷ **small** /smɔːl/ adj. **1** (abbr. **S**) not large in size, number, amount, etc.: *a small car/flat/town* ◇ *a small group of people* ◇ *a small amount of money* ◇ *That dress is too small for you.* ▶ **mały** **2** young: *He has a wife and three small children.* ◇ *When I was small we lived in a big old house.* ▶ **mały** **3** not important or serious; slight: *Don't worry. It's only a small problem.* ▶ **mały**

> **small**
> **Small** jest najczęściej używanym antonimem przymiotników **big** lub **large**. **Little** używa się z innymi przymiotnikami w celu wyrażenia emocji oraz podkreślenia, że coś/ktoś jest mały: *a horrible little man* ◇ *a lovely little girl* ◇ *a nice little house.* Formy stopnia wyższego i najwyższego **smaller** oraz **smallest** są często używane. **Small** często występuje z takimi słowami jak **rather**, **quite** i **very**: *My flat is smaller than yours.* ◇ *The village is quite small.* ◇ *a very small car.* **Little** rzadko występuje z tymi słowami i zwykle nie podlega stopniowaniu. Wyrazy **tiny** oraz **minute** /maɪˈnjuːt/ oznaczają „bardzo mały".

IDM **in a big/small way** → WAY[1]
■ **small** adv. in a small size: *She's painted the picture far too small.* ▶ **w małym rozmiarze**

ˈsmall ad (Brit., informal) = CLASSIFIED ADVERTISEMENT

ˌsmall ˈchange noun [U] coins that have a low value ▶ **drobne (pieniądze)**

the ˈsmall hours noun [pl.] the early morning hours soon after midnight ▶ **pierwsze godziny po północy**

smallpox /ˈsmɔːlpɒks/ noun [U] a serious infectious disease that causes a high temperature and leaves marks on the skin. In past times many people died from **smallpox.** ▶ **ospa**

the ˌsmall ˈprint (US **the ˌfine ˈprint**) noun [U] the important details of a legal document, contract, etc. that are usually printed in small type and are therefore easy to miss: *Make sure you read the small print before you sign anything.* ▶ **ważne szczegóły umowy itp.** (*zwykle drukowane bardzo małym drukiem*), **mały druk**

ˌsmall-ˈscale adj. (used about an organization or activity) not large; limited in what it does ▶ **na małą skalę**

ˈsmall talk noun [U] polite conversation, for example at a party, about unimportant things: *We had to **make small talk** for half an hour.* ▶ **rozmowa towarzyska**

⚷ **smart¹** /smɑːt/ adj. **1** (especially Brit.) (used about a person) having a clean and tidy appearance: *You look smart. Are you going somewhere special?* ▶ **elegancki, wytworny** **2** (especially Brit.) (used about a piece of clothing, etc.) good enough to wear on a formal occasion: *a smart suit* ▶ **szykowny, elegancki** **3** (especially US) clever; intelligent: *He's not smart enough to be a politician.* ▶ **bystry, inteligentny** ➲ note at **intelligent** **4** (especially Brit.) fashionable and usually expensive: *a smart restaurant/hotel* ▶ **elegancki, wytworny** **5** (used about a movement or action) quick and usually done with force: *We set off at a smart pace.* ▶ **szybki, żwawy**
■ **smartly** adv.: *She's always smartly dressed.* ▶ **elegancko, wytwornie**

smart² /smɑːt/ verb [I] **1 smart (from sth)** to feel a stinging pain in your body ▶ **piec, szczypać** **2 smart (from/over sth)** to feel upset or offended because of a criticism, failure, etc.: *He was still smarting from her insult.* ▶ **boleśnie odczuwać/odbierać** (*np. krytykę*)

smart alec (US **smart aleck**) /ˈsmɑːt ælɪk/ (also **ˈsmarty pants**; **ˈsmart-arse**; US **ˈsmart-ass**) noun [C] (informal) a person who thinks they are very clever and likes to show people this in an annoying way ▶ **mądrala**

ˈsmart card noun [C] a small plastic card on which information can be stored in electronic form ▶ **karta magnetyczna**

smarten /ˈsmɑːtn/ verb
PHR V **smarten (yourself/sb/sth) up** (especially Brit.) to make yourself/sb/sth look tidy and more attractive ▶ **wystroić (się), dodawać szyku**

⚷ **smash¹** /smæʃ/ verb **1** [I,T] to break sth, or to be broken violently and noisily into many pieces: *The glass smashed into a thousand pieces.* ◇ *The police had to smash the door open.* ▶ **rozbijać (się), rozwalać (się)** **2** [I,T] **smash (sth) against, into, through, etc.** to move with great force in a particular direction; to hit sth very hard: *The car smashed into a tree.* ◇ *He smashed his fist through the window.* ▶ **walnąć (się)** (*np. w coś/o coś*), **rąbnąć (się)** **3** [T] **smash sth (up)** to crash a vehicle, usually causing a lot of damage: *I smashed up my father's car.* ▶ **rozbić** (*np. samochód*) **4** [T] (in sports such as **tennis**) to hit a ball that is high in the air downwards very hard over the net ▶ **smeczować**

⚷ **smash²** /smæʃ/ noun **1** [sing.] the action or the noise of sth breaking violently: *I heard the smash of breaking glass.* ▶ **rozbijanie, roztrzaskiwanie** **2** [C] (in sports such as **tennis**) a way of hitting a ball that is high in the air downwards very hard over the net ▶ **smeczowanie** **3** (also ˌ**smash ˈhit**) [C] (informal) a song, play, film, etc. that is very successful: *her latest chart smash* ▶ **przebój** **4** a car crash ▶ **kraksa**

smashing /ˈsmæʃɪŋ/ adj. (Brit., old-fashioned, informal) very good or enjoyable: *We had a smashing time.* ▶ **kapitalny, bombowy**

smattering /ˈsmætərɪŋ/ noun [sing.] **smattering (of sth)** a small amount of sth, especially knowledge of a language: *He only has a smattering of French.* ▶ **powierzchowna znajomość (czegoś)**

smear¹ /smɪə(r)/ verb [T] **smear sth on/over sth/sb; smear sth/sb with sth** to spread a sticky substance across sth/sb: *Her face was smeared with blood.* ▶ **smarować, paćkać**

smear² /smɪə(r)/ noun [C] **1** a dirty mark made by spreading a substance across sth: *a smear of oil* ▶ **maźnięcie, plama** **2** something that is not true that is said or written about an important person and that is intended to damage people's opinion about them, especially in politics: *He was the victim of a **smear campaign.*** ▶ **potwarz**

'smear test (also ˌcervical 'smear; US 'Pap smear) noun [C] a medical test in which a very small amount of **tissue** from a woman's **cervix** is removed and examined for cancer cells ▶ **badanie cytologiczne** (*szyjki macicy*)

smell¹ /smel/ verb (pt, pp **smelt** /smelt/ or **smelled** /smeld/) **1** [I] **smell (of sth)** to have a particular smell: *Dinner smells good!* ◇ *This perfume smells of roses.* ◇ *His breath smelt of whisky.* ▶ **pachnieć 2** [T] to notice or recognize sb/sth by using your nose: *He could smell something burning.* ◇ *Can you smell gas?* ◇ *I could still smell her perfume in the room.* ▶ **czuć zapach** ➲ note at **can¹** (2) **3** [T] to put your nose near sth and breathe in so that you can discover or identify its smell: *I smelt the milk to see if it had gone off.* ▶ **wąchać 4** [I] to have a bad smell: *Your feet smell.* ▶ **śmierdzieć 5** [I] to be able to smell: *I can't smell properly because I've got a cold.* ▶ **czuć zapach**

smell² /smel/ noun **1** [C] the impression that you get of sth by using your nose; the thing that you smell: *What's that smell?* ◇ *a sweet/musty/fresh/sickly smell* ◇ *a strong/faint smell of garlic* ▶ **zapach**, **woń 2** [sing.] an unpleasant smell: *Ugh! What's that smell?* ▶ **nieprzyjemny zapach 3** [U] the ability to sense things with the nose: *Dogs have a very good **sense of smell**.* ▶ **węch**, **powonienie 4** [C] the act of putting your nose near sth to smell it: *Have a smell of this milk* (powąchaj to mleko)*; is it all right?* ▶ **wąchanie** ➲ note at **feel¹**

> **Stink, stench, odour** i **pong** oznaczają nieprzyjemne zapachy. **Aroma, fragrance, perfume** i **scent** oznaczają przyjemne zapachy.

smelly /'smeli/ adj. (**smellier**; **smelliest**) (informal) having a bad smell: *smelly feet* ▶ **śmierdzący**

smile¹ /smaɪl/ verb **1** [I] **smile (at sb/sth)** to make a smile appear on your face: *to smile sweetly/faintly/broadly* ◇ *She smiled at the camera.* ▶ **uśmiechać się 2** [T] to say or express sth with a smile: *I smiled a greeting to them.* Przywitałem ich uśmiechem. ▶ **wyrażać coś uśmiechem**

smile² /smaɪl/ noun [C] an expression on your face in which the corners of your mouth turn up, showing happiness, pleasure, etc.: *to have a smile on your face* ◇ *'It's nice to see you,' he said with a smile.* ▶ **uśmiech** ➲ look at **beam**, **grin**, **smirk**

smirk /smɜːk; US smɜːrk/ noun [C] an unpleasant smile which you have when you are pleased with yourself or think you are very clever ▶ **uśmieszek samozadowolenia**
■ **smirk** verb [I] ▶ **uśmiechać się** (*z samozadowoleniem*)

smock /smɒk/ noun [C] **1** a type of long loose shirt that was once worn by farmers but is now usually worn by women ▶ **kitel**, **luźna bluza** (*np. dla kobiety w ciąży*) **2** a long loose piece of clothing worn over other clothes to protect them from dirt, etc.: *an artist's smock* ▶ **kitel**

smog /smɒg/ noun [U] dirty, poisonous air that can cover a whole city ▶ **smog** ➲ note at **fog**

smoke¹ /sməʊk/ noun **1** [U] the grey, white or black gas that you can see in the air when sth is burning: *Thick smoke poured from the chimney.* ◇ *a room full of cigarette smoke* ▶ **dym 2** [C, usually sing.] an action of smoking a cigarette, etc.: *He went outside for a quick smoke* (wyszedł na papierosa). ▶ **palenie** (*papierosa*)
IDM **go up in smoke 1** to be completely burnt: *The whole house went up in smoke.* ▶ **pójść z dymem 2** if your plans, hopes, etc. go up in smoke, they fail completely ▶ **spełznąć na niczym**

smoke² /sməʊk/ verb **1** [I,T] to breathe in smoke through a cigarette, etc. and let it out again; to use cigarettes, etc. in this way, as a habit: *Do you mind if I smoke?* ◇ *I used to smoke 20 cigarettes a day.* ▶ **palić (tytoń) 2** [I] to send out smoke: *The oil in the pan started to smoke.* ▶ **dymić**
■ **smoker** noun [C]: *She's a **chain smoker**.* Jest nałogową palaczką. ▶ **palacz/ka** (*papierosów*) OPP **non-smoker** | **smoking** noun [U]: *My doctor has advised me to give up smoking.* ◇ *Would you like a table in the smoking or non-smoking section?* ▶ **palenie** (*tytoniu*)

smoked /sməʊkt/ adj. (used of certain types of food) given a special taste by being hung for a period of time in smoke from wood fires: *smoked salmon/ham/cheese* ▶ **wędzony**

smoky /'sməʊki/ adj. (**smokier**; **smokiest**) **1** full of smoke; producing a lot of smoke: *a smoky room/fire* ▶ **zadymiony**; **dymiący 2** with the smell, taste or appearance of smoke ▶ **wędzony**, **zadymiony**

smolder (US) = SMOULDER

smooth¹ /smuːð/ adj. **1** having a completely flat surface with no lumps or holes or rough areas: *smooth skin* ◇ *a smooth piece of wood* ▶ **gładki**, **wygładzony** OPP **rough 2** (used about a liquid mixture) without lumps: *Stir the sauce until it is smooth.* ▶ (*płyn*) **rzadki** OPP **lumpy 3** without difficulties: *The transition from the old method to the new has been very smooth.* ▶ **gładki 4** (used about a journey in a car, etc.) with an even, comfortable movement: *You get a very smooth ride in this car.* ▶ **gładki**, **miękki** OPP **bumpy 5** (used in a critical way, usually about a man) too pleasant or polite to be trusted: *I don't like him. He's far too smooth.* ▶ **gładki**, **słodki**
■ **smoothness** noun [U] ▶ **gładkość**
IDM **take the rough with the smooth** → ROUGH²

smooth² /smuːð/ verb [T] **smooth sth (away, back, down, out, etc.)** to move your hands in the direction mentioned over a surface to make it smooth ▶ **wygładzać**, **wyrównywać**

smoothie /'smuːði/ noun [C] **1** (informal) a man who dresses well and talks very politely in a confident way, but who is often not honest or sincere ▶ **czarujący, ale nieuczciwy/nieszczery mężczyzna 2** a drink made of fruit or fruit juice, sometimes mixed with milk or ice cream ▶ **smoothie**

smoothly /'smuːðli/ adv. without any difficulty: *My work has been going quite smoothly.* ▶ **gładko**

smother /'smʌðə(r)/ verb [T] **1 smother sb (with sth)** to kill sb by covering their face so that they cannot breathe: *She was smothered with a pillow.* ▶ **dusić 2 smother sth/sb in/with sth** to cover sth/sb with too much of sth: *The salad was smothered in oil.* ◇ *He smothered* (oblał) *his cake with cream.* ▶ **pokrywać 3** to stop a feeling, etc. from being expressed ▶ **tłumić 4** to stop sth burning by covering it: *to smother the flames with a blanket* ▶ **tłumić** (*np. uczucie*)

smoulder (US **smolder**) /'sməʊldə(r)/ verb [I] to burn slowly without a flame: *a cigarette smouldering in an ashtray* ▶ **tlić się**

SMS /ˌes em 'es/ noun [U] **short message service**; a system for sending short written messages from one mobile phone to another ▶ **SMS** ➲ look at **text message**

smudge /smʌdʒ/ verb **1** [I] to become untidy, without a clean line around it: *Her lipstick smudged when she kissed him.* ▶ **rozmazywać się 2** [T] to make sth dirty or untidy by touching it: *Leave your painting to dry or you'll smudge it.* ▶ **plamić**, **paćkać**
■ **smudge** noun [C] ▶ **plama**, **kleks**

smug /smʌg/ adj. too happy or satisfied with yourself: *Don't look so smug.* ▶ **zadowolony z siebie**
■ **smugly** adv.: *He smiled smugly as the results were announced.* ▶ **z samozadowoleniem** | **smugness** noun [U] ▶ **samozadowolenie**

smuggle /'smʌgl/ verb [T] to take things into or out of a country secretly in a way that is not allowed by the law; to take a person or a thing secretly into or out of a place: *The drugs had been smuggled through customs.* ▶ **przemycać**

■ **smuggler** noun [C]: *a drug smuggler* ▶ **przemytnik** | **smuggling** noun ▶ **przemyt**

snack /snæk/ noun [C] food that you eat quickly between main meals: *I had a snack on the train.* ▶ **przekąska** ➲ note at **meal**
■ **snack** verb [I] (informal) **snack on sth** ▶ **przekąsić**

'**snack bar** noun [C] a place where you can buy a small quick meal, such as a **sandwich** ▶ **bar szybkiej obsługi**

snag[1] /snæg/ noun [C] a small difficulty or disadvantage that is often unexpected or hidden: *His offer is very generous – are you sure there isn't a snag?* ▶ **haczyk**

snag[2] /snæg/ verb [T] (**snagging**; **snagged**) to catch a piece of clothing, etc. on sth sharp and tear it ▶ **rozdzierać** (*np. na wystającym gwoździu*)

snail /sneɪl/ noun [C] a type of animal with a soft body and no legs that is covered by a shell. **Snails** move very slowly. ▶ **ślimak**

'**snail mail** noun [U] (informal) (used by people who use email to describe the system of sending letters by ordinary post) ▶ **zwykła poczta**

⚷ **snake**[1] /sneɪk/ noun [C] a type of long thin animal with no legs that slides along the ground by moving its body from side to side ▶ **wąż** ➲ picture on **page A11**

snake[2] /sneɪk/ verb [I] (formal) to move like a snake in long curves from side to side ▶ **wić się**

snap[1] /snæp/ verb (**snapping**; **snapped**) **1** [I,T] to break or be broken suddenly, usually with a sharp noise: *The top has snapped off my pen.* ◇ *The branch snapped.* ◇ *I snapped* (urwałem) *my shoelace when I was tying it.* ▶ **łamać (się) z trzaskiem 2** [I,T] to move or be moved into a particular position, especially with a sharp noise: *He snapped to attention* (stanął na baczność) *when the boss walked in.* ◇ *She snapped the bag shut and walked out.* ▶ **przesuwać się/coś pospiesznie i z trzaskiem 3** [I,T] **snap (sth) (at sb)** to speak or say sth in a quick angry way: *Why do you always snap at me?* ▶ **warczeć (na kogoś) 4** [I] to try to bite sb/sth: *The dog snapped at the child's hand.* ▶ **kłapać zębami 5** [I,T] (informal) to take a quick photograph of sb/sth: *A tourist snapped the plane as it crashed.* ▶ **pstrykać** (*zdjęcia*) **6** [I] to suddenly be unable to control your feelings any longer: *Suddenly something just snapped* (nagle coś we mnie po prostu pękło) *and I lost my temper with him.* ▶ **stracić panowanie nad sobą**
IDM **snap your fingers** to make a sharp noise by moving your middle finger quickly against your thumb, especially when you want to attract sb's attention ▶ **pstrykać** (*palcami*)
PHR V **snap sth up** to buy or take sth quickly, especially because it is very cheap ▶ **rwać** (*kupować*)

snap[2] /snæp/ noun **1** [C] a sudden sharp sound of sth breaking ▶ **trzask**, **pstryknięcie 2** (also **snapshot** /'snæpʃɒt/) [C] a photograph that is taken quickly and in an informal way: *I showed them some holiday snaps.* ▶ **fotka 3** [U] (Brit.) a card game where players call out '**Snap**' when two cards that are the same or similar are put down by different players ▶ **rodzaj gry w karty 4** [C] (US) = POPPER

snap[3] /snæp/ adj. [only before a noun] (informal) done quickly and suddenly, often without any careful thought: *a snap decision/judgement* ▶ **pośpieszny**

snappy /'snæpi/ adj. (**snappier**; **snappiest**) **1** (used about a remark, title, etc.) clever or amusing and short: *a snappy slogan* ▶ **błyskotliwy i zwięzły 2** [usually before a noun] (informal) attractive and fashionable: *a snappy outfit* ◇ *She's a **snappy dresser.*** ▶ **szykowny 3** (used about people or their behaviour) tending to speak to people in a bad-tempered, impatient way: *Interruptions make her snappy and nervous.* ▶ **opryskliwy 4** lively; quick: *a snappy tune* ▶ (*melodia*) **żywy**, **szybki**
■ **snappily** adv. ▶ **szybko**; **błyskotliwie**; **szykownie**; **opryskliwie** | **snappiness** noun [U] ▶ **błyskotliwość**; **elegancja**; **opryskliwość**
IDM **make it snappy** (informal) (used to tell sb to do sth quickly or to hurry): *Come in, but make it snappy. I've got a meeting to go to.* ▶ **pośpiesz/cie się**

snapshot /'snæpʃɒt/ noun [C] **1** = SNAP[2] (2) **2** a short description or a small amount of information that gives you an idea of what sth is like ▶ **migawki**

snare /sneə(r)/ noun [C] a piece of equipment used to catch birds or small animals ▶ **sidła**
■ **snare** verb [T] ▶ **zastawiać sidła**

snarl /snɑːl/ verb [I,T] **snarl (sth) (at sb)** (used about an animal) to make an angry sound while showing its teeth: *The dog snarled at the stranger.* ▶ **warczeć**, **burczeć**
■ **snarl** noun [C, usually sing.] ▶ **warczenie**, **burczenie**

snatch[1] /snætʃ/ verb **1** [I,T] to take sth with a quick rough movement: *A boy snatched her handbag and ran off.* ◇ *My bag was snatched.* Wyrwali mi torebkę. ▶ **wyrywać**, **chwytać**, **łapać** SYN **steal** ➲ look at **grab 2** [T] to take or get sth quickly using the only time or chance that you have: *I managed to snatch some sleep on the train.* ◇ *The team snatched a 2-1 victory.* Zespołowi cudem udało się wygrać dwa do jednego. ▶ **łapać** (*np. trochę snu*)
PHR V **snatch at sth** to try to take hold of sth suddenly: *The man snatched at my wallet but I didn't let go of it.* ▶ **chwytać/łapać coś**, **rwać się do czegoś**

snatch[2] /snætʃ/ noun **1** [C, usually pl.] a short part or period of sth: *I heard snatches of conversation from the next room.* ▶ **strzęp**, **urywek 2** [sing.] a sudden movement that sb makes when trying to take hold of sth: *I made a snatch at the ball.* Chwyciłem piłkę. ▶ **chwytanie**, **łapanie**

sneak[1] /sniːk/ verb **1** [I] **sneak into, out of, past, etc. sth**; **sneak in, out, away, etc.** to go very quietly in the direction mentioned, so that nobody can see or hear you: *The prisoner sneaked past the guards.* ◇ *Instead of working, he sneaked out to play football.* ▶ **wymykać się**, **przekradać się 2** [T] (informal) to do or take sth secretly: *I tried to **sneak a look*** (zerknąć ukradkiem) *at the test results in the teacher's bag.* ◇ *They managed to sneak a note to him/sneak him a note in prison* (przemycić mu wiadomość do więzienia). ▶ **robić coś ukradkiem**
PHR V **sneak up (on sb/sth)** to go near sb very quietly, especially so that you can surprise them ▶ **podkradać się (do kogoś/czegoś)**

sneak[2] /sniːk/ noun [C] (Brit., old-fashioned) (used in a critical way) a person, especially a child, who tells sb about the bad things another person has done ▶ **kabel** ⓘ Wyraża dezaprobatę.

sneaker (US) = TRAINER (1)

sneaking /'sniːkɪŋ/ adj. [only before a noun] (used about feelings) not expressed; secret: *I've a sneaking suspicion that he's lying.* ▶ **utajony**, **skrywany**

sneer /snɪə(r)/ verb [I] **1** to smile unpleasantly with one side of your mouth raised to show that you dislike sb/sth ▶ **uśmiechać się drwiąco/szyderczo 2 sneer (at sb/sth)** to behave or speak as if sth is not good enough for you: *She sneered at his attempts to speak French.* ▶ **drwić**, **szydzić**
■ **sneer** noun [C] ▶ **drwiący/szyderczy uśmiech**; **szyderstwo**

sneeze /sniːz/ verb [I] to make air come out of your nose suddenly and noisily in a way that you cannot control, for example because you have a cold: *Dust makes me sneeze.* ▶ **kichać**
■ **sneeze** noun [C] ▶ **kichnięcie**

snide /snaɪd/ adj. (used about an expression or a comment) critical in an unpleasant way ▶ **uszczypliwy**

sniff /snɪf/ verb **1** [I] to breathe air in through the nose in a way that makes a sound, especially because you have a cold or you are crying: *Stop sniffing and blow your nose.* ▶ **pociągać nosem 2** [I,T] **sniff (at) sth** to smell sth by sniffing: *'I can smell gas,' he said, sniffing the air.* ◇ *The dog sniffed at the bone.* ▶ **węszyć, wąchać**
■ **sniff** noun [C]: *Have a sniff of this milk and tell me if it's still OK.* ▶ **pociąganie nosem; węszenie**

sniffle /ˈsnɪfl/ verb [I] to make noises by breathing air suddenly up your nose, especially because you have a cold or you are crying ▶ **siąkać nosem**

snigger /ˈsnɪɡə(r)/ verb [I] **snigger (at sb/sth)** to laugh quietly and secretly in an unpleasant way ▶ **chichotać**
■ **snigger** noun [C] ▶ **chichot**

snip[1] /snɪp/ verb [I,T] (**snipping**; **snipped**) **snip (sth) (off, out, in, etc.)** to cut using scissors, with a short quick action: *He sewed on the button and snipped off the ends of the cotton.* ◇ *to snip a hole in something* ▶ **ciachać nożyczkami**

snip[2] /snɪp/ noun [C] **1** a small cut made with scissors: *She made a row of small snips in the cloth.* ▶ **ciachnięcie nożyczkami 2** (Brit., informal) something that is much cheaper than expected ▶ **wyjątkowa okazja**

sniper /ˈsnaɪpə(r)/ noun [C] a person who shoots at sb from a hidden position ▶ **snajper**

snippet /ˈsnɪpɪt/ noun [C] a small piece of sth, especially information or news ▶ **skrawek, urywek**

snivel /ˈsnɪvl/ verb [I] (**snivelling**; **snivelled**; US **sniveling**; **sniveled**) to keep crying quietly in a way that is annoying ▶ **pochlipywać**

snob /snɒb/ noun [C] a person who thinks they are better than sb of a lower social class and who admires people who have a high social position: *He's such a snob – he wears his Oxford University tie all the time.* ▶ **snob/ka**
■ **snobbish** adj. ▶ **snobistyczny** | **snobbishly** adv. ▶ **snobistycznie** | **snobbishness** noun [U] ▶ **snobowanie się**

snobbery /ˈsnɒbəri/ noun [U] behaviour or attitudes typical of people who think they are better than other people in society, for example because they have more money, better education, etc.: *To say that 'all pop music is rubbish' is just snobbery.* ▶ **snobizm**

snog /snɒɡ/ verb [I,T] (**snogging**; **snogged**) (Brit., informal) (used about a couple) to kiss each other for a long period of time ▶ **całować się**
■ **snog** noun [sing.] ▶ **całowanie się**

snooker /ˈsnuːkə(r)/ noun [U] a game in which two players try to hit a number of coloured balls into pockets at the edges of a large table using a **cue**: *to play snooker* ▶ **rodzaj bilardu** (*z użyciem 22 bil o różnych barwach*) ➲ look at **billiards**, **pool**

snoop /snuːp/ verb [I] **snoop (around)**; **snoop (on sb)** to look around secretly and without permission in order to find out information, etc.: *She suspected that her neighbours visited just to snoop on her.* ▶ **myszkować**

snooty /ˈsnuːti/ adj. (**snootier**; **snootiest**) (informal) acting in a rude way because you think you are better than other people ▶ **bubkowaty, nadęty**

snooze /snuːz/ verb [I] (informal) to have a short sleep, especially during the day ▶ **zdrzemnąć się**
■ **snooze** noun [C, usually sing.]: *I had a bit of a snooze on the train.* ▶ **drzemka** ➲ look at **nap**

snore /snɔː(r)/ verb [I] to breathe noisily through your nose and mouth while you are asleep: *She heard her father snoring in the next room.* ▶ **chrapać**
■ **snore** noun [C]: *He has the loudest snore I've ever heard.* ▶ **chrapanie**

snorkel /ˈsnɔːkl/ noun [C] a short tube that a person swimming just below the surface of the water can use to breathe through ▶ **rurka do nurkowania**
■ **snorkelling** (US **snorkeling**) noun [U]: *to go snorkelling* ▶ **nurkowanie z rurką**

snort /snɔːt/ verb [I] **1** (used about animals) to make a noise by blowing air through the nose and mouth: *The horse snorted in fear.* ▶ **parskać 2** (used about people) to blow out air noisily as a way of showing that you do not like sth, or that you are impatient ▶ **prychać**
■ **snort** noun [C] ▶ **prychnięcie**

snot /snɒt/ noun [U] (informal) the liquid produced by the nose ▶ **glut/y, smark/i**

snout /snaʊt/ noun [C] the long nose of certain animals: *a pig's snout* ▶ **ryj, pysk**

⚷ **snow[1]** /snəʊ/ noun [U] small, soft, white pieces of frozen water that fall from the sky in cold weather: *Three inches of snow fell during the night.* ◇ *The snow melted before it could settle.* ▶ **śnieg** ➲ note at **weather** ➲ picture on **page A16**

⚷ **snow[2]** /snəʊ/ verb [I] (used about snow) to fall from the sky: *It snowed all night.* ▶ (*śnieg*) **padać**

snowball[1] /ˈsnəʊbɔːl/ noun [C] a lump of snow that is pressed into the shape of a ball and used by children for playing ▶ **śnieżka**

snowball[2] /ˈsnəʊbɔːl/ verb [I] to quickly grow bigger and bigger or more and more important ▶ **rosnąć lawinowo**

snowboard /ˈsnəʊbɔːd/ noun [C] a type of board that you fasten to both your feet and use for moving down mountains that are covered with snow ▶ **snowboard**
■ **snowboarder** noun [C] ▶ **snowboardzist(k)a** | **snowboarding** noun [U]: *Have you ever been snowboarding?* ▶ **snowboarding**

snowdrift /ˈsnəʊdrɪft/ noun [C] a deep pile of snow that has been made by the wind: *The car got stuck in a snowdrift.* ▶ **zaspa śnieżna**

snowdrop /ˈsnəʊdrɒp/ noun [C] a type of small white flower that appears at the end of winter ▶ **śnieżyczka** ➲ picture on **page A15**

ˌsnowed ˈin adj. not able to leave home or travel because the snow is too deep ▶ **zasypany śniegiem**

ˌsnowed ˈunder adj. with more work, etc. than you can deal with ▶ **zawalony** (*np. pracą*)

snowfall /ˈsnəʊfɔːl/ noun **1** [C] the snow that falls on one occasion: *heavy snowfalls* ▶ **opad śniegu 2** [U] the amount of snow that falls in a particular place ▶ **opady śniegu**

snowflake /ˈsnəʊfleɪk/ noun [C] one of the small, soft, white pieces of frozen water that fall together as snow ▶ **płatek śniegu**

snowman /ˈsnəʊmæn/ noun [C] (pl. **-men** /-men/) the figure of a person made out of snow ▶ **bałwan śniegowy**

snow pea (US) = MANGETOUT

snowplough (US **snowplow**) /ˈsnəʊplaʊ/ noun [C] a vehicle that is used to clear snow away from roads or railways ▶ **pług śnieżny** ➲ look at **plough**

snowy /ˈsnəʊi/ adj. (**snowier**; **snowiest**) with a lot of snow: *snowy weather* ◇ *a snowy scene* ▶ **śnieżny, śniegowy**

Snr (especially US) = SENIOR[1] (2)

snub[1] /snʌb/ verb [T] (**snubbing**; **snubbed**) to treat sb rudely, for example by refusing to look at or speak to them ▶ **ucierać komuś nosa, robić komuś afront**
■ **snub** noun [C]: *When they weren't invited to the party, they felt it was a snub.* ▶ **afront**

snub[2] /snʌb/ adj. (used about a nose) short, flat and turned up at the end ▶ **zadarty**

■ ˌ**snub-ˈnosed** adj. ▶ **z zadartym nosem**

snuff /snʌf/ noun [U] (especially in past times) **tobacco** which people breathe up into the nose in the form of a powder ▶ **tabaka**

snuffle /ˈsnʌfl/ verb [I] (used about people and animals) to make a noise through your nose: *The dog snuffled around the lamp post.* ▶ **mówić przez nos**, **węszyć**

snug /snʌg/ adj. **1** warm and comfortable: *a snug little room* ◇ *The children were snug in bed.* ▶ **przytulny**, **wygodny 2** fitting sb/sth closely: *Adjust the safety belt to give a snug fit.* ▶ **(dobrze) dopasowany**
■ **snugly** adv. **1** warmly and comfortably ▶ **przytulnie**, **ciepło 2** tidily and tightly ▶ **jak ulał**

snuggle /ˈsnʌgl/ verb [I] **snuggle (up to sb)**; **snuggle (up/down)** to get into a position that makes you feel safe, warm and comfortable, usually next to another person: *She snuggled up to her mother.* ◇ *I snuggled down under the blanket to get warm.* ▶ **przytulać się**, **układać się wygodnie**

So. (US) = SOUTH, SOUTHERN

⚷**so¹** /səʊ/ adv. **1** (used to emphasize an adjective or adverb, especially when this produces a particular result): *She's so ill (that) she can't get out of bed.* ◇ *He was driving so fast that he couldn't stop.* ◇ *You've been so kind. How can I thank you?* ▶ **tak** ➲ note at **such 2** (used in negative sentences for comparing people or things): *She's not so clever as we thought.* ▶ **(nie) tak (…jak) 3** (used in place of sth that has been said already, to avoid repeating it): *Are you coming by plane? If so, I can meet you at the airport.* ◇ *'I failed, didn't I?' 'I'm afraid so* (obawiam się, że tak), *Susan.'* ▶ **tak** ⓘ W języku formalnym, nawiązując do tego, co ktoś zrobił, stosuje się **do** razem z **so**: *He asked me to write to him and **I did so*** (zrobiłem to). **4** [not with verbs in the negative] also; too: *He's a teacher and **so is** his wife.* ◇ *'I've been to New York.' '**So have I.**'* ◇ *I like singing and **so does** Helen.* ▶ **też** ⓘ Por. **neither** w zdaniach przeczących. **5** (used to show that you agree that sth is true, especially when you are surprised): *'It's getting late.' 'So it is. We'd better go.'* ▶ **tak jest**, **rzeczywiście 6** (formal) (used when you are showing sb sth) in this way; like this: *It was a black insect, about so big.* ◇ *Fold the paper in two diagonally, **like so.*** ▶ **właśnie tak**
IDM **and so on (and so forth)** (used at the end of a list to show that it continues in the same way): *They sell pens, pencils, paper and so on.* ▶ **i tak dalej**
I told you so → TELL
it (just) so happens (used to introduce a surprising fact) by chance: *It just so happened that we were going the same way, so he gave me a lift.* ▶ **tak się zdarzyło (że)**
just so → JUST¹
or so (used to show that a number, time, etc. is not exact) approximately; about: *A hundred or so people came to the meeting.* ▶ **lub coś koło tego**
so as to do sth with the intention of doing sth; in order to do sth ▶ **tak, żeby**
so much for (used for saying that sth was not helpful or successful): *So much for that diet* (koniec z dietą)*! I didn't lose any weight at all.* ▶ **i tyle!**
that is so (formal) that is true ▶ **tak jest!**

⚷**so²** /səʊ/ conj. **1 so (that …)** with the purpose that; in order that: *She wore dark glasses so (that) nobody would recognize her.* ▶ **tak, żeby 2** with the result that; therefore: *She felt very tired so she went to bed early.* ▶ **(a) więc 3** (used to show how one part of a story follows another): *So what happened next?* ▶ **tak więc**
IDM **so what?** (informal) (showing that you think sth is not important) Who cares?: *'It's late.' 'So what? We don't have to go to school tomorrow.'* ▶ **(i) co z tego?**

soak /səʊk/ verb **1** [I,T] to become or make sth completely wet: *Leave the dishes to soak for a while.* ◇ *The dog came out of the river and shook itself, soaking everyone.* ▶ **moczyć (się) 2** [I] **soak into/through sth**; **soak in** (used about a liquid) to pass into or through sth: *Blood had soaked right through the bandage.* ▶ **przesiąkać**
PHR V **soak sth up** to take sth in (especially a liquid): *I soaked the water up with a cloth.* Zebrałem wodę ścierką. ◇ *She loves to lie on a beach, soaking up the sun* (kąpać się w słońcu). ▶ **wchłaniać**

soaked /səʊkt/ adj. [not before a noun] extremely wet: *I got **soaked** waiting for my bus in the rain.* ▶ **przemoczony**, **zmoknięty**

soaking /ˈsəʊkɪŋ/ (also ˌ**soaking** ˈ**wet**) adj. extremely wet ▶ **przemoczony do suchej nitki**

ˈ**so-and-so** noun [C] (pl. **so-and-sos**) (informal) **1** a person who is not named: *Imagine a Mrs So-and-so telephones. What would you say?* ▶ **taki a taki 2** a person that you do not like: *He's a bad-tempered old so-and-so.* ▶ **taki owaki**, **jak mu tam**

⚷**soap** /səʊp/ noun **1** [U,C] a substance that you use for washing and cleaning: *He washed his hands with soap.* ◇ *a bar of soap* ◇ *soap powder* proszek do prania ▶ **mydło** ➲ picture at **bar 2** [C] (informal) = SOAP OPERA
■ **soapy** adj. ▶ **mydlany**

ˈ**soap opera** (also informal **soap**) noun [C] a story about the lives and problems of a group of people, which continues several times a week on TV or radio ▶ **telenowela** ➲ look at **opera**

soar /sɔː(r)/ verb [I] **1** to rise very fast: *Prices are soaring because of inflation.* ▶ **szybować 2** to fly high in the air: *an eagle soaring above us* ▶ **wzbijać się**; **zwyżkować**

sob /sɒb/ verb [I] (so**bb**ing; so**bb**ed) to cry while taking in sudden, sharp breaths; to speak while you are crying: *The child was sobbing because he'd lost his toy.* ▶ **łkać**, **szlochać**
■ **sob** noun [C]: *It was heartbreaking to listen to her sobs.* ▶ **łkanie**, **szlochanie**

sober¹ /ˈsəʊbə(r)/ adj. **1** (used about a person) not affected by alcohol: *He'd been drunk the first time he'd met her, but this time he was **stone-cold sober*** (zupełnie trzeźwy). ▶ **trzeźwy 2** not funny; serious: *a sober expression* ◇ *Her death is a sober reminder of just how dangerous drugs can be.* ▶ **poważny**, **zamyślony 3** (used about a colour) not bright or likely to be noticed: *a sober grey suit* ▶ **dyskretny**, **stonowany**

sober² /ˈsəʊbə(r)/ verb
PHR V **sober (sb) up** to become or make sb become normal again after being affected by alcohol: *I need a cup of black coffee to sober me up.* ◇ *There's no point talking to him until he's sobered up.* ▶ **otrzeźwić (się)**

sobering /ˈsəʊbərɪŋ/ adj. making you feel serious: *It is **a sobering thought** that over 25 million people have been killed in car accidents.* ▶ **otrzeźwiający**

ˈ**sob story** noun [C] (informal) a story that sb tells you just to make you feel sorry for them, especially one that does not have that effect or is not true ▶ **(często nieprawdziwa) historia mająca na celu wzbudzenie czyjegoś współczucia**

Soc. = SOCIETY (2): *the Amateur Dramatic Soc.*

ˌ**so-ˈcalled** adj. **1** [only before a noun] (used to show that the words you describe sb/sth with are not correct): *She realized that her so-called friends only wanted her money.* ▶ **tak zwany 2** (used to show that a special name has been given to sb/sth): *Stephens, the so-called 'Blackpool butcher' pleaded guilty to the murders.* ▶ **tak zwany**

soccer (especially US) = FOOTBALL (1)

sociable /ˈsəʊʃəbl/ adj. enjoying being with other people; friendly ▶ **towarzyski**

🔑**social** /'səʊʃl/ adj. [only before a noun] **1** connected with society and the way it is organized: *social problems/issues/reforms* ▶ **społeczny, socjalny 2** connected with the position of people in society: *We share the same social background.* ▶ **społeczny 3** connected with meeting people and enjoying yourself: *a social club* ◇ *She has a busy* ***social life.*** ◇ *Children have to develop their* ***social skills*** (umiejętności życia w społeczeństwie) *when they start school.* ▶ **towarzyski 4** (used about animals) living in groups: *Lions are social animals.* ▶ **stadny, gromadny**
■ **socially** /-ʃəli/ adv.: *We work together but I don't know him socially.* ▶ **towarzysko, na stopie towarzyskiej**

socialism /'səʊʃəlɪzəm/ noun [U] the political idea that is based on the belief that all people are equal and that money and property should be equally divided ▶ **socjalizm**
■ **socialist** /-ɪst/ **1** adj.: *socialist beliefs/policies/writers* ▶ **socjalistyczny 2** noun [C]: *Tony was a socialist when he was younger.* ▶ **socjalist(k)a**

socialize (also **-ise**) /'səʊʃəlaɪz/ verb [I] **socialize (with sb)** to meet and spend time with people in a friendly way, in order to enjoy yourself: *I enjoy socializing with the other students.* ▶ **udzielać się towarzysko** ➲ look at **go out**

ˌsocial 'science noun [C,U] the study of people in society ▶ **nauki społeczne**

ˌsocial se'curity (US **welfare**) noun [U] money paid regularly by the government to people who are poor, old, ill, or who have no job: *to live on social security* ▶ **opieka społeczna**

ˌsocial 'services noun [pl.] a group of services organized by local government to help people who have money or family problems ▶ **świadczenia socjalne**

'social work noun [U] work that involves giving help and advice to people with money or family problems ▶ **praca społeczna**
■ **'social worker** noun [C] ▶ **pracownik socjalny**

🔑**society** /sə'saɪəti/ noun (pl. **societies**) **1** [C,U] the people in a country or an area, thought of as a group, who have shared customs and laws: *a civilized society* ◇ *Society's attitude to women has changed considerably this century.* ◇ *The role of men* ***in society*** *is changing.* ▶ **społeczeństwo 2** [C] (abbr. **Soc.**) an organization of people who share a particular interest or purpose; a club: *a drama society* kółko dramatyczne ▶ **towarzystwo**

sociologist /ˌsəʊsi'ɒlədʒɪst/ noun [C] a student of or an expert in **sociology** ▶ **socjolog**

sociology /ˌsəʊsi'ɒlədʒi/ noun [U] the study of human societies and social behaviour ▶ **socjologia**
■ **sociological** /ˌsəʊsiə'lɒdʒɪkl/ adj. ▶ **socjologiczny**

🔑**sock** /sɒk/ noun [C] a piece of clothing that you wear on your foot and lower leg, inside your shoe: *a pair of socks* ▶ **skarpet(k)a**
IDM **pull your socks up** → PULL[1]

socket /'sɒkɪt/ noun [C] **1** (also **'power point**) (Brit.) a place in a wall where a piece of electrical equipment can be connected to the electricity supply ▶ **gniazdko (elektryczne)** ➲ picture at **plug 2** a hole in a piece of electrical equipment where another piece of equipment can be connected ▶ **wejście 3** a hole that sth fits into: *your eye socket* oczodół ◇ *A dislocation happens when a bone comes out of its socket* (kość wypada ze stawu). ▶ **wklęsłość, łożysko**

soda /'səʊdə/ noun **1** (also **'soda water**) [U] water that has bubbles in it and is usually used for mixing with other drinks: *a whisky and soda* ▶ **woda sodowa 2** [C] (US) = FIZZY DRINK

sodium /'səʊdiəm/ noun [U] (symbol **Na**) a chemical element that exists as a soft, silver-white metal and combines with other elements, for example to make salt ▶ **sód**

sodium bicarbonate /ˌsəʊdiəm baɪ'kɑːbənət/ (also **biˌcarbonate of 'soda**; **'baking soda**) noun [U] (symbol **NaHCO3**) a chemical in the form of a white powder that dissolves and is used in baking to make cakes, etc. rise and become light, and in making **fizzy** drinks and some medicines ▶ **wodorowęglan sodowy**

sofa /'səʊfə/ noun [C] a comfortable seat with a back and arms for two or more people to sit on ▶ **kanapa** SYN **settee**

'sofa bed noun [C] a **sofa** that can be folded out to form a bed ▶ **wersalka**

🔑**soft** /sɒft/ adj. **1** not hard or firm: *a soft bed/seat* ◇ *The ground is very soft after all that rain.* ▶ **miękki** OPP **hard 2** smooth and pleasant to touch: *soft skin/hands* ◇ *a soft towel* ▶ **miękki, delikatny** OPP **rough 3** gentle and pleasant: *The room was decorated in soft pinks and greens.* ▶ **łagodny, stonowany** OPP **bright 4** (used about sounds, voices, words, etc.) quiet or gentle; not angry: *She spoke in a soft whisper.* ▶ **cichy** OPP **loud, harsh 5** (used about people) kind and gentle, sometimes too much so: *A good manager can't afford to be too soft.* ▶ **łagodny** OPP **hard, strict 6** less dangerous and serious than the type of illegal drugs which can kill people: *soft drugs such as marijuana* ▶ **miękki** ➲ look at **hard drug**
■ **softly** adv.: *He closed the door softly behind him.* ▶ **cicho** | **softness** noun [U] ▶ **miękkość, delikatność**
IDM **have a soft spot for sb/sth** (informal) to have good or loving feelings towards sb/sth ▶ **mieć do kogoś/czegoś słabość**

ˌsoft 'drink noun [C] a cold drink that contains no alcohol ▶ **napój bezalkoholowy** ➲ look at **alcoholic**

soften /'sɒfn/ verb **1** [I,T] to become softer or gentler; to make sb/sth softer or gentler: *a lotion to soften the skin* ▶ **łagodnieć, mięknąć; zmiękczać 2** [T] to make sth less shocking and unpleasant: *Her letter sounded too angry so she softened the language.* ◇ *The airbag softened the impact of the crash.* ▶ **łagodzić**

ˌsoft-'hearted adj. kind and good at understanding other people's feelings ▶ **o miękkim sercu** OPP **hard-hearted**

ˌsoft 'option noun [C] the easier thing to do of two or more possibilities, but not the best one: *The government has taken the soft option of agreeing to their demands.* ▶ **łatwiejsze wyjście** (*z sytuacji*)

ˌsoft-'spoken adj. having a gentle, quiet voice: *He was a kind, soft-spoken man.* ▶ **o łagodnym głosie**

🔑**software** /'sɒftweə(r)/ noun [U] the programs, etc. used to operate a computer: *There's a lot of new educational software available now.* ▶ **oprogramowanie** ➲ look at **hardware**

soggy /'sɒgi/ adj. (**soggier**; **soggiest**) very wet and soft and so unpleasant ▶ **rozmokły**

🔑**soil[1]** /sɔɪl/ noun **1** [C,U] the substance that plants, trees, etc. grow in; earth: *poor/dry/acid/sandy soil* ▶ **gleba, ziemia** ➲ note at **ground[1]** **2** [U] (formal) the land that is part of a country: *to set foot on British soil* ▶ **ziemia**

soil[2] /sɔɪl/ verb [T, often passive] (formal) to make sth dirty ▶ **brudzić, plamić**

solace /'sɒləs/ noun [U, sing.] (formal) **solace (in sth)** a person or thing that makes you feel better or happier when you are sad or disappointed: *to find/seek solace in somebody/something* ▶ **pocieszenie, ukojenie** SYN **comfort**

solar /'səʊlə(r)/ adj. [only before a noun] **1** connected with the sun: *a solar eclipse* ▶ **słoneczny 2** using the sun's energy: *solar power* ▶ **słoneczny** ➲ note at **environment**

the 'solar system noun [sing.] the sun and the planets that move around it ▶ **układ słoneczny**

sold past tense, past participle of **sell**

soldier /'səʊldʒə(r)/ noun [C] a member of an army: *The soldiers marched past.* ▶ **żołnierz**

sole[1] /səʊl/ adj. [only before a noun] **1** only; single: *His sole interest is football.* ▶ **jedyny 2** belonging to one person only; not shared ▶ **wyłączny**

■ **solely** adv.: *I agreed to come solely because of your mother.* ▶ **jedynie, wyłącznie**

sole[2] /səʊl/ noun **1** [C] the bottom surface of your foot ▶ **stopa, podeszwa** ➲ picture at **body 2** [C] the part of a shoe or sock that covers the bottom surface of your foot ▶ **podeszwa, zelówka** ➲ picture at **shoe 3** [C,U] (pl. **sole**) a flat sea fish that we eat ▶ *(ryba)* **sola**

solemn /'sɒləm/ adj. **1** (used about a person) very serious; not happy or smiling: *Her solemn face told them that the news was bad.* ▶ **poważny, namaszczony** OPP **cheerful 2** sincere; done or said in a formal way: *to make a solemn promise* ▶ **uroczysty, poważny** SYN **serious**

■ **solemnity** /sə'lemnəti/ noun [U] ▶ **powaga, namaszczenie** | **solemnly** adv.: *'I have something very important to tell you,' she began solemnly.* ▶ **z powagą**

solicit /sə'lɪsɪt/ verb **1** [T] (formal) to ask sb for money, help, support, etc.: *They tried to solicit support for the proposal.* ▶ **zabiegać o coś, starać się o coś 2** [I,T] (used about a woman who has sex for money) to go to sb, especially in a public place, and offer sex in return for money ▶ **nagabywać**

solicitor /sə'lɪsɪtə(r)/ noun [C] (Brit.) a lawyer whose job is to give legal advice, prepare legal documents and arrange the buying and selling of land, etc. ▶ **notariusz, adwokat** ➲ note at **lawyer**

solid[1] /'sɒlɪd/ adj. **1** hard and firm; not in the form of liquid or gas: *It was so cold that the village pond had **frozen solid*** (zamarzł na dobre). ◇ *Our central heating runs on **solid fuel*** (na paliwo stałe). ▶ **stały 2** having no holes or empty spaces inside: *a solid mass of rock* ◇ *The briefcase was **packed solid with*** (wypchana) *£50 notes.* ▶ **jednolity, solidny 3** strong, firm and well made: *a solid little car* ◇ (figurative) *They built up a solid friendship over the years.* ▶ **solidny 4** of good enough quality; that you can trust: *The police cannot make an arrest without solid evidence.* ▶ **konkretny 5** [only before a noun] made completely of one substance, both on the inside and outside: *a **solid gold** chain* ▶ **lity, masywny 6** (informal) without a break or pause: *I was so tired that I slept for twelve solid hours/twelve hours solid* (dwanaście bitych godzin). ▶ **nieprzerwany**

■ **solidity** /sə'lɪdəti/ noun [U] ▶ **solidność, masywność**

solid[2] /'sɒlɪd/ noun [C] **1** a substance or object that is hard; not a liquid or gas: *Liquids become solids when frozen.* ◇ *The baby is not yet on solids* (nie przeszło jeszcze na pokarm stały). ▶ **ciało stałe 2** an object that has length, width and height, not a flat shape: *A cube is a solid.* ▶ **bryła**

solidarity /ˌsɒlɪ'dærəti/ noun [U] **solidarity (with sb)** the support of one group of people for another, because they agree with their aims: *Many local people expressed solidarity with the strikers.* ▶ **solidarność**

solidify /sə'lɪdɪfaɪ/ verb [I] (**solidifying**; **solidifies**; pt, pp **solidified**) to become hard or solid ▶ **krzepnąć, tężeć**

solidly /'sɒlɪdli/ adv. **1** strongly: *a solidly built house* ▶ **solidnie, masywnie 2** without stopping: *It rained solidly all night.* ▶ **bez przerwy**

solitaire /ˌsɒlɪ'teə(r); US 'sɒləter/ noun [U] **1** a game for one person in which you remove pieces from a special board by moving other pieces over them until you have only one piece left ▶ *(gra planszowa)* **samotnik 2** (US) = PATIENCE (2)

solitary /'sɒlətri; US -teri/ adj. **1** done alone, without other people: *Writing novels is a solitary occupation.* ▶ **samotny, odludny 2** (used about a person or an animal) enjoying being alone; often spending time alone: *She was always a solitary child.* ▶ **samotniczy 3** [only before a noun] alone; with no others around: *a solitary figure walking up the hillside* ▶ **pojedynczy, samotny** SYN **lone 4** [only before a noun; usually in negative sentences or questions] only one; single: *I can't think of a solitary example.* ▶ **pojedynczy**

ˌsolitary con'finement noun [U] a punishment in which a person in prison is kept completely alone in a separate cell away from the other prisoners ▶ **osadzenie w separatce**

solitude /'sɒlɪtjuːd; US -ətuːd/ noun [U] the state of being alone, especially when you find this pleasant: *She longed for peace and solitude.* ▶ **samotność, osamotnienie** ➲ look at **loneliness, isolation**

solo[1] /'səʊləʊ/ adj. [only before a noun], adv. **1** (done) alone; by yourself: *a solo flight* ◇ *to fly solo* ▶ **w pojedynkę 2** connected with or played as a musical **solo**: *a solo artist* ▶ **solowy**

solo[2] /'səʊləʊ/ noun [C] (pl. **solos**) a piece of music for only one person to play or sing ▶ **solo, solówka** ➲ look at **duet**

■ **soloist** /-ɪst/ noun [C] ▶ **solist(k)a**

solstice /'sɒlstɪs/ noun [C] the longest or the shortest day of the year: *the summer/winter solstice* ▶ **przesilenie** *(letnie/zimowe)*

soluble /'sɒljəbl/ adj. **1 soluble (in sth)** that will dissolve in liquid: *These tablets are soluble in water.* ▶ **rozpuszczalny 2** (formal) (used about a problem, etc.) that has an answer; that can be solved ▶ **rozwiązywalny** OPP for both meanings **insoluble**

solution /sə'luːʃn/ noun **1** [C] **a solution (to sth)** a way of solving a problem, dealing with a difficult situation, etc.: *a solution to the problem of unemployment* ▶ **rozwiązanie 2** [C] **the solution (to sth)** the answer (to a game, competition, etc.): *The solution to the quiz will be published next week.* ▶ **rozwiązanie 3** [C,U] (a) liquid in which sth solid has been dissolved: *saline solution* ▶ **roztwór**

solve /sɒlv/ verb [T] **1** to find a way of dealing with a problem or difficult situation: *The government is trying to solve the problem of inflation.* ◇ *The police have not managed to solve the crime.* ◇ *to solve a mystery* ▶ **rozwiązywać 2** to find the correct answer to a competition, a problem in mathematics, a series of questions, etc.: *to solve a puzzle/an equation/a riddle* ▶ **rozwiązywać** ➲ noun **solution** ➲ adjective **soluble**

solvent /'sɒlvənt/ noun [C,U] a liquid that can dissolve another substance ▶ **rozpuszczalnik**

sombre (US **somber**) /'sɒmbə(r)/ adj. **1** dark in colour ▶ **ciemny, mroczny** SYN **dull 2** sad and serious: *a sombre occasion* ▶ **ponury, posępny**

■ **sombrely** adv. ▶ **ciemno; ponuro**

some /səm; strong form sʌm/ determiner, pron. **1** [before uncountable nouns and plural countable nouns] a certain amount of or a number of: *We need some butter and some potatoes.* ◇ *I don't need any more money – I've still got some.* ▶ **trochę, nieco**

> W zdaniach przeczących i pytających zamiast **some** używa się **any**: *Do we need any butter?* ◇ *I need some more money. I haven't got any.* Zob. przykł. w znaczeniu 2, gdzie **some** jest użyte w zdaniach pytających (gdy spodziewana jest odpowiedź twierdząca).

2 (used in questions when you expect or want the answer 'yes'): *Would you like some more cake?* ◇ *Can I take some of this paper?* ▶ **trochę 3 some (of sb/sth)** (used when you are referring to certain members of a group or certain types of a thing, but not all of them): *Some pupils enjoy this kind of work, some don't.* ◇ *Some of his books are very exciting.* ◇ *Some of us are going to* *the park.* ▶ **niektóry 4** (used with singular countable nouns for talking about a person or thing without saying any details): *I'll see you again some time, I expect.* ◇ *There must be some mistake.* ◇ *I read about it in **some** newspaper **or other**.* ▶ **jakiś, taki lub inny**

somebody /ˈsʌmbədi/ (also **someone** /ˈsʌmwʌn/) pron. a person who is not known or not mentioned by name: *How are you? Somebody said that you'd been ill.* ◇ *She's getting married to someone she met at work.* ◇ *There's somebody at the door.* ◇ *I think you should talk to **someone else*** (z kimś innym) *about this problem.* ▶ **ktoś**

> **Somebody**, **anybody** i **everybody** łączą się z czasownikiem w lp, ale często zastępowane są zaimkiem osobowym w lm (z wyjątkiem języka formalnego, gdzie używa się **his/her** lub **him/her**): *Somebody is coming.* ◇ *Has everybody got something to eat?* ◇ *Somebody has left **their** coat behind.* ◇ *Has anyone not brought **their** books?* ◇ *I'll see everybody concerned and tell **them** the news.* Różnica między **somebody** i **anybody** jest taka sama, jak między **some** i **any**. ➲ note at **some**

ˈ**some day** (also **someday**) adv. at a time in the future that is not yet known: *I hope you'll come and visit me some day.* ▶ **któregoś dnia, kiedyś**

somehow /ˈsʌmhaʊ/ adv. **1** in a way that is not known or certain: *The car's broken down but I'll get to work somehow.* ◇ *Somehow we had got completely lost.* ▶ **jakoś 2** for a reason you do not know or understand: *I somehow get the feeling that I've been here before.* ▶ **jakoś, z jakiejś przyczyny**

someone = SOMEBODY

someplace (US) = SOMEWHERE

somersault /ˈsʌməsɔːlt/ noun [C] a movement in which you roll right over with your feet going over your head ▶ **salto, koziołek**

something /ˈsʌmθɪŋ/ pron. **1** a thing that is not known or not named: *I've got something in my eye.* ◇ *Wait a minute – I've forgotten something.* ◇ *Would you like **something else*** (coś innego) *to drink?* ▶ **coś** ⓘ Różnica między **something** i **anything** jest taka sama, jak między **some** i **any**. ➲ note at **some 2** a thing that is important, useful or worth considering: *There's **something in** what your mother says.* ◇ *I think you've got something there* (w tym, co mówisz, jest coś) – *I like that idea.* ▶ **coś 3** (informal) (used to show that a description, an amount, etc. is not exact): *a new comedy series aimed at **thirty-somethings*** (ludzi w wieku 30-40 lat). ▶ **około**

IDM **or something** (informal) (used for showing that you are not sure about what you have just said): *'What's his job?' 'I think he's a plumber, or something.'* ▶ **coś w tym rodzaju**

something like 1 about; approximately: *The cathedral took something like 200 years to build.* ▶ **(coś) około 2** similar to: *A loganberry is something like a raspberry.* ▶ **coś w rodzaju (czegoś)**

something to do with sth connected or involved with sth: *The programme's something to do with the environment.* ▶ **związek z czymś**

sometime (also **some time**) /ˈsʌmtaɪm/ adv. at a time that you do not know exactly or have not yet decided: *I'll phone you sometime this evening.* ◇ *I must go and see her sometime.* ▶ **któregoś dnia, kiedyś**

sometimes /ˈsʌmtaɪmz/ adv. on some occasions; now and then: *Sometimes I drive to work and sometimes I go by bus.* ◇ *I sometimes watch TV in the evenings.* ▶ **czasem, czasami**

somewhat /ˈsʌmwɒt; US -wʌt/ adv. rather; to some degree: *We missed the train, which was somewhat unfortunate.* ▶ **nieco**

somewhere /ˈsʌmweə(r)/ (US also **someplace** /ˈsʌmpleɪs/) adv. at, in or to a place that you do not know or do not mention by name: *I've seen your glasses somewhere downstairs.* ◇ *'Have they gone to France?' 'No, I think they've gone **somewhere else*** (gdzie indziej) *this year.'* ▶ **gdzieś** ⓘ Różnica między **somewhere** i **anywhere** jest taka sama, jak między **some** i **any**. ➲ note at **some**

IDM **get somewhere/nowhere (with sb/sth)** → GET

somewhere along/down the line at some time; sooner or later ▶ **kiedyś, wcześniej czy później**

somewhere around (used when you do not know an exact time, number, etc.): *Your ideal weight should probably be **somewhere around** 70 kilos.* ▶ **gdzieś około**

son /sʌn/ noun [C] a male child ▶ **syn** ➲ look at **daughter**

sonata /səˈnɑːtə/ noun [C] a piece of music written for the piano, or for another instrument together with the piano ▶ **sonata**

song /sɒŋ/ noun **1** [C] a piece of music with words that you sing: *a folk/love/pop song* ▶ **piosenka, pieśń** ➲ note at **pop 2** [U] songs in general; music for singing: *to burst/break into song* zaśpiewać ▶ **śpiew 3** [U,C] the musical sounds that birds make: *birdsong* ▶ **śpiew**

songwriter /ˈsɒŋraɪtə(r)/ noun [C] a person whose job is to write songs ▶ **twórca piosenek**

sonic /ˈsɒnɪk/ adj. (technical) connected with sound waves ▶ **dźwiękowy**

ˈ**son-in-law** noun [C] (pl. **sons-in-law**) the husband of your daughter ▶ **zięć**

sonnet /ˈsɒnɪt/ noun [C] a type of poem that has 14 lines that **rhyme** in a fixed pattern: *Shakespeare's sonnets* ▶ **sonet**

soon /suːn/ adv. **1** in a short time from now; a short time after sth else has happened: *It will soon be dark.* ◇ *He left soon after me.* ◇ *We should arrive at your house soon after twelve.* ◇ (informal) *See you soon.* ▶ **wkrótce, niedługo, zaraz 2** early; quickly: *Don't leave so soon. Stay for tea.* ◇ *How soon can you get here?* ▶ **szybko**

IDM **as soon as** at the moment (that); when: *Phone me as soon as you hear some news.* ◇ *I'd like your reply **as soon as possible*** (jak najwcześniej). ▶ **gdy tylko**

no sooner ... than (formal) immediately when or after: *No sooner had I shut the door than I realized* (jak tylko zamknąłem drzwi, zdałem sobie sprawę z tego, że) *I'd left my keys inside.* ⓘ Zwróć uwagę na szyk zdania. Wyrażenie **no sooner** wymaga inwersji, tj. najpierw występuje czasownik, a po nim podmiot zdania. ▶ **gdy tylko ... wówczas/wtedy ...**

sooner or later at some time in the future; one day ▶ **wcześniej czy później**

soot /sʊt/ noun [U] black powder that is produced when wood, coal, etc. is burnt ▶ **sadza**

soothe /suːð/ verb [T] **1** to make sb calmer or less upset ▶ **koić, uspokajać** SYN **comfort 2** to make a part of the body or a feeling less painful: *The doctor gave me some skin cream to soothe the irritation.* ▶ **łagodzić, uśmierzać**

■ **soothing** adj.: *soothing music* ◇ *a soothing massage* ▶ **kojący, uspokajający** | **soothingly** adv. ▶ **łagodnie, uspokajająco**

sophisticated /səˈfɪstɪkeɪtɪd/ adj. **1** having or showing a lot of experience of the world and social situations; knowing about fashion, culture, etc.: *She's a very sophisticated young woman* (światowa młoda dama). ▶ **wytworny, bywały 2** (used about machines, systems, etc.) advanced and complicated ▶ **skomplikowany 3** able to understand difficult or complicated things: *Voters are much more sophisticated these days.* ▶ **wyrobiony, doświadczony**

■ **sophistication** /səˌfɪstɪˈkeɪʃn/ noun [U] ▶ **wyrafinowanie; wyrobienie**

S

sophomore /ˈsɒfəmɔː(r)/ noun [C] (US) **1** a student in the second year of a course of study at a college or university ▶ **student/ka drugiego roku 2** a high school student in the 10th grade ▶ **uczeń/uczennica drugiej klasy liceum/technikum**

soppy /ˈsɒpi/ adj. (**soppier**; **soppiest**) (informal) full of unnecessary emotion; silly: *a soppy romantic film* ▶ **ckliwy**

soprano /səˈprɑːnəʊ; US also -ˈpræn-/ noun [C] (pl. **sopranos** /-nəʊz/) the highest singing voice; a woman, girl or boy with this voice ▶ **sopran**

soˌprano reˈcorder (US) = DESCANT RECORDER

sorcerer /ˈsɔːsərə(r)/ noun [C] (in stories) a man with magic powers, who is helped by evil spirits ▶ **czarnoksiężnik**

sorceress /ˈsɔːsərəs/ noun [C] (in stories) a woman with magic powers, who is helped by evil spirits ▶ **czarownica**

sordid /ˈsɔːdɪd/ adj. **1** unpleasant; not honest or moral: *We discovered the truth about his sordid past.* ◇ *The newspapers were full of* ***the sordid details*** (obrzydliwych szczegółów) *of their affair.* ▶ **niecny, nikczemny 2** very dirty and unpleasant ▶ **obskurny, nędzny**

⚷ **sore**[1] /sɔː(r)/ adj. (used about a part of the body) painful, especially when touched: *to have a sore throat* ◇ *My feet were sore from walking so far.* ◇ *I feel all right after the operation but my stomach is still very sore* (brzuch jeszcze bardzo mnie boli). ▶ **bolący, bolesny**

■ **soreness** noun [U]: *a cream to reduce soreness and swelling* ▶ **zaczerwienienie, obrzmienie**

IDM **a sore point** a subject that is likely to make sb upset or angry when mentioned ▶ **czułe miejsce**

stand/stick out like a sore thumb to be extremely obvious, especially in a negative way: *A big new office block would stand out like a sore thumb in the old part of town.* ▶ **zbytnio rzucać się w oczy** (*w sposób negatywny*)

sore[2] /sɔː(r)/ noun [C] a painful, often red place on your body where the skin is cut or infected ▶ **owrzodzenie**

sorely /ˈsɔːli/ adv. (formal) very much; seriously: *You'll be* ***sorely missed*** *when you leave.* ▶ **bardzo, wielce**

sorrow /ˈsɒrəʊ/ noun (formal) **1** [U] a feeling of great sadness because sth bad has happened ▶ **smutek, żal 2** [C] a very sad event or situation ▶ **bolesny cios**

■ **sorrowful** /-fl/ adj. ▶ **zasmucony, żałosny** | **sorrowfully** /-fəli/ adv. ▶ **ze smutkiem, żałośnie**

⚷ **sorry**[1] /ˈsɒri/ adj. (**sorrier**; **sorriest**) **1** [not before a noun] **sorry (to see, hear, etc.)**; **sorry that…** sad or disappointed: *I was sorry to hear that you've been ill.* ◇ *I am sorry that we have to leave so soon.* ◇ *'Simon's mother died last week.' 'Oh, I am sorry.'* (współczuję) ▶ **przykro mi, jaka szkoda 2** [not before a noun] **sorry (for/about sth)**; **sorry (to do sth/that…)** (used for excusing yourself for sth that you have done): *I'm awfully sorry for spilling that coffee.* ◇ *I'm sorry I've kept you all waiting.* ◇ *I'm sorry to disturb you so late in the evening, but I wonder if you can help me.* ▶ **przepraszać, przykro mi 3** [only before a noun] very bad: *The house was in a* ***sorry state*** *when we first moved in.* ◇ *They were a* ***sorry sight*** *when they finally got home.* ▶ **opłakany**

IDM **be/feel sorry for sb** to feel sadness or pity for sb: *I feel very sorry for* (bardzo współczuję) *the families of the victims.* ◇ *Stop feeling sorry for yourself!* ▶ **współczuć komuś**

I'm sorry (used for politely saying 'no' to sth, disagreeing with sth or introducing bad news): *'Would you like to come to dinner on Friday?' 'I'm sorry, I'm busy that evening.'* ◇ *I'm sorry, I don't agree with you. I think we should accept the offer.* ◇ *I'm sorry to tell you that your application has been unsuccessful.* ▶ **przykro mi, przepraszam**

sorry[2] /ˈsɒri/ interj. **1** (used for making excuses, apologizing, etc.): *Sorry, I didn't see you standing behind me.* ◇ *Sorry I'm late – the bus didn't come on time.* ◇ *He didn't even* ***say sorry.*** Nawet nie przeprosił. ▶ **przepraszam 2** (especially Brit.) (used for asking sb to repeat sth that you have not heard correctly): *'My name's Dave Harries.' 'Sorry? Dave who?'* (przepraszam, kto) ▶ **słucham? 3** (used for correcting yourself when you have said sth wrong): *Take the second turning, sorry, the third turning on the right.* ▶ **przepraszam**

⚷ **sort**[1] /sɔːt/ noun **1** [C] **a sort of sb/sth** a type or kind: *What sort of music do you like?* ◇ *She's got* ***all sorts of*** *problems at the moment.* ◇ *There were snacks – peanuts, olives,* ***that sort of thing.*** ▶ **gatunek, rodzaj 2** [sing.] (especially Brit.) a particular type of character; a person: *My brother would never cheat on his wife – he's not that sort* (on nie jest tego typu człowiekiem). ▶ **facet, gość**

SYN for both meanings **kind**

IDM **a sort of sth** (informal) a type of sth; sth that is similar to sth: *Can you hear a sort of ticking noise?* ▶ **coś w rodzaju**

sort of (informal) rather; in a way: *'Do you see what I mean?' 'Sort of.'* ◇ *I'd sort of like to go, but I'm not sure.* ▶ **trochę, jakoś**

⚷ **sort**[2] /sɔːt/ verb [T] **1 sort sth (into sth)** to put things into different groups or places, according to their type, etc.; to separate things of one type from others: *I'm just sorting these papers into the correct files.* ▶ **segregować, porządkować 2** [often passive] (especially Brit., informal) to find an answer to a problem or difficult situation; to organize sth/sb: *It's our problem. We'll* ***get it sorted*** (zajmiemy się nim). ◇ *It's time you* ***got yourself sorted*** (żebyś uporządkował swoje sprawy). ◇ *I'll have more time when I've got things sorted at home* (kiedy uporządkuję sprawy domowe). ▶ **doprowadzać do ładu, porządkować**

PHR V **sort sth out** to tidy or organize sth: *The toy cupboard needs sorting out.* ▶ **porządkować coś**

sort sth/sb/yourself out (especially Brit.) to deal with sb's/your own problems successfully: *If you can wait a moment, I'll sort it all out for you.* ◇ *You load up the car and I'll sort the kids out.* ▶ **załatwiać czyjeś/swoje sprawy**

sort through sth (for sth) to look through a number of things, in order to find sth that you are looking for or to put them in order ▶ **przeglądać (*np. dokumenty*) w poszukiwaniu czegoś**; **porządkować** (*np. dokumenty*)

ˈsort code (US **ˈrouting number**) noun [C] a number that is used to identify a particular bank ▶ **kod bankowy**

ˌso-ˈso adj., adv. (informal) all right but not particularly good/well: *'How are you feeling today?' 'So-so.'* ▶ **jako tako, tak sobie**

soufflé /ˈsuːfleɪ; US suːˈfleɪ/ noun [C,U] a type of food made mainly from egg whites, flour and milk, beaten together and baked until it rises ▶ **suflet**

sought past tense, past participle of **seek**

ˈsought after adj. that people want very much, because it is of high quality or rare ▶ **poszukiwany, wzięty**

⚷ **soul** /səʊl/ noun **1** [C] the spiritual part of a person that is believed to continue to exist after the body is dead: *Christians believe that your soul goes to heaven when you die.* ▶ **dusza 2** [C] the inner part of a person containing their deepest thoughts and feelings: *There was a feeling of restlessness deep in her soul.* ▶ **dusza** ➲ look at **spirit 3** [C,U] deep feeling and thought: *The music was performed perfectly but it lacked soul.* ▶ **uczucie 4** [C] [used with adjectives] (old-fashioned) a particular type of person: *She's a kind old soul.* ▶ **dusza 5** [sing.] [in negative sentences] a person: *There wasn't a soul in sight* (ani żywego ducha). ◇ *Promise me you won't tell a soul.* Obiecaj, że nie powiesz nikomu. ▶ **dusza 6** (also **ˈsoul music**) [U] a type of

popular African-American music: *a soul singer* ▶ **muzyka soul**
IDM **heart and soul** → HEART

'soul-destroying adj. (used about a job or task) very dull and boring, because it has to be repeated many times or because there will never be any improvement ▶ (*praca/zadanie*) **śmiertelnie nudny**

soulful /'səʊlfl/ adj. having or showing deep feeling: *a soulful expression* ▶ **pełen uczucia/wyrazu**

soulless /'səʊlləs/ adj. without feeling, warmth or interest: *They live in soulless concrete blocks.* ▶ **bezduszny** SYN **depressing**

'soul music = SOUL (5)

'soul-searching noun [U] the careful examination of your thoughts and feelings, for example in order to reach the correct decision or solution to sth: *After much soul-searching* (po długim i wnikliwym namyśle) *she decided to leave.* ▶ **głębokie zastanawianie się**

sound[1] /saʊnd/ noun **1** [C,U] something that you hear or that can be heard: *the sound of voices* ◇ *a clicking/buzzing/scratching sound* ◇ *After that, he didn't **make a sound.*** ◇ *She opened the door without a sound* (bezszelestnie). ◇ *Light travels faster than sound.* ◇ *sound waves* ▶ **dźwięk**, **odgłos** SYN **noise** **2** [U] what you can hear coming from a TV, radio, etc.: *Can you turn the sound up/down* (zgłośnić/przyciszyć)*?* ◇ *to sound the horn* (naciskać klakson) *of your car* ▶ **fonia**
IDM **by the sound of it/things** judging from what sb has said or what you have read about sb/sth: *She must be an interesting person, by the sound of it.* ▶ **z tego co słyszę**, **wygląda na to, że**
like the look/sound of sb/sth → LIKE[2]

sound[2] /saʊnd/ verb **1** [I] [not usually used in the continuous tenses] to give a particular impression when heard or read about; to seem: *That **sounds like** a child crying.* ◇ *She sounded upset and angry on the phone.* ◇ *You sound like your father when you say things like that!* ◇ *He sounds a very nice person from his letter.* ◇ *Does she sound like the right person for the job?* ◇ *It doesn't **sound as if/though*** (nie wygląda na to, że) *he's very reliable.* ◇ *A party on the beach **sounds fun*** (brzmi nieźle). ▶ **brzmieć** ℹ W języku mówionym, zwłaszcza w Amer. ang., często używa się **like** zamiast **as if** lub **as though**: *It sounds like you had a great time.* W Br. ang. pisanym jest to uważane za nieprawidłowe. ➲ note at **feel**[1] **2** (**-sounding**) [in compounds] seeming to be of the type mentioned, from what you have heard or read: *a Spanish-sounding surname* ▶ **brzmiący** **3** [T] to cause sth to make a sound; to give a signal by making a sound: *to sound the horn of your car* ◇ *A student on one of the upper floors **sounded the alarm.*** ▶ **włączać coś, co wydaje dźwięk**
PHR V **sound sb out (about sth)** to ask sb questions in order to find out what they think or intend to do ▶ **sondować (kogoś)**, **wybadać**

sound[3] /saʊnd/ adj. **1** sensible; that you can depend on and that will probably give good results: *sound advice* ◇ *a sound investment* ▶ **rozsądny**; **pewny** **2** healthy and strong; in good condition: *The structure of the bridge is basically sound.* ▶ **dobry**, **w dobrym stanie** OPP for both meanings **unsound**
■ **soundness** noun [U] ▶ **wytrzymałość**, **dobry stan**

sound[4] /saʊnd/ adv.
IDM **be sound asleep** to be deeply asleep ▶ **spać głęboko**

'sound bite noun [C] a short phrase or sentence taken from a longer speech, especially a speech made by a politician, that is considered to be particularly effective or appropriate ▶ **efektowny fragment przemówienia** (*trafiający w sedno sprawy*)

'sound effect noun [C, usually pl.] a sound, for example the sound of the wind, that is made in an artificial way and used in a play, film or computer game to make it more realistic ▶ **efekt dźwiękowy**

soundly /'saʊndli/ adv. completely or deeply: *The children were sleeping soundly.* ▶ **dotkliwie**; **głęboko**

soundproof /'saʊndpru:f/ adj. made so that no sound can get in or out: *a soundproof room* ▶ **dźwiękoszczelny**, **wyciszony**

soundtrack /'saʊndtræk/ noun [C] the recorded sound and music from a film or computer game ▶ **ścieżka dźwiękowa** ➲ note at **film** ➲ look at **track**

soup /su:p/ noun [U,C] liquid food made by cooking meat, vegetables, etc. in water: *a tin of chicken soup* ◇ *chicken soup* rosół ▶ **zupa** ➲ picture on **page A14**

sour /'saʊə(r)/ adj. **1** having a sharp taste like that of a lemon: *This sauce is quite sour.* ▶ **kwaśny** ➲ look at **bitter**, **sweet** **2** (used especially about milk) tasting or smelling unpleasant because it is no longer fresh: *This cream has **gone sour.*** ▶ **skwaśniały**; **zsiadły** **3** (used about people) angry and unpleasant: *a sour expression* ◇ *a **sour-faced** old woman* ◇ *a sour expression* kwaśna mina ▶ **w złym humorze**
■ **sour** verb [T] (formal): *The disagreement over trade tariffs has soured relations between the two countries.* ▶ **psuć** (*np. stosunki*) | **sourly** adv. ▶ **kwaśno**, **zgorzkniale** | **sourness** noun [U] ▶ **cierpkość**; **zgorzknienie**
IDM **go/turn sour** to stop being pleasant or friendly: *Their relationship turned sour after a few months.* Po paru miesiącach w ich związku coś się popsuło. ▶ **psuć się**
sour grapes pretending to not want sth that in fact you secretly want, because you cannot have it ▶ **kwaśne winogrona**

source /sɔ:s/ noun [C] a place, person or thing where sth comes or starts from or where sth is obtained: *Britain's oil reserves are an important **source of income.*** ◇ *The TV is a great source of entertainment.* ◇ *Police have refused to reveal the source of their information.* ◇ *He set out to discover the source of the river* ▶ **źródło**

,sour 'cream noun [U] cream that has been deliberately made sour by the addition of bacteria, and is used in cooking ▶ **kwaśna śmietana**

south[1] /saʊθ/ noun [sing.] (abbr. **S**; **So.**) **1** (also **the south**) the direction that is on your right when you watch the sun rise; one of the **points of the compass**: *warm winds from the south* ◇ *Which way is south?* ◇ *We live **to the south of** London.* ▶ **południe** **2** (**the south**; **the South**) the southern part of a country, a city, a region or the world: *Nice is in the South of France.* ▶ **południe** ➲ look at **north**, **east**, **west**

south[2] /saʊθ/ adj. **1** (also **South**) [only before a noun] in the south: *the south coast of Cornwall* ▶ **południowy** **2** (used about a wind) coming from the south ▶ **południowy**, **z południa**
■ **south** adv. to or towards the south: *The house faces south.* ◇ *We live just south of Birmingham.* ◇ *Brighton is south of London.* ▶ **na połud-nie/niu**

southbound /'saʊθbaʊnd/ adj. travelling or leading towards the south ▶ (*jadący/idący itp.*) **w kierunku południowym/na południe**

,south-'east[1] (also **the ,South-'East**) noun [sing.] (abbr. **SE**) the direction or a region that is an equal distance between south and east ▶ **południowy wschód**

,south-'east[2] adj. in, from or to the **south-east** of a place or country: *the south-east coast of Spain* ▶ **południowo-wschodni**
■ **,south-'east** adv. ▶ **w kierunku południowo-wschodnim**

,south-'easterly adj. **1** [only before a noun] towards the south-east: *in a south-easterly direction* ▶ **południowo-wschodni**; **w kierunku południowo-wschodnim** **2**

S

(used about a wind) coming from the south-east ▶ **południowo-wschodni**

ˌsouth-ˈeastern adj. (abbr. **SE**) [only before a noun] connected with the south-east of a place or country: *the south-eastern states of the US* ▶ **południowo-wschodni**

ˌsouth-ˈeastwards (also **ˌsouth-ˈeastward**) adv. towards the south-east ▶ **w kierunku południowo-wschodnim**

southerly /ˈsʌðəli/ adj. **1** [only before a noun] to, towards or in the south: *Keep going in a southerly direction.* ▶ **południowy 2** (used about a wind) coming from the south ▶ **południowy, z południa**

southern (also **Southern**) /ˈsʌðən/ adj. (abbr. **S**) of, in or from the south of a place: *a man with a southern accent* ◇ *Greece is in Southern Europe.* ▶ **południowy**

southerner (also **Southerner**) /ˈsʌðənə(r)/ noun [C] a person who was born in or lives in the southern part of a country ▶ **osoba pochodząca z południa kraju/mieszkająca na południu kraju** OPP **northerner**

the ˌSouth ˈPole noun [sing.] the point on the Earth's surface which is furthest south ▶ **biegun południowy**

southwards /ˈsaʊθwədz/ (also **southward**) adv. towards the south ▶ **na południe**
■ **southward** adj. ▶ **południowy**

ˌsouth-ˈwest¹ (also **the ˌSouth-ˈWest**) noun [sing.] (abbr. **SW**) the direction or a region that is an equal distance between south and west ▶ **południowy zachód**

ˌsouth-ˈwest² adj. in, from or to the **south-west** of a place or country: *the south-west coast of France* ▶ **południowo-zachodni**
■ **ˌsouth-ˈwest** adv.: *Our garden faces south-west.* ▶ **w kierunku południowo-zachodnim**

ˌsouth-ˈwesterly adj. **1** [only before a noun] towards the south-west: *in a south-westerly direction* ▶ **południowo-zachodni 2** (used about a wind) coming from the south-west ▶ **południowo-zachodni**

ˌsouth-ˈwestern adj. (abbr. **SW**) [only before a noun] connected with the south-west of a place or country ▶ **południowo-zachodni**

ˌsouth-ˈwestwards (also **ˌsouth-ˈwestward**) adv. towards the south-west: *Follow the B409 south-westwards for twenty miles.* ▶ **w kierunku południowo-zachodnim**

souvenir /ˌsuːvəˈnɪə(r); US also ˈsuːvənɪr/ noun [C] something that you keep to remind you of somewhere you have been on holiday or of a special event: *I brought back a menu as a souvenir of my trip.* ▶ **pamiątka** SYN **memento**

sovereign¹ /ˈsɒvrɪn; US -rən/ noun [C] a king or queen ▶ **monarch-a/ini**

sovereign² /ˈsɒvrɪn; US -rən/ adj. **1** [only before a noun] (used about a country) not controlled by any other country; independent ▶ **suwerenny 2** having complete power or the greatest power in the country ▶ (*władza itp.*) **nieograniczony; najwyższy**

sovereignty /ˈsɒvrənti/ noun [U] the power that a country has to control its own government ▶ **suwerenność**

Soviet /ˈsəʊviət; ˈsɒv-/ adj. [usually before a noun] connected with the former USSR: *Soviet Russia* ▶ **radziecki**

sow¹ /səʊ/ verb [T] (pt **sowed**; pp **sown** /səʊn/ or **sowed**) **sow A (in B); sow B (with A)** to plant seeds in the ground: *to sow seeds in pots* ◇ *to sow a field with wheat* obsiać pole pszenicą ▶ **siać**

sow² /saʊ/ noun [C] an adult female pig ▶ **maciora** ➲ note at **pig**

soya /ˈsɔɪə/ (US **soy** /sɔɪ/) noun [U] the plant on which **soya beans** grow; the food obtained from **soya beans**: *a soya crop* ◇ *soya flour* ▶ **soja**

soya bean (US **soybean** /ˈsɔɪbiːn/) noun [C] a type of **bean** that can be cooked and eaten or used to make many different types of food, for example flour, oil and a type of milk ▶ **soja**

soy sauce /ˌsɔɪ ˈsɔːs/ (also **ˌsoya ˈsauce**) noun [U] a dark brown sauce that is made from **soya beans** and that you add to food to make it taste better ▶ **sos sojowy**

spa /spɑː/ noun [C] **1** a place where mineral water comes out of the ground and where people go to drink this water because it is considered to be healthy ▶ **uzdrowisko 2** a place where people can relax and improve their health: *a superb* ***health spa*** *which includes sauna, Turkish bath and fitness rooms* ▶ **spa, uzdrowisko**

space¹ /speɪs/ noun **1** [C,U] **space (for sb/sth) (to do sth)** a place or an area that is empty or not used: *Is there enough space for me to park the car there?* ◇ *Shelves would* ***take up*** *less* ***space*** *than a cupboard.* ◇ *a parking space* ◇ *We're a bit short of space.* ◇ *There's a space here for you to write your name.* ◇ *Leave a space after the comma.* ◇ *wide open spaces* otwarta przestrzeń ▶ **miejsce, przestrzeń** SYN **room** ➲ note at **place¹ 2** [U] (also **ˌouter ˈspace**) [in compounds] the area which surrounds the planet Earth and the other planets and stars: *space travel* ◇ *a spaceman/spacewoman* ▶ **przestrzeń kosmiczna, kosmos 3** [C, usually sing.] a period of time: *Priti had been ill three times* ***in/within the space of*** *four months.* ◇ *He's achieved a lot in* ***a short space of time.*** ▶ **okres 4** [U] time and freedom to think and do what you want: *I need some space to think.* ▶ **czas**

> **space**
>
> The **Earth** and other **planets** form the **solar system**. The Earth **orbits** the **sun** and the **moon** orbits the Earth. Everything beyond the Earth's **atmosphere** is **outer space** and the Earth, the planets and the whole of space make up the **universe**. **Astronomers** study the sun, planets and stars; the subject is called **astronomy**. **Astronauts** travel into space in a **space shuttle**. **Satellites** are **launched** into space and are used to send back information, television pictures, etc.
>
> Some people believe that there is life on other planets and that these **aliens** are trying to contact us. Some people who see **UFOs** think that they may be alien **spaceships**.

space² /speɪs/ verb [T] **space sth (out)** to arrange things so that there are empty spaces between them ▶ **rozstawiać, rozkładać**

ˈspace bar noun [C] a bar on the keyboard of a computer or **typewriter** that you press to make spaces between words ▶ **klawisz spacji**

spacecraft /ˈspeɪskrɑːft; US -kræft/ noun [C] (pl. **spacecraft**) a vehicle that travels in space ▶ **pojazd kosmiczny**

ˌspaced ˈout adj. (informal) not completely conscious of what is happening around you, often because of taking drugs ▶ **półprzytomny, przymulony**

spaceman /ˈspeɪsmən/, **spacewoman** /ˈspeɪswʊmən/ noun [C] (pl. **-men** /-mən/; **-women** /-wɪmɪn/) a person who travels in space ▶ **kosmonaut(k)a**

spaceship /ˈspeɪsʃɪp/ noun [C] a vehicle that travels in space, carrying people ▶ **statek kosmiczny**

ˈspace shuttle noun [C] a vehicle that can travel into space and land like a plane when it returns to Earth ▶ **prom kosmiczny**

spacious /ˈspeɪʃəs/ adj. having a lot of space; large in size: *a spacious flat* ▶ **obszerny, przestronny** SYN **roomy**
■ **spaciousness** noun [U] ▶ **obszerność**

spade /speɪd/ noun **1** [C] a tool that you use for digging ▶ **łopata** ➲ look at **shovel** ➲ picture at **garden 2** (**spades**) [pl.]

in a pack of playing cards, the **suit** with pointed black symbols on them: *the king of spades* ▶ **piki** ➲ note at **card 3** [C] one of the cards from this suit: *Have you got a spade?* ▶ **pik**

spaghetti /spəˈgeti/ noun [U] a type of **pasta** that looks like long strings: *How long does spaghetti take to cook?* ▶ **spaghetti** ➲ note at **pasta** ➲ picture on **page A14**

spam /spæm/ noun [U] advertising material sent by email to people who have not asked for it ▶ **spam** ➲ look at **junk mail**

span[1] /spæn/ noun [C] **1** the length of time that sth lasts or continues: *Young children have a short attention span* (małą rozpiętość uwagi). ▶ **rozpiętość 2** the length of sth from one end to the other: *the wingspan* (rozpiętość skrzydeł) *of a bird* ▶ **okres**, **długość** (*czasu, życia*)

span[2] /spæn/ verb [T] (**spanning**; **spanned**) **1** to form a bridge over sth ▶ **łączyć brzegi**, **rozciągać się 2** to last or continue for a particular period of time ▶ **obejmować** (*np. okres*)

spaniel /ˈspænjəl/ noun [C] a dog with large ears which hang down. There are several breeds of spaniel: *a cocker spaniel* ▶ **spaniel**

spank /spæŋk/ verb [T] to hit a child on their bottom with an open hand as a punishment ▶ **dawać klapsa**

spanner /ˈspænə(r)/ (US **wrench**) noun [C] a metal tool with an end shaped for turning **nuts** and **bolts** ▶ **klucz (płaski)** ➲ picture at **tool**

🔑 **spare[1]** /speə(r)/ adj. **1** [only before a noun] not needed now but kept because it may be needed in the future: *The spare tyre is kept in the boot.* ◇ *a spare room* ▶ **pokój gościnny**; **zapasowy 2** not being used; free: *There were no seats spare so we had to stand.* ◇ *Have you got any spare change* (drobne)? ◇ *Are there any tickets* ***going spare?*** Czy są jakieś wolne bilety? ▶ **wolny 3** not used for work: *What do you do in your* ***spare time?*** ▶ **wolny**

■ **spare** noun [C]: *The fuse has blown. Where do you keep your spares?* ▶ **zapasowy bezpiecznik itp.**

spare[2] /speə(r)/ verb [T] **1 spare sth (for sb)**; **spare (sb) sth** to be able to give sth to sb: *I suppose I can spare you a few minutes.* ▶ **darowywać**, **poświęcać 2 spare sb (from) sth/doing sth** to save sb from having an unpleasant experience: *You could spare yourself waiting if you book in advance.* ▶ **oszczędzać 3 spare sb/sth (from sth)** to not hurt or damage sb/sth ▶ **oszczędzać**, **darowywać 4 spare no effort, expense, etc.** to do sth as well as possible without limiting the time, money, etc. involved: *No expense was spared at the wedding.* Nie pożałowano pieniędzy na wesele. ◇ *He spared no effort in trying to find a job.* ▶ **oszczędzać**

IDM **to spare** more than is needed: *There's no time to spare. We must leave straight away.* ▶ (*mieć*) **do stracenia**, (*mieć*) **na zbyciu**

ˌspare ˈpart noun [C] a part for a machine, an engine, etc. that you can use to replace an old part which is damaged or broken ▶ **część zapasowa**

sparing /ˈspeərɪŋ/ adj. (formal) using only a little of sth; careful: *Try to be sparing with the salt.* Nie używaj zbyt dużo soli. ▶ **oszczędny**

■ **sparingly** adv. ▶ **oszczędnie**

spark[1] /spɑːk/ noun **1** [C] a very small bright piece of burning material: *A spark set fire to the carpet.* ▶ **iskra 2** [C] a flash of light that is caused by electricity: *A spark ignites the fuel in a car engine.* ▶ **iskra**; **błysk 3** [C,U] an exciting quality that sb/sth has ▶ **polot**, **przebłysk**

spark[2] /spɑːk/ verb

PHR V **spark sth off** to cause sth: *Eric's comments sparked off a tremendous argument.* ▶ **wywoływać**

sparkle /ˈspɑːkl/ verb [I] to shine with many small points of light: *The river sparkled in the sunlight.* ▶ **skrzyć się**, **iskrzyć się**

■ **sparkle** noun [C,U] ▶ **iskra**

sparkling /ˈspɑːklɪŋ/ adj. **1** shining with many small points of light: *sparkling blue eyes* ▶ **iskrzący (się) 2** (used about a drink) containing bubbles of gas: *sparkling wine/mineral water* ▶ (*wino*) **musujący**, (*woda, napój*) **gazowany** SYN **fizzy** ➲ look at **still 3** full of life; appearing interesting and intelligent: *a sparkling, witty speech* ▶ **ognisty**, **pełen werwy**

ˈspark plug noun [C] a small piece of equipment in an engine that produces a **spark** of electricity to make the fuel burn and start the engine ▶ **świeca zapłonowa**

sparrow /ˈspærəʊ/ noun [C] a small brown and grey bird that is common in many parts of the world ▶ **wróbel**

sparse /spɑːs/ adj. small in quantity or amount: *a sparse crowd* ◇ *He just had a few sparse hairs on his head.* ▶ **rzadki**

■ **sparsely** adv.: *a sparsely populated area* ▶ **rzadko** | **sparseness** noun [U] ▶ **rzadkość**

spartan /ˈspɑːtn/ adj. (formal) very simple and not comfortable: *spartan living conditions* ▶ **spartański**

spasm /ˈspæzəm/ noun [C,U] a sudden movement of a muscle that you cannot control: *He had painful muscular spasms in his leg.* ▶ **kurcz**, **skurcz**

spasmodic /spæzˈmɒdɪk/ adj. **1** happening suddenly for short periods of time; not regular or continuous: *There was spasmodic fighting in the area yesterday.* ▶ **podejmowany zrywami**; **nieregularny 2** caused by your muscles becoming tight in a way that you cannot control: *spasmodic movements* ▶ **spazmatyczny**

■ **spasmodically** /-kli/ adv. ▶ **zrywami**; **spazmatycznie**

spat past tense, past participle of **spit[1]**

spate /speɪt/ noun [sing.] a large number or amount of sth happening at one time: *There has been a spate of burglaries* (seria włamań) *in the area recently.* ▶ **napływ**, **natłok**

spatial /ˈspeɪʃl/ adj. (formal) connected with the size or position of sth ▶ **przestrzenny**

spatter /ˈspætə(r)/ verb [T] **spatter sb/sth (with sth)**; **spatter sth (on sb/sth)** to cover sb/sth with small drops of sth wet ▶ **opryskiwać**

spatula /ˈspætʃələ/ noun [C] a tool with a wide flat part, used in cooking for mixing and spreading things ▶ **łopatka**, **szpachelka** ➲ picture at **kitchen**, **laboratory**

🔑 **speak** /spiːk/ verb (pt **spoke** /spəʊk/, pp **spoken** /ˈspəʊkən/) **1** [I] **speak (to sb) (about sb/sth)**; **speak (of sth)** to talk or say things: *I'd like to speak to the manager, please.* ◇ *Could you speak more slowly?* ◇ *I was so angry I could hardly speak.* ▶ **mówić**, **rozmawiać**

> **Speak** i **talk** mają prawie takie samo znaczenie, chociaż **speak** jest nieco bardziej formalne. **Talk** odnosi się raczej do rozmowy, podczas gdy **speak** często używa się w sytuacji, kiedy mówi tylko jedna osoba: *We talked all night.* ◇ *Speaking personally, I'm all in favour of the idea.* ◇ *The head teacher spoke to the class about university courses.* ◇ *I'd like to speak to the manager, please.*

2 [T] [not used in the continuous tenses] to know and be able to use a language: *Does anyone here speak German?* ◇ *She speaks (in) Greek to her parents.* ◇ *a French-speaking guide* ▶ (*np. po angielsku*) **mówić 3** [I] **speak (on/about sth)** to make a speech to a group of people: *Professor Hurst has been invited to speak on American foreign policy.* ▶ **przemawiać (na jakiś temat)**

IDM **be on speaking terms (with sb)** to be friendly with sb again after an argument: *Thankfully they are back on speaking terms again.* ▶ **pogodzić się**

be speaking (to sb) (informal) to be friendly with sb again after an argument ▶ **rozmawiać (z kimś)**

so to speak (used when you are describing sth in a way that sounds strange): *She turned green, so to speak, after watching a TV programme about the environment.* ▶ **że tak powiem**
speak for itself to be very clear so that no other explanation is needed: *The statistics speak for themselves.* ▶ **mówić samo za siebie**
speak/talk of the devil → DEVIL
speak your mind to say exactly what you think, even though you might offend sb ▶ **wypowiadać swoje zdanie** (*bez ogródek*)
strictly speaking → STRICTLY
PHR V **speak for sb** to express the thoughts or opinions of sb else ▶ **mówić za kogoś**
speak out (against sth) to say publicly that you think sth is bad or wrong ▶ **mówić otwarcie (przeciwko czemuś)**
speak up to speak louder ▶ **mówić głośniej**

speaker /'spi:kə(r)/ noun [C] **1** a person who makes a speech to a group of people: *Tonight's speaker is a well-known writer and journalist.* ▶ **mów-ca/czyni 2** a person who speaks a particular language: *She's a fluent Russian speaker.* ▶ **osoba mówiąca określonym językiem 3** (also **loudspeaker**) the part of a radio, computer or piece of musical equipment that the sound comes out of ▶ **głośnik**

spear /spɪə(r)/ noun [C] a long pole with a sharp point at one end, used for hunting or fighting ▶ **włócznia**

spearhead /'spɪəhed/ noun [C, usually sing.] a person or group that begins or leads an attack ▶ **osoba lub grupa rozpoczynająca lub przeprowadzająca atak**
■ **spearhead** verb [T] ▶ **przewodzić, stawać na czele**

spearmint /'spɪəmɪnt/ noun [U] a type of leaf with a strong fresh taste that is used in sweets, etc.: *spearmint chewing gum* ▶ **mięta zielona** ➲ look at **peppermint**

special¹ /'speʃl/ adj. **1** not usual or ordinary; important for some particular reason: *a special occasion* ◇ *Please take special care of it.* ◇ *Are you doing anything special tonight?* ▶ **specjalny, szczególny 2** [only before a noun] for a particular purpose: *Andy goes to a special school for the deaf.* ◇ *There's a special tool for doing that.* ▶ **specjalny**

special² /'speʃl/ noun [C] something that is not of the usual or ordinary type: *I'm going to cook one of my specials tonight.* ◇ *the all-night election special* (specjalny program wyborczy) *on TV* ▶ **nadzwyczajne wydarzenie**

ˌspecial efˈfects noun [pl.] unusual or exciting pieces of action in films/movies or television programmes, that are created by computers or clever photography to show things that do not normally exist or happen ▶ **efekty specjalne**

specialism /'speʃəlɪzəm/ noun **1** [C] an area of study or work that sb **specializes** in: *a business degree with a specialism in computing* ▶ **specjalizacja 2** [U] the fact of **specializing** in a particular subject ▶ **specjalizacja**

specialist /'speʃəlɪst/ noun [C] a person with special or deep knowledge of a particular subject: *She's a specialist in diseases of cattle.* ◇ *I have to see a heart specialist.* ◇ *to give specialist advice* udzielić specjalistycznej porady ▶ **specjalist(k)a**

speciality /ˌspeʃi'æləti/ noun [C] (pl. **specialities**) (US **specialty** /'speʃəlti/, pl. **specialties**) **1** something made by a person, place, business, etc. that is very good and that he/she/it is known for: *The cheese is a speciality of the region.* ▶ **specjalność 2** an area of study or a subject that you know a lot about ▶ **specjalizacja**

specialize (also **-ise**) /'speʃəlaɪz/ verb [I] **specialize (in sth)** to give most of your attention to one subject, type of product, etc.: *This shop specializes in clothes for taller men.* ▶ **specjalizować się (w czymś)**
■ **specialization** (also **-isation**) /ˌspeʃəlaɪ'zeɪʃn; US -lə'z-/ noun [U] ▶ **specjalizacja**

specialized (also **-ised**) /'speʃəlaɪzd/ adj. **1** to be used for a particular purpose: *a specialized system* ▶ **wyspecjalizowany 2** having or needing deep or special knowledge of a particular subject: *We have specialized staff to help you with any problems.* ▶ **wyspecjalizowany**

specially /'speʃəli/ (also **especially**) adv. **1** for a particular purpose or reason: *I made this specially for you.* ▶ **specjalnie 2** particularly; very; more than usual: *The restaurant has a great atmosphere but the food is not specially good.* ◇ *It's not an especially difficult exam.* ▶ **szczególnie**

ˌspecial 'school noun [C] a school for children who have physical or learning problems ▶ **szkoła specjalna**

specialty (US) = SPECIALITY

species /'spi:ʃi:z/ noun [C] (pl. **species**) a group of plants or animals that are all the same and that can breed together: *This conservation group aims to protect endangered species.* ◇ *a rare species of frog* ▶ **gatunek**

specific /spə'sɪfɪk/ adj. **1 specific (about sth)** detailed or exact: *You must give the class specific instructions on what they have to do.* ◇ *Can you be more specific about what the man was wearing?* ▶ **ścisły, szczegółowy 2** particular; not general: *Everyone has been given a specific job to do.* ▶ **specyficzny**
■ **specifically** /-kli/ adv.: *a play written specifically for radio* ▶ **specjalnie**

specification /ˌspesɪfɪ'keɪʃn/ noun [C,U] detailed information about how sth is or should be built or made ▶ **specyfikacja**

specify /'spesɪfaɪ/ verb [T] (**specifying**; **specifies**; pt, pp **specified**) to say or name sth clearly or in detail: *The fire regulations specify the maximum number of people allowed in.* ▶ **wymieniać, precyzować**

specimen /'spesɪmən/ noun [C] **1** a small amount of sth that is tested for medical or scientific purposes: *Specimens of the patient's blood were tested in the hospital laboratory.* ▶ **okaz 2** an example of a particular type of thing, especially intended to be studied by experts or scientists ▶ **próbka** SYN for both meanings **sample**

speck /spek/ noun [C] a very small spot or mark: *a speck of dust/dirt* ▶ **pyłek, punkcik**

speckled /'spekld/ adj. with small marks or spots: *a speckled hen* ◇ *speckled eggs* ▶ **nakrapiany**

specs (informal) = GLASSES

spectacle /'spektəkl/ noun [C] something that is impressive or shocking to look at ▶ **widowisko**

spectacles (formal) = GLASSES

spectacular /spek'tækjələ(r)/ adj. very impressive to see: *The view from the top of the hill is quite spectacular.* ▶ **widowiskowy, okazały**
■ **spectacularly** adv. ▶ **widowiskowo, okazale**

spectator /spek'teɪtə(r); US 'spekteɪ-/ noun [C] a person who is watching an event, especially a sports event ▶ **widz**

spec'tator sport noun [C] a sport that many people watch; a sport that is interesting to watch ▶ **sport widowiskowy**

spectre (US **specter**) /'spektə(r)/ noun [C] **1** something unpleasant that people are afraid might happen in the future: *the spectre of unemployment* ▶ **widmo, upiór 2** (old-fashioned) = GHOST

spectrum /'spektrəm/ noun [C, usually sing.] (pl. **spectra** /'spektrə/) **1** the set of seven colours into which white light can be separated: *You can see the colours of the spectrum in a rainbow.* ▶ **widmo** (*fizyczne*) **2** all the possible varieties of sth: *The speakers represented the whole spectrum of political opinions.* ▶ **spektrum**

speculate /ˈspekjuleɪt/ verb **1** [I,T] **speculate (about/on sth); speculate that...** to make a guess about sth: *to speculate about the result of the next election* ▶ **spekulować 2** [I] to buy and sell with the aim of making money but with the risk of losing it: *to speculate on the stock market* ▶ **spekulować**
■ **speculation** /ˌspekjuˈleɪʃn/ noun [U,C] ▶ **spekulacja** | **speculator** /ˈspekjuleɪtə(r)/ noun [C] ▶ **spekulant/ka**

speculative /ˈspekjələtɪv/ adj. **1** based on guessing or on opinions that have been formed without knowing all the facts ▶ **spekulatywny 2** (used in business) done in the hope of making money, but involving the risk of losing it ▶ **spekulacyjny**

sped past tense, past participle of **speed**[2]

speech /spiːtʃ/ noun **1** [C] a formal talk that you give to a group of people: *The Chancellor is going to make a speech* (wygłosić mowę) *to city businessmen.* ▶ **przemówienie, mowa 2** [U] the ability to speak: *He lost the* ***power of speech*** *after the accident.* ◇ *freedom of speech* wolność słowa ▶ **mowa 3** [U] the particular way of speaking of a person or group of people: *She's doing a study of children's speech.* ▶ **mowa 4** [C] a group of words that one person must say in a play: *This character has the longest speech in the play.* ▶ **mowa**

speechless /ˈspiːtʃləs/ adj. not able to speak, for example because you are shocked, angry, etc.: *He was speechless with rage.* ▶ **oniemiały**

ˌspeech ˈtherapy noun [U] special treatment to help people who have problems in speaking clearly, for example in pronouncing particular sounds ▶ **terapia logopedyczna**
■ **ˌspeech ˈtherapist** noun [C] ▶ **logopeda**

speed[1] /spiːd/ noun **1** [U] fast movement: *I intend to start the race slowly and gradually* ***pick up speed*** (nabierać prędkości). ◇ *With* ***a burst of speed*** (zrywając się), *the rabbit got away from the dog.* ◇ *The bus was travelling* ***at speed*** (bardzo szybko) *when it hit the wall.* ▶ **szybkość, prędkość 2** [C,U] the rate at which sb/sth moves or travels: *The car was travelling* ***at a speed of*** *140 kilometres an hour.* ◇ *to travel* ***at top/high/full/maximum speed*** ▶ **prędkość, szybkość**

speed[2] /spiːd/ verb [I] (pt, pp **sped** /sped/) **1** to go or move very quickly: *He sped round the corner on his bicycle.* ▶ **pędzić, mknąć 2** [only used in the continuous tenses] to drive a car, etc. faster than the legal speed limit: *The police said she had been speeding.* ▶ **przekraczać dozwoloną przepisami szybkość**
PHR V **speed (sth) up** (pt, pp **speeded**) to go or make sth go faster: *The new computer system should speed up production in the factory.* ▶ **przyśpieszać**

speedboat /ˈspiːdbəʊt/ noun [C] a small fast boat with an engine ▶ **ślizgacz**

speeded past tense, past participle of **speed**[2]

ˈspeed hump (US usually **ˈspeed bump**) noun [C] a raised area across a road that is put there to make traffic go slower ▶ **poprzeczny garb na jezdni** (*stosowany w celu zmniejszenia szybkości pojazdów*), **szykana**

speeding /ˈspiːdɪŋ/ noun [U] driving a car, etc. faster than the legal speed limit ▶ **przekraczanie dozwolonej prędkości**

ˈspeed limit noun [C, usually sing.] the highest speed that you may drive without breaking the law on a particular road: *He was going way* ***over the speed limit*** *when the police stopped him.* ▶ **ograniczenie prędkości** ➲ note at **driving**

speedometer /spiːˈdɒmɪtə(r)/ noun [C] a piece of equipment in a vehicle that tells you how fast you are travelling ▶ **szybkościomierz** ➲ picture at **car**

speedway /ˈspiːdweɪ/ noun [U] the sport of racing motorbikes around a special track ▶ **żużel**

speedy /ˈspiːdi/ adj. (**speedier**; **speediest**) fast; quick: *a speedy response/reply* ◇ *to make a speedy recovery from an illness* szybko wyzdrowieć ▶ **szybki**
■ **speedily** adv. ▶ **szybko** | **speediness** noun [U] ▶ **szybkość, prędkość**

spell[1] /spel/ verb (pt, pp **spelled** /speld/ or **spelt** /spelt/) **1** [I,T] to write or say the letters of a word in the correct order: *I could never spell very well at school.* ◇ ***How do you spell your surname?*** ◇ *His name is spelt P-H-I-L-I-P.* ▶ **literować 2** [T] (used about a set of letters) to form a particular word: *If you add an 'e' to 'car', it spells 'care'.* ▶ **pisać (się) 3** [T] to mean sth; to have sth as a result: *Another poor harvest would* ***spell disaster*** *for the region.* ▶ **znaczyć**
PHR V **spell sth out 1** to express sth in a very clear and direct way: *Although she didn't spell it out, it was obvious she wasn't happy.* ▶ **precyzować coś 2** to write or say the letters of a word or name in the correct order: *I have an unusual name, so I always have to spell it out to people.* ▶ **przeliterowywać coś**

spell[2] /spel/ noun [C] **1** a short period of time: *a spell of cold weather* ▶ **krótki okres 2** (especially in stories) magic words or actions that cause sb to be in a particular state or condition: *The witch* ***put/cast a spell on*** *the prince.* ◇ (figurative) *He's completely* ***under her spell.*** ▶ **urok, czar; zaklęcie**

spellbinding /ˈspelbaɪndɪŋ/ adj. holding your attention completely: *a spellbinding performance* ▶ **urzekający** SYN **enthralling**

spellcheck /ˈspeltʃek/ verb [T] to use a computer program to check your writing to see if your spelling is correct ▶ (*komput.*) **stosować funkcję sprawdzania pisowni**
■ **spellcheck** = SPELLCHECKER

spellchecker /ˈspeltʃekə(r)/ noun [C] a computer program that checks your writing to see if your spelling is correct ▶ (*komput.*) **program do sprawdzania pisowni**

spelling /ˈspelɪŋ/ noun **1** [U] the ability to write the letters of a word correctly: *Roger is very poor at spelling.* ▶ **ortografia 2** [C,U] the way that letters are arranged to make a word: *'Center' is the American spelling of 'centre'.* ▶ **pisownia**

spelt past tense, past participle of **spell**[1]

spend /spend/ verb (pt, pp **spent** /spent/) **1** [I,T] **spend (sth) (on sth)** to give or pay money for sth: *How much do you spend on food each week?* ◇ *You shouldn't go on spending like that.* ▶ **wydawać 2** [T] **spend sth (on sth/doing sth)** to pass time: *I spent a whole evening writing letters.* ◇ *I'm spending the weekend at my parents' house.* ◇ *He spent two years in Rome.* ◇ *I don't want to spend too much time on this project.* ▶ **spędzać**

spending /ˈspendɪŋ/ noun [U] the amount of money that is spent by a government or an organization ▶ **nakłady**

spendthrift /ˈspendθrɪft/ noun [C] a person who spends too much money or who wastes money ▶ **rozrzutni-k/ca**
■ **spendthrift** adj. [usually before a noun] ▶ **rozrzutny**

spent past tense, past participle of **spend**

sperm /spɜːm/ noun **1** [C] (pl. **sperm** or **sperms**) a cell that is produced in the sex organs of a male and that can join with a female egg to produce young ▶ **plemnik 2** [U] the liquid that contains **sperms** ▶ **sperma, nasienie**

spew /spjuː/ verb [I,T] **1** [I] to flow out quickly, or to make sth flow out quickly, in large amounts: *Flames spewed* (buchały) *from the aircraft's engine.* ◇ *Massive chimneys were spewing out smoke.* ▶ **wypływać** (*z dużą szybkoś-*

S

cią), **wypluwać 2 spew (sth) (up)** (Brit., informal) to **vomit**: *He spewed up on the pavement.* ◇ *He makes me want to spew.* ▶ **wyrzygać (się)**

sphere /sfɪə(r)/ noun [C] **1** any round object shaped like a ball ▶ **kula 2** an area of interest or activity ▶ **sfera, dziedzina**
■ **spherical** /'sferɪkl/ adj. ▶ **kulisty**

spice¹ /spaɪs/ noun **1** [C,U] a substance, especially a powder, that is made from a plant and used to give flavour to food: *I use a lot of herbs and spices in my cooking.* ◇ *Pepper and paprika are two common spices.* ▶ **przyprawa** ➲ look at **herb 2** [U] excitement and interest: *to **add spice** to a situation* ▶ **pikanteria**
■ **spicy** adj. (**spicier**; **spiciest**): *Do you like spicy food?* ▶ **ostry, pikantny**

spice² /spaɪs/ verb [T] **spice sth (up) (with sth) 1** to add spice to food: *He always spices his cooking with lots of chilli powder.* ▶ **doprawiać (potrawę) 2** to add excitement to sth ▶ **nadawać pikanterii**

spider /'spaɪdə(r)/ noun [C] a small creature with eight thin legs ▶ **pająk**

Spiders **spin webs** to catch insects for food.

spies → SPY

spike /spaɪk/ noun [C] a piece of metal, wood, etc. that has a sharp point at one end ▶ **szpic, kolec**

spiky /'spaɪki/ adj. (**spikier**; **spikiest**) **1** having sharp points: *spiky plants, such as cacti* ▶ **kolczasty 2** (used about hair) sticking straight up from the head ▶ **sterczący 3** (Brit.) (used about people) easily annoyed or offended ▶ **wybuchowy, drażliwy**

spill /spɪl/ verb [I,T] (pt, pp **spilt** /spɪlt/ or **spilled**) **1** (used especially about a liquid) to accidentally come out of a container; to make a liquid, etc. do this: *Some water had spilled out of the bucket onto the floor.* ◇ *The bag split, and sugar spilled everywhere.* ◇ *I've spilt some coffee on the desk.* ▶ **rozlewać (się) 2** [I] **spill out, over, into, etc.** (used about people) to come out of a place suddenly and go in different directions: *The train stopped and everyone spilled out.* ◇ *There were so many people that the party spilled over into the garden.* ▶ (*przen.*) **wysypywać/wylewać się**
■ **spill** noun [C]: *Many seabirds died as a result of the oil spill.* ▶ **wyciek**
IDM **spill the beans** (informal) to tell a person about sth that should be a secret ▶ **wygadać się, puszczać farbę**

spin¹ /spɪn/ verb (**spinning**; pt, pp **spun** /spʌn/) **1** [I,T] **spin (sth) (round)** to turn or to make sth turn round quickly: *Mary spun round when she heard someone call her name.* ◇ *to spin a ball/wheel* ◇ *to spin a coin* podrzucać monetę (żeby zawirowała) ◇ *After three glasses of wine **my head was spinning*** (kręciło mi się w głowie). ▶ **obracać (się) 2** [I,T] to make thread from a mass of wool, cotton, etc.: *She spun and dyed the wool herself.* ▶ **prząść 3** [T] to remove water from clothes that have just been washed in a washing machine by turning them round and round very fast ▶ **odwirowywać**
PHR V **spin sth out** to make sth last as long as possible ▶ **rozciągać, przedłużać**

spin² /spɪn/ noun [C,U] **1** an act of making sth **spin¹** (1): *to **put** some **spin on** a ball* podkręcać piłkę ▶ **wirowanie, kręcenie się 2** (especially in politics) a way of talking publicly about a difficult situation, a mistake, etc. that makes it sound positive for you ▶ **korzystne dla siebie przedstawienie popełnionego błędu/zaistniałej sytuacji**
IDM **go/take sb for a spin** to go/take sb out in a car or other vehicle ▶ **jechać/zabierać kogoś na przejażdżkę**

spina bifida /ˌspaɪnə 'bɪfɪdə/ noun [U] a medical condition in which some bones in the **spine** have not developed normally at birth, often causing **paralysis** in the legs ▶ **rozszczep kręgosłupa**

spinach /'spɪnɪtʃ; -ɪdʒ/ noun [U] a plant with large dark green leaves that can be cooked and eaten as a vegetable ▶ **szpinak**

spinal /'spaɪnl/ adj. connected with the **spine** ▶ **kręgowy, rdzeniowy**

ˌspinal 'cord noun [C, usually sing.] a mass of nerve fibres that are in the **spine**, connecting all parts of the body with the brain ▶ **rdzeń kręgowy**

'spin doctor noun [C] (especially in politics) a person who finds ways of talking about difficult situations, mistakes, etc. in a positive way ▶ **osoba, która zawsze usprawiedliwia czyjeś błędy, znajduje pozytywne strony trudności itp.**

ˌspin 'dryer noun [C] (Brit.) a machine that removes water from wet clothes by turning them round and round very fast ▶ **wirówka**
■ **ˌspin-'dry** verb [T] ▶ **wirować**

spine /spaɪn/ noun [C] **1** the row of small bones that are connected together down the middle of your back ▶ **kręgosłup** SYN **backbone** ➲ picture at **body 2** one of the sharp points like needles on some plants and animals: *Porcupines use their spines to protect themselves.* ▶ **kolec, cierń** ➲ look at **prickle 3** the narrow part of the cover of a book that you can see when it is on a shelf ▶ **grzbiet**

spineless /'spaɪnləs/ adj. weak and easily frightened ▶ (*osoba*) **bez kręgosłupa**

'spinning wheel noun [C] a simple machine that people used in their homes in the past for twisting wool, etc. It has a large wheel operated with the foot. ▶ **kołowrotek**

'spin-off noun [C] **a spin-off (from/of sth)** something unexpected and useful that develops from sth else ▶ **efekt uboczny**

spinster /'spɪnstə(r)/ noun [C] (old-fashioned) a woman, especially an older woman, who has never been married ▶ **stara panna** ➲ look at **bachelor** ⓘ Mówiąc o nieżonatym mężczyźnie lub niezamężnej kobiecie, obecnie najczęściej używa się słowa **single**: *a single woman.*

spiral /'spaɪrəl/ noun [C] a long curved line that moves round and round away from a central point ▶ **spirala**
■ **spiral** adj.: *a spiral staircase* kręcone schody ▶ **spiralny** | **spiral** verb [I] (**spiralling**; **spiralled**; US **spiraling**; **spiraled**): *The plane spiralled to the ground.* ▶ **wznosić się; opadać**

spire /'spaɪə(r)/ noun [C] a tall pointed tower on the top of a church ▶ **iglica**

spirit¹ /'spɪrɪt/ noun **1** [sing.] the part of a person that is not physical; your thoughts and feelings, not your body: *the power of the human spirit to overcome difficulties* ▶ **duch 2** [C] the mood, attitude or state of mind of sb/sth: *to be **in high/low spirits*** być w dobrym/złym nastroju ◇ *Everyone **entered into the spirit** of the party.* Wszyscy poddali się nastrojowi przyjęcia. ▶ **duch, nastrój 3** (**-spirited**) [in compounds] having the mood or attitude of mind mentioned: *a group of high-spirited teenagers* grupa pełnych werwy nastolatków ▶ **(***określa nastrój***) 4** [U] energy, strength of mind or determination: *The group had plenty of **team spirit**.* ▶ **duch, animusz 5** [sing.] the typical or most important quality of sth: *the pioneer spirit* ◇ *The painting perfectly captures the spirit of the times.* ▶ **duch 6** [C] a being without a body; the part of a person that many people believe still exists after their body is dead: *It was believed that people could be possessed by **evil spirits**.* ◇ *the Holy Spirit* Duch Święty ▶ **duch** ➲ look at **ghost, soul 7** (**spirits**) [pl.] (especially Brit.) strong alcoholic drinks, for example **whisky** and **vodka**: *I never drink spirits.* ▶ **mocny alkohol**

spirit² /ˈspɪrɪt/ verb
PHR V **spirit sb/sth away/off** to take sb/sth away secretly ▶ **zabierać/wywozić (kogoś/coś) po kryjomu**

spirited /ˈspɪrɪtɪd/ adj. full of energy, determination and courage ▶ **ożywiony, porywający**

ˈ**spirit level** noun [C] a glass tube partly filled with liquid, with a bubble of air inside. **Spirit levels** are used to test whether a surface is level, by the position of the bubble. ▶ **poziomnica**

spiritual¹ /ˈspɪrɪtʃuəl/ adj. **1** connected with deep thoughts, feelings or emotions rather than the body or physical things: *spiritual development/growth/needs* ▶ **duchowy** ➲ look at **material 2** connected with religion: *a spiritual leader* ▶ **duchowy**
■ **spiritually** /-tʃuəli/ adv. ▶ **duchowo**

spiritual² /ˈspɪrɪtʃuəl/ (also ˌ**Negro ˈspiritual** /ˈniːgrəʊ/) noun [C] a religious song of the type originally sung by black **slaves** in America ▶ **negro spiritual**

spiritualism /ˈspɪrɪtʃuəlɪzəm/ noun [U] the belief that people who have died can get messages to living people, usually through a **medium** ▶ **spirytyzm**
■ **spiritualist** /-ɪst/ noun [C] ▶ **spirytyst(k)a**

spit¹ /spɪt/ verb [I,T] (**spitting**; pt, pp **spat** /spæt/) ❶ W Amer. ang. czas przeszły i imiesłów bierny czasu przeszłego też mogą przyjmować formę **spit**. **spit (sth) (out)** to force liquid, food, etc. out from your mouth: *He took one sip of the wine and spat it out.* ▶ **pluć**

spit² /spɪt/ noun **1** [U] (informal) the liquid in your mouth ▶ **ślina, plwocina** ➲ look at **saliva 2** [C] a long, thin piece of land that sticks out into the sea, a lake, etc. ▶ **cypel, mierzeja 3** [C] a long thin metal stick that you put through meat to hold it when you cook it over a fire: *chicken roasted **on a spit*** ▶ **rożen**

spite /spaɪt/ noun [U] the desire to hurt or annoy sb: *He stole her letters **out of spite**.* ▶ **złośliwość**
■ **spite** verb [T]: *I think he only said it to spite me* (na złość). ▶ **urażać**
IDM **in spite of** (used to show that sth happened although you did not expect it): *In spite of all her hard work, Sue failed her exam.* ◇ *Ben lost the race, in spite of running fast.* ▶ **pomimo, wbrew** SYN **despite**

spiteful /ˈspaɪtfl/ adj. behaving in a cruel or unkind way in order to hurt or upset sb: *He's been saying a lot of spiteful things about his ex-girlfriend.* ▶ **złośliwy**
■ **spitefully** /-fəli/ adv. ▶ **złośliwie**

ˌ**spitting ˈimage** noun
IDM **be the spitting image of sb** to look exactly like sb else: *She's the spitting image of her mother.* Jest podobna do swojej matki jakby skórę zdjął. ▶ **być bardzo podobnym do kogoś**

splash¹ /splæʃ/ verb [I,T] (used about a liquid) to fall or to make liquid fall noisily or fly in drops onto a person or thing: *Rain splashed against the windows.* ◇ *The children were splashing each other with water.* ◇ *Be careful not to splash paint onto the floor.* ▶ **chlapać**
PHR V **splash out (on sth)** (Brit., informal) to spend money on sth that is expensive and that you do not really need ▶ **wykosztować się**

splash² /splæʃ/ noun [C] **1** the sound of liquid hitting sth or of sth hitting liquid: *Paul jumped into the pool with a big splash.* ▶ **plusk 2** a small amount of liquid that falls onto sth: *splashes of oil on the cooker* ▶ **plama 3** a small bright area of colour: *Flowers add **a splash of colour** to a room.* ▶ **plama**

splatter /ˈsplætə(r)/ verb [I,T] (used about a liquid) to fly about in large drops and hit sb/sth noisily: *The paint was splattered all over the floor.* ◇ *Heavy rain splattered on the roof.* ▶ **ochlapywać, obryzgiwać**

splay /spleɪ/ verb [I,T] **splay (sth) (out)** to make fingers, legs, etc. become further apart from each other or spread out; to become spread out wide apart: *splayed fingers* ▶ **rozcapierzać, rozszerzać**

splendid /ˈsplendɪd/ adj. **1** very good; excellent: *What a splendid idea!* ▶ **doskonały, wspaniały** SYN **great 2** very impressive: *the splendid royal palace* ▶ **okazały, świetny**
■ **splendidly** adv. ▶ **doskonale, wspaniale**

splendour (US **splendor**) /ˈsplendə(r)/ noun [U] very impressive beauty ▶ **wspaniałość, okazałość**

splint /splɪnt/ noun [C] a piece of wood or metal that is tied to a broken arm or leg to keep it in the right position ▶ **szyna chirurgiczna, łupek**

splinter /ˈsplɪntə(r)/ noun [C] a small thin sharp piece of wood, metal or glass that has broken off a larger piece: *I've got a splinter in my finger.* ▶ **drzazga, odłamek**
■ **splinter** verb [I,T] ▶ **rozłupywać (się), rozszczepiać (się)**

split¹ /splɪt/ verb (**splitting**; pt, pp **split**) **1** [I,T] **split (sb) (up) (into sth)** to divide or to make a group of people divide into smaller groups: *Let's split into two groups.* ◇ *A debate that has **split** the country **down the middle*** (podzieliła kraj na połowę). ▶ **(po)dzielić (się) 2** [T] **split sth (between sb/sth); split sth (with sb)** to divide or share sth: *We split the cost of the meal between the six of us.* ▶ **dzielić (się) (czymś) 3** [I,T] **split (sth) (open)** to break or make sth break along a straight line: *My jeans have split.* ▶ **rozdzierać (się), rozłupywać (się)**
IDM **split the difference** (used when discussing a price) to agree on an amount that is at an equal distance between the two amounts that have been suggested ▶ **dojść do porozumienia krakowskim targiem** (*w sprawie ceny/płatności*)
split hairs (usually used in a critical way) to pay too much attention in an argument to details that are very small and not important ▶ **dzielić włos na czworo**
PHR V **split away/off (from sth); split sth away/off (from sth)** to separate from, or to separate sth from, a larger object or group: *A rebel faction has split away from the main group.* ◇ *The storm split a branch off from the main trunk.* ▶ **oderwać się (od czegoś)**
split up (with sb) to end a marriage or relationship: *He's split up with his girlfriend.* ▶ **rozchodzić się (z kimś)**
split sth up to divide sth into smaller parts: *The day was split up into 6 one-hour sessions.* ▶ **dzielić coś**

split² /splɪt/ noun [C] **1** a disagreement that divides a group of people: *Disagreement about European policy led to a split within the Conservative party.* ▶ **rozłam, podział 2** a long cut or hole in sth: *There's a big split in the tent.* ▶ **rysa, pęknięcie**

ˌ**split ˈsecond** noun [C] a very short period of time ▶ **ułamek sekundy**
■ **split-ˈsecond** adj. [only before a noun] done very quickly or very accurately ▶ **błyskawiczny; bardzo dokładny**

splurge /splɜːdʒ/ noun [usually sing.] (informal) an act of spending a lot of money on sth that you do not really need ▶ **szastanie pieniędzmi**
■ **splurge** verb [T,I] **splurge (sth) (on sth)** (informal) to spend a lot of money on sth that you do not really need ▶ **szastać pieniędzmi**

splutter /ˈsplʌtə(r)/ verb **1** [I,T] to speak with difficulty, for example because you are very angry or embarrassed: *'How dare you!' she spluttered indignantly.* ▶ **wykrztusić 2** [I] to make a series of sounds like a person coughing ▶ **prychać**
■ **splutter** noun [C] ▶ **bełkot, prychanie**

spoil /spɔɪl/ verb [T] (pt, pp **spoilt** /spɔɪlt/ or **spoiled** /spɔɪld/) **1** to change sth good into sth bad, unpleasant, useless, etc.; to ruin sth: *The new office block will spoil the view.* ◇ *Our holiday was spoilt by bad weather.* ◇ *Eating*

S

between meals will ***spoil*** *your* ***appetite.*** ▶ **psuć 2** to do too much for sb, especially a child, so that you have a bad effect on their character: *a spoilt child* ▶ **psuć, rozpieszczać 3 spoil sb/yourself** to do sth special or nice to make sb/yourself happy: *Why not spoil yourself with one of our new range of beauty products?* ▶ **dogadzać, rozpieszczać**

spoils /spɔɪlz/ noun [pl.] (formal) things that have been stolen by thieves, or taken in a war or battle: *the spoils of war* ▶ **łup, zdobycz**

spoilsport /ˈspɔɪlspɔːt/ noun [C] (informal) a person who tries to stop other people enjoying themselves, for example by not taking part in an activity ▶ **osoba psująca innym zabawę**

spoilt past tense, past participle of **spoil**

spoke¹ /spəʊk/ noun [C] one of the thin pieces of metal that connect the centre of a wheel to the outside edge ▶ **szprycha** ➲ picture at **bicycle**

spoke² past tense of **speak**

⚷ **spoken** past participle of **speak**

spokesman /ˈspəʊksmən/, **spokeswoman** /ˈspəʊkswʊmən/, **spokesperson** /ˈspəʊkspɜːsn/ noun [C] (pl. **-men** /-mən/; **-women** /-wɪmɪn/; **-persons** or **-people** /-ˈpiːpl/) a person who is chosen to speak for a group or an organization ▶ **rzeczni-k/czka** ⓘ Obecnie istnieje tendencja do używania słowa **spokesperson**, ponieważ można je używać zarówno w odniesieniu do kobiety, jak i mężczyzny.

sponge¹ /spʌndʒ/ noun [C,U] **1** a piece of artificial or natural material that is soft and light and full of holes and can hold water easily, used for washing yourself or cleaning sth ▶ **gąbka 2** = SPONGE CAKE

sponge² /spʌndʒ/ verb [T] to remove or clean sth with a wet **sponge¹** (1) or cloth ▶ **myć/wycierać gąbką**

PHR V **sponge off sb** (informal) to get money, food, etc. from sb without paying or doing anything in return ▶ **pasożytować na kimś**

ˈ**sponge bag** (Brit. ˈ**toilet bag**; US ˈ**toiletry bag**) noun [C] a small bag that you use when travelling to carry the things you need to wash, clean your teeth, etc. ▶ **kosmetyczka**

ˈ**sponge cake** (also **sponge**) noun [C,U] a light cake made from eggs, flour and sugar, with or without fat ▶ **biszkopt**

sponsor /ˈspɒnsə(r)/ noun [C] **1** a person or an organization that helps to pay for a special sports event, etc. (usually so that it can advertise its products) ▶ **sponsor/ka** ➲ look at **patron 2** a person who agrees to pay money to a charity if sb else completes a particular activity ▶ **sponsor/ka**

■ **sponsor** verb [T]: *a sponsored walk to raise money for children in need* ▶ **sponsorować** | **sponsorship** noun [U]: *Many theatres depend on industry for sponsorship.* ▶ **sponsorowanie**

spontaneous /spɒnˈteɪniəs/ adj. done or happening suddenly; not planned: *a spontaneous burst of applause* ▶ **spontaniczny**

■ **spontaneously** adv. ▶ **spontanicznie** | **spontaneity** /ˌspɒntəˈneɪəti/ noun [U] ▶ **spontaniczność**

spoof /spuːf/ noun [C] (informal) an amusing copy of a film, TV programme, etc. that exaggerates its main characteristics: *It's a spoof on horror movies.* ▶ **parodia** (*np. filmu, powieści*)

spook /spuːk/ noun [C] (informal) **1** a ghost ▶ **duch 2** (especially US) a **spy**: *a CIA spook* ▶ **szpieg**

■ **spook** verb [I,T] (especially US, informal) to frighten a person or an animal; to become frightened: *We were spooked by the strange noises and lights.* ◇ *The horse spooked at the siren.* ▶ **wystraszyć**

spooky /ˈspuːki/ adj. (**spookier**; **spookiest**) (informal) strange and frightening: *It's spooky* (strasznie) *in the house alone at nights.* ▶ **straszny** SYN **creepy**

spool /spuːl/ noun [C] a round object which thread, film, wire, etc. is put around ▶ **szpula, szpulka** ➲ look at **reel**

⚷ **spoon** /spuːn/ noun [C] an object with a round end and a long handle that you use for eating, mixing or serving food: *Give each person a* ***knife, fork and spoon.*** ◇ *a wooden spoon for cooking* ▶ **łyżka** ➲ picture at **kitchen**

■ **spoon** verb [T]: *Next, spoon the mixture onto a baking tray.* ▶ **czerpać/nalewać/nakładać łyżką**

spoonful /ˈspuːnfʊl/ noun [C] the amount that one spoon can hold: *Add two spoonfuls of sugar.* ▶ **(pełna) łyżka/łyżeczka** (*czegoś*)

sporadic /spəˈrædɪk/ adj. not done or happening regularly ▶ **sporadyczny, rzadki**

■ **sporadically** /-kli/ adv. ▶ **sporadycznie, rzadko**

⚷ **sport** /spɔːt/ noun **1** [U] a physical game or activity that you do for exercise or because you enjoy it: *John* ***did*** *a lot of* ***sport*** *when he was at school.* ◇ *Do you like sport?* ◇ *And now with the news, sport and weather here's Mark Foster.* (mówiono w radiu/TV) ▶ **sport** ➲ picture on **page A8 2** [C] a particular game or type of sport: *What's your favourite sport?* ◇ ***winter sports*** sporty zimowe ▶ **sport 3** [C] (informal) a person who does not get angry or upset if they lose a game or if sb plays a joke on them ▶ **równy facet, równa dziewczyna** ➲ look at **spoilsport**

■ **sporting** adj.: *a major sporting event* ▶ **sportowy**

> **sport**
>
> You can **play** particular sports (without 'the'): *I play football every Saturday*. In **team sports** one team **plays** or **plays against** another team: *Who are you playing against next week?* Other sports and activities can take the verbs **do** or **go**: *I do gymnastics and yoga.* ◇ *I go swimming twice a week.*
>
> Sports that are played outside on grass, like **football**, **cricket** and **rugby**, are played on a **pitch**. Some other sports, for example **tennis** and **basketball**, are played on a **court**. **Athletics** is made up of **track events** (sports that involve running on a track, such as **sprinting** and **hurdling**) and **field events** (sports that involve jumping and throwing, such as the **high jump** and **javelin**). Sports that take place on snow or ice, such as **skiing**, **snowboarding** and **skating**, are called **winter sports**. Dangerous activities, such as **bungee jumping**, are often called **extreme sports**.
>
> A person who trains people to compete in certain sports is a **coach**. The official person who controls a **match** and makes sure that players do not break the rules is a **referee** (in football, rugby, etc.) or an **umpire** (in tennis, cricket, etc.).

ˈ**sports car** noun [C] a low, fast car often with a roof that you can open ▶ **sportowy samochód** ➲ picture on **page A7**

ˈ**sports centre** noun [C] (Brit.) a building where the public can go to play many different kinds of sports, swim, etc. ▶ **ośrodek sportowy**

sportsman /ˈspɔːtsmən/ noun [C] (pl. **-men** /-mən/) a man who does a lot of sport or who is good at sport: *a keen sportsman* ▶ **sportowiec**

sportsmanlike /ˈspɔːtsmənlaɪk/ adj. behaving in a fair, generous and polite way when you are playing a game or doing sport ▶ **godny prawdziwego sportowca**

sportsmanship /ˈspɔːtsmənʃɪp/ noun [U] the quality of being fair, generous and polite when you are playing a game or doing sport ▶ **godne sportowe zachowanie**

sportswoman /ˈspɔːtswʊmən/ noun [C] (pl. **-women** /-wɪmɪn/) a woman who does a lot of sport or who is good at sport ▶ **sportsmenka**

sporty /ˈspɔːti/ adj. (**sportier**; **sportiest**) liking or good at sport ▶ **wysportowany**

spot¹ /spɒt/ noun [C] **1** a small round mark on a surface: *a blue skirt with red spots on it* ◇ *Leopards have dark spots.* Lamparty są w ciemne cętki. ▶ **plamka**, **kropka** ➲ adjective **spotted** **2** a small dirty mark on sth: *grease/rust spots* ▶ **plama** **3** a small red or yellow lump that appears on your skin: *Many teenagers* ***get spots.*** ▶ **krosta**, **pryszcz** ➲ adjective **spotty** **4** a particular place or area: *a quiet/lonely/secluded spot* ▶ **miejsce** **5** [usually sing.] (Brit., informal) **a spot of sth** a small amount of sth: *Can you help me? I'm having a spot of trouble.* ▶ **odrobina**, **krzta** **6** = SPOTLIGHT (1)

IDM **have a soft spot for sb/sth** → SOFT

on the spot **1** immediately: *Paul was caught stealing money and was dismissed on the spot.* ▶ **z miejsca**, **natychmiast** **2** at the place where sth happened or where sb/sth is needed: *The fire brigade were on the spot within five minutes.* ▶ **na miejscu**

put sb on the spot to make sb answer a difficult question or make a difficult decision without having much time to think ▶ **stawiać kogoś w kłopotliwym położeniu, zadając trudne pytanie lub wymagając natychmiastowej decyzji bez zastanowienia**

spot² /spɒt/ verb [T] (**spotting**; **spotted**) [not used in the continuous tenses] to see or notice sb/sth, especially suddenly or when it is not easy to do: *I've spotted a couple of spelling mistakes.* ▶ **spostrzegać**, **zauważać** ℹ Czasownika **spot** nie używa się w czasach *continuous*. Natomiast często spotyka się go w *present participle* (formie *-ing*): *Spotting a familiar face in the crowd, he began to push his way towards her.*

ˌspot ˈcheck noun [C] a check that is made suddenly and without warning on a few things or people chosen from a group ▶ **wyrywkowa kontrola**

spotless /ˈspɒtləs/ adj. perfectly clean ▶ **nieskazitelny**

spotlight /ˈspɒtlaɪt/ noun **1** (also **spot**) [C] a lamp that can send a single line of bright light onto a small area. **Spotlights** are often used in theatres. ▶ **reflektor punktowy (wąskostrumieniowy)** ➲ picture at **light** **2** (**the spotlight**) [sing.] the centre of public attention or interest: *to be* ***in the spotlight*** ▶ **centrum uwagi/powszechnego zainteresowania**

ˌspot ˈon adj. [not before a noun] (Brit., informal) exactly right: *Your estimate was spot on.* ▶ **dokładny**, **precyzyjny**

spotted /ˈspɒtɪd/ adj. (used about clothes, cloth, etc.) covered with round shapes of a different colour: *a spotted blouse* ▶ **cętkowany**, **nakrapiany**

spotty /ˈspɒti/ adj. (**spottier**; **spottiest**) having small red or yellow lumps on your skin ▶ **krostowaty**, **pryszczaty**

spouse /spaʊs/ noun [C] (formal) your husband or wife ▶ **małżon-ek/ka** ℹ **Spouse** jest formalnym słowem, używanym w formularzach, dokumentach itp.

spout¹ /spaʊt/ noun [C] a tube or pipe through which liquid comes out: *the spout of a teapot* ▶ **dziób**, **rura spustowa**

spout² /spaʊt/ verb [I,T] **1** to send out a liquid with great force; to make a liquid do this ▶ **tryskać**, **sikać**, **wyrzucać/wypluwać z siebie** **2** (informal) **spout (on/off) (about sth)** to say sth, using a lot of words, in a way that is boring or annoying ▶ **zalewać potokiem słów**

sprain /spreɪn/ verb [T] to injure part of your body, especially your wrist or your ankle, by suddenly bending or turning it: *I've sprained my ankle.* ▶ **zwichnąć**, **skręcić**
■ **sprain** noun [C] ▶ **zwichnięcie**

sprang past tense of **spring²**

sprawl /sprɔːl/ verb [I] **1** to sit or lie with your arms and legs spread out in an untidy way: *People lay sprawled out in the sun.* ▶ **rozwalać się** (*np. na krześle*) **2** to cover a large area of land ▶ (*zabudowania itp.*) **rozciągać się**, **ciągnąć się** (*na dużej przestrzeni*)
■ **sprawling** adj.: *the sprawling city suburbs* niekończące się przedmieścia ▶ **rozciągnięty**

spray¹ /spreɪ/ noun **1** [U] liquid in very small drops that is sent through the air: *clouds of spray from the waves* ▶ **rozpylona ciecz**, **pył wodny** **2** [C,U] liquid in an **aerosol** that is forced out under pressure when you push a button: *hairspray* ▶ **spray** ➲ picture at **container**

spray² /spreɪ/ verb [I,T] (used about a liquid) to be forced out of a container or sent through the air in very small drops; to send a liquid out in this way: *The crops are regularly sprayed with pesticide.* ▶ **rozpylać (się)**, **pryskać**

ˈspray can noun [C] a small metal container that has paint in it under pressure and that you use to spray paint onto sth ▶ **pojemnik ze sprayem**

ˈspray paint noun [U] paint that is kept in a container under pressure and that you can spray onto sth: *a can of red spray paint* ▶ **farba w sprayu**
■ **ˈspray-paint** verb [T]: *The walls were spray-painted with slogans.* ▶ **malować farbą w sprayu**

spread¹ /spred/ verb (pt, pp **spread**) **1** [T] **spread sth (out) (on/over sth)** to open sth that has been folded so that it covers a larger area; to move things so that they cover a larger area: *Spread the map out on the table so we can all see it!* ▶ **rozkładać** **2** [I,T] to affect a larger area or a bigger group of people; to make sth do this: *Fear spread through* (strach ogarnął) *the village.* ◇ *The fire spread rapidly because of the strong wind.* ◇ *Rats and flies* ***spread disease.*** ◇ *to* ***spread rumours*** *about somebody* ▶ **rozprzestrzeniać (się)**, **roznosić (się)** **3** [T] **spread A on/over B**; **spread B with A** to cover a surface with a layer of a soft substance: *to spread jam on bread* ◇ *to spread bread with jam* ▶ **smarować**, **rozsmarowywać** **4** [I] to continue for a great distance: *The swamp spreads for several miles among the coast.* ▶ **ciągnąć się** **4** [T] **spread sth (out) (over sth)** to separate sth into parts and divide them between different times or people: *You can spread your repayments over a period of three years.* ▶ **rozkładać**

PHR V **spread (yourself) out** to move away from the others in a group of people in order to cover a larger area: *The police spread out to search the whole area.* ▶ **rozpraszać się**

spread² /spred/ noun **1** [U] an increase in the amount or number of sth that there is, or in the area that is affected by sth: *Dirty drinking water encourages* ***the spread of disease.*** ▶ **rozszerzanie (się)**, **rozprzestrzenianie (się)** **2** [C,U] a soft food that you put on bread: *cheese spread* serek topiony ▶ **produkt do smarowania pieczywa** **3** [C] a newspaper or magazine article that covers one or more pages: *a double-page spread* ▶ **rozkładówka**

spreadsheet /ˈspredʃiːt/ noun [C] a computer program for working with rows of numbers, used especially for doing accounts ▶ **arkusz kalkulacyjny**

spree /spriː/ noun [C] (informal) a short time that you spend doing sth you enjoy, often doing too much of it: *to* ***go on a*** *shopping/spending* ***spree*** ▶ **hulanka**, **szaleństwo**

sprig /sprɪɡ/ noun [C] a small piece of a plant with leaves on it ▶ **gałązka**

spring¹ /sprɪŋ/ noun **1** [C,U] the season of the year between winter and summer when the weather gets warmer and plants begin to grow: *Daffodils bloom* ***in spring.*** ▶ **wiosna** ➲ picture on **page A16** **2** [C] a long piece of thin metal or wire that is bent round and round. After you push or pull a spring it goes back to its original shape and size: *bed springs* ▶ **sprężyna** ➲ picture at **coil**

3 [C] a place where water comes up naturally from under the ground: *a hot spring* ▶ **źródło 4** [C] a sudden jump upwards or forwards ▶ **skok**

spring² /sprɪŋ/ verb [I] (pt **sprang** /spræŋ/, pp **sprung** /sprʌŋ/) **1** to jump or move quickly: *When the alarm went off, Ray sprang out of bed.* ◇ *to spring to your feet* zerwać się na (równe) nogi ◇ (figurative) *to spring to somebody's defence/assistance* ▶ **skakać**; **rzucać się** (*np. na pomoc*) **2** (used about an object) to move suddenly and violently: *The door sprang open* (gwałtownie się otworzyły) *and Bella walked in.* ◇ *The branch sprang back* (nagle odskoczyła) *and hit him in the face.* ▶ **nagle i/lub gwałtownie wykonać jakiś ruch 3** to appear suddenly: *Tears sprang to her eyes.* ▶ **nagle przybyć/pojawić się**

IDM **come/spring to mind** → MIND¹

PHR V **spring from...** (informal) to appear suddenly and unexpectedly from a particular place: *Where on earth did you spring from?* Skąd się u diabła wziąłeś? ▶ **wyskakiwać skądś**

spring from sth (formal) to be the result of sth: *The idea for the book sprang from an experience she had while travelling in India.* ▶ **mieć swoje źródło w czymś, zrodzić się z czegoś**

spring sth on sb (informal) to do or say sth that sb is not expecting ▶ **zaskakiwać (czymś kogoś), zastrzelić** (*np. wiadomością*)

spring up to appear or develop quickly or suddenly: *Play areas for children are springing up everywhere.* ▶ **wyskakiwać** (*np. jak grzyby po deszczu*)

springboard /ˈsprɪŋbɔːd/ noun [C] **1** a low board that bends and that helps you jump higher, for example before you jump into a swimming pool ▶ **trampolina 2 a springboard (for/to sth)** something that helps you start an activity, especially by giving you ideas ▶ **odskocznia (dla/do czegoś)**

ˌspring-ˈclean verb [T] to clean a house, room, etc. very well, including the parts that you do not usually clean ▶ **robić wiosenne porządki**

ˌspring ˈonion (US ˌ**green ˈonion**; **scallion** /ˈskæliən/) noun [C,U] a type of small onion with a long green central part and leaves ▶ **dymka** ➲ picture on **page A13**

springtime /ˈsprɪŋtaɪm/ noun [U] (formal) the season of spring ▶ **wiosna**

springy /ˈsprɪŋi/ adj. (**springier**; **springiest**) going quickly back to its original shape or size after being pushed, pulled, etc.: *soft springy grass* ▶ **sprężysty**

sprinkle /ˈsprɪŋkl/ verb [T] **sprinkle A (on/onto/over B)**; **sprinkle B (with A)** to throw drops of water or small pieces of sth over a surface: *to sprinkle sugar on a cake* ◇ *to sprinkle a cake with sugar* ▶ **posypywać, kropić**

sprinkler /ˈsprɪŋklə(r)/ noun [C] a device with holes in it that sends out water in small drops. **Sprinklers** are used in gardens to keep the grass green, and in buildings to stop fires from spreading. ▶ **zraszacz, instalacja tryskaczowa** (*do gaszenia pożaru*)

sprinkling /ˈsprɪŋklɪŋ/ (also **sprinkle**) noun [C] a small amount of a substance that is dropped somewhere, or a number of things or people that are spread or included somewhere: *Add a sprinkling of pepper.* ◇ *Most were men, but there was also a sprinkling* (garstka) *of young women.* ▶ **szczypta, odrobina**

sprint /sprɪnt/ verb [I,T] to run a short distance as fast as you can ▶ **biec sprintem**

■ **sprint** noun [C] ▶ **sprint**

sprout¹ /spraʊt/ verb [I,T] (used about a plant) to begin to grow or to produce new leaves: *The seeds are sprouting.* ▶ **kiełkować, puszczać pędy**

sprout² /spraʊt/ noun [C] **1** = BRUSSELS SPROUT **2** a new part that has grown on a plant ▶ **kiełek, pęd**

spruce¹ /spruːs/ verb

PHR V **spruce (sb/yourself) up** to make sb/yourself clean and tidy ▶ **wyelegantować (się)**

spruce² /spruːs/ noun [C] a fir tree with many leaves like needles ▶ **świerk**

sprung past participle of **spring²**

spud /spʌd/ noun [C] (informal) a potato ▶ **ziemniak, kartofel**

spun past tense, past participle of **spin¹**

spur¹ /spɜː(r)/ noun [C] **1** a piece of metal that a rider wears on the back of their boots to encourage the horse to go faster ▶ **ostroga** ➲ picture at **horse 2 a spur (to sth)** something that encourages you to do sth or that makes sth happen more quickly: *My poor exam results acted as a spur to make me study harder.* ▶ **bodziec, zachęta**

IDM **on the spur of the moment** without planning; suddenly ▶ **spontanicznie, bez namysłu**

spur² /spɜː(r)/ verb [T] (**spurring**; **spurred**) **spur sb/sth (on/onto sth) 1** to encourage sb or make them work harder or faster: *The letter spurred me into action.* ◇ *We were spurred on by the positive feedback from customers.* ▶ **zagrzewać (kogoś do czegoś), przynaglać 2** to make a horse go faster by using spurs ▶ **spinać ostrogami** (*konia*)

spurious /ˈspjʊəriəs/ adj. **1** false, although seeming to be genuine: *He had managed to create the entirely spurious impression that the company was thriving.* ▶ **fałszywy** (*wbrew pozorom*) **2** based on false ideas or ways of thinking: *a spurious argument* ▶ **błędny**

■ **spuriously** adv. ▶ **fałszywie; błędnie**

spurn /spɜːn/ verb [T] (formal) to refuse sth that sb has offered to you: *She spurned his offer of friendship.* ▶ **odtrącać/odrzucać z pogardą**

spurt /spɜːt/ verb **1** [I,T] (used about a liquid) to come out quickly with great force; to make a liquid do this: *Blood spurted from the wound.* ▶ **tryskać 2** [I] to increase your speed for a short time to get somewhere faster: *The Moroccan athlete suddenly spurted clear of the other runners* (nagle przyśpieszył i wyprzedził innych biegaczy).

■ **spurt** noun [C] **1** when a liquid comes out in a spurt, it comes out suddenly and with great force ▶ **struga, fontanna** (*np. krwi z rany*) **2** a sudden increase in speed or effort: *If we **put on a spurt*** (jeśli się pośpieszymy), *we might finish the job on schedule.* ◇ *a growth spurt* gwałtowny wzrost ◇ *a sudden spurt of* (atak) *anger* ▶ **zryw**

spy¹ /spaɪ/ noun [C] (pl. **spies**) a person who tries to get secret information about another country, person or organization ▶ **szpieg**

spy² /spaɪ/ verb (**spying**; **spies**; pt, pp **spied**) **1** [I] to try to get secret information about sb/sth ▶ **szpiegować** ➲ look at **espionage 2** [T] (formal) to see ▶ **dostrzegać, ujrzeć**

IDM **spy on sb/sth** to watch sb/sth secretly: *The man next door is spying on us.* ▶ **szpiegować kogoś/coś**

spyhole /ˈspaɪhəʊl/ noun [C] a small hole in a door for looking at the person on the other side before deciding to let them in ▶ **wizjer**

sq 1 = SQUARE¹ (3): *10 sq cm* **2** (**Sq**) = SQUARE² (2): *6 Hanover Sq*

squabble /ˈskwɒbl/ verb [I] **squabble (over/about sth)** to argue in a noisy way about sth that is not very important ▶ **handryczyć się**

■ **squabble** noun [C] ▶ **handryczenie się**

squad /skwɒd/ noun [C, with sing. or pl. verb] a group of people who work as a team: *He's a policeman with the drugs squad.* ▶ **oddział, brygada**

squadron /ˈskwɒdrən/ noun [C, with sing. or pl. verb] a group of military aircraft or ships ▶ **szwadron, eskadra**

squalid /ˈskwɒlɪd/ adj. very dirty, untidy and unpleasant: *squalid housing conditions* ▶ **nędzny**, **niechlujny**

squall /skwɔːl/ noun [C] a sudden storm with strong winds ▶ **nawałnica**

squalor /ˈskwɒlə(r)/ noun [U] the state of being very dirty, untidy or unpleasant: *to live **in squalor*** ▶ **nędza**, **niechlujstwo**

squander /ˈskwɒndə(r)/ verb [T] **squander sth (on sth)** to waste time, money, etc.: *He squanders his time on TV and computer games.* ▶ **trwonić**, **marnotrawić**

square¹ /skweə(r)/ adj. **1** having four straight sides of the same length and corners of 90°: *a square tablecloth* ▶ **kwadratowy 2** shaped like a square or forming an angle of about 90°: *a square face* ◇ *square shoulders* barczyste ramiona ▶ **kwadratowy 3** (abbr. **sq**) (used for talking about the area of sth): *If a room is 5 metres long and 4 metres wide, its area is 20 square metres.* ▶ **kwadratowy 4** (used about sth that is square in shape) having sides of a particular length: *The picture is twenty centimetres square* (jest kwadratem o długości boku wynoszącej 20 cm). ▶ **kwadratowy 5** [not before a noun] not owing any money: *Here is the money I owe you. Now we're (all) square.* ▶ **(być) kwita 6** [not before a noun] having equal points (in a game, etc.): *The teams were **all square** at half-time.* Do przerwy był remis. ▶ (*wynik*) **remisowy 7** fair or honest, especially in business matters: *a square deal* ▶ **sprawiedliwy i uczciwy**

IDM **a square meal** a good meal that makes you feel satisfied ▶ **solidny posiłek**

■ **square** adv. (also **squarely** /ˈskweəli/) in an obvious and direct way: *to look somebody square in the eye* ◇ *I think the blame falls squarely on her.* ▶ **prosto**, **bezpośrednio**

square² /skweə(r)/ noun [C] **1** a shape that has four sides of the same length and four **right angles**: *There are 64 squares* (pola) *on a chess board.* ▶ **kwadrat**, **czworobok 2** (also **Square**) (abbr. **Sq**) an open space in a town or city that has buildings all around it: *Protesters gathered in the town square.* ◇ *Trafalgar Square* ◇ *the market square* rynek ▶ **plac 3** the number that you get when you multiply another number by itself: *Four is the square of two.* ▶ **kwadrat** ➲ look at **square root**

square³ /skweə(r)/ verb [I,T] **square (sth) with sb/sth** to agree with sth; to make sure that sb/sth agrees with sth: *Your conclusion doesn't really square with the facts.* ◇ *If you want time off you'll have to square it with the boss.* ▶ **zgadzać się**

PHR V **square up (with sb)** to pay sb the money that you owe them ▶ **rozliczać się (z kimś)**

squared /skweəd/ adj. (used about a number) multiplied by itself: *Four squared is sixteen.* ▶ **podniesiony do kwadratu** ➲ look at **square root**

squarely = SQUARE¹

ˌsquare ˈroot noun [C] a number that produces another particular number when it is multiplied by itself: *The square root of sixteen is four.* ▶ **pierwiastek kwadratowy** ➲ look at **square**, **squared**, **root**

squash¹ /skwɒʃ/ verb **1** [T] to press sth so that it is damaged, changes shape or becomes flat: *The fruit at the bottom of the bag will **get squashed**.* ◇ *Move up – you're squashing me!* ▶ **gnieść**; **dławić 2** [I,T] to go into a place, or move sb/sth to a place, where there is not much space: *We all squashed into the back of the car.* ▶ **tłoczyć (się) 3** [T] to destroy sth because it is a problem: *to squash somebody's suggestion/plan/idea* ▶ **niweczyć** (*np. czyjeś plany, zamiary*), **rujnować** (*np. plany*)

squash² /skwɒʃ/ noun **1** [C, usually sing.] a lot of people in a small space: *We can get ten people around the table, but it's **a bit of a squash**.* ▶ **tłok**, **ścisk 2** [U,C] (Brit.) a drink that is made from fruit juice and sugar. You add water to **squash** before you drink it: *orange squash* ▶ **sok owocowy zagęszczony z cukrem** (*do rozcieńczania wodą*) **3** [U] a game for two people, played in a court. You play **squash** by hitting a small rubber ball against any one of the walls of the court: *a squash racket* ▶ **squash**

squat¹ /skwɒt/ verb [I] (**squatting**; **squatted**) **1** to rest with your weight on your feet, your legs bent and your bottom just above the ground ▶ **kucać** ➲ picture at **kneel 2** to go and live in an empty building without permission from the owner ▶ **mieszkać na dziko**

squat² /skwɒt/ adj. short and fat or thick: *a squat ugly building* ▶ **przysadzisty**, **pękaty**

squatter /ˈskwɒtə(r)/ noun [C] a person who is living in an empty building without the owner's permission ▶ **osoba osiedlająca się bezprawnie w niezamieszkałym budynku**

squawk /skwɔːk/ verb [I] (used especially about a bird) to make a loud unpleasant noise ▶ **skrzeczeć**, **gdakać**

■ **squawk** noun [C] ▶ **skrzek**

squeak /skwiːk/ noun [C] a short high noise that is not very loud: *the squeak of a mouse* ◇ *She gave a little squeak of surprise.* ▶ **(cichy) pisk/kwik**

■ **squeak** verb [I,T] ▶ **(cicho) piszczeć/kwiczeć** | **squeaky** adj.: *a squeaky floorboard* ◇ *a squeaky voice* ▶ **piskliwy**, **skrzypiący**

squeal /skwiːl/ verb [I,T] to make a loud high noise because of pain, fear or enjoyment: *The baby squealed in delight at the new toy.* ▶ **piszczeć**

Squeal jest głośniejszy i dłuższy od **squeak**, ale nie tak głośny jak **scream**.

■ **squeal** noun [C] ▶ **pisk**

squeamish /ˈskwiːmɪʃ/ adj. easily upset by unpleasant sights, especially blood ▶ **wrażliwy** (*np. na widok krwi*)

squeeze¹ /skwiːz/ verb **1** [T] **squeeze sth (out)**; **squeeze sth (from/out of sth)** to press sth hard for a particular purpose: *She squeezed his hand as a sign of affection.* ◇ *to squeeze a tube of toothpaste* ◇ *Squeeze a lemon/the juice of a lemon into a glass.* ◇ *I squeezed the water out of the cloth.* ▶ **ściskać**, **wyciskać**, **zgniatać 2** [I,T] **squeeze (sb/sth) into, through, etc. sth**; **squeeze (sb/sth) through, in, past, etc.** to force sb/sth into or through a small space: *We can squeeze another person into the back of the car.* ◇ *There was just room for the bus to squeeze past.* ▶ **przeciskać (się)**, **wciskać (się)**

squeeze² /skwiːz/ noun **1** [C] an act of pressing sth firmly: *He gave her hand a squeeze and told her he loved her.* ▶ **uścisk** ➲ look at **hug 2** [C] the amount of liquid that you get from squeezing an orange, a lemon, etc.: *a squeeze of lemon* ▶ **parę wyciśniętych kropli 3** [sing.] a situation where there is not much space: *It was **a tight squeeze** to get twelve people around the table.* ▶ **ścisk**, **tłok 4** [C, usually sing.] an effort to use less money, time, etc., especially with the result that there is not enough: *a government squeeze on spending* ograniczenie wydatków rządowych ◇ *We're really been feeling the squeeze* (mamy dotkliwe problemy finansowe) *since I lost my job.*

squelch /skweltʃ/ verb [I] to make the sound your feet make when you are walking in deep wet mud ▶ **chlupotać**, **chlupać** (*nogami*)

squid /skwɪd/ noun [C,U] (pl. **squid** or **squids**) a sea animal that you can eat, with a long soft body and ten **tentacles** ▶ **kałamarnica**

squiggle /ˈskwɪgl/ noun [C] (informal) a quickly drawn line that goes in all directions ▶ **zakrętas**

squint /skwɪnt/ verb [I] **1 squint (at sth)** to look at sth with your eyes almost closed: *to squint in bright sunlight* ▶ **patrzeć spod przymkniętych powiek 2** to have eyes that appear to look in different directions at the same time ▶ **zezować**

■ **squint** noun [C] ▶ **zez**

squire /ˈskwaɪə(r)/ noun [C] (in the past) a man who owned land in a country area ▶ **dziedzic**

squirm /skwɜːm/ verb [I] to move around in your chair because you are nervous, uncomfortable, etc. ▶ **kręcić się, wiercić się**

squirrel /ˈskwɪrəl/ noun [C] a small grey or red animal with a long thick tail that lives in trees and eats nuts ▶ **wiewiórka**

squirt /skwɜːt/ verb [I,T] if a liquid **squirts** or if you **squirt** it, it is suddenly forced out of sth in a particular direction: *I cut the orange and juice squirted out.* ◇ *She squirted water on the flames.* ◇ *He squirted me with water.* ▶ **tryskać, sikać**
■ **squirt** noun [C]: *a squirt of lemon juice* ▶ **kilka kropel**

Sr = SENIOR[1] (2)

St **1** = STREET (2): *20 Swan St* **2** = SAINT (1): *St Peter*

st = STONE (5)

stab[1] /stæb/ verb [T] (**stabbing**; **stabbed**) to push a knife or other pointed object into sb/sth: *The man had been stabbed in the back.* ◇ *He stabbed a potato with his fork.* ▶ **kłuć, dźgać**

stab[2] /stæb/ noun [C] **1** an injury that was caused by a knife, etc.: *a stab wound* rana kłuta ▶ **pchnięcie nożem** **2** a sudden sharp pain: *a stab of pain* kłujący ból ▶ **ukłucie, dźgnięcie**
IDM **have a stab at sth/doing sth** (informal) to try to do sth ▶ **próbować (czegoś)**

stabbing[1] /ˈstæbɪŋ/ noun [C] an occasion when sb is injured or killed with a knife or other sharp object ▶ **napad z nożem itp.**

stabbing[2] /ˈstæbɪŋ/ adj. [only before a noun] (used about a pain) sudden and strong ▶ **kłujący**

stability /stəˈbɪləti/ noun [U] the state or quality of being steady and not changing: *After so much change we now need a period of stability.* ◇ *The ladder is slightly wider at the bottom for greater stability.* ▶ **stabilizacja, stabilność** OPP **instability** ➲ adjective **stable**

stabilize (also -ise) /ˈsteɪbəlaɪz/ verb [I,T] to become or to make sth firm, steady and unlikely to change: *The patient's condition has stabilized.* ▶ **stabilizować** ➲ look at **destabilize**

stable[1] /ˈsteɪbl/ adj. steady, firm and unlikely to change: *This ladder doesn't seem very stable.* ◇ *The patient is **in a stable condition**.* ▶ **stabilny, trwały** OPP **unstable** ➲ noun **stability**

stable[2] /ˈsteɪbl/ noun [C] a building where horses are kept ▶ **stajnia**

stack[1] /stæk/ noun [C] **1** a tidy pile of sth: *a stack of plates/books/chairs* ▶ **stos** **2** [often plural] (informal) a lot of sth: *I've still got stacks of work to do.* ▶ **mnóstwo, kupa**

stack[2] /stæk/ verb [T] **stack sth (up)** to put sth into a tidy pile: *Could you stack those chairs?* ▶ **układać w stos**

stacked /stækt/ adj. full of piles of things: *The room was stacked high with books.* ▶ **założony/pokryty (stosem czegoś)**

stadium /ˈsteɪdiəm/ noun [C] (pl. **stadiums** or **stadia** /-diə/) a large structure, usually with no roof, where people can sit and watch sport ▶ **stadion**

staff /stɑːf; US stæf/ noun [C, usually sing., U] the group of people who work for a particular organization: *hotel/library/medical staff* ◇ *The hotel has over 200 people **on its staff**.* ◇ *a staffroom* pokój nauczycielski ▶ **personel**

> Mówi się **a member of staff** (nie ~~a staff~~), w odniesieniu do jednej osoby z personelu: *Two **members of staff** will accompany the students on the school trip.*
>
> **Staff** zwykle używa się tylko w lp i przeważnie z czasownikiem w lm: *The staff all speak good English.* ◇ *The staff are all English.*

■ **staff** verb [T, usually passive]: *The office is staffed 24 hours a day.* ▶ **obsadzać** (*personelem*)

staffroom /ˈstɑːfruːm; -rʊm; US ˈstæf-/ noun [C] (Brit.) a room in a school where teachers can go when they are not teaching ▶ **pokój nauczycielski**

stag /stæg/ noun [C] a male **deer** ▶ **jeleń** ➲ note at **deer** ➲ picture on **page A10**

stage[1] /steɪdʒ/ noun **1** [C] one part of the progress or development of sth: *The first stage of the course lasts for three weeks.* ◇ *I suggest we do the journey **in two stages**.* ◇ ***At this stage** it's too early to say what will happen.* ▶ **etap, faza** **2** [C] a platform in a theatre, concert hall, etc. on which actors, musicians, etc. perform: *There were more than 50 people on stage in one scene.* ▶ **scena, estrada** **3** [sing., U] the theatre and the world of acting as a form of entertainment: *Her parents didn't want her to **go on the stage*** (aby została aktorką). ◇ *an actor of stage and screen* ▶ **teatr**

stage[2] /steɪdʒ/ verb [T] **1** to organize a performance of a play, concert, etc. for the public ▶ **wystawiać** **2** to organize an event: *They have decided to stage a 24-hour strike.* ▶ **organizować**

ˈstage fright noun [U] nervous feelings felt by performers before they appear in front of an audience ▶ **trema**

stagehand /ˈsteɪdʒhænd/ noun [C] a person whose job is to help move **scenery**, etc. in a theatre, to prepare the stage for the next play or the next part of a play ▶ **pomocni-k/ca przy zmianie dekoracji w teatrze**

ˌstage ˈmanager noun [C] the person who is responsible for the stage, lights, etc. during a theatre performance ▶ **inspicjent/ka**

stagger /ˈstægə(r)/ verb [I] to walk with short steps as if you could fall at any moment, for example because you are ill, drunk or carrying sth heavy: *He staggered across the finishing line and collapsed.* ▶ **zataczać się**

staggered /ˈstægəd/ adj. **1** [not before a noun] (informal) very surprised: *I was absolutely staggered when I heard the news.* ▶ **oszołomiony** **2** (used about a set of times, payments, etc.) arranged so that they do not all happen at the same time: *staggered working hours* zróżnicowane godziny pracy ▶ **niejednoczesny** (*rozłożony w czasie*)

staggering /ˈstægərɪŋ/ adj. that you find difficult to believe ▶ **niewiarygodny**
■ **staggeringly** adv. ▶ **niewiarygodnie**

stagnant /ˈstægnənt/ adj. **1** (used about water) not flowing and therefore dirty and having an unpleasant smell ▶ (*woda*) **stojący** **2** (used about business, etc.) not active; not developing: *a stagnant economy* ▶ **w zastoju**

stagnate /stægˈneɪt; US ˈstægn-/ verb [I] **1** to stop developing, changing or being active: *a stagnating economy* ▶ **być w stagnacji** **2** (used about water) to be or become **stagnant** ▶ **stać w bezruchu**
■ **stagnation** /stægˈneɪʃn/ noun [U] ▶ **zastój**

ˈstag night (also **ˈstag party**) noun [C] a party for men only that is given for a man just before his wedding day ▶ **wieczór kawalerski** ➲ look at **hen party**

staid /steɪd/ adj. serious, old-fashioned and rather boring ▶ **stateczny**

stain /steɪn/ verb [I,T] to leave a coloured mark that is difficult to remove: *Don't spill any of that red wine – it'll stain the carpet.* ▶ **plamić (się)**
■ **stain** noun [C]: *The blood had left a stain on his shirt.* ▶ **plama**

ˌstained ˈglass noun [U] pieces of coloured glass that are used in church windows, etc.: *a stained-glass window* ▶ **witraż**

ˌ**stainless ˈsteel** noun [U] a type of steel that does not change colour or **rust**: *a stainless steel pan* ▶ **stal nierdzewna**

stair /steə(r)/ noun **1** (**stairs**) [pl.] a series of steps inside a building that lead from one level to another: ***a flight of stairs*** kondygnacja schodów ◇ *I heard somebody coming* ***down the stairs.*** ◇ *She ran* ***up the stairs.*** ▶ **schody** ➲ look at **downstairs**, **upstairs**

> Por. **stair** z **step**. **Stairs** lub **flights of stairs** są zwykle w budynkach. **Steps** zazwyczaj znajdują się poza budynkami i są zrobione z kamienia lub betonu.

2 [C] one of the steps in a series inside a building: *She sat down on the bottom stair to read the letter.* ▶ **schodek**

staircase /ˈsteəkeɪs/ (also **stairway**) noun [C] a set of stairs with rails on each side that you can hold on to ▶ **klatka schodowa** ➲ look at **escalator**

stairway /ˈsteəweɪ/ noun [C] a set of stairs inside or outside a building ▶ **klatka schodowa**; **schody zewnętrzne**

stairwell /ˈsteəwel/ noun [usually sing.] the space in a building in which the stairs are built ▶ **klatka schodowa**

stake¹ /steɪk/ noun **1** [C] a wooden or metal pole with a point at one end that you push into the ground ▶ **palik** **2** [C] a part of a company, etc. that you own, usually because you have put money into it: *Foreign investors now* ***have a 20% stake in*** *the company.* ▶ **udział** (*w firmie*) **3** (**stakes**) [pl.] the things that you might win or lose in a game or in a particular situation: *We play cards for money, but never for very high stakes.* ▶ **stawka**

IDM **be at stake** to be in danger of being lost; at risk: *He thought very carefully about the decision because he knew his future was at stake.* ▶ **wchodzić w grę**, **być zagrożonym**

stake² /steɪk/ verb [T] **stake sth (on sth)** to put your future, etc. in danger by doing sth, because you hope that it will bring you a good result: *He is staking his political reputation on this issue.* ▶ **ryzykować (coś)** SYN **bet**

IDM **stake a/your claim (to sth)** to say that you have a right to have sth ▶ **rościć sobie prawo do czegoś**

PHR V **stake sth out** **1** to clearly mark an area of land that you are going to use ▶ **palikować**, **wytyczać granicę** **2** to make your position, opinion, etc. clear to everyone: *In his speech, the President staked out his position on tax reform.* ▶ **przedstawiać** (*np. swoje stanowisko*) **3** to watch a place secretly for a period of time: *The police had been staking out the house for months.* ▶ **obserwować** (*z ukrycia*)

stakeholder /ˈsteɪkhəʊldə(r)/ noun [C] **1** a person or company that is involved in a particular organization, project, system, etc., especially because they have invested money in it: *All our employees are stakeholders in the company.* ▶ **udziałowiec** **2** a person who holds all the bets placed on a game or race and who pays the money to the winner ▶ **bukmacher**

stale /steɪl/ adj. **1** (used about food or air) old and not fresh any more: *The bread will* ***go stale*** (szczerstwieje) *if you don't put it away.* ▶ **czerstwy**, **stęchły** **2** not interesting or exciting any more: *She says her marriage has gone stale* (się zużyło). ▶ **już nieciekawy**, **oklepany**, **stary** ➲ look at **fresh**

stalemate /ˈsteɪlmeɪt/ noun [sing., U] **1** a situation in an argument in which neither side can win or make any progress ▶ **sytuacja patowa** **2** (in the game of **chess**) a position in which a game ends without a winner because neither side can move ▶ **pat**

stalk¹ /stɔːk/ noun [C] one of the long thin parts of a plant which the flowers, leaves or fruit grow on ▶ **łodyga** ➲ picture on **page A12**

stalk² /stɔːk/ verb **1** [T] to move slowly and quietly towards an animal in order to catch or kill it: *a lion stalking its prey* ▶ **podchodzić** (*zwierzynę*) **2** [T] to follow a person over a period of time in a frightening or annoying way: *The actress claimed the man had been stalking her for two years.* ▶ **śledzić** **3** [I] to walk in an angry way ▶ **kroczyć sztywno** (*z dumą/złością*)

stall¹ /stɔːl/ noun **1** [C] a small shop with an open front or a table with things for sale: *a market stall* ◇ *a bookstall at the station* ▶ **stragan**, **stoisko** ➲ picture on **page A5** **2** (**stalls**) [pl.] the seats nearest the front in a theatre or cinema ▶ **miejsca na parterze** **3** [C, usually sing.] a situation in which a vehicle's engine suddenly stops because it is not receiving enough power: *The plane went into a stall* (silnik samolotu zgasł) *and almost crashed.*

stall² /stɔːl/ verb [I,T] **1** (used about a vehicle) to stop suddenly because the engine is not receiving enough power; to make a vehicle do this accidentally: *The bus often stalls on this hill.* ◇ *I kept stalling the car.* Tak jechałem, że ciągle gasł mi silnik. ▶ **stawać**, **gasnąć**; **powodować stawanie/gaśnięcie silnika**, **nagłe zatrzymanie pojazdu** **2** to avoid doing sth or to try to stop sth happening until a later time ▶ **działać/odpowiadać wymijająco**

stallion /ˈstæliən/ noun [C] an adult male horse, especially one that is kept for breeding ▶ **ogier** ➲ note at **horse**

stalwart /ˈstɔːlwət/ adj. always loyal to the same organization, team, etc.: *a stalwart supporter of the club* ▶ **oddany**, **wierny**

■ **stalwart** noun [C] ▶ **lojaln-y/a zwolenni-k/czka**

stamina /ˈstæmɪnə/ noun [U] the ability to do sth that involves a lot of physical or mental effort for a long time: *You need a lot of stamina to run long distances.* ▶ **wytrzymałość**

stammer /ˈstæmə(r)/ verb [I,T] to speak with difficulty, repeating sounds and pausing before saying things correctly: *He stammered an apology and left quickly.* ▶ **jąkać się**; **wyjąkiwać**

■ **stammer** noun [sing.]: *to have a stammer* jąkać się ▶ **jąkanie się**

stamp¹ /stæmp/ noun [C] **1** (also ˈ**postage stamp**) a small piece of paper that you stick onto a letter or package to show that you have paid for it to be posted: *a first-class/second-class stamp* ◇ *John's hobby is collecting stamps.* ▶ **znaczek pocztowy** ➲ note at **post** ➲ look at **first class**

> Poczta brytyjska stosuje dwa rodzaje znaczków na przesyłki krajowe: **first-class** i **second-class**. Przesyłki ofrankowane znaczkami pierwszej klasy są droższe i szybciej dostarczane.

2 a small object that prints some words, a design, the date, etc. when you press it onto a surface: *a date stamp* datownik ▶ **stempel**, **pieczęć** **3** the mark made by stamping sth onto a surface: *Have you got any visa stamps in your passport?* ◇ (figurative) *The government has given the project its* ***stamp of approval.*** ▶ **stempel**, **pieczęć** **4** [usually sing.] **the stamp of sth** something that shows a particular quality or that sth was done by a particular person: *Her novels have the stamp of genius.* ▶ **piętno (czegoś)**

stamp² /stæmp/ verb **1** [I,T] **stamp (on sth)** to put your foot down very heavily and noisily: *He stamped on the spider and squashed it.* ◇ *It was so cold that I had to stamp my feet to keep warm.* ◇ *She stamped her foot in anger.* ▶ **tupać** **2** [I] to walk with loud heavy steps: *She stamped around the room, shouting angrily.* ▶ **ciężko stąpać** **3** [T] **stamp A (on B)**; **stamp B (with A)** to print some words, a design, the date, etc. by pressing a **stamp¹** (2) onto a surface: *to stamp a passport* ▶ **stemplować**, **pieczętować** **4** [T, usually passive] to stick a stamp on a letter or package: *Please enclose a stamped addressed envelope with your application.* ▶ **naklejać znaczek**

S

PHR V **stamp sth out** to put an end to sth completely: *The police are trying to stamp out this kind of crime.* ▶ **wykorzeniać coś**

ˈ**stamp album** noun [C] a book in which you put stamps that you have collected ▶ **klaser**

ˈ**stamp collecting** noun [U] the hobby of collecting stamps from different countries ▶ **filatelistyka**
■ ˈ**stamp collector** noun [C] ▶ **filatelist(k)a**

ˈ**stamp duty** noun [U] a tax in Britain on some legal documents ▶ **opłata skarbowa** (*stosowana przy wydawaniu dokumentów sądowych*)

ˌ**stamped addressed ˈenvelope** (also ˌ**self-addressed ˈenvelope**) noun [C] (abbr. **sae** /ˌes eɪ ˈiː/) an empty envelope with your own name and address and a stamp on it that you send to a company, etc. when you want sth to be sent back to you ▶ **zaadresowana do siebie koperta ze znaczkiem**

stampede /stæmˈpiːd/ noun [C] a situation in which a large number of animals or people start running in the same direction, for example because they are frightened or excited ▶ **masowy pęd (na oślep)**
■ **stampede** verb [I] ▶ **pędzić na oślep**

stance /stæns; stɑːns/ noun [C, usually sing.] **1 stance (on sth)** the opinions that sb expresses publicly about sth: *the Prime Minister's stance on foreign affairs* ▶ **stanowisko** (*w sprawie*) **2** the position in which sb stands, especially when playing a sport ▶ **pozycja**

stand¹ /stænd/ verb [I,T] (pt, pp **stood** /stʊd/) **1** [I] to be on your feet, not sitting or lying down; to be in a vertical position: *He was standing near the window.* ◇ ***Stand still*** *– I'm trying to draw you!* ◇ *Only a few houses were left standing after the earthquake.* ▶ **stać 2** [I] **stand (up)** to rise to your feet from another position: *He stood up when I entered the room.* ▶ **wstawać 3** [T] to put sb/sth in a particular place or position: *We stood the mirror against the wall while we decided where to hang it.* ▶ **stawiać 4** [I] to be or to stay in a particular position or situation: *The castle stands on a hill.* ◇ *The house has stood empty for ten years.* ◇ *He was very critical of the law* ***as it stands*** (w obecnej formie). ▶ **stać 5** [I] **stand (at) sth** to be of a particular height, level, amount, etc.: *The world record stands at* (wynosi) *6.59 metres.* ◇ *The world record has stood for ten years.* ◇ *The building stands nearly 60 metres high.* ▶ **pozostawać (na czymś) 6** [I] to stay the same as before, without being changed: *Does your decision still stand?* ▶ **pozostawać bez zmian 7** [I] **stand (on sth)** to have an opinion or view about sth: *Where do you stand on euthanasia?* ▶ **stać na stanowisku** (*w jakiejś sprawie*), **zajmować stanowisko** (*w jakiejś sprawie*) **8** [I] **stand to do sth** to be in a situation where you are likely to do sth: *If he has to sell the company, he stands to lose a lot of money.* ▶ **mieć szanse wygrania/coś do stracenia 9** [T] [in negative sentences and questions, with *can/could*] to be able to bear or **tolerate** sb/sth: *I can't stand that woman – she's so rude.* ◇ *I couldn't* ***stand the thought of*** *waiting another two hours so I went home.* ▶ **znosić** ➲ note at **dislike 10** [T] [used especially with *can/could*] to be able to survive difficult conditions: *Camels can stand extremely hot and cold temperatures.* ▶ **wytrzymywać**, **przetrwać** SYN **bear**, **take 11** [I] **stand (for/as sth)** to be one of the people who hopes to be chosen in an election: *She's standing for the European Parliament.* ▶ **kandydować**
ℹ **Stand** używa się w idiomach, np. **it stands to reason**. Zob. hasła odpowiednich rzeczowników, przymiotników itp.

PHR V **stand around** to stand somewhere not doing anything: *A lot of people were just standing around outside.* ▶ **stać sobie**

stand aside to move to one side: *People stood aside to let the police pass.* ▶ **odsuwać się na bok**

stand back (from sth) to move back: *The policeman told everybody to stand back.* ▶ **cofać się (skądś)**

stand between sb/sth and sth to prevent sb from getting or achieving sth: *Only one game stood between him and victory.* ▶ **stać między kimś/czymś a czymś**

stand by 1 to be present, but do nothing in a situation: *How can you stand by and let them treat their animals like that?* ▶ **stać bezczynnie 2** to be ready to act: *The police are standing by in case there's trouble.* ▶ **stać/być w gotowości**

stand by sb to help sb or be friends with them, even in difficult situations ▶ **stać przy kimś**, **być wiernym/oddanym komuś**

stand by sth to still believe or agree with sth you said, decided or agreed earlier: *She still stands by every word she said.* ▶ **trzymać się czegoś**

stand down 1 stand down (as sth) to leave a job or position: *He stood down to make way for someone younger.* ▶ **ustępować (ze stanowiska) 2** (used about a witness) to leave the **witness box/stand** in court after giving evidence ▶ (*świadek w sądzie*) **być wolnym**

stand for sth 1 to be a short form of sth: *What does BBC stand for?* ▶ **oznaczać coś 2** to support sth (such as an idea or opinion): *I hate everything that the party stands for.* ▶ **popierać coś**

stand in (for sb) to take sb's place for a short time ▶ **zastępować (kogoś) czasowo**

stand out (from/against sth) to be easily seen or noticed ▶ **wyróżniać się (od czegoś)**

stand up to be or become vertical: *You'll look taller if you stand up straight.* ▶ **wstawać**, **powstawać**

stand sb up (informal) to not appear when you have arranged to meet sb, especially a boyfriend or girlfriend ▶ **wystawiać kogoś do wiatru**, **nie przyjść na spotkanie z kimś**

stand up for sb/sth to say or do sth which shows that you support sb/sth: *I admire him. He really stands up for his rights.* ▶ **stawać w obronie kogoś/czegoś**

stand up to sb/sth to defend yourself against sb/sth that is stronger or more powerful ▶ **stawiać komuś/czemuś czoło**

stand² /stænd/ noun [C] **1 a stand (on/against sth)** a strong effort to defend yourself or sth that you have a strong opinion about: *The workers have decided to* ***take/make a stand*** (stawiać opór) *against further job losses.* ▶ **opór**, **stanowisko 2** a table or small shop in the street or in a large public building from which you can buy things or get information: *a newspaper/hamburger stand* ◇ *a company stand at a trade fair* ▶ **stoisko**, **stragan 3** a piece of equipment or furniture that you use for holding a particular type of thing: *a music stand* pulpit ▶ **stojak**, **podstawa** ➲ picture at **bicycle 4** a large structure where people can watch sport from seats arranged in rows that are low near the front and high near the back ▶ **trybuna**

ˈ**stand-alone** adj. [usually before a noun] (especially used about a computer) able to be operated on its own without being connected to a larger system ▶ (*zwł. komput.*) **niezależny**

standard¹ /ˈstændəd/ noun [C] **1** a level of quality that you compare sth else with: ***By European standards*** *this is a very expensive city.* ◇ *He is a brilliant player* ***by any standard.*** ▶ **kryterium 2** a level of quality: *We complained about the low standard of service in the hotel.* ◇ *This work is not* ***up to*** *your usual* ***standard*** (nie jest na twoim poziomie). ▶ **poziom**, **standard 3** [usually pl.] a level of behaviour that is morally acceptable: *Many people are worried about falling standards in modern society.* ▶ **norma zachowania**

standard² /ˈstændəd/ adj. **1** normal or average; not special or unusual: *He's got long arms, so standard sizes of shirt don't fit him.* ▶ **podstawowy**, **zwykły 2** that people generally accept as normal and correct: *standard*

English ◇ *The standard argument is* (typowym argumentem jest to) *that it would be too difficult to change things now.* ▶ **standardowy**

ˈstandard class = SECOND CLASS[1] (1)

standardize (also -ise) /ˈstændədaɪz/ verb [T] to make things that are different the same: *Safety tests on old cars have been standardized throughout Europe.* ▶ **normalizować, ujednolicać**
■ **standardization** (also -isation) /stændədaɪˈzeɪʃn; US -dəˈz-/ noun [U] ▶ **normalizacja, ujednolicenie**

ˌstandard of ˈliving noun [C] the amount of money and level of comfort that a particular person or group has: *There is a higher standard of living in the north than in the south.* ▶ **poziom życia** ⓘ Zwrot o podobnym znaczeniu to **living standards**, którego używa się w lm: *Living standards have improved.*

standby /ˈstændbaɪ/ noun **1** [C] (pl. **standbys**) a thing or person that can be used if needed, for example if sb/sth is not available or in an emergency: *We always keep candles* ***as a standby*** *in case there is a power cut.* ▶ **zapas, rezerwa 2** [U] the state of being ready to do sth immediately if needed, or if a ticket becomes available: *Ambulances were* ***on standby*** (w gotowości) *along the route of the marathon.* ◇ *We were* ***put on standby*** (na liście rezerwowej) *for the flight to Rome.*
■ **standby** adj. [only before a noun]: *a standby ticket/passenger* ▶ **zapasowy, awaryjny**

standing[1] /ˈstændɪŋ/ adj. [only before a noun] that always exists; permanent ▶ **stały**

standing[2] /ˈstændɪŋ/ noun [U] **1** the position that sb/sth has, or how people think of them or it: *The agreement has no legal standing* (nie ma mocy prawnej). ▶ **pozycja** SYN **status 2** the amount of time during which sth has continued to exist: *a problem of many years' standing* wieloletni problem ▶ **czas trwania**

ˌstanding ˈorder noun [C] an instruction to your bank to make a regular payment to sb from your account ▶ **zlecenie stałe** ➲ look at **direct debit**

standpoint /ˈstændpɔɪnt/ noun [C] a particular way of thinking about sth ▶ **punkt widzenia** SYN **point of view**

standstill /ˈstændstɪl/ noun [sing.] a situation when there is no movement, progress or activity: *The traffic* ***is at/has come to a complete standstill*** (stanął w miejscu). ▶ **unieruchomienie, martwy punkt**
IDM **grind to a halt/standstill** → GRIND[1]

stank past tense of **stink**

stanza /ˈstænzə/ noun [C] a group of lines that form a unit in some types of poem ▶ **strofa** SYN **verse** ⓘ **Stanza** to termin fachowy. Powszechnie na określenie strofy wiersza stosuje się słowo **verse**.

staple /ˈsteɪpl/ noun [C] a small thin piece of bent wire that you push through pieces of paper using a **stapler** to fasten them together ▶ **zszywka**
■ **staple** verb [T]: *Staple the letter to the application form.* ▶ **zszywać** (*zszywaczem*) | **stapler** noun [C] small device used for putting **staples** into paper, etc. ▶ **zszywacz** ➲ picture at **stationery**

ˌstaple ˈdiet noun [C, usually sing.] the main food that a person or an animal normally eats: *a staple diet of rice and fish* ▶ **podstawowe pożywienie**

🔑 **star[1]** /stɑː(r)/ noun **1** [C] a large ball of burning gas in space that you see as a small point of light in the sky at night: *It was a clear night and the stars were shining brightly.* ▶ **gwiazda 2** [C] a shape, decoration, mark, etc. with five or six points sticking out in a regular pattern: *I've marked the possible candidates on the list with a star.* ▶ **gwiazd(k)a 3** [C] a mark that represents a star that is used for telling you how good sth is, especially a hotel or restaurant: *a five-star hotel* ▶ **gwiazdka 4** [C] a famous person in acting, music or sport: *a pop/rock/film/movie star* ◇ *a football/tennis star* ▶ **gwiazd-or/a 5** (**stars**) [pl.] = HOROSCOPE

🔑 **star[2]** /stɑː(r)/ verb (**starring**; **starred**) **1** [I] **star (in sth)** to be one of the main actors in a play, film, etc.: *Gwyneth Paltrow is to star in a new romantic comedy.* ▶ **grać główną rolę 2** [T] to have sb as a star: *The film stars* (w filmie występuje) *Jane Fonda as a teacher in Mexico.* ▶ **obsadzać w głównej roli**

starboard /ˈstɑːbəd/ noun [U] the side of a ship that is on the right when you are facing towards the front of it ▶ **prawa burta** OPP **port** ➲ note at **boat**

starch /stɑːtʃ/ noun [C,U] **1** a white substance that is found in foods such as potatoes, rice and bread ▶ **skrobia 2** a substance that is used for making cloth stiff ▶ **krochmal**
■ **starch** verb [T, usually passive] to make clothes, sheets, etc. stiff using starch: *a starched* (wykrochmalony) *white shirt* ▶ **krochmalić**

stardom /ˈstɑːdəm/ noun [U] the state of being a famous person in acting, music or sport: *She* ***shot to stardom*** (osiągnęła sławę) *in a Broadway musical.* ▶ **gwiazdorstwo**

🔑 **stare** /steə(r)/ verb [I] **stare (at sb/sth)** to look at sb/sth for a long time because you are surprised, shocked, etc.: *Everybody stared at his hat.* ◇ *He didn't reply, he just stared into the distance.* ▶ **gapić się, patrzeć uporczywie, wpatrywać się**
■ **stare** noun [C]: *She gave him a blank stare.* Popatrzyła na niego obojętnym wzrokiem. ▶ **(utkwione) spojrzenie**

starfish /ˈstɑːfɪʃ/ noun [C] (pl. **starfish**) a flat sea animal in the shape of a star with five or more arms ▶ **rozgwiazda** ➲ picture on **page A11**

stark[1] /stɑːk/ adj. **1** very empty and without decoration and therefore not attractive: *a stark landscape* ▶ **nagi, surowy 2** unpleasant and impossible to avoid: *He now faces the* ***stark reality*** (brutalną rzeczywistość) *of life in prison.* ▶ **bardzo nieprzyjemny i nieunikniony 3** very different to sth in a way that is easy to see ▶ **skrajnie kontrastujący**

stark[2] /stɑːk/ adv. completely; extremely: *stark naked* ◇ *Have you gone stark raving mad?* ▶ **zupełnie**

starlight /ˈstɑːlaɪt/ noun [U] the light that is sent out by stars in the sky ▶ **światło gwiazd**

starling /ˈstɑːlɪŋ/ noun [C] a small noisy bird with dark shiny feathers ▶ **szpak**

starry /ˈstɑːri/ adj. full of stars: *a starry night* ▶ **gwiaździsty**

ˈstar sign (also informal **sign**) one of the twelve divisions of the **zodiac**: *'What's your star sign?' 'Leo.'* ▶ **znak zodiaku**

🔑 **start[1]** /stɑːt/ verb **1** [I,T] **start (sth/to do sth/doing sth)** to begin doing sth: *Turn over your exam papers and start now.* ◇ *We'll have to start early* (wcześnie wyruszyć) *if we want to be in Dover by 10.* ◇ *Prices start at £5.* ◇ *After waiting for an hour, the customers started to complain.* ◇ *She started playing the piano when she was six.* ◇ *What time do you have to* ***start work*** *in the morning?* ▶ **zaczynać (się), rozpoczynać 2** [I,T] to begin or to make sth begin to happen: *What time does the concert start?* ◇ *I'd like to start the meeting now.* ◇ *The police think a young woman may have started the fire* (wywołać pożar). ▶ **rozpoczynać (się)** ➲ note at **begin 3** [I,T] **start (sth) (up)** to make an engine, a car, etc. begin to work; (used about an engine, a car, etc.) to begin to work: *The car won't start* (nie chce zapalić). ◇ *We heard an engine starting up in the street.* ◇ *He got onto his motor bike, started the engine and rode away.* ▶ **uruchamiać (się) 4** [I,T] **start (sth) (up)** to create a company, an organiza-

S

tion, etc.; to begin to exist: *They've decided to start their own business.* ◇ *There are a lot of new companies starting up in that area now.* ▶ **uruchamiać, rozpoczynać (się)** **5** [I] to make a sudden, quick movement because you are surprised or afraid: *A loud noise outside made me start.* ▶ **wzdrygać się**

IDM **get/start off on the right/wrong foot (with sb)** → FOOT[1]

set/start the ball rolling → BALL

to start (off) with 1 (used for giving your first reason for sth): *'Why are you so angry?' 'Well, to start off with, you're late, and secondly you've lied to me.'* ▶ **po pierwsze 2** in the beginning; at first: *Everything was fine to start with, but the marriage quickly deteriorated.* ▶ **na początku**

PHR V **start off** to begin in a particular way: *I'd like to start off by welcoming you all to Leeds.* ▶ **zaczynać od czegoś**

start on sth to begin doing sth that needs to be done ▶ **zaczynać (coś robić)**

start out to begin your life, career, etc. in a particular way that changed later: *She started out as a teacher in Glasgow.* ▶ **rozpoczynać** (*np. karierę*)

start over (US) to begin again ▶ **zaczynać od początku/na nowo**

start² /stɑːt/ noun **1** [C, usually sing.] the point at which sth begins: *The chairman made a short speech **at the start of** the meeting.* ◇ *I told you it was a bad idea **from the start**.* ▶ **początek 2** [C, usually sing.] the action or process of starting: *We've got a lot of work to do today, so let's **make a start on*** (zacznijmy od) *those files.* ◇ *to make a fresh start* zaczynać wszystko od początku ▶ **początek, rozpoczęcie 3** (**the start**) [sing.] the place where a race begins: *The athletes are now lining up at the start.* ▶ **start 4** [C, usually sing.] an amount of time or distance that you give to a weaker person at the beginning of a race, game, etc.: *I gave the younger children a start.* ▶ **fory** ➲ look at **head start 5** [C, usually sing.] a sudden quick movement that your body makes because you are surprised or afraid: *She woke up **with a start**.* Zerwała się ze snu. ▶ **wzdrygnięcie**

IDM **for a start** (informal) (used to emphasize your first reason for sth): *'Why can't we go on holiday?' 'Well, for a start we can't afford it...'* ▶ **po pierwsze**

get off to a flying start → FLYING

get off to a good, bad, etc. start to start well, badly, etc. ▶ **dobrze/źle się rozpoczynać**

starter /ˈstɑːtə(r)/ (US usually **appetizer** /ˈæpɪtaɪzə(r)/) noun [C] a small amount of food that is served before the main course of a meal ▶ **przystawka** ➲ note at **restaurant** ➲ look at **hors d'oeuvre**

ˈstarting point noun [C] **starting point (for sth) 1** an idea or a topic that you use to begin a discussion with ▶ **punkt wyjścia 2** the place where you begin a journey ▶ **miejsce rozpoczęcia**

startle /ˈstɑːtl/ verb [T] to surprise sb/sth in a way that slightly shocks or frightens them or it: *The gunshot startled the horses.* ▶ **przestraszyć, zaskoczyć** (*tak, że aż drgnie*)

■ **startled** adj. ▶ **przestraszony, wstrząśnięty** | **startling** adj. ▶ **wstrząsający**

starvation /stɑːˈveɪʃn/ noun [U] suffering or death because there is not enough food: *to die of starvation* ▶ **głód, śmierć z głodu**

starve /stɑːv/ verb [I,T] to suffer or die because you do not have enough food to eat; to make sb/sth suffer or die in this way: *Millions of people are starving in the poorer countries of the world.* ◇ *That winter many animals **starved to death**.* ▶ **głodować, głodzić (się)**

IDM **be starved of sth** to suffer because you are not getting enough of sth that you need: *The children had been starved of love and affection for years.* ▶ **być spragnionym czegoś**

be starving (informal) to be extremely hungry ▶ **umierać z głodu**

stash /stæʃ/ verb [T,I] (informal) to store sth in a safe or secret place: *She has a fortune **stashed away** in various bank accounts.* ▶ **ukrywać**

■ **stash** noun [usually sing.] (informal) an amount of sth that is kept secretly: *a stash of money* ▶ **ukryty zapas**

state¹ /steɪt/ noun **1** [C] the mental, emotional or physical condition that sb/sth is in at a particular time: *the state of the economy* ◇ *He is in a **state of shock**.* ◇ *The house is in a terrible state.* ▶ **stan 2** (also **State**) [C] a country considered as an organized political community controlled by one government: *Pakistan has been an independent state since 1947.* ▶ **państwo** ➲ note at **country 3** (also **State**) [C] an organized political community forming part of a country: *the southern States of the US* ▶ **stan** ➲ look at **county, province 4** (often **the State**) [U] the government of a country: *affairs/matters of state* ◇ *the relationship between the Church and the State* ◇ *a state-owned company* ◇ *heads of State* głowy państw ▶ **państwo 5** [U] the formal ceremonies connected with high levels of government or with the leaders of countries: *The President was driven in state* (uroczyście) *through the streets.* **6** (**the States**) [pl.] (informal) the United States of America: *We lived in the States for about five years.* ▶ **Stany**

IDM **be in/get into a state** (especially Brit., informal) to be or become very nervous or upset: *Now don't get into a state! I'm sure everything will be all right.* ▶ **bardzo się (z)denerwować**

state of affairs a situation: *This state of affairs must not be allowed to continue.* ▶ **stan rzeczy**

state of mind mental condition: *She's in a very confused state of mind.* ▶ **stan umysłu**

state² adj. [only before a noun] **1** provided or controlled by the government of a country: *She went to a state school.* ▶ **państwowy 2** connected with the leader of a country attending an official ceremony: *The Queen is going on a **state visit** to Moscow.* ▶ **państwowy 3** connected with a particular state of a country, especially in the US: *a state prison/hospital/university* ▶ **stanowy**

state³ /steɪt/ verb [T] to say or write sth, especially formally: *Your letter states that you sent the goods on 31 March, but we have not received them.* ▶ **oznajmiać, oświadczać**

the ˈState Department noun [sing.] the US government department of foreign affairs: *senior US Defence and State Department officials* ▶ **Departament Stanu**

stately /ˈsteɪtli/ adj. formal and impressive: *a stately old building* ▶ **majestatyczny**

ˌstately ˈhome noun [C] (Brit.) a large old house that has historical interest and can be visited by the public ▶ **budynek o historycznym znaczeniu, dostępny dla zwiedzających** ➲ picture on **page A3**

statement /ˈsteɪtmənt/ noun [C] **1** something that you say or write, especially formally: *The Prime Minister will **make a statement** about the defence cuts today.* ▶ **oświadczenie 2** = BANK STATEMENT

ˌstate of the ˈart adj. using the most modern or advanced methods; as good as it can be at the present time: *The system was state of the art.* ◇ *a state-of-the-art system* najnowocześniejszy system ▶ **zgodny z najnowszymi osiągnięciami wiedzy**

statesman /ˈsteɪtsmən/ noun [C] (pl. **-men** /-mən/) an important and experienced politician who has earned public respect ▶ **mąż stanu**

static¹ /ˈstætɪk/ adj. not moving, changing or developing: *House prices are static.* ▶ **statyczny**

static² /ˈstætɪk/ noun [U] **1** sudden noises that disturb radio or TV signals, caused by electricity in the atmosphere ▶ **zakłócenia atmosferyczne** (*w radiu/TV*) **2** (also ˌstatic elecˈtricity) electricity that collects on a surface: *My hair gets full of static when I brush it.* ▶ **elektryczność statyczna**

station¹ /ˈsteɪʃn/ noun [C] **1** (also ˈrailway station) a building on a railway line where trains stop so that passengers can get on and off: *I get off at the next station.* ▶ **dworzec kolejowy** ➲ note at **train 2** [in compounds] a building from which buses begin and end journeys: *The coach leaves the bus/coach station at 9.30 a.m.* ▶ **dworzec autobusowy 3** [in compounds] a building where a particular service or activity is based: *a fire station* remiza strażacka ◇ *a petrol station* stacja benzynowa ◇ *a police station* komenda/posterunek policji ◇ *a power station* elektrownia ▶ **budynek specjalnego (określonego nazwą) przeznaczenia 4** [in compounds] a radio or TV company and the programmes it sends out: *a local radio/TV station* ◇ *He tuned in to another station.* ▶ **stacja** ➲ look at **channel**

station² /ˈsteɪʃn/ verb [T, often passive] to send sb, especially members of the armed forces, to work in a place for a period of time ▶ **stacjonować, rozstawiać** (*wojsko*)

stationary /ˈsteɪʃənri; US -neri/ adj. not moving: *He crashed into the back of a stationary vehicle.* ▶ **nieruchomy**

stationer's /ˈsteɪʃənəz/ noun [sing.] a shop that sells writing equipment, such as paper, pens, envelopes, etc. ▶ **sklep papierniczy**

stationery /ˈsteɪʃənri; US -neri/ noun [U] writing equipment, for example pens, pencils, paper, envelopes, etc. ▶ **przybory/materiały piśmienne**

ˈstation wagon (US) = ESTATE CAR

statistician /ˌstætɪsˈtɪʃn/ noun [C] a person who studies or works with statistics ▶ **statystyk**

statistics /stəˈtɪstɪks/ noun **1** [pl.] numbers that have been collected in order to provide information about sth: *Statistics indicate that 90% of homes in this country have a TV.* ◇ *crime statistics* ▶ **dane statystyczne 2** [U] the science of collecting and studying these numbers ▶ **statystyka**
■ **statistical** /stəˈtɪstɪkl/ adj.: *statistical information* ▶ **statystyczny** | **statistically** /-kli/ adv. ▶ **statystycznie**

statue /ˈstætʃuː/ noun [C] a figure of a person or an animal that is made of stone or metal and usually put in a public place: *the Statue of Liberty* (Statua Wolności) *in New York* ▶ **posąg**

stature /ˈstætʃə(r)/ noun [U] (formal) **1** the importance and respect that sb has because people have a high opinion of their skill or of what they have done ▶ **(ważna/wysoka) pozycja, format/kaliber** (*człowieka*) **2** the height of a person: *He's quite small* ***in stature.*** ▶ **wzrost**

status /ˈsteɪtəs/ noun **1** [U] the legal position of a person, group or country: *Please indicate your name, age and* ***marital status.*** ◇ *They were granted refugee status.* ▶ **stan (cywilny) 2** [sing.] your social or professional position in relation to other people: *Teachers don't have a very high status in this country.* ▶ **pozycja społeczna/zawodowa 3** [U] a high social position: *The new job gave him much more status.* ▶ **pozycja społeczna**

the **status quo** /ˌsteɪtəs ˈkwəʊ/ noun [sing.] the situation as it is now, or as it was before a recent change ▶ **istniejący stan rzeczy**

stationery

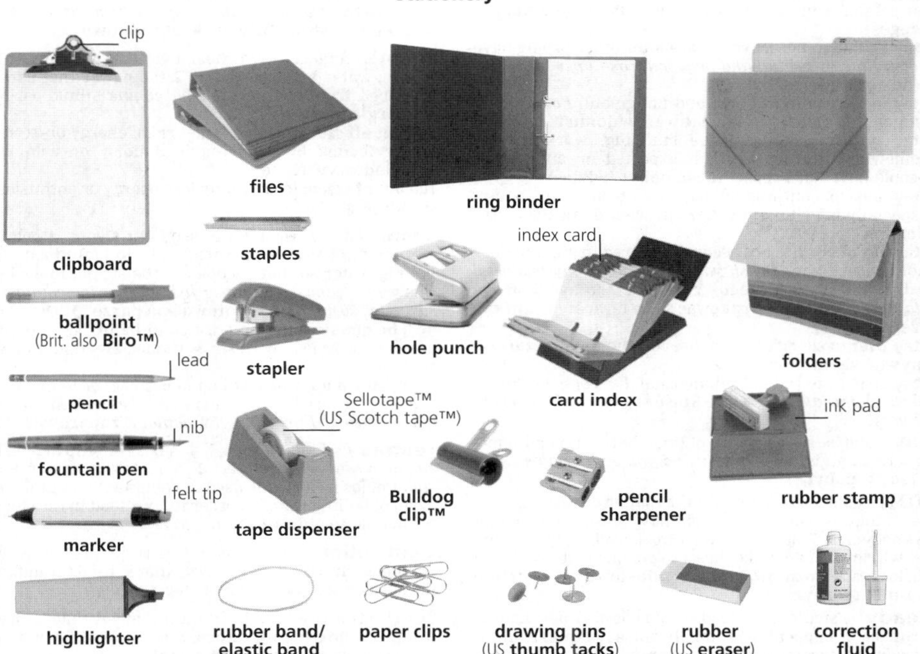

S

ˈ**status symbol** noun [C] something that a person owns that shows that they have a high position in society and a lot of money ▶ **oznaka statusu społecznego**

statute /ˈstætʃuːt/ noun [C] (formal) a law or a rule ▶ **ustawa, prawo**

statutory /ˈstætʃətri; US -tɔːri/ adj. (formal) decided by law: *a statutory right* ▶ **ustawowy**

staunch /stɔːntʃ/ adj. believing in sb/sth or supporting sb/sth very strongly; loyal ▶ **zagorzały; oddany**

stave[1] /steɪv/ noun [C] a set of five lines on which music is written ▶ **pięciolinia** ➲ picture at **music**

stave[2] /steɪv/ verb

PHR V **stave sth off** to stop sth unpleasant from happening now, although it may happen at a later time; to delay sth: *to stave off illness/inflation/bankruptcy* ◇ *to stave off hunger* oszukać głód ▶ **oddalać na jakiś czas** (*np. niebezpieczeństwo, choroby*)

⚷ **stay**[1] /steɪ/ verb [I] **1** to continue to be somewhere and not go away: *Patrick stayed in bed until 11 o'clock.* ◇ *I can't stay long.* ◇ *Stay on this road until you get to Wells.* ◇ *Pete's staying late at the office tonight.* ▶ **zostawać** **2** to continue to be in a particular state or situation without change: *I can't* ***stay awake*** *any longer.* ◇ *I don't know why they stay together.* ▶ **zostawać, pozostawać** ⓘ **Remain** i **stay** mają podobne znaczenie, ale **remain** jest bardziej formalne. **3** to live in a place temporarily as a visitor or guest: *We stayed with friends in France.* ◇ *Which hotel are you* ***staying at?*** ◇ *Can you stay for lunch?* ◇ *Why don't you* ***stay the night?*** ▶ **zatrzymywać się, mieszkać** (*np. w hotelu*), **zostawać** (*np. na noc/obiad*)

IDM **keep/stay/steer clear (of sb/sth)** → CLEAR[3]

stay put (informal) to continue in one place; to not leave ▶ **zostawać na miejscu**

PHR V **stay away (from sb/sth)** to not go near a particular person or place ▶ **trzymać się z daleka (od kogoś/czegoś)**

stay behind to not leave a place after other people have gone: *I'll stay behind and help you wash up.* ▶ **pozostawać** (*np. dłużej, w tyle*)

stay in to remain at home and not go out: *I'm going to stay in and watch TV.* ▶ **zostawać w domu**

stay on (at...) to continue studying, working, etc. somewhere for longer than expected or after other people have left ▶ **przedłużać pobyt (gdzieś)**

stay out to continue to be away from your house, especially late at night ▶ **pozostawać (do późna) poza domem**

stay out of sth 1 to not become involved in sth that does not concern you: *I wish you'd stay out of my business!* ▶ **trzymać się od czegoś z daleka** **2** to avoid sth: *to stay out of trouble* nie pakować się w tarapaty ▶ **unikać czegoś**

stay over to sleep at sb's house for one night ▶ **zatrzymywać się na noc**

stay up to go to bed later than usual: *I'm going to stay up to watch the late film.* ▶ **nie kłaść się, czuwać** (*do późna w nocy*)

⚷ **stay**[2] /steɪ/ noun [C] a period of time that you spend somewhere as a visitor or guest: *Did you enjoy your stay in Crete?* ▶ **pobyt**

STD /ˌes tiː ˈdiː/ abbr. **1 sexually transmitted disease**; any disease that is spread through having sex ▶ **choroba weneryczna** **2** (Brit.) **subscriber trunk dialling**; the system by which you can make direct telephone calls over long distances ▶ **rozmowa międzymiastowa w systemie automatycznym**

⚷ **steady**[1] /ˈstedi/ adj. (**steadier**; **steadiest**) **1** developing, growing or happening gradually and at a regular rate: *a steady increase/decline* ▶ **równomierny** **2** staying the same; not changing and therefore safe: *a steady job/income* ◇ *His breathing was steady* (miarowy). ◇ *She drove at a steady* (ze stałą prędkością) *50 mph.* ▶ **stały** **3** firmly fixed, supported or balanced; not shaking or likely to fall down: *You need* ***a steady hand*** *to take good photographs.* ◇ *He held the ladder steady as she climbed up it.* ▶ **pewny, ustabilizowany**

■ **steadily** adv.: *Unemployment has risen steadily since April 1998.* ▶ **równomiernie**

steady[2] /ˈstedi/ verb [I,T] (**steadying**; **steadies**; pt, pp **steadied**) to stop yourself/sb/sth from moving, shaking or falling; to stop moving, shaking or falling: *She thought she was going to fall, so she put out a hand to steady herself.* ◇ *He had to* ***steady*** *his* ***nerves/voice*** *before beginning his speech.* ▶ **odzyskiwać równowagę; opanowywać** (*np. nerwy, drżenie głosu*); (*nerwy, drżenie serca*) **uspokajać się**

steak /steɪk/ noun [C,U] a thick flat piece of meat or fish: *a piece of steak* ◇ *a cod/salmon steak* ▶ **płat, stek** ➲ look at **chop**

⚷ **steal** /stiːl/ verb (pt **stole** /stəʊl/, pp **stolen** /ˈstəʊlən/) **1** [I,T] **steal (sth) (from sb/sth)** to take sth from a person, shop, etc. without permission and without intending to return it or pay for it: *The terrorists were driving a stolen car.* ◇ *We found out she had been stealing from us for years.* ▶ **kraść** ➲ note at **thief**

> Dopełnieniami czasownika **steal** są przedmioty – a czasownika **rob** osoby lub instytucje, np. banki: *My camera has been stolen!* ◇ *I've been robbed!* ◇ *to rob a bank* ◇ *They robbed me of all my money!*

2 [I] **steal away, in, out, etc.** to move somewhere secretly and quietly: *She stole out of the room.* ▶ **wynosić się ukradkiem; wkradać się**

stealth /stelθ/ noun [U] (formal) behaviour that is secret or quiet: *The terrorists operate* ***by stealth.*** Terroryści działają skrycie. ▶ **potajemne działanie**

■ **stealthy** adj.: *a stealthy approach/movement* ▶ **ukradkowy** | **stealthily** adv. ▶ **ukradkowo**

⚷ **steam**[1] /stiːm/ noun [U] **1** the hot gas that is produced by boiling water ▶ **para** (*wodna*) **2** the power that can be produced from steam: *a steam engine* silnik parowy ▶ **energia parowa**

IDM **let off steam** (informal) to get rid of energy or express strong feeling by behaving in a noisy or wild way ▶ **wyładowywać się**

run out of steam to gradually lose energy or enthusiasm ▶ **oklapnąć**

steam[2] /stiːm/ verb **1** [I,T] to send out steam: *a bowl of steaming hot soup* ▶ **parować** **2** [T] to place food over boiling water so that it cooks in the steam; to cook in this way: *steamed vegetables/fish* ◇ *Leave the potatoes to steam for 30 minutes.* ▶ **gotować na parze** ➲ note at **cook**

IDM **be/get steamed up** (informal) to be or become very angry or worried about sth ▶ **wściec się; (z)denerwować się**

PHR V **steam up; steam sth up** to become, or to make sth become, covered with steam: *As he walked in, his glasses steamed up.* ▶ (*szyby, okulary*) **zaparować**

steamer /ˈstiːmə(r)/ noun [C] **1** a boat or ship driven by steam power ▶ **parowiec** **2** a metal container with small holes in it that is used in cooking. You put it over a pan of boiling water in order to cook food in the steam. ▶ **garnek do gotowania na parze**

steamroller /ˈstiːmrəʊlə(r)/ noun [C] a big heavy vehicle with wide heavy wheels that is used for making the surface of a road flat ▶ **walec drogowy**

⚷ **steel**[1] /stiːl/ noun [U] a very strong metal that is made from iron mixed with **carbon**. Steel is used for making knives, tools, machines, etc. ▶ **stal**

steel[2] /stiːl/ verb [T] **steel yourself** to prepare yourself to deal with sth difficult or unpleasant: *Steel yourself for a shock.* ▶ **nastawiać się (na coś)**

steelworks /ˈstiːlwɜːks/ noun [C, with sing. or pl. verb] (pl. **steelworks**) a factory where steel is made ▶ **huta stali**

steep /stiːp/ adj. **1** (used about a hill, mountain, street, etc.) rising or falling quickly; at a sharp angle: *I don't think I can cycle up that hill. It's too steep.* ▶ **stromy** **2** (used about an increase or fall in sth) very big: *a steep rise in unemployment* ▶ **ostry** **3** (informal) too expensive: *£2 for a cup of coffee seems a little steep to me.* ▶ (*koszt itp.*) **wygórowany**
■ **steeply** adv.: *House prices have risen steeply this year.* ▶ **gwałtownie** | **steepness** noun [U] ▶ **stromość**

steeped /stiːpt/ adj. **steeped in sth** having a lot of sth; full of sth: *a city steeped in history* ▶ **przesiąknięty**, **nasycony**

steepen /ˈstiːpən/ verb [I,T] to become or to make sth become steeper: *After a mile, the slope steepened.* ▶ **stać się bardziej stromym**; **powodować, że coś staje się bardziej strome**

steeple /ˈstiːpl/ noun [C] a tower on the roof of a church, often with a **spire** ▶ **strzelista wieża**, **iglica**

steer /stɪə(r)/ verb **1** [I,T] to control the direction that a vehicle is going in: *Can you push the car while I steer?* ◇ *to steer a boat/ship/bicycle/motorbike* ▶ **kierować**, **sterować** **2** [T] to take control of a situation and try to influence the way it develops: *She tried to steer the conversation away from the subject of money.* ▶ **sprowadzać** (*np. na inny temat*)
IDM **keep/stay/steer clear (of sb/sth)** → CLEAR[3]

steering /ˈstɪərɪŋ/ noun [U] the parts of a vehicle that control the direction that it moves in: *a car with power steering* ▶ **układ kierowniczy**

ˈ**steering wheel** (also **wheel**) noun [C] the wheel that the driver turns in a vehicle to control the direction that it moves in ▶ **kierownica** ➲ picture at **car**

stem[1] /stem/ noun [C] **1** the main central part of a plant above the ground from which the leaves or flowers grow ▶ **łodyga** **2** the main part of a word onto which other parts are added: *'Writ-' is the stem of the words 'write', 'writing', 'written' and 'writer'.* ▶ **temat** **3** the long thin part of a wine glass between the bowl and the base ▶ **nóżka** (*kieliszka*)

stem[2] /stem/ verb [T] (**stemming**; **stemmed**) to stop sth that is increasing or spreading ▶ **tamować**
PHR V **stem from sth** [not used in the continuous tenses] to be the result of sth ▶ **wywodzić się skądś/z czegoś**
ℹ Czasownika **stem** nie używa się w czasach *continuous*. Natomiast często spotyka się go w *present participle* (formie *-ing*): *He was treated for depression stemming from his domestic and business difficulties.*

ˈ**stem cell** noun [C] a basic type of cell which can divide and develop into cells with particular functions. All the different kinds of cells in the human body develop from **stem cells**. ▶ **komórka macierzysta**

stench /stentʃ/ noun [sing.] a very unpleasant smell ▶ **odór** ➲ note at **smell**[2]

stencil /ˈstensl/ noun [C] a thin piece of metal, plastic or card with a design cut out of it, that you put onto a surface and paint over so that the design is left on the surface; the pattern or design that is produced in this way ▶ **szablon**
■ **stencil** verb [I,T] (**stencilling**; **stencilled**; US also **stenciling**; **stenciled**) ▶ **malować przez szablon**

step[1] /step/ noun [C] **1** the act of lifting one foot and putting it down in a different place: *Nick **took a step** forward and then stopped.* ◇ *I heard steps outside the window.* ◇ *We were obviously lost so we decided to **retrace our steps*** (wrócić tą samą drogą). ▶ **krok** **2** one action in a series of actions that you take in order to achieve sth: *This will not solve the problem completely, but it is **a step in the right direction.*** ▶ **krok do czegoś** **3** one of the surfaces on which you put your foot when you are going up or down stairs: *on the top/bottom step* ◇ *a flight of steps* kondygnacja schodów ▶ **schodek** ➲ note at **stair**
IDM **be in/out of step (with sb/sth)** to move/not move your feet at the same time as other people when you are marching, dancing, etc. ▶ **iść w takt**; **gubić krok**
step by step (used for talking about a series of actions) moving slowly and gradually from one action or stage to the next: *clear step-by-step instructions* ▶ **stopniowo**, **krok po kroku**
take steps to do sth to take action in order to achieve sth ▶ **podejmować kroki, aby coś zrobić**
watch your step → WATCH[1]

step[2] /step/ verb [I] (**stepping**; **stepped**) **1** to lift one foot and put it down in a different place when you are walking: *Be careful! Don't step in the mud.* ◇ *to step forward/back* ◇ *Ouch! You stepped on my foot!* ▶ **stąpać**, **kroczyć** **2** to move a short distance; to go somewhere: *I stepped outside for a minute to get some air.* ◇ *Could you step out of the car* (wysiąść z samochodu) *please, sir?* ▶ **wychodzić** (*np. na zewnątrz*)
PHR V **step aside/down** to leave an important job or position and let sb else take your place ▶ **ustępować** (*ze stanowiska*)
step in to help sb in a difficult situation or to become involved in a disagreement ▶ **wkraczać w coś**
step sth up to increase the amount, speed, etc. of sth: *The Army has decided to step up its security arrangements.* ▶ **podnosić (stopniowo)**, **intensyfikować**

step- /step-/ [in compounds] related as a result of one parent marrying again ▶ **przyrodni, spokrewniony po linii jednego rodzica**

stepbrother /ˈstepbrʌðə(r)/ noun [C] a son from an earlier marriage of sb who has married your mother or father ▶ **przyrodni brat** ➲ look at **half-brother**

stepchild /ˈsteptʃaɪld/ noun [C] (pl. **stepchildren**) a child from an earlier marriage of your husband or wife ▶ **pasierb/ica** ➲ note at **child**

stepdaughter /ˈstepdɔːtə(r)/ noun [C] a daughter from an earlier marriage of your husband or wife ▶ **pasierbica**

stepfather /ˈstepfɑːðə(r)/ noun [C] a man who has married your mother when your parents are divorced or your father is dead ▶ **ojczym**

stepladder /ˈsteplædə(r)/ noun [C] a short **ladder** with two parts, one with steps. The parts are joined together at the top so that it can stand on its own and be folded up when you are not using it. ▶ **drabina składana**

stepmother /ˈstepmʌðə(r)/ noun [C] a woman who has married your father when your parents are divorced or your mother is dead ▶ **macocha**

ˈ**stepping stone** noun [C] **1** one of a line of flat stones that you can step on in order to cross a river ▶ **płaski kamień, umożliwiający przejście przez strumień itp.** **2** something that allows you to make progress or helps you to achieve sth ▶ **odskocznia w czymś**

stepsister /ˈstepsɪstə(r)/ noun [C] a daughter from an earlier marriage of sb who has married your mother or father ▶ **przyrodnia siostra** ➲ look at **half-sister**

stepson /ˈstepsʌn/ noun [C] a son from an earlier marriage of your husband or wife ▶ **pasierb**

stereo /ˈsteriəʊ/ noun (pl. **stereos**) **1** (also ˈ**stereo system**) [C] a machine that plays CDs, tapes, etc., sometimes with a radio, that has two separate speakers so that you hear sounds from each: *a car/personal stereo* ▶ **zestaw stereo(foniczny)** ➲ note at **listen** ➲ picture at **car** **2** [U] the system for playing recorded music, speech, etc. in which

the sound is divided into two parts: *This programme is broadcast **in stereo**.* ▶ **stereo(fonia)** ➲ look at **mono**
■ **stereo** adj. [only before a noun]: *a stereo TV* ▶ **stereofoniczny**

stereotype /ˈsteriətaɪp/ noun [C] a fixed idea about a particular type of person or thing, which is often not true in reality ▶ **stereotyp**
■ **stereotype** verb [T]: *In advertisements, women are often stereotyped as housewives.* ▶ **myśleć/przedstawiać stereotypowo** | **stereotypical** /ˌsteriəˈtɪpɪkl/ adj. ▶ **stereotypowy**

sterile /ˈsteraɪl; US ˈsterəl/ adj. **1** not able to produce young animals or babies ▶ **bezpłodny 2** completely clean and free from bacteria: *All equipment used during a medical operation must be sterile.* ▶ **sterylny 3** not producing any useful result: *a sterile discussion/argument* ▶ **jałowy**
■ **sterility** /stəˈrɪləti/ noun [U] ▶ **bezpłodność**

sterilize (also -ise) /ˈsterəlaɪz/ verb [T] **1** to make sb/sth completely clean and free from bacteria ▶ **sterylizować 2** [usually passive] to perform an operation on a person or an animal so that they or it cannot have babies ▶ **sterylizować**
■ **sterilization** (also -isation) /ˌsterəlaɪˈzeɪʃn; US -ləˈz-/ noun [U] ▶ **sterylizacja**

sterling[1] /ˈstɜːlɪŋ/ noun [U] the system of money used in Britain, that uses the pound as its basic unit ▶ **szterling**

sterling[2] /ˈstɜːlɪŋ/ adj. of very high quality: *sterling work* ▶ **doskonały**, **rzetelny**

stern[1] /stɜːn/ adj. very serious; not smiling: *a stern expression/warning* ▶ **srogi**; **surowy**
■ **sternly** adv. ▶ **srogo**, **surowo**

stern[2] /stɜːn/ noun [C] the back end of a ship or boat ▶ **rufa** OPP **bow** ➲ note at **boat** ➲ picture on **page A6**

sternum /ˈstɜːnəm/ noun [C] (pl. **sternums** or **sterna**) the **breastbone** ▶ (*anat.*) **mostek**

steroid /ˈsterɔɪd/ noun [C] a chemical substance produced naturally in the body. There are many different **steroids** and they can be used to treat diseases and are sometimes used illegally by people playing sports. ▶ **steryd**

stethoscope /ˈsteθəskəʊp/ noun [C] the piece of equipment that a doctor uses for listening to your breathing and heart ▶ **słuchawka lekarska**

stew /stjuː; US stuː/ noun [C,U] a type of food that you make by cooking meat and/or vegetables in liquid for a long time ▶ **gulasz**
■ **stew** verb [I,T] ▶ **dusić** ➲ note at **cook**

steward /ˈstjuːəd; US ˈstuː-/ noun [C] **1** a man whose job is to look after passengers on an aircraft, a ship or a train ▶ **steward 2** (Brit.) a person who helps to organize a large public event, for example a race ▶ **osoba utrzymująca porządek na publicznych imprezach lub nadzorująca ich organizację**

stewardess /ˌstjuːəˈdes; ˈstjuːə-; US ˈstuːə-/ noun [C] **1** (old-fashioned) a woman whose job is to look after passengers on an aircraft ▶ **stewardesa 2** a woman who looks after the passengers on a ship or train ▶ **stewardesa**

🔑 **stick**[1] /stɪk/ verb (pt, pp **stuck** /stʌk/) **1** [I,T] **stick (sth) in/into (sth)** to push a pointed object into sth; to be pushed into sth: *Stick a fork into the meat to see if it's ready.* ▶ **wbijać**, **wtykać 2** [I,T] to fix sth to sth else by using a sticky substance; to become fixed to sth else: *I stuck a stamp on the envelope.* ◇ *We used glue to stick the pieces together.* ▶ **lepić (się) 3** [T] (informal) to put sth somewhere, especially quickly or carelessly: *Stick* (rzuć) *your bags in the bedroom.* ◇ *Just at that moment James stuck* (wystawił) *his head round the door.* ◇ *Can you stick this on* (wywiesić na) *the noticeboard?* **4** [I] **stick (in sth)** (used about sth that can usually be moved) to become fixed in one position so that it cannot be moved: *The car was stuck* (ugrzązł) *in the mud.* ◇ *This drawer keeps sticking* (zacina się). ▶ **tkwić 5** [T] [often in negative sentences and questions] (informal) to stay in a difficult or unpleasant situation: *I can't stick this job much longer.* ▶ **znosić**
IDM **poke/stick your nose into sth** → NOSE[1]
put/stick your tongue out → TONGUE
stand/stick out like a sore thumb → SORE[1]
PHR V **stick around** (informal) to stay somewhere, waiting for sth to happen or for sb to arrive ▶ **być/kręcić się w pobliżu**
stick at sth (informal) to continue working at sth even when it is difficult ▶ **wytrwale dalej coś robić**
stick by sb (informal) to continue to give sb help and support even in difficult times ▶ **pozostawać komuś wiernym**, **nie opuszczać kogoś** (*w kłopotach*)
stick sth down (informal) to write sth somewhere: *I think I'll stick my name down on the list.* ▶ **zapisać coś**
stick out (informal) to be very noticeable and easily seen: *The new office block really sticks out from the older buildings around it.* ▶ **sterczeć**
stick (sth) out (of sth) to be further out than sth else; to push sth further out than sth else: *The boy's head was sticking out of the window.* ▶ **wystawiać**, **odstawiać**; **wystawać**, **odstawać**
stick it/sth out (informal) to stay in a difficult or unpleasant situation until the end ▶ **znosić do końca**
stick to sth (informal) to continue with sth and not change to anything else ▶ **trzymać się (czegoś)**
stick together (informal) (used about a group of people) to stay friendly and loyal to each other ▶ **trzymać się razem**
stick up to point upwards: *You look funny. Your hair's sticking up!* ◇ *The branch was sticking up out of the water.* ▶ **sterczeć do góry**
stick up for yourself/sb/sth (informal) to support or defend yourself/sb/sth: *Don't worry. I'll stick up for you if there's any trouble.* ▶ **bronić (się)**, **ujmować się za kimś**
stick with sb [no passive] (informal) to stay close to sb so that they can help you: *Stick with me and I'll make you a millionaire!* ▶ **trzymać się kogoś**
stick with sth [no passive] (informal) to continue with sth or continue doing sth: *They decided to stick with their original plan.* ▶ **trzymać się czegoś**

🔑 **stick**[2] /stɪk/ noun [C] **1** a small thin piece of wood from a tree: *We collected dry sticks to start a fire.* ▶ **patyk 2** (especially Brit.) = WALKING STICK **3** a long thin piece of wood that you use for hitting the ball in some sports: *a hockey stick* ▶ **kij** ➲ look at **bat**, **club**, **racket 4** a long thin piece of sth: *a stick of celery/dynamite* ▶ **laska**

sticker /ˈstɪkə(r)/ noun [C] a piece of paper with writing or a picture on one side that you can stick onto sth ▶ **nalepka**

ˈsticking plaster = PLASTER[1] (3)

🔑 **sticky** /ˈstɪki/ adj. (**stickier**; **stickiest**) **1** (used for describing a substance that easily becomes joined to things that it touches, or sth that is covered with this kind of substance): *These sweets are very sticky.* ▶ **lepki**, **lepiący się 2** (informal) (used about a situation) difficult or unpleasant: *There were a few sticky moments in the meeting.* ▶ **kłopotliwy**

ˈsticky tape (Brit.) = SELLOTAPE

🔑 **stiff**[1] /stɪf/ adj. **1** (used about material, paper, etc.) firm and difficult to bend or move: *My new shoes feel rather stiff.* ◇ *The door handle is stiff* (klamka nie chce się ruszyć) *and I can't turn it.* ▶ **sztywny**, **twardy**; **ciężko chodzący/działający 2** not easy to move: *My arm feels really stiff after playing tennis yesterday.* ▶ **zesztywniały 3** (used about a liquid) very thick; almost solid:

Beat the egg whites until they are stiff. Ubij białko na sztywną pianę. ▶ **ścięty, gęsty** **4** more difficult or stronger than usual: *The firm faces stiff competition from its rivals.* ◇ *a stiff breeze/wind* ◇ *stiff opposition to the plan* zaciekły sprzeciw wobec planu ▶ **trudny, silny** **5** not relaxed or friendly; formal: *The speech he made to welcome them was stiff and formal.* ▶ **sztywny** **6** [only before a noun] strong: *a stiff whisky* ▶ **mocny**
■ **stiffness** noun [U] ▶ **sztywność, zesztywnienie**

stiff² /stɪf/ adv. (informal) extremely: *to be bored/frozen/scared/worried stiff* ▶ **śmiertelnie**

stiffen /ˈstɪfn/ verb **1** [I] (used about a person) to suddenly stop moving and hold your body very straight, usually because you are afraid or angry ▶ **sztywnieć** **2** [I,T] to become, or to make sth become, difficult to bend or move ▶ **sztywnieć; usztywniać**

stiffly /ˈstɪfli/ adv. in an unfriendly formal way: *He smiled stiffly.* ▶ **sztywno**

stifle /ˈstaɪfl/ verb **1** [T] to stop sth happening, developing or continuing: *Her strict education had stifled her natural creativity.* ◇ *to stifle a yawn/cry/giggle* ▶ **tłumić; dławić** **2** [I,T] to be or to make sb unable to breathe because it is very hot and/or there is no fresh air: *Fergus was almost stifled by the smoke.* ▶ **dusić (się)**
■ **stifling** adj.: *The heat was stifling.* ▶ **duszący, dławiący**

stigma /ˈstɪgmə/ noun [C,U] bad and often unfair feelings that people in general have about a particular illness, way of behaving, etc.: *There is still a lot of stigma attached to being unemployed.* ▶ **piętno**

stigmatize (also -ise) /ˈstɪgmətaɪz/ verb [T, usually passive] (formal) to treat sb in a way that makes them feel that they are very bad or unimportant ▶ **piętnować**
■ **stigmatization** (also -isation) /ˌstɪgmətaɪˈzeɪʃn; US -təˈz-/ noun [U] ▶ **napiętnowanie**

stiletto /stɪˈletəʊ/ (pl. **-os** or **-oes**) (also ˌstiletto ˈheel) noun [C] (especially Brit.) a woman's shoe with a very high narrow heel; the heel on such a shoe ▶ **szpilka** (*but lub obcas*)

still¹ /stɪl/ adv. **1** continuing until now or until the time you are talking about and not finishing: *Do you still live in London?* ◇ *It's still raining.* ◇ *I've eaten all the food but I'm still hungry.* ◇ *In 1997 Zoran was still a student.* ▶ **nadal, wciąż** **2** in spite of what has just been said: *He had a bad headache but he still went to the party.* ▶ **mimo to** **3** (used for making a comparative adjective stronger): *It was very cold yesterday, but today it's colder still.* ◇ *There was still more bad news to come.* ▶ **jeszcze/nawet bardziej, więcej itp.** **4** in addition; more: *There are still ten days to go until my holiday.* ▶ **jeszcze**

still² /stɪl/ adj. **1** not moving: *Stand still! I want to take a photograph!* ◇ *Children find it hard to* ***keep/stay still*** *for long periods.* ▶ **nieruchomy; nieruchomo** **2** quiet or calm: *The water was perfectly still.* ◇ *a still evening* bezwietrzny wieczór ▶ (*woda itp.*) **spokojny,** (*woda itp.*) **niezmącony** **3** (used about a drink) not containing gas: *still mineral water* ▶ **niegazowany** ⊃ look at **fizzy, sparkling**
■ **stillness** noun [U] ▶ **bezruch**

still³ /stɪl/ noun [C] a single photograph that is taken from a film or video ▶ **kadr z filmu**

stillborn /ˈstɪlbɔːn/ adj. (used about a baby) dead when it is born ▶ (*dziecko*) **martwo urodzony**

ˌstill ˈlife noun [U,C] (pl. **still lifes**) the representation in painting or drawing of objects which are not living, e.g. fruit, flowers, etc.; a picture of this type ▶ **martwa natura**

stilt /stɪlt/ noun [C] **1** one of two long pieces of wood, with places to rest your feet on, on which you can walk above the ground: *Have you tried walking* ***on stilts?*** ▶ **szczudło** **2** one of a set of poles that supports a building above the ground or water ▶ **pal**

stilted /ˈstɪltɪd/ adj. (used about a way of speaking or writing) not natural or relaxed; too formal ▶ (*wypowiedź, tekst*) **sztywny, bardzo formalny**

stimulant /ˈstɪmjələnt/ noun [C] a drug or medicine that makes you feel more active ▶ **środek pobudzający**

stimulate /ˈstɪmjuleɪt/ verb [T] **1** to make sth active or more active: *Exercise stimulates the blood circulation.* ◇ *The government has decided to cut taxes in order to stimulate the economy.* ▶ **pobudzać, ożywiać** **2** to make sb feel interested and excited about sth: *The lessons don't really stimulate him.* ▶ **inspirować, podniecać**
■ **stimulation** /ˌstɪmjuˈleɪʃn/ noun [U] ▶ **stymulacja, bodziec**

stimulating /ˈstɪmjuleɪtɪŋ/ adj. interesting and exciting: *a stimulating discussion* ▶ **pobudzający**

stimulus /ˈstɪmjələs/ noun [C,U] (pl. **stimuli** /-laɪ/) something that causes activity, development or interest: *Books provide children with ideas and a stimulus for play.* ▶ **bodziec**

sting¹ /stɪŋ/ verb [I,T] (pt, pp **stung** /stʌŋ/) **1** (used about an insect, a plant, etc.) to make a person or an animal feel a sudden pain by pushing sth sharp into their skin and sending poison into them: *Ow! I've been stung by a bee!* ◇ *Be careful. Those plants sting.* ▶ **żądlić, parzyć** ⊃ look at **bite** **2** to make sb/sth feel a sudden, sharp pain: *Soap stings if it gets in your eyes.* ▶ **szczypać, kłuć** **3** to make sb feel very hurt and upset because of sth you say: *Kate was stung by her father's criticism.* ▶ **ranić, dotykać**

sting² /stɪŋ/ noun [C] **1** the sharp pointed part of some insects and animals that is used for pushing into the skin of a person or an animal and putting in poison: *the sting of a bee* ▶ **żądło** ⊃ picture at **insect** **2** the pain that you feel when an animal or insect pushes its sting into you: *I got a wasp sting on the leg.* ▶ **użądlenie** **3** a sharp pain that feels like a sting: *the sting of soap in your eyes* ▶ **szczypanie, kłucie, parzenie**

stingy /ˈstɪndʒi/ adj. (**stingier**; **stingiest**) (informal) not given or giving willingly; not generous, especially with money: *Don't be so stingy with the cream!* ▶ **skąpy** SYN **mean**
■ **stinginess** noun [U] ▶ **skąpstwo**

stink /stɪŋk/ verb [I] (pt **stank** /stæŋk/ or **stunk** /stʌŋk/, pp **stunk**) (informal) **stink (of sth)** **1** to have a very strong and unpleasant smell: *It stinks in here – open a window!* ◇ *to stink of fish* ▶ **śmierdzieć** ⊃ note at **smell²** **2** to seem to be very bad, unpleasant or dishonest: *The whole business stinks of corruption.* ▶ (*przen.*) **śmierdzieć (czymś)**
■ **stink** noun [C] ▶ **smród**

stinky /ˈstɪŋki/ adj. (**stinkier**; **stinkiest**) (informal) **1** having an extremely bad smell ▶ **śmierdzący** **2** extremely unpleasant or bad ▶ (*interes itp.*) **śmierdzący**

stint /stɪnt/ noun [C] a fixed period of time that you spend doing sth: *He did a brief stint in the army after leaving school.* ▶ **okres jakiejś działalności**

stipend /ˈstaɪpend/ noun [C] (formal) an amount of money that is paid regularly to sb, especially a priest, as wages or money to live on: *a monthly stipend* ◇ (especially US) *a summer internship with a small stipend* ▶ **uposażenie** (*zwł. osoby duchownej*)

stipulate /ˈstɪpjuleɪt/ verb [T] (formal) to say exactly and officially what must be done: *The law stipulates that all schools must be inspected every three years.* ▶ **zastrzegać**
■ **stipulation** /ˌstɪpjuˈleɪʃn/ noun [C,U] ▶ **wymóg**

stir¹ /stɜː(r)/ verb (**stirring**; **stirred**) **1** [T] to move a liquid, etc. round and round, using a spoon, etc.: *She stirred her coffee with a teaspoon.* ▶ **mieszać** **2** [I,T] to move or make sb/sth move slightly: *She heard the baby stir in the next room.* ▶ **lekko poruszać (się)** **3** [T] to make sb feel a strong emotion: *The story stirred Carol's imagination.*

S

◇ *a stirring speech* poruszająca przemowa ▶ **poruszyć (kogoś)**

PHR V **stir sth up** to cause problems, or to make people feel strong emotions: *He's always trying to* ***stir up trouble.*** ◇ *The article stirred up a lot of anger among local residents.* ▶ **wzniecać**

stir² /stɜː(r)/ noun **1** [sing.] something exciting or shocking that everyone talks about ▶ **(ogólne) poruszenie**, **(ogólne) podniecenie** **2** [C] the action of stirring sth: *Give the soup a stir.* ▶ **mieszanie**; **poruszanie**

'stir-fry verb [T] to cook thin strips of vegetables or meat quickly in a small amount of very hot oil ▶ **smażyć metodą stir-fry**

■ **stir-fry** noun [C] ▶ **danie smażone metodą stir-fry**

stirring /'stɜːrɪŋ/ noun [C] **stirring (of sth)** the beginning of a feeling, an idea or a development: *She felt a stirring of anger.* ◇ *the first stirrings of spring in the air* ▶ **przypływ** (*uczucia*), **oznaka**

■ **stirring** adj. [usually before a noun] causing strong feelings; exciting: *a stirring performance* ▶ **pasjonujący**, **porywający**

stirrup /'stɪrəp/ noun [C] one of the two metal objects that you put your feet in when you are riding a horse ▶ **strzemię** ➲ picture at **horse**

stitch¹ /stɪtʃ/ noun [C] **1** one of the small lines of thread that you can see on a piece of cloth after it has been sewn ▶ **ścieg** **2** one of the small circles of wool that you put round a needle when you are knitting ▶ **oczko** **3** one of the small pieces of thread that a doctor uses to sew your skin together if you cut yourself very badly, or after an operation: *How many stitches did you have in your leg?* ▶ **szew (chirurgiczny)** **4** [usually sing.] a sudden pain that you get in the side of your body when you are running ▶ **kłujący ból**

IDM **in stitches** (informal) laughing so much that you cannot stop

stitch² /stɪtʃ/ verb [I,T] to sew ▶ **szyć**

stoat /stəʊt/ noun [C] a small animal with brown fur that turns mainly white in winter. The white fur is called **ermine.** ▶ **gronostaj**

stock¹ /stɒk/ noun **1** [U,C] the supply of things that a shop, etc. has for sale: *We'll have to order extra stock if we sell a lot more this week.* ◇ *I'll see if we have your size* ***in stock*** (na składzie (towaru)). ◇ *'Have you got the Polish edition of the Oxford Wordpower Dictionary?' 'I'm afraid we're temporarily* ***out of stock*** (niestety nakład jest wyczerpany). *Shall I order it for you?'* ▶ **towar**, **zapas** (*towaru*) **2** [C] an amount of sth that has been kept ready to be used: *Food stocks in the village were very low.* ▶ **zapas** **3** [C,U] a share that sb has bought in a company, or the value of a company's shares: *to invest in stocks and shares* ▶ **udział**, **obligacja** **4** [C,U] a liquid that is made by boiling meat, bones, vegetables, etc. in water, used especially for making soups and sauces: *vegetable/chicken stock* ▶ **wywar**

IDM **take stock (of sth)** to think about sth very carefully before deciding what to do next ▶ **zastanawiać się (nad czymś)**

stock² /stɒk/ verb [T] **1** (usually used about a shop) to have a supply of sth: *They stock food from all over the world.* ▶ **mieć na składzie** **2** to fill a place with sth: *a well-stocked library* ▶ **zaopatrywać**

PHR V **stock up (on/with sth)** to collect a large supply of sth for future use: *to stock up with food for the winter* ▶ **gromadzić** (*np. zapasy*)

stock³ /stɒk/ adj. [only before a noun] (used for describing sth that sb says) used so often that it does not have much meaning: *He always gives the same stock answers.* ▶ **szablonowy**

stockbroker /'stɒkbrəʊkə(r)/ (also **broker**) noun [C] a person whose job is to buy and sell shares in companies for other people ▶ **makler/ka giełdow-y/a**

'stock exchange noun [C] **1** a place where shares in companies are bought and sold: *the Tokyo Stock Exchange* ▶ **giełda** (*papierów wartościowych*) **2** (also **'stock market**) the business or activity of buying and selling shares in companies ▶ **rynek papierów wartościowych** ➲ note at **money** ➲ look at **exchange**

stocking /'stɒkɪŋ/ noun [C] one of a pair of thin pieces of clothing that fit tightly over a woman's feet and legs: *a pair of stockings* ▶ **pończocha** ➲ look at **tights**

stockist /'stɒkɪst/ noun [C] a shop that sells goods made by a particular company ▶ **sklep prowadzący sprzedaż towarów określonej firmy**

'stock market = STOCK EXCHANGE (2)

stockpile /'stɒkpaɪl/ verb [T] to collect and keep a large supply of sth ▶ **gromadzić (duże) zapasy**

■ **stockpile** noun [C]: *a stockpile of weapons* ▶ **duże zapasy**

stocktaking /'stɒkteɪkɪŋ/ noun [U] the activity of counting the total supply of things that a shop or business has at a particular time: *They close for an hour a month to do the stocktaking.* ▶ **remanent**, **inwentaryzacja**

stocky /'stɒki/ adj. (**stockier**; **stockiest**) (used about sb's body) short but strong and heavy ▶ **krępy**

stodgy /'stɒdʒi/ adj. (informal) (especially Brit.) **1** (used about food) heavy and making you feel very full: *stodgy puddings* ▶ (*jedzenie*) **ciężki**, **zapychający** **2** serious and boring; not exciting: *The article was rather stodgy– it contained too many facts.* ▶ (*styl pisania*) **ciężki**

stoic /'stəʊɪk/ (also **stoical** /-kl/) adj. (formal) suffering pain or difficulty without complaining ▶ **stoicki**

■ **stoically** /-kli/ adv. ▶ **stoicko** | **stoicism** /'stəʊɪsɪzəm/ noun [U] ▶ **stoicyzm**

stoke /stəʊk/ verb [T] **1 stoke sth (up) (with sth)** to add fuel to a fire: *to stoke up a fire with more coal* ◇ *to stoke a furnace* palić w piecu ▶ **dokładać** (*np. węgla do ognia*) **2 stoke sth (up)** to make people feel sth more strongly: *to stoke up envy* ▶ **podsycać**

stole past tense of **steal**

stolen past participle of **steal**

stolid /'stɒlɪd/ adj. (used about a person) showing very little emotion or excitement ▶ **powściągliwy**

■ **stolidly** adv. ▶ **powściągliwie**

stomach¹ /'stʌmək/ (also informal **tummy** /'tʌmi/, pl. **tummies**) noun [C] **1** the organ in your body where food goes after you have eaten it: *He went to the doctor with stomach pains.* ▶ **żołądek** **2** the front part of your body below your chest and above your legs: *She turned over onto her stomach.* ▶ **brzuch** ➲ picture at **body**

stomach² /'stʌmək/ verb [T] [usually in negative sentences and questions] (informal) to be able to watch, listen to, accept, etc. sth that you think is unpleasant: *I can't stomach too much violence in films.* ▶ **znosić**

'stomach ache noun [C,U] a pain in your stomach: *I've got terrible stomach ache.* ▶ **ból żołądka** ➲ note at **ache**

stomp /stɒmp/ verb [I] (informal) to walk with heavy steps ▶ **ciężko stąpać**

stone /stəʊn/ noun **1** [U] a hard solid substance that is found in the ground: *The house was built of grey stone.* ◇ *a stone wall* ▶ **kamień** **2** [C] a small piece of rock: *The boy picked up a stone and threw it into the river.* ▶ **kamyk** **3** [C] = PRECIOUS STONE **4** [C] the hard seed inside some types of fruit: *Peaches, plums, cherries and olives all have stones.* ▶ **pestka** ➲ picture on **page A12** **5** [C] (pl. **stone**) (abbr. **st**) a measure of weight; 6.35 kilograms. There are 14 pounds in a stone: *I weigh eleven stone two.* ▶ **miara wagi** (*=6,35 kg*)

IDM **kill two birds with one stone** → KILL[1]

■ **stone** verb [T] to throw stones at sb/sth, e.g. as a punishment: *The two women were stoned to death.* ▶ **kamienować**

stoned /stəʊnd/ adj. (slang) not behaving or thinking normally because of drugs or alcohol ▶ **naćpany**; **zalany (w pestkę)**

stonemason /ˈstəʊnmeɪsn/ noun [C] a person who cuts and prepares stone or builds with stone ▶ **kamieniarz**

stony /ˈstəʊni/ adj. (**stonier**; **stoniest**) **1** (used about the ground) having a lot of stones in it, or covered with stones ▶ **kamienisty 2** not friendly: *There was a stony silence as he walked into the room.* ▶ **kamienny**

stood past tense, past participle of **stand**[1]

stool /stuːl/ noun [C] a seat that does not have a back or arms: *a piano stool* ▶ **stołek**, **taboret**

stoop /stuːp/ verb [I] to bend your head and shoulders forwards and downwards: *He had to stoop to get through the low doorway.* ▶ **schylać się**

■ **stoop** noun [sing.]: *to walk with a stoop* ▶ **przygarbienie**

PHR V **stoop to sth/doing sth** to do sth bad or wrong that you would normally not do ▶ **poniżać się do tego stopnia, aby coś zrobić**

stop[1] /stɒp/ verb (**stopping**; **stopped**) **1** [I,T] to finish moving or make sth finish moving: *He walked along the road for a bit, and then stopped.* ◇ *Does this train stop at Didcot?* ◇ *My watch has stopped.* ◇ *I stopped someone in the street to ask the way to the station.* ▶ **stawać**, **zatrzymywać (się) 2** [I,T] to no longer continue or to make sth not continue: *I think the rain has stopped.* ◇ *It's stopped raining now.* ◇ *Stop making that terrible noise!* ◇ *The bus service stops at midnight.* ◇ *We tied a bandage round his arm to stop the bleeding.* ▶ **przestawać**, **tamować** (*np. krawienie*), **kończyć (się)** ℹ **Stop to do sth** oznacza zatrzymanie się w celu zrobienia czegoś: *On the way home I stopped to buy a newspaper.* **Stop doing sth** oznacza przestanie robienia czegoś: *I stopped smoking 3 months ago.* **3** [T] **stop sb/sth (from) doing sth** to make sb/sth end or finish an activity; to prevent sb/sth from doing sth: *They've built a fence to stop the dog getting out.* ◇ *I'm going to go and you can't stop me.* ◇ *Can't you stop the car making that noise?* Zrób coś, żeby ten samochód przestał tak hałasować. ▶ **kłaść kres czemuś**; **powstrzymywać kogoś/coś od czegoś 4** [I,T] **stop (for sth)**; **stop (and do/to do sth)** to end an activity for a short time in order to do sth: *Shall we stop for lunch now?* ◇ *Let's stop and look at the map.* ◇ *We stopped work for half an hour to have a cup of coffee.* ◇ *Stop it* (przestań)*! You're hurting me.* ▶ **przestawać**, **zatrzymywać się 5** [T] to prevent money from being paid ▶ **wstrzymywać** (*np. wypłatę*)

IDM **stop at nothing** to do anything to get what you want, even if it is wrong or dangerous ▶ **nie cofać się przed niczym**

stop short of sth/doing sth to almost do sth, but then decide not to do it at the last minute ▶ **powstrzymać się od czegoś w ostatniej chwili**

PHR V **stop by (sth)** to make a short visit somewhere: *I'll stop by this evening for a chat.* ▶ **wstąpić gdzieś**

stop off (at/in ...) to stop during a journey to do sth ▶ **przerywać podróż gdzieś**

stop over (at/in ...) to stay somewhere for a short time during a long journey ▶ **zatrzymać się** (*na krótki postój*)

stop[2] /stɒp/ noun [C] **1** an act of stopping or the state of being stopped: *Our first stop will be in Edinburgh.* ◇ *Production at the factory will* ***come to a stop*** (zostanie wstrzymana) *at midnight tonight.* ◇ *The lift* ***came to a stop*** (winda zatrzymała się) *on the third floor.* ◇ *I managed to* ***bring*** *the car* ***to a stop*** *just in time.* ▶ **postój**, **zatrzymanie się 2** the place where a bus, train, etc. stops so that people can get on and off: *a bus stop* ◇ *I'm getting off at the next stop.* ▶ **przystanek** (*autobusowy*), **stacja** (*kolejowa*)

IDM **pull out all the stops** → PULL[1]

put a stop to sth to prevent sth bad or unpleasant from continuing ▶ **położyć czemuś kres**

stopgap /ˈstɒpgæp/ noun [C] a person or a thing that does a job for a short time until sb/sth permanent can be found ▶ **zatkajdziura**

stopover /ˈstɒpəʊvə(r)/ (also **layover** /ˈleɪəʊvə(r)/) noun [C] a short stop in a journey ▶ **przerwa w podróży**

stoppage /ˈstɒpɪdʒ/ noun [C] **1** a situation in which people stop working as part of a protest ▶ **przestój w pracy** (*zwł. z powodu strajku*) **2** (in sport) an interruption in a game for a particular reason ▶ **wstrzymanie gry**

stopper /ˈstɒpə(r)/ noun [C] an object that you put into the top of a bottle in order to close it ▶ **zatyczka**

stopwatch /ˈstɒpwɒtʃ/ noun [C] a watch which can be started and stopped by pressing a button, so that you can measure exactly how long sth takes ▶ **stoper**

storage /ˈstɔːrɪdʒ/ noun [U] the process of keeping things until they are needed; the place where they are kept: *This room is being used for storage at the moment.* ▶ **magazynowanie**

store[1] /stɔː(r)/ noun [C] **1** a large shop: *She's a sales assistant in a large department store.* ◇ *a furniture store* ▶ **dom towarowy**, **magazyn** ➲ look at **chain store 2** (US) = SHOP[1] (1) **3** a supply of sth that you keep for future use; the place where it is kept: *a good store of food for the winter* ◇ *Police discovered a weapons store in the house.* ▶ **zapas**; **skład**

IDM **be in store (for sb/sth)** to be going to happen in the future: *There's a surprise in store for you* (czeka cię niespodzianka) *when you get home!* ▶ **być przygotowanym (dla kogoś)**, (*coś*) **mieć nastąpić w przyszłości**

set ... store by sth to consider sth to be important: *Nick sets great store by his mother's opinion.* ▶ **przywiązywać wielką wagę do czegoś**

store[2] /stɔː(r)/ verb [T] to keep sth or a supply of sth for future use: *to store information on a computer* ▶ **przechowywać** (*np. w komputerze, magazynie*)

ˈ**store card** noun [C] a card that a particular shop provides for regular customers so that they can use it to buy goods that they will pay for later ▶ **karta kredytowa** (*wydawana przez sklep*) ➲ look at **credit card**

storekeeper (US) = SHOPKEEPER

storeroom /ˈstɔːruːm; -rʊm/ noun [C] a room where things are kept until they are needed ▶ **składnica**, **magazyn/ek**

storey (US **story**) /ˈstɔːri/ noun [C] (pl. **storeys**; US **stories**) one floor or level of a building: *The building will be five storeys high.* ◇ *a two-storey house* ◇ *a multi-storey car park* parking wielopoziomowy ▶ **piętro**

stork /stɔːk/ noun [C] a large white bird with a long beak, neck and legs. **Storks** often make their nests on the top of buildings. ▶ **bocian**

storm[1] /stɔːm/ noun [C] very bad weather with strong winds and rain: *Look at those black clouds. I think there's going to be a storm.* ◇ *a thunderstorm* burza z piorunami ◇ *a snowstorm* burza śnieżna ◇ *a hailstorm* burza gradowa ◇ *a sandstorm* burza piaskowa ▶ **burza** ➲ note at **weather**

storm

During a **thunderstorm** you hear **thunder** and see flashes of **lightning** in the sky. Large, violent storms with very strong winds are called **cyclones. Hurricanes** (or **typhoons**) are a type of cyclone. A storm with

S

a very strong circular wind is called a **tornado**. A **blizzard** is a very bad snowstorm.

storm² /stɔːm/ verb **1** [T] to attack a building, town, etc. suddenly and violently in order to take control of it ▶ **szturmować 2** [I] to enter or leave somewhere in a very angry and noisy way: *He threw down the book and stormed out of the room.* ▶ **wpadać/wypadać (skądś) z hałasem/furią**

stormy /ˈstɔːmi/ adj. (**stormier**; **stormiest**) **1** (used for talking about very bad weather, with strong winds, heavy rain, etc.): *a stormy night* ◇ *stormy weather* ▶ **burzowy**, (*morze*) **wzburzony 2** involving a lot of angry argument and strong feeling: *a stormy relationship* ▶ **burzliwy**

story /ˈstɔːri/ noun [C] (pl. **stories**) **1 a story (about sb/sth)** a description of people and events that are not real: *I'll tell you* ***a story*** *about the animals that live in that forest.* ◇ *I always read the children* ***a bedtime story.*** ◇ *a detective story* kryminał ◇ *a fairy story* bajka ◇ *a ghost story* opowieść o duchach ◇ *a love story* romans ◇ *a short story* nowela/opowiadanie ▶ **opowieść** ➲ note at **history 2** an account, especially a spoken one, of sth that has happened: *The police didn't believe his story.* ▶ **relacja**, **wersja** (*wydarzeń*) **3** a description of true events that happened in the past: *He's writing his life story.* ▶ **historia** (*prawdziwa relacja*) **4** an article or a report in a newspaper or a magazine: *The plane crash was the front-page story in most newspapers.* ▶ **relacja (prasowa) 5** (US) = STOREY

stout /staʊt/ adj. **1** (used about a person) rather fat ▶ **tęgi 2** strong and thick: *stout walking boots* ▶ **solidny**

stove /stəʊv/ noun [C] **1** a closed metal box in which you burn wood, coal, etc. for heating: *a wood-burning stove* ▶ **piec/yk metalowy 2** the top part of a cooker that has gas or electric rings: *He put a pan of water to boil on the stove.* ▶ **kuchenka** (*elektryczna/gazowa*)

stovetop (US) = HOB

stow /stəʊ/ verb [T] **stow sth (away)** to put sth away in a particular place until it is needed ▶ **chować** (*na później*)

stowaway /ˈstəʊəweɪ/ noun [C] a person who hides in a ship or plane so that they can travel without paying ▶ **pasażer/ka na gapę**

straddle /ˈstrædl/ verb [T] **1** (used about a person) to sit or stand with your legs on each side of sth: *to straddle a chair* ▶ **stać/siedzieć okrakiem 2** (used about a building, bridge, etc.) to be on both sides of sth: *The village straddles the border* (leży na samej granicy) *between the two states.* ▶ **obejmować dwie części/połowy czegoś**

straggle /ˈstræɡl/ verb [I] **1** to grow, spread or move in an untidy way or in different directions: *Her wet hair straggled across her forehead.* ◇ *a straggling moustache* sumiaste wąsy ▶ **rosnąć dziko**, **zarastać 2** to walk, etc. more slowly than the rest of the group: *The children straggled along behind their parents.* ▶ **wlec się w tyle za innymi**

■ **straggler** noun [C] ▶ **maruder** | **straggly** adj.: *long straggly hair* ▶ **rozczochrany**

straight¹ /streɪt/ adv. **1** not in a curve or at an angle; in a straight line: *Go* ***straight on*** *for about two miles until you come to some traffic lights.* ◇ *He was looking* ***straight ahead.*** ◇ *to sit up straight* ▶ **prosto 2** without stopping: *I took the children straight home after school.* ◇ *I'm going straight to bed when I get home.* ◇ *He joined the army straight from school.* ◇ *to walk straight past sb/sth* iść bez zatrzymywania się koło/obok kogoś/czegoś ▶ **prosto** (*nie zbaczając*), **bezpośrednio 3** in an honest and direct way: *Tell me straight, doctor – is it serious?* ▶ **uczciwie**, **otwarcie**

IDM **go straight** to become honest after being a criminal ▶ **wstępować na uczciwą drogę**

right/straight away → AWAY

straight out in an honest and direct way: *I told Asif straight out that I didn't want to see him any more.* ▶ **prosto z mostu**

straight² /streɪt/ adj. **1** with no bends or curves; going in one direction only: *He's got straight dark hair.* ◇ *Keep your back straight!* ◇ *He was so drunk he couldn't walk* ***in a straight line.*** ▶ **prosty** ➲ picture at **hair 2** [not before a noun] in an exactly horizontal or vertical position: *That picture isn't straight.* ▶ **prosty 3** tidy or organized as it should be: *It took ages to* ***put*** *the room* ***straight*** (aby doprowadzić pokój do porządku) *after we'd decorated it.* ▶ **uporządkowany 4** honest and direct: *Politicians never give* ***a straight answer.*** ◇ *Are you being straight with me?* ▶ **prosty**, **szczery 5** (US) = NEAT (5) **6** (informal) (used to describe a person who you think is too serious and boring) ▶ **sztywny 7** (informal) attracted to people of the opposite sex ▶ **heteroseksualny** SYN **heterosexual** OPP **gay**

IDM **get sth straight** to make sure that you understand sth completely ▶ **wyjaśniać coś**

keep a straight face to stop yourself from smiling or laughing ▶ **zachowywać powagę**

put/set the record straight → RECORD¹

straighten /ˈstreɪtn/ verb [I,T] **straighten (sth) (up/out)** to become straight or to make sth straight: *The road straightens out at the bottom of the hill.* ◇ *to straighten your tie* poprawiać krawat ▶ **prostować (się)**

PHR V **straighten sth out** to remove the confusion or difficulties from a situation ▶ **wyjaśniać coś**, **doprowadzać coś do porządku**

straighten up to make your body straight and vertical ▶ **prostować się**

ˌstraight-ˈfaced adj. without laughing or smiling, even though you may be amused ▶ **z poważną miną**

straightforward /ˌstreɪtˈfɔːwəd/ adj. **1** easy to do or understand; simple: *straightforward instructions* ▶ **łatwy (do zrozumienia)**, **prosty** (*nieskomplikowany*) **2** honest and open: *a straightforward person* ▶ **prostolinijny**

straightjacket = STRAITJACKET

strain¹ /streɪn/ noun **1** [C,U] worry or pressure caused by having too much to deal with: *to be* ***under*** *a lot of* ***strain*** *at work* ▶ **napięcie (emocjonalne) 2** [C] something that makes you feel worried and tense: *I always find exams a terrible strain.* ▶ **napięcie (emocjonalne) 3** [U] pressure that is put on sth when it is pulled or pushed by a physical force: *Running downhill puts strain on the knees.* ◇ *The rope finally broke* ***under the strain.*** ▶ **napięcie**; **obciążenie 4** [C,U] an injury to part of your body that is caused by using it too much: *He is out of today's game with a back strain.* ▶ **nadwerężenie**, **naciągnięcie** (*np. mięśnia*) **5** [C] one type of animal, plant or disease that is slightly different from the other types: *This new strain of the disease is particularly dangerous.* ▶ **odmiana**, **szczep**

strain² /streɪn/ verb **1** [T] to injure a part of your body by using it too much: *Don't read in the dark. You'll strain your eyes.* ◇ *I think I've strained a muscle in my neck.* ▶ **naciągać** (*np. mięsień*) **2** [I,T] to make a great effort to do sth: *I was straining to see what was happening.* ◇ *Bend down as far as you can without straining.* ◇ *I had to strain my ears* (wytężać słuch) *to catch what they were saying.* ▶ **wytężać**, **wysilać się 3** [T] to put a lot of pressure on sth: *Money problems have strained their relationship.* ▶ **napinać 4** [T] to separate a solid and a liquid by pouring them into a special container with small holes in it: *to strain tea/vegetables/spaghetti* ▶ **cedzić**

strained /streɪnd/ adj. **1** worried because of having too much to deal with: *Martin looked tired and strained.* ▶ (*wzajemne stosunki itp.*) **napięty 2** not natural or friendly: *Relations between the two countries are strained.* ▶ **napięty (emocjonalnie)**

strait /streɪt/ noun **1** [C, usually pl.] a narrow piece of sea that joins two larger seas: *the straits of Gibraltar* ▶ **cieśnina 2** (**straits**) [pl.] a very difficult situation, especially one caused by having no money: *The company is in desperate financial straits.* ▶ **tarapaty**
IDM **be in dire straits** → DIRE

straitened /ˈstreɪtnd/ adj. [only before a noun] (formal) without enough money or as much money as there was before: *The family of eight was living **in straitened circumstances.*** ▶ **trudny** (*finansowo*)

straitjacket (also **straightjacket**) /ˈstreɪtdʒækɪt/ noun [C] a piece of clothing like a jacket with long arms which are tied to prevent the person wearing it from behaving violently. **Straitjackets** are sometimes used to control people who are mentally ill. ▶ **kaftan bezpieczeństwa**

strait-laced (also **straight-laced**) /ˌstreɪt ˈleɪst/ adj. having strict or old-fashioned ideas about people's moral behaviour ▶ **purytański** ℹ Wyraża dezaprobatę.

strand /strænd/ noun [C] **1** a single piece of cotton, wool, hair, etc. ▶ **włos**, **nić 2** one part of a story, a situation or an idea ▶ **wątek**, **splot** (*np. zagadnień*)

stranded /ˈstrændɪd/ adj. left in a place that you cannot get away from: *We were left stranded when our car broke down in the mountains.* ▶ **pozostawiony** (*np. na lodzie*)

⚷ **strange** /streɪndʒ/ adj. **1** unusual or unexpected: *A very strange thing happened to me on the way home.* ◇ *a strange noise* ▶ **dziwny**, **niezwykły 2** that you have not seen, visited, met, etc. before: *a strange town* ◇ *Do not talk to strange men.* ▶ **dziwny**, **obcy** ➲ look at **foreign**

Mówiąc o osobie lub rzeczy pochodzącej z innego kraju nie używa się **strange**, lecz **foreign**.

■ **strangely** adv.: *The streets were strangely quiet.* ◇ *He's behaving strangely at the moment.* ▶ **dziwnie**, **niezwykle** | **strangeness** noun [U] ▶ **obcość**; **dziwność**

⚷ **stranger** /ˈstreɪndʒə(r)/ noun [C] **1** a person that you do not know: *I had to ask a **complete stranger** to help me with my suitcase.* ▶ **osoba obca**, **nieznajom-y/a**

Mówiąc o osobie pochodzącej z innego kraju nie używa się **stranger**, lecz **foreigner**.

2 a person who is in a place that they do not know: *I'm a stranger to this part of the country.* Zupełnie nie znam tej części kraju. ▶ **obcy**

strangle /ˈstræŋgl/ verb [T] **1** to kill sb by squeezing their neck or throat with your hands, a rope, etc. ▶ **dusić** SYN **throttle** ➲ look at **choke 2** to prevent sth from developing ▶ **tłumić** (*np. inicjatywę*)

strap /stræp/ noun [C] a long narrow piece of leather, cloth, plastic, etc. that you use for carrying sth or for keeping sth in position: *a watch with a leather strap* ▶ **pasek**, **rzemyk**, **uchwyt** ➲ picture at **bag**
■ **strap** verb [T] (**strapping**; **strapped**): *The racing driver was securely strapped into the car.* ▶ **przymocowywać** (*pasem*)

strapless /ˈstræpləs/ adj. (especially used about a dress or **bra**) without **straps** ▶ **bez ramiączek**

strategic /strəˈtiːdʒɪk/ (also **strategical** /-kl/) adj. **1** helping you to achieve a plan; giving you an advantage: *They made a strategic decision to sell off part of the company.* ▶ **strategiczny 2** connected with a country's plans to achieve success in a war or in its defence system ▶ (*plany wojskowe*) **strategiczny 3** (used about bombs and other weapons) intended to be fired at the enemy's country rather than be used in battle ▶ **strategiczny**
■ **strategically** /-kli/ adv.: *The island is strategically important.* ▶ **strategicznie**

strategist /ˈstrætədʒɪst/ noun [C] a person who is skilled at planning things, especially military activities: *a military strategist* ▶ **strateg**

⚷ **strategy** /ˈstrætədʒi/ noun (pl. **strategies**) **1** [C] a plan that you use in order to achieve sth: *What's your strategy for this exam?* ▶ **strategia 2** [U] the act of planning how to do or achieve sth: *military strategy* ▶ **strategia**

stratify /ˈstrætɪfaɪ/ verb (**stratifies**; **stratifying**; **stratified**; **stratified**) [T, usually passive] (formal or technical) to arrange sth in layers: *a highly stratified society* ◇ *stratified rock* ▶ **rozwarstwiać** (*np. społeczeństwo*), **uwarstwiać**

straw /strɔː/ noun **1** [U] the long thin parts of some plants, for example **wheat**, which are dried and then used for animals to sleep on or for making hats, covering a roof, etc.: *a straw hat* ▶ **słoma 2** [C] one piece of **straw** ▶ **źdźbło słomy 3** [C] a long plastic or paper tube that you can use for drinking through ▶ **słomka**
IDM **the last/final straw** the last in a series of bad things that happen to you and that makes you decide that you cannot accept the situation any longer: *That's the last straw!* Tego już za wiele!

strawberry /ˈstrɔːbəri; US -beri/ noun [C] (pl. **strawberries**) a small soft red fruit with small white seeds on it: *strawberries and cream* ◇ *a wild strawberry* poziomka ▶ **truskawka** ➲ picture on **page A12**

ˌ**straw ˈpoll** noun [C] a survey of public opinion that is not official ▶ **nieoficjalny sondaż**

stray[1] /streɪ/ verb [I] **1** to go away from the place where you should be: *The sheep had strayed onto the road.* ▶ **błąkać się**, **zbaczać 2** to not keep to the subject you should be thinking about or discussing: *My thoughts strayed for a few moments.* ▶ **zbaczać z tematu**

stray[2] /streɪ/ noun [C] a dog, cat, etc. that does not have a home ▶ **zabłąkane zwierzę**
■ **stray** adj. [only before a noun]: *a stray dog* ▶ **zabłąkany**

streak[1] /striːk/ noun [C] **1 streak (of sth)** a thin line or mark: *The cat had brown fur with streaks of white in it.* ▶ **pasek 2** a part of sb's character that sometimes shows in the way they behave: *Ania's a very caring girl, but she does have a selfish streak* (ale bywa samolubna). ▶ **cecha charakteru 3** a continuous period of bad or good luck in a game or sport: *The team is **on a losing/winning streak** at the moment.* ▶ (*dobra/zła*) **passa**

streak[2] /striːk/ verb [I] (informal) to run fast ▶ **pędzić**

streaked /striːkt/ adj. **streaked (with sth)** having lines of a different colour: *black hair streaked with grey* ▶ **z domieszką (czegoś)**, **pręgowany**

⚷ **stream**[1] /striːm/ noun [C] **1** a small river: *I waded across the shallow stream.* ▶ **strumień 2** the continuous movement of a liquid or gas: *a stream of blood* ▶ **przepływ** (*np. wody, gazu*) **3** a continuous movement of people or things: *a stream of traffic* ▶ **strumień 4** a large number of things which happen one after another: *a stream of letters/telephone calls/questions* ▶ (*przen.*) **rzeka 5** a group of schoolchildren who are in the same class because they have similar abilities ▶ **klasa profilowana**

stream[2] /striːm/ verb [I] **1** (used about a liquid, gas or light) to flow in large amounts: *Tears were streaming down his face.* ◇ *Sunlight was streaming in through the windows.* ▶ **przepływać**, **lać się** (*strumieniami*) **2** (used about people or things) to move somewhere in a continuous flow: *People were streaming out of the station.* ▶ (*ludzie, rzeczy*) **spływać obficie 3** [T, usually passive] to put schoolchildren into groups of similar ability ▶ **przydzielać uczniów do klasy profilowanej**

streamer /ˈstriːmə(r)/ noun [C] a long piece of coloured paper that you use for decorating a room before a party, etc. ▶ **serpentyna** (*papierowa*)

S

streamline /ˈstriːmlaɪn/ verb [T] **1** to give a vehicle, etc. a long smooth shape so that it will move easily through air or water ▶ **nadawać (czemuś) kształt/linię opływow-y/ą** **2** to make an organization, a process, etc. work better by making it simpler ▶ **usprawniać, optymalizować**
■ **streamlined** adj. ▶ **opływowy; usprawniony**

street /striːt/ noun [C] **1** a public road in a city or town that has houses and buildings on one side or both sides: *to walk **along/down the street*** iść ulicą ◇ *to **cross the street*** ◇ *I met Karen **in the street*** (na ulicy) *this morning.* ◇ *a narrow street* ◇ *a street map* plan miasta ▶ **ulica** ➲ note at **road 2** (**Street**) (abbr. **St**) [sing.] (used in the names of streets): *64 High Street* ◇ *The post office is in Sheep Street.* ▶ **ulica**
IDM **the man in the street** → MAN[1]
streets ahead (of sb/sth) (informal) much better than sb/sth ▶ **o niebo lepszy**
(right) up your street (informal) (used about an activity, a subject, etc.) exactly right for you because you know a lot about it, like it very much, etc. ▶ **dokładnie (czyjaś) działka, ulubiony** (*np. temat*)

streetcar (US) = TRAM

street cred /ˈstriːt kred/ (informal) (also ˈ**street credibility**) noun [U] a way of behaving and dressing that is acceptable to young people, especially those who live in cities: *Those clothes do nothing for your street cred.* ▶ **styl/zachowanie modn-y/e wśród młodzieży**

strength /streŋθ/ noun **1** [U] the quality of being physically strong; the amount of this quality that you have: *He pulled with all his strength but the rock would not move.* ◇ *I didn't have the strength to walk any further.* ▶ **siła; siły** **2** [U] the ability of an object to hold heavy weights or not to break or be damaged easily: *All our suitcases are tested for strength before they leave the factory.* ▶ **wytrzymałość** **3** [U] the power and influence that sb has: *Germany's economic strength* ▶ **potęga** **4** [U] how strong a feeling or opinion is: *The government has misjudged the strength of public feeling on this issue.* ◇ *There is great strength of feeling against* (jest silny sprzeciw opinii publicznej przeciwko) *nuclear weapons in this country.* ▶ **siła** **5** [C,U] a good quality or ability that sb/sth has: *His greatest strength is his ability to communicate with people.* ◇ *the strengths and weaknesses of a plan* ▶ **mocna strona** OPP **weakness**
IDM **at full strength** → FULL[1]
below strength (used about a group) not having the number of people it needs or usually has ▶ **nie w pełnej obsadzie**
on the strength of sth as a result of information, advice, etc. ▶ **w oparciu o coś**

strengthen /ˈstreŋθn/ verb [I,T] to become stronger or to make sth stronger: *exercises to strengthen your muscles* ▶ **wzmacniać (się)** OPP **weaken**

strenuous /ˈstrenjuəs/ adj. needing or using a lot of effort or energy: *Don't do **strenuous exercise** after eating.* ◇ *a strenuous climb* ◇ *She's making a **strenuous effort*** (czyni usilne starania) *to be on time every day.* ▶ **forsowny**
■ **strenuously** adv. ▶ **z wysiłkiem**

stress[1] /stres/ noun **1** [C,U] worry and pressure that is caused by having too much to deal with: *He's been **under a lot of stress** since his wife went into hospital.* ▶ **stres** ➲ look at **trauma** **2** [C,U] a physical force that may cause sth to bend or break: *Heavy lorries **put** too much **stress** on this bridge.* ▶ **nacisk** **3** [U] **stress (on sth)** the special attention that you give to sth because you think it is important: *We should **put** more **stress** on preventing crime.* ▶ **nacisk** **4** [C,U] **(a) stress (on sth)** the force that you put on a particular word or part of a word when you speak: *In the word 'dictionary' the stress is on the first syllable, 'dic'.* ▶ **akcent**

stress[2] /stres/ verb [T] **1** to give sth attention because it is important: *The minister stressed the need for a peaceful solution.* ▶ **podkreślać** SYN **emphasize** **2** to give extra force to a word or syllable when saying it: *You stress the first syllable in this word.* ▶ **akcentować**

stressed /strest/ adj. [not before a noun] (informal) (also ˌ**stressed** ˈ**out**) too anxious and tired to be able to relax: *He was feeling very stressed and tired.* ▶ **zestresowany**

stressful /ˈstresfl/ adj. causing worry and pressure: *a stressful job* ▶ **stresujący**

stretch[1] /stretʃ/ verb **1** [I,T] to pull sth so that it becomes longer or wider; to become longer or wider in this way: *The artist stretched the canvas tightly over the frame.* ◇ *My T-shirt stretched when I washed it.* ▶ **rozciągać (się)** **2** [I,T] **stretch (sth) (out)** to push out your arms, legs, etc. as far as possible: *He switched off the alarm clock, yawned and stretched.* ◇ *She stretched out on the sofa and fell asleep.* ◇ *She stretched out her arm to take the book.* ▶ **przeciągać się; wyciągać (się)** **3** [I] to cover a large area of land or a long period of time: *The long white beaches stretch for miles along the coast.* ▶ **rozciągać się (dokądś)** **4** [T] to make use of all the money, ability, time, etc. that sb has available for use: *The test has been designed to really stretch students' knowledge.* ▶ **zmuszać do wysiłku, wyczerpywać**
IDM **stretch your legs** to go for a walk after sitting down for a long time ▶ **rozprostowywać nogi**
stretch a point to agree to sth that you do not normally allow ▶ **robić ustępstwo, robić wyjątek**

stretch[2] /stretʃ/ noun [C] **1 a stretch (of sth)** an area of land or water: *a dangerous stretch of road* ▶ **obszar, przestrzeń, odcinek** (*drogi*) **2** [usually sing.] the act of making the muscles in your arms, legs, back, etc. as long as possible: *Stand up, everybody, and have a good stretch* (i rozprostujcie kości). ▶ **przeciąganie się**
IDM **at full stretch** → FULL[1]
at a stretch without stopping: *We travelled for six hours at a stretch.* ▶ **bez przerwy**

stretcher /ˈstretʃə(r)/ noun [C] a piece of cloth supported by two poles that is used for carrying a person who has been injured ▶ **nosze**

stretchy /ˈstretʃi/ adj. (**stretchier**; **stretchiest**) that can easily be made longer or wider without tearing or breaking: *stretchy fabric* ▶ **elastyczny, rozciągliwy**

strict /strɪkt/ adj. **1** that must be obeyed completely: *I gave her strict instructions to be home before 9.00.* ▶ **ścisły** **2** not allowing people to break rules or behave badly: *Samir's very strict with his children.* ◇ *I went to an extremely strict school.* ▶ **surowy, srogi** **3** exactly correct; accurate: *a strict interpretation of the law* ▶ **ścisły**

strictly /ˈstrɪktli/ adv. **1** with a lot of control and rules that must be obeyed: *She was brought up very strictly.* ▶ **surowo** **2** (used to emphasize that sth happens or must happen in all circumstances): *Smoking is strictly forbidden.* ▶ **ściśle**
IDM **strictly speaking** to be exactly correct or accurate: *Strictly speaking, the tomato is not a vegetable. It's a fruit.* ▶ **ściśle mówiąc, dokładnie mówiąc**

stride[1] /straɪd/ verb [I] (pt **strode** /strəʊd/) [not used in the perfect tenses] to walk with long steps, often because you feel very confident or determined: *He strode up to the house and knocked on the door.* ▶ **iść zdecydowanie/pewnie/zamaszyście**

stride[2] /straɪd/ noun [C] a long step ▶ **wielki krok**
IDM **get into your stride** to start to do sth in a confident way and well after an uncertain beginning ▶ **wciągać się** (*w normalny tok pracy*)
make great strides → GREAT[1]

take sth in your stride to deal with a new or difficult situation easily and without worrying ▶ **radzić sobie** (*z łatwością*)

strident /ˈstraɪdnt/ adj. (used about a voice or a sound) loud and unpleasant ▶ **ostry, przeraźliwy**

strife /straɪf/ noun [U] (formal) trouble or fighting between people or groups ▶ **zmagania, niesnaski**

strike¹ /straɪk/ verb (pt, pp **struck** /strʌk/) **1** [T] (formal) to hit sb/sth: *The stone struck her on the head.* ◇ *The boat struck a rock and began to sink.* ▶ **uderzać, walić** ➲ note at **hit 2** [I,T] to attack and harm sb/sth suddenly: *The earthquake struck Kobe in 1995.* ◇ *The building had been* ***struck by lightning.*** ▶ **atakować, uderzać 3** [T] to come suddenly into sb's mind: *It suddenly struck me that she would be the ideal person for the job.* ▶ **wpadać do głowy 4** [T] **strike sb (as sth)** to give sb a particular impression: *Does anything here strike you as unusual?* ◇ *He strikes me as a very caring man.* ▶ **uderzać, wywierać wrażenie 5** [I] to stop work as a protest: *The workers voted to strike for more money.* ▶ **zaczynać strajk 6** [T] to produce fire by rubbing sth, especially a match, on a surface: *She struck a match and lit her cigarette.* ▶ **zapalać, krzesać 7** [I,T] to ring a bell so that people know what time it is: *The church clock struck three.* ▶ **wybijać** (*godziny*) **8** [T] to discover gold, oil, etc. in the ground: *They had struck oil!* ▶ **natrafiać na coś**

IDM **strike a balance (between A and B)** to find a middle way between two extremes ▶ **znajdować złoty środek**

strike a bargain (with sb) to make an agreement with sb ▶ **dobijać targu (z kimś)**

strike a chord (with sb) to say or do sth that makes other people feel sympathy, excitement, etc. ▶ **uderzyć w czyjąś czułą/właściwą strunę**

within striking distance near enough to be reached or attacked easily ▶ **w zasięgu ręki/strzału itp.**

PHR V **strike back (at/against sb)** to attack sb/sth that has attacked you ▶ **kontratakować (kogoś)**

strike sb/sth off (sth) to remove sb/sth's name from sth, such as the list of members of a professional group: *Strike her name off the list.* ◇ *The doctor was struck off for incompetence.* ▶ **usuwać kogoś/coś (z czegoś)**

strike up sth (with sb) to start a conversation or friendship with sb ▶ **nawiązywać (z kimś) rozmowę; zawierać (z kimś) znajomość**

strike² /straɪk/ noun [C] **1** a period of time when people refuse to go to work, usually because they want more money or better working conditions: *a one-day strike* ◇ *Union members voted to* ***go on strike*** (rozpocząć strajk) *for better working conditions.* ◇ *The workers have been* ***on strike*** (strajkują) *for two weeks now.* ◇ *to take strike action* podejmować akcję strajkową ▶ **strajk 2** a sudden military attack, especially by aircraft: *an air strike* ▶ **uderzenie**

striker /ˈstraɪkə(r)/ noun [C] **1** a person who has stopped working as a protest ▶ **(pracownik) strajkujący 2** (in football) a player whose job is to score goals ▶ **napastni-k/czka**

striking /ˈstraɪkɪŋ/ adj. very noticeable; making a strong impression: *There was a striking similarity between the two men.* ▶ **uderzający**

■ **strikingly** adv.: *She is strikingly beautiful.* ▶ **uderzająco**

string¹ /strɪŋ/ noun **1** [C,U] a piece of long, strong material like very thin rope, that you use for tying things: *a ball/piece/length of string* ◇ *The key is hanging on a string.* ▶ **sznurek** ➲ picture at **cable 2** [C] **a string of sth** a line of things that are joined together on the same piece of thread: *a string of beads* ▶ **sznur 3** [C] **a string of sth** a series of people, things or events that follow one after another: *a string of visitors* ▶ **sznur, ciąg 4** [C] one of the pieces of thin wire, etc. that produce the sound on some musical instruments: *A guitar has six strings.* ▶ **struna 5 (the strings)** [pl.] (in an **orchestra**) the instruments that have strings ▶ **instrumenty smyczkowe** ➲ note at **instrument 6** [C] one of the pieces of thin material that is stretched across a **racket** ▶ **struna**

IDM **(with) no strings attached; without strings** with no special conditions ▶ **nie stawiając warunków, bez żadnych zobowiązań**

pull strings → PULL¹

string² /strɪŋ/ verb [T] (pt, pp **strung** /strʌŋ/) **string sth (up)** to hang up a line of things with a piece of string, etc. ▶ **rozwieszać**

PHR V **string sb along** (informal) to allow sb to believe sth that is not true, for example that you love them, intend to help them, etc.: *She has no intention of giving you a divorce; she's just stringing you along.* ▶ **nabierać kogoś**

string sb/sth out to make people or things form a line with spaces between each person or thing ▶ **rozstawiać (kogoś/coś) z odstępami w rzędzie**

string sth out to make sth last longer than expected or necessary: *They seem determined to string the talks out for an indefinite period.* ▶ **przeciągać coś**

string sth together to put words or phrases together to make a sentence, speech, etc.: *I can barely string two words together in Japanese.* ▶ **sklecić** (*np. zdanie*)

ˌstringed ˈinstrument noun [C] any musical instrument with strings that you play with your fingers or with a **bow** ▶ **instrument strunowy**

stringent /ˈstrɪndʒənt/ adj. (used about a law, rule, etc.) very strict ▶ **surowy, ścisły**

strip¹ /strɪp/ verb (**stripping**; **stripped**) **1** [I,T] **strip (sth) (off)** to take off your clothes; to take off sb else's clothes: *The doctor asked him to strip to the waist.* ◇ *I was stripped and searched at the airport by two customs officers.* ▶ **rozbierać (się) 2** [T] **strip sth (off)** to remove sth that is covering a surface: *to strip the paint off a door* ◇ *to strip wallpaper* ▶ **zdzierać, zdejmować** (*np. farbę, warstwę*) **3** [T] **strip sb/sth (of sth)** to take sth away from sb/sth: *They stripped the house of all its furniture.* ▶ **pozbawiać (kogoś/coś) czegoś**

strip² /strɪp/ noun [C] a long narrow piece of sth: *a strip of paper* ▶ **pasek, pasmo**

ˌstrip carˈtoon = COMIC STRIP

stripe /straɪp/ noun [C] a long narrow line of colour: *Zebras have black and white stripes.* ▶ **pasek, pręga, lampas**

■ **striped** adj.: *a red and white striped dress* ▶ **w paski, pręgowany** ➲ picture on **page A1**

stripper /ˈstrɪpə(r)/ noun [C] a person whose job is to take off their clothes in order to entertain people ▶ **striptizer/ka**

striptease /ˈstrɪptiːz/ noun [C,U] entertainment in which sb takes off their clothes, usually to music ▶ **striptiz**

strive /straɪv/ verb [I] (pt **strove** /strəʊv/, pp **striven** /ˈstrɪvn/) (formal) **strive (for sth/to do sth)** to try very hard to do or get sth: *to strive for perfection* ▶ **usiłować** (*coś zrobić*)

strode past tense of **stride¹**

stroke¹ /strəʊk/ noun **1** [C] one of the movements that you make when you are swimming, **rowing**, playing golf, etc.: *Woods won by three strokes.* ▶ **ruch** (*rąk w pływaniu*), **uderzenie** (*np. wiosłem, rakietą*) **2** [C,U] [in compounds] one of the styles of swimming: *I can do backstroke and breaststroke, but not front crawl.* ▶ **styl** (*pływania*) ➲ look at **crawl 3** [C] one of the movements that you make when you are writing or painting: *a brush stroke* ▶ **pociągnięcie** (*np. pióra, pędzla*) **4** [sing.] **a stroke of sth** a sudden successful action or event: *It was* ***a stroke of luck*** (uśmiech losu) *finding your ring on the beach, wasn't it?* ◇ *a* ***stroke of bad luck*** pech ◇ *It took* ***a stroke of genius***

to solve the puzzle. Rozwiązanie tej zagadki wymagało przebłysku geniuszu. **5** [C] a sudden illness which attacks the brain and can leave a person unable to move part of their body, speak clearly, etc.: *to* ***have a stroke*** ▶ **wylew krwi do mózgu**

IDM **at a/one stroke** with a single action ▶ **jednym pociągnięciem**

not do a stroke (of work) to not do any work at all ▶ **nie kiwnąć palcem**

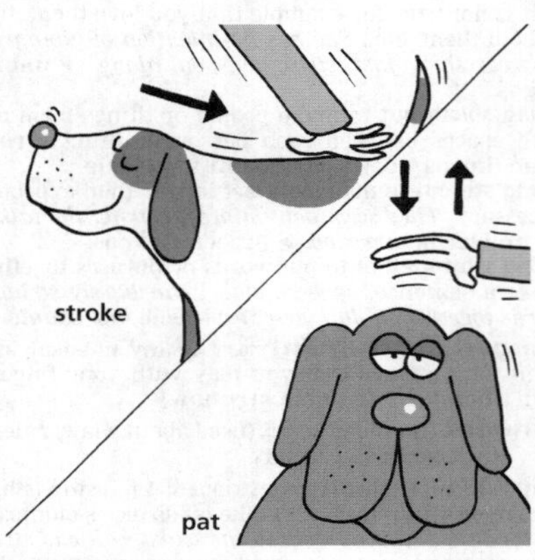

stroke² /strəʊk/ verb [T] **1** to move your hand gently over sb/sth: *She stroked his hair affectionately.* ◇ *to stroke a dog* ▶ **gładzić 2** to move sth somewhere with a smooth movement: *He stroked the ball just wide of the hole.* ◇ *She stroked away his tears.* Delikatnie otarła mu łzy. ▶ **delikatnie przesuwać**

stroll /strəʊl/ noun [C] a slow walk for pleasure: *to* ***go for a stroll*** *along the beach* ▶ **przechadzka**

■ **stroll** verb [I] ▶ **przechadzać się**

stroller (US) = PUSHCHAIR

strong /strɒŋ/ adj. **1** (used about a person) able to lift or carry heavy things: *I need someone strong to help me move this bookcase.* ◇ *to have strong arms/muscles* ▶ **silny** OPP **weak 2** powerful: *strong winds/currents/sunlight* ▶ **silny 3** having a big effect on the mind, body or senses: *a* ***strong smell*** *of garlic* ◇ *strong coffee* ◇ *a strong drink* ◇ *I have the* ***strong impression*** *that they don't like us.* ▶ **intensywny**, **mocny 4** difficult to fight against: *There was* ***strong opposition*** *to the idea.* ◇ ***strong support*** *for the government's plan* ▶ **silny**; **stanowczy** SYN **firm 5** (used about an object) not easily broken or damaged: *That chair isn't strong enough for you to stand on.* ▶ **wytrzymały**; **solidny** ➲ look at **fragile 6** powerful and likely to succeed: *She's a strong candidate for the job.* ◇ *a strong team* ▶ **mający duże szanse** OPP **weak 7** [used after a noun] having a particular number of people: *The army was 50 000 strong.* ▶ **w sile** ➲ noun **strength**

■ **strongly** adv.: *The directors are strongly opposed to the idea.* ◇ *to feel very strongly about something* ▶ **silnie**, **głęboko**

IDM **going strong** (informal) continuing, even after a long time: *The company was formed in 1851 and is still going strong.* ▶ **być nadal w dobrej formie/kondycji**

sb's strong point something that a person is good at: *Maths is not my strong point.* ▶ **czyjaś mocna strona**

stronghold /'strɒŋhəʊld/ noun [C] an area in which there is a lot of support for a particular belief or group of people, especially a political party: *a Republican stronghold/a stronghold of Republicanism* ◇ *The Labour Party retained its traditional stronghold in the north.* ◇ *The college is a stronghold of the child-centred approach to teaching.* ▶ **bastion**

ˌstrong-'minded adj. having firm ideas or beliefs ▶ **o zdecydowanych poglądach** SYN **determined**

stroppy /'strɒpi/ adj. (**stroppier**; **stroppiest**) (Brit., slang) (used about a person) easily annoyed and difficult to deal with ▶ **kłótliwy**; **humorzasty**

strove past tense of **strive**

struck past tense, past participle of **strike¹**

structure¹ /'strʌktʃə(r)/ noun **1** [C,U] the way that the parts of sth are put together or organized: *the political and social structure of a country* ◇ *the grammatical structures of a language* ▶ **budowa**, **struktura 2** [C] a building or sth that has been built or made from a number of parts: *The old office block had been replaced by a modern glass structure.* ▶ **budowla**, **struktura**

■ **structural** /'strʌktʃərəl/ adj. ▶ **strukturalny**

structure² /'strʌktʃə(r)/ verb [T] to arrange sth in an organized way: *a carefully-structured English course* ▶ **konstruować**

struggle¹ /'strʌgl/ verb [I] **1 struggle (with sth/for sth/to do sth)** to try very hard to do sth, especially when it is difficult: *We struggled up the stairs with our heavy suitcases.* ◇ *Maria was struggling with her English homework.* ◇ *The country is struggling for independence.* ▶ **szarpać się 2 struggle (with sb/sth)**; **struggle (against sth)** to fight in order to prevent sth or to escape from sb: *He shouted and struggled but he couldn't get free.* ◇ *A passer-by was struggling with one of the robbers on the ground.* ◇ *He has been struggling against cancer for years.* ▶ **szamotać się**

PHR V **struggle along/on** to continue to do sth although it is difficult: *I felt terrible but managed to struggle on to the end of the day.* ▶ **z trudem dalej coś robić**

struggle² /'strʌgl/ noun [C] **1** a fight in which sb tries to do or get sth when this is difficult: *All countries should join together in the struggle against terrorism.* ◇ *He will not give up the presidency without a struggle.* ◇ *a struggle for independence* ▶ **walka 2** [usually sing.] sth that is difficult to achieve: *It will be a struggle* (trudno będzie) *to get there on time.* ▶ **wysiłek** SYN **effort**

strum /strʌm/ verb [I,T] (**strumming**; **strummed**) to play a **guitar** by moving your hand up and down over the strings ▶ **brzdąkać**

strung past tense, past participle of **string²**

strut /strʌt/ verb [I] (**strutting**; **strutted**) to walk in a proud way ▶ **chodzić/kroczyć dumnie jak paw**

stub /stʌb/ noun [C] the short piece of a cigarette or pencil that is left after the rest of it has been used ▶ **niedopałek**; **resztka**

■ **stub** verb [T] to hurt your toe by accidentally hitting it against sth hard ▶ **uderzyć się** (*w palec u nogi*)

PHR V **stub sth out** to stop a cigarette, etc. from burning by pressing the end against sth hard ▶ **gasić** (*np. papierosa*)

stubble /'stʌbl/ noun [U] **1** the short parts of crops such as **wheat** that are left standing after the rest has been cut ▶ **ścierń 2** the short hairs that grow on a man's face when he has not shaved for some time ▶ **szczecina** (*na brodzie*) ➲ picture at **hair**

stubborn /'stʌbən/ adj. not wanting to do what other people want you to do; refusing to change your plans or decisions: *She's too stubborn to apologize.* ▶ **uparty**; **nieustępliwy** SYN **obstinate** ➲ look at **pig-headed**

■ **stubbornly** adv.: *He stubbornly refused to apologize so he was sacked.* ▶ **uparcie**; **nieustępliwie** | **stubbornness** noun [U] ▶ **upór**; **nieustępliwość**

stucco /ˈstʌkəʊ/ noun [U] plaster or cement that is used for covering or decorating walls or ceilings ▶ **stiuk**

stuck[1] past tense, past participle of **stick[2]**

stuck[2] /stʌk/ adj. [not before a noun] **be/get stuck 1** not able to move: *This drawer's stuck. I can't open it at all.* ◇ *We were stuck in traffic for over two hours.* ▶ **zacinać się, zaklinowywać się 2** not able to continue with an exercise, etc. because it is too difficult: *If you* ***get stuck****, ask your teacher for help.* ▶ **utknąć**

stud /stʌd/ noun **1** [C] a small, round, solid piece of metal that you wear through a hole in your ear or other part of the body ▶ **kolczyk** (*typu kuleczka lub wkrętka*) **2** [C] a small piece of metal that sticks out from the rest of the surface that it is fixed to: *a black leather jacket with studs all over it* ▶ **ćwiek, spinka** (*do kołnierzyka*) **3** [C] one of the pieces of plastic or metal that stick out from the bottom of football boots, etc. and that help you stand up on wet ground ▶ **korek** (*w podeszwie buta sportowego*) **4** [C,U] a number of high quality horses or other animals that are kept for breeding young animals; the place where these animals are kept: *to keep a stallion at stud* (jako reproduktora) ◇ *a stud farm* ▶ **stadnina**

studded /ˈstʌdɪd/ adj. **1** covered or decorated with small pieces of metal that stick out from the rest of the surface ▶ **wysadzany, nabijany (czymś) 2 studded (with sth)** containing a lot of sth: *a star-studded cast* gwiazdorska obsada ◇ *a sky studded with stars* niebo usiane gwiazdami ▶ **pełen czegoś**

student /ˈstjuːdnt; US ˈstuː-/ noun [C] a person who is studying at a school, college or university: *Paola is a medical student at Bristol University.* ◇ *a full-time/part-time student* student/ka studiując-y/a w pełnym/niepełnym wymiarze godzin ◇ *a postgraduate/research student* ◇ *a student teacher* słuchacz szkoły pedagogicznej lub praktykant w szkole ▶ **student/ka** ➲ note at **school**, **university** ➲ look at **graduate**, **pupil**, **scholar**, **undergraduate**

studied /ˈstʌdid/ adj. [only before a noun] (formal) carefully planned or done, especially when you are trying to give a particular impression ▶ **wystudiowany** (*np. gest, uśmiech*)

studio /ˈstjuːdiəʊ; US ˈstuː-/ noun [C] (pl. **studios**) **1** a room or building where films or TV programmes are made, or where music, radio programmes, etc. are recorded: *a film/TV/recording studio* ▶ **studio, wytwórnia filmowa 2** a room where an artist or a photographer works: *a sculptor's studio* ▶ **pracownia** (*artystyczna*), **atelier 3** (Brit. also ˈ**studio flat**; US also ˈ**studio apartment**) a small flat with one main room for living and sleeping in and usually a kitchen and bathroom ▶ **mieszkanie typu kawalerka**

studious /ˈstjuːdiəs; US ˈstuː-/ adj. (used about a person) spending a lot of time studying ▶ **pilny**

studiously /ˈstjuːdiəsli; US ˈstuː-/ adv. with great care ▶ **starannie, skrupulatnie**

study[1] /ˈstʌdi/ noun (pl. **studies**) **1** [U] the activity of learning about sth: *One hour every afternoon is left free for individual study.* ◇ *Physiology is the study of how living things work.* ◇ *study skills* umiejętności uczenia się ▶ **nauka, uczenie się 2 (studies)** [pl.] the subjects that you study: *business/media/Japanese studies* ▶ **studia, badania 3** [C] a piece of research that examines a question or a subject in detail: *They are doing a study of the causes of heart disease.* ▶ **praca naukowa, studium 4** [C] a room in a house where you go to read, write or study ▶ **gabinet, pracownia**

study[2] /ˈstʌdi/ verb (**studying**; **studies**; pt, pp **studied**) **1** [I,T] **study (sth/for sth)** to spend time learning about sth: *to study French at university* ◇ *Leon has been studying hard for his exams.* ▶ **uczyć się, studiować 2** [T] to look at sth very carefully: *to study a map* ▶ **wpatrywać się (w coś)**

> **studying**
>
> If you want to **study** sth or **learn about** sth, you can **teach yourself** or you can take a **course**. This will be **full-time** or **part-time**, perhaps with **evening classes**. You will need to **take notes**, and you might have to **write essays** or **do a project**. You should **hand** these **in** to your **teacher**/**tutor** before the **deadline**. Before you take **exams** you'll need to **revise**.

stuff[1] /stʌf/ noun [U] (informal) **1** (used to refer to sth without using its name): *What's that green stuff at the bottom of the bottle?* ◇ *The shop was burgled and a lot of stuff was stolen.* ◇ *They sell stationery and stuff (like that).* ◇ *I'll put the swimming stuff in this bag.* ▶ **rzeczy, coś 2** (used to refer in general to things that people do, say, think, etc.): *I've got lots of stuff* (mnóstwo rzeczy) *to do tomorrow so I'm going to get up early.* ◇ *I don't believe all that stuff* (w to wszystko) *about him being robbed.* ◇ *I like reading and stuff* (i tego rodzaju rzeczy). ▶ **rzeczy**

stuff[2] /stʌf/ verb **1** [T] **stuff sth (with sth)** to fill sth with sth: *The pillow was stuffed with feathers.* ◇ *red peppers stuffed with rice* ▶ **wypychać/napychać; faszerować, nadziewać 2** [T] (informal) **stuff sth into sth** to put sth into sth else quickly or carelessly: *He quickly stuffed a few clothes into a suitcase.* ▶ **wpychać 3** [T] (informal) **stuff yourself (with sth)** to eat too much of sth: *Barry just sat there stuffing himself with sandwiches.* ▶ **obżerać się 4** [T] to fill the body of a dead bird or animal with special material so that it looks as if it is alive: *They've got a stuffed crocodile in the museum.* ▶ **wypychać**

IDM **get stuffed** (Brit., informal) (a rude expression used when you are angry with sb) ▶ **wypchać się**

stuffing /ˈstʌfɪŋ/ noun [U] **1** a mixture of small pieces of food that you put inside a chicken, vegetable, etc. before you cook it ▶ **farsz, nadzienie 2** the material that you put inside **cushions**, soft toys, etc. ▶ **wypełnienie, wyściółka**

stuffy /ˈstʌfi/ adj. (**stuffier**; **stuffiest**) **1** (used about a room) too warm and having no fresh air ▶ **duszny 2** (informal) (used about a person) formal and old-fashioned ▶ **staroświecki, nudny**

stumble /ˈstʌmbl/ verb [I] **1 stumble (over/on sth)** to hit your foot against sth when you are walking or running and almost fall over ▶ **potykać się** SYN **trip 2 stumble (over/through sth)** to make a mistake when you are speaking, playing music, etc.: *The newsreader stumbled over the name of the Russian tennis player.* ▶ **zająknąć się, dukać**

PHR V **stumble across/on/upon sb/sth** to meet or find sb/sth by chance ▶ **natykać się na kogoś/coś**

ˈ**stumbling block** noun [C] something that causes trouble or a problem, so that you cannot achieve what you want: *Money is still the stumbling block to settling the dispute.* ▶ **szkopuł, przeszkoda**

stump[1] /stʌmp/ noun [C] the part that is left after sth has been cut down, broken off, etc.: *a tree stump* ▶ **pniak, kikut**

stump[2] /stʌmp/ verb **1** [T] (informal) to cause sb to be unable to answer a question or find a solution to a problem: *I was completely stumped by question* (zbaraniałem przy pytaniu numer) *14.* ▶ **zbić z tropu 2** [I] to walk with slow heavy steps ▶ **stąpać** (*sztywno*)

stun /stʌn/ verb [T] (**stunning**; **stunned**) **1** to make a person or an animal unconscious or confused by hitting them or it on the head ▶ **ogłuszać 2** to make a person very surprised by telling them some unexpected news: *His sudden death stunned his friends.* ▶ **ogłuszać, oszałamiać** SYN **astound**

S

■ **stunned** adj.: *There was a stunned silence* (zapadła grobowa cisza) *after Margaret announced her resignation.* ▶ **oszołomiony**

stung past tense, past participle of **sting**[1]

stunk past participle of **stink**

stunning /ˈstʌnɪŋ/ adj. (informal) very attractive, impressive or surprising: *a stunning view* ▶ **olśniewający**, **urzekający** SYN **beautiful**

stunt[1] /stʌnt/ noun [C] **1** a very difficult or dangerous thing that sb does to entertain people or as part of a film: *Some actors do their own stunts, others use a stuntman.* ▶ **wyczyn kaskaderski 2** something that you do to get people's attention: *a publicity stunt* chwyt reklamowy ▶ **sztuczka**, **trik**

stunt[2] /stʌnt/ verb [T] to stop sb/sth growing or developing properly: *A poor diet can stunt a child's growth.* ▶ **hamować** (*rozwój czegoś*), **powstrzymywać**

stunted /ˈstʌntɪd/ adj. that has not been able to grow or develop as much as it should: *stunted trees* skarłowaciałe drzewa ◇ *the stunted lives of children deprived of education* ▶ **zdeformowany**, **opóźniony w rozwoju**

stuntman /ˈstʌntmæn/, **stuntwoman** /ˈstʌntwʊmən/ noun [C] (pl. **-men** /-men/; **-women** /-wɪmɪn/) a person who does sth dangerous in a film in the place of an actor ▶ **kaskader/ka**

stupefy /ˈstjuːpɪfaɪ; US ˈstuː-/ verb [T] (**stupefies**; **stupefying**; **stupefied**; **stupefied**) [often passive] to surprise or shock sb; to make sb unable to think clearly: *He was stupefied by the amount they had spent.* ◇ *She was stupefied with cold.* ▶ **wprawiać w osłupienie**, **oszałamiać**

■ **stupefaction** /ˌstjuːpɪˈfækʃn; US ˌstuː-/ noun [U] ▶ **osłupienie**, **oszołomienie**

stupendous /stjuːˈpendəs; US stuː-/ adj. very large or impressive: *a stupendous achievement* ▶ **niesłychany**, **zdumiewający**

stupid /ˈstjuːpɪd; US ˈstuː-/ adj. **1** not intelligent or sensible: *Don't be so stupid, of course I'll help you!* ◇ *He was stupid to trust her.* ◇ *a stupid mistake/suggestion/question* ▶ **głupi**, **idiotyczny** SYN **silly 2** [only before a noun] (informal) (used to show that you are angry or do not like sb/sth): *I'm tired of hearing about his stupid car.* ▶ **głupi**

■ **stupidity** /stjuːˈpɪdəti; US stuː-/ noun [U] ▶ **głupota** | **stupidly** adv. ▶ **głupio**, **idiotycznie**

stupor /ˈstjuːpə(r); US ˈstuː-/ noun [sing., U] the state of being nearly unconscious or being unable to think properly: *He was lying on the ground* ***in a drunken stupor*** (pijany do nieprzytomności). ▶ **zamroczenie**, **otępienie**

sturdy /ˈstɜːdi/ adj. (**sturdier**; **sturdiest**) strong and healthy; that will not break easily: *sturdy legs* ◇ *sturdy shoes* ▶ **krzepki**; **mocny**, **wytrzymały**

■ **sturdily** adv. ▶ **krzepko**; **mocno**, **wytrzymale** | **sturdiness** noun [U] ▶ **krzepkość**, **wytrzymałość**

sturgeon /ˈstɜːdʒən/ noun [C,U] (pl. **sturgeon** or **sturgeons**) a large fish found in rivers. **Sturgeons** are eaten as food and also caught for their eggs (**caviar**). ▶ **jesiotr**

stutter /ˈstʌtə(r)/ verb [I,T] to have difficulty when you speak, so that you keep repeating the first sound of a word ▶ **jąkać się**

■ **stutter** noun [C]: *to have a stutter* ▶ **jąkanie się**

sty (also **stye**) /staɪ/ noun [C] (pl. **sties** or **styes**) **1** = PIGSTY **2** a painful spot on your **eyelid** ▶ **jęczmień** (*na powiece*)

style /staɪl/ noun **1** [C,U] the way that sth is done, built, etc.: *a new style of architecture* ◇ *The writer's style is very clear and simple.* ◇ *an American-style education system* ▶ **styl 2** [C,U] the fashion, shape or design of sth: *We stock all the latest styles.* ◇ *a hairstyle* fryzura ▶ **styl** (*mody*), **fason 3** [U] the ability to do things in a way that other people admire: *He's got no sense of style.* ▶ **(dobry) styl**, **szyk**

stylish /ˈstaɪlɪʃ/ adj. fashionable and attractive: *She's a stylish dresser.* ▶ **stylowy**, **szykowny**

stylist /ˈstaɪlɪst/ noun [C] a person whose job is cutting and shaping people's hair ▶ **fryzjer/ka**, **stylist(k)a**

stylistic /staɪˈlɪstɪk/ adj. [only before a noun] connected with the style an artist uses in a particular piece of art, writing or music: *stylistic analysis* ◇ *stylistic features* ▶ **stylistyczny**

■ **stylistically** /-kli/ adv.: *The works are stylistically related.* ▶ **stylistycznie**

suave /swɑːv/ adj. (usually used about a man) confident, elegant and polite, sometimes in a way that does not seem sincere ▶ **szarmancki**, **z ogładą**

subconscious /ˌsʌbˈkɒnʃəs/ (also **unconscious**) noun (**the subconscious**) [sing.] the hidden part of your mind that can affect the way that you behave without you realizing ▶ **podświadomość**

■ **subconscious** adj.: *the subconscious mind* ◇ *Many advertisements work on a subconscious level.* ▶ **podświadomy** | **subconsciously** adv. ▶ **podświadomie**

subcontinent /ˌsʌbˈkɒntɪnənt/ noun [sing.] a large area of land that forms part of a continent, especially the part of Asia that includes India, Pakistan and Bangladesh: *the Indian subcontinent* ▶ **subkontynent**

subculture /ˈsʌbkʌltʃə(r)/ noun [C] the behaviour and beliefs of a particular group of people in society that are different from those of most people: *the* ***criminal/drug/youth, etc. subculture*** ▶ **subkultura** ℹ Czasami wyraża dezaprobatę.

subdivide /ˌsʌbdɪˈvaɪd/ verb [I,T] to divide or be divided into smaller parts ▶ **dzielić (się)** (*na mniejsze części/jednostki*)

■ **subdivision** /ˈsʌbdɪvɪʒn/ noun [C,U] ▶ **podział** (*na mniejsze części/jednostki*)

subdue /səbˈdjuː; US -ˈduː/ verb [T] to defeat sb/sth or bring sb/sth under control ▶ **ujarzmiać**, **poskramiać**

subdued /səbˈdjuːd; US -ˈduː-/ adj. **1** (used about a person) quieter and with less energy than usual ▶ **przyćmiony**, **stonowany 2** not very loud or bright: *subdued laughter/lighting* ▶ **przygnębiony**, **przygaszony**

subheading /ˈsʌbhedɪŋ/ noun [C] a title given to any of the sections into which a longer piece of writing has been divided ▶ **podtytuł**

subject[1] /ˈsʌbdʒɪkt/ noun [C] **1** a person or thing that is being considered, shown or talked about: *What subject is the lecture on?* ◇ *What are your views on this subject?* ◇ *I've tried several times to* ***bring up/raise the subject*** (poruszyć temat) *of money.* ▶ **temat**, **przedmiot 2** an area of knowledge that you study at school, university, etc.: *My favourite subjects at school are Biology and French.* ▶ **przedmiot 3** the person or thing that does the action described by the verb in a sentence: *In the sentence 'The cat sat on the mat', 'the cat' is the subject.* ▶ **podmiot** ➲ look at **object 4** a person from a particular country, especially one with a king or queen; a citizen: *a British subject* ▶ **poddan-y/a**

IDM **change the subject** → CHANGE[1]

subject[2] /ˈsʌbdʒekt/ adj. **subject to sth 1** likely to be affected by sth: *The area is subject to regular flooding.* ◇ *Smokers are more subject to heart attacks than non-smokers.* ▶ **narażony**, **podatny 2** depending on sth as a condition: *The plan for new housing is still subject to approval by the minister.* ▶ **uwarunkowany czymś 3** controlled by or having to obey sb/sth ▶ **podlegający**, **podległy**

subject[3] /səbˈdʒekt/ verb

PHR V **subject sb/sth to sth** to make sb/sth experience sth unpleasant: *He was subjected to verbal and physical* *abuse from the other boys.* ▶ **narażać kogoś/coś na coś, poddawać kogoś czemuś**

subjective /səbˈdʒektɪv/ adj. based on your own tastes and opinions instead of on facts: *Try not to be so subjective in your essays.* ▶ **subiektywny** OPP **objective**
■ **subjectively** adv. ▶ **subiektywnie**

ˈ**subject matter** noun [U] the ideas or information contained in a book, speech, painting, etc.: *I don't think the* ***subject matter*** *of this programme is suitable for children.* ▶ **temat**

subjugate /ˈsʌbdʒugeɪt/ verb [T, usually passive] (formal) to defeat sb/sth; to gain control over sb/sth: *Her personal ambitions had been subjugated to the needs of her family.* ▶ **ujarzmiać, podporządkowywać**
■ **subjugation** /ˌsʌbdʒuˈgeɪʃn/ noun (formal): *the subjugation of Ireland by England* ▶ **ujarzmienie, podporządkowanie**

subjunctive /səbˈdʒʌŋktɪv/ noun [sing.] the form of a verb in certain languages that expresses doubt, possibility, a wish, etc. ▶ **tryb łączący**
■ **subjunctive** adj. ▶ **łączący**

sublet /ˌsʌbˈlet/ verb [T,I] (**subletting**; pt, pp **sublet**) **sublet (sth) (to sb)** to rent to sb else all or part of a property that you rent from the owner ▶ **poddzierżawiać (coś) (komuś), podnajmować (coś) (komuś)**

sublimate /ˈsʌblɪmeɪt/ verb [T] to direct your energy, especially sexual energy, to socially acceptable activities such as work, exercise, art, etc. ▶ **sublimować** SYN **channel**
■ **sublimation** /ˌsʌblɪˈmeɪʃn/ noun [U] ▶ **sublimacja**

sublime /səˈblaɪm/ adj. (formal) of extremely high quality that makes you admire sth very much ▶ **wzniosły, podniosły**
■ **sublimely** adv. ▶ **wzniośle, podniośle**

subliminal /ˌsʌbˈlɪmɪnl/ adj. affecting your mind even though you are not aware of it: *subliminal advertising* ◇ *music containing subliminal messages* ▶ **podprogowy**
■ **subliminally** adv. ▶ **podprogowo**

submarine /ˌsʌbməˈriːn/ noun [C] a type of ship that can travel under the water as well as on the surface ▶ **łódź podwodna** ➲ picture on **page A6**

submerge /səbˈmɜːdʒ/ verb [I,T] to go or make sth go underwater: *The fields were submerged by the floods.* ▶ **zanurzać (się), zalewać**
■ **submerged** adj. ▶ **zanurzony**

submission /səbˈmɪʃn/ noun **1** [U] the accepting of sb else's power or control because they have defeated you ▶ **uległość, pokora 2** [U,C] the act of giving a plan, document, etc. to an official organization so that it can be studied and considered; the plan, document, etc. that you send ▶ **przedłożenie, złożenie**

submissive /səbˈmɪsɪv/ adj. ready to obey other people and do whatever they want ▶ **uległy, pokorny**

submit /səbˈmɪt/ verb (**submitting**; **submitted**) **1** [T] **submit sth (to sb/sth)** to give a plan, document, etc. to an official organization so that it can be studied and considered: *to submit an application/a complaint/a claim* ▶ **przedkładać, składać 2** [I] **submit (to sb/sth)** to accept sb/sth's power or control because they have defeated you ▶ **poddawać się, ulegać**

subnormal /ˌsʌbˈnɔːml/ adj. **1** (technical) lower than normal: *subnormal temperatures* ▶ **poniżej normy 2** having a very low level of intelligence ▶ **opóźniony w rozwoju, niedorozwinięty (umysłowo)** ⓘ W tym znaczeniu to słowo może być obraźliwe.

subordinate¹ /səˈbɔːdɪnət/ adj. **subordinate (to sb/sth)** having less power or authority than sb else; less important than sth else ▶ **drugorzędny, drugoplanowy**
■ **subordinate** noun [C]: *the relationship between superiors and their subordinates* ▶ **podwładn-y/a**

subordinate² /səˈbɔːdɪneɪt/ verb [T] to treat one person or thing as less important than another ▶ **podporządkowywać sobie, uzależniać**

suˌ**bordinate** ˈ**clause** noun [C] a group of words that is not a sentence but that adds information to the main part of the sentence ▶ **zdanie podrzędne**

subscribe /səbˈskraɪb/ verb [I] **subscribe (to sth)** to pay for a newspaper or magazine to be sent to you regularly ▶ **prenumerować**
PHR V **subscribe to sth** to agree with an idea, a belief, etc.: *I don't subscribe to the view that all war is wrong.* ▶ **zgadzać się z czymś, podpisywać się pod czymś**

subscriber /səbˈskraɪbə(r)/ noun [C] a person who pays to receive a newspaper or magazine regularly or to use a particular service: *subscribers to satellite and cable TV* ▶ **prenumerator/ka; abonent/ka**

subscription /səbˈskrɪpʃn/ noun [C] an amount of money that you pay, usually once a year, to receive a newspaper or magazine regularly or to belong to an organization ▶ **prenumerata**

subsection /ˈsʌbsekʃn/ noun [C] a part of a section, especially of a legal document ▶ **podpunkt**

subsequent /ˈsʌbsɪkwənt/ adj. [only before a noun] (formal) coming after or later: *I thought that was the end of the matter but subsequent events proved me wrong.* ▶ **dalszy, późniejszy**
■ **subsequently** adv.: *The rumours were subsequently found to be untrue.* ▶ **następnie, później**

subservient /səbˈsɜːviənt/ adj. **1 subservient (to sb/sth)** too ready to obey other people ▶ **służalczy 2** (formal) **subservient (to sth)** considered to be less important than sb/sth else ▶ **pomocniczy**
■ **subservience** noun [U] ▶ **wiernopoddańczość, służalczość**

subset /ˈsʌbset/ noun [C] a smaller group of people or things formed from the members of a larger group ▶ **podgrupa**

subside /səbˈsaɪd/ verb [I] **1** to become calmer or quieter: *The storm seems to be subsiding.* ▶ **uciszać się, ustawać 2** (used about land, a building, etc.) to sink down into the ground ▶ **obsuwać się, osiadać**
■ **subsidence** /ˈsʌbsɪdns; səbˈsaɪdns/ noun [U] ▶ **obsunięcie się, zapadnięcie się**

subsidiary¹ /səbˈsɪdiəri; US -dieri/ adj. connected with sth but less important than it ▶ **pomocniczy, dodatkowy**

subsidiary² /səbˈsɪdiəri; US -dieri/ noun [C] (pl. **subsidiaries**) a business company that belongs to and is controlled by another larger company ▶ **filia** (*spółki*)

subsidize (also **-ise**) /ˈsʌbsɪdaɪz/ verb [T] (used about a government, etc.) to give money in order to keep the cost of a service low: *Public transport should be subsidized.* ▶ **dotować, subsydiować**

subsidy /ˈsʌbsədi/ noun [C,U] (pl. **subsidies**) money that the government, etc. pays to help an organization or to keep the cost of a service low: *agricultural/state/housing subsidies* ▶ **dotacja, subwencja**

subsist /səbˈsɪst/ verb [I] (formal) **subsist (on sth)** to manage to live with very little food or money ▶ **egzystować, trwać**
■ **subsistence** noun [U] ▶ **egzystencja, przetrwanie**

🔑 **substance** /ˈsʌbstəns/ noun **1** [C] a solid or liquid material: *poisonous substances* ◇ *The cloth is coated in a new waterproof substance.* ▶ **substancja, tworzywo, masa 2** [U] importance, value or truth: *It was malicious gossip, completely without substance.* ◇ *The commissioner's report* ***gives substance to*** (potwierdził) *these allegations.* ◇ *There's little substance* (mało treści) *to the film but it's* *very entertaining.* ▶ **podstawa, znaczenie 3** [U] the most important or main part of sth: *What was the substance of his argument?* ▶ **sedno, sens**

substandard /ˌsʌbˈstændəd/ adj. of poor quality; not as good as usual or as it should be ▶ **podrzędny, lichy**

substantial /səbˈstænʃl/ adj. **1** large in amount: *The storms caused substantial damage.* ◇ *a substantial sum of money* ▶ **znaczny, pokaźny 2** large or strong: *The furniture was cheap and not very substantial.* ▶ **solidny, trwały** OPP for both meanings **insubstantial**

substantially /səbˈstænʃəli/ adv. **1** very much: *House prices have fallen substantially.* ▶ **znacznie, pokaźnie** SYN **greatly 2** generally; in most points: *The landscape of Wales has remained substantially the same for centuries.* ▶ **ogólnie, przeważnie**

substitute /ˈsʌbstɪtjuːt; US -tuːt/ noun [C] **a substitute (for sb/sth)** a person or thing that takes the place of sb/sth else: *One player was injured so the substitute* (gracz/zawodnik rezerwowy) *was sent on to play.* ▶ **namiastka, zastęp-ca/czyni**

■ **substitute** verb [T] **substitute sb/sth (for sb/sth); substitute for sb/sth**: *You can substitute margarine for butter.* ▶ **zastępować kogoś/coś (kimś/czymś innym); pełnić czyjąś funkcję** | **substitution** /ˌsʌbstɪˈtjuːʃn; US -ˈtuː-/ noun [C,U] ▶ **zastępowanie kogoś/czegoś (kimś/czymś)**

subterranean /ˌsʌbtəˈreɪniən/ adj. (formal) under the ground: *a subterranean cave* ▶ **podziemny**

subtext /ˈsʌbtekst/ noun [C] a hidden meaning or reason for doing sth ▶ **podtekst**

subtitle /ˈsʌbtaɪtl/ noun [C, usually pl.] the words at the bottom of the picture on TV or at the cinema. The **subtitles** translate the words that are spoken, or show them to help people with hearing problems: *a Polish film with English subtitles* ▶ **napisy** (*na filmie*) ➲ look at **dub**

subtle /ˈsʌtl/ adj. **1** not very noticeable; not very strong or bright: *subtle colours* ◇ *I noticed a subtle difference in her.* ▶ **subtelny, delikatny 2** very clever, and using indirect methods to achieve sth: *Advertisements persuade us to buy things in very subtle ways.* ▶ **wyrafinowany, subtelny**

■ **subtlety** /ˈsʌtlti/ noun [C,U] (pl. **subtleties**) ▶ **subtelność, wyrafinowanie** | **subtly** /ˈsʌtli/ adv. ▶ **subtelnie, ledwo zauważalnie**

subtract /səbˈtrækt/ verb [T] **subtract sth (from sth)** to take one number or quantity away from another: *If you subtract five from nine you get four.* ▶ **odejmować** OPP **add**

■ **subtraction** /səbˈtrækʃn/ noun [C,U] ▶ **odejmowanie**

suburb /ˈsʌbɜːb/ noun [C] an area where people live that is outside the central part of a town or city: *Most people live **in the suburbs** and work in the centre of town.* ▶ **przedmieście, peryferie**

■ **suburban** /səˈbɜːbən/ adj. ▶ **podmiejski, peryferyjny** ℹ Życie podmiejskie często uważa się za nudne, stąd też **suburban** często oznacza „nudny". | **suburbia** /səˈbɜːbiə/ noun [U] ▶ **przedmieścia, mieszkańcy przedmieść**

subversive /səbˈvɜːsɪv/ adj. trying to destroy or damage a government, religion or political system by attacking it secretly and in an indirect way: *subversive literature* ▶ **wywrotowy**

■ **subversive** noun [C] ▶ **wywrotowiec** | **subversion** /səbˈvɜːʃn; US -ʒn/ noun [U] ▶ **działalność wywrotowa**

subvert /səbˈvɜːt/ verb [T] to try to destroy or damage a government, religion or political system by attacking it secretly and in an indirect way ▶ **obalać, wywracać**

subway /ˈsʌbweɪ/ noun [C] **1** a tunnel under a busy road or railway that people can walk through to cross to the other side ▶ **przejście podziemne 2** (US) = UNDERGROUND[3]

succeed /səkˈsiːd/ verb **1** [I] **succeed (in sth/doing sth)** to manage to achieve what you want; to do well: *Our plan succeeded.* ◇ *A good education will help you succeed in life.* ◇ *to succeed in passing an exam* ◇ *He succeeded in* (udało mu się) *getting a place at art school.* ▶ **powieść się, odnosić sukces** OPP **fail 2** [I,T] to have a job or important position after sb else: *Tony Blair succeeded John Major as British Prime Minister in 1997.* ▶ **następować po kimś**

success /səkˈses/ noun **1** [U] the fact that you have achieved what you want; doing well and becoming famous, rich, etc.: *Hard work is **the key to success**.* ◇ *Her attempts to get a job for the summer have not **met with** much **success*** (nie powiodły się). ◇ *What's the secret of your success?* ▶ **powodzenie, sukces 2** [C] the thing that you achieve; sth that becomes very popular: *He really tried to **make a success of** the business.* ◇ *The film 'Titanic' was a huge success* (cieszył się olbrzymim powodzeniem). ◇ *You must try to make a success of your marriage* (żeby twoje małżeństwo było udane). ▶ **sukces** OPP for both meanings **failure**

successful /səkˈsesfl/ adj. having achieved what you wanted; having become popular, rich, etc.: *a successful attempt to climb Mount Everest* ◇ *a successful actor* wzięty aktor ▶ **pomyślny, dobrze prosperujący, zwycięski, udany** OPP **unsuccessful**

■ **successfully** /-fəli/ adv. ▶ **pomyślnie, szczęśliwie**

succession /səkˈseʃn/ noun **1** [C] a number of people or things that follow each other in time or order; a series: *a succession of events/problems/visitors* ▶ **szereg, seria 2** [U] the right to have an important position after sb else ▶ **następstwo tronu, sukcesja**

IDM **in succession** following one after another: *There have been three deaths in the family in quick succession* (w krótkich odstępach czasu). ▶ **pod rząd, kolejno, raz za razem**

successive /səkˈsesɪv/ adj. [only before a noun] following immediately one after the other: *This was their fourth successive win.* ◇ *Successive governments have tried to tackle the problem.* ▶ **kolejny** SYN **consecutive**

successor /səkˈsesə(r)/ noun [C] a person or thing that comes after sb/sth else and takes their or its place ▶ **następ-ca/czyni, spadkobier-ca/czyni** ➲ look at **predecessor**

succinct /səkˈsɪŋkt/ adj. said clearly, in a few words ▶ **zwięzły, treściwy**

■ **succinctly** adv. ▶ **zwięźle, treściwie**

succulent /ˈsʌkjələnt/ adj. (used about fruit, vegetables and meat) containing a lot of juice and tasting very good ▶ **soczysty, mięsisty**

succumb /səˈkʌm/ verb [I] (formal) **succumb (to sth)** to stop fighting against sth: *to succumb to an illness* umrzeć ▶ **ulegać** (*np. pokusie*)

such /sʌtʃ/ determiner **1** (used for referring to sb/sth that you mentioned earlier) of this or that type: *I don't believe in ghosts. There's **no such thing**.* ▶ **taki 2** (used to describe the result of sth): *The statement was worded **in such a way that** it did not upset anyone.* ▶ **taki 3** (used for emphasizing the degree of sth): *It was such a fascinating book that I couldn't put it down.* ◇ *It seems such a long time since we last saw each other.* ▶ **taki**

> **Such** występuje przed rzeczownikiem lub przed rzeczownikiem poprzedzonym przymiotnikiem: *Simon is such a bore!* ◇ *Susan is such a boring woman.* **So** występuje przed przymiotnikiem (bez rzeczownika): *Don't be so boring.* Por. następujące zdania: *It was so cold we stayed at home.* ◇ *It was such a cold night that we stayed at home.*

■ **such** pron.: *The economic situation is such that we all have less money to spend.* ▶ **taki**

IDM **as such** as the word is usually understood; exactly: *It's not a promotion as such, but it will mean more money.* ▶ **jako taki, sam w sobie**

such as for example: *Fatty foods such as chips are bad for you.* ▶ **jak na przykład; taki jak**

suck /sʌk/ verb **1** [I,T] to pull a liquid into your mouth: *to suck milk up through a straw* ▶ **ssać, wsysać, wysysać** **2** [I,T] to have sth in your mouth and keep touching it with your tongue: *He was noisily sucking (on) a sweet.* ▶ **ssać** **3** [T] to pull sth in a particular direction, using force: *Vacuum cleaners suck up the dirt.* ▶ **wsysać, pochłaniać**

PHR V **suck up (to sb)** (informal) to try to please sb in authority by praising them too much, helping them, etc., in order to gain some advantage for yourself ▶ **podlizywać się (komuś)**

sucker /ˈsʌkə(r)/ noun [C] **1** (informal) a person who believes everything that you tell them and who is easy to trick or persuade to do sth ▶ **naiwnia-k/czka, frajer/ka** **2** a part of some plants, animals or insects that is used for helping them stick onto a surface ▶ **odrost korzeniowy, ssawka** (*np. owada*)

suction /ˈsʌkʃn/ noun [U] the act of removing air or liquid from a space or container so that sth else can be pulled into it or so that two surfaces can stick together: *A vacuum cleaner works by suction.* ◇ *The hook is attached to the wall by a suction pad* (za pomocą przyssawki). ▶ **ssanie, wsysanie; przyssanie się**

sudden /ˈsʌdn/ adj. done or happening quickly, or when you do not expect it: *a sudden decision/change* ▶ **nagły, niespodziewany**

■ **suddenly** adv.: *Suddenly, everybody started shouting.* ◇ *It all happened so suddenly.* ▶ **nagle, niespodziewanie** | **suddenness** noun [U] ▶ **raptowność, nagłość**

IDM **all of a sudden** quickly and unexpectedly: *All of a sudden the lights went out.* ▶ **nagle**

sudden death a way of deciding who wins a game where the score is equal by continuing to play until one side gains the lead ▶ (*przy remisie*) **dogrywka do pierwszego punktu**

suds /sʌdz/ noun [pl.] the bubbles that you get when you mix soap and water ▶ **mydliny**

sue /suː/ verb [I,T] **sue (sb) (for sth)** to go to a court of law and ask for money from sb because they have done sth bad to you, or said sth bad about you: *to sue somebody for libel/breach of contract/damages* ▶ **skarżyć (kogoś o coś), podawać kogoś do sądu**

suede /sweɪd/ noun [U] a type of soft leather which does not have a smooth surface and feels a little like cloth ▶ **zamsz**

suet /ˈsuːɪt/ noun [U] a type of hard animal fat that is used in cooking ▶ **łój**

suffer /ˈsʌfə(r)/ verb **1** [I,T] **suffer (from sth)**; **suffer (for sth)** to experience sth unpleasant, for example pain, sadness, difficulty, etc.: *Mary often suffers from severe headaches.* ◇ *Our troops suffered heavy losses.* ◇ *He made a rash decision and now he's suffering for it.* ▶ **cierpieć (z powodu czegoś)** **2** [I] to become worse in quality: *My work is suffering as a result of problems at home.* ▶ **ucierpieć** (*na skutek czegoś*), **pogarszać się**

■ **sufferer** noun [C]: *asthma sufferers* chorzy na astmę ▶ **osoba cierpiąca, osoba chora** (*na jakąś chorobę*) | **suffering** noun [U] ▶ **cierpienie, ból**

sufferance /ˈsʌfərəns/ noun [U]

IDM **on sufferance** if you do sth **on sufferance**, sb allows you to do it although they do not really want you to: *He's only staying here on sufferance.* ▶ **z łaski**

suffice /səˈfaɪs/ verb [I,T] (formal) [not used in the progressive tenses] to be enough for sb/sth: *Generally a brief note or a phone call will suffice.* ◇ *One example will suffice to illustrate the point.* ▶ **wystarczać**

IDM **suffice (it) to say (that)...** (used to suggest that although you could say more, what you do say will be enough to explain what you mean): *I won't go into all the details. Suffice it to say that the whole event was a complete disaster.* ▶ **wystarczy powiedzieć, że**

sufficient /səˈfɪʃnt/ adj. (formal) as much as is necessary; enough: *We have sufficient oil reserves to last for three months.* ▶ **wystarczający, dostateczny** OPP **insufficient**

■ **sufficiently** adv. ▶ **wystarczająco, dostatecznie**

suffix /ˈsʌfɪks/ noun [C] a letter or group of letters that you add at the end of a word, and that changes the meaning of the word or the way it is used: *To form the noun from the adjective 'sad', add the suffix 'ness'.* ▶ **przyrostek** ➲ look at **prefix**

suffocate /ˈsʌfəkeɪt/ verb [I,T] to die because there is no air to breathe; to kill sb in this way ▶ **dusić (się)**

■ **suffocating** adj. ▶ **duszący, dławiący** | **suffocation** /ˌsʌfəˈkeɪʃn/ noun [U] ▶ **uduszenie (się)**

suffuse /səˈfjuːz/ verb [T, often passive] **suffuse sb/sth (with sth)** (literary) (especially used about a colour, light or feeling) to spread all over or through sb/sth: *Her face was suffused with colour.* ◇ *Colour suffused her face.* ◇ *The room was suffused with a soft golden light.* ▶ **zalewać kogoś/coś (czymś), przesycać kogoś/coś (czymś)**

sugar /ˈʃʊgə(r)/ noun **1** [U] a sweet substance that you get from certain plants: *Do you **take sugar** in tea?* Czy słodzisz herbatę? ◇ *caster sugar* rodzaj drobnego cukru ◇ *icing sugar* cukier puder ▶ **cukier** **2** [C] (in a cup of tea, coffee, etc.) the amount of sugar that a small spoon can hold; a lump of sugar: *Two sugars, please.* ▶ **łyżeczka/kostka cukru**

ˈ**sugar beet** noun [U] a plant with a large round root from which sugar is made ▶ **burak cukrowy**

ˈ**sugar cane** noun [U] a tall tropical grass with thick stems from which sugar is made ▶ **trzcina cukrowa**

sugary /ˈʃʊgəri/ adj. very sweet ▶ **przesłodzony, (obficie) ocukrzony**

suggest /səˈdʒest/ verb [T] **1 suggest sth (to sb)**; **suggest doing sth**; **suggest that...** to mention a plan or an idea that you have for sb to discuss or consider: *Can anybody suggest ways of raising more money?* ◇ *Kate suggested going out for a walk.* ◇ *Kate suggested (that) we go out for a walk.* ◇ *Kate suggested a walk.* ◇ *How do you suggest* (jak, twoim zdaniem) *we get out of this mess?* ▶ **proponować, sugerować** **2 suggest sb/sth (for/as sth)** to say that a person, thing or place is suitable: *Who would you suggest for the job?* ▶ **proponować** SYN **recommend**

> Uwaga! Jedyna poprawna konstrukcja z tym czasownikiem to **suggest something to somebody.** Nie można powiedzieć ~~*suggest somebody something*~~.

3 to say or show sth in an indirect way: *Are you suggesting the accident was my fault?* ▶ **sugerować**

suggestion /səˈdʒestʃən/ noun **1** [C] a plan or idea that sb mentions for sb else to discuss and consider: *May I **make a suggestion**?* ◇ *Has anyone got any suggestions for how to solve this problem?* ▶ **propozycja** **2** [sing.] a slight amount or sign of sth: *He spoke with **a suggestion of** a Scottish accent.* ▶ **naleciałość, odrobina** SYN **hint** **3** [U] putting an idea into sb's mind; giving advice about what to do: *I came **at** Tim's **suggestion**.* ▶ **porada, sugestia**

suggestive /səˈdʒestɪv/ adj. **1 suggestive (of sth)** making you think of sth; being a sign of sth: *Your symptoms are more suggestive of an allergy than a virus.* ▶ **przypominający** **2** making you think about sex: *a suggestive dance/remark/posture* ▶ **dwuznaczny**

S

■ **suggestively** adv. ▶ **dwuznacznie**

suicidal /ˌsuːɪˈsaɪdl/ adj. **1** people who are **suicidal** want to kill themselves: *to be/feel suicidal* ▶ **samobójczy** **2** likely to have a very bad result; extremely dangerous ▶ **samobójczy**

suicide /ˈsuːɪsaɪd/ noun [U,C] the act of killing yourself deliberately: *Ben has tried to* ***commit suicide*** *several times.* ◇ *There have been three suicides by university students this year.* W tym roku trzech studentów popełniło samobójstwo. ◇ *a suicide note* list pożegalny (samobójcy) ▶ **samobójstwo**

suit[1] /suːt/ noun [C] **1** a formal set of clothes that are made of the same cloth, consisting of a jacket and either trousers or a skirt: *He always wears a suit and tie to work.* ▶ **garnitur** (*męski*), **kostium** (*damski*) ➲ picture on **page A1** **2** a piece of clothing or set of clothes that you wear for a particular activity: *a swimsuit* kostium kąpielowy ◇ *a spacesuit* kombinezon kosmonauty ◇ *a tracksuit* dres ◇ *a suit of armour* zbroja ▶ **kombinezon** **3** one of the 4 sets of 13 playing cards that form a pack: *The four suits are hearts, clubs, diamonds and spades.* ▶ **kolor** (*w kartach*) ➲ note at **card**
IDM **follow suit** → FOLLOW

suit[2] /suːt/ verb [T] [not used in the continuous tenses] **1** to be convenient or useful for sb/sth: *Would Thursday at 9.30 suit you?* ◇ *He will help around the house, but only when it suits him.* ▶ **odpowiadać**, **być dogodnym** ➲ note at **match**[2] **2** (used about clothes, colours, etc.) to make you look attractive: *That dress really suits you.* ▶ **pasować**, **być do twarzy**

suitable /ˈsuːtəbl/ adj. **suitable (for sb/sth)**; **suitable (to do sth)** right or appropriate for sb/sth: *The film isn't suitable for children.* ◇ *I've got nothing suitable to wear for a wedding.* ▶ **odpowiedni**, **stosowny** OPP **unsuitable**
■ **suitability** /ˌsuːtəˈbɪləti/ noun [U] ▶ **stosowność**, **właściwość** | **suitably** /-əbli/ adv. ▶ **stosownie**, **właściwie**

suitcase /ˈsuːtkeɪs/ (also **case**) noun [C] a box with a handle that you use for carrying your clothes, etc. in when you are travelling ▶ **waliz(k)a** ➲ picture at **bag**

suite /swiːt/ noun [C] **1** a set of rooms, especially in a hotel: *the honeymoon/penthouse suite* ◇ *a suite of rooms/offices* ▶ **apartament** ➲ look at **en suite** **2** a set of two or more pieces of furniture of the same style or covered in the same material: *a three-piece suite* kanapa i dwa fotele ▶ **zestaw wypoczynkowy**

suited /ˈsuːtɪd/ adj. **suited (for/to sb/sth)** appropriate or right for sb/sth ▶ **dobrany**, **odpowiedni**

suitor /ˈsuːtə(r)/ noun [C] (old-fashioned) a man who wants to marry a particular woman ▶ **konkurent**

sulk /sʌlk/ verb [I] to refuse to speak or smile because you want people to know that you are angry about sth ▶ **dąsać się**
■ **sulky** adj. ▶ **nadąsany** | **sulkily** /-ɪli/ adv. ▶ **z naburmuszoną miną**

sullen /ˈsʌlən/ adj. looking bad-tempered and not wanting to speak to people: *a sullen face/expression/glare* ▶ **posępny**
■ **sullenly** adv. ▶ **posępnie**

sulphur (US **sulfur**) /ˈsʌlfə(r)/ noun [U] (symbol **S**) a natural yellow substance with a strong unpleasant smell ▶ **siarka**

sultan (also **Sultan**) /ˈsʌltən/ noun [C] the ruler in some Muslim countries ▶ **sułtan**

sultana /sʌlˈtɑːnə; US -ˈtænə/ noun [C] a dried **grape** with no seeds in it that is used in cooking ▶ **rodzynka sułtańska** ➲ look at **raisin**

sultry /ˈsʌltri/ adj. (**sultrier**; **sultriest**) **1** (used about the weather) hot and uncomfortable ▶ **parny** **2** (used about a woman) behaving in a way that makes her sexually attractive ▶ **ponętna**

sum[1] /sʌm/ noun [C] **1** an amount of money: *The industry has spent huge* ***sums of money*** *modernizing its equipment.* ▶ **suma** **2** [usually sing.] **the sum (of sth)** the amount that you get when you add two or more numbers together: *The sum of two and five is seven.* ◇ *A photo, a few letters and a gold ring – that was* ***the sum total*** (to wszystko) *of what was left of his married life.* ▶ **suma** **4** a simple problem that involves calculating numbers: *to* ***do sums*** *in your head* policzyć w pamięci ▶ **zadanie arytmetyczne**

sum[2] /sʌm/ verb (**summing**; **summed**)
PHR V **sum (sth) up** to describe in a few words the main ideas of what sb has said or written: ***To sum up****, there are three options here ...* ▶ **reasumować**
sum sb/sth up to form an opinion about sb/sth: *He summed the situation up immediately.* ▶ **oceniać**

summary[1] /ˈsʌməri/ noun [C] (pl. **summaries**) a short description of the main ideas or points of sth but without any details: *A brief summary of the experiment is given at the beginning of the report.* ▶ **streszczenie**, **skrót** SYN **precis**
■ **summarize** (also **-ise**) /ˈsʌməraɪz/ verb [T]: *Could you summarize the story so far?* ▶ **streszczać**

summary[2] /ˈsʌməri/ adj. [only before a noun] (formal) done quickly and without taking time to consider if it is the right thing to do or following the right process: *a summary judgment* ▶ **doraźny**

summer /ˈsʌmə(r)/ noun [C,U] one of the four seasons of the year, after spring and before autumn. Summer is the warmest season of the year: *Is it very hot here* ***in summer****?* ◇ *a summer's day* ▶ **lato** ➲ picture on **page A16**
■ **summery** /ˈsʌməri/ adj.: *summery weather* ◇ *a summery dress* ▶ **letni**

ˈsummer time (US ˌ**daylight ˈsaving time**) noun [U] the period between March and October during which in some countries the clocks are put forward one hour, so that it is light for an extra hour in the evening ▶ **czas letni**

summertime /ˈsʌmətaɪm/ noun [U] the season of summer: *It's busy here in the summertime.* ▶ **sezon letni**

ˌsumming-ˈup noun [C] (pl. **summings-up**) a speech in which a judge gives a **summary** of what has been said in a court of law before a **verdict** is reached ▶ **podsumowanie**

summit /ˈsʌmɪt/ noun [C] **1** the top of a mountain ▶ **szczyt** **2** an important meeting or series of meetings between the leaders of two or more countries ▶ **szczyt**

summon /ˈsʌmən/ verb [T] **1** (formal) to order a person to come to a place: *The boys were summoned to the head teacher's office.* ▶ **wzywać** **2** **summon sth (up)** to find strength, courage or some other quality that you need even though it is difficult to do so: *She couldn't summon up the courage to leave him.* ▶ **zbierać** (*np. siły*)

summons /ˈsʌmənz/ noun [C] an order to appear in a court of law ▶ **wezwanie**

sumptuous /ˈsʌmptʃuəs/ adj. (formal) very expensive and looking very impressive: *We dined in sumptuous surroundings.* ▶ **wystawny**, **okazały**
■ **sumptuously** adv. ▶ **wystawnie**, **okazale**

Sun. = SUNDAY: *Sun. 5 April*

sun[1] /sʌn/ noun **1** (**the sun**) [sing.] the star that shines in the sky during the day and that gives the earth heat and light: *The sun rises in the east and sets in the west.* ◇ *the rays of the sun* ▶ **słońce** ➲ note at **space** **2** [sing., U] light and heat from the sun: *Don't sit* ***in the sun*** *too long.* ◇ *Too much sun can be harmful.* ▶ **słońce**, **promienie słoneczne**

IDM **catch the sun** → CATCH[1]

sun² /sʌn/ verb [T] (**sunning**; **sunned**) **sun yourself** to sit or lie outside when the sun is shining in order to enjoy the heat ▶ **opalać się**

sunbathe /ˈsʌnbeɪð/ verb [I] to take off most of your clothes and sit or lie in the sun in order to get a **tan** ▶ **opalać się** ➲ look at **bathe**

sunbeam /ˈsʌnbiːm/ noun [C] a line of light from the sun ▶ **promień słońca**

sunblock /ˈsʌnblɒk/ noun [U,C] a cream that you put on your skin to protect it completely from the harmful effects of the sun ▶ **krem z filtrem przeciwsłonecznym o najwyższym czynniku ochrony**

sunburn /ˈsʌnbɜːn/ noun [U] red painful skin caused by spending too long in the sun ▶ **oparzenie słoneczne**
■ **sunburned** (also **sunburnt** /ˈsʌnbɜːnt/) adj. ▶ **poparzony** (*po intensywnym opalaniu*)

suncream /ˈsʌnkriːm/ noun [U,C] cream that you put on your skin to protect it from the harmful effects of the sun ▶ **krem z filtrem przeciwsłonecznym**

sundae /ˈsʌndeɪ; -di/ noun [C] a type of food that consists of ice cream with fruit, nuts, etc. on the top ▶ **lody z owocami, orzechami itp.**

Sunday /ˈsʌndeɪ; -di/ noun [C,U] (abbr. **Sun.**) the day of the week after Saturday ▶ **niedziela** ➲ note at **Monday**

ˈ**Sunday school** noun [C, U] a class that is organized by a church or **synagogue** where children can go for a short time on Sundays to learn about the Christian or Jewish religion ▶ **szkółka niedzielna**

sundial /ˈsʌndaɪəl/ noun [C] a type of clock used in past times that uses the sun and a pointed piece of metal to show what the time is ▶ **zegar słoneczny**

sundry /ˈsʌndri/ adj. [only before a noun] of various kinds that are not important enough to be named separately ▶ **rozmaity**
IDM **all and sundry** (informal) everyone ▶ **wszyscy (bez wyjątku)**

sunflower /ˈsʌnflaʊə(r)/ noun [C] a very tall plant with large yellow flowers, often grown for its seeds and their oil, which is used in cooking ▶ **słonecznik** ➲ picture on **page A15**

sung past participle of **sing**

sunglasses /ˈsʌŋɡlɑːsɪz; US -ɡlæs-/ (also ˌ**dark** ˈ**glasses**) (informal **shades**) noun [pl.] a pair of dark glasses which you wear to protect your eyes from bright **sunlight** ▶ **okulary przeciwsłoneczne**

sunk past participle of **sink¹**

sunken /ˈsʌŋkən/ adj. **1** [only before a noun] below the water: *a sunken ship* ▶ **zatopiony 2** (used about cheeks or eyes) very far into the face as a result of illness or age ▶ **zapadnięty 3** at a lower level than the surrounding area: *a sunken bath/garden* ▶ **wpuszczony** (*np. w podłogę*), (*ogród itp.*) **obniżony**

sunlight /ˈsʌnlaɪt/ noun [U] the light from the sun: *a ray/pool of sunlight* ▶ **światło słoneczne**

sunlit /ˈsʌnlɪt/ adj. having bright light from the sun: *a sunlit terrace* ▶ **nasłoneczniony**

sunny /ˈsʌni/ adj. (**sunnier**; **sunniest**) having a lot of light from the sun: *a sunny garden* ◇ *a sunny day* ▶ **słoneczny**

sunrise /ˈsʌnraɪz/ noun [C,U] the time when the sun comes up in the morning: *to get up **at sunrise*** ▶ **wschód słońca** ➲ look at **dawn**, **sunset**

sunscreen /ˈsʌnskriːn/ noun [C, U] a cream or liquid that you put on your skin to protect it from the harmful effects of the sun: *a high factor sunscreen* ▶ **krem/mleczko z filtrem przeciwsłonecznym**

sunset /ˈsʌnset/ noun [C,U] the time when the sun goes down in the evening: *The park closes **at sunset.*** ◇ *a beautiful sunset* ▶ **zachód słońca** ➲ picture on **page A16**

sunshine /ˈsʌnʃaɪn/ noun [U] heat and light from the sun: *We sat down **in the sunshine** and had lunch.* ▶ **światło słoneczne**, **słońce**

sunstroke /ˈsʌnstrəʊk/ noun [U] an illness that is caused by spending too much time in very hot, strong sun: *Keep your head covered or you'll **get sunstroke.*** ▶ **porażenie słoneczne**

suntan /ˈsʌntæn/ (also **tan**) noun [C] when you have a **suntan**, your skin is darker than usual because you have spent time in the sun: *to have/get a suntan* ◇ *suntan oil* olejek do opalania ▶ **opalenizna**
■ **suntanned** (also **tanned**) adj. ▶ **opalony**

super /ˈsuːpə(r)/ adj. **1** (old-fashioned) very good; wonderful: *We had a super time.* ▶ **wspaniały 2** [in compounds] bigger, better, stronger, etc. than other things of the same type: *super-rich* ◇ *superglue* ▶ **wspaniały**
■ **super** adv. (informal) especially; particularly: *She's super fit.* ▶ **wspaniale**, **super**

superb /suːˈpɜːb; Brit. also sjuː-/ adj. extremely good, excellent ▶ **znakomity**
■ **superbly** adv. ▶ **znakomicie**

supercilious /ˌsuːpəˈsɪliəs; Brit. also ˌsjuː-/ adj. showing that you think that you are better than other people: *She gave a supercilious smile.* ▶ **wyniosły**
■ **superciliously** adv. ▶ **wyniośle**

superficial /ˌsuːpəˈfɪʃl; Brit. also ˌsjuː-/ adj. **1** not studying or thinking about sth in a deep or complete way: *a superficial knowledge of the subject* ▶ **powierzchowny 2** only on the surface, not deep: *a superficial wound/cut/burn* ▶ **powierzchowny 3** (used about people) not caring about serious or important things: *He's a very superficial sort of person.* ▶ **powierzchowny**
■ **superficiality** /ˌsuːpəˌfɪʃiˈæləti; Brit. also ˌsjuː-/ noun [U] ▶ **powierzchowność** (*np. zainteresowań*) | **superficially** /-ʃəli/ adv. ▶ **powierzchownie**

superfluous /suːˈpɜːfluəs; Brit. also sjuː-/ adj. more than is wanted; not needed ▶ **zbyteczny**

superhuman /ˌsuːpəˈhjuːmən; Brit. also ˌsjuː-/ adj. much greater than is normal: *superhuman strength* ▶ **nadludzki**

superimpose /ˌsuːpərɪmˈpəʊz/ verb [T] **superimpose sth (on sth)** to put sth on top of sth else so that what is underneath can still be seen: *The old street plan was superimposed on a map of the modern city.* ▶ **nakładać** (*jedno na drugie*)

superintendent /ˌsuːpərɪnˈtendənt/ noun [C] **1** a police officer with a high position: *Detective Superintendent Waters* ▶ **nadinspektor 2** a person who looks after a large building ▶ **dozor-ca/czyni**

superior¹ /suːˈpɪəriə(r); Brit. also sjuː-/ adj. **1 superior (to sb/sth)** better than usual or than sb/sth else: *He is clearly superior to all the other candidates.* ▶ (*o wiele*) **lepszy** OPP **inferior 2 superior (to sb)** having a more important position: *a superior officer* ▶ **wyższy** (*rangą*) **3** thinking that you are better than other people: *There's no need to be so superior.* ▶ **wyniosły**
■ **superiority** /suːˌpɪəriˈɒrəti; Brit. also sjuː-/ noun [U] ▶ **wyższość**

superior² /suːˈpɪəriə(r)/ noun [C] a person of higher position: *Report any accidents to your superior.* ▶ **przełożon-y/a** OPP **inferior**

superlative /suˈpɜːlətɪv; Brit. also sjuː-/ noun [C] the form of an adjective or adverb that expresses its highest degree: *'Most beautiful', 'best' and 'fastest' are all super-*

latives. ▶ **stopień najwyższy przymiotnika i przysłówka**

supermarket /ˈsuːpəmɑːkɪt; ˈsjuː-; US -kət/ noun [C] a very large shop that sells food, drink, goods used in the home, etc. ▶ **supersam**

At a supermarket, you put your **shopping** in a **basket** or a **trolley** (US **cart**). Then you **queue** at the **checkout**, where you **pack** everything into **carrier bags**.

supermodel /ˈsuːpəmɒdl/ noun [C] a very famous and highly paid fashion model ▶ **supermodel/ka**

supernatural /ˌsuːpəˈnætʃrəl; Brit. also ˌsjuː-/ adj. that cannot be explained by the laws of science: *a creature with supernatural powers* ▶ **nadprzyrodzony**
■ **the supernatural** noun [sing.] events, forces or powers that cannot be explained by the laws of science: *I don't believe in the supernatural.* ▶ **zjawiska/siły nadprzyrodzone**

superpower /ˈsuːpəpaʊə(r); Brit. also ˈsjuː-/ noun [C] one of the countries in the world that has very great military or economic power, for example the US ▶ **supermocarstwo** ➲ look at **power**[1] (5)

supersede /ˌsuːpəˈsiːd; Brit. also ˌsjuː-/ verb [T] to take the place of sb/sth which existed or was used before and which has become old-fashioned: *The old software has been superseded by a new package.* ▶ **wypierać**

supersonic /ˌsuːpəˈsɒnɪk; Brit. also ˌsjuː-/ adj. faster than the speed of sound ▶ **(po)naddźwiękowy**

superstar /ˈsuːpəstɑː(r); Brit. also ˈsjuː-/ noun [C] a singer, film star, etc. who is very famous and popular ▶ **wielka gwiazda**

superstition /ˌsuːpəˈstɪʃn; Brit. also ˌsjuː-/ noun [C,U] a belief that cannot be explained by reason or science: *According to superstition, it's unlucky to walk under a ladder.* ▶ **przesąd**
■ **superstitious** /ˌsuːpəˈstɪʃəs; Brit. also ˌsjuː-/ adj.: *I never do anything important on Friday 13th – I'm superstitious.* ▶ **przesądny**

superstore /ˈsuːpəstɔː(r); Brit. also ˈsjuː-/ noun [C] a very large shop that sells food or a wide variety of one particular type of goods ▶ **wielki dom handlowy** (*sprzedający artykuły jednej branży*)

supervise /ˈsuːpəvaɪz; Brit. also ˈsjuː-/ verb [I,T] to watch sb/sth to make sure that work is being done properly or that people are behaving correctly: *Your job is to supervise the building work.* ▶ **nadzorować**
■ **supervision** /ˌsuːpəˈvɪʒn; Brit. also ˌsjuː-/ noun [U]: *Children should not play here without supervision* (bez opieki). ▶ **nadzór** | **supervisor** /ˈsuːpəvaɪzə(r)/ noun [C] ▶ **nadzorca, kierowni-k/czka**

supper /ˈsʌpə(r)/ noun [C,U] the last meal of the day, either the main meal of the evening or a small meal that you eat quite late, not long before you go to bed ▶ **kolacja** ➲ note at **meal**, **dinner**

supple /ˈsʌpl/ adj. that bends or moves easily; not stiff: *Children are generally far more supple than adults.* ▶ **giętki, elastyczny**
■ **suppleness** noun [U] ▶ **giętkość, elastyczność**

supplement /ˈsʌplɪmənt/ noun [C] something that is added to sth else: *You have to pay a small supplement if you travel on a Saturday.* ◇ *There is a £10 supplement* (dopłata) *for a single room.* ◇ *a Sunday newspaper with a colour supplement* (z ilustrowanym magazynem) ▶ **dodatek**
■ **supplement** /ˈsʌplɪment/ verb [T] **supplement sth (with sth)**: *to supplement your diet with vitamins* ▶ **uzupełniać** | **supplementary** /ˌsʌplɪˈmentri/ adj.: *supplementary exercises at the back of the book* ▶ **dodatkowy**

supplier /səˈplaɪə(r)/ noun [C] a person or company that supplies goods ▶ **dostawca**

supply[1] /səˈplaɪ/ noun [C,U] (pl. **supplies**) a store or amount of sth that is provided or available to be used: *The water supply was contaminated.* ◇ *Food supplies were dropped by helicopter.* ◇ *In many parts of the country water is* ***in short supply*** (brakuje wody). ◇ ***supply and demand*** podaż i popyt ▶ **zasób, dostawa**

supply[2] /səˈplaɪ/ verb [T] (**supplying**; **supplies**; pt, pp **supplied**) **supply sth (to sb)**; **supply sb (with sth)** to give or provide sth: *The farmer supplies eggs to the surrounding villages.* ◇ *He supplies the surrounding villages with eggs.* ▶ **zaopatrywać**

support[1] /səˈpɔːt/ verb [T] **1** to help sb/sth by saying that you agree with them or it, and sometimes giving practical help such as money: *Several large companies are supporting the project.* ◇ *Which political party do you support?* ▶ **popierać 2** to give sb the money they need for food, clothes, etc.: *Jim has to support two children from his previous marriage.* ▶ **utrzymywać** (*np. rodzinę*) **3** to carry the weight of sb/sth: *Large columns support the roof.* ▶ **podtrzymywać 4** to show that sth is true or correct: *What evidence do you have to support what you say* (na potwierdzenie tego, co mówisz)*?* ▶ **popierać, potwierdzać 5** to have a particular sports team that you like more than any other: *Which football team do you support?* ▶ **kibicować**

support[2] /səˈpɔːt/ noun **1** [U] **support (for sb/sth)** help and confidence that you give in order to encourage a person or thing: *public support for the campaign* ◇ *Steve spoke* ***in support of*** (przemawiał za) *the proposal.* ▶ **poparcie, wsparcie 2** [U] money to buy food, clothes, etc.: *She has no home and no means of support.* ▶ **utrzymanie 3** [C,U] something that carries the weight of sb/sth or holds sth firmly in place: *a roof support* ◇ *She held on to his arm for support.* ▶ **podpora**
IDM **moral support** → MORAL[1]

supporter /səˈpɔːtə(r)/ noun [C] a person who supports a political party, sports team, etc.: *football supporters* ▶ **kibic, stronni-k/czka**

supportive /səˈpɔːtɪv/ adj. giving help or support to sb in a difficult situation: *Everyone was very supportive* (wszyscy mnie wspierali) *when I lost my job.* ▶ **pomocny, wspierający**

suppose /səˈpəʊz/ verb [T] **1** to think that sth is probable: *I don't suppose that they're coming now.* ◇ *What do you suppose* (co, twoim zdaniem) *could have happened?* ▶ **przypuszczać, sądzić 2** to pretend that sth will happen or is true: *Suppose you won the lottery. What would you do?* ▶ **gdyby; przypuśćmy, że 3** (used to make a suggestion, request or statement less strong): *I don't suppose you'd lend me* (chyba nie pożyczysz mi) *your car tonight, would you?* ◇ *What I'm saying, I suppose, is* (to, co staram się chyba powiedzieć, to to, że) *your work is not good enough.* **4** (used when you agree with sth, but are not very happy about it): *'Can we give Andy a lift?' 'Yes,* ***I suppose so****, if we must.'* ▶ **chyba tak**
IDM **be supposed to do sth 1** to be expected to do sth or to have to do sth: *The train was supposed to arrive ten minutes ago.* ◇ *This is secret and I'm not supposed to talk about it.* ▶ **mieć/musieć coś zrobić 2** (informal) to be considered or thought to be sth: *This is supposed to be* (to podobno jest) *the oldest building in the city.* ◇ *I haven't seen it, but it's supposed to be* (to ma być) *a good play.* ▶ **przypuszcza się, że**
I suppose (used to show that you are not certain about sth): *I suppose it's all right, but I'm not sure.* ◇ *It's about ten years old, I suppose.* ▶ **chyba, o ile się nie mylę**

supposedly /səˈpəʊzɪdli/ adv. according to what many people believe ▶ **podobno**

supposing /sə'pəʊzɪŋ/ conj. if sth happens or is true; what if: *Supposing the plan goes wrong, what will we do then?* ▶ **a jeśli**

supposition /ˌsʌpə'zɪʃn/ noun [C,U] an idea that a person thinks is true but which has not been shown to be true ▶ **domniemanie**

suppress /sə'pres/ verb [T] **1** to stop sth by using force ▶ **tłumić 2** to stop sth from being seen or known: *to suppress the truth* ▶ **taić 3** to stop yourself from expressing your feelings, etc.: *to suppress laughter/a yawn* ▶ **tłumić**

■ **suppression** /sə'preʃn/ noun [U] ▶ **(s)tłumienie; zatajenie; powstrzymywanie**

supremacy /su:'preməsi/ noun [U] **supremacy (over sb/sth)** the state of being the most powerful ▶ **przewaga**

supreme /su:'pri:m/ adj. the highest or greatest possible ▶ **najwyższy, olbrzymi**

supremely /su:'pri:mli/ adv. extremely ▶ **niezwykle**

surcharge /'sɜ:tʃɑ:dʒ/ noun [C] an extra amount of money that you have to pay for sth ▶ **dopłata**

⚷ **sure**[1] /ʃʊə(r); Brit. also ʃɔ:(r)/ adj. **1** [not before a noun] having no doubt about sth; certain: *You must be sure of your facts before you make an accusation.* ◇ *I'm not sure what to do next.* ◇ *Craig was sure that he'd made the right decision.* ◇ *I think I had my bag when I got off the bus but I'm not sure.* ▶ **pewny** OPP **unsure**

> **Sure** i **certain** mają bardzo podobne znaczenie. Jednak w wyrażeniu **It is certain that...** nie można stosować ich wymiennie: *It is certain that* (na pewno) *there will be an election next year.* Chcąc użyć **sure** należy powiedzieć: ***There is sure to be** an election next year.*

2 [not before a noun] **sure of sth; sure to do sth** that you will definitely get or do, or that will definitely happen: *If you go and see them you can be sure of* (możesz liczyć na) *a warm welcome.* ◇ *If you work hard you are sure to pass* (na pewno zdasz) *the exam.* ▶ **niezawodnie mający coś zrobić/osiągnąć itp.; pewny 3** that you can be certain of: *A noise like that is a sure sign of engine trouble.* ▶ **pewny**

IDM **be sure to do sth** (used for telling sb to do sth) do not forget to do sth: *Be sure to write and tell me what happens.* ▶ **koniecznie coś zrobić**

for sure without doubt: *Nobody knows for sure what happened.* ▶ **z (całą) pewnością, na pewno**

make sure 1 to take the action that is necessary: *Make sure you are back home by 11 o'clock.* Koniecznie wróć przed jedenastą. ▶ **upewniać się 2** to check that sth is in a particular state or has been done: *I must go back and make sure I closed the window.* ▶ **sprawdzać, czy**

sure thing (US, informal) yes: *'Can I borrow this book?' 'Sure thing.'* ▶ **pewnie!**

sure of yourself confident about your opinions, or about what you can do ▶ **pewny siebie**

sure[2] /ʃʊə(r) (Brit. also) ʃɔ:(r); US / adv. (informal) (especially US) yes: *'Can I have a look at your newspaper?' 'Sure.'* ▶ **pewnie!**

IDM **sure enough** as was expected: *I expected him to be early, and sure enough he arrived five minutes before the others.* ▶ **rzeczywiście**

⚷ **surely** /'ʃʊəli; Brit. also 'ʃɔ:li/ adv. **1** without doubt: *This will surely cause problems.* ▶ **z (całą) pewnością 2** (used for expressing surprise at sb else's opinions, plans, actions, etc.): *'Meena's looking for another job.' 'Surely not* (chyba żartujesz).*'* ◇ *Surely you're not going to* (chyba nie zamierzasz) *walk home in this rain?* ▶ **chyba 3** (US, informal) yes; of course ▶ **tak, oczywiście, pewnie że tak**

surf[1] /sɜ:f/ noun [U] the white part on the top of waves in the sea ▶ **czoło fali morskiej**

surf[2] /sɜ:f/ verb [I] to stand or lie on a **surfboard** and ride on a wave towards the beach ▶ **pływać na desce surfingowej** ➲ picture on **page A8**

IDM **surf the net** to use the Internet ▶ **surfować po internecie**

⚷ **surface**[1] /'sɜ:fɪs/ noun **1** (**the surface**) [sing.] the top part of an area of water: *The submarine slowly rose to the surface* (powoli wypływała na powierzchnię). ◇ *leaves floating on the surface of a pond* ▶ **powierzchnia 2** [C] the outside part of sth: *the earth's surface* ◇ *Teeth have a hard surface called enamel.* ◇ *This tennis court has a very uneven surface.* ▶ **zewnętrzna warstwa, powierzchnia, nawierzchnia 3** [C] the flat top part of a piece of furniture, used for working on: *a work surface* ◇ *kitchen surfaces* ▶ **blat 4** [sing.] the qualities of sb/sth that you see or notice, that are not hidden: *Everybody seems very friendly but there are a lot of tensions **below/beneath the surface*** (istnieje wiele skrywanych napięć). ▶ **powierzchowność, wygląd zewnętrzny**

surface[2] /'sɜ:fɪs/ verb **1** [I] to come up to the surface of water ▶ **wynurzać się 2** [I] to appear again: *All the old arguments surfaced again in the discussion.* ▶ **wyłaniać się 3** [T] to cover the surface of sth: *to surface a road with tarmac* asfaltować drogę ▶ **pokrywać** (*nawierzchnię*)

'**surface mail** noun [U] letters, packages, etc. that go by road, rail or sea, not by air ▶ **poczta lądowo-morska** ➲ look at **airmail**

surfboard /'sɜ:fbɔ:d/ noun [C] a long narrow board used for **surfing** ▶ **deska surfingowa** ➲ picture on **page A8**

surfeit /'sɜ:fɪt/ noun [sing.] (formal) **a surfeit (of sth)** too much of sth ▶ **nadmiar**

surfer /'sɜ:fə(r)/ noun [C] **1** a person who rides on waves standing on a special board ▶ **osoba pływająca na desce** ➲ picture on **page A8 2** (also **'Net surfer**) (informal) a person who spends a lot of time using the Internet ▶ **surfer po internecie**

surfing /'sɜ:fɪŋ/ noun [U] **1** the sport of riding on waves while standing or lying on a **surfboard**: *to go surfing* iść surfować ▶ **surfing 2** the activity of looking at different things on the Internet, or of looking quickly at different TV programmes, in order to find sth interesting ▶ **szybkie surfowanie po stronach internetowych; przeskakiwanie po kanałach telewizji**

surge /sɜ:dʒ/ noun [C, usually sing.] **a surge (of/in sth) 1** a sudden strong movement in a particular direction by a large number of people or things: *a surge of interest* ◇ *a surge* (nagły wzrost) *in the demand for electricity* ▶ **nagłe poruszenie się; nagły skok 2** a sudden strong feeling ▶ **nagły przypływ**

■ **surge** verb [I]: *The crowd surged forward* (ruszył naprzód). ▶ **wzbierać**

surgeon /'sɜ:dʒən/ noun [C] a doctor who performs medical operations: *a brain surgeon* neurochirurg ▶ **chirurg**

surgery /'sɜ:dʒəri/ noun (pl. **surgeries**) **1** [U] medical treatment in which your body is cut open so that part of it can be removed or repaired: *to undergo emergency surgery* ▶ **operacja, zabieg chirurgiczny** ➲ look at **plastic surgery, operation 2** [C,U] the place or time when a doctor or dentist sees patients: *Surgery hours are from 9.00 to 11.30.* ▶ **gabinet (lekarski); godziny przyjęć** ➲ note at **doctor**

surgical /'sɜ:dʒɪkl/ adj. [only before a noun] connected with medical operations: *surgical instruments* ▶ **chirurgiczny**

■ **surgically** /-kli/ adv. ▶ **chirurgicznie**

surly /'sɜ:li/ adj. (**surlier; surliest**) unfriendly and rude: *a surly expression* ▶ **gburowaty, opryskliwy**

surmount /sə'maʊnt/ verb [T] to deal successfully with a problem or difficulty ▶ **pokonywać** ➲ look at **insurmountable**

🔑**surname** /'sɜːneɪm/ (also **'last name**; **'second name**) noun [C] the name that you share with other people in your family: *'What's your surname?' 'Jones.'* ▶ **nazwisko** ➲ note at **name**

surpass /sə'pɑːs; US -'pæs/ verb [T] (formal) to do sth better than sb/sth else or better than expected: *The success of the film surpassed all expectations.* ▶ **przewyższać**

surplus /'sɜːpləs/ noun [C,U] an amount that is extra or more than you need: *the food surplus in Western Europe* ▶ **nadwyżka**
■ **surplus** adj.: *They sell their surplus grain to other countries.* ▶ **nadmierny**, **zbyteczny**

🔑**surprise**[1] /sə'praɪz/ noun **1** [C] something that you did not expect or know about: *What a pleasant surprise to see you again!* ◇ *The news came as a complete surprise.* ◇ *a surprise visit/attack/party* ▶ **niespodzianka 2** [U] the feeling that you have when sth happens that you do not expect: *They looked up* ***in surprise*** *when she walked in.* ◇ ***To my surprise*** *they all agreed with me.* ▶ **zdziwienie**
IDM **take sb by surprise** to happen or do sth when sb is not expecting it ▶ **zaskakiwać**

🔑**surprise**[2] /sə'praɪz/ verb [T] **1** to make sb feel surprised: *It wouldn't surprise me if you got the job.* ▶ **dziwić**, **zaskakiwać 2** to attack or find sb suddenly and unexpectedly ▶ **zaskakiwać**

🔑**surprised** /sə'praɪzd/ adj. feeling or showing surprise: *I was very surprised to see Cara there. I thought she was still abroad.* ▶ **zdziwiony**, **zaskoczony**

🔑**surprising** /sə'praɪzɪŋ/ adj. that causes surprise: *It's surprising how many adults can't read or write.* ▶ **zadziwiający**, **zaskakujący**
■ **surprisingly** adv.: *Surprisingly few people got the correct answer.* ▶ **zadziwiająco**, **zaskakująco**

surreal /sə'riːəl/ (also **surrealistic** /səˌriːə'lɪstɪk/) adj. very strange; with images mixed together in a strange way like in a dream: *a surreal film/painting/situation* ▶ **surrealistyczny**

surrender /sə'rendə(r)/ verb **1** [I,T] **surrender (yourself) (to sb)** to stop fighting and admit that you have lost ▶ **poddawać się** SYN **yield 2** [T] (formal) **surrender sb/sth (to sb)** to give sb/sth to sb else: *The police ordered them to surrender their weapons* (oddać broń). ▶ **zrzekać się (czegoś)**
■ **surrender** noun [C,U] ▶ **poddawanie się**, **oddawanie (się)**

surreptitious /ˌsʌrəp'tɪʃəs; US ˌsɜːr-/ adj. done secretly: *I had a surreptitious look at what she was writing.* ▶ **ukradkowy**
■ **surreptitiously** adv. ▶ **ukradkiem**

surrogate /'sʌrəgət; US 'sɜːr-/ noun [C], adj. (a person or thing) that takes the place of sb/sth else: *a surrogate mother* matka zastępcza ▶ **zastępca**; **namiastka**

🔑**surround** /sə'raʊnd/ verb [T] **surround sb/sth (by/with sth)** to be or go all around sb/sth: *The garden is surrounded by a high wall.* ◇ *Troops have surrounded the parliament building.* ▶ **otaczać**, **okrążać**

🔑**surrounding** /sə'raʊndɪŋ/ adj. [only before a noun] that is near or around sth ▶ **okoliczny**, **otaczający**

🔑**surroundings** /sə'raʊndɪŋz/ noun [pl.] everything that is near or around you; the place where you live: *to live in pleasant surroundings* ◇ *animals living in their natural surroundings* ▶ **otoczenie**, **środowisko** ➲ look at **environment**

surveillance /sɜː'veɪləns/ noun [U] the careful watching of sb who may have done sth wrong: *The building is protected by surveillance cameras.* ▶ **nadzór**

🔑**survey**[1] /'sɜːveɪ/ noun [C] **1** a study of the opinions, behaviour, etc. of a group of people: *Surveys have shown that more and more people are getting into debt.* ◇ *to carry out/conduct/do a survey* ▶ **badanie 2** the act of examining an area of land and making a map of it: *a geological survey* ▶ **pomiary terenu i sporządzenie mapy 3** the act of examining a building in order to find out if it is in good condition ▶ **ekspertyza**

🔑**survey**[2] /sə'veɪ/ verb [T] **1** to look carefully at the whole of sth: *We stood at the top of the hill and surveyed the countryside.* ▶ **obserwować**; **analizować 2** to carefully measure and make a map of an area of land ▶ **dokonywać pomiarów terenu i sporządzać mapę 3** to examine a building carefully in order to find out if it is in good condition ▶ **przeprowadzać ekspertyzę**

surveyor /sə'veɪə(r)/ noun [C] **1** a person whose job is to examine and record the details of a piece of land ▶ **geodet(k)a**, **mierniczy 2** (US **inspector**) a person whose job is to examine a building to make sure it is in good condition, usually done for sb who wants to buy it ▶ **rzeczoznawca budowlany**

survival /sə'vaɪvl/ noun **1** [U] the state of continuing to live or exist: *the struggle for survival* ▶ **przetrwanie**, **przeżycie 2** [C] a person or a thing that has continued to exist from an earlier time ▶ **relikt**

🔑**survive** /sə'vaɪv/ verb **1** [I,T] to continue to live or exist in or after a difficult or dangerous situation: *More than a hundred people were killed in the crash and only five passengers survived.* ◇ *How can she survive on such a small salary?* ◇ *to survive a plane crash* ◇ *Not many buildings survived the bombing.* ▶ **przeżyć 2** [T] to live longer than sb/sth: *The old man survived all his children.* ▶ **przeżyć**
■ **survivor** /sə'vaɪvə(r)/ noun [C]: *There were five survivors of* (pięć osób przeżyło) *the crash.* ▶ **osoba pozostała przy życiu** (*np. po wypadku*)

sus = SUSS

susceptible /sə'septəbl/ adj. [not before a noun] **susceptible to sth** easily influenced, damaged or affected by sb/sth: *People in a new country are highly susceptible to illness.* ▶ **podatny** (*np. na wpływy*), **wrażliwy na coś**

🔑**suspect**[1] /sə'spekt/ verb [T] **1** to believe that sth may happen or be true, especially sth bad: *The situation is worse than we first suspected.* ◇ *Nobody suspected that she was thinking of leaving.* ▶ **podejrzewać** ➲ look at **unsuspecting 2** to not be sure that you can trust sb or believe sth: *I rather suspect his motives for offering to help.* ▶ **podejrzewać 3 suspect sb (of sth/of doing sth)** to believe that sb is guilty of sth: *I suspect Laura of taking the money.* ◇ *She strongly suspected that he was lying.* ▶ **podejrzewać (kogoś o coś)** ➲ noun **suspicion**

🔑**suspect**[2] /'sʌspekt/ noun [C] a person who is thought to be guilty of a crime: *The suspects are being questioned by police.* ▶ (*osoba*) **podejrzan-y/a** ➲ note at **crime**

suspect[3] /'sʌspekt/ adj. possibly not true or not to be trusted: *to have suspect motives* ◇ *a suspect parcel* ▶ **podejrzany**

suspend /sə'spend/ verb [T] **1 suspend sth (from sth) (by/on sth)** to hang sth from sth else: *The huge skeleton is suspended from the museum's ceiling on chains.* ▶ **zawieszać 2** to stop or delay sth for a time: *Some rail services were suspended during the strike.* ◇ *The young man was given a* ***suspended sentence*** (wyrok w zawieszeniu). ▶ **zawieszać**, **wstrzymywać**, **odraczać 3 suspend sb (from sth)** to send sb away from their school, job, position, etc. for a period of time, usually as a punishment: *He was suspended from school for a week for stealing.* ▶ **zawieszać** ➲ noun **suspension**

suspender /sə'spendə(r)/ noun **1** [C, usually pl.] (Brit.) a short piece of **elastic** that women use to hold up their **stockings** ▶ **podwiązka 2** (**suspenders**) [pl.] (US) = BRACE[1] (2)

su'spender belt (also 'garter belt) noun [C] a piece of women's underwear like a belt, with fastenings for holding stockings up ▶ **pas do pończoch**

suspense /sə'spens/ noun [U] the feeling of excitement or worry that you have when you feel sth is going to happen, when you are waiting for news, etc.: *Don't keep us **in suspense.** Tell us what happened.* ▶ **niepewność**, **napięcie**

suspension /sə'spenʃn/ noun **1** [C,U] not being allowed to do your job or go to school for a period of time, usually as a punishment: *suspension on full pay* ▶ **zawieszenie** (*kogoś w czynnościach służbowych*) **2** [U] delaying sth for a period of time ▶ **zawieszenie**, **wstrzymywanie**, **odraczanie** ➲ verb **suspend 3** (**the suspension**) [U] the parts that are connected to the wheels of a car, etc. that make it more comfortable to ride in ▶ **zawieszenie**

🔑 **suspicion** /sə'spɪʃn/ noun **1** [C,U] a feeling or belief that sth is wrong or that sb has done sth wrong: *I always treat smiling politicians with suspicion.* ◇ *She was arrested on suspicion of murder* (pod zarzutem morderstwa). ◇ *He is **under suspicion of*** (podejrzany o) *being involved in drug smuggling.* ▶ **podejrzliwość**, **podejrzenie 2** [C] a feeling that sth may happen or be true: *I have a suspicion that he's forgotten he invited us.* ▶ **podejrzenie** ➲ verb **suspect**

🔑 **suspicious** /sə'spɪʃəs/ adj. **1 suspicious (of/about sb/sth)** feeling that sb has done sth wrong, dishonest or illegal: *We became suspicious of his behaviour and alerted the police.* ◇ *His strange behaviour made the police suspicious* (wzbudziło podejrzenia policji). ▶ **podejrzliwy 2** that makes you feel that sth is wrong, dishonest or illegal: *The old man died **in suspicious circumstances.*** ◇ *It's very suspicious that she was not at home on the evening of the murder.* ◇ *a suspicious-looking person* ▶ **podejrzany**

■ **suspiciously** adv.: *to behave suspiciously* ◇ *The house was suspiciously quiet.* W domu było podejrzanie cicho. ▶ **podejrzanie**

suss (also sus) /sʌs/ verb [I,T] **suss (sb/sth) (out)** (Brit., informal) to realize sth; to understand the important things about sb/sth: *I think I've **got him sussed.*** ◇ *If you want to succeed in business, you have to suss out the competition.* ▶ **rozgryźć kogoś/coś**; **połapać się w czymś**

sustain /sə'steɪn/ verb [T] **1** to keep sb/sth alive or healthy: *Oxygen sustains life.* ▶ **podtrzymywać 2** to make sth continue for a long period of time without becoming less: *It's hard to sustain interest for such a long time.* ▶ **podtrzymywać 3** (formal) to experience sth bad: *to sustain damage/an injury/a defeat* ▶ **odnosić** (*np. obrażenia*), **ponosić** (*np. klęskę*), **ulegać** (*np. zniszczeniu*)

SW = SOUTH-WEST[1], SOUTH-WESTERN: *SW Australia*

swab /swɒb/ noun [C] **1** a piece of soft material used by a doctor, nurse, etc. for cleaning wounds or taking a small amount of a substance from sb's body for testing ▶ **wacik**, **gazik 2** an act of taking a small amount of a substance from sb's body, with a **swab**: *to take a throat swab* pobierać wymaz z gardła ▶ **wymaz**

■ **swab** verb [T] (**swabbing**; **swabbed**) ▶ **oczyszczać wacikiem** (*np. ranę*)

swagger /'swægə(r)/ verb [I] to walk in a way that shows that you are too confident or proud ▶ **kroczyć dumnie**

■ **swagger** noun [sing.] ▶ **dumny krok**

🔑 **swallow[1]** /'swɒləʊ/ verb **1** [T] to make food, drink, etc. go down your throat to your stomach: *It's easier to swallow pills if you take them with water.* ▶ **połykać**; **pochłaniać 2** [I] to make a movement in your throat, often because you are afraid or surprised, etc.: *She swallowed hard and tried to speak, but nothing came out.* ▶ **przełykać 3** [T] **swallow sth (up)** to use all of sth, especially money: *The rent swallows up most of our monthly income.* ▶ **pochłaniać** (*np. oszczędności*) **4** [T] to accept or believe sth too easily: *You shouldn't swallow everything they tell you!* ▶ **dawać wiarę 5** [T] to accept an insult, etc. without complaining: *I find her criticisms very **hard to swallow.*** ▶ **chować do kieszeni** (*np. obrazę*), **przełknąć** (*gorzką pigułkę*)

swallow[2] /'swɒləʊ/ noun [C] **1** an act of swallowing; an amount of food or drink that is swallowed at one time ▶ **połykanie**, **przełykanie 2** a small bird that eats insects and has long wings and a forked tail ▶ **jaskółka**

swam past tense of **swim**

swamp[1] /swɒmp/ noun [C,U] an area of soft wet land ▶ **bagno**, **moczary**

swamp[2] /swɒmp/ verb [T] **1** [usually passive] **swamp sb/sth (with sth)** to give sb so much of sth that they cannot deal with it: *We've been swamped with applications for the job.* ▶ **zalewać**, **zasypywać** SYN **inundate 2** to cover or fill sth with water: *The fishing boat was swamped by enormous waves.* ▶ **zalewać**

swan /swɒn/ noun [C] a large, usually white, bird with a very long neck that lives on lakes and rivers ▶ **łabędź**

swanky /'swæŋki/ (**swankier**; **swankiest**) (especially Brit.) (especially US **swank**) adj. (informal) fashionable and expensive in a way that is intended to impress people: *a swanky hotel* ▶ **elegancki i drogi** SYN **posh**

swap (also swop) /swɒp/ verb [I,T] (**swapping**; **swapped**) **swap (sth) (with sb)**; **swap A for B** to give sth for sth else; to exchange: *When we finish these books shall we swap?* ◇ *Would you swap seats with me?* ◇ *I'd swap my job for hers any day.* ▶ **zamieniać (się)**, **wymieniać** (*coś na coś innego*)

■ **swap** noun [sing.]: *Let's **do a swap.*** ▶ **zamiana**, **wymiana**

IDM **change/swap places (with sb)** → PLACE[1]

swarm[1] /swɔːm/ noun [C] **1** a large group of insects moving around together: *a swarm of bees/locusts/flies* ▶ **rój 2** a large number of people together ▶ **mrowie**, **chmara**

swarm[2] /swɔːm/ verb [I] to fly or move in large numbers ▶ **wyrajać się**, **wylegać**

PHR V **swarm with sb/sth** to be too crowded or full ▶ **roić się od czegoś**

swarthy /'swɔːði/ adj. (especially used about a person or their face) having dark skin: *a swarthy complexion* ▶ **śniady**

swat /swɒt/ verb [T] (**swatting**; **swatted**) to hit sth, especially an insect, with sth flat ▶ **pacnąć coś czymś płaskim**

swathe /sweɪð/ noun [C] (also **swath** /swɒθ/) (formal) **1** a long strip of land, especially one on which the plants or crops have been cut: *The combine had cut a swathe around the edge of the field.* ◇ *Development has affected vast swathes of our countryside.* ▶ **pas ziemi** (*zwł. zebranych plonów/ściętych roślin*), **połać 2** a large strip or area of sth: *The mountains rose above a swathe of thick cloud.* ▶ **duży obszar**

IDM **cut a swathe through sth** (used about a person, fire, etc.) to pass through a particular area destroying a large part of it: *Building the tunnel would involve cutting a great swathe through the forest.* ▶ **zniszczyć duży fragment terenu**

■ **swathe** verb [T, usually passive] **swathe sb/sth (in sth)** (formal) to wrap or cover sb/sth in sth: *He was lying on the hospital bed, swathed in bandages.* ◇ *The village was swathed in early morning mist.* Wioskę spowijała poranna mgła. ▶ **owijać kogoś/coś (w coś)**

sway /sweɪ/ verb **1** [I] to move slowly from side to side: *The trees were swaying in the wind.* ▶ **kołysać (się) 2** [T] to influence sb: *Many people were swayed by his convin-*

cing arguments. ▶ **wywierać wpływ na kogoś, przechylać szalę na (czyjąś/swoją) stronę**

swear /sweə(r)/ verb (pt **swore** /swɔː(r)/, pp **sworn** /swɔːn/) **1** [I] **swear (at sb/sth)** to use rude or bad language: *He hit his thumb with the hammer and swore loudly.* ◇ *There's no point in swearing at the car just because it won't start!* ▶ **kląć, przeklinać** ➲ look at **curse 2** [I,T] **swear (to do sth); swear that...** to make a serious promise: *When you give evidence in court you have to swear to tell the truth.* ◇ *Will you swear not to tell anyone?* ▶ **przysięgać**
PHR V **swear by sb/sth** to believe completely in the value of sb/sth ▶ **(głęboko/święcie) wierzyć w kogoś/coś**
swear sb in [usually passive] to make sb say officially that they will accept the responsibility of a new position: *The President will be sworn in next week.* ▶ **zaprzysięgać kogoś**

swearing /ˈsweərɪŋ/ noun [U] rude language that may offend people: *I was shocked at the swearing.* ▶ **przekleństwa**

ˈswear word (also old-fashioned **oath**) noun [C] a word that is considered rude or bad and that may offend people ▶ **przekleństwo, ordynarne słowo**

sweat /swet/ verb [I] **1** to produce liquid through your skin because you are hot, ill or afraid: *to sweat heavily* ▶ **pocić się 2 sweat (over sth)** to work hard: *I've been sweating over that problem all day.* ▶ **pocić się (nad czymś)**
■ **sweat** noun [C,U]: *He stopped digging and wiped the sweat from his forehead.* ◇ *He woke up* ***in a sweat.*** Obudził się cały spocony. ▶ **pot** ➲ look at **perspiration**
IDM **work/sweat your guts out** → GUT[1]

sweatband /ˈswetbænd/ noun [C] a band of cloth worn around the head or wrist, for absorbing sweat ▶ **opaska przeciwpotowa**

sweater /ˈswetə(r)/ noun [C] a warm piece of clothing with long sleeves, often made of wool, which you wear on the top half of your body ▶ **sweter** ➲ picture on **page A1**

> **sweater**
> **Sweater, jumper, pullover** i **jersey** wszystkie oznaczają „sweter". Są najczęściej wykonane z wełny lub innej dzianiny. **Cardigan** to sweter rozpinany. **Sweatshirt** to bluza sportowa, zwykle bawełniana, zaś **fleece** to polar.

sweatshirt /ˈswetʃɜːt/ noun [C] a warm piece of cotton clothing with long sleeves, which you wear on the top half of your body ▶ **bluza (sportowa)** ➲ note at **sweater**

sweatshop /ˈswetʃɒp/ noun [C] a place where people work for low wages in poor conditions ▶ **zakład wyzyskujący pracowników**

sweaty /ˈsweti/ adj. (**sweatier**; **sweatiest**) **1** wet with sweat: *I was hot and sweaty after the match and needed a shower.* ▶ **spocony, oblany potem 2** [only before a noun] causing you to sweat: *a hot sweaty day* ▶ **parny, gorący** (*powodujący pocenie się*)

swede /swiːd/ noun [C,U] a large, round, yellow vegetable that grows under the ground ▶ **brukiew**

sweep[1] /swiːp/ verb (pt, pp **swept** /swept/) **1** [I,T] to clean the floor, etc. by moving dust, dirt, etc. away with a brush: *to sweep the floor* ◇ *I'm going to sweep the leaves off the path.* Zmiotę liście ze ścieżki. ▶ **zamiatać** ➲ note at **clean[2] 2** [T] to remove sth from a surface using your hand, etc.: *He swept the books angrily off the table.* ▶ **zgarniać 3** [T] to move or push sb/sth with a lot of force: *The huge waves swept her overboard.* ◇ *He was swept along by the huge crowd.* ▶ **porywać, znosić** (*np. z pokładu*) **4** [I,T] to move quickly and smoothly over the area or in the direction mentioned: *Fire swept through the building.* ▶ **rozprzestrzeniać się; ogarniać 5** [I] to move in a way that impresses or is intended to impress people: *Five big black Mercedes swept past us.* ◇ *She swept angrily out of the room.* Z gniewem i energicznie opuściła pokój. ▶ **poruszać się dumnie/majestatycznie 6** [I,T] to move over an area, especially in order to look for sth: *The army were sweeping* (przeczesywało) *the fields for mines.* ◇ *His eyes swept quickly* (wodził wzrokiem) *over the page.* ▶ **przesuwać się**
PHR V **sweep sb/sth aside** to not allow sb/sth to affect your progress or plans ▶ **odsuwać kogoś/coś**
sweep sth out to remove dirt and dust from the floor of a room or building using a brush ▶ **zamiatać podłogę**
sweep over sb (used about a feeling) to suddenly affect sb very strongly ▶ (*uczucie*) **ogarniać kogoś**
sweep (sth) up to remove dirt, dust, leaves, etc. using a brush ▶ **zamiatać**

sweep[2] /swiːp/ noun [C] **1** [usually sing.] the act of moving dirt and dust from a floor or surface using a brush: *I'd better give the floor a sweep.* Lepiej pozamiataj podłogę. ▶ **zamiatanie 2** a long, curving shape or movement: *He showed us which way to go with a sweep of his arm.* ▶ **długi łuk** (*np. plaży, drogi*); **szeroki zamaszysty ruch 3** a movement over an area, especially in order to look for sth ▶ **przeczesywanie** (*terenu*) **4** = CHIMNEY SWEEP
IDM **a clean sweep** → CLEAN[1]

sweeper /ˈswiːpə(r)/ noun [C] **1** a person or thing that cleans surfaces with a brush: *He's a road sweeper.* ◇ *Do you sell carpet sweepers* (szczotki do dywanów)*?* ▶ **zamiatacz/ka; zamiatarka 2** (in football) the defending player who plays behind the other defending players ▶ **obrońca**

sweeping /ˈswiːpɪŋ/ adj. **1** having a great and important effect: *sweeping reforms* ▶ **gruntowny, generalny 2** (used about statements, etc.) too general and not accurate enough: *He made a sweeping statement about all politicians being dishonest.* ▶ (*zmiany itp.*) **uogólniający, generalizujący**

sweet[1] /swiːt/ adj. **1** containing, or tasting as if it contains, a lot of sugar: *Children usually like sweet things.* ◇ *This cake's too sweet.* ▶ **słodki** ➲ look at **savoury**, **sour 2** (used about a smell or a sound) pleasant: *the sweet sound of children singing* ▶ **słodki, melodyjny, rozkoszny 3** (used especially about children and small things) attractive: *a sweet little kitten* ◇ *Isn't that little girl sweet?* ▶ **słodki; przemiły** SYN **cute 4** having or showing a kind character: *a sweet smile* ◇ *It's very sweet* (bardzo miło) *of you to remember my birthday!* ▶ **miły**
■ **sweetness** noun [U] ▶ **słodycz**
IDM **have a sweet tooth** to like eating sweet things ▶ **lubić słodycze**

sweet[2] /swiːt/ noun **1** [C, usually pl.] (US **candy** /ˈkændi/ (pl. **candies**) [U,C]) a small piece of boiled sugar, chocolate, etc., eaten between meals: *He was sucking a sweet.* ◇ *a sweet shop* sklep ze słodyczami ▶ **cukierek 2** [C,U] sweet food served at the end of a meal: *As a sweet/For sweet there is ice cream or chocolate mousse.* ▶ **deser** ➲ look at **pudding**, **dessert**

sweetcorn /ˈswiːtkɔːn/ (US **corn**) noun [U] the yellow grains of a type of **maize** that you cook and eat as a vegetable: *tinned sweetcorn* ▶ **kukurydza** ➲ picture on **page A13**

sweeten /ˈswiːtn/ verb [T] to make sth sweet by adding sugar, etc. ▶ **słodzić**

sweetener /ˈswiːtnə(r)/ noun [C,U] a substance used instead of sugar for making food or drink sweet: *artificial sweeteners* ▶ **słodzik**

sweetheart /ˈswiːthɑːt/ noun [C] **1** (used when speaking to sb, especially a child, in a very friendly way): *Do you want a drink, sweetheart?* ▶ **skarbie, kochanie 2** (old-fashioned) a boyfriend or girlfriend: *They were childhood* *sweethearts.* W dzieciństwie byli parą narzeczonych. ▶ **sympatia**

sweetly /ˈswiːtli/ adv. in an attractive, kind or pleasant way: *She smiled sweetly.* ◇ *sweetly-scented flowers* ▶ **słodko**

swell[1] /swel/ verb (pt **swelled** /sweld/, pp **swollen** /ˈswəʊlən/ or **swelled**) **1** [I,T] **swell (up)** to become or to make sth bigger, fuller or thicker: *After the fall her ankle began to swell up.* ◇ *Heavy rain had swollen the rivers* (spowodował wezbranie rzeki). ▶ **puchnąć**; (*rzeka*) **wzbierać, przybierać 2** [I,T] to increase or make sth increase in number or size: *The crowd swelled to 600 by the end of the evening.* ▶ **powiększać się 3** [I] (formal) (used about feelings or sound) to suddenly become stronger or louder: *Hatred swelled inside him.* ▶ **wzmagać się** ▶ (*muz.*) **przybierać na sile**

swell[2] /swel/ noun [sing.] the slow movement up and down of the surface of the sea ▶ **(łagodne) falowanie morza**

swelling /ˈswelɪŋ/ noun **1** [U] the process of becoming swollen: *The disease often causes swelling of the ankles and knees.* ▶ **obrzęk, opuchlizna 2** [C] a place on your body that is bigger or fatter than usual because of an injury or illness: *I've got a nasty swelling under my eye.* ▶ **obrzęk, opuchlizna**

swelter /ˈsweltə(r)/ verb [I] to be very hot in a way that makes you feel uncomfortable: *Passengers sweltered in temperatures of over 30° C.* ▶ **umierać z gorąca**
■ **sweltering** adj. much too hot: *sweltering heat* ◇ *It was sweltering* (strasznie gorąco) *in the office today.* ▶ **upalny**

swept past tense, past participle of **sweep**[1]

swerve /swɜːv/ verb [I] to change direction suddenly: *The car swerved to avoid the child.* ▶ **nagle/gwałtownie skręcić** (*np. z drogi*)
■ **swerve** noun [C] ▶ **nagłe/gwałtowne skręcanie** (*np. z drogi*)

swift /swɪft/ adj. happening without delay; quick: *a swift reaction/decision/movement* ◇ *a swift runner* ▶ **szybki, rychły**
■ **swiftly** adv. ▶ **szybko, rychle**

swig /swɪɡ/ verb [I,T] (**swigging**; **swigged**) (informal) to take a quick drink of sth, especially alcohol ▶ **wypić coś haustem**
■ **swig** noun [C] ▶ **haust**

swill /swɪl/ verb [T] **swill sth (out/down)** to wash sth by pouring large amounts of water, etc. into, over or through it ▶ **płukać, zmywać**

swim /swɪm/ verb (**swimming**; pt **swam** /swæm/, pp **swum** /swʌm/) **1** [I,T] to move your body through water: *How far can you swim?* ◇ *Hundreds of tiny fish swam past.* ◇ *I swam* (przepłynąłem) *25 lengths of the pool.* ▶ **pływać**
Go swimming to potoczny zwrot oznaczający pływanie rekreacyjne: *We go swimming every Saturday.* ◇ *They went swimming before breakfast.* Można też powiedzieć **go for a swim**, mówiąc o jednorazowym zażywaniu kąpieli: *I went for a swim this morning.* **2** [I] **be swimming (in/with sth)** to be covered with a lot of liquid: *The salad was swimming in oil.* ▶ (*przen.*) **pływać w czymś 3** [I] to seem to be moving or turning: *The floor began to swim before my eyes and I fainted.* ▶ **wirować** (*np. przed oczami*) **4** [I] (used about your head) to feel confused: *My head was swimming with so much new information.* ▶ **kręcić się** (*w głowie*)
■ **swim** noun [sing.]: *to go for/have a swim* ▶ **pływanie** | **swimmer** noun [C]: *a strong/weak swimmer* ▶ **pływa-k/czka**

ˈswimming bath noun [C] (also **swimming baths** [pl.]) a public swimming pool, usually inside a building ▶ **pływalnia, basen kryty**

ˈswimming cap (also **ˈswimming hat**; especially US **ˈbathing cap**) noun [C] a soft rubber or plastic cap that fits closely over your head to keep your hair dry while you are swimming ▶ **czepek kąpielowy**

ˈswimming costume (Brit.) = SWIMSUIT

ˈswimming pool (also **pool**) noun [C] a pool that is built especially for people to swim in: *an indoor/outdoor/open-air swimming pool* ▶ **basen**

ˈswimming trunks noun [pl.] a piece of clothing like short trousers that a man wears to go swimming: *a pair of swimming trunks* ▶ **kąpielówki**

swimsuit /ˈswɪmsuːt/ (Brit. **ˈswimming costume**; **costume**) noun [C] a piece of clothing that a woman wears to go swimming ▶ **kostium kąpielowy** ➲ look at **bikini**

swindle /ˈswɪndl/ verb [T] **swindle sb/sth (out of sth)** to trick sb in order to get money, etc. ▶ **wyłudzać**
■ **swindle** noun [C]: *a tax swindle* oszustwo podatkowe ▶ **szwindel, szachrajstwo** | **swindler** noun [C] a person who **swindles** ▶ **oszust/ka**; **szachraj/ka**

swine /swaɪn/ noun **1** [C] (informal) a very unpleasant person ▶ **świnia 2** [pl.] (old-fashioned) pigs ▶ **świnie**

swing[1] /swɪŋ/ verb (pt, pp **swung** /swʌŋ/) **1** [I,T] to move backwards and forwards or from side to side while hanging from sth; to make sb/sth move in this way: *The rope was swinging from a branch.* ◇ *She sat on the wall, swinging her legs.* ▶ **huśtać (się), kołysać (się) 2** [I] to move or change from one position or situation towards the opposite one: *She swung round when she heard the door open.* ◇ (figurative) *His moods swing from one extreme to the other.* ▶ **obracać się** (*np. na pięcie*); **wahać się 3** [I,T] to move or make sb/sth move in a curve: *The door swung open and Rudi walked in.* ◇ *He swung the child up onto his shoulders.* ▶ **poruszać się/coś, wykonując ruch po łuku 4** [I,T] **swing (sth) (at sb/sth)** to try to hit sb/sth: *He swung violently at the other man but missed.* ▶ **zamachnąć się ręką (na kogoś/coś)**

swing[2] /swɪŋ/ noun **1** [sing.] a **swinging** movement or rhythm: *He took a swing at the ball.* ▶ **zamachnięcie się 2** [C] a change from one position or situation towards the opposite one: *Opinion polls indicate a significant swing towards the right.* ▶ **zwrot 3** [C] a seat, a piece of rope, etc. that is hung from above so that you can **swing** backwards and forwards on it: *Some children were playing on the swings.* ▶ **huśtawka**
IDM **in full swing** → FULL[1]

S

swipe /swaɪp/ verb **1** [I,T] (informal) **swipe (at) sb/sth** to hit or try to hit sb/sth by moving your arm in a curve: *He swiped at the wasp with a newspaper but missed.* ▶ **(próbować) walić (w kogoś/coś) na oślep/na chybił trafił 2** [T] (informal) to steal sth ▶ **podwędzić, gwizdnąć 3** [T] to pass the part of a plastic card on which information is stored through a special machine for reading it: *The receptionist swiped my credit card and handed me the slip to sign.* ▶ **wczytywać**
■ **swipe** noun [C]: *She took a swipe at him with her handbag.* ▶ **cios na oślep/na chybił trafił**

ˈswipe card noun [C] a small plastic card on which information is stored which can be read by an electronic machine ▶ **karta magnetyczna**

swirl /swɜːl/ verb [I,T] to move or to make sth move around quickly in a circle: *Her long skirt swirled round her legs as she danced.* ◇ *He swirled some water round in his mouth and spat it out.* ▶ **wirować, kręcić (się)**
■ **swirl** noun [C] ▶ **wirowanie, kręcenie (się)**

switch[1] /swɪtʃ/ noun [C] **1** a small button or sth similar that you press up or down in order to turn on electricity: *a light switch* ▶ **przełącznik 2** a sudden change: *a switch in policy* ▶ **nagła zmiana 3** (US) = POINT[1] (12)

switch[2] /swɪtʃ/ verb [I,T] **1 switch (sth) (over) (from sth) (to sth)**; **switch (between A and B)** to change or be changed from one thing to another: *I'm fed up with my glasses –*

I'm thinking of switching over to contact lenses. ◇ *Press these two keys to switch between documents on screen.* ◇ *The match has been switched from Saturday to Sunday.* ▶ **przerzucać się (z czegoś na coś), przenosić coś** (*np. na inny termin*) **2 switch (sth) (with sb/sth); switch (sth) (over/round)** to exchange positions, activities, etc.: *This week you can have the car and I'll go on the bus, and next week we'll switch over.* ◇ *Someone switched the signs round* (ktoś odwrócił znaki) *and everyone went the wrong way.* ▶ **zamieniać się**

PHR V **switch (sth) off/on** to press a switch in order to stop/start electric power: *Don't forget to switch off the cooker.* ▶ **wyłączać; włączać**

switch (sth) over to change to a different TV programme ▶ **przełączać (się) na inny program**

switchboard /ˈswɪtʃbɔːd/ noun [C] the place in a large company, etc. where all the telephone calls are connected ▶ **centrala telefoniczna**

swivel /ˈswɪvl/ verb [I,T] (**swivelling**; **swivelled**; US **swiveling**; **swiveled**) **swivel (sth) (round)** to turn around a central point; to make sth do this: *She swivelled round to face me.* ◇ *He swivelled his chair towards the door.* ▶ **obracać (się)** (*np. na osi*)

swollen[1] past participle of **swell**[1]

⚷ **swollen**[2] /ˈswəʊlən/ adj. thicker or wider than usual: *Her ankle was badly swollen after she twisted it.* ▶ **spuchnięty**

swoon /swuːn/ verb [I] **1 swoon (over sb)** to feel very excited, emotional, etc. about sb that you think is sexually attractive, so that you almost become unconscious: *He's used to having women swooning over him.* ▶ **zachwycać się (kimś), wpadać w uniesienie (z powodu kogoś) 2** (old-fashioned) to become unconscious ▶ **zemdleć** SYN **faint**

■ **swoon** noun (old-fashioned): *to go into a swoon* zemdleć ▶ **omdlenie**

swoop /swuːp/ verb [I] **1** to fly or move down suddenly: *The bird swooped down on its prey.* ▶ **runąć, rzucać się (na kogoś/coś) 2** (used especially about the police or the army) to visit or capture sb/sth without warning: *Police swooped at dawn and arrested the man at his home.* ▶ **zrobić nalot**

■ **swoop** noun [C] **a swoop (on sb/sth)** ▶ **napaść**

swop = SWAP

sword /sɔːd/ noun [C] a long, very sharp metal weapon, like a large knife ▶ **miecz, szpada**

swore past tense of **swear**

sworn past participle of **swear**

swot[1] /swɒt/ noun [C] (informal) a person who studies too hard ▶ **kujon**

swot[2] /swɒt/ verb [I,T] (**swotting**; **swotted**) **swot (up) (for/on sth)**; **swot sth up** to study sth very hard, especially to prepare for an exam: *She's swotting for her final exams.* ▶ **wkuwać** (*np. do egzaminu*)

swum past participle of **swim**

swung past tense, past participle of **swing**[1]

sycamore /ˈsɪkəmɔː(r)/ noun [C] **1** (especially Brit.) a large tree of the **maple** family ▶ **jawor 2** (especially US) an American **plane tree** ▶ **platan**

sycophant /ˈsɪkəfænt/ noun [C] (formal) a person who praises important or powerful people too much and in a way that is not sincere, especially in order to get sth from them ▶ **pochlebca**

■ **sycophancy** /ˈsɪkəfənsi/ noun [U] ▶ **czołobitność** | **sycophantic** /ˌsɪkəˈfæntɪk/ adj.: *a sycophantic review* ▶ **czołobitny**

syllable /ˈsɪləbl/ noun [C] a word or part of a word which contains one vowel sound: *'Mat' has one syllable and 'mattress' has two syllables.* ◇ *The stress in 'international' is on the third syllable.* ▶ **sylaba**

syllabus /ˈsɪləbəs/ noun [C] a list of subjects, etc. that are included in a course of study ▶ **program nauczania**

➲ look at **curriculum**

symbiosis /ˌsɪmbaɪˈəʊsɪs/ noun [U,C] (pl. **symbioses** /-ˈəʊsiːz/) **1** the relationship between two different living creatures that live close together and depend on each other in particular ways, each getting particular benefits from the other ▶ **symbioza 2** a relationship between people, companies, etc. that is to the advantage of both ▶ **symbioza**

■ **symbiotic** /-ˈɒtɪk/ adj.: *a symbiotic relationship* ▶ **symbiotyczny**

⚷ **symbol** /ˈsɪmbl/ noun [C] **1 a symbol (of sth)** a sign, object, etc. which represents sth: *The cross is the symbol of Christianity.* ▶ **symbol 2 a symbol (for sth)** a letter, number or sign that has a particular meaning: *O is the symbol for oxygen.* ▶ **symbol/znak (czegoś)**

symbolic /sɪmˈbɒlɪk/ (also **symbolical** /-kl/) adj. (used or seen to represent sth): *The white dove is symbolic of peace.* ▶ **symboliczny, umowny**

■ **symbolically** /-kli/ adv. ▶ **symbolicznie**

symbolism /ˈsɪmbəlɪzəm/ noun [U] the use of symbols to represent things, especially in art and literature ▶ **symbolizm**

symbolize (also **-ise**) /ˈsɪmbəlaɪz/ verb [T] to represent sth: *The deepest notes in music are often used to symbolize danger or despair.* ▶ **symbolizować, oznaczać**

symmetrical /sɪˈmetrɪkl/ (also **symmetric**) adj. having two halves that match each other exactly in size, shape, etc. ▶ **symetryczny**

■ **symmetrically** /-kli/ adv. ▶ **symetrycznie**

symmetry /ˈsɪmətri/ noun [U] the state of having two halves that match each other exactly in size, shape, etc. ▶ **symetria**

⚷ **sympathetic** /ˌsɪmpəˈθetɪk/ adj. **1 sympathetic (to/towards sb)** showing that you understand other people's feelings, especially their problems: *When Suki was ill, everyone was very sympathetic.* ◇ *I felt very sympathetic towards him.* ◇ *If you need **a sympathetic ear*** (życzliwego słuchacza), *give me a call.* ▶ **współczujący, pełen zrozumienia**

> Uwaga! W jęz. ang. **sympathetic** nie oznacza „sympatyczny". Mówiąc o osobie, że jest sympatyczna, używa się słowa **nice**: *I met Alex's sister yesterday. She's very nice.*

2 sympathetic (to sb/sth) being in agreement with or supporting sb/sth: *I explained our ideas but she wasn't sympathetic to them.* ▶ **życzliwy, popierający**

■ **sympathetically** /-kli/ adv. ▶ **współczująco; życzliwie**

sympathize (also **-ise**) /ˈsɪmpəθaɪz/ verb [I] **sympathize (with sb/sth) 1** to feel sorry for sb; to show that you understand sb's problems: *I sympathize with her, but I don't know what I can do to help.* ▶ **współczuć 2** to support sb/sth: *I find it difficult to sympathize with his opinions.* ▶ **podzielać** (*np. czyjeś poglądy*)

sympathizer (also **-iser**) /ˈsɪmpəθaɪzə(r)/ noun [C] a person who agrees with and supports an idea or aim ▶ **sympaty-k/czka, zwolenni-k/czka**

⚷ **sympathy** /ˈsɪmpəθi/ noun (pl. **sympathies**) **1** [U] **sympathy (for/towards sb)** an understanding of other people's feelings, especially their problems: *Everyone **feels** great **sympathy** for the victims of the attack.* ◇ *I don't expect any sympathy from you.* ◇ *I **have** no **sympathy** for Mark – it's his own fault.* ◇ *When his wife died he received dozens of letters of sympathy* (listów kondolencyjnych). ▶ **współczucie 2** (**sympathies**) [pl.] feelings of support or

agreement: *Some members of the party have nationalist sympathies.* ▶ **inklinacja**
IDM **be in sympathy (with sb/sth)** to be in agreement, showing that you support or approve of sb/sth: *He is not in sympathy with all the ideas of the party.* ◇ *Taxi drivers stopped work in sympathy with the striking bus drivers.* ▶ **popierać (kogoś/coś), solidaryzować się (z kimś)**

symphony /ˈsɪmfəni/ noun [C] (pl. **symphonies**) a long piece of music written for a large **orchestra**: ***a symphony orchestra*** orkiestra symfoniczna ▶ **symfonia**

symptom /ˈsɪmptəm/ noun [C] **1** a change in your body that is a sign of illness: *The symptoms of flu include a headache, a high temperature and aches in the body.* ▶ **symptom, objaw** (*choroby*) ➲ note at **ill 2** a sign (that sth bad is happening or exists) ▶ **symptom, objaw**
■ **symptomatic** /ˌsɪmptəˈmætɪk/ adj. ▶ **symptomatyczny, znamienny**

synagogue /ˈsɪnəɡɒɡ/ noun [C] a building where Jewish people go to worship or to study their religion, etc. ▶ **synagoga**

synchronize (also -ise) /ˈsɪŋkrənaɪz/ verb [T] to make sth happen or work at the same time or speed: *We synchronized our watches to make sure we agreed what the time was.* ▶ **synchronizować**

syncopated /ˈsɪŋkəpeɪtɪd/ adj. in **syncopated** rhythm the strong beats are made weak and the weak beats are made strong ▶ **synkopowy**
■ **syncopation** /ˌsɪŋkəˈpeɪʃn/ noun [U] ▶ **synkopa**

syndicate /ˈsɪndɪkət/ noun [C] a group of people or companies that work together in order to achieve a particular aim ▶ **syndykat**

syndrome /ˈsɪndrəʊm/ noun [C] **1** a group of signs or changes in the body that are typical of an illness: *Down's syndrome* ◇ *Acquired Immune Deficiency Syndrome (AIDS)* ▶ **syndrom** (*zespół objawów choroby*) **2** a set of opinions or a way of behaving that is typical of a particular type of person, attitude or social problem ▶ **syndrom**

synergy /ˈsɪnədʒi/ noun [U,C] (pl. **-ies**) the extra energy, power, success, etc. that is achieved by two or more people or companies working together, instead of on their own: *Managing effective teams is a matter of achieving synergy between the individual members.* ◇ *attempts to re-establish synergy between mankind and nature* ▶ **synergia**

synonym /ˈsɪnənɪm/ noun [C] a word or phrase that has the same meaning as another word or phrase in the same language: *'Big' and 'large' are synonyms.* ▶ **synonim**
■ **synonymous** /sɪˈnɒnɪməs/ adj. **synonymous (with sth)** (figurative): *Wealth is not always synonymous with happiness.* ▶ **tożsamy z czymś, jednoznaczny z czymś** ➲ look at **antonym**

synopsis /sɪˈnɒpsɪs/ noun [C] (pl. **synopses** /-siːz/) a short description of a piece of writing, a play, etc.: *The programme gives a brief synopsis of the plot.* ▶ **streszczenie** SYN **summary**

syntax /ˈsɪntæks/ noun [U] the system of rules for the structure of a sentence in a language ▶ **składnia**

synthesis /ˈsɪnθəsɪs/ noun (pl. **syntheses** /-siːz/) **1** [C,U] **synthesis (of sth)** the act of combining separate ideas, beliefs, styles, etc.; a mixture or combination of ideas, beliefs, styles, etc.: *the synthesis of art with everyday life* ◇ *a synthesis of traditional and modern values* ▶ **synteza 2** [U] (technical) the natural chemical production of a substance in animals and plants, or the artificial production of such a substance: *protein synthesis* ▶ **synteza 3** [U] (technical) the production of sounds, music or speech using electronic equipment: *speech synthesis* ▶ **synteza**
■ **synthesize** (also -ise) /ˈsɪnθəsaɪz/ verb [T] **1** (technical) to produce a substance by means of chemical processes ▶ **syntetyzować 2** to produce sounds, music or speech using electronic equipment ▶ **syntetyzować 3** to combine separate ideas, beliefs, styles, etc. ▶ **syntetyzować**

synthesizer (also -iser) /ˈsɪnθəsaɪzə(r)/ noun [C] an electronic musical instrument that can produce a wide variety of different sounds ▶ **syntetyzator**

synthetic /sɪnˈθetɪk/ adj. made by a chemical process; not natural: *synthetic materials/fibres* ▶ **syntetyczny, sztuczny**
■ **synthetically** /-kli/ adv. ▶ **syntetycznie; sztucznie**

syphilis /ˈsɪfɪlɪs/ noun [U] a serious disease that passes from one person to another by sexual contact ▶ **syfilis**

syphon = SIPHON

syringe /sɪˈrɪndʒ/ noun [C] a plastic or glass tube with a needle that is used for taking a small amount of blood out of the body or for putting drugs into the body ▶ **strzykawka** ➲ picture at **laboratory**

syrup /ˈsɪrəp/ noun [U] thick sweet liquid made by boiling sugar with water or fruit juice: *peaches in syrup* ▶ **syrop** ➲ look at **treacle**

system /ˈsɪstəm/ noun **1** [C] a set of ideas or rules for organizing sth; a particular way of doing sth: *We have a new computerized system in the library.* ◇ *The government is planning to reform the education system.* ▶ **system 2** [C] a group of things or parts that work together: *a central heating system* ◇ *a transport system* ▶ **system, układ 3** [C] the body of a person or an animal; parts of the body that work together: *the central nervous system* ▶ **organizm** (*człowieka*); **układ** (*np. nerwowy*) **4** (**the system**) [sing.] (informal) the traditional methods and rules of a society: *You can't* ***beat the system.*** ▶ **ustrój/system (społeczny)**
IDM **get sth out of your system** (informal) to do sth to free yourself of a strong feeling or emotion ▶ **mieć (coś) z głowy**

systematic /ˌsɪstəˈmætɪk/ adj. done using a fixed plan or method: *a systematic search* ▶ **systematyczny**
■ **systematically** /-kli/ adv. ▶ **systematycznie**

systematize (also -ise) /ˈsɪstəmətaɪz/ verb [T] (formal) to arrange sth according to a system ▶ **systematyzować** SYN **organize**
■ **systematization** (also -isation) /ˌsɪstəmətaɪˈzeɪʃn; US -təˈz-/ noun [U] ▶ **usystematyzowanie**

systemic /sɪˈstemɪk; sɪˈstiːmɪk/ adj. **1** affecting or connected with the whole of sth, especially the human body: *a systemic disease* ▶ **ogólnoustrojowy 2 systemic** chemicals or drugs that are used to treat diseases in plants or animals enter the body of the plant or animal and spread to all parts of it: *systemic weedkillers* ▶ **systemiczny**
■ **systemically** adv.: *substances that are absorbed systemically* ▶ **systemicznie**

ˈsystems analyst noun [C] a person whose job is to look carefully at the needs of a business company or an organization and then design the best way of working and completing tasks using computer programs ▶ **analityk systemów**

Tt

T, t /tiː/ noun [C,U] (pl. **Ts**; **ts**; **T's**; **t's** /tiːz/) the 20th letter of the English alphabet: *'Table' begins with (a) 'T'.* ▶ **litera** *t*

t = TON (1), TONNE: *5t coal*

ta /tɑː/ interj. (Brit., informal) thank you ▶ **dzięki**

tab /tæb/ noun [C] **1** a small piece of cloth, metal or paper that is fixed to the edge of sth to help you open, hold or identify it: *You open the tin by pulling the metal tab.* ▶ **uchwyt**, **uszko** (*np. do otwierania puszki*) **2** the money that you owe for food, drink, etc. that you receive in a bar, restaurant, etc. but pay for later ▶ **rachunek** **3** = TAB KEY

IDM **keep tabs on sb/sth** (informal) to watch sb/sth carefully; to check sth ▶ **mieć kogoś/coś na oku**

tabby /ˈtæbi/ noun [C] (pl. **tabbies**) (also ˈ**tabby cat**) a cat with grey or brown fur and dark stripes ▶ **szary pręgowany kot**

ˈ**tab key** (also **tab**) noun [C] a button on a keyboard that you use to move to a certain fixed position in a line of a document that you are typing ▶ **klawisz tabulacji**

⚷ **table** /ˈteɪbl/ noun [C] **1** a piece of furniture with a flat top supported by legs: *Could you **lay/set the table*** (nakryć do stołu) *for lunch?* ◇ *Let me help you **clear the table*** (posprzątać ze stołu). ◇ *Don't read the newspaper at the table* (przy stole). ◇ *a dining table* stół w jadalni ◇ *a bedside table* szafka nocna ◇ *a kitchen table* stół kuchenny ◇ *a coffee table* stolik do kawy ▶ **stół**, **stolik**

We put things **on the table** but we sit **at the table**.

2 a list of facts or figures, usually arranged in rows and columns down a page: *the table of contents* spis treści ◇ *Table 3 shows the results.* ▶ **tabela** **3** = MULTIPLICATION TABLE

tablecloth /ˈteɪblklɒθ/ noun [C] a piece of cloth that you use for covering a table, especially when having a meal ▶ **obrus**

ˈ**table manners** noun [pl.] behaviour that is considered correct while you are having a meal at a table with other people ▶ **zachowanie się przy stole**

tablespoon /ˈteɪblspuːn/ noun [C] **1** a large spoon used for serving or measuring food ▶ **łyżka stołowa** (*czegoś*) **2** (also **tablespoonful** /-fʊl/) (abbr. **tbsp**) the amount that a **tablespoon** holds: *Add two tablespoons of sugar.* ▶ **pełna łyżka stołowa**

⚷ **tablet** /ˈtæblət/ noun [C] a small amount of medicine in solid form that you swallow: ***Take two tablets** with water before meals.* ▶ **tabletka**, **pastylka** SYN **pill**

ˈ**table tennis** (also informal **ping-pong**) noun [U] a game with rules like **tennis** in which you hit a light plastic ball across a table with a small round **bat** ▶ **tenis stołowy**, **ping-pong**

tabloid /ˈtæblɔɪd/ noun [C] a newspaper with small pages, a lot of pictures and short articles, especially ones about famous people ▶ **brukowiec** ➲ note at **newspaper**

taboo /təˈbuː/ noun [C] (pl. **taboos**) something that you must not say or do because it might shock, offend or embarrass people ▶ **tabu**
■ **taboo** adj.: *a taboo subject/word* ▶ **tabu**, **zakazany**

tabulate /ˈtæbjuleɪt/ verb [T] to arrange facts or figures in columns or lists so that they can be read easily ▶ **zestawiać w formie tabeli**
■ **tabulation** /ˌtæbjuˈleɪʃn/ noun [U,C] ▶ **zestawienie tabularyczne**

tacit /ˈtæsɪt/ adj. (formal) understood but not actually said ▶ **milczący**, **niewypowiedziany**
■ **tacitly** adv. ▶ **milcząco**

tack¹ /tæk/ noun **1** [sing.] a way of dealing with a particular situation: *If people won't listen we'll have to try a different tack.* ▶ **taktyka** **2** [C] a small nail with a sharp point and a flat head ▶ **pinezka**, **pluskiewka**

tack² /tæk/ verb [T] **1** to fasten sth in place with **tacks¹** (2) **2** to fasten cloth together temporarily with long **stitches** that can be removed easily ▶ **fastrygować**

PHR V **tack sth on (to sth)** to add sth extra on the end of sth ▶ **doczepiać**, **dołączać**

⚷ **tackle¹** /ˈtækl/ verb **1** [T] to make an effort to deal with a difficult situation or problem: *The government must tackle the problem of rising unemployment.* ◇ *Firemen were brought in to tackle the blaze* (opanować pożar). ▶ **rozprawiać się z czymś** **2** [T] **tackle sb about sth** to speak to sb about a difficult subject: *I'm going to tackle Henry about the money he owes me.* ▶ **konfrontować czyjeś stanowisko** (*w jakiejś sprawie*) **3** [I,T] (in football, etc.) to try to take the ball from sb in the other team: *He was tackled just outside the penalty area.* ▶ (*sport*) **blokować**, (*rugby*) **chwytać** **4** [T] to stop sb running away by pulling them down: *The police officer tackled one of the robbers as he ran out.* ▶ **przytrzymywać**, **blokować** (*przeciwnika*)

⚷ **tackle²** /ˈtækl/ noun **1** [C] the act of trying to get the ball from another player in football, etc. ▶ (*sport*) **blok(owanie)**, (*rugby*) **chwyt** **2** [U] the equipment you use in some sports, especially fishing: *fishing tackle* ▶ **sprzęt sportowy** (*zwł. wędkarski*)

tacky /ˈtæki/ adj. (**tackier**; **tackiest**) **1** (informal) cheap and of poor quality and/or not in good taste: *a shop selling tacky souvenirs* ▶ **tandetny** **2** (used about paint, etc.) not quite dry; sticky ▶ **lepki**, **kleisty**

tact /tækt/ noun [U] the ability to deal with people without offending or upsetting them: *She handled the situation with great tact and diplomacy.* ▶ **takt**

tactful /ˈtæktfl/ adj. careful not to say or do things that could offend people ▶ **taktowny** SYN **diplomatic** OPP **tactless**
■ **tactfully** /-fəli/ adv. ▶ **taktownie**

tactic /ˈtæktɪk/ noun **1** [C, usually pl.] the particular method you use to achieve sth: *We must decide what our tactics are going to be at the next meeting.* ◇ *I don't think this tactic will work.* ▶ **taktyka**, **metoda działania** **2** (**tactics**) [pl.] the skilful arrangement and use of military forces in order to win a battle ▶ **taktyka wojskowa**

tactical /ˈtæktɪkl/ adj. **1** connected with the particular method you use to achieve sth: *I made a tactical error.* ◇ *tactical planning* ▶ **taktyczny** **2** designed to bring a future advantage: *a tactical decision* ▶ **taktyczny**, **przebiegły**
■ **tactically** /-kli/ adv. ▶ **taktycznie**

tactile /ˈtæktaɪl; US -tl/ adj. [usually before a noun] connected with the sense of touch; using your sense of touch: *tactile stimuli* ◇ *tactile fabric* tkanina, która jest przyjemna w dotyku ◇ *tactile maps* ◇ *He's a very tactile man.* (używane w społeczeństwie anglosaskim, w ktorym zwł. mężczyźni z reguły mało dotykają swoich przyjaciół) Ten mężczyzna jest bardzo wylewny i lubi lekko dotykać lub poklepywać innych ludzi (np. w czasie rozmowy). ▶ **dotykowy**

tactless /ˈtæktləs/ adj. saying and doing things that are likely to offend and upset other people: *It was rather tactless of you to ask her how old she was.* ▶ **nietaktowny** OPP **tactful**
■ **tactlessly** adv. ▶ **nietaktownie**

tadpole /ˈtædpəʊl/ noun [C] a young form of a **frog** when it has a black head and a long tail ▶ **kijanka** ➲ picture on page A11

tag¹ /tæg/ noun [C] **1** [in compounds] a small piece of card, cloth, etc. fastened to sth to give information about it: *How much is this dress? There isn't a* ***price tag*** *on it.* ▶ **metka, etykieta 2** = QUESTION TAG

tag² /tæg/ verb [T] (**tagging**; **tagged**) to fasten a **tag** onto sb/sth ▶ **przymocowywać metkę/etykietę**

PHR V **tag along (behind/with sb)** to follow or go somewhere with sb, especially when you have not been invited ▶ **iść (za kimś) jak cień**

tail¹ /teɪl/ noun **1** [C] the part at the end of the body of an animal, bird, fish, etc.: *The dog barked and wagged its tail.* ▶ **ogon** ➲ picture at **horse** ➲ picture on **page A10**, **page A11 2** [C] the back part of an aircraft, etc.: *the tail wing* ▶ **ogon 3** (**tails**) [pl.] a man's formal coat that is short at the front but with a long, divided piece at the back, worn especially at weddings: *The men all wore top hat and tails.* ▶ **frak 4** (**tails**) [U] the side of a coin that does not have the head of a person on it: *'We'll toss a coin to decide,' said my father. '****Heads or tails?****'* ▶ **reszka 5** [C] (informal) a person who is sent to follow sb secretly to get information about them: *The police have* ***put a tail on*** *him.* Śledzi go policja. ▶ (*tajniak*) **ogon**

IDM **make head or tail of sth** → HEAD¹

tail² /teɪl/ verb [T] to follow sb closely, especially to watch where they go ▶ **śledzić** (*krok po kroku*)

PHR V **tail away/off** (especially Brit.) to become less or weaker ▶ **zamierać, słabnąć**

tailback /ˈteɪlbæk/ noun [C] (Brit.) a long line of traffic that is moving slowly or not moving at all, because sth is blocking the road: *It took a couple of hours for the two-mile tailback to clear.* ▶ **korek (komunikacyjny)**

tailbone /ˈteɪlbəʊn/ noun [C] the small bone at the bottom of the **spine** ▶ **kość ogonowa** SYN **coccyx**

tailor¹ /ˈteɪlə(r)/ noun [C] a person whose job is to make clothes, especially for men ▶ **krawiec** (*męski*)

tailor² /ˈteɪlə(r)/ verb [T, usually passive] **1 tailor sth to/for sb/sth** to make or design sth for a particular person or purpose: *programmes tailored to the needs of specific groups* ▶ **projektować coś na specjalne zamówienie, przystosowywać 2** to make clothes: *a well-tailored coat* ▶ **szyć ubrania**

ˌtailor-ˈmade adj. **tailor-made (for sb/sth)** made for a particular person or purpose and therefore very suitable ▶ **zrobiony na miarę, w sam raz**

tailpipe (US) = EXHAUST¹ (2)

tailplane /ˈteɪlpleɪn/ noun [C] a small horizontal wing at the back of an aircraft ▶ **statecznik poziomy** ➲ picture at **plane**

taint /teɪnt/ noun [usually sing.] (formal) the effect of sth bad or unpleasant that spoils the quality of sb/sth: *the taint of corruption* ▶ **skaza, ślad**

■ **taint** verb [T, usually passive]: *Her reputation was tainted by the scandal.* ▶ **plamić; psuć**

take /teɪk/ verb [T] (pt **took** /tʊk/, pp **taken** /ˈteɪkən/) **1** to carry or move sb/sth; to go with sb from one place to another: *Take your coat with you – it's cold.* ◇ *Could you take this letter home to your parents?* ◇ *The ambulance took him to hospital.* ◇ *I'm taking the children swimming this afternoon.* ▶ **brać, zabierać** ➲ picture at **bring 2** to put your hand round sth and hold it (and move it towards you): *She held out the keys, and I took them.* ◇ *He took a sweater out of the drawer.* ◇ *She* ***took*** *my* ***hand****/me by the hand.* ▶ **brać 3** to remove sth from a place or a person, often without permission: *Who's taken my pen?* ◇ *My name had been taken off the list.* ◇ *The burglars took all my jewellery.* ▶ **zabierać** (*bez pozwolenia*) **4** to capture a place by force; to get control of sb/sth: *The state will* ***take control of*** *the company.* ▶ **brać 5** to swallow sth: ***Take*** *two* ***tablets*** *four times a day.* ◇ *Do you* ***take sugar*** *in (your) tea?* ▶ **brać 6** to write or record sth: *She* ***took notes*** (robiła notatki) *during the lecture.* ◇ *The police officer took my name and address.* ▶ **zapisywać 7** to photograph sth: *I* ***took*** *some nice* ***photos*** *of the wedding.* ▶ **robić zdjęcia 8** to measure sth: *The doctor* ***took*** *my* ***temperature****/pulse/blood pressure.* ▶ **mierzyć 9** to accept or receive sth: *If you* ***take*** *my* ***advice*** (jeśli skorzystasz z mojej rady), *you'll forget all about him.* ◇ *Do you take credit cards?* ◇ *What coins does the machine take?* ◇ *She's not going to* ***take the job.*** ◇ *I'm not going to* ***take the blame*** (nie wezmę na siebie winy) *for the accident.* ▶ **brać, przyjmować 10** to understand sth or react to sth in a particular way: *She took what he said as a compliment.* ◇ *I wish you would* ***take*** *things more* ***seriously.*** ▶ **brać, przyjmować** (*np. wiadomość*) **11** to be able to deal with sth difficult or unpleasant: *I can't take much more of this heat.* ▶ **znosić** SYN **stand 12** to get a particular feeling from sth: *He* ***takes*** *great* ***pleasure in*** *his grandchildren.* Wnuki sprawiają mu wiele radości. ◇ *When she failed the exam she* ***took comfort from*** *the fact that it was only by a few marks.* ▶ **brać 13** (used with nouns to say that sb is performing an action): ***Take a look*** *at this article.* Zerknij na ten artykuł. ◇ *We have to* ***take a decision.*** Musimy podjąć decyzję. **14** to need sth/sb: *It took three people* (potrzeba było trzech ludzi) *to move the piano.* ◇ *How long did the journey take?* Jak długo trwała podróż? ◇ *It took a lot of courage* (wymagało dużo odwagi) *to say that.* **15** [not used in the continuous tenses] to have a certain size of shoes or clothes: *What size shoes do you take?* ▶ **nosić** (*rozmiar ubrania*) **16** [not used in the continuous tenses] to have enough space for sb/sth: *How many passengers can this bus take?* ▶ **mieścić 17 take sb (for sth)** to give lessons to sb: *Who takes you for History?* Kto cię uczy historii? **18** to study a subject for an exam; to do an exam: *I'm taking the advanced exam this summer.* ▶ **uczyć się do egzaminu; zdawać egzamin 19** to use a form of transport; to use a particular route: *I always* ***take the train*** *to York.* ◇ *Which road do you take to Hove?* ◇ *Take the second turning on the right.* ▶ **jechać; wybierać 20** [not used in the continuous tenses] to have or need a word to go with it in a sentence or other structure: *The verb 'depend' takes the preposition 'on'.* ▶ **występować/łączyć się** (*z innym słowem w zdaniu*)

IDM **be taken with sb/sth** to find sb/sth attractive or interesting ▶ **być zauroczonym/zainteresowanym (kimś/czymś)**

I take it (that ...) (used to show that you understand sth from a situation, even though you have not been told) I suppose: *I take it that you're not coming?* ▶ **zakładać, że**

take it from me believe me ▶ **uwierz/cie mi**

take a lot out of sb to make sb very tired ▶ **wyczerpywać kogoś**

take a lot of/some doing to need a lot of work or effort ▶ **wymagać dużo pracy/wysiłku**

ⓘ **Take** używa się w innych idiomach, np. **take place**. Zob. hasła odpowiednich rzeczowników, przymiotników itp.

PHR V **take sb aback** [usually passive] to surprise or shock sb ▶ **zaskakiwać**

take after sb [not used in the continuous tenses] to look or behave like an older member of your family, especially a parent ▶ **być podobnym do kogoś w rodzinie**

take sth apart to separate sth into the different parts it is made of ▶ **rozkładać na części**

take sth away 1 to cause a feeling, etc. to disappear: *These aspirins will take the pain away.* ▶ **usuwać 2** to buy cooked food at a restaurant, etc. and carry it out to eat somewhere else, for example at home ▶ **kupować posiłek na wynos** ➲ noun **takeaway**

take sb/sth away (from sb) to remove sb/sth: *She took the scissors away from the child.* ▶ **zabierać/odbierać (kogoś/coś komuś)**

T

take sth back **1** to return sth to the place that you got it from ▶ **oddawać, zwracać** ➲ note at **shopping** **2** to admit that sth you said was wrong ▶ **cofać** (*np. pomówienie*)
take sth down **1** to remove a structure by separating it into the pieces it is made of: *They took the tent down and started the journey home.* ▶ **rozbierać** **2** to write down sth that is said ▶ **notować**
take sb in **1** to invite sb who has no home to live with you: *Her parents were killed in a crash so she was taken in by her grandparents.* ▶ **przyjmować kogoś pod swój dach** **2** to make sb believe sth that is not true: *I was completely taken in by her story.* ▶ **nabierać (kogoś na coś)**
take sth in **1** to understand what you see, hear or read: *There was too much in the museum to take in at one go.* ▶ **zrozumieć, obejmować** (*np. umysłem*) **2** to make a piece of clothing narrower or tighter ▶ **zwężać** (*ubranie*) OPP **let sth out**
take off **1** (used about an aircraft) to leave the ground and start flying ▶ **startować** OPP **land** **2** (used about an idea, a product, etc.) to become successful or popular very quickly or suddenly ▶ (*przen.*) **chwycić, odnosić sukces**
take sb off to copy the way sb speaks or behaves in an amusing way ▶ **naśladować, parodiować**
take sth off **1** to remove sth, especially clothes: *Come in and take your coat off.* ▶ **zdejmować** OPP **put sth on** **2** to have the period of time mentioned as a holiday: *I'm going to take a week off.* ▶ **brać urlop**
take sb on to start to employ sb: *The firm is taking on new staff.* ▶ **zatrudniać kogoś**
take sth/sb on **1** to decide to do sth; to agree to be responsible for sth/sb: *I can't take on any extra work.* ◇ *We're not taking on any new clients at present.* ▶ **przyjmować coś/kogoś, brać coś na siebie** **2** (used about a bus, plane or ship) to allow sb/sth to enter: *The bus stopped to take on more passengers.* ▶ **zabierać coś/kogoś, nabierać czegoś**
take sb out to go out with sb you have invited (for a social occasion): *I'm taking Angela out for a meal tonight.* ▶ **zabierać kogoś** (*np. na przyjęcie*)
take sth out **1** to remove sth from inside your body: *He's having two teeth taken out.* ▶ **usuwać** (*np. ząb, wyrostek robaczkowy*) **2** to obtain a service: *to take out a mortgage/loan* ▶ **uzyskać** (*np. pożyczkę*)
take sth out (of sth) to remove sth from sth: *He took a notebook out of his pocket.* ◇ *I need to take some money out* (wypłacić pieniądze (z konta)) *of the bank.* ▶ **wyjmować coś (skądś)**
take it/sth out on sb to behave badly towards sb because you are angry or upset about sth, even though it is not this person's fault ▶ **wyładowywać się/coś (na kimś)**
take (sth) over (from sb) to get control of sth or responsibility for sth: *The firm is being taken over by a large company.* ◇ *Who's going to take over as assistant* (przejąć obowiązki asystenta) *when Tim leaves?* ▶ **przejmować** (*np. kontrolę nad czymś*)
take sb through sth to help sb learn or become familiar with sth, for example by talking about each part in turn: *The director took us through the play scene by scene.* ◇ *I still don't understand the contract. Can you take me through it again?* ▶ **zaznajamiać kogoś z czymś**
take to sb/sth to start liking sb/sth ▶ **polubić kogoś/coś**
take to sth/doing sth to begin doing sth regularly as a habit ▶ **nabierać zwyczaju robienia czegoś**
take sth up **1** to make sth such as a piece of clothing shorter: *The skirt needs taking up.* ▶ **skracać** (*ubranie*) OPP **let sth down** **2** to start doing sth regularly (for example as a hobby): *I've taken up yoga recently.* ▶ **zabrać się za coś, zainteresować się czymś, podjąć** (*np. hobby*)
take up sth to use or fill an amount of time or space: *All her time is taken up looking after the new baby.* ▶ **zajmować czas, pochłaniać** (*np. czas, energię*) SYN **occupy**
take sb up on sth **1** to say that you disagree with sth that sb has just said, and ask them to explain it: *I must take you up on that last point.* ▶ **zgłaszać zastrzeżenia wobec czyjejś wypowiedzi** **2** (informal) to accept an offer that sb has made: *'Come and stay with us any time.' 'We'll take you up on that!'* ▶ **trzymać za słowo**
take sth up with sb to ask or complain about sth: *I'll take the matter up with my MP.* ▶ **poruszać temat (z kimś); składać skargę u kogoś**

takeaway /ˈteɪkəweɪ/ (US **takeout** /ˈteɪkaʊt/, ˈcarry-out) noun [C] **1** a restaurant that sells food that you can eat somewhere else ▶ **restauracja oferująca potrawy na wynos** **2** the food that such a restaurant sells: *Let's have a takeaway.* ▶ **potrawy na wynos** ➲ note at **meal**

taken past participle of **take**

ˈ**take-off** noun [U,C] the moment when an aircraft leaves the ground and starts to fly: *The plane is ready for take-off.* ▶ **start** OPP **landing**

takeout (US) = TAKEAWAY

takeover /ˈteɪkəʊvə(r)/ noun [C] the act of taking control of sth: *They made a takeover bid for the company.* ◇ *a military takeover* (przewrót wojskowy) *of the government* ▶ **przejęcie**

takings /ˈteɪkɪŋz/ noun [pl.] the amount of money that a shop, theatre, etc. gets from selling goods, tickets, etc. ▶ **wpływy kasowe**

talcum powder /ˈtælkəm paʊdə(r)/ (also **talc** /tælk/) noun [U] a soft powder which smells nice. People often put it on their skin after a bath. ▶ **talk kosmetyczny**

tale /teɪl/ noun [C] **1** a story about events that are not real: *a fairy tale* bajka ▶ **(o)powiastka, baśń** **2** a report or description of sb/sth that may not be true: *I've heard tales of people seeing ghosts in that house.* ▶ **opowieść, bajda**

talent /ˈtælənt/ noun [C,U] **(a) talent (for sth)** a natural skill or ability: *She has a talent for painting.* ◇ *His work shows great talent.* ▶ **talent, zdolność**
■ **talented** adj.: *a talented musician* ▶ **utalentowany, zdolny**

🔑 **talk**[1] /tɔːk/ verb **1** [I] **talk (to/with sb) (about/of sb/sth)** to say things; to speak in order to give information or to express feelings, ideas, etc.: *I could hear them talking downstairs.* ◇ *Can I talk to you for a minute?* ◇ *Nasreen is not an easy person to talk to.* ◇ *We need to talk about the plans for the weekend.* ◇ *He's been talking of going to Australia for some time now.* ◇ *Dr Impey will be talking about Japanese Art in his lecture.* ▶ **rozmawiać, mówić** ➲ note at **speak** **2** [I,T] to discuss sth serious or important: *We can't go on like this. We need to talk.* ◇ *Could we **talk business** after dinner?* ▶ **rozmawiać** **3** [I] to discuss people's private lives: *His strange lifestyle and appearance started the local people talking.* ▶ **mówić, plotkować** SYN **gossip** **4** [I] to give information to sb, especially when you do not want to: *The police questioned him for hours but he refused to talk* (nie chciał nic powiedzieć). ▶ **mówić**
IDM **know what you are talking about** → KNOW[1]
speak/talk of the devil → DEVIL
talk sense to say things that are correct or sensible: *He's the only politician who talks any sense.* ▶ **mówić do rzeczy/z sensem**
talk shop to talk about your work with the people you work with, outside working hours ▶ **rozmawiać o sprawach zawodowych (poza pracą)**
PHR V **talk back (to sb)** to answer sb rudely, especially sb in authority ▶ **niegrzecznie odpowiadać (komuś)**

talk down to sb to talk to sb as if they are less intelligent or important than you ▶ **mówić (do kogoś) protekcjonalnie/z lekceważeniem**
talk sb into/out of doing sth to persuade sb to do/not to do sth: *She tried to talk him into buying a new car.* ▶ **namawiać (kogoś do czegoś)**; **wyperswadowywać (coś komuś)**
talk sth over (with sb) to discuss sth with sb, especially in order to reach an agreement or make a decision ▶ **przedyskutować coś (z kimś)**
talk sth through to discuss sth thoroughly until you are sure you understand it: *It sounds like a good idea but we'll need to talk it through.* ▶ **omawiać coś**

talk² /tɔːk/ noun **1** [C] **a talk (with sb) (about sth)** a conversation or discussion: *Charles and Anne had a long talk about the problem.* ▶ **rozmowa 2** (**talks**) [pl.] formal discussions between governments: *The Foreign Ministers of the two countries will meet for talks next week.* ◇ *arms/pay/peace talks* ▶ **rozmowy 3** [C] **a talk (on sth)** a formal speech on a particular subject: *He's giving a talk on 'Our changing world'.* ▶ **prelekcja**, **wykład** SYN **lecture 4** [U] (informal) things that people say that are not based on facts or reality: *He says he's going to resign but it's just talk.* ▶ **gadanie**, **(puste) słowa** ➲ look at **small talk**

talkative /ˈtɔːkətɪv/ adj. liking to talk a lot ▶ **rozmowny**, **gadatliwy**

ˈ**talk show** noun [C] **1** (especially US) : *a talk-show host* = CHAT SHOW **2** a television or radio programme in which a **presenter** introduces a particular topic which is then discussed by the audience ▶ **talk show**

tall /tɔːl/ adj. **1** (used about people or things) of more than average height; not short: *a tall young man* ◇ *a tall tree/tower/chimney* ◇ *Nick is taller than his brother.* ▶ **wysoki** OPP **short 2** (used to describe the height of sb/sth): *Claire is five feet tall.* Claire ma pięć stóp wzrostu. ◇ *How tall are you?* Jakiego jesteś wzrostu? ▶ **wysoki** ➲ noun **height**

> **Tall** i **high** mają podobne znaczenie. **Tall** używa się w celu opisania ludzkiego wzrostu: *He is six foot three inches tall*; wysokości drzew: *A tall oak tree stood in the garden*; a także często do określenia wąskich i wysokich przedmiotów: *the tall skyscrapers of Manhattan*. **High** używa się do opisania miary czegoś: *The fence is two metres high.* lub odległości w pionie: *a room with high ceilings*.

tally /ˈtæli/ noun [C] (pl. **-ies**) a record of the number or amount of sth, especially one that you can keep adding to: *He hopes to improve on his tally* (uzyskać lepszy wynik) *of three goals in the past nine games.* ◇ ***Keep a tally*** (prowadź rejestr) *of how much you spend while you're away.* ◇ *With 85% of the vote counted, unofficial tallies* (nieoficjalne wyniki) *showed Ramos leading his closest rivals.* ▶ **rejestrowanie**, (*sport*) **wynik**
■ **tally** verb (**tallies**; **tallying**; pt, pp **tallied**) **1** [I] **tally (with sth)** to be the same as or to match another person's account of sth, another set of figures, etc.: *Her report of what happened tallied exactly with the story of another witness.* ▶ **zgadzać się (z czymś)** SYN **match up (with sth) 2** [T] **tally sth (up)** to calculate the total number, cost, etc. of sth ▶ **obliczać**, **przeprowadzać kalkulację czegoś**

talon /ˈtælən/ noun [C] a long sharp curved nail on the feet of some birds, used to catch other animals for food ▶ **szpon**, **pazur** ➲ picture on **page A11**

tambourine /ˌtæmbəˈriːn/ noun [C] a musical instrument that has a round frame covered with plastic or skin, with small flat pieces of metal around the edge. To play it, you hit it or shake it with your hand. ▶ **tamburyn**

tame¹ /teɪm/ adj. **1** (used about animals or birds) not wild or afraid of people: *The birds are so tame they will eat from your hand.* ▶ **oswojony 2** boring; not interesting or exciting: *After the big city, you must find village life very tame.* ▶ **nudny**, **nijaki**

tame² /teɪm/ verb [T] to bring sth wild under your control; to make sth **tame** ▶ **oswajać**

tamper /ˈtæmpə(r)/ verb
PHR V **tamper with sth** to make changes to sth without permission, especially in order to damage it: *Don't eat the sweets if the packaging has been tampered with* (zostało naruszone). ▶ **dobierać się (do czegoś)**, **manipulować czymś**

tampon /ˈtæmpɒn/ noun [C] a piece of cotton material that a woman puts inside her body to absorb the blood that she loses once a month ▶ **tampon** ➲ look at **sanitary towel**

tan¹ /tæn/ verb [I,T] (**tanning**; **tanned**) (used about sb's skin) to become brown as a result of spending time in the sun: *Do you tan easily?* ▶ **opalać (się)**
■ **tanned** adj.: *You're looking very tanned – have you been on holiday?* ▶ **opalony**

tan² /tæn/ noun **1** [U] a colour between yellow and brown ▶ **kolor jasnobrązowy** (*naturalnej skóry*) **2** [C] = SUNTAN
■ **tan** adj. ▶ **koloru jasnobrązowego**

tandem /ˈtændəm/ noun [C] a bicycle with seats for two people, one behind the other ▶ (*rower*) **tandem**
IDM **in tandem (with sb/sth)** working together with sth/sb else; happening at the same time as sth else ▶ **w parze (z kimś/czymś)**; **jednocześnie (z czymś)**; **tandem**

tang /tæŋ/ noun [usually sing.] a sharp taste, flavour or smell: *a sauce with a tang of lemon juice* ▶ **wyrazisty smak**
■ **tangy** /ˈtæŋi/ adj. ▶ **kwaskowy**

tangent /ˈtændʒənt/ noun [C] a straight line that touches a curve but does not cross it ▶ **styczna**
IDM **go off at a tangent** (US) to suddenly start saying or doing sth that seems to have no connection with what has gone before ▶ **nagle zmieniać** (*np. temat*)

tangerine /ˌtændʒəˈriːn; US ˈtændʒəriːn/ noun **1** [C] a fruit like a small sweet orange with a skin that is easy to take off ▶ **rodzaj mandarynki 2** [U] a deep orange colour ▶ **kolor ciemnopomarańczowy**
■ **tangerine** adj. ▶ **ciemnopomarańczowy**

tangible /ˈtændʒəbl/ adj. that can be clearly seen to exist: *There are tangible benefits in the new system.* ▶ **namacalny**, **dotykalny**, **faktyczny** OPP **intangible**

tangle /ˈtæŋgl/ noun [C] a confused mass, especially of threads, hair, branches, etc. that cannot easily be separated from each other: *My hair's full of tangles.* ◇ *This string's **in a tangle**.* ▶ **kołtun**, **plątanina**
■ **tangled** adj.: *The wool was all tangled up.* ▶ **poplątany**, **skołtuniony**

tango /ˈtæŋgəʊ/ noun [C] (pl. **tangos** /-gəʊz/) a fast South American dance with a strong beat, in which two people hold each other closely; a piece of music for this dance ▶ **tango**
■ **tango** verb [I] (**tangoing**; **tangoes**; pt, pp **tangoed**) ▶ **tańczyć tango**

tank /tæŋk/ noun [C] **1** a container for holding liquids or gas; the amount that a tank will hold: *a water/fuel/petrol/fish tank* ◇ *We drove there and back on one tank of petrol.* ◇ *How many litres does the petrol tank* (bak) *hold?* ▶ **zbiornik**, **cysterna 2** a large, heavy military vehicle covered with strong metal and armed with guns, that moves on special wheels ▶ **czołg**

T

tanker /ˈtæŋkə(r)/ noun [C] a ship or lorry that carries oil, petrol, etc. in large amounts: *an oil tanker* ▶ **tankowiec**; **cysterna** ➲ picture on **page A6**

Tannoy™ /ˈtænɔɪ/ noun [C] a system used for giving spoken information in a public place: *They announced over the Tannoy* (przez megafon) *that our flight was delayed.* ▶ **system nagłaśniający**

tantalizing (also **-ising**) /ˈtæntəlaɪzɪŋ/ adj. making you want sth that you cannot have or do: *A tantalizing aroma of cooking was coming from the kitchen next door.* ▶ **pociągający**, **kuszący**
■ **tantalizingly** (also **-isingly**) adv. ▶ **dręcząco**, **pociągająco**

tantamount /ˈtæntəmaʊnt/ adj. [not before a noun] **tantamount to sth** equal in effect to sth ▶ **równoznaczny z czymś**, **sprowadzający się do czegoś**

tantrum /ˈtæntrəm/ noun [C] a sudden explosion of anger, especially by a child: *The little boy chose that moment to* ***throw a tantrum.*** Chłopczyk właśnie wtedy dostał napadu złości. ▶ **napad złości**

tap¹ /tæp/ verb (**tapping**; **tapped**) **1** [I,T] **tap (at/on sth)**; **tap sb/sth (on/with sth)** to touch or hit sb/sth quickly and lightly: *Their feet were tapping in time to the music.* ◇ *She tapped me on the shoulder.* ▶ **(lekko) stukać/pukać** **2** [I,T] **tap (into) sth** to make use of a source of energy, knowledge, etc. that already exists: *to tap the skills of young people* ▶ **wykorzystywać** (*zasoby*) **3** [T] to fit a device to sb's telephone so that their calls can be listened to secretly: *She was convinced that the police had tapped her phone.* ▶ **zakładać podsłuch telefoniczny**

tap² /tæp/ noun [C] **1** (US **faucet** /ˈfɔːsɪt/) a type of handle that you turn to let water, gas, etc. out of a pipe or container: *Turn the hot/cold tap on/off.* ▶ **kran**, **kurek** **2** a light hit with your hand or fingers: *a tap on the shoulder* ▶ **puknięcie**, **stuknięcie**, **pukanie** **3** a device that is fitted to sb's telephone so that their calls can be listened to secretly: *a phone tap* ▶ **podsłuch**

ˈtap dance noun [C] a style of dancing in which you tap the rhythm of the music with your feet, wearing special shoes with pieces of metal on them ▶ (*taniec*) **step**
■ **ˈtap dance** verb [I] ▶ **stepować**

tape¹ /teɪp/ noun **1** [U] a long thin band of plastic material used for recording sound, pictures or information: *I've got the whole concert* ***on tape.*** ▶ **taśma/kaseta magnetofonowa/magnetowidowa/magnetyczna** **2** [C] a small flat plastic case containing tape for playing or recording music or sound: *to rewind a tape* ◇ *a* ***blank*** (pusta) *tape* ◇ *We've made a tape* (nakręciliśmy film) *of the children playing in the garden.* ▶ **taśma magnetofonowa/magnetowidowa/magnetyczna** ➲ note at **cassette** **3** [U] a long narrow band of plastic, etc. with a sticky substance on one side that is used for sticking things together, covering electric wires, etc.: *sticky/adhesive tape* ▶ **taśma** ➲ look at **Sellotape** ➲ picture at **stationery** **4** [C,U] a narrow piece of cloth that is used for tying things together: *The papers were in a pile, bound with blue tape.* ▶ **tasiemka**, **wstążeczka** ➲ look at **red tape** **5** [C] a piece of material stretched across a race track to mark where the race finishes: *the finishing tape* ▶ **taśma**

tape² /teɪp/ verb [T] **1** to record sound, music, TV programmes, etc. using a **cassette** ▶ **nagrywać na taśmę**, **nakręcać** (*film*) **2** **tape sth (up)** to fasten sth by sticking or tying sth with **tape¹** (3) ▶ **przymocowywać taśmą klejącą**

ˈtape deck noun [C] the part of a hi-fi system on which you play tapes ▶ **magnetofon** (*bez wzmacniacza*)

ˈtape measure (also **ˈmeasuring tape**) noun [C] a long thin piece of plastic, cloth or metal with centimetres, etc. marked on it. It is used for measuring things. ▶ **taśma miernicza** ➲ look at **tape**

ˈtape recorder noun [C] a machine that is used for recording and playing sounds on tape ▶ **magnetofon**
■ **ˈtape recording** noun [C]: *We made a tape recording of the interview.* ▶ **nagranie na taśmę**

tapestry /ˈtæpəstri/ noun [C,U] (pl. **tapestries**) a piece of heavy cloth with pictures or designs sewn on it in coloured thread ▶ **gobelin**, **arras**

ˈtap water noun [U] water that comes through pipes and out of taps, not water sold in bottles ▶ **woda z kranu**

tar /tɑː(r)/ noun [U] **1** a thick black sticky liquid that becomes hard when it is cold. **Tar** is obtained from coal and is used for making roads, etc. ▶ **smoła** ➲ look at **Tarmac** **2** a similar substance formed by burning **tobacco**: *low-tar cigarettes* ▶ **substancja smolista** (*w papierosie*)

target¹ /ˈtɑːɡɪt/ noun [C] **1** a result that you try to achieve: *Our target is to finish the job by Friday.* ◇ *a target* (docelowa) *area/audience/group* ◇ *So far we're right* ***on target*** (dążymy prosto do wyznaczonego celu). ▶ **cel** **2** a person, place or thing that you try to hit when shooting or attacking: *Doors and windows are* ***an easy target*** *for burglars.* ▶ **cel** **3** a person or thing that people criticize, laugh at, etc.: *The education system has been the target of heavy criticism.* ▶ **cel** **4** an object, often a round board with circles on it, that you try to hit in shooting practice: *to aim at/hit/miss a target* ▶ **tarcza (strzelnicza)**

target² /ˈtɑːɡɪt/ verb [T, usually passive] **target sb/sth**; **target sth at/on sb/sth** to try to have an effect on a particular group of people; to try to attack sb/sth: *The advertising campaign is targeted at teenagers.* ▶ **obierać (kogoś/coś) za cel** (*np. działania, ataku*)

tariff /ˈtærɪf/ noun [C] **1** a tax that has to be paid on goods coming into a country ▶ **cło** **2** a list of prices, especially in a hotel ▶ **taryfa**

Tarmac™ /ˈtɑːmæk/ (also **blacktop** /ˈblæktɒp/) noun **1** [U] a black material used for making the surfaces of roads ▶ **rodzaj asfaltowej nawierzchni drogowej** ➲ look at **tar** **2** (**the tarmac**) [sing.] an area covered with a **Tarmac** surface, especially at an airport ▶ **nawierzchnia pokryta tarmakadamem**

tarnish /ˈtɑːnɪʃ/ verb **1** [I,T] (used about metal, etc.) to become or to make sth less bright and shiny ▶ **matowieć**; **czynić matowym** **2** [T] to spoil the good opinion people have of sb/sth ▶ **plamić/szargać reputację**

tarpaulin /tɑːˈpɔːlɪn/ noun [C,U] strong material that water cannot pass through, which is used for covering things to protect them from the rain ▶ **brezent**

tart¹ /tɑːt/ noun **1** [C,U] an open **pie** filled with sweet food such as fruit or jam ▶ **ciasto/placek z owocami** ➲ note at **pie** **2** [C] (Brit., informal) a woman who dresses or behaves in a way that people think is immoral ▶ **dziwka**

tart² /tɑːt/ verb
PHR V **tart sb/sth up** (Brit., informal) to decorate and improve the appearance of sb/sth ▶ **odstawiać (się)**

tartan /ˈtɑːtn/ noun [U,C] **1** a traditional Scottish pattern of coloured squares and lines that cross each other ▶ **wzór szkockiej kraty** **2** cloth made from wool with this pattern on it ▶ **materiał w szkocką kratę**

task /tɑːsk; US tæsk/ noun [C] a piece of work that has to be done, especially an unpleasant or difficult one: *Your first task will be to type these letters.* ◇ *to perform/carry out/undertake a task* ▶ **zadanie**, **przedsięwzięcie**

tassel /ˈtæsl/ noun [C] a bunch of threads that are tied together at one end and hang from curtains, clothes, etc. as a decoration ▶ **frędzel**

taste¹ /teɪst/ noun **1** [sing.] the particular quality of different foods or drinks that allows you to recognize them when you put them in your mouth; flavour: *I don't like* *the taste of this coffee.* ◇ *a sweet/bitter/sour/salty taste* ◇ *taste buds* kubki smakowe ▶ **smak** **2** [U] the ability to recognize the flavour of food or drink: *I've got such a bad cold that I seem to have lost my sense of taste.* ▶ **zmysł smaku** **3** [C, usually sing.] **a taste (of sth)** a small amount of sth to eat or drink that you have in order to see what it is like: *Have a taste of* (spróbuj) *this cheese to see if you like it.* ▶ **odrobina** **4** [sing.] a short experience of sth: *That was my **first taste** of success.* ▶ (*przen.*) **smak** **5** [U] the ability to decide if things are suitable, of good quality, etc.: *He has excellent **taste in** music.* ▶ **wyczucie**, **gust** **6** [sing.] **a taste (for sth)** what a person likes or prefers: *She has developed a taste for modern art.* ▶ **smak**

IDM **(be) in bad, poor, etc. taste** (used about sb's behaviour) (to be) unpleasant and not suitable: *Some of his comments were in very bad taste.* ▶ **(być) w złym guście**

taste[2] /teɪst/ verb **1** [I] **taste (of sth)** to have a particular flavour: *The pudding tasted of oranges.* ◇ *to taste sour/sweet/delicious* ▶ **mieć smak (czegoś)**, **smakować** **2** [T] to notice or recognize the flavour of food or drink: *Can you taste the garlic in this soup?* ▶ **czuć/rozpoznawać smak** ➲ note at **can**[1] (2) **3** [T] to try a small amount of food and drink; to test the flavour of sth: *Can I taste a piece of that cheese to see what it's like?* ▶ **kosztować**, **próbować** ➲ note at **feel**

'taste bud noun [usually pl.] one of the small structures on the tongue that allow you to recognize the flavours of food and drink ▶ **kubek smakowy**

tasteful /'teɪstfl/ adj. (used especially about clothes, furniture, decorations, etc.) attractive and well chosen ▶ **w dobrym guście** OPP **tasteless**

■ **tastefully** /-fəli/ adv. ▶ **gustownie**

tasteless /'teɪstləs/ adj. **1** having little or no flavour: *This sauce is rather tasteless.* ▶ **bez gustu** OPP **tasty** **2** likely to offend people: *His joke about the funeral was particularly tasteless.* ▶ **w złym guście**, **bez wyczucia** **3** (used especially about clothes, furniture, decorations, etc.) not attractive; not well chosen ▶ **niesmaczny** OPP **tasteful**

tasty /'teɪsti/ adj. (**tastier**; **tastiest**) having a good flavour: *spaghetti with a tasty sauce* ▶ **smaczny**, **smakowity**

tattered /'tætəd/ adj. old and torn; in bad condition: *a tattered coat* ▶ **w strzępach**

tatters /'tætəz/ noun

IDM **in tatters** badly torn or damaged: *Her dress was in tatters.* ▶ **w strzępach**

tattoo /tə'tuː; US tæ-/ noun [C] (pl. **tattoos**) a picture or pattern that is marked permanently on sb's skin ▶ **tatuaż**

■ **tattoo** verb [T] (**tattooing**; **tattoos**; pt, pp **tattooed**): *She had a butterfly tattooed on her back.* ▶ **tatuować**

tatty /'tæti/ adj. (**tattier**; **tattiest**) (informal) in bad condition: *tatty old clothes* ▶ **sfatygowany**

taught past tense, past participle of **teach**

taunt /tɔːnt/ verb [T] to try to make sb angry or upset by saying unpleasant or cruel things ▶ **szydzić**

■ **taunt** noun [C] ▶ **szyderstwo**

Taurus /'tɔːrəs/ noun [C,U] the 2nd sign of the **zodiac**, the Bull; a person born under this sign: *I'm a Taurus* ▶ **Byk**; **zodiakalny Byk**

taut /tɔːt/ adj. (used about rope, wire, etc.) stretched very tight; not loose ▶ **naprężony**

tavern /'tævən/ noun [C] (old-fashioned) a pub ▶ **tawerna**

tawdry /'tɔːdri/ adj. **1** intended to be bright and attractive but cheap and of low quality: *tawdry jewellery* ▶ **tandetny** **2** involving low moral standards; extremely unpleasant or offensive: *a tawdry affair* ▶ **brudny** (*moralnie*), **odrażający**

■ **tawdriness** noun [U] ▶ **jarmarczność**; **brud** (*moralny*)

tax /tæks/ noun [C,U] **(a) tax (on sth)** the money that you have to pay to the government so that it can provide public services: ***income tax*** ◇ ***direct/indirect tax*** ◇ *There used to be a tax on windows.* ◇ *the tax office* urząd skarbowy ▶ **podatek**

■ **tax** verb [T, often passive]: *Alcohol, cigarettes and petrol are heavily taxed.* ▶ **opodatkowywać**

taxable /'tæksəbl/ adj. on which you have to pay tax: *taxable income* ▶ **podlegający opodatkowaniu**

taxation /tæk'seɪʃn/ noun [U] **1** the amount of money that people have to pay in tax: *to increase/reduce taxation* ◇ *high/low taxation* ▶ **opodatkowanie** **2** the system by which a government takes money from people so that it can pay for public services: *direct/indirect taxation* ▶ **opodatkowanie**

'tax avoidance noun [U] ways of paying only the smallest amount of tax that you legally have to ▶ **unikanie płacenia podatku** ➲ look at **tax evasion**

ˌtax-de'ductible adj. (used about costs) that can be taken off your income before the amount of tax that you have to pay is calculated ▶ **odliczany od podatku**

'tax evasion noun [U] the crime of deliberately not paying all the taxes that you should pay ▶ **uchylanie się od płacenia podatków** ➲ look at **tax avoidance**

ˌtax-'free adj. on which you do not have to pay tax: *a tax-free allowance* ▶ **wolny od podatku** ➲ look at **duty-free**

taxi[1] /'tæksi/ (also **taxicab** /'tæksikæb/ especially US **cab**) noun [C] (pl. **taxis**) a car with a driver whose job is to take you somewhere in exchange for money: *Shall we go by bus or **get/take a taxi**?* ▶ **taksówka**

> You **hail** a taxi to stop it so that you can get in. The amount of money that you have to pay (your **fare**) is shown on a **meter**. ➲ picture on **page A7**

taxi[2] /'tæksi/ (**taxiing**; **taxies**; pt, pp **taxied**) verb [I] (used about an aircraft) to move slowly along the ground before or after flying ▶ **kołować**

taxing /'tæksɪŋ/ adj. difficult; needing a lot of effort: *a taxing exam* ▶ **wyczerpujący**, **wystawiający na próbę**

'taxi rank noun [C] a place where taxis park while they are waiting for customers ▶ **postój taksówek**

taxpayer /'tækspeɪə(r)/ noun [C] a person who pays tax to the government, especially on the money that they earn ▶ **podatnik**

'tax return noun [C] an official document in which you give details of the amount of money that you have earned so that the government can calculate how much tax you have to pay ▶ **zeznanie podatkowe**

'tax year (Brit.) = FINANCIAL YEAR

TB = TUBERCULOSIS

tbsp = TABLESPOON (2): *Add 3 tbsp sugar.*

tea /tiː/ noun **1** [U] the dried leaves of the tea plant: *a packet of tea* ◇ *Do you drink tea?* ▶ **herbata** ℹ Z wyrażeniem **a cup of tea** używa się zwykle czasownika **have**, a nie **drink**: *I had three cups of tea this morning.* **2** [C,U] a hot drink made by pouring boiling water onto the dried leaves of the tea plant or of some other plants; a cup of this drink: *a cup/pot of tea* ◇ *weak/strong tea* ◇ *herb/mint/camomile tea* ◇ *Three teas and one coffee, please.* ▶ **herbata** ➲ picture on **page A14** **3** [C,U] (especially Brit.) a small afternoon meal of **sandwiches**, cakes, etc. and tea to drink, or a cooked meal eaten at 5 or 6 o'clock: *The kids have their tea as soon as they get home from school.* ▶ **podwieczorek**, **herbatka**, **kolacja** ➲ note at **meal**, **dinner**

IDM **not sb's cup of tea** → CUP[1]

'tea bag noun [C] a small paper bag with tea leaves in it, that you use for making tea ▶ **torebka herbaty**

T

teach /tiːtʃ/ verb (pt, pp **taught** /tɔːt/) **1** [I,T] **teach sb (sth/to do sth); teach sth (to sb)** to give sb lessons or instructions so that they know how to do sth: *My mother taught me to play the piano.* ◇ *He is teaching us how to use the computer.* ◇ *Jeremy teaches English to foreign students.* ◇ *I teach in a primary school.* ▶ **uczyć 2** [T] to make sb believe sth or behave in a certain way: *The story teaches us that history often repeats itself.* ◇ *My parents taught me always to tell the truth.* ▶ **uczyć, nauczać 3** [T] to make sb have a bad experience so that they are careful not to do the thing that caused it again: *A week in prison? That'll teach him to drink and drive!* ▶ **nauczyć kogoś, aby czegoś nie robił**

IDM **teach sb a lesson** to make sb have a bad experience so that they will not do the thing that caused it again ▶ **dawać komuś nauczkę**

teacher /ˈtiːtʃə(r)/ noun [C] a person whose job is to teach, especially in a school or college: *He's a teacher at a primary school.* ◇ *a chemistry/music teacher* ▶ **nauczyciel/ka** ➲ note at **school** ➲ look at **head** ➲ picture on **page A4**

teaching /ˈtiːtʃɪŋ/ noun **1** [U] the work of a teacher: *My son went into teaching.* ◇ *teaching methods* ▶ **nauczanie, zawód nauczyciela 2** [C, usually pl.] ideas and beliefs that are taught by sb/sth: *the teachings of Gandhi* ▶ **nauki**

'tea cloth = TEA TOWEL

teacup /ˈtiːkʌp/ noun [C] a cup that you drink tea from ▶ **filiżanka do herbaty**

teak /tiːk/ noun [U] the strong hard wood of a tall Asian tree, used for making furniture ▶ **tek, drzewo tekowe**

'tea leaves noun [pl.] the small leaves that are left in a cup after you have drunk the tea ▶ **listki herbaty**

team[1] /tiːm/ noun [C, with sing. or pl. verb] **1** a group of people who play a sport or game together against another group: *a football team* ◇ *Are you **in/on the team**?* ▶ **drużyna, zespół 2** a group of people who work together: *a team of doctors* ▶ **zespół** ℹ Jeżeli słowo **team** występuje w lp, następujący po nim czasownik może mieć formę lp lub lm: *The team play/plays two matches every week.*

team[2] /tiːm/ verb

PHR V **team up (with sb)** to join sb in order to do sth together: *I teamed up with Irena to plan the project.* ▶ **łączyć siły/się (z kimś)**

teamwork /ˈtiːmwɜːk/ noun [U] the ability of people to work together: *Teamwork is a key feature of the training programme.* ▶ **praca zespołowa, współpraca**

teapot /ˈtiːpɒt/ noun [C] a container that you use for making tea in and for serving it ▶ **imbryczek** ➲ picture at **pot**, picture on **page A14**

tear[1] /tɪə(r)/ noun [C, usually pl.] a drop of water that comes from your eye when you are crying, etc.: *I was **in tears** at the end of the film.* ◇ *The little girl **burst into tears*** (wybuchnęła płaczem). ▶ **łza**

IDM **shed tears** → SHED[2]

tear[2] /teə(r)/ verb (pt **tore** /tɔː(r)/, pp **torn** /tɔːn/) **1** [T,I] to damage sth by pulling it apart or into pieces; to become damaged in this way: *I tore my shirt on that nail.* ◇ *She tore the letter in half.* ◇ *I tore a page out* (wydarłem kartkę) *of my notebook.* ◇ *This material doesn't tear easily.* ▶ **drzeć (się), rwać (się)** SYN **rip 2** [T] to make a hole in sth by force: *The explosion tore a hole in the wall.* ▶ **wydzierać** (*dziurę*) SYN **rip 3** [T] to remove sth by pulling violently and quickly: *Paul tore the poster down from the wall.* ◇ *He tore the bag out of her hands.* ▶ **zrywać, wyrywać** SYN **rip 4** [I] **tear along, up, down, past, etc.** to move very quickly in a particular direction: *An ambulance went tearing past.* ▶ **pędzić**

■ **tear** noun [C]: *You've got a tear in the back of your trousers.* ▶ **rozdarcie**

IDM **wear and tear** → WEAR[2]

PHR V **tear sth apart 1** to pull sth violently into pieces: *The bird was torn apart by the two dogs.* ▶ **rozdzierać, rozszarpywać 2** to destroy sth completely: *The country has been torn apart by the war.* ▶ **niszczyć, rozdzierać**

tear yourself away (from sb/sth) to make yourself leave sb/sth or stop doing sth ▶ **odrywać się (od kogoś/czegoś)**

be torn between A and B to find it difficult to choose between two things or people ▶ **być w rozterce między jednym a drugim**

tear sth down (used about a building) to destroy it: *They tore down the old houses and built a shopping centre.* ▶ **burzyć**

tear sth up to pull sth into pieces, especially sth made of paper: *'I hate this photograph,' she said, tearing it up.* ▶ **drzeć, rwać na kawałki**

tear duct /ˈtɪə dʌkt/ noun [C] a tube through which tears pass from the tear **glands** to the eye, or from the eye to the nose ▶ **kanalik łzowy**

tearful /ˈtɪəfl/ adj. crying or nearly crying ▶ **zapłakany; płaczliwy, łzawy**

tear gas /ˈtɪə gæs/ noun [U] a type of gas that hurts the eyes and throat, and is used by the police, etc. to control large groups of people ▶ **gaz łzawiący**

tear jerker /ˈtɪə dʒɜːkə(r)/ noun [C] (informal) a film, story, etc. that is designed to make people feel sad ▶ **wyciskacz łez**

'tea room (also **'tea shop**) noun [C] (Brit.) a small restaurant which serves tea, coffee, etc., and also cakes and light meals ▶ **herbaciarnia**

tease /tiːz/ verb [I,T] to laugh at sb either in a friendly way or in order to upset them: *Don't pay any attention to those boys. They're only teasing.* ◇ *They teased her about being fat.* ▶ **drażnić, droczyć się**

teaspoon /ˈtiːspuːn/ noun [C] **1** a small spoon used for putting sugar in tea, coffee, etc. ▶ **łyżeczka do herbaty 2** (also **teaspoonful** /-fʊl/) (abbr. **tsp**) the amount that a teaspoon can hold ▶ **(pełna) łyżeczka do herbaty**

teat /tiːt/ noun [C] **1** (US **nipple**) the soft rubber part at the end of a baby's bottle ▶ **smoczek 2** one of the parts of a female animal's body that the young animals suck in order to get milk ▶ (*u wymion zwierząt*) **cycek** ➲ look at **nipple**

'tea towel (also **'tea cloth**) noun [C] (US **dishtowel** /ˈdɪʃtaʊəl/) a small piece of cloth that is used for drying plates, knives, forks, etc. ▶ **ścierka do naczyń** (*do osuszania naczyń*)

'tea tree noun [C] a small Australian and New Zealand tree. The oil from its leaves can be used to treat wounds and skin problems. ▶ **drzewo herbaciane**

technical /ˈteknɪkl/ adj. **1** connected with the practical use of machines, methods, etc. in science and industry: *The train was delayed due to a technical problem.* ▶ **techniczny, fachowy 2** connected with the skills involved in a particular activity or subject: *This computer magazine is too technical for me.* ▶ **techniczny 3** [only before a noun] relating to a particular subject: *the technical terms connected with computers* ▶ **fachowy, techniczny**

'technical college noun [C] a college where students can study mainly practical subjects ▶ **uczelnia techniczna**

technicality /ˌteknɪˈkæləti/ noun [C] (pl. **technicalities**) one of the details of a particular subject or activity ▶ **szczegół techniczny/fachowy**

technically /ˈteknɪkli/ adv. **1** according to the exact meaning, facts, etc.: *Technically, you should pay by August 1st, but it doesn't matter if it's a few days late.* ▶ **formalnie/technicznie rzecz biorąc 2** (used about sb's practical ability in a particular activity): *He's a technically brilliant dancer.* ▶ **technicznie 3** in a way that involves detailed knowledge of the machines, etc. that are used in industry or science: *The country is technically* (w zakresie wiedzy fachowej) *not very advanced.* ▶ **technicznie**

technician /tek'nɪʃn/ noun [C] a person whose work involves practical skills, especially in industry or science: *a laboratory technician* ▶ **technik**

technique /tek'ni:k/ noun **1** [C] a particular way of doing sth: *new techniques for teaching languages* ◇ *marketing/management techniques* ▶ **technika**, **sposób** **2** [U] the practical skill that sb has in a particular activity: *He's a naturally talented runner, but he needs to work on his technique.* ▶ **technika**

technology /tek'nɒlədʒi/ noun [C,U] (pl. **technologies**) the scientific knowledge and/or equipment that is needed for a particular industry, etc.: *developments in computer technology* ▶ **technika**, **technologia**
■ **technological** /ˌteknə'lɒdʒɪkl/ adj.: *technological developments* ▶ **techniczny**, **technologiczny** | **technologist** /tek'nɒlədʒɪst/ noun [C]: *Technologists are developing a computer that can perform surgery.* ▶ **technolog**

'**teddy bear** /'tedi beə(r)/ (also **teddy** pl. **teddies**) noun [C] a toy for children that looks like a bear ▶ **miś** (*pluszowy*)

tedious /'ti:diəs/ adj. boring and lasting for a long time: *a tedious train journey* ▶ **długi**, **nudny**, **nużący** SYN **boring**

teem /ti:m/ verb [I] **teem with sth** (used about a place) to have a lot of people or things moving about in it: *The streets were teeming with people.* ▶ **roić się**; **obfitować**

teenage /'ti:neɪdʒ/ adj. [only before a noun] **1** between 13 and 19 years old: *teenage children* ▶ **nastoletni** **2** typical of or suitable for people between 13 and 19 years old: *teenage magazines/fashion* ▶ **dla nastolatków**

teenager /'ti:neɪdʒə(r)/ noun [C] a person aged between 13 and 19 years old: *The band's music is very popular with teenagers.* ▶ **nastolat-ek/ka** ➲ look at **adolescent**

teens /ti:nz/ noun [pl.] the years of a person's life when they are between 13 and 19 years old: *She began writing poetry **in her teens*** (kiedy była nastolatką). ◇ *to be **in your** early/late **teens*** mieć dopiero kilkanaście/prawie dwadzieścia lat ▶ **„naście" lat**, **wiek dojrzewania** (*od 13 do 19 lat*)

'**tee shirt** = T-SHIRT

teeth plural of **tooth**

teethe /ti:ð/ verb [I] [usually in the *-ing* forms] (used about a baby) to start growing its first teeth ▶ **ząbkować**

'**teething troubles** (also '**teething problems**) noun [pl.] the problems that can develop when a person, system, etc. is new: *We've just installed this new software and are having a few teething troubles with it.* ▶ **początkowe trudności**

teetotal /ˌti:'təʊtl/ adj. [not before a noun] (used about a person) never drinking alcohol: *Simon is teetotal* (jest abstynentem). ▶ **nie używający napojów alkoholowych**
■ **teetotaller** (US **teetotaler**) /-'təʊtlə(r)/ noun [C] ▶ **abstynent/ka** ➲ look at **alcoholic**

TEFL /'tefl/ abbr. **Teaching English as a Foreign Language** ▶ **nauka języka angielskiego jako języka obcego**

tel. abbr. **telephone** (number): *tel. 01865 556767* ▶ **tel.**

telecast /'telikɑ:st; US -kæst/ noun [C] (especially US) a broadcast on television ▶ **program telewizyjny**
■ **telecast** verb [T] (**telecast**; **telecast**) [usually passive] ▶ **nadawać w telewizji**

telecommunications /ˌtelikəˌmju:nɪ'keɪʃnz/ noun [pl.] the technology of sending signals, images and messages over long distances by radio, telephone, TV, etc. ▶ **telekomunikacja**

telegram /'telɪgræm/ noun [C] a message that is sent by a system that uses electrical signals and that is then printed and given to sb ▶ **telegram**

telegraph /'telɪgrɑ:f; US -græf/ noun [U] a method of sending messages over long distances, using wires that carry electrical signals ▶ **telegraf**

'**telegraph pole** noun [C] a tall wooden pole that is used for supporting telephone wires ▶ **słup telegraficzny**

telemarketing = TELESALES

telepathy /tə'lepəθi/ noun [U] the communication of thoughts between people's minds without using speech, writing or other normal methods ▶ **telepatia**

telephone /'telɪfəʊn/ (also informal **phone**) noun **1** [U] an electrical system for talking to sb in another place by speaking into a special piece of equipment: *Can I contact you **by telephone**?* ◇ *to **make a phone call*** ◇ *What's your **telephone number**?* ▶ **telefon** ℹ Częściej używa się słowa **phone**, zwł. w języku mówionym. **2** [C] the piece of equipment that you use when you talk to sb by telephone: *Could I use your telephone?* ◇ *a mobile phone* ◇ *Where's the nearest public telephone* (automat telefoniczny)*?* ▶ **telefon**
■ **telephone** (also **phone**) verb [I,T] ▶ **dzwonić**
IDM **on the phone/telephone** → PHONE

using the telephone

When you **call** sb or **phone** sb (not ~~*to sb*~~), his/her phone **rings** and he/she **answers** it. Sometimes the phone is **engaged** (US **busy**) or there is **no answer**. You might need to **leave a message**, either on an **answering machine**, or with sb else: *Could you please ask her to call me back?* Introduce yourself by saying **It's...** or **This is...** (not ~~*Here is...*~~). If you phone sb by mistake, you can say: *I'm sorry, I've **dialled the wrong number**.* The number that you dial before the telephone number if you are telephoning a different area or country is called the **code**: *What's the code for Spain?* When you finish speaking you **put the phone down/hang up**. You can use a telephone line to send a copy of a letter, etc. using a **fax machine**.

'**telephone booth** = PHONE BOOTH

'**telephone box** (also '**phone box**; '**call box**) noun [C] a small covered place in a street, etc. that contains a telephone for public use ▶ **budka telefoniczna**

'**telephone directory** (also '**phone book**) noun [C] a book that gives a list of the names, addresses and telephone numbers of the people in a particular area ▶ **książka telefoniczna**

'**telephone exchange** (also **exchange**) noun [C] a place belonging to a telephone company where telephone lines are connected to each other ▶ **centrala telefoniczna**

telephonist (Brit.) = OPERATOR

telephoto lens /ˌtelifəʊtəʊ 'lenz/ noun [C] a camera **lens** that produces a large image of an object that is far away and allows you to take photographs of it ▶ **teleobiektyw**

teleprompter (especially US) = AUTOCUE

telesales /'teliseɪlz/ (also **telemarketing** /'telimɑ:kɪtɪŋ/) noun [U] a method of selling things by telephone: *He works in telesales.* ▶ **zakupy przez telefon**

telescope /'telɪskəʊp/ noun [C] an instrument in the shape of a tube with special glass inside it. You look through it to make things that are far away appear bigger and nearer. ▶ **teleskop**

teleshopping /'telifɒpɪŋ/ noun [U] shopping that is done using the telephone or television ▶ **telezakupy**

teletext /ˈtelitekst/ noun [U] a service that provides news and other information in written form on TV ▶ **telegazeta**

telethon /ˈteləθɒn/ noun [C] a very long television show, broadcast to raise money for charity ▶ **wielogodzinna akcja charytatywna w telewizji**

televise /ˈtelɪvaɪz/ verb [T] to show sth on TV: *a televised concert* ▶ **nadawać w telewizji**

television /ˈtelɪvɪʒn/ (also **TV** /ˌtiː ˈviː/) (Brit., informal **telly** /ˈteli/, pl. **tellies**) noun **1** (also **ˈtelevision set**) [C] a piece of electrical equipment with a screen on which you can watch programmes with moving pictures and sounds: *a colour television* ◇ *to switch/turn the television on/off* ▶ **telewizor 2** [U] the programmes that are shown on a television set: *Paul's watching television.* ▶ **telewizja 3** [U] the system, process or business of sending out television programmes: *a television presenter/series/documentary* ◇ *cable/satellite/digital television* ◇ *She works in television.* ▶ **telewizja**

IDM **on television** being shown by television; appearing in a television programme: *What's on television tonight?* ▶ **w telewizji** ➲ look at **media**

> **television**
>
> If you have **digital** or **satellite TV**, you can watch **programmes** on lots of different **channels**. You use the **remote control** to change channels without having to leave your seat. **Independent** TV channels have a lot of **commercials/adverts**. They **broadcast** programmes that get good **ratings**. These include **dramas**, **quiz programmes** and **soap operas**. A TV **serial** has a number of **episodes** which tell one story over a period of time.

teleworker /ˈteliwɜːkə(r)/ noun [C] a person who works from home and communicates with his/her office, customers and others by telephone ▶ **osoba pracująca w domu** (*kontaktująca się z firmą przez telefon/e-mail*)

telex /ˈteleks/ noun **1** [U] a system of sending written messages using special machines. The message is typed on a machine in one place, and then sent by telephone to a machine in another place, which immediately prints it out. ▶ **teleks 2** [C] a machine for sending out such messages; a message that is sent or received by telex ▶ **teleks** ➲ look at **fax**

tell /tel/ verb (pt, pp **told** /təʊld/) **1** [T] **tell sb (sth/that ...)**; **tell sb (about sth)**; **tell sth to sb** to give information to sb by speaking or writing: *She told me her address but I've forgotten it.* ◇ *He wrote to tell me that his mother had died.* ◇ *Tell us about your holiday.* ◇ *to* ***tell the truth/a lie*** ◇ *He tells* (opowiada) *that story to everyone he sees.* ◇ *Excuse me, could you tell me where the station is?* ▶ **powiedzieć**, **mówić**, **informować** ➲ note at **say 2** [T] (used about a thing) to give information to sb: *This book will tell you all you need to know.* ▶ **dostarczać informacji 3** [I] to not keep a secret: *Promise you won't tell!* ▶ **zdradzić** (*sekret*) **4** [T] **tell sb to do sth** to order or advise sb to do sth: *The policewoman told us to get out of the car.* ▶ **powiedzieć**, **kazać**, **poradzić 5** [I,T] to know, see or judge (sth) correctly: *'What do you think Jenny will do next?'* ***'It's hard to tell.'*** ◇ *I could tell* (widziałem) *that he had enjoyed the evening.* ◇ ***You can never tell*** *what he's going to say next.* ◇ *I can't* ***tell the difference between*** *Dan's sisters.* ◇ ***There's no telling*** (nigdy nie wiadomo) *what time Jan will arrive.* ▶ **powiedzieć**, **wiedzieć**, **orientować się 6** [I] **tell (on sb/sth)** to have a noticeable effect: *I can't run as fast as I could – my age is beginning to tell* (być widoczny)*!* ▶ **mieć widoczny skutek**

IDM **all told** with everyone or everything counted and included ▶ **w sumie**

(I'll) tell you what (informal) (used to introduce a suggestion): *I'll tell you what – let's ask Diane to take us.* ▶ **posłuchaj**

I told you so (informal) I warned you that this would happen: *'I missed the bus.' 'I told you so. I said you needed to leave earlier.'* ▶ **mówiłem ci, że tak będzie**

tell A and B apart to see the difference between A and B: *It's very difficult to tell Tom and James apart.* ▶ **odróżniać (od siebie)**

tell the time to read the time from a clock or watch ▶ **podawać czas**

PHR V **tell sb off (for sth/for doing sth)** to speak to sb angrily because they have done sth wrong: *The teacher told me off for not doing my homework.* ▶ **ganić**

tell on sb to tell a parent, teacher, etc. about sth bad that sb has done ▶ **skarżyć na kogoś**

telling /ˈtelɪŋ/ adj. **1** having a great effect: *That's quite a telling argument.* ▶ **skuteczny 2** showing, without intending to, what sb/sth is really like: *The number of homeless people is a telling comment on today's society.* ▶ **wymowny**

telltale /ˈtelteɪl/ adj. [only before a noun] giving information about sth secret or private: *He said he was fine, but there were telltale signs of worry on his face.* ▶ **zdradzający**

telly (Brit., informal) = TELEVISION

temp /temp/ noun [C] (informal) a temporary employee, especially in an office, who works somewhere for a short period of time when sb else is ill or on holiday ▶ **pracownik (zwł. biurowy) zatrudniony tymczasowo**

■ **temp** verb [I] ▶ **pracować jako pracownik zatrudniony tymczasowo**

temp. = TEMPERATURE: *temp. 15 °C*

temper /ˈtempə(r)/ noun **1** [C,U] if you have a **temper**, you get angry very easily: *Be careful of Paul. He's got quite a temper!* ◇ *You must learn to control your temper* (panować nad sobą). ▶ **gwałtowny charakter**, **wybuchy złości 2** [C] the way you are feeling at a particular time: *It's no use talking to him when he's* ***in a bad temper.*** ▶ **humor** SYN **mood**

IDM **in a temper** feeling very angry and not controlling your behaviour ▶ **rozzłoszczony**

keep your temper to stay calm ▶ **zachowywać spokój**

lose your temper to become angry ▶ **złościć się** ➲ look at **bad-tempered**

temperament /ˈtemprəmənt/ noun [C,U] sb's character, especially as it affects the way they behave and feel: *to have an artistic/a fiery/a calm temperament* ▶ **usposobienie** SYN **disposition**

temperamental /ˌtemprəˈmentl/ adj. often and suddenly changing the way you behave or feel: *a temperamental character* ▶ **ulegający nastrojom**, **wybuchowy**

temperate /ˈtempərət/ adj. (used about a climate) not very hot and not very cold ▶ **umiarkowany**

temperature /ˈtemprətʃə(r)/ noun (abbr. **temp.**) **1** [C,U] how hot or cold sth is: *Heat the oven to a temperature of 200° C.* ◇ *a high/low temperature* ◇ *an increase in temperature* ▶ **temperatura** ➲ note at **cold 2** [C] how hot or cold sb's body is ▶ **temperatura** (*ciała*)

IDM **have a temperature** to be hotter than normal because you are ill ▶ **mieć gorączkę** ➲ look at **fever**

take sb's temperature to measure the temperature of sb's body with a **thermometer** ▶ **mierzyć komuś temperaturę**

template /ˈtempleɪt/ noun [C] a piece of card, metal or thin wood that is made in a particular shape and used as a guide for cutting metal, stone, wood, cloth, etc. ▶ **szablon**, **forma**

temple /ˈtempl/ noun [C] **1** a building where people worship: *a Buddhist/Hindu temple* ▶ **świątynia 2** one of the flat parts on each side of your head, at the same level as your eyes and higher ▶ **skroń** ➲ picture at **body**

tempo /ˈtempəʊ/ noun (pl. **tempos** /ˈtempəʊz/) **1** [C,U] the speed of a piece of music: *a fast/slow tempo* ▶ **tempo** **2** [sing., U] the speed of an activity or event ▶ **tempo**

⚷ **temporary** /ˈtemprəri; US -pəreri/ adj. lasting for a short time: *a temporary job* ◇ *This arrangement is only temporary.* ▶ **tymczasowy, prowizoryczny** OPP **permanent**
■ **temporarily** /ˈtemprərəli; US -pəˈrerəli/ adv. ▶ **tymczasowo, prowizorycznie**

tempt /tempt/ verb [T] **tempt sb (into sth/into doing sth)**; **tempt sb (to do sth)** to try to persuade or attract sb to do sth, even if it is wrong: *His dream of riches had tempted him into a life of crime.* ◇ *She was tempted to stay in bed all day.* ▶ **kusić**

temptation /tempˈteɪʃn/ noun **1** [U] a feeling that you want to do sth, even if you know that it is wrong: *I managed to **resist the temptation** to tell him what I really thought.* ◇ *She wanted a cigarette badly, but didn't **give in to temptation**.* ▶ **pokusa** **2** [C] a thing that attracts you to do sth wrong or silly: *All that money is certainly a big temptation.* ▶ **pokusa**

tempting /ˈtemptɪŋ/ adj. attractive in a way that makes you want to do or have sth: *a tempting offer* ▶ **kuszący**

⚷ **ten** /ten/ number 10 ▶ **dziesięć** ➲ note at **six**

tenacious /təˈneɪʃəs/ adj. not likely to give up or let sth go; determined ▶ **nieustępliwy**
■ **tenacity** /təˈnæsəti/ noun [U] ▶ **nieustępliwość**

tenancy /ˈtenənsi/ noun [C,U] (pl. **tenancies**) the use of a room, flat, building or piece of land, for which you pay rent to the owner: *a six-month tenancy* ◇ *It says in the tenancy agreement that you can't keep pets.* ▶ **najem; dzierżawa**

tenant /ˈtenənt/ noun [C] a person who pays rent to the owner of a room, flat, building or piece of land so that they can live in it or use it ▶ **lokator/ka; dzierżawca/czyni** ➲ look at **landlord**

⚷ **tend** /tend/ verb **1** [I] **tend to do sth** to usually do or be sth: *Women tend to live* (na ogół żyją) *longer than men.* ◇ *There tends to be a lot of heavy traffic on that road.* ◇ *My brother tends to talk a lot when he's nervous.* ▶ **mieć skłonność/tendencję do czegoś** ℹ Często tłumaczy się „zwykle" + czasownik. **2** [I] (used for giving your opinion in a polite way): *I **tend to think** that we shouldn't interfere.* ▶ **skłaniać się ku czemuś** **3** [I,T] (formal) **tend (to) sb/sth** to look after sb/sth: *Paramedics tended (to) the injured.* ▶ **opiekować się, pielęgnować**

⚷ **tendency** /ˈtendənsi/ noun [C] (pl. **tendencies**) **a tendency (to do sth/towards sth)** something that a person or thing usually does; a way of behaving: *They both **have a tendency** to be late for appointments.* ◇ *The dog began to show vicious tendencies.* ◇ *She seems to have a tendency towards depression.* ▶ **skłonność, tendencja**

tendentious /tenˈdenʃəs/ adj. (formal) (used about a speech, piece of writing, theory, etc.) expressing a strong opinion that people are likely to disagree with: *tendentious political memoirs* ▶ **tendencyjny** ℹ Zwykle wyraża dezaprobatę. SYN **controversial**
■ **tendentiously** adv. ▶ **tendencyjnie** | **tendentiousness** noun [U] ▶ **tendencyjność**

tender¹ /ˈtendə(r)/ adj. **1** kind and loving: *tender words/looks/kisses* ▶ **czuły** **2** (used about food) soft and easy to cut or bite: *The meat should be nice and tender.* ▶ **kruchy, miękki** OPP **tough** **3** (used about a part of the body) painful when you touch it ▶ **wrażliwy**
■ **tenderly** adv. ▶ **czule** | **tenderness** noun [U] ▶ **czułość; wrażliwość**
IDM **at a tender age; at the tender age of...** when still young and without much experience: *She went to live in London at the tender age of 15.* ▶ **młody, niedojrzały**

tender² /ˈtendə(r)/ verb **1** [I] **tender (for sth)** to make a formal offer to supply goods or do work at a stated price: *Five different companies tendered for the building contract.* ▶ **brać udział w przetargu** **2** [T] **tender sth (to sb)** (formal) to to offer or give sth to sb: *After the scandal the Foreign Minister was forced to **tender her resignation**.* ▶ **składać** (*rezygnację*), **przedkładać** (*ofertę*)
■ **tender** (especially US **bid**) noun [C]: *Several firms submitted a tender for the catering contract.* ▶ **oferta** (*przetargowa*)

tendon /ˈtendən/ noun [C] a strong, thin part inside the body that joins a muscle to a bone ▶ **ścięgno** ➲ look at **ligament**

tenement /ˈtenəmənt/ noun [C] a large building that is divided into small flats, especially in a poor area of a city ▶ **dom czynszowy**

tenner /ˈtenə(r)/ noun [C] (Brit., informal) £10 or a ten-pound note ▶ **dziesięć funtów; banknot dziesięciofuntowy**

tennis /ˈtenɪs/ noun [U] a game for two or four players who hit a ball over a net using a **racket**: *Let's play tennis.* ◇ *to have a game of tennis* ◇ *a tennis match* ▶ **tenis** ➲ note at **sport** ➲ picture on **page A8**

> In tennis you can play **singles** (a game between two people) or **doubles** (a game between two teams of two people).

tenor /ˈtenə(r)/ noun [C] a fairly high singing voice for a man; a man with this voice: *Pavarotti is a famous Italian tenor.* ▶ **tenor**
■ **tenor** adj. [only before a noun]: *a tenor saxophone/trombone* ▶ **tenorowy**

tenpin bowling /ˌtenpɪn ˈbəʊlɪŋ/ noun [U] a game in which you roll a heavy ball towards ten **tenpins** and try to knock them down ▶ **gra w kręgle**

tense¹ /tens/ adj. **1** (used about a person) not able to relax because you are worried or nervous: *She looked pale and tense.* ▶ **spięty** **2** (used about an atmosphere or a situation) in which people feel worried and not relaxed ▶ **napięty** **3** (used about a muscle or a part of the body) tight; not relaxed ▶ **naprężony**

tense² /tens/ noun [C,U] a form of a verb that shows if sth happens in the past, present or future ▶ (*gram.*) **czas**

tense³ /tens/ verb [I,T] **tense (sth) (up)** if you **tense** your muscles, or you or your muscles **tense**, they become tight or stiff, especially because you are not relaxed ▶ **stawać się spiętym; naprężać**

⚷ **tension** /ˈtenʃn/ noun **1** [C,U] bad feeling and lack of trust between people, countries, etc.: *There are signs of growing tensions between the two countries.* ▶ **napięcie** **2** [U] the condition of not being able to relax because you are worried or nervous: *I could hear the tension in her voice as she spoke.* ▶ **napięcie** **3** [U] (used about a rope, muscle, etc.) the state of being stretched tight; how tightly sth is stretched: *The massage relieved the tension in my neck.* ▶ **naprężenie**

⚷ **tent** /tent/ noun [C] a small structure made of cloth that is held up by poles and ropes. You use a tent to sleep in when you go camping: *to put up/take down a tent* ▶ **namiot** ➲ look at **marquee**

tentacle /ˈtentəkl/ noun [C] one of the long thin soft parts like legs that some sea animals have: *An octopus has eight tentacles.* ▶ **macka, czułek**

tentative /ˈtentətɪv/ adj. **1** (used about plans, etc.) uncertain; not definite ▶ **prowizoryczny** **2** (used about a person or their behaviour) not confident about what you are saying or doing: *a tentative smile/suggestion* ▶ **niepewny**
■ **tentatively** adv. ▶ **tytułem próby; niepewnie**

tenterhooks /ˈtentəhʊks/ noun

T

IDM **(be) on tenterhooks** (to be) in a very nervous or excited state because you are waiting to find out what is going to happen ▶ **umierać z ciekawości**

tenth /tenθ/ ordinal number 10th ▶ **dziesiąty** ➲ note at **sixth**
■ **tenth** noun [C] ¹⁄₁₀; one of ten equal parts of sth ▶ **(jedna) dziesiąta**

'tent peg = PEG[1] (2)

tenuous /'tenjuəs/ adj. very weak or uncertain: *The connection between Joe's story and what actually happened was tenuous.* ▶ **wątły, nieistotny**

tenure /'tenjə(r)/ noun [U] a legal right to live in a place, hold a job, use land, etc. for a certain time ▶ **tytuł prawny posiadania** (*nieruchomości*); **piastowanie** (*urzędu*)

tenured /'tenjəd/ adj. [usually before a noun] **1** (used about an official job) that you can keep permanently: *a tenured post* ▶ **stały 2** (used about a person, especially a teacher at a university) having the right to keep their job permanently: *a tenured professor* ▶ **na etacie**

tepid /'tepɪd/ adj. (used about liquids) only slightly warm ▶ **letni**

term[1] /tɜːm/ noun **1** [C] a word or group of words with a particular meaning: *What exactly do you mean by the term 'racist'? ◇ a technical term in computing* ▶ **określenie, termin 2** (**terms**) [pl.] **in terms of …**; **in … terms** (used for showing which particular way you are thinking about sth or from which point of view): *The flat would be ideal in terms of* (pod względem) *size, but it is very expensive.* ▶ **w kategoriach 3** (**terms**) [pl.] the conditions of an agreement: ***Under the terms of*** *the contract you must give a week's notice. ◇ Both sides agreed to the peace terms.* ▶ **warunki 4** [C] a period of time that the school or university year is divided into: *the autumn/spring/summer term ◇ an end-of-term test* ▶ **semestr, okres, trymestr** ➲ look at **semester 5** [C] a period of time for which sth lasts: *The US President is now in his second term of office.* ▶ **kadencja**

IDM **be on equal terms (with sb)** → EQUAL[1]

be on good, friendly, etc. terms (with sb) to have a friendly relationship with sb ▶ **być w dobrych/przyjaznych stosunkach (z kimś)**

be on speaking terms (with sb) → SPEAK

come to terms with sth to accept sth unpleasant or difficult ▶ **pogodzić się z czymś**

in the long/short term over a long/short period of time in the future ▶ **w dłuższym/krótszym okresie**

term[2] /tɜːm/ verb [T] to describe sb/sth by using a particular word or expression: *the period of history that is often termed the 'Dark Ages'* ▶ **określać, nazywać**

terminal[1] /'tɜːmɪnl/ noun [C] **1** a large railway station, bus station or building at an airport where journeys begin and end: *the bus terminal ◇ Which terminal are you flying from?* ▶ **dworzec, terminal 2** the computer that one person uses for getting information from a central computer or for putting information into it ▶ (*komput.*) **terminal**

terminal[2] /'tɜːmɪnl/ adj. (used about an illness) slowly causing death: *terminal cancer* ▶ **nieuleczalny, śmiertelny**
■ **terminally** /-nəli/ adv.: *a terminally ill patient* ▶ **nieuleczalnie, śmiertelnie**

terminate /'tɜːmɪneɪt/ verb [I,T] (formal) to end or to make sth end: *to terminate a contract/an agreement* ▶ **kończyć (się), rozwiązywać** (*umowę*)
■ **termination** /ˌtɜːmɪ'neɪʃn/ noun [U] ▶ **zakończenie, rozwiązanie**

terminology /ˌtɜːmɪ'nɒlədʒi; US -mə'n-/ noun [U] the special words and expressions that are used in a particular profession, subject or activity ▶ **terminologia**

terminus /'tɜːmɪnəs/ noun [C] the last stop or station at the end of a bus route or railway line ▶ **końcow-a/y stacja/przystanek**

termite /'tɜːmaɪt/ noun [C] an insect that lives in hot countries and does a lot of damage by eating the wood of trees and buildings ▶ **termit**

terrace /'terəs/ noun **1** (Brit.) [C] a line of similar houses that are all joined together ▶ **domy jednorodzinne w zabudowie szeregowej 2** [C] a flat area of stone next to a restaurant or large house where people can have meals, sit in the sun, etc. ▶ **taras** ➲ look at **patio**, **veranda**, **balcony 3** (**terraces**) [pl.] the wide steps that people stand on to watch a football match ▶ **trybuny** (*z miejscami stojącymi*) **4** [C, usually pl.] one of a series of steps that are cut into the side of a hill so that crops can be grown there ▶ **taras**

terraced /'terəst/ adj. **1** (Brit.) (used about a house) forming part of a line of similar houses that are all joined together ▶ (*dom*) **szeregowy** ➲ picture on **page A3 2** (used about a hill) having steps cut out of it so that crops can be grown there ▶ **tarasowy, tarasowaty**

terracotta /ˌterə'kɒtə/ noun [U] **1** clay that has been baked but not glazed, used for making pots, etc. ▶ **terakota 2** the reddish-brown colour of terracotta ▶ **koloru terakoty**

terrain /tə'reɪn/ noun [U] land of the type mentioned: *mountainous/steep/rocky terrain* ▶ **teren**

terrestrial /tə'restriəl/ adj. **1** connected with, or living on, the earth ▶ **lądowy 2** (used about television, etc.) operating on earth rather than from a **satellite** ▶ **naziemny**

terrible /'terəbl/ adj. **1** ill or very upset: *I **feel terrible*** (okropnie). *I think I'm going to be sick. ◇ He **felt terrible*** (podle) *when he realized what he had done.* ▶ **straszny, okropny 2** very unpleasant; causing great shock or injury: *a terrible accident ◇ terrible news ◇ What a terrible thing to do!* ▶ **okropny**; **straszny 3** very bad; of poor quality: *a terrible hotel/book/memory/driver* ▶ **straszny, okropny** ➲ note at **bad 4** [only before a noun] (used to emphasize how bad sth is): *in terrible pain/trouble ◇ The room was in a terrible mess. ◇ It was a terrible shame* (wielka szkoda) *that you couldn't come.* ▶ **wielki**

terribly /'terəbli/ adv. **1** very: *I'm terribly sorry.* Ogromnie mi przykro. ▶ **ogromnie, bardzo 2** very badly: *I played terribly. ◇ The experiment went terribly wrong.* ▶ **strasznie, okropnie**

terrier /'teriə(r)/ noun [C] a type of small dog ▶ **terier**

terrific /tə'rɪfɪk/ adj. **1** (informal) extremely nice or good; excellent: *You're doing a terrific job!* ▶ **wspaniały, świetny** ➲ note at **good 2** [only before a noun] very great: *I've got a terrific amount of work to do.* ▶ **wspaniały, świetny**
■ **terrifically** /-kli/ adv.: *terrifically expensive* ▶ **strasznie, przeraźliwie**

terrified /'terɪfaɪd/ adj. **terrified (of sb/sth)** very afraid: *I'm absolutely terrified* (przeraźliwie boję się) *of snakes. ◇ What's the matter? You look terrified.* ▶ **przerażony, przestraszony**

terrify /'terɪfaɪ/ verb [T] (**terrifying**; **terrifies**; pt, pp **terrified**) to frighten sb very much ▶ **przerażać, straszyć**
■ **terrifying** adj. ▶ **przerażający**

territorial /ˌterə'tɔːriəl/ adj. [only before a noun] connected with the land or area of sea that belongs to a country: *territorial waters* ▶ **terytorialny**

territory /'terətri; US -tɔːri/ noun (pl. **territories**) **1** [C,U] an area of land that belongs to one country: *to fly over enemy territory* ▶ **terytorium, obszar 2** [C,U] an area that an animal has as its own ▶ **terytorium 3** [U] an area of knowledge or responsibility: *Computer programming is Frank's territory.* ▶ **teren** (*np. działania*)

terror /ˈterə(r)/ noun **1** [U] very great fear: *He screamed **in terror*** (przerażony) *as the rats came towards him.* ▶ **przerażenie, paniczny strach 2** [C] a person or thing that makes you feel afraid: *the terrors of the night* ▶ **strach, postrach 3** [U] violence and the killing of ordinary people for political purposes: *a campaign of terror* ◇ *a terror campaign* kampania terrorystyczna ▶ **terror 4** [C] a person (especially a child) or an animal that is difficult to control: *Joey's a little terror.* ▶ (*przen.*) **diabełek**

terrorism /ˈterərɪzəm/ noun [U] the killing of ordinary people for political purposes: *an act of terrorism* ▶ **terroryzm** ➲ note at **crime**
■ **terrorist** /-ɪst/ noun [C] ▶ **terroryst(k)a** | **terrorist** /-ɪst/ adj. ▶ **terrorystyczny**

terrorize (also -ise) /ˈterəraɪz/ verb [T] to make sb feel frightened by using or threatening to use violence against them: *The gang has terrorized the neighbourhood for months.* ▶ **terroryzować**

terse /tɜːs/ adj. said in few words and in a not very friendly way: *a terse reply* ▶ **lapidarny, zwięzły**

tertiary /ˈtɜːʃəri; US also -ʃieri/ adj. (used about education) at university or college level: *a tertiary college* szkoła pomaturalna ▶ **pomaturalny**

TESL /ˈtesl/ abbr. **Teaching English as a Second Language** ▶ **nauka języka angielskiego jako drugiego języka**

⚷ **test¹** /test/ noun [C] **1** a short exam to measure sb's knowledge or skill in sth: *We have a spelling test* (test ortograficzny) *every Friday.* ▶ **test, egzamin** ➲ note at **exam** ➲ look at **driving**

When you **take** a test you can either **pass** it or **fail** it.

2 a short medical examination of a part of your body: *to have an eye test* ▶ **badanie 3** an experiment to find out if sth works or to find out more information about it: *Tests show that the new drug is safe and effective.* ◇ *to carry out/perform/do a test* ▶ **test, badanie 4** a situation or event that shows how good, strong, etc. sb/sth is: *The local elections will be a good test of the government's popularity.* ▶ **test, próba**
IDM **put sb/sth to the test** to do sth to find out how good, strong, etc. sb/sth is ▶ **poddawać kogoś/coś próbie**

⚷ **test²** /test/ verb [T] **1 test sb (on sth)** to examine sb's knowledge or skill in sth: *We're being tested on irregular verbs this morning.* ▶ **egzaminować (z czegoś) 2** to examine a part of the body to find out if it is healthy: *to have your eyes tested* przechodzić badanie wzroku ▶ **badać 3 test sb/sth (for sth)**; **test sth (on sb/sth)** to try, use or examine sth carefully to find out if it is working properly or what it is like: *These cars have all been tested for safety.* ◇ *Do you think drugs should be tested on animals?* ▶ **sprawdzać, wypróbowywać, testować**

testament /ˈtestəmənt/ noun [C, usually sing.] (formal) **a testament (to sth)** something that shows that sth exists or is true: *Her new film is a testament to* (świadczy o) *her talent and experience.* ▶ **świadectwo, dowód** ➲ look at **testimony**

testicle /ˈtestɪkl/ noun [C] one of the two male sex organs that produce **sperm** ▶ **jądro**

testify /ˈtestɪfaɪ/ verb [I,T] (**testifying**; **testifies**; pt, pp **testified**) to make a formal statement that sth is true, especially in a court of law ▶ **zeznawać**

testimony /ˈtestɪməni; US -məʊni/ noun (pl. **testimonies**) **1** [U, sing.] (formal) something that shows that sth else exists or is true ▶ **świadectwo, dowód** ➲ look at **testament 2** [C,U] a formal statement that sth is true, especially one that is made in a court of law ▶ **zeznanie**

testosterone /teˈstɒstərəʊn/ noun [U] a **hormone** produced in men's **testicles** that causes them to develop the physical and sexual features that are characteristic of the male body ▶ **testosteron** ➲ look at **oestrogen, progesterone**

ˌ**test ˈrun** = TRIAL RUN

ˈ**test tube** noun [C] a thin glass tube that is used in chemical experiments ▶ **probówka** ➲ picture at **laboratory**

ˈ**test-tube baby** noun [C] a baby that develops from an egg which has been taken out of the mother's body. The egg is **fertilized** and then put back inside to develop normally. ▶ **dziecko z probówki**

tetanus /ˈtetənəs/ noun [U] a serious disease that makes your muscles, especially the muscles of your face, hard and impossible to move. You can get **tetanus** by cutting yourself on sth dirty. ▶ **tężec**

tether¹ /ˈteðə(r)/ verb [T] to tie an animal to sth with a rope, etc. ▶ **pętać**

tether² /ˈteðə(r)/ noun
IDM **at the end of your tether** → END¹

⚷ **text¹** /tekst/ noun **1** [U] the main written part of a book, newspaper, etc. (not the pictures, notes, etc.): *My job is to lay out the text on the page.* ▶ **tekst 2** [C] the written form of a speech, etc.: *The newspaper printed the complete text of the interview.* ▶ **tekst 3** [C] = TEXT MESSAGE **4** [C] a book or a short piece of writing that people study as part of a literature or language course: *a set text* lektura obowiązkowa ▶ **lektura**

text² /tekst/ (also ˈ**text-message**) verb [T,I] to send sb a written message using a mobile phone: *I texted him to say we were waiting in the pub.* ▶ **przesyłać wiadomość tekstową (SMS)** ➲ note at **mobile phone**

textbook /ˈtekstbʊk/ noun [C] a book that teaches a particular subject and that is used especially in schools: *a history textbook* ▶ **podręcznik**

texter /ˈtekstə(r)/ noun [C] (especially Brit.) a person who sends **text messages** ▶ **osoba wysyłająca wiadomości tekstowe**

textile /ˈtekstaɪl/ noun [C] any cloth made in a factory: *cotton textiles* ◇ *the textile industry* ▶ **tkanina**

ˈ**text message** (also **text**) noun [C] a written message that you send using a mobile phone: *Send a text message to this number to vote for the winner.* ▶ **wiadomość tekstowa, SMS** ➲ look at **SMS** ➲ note at **mobile phone**
■ ˈ**text-messaging** (also **texting** /ˈtekstɪŋ/) noun [U] ▶ **SMS-owanie**

texture /ˈtekstʃə(r)/ noun [C,U] the way that sth feels when you touch it: *a rough/smooth/coarse texture* ◇ *cheese with a very creamy texture* ◇ *material with a silky texture* (jedwabisty w dotyku) ▶ **faktura, wrażenie w dotyku**

textured /ˈtekstʃəd/ adj. with a surface that is not smooth, but has a particular **texture**: *textured wallpaper* ▶ **z fakturą**

⚷ **than** /ðən; strong form ðæn/ conj., prep. **1** (used when you are comparing two things): *He's taller than me.* ◇ *He's taller than I am.* ◇ *London is more expensive than Madrid.* ◇ *You speak French much better than she does/than her.* ◇ *I'd rather play tennis than football.* ▶ **niż, od 2** (used with 'more' and 'less' before numbers, expressions of time, distances, etc.): *I've worked here for more than three years.* ▶ **niż, od**

⚷ **thank** /θæŋk/ verb [T] **thank sb (for sth/for doing sth)** to tell sb that you are grateful: *I'm writing to thank you for the present you sent me.* ◇ *I'll go and thank him for offering to help.* ▶ **dziękować**

Zarówno **thank you**, jak i **thanks** używa się, aby komuś za coś podziękować. **Thanks** jest mniej formalne: *Thank you very much for your letter.* ◇ *'How are you, Rachel?' 'Much better, thanks.'* Obu wyrażeń można też użyć, aby podziękować komuś za poczęstunek: *'Have a piece of cake.' 'Thank you. That would be nice.'* Jeśli chce się grzecznie odmówić, wówczas można powiedzieć **no, thank you** lub **no, thanks**: *'Would you like some more tea?' 'No, thanks.'*

IDM **thank God, goodness, heavens, etc.** (used for expressing happiness that sth unpleasant has stopped or will not happen): *Thank goodness it's stopped raining.* ▶ **dzięki Bogu!**

thankful /ˈθæŋkfl/ adj. [not before a noun] **thankful (for sth/to do sth/that ...)** pleased and grateful: *I was thankful to hear that you got home safely.* ◇ *I was thankful for my thick coat when it started to snow.* ▶ **wdzięczny**

thankfully /ˈθæŋkfəli/ adv. **1** (used for expressing happiness that sth unpleasant did not or will not happen): *Thankfully, no one was injured in the accident.* ▶ **na szczęście** SYN **fortunately** **2** in a pleased or grateful way: *I accepted her offer thankfully.* ▶ **z wdzięcznością**

thankless /ˈθæŋkləs/ adj. involving hard work that other people do not notice or thank you for ▶ **niewdzięczny**

⚷ **thanks** /θæŋks/ noun [pl.] words which show that you are grateful: *I'd like to express my thanks to all of you for coming here today.* ▶ **podziękowanie**

IDM **thanks to sb/sth** because of sb/sth: *We're late, thanks to you!* ▶ **dzięki komuś/czemuś**

a vote of thanks → VOTE[1]

Thanksgiving (Day) /ˌθæŋksˈɡɪvɪŋ deɪ/ noun [U,C] a public holiday in the US and in Canada ▶ **Święto Dziękczynienia**

Thanksgiving Day wypada w ostatni czwartek listopada w USA i w drugi poniedziałek października w Kanadzie. Początkowo był to dzień, w którym ludzie dziękowali Bogu za pomyślne zbiory, a także Indianom za pomoc, jakiej udzielili im podczas pierwszych zasiewów.

⚷ **ˈthank you** noun [C] an expression of thanks: *Let's have a big thank-you* (podziękujmy gorąco) *to everybody who worked so hard.* ▶ **podziękowanie**

⚷ **that** /ðæt/ determiner, pron., conj., adv. **1** (pl. **those** /ðəʊz/) (used to refer to a person or thing, especially when he/she/it is not near the person speaking): *I like that house over there.* ◇ *What's that* (a cóż to takiego) *in the road?* ◇ *'Could you pass me the book?' 'This one?' 'No, that one over there.'* ▶ **ten/tamten** (*wskazując na coś*) **2** (pl. **those**) (used for talking about a person or thing already known or mentioned): *That was the year* (to był ten rok, kiedy) *we went to Spain, wasn't it?* ◇ *Can you give me back that money I lent you last week?* ▶ **to**, **ten** **3** /ðət; strong form ðæt/ [used for introducing a relative clause] the person or thing already mentioned: *I'm reading the book that won the Booker prize.* ◇ *The people that live next door are French.* ▶ **który** ⮌ note at **which** ⓘ Kiedy **that** jest dopełnieniem zdania względnego, wówczas można je pominąć: *I want to see the doctor (that) I saw last week.* ◇ *I wore the dress (that) I bought in Paris.* **4** /ðət; strong form ðæt/ (used after certain verbs, nouns and adjectives to introduce a new part of the sentence): *She told me that she was leaving.* ◇ *I hope that you feel better soon.* ◇ *I'm certain that he will come.* ◇ *It's funny that you should say that.* ▶ **że** ⓘ W zdaniach typu *I thought (that) you would like it.* **that** jest często pomijane. **5** [used with adjectives and adverbs] as much as that: *30 miles? I can't walk that far.* ▶ **(aż) tak**

IDM **that is (to say)** (used when you are giving more information about sb/sth): *I'm on holiday next week. That's to say, from Tuesday.* ▶ **to znaczy**, **to jest**

that's that there is nothing more to say or do: *I'm not going and that's that* (i tyle). ▶ **to tyle (na razie)**

thatched /θætʃt/ adj. (used about a building) having a roof made of **straw** ▶ **pokryty strzechą** ⮌ picture on **page A3**

thaw /θɔː/ verb [I,T] **thaw (sth) (out)** to become or to make sth become soft or liquid again after freezing: *Is the snow thawing?* ◇ *Always thaw chicken thoroughly before you cook it.* ◇ *It's starting to thaw.* Zaczyna się odwilż. ▶ **topnieć**; **rozmrażać** ⮌ look at **melt**

■ **thaw** noun [C, usually sing.] ▶ **odwilż**

⚷ **the** /ðə; ði; strong form ðiː/ definite article ⓘ Najczęściej nie tłumaczy się. **1** (used for talking about a person or thing that is already known or that has already been mentioned): *I took the children to the dentist.* ◇ *We met the man who bought your house.* ◇ *The milk is in the fridge.* **2** (used when there is only one of sth): *The sun is very strong today.* ◇ *Who won the World Cup?* ◇ *the government* **3** (used with numbers and dates): *This is the third time I've seen this film.* ◇ *Friday the thirteenth* piątek trzynastego ◇ *I grew up in the sixties* (w latach sześćdziesiątych). **4** (formal) (used with a singular noun when you are talking generally about sth): *The dolphin is an intelligent animal.* **5** with musical instruments: *Do you play the piano* (na pianinie)? **6** (used with adjectives to name a group of people): *the French* Francuzi ◇ *the poor* biedni ⓘ Nadaje przymiotnikowi funkcję rzeczownika w lm. **7** with units of measurement, meaning 'every': *Our car does forty miles to the gallon.* ▶ **na**, **za** **8** the well-known or important one: *'My best friend at school was Tony Blair.' 'You mean the Tony Blair?'* ▶ **ten (sławny)** ⓘ **The** wymawia się /ðiː/ w tym znaczeniu. **9 the ... the ...** (used for saying that the way in which two things change is connected): *The more you eat, the fatter you get.* ▶ **im ... tym ...**

⚷ **theatre** (US **theater**) /ˈθɪətə(r); US ˈθiːət-/ noun **1** [C] a building where you go to see plays, shows, etc.: *How often do you go to the theatre?* ▶ **teatr** **2** [U] plays in general: *He's studying modern Irish theatre.* ▶ **teatr**, **dramat** SYN **drama** **3** [sing., U] the work of acting in or producing plays: *He's worked in (the) theatre for thirty years.* ▶ **teatr** **4** [C,U] = OPERATING THEATRE: *He's still in theatre.*

theatre

A **play** is performed in a **theatre**, on a **stage**. A theatre company, drama group, etc. **produces** the play. The furniture, etc. on the stage is the **scenery**. If an **actor**/**actress** wants a **part** in a play, he/she may need to have an **audition**, so the **director** can decide if he/she is good enough. Before they **put on** a play, **the cast** has to **rehearse** it. If the **audience** like the play, they **clap**/**applaud** at the end of the **performance**.

theatregoer (US **theatergoer**) /ˈθɪətəɡəʊə(r); US ˈθiːə-/ noun [C] a person who goes regularly to the theatre ▶ **teatroman/ka**

theatrical /θiˈætrɪkl/ adj. **1** [only before a noun] connected with the theatre ▶ **teatralny**, **dramatyczny** **2** (used about behaviour) exaggerated or showing feelings, etc. in a very obvious way because you want people to notice you ▶ **teatralny**, **dramatyczny**

theft /θeft/ noun [C,U] the crime of stealing sth: *There have been a lot of thefts in this area recently.* ◇ *The woman was arrested for theft.* ▶ **kradzież** ⮌ note at **thief**

⚷ **their** /ðeə(r)/ determiner **1** of or belonging to them: *The children picked up their books and left.* ▶ **ich**, **swój** **2** (informal) (used instead of *his* or *her*): *Has everyone got their book?* ▶ **jego**, **jej**, **swój** ⮌ note at **he**

⚷ **theirs** /ðeəz/ pron. of or belonging to them: *Our flat isn't as big as theirs.* ▶ **ich**

⚷ **them** /ðəm; strong form ðem/ pron. [the object of a verb or preposition] **1** the people or things mentioned earlier: *I'll phone them now.* ◇ *'I've got the keys here.' 'Oh good. Give them to me.'* ◇ *We have students from several countries but*

***most of them** are Italian.* ◇ *They asked for your address so I gave it to them.* ▶ **(*przypadek zależny słowa* they)**

Czasem spotyka się pisownię **'em**, która odzwierciedla wymowę **them** w języku potocznym.

2 (informal) him or her: *If anyone phones, tell them* (to powiedz) *I'm busy.* ▶ **(*przypadek zależny słów* he/she)** ➲ note at **he**

thematic /θɪ'mætɪk; θiː-/ adj. [usually before a noun] connected with the theme or themes of sth: *the thematic structure of a text* ▶ **tematyczny**
■ **thematically** /-kli/ adv.: *The books have been grouped thematically.* ▶ **tematycznie**

⚷ **theme** /θiːm/ noun [C] the subject of a talk, a piece of writing or a work of art: *The theme of today's discussion will be 'Our changing cities'.* ▶ **temat**; **motyw**

'theme park noun [C] a park where people go to enjoy themselves, for example by riding on **roller coasters**, and where the entertainment is based on a single idea ▶ **park rozrywki** (*oparty na jednym pomyśle/temacie*)

⚷ **themselves** /ðəm'selvz/ pron. **1** (used when the people or things who do an action are also affected by it): *Susie and Angela seem to be enjoying themselves.* ◇ *People often talk to themselves when they are worried.* ▶ **się**, **siebie** **2** (used to emphasize the people who do the action): *They themselves say that the situation cannot continue.* ◇ *Did they paint the house themselves?* ▶ **sami**, **osobiście**
IDM **(all) by themselves 1** alone: *The boys are too young to go out by themselves.* ▶ **sami**, **samotnie** ➲ note at **alone 2** without help: *The children cooked the dinner all by themselves.* ▶ **sami**, **samodzielnie**

⚷ **then** /ðen/ adv. **1** (at) that time: *In 1990? I was at university then.* ◇ *I spoke to him on Wednesday, but I haven't seen him **since then*** (od tamtej pory). ◇ *They met in 1941 and remained close friends **from then on**.* ◇ *I'm going tomorrow. Can you wait **until then*** (do tego czasu)? ◇ *Phone me tomorrow – I will have decided **by then**.* ▶ **wtedy**, **wówczas 2** next; after that: *I'll have a shower and get changed, then we'll go out.* ◇ *There was silence for a minute. Then he replied.* ▶ **potem**, **następnie 3** (used to show the logical result of a statement or situation): *'I don't feel at all well.' 'Why don't you go to the doctor then?'* ◇ *If you don't do any work then you'll fail the exam.* ▶ **w takim razie**, **wobec tego 4** (informal) (used after words like *now*, *right*, *well*, etc. to show the beginning or end of a conversation or statement): *Now then, are we all ready to go?* ◇ *OK then, I'll see you tomorrow.* ▶ **dobra**
IDM **then/there again** → AGAIN
there and then; **then and there** → THERE

thence /ðens/ adv. (old-fashioned) from there ▶ **stamtąd**

theologian /ˌθiːə'ləʊdʒən/ noun [C] a person who studies **theology** ▶ **teolog**

theology /θi'ɒlədʒi/ noun [U] the study of religion ▶ **teologia**
■ **theological** /ˌθiːə'lɒdʒɪkl/ adj. ▶ **teologiczny**

theorem /'θɪərəm; US also 'θiːə-/ noun [C] (technical) a rule or principle, especially in mathematics, that can be proved to be true: *a mathematical theorem* ◇ *Pythagoras' theorem* ▶ **teoremat**, **twierdzenie** (*zwł. matematyczne*)

theoretical /ˌθɪə'retɪkl; US ˌθiːə-/ adj. **1** based on ideas and principles, not on practical experience: *A lot of university courses are still far too theoretical.* ▶ **teoretyczny** ➲ look at **practical 2** that may possibly exist or happen, although it is unlikely: *There is a theoretical possibility that the world will end tomorrow.* ▶ **teoretyczny**
■ **theoretically** /-kli/ adv. ▶ **teoretycznie**

theorist /'θɪərɪst; US also 'θiːə-/ noun [C] a person who develops ideas and principles about a particular subject in order to explain why things happen or exist: *a political theorist* ▶ **teoretyk**

theorize (also -ise) /'θɪəraɪz; US 'θiːə-/ verb [I,T] **theorize (about/on sth)** to suggest facts and ideas to explain sth; to form a theory or theories about sth: *The study theorizes about the role of dreams in people's lives.* ▶ **teoretyzować**; **formułować teorie (na temat czegoś)**

⚷ **theory** /'θɪəri; US also 'θiːəri/ noun (pl. **theories**) **1** [C] an idea or set of ideas that try to explain sth: *the theory about how life on earth began* ▶ **teoria**, **koncepcja 2** [U] the general idea or principles of a particular subject: *political theory* ◇ *the theory and practice of language teaching* ▶ **teoria 3** [C] an opinion or a belief that has not been shown to be true: *He has this theory that drinking whisky helps you live longer.* ▶ **teoria**
IDM **in theory** as a general idea which may not be true in reality: *Your plan sounds fine in theory, but I don't know if it'll work in practice.* ▶ **teoretycznie**

therapeutic /ˌθerə'pjuːtɪk/ adj. **1** helping to cure an illness: *therapeutic drugs* ▶ **leczniczy**, **terapeutyczny 2** helping you to relax and feel better: *I find listening to music very therapeutic.* ▶ **kojący**, **leczniczy**

therapy /'θerəpi/ noun [U] treatment to help or cure a mental or physical illness, usually without drugs or medical operations: *to have/undergo therapy* ◇ *speech therapy* logopedia ▶ **terapia**, **leczenie**
■ **therapist** /-pɪst/ noun [C]: *a speech therapist* logopeda ▶ **terapeut(k)a**

⚷ **there** /ðeə(r)/ adv. **1** (used as the subject of *be*, *seem*, *appear*, etc. to say that sth exists): *There's a man at the door.* Przy drzwiach jest jakiś mężczyzna. ◇ *There's somebody singing* (ktoś śpiewa) *outside our house.* ◇ *Is there a god?* Czy Bóg istnieje? ◇ *There wasn't* (nie było) *much to eat.* ◇ *There seems to be* (wygląda na to, że jest) *a mistake here.* ℹ **There is/are** często tłumaczy się „jest/są". **2** in, at or to that place: *Could you put the table there, please?* ◇ *I like Milan. My husband and I met there.* ◇ *Have you been to Bonn? We're going there next week.* ◇ *Have you looked under there?* ▶ **tam 3** available if needed: *Her parents are always there if she needs help.* ▶ **dostępny**, **do dyspozycji 4** at that point (in a conversation, story, etc.): *Could I interrupt you there for a minute?* ▶ **tutaj**, **w tym momencie 5** (used for calling attention to sth): *Oh look, there's* (oto) *Kate!* ◇ *Hello there* (halo)! *Can anyone hear me?*
IDM **be there for sb** to be available to help and support sb when they have a problem: *Whenever I'm in trouble, my sister is always there for me.* ▶ **być gotowym komuś pomóc**
then/there again → AGAIN
there and then; **then and there** at that time and place; immediately ▶ **od ręki**, **z miejsca**
there you are 1 (used when you give sth to sb): *There you are. I've bought you a newspaper.* ▶ **proszę**, **masz 2** (used when you are explaining sth to sb): *Just press the switch and there you are!* ▶ **i proszę 3** (used for saying that you are not surprised) ▶ **masz ci los**, **no i proszę**

thereabouts /ˌðeərə'baʊts/ (US **thereabout** /ˌðeərə'baʊt/) adv. [usually after *or*] somewhere near a number, time or place: *There are 100 students, or thereabouts.* ◇ *She lives in Sydney, or thereabouts.* ▶ **mniej więcej**, **w pobliżu**

thereafter /ˌðeər'ɑːftə(r); US -'æf-/ adv. (formal) after that ▶ **od tego czasu**, **później**

thereby /ˌðeə'baɪ/ adv. (formal) in that way ▶ **tym samym**, **w ten sposób**

⚷ **therefore** /'ðeəfɔː(r)/ adv. for that reason: *The new trains have more powerful engines and are therefore faster.* ▶ **dlatego**, **zatem** SYN **thus**

therein /ˌðeər'ɪn/ adv. (formal) because of sth that has just been mentioned ▶ **w tym/nim itp.**

T

thereupon /ˌðeərəˈpɒn/ adv. (formal) immediately after that and often as the result of sth ▶ **po czym, wskutek tego**

thermal[1] /ˈθɜːml/ adj. [only before a noun] **1** connected with heat: *thermal energy* ▶ **cieplny, termiczny 2** (used about clothes) made to keep you warm in cold weather: *thermal underwear* ▶ (*ubranie*) **ciepły, ocieplany**

thermal[2] /ˈθɜːml/ noun **1** [C] a flow of rising warm air ▶ **prąd termiczny 2** (**thermals**) [pl.] clothes, especially underwear, made to keep you warm in cold weather ▶ **bielizna ocieplana, ubranie ocieplane**

thermometer /θəˈmɒmɪtə(r)/ noun [C] an instrument for measuring the temperature of sb's body or of a room ▶ **termometr**

Thermos™ /ˈθɜːməs/ (also **ˈThermos flask**; Brit. also **flask**) noun [C] a type of container used for keeping a liquid hot or cold ▶ **termos**

thermostat /ˈθɜːməstæt/ noun [C] a device that controls the temperature in a house or machine by switching the heat on and off as necessary ▶ **termostat**

thesaurus /θɪˈsɔːrəs/ noun [C] a book that contains lists of words and phrases with similar meanings ▶ **leksykon, tezaurus**

these plural of **this**

thesis /ˈθiːsɪs/ noun [C] (pl. **theses** /ˈθiːsiːz/) **1** a long piece of writing on a particular subject that you do as part of a university degree: *He did his thesis on Japanese investment in Europe.* ▶ **dysertacja** ➲ look at **dissertation 2** an idea that is discussed and presented with evidence in order to show that it is true ▶ **teza**

⚷ **they** /ðeɪ/ pron. [the subject of a verb] **1** the people or things that have been mentioned: *We've got two children. They're both boys.* ◇ *'Have you seen my keys?' 'Yes, they are on the table.'* ▶ **oni, one 2** (informal) (used instead of *he* or *she*): *Somebody phoned for you but they didn't leave their name.* ▶ **ta osoba** ➲ note at **he 3** people in general or people whose identity is not known or stated: *They say* (podobno) *it's going to be a hard winter.* ▶ **ludzie**

they'd /ðeɪd/ short for **they had; they would**

they'll /ðeɪl/ short for **they will**

they're /ðeə(r)/ short for **they are**

they've /ðeɪv/ short for **they have**

⚷ **thick**[1] /θɪk/ adj. **1** (used about sth solid) having a large distance between its opposite sides; not thin: *a thick black line* ◇ *a thick coat/book* ◇ *These walls are very thick.* ▶ **gruby** OPP **thin 2** (used for saying what the distance is between the two opposite sides of sth): *The ice was three inches thick* (miał trzy cale grubości). ▶ **gruby 3** having a lot of things close together: *a thick forest* ◇ *thick hair* ▶ **gęsty** OPP **thin 4** that does not flow easily: *thick cream* ◇ *This paint is too thick.* ▶ **gęsty** OPP **thin 5** difficult to see through: *There'll be a thick fog tonight.* ◇ *thick clouds of smoke* ▶ **gęsty 6 thick (with sth)** containing a lot of sth/sb close together: *The air was thick with dust.* ◇ *The streets were thick with shoppers.* ▶ **pełen (czegoś), zapchany (czymś) 7** (informal) slow to learn or understand; stupid: *He's thick.* On jest głupolem. ▶ **głupi, tępy 8** easily recognized as being from a particular country or area: *a thick Brooklyn accent* ▶ **silny** SYN **strong**

■ **thick** adv.: *Snow lay thick* (leżał grubą warstwą) *on the ground.* ▶ **grubo, gęsto** | **thickly** adv.: *Spread the butter thickly.* ◇ *a thickly wooded* (gęsto zalesiony) *area* ▶ **grubo, gęsto**

IDM **have a thick skin** to be not easily upset or worried by what people say about you ▶ **być gruboskórnym**

thick[2] /θɪk/ noun

IDM **in the thick of sth** in the most active or crowded part of sth; very involved in sth ▶ **w wirze (czegoś), w samym środku czegoś**

through thick and thin through difficult times and situations ▶ **na dobre i na złe**

thicken /ˈθɪkən/ verb [I,T] to become or to make sth thicker ▶ **gęstnieć, zagęszczać (się)**

thickener /ˈθɪkənə(r)/ noun [C] a substance used to make a liquid thicker ▶ **zagęszczacz**

⚷ **thickness** /ˈθɪknəs/ noun [C,U] the quality of being thick or how thick sth is ▶ **grubość, gęstość** ➲ look at **width**

ˌthick-ˈskinned adj. not easily worried or upset by what other people say about you: *Politicians have to be thick-skinned.* ▶ **gruboskórny**

⚷ **thief** /θiːf/ noun [C] (pl. **thieves** /θiːvz/) a person who steals things from another person ▶ **złodziej/ka** ➲ note at **steal**

> **thief**
>
> **Thief** to ogólne słowo określające złodzieja, osobę, która kradnie, zwykle potajemnie i bez użycia przemocy. Zwykła kradzież to **theft. Robber** okrada bank lub sklep, często z użyciem przemocy lub groźby. **Burglar** w celu kradzieży włamuje się do domu, sklepu itp., zwykle w nocy. **Shoplifter** natomiast wykrada rzeczy ze sklepu w czasie godzin jego otwarcia. **Mugger** okrada ludzi na ulicy, często stosując przemoc i pogróżki.

thigh /θaɪ/ noun [C] the top part of your leg, above your knee ▶ **udo, udko** ➲ picture at **body**

ˈthigh bone noun [C] the large thick bone in the top part of the leg between the hip and the knee ▶ **kość udowa**

thimble /ˈθɪmbl/ noun [C] a small metal or plastic object that you wear on the end of your finger to protect it when you are sewing ▶ **naparstek**

⚷ **thin**[1] /θɪn/ adj. (**thinner**; **thinnest**) **1** (used about sth solid) having a small distance between the opposite sides: *a thin book/shirt* ◇ *a thin slice of meat* ▶ **cienki** OPP **thick 2** having very little fat on the body: *You need to eat more. You're too thin!* ▶ **chudy** OPP **fat**

> **Thin, skinny, slim** i **underweight** mają podobne znaczenie. **Thin** to najbardziej ogólne określenie ludzi szczupłych. **Slim** odnosi się do osób, które są szczupłe i przez to atrakcyjne. Jeśli natomiast mówi się o kimś, że jest **skinny**, oznacza to, że dana osoba jest bardzo chuda i przez to nieatrakcyjna. **Underweight** to słowo bardziej formalne; często używa się go w odniesieniu do ludzi z niedowagą z punktu widzenia medycznego.

3 that flows easily; not thick: *a thin sauce* ▶ **rzadki, wodnisty** OPP **thick 4** not difficult to see through: *They fought their way through where the smoke was thinner.* ▶ **rzadki, rozrzedzony** OPP **thick 5** having only a few people or things with a lot of space between them: *The population is rather thin in this part of the country.* Ta część kraju jest dość rzadko zaludniona. ▶ **rzadki**

■ **thin** adv.: *Don't slice the onion too thin.* ▶ **cienko** | **thinly** adv.: *thinly sliced bread* ◇ *thinly populated areas* ▶ **cienko, rzadko**

IDM **thin on the ground** difficult to find; not common: *Jobs for people with my skills are fairly thin on the ground these days.* ▶ **rzadko spotykany**

through thick and thin → THICK[2]

vanish, etc. into thin air to disappear completely ▶ **znikać jak kamfora**

wear thin → WEAR[1]

thin[2] /θɪn/ verb [I,T] (**thinning**; **thinned**) **thin (sth) (out)** to become thinner or fewer in number; to make sth thinner: *The trees thin out towards the edge of the forest.* ◇ *Thin the sauce by adding milk.* ▶ **rzednąć, przerzedzać się; rozrzedzać**

thing /θɪŋ/ noun **1** [C] an object that is not named: *What's that red thing on the table?* ◇ *A pen is a thing you use for writing with.* ◇ *I need to get a few things at the shops.* ▶ **rzecz, przedmiot 2** (**things**) [pl.] clothes or tools that belong to sb or are used for a particular purpose: *I'll just go and pack my things.* ◇ *We keep all the cooking things in this cupboard.* ▶ **rzeczy, odzież 3** [C] an action, event or statement: *When I get home the first thing I do* (pierwsze, co robię) *is have a cup of tea.* ◇ *A strange thing* (coś dziwnego) *happened to me yesterday.* ◇ *What a nice thing to say!* Jak to miło z twojej (jego itd.) strony! ▶ **coś 4** [C] a fact, subject, etc.: *He told me a few things that I didn't know before.* ▶ **rzecz, fakt 5** [C] a quality or state: *There's **no such thing** as evil.* Zło nie istnieje. ◇ *The best thing about my job is the way* (najlepsze w mojej pracy jest to, że) *it changes all the time.* ▶ **rzecz, coś 6** (**things**) [pl.] the situation or conditions of your life: *Things seem to be going very well for him at the moment.* Chwilowo wszystko układa się (dla niego) pomyślnie. ◇ *How are things?* Co słychać? ◇ *to talk things over* omawiać sprawy ▶ **sytuacja, okoliczności 7** (**the thing**) [sing.] exactly what is wanted or needed: *That's just the thing I was looking for!* ◇ *A week in our hotel is just the thing* (to jest to) *for tired business people.* ▶ **to, co jest wskazane lub modne 8** [C] (used for expressing how you feel about a person or an animal): *You've broken your finger? You poor thing* (biedactwo)*!* ◇ *Look how thin that cat is! Poor little thing* (biedactwo)*!*

IDM **a close shave/thing** → CLOSE[3]

be a good thing (that) to be lucky that: *It's a good thing you remembered your umbrella.* ▶ **na szczęście**

do your own thing to do what you want to do, without thinking about other people: *I like to spend time alone, just doing my own thing.* ▶ **robić swoje**

first/last thing as early/late as possible: *I'll telephone her first thing tomorrow morning* (z samego rana). ◇ *I saw him last thing on Friday evening* (tuż przed snem). ▶ **jak najwcześniej; jak najpóźniej**

for one thing (used for introducing a reason for sth): *I think we should go by train. For one thing it's cheaper.* ▶ **po pierwsze**

have a thing about sb/sth (informal) to have strong feelings about sb/sth ▶ **mieć bzika na czyimś/jakimś punkcie**

to make matters/things worse → WORSE

the real thing → REAL[1]

take it/things easy → EASY[2]

think /θɪŋk/ verb (pt, pp **thought** /θɔːt/) **1** [I,T] **think (sth) (of/about sb/sth); think that…** to have a particular idea or opinion about sth/sb; to believe sth: *'Do you think (that) we'll win?' 'No, I **don't think so.**'* ◇ *'Jay's coming tomorrow, isn't he?' 'Yes, I **think so.**'* ◇ *I think (that) they've moved to York but I'm not sure.* ◇ *What did you think of* (jak ci się podobał) *the film?* ◇ *What do you think about going out tonight?* ▶ **myśleć, sądzić 2** [I] **think (about sth)** to use your mind to consider sth or to form connected ideas: *Think before you speak.* ◇ *What are you thinking about?* ◇ *He had to think hard* (intensywnie pomyśleć) *about the question.* ▶ **myśleć 3** [I] to form an idea of sth; to imagine sth: ***Just think** what we could do with all that money!* ▶ **pomyśleć, wyobrazić sobie 4** [T] to expect sth: *The job took longer than we thought.* ▶ **spodziewać się, oczekiwać 5** [I] to think in a particular way: *We've got to **think positive.*** ◇ *If you want to be successful, you have to **think big*** (musisz mieć ambitne plany). ▶ **myśleć 6** [I] **think of/about doing sth; think (that)…** to intend or plan to do sth: *We're thinking of moving house.* ◇ *I think (that) I'll go for a swim.* ▶ **zamierzać 7** [T] to remember sth; to have sth come into your mind: *Can you think where you left the keys?* ◇ *I didn't think to ask him his name.* ▶ **przypominać sobie**

■ **think** noun [sing.]: *I'm not sure. I'll have to **have a think** about it.* Będę musiał to sobie przemyśleć. ▶ **rozważanie**

IDM **think better of (doing) sth** to decide not to do sth; to change your mind ▶ **rozmyślić się, zmienić zdanie**

think highly, a lot, not much, etc. of sb/sth to have a good, bad, etc. opinion of sb/sth: *I didn't think much of that film.* ▶ **mieć o kimś dobre/złe itp. zdanie**

think the world of sb/sth to love and admire sb/sth very much ▶ **świata poza kimś nie widzieć**

PHR V **think about/of sb** to consider the feelings of sb else: *She never thinks about anyone but herself.* ▶ **myśleć o kimś, troszczyć się o kogoś**

think of sth to create an idea in your imagination: *Who first thought of the plan?* ▶ **wymyślić coś**

think sth out to consider carefully all the details of a plan, idea, etc.: *a well-thought-out scheme* dobrze obmyślony plan ▶ **obmyślać/przemyśleć coś**

think sth over to consider sth carefully: *I'll think your offer over and let you know tomorrow.* ▶ **przemyśleć coś**

think sth through to consider every detail of sth carefully: *He made a bad decision because he didn't think it through.* ▶ **przemyśleć coś**

think sth up to create sth in your mind; to invent: *to think up a new advertising slogan* ▶ **wymyślić coś**

> **think**
> Kiedy chce się przedstawić swoje zdanie, można rozpocząć od '**I think** (that) …' lub '**Personally, I think** (that) …' lub od wyrażenia **In my opinion/As far as I'm concerned/It seems to me that…** W języku potocznym często używa się czasownika **reckon**, aby powiedzieć, że uważa się coś za prawdziwe lub prawdopodobne/możliwe: *I reckon (that) I'm going to get that job.* Kiedy chce się przedstawić swoje prywatne zdanie dotyczące tematów etycznych, można użyć czasownika **believe**: *She believes (that) killing animals is wrong.* Podczas formalnej rozmowy można zadać pytanie: *What is your opinion of/on/about…?* lub: *How do you feel about…?*

thinker /ˈθɪŋkə(r)/ noun [C] **1** a person who thinks about serious and important subjects ▶ **myśliciel/ka, intelektualist(k)a 2** a person who thinks in a particular way: *a quick/creative/clear thinker* ▶ **osoba myśląca w określony sposób**

thinking[1] /ˈθɪŋkɪŋ/ noun [U] **1** using your mind to think about sth: *We're going to have to do some quick thinking.* ◇ *clear thinking* klarowność myślenia ▶ **myślenie 2** ideas or opinions about sth: *This accident will make them change their thinking on safety matters.* ▶ **opinia, zdanie** ➲ look at **wishful thinking**

thinking[2] /ˈθɪŋkɪŋ/ adj. [only before a noun] intelligent and using your mind to think about important subjects ▶ **myślący, inteligentny**

ˈ**think tank** noun [C] a group of experts who provide advice and ideas on political, social or economic matters ▶ **sztab ekspertów**

third[1] /θɜːd/ ordinal number 3rd ▶ **trzeci** ➲ note at **sixth**

third[2] /θɜːd/ noun [C] **1** ⅓; one of three equal parts of sth ▶ **(jedna) trzecia 2** (Brit.) a result in final university exams, below first and second class degrees ▶ **dyplom trzeciej kategorii**

thirdly /ˈθɜːdli/ adv. (used to introduce the third point in a list): *We have made savings in three areas: firstly, defence, secondly, education and thirdly, health.* ▶ **po trzecie**

ˌ**third ˈparty** noun [C] a person who is involved in a situation in addition to the two main people involved ▶ **ktoś/osoba trzeci/a, osoba postronna**

the ˌ**Third ˈWorld** noun [sing.] the poorer countries of Asia, Africa and South America ▶ **trzeci świat** ➲ look at **developing**

T

thirst /θɜːst/ noun **1** [U, sing.] the feeling that you have when you want or need a drink: *Cold tea really quenches your thirst.* ◇ *to die of thirst* ▶ **pragnienie 2** [sing.] **a thirst for sth** a strong desire for sth ▶ **pragnienie**, **żądza** ➲ look at **hunger**

thirsty /ˈθɜːsti/ adj. (**thirstier**; **thirstiest**) wanting or needing a drink: *I'm thirsty. Can I have a drink of water, please?* ▶ **spragniony** ➲ look at **hungry**
■ **thirstily** adv. ▶ **łapczywie**

thirteen /ˌθɜːˈtiːn/ number 13 ▶ **trzynaście** ➲ note at **six**
■ **thirteenth** /ˌθɜːˈtiːnθ/ **1** ordinal number 13th ▶ **trzynasty** ➲ note at **sixth 2** noun [C] 1/13; one of thirteen equal parts of sth ▶ **(jedna) trzynasta**

thirty /ˈθɜːti/ number 30 ▶ **trzydzieści** ➲ note at **sixty**
■ **thirtieth** /ˈθɜːtiəθ/ **1** ordinal number 30th ▶ **trzydziesty** ➲ note at **sixth 2** noun [C] 1/30; one of thirty equal parts of sth ▶ **(jedna) trzydziesta**

ˌthirty-ˈsecond note (US) = DEMISEMIQUAVER

this /ðɪs/ determiner, pron. (pl. **these** /ðiːz/) **1** (used for talking about sb/sth that is close to you in time or space): *Have a look at this photo.* ◇ *These boots are really comfortable. My old ones weren't.* ◇ *Is this the book you asked for?* ◇ *These are the letters to be filed, not those over there.* ◇ *This chair's softer than that one, so I'll sit here.* ▶ **ten 2** (used for talking about sth that was mentioned or talked about earlier): *Where did you hear about this?* ▶ **to 3** (used for introducing sb or showing sb sth): *This is my wife, Claudia, and these are our children, David and Vicky.* ◇ *It's easier if you do it like this.* ▶ **to 4** (used with days of the week or periods of time) of today or the present week, year, etc.: *Are you busy this afternoon?* ◇ *this Friday* ▶ **ten 5** (informal) (used when you are telling a story) a certain: *Then this woman said ...* ▶ **ten**
■ **this** adv.: *The road is not usually this busy.* ▶ **(aż) tak**
IDM **this and that**; **this, that and the other** various things: *We chatted about this and that.* ▶ **to i owo**

thistle /ˈθɪsl/ noun [C] a wild plant with purple flowers and sharp points on its leaves ▶ **oset**

> Thistle to godło Szkocji.

thong (US) = FLIP-FLOP

thorax /ˈθɔːræks/ noun [C] **1** the middle part of your body between your neck and your waist ▶ **klatka piersiowa 2** the middle section of an insect's body, to which the legs and wings are connected ▶ **tułów** (*owada*) ➲ picture at **insect**

thorn /θɔːn/ noun [C] one of the hard sharp points on some plants and bushes, for example on rose bushes ▶ **cierń**, **kolec**

thorny /ˈθɔːni/ adj. (**thornier**; **thorniest**) **1** causing difficulty or disagreement: *a thorny problem/question* ▶ **drażliwy 2** having **thorns** ▶ **ciernisty**, **kolczasty**

thorough /ˈθʌrə; US ˈθɜːrəʊ/ adj. **1** careful and complete: *The police made a thorough search of the house.* ▶ **gruntowny**, **drobiazgowy 2** doing things in a very careful way, making sure that you look at every detail: *Pam is slow but she is very thorough.* ▶ **sumienny**
■ **thoroughness** noun [U]: *I admire his thoroughness.* ▶ **drobiazgowość**; **sumienność**

thoroughbred /ˈθʌrəbred; US ˈθɜːrəʊb-/ noun [C] an animal, especially a horse, of high quality, that has parents that are both of the same breed ▶ **koń czystej krwi**
■ **thoroughbred** adj.: *a thoroughbred mare* ▶ (*koń itp.*) **czystej krwi**

thoroughfare /ˈθʌrəfeə(r); US ˈθɜːrəʊf-/ noun [C] a public road or street used by traffic, especially a main road in a city or town ▶ **główna ulica/droga**

thoroughly /ˈθʌrəli; US ˈθɜːr-/ adv. **1** completely; very much: *We thoroughly enjoyed our holiday.* ▶ **całkowicie**, **zupełnie 2** in a careful and complete way: *to study a subject thoroughly* ▶ **gruntownie**, **drobiazgowo**

those plural of **that** (1, 2)

though /ðəʊ/ conj., adv. **1** in spite of the fact that: *Though he had very little money, Neil always managed to dress smartly.* ◇ *She still loved him **even though** he had treated her so badly.* ▶ **chociaż**, **choć** SYN **although 2** but: *I'll come as soon as I can, though I can't promise to be on time.* ▶ **chociaż**, **choć 3** (informal) however: *I quite like him. I don't like his wife, though.* ▶ **chociaż**, **niemniej jednak** ➲ note at **although**
IDM **as though** → AS

thought[1] past tense, past participle of **think**

thought[2] /θɔːt/ noun **1** [C] an idea or opinion: *What are your thoughts on this subject?* ◇ *The thought of living alone filled her with fear.* ◇ *I've just had a thought.* ▶ **zdanie**, **pomysł 2** (**thoughts**) [pl.] sb's mind and all the ideas that are in it: *You are always **in my thoughts**.* Zawsze o tobie myślę. **3** [U] the power or process of thinking: *I need to **give** this problem **some thought**.* Zastanowię się nad tym problemem. ◇ *You haven't put enough thought into this work.* Niedostatecznie dobrze przemyślałeś tę pracę. ▶ **myślenie 4** [sing.] a feeling of care or worry: *They sent me flowers. What a kind thought* (jak to miło z ich strony)*!* ◇ *We should **spare a thought for*** (pomyślmy o) *Joe, who is in hospital now.* **5** [U] particular ideas or a particular way of thinking: *a change in medical thought on the subject* ▶ **opinia**, **zdanie**
IDM **deep in thought/conversation** → DEEP[1]
a school of thought → SCHOOL
second thoughts → SECOND[1]

thoughtful /ˈθɔːtfl/ adj. **1** thinking deeply: *a thoughtful expression* ▶ **zamyślony**, **zadumany 2** thinking about what other people want or need: *It was very thoughtful of you* (to bardzo miło z twojej strony) *to send her some flowers.* ▶ **troskliwy** SYN **kind**
■ **thoughtfully** /-fəli/ adv. ▶ **w zamyśleniu**; **troskliwie** | **thoughtfulness** noun [U] ▶ **troskliwość**

thoughtless /ˈθɔːtləs/ adj. not thinking about what other people want or need or what the result of your actions will be: *a thoughtless remark* ▶ **bezmyślny**, **nieprzemyślany** SYN **inconsiderate**
■ **thoughtlessly** adv. ▶ **bezmyślnie**, **nierozważnie** | **thoughtlessness** noun [U] ▶ **bezmyślność**, **brak rozwagi**

ˈthought-provoking adj. making people think seriously about a particular subject or issue ▶ **skłaniający do refleksji**

thousand /ˈθaʊznd/ number 1000 ▶ **tysiąc**

> Zwróć uwagę, że mówiąc o liczbach używa się **thousand** w lp: *There were over seventy thousand spectators at the match.* **Thousands** oznacza „mnóstwo": *Thousands of people attended the meeting.*

ℹ Więcej o liczebnikach w dodatku *Wyrażenia liczbowe* na końcu słownika.

thousandth /ˈθaʊznθ/ ordinal number 1000th ▶ **tysięczny**
■ **thousandth** noun [C] 1/1000; one of a thousand equal parts of sth ▶ **(jedna) tysięczna**

thrash /θræʃ/ verb **1** [T] to hit sb/sth many times with a stick, etc. as a punishment ▶ **bić**, **chłostać 2** [I,T] **thrash (sth) (about/around)** to move or make sth move in a wild way without any control ▶ **rzucać się**, **wić się 3** [T] to defeat sb easily in a game, competition, etc.: *I thrashed Leo at tennis yesterday.* ▶ **rozgromić** (*przeciwnika*), **pokonać**
PHR V **thrash sth out** to talk about sth with sb until you reach an agreement ▶ **debatować nad czymś**, **dochodzić do porozumienia w jakiejś sprawie**

thrashing /ˈθræʃɪŋ/ noun [C] **1** the act of hitting sb/sth many times with a stick, etc. as a punishment ▶ **lanie 2** (informal) a bad defeat in a game ▶ **rozgromienie przeciwnika**

thread¹ /θred/ noun **1** [C,U] a long thin piece of cotton, wool, etc. that you use for sewing or making cloth: *a needle and thread* ▶ **nić**, **nitka** ➲ picture at **cable 2** [C] the connection between ideas, the parts of a story, etc.: *I've lost the thread of this argument.* ▶ **wątek**

thread² /θred/ verb [T] **1** to put sth long and thin, especially thread, through a narrow opening or hole: *to thread a needle* ◇ *He threaded the belt through the loops on his trousers.* ▶ **nawlekać**; **przewlekać (coś przez coś) 2** to join things together by putting them onto a string, etc.: *to thread beads onto a string* ▶ **nizać**
IDM **thread your way through sth** to move through sth with difficulty, going around things or people that are in your way ▶ **brnąć/przedostawać się przez coś**

threadbare /ˈθredbeə(r)/ adj. (used about cloth or clothes) old and very thin ▶ **wytarty**

threat /θret/ noun **1** [C] a warning that sb may hurt, kill or punish you if you do not do what they want: *to* ***make threats*** *against somebody* grozić komuś ◇ *He keeps saying he'll resign, but he won't* ***carry out*** *his* ***threat*** (ale nie spełni swoich gróźb). ▶ **groźba**, **pogróżka 2** [U, sing.] the possibility of trouble or danger: *The forest is under threat* (zagrożony) *from building developments.* ▶ **zagrożenie 3** [C] a person or thing that may damage sth or hurt sb; something that indicates future danger: *a threat to national security* ▶ **zagrożenie**

threaten /ˈθretn/ verb **1** [T] **threaten sb (with sth)**; **threaten (to do sth)** to warn that you may hurt, kill or punish sb if they do not do what you want: *The boy threatened him with a knife.* ◇ *She was threatened with dismissal.* ◇ *The man threatened to kill her if she didn't tell him where the money was.* ▶ **grozić**, **straszyć 2** [I,T] to seem likely to do sth unpleasant: *The strong wind was threatening to destroy the bridge.* ▶ **zagrażać**, **grozić**
■ **threatening** adj. ▶ **grożący**, **groźny** | **threateningly** adv. ▶ **groźnie**, **surowo**

three /θriː/ number **1** 3 ▶ **trzy** ➲ note at **six** ➲ look at **third 2** [in compounds] having three of the thing mentioned: *a three-legged stool* taboret o trzech nogach ◇ *a three-bedded room* pokój z trzema łóżkami ▶ **trzy-**, **trój-**

ˌthree-diˈmensional (also ˌ3-ˈD; ˌthree-ˈD) adj. having length, width and height: *a three-dimensional model* ▶ **trójwymiarowy**

threshold /ˈθreʃhəʊld/ noun [C] **1** the ground at the entrance to a room or building: *She stood on the threshold* (w przedsionku). ▶ **próg**; **przedsionek 2** the level at which sth starts to happen: *Young children have a low boredom threshold.* Małe dzieci szybko się nudzą. ▶ **próg 3** the time when you are just about to start sth or find sth: *We could be* ***on the threshold of*** *a scientific breakthrough.* ▶ **próg**, **granica**

threw past tense of **throw**

thrift /θrɪft/ noun [U] the quality of being careful not to spend too much money ▶ **oszczędność**
■ **thrifty** adj. ▶ **oszczędny**

ˈthrift shop (also ˈ**thrift store**) (US) = CHARITY SHOP

thrill /θrɪl/ noun [C] a sudden strong feeling of pleasure or excitement ▶ **dreszcz/yk** (*np. rozkoszy, emocji*), **mocne wrażenie**
■ **thrill** verb [T]: *His singing thrilled the audience.* ▶ **wzruszać**, **zachwycać** | **thrilled** adj.: *He was thrilled with my present.* ▶ **zachwycony**, **urzeczony** | **thrilling** adj. ▶ **porywający**, **pasjonujący**

thriller /ˈθrɪlə(r)/ noun [C] a play, film, book, etc. with a very exciting story, often about a crime ▶ **dreszczowiec**

thrive /θraɪv/ verb [I] (pt **thrived** or **throve** /θrəʊv/, pp **thrived**) to grow or develop well ▶ **doskonale prosperować**, **doskonale się rozwijać**
■ **thriving** adj.: *a thriving industry* ▶ **doskonale prosperujący**, **kwitnący**

throat /θrəʊt/ noun [C] **1** the front part of your neck: *The attacker grabbed the man by the throat.* ▶ **gardło 2** the back part of your mouth and the passage down your neck through which air and food pass: *She got a piece of bread stuck in her throat.* ◇ *I've got a terrible sore throat.* Strasznie boli mnie gardło. ▶ **gardło** ➲ picture at **body**
IDM **clear your throat** → CLEAR²
have/feel a lump in your throat → LUMP¹

throb /θrɒb/ verb [I] (**throbbing**; **throbbed**) to make strong regular movements or noises; to beat strongly: *Her finger throbbed with pain.* Czuła rwący ból w palcu. ▶ **tętnić**, **pulsować**
■ **throb** noun [C] ▶ **warkot**, **pulsowanie**

thrombosis /θrɒmˈbəʊsɪs/ noun [C,U] (pl. **thromboses** /-siːz/) a serious condition caused by a blood **clot** forming in the heart or in a tube that carries blood ▶ **zakrzepica** ➲ look at **deep vein thrombosis**

throne /θrəʊn/ noun **1** [C] the special chair where a king or queen sits ▶ **tron 2** (**the throne**) [sing.] the position of being king or queen ▶ **tron**

throng¹ /θrɒŋ/ noun [C] (formal) a large crowd of people ▶ **tłok**, **ciżba**

throng² /θrɒŋ/ verb [I,T] (formal) (used about a crowd of people) to move into or fill a particular place: *Crowds were thronging into the square, keen to catch a glimpse of the band.* ▶ **zapełniać** (*np. ulice*), **tłoczyć się**

throttle¹ /ˈθrɒtl/ verb [T] to hold sb tightly by the throat and stop them breathing ▶ **dusić**, **dławić** SYN **strangle**

throttle² /ˈθrɒtl/ noun [C] the part in a vehicle that controls the speed by controlling how much fuel goes into the engine ▶ **przepustnica**

through /θruː/ prep., adv. **1** from one end or side of sth to the other: *We drove through the centre of London.* ◇ *to look through a telescope* ◇ *She cut through the rope* (przecięła linę). ◇ *to push through a crowd of people* ▶ **przez**, **poprzez 2** from the beginning to the end of sth: *Food supplies will not last through the winter.* ◇ *He read the letter through and handed it back.* ◇ *We're halfway through the book* (w połowie książki). ▶ **przez**, **od początku do końca 3** past a limit, stage or test: *She didn't get through the first interview.* ◇ *He lifted the rope to let us through* (aby nas przepuścić). ▶ **przez 4** (also thru) (US) until, and including: *They are staying Monday through Friday.* ▶ **(aż) do 5** because of; with the help of: *Errors were made through bad organization.* ◇ *David got the job through his uncle.* ▶ **za pośrednictwem**, **z powodu 6** (Brit.) connected by telephone: *Can you put me through to extension* (połączyć z numerem wewnętrznym) *5678, please?* ▶ **połączony** ℹ Wyrażenie **through train** oznacza pociąg bezpośredni. Znak **No through road** oznacza ulicę bez przejazdu.
PHR V **be through (with sb/sth)** to have finished with sb/sth ▶ **skończyć z kimś/czymś**

throughout /θruːˈaʊt/ prep. **1** in every part of sth: *The match can be watched live on TV throughout the world.* ▶ **na/po całym 2** from the beginning to the end of sth ▶ **przez cały** (*np. czas*)
■ **throughout** adv. **1**: *The house is beautifully decorated throughout.* Cały dom jest pięknie odnowiony. ▶ **wszędzie 2**: *We didn't enjoy the holiday because it rained throughout.* ▶ **przez cały czas**

throve past tense of **thrive**

throw /θrəʊ/ verb (pt **threw** /θruː/, pp **thrown** /θrəʊn; US θroʊn/) **1** [I,T] **throw (sth) (to/at sb)**; **throw sb sth** to send

T

sth from your hand through the air by moving your hand or arm quickly: *How far can you throw?* ◇ *Throw the ball to me.* ◇ *Throw me the ball.* ◇ *Don't throw stones at people.* ▶ **rzucać** **2** [T] to put sth somewhere quickly or carelessly: *He threw his bag down in a corner.* ◇ *She threw on a sweater and ran out of the door.* ▶ **rzucać, ciskać** **3** [T] to move your body or part of it quickly or suddenly: *Jenny threw herself onto the bed and sobbed.* ◇ *Lee threw back his head* (odrzucił głowę do tyłu) *and roared with laughter.* ▶ **rzucać** **4** [T] to cause sb to fall down quickly or violently: *The bus braked and we were thrown to the floor.* ▶ **rzucać, ciskać** **5** [T] to put sb in a particular (usually unpleasant) situation: *Many people were thrown out of work in the recession.* ◇ *We were thrown into confusion by the news.* Ta wiadomość wywołała wśród nas zamieszanie. ▶ **rzucać, wyrzucać** **6** [T] (informal) to make sb feel upset, confused or surprised: *The question threw me and I didn't know what to reply.* ▶ **zbijać z tropu** **7** [T] to send light or shade onto sth: *The tree threw a long shadow across the lawn in the late afternoon.* ▶ **rzucać**

■ **throw** noun [C]: *It's your throw.* ◇ *a throw of 97 metres* ▶ **rzut**

PHR V **throw sth away** **1** (also **throw sth out**) to get rid of rubbish or sth that you do not want: *I threw his letters away.* ▶ **wyrzucać** **2** to waste or not use sth useful: *to throw away an opportunity* ▶ **przepuszczać**

throw sth in (informal) to include sth extra without increasing the price ▶ **dorzucać (coś gratis)**

throw yourself/sth into sth to begin to do sth with energy and enthusiasm ▶ **rzucać się w wir czegoś, zabierać się energicznie do czegoś**

throw sb out (of…) to force sb to leave a place ▶ **wyrzucać kogoś skądś**

throw sth out **1** to decide not to accept sb's idea or suggestion ▶ **odrzucać** (*np. propozycję*) **2** = THROW STH AWAY (1)

throw up (informal) to be sick ▶ **wymiotować** SYN **vomit**

throw sth up **1** to be sick: *The baby's thrown up her dinner.* ▶ **wymiotować** SYN **vomit** **2** to produce or show sth: *Our research has thrown up some interesting facts.* ▶ **przynosić, dawać** **3** to leave your job, career, studies, etc. ▶ **rezygnować z czegoś**

thru (US) = THROUGH (4)

thrush /θrʌʃ/ noun [C] a bird with a brownish back and brown spots on its breast ▶ **drozd**

thrust[1] /θrʌst/ verb [I,T] (pt, pp **thrust**) **1** to push sb/sth suddenly or violently; to move quickly and suddenly in a particular direction: *The man thrust his hands deeper into his pockets.* ◇ *She thrust past him and ran out of the room.* ▶ **popychać, wpychać** **2** to make a sudden forward movement with a knife, etc. ▶ **dźgać, pchać**

PHR V **thrust sb/sth upon sb** to force sb to accept or deal with sb/sth ▶ **narzucać (coś/kogoś komuś)**

thrust[2] /θrʌst/ noun **1** (**the thrust**) [sing.] the main part or point of an argument, policy, etc. ▶ **cel, istota** **2** [C] a sudden strong movement forward ▶ **pchnięcie; dźgnięcie**

thud /θʌd/ noun [C] the low sound that is made when a heavy object hits sth else: *She fell to the ground and her head hit the floor with a dull thud.* ▶ **głuchy odgłos, łomot**

■ **thud** verb [I] (**thudding**; **thudded**) ▶ **uderzać w coś** (*z głuchym odgłosem*), **łomotać**

thug /θʌg/ noun [C] a violent person who may harm other people ▶ **zbir, opryszek**

thumb[1] /θʌm/ noun [C] **1** the short thick finger at the side of each hand: *She sucks her thumb.* ▶ **kciuk** ➲ note at **finger** ➲ picture at **body** **2** the part of a glove, etc. that covers your thumb ▶ **duży palec** (*w rękawiczce*)

IDM **a rule of thumb** → RULE[1]

have a green thumb → GREEN[1]

stand/stick out like a sore thumb → SORE[1]

the thumbs up/down a sign or an expression that shows approval/disapproval: *The new proposal was given the thumbs up by* (dostała zielone światło od) *the City Council.* ▶ **znak aprobaty/dezaprobaty**

under sb's thumb (used about a person) completely controlled by sb: *She's got him under her thumb.* ▶ **pod czyimś pantoflem**

thumb[2] /θʌm/ verb [I,T] **thumb (through) sth** to turn the pages of a book, etc. quickly ▶ **przerzucać (szybko) kartki, kartkować**

IDM **thumb a lift** to hold out your thumb to cars going past, to ask sb to give you a free ride ▶ **zatrzymywać samochód (prosząc o podwiezienie)** ➲ note at **hitchhike**

thumbtack (US) = DRAWING PIN

thump /θʌmp/ verb **1** [T] to hit sb/sth hard with sth, usually your **fist**: *He started coughing and Jo thumped him on the back.* ▶ **uderzać, grzmocić** **2** [I,T] to make a loud sound by hitting sth or by beating hard: *His heart was thumping with excitement.* ▶ **walić, bić**

■ **thump** noun [C] ▶ **uderzenie, walnięcie**

thunder[1] /ˈθʌndə(r)/ noun [U] the loud noise in the sky that you can hear when there is a storm: *a clap/crash/roll of thunder* ▶ **grzmot, grom** ➲ note at **storm** ➲ look at **lightning**

thunder[2] /ˈθʌndə(r)/ verb [I] **1** [used with *it*] to make a loud noise in the sky during a storm: *The rain poured down and it started to thunder.* ▶ **grzmieć** **2** to make a loud deep noise like **thunder**: *Traffic thundered across the bridge.* ▶ **grzmieć, przejeżdżać itp. z hukiem**

thunderstorm /ˈθʌndəstɔːm/ noun [C] a storm with **thunder** and **lightning** ▶ **burza z piorunami** ➲ note at **storm**

Thur. (also **Thurs.**) = THURSDAY: *Thur. 26 September*

Thursday /ˈθɜːzdeɪ; -di/ noun [C,U] (abbr. **Thur.**) the day of the week after Wednesday ▶ **czwartek** ➲ note at **Monday**

thus /ðʌs/ adv. (formal) **1** like this; in this way: *Thus began the series of incidents which changed her life.* ▶ **w ten sposób, tak** **2** because of or as a result of this: *He is the eldest son and thus heir to the throne.* ▶ **a zatem, tak więc** SYN **therefore**

thwart /θwɔːt/ verb [T] **thwart sth**; **thwart sb (in sth)** to stop sb doing what they planned to do; to prevent sth happening: *to thwart somebody's plans/ambitions/efforts* ◇ *She was thwarted in her attempt to gain control.* ▶ **krzyżować (plany); udaremniać**

thyme /taɪm/ noun [U] a **herb** that is used in cooking and has small leaves and a sweet smell ▶ **tymianek** ➲ picture on **page A12**

thyroid /ˈθaɪrɔɪd/ (also ˈ**thyroid gland**) noun [C] a small organ at the front of the neck that produces **hormones** that control the way in which the body grows and functions: ***an underactive/overactive thyroid*** ▶ **tarczyca**

tibia /ˈtɪbiə/ noun [C] the inner and larger bone of the two bones in the lower part of the leg between your knee and foot ▶ **kość piszczelowa** SYN **shin** ➲ look at **fibula** ➲ picture at **body**

tic /tɪk/ noun [C] a sudden quick movement of a muscle, especially in your face or head, that you cannot control: *He has a nervous tic.* ▶ **tik**

tick[1] /tɪk/ verb **1** [I] (used about a clock or watch) to make regular short sounds ▶ **tykać** **2** (US **check**) [T] to put a mark (✓) next to a name, an item on a list, etc. to show that sth has been dealt with or chosen, or that it is correct: *Please tick the appropriate box.* ▶ **odfajkowywać, stawiać ptaszek, zaznaczać** ➲ note at **tick**[2] (2)

IDM **what makes sb/sth tick** the reasons why sb behaves or sth works in the way he/she/it does: *He has a strong*

interest in people and what makes them tick. ▶ **co jest motywem/motorem czegoś/czyjegoś działania**
PHR V **tick away/by/past** (used about time) to pass ▶ **mijać**
tick sb off (Brit., informal) to speak angrily to sb, especially a child, because they have done sth wrong: *I was always being ticked off for messy work.* ▶ **objeżdżać kogoś, rugać kogoś** SYN **tell sb off (for sth/doing sth)**
tick sb/sth off to put a mark (✓) next to a name, an item on a list, etc. to show that sth has been done or sb has been dealt with ▶ **odhaczać kogoś/coś** (*na liście*)
tick over [usually used in the continuous tenses] (informal) **1** (used about an engine) to run slowly while the vehicle is not moving ▶ **chodzić na jałowym biegu 2** to keep working slowly without producing or achieving very much ▶ **chodzić na zwolnionych obrotach**

tick[2] /tɪk/ noun [C] **1** (US **check mark**; **check**) a mark (✓) next to an item on a list that shows that sth has been done or next to an answer to show that it is correct: *Put a tick after each correct answer.* ▶ **fajka** ⓘ W Amer. ang. postawienie fajki na marginesie wypracowania lub testu może oznaczać, że w tym miejscu jest błąd. W Br. ang. fajka zwykle oznacza, że dany fragment tekstu jest poprawny, a błąd zaznacza się krzyżykiem ✘. **2** (also **ticking**) the regular short sound that a watch or clock makes when it is working ▶ **tykanie 3** (Brit., informal) a moment ▶ **moment, chwilka 4** a small insect that sucks blood ▶ **kleszcz**

tickbox (Brit.) = CHECKBOX

⚷ **ticket** /ˈtɪkɪt/ noun [C] **1 a ticket (for/to sth)** a piece of paper or card that shows you have paid for a journey, or allows you to enter a theatre, cinema, etc.: *two tickets for the Cup Final* ◇ *I'd like a single/return ticket* (bilet w jedną stronę/powrotny) *to London.* ◇ *a ticket office/machine/collector* ▶ **bilet** ➲ look at **season ticket** ➲ picture at **label 2** a piece of paper fastened to sth in a shop that shows its price, size, etc. ▶ **metka 3** an official piece of paper that you get when you have parked illegally or driven too fast telling you that you must pay money as a punishment: *a parking ticket* ▶ **mandat**
IDM **just the job/ticket** → JOB

ticking = TICK[2] (2)

tickle /ˈtɪkl/ verb **1** [T] to touch sb lightly with your fingers or with sth soft so that they laugh: *She tickled the baby's toes.* ▶ **łaskotać 2** [I,T] to produce or to have an uncomfortable feeling in a part of your body: *The woollen scarf tickled her neck.* ◇ *My nose tickles/is tickling.* Swędzi mnie nos. ▶ **swędzić, łaskotać 3** [T] (informal) to amuse and interest sb: *That joke really tickled me.* ▶ **bawić, cieszyć**
■ **tickle** noun [C]: *I've got a tickle* (swędzi mnie) *in my throat.* ▶ **swędzenie, łaskotanie**

ticklish /ˈtɪklɪʃ/ adj. if a person is **ticklish**, they laugh when sb **tickles** them: *Are you ticklish?* ▶ **mający łaskotki, łaskotliwy**

tidal /ˈtaɪdl/ adj. connected with the **tides** of the sea: *tidal forces* ◇ *a tidal river* ▶ **pływowy, dotyczący przypływu/odpływu**

ˌ**tidal ˈwave** noun [C] a very large wave in the sea which destroys things when it reaches the land, and is often caused by an **earthquake** ▶ **fala pływowa** ➲ look at **tsunami**

tidbit (US) = TITBIT

tide[1] /taɪd/ noun [C] **1** the regular change in the level of the sea caused by the moon and the sun. At *high tide* the sea is closer to the land, at *low tide* it is further away and more of the beach can be seen: *The tide is **coming in/going out.*** Nadchodzi przypływ/odpływ. ◇ *The tide is in/out.* Jest przypływ/odpływ. ▶ **przypływ, odpływ** ➲ note at **ebb 2** [usually sing.] the way that most people think or feel about sth at a particular time: *It appears that **the tide has turned** in the government's favour.* ▶ **opinia publiczna**

tide[2] /taɪd/ verb
PHR V **tide sb over (sth)** to give sb sth to help them through a difficult time ▶ **pomagać komuś przetrwać trudne chwile**

⚷ **tidy**[1] /ˈtaɪdi/ adj. (**tidier**; **tidiest**) **1** (especially Brit.) arranged with everything in good order: *If you keep your room tidy it is easier to find things.* ▶ **uporządkowany, czysty 2** (used about a person) liking to keep things in good order: *Mark is a very tidy boy.* ▶ **staranny** SYN for both meanings **neat** OPP for both meanings **untidy**
■ **tidily** adv. ▶ **porządnie, starannie** | **tidiness** noun [U] ▶ **staranność, schludność**

⚷ **tidy**[2] /ˈtaɪdi/ verb [I,T] (**tidying**; **tidies**; pt, pp **tidied**) **tidy (sb/sth/yourself) (up)** to make sb/sth/yourself look in order and well arranged: *We must tidy this room up before the visitors arrive.* ▶ **doprowadzać do porządku, sprzątać**
PHR V **tidy sth away** to put sth into the drawer, cupboard, etc. where it is kept so that it cannot be seen ▶ **odkładać (coś) na miejsce**

⚷ **tie**[1] /taɪ/ verb (**tying**; **ties**; pt, pp **tied**) **1** [T] to fasten sb/sth or fix sb/sth in position with rope, string, etc.; to make a knot in sth: *The prisoner was tied to a chair.* ◇ *Kay tied her hair back with a ribbon.* ◇ *to tie something in a knot* ◇ *to tie your shoelaces* ▶ **przywiązywać, związywać** (*włosy*) OPP **untie 2** [T, usually passive] **tie sb (to sth/to doing sth)** to limit sb's freedom and make them unable to do everything they want to: *I don't want to be tied to staying in this country permanently.* ▶ **ograniczać kogoś (do czegoś) 3** [I] **tie (with sb) (for sth)** to have the same number of points as another player or team at the end of a game or competition: *England tied with Italy for third place.* ▶ **remisować (z kimś)**
IDM **your hands are tied** → HAND[1]
PHR V **tie sb/yourself down** to limit sb's/your freedom: *Having young children really ties you down.* ▶ **krępować (się), wiązać (się)**
tie in (with sth) to agree with other facts or information that you have; to match: *The new evidence seems to tie in with your theory.* ▶ **wiązać się (z czymś)**
tie sb up [usually passive] to keep sb busy: *Mr Jones is tied up* (jest zajęty) *in a meeting.*
tie sb/sth up to fix sb/sth in position with rope, string, etc.: *The dog was tied up in the back garden.* ▶ **uwiązywać/przywiązywać kogoś/coś** OPP **untie**

⚷ **tie**[2] /taɪ/ noun [C] **1** (US also **necktie** /ˈnektaɪ/) a long thin piece of cloth worn round the neck, especially by men, with a knot at the front. A tie is usually worn with a shirt: *a striped silk tie* ▶ **krawat** ➲ look at **bow tie** ➲ picture on **page A1 2** [usually pl.] a strong connection between people or organizations: *personal/emotional ties* ◇ *family ties* ▶ **więź 3** something that limits your freedom: *He never married because he didn't want any ties.* ▶ **więzy, skrępowanie 4** a situation in a game or competition in which two or more teams or players get the same score: *There was a tie for first place.* ▶ **remis**

tier /tɪə(r)/ noun [C] one of a number of levels ▶ **kondygnacja, rząd** (*np. krzeseł*), **poziom**

tiff /tɪf/ noun [C] a slight argument between close friends or lovers: *to have a tiff with sb* ▶ **sprzeczka**

tiger /ˈtaɪgə(r)/ noun [C] a large wild cat that has yellow fur with black lines. **Tigers** live in parts of Asia. ▶ **tygrys**

> A female tiger is called a **tigress** and a baby is called a **cub**.

⚷ **tight** /taɪt/ adj. **1** fixed firmly in position and difficult to move or open: *a tight* (mocno zaciśnięty) *knot* ◇ *Keep a **tight grip/hold** on this rope.* ▶ **mocny, zwarty 2** fit-

T

ting very closely in a way that is often uncomfortable: *These shoes hurt. They're too tight.* ▶ **ciasny**, **wąski** OPP **loose 3** controlled very strictly and firmly: *Security is very tight at the airport.* ▶ **zaostrzony**, **ściśle kontrolowany 4** stretched or pulled hard so that it cannot be stretched further: *The rope was stretched tight.* ▶ **napięty**, **naprężony 5** not having much free time or space: *My schedule this week is very tight.* ▶ (*harmonogram itp.*) **napięty**, (*przestrzeń itp.*) **ciasny 6 (-tight)** [in compounds] not allowing sth to get in or out: *an airtight* (hermetyczny)/*watertight* (wodoszczelny) *container* ▶ **szczelny**

■ **tight** adv. firmly; closely: ***Hold tight**, please!* (w autobusie) Proszę trzymać się poręczy! ◇ *a tight-fitting skirt* obcisła spódnica ▶ **mocno**; **ciasno** | **tightly** adv.: *Screw the lid on tightly.* ◇ *She kept her eyes tightly closed.* ▶ **mocno**, **ciasno** ℹ Przed imiesłowem biernym używa się **tightly**, a nie **tight**: *The van was packed tight with boxes.* ◇ *The van was tightly packed with boxes.*

■ **tightness** noun [U] ▶ **napięcie**, **ściśnięcie**

tighten /ˈtaɪtn/ verb [I,T] **tighten (sth) (up)** to become or to make sth tight or tighter: *His grip on her arm tightened.* ◇ *He tightened the screws as far as they would go.* Dokręcił śruby aż do oporu. ▶ **zaciskać**, **zacieśniać**

IDM **tighten your belt** to spend less money because you have less than usual available ▶ (*przen.*) **zacisnąć pasa**

PHR V **tighten up (on) sth** to cause sth to become stricter: *to tighten up security/a law* ▶ **zaostrzyć** (*np. restrykcje*)

tightrope /ˈtaɪtrəʊp/ noun [C] a rope or wire that is stretched high above the ground and that people walk along, especially as a form of entertainment ▶ **lina**

tights /taɪts/ (US **pantyhose** /ˈpæntihəʊz/) noun [pl.] a piece of thin clothing, usually worn by women, that fits tightly from the waist over the legs and feet: *a pair of tights* ▶ **rajstopy** ➲ look at **stocking** ➲ picture on **page A1**

tile /taɪl/ noun [C] one of the flat, square objects that are arranged in rows to cover roofs, floors, bathroom walls, etc.: *carpet tiles* kwadraty wykładziny dywanowej ▶ **dachówka**, **płytka**, **kafel**

■ **tile** verb [T]: *a tiled bathroom* ▶ **wykładać kafelkami**, **pokrywać dachówką**

till¹ (informal) = UNTIL

till² /tɪl/ (also ˈ**cash register**) noun [C] the machine or drawer where money is kept in a shop, etc.: *Please pay at the till.* ▶ **kasa**

tilt /tɪlt/ verb [I,T] to move, or make sth move, into a position with one end or side higher than the other: *The front seats of the car tilt forward.* ◇ *She tilted her head to one side.* ▶ **nachylać (się)**, **przechylać (się)**

■ **tilt** noun [sing.] ▶ **nachylenie**, **przechylenie**

timber /ˈtɪmbə(r)/ noun **1** (especially US **lumber** /ˈlʌmbə(r)/) [U] wood that is going to be used for building ▶ **drewno**, **budulec 2** [C] a large piece of wood: *roof timbers* ▶ **belka**

timbre /ˈtæmbə(r)/ noun [C] (formal) the quality of sound that is produced by a particular voice or musical instrument ▶ **barwa** (*głosu*)

time¹ /taɪm/ noun **1** [U, sing.] a period of minutes, hours, days, etc.: *As time passed and there was still no news, we got more worried.* ◇ *You're **wasting time** – get on with your work!* ◇ *I'll go by car to **save time**.* ◇ *free/spare time* ◇ *We haven't got time to stop now.* ◇ *I've been waiting **a long time*** (długo). ◇ *Learning a language **takes time**.* ▶ **czas 2** [U,C] **time (to do sth)**; **time (for sth)** the time in hours and minutes shown on a clock; the moment when sth happens or should happen: *What's the time?/What time is it?* Która godzina? ◇ *Look at the time!* Spójrz, która godzina! ◇ *It's time to go home.* ◇ *It's time for lunch.* ◇ ***By the time*** (gdy dotrę do domu) *I get home, Mark will have cooked the dinner.* ◇ ***This time tomorrow** I'll be on the plane.* ◇ *Can Mark tell the time* (umie powiedzieć, która godzina) *yet?* ◇ *Can you tell me the times* (godziny odjazdu) *of trains to Bristol, please?* ▶ **czas**, **pora**, **godzina 3** [sing.] a system for measuring time in a particular part of the world: *We arrive in Atlanta at eleven, **local time*** (czasu miejscowego). ▶ **czas 4** [C] a period in the past; a part of history: *In Shakespeare's times, few people could read.* ◇ *The 19th century was a time of great industrial change.* ▶ **czas/y 5** [C] an occasion when you do sth or when sth happens: *I phoned them three times.* ◇ *I'll do it better **next time**.* ◇ ***Last time** I saw him, he looked ill.* ◇ ***How many times** have I told you not to touch that?* ▶ **raz 6** [C] an event or an occasion that you experience in a certain way: ***Have a good time*** (baw się dobrze) *tonight.* ◇ *We had a terrible time* (przeżyliśmy okropne chwile) *at the hospital.* ▶ **czas 7** [C,U] the number of minutes, etc., taken to complete a race or an event: *What was his time in* (jaki miał czas na) *the hundred metres?* ▶ **czas**

IDM **(and) about time (too)**; **(and) not before time** (informal) (used to say that sth should already have happened) ▶ **najwyższy czas**

ahead of your time → AHEAD

all the time/the whole time during the period that sb was doing sth or that sth was happening: *I searched everywhere for my keys and they were in the door all the time.* ▶ **(przez) cały czas**

at the same time → SAME

at a time on each occasion: *The lift can hold six people at a time.* ◇ *She ran down the stairs two at a time.* ▶ **jednocześnie**, **na raz**

at one time in the past ▶ **kiedyś**, **dawno temu** SYN **previously**

at the time at a particular moment or period in the past; then: *I agreed at the time but later changed my mind.* ▶ **wtedy**, **wówczas**

at times sometimes: *At times I wish we'd never moved house.* ▶ **czasami**, **niekiedy** SYN **occasionally**

before your time before you were born ▶ **kiedy cię jeszcze na świecie nie było**

behind the times not modern or fashionable ▶ **zacofany**

bide your time → BIDE

buy time → BUY¹

for the time being just for the present; not for long ▶ **na razie**, **chwilowo**

from time to time sometimes; not often ▶ **czasami**, **od czasu do czasu**

give sb a hard time → HARD¹

have a hard time doing sth → HARD¹

have no time for sb/sth to not like sb/sth: *I have no time for lazy people.* ▶ **nie mieć czasu dla kogoś/czegoś**

have the time of your life to enjoy yourself very much ▶ **świetnie się bawić**

in the course of time → COURSE

in good time early; at the right time ▶ **przed czasem**; **na czas**

in the nick of time → NICK¹

in time (for sth/to do sth) not late; with enough time to be able to do sth: *Don't worry. We'll get to the station in time for your train.* ▶ **na czas**, **przed czasem**

it's about/high time (informal) (used to say that you think sb should do sth very soon): *It's about time you told him what's going on.* ▶ **najwyższy czas**

once upon a time → ONCE

on time not too late or too early: *The train left the station on time.* ▶ **na czas**

> Zwróć uwagę na różnicę między **in time (for sth/to do sth)** oraz **on time**. **In time** oznacza, że coś wydarzyło się o dokładnie wyznaczonej porze lub wcześniej. Natomiast **on time** oznacza, że coś wydarzyło się o dokładnie wyznaczonej porze: *I arrived at the station at 6.55, in time for the train, which left on time, at 7.00.*

one at a time → ONE[1]
take your time to do sth without hurrying ▶ **nie śpieszyć się**
tell the time → TELL
time after time; **time and (time) again** again and again ▶ **raz za razem** SYN **repeatedly**

time² /taɪm/ verb [T] **1** [often passive] to arrange to do sth or arrange for sth to happen at a particular time: *Their request was badly timed.* ◇ *She timed her arrival for shortly after three.* ▶ **wybierać czas, synchronizować czas** (*jakiegoś wydarzenia z czymś*) **2** to measure how long sb/sth takes: *Try timing yourself when you write your essay.* ▶ **mierzyć czas**

'time-consuming adj. that takes or needs a lot of time ▶ **czasochłonny**

'time lag = LAG[2]

timeless /'taɪmləs/ adj. (formal) that does not seem to be changed by time or affected by changes in fashion ▶ **wieczny**

'time limit noun [C] a time during which sth must be done: *We have to **set a time limit** for the work.* ▶ **(określony) termin**

timeline /'taɪmlaɪn/ noun [C] a horizontal line that is used to represent time, with the past towards the left and the future towards the right ▶ **linia czasu**

timely /'taɪmli/ adj. happening at exactly the right time: *The accident was a timely reminder of the dangers involved.* Wypadek ten wydarzył się w samą porę, aby przypomnieć o zagrożeniach związanych z motoryzacją. ▶ **zachodzący w samą porę**

'time machine noun [C] (in science fiction stories) a machine that enables you to travel in time to the past or the future ▶ **wehikuł czasu**

timer /'taɪmə(r)/ noun [C] a person or machine that measures time: *an oven timer* ◇ *an egg timer* klepsydra (do mierzenia czasu na gotowanie jajek) ▶ **chronometrażyst(k)a; regulator czasowy**

times¹ /taɪmz/ prep. (symbol ×) (used when you are multiplying one figure by another): *Three times four is twelve.* ▶ **razy**

times² /taɪmz/ noun [pl.] (used for comparing amounts): *Tea is **three times as*** (trzy razy droższa) *expensive in Spain as in England.* ◇ *Tea is **three times more*** (trzy razy droższa) *expensive in Spain than in England.* ▶ **razy**

'time signature noun [C] a sign at the start of a piece of music, usually in the form of numbers, showing the number of beats in each bar ▶ **znak metryczny** ➲ picture at **music**

⚷ **timetable** /'taɪmteɪbl/ (US **schedule**) noun [C] a list that shows the times at which sth happens: *a bus/train/school timetable* ▶ **rozkład, plan lekcji**

'time zone noun [C] one of the 24 areas that the world is divided into, each with its own time that is one hour earlier than that of the **time zone** immediately to the east: *a flight crossing several time zones* ▶ **strefa czasu**

timid /'tɪmɪd/ adj. easily frightened; shy and nervous: *as timid as a rabbit* ▶ **bojaźliwy, nieśmiały**
■ **timidity** /tɪ'mɪdəti/ noun [U] ▶ **bojaźliwość, nieśmiałość** | **timidly** adv. ▶ **bojaźliwie, nieśmiało**

timing /'taɪmɪŋ/ noun [U] **1** the time when sth is planned to happen: *The manager was careful about the timing of his announcement.* ▶ **(określony/proponowany) czas** (*np. spotkania*) **2** the skill of doing sth at exactly the right time: *The timing of her speech was perfect.* ▶ **umiejętność planowania w czasie**

timpani /'tɪmpəni/ noun [pl.] a set of large metal drums (also called **kettledrums**) ▶ (*muz.*) **kotły**
■ **timpanist** /-nɪst/ noun [C] ▶ **kotlist(k)a**

⚷ **tin** /tɪn/ noun **1** [U] (symbol **Sn**) a soft silver-white metal that is often mixed with other metals: *a tin mine* ▶ **cyna** **2** (also ˌ**tin 'can**; especially US **can**) [C] a closed metal container in which food, paint, etc. is stored and sold; the contents of one of these containers: *a tin of peas/beans/soup* ◇ *a tin of paint/varnish* ▶ **(blaszana) puszka** ➲ note at **can** ➲ picture at **container** **3** [C] a metal container with a lid for keeping food in: *a biscuit/cake tin* ▶ **(blaszana) puszka z przykrywką**
■ **tinned** adj.: *tinned peaches/peas/soup* ▶ **konserwowy**

tinder /'tɪndə(r)/ noun [U] dry material, especially wood or grass, that burns easily and can be used to light a fire: *The fire started late Saturday in tinder-dry grass near the Snake River.* ▶ **podpałka**

tinfoil = FOIL[1]

tinge /tɪndʒ/ noun [C, usually sing.] a small amount of a colour or a feeling: *a tinge of sadness* ▶ **zabarwienie; odcień**
■ **tinged** adj. **tinged (with sth)**: *Her joy at leaving was tinged with regret.* ▶ **zabarwiony; z odcieniem**

tingle /'tɪŋgl/ verb [I] (used about a part of the body) to feel as if a lot of small sharp points are pushing into it: *His cheeks tingled as he came in from the cold.* ▶ **odczuwać mrowienie, świerzbić**
■ **tingle** noun [usually sing.]: *a tingle of excitement/anticipation/fear* ▶ **mrowienie, szczypanie** (*np. mrozu*)

tinker /'tɪŋkə(r)/ verb [I] **tinker (with sth)** to try to repair or improve sth without having the proper skill or knowledge ▶ **majstrować**

tinkle /'tɪŋkl/ verb [I] to make a light high ringing sound, like that of a small bell ▶ **delikatnie dzwonić**
■ **tinkle** noun [C, usually sing.] ▶ **delikatne dzwonienie**

'tin-opener (especially US **'can-opener**) noun [C] a tool that you use for opening a tin of food ▶ **otwieracz do konserw** ➲ picture at **kitchen**

tinsel /'tɪnsl/ noun [U] long strings of shiny coloured paper, used as a decoration to hang on a Christmas tree ▶ **lameta**

T

tint /tɪnt/ noun [C] a shade or a small amount of a colour: *white paint with a pinkish tint* ▶ **zabarwienie**
■ **tint** verb [T]: *tinted glasses* ◇ *She had her hair tinted.* ▶ **barwić, farbować**

⚷ **tiny** /'taɪni/ adj. (**tinier**; **tiniest**) very small: *the baby's tiny fingers* ▶ **malutki**

⚷ **tip¹** /tɪp/ noun [C] **1** the thin or pointed end of sth: *the tips of your toes/fingers* ◇ *the tip of your nose* ◇ *the southernmost tip* (najbardziej na południe wysunięty punkt) *of South America* ▶ **koniuszek, koniec** (*np. palca*) **2 a tip (on/for sth/doing sth)** a small piece of useful advice about sth practical: *useful tips on how to save money* ▶ **dobra rada, wskazówka** **3** a small amount of extra money that you give to sb who serves you, for example in a restaurant: *to leave a tip for the waiter* ◇ *I gave the porter a $5 tip.* ▶ **napiwek** **4** (Brit.) (also **'rubbish tip**) a place where you can take rubbish and leave it: *We took the old and broken furniture to the tip.* ▶ **śmietnik, śmietnisko** SYN **dump** **5** (Brit., informal) a place that is very dirty or untidy: *The house was a tip!* ▶ **śmietnik**
IDM **on the tip of your tongue** if a word or name is **on the tip of your tongue** you are sure that you know it but you cannot remember it ▶ **mieć coś na końcu języka**
the tip of the iceberg only a small part of a much larger problem ▶ **wierzchołek góry lodowej**

⚷ **tip²** /tɪp/ verb (**tipping**; **tipped**) **1** [I,T] **tip (sth) (up/over)** to move so that one side is higher than the other; to make sth move in this way: *When I stood up, the bench tipped up and the person on the other end fell off.* ▶ **przechylać/podnosić (się) jednym końcem w górę**, (*ławka, deska* *itp.*) **przeważać 2** [T] to make sth come out of a container by holding or lifting it at an angle: *Tip the dirty water down the drain.* ◇ *The child tipped all the toys onto the floor.* ▶ **wylewać; wysypywać 3** [I,T] to give sb a small amount of extra money (in addition to the normal charge) to thank them for a service: *She tipped the taxi driver generously.* ▶ **dawać napiwek 4** [T] **tip sb/sth (as sth/to do sth)** to think or say that sb/sth is likely to do sth: *This horse is tipped to win the race.* Ten koń jest typowany na zwycięzcę. ◇ *He is widely tipped as* (prawie wszyscy typują go na) *the next leader of the Labour Party.* ▶ **typować**

PHR V **tip sb off (about sth)** to give sb secret information ▶ **udzielać poufnej informacji**

tip (sth) up/over to fall or turn over; to make sth do this: *An enormous wave crashed into the little boat and it tipped over.* ▶ **wywracać (się)**

'tip-off noun [C] secret information that sb gives, for example to the police, about an illegal activity that is going to happen: *Acting on a tip-off, the police raided the house.* ▶ **poufna informacja**

Tippex™ /'tɪpeks/ noun [U] (Brit.) a liquid, usually white, that you use to cover mistakes that you make when you are writing or typing, and that you can write on top of; a type of **correction fluid** ▶ **korektor** (*w płynie*)

■ **tippex** verb [T] **tippex sth out**: *I tippexed out the mistakes.* ▶ **poprawić coś za pomocą korektora**

tipsy /'tɪpsi/ adj. (informal) slightly drunk ▶ **podchmielony**

tiptoe[1] /'tɪptəʊ/ noun

IDM **on tiptoe** standing or walking on the ends of your toes with the back part of your foot off the ground, in order not to make any noise or to reach sth high up ▶ (*stawać/chodzić*) **na palcach**

tiptoe[2] /'tɪptəʊ/ verb [I] to walk on your toes with the back part of your foot off the ground ▶ **chodzić na palcach**

tirade /taɪ'reɪd; US 'taɪr-/ noun [C] **tirade (against sb/sth)** a long angry speech criticizing sb/sth or accusing sb of sth: *She launched into a tirade of abuse against politicians.* ▶ **tyrada**

⚷ **tire**[1] /'taɪə(r)/ verb [I,T] to feel that you need to rest or sleep; to make sb feel like this ▶ **męczyć (się)**

PHR V **tire of sth/sb** to become bored or not interested in sth/sb any more ▶ **nudzić się (czymś/kimś)**

tire sb/yourself out to make sb/yourself very tired: *The long country walk tired us all out.* ▶ **wyczerpywać kogoś; przemęczać się** SYN **exhaust**

⚷ **tire**[2] (US) = TYRE

⚷ **tired** /'taɪəd/ adj. feeling that you need to rest or sleep: *She was tired after a hard day's work.* ◇ *I was completely **tired out*** (wykończony) *after all that.* ▶ **zmęczony** ➲ note at **sleep**

■ **tiredness** noun [U] ▶ **zmęczenie**

IDM **be tired of sb/sth/doing sth** to be bored with or annoyed by sb/sth/doing sth: *I'm tired of this game. Let's play something else.* ◇ *I'm **sick and tired** of* (mam powyżej uszu) *listening to the same thing again and again.* ▶ **być zmęczonym (kimś/czymś/robieniem czegoś)**

tireless /'taɪələs/ adj. putting a lot of hard work and energy into sth over a long period of time without stopping or losing interest ▶ **niezmordowany**

tiresome /'taɪəsəm/ adj. (formal) that makes you angry or bored; annoying ▶ (*osoba*) **męczący, nieznośny**

⚷ **tiring** /'taɪərɪŋ/ adj. making you want to rest or sleep: *a tiring journey/job* ▶ **męczący** SYN **exhausting**

tissue /'tɪʃuː; 'tɪsjuː/ noun **1** [U, pl.] the mass of cells that form the bodies of humans, animals and plants: *muscle/brain/nerve/scar tissue* ◇ *Radiation can destroy the body's tissues.* ▶ **tkanka 2** [C] a thin piece of soft paper that you use to clean your nose and throw away after you have used it: *a box of tissues* ▶ **chusteczka higieniczna** ➲ note at **handkerchief 3** (also **'tissue paper**) [U] thin soft paper that you use for putting around things that may break ▶ **bibuł(k)a**

tit /tɪt/ noun [C] **1** (slang) a woman's breast ▶ **cyc/ek** ℹ Uwaga! Niektórzy uważają to słowo za obraźliwe. **2** a small bird, often with a dark top to the head. There are several types of tit: *a blue tit* ▶ **sikorka**

IDM **tit for tat** a situation in which you do something bad to sb because they have done the same to you ▶ **wet za wet**

titbit /'tɪtbɪt/ (US **tidbit** /'tɪdbɪt/) noun [C] **1** a small but very nice piece of food ▶ **smakowity kąsek 2** an interesting piece of information ▶ **rodzynek**

titillate /'tɪtɪleɪt/ verb [I,T] to interest or excite sb, especially in a sexual way: *titillating pictures* ▶ **podniecać** (*zwł. seksualnie*) ℹ Często wyraża dezaprobatę.

■ **titillation** /ˌtɪtɪ'leɪʃn/ noun [U] ▶ **podniecanie**

⚷ **title** /'taɪtl/ noun [C] **1** the name of a book, play, film, picture, etc.: *I know the author's name but I can't remember the title of the book.* ▶ **tytuł 2** a word that shows sb's position, profession, etc.: *'Lord', 'Doctor', 'Reverend', 'Mrs' and 'General' are all titles.* ▶ **tytuł 3** the position of being the winner of a competition, especially a sports competition: *Sue is playing this match to defend her title.* ▶ **tytuł**

titled /'taɪtld/ adj. having a word, for example 'Duke', 'Lady', etc. before your name that shows that your family has an important position in society ▶ (*arystokrata*) **utytułowany**

'title-holder noun [C] the person or team who won a sports competition the last time it took place ▶ **rekordzist(k)a, medalist(k)a**

'title role noun [C] the main character in a film, book, etc. whose name is the same as the title ▶ **tytułowa rola**

titter /'tɪtə(r)/ verb [I] to laugh quietly, especially in an embarrassed or nervous way ▶ **chichotać**

■ **titter** noun [C] ▶ **chichot**

'T-junction noun [C] a place where two roads join to form the shape of a T ▶ **skrzyżowanie dwóch dróg w kształcie litery** *T*

TM = TRADEMARK

TNT /ˌtiː en 'tiː/ noun [U] a substance used to cause powerful explosions ▶ **trotyl**

⚷ **to** /tə; before vowels tu; strong form tuː/ prep. **1** in the direction of; as far as: *She's going to London.* ◇ *Turn to the left* (w lewo). ◇ *Pisa is to the west of* (na zachód od) *Florence.* ◇ *He has gone to school.* ▶ **do 2** reaching a particular state: *The meat was cooked to perfection* (było idealnie wypieczone). ◇ *His speech reduced her to tears* (doprowadziło ją do łez). **3** (used to show the end or limit of a series of things or period of time): ***from** Monday **to** Friday* od poniedziałku do piątku ◇ *from beginning to end* ▶ **do, po 4** (used to say what time it is) before: *It's ten to three.* ▶ **za 5** (used to show the person or thing that receives sth): *Give that to me.* Daj mi to. ◇ *I am very grateful to my parents.* Jestem wdzięczny moim rodzicom. ◇ *What have you done to your hair?* Coś ty zrobił z włosami? ◇ *Sorry, I didn't realize you were talking to me* (że mówiłeś do mnie). ◇ *You must be kind to animals.* Musisz być dobry dla zwierząt. ℹ Często nie tłumaczy się. Wówczas w tłumaczeniu stosuje się rzeczownik w celowniku. **6** (nearly) touching sth: *He put his hands to his ears.* Zatkał uszy rękami. ◇ *They sat back to back.* Siedzieli plecami do siebie. ▶ **przy, do 7** directed towards sth: *She made no reference to her personal problems.* ▶ **do 8** (used to introduce the second part of a comparison): *I prefer theatre to opera.* ▶ **od, niż 9** (used for expressing quantity) for each unit of money, measurement, etc.: *How many dollars are there to the euro?* ▶ **(w stosunku) do** **10** (used for expressing a reaction or attitude to sth): *To my surprise, I saw two strangers coming out of my house.* ◇ *His paintings aren't really to my taste* (nie są w moim guście). ▶ **ku, z** **11** (used to express sb's opinion or feeling about sth): *To me, it was the wrong decision.* ◇ *It sounded like a good idea to me.* ◇ *I don't think our friendship means anything to him.* ▶ **według** **12** (used with verbs to form the infinitive): *I want to go* (iść) *home now.* ◇ *He asked me to go* (poprosił, żebym sobie poszła) *but I didn't want to.* ◇ *Don't forget to write.* ◇ *I didn't know what to do.* ⓘ Nie tłumaczy się.

■ **to** /tu:/ adv. (used about a door) in or into a closed position: *Push the door to.* Zamknij drzwi.

IDM **to and fro** backwards and forwards ▶ **tam i z powrotem**

toad /təʊd/ noun [C] a small animal with rough skin and long back legs that it uses for jumping, that lives both on land and in water ▶ **ropucha** ➲ picture on **page A11**

toadstool /ˈtəʊdstu:l/ noun [C] a plant without leaves, flowers or green colouring, with a flat or curved top and that is usually poisonous ▶ **muchomor, grzyb trujący** ➲ note at **mushroom** ➲ look at **fungus**

toast /təʊst/ noun **1** [U] a thin piece of bread that is heated on both sides to make it brown ▶ **grzanka** ⓘ Wyraz **toast** w tym znaczeniu jest niepoliczalny. Jedna grzanka to **a piece/a slice of toast** (a nie ~~a toast~~). **2** [C] **a toast (to sb/sth)** an occasion at which a group of people wish sb happiness, success, etc., by drinking a glass of wine, etc. at the same time: *I'd like to **propose a toast to** the happy couple.* ▶ **toast** ➲ look at **drink**

■ **toast** verb **1** [T] to hold up your glass and wish sb success, happiness, etc. before you drink ▶ **wznosić toast** **2** [I,T] to make sth, especially bread, turn brown by heating it in a toaster or close to heat; to turn brown in this way ▶ (*kromka chleba itp.*) **przypiekać się; piec grzanki** ➲ note at **cook**

toaster /ˈtəʊstə(r)/ noun [C] an electrical machine for making bread turn brown by heating it on both sides ▶ **toster**

tobacco /təˈbækəʊ/ noun [U] the dried leaves of the **tobacco** plant that people smoke in cigarettes and pipes ▶ **tytoń**

tobacconist /təˈbækənɪst/ noun **1** [C] a person who sells cigarettes, matches, etc. ▶ **osoba prowadząca sklep z/handlująca wyrobami tytoniowymi** **2** (also **the tobacconist's**) [sing.] a shop where you can buy cigarettes, matches, etc. ▶ **sklep z wyrobami tytoniowymi**

toboggan /təˈbɒgən/ noun [C] a type of flat board with flat pieces of metal underneath, that people use for travelling down hills on snow for fun ▶ **saneczki** ➲ look at **bobsleigh, sledge**

⚷ **today** /təˈdeɪ/ noun [U], adv. **1** (on) this day: *Today is Monday.* ◇ *What shall we do today?* ◇ *School ends **a week today.*** Szkoła kończy się od dziś za tydzień. ◇ *Where is today's paper* (dzisiejsza gazeta)? ▶ **dziś, dzisiaj** **2** (in) the present age; these days: *Young people today have far more freedom.* ◇ *Today's* (dzisiejsze) *computers are much smaller than the early models.* ▶ **teraz** SYN **nowadays**

toddle /ˈtɒdl/ verb [I] **1** to walk with short steps like a very young child ▶ **chodzić niepewnym krokiem** **2** (informal) to walk or go somewhere

toddler /ˈtɒdlə(r)/ noun [C] a young child who has only just learnt to walk ▶ **małe dziecko dopiero uczące się chodzić**

⚷ **toe**[1] /təʊ/ noun [C] **1** one of the small parts like fingers at the end of each foot: *the big/little toe* ▶ **palec** ➲ note at **finger** ➲ picture at **body**, picture on **page A10** **2** the part of a sock, shoe, etc. that covers your toes ▶ **palce**

toe[2] /təʊ/ verb (**toeing**; **toed**)

IDM **toe the (party) line** to do what sb in authority tells you to do, even if you do not agree with them ▶ **iść po linii** (*np. partyjnej*)

TOEFL /ˈtəʊfl/ abbr. **Test of English as a Foreign Language**; the examination for foreign students who want to study at an American university ▶ **egzamin z języka angielskiego dla obcokrajowców pragnących studiować w USA**

toenail /ˈtəʊneɪl/ noun [C] one of the hard flat parts that cover the end of your toes ▶ **paznokieć u nogi** ➲ picture at **body**

toffee /ˈtɒfi/ noun [C,U] a hard sticky sweet that is made by cooking sugar and butter together ▶ **toffi**

⚷ **together**[1] /təˈgeðə(r)/ adv. **1** with or near each other: *Can we have lunch together?* ◇ *They walked home together.* ◇ *I'll get all my things together tonight because I want to leave early.* ◇ *Stand with your feet together.* Stań ze złączonymi stopami. ▶ **razem, wspólnie** **2** so that two or more things are mixed or joined to each other: *Tie the two ends together.* ◇ *Add these numbers together to find the total.* ◇ *Mix the butter and sugar together.* Zmieszaj masło z cukrem. ▶ **razem (z czymś)** **3** at the same time: *Don't all talk together.* ▶ **na raz**

IDM **get your act together** → ACT[1]

put together [used after a noun or nouns referring to a group of people or things] combined; in total: *You got more presents than the rest of the family put together.* ▶ **razem wzięty**

put/get your heads together → HEAD[1]

together with sb/sth in addition to; as well as: *I enclose my order together with a cheque for £15.* ▶ **razem z kimś/czymś**

together[2] /təˈgeðə(r)/ adj. (informal) (used about a person) organized, capable: *I'm not very together this morning.* ▶ **zorganizowany, zdolny**

togetherness /təˈgeðənəs/ noun [U] a feeling of friendship ▶ **wspólnota** (*np. rodzinna*)

toil /tɔɪl/ verb [I] (formal) to work very hard or for a long time at sth ▶ **mozolić się**

■ **toil** noun [U] ▶ **trud**

⚷ **toilet** /ˈtɔɪlət/ noun [C] a large bowl with a seat, connected to a water pipe, that you use when you need to get rid of waste material from your body; the room containing this: *I need to **go to the toilet.*** ◇ *to flush the toilet* spuszczać wodę w ubikacji ▶ **toaleta; ubikacja**

> O ubikacji w domu mówi się zwykle **toilet** (lub potocznie **loo**). **Lavatory** i **WC** to słowa używane w języku formalnym, które wychodzą z użycia. Toalety w miejscach publicznych to **Public Conveniences** lub **ladies/gents**. W Amer. ang. używa się też słowa **bathroom** (o ubikacji w domu), natomiast o toaletach w miejscach publicznych mówi się **restroom** lub **ladies'/men's room**.

ˈ**toilet bag** (Brit.) = SPONGE BAG

ˈ**toilet paper** (also ˈ**toilet tissue**) noun [U] soft, thin paper that you use to clean yourself after going to the toilet ▶ **papier toaletowy**

toiletries /ˈtɔɪlətriz/ noun [pl.] things such as soap or **toothpaste** that you use for washing, cleaning your teeth, etc. ▶ **przybory toaletowe** ➲ look at **sponge bag, toilet bag**

ˈ**toilet roll** noun [C] (Brit.) a long piece of toilet paper rolled round a tube ▶ **rolka papieru toaletowego**

ˈ**toiletry bag** (US) = SPONGE BAG

ˈ**toilet tissue** = TOILET PAPER

ˈ**toilet-train** verb [T, usually passive] to teach a small child to use the toilet ▶ **uczyć dziecko siadać na nocniku**

token¹ /ˈtəʊkən/ noun [C] **1** a round piece of metal, plastic, etc. that you use instead of money to operate some machines or as a form of payment ▶ **żeton 2** (Brit.) a piece of paper that you can use to buy sth of a certain value in a particular shop. **Tokens** are often given as presents: *a gift token* prezent w postaci bonu towarowego ◇ *a £10 book/CD token* ▶ **bon towarowy** ➲ look at **voucher** **3** something that represents or is a symbol of sth: *We would like you to accept this gift* ***as a token of*** *our gratitude.* ▶ **znak**

token² /ˈtəʊkən/ adj. [only before a noun] **1** done, chosen, etc. in a very small quantity, and only in order not to be criticized: *There is a token woman on the board.* W radzie nadzorczej znajduje się jedna kobieta, ponieważ wypadało przyznać chociać jedno miejsce osobie takiej płci. ◇ *The troops put up only token resistance.* ▶ **na pokaz, pozorny 2** small, but done or given to show that you are serious about sth and will keep a promise or an agreement: *a token payment* ▶ **symboliczny**

told past tense, past participle of **tell**

tolerable /ˈtɒlərəbl/ adj. **1** quite good, but not of the best quality **2** of a level that you can accept or deal with, although unpleasant or painful: *Drugs can reduce the pain to a tolerable level.* ▶ **znośny** OPP **intolerable**

tolerant /ˈtɒlərənt/ adj. **tolerant (of/towards sb/sth)** able to allow or accept sth that you do not like or agree with: *He's not very tolerant of dogs.* ▶ **tolerancyjny (dla/w stosunku do kogoś/czegoś)** OPP **intolerant**

■ **tolerance** noun [U] **tolerance (of/for sb/sth)**: *religious/racial tolerance* ▶ **tolerancja** OPP **intolerance**

tolerate /ˈtɒləreɪt/ verb [T] **1** to allow or accept sth that you do not like or agree with: *In a democracy we must tolerate opinions that are different from our own.* ▶ **tolerować 2** to accept or be able to deal with sb/sth unpleasant without complaining: *The noise was more than she could tolerate.* ▶ **znosić**

■ **toleration** /ˌtɒləˈreɪʃn/ = TOLERANCE

toll /təʊl/ noun **1** [C] money that you pay to use a road or bridge: *motorway tolls* ◇ *a toll bridge* ▶ **myto, opłata targowa 2** [C, usually sing.] the amount of damage done or the number of people who were killed or injured by sth: *The official death toll* (liczba ofiar śmiertelnych) *has now reached 5 000.* ▶ **liczba** (*np. ofiar*)

IDM **take a heavy toll/take its toll (on sth)** to cause great loss, damage, suffering, etc. ▶ **zbierać obfite żniwo (czegoś)**

tom = TOMCAT

tomato /təˈmɑːtəʊ; US -ˈmeɪ-/ noun [C] (pl. **tomatoes**) a soft red fruit that is often eaten without being cooked in salads, or cooked as a vegetable: *tomato juice/soup/sauce* ▶ **pomidor** ➲ picture on **page A13**, picture at **salad**

tomb /tuːm/ noun [C] a large place, usually built of stone under the ground, where the body of an important person is buried: *the tombs of the Pharaohs* ▶ **grobowiec** ➲ look at **grave**

tomboy /ˈtɒmbɔɪ/ noun [C] a young girl who likes the same games and activities that are traditionally considered to be for boys ▶ **chłopczyca**

tombstone /ˈtuːmstəʊn/ noun [C] a large flat stone that lies on or stands at one end of the place where sb is buried and shows the name, dates, etc. of the dead person ▶ **kamień nagrobny** ➲ look at **gravestone, headstone**

tomcat /ˈtɒmkæt/ (also **tom**) noun [C] a male cat ▶ **kot, kocur** ➲ note at **cat**

tomorrow /təˈmɒrəʊ/ noun [U], adv. **1** (on) the day after today: *Today is Friday so tomorrow is Saturday.* ◇ *See you tomorrow.* ◇ *I'm going to bed. I've got to get up early tomorrow morning.* ◇ *a week tomorrow* od jutra za tydzień ◇ *The advertisement will appear in tomorrow's papers* (w jutrzejszych gazetach). ▶ **jutro** ➲ note at **morning** ℹ Zwróć uwagę, że mówi się **tomorrow morning, tomorrow afternoon** itp., a nie ~~*tomorrow in the morning*~~ itp. **2** the future: *The schoolchildren of today are tomorrow's workers* (jutrzejsi pracownicy). ▶ **jutro**

ton /tʌn/ noun **1** [C] (informal) (abbr. **t**) a measure of weight; 2 240 pounds: *What have you got in this bag? It weighs a ton!* ▶ **tona** (*= 2 200 funtów ang.*) ℹ Nie należy mylić **ton** z **tonne** (tj. toną metryczną = 1 000 kg). **Ton** odpowiada 1,016 tony metrycznej. Tona amer. odpowiada 2 000 funtów ang. lub 0,907 tony metrycznej. **2** (**tons**) [pl.] (informal) a lot: *I've got tons of homework to do.* ▶ **kupa**

tonal /ˈtəʊnl/ adj. **1** (technical) relating to tones of sound or colour ▶ **tonowy 2** (used about music) having a particular **key** ▶ **tonalny** OPP **atonal**

tonality /təʊˈnæləti/ noun [U,C] (pl. **-ies**) the quality of a piece of music that depends on the **key** in which it is written ▶ **tonacja**

tone¹ /təʊn/ noun **1** [C,U] the quality of a sound or of sb's voice, especially expressing a particular emotion: *'Do you know each other?' she asked in a casual tone of voice.* ▶ **ton 2** [sing.] the general quality or style of sth: *The tone of the meeting was optimistic.* ▶ **atmosfera** (*np. zebrania*) **3** [C] a shade of a colour: *warm tones of red and orange* ▶ **odcień** (*koloru*) **4** [C] a sound that you hear on the telephone: *Please speak after the tone.* ▶ **sygnał telefoniczny**

tone² /təʊn/ verb [T] **tone sth (up)** to make your muscles, skin, etc. firmer, especially by doing exercise ▶ **wzmacniać, ujędrniać**

PHR V **tone sth down** to change sth that you have said, written, etc., to make it less likely to offend ▶ **stonować/złagodzić coś**

ˌtone-ˈdeaf adj. not able to sing or hear the difference between notes in music ▶ **nie mający słuchu muzycznego**

toner /ˈtəʊnə(r)/ noun [U,C] **1** a type of ink used in machines that print or photocopy ▶ **toner 2** a liquid or cream used for making the skin on your face firm and smooth ▶ **tonik**

tongs /tɒŋz/ noun [pl.] a tool that looks like a pair of scissors but that you use for holding or picking things up ▶ **szczypce** ➲ picture at **laboratory**

tongue /tʌŋ/ noun **1** [C] the soft part inside your mouth that you can move. You use your tongue for speaking, tasting things, etc. ▶ **język** ➲ picture at **body 2** [C,U] the tongue of some animals, cooked and eaten: *a slice of ox tongue* ▶ (*potrawa*) **ozór, ozorek 3** [C] (formal) a language: ***your mother tongue*** język ojczysty ▶ **język**

IDM **on the tip of your tongue** → TIP¹

put/stick your tongue out to put your tongue outside your mouth as a rude sign to sb ▶ **pokazywać język**

a slip of the tongue → SLIP²

(with) tongue in cheek done or said as a joke; not intended seriously ▶ (*mówić/robić coś*) **ironicznie**

ˈtongue-tied adj. not saying anything because you are shy or nervous ▶ **oniemiały**

ˈtongue-twister noun [C] a phrase or sentence with many similar sounds that is difficult to say correctly when you are speaking quickly ▶ **zdanie/wyraz trudny do wypowiedzenia, łamaniec językowy**

tonic /ˈtɒnɪk/ noun **1** (also **ˈtonic water**) [U,C] a type of water with bubbles in it and a rather bitter taste that is often added to alcoholic drinks: *a gin and tonic* ▶ **tonik 2** [C,U] a medicine or sth you do that makes you feel stronger, healthier, etc., especially when you are very tired: *A relaxing holiday is a wonderful tonic.* ▶ **środek tonizujący** (*np. wzmacniający/ożywiający*)

tonight /təˈnaɪt/ noun [U], adv. (on) the evening or night of today: *Tonight is the last night of our holiday.* ◇ *What's on TV tonight?* ◇ *We are staying with friends tonight and* *going home tomorrow.* ▶ **dzisiejsz-y/a wieczór/noc, dziś wieczorem**

tonne /tʌn/ noun [C] (abbr. **t**) a measure of weight; 1 000 kilograms ▶ **tona** (*metryczna*) ➲ look at **ton**

tonsil /ˈtɒnsl/ noun [C] one of the two soft lumps in your throat at the back of your mouth: *She had to **have** her **tonsils out**.* Musiała usunąć migdałki. ▶ **migdał/ek**

tonsillitis /ˌtɒnsəˈlaɪtɪs/ noun [U] an illness in which the **tonsils** become very sore and swollen ▶ **zapalenie migdałków**

too /tuː/ adv. **1** [used before adjectives and adverbs] more than is good, allowed, possible, etc.: *These boots are too small.* ◇ *It's far too cold to go out without a coat.* ◇ *It's too long a journey* (to zbyt długa podróż) *for you to make alone.* ▶ **za, zbyt** ℹ Zwróć uwagę, że nie można powiedzieć ~~*It's a too long journey*~~. **2** [not with negative statements] in addition; also: *Red is my favourite colour but I like blue, too.* ◇ *Phil thinks you're right and I do too.* ▶ **też, także** ➲ note at **also** ℹ Zwróć uwagę, że mówi się: *There were lions and tigers at the zoo. There were elephants too*; ale: *There were no zebras and there were no giraffes, either.* **3** (used to add sth which makes a situation even worse): *Her purse was stolen. And on her birthday too* (i to w dniu jej urodzin). ▶ **na dodatek 4** [usually used in negative sentences] very: *The weather is not too bad* (nie najgorsza) *today.* ▶ **(nie) zbyt**

took past tense of **take**

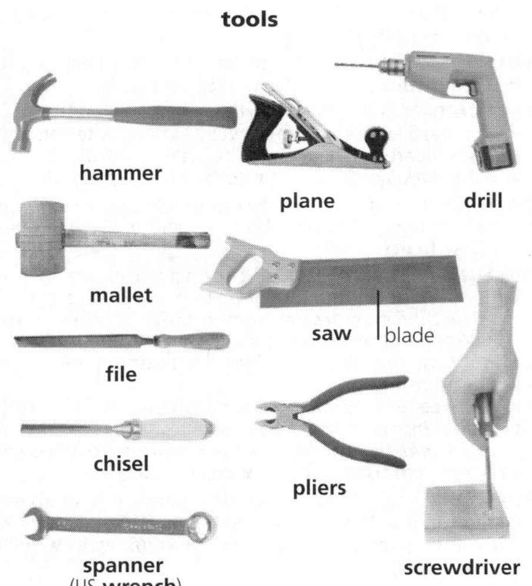

tool /tuːl/ noun [C] a piece of equipment such as a hammer, that you hold in your hand(s) and use to do a particular job: *Hammers, screwdrivers and saws are all carpenter's tools.* ◇ *garden tools* ◇ *a tool kit* zestaw narzędzi ▶ **narzędzie** (*np. pracy*)

tool

Tool oznacza zwykle coś, co można trzymać w ręce, np. **spanner** lub **hammer**. **Implement** oznacza narzędzie często używane poza domem, np. w rolnictwie lub ogrodnictwie. **Machine** to narzędzie zasilane energią elektryczną, wyposażone w silnik, mające ruchome części itp. **Instrument** często używa się, mówiąc o narzędziach stosowanych w pracy technicznej lub precyzyjnej: *a dentist's instruments* ◇ *precision instruments*. **Device** to słowo ogólne oznaczające jakieś przydatne urządzenie do wykonywania konkretnej czynności: *The machine has a safety device which switches the power off if there is a fault.*

toolbar /ˈtuːlbɑː(r)/ noun [C] a row of symbols on a computer screen that show the different things that the computer can do ▶ **pasek narzędzi**

toot /tuːt/ noun [C] the short high sound that a car horn makes ▶ **gwizd; trąbienie**
■ **toot** verb [I,T]: *Toot your horn* (zatrąb) *to let them know we're here.* ▶ **trąbić; gwizdać**

tooth /tuːθ/ noun [C] (pl. **teeth** /tiːθ/) **1** one of the hard white things in your mouth that you use for biting: *She's got beautiful teeth.* ◇ *I've just **had a tooth out*** (właśnie wyrwałem ząb) *at the dentist's.* ◇ *The old man took out his **false teeth*** (sztuczną szczękę). ▶ **ząb** ➲ look at **wisdom tooth** ➲ picture at **body 2** one of the long narrow pointed parts of an object such as a **comb** ▶ **ząb**
IDM **by the skin of your teeth** → SKIN[1]
gnash your teeth → GNASH
grit your teeth → GRIT[2]
have a sweet tooth → SWEET[1]

teeth

You **brush/clean** your teeth with a **toothbrush**. You clean between your teeth with special string called **dental floss**. If you have **toothache** or **tooth decay**, you should see a **dentist**. You might need a **filling**, or you can have the tooth **out/extracted**. Some children have a **brace** to straighten their teeth, and people with no teeth can have **false teeth** or **dentures**.

toothache /ˈtuːθeɪk/ noun [U,C, usually sing.] a pain in your tooth or teeth ▶ **ból zęba** ➲ note at **ache**

toothbrush /ˈtuːθbrʌʃ/ noun [C] a small brush with a handle that you use for cleaning your teeth ▶ **szczoteczka do zębów** ➲ picture at **brush**

toothpaste /ˈtuːθpeɪst/ noun [U] a substance that you put on a brush and use for cleaning your teeth ▶ **pasta do zębów**

toothpick /ˈtuːθpɪk/ noun [C] a short pointed piece of wood that you use for getting pieces of food out from between your teeth ▶ **wykałaczka**

top[1] /tɒp/ noun **1** [C] the highest part or point of sth: *The flat is **at the top of** the stairs.* ◇ *Snow was falling on the mountain tops.* ◇ *Start reading at the top of the page.* ▶ **szczyt, góra** OPP **foot 2** [C] the flat upper surface of sth: *a bench top* ◇ *a desk/table top* blat biurka/stołu ▶ **wierzch 3** [sing.] **the top (of sth)** the highest or most important position: *to be at the top of your profession* ▶ **szczyt 4** [C] the cover that you put onto sth in order to close it: *Put the tops back on the pens or they will dry out.* ▶ **zatyczka, zakrętka, skuwka** ➲ picture at **container**

Top, cap czy **lid**? **Top** i **cap** są zazwyczaj małe oraz okrągłe i można je zdjąć przez odkręcenie: *a bottle top* ◇ *Unscrew cap to open.* **Lid** to może być większa przykrywka, którą można podnosić: *a saucepan lid* ◇ *Put the lid back on the box.*

5 [C] a piece of clothing that you wear on the upper part of your body: *a tracksuit/bikini/pyjama top* ◇ *I need a top to match my new skirt.* ▶ **bluzka, koszula itp.** ➲ picture on **page A1 6** [C] a child's toy that turns round very quickly on a point: *a spinning top* ▶ **bąk**
IDM **at the top of your voice** as loudly as possible ▶ **na całe gardło**
get on top of sb (informal) to be too much for sb to manage or deal with: *I've got so much work to do. It's really getting on top of me.* ▶ **wchodzić komuś na głowę, dawać się komuś we znaki**

T

off the top of your head (informal) just guessing or using your memory without preparing or thinking about sth first ▶ **bez przygotowania**
on top 1 on or onto the highest point: *a mountain with snow on top* ▶ (*kłaść/leżeć itp.*) **na wierzch/u 2** in control; in a leading position: *Josie always seems to come out on top.* ▶ **(być) górą**
on top of sb/sth 1 on, over or covering sb/sth else: *Books were piled on top of one another.* ◇ *The remote control is on top of the TV.* ▶ **na 2** in addition to sb/sth else: *On top of everything else, the car's broken down.* ▶ **w dodatku 3** (informal) very close to sb/sth: *We were all living on top of each other in that tiny flat.* ◇ *modern houses built on top of each other* nowoczesne domy stoją prawie jeden na drugim ▶ **stłoczony**
over the top; **OTT** (especially Brit., informal) exaggerated or done with too much effort ▶ **przegięcie (pały)**

top² /tɒp/ adj. highest in position or degree: *one of Britain's top businessmen* ◇ *at the top speed* z największą szybkością ◇ *the top floor of the building* ◇ *She got top marks for her essay.* ▶ **najwyższy, najlepszy**

top³ /tɒp/ verb [T] (**topping**; **topped**) **1** to be higher or greater than a particular amount: *Inflation has topped* (przekroczyła) *the 10% mark.* ▶ **przewyższać, przerastać 2** to be in the highest position on a list because you are the most important, successful, etc. ▶ **znajdować się na szczycie** (*np. listy przebojów*) **3** [usually passive] **top sth (with sth)** to put sth on the top of sth: *cauliflower topped with cheese sauce* (polany sosem serowym) ▶ **nakrywać**
PHR V **top (sth) up** to fill sth that is partly empty: *I need to top up my mobile phone.* ▶ **dopełniać**

ˌtop-ˈclass adj. of the highest quality or standard: *a top-class performance* ▶ **najwyższej klasy**

ˌtop ˈhat noun [C] the tall black or grey hat that a man wears on formal occasions ▶ **cylinder**

ˌtop-ˈheavy adj. heavier at the top than the bottom and likely to fall over ▶ **przeciążony u góry**

topic /ˈtɒpɪk/ noun [C] a subject that you talk, write or learn about ▶ **temat**

topical /ˈtɒpɪkl/ adj. connected with sth that is happening now; that people are interested in at the present time ▶ **aktualny**

topless /ˈtɒpləs/ adj. (used about a woman) not wearing any clothes on the upper part of the body so that her breasts are not covered: *a topless swimsuit* kostium kąpielowy typu toples ▶ **toples, topless** (*bez stanika*)
■ **topless** adv.: *to sunbathe topless* (w stroju kąpielowym bez stanika) ▶ **w toplessie** (*bez stanika*)

topmost /ˈtɒpməʊst/ adj. [only before a noun] highest: *the topmost branches of the tree* ▶ **najwyższy**

ˌtop-ˈnotch adj. (informal) excellent; of the highest quality ▶ **doskonały**

topping /ˈtɒpɪŋ/ noun [C,U] something such as cream or a sauce that is put on the top of food to decorate it or make it taste nicer ▶ **wierzch, dekoracja**

topple /ˈtɒpl/ verb **1** [I] **topple (over)** to become less steady and fall down: *Don't add another book to the pile or it will topple over.* ▶ **przewracać się 2** [T] to cause a leader of a country, etc. to lose his or her position of power or authority ▶ **obalać**

ˌtop-ˈranking adj. [only before a noun] of the highest rank, status or importance in an organization, a sport, etc.: *top-ranking officials* ▶ **wysokiej rangi, wysoko notowany**

ˌtop ˈsecret adj. that must be kept very secret, especially from other governments ▶ **ściśle tajny**

the Torah noun [sing.] (in the Jewish religion) the law of God as given to Moses and recorded in the first five books of the Bible ▶ **Tora**

torch /tɔːtʃ/ noun [C] **1** (US **flashlight** /ˈflæʃlaɪt/) a small electric light that you carry in your hand: *Shine the torch under the sofa and see if you can find my ring.* ▶ **latarka (elektryczna)** ➲ picture at **light 2** a long piece of wood with burning material at the end that you carry to give light: *the Olympic torch* ▶ **pochodnia**

tore past tense of **tear²**

torment /ˈtɔːment/ noun [U,C] great pain and suffering in your mind or body; sb/sth that causes this: *to be **in torment*** cierpieć katusze ▶ **męka**
■ **torment** /tɔːˈment/ verb [T] ▶ **dręczyć**

torn past participle of **tear²**

tornado /tɔːˈneɪdəʊ/ noun [C] (pl. **tornados** or **tornadoes**) a violent storm with very strong winds that move in a circle. **Tornadoes** form a tall column of air which is narrower at the bottom than at the top. ▶ **tornado** ➲ note at **storm**

torpedo /tɔːˈpiːdəʊ/ noun [C] (pl. **torpedoes**) a bomb, shaped like a long narrow tube, that is fired from a **submarine** and explodes when it hits another ship ▶ **torpeda**

torrent /ˈtɒrənt/ noun [C] a strong fast flow of sth, especially water: *The rain was coming down **in torrents*** (lał się strumieniami). ▶ **potok** (*wody, obelg*)

torrential /təˈrenʃl/ adj. (used about rain) very great in amount ▶ **ulewny**

torso /ˈtɔːsəʊ/ noun [C] (pl. **torsos**) the main part of your body, not your head, arms and legs ▶ **tułów**

tortoise /ˈtɔːtəs/ (US also **turtle**) noun [C] a small animal with a hard shell that moves very slowly. A **tortoise** can pull its head and legs into its shell to protect them. ▶ **żółw** (*lądowy*) ➲ look at **turtle** ➲ picture on **page A11**

tortuous /ˈtɔːtʃuəs/ adj. **1** complicated, not clear and simple ▶ **kręty 2** (used about a road, etc.) with many bends ▶ **kręty**

torture /ˈtɔːtʃə(r)/ noun [U,C] **1** the act of causing sb great pain either as a punishment or to make them say or do sth: *His confession was extracted **under torture**.* ▶ **tortury 2** mental or physical suffering: *It's torture having to sit here and listen to him complaining for hours.* ▶ **męczarnie**
■ **torture** verb [T]: *Most of the prisoners were tortured into making a confession.* ◇ *She was tortured by the thought that the accident was her fault.* ▶ **torturować; dręczyć** | **torturer** noun [C] ▶ **dręczyciel/ka**

Tory /ˈtɔːri/ noun [C], adj. (pl. **Tories**) a member of, or sb who supports, the British Conservative Party; connected with this party: *the Tory Party conference* ▶ **torys** ➲ note at **party**

tosh /tɒʃ/ noun [U] (Brit., old-fashioned, slang) nonsense ▶ **bzdury** SYN **rubbish**

toss /tɒs/ verb **1** [T] to throw sth lightly and carelessly: *Rhodri opened the letter and tossed the envelope into the bin.* ▶ **rzucać (lekko) 2** [T] to move your head back quickly especially to show you are annoyed or impatient: *I tried to apologise but she just **tossed** her **head** and walked away.* ▶ **odrzucać** (*głowę do tyłu*) **3** [I,T] to move, or make sb/sth move, up and down or from side to side: *He lay **tossing and turning** in bed, unable to sleep.* ◇ *The ship was tossed about by huge waves.* ▶ **rzucać się** (*z boku na bok*), **kołysać (się) 4** [I,T] **toss (up) (for sth)** to throw a coin into the air in order to decide sth, by guessing which side of the coin will land facing upwards: *to toss a coin* ▶ **grać w orła i reszkę**

Por. **heads i tails**. Słowa te znaczą „orzeł" i „reszka". Rzucając monetę, mówi się **heads** lub **tails** zgadując, którą stroną moneta upadnie: *Let's toss to see who* *does the washing-up. Heads or tails? ◇ There's only one cake left. I'll toss you for it. Heads or tails?* Zagrajmy o nie w orła i reszkę.

■ **toss** noun [C]: *She left with an angry toss of the head* (potrząsając głową). ▶ **rzucenie**, **podrzucenie**
IDM **win/lose the toss** to guess correctly/wrongly which side of a coin will face upwards when it lands: *Ms Williams won the toss and chose to serve first.* ▶ **zgadywać/nie zgadywać, czy wypadnie orzeł, czy reszka**

'toss-up noun [sing.] (informal) a situation in which either of two choices, results, etc. is equally possible: *'Have you decided on the colour yet?' '**It's a toss-up** between the blue and the green* (możliwy do wyboru jest kolor niebieski lub zielony).*'*

tot[1] /tɒt/ noun [C] **1** (informal) a very small child ▶ **berbeć 2** (especially Brit.) a small glass of a strong alcoholic drink ▶ **szklaneczka** (*np. whisky*)

tot[2] /tɒt/ verb (**totting**; **totted**)
PHR V **tot (sth) up** (informal) to add numbers together to form a total ▶ **zliczać**

total[1] /'təʊtl/ adj. being the amount after everyone or everything is counted or added together: *What was the total number of people there? ◇ a total failure ◇ The couple ate in total silence.* ▶ **całkowity**, **kompletny** SYN **complete**

total[2] /'təʊtl/ noun [C] the number that you get when you add two or more numbers or amounts together ▶ **ogólna suma**
■ **total** verb [T] (**totalling**; **totalled**; US **totaling**; **totaled**): *His debts totalled more than £10 000. ◇ Each student's points were totalled and entered in a list.* ▶ (*suma*) **wynosić**; **sumować**
IDM **in total** when you add two or more numbers or amounts together: *The appeal raised £4 million in total.* ▶ **w sumie**

totalitarian /təʊˌtælə'teəriən/ adj. (used about a country or system of government) in which there is only one political party that has complete power and control over the people ▶ **totalitarny**
■ **totalitarianism** /-ɪzəm/ noun [U] ▶ **totalitaryzm**

totally /'təʊtəli/ adv. completely: *I totally agree with you.* ▶ **całkowicie**

totter /'tɒtə(r)/ verb [I] to stand or move in a way that is not steady, as if you are going to fall, especially because you are drunk, ill or weak ▶ **stać/iść na chwiejnych nogach**

touch[1] /tʌtʃ/ verb **1** [T] to put your hand or fingers onto sb/sth: *It's very delicate so don't touch it. ◇ He touched her gently on the cheek. ◇ The police asked us not to touch anything.* ▶ **dotykać 2** [I,T] (used about two or more things, surfaces, etc.) to be or move so close together that there is no space between them: *They were sitting so close that their shoulders touched. ◇ This bicycle is too big. My feet don't **touch the ground**.* ▶ **dotykać (się)**, **stykać (się) 3** [T] to make sb feel sad, sorry for sb, grateful, etc. ▶ **wzruszać** ➲ look at **touched 4** [T] [in negative sentences] to be as good as sb/sth in skill, quality, etc.: *He's a much better player than all the others. No one else can touch him.* ▶ **(nie) dorównywać (komuś)**
IDM **touch wood**; **knock on wood** → WOOD
PHR V **touch down** (used about an aircraft) to land ▶ **lądować**
touch sth up to improve sth by changing or adding to it slightly: *She was busy touching up her make-up in the mirror.* ▶ **dokonywać drobnych poprawek**
touch on/upon sth to mention or refer to a subject for only a short time ▶ **dotykać czegoś**

touch[2] /tʌtʃ/ noun **1** [U] one of the five senses: the ability to feel things and know what they are like by putting your hands or fingers on them: *The **sense of touch** is very important to blind people.* ▶ **dotyk 2** [C, usually sing.] the act of putting your hands or fingers onto sb/sth: *I felt the touch of her hand on my arm.* ▶ **dotknięcie 3** [U] the way sth feels when you touch it: *Marble is cold to the touch* (zimny w dotyku). ▶ **dotyk 4** [C] a small detail that is added to improve sth: *The flowers in our room were **a nice touch**. ◇ She's just **putting the finishing touches to** the cake.* ▶ **dodatek 5** [sing.] a way or style of doing sth: *She prefers to write her letters by hand for a more **personal touch*** (dla nadania im bardziej prywatnego charakteru). ▶ **efekt 6** [sing.] **a touch (of sth)** a small amount of sth: *He's not very ill. It's just a touch of flu.* To tylko lekka grypa. ▶ **odrobina**
IDM **in/out of touch (with sb)** being/not being in contact with sb by speaking or writing to them: *During the year she was abroad, they **kept in touch** by letter.* ▶ (*być/nie być*) **w kontakcie**
in/out of touch with sth having/not having recent information about sth: *We're out of touch with what's going on.* ▶ (*być/nie być*) **na bieżąco**
lose touch → LOSE
lose your touch → LOSE

touchdown /'tʌtʃdaʊn/ noun [C,U] the moment when a plane or spacecraft lands ▶ **lądowanie**

touched /tʌtʃt/ adj. [not before a noun] **touched (by sth)**; **touched that...** made to feel sad, sorry for sb, grateful, etc.: *We were very touched by the plight of the refugees. ◇ I was touched that he offered to help.* ▶ **wzruszony**

touching /'tʌtʃɪŋ/ adj. that makes you feel sad, sorry for sb, grateful, etc. ▶ **wzruszający** SYN **moving**

'touch screen noun [C] a computer screen which shows information when you touch it: *touch-screen technology* ▶ **ekran dotykowy**

'Touch-Tone™ adj. (used about a telephone or telephone system) producing different sounds when different numbers are pushed ▶ **działający w systemie tonowym**

touchy /'tʌtʃi/ adj. (**touchier**; **touchiest**) **1 touchy (about sth)** easily upset or made angry: *He's a bit touchy about his weight.* ▶ **drażliwy 2** (used about a subject, situation, etc.) that may easily upset people or make them angry: *Don't mention the exam. It's a very touchy subject.* ▶ **drażliwy**, **obraźliwy** SYN for both meanings **sensitive**

tough /tʌf/ adj. **1** having or causing problems: *It will be a tough decision to make. ◇ He's had **a tough time of it** recently.* Ostatnio miał ciężki okres. ▶ **ciężki 2 tough (on/with sb/sth)** not feeling sorry for anyone: *The government plans to **get tough with** people who drink and drive. ◇ Don't be too tough on them – they were trying to help.* ▶ **surowy 3** strong enough to deal with difficult conditions or situations: *You need to be tough to go climbing in winter.* ▶ **wytrzymały**, **bardzo mocny 4** not easily broken, torn or cut; very strong: *a tough pair of boots* ▶ **solidny**, **bardzo mocny 5** difficult to cut and eat ▶ **żylasty 6** (informal) **tough (on sb)** bad luck in a way that seems unfair: *It's tough on her that she lost her job. ◇ That's tough!* To pech! ▶ **trudny**, **pechowy**
■ **toughness** noun [U] ▶ **wytrzymałość**; **twardość**; **trudność**; **surowość**

toughen /'tʌfn/ verb [I,T] **toughen (sb/sth) (up)** to make sb/sth tough ▶ **wzmacniać (się)**; **utwardzać (się)**; **hartować (się)**

ˌtough-'minded adj. dealing with problems and situations in a determined way without being influenced by emotions ▶ (*osoba*) **twardy** SYN **hard-headed**

toupee /'tu:peɪ; US tu:'peɪ/ noun [C] a small section of artificial hair, worn by a man to cover an area of his head where hair no longer grows ▶ **tupecik**

tour /tʊə(r); Brit. also tɔ:(r)/ noun **1** [C] **a tour (of/round/around sth)** a journey that you make for pleasure during

T

which you visit many places: *to* **go on a** *ten-day coach* **tour** *of/around Scotland* ◇ *a sightseeing tour* ◇ *a tour operator* organizator (osoba lub firma) wycieczki ▶ **wycieczka turystyczno-krajoznawcza** ➲ note at **travel** **2** [C] a short visit around a city, famous building, etc.: *a* ***guided tour*** (zwiedzanie z przewodnikiem) *round St Paul's Cathedral* ▶ **wycieczka, zwiedzanie** ➲ note at **travel** **3** [C,U] an official series of visits that singers, musicians, sports players, etc. make to different places to perform, play, etc.: *The band is currently* ***on tour*** *in America.* ◇ *a concert/cricket tour* ▶ **tournée**
■ **tour** verb [I,T]: *We toured southern Spain for three weeks.* ▶ **jechać na wycieczkę objazdową; objeżdżać**

tourism /ˈtʊərɪzəm; Brit. also ˈtɔːr-/ noun [U] the business of providing and arranging holidays and services for people who are visiting a place: *The country's economy relies heavily on tourism.* ▶ **turystyka**

⚷ **tourist** /ˈtʊərɪst; Brit. also ˈtɔːr-/ noun [C] a person who visits a place for pleasure ▶ **turyst(k)a** ➲ look at **sightseer**

tournament /ˈtʊənəmənt; ˈtɜːn-; Brit. also ˈtɔːn-/ noun [C] a competition in which many players or teams play games against each other ▶ **zawody sportowe**

tourniquet /ˈtʊənɪkeɪ; US ˈtɜːnəkət/ noun [C] a band of cloth that is tied tightly around an arm or a leg to stop the loss of blood from a wound ▶ (*med.*) **opaska uciskowa**

tousled /ˈtaʊzld/ adj. (used about hair) untidy, often in an attractive way ▶ **potargany**

tow /təʊ/ verb [T] to pull a car or boat behind another vehicle, using a rope or chain: *My car was towed away by the police.* ▶ **holować**
■ **tow** noun [sing.] ▶ **holowanie**
IDM **in tow** (informal) following closely behind: *He arrived with his wife and five children in tow.* ▶ **holując (kogoś za sobą)**

⚷ **towards** /təˈwɔːdz; US tɔːdz/ (also **toward** /təˈwɔːd; US tɔːd/) prep. **1** in the direction of sb/sth: *I saw Ken walking towards the station.* ◇ *a first step towards world peace* ◇ *She had her back towards me.* Była odwrócona do mnie tyłem. ▶ **w kierunku, ku 2** near or nearer a time or date: *It gets cool towards evening.* ◇ *The shops get very busy towards Christmas.* ▶ **koło, pod 3** (used when you are talking about your feelings about sb/sth) in relation to: *Patti felt very protective towards her younger brother.* ◇ *What is your attitude towards this government?* ▶ **(w stosunku) do kogoś/czegoś 4** as part of the payment for sth: *The money will* ***go towards*** *the cost of a new minibus.* ▶ (*wpłata*) **na jakiś cel**

⚷ **towel** /ˈtaʊəl/ noun [C] a piece of cloth or paper that you use for drying sb/sth/yourself: *a bath/hand/beach towel* ◇ *kitchen/paper towels* ▶ **ręcznik** ➲ look at **sanitary towel, tea towel**

⚷ **tower¹** /ˈtaʊə(r)/ noun [C] a tall narrow building or part of a building such as a church or castle: *the Eiffel Tower* ◇ *a church tower* ◇ *a control tower* wieża kontrolna ▶ **wieża** ➲ picture on **page A2**

tower² /ˈtaʊə(r)/ verb
PHR V **tower over/above sb/sth 1** to be much higher or taller than the people or things that are near: *The cliffs towered above them.* ◇ *He towered over his classmates.* ▶ **górować nad kimś/czymś 2** to be much better than others in ability, quality, etc.: *She towers over other dancers of her generation.* ▶ (*przen.*) **górować nad kimś**

ˈ**tower block** noun [C] (Brit.) a very tall building consisting of flats or offices ▶ **wieżowiec**

⚷ **town** /taʊn/ noun **1** [C] a place with many streets and buildings. A town is larger than a village but smaller than a city: *Romsey is a small market town.* ◇ *After ten years away, she decided to move back to her* ***home town*** (do swojego miasta rodzinnego). ▶ **miasto 2** (**the town**) [sing.] all the people who live in a town: *The whole town is talking about it.* ▶ **miasto 3** [U] the main part of a town, where the shops, etc. are: *I've got to go into town this afternoon.* ▶ **miasto, centrum**
IDM **go to town (on sth)** (informal) to do sth with a lot of energy and enthusiasm; to spend a lot of money on sth ▶ **zaszaleć** (*np. z zakupami*)
(out) on the town (informal) going to restaurants, theatres, clubs, etc., for entertainment, especially at night ▶ (*np. ruszać*) **w miasto,** (*bawić się*) **w mieście**

ˌ**town ˈcouncil** noun [C] (Brit.) a group of people who are responsible for the local government of a town ▶ **rada miejska**

ˌ**town ˈhall** noun [C] a large building that contains the local government offices and often a large room for public meetings, concerts, etc. ▶ **ratusz** ➲ look at **hall**

ˌ**town ˈplanning** noun [U] the control of the growth and development of a town, including its buildings, roads, etc. ▶ **urbanistyka**
■ ˌ**town ˈplanner** = PLANNER

toxic /ˈtɒksɪk/ adj. poisonous ▶ **trujący**

toxin /ˈtɒksɪn/ noun [C] a poisonous substance, especially one that is produced by bacteria in plants and animals ▶ **toksyna**

⚷ **toy¹** /tɔɪ/ noun [C] an object for a child to play with: *The children were playing happily with their toys.* ◇ *a toyshop* sklep z zabawkami ▶ **zabawka**
■ **toy** adj. [only before a noun]: *a toy car* samochodzik ◇ *a toy soldier* żołnierzyk ◇ *a toy farm* model gospodarstwa wiejskiego do zabawy

toy² /tɔɪ/ verb
PHR V **toy with sth 1** to think about doing sth, perhaps not very seriously: *She's* ***toying with the idea of*** *going abroad for a year.* ▶ **luźno rozważać** (*możliwość zrobienia czegoś*) **2** to move sth about without thinking about what you are doing, often because you are nervous or upset: *He toyed with his food* (podziobał widelcem w jedzeniu) *but hardly ate any of it.* ▶ **ruszać czymś bezwiednie**

⚷ **trace¹** /treɪs/ verb [T] **1 trace sb/sth (to sth)** to find out where sb/sth is by following marks, signs or other information: *The wanted man was traced to an address in Amsterdam.* ▶ **odszukiwać 2 trace sth (back) (to sth)** to find out where sth came from or what caused it; to describe the development of sth: *She traced her family tree* (wywiodła swoje drzewo genealogiczne) *back to the 16th century.* ◇ *The police were unable to* ***trace the call*** (namierzyć numeru). ▶ **iść śladem, dochodzić do źródła 3** to make a copy of a map, plan, etc. by placing a piece of **tracing paper** over it and drawing over the lines ▶ **kalkować**

⚷ **trace²** /treɪs/ noun **1** [C,U] a mark, an object or a sign that shows that sb/sth existed or happened: *traces of an earlier civilization* ◇ *The man* ***disappeared/vanished without trace.*** ▶ **ślad 2** [C] **a trace (of sth)** a very small amount of sth: *Traces of blood were found under her fingernails.* ▶ **pozostałość, resztka**

trachea /trəˈkiːə/ noun [C] (pl. **tracheae** /-kiːiː/ or **tracheas**) the tube in your throat that carries air to the lungs ▶ **tchawica** SYN **windpipe** ➲ picture at **body**

ˈ**tracing paper** noun [U] strong transparent paper that is placed on top of a drawing, etc. so that you can follow the lines with a pen or pencil in order to make a copy of it ▶ **kalka kreślarska**

⚷ **track¹** /træk/ noun **1** [C] a natural path or rough road: *Follow the dirt track through the forest.* ▶ **szlak 2** [C, usually pl.] marks that are left on the ground by a person, an animal or a moving vehicle: *The hunter followed the* *tracks of a deer.* ◇ *tyre tracks* ▶ **trop** ➲ look at **footprint** **3** [C,U] the two metal rails on which a train runs: *The train stopped because there was a tree across the track.* ▶ **tor** (*kolejowy, tramwajowy*) **4** [C] a piece of ground, often in a circle, for people, cars, etc. to have races on: *a running track* ▶ **tor wyścigowy** **5** [C] one song or piece of music on a tape, CD or record: *the first track from her latest album* ▶ **jeden utwór muzyczny** ➲ look at **soundtrack**

IDM **keep/lose track of sb/sth** to have/not have information about what is happening or where sb/sth is: *I lost all track of time.* Straciłem rachubę czasu. ▶ **śledzić; tracić ślad/kontakt**

off the beaten track → BEAT[1]

on the right/wrong track having the right/wrong idea about sth: *That's not the answer but you're on the right track.* ▶ **na dobrym/złym tropie**

track² /træk/ verb [T] to follow the movements of sb/sth: *to track enemy planes on a radar screen* ▶ **śledzić**

PHR V **track sb/sth down** to find sb/sth after searching for them or it ▶ **wytropić kogoś/coś**

ˌtrack and ˈfield (US) = ATHLETICS

ˈtrack event noun [C] a sports event that consists of running round a track in a race, rather than throwing sth or jumping ▶ **bieg lekkoatletyczny** ➲ look at **field event**

ˈtrack record noun [sing.] all the past successes or failures of a person or organization ▶ **osiągnięcia w pracy jednostki/organizacji**

tracksuit /ˈtræksuːt/ noun [C] a warm pair of soft trousers and a matching jacket that you wear for sports practice ▶ **dres**

tractor /ˈtræktə(r)/ noun [C] a large vehicle that is used on farms for pulling heavy pieces of machinery ▶ **traktor**

⚷ **trade¹** /treɪd/ noun **1** [U] the buying or selling of goods or services between people or countries: *an international trade agreement* ◇ *Trade is not very good at this time of year.* ▶ **handel** ➲ look at **commerce** **2** [C] a particular type of business: *the tourist/building/retail trade* ◇ *the book trade* księgarstwo ◇ *Many seaside resorts depend on the tourist trade* (zależy od rozwoju turystyki). ▶ **działalność gospodarcza** **3** [C,U] a job for which you need special skill, especially with your hands: *Jeff is a plumber **by trade**.* ◇ *to learn a trade* ▶ **fach, rzemiosło** ➲ note at **work**

⚷ **trade²** /treɪd/ verb **1** [I] **trade (in sth) (with sb)** to buy or sell goods or services: *We no longer trade with that country.* ◇ *to trade in arms* handlować bronią ◇ *to trade in stocks and shares* ▶ **handlować** **2** [T] **trade sth (for sth)** to exchange sth for sth else: *He traded his CD player for his friend's bicycle.* ▶ **przehandlowywać**

■ **trading** noun [U] ▶ **handel**

PHR V **trade sth in (for sth)** to give sth old in part payment for sth new or newer: *We traded in our old car for a van.* ▶ **handlować wymiennie** (*np. kupić nowy samochód, pozostawiając w rozliczeniu stary*)

ˈtrade deficit (also **ˈtrade gap**) noun [usually sing.] a situation in which the value of a country's imports is greater than the value of its exports ▶ **deficyt bilansu handlowego**

trademark /ˈtreɪdmɑːk/ noun [C] (abbr. **TM** /ˌtiː ˈem/) a special symbol, design or name that a company puts on its products and that cannot be used by any other company: *a registered trademark* ▶ **chroniony znak handlowy**

ˈtrade name noun [C] **1** = BRAND NAME **2** a name that is taken and used by a company for business purposes: *The company uses the trade name Marubeni in the US.* ▶ **nazwa handlowa**

ˈtrade-off noun [C] **trade-off (between sth and sth)** the act of balancing two things that you need or want but which are opposed to each other: *There is a trade-off between the benefits of the drug and the risk of side effects.* ▶ **bilans, kompromis**

trader /ˈtreɪdə(r)/ noun [C] a person who buys and sells things, especially goods in a market or company shares ▶ **handla-rz/rka**

tradesman /ˈtreɪdzmən/ noun [C] (pl. **-men** /-mən/) a person who brings goods to people's homes to sell them or who has a shop ▶ **dostawca; kupiec**

ˌtrade ˈunion (also **ˌtrades ˈunion; union**) noun [C] an organization for people who all do the same type of work. **Trade unions** try to get better pay and working conditions for their members. ▶ **związek zawodowy**

ˌtrade ˈunionist (also **ˌtrades ˈunionist; unionist**) noun [C] a member of a **trade union** ▶ **związkowiec**

⚷ **tradition** /trəˈdɪʃn/ noun [C,U] a custom, belief or way of doing sth that has continued from the past to the present: *religious/cultural/literary traditions* ◇ ***By tradition*** (zgodnie z tradycją), *the bride's family pays the costs of the wedding.* ▶ **tradycja**

■ **traditional** /-ʃənl/ adj.: *It is traditional in Britain to eat turkey at Christmas.* ▶ **tradycyjny** | **traditionally** /-ʃənəli/ adv. ▶ **tradycyjnie**

⚷ **traffic** /ˈtræfɪk/ noun [U] **1** all the vehicles that are on a road at a particular time: *heavy/light traffic* ◇ *We got stuck **in traffic** and were late for the meeting.* ▶ **ruch** **2** the movement of ships, aircraft, etc.: *air traffic control* ▶ **ruch** **3 traffic (in sth)** the illegal buying and selling of sth: *the traffic in drugs/firearms* ▶ **nielegalny handel**

■ **traffic** verb (**trafficking; trafficked**)

PHR V **traffic in sth** to buy and sell sth illegally ▶ **nielegalnie handlować czymś**

ˈtraffic island (Brit. **island**) noun [C] a higher area in the middle of the road, where you can stand and wait for the traffic to pass when you want to cross ▶ **wysepka uliczna**

ˈtraffic jam noun [C] a long line of cars, etc. that cannot move or that can only move very slowly: *We were stuck in a terrible traffic jam.* ▶ **korek** (*uliczny*) ➲ note at **driving**

trafficking /ˈtræfɪkɪŋ/ noun [U] the activity of buying and selling sth illegally: *drug trafficking* ▶ **nielegalny handel**

■ **trafficker** noun [C]: *a drugs trafficker* ▶ **handlarz nielegalnym towarem**

ˈtraffic light noun [C, usually pl.] a sign with red, orange and green lights that is used for controlling the traffic where two or more roads meet ▶ **światło sygnalizacyjne** (*na skrzyżowaniu*)

ˈtraffic warden noun [C] (Brit.) a person whose job is to check that cars are not parked in the wrong place or for longer than is allowed ▶ **kontroler poprawnego parkowania pojazdów** ➲ note at **parking**

tragedy /ˈtrædʒədi/ noun (pl. **tragedies**) **1** [C,U] a very sad event or situation, especially one that involves death: *It's a tragedy that he died so young.* ▶ **tragedia** **2** [C] a serious play that has a sad ending: *Shakespeare's 'King Lear' is a tragedy.* ▶ **tragedia** ➲ look at **comedy**

tragic /ˈtrædʒɪk/ adj. **1** that makes you very sad, especially because it involves death: *It's tragic that she lost her only child.* ◇ *a tragic accident* ▶ **tragiczny** **2** [only before a noun] (formal) (used about literature) in the style of **tragedy**: *a tragic actor/hero* ▶ **tragiczny**

■ **tragically** /-kli/ adv. ▶ **tragicznie**

trail¹ /treɪl/ noun [C] **1** a series of marks in a long line that is left by sb/sth as he/she/it moves: *a trail of blood/footprints* ▶ **ślad** **2** a track, sign or smell that is left behind and that you follow when you are hunting sb/sth: *The*

T

dogs ran off ***on the trail of*** *the fox.* ▶ **trop 3** a path through the country ▶ **szlak**

trail² /treɪl/ verb **1** [I,T] to pull or be pulled along behind sb/sth: *The skirt was too long and trailed along the ground.* ◇ *Her long hair trailed behind her in the wind* (powiewały za nią jak tren na wietrze). ▶ **ciągnąć (się) za kimś/czymś 2** [I] to move or walk slowly behind sb/sth else, usually because you are tired or bored: *It was impossible to do any shopping with the kids trailing around after me.* ▶ **wlec się za kimś/czymś 3** [I,T] [usually used in the continuous tenses] **trail (by/in sth)** to be in the process of losing a game or a competition: *At half-time Liverpool were trailing by two goals to three.* ▶ **pozostawać w tyle** (*w punktacji*), **przegrywać 4** [I] (used about plants or sth long and thin) to grow over sth and hang downwards; to lie across a surface: *Computer wires trailed across the floor.* ▶ **piąć się**; **wlec się**

PHR V **trail away/off** (used about sb's voice) to gradually become quieter and then stop ▶ **zanikać**

trailblazer /ˈtreɪlbleɪzə(r)/ noun [C] a person who is the first to do or discover sth and so makes it possible for others to follow: *a trailblazer in the field of genetic engineering* ▶ **pionier/ka**

■ **trailblazing** adj. [usually before a noun]: *trailblazing scientific research* ▶ **pionierski**

trailer /ˈtreɪlə(r)/ noun [C] **1** a type of container with wheels that is pulled by vehicle: *a car towing a trailer with a boat on it* ▶ **przyczepa 2** (US) = CARAVAN (1) **3** (US) = MOBILE HOME **4** (especially Brit.) a series of short pieces taken from a film and used to advertise it ▶ **zwiastun** ➲ look at **clip**

ˈ**trail riding** (US) = PONY-TREKKING

train¹ /treɪn/ noun [C] **1** a type of transport that is pulled by an engine along a railway line. A train is divided into **carriages** and **coaches** and **wagons**: *to catch/take/get the train to London* ◇ *the 12 o'clock train to Bristol* ◇ *to get on/off a train* ◇ *Hurry up or we'll* ***miss the train.*** ◇ *a passenger train* pociąg osobowy ◇ *a goods/freight train* pociąg towarowy ◇ *a fast/slow train* pociąg pośpieszny/osobowy ◇ *an express/a stopping train* pociąg ekspresowy/osobowy ◇ *You have to change trains* (masz przesiadkę) *at Reading.* ▶ **pociąg** ➲ picture on **page A7**

> Uwaga! Mówiąc ogólnie o podróżowaniu pociągiem, używamy wyrażenia **by train**. Kiedy mówimy o jednej konkretnej podróży, wówczas używamy wyrażenia **on the train**: *Victoria travels to work by train.* ◇ *Yesterday she fell asleep on the train and missed her station.*

2 [usually sing.] a series of thoughts or events that are connected: *A knock at the door interrupted my* ***train of thought.*** ▶ **ciąg**

> **travelling by train**
>
> You go to the **station** to **catch** a train. You can buy a **single** or a **return**. In American English these are called a **one-way ticket** and a **round-trip ticket**. A **first-class** ticket is the most expensive type of ticket. A **timetable** is the list that shows the times when trains **arrive** and **depart**. You wait on the **platform** to get on your train. If the weather is bad, it might be **delayed** or even **cancelled**. If you are late and the train is **on time**, you will **miss** it. If there is no **direct** service, you will have to **change**.

train² /treɪn/ verb **1** [T] **train sb (as sth/to do sth)** to teach a person to do sth which is difficult or which needs practice: *The organization trains guide dogs for the blind.* ◇ *There is a shortage of trained teachers.* ▶ **szkolić**; **tresować 2** [I,T] **train (as/in sth) (to do sth)** to learn how to do a job: *She trained as an engineer.* ◇ *He's not trained in anything.* ◇ *He's training to be a doctor.* ▶ **szkolić się 3** [I,T] **train (for sth)** to prepare yourself, especially for a sports event, by practising; to help a person or an animal to do this: *I'm training for the London Marathon.* ◇ *to train racehorses* ▶ **trenować**; **tresować 4** [T] **train sth (at/on sb/sth)** to point a gun, camera, etc. at sb/sth ▶ **wycelować**

ˈ**train driver** = ENGINE DRIVER

trainee /ˌtreɪˈniː/ noun [C] a person who is being taught how to do a particular job ▶ **osoba będąca w trakcie szkolenia**

trainer /ˈtreɪnə(r)/ noun [C] **1** (US **sneaker** /ˈsniːkə(r)/) [usually pl.] a shoe that you wear for doing sport or as informal clothing ▶ **but sportowy do biegania** ➲ look at **plimsoll** ➲ picture at **shoe**, picture on **page A1 2** a person who teaches people or animals how to do a particular job or skill well, or to do a particular sport: *teacher trainers* ◇ *a racehorse trainer* ▶ **trener/ka**; **treser/ka**

training /ˈtreɪnɪŋ/ noun [U] **1 training (in sth/in doing sth)** the process of learning the skills that you need to do a job: *Few candidates had received any training in management.* ◇ *a training course* ▶ **szkolenie 2** the process of preparing to take part in a sports competition by doing physical exercises: *to be* ***in training*** *for* (trenować przed) *the Olympics* ▶ **trening**

trainspotter /ˈtreɪnspɒtə(r)/ noun [C] (Brit.) **1** a person who collects the numbers of railway engines as a hobby ▶ **kolekcjoner/ka numerów lokomotyw 2** a person who has a boring hobby or who is interested in the details of a subject that other people find boring ▶ **osoba o nieciekawych zainteresowaniach lub nieinteresującym dla innych hobby**

■ **trainspotting** noun [U] **1** ▶ **kolekcjonowanie numerów lokomotyw 2** ▶ **nudne hobby**, **nieciekawe zainteresowania**

traipse /treɪps/ verb [I] (informal) to walk somewhere slowly when you are tired and unwilling: *We spent the afternoon traipsing around the town.* ▶ **wlec się**

trait /treɪt/ noun [C] a quality that forms part of your character ▶ **cecha**, **rys charakteru**

traitor /ˈtreɪtə(r)/ noun [C] **a traitor (to sb/sth)** a person who is not loyal to their country, friends, etc. ▶ **zdrajca/czyni**

> A traitor **betrays** his/her friends, country, etc. and the crime against his/her country is called **treason**.

tram /træm/ (US **streetcar** /ˈstriːtkɑː(r)/, **trolley** /ˈtrɒli/) noun [C] a type of bus that works by electricity and that moves along special rails in the road carrying passengers ▶ **tramwaj** ➲ picture on **page A7**

tramp¹ /træmp/ noun **1** [C] a person who has no home or job and who moves from place to place ▶ **włóczęga 2** [sing.] the sound of people walking with heavy or noisy steps ▶ **stąpanie ciężkimi krokami**

tramp² /træmp/ verb [I,T] to walk with slow heavy steps, especially for a long time ▶ **stąpać ciężkimi krokami**

trample /ˈtræmpl/ verb [I,T] **trample on/over sb/sth** to walk on sb/sth and damage or hurt them or it: *The boys trampled on the flowers.* ▶ **deptać**

trampoline /ˈtræmpəliːn/ noun [C] a piece of equipment for jumping up and down on, made of a piece of strong cloth fixed to a metal frame by springs ▶ **batut** ➲ look at **springboard**

trance /trɑːns; US træns/ noun [C] a mental state in which you do not notice what is going on around you: *to go/fall into a trance* ▶ **trans**

tranquil /ˈtræŋkwɪl/ adj. (formal) calm and quiet ▶ **spokojny**, **cichy**

tranquillize (also **-ise**; US **tranquilize**) /ˈtræŋkwəlaɪz/ verb [T] to make a person or an animal calm or unconscious, especially by giving them a drug ▶ **podawać środek uspokajający**

tranquillizer (also -iser; US also tranquilizer) /ˈtræŋkwəlaɪzə(r)/ noun [C] a drug that is used for making people or animals calm or unconscious ▶ **środek uspokajający** ➲ look at **sedative**

transaction /trænˈzækʃn/ noun [C] a piece of business that is done between people: *financial transactions* ▶ **operacja handlowa**

transatlantic /ˌtrænzətˈlæntɪk/ adj. [only before a noun] to or from the other side of the Atlantic Ocean; across the Atlantic: *a transatlantic flight/voyage* ▶ **transatlantycki**

transcend /trænˈsend/ verb [T] (formal) to go further than the usual limits of sth ▶ **przekraczać; przewyższać**

transcribe /trænˈskraɪb/ verb [T] **transcribe sth (into sth)** to record thoughts, speech or data in a written form, or in a different written form from the original: *The interview was recorded and then transcribed.* ▶ **przepisywać** (*np. tekst mówiony na pisany*)

transcript /ˈtrænskrɪpt/ (also **transcription** /trænˈskrɪpʃn/) noun [C] a written or printed copy of what sb has said: *a transcript of the interview/trial* ▶ **zapis** (*rozmowy*)

transexual = TRANSSEXUAL

transfer¹ /trænsˈfɜː(r)/ verb (**transferring**; **transferred**) **1** [I,T] **transfer (sb/sth) (from ...) (to ...)** to move, or to make sb/sth move, from one place to another: *He's transferring to our Tokyo branch next month.* ◇ *I'd like to transfer £1 000 from my deposit account.* ◇ *Transfer the data onto a disk.* ▶ **przenosić (się)**, **przelewać** (*pieniądze*) **2** [T] to officially arrange for sth to belong to, or be controlled by, sb else: *She transferred the property to her son.* ▶ (*prawn.*) **cedować**

■ **transferable** adj.: *This ticket is not transferable.* ▶ **z prawem odstąpienia drugiej osobie**

transfer² /ˈtrænsfɜː(r)/ noun **1** [C,U] moving or being moved from one place, job or state to another: *Paul is not happy here and has asked for a transfer.* ▶ **przeniesienie**, **transfer** **2** [U] changing to a different vehicle or route during a journey: *Transfer from the airport to the hotel is included.* ▶ **zmiana** **3** [C] (US) a ticket that allows you to continue your journey on another bus or train ▶ **bilet przesiadkowy** **4** [C] (especially Brit.) a piece of paper with a picture or writing on it that you can stick onto another surface by pressing or heating it ▶ **kalkomania**

transform /trænsˈfɔːm/ verb [T] **transform sb/sth (from sth) (into sth)** to change sb/sth completely, especially in a way which improves sb/sth ▶ **odmieniać**, **przekształcać**

■ **transformation** /ˌtrænsfəˈmeɪʃn/ noun [C,U] ▶ **odmiana**, **przekształcenie**

transformer /trænsˈfɔːmə(r)/ noun [C] a device for reducing or increasing the strength of a supply of electricity, usually to allow a particular piece of electrical equipment to be used ▶ **transformator**

transfusion /trænsˈfjuːʒn/ noun [C] the act of putting new blood into sb's body instead of their own because they are ill: *a blood transfusion* ▶ **transfuzja krwi**

transistor /trænˈzɪstə(r)/ noun [C] **1** a small piece of electronic equipment that is used in computers, radios, TVs, etc. ▶ **tranzystor** **2** (also tranˌsistor ˈradio) a small radio that you can carry easily ▶ **tranzystor**

transit /ˈtrænzɪt/ noun [U] **1** the act of being moved or carried from one place to another: *The goods had been damaged **in transit*** (podczas transportu). ▶ **przewóz** **2** going through a place on the way to somewhere else: *the transit lounge* hala tranzytowa ▶ **tranzyt**

transition /trænˈzɪʃn/ noun [C,U] **(a) transition (from sth) (to sth)** a change from one state or form to another: *the transition from childhood to adolescence* ▶ **przejście**, **przemiana**

■ **transitional** /-ʃənl/ adj.: *a transitional stage/period* ▶ **przejściowy**

transitive /ˈtrænsətɪv/ adj. (used about a verb) that has a direct object. Transitive verbs are marked '[T]' in this dictionary. ▶ **przechodni** OPP **intransitive**

translate /trænsˈleɪt; trænz-/ verb [I,T] **translate (sth) (from sth) (into sth)** to change sth written or spoken from one language to another: *This book has been translated from Czech into English.* ▶ **przekładać**, **(prze)tłumaczyć** ➲ look at **interpret**

■ **translation** /trænsˈleɪʃn; trænz-/ noun [C,U]: *The book loses something **in translation**.* ◇ *a word-for-word* (dosłowny) *translation* ▶ **przekład**, **tłumaczenie**

translator /trænsˈleɪtə(r); trænz-/ noun [C] a person who changes sth that has been written or spoken from one language to another ▶ **tłumacz/ka** ➲ look at **interpreter**

translucent /trænsˈluːsnt; trænz-/ adj. (formal) that light can pass through but not transparent ▶ **półprzezroczysty** ➲ look at **opaque**, **transparent**

■ **translucence** (also **translucency** /-snsi/) noun [U] ▶ **półprzezroczystość**

transmission /trænsˈmɪʃn; trænz-/ noun **1** [U] sending sth out or passing sth on from one person, place or thing to another: *the transmission of TV pictures by satellite* ◇ *the transmission of a disease/virus* ▶ **transmisja**, **przenoszenie** **2** [C] a TV or radio programme ▶ **transmisja** **3** [U,C] the system in a car, etc. by which power is passed from the engine to the wheels ▶ **napęd**

transmit /trænsˈmɪt; trænz-/ verb [T] (**transmitting**; **transmitted**) **1** to send out TV or radio programmes, electronic signals, etc.: *The match was transmitted live all over the world.* ▶ **transmitować** **2** to send or pass sth from one person or place to another: *a sexually transmitted disease* ▶ **przenosić**

transmitter /trænsˈmɪtə(r); trænz-/ noun [C] a piece of equipment that sends out electronic signals, TV or radio programmes, etc. ▶ **nadajnik**

transparency /trænsˈpærənsi/ noun [C] (pl. **transparencies**) a piece of plastic on which you can write or draw or that has a picture, etc. on it that you look at by putting it on a **projector** and shining light through it: *a transparency for the overhead projector* ▶ **przeźrocze**, **folia do rzutnika** ➲ look at **slide**

transparent /trænsˈpærənt/ adj. that you can see through: *Glass is transparent.* ▶ **przezroczysty** OPP **opaque** ➲ look at **translucent**

transplant¹ /trænsˈplɑːnt; trænz-; US -ˈplænt/ verb [T] **1** to take out an organ or other part of sb's body and put it into another person's body ▶ **przeszczepiać** ➲ look at **graft** **2** to move a growing plant and plant it somewhere else ▶ **przesadzać**

transplant² /ˈtrænsplɑːnt; ˈtrænz-; US -plænt/ noun [C] a medical operation in which an organ, etc. is taken out of sb's body and put into another person's body: *to have a heart/kidney transplant* ▶ **przeszczep**

transport /ˈtrænspɔːt/ (especially US **transportation** /ˌtrænspɔːˈteɪʃn/) noun [U] **1** the act of carrying or taking people or goods from one place to another: *road/rail/sea transport* ▶ **przewóz**, **transport** **2** vehicles that you travel in; a method of travel: *Do you have your own transport?* ◇ *I travel to school by **public transport**.* Jeżdżę do szkoły środkami komunikacji miejskiej. ◇ *His bike is his only **means of transport**.* ▶ **środek transportu**

■ **transport** /trænˈspɔːt/ verb [T] to move sb/sth from one place to another in a vehicle ▶ **transportować**

transpose /trænˈspəʊz/ verb [T] (formal) **1** to change the order of two or more things: *Two letters were accidental-*

T

ly transposed and 'gun' was printed as 'gnu'. ▶ **przestawiać** (*zwł. słowa lub litery*) **2** to move or change sth to a different place or into a different form: *The director transposes Shakespeare's play from 16th-century Italy to modern England.* ▶ **transponować 3** to write or play a piece of music or a series of notes in a different key ▶ **transponować**

■ **transposition** /ˌtrænspəˈzɪʃn/ noun [C,U] ▶ **przestawienie**; **transpozycja**

transsexual (also **transexual**) /trænzˈsekʃuəl; træns-/ noun [C] a person who feels emotionally that they want to live, dress, etc. as a member of the opposite sex, especially one who has a medical operation to change their sexual organs ▶ **transeksualist(k)a**

transvestite /trænzˈvestaɪt/ noun [C] a person, especially a man, who enjoys dressing like a member of the opposite sex ▶ **transwestyt(k)a**

trap¹ /træp/ noun [C] **1** a piece of equipment that you use for catching animals: *a mousetrap* ◇ *The rabbit's leg was caught in the trap.* ▶ **pułapka 2** a clever plan that is designed to trick sb: *She **walked straight into the trap**.* Łatwo dała się złapać w pułapkę. ◇ *He **fell into the trap of** thinking* (błędnie przyjął, że) *she would always be there.* ▶ (*przen.*) **pułapka**, **podstęp 3** an unpleasant situation from which it is hard to escape: *He thought of marriage as a trap.* ▶ (*przen.*) **pułapka**

trap² /træp/ verb [T] (**trapping**; **trapped**) **1** [often passive] to keep sb in a dangerous place or a bad situation from which they cannot escape: *The door closed behind them and they were trapped.* ◇ *Many people are trapped* (uwięzionych) *in low-paid jobs.* ▶ **łapać w pułapkę 2** to catch and keep or store sth: *Special glass panels trap heat from the sun.* ▶ **zatrzymywać 3** to force sb/sth into a place or situation from which they or it cannot escape: *Police believe this new evidence could help trap the killer.* ▶ (*przen.*) **łapać w pułapkę 4** to catch an animal, etc. in a **trap**: *Raccoons used to be trapped for their fur.* ▶ **łapać w pułapkę 5 trap sb (into sth/into doing sth)** to make sb do sth by tricking them: *She had been trapped into revealing her true identity.* ▶ **usidlać**

trapdoor /ˈtræpdɔː(r)/ noun [C] a small door in a floor or ceiling ▶ **drzwi zapadowe**, **zapadnia**

trapeze /trəˈpiːz; US træ-/ noun [C] a wooden or metal bar hanging from two ropes high above the ground, used by **acrobats** ▶ **trapez**

trappings /ˈtræpɪŋz/ noun [pl.] clothes, possessions, etc. which are signs of a particular social position ▶ **oznaki** (*np. urzędu, zamożności*)

trash (US) = RUBBISH

ˈ**trash can** (US) = DUSTBIN

trashy /ˈtræʃi/ adj. (**trashier**; **trashiest**) of poor quality: *trashy novels* ▶ **lipny**

trauma /ˈtrɔːmə; US ˈtraʊmə/ noun [C,U] (an event that causes) a state of great shock or sadness: *the trauma of losing your parents* ▶ **trauma** ➲ look at **stress**

■ **traumatic** /trɔːˈmætɪk; US traʊˈm-/ adj. ▶ **traumatyczny**

traumatize (also **-ise**) /ˈtrɔːmətaɪz; US ˈtraʊm-/ verb [T, usually passive] to shock and upset sb very much, often making them unable to think or work normally ▶ **niszczyć psychicznie**

travel¹ /ˈtrævl/ verb (**travelling**; **travelled**; US **traveling**; **traveled**) **1** [I] to go from one place to another, especially over a long distance: *Charles travels a lot on business.* ◇ *to travel abroad* ◇ *to travel by sea/air/car* ◇ *to travel to work* ◇ *travelling expenses* wydatki na podróż ◇ *News travels fast* (wiadomości szybko się rozchodzą) *in this company.* ▶ **podróżować** ➲ note at **plane**, **train 2** [T] to make a journey of a particular distance: *They travelled 60 kilometres to come and see us.* ▶ **przebywać** (*daną odległość*)

IDM **travel light** to take very few things with you when you travel ▶ **podróżować z małą ilością bagażu**

travel² /ˈtrævl/ noun **1** [U] the act of going from one place to another: *air/rail/space travel* ◇ *a travel bag/clock/iron* ▶ **podróż 2** (**travels**) [pl.] time spent travelling, especially to places that are far away ▶ **podróże**

> **Travel** jest rzeczownikiem niepoliczalnym i można go używać tylko mówiąc o ogólnym procesie przenoszenia się z miejsca na miejsce: *Foreign travel is very popular these days.* Mówiąc o podróżowaniu z jednego miejsca do innego, używa się rzeczownika **journey** oznaczającego podróż, która może być długa (*the journey across Canada*), lub krótka, ale powtarzająca się (*the journey to work*). **Tour** to podróż wycieczkowa lub spacer, kiedy odwiedza się różne miejsca: *We went on a three-week tour around Italy.* ◇ *a guided tour of the castle.* Często używa się też słowa **trip** w znaczeniu całej wizyty, wliczając w to pobyt na miejscu i podróż w obie strony: *We're just back from a trip to Japan. We had a wonderful time.* (Por. użycie słowa **journey** w następnym pytaniu: *'How was the journey back?' 'Awful – the plane was delayed!'*) **Trip** może oznaczać krótką podróż (*a day trip*), lub dłuższą (*a trip round the world*), i może odbywać się w interesach lub dla przyjemności: *How about a trip to the seaside this weekend?* ◇ *He's on a trip to New York to meet a client.* **Excursion** to zorganizowana, wieloosobowa wycieczka: *The holiday includes a full day excursion by coach to the Lake District.* Zwróć uwagę na zwrot **go on**: *to go on a journey/trip/excursion.*

ˈ**travel agency** noun [C] (pl. **travel agencies**) a company that makes travel arrangements for people (arranging tickets, flights, hotels, etc.) ▶ **biuro podróży**

ˈ**travel agent** noun **1** [C] a person whose job is to make travel arrangements for people ▶ **pracownik biura podróży 2** (**the travel agent's**) [sing.] the shop where you can go to make travel arrangements, buy tickets, etc. ▶ **biuro podróży** ➲ note at **holiday**

traveller (US **traveler**) /ˈtrævələ(r)/ noun [C] **1** a person who is travelling or who often travels: *She is a frequent traveller to Belgium.* ▶ **podróżni-k/czka 2** (Brit.) a person who travels around the country in a large vehicle and does not have a permanent home anywhere: *New Age travellers* ▶ **wędrowiec** ➲ look at **Gypsy**

ˈ**traveller's cheque** (US ˈ**traveler's check**) noun [C] a cheque that you can change into foreign money when you are travelling in other countries ▶ **czek podróżny**

ˈ**travel-sick** adj. feeling sick or **vomiting** because of the movement of the vehicle you are travelling in ▶ **cierpiący na chorobę lokomocyjną** ➲ look at **airsick**, **carsick**, **seasick**

travesty /ˈtrævəsti/ noun (pl. **-ies**) **travesty (of sth)** something that does not have the qualities or values that it should have, and as a result is often shocking or offensive: *The trial was a **travesty of justice**.* ◇ *His claim is a travesty of the facts.* ▶ **parodia**, **karykatura** SYN **parody**

trawl /trɔːl/ verb **1** [I,T] **trawl (through sth) (for sth/sb)**; **trawl sth (for sth/sb)** to search through a large amount of information or a large number of people, places, etc. looking for a particular thing or person: *The police are trawling through their files for similar cases.* ◇ *She trawled the shops for bargains.* ▶ **poszukiwać czegoś (aby znaleźć kogoś/coś) 2** [I] **trawl (for sth)** to try to catch fish by pulling a large net with a wide opening through the water ▶ **poławiać**

trawler /ˈtrɔːlə(r)/ noun [C] a fishing boat that uses large nets that it pulls through the sea behind it ▶ **trawler**, **statek rybacki** ➲ picture at **boat**

tray /treɪ/ noun [C] **1** a flat piece of wood, plastic, metal, etc. with slightly higher edges that you use for carrying food, drink, etc. on ▶ **taca 2** a flat container with low edges in which you put papers, etc. on a desk ▶ **płaski, otwarty pojemnik**

treacherous /ˈtretʃərəs/ adj. **1** (used about a person) that you cannot trust and who may do sth to harm you: *He was cowardly and treacherous.* ▶ **zdradziecki 2** dangerous, although seeming safe ▶ **zdradliwy**

treachery /ˈtretʃəri/ noun [U] the act of causing harm to sb who trusts you ▶ **zdradliwość**

treacle /ˈtriːkl/ (US **molasses** /məˈlæsɪz/) noun [U] a thick, dark, sticky liquid that is made from sugar ▶ **melasa** ➲ look at **syrup**

tread¹ /tred/ verb (pt **trod** /trɒd/, pp **trodden** /ˈtrɒdn/) **1** [I] **tread (on/in/over sb/sth)** to put your foot down while you are walking: *Don't tread in the puddle!* ◇ *He trod on my toe* (nadepnął mi na palec) *and didn't even say sorry!* ◇ (figurative) *We must **tread carefully*** (postępować dyplomatycznie) *or we'll offend him.* ▶ **stąpać 2** [T] **tread sth (in/into/down)** to press down on sth with your foot: *This wine is still made by treading grapes in the traditional way.* ▶ **wdeptać, przydeptać 3** [T] to walk on sth: *He walked down the path he had trodden so many times before.* ▶ **przemierzać**

tread² /tred/ noun **1** [sing.] the sound you make when you walk; the way you walk ▶ **odgłos kroków 2** [C,U] the pattern on the surface of a tyre on a vehicle which is slightly higher than the rest of the surface ▶ **bieżnik**

treason /ˈtriːzn/ noun [U] the criminal act of causing harm to your country, for example by helping its enemies ▶ **zdrada** ➲ note at **traitor**

treasure¹ /ˈtreʒə(r)/ noun **1** [U] a collection of very valuable objects, for example gold, silver, jewellery, etc.: *to find buried treasure* ▶ **skarb 2** [C] something that is very valuable: *the nation's art treasures* (bezcenne dzieła sztuki) ▶ **skarb, bogactwa**

treasure² /ˈtreʒə(r)/ verb [T] to consider sb/sth to be very special or valuable: *I will treasure those memories forever.* ▶ **zachowywać w sercu, cenić**

ˈtreasure hunt noun [C] a game in which people try to find a hidden prize by answering a series of questions that have been left in different places ▶ **zabawa w poszukiwanie skarbów**

treasurer /ˈtreʒərə(r)/ noun [C] the person who looks after the money and accounts of a club or an organization ▶ **skarbni-k/czka**

the Treasury /ˈtreʒəri/ noun [sing., with sing. or pl. verb] the government department that controls public money ▶ **ministerstwo skarbu państwa**

⚷ **treat¹** /triːt/ verb [T] **1 treat sb/sth (with/as/like sth)** to act or behave towards sb/sth in a particular way: *Teenagers hate being treated like children.* ◇ (informal) *You should treat older people with respect.* ◇ *to treat somebody badly/fairly/well* ▶ **traktować 2 treat sth as sth** to consider sth in a particular way: *I decided to treat his comment as a joke.* ▶ **traktować 3** to deal with or discuss sth in a particular way: *The article treats this question in great detail.* ▶ **omawiać** (*książkę itp.*) **4 treat sb/sth (for sth)** to use medicine or medical care to try to make a sick or injured person well again: *The boy was treated for burns at the hospital.* ◇ *a new drug to treat cancer* (na leczenie raka) ▶ **leczyć 5 treat sth (with sth)** to put a chemical substance onto sth in order to protect it from damage, clean it, etc.: *Most vegetables are treated* (spryskuje się) *with insecticide.* ▶ **zabezpieczać (coś czymś) 6 treat sb/yourself (to sth)** to pay for sth or give sb/yourself sth that is very special or enjoyable: *Clare treated the children to an ice cream.* ▶ **fundować coś (sobie/komuś), częstować (się) czymś**

treat² /triːt/ noun [C] something special or enjoyable that you pay for or give to sb/yourself: *I've brought some cream cakes as a treat.* ◇ *It's a real treat for me to stay in bed late.* ◇ *Let's go out for dinner – **my treat*** (ja stawiam). ▶ **poczęstunek, duża przyjemność**
IDM **trick or treat** → TRICK

⚷ **treatment** /ˈtriːtmənt/ noun **1** [U,C] **treatment (for sth)** the use of medicine or medical care to cure an illness or injury; sth that is done to make sb feel and look good: *to require hospital/medical treatment* ▶ **leczenie 2** [U] the way that you behave towards sb or deal with sth: *The treatment of the prisoners of war was very harsh.* ▶ **traktowanie 3** [U,C] **treatment (for sth)** a process by which sth is cleaned, protected from damage, etc.: *an effective treatment for dry rot* ▶ **oczyszczanie, ochrona (przed czymś)**

treaty /ˈtriːti/ noun [C] (pl. **treaties**) a written agreement between two or more countries: *to sign a peace treaty* ▶ **traktat**

treble¹ /ˈtrebl/ noun [C] **1** a high singing voice, especially that of a young boy ▶ **dyszkant 2** a boy who has a high singing voice ▶ **chłopiec śpiewający dyszkantem**

treble² /ˈtrebl/ verb [I,T] to become or to make sth three times bigger: *Prices have trebled in the past ten years.* ▶ **potrajać (się)**
■ **treble** determiner: *This figure is treble* (trzykrotnie większy od) *the number five years ago.* ▶ **potrójny**

⚷ **tree** /triː/ noun [C] a tall plant that can live for a long time. Trees have a thick wooden central part from which branches grow: *an apple tree* jabłoń ◇ *an elm tree* wiąz ◇ *an oak tree* dąb ▶ **drzewo** ➲ look at **Christmas tree, family tree**

> The stem of a tree is called a **trunk**. The outer surface of this is **bark**. The **branches** grow out from the trunk. A tree may have **leaves** or **needles**.

trek /trek/ noun [C] **1** a long hard walk, lasting several days or weeks, usually in the mountains ▶ **długa piesza wędrówka 2** (informal) a long walk ▶ **kawałek drogi**
■ **trek** verb [I] (tre**kk**ing; tre**kk**ed) ▶ **wędrować** ⓘ Mówiąc o długiej pieszej wędrówce dla przyjemności, używa się zwrotu **go trekking**: *Last summer we went trekking in Nepal.*

trellis /ˈtrelɪs/ noun [C,U] a light wooden frame used to support climbing plants ▶ **treliaż**

tremble /ˈtrembl/ verb [I] **tremble (with sth)** to shake, for example because you are cold, frightened, etc.: *She was pale and trembling with shock.* ◇ *His hand was trembling as he picked up his pen to sign.* ▶ **drżeć**
■ **tremble** noun [C] ▶ **drżenie**

tremendous /trəˈmendəs/ adj. **1** very large or great: *a tremendous amount of work* ▶ **olbrzymi** SYN **huge 2** (informal) very good: *It was a tremendous experience.* ▶ **kapitalny** SYN **great**

tremendously /trəˈmendəsli/ adv. very; very much: *tremendously exciting* ◇ *Prices vary tremendously from one shop to another.* ▶ **niesamowicie, ogromnie**

tremor /ˈtremə(r)/ noun [C] a slight shaking movement: *There was a tremor in his voice.* ◇ *an earth tremor* lekki wstrząs ziemi ▶ **drżenie**

trench /trentʃ/ noun [C] **1** a long narrow hole dug in the ground for water to flow along ▶ **rów 2** a long deep hole dug in the ground for soldiers to hide in during enemy attacks ▶ **okop**

⚷ **trend** /trend/ noun [C] **a trend (towards sth)** a general change or development: *The current trend is towards smaller families.* ◇ *He always followed the latest trends in fashion.* ▶ **kierunek/trend mody, tendencja**

T

IDM **set a/the trend** to start a new style or fashion ▶ **nadawać styl, wylansować nowy kierunek mody**

trendy /ˈtrendi/ adj. (**trendier**; **trendiest**) (informal) fashionable ▶ **modny**

trespass /ˈtrespəs/ verb [I] to go onto sb's land or property without permission ▶ **wkraczać bez pozwolenia na czyjś grunt**

■ **trespasser** noun [C] ▶ **osoba wkraczająca bez pozwolenia na czyjś grunt**

ˈ**trestle table** noun [C] a table that consists of a wooden top supported by two or more structures with two pairs of sloping legs (**trestles**) ▶ **stół na kozłach**

trial /ˈtraɪəl/ noun [C,U] **1** the process in a court of law where a judge, etc. listens to evidence and decides if sb is guilty of a crime or not: *Everyone has the right to a fair trial.* ◇ *He was* ***on trial for*** (miał proces) *murder.* ◇ *trial by jury* sądzenie przez ławę przysięgłych ▶ **rozprawa sądowa** ➲ note at **court 2** an act of testing sb/sth: *New drugs must go through extensive trials.* ◇ *a* ***trial period*** *of three months* trzymiesięczny okres próbny ▶ **próba**

IDM **trial and error** trying different ways of doing sth until you find the best one ▶ **metoda prób i błędów**

ˌ**trial ˈrun** noun [C] an occasion when you practise doing sth in order to make sure you can do it correctly later on ▶ **próba (czegoś)**

triangle /ˈtraɪæŋgl/ noun [C] **1** a shape that has three straight sides: *a right-angled triangle* trójkąt prostokątny ▶ **trójkąt 2** a metal musical instrument in the shape of a triangle that you play by hitting it with a metal stick ▶ (*instrument muzyczny*) **trójkąt**

triangular /traɪˈæŋgjələ(r)/ adj. shaped like a triangle ▶ **trójkątny**

tribe /traɪb/ noun [C] a group of people who have the same language and customs and who live in a particular area, often with one of the group as an official leader: *tribes living in the Amazonian rainforest* ▶ **plemię**

■ **tribal** /ˈtraɪbl/ adj.: *tribal art* ▶ **plemienny**

tribunal /traɪˈbjuːnl/ noun [C] a type of court with the authority to decide who is right in particular types of disagreement: *an industrial tribunal* komisja arbitrażu przemysłowego ▶ **trybunał, sąd (trybunalski)**

tributary /ˈtrɪbjətri; US -teri/ noun [C] (pl. **tributaries**) a small river that flows into a larger river ▶ **rzeka/strumień dopływow-a/y**

tribute /ˈtrɪbjuːt/ noun **1** [C,U] **tribute (to sb/sth)** something that you say or do to show that you respect or admire sb/sth, especially sb who has died: *A special concert was held as a tribute to the composer.* ▶ **hołd 2** [sing.] **be a tribute to sb/sth** to be a sign of how good sb/sth is: *The success of the festival is a tribute to the organizers.* ▶ **wystawiać komuś/czemuś wyśmienite świadectwo**

IDM **pay tribute to sb/sth** → PAY[1]

trick /trɪk/ noun [C] **1** something that you do to make sb believe sth that is not true or a joke that you play to annoy sb: *The thieves used a trick to get past the security guards.* ▶ **podstęp; psikus 2** something that confuses you so that you see, remember, understand, etc. things in the wrong way: *The special effects in the film are all done using* ***trick photography*** (zdjęcia trikowe). ◇ *It was a* ***trick question*** (podchwytliwe pytanie). ▶ **coś sprytnego 3** an action that uses special skills to make people believe sth which is not true or real as a form of entertainment: *The magician* ***performed a trick*** *in which he made a rabbit disappear.* ◇ *a card trick* ▶ **trik, sztuczka (magiczna) 4** [usually sing.] a clever or the best way of doing sth: *I can't get the top off this jar.* ***Is there a trick to it*** (czy jest na to jakiś sposób)*?* ▶ **sztuka (robienia czegoś)**

■ **trick** verb [T]: *I'd been tricked and I felt like a fool.* ▶ **naciągać (kogoś na coś)**

IDM **do the job/trick** → JOB

play a joke/trick on sb → PLAY[1]

trick or treat (especially US) a custom in which children dress up in strange clothes and go to people's houses on Halloween and threaten to do sth bad to them if they do not give them sweets, etc.: *to go trick or treating* ▶ **tradycja przestrzegana w wigilię Wszystkich Świętych**

PHR V **trick sb into sth/doing sth** to persuade sb to do sth by making them believe sth that is not true: *He tricked me into lending him money.* ▶ **naciągać kogoś na coś**

trick sb out of sth to get sth from sb by making them believe sth that is not true: *Stella was tricked out of her share of the money.* ▶ **wyłudzać coś od kogoś**

trickery /ˈtrɪkəri/ noun [U] the use of dishonest methods to trick sb in order to get what you want ▶ **oszukaństwo**

trickle /ˈtrɪkl/ verb [I] **1** (used about a liquid) to flow in a thin line: *Raindrops trickled down the window.* ▶ **sączyć się 2** to go somewhere slowly and gradually: *At first no one came, but then people began to trickle in.* ◇ *News is starting to trickle out.* ▶ **powoli napływać gdzieś**

■ **trickle** noun [C, usually sing.]: *a trickle of water* ◇ *The flood of refugees had been reduced to a trickle* (ograniczono do małego strumienia). ▶ **wąska struga**

tricky /ˈtrɪki/ adj. (**trickier**; **trickiest**) difficult to do or deal with: *a tricky situation* ▶ **zawiły, delikatny, trudny**

tricycle /ˈtraɪsɪkl/ noun [C] a bicycle that has one wheel at the front and two at the back ▶ **trójkołowiec**

trifle /ˈtraɪfl/ noun **1** (**a trifle**) [sing.] (formal) slightly; rather ▶ **trochę 2** [C] something that is of little value or importance: *£5 000 is* ***a mere trifle*** (zwykła błahostka) *to her.* ▶ **błahostka 3** [C,U] (Brit.) a type of cold **dessert** made from cake and fruit covered with **custard** and cream ▶ **ciasto deserowe z owocami w galaretce, pokryte kremem i bitą śmietaną**

trifling /ˈtraɪflɪŋ/ adj. very unimportant or small SYN trivial ▶ **błahy**

trigger[1] /ˈtrɪgə(r)/ noun [C] **1** the part of a gun that you press to fire it: *to pull the trigger* ▶ **cyngiel 2** the cause of a particular reaction or event, especially a bad one ▶ **powód**

trigger[2] /ˈtrɪgə(r)/ verb [T] **trigger sth (off)** to make sth happen suddenly: *Her cigarette smoke triggered off the fire alarm.* ▶ **uruchamiać, wywoływać natychmiastową reakcję**

trill /trɪl/ noun [C] **1** a repeated short high sound made, for example, by sb's voice or by a bird ▶ **trel 2** the sound made when two notes next to each other in the musical **scale** are played or sung quickly several times one after the other ▶ **tryl 3** (also **roll**) a sound, usually an /r/, produced by making the tongue **vibrate** against a part of the mouth ▶ **drżące** *r*

■ **trill** verb **1** [I] to make repeated short high sounds: *The canary was trilling away happily.* ▶ **trylować** SYN **warble 2** [T] to say sth in a high cheerful voice: *'How wonderful!' she trilled.* ▶ **szczebiotać** SYN **warble 3** [T] to pronounce an 'r' sound by making a **trill** (3) ➲ look at **roll** (10) ▶ **wymawiać drżące** *r*

trillion /ˈtrɪljən/ number one million million ▶ **trylion**
ℹ Więcej o liczbach w dodatku *Wyrażenia liczbowe* na końcu słownika.

trilogy /ˈtrɪlədʒi/ noun [C] (pl. **trilogies**) a group of three novels, plays, etc. that form a set ▶ **trylogia**

trim[1] /trɪm/ verb [T] (**trimming**; **trimmed**) **1** to cut a small amount off sth so that it is tidy: *to trim your hair/fringe/beard* ◇ *The hedge needs trimming.* ▶ **przycinać 2 trim sth (off sth)** to cut sth off because you do not need it: *Trim the fat off the meat.* ▶ **odcinać 3 trim sth (with**

sth) to decorate the edge of sth with sth ▶ **ozdabiać brzegi, garnirować potrawę**
■ **trim** noun [C, usually sing.]: *My hair needs a trim.* ▶ **podstrzyganie**

trim² /trɪm/ adj. **1** (used about a person) looking thin, healthy and attractive ▶ **szczupły 2** well cared for; tidy ▶ **uporządkowany**; **schludny**

trimming /ˈtrɪmɪŋ/ noun **1** (**trimmings**) [pl.] extra things which you add to sth to improve its appearance, taste, etc. ▶ **przybranie**, **garnirunek** (*potrawy*) **2** [C,U] material that you use for decorating the edge of sth ▶ **przybranie**

the **Trinity** /ˈtrɪnəti/ noun [sing.] (in Christianity) the union of Father, Son and Holy Spirit as one God ▶ **Trójca Święta**

trinket /ˈtrɪŋkɪt/ noun [C] a piece of jewellery or an attractive small object that is not worth much money ▶ **świecidełko**

trio /ˈtriːəʊ/ noun (pl. **trios**) **1** [C, with sing. or pl. verb] a group of three people who play music or sing together ▶ **trio 2** [C] a piece of music for three people to play or sing ▶ **trio**

trip¹ /trɪp/ noun [C] a journey to a place and back again, either for pleasure or for a particular purpose: *How was your trip to Turkey?* ◇ *We had to make several trips to move all the furniture.* ◇ *to* ***go on a*** *shopping* ***trip*** pojechać (do innego miasta itp.) na zakupy ◇ *a business trip* (podróż służbowa) *to Brussels* ▶ **wycieczka**, **podróż** ➲ note at **travel**
■ **tripper** noun [C]: *Brighton was full of* ***day trippers*** *from London.* ▶ **wycieczkowicz/ka**, **turyst(k)a**

trip² /trɪp/ verb (**tripping**; **tripped**) **1** [I] **trip (over/up)**; **trip (over/on sth)** to catch your foot on sth when you are walking and fall or nearly fall: *Don't leave your bag on the floor. Someone might trip over it.* ◇ *She tripped up on a loose paving stone.* ▶ **potykać się (o coś) 2** [T] **trip sb (up)** to catch sb's foot and make them fall or nearly fall: *Linda stuck out her foot and tripped Barry up.* ▶ **podstawiać komuś nogę**
PHR V **trip (sb) up** to make a mistake; to make sb say sth that they did not want to say: *The journalist asked a difficult question to try to trip the politician up.* ▶ **łapać kogoś na błędzie/pomyłce**; **popełniać błąd/pomyłkę**

tripe /traɪp/ noun [U] **1** the lining of a cow's stomach used as food ▶ **flaki 2** (informal) nonsense ▶ **bzdury 3** (informal) writing, music, etc. of low quality: *I don't read any old tripe* (byle co). ▶ **miernota**

triple /ˈtrɪpl/ adj. [only before a noun] having three parts, happening three times or containing three times as much as usual: *You'll receive triple pay if you work over the New Year.* ▶ **potrójny**, **trzykrotny**
■ **triple** verb [I,T] ▶ **potrajać (się)**

the ˈ**triple jump** noun [sing.] a sporting event in which people try to jump as far forward as possible with three jumps. The first jump lands on one foot, the second on the other, and the third on both feet. ▶ **trójskok**

triplet /ˈtrɪplət/ noun [C] one of three children or animals that are born to one mother at the same time ▶ **trojaczek** ➲ look at **twin**

tripod /ˈtraɪpɒd/ noun [C] a piece of equipment with three legs that you use for putting a camera, etc. on ▶ **statyw** ➲ picture at **laboratory**

trite /traɪt/ adj. (used about a remark, an opinion, etc.) dull and boring because it has been expressed so many times before; not original ▶ **wyświechtany**, **banalny**
SYN **banal**
■ **tritely** adv. ▶ **banalnie** | **triteness** noun [U] ▶ **szablonowość**

triumph¹ /ˈtraɪʌmf/ noun [C,U] a great success or victory; the feeling of happiness that you have because of this: *The team returned home* ***in triumph.*** ◇ *The new programme was a triumph with the public* (święcił tryumf wśród publiczności). ▶ **tryumf**; **tryumfowanie**

triumph² /ˈtraɪʌmf/ verb [I] **triumph (over sb/sth)** to achieve success; to defeat sb/sth: *France triumphed over Brazil in the final.* ▶ **tryumfować (nad kimś/czymś)**, **odnosić zwycięstwo (nad kimś/czymś)**

triumphant /traɪˈʌmfənt/ adj. feeling or showing great happiness because you have won or succeeded at sth: *a triumphant cheer* ▶ **tryumfalny**
■ **triumphantly** adv. ▶ **tryumfalnie**

trivia /ˈtrɪviə/ noun [U] **1** unimportant matters, details or information ▶ **błahostki 2** [usually in compounds] facts about many subjects that are used in a game to test people's knowledge: *a trivia quiz* ▶ **wiedza ogólna**

trivial /ˈtrɪviəl/ adj. of little importance; not worth considering: *a trivial detail/problem* ▶ **trywialny**
■ **triviality** /ˌtrɪviˈæləti/ noun [C,U] (pl. **trivialities**) ▶ **trywialność**

trivialize (also **-ise**) /ˈtrɪviəlaɪz/ verb [T] to make sth seem less important, serious, etc. than it really is ▶ **trywializować**

trod past tense of **tread¹**

trodden past participle of **tread¹**

trolley /ˈtrɒli/ noun [C] **1** (US **cart**) a piece of equipment on wheels that you use for carrying things: *a supermarket/shopping/luggage trolley* ▶ **wózek 2** (Brit.) a small table with wheels that is used for carrying or serving food and drinks: *a tea/sweet/drinks trolley* ▶ **stolik na kółkach** (*z którego podaje się jedzenie lub napoje*) **3** (US) = TRAM

trolleybus /ˈtrɒlibʌs/ noun [C] a bus that gets power from an electric cable above the street ▶ **trolejbus**

trombone /trɒmˈbəʊn/ noun [C] a large musical instrument made of **brass** that you play by blowing into it and moving a long tube backwards and forwards ▶ **puzon**

troop /truːp/ noun **1** (**troops**) [pl.] soldiers ▶ **wojsko 2** [C] a large group of people or animals ▶ **gromada**
■ **troop** verb [I]: *When the bell rang everyone trooped into the hall.* ▶ **przemieszczać się gromadnie**

trophy /ˈtrəʊfi/ noun [C] (pl. **trophies**) a large silver cup, etc. that you get for winning a competition or race ▶ **trofeum** ➲ picture at **medal**

tropic /ˈtrɒpɪk/ noun **1** [C, usually sing.] one of the two lines around the earth that are 23° 26′ north and south of the **equator**. The lines are called the Tropic of Cancer and the Tropic of Capricorn. ▶ **zwrotnik 2** (**the tropics**) [pl.] the part of the world that is between these two lines, where the climate is hot and wet ▶ **tropik**
■ **tropical** /-kl/ adj.: *tropical fruit* ◇ *tropical rainforest* ▶ **tropikalny**

trot¹ /trɒt/ verb [I] (**trotting**; **trotted**) **1** (used about a horse and its rider) to move forward at a speed that is faster than a walk ▶ **kłusować**, **biec truchtem** ➲ look at **canter**, **gallop 2** (used about a person or an animal) to walk fast, taking short quick steps ▶ **truchtać**
PHR V **trot sth out** (informal) to repeat an old idea rather than thinking of sth new to say: *to trot out the same old story* ▶ **odgrzebywać** (*stare pomysły*)

trot² /trɒt/ noun [sing.] a speed that is faster than a walk ▶ **kłus**; **jazda kłusem**
IDM **on the trot** (informal) one after another; without stopping: *We worked for six hours on the trot.* ▶ **ciągiem**, **bez przerwy**

trouble¹ /ˈtrʌbl/ noun **1** [U,C] **trouble (with sb/sth)** (a situation that causes) a problem, difficulty or worry: *If I don't get home by 11 o'clock I'll* ***be in trouble.*** ◇ *I'm* ***having trouble*** *getting the car started.* ◇ *I'm having trouble with my car.* ◇ *financial troubles* ◇ *Marie is clever.* ***The trouble is*** *she's very lazy.* ▶ **kłopot 2** [U] illness or pain:

back/heart trouble ▶ **dolegliwość** **3** [C,U] a situation where people are fighting or arguing with each other: *There's often trouble in town on Saturday night after the bars have closed.* ▶ **rozróba** **4** [U] extra work or effort: *Why don't you stay the night with us. **It's no trouble.*** ◇ *I'm sorry to **put you to** so much **trouble.*** ◇ *Let's eat out tonight. It will **save you the trouble** of cooking.* ▶ **kłopot**

IDM **ask for trouble/it** → ASK

get into trouble to get into a situation which is dangerous or in which you may be punished ▶ **wpadać w tarapaty**

go to a lot of trouble (to do sth) to put a lot of work or effort into sth: *They went to a lot of trouble to make us feel welcome.* ▶ **zadawać sobie wiele trudu**

take trouble over/with sth; **take trouble to do sth/doing sth** to do sth with care ▶ **bardzo się starać**

take the trouble to do sth to do sth even though it means extra work or effort ▶ **zadawać sobie trud**

trouble² /ˈtrʌbl/ verb [T] **1** to make sb worried, upset, etc.: *Is there something troubling you?* ▶ **kłopotać** **2** (formal) **trouble sb (for sth)** (used when you are politely asking sb for sth or to do sth) to disturb sb: *Sorry to trouble you, but would you mind answering a few questions?* ◇ *Could I trouble you for some change?* Czy mógłbym pana prosić o drobne? ▶ **prosić kogoś o coś, fatygować (kogoś)** SYN for both meanings **bother**

troublemaker /ˈtrʌblmeɪkə(r)/ noun [C] a person who often deliberately causes trouble ▶ **osoba sprawiająca kłopoty**

troubleshooter /ˈtrʌblʃuːtə(r)/ noun [C] a person who helps to solve problems in a company or an organization ▶ **specjalista rozpoznający i usuwający np. usterki techniczne dla firmy/organizacji.**

■ **troubleshooting** noun [U] ▶ **rozwiązywanie problemów technicznych itp.**

troublesome /ˈtrʌblsəm/ adj. causing trouble, pain, etc. over a long period of time ▶ **kłopotliwy** SYN **annoying**

ˈ**trouble spot** noun [C] a place or country where trouble often happens, especially violence or war ▶ **punkt zapalny**

trough /trɒf/ noun [C] **1** a long narrow container from which farm animals eat or drink ▶ **żłób, koryto** **2** a low area or point, between two higher areas ▶ **dolina**

trounce /traʊns/ verb [T] (formal) to defeat sb completely: *Brazil trounced Italy 5-1 in the final.* ▶ **pokonać kogoś**

troupe /truːp/ noun [C, with sing. or pl. verb] a group of actors, singers, etc. who work together ▶ **trupa**

⚷ **trousers** /ˈtraʊzəz/ (US **pants** /pænts/) noun [pl.] a piece of clothing that covers the whole of both your legs ▶ **spodnie** ℹ Zwróć uwagę, że słowo **trousers** występuje tylko w lm, a zatem nie można powiedzieć, np. ~~*a new trouser*~~. Można stosować następujące formy: *I need some new trousers.* ◇ *I need a new pair of trousers.* ◇ *These trousers are too tight.* Słowa **trouser** używa się w roli przymiotnika: *a trouser leg* ◇ *a trouser suit.* ➲ picture on **page A1**

trout /traʊt/ noun [C,U] (pl. **trout**) a type of fish that lives in rivers and that we eat ▶ **pstrąg**

trowel /ˈtraʊəl/ noun [C] **1** a small garden tool used for lifting plants, digging small holes, etc. ▶ **rydelek ogrodniczy** ➲ picture at **garden** **2** a small tool with a flat blade, used in building ▶ **kielnia**

truant /ˈtruːənt/ noun [C] a child who stays away from school without permission ▶ **wagarowicz/ka**

■ **truancy** /-ənsi/ noun [U] ▶ (*chodzenie na*) **wagary**

IDM **play truant**; US **play hooky** to stay away from school without permission ▶ **chodzić na wagary**

truce /truːs/ noun [C] an agreement to stop fighting for a period of time ▶ **zawieszenie broni** ➲ look at **ceasefire**

trucks

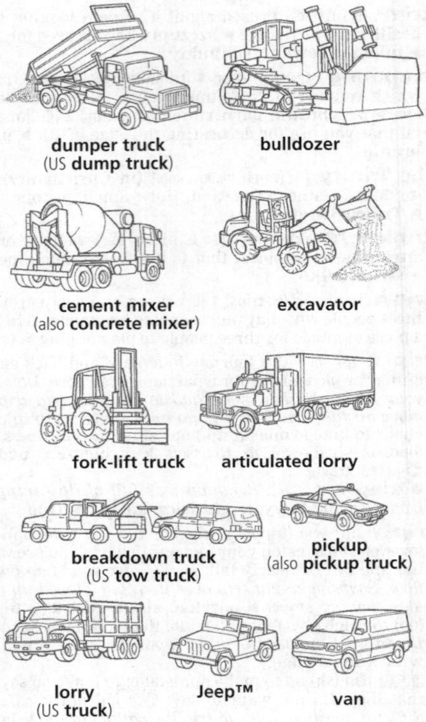

dumper truck (US **dump truck**)
bulldozer
cement mixer (also **concrete mixer**)
excavator
fork-lift truck
articulated lorry
breakdown truck (US **tow truck**)
pickup (also **pickup truck**)
lorry (US **truck**)
Jeep™
van

⚷ **truck** /trʌk/ noun [C] **1** (especially US) = LORRY: *a truck driver* **2** (Brit.) a section of a train that is used for carrying goods or animals: *a cattle truck* ▶ **odkryty wagon kolejowy, platforma kolejowa** **3** [in compounds] a large heavy vehicle, used for a particular purpose: *a fork-lift truck* podnośnik widłowy ▶ **pojazd specjalnego przeznaczenia**

trudge /trʌdʒ/ verb [I] to walk with slow, heavy steps, for example because you are very tired ▶ **iść ciężkimi krokami/z trudem**

⚷ **true** /truː/ adj. **1** right or correct: *Is it true that Adam is leaving?* ◇ *I didn't think the film was at all **true to life*** (pokazywał prawdziwe życie). ◇ *Read the statements and decide if they are true or false.* ▶ **prawdziwy** OPP **untrue**, **false** **2** real or genuine, often when this is different from how sth seems: *The novel was based on **a true story.*** ▶ **prawdziwy** OPP **false** **3** having all the typical qualities of the thing mentioned: *How do you know when you have found **true love?*** ▶ **prawdziwy** **4** **true (to sb/sth)** behaving as expected or as promised: *He was **true to his word.*** Dotrzymał słowa. ◇ *She has been a true friend to me.* ▶ **zgodny z oczekiwaniami** ➲ noun **truth**

IDM **come true** to happen in the way you hoped or dreamed: *Winning was like a dream come true!* ▶ **spełniać się**

too good to be true (used to say that you cannot believe that sth is as good as it seems) ▶ **zbyt piękne, aby było prawdziwe**

true to form typical; as usual ▶ **w sposób charakterystyczny dla kogoś**

truly /'tru:li/ adv. **1** (used to emphasize a feeling, statement) really; completely: *We are truly grateful to you for your help.* ▶ **naprawdę, zupełnie 2** (used to emphasize that sth is correct or accurate): *I cannot truly say that I was surprised at the news.* ▶ **naprawdę**

Yours truly ...(szczerze oddany) jest zwrotem grzecznościowym używanym na zakończenie listu w Amer. ang.

IDM **well and truly** → WELL[1]

trump /trʌmp/ noun [C] (in some card games) a card of the chosen **suit** that has a higher value than cards of the other three **suits** during a particular game: *Spades are trumps.* ▶ **atut**

'trump card noun [C] a special advantage you have over other people that you keep secret until you can surprise them with it: *It was time for her to* ***play*** *her* ***trump card*** (aby wyciągnąć asa z rękawa). ▶ **atut**

trumpet /'trʌmpɪt/ noun [C] a musical instrument made of **brass** that you play by blowing into it. There are three buttons on it which you press to make different notes. ▶ **trąbka** ➲ note at **music**, **piano**

truncate /trʌŋ'keɪt; US 'trʌŋkeɪt/ verb [T] (formal) to make sth shorter: *My article was published in truncated form.* ◇ *Further discussion was truncated by the arrival of tea.* ▶ **skracać, przycinać**

truncheon /'trʌntʃən/ (especially Brit.) (also **baton**; US usually **nightstick** /'naɪtstɪk/) noun [C] (old-fashioned) a short thick stick that a police officer carries as a weapon ▶ **pałka policyjna**

trundle /'trʌndl/ verb [I,T] to move, or make sth heavy move, slowly and noisily: *A lorry trundled down the hill.* ▶ **toczyć się; wolno popychać/ciągnąć** (*coś na kołach*)

trunk /trʌŋk/ noun **1** [C] the thick central part of a tree that the branches grow from ▶ **pień 2** [C] (US) = BOOT[1] (2) **3** [C] the long nose of an **elephant** ▶ **trąba słonia** ➲ picture on **page A10 4** (**trunks**) [pl.] = SWIMMING TRUNKS **5** [C] a large box that you use for storing or transporting things ▶ **kufer 6** [usually sing.] the main part of your body (not including your head, arms and legs) ▶ **tułów**

trust[1] /trʌst/ noun **1** [U] **trust (in sb/sth)** the belief that sb is good, honest, sincere, etc. and will not try to harm or trick you: *Our marriage is based on love and trust.* ◇ *I* ***put my trust in*** *him* (zaufałem mu), *but he failed me.* ◇ *As a teacher you are in* ***a position of trust*** (masz moralnie odpowiedzialne stanowisko). ▶ **zaufanie** ➲ look at **distrust**, **mistrust 2** [C,U] a legal arrangement by which a person or organization looks after money and property for sb else until that person is old enough to control it: *The money was put into (a) trust for the children.* ▶ **powiernictwo**

IDM **take sth on trust** to believe what sb says without having proof that it is true: *I can't prove it. You must take it on trust.* ▶ **wierzyć komuś na słowo**

trust[2] /trʌst/ verb [T] **trust sb (to do sth)**; **trust sb (with sth)** to believe that sb is good, sincere, honest, etc. and that they will not trick you or try to harm you: *He said the car was safe but I just don't trust him.* ◇ *You can't trust her with money.* Nie można jej powierzać pieniędzy. ◇ *I don't trust that dog. It looks dangerous.* ▶ **ufać** ➲ look at **mistrust**, **distrust**

IDM **Trust sb (to do sth)** (informal) it is typical of sb to do sth: *Trust Alice to be late.* (Możesz być pewien, że Alice się spóźni.) *She's never on time!* ▶ **być przekonanym/pewnym (że ktoś coś zrobi)**

PHR V **trust in sb/sth** (formal) to have confidence in sb/sth; to believe that sb/sth is good and can be relied on: *She needs to trust more in her own abilities.* ▶ **zaufać komuś/czemuś**

trustee /trʌ'sti:/ noun [C] a person who looks after money or property for sb else ▶ **powierni-k/czka**

trusting /'trʌstɪŋ/ adj. believing that other people are good, sincere, honest, etc. ▶ **ufny**

trustworthy /'trʌstwɜ:ði/ adj. that you can depend on to be good, sincere, honest, etc. ▶ **godny zaufania**

truth /tru:θ/ noun (pl. **truths** /tru:ðz/) **1** (**the truth**) [sing.] what is true; the facts: *Please* ***tell me the truth.*** ◇ *Are you telling me* ***the whole truth*** *about what happened?* ◇ ***The truth is,*** *we can't afford to live here any more.* ▶ **prawda 2** [U] the state or quality of being true: *There's a lot of truth in what she says.* ▶ **prawda 3** [C] a fact or idea that is believed by most people to be true: *scientific/universal truths* ▶ **prawda** ➲ adjective **true**

truthful /'tru:θfl/ adj. **1 truthful (about sth)** (used about a person) who tells the truth: *I don't think you're being truthful with me.* ▶ **prawdomówny, szczery** SYN **honest 2** (used about a statement) true or correct: *a truthful account* ▶ **zgodny z prawdą, prawidłowy**
■ **truthfully** /-fəli/ adv. ▶ **zgodnie z prawdą; prawdziwie**

try[1] /traɪ/ verb (**trying**; **tries**; pt, pp **tried**) **1** [I] **try (to do sth)** to make an effort to do sth: *I tried to phone you but I couldn't get through.* ◇ *She was* ***trying hard*** *not to laugh.* ◇ *She'll* ***try her best/hardest*** (spróbuje z całych sił) *to help you.* ◇ *I'm sure you can do it if you try.* ▶ **próbować, starać się**

W języku codziennym często używa się **try and** zamiast **try to**: *I'll try to get there on time.* ◇ (informal) *I'll try and get there on time.* Nie można jednak używać **try and** w czasie przeszłym. W tym czasie poprawna forma to **try to**: *I tried to get there on time.*

2 [T] **try (doing) sth** to do, use or test sth in order to see how good or successful it is: *'I've tried everything but I can't get the baby to sleep.' 'Have you tried taking her out in the car?'* ◇ *Have you ever tried raw fish?* ◇ *He tried several bookshops* (sprawdzał w kilku księgarniach) *but none of them had the books he wanted.* ◇ *We tried the door* (próbowaliśmy otworzyć drzwi) *but it was locked.* ▶ **próbować, sprawdzać**

Por. **try do to sth** oraz **try doing sth**: *I've tried to give up smoking many times.* Wiele razy próbowałem rzucić palenie. ◇ *'I've got a sore throat.' 'You should try taking some medicine* (może spróbuj wziąć jakieś lekarstwo).*'*

3 [T] **try sb (for sth)** to examine sb in a court of law in order to decide if they are guilty of a crime or not: *He was tried for murder.* ▶ **sądzić kogoś za coś**

IDM **try your hand at sth** to do sth such as an activity or a sport for the first time ▶ **próbować coś robić po raz pierwszy**

try sb's patience to make sb feel impatient ▶ **nadużywać czyjejś cierpliwości**

PHR V **try for sth** to make an attempt to get or win sth ▶ **starać się o coś**

try sth on to put on a piece of clothing to see if it fits you properly: *Can I try these jeans on, please?* ▶ **przymierzać** ➲ note at **clothes**

try out for sth (especially US) to compete for a position or place in sth, or to be a member of a team: *She's trying out* (ubiega się o rolę) *for the school play.* ▶ **starać się dostać do czegoś**

try sb/sth out (on sb) to test sb/sth to find out if he/she/it is good enough ▶ **wypróbowywać**

try[2] /traɪ/ noun [C] (pl. **tries**) an occasion when you try to do sth: *I don't know if I can move it by myself, but I'll* ***give it a try*** (spróbuję). ▶ **próba** SYN **attempt**

trying /ˈtraɪɪŋ/ adj. that makes you tired or angry: *a trying journey* ▶ **męczący; dokuczliwy**

tsar (also czar, tzar) /zɑː(r)/ noun [C] **1** the title of the ruler of Russia in the past: *Tsar Nicholas II* ▶ **car 2** an expert usually chosen by a government with responsibility for sth important: *the Government's drugs tsar* ▶ **rzeczoznawca** (*zwł. powołany przez rząd i odpowiedzialny za istotne sprawy*)

tsarina (also czarina, tzarina) /zɑːˈriːnə/ noun [C] the title of the female ruler of Russia in the past ▶ **caryca**

ˈT-shirt (also teeshirt) noun [C] a shirt with short sleeves and without buttons or a **collar** ▶ **koszulka z krótkim rękawem bez guzików i kołnierzyka**

tsp = TEASPOON (2): *Add 1 tsp salt.*

tub /tʌb/ noun [C] **1** a large round container ▶ **balia, kadź, wanienka (na coś) 2** a small plastic container with a lid that is used for holding food: *a tub of margarine/ice cream* ▶ **plastikowe pudełko z przykrywką** ➲ picture at **container**

tuba /ˈtjuːbə; US ˈtuː-/ noun [C] a large musical instrument made of **brass** that makes a low sound ▶ **tuba**

⚷ **tube** /tjuːb; US tuːb/ noun **1** [C] a long empty pipe: *Blood flowed along the tube into the bottle.* ◇ *the inner tube of a bicycle tyre* dętka rowerowa ◇ *a laboratory test-tube* probówka ▶ **rur(k)a, wąż/wężyk** ➲ look at **test tube 2** [C] **a tube (of sth)** a long thin container with a lid at one end made of soft plastic or metal. Tubes are used for holding thick liquids that can be squeezed out of them: *a tube of toothpaste* ▶ **tubka** ➲ picture at **container 3** (**the tube**) [sing.] (Brit., informal) = UNDERGROUND[3]

tuberculosis /tjuːˌbɜːkjuˈləʊsɪs; US tuːˌbɜːkjəˈl-/ noun [U] (abbr. **TB** /ˌtiː ˈbiː/) a serious disease that affects the lungs ▶ **gruźlica**

tubing /ˈtjuːbɪŋ; US ˈtuːb-/ noun [U] a long piece of metal, rubber, etc. in the shape of a tube ▶ **rur-y/ki**

TUC /ˌtiː juː ˈsiː/ abbr. the **Trades Union Congress**; the association of British **trade unions** ▶ **Zjednoczenie Brytyjskich Związków Zawodowych**

tuck /tʌk/ verb [T] **1 tuck sth in, under, round, etc. (sth)** to put or fold the ends or edges of sth into or round sth else so that it looks tidy: *Tuck your shirt in* (włóż koszulę w spodnie) *– it looks untidy like that.* ▶ **owijać, podwijać 2 tuck sth (away)** to put sth into a small space, especially to hide it or to keep it safe: *The letter was tucked behind a pile of books.* ▶ **chować (starannie/dokładnie), wtykać**

PHR V **tuck sth away 1** [only in the passive form] to be hidden: *The house was tucked away among the trees.* ▶ **chować 2** to hide sth somewhere; to keep sth in a safe place: *He tucked his wallet away in his inside pocket.* ▶ **chować coś gdzieś**

tuck sb in/up to make sb feel comfortable in bed by pulling the covers up around them ▶ **otulać kogoś**

tuck in; tuck into sth (especially Brit., informal) to eat with pleasure ▶ **wcinać** (*jedzenie*)

Tue. (also Tues.) = TUESDAY: *Tue. 9 March*

⚷ **Tuesday** /ˈtjuːzdeɪ; -di; US ˈtuː-/ noun [C,U] (abbr. **Tue.**; **Tues.**) the day of the week after Monday ▶ **wtorek** ➲ note at **Monday**

tuft /tʌft/ noun [C] a small amount of hair, grass, etc. growing together ▶ **kępka**

tug¹ /tʌg/ verb [I,T] (**tugging**; **tugged**) **tug (at/on sth)** to pull sth hard and quickly, often several times: *The boy tugged at his father's trouser leg.* ▶ **szarpać**

tug² /tʌg/ noun [C] **1** (also **tugboat** /ˈtʌgbəʊt/) a small powerful boat that is used for pulling ships into a port, etc. ▶ **holownik 2** a sudden hard pull: *She gave the rope a tug.* Szarpnęła za sznur. ▶ **szarpnięcie** ➲ picture at **boat**

tuition /tjuˈɪʃn; US tu-/ noun [U] **tuition (in sth)** teaching, especially to a small group of people: *private tuition in Italian* ◇ *tuition fees* czesne ▶ **nauczanie, korepetycje**

tulip /ˈtjuːlɪp; US ˈtuː-/ noun [C] a brightly coloured flower, shaped like a cup, that grows in the spring ▶ **tulipan** ➲ picture on **page A15**

tumble /ˈtʌmbl/ verb [I] **1** to fall down suddenly but without serious injury: *He tripped and tumbled all the way down the steps* (stoczył się ze schodów). ▶ **upaść, runąć 2** to fall suddenly in value or amount: *House prices have tumbled.* ▶ **gwałtownie spadać 3** to move or fall somewhere in an untidy way: *She opened her bag and all her things tumbled out of it.* ▶ **gramolić się, wysypywać się** ■ **tumble** noun [C, usually sing.] ▶ **gwałtowny upadek**

PHR V **tumble down** to fall down: *The walls of the old house were tumbling down.* ▶ **przewracać się** (*z hukiem*), **walić się**

ˌtumble ˈdryer (also **tumble-drier**) noun [C] (Brit.) a machine that dries clothes by moving them about in hot air ▶ **suszarka do bielizny**

tumbler /ˈtʌmblə(r)/ noun [C] a glass for drinking out of with straight sides and no handle ▶ **szklanka**

tummy (informal) = STOMACH[1]

tumour (US **tumor**) /ˈtjuːmə(r); US ˈtuː-/ noun [C] a mass of cells that are not growing normally in the body as the result of a disease: *a brain tumour* ▶ **guz**

tumultuous /tjuːˈmʌltʃuəs; US tuː-/ adj. very noisy, because people are excited: *a tumultuous welcome* ◇ *tumultuous applause* ▶ **wrzaskliwy**

tuna /ˈtjuːnə; US ˈtuː-/ (also **ˈtuna fish**) noun [C,U] (pl. **tuna**) a large sea fish that we eat: *a tin of tuna* ▶ **tuńczyk; mięso z tuńczyka**

⚷ **tune¹** /tjuːn; US tuːn/ noun [C,U] a series of musical notes that are sung or played to form a piece of music: *The children **played** us **a tune** on their recorders.* ◇ *Some people complain that modern music has no tune to it.* ◇ *a signature tune* sygnał rozpoznawczy (programu telewizyjnego/radiowego) ▶ **melodia**

IDM **call the shots/tune** → CALL[1]

change your tune → CHANGE[1]

in/out of tune 1 (not) singing or playing the correct musical notes to sound pleasant: *You're singing out of tune.* ▶ (*śpiewać/grać*) **czysto/nieczysto 2** having/not having the same opinions, interests, feelings, etc. as sb/sth: *The President doesn't seem to be in tune with* (chyba nie rozumie) *what ordinary people are thinking.* ▶ **(nie) w zgodzie z kimś/czymś**

⚷ **tune²** /tjuːn; US tuːn/ verb **1** [T] to make small changes to the sound a musical instrument makes so that it plays the correct notes: *to tune a piano/guitar* ▶ **stroić 2** [T] to make small changes to an engine so that it runs well ▶ **regulować 3** [T, usually passive] **tune sth (in) (to sth)** to move the controls on a radio or TV so that you can receive a particular station ▶ **nastrajać na daną stację/kanał**

PHR V **tune in (to sth)** to listen to a radio programme or watch a TV programme: ***Stay tuned** to this station* (proszę słuchać dalej naszej stacji) *for the latest news.* ▶ **nastawiać radio/tv na jakąś stację**

tune (sth) up to make small changes to a group of musical instruments so that they sound pleasant when played together ▶ **zestrajać się; stroić**

tuneful /ˈtjuːnfl; US ˈtuː-/ adj. (used about music) nice or pleasant to listen to ▶ **melodyjny**

tuner /ˈtjuːnə(r); US ˈtuː-/ noun [C] **1** [especially in compounds] a person who tunes musical instruments, especially pianos ▶ **stroiciel/ka 2** the part of a radio, television, etc. that you move in order to change the signal and receive the radio or television station that you want ▶ **regulator strojenia 3** an electronic device that receives a radio signal and sends it to an **amplifier** so that it can be heard ▶ **tuner**

tunic /ˈtjuːnɪk; US ˈtuː-/ noun [C] **1** a piece of women's clothing, usually without sleeves, that is long and not tight ▶ **tunika** **2** (Brit.) the jacket that is part of the uniform of police officers, soldiers, etc. ▶ **górna część munduru**

tunnel /ˈtʌnl/ noun [C] a passage under the ground: *The train disappeared into a tunnel.* ◇ *the Channel Tunnel* tunel pod kanałem La Manche ▶ **tunel**

■ **tunnel** verb [I,T] (**tunnelling**; **tunnelled**; US **tuneling**; **tunneled**) ▶ **drążyć tunel**

turban /ˈtɜːbən/ noun [C] a covering for the head worn especially by Sikh and Muslim men. A **turban** is made by folding a long piece of cloth around the head. ▶ **turban**

turbine /ˈtɜːbaɪn/ noun [C] a machine or an engine that receives its power from a wheel that is turned by the pressure of water, air or gas ▶ **turbina**

turbulent /ˈtɜːbjələnt/ adj. **1** in which there is a lot of sudden change, confusion, disagreement, and sometimes violence ▶ **burzliwy** **2** (used about water or air) moving in a violent way ▶ **rwący**

■ **turbulence** noun [U] ▶ (*podczas lotu samolotem*) **turbulencja**; (*sytuacja polityczna*) **niepokój**, **zamieszki**

turf[1] /tɜːf/ noun [U,C] (a piece of) short thick grass and the layer of soil underneath it ▶ **darń**

turf[2] /tɜːf/ verb [T] to cover ground with **turf** ▶ **pokrywać darnią**

PHR V **turf sb out (of sth)** (Brit., informal) to force sb to leave a place ▶ **wywalać (kogoś skądś)**

turkey /ˈtɜːki/ noun [C,U] a large bird that is kept on farms for its meat. Turkeys are usually eaten at Christmas in Britain and at Thanksgiving in the US. ▶ **indyk**

IDM **cold turkey** → COLD[1]

turmoil /ˈtɜːmɔɪl/ noun [U, sing.] a state of great noise or confusion: *His statement **threw** the court **into turmoil*** (wywołało zamieszanie w sądzie). ◇ *Her mind was **in (a) turmoil**.* Miała zupełny mętlik w głowie. ▶ **zgiełk**

turn[1] /tɜːn/ verb **1** [I,T] to move or make sth move round a fixed central point: *The wheels turned faster and faster.* ◇ *She turned the key in the lock.* ◇ *Turn the steering wheel to the right.* ▶ **kręcić (się)**, **obracać (się)** **2** [I,T] to move your body, or part of your body, so that you are facing in a different direction: *He turned round when he heard my voice.* ◇ *She **turned** her **back on** me.* ▶ **odwracać (się)** **3** [I,T] to change the position of sth: *I turned the box upside down.* ◇ *He turned the page and started the next chapter.* ▶ **przekręcać**, **odwracać**, **przewracać** **4** [I,T] to change direction when you are moving: *Go straight on and **turn left** at the church.* ◇ *The car **turned the corner*** (skręcił na rogu). ▶ **skręcać** **5** [T] to point or aim sth in a particular direction: *She turned her attention back to me.* ▶ **skierować** **6** [I,T] (to cause) to become: *He **turned** very **red** when I asked him about the money.* ◇ *These caterpillars will turn into butterflies.* ▶ **stawać się**; **zamieniać (kogoś/się w coś)** **7** [T] [not used in the continuous tenses] to reach or pass a particular age or time: *It's turned midnight.* Minęła północ. ▶ **mijać**; **skończyć** (*ileś lat*)

ⓘ **Turn** używa się w idiomach, np. **turn a blind eye**. Zob. hasła odpowiednich rzeczowników, przymiotników itp.

PHR V **turn (sb/sth) around/round** to change position or direction in order to face the opposite way, or to return the way you came; to make sb/sth do this: *This road is a dead end. We'll have to turn round and go back to the main road.* ◇ *He turned the car around and drove off.* ▶ **zawracać (kogoś/coś)**, **odwracać/obracać (kogoś/się/coś)**

turn away to stop looking at sb/sth: *She turned away in horror at the sight of the blood.* ▶ **odwracać się**

turn sb away to refuse to allow a person to go into a place ▶ **odprawiać kogoś (z kwitkiem)**

turn back; **turn sb/sth back** to return the way you have come; to make sb/sth do this: *We've come so far already, we can't turn back now.* ◇ *The weather became so bad that they had to turn back.* ◇ (figurative) *We said we would do it – there can be no turning back* (nie ma odwrotu). ▶ **zawracać (kogoś/coś)** ➲ note at **return**

turn sb/sth down to refuse an offer, etc. or the person who makes it: *Why did you turn that job down?* ◇ *He asked her to marry him, but she turned him down.* ▶ **odrzucać kogoś/coś**, **odmawiać komuś**

turn sth down to reduce the sound or heat that sth produces: *Turn the TV down!* ▶ **przyciszać/zmniejszać coś**

turn sb/sth (from sth) into sth to make sb/sth become sth: *Ten years of prison had turned him into an old man.* ◇ *The prince was turned into a frog by the witch.* ▶ **zmieniać/przemieniać kogoś/coś (z czegoś) w coś**

turn off (sth) to leave one road and go on another ▶ **skręcać/zjeżdżać z czegoś**

turn sth off to stop the flow of electricity, water, etc. by moving a switch, tap, etc.: *He turned the TV off.* ▶ **wyłączać coś**

turn sb on to make sb excited or interested, especially sexually ▶ **podniecać kogoś**

turn sth on to start the flow of electricity, water, etc. by moving a switch, tap, etc.: *to turn the lights on* ▶ **włączać**

turn out (for sth) to be present at an event ▶ **wylegać** (*np. na ulice*), **pojawiać się gdzieś**

turn out (to be sth) to be in the end: *The weather turned out fine.* ◇ *The house that they had promised us turned out to be a tiny flat.* ▶ **okazywać się (być jakimś/czymś)**

turn sth out to move the switch, etc. on a light or a source of heat to stop it: *Turn the lights out before you go to bed.* ▶ **gasić coś**

turn over **1** to change position so that the other side is facing out or upwards: *He turned over and went back to sleep.* ▶ **przewracać się** (*na drugi bok*) **2** (used about an engine) to start or to continue to run ▶ **zapalać**; (*przen.*) **chodzić**

turn over (to sth) (Brit.) to change to another programme when you are watching television: *This film's awful. Shall I turn over?* ▶ **przełączać się (na coś)**

turn sth over **1** to make sth change position so that the other side is facing out or upwards: *You may now turn over your exam papers and begin.* ▶ **odwracać coś** **2** to keep thinking about sth carefully: *She kept turning over what he'd said in her mind.* ▶ **przemyśliwać coś**

turn to sb/sth to go to sb/sth to get help, advice, etc. ▶ **zwracać się do kogoś/czegoś (z prośbą)**; **otwierać książkę na danej stronie**

turn up **1** to arrive; to appear: *What time did they finally turn up?* ▶ **pojawiać się** **2** to be found, especially by chance: *I lost my glasses a week ago and they haven't turned up yet.* ▶ **znaleźć się**

turn sth up to increase the sound or heat that sth produces: *Turn the heating up – I'm cold.* ▶ **podkręcać** (*np. ogrzewanie*), **zwiększać** (*np. głośność*)

turn[2] /tɜːn/ noun [C] **1** the act of turning sb/sth round: *Give the screw another couple of turns to make sure it is really tight.* ▶ **obrót** **2** a change of direction in a vehicle: *to make a **left/right turn*** ◇ *a U-turn* zwrot o 180 stopni ▶ **skręt** **3** (Brit. also **turning**) a bend or corner in a road, river, etc.: *Take the next turn* (skręć w następną ulicę) *on the left.* ▶ **ulica**, **zakręt** **4** [usually sing.] the time when sb in a group of people should or is allowed to do sth: *Please wait in the queue until it is your turn.* ◇ *Whose turn is it to do the cleaning?* ◇ *to miss a turn* stracić kolejkę ◇ *to take turns* zmieniać się ▶ **kolej** SYN **go** **5** an unusual or unexpected change: *The patient's condi-*

tion has taken a turn for the worse (pogorszył się). ▶ **zmiana**

IDM **(do sb) a good turn** (to do) sth that helps sb: *Well, that's my good turn for today.* ▶ **wyświadczać komuś przysługę**

in turn one after the other: *I spoke to each of the children in turn.* ▶ **po kolei**

take turns (at sth) to do sth one after the other to make sure it is fair ▶ **robić coś kolejno**

the turn of the century/year the time when a new century/year starts ▶ **przełom wieku, koniec roku**

wait your turn → WAIT[1]

turning /ˈtɜːnɪŋ/ (Brit.) (also **turn**) noun [C] a place where one road leads off from another: *We must have taken a wrong turning.* ◇ *Take the third turning* (skręć w trzecią ulicę) *on the right.* ▶ **ulica, przecznica**

ˈ**turning point** noun [C] **a turning point (in sth)** a time when an important change happens, usually a good one ▶ **punkt zwrotny**

turnip /ˈtɜːnɪp/ noun [C,U] a round white vegetable that grows under the ground ▶ **rzepa**

ˈ**turn-off** noun [C] the place where a road leads away from a larger or more important road: *This is the turn-off for York.* ▶ **zjazd z głównej drogi**

ˈ**turn-on** noun [usually sing.] (informal) a person or thing that people find sexually exciting: *He finds leather a real turn-on.* ▶ **osoba/rzecz działając-a/y na kogoś podniecająco**

turnout /ˈtɜːnaʊt/ noun [C, usually sing.] the number of people who go to a meeting, sports event, etc. ▶ **frekwencja**

turnover /ˈtɜːnəʊvə(r)/ noun [sing.] **a turnover (of sth)** **1** the amount of business that a company does in a particular period of time: *The firm has an annual turnover of $50 million.* ▶ **obrót** (*handlowy*) **2** the rate at which workers leave a company and are replaced by new ones: *a high turnover of staff* ▶ **rotacja pracowników**

ˈ**turn signal** (US) = INDICATOR (2)

turnstile /ˈtɜːnstaɪl/ noun [C] a metal gate that moves round in a circle when it is pushed, and allows one person at a time to enter a place ▶ **kołowrót u wejścia**

turntable /ˈtɜːnteɪbl/ noun [C] the round surface on a record player that you place the record on to be played ▶ **talerz obrotowy**

turpentine /ˈtɜːpəntaɪn/ noun [U] a clear liquid with a strong smell that you use for removing paint or for making paint thinner ▶ **terpentyna**

turquoise /ˈtɜːkwɔɪz/ noun **1** [C,U] a blue or greenish-blue **precious stone** ▶ (*geol.*) **turkus 2** [U] a greenish-blue colour ▶ **kolor turkusowy**

■ **turquoise** adj. ▶ **turkusowy**

turret /ˈtʌrət; US ˈtɜːrət/ noun [C] a small tower on the top of a large building ▶ **wieżyczka** ➲ picture on **page A3**

turtle /ˈtɜːtl/ noun [C] **1** an animal with a thick shell and a skin covered in scales that lives in the sea ▶ **żółw morski 2** (US) = TORTOISE ➲ picture on **page A11**

tusk /tʌsk/ noun [C] one of the two very long pointed teeth of an **elephant**, etc. Elephants' **tusks** are made of **ivory**. ▶ **kieł** ➲ picture on **page A10**

tussle /ˈtʌsl/ noun [C] (informal) **a tussle (for/over sth)** a fight, for example between two or more people who want to have the same thing ▶ **szamotanina**

tut /tʌt/ (also ˌ**tut-ˈtut**) interj. (the way of writing the sound that people make to show disapproval of sb/sth) ▶ (*wyrażenie w formie pisemnej odgłosu oznaczającego dezaprobatę itp.*)

tutor /ˈtjuːtə(r); US ˈtuː-/ noun [C] **1** a private teacher who teaches one person or a very small group ▶ **korepetytor/ka 2** (Brit.) a teacher who is responsible for a small group of students at school, college or university. A **tutor** advises students on their work or helps them if they have problems in their private life. ▶ **wychowaw-ca/czyni, opiekun/ka grupy (studentów)**

tutorial /tjuːˈtɔːriəl; US tuː-/ noun [C] a lesson at a college or university for an individual student or a small group of students ▶ **korepetycja**

tuxedo (also informal **tux**) (US) = DINNER JACKET

⚷ **TV** = TELEVISION

twang /twæŋ/ noun [C] the sound that is made when you pull a tight string or wire, etc. and then let it go suddenly ▶ **brzdęk**

■ **twang** verb [I,T] ▶ **brzdąkać**

tweak /twiːk/ verb [T] **1** to pull or twist sth suddenly: *She tweaked his ear playfully.* ▶ **pociągnąć; wykręcać 2** to make slight changes to a machine, system, etc. to improve it: *I think you'll have to tweak these figures a little before you show them to the boss.* ▶ **ulepszać** (*nieznacznie*), **naciągać** (*np. wyniki*)

■ **tweak** noun [C] **1** a sharp pull or twist: *She gave his ear a tweak.* ▶ **pociągnięcie; wykręcenie 2** a slight change that you make to a machine, system, etc. to improve it: *With a few tweaks this venue will be perfect.* ▶ **mała poprawka**

tweed /twiːd/ noun [U] a type of thick rough cloth that is made from wool and used for making clothes ▶ **tweed**

tweet /twiːt/ noun [C] the short high sound made by a small bird ▶ **ćwierkanie**

tweezers /ˈtwiːzəz/ noun [pl.] a small tool consisting of two pieces of metal that are joined at one end. You use **tweezers** for picking up or pulling out very small things: *a pair of tweezers* pęseta ▶ **pęseta**

⚷ **twelve** /twelv/ number 12 ▶ **dwanaście** ➲ note at **six** ➲ look at **dozen**

■ **twelfth** /twelfθ/ **1** ordinal number 12th ▶ **dwunasty** ➲ note at **sixth 2** noun [C] 1/12; one of twelve equal parts of sth ▶ **(jedna) dwunasta**

⚷ **twenty** /ˈtwenti/ number 20 ▶ **dwadzieścia** ➲ note at **sixty**

■ **twentieth** /ˈtwentiəθ/ **1** ordinal number 20th ▶ **dwudziesty** ➲ note at **sixth 2** noun [C] 1/20; one of twenty equal parts of sth ▶ **(jedna) dwudziesta**

⚷ **twice** /twaɪs/ adv. two times: *I've been to Egypt twice – once last year and once in 1994.* ◇ *The film will be shown twice daily.* ◇ *Take the medicine twice a day.* ◇ *Prices have risen twice as fast in this country as in Japan.* ▶ **dwa razy, podwójnie**

twiddle /ˈtwɪdl/ verb [I,T] (Brit.) **twiddle (with) sth** to keep turning or moving sth with your fingers, often because you are nervous or bored ▶ **kręcić palcami** (*np. nerwowo/w roztargnieniu*), **bawić się (czymś) używając palców**

twig /twɪg/ noun [C] a small thin branch on a tree or bush ▶ **gałązka**

twilight /ˈtwaɪlaɪt/ noun [U] the time after the sun has set and before it gets completely dark ▶ **zmrok** ➲ look at **dusk**

⚷ **twin** /twɪn/ noun [C] **1** one of two children or animals that are born to one mother at the same time: *They're very alike. Are they twins?* ◇ *a twin brother/sister* ◇ *identical twins* ▶ **bliźnia-k/czka** ➲ look at **triplet 2** one of a pair of things that are the same or very similar: *twin-engined* dwusilnikowy ◇ *a twin-bedded room* pokój z dwoma pojedynczymi łóżkami ➲ note at **bed**[1]

■ **twin** verb [T] (**twinning**; **twinned**) to join two towns in different countries together in a special relationship ▶ **tworzyć bliźniacze miasta**

ˌ**twin ˈbed** noun [C] **1** [usually pl.] one of a pair of single beds in a room: *Would you prefer twin beds or a double?* ▶ **dwa pojedyncze łóżka** (*w jednym pokoju*) **2** (US) a bed big enough for one person: *sheets to fit a twin bed* ▶ **pojedyncze łóżko**

twinge /twɪndʒ/ noun [C] **1** a sudden short pain: *He kicked the ball and suddenly felt a twinge in his back.* ▶ **nagły ból 2 a twinge (of sth)** a sudden short feeling of an unpleasant emotion ▶ **nagłe uczucie** (*czegoś nieprzyjemnego*)

twinkle /ˈtwɪŋkl/ verb [I] **1** to shine with a light that seems to go on and off: *Stars twinkled in the sky.* ▶ **migotać 2** (used about your eyes) to look bright because you are happy ▶ **iskrzyć się**
■ **twinkle** noun [sing.] ▶ **iskrzenie się**

ˌ**twin ˈtown** noun [C] one of two towns in different countries that have a special relationship: *Grenoble is Oxford's twin town.* ▶ **miasto bliźniacze**

twirl /twɜːl/ verb [I,T] **twirl (sb/sth) (around/round)** to turn round and round quickly; to make sb/sth do this ▶ **wirować (czymś)**

twist¹ /twɪst/ verb **1** [I,T] to bend or turn sth into a particular shape, often one it does not go in naturally; to be bent in this way: *Her face twisted in anger.* ◇ *She twisted* (upięła) *her long hair into a knot.* ▶ **wykręcać (się), wykrzywiać (się), skręcać (się) 2** [I,T] to turn a part of your body while the rest stays still: *She twisted round to see where the noise was coming from.* ◇ *He kept twisting his head from side to side.* ▶ **kręcić (się), wykręcać (się) 3** [T] to turn sth around in a circle with your hand: *She twisted the ring on her finger nervously.* ◇ *Most containers have twist-off caps.* ▶ **kręcić, obracać 4** [I] (used about rivers and roads) to change direction often: *a narrow twisting lane* ◇ *The road **twists and turns** along the coast.* ▶ (*droga itp.*) **wić się 5** [I,T] **twist (sth) (round/around sth)** to put sth round another object; to be round another object: *The telephone wire has **got twisted** round the table leg.* ▶ **okręcać (się) (wokół czegoś), owijać (się) (wokół czegoś) 6** [T] to change the meaning of what sb has said: *Journalists often **twist your words**.* ▶ **przekręcać** (*znaczenie*)
IDM **twist sb's arm** (informal) to force or persuade sb to do sth ▶ **przyciskać kogoś** (*żeby coś zrobił*)
PHR V **twist sth off** to turn and pull sth with your hand to remove it from sth: *I twisted off the lid and looked inside.* ▶ **odkręcać coś**

twist² /twɪst/ noun [C] **1** the act of turning sth with your hand, or of turning part of your body: *She killed the chicken with one twist of its neck.* ▶ **skręcenie, wykręcenie 2** an unexpected change or development in a story or situation: *There's a brilliant twist at the end of the film.* ▶ **(nieoczekiwan-a/y) zmiana/zwrot w wydarzeniach/sprawach 3** a place where a road, river, etc. bends or changes direction: *the **twists and turns** of the river* ▶ **skręt, zakręt, kolano** (*rzeki*) **4** something that has become or been bent into a particular shape: *Straighten out the wire so that there are no twists in it.* ▶ **skręt**

twisted /ˈtwɪstɪd/ adj. **1** bent or turned so that the original shape is lost: *After the crash the car was a mass of twisted metal.* ◇ *a twisted ankle* skręcona kostka ▶ **poskręcany 2** (used about a person's mind or behaviour) not normal; strange in an unpleasant way: *Her experiences had left her **bitter and twisted**.* ▶ (*psychika itp.*) **skrzywiony**

twit /twɪt/ noun [C] (Brit., informal) a stupid or annoying person ▶ **głupek**

twitch /twɪtʃ/ verb [I,T] to make a quick sudden movement, often one that you cannot control; to cause sth to make a sudden movement: *The rabbit twitched and then lay still.* ◇ *He twitched his nose.* ◇ *Can you twitch* (ruszać) *your ears?* ▶ **drgać**
■ **twitch** noun [C]: *He has a nervous twitch.* ▶ **drgnięcie**

twitter /ˈtwɪtə(r)/ verb [I] (used about birds) to make a series of short high sounds ▶ **ćwierkać**

two /tuː/ number **1** 2 ▶ **dwa** ➲ note at **six** ➲ look at **second 2** (**two-**) [in compounds] having two of the thing mentioned: *a two-week holiday* ▶ **dwu-, dwa**
IDM **be in two minds (about sth/doing sth)** to not feel sure of sth: *I'm in two minds about leaving Will alone in the house while we're away.* ▶ **być niezdecydowanym**
in two in or into two pieces: *The plate fell on the floor and broke in two.* ▶ **na dwoje**

ˌ**two-diˈmensional** adj. flat; having no depth; appearing to have only two **dimensions**: *a two-dimensional drawing* ◇ (figurative) *The novel was criticized for its two-dimensional characters.* ▶ **dwuwymiarowy; płytki**

ˌ**two-ˈfaced** adj. (informal) not sincere; not acting in a way that supports what you say that you believe; saying different things to different people about a particular subject ▶ **dwulicowy** SYN **hypocritical**

ˌ**two-ˈway** adj. [usually before a noun] **1** moving in two different directions; allowing sth to move in two different directions: *two-way traffic* ◇ *two-way trade* ◇ *a two-way switch* wyłącznik dwupozycyjny ▶ **dwukierunkowy, dwustronny 2** (used about communication between people) needing equal effort from both people or groups involved: *Friendship is a two-way process.* ▶ **obustronny 3** (used about radio equipment, etc.) used both for sending and receiving signals ▶ **nadawczo-odbiorczy**

tycoon /taɪˈkuːn/ noun [C] a person who is very successful in business or industry and who has become rich and powerful: *a business/property/media tycoon* ▶ **magnat/ka** (*np. handlowy*), **potentat/ka**

type¹ /taɪp/ noun **1** [C] **a type (of sth)** a group of people or things that share certain qualities and that are part of a larger group: *Which type of paint should you use on metal?* ◇ *Spaniels are a type of dog.* ◇ *You meet all types of people in this job.* ◇ *the first building of its type in the world* ◇ *I love this type/these types of movie.* ▶ **rodzaj** SYN **kind, sort 2** [C] a person of a particular kind: *She's **not the type to** do anything silly.* ◇ *He's the careful type.* On jest jednym z tych ludzi, którzy są zbyt ostrożni. ▶ **typ** (*człowieka*) ➲ look at **typical 3** (**-type**) [in compounds] having the qualities, etc. of the group, person or thing mentioned: *a ceramic-type material* ◇ *a police-type badge* ▶ **typu 4** [U] letters that are printed or typed: *The type is too small to read.* ▶ **litery drukowane**

type² /taɪp/ verb [I,T] to write sth using a computer or **typewriter**: *How fast can you type?* ◇ *Type (in) the filename, then press 'Return'.* ▶ **pisać na maszynie/komputerze itp.**
■ **typing** noun [U]: *typing skills* ◇ *There is still a lot of typing to be done.* Zostało jeszcze dużo do napisania (na maszynie). ▶ **pisanie na maszynie; maszynopis**

typecast /ˈtaɪpkɑːst; US -kæst/ verb [T] (pp, pt **typecast**) [usually passive] **typecast sb (as sth)** if an actor is **typecast**, he or she is always given the same kind of character to play ▶ **zaszufladkować**

typewriter /ˈtaɪpraɪtə(r)/ noun [C] a machine that you use for writing in print ▶ **maszyna do pisania**

typewritten /ˈtaɪprɪtn/ adj. written using a **typewriter** or computer ▶ **napisany na maszynie lub komputerze**

typhoid /ˈtaɪfɔɪd/ noun [U] a serious disease that can cause death. People get **typhoid** from bad food or water. ▶ **tyfus**

typhoon /taɪˈfuːn/ noun [C] a violent tropical storm with very strong winds ▶ **tajfun** ➲ note at **storm**

T

typical /ˈtɪpɪkl/ adj. **typical (of sb/sth) 1** having or showing the usual qualities of a particular person, thing or type: *a typical Italian village* ◇ *There's no such thing as a typical American.* ▶ **typowy** SYN **normal** OPP **untypical, atypical 2** behaving in the way you expect: *It was absolutely typical of him not to reply to my letter.* ▶ **typowy**

typically /ˈtɪpɪkli/ adv. **1** in a typical case; that usually happens in this way: *Typically it is the girls who offer to help, not the boys.* ▶ **zwykle, typowo 2** in a way that shows the usual qualities of a particular person, type or thing: *typically British humour* ▶ **typowo**

typify /ˈtɪpɪfaɪ/ verb [T] (**typifying**; **typifies**; pt, pp **typified**) to be a typical mark or example of sb/sth: *This film typified the Hollywood westerns of that time.* ▶ **być typowym przykładem/znakiem/wzorem**

typist /ˈtaɪpɪst/ noun [C] a person who works in an office typing letters, etc. ▶ **maszynist(k)a**

tyranny /ˈtɪrəni/ noun [U] the cruel and unfair use of power by a person or small group to control a country or state ▶ **tyrania**
■ **tyrannical** /tɪˈrænɪkl/ adj.: *a tyrannical ruler* ▶ **tyrański** | **tyrannize** (also -ise) /ˈtɪrənaɪz/ verb [I,T] ▶ **tyranizować**

tyrant /ˈtaɪrənt/ noun [C] a cruel ruler who has complete power over the people in his or her country ▶ **tyran** ➲ look at **dictator**

tyre (US tire) /ˈtaɪə(r)/ noun [C] the thick rubber ring that fits around the outside of a wheel: *a **flat tyre*** flak ▶ **opona** ➲ picture at **bicycle**, **car**, picture on **page A7**

tzar, tzarina = TSAR, TSARINA

Uu

U, u /juː/ noun [C,U] (pl. **Us**; **us**; **U's**; **u's** /juːz/) the 21st letter of the English alphabet: *'Understand' begins with (a) 'U'.* ▶ **litera** *u*

U /juː/ abbr. (Brit.) (used about films that are suitable for anyone, including children) **universal** ▶ **kategoria filmu „Dozwolony bez ograniczeń wieku"**

ubiquitous /juːˈbɪkwɪtəs/ adj. (formal) seeming to be everywhere or in several places at the same time; very common: *the ubiquitous mobile phone* ▶ **wszechobecny**; **powszechnie używany**

udder /ˈʌdə(r)/ noun [C] the part of a female cow, etc. that hangs under its body and produces milk ▶ **wymię**

UEFA /juˈeɪfə/ abbr. the **Union of European Football Associations**: *the UEFA cup* ▶ **Europejski Związek Piłki Nożnej**

UFO (also **ufo**) /ˌjuː ef ˈəʊ; ˈjuːfəʊ/ abbr. (pl. **UFOs**) an **unidentified flying object** ▶ **UFO, latający talerz** ➲ look at **flying saucer**

ugh /ɜː/ interj. (used in writing to express the sound that you make when you think sth is disgusting) ▶ **fuj!**

ugly /ˈʌgli/ adj. (**uglier**; **ugliest**) **1** unpleasant to look at or listen to: *The burn left an ugly scar on her face.* ◇ *an ugly modern office block* ▶ **brzydki** SYN **unattractive 2** (used about a situation) dangerous or threatening: *The situation **turned ugly** when people started throwing stones.* ▶ **niebezpieczny**
■ **ugliness** noun [U] ▶ **brzydota**

UHT /ˌjuː eɪtʃ ˈtiː/ abbr. **ultra heat treated**; used about foods such as milk that are treated to last longer: *UHT milk* ▶ **poddany działaniu bardzo wysokiej temperatury**

UK = UNITED KINGDOM: *She is Kenyan by birth but is now a UK citizen*

ulcer /ˈʌlsə(r)/ noun [C] a painful area on your skin or inside your body, which may lose blood or produce a poisonous substance: *a mouth/stomach ulcer* ▶ **wrzód**

ulna /ˈʌlnə/ noun [C] the longer bone of the two bones in the lower part of your arm between your wrist and your elbow ▶ **kość łokciowa** ➲ look at **radius** ➲ picture at **body**

ulterior /ʌlˈtɪəriə(r)/ adj. [only before a noun] that you keep hidden or secret: *Why is he suddenly being so nice to me? He must have an **ulterior motive**.* ▶ **ukryty**

ultimate[1] /ˈʌltɪmət/ adj. [only before a noun] **1** being or happening at the end; last or final: *Our ultimate goal is complete independence.* ▶ **ostateczny**; **ostatni 2** the greatest, best or worst: *For me the ultimate luxury is to stay in bed till 10 o'clock on a Sunday.* ▶ **krańcowy**

ultimate[2] /ˈʌltɪmət/ noun [sing.] (informal) **the ultimate (in sth)** the greatest or best: *This new car is the ultimate in comfort.* ▶ **szczyt** (*np. wygody*)

ultimately /ˈʌltɪmətli/ adv. **1** in the end: *Ultimately, the decision is yours.* ▶ **ostatecznie 2** at the most basic level; most importantly: *Ultimately, this discussion is not about quality but about money.* ▶ **w zasadzie**

ultimatum /ˌʌltɪˈmeɪtəm/ noun [C] (pl. **ultimatums**) a final warning to sb that, if they do not do what you ask, you will use force or take action against them: *I gave him an ultimatum – either he paid his rent or he was out.* ▶ **ultimatum**

ultra- /ˈʌltrə/ [in compounds] extremely: *ultra-modern* ultranowoczesny ▶ **ultra-**

ultrasound /ˈʌltrəsaʊnd/ noun **1** [U] sound that is higher than humans can hear ▶ **ultradźwięk 2** [U,C] a medical process that produces an image of what is inside your body: *Ultrasound showed she was expecting twins.* ◇ *an ultrasound scan* badanie ultrasonograficzne ▶ **ultrasonografia**

ultraviolet /ˌʌltrəˈvaɪələt/ adj. (used about light) that causes your skin to turn darker and that can be dangerous in large amounts: *ultraviolet radiation* ▶ **ultrafioletowy** ➲ look at **infrared**

um exclamation (the way of writing the sound /ʌm/ or /əm/ that people make when they hesitate, or do not know what to say next): *Um, I'm not sure how to ask you this ...* ▶ **ee**

umbilical cord /ʌmˌbɪlɪkl ˈkɔːd/ noun [C] the tube that connects a baby to its mother before it is born ▶ **pępowina**

umbrella /ʌmˈbrelə/ (Brit., informal **brolly** /ˈbrɒli/, pl. **brollies**) noun [C] an object that you open and hold over your head to keep yourself dry when it is raining: *to put an umbrella up/down* otwierać/zamykać parasol ▶ **parasol/ka** (*od deszczu*)

umpire /ˈʌmpaɪə(r)/ noun [C] a person who watches a game such as **tennis** or **cricket** to make sure that the players obey the rules ▶ **sędzia sportowy** ➲ look at **referee** ➲ picture on **page A8**
■ **umpire** verb [I,T] ▶ **sędziować** (*np. w tenisie/krykiecie*)

umpteen /ˌʌmpˈtiːn/ pron., determiner (informal) very many; a lot ▶ **x razy**
■ **umpteenth** /ˌʌmpˈtiːnθ/ pron., determiner: *For the umpteenth time – phone if you're going to be late!* ▶ (*po raz*) **setny**

UN = UNITED NATIONS

unable /ʌnˈeɪbl/ adj. **unable to do sth** not having the time, knowledge, skill, etc. to do sth; not able to do sth: *She lay there, unable to move.* ▶ **niezdolny (do zrobienia czegoś)** OPP **able** ➲ noun **inability**

unacceptable /ˌʌnəkˈseptəbl/ adj. that you cannot accept or allow ▶ **nie do przyjęcia** OPP **acceptable**
■ **unacceptably** /-əbli/ adv. ▶ **w sposób niemożliwy do przyjęcia**

unaccompanied /ˌʌnəˈkʌmpənid/ adj. alone, without sb/sth else with you: *Unaccompanied children are not allowed in the bar.* ▶ **bez opieki, bez towarzystwa**

unadulterated /ˌʌnəˈdʌltəreɪtɪd/ adj. **1** (used to emphasize that sth is complete or total): *For me, the holiday was sheer unadulterated pleasure.* ▶ **czysty** (*np. przyjemność*) **2** not mixed with other substances: *unadulterated foods* ▶ **nieskażony, nierozcieńczony** SYN **pure**

unaffected /ˌʌnəˈfektɪd/ adj. **1** not changed by sth ▶ **niedotknięty 2** behaving in a natural way without trying to impress anyone ▶ **bezpretensjonalny, bez afektacji** OPP for both meanings **affected**

unaided /ʌnˈeɪdɪd/ adv. without any help ▶ **bez pomocy, zdany na siebie**

unanimous /juˈnænɪməs/ adj. **1** (used about a decision, etc.) agreed by everyone: *The jury reached a unanimous verdict of guilty.* ▶ **jednomyślny 2** (used about a group of people) all agreeing about sth: *The judges were unanimous in their decision.* ▶ **jednomyślny**
■ **unanimously** adv. ▶ **jednomyślnie**

unarmed /ˌʌnˈɑːmd/ adj. having no guns, knives, etc.; not armed ▶ **nieuzbrojony** OPP **armed**

unashamed /ˌʌnəˈʃeɪmd/ adj. not feeling sorry or embarrassed about sth bad that you have done ▶ **bezwstydny** OPP **ashamed**
■ **unashamedly** /ˌʌnəˈʃeɪmɪdli/ adv. ▶ **bezwstydnie**

unˈasked-for adj. that has not been asked for or requested: *unasked-for advice* ▶ **nieproszony**

unassuming /ˌʌnəˈsjuːmɪŋ; US -ˈsuː-/ adj. not wanting people to notice how good, important, etc. you are ▶ **bezpretensjonalny** SYN **modest**

unattached /ˌʌnəˈtætʃt/ adj. **1** not married; without a regular partner ▶ **nieżonaty, niezamężna; samotny** SYN **single 2** not connected to sb/sth else ▶ **nie związany, nie złączony**

unattended /ˌʌnəˈtendɪd/ adj. not watched or looked after: *Do not leave bags unattended.* ▶ **bez dozoru; bez opieki**

unattractive /ˌʌnəˈtræktɪv/ adj. **1** not attractive or pleasant to look at ▶ **nieatrakcyjny, nieładny 2** not good, interesting or pleasant ▶ **nieciekawy, nieinteresujący** OPP **attractive**

unauthorized /ʌnˈɔːθəraɪzd/ adj. done without permission ▶ **nieupoważniony**

unavoidable /ˌʌnəˈvɔɪdəbl/ adj. that cannot be avoided or prevented ▶ **nieunikniony** OPP **avoidable**
■ **unavoidably** /-əbli/ adv. ▶ **niechybnie**

unaware /ˌʌnəˈweə(r)/ adj. [not before a noun] **unaware (of sth); unaware that...** not knowing about or not noticing sth: *She seemed unaware of all the trouble she had caused.* ▶ **nieświadomy (czegoś)** OPP **aware**

unawares /ˌʌnəˈweəz/ adv. by surprise; without expecting sth or being prepared for it: *I was* ***taken*** *completely* ***unawares*** (zostałem całkowicie zaskoczony) *by his suggestion.* ◇ *The goalkeeper was* ***caught unawares*** (został znienacka zaskoczony) *by a long shot.* ▶ **niespodziewanie**

unbalanced /ˌʌnˈbælənst/ adj. **1** (used about a person) slightly crazy ▶ **niezrównoważony 2** not fair to all ideas or sides of an argument ▶ **niewyważony** OPP **balanced**

unbearable /ʌnˈbeərəbl/ adj. too unpleasant, painful, etc. for you to accept ▶ **nieznośny** SYN **intolerable** OPP **bearable**
■ **unbearably** /-əbli/ adv.: *It was unbearably hot.* ▶ **nieznośnie**

unbeatable /ʌnˈbiːtəbl/ adj. that cannot be defeated or improved on: *unbeatable prices* ▶ **niepokonany,** (*cena itp.*) **nie do pobicia**

unbeaten /ʌnˈbiːtn/ adj. that has not been beaten or improved on ▶ (*rekord itp.*) **niepobity**

unbelievable /ˌʌnbɪˈliːvəbl/ adj. very surprising; difficult to believe ▶ **nieprawdopodobny; niewiarygodny** OPP **believable** ➲ look at **incredible**
■ **unbelievably** /-əbli/ adj.: *His work was unbelievably bad.* ▶ **nieprawdopodobnie; niewiarygodnie**

unblemished /ʌnˈblemɪʃt/ adj. not spoiled, damaged or marked in any way: *The new party leader has an unblemished reputation.* ▶ **nieposzlakowany**

unborn /ˌʌnˈbɔːn/ adj. not yet born ▶ **nienarodzony**

unbroken /ʌnˈbrəʊkən/ adj. **1** continuous; not interrupted: *a period of unbroken silence* ▶ **nieprzerwany 2** that has not been beaten: *His record for the 1500 metres remains unbroken.* ▶ **nie pobity**

unbutton /ˌʌnˈbʌtn/ verb [T] to undo the buttons on a piece of clothing ▶ **rozpinać**

uncalled for /ʌnˈkɔːld fɔː(r)/ adj. (used about sth sb says or does) not fair or appropriate: *His comments were uncalled for.* ◇ *uncalled-for comments* ▶ **niestosowny** SYN **unnecessary**

uncanny /ʌnˈkæni/ adj. very strange; that you cannot easily explain: *an uncanny coincidence* ▶ **niesamowity, zagadkowy**

⚷ **uncertain** /ʌnˈsɜːtn/ adj. **1 uncertain (about/of sth)** not sure; not able to decide: *She was still uncertain of his true feelings for her.* ▶ **niepewny, niezdecydowany 2** not known exactly or not decided: *He's lost his job and his future seems very uncertain.* ▶ **niepewny, nieokreślony** OPP for both meanings **certain**
■ **uncertainly** adv. ▶ **niepewnie, niezdecydowanie** | **uncertainty** noun [C,U] (pl. **uncertainties**): *Today's decision will put an end to all the uncertainty.* ▶ **niepewność, niezdecydowanie** OPP **certainty**

unchanged /ʌnˈtʃeɪndʒd/ adj. staying the same; not changed: *The town has remained almost unchanged* (prawie się nie zmienił) *since the 18th century.* ▶ **niezmieniony**

uncharacteristic /ˌʌnˌkærəktəˈrɪstɪk/ adj. not typical or usual ▶ **nietypowy** OPP **characteristic**
■ **uncharacteristically** /-kli/ adv. ▶ **nietypowo**

unchecked /ˌʌnˈtʃekt/ adj. (used about sth harmful) not controlled or stopped from getting worse: *The fire was allowed to burn unchecked.* ◇ *The rise in violent crime must not* ***go unchecked.*** ◇ *The plant will soon choke ponds and waterways if* ***left unchecked*** (pozostawiona bez kontroli). ▶ **niekontrolowany, niepohamowany**

⚷ **uncle** /ˈʌŋkl/ noun [C] the brother of your father or mother; the husband of your aunt: *Uncle Steven* ▶ **stryj/ek; wuj/ek**

⚷ **uncomfortable** /ʌnˈkʌmftəbl/ adj. **1** not pleasant to wear, sit in, lie on, etc.: *uncomfortable shoes* ▶ **niewygodny 2** not able to sit, lie, etc. in a position that is pleasant: *I was very uncomfortable* (było mi bardzo niewygodnie) *for most of the journey.* ▶ **niewygodny 3** feeling or causing worry or embarrassment: *I felt very uncomfortable when they started arguing in front of me.* ▶ **nieswój, skrępowany** OPP for all meanings **comfortable**
■ **uncomfortably** /-əbli/ adv. ▶ **niewygodnie**

uncommon /ʌnˈkɒmən/ adj. unusual ▶ **niezwykły** SYN **rare** OPP **common**

uncompromising /ʌnˈkɒmprəmaɪzɪŋ/ adj. refusing to discuss or change a decision ▶ **bezkompromisowy**

unconcerned /ˌʌnkənˈsɜːnd/ adj. **unconcerned (about/by/with sth)** not interested in sth or not worried about it ▶ **obojętny** OPP **concerned**

U

unconditional /ˌʌnkənˈdɪʃənl/ adj. without limits or conditions: *the unconditional surrender of military forces* ▶ **bezwarunkowy** OPP **conditional**
■ **unconditionally** /-ʃənəli/ adv. ▶ **bezwarunkowo**

unconscious /ʌnˈkɒnʃəs/ adj. **1** in a state that is like sleep, for example because of injury or illness: *He was found lying unconscious on the kitchen floor.* ▶ **nieprzytomny 2 unconscious of sb/sth** not knowing about or not noticing sb/sth: *He seemed unconscious of everything that was going on around him.* ▶ **nieświadomy** SYN **unaware 3** done, spoken, etc. without you thinking about it or realizing it: *The article was full of unconscious humour.* ▶ (*humor itp.*) **niezamierzony** OPP **conscious 4** (**the unconscious**) noun [sing.] = SUBCONSCIOUS
■ **unconsciously** adv. ▶ **nieświadomie** | **unconsciousness** noun [U] ▶ **nieprzytomność**

uncontrollable /ˌʌnkənˈtrəʊləbl/ adj. that you cannot control: *I had an uncontrollable urge to laugh.* ▶ **niepohamowany**, **nieopanowany**
■ **uncontrollably** /-əbli/ adv. ▶ **niepohamowanie**, **nieopanowanie**

uncontrolled /ˌʌnkənˈtrəʊld/ adj. **1** (used about emotions, behaviour, etc.) that sb cannot control or stop: *uncontrolled anger* ▶ (*śmiech itp.*) **nieopanowany 2** that is not limited or managed by law or rules: *the uncontrolled growth of cities* ◇ *uncontrolled dumping of toxic waste* ▶ (*rozwój itp.*) **niekontrolowany** ➲ look at **controlled**

uncountable /ʌnˈkaʊntəbl/ adj. an uncountable noun cannot be counted and so does not have a plural. In this dictionary uncountable nouns are marked '[U]'. ▶ **niepoliczalny** OPP **countable**

> W celu oznaczenia ilości rzeczy niepoliczalnych używa się takich słów jak **piece** i **bit** z przyimkiem **of**: *a piece of cake* ◇ *some bits of paper*. Niektóre rzeczowniki występują w specyficznym połączeniu z jeszcze innymi słowami: *a bar of soap* ◇ *a drop of water* ◇ *a loaf of bread* ◇ *a speck of dust*.

uncouth /ʌnˈkuːθ/ adj. rude or socially unacceptable: *an uncouth young man* ▶ **nieokrzesany**

uncover /ʌnˈkʌvə(r)/ verb [T] **1** to remove the cover from sth ▶ **odkrywać**, **odsłaniać** OPP **cover 2** to find out or discover sth: *Police have uncovered a plot to murder a top politician.* ▶ **demaskować**; **odkrywać** (*np. tajemnicę*)

undecided /ˌʌndɪˈsaɪdɪd/ adj. **1** not having made a decision: *I'm still undecided about whether to take the job or not.* ▶ **niezdecydowany 2** without any result or decision ▶ **niepewny**

undeniable /ˌʌndɪˈnaɪəbl/ adj. clear, true or certain ▶ **niezaprzeczalny**
■ **undeniably** /-əbli/ adv. ▶ **niezaprzeczalnie**

under /ˈʌndə(r)/ prep. **1** in or to a position that is below sth: *We found him hiding under the table.* ◇ *The dog crawled under the gate and ran into the road.* ▶ **pod 2** below the surface of sth; covered by sth: *Most of an iceberg is under the water.* ◇ *He was wearing a vest under his shirt.* ▶ **poniżej**; **pod 3** less than a certain number; younger than a certain age: *People working under 20 hours a week will pay no extra tax.* ◇ *Nobody under eighteen is allowed to buy alcohol.* ▶ (*zarabiać itp.*) **poniżej/mniej niż**; (*wiek*) **poniżej 4** governed or controlled by sb/sth: *The country is now under martial law.* ▶ **pod** (*np. kierownictwem*) **5** according to a law, agreement, system, etc.: *Under English law you are innocent until you are proved guilty.* ▶ **stosownie** (*np. do prawa*) **6** experiencing a particular feeling, process or effect: *He was jailed for driving under the influence of alcohol.* ◇ *a building under construction* (w trakcie budowy) ◇ *The manager is **under pressure** to resign.* ◇ *I was **under the impression that** Bill was not very happy there.* ▶ **w trakcie** (*budowy*) **7** using a particular name: *to travel under a false name* ▶ **pod** (*np. pseudonimem*) **8** found in a particular part of a book, list, etc.: *You'll find some information on rugby under 'team sports'.* ▶ **pod** (*np. hasłem*)

> **Under** używa się w celu powiedzenia, że jakaś rzecz znajduje się bezpośrednio pod drugą. Między nimi może być odstęp (*The cat is asleep under the table.*) lub jedna rzecz może dotykać innej bądź przykrywać inną rzecz (*I think your letter is under that book*). Słowa **below** można użyć w celu powiedzenia, że jedna rzecz znajduje się poniżej innej rzeczy, wówczas gdy są w tym samym budynku, na tym samym wzgórzu, w tej samej części ciała itp: *They live on the floor below us.* ◇ *We could see a few houses below the castle.* ◇ *It hurts here – just below the knee.* ◇ *The skirt comes down to just below the knee.* Mówiąc o ruchu z jednej strony czegoś na drugą trzeba użyć **under** (nie **below**): *We swam under the bridge.* Czasem stosuje się **beneath** w celu powiedzenia, że jedna rzecz znajduje się bezpośrednio pod drugą, ale **under** jest częściej używane. **Beneath** jest słowem literackim. Można zastosować **underneath** zamiast **under**, kiedy chce się podkreślić, że coś jest przykryte inną rzeczą lub schowane pod nią: *Have you looked underneath the sofa as well as behind it?*

■ **under** adv. **1** under water: *How long can you stay under for?* ▶ **pod wodą 2** less; younger ▶ (*wiek*) **poniżej**

under- /ˈʌndə(r)/ [in compounds] **1** lower in level or position: *the minister's under-secretary* podsekretarz stanu ▶ **pod- 2** not enough: *undercooked food* ◇ *underdeveloped countries* kraje słabo/mało rozwinięte ▶ **nie-**, **niewystarczająco**

underarm /ˈʌndərɑːm/ adj. [only before a noun] connected with the part of the body under the arm where it meets the shoulder: *underarm deodorant* ▶ **pacha** ➲ look at **armpit**

undercarriage /ˈʌndəkærɪdʒ/ (also ˈ**landing gear**) noun [C] the part of an aircraft, including the wheels, that supports it when it is landing and taking off ▶ **podwozie** (*samolotu*) ➲ picture at **plane**, picture on **page A6**

underclothes (formal) = UNDERWEAR

undercover /ˌʌndəˈkʌvə(r)/ adj. working or happening secretly: *an undercover reporter/detective* ▶ **tajny**

undercurrent /ˈʌndəkʌrənt; US -kɜːr-/ noun [C] **undercurrent (of sth)** a feeling, especially a negative one, that is hidden but whose effects are felt: *I detect an undercurrent of resentment* (wyczuwam, wbrew zewnętrznym pozorom, niechętny stosunek) *towards the new proposals.* ▶ **nieczytelna od razu tendencja**, **nuta** (*np. goryczy*)

undercut /ˌʌndəˈkʌt/ verb [T] (**undercutting**; pt, pp **undercut**) to sell sth at a lower price than other shops, etc. ▶ **podcinać działalność konkurencji metodą wojny cenowej**

underdeveloped /ˌʌndədɪˈveləpt/ adj. (used about a country, society, etc.) having few industries and a low standard of living ▶ (*kraj*) **słabo rozwinięty** ➲ look at **developed**, **developing** ℹ Obecnie częściej mówi się **a developing country.**
■ **underdevelopment** noun [U] ▶ **słaby rozwój**

underdog /ˈʌndədɒg/ noun [C] a person, team, etc. who is weaker than others, and not expected to be successful: *San Marino were the underdogs, but managed to win the game 2-1.* ▶ **osoba/drużyna na przegranej pozycji**

underestimate /ˌʌndərˈestɪmeɪt/ verb [T] **1** to guess that the amount, etc. of sth will be less than it really is ▶ **za nisko szacować 2** to think that sb/sth is not as

strong, good, etc. as he/she/it really is: *Don't underestimate your opponent. He's a really good player.* ▶ **nie doceniać** OPP for both meanings **overestimate**
■ **underestimate** /-mət/ noun [C] ▶ **niedocenianie**

underfoot /ˌʌndəˈfʊt/ adv. under your feet; where you are walking: *It's very wet underfoot.* ▶ **pod stopami/nogami**

undergo /ˌʌndəˈgəʊ/ verb [T] (**undergoing**; **undergoes** /-ˈgəʊz/, pt **underwent** /-ˈwent/, pp **undergone** /-ˈgɒn/) to have a difficult or unpleasant experience: *She underwent a five-hour operation.* ▶ **przechodzić, poddawać się (czemuś)**

undergraduate /ˌʌndəˈgrædʒuət/ noun [C] a university student who is studying for their first degree ▶ **student/ka** ➲ look at **graduate**, **postgraduate**

underground[1] /ˈʌndəgraʊnd/ adj. [only before a noun] **1** under the surface of the ground: *an underground car park* ▶ **podziemny 2** secret or illegal: *an underground radio station* ▶ **podziemny**

underground[2] /ˌʌndəˈgraʊnd/ adv. **1** under the surface of the ground: *The cables all run underground.* ▶ **pod ziemią 2** into a secret place: *She went underground to escape from the police.* ▶ (*przen.*) **w podziemie**

underground[3] /ˈʌndəgraʊnd/ (US **subway**) noun [sing.] a railway system under the ground ▶ **metro** ➲ picture on **page A7**

Metro londyńskie nazywa się **the underground** lub **the tube**.

undergrowth /ˈʌndəgrəʊθ/ noun [U] bushes and plants that grow around and under trees ▶ **podszycie** (*lasu*)

underhand /ˌʌndəˈhænd/ adj. secret or not honest ▶ **potajemny, podstępny**

underlie /ˌʌndəˈlaɪ/ verb [T] (**underlying**; **underlies**; pt **underlay** /ˈʌndəleɪ/, pp **underlain** /-ˈleɪn/) (formal) to be the reason for or cause of sth: *It is a principle that underlies all the party's policies.* ▶ **leżeć u podstaw czegoś, być podłożem czegoś**

underline /ˌʌndəˈlaɪn/ (especially US **underscore** /ˌʌndəˈskɔː(r)/) verb [T] **1** to draw a line under a word, etc. ▶ **podkreślać 2** to show sth clearly or to emphasize sth: *This accident underlines the need for greater care.* ▶ **podkreślać**

underlying /ˌʌndəˈlaɪɪŋ/ adj. [only before a noun] important but hidden: *the underlying causes of the disaster* ▶ **ukryty, leżący u podstaw**

undermine /ˌʌndəˈmaɪn/ verb [T] to make sth weaker: *The public's confidence in the government has been undermined by the crisis.* ▶ **podrywać** (*np. autorytet*), **osłabiać** (*np. zaufanie*)

underneath /ˌʌndəˈniːθ/ prep., adv. under; below: *The coin rolled underneath the chair.* ▶ **pod** ➲ note at **under**

the **underneath** /ˌʌndəˈniːθ/ noun [sing.] the bottom or lowest part of something: *There is a lot of rust on the underneath of the car.* ▶ **spód, dół**

underpaid past tense, past participle of **underpay**

underpants /ˈʌndəpænts/ (Brit. also **pants** /pænts/) noun [pl.] a piece of clothing that men or boys wear under their trousers ▶ **slipy męskie**

underpass /ˈʌndəpɑːs; US -pæs/ noun [C] a road or path that goes under another road, railway, etc. ▶ **przejazd/przejście podziemn-y/e**

underpay /ˌʌndəˈpeɪ/ verb [T] (pt, pp **underpaid**) to pay sb too little ▶ **źle wynagradzać** OPP **overpay**

underprivileged /ˌʌndəˈprɪvəlɪdʒd/ adj. having less money, rights, opportunities, etc. than other people in society ▶ (*warstwa społeczna itp.*) **upośledzony** OPP **privileged**

underrate /ˌʌndəˈreɪt/ verb [T] to think that sb/sth is less clever, important, good, etc. than he/she/it really is ▶ **nie doceniać** OPP **overrate**

underscore[1] (especially US) = UNDERLINE

underscore[2] /ˈʌndəskɔː(r)/ noun [C] the symbol (_) that is used to draw a line under a letter or word and used in computer commands and in Internet addresses ▶ (*symbol*) **podkreślenie**

undershirt (US) = VEST (1)

underside /ˈʌndəsaɪd/ noun [C] the side or surface of sth that is underneath ▶ **spód, dół** SYN **bottom**

understand /ˌʌndəˈstænd/ verb (pt, pp **understood** /-ˈstʊd/) **1** [I,T] to know or realize the meaning of sth: *I'm not sure that I really understand.* ◇ *I didn't understand the instructions.* ◇ *Please speak more slowly. I can't understand you.* ◇ *Do you understand what I'm asking you?* ▶ **rozumieć 2** [T] to know how or why sth happens or why it is important: *I can't understand why the engine won't start.* ◇ *As far as I understand it, the changes won't affect us.* ▶ **rozumieć, wnioskować 3** [T] to know sb's character and why they behave in a particular way: *It's easy to understand why she felt so angry.* ▶ **rozumieć 4** [T] (formal) to have heard or been told sth: *I understand that you have decided to leave.* ▶ **rozumieć**
IDM **give sb to believe/understand (that)** → BELIEVE
make yourself understood to make your meaning clear: *I can just about make myself understood in Finnish.* ▶ **porozumiewać się** (*np. w obcym języku*)

understandable /ˌʌndəˈstændəbl/ adj. that you can understand: *It was an understandable mistake to make.* ▶ **zrozumiały**
■ **understandably** /-əbli/ adv.: *She was understandably angry* (to zrozumiałe, że była zła) *at the decision.* ▶ **w sposób zrozumiały**

understanding[1] /ˌʌndəˈstændɪŋ/ noun **1** [U] the ability to think or learn about sth: *The book is beyond the understanding of most ten-year-olds.* ▶ **zdolność pojmowania 2** [U, sing.] the knowledge that sb has of a particular subject or situation: *A basic understanding of physics is necessary for this course.* ◇ *He has little understanding of how computers work.* ▶ **znajomość** (*tematu*) **3** [C, usually sing.] an informal agreement: *I'm sure we can **come to/reach an understanding** about the money I owe him.* ▶ **porozumienie 3** [U] the ability to know why people behave in a particular way and to forgive them if they do sth wrong or bad: *She apologized for her actions and her boss showed great understanding.* ▶ **zrozumienie 4** [U] the way in which you think sth is meant: *My understanding of the arrangement is that* (rozumiem umowę w ten sposób, że) *he will only phone if there is a problem.* ▶ **zrozumienie**
IDM **on the understanding that…** only if…; because it was agreed that…: *We let them stay in our house on the understanding that it was only for a short period.* ▶ **pod warunkiem, że**

understanding[2] /ˌʌndəˈstændɪŋ/ adj. showing kind feelings towards sb ▶ **wyrozumiały** SYN **sympathetic**

understate /ˌʌndəˈsteɪt/ verb [T] to say that sth is smaller or less important than it really is ▶ **pomniejszać** (*np. fakty*) OPP **overstate**
■ **understatement** noun [C]: *'Is she pleased?' 'That's an understatement* (to za mało powiedziane). *She's delighted.'* ▶ **umniejszanie** (*np. faktów*)

understood past tense, past participle of **understand**

understudy /ˈʌndəstʌdi/ noun [C] (pl. **understudies**) an actor who learns the role of another actor and replaces them if they are ill ▶ **dubler/ka** (*w teatrze*)

undertake /ˌʌndəˈteɪk/ verb [T] (pt **undertook** /-ˈtʊk/, pp **undertaken** /-ˈteɪkən/) **1** to decide to do sth and start

U

doing it: *The company is undertaking a major programme of modernization.* ▶ **przeprowadzać** **2** to agree or promise to do sth ▶ **podejmować się (wykonania czegoś)**, **zobowiązywać się**

undertaker /ˈʌndəteɪkə(r)/ (also **funeral director**; US also **mortician** /mɔːˈtɪʃn/) noun [C] a person whose job is to prepare dead bodies to be buried and to arrange funerals ▶ **osoba prowadząca przedsiębiorstwo pogrzebowe**

undertaking /ˌʌndəˈteɪkɪŋ/ noun [C, usually sing.] **1** a piece of work or business: *Buying the company would be a very risky undertaking.* ▶ **przedsięwzięcie** **2 undertaking (that .../to do sth)** a formal or legal promise to do sth: *He gave an undertaking that* (zaręczył, że) *he would not leave the country.* ▶ **zobowiązanie**

undertone /ˈʌndətəʊn/ noun [C] **1** a feeling, quality or meaning that is not expressed in a direct way ▶ **podtekst**, **zabarwienie** **2** a low, quiet voice ▶ **półgłos**
IDM **in an undertone**; **in undertones** in a quiet voice ▶ **półgłosem**

undertook past tense of **undertake**

undervalue /ˌʌndəˈvæljuː/ verb [T] to place too low a value on sb/sth ▶ **nie doceniać**

⚷ **underwater** /ˌʌndəˈwɔːtə(r)/ adj. existing, happening or used below the surface of water: *underwater exploration* ◇ *an underwater camera* ▶ **podwodny**
■ **underwater** adv.: *Can you swim underwater?* ▶ **pod wodą**

⚷ **underwear** /ˈʌndəweə(r)/ noun [U] clothing that is worn next to the skin under other clothes ▶ **bielizna** ℹ Słowo **underclothes** /ˈʌndəkləʊðz/ ma to samo znaczenie, ale jest bardziej formalne i występuje tylko w lm.

underweight /ˌʌndəˈweɪt/ adj. (used especially about a person) weighing less than is normal or correct ▶ (*osoba*) **mający niedowagę** OPP **overweight** ➲ note at **thin**

underwent past tense of **undergo**

the underworld /ˈʌndəwɜːld/ noun [sing.] people who are involved in organized crime ▶ **świat przestępczy**

undesirable /ˌʌndɪˈzaɪərəbl/ adj. unpleasant or not wanted; likely to cause problems ▶ **niepożądany** OPP **desirable**

undid past tense of **undo**

undignified /ʌnˈdɪɡnɪfaɪd/ adj. causing you to look silly and to lose the respect of other people ▶ **pozbawiony godności**, **żenujący** OPP **dignified**

undivided /ˌʌndɪˈvaɪdɪd/ adj.
IDM **get/have sb's undivided attention** to receive all sb's attention ▶ **skupiać na sobie czyjąś całkowitą uwagę**
give your undivided attention (to sb/sth) to give all your attention to sb/sth ▶ **poświęcać (komuś/czemuś) całkowitą uwagę**

⚷ **undo** /ʌnˈduː/ verb [T] (**undoing**; **undoes** /ʌnˈdʌz/, pt **undid** /ʌnˈdɪd/, pp **undone** /ʌnˈdʌn/) **1** to open sth that was tied or fastened: *to undo a knot/zip/button* ▶ **rozwiązywać**, **rozpinać** **2** to destroy the effect of sth that has already happened: *His mistake has undone all our good work.* ▶ **naprawiać** (*zło*), **unieważniać**

undone /ʌnˈdʌn/ adj. **1** open; not fastened or tied: *I realized that my zip was undone.* ▶ **rozpięty**, **rozwiązany** **2** not done: *I left the housework undone.* ▶ **niezrobiony**, **niewykonany**

undoubted /ʌnˈdaʊtɪd/ adj. definite; accepted as being true ▶ **niewątpliwy**
■ **undoubtedly** adv. ▶ **niewątpliwie**

undress /ʌnˈdres/ verb **1** [I] to take off your clothes ▶ **rozbierać się** ℹ Częściej używa się zwrotu **get undressed**: *He got undressed and had a shower.* **2** [T] to take off sb's clothes ▶ **rozbierać** OPP for both meanings **dress**
■ **undressed** adj. ▶ **rozebrany**

undue /ˌʌnˈdjuː; US -ˈduː/ adj. [only before a noun] more than is necessary or reasonable: *The police try not to use undue force when arresting a person.* ▶ **nadmierny**
■ **unduly** adv.: *She didn't seem unduly worried by their unexpected arrival.* ▶ **nadmiernie**

unearth /ʌnˈɜːθ/ verb [T] to dig sth up out of the ground; to discover sth that was hidden: *Archaeologists have unearthed a Roman tomb.* ▶ **wykopywać**; **wydobywać na światło dzienne**

unearthly /ʌnˈɜːθli/ adj. strange or frightening: *an unearthly scream* ▶ **niesamowity**, **nie z tej ziemi**
IDM **at an unearthly hour** (informal) extremely early in the morning ▶ **nieprzyzwoicie wcześ-nie/ny**

unease /ʌnˈiːz/ (also **uneasiness** /ʌnˈiːzinəs/) noun [U] a worried or uncomfortable feeling ▶ **zaniepokojenie**, **skrępowanie** OPP **ease**

uneasy /ʌnˈiːzi/ adj. **1 uneasy (about sth/doing sth)** worried; not feeling relaxed or comfortable ▶ **zaniepokojony**, **niespokojny** **2** not settled; unlikely to last: *an uneasy compromise* ▶ **wątpliwy**
■ **uneasily** adv. ▶ **z zakłopotaniem**

uneconomic /ˌʌnˌiːkəˈnɒmɪk; ˌʌnˌek-/ adj. (used about a company, etc.) not making or likely to make a profit ▶ **nieopłacalny** OPP **economic**

uneconomical /ˌʌnˌiːkəˈnɒmɪkl; ˌʌnˌek-/ adj. wasting money, time, materials, etc. ▶ **nieoszczędny** OPP **economical**
■ **uneconomically** /-kli/ adv. ▶ **nieoszczędnie**

uneducated /ʌnˈedʒukeɪtɪd/ adj. having had little or no formal education at a school; showing a lack of education ▶ **niewykształcony**, **bez wykształcenia** OPP **educated**

⚷ **unemployed** /ˌʌnɪmˈplɔɪd/ adj. **1** not able to find a job; out of work: *She has been unemployed for over a year.* ▶ **bezrobotny** SYN **jobless** ➲ look at **work** **2** (**the unemployed**) noun [pl.] people who cannot find a job: *the long-term unemployed* ▶ **bezrobotni**

⚷ **unemployment** /ˌʌnɪmˈplɔɪmənt/ noun [U] **1** the number of people who are unemployed: *The economy is doing very badly and unemployment is rising.* ▶ **bezrobocie** SYN **joblessness** ➲ look at **dole** **2** the situation of not being able to find a job: *The number of people claiming* ***unemployment benefit*** (zasiłek dla bezrobotnych) *has gone up.* ▶ **bezrobocie** OPP **employment**

unending /ʌnˈendɪŋ/ adj. having or seeming to have no end ▶ **niekończący się**

unequal /ʌnˈiːkwəl/ adj. **1** not fair or balanced: *an unequal distribution of power* ▶ **nierówny** **2** different in size, amount, level, etc. ▶ **nierówny** OPP for both meanings **equal**
■ **unequally** /ʌnˈiːkwəli/ adv. ▶ **niejednakowo**

uneven /ʌnˈiːvn/ adj. **1** not completely smooth, level or regular: *The sign was painted in rather uneven letters.* ▶ **nierówny** OPP **even** **2** not always of the same level or quality ▶ **nierówny**
■ **unevenly** adv.: *The country's wealth is unevenly distributed.* ▶ **nierówno**

⚷ **unexpected** /ˌʌnɪkˈspektɪd/ adj. not expected and therefore causing surprise ▶ **niespodziewany**
■ **unexpectedly** adv.: *I got there late because I was unexpectedly delayed.* ▶ **niespodziewanie**

unfailing /ʌnˈfeɪlɪŋ/ adj. that you can be sure will always be there and always be the same: *unfailing support* ▶ (*optymizm itp.*) **niewyczerpany**, (*wsparcie itp.*) **niezawodny**
■ **unfailingly** adv. ▶ **niewyczerpanie**, **niezawodnie**

🔑**unfair** /ˌʌnˈfeə(r)/ adj. **1 unfair (on/to sb)** not dealing with people as they deserve; not treating each person equally: *This law is unfair to women.* ◇ *The tax is unfair on people with low incomes.* ▶ **niesprawiedliwy 2** not following the rules and therefore giving an advantage to one person, team, etc.: *The referee warned him for unfair play.* ▶ **nieuczciwy** OPP for both meanings **fair**
■ **unfairly** adv. ▶ **niesprawiedliwie**; **nieuczciwie** | **unfairness** noun [U] ▶ **niesprawiedliwość**; **nieuczciwość**

unfaithful /ʌnˈfeɪθfl/ adj. **unfaithful (to sb/sth)** having a sexual relationship with sb who is not your husband, wife or partner: *She discovered that her husband was being unfaithful to her* (zdradzał ją). ▶ **niewierny** OPP **faithful**
■ **unfaithfulness** noun [U] ▶ **niewierność**

unfamiliar /ˌʌnfəˈmɪliə(r)/ adj. **1 unfamiliar (to sb)** that you do not know well: *an unfamiliar part of town* ▶ **nieznany 2 unfamiliar (with sb/sth)** not having knowledge or experience of sth: *I'm unfamiliar with this author.* ▶ **nieobeznany z czymś** OPP for both meanings **familiar**

unfashionable /ʌnˈfæʃnəbl/ adj. sth that was popular in the past but is not popular now: *unfashionable ideas/clothes* ▶ **niemodny** OPP **fashionable** ➲ look at **old-fashioned**

unfasten /ʌnˈfɑːsn; US -ˈfæsn/ verb [T] to open sth that is fastened: *to unfasten a belt/button, etc.* ▶ **rozpinać** OPP **fasten** ➲ look at **undo**

unfavourable (US **unfavorable**) /ʌnˈfeɪvərəbl/ adj. **1** not good and likely to cause problems or make sth difficult ▶ **niekorzystny**, (*pogoda*) **niesprzyjający 2** showing that you do not like or approve of sb/sth ▶ **nieprzychylny** OPP for both meanings **favourable** ➲ look at **adverse**

unfinished /ʌnˈfɪnɪʃt/ adj. not complete; not finished: *We have some* ***unfinished business*** *to settle.* ▶ **niedokończony**

unfit /ʌnˈfɪt/ adj. **1 unfit (for sth/to do sth)** not suitable or not good enough for sth: *His criminal past makes him unfit to be a politician.* ▶ **nie nadający się 2** not in good physical health, especially because you do not get enough exercise ▶ **w słabej kondycji** OPP for both meanings **fit**

unfold /ʌnˈfəʊld/ verb [I,T] **1** to open out and become flat; to open out sth that was folded: *The sofa unfolds into a spare bed.* ◇ *I unfolded the letter and read it.* ▶ **rozkładać (się)** OPP **fold 2** to become known, or to allow sth to become known a little at a time: *As the story unfolded* (w miarę rozwoju akcji), *more and more surprising things were revealed.* ▶ **rozwijać (się)**

unforeseen /ˌʌnfɔːˈsiːn/ adj. not expected: *an unforeseen problem* ▶ **nieprzewidziany**

unforgettable /ˌʌnfəˈgetəbl/ adj. making such a strong impression that you cannot forget it ▶ **niezapomniany** SYN **memorable**

🔑**unfortunate** /ʌnˈfɔːtʃənət/ adj. **1** not lucky: *The unfortunate people* (ci pechowcy) *who lived near the river lost their homes in the flood.* ▶ **nieszczęśliwy** SYN **unlucky** OPP **fortunate 2** that you feel sorry about: *I would like to apologize for this unfortunate mistake.* ▶ **niefortunny**
■ **unfortunately** adv.: *I'd like to help you but unfortunately there's nothing I can do.* ▶ **niestety**

unfounded /ʌnˈfaʊndɪd/ adj. not based on or supported by facts: *unfounded allegations* ▶ **bezpodstawny**

🔑**unfriendly** /ʌnˈfrendli/ adj. **unfriendly (to/towards sb)** unpleasant or not polite to sb ▶ **nieprzyjazny**, **nieżyczliwy** OPP **friendly**

ungainly /ʌnˈgeɪnli/ adj. moving in a way that is not smooth or elegant ▶ **niezdarny**

ungrateful /ʌnˈgreɪtfl/ adj. not feeling or showing thanks to sb ▶ **niewdzięczny** OPP **grateful**
■ **ungratefully** /-fəli/ adv. ▶ **niewdzięcznie**

unguarded /ʌnˈgɑːdɪd/ adj. **1** not protected or guarded ▶ **niestrzeżony 2** saying more than you wanted to: *He admitted the truth in an unguarded moment* (w chwili nieuwagi). ▶ **nierozważny** OPP for both meanings **guarded**

unhappily /ʌnˈhæpɪli/ adv. **1** in a sad way ▶ **nieszczęśliwie** SYN **sadly 2** unfortunately ▶ **niestety** OPP for both meanings **happily**

🔑**unhappy** /ʌnˈhæpi/ adj. (**unhappier**; **unhappiest**) **1 unhappy (about sth)** sad: *She's terribly unhappy about losing her job.* ◇ *He had a very unhappy childhood.* ▶ **przygnębiony**, **nieszczęśliwy** ➲ note at **sad 2 unhappy (about/at/with sth)** not satisfied or pleased; worried: *They're unhappy at having to accept a pay cut.* ▶ **niezadowolony**, **zmartwiony** OPP for both meanings **happy**
■ **unhappiness** noun [U] ▶ **nieszczęście**

unhealthy /ʌnˈhelθi/ adj. **1** not having or showing good health: *He looks pale and unhealthy.* ▶ **niezdrowy 2** likely to cause illness or poor health: *unhealthy conditions* ▶ **niezdrowy 3** not natural: *an unhealthy interest in death* ▶ **niezdrowy** OPP for all meanings **healthy**

unheard /ʌnˈhɜːd/ adj. [not before a noun] not listened to or given any attention: *My suggestions went unheard* (przeszły niezauważone). ▶ **niewysłuchany**

unˈheard-of adj. not known; never having happened before ▶ **niesłychany**, **niespotykany**

unicorn /ˈjuːnɪkɔːn/ noun [C] (in stories) an animal that looks like a white horse with a long straight horn on its head ▶ **jednorożec**

unidentified /ˌʌnaɪˈdentɪfaɪd/ adj. whose identity is not known: *An unidentified body has been found in the river.* ▶ **niezidentyfikowany**

🔑**uniform**[1] /ˈjuːnɪfɔːm/ noun [C,U] the set of clothes worn at work by the members of an organization or a group, or by children at school: *I didn't know he was a policeman because he wasn't* ***in uniform.*** ▶ **mundurek (szkolny)**, **mundur** ➲ note at **clothes**
■ **uniformed** adj. ▶ **umundurowany**

🔑**uniform**[2] /ˈjuːnɪfɔːm/ adj. not varying; the same in all cases or at all times ▶ **jednolity**
■ **uniformity** /ˌjuːnɪˈfɔːməti/ noun [U] ▶ **identyczność**

unify /ˈjuːnɪfaɪ/ verb [T] (**unifying**; **unifies**; pt, pp **unified**) to join separate parts together to make one unit, or to make them similar to each other ▶ **jednoczyć**, **łączyć**
■ **unification** /ˌjuːnɪfɪˈkeɪʃn/ noun [U] ▶ **zjednoczenie**

unilateral /ˌjuːnɪˈlætrəl/ adj. done or made by one person who is involved in sth without the agreement of the other person or people: *a unilateral declaration of independence* ▶ **jednostronny** ➲ look at **multilateral**
■ **unilaterally** /-rəli/ adv. ▶ **jednostronnie**

unimportant /ˌʌnɪmˈpɔːtnt/ adj. not important: *unimportant details* ◇ *They dismissed the problem as unimportant.* ▶ **nieistotny**

uninhabitable /ˌʌnɪnˈhæbɪtəbl/ adj. not possible to live in ▶ **nie nadający się do zamieszkania** OPP **habitable**

uninhabited /ˌʌnɪnˈhæbɪtɪd/ adj. (used about a place or a building) with nobody living in it ▶ **niezamieszkały**, **bezludny**

uninhibited /ˌʌnɪnˈhɪbɪtɪd/ adj. behaving in a free and natural way, without worrying what other people think of you ▶ **bez zahamowań** OPP **inhibited**

unintelligent /ˌʌnɪnˈtelɪdʒənt/ adj. not intelligent ▶ **nieinteligentny**

unintelligible /ˌʌnɪnˈtelɪdʒəbl/ adj. impossible to understand ▶ **niezrozumiały**, **nieczytelny** OPP **intelligible**

U

uninterested /ʌnˈɪntrəstɪd/ adj. **uninterested (in sb/sth)** having or showing no interest in sb/sth: *She seemed uninterested in anything I had to say.* ▶ **obojętny** OPP **interested** ⓘ Por. **disinterested**, które ma inne znaczenie.

union /ˈjuːniən/ noun **1** = TRADE UNION **2** [C] an organization for a particular group of people: *the Athletics Union* ▶ **związek 3** [C] a group of states or countries that have joined together to form one country or group: *the European Union* Unia Europejska ▶ **związek 4** [U, sing.] the act of joining or the situation of being joined: *the union of the separate groups into one organization* ▶ **zjednoczenie**

unionist = TRADE UNIONIST

the ˌ**Union 'Jack** noun [sing.] the national flag of the United Kingdom, with red and white crosses on a dark blue background ▶ **flaga brytyjska**

unique /juˈniːk/ adj. **1** not like anything else; being the only one of its type: *Shakespeare made a unique contribution to the world of literature.* ▶ **unikatowy 2** very unusual: *There's nothing unique about that sort of crime.* ▶ **niezwykły 3 unique to sb/sth** connected with only one place, person or thing: *This dance is unique to this region.* ▶ **jedyny w swoim rodzaju**

unisex /ˈjuːnɪseks/ adj. designed for and used by both sexes: *unisex fashions* ▶ **dla kobiet i mężczyzn**

unison /ˈjuːnɪsn/ noun

IDM **in unison** saying, singing or doing the same thing at the same time as sb else: *'No, thank you,' they said **in unison**.* ▶ **zgodnie**, **unisono**

unit /ˈjuːnɪt/ noun [C] **1** a single thing which is complete in itself, although it can be part of sth larger: *The book is divided into ten units.* ▶ **część 2** a group of people who perform a certain function within a larger organization: *army/military units* ▶ **oddział 3** a fixed amount or number used as a standard of measurement: *a unit of currency* ▶ **jednostka 4** a piece of furniture that fits with other pieces of furniture and has a particular use: *kitchen units* ▶ **element 5** a small machine that performs a particular task or that is part of a larger machine: *The heart of a computer is the central processing unit.* ▶ **mechanizm**

unite /juˈnaɪt/ verb **1** [I] **unite (in sth/in doing sth)** to join together for a particular purpose: *We should all unite in seeking a solution to this terrible problem.* ▶ **jednoczyć (się) 2** [I,T] to join together and act in agreement; to make this happen: *Unless we unite, our enemies will defeat us.* ▶ **jednoczyć się**

united /juˈnaɪtɪd/ adj. joined together by a common feeling or aim ▶ **zjednoczony**

the **U**ˌ**nited 'Kingdom** noun [sing.] (abbr. **(the) UK** /ˌjuː ˈkeɪ/) England, Scotland, Wales and Northern Ireland ▶ **Zjednoczone Królestwo**

> **The UK** to polityczna całość, która składa się z Anglii, Szkocji, Walii i Irlandii Północnej, ale nie z Republiki Irlandii (Eire), która stanowi odrębne państwo. **Great Britain** to Anglia, Szkocja i Walia. **The British Isles** to kraina geograficzna, w skład której wchodzi Zjednoczone Królestwo i Republika Irlandii.

the **U**ˌ**nited 'Nations** noun [sing., with sing. or pl. verb] (abbr. **UN** /ˌjuː ˈen/) the organization formed to encourage peace in the world and to deal with problems between countries ▶ **Organizacja Narodów Zjednoczonych**

the **U**ˌ**nited 'States (of A'merica)** noun [sing., with sing. or pl. verb] (abbr. **US**; **USA**) a large country in North America made up of 50 states and the District of Columbia ▶ **Stany Zjednoczone (Ameryki)**

unity /ˈjuːnəti/ noun [U] the situation in which people are in agreement and working together ▶ **jedność**; **zgoda**

universal /ˌjuːnɪˈvɜːsl/ adj. connected with, done by or affecting everyone in the world or everyone in a particular group: *The environment is a universal issue.* ▶ **powszechny** ➲ note at **PG**
■ **universally** /-səli/ adv. ▶ **powszechnie**

the **universe** /ˈjuːnɪvɜːs/ noun [sing.] everything that exists, including the planets, stars, space, etc. ▶ **wszechświat**

university /ˌjuːnɪˈvɜːsəti/ noun [C] (pl. **universities**) an institution that provides the highest level of education, in which students study for degrees and in which academic research is done: *Which university did you go to?* ◇ *I did History **at university**.* ◇ *a university lecturer* ▶ **uniwersytet** ➲ note at **study** ➲ look at **red-brick**

> Wyrażenia **at university** i **to go to university** stosuje się bez przedimka, mówiąc o kimś, kto uczęszcza na uniwersytet jako student: *He's hoping to go to university next year.*; w sytuacjach, gdy ktoś udaje się na teren uniwersytetu w innym celu niż edukacyjny stosuje się przedimek **the**: *I'm going to a conference at the university in July.*

> **university**
>
> People who want to **go to university** in Britain have to **apply** and they may have to take an **entrance exam.** Some also apply for a **scholarship** in order to pay their **tuition fees.** University **students** attend classes such as **lectures, seminars** and **tutorials.** They are taught by **professors, lecturers** and **tutors.** They may have to **do research** and **write a thesis.** People studying for their first degree are called **undergraduates** and those doing further studies after their first degree are called **postgraduates.** If undergraduates pass their **finals,** they will **graduate** (/ˈɡrædʒueɪt/) with a **degree.** A person who has graduated is called a **graduate** (/ˈɡrædʒuət/).

unkempt /ˌʌnˈkempt/ adj. (especially of sb's hair or general appearance) not well cared for; not tidy: *greasy, unkempt hair* ▶ **rozczochrany**, **zaniedbany** SYN **dishevelled**

unkind /ˌʌnˈkaɪnd/ adj. unpleasant and not friendly: *That was an unkind thing to say.* ◇ *It would be unkind to go without him.* ▶ **niegrzeczny**; **okrutny** OPP **kind**
■ **unkindly** adv. ▶ **niegrzecznie**; **okrutnie** | **unkindness** noun [U] ▶ **nieżyczliwość**, **niegrzeczność**

unknown[1] /ˌʌnˈnəʊn/ adj. **1 unknown (to sb)** that sb does not know; without sb knowing: *Unknown to the boss,* (bez wiedzy szefa) *she went home early.* ▶ **nieznany 2** not famous or familiar to other people: *an unknown actress* ▶ **nieznany** OPP **well known**, **famous**

IDM **an unknown quantity** a person or thing that you know very little about ▶ **niewiadoma**

unknown[2] /ˌʌnˈnəʊn/ noun **1** (usually **the unknown**) [sing.] a place or thing that you know nothing about: *a fear of the unknown* ▶ **nieznane 2** [C] a person who is not well known: *A complete unknown* (zupełnie nieznany zawodnik) *won the tournament.* ▶ **nieznajom-y/a**

unleaded /ˌʌnˈledɪd/ adj. not containing lead: *unleaded petrol* ▶ **bezołowiowy**

unleash /ʌnˈliːʃ/ verb [T] **unleash sth (on/upon sb/sth)** to suddenly let a strong force, emotion, etc., be felt or have an effect: *The new government proposals unleashed a storm of protest in the press.* ▶ **wywoływać** (*np. burzę emocji*)

unless /ənˈles/ conj. if ... not; except if: *I was told that unless my work improved, I would lose the job.* ◇ *'Would you like a cup of coffee?' 'Not unless you've already made some.'* ◇ *Unless anyone has anything else to say, the meet-*

ing is closed. ◇ *Don't switch that on unless I'm here.* ▶ **jeżeli nie, o ile nie, chyba że**

⚷ **unlike** /ˌʌnˈlaɪk/ prep. **1** different from a particular person or thing; (used to contrast sb/sth with another person or thing): *She's unlike anyone else I've ever met.* ◇ *Unlike most systems, this one is very easy to install.* ◇ *He's extremely ambitious, unlike me.* ◇ *The film is not unlike* (trochę przypomina) *several others I've seen.* ▶ **niepodobny; w przeciwieństwie do kogoś/czegoś** **2** not typical of sb/sth: *It's unlike him to be so rude.* ▶ **niepodobne do kogoś/czegoś** OPP **like**
■ **unlike** adj. [not before a noun] (used about two people or things) different from each other: *They are both teachers. Otherwise they are quite unlike.* ▶ **inny niż**

⚷ **unlikely** /ʌnˈlaɪkli/ adj. (**unlikelier**; **unlikeliest**) **1 unlikely (to do sth/that...)** not likely to happen; not expected; not probable: *He is seriously ill and unlikely to recover* (nie zanosi się na to, żeby wyzdrowiał). ◇ *I suppose she might win but I think it's very unlikely.* ◇ *It's **highly unlikely** that I'll have any free time next week.* ▶ **mało prawdopodobny, nieprawdopodobny** OPP **likely** **2** [only before a noun] difficult to believe: *an unlikely excuse* ▶ **mało prawdopodobny, nieprawdopodobny** SYN for both meanings **improbable**

unlimited /ʌnˈlɪmɪtɪd/ adj. without limit; as much or as great as you want ▶ **nieograniczony** OPP **limited**

⚷ **unload** /ˌʌnˈləʊd/ verb **1** [I,T] **unload (sth) (from sth)** to take things that have been transported off or out of a vehicle: *We unloaded the boxes from the back of the van.* ▶ **wyładowywać, rozładowywać** **2** [I,T] (used about a vehicle) to have the things removed that have been transported: *Parking here is restricted to vehicles that are loading or unloading.* ▶ **rozładowywać** OPP **load** **3** [T] (informal) **unload sb/sth (on/onto sb)** to get rid of sth you do not want or to pass it to sb else: *He shouldn't try and unload the responsibility onto you.* ▶ **zrzucać na kogoś** (*np. obowiązki*)

unlock /ˌʌnˈlɒk/ verb [I,T] to open the lock on sth using a key; to be opened with a key: *I can't unlock this door.* ◇ *This door won't unlock.* ▶ **otwierać kluczem** OPP **lock**

⚷ **unlucky** /ʌnˈlʌki/ adj. (**unluckier**; **unluckiest**) having or causing bad luck: *They were unlucky to lose* (mieli pecha, że przegrali) *because they played so well.* ◇ *Thirteen is often thought to be an unlucky number.* ▶ **pechowy, nieszczęśliwy** SYN **unfortunate** OPP **lucky**
■ **unluckily** adv. ▶ **na nieszczęście, niestety**

unmanned /ˌʌnˈmænd/ adj. if a machine, a vehicle, a place or an activity is **unmanned**, it does not have or need a person to control or operate it: *an unmanned spacecraft* ▶ **bezzałogowy**

unmarried /ˌʌnˈmærid/ adj. not married ▶ **niezamężna, nieżonaty** SYN **single** OPP **married**

unmistakable /ˌʌnmɪˈsteɪkəbl/ adj. that cannot be confused with anything else; easy to recognize: *She had an unmistakable French accent.* ▶ **niewątpliwy**
■ **unmistakably** /-əbli/ adv. ▶ **niewątpliwie**

unmoved /ˌʌnˈmuːvd/ adj. not affected in an emotional way: *The judge was unmoved by the boy's sad story, and sent him to jail.* ▶ **niewzruszony**

unnatural /ʌnˈnætʃrəl/ adj. different from what is normal or expected ▶ **nienaturalny** OPP **natural**
■ **unnaturally** /-rəli/ adv.: *It's unnaturally quiet in here.* ◇ *Not unnaturally* (jak można było się spodziewać), *she was delighted by the news.* ▶ **nienaturalnie**

⚷ **unnecessary** /ʌnˈnesəsəri; US -seri/ adj. more than is needed or acceptable: *We should try to avoid all unnecessary expense.* ▶ **niekonieczny, niepotrzebny** OPP **necessary** ⓘ Wyraz **needless** ma inne znaczenie.
■ **unnecessarily** /ʌnˈnesəsərəli; ˌʌnˌnesəˈserəli/ adv.: *His explanation was unnecessarily complicated.* ▶ **niekoniecznie; niepotrzebnie**

unnerve /ˌʌnˈnɜːv/ verb [T] to make sb feel nervous or frightened or lose confidence: *His silence unnerved us.* ▶ **wytrącać z równowagi**
■ **unnerving** adj. ▶ **wytrącający z równowagi**

unnoticed /ˌʌnˈnəʊtɪst/ adj. [not before a noun] not noticed or seen: *He didn't want his hard work to **go unnoticed*** (aby jego ciężka praca pozostała niezauważona). ▶ **niezauważony**

unobtrusive /ˌʌnəbˈtruːsɪv/ adj. avoiding being noticed; not attracting attention ▶ **dyskretny; nie rzucający się w oczy**
■ **unobtrusively** adv.: *He tried to leave as unobtrusively as possible.* ▶ **dyskretnie**

unofficial /ˌʌnəˈfɪʃl/ adj. not accepted or approved by a person in authority: *an unofficial strike* ◇ *Unofficial reports say that four people died in the explosion.* ▶ **nieoficjalny; niepotwierdzony** (*urzędowo*) OPP **official**
■ **unofficially** /-ʃəli/ adv. ▶ **nieoficjalnie**

unorthodox /ʌnˈɔːθədɒks/ adj. different from what is generally accepted, usual or traditional ▶ **nieszablonowy, niekonwencjonalny** OPP **orthodox**

unpack /ˌʌnˈpæk/ verb [I,T] to take out the things that were in a bag, suitcase, etc.: *When we arrived at the hotel we unpacked and went to the beach.* ▶ **rozpakowywać (się)** OPP **pack**

unpaid /ˌʌnˈpeɪd/ adj. **1** not yet paid: *an unpaid bill* ▶ **niezapłacony** **2** (used about work) done without payment: *unpaid overtime* ▶ **niepłatny** **3** not receiving money for work done: *an unpaid assistant* ▶ **nieopłacany**

⚷ **unpleasant** /ʌnˈpleznt/ adj. **1** causing you to have a bad feeling; not nice: *This news has come as an unpleasant surprise.* ▶ **niemiły** OPP **pleasant** **2** unfriendly; not polite: *There's no need to get unpleasant* (nie ma sensu się kłócić), *we can discuss this in a friendly way.* ▶ **nieprzyjemny; niegrzeczny**
■ **unpleasantly** adv. ▶ **nieprzyjemnie**

unplug /ˌʌnˈplʌɡ/ verb [T] (**unplugging**; **unplugged**) to remove a piece of electrical equipment from the electricity supply: *Could you unplug the printer, please?* ▶ **wyłączać** (*wtyczkę z kontaktu, drukarkę itp.*) OPP **plug sth in**

U

unpopular /ʌnˈpɒpjələ(r)/ adj. **unpopular (with sb)** not liked by many people: *Her methods made her very unpopular with the staff.* ▶ **niepopularny** OPP **popular**
■ **unpopularity** /ˌʌnˌpɒpjuˈlærəti/ noun [U] ▶ **brak/utrata popularności**

unprecedented /ʌnˈpresɪdentɪd/ adj. never having happened or existed before ▶ **bez precedensu, niespotykany** ➔ look at **precedent**

unpredictable /ˌʌnprɪˈdɪktəbl/ adj. that cannot be predicted because it changes a lot or depends on too many different things: *unpredictable weather* ◇ *The result is entirely unpredictable.* ▶ **nieprzewidywalny** OPP **predictable**
■ **unpredictability** /ˌʌnprɪˌdɪktəˈbɪləti/ noun [U] ▶ **nieprzewidywalność** | **unpredictably** /ˌʌnprɪˈdɪktəbli/ adv. ▶ **nieprzewidywalnie**

unprovoked /ˌʌnprəˈvəʊkt/ adj. (used especially about an attack) not caused by anything the person who is attacked has said or done ▶ **niczym nie sprowokowany**

unqualified /ˌʌnˈkwɒlɪfaɪd/ adj. **1** not having the knowledge or not having passed the exams that you need for sth: *I'm unqualified to offer an opinion on this matter.* ▶ **niewykwalifikowany, niekompetentny** OPP **qualified** **2** complete; total: *an unqualified success* ▶ **pełny, zupełny**

unquestionable /ʌn'kwestʃənəbl/ adj. certain; that cannot be doubted ▶ **bezsprzeczny** OPP **questionable**
■ **unquestionably** /-əbli/ adv.: *She is unquestionably the most famous opera singer in the world.* ▶ **bezsprzecznie**

unravel /ʌn'rævl/ verb [I,T] (**unravelling**; **unravelled**; US **unraveling**; **unraveled**) **1** to remove the knots from a piece of string, thread, etc., or to make them loose; to become loose in this way: *I unravelled the tangled string and wound it into a ball.* ◇ *The knitting I was doing started to unravel* (zaczęła się pruć). ▶ **rozplątywać (się) 2** (used about a complicated story, etc.) to become or to make sth become clear ▶ **wyjaśniać (się)**

unreal /ˌʌn'rɪəl; US -'ri:əl/ adj. **1** very strange and seeming more like a dream than reality: *Her voice had an unreal quality about it* ▶ **nieprawdziwy**, **nierzeczywisty 2** not connected with reality: *Some people have unreal expectations of marriage.* ▶ **nierealny**

unrealistic /ˌʌnrɪə'lɪstɪk; US -ri:ə-/ adj. not showing or accepting things as they are: *unrealistic expectations* ◇ ***It is unrealistic to** expect them to be able to solve the problem immediately.* ▶ **nierealny** OPP **realistic**
■ **unrealistically** /-kli/ adv. ▶ **nierealnie**

unreasonable /ʌn'ri:znəbl/ adj. **1** not willing to listen to other people; acting without good reasons: *I think she is being totally unreasonable about it.* ▶ **nierozsądny**, **niedorzeczny 2** too great; expecting too much: *He makes unreasonable demands on his staff.* ▶ **wygórowany** OPP for both meanings **reasonable**
■ **unreasonably** /-əbli/ adv. ▶ **nierozsądnie**, **niedorzecznie**

unrelenting /ˌʌnrɪ'lentɪŋ/ adj. continuously strong, not becoming weaker or stopping ▶ **bezustanny**, **nieustępliwy**

unreliable /ˌʌnrɪ'laɪəbl/ adj. that cannot be trusted or depended on: *The trains are notoriously unreliable.* ◇ *an unreliable witness* ◇ *He's totally unreliable as a source of information.* ▶ **niesolidny**, **zawodny** OPP **reliable**
■ **unreliability** /ˌʌnrɪˌlaɪə'bɪləti/ noun [U] ▶ **niesolidność**, **zawodność**

unreserved /ˌʌnrɪ'zɜ:vd/ adj. **1** (used about seats in a theatre, etc.) not kept for the use of a particular person ▶ **niezarezerwowany** OPP **reserved 2** without limit; complete: *The government's action received the unreserved support of all parties.* ▶ **nieograniczony**; **zupełny**
■ **unreservedly** /ˌʌnrɪ'zɜ:vɪdli/ adv. ▶ **bez zastrzeżeń**, **całkowicie**

unrest /ʌn'rest/ noun [U] a situation in which people are angry or not happy and likely to protest or fight: *social unrest* niezadowolenie społeczne ▶ **niepokój**, **zamieszki**

unrivalled (US **unrivaled**) /ʌn'raɪvld/ adj. much better than any other of the same type: *His knowledge of Greek theology is unrivalled.* ▶ **niezrównany**

unroll /ʌn'rəʊl/ verb [I,T] to open from a rolled position: *He unrolled the poster and stuck it on the wall.* ▶ (*coś zwiniętego*) **rozwijać (się)** OPP **roll up**

unruly /ʌn'ru:li/ adj. difficult to control; without discipline: *an unruly crowd* ▶ **nieposłuszny**, **nieopanowany**, **awanturniczy**
■ **unruliness** noun [U] ▶ **chuligańskie zachowanie**, **krnąbrność**

unsavoury (US **unsavory**) /ʌn'seɪvəri/ adj. unpleasant; not morally acceptable: *His friends are all unsavoury characters.* ▶ **nieprzyjemny**; **podejrzany**

unscathed /ʌn'skeɪðd/ adj. [not before a noun] not hurt, without injury: *He came out of the fight unscathed.* ▶ **bez szwanku**

unscrew /ˌʌn'skru:/ verb [T] **1** to open or remove sth by turning it: *Could you unscrew the top of this bottle for me?* ▶ **odkręcać 2** to remove the screws from sth ▶ **odkręcać śruby**, **odśrubowywać**

unscrupulous /ʌn'skru:pjələs/ adj. being dishonest, cruel or unfair in order to get what you want ▶ **niegodziwy** OPP **scrupulous**

unselfish /ʌn'selfɪʃ/ adj. giving more time or importance to other people's needs or wishes than to your own ▶ **bezinteresowny** OPP **selfish** ➲ look at **selfless**

unsettle /ˌʌn'setl/ verb [T] to make sb feel upset or worried, especially because a situation has changed: *Changing schools might unsettle the kids.* ▶ **niepokoić**, **stresować**

unsettled /ʌn'setld/ adj. **1** (used about a situation) that may change; making people uncertain about what might happen: *These were difficult and unsettled times.* ◇ *The weather has been very unsettled* (zmienna). ▶ **niespokojny**, **niepewny 2** not calm or relaxed: *They all felt restless and unsettled.* ▶ **niespokojny 3** (used about an argument, etc.) that continues without any agreement being reached ▶ (*spór itp.*) **nierozstrzygnięty 4** (used about a bill, etc.) not yet paid ▶ (*rachunek*) **nieuregulowany**

unsettling /ʌn'setlɪŋ/ adj. making you feel upset, nervous or worried ▶ **niepokojący**

unsightly /ʌn'saɪtli/ adj. very unpleasant to look at: *an unsightly new building* ▶ **szpetny** SYN **ugly**

unskilled /ˌʌn'skɪld/ adj. not having or needing special skill or training: *an unskilled job/worker* ▶ **niewykwalifikowany** OPP **skilled**

unsolicited /ˌʌnsə'lɪsɪtɪd/ adj. not asked for: *unsolicited praise/advice* ▶ **spontaniczny**

unsound /ˌʌn'saʊnd/ adj. **1** based on wrong ideas and therefore not correct or sensible ▶ **wadliwy 2** in poor condition; weak: *The building is structurally unsound* (ma niepewną konstrukcję). ▶ **niepewny**, **niesolidny** OPP for both meanings **sound**

unstable /ʌn'steɪbl/ adj. **1** likely to change or fail: *a period of unstable government* ▶ **niestabilny 2** (used about sb's moods or behaviour) likely to change suddenly or often ▶ **chwiejny 3** likely to fall down or move; not firmly fixed ▶ **niepewny**, **chwiejny** OPP for all meanings **stable** ➲ noun **instability**

unsteady /ʌn'stedi/ adj. **1** not completely in control of your movements so that you might fall: *She is still a little* ***unsteady on her feet*** (nadal stoi niepewnie na własnych nogach) *after the operation.* ▶ (*krok itp.*) **niepewny 2** shaking or moving in a way that is not controlled: *His writing is untidy because he has an unsteady hand.* ▶ (*ruch ręki itp.*) **drżący** OPP for both meanings **steady**
■ **unsteadily** adv. ▶ **niepewnie**; **drżąco**

unstuck /ˌʌn'stʌk/ adj. no longer stuck together or stuck down: *The label on the parcel is about to **come unstuck*** (wkrótce się odklei). ▶ **odklejony**
IDM **come unstuck** to fail badly; to go wrong: *His plan came unstuck when he realized he didn't have enough money.* ▶ **nie powieść się**

unsuccessful /ˌʌnsək'sesfl/ adj. not successful; not achieving what you wanted to: *His efforts to get a job proved unsuccessful.* ◇ *She made several unsuccessful attempts to see him.* ▶ **nieudany** OPP **successful**
■ **unsuccessfully** /-fəli/ adv. ▶ **bez powodzenia**

unsuitable /ʌn'su:təbl/ adj. not right or appropriate for sb/sth: *This film is unsuitable for children under 12.* ▶ **nieodpowiedni** OPP **suitable** ➲ look at **inappropriate**

unsure /ˌʌn'ʃʊə(r); Brit. also -'ʃɔ:(r)/ adj. **1 unsure (about/of sth)** not certain; having doubts: *I didn't argue because I was unsure of the facts.* ▶ **niepewny (czegoś) 2 unsure of yourself** not feeling confident about yourself: *He's young* *and still quite unsure of himself.* ▶ **niepewny siebie** OPP for both meanings **sure**

unsuspecting /ˌʌnsəˈspektɪŋ/ adj. not realizing that there is danger ▶ **niczego nie podejrzewający** ➲ look at **suspect**, **suspicious**

unsympathetic /ˌʌnˌsɪmpəˈθetɪk/ adj. not feeling or showing any sympathy ▶ **obojętny**

untangle /ˌʌnˈtæŋgl/ verb [T] to separate threads which have become tied together in a confused way: *The wires got mixed up and it took me ages to untangle them.* ▶ **rozplątywać**

unthinkable /ʌnˈθɪŋkəbl/ adj. impossible to imagine or accept: *It was unthinkable that he would never see her again.* ▶ **nie do pomyślenia**

unthinking /ʌnˈθɪŋkɪŋ/ adj. done, said, etc. without thinking carefully ▶ **bezmyślny**
■ **unthinkingly** adv. ▶ **bezmyślnie**

⚷ **untidy** /ʌnˈtaɪdi/ adj. (**untidier**; **untidiest**) **1** not tidy or well arranged: *an untidy bedroom* nieposprzątana sypialnia ◇ *untidy hair* rozczochrane włosy ▶ **nieporządny 2** (used about a person) not keeping things tidy or in good order: *My flatmate is so untidy!* ▶ **niechlujny** OPP for both meanings **tidy**, **neat**
■ **untidily** adv. ▶ **niechlujnie** | **untidiness** noun [U] ▶ **nieład**

untie /ʌnˈtaɪ/ verb [T] (**untying**; **unties**; pt, pp **untied**) to remove a knot; to free sb/sth that is tied by a rope, etc. ▶ **rozwiązywać**; **uwalniać** OPP **tie**, **tie sb/sth up**, **fasten**

⚷ **until** /ənˈtɪl/ (also informal **till** /tɪl/) conj. up to the time or the event mentioned: *We won't leave until the police get here.* ◇ *She waited until he had finished.* ▶ **dopóki (nie)**
■ **until** prep. up to the time or the event mentioned: *The restaurant is open until midnight.* ◇ *Until that moment she had been happy.* ◇ *We can't leave until 10 o'clock.* Nie możemy stąd wyjść przed dziesiątą. ▶ **(aż) do**

> **until**
>
> **Until** można użyć zarówno w formalnej, jak i codziennej angielszczyźnie. **Till** częściej występuje w codziennej angielszczyźnie i zwykle nie na początku zdania. Trzeba pamiętać, że w zwrotach dotyczących czasu używa się wyłącznie **till** i **until**. Z kolei **as far as** używa się w odniesieniu do odległości: *I walked as far as the shops.* Mówiąc o jakiejś liczbie, używa się **up to**: *You can take up to 20 kilos of luggage.*

untold /ˌʌnˈtəʊld/ adj. [only before a noun] very great; so big, etc. that you cannot count or measure it: *untold suffering* ▶ **niewypowiedziany**; **niezliczony**

untoward /ˌʌntəˈwɔːd; US ʌnˈtɔːd/ adj. (used about an event, etc.) unexpected and unpleasant: *The security guard noticed nothing untoward.* ▶ **niefortunny**

untrue /ʌnˈtruː/ adj. not true; not based on facts ▶ **nieprawdziwy** SYN **false** OPP **true**

untruth /ˌʌnˈtruːθ/ noun [C] (pl. **untruths** /ˌʌnˈtruːðz/) (formal) something that is not true; a lie ▶ **nieprawda**
■ **untruthful** /-fl/ adj.: *I don't like being untruthful.* Nie lubię mijać się z prawdą. ▶ **mijający się z prawdą** | **untruthfully** /-fəli/ adv. ▶ **kłamliwie**, **nieprawdziwie**

untypical /ʌnˈtɪpɪkl/ adj. not typical or usual: *an untypical example* ▶ **nietypowy** OPP **typical** ➲ look at **atypical**

unused[1] /ˌʌnˈjuːzd/ adj. that has not been used ▶ **(jeszcze) nie używany**

unused[2] /ʌnˈjuːst/ adj. **unused to sth/to doing sth** not having any experience of sth: *She was unused to getting such a lot of attention.* ▶ **nieprzyzwyczajony**, **nienawykły**

⚷ **unusual** /ʌnˈjuːʒuəl; -ʒəl/ adj. **1** not expected or normal: *It's unusual for Joe to be late.* Rzadko się zdarza, żeby Joe się spóźnił. ▶ **rzadki** OPP **usual 2** interesting because it is different: *What an unusual hat!* ▶ **niezwykły**

⚷ **unusually** /ʌnˈjuːʒuəli; -ʒəli/ adv. **1** more than is common; extremely: *an unusually hot summer* ▶ **wyjątkowo 2** in a way that is not normal or typical of sb/sth: *Unusually for her, she forgot his birthday.* Wyjątkowo tak się zdarzyło, że zapomniała o jego urodzinach. ▶ **nietypowo** OPP **usually**

unveil /ˌʌnˈveɪl/ verb [T] to show sth new to the public for the first time: *The President unveiled a memorial to those who died in the war.* ▶ **odsłaniać**

unwanted /ˌʌnˈwɒntɪd/ adj. not wanted: *an unwanted gift* ▶ **niechciany**, **zbyteczny**

unwarranted /ʌnˈwɒrəntɪd/ adj. that is not deserved or for which there is no good reason: *unwarranted criticism* ▶ **(niczym) nieusprawiedliwiony**, **bezpodstawny**

unwell /ʌnˈwel/ adj. [not before a noun] ill; sick: *to feel unwell* ▶ **niezdrów** OPP **well**

unwieldy /ʌnˈwiːldi/ adj. difficult to move or carry because it is too big, heavy, etc. ▶ **(zbyt) ciężki**, **nieporęczny**

⚷ **unwilling** /ʌnˈwɪlɪŋ/ adj. not wanting to do sth but often forced to do it by other people ▶ **niechętny**, **niesklonny** OPP **willing**
■ **unwillingly** adv. ▶ **niechętnie**

unwind /ˌʌnˈwaɪnd/ verb (pt, pp **unwound** /ˌʌnˈwaʊnd/) **1** [I,T] if you **unwind** sth or if sth **unwinds**, it comes away from sth that it had been put round: *The bandage had unwound.* ▶ **rozwijać (się) 2** [I] (informal) to relax, especially after working hard: *After a busy day, it takes me a while to unwind.* ▶ **rozluźniać się** ➲ look at **wind**

unwise /ˌʌnˈwaɪz/ adj. showing a lack of good judgement; silly: *I think it would be unwise to tell anyone about our plan yet.* ▶ **niemądry** OPP **wise**
■ **unwisely** adv. ▶ **niemądrze**

unwitting /ʌnˈwɪtɪŋ/ adj. [only before a noun] not realizing sth; not intending to do sth: *an unwitting accomplice to the crime* ▶ **nieświadomy**; **mimowolny**
■ **unwittingly** adv. ▶ **nieświadomie**; **mimowolnie**

unwound past tense, past participle of **unwind**

unwrap /ʌnˈræp/ verb [T] (**unwrapping**; **unwrapped**) to take off the paper, etc. that covers or protects sth ▶ **rozpakowywać**

unzip /ˌʌnˈzɪp/ verb [I,T] (**unzipping**; **unzipped**) if a bag, piece of clothing, etc. **unzips**, or you **unzip** it, you open it by pulling on the **zip** ▶ **rozpinać** (*zamek błyskawiczny*) OPP **zip**

⚷ **up** /ʌp/ prep., adv. **1** at or to a high or higher level or position: *The monkey* ***climbed up*** (wspięła się na drzewo) *the tree.* ◇ *I walked up the hill.* ◇ *I carried her suitcase up to the third floor.* ◇ ***Put*** *your* ***hand up*** *if you know the answer.* ▶ **do góry 2** in or into a vertical position: *Stand up, please.* Proszę wstać. ◇ *Is he up yet?* Czy już wstał (z łóżka)? ◇ *I had to get up early* (wcześnie wstać). **3** (used for showing an increase in sth): *Prices have* ***gone up.*** ◇ *Turn the volume up.* Nastaw głośniej. ▶ **w górę 4** to the place where sb/sth is: *She ran up to* (podbiegła do) *her mother and kissed her.* ◇ *A car drove up and two men got out.* ▶ **blisko (do) 5** in or to the north: *My parents have just moved* ***up north.*** ◇ *When are you going up to Scotland?* ◇ *We're going up to Leeds tomorrow.* Jutro jedziemy do Leeds. ▶ **do** (*w kierunku północnym*), **na 6** into pieces: *We chopped the old table up and used it for firewood.* ◇ *She* ***tore up*** *the letter and threw it away.* ▶ **na kawałki 7** (used for showing that an action continues until it is completed): ***Eat up*** (zjedzcie wszystko), *everybody, I want you to finish everything on the table.* ◇ *Can you help me* ***clean up*** *the kitchen?* ▶ **do końca 8** coming or being put together: *The teacher collected up* (zebrała) *our exam papers.* ◇ *Keiko and Jos teamed up* (połączyli

U

siły) *in the doubles competition.* **9** (used about a period of time) finished: *Stop writing. Your time's up.* Skończył się czas. ▶ **zakończony** **10** (used with verbs of closing or covering): ***Do up*** (zapnij) *your coat. It's cold.* ◇ *She tied the parcel up* (związała paczkę) *with string.* ◇ *I found some wood to **cover up*** (aby zakryć) *the hole.* **11** in a particular direction: *I live just **up the road*** (trochę dalej na tej samej ulicy). ◇ ***Move up*** (posuń się) *a little and let me sit down.* ▶ **dalej** **12** (used about computers) working; in operation: *Are the computers back up yet?* Czy komputery już działają? ▶ **działający** **13** (informal) (used for showing that sth is spoiled): *I really messed up* (zawaliłem sprawę) *when I told the interviewer I liked sleeping.*

IDM **be up for sth** **1** to be available to be bought or chosen: *That house is up for sale.* ◇ *How many candidates are up for election?* ▶ **być na sprzedaż/do wyboru** **2** (informal) to be enthusiastic about doing sth: *Is anyone up for a swim?* ▶ **mieć wielką ochotę na coś**

be up to sb to be sb's responsibility: *I can't take the decision. It's not up to me.* ▶ **zależeć od kogoś**

not up to much (informal) not very good: *The programme wasn't up to much.* ▶ **niewiele wart**

be up against sth/sb to face sth/sb that causes problems ▶ **stawić czoła czemuś/komuś**

up and down backwards and forwards, or rising and falling: *He was nervously walking up and down outside the interview room.* ▶ **tam i z powrotem**; **do góry i na dół**

up and running (used about sth new) working well: *The new system is already up and running* (już jest sprawny). ▶ **działający**

up to sth **1** as much/many as: *We're expecting up to 100 people at the meeting.* ▶ **aż do** (*pewnej sumy/liczby*) **2** as far as now: *Up to now, things have been easy.* ▶ **dotychczas** **3** capable of sth: *I don't feel up to cooking this evening. I'm too tired.* ▶ **na siłach czegoś**; **w stanie, aby coś zrobić** **4** doing sth secret and perhaps bad: *What are the children up to* (co te dzieci nam szykują)*? Go and see.* ▶ **robiący coś potajemnie**

what's up? (informal) what's the matter? ▶ **co jest (grane)?** ⓘ **Up** używa się w czasownikach złożonych. Zob. hasła przy odpowiednich czasownikach, np. **pick sth up**.

upbeat /ˈʌpbiːt/ adj. (informal) positive and enthusiastic; making you feel that the future will be good: *The meeting ended on an upbeat note.* ▶ **optymistyczny**, **entuzjastyczny** SYN **optimistic** OPP **downbeat**

upbringing /ˈʌpbrɪŋɪŋ/ noun [sing.] the way a child is treated and taught how to behave by their parents: *a strict upbringing* ▶ **wychowanie**

update /ˌʌpˈdeɪt/ verb [T] **1** to make sth more modern ▶ **unowocześniać** **2** to put the most recent information into sth; to give sb the most recent information: *Our database of addresses is updated regularly.* ▶ **uaktualniać**; **podawać ostatnie/aktualne wiadomości**

■ **update** /ˈʌpdeɪt/ noun [C]: *an update on a news story* aktualizacja wiadomości ▶ **aktualizacja**

upgrade /ˌʌpˈɡreɪd/ verb [T] to change sth so that it is of a higher standard: *Upgrading your computer software can be expensive.* ▶ **ulepszać**, **uaktualniać** (*np. komputer, oprogramowanie itp.*)

■ **upgrade** /ˈʌpɡreɪd/ noun [C]: *I managed to get an upgrade to business class* (uzyskać (darmową) zamianę biletu na bilet klasy business) *on the plane.* ▶ **ulepszenie**; (*komput.*) **upgrade**

upheaval /ʌpˈhiːvl/ noun [C,U] a sudden big change, especially one that causes a lot of trouble ▶ **wstrząs**

upheld past tense, past participle of **uphold**

uphill /ˌʌpˈhɪl/ adj. **1** going towards the top of a hill ▶ **pod górę** **2** (**an uphill battle, struggle, task, etc.**) needing a lot of effort: *It was an uphill struggle to find a job.* ▶ **uciążliwy**

■ **uphill** adv. ▶ **pod górę**; **uciążliwie** OPP **downhill**

uphold /ʌpˈhəʊld/ verb [T] (pt, pp **upheld** /-ˈheld/) to support a decision, etc. especially when other people are against it ▶ **podtrzymywać**

upholstered /ʌpˈhəʊlstəd/ adj. (used about a chair, etc.) covered with a soft thick material ▶ **obity**

upholstery /ʌpˈhəʊlstəri/ noun [U] the thick soft materials used to cover chairs, car seats, etc. ▶ **obicie**

upkeep /ˈʌpkiːp/ noun [U] **1** the cost or process of keeping sth in a good condition; the cost or process of providing children or animals with what they need to live: *The landlord pays for the upkeep of the building.* ▶ **utrzymanie**, **koszt utrzymania**

upland /ˈʌplənd/ adj. [only before a noun] consisting of hills and mountains ▶ **wyżynny**

■ **upland** noun [C, usually pl.] ▶ **wyżyna**

uplifting /ˌʌpˈlɪftɪŋ/ adj. producing a feeling of hope and happiness: *an uplifting speech* ▶ **podnoszący na duchu**

upload /ˌʌpˈləʊd/ verb [T] to move data to a larger computer system from a smaller one ▶ **ściągać** (*dane z mniejszego systemu komputerowego na większy*) OPP **download**

■ **upload** /ˈʌpləʊd/ noun [C] ▶ **ściągnięte dane**

upmarket /ˌʌpˈmɑːkɪt/ (US ˌup'scale /ˌʌpˈskeɪl/) adj. [usually before a noun] designed to appeal to or to satisfy people in the higher social classes: *an upmarket restaurant* ▶ **ekskluzywny** OPP **downmarket**

■ **upmarket** (US **upscale**) adv.: *The company has been forced to move more upmarket* (poszukać bardziej wyrafinowanej klienteli).

⚷ **upon** (formal) = ON (1)

⚷ **upper** /ˈʌpə(r)/ adj. [only before a noun] in a higher position than sth else; above sth: *He had a cut on his upper lip.* ▶ **wyższy** OPP **lower**

IDM **get, have, etc. the upper hand** to get into a stronger position than another person; to gain control over sb ▶ **zdobywać przewagę/kontrolę**

ˌupper ˈcase noun [U] letters that are written or printed in their large form: *'BBC' is written in upper case.* ▶ **duże litery** SYN **capital** OPP **lower case**

the ˌupper ˈclass noun [sing., with sing. or pl. verb] (also **the ˌupper ˈclasses** [pl.]) the groups of people that are considered to have the highest social position and that have more money and/or power than other people in society: *a member of the upper class/upper classes* ▶ **klasa wyższa społeczeństwa** ➲ look at **middle class**, **working class**

■ **ˌupper ˈclass** adj.: *Her family is very upper class.* ◇ *an upper-class accent* ▶ **wyższej klasy** (*społecznej*), **wyższych sfer**

uppermost /ˈʌpəməʊst/ adj. in the highest or most important position: *Concern for her family was **uppermost in her mind.*** ▶ **najważniejszy**, **najwyższy**

upright /ˈʌpraɪt/ adj. **1** in or into a vertical position ▶ **pionowy** SYN **erect** **2** honest and responsible ▶ **prawy**, **odpowiedzialny**

IDM **bolt upright** → BOLT[3]

■ **upright** adv. with a straight back; into a vertical position: *I was so tired I could hardly stay upright.* ▶ **prosto**, **pionowo**

ˌupright piˈano (also **upright**) noun [C] a piano in which the strings are vertical ▶ **pianino** ➲ look at **grand piano**

uprising /ˈʌpraɪzɪŋ/ noun [C] a situation in which a group of people start to fight against the people in power in their country ▶ **powstanie**

uproar /ˈʌprɔː(r)/ noun [U, sing.] a lot of noise, confusion, anger, etc.; an angry discussion about sth: *The meeting ended **in uproar.*** ▶ **zgiełk**; **awantura**

■ **uproarious** /ʌp'rɔːriəs/ adj. [usually before a noun] very noisy: *uproarious laughter* ▶ **wrzaskliwy**

uproot /ˌʌp'ruːt/ verb [T] to pull up a plant by the roots: *Strong winds had uprooted the tree.* ◇ *Many people have to uproot themselves* (przesiedlać się) *when they change jobs.* ▶ **wykorzeniać**

ups /ʌps/ noun
IDM **ups and downs** both good times and bad times: *We're happy together but we've had our ups and downs.* ▶ **powodzenia i klęski**

upscale (US) = UPMARKET

upset[1] /ˌʌp'set/ verb [T] (**upsetting**; pt, pp **upset**) **1** to make sb worry or feel unhappy: *The pictures of starving children upset her.* ▶ **niepokoić, wytrącać kogoś z równowagi** ➲ note at **sad** **2** to make sth go wrong: *to upset someone's plans* ▶ **pokrzyżować** (*plany*), **psuć** (*np. zabawę*) **3** to make sb ill in the stomach: *Rich food usually upsets me.* ▶ **rozstrajać żołądek** **4** to knock sth over: *I upset a cup of tea all over the tablecloth.* ▶ **przewracać**

upset[2] /ˌʌp'set/ adj. **1** [not before a noun] worried and unhappy: *She was looking very upset about something.* ▶ **zaniepokojony, wytrącony z równowagi** ➲ note at **sad** **2** slightly ill: *I've got **an upset stomach**.* ▶ (*żołądek*) **rozstrojony**

Zwróć uwagę, że przymiotnik **upset** wymawia się /'ʌpset/ w pozycji przed rzeczownikiem, ale /ˌʌp'set/ w każdej innej pozycji w zdaniu.

upset[3] /'ʌpset/ noun **1** [C,U] a situation in which there are unexpected problems or difficulties: *The company survived the recent upset in share prices.* ▶ **zawirowanie** **2** [C,U] a situation that causes worry and sadness: *She's had a few upsets recently.* ◇ *It had been the cause of much emotional upset.* ▶ **zmartwienie, wytrącenie z równowagi** **3** [C] a slight illness in your stomach: *a stomach upset* ▶ **rozstrój żołądka**

upshot /'ʌpʃɒt/ noun [sing.] **the upshot (of sth)** the final result, especially of a conversation or an event ▶ **wynik**

upside down /ˌʌpsaɪd 'daʊn/ adv. with the top part turned to the bottom: *You're holding the picture upside down.* ▶ **do góry nogami** ➲ picture at **back**
IDM **turn sth upside down** **1** (informal) to make a place untidy when looking for sth: *I had to turn the house upside down looking for my keys.* ▶ **przewracać coś do góry nogami** **2** to cause large changes and confusion in sb's life: *His sudden death turned her world upside down.* ▶ **przewracać coś do góry nogami**

upstairs /ˌʌp'steəz/ adv. to or on a higher floor of a building: *to **go upstairs*** ◇ *She's sleeping upstairs.* ▶ **na górę/górze** OPP **downstairs**
■ **upstairs** /'ʌpsteəz/ adj. [only before a noun]: *an upstairs window* ▶ **na górnym piętrze** | **the upstairs** noun (informal): *We're going to paint the upstairs.* ▶ **górne piętro**

upstream /ˌʌp'striːm/ adv. **upstream (of/from sth)** in the direction that a river flows from: *He found it hard work swimming upstream.* ▶ **pod prąd** OPP **downstream**

upsurge /'ʌpsɜːdʒ/ noun [C, usually sing.] **an upsurge (in sth)** a sudden increase of sth ▶ **nagły wzrost**

uptake /'ʌpteɪk/ noun
IDM **quick/slow on the uptake** quick/slow to understand the meaning of sth: *I gave him a hint but he's slow on the uptake.* ▶ **szybko/powoli pojmować**

uptight /ˌʌp'taɪt/ adj. (informal) nervous and not relaxed: *He gets uptight before an exam.* ▶ **spięty, zdenerwowany**

ˌup to 'date adj. **1** modern ▶ **nowoczesny** **2** having the most recent information ▶ **aktualny, na bieżąco**

ˌup-to-the-'minute adj. having the most recent information possible ▶ **najświeższy**

upturn /'ʌptɜːn/ noun [C] **an upturn (in sth)** an improvement in sth: *an upturn in support for the government* ▶ **poprawa** OPP **downturn**

upturned /ˌʌp'tɜːnd/ adj. **1** pointing upwards: *an upturned nose* ▶ **zadarty** **2** with the top part turned to the bottom ▶ **do góry dnem/nogami, wywrócony**

upward /'ʌpwəd/ adj. [only before a noun] moving or directed towards a higher place: *an upward trend* (tendencja zwyżkowa) *in exports* ▶ **w górę, skierowany ku górze** OPP **downward**
■ **upward** (also **upwards** /'ʌpwədz/) adv. ▶ **w górę**

'upwards of prep. more than the number mentioned: *They've invited upwards of a hundred guests.* ▶ **ponad**

uranium /ju'reɪniəm/ noun [U] (symbol **U**) a metal that can be used to produce nuclear energy: *Uranium is highly radioactive.* ▶ **uran**

Uranus /'jʊərənəs; jʊ'reɪnəs; US jʊ'r-/ noun [sing.] the planet that is 7th in order from the sun ▶ **Uran**

urban /'ɜːbən/ adj. connected with a town or city: *urban development* ▶ **miejski, wielkomiejski** ➲ look at **rural**

urbane /ɜː'beɪn/ adj. (especially used about a man) good at knowing what to say and how to behave in social situations; appearing relaxed and confident: *He was charming and urbane, full of witty conversation.* ▶ (*zwł. mężczyzna*) **wytworny i elegancki, o doskonałych manierach**
■ **urbanely** adv. ▶ **wytwornie, elegancko** | **urbanity** /ɜː'bænəti/ noun [U] ▶ **wytworność, dobre wychowanie**

Urdu /'ʊəduː; 'ɜːduː/ noun [U] the official language of Pakistan, also widely used in India ▶ **język urdu**

urethra /jʊ'riːθrə/ noun [C] the tube that carries liquid waste out of the body. In men and male animals **sperm** also flows along this tube. ▶ **cewka moczowa**

urge[1] /ɜːdʒ/ verb [T] **1 urge sb (to do sth)**; **urge sth** to advise or try hard to persuade sb to do sth: *I urged him to fight the decision.* ◇ *Drivers are urged to take care on icy roads.* ◇ *Police urge caution on the icy roads.* ▶ **zalecać; usilnie namawiać** **2** to force sb/sth to go in a certain direction: *He urged his horse over the fence.* ▶ **zmuszać do przemieszczenia się, kierować w określonym kierunku**
PHR V **urge sb on** to encourage sb: *The captain urged his team on.* ▶ **dopingować kogoś**

urge[2] /ɜːdʒ/ noun [C] a strong need or desire: *sexual/creative urges* ▶ **pobudka**

urgent /'ɜːdʒənt/ adj. needing immediate attention: *an urgent message* ▶ **pilny**
■ **urgency** /'ɜːdʒənsi/ noun [U]: *a matter of the greatest urgency* ▶ **nagła potrzeba** | **urgently** adv.: *I must see you urgently.* ▶ **pilnie**

urinal /jʊə'raɪnl; 'jʊərɪnl; US 'jʊərənl/ noun [C] a type of toilet for men that is attached to the wall; a room or building containing **urinals** ▶ **pisuar**

urinary /'jʊərɪnəri; US -rəneri/ adj. [usually before a noun] connected with **urine** or the parts of the body through which it passes: *a urinary infection* ◇ *the urinary tract* ▶ **moczowy**

urinate /'jʊərɪneɪt/ verb [I] (formal) to pass **urine** from the body ▶ **oddawać mocz**

urine /'jʊərɪn; -raɪn; US -rən/ noun [U] the yellowish liquid that is passed from your body when you go to the toilet ▶ **mocz**

URL /ˌjuː ɑːr 'el/ abbr. **uniform/universal resource locator**; the address of a World Wide Web page ▶ **URL** ➲ note at **Internet**

urn /ɜːn/ noun [C] **1** a special container, used especially to hold the **ashes** that are left when a dead person has been **cremated** ▶ **urna** **2** a large metal container used for

U

making a large quantity of tea or coffee and for keeping it hot ▶ **termos (bufetowy)**

US /ˌjuː ˈes/ abbr. the **United States** (of America) ▶ **USA**

🔑 **us** /əs; strong form ʌs/ pron. [used as the object of a verb, or after *be*] me and another person or other people; me and you: *Come with us.* ◇ *Leave us alone.* ◇ *Will you write to us?* ▶ *(przypadek zależny od* **we**)

USA /ˌjuː es ˈeɪ/ abbr. the **United States** (of America) ▶ **USA**

usable /ˈjuːzəbl/ adj. that can be used ▶ **używalny**

usage /ˈjuːsɪdʒ/ noun **1** [U] the way that sth is used; the amount that sth is used ▶ **użytkowanie**; **zużycie 2** [C,U] the way that words are normally used in a language: *a guide to English grammar and usage* ▶ **używanie**

USˈB stick (also ˈ**Memory Stick™**) noun [C] a small device that you can carry around with you which is used for storing and moving data onto a computer ▶ **pamięć przenośna**, **karta pamięci**

🔑 **use¹** /juːz/ verb [T] (**using**; pt, pp **used** /juːzd/) **1 use sth (as/for sth)**; **use sth (to do sth)** to do sth with a machine, an object, a method, etc. for a particular purpose: *The building was used as a shelter for homeless people.* ◇ *A gun is used for shooting with.* ◇ *What's this used for?* ◇ *We used the money to buy a house.* ◇ *That's a word I never use.* ◇ *Could I use your phone* (skorzystać z twojego telefonu)*?* ◇ *Use your imagination!* Pobudź swą wyobraźnię! ▶ **używać 2** to need or to take sth: *Don't use all the milk.* ▶ **używać**, **zużywać 3** to treat sb/sth in an unfair way in order to get sth that you want: *I felt used.* ▶ **wykorzystywać**

PHR V **use sth up** to use sth until no more is left ▶ **zużyć**

Zwróć uwagę na różnicę w wymowie słowa: **use** czasownik = /juːz/; rzeczownik = /juːs/.

🔑 **use²** /juːs/ noun **1** [U] the act of using sth or of being used: *The use of computers is now widespread.* ◇ *She kept the money for use in an emergency.* ▶ **użycie 2** [C,U] the purpose for which sth is used: *This machine has many uses.* ▶ **zastosowanie 3** [U] the ability or permission to use sth: *He lost the use of his hand* (stracił władzę w ręce) *after the accident.* ◇ *She offered them the use of her car.* ▶ **(możliwość/prawo) używania 4** [U] the advantage of sth; how useful sth is: ***It's no use*** (nie ma sensu) *studying for an exam at the last minute.* ◇ ***What's the use of** trying?* Po co próbować? ◇ *Will this jumper **be of use to** you or should I get rid of it?* ▶ **pożytek**

IDM **come into/go out of use** to start/stop being used regularly or by a lot of people: *Email came into widespread use in the 1990s.* ▶ **zacząć być używanym**, **wychodzić z użycia**

make use of sth/sb to use sth/sb in a way that will give you an advantage ▶ **wykorzystywać coś/kogoś**, **używać czegoś**

🔑 **used** adj. **1** /juːzd/ that has had another owner before: *a garage selling used cars* ▶ **używany** SYN **second-hand 2** /juːst/ **used to sth/to doing sth** familiar with sth because you do it or experience it often: *He's used to the heat.* ◇ *I'll never get used to getting up at five* (nigdy nie przyzwyczaję się do wstawania o piątej rano). ▶ **przyzwyczajony**

🔑 **used to** /ˈjuːst tə; before a vowel and in final position ˈjuːst tu/ modal verb (for talking about sth that happened often or continuously in the past or about a situation which existed in the past): *You used to work* (kiedyś pracowałeś) *in Glasgow, didn't you?* ◇ *Did you use to smoke?* Czy kiedyś paliłeś? ◇ *He didn't use to speak to me.* Nie miał zwyczaju ze mną rozmawiać. ▶ **zwykł coś robić** (*kiedyś, ale już nie teraz*) ➲ look at **would** (8)

Do tworzenia pytań z **used to** zwykle używa się **did**: *Did she use to be in your class?* Do tworzenia zaprzeczeń używa się **didn't use to** lub **never used to**: *I never used to like jazz.* ◇ *I didn't use to like jazz.* Następujące formy przeczeń i pytań są bardziej formalne i dość rzadko używane: *He used not to drive a car.* ◇ *Used they to work here?* Zwróć uwagę na różnicę między zwrotem **used to** + bezokolicznik, odnoszącym się tylko do przeszłości, a zwrotem **be used to (doing) sth**, który ma inne znaczenie i może odnosić się do przeszłości, teraźniejszości lub przyszłości: *I used to live* (kiedyś mieszkałem) *with my parents, but now I live on my own.* ◇ *I'm used to living on my own* (przyzwyczaiłem się do tego, że mieszkam sam), *so I don't feel lonely.* Wyrażenie **get used to doing sth** używane jest do opisania nowych sytuacji, do których się jeszcze nie przyzwyczailiśmy: *I'm still getting used to my new job.*

🔑 **useful** /ˈjuːsfl/ adj. having some practical use; helpful: *a useful tool* ◇ *useful advice* ▶ **użyteczny**, **pomocny**
■ **usefully** /-fəli/ adv. ▶ **pożytecznie** | **usefulness** noun [U] ▶ **pożytek**, **przydatność**

IDM **come in useful** to be of practical help in a certain situation: *Don't throw that box away – it might come in useful for something.* ▶ **przydawać się**

🔑 **useless** /ˈjuːsləs/ adj. **1** that does not work well, that does not achieve anything: *This new machine is useless* (do niczego). ◇ *It's useless complaining/to complain – you won't get your money back.* ▶ **bezużyteczny**, **niepotrzebny 2** (informal) **useless (at sth/at doing sth)** (used about a person) weak or not successful at sth: *I'm useless at sport.* ▶ **kiepski**
■ **uselessly** adv. ▶ **bezużytecznie**, **bezcelowo** | **uselessness** noun [U] ▶ **bezużyteczność**, **bezcelowość**

Usenet /ˈjuːznet/ noun [U] a service on the Internet used by groups of users who email each other because they share a particular interest ▶ **Usenet** (*usługa group dyskusyjnych w internecie*)

🔑 **user** /ˈjuːzə(r)/ noun [C] [in compounds] a person who uses a service, machine, place, etc.: *users of public transport* ◇ *computer software users* ▶ **użytkowni-k/czka**

ˌ**user-ˈfriendly** adj. (used about computers, books, machines, etc.) easy to understand and use ▶ **łatwy w użyciu**, **przyjazny**

ˈ**user group** noun [C] a group of people who use a particular thing and who share information about it, especially people who share information about computers on the Internet ▶ **grupa użytkownika**

username /ˈjuːzəneɪm/ noun [C] the name you use in order to be able to use a computer program or system: *Please enter your username.* ▶ **nazwa użytkownika**

usher¹ /ˈʌʃə(r)/ noun [C] a person who shows people to their seats in a theatre, church, etc. ▶ **bileter/ka**; **mistrz ceremonii**

usher² /ˈʌʃə(r)/ verb [T] to take or show sb where to go: *I was ushered into an office.* ▶ **wprowadzać** (*np. do salonu, sali*)

PHR V **usher sth in** to be the beginning of sth new or to make sth new begin: *The agreement ushered in a new period of peace for the two countries.* ▶ **zapoczątkowywać** (*np. okres pokoju*)

usherette /ˌʌʃəˈret/ noun [C] (especially Brit.) a woman who shows people to their seats in a cinema or theatre ▶ **bileterka**

USSR /ˌjuː es es ˈɑː(r)/ abbr. (the former) Union of Soviet Socialist Republics ▶ **ZSRR**

🔑 **usual** /ˈjuːʒuəl; -ʒəl/ adj. **usual (for sb/sth) (to do sth)** happening or used most often: *It's usual for her to work at weekends.* Ona zwykle pracuje w weekendy. ◇ *He got home later than usual* (później niż zwykle). ◇ *I sat in* *my usual seat* (na krześle, na którym zwykle siadam). ▶ **zwykły** OPP **unusual**

IDM **as usual** in the way that has often happened before: *Here's Dylan, late as usual!* ▶ **jak zwykle**

usually /ˈjuːʒuəli; -ʒəli/ adv. in the way that is usual; most often: *She's usually home by six.* ◇ *Usually, we go out on Saturdays.* ▶ **zwykle**, **zazwyczaj**

usurp /juːˈzɜːp/ verb [T] (formal) to take sb's position and/or power without having the right to do this ▶ **uzurpować sobie**

■ **usurper** noun [C] ▶ **uzurpator/ka**

utensil /juːˈtensl/ noun [C] a type of tool that is used in the home: *kitchen/cooking utensils* ▶ **sprzęt kuchenny** (*np. łyżka drewniana, nóż*)

uterus /ˈjuːtərəs/ noun [C] (pl. **uteruses** in scientific use **uteri** /-raɪ/) (formal) the part of a woman or female animal where a baby develops before it is born ▶ **macica** ℹ Mniej formalne słowo to **womb**.

utilitarian /ˌjuːtɪlɪˈteəriən/ adj. (formal) designed to be useful and practical rather than attractive ▶ **funkcjonalny**, **praktyczny**

utility /juːˈtɪləti/ noun (pl. **utilities**) **1** [C] (especially US) a service provided for the public, such as a water, gas or electricity supply: *the administration of* ***public utilities*** ▶ **zakład użyteczności publicznej 2** [U] (formal) the quality of being useful ▶ **pożytek 3** [C] a computer program or part of a program that does a particular task: *a utility program* ▶ **program użytkowy**

uˈtility room noun [C] a small room in some houses, often next to the kitchen, where people keep large pieces of kitchen equipment, such as a washing machine ▶ **pomieszczenie gospodarcze**

utilize (also **-ise**) /ˈjuːtəlaɪz/ verb [T] (formal) to make use of sth: *to utilize natural resources* ▶ **wykorzystywać**

utmost¹ /ˈʌtməʊst/ adj. [only before a noun] (formal) greatest: *a message* ***of the utmost importance*** ▶ **najwyższy**

utmost² /ˈʌtməʊst/ noun [sing.] the greatest amount possible: *Resources have been exploited* ***to the utmost*** (maksymalnie wykorzystane). ◇ *I will* ***do my utmost*** *to help.* Zrobię wszystko, co w mojej mocy.

utopia (also **Utopia**) /juːˈtəʊpiə/ noun [C,U] a place or state that exists only in the imagination, where everything is perfect ▶ **utopia**

■ **utopian** (also **Utopian**) /juːˈtəʊpiən/ adj. ▶ **utopijny**

utter¹ /ˈʌtə(r)/ adj. [only before a noun] complete; total: *He felt an utter fool.* ▶ **zupełny**, **całkowity**

■ **utterly** adv.: *It's utterly impossible.* ▶ **zupełnie**

utter² /ˈʌtə(r)/ verb [T] to say sth or make a sound with your voice: *She did not* ***utter a word*** *in the meeting.* ◇ *She left without uttering a word.* Wyszła bez słowa. ▶ **wypowiadać** (*słowa*), **wydawać głos**

■ **utterance** /ˈʌtərəns/ noun [C] (formal) ▶ **wypowiedź**, **wyrażenie**

U-turn /ˈjuː tɜːn/ noun [C] **1** a type of movement where a car, etc. turns round so that it goes back in the direction it came from ▶ **zawracanie pojazdu 2** (informal) a sudden change from one plan or policy to a completely different or opposite one ▶ **całkowita zmiana planu** ➲ look at **about-turn**

uvula /ˈjuːvjələ/ noun [C] (pl. **uvulae** /-liː/) a small piece of flesh that hangs from the top of the inside of the mouth just above the throat ▶ (*anat.*) **języczek** ➲ picture at **body**

V v

V, v /viː/ noun [C,U] (pl. **Vs**; **vs**; **V's**; **v's** /viːz/) **1** the 22nd letter of the English alphabet: *'Velvet' begins with (a) 'V'.* ▶ **litera** *v* **2** the shape of a V: *a V-neck sweater* ◇ *The birds were flying in a V* (kluczem). ▶ **kształt litery** *v* ➲ picture on **page A1**

V 1 = VERSUS (1): *Liverpool v Everton* **2** (**V**) = VOLT: *a 9V battery* **3** = VERSE (2) **4** (informal) = VERY (1): *v good*

vacancy /ˈveɪkənsi/ noun [C] (pl. **vacancies**) **1 a vacancy (for sb/sth)** a job that is available for sb to do: *We have a vacancy for a secretary.* ▶ **wakat 2** a room in a hotel, etc. that is available: *The sign outside the hotel said 'No Vacancies'.* ▶ **wolny pokój** (*np. w hotelu*)

vacant /ˈveɪkənt/ adj. **1** (used about a house, hotel room, seat, etc.) not being used; empty ▶ **wolny 2** (used about a job in a company, etc.) that is available for sb to take: *the 'Situations Vacant' page* strona gazety z ogłoszeniami o pracę ▶ **wolny**, **wakujący 3** showing no sign of intelligence or understanding: *a vacant expression* ▶ **bezmyślny**

■ **vacantly** adv.: *She stared at him vacantly.* ▶ **bezmyślnie**

vacate /veˈkeɪt; vəɪˈk-/ verb [T] (formal) to leave a building, a seat, a job, etc. so that it is available for sb else ▶ **zwalniać** (*np. mieszkanie, stanowisko*)

vacation /vəˈkeɪʃn/ noun **1** [C] (Brit.) any of the periods of time when universities or courts of law are closed: *the Christmas/Easter vacation* ▶ **wakacje**; **ferie uniwersyteckie 2** (US) : *The boss is* ***on vacation.*** = HOLIDAY (1)

vaccinate /ˈvæksɪneɪt/ verb [T, often passive] **vaccinate sb (against sth)** to protect a person or an animal against a disease by giving them a mild form of the disease with an **injection**: *Were you vaccinated against measles as a child?* ▶ **szczepić** ➲ look at **immunize**, **inoculate**

■ **vaccination** /ˌvæksɪˈneɪʃn/ noun [C,U] ▶ **szczepienie**

vaccine /ˈvæksiːn; US vækˈsiːn/ noun [C] a mild form of a disease that is put into a person or an animal's blood by an **injection** in order to protect the body against that disease ▶ **szczepionka**

vacillate /ˈvæsəleɪt/ verb [I] (formal) to keep changing your opinion or thoughts about sth, especially in a way that annoys other people: *The country's leaders are still vacillating between confrontation and compromise.* ▶ **nie móc się zdecydować**, **wahać się** SYN **waver**

■ **vacillation** /ˌvæsəˈleɪʃn/ noun [U,C] ▶ **niezdecydowanie**, **wahanie**

vacuous /ˈvækjuəs/ adj. (formal) showing no sign of intelligence or sensitive feelings: *a vacuous expression* ▶ **bezmyślny**

■ **vacuously** adv. ▶ **bezmyślnie**

vacuum¹ /ˈvækjuəm/ noun [C] **1** a space that is completely empty of all substances, including air or other gases: *vacuum-packed foods* ▶ **próżnia 2** [usually sing.] a situation from which sth is missing or lacking: *a vacuum in her life* ▶ **poczucie pustki 3** (informal) = VACUUM CLEANER **4** [usually sing.] the act of cleaning sth with a **vacuum cleaner**: *to give a room a quick vacuum* poodkurzać pokój ▶ **odkurzanie**

vacuum² /ˈvækjuəm/ verb [I,T] to clean sth using a **vacuum cleaner** ▶ **odkurzać**

ˈvacuum cleaner (also informal **vacuum**; Brit. also **Hoover™** /ˈhuːvə(r)/) noun [C] an electric machine that cleans carpets, etc. by sucking up dirt ▶ **odkurzacz** ➲ look at **cleaner**

'vacuum flask noun [C] a type of container used for keeping a liquid hot or cold ▶ **termos** ⓘ **Vaccuum flask**, w którym trzyma się gorące/zimne napoje, może również być nazywany **flask**. ➲ look at **Thermos**

vagabond /ˈvægəbɒnd/ noun [C] (old-fashioned) a person who has no home or job and who travels from place to place ▶ **włóczęga** ⓘ Wyraża dezaprobatę.

vagina /vəˈdʒaɪnə/ noun [C] the passage in the body of a woman or female animal that connects the outer sex organs to the **womb** ▶ **pochwa**

vagrant /ˈveɪɡrənt/ noun [C] a person who has no home and no job, especially one who asks people for money ▶ **włóczęga**

vague /veɪɡ/ adj. **1** not clear or definite: *He was very vague about how much money he'd spent.* ◇ *a vague shape in the distance* ▶ (*wspomnienie itp.*) **mglisty**, **niewyraźny** **2** (used about a person) not thinking or understanding clearly: *She looked vague when I tried to explain.* Wyglądało na to, że nie pojmuje tego, co starałem się jej wytłumaczyć. ▶ **nie pojmujący**
■ **vagueness** noun [U] ▶ **nieprecyzyjność**, **nieświadomość**

vaguely /ˈveɪɡli/ adv. **1** in a way that is not clear; slightly: *Her name is vaguely familiar* (brzmi znajomo). ▶ **niewyraźnie**; **nieco** **2** without thinking about what is happening: *He smiled vaguely and walked away.* ▶ **nieprzytomnie**

vain /veɪn/ adj. **1** failing to produce the result you want: *She turned away* ***in a vain attempt to*** *hide her tears* (nadaremnie próbując ukryć łzy). ▶ (*wysiłek itp.*) **próżny** SYN **useless** **2** (used about a person) too proud of your own appearance, abilities, etc.: *He's so vain – he looks in every mirror he passes.* ▶ **próżny** ➲ noun **vanity**
■ **vainly** adv. ▶ **bezcelowo**, **bezskutecznie**
IDM **in vain** without success: *The firemen tried in vain to put out the fire.* ▶ **na próżno**

vale /veɪl/ noun [C] (used in place names and poetry) a valley: *the Vale of York* ▶ **dolina** ⓘ Tego słowa używa się tylko w nazwach miejsc i w poezji.

valedictory /ˌvælɪˈdɪktəri/ adj. [usually before a noun] (formal) connected with saying goodbye, especially at a formal occasion: *a valedictory speech* ▶ **pożegnalny**

valentine /ˈvæləntaɪn/ noun [C] **1** (also **'valentine card**) a card that you send, usually without putting your name on it, to sb you love ▶ **walentynka** **2** the person you send this card to ▶ **osoba otrzymująca walentynkę**

valiant /ˈvæliənt/ adj. (formal) full of courage and not afraid ▶ **mężny**
■ **valiantly** adv. ▶ **mężnie**

⚷ **valid** /ˈvælɪd/ adj. **1 valid (for sth)** legally or officially acceptable: *This passport is valid for one year only.* ▶ **ważny (mający moc prawną)** **2** based on what is logical or true; acceptable: *I could raise no valid objections to the plan.* ◇ *Jeff's making a perfectly valid point.* ▶ (*argument itp.*) **trafny**; **uzasadniony** OPP for both meanings **invalid**
■ **validity** /vəˈlɪdəti/ noun [U] ▶ **ważność**; **moc prawna**; **słuszność**

validate /ˈvælɪdeɪt/ verb [T] (formal) **1** to prove that sth is true: *to validate a theory* ▶ **potwierdzać** (*np. teorię*) OPP **invalidate** **2** to make sth legally or officially valid or acceptable: *to validate a contract* ▶ **uprawomocniać**, **nadawać ważność** OPP **invalidate** **3** to state officially that sth is useful and of an acceptable standard: *Check that their courses have been validated by a reputable organization.* ▶ **zatwierdzać**
■ **validation** /ˌvælɪˈdeɪʃn/ noun [C,U] ▶ **potwierdzenie**; **uprawomocnienie**, **nadanie ważności**; **zatwierdzenie**

⚷ **valley** /ˈvæli/ noun [C] the low land between two mountains or hills, which often has a river flowing through it ▶ **dolina**

valour (US **valor**) /ˈvælə(r)/ noun [U] (formal, old-fashioned) great courage, especially in war ▶ **męstwo** ⓘ Tego słowa używa się w starych, formalnych lub poetyckich tekstach.

⚷ **valuable** /ˈvæljuəbl/ adj. **1** very useful: *a valuable piece of information* ▶ **cenny** **2** worth a lot of money: *Is this ring valuable?* ▶ **cenny**

> Uwaga! Antonimem wyrazu **valuable** nie jest **invaluable**, który znaczy „bezcenny", ale **valueless** lub **worthless**.

valuables /ˈvæljuəblz/ noun [pl.] the small things that you own that are worth a lot of money, such as jewellery, etc.: *Please put your valuables in the hotel safe.* ▶ **kosztowności**

valuation /ˌvæljuˈeɪʃn/ noun [C] a professional judgement about how much money sth is worth ▶ **wycena**

⚷ **value**[1] /ˈvæljuː/ noun **1** [U,C] the amount of money that sth is worth: *The thieves stole goods with a total value of $10 000.* ◇ *to go up/down in value* ▶ **wartość** ➲ look at **face value** **2** [U] (Brit.) how much sth is worth compared with its price: *The hotel was* ***good/excellent value.*** ◇ *Package holidays give the best* ***value for money*** (są warte swojej ceny). ▶ **wartość** **3** [U] the importance of sth: *to be of great/little/no value to somebody* ◇ *This bracelet is of great* ***sentimental value*** *to me.* ▶ **wartość** **4** (**values**) [pl.] beliefs about what is the right and wrong way for people to behave; moral principles: *a return to traditional values* ◇ *Young people have a completely different* ***set of values*** *and expectations.* ▶ **wartości**

⚷ **value**[2] /ˈvæljuː/ verb [T] (**valuing**) **1 value sb/sth (as sth)** to think sb/sth is very important: *Sandra has always valued her independence.* ◇ *I really value her as a friend.* ▶ **cenić** **2** [usually passive] **value sth (at sth)** to decide the amount of money that sth is worth: *The house was valued at $150 000.* ▶ **wyceniać**

ˌvalue 'added tax noun [U] (abbr. **VAT**) (also **Vat**) /ˌviː eɪ ˈtiː; væt/ a tax on the increase in value of sth at each stage of its production ▶ **podatek VAT**

valueless /ˈvæljuːləs/ adj. without value or use ▶ **bezwartościowy** SYN **worthless** OPP **valuable** ➲ look at **invaluable**

valve /vælv/ noun [C] a device in a pipe or tube which controls the flow of air, liquid or gas, letting it move in one direction only: *a radiator valve* ◇ *the valve on a bicycle tyre* ▶ **zawór**, **wentyl** ➲ picture at **bicycle**

vampire /ˈvæmpaɪə(r)/ noun [C] (in stories) a dead person who comes out at night and drinks the blood of living people ▶ **wampi-r/rzyca**

⚷ **van** /væn/ noun [C] a road vehicle that is used for transporting things ▶ **furgon** ➲ picture at **lorry** ⓘ **Van** czy **lorry**? **Van** jest mniejszy niż **lorry** i ma dach. ➲ picture on **page A7**

vandal /ˈvændl/ noun [C] a person who damages sb else's property on purpose and for no reason ▶ **wandal**
■ **vandalism** /ˈvændəlɪzəm/ noun [U]: *acts of vandalism* ▶ **wandalizm** | **vandalize** (also **-ise**) /ˈvændəlaɪz/ verb [T, usually passive]: *All the phone boxes in this area have been vandalized.* ▶ **dewastować**, **niszczyć** ➲ note at **crime**

vanilla /vəˈnɪlə/ noun [U] a substance from a plant that is used for giving flavour to sweet food: *vanilla ice cream* ▶ **wanilia**

vanish /ˈvænɪʃ/ verb [I] **1** to disappear suddenly or in a way that you cannot explain: *When he turned round, the two men had* ***vanished without trace.*** ▶ **znikać** **2** to stop existing: *This species of plant is vanishing from our countryside.* ▶ **zanikać**

vanity /ˈvænəti/ noun [U] the quality of being too proud of your appearance or abilities ▶ **próżność, zarozumiałość** ➲ adjective **vain**

vantage point /ˈvɑːntɪdʒ pɔɪnt; US ˈvæn-/ noun [C] a place from which you have a good view of sth: (figurative) *From our modern vantage point, we can see why the Roman Empire collapsed.* ▶ **punkt obserwacyjny; punkt widzenia**

vapour (US **vapor**) /ˈveɪpə(r)/ noun [C,U] a mass of very small drops of liquid in the air, for example steam: *water vapour* ▶ **para**

variable /ˈveəriəbl; US also ˈvær-/ adj. not staying the same; often changing ▶ **zmienny**
■ **variability** /ˌveəriəˈbɪləti; US also ˌvær-/ noun [U] ▶ **zmienność**

variant /ˈveəriənt; US also ˈvær-/ noun [C] a slightly different form or type of sth ▶ **wariant**

⚷ **variation** /ˌveəriˈeɪʃn/ noun **1** [C,U] **(a) variation (in sth)** a change or difference in the amount or level of sth: *There was a lot of variation in the examination results.* Wyniki egzaminu były zróżnicowane. ◇ *There may be a slight variation in price from shop to shop.* ▶ **różnica 2** [C] **a variation (on/of sth)** a thing that is slightly different from another thing in the same general group: *All her films are just variations on a basic theme.* ▶ **wariant**

varicose vein /ˌværɪkəʊs ˈveɪn/ noun [C, usually pl.] a **vein**, especially one in the leg, which has become swollen and painful ▶ **żylak**

⚷ **varied** /ˈveərid; US also ˈvær-/ adj. having many different kinds of things or activities: *I try to make my classes as varied as possible.* ▶ **urozmaicony** ➲ look at **different**

⚷ **variety** /vəˈraɪəti/ noun (pl. **varieties**) **1** [sing.] **a variety (of sth)** a number of different types of the same thing: *There is a **wide variety** of dishes to choose from.* ◇ *You can take evening classes in a variety of subjects* (z różnych przedmiotów) *including photography, Spanish and computing.* ▶ **rozmaitość 2** [U] the quality of not being or doing the same all the time: *There's so much variety in my new job. I do something different every day!* ▶ **urozmaicenie 3** [C] **a variety (of sth)** a type of sth: *a new variety of apple called 'Perfection'* ▶ **odmiana, typ 4** (US **vaudeville** /ˈvɔːdəvɪl/) [U] a form of theatre or television entertainment that consists of a series of short performances, such as singing, dancing and funny acts: *a variety show* program rozrywkowy ◇ *a variety theatre* teatr rozrywki ▶ **wodewil**

⚷ **various** /ˈveəriəs; US also ˈvær-/ adj. several different: *I decided to leave London for various reasons.* ▶ **rozmaity, różny; wiele** ➲ look at **different**

varnish /ˈvɑːnɪʃ/ noun [U] a clear liquid that you paint onto hard surfaces, especially wood, to protect them and make them shine ▶ **lakier** ➲ look at **nail polish**
■ **varnish** verb [T] ▶ **lakierować**

⚷ **vary** /ˈveəri; US also ˈværi/ verb (**varying**; **varies**; pt, pp **varied**) **1** [I] **vary (in sth)** (used about a group of similar things) to be different from each other: *The hotel bedrooms vary in size from medium to very large.* ◇ *The experiments were carried out with **varying degrees of** success* (z mniejszym lub większym powodzeniem). ▶ **różnić się 2** [I] **vary (from ... to ...)** to be different or to change according to the situation, etc.: *The price of the holiday varies from £500 to £1200, depending on the time of year.* ▶ **zmieniać się, różnić się 3** [T] to make sth different by changing it often in some way: *I try to vary my work as much as possible so I don't get bored.* ▶ **urozmaicać**

vase /vɑːz; US veɪs; veɪz/ noun [C] a container that is used for holding cut flowers ▶ **wazon**

vasectomy /vəˈsektəmi/ noun [C] (pl. **vasectomies**) a medical operation to stop a man being able to have children ▶ **wycięcie nasieniowodu**

⚷ **vast** /vɑːst; US væst/ adj. extremely big: *a vast sum of money* ◇ *a vast country* ▶ **ogromny** SYN **huge**
■ **vastly** adv.: *a vastly improved traffic system* ▶ **ogromnie**

VAT = VALUE ADDED TAX: *prices include VAT*

vat /væt/ noun [C] a large container for holding liquids, especially in industrial processes: *distilling vats* ◇ *a vat of whisky* ▶ **kadź**

vaudeville = VARIETY (4)

vault¹ /vɔːlt/ noun [C] **1** a room with a strong door and thick walls in a bank, etc. that is used for keeping money and other valuable things safe ▶ **skarbiec 2** a room under a church where dead people are buried: *a family vault* ▶ **krypta 3** a high roof or ceiling in a church, etc., made from a number of **arches** joined together at the top ▶ **sklepienie**

vault² /vɔːlt/ verb [I,T] **vault (over) sth** to jump over or onto sth in one movement, using your hands or a pole to help you: *The boy vaulted over the wall.* ◇ *to pole vault* skok o tyczce ▶ **skakać** (*z podparciem rąk lub tyczki*)

VCR = VIDEO CASSETTE RECORDER

VD = VENEREAL DISEASE

VDU /ˌviː diː ˈjuː/ noun [C] **visual display unit**; a screen on which you can see information from a computer ▶ **monitor komputera**

veal /viːl/ noun [U] the meat from a **calf** ▶ **cielęcina** ➲ note at **meat**

veer /vɪə(r)/ verb [I] (used about vehicles) to change direction suddenly: *The car veered across the road and hit a tree.* ▶ **nagle zmieniać kierunek jazdy**

veg¹ (Brit., informal) = VEGETABLE: *a fruit and veg stall*

veg² /vedʒ/ verb (**vegging**; **vegged**)
PHR V **veg out** (Brit., slang) to relax and do nothing that needs thought or effort: *I'm just going to go home and veg out in front of the telly.* ▶ **obijać się**

vegan /ˈviːɡən/ noun [C] a person who does not eat meat or any other animal products at all ▶ **wegan-in/ka** ➲ look at **vegetarian**
■ **vegan** adj. ▶ **wegański**

⚷ **vegetable** /ˈvedʒtəbl/ (Brit., informal **veg** /vedʒ/, **veggie** /ˈvedʒi/) noun [C] a plant or part of a plant that we eat: *Potatoes, beans and onions are all vegetables.* ◇ *vegetable soup* ▶ **jarzyna, warzywo**

vegetarian /ˌvedʒəˈteəriən/ (Brit., informal **veggie** /ˈvedʒi/) noun [C] a person who does not eat meat or fish ▶ **wegetarian-in/ka** ➲ look at **vegan**
■ **vegetarian** adj.: *a vegetarian cookery book* ▶ **wegetariański**

vegetation /ˌvedʒəˈteɪʃn/ noun [U] (formal) plants in general; all the plants that are found in a particular place: *tropical vegetation* ▶ **wegetacja**

veggie noun [C] (Brit., informal) **1** = VEGETARIAN **2** = VEGETABLE
■ **veggie** adj.: *a veggie burger* ▶ **wegetariański**

vehement /ˈviːəmənt/ adj. showing very strong (often negative) feelings, especially anger: *a vehement attack on the government* ▶ **gwałtowny**

⚷ **vehicle** /ˈviːəkl/ noun [C] **1** something which transports people or things from place to place, especially on land, for example cars, bicycles, lorries and buses: *Are you the owner of this vehicle?* ▶ **pojazd 2** something which is used for communicating particular ideas or opinions: *This newspaper has become a vehicle for Conservative opinion.* ▶ **nośnik, organ**

veil /veɪl/ noun [C] a piece of thin material for covering the head and face of a woman: *a bridal veil* ▶ **welon, woalka**

vein /veɪn/ noun **1** [C] one of the tubes which carry blood from all parts of your body to your heart ▶ **żyła** ➲ look at

V

artery **2** [sing., U] a particular style or quality: *After a humorous beginning, the programme continued in a more serious vein.* ▶ **nastrój**

Velcro™ /ˈvelkrəʊ/ noun [U] a material for fastening parts of clothes together. **Velcro** is made of **nylon** and is used in small pieces, one rough and one smooth, that can stick together and be pulled apart. ▶ **rzep** (*rodzaj zapięcia*) ➲ picture at **button**

velocity /vəˈlɒsəti/ noun [U] (technical) the speed at which sth moves ▶ **prędkość** ℹ **Velocity** to termin techniczny. W języku codziennym używa się **speed**.

velour /vəˈlʊə(r)/ noun [U] a type of silk or cotton cloth with a thick soft surface like **velvet** ▶ **welur**

velvet /ˈvelvɪt/ noun [U] a type of cloth made of cotton or other material, with a soft thick surface on one side only: *black velvet trousers* ▶ **aksamit**

vendetta /venˈdetə/ noun [C] a serious argument or disagreement between two people or groups which lasts for a long time ▶ **wendeta**

vending machine /ˈvendɪŋ məʃiːn/ noun [C] a machine from which you can buy drinks, cigarettes, etc. by putting coins in it ▶ **automat** (*np. z napojami*)

vendor /ˈvendə(r)/ noun [C] (formal) a person who is selling sth ▶ **sprzedaw-ca/czyni** ➲ look at **purchaser**

veneer /vəˈnɪə(r)/ noun **1** [C,U] a thin layer of wood or plastic that is stuck onto the surface of a cheaper material, especially wood, to give it a better appearance ▶ **fornir 2** [sing.] (formal) **a veneer (of sth)** a part of sb's behaviour or of a situation which hides what it is really like underneath: *a thin veneer of politeness* ▶ **warstewka** (*np. ogłady, grzeczności*)

venerable /ˈvenərəbl/ adj. (formal) **venerable** people or things deserve respect because they are old, important, wise, etc.: *a venerable old man* ◇ *a venerable institution* ▶ **czcigodny**

venerate /ˈvenəreɪt/ verb [T] **venerate sb/sth (as sth)** (formal) to have and show a lot of respect for sb/sth, especially sb/sth that is considered to be holy or very important ▶ **czcić** SYN **revere**

■ **veneration** /ˌvenəˈreɪʃn/ noun [U]: *The relics were objects of veneration.* ▶ **cześć**

venereal disease /vəˌnɪəriəl dɪˈziːz/ noun [C, U] (abbr. **VD** /ˌviː ˈdiː/) a disease that is caught by having sex with an infected person ▶ **choroba weneryczna**

venetian blind /vəˌniːʃn ˈblaɪnd/ noun [C] a covering for a window that is made of horizontal pieces of flat plastic, etc. which can be turned to let in as much light as you want ▶ **żaluzja** (*z poziomych listewek*)

vengeance /ˈvendʒəns/ noun [U] (formal) **vengeance (on sb)** the act of punishing or harming sb in return for sth bad they have done to you, your friends or family: *He felt a terrible desire for vengeance on the people who had destroyed his career.* ▶ **zemsta** ➲ look at **revenge**

IDM **with a vengeance** to a greater degree than is expected or usual: *After a week of good weather winter returned with a vengeance.* ▶ **z podwójną siłą**

vengeful /ˈvendʒfl/ adj. (formal) showing a desire to punish sb who has harmed you ▶ **mściwy**

■ **vengefully** /-fəli/ adv. ▶ **mściwie**

venison /ˈvenɪsn/ noun [U] the meat from a **deer** ▶ **dziczyzna** ➲ note at **deer**

venom /ˈvenəm/ noun [U] **1** the poisonous liquid that some snakes, spiders, etc. produce when they bite or sting you ▶ **jad 2** extreme anger or hatred and a desire to hurt sb: *a look of pure venom* ▶ **jad**

venomous /ˈvenəməs/ adj. **1** (used about a snake, etc.) producing **venom** ▶ **jadowity 2** (formal) full of bitter feeling or hatred: *a venomous look* ◇ *a venomous attack on his political enemies* ▶ (*przen.*) **jadowity, złośliwy**

■ **venomously** adv.: *She glared at him venomously.* ▶ (*przen.*) **jadowicie**

vent /vent/ noun [C] an opening in the wall of a room or machine which allows air to come in, and smoke, steam or smells to go out: *an air vent* ◇ *a heating vent* ▶ **otwór wentylacyjny, kanał, wylot**

ventilate /ˈventɪleɪt/ verb [T] to allow air to move freely in and out of a room or building: *The office is badly ventilated.* ▶ **wietrzyć**

■ **ventilation** /ˌventɪˈleɪʃn/ noun [U]: *There was no ventilation in the room except for one tiny window.* ▶ **przewietrzenie**

ventilator /ˈventɪleɪtə(r)/ noun [C] **1** a device or an opening for letting fresh air come into a room ▶ **wentylator, wywietrznik 2** a piece of equipment that helps sb to breathe by sending air in and out of their lungs: *He was put on a ventilator.* ▶ **respirator**

ventricle /ˈventrɪkl/ noun [C] **1** either of the two lower spaces in the heart that **pump** blood to the **lungs** or around the body ▶ **komora** (*serca*) **2** any hollow space in the body, especially one of four main hollow spaces in the brain ▶ **komora** (*zwł. w mózgu*)

⚷ **venture¹** /ˈventʃə(r)/ noun [C] a project which is new and possibly dangerous, because you cannot be sure that it will succeed: *a business venture* ▶ **(nowe, często ryzykowne) przedsięwzięcie**

⚷ **venture²** /ˈventʃə(r)/ verb [I] to do sth or go somewhere new and dangerous, when you are not sure what will happen: *He ventured out into the storm* (odważył się wyjść w czasie burzy) *in a thick coat, hat and scarf.* ◇ *The company has decided to venture into* (zaryzykować) *computer production as well as design.* ▶ **ponosić ryzyko**

venue /ˈvenjuː/ noun [C] the place where people meet for an organized event, for example a concert or a sports event ▶ **miejsce** (*np. koncertu*)

Venus /ˈviːnəs/ noun [sing.] the planet that is second in order from the sun and nearest to the earth ▶ **Wenus**

veranda (also **verandah**) /vəˈrændə/ (US also **porch**) noun [C] a platform joined to the side of a house, with a roof and floor but no outside wall ▶ **weranda** ➲ look at **balcony, patio, terrace**

verb /vɜːb/ noun [C] a word or group of words that is used to indicate that sth happens or exists, for example *bring, happen, be, do*. ▶ **czasownik** ➲ look at **phrasal verb**

verbal /ˈvɜːbl/ adj. (formal) **1** connected with words, or the use of words: *verbal skills* ▶ **werbalny 2** spoken, not written: *a verbal agreement/warning* ▶ **ustny**

■ **verbally** /ˈvɜːbəli/ adv. ▶ **ustnie; werbalnie**

verbalize (also -ise) /ˈvɜːbəlaɪz/ verb [I,T] (formal) to express your feelings or ideas in words: *He's a real genius but he has difficulty verbalizing his ideas.* ▶ **wyrażać słowami** SYN **put sth into words** at **put**

verbatim /vɜːˈbeɪtɪm/ adj. exactly as spoken or written; word for word ▶ **dosłowny**

■ **verbatim** adv. ▶ **słowo w słowo**

verdict /ˈvɜːdɪkt/ noun [C] **1** the decision that is made by the **jury** in a court of law, which states if a person is guilty of a crime or not: *The jury* ***returned a verdict*** *of 'not guilty'* (wydała werdykt „niewinny"). ◇ *Has the jury* ***reached a verdict*** (uzgodniła werdykt)? ▶ **werdykt** ➲ note at **court 2 a verdict (on sb/sth)** a decision that you make or an opinion that you give after testing sth or considering sth carefully: *The general verdict was that the restaurant was too expensive.* ▶ **sąd**

verge¹ /vɜːdʒ/ noun [C] (Brit.) the narrow piece of land at the side of a road, railway line, etc. that is usually covered in grass ▶ **pobocze drogi**

IDM **on the verge of sth/doing sth** very near to doing sth, or to sth happening: *He was on the verge of a nervous breakdown.* ◇ *Scientists are on the verge of discovering a cure.* ▶ **u progu, na skraju czegoś**

verge² /vɜːdʒ/ verb
PHR V **verge on sth** to be very close to an extreme state or condition: *What they are doing verges on the illegal.* ▶ **graniczyć z czymś, zbliżać się do czegoś**

verify /ˈverɪfaɪ/ verb [T] (**verifying**; **verifies**; pt, pp **verified**) (formal) to check or state that sth is true: *to verify a statement* ▶ **sprawdzać**
■ **verification** /ˌverɪfɪˈkeɪʃn/ noun [U] ▶ **sprawdzenie**

veritable /ˈverɪtəbl/ adj. [only before a noun] (formal) (used to emphasize that sb/sth can be compared to sb/sth else that is more exciting, more impressive, etc.): *The meal he cooked was a veritable banquet.* ▶ **prawdziwy, istny**

vermin /ˈvɜːmɪn/ noun [pl.] small wild animals (for example mice) that carry disease and destroy plants and food ▶ **szkodniki**

vernacular /vəˈnækjələ(r)/ noun [C] (**the vernacular**) [sing.] the language spoken in a particular area or by a particular group, especially one that is not the official or written language ▶ **język miejscowy, dialekt; żargon**

versatile /ˈvɜːsətaɪl; US -sətl/ adj. **1** (used about a person) able to do many different things: *Ela is so versatile! She can dance, sing, act and play the guitar!* ▶ **wszechstronny 2** (used about an object) having many different uses: *a versatile tool that drills, cuts or polishes* ▶ **uniwersalny**

verse /vɜːs/ noun **1** [U] writing arranged in lines which have a definite rhythm and often **rhyme**: *He wrote his valentine's message in verse.* ▶ **wiersz** SYN **poetry 2** [C] (abbr. **v**) a group of lines which form one part of a song or poem: *This song has five verses.* ▶ **zwrotka**; **strofa** ➲ look at **chorus**

⚷ **version** /ˈvɜːʃn; -ʒn/ noun [C] **1** a thing which has the same basic content as sth else but which is presented in a different way: *Have you heard the live version of this song?* ▶ **wersja 2** sb's description of sth that has happened: *The two drivers gave very different versions of the accident.* ▶ **wersja**

versus /ˈvɜːsəs/ prep. **1** (abbr. **v**; **vs**) (used in sport for showing that two teams or people are playing against each other): *England versus Argentina* ▶ **przeciw**, **kontra 2** (used for showing that two ideas or things that are opposite to each other, especially when you are trying to choose one of them): *It's a question of quality versus price.* ▶ **w opozycji do czegoś**

vertebra /ˈvɜːtɪbrə/ noun [C] (pl. **vertebrae** /-breɪ; -briː/) any of the small bones that are connected together in a row down the middle of your back ▶ (*med.*) **kręg** ➲ picture at **body** ➲ look at **spine**

vertebrate /ˈvɜːtɪbrət/ noun [C] an animal with a backbone ▶ (*biol.*) **kręgowiec**

⚷ **vertical** /ˈvɜːtɪkl/ adj. going straight up at an angle of 90° from the ground: *a vertical line* ◇ *The cliff was almost vertical.* ▶ **pionowy** ➲ look at **horizontal**, **perpendicular**
■ **vertically** /-kli/ adv. ▶ **pionowo**

vertigo /ˈvɜːtɪɡəʊ/ noun [U] the feeling of **dizziness** and fear, and of losing your balance, that is caused in some people when they look down from a very high place ▶ **zawroty głowy** (*spowodowane lękiem wysokości*)

verve /vɜːv/ noun [U, sing.] energy, excitement or enthusiasm: *It was a performance of verve and vitality.* ▶ **werwa** SYN **gusto**

⚷ **very** /ˈveri/ adv. (abbr. **v**) (used with an adjective or adverb to make it stronger): *very small* ◇ *very slowly* ◇ *I don't like milk very much.* ◇ *'Are you hungry?' 'Not very* (niezbyt).' ▶ **bardzo**

Very używa się z przymiotnikami w stopniu najwyższym: *the very best/youngest*. Natomiast z przymiotnikami w stopniu wyższym używa się **much** lub **very much**: *much/very much better* ◇ *much/very much younger*.

IDM **very well** (used for showing that you agree to do sth): *Very well, Mrs Dawson, we'll replace your shoes with a new pair.* ▶ **tak jest**, **zgoda**
■ **very** adj. (used to emphasize a noun): *We climbed to the very top* (na sam szczyt) *of the mountain.* ◇ *You're the very person* (dokładnie tą osobą) *I wanted to talk to.*

vessel /ˈvesl/ noun [C] **1** (formal) a ship or large boat ▶ **statek**, **okręt 2** (old-fashioned) a container for liquids, for example a bottle, cup or bowl: *ancient drinking vessels* ▶ **naczynie**

vest /vest/ noun [C] **1** (US **undershirt** /ˈʌndəʃɜːt/) a piece of clothing that you wear under your other clothes, on the top part of your body ▶ **podkoszulek** ➲ picture on **page A1**
2 (US) = WAISTCOAT

vested interest /ˌvestɪd ˈɪntrest/ noun [C] a strong and often secret reason for doing sth that will bring you an advantage of some kind, for example more money or power ▶ **żywotny, często skrywany interes**

vestige /ˈvestɪdʒ/ noun [C] a small part of sth that is left after the rest of it has gone: *the last vestige of the old system* ▶ **pozostałość** SYN **trace**

vet¹ /vet/ (also formal **ˈveterinary surgeon**; US **veterinarian** /ˌvetərɪˈneəriən/) noun [C] a doctor for animals: *We took the cat to the vet/to the vet's.* ▶ **weterynarz** ➲ note at **pet**

vet² /vet/ verb [T] (**vetting**; **vetted**) to do careful and secret checks before deciding if sb/sth can be accepted or not: *All new employees at the Ministry of Defence are carefully vetted.* ▶ **sprawdzać wnikliwie** (*czyjąś przeszłość itp.*)

veteran /ˈvetərən/ noun [C] **1** a person who has very long experience of a particular job or activity ▶ **weteran 2** a person who has served in the army, navy or air force, especially during a war ▶ **kombatant/ka**

veterinarian (US) = VET¹

veterinary /ˈvetnri; ˈvetrənəri; US ˈvetərəneri/ adj. [only before a noun] connected with the medical treatment of sick or injured animals: *a veterinary practice* ◇ *a veterinary surgeon* weterynarz ▶ **weterynaryjny** ➲ look at **vet**

ˈveterinary surgeon (formal) = VET¹

veto /ˈviːtəʊ/ verb [T] (**vetoing**; **vetoes**; pt, pp **vetoed**) to refuse to give official permission for an action or plan, when other people have agreed to it: *The Prime Minister vetoed the proposal to reduce taxation.* ▶ **zakładać weto**
■ **veto** noun [C,U] (pl. **vetoes**) **1** the official power to refuse permission for an action or a plan ▶ **sprzeciw 2** the act of vetoing on a particular occasion: *the right of veto* ▶ **weto**

vexed /vekst/ adj. causing difficulty, worry, and a lot of discussion: *the vexed question of our growing prison population* ▶ (*pytanie*) **niewygodny**, (*problem*) **stale powracający**

⚷ **via** /ˈvaɪə/ prep. **1** going through a place: *We flew from Paris to Sydney via Bangkok.* ▶ **przez** (*wymienioną miejscowość*) **2** by means of sth; using sth: *These pictures come to you via our satellite link.* ▶ **poprzez**

viable /ˈvaɪəbl/ adj. that can be done; that will be successful: *I'm afraid your idea is not commercially viable.* ▶ **rokujący powodzenie**
■ **viability** /ˌvaɪəˈbɪləti/ noun [U] ▶ **czynnik rokujący powodzenie**

viaduct /ˈvaɪədʌkt/ noun [C] a long, high bridge which carries a railway or road across a valley ▶ **wiadukt**

V

vibes /vaɪbz/ noun [pl.] (also **vibe** [sing.]) (informal) a mood or an atmosphere produced by a particular person, thing or place: ***good/bad vibes*** ◇ *The vibes weren't right.* ▶ **atmosfera**

vibrant /ˈvaɪbrənt/ adj. **1** full of life and energy: *a vibrant city/atmosphere/personality* ▶ **tętniący życiem, entuzjastyczny, bardzo żywy** SYN **exciting** **2** (used about colours) bright and strong ▶ **żywy**

vibrate /vaɪˈbreɪt/ verb [I] to make continuous very small and fast movements from side to side: *When a guitar string vibrates it makes a sound.* ▶ **wibrować**
■ **vibration** /vaɪˈbreɪʃn/ noun [C,U] ▶ **drganie, wibracja**

vicar /ˈvɪkə(r)/ noun [C] a priest of the Church of England. A **vicar** looks after a church and its **parish**. ▶ **proboszcz** ➲ look at **minister, priest**

vicarage /ˈvɪkərɪdʒ/ noun [C] the house where a **vicar** lives ▶ **plebania**

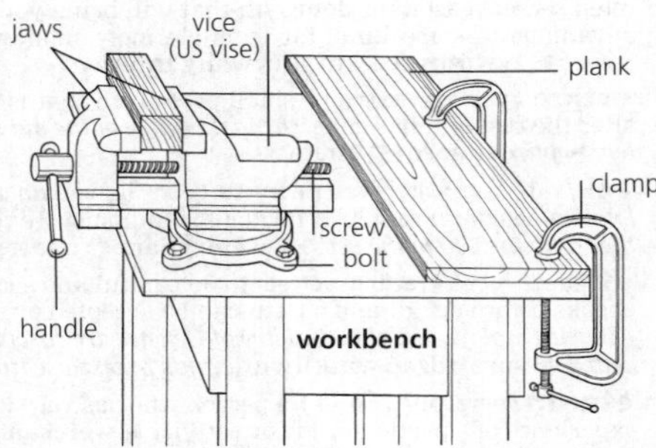

vice /vaɪs/ noun **1** [U] criminal activities involving sex or drugs ▶ **występek, rozpusta** **2** [C] a moral weakness or bad habit: *My only vice is smoking.* ◇ *Greed and envy are terrible vices.* ▶ **wada** ➲ look at **virtue** **3** (US **vise**) [C] a tool that you use to hold a piece of wood, metal, etc. firmly while you are working on it: (figurative) *He held my arm in a vice-like grip.* ▶ **imadło**

vice- /vaɪs/ [in compounds] having a position second in importance to the position mentioned: *Vice-President* ◇ *the vice-captain* ▶ **wice-**

vice versa /ˌvaɪs ˈvɜːsə; ˌvaɪsi/ adv. in the opposite way to what has just been said: *Anna ordered fish and Maria chicken – or was it vice versa?* ▶ **(i) odwrotnie**

vicinity /vəˈsɪnəti/ noun
IDM **in the vicinity (of sth)** (formal) in the surrounding area: *There's no bank in the immediate vicinity.* ▶ **w sąsiedztwie (czegoś), w pobliżu (czegoś)**

vicious /ˈvɪʃəs/ adj. **1** cruel; done in order to hurt sb/sth: *a vicious attack* ▶ **okrutny; zjadliwy** **2** (used about an animal) dangerous; likely to hurt sb: *a vicious dog* ▶ **niebezpieczny**
■ **viciously** adv. ▶ **okrutnie; zjadliwie**
IDM **a vicious circle** a situation in which one problem leads to another and the new problem makes the first problem worse ▶ **błędne koło**

🔑 **victim** /ˈvɪktɪm/ noun [C] a person or an animal that is injured, killed or hurt by sb/sth: *a murder victim* ◇ *The children are often the innocent victims of a divorce.* ▶ **ofiara**

victimize (also **-ise**) /ˈvɪktɪmaɪz/ verb [T] to punish or make sb suffer unfairly ▶ **gnębić, stosować represje**
■ **victimization** (also **-isation**) /ˌvɪktɪmaɪˈzeɪʃn; US -məˈz-/ noun [U] ▶ **tyranizowanie, stosowanie represji, gnębienie**

victor /ˈvɪktə(r)/ noun [C] (formal) the person who wins a game, competition, battle, etc. ▶ **zwycię-zca/żczyni**

Victorian /vɪkˈtɔːriən/ adj. **1** connected with the time of the British queen Victoria (1837–1901): *Victorian houses* ▶ **wiktoriański** **2** having attitudes that were typical in the time of Queen Victoria ▶ **wiktoriański**
■ **Victorian** noun [C] ▶ **osoba żyjąca w epoce wiktoriańskiej**

🔑 **victory** /ˈvɪktəri/ noun [C,U] (pl. **victories**) success in winning a battle, game, competition, etc.: *Keane led his team to victory in the final.* ▶ **zwycięstwo**
■ **victorious** /vɪkˈtɔːriəs/ adj.: *the victorious team* ▶ **zwycięski**
IDM **romp home/to victory** → ROMP

🔑 **video** /ˈvɪdiəʊ/ noun (pl. **videos**) **1** (also ˌ**video casˈsette**; **videotape** /ˈvɪdiəʊteɪp/) [C] a tape used for recording moving pictures and sound; a plastic case containing this tape: *Would you like to see the video we made on holiday?* ◇ *to rent a video* ◇ *a video (rental) shop* wypożyczalnia kaset wideo ▶ **wideokaseta** **2** = VIDEO CASSETTE RECORDER **3** [U] the system of recording moving pictures and sound using a camera, and showing them with a **video cassette recorder** and a TV: *We recorded the wedding* ***on video.*** ▶ **wideo**
■ **video** (also **videotape**) verb [T] (**videoing**; **videos**; pt, pp **videoed**): *We hired a camera to video the school play.* ▶ **rejestrować na wideo**

ˌ**video casˈsette recorder** (also **video**; ˈ**video recorder**) noun [C] (abbr. **VCR** /ˌviː siː ˈɑː(r)/) a machine that is connected to a TV on which you can record or play back a film or TV programme ▶ **magnetowid**

videoconferencing /ˈvɪdiəʊkɒnfərənsɪŋ/ noun [U] a system that people in different parts of the world can use to have a meeting, by watching and listening to each other using video screens ▶ **wideokonferencja**

ˈ**video game** noun [C] a game in which you press buttons to control and move images on a screen ▶ **gra komputerowa/wideo**

videotape noun = VIDEO (1)
■ **videotape** verb = VIDEO: *a videotaped interview*

vie /vaɪ/ verb [I,T] (**vying** /ˈvaɪɪŋ/, pt, pp **vied**) **vie (with sb) (for sth)** (formal) to compete strongly with sb in order to obtain or achieve sth: *She was surrounded by men all vying for her attention.* ◇ *a row of restaurants vying with each other for business* ◇ *Screaming fans vied to get closer to their idol.* ▶ **rywalizować (z kimś) (o coś)** SYN **compete**

🔑 **view**[1] /vjuː/ noun **1** [C] **a view (about/on sth)** an opinion or a particular way of thinking about sth: *He expressed the view that standards were falling.* ◇ ***In my view*** (moim zdaniem), *she has done nothing wrong.* ◇ *She has* ***strong views*** *on the subject.* ▶ **pogląd, opinia** **2** [U] the ability to see sth or to be seen from a particular place: *The garden was hidden from view behind a high wall.* ◇ *to come into view* ◇ *to disappear from view* ▶ **pole widzenia, widok** **3** [C] what you can see from a particular place: *There are* ***breathtaking views*** *from the top of the mountain.* ◇ *a room with* ***a sea view*** (z widokiem na morze) ▶ **widok** ➲ note at **scenery**
IDM **have, etc. sth in view** (formal) to have sth as a plan or idea in your mind ▶ **mieć coś na celu**
in full view (of sb/sth) → FULL[1]
in view of sth because of sth; as a result of sth: *In view of her apology we decided to take no further action.* ▶ **ze względu na coś**
point of view → POINT[1]
with a view to doing sth (formal) with the aim or intention of doing sth ▶ **mając na celu zrobienie czegoś**

🔑 **view²** /vjuː/ verb [T] (formal) **1 view sth (as sth)** to think about sth in a particular way: *She viewed holidays as a waste of time.* ▶ **uważać (coś za coś) 2** to watch or look at sth: *Viewed from this angle, the building looks much taller than it really is.* ▶ **oglądać, patrzeć**

viewer /ˈvjuːə(r)/ noun [C] a person who watches TV ▶ **telewidz**

viewpoint /ˈvjuːpɔɪnt/ noun [C] a way of looking at a situation; an opinion: *Let's look at this problem from the customer's viewpoint.* ▶ **punkt widzenia** SYN **point of view**

vigil /ˈvɪdʒɪl/ noun [C,U] a period when you stay awake all night for a special purpose: *All night she* ***kept vigil*** *over* (czuwała nad) *the sick child.* ▶ **czuwanie całonocne**

vigilant /ˈvɪdʒɪlənt/ adj. (formal) careful and looking out for danger ▶ **czujny**
■ **vigilance** noun [U]: *the need for constant vigilance* ▶ **czujność**

vigilante /ˌvɪdʒɪˈlænti/ noun [C] a member of a group of people who try to prevent crime or punish criminals in a community, especially because they believe the police are not doing this ▶ **członek (nieoficjalnej) straży obywatelskiej**

vigour (US **vigor**) /ˈvɪɡə(r)/ noun [U] strength or energy: *After the break we started work again with renewed vigour.* ▶ **energia**
■ **vigorous** /ˈvɪɡərəs/ adj.: *vigorous exercise* ▶ **energiczny** | **vigorously** adv. ▶ **energicznie**

Viking /ˈvaɪkɪŋ/ noun [C] a member of a race of Scandinavian people who attacked and sometimes settled in parts of NW Europe, including Britain, in the 8th to the 11th centuries ▶ **wiking**

vile /vaɪl/ adj. very bad or unpleasant: *She's in a vile mood.* ◇ *a vile smell* ▶ **parszywy, ohydny** SYN **terrible**

villa /ˈvɪlə/ noun [C] **1** a house that people rent and stay in on holiday ▶ **letni dom do wynajęcia 2** a large house in the country, especially in Southern Europe ▶ **duży dom letni na wsi** (*zwł. na południu Europy*)

🔑 **village** /ˈvɪlɪdʒ/ noun **1** [C] a group of houses with other buildings, for example a shop, school, etc., in a country area. A village is smaller than a town: *a small fishing village* ◇ *the village shop* ▶ **wieś 2** [sing., with sing. or pl. verb] all the people who live in a village: *All the village is/are taking part in the carnival.* ▶ **wieś** (*mieszkańcy wsi*)

villager /ˈvɪlɪdʒə(r)/ noun [C] a person who lives in a village ▶ **osoba mieszkająca we wsi**

villain /ˈvɪlən/ noun [C] **1** an evil person, especially in a book or play: *In most of his films he has played villains, but in this one he's a good guy.* ▶ **czarny charakter** ➲ look at **hero 2** (informal) a criminal: *The police caught the villains who robbed the bank.* ▶ **zbir, łot-r/rzyca**

vindicate /ˈvɪndɪkeɪt/ verb [T] (formal) **1** to prove that sth is true or that you were right to do sth, especially when other people had a different opinion: *I have every confidence that this decision will be fully vindicated.* ▶ **dowodzić słuszności 2** to prove that sb is not guilty when they have been accused of doing sth wrong or illegal: *New evidence emerged, vindicating him completely.* ▶ **dowodzić czyjejś niewinności**

vindictive /vɪnˈdɪktɪv/ adj. wanting or trying to hurt sb without good reason: *a vindictive comment/person* ▶ **mściwy, złośliwy**
■ **vindictiveness** noun [U] ▶ **mściwość, złośliwość**

vine /vaɪn/ noun [C] the climbing plant that **grapes** grow on ▶ **winorośl**

vinegar /ˈvɪnɪɡə(r)/ noun [U] a liquid with a strong sharp taste that is made from wine. **Vinegar** is often mixed with oil and put onto salads. ▶ **ocet**

vineyard /ˈvɪnjəd/ noun [C] a piece of land where **grapes** are grown in order to produce wine ▶ **winnica**
ℹ Zwróć uwagę na inną wymowę tego słowa w porównaniu z rzeczownikiem **vine**.

vintage¹ /ˈvɪntɪdʒ/ noun [C] the wine that was made in a particular year: *1999 was an excellent vintage.* ▶ **rocznik** (*wina*)

vintage² /ˈvɪntɪdʒ/ adj. [only before a noun] **1** (used about wine) that was produced in a particular year and district: *a bottle of vintage champagne* ▶ **danego rocznika i obszaru 2** of very high quality: *a vintage performance by Robert De Niro* ▶ **doskonały**

vinyl /ˈvaɪnl/ noun [C,U] a strong plastic that can bend easily and is used to cover walls, floors, furniture, books, etc. ▶ **winyl**

viola /viˈəʊlə/ noun [C] a musical instrument with strings, that you hold under your chin and play with a **bow**: *A viola is like a large violin.* ▶ **altówka** ➲ note at **music**, **piano**

violate /ˈvaɪəleɪt/ verb [T] (formal) **1** to break a rule, an agreement, etc.: *to violate a peace treaty* ▶ **naruszać, gwałcić 2** to not respect sth; to spoil or damage sth: *to violate somebody's privacy/rights* ▶ **zakłócać, naruszać**
■ **violation** /ˌvaɪəˈleɪʃn/ noun [C,U]: *(a) violation of human rights* ▶ **naruszenie**

🔑 **violence** /ˈvaɪələns/ noun [U] **1** behaviour which harms or damages sb/sth physically: *They threatened to* ***use violence*** *if we didn't give them the money.* ◇ *an* ***act of violence*** ▶ **przemoc, gwałtowne zachowanie 2** great force or energy: *the violence of the storm* ▶ **gwałtowność, pasja**

🔑 **violent** /ˈvaɪələnt/ adj. **1** using physical strength to hurt or kill sb; caused by this behaviour: *The demonstration started peacefully but later turned violent.* ◇ *a violent crime/death* ▶ **brutalny, gwałtowny; zadany przemocą 2** very strong and impossible to control: *a violent collision* ◇ *a violent storm* ◇ *He has a violent temper* (wybuchowy charakter). ▶ **gwałtowny, nieokiełznany**
■ **violently** adv.: *The ground shook violently and buildings collapsed in the earthquake.* ▶ **gwałtownie, niepohamowanie; brutalnie**

violet /ˈvaɪələt/ noun **1** [C] a small plant that grows wild or in gardens and has purple or white flowers and a pleasant smell ▶ **fiołek 2** [U] a bluish-purple colour ▶ **kolor fioletowy**
■ **violet** adj. ▶ **fioletowy**

violin /ˌvaɪəˈlɪn/ noun [C] a musical instrument with strings, that you hold under your chin and play with a **bow** ▶ **skrzypce** ➲ note at **music**, **piano**
■ **violinist** noun [C] a person who plays the violin ▶ **skrzy-pek/paczka**

VIP /ˌviː aɪ ˈpiː/ abbr. (informal) **very important person**: *the VIP lounge at the airport* ◇ *to give someone the VIP treatment* przyjąć kogoś z honorami należnymi VIP-owi ▶ **VIP**

viral /ˈvaɪrəl/ adj. like or caused by a virus: ***a viral infection*** ◇ ***viral marketing*** ▶ **wirusowy**

virgin¹ /ˈvɜːdʒɪn/ noun [C] a person who has never had sex ▶ **dziewica, prawiczek**

virgin² /ˈvɜːdʒɪn/ adj. that has not yet been used, touched, damaged, etc.: *virgin forest* ▶ **dziewiczy**

virginity /vəˈdʒɪnəti/ noun [U] the state of never having had sex: *to lose your virginity* ▶ **dziewictwo**

Virgo /ˈvɜːɡəʊ/ noun [C,U] (pl. **Virgos**) the 6th sign of the **zodiac**, the **Virgin**; a person born under this sign: *I'm a Virgo* ▶ **Panna; zodiakalna Panna**

virile /ˈvɪraɪl; US -rəl/ adj. (used about a man) strong and having great sexual energy ▶ **męski, jurny**

V

virility /vəˈrɪləti/ noun [U] a man's sexual power and energy ▶ **męskość**

virtual /ˈvɜːtʃuəl/ adj. [only before a noun] **1** being almost or nearly sth: *The country is in a state of virtual civil war.* ▶ **faktyczny 2** made to appear to exist by using a computer: *virtual reality* wirtualna rzeczywistość ▶ **wirtualny**

■ **virtually** /-ʃuəli/ adv.: *The building is virtually finished* (prawie skończony). ▶ **prawie (że)**

virtue /ˈvɜːtʃuː/ noun **1** [U] behaviour which shows high moral standards: *to lead a life of virtue* (cnotliwe życie) ▶ **cnota** SYN **goodness 2** [C] a good quality or habit: *Patience is a great virtue.* ▶ **zaleta** ➲ look at **vice 3** [C,U] **the virtue (of sth/of being/doing sth)** an advantage or a useful quality of sth: *This new material **has the virtue** of being* (ma tę zaletę, że jest) *strong as well as very light.* ▶ **zaleta**

IDM **by virtue of sth** (formal) by means of sth or because of sth ▶ **z powodu czegoś, z racji czegoś**

virtuoso /ˌvɜːtʃuˈəʊsəʊ; -ˈəʊzəʊ/ noun [C] (pl. **virtuosos** or **virtuosi** /-siː; -ziː/) a person who is extremely skilful at sth, especially playing a musical instrument ▶ **wirtuoz/ka**

virtuous /ˈvɜːtʃuəs/ adj. behaving in a morally good way ▶ **cnotliwy, zacny**

virulent /ˈvɪrələnt; -rjəl-/ adj. **1** (used about a poison or a disease) very strong and dangerous: *a particularly virulent form of influenza* ▶ **bardzo silny; złośliwy 2** (formal) very strong and full of anger: *a virulent attack on the leader* ▶ **jadowity**

⚷ **virus** /ˈvaɪrəs/ noun [C] **1** a living thing, too small to be seen without a **microscope**, that causes disease in people, animals and plants: *HIV, the virus that can cause AIDS* ◇ *to catch a virus* ▶ **wirus** ➲ look at **bacteria**, **germ 2** instructions that are put into a computer program in order to stop it working properly and destroy information ▶ **wirus komputerowy**

visa /ˈviːzə/ noun [C] an official mark or piece of paper that shows you are allowed to enter, leave or travel through a country: *His passport was full of visa stamps.* ◇ *a tourist/work/student visa* ▶ **wiza**

viscount /ˈvaɪkaʊnt/ noun [C] a member of the British aristocracy who is higher in rank than a baron but lower than an earl ▶ **wicehrabia**

viscous /ˈvɪskəs/ adj. (technical) (used about a liquid) thick and sticky; not flowing freely ▶ **lepki, kleisty**

■ **viscosity** /vɪˈskɒsəti/ noun [U] ▶ **lepkość, kleistość**

vise (US) = VICE (3)

visibility /ˌvɪzəˈbɪləti/ noun [U] the distance that you can see in particular light or weather conditions: *In the fog visibility was down to 50 metres.* ◇ *poor/good visibility* ▶ **widoczność**

⚷ **visible** /ˈvɪzəbl/ adj. that can be seen or noticed: *The church tower was visible from the other side of the valley.* ◇ *a visible improvement in his work* ▶ **widoczny** OPP **invisible**

■ **visibly** /-əbli/ adv.: *Rosa was visibly upset.* ▶ **widocznie, wyraźnie**

⚷ **vision** /ˈvɪʒn/ noun **1** [U] the ability to see; sight: *to have good/poor/normal/perfect vision* ▶ **wzrok 2** [C] a picture in your imagination: *They have a vision of a world without weapons.* ◇ *I **had visions of** being left behind* (wyobrażałem sobie, że będę iść w tyle za innymi), *but in fact the others had waited for me.* ▶ **wyobrażenie, wizja 3** [C] a dream or similar experience often connected with religion: *God appeared to Paul in a vision.* ▶ **objawienie 4** [U] the ability to make great plans for the future: *a leader of great vision* ▶ **wyobraźnia, wizja 5** [U] the picture on a TV or cinema screen: *a temporary loss of vision* ▶ **wizja**

visionary /ˈvɪʒənri; US -neri/ adj. having great plans for the future: *He was a visionary leader.* ▶ **wizjonerski**

■ **visionary** noun [C] ▶ **wizjoner/ka**

⚷ **visit** /ˈvɪzɪt/ verb [I,T] to go to see a person or place for a period of time: *I don't live here. I'm just visiting.* ◇ *We often visit relatives at the weekend.* ◇ *She's going to visit her son in hospital.* ◇ *When you go to London you must visit the Science Museum.* ▶ **składać wizytę, odwiedzać, zwiedzać** ➲ note at **know**

■ **visit** noun [C]: *The Prime Minister is **on a visit** to* (pojechał z wizytą w) *Germany.* ◇ *We had a flying visit from Richard* (Richard złożył nam przelotną wizytę) *on Sunday.* ◇ *They said they are going to **pay us a visit*** (że złożą nam wizytę). ▶ **wizyta**

⚷ **visitor** /ˈvɪzɪtə(r)/ noun [C] a person who visits sb/sth: *visitors to London from overseas* ▶ **gość, przyjezdny**

visor /ˈvaɪzə(r)/ noun [C] **1** the part of a **helmet** that you can pull down to protect your eyes or face ▶ **przyłbica 2** a piece of plastic, cloth, etc. on a hat or in a car, which stops the sun shining into your eyes ▶ **daszek** (*u czapki*); **osłona przeciwsłoneczna** (*w samochodzie*)

vista /ˈvɪstə/ noun [C] (formal) a beautiful view, for example of the countryside, a city, etc. ▶ **piękny widok**

visual /ˈvɪʒuəl/ adj. connected with seeing: *the visual arts* (np. malarstwo, rzeźba, sztuka filmowa) ▶ **wzrokowy, wizualny**

■ **visually** /ˈvɪʒuəli/ adv.: *The film is visually stunning.* ◇ *to be visually handicapped* być niewidomym ▶ **wzrokowo; widocznie**

ˌvisual ˈaid noun [C] a picture, film, map, etc. that helps a student to learn sth ▶ **pomoc wizualna**

ˌvisual ˈfield = FIELD OF VISION

visualize (also -ise) /ˈvɪʒuəlaɪz/ verb [T] to imagine or have a picture in your mind of sb/sth: *It's hard to visualize what this place looked like before the factory was built.* ▶ **uzmysławiać sobie**

⚷ **vital** /ˈvaɪtl/ adj. **1** very important or necessary: *Practice is vital if you want to speak a language well.* ◇ *vital information* ▶ **niezbędny; podstawowy** ➲ note at **important 2** full of energy ▶ **witalny** SYN **lively**

■ **vitally** /-təli/ adv.: *vitally important* ▶ **niezbędnie**

vitality /vaɪˈtæləti/ noun [U] the state of being full of energy ▶ **witalność**

vitamin /ˈvɪtəmɪn; US ˈvaɪt-/ noun [C] one of several natural substances in certain types of food that are important to help humans and animals grow and stay healthy: *Oranges are rich in vitamin C.* ▶ **witamina**

vitriolic /ˌvɪtriˈɒlɪk/ adj. (formal) (used about language or comments) full of anger and hatred: *The newspaper launched a vitriolic attack on the president.* ▶ (*przen.*) **jadowity** SYN **bitter**

vivacious /vɪˈveɪʃəs/ adj. (used about a person, usually a woman) full of energy; happy ▶ **pełen życia** SYN **lively**

vivid /ˈvɪvɪd/ adj. **1** having or producing a strong, clear picture in your mind: *vivid dreams/memories* ▶ **barwny 2** (used about light or a colour) strong and very bright: *the vivid reds and yellows of the flowers* ▶ **żywy**

■ **vividly** adv. ▶ **barwnie**

vivisection /ˌvɪvɪˈsekʃn/ noun [U] doing scientific experiments on live animals ▶ **wiwisekcja**

vixen /ˈvɪksn/ noun [C] a female **fox** ▶ **lisica** ➲ note at **fox**

viz. /vɪz/ abbr. [often read out as *namely*] (used to introduce a list of things that explain sth more clearly or are given as examples) ▶ **tj., tzn.**

⚷ **vocabulary** /vəˈkæbjələri; US -leri/ noun (pl. **vocabularies**) **1** [C,U] all the words that sb knows or that are used in a particular book, subject, etc.: *He has an amazing* *vocabulary for a five-year-old.* ◇ *Reading will increase your English vocabulary.* ▶ **słownictwo 2** [sing.] all the words in a language: *New words are always entering the vocabulary.* ▶ **słownictwo**

vocal /ˈvəʊkl/ adj. **1** [only before a noun] connected with the voice ▶ **głosowy 2** expressing your ideas or opinions loudly or freely: *a small but vocal group of protesters* ▶ **głośno/swobodnie wyrażający swoje poglądy, wymowny**

ˌvocal ˈcords noun [pl.] the thin strips of **tissue** in the throat that are moved by the flow of air to produce the voice ▶ **struny głosowe**

vocalist /ˈvəʊkəlɪst/ noun [C] a singer, especially in a band: *a lead/backing vocalist* ▶ **wokalist(k)a**

vocation /vəʊˈkeɪʃn/ noun [C,U] a type of work or a way of life that you believe to be especially suitable for you: *Peter has finally found his vocation in life.* ▶ **powołanie**

vocational /vəʊˈkeɪʃənl/ adj. connected with the skills, knowledge, etc. that you need to do a particular job: *vocational training* szkolenie zawodowe ▶ **zawodowy**

voˈcational school noun [C, U] (in the US) a school that teaches skills that are necessary for particular jobs ▶ **szkoła zawodowa**

vociferous /vəˈsɪfərəs; US vəʊˈs-/ adj. (formal) expressing your opinions or feelings in a loud and confident way ▶ **głośny, krzykliwy**
■ **vociferously** adv. ▶ **głośno, krzykliwie**

vodka /ˈvɒdkə/ noun [C,U] a strong clear alcoholic drink originally from Russia ▶ **wódka**

vogue /vəʊg/ noun [C,U] **a vogue (for sth)** a fashion for sth: *a vogue for large cars* ◇ *That hairstyle is **in vogue** at the moment.* ▶ **moda, wzięcie**

voice¹ /vɔɪs/ noun **1** [C] the sounds that you make when you speak or sing; the ability to make these sounds: *He had a bad cold and **lost** his **voice**.* ◇ *to lower/raise your voice* ◇ *to speak in a loud/soft/low/hoarse voice* mówić głośnym/miękkim/cichym/ochrypłym głosem ◇ *Shh! **Keep your voice down**!* Mów cicho! ◇ *Alan's **voice is breaking*** (przechodzi mutację). ▶ **głos 2** (**-voiced**) [in compounds] having a voice of the type mentioned: *husky-voiced* o chrypiącym głosie ▶ (*określa rodzaj głosu*) **3** [sing.] **a voice (in sth)** (the right to express) your ideas or opinions: *The workers want more of a voice in the running of the company.* ▶ **prawo głosu 4** [C] a particular feeling, attitude or opinion that you have or express: *You should listen to the voice of reason and apologise.* ▶ **głos 5** [sing.] the form of a verb that shows if a sentence is active or passive: *'Keats wrote this poem' is in the **active voice**.* ◇ *'This poem was written by Keats' is in the **passive voice**.* ▶ **strona** (*czynna/bierna*)
IDM **at the top of your voice** → TOP¹

voice² /vɔɪs/ verb [T] to express your opinions or feelings: *to voice complaints/criticisms* ▶ **wyrażać (pogląd)**

ˈvoice box noun [C] the area at the top of the throat that contains the **vocal cords** ▶ **krtań** SYN **larynx**

voicemail /ˈvɔɪsmeɪl/ noun [U] an electronic system which can store telephone messages, so that you can listen to them later ▶ **poczta głosowa** ➲ note at **mobile phone**

ˈvoice-over noun [C] information or comments in a film/movie, television programme, etc. that are given by a person who is not seen on the screen: *She earns a lot of money doing voice-overs* (pracując jako lektorka) *for TV commercials.* ▶ **komentarz/dialog czytany przez lektora**

void¹ /vɔɪd/ noun [C, usually sing.] (formal) a large empty space: *Her death left a void in their lives.* ▶ **próżnia, pustka**

void² /vɔɪd/ adj. **1** (formal) **void (of sth)** completely lacking sth: *This book is totally void of interest for me.* ▶ **próżny; pozbawiony czegoś 2** (used about a ticket, contract, decision, etc.) that can no longer be accepted or used: *The agreement was declared void.* ▶ **nieważny, nie mający mocy prawnej**

vol. = VOLUME: *The Complete Works of Byron, Vol. 2*

volatile /ˈvɒlətaɪl; US -lətl/ adj. **1** that can change suddenly and unexpectedly: *a highly volatile situation which could easily develop into rioting* ◇ *a volatile personality* ▶ **zmienny 2** (used about a liquid) that can easily change into a gas ▶ **lotny**

volcano /vɒlˈkeɪnəʊ/ noun [C] (pl. **volcanoes** or **volcanos**) a mountain with a **crater** at the top through which steam, **lava**, fire, etc. sometimes come out: *When did the volcano last erupt?* ◇ *an active/dormant/extinct volcano* czynny/drzemiący/wygasły wulkan ▶ **wulkan**
■ **volcanic** /vɒlˈkænɪk/ adj.: *volcanic rock/ash* ▶ **wulkaniczny**

volition /vəˈlɪʃn/ noun [U] (formal) the power to choose sth freely or to make your own decisions: *They left entirely **of their own volition*** (z własnej woli). ▶ **wola**

volley /ˈvɒli/ noun [C] **1** (in sports such as football, **tennis**, etc.) a hit or kick of the ball before it touches the ground: *a forehand/backhand volley* ▶ **wolej 2** a number of stones, bullets, etc. that are thrown or shot at the same time: *The soldiers fired a volley over the heads of the crowd.* ▶ **salwa 3** a lot of questions, insults, etc. that are directed at one person very quickly, one after the other: *a volley of abuse* ▶ **stek** (*np. przekleństw*)
■ **volley** verb [I,T]: *Rios volleyed the ball into the net.* ▶ **uderzać piłkę z woleja**

volleyball /ˈvɒlibɔːl/ noun [U] a game in which two teams of six players hit a ball over a high net with their hands while trying not to let the ball touch the ground on their own side ▶ **siatkówka**

volt /vəʊlt; vɒlt/ noun [C] (abbr. **V**) a measure of electric force ▶ **wolt**

voltage /ˈvəʊltɪdʒ/ noun [C,U] an electrical force measured in **volts** ▶ **napięcie, woltaż**

volume /ˈvɒljuːm; US also -jəm/ noun **1** [U,C] (abbr. **vol.**, pl. **vols**) the amount of space that sth contains or fills: *What is the volume of this sphere?* ▶ **objętość** ➲ look at **area 2** [C,U] the large quantity or amount of sth: *the **sheer volume** of traffic* (samo natężenie ruchu) *on the roads* ◇ *I've got volumes of work to get through.* ▶ **ilość, wielkość 3** [U, sing.] how loud a sound is: *to turn the volume on a radio up/down* pogłaśniać/przyciszać radio ◇ *the volume control/dial* przycisk głośności ◇ *a low/high volume* ▶ **głośność** ➲ note at **listen 4** [C] (abbr. **vol.**) a book, especially one of a set or series: *The dictionary comes in three volumes.* ▶ **książka, tom**

voluminous /vəˈluːmɪnəs/ adj. (formal) (used about clothing, furniture, etc.) very large; having plenty of space: *a voluminous skirt* ▶ **obszerny**

voluntary /ˈvɒləntri; US -teri/ adj. **1** done or given because you want to do it, not because you have to do it: *He took **voluntary redundancy*** (dobrowolnie zrezygnował z pracy) *and left the firm last year.* ▶ **dobrowolny** OPP **compulsory 2** done or working without payment: *She does some **voluntary work** at the hospital.* ▶ **ochotniczy 3** (used about movements of the body) that you can control ▶ **świadomy** OPP **involuntary**
■ **voluntarily** /ˈvɒləntrəli; US -ˈterəli/ adv.: *She left the job voluntarily, she wasn't sacked.* ▶ **dobrowolnie**

volunteer¹ /ˌvɒlənˈtɪə(r)/ noun [C] **1** a person who offers or agrees to do sth without being forced or paid to do it: *Are there any volunteers to do the washing up?* ▶ **ochotni-k/czka, wolontariusz/ka 2** a person who joins the armed forces without being ordered to ▶ **ochotni-k/czka do wojska** ➲ look at **conscript**

V

volunteer² /ˌvɒlənˈtɪə(r)/ verb **1** [I,T] **volunteer (sth); volunteer (to do sth)** to offer sth or to do sth which you do not have to do or for which you will not be paid: *They volunteered* (zaoferowali) *their services free.* ◇ *She frequently volunteers* (zgłasza się na ochotnika) *for extra work because she really likes her job.* ◇ *One of my friends volunteered* (zaproponował) *to take us all in his car.* ▶ **podjąć się dobrowolnie coś zrobić** **2** [T] to give information, etc. or to make a comment or suggestion without being asked to: *I volunteered a few helpful suggestions.* ▶ **dobrowolnie udzielać informacji** **3** [I] **volunteer (for sth)** to join the armed forces without being ordered ▶ **ochotniczo wstępować do wojska**

voluptuous /vəˈlʌptʃuəs/ adj. **1** (formal) (used about a woman) attractive in a sexual way with large breasts and hips ▶ (*kobieta*) **o obfitych i ponętnych kształtach** SYN **buxom** **2** (literary) giving you physical pleasure: *voluptuous perfume* ▶ **zmysłowy** SYN **sensual**
■ **voluptuously** adv.: *She yawned and stretched voluptuously.* ▶ **zmysłowo**

vomit /ˈvɒmɪt/ verb [I,T] to bring food, etc. up from the stomach and out of the mouth ▶ **wymiotować** ⓘ W codziennym Br. ang. mówi się **be sick**: *I ate too much last night and I was sick.*
■ **vomit** noun [U] ▶ **wymiociny**

voracious /vəˈreɪʃəs/ adj. (formal) **1** eating or wanting large amounts of food: *a voracious eater* obżartuch ◇ *to have a* ***voracious appetite*** (wilczy apetyt) ▶ **żarłoczny** SYN **greedy** **2** wanting a lot of new information and knowledge: *a voracious reader* ◇ *a boy with a voracious and undiscriminating appetite for facts* ▶ **nienasycony** SYN **avid**
■ **voraciously** adv. ▶ **żarłocznie**; **zachłannie**

vote¹ /vəʊt/ noun **1** [C] **a vote (for/against sb/sth)** a formal choice in an election or at a meeting, which you show by holding up your hand or writing on a piece of paper: *The votes are still being counted.* ◇ *There were 10* ***votes for,*** *and 25* ***against,*** *the motion.* ▶ **głos** **2** [C] **a vote (on sth)** a method of deciding sth by asking people to express their choice and finding out what most people want: *Let's* ***have a vote*** (zagłosujmy)/***put it to the vote*** (poddajmy pod głosowanie). *All those in favour, raise your hands.* ◇ *The democratic way to decide this would be to* ***take a vote*** (przeprowadzić głosowanie). ▶ **głosowanie** **3** (**the vote**) [sing.] the total number of votes in an election: *She obtained 30% of the vote.* ▶ **liczba głosów** **4** (**the vote**) [sing.] the legal right to vote in political elections: *Women did not get the vote in this country until the 1920s.* ▶ **prawo głosu**
IDM **cast a/your vote** → CAST¹
a vote of thanks a short speech to thank sb, usually a guest at a meeting, etc.: *The club secretary proposed a vote of thanks to the guest speaker.* ▶ **krótka mowa dziękczynna**

vote² /vəʊt/ verb **1** [I,T] **vote (for/against sb/sth); vote (on sth); vote to do sth** to show formally a choice or opinion by marking a piece of paper or by holding up your hand: *Who did you vote for in the last general election?* ◇ *46%* ***voted in favour of*** *the proposed change.* ◇ *Very few MPs voted against the new law.* ◇ *After the debate we'll vote on the motion* (zagłosujemy wniosek). ◇ *They voted to change the rules of the club.* ◇ *I voted Liberal Democrat.* ▶ **głosować** ➲ note at **politics** **2** [T, usually passive] to choose sb for a particular position or prize: *He was voted best actor at the Oscars.* ▶ **ogłaszać (kogoś czymś)** **3** [T] (informal) to decide and state that sth is/was good or bad: *We all voted the trip a success.* ▶ **orzekać**
■ **voter** noun [C] ▶ **wyborca**

ˌvote of ˌno ˈconfidence noun [usually sing.] a formal vote to show that people do not support a leader, a political party, an idea, etc.: *The assembly passed a vote of no confidence in the government.* ▶ **wotum nieufności**

vouch /vaʊtʃ/ verb [I] **vouch for sb/sth** to say that a person is honest or good or that sth is true or genuine ▶ **ręczyć (za kogoś/coś)**

voucher /ˈvaʊtʃə(r)/ noun [C] (Brit.) a piece of paper that you can use instead of money to pay for all or part of sth ▶ **kwit**, **bon** ➲ look at **token**

vow /vaʊ/ noun [C] a formal and serious promise (especially in a religious ceremony): *to keep/break your marriage vows* ▶ **przysięga**
■ **vow** verb [T]: *We vowed never to discuss the subject again.* ▶ **ślubować**, **przyrzekać**

vowel /ˈvaʊəl/ noun [C] any of the sounds represented in English by the letters *a, e, i, o* or *u* ▶ **samogłoska** ➲ look at **consonant**

voyage /ˈvɔɪɪdʒ/ noun [C] a long journey by sea or in space: *an around-the-world voyage* ◇ *a voyage to Jupiter* ▶ **podróż** (*morska lub w kosmos*) ➲ note at **journey**
■ **voyager** noun [C] ▶ **podróżni-k/czka**

voyeur /vwaɪˈɜː(r); vɔɪˈɜː(r)/ noun [C] a person who gets pleasure from secretly watching other people have sex ▶ **podglądacz/ka** ⓘ Wyraża dezaprobatę.
■ **voyeurism** /vwaɪˈɜːrɪzəm; vɔɪˈɜː-/ noun [U] ▶ **podglądanie**, **voyeuryzm** | **voyeuristic** /ˌvwaɪəˈrɪstɪk; ˌvɔɪəˈr-/ adj.: *a voyeuristic interest in other people's lives* ▶ **voyerystyczny**, **dot. podglądania**

vs = VERSUS (1)

VSO /ˌviː es ˈəʊ/ abbr. (Brit.) **Voluntary Service Overseas**; an organization that sends people to go to work in developing countries ▶ **Ochotnicza Służba Zagraniczna**

vulgar /ˈvʌlɡə(r)/ adj. **1** not having or showing good judgement about what is attractive or appropriate; not polite or well behaved: *vulgar furnishings* ◇ *a vulgar man/woman* ▶ **prostacki**; **niewykształcony** **2** rude or likely to offend people: *a vulgar joke* ▶ **wulgarny**
■ **vulgarity** /vʌlˈɡærəti/ noun [C,U] (pl. **vulgarities**) ▶ **wulgarność**

vulnerable /ˈvʌlnərəbl/ adj. **vulnerable (to sth/sb)** weak and easy to hurt in a physical or emotional way: *Poor organization left the troops vulnerable to enemy attack* (pozostawiła żołnierzy bez zabezpieczenia przed atakiem wroga). ▶ **nie zabezpieczony**, **podatny (na coś)**
■ **vulnerability** /ˌvʌlnərəˈbɪləti/ noun [U] ▶ **brak zabiezpieczenia**, **podatność (na coś)**

vulture /ˈvʌltʃə(r)/ noun [C] a large bird with no feathers on its head or neck that eats dead animals ▶ **sęp**

vulva /ˈvʌlvə/ noun [C] the outer opening of the female sex organs ▶ **srom**

Ww

W, w /ˈdʌbljuː/ noun [C,U] (pl. **Ws**; **ws**; **W's**; **w's** /ˈdʌbljuːz/) the 23rd letter of the English alphabet: *'Water' begins with (a) 'W'.* ▶ **litera** *w*

W **1** = WATT: *a 60W light bulb* **2** = WEST¹, WESTERN¹ (1): *W Cumbria*

wacky (also **whacky**) /ˈwæki/ adj. (**wackier**; **wackiest**) (informal) amusing or funny in a slightly crazy way ▶ **zwariowany**; **niesamowity**

wad /wɒd/ noun [C] **1** a large number of papers, paper money, etc. folded or rolled together: *He pulled a wad of £20 notes out of his pocket.* ▶ **plik**, **zwój** **2** a mass of soft material that is used for blocking sth or keeping sth in place: *The nurse used a wad of cotton wool to stop the bleeding.* ▶ **tampon**, **podkład** (*np. z waty*)

waddle /ˈwɒdl/ verb [I] to walk with short steps, moving the weight of your body from one side to the other, like a **duck** ▶ **chodzić (drobnymi kroczkami) kolebiąc się**

wade /weɪd/ verb [I] to walk with difficulty through fairly deep water, mud, etc. ▶ **brnąć**
PHR V **wade through sth** to deal with or read sth that is boring and takes a long time ▶ (*przen.*) **brnąć przez coś**

wafer /ˈweɪfə(r)/ noun [C] a very thin, dry biscuit often eaten with ice cream ▶ **cienki wafel, opłatek**

waffle[1] /ˈwɒfl/ noun **1** [C] a flat cake with a pattern of squares on it that is often eaten warm with **syrup** ▶ **gofr** ➲ picture on **page A14** **2** [U] (Brit., informal) language that uses a lot of words but that does not say anything important or interesting: *The last two paragraphs of your essay are just waffle.* ▶ **lanie wody**

waffle[2] /ˈwɒfl/ verb [I] (Brit., informal) **waffle (on) (about sth)** to talk or write for much longer than necessary without saying anything important or interesting ▶ **lać wodę**

waft /wɒft; US also wæft/ verb [I,T] to move, or make sth move, gently through the air: *The smell of her perfume wafted across the room.* ▶ **unosić się**; **nieść** (*w powietrzu*)

wag /wæg/ verb [I,T] (**wagging**; **wagged**) to shake up and down or move from side to side; to make sth do this: *The dog wagged its tail.* ▶ **merdać, machać**

⚷ **wage**[1] /weɪdʒ/ noun [sing.] (also **wages** [pl.]) the regular amount of money that you earn, usually every week, for work or services: *a weekly wage of £200* ◇ *What's the national **minimum wage**?* ◇ *Our wages are paid every Thursday.* ▶ **zapłata tygodniowa, wypłata** ➲ look at **salary** ➲ note at **pay**[2]

> **Wage** w lp używa się zwykle, mówiąc o sumie zapłaconych pieniędzy, lub kiedy słowo to łączy się z innym, np. **wage packet**, **wage rise** itp. **Wages** w lm oznacza same pieniądze (zarobki): *I have to pay the rent out of my wages.*

wage[2] /weɪdʒ/ verb [T] **wage sth (against/on sb/sth)** to begin and then continue a war, battle, etc.: *to wage war on your enemy* ▶ **prowadzić**

wager /ˈweɪdʒə(r)/ noun [C] (old-fashioned or formal) an arrangement to risk money on the result of a particular event ▶ **zakład** SYN **bet**
■ **wager** verb (old-fashioned or formal) **1** [I,T] **wager (sth) (on sth)**; **wager sth/sb that...** to bet money: *to wager £50 on a horse* ◇ *She always wagered on an outsider.* ▶ **stawiać coś (na coś)**; **zakładać się (z kimś)** SYN **bet** **2** [T] (used to say that you are so confident that sth is true or will happen that you would be willing to bet money on it): *I'll wager that she knows more about it than she's saying.* ▶ **zakładać się, że** SYN **bet**

waggle /ˈwægl/ verb [I,T] (informal) to move up and down or from side to side with quick, short movements; to make sth do this ▶ **trząść (się)**

wagon /ˈwægən/ noun [C] **1** (US ˈ**freight car**) an open section of a train, used for carrying goods or animals: *coal transported in goods wagons* ▶ **wagon towarowy** ➲ look at **truck** **2** a vehicle with four wheels that is pulled by horses, etc. and used for transporting things ▶ **fura, wóz**

waif /weɪf/ noun [C] a small thin person, usually a child, who seems to have no home ▶ **porzucone dziecko**

wail /weɪl/ verb **1** [I,T] to cry or complain in a loud, high voice, especially because you are sad or in pain ▶ **jęczeć** **2** [I] (used about things) to make a sound like this: *sirens wailing in the streets outside* ▶ **wyć, brzmieć żałośnie**
■ **wail** noun [C]: *a wail of anguish/despair/distress* ◇ *the wail of sirens* ▶ **jęk, wycie**

⚷ **waist** /weɪst/ noun [C, usually sing.] **1** the narrowest part around the middle of your body: *She put her arms around his waist.* ◇ *He was paralysed **from the waist down*** (od pasa w dół). ▶ **talia** ➲ picture at **body** **2** the part of a piece of clothing that goes round the waist: *The trousers are too baggy round the waist* (zbyt luźne w pasie). ▶ **talia, pas**

waistband /ˈweɪstbænd/ noun [C] the narrow piece of cloth at the waist of a piece of clothing, especially trousers or a skirt ▶ **pasek** (*wszyty*)

waistcoat /ˈweɪskəʊt/ (US **vest**) noun [C] a piece of clothing with buttons down the front and no sleeves that is often worn over a shirt and under a jacket as part of a man's suit ▶ **kamizelka**

waistline /ˈweɪstlaɪn/ noun [C, usually sing.] **1** (used to talk about how fat or thin a person is) the measurement or size of the body around the waist ▶ **rozmiar w talii** **2** the place on a piece of clothing where your waist is: *a dress with a high waistline* sukienka wysoka w talii ▶ **talia, pas, stan**

⚷ **wait**[1] /weɪt/ verb [I] **1 wait (for sb/sth) (to do sth)** to stay in a particular place, and not do anything until sb/sth arrives or until sth happens: *Wait here. I'll be back in a few minutes.* ◇ *Have you been waiting long?* ◇ *If I'm a bit late, can you wait for me?* ◇ *I'm waiting to see the doctor.* ▶ **czekać**

> Por. **wait** z **expect**: *I was expecting him to be there at 7.30 but at 8 I was still waiting.* ◇ *I'm waiting for the exam results but I'm not expecting to pass.* Kiedy mamy nadzieję, że coś się wydarzy, używamy czasownika **hope** a nie ~~*expect*~~ ◇ *I hope you will have a good party.* Kiedy cieszymy się na przyszłe wydarzenie, używamy wyrażenia **look forward to**: *I'm looking forward to your visit.*

2 to be left or delayed until a later time: *Is this matter urgent or **can it wait**?* ▶ **czekać**
IDM **can't wait/can hardly wait** (used when you are emphasizing that sb is very excited and enthusiastic about doing sth): *I can't wait* (nie mogę doczekać się) *to find out what happens at the end.* ◇ *The kids can't wait to see their father again.* ▶ **nie móc się czegoś doczekać**
keep sb waiting to make sb wait or be delayed, especially because you arrive late: *I'm sorry if I've kept you waiting.* ▶ **kazać komuś (na siebie itp.) czekać**
wait and see to be patient and find out what will happen later (perhaps before deciding to do sth): *Let's wait and see* (poczekamy, zobaczymy) – *there's nothing more we can do.* ▶ **czekać cierpliwie**
wait your turn to wait until the time when you are allowed to do sth ▶ **czekać na swoją kolej**
(just) you wait (used to emphasize a threat, warning or promise): *I'll be famous one day – just you wait!* ▶ **zobaczysz!**
PHR V **wait about/around** to stay in a place doing nothing because sb or sth is late ▶ **czekać bezczynnie** (*ponieważ ktoś/coś się spóźnia*)
wait behind to stay in a place after others have left it: *She waited behind after class to speak to her teacher.* ▶ **zostawać** (*gdzieś po odejściu innych*)
wait in to stay at home because you are expecting sb to come or sth to happen ▶ **zostawać w domu** (*w oczekiwaniu na coś*)
wait on sb to serve food, drink, etc. to sb, usually in a restaurant ▶ **podawać do stołu** (*zwykle w restauracji*), **usługiwać przy stole**
wait up (for sb) to not go to bed because you are waiting for sb to come home ▶ **czekać do późna**

wait[2] /weɪt/ noun [C, usually sing.] **a wait (for sth/sb)** a period of time when you wait ▶ **oczekiwanie**
IDM **lie in wait (for sb)** → LIE[2]

W

waiter /ˈweɪtə(r)/ noun [C] a man whose job is to serve customers at their tables in a restaurant, etc. ▶ **kelner**

ˈ**waiting list** noun [C] a list of people who are waiting for sth, for example a service or medical treatment, that will be available in the future: *to put your name* ***on a waiting list*** ▶ **lista osób oczekujących (na coś)**

ˈ**waiting room** noun [C] a room where people can sit while they are waiting, for example for a train, or to see a doctor or dentist ▶ **poczekalnia**

ˈ**wait list** (US) = WAITING LIST

ˈ**wait-list** verb [T] (US) to put sb's name on a **waiting list**: *He's been wait-listed for a football scholarship to Stanford.* ▶ **wpisywać kogoś na listę oczekujących**

waitress /ˈweɪtrəs/ noun [C] a woman whose job is to serve customers at their tables in a restaurant, etc. ▶ **kelnerka**

waitressing /ˈweɪtrəsɪŋ/ noun [U] the job of being a waitress: *I did some waitressing* (pracowałam jako kelnerka) *when I was a student.* ▶ **praca kelnerki**

waive /weɪv/ verb [T] (formal) to say officially that a rule, etc. need not be obeyed; to say officially that you no longer have a right to sth: *In your case, we will waive your tuition fees.* ▶ **uchylać** (*np. przepis*); **zrzekać się**

wake[1] /weɪk/ verb [I,T] (pt **woke** /wəʊk/, pp **woken** /ˈwəʊkən/) **wake (sb) (up)** to stop sleeping; to make sb stop sleeping: *I woke early in the morning and got straight out of bed.* ◇ *Wake up! It's nearly 8 o'clock!* ◇ *Could you wake me at 7.30, please?* ▶ **budzić się**; **budzić** ➲ note at **sleep** ➲ adjective **awake**

PHR V **wake sb up** to make sb become more active or full of energy: *She always has some coffee to wake her up* (na rozbudzenie) *when she gets to work.* ▶ **rozbudzać kogoś**

wake up to sth to realize sth; to notice sth ▶ **uprzytamniać sobie coś**

wake[2] /weɪk/ noun [C] **1** an occasion before a funeral when people meet to remember the dead person, traditionally held at night to watch over the body before it is buried ▶ **czuwanie** (*przy zwłokach*) **2** the track that a moving ship leaves behind on the surface of the water ▶ **kilwater**

IDM **in the wake of sb/sth** following or coming after sb/sth: *The floods left a great deal of suffering in their wake* (pozostawiły po sobie wiele cierpienia). ▶ **śladem kogoś/czegoś**

waken /ˈweɪkən/ verb [I,T] (old-fashioned, formal) to stop sleeping or to make sb/sth stop sleeping: *She wakened from a deep sleep.* ▶ **budzić (się)**

walk[1] /wɔːk/ verb **1** [I] to move or go somewhere by putting one foot in front of the other on the ground, but without running: *The door opened and Billy walked in.* ◇ *I walk to work every day.* ◇ *He walked with a limp.* Kulał. ◇ *Are the shops* ***within walking distance?*** Czy do sklepów można dojść na piechotę? ◇ *'How did you get here? By bus?' 'No, I walked* (przyszedłem piechotą).*'* ▶ **chodzić, iść 2** [I] to move in this way for exercise or pleasure ▶ **przechadzać się** ➲ note at **walk**[2] **3** [T] to go somewhere with sb/sth on foot, especially to make sure they get there safely: *I'll* ***walk you home*** *if you don't want to go on your own.* ◇ *He walked me to my car.* ▶ **odprowadzać, zaprowadzać 4** [T] to take a dog out for exercise: *I'm just going to* ***walk the dog.*** ▶ **wyprowadzać** (*psa na spacer*) **5** [T] to go along or through sth on foot: *He walked the streets all night.* ▶ **chodzić po czymś**

■ **walker** noun [C]: *She's a fast walker.* ◇ *This area is very popular with walkers.* ▶ **piechur, spacerowicz/ka** | **walking** noun [U]: *to* ***go walking*** ◇ *a walking holiday* (obóz wędrowny) *in Wales* ▶ **piesze wycieczki, wędrówka**

PHR V **walk off with sth 1** to win sth easily: *She walked off with all the prizes.* ▶ **odnieść łatwe zwycięstwo 2** to steal sth; to take sth that does not belong to you by mistake: *When I got home I realized that I had walked off with her pen.* ▶ **kraść**; **zabierać cudzą rzecz przez pomyłkę**

walk out (of sth) to leave suddenly and angrily: *She walked out of the meeting in disgust.* ▶ **wychodzić ostentacyjnie**

walk out on sb (informal) to leave sb for ever: *He walked out on his wife and children after 15 years of marriage.* ▶ **rzucać kogoś**

walk (all) over sb (informal) **1** to treat sb badly, without considering their needs or feelings: *I don't know why she lets her husband walk all over her like that.* ▶ **poniewierać kimś 2** to defeat sb completely: *He played brilliantly and walked all over his opponent.* ▶ **zniszczyć kogoś**

walk up (to sb/sth) to walk towards sb/sth, especially in a confident way ▶ **podchodzić (do kogoś/czegoś)**

walk[2] /wɔːk/ noun **1** [C] going somewhere on foot for pleasure, exercise, etc.: *We went for a walk in the country.* ◇ *I'm just going to take the dog for a walk.* ◇ *The beach is five minutes' walk/a five-minute walk* (w odległości pięciu minut piechotą) *from the hotel.* ▶ **spacer**

> Zwrotu **go for a walk** używa się, mówiąc o krótkim spacerze dla przyjemności. Mówiąc o długim spacerze lub o parodniowej pieszej wycieczce, używa się zwrotu **go walking**.

2 [C] a path or route for walking for pleasure: *From here there's a lovely walk through the woods.* ▶ **trasa spacerowa 3** [sing.] a way or style of walking: *He has a funny walk.* ▶ **chód 4** [sing.] the speed of walking: *She slowed to a walk.* ▶ **krok spacerowy**

IDM **a walk of life** sb's job or position in society: *She has friends from all walks of life.* ▶ (*warstwa społeczna*) **sfera**

walkie-talkie /ˌwɔːki ˈtɔːki/ noun [C] (informal) a small radio that you can carry with you to send or receive messages ▶ **krótkofalówka**

ˈ**walking stick** (especially Brit. **stick**) noun [C] a stick that you carry and use as a support to help you walk ▶ **laska** ➲ look at **crutch**

walkover /ˈwɔːkəʊvə(r)/ noun [C] an easy win or victory in a game or competition ▶ **łatwa wygrana**

wall /wɔːl/ noun [C] **1** a solid, vertical structure made of stone, brick, etc. that is built round an area of land to protect it or to divide it: *There is a high wall all around the prison.* ▶ **mur 2** one of the sides of a room or building joining the ceiling and the floor: *He put the picture up* ***on the wall.*** ▶ **ściana**

IDM **up the wall** (informal) crazy or angry: *She went up the wall* (strasznie się wściekła) *when I turned up an hour late.* ◇ *That noise is driving me up the wall* (doprowadza mnie do szału). ▶ **wściekły**

walled /wɔːld/ adj. surrounded by a wall ▶ **obwarowany murem**

wallet /ˈwɒlɪt/ (US **billfold** /ˈbɪlfəʊld/) noun [C] a small, flat, folding case in which you keep paper money, plastic cards, etc. ▶ **portfel** ➲ look at **purse**

wallop /ˈwɒləp/ verb [T] (informal) to hit sb/sth very hard ▶ **walić**

wallow /ˈwɒləʊ/ verb [I] **wallow (in sth) 1** (used about people and large animals) to lie and roll around in water, etc. in order to keep cool or for pleasure: *I spent an hour wallowing in the bath.* ▶ **pławić się 2** to enjoy sth that causes you pleasure: *to wallow in self-pity* demonstracyjnie użalać się nad sobą ▶ **pławić się (w czymś)**

wallpaper /ˈwɔːlpeɪpə(r)/ noun [U] **1** paper that you stick to the walls of a room to decorate or cover them

▶ **tapeta 2** the background pattern or picture that you choose to have on your computer screen ▶ (*komput.*) **tapeta**

■ **wallpaper** verb [I,T] ▶ **tapetować**

ˌwall-to-ˈwall adj. [only before a noun] (used especially about a carpet) covering the floor of a room completely ▶ **od ściany do ściany**

wally /ˈwɒli/ noun [C] (pl. **wallies**) (Brit., slang) a silly or stupid person ▶ **głupek**, **głupiec**

walnut /ˈwɔːlnʌt/ noun **1** [C] a nut that we eat, with a rough surface and a hard brown shell that is in two halves ▶ **orzech włoski 2** (also ˈ**walnut tree**) [C] the tree on which these nuts grow ▶ **orzech włoski** (*drzewo*) **3** [U] the wood from the **walnut** tree, used in making furniture ▶ **orzech włoski** (*drewno*)

walrus /ˈwɔːlrəs/ noun [C] a large animal with two **tusks** that lives in or near the sea in Arctic regions ▶ **mors**

waltz[1] /wɔːls; -lts/ noun [C] an elegant dance that you do with a partner, to music which has a rhythm of three beats; the music for this dance: *a Strauss waltz* ▶ **walc**

waltz[2] /wɔːls; -lts/ verb **1** [I,T] to dance a **waltz**: *They waltzed around the floor.* ◇ *He waltzed her round the room.* ▶ **tańczyć walca 2** [I] (informal) to go somewhere in a confident way: *You can't just waltz in* (nie możesz tak sobie wejść do pokoju jakby nigdy nic) *and expect your meal to be ready for you.* ▶ **chodzić nonszalancko**

WAN /wæn/ abbr. **wide area network**; a system in which computers in different places are connected, usually over a large area ▶ **WAN** ➲ look at **LAN**

wan /wɒn/ adj. looking pale and ill or tired ▶ **mizerny**, **blady**, **wyczerpany**

wand /wɒnd/ noun [C] a thin stick that people hold when they are doing magic tricks: *I wish I could* ***wave a magic wand*** *and make everything better.* ▶ **różdżka**

⚷ **wander** /ˈwɒndə(r)/ verb **1** [I,T] to walk somewhere slowly with no particular sense of direction or purpose: *We spent a pleasant day wandering around the town.* ◇ *He was found in a confused state, wandering the streets.* ▶ **wędrować**, **tułać się 2** [I] **wander (away/off) (from sb/sth)** to walk away from a place where you ought to be or the people you were with: *We must stay together while visiting the town so I don't want anybody to wander off.* ◇ *Don't wander away from the main road.* ▶ **zbaczać z właściwej drogi**; **odbiegać od tematu 3** [I] (used about sb's mind, thoughts, etc.) to stop paying attention to sth; to be unable to stay on one subject: *The lecture was so boring that my attention began to wander.* ▶ (*myśli, wzrok itp.*) **błądzić**; **schodzić** (*z tematu*)

■ **wander** noun [sing.]: *I went to the park for a wander.* ▶ **przechadzka**

wane[1] /weɪn/ verb [I] **1** (formal) to become gradually weaker or less important: *My enthusiasm was waning rapidly.* ▶ **maleć**, **słabnąć 2** (used about the moon) to appear slightly smaller each day after being full and round ▶ **ubywać**

wane[2] /weɪn/ noun

IDM **on the wane** (formal) becoming smaller, less important or less common: *The singer's popularity seems to be on the wane these days.* ▶ **w zaniku**

wangle /ˈwæŋgl/ verb [T] (informal) to get sth that you want by persuading sb or by having a clever plan: *Somehow he wangled a day off to meet me.* ▶ **wyłudzić**, **skombinować**

wanna /ˈwɒnə; US also ˈwʌnə/ a way of writing 'want to' or 'want a' to show that sb is speaking in an informal way: *I wanna go home now.* ➲ note at **gonna**

wannabe /ˈwɒnəbi; US also ˈwʌn-/ noun [C] (informal) a person who behaves, dresses, etc. like a famous person because they want to be like them ▶ **osoba naśladująca kogoś sławnego**

⚷ **want**[1] /wɒnt/ verb [T] [not used in the continuous tenses] **1 want sth (for sth)**; **want (sb) to do sth**; **want sth (to be) done** to have a desire or a wish for sth: *He wants a new bike.* ◇ *What do they want for breakfast?* ◇ *I don't want to discuss it now.* ◇ *They want Stevens as captain.* Chcą, żeby Stevens był kapitanem. ◇ *I want you to phone me* (chcę, żebyś do mnie zadzwonił) *when you get there.* ◇ *The boss wants this letter typed.* ▶ **chcieć**

> **Want** i **would like** mają podobne znaczenie, ale **would like** jest grzeczniejsze: *'I want a drink!' screamed the child.* ◇ *'Would you like some more tea, Mrs Jones?'*

2 (informal) (used to say that sth needs to be done): *The house wants a new coat of paint.* ◇ *The button on my shirt wants sewing on* (wymaga przyszycia). ▶ **wymagać**, **potrzebować 3** [usually passive] to need sb to be in a particular place or for a particular reason: *Mrs Dawson, you are wanted on the phone* (proszą panią do telefonu). ◇ *She is* ***wanted by the police*** (jest poszukiwana). ▶ **chcieć 4** (informal) (used to give advice to sb) should or ought to: *He wants to be more careful about* (powinien bardziej uważać na to) *what he tells people.* ◇ *If you're bored, you want to go out more often* (to musisz częściej wychodzić z domu). ▶ **potrzebować**, **musieć 5** to feel sexual desire for sb ▶ **pragnąć kogoś** ℹ Czasownika **want** nie używa się w czasach *continuous*. Natomiast często spotyka się go w *present participle* (formie *-ing*): *She kept her head down, not wanting to attract attention.*

want[2] /wɒnt/ noun (formal) **1** (**wants**) [pl.] sth you need or want: *All our wants were satisfied.* ▶ **potrzeba**, **wymaganie 2** [sing.] a lack of sth: *He's suffering due to a want of care.* ▶ **brak**, **niedostatek**

IDM **for (the) want of sth** because of a lack of sth; because sth is not available: *I took the job for want of a better offer* (z braku lepszej oferty). ▶ **z braku czegoś**

wanting /ˈwɒntɪŋ/ adj. (formal) [not before a noun] **wanting (in sth) 1** not having enough of sth; lacking: *The children were certainly not wanting in enthusiasm.* ▶ **brakować 2** not good enough: *The new system* ***was found wanting.*** ▶ **niedoskonały**

wanton /ˈwɒntən/ adj. (formal) (used about an action) done in order to hurt sb or damage sth for no good reason: *wanton vandalism* ▶ **złośliwy**, **nieusprawiedliwiony**

WAP /wæp/ abbr. **wireless application protocol**; a technology that connects devices such as mobile phones to the Internet: *a WAP-enabled phone* ▶ **WAP** (*system telefonii*)

⚷ **war** /wɔː(r)/ noun **1** [U,C] a state of fighting between different countries or groups within countries using armies and weapons: *The Prime Minister announced that the country was* ***at war*** (że państwo jest w stanie wojny). ◇ *to* ***declare war on*** (wypowiadać wojnę) *another country* ◇ *When* ***war broke out*** (kiedy wybuchła wojna), *thousands of men volunteered for the army.* ◇ *a* ***civil war*** wojna domowa ◇ *to* ***go to war*** *against somebody* ◇ *to fight a war* toczyć wojnę ◇ *He was killed in the war* (na wojnie). ▶ **wojna 2** [C,U] aggressive competition between groups of people, companies, countries, etc.: *a price war among oil companies* ▶ **zmaganie**, **wojna** (*np. cenowa*) **3** [U, sing.] **war (against/on sb/sth)** efforts to end or get rid of sth: *We seem to be winning the war against organized crime.* ▶ **walka (z czymś)**

> **war**
>
> The three main parts of a country's **armed forces** are the **army**, the **navy** and the **air force**. **Officers** in the forces give orders to their **troops**. When a war **breaks out** two or more countries are **at war**. A war between different groups in the same country is called a **civil war**. A country's **enemies** are the countries it is fighting against and its **allies** are countries which

W

support it. If armed forces from one country enter another country, they **invade** it. If they stay there and take control of the country, they **occupy** it. A country will try to **defend** itself against **attack** from another country. At the end of a war one country is **defeated** and **surrenders**.

warble /ˈwɔːbl/ verb [I] (used usually about a bird) to sing gently, varying the notes up and down ▶ **wywodzić trele, świergotać**

ˈ**war crime** noun [C] a cruel act that is committed during a war and that is against the international rules of war ▶ **zbrodnia wojenna**

ward[1] /wɔːd/ noun [C] **1** a separate part or room in a hospital for patients with the same kind of medical condition: *the maternity/psychiatric/surgical ward* ▶ **oddział szpitalny, izolatka 2** (Brit.) one of the sections into which a town is divided for elections ▶ **okręg wyborczy 3** a child who is under the protection of a court of law; a child whose parents are dead and who is cared for by a **guardian**: *The child was made a ward of court.* ▶ **dziecko znajdujące się pod kuratelą; wychowanek/ka**

ward[2] /wɔːd/ verb

PHR V **ward sb/sth off** to protect or defend yourself against danger, illness, attack, etc. ▶ **odpędzać, chronić (się) przed niebezpieczeństwem/nieprzyjemnością**

warden /ˈwɔːdn/ noun [C] **1** sb whose job is to check that rules are obeyed or to look after the people in a particular place: *a* ***traffic warden*** osoba kontrolująca poprawne parkowanie samochodów ▶ **inspektor/ka, nadzor-ca/czyni 2** (especially US) the person in charge of a prison ▶ **naczelnik więzienia**

warder /ˈwɔːdə(r)/ noun [C] (Brit.) a person whose job is to guard prisoners ▶ **strażnik więzienny** ➲ look at **guard**

wardrobe /ˈwɔːdrəʊb/ noun [C] **1** a large cupboard in which you can hang your clothes ▶ **szafa** (*na ubrania*) **2** sb's collection of clothes: *I need a whole new summer wardrobe.* ▶ **garderoba 3** [usually sing.] the department in a theatre or television company that takes care of the clothes that actors wear ▶ **garderoba**

ware /weə(r)/ noun **1** [U] [in compounds] things made from a particular type of material or suitable for a particular use: *glassware* ◇ *kitchenware* ◇ *a hardware shop* sklep z towarami żelaznymi (np. narzędziami) ◇ *an earthenware pot* gliniany garnek ▶ **towary, wyroby 2** (**wares**) [pl.] (old-fashioned) goods offered for sale ▶ **towary na sprzedaż**

warehouse /ˈweəhaʊs/ noun [C] a building where large quantities of goods are stored before being sent to shops ▶ **magazyn** ➲ picture on **page A2**

warfare /ˈwɔːfeə(r)/ noun [U] methods of fighting a war; types of war: *guerrilla warfare* wojna partyzancka ◇ *biological/nuclear warfare* wojna biologiczna/jądrowa ▶ **działania wojenne; rodzaj akcji wojennej**

warhead /ˈwɔːhed/ noun [C] the **explosive** part of a **missile**: *nuclear warheads* ▶ **głowica** (*bojowa*)

warily → WARY

warlike /ˈwɔːlaɪk/ adj. liking to fight or good at fighting: *a warlike nation* ▶ **wojowniczy**

⚷ **warm**[1] /wɔːm/ adj. **1** having a pleasant temperature that is fairly high, between cool and hot: *It's quite warm in the sunshine.* ◇ *Are you warm enough* (czy jest ci dość ciepło) *or would you like me to put the heating on?* ◇ *I jumped up and down to keep my feet warm* (żeby mi było ciepło w nogi). ▶ **ciepły** ➲ note at **cold**[1] **2** (used about clothes) preventing you from getting cold: *Take plenty of warm clothes.* ▶ **ciepły 3** friendly, kind and pleasant: *I was given a very warm welcome.* ▶ **ciepły, serdeczny 4** creating a pleasant, comfortable feeling: *warm colours* ▶ **ciepły**

■ **the warm** noun [sing.]: *It's awfully cold out here – I want to go back into the warm.* ▶ **ciepło, ciepłe miejsce** | **warmly** adv.: *warmly dressed* ◇ *She thanked him warmly for his help.* ▶ **ciepło; gorąco**

⚷ **warm**[2] /wɔːm/ verb [I,T] **warm (sb/sth) (up)** to become or to make sb/sth become warm or warmer: *It was cold earlier but it's beginning to warm up now.* ◇ *I sat by the fire to warm up.* ▶ **ocieplać (się), ogrzewać się, podgrzewać**

PHR V **warm to/towards sb** to begin to like sb that you did not like at first ▶ **polubić (kogoś)**

warm to sth to become more interested in sth ▶ **polubić**

warm up to prepare to do an activity or sport by practising gently: *The team warmed up before the match.* ▶ **rozgrzewać się**

ˌ**warm-ˈblooded** adj. (used about animals) having a warm blood temperature that does not change if the temperature around them changes ▶ **stałocieplny** ➲ look at **cold-blooded**

ˌ**warm-ˈhearted** adj. kind and friendly ▶ **serdeczny**

⚷ **warmth** /wɔːmθ/ noun [U] **1** a fairly high temperature or the effect created by this, especially when it is pleasant: *She felt the warmth of the sun on her face.* ▶ **ciepło 2** the quality of being kind and friendly: *I was touched by the warmth of their welcome.* ▶ **ciepło**

ˈ**warm-up** noun [C, usually sing.] **1** a short practice or a series of gentle exercises that you do to prepare yourself for doing a particular sport or activity: *warm-up exercises* ćwiczenia rozgrzewające ▶ **rozgrzewka 2** a short performance of music, comedy, etc. that is intended to prepare the audience for the main show: *a warm-up act* akt wprowadzający ▶ **rozgrzewka**

⚷ **warn** /wɔːn/ verb [T] **1 warn sb (of sth); warn sb (about sb/sth)** to tell sb about sth unpleasant or dangerous that exists or might happen, so that they can avoid it: *When I saw the car coming I tried to warn him, but it was too late.* ◇ *The government is warning the public of possible terrorist attacks.* ◇ *He warned me about the danger of walking home alone at night.* ▶ **ostrzegać 2 warn (sb) against doing sth; warn sb (not to do sth)** to advise sb not to do sth: *The radio warned people against going out during the storm.* ◇ *I warned you not to trust him.* ▶ **ostrzegać**

⚷ **warning** /ˈwɔːnɪŋ/ noun [C,U] something that tells you to be careful or tells you about sth, usually sth bad, before it happens: *Your employers can't dismiss you* ***without warning.*** ◇ *You could have given me some warning that your parents were coming to visit.* ▶ **ostrzeżenie, uprzedzenie (o czymś)**

warp /wɔːp/ verb **1** [I,T] to become bent into the wrong shape, for example as a result of getting hot or wet; to make sth become like this: *The window frame was badly warped and wouldn't shut.* ▶ **paczyć (się) 2** [T] to influence sb so that they start behaving in an unusual or shocking way: *His experiences in the war had warped him.* ▶ **wypaczać**

■ **warped** adj. ▶ **wypaczony**

warpath /ˈwɔːpɑːθ; US -pæθ/ noun

IDM **(be/go) on the warpath** (informal) to be very angry and want to fight or punish sb ▶ **być na ścieżce wojennej; wchodzić na ścieżkę wojenną**

warrant[1] /ˈwɒrənt/ noun [C] an official written statement that gives sb permission to do sth: *a search warrant* nakaz rewizji ▶ **nakaz, upoważnienie**

warrant[2] /ˈwɒrənt/ verb [T] (formal) to make sth seem right or necessary; to deserve sth: *Her behaviour does not warrant such criticism.* ▶ **dawać podstawę do czegoś, zasługiwać**

warranty /ˈwɒrənti/ noun [C,U] (pl. **warranties**) a written statement that you get when you buy sth, which promises to repair or replace it if it is broken or does not work: *Fortunately my washing machine is still **under warranty*** (na gwarancji). ▶ **gwarancja** (*na zakupiony towar*) ➲ look at **guarantee**

warren = RABBIT WARREN

warrior /ˈwɒriə(r)/ noun [C] (old-fashioned) a person who fights in a battle; a soldier ▶ **wojownik**

warship /ˈwɔːʃɪp/ noun [C] a ship for use in war ▶ **okręt wojenny**

wart /wɔːt/ noun [C] a small hard dry lump that sometimes grows on the face or body ▶ **kurzajka**

wartime /ˈwɔːtaɪm/ noun [U] a period of time during which there is a war ▶ **okres wojenny**

wary /ˈweəri/ adj. (**warier** no superlative) **wary (of sb/sth)** careful because you are uncertain or afraid of sb/sth: *Since becoming famous, she has grown wary of journalists.* ◇ *He was wary of* (wystrzegał się) *accepting the suggestion in case it meant more work for him.* ▶ **ostrożny**
■ **warily** adv. ▶ **ostrożnie**

was → BE

⚷ **wash**[1] /wɒʃ/ verb **1** [I,T] to clean sb/sth/yourself with water and often soap: *to wash your hands/face/hair* ◇ *That shirt needs washing.* ◇ *Wash and dress quickly or you'll be late!* ◇ *I'll wash* (pozmywam), *you dry.* ▶ **prać**; **myć (się)**; **zmywać** ➲ note at **clean**[2] **2** [I] to be able to be washed without being damaged: *Does this material wash well, or does the colour come out?* ▶ **prać się 3** [I,T] (used about water) to flow or carry sth/sb in the direction mentioned: *I let the waves wash over my feet.* ◇ *The current washed the ball out to sea.* ▶ **obmywać**; **porywać**
IDM **wash your hands of sb/sth** to refuse to be responsible for sb/sth any longer: *They washed their hands of their son when he was sent to prison.* ▶ **umywać ręce od kogoś/czegoś**
PHR V **wash sb/sth away** (used about water) to carry sb/sth away: *The floods had washed away the path.* ▶ **znosić kogoś/coś**
wash (sth) off (sth) to (make sth) disappear by washing: *The writing has washed off and now I can't read it.* ◇ *Go and wash that make-up off!* ▶ **zmywać (coś/się) (skądś)**
wash out to be removed from a material by washing: *These grease marks won't wash out* (nie dają się sprać). ▶ **sprać się**
wash sth out to wash sth or the inside of sth in order to remove dirt: *I'll just wash out this bowl and then we can use it.* ▶ **wyprać/wypłukiwać coś**
wash (sth) up 1 (Brit.) to wash the plates, knives, forks, etc. after a meal: *Whose turn is it to wash up?* ▶ **zmywać** (*naczynia*) **2** (US) to wash your face and hands: *Go and wash up quickly and put on some clean clothes.* ▶ **myć twarz i ręce 3** [often passive] (used about water) to carry sth to land and leave it there: *Police found the girl's body washed up on the beach.* ▶ **wyrzucać coś na brzeg**

wash[2] /wɒʃ/ noun **1** [C, usually sing.] an act of cleaning or being cleaned with water: *I'd better go and **have a wash** before we go out.* ▶ **mycie się**, **pranie**, **zmywanie 2** [sing.] the waves caused by the movement of a ship through water ▶ **kilwater**
IDM **in the wash** (used about clothes) being washed: *'Where's my red T-shirt?' 'It's in the wash.'* ▶ **w praniu**

washable /ˈwɒʃəbl/ adj. that can be washed without being damaged ▶ **nadający się do prania**

washbasin /ˈwɒʃbeɪsn/ (also **basin**) noun [C] a large bowl for water that has taps and is fixed to a wall, in a bathroom, etc. ▶ **umywalka** ➲ look at **sink**

washcloth (US) = FACECLOTH

ˌ**washed ˈout** adj. tired and pale: *They arrived looking washed out after their long journey.* ▶ **wymęczony**

washer /ˈwɒʃə(r)/ noun [C] a small flat ring placed between two surfaces to make a connection tight ▶ **podkładka**, **uszczelka** ➲ picture at **bolt**

⚷ **washing** /ˈwɒʃɪŋ/ noun [U] **1** the act of cleaning clothes, etc. with water: *I usually **do the washing** on Mondays.* ▶ **pranie** (*brudna bielizna*) **2** clothes that need to be washed or are being washed: *Could you put the washing in the machine?* ◇ *a pile of dirty washing* ▶ **pranie**

ˈ**washing line** (Brit.) = CLOTHES LINE

ˈ**washing machine** noun [C] an electric machine for washing clothes ▶ **pralka**

ˈ**washing powder** noun [U] soap in the form of powder for washing clothes ▶ **proszek do prania**

ˌ**washing-ˈup** noun [U] **1** the work of washing the plates, knives, forks, etc. after a meal: *I'll **do the washing-up**.* **2** plates, etc. that need washing after a meal: *Put the washing-up next to the sink.* ▶ **zmywanie naczyń**

washing-ˈup liquid noun [U] (Brit.) liquid soap for washing dishes, pans, etc. ▶ **płyn do zmywania naczyń**

washout /ˈwɒʃaʊt/ noun [C] (informal) an event that is a complete failure, especially because of rain ▶ **klapa**

washroom /ˈwɒʃruːm; -rʊm/ noun [C] (US) a toilet, especially in a public building ▶ **toaleta**

wasn't /ˈwɒznt/ short for **was not**

wasp /wɒsp/ noun [C] a small black and yellow flying insect that can sting ▶ **osa** ➲ look at **bee** ➲ picture at **insect**

wastage /ˈweɪstɪdʒ/ noun [U] (formal) using too much of sth in a careless way; the amount of sth that is wasted ▶ **marnotrawstwo**; **straty**

⚷ **waste**[1] /weɪst/ verb [T] **1 waste sth (on sb/sth)**; **waste sth (in doing sth)** to use or spend sth in a careless way or for sth that is not necessary: *She wastes a lot of money on cigarettes.* ◇ *He wasted his time at university because he didn't work hard.* ◇ *She wasted no time in decorating her new room.* ▶ **trwonić 2** [usually passive] to give sth to sb who does not value it: *Expensive wine is wasted on me. I don't even like it.* ▶ **marnować**

⚷ **waste**[2] /weɪst/ noun **1** [sing.] **a waste (of sth)** using sth in a careless and unnecessary way: *The seminar was **a waste of time** – I'd heard it all before.* ◇ *It seems a waste to throw away all these old newspapers.* ▶ **strata 2** [U] material, food, etc. that is not needed and is therefore thrown away: *nuclear waste* ◇ *A lot of household waste can be recycled and reused.* ▶ **odpady**, **odpadki** ➲ look at **rubbish 3** (**wastes**) [pl.] (formal) large areas of land that are not lived in and not used: *the wastes of the Sahara desert* ▶ **nieużytki**
IDM **go to waste** to not be used and so thrown away and wasted: *I can't bear to see good food going to waste!* ▶ **marnować się**

⚷ **waste**[3] /weɪst/ adj. [only before a noun] **1** (used about land) not used or not suitable for use; not looked after: *There's an area of waste ground* (obszar niewykorzystanego terenu) *outside the town where people dump their rubbish.* ▶ **leżący odłogiem**, **nieuprawny**; **zapuszczony 2** no longer useful; that is thrown away: *waste paper* zużyty papier ◇ *waste material* ▶ **odpadkowy**

wastebasket (US) = WASTE-PAPER BASKET

wasted /ˈweɪstɪd/ adj. **1** [only before a noun] not necessary or successful: *a wasted journey* ▶ **zmarnowany 2** very thin, especially because of illness ▶ **wychudzony**, **wymizerowany 3** (slang) suffering from the effects of drugs or alcohol ▶ **zmarnowany**

wasteful /ˈweɪstfl/ adj. using more of sth than necessary; causing waste ▶ **marnotrawny**

W

wasteland /ˈweɪstlænd/ noun [C, U] an area of land that cannot be used or that is no longer used for building or growing things on: *industrial wasteland* ◇ *the desert wastelands of Arizona* ◇ (figurative) *The mid 1970s are seen as a cultural wasteland for rock music.* ▶ **teren niezagospodarowany**; (*przen.*) **pustynia**

ˌwaste-ˈpaper basket noun [C] (US **wastebasket** /ˈweɪstbɑːskɪt; US -bæs-/) a container in which you put paper, etc. that is to be thrown away ▶ **kosz na śmieci** ➲ picture at **bin**

ˈwaste product noun [C] a useless material or substance produced while making sth else ▶ **produkt odpadowy**

watch¹ /wɒtʃ/ verb **1** [I,T] to look at sb/sth for a time, paying attention to what happens: *I* ***watched in horror*** *as the car swerved and crashed.* ◇ *I'm watching to see how you do it.* ◇ *We* ***watch TV*** *most evenings.* ◇ *Watch what she does next.* ◇ *I watched him open the door and walk away.* ◇ *We went to watch John rowing.* Poszliśmy zobaczyć, jak John wiosłuję. ▶ **przyglądać się**, **patrzeć na kogoś/coś**, **oglądać** ➲ note at **look 2** [T] **watch sb/sth (for sth)** to take care of sth for a short time: *Could you watch my bag for a second while I go and get a drink?* ▶ **(po)pilnować 3** [T] to be careful about sb/sth; to pay careful attention to sth/sb: *You'd better* ***watch what you say*** *to her. She gets upset very easily.* ◇ *Watch that boy – he's acting suspiciously.* ◇ *Doctors are watching for further signs of the disease.* ▶ **uważać**; **baczyć (na coś)**, **obserwować**

IDM **watch your step 1** to be careful about where you are walking: *The path's very slippery here so watch your step.* ▶ **uważać jak się idzie 2** to be careful about how you behave ▶ **uważać co się robi**

PHR V **watch out** to be careful because of possible danger or trouble: *Watch out* (uwaga)*! There's a car coming.* ◇ *If you don't watch out you'll lose your job.* ▶ **uważać**

watch out for sb/sth to look carefully and be ready for sb/sth: *Watch out for snakes if you walk through the fields.* ▶ **strzec się kogoś/czegoś**

watch over sb/sth to look after or protect sb/sth: *For two weeks she watched over the sick child.* ▶ **czuwać nad kimś/czymś**

watch² /wɒtʃ/ noun **1** [C] a type of small clock that you usually wear around your wrist: *a digital watch* ◇ *My watch is a bit fast/slow* (trochę się śpieszy/spóźnia). ◇ *to wind up/set your watch* nakręcać/nastawiać zegarek ▶ **zegarek** ➲ look at **clock 2** [sing., U] the act of watching sb/sth in case of possible danger or problems: *Tour companies have to* ***keep a close watch on*** (dobrze obserwować) *the political situation in the region.* ◇ *You* ***keep watch*** *for her* (wypatruj jej) *and I'll go inside to make sure everything is ready.* ▶ **obserwacja**, **pilnowanie 3** [sing.] a person or group of people whose job is to guard and protect a place or a person ▶ **straż**

watchband (US) = WATCH STRAP

watchdog /ˈwɒtʃdɒg/ noun [C] a person or group whose job is to make sure that large companies respect people's rights: *a consumer watchdog* ▶ **organizacja śledząca politykę rynkową, zwł. (dużych) firm, w celu zabezpieczenia praw konsumentów**

watchful /ˈwɒtʃfl/ adj. careful to notice things ▶ **baczny**

ˈwatch strap (US **ˈwatchband** /ˈwɒtʃbænd/) noun [C] a thin strip of leather, etc. for fastening your watch around your wrist ▶ **pasek do zegarka**

watchtower /ˈwɒtʃtaʊə(r)/ noun [C] a tall tower from which soldiers, etc. watch when they are guarding a place ▶ **wieża obserwacyjna**

water¹ /ˈwɔːtə(r)/ noun **1** [U] the clear liquid that falls as rain and is in rivers, seas and lakes ➲ picture at **bar**: *All the rooms have hot and cold running water* (bieżącą wodę). ◇ *a glass of water* ◇ *drinking water* woda pitna ◇ *tap water* woda z kranu ▶ **woda** ➲ look at **freeze**, **steam 2** [U] a large amount of water, especially the water in a lake, river or sea: *Don't go too near the edge or you'll fall in the water!* ◇ *After the heavy rain several fields were* ***under water*** (zalane powodzią). ▶ **woda 3** (**waters**) [pl.] the water in a particular sea, lake, etc. or near a particular country: *The ship was still in British waters.* ▶ **wody (terytorialne) 4** [U] the surface of an area of water: *Can you swim* ***under water****?* ◇ *I can see my reflection in the water.* ▶ **woda**

IDM **keep your head above water** → HEAD¹

pass water → PASS¹

When water is **heated** to 100° Celsius, it **boils** and becomes **steam**. When steam touches a cold surface, it **condenses** and becomes water again. When water is **cooled** below 0° Celsius, it **freezes** and becomes **ice**. If the temperature increases, the ice **melts**. When talking about **icy** weather becoming warmer, we say it **thaws**. Frozen food **thaws** or **defrosts** when we take it out of the freezer.

water² /ˈwɔːtə(r)/ verb **1** [T] to give water to plants ▶ **podlewać 2** [I] (used about the eyes or mouth) to fill with liquid: *The smoke in the room was starting to* ***make*** *my* ***eyes water.*** ◇ *The food smelled so delicious that it* ***made*** *my* ***mouth water*** (że aż ślinka napłynęła mi do ust). ▶ **łzawić**, **ślinić się**

PHR V **water sth down 1** to add water to a liquid in order to make it weaker ▶ **rozwadniać 2** to change a statement, report, etc. so that the meaning is less strong or direct ▶ **osłabiać**

watercolour /ˈwɔːtəkʌlə(r); US also ˈwɑːt-/ noun **1** (**watercolours**) [pl.] paints that are mixed with water, not oil ▶ **akwarela 2** [C] a picture that has been painted with **watercolours** ▶ **akwarela**

ˈwater cooler noun [C] a machine, for example in an office, that cools water and supplies it for drinking ▶ **automat z chłodzoną wodą**

watercress /ˈwɔːtəkres; US also ˈwɑːt-/ noun [U] a type of plant with small round green leaves which have a strong taste and are often eaten in salads ▶ **rukiew wodna**

waterfall /ˈwɔːtəfɔːl; US also ˈwɑːt-/ noun [C] a river that falls from a high place, for example over a rock, etc. ▶ **wodospad**

ˈwatering can noun [C] a container with a long tube on one side which is used for pouring water on plants ▶ **konewka** ➲ picture at **garden**

ˈwater lily noun [C] a plant that floats on the surface of water, with large round flat leaves and white, yellow or pink flowers ▶ **lilia wodna**, **grążel** ➲ picture on **page A15**

waterlogged /ˈwɔːtəlɒgd; US also ˈwɑːt-; -lɑːgd/ adj. **1** (used about the ground) extremely wet: *Our boots sank into the waterlogged ground.* ▶ (*teren*) **rozmokły 2** (used about a boat) full of water and likely to sink ▶ **pełen wody**

watermelon /ˈwɔːtəmelən; US also ˈwɑːt-/ noun [C,U] a large, round fruit with a thick, green skin. It is pink or red inside with a lot of black seeds. ▶ **arbuz** ➲ picture on **page A12**

waterproof /ˈwɔːtəpruːf; US also ˈwɑːt-/ adj. that does not let water go through: *a waterproof jacket* ▶ **nieprzemakalny**

watershed /ˈwɔːtəʃed; US also ˈwɑːt-/ noun [C] an event or time which is important because it marks the beginning of sth new or different ▶ **wydarzenie przełomowe**, **moment zwrotny**

waterski /ˈwɔːtəskiː; US also ˈwɑːt-/ verb [I] to move across the surface of water standing on **waterskis** and being pulled by a boat ▶ **jeździć na nartach wodnych** ➲ picture on **page A8**
■ **waterski** noun [C] either of the pair of long flat boards on which a person stands in order to waterski ▶ **narta wodna**

ˈ**water sports** noun [pl.] sports that are carried out on water ▶ **sporty wodne**

watertight /ˈwɔːtətaɪt; US also ˈwɑːt-/ adj. **1** made so that water cannot get in or out: *Store in a watertight container.* ▶ **wodoszczelny 2** (used about an excuse, opinion, etc.) impossible to prove wrong; without any faults: *His alibi was absolutely watertight.* ▶ **niezbity**

waterway /ˈwɔːtəweɪ; US also ˈwɑːt-/ noun [C] a river, **canal**, etc. along which boats can travel ▶ **droga wodna**

watery /ˈwɔːtəri; US ˈwɑːt-/ adj. **1** containing mostly water: *watery soup* ◇ *A watery liquid came out of the wound.* ▶ **wodnisty**, **rzadki 2** weak and pale: *watery sunshine* ◇ *a watery* (wyblakły) *smile* ▶ **słaby**, **blady**

watt /wɒt/ noun [C] (abbr. **W**) a unit of electric power: *a 60-watt light bulb* ▶ **wat**

wave¹ /weɪv/ noun [C] **1** a line of water moving across the surface of water, especially the sea, that is higher than the rest of the surface: *We watched the waves roll in and break on the shore.* ▶ **fala** ➲ look at **tidal wave 2** a sudden increase or spread of a feeling or type of behaviour: *There has been a wave of sympathy for the refugees.* ◇ *a crime wave* ◇ *The pain came* ***in waves.*** ▶ **fala** ➲ look at **heatwave 3** a large number of people or things suddenly moving or appearing somewhere: *There is normally a wave of tourists in August.* ▶ **fala 4** a movement of sth, especially your hand, from side to side in the air: *With a wave of his hand, he said goodbye and left.* ▶ **machnięcie (ręką) 5** the form that some types of energy such as sound, light, heat, etc. take when they move: *sound waves* ◇ *shock waves from the earthquake* ➲ look at **LW**, **MW 6** a gentle curve in your hair ▶ **fala** ➲ look at **perm**

wave² /weɪv/ verb **1** [I,T] to move your hand from side to side in the air, usually to attract sb's attention or as you meet or leave sb: *She waved to her friends.* ◇ *He leant out of the window and* ***waved goodbye*** *to her as the train left the station.* ▶ **machać (ręką)**; **witać/żegnać machaniem ręki 2** [T] **wave sb/sth away, on, through, etc.** to move your hand in a particular direction to show sb/sth which way to go: *There was a policeman in the middle of the road, waving us on.* ▶ **machnięciem ręki kazać komuś podjechać/podejść lub odjechać/odejść 3** [T] **wave sth (at sb)**; **wave sth (about)** to hold sth in the air and move it from side to side: *The crowd waved flags as the President came out.* ◇ *She was talking excitedly and waving her arms about.* ▶ **machać 4** [I] to move gently up and down or from side to side: *The branches of the trees waved gently in the breeze.* ▶ **kołysać się**
PHR V **wave sth aside/away** to decide not to pay attention to sb/sth because you think he/she/it is not important ▶ **machnąć na coś ręką**
wave sb off to wave to sb who is leaving ▶ **machać komuś na pożegnanie**

waveband /ˈweɪvbænd/ (also **band**) noun [C] a set of radio waves of similar length ▶ **zakres fal radiowych**

wavelength /ˈweɪvleŋθ/ noun [C] **1** the distance between two sound waves ▶ **odległość między falami dźwiękowymi 2** the length of wave on which a radio station sends out its programmes ▶ **długość fali radiowej**
IDM **on the same wavelength** → SAME

waver /ˈweɪvə(r)/ verb [I] **1** to become weak or uncertain, especially when making a decision or choice: *He never wavered in his support.* ▶ **wahać się**; **być niezdecydowanym 2** to move in a way that is not firm or steady: *His hand wavered* (zadrżała) *as he reached for the gun.* ▶ **zachwiać się**

wavy /ˈweɪvi/ adj. (**wavier**; **waviest**) having curves; not straight: *wavy hair* ◇ *a wavy line* ▶ **falisty** ➲ picture at **hair**

wax¹ /wæks/ noun [U] **1** a substance made from fat or oil that melts easily and is used for making polish, **candles**, etc. ▶ **wosk 2** a yellow substance that is found in your ears ▶ **woskowina**

wax² /wæks/ verb **1** [T] to polish sth with **wax** ▶ **woskować 2** [T, usually passive] to cover sth with wax: *waxed paper* ▶ **woskować 3** [T, often passive] to remove hair from a part of your body using **wax**: *to wax your legs/to have your legs waxed* ▶ **depilować woskiem 4** [I] (used about the moon) to seem to get gradually bigger until its form is visible ▶ (*księżyc*) **przybywać** OPP **wane 5** (**wax lyrical, eloquent, sentimental, etc.**) [I] (formal) to become **lyrical**, etc. when speaking or writing: *He waxed lyrical on the food at the new restaurant.* Rozpływał się nad jedzeniem w nowej restauracji. ▶ **popadać** (*np. w sentymentalizm*), **zrobić się lirycznym, elokwentnym**

waxwork /ˈwækswɜːk/ noun [C] **1** a model of sb/sth, especially of a famous person, made of **wax** ▶ **figura woskowa 2** (**waxworks**) [sing.] a place where **wax** models of famous people are shown to the public ▶ **gabinet figur woskowych**

way¹ /weɪ/ noun **1** [C] **a way (to do sth/of doing sth)** a particular method, style or manner of doing sth: *What is the* ***best way*** *to learn a language?* ◇ *I've discovered a brilliant way of saving paper!* ◇ *They'll have to find the money* ***one way or another.*** ◇ *He always* ***does things his own way.*** ◇ *She smiled* ***in a friendly way.*** ◇ *As you get older, it becomes more difficult to change your ways* (zmienić zwyczaje). ▶ **sposób**; **nawyk 2** [C, usually sing.] the route you take to reach somewhere; the route you would take if nothing were stopping you: ***the way in/out*** *of somewhere* wejście, wjazd/wyjście, wyjazd ◇ *Can you tell me* ***the way to*** *James Street?* ◇ *Which way should I go to get to the town centre?* ◇ *If you* ***lose*** *your* ***way,*** *phone me.* ◇ *We stopped* ***on the way to*** *Leeds for a meal.* ◇ *Can I drive you home? It's* ***on my way*** (jest po drodze). ◇ *These birds find their way* (trafią) *to Africa every winter.* ◇ *Get out of my way!* ◇ *Can you move that box – it's* ***in my/the way.*** ▶ **droga 3** [C] a path, road, route, etc. that you can travel along: *There's a way across the fields.* ▶ **droga** ➲ look at **highway**, **motorway**, **railway 4** [sing.] a direction or position: *Look this way!* ◇ *That painting is* ***the wrong way up*** (wisi do góry nogami). ◇ *Are you sure these two words are* ***the right way round*** (w dobrej kolejności)*?* ◇ *Shouldn't you be wearing that hat* ***the other way round*** (odwrotnie)*?* ◇ *He thought I was older than my sister but in fact it's* ***the other way round*** (odwrotnie). ▶ **kierunek** ➲ look at **back to front 5** [sing.] a distance in space or time: ***It's a long way from*** *London* ***to*** *Edinburgh.* ◇ *Christmas is still a* ***a long way off.*** Jeszcze daleko do Świąt Bożego Narodzenia. ◇ *We came all this way to see him and he's not at home!* ▶ **odległość**
IDM **be set in your ways** to be unable to change your habits, attitudes, etc. ▶ **mieć ustalone nawyki**
bluff your way in, out, through, etc. sth → BLUFF¹
by the way (used for adding sth to the conversation) on a new subject: *Oh, by the way, I saw Mario in town yesterday.* ▶ **przy okazji**
change your ways → CHANGE¹
get/have your own way to get or do what you want, although others may want sth else ▶ **postawić na swoim, robić po swojemu**
give way to break or fall down: *The branch of the tree suddenly gave way and he fell.* ▶ **łamać się**, **spadać**

W

give way (to sb/sth) **1** to stop or to allow sb/sth to go first: *Give way to traffic coming from the right.* ▶ **przepuszczać, dawać pierwszeństwo przejazdu** **2** to allow sb to have what they want although you did not at first agree with it: *We shall not give way to the terrorists' demands.* ▶ **poddawać się**
go a long way → LONG[1]
go out of your way (to do sth) to make a special effort to do sth ▶ **bardzo się starać**
have a long way to go → LONG[1]
in a/one/any way; in some ways to a certain degree but not completely: *In a way, I rather like him.* ◇ *In some ways the meeting was very useful.* ▶ **w pewnym sensie, pod pewnym względem**
in a big/small way (used for expressing the size or importance of an activity): *'Have you done any acting before?' 'Yes, but in a very small way.'* ▶ **na małą/dużą skalę**
in the way **1** blocking the road or path: *I can't get past. There's a big lorry in the way.* ▶ **na drodze** **2** not needed or wanted: *I felt rather in the way* (czułem, że zawadzam) *at my daughter's party.* ▶ **nie na miejscu**
learn the hard way → LEARN
no way (informal) definitely not: *'Can I borrow your car?' 'No way!'* ▶ **wykluczone!**
the other way round → OTHER
out of harm's way → HARM[1]
thread your way through sth → THREAD[2]
under way having started and making progress: *Discussions between the two sides are now under way.* ▶ **w toku**
a/sb's way of life the behaviour and customs that are typical of a person or group of people ▶ **styl życia**

way[2] /weɪ/ adv. (informal) very far; very much: *I finally found his name way down at the bottom of the list* (na samym końcu listy). ◇ *Matt's got way more experience than me.* ▶ **bardzo daleko; dużo** (*więcej/bardziej*)

ˌway ˈout noun [C] **1** (Brit.) a door used for leaving a building SYN **exit** ▶ **wyjście** **2** a way of escaping from a difficult situation: *She was in a mess and could see no way out.* ▶ **wyjście**
IDM **on the way out** **1** as you are leaving ▶ **wychodząc** **2** going out of fashion ▶ **wychodzący z mody**

WC /ˌdʌblju: ˈsi:/ abbr. **water closet**; toilet ▶ **WC**

we /wi:/ pron. the subject of a verb; used for talking about the speaker and one or more other people: *We're going to the cinema.* ◇ *We are both very pleased with the house.* ▶ **my**

weak /wi:k/ adj. **1** (used about the body) having little strength or energy: *The child was weak with hunger.* ◇ *Her legs felt weak.* ▶ **słaby** **2** that cannot support a lot of weight; likely to break: *That bridge is too weak to take heavy traffic.* ▶ **słaby** **3** easy to influence; not firm: *He is too weak to be a good leader.* ◇ *a weak character* ▶ **słaby** **4** not having economic success: *a weak currency/economy/market* ▶ **słaby** **5** **weak (at/in/on sth)** not very good at sth: *a weak team* ◇ *He's weak at maths./His maths is weak.* Jest słaby z matematyki. ▶ **słaby** OPP **strong** **6** not easy to believe: *She made some weak excuse about washing her hair tonight.* ▶ **słaby** **7** not easy to see or hear; not definite or strong: *a weak voice* ◇ *She gave a weak smile.* ▶ **słaby, mdły** **8** containing a lot of water, not strong in taste: *weak coffee* ◇ *I like my tea quite weak.* ▶ **słaby**
■ **weakly** adv. ▶ **słabo**

weaken /ˈwi:kən/ verb [I,T] **1** to become less strong; to make sb/sth less strong: *The illness had left her weakened.* ◇ *The building had been weakened by the earthquake.* ▶ **osłabiać; słabnąć** OPP **strengthen** **2** to become, or make sb become, less certain or firm about sth: *She eventually weakened and allowed him to stay.* ▶ **ulegać, słabnąć**

ˈweak form noun [C] a way of pronouncing a word when it is not emphasized ▶ (*fonetyka*) **słaba forma**

weakness /ˈwi:knəs/ noun **1** [U] the state of being weak: *He thought that crying was a sign of weakness.* ▶ **słabość** OPP **strength** **2** [C] a fault or lack of strength, especially in sb's character: *It's important to know your own strengths and weaknesses.* ▶ **słaba strona** OPP **strength** **3** [C, usually sing.] **a weakness for sth/sb** a particular and often silly liking for sth/sb: *I have a weakness for chocolate.* ▶ **słabość (do czegoś/kogoś)**

wealth /welθ/ noun **1** [U] a lot of money, property, etc. that sb owns; the state of being rich: *They were a family of enormous wealth.* ▶ **zamożność** SYN **riches** **2** [sing.] **a wealth of sth** a large number or amount of sth: *a wealth of information/experience/talent* ▶ **bogactwo, mnóstwo**

wealthy /ˈwelθi/ adj. (**wealthier**; **wealthiest**) having a lot of money, property, etc. ▶ **zamożny** SYN **rich, well-to-do** OPP **poor**

wean /wi:n/ verb [T] to gradually stop feeding a baby or young animal with its mother's milk and start giving it solid food ▶ **odstawiać od piersi**
PHR V **wean sb off/from sth** to make sb gradually stop doing or using sth: *The doctor tried to wean her off sleeping pills.* ▶ **odzwyczajać kogoś od czegoś**

weapon /ˈwepən/ noun [C] an object which is used for fighting or for killing people, such as a gun, knife, bomb, etc. ▶ **broń**

ˌweapon of ˌmass deˈstruction noun [C] (abbr. **WMD**) a weapon such as a nuclear weapon, a **chemical weapon** or a **biological weapon** that can cause a lot of destruction and kill many people ▶ **broń masowego rażenia**

wear[1] /weə(r)/ verb (pt **wore** /wɔ:(r)/, pp **worn** /wɔ:n/) **1** [T] to have clothes, jewellery, etc. on your body: *He was wearing* (miał na sobie) *a suit and tie.* ◇ *I wear glasses for reading.* ◇ *to wear your hair short* mieć krótkie włosy ▶ **nosić** (*np. ubranie, biżuterię*) ➲ note at **carry** **2** [T] to have a certain look on your face: *His face wore a puzzled look.* ▶ **mieć (jakiś) wyraz twarzy** **3** [I,T] to become or make sth become thinner, smoother or weaker because of being used or rubbed a lot: *These tyres are badly worn.* ◇ *The soles of his shoes had worn smooth.* ▶ **zużywać się** **4** [T] to make a hole, path, etc. in sth by rubbing, walking, etc.: *Put some slippers on or you'll wear a hole in your socks!* ▶ **wydzierać** (*np. dziurę w skarpetce*); **wydeptywać ścieżkę** **5** [I] to last for a long time without becoming thinner or damaged: *This material wears well.* ▶ **nosić się**
IDM **wear thin** to have less effect because of being used too much: *We've heard that excuse so often that it's beginning to wear thin.* ▶ **tracić na znaczeniu**
PHR V **wear (sth) away** to damage sth or to make it disappear over a period of time, by using or touching it a lot; to disappear or become damaged in this way: *The sea had worn* (morze podmyło) *the bottom of the cliffs away.* ▶ **niszczyć** (*przez częste używanie*), **zdzierać coś (się)**
wear (sth) down to become or to make sth smaller or smoother: *The heels on these shoes have worn right down.* ▶ **zmniejszać (się), skracać (się)**
wear sb/sth down to make sb/sth weaker by attacking, persuading, etc.: *They wore him down with constant arguments until he changed his mind.* ▶ **osłabiać kogoś/coś**
wear off to become less strong or to disappear completely: *The effects of the drug wore off after a few hours.* ▶ **słabnąć; niknąć, mijać**
wear on (used about time) to pass slowly ▶ **wolno upływać**

wear (sth) out to become too thin or damaged to use any more; to cause sth to do this: *Children's shoes wear out very quickly.* ▶ **zdzierać coś/się**

wear yourself/sb out to make yourself/sb very tired: *She wore herself out walking home with the heavy bags.* ▶ **wyczerpywać/męczyć kogoś/się** ➲ look at **worn out**

wear² /weə(r)/ noun [U] **1** wearing or being worn; use as clothing: *You'll need jeans and jumpers for everyday wear.* ▶ **noszenie (na sobie) 2** [in compounds] (used especially in shops to describe clothes for a particular purpose or occasion): *casual/evening/sports wear* ◇ *children's wear* ◇ *menswear* odzież męska ◇ *underwear* bielizna (osobista) ▶ **ubranie 3** long use which damages the quality or appearance of sth: *The engine is checked regularly for signs of wear.* ▶ **znoszenie** (*ubrania*), **zdarcie**

IDM **wear and tear** the damage caused by ordinary use ▶ **zużywanie się**

the worse for wear → WORSE

weary /ˈwɪəri/ adj. (**wearier**; **weariest**) very tired, especially after you have been doing sth for a long time: *He gave a weary smile.* Uśmiechnął się blado (z powodu zmęczenia). ▶ **zmęczony**

■ **wearily** adv. ▶ **ze zmęczeniem** | **weariness** noun [U] ▶ **zmęczenie**

weasel /ˈwiːzl/ noun [C] a small wild animal with reddish-brown fur, a long thin body and short legs ▶ **łasica**

weather¹ /ˈweðə(r)/ noun [U] the condition of the atmosphere at a particular place and time, including how much wind, rain, sun, etc. there is, and how hot or cold it is: ***What's the weather like*** *where you are?* ◇ *hot/warm/sunny/fine weather* ◇ *cold/wet/windy/wintry weather* ◇ *I'm not going for a run* ***in this weather!*** ▶ **pogoda** ➲ note at **cold**, **fog**, **storm**

> When we talk about the weather, we often say 'It's a **lovely**/**beautiful**/**horrible**/**terrible** day, isn't it?' If you want to know what the weather is going to be like, you can watch or listen to the **weather forecast**.

IDM **make heavy weather of sth** → HEAVY

under the weather (informal) not very well ▶ **o kiepskim zdrowiu/samopoczuciu**

weather² /ˈweðə(r)/ verb **1** [I,T] to change or make sth change in appearance because of the effect of the sun, air or wind: *The farmer's face was weathered by the sun.* ▶ **zmieniać wygląd pod wpływem warunków atmosferycznych**; **sezonować** (*drewno*); (*skały*) **wietrzeć 2** [T] to come safely through a difficult time or experience: *Their company managed to weather the recession and recover.* ▶ **przetrwać burzę/trudny okres**

ˈ**weather-beaten** adj. (used especially about sb's face or skin) made rough and damaged by the sun and wind ▶ **ogorzały**, **osmagany** (*wiatrem*)

ˈ**weather forecast** (also **forecast**) noun [C] a description of the weather that is expected for the next day or next few days ▶ **prognoza pogody**

weave /wiːv/ verb [I,T] (pt **wove** /wəʊv/ or in sense 2 **weaved**; pp **woven** /ˈwəʊvn/ or in sense 2 **weaved**) **1** to make cloth, etc. by passing threads under and over a set of threads that is fixed to a **loom**: *woven cloth* ▶ **tkać 2** to change direction often when you are moving so that you are not stopped by anything: *The cyclist weaved in and out of the traffic.* ▶ **kluczyć**, **przewijać się**

web /web/ noun **1** [C] a type of fine net that a spider makes in order to catch small insects: *A spider spins webs.* ▶ **pajęczyna** ➲ look at **cobweb 2** (**the Web**): *I looked it up on the Web.* = WORLD WIDE WEB

webbed /webd/ adj. [only before a noun] (used about the feet of some birds or animals) having the toes connected by pieces of skin ▶ **złączony błoną** ➲ picture on **page A11**

webcam (US **Webcam™**) /ˈwebkæm/ noun [C] a video camera that is connected to a computer so that what it records can be seen on a website as it happens ▶ **kamera internetowa**

weblog = BLOG

webmaster /ˈwebmɑːstə(r); US -mæs-/ noun [C] a person who is responsible for particular pages of information on the World Wide Web ▶ **twórca strony www**

ˈ**web page** noun [C] a document connected to the World Wide Web, usually forming part of a website, that anyone with an Internet connection can see: *We learned how to create and register a new web page.* ▶ **strona internetowa**

website /ˈwebsaɪt/ (also **site**) noun [C] a place connected to the Internet where a company, an organization or an individual person puts information: *I found it on their website.* ◇ *Visit our website to learn more.* ▶ **miejsce internetowe** ➲ note at **Internet**

webzine /ˈwebziːn/ noun [C] a magazine published on the Internet, not on paper ▶ **czasopismo internetowe**

Wed. (also **Weds.**) = WEDNESDAY: *Wed. 4 May*

we'd /wiːd/ short for **we had**; **we would**

wed /wed/ verb [I,T] (pt, pp **wedded**) or (**wed**) [not used in the progressive tenses; old-fashioned or used in newspapers] to marry ▶ **poślubiać**; **pobierać się**

wedding /ˈwedɪŋ/ noun [C] a marriage ceremony and often the **reception**: *I've been invited to their wedding.* ◇ *a wedding dress/present* ◇ *a wedding ring* obrączka ślubna ◇ *All her friends could hear wedding bells* (dzwony weselne). ▶ **ślub**, **wesele** ⓘ W krajach anglosaskich obrączkę ślubną nosi się na lewej ręce.

> **weddings**
>
> At a **wedding**, two people **get married**. The woman is called the **bride** and the man is the **groom** (or **bridegroom**). They are helped during the **wedding ceremony** by the **best man** and the **bridesmaids**. A wedding can take place in church (a **church wedding**) or in a **registry office**. After the ceremony there is usually a **wedding reception**. Many **couples** go on a **honeymoon** after getting married. **Marriage** refers to the relationship between a **husband** and **wife**: *They have a happy marriage.* A couple celebrate their **silver wedding anniversary** when they have been married for 25 years, their **golden wedding** after 50 years and their **diamond wedding** after 60.

wedge¹ /wedʒ/ noun [C] a piece of wood, etc. with one thick and one thin pointed end that you can push into a small space, for example to keep things apart: *The door was kept open with a wedge.* ▶ **klin**

wedge² /wedʒ/ verb [T] **1** to force sth/sb to fit into a small space: *The cupboard was wedged between the table and the door.* ▶ **wciskać 2** to force sth apart or to prevent sth from moving by using a **wedge**: *to wedge a door open* ▶ **klinować**

Wednesday /ˈwenzdeɪ; -di/ noun [C,U] (abbr. **Wed.**) the day of the week after Tuesday ▶ **środa** ➲ note at **Monday**

wee¹ /wiː/ (also ˈ**wee-wee**) noun [C,U] (informal) (used by young children or when you are talking to them) water that you pass from your body ▶ **siusiu** SYN **urine**

■ **wee** verb [I] ▶ **siusiać**

wee² /wiː/ adj. little, small: *a wee boy* ◇ *I'm a wee bit* (odrobinę) *tired.* ▶ **maleńki** ⓘ Słowa tego używają zwłaszcza Szkoci.

weed¹ /wiːd/ noun **1** [C] a wild plant that is not wanted in a garden because it prevents other plants from growing properly ▶ **chwast 2** [U] a mass of very small green plants that floats on the surface of an area of water

W

▶ **rzęsa** (*np. na stawie*) **3** [C] (informal) a thin, weak person or sb who has a weak character ▶ **cherlak**; (*osoba*) **chorągiewka**

weed² /wi:d/ verb [I,T] to remove **weeds** from a piece of ground, etc. ▶ **pielić**

PHR V **weed sth/sb out** to remove the things or people that you do not think are good enough: *He weeded out all the letters with spelling mistakes in them.* ▶ **przesiewać** (*np. kandydatów*)

weedkiller /ˈwi:dkɪlə(r)/ noun [U,C] a substance that is used to destroy **weeds**: *a can of weedkiller* ▶ **środek chwastobójczy**

weedy /ˈwi:di/ adj. (**weedier**; **weediest**) (informal) small and weak: *a small weedy man* ▶ **cherlawy**; **słabego charakteru**

week /wi:k/ noun [C] **1** (abbr. **wk**, pl. **wks**) a period of seven days, especially from Monday to Sunday or from Sunday to Saturday: *We arrived* ***last week.*** ◇ *He left two weeks ago.* ◇ *I haven't seen her for a week.* ◇ *I go there twice a week.* ◇ *They'll be back in a week/in a week's time.* ▶ **tydzień** ⓘ W Br. ang. okres dwóch tygodni zwykle nazywa się **fortnight**. **2** the part of the week when people go to work, etc. usually from Monday to Friday: *She works hard during the week so that she can enjoy herself at the weekend.* ◇ *I work a 40-hour week.* ▶ **tydzień (pracy)**

IDM **today, tomorrow, Monday, etc. week** seven days after today, tomorrow, Monday, etc. ▶ **za tydzień** (*np. od dziś, jutra*)

week in, week out every week without a rest or change: *He's played for the same team week in, week out for 20 years.* ▶ **tydzień za tygodniem**

a week yesterday, last Monday, etc. seven days before yesterday, Monday, etc.: *They got married a week last Saturday.* Zeszłej soboty minął tydzień od ich ślubu. ▶ **tydzień przed** (*licząc od wczoraj, zeszłego poniedziałku itp.*)

weekday /ˈwi:kdeɪ/ noun [C] any day except Saturday or Sunday: *I only work on weekdays.* ▶ **dzień powszedni** ➲ note at **routine**

■ **weekdays** adv.: *open weekdays from 9 a.m. to 6 p.m.* ▶ **dzień powszedni**

weekend /ˌwi:kˈend; US ˈwi:kend/ noun [C] Saturday and Sunday: *What are you doing* ***at the weekend?*** ⓘ W Br. ang. mówi się **at the weekend**, natomiast w Amer. ang. **on the weekend**. ▶ **sobota i niedziela**

weekly¹ /ˈwi:kli/ adj., adv. happening or appearing once a week or every week: *a weekly report* ◇ *We are paid weekly.* ▶ **tygodniowy**, **cotygodniowy**; **tygodniowo**, **co tydzień**

weekly² /ˈwi:kli/ noun [C] (pl. **weeklies**) a newspaper or magazine that is published every week ▶ **tygodnik**

weeknight /ˈwi:knaɪt/ noun [C] any night of the week except Saturday, Sunday and sometimes Friday night: *I have to stay in on weeknights.* ▶ **wieczór dnia powszedniego**

weep /wi:p/ verb [I,T] (pt, pp **wept** /wept/) (formal) to let tears fall because of strong emotion; to cry: *She wept at the news of his death.* ▶ **płakać**

weevil /ˈwi:vl/ noun [C] a small insect with a hard shell, that eats grain, nuts and other seeds and destroys crops ▶ **chrząszcz ryjkowiec**

weigh /weɪ/ verb **1** [T] to have or show a certain weight: *I weigh 56 kilos.* ◇ *How much does this weigh?* ▶ **ważyć** **2** [T] to measure how heavy sth is, especially by using **scales**: *I weigh myself every week.* ◇ *Can you weigh this parcel for me, please?* ▶ **ważyć** **3** [T] **weigh sth (up)** to consider sth carefully: *You need to weigh up your chances of success.* ▶ **rozważać** **4** [T] **weigh sth (against sb/sth)** to consider if one thing is better, more important, etc. than another or not: *We shall weigh the advantages of the plan against the risks.* ▶ **porównywać z czymś** **5** [I] **weigh against (sb/sth)** to be considered as a disadvantage when sb/sth is being judged: *She didn't get the job because her lack of experience weighed against her.* ▶ **zaważyć na czymś**

PHR V **weigh sb down** to make sb feel worried and sad: *He felt weighed down by all his responsibilities.* ▶ **przytłaczać kogoś**

weigh sb/sth down to make it difficult for sb/sth to move (by being heavy): *I was weighed down by heavy shopping.* ▶ **przytłaczać kogoś/coś**

weigh on sb/sth to make sb worry: *The responsibilities* ***weigh heavily*** *on him.* ◇ *That problem has been* ***weighing on my mind*** *for a long time.* ▶ **przytłaczać kogoś/coś**

weigh sb/sth up to consider sb/sth carefully and form an opinion: *I weighed up my chances and decided it was worth applying.* ▶ **szacować coś**; **oceniać kogoś**

weight¹ /weɪt/ noun (abbr. **wt**) **1** [U] how heavy sth/sb is; the fact of being heavy: *The doctor advised him to* ***lose weight*** (aby stracił na wadze). ◇ *You've* ***lost weight.*** Schudłeś. ◇ *He's* ***put on weight.*** Utył. ◇ *The weight of the snow broke the branch.* Gałąź złamała się pod ciężarem śniegu. ▶ **waga** **2** [C] a heavy object: *The doctor has told me not to lift heavy weights.* ▶ **ciężar** **3** [C] a piece of metal that weighs a known amount that can be used to measure an amount of sth, or that can be lifted as a form of exercise: *a 500-gram weight* ◇ *She lifts weights in the gym as part of her daily training.* ▶ **odważnik** **4** [sing.] something that you are worried about: *Telling her the truth took* ***a weight off*** *his* ***mind.*** Gdy powiedział jej prawdę, spadł mu kamień z serca. ▶ **ciężar**

IDM **carry weight** → CARRY

pull your weight → PULL[1]

weight² /weɪt/ verb [T] **1** **weight sth (down) (with sth)** to hold sth down with a heavy object or objects: *to weight down a fishing net* ▶ **obciążać** **2** [usually passive] to organize sth so that a particular person or group has an advantage/disadvantage: *The system is* ***weighted in favour of/against*** (daje przewagę/działa na niekorzyść) *people with children.*

weightless /ˈweɪtləs/ adj. having no weight, for example when travelling in space ▶ **nic nie ważący**

■ **weightlessness** noun [U] ▶ **nieważkość**

weightlifting /ˈweɪtlɪftɪŋ/ noun [U] a sport in which heavy metal objects are lifted ▶ **podnoszenie ciężarów** ➲ picture on **page A9**

■ **weightlifter** noun [C] ▶ (*sport*) **ciężarowiec**

ˈweight training noun [U] the activity of lifting **weights** as a form of exercise: *I do* ***weight training*** *to keep fit.* ▶ **ćwiczenia z użyciem ciężarków**

weighty /ˈweɪti/ adj. (**weightier**; **weightiest**) serious and important: *a weighty question* ▶ **ważki**

weir /wɪə(r)/ noun [C] a type of wall that is built across a river to stop or change the direction of the flow of water ▶ **grobla**

weird /wɪəd/ adj. strange and unusual: *a weird noise/experience* ◇ *weird clothes/ideas* ▶ **niesamowity**, **dziwaczny** SYN **bizarre**, **strange**

■ **weirdly** adv. ▶ **dziwnie**, **dziwacznie**

weirdo /ˈwɪədəʊ/ noun [C] (pl. **-os** /-əʊz/) (informal) a person who looks strange and/or behaves in a strange way ▶ **dziwa-k/czka**

welcome¹ /ˈwelkəm/ verb [T] **1** to be friendly to sb when they arrive somewhere: *Everyone came to the door to welcome us.* ▶ **witać** **2** to be pleased to receive or accept sth: *I've no idea what to do next, so I'd welcome any suggestions.* ▶ **przyjmować z radością**

■ **welcome** noun [C]: *Let's give a warm welcome to our next guest.* ▶ **powitanie**

welcome² /ˈwelkəm/ adj. **1** received with pleasure; giving pleasure: *You're always welcome here.* ◇ *welcome news* ▶ **mile widziany**, **pożądany** **2 welcome to sth/to do sth** allowed to do sth: *You're welcome to use our swimming pool.* Proszę korzystać z naszego basenu. ▶ **zapraszać do robienia czegoś/korzystania z czegoś** **3** (used to say that sb can have sth that you do not want yourself): *Take the car if you want. You're welcome to it* (możesz go sobie wziąć). *It's always breaking down.*

■ **welcome** interj.: *Welcome to London!* ◇ *Welcome home!* ▶ **witaj/cie!**

IDM **make sb welcome** to receive sb in a friendly way ▶ **serdecznie witać**, **zgotować serdeczne przyjęcie**

you're welcome (informal) you do not need to thank me: *'Thank you for your help.' 'You're welcome.'* ▶ (*odpowiedź na czyjeś podziękowanie*) **proszę bardzo**, **cała przyjemność po mojej stronie**

weld /weld/ verb [I,T] to join pieces of metal by heating them and pressing them together ▶ **spawać**

welfare /ˈwelfeə(r)/ noun [U] **1** the general health, happiness of a person, an animal or a group: *The doctor is concerned about the child's welfare.* ▶ **pomyślność** SYN **well-being** **2** the help and care that is given to people who have problems with health, money, etc.: *education and welfare services* ▶ **opieka społeczna** **3** (US) = SOCIAL SECURITY

ˌwelfare ˈstate noun [sing.] a system organized by a government to provide free services and money for people who have no job, who are ill, etc.; a country that has this system ▶ **państwo opiekuńcze**

we'll /wiːl/ short for **we shall; we will**

well¹ /wel/ adv. (**better** /ˈbetə(r)/; **best** /best/) **1** in a good way: *You speak English very well.* ◇ *I hope your work is* ***going well.*** ◇ *You passed your exam!* ***Well done*** (brawo)*!* ◇ *He took it well when I told him he wasn't on the team.* ▶ **dobrze** OPP **badly** **2** completely or fully: *Shake the bottle well before opening.* ◇ *How well do you know Henry?* ▶ **dobrze**, **mocno**, **dokładnie** **3** very much: *They arrived home well past midnight.* ◇ *She says she's 32 but I'm sure she's well over 40.* ◇ *This book is* ***well worth reading*** (naprawdę warta przeczytania). ▶ **bardzo**; **dobrze** **4** [used with *can, could, may* or *might*] probably or possibly: *He might well be right.* ▶ **prawdopodobnie** **5** [used with *can, could, may* or *might*] with good reason: *I can't very well refuse to help them* (nie mogę tak po prostu im odmówić pomocy) *after all they've done for me.* ◇ *'Where's Bill?' 'You may well ask!* (pyta mnie, a ja mogę zapytać o to samo)*'*

IDM **as well (as sb/sth)** in addition to sb/sth: *Can I come as well?* ◇ *He's worked in Japan as well as Italy.* ▶ **też**, **jak i**, **także** ➲ note at **also**

augur well/ill for sb/sth → AUGUR

bode well/ill (for sb/sth) → BODE

do well **1** to be successful: *Their daughter has done well at university.* ▶ **odnosić sukces** **2** to be getting better after an illness: *Mr Singh is doing well after his operation.* ▶ (*zdrowie*) **poprawiać się**

do well to do sth (used to say that sth is the right and sensible thing to do): *He would do well to check* (lepiej byś najpierw sprawdził) *the facts before accusing people.* ◇ *You did very well to buy* (dobrze zrobiłeś, że kupiłeś) *this house before prices went up.*

it is just as well (that ...) → JUST¹

may/might (just) as well (used for saying that sth is the best thing you can do in the situation, even though you may not want to do it): *I may as well tell you the truth – you'll find out anyway.* ▶ **równie dobrze**

mean well → MEAN¹

well and truly completely: *We were well and truly lost.* ▶ **zupełnie**

well/badly off → OFF¹

be well out of sth to be lucky because you are not involved in sth: *They're still arguing – I'm glad we're well out of it* (że nas to już nie dotyczy). ▶ **już kogoś nie dotyczyć**

well² /wel/ adj. (**better** /ˈbetə(r)/; **best** /best/) [not before a noun] **1** in good health: *'How are you?' 'I'm very well* (czuję się bardzo dobrze)*, thanks.'* ◇ *This medicine will make you* ***feel better.*** ◇ ***Get well soon.*** (Życzymy) szybkiego powrotu do zdrowia. ▶ **zdrowy**, **dobrze się czujący/wyglądający** **2** in a good state: *I hope all is well with you* (u ciebie/was wszystko w porządku). ▶ **zadowalający**

IDM **all very well (for sb)** (informal) (used for showing that you are not happy or do not agree with sth): *It's all very well for her to criticize but it doesn't help the situation.* ▶ **łatwo/dobrze (komuś coś robić)**

be (just) as well (to do sth) to be sensible; to be a good idea: *It would be just as well to ask his permission.* ▶ **dobrze byłoby** ℹ Por. **it is just as well (that)** przy **just**.

> **well**
>
> Na pytanie **How are you?** jest wiele odpowiedzi. Kiedy chcemy odpowiedzieć, że się mamy dobrze, możemy użyć wyrażeń: *I'm* ***very well.*** ◇ *I'm* ***great.*** ◇ *I'm* ***good.*** Inne wyrażenia to: *I'm* ***OK.*** ◇ *I'm* ***fine.*** Jeśli nie jest się w najlepszym stanie zdrowia, można powiedzieć: *I'm* ***not (too) bad.*** ◇ ***So-so.***

well³ /wel/ interj. **1** (used for showing surprise, anger or relief): *Well, thank goodness you've arrived.* ▶ **no!**; **nareszcie!** **2** (also **oh well**) (used for showing that you know there is nothing you can do to change a situation): *Oh well, there's nothing we can do.* ▶ **(no) cóż**, **niech będzie** **3** (used when you begin the next part of a story or when you are thinking about what to say next): *Well, the next thing that happened was ...* ◇ *Well now, let me see ...* ▶ **zatem**, **otóż** **4** (used when you feel uncertain about sth): *'Do you like it?' 'Well, I'm not really sure.'* ▶ **hm**, **cóż** **5** (used to show that you are waiting for sb to say sth): *Well? Are you going to tell us what happened?* ▶ **a więc** **6** (used to show that you want to finish a conversation): *Well, it's been nice talking to you.* ▶ **(no) cóż**

well⁴ /wel/ noun [C] **1** a deep hole in the ground from which water is obtained: *to draw water from a well* ▶ **studnia** **2** = OIL WELL

well⁵ /wel/ verb [I] **well (out/up)** (used about a liquid) to come to the surface: *Tears welled up* (pojawiły się) *in her eyes.* ▶ **wypływać**

ˌwell adˈjusted adj. (used about a person) able to deal with people, problems and life in general in a normal, sensible way: *The school aims to produce well-adjusted members of society.* ▶ **przystosowany**, **zrównoważony** ➲ look at **maladjusted**

ˌwell ˈbalanced adj. **1** (used about a meal, etc.) containing enough of the healthy types of food your body needs: *a well-balanced diet* ▶ **zrównoważony** **2** (used about a person or their behaviour) calm and sensible: *His response was well balanced.* ▶ **dobrze wyważony**

ˌwell beˈhaved adj. behaving in a way that most people think is correct ▶ **dobrze wychowany**, **z dobrymi manierami**

ˈwell-being noun [U] a state of being healthy and happy ▶ **dobro (czyjeś/ogółu)**, **pomyślność**

ˌwell ˈdone adj. (used about meat, etc.) cooked for a long time ▶ **dobrze wypieczony/wysmażony** ➲ look at **rare**, **medium**

ˌwell ˈdressed adj. wearing attractive and fashionable clothes ▶ **dobrze ubrany**

ˌwell ˈearned adj. that you deserve, especially because you have been working hard: *She's having a well earned holiday.* ▶ (*nagroda itp.*) **zasłużony**, **słuszny**

W

ˌ**well ˈfed** adj. having good food regularly ▶ **dobrze odżywiony**

ˌ**well inˈformed** adj. knowing a lot about one or several subjects ▶ **dobrze poinformowany**

wellington /ˈwelɪŋtən/ (also informal **welly** /ˈweli/, pl. **wellies**) noun [C] (Brit.) one of a pair of long rubber boots that you wear to keep your feet and the lower part of your legs dry: *a pair of wellingtons* ▶ **gumiak** ➲ picture at **shoe**

ˌ**well ˈkept** adj. looked after very carefully so that it has a tidy appearance: *a well-kept garden* ▶ **dobrze utrzymany**

⚷ˌ**well ˈknown** adj. known by a lot of people ▶ **powszechnie znany; sławny** SYN **famous** OPP **unknown**

ˌ**well ˈmannered** adj. (formal) having good manners ▶ **dobrze wychowany** SYN **polite**

ˌ**well ˈmatched** adj. able to live together, play or fight each other, etc. because they are similar in character, ability, etc.: *a well-matched couple* ◇ *The two teams were well matched.* ▶ **(dobrze) dobrany**

ˌ**well ˈmeaning** adj. (used about a person) wanting to be kind or helpful, but often not having this effect ▶ **mający jak najlepsze intencje**

ˌ**well ˈmeant** adj. intended to be kind or helpful but not having this result ▶ **w najlepszej intencji**

ˌ**well ˈpaid** adj. earning or providing a lot of money: *well-paid managers* ▶ **dobrze płatny**

ˌ**well ˈread** adj. having read many books and therefore having gained a lot of knowledge ▶ **oczytany**

ˌ**well ˈrounded** adj. **1** having a variety of experiences and abilities and a fully developed personality: *well-rounded individuals* ▶ **wszechstronnie wykształcony** **2** providing or showing a variety of experience, ability, etc.: *a well-rounded education* ▶ **wszechstronny** **3** (used about a person's body) pleasantly round in shape ▶ **zaokrąglony**

ˌ**well ˈspoken** adj. having a way of speaking that is considered correct or elegant ▶ **mówiący poprawnym/eleganckim językiem**

ˌ**well-to-ˈdo** adj. having a lot of money, property, etc. ▶ **zamożny** SYN **rich, wealthy**

ˌ**well ˈtravelled** (Brit.) (US ˌ**well ˈtraveled**) adj. **1** (used about a person) having travelled to many different places: *She is a well-travelled woman.* Dużo podróżowała. **2** (used about a route) used by a lot of people ▶ (*droga*) **uczęszczany**

ˈ**well-wisher** noun [C] a person who hopes that sb/sth will be successful: *She received lots of letters from well-wishers.* ▶ **życzliwa osoba**

welly (Brit., informal) = WELLINGTON

Welsh /welʃ/ adj. from Wales ▶ **walijski** ❶ Więcej w dodatku *Nazwy geograficzne i mapy* na końcu słownika.
■ **Welsh** noun **1** [U] the language of Wales ▶ **walijski (język)** ❶ **Welsh** jest językiem celtyckim, zupełnie innym niż angielski. **2** (**the Welsh**) [pl.] the people of Wales ▶ **Walijczycy**

Wendy house (Brit.) = PLAYHOUSE

went past tense of **go**[1]

wept past tense, past participle of **weep**

we're /wɪə(r)/ short for **we are**

were → BE

weren't /wɜːnt/ short for **were not**

⚷**west**[1] /west/ noun [sing.] (abbr. **W**) **1** (also **the west**) the direction you look towards in order to see the sun go down; one of the four **points of the compass**: *Which way is west?* ◇ *Rain is spreading from the west.* ◇ *There's a road* **to the west of** *here.* ▶ **zachód** **2** (**the west**; **the West**) the part of any country, city, etc. that is further to the west than other parts: *I live in the west of Scotland.* ▶ **zachód** **3** (**the West**) [sing.] the countries of North America and Western Europe ▶ **Zachód**

⚷**west**[2] /west/ adj. **1** (also **West**) [only before a noun] in the west: *West London* ▶ **zachodni** **2** (used about a wind) coming from the west ▶ **zachodni, z zachodu** **3** to or towards the west
■ **west** adv. to or towards the west: *to travel west* ◇ *The island is five miles west of here.* ◇ *We live west of the city.* ▶ **na zachód/zachodzie**

westbound /ˈwestbaʊnd/ adj. travelling or leading towards the west: *the westbound carriageway of the motorway* ▶ (*jadący/idący itp.*) **w kierunku zachodnim/na zachód**

the ˌ**West ˈEnd** noun [sing.] the western area of central London where there are many theatres, shops and hotels ▶ **West End** (*dzielnica eleganckich sklepów, hoteli i teatrów w zachodniej części Londynu*)

westerly /ˈwestəli/ adj. **1** [only before a noun] to, towards or in the west: *in a westerly direction* ▶ **zachodni** **2** (used about winds) coming from the west ▶ **zachodni, z zachodu**

⚷**western**[1] (also **Western**) /ˈwestən/ adj. **1** [only before a noun] (abbr. **W**) in or of the west: *western France* ▶ **zachodni** **2** from or connected with the western part of the world, especially Europe or North America: *the Western way of life* ▶ **zachodni**

western[2] /ˈwestən/ noun [C] a film or book about life in the past in the west of the United States ▶ **western (gatunek filmu)**

westerner /ˈwestənə(r)/ noun [C] a person who was born or who lives in the western part of the world, especially Europe or North America: *Westerners arriving in China usually experience culture shock.* ▶ **osoba pochodząca z Zachodu**

westernize (also **-ise**) /ˈwestənaɪz/ verb [T, usually passive] to make a country or people more like Europe and North America: *Young people in our country are becoming westernized* (ulegają wpływowi kultury zachodniej) *through watching American television programmes.* ▶ **szerzyć kulturę Zachodu, europeizować**

the ˌ**West ˈIndies** noun [pl.] a group of islands in the Caribbean Sea that consists of the Bahamas, the Antilles and the Leeward and Windward Islands ▶ **Indie Zachodnie**
■ ˌ**West ˈIndian** noun [C]: *The West Indians won their match against Australia.* ▶ **mieszka-niec/nka Indii Zachodnich** | ˌ**West ˈIndian** adj. ▶ **antylski**

westwards /ˈwestwədz/ (also **westward**) adv.: *to fly westwards* ▶ **na zachód**
■ **westward** adj. towards the west: *in a westward direction* ▶ **zachodni**

⚷**wet**[1] /wet/ adj. (**wetter**; **wettest**) **1** covered in a liquid, especially water: *wet clothes/hair/grass/roads* ◇ *Don't get your feet wet.* ▶ **mokry** OPP **dry**

> **Moist** znaczy „lekko wilgotny". **Damp** znaczy „wilgotny w nieprzyjemny sposób ...: *Don't sit on the grass. It's damp.* Wyrazu **humid** używa się do opisania ciepłej i jednocześnie wilgotnej pogody lub powietrza.

2 (used about the weather, etc.) with a lot of rain: *a wet day* ▶ **słotny** OPP **dry** **3** (used about paint, etc.) not yet dry or hard: *The ink is still wet.* ▶ **mokry, wilgotny** OPP **dry** **4** (used about a person) without energy or enthusiasm: *'Don't be so wet,' she laughed.* ▶ **niemrawy, miękki, bojaźliwy**
■ **the wet** noun [sing.]: *Come in out of the wet.* Wyjdź z deszczu. ▶ **deszcz**
IDM **a wet blanket** (informal) a person who spoils other people's fun, especially because they refuse to take part

in sth ▶ **osoba psująca innym zabawę/nie biorąca udziału w ogólnej zabawie**
wet through extremely wet ▶ **przemoczony do suchej nitki**

wet² /wet/ verb [T] (**wetting**; pt, pp **wet** or **wetted**) **1** to make sth wet ▶ **moczyć 2** (used especially of young children) to make yourself or your bed, clothes, etc. wet by letting **urine** escape from your body ▶ **moczyć się**

wetsuit /ˈwetsuːt/ noun [C] a piece of clothing made of rubber that fits the whole body closely, worn by people swimming underwater or sailing ▶ **strój nurka**

wetted past tense, past participle of **wet²**

we've /wiːv/ short for **we have**

whack /wæk/ verb [T] (informal) to hit sb/sth hard ▶ **walić**

whacky = WACKY

whale /weɪl/ noun [C] a very large animal that lives in the sea and looks like a very large fish ▶ **wieloryb** ➲ picture on **page A10**

whaling /ˈweɪlɪŋ/ noun [U] the hunting of **whales** ▶ **wielorybnictwo**

wharf /wɔːf/ noun [C] (pl. **wharves** /wɔːvz/) a platform made of stone or wood at the side of a river where ships and boats can be tied up ▶ **nabrzeże**

⚷ **what** /wɒt; US also wʌt/ determiner, pron. **1** (used for asking for information about sb/sth): *What time is it?* Która godzina? ◇ *What kind of music do you like?* ◇ *She asked him what he was doing.* ◇ *What's their phone number?* ▶ **jaki, co** ➲ note at **which 2** the thing or things that have been mentioned or said: *What he says is true.* ◇ *I haven't got much, but you can borrow what money I have.* ▶ **(wszystko) to, co 3** (used for emphasizing sth): *What strange eyes she's got!* ◇ *What a kind thing to do!* ◇ *What awful weather!* ▶ **co (za)?**
IDM **how/what about...?** → ABOUT²
what? (used to express surprise or to tell sb to say or repeat sth): *'I've asked Alice to marry me.' 'What?'* ▶ **co takiego?**
what for for what purpose or reason: *What's this little switch for?* ◇ *What did you say that for?* ▶ **po co, na co, dlaczego**
what if...? what would happen if...?: *What if the car breaks down?* ▶ **co będzie, jeżeli**

⚷ **whatever** /wɒtˈevə(r); US also wət-/ determiner, pron. **1** any or every; anything or everything: *You can say whatever you like.* ◇ *He took whatever help he could get.* ▶ **cokolwiek, jakikolwiek, każdy, wszystko (to) co 2** (used to say that it does not matter what happens or what sb does, because the result will be the same): *I still love you, whatever you may think.* ◇ *Whatever she says, she doesn't really mean it.* ▶ **cokolwiek, bez względu na to co 3** (used for expressing surprise or worry) what: *Whatever could have happened to them?* ▶ **co (za), cóż**
■ **whatever** (also **whatsoever** /wɒtsəʊˈevə(r)/) adv. at all: *I've no reason whatever to doubt him.* ◇ *'Any questions?' 'None whatsoever.'* ▶ **w ogóle (żaden), wcale**
IDM **or whatever** (informal) or any other or others of a similar kind: *You don't need to wear anything smart – jeans and a sweater or whatever.* ▶ **czy cokolwiek** (*innego itp.*)
whatever you do (used to emphasize that sb must not do sth): *Don't touch the red switch, whatever you do.* ▶ **w żadnym wypadku** (*nie wolno czegoś robić*)

wheat /wiːt/ noun [U] **1** a type of grain which can be made into flour ▶ **pszenica 2** the plant which produces this grain: *a field of wheat* ▶ **pszenica**

⚷ **wheel¹** /wiːl/ noun [C] **1** one of the round objects under a car, bicycle, etc. that turns when it moves ➲ picture at **bicycle**: *His favourite toy is a dog on wheels.* ◇ *By law, you have to carry a spare wheel in your car.* ◇ *a set of wheels* cztery kółka ▶ **koło** ➲ picture on **page A7 2** [usually sing.] = STEERING WHEEL: *Her husband was **at the wheel** when the accident happened.*

wheel² /wiːl/ verb **1** [T] to push along an object that has wheels; to move sb about in/on a vehicle with wheels: *She was wheeled back to her bed on a trolley.* ◇ *He wheeled his bicycle* (poprowadził rower) *up the hill.* ▶ **toczyć, wozić 2** [I] to fly round in circles: *Birds wheeled above the ship.* ▶ **krążyć w powietrzu 3** [I] to turn round suddenly: *Eleanor wheeled round, with a look of horror on her face.* ▶ **obracać się**

wheelbarrow /ˈwiːlbærəʊ/ (also **barrow**) noun [C] a type of small open container with one wheel and two handles that you use outside for carrying things ▶ **taczka** ➲ picture at **garden**

wheelchair /ˈwiːltʃeə(r)/ noun [C] a chair with large wheels that a person who cannot walk can move or be pushed about in ▶ **wózek inwalidzki**

ˈ**wheel clamp** = CLAMP² (2)

ˈ**wheelie bin** noun [C] (Brit., informal) a large container with a lid and wheels, that you keep outside your house and use for putting rubbish in ▶ **pojemnik na śmieci** (*na kółkach*)

wheeze /wiːz/ verb [I] to breathe noisily, for example if you have a chest illness ▶ **charczeć, sapać**

⚷ **when** /wen/ adv., conj. **1** at what time: *When did she arrive?* ◇ *I don't know when she arrived.* ▶ **kiedy 2** (used for talking about the time at which sth happens or happened): *Sunday is the day when I can relax.* ◇ *I last saw her in May, when she was in London.* ◇ *He jumped up when the phone rang.* ▶ **kiedy, gdy**

> Zwróć uwagę, że mówiąc o przyszłości używa się po **when** czasu teraźniejszego: *I'll call you when I'm ready.*
>
> **When** używa się, gdy mówiący jest przekonany, że to, o czym mówi, na pewno się wydarzy, zaś **if** – gdy takiej pewności nie ma. Porównaj następujące zdania: *I'll ask her when (gdy) she comes.* (Jestem pewien, że przyjdzie.) ◇ *I'll ask her if (jeżeli) she comes.* (Nie jestem pewien, czy przyjdzie.)

3 since; as; considering that: *Why do you want more money when you've got enough already?* ▶ **kiedy, podczas gdy**

whence /wens/ adv. (old-fashioned) (from) where: *They returned whence they had come.* ▶ **skąd**

⚷ **whenever** /wenˈevə(r)/ conj., adv. at any time; no matter when: *You can borrow my car whenever you want.* ◇ *Don't worry. You can give it back the next time you see me, or whenever.* ▶ **kiedykolwiek, kiedy tylko**
■ **whenever** adv. (used in questions when you are showing that you are surprised or impatient) when: *Whenever did you find time to do all that cooking?* ▶ **(a) kiedyż to**

⚷ **where** /weə(r)/ adv., conj. **1** in or to what place or position: *Where can I buy a paper?* ◇ *I asked him where he lived.* ▶ **gdzie, dokąd 2** in or to the place or situation mentioned: *the town where you were born* ◇ *She ran to where* (tam/do tego miejsca) *they were standing.* ◇ *Where possible* (kiedy (to) możliwe), *you should travel by bus, not taxi.* ◇ *We came to a village, where we stopped for lunch.* ◇ ***Where maths is concerned*** (jeśli chodzi o matematykę), *I'm hopeless.* ▶ **gdzie**

whereabouts¹ /ˈweərəbaʊts/ noun [pl.] the place where sb/sth is: *The whereabouts of the stolen painting are unknown.* ▶ **miejsce przebywania**

whereabouts² /ˌweərəˈbaʊts/ adv. where; in or near what place: *Whereabouts did you lose your purse?* ▶ **w jakim miejscu**

W

whereas /ˌweərˈæz/ conj. (used for showing a fact that is different): *He eats meat, whereas she's a vegetarian.* ▶ **podczas gdy** SYN **while**

whereby /weəˈbaɪ/ adv. (formal) by which; because of which: *These countries have an agreement whereby foreign visitors can have free medical care.* ▶ **mocą którego**

whereupon /ˌweərəˈpɒn; US also ˈwerə-/ conj. (formal) after which: *He fell asleep, whereupon she walked quietly from the room.* ▶ **po czym, na co**

wherever /weərˈevə(r)/ conj. **1** in or to any place: *You can sit wherever you like.* ◇ *She comes from Omiya, wherever that is.* ▶ **gdziekolwiek, dokądkolwiek** **2** everywhere, in all places that: *Wherever I go, he goes.* ▶ **gdziekolwiek, dokądkolwiek**
■ **wherever** adv. (used in questions for showing surprise): *Wherever did you learn to cook like that?* ▶ **(a) gdzież**
IDM **or wherever** or any other place: *The students might be from Sweden, Denmark or wherever* (czy skądkolwiek). ▶ **czy gdziekolwiek**

whet /wet/ verb (whetting; whetted)
IDM **whet sb's appetite** to make sb want more of sth: *Our short stay in Prague whetted our appetite to spend more time there.* ▶ **pobudzać/zaostrzać apetyt**

whether /ˈweðə(r)/ conj. **1** [used after verbs like *ask, doubt, know*, etc.] if: *He asked me whether we would be coming to the party.* ▶ **czy** **2** (used for expressing a choice or doubt between two or more possibilities): *I can't make up my mind **whether** to go **or not**.* ▶ **czy**

> **Whether** i **if** można używać wymiennie w znaczeniu 1. Natomiast tylko **whether** może występować przed **to** + czasownik: *Have you decided whether to accept the offer yet?* Również po przyimku używa się tylko **whether**: *the problem of whether to accept the offer*.

IDM **whether or not** (used to say that sth will be true in either of the situations that are mentioned): *We shall play on Saturday whether it rains or not.* ◇ *Whether or not it rains, we shall play on Saturday.* ▶ **(bez względu na to) czy ... czy też nie**

whey /weɪ/ noun [U] the thin liquid that remains after sour milk has formed curds ▶ **serwatka**

which /wɪtʃ/ determiner, pron. **1** (used in questions to ask sb to be exact, when there are a number of people or things to choose from): *Which hand do you write with?* ◇ *Which is your bag?* ◇ *She asked me which book I preferred.* ◇ *I can't remember which of the boys is the older.* ▶ **który, jaki**

> **Which** czy **what**? Słowa **which** używa się, kiedy wybór dotyczy małej liczby rzeczy: *Which car is yours? The Ford or the Volvo?* Natomiast **what** stosuje się, gdy wybór jest nieograniczony: *What car would you choose, if you could have any one you wanted?* ◇ *What is your name?*

2 (used for saying exactly what thing or things you are talking about): *Cars which use unleaded petrol are more eco-friendly.* ▶ **który, jaki**

> W przykładzie powyżej fraza *which use unleaded petrol* zawiera niezbędne informacje na temat samochodów. Część zdania po **which** to **defining relative clause** (zdanie względne określające). W takim zdaniu można również zamiast **which** użyć **that**: *Cars that use unleaded petrol ...* Uwaga! W takich zdaniach przed **which** czy **that** nie stawia się przecinka: *The situation **which** he found himself **in** was very difficult.*
>
> W języku formalnym pisze się: *The situation **in which** he found himself was very difficult.* W języku nieformalnym zaimek **which** jest często pomijany: *The situation he found himself in ...*

3 (used for giving more information about a thing or an animal): *My first car, which I bought as a student, was a Renault.* ▶ **który** (*w zdaniu wtrąconym*)

> W zdaniu powyżej fraza *which I bought as a student* dostarcza nam dodatkowych informacji na temat samochodu. Część zdania po **which** nazywa się **non-defining relative clause** (zdanie względne nieokreślające). W takich zdaniach nie można używać zaimka **that**. Trzeba też postawić przecinek przed zaimkiem **which** oraz na końcu tego zdania względnego.

4 (used for making a comment on what has just been said): *We had to wait 16 hours for our plane, which was really annoying* (co było bardzo denerwujące). ▶ **co** (*w zdaniu uzupełniającym*) ⓘ Uwaga! W tego typu zdaniach zaimek **which** poprzedzony jest przecinkiem.

whichever /wɪtʃˈevə(r)/ determiner, pron. **1** (used to say what feature or quality is important in deciding sth): *You can choose whichever book you want.* ◇ *Pensions should be increased annually in line with earnings or prices, whichever is the higher.* ▶ **którykolwiek** **2** (used to say that it does not matter which, as the result will be the same): *It takes three hours, whichever route you take.* ▶ **którykolwiek, jakikolwiek** **3** (used for expressing surprise) which: *You're very late. Whichever way did you come?* ▶ **(a) który, (a) jaki(ż)**

whiff /wɪf/ noun [usually sing.] **a whiff (of sth)** a smell, especially one which only lasts for a short time: *He **caught a whiff*** (poczuł zapach) *of her perfume.* ▶ **(ulotny) zapach**

while¹ /waɪl/ (also formal **whilst** /waɪlst/) conj. **1** during the time that; when: *He always phones while we're having lunch.* ▶ **(podczas) gdy; w czasie, kiedy** **2** at the same time as: *He always listens to the radio while he's driving to work* (jadąc do pracy). ▶ **podczas gdy, w czasie** **3** (formal) (used when you are contrasting two ideas): *Some countries are rich, while others are extremely poor.* ▶ **podczas gdy, natomiast** SYN **whereas**

while² /waɪl/ noun [sing.] a (usually short) period of time: *Let's sit down here for a while.* ▶ **chwila**
IDM **once in a while** → ONCE
worth sb's while → WORTH[1]

while³ /waɪl/ verb
PHR V **while sth away** to pass time in a lazy or relaxed way: *We whiled away the evening chatting and listening to music.* ▶ **zabijać czas, skracać sobie czas**

whim /wɪm/ noun [C] a sudden idea or desire to do sth (often sth that is unusual or not necessary): *We bought the house **on a whim*** (pod wpływem kaprysu). ▶ **kaprys, zachcianka**

whimper /ˈwɪmpə(r)/ verb [I] to make weak crying sounds, especially with fear or pain ▶ **kwilić, skomleć**
■ **whimper** noun [C] ▶ **kwilenie, skomlenie**

whimsical /ˈwɪmzɪkl/ adj. unusual and not serious in a way that is either amusing or annoying: *to have a whimsical sense of humour* ▶ **figlarny; kapryśny**
■ **whimsically** /-kli/ adv. ▶ **figlarnie; kapryśnie**

whine /waɪn/ verb **1** [I,T] to complain about sth in an annoying, crying voice: *The children were whining all afternoon.* ▶ **jęczeć** **2** [I] to make a long high unpleasant sound because you are in pain or unhappy: *The dog is whining to go out.* ▶ **skowyczeć, jęczeć**
■ **whine** noun [C] ▶ **jęk, skowyt**

whinge /wɪndʒ/ verb [I] (**whingeing** or **whinging**) (Brit., informal) **whinge (about sb/sth)** to complain in an annoying way: *She's always whingeing about how unfair everything is.* ▶ **biadolić** ⊃ note at **grumble**
■ **whinge** noun [C] ▶ **biadolenie** | **whinger** noun [C] ▶ **malkontent/ka**

whip¹ /wɪp/ noun [C] **1** a long thin piece of leather, etc. with a handle, that is used for making animals go faster and for hitting people as a punishment: *He **cracked the whip*** (trzasnął z bicza) *and the horse leapt forward.* ▶ **bat, bicz 2** (in Britain and the US) an official of a political party who makes sure that all members vote on important matters ▶ **osoba wyznaczona przez partię polityczną do przestrzegania dyscypliny partyjnej, zwłaszcza podczas głosowania w parlamencie**

whip² /wɪp/ verb (**whipping**; **whipped**) **1** [T] to hit a person or an animal hard with a **whip**, as a punishment or to make them or it go faster or work harder ▶ **biczować, chłostać, zacinać** (*konia*) **2** [I] (informal) to move quickly, suddenly or violently: *She whipped round to see what had made the noise behind her.* ▶ **wykonywać błyskawiczny ruch; przemieszczać coś błyskawicznym ruchem 3** [T] to remove or pull sth quickly and suddenly: *He whipped out a pen* (błyskawicznie wyciągnął pióro) *and made a note of the number.* **4** [T] **whip sth (up)** to mix the white part of an egg, cream, etc. until it is light and thick: *whipped cream* ▶ **ubijać 5** [T] (Brit., informal) to steal sth: *Who's whipped my pen?* ▶ **gwizdnąć**
PHR V **whip through sth** (informal) to do or finish sth very quickly: *I whipped through my homework in ten minutes.* ▶ **zrobić/zakończyć coś bardzo szybko** (*jak z bicza strzelił*)
whip sb/sth up to deliberately try to make people excited or feel strongly about sth: *to whip up excitement* ▶ **wprawiać w stan podniecenia, rozgrzewać** (*np. emocje*)
whip sth up (informal) to prepare food quickly: *to whip up a quick snack* ▶ **pichcić coś**

whir (especially US) = WHIRR

whirl¹ /wɜːl/ verb [I,T] to move, or to make sb/sth move, round and round very quickly in a circle: *The dancers whirled round the room.* ◇ (figurative) *I couldn't sleep. My mind was whirling after all the excitement.* ▶ **wirować, kręcić (się)**

whirl² /wɜːl/ noun [sing.] **1** the action or sound of sth moving round and round very quickly: *the whirl of the helicopter's blades* ▶ **wirowanie 2** a state of confusion or excitement: *My head's in a whirl* (kręci mi się w głowie) *– I'm so excited.* ▶ **wirowanie, wir 3** a number of events or activities happening one after the other: *The next few days passed in a whirl of activity.* ▶ **wir** (*zdarzeń*)
IDM **give sth a whirl** (informal) to try sth to see if you like it or can do it ▶ **próbować**

whirlpool /ˈwɜːlpuːl/ noun [C] a place in a river or the sea where currents in the water move very quickly round in a circle ▶ **wir** (*wodny*)

whirlwind /ˈwɜːlwɪnd/ noun [C] a very strong wind that moves very fast in a circle ▶ **trąba powietrzna** SYN **tornado** ➲ note at **storm**

whirr (especially US **whir**) /wɜː(r)/ verb [I] to make a continuous low sound like the parts of a machine moving: *The noise of the fan whirring kept me awake.* ▶ **furkotać, warkotać**
■ **whirr** (especially US **whir**) noun [C, usually sing.] ▶ **furkot, warkot**

whisk¹ /wɪsk/ verb [T] **1** to beat or mix eggs, cream, etc. very fast using a fork or a **whisk**: *Whisk the egg whites until stiff.* ▶ **ubijać** SYN **beat 2** to take sb/sth somewhere very quickly: *The prince was whisked away* (błyskawicznie wywieziono księcia) *in a black limousine.* ▶ **przewozić (kogoś/coś) błyskawicznie**

whisk² /wɪsk/ noun [C] a tool that you use for beating eggs, cream, etc. very fast ▶ **trzepaczka** (*np. do piany*) ➲ picture at **kitchen, mixer**

whisker /ˈwɪskə(r)/ noun **1** [C] one of the long thick hairs that grow near the mouth of some animals such as a mouse, cat, etc. ▶ **wąs** ➲ picture on **page A10 2** (**whiskers**) [pl.] (old-fashioned or humorous) the hair that is growing on a man's face ▶ **bokobrody, broda**

whisky /ˈwɪski/ noun (pl. **whiskies**) **1** [U] a strong alcoholic drink that is made from grain and is sometimes drunk with water and/or ice: *Scotch whisky* ▶ **whisky 2** [C] a glass of **whisky** ▶ **whisky** ℹ W USA i Irlandii stosuje się pisownię **whiskey**.

whisper /ˈwɪspə(r)/ verb [I,T] to speak very quietly into sb's ear, so that other people cannot hear what you are saying ▶ **szeptać**
■ **whisper** noun [C]: *to speak **in a whisper*** ▶ **szept**

whistle¹ /ˈwɪsl/ noun [C] **1** a small metal or plastic tube that you blow into to make a long high sound or music: *The referee blew his whistle to stop the game.* ▶ **gwizdek 2** the sound made by blowing a **whistle** or by blowing air out between your lips: *United scored just moments before **the final whistle.*** ◇ *He gave a low whistle of surprise.* ▶ **gwizd**

whistle² /ˈwɪsl/ verb **1** [I,T] to make a musical or a high sound by forcing air out between your lips or by blowing a **whistle**: *He whistled a tune to himself.* ▶ **gwizdać 2** [I] to move somewhere quickly making a sound like a **whistle**: *A bullet whistled past his head.* ▶ **gwizdać**

ˈwhistle-blower noun [C] [used especially in newspapers] a person who informs people in authority or the public that the company they work for is doing sth wrong or illegal ▶ **informator/ka**

white¹ /waɪt/ adj. **1** having the very light colour of fresh snow or milk: *a white shirt* ◇ *white coffee* kawa z mlekiem ▶ **biały 2** (used about a person) belonging to or connected with a race of people who have pale skin: *white middle-class families* ▶ **biały 3 white (with sth)** (used about a person) very pale because you are ill, afraid, etc.: *to be white with shock/anger/fear* ◇ *She went **white as a sheet** when they told her.* ▶ **biały**
IDM **black and white** → BLACK¹

white² /waɪt/ noun **1** [U] the very light colour of fresh snow or milk: *She was dressed **in white.*** ▶ **biel, kolor biały 2** [C, usually pl.] a member of a race of people with pale skin ▶ **człowiek białej rasy 3** [C,U] the part of an egg that surrounds the **yolk** and that becomes white when it is cooked: *Beat the whites of four eggs.* ▶ **białko 4** [C] the white part of the eye: *The whites of her eyes were bloodshot.* ▶ **białko**
IDM **in black and white** → BLACK²

ˌwhite ˈblood cell noun [C] any of the clear cells in the blood that help to fight disease ▶ **krwinka biała**

whiteboard /ˈwaɪtbɔːd/ noun [C] a large board with a smooth white surface that teachers, etc. write on with special pens: *an **interactive whiteboard*** tablica interaktywna typu whiteboard ▶ **tablica typu whiteboard** (*biała, na której pisze się specjalnymi, łatwo ścieralnymi markerami*)

ˈwhite-collar adj. (used about work) done in an office not a factory; (used about people) who work in an office ▶ **biurowy** ➲ look at **blue-collar**

ˌwhite ˈelephant noun [sing.] something that you no longer need and that is not useful any more, although it cost a lot of money ▶ **piąte koło u wozu**

the ˈWhite House noun [sing.] **1** the large house in Washington D.C. where the US president lives and works ▶ **Biały Dom 2** (used to refer to the US president and the other people in the government who work with him or her) ▶ (*instytucja*) **Biały Dom**

ˌwhite ˈlie noun [C] a lie that is not very harmful or serious, especially one that you tell because the truth would hurt sb ▶ **niewinne/nieszkodliwe kłamstwo**

W

whiten /ˈwaɪtn/ verb [I,T] to become white or whiter; to make sth white or whiter: *He gripped the wheel until his knuckles whitened.* ◇ *Her face whitened when she heard the news.* ◇ *Snow had whitened the tops of the trees.* ▶ **zbieleć**; **pobielać**

ˌ**White ˈPaper** noun [C] (Brit.) an official government report on a particular subject that will later be discussed in Parliament ▶ **oficjalne sprawozdanie rządowe**

whitewash¹ /ˈwaɪtwɒʃ/ noun [U] **1** a white liquid that you use for painting walls ▶ **wapno** (*malarskie*) **2** [sing.] trying to hide unpleasant facts about sb/sth: *The opposition say the report is a whitewash.* ▶ **wybielenie**

whitewash² /ˈwaɪtwɒʃ/ verb [T] **1** to paint **whitewash** onto a wall ▶ **bielić wapnem 2** to try to hide sth bad or wrong that you have done ▶ **wybielać** (*np. osobę*)

ˌ**white-water ˈrafting** noun the sport of travelling down a fast rough section of a river, lake, etc. in a rubber boat ▶ **spływ górski** ➲ picture on **page A8**

Whitsun /ˈwɪtsn/ (also **Whit** /wɪt/) noun [sing.] the seventh Sunday after Easter and the days close to it ▶ **Zielone Świątki**

whizz¹ (especially US **whiz**) /wɪz/ verb [I] (informal) to move very quickly, often making a high continuous sound: *The racing cars went whizzing by.* Samochody wyścigowe przeleciały ze świstem. ▶ **pędzić**, **lecieć**

whizz² (especially US **whiz**) /wɪz/ noun [sing.] a person who is very good and successful at sth: *She's a whizz at crosswords.* ◇ *He's our new marketing* ***whizz-kid***. ▶ **geniusz**

🔑 **who** /huː/ pron. **1** (used in questions to ask sb's name, identity, position, etc.): *Who was on the phone?* ◇ *Who's that woman in the grey suit?* ◇ *She wondered who he was.* ▶ **kto 2** (used for saying exactly which person or what kind of person you are talking about): *I like people who say what they think.* ◇ *That's the man who I met at Ann's party.* ◇ *The woman who I work for is very nice.* ▶ **(ten) który**, **(ten) co** ℹ W ostatnich dwóch przykładach, tzn. kiedy **who** jest dopełnieniem lub gdy występuje z przyimkiem, można je opuścić: *That's the man I met at Ann's party.* ◇ *The woman I work for is very nice.* **3** (used for giving extra information about sb): *My mother, who's over 80* (która ma ponad 80 lat), *still drives a car.* ℹ Zwróć uwagę, że dodatkowa informacja jest oddzielona od reszty zdania przecinkami. ▶ **który** ➲ note at **whom**

who'd /huːd/ short for **who had; who would**

ˌ**whoˈdunnit** (especially US **whodunit**) /ˌhuːˈdʌnɪt/ noun [C] (informal) a story, play, etc. about a murder in which you do not know who did the murder until the end ▶ **kryminał**

🔑 **whoever** /huːˈevə(r)/ pron. **1** the person or people who; any person who: *I want to speak to whoever is in charge.* ▶ **ktokolwiek**, **każdy**, **kto 2** it does not matter who: *She doesn't want to see anybody – whoever it is.* ▶ **ktokolwiek**, **obojętne kto 3** (used for expressing surprise) who: *Whoever could have done that?* ▶ **kto/któż (to)**

🔑 **whole¹** /həʊl/ adj. **1** [only before a noun] complete; full: *I drank a whole bottle of water.* ◇ *Let's just forget* ***the whole thing***. ◇ *She wasn't telling me* ***the whole truth***. ▶ **cały**; **pełny 2** not broken or cut: *Snakes swallow their prey whole* (w całości). ▶ **cały** ➲ adverb **wholly**

🔑 **whole²** /həʊl/ noun [sing.] **1** a thing that is complete or full in itself: *Two halves make a whole.* ▶ **całość 2 the whole of sth** all that there is of sth: *I spent the whole of the morning* (cały ranek) *cooking.* ▶ **całość**

IDM **as a whole** as one complete thing or unit and not as separate parts: *This is true in Britain, but also in Europe as a whole.* ▶ **w całości**

on the whole generally, but not true in every case: *On the whole I think it's a very good idea.* ▶ **na ogół**

wholefood /ˈhəʊlfuːd/ noun [U] (**wholefoods**) [pl.] food that is considered healthy because it does not contain artificial substances and is produced as naturally as possible ▶ **zdrowa żywność**

wholegrain /ˈhəʊlgreɪn/ adj. made with or containing whole grains, for example of **wheat** ▶ **pełnoziarnisty**

wholehearted /ˌhəʊlˈhɑːtɪd; US -təd/ adj. complete and enthusiastic: *to give sb your wholehearted support* (pełne poparcie) ▶ **niekłamany**, **z głębi serca płynący**
■ **wholeheartedly** adv. ▶ **z całego serca**, **w pełni**

wholemeal /ˈhəʊlmiːl/ (also **wholewheat** /ˈhəʊlwiːt/) adj. (made from flour) that contains all the grain including the outside layer: *wholemeal bread/flour* ▶ **razowy**

ˈ**whole note** (US) = SEMIBREVE

wholesale /ˈhəʊlseɪl/ adj. [only before a noun] **1** connected with buying and selling goods in large quantities, especially in order to sell them again and make a profit: *wholesale goods/prices* ▶ **hurtowy** ➲ look at **retail 2** (usually about sth bad) very great; on a very large scale: *the wholesale slaughter of wildlife* ▶ **masowy**
■ **wholesale** adv.: *They get all their building materials wholesale.* ▶ **hurtowo**; **masowo**

wholesome /ˈhəʊlsəm/ adj. **1** good for your health: *simple wholesome food* ▶ **zdrowy 2** having a moral effect that is good: *clean wholesome fun* ▶ **(moralnie) zdrowy**

who'll /huːl/ short for **who will**

wholly /ˈhəʊlli/ adv. completely; fully: *George is not wholly to blame for the situation.* ▶ **całkowicie**, **zupełnie**

🔑 **whom** /huːm/ pron. (formal) (used instead of 'who' as the object of a verb or preposition): *Whom did you meet there?* ◇ *He asked me whom I had met.* ◇ *To whom am I speaking?* ▶ *(przypadek zależny od* **kto/który)**

> Stosowanie **whom** zamiast **who** jest charakterystyczne dla bardzo formalnego języka. Zwykle takie zdanie jak *He asked me with whom I had discussed it* wyraża się w postaci *He asked me who I had discussed it with.* (Zwróć uwagę, że przyimek stoi wówczas na końcu zdania).

whooping cough /ˈhuːpɪŋ kɒf/ noun [U] a serious disease, especially of children, which makes them cough loudly and not be able to breathe easily ▶ **koklusz**

whoops /wʊps/ interj. (used when you have, or nearly have, a small accident): *Whoops! I nearly dropped the cup.* ▶ **o rety!**

whoosh /wʊʃ/ noun [usually sing.] the sudden movement and sound of air or water going past very fast ▶ **świst**, **szust**
■ **whoosh** verb [I] ▶ **przemieszczać się ze świstem**

whopper /ˈwɒpə(r)/ noun [C] (informal) **1** something that is very big for its type ▶ **olbrzym 2** a lie ▶ **wierutne kłamstwo**

whopping /ˈwɒpɪŋ/ (also ˈ**whopping great**) adj. [only before a noun] (informal) very big: *The company made a whopping 75 million dollar loss.* ▶ **gigantyczny**

who're /ˈhuːə(r)/ short for **who are**

whore /hɔː(r)/ noun [C] (old-fashioned) a female **prostitute** ▶ **dziwka**

who's /huːz/ short for **who is; who has**

🔑 **whose** /huːz/ determiner, pron. **1** (used in questions to ask who sth belongs to) of whom?: *Whose car is that?* ◇ *Whose is that car?* ◇ *Those are nice shoes – I wonder whose they are.* ▶ **czyj 2** (used to say exactly which person or thing you mean, or to give extra information about a person or thing) of whom; of which: *That's the boy whose mother I met.* ◇ *My neighbours, whose house is up for sale, are splitting up.* ▶ *(przypadek zależny od* **który)** ℹ W niektórych zdaniach za pomocą **whose** wprowadza się dodatkową informację o podmiocie (osobie lub rzeczy). Jest to tzw. zdanie wtrącone (bez niego zdanie główne też będzie miało sens). W takich wypadkach przed **whose** oraz na końcu zdania wtrąconego stawiamy przecinki.

who've /huːv/ short for **who have**

why /waɪ/ adv. **1** for what reason: *Why was she so late?* ◇ *I wonder why they went.* ◇ *'I'm not staying any longer.' 'Why not?'* ▶ **dlaczego**, **czemu 2** (used for giving or talking about a reason for sth): ***The reason why*** *I'm leaving you* (powód, dla którego odchodzę) *is obvious.* ◇ *I'm tired and* ***that's why*** (i dlatego) *I'm in such a bad mood.* ▶ **dlatego**

IDM **why ever** (used to show that you are surprised or angry): *Why ever didn't you phone?* ▶ **(a) dlaczego(ż)**
why not? (used for making or agreeing to a suggestion): *Why not phone her tonight?* ◇ *'Shall we go out tonight?' 'Yes, why not?'* ▶ **dlaczego/czemu nie?**, **może by**

wick /wɪk/ noun [C] the piece of string that burns in the middle of a **candle** ▶ **knot**

wicked /ˈwɪkɪd/ adj. **1** morally bad; evil ▶ **nikczemny**, **zły** ➲ note at **evil 2** (informal) slightly bad but in a way that is amusing and/or attractive: *a wicked sense of humour* ▶ **figlarny 3** (slang) very good: *This song's wicked.* ▶ **odjazdowy**, **bombowy**
■ **wickedly** adv. ▶ **figlarnie** | **wickedness** noun [U] ▶ **nikczemność**, **zło**

wicker /ˈwɪkə(r)/ noun [U] thin sticks of wood that bend easily and are crossed over and under each other to make furniture and other objects: *a wicker basket* ▶ **wiklina**

wicket /ˈwɪkɪt/ noun [C] **1** (in the sport of **cricket**) either of the two sets of three vertical sticks that the player throwing the ball tries to hit ▶ (*w krykiecie*) **bramka 2** (in the sport of **cricket**) the area of ground between the two **wickets** ▶ (*w krykiecie*) **obszar pomiędzy bramkami**

wide[1] /waɪd/ adj. **1** measuring a lot from one side to the other: *The road was not wide enough for two cars to pass.* ◇ *a wide river* ▶ **szeroki** OPP **narrow** ➲ note at **broad** ➲ noun **width 2** measuring a particular distance from one side to the other: *The box was only 20 centimetres wide.* ◇ *How wide is the river?* ▶ **szeroki**, **mający (x m itd.) szerokości 3** including a large number or variety of different people or things; covering a large area: *You're the nicest person in* ***the whole wide world!*** ◇ *a* ***wide range/choice/variety*** *of goods* ◇ *a manager with wide experience of industry* ▶ **bezmierny**, **rozległy 4** fully open: *The children's eyes were wide with excitement.* ▶ **szeroko otwarty 5** not near what you wanted to touch or hit: *His first serve was wide.* ▶ **daleko (od celu)**
■ **widely** adv. **1** to a large degree; a lot: *Their opinions differ widely.* ▶ **znacznie**, **bardzo 2** over a large area or range: *Steve travelled widely* (dużo podróżował) *in his youth.* ▶ **szeroko**, **rozlegle**

wide[2] /waɪd/ adv. as far or as much as possible; completely: *Open your mouth wide.* Otwórz szeroko usta. ◇ *It was late but she was still* ***wide awake*** (wcale nie chciało jej się spać). ◇ *The front door was* ***wide open*** (były otwarte na oścież).

ˌwide-angle ˈlens noun [C] a camera **lens** that can give a wider view than a normal **lens** ▶ **obiektyw szerokokątny**

widen /ˈwaɪdn/ verb [I,T] to become wider; to make sth wider: *The road widens just up ahead.* ▶ **poszerzać (się)**, **rozszerzać (się)**

ˌwide-ˈranging adj. covering a large area or many subjects: *a wide-ranging discussion* ▶ **obejmujący szeroki zakres** (*np. zagadnień*), **obszerny**

widescreen /ˈwaɪdskriːn/ noun [U] a way of presenting images on television with the width a lot greater than the height ▶ **szeroki ekran** SYN **letter box**

widespread /ˈwaɪdspred/ adj. found or happening over a large area; affecting a large number of people: *The storm has caused widespread damage.* ▶ **rozległy**

widow /ˈwɪdəʊ/ noun [C] a woman whose husband has died and who has not married again ▶ **wdowa**
■ **widowed** adj.: *She's been widowed for ten years now.* ▶ **owdowiał-y/a**

widower /ˈwɪdəʊə(r)/ noun [C] a man whose wife has died and who has not married again ▶ **wdowiec**

width /wɪdθ/ noun **1** [C,U] the amount that sth measures from one side or edge to the other: *The room is eight metres* ***in width.*** ◇ *The carpet is available in two different widths.* ▶ **szerokość** ➲ adjective **wide** ➲ picture at **dimension 2** [C] the distance from one side of a swimming pool to the other: *How many widths can you swim?* ▶ **szerokość (basenu)** ➲ look at **length**, **breadth**

wield /wiːld/ verb [T] **1** to have and use power, authority, etc.: *She wields enormous power in the company.* ▶ **mieć** (*władzę*) **2** to hold and be ready to use a weapon: *Some of the men were wielding knives.* ▶ **władać**, **dzierżyć**

wiener (US) = FRANKFURTER

wife /waɪf/ noun [C] (pl. **wives** /waɪvz/) the woman to whom a man is married ▶ **żona**

wig /wɪg/ noun [C] a covering made of real or false hair that you wear on your head ▶ **peruka**

wiggle /ˈwɪgl/ verb [I,T] (informal) to move from side to side with small quick movements; to make sth do this: *You have to wiggle your hips in time to the music.* ▶ **poruszać (czymś/się) w prawo i w lewo**
■ **wiggle** noun [C] ▶ **kręcenie biodrami** | **wiggly** /ˈwɪgli/ adj. ▶ **poruszający się**

wild[1] /waɪld/ adj. **1** living or growing in natural conditions, not looked after by people: *wild animals/flowers/strawberries* ▶ **dziki 2** in its natural state; not changed by people: *the wild plains of Siberia* ▶ **dziki 3** (used about a person or their behaviour or emotions) without control or discipline; slightly crazy: *The crowd* ***went wild*** (oszalał) *with excitement.* ◇ *He had a wild look in his eyes.* Patrzył szalonym wzrokiem. ◇ *They let their children* ***run wild*** (wyszaleć się). ▶ **szalony 4** not carefully planned; not sensible or accurate: *She made* ***a wild guess.*** ◇ *wild accusations/rumours* ▶ **na ślepo**, **na chybił trafił 5** (informal) **be wild (about sb/sth)** to like sb/sth very much: *I'm not wild about their new house.* ▶ **szaleć/przepadać (za kimś/czymś) 6** with strong winds or storms: *It was a wild night last night.* ▶ **burzliwy**
■ **wildly** adv. ▶ **dziko**, **szaleńczo** | **wildness** noun [U] ▶ **obłąkanie**, **dzikość**

wild[2] /waɪld/ noun **1** (**the wild**) [sing.] a natural environment that is not controlled by people: *the thrill of seeing elephants in the wild* (na wolności) ▶ **naturalne otoczenie/środowisko 2** (**the wilds**) [pl.] places that are far away from towns, where few people live: *They live somewhere out in the wilds.* ▶ **odludzie**

wilderness /ˈwɪldənəs/ noun [C, usually sing.] **1** a large area of land that has never been used for building on or for growing things: *The Antarctic is the world's last great wilderness.* ▶ **pustkowie**, **pustynia 2** a place that people do not take care of or control: *Their garden is a wilderness.* ▶ **puszcza**, **chaszcze**

ˌwild ˈgoose chase noun [C] a search for sth that is impossible for you to find or that does not exist, that makes you waste a lot of time: *The police had been sent on a wild goose chase.* ▶ **szukanie wiatru w polu**

wildlife /ˈwaɪldlaɪf/ noun [U] animals, birds, insects, etc. that are wild and live in a natural environment ▶ **dzika fauna i flora**

wilful (US also willful) /ˈwɪlfl/ adj. **1** done deliberately although the person doing it knows that it is wrong: *wilful damage/neglect* ▶ **rozmyślny, z premedytacją** **2** doing exactly what you want, no matter what other people think or say: *a wilful child* ▶ **samowolny**
■ **wilfully** /-fəli/ adv. ▶ **rozmyślnie, z premedytacją; samowolnie**

will[1] /wɪl/ modal verb (short form **'ll** /l/, negative **will not**; short form **won't** /wəʊnt/, pt **would** /wəd; strong form wʊd/, short form **'d** /d/, negative **would not**; short form **wouldn't** /ˈwʊdnt/) **1** (used in forming the future tenses): *He will be* (będzie) *here soon.* ◇ *I'm sure you'll pass* (zdasz) *your exam.* ◇ *I'll be* (będę) *sitting on the beach this time next week.* ◇ *Next Sunday, she will have been in England for a year.* W przyszłą niedzielę minie rok od jej przyjazdu do Anglii. **2** (used for showing that sb is offering sth or wants to do sth, or that sth is able to do sth): *'We need some more milk.' 'OK, I'll get it* (przyniosę je)*.'* ◇ *Why won't you tell me* (powiedz mi) *where you were last night?* ◇ *I'll carry* (poniosę) *your case for you.* ◇ *My car won't start* (nie chce zapalić). ◇ *Will you have a cup of tea?* Czy napijesz się herbaty? **3** (used for asking sb to do sth): *Will you sit down, please?* Proszę usiąść. **4** (used for ordering sb to do sb): *Will you all be quiet!* Proszę wszystkich o spokój! **5** (used for saying that you think sth is probably true): *That will be the postman at the door.* To na pewno listonosz. ◇ *He'll have left work by now, I suppose.* Chyba już wyszedł do pracy. **6** [only in positive sentences] (used for talking about habits): *She'll listen to music, alone in her room, for hours.* Godzinami słucha muzyki, siedząc sama w pokoju. ⓘ Jeśli zaakcentuje się mocniej **will**, oznacza to, że dany nawyk jest denerwujący: *He **will** keep interrupting me when I'm trying to work.* Ciągle mi przeszkadza, kiedy próbuję pracować.

will[2] /wɪl/ verb [T] to use the power of your mind to do sth or to make sth happen: *He willed himself to carry on to the end of the race.* ▶ **zmuszać się/kogoś siłą woli**

will[3] /wɪl/ noun **1** [C,U] the power of the mind to choose what to do; a feeling of strong determination: *Both her children have got very strong wills.* ◇ *My father seems to have lost **the will to live**.* ▶ **wola** **2** [sing.] what sb wants to happen in a particular situation: *My mother doesn't want to sell the house and I don't want to **go against** her **will**.* ▶ **wola, życzenie** **3** [C] a legal document in which you write down who should have your money and property after your death: *You really ought to **make a will**.* ◇ *Gran left us some money **in** her **will**.* ▶ **testament** **4** (**-willed**) [in compounds] having the type of will mentioned: *a strong-willed/weak-willed person* osoba o silnej/słabej woli
IDM **of your own free will** → FREE[1]

willing /ˈwɪlɪŋ/ adj. **1** [not before a noun] **willing (to do sth)** happy to do sth; having no reason for not doing sth: *Are you willing to help us?* ◇ *She's **perfectly willing** to lend me her car.* ◇ *I'm not willing to take any risks.* ▶ **skłonny, gotów (coś zrobić)** **2** ready or pleased to help and not needing to be persuaded; enthusiastic: *a willing helper/volunteer* ▶ **chętny, ochoczy** OPP for both meanings **unwilling**
■ **willingly** adv. ▶ **chętnie, z własnej woli** | **willingness** noun [U, sing.] ▶ **gotowość, ochota**

willow /ˈwɪləʊ/ (also ˈwillow tree) noun [C] a tree with long thin branches that hang down which grows near water: *weeping willow* wierzba płacząca ▶ **wierzba**

willpower /ˈwɪlpaʊə(r)/ noun [U] determination to do sth; strength of mind: *It takes a lot of willpower to give up smoking.* ▶ **siła woli**

willy /ˈwɪli/ noun [C] (pl. **willies**) (informal) a word used to refer to the **penis** ▶ **siusiak** ⓘ Słowo używane przez dzieci lub w rozmowie z dziećmi.

willy-nilly /ˌwɪli ˈnɪli/ adv. **1** if you want to or not ▶ **chcąc nie chcąc** **2** in a careless way without planning: *Don't spend your money willy-nilly.* ▶ **bez ładu i składu**

wilt /wɪlt/ verb [I] (used about a plant or flower) to bend and start to die, because of heat or a lack of water ▶ **więdnąć, marnieć**

wily /ˈwaɪli/ adj. (**wilier**; **wiliest**) clever at getting what you want ▶ **chytry, przebiegły** SYN **cunning**

wimp /wɪmp/ noun [C] (informal) a weak person who has no courage or confidence: *Don't be such a wimp!* ▶ **słabeusz, mięczak**
■ **wimpish** adj. ▶ **słabowity, mięczakowaty**

win /wɪn/ verb (**winning**; pt, pp **won** /wʌn/) **1** [I,T] to be the best, first or strongest in a race, game, competition, etc.: *to win a game/match/championship* ◇ *I never win at table tennis.* ◇ *Which party do you think will win the next election?* ▶ **wygrywać, zwyciężać** **2** [T] to get money, a prize, etc. as a result of success in a competition, race, etc.: *We won a trip to Australia.* ◇ *Who won the gold medal?* ◇ *He won the jackpot in the lottery.* ▶ **wygrywać** **3** [T] to get sth by hard work, great effort, etc.: *Her brilliant performance won her a great deal of praise.* ◇ *to win support for a plan* ▶ **zdobywać**
■ **win** noun [C]: *We have had two wins and a draw so far this season.* ▶ **wygrana** | **winning** adj.: *The winning ticket is number 65.* ▶ **wygrywający, zwycięski**
IDM **win/lose the toss** → TOSS
you can't win (informal) there is no way of being completely successful or of pleasing everyone: *Whatever you do you will upset somebody. You can't win.* ▶ **i tak źle, i tak niedobrze**
PHR V **win sb over/around/round (to sth)** to persuade sb to support or agree with you: *They're against the proposal at the moment, but I'm sure we can win them over.* ▶ **pozyskiwać (kogoś do czegoś)**

wince /wɪns/ verb [I] to make a sudden quick movement (usually with a part of your face) to show you are feeling pain or embarrassment ▶ **drgnąć, krzywić się** (*np. z bólu*)

winch /wɪntʃ/ noun [C] a machine that lifts or pulls heavy objects using a thick chain, rope, etc. ▶ **wciągarka, wyciągarka**
■ **winch** verb [T]: *The injured climber was winched up into a helicopter.* ▶ **wciągać, wyciągać** (*za pomocą w(y)ciągarki*)

wind[1] /wɪnd/ noun **1** [C,U] air that is moving across the surface of the earth: *There was a strong wind blowing.* ◇ *high winds* silne wiatry ◇ *A **gust of wind** blew his hat off.* ▶ **wiatr** **2** [U] gas that is formed in your stomach: *The baby cries when he has wind.* ▶ **wiatry, wzdęcie** **3** [U] the breath that you need for doing exercise or playing a musical instrument: *She stopped running to get her wind back.* ▶ **oddech, dech** **4** [U] (in an **orchestra**) the group of instruments that you play by blowing into them: *the wind section* ▶ **instrumenty dęte**
IDM **get wind of sth** to hear about sth that is secret ▶ **wywęszyć**

wind[2] /wɪnd/ verb [T] **1** to cause sb to have difficulty in breathing: *The punch in the stomach winded her.* ▶ **pozbawiać tchu** **2** to help a baby get rid of painful gas in the stomach by rubbing or gently hitting its back ▶ **pomóc dziecku, aby mu się odbiło po jedzeniu**

wind[3] /waɪnd/ verb (pt, pp **wound** /waʊnd/) **1** [I] (used about a road, path, etc.) to have a lot of bends or curves in it: *The path winds down the cliff to the sea.* ▶ **kręcić się, wić się** **2** [T] to put sth long round sth else several times: *She wound the bandage around his arm.* ▶ **nawijać, zwijać, owijać** **3** [T] to make sth work or move by turning a key, handle, etc.: *He wound the car window down* (opuścił szybę) *and shouted at the other driver.* ◇ *Wind the tape on a bit to the next song.* ▶ **kręcić** (*np. korbką*), **przewijać** (*np. taśmę*)

PHR V **wind down** (about a person) to rest and relax after a period of hard work, worry, etc. ▶ **odprężać się** ➲ look at **unwind**

wind sth down **1** to bring a business, an activity, etc. to an end gradually over a period of time: *The government is winding down its nuclear programme.* ◇ *The department is being wound down after the election.* ▶ **kończyć** (*jakąś działalność, program*), **zwijać** (*interes*) **2** to make sth such as the window of a car move downwards by turning a handle, pressing a button, etc.: *Can I wind my window down?* ▶ **otwierać okno** (*w samochodzie*)

wind up to find yourself in a place or situation that you did not intend to be in: *We got lost and wound up in a dangerous-looking part of town.* ◇ *You'll wind up failing your exams if you go on like this.* Jeżeli będziesz tak dalej robił, to w końcu oblejesz egzaminy. ▶ **znaleźć się gdzieś/w pewnej sytuacji**

wind sb up to annoy sb until they become angry ▶ **rozzłościć kogoś**

wind sth up to finish, stop or close sth: *The company was losing money and had to be wound up.* ▶ **kończyć** (*działalność*), **zamykać**

windbreak /ˈwɪndbreɪk/ noun [C] a row of trees, a fence, etc. that provides protection from the wind ▶ **wiatrochron**

windfall /ˈwɪndfɔːl/ noun [C] an amount of money that you win or receive unexpectedly ▶ **gratka**, **nieoczekiwane szczęście/powodzenie**

winding /ˈwaɪndɪŋ/ adj. with bends or curves in it: *a winding road through the hills* ▶ **kręty**, **wijący się**

ˈ**wind instrument** noun [C] a musical instrument that you play by blowing through it ▶ **instrument dęty**

windmill /ˈwɪndmɪl/ noun [C] a tall building or structure with long parts called **sails** that turn in the wind. In past times **windmills** were used for making flour from grain, but now they are used mainly for producing electricity. ▶ **wiatrak**

⚷ **window** /ˈwɪndəʊ/ noun [C] **1** the opening in a building, car, etc. that you can see through and that lets light in. A window usually has glass in it: *Open the window. It's hot in here.* ◇ *a shop window* wystawa sklepowa ◇ *a window seat* miejsce przy oknie ▶ **okno 2** the glass in a window: *to break a window* ▶ **szyba 3** an area on a computer screen that has a particular type of information in it ▶ **okno 4** a time when you have not arranged to do anything and so are free to meet sb, etc.: *I'm busy all Tuesday morning, but I've got a window from 2 until 3.* ▶ **okienko** (*w harmonogramie*)

ˈ**window box** noun a long narrow box outside a window, in which plants are grown ▶ **skrzynka na kwiaty umieszczana na zewnątrz okna**

ˈ**window ledge** = WINDOWSILL

windowpane /ˈwɪndəʊpeɪn/ noun [C] one piece of glass in a window ▶ **szyba**

ˈ**window-shopping** noun [U] looking at things in shop windows without intending to buy anything ▶ **oglądanie wystaw sklepowych**

windowsill /ˈwɪndəʊsɪl/ (also ˈ**window ledge**) noun [C] the narrow shelf at the bottom of a window, either inside or outside ▶ **parapet okienny**

windpipe /ˈwɪndpaɪp/ noun [C] the tube that takes air from the throat to the lungs ▶ **tchawica** ℹ Określenie naukowe to **trachea**. SYN **trachea** ➲ picture at **body**

windscreen /ˈwɪndskriːn/ (US **windshield** /ˈwɪndʃiːld/) noun [C] the window in the front of a vehicle ▶ **przednia szyba** ➲ picture at **car**, picture on **page A7**

ˈ**windscreen wiper** (also **wiper** /ˈwaɪpə(r)/; US **windshield wiper**) noun [C] one of the two blades with rubber edges that move across a **windscreen** to make it clear of water, snow, etc. ▶ **wycieraczka (szyby samochodowej)** ➲ picture at **car**

windshield (US) = WINDSCREEN

ˈ**windshield wiper** (US) = WINDSCREEN WIPER

windsurf /ˈwɪndsɜːf/ verb [I] to move over water standing on a special board with a sail ▶ **uprawiać windsurfing** ℹ Zwykle mówi się **go windsurfing**: *Have you ever been windsurfing?*

■ **windsurfing** noun [U] ▶ **windsurfing** ➲ picture on **page A8**

windsurfer /ˈwɪndsɜːfə(r)/ noun [C] **1** (also **sailboard** /ˈseɪlbɔːd/) a board with a sail that you stand on as it moves over the surface of the water, pushed by the wind ▶ **deska windsurfingowa 2** a person who rides on a board like this ▶ **osoba uprawiająca windsurfing**

windswept /ˈwɪndswept/ adj. **1** (used about a place) that often has strong winds: *a windswept coastline* ▶ **wystawiony na wiatr**, **wietrzny 2** looking untidy because you have been in a strong wind: *windswept hair* ▶ **rozczochrany/potargany (na wietrze)**

windy /ˈwɪndi/ adj. (**windier**; **windiest**) with a lot of wind: *a windy day* ▶ **wietrzny** ➲ picture on **page A16**

⚷ **wine** /waɪn/ noun [C,U] an alcoholic drink that is made from **grapes**, or sometimes other fruit: *sweet* (słodkie)/ *dry* (wytrawne) *wine* ◇ *German wines* ▶ **wino** ➲ look at **beer**

> Wine is made in three colours: **red**, **white** and **rosé**. The grapes are grown in a **vineyard** (/ˈvɪnjəd/).

ˈ**wine bar** noun [C] a place where you can go to drink wine and have sth to eat ▶ **winiarnia** ➲ note at **bar**

⚷ **wing** /wɪŋ/ noun **1** [C] one of the two parts that a bird, insect, etc. uses for flying: *The chicken ran around flapping its wings.* ▶ **skrzydło** ➲ picture at **insect**, picture on **page A11**, picture at **fairy 2** [C] one of the two long parts that stick out from the side of a plane and support it in the air ▶ **skrzydło** ➲ picture at **plane**, picture on **page A6 3** [C] a part of a building that sticks out from the main part or that was added on to the main part: *the maternity wing of the hospital* ▶ **skrzydło 4** (US **fender**) [C] the part of the outside of a car that covers the top of the wheels: *There was a dent in the wing.* ▶ **błotnik** ➲ picture on **car 5** [C, usually sing.] a group of people in a political party that have particular beliefs or opinions: *He's on the right wing of the Conservative Party* ▶ **skrzydło** ➲ look at **left wing**, **right wing 6** [C] the part at each side of the area where the game is played: *to play on the wing* ▶ **skrzydło 7** (also **winger** /wɪŋə(r)/) [C] a person who plays in an attacking position at one of the sides of the field ▶ **skrzydłowy/a 8** (**the wings**) [pl.] the area at the sides of the stage where the actors cannot be seen by the audience ▶ **kulisy**

IDM **take sb under your wing** to take care of and help sb who has less experience than you ▶ **wziąć kogoś pod swoje skrzydła**

wink /wɪŋk/ verb [I] **wink (at sb)** to close and open one eye very quickly, usually as a signal to sb ▶ **mrugać** ➲ picture at **blink**

■ **wink** noun [C]: *He smiled and gave the little girl a wink.* ◇ *I didn't sleep a wink.* Nie zmrużyłem oka. ▶ **mrugnięcie**

IDM **forty winks** → FORTY

⚷ **winner** /ˈwɪnə(r)/ noun [C] **1** a person or an animal that wins a competition, game, race, etc.: *The winner of the competition will be announced next week.* ▶ **zwycię-**

W

zca/żczyni 2 (informal) something that is likely to be successful: *I think your idea is a winner.* ▶ **pewniak 3** (in sport) a goal that wins a match, a hit that wins a point, etc.: *Henry scored the winner in the last minute.* ▶ **zwycięski gol itp.**

winning → WIN

winnings /ˈwɪnɪŋz/ noun [pl.] money that you win in a competition or game ▶ **wygrana**

winter /ˈwɪntə(r)/ noun [C,U] the coldest season of the year between autumn and spring: *It snows a lot here* ***in winter.*** ◇ *a cold winter's day* ◇ *We went skiing in France last winter.* ▶ **zima** ➲ picture on **page A16**
■ **wintry** /ˈwɪntri/ adj.: *wintry weather* ▶ **zimowy**

ˌ**winter ˈsports** noun [pl.] sports which take place on snow or ice, for example **skiing** and **skating** ▶ **sporty zimowe**

wintertime /ˈwɪntətaɪm/ noun [U] the period or season of winter ▶ **zima**, **okres zimowy**

wipe¹ /waɪp/ verb [T] **1** to clean or dry sth by rubbing it with a cloth, etc.: *She stopped crying and wiped her eyes with a tissue.* ◇ *Could you wipe the table, please?* ▶ **wycierać**, **obcierać** ➲ note at **clean² 2 wipe sth from/off sth**; **wipe sth away/off/up** to remove sth by rubbing it: *He wiped the sweat from his forehead.* ◇ *Wipe up the milk you spilled.* ▶ **ścierać**, **wycierać 3 wipe sth (off) (sth)** to remove sound, information or images from sth: *I accidentally wiped the tape.* ◇ *I tried to wipe the memory from my mind.* ▶ **wymazać**, **zmazać**
PHR V **wipe sth down** to clean a surface completely, using a wet cloth: *She took a cloth and wiped down the kitchen table.* ▶ **wycierać coś na mokro**
wipe sth out to destroy sth completely: *Whole villages were wiped out in the bombing raids.* ▶ **zmiatać coś** (*np. z powierzchni ziemi*), **zniszczyć coś**

wipe² /waɪp/ noun [C] **1** the act of **wiping**: *He gave the table a quick wipe.* ▶ **wytarcie**, **starcie 2** a piece of paper or thin cloth that has been made wet with a special liquid and is used for cleaning sth: *a box of baby wipes* ▶ **chusteczka higieniczna** (*nasączona emulsją do mycia*), **ściereczka czyszcząca** (*nasączona płynem/mleczkiem do czyszczenia*)

wiper = WINDSCREEN WIPER

wire¹ /ˈwaɪə(r)/ noun [C,U] **1** metal in the form of thin thread; a piece of this: *a piece of wire* ◇ *a wire fence* ogrodzenie z siatki metalowej ◇ *barbed wire* drut kolczasty ▶ **drut 2** a piece of wire that is used to carry electricity: *telephone wires* ▶ **przewód**, **kabel** ➲ picture at **cable**

wire² /ˈwaɪə(r)/ verb [T] **1 wire sth (up) (to sth)** to connect sth to a supply of electricity or to a piece of electrical equipment by using wires: *to wire a plug* ◇ *The microphone was wired up to a loudspeaker.* ▶ **zakładać przewody elektryczne**, **zakładać instalację elektryczną 2 wire sth (to sb)**; **wire sb sth** to send money to sb's bank account using an electronic system: *The bank's going to wire me the money.* ▶ **przesyłać pieniądze drogą elektroniczną 3** to join two things together using wire ▶ **drutować**

wired /ˈwaɪəd/ adj. connected to a system of computers: *Many colleges now have wired dormitories.* ▶ **skomputeryzowany**

wireless /ˈwaɪələs/ adj. not using wires: *wireless technology/communications* ▶ **bezprzewodowy**, **radiowy**

wiring /ˈwaɪərɪŋ/ noun [U] the system of wires that supplies electricity to rooms in a building ▶ **instalacja elektryczna**

wiry /ˈwaɪəri/ adj. (**wirier**; **wiriest**) (used about a person) small and thin but strong ▶ **żylasty**

wisdom /ˈwɪzdəm/ noun [U] the ability to make sensible decisions and judgements because of your knowledge or experience: *I doubt the wisdom of taking a decision too early.* Wątpię, czy rozsądne jest zbyt wczesne podejmowanie decyzji. ◇ *I don't see the wisdom of this plan.* Nie uważam, aby ten plan miał sens. ▶ **mądrość** ➲ adjective **wise**

ˈ**wisdom tooth** noun [C] one of the four teeth at the back of your mouth that do not grow until you are an adult ▶ **ząb mądrości**

wise /waɪz/ adj. **1** (used about people) able to make sensible decisions and give good advice because of the experience and knowledge that you have: *a wise old man* ▶ **mądry 2** (used about actions) sensible; based on good judgement: *a wise decision* ◇ *It would be wiser to wait for a few days.* ▶ **mądry**, **roztropny**
■ **wisely** adv. ▶ **mądrze**, **roztropnie**
IDM **none the wiser/worse** → NONE²

wish¹ /wɪʃ/ verb **1** [T] [often with a verb in the past tense] **wish (that ...)** to want sth that cannot now happen or that probably will not happen: *I wish I was taller.* Chciałbym być wyższy. ◇ *I wish I could help you.* Chciałbym ci pomóc. ◇ *I wish (that) I had listened more carefully.* Szkoda, że nie słuchałem dokładniej. ◇ *I wish (that) I knew what was going to happen.* Szkoda, że nie wiedziałem, co ma się wydarzyć. ◇ *My father wishes (that) he had gone to university.* Mój ojciec żałuje, że nie poszedł na studia. ▶ **życzyć (sobie)**, **chcieć** ℹ Zwróć uwagę, że w formalnym angielskim używa się **were** zamiast **was** z **I** lub **he/she**: *I wish I were rich.* Chciałbym być bogaty. ◇ *She wishes she were in a different class.* Chciałaby być w innej klasie. **2** [I,T] (formal) **wish (to do sth)** to want to do sth: *I wish to make a complaint about one of the doctors.* ▶ **pragnąć**, **mieć życzenie 3** [I] **wish for sth** to say to yourself that you want sth that can only happen by good luck or chance: *She wished for her mother to get better.* ▶ **życzyć sobie (żeby) 4** [T] to say that you hope sb will have sth: *I rang him up to* ***wish*** *him* ***a happy birthday.*** ◇ *We* ***wish*** *you* ***all the best*** *for your future career.* ▶ **życzyć (czegoś komuś)**, **składać życzenia**

wish² /wɪʃ/ noun **1** [C] a feeling that you want to have sth or that sth should happen: *I have no wish to see her ever again.* ◇ *Doctors should respect the patient's wishes.* ▶ **życzenie 2** [C] a try at making sth happen by thinking hard about it, especially in stories when it often happens by magic: *Throw a coin into the fountain and* ***make a wish.*** ◇ *My wish came true.* Spełniło się moje życzenie. ▶ **życzenie 3** (**wishes**) [pl.] a hope that sb will be happy or have good luck: *Please* ***give*** *your parents* ***my best wishes.*** ◇ *Best Wishes* Wszystkiego dobrego! (formuła kończąca list) ▶ **życzenia**

ˌ**wishful ˈthinking** noun [U] ideas that are based on what you would like, not on facts ▶ **pobożne życzenia** ➲ look at **thinking**

ˈ**wish list** noun [C] (informal) all the things that you would like to have, or that you would like to happen

wishy-washy /ˈwɪʃi wɒʃi/ adj. (informal) ℹ Wyraża dezaprobatę. **1** not having clear or firm ideas or beliefs: *a wishy-washy liberal* ▶ (*osoba*) **mętny 2** not bright in colour: *a wishy-washy blue* ▶ (*kolor*) **rozmyty**

wisp /wɪsp/ noun [C] **1** a few pieces of hair that are together ▶ **kosmyk 2** a small amount of smoke ▶ **wstęga** (*dymu*)

wispy /ˈwɪspi/ adj. consisting of small, thin pieces; not thick: *wispy hair/clouds* ▶ **rzadki i postrzępiony**; (*chmura itp.*) **strzępiasty**; (*mgła*) **zwiewny**

wistful /ˈwɪstfl/ adj. feeling or showing sadness because you cannot have what you want: *a wistful sigh* ▶ **tęskny**, **pełen tęsknoty**
■ **wistfully** /-fəli/ adv. ▶ **z tęsknotą**

wit /wɪt/ noun [U] **1** the ability to use words in a clever and amusing way ▶ **błyskotliwość** ➲ adjective **witty 2** (**wits**) [pl.] your ability to think quickly and clearly and to make good decisions: *The game of chess is essentially **a battle of wits.*** ▶ **bystrość umysłu, rozum 3 (-witted)** [in compounds] having a particular type of intelligence: *quick-witted* o bystrym umyśle ◇ *slow-witted* o tępym umyśle ▶ **(***określa umysł***)**

IDM **be at your wits' end** to not know what to do or say because you are very worried ▶ **znaleźć się w kropce** **keep your wits about you** to be ready to act in a difficult situation ▶ **nie być w ciemię bitym**

witch /wɪtʃ/ noun [C] (in past times and in stories) a woman who is thought to have magic powers ▶ **wiedźma, czarownica** ➲ look at **wizard**

witchcraft /ˈwɪtʃkrɑːft; US -kræft/ noun [U] the use of magic powers, especially evil ones ▶ **czary**

ˈwitch-hunt noun [C] an attempt to find and punish people who hold opinions that are thought to be unacceptable or dangerous to society ▶ **polowanie na czarownice** ⓘ Zwykle wyraża dezaprobatę.

with /wɪð; wɪθ/ prep. **1** in the company of sb/sth; in or to the same place as sb/sth: *I live with my parents.* ◇ *Are you coming with us?* ◇ *I talked about the problem with my tutor.* ◇ *Does this tie go with* (pasuje do) *this shirt?* ◇ *Could you put this book with* (razem z) *the others?* ▶ **z 2** having or carrying sth: *a girl with red hair* ◇ *a house with a garden* ◇ *the man with the suitcase* ▶ **z 3** using sth: *Cut it with a knife* (nożem). ◇ *I did it with his help.* ▶ **za** (*pomocą czegoś*), **przy** (*pomocy kogoś*) **4** (used for saying what fills, covers, etc. sth): *Fill the bowl with water* (wodą). ◇ *His hands were covered with oil.* Jego ręce były pokryte olejem. ⓘ **With** + rzeczownik często tłumaczy się rzeczownikiem w narzędniku. **5** in competition with sb/sth; against sb/sth: *He's always arguing with his brother.* ◇ *I usually play tennis with my sister.* ▶ (*rywalizacja*) **z kimś/czymś 6** towards, concerning or compared with sb/sth: *There's a problem with my visa.* ◇ *Compared with Canada* (w porównaniu z Kanadą), *England has mild winters.* ◇ *Is he angry with us?* Czy on się na nas gniewa? ▶ **z 7** including sth: *The price is for two people with all meals.* ▶ **wraz z czymś 8** (used to say how sth happens or is done): *Open this parcel with care* (ostrożnie). ◇ *to greet somebody with a smile* ▶ **z 9** because of sth; as a result of sth: *We were shivering with cold.* ◇ *With all the problems we've got, we're not going to finish on time.* ▶ **ze względu na coś; z 10** in the care of sb: *We left the keys with the neighbours.* ▶ **u kogoś (pod czyjąś opieką) 11** agreeing with or supporting sb/sth: *We've got everybody with us* (wszyscy zgadzają się z nami) *on this issue.* ▶ **(w zgodzie) z (kimś)** OPP **against 12** at the same time as sth: *I can't concentrate with you watching me all the time.* ▶ **kiedy, podczas gdy**

IDM **be with sb** to be able to follow what sb is saying: *I'm not quite with you. Say it again.* ▶ **nadążać za kimś** (*w rozumieniu tego, co ktoś mówi*)

withdraw /wɪðˈdrɔː/ verb (pt **withdrew** /-ˈdruː/, pp **withdrawn** /-ˈdrɔːn/) **1** [I,T] **withdraw (sb/sth) (from sth)** to move sb/sth or order sb to move back or away from a place: *The troops withdrew from the town.* ▶ **wycofywać (się) 2** [T] to remove sth or take sth away: *to withdraw an offer/a statement* ▶ **wycofywać, cofać 3** [I] to decide not to take part in sth: *Jackson withdrew from the race at the last minute.* ▶ **wycofywać się 4** [T] to take money out of a bank account: *How much would you like to withdraw?* ▶ **podejmować, wypłacać** (*pieniądze z banku*) ➲ note at **money** ➲ look at **deposit**

withdrawal /wɪðˈdrɔːəl/ noun **1** [C,U] moving or being moved back or away from a place: *the withdrawal of troops from the war zone* ▶ **wycofywanie 2** [C] taking money out of your bank account; the amount of money that you take out: *to **make a withdrawal*** ▶ **podejmowanie** (*pieniędzy z banku*), **wypłata 3** [U] the act of stopping doing sth, especially taking a drug: *When he gave up alcohol he suffered severe **withdrawal symptoms.*** ▶ **odwyk**

withdrawn[1] past participle of **withdraw**

withdrawn[2] /wɪðˈdrɔːn/ adj. (used about a person) very quiet and not wanting to talk to other people ▶ **zamknięty w sobie, markotny**

withdrew past tense of **withdraw**

wither /ˈwɪðə(r)/ verb **1** [I,T] **wither (sth) (away)** (used about plants) to become dry and die; to make a plant do this: *The plants withered in the hot sun.* ▶ **usychać, więdnąć; powodować usychanie/więdnięcie 2** [I] **wither (away)** to become weaker and then disappear: *This type of industry will wither away in the years to come.* ▶ **zanikać, więdnąć**

withering /ˈwɪðərɪŋ/ adj. done to make sb feel silly or embarrassed: *a withering look* ▶ (*spojrzenie itp.*) **miażdżący, ośmieszający**

withhold /wɪðˈhəʊld; wɪθˈh-/ verb [T] (pt, pp **withheld** /-ˈheld/) (formal) **withhold sth (from sb/sth)** to refuse to give sth to sb: *to withhold information from the police* ▶ **wstrzymywać, nie udzielać**

within /wɪˈðɪn/ prep., adv. **1** in a period not longer than a particular length of time: *I'll be back within an hour.* ◇ *She got married, found a job and moved house, all within a week.* ▶ **w ciągu 2 within sth (of sth)** not further than a particular distance from sth: *The house is within a kilometre of the station.* Dom jest w odległości kilometra od stacji. ▶ **w odległości 3** not outside the limits of sb/sth: *Each department must keep within its budget.* ▶ **w obrębie, w granicach 4** (formal) inside sb/sth: *The anger was still there deep within him.* ▶ **wewnątrz, w środku**

■ **within** adv. inside ▶ **we wnętrzu, w środku**

without /wɪˈðaʊt/ prep., adv. **1** not having or showing sth: *Don't go out without a coat on.* ◇ *If there's no salt, we'll have to manage without.* ▶ **bez 2** not using or being with sb/sth: *I drink my coffee without milk.* ◇ *Don't leave without me.* ▶ **bez 3** (used with a verb in the *-ing* form to mean 'not'): *She left without saying goodbye* (bez pożegnania). ◇ *I used her phone without her knowing* (bez jej wiedzy). ▶ **bez**

withstand /wɪðˈstænd/ verb [T] (pt, pp **withstood** /-ˈstʊd/) (formal) to be strong enough not to break, give up, be damaged, etc.: *These animals can withstand very high temperatures.* ▶ **wytrzymywać, opierać się**

witless /ˈwɪtləs/ adj. silly or stupid; not sensible ▶ **głupi; bezmyślny** SYN **foolish**

IDM **be scared/bored witless** (informal) to be extremely frightened or bored ▶ **być śmiertelnie przerażonym; śmiertelnie się nudzić**

witness[1] /ˈwɪtnəs/ noun [C] **1** (also **eyewitness** /ˈaɪwɪtnəs/) **a witness (to sth)** a person who sees sth happen and who can tell other people about it later: *There were two witnesses to the accident.* ▶ **świadek 2** a person who appears in a court of law to say what they have seen or what they know about sb/sth: *a witness for the defence/prosecution* świadek obrony/oskarżenia ▶ **świadek** ➲ note at **court 3** a person who sees sb sign an official document and who then signs it himself or herself: *Mary was one of the witnesses at our wedding.* ▶ **świadek, osoba poświadczająca**

IDM **bear witness (to sth)** → BEAR[1]

witness[2] /ˈwɪtnəs/ verb [T] **1** to see sth happen and be able to tell other people about it later: *to witness a murder* ▶ **być świadkiem (czegoś) 2** to see sb sign an official document and then sign it yourself: *to witness a will* ▶ **poświadczać**

ˈwitness box (US ˈwitness-stand) noun [C] the place in a court of law where a **witness** stands when he or she is giving evidence ▶ **miejsce dla świadków w sądzie**

W

wittily → WITTY

witty /ˈwɪti/ adj. (**wittier**; **wittiest**) clever and amusing; using words in a clever way: *a very witty speech* ▶ **błyskotliwy, dowcipny** ➲ noun **wit** ➲ note at **humour**
■ **wittily** adv. ▶ **błyskotliwie, dowcipnie**

wives plural of **wife**

wizard /ˈwɪzəd/ noun [C] (in stories) a man who is believed to have magic powers ▶ **czarodziej, czarnoksiężnik** ➲ look at **witch, magician**

wk = WEEK (1)

wobble /ˈwɒbl/ verb [I,T] to move from side to side in a way that is not steady; to make sb/sth do this: *Put something under the leg of the table. It's wobbling.* ◇ *Stop wobbling the desk. I can't write.* ▶ **chwiać (się), chybotać (się)**
■ **wobbly** /ˈwɒbli/ adj. ▶ **chwiejny, chybotliwy**

woe /wəʊ/ noun (formal) **1** (**woes**) [pl.] the problems that sb has ▶ **kłopoty 2** [U] (old-fashioned) great unhappiness ▶ **niedola**
IDM **woe betide sb** (used as a warning that there will be trouble if sb does/does not do a particular thing): *Woe betide anyone who yawns while the boss is talking.* ▶ **biada temu, kto**

wok /wɒk/ noun [C] a large pan that is shaped like a bowl and used for cooking Chinese food ▶ **wok** ➲ picture at **pan**

woke past tense of **wake**[1]

woken past participle of **wake**[1]

wolf /wʊlf/ noun [C] (pl. **wolves** /wʊlvz/) a wild animal that looks like a dog and that lives and hunts in a group called a **pack** ▶ **wilk** ➲ picture on **page A10**

woman /ˈwʊmən/ noun [C] (pl. **women** /ˈwɪmɪn/) **1** an adult female person: *men, women and children* ◇ *Would you prefer to see a woman doctor?* ▶ **kobieta 2** (**-woman**) [in compounds] a woman who does a particular activity: *a businesswoman* kobieta interesu ▶ **kobieta**

womanhood /ˈwʊmənhʊd/ noun [U] the state of being a woman ▶ **kobiecość** ➲ look at **femininity**

womanizing (also **-ising**) /ˈwʊmənaɪzɪŋ/ noun [U] the fact of having sexual relationships with many different women ▶ **uganianie się za spódniczkami** ℹ Wyraża dezaprobatę.
■ **womanizer** (also **-iser**) noun [C]: *He has a reputation for being a womanizer.* ▶ **kobieciarz**

womanly /ˈwʊmənli/ adj. having qualities considered typical of a woman ▶ **kobiecy**

womb /wuːm/ noun [C] the part of a woman or female animal where a baby grows before it is born ▶ **łono** ℹ Bardziej formalne słowo to **uterus**.

won past tense, past participle of **win**

wonder[1] /ˈwʌndə(r)/ verb **1** [I,T] **wonder (about sth)** to want to know sth; to ask yourself questions about sth: *I wonder what the new teacher will be like.* ◇ *It was something that she had been wondering about for a long time.* ▶ **zastanawiać się, być ciekawym (czegoś) 2** [T] (used as a polite way of asking a question or of asking sb to do sth): *I wonder if you could help me.* ◇ *I was wondering if you'd like to come to dinner at our house.* ▶ **zastanawiać się, czy 3** [I,T] **wonder (at sth)** to feel great surprise or admiration: *We wondered at the speed with which he worked.* ◇ *'She was very angry.' 'I don't wonder. She had a right to be.'* ▶ **zdumiewać się, podziwiać**

wonder[2] /ˈwʌndə(r)/ noun **1** [U] a feeling of surprise and admiration: *The children just stared* ***in wonder*** *at the acrobats.* ▶ **zdumienie, podziw 2** [C] something that causes you to feel surprise or admiration: *the wonders of modern technology* ▶ **cud**
IDM **do wonders (for sb/sth)** to have a very good effect on sb/sth: *Working in Mexico did wonders for my Spanish.* ▶ **doskonale wpływać na kogoś/coś**
it's a wonder (that)... it's surprising that...: *It's a wonder we managed to get here on time, with all the traffic.* ▶ **zadziwiające/zdumiewające, że**
no wonder it is not surprising: *You've been out every evening this week. No wonder you're tired.* ▶ **nic dziwnego**

wonderful /ˈwʌndəfl/ adj. extremely good; great: *What wonderful weather!* ◇ *It's wonderful to see you again.* ▶ **cudowny** ➲ note at **good, nice**
■ **wonderfully** /-fəli/ adv. ▶ **cudownie**

wonderland /ˈwʌndəlænd/ noun [usually sing.] **1** an imaginary place in children's stories ▶ **kraina z bajki 2** a place that is exciting and full of beautiful and interesting things ▶ **kraina jak z bajki**

won't /wəʊnt; US / short for **will not**

wood /wʊd/ noun **1** [U,C] the hard substance that trees are made of: *He chopped some wood for the fire.* ▶ **drewno 2** [C, often plural] an area of land that is covered with trees. A wood is smaller than a forest: *a walk in the woods* ▶ **las** ➲ note at **forest**
IDM **touch wood**; US **knock on wood** an expression that people use (often while touching a piece of wood) to prevent bad luck: *I've been driving here for 20 years and I haven't had an accident yet – touch wood!* ▶ **odpukać** (*w niemalowane drewno*)

wooded /ˈwʊdɪd/ adj. (used about an area of land) having a lot of trees growing on it ▶ **zalesiony, lesisty**

wooden /ˈwʊdn/ adj. made of wood ▶ **drewniany**

ˌwooden ˈspoon = BOOBY PRIZE

woodland /ˈwʊdlənd/ noun [C,U] land that has a lot of trees growing on it: *The village is surrounded by woodland.* ◇ *woodland birds* ▶ **las**

woodpecker /ˈwʊdpekə(r)/ noun [C] a bird that climbs trees and taps them rapidly with its beak to find insects ▶ **dzięcioł**

woodwind /ˈwʊdwɪnd/ noun [sing., with sing. or pl. verb] the group of musical instruments that you play by blowing into them: *the woodwind section of the orchestra* ▶ **drewniane instrumenty dęte** ➲ note at **instrument**

woodwork /ˈwʊdwɜːk/ noun [U] **1** the parts of a building that are made of wood such as the doors, stairs, etc. ▶ **stolarka 2** the activity or skill of making things out of wood ▶ **stolarstwo**

woof /wʊf/ noun [C] (informal) (used for describing the sound that a dog makes) ▶ **hau, hau!** ➲ look at **bark**

wool /wʊl/ noun [U] **1** the soft thick hair of sheep ▶ **wełna 2** thick thread or cloth that is made from wool ▶ **wełna** ➲ look at **cotton wool**

woollen (US **woolen**) /ˈwʊlən/ adj. made of wool ▶ **wełniany**

woolly (US **wooly**) /ˈwʊli/ adj. (**woollier**; **woolliest**) like wool or made of wool: *The dog had a thick woolly coat.* ◇ *long woolly socks* ▶ **wełnisty**

word[1] /wɜːd/ noun **1** [C] a sound or letter or group of sounds or letters that expresses a particular meaning: *What's the Greek word for 'mouth'?* ◇ *What does this word mean?* ▶ **słowo, wyraz 2** [C] a thing that you say; a short statement or comment: *Could I* ***have a word*** *with you in private?* ◇ *Don't say a word* (ani słowa) *about this to anyone.* ▶ **parę słów 3** [sing.] a promise: ***I give you my word*** *that I won't tell anyone.* ◇ *I'll* ***keep my word*** *to her and lend her the money.* ◇ *You'll just have to trust him not* ***to go back on his word.*** ▶ **słowo, obietnica**
IDM **a dirty word** → DIRTY[1]
not breathe a word (of/about sth) (to sb) → BREATHE
the last/final word (on sth) the last comment or decision about sth ▶ **ostatnie słowo** (*w jakiejś sprawie*)

not get a word in edgeways to not be able to interrupt when sb else is talking so that you can say sth yourself ▶ **nie dochodzić do słowa**
have, etc. the last word → LAST[1]
in other words → OTHER
lost for words → LOST[2]
put in a (good) word for sb to say sth good about sb to sb else: *If you could put in a good word for me I might stand a better chance of getting the job.* ▶ **szepnąć słówko za kimś**
take sb's word for it to believe what sb says without any proof ▶ **wierzyć komuś na słowo**
word for word 1 repeating sth exactly: *Sharon repeated word for word what he had told her.* ▶ **słowo w słowo, dosłownie 2** translating each word separately, not looking at the general meaning: *a word-for-word translation* ▶ **słowo w słowo, dosłownie**

word[2] /wɜːd/ verb [T, often passive] to choose carefully the words that you use to express sth: *The statement was carefully worded so that nobody would be offended by it.* ▶ **formułować, redagować**

wording /ˈwɜːdɪŋ/ noun [sing.] the words that you use to express sth: *The wording of the contract was vague.* ▶ **sformułowanie, dobór słów**

ˌword-ˈperfect adj. able to say sth that you have learnt from memory, without making a mistake ▶ **doskonale wyuczony na pamięć**

ˈwordpower /ˈwɜːdpaʊə(r)/ noun [U] the ability to use language well; the number of words you know ▶ **dobra znajomość języka, zasób wyrazów danego języka**

ˌword ˈprocessor noun [C] (abbr. **WP**) a type of computer that you can use for writing letters, reports, etc. You can correct or change what you have written before you print it out. ▶ **edytor tekstu**
■ **word processing** noun [U] ▶ **komputerowe przetwarzanie/redagowanie tekstu**

wore past tense of **wear[1]**

work[1] /wɜːk/ verb **1** [I,T] **work (as sth) (for sb)** ; **work (at/on sth)**; **work (to do sth)** to do sth which needs physical or mental effort, in order to earn money or to achieve sth: *She's working for a large firm in Glasgow.* ◇ *I'd like to work as a newspaper reporter.* ◇ *Doctors often work extremely long hours.* ◇ *My teacher said that I wouldn't pass the exam unless I worked harder.* ◇ *I hear she's working on a new novel.* ◇ *I'm going to stay in tonight and work at my project.* ▶ **pracować** ➲ note at **job**, **office 2** [T] to make yourself/sb work, especially very hard: *The coach works the players very hard in training.* ▶ **eksploatować 3** [I,T] to function; to make sth function; to operate: *Our telephone hasn't been working for several days.* ◇ *We still don't really understand how the brain works.* ◇ *Can you show me how to work the photocopier?* ▶ **działać, pracować; obsługiwać 4** [I] to have the result or effect that you want; to be successful: *Your idea sounds good but I don't think it will really work.* ◇ *The heat today could work in favour of* (to, że dzisiaj mamy upał, może działać na korzyść) *the African runners.* ▶ (*idea itp.*) **działać**, (*pomysł*) **wychodzić 5** [I,T] to use materials to make a model, a picture, etc.: *He worked the clay into the shape of a horse.* ◇ *She usually works in/with oils or acrylics.* ▶ **pracować** (*np. w glinie*), **używać** (*np. farb olejnych*) **6** [I,T] to move gradually to a new position or state: *Engineers check the plane daily, because nuts and screws can **work loose*** (mogą się wyrobić). ◇ *I watched the snail **work its way** up the wall* (jak ślimak powoli wchodził po ścianie). ▶ **przemieszczać się**
IDM **work/perform miracles** → MIRACLE
work/sweat your guts out → GUT[1]
work to rule to follow the rules of your job in a very strict way in order to cause delay, as a form of protest against your employer or your working conditions ▶ **strajk włoski**
PHR V **work out 1** to develop or progress, especially in a good way: *I hope things work out for you.* ▶ **(dobrze komuś) wychodzić 2** to do physical exercises in order to keep your body fit: *We work out to music at my exercise class.* ▶ **gimnastykować się**
work out (at sth) to come to a particular result or total after everything has been calculated: *If we divide the work between us, it'll work out at about four hours each.* ▶ (*koszt*) **wynosić (ileś)**
work sb out to understand sb: *I've never been able to work her out.* ▶ **zrozumieć kogoś**
work sth out 1 to find the answer to sth; to solve sth: *I can't work out how to do this.* ▶ **wykombinować coś, znaleźć sposób na coś, rozwiązać coś 2** to calculate sth: *I worked out the total cost.* ▶ **obliczać coś 3** to plan sth: *Have you worked out the route through France?* ▶ **opracowywać/planować coś**
work up to sth to develop or progress to sth: *Start with 15 minutes' exercise and gradually work up to 30.* ▶ **stopniowo doprowadzać/dochodzić do czegoś**
work sth up to develop or improve sth with effort: *I'm trying to work up the energy to go out.* Usiłuję zmobilizować się do wyjścia. ▶ **wypracowywać coś**
work sb/yourself up (into sth) to make sb/yourself become angry, excited, upset, etc.: *He had worked himself up into a state of anxiety about his interview.* ▶ **stopniowo doprowadzać (się)** (*np. do złości*)

work[2] /wɜːk/ noun **1** [U] the job that you do, especially in order to earn money; the place where you do your job: *It is very difficult to **find work** in this city.* ◇ *He's been **out of work*** (nie miał pracy) *for six months.* ◇ *When do you **start work**?* ◇ *I'll ask if I can **leave work** early today.* ◇ ***I go to work** at 8 o'clock.* ◇ *The people **at work*** (w pracy) *gave me some flowers for my birthday.* ◇ *Police work is not as exciting as it looks on TV.* ◇ *a work permit* pozwolenie na pracę ▶ **praca** ➲ note at **job**, **routine** ➲ look at **employment 2** [U] something that needs physical or mental effort that you do in order to achieve sth: *Her success is due to sheer **hard work**.* ◇ *I've got a lot of work to do today.* ◇ *We hope to **start work on** the project next week.* ◇ *Students do work experience* (odbywają praktykę zawodową) *in local firms.* ▶ **praca 3** [U] something that you are working on or have produced: *a piece of written work* ◇ *The teacher marked their work.* ◇ *Is this all your own work?* ▶ **praca, zadanie 4** [C] a book, painting, piece of music, etc.: *an early work by Picasso* ◇ *the complete works of Shakespeare* ▶ **utwór, dzieło 5** (**works**) [pl.] the act of building or repairing sth: *The roadworks are causing long traffic jams.* ▶ **roboty** (*np. drogowe*), **prace** (*np. ziemne*) **6** (**works**) [C, with sing. or pl. verb] [in compounds] a factory: *The steelworks* (stalownia) *is/are closing down.* ▶ **fabryka, zakład (produkcyjny)**
IDM **get/go/set to work (on sth)** to begin; to make a start (on sth) ▶ **zabierać się do pracy**

work

Work jest rzeczownikiem niepoliczalnym i dlatego nie można powiedzieć ~~*a work*~~ lub ~~*works*~~ ◇ *I've found work at the hospital.*. W niektórych kontekstach trzeba używać policzalnego słowa **job**: *I've got a new job at the hospital.* Rzeczownik niepoliczalny **employment** (zatrudnienie) jest słowem bardziej oficjalnym niż **work** lub **job**: *Many married women are in part-time employment.* **Occupation** stosuje się w formularzach przy pytaniach o wykonywane zajęcie lub zawód: *Occupation: student. Occupation: bus driver.* **Profession** oznacza pracę wymagającą specjalnego wykształcenia i studiów wyższych: *the medical profession.* **Trade** oznacza pracę fizyczną wymagającą umiejętności zawodowych: *He's a carpenter by trade.*

W

workable /ˈwɜːkəbl/ adj. that can be used successfully: *a workable idea/plan/solution* ▶ **wykonalny** SYN **practical**

workaholic /ˌwɜːkəˈhɒlɪk/ noun [C] a person who loves work and does too much of it ▶ **pracoholi-k/czka**

workbench /ˈwɜːkbentʃ/ noun [C] a long heavy table used for doing practical jobs, working with tools, etc. ▶ **stół warsztatowy**

workbook /ˈwɜːkbʊk/ noun [C] a book with questions and exercises in it that you use when you are studying sth ▶ **podręcznik**

workday 1 (US) = WORKING DAY (1): *an 8-hour workday* 2 = WORKING DAY (2): *workday traffic*

ˌworked ˈup adj. [not before a noun] **worked up (about sth)** (informal) very excited or upset about sth: *There's no point in* ***getting worked up*** *about it.* Nie ma sensu tym się denerwować. ▶ **zdenerwowany, zmartwiony**

worker /ˈwɜːkə(r)/ noun [C] 1 [in compounds] a person who works, especially one who does a particular kind of work: *factory/office/farm workers* ◇ *skilled/manual workers* ▶ **pracowni-k/-ca/-czka, robotni-k/ca** 2 a person who is employed to do physical work rather than organizing things or managing people: *Workers' representatives will meet management today to discuss the pay dispute.* ▶ **robotni-k/ca** 3 a person who works in a particular way: *a slow/fast worker* ▶ **pracowni-k/ca**

ˈwork experience noun [U] 1 the work or jobs that you have done in your life so far ▶ **doświadczenie zawodowe** 2 (Brit.) a period of time that a young person, especially a student, spends working in a company as a form of training ▶ **staż** ⮌ look at **internship**

workforce /ˈwɜːkfɔːs/ noun [C, with sing. or pl. verb] 1 the total number of people who work in a company, factory, etc. ▶ **załoga, personel** 2 the total number of people in a country who are able to work: *Ten per cent of the workforce is/are unemployed.* ▶ **siła robocza**

working /ˈwɜːkɪŋ/ adj. [only before a noun] 1 employed; having a job: *the problems of childcare for working mothers* ▶ **pracujący** 2 connected with your job: *He stayed with the same company for the whole of his* ***working life.*** ◇ *The company offers excellent working conditions* (warunki pracy). ▶ **zawodowy, pracowniczy** 3 good enough to be used, although it could be improved: *We are looking for someone with* ***a working knowledge*** *of French.* ▶ **praktyczny**

IDM **in working order** (used about machines, etc.) working properly, not broken ▶ **sprawny**

the **ˌworking ˈclass** noun [sing., with sing. or pl. verb] (also **the ˌworking ˈclasses** [pl.]) the group of people in society who do not have much money or power and who usually do physical work, especially in industry: *unemployment among the working class* ▶ **klasa robotnicza/pracująca** ⮌ look at **middle class, upper class**

■ **ˌworking-ˈclass** adj.: *a working-class area/family* ▶ **klasy robotniczej/pracującej**

ˌworking ˈday noun [C] (Brit.) 1 (US **workday** /ˈwɜːkdeɪ/) the part of a day during which you work: *I spend most of my working day sitting at a desk.* ▶ **dzień pracy** 2 (also **workday**) a day on which you usually work or on which most people usually work: *Sunday is a normal working day for me.* ▶ **dzień roboczy**

workings /ˈwɜːkɪŋz/ noun [pl.] the way in which a machine, an organization, etc. operates: *It's very difficult to understand the workings of the legal system.* ▶ **działanie, funkcjonowanie**

workload /ˈwɜːkləʊd/ noun [C] the amount of work that you have to do: *She often gets home late when she has a* ***heavy workload*** (ma wiele obowiązków w pracy). ▶ **ilość pracy do wykonania**

workman /ˈwɜːkmən/ noun [C] (pl. **-men** /-mən/) a man who works with his hands, especially at building or making things ▶ **robotnik**

workmanlike /ˈwɜːkmənlaɪk/ adj. done, made, etc. very well, but not original or exciting: *a workmanlike performance* ▶ **fachowy**

workmanship /ˈwɜːkmənʃɪp/ noun [U] the skill with which sth is made ▶ **fachowość**

workmate /ˈwɜːkmeɪt/ noun [C] (especially Brit.) a person that you work with, often doing the same job, in an office, a factory, etc. ▶ **kole-ga/żanka z pracy** SYN **colleague**

ˌwork of ˈart noun [C] (pl. **works of art**) a very good painting, book, piece of music, etc. ▶ **dzieło sztuki** ⮌ look at **art**

workout /ˈwɜːkaʊt/ noun [C] a period of physical exercise, for example when you are training for a sport or keeping fit: *She does a twenty-minute workout every morning.* ▶ **trening, zaprawa fizyczna**

workplace /ˈwɜːkpleɪs/ noun [C] (often **the workplace**) [sing.] the office, factory, etc. where people work: *the introduction of new technology into the workplace* ▶ **miejsce pracy**

worksheet /ˈwɜːkʃiːt/ noun [C] a piece of paper with questions or exercises on it that you use when you are studying sth ▶ **kartka z ćwiczeniami/zadaniami (do nauki)**

workshop /ˈwɜːkʃɒp/ noun [C] 1 a place where things are made or repaired ▶ **zakład** (*produkcyjny/remontowy*), **warsztat** 2 a period of discussion and practical work on a particular subject, when people share their knowledge and experience: *a drama/writing workshop* ▶ **warsztaty** (*seminarium dyskusyjne*)

workstation /ˈwɜːksteɪʃn/ noun [C] the desk and computer at which a person works; one computer that is part of a system of computers ▶ **stanowisko komputerowe**

worktop /ˈwɜːktɒp/ (also **ˈwork surface**) noun [C] a flat surface in a kitchen, etc. that you use for preparing food, etc. on ▶ **blat (kuchenny)**

world /wɜːld/ noun 1 (**the world**) [sing.] the earth with all its countries and people: *a map of the world* ◇ *the most beautiful place* ***in the world*** ◇ *I took a year off work to travel* ***round the world.*** ◇ *She is famous* ***all over the world.*** ◇ *People are basically the same* ***the world over*** (na całym świecie). ▶ **świat, ziemia** 2 [sing.] a particular part of the earth or group of countries: *the western world* ◇ *the Arab world* ◇ *the Third World* ▶ **świat** 3 [C] a planet with life on it: *Do you believe there are other worlds out there, like ours?* ▶ **świat** 4 [C] [in compounds] a particular area of activity or group of people or things: *the world of sport/fashion/politics* ◇ *the medical/business/animal/natural world* ▶ **świat** 5 [sing.] the life and activities of people; their experience: *It's time you learned something about the real world!* ◇ *the modern world* ▶ **świat** 6 [sing.] the people in the world: ***The whole world*** *was waiting for news of the astronauts.* ▶ **świat**

IDM **do sb a/the world of good** (informal) to have a very good effect on sb: *The holiday has done her the world of good.* ▶ **być dla kogoś/czegoś korzystnym**

in the world (used to emphasize what you are saying): *Everyone else is stressed but he doesn't seem to have a care in the world* (żadnych zmartwień). ◇ *There's no need to rush – we've got all the time in the world* (mnóstwo czasu). ◇ *What in the world* (u licha) *are you doing?*

the outside world → OUTSIDE[2]

think the world of sb/sth → THINK

out of this world (informal) (used to emphasize how good, beautiful, etc. sth is) ▶ (*przen.*) **nie z tej ziemi**

ˌ**world-'class** adj. as good as the best in the world: *a world-class athlete* ▶ **światowej klasy**

ˌ**world-'famous** adj. known all over the world ▶ **światowej sławy**

worldly /'wɜːldli/ adj. **1** [only before a noun] connected with ordinary life, not with the spirit: *He left all his worldly possessions to his nephew.* ▶ **materialny, doczesny 2** having a lot of experience and knowledge of life and people: *a sophisticated and worldly man* ▶ **światowy**

'**world music** noun [U] a type of pop music that includes influences from different parts of the world, especially Africa and Asia ▶ **muzyka pop z różnych stron świata**

ˌ**world 'war** noun [C] a war that involves a lot of different countries: *the Second World War* ◇ *World War One* ▶ **wojna światowa**

worldwide /'wɜːldwaɪd/ adj. (happening) in the whole world: *The situation has caused worldwide concern.* ▶ **ogólnoświatowy**
■ **worldwide** adv.: *The product will be marketed worldwide.* ▶ **na całym świecie**

the ˌ**World Wide 'Web** (also the Web) noun [sing.] (abbr. **WWW** /ˌdʌblju: dʌblju: 'dʌblju:/) the international system of computers that makes it possible for you to see information from around the world on your computer ▶ **światowa sieć komputerowa, Internet** ➲ look at **Internet**

worm[1] /wɜːm/ noun [C] **1** a small animal with a long thin body and no eyes, bones or legs: *an earthworm* dżdżownica ▶ **robak 2** (**worms**) [pl.] one or more **worms** that live inside a person or an animal and may cause disease: *He's got worms.* ▶ **robaki**

worm[2] /wɜːm/ verb [T] **worm your way/yourself along, through, etc.** to move slowly or with difficulty in the direction mentioned: *I managed to worm my way through the crowd.* ▶ **przeciskać/przesuwać się powoli w jakimś kierunku**
PHR V **worm your way/yourself into sth** to make sb like you or trust you, in order to dishonestly gain an advantage for yourself ▶ **wkradać się** (*np. w czyjeś łaski*)

worn past participle of **wear**[1]

ˌ**worn 'out** adj. **1** too old or damaged to use any more: *My shoes are completely worn out.* ▶ **zdarty, znoszony 2** extremely tired: *I'm absolutely worn out. I think I'll go to bed early.* ▶ **wyczerpany** ➲ look at **wear**

⚷ **worried** /'wʌrid; US 'wɜːr-/ adj. **worried (about sb/sth); worried (that ...)** thinking that sth bad might happen or has happened: *Don't look so worried. Everything will be all right.* ◇ *I'm* ***worried sick*** *about the exam.* ◇ *We were* ***worried stiff*** (strasznie się martwiliśmy) *that you might have had an accident.* ▶ **zmartwiony**

⚷ **worry**[1] /'wʌri; US 'wɜːri/ verb (**worrying; worries**; pt, pp **worried**) **1** [I] **worry (about sb/sth)** to think that sth bad might happen or has happened: *Don't worry – I'm sure everything will be all right.* ◇ *There's nothing to worry about.* ◇ *He worries if I don't phone every weekend.* ▶ **martwić się 2** [T] **worry sb/yourself (about sb/sth)** to make sb/yourself think that sth bad might happen or has happened: *What worries me is how are we going to get home?* ◇ *She worried herself sick when he was away in the army.* ▶ **martwić (się) 3** [T] **worry sb (with sth)** to disturb sb: *Don't keep worrying him with questions.* ▶ **niepokoić kogoś** SYN **bother**
■ **worrying** adj.: *a worrying situation* ▶ **niepokojący**
IDM **not to worry** it is not important; it does not matter ▶ **nieważne**

⚷ **worry**[2] /'wʌri; US 'wɜːri/ noun (pl. **worries**) **1** [U] the state of worrying about sth: *His son has caused him a lot of worry recently.* ▶ **zmartwienie 2** [C] something that makes you worry; a problem: *Crime is a real worry for old people.* ◇ *financial worries* ▶ **zmartwienie, kłopot**

⚷ **worse** /wɜːs/ adj. [the comparative of *bad*] **1** not as good or as well as sth else: *My exam results were* ***far/much worse*** *than I thought they would be.* ▶ **gorszy 2** [not before a noun] more ill; less well: *If you* ***get any worse*** (jeśli twój stan się pogorszy), *we'll call the doctor.* ▶ (*chora osoba*) **czujący się gorzej**
■ **worse** adv. [the comparative of *badly*] less well: *She speaks German* ***even worse than I do.*** ▶ **gorzej** | **worse** noun [U]: *The situation was already bad but there was worse to come.* ▶ **coś gorszego**
IDM **a change for the better/worse** → CHANGE[2]
none the wiser/worse → NONE[2]
to make matters/things worse to make a situation, problem, etc. even more difficult or dangerous than before ▶ **na domiar złego**
the worse for wear (informal) damaged; not in good condition: *This suitcase looks a bit the worse for wear.* ▶ **podniszczony, w kiepskim stanie**
worse luck! (informal) unfortunately: *The dentist says I need three fillings, worse luck!* ▶ **na nieszczęście**

worsen /'wɜːsn/ verb [I,T] to become worse or to make sth worse: *Relations between the two countries have worsened.* ▶ **pogarszać (się)**

⚷ **worship** /'wɜːʃɪp/ verb (**worshipping; worshipped**; US **worshiping; worshiped**) **1** [I,T] to show respect for God or a god, by saying prayers, singing with others, etc.: *People travel from all over the world to worship at this shrine.* ▶ **modlić się, oddawać cześć boską 2** [T] to love or admire sb/sth very much: *She worshipped her husband.* ▶ **uwielbiać**
■ **worship** noun [U]: *Different religions have different forms of worship.* ▶ **oddawanie czci boskiej, modlitwa, nabożeństwo** | **worshipper** noun [C] ▶ **wiern-y/a**

⚷ **worst**[1] /wɜːst/ adj. [the superlative of *bad*] the least pleasant or suitable; the least well: *It's been the worst winter that I can remember.* ▶ **najgorszy**
■ **worst** adv. [the superlative of *badly*] least well: *A lot of the children behaved badly but my son behaved worst of all!* ▶ **najgorzej**

worst[2] /wɜːst/ noun [sing.] something that is as bad as it can be: *My parents always expect the worst if I'm late.* ▶ **najgorsze**
IDM **at (the) worst** if the worst happens or if you consider sb/sth in the worst way: *The problem doesn't look too serious. At worst we'll have to make a few small changes.* ▶ **w najgorszym razie**
bring out the best/worst in sb → BEST[3]
if the worst comes to the worst if the worst possible situation happens ▶ **w najgorszym wypadku**

'**worst-case** adj. [only before a noun] involving the worst situation that could happen: *In the* ***worst-case scenario*** *more than ten thousand people might be affected.* ▶ **najgorszy**

⚷ **worth**[1] /wɜːθ/ adj. [not before a noun] **1** having a particular value (in money): *How much do you think that house is worth?* ▶ **wart 2 worth doing, etc.** (used as a way of recommending or advising): *That museum's* ***well worth*** *visiting if you have time.* ◇ *It's already four o'clock. It's* ***not worth*** *going shopping now* (nie warto już iść na zakupy). ▶ **wart** (*np. odwiedzenia*) ℹ Można powiedzieć: *It isn't worth repairing the car.* lub: *The car isn't worth repairing.* **3** enjoyable or useful to do or have, even if it means extra cost, effort, etc.: *It takes a long time to walk to the top of the hill but it's worth the effort.* ◇ *Don't bother cooking a big meal. It isn't* ***worth it*** (nie warto) – *we're not hungry.* ▶ **warto** (*np. coś robić*)
IDM **get your money's worth** → MONEY

W

worth sb's while helpful, useful or interesting to sb ▶ **wart** *(np. czyjegoś czasu)*

worth² /wɜːθ/ noun [U] **1** the amount of sth that the money mentioned will buy: *ten pounds' worth of petrol* paliwo za równowartość dziesięciu funtów ▶ **równowartość 2** the amount of sth that will last for the time mentioned: *two days' worth of food* jedzenie na dwa dni ▶ **równowartość (danego czasu) 3** the value of sb/sth; how useful sb/sth is: *She has proved her worth as a member of the team.* ▶ **wartość**

worthless /ˈwɜːθləs/ adj. **1** having no value or use: *It's worthless – it's only a bit of plastic!* ▶ **bezwartościowy 2** (used about a person) having bad qualities ▶ **bezwartościowy** ➲ look at **priceless**, **valuable**, **invaluable**

worthwhile /ˌwɜːθˈwaɪl/ adj. important, enjoyable or interesting enough to be worth the cost or effort: *Working for so little money just isn't worthwhile.* ▶ **wart zachodu**, **opłacający się**

worthy /ˈwɜːði/ adj. (**worthier**; **worthiest**) **1 worthy of sth/ to do sth** good enough for sth or to have sth: *He felt he was not worthy to accept such responsibility.* ▶ **wart (czegoś)**, **zasługujący na coś 2** that should receive respect, support or attention: *a worthy leader* ◇ *a worthy cause* ▶ **godny**, **szanowany**

⚷ **would** /wəd/ strong form /wʊd/ modal verb (short form **'d**; negative **would not**; short form **wouldn't** /ˈwʊdnt/) **1** (used as the past form of 'will' when you report what sb says or thinks): *They said that they would help us* (że nam pomogą). ◇ *She didn't think that he would do* (że on może zrobić) *a thing like that.* ▶ *(czas przeszły od* **will**, *używany w mowie zależnej)* **2** (used when talking about the result of an event that you imagine): *He would be delighted if you went to see him.* ◇ *She'd be stupid not to accept.* ◇ *I would have done more, if I'd had the time.* ▶ **byłby 3** (used after 'wish'): *I wish the sun would come out.* Chciałbym, żeby wyszło słońce. **4** to agree or be ready to do sth: *She just wouldn't* (nie chciała) *do what I asked her.* ▶ **chcieć 5** (used when you are giving your opinion but are not certain that you are right): *I'd say* (powiedziałbym) *she's about 40.* **6** (used for asking sb politely to do sth): *Would you come this way, please?* Bardzo proszę iść tędy. **7** (used with 'like' or 'love' as a way of asking or saying what sb wants): ***Would you like*** (czy chciałbyś) *to come with us?* ◇ ***I'd love*** (bardzo chciałbym) *a piece of cake.* ℹ Po wyrażeniach **would like** oraz **would love** używa się czasowników w formie bezokolicznika, a nie w formie *-ing*. ➲ note at **want 8** (used for talking about things that often happened in the past): *When he was young he would often walk* (często spacerował) *in these woods.* ➲ look at **used to 9** (used for commenting on behaviour that is typical of sb): *You would say that* (wiedziałem, że to powiesz). *You always support him.*

ˈ**would-be** adj. [only before a noun] (used to describe sb who is hoping to become the type of person mentioned): *a would-be actor* ◇ *advice for would-be parents* ▶ **niedoszły**; **potencjalny**

⚷ **wound¹** /wuːnd/ noun [C] an injury to part of your body, especially a cut, often one received in fighting: *a bullet wound* ▶ **rana**

IDM **rub salt into the wound/sb's wounds** → RUB

⚷ **wound²** /wuːnd/ verb [T, usually passive] **1** to injure sb's body with a weapon: *He was wounded in the leg during the war.* ▶ **ranić** ➲ note at **hurt 2** (formal) to hurt sb's feelings deeply: *I was wounded by his criticism.* ▶ **urażać**

■ **wounded** adj.: *a wounded soldier* ▶ **ranny** | **the wounded** noun [pl.]: *Paramedics tended to the wounded at the scene of the explosion.* ▶ **ranni**

wound³ past tense, past participle of **wind³**

wove past tense of **weave**

woven past participle of **weave**

wow /waʊ/ interj. (informal) (used for showing that you find sth impressive or surprising): *Wow! What a fantastic boat!* ▶ **o rany!**, **ho, ho!**

WP = WORD PROCESSOR, WORD PROCESSING

wrack = RACK

wrangle /ˈræŋgl/ noun [C] a noisy or complicated argument: *The company is involved in **a legal wrangle*** (spór prawny) *over copyright.* ▶ **awantura**

■ **wrangle** verb [I] ▶ **awanturować się**

⚷ **wrap** /ræp/ verb [T] (**wrapping**; **wrapped**) **1 wrap sth (up) (in sth)** to put paper or cloth around sb/sth as a cover: *to wrap up a present* ◇ *The baby was found wrapped in a blanket.* ▶ **pakować**, **zawijać 2 wrap sth round/around sb/sth** to tie sth such as paper or cloth around an object or a part of the body: *The man had a bandage wrapped round his head.* ▶ **owijać**, **zakutać**

IDM **be wrapped up in sb/sth** to be very involved and interested in sb/sth: *They were completely wrapped up in each other. They didn't notice I was there.* ▶ **być zapatrzonym w kogoś/coś**

PHR V **wrap (sb/yourself) up** to put warm clothes on sb/ yourself ▶ **opatulać (się) (w coś)**

wrapper /ˈræpə(r)/ noun [C] the piece of paper or plastic which covers sth when you buy it: *a sweet/chocolate wrapper* ▶ **opakowanie**, **obwoluta**, **opaska**

⚷ **wrapping** /ˈræpɪŋ/ noun [C,U] paper, plastic, etc. that is used for covering sth in order to protect it: *She tore off the wrapping.* ▶ **opakowanie**

ˈ**wrapping paper** noun [U] paper which is used for putting round presents ▶ **papier pakowy**

wrath /rɒθ; US ræθ/ noun [U] (formal) very great anger ▶ **wielki gniew**

wreak /riːk/ verb [T] (formal) **wreak sth (on sb/sth)** to cause great damage or harm to sb/sth: *Fierce storms **wreak havoc*** (powodują spustoszenie) *at this time of year.* ▶ **wywrzeć na kimś** *(np. zemstę)*, **powodować** *(np. szkodę)*, **wymierzać** *(np. karę)*

wreath /riːθ/ noun [C] (pl. **wreaths** /riːðz/) a circle of flowers and leaves, especially one that you give to the family of sb who has died ▶ **wieniec**

wreck /rek/ noun **1** [C] a ship that has sunk or been badly damaged at sea: *Divers searched the wreck.* ▶ **wrak statku 2** [C] a car, plane, etc. which has been badly damaged, especially in an accident: *The car was a wreck but the lorry escaped almost without damage.* ▶ **wrak 3** [C, usually sing.] (informal) a person or thing that is in a very bad condition: *He drove so badly I was **a nervous wreck** when we got there.* ▶ **rozbitek**

■ **wreck** verb [T]: *Vandals had wrecked the school hall.* ◇ *The strike wrecked all our holiday plans.* ▶ **rujnować**, **rozbijać**

wreckage /ˈrekɪdʒ/ noun [U] the broken pieces of sth that has been destroyed: *They searched the wreckage of the plane for evidence.* ▶ **szczątki**, **wrak**

wrench¹ /rentʃ/ verb [T] **1 wrench sb/sth (away, off, etc.)** to pull or turn sb/sth strongly and suddenly: *They had to wrench the door off* (wyrwać drzwi) *the car to get the driver out.* ◇ (figurative) *The film was so exciting that I could hardly wrench myself away* (trudno było się oderwać). ▶ **pociągnąć/skręcić gwałtownie 2** to injure part of your body by turning it suddenly ▶ **skręcić**, **zwichnąć** *(np. nogę)*

wrench² /rentʃ/ noun **1** [C] (US) = SPANNER **2** [sing.] the sadness you feel because you have to leave sb/sth ▶ **ból** *(np. rozstania)* **3** [C] a sudden, violent pull or turn: *With a wrench I managed to open the door.* ▶ **gwałtowne szarpnięcie/skręcenie**

wrestle /ˈresl/ verb **1** [I,T] **wrestle (with) sb** to fight by trying to get hold of your opponent's body and throw them to the ground. People **wrestle** as a sport: *He managed to wrestle the man to the ground and take the knife from him.* ▶ **prowadzić walkę** (*w zapasach*) **2** [I] **wrestle (with sth)** to try hard to deal with sth that is difficult ▶ **zmagać się (z czymś)**

wrestling /ˈreslɪŋ/ noun [U] a sport in which two people fight and try to throw each other to the ground: *a wrestling match* ▶ **zapasy**

■ **wrestler** noun [C] ▶ **zapaśni-k/czka**

wretch /retʃ/ noun [C] (old-fashioned) a poor, unhappy person: *The poor wretch was clearly starving.* ▶ **bieda-k/czka**

wretched /ˈretʃɪd/ adj. **1** very unhappy ▶ **nieszczęsny**; **żałosny** SYN **awful 2** [only before a noun] (informal) (used for expressing anger): *That wretched dog has chewed up my slippers again!* ▶ **cholerny**

wriggle /ˈrɪɡl/ verb [I,T] **1 wriggle (sth) (about /around)** to move about, or to move a part of your body, with short, quick movements, especially from side to side: *The baby was wriggling around on my lap.* ◇ *She wriggled her fingers about in the hot sand.* ▶ **wiercić się**, **kręcić (się) 2** to move in the direction mentioned by making quick turning movements: *The worm wriggled back into the soil.* ▶ **wkręcać się**

PHR V **wriggle out of sth/doing sth** (informal) to avoid sth by making clever excuses: *It's your turn to wash up – you can't wriggle out of it this time!* ▶ **wykręcać się z czegoś**

wring /rɪŋ/ verb [T] (pt, pp **wrung** /rʌŋ/) **wring sth (out)** to press and squeeze sth in order to remove water from it ▶ **wykręcać** (*bieliznę*)

wrinkle[1] /ˈrɪŋkl/ noun [C] a small line in sth, especially one on the skin of your face which you get as you grow older: *She's got fine wrinkles around her eyes.* ◇ *Smooth out the wrinkles in the fabric.* ▶ **zmarszczka** ➲ look at **furrow**

■ **wrinkled** adj. ▶ **pomarszczony**

wrinkle[2] /ˈrɪŋkl/ verb [I,T] **wrinkle (sth) (up)** to form small lines and folds in sth: *She wrinkled her nose at the nasty smell.* ◇ *My skirt had wrinkled up on the journey.* ▶ **marszczyć (się)**

⚷ **wrist** /rɪst/ noun [C] the narrow part at the end of your arm where it joins your hand ▶ **nadgarstek** ➲ picture at **body**

wristwatch /ˈrɪstwɒtʃ/ noun [C] a watch that you wear on your wrist ▶ **zegarek na rękę**

writ /rɪt/ noun [C] a legal order to do or not to do sth, given by a court of law ▶ **nakaz sądowy**

⚷ **write** /raɪt/ verb (pt **wrote** /rəʊt/, pp **written** /ˈrɪtn/) **1** [I,T] to make words, letters, etc., especially on paper using a pen or pencil: *I can't write with this pen.* ◇ *Write your name and address on the form.* ▶ **pisać 2** [T] to create a book, story, song, etc. in written form for people to read or use: *Tolstoy wrote 'War and Peace'.* ◇ *He wrote his wife a poem.* ◇ *Who wrote the music for that film?* ▶ **pisać**, **komponować 3** [I,T] **write (sth) (to sb)**; **write (sb) sth** to write and send a letter, etc. to sb: *She wrote that they were all well and would be home soon.* ◇ *She phones every week and writes occasionally.* ◇ *I've written a letter to my son./I've written my son a letter.* ◇ *I've written to him.* ▶ **pisać** ℹ W Amer. ang. można powiedzieć *I've written him.* **4** [T] **write sth (out) (for sb)** to fill or complete a form, cheque, document, etc. with the necessary information: *I wrote out a cheque for £10.* ▶ **wypisywać** (*np. czek, receptę*)

PHR V **write back (to sb)** to send a reply to sb ▶ **odpisywać (komuś)** SYN **reply**

write sth down to write sth on paper, especially so that you can remember it: *Did you write down Jon's address?* ▶ **zapisywać coś**

write in (to sb/sth) (for sth) to write a letter to an organization, etc. to ask for sth, give an opinion, etc. ▶ **prosić listownie o coś**; **posyłać do jakiejś instytucji** (*np. swoje postulaty*)

write off/away (to sb/sth) (for sth) to write a letter to an organization, etc. to order sth or ask for sth ▶ **prosić listownie o informacje**, **składać listownie zamówienie** (*na towary*)

write sb/sth off (as sth) to decide that sb/sth is a failure or not worth paying any attention to ▶ **spisywać kogoś/coś na straty (jako coś)** SYN **dismiss**

write sth off to accept that you will not get back an amount of money you have lost or spent: *to write off a debt* ▶ **wyksięgować**, **spisywać coś na straty**

write sth out to write the whole of sth on paper: *Can you write out that recipe for me?* ▶ **napisać coś w całości**, **przepisywać coś**

write sth up to write sth in a complete and final form, often using notes that you have made: *to write up lecture notes* ▶ **pisać na czysto**

ˈ**write-off** noun [C] a thing, especially a vehicle, that is so badly damaged that it is not worth repairing ▶ **przedmiot spisany na straty**, **wrak** (*samochód nie nadający się do naprawy*)

⚷ **writer** /ˈraɪtə(r)/ noun [C] a person who writes, especially one whose job is to write books, articles, stories, etc. ▶ **pisa-rz/rka**

ˈ**write-up** noun [C] an article in a newspaper or magazine in which sb writes what they think about a new book, play, product, etc.: *The performance got a good write-up in the local paper.* ▶ **omówienie**, **recenzja**

writhe /raɪð/ verb [I] to turn and roll your body about: *She was writhing in pain.* ▶ **wić się**

⚷ **writing** /ˈraɪtɪŋ/ noun [U] **1** the skill or activity of writing words: *He had problems with his reading and writing at school.* ▶ **pisanie 2** the activity or job of writing books, etc.: *It's difficult to earn much money from writing.* ▶ **pisarstwo 3** the books, etc. that sb has written or the style in which sb writes: *Love is a common theme in his early writing.* ▶ **twórczość literacka**; **pisarstwo** (*charakter literacki*) **4** words that have been written or printed; the way a person writes: *This card's got no writing inside. You can put your own message.* ◇ *I can't read your writing, it's too small.* ▶ **napis**; **charakter pisma**

IDM **in writing** in written form: *I'll confirm the offer in writing next week.* ▶ **na piśmie**

ˈ**writing paper** noun [U] paper for writing letters on ▶ **papier listowy**

written[1] past participle of **write**

⚷ **written**[2] /ˈrɪtn/ adj. expressed on paper; not just spoken: *a written agreement* ▶ **pisemny**, **na piśmie**

⚷ **wrong**[1] /rɒŋ/ adj. **1** not correct; in a way that is not correct: *the wrong answer* ◇ *You've got the wrong number.* Pomyłka (telefoniczna). ◇ *I think you're wrong about Nicola – she's not lazy.* OPP **right** ▶ **zły**, **błędny 2** [not before a noun] **wrong (with sb/sth)** causing problems or difficulties; not as it should be: *You look upset. Is something wrong?* ◇ ***What's wrong** with the car this time?* Co się znowu stało z samochodem? ◇ *She's got something wrong with her leg.* ▶ **nie w porządku**, **niesprawny 3** not the best; not suitable: *That's the wrong way to hold the bat.* ◇ *I think she married the wrong man.* ◇ *I like him – I just think he's wrong for the job.* ▶ **nieprawidłowy**, **nieodpowiedni 4 wrong (to do sth)** not morally right or honest: *It's wrong to tell lies.* ◇ *The man said that he had done nothing wrong.* ◇ *I think it was wrong of us* (to niełądnie z naszej strony) *not to invite him.* ▶ **zły** (*nielegalny/przestępczy*), **niełądny**

IDM **get (hold of) the wrong end of the stick** (Brit., informal) to misunderstand completely what has been said: *You must have got the wrong end of the stick. We're not going there – they're coming here.* ▶ **opacznie coś zrozumieć**

get on the right/wrong side of sb → SIDE[1]
get/start off on the right/wrong foot (with sb) → FOOT[1]
on the right/wrong track → TRACK[1]

wrong[2] /rɒŋ/ adv. in an incorrect way: *I always pronounce that word wrong.* ▶ **źle**
IDM **get sb wrong** (informal) to not understand sb: *Don't get me wrong! I don't dislike him.* ▶ **opacznie kogoś zrozumieć**
go wrong 1 to make a mistake: *I'm afraid we've gone wrong. We should have taken the other road.* ▶ **mylić się** **2** to stop working properly or to stop developing well: *My computer keeps going wrong.* ▶ **psuć się, źle chodzić**

wrong[3] /rɒŋ/ noun **1** [U] things that are morally bad or dishonest: *Children quickly learn the difference between right and wrong.* ▶ **zło 2** [C] an action or situation which is not fair: *A terrible wrong has been done. Those men should never have gone to prison.* ▶ **niesprawiedliwość**
IDM **in the wrong** (used about a person) having made a mistake ▶ **winny**
right a wrong → RIGHT[4]

wrong[4] /rɒŋ/ verb [T] (formal) to do sth to sb which is bad or unfair: *I wronged her when I said she was lying.* ▶ **krzywdzić**

wrongful /ˈrɒŋfl/ adj. [only before a noun] (formal) not fair, not legal or not moral: *He sued the company for wrongful dismissal.* ▶ **niesprawiedliwy; bezprawny**

wrongly /ˈrɒŋli/ adv. in a way that is wrong or not correct: *He was wrongly accused of stealing money.* ▶ **błędnie**

Przysłówek **wrong** stawia się po czasowniku lub po dopełnieniu czasownika, zwłaszcza w rozmowie: *He's spelt my name wrong.* Przysłówka **wrongly** używa się zwykle przed imiesłowem biernym czasu przeszłego lub przed czasownikiem: *My name's been wrongly spelt.*

wrote past tense of **write**

wrought iron /ˌrɔːt ˈaɪən/ noun [U] a form of iron used to make fences, gates, etc.: *wrought-iron gates* ▶ **kute żelazo** ⊃ look at **cast iron**

wrung past tense, past participle of **wring**

wry /raɪ/ adj. showing that you are both disappointed and amused: *'Never mind,' she said with a wry grin. 'At least we got one vote.'* ▶ (*uśmiech itp.*) **kwaśny, krzywy**
■ **wryly** adv. ▶ **kwaśno, krzywo** (*np. uśmiechać się*)

wt = WEIGHT[1]: *net wt 500g*

WWW = WORLD WIDE WEB

X, x /eks/ noun [C,U] (pl. **Xs**; **xs**; **X's**; **x's** /ˈeksɪz/) the 24th letter of the English alphabet: *'Xylophone' begins with (an) 'X'.* ▶ **litera** *x*

Litera **x** jest używana przez nauczycieli do zaznaczenia błędnej odpowiedzi. Stosuje się ją również zamiast nazwiska nieznanej osoby: *Mr and Mrs X.* Na końcu listu litera **x** symbolizuje przesłany pocałunek: *Lots of love, Mary XX.*

xenophobia /ˌzenəˈfəʊbiə/ noun [U] a fear or hatred of foreign people and cultures ▶ **ksenofobia**
■ **xenophobic** adj. ▶ **ksenofobiczny**

Xerox™ /ˈzɪərɒks/ noun [C] **1** a process for producing copies of letters, documents, etc. using a special machine ▶ **kopiowanie na kserografie/fotokopiarce** **2** a copy produced by a **Xerox** or similar process ▶ **ksero**
SYN **photocopy**
■ **xerox** verb [T] ▶ **kserować**

XL abbr. **extra large** (size) ▶ **bardzo duży (rozmiar)**

Xmas /ˈkrɪsməs; ˈeksməs/ noun [C,U] (informal) (used as a short form in writing) Christmas: *Happy Xmas* ▶ **Boże Narodzenie**

ˈ**X-ray** noun [C] **1** [usually pl.] a type of light that makes it possible to see inside solid objects, for example the human body, so that they can be examined and a photograph of them can be made ▶ **promieniowanie rentgenowskie 2** a photograph that is made with an **X-ray** machine: *The X-ray showed that the bone was not broken.* ▶ **rentgen** (*zdjęcie rentgenowskie*) ⊃ look at **ray**
■ **X-ray** verb [T]: *She had her chest X-rayed.* ▶ **robić zdjęcie rentgenowskie**

xylophone /ˈzaɪləfəʊn/ noun [C] a musical instrument that consists of a row of wooden bars of different lengths. You play it by hitting these bars with a small hammer. ▶ **ksylofon**

Y, y /waɪ/ noun [C,U] (pl. **Ys**; **ys**; **Y's**; **y's** /waɪz/) the 25th letter of the English alphabet: *'Yesterday' begins with (a) 'Y'.* ▶ **litera** *y*

yacht /jɒt/ noun [C] **1** a boat with sails, used for pleasure: *a yacht race* regaty jachtowe ▶ **jacht** ⊃ note at **boat** ⊃ picture on **page A6 2** a large boat with a motor, used for pleasure ▶ **jacht motorowy** ⊃ picture at **boat**

yachting /ˈjɒtɪŋ/ noun [U] the activity or sport of sailing or racing **yachts** ▶ **żeglowanie** (*jachtem*)

yachtsman /ˈjɒtsmən/, **yachtswoman** /-wʊmən/ noun [C] (pl. **-men** /-mən/; **-women** /-wɪmɪn/) a person who sails a **yacht** in races or for pleasure ▶ **żegla-rz/rka**

Yank /jæŋk/ noun [C] (Brit., informal) a person from the US; an American ▶ **Jankes/ka** ℹ Czasami słowa tego używa się w znaczeniu obraźliwym.

yank /jæŋk/ verb [I,T] (informal) to pull sth suddenly, quickly and hard: *She yanked at the door handle.* ▶ **szarpać**
■ **yank** noun [C] ▶ **szarpnięcie**

yap /jæp/ verb [I] (**yapping**; **yapped**) (used about dogs, especially small ones) to make short, loud noises in an excited way ▶ **szczekać piskliwie**

yard /jɑːd/ noun [C] **1** (Brit.) an area outside a building, usually with a hard surface and a wall or fence around it: *a school/prison yard* ▶ **podwórze, boisko** ⊃ look at **courtyard, churchyard 2** (US) = GARDEN[1] (1) **3** [in compounds] an area, usually without a roof, used for a particular type of work or purpose: *a shipyard* stocznia ◇ *a builder's yard* skład materiałów budowlanych ▶ **otwarta przestrzeń szczególnego przeznaczenia**

W Br. ang. przydomowy ogródek nazywa się **garden**, jeżeli jest porośnięty trawą, kwiatami itp., natomiast **yard** oznacza kamienny lub wybetonowany plac przed domem lub wokół domu. W Amer. ang. przydomowy ogródek nazywa się **yard** bez względu na to, czy jest porośnięty trawą, czy nie.

4 (abbr. **yd**, pl. **yds**) a measure of length; 0.914 of a metre. There are 3 feet in a yard. ▶ **jard** ℹ Więcej o miarach w dodatku *Wyrażenia liczbowe* na końcu słownika.

yardstick /ˈjɑːdstɪk/ noun [C] a standard with which things can be compared: *Exam results should not be the only yardstick by which pupils are judged.* ▶ **miara**

yarn /jɑːn/ noun **1** [U] thread (usually of wool or cotton) that is used for knitting, etc. ▶ **przędza 2** [C] (informal) a long story that sb tells, especially one that is invented or exaggerated ▶ **historyjka**

yawn /jɔːn/ verb [I] **1** to open your mouth wide and breathe in deeply, especially when you are tired or bored: *I kept yawning all through the lecture.* ▶ **ziewać** **2** (used about a hole, etc.) to be wide open ▶ **zionąć**
■ **yawn** noun [C]: *'How much longer will it take?' he said with a yawn.* ▶ **ziewnięcie**

yd = YARD (4)

yeah /jeə/ interj. (informal) yes ▶ **tak**

year /jɪə(r); jɜː(r)/ noun **1** [C] (also 'calendar year) (abbr. **yr**, pl. **yrs**) the period from 1 January to 31 December, 365 or 366 days divided into 12 months or 52 weeks: *last year/this year/next year* ◇ *The population of the country will be 70 million by the year 2010.* ◇ *Interest is paid on this account once a year.* ◇ *a **leap year*** rok przestępny ◇ *the **New Year*** ▶ **rok kalendarzowy** **2** [C] any period of 12 months, measured from any date: *She worked here for twenty years.* ◇ *He left school just over a year ago.* ◇ *In a year's time* (za rok), *you'll be old enough to vote.* ▶ **rok** **3** [C] a period of 12 months in connection with schools, the business world, etc.: *the academic/school year* ◇ *the tax/financial year* ▶ **rok** (*np. szkolny, budżetowy*) **4** [C] (especially Brit.) the level that a particular student is at: *My son is in year ten now.* ◇ *The first-years do French as a compulsory subject.* ◇ *He was a year below me at school.* ▶ **rok** **5** [C, usually pl.] (used in connection with the age of sb/sth) a period of 12 months: *He's ten years old* (kończy dziesięć lat) *today.* ◇ *a six-year-old* (sześcioletnia) *daughter* ◇ *The company is now in its fifth year.* ▶ **wiek** (*np. osoby, organizacji*) ➲ note at **age**

Zwróć uwagę, że można powiedzieć **He's ten** lub **He's ten years old**, ale nie ~~*He's ten years*~~ ani ~~*a ten-years-old boy*~~.

6 (**years**) [pl.] a long time: *It happened years ago.* ◇ *I haven't seen him for years.* ▶ **wiele lat**
IDM **all year round** for the whole year ▶ **przez cały rok**
donkey's years → DONKEY
take a year out to go away or stop doing sth for a year, especially between leaving school and starting university, or between leaving university and starting work: *I decided to take a year out of university to travel.* ▶ **mieć rok przerwy** (*np. w nauce*), **wyjechać na rok**
the turn of the century/year → TURN[2]
year after year; **year in year out** every year for many years ▶ **rok po roku**

yearbook /ˈjɪəbʊk/ noun [C] **1** a book published once a year, giving details of events, etc. of the previous year, especially those connected with a particular area of activity ▶ **rocznik** **2** (especially US) a book that is produced by students in their final year of school or college, containing photographs of students and details of school activities ▶ **kronika szkolna**

yearly /ˈjɪəli; Brit. also ˈjɜːli/ adj. (happening) every year or once a year: *a yearly pay increase* ▶ **doroczny**
■ **yearly** adv.: *The conference is held yearly.* ▶ **rokrocznie**

yearn /jɜːn/ verb [I] (formal) **yearn (for sb/sth)**; **yearn (to do sth)** to want sb/sth very much, especially sb/sth that you cannot have ▶ **tęsknić (za kimś/czymś)** SYN **long**
■ **yearning** noun [C,U] ▶ **pragnienie (czegoś)**, **tęsknota (za kimś/czymś)**

yeast /jiːst/ noun [U] a substance used for making bread rise and for making beer, wine, etc. ▶ **drożdże**

yell /jel/ verb [I,T] **yell (out) (sth)**; **yell (sth) (at sb/sth)** to shout very loudly, often because you are angry, excited or in pain: *She yelled out his name.* ◇ *There's no need to yell at me – I can hear you perfectly well.* ▶ **wrzeszczeć**, **wyć** (*np. z bólu*)
■ **yell** noun [C] ▶ **wrzask**, **wycie** (*np. z bólu*)

yellow /ˈjeləʊ/ adj. having the colour of lemons or butter: *a pale/light yellow dress* ▶ **żółty**
■ **yellow** noun [C,U]: *a bright shade of yellow* ▶ **żółty kolor**

ˌyellow ˈcard noun [C] (in football) a card that is shown to a player as a warning that he or she will be sent off the field if he or she behaves badly again ▶ **żółta kartka** ➲ look at **red card**

yellowish /ˈjeləʊɪʃ/ adj. (also **yellowy** /ˈjeləʊi/) slightly yellow in colour ▶ **żółtawy**

ˌyellow ˈline noun [C] (Brit.) a yellow line at the side of a road to show that you can only park there for a limited time: ***double yellow lines*** ▶ **żółta linia**

the **ˌYellow ˈPages™** noun [pl.] a telephone book (on yellow paper) that lists all the business companies, etc. in a certain area in sections according to the goods or services they provide ▶ **książka telefoniczna firm**

yellowy = YELLOWISH

yelp /jelp/ verb [I] to give a sudden short cry, especially of pain ▶ **skamleć**
■ **yelp** noun [C] ▶ **skamlenie**

yep /jep/ exclamation (informal) (used to say 'yes'): *'Are you ready?' 'Yep.'* ▶ **tak**

yes /jes/ interj. **1** (used to give a positive answer to a question, for saying that sth is true or correct or for saying that you want sth): *'Are you having a good time?' 'Yes, thank you.'* ◇ *'You're married, aren't you?' 'Yes, I am.'* ◇ *'May I sit here?' 'Yes, of course.'* ◇ *'More coffee?' 'Yes, please.'* ▶ **tak**, **owszem** OPP **no** **2** (used when saying that a negative statement that sb has made is not true): *'You don't care about anyone but yourself.' 'Yes, I do.'* ▶ **tak** OPP **no** **3** (used for showing you have heard sb or will do what they ask): *'Waiter!' 'Yes, madam.'* ▶ **tak**
■ **yes** noun [C]: *Was that a yes or a no?* ▶ **odpowiedź twierdząca**

yesterday /ˈjestədeɪ; ˈjestədi/ adv., noun [C,U] (on) the day before today: *Did you watch the film on TV yesterday?* ◇ *yesterday morning/afternoon/evening* ◇ *I posted the form **the day before yesterday*** (przedwczoraj). ◇ *Have you still got yesterday's paper* (wczorajszą gazetę)*?* ◇ *I spent the whole of yesterday* (cały wczorajszy dzień) *walking round the shops.* ▶ **wczoraj**

yet /jet/ adv. **1** (used with negative verbs or in questions for talking about sth that has not happened but that you expect to happen): *I haven't seen that film yet.* Jeszcze nie widziałem tego filmu. ℹ W Amer. ang. można powiedzieć: *I didn't see that film yet.* ◇ *We haven't had any serious problems yet.* Dotychczas nie mieliśmy żadnych poważnych kłopotów. ◇ *Has it stopped raining yet?* Czy już przestało padać? ◇ *There was a pile of work on my desk which I hadn't yet done* (wciąż jeszcze nie zrobiłem). ▶ **(wciąż) jeszcze** (*w zdaniach przeczących*), **już** (*w pytaniach*) **2** [used with negative verbs] now; as early as this: *You don't have to leave yet – your train isn't for another hour.* ▶ **jeszcze (teraz)** **3** from now until the period of time mentioned has passed: *She isn't all that old – she'll live for years yet* (pożyje jeszcze wiele lat). ▶ **jeszcze** **4** [used especially with *may* or *might*] at some time in the future: *With a bit of luck, they may yet win.* ▶ **(wciąż) jeszcze** **5** [used with superlatives] until now/until then; so far: *This is her best film yet.* ▶ **dotychczas** **6** (used with comparatives to emphasize an increase in the degree of sth): *a recent and yet more improbable theory* ▶ **jeszcze** **7** but; in spite of that ▶ **ale**, **a jednak**
IDM **as yet** until now: *As yet little is known about the disease.* ▶ **dotychczas**
yet again (used for expressing surprise or anger that sth happens again) once more; another time: *I found out that he had lied to me yet again.* ▶ **znowu**

Y

yet another (used for expressing surprise that there is one more of sth): *They're opening yet another fast food restaurant in the square.* ▶ **jeszcze jeden**
yet to do, etc. that has not been done and is still to do in the future: *The final decision has yet to be made.* ▶ **jeszcze do** (*zrobienia itp.*)
■ **yet** conj. but (when sth is surprising after the first part of the statement): *He seems pleasant, yet there's something about him I don't like.* ▶ **ale (jednak)**

yew /juː/ noun **1** [C,U] (also 'yew tree) a tree with dark green leaves and small round red fruit which are poisonous ▶ **cis 2** [U] the wood from the **yew tree** ▶ **cis**

'**Y-fronts**™ noun [pl.] (Brit.) a type of men's underwear with an opening in the front sewn in the shape of a Y ▶ **slipy** (*z frontem uformowanym w kształcie litery Y*)

YHA /ˌwaɪ eɪtʃ 'eɪ/ abbr. (Brit.) **Youth Hostels Association** ▶ **Stowarzyszenie Schronisk Młodzieżowych**

Yiddish /'jɪdɪʃ/ noun [U] a Jewish language, originally used in central and eastern Europe, based on a form of German with words from Hebrew and several modern languages ▶ **jidysz**

yield[1] /jiːld/ verb **1** [T] to produce or provide crops, profits or results: *How much wheat does each field yield?* ◇ *Did the experiment yield any new information?* ▶ **dostarczać 2** [I] (formal) **yield (to sb/sth)** to stop refusing to do sth or to obey sb: *The government refused to yield to the hostage takers' demands.* ▶ **ulegać** ℹ Zwrot **give in** jest mniej formalny. **3** [T] **yield sb/sth (up) (to sb/sth)** to allow sb to have control of sth that you were controlling: *The army has yielded power to the rebels.* ▶ **oddawać** (*np. władzę*) **4** [I] (formal) to move, bend or break because of pressure: *The dam finally yielded under the weight of the water.* ▶ **załamywać się** ℹ Zwrot **give way** jest mniej formalny. **5** [I] (US) **yield (to sb/sth)** to allow other vehicles on a bigger road to go first: *You have to yield to traffic from the left here.* ▶ **dawać pierwszeństwo przejazdu** ℹ W Br. ang. używa się **give way**.
PHR V **yield to sth** (formal) to be replaced by sth, especially sth newer: *Old-fashioned methods have yielded to new technology.* ▶ **ustępować** (*np. nowemu*) ℹ Zwrot **give way** jest mniej formalny.

yield[2] /jiːld/ noun [C] the amount that is produced: *Wheat yields were down 5% this year.* ◇ *This investment has an annual yield of 12%.* ▶ **plon, wydajność, zysk**

yo /jəʊ/ interj. (especially US, slang) (used by some people when they see a friend) hello ▶ **cześć!**

yob /jɒb/ noun [C] (Brit., slang) a boy or young man who is rude, loud and sometimes violent or aggressive ▶ **łobuz** ➲ look at **lout, hooligan**

yoga /'jəʊgə/ noun [U] a system of exercises for the body that helps you control and relax both your mind and your body ▶ **joga**

yogurt (also **yoghurt**) /'jɒgət/ noun [C,U] a slightly sour, thick liquid food made from milk: *plain/banana/strawberry yogurt* ▶ **jogurt**

yoke /jəʊk/ noun **1** [C] a long piece of wood fixed across the necks of two animals so that they can pull heavy loads together ▶ **jarzmo 2** [sing.] something that limits your freedom and makes your life difficult: *the yoke of parental control* ▶ (*przen.*) **jarzmo**

yolk /jəʊk/ noun [C,U] the yellow part in the middle of an egg ▶ **żółtko**

yonks /jɒŋks/ noun [U] (slang) a very long time: *I haven't been to the theatre for yonks.* ▶ **wieki**

ˌ**Yorkshire 'pudding** /ˌjɔːkʃə 'pʊdɪŋ/ noun [U,C] a type of British food made from batter that is baked until it rises, traditionally eaten with roast beef ▶ **rodzaj potrawy**

🔑 **you** /ju; US jə; strong form juː/ pron. **1** (used as the subject or object of a verb, or after a preposition to refer to the person or people being spoken or written to): *You can play the guitar, can't you?* ◇ *I've told you about this before.* ◇ *Bring all your photos with you.* ▶ **ty, wy, pan/i, państwo 2** (used with a noun, adjective or phrase when calling sb sth): *You idiot! What do you think you're doing?* ▶ **ty, wy 3** (used for referring to people in general): *The more you earn, the more tax you pay.* ◇ *You don't see many tourists* (nie widzi się wielu turystów) *here at this time of year.* ℹ **One** ma takie samo znaczenie, ale jest o wiele bardziej formalne: *One tries to help as much as one can.* ▶ *(tłumaczy się formą bezosobową)*

you'd /juːd/ short for **you had; you would**

you'll /juːl/ short for **you will**

🔑 **young**[1] /jʌŋ/ adj. (**younger** /'jʌŋgə(r)/; **youngest** /'jʌŋgɪst/) not having lived or existed for very long; not old: *I'm a year younger than her.* ◇ *my younger brothers* ◇ *My father was the youngest of eight children.* ◇ *They have two young children* (dwoje małych dzieci). ◇ *young fashion* moda młodzieżowa ▶ **młody** OPP **old**
IDM **young at heart** behaving or thinking like a young person, although you are old ▶ **młody duchem**

young[2] /jʌŋ/ noun [pl.] **1** (**the young**) young people considered as a group: *The young of today are more ambitious than their parents.* ▶ **młodzież 2** young animals: *Swans will attack to protect their young.* ▶ **młode** (*zwierząt*)

youngish /'jʌŋɪʃ/ adj. quite young ▶ **dość młody**

youngster /'jʌŋstə(r)/ noun [C] a young person: *There is very little entertainment for youngsters in this town.* ▶ **młoda osoba**

🔑 **your** /jə(r); jɔː(r); US jʊr/ determiner **1** of or belonging to the person or people being spoken to: *What's your flat like?* ◇ *Thanks for all your help.* ◇ *How old are your children now?* ◇ *It would be helpful if you could all give me your addresses* (swoje adresy). ▶ **twój, wasz, pan-a/i, pański, państwa 2** belonging to or connected with people in general: *When your life is* (kiedy czyjeś życie jest) *as busy as mine, you have little time to relax.* ▶ **czyjś** (*używa się w znaczeniu bezosobowym*) **3** (informal) (used for saying that sth is well known to people in general): *So this is your typical English pub, is it?* ▶ **taki, ten słynny 4** (**Your**) (used in some titles): *Your Highness* ◇ *Your Majesty* wasza królewska mość ▶ (*w tytułach*) **wasza** (*wysokość itp.*)

you're /jʊə(r); Brit. also jɔː(r); US also jər/ short for **you are**

🔑 **yours** /jɔːz; US jəz; jʊz/ pron. **1** of or belonging to you: *Is this bag yours or mine?* ◇ *I was talking to a friend of yours* (z jednym z twoich znajomych) *the other day.* ▶ **twój, wasz, pan-a/i, pański, państwa 2** (**Yours**) (used at the end of a letter): *Yours sincerely.../faithfully...* ◇ *Yours...* ▶ **z poważaniem**

> **Yours sincerely** używa się, kiedy nazwisko adresata jest znane i wymienione na początku listu, np. **Dear Mrs Smith. Yours faithfully** stosuje się, kiedy nazwisko adresata nie jest znane. Wówczas list zaczyna się zwrotem **Dear Sir, Dear Madam** lub **Dear Sir/Madam**.

🔑 **yourself** /jɔː'self; weak form jə-; US also jʊə-/ pron. (pl. **yourselves** /-'selvz/) **1** (used when the person or people being spoken to both do an action and are also affected by the action): *Be careful or you'll hurt yourself.* ◇ *Here's some money. Buy yourselves a present.* ◇ *You're always talking about yourself!* ▶ **się, siebie 2** (used to emphasize the person or people who do the action): *You yourself told me there was a problem last week.* ◇ *Did you repair the car yourselves?* ▶ **sam, osobiście 3** you: *'How are you?' 'Not too bad, thanks. And yourself?'* ▶ **ty/wy 4** in your normal state; healthy: *You don't look yourself today.* Wyglądasz dziś nieswojo. ▶ **tak jak zwykle; zdrowy**

IDM **(all) by yourself/yourselves 1** alone: *Do you live by yourself?* ➲ note at **alone** ▶ **sam** (*bez towarzystwa*) **2** without help: *You can't cook dinner for ten people by yourself.* ▶ **samemu**

⚷ **youth** /ju:θ/ noun (pl. **youths** /ju:ðz/) **1** [U] the period of your life when you are young, especially the time before a child becomes an adult: *He was quite a good sportsman **in his youth.*** ▶ **młodość 2** [U] the fact or state of being young: *I think that her youth will be a disadvantage in this job.* ▶ **młodość** ➲ look at **age 3** [C] a young person (usually a young man, and often one that you do not have a good opinion of): *a gang of youths* ▶ **młody człowiek, młodzieniec 4** (**the youth**) [U] young people considered as a group: *the youth of today* ▶ **młodzież** ➲ look at **age, old age**

'youth club noun [C] (in Britain) a club where young people can meet each other and take part in various activities ▶ **klub młodzieżowy**

youthful /'ju:θfl/ adj. **1** typical of young people: *youthful enthusiasm* ▶ **młodzieńczy 2** seeming younger than you are: *She's a youthful fifty-year-old.* ▶ **młodociany, młody**

'youth hostel noun [C] a cheap and simple place to stay, especially for young people, when they are travelling ▶ **schronisko młodzieżowe**

you've /ju:v/ short for **you have**

'Yo Yo™ (also **'yo-yo**) noun [C] (pl. **Yo Yos**; **yo-yos**) a toy which is a round piece of wood or plastic with a string round the middle. You put the string round your finger and can make the **yo-yo** go up and down it. ▶ **jo-jo**

yr = YEAR

yuck /jʌk/ interj. (informal) (used for saying that you think sth is disgusting or very unpleasant): *It's filthy! Yuck!*
■ **yucky** adj.: *a yucky colour* ▶ **paskudny** ▶ **fu!**

yum /jʌm/ (also **,yum-'yum**) exclamation (informal) (used to show that you think sth tastes or smells very nice) ▶ **mmm ...** (*to jest pyszne!*)

yummy /'jʌmi/ adj. (informal) tasting very good: *a yummy cake* **SYN** **delicious** ▶ **pyszny**

yuppie (also **yuppy**) /'jʌpi/ noun [C] (pl. **yuppies**) a successful young professional person who lives in a city, earns a lot of money and spends it on fashionable things ▶ **yuppie**

Zz

Z, z /zed/ noun [C,U] (pl. **Zs**; **zs**; **Z's**; **z's** /zedz; US zi:z/) the 26th letter of the English alphabet: *'Zero' begins with (a) 'Z'.* ▶ **litera** *z* ℹ Zwróć uwagę na inną wymowę amerykańską.

zany /'zeɪni/ adj. (**zanier**; **zaniest**) funny in an unusual and crazy way: *a zany comedian* ▶ **zwariowany**

zap /zæp/ verb (**zapping**; **zapped**) (informal) **1** [T] **zap sb/sth (with sth)** to destroy, hit or kill sb, usually with a gun or other weapon: *It's a computer game where you have to zap aliens with a laser.* **2** [I,T] to change TV programmes very quickly using a **remote control** ▶ **załatwiać kogoś**

zeal /zi:l/ noun [U] (formal) great energy or enthusiasm: *religious zeal* ▶ **gorliwość**

zealot /'zelət/ noun [C] a person who is extremely enthusiastic about sth, especially religion or politics ▶ **fanaty-k/czka** ℹ Często wyraża dezaprobatę. **SYN** **fanatic**

zealous /'zeləs/ adj. using great energy and enthusiasm ▶ **gorliwy**
■ **zealously** adv. ▶ **gorliwie**

zebra /'zebrə/ noun [C] (pl. **zebra** or **zebras**) an African wild animal that looks like a horse, with black and white lines all over its body ▶ **zebra**

,zebra 'crossing noun [C] (Brit.) a place where the road is marked with black and white lines and people can cross safely because cars must stop to let them do this ➲ look at **pedestrian crossing** ▶ **zebra** (*przejście dla pieszych*)

zenith /'zenɪθ/ noun [sing.] **1** the highest point that the sun or moon reaches in the sky, directly above you ▶ (*astr.*) **zenit 2** (formal) the time when sth is strongest and most successful: *The rock band was **at the zenith** of its creative powers.* ▶ (*przen.*) **szczyt**

⚷ **zero¹** /'zɪərəʊ; US also 'zi:-/ number (pl. **zeros**) **1** [C] the figure 0 ▶ **zero** ➲ note at **six 2** [U] freezing point; 0°C: *The temperature is likely to fall to five degrees **below zero.*** ▶ **zero 3** [U] the lowest possible amount or level; nothing at all: *zero growth/inflation/profit* ▶ **zerowy**

> **zero**
>
> W Br. ang. cyfra **0** ma kilka różnych nazw. **Zero** najczęściej używa się w języku naukowym lub technicznym, **nil** najczęściej spotyka się w języku mówionym przy podawaniu wyników sportowych, zwł. w piłce nożnej. **Nought** używa się w odniesieniu do cyfry **0** tworzącej jakąś liczbę: *a million is one followed by six noughts.* **0** (wymawiane /əʊ/) na ogół używa się w języku mówionym przy podawaniu numeru telefonu, lotu itp.

zero² /'zɪərəʊ; US also 'zi:-/ verb [T] (**zeroing**; **zeroes**; pt, pp **zeroed**) to turn an instrument, control, etc. to zero
PHR V **zero in on sb/sth 1** to fix all your attention on the person or thing mentioned: *They zeroed in on the key issues.* ▶ **skupiać się na kimś/czymś** (*np. na zadaniu, sprawie*) **2** to aim guns, etc. at the person or thing mentioned ▶ **celować do kogoś/czegoś**

'zero hour noun [U] the time when an important event, an attack, etc. is planned to start ▶ **godzina zero**

,zero 'tolerance noun [U] the policy of applying laws very strictly so that people are punished even for offences that are not very serious ▶ **zero tolerancji**

zest /zest/ noun [U, sing.] **zest (for sth)** a feeling of enjoyment, excitement and enthusiasm: *She has a great **zest for life.*** ▶ **werwa, zapał**

zigzag /'zɪgzæg/ noun [C], adj. [only before a noun] (consisting of) a line with left and right turns, like a lot of letter Ws, one after the other: *The skier came down the slope in a series of zigzags.* ◇ *a zigzag pattern/line* ▶ **zygzak** ➲ picture on **page A1**
■ **zigzag** verb [I] (**zigzagging**; **zigzagged**) ▶ **ciągnąć się/posuwać się zygzakiem**

zilch /zɪltʃ/ noun [U] (informal) nothing: *I arrived in this country with zilch.* ▶ **absolutnie nic**

zillion /'zɪljən/ noun [C] (especially US, informal) a very large number: *There were zillions of people waiting outside the theatre.* ▶ (*mnóstwo*) **milion**

zinc /zɪŋk/ noun [U] (symbol **Zn**) a silver-grey metal, often put on the surface of iron and steel as protection against water ▶ **cynk**

zip /zɪp/ (US **zipper** /'zɪpə(r)/) noun [C] a device consisting of two rows of metal or plastic teeth, that you use for fastening clothes, bags, etc.: *to do up/undo a zip* ▶ **zamek błyskawiczny** ➲ picture at **button**, picture on **page A1**
■ **zip** verb [T] **zip sth (up)** (**zipping**; **zipped**) **zip sth (up)**: *There was so much in the bag that it was difficult to zip it up.* ▶ **zapinać na zamek błyskawiczny** **OPP** **unzip**

'zip code (also **ZIP code**) (US) = POSTCODE

zipper (US) = ZIP

zit /zɪt/ noun [C] (informal) a spot on the skin, especially on the face ▶ **pryszcz** (*zwł. na twarzy*), **wyprysk**

the zodiac /'zəʊdiæk/ noun [sing.] a diagram of the positions of the sun, moon and planets, which is divided into twelve equal parts, each with a special name and symbol called a **sign of the zodiac**

> The signs of the zodiac are used in **astrology** and **horoscopes** (often called **the stars**) in newspapers and magazines. People often refer to the signs and to the influence that they think these have on sb's personality and future: *Which sign (of the zodiac) are you?*

▶ **zodiak**

zombie /ˈzɒmbi/ noun [C] (informal) a person who seems only partly alive, without any feeling or interest in what is happening ▶ **zombi**

zone /zəʊn/ noun [C] an area that is different from those around it for example because sth special happens there: *a war zone* ▶ **strefa**

zonked /zɒŋkt/ adj. [not before a noun] **zonked (out)** (slang) extremely tired or suffering from the effects of alcohol or drugs ▶ **padnięty**; **nawalony**; **naćpany**

zoo /zuː/ noun [C] (pl. **zoos**) a park where many kinds of wild animals are kept so that people can look at them and where they are bred, studied and protected ▶ **zoo**

zookeeper /ˈzuːkiːpə(r)/ noun [C] a person who works in a **zoo**, taking care of the animals ▶ **dozorca** (*w zoo*)

zoology /zəʊˈɒlədʒi; Brit. also zuˈɒl-/ noun [U] the scientific study of animals ▶ **zoologia**
■ **zoological** /ˌzəʊəˈlɒdʒɪkl; Brit. also ˌzuːəˈl-/ adj.: *zoological illustrations* ▶ **zoologiczny** | **zoologist** /-dʒɪst/ noun [C] ▶ **zoolog**

zoom /zuːm/ verb [I] to move or go somewhere very fast: *Traffic zoomed past us.* ▶ **mknąć z hałasem**
PHR V **zoom in/out** (used about a camera) to show the object that is being photographed from closer/further away, with the use of a **zoom lens**: *The camera zoomed in on the actor's face.* ▶ **robić najazd/odjazd kamerą**

ˌzoom ˈlens noun [C] a device on a camera that makes an object being photographed appear gradually bigger or smaller so that it seems to be getting closer or further away ▶ **obiektyw ze zmienną ogniskową**

zucchini (especially US) = COURGETTE

Study pages

Prepositions of place
Przyimki określające miejsce

The lamp is **above** the table.

The meat is **on** the table.

The cat is **under** the table.

The lorry is **in front of** the car.

The car is **behind** the lorry.

The bird is **in/inside** the cage.

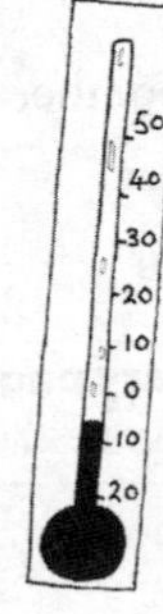

The temperature is **below** zero.

Kim is **next to/beside** Sam.

Sam is **between** Tom and Kim.

Tom is **opposite** Kim.

The house is **among** the trees.

The girl is leaning **against** the wall.

Prepositions of movement
Przyimki określające ruch

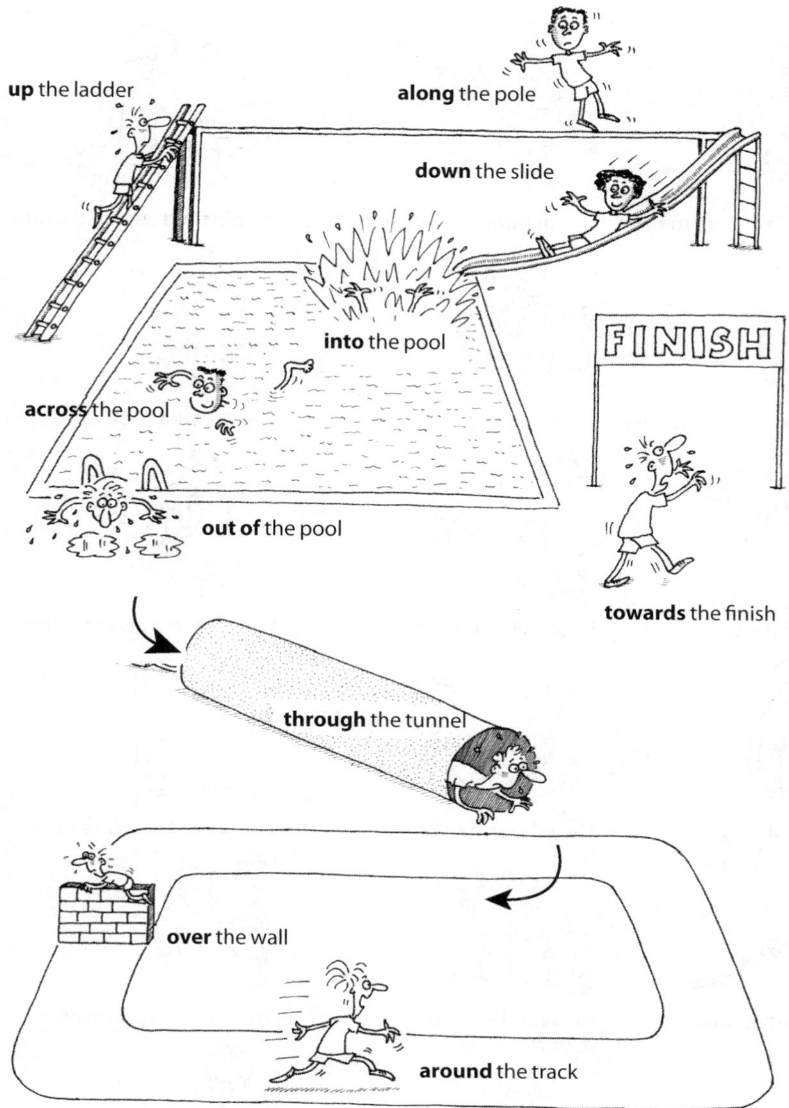

Action verbs
Czasowniki ruchu

He **punched** him in the stomach.

She **slapped** her across the face.

He **pinched** him on the arm.

He **tapped** him on the shoulder.

She **nudged** her.

He **elbowed past**.

He **nodded** his head.

He **shook his head**.

He **shrugged** his shoulders.

They **held hands**.

They **shook hands**.

She **waved** goodbye to him.

She **poked** the fire with a stick.

He **poked** the stick down the hole.

They **walked** arm in arm.

He **folded** his arms.

He **sat cross-legged**.

She **crossed her legs**.

Words that go together
Związki wyrazowe

Niektóre słowa bardzo często występują w parach czy nawet większych grupach z innymi wyrazami. Takie pary czy grupy nazywamy związkami wyrazowymi (**collocations**). Popatrz na hasło rzeczownika **work**, aby zobaczyć, jak w tym słowniku są podane najczęściej spotykane związki wyrazowe. Im częściej będziesz używać takich związków wyrazowych, tym bardziej naturalnie będą brzmieć twoje wypowiedzi. Zbieraj pary i grupy wyrazów, które cię szczególnie zainteresują lub które uznasz za przydatne.

work[2] /wɜːk/ noun **1** [U] the job that you do, especially in order to earn money; the place where you do your job: *It is very difficult to* ***find work*** *in this city.* ◇ *He's been* ***out of work*** (nie miał pracy) *for six months.* ◇ *When do you* ***start work****?* ◇ *I'll ask if I can* ***leave work*** *early today.* ◇ *I* ***go to work*** *at 8 o'clock.* ◇ *The people* ***at work*** (w pracy) *gave me some flowers for my birthday.* ◇ *Police work is not as exciting as it looks on TV.* ◇ *a work permit* pozwolenie na pracę ▶ **praca** ➲ note at **job**, **routine** ➲ look at **employment** **2** [U] something that needs physical or mental effort that you do in order to achieve sth: *Her success is due to sheer* ***hard work.*** ◇ *I've got a lot of work to do today.* ◇ *We hope to* ***start work on*** *the project next week.* ◇ *Students do work experience* (odbywają praktykę zawodową) *in local firms.* ▶ **praca**

Wyrażenia z czasownikami **do, make** i **give**

Jedyną skuteczną metodą opanowania tych wyrażeń jest zbieranie ich i ciągłe ich powtarzanie, ale podajemy tu kilka wskazówek, które mogą być pomocne w wyborze prawidłowego czasownika.

Do używa się często w wypadku czynności czy obowiązków, które – choć wymagają wykonania – to jednak nie mają charakteru czynności twórczych, a także w wyrażeniach zawierających słowa **thing**, **nothing**, **anything**, itd.:

do the cleaning
do an exam
do a job
do something wrong
do things your own way
nothing to do

Make używa się często, kiedy wykonujesz czynność lub tworzysz coś, wykorzystując swoje umiejętności, zdolności wypowiedzi:

make dinner
make a movie
make an excuse
make a decision
make a judgement
make a guess
make a comment
make a suggestion
make a promise
make a model
(ale *do a painting*)

Give używa się w wielu wyrażeniach związanych z użyciem słów, a także w wyrażeniach opisujących czynności fizyczne:

give (sb) advice
give (sb) your word
give a reason
give a lecture
give evidence
give sth a kick/a twist/a push
give sb a slap/a kiss/a hug

Wydziel część zeszytu słowniczka na swój własny zbiór związków wyrazowych. Najlepiej utwórz dwie listy: wyrażeń, które według ciebie mają wydźwięk pozytywny, oraz takich, które twoim zdaniem mają znaczenie negatywne. Decydując, na którą listę wpisać dany związek wyrazowy, lepiej go zapamiętasz.

Na którą listę wpisałbyś związek **take a risk**?

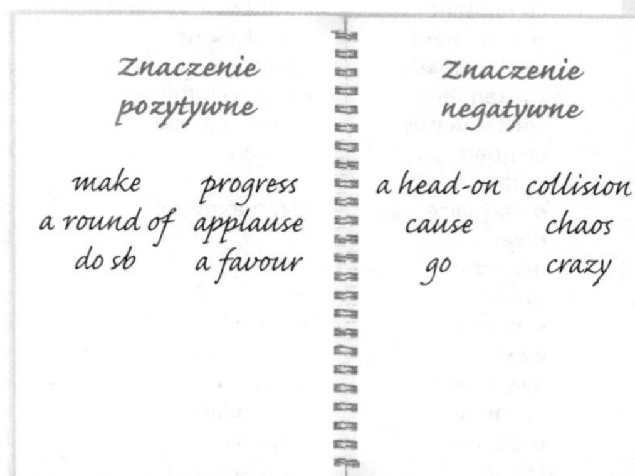

Znaczenie pozytywne
make progress
a round of applause
do sb a favour
Znaczenie negatywne
a head-on collision
cause chaos
go crazy

False friends Fałszywi przyjaciele

Mimo znacznych różnic między językiem polskim i angielskim, w obu językach występują słowa, które wyglądają (a czasem również brzmią) bardzo podobnie, jednak różnią się całkowicie (lub przynajmniej częściowo) znaczeniem. Takie pary wyrazów określa się nazwą **false friends** (fałszywi przyjaciele). Oto kilka przykładów.

Angielskie słowo **adaptor** wygląda jak polskie słowo „adapter", lecz ma zupełnie inne znaczenie. Prawidłowy polski odpowiednik angielskiego **adaptor** to „rozgałęziacz". Podobnie słowa **conductor** i „konduktor": obydwa mogą oznaczać osobę sprzedającą bilety, np. w autobusie, jednak słowo angielskie znaczy także „dyrygent". Angielskie słowo **marmalade** kojarzy się Polakom ze słowem „marmolada", jednak oznacza dżem z owoców cytrusowych.

Zamieszczone poniżej tabele zawierają pary **false friends** z podaniem różnic znaczeniowych.

A Słowo	Nie oznacza	Oznacza
accord	akord	porozumienie
actual	aktualny	rzeczywisty, faktyczny
actually	aktualnie	faktycznie, prawdę powiedziawszy
adaptor	adapter	rozgałęziacz
agenda	agenda	porządek dzienny
audition	audycja	przesłuchanie do roli
baton	baton	batuta; pałeczka sztafetowa
boot	but	but z cholewą, botek
brunette	brunetka	szatynka
caravan	karawan	przyczepa kempingowa
carnation	karnacja	goździk
census	cenzus	spis ludności
central	centrala	centralny, środkowy
chalet	szalet	domek letniskowy/kempingowy
chef	szef	szef kuchni
civil	cywil	społeczny, obywatelski; cywilny; poprawny, uprzejmy
closet	klozet	szafa w ścianie
combatant	kombatant	żołnierz, bojownik
complement	komplement	uzupełnienie; komplet; dopełnienie
confectionery	konfekcja	słodycze, wyroby cukiernicze
consequent	konsekwentny	wynikający, następujący
consequently	konsekwentnie	w konsekwencji, wskutek (czegoś)
cymbals	cymbały	czynele
data	data	dane
demoralize	demoralizować	działać demobilizująco, zniechęcać do dalszego działania
divan	dywan	tapczan
diversion	dywersja	odwrócenie kierunku; objazd
dress	dres	suknia, sukienka
economy	ekonomia	gospodarka; oszczędność
eventual	ewentualny	końcowy, ostateczny
eventually	ewentualnie	w końcu, ostatecznie
example	egzemplarz	przykład; wzór
expertise	ekspertyza	biegłość, znawstwo
fabric	fabryka	tkanina, materiał
genial	genialny	dobroduszny, towarzyski
gymnasium	gimnazjum	sala gimnastyczna, siłownia
lecture	lektura	wykład
lunatic	lunatyk	wariat/ka
manifestation	manifestacja	dowód (czegoś/na coś), ujawnienie (się)
mark	marka	plama, znak, ślad
marmalade	marmolada	dżem pomarańczowy/cytrynowy
novel	nowela	powieść
obscure	obskurny	niejasny; nieznany
operator	operator	telefonist-a/ka

ordinary	ordynarny	zwykły, normalny
pamphlet	pamflet	broszura, prospekt
pantomime	pantomima	przedstawienie dla dzieci urządzane po Bożym Narodzeniu
paragraph	paragraf	akapit, nowy wiersz (*w tekście*)
pasta	pasta	makaron
pension	pensja	emerytura, renta
preservative	prezerwatywa	środek konserwujący
prospect	prospekt	szansa; perspektywa (na coś); widoki
receipt	recepta	pokwitowanie, paragon
rent	renta	czynsz, komorne
revenge	rewanż	zemsta
rumour	rumor	pogłoska, plotka
smoking	smoking	palenie (*tytoniu*)
speaker	spiker (*w radiu/telewizji*)	mów-ca/czyni; głośnik
sympathetic	sympatyczny	współczujący
tobacco	tabaka	tytoń
wagon	wagon	fura, wóz

B

Angielskie słowo	Nie zawsze oznacza	Może też oznaczać
advocate	adwokat	zwolenni-k/czka
affair	afera	romans
argument	argument	sprzeczka, spór
chips	czipsy	frytki (*Br. ang.*)
conductor	konduktor	dyrygent; przewodnik
hysterical	histeryczny	bardzo śmieszny
interpret	interpretować	tłumaczyć na żywo
invalid	inwalida	nieważny; nieprawidłowy
medicine	medycyna	lekarstwo
pathetic	patetyczny	żałosny; żenująco kiepski
propose	proponować	oświadczać się
romance	romans	romantyczność

C

Polskie słowo	Nie zawsze oznacza	Może też znaczyć
artysta	**artist**	**actor, performer**
gabinet	**cabinet**	**study; surgery**
kadencja	**cadence**	**term of office**
kalendarz(yk)	**calendar**	**diary**
klient	**client**	**customer**
kolega	**colleague**	**friend**
komunikacja	**communication**	**public transport**
dekada	**decade**	**ten days**
delegacja	**delegation**	**business trip**
dyplom	**diploma**	**degree**
emisja	**emission**	**broadcast**
fatalny	**fatal**	**abysmal**
golf	**golf**	**polo neck**
hazard	**hazard**	**gambling**
historia	**history**	**story**
humor	**humour**	**mood**
mandat	**mandate**	**fine**
okazja	**occasion**	**bargain**
perspektywa	**perspective**	**prospect**
problem	**problem**	**concern, reponsibility**
proces	**process**	**trial, lawsuit**
prognoza	**prognosis**	**(weather) forecast**
program	**programme**	**(TV) channel**
rasa	**race**	**breed**
scena	**scene**	**stage**
technika	**technique**	**technology**
trywialny	**trivial**	**common, vulgar**

American English
Amerykańska odmiana języka angielskiego

I just saw a man fall on the sidewalk in front of my neighbor's house!

Czy to mówi Anglik czy Amerykanin? Odmianę angielskiego można rozpoznać po słownictwie, pisowni, gramatyce oraz wymowie. Dlatego łatwo ustalić, że autorem powyższego zdania jest Amerykanin!

Słownictwo

Słownik podaje wiele przykładów słów używanych wyłącznie w amerykańskiej angielszczyźnie. Podane są również słowa, które w obu odmianach mają różne znaczenie, np.:

US **elevator** = Brit. **lift**
US **gas** = Brit. **petrol**

Sprawdź w słowniku znaczenie następujących wyrazów: **expressway**, **cab**, **rest room**, **purse**, **flat**[2], **pants**.

Pisownia

Słownik podaje różnice w pisowni między angielszczyzną brytyjską i amerykańską. Oto przykłady najczęściej spotykanych wyrazów o odmiennej pisowni:

	Brit.	US
a	travel**l**ed	travel**e**d
	cancel**l**ing	cancel**i**ng
b	met**re**	met**er**
	cent**re**	cent**er**
c	col**ou**r	col**o**r
	hon**ou**r	hon**o**r
d	defen**c**e	defen**s**e
	licen**c**e	licen**s**e
e	dialo**gue**	dialo**g**
	catalo**gue**	catalo**g**

Gramatyka

1 Tam, gdzie w brytyjskiej angielszczyźnie używa się czasu **Present Perfect**, w odmianie amerykańskiej najczęściej stosuje się czas **Simple Past:**

Brit. *I**'ve** just **seen** her.*
US *I just **saw** her.*
Brit. ***Have** you **heard** the news?*
US ***Did** you **hear** the news?*

2 Amerykanie często używają **have** w zdaniach, w których Brytyjczycy stosują wyrażenie **have got**:

Brit. *I **haven't got** much time.*
US *I **don't have** much time.*
Brit. ***Have** you **got** a camera?*
US ***Do** you **have** a camera?*

3 W obu odmianach występują drobne różnice w użyciu przyimków i przysłówków:

Brit. *stay **at** home*
US *stay home*
Brit. *Monday **to** Friday*
US *Monday **through** Friday*

Wymowa

W wypadku występującej różnicy w wymowie jakiegoś słowa, wymowa amerykańska podana jest w słowniku po wymowie brytyjskiej:
tomato /tə'mɑːtəʊ; US tə'meɪtəʊ/

A oto najważniejsze różnice dotyczące wymowy:

1 Samogłoski akcentowane są zwykle dłuższe w amerykańskim niż w brytyjskim angielskim, np. dźwięk /æ/ w słowie **packet**. Litera *o*, np. w słowie **shop,** jest w amerykańskim angielskim wymawiana jako /ɑː/: lub /ɔː/:
shop /Brit. ʃɒp; US ʃɑːp/
off /Brit. ɒf; US ɔːf, ɑːf/

Niektóre wyrazy wymawia się z dyftongiem w brytyjskim angielskim, a z pojedynczą samogłoską w amerykańskim angielskim:
near /Brit. nɪə(r); US nɪr/
hair /Brit. heə(r); US her/
pure /Brit. pjʊə(r); US pjʊr/

Tego typu regularne różnice wymowy nie są pokazane w słowniku.

2 Litera *r* w brytyjskim angielskim wymawiana jest tylko przed samogłoską (np. w słowie **red** czy **bedroom**), natomiast w pozostałych wypadkach jest niema (np. w słowie **learn**). W standardowym amerykańskim *r* jest zawsze wymawiane.

3 Wymowa *t* i *d* w pozycji między dwiema samogłoskami w amerykańskiem angielskim jest prawie identyczna i brzmi jak /d/. Tak więc słowa **writer** i **rider** brzmią prawie identycznie.

Clothes Ubranie

cap
czapka

V-neck
wycięcie w szpic

vest (US **undershirt**)
podkoszulek

sweater (Brit. also **jumper**)
sweter

trainers (US **sneakers**)
buty sportowe

rucksack (also **backpack**)
plecak

coat
płaszcz

glove
rękawiczka

jeans
dżinsy

walking boots
buty turystyczne

zip (US **zipper**)
zamek błyskawiczny

button
guzik

top
bluzka

denim jacket
kurtka dżinsowa

shoulder bag
torba na ramię

skirt
spódnica

tights (US **pantyhose**)
rajstopy

collar
kołnierz/yk

tie
krawat

shirt
koszula

sleeve
rękaw

cuff
mankiet

trousers (US **pants**)
spodnie

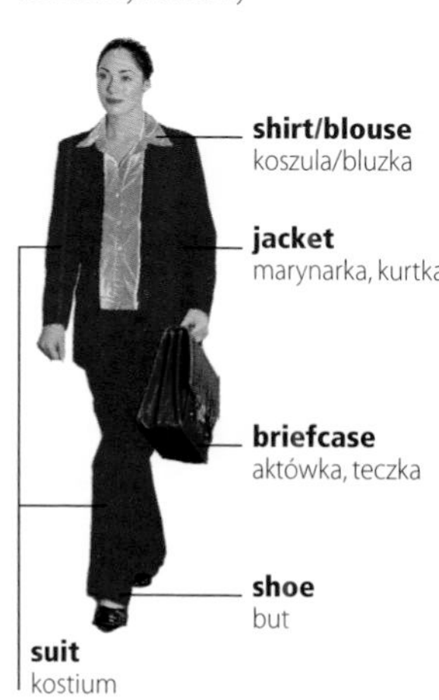

shirt/blouse
koszula/bluzka

jacket
marynarka, kurtka

briefcase
aktówka, teczka

shoe
but

suit
kostium

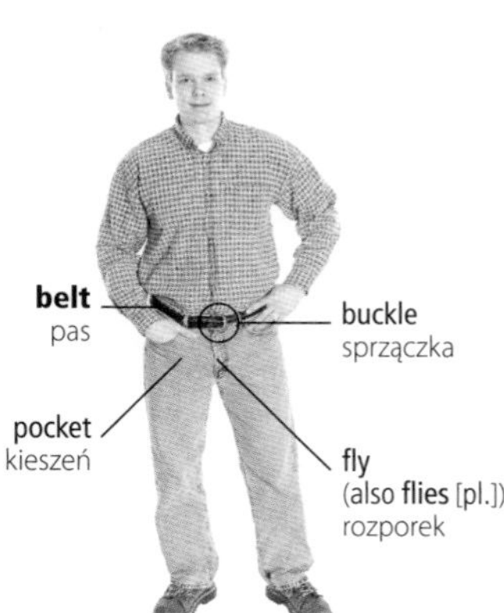

belt
pas

buckle
sprzączka

pocket
kieszeń

fly
(also flies [pl.])
rozporek

pyjamas (US **pajamas**)
piżama

SPRAWDŹ TAKŻE

bag
button
cardigan
dress
hat
lace
overall
raincoat
sari
scarf
shoe
sock
stocking
sweater
swimsuit
underwear

Patterns
Wzory

zigzag
zygzakowaty

patterned
wzorzysty

plain
gładki

floral
kwiatowy

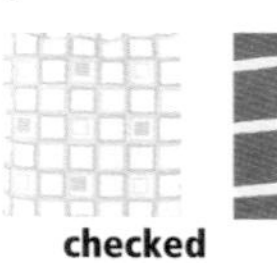

checked (also **check**)
w krat(k)ę, kraciasty

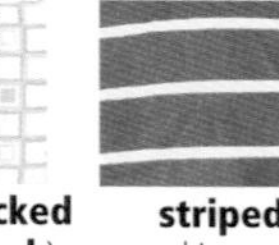

striped
w paski

Buildings Budynki

church kościół

monument pomnik, monument

ruin ruiny

pub bar, pub

tower wieża

office block (US **office building**) biurowiec

SPRAWDŹ TAKŻE

brick
cathedral
concrete
library
mosque
police station
power station
skyscraper
steel
stone
synagogue
temple
tower block
town hall

dam tama

stadium stadion

lighthouse latarnia morska

bridge most

warehouse magazyn

Homes in Britain
Domy w Wielkiej Brytanii

SPRAWDŹ TAKŻE

bedsit	maisonette
chalet	palace
estate	property
flat	studio
hut	yard

terraced house dom szeregowy

block of flats (especially US **apartment block**) blok mieszkalny

detached house dom wolno stojący

bay window okno wykuszowe

semi-detached house dom typu bliźniak

bungalow dom parterowy

lawn trawnik

thatch strzecha

thatched cottage dom kryty strzechą

castle zamek

moat fosa

stately home budynek o historycznym znaczeniu

Jobs Zawody

fisherman rybak

SPRAWDŹ TAKŻE

apprentice	**doctor**	**postman**
assistant	**dustman**	**secretary**
baker	**manager**	**shop**
designer	**plumber**	**technician**

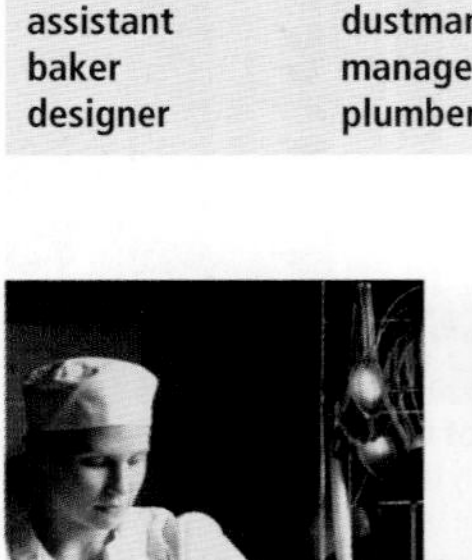

cook kucha-rz/rka

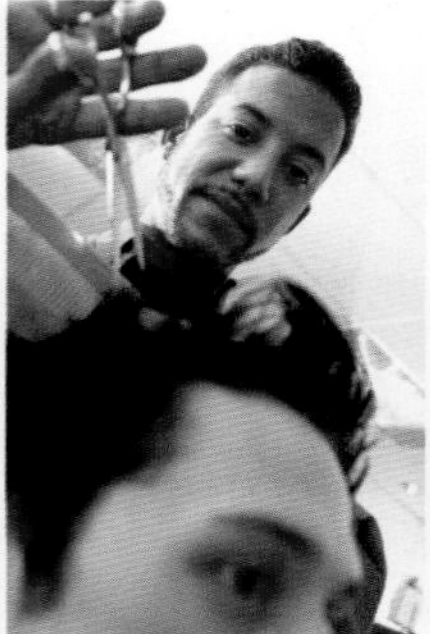

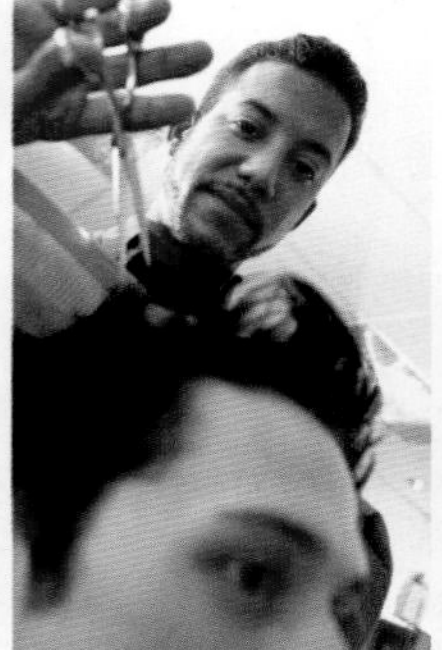

hairdresser fryzjer/ka

farmer rolni-k/czka

carpenter stolarz

teacher nauczyciel/ka

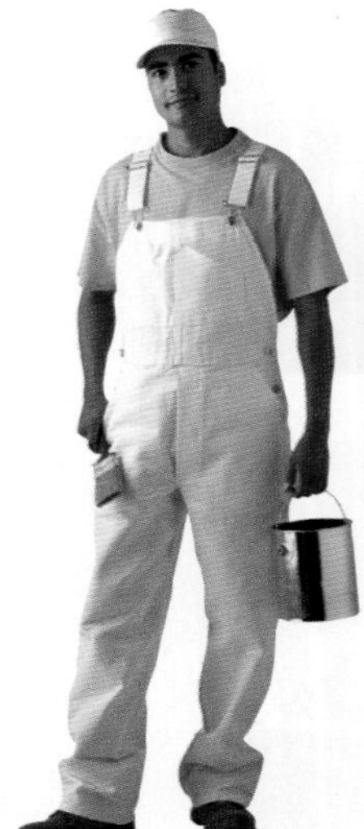

painter
malarz pokojowy

pilot
pilot/ka

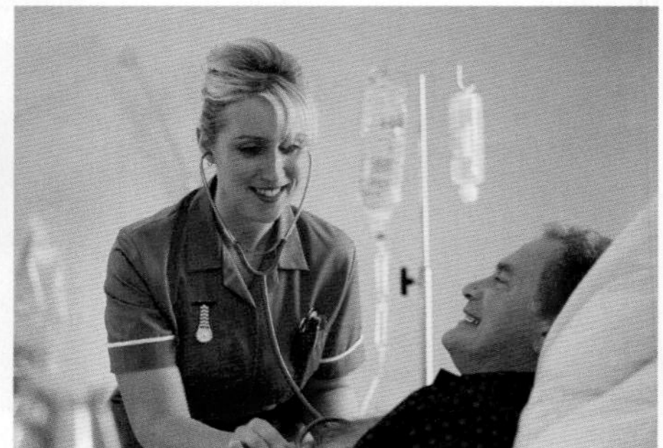

nurse pielęgnia-rz/rka

Shops Sklepy

grocer's (US **grocery store**)
sklep spożywczy

baker's (especially US **bakery**)
sklep z pieczywem, piekarnia

fish and chip shop
sklep sprzedający smażone ryby z frytkami

optician's optyk

market targ

butcher sklep mięsny

flower stall
stragan z kwiatami

SPRAWDŹ TAKŻE

bill	**chemist's**	**newsagent**
bookshop	**counter**	**receipt**
carrier bag	**customer**	**takeaway**
change	**florist**	**till**
checkout	**launderette**	**trolley**

dry-cleaner's
pralnia chemiczna

clothes shop
(US **clothes store**)
sklep odzieżowy

shopping centre (US **shopping center**)
centrum handlowe

garden centre
centrum ogrodnicze

Transport
Środki transportu

Aircraft Samoloty

aeroplane (US **airplane**) samolot

helicopter helikopter

glider szybowiec

Boats Statki i łodzie

oil tanker tankowiec

liner statek dalekomorski

hovercraft poduszkowiec

lifeboat łódź ratownicza

ferry prom

submarine łódź podwodna

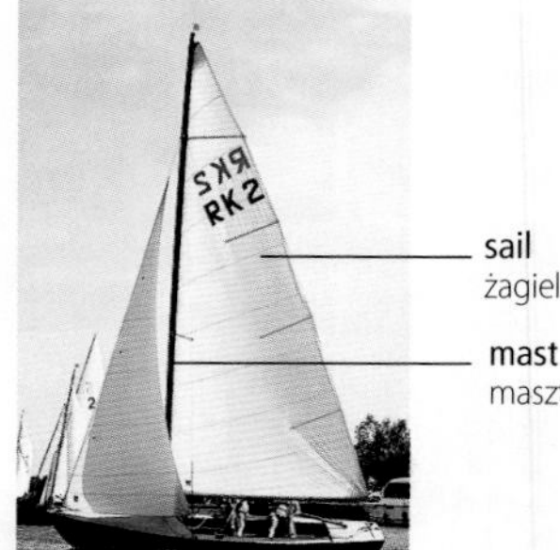

yacht jacht

SPRAWDŹ TAKŻE

barge	**cruiser**	**fender**	**plane**
bicycle	**dinghy**	**moped**	**raft**
bike	**driving**	**motor**	**sail**
boat	**engine**	**parking**	**travel**

Rail transport
Transport szynowy

tram (US **streetcar, trolley**)
tramwaj

train pociąg

underground (US **subway**)
metro

monorail kolejka jednoszynowa

Road vehicles
Pojazdy drogowe

exhaust (US **tailpipe**) spaliny

sports car
samochód sportowy

estate car (US **station wagon**)
kombi

boot (US **trunk**) bagażnik

saloon (US **sedan**)
samochód typu sedan

people carrier (also **minivan**)
samochód rodzinny typu minivan

taxi (also **taxicab,** especially US **cab**)
taksówka

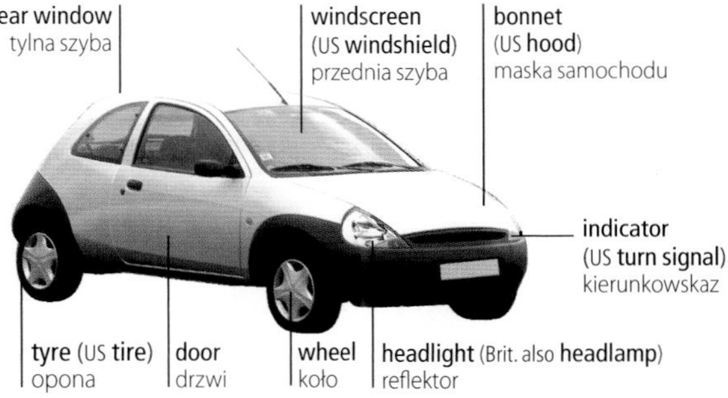

hatchback samochód typu hatchback

motorbike (formal **motorcycle**)
motocykl

van
furgon, furgonetka

bus
autobus

scooter skuter

coach (US **bus**)
autokar

cab
szoferka

lorry (especially US **truck**)
ciężarówka

Sports Sport

umpire
sędzia sportowy

bowler
gracz serwujący piłkę

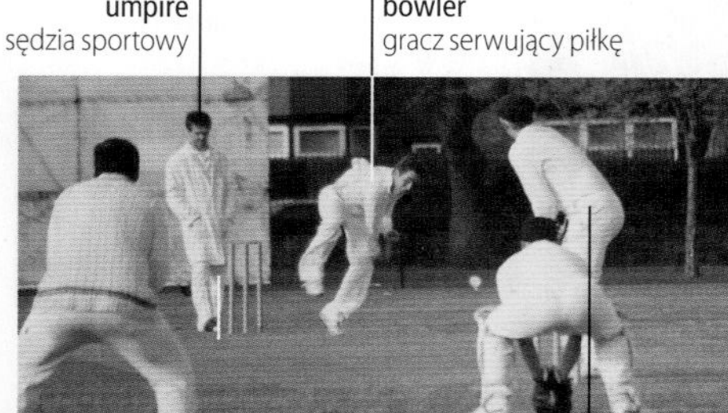

cricket
krykiet

batsman
gracz , który uderza piłkę

ne
sia

tennis tenis

court
kort

racket
rakieta

basketball
koszykówka

basket
kosz

rugby rugby

baseball baseball

ice hockey (US **hockey**)
hokej na lodzie

hockey (US **field hockey**)
hokej na trawie

boxing boks

SPRAWDŹ TAKŻE

amateur	**netball**	**sport**
badminton	**parachute**	**squash**
exercise	**professional**	**swim**
football	**score**	**table tennis**
hobby	**shot-put**	**trampoline**
martial arts	**skate**	**volleyball**

jockey
dżokej

horse racing (also **racing**)
wyścigi konne

jump
przeszkoda

rider
jeździec

showjumping
konkurs jazdy konnej z przeszkodami

skiing narciarstwo

skier narcia-rz/rka

skating jazda szybka na łyżwach

gymnastics gimnastyka

gymnast gimnasty-k/czka

foil floret

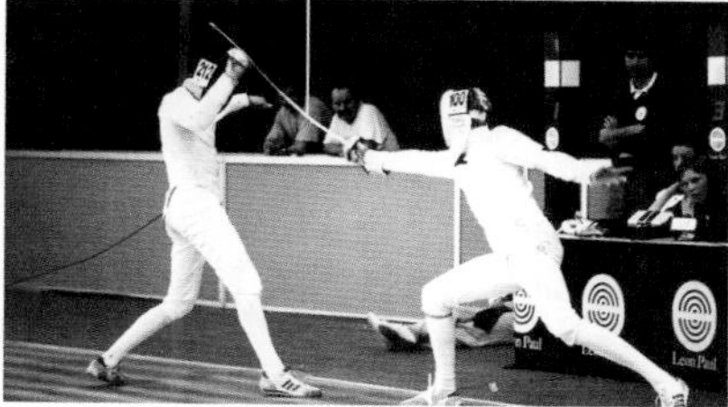

fencing szermierka

mask maska

athletics (US **track and field**) lekkoatletyka

weightlifting podnoszenie ciężarów

golfer gracz w golfa

golf golf

golf club kij golfowy

judo dżudo

Extreme sports Sporty ekstremalne

waterskiing jazda na nartach wodnych

bungee jumping skoki na bungee

surfer osoba pływająca na desce

surfing surfing

surfboard deska surfingowa

abseiling (US **rappelling**) spuszczanie się po linie

white-water rafting spływ górski

windsurfing windsurfing

Animals Zwierzęta

Mammals Ssaki

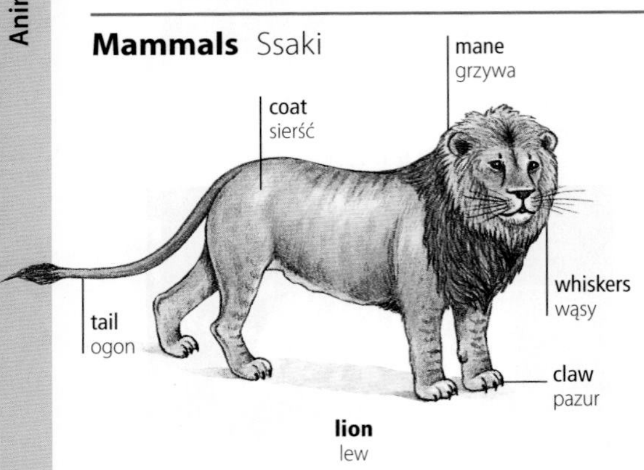

lion
lew

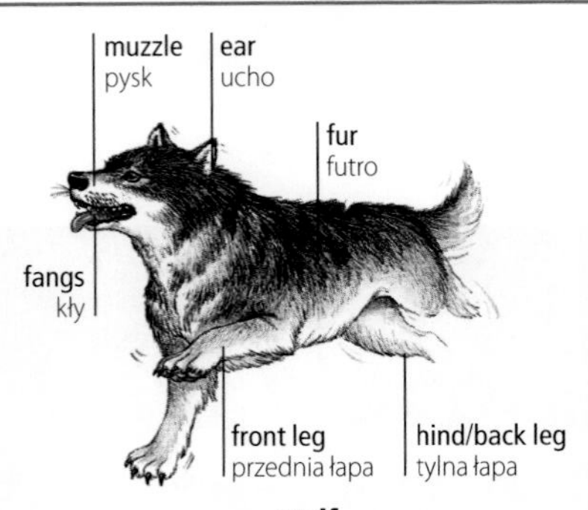

wolf
wilk

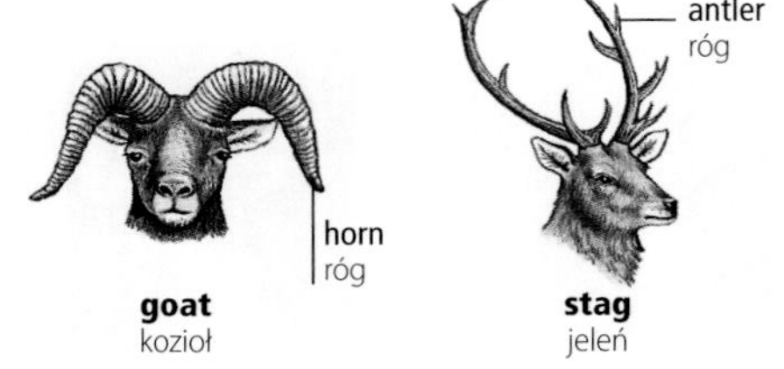

goat
kozioł

stag
jeleń

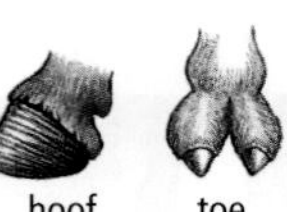

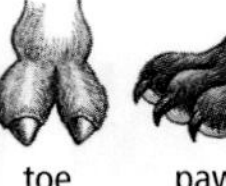

hoof
kopyto

toe
palec

paw
łapa

elephant
słoń

koala
miś koala

kangaroo
kangur

bat
nietoperz

SPRAWDŹ TAKŻE

alligator	**duck**	**monkey**
bee	**fawn**	**pet**
calf	**foal**	**pig**
chicken	**fox**	**rabbit**
cow	**hen**	**sheep**
deer	**horse**	**snail**

whale
wieloryb

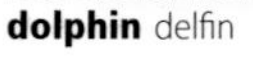

dolphin delfin

seal foka

Amphibians Płazy

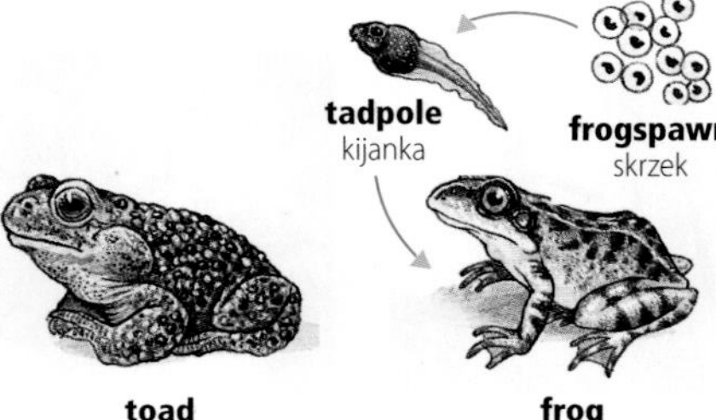

tadpole
kijanka

frogspawn
skrzek

toad
ropucha

frog
żaba

Birds Ptaki

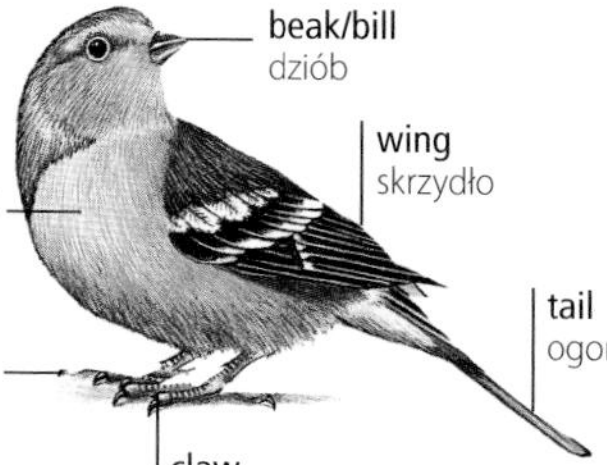

beak/bill
dziób
wing
skrzydło
breast
pierś
tail
ogon
toe
palec
claw
pazur

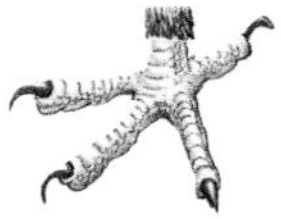

talon
szpon

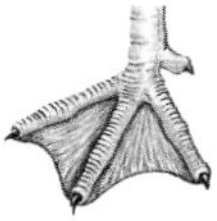

webbed foot
palce złączone błoną

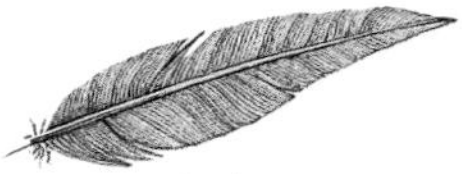

feather
pióro

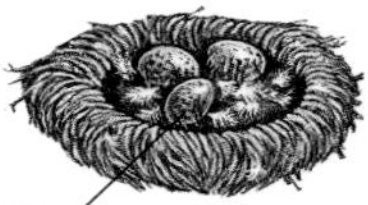

egg
jajko

nest
gniazdo

Reptiles Gady

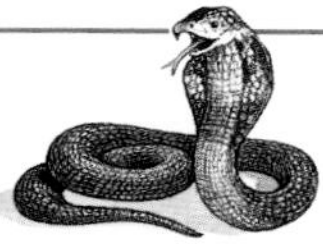

snake
wąż

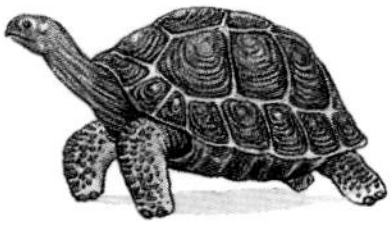

tortoise (US also **turtle**)
żółw lądowy

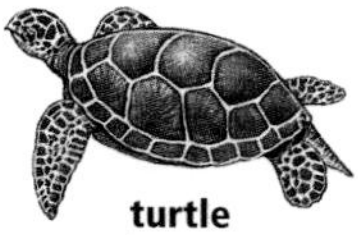

turtle
żółw morski

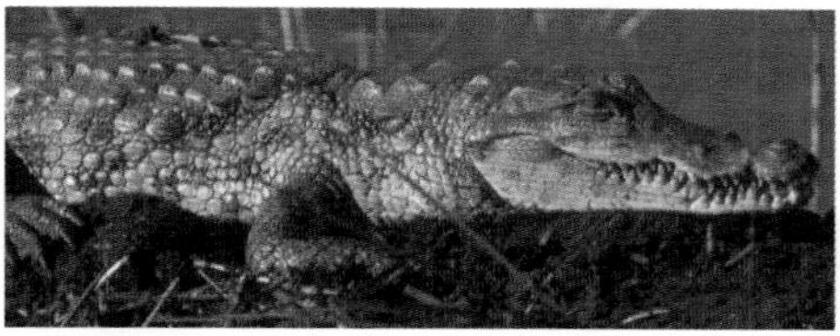

crocodile krokodyl

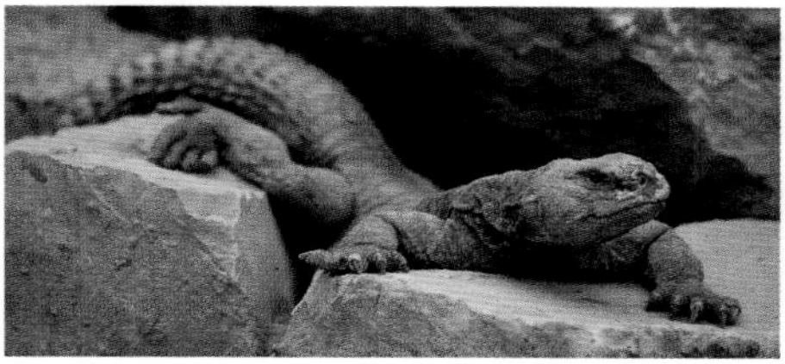

lizard jaszczurka

Fish Ryby

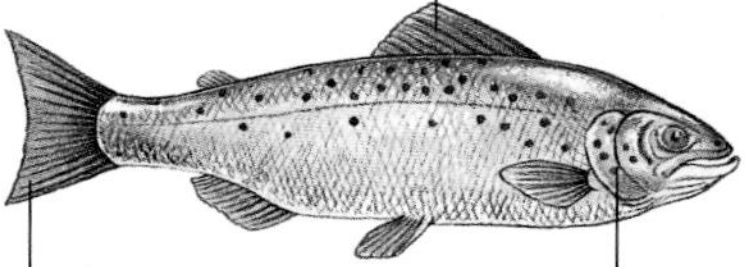

fin
płetwa
tail
płetwa
gills
skrzele

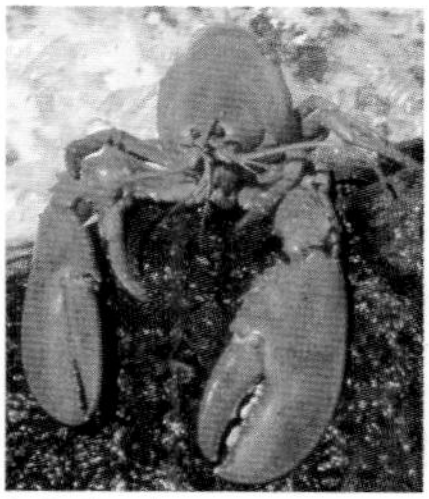

lobster homar

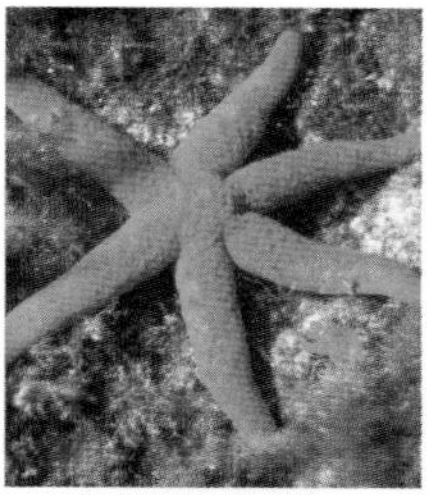

starfish rozgwiazda

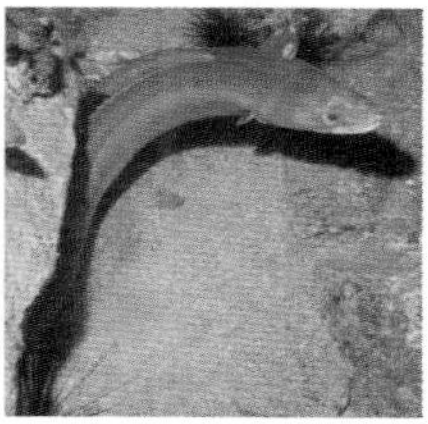

eel węgorz

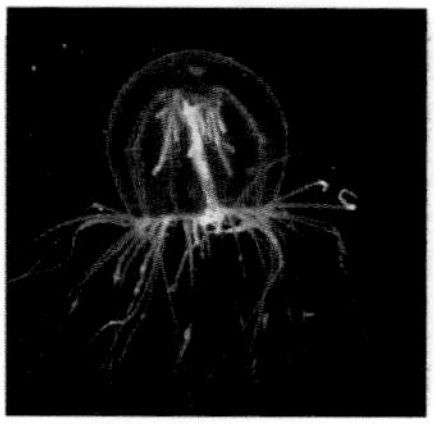

jellyfish meduza

Shellfish Skorupiaki

antenna
czułek

prawn (US **shrimp**)
krewetka

claw/pincer
szczypce
shell
skorupa

crab
krab

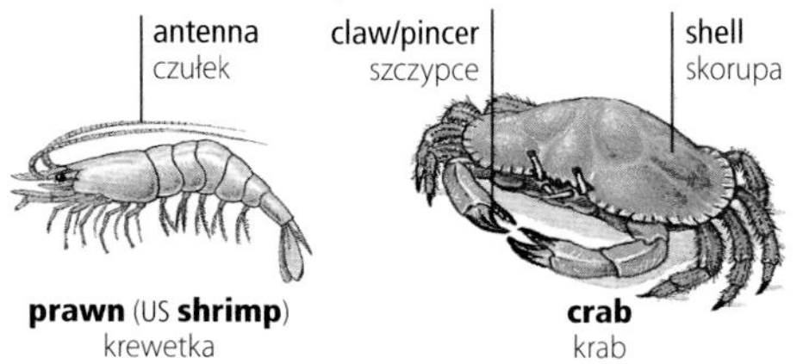

Fruit Owoce

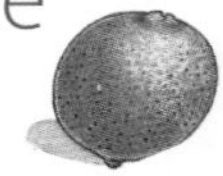

lime limona, limeta

lemon cytryna

orange pomarańcza

grapefruit grejpfrut
peel skórka
segment cząstka

apple jabłko
core środek owocu
pip pestka

pear gruszka

fig figa

plum śliwka

peach brzoskwinia
stone pestka

papaya (also **pawpaw**) papaja
skin skórka
flesh miąższ

kiwi (also **kiwi fruit**) kiwi

apricot morela

mango mango

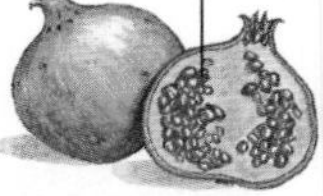

pomegranate granat
seeds ziarna

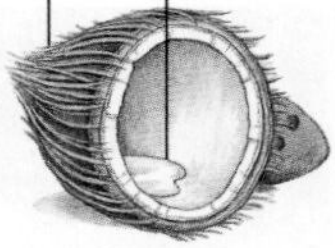

coconut kokos
shell łupina
milk mleczko

melon melon

watermelon arbuz

banana banan

avocado awokado

cherries czereśnie, wiśnie
stalk łodyżka

strawberries truskawki

grapes winogrona

pineapple ananas

gooseberries agrest

raspberries maliny

blackberries jeżyny

Herbs and spices Zioła i przyprawy

thyme tymianek

parsley pietruszka

basil bazylia

mint mięta

ginger imbir

cloves goździki

cinnamon cynamon

Vegetables Warzywa

asparagus
szparagi

brussels sprouts
brukselka

parsnip
pasternak

carrot
marchew

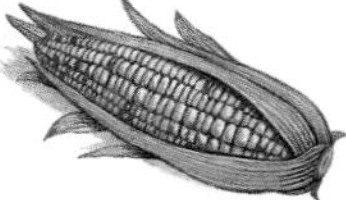

sweetcorn (US **corn**)
kukurydza

potato
ziemniak

broccoli
brokuły

artichoke
karczoch

aubergine (US **eggplant**)
bakłażan

cabbage
kapusta

cauliflower
kalafior

marrow
kabaczek

celery
seler (naciowy)

courgette (US **zucchini**)
cukinia

leek
por

pumpkin
dynia

mushrooms
pieczarki

peas
groszek

spring onions
(US **green onions, scallions**)
dymka

radishes
rzodkiewki

lettuce
sałata

beans
fasolka

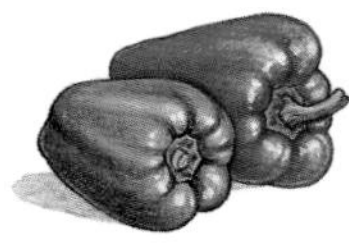

peppers (US **bell peppers**)
papryka

onion
cebula

garlic
czosnek

cucumber
ogórek

tomato
pomidor

chilli (US **chili**)
papryka chilli

Food and drink Potrawy i napoje

hamburger (also **burger**)
hamburger

salad
sałatka

filling
nadzienie

sandwich
kanapka

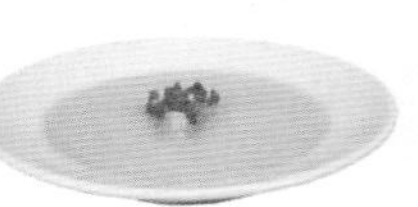
soup
zupa

hot dog
hot dog

pizza
pizza

kebab
szaszłyk

pasta
makaron

fish and chips
smażona ryba z frytkami

roast beef
pieczeń wołowa

sauce
sos

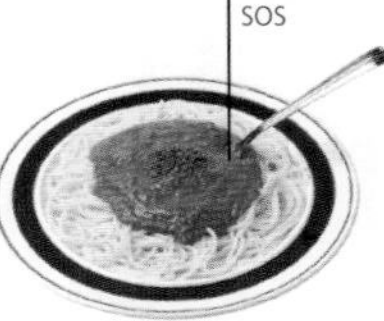

spaghetti
spaghetti

quiche
słona tarta z serem itp.

baked beans
fasolka w sosie pomidorowym

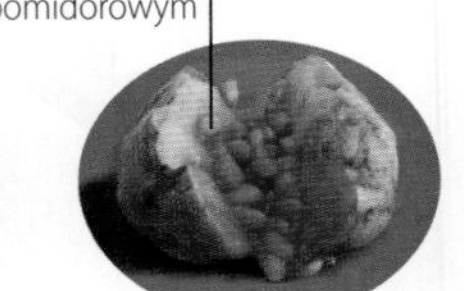
jacket potato/baked potato
ziemniak w mundurku

apple pie
szarlotka

ice cream
lody

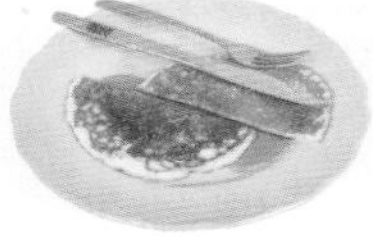
pancake
naleśnik

cheese
ser

eggs
jajka

jam
dżem

honey
miód

cream
śmietan-a/ka

waffle
gofr

cereal
płatki zbożowe

teapot
imbryczek

cup of tea
herbata

black coffee
czarna kawa

milkshake
koktajl mleczny

SPRAWDŹ TAKŻE

cake	**pudding**
fizzy	**sausage**
meat	**shellfish**
nuts	**still**
porridge	**takeaway**

Flowers Kwiaty

lily lilia

water lily nenufar

sunflower słonecznik

daffodil żonkil

snowdrop śnieżyczka

geranium geranium, pelargonia

carnation goździk

primrose pierwiosnek

rose róża

SPRAWDŹ TAKŻE

bud	orchid
bulb	petal
buttercup	seed
crocus	stalk
daisy	sweet pea
dandelion	violet

poppy mak

tulip tulipan

pansy bratek

Weather and seasons
Pogoda i pory roku

autumn jesień

winter zima

summer lato

spring wiosna

rainbow tęcza

snow śnieg

sunset zachód słońca

clouds chmury

lightning piorun

it's raining pada deszcz

it's windy wiatr wieje

SPRAWDŹ TAKŻE

boiling	**mist**
chilly	**sleet**
fog	**storm**
freezing	**sunny**
hail	**thunder**

Computers Komputery

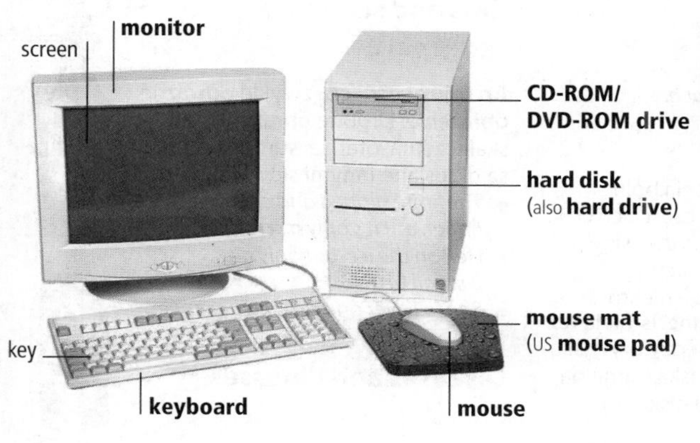

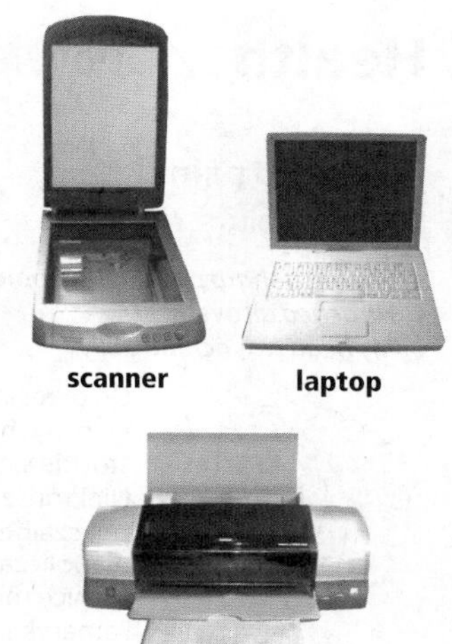

installing software
instalacja oprogramowania

- ***boot up/start up** the computer*
- ***insert** the **CD-ROM***
- ***follow** the set-up **instructions***
- ***reboot/restart** the computer*

creating a document
tworzenie dokumentu

- ***select** the new document **option** from the **pull-down menus** or **click on** the new document **icon***
- ***type**, **edit** and **format** the document*
- ***print out** the document*
- ***save** and **close** the document*

cutting and pasting text
wycinanie i wklejanie tekstu

- ***scroll down** the **text** to find the **block** of text you want to **move***
- ***position** the **cursor** at the beginning of the block of text*
- ***hold down** the **left mouse button** and **drag** the mouse to **highlight** the block of text*
- ***release** the left mouse button*
- ***click on** the **right mouse button** and **select** the cut text **option** from the **pop-up menu***
- ***move** the **cursor** to where you want the text to go*
- ***select** the paste text **option***

looking up something on the Internet
wyszukiwanie informacji w internecie

- ***connect to** the **Internet***
- ***type in** the **website address** or **click (on)/ follow** a **link***
- ***access** the **website***
- ***browse/search** the **website** to find the information*
- *if necessary, **download** the information*

running several applications at the same time
uruchamianie kilku programów równocześnie

- ***double-click on** the different program **icons***
- ***move** and **mimimize** the program **windows** as required*
- ***click on** a program's **window** to use that program*
- *when finished, **close** the **windows***

backing up a file onto a USB stick
tworzenie zapasowej kopii pliku na pamięci przenośnej

- ***insert** a **USB stick** and **format** it, if necessary*
- ***compress/zip** the **file** if it is too large*
- ***copy/save** the **file** onto the **USB stick***
- *if necessary, **rename** the backed-up **file***
- ***remove/take out** the **USB stick***

Health Zdrowie

Aches and pains
Rodzaje bólu

- *She felt a sharp pain in her stomach.*
- *He ached all over.*
- *My head was aching dully.*

Do określenia bólu w różnych częściach ciała stosuje się różne słowa. Niektóre z nich są policzalne, a niektóre niepoliczalne. Istnieją też różnice między brytyjską i amerykańską odmianą języka angielskiego:

headache [C]
- *She told us she had a headache.*

stomach ache [C], Brit. also [U]
- *He went to bed early with (a) stomach ache.*

backache, earache i **toothache** [U], especially US [C]
- *He's in excellent health except for occasional backache.* (Brit.)
- *I've got earache/toothache.* (Brit.)
- *He's in excellent health except for an occasional backache.* (US)
- *I have an earache/a toothache.* (US)

Accidents and injuries
Wypadki i obrażenia ciała

Injury [U] lub **an injury** [C] to zranienie lub inne obrażenie ciała, doznane np. w wyniku wypadku:
- *A local man suffered serious injuries when his car went off the road and ran into a tree.*
- *Two drivers escaped injury when their vehicles collided.*

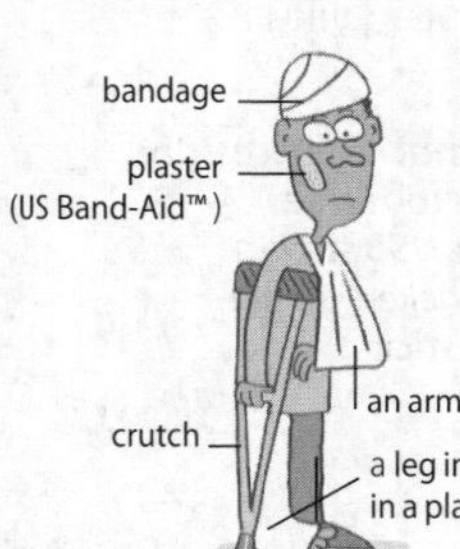

A wound to rana, miejsce obrażenia ciała, najczęściej zewnętrzne:
- *The nurse changed the bandage on the wound every day.*

Cuts and scratches
Skaleczenia i otarcia

An injury oznacza zwykle poważne obrażenie. Drobne obrażenia, jak skaleczenia, otarcia, stłuczenia itp. są określane innymi słowami:
- *The knife slipped and cut my finger, but it's only **a scratch**.*
- *I fell on the ice, but only got **a** small **bruise**.*
- *She fell over and **grazed** her knees.*

Diseases and illnesses
Choroby

Illness to ogólne słowo określające chorobę/stan chorobowy:
- *He died unexpectedly after a short illness.*
- *The doctor asked whether she had a history of any serious illness.*

Disease to ciężka choroba, która ma swoją nazwę lub choroba, która dotyczy konkretnej części ciała:
- *Measles is the most devastating of all the major childhood diseases.*
- *A healthy diet and regular exercise can help prevent heart disease.*

Condition to choroba przewlekła, która dotyczy konkretnej części ciała:
- *Asthma can be a very frightening condition, especially in a child.*
- *She suffers from a heart condition.*

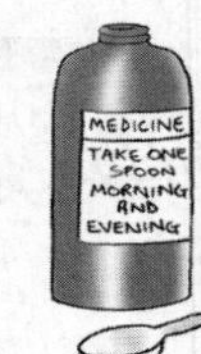

medicine

pills
(Brit. also **tablets**)

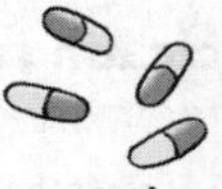

capsules

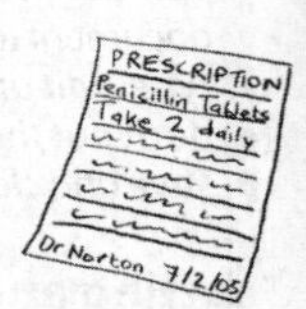

prescription

ointment

have an injection

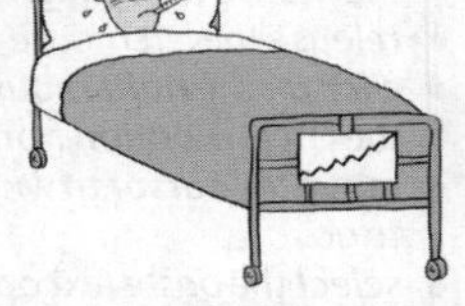

He's got a temperature. (Brit.)/ **He has a fever**. (US)

cough

sneeze

Talking about diseases or illnesses

Jak mówimy o chorobach

Mówiąc, że ktoś cierpi na jakąś chorobę, używa się czasownika **have**:

- *I'm warning you – I have a bad cold.*
- *Have the kids had chickenpox yet?*

Mówiąc o zachorowaniu na jakąś chorobę, używa się czasownika **catch**, **get** lub **come down with**:

- *I must have caught this cold from you.*
- *He gets really bad hay fever every summer.*
- *I've been sneezing and coughing all day – I must be coming down with something.*

W języku formalnym, a także mówiąc o ciężkich chorobach, używa się czasownika **suffer from** lub **contract**:

- *This medicine is often recommended by doctors for their patients who suffer from arthritis.*
- *people who have contracted AIDS*

O tym, że ktoś zachorował lub jest chory, mówi się inaczej w brytyjskiej angielszczyźnie, a inaczej w amerykańskiej:

- *I've never **been** so **ill** in my life.* (Brit.)
- *What's wrong? Are you **feeling unwell**?* (Brit.)
- *He's not in the office today – he**'s sick**.* (US)
- *She **was taken ill** with severe pains in the stomach.* (Brit.)
- *I just can't afford to **get sick**.* (US)

Feel sick ma inne znaczenie w brytyjskiej angielszczyźnie, a inne w amerykańskiej. W amerykańskiej odmianie języka angielskiego wyrażenie to oznacza, że ktoś czuje się chory:

- *He began feeling sick Friday afternoon and was diagnosed as having suffered a minor heart attack.*

W brytyjskiej angielszczyźnie **feel sick** znaczy, że komuś jest niedobrze i zbiera mu się na wymioty:

- *The smell of stale cigarettes always makes me feel sick.*

Aby to samo wyrazić w amerykańskiej angielszczyźnie, mówi się **sick to your stomach**:

- *The smell of stale cigarettes always makes me sick to my stomach.*

Staying healthy

Utrzymywanie się w dobrym zdrowiu

Mówiąc o osobie, która jest zdrowa, silna i w dobrej kondycji fizycznej, zwłaszcza w wyniku stosowania diety i regularnych ćwiczeń, stosuje się wyrażenia **fit** (Brit.), **physically fit**, lub **in shape** (especially US):

- *Top athletes have to be very fit.* (Brit.)
- *People who are physically fit have a lower risk of heart disease.*
- *After my heart attack, the doctor advised me to get in shape and stay that way.*
- *The doctor said I should **get** more **exercise*** (Brit. also ***take** more **exercise***).
- *No cream for me – I'm **on a diet**.*
- *I need to **go on a diet**.*
- *She cycles up to 90 miles a day to **keep fit**.* (Brit.)
- *She rides her bike up to 90 miles a day to **stay in shape**.* (especially US)

The National Health Service (NHS)

Narodowa Służba Zdrowia

Most medical care in Britain is provided by the **National Health Service**, or **NHS**, though some people do pay for private medical insurance. The **NHS** is paid for by the government through taxation, and treatment by doctors and in hospitals is free. You do, however, have to pay for medicines and also for dental treatment.

When you register at a **health centre**, you are given a **medical card** and allotted a **GP** (**general practitioner**). A **GP** is normally based in a specific **surgery**, though it is also possible to arrange home visits. When you have a health problem, you normally make an appointment with your **GP**, unless it is an emergency. The **GP** can write **prescriptions** for medicines, or, if the problem could be more serious, (s)he may recommend that you should visit a **specialist** in a particular field.

Informal English
W towarzystwie anglojęzycznych znajomych

W tym rozdziale zobaczymy, jak naprawdę mówią Anglicy i jakich zwrotów czy słów (przynajmniej niektórych) szczególnie ludzie młodzi najczęściej używają w rozmowie. Pamiętaj, że jest to sekcja poświęcona językowi mówionemu. Większość z podanych tu zwrotów używana jest wyłącznie w języku potocznym, a nie w bardziej formalnych sytuacjach, takich jak pisanie listów czy rozmowy kwalifikacyjne.

Jak mówią młodzi Anglicy

- Pytając „dlaczego?" często mówią **How come?** albo **How's that?**:

  How come *you didn't tell me?*
  'I'm going home early today.' ***'How's that?'***

- Wyrażając opinię, używają zwrotów **I reckon** albo **I bet**:

  I reckon *she'll pass the exam.*
  I bet *they're late.*

- Sugerując/proponując coś, mówią **Do you fancy ...?** albo **How about ...?**:

  Do you fancy *going for a pizza?*
  How about *meeting up at the cinema?*

- Jeżeli ktoś o coś prosi, często odpowiadają **No problem** albo **Not a problem**:

  'Can I have a Coke?' 'Yes, ***no problem****.'*

- Aby powiedzieć „dużo" często używają zwrotów **loads/masses/tons (of)** albo **an awful lot (of)**:

  She gave me ***loads*** *to do.*
  There were ***masses*** *of people at the concert.*
  I've got an ***awful lot*** *of homework.*

Jak powiedzieć:

Tak!	Yeah! OK! You bet!	Yep! Right! Sure!
(Absolutnie) nie!	No way! You must be joking!	Nope!
Dziękuję!	Thanks! Cheers!	Ta!
W porządku!	No problem!	
Cześć! (na powitanie)	Hi (there)! What's new!	Hiya!
Na razie!	See you (in a bit)! See you later!	
Cześć! (na pożegnanie)	Bye!	Cheers!

Kiedy Anglikom coś się podoba

- Aby powiedzieć, że coś jest dobre, wspaniałe itp. mówią:

Cool! *It's brilliant!* *Excellent!* *It's magic!* *Wicked!*

- Jeżeli uważają, że ktoś jest wspaniały, naprawdę zna się na czymś czy dobrze pracuje, wtedy mówią:

  You're a ***star****!*
  She's a ***genius****!*

- Jeżeli podoba im się jakiś pomysł czy plan, używają wyrażeń **cool** albo **great**:

  *'Let's go and see a film.' '****Cool****!'*
  *'I'll ring you tonight.' '****Great****!'*

- Opisując coś modnego, często mówią:

  I know a really ***hip/cool*** *bar.*
  Those shoes are very ***trendy****.*
  What a ***groovy*** *jacket!*

- O osobie, która im się podoba, mówią:

  He's ***drop-dead*** *gorgeous!*
  She's ***fit****!*

Kiedy Anglikom coś się nie podoba

- Jeżeli coś nie jest dobre albo coś się im nie podoba, mówią często:

  It's ***rubbish****/(****a pile of****)* ***pants****/(****a load of****)* ***crap****.* (Zwróć uwagę, że niektórzy uważają słowo **crap** za obraźliwe).

- Aby stwierdzić, że ktoś źle pracuje lub nie ma o czymś pojęcia, mówią:

  You're ***useless****!*
  What a ***loser****!*
  She's a real ***waste of space****!*

- Jeżeli ktoś lub coś jest niemodne lub nieciekawe, używają przymiotnika **naff**. Aby określić niemodne, nudne zajęcie czy osoby, często stosują **sad**:

  That's a rather ***naff*** *shirt!*
  He's just a ***sad*** *old man.*
  Staying at home all weekend watching TV is pretty ***sad****.*

- Aby powiedzieć, że ktoś jest głupi, często używają wyrażeń:

You dummy! *What a moron!*

- Jeżeli nudzi ich wykonywane zajęcie, mówią:

  It's a ***pain in the neck*** *having to stay indoors and work!*
  That's a real ***drag****.*

Trochę słownictwa

guy, **bloke**, **mate**, **buddy** (especially US) = facet, kumpel

kid = dziecko, dzieciak

cash = gotówka, pieniądze

booze = gorzał(k)a, wóda

the box/telly = telewizor, telewizja

check out that car! = popatrz na ten samochód!

get lost! = spływaj!, zjeżdżaj!

hang on/hold on! = poczekaj (przez chwilę)!

to crash out = paść i usnąć, przespać się

to flip = wkurzać się

to hang out = przesiadywać

to skive/bunk off = bumelować

to throw a wobbly = wściekać się, histeryzować

to veg out = obijać się

Learning vocabulary
Jak uczyć się nowych słówek

1 Mind Maps Mapy myśli

W uczeniu się słownictwa bardzo pomocne są **mind maps** („mapy myśli" lub „mapy umysłu"). Pośrodku mapy wpisz słowo główne (na rysunku **human**) i dopisz do niego jak najwięcej słów-skojarzeń. Przyjrzyj się rysunkowi poniżej, a następnie narysuj podobną mapę myśli i umieść na niej osiem słów kojarzących ci się ze słowem głównym.

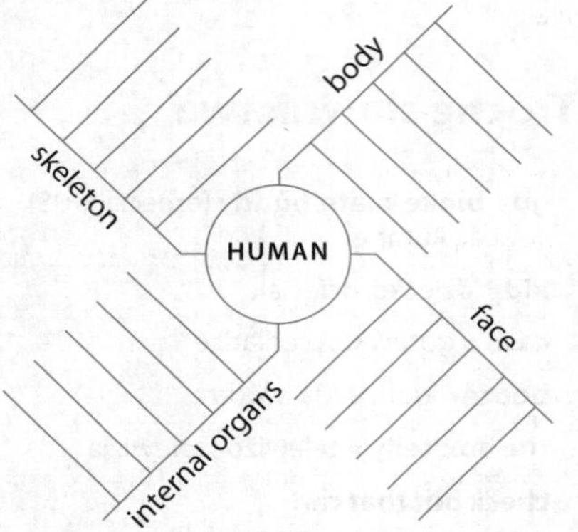

Narysuj jeszcze dwie mapy myśli dla dowolnych słów z ramki.

stationery	kitchen utensils
car	containers
garden	equipment

2 Categorization
Podział słów na kategorie

1 Wyszukaj w słowniku **laboratory**, znajdź ilustrację przedstawiającą aparaturę laboratoryjną i zapoznaj się ze słownictwem na ten temat, a następnie podziel słówka na dwie kategorie. Narysuj tabelkę i wpisz do niej słówka odnoszące się do laboratorium w dwóch kolumnach.

Laboratory Apparatus	
containers	non-containers

2 Wykonaj podobne ćwiczenie z następującymi słowami:
- **Bags** (podziel na kategorie: **shopping, travelling i work**)
- **Insects** (podziel na kategorie: **winged i non-winged**)
- **Plane** (podziel na kategorie: **exterior i interior**)

3 Parts of speech Części mowy

Przeczytaj uważnie tekst, którego się ostatnio uczyłeś i wybierz z niego sześć lub siedem ważnych czasowników. Wpisz je do poniższej tabelki, a następnie sprawdź w słowniku, czy istnieją ich przymiotniki i rzeczowniki pochodne. Dla niektórych czasowników znajdziesz tylko przymiotnik lub tylko rzeczownik.

verb	adjective	noun
1 *pollute*	*polluted*	*pollution*
2		
3		
4		
5		
6		
7		

4 Word families Grupy tematyczne wyrazów

Przeczytaj listę zwierząt, a następnie wyszukaj jak najwięcej dodatkowych słówek na ich temat (jak nazywa się samiec, samica, młode, dźwięk, który dane zwierzę wydaje, grupa tych zwierząt, mieso itp.) i uzupełnij tabelę według przykładu.

Animal	Male	Female	Young	Sound	Group Name	Meat
cow	*bull*	*cow*	*heifer*	*moo*	*cattle/ herd*	*beef*
sheep						
goat						
chicken						
pig						
horse						

5 Which word? Jakie słowa występują razem?

W słowniku znajdziesz informacje o tym, jakie słowa występują razem z innymi słowami w związkach wyrazowych. Wyszukaj hasła następujących rzeczowników i napisz we właściwym miejscu w tabelce, które z nich występują razem z czasownikiem **give**, a które z czasownikiem **take**.

Przykład: *to* ***give*** *sb a* ***push***

hint, risk, bath, break, push, hug, OK, lecture, photograph, ring, lift, joke

give	take

6 Acronyms and abbreviations Skrótowce

Co oznaczają podane w ramce skrótowce i jakiej tematyki dotyczą? Wpisz w tabelce skrótowce podane w ramce oraz ich pełne nazwy. Spróbuj znaleźć więcej skrótowców w słowniku.

GNP	BC	FAQ	CIA	DIY	ISP
BBC	CD	UFO	MD	VIP	EU
WAP	VDU	NGO	GMT	HGV	CCTV

Acronyms and abbreviations

Short form	Full form
GNP	*Gross National Product*
BC	

Odpowiedzi

4 sheep: ram, ewe, lamb, baa/bleat, flock, lamb/mutton
goat: billy goat, nanny goat, kid, bleat, herd, goat
chicken: cock, hen, chick, cluck, flock, chicken
pig: boar, sow, piglet, grunt/squeal, herd, pork/ham/bacon
horse: stallion, mare, colt/filly, neigh, herd, horse
5 give: push, ring, lecture, lift, hug, OK
take: bath, photograph, hint, risk, break, joke

Letter writing Pisanie listów

Formal Letters Listy formalne

Applying for a job – *British style*
Podanie o pracę – *styl korespondencji stosowany w brytyjskiej angielszczyźnie*

Tu wpisz adres, imię i nazwisko oraz stanowisko osoby, do której kierujesz list/podanie.

Nigdy nie pisz swojego imienia i nazwiska u góry listu.

Rocks Lane
Bristol BS8 9DF

Wpisz swój adres w prawym górnym rogu.

20 April 2005

Datę możesz wpisać z lewej lub z prawej strony listu.

Ms Patricia Wright
Personnel Department
Multimedia Design
4 Albion Road
London SE1 4DD

Dział **Personnel** czasem nazywa się **Human Resources**.

Dear Ms Wright

Jeśli nie znasz nazwiska osoby, do której piszesz, napisz na początku listu **Dear Sir** lub **Dear Madam**. Jeśli znasz nazwisko, napisz **Dear Mr/Ms** itp. i nazwisko.

I am writing to apply for the **post** of assistant designer advertised in the Evening Post of 18 May. Please find enclosed a copy of my CV. ❶

W podaniu o pracę używaj słów **post**, **position** lub **vacancy**, a nie *job*.

Since graduating from Cardiff University I have been working for EMS Corporate Imaging on a contract basis. I have become particularly interested in interactive and multimedia work and now wish to develop my career in that direction. ❷

Używaj słów i zwrotów stosowanych w języku formalnym.

I would welcome the chance to work as part of a small dynamic team where I could make a significant contribution while developing my skills yet further. I would be happy to show you a portfolio of my work. ❸

I am available for interview next week and look forward to hearing from you. ❹

Nie stosuj form skróconych (np. pisz **I am**, a nie *I'm*).

Yours sincerely

W brytyjskiej angielszczyźnie na końcu listu napisz **Yours sincerely**, jeżeli na początku został użyty tytuł **Mr/Ms** itp. i nazwisko osoby. Jeśli jednak na początku listu został użyty zwrot **Dear Sir** lub **Dear Madam,** wówczas na zakończenie listu napisz **Yours faithfully**.

Mark Wallace

Mark Wallace

Podpisz się pełnym imieniem i nazwiskiem, a pod podpisem napisz dodatkowo drukiem swoje imię i nazwisko.

Enc. CV

Skróty **encl.** lub **enc.** na końcu listu oznaczają, że do listu dołączasz załącznik(i).

akapit ❶ wyjaśnij, o jaką pracę się ubiegasz oraz jak/skąd się o niej dowiedziałeś

akapit ❷ napisz krótko, jakie masz wykształcenie/ kwalifikacje i/lub doświadczenie zawodowe

akapit ❸ wyjaśnij, dlaczego starasz się o tę pracę i dlaczego sądzisz, że będziesz w niej dobry

akapit ❹ napisz, jak można się z tobą skontaktować i/lub kiedy możesz przyjść na rozmowę kwalifikacyjną

Inne użyteczne zwroty stosowane w podaniach o pracę:

akapit ❶

- *I noted with interest your advertisement for a … in today's edition of …*
- *I am writing in response to your advertisement in … for the position of …*
- *I would like to apply for the vacancy advertised in …*
- *With reference to your advertisement in …*
- *I am interested in applying for the post of …*
- *As you will see from my CV …*
- *I have enclosed a copy of my CV, from which you will see …*
- *Please find enclosed a copy of my CV.*

akapit ❷

- *I am currently studying … at …*
- *After graduating from …, I …*
- *Since leaving university, I have …*
- *On leaving school, I …*
- *Having gained a degree, I …*
- *While I was working at …*
- *During my employment at …*
- *I am currently employed as …*

akapit ❸

- *This post interests me because …*
- *I would welcome the chance to gain more experience of …*
- *I would be grateful for the opportunity to improve my … skills.*
- *I have extensive experience of …*

akapit ❹

- *If you consider that my experience and qualifications are suitable …*
- *I am available for interview any afternoon and would be pleased to discuss the post in person.*
- *I will be available for interview from … to …*
- *I can arrange to attend an interview whenever is convenient for you.*

A letter of complaint Skargi, zażalenia, reklamacje

17 Wolfson Close
Reigate
Surrey RH6 3KE
Tel: 0116 587392
12 December 2005

Customer Services
Mainrail
Carbis House
London WC1 5NR

Dear Sir or Madam

I am writing to complain about the poor service provided by your train company. ❶

Yesterday I travelled on the 7.20 from Oxford to London Paddington. Not only was the train thirty minutes late leaving Oxford but we were further delayed at Reading and no explanation or apology was offered. Furthermore, the heating broke down and the train got colder and colder. I complained to a member of staff, who was most unhelpful and unsympathetic. ❷

As a result of the delays I was two hours late for an important meeting with a valuable client, which caused considerable difficulty and embarrassment. ❸

In the circumstances I believe I am entitled to compensation. I look forward to hearing from you very soon. ❹

Yours faithfully

John Holland

John Holland

Większość listów dotyczących skarg, zażaleń lub reklamacji pisze się językiem formalnym. Przedstawione w nich sprawy są prezentowane w pewnym ustalonym porządku:

akapit ❶ napisz, czego dotyczy skarga, zażalenie lub reklamacja

akapit ❷ wyjaśnij, na czym polega problem i napisz, co zrobiłeś w związku z nim

akapit ❸ napisz, jakie negatywne skutki miała ta sprawa dla ciebie

akapit ❹ napisz, jakiego rozwiązania sprawy oczekujesz w związku z zaistniałym problemem

Inne użyteczne zwroty stosowane w skargach, zażaleniach i reklamacjach:

- *I am writing to express my dissatisfaction with/at …*
- *I was surprised/shocked/horrified to find …*
- *I returned/explained/requested …*
- *What made matters worse was that …*
- *Furthermore/in addition/what's more …*
- *As if this was/were not enough …*
- *On top of all this …*
- *As a consequence …*
- *This caused me to …*
- *I am sure you will appreciate that this level of service is unacceptable.*
- *I expect to be compensated for the inconvenience I have been caused.*
- *I expect better service from a company of your reputation.*
- *Please replace the goods as soon as possible.*
- *I would like a full refund.*
- *I would like to know what action you will take to rectify this situation.*
- *In future I shall take my custom elsewhere.*
- *I look forward to a prompt reply/a full explanation.*
- *I await your response/comments.*

Asking for information – *American style*

Prośba o udzielenie informacji
– styl korespondencji stosowany w amerykańskiej odmianie języka angielskiego

179 San Jacinto Blvd
San Antonio TX 78210
September 3, 2005

Southern Sports Holidays
142 Woodbridge Road
Denver CO 80201-1023

To whom it may concern:

I am interested in language and sports holidays as advertised in your brochure and I would appreciate it if you could send me further information about prices and facilities.

Could you tell me how many hours a week of language tuition are offered and how large the groups are? I would also like to know whether special diets are catered for, as one of my friends is a vegetarian.

Thank you.

Sincerely,

GLORIA RODRIGUEZ

Gloria Rodriguez

- Wyrażenie **To whom it may concern** jest używane zwłaszcza w amerykańskiej odmianie języka angielskiego, w sytuacji gdy nie znasz nazwiska osoby, do której piszesz.
- W amerykańskiej odmianie języka angielskiego na zakończenie listu napisz **Sincerely**, **Sincerely yours** lub **Yours truly**.

Inne użyteczne zwroty stosowane w listach, w których prosisz o podanie informacji:

- *It would also be helpful to know what/when/etc. ...*
- *I would be interested to know ...*
- *Please let me know ...*
- *Would you send me details of ...*
- *I would be grateful if you could let me have ...*

Informal Letters Listy nieformalne

A letter of thanks List z podziękowaniami

Nie musisz wpisywać adresu osoby, do której piszesz.

W prawym górnym rogu zwykle pisze się swój adres. W liście nieformalnym można go opuścić.

4 Longton Avenue
Exeter
Devon EX3 8NS

28 June 2005

Na początku listu napisz **Dear** i imię bliskiej osoby.

Dear Lucy

Just a note to say a big thank you for giving us such a fab time in the Lake District. Bill and I were so pleased to meet your family, and they made us really welcome.

Możesz stosować język nieformalny i formy skrócone (*I'll*, *we're*, itp.).

I'll never forget climbing Helvellyn. My legs ached for days, but it was worth it for the fantastic views!

We're both back at work now and very busy. However, this weekend we're going to decorate the spare room so I hope you'll come and visit us soon.

W listach do bliskich przyjaciół lub członków rodziny napisz na zakończenie **Love**, **Love from** lub **Lots of love**. W innych wypadkach napisz **Best wishes**, **All the best** lub **Take care**.

Love,
Ellie

Jeśli po zakończeniu listu chcesz dopisać jakąś informację lub dodać coś, o czym zapomniałeś wcześniej, możesz po podpisie wstawić dopisek **PS** (postscriptum).

PS I found that CD you told me about. Great band!

Writing emails, faxes and memos
Pisanie e-maili, faksów i notatek służbowych

Listy przesyłane e-mailem lub faksem lub jako notatki służbowe mogą mieć podobny styl. Notatki służbowe i e-maile do kolegów z pracy mogą być nieformalne, jednak faksy i e-maile wysyłane do partnerów biznesowych są na ogół półformalne lub formalne, zależnie od stopnia znajomości osób korespondujących oraz treści listu. Listy biznesowe są często przesyłane faksem.

Jest kilka podstawowych zasad pisania faksów, notatek służbowych i e-maili:

- Nie musisz pisać **Dear Sir/Madam/Mrs Smith** itp. na początku ani używać specjalnego zwrotu na zakończenie: wystarczy podpis.
- Stosuj jednolity styl: formalny lub nieformalny.
- Wygląd e-maila, faksu czy notatki jest równie ważny jak innego listu - pisz poprawne zdania i stosuj podział na akapity.
- Pisz krótko i na temat.
- Zawsze wpisuj temat w przeznaczonej do tego rubryce, aby odbiorca wiedział, czego dotyczy e-mail, faks czy notatka.

Email E-maile

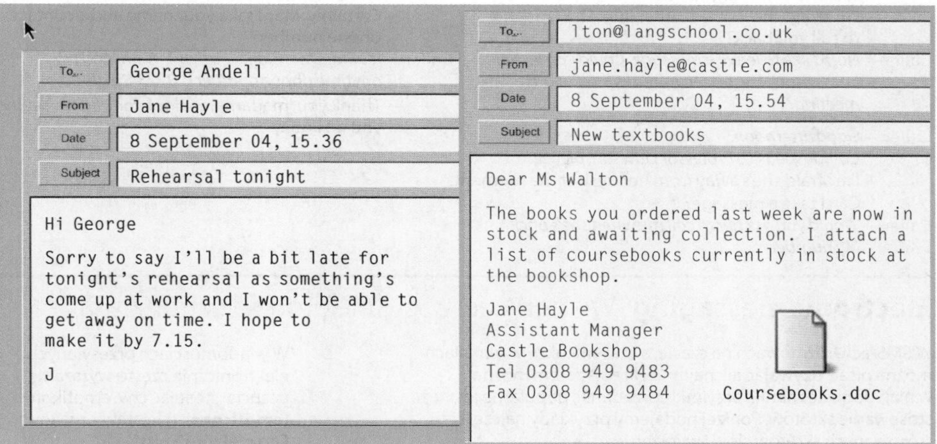
To... George Andell
From Jane Hayle
Date 8 September 04, 15.36
Subject Rehearsal tonight

Hi George

Sorry to say I'll be a bit late for tonight's rehearsal as something's come up at work and I won't be able to get away on time. I hope to make it by 7.15.

J

To... lton@langschool.co.uk
From jane.hayle@castle.com
Date 8 September 04, 15.54
Subject New textbooks

Dear Ms Walton

The books you ordered last week are now in stock and awaiting collection. I attach a list of coursebooks currently in stock at the bookshop.

Jane Hayle
Assistant Manager
Castle Bookshop
Tel 0308 949 9483
Fax 0308 949 9484

Coursebooks.doc

Fax Faksy

Falcon Publishing
354 Walnut Street, Philadelphia, PA 19106
Tel 0049 3492945, Fax 215 925 8722
Email a.carroll@falcpub.com

Fax
To Ian Jenkins, Hedgerow Books
From Alice Carroll
Fax no. 202 736 5412
Subject Publicity Material
Date 8 March 2005
Pages including this page: 1

Following our phone conversation yesterday I am sorry to say that the publicity material for The Magic Pineapple will not be available until next week. I will arrange for it to be sent to you as soon as we receive it from the printers.

Alice Carroll
Publicity Assistant

Memo Notatki służbowe

Falcon Publishing
Children's Books

Memorandum

To: All editors
From: Frank Digby
Subject: Sales figures
Date: 8 October 2005

Please see the attached sales figures for September. A meeting to discuss these will be held on Tuesday 12 October at 10.30 a.m. in the Conference Room.

Frank

Telephoning and electronic messaging

Rozmowy telefoniczne i SMS-y

Telephoning Rozmowy telefoniczne

— Hello.
Caller — *Hello, is that Rachel Davies?*
— Yes, speaking.
Caller — *Oh, hello, it's Mark Turnbull from Print Systems here. I'm calling about the order you placed last week.*

Caller — *Hello, could I speak to Amy, please?*
— Yes, of course. May I ask who's calling?
Caller — *It's Kate.*
— OK, just a minute, please...

Caller — *Good morning. This is Alison Savage. Could I speak to Tina Marks, please?*
— I'm afraid she's on the other line. Shall I ask her to call you back?
Caller — *No, I'd like to leave a message. Could you let her know that I'll be fifteen minutes late for our meeting?*

Caller — *Good afternoon. Could I speak to Professor Dawson, please?*
— I'm afraid she's away from her desk at the moment. Can I take a message?
Caller — *Would you ask her to call me when she's back? My number is...*

— Good afternoon. Planet Warehouse. How can I help you?
Caller — *Could you put me through to Customer Services, please?*
— Yes, hold the line please.

— Good afternoon, Customer Services. Shelley speaking. How may I help you?
Caller — *Hello, I'm having trouble with the fridge I bought from you yesterday.*

— Good morning. Bistro 21. Can I help you?
Caller — *Good morning. I'd like to book a table for two for 8.30 on Friday please.*
— Certainly. May I take your name and a contact phone number?
Caller — *It's Blair, Mrs Blair. That's B-L-A-I-R, and my daytime phone number is 02234 659920.*
— Thank you, madam – we look forward to seeing you on Friday.

Electronic messaging Wiadomości wysyłane drogą elektroniczną

W SMS-ach, rozmowach na czacie, a czasem także w e-mailach można pisać, używając jak najmniej liter. A zatem można w nich pomijać zaimki, przyimki i przedimki, popularne jest też stosowanie skrótów. Poniżej podajemy przykłady najczęściej stosowanych skrótów słów i wyrażeń:

2DAY	today
2MORO	tomorrow
2NITE	tonight
ASAP	as soon as possible
ATB	all the best
B4	before
B4N	bye for now
BBL	be back later
BTW	by the way
CUL8R	see you later
F2F	face to face
FWIW	for what it's worth
FYI	for your information
GR8	great
HAND	have a nice day
ILU	I love you
IMHO	in my humble opinion
KIT	keep in touch
LOL	lots of love / luck / laughing out loud
MSG	message
MYOB	mind your own business
NO1	no one
PCM	please call me
PLS	please
SOM1	someone
SPK	speak
THX	thanks
WAN2	want to
WKND	weekend
X	kiss
XLNT	excellent
XOXO	hugs and kisses
YR	your/you're

W wiadomościach przesyłanych elektronicznie często wyraża się uczucia, stosując tzw. emotikony (**emoticons**), tj. zestawy znaków. Oto niektóre z nich:

:-)	wesoły
:-(	smutny
;-)	mrugnięcie
:-D	śmiech
:-Q	nie rozumiem
:'-(	płacz
:-|	znudzony
:-*	pocałunek
:-O	zdziwiony
:-X	nic nie mowię

Użyteczne słowa i zwroty

My life

Personal details

- *My surname* (lub *family name*) *is ...*
- *My first name/middle name is ...*
- *I'm sixteen years old.*
- *My birthday is 11th November.* (mówi się: *My birthday is the 11th of November.*)
- *I was born in Warsaw in 1993.*
- *My date of birth is ...*
- *I'm Polish.*
- *I come from Poland.*
- *My family originally came from Latvia.*
- *I'm half Polish and half Ukrainian.*
- *I speak Polish, English and German.*
- *Polish is my mother tongue.*
- *I'm fluent in two languages.*
- *I speak fluent/basic/a little Italian.*
- *I have some knowledge of French.*
- *I'm bilingual (in Polish and Czech).*

My appearance

- *I'm tall/short.*
- *I'm quite/very slim.*
- *I'm 5 foot 6 inches/1.67 metres tall.*
- *I weigh 8 stone 5 pounds/53 kilos.*
- *I've got — long/short/shoulder-length/cropped*
  — black/brown/dark/blond/fair/red
  — straight/wavy/curly/frizzy hair.
- *I've got fair/dark skin.*
- *I've got freckles.*

My home

- *I live in Lublin.*
- *My address is ...*
- *I live in the country/on a farm/in a city/in an industrial town/in a village.*
- *I live in the centre of town/in the suburbs/in a quiet residential area/on the outskirts of town.*
- *I live in a large/small one-/two-/three-bedroom flat/house.*
- *There are five of us living in the house.*
- *My family owns our flat/house.*
- *We rent a furnished/unfurnished flat.*
- *We have a small garden/a lot of land/an allotment.*
- *I share a bedroom with my brother/sister.*
- *I have my own bedroom.*

My family

- *I come from a large/small family.*
- *I've got one brother and one sister.*
- *I haven't got any brothers or sisters. I'm an only child.*
- *I am the youngest/the oldest/in the middle.*
- *I was adopted.*
- *My parents are divorced/separated.*
- *I live with my mother/father/grandparents.*
- *I've got lots of cousins.*
- *My maternal/paternal grandparents are still alive.*
- *I often/never fight with my brothers and sisters.*
- *We (don't) get on very well.*
- *We often argue/fall out with each other.*
- *We are (not) very close.*
- *We look after each other.*
- *I get on well with my parents.*
- *My parents are very understanding and supportive.*
- *I can/can't talk to my parents about my problems.*
- *My parents are too strict.*
- *My mother/father is a doctor/plumber/civil servant.*
- *She/he works for a big company/a local firm.*
- *She/he works from home.*
- *My sister is training to be a nurse.*
- *My elder brother is studying law at university.*
- *My younger/elder brother is in the army.*

Pets

- *I have two pets.*
- *I have a pet dog/cat/rabbit.*
- *Every day I have to take it for a walk/feed it/clean its cage.*

My daily routine

- *Every day I get up at 6 o'clock.*
- *I wash/have a shower and get dressed.*
- *I always/usually/sometimes have ... for breakfast.*
- *After breakfast I go to school.*
- *After school I play football/go swimming/meet my friends.*
- *I sometimes do extra-curricular activities after school.*

- *In the evening I do my homework and then watch TV.*
- *Twice a week I go out with my friends.*
- *I visit my grandparents every other weekend.*
- *I have a part-time job on a Saturday.*
- *At home I help with the cooking/cleaning/washing-up/housework.*
- *I help look after my younger brothers/sisters.*
- *It's my job to clean the car/dust the living room/weed the garden.*

My personality

- *I would describe myself as adventurous/ambitious/energetic/extrovert/lively.*
- *I'm rather introverted/quiet/shy.*
- *I like to be the leader.*
- *I don't like making decisions.*
- *I'm flexible/friendly/sociable/easy to get on with.*
- *I'm a bit stubborn.*
- *I think my strongest point is … and my weakest point is …*
- *People like me because I'm funny/interesting.*
- *I like to make people laugh.*
- *People often say I'm …*

My friends

- *I have lots of/a few friends.*
- *My friends are important to me because …*
- *My best friend is … I like him/her because …*
- *We've been friends since 2003/for five years.*
- *His/her best characteristic is …*
- *He/she is very funny/generous/honest/kind/loyal/trustworthy/understanding.*
- *I'd say his/her faults are …*
- *We tell each other everything/share secrets/enjoy doing the same things.*
- *We have a lot of things in common.*
- *I know I can turn to … when I have a problem.*
- *I have an American penfriend.*

My aims and ambitions

- *The most important thing in my life is …*
- *It is important to me because …*
- *I think we are on this earth to …*
- *It is everyone's duty to …*
- *My aim in life is to …*
- *I am ambitious. My ambitions are to …*
- *When I'm older I'd (really) like to …*

My feelings

- *What I enjoy most in life is …*
- *The happiest/saddest time in my life was when …*
- *The best/worst thing that ever happened to me was …*
- *My greatest worry/fear is that …*
- *My biggest achievement/disappointment has been …*
- *I'm most proud of …*
- *The thing I'm most ashamed of is …*

Special times

- *My favourite time of year is spring/summer/autumn/winter.*
- *I like this season because it's warm/hot/cold and I can go hiking/swimming/skiing.*
- *At this time of year we like to …*
- *At this time we always eat … and …*
- *Christmas/Easter is a special time in my country/for my family.*
- *My whole family gets together.*
- *We give each other presents.*

Lifestyle

Free time

- *What do you do in your free time?*
- *Do you have any hobbies?*
- *What are your interests?*
- *I like reading/painting/hiking in the mountains/fishing.*
- *My hobbies are stamp collecting/mountain biking/acting.*
- *I'm in the school football/badminton/hockey team.*
- *I go bowling/sailing/camping/skiing every week/in the summer/twice a year.*
- *I spend a lot of time with my friends/family/at the library/in the park.*
- *I sometimes go out to a restaurant with my family.*
- *I love shopping/going to the cinema/going camping.*
- *I'm interested in acting/animals/science.*
- *I'm a member of the Scouts/Guides.*
- *In the evenings I often watch TV/go out with my friends/go dancing/read a book.*
- *My favourite TV programme/film/book/ magazine/actor/writer is …*
- *I particularly like comedies/horror films/ romances /thrillers.*
- *I find reading/watching TV/making models very relaxing.*
- *I do voluntary work at an old people's home.*
- *I help out at a kindergarten/vet's.*
- *I have a part-time job at …*

Do

jigsaws/
puzzles

flower
arranging
embroidery

aerobics
karate
judo

Make

models
clothes

Keeping fit

She's doing **sit-ups**.

He's doing **press-ups** (US **push-ups**).

She's **bending**.

He's **stretching**.

She's **touching her toes**.

Swimming

the crawl

backstroke

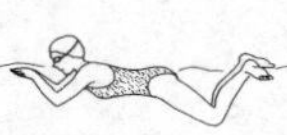

breaststroke

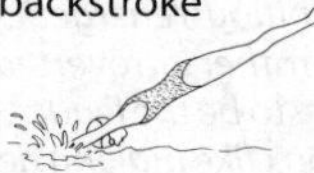

diving

Play

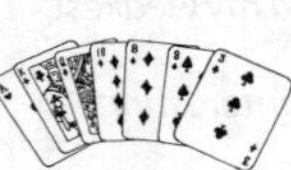

cards
games

hockey
football
tennis

the flute
the piano
the saxophone

Go

swimming
running
climbing

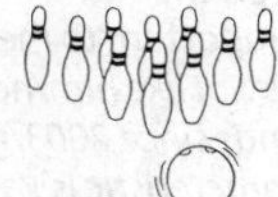

bowling
skating
fishing

mountain biking
sailing
skiing

She **paints**.

He **works out**.

He **collects stamps**.

They **act**.

She **knits**.

Food

Meals

- *breakfast*
- *lunch*
- *coffee break*
- *dinner*
- *supper*
- *snack*
- *I eat/have toast, cereal and a boiled egg for breakfast.*
- *We have a coffee break at 11 o'clock.*
- *I eat/have lunch at 1 o'clock.*
- *I often/rarely eat snacks between meals.*

Likes and dislikes

- *I like Polish/Italian/Chinese food.*
- *My favourite food is pasta/hamburgers/ice cream.*
- *I love home-made cakes and biscuits.*
- *I like spicy/hot food.*
- *I don't like … because it tastes too …*
- *That smells/looks/tastes delicious.*
- *I'm a vegetarian/vegan. I don't eat meat or fish.*
- *I'm hungry/a bit peckish/starving/full.*

Eating out

- *I sometimes eat out/go to a restaurant.*
- *to order a meal*
- *to ask for the bill*
- *to leave a tip/to tip the waiter*
- *We sometimes get/order a takeaway.*
- *The most popular fast food in my country is …*
- *In Britain, a popular type of fast food is fish and chips/a Chinese takeaway.*

ℹ Zwróć uwagę, że w brytyjskim angielskim słowo **dessert** stosuje się przede wszystkim w jadłospisach i w książkach kucharskich. W języku mówionym najczęściej używa się słowa **pudding**. Powszechnie używane jest także słowo **sweet**.

Drinks

- *Would you like something to drink?*
- *Yes, please. I'd like:*
  - *— a cold/hot drink*
  - *— a fizzy drink*
  - *— a coffee/tea*
  - *— a milkshake*
  - *— a cocoa/hot chocolate*
  - *— a soft drink/non-alcoholic drink*
  - *— some sparkling/still water*
  - *— a glass of red/white/dry/sweet wine*
  - *— a gin and tonic*
  - *— a cocktail.*
- *a cup of instant/filter/decaffeinated coffee*
- *I take my coffee black/white.*
- *Do you take sugar/milk in your tea?*
- *tea with milk/lemon*
- *alcohol/an alcoholic drink*
- *I don't drink (= alcohol).*
- *He's teetotal/a teetotaller.*
- *She's a heavy drinker.*

Diet

- *I have/eat a healthy/balanced/unhealthy diet.*
- *I eat plenty of … /too much …*
- *I don't eat much fast food/junk food.*
- *Fruit and vegetables are nutritious/good for you.*
- *Too many fatty foods are unhealthy/bad for you.*
- *If you want to lose weight, you should eat low-fat/low-calorie foods.*
- *to put on weight*
- *Meat contains a lot of protein.*
- *You get vitamins from fresh foods such as fruit and vegetables.*
- *Eggs and spinach are high in iron.*
- *Tea and coffee can be bad for you because they contain a lot of caffeine.*
- *dairy products*
- *carbohydrates*
- *food containing a lot of fibre, such as wholemeal bread*

Cooking

- *I like cooking./I'm (not) a good cook./I can't cook.*
- *The main ingredient in this recipe is …*
- *The ingredients I need to make this dish are:*

a packet/tin/sachet of …
a kilo/500 grams of pork
200 millilitres of water
a tablespoon of flour
a teaspoon of sugar
a pinch of salt

Mix the ingredients.
Melt the butter.
Heat the oil.
Stir gently.
Bring to the boil.
Cover the pan.
Simmer for10 minutes.
Sift the flour.
Beat the egg.
Allow to cool.
Whip the cream.
Decorate the cake.

ℹ Zob. też uwagę, przy **cook**.

Education and work

The British education system

Children usually start **primary school** at the age of five and move on to **secondary school** at eleven. Compulsory education ends at sixteen but many students stay on until they are eighteen to gain further qualifications.

Secondary schools

Most secondary schools are **comprehensive schools**. They offer a general education to children of all abilities. There are **grammar schools** in some parts of the country. They select their pupils according to ability and aim to provide a more academic education.

Education in Britain is free, and most children go to state schools. However, some parents pay to send their children to **independent schools**. In England and Wales some of the more traditional independent schools are called **public schools**, though they are in fact private. Many of these are **boarding schools**, where children live and sleep during term.

The curriculum

The **national curriculum** is the group of subjects that must be taught in schools in England and Wales. The core subjects are English, Mathematics and Science. The non-core subjects are History, Geography, Modern Foreign Languages, Art and Design, Music, Design and Technology, ICT (Information and Communication Technology), Physical Education (PE) and Citizenship.

Exams

In England, Wales and Northern Ireland pupils take **GCSEs** at the age of 16. At 17 they take **AS levels** and the following year **A2 levels**. AS and A2 levels together form **A levels**, which are needed for entrance to university. Scotland has a different system with exams called **National Qualifications**. Students sit exams at Standard Grade at about 16 and progress to other levels such as Intermediate 1, Intermediate 2, Higher or Advanced Higher. Students in their final year do their **highers**.

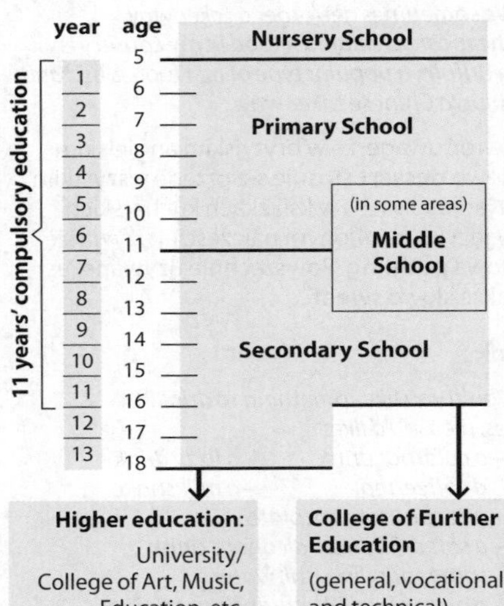

This chart shows how education is organized in England and Wales. The system is a little different in Scotland and Northern Ireland.

The American education system

Schools

Education is compulsory in the US for children between the ages of 6 and 16.

Most children go to **public schools**, which are free. (Don't confuse them with British public schools!) There are some **private schools**, which charge fees, as well as **parochial schools**, which are supported by local religious organizations and churches.

Assessment

There are no national exams, although some schools and states have their own exams. Students receive **grades** based on how well they do in tests, in classroom discussions and in their homework throughout the year. If students want to go on to higher education, most colleges and universities require them to take the **SAT** (**Scholastic Aptitude Test**).

Graduation

Students **graduate** from high school if they have enough **credits**, which they receive when they pass a course. Students usually take a combination of basic subjects called **requirements** (e.g. English and Mathematics) and a smaller number of specialized subjects called **electives** (e.g. a foreign language and art).

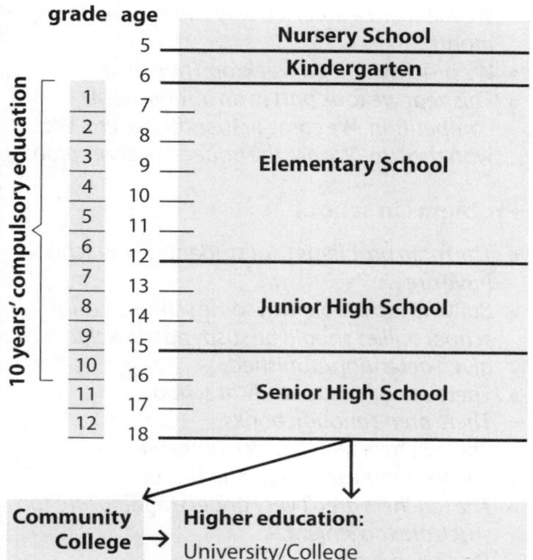

This chart shows how education is organized in the US, although in some states the system may be different.

My school

- *I'm a secondary school/college/university student.*
- *I'm at secondary school/college/university.*
- *I go to Warsaw University/Chopin Grammar School/Copernicus College.*
- *I'm in year/grade three.*

ⓘ Nauka w szkole podstawowej i pełnej średniej w Wlk. Br. trwa 13 lat. Odpowiednik klasy jako kolejnego etapu nauki to **year**. Czternastoletni uczeń powie: *I'm in year ten* i *I'm a year-ten student*. Słowa **year** używa się także, mówiąc o studiach wyższych, ale student powie: *I'm in my second year* (nie ~~*I'm in year two*~~) i *I'm a second-year student*.

My school day

- *I go to school by bus/car/bike.*
- *I walk to school.*
- *My lessons start at 8.00 a.m. three days a week and at 8.50 p.m. on the other two days.*
- *Students go to their class when they arrive and the teacher takes the register.*
- *Lessons last forty-five minutes.*
- *There are breaks of five or ten minutes between lessons and a longer break for lunch.*
- *I have lunch in the school canteen/cafeteria.*
- *I chat with my friends in the playground/in the corridor/in the common room during breaks.*
- *We are given homework most days.*
- *I do about one hour's homework a night.*

The school year

- *The autumn/winter term starts on ...*
- *We break up for the summer holidays on ...*
- *We have mock matura exams in April.*
- *We sit our matura exams in May.*
- *I revised for my exams during the Easter holidays.*
- *In some subjects we are graded by continuous assessment.*

Subjects

- *Polish*
- *Maths*
- *Physics*
- *Chemistry*
- *Biology*
- *Cooking*
- *Geography*
- *PE*
- *extra-curricular activities such as music, sport, drama*
- *English/German/French* itp.
- *Music*
- *Art*
- *Craft*
- *Woodwork*
- *History*
- *ICT*
- *RE* (= **religious education**, tj. przedmiot omawiający chrześcijaństwo i inne religie świata)

ℹ Zwróć uwagę, że przedmioty pisze się albo dużą literą, albo małą, z wyjątkiem języków, które zawsze pisze się dużą literą:

- *I'm good at Maths and English.*
- *I'm not very good at History.*
- *My favourite/best subject is Chemistry.*
- *My worst/weakest subject is Physics.*
- *I like studying German but I hate grammar.*
- *I've been studying English for six years.*

Places in a school

a classroom	*a tennis court*
the library	*a gymnasium*
a science laboratory	*the playground*
a music room	*the school/main hall*
a workshop	*the common room*
a sports field	*the staff room*
a football pitch	*a corridor*
a language laboratory	

ℹ Sala wykładowa/aula to **lecture theatre**.

Students

ℹ Słowa **pupil** używa się jeszcze w Wlk. Br. w odniesieniu do dzieci w szkołach podstawowych, ale powoli wychodzi ono z użycia. Słowo **student** stosuje się, opisując każdą uczącą się osobę.

School staff

- *head teacher*
- *secretary*
- *caretaker*
- *deputy head teacher*
- *school counsellor*
- *head of English/Science/Maths*, etc.
- *English/Maths/Chemistry*, etc. *teacher*

ℹ W szkołach brytyjskich, oprócz dyplomowanych nauczycieli, zajęcia z języków obcych prowadzą także asystenci, zwani **language assistants**. Są to obcokrajowcy, najczęściej studenci uniwersytetu lub kolegium, którzy uczą w szkole swojego ojczystego języka.

- *My favourite teacher is the English/Maths/Geography teacher.*
- *I think it's important for a teacher to be approachable/respected/strict/understanding.*

School clubs/teams

- *I'm a member of the chess/model/music club.*
- *I'm in the school choir.*
- *I'm in the school football/badminton/running team.*
- *We meet once a week/every Tuesday/once a month.*
- *We practise twice a week/on Thursdays.*
- *This year we took part in an inter-schools competition. We came first/second/third. We won the cup./We are the under-17s champions.*

Problems in school

- *The main problems that students in my school have are …*
- *Bullying is a problem in some schools. I think school bullies should be suspended/excluded/given detention/punished.*
- *There's nowhere to study at school.*
- *There aren't enough books.*
- *The teachers set too much homework.*
- *The teachers expect too much of us.*
- *The teachers aren't very understanding/are too strict/are too lenient.*
- *Discipline is poor.*
- *If you have a problem, you should talk to your class teacher/the school counsellor/your parents/your classmates/your friends.*

Work

- *When I leave school, I want to be a teacher/ farmer/fashion designer.*
- *I want to study English/Maths/Chemistry at university.*
- *I'd like to take a year off/travel/get some work experience.*
- *If you want to be a …, you have to be good at …/you need to study …*
- *The best university to study Maths/Medicine/ Physics at is …*
- *It takes six years to train to be a doctor/an architect/a lawyer.*

- *The minimum wage in Poland is …*
- *I'd like a starting salary of …*
- *Lawyers/stockbrokers,* etc. *are well-paid in Poland.*
- *Nurses/teachers/office workers don't earn much.*
- *It's easy/difficult to find work as a …*
- *There's a lot of competition to become a …*

- *to look for a job*
- *to apply for a job*
- *to write a job application*
- *to enclose/attach your CV*
- *My qualifications are …*
- *The best place to look for a job is at the job centre/ in the newspaper/on the Internet.*

- *I want to work full-time/part-time/freelance.*
- *I'd like to be part of a team/work independently/ work from home.*

- *to get promoted*
- *to get an annual pay rise/a bonus/benefits/perks*
- *The perks of this job are …*

- *Unemployment is high/low in my region.*
- *If you are unemployed, you can get state benefits/ the dole.*

CURRICULUM VITAE

Name	Peter James Green
Address	26 Windmill Road, Bristol BS2 6DP
Telephone	0117 945649
Nationality	British
Date of birth	11 March 1977
Marital status	Single

Education / Qualifications

1996–99	Anglia Polytechnic University: BA in Graphic Design (First Class Hons)
1988–95	Clifton School, 3 A levels: Art (A); Design and Technology (A); Mathematics (C) 10 GCSEs

Employment to date

1999–present	EMS Corporate Imaging, Design Department, Riverside House, 22 Charles St, Bristol
Skills	Computer literate: familiar with a number of design and DTP packages; clean driving licence
Foreign languages	French
Interests	Tennis, swimming, jazz

Useful phrases for a CV

- *Native Polish speaker*
- *Near-native command of English*
- *Adequate spoken French and German*
- *Matura 5 (equivalent of A levels)*
- *The qualifications described below do not have exact equivalents in the British system.*
- *I enclose photocopies of my certificates with English translations.*

Politics and the economy

Poland: some facts and figures

- *The population of Poland is approximately 39 million.*
- *The capital of Poland is Warsaw. It has a population of approximately two million people.*
- *Other large cities include Łódź, Katowice, Gdańsk, Wrocław, Poznań and Kraków.*
- *The main religion in Poland is Catholicism.*
- *The currency of Poland is the złoty.*
- *Poland has a system of social security.*
- *The State provides benefits for the unemployed and housing for people with low incomes.*
- *There is a public health care system.*
- *Education is compulsory until the age of 18.*
- *Men between the ages of 19 and 29 have to do one year's military service.*

Politics

	Poland	**Britain**	**US**
Political system	Democracy/Republic	Democracy/Constitutional Monarchy	Democracy/Republic
Parliamentary structure — lower house: — upper house:	 Sejm Senat	 House of Commons House of Lords	 House of Representatives Senate
General elections	every 4 years	every 5 years	Presidential elections: every 4 years House of Representatives and Senate elections: every 2 years (one third of senators are elected to the Senate every two years for a six-year term)
Leaders — head of state — head of government	 President Prime Minister	 Queen/King Prime Minister	 President President

Britain

General elections are held every five years in Britain. You are eligible to vote once you are 18. Voting in Britain is not compulsory.

There are three main political parties: **the Labour Party**, **the Conservative Party** and **the Liberal Democrats**.

There are two **Houses of Parliament**: **the House of Commons** and **the House of Lords**. Elections are held every five years to choose Members of Parliament (**MPs**) who will sit in the House of Commons. The members of the House of Lords are called **peers**. They are not elected. There are hereditary peers and life peers, who are appointed by the government. The Labour

Government of Tony Blair began reforming the House of Lords by phasing out hereditary peers. The issue of how future peers will be selected is still controversial.

The head of the government is the **Prime Minister**. Some other important politicians are: the **Chancellor of the Exchequer** (Minister Finansów/Skarbu), **the Home Secretary** (Minister Spraw Wewnętrznych), **the Foreign Secretary** (Minister Spraw Zagranicznych) and the Speaker (Marszałek) of the House of Commons. The most senior politicians in the government form **the Cabinet**.

The United States

The US system of government is divided between the federal and state governments as laid down in the US constitution. The federal government has three branches: the Legislative (władza ustawodawcza) (i.e. **Congress**), the Executive (władza wykonawcza) (led by the President), and the Judicial (władza sądowa) (i.e. the Supreme Court and other federal courts). Each state also has its own government.

The two main political parties in the United States are **the Democratic Party** and **the Republican Party**. The US parliament is called the **Congress** and is made up of **the House of Representatives** and **the Senate**.

The President is the Head of State and head of the executive branch of government. He decides US policy on foreign affairs and is the commander-in-chief of the armed forces.

Some other important politicians are the **Vice-President**, who is second in command and presides over the Senate, the **Secretary of State** (Minister Spraw Zagranicznych) and the Speaker of the House of Representatives.

The heads of government departments are called secretaries, with the exception of the head of the Justice Department, who is the **Attorney General**. Together the heads of departments make up **the Cabinet**.

Poland

- *The party currently in power is the ... Party.*
- *It is a left-wing/right-wing/centre-left/centre-right party.*
- *The main policies of the party are ...*
- *The government has a large/small majority.*
- *The ... Party has formed a coalition with the ... Party.*
- *Poland has a coalition government.*
- *The main opposition party is ...*
- *It has/holds X seats in parliament.*

Economy

- *Economic growth will be at the rate of 2% this year.*
- *The economy is growing/slowing.*
- *The economy is in recession.*
- *a strong/weak economy*
- *The rate of inflation is ...*
- *8% of the workforce is unemployed.*
- *The government intends to raise/lower taxes.*
- *The government plans to increase/reduce spending on health and education.*
- *the defence/transport/education budget*
- *a budget/trade deficit*

Industry and agriculture

- *The main industries in Poland are iron, copper, and ...*
- *It also manufactures machines and ..., and builds ships, ...*
- *Poland exports coal, ...*
- *Its exports include ham, ...*
- *Poland trades with the EU, ...*
- *The main crops are grain, ...*
- *Poland farms dairy cattle, sheep, pigs and poultry.*
- *Poland joined the European Union in 2004.*

The world around us

Climate

- *The climate in Poland is temperate.*
- *Some other types of climate are: continental, tropical, dry, wet, humid, mild.*
- *Poland is cold in winter and warm in summer.*
- *In January temperatures are usually below freezing.*
- *Summer temperatures are generally moderate/ warm/mild.*
- *The Polish climate is similar to/warmer than/ colder than the climate in Britain/Florida/ Alaska.*
- *This region gets a lot of snow/floods/strong winds/rain/storms.*
- *The climate in Poland is changing because of global warming. We have more droughts and flooding.*
- *We don't usually suffer from extreme weather like hurricanes.*

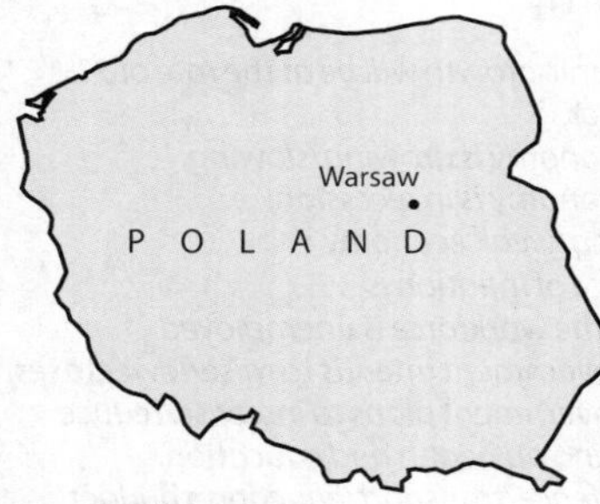

Geography

- *Poland has borders with the Russian Federation, Lithuania, Belarus, Ukraine, Slovakia, the Czech Republic and Germany.*
- *Poland is on the Baltic Sea.*
- *Two thirds of the country is flat/a plain.*
- *Forests cover about one quarter of the country.*
- *Most of the trees are evergreens.*
- *One of the common deciduous trees is the birch.*
- *In the south there are hills and mountains, including the Tatra and western Carpathian Mountains.*
- *The longest river in Poland is the Vistula. It is 678 miles long. It flows through Warsaw.*
- *Poland has almost 10 000 lakes.*

Nature

- *There are 22 national parks in Poland with a total area of about 300 000 hectares.*
- *In the national parks, you can go hiking, skiing, mountain climbing, canoeing and cycling.*
- *Poland also has areas of protected natural landscape.*
- *There are many wild animals in Poland, including deer, wild boar, beavers, elk and bears.*
- *European bison are a protected species in Poland.*
- *If we don't protect endangered species, they will die out/become extinct.*

Threats to the modern world

Threats to the environment

- *Natural disasters include: floods, droughts, earthquakes, cyclones, bush fires.*
- *The last major natural disaster in Poland was in … It was a …*
- *Many natural habitats were destroyed.*
- *People were killed/injured/lost their homes.*
- *Threats to the environment in Poland include: pollution, acid rain, global warming, the hole in the ozone layer, and deforestation.*
- *The Polish countryside/forest/wildlife is being harmed by …*
- *Air/water pollution is mainly caused by emissions from factories, …*
- *Farmers should use organic fertilizers instead of chemical ones.*
- *Organic farming is more eco-friendly.*
- *Genetic engineering is a good/bad thing because …*
- *GM crops produce a higher yield but can contaminate organic crops.*
- *We should use renewable sources of energy such as wind power and solar power.*
- *Soon there won't be any fossil fuels left to burn.*
- *Burning fossil fuels releases carbon dioxide into the atmosphere, which adds to global warming.*
- *I think international agreements on climate change are good/bad because …*
- *Burying rubbish in landfills is bad for the environment.*
- *We should use more biodegradable products that won't pollute the environment.*
- *We should recycle our rubbish.*

Threats to people's health

- *alcoholism*
- *drug-taking*
- *smoking*
- *dangerous driving*
- *Many people die of alcohol-related problems each year.*
- *Heavy drinking can lead to violence/car accidents.*
- *In Britain, you can legally buy alcohol when you are eighteen; in the US you have to be twenty-one. I think this is better/worse than the law in Poland because ...*
- *Smoking is bad for you because it can cause lung cancer and heart disease.*
- *Smoking should (not) be allowed in public places.*
- *to give up smoking*
- *to be a heavy smoker/a chain-smoker*
- *Drug addiction can harm people's health and ruin their lives.*
- *Swapping needles can spread diseases such as HIV.*
- *Drugs-related crimes include mugging/burglary/robbery.*
- *There are rehabilitation centres to help people overcome their addictions.*
- *Some of the reasons people take drugs are ...*
- *hard drugs such as heroin, cocaine, crack*
- *soft drugs such as marijuana and Ecstasy*
- *Dangerous driving is the cause of many deaths/injuries each year.*
- *Driving under the influence of alcohol/drink driving is especially dangerous.*
- *The speed limit on main roads/motorways/in towns is ...*
- *to break the speed limit*
- *to wear a seat belt/a helmet*

Threats to society

- *There is little/a lot of crime in my area/town/city.*
- *The most common type of crime is burglary/shoplifting/theft/violence/mugging/vandalism.*
- *The punishment for this crime is a fine/prison sentence.*
- *I think this is too lenient/severe because ...*
- *Acts of terrorism include bombing/hijacking/kidnapping/taking hostages.*
- *Some people think the decline of the traditional two-parent family is a negative influence on society.*
- *The increase in out-of-town superstores is bad for our towns.*

Science

- *Scientific advances over the last century mean we now know much more than our ancestors about ...*
- *In my opinion, the most important scientific discovery of the last century was ...*
- *Scientists are still looking for a cure for cancer/AIDS/Alzheimer's disease.*
- *They are doing research into the causes of ME.*
- *It is now possible to clone animals and humans.*
- *The computer and the Internet have revolutionized the way we live and work.*
- *Ethical questions relating to the use of science, e.g. in the areas of genetics, are being hotly debated.*
- *In the future there will be many new technologies that will change our lives.*
- *Change is happening so fast that it's hard to imagine the world in twenty years' time.*

Shopping

- *a clothes/furniture/hardware/shoe/souvenir, etc. shop*
- *a bookshop*
- *a baker's/butcher's/greengrocer's*
- *a chemist's/chemist shop/pharmacy*
- *a flower shop/florist's/flower stall*
- *a supermarket*
- *a superstore*
- *a clothes boutique*
- *a department store*
- *a garden centre*
- *a market*
- *a book/computer/ski, etc. fair*
- *a shopping arcade*
- *a shopping centre*
- *a (shopping) mall*

- *I usually shop at the market/supermarket.*
- *Take this prescription to the chemist's.*
- *Hello, can I help you?*
- *I'm just looking/browsing.*
- *I'm looking for ...*
- *This shirt is available in small/medium/large/ extra large.*
- *I'm a size 40.*
- *I take size 38 shoes.*
- *Do you have this in a different size/colour?*
- *Would you like to pay with cash or by credit card?*
- *There's a special offer on soap: two for the price of one/buy one, get one free.*
- *Oranges are on offer this week.*
- *Can I have a discount?*
- *This skirt is a bargain - it only costs £10.*
- *There's a sale at the department store.*

- *You can get up to 50% off.*
- *I'd like to exchange this shirt for a bigger size/ different colour.*
- *I'd like a refund.*
- *This dress is torn/stained/the wrong size.*
- *The zip is broken.*
- *There's a button missing.*
- *How much are cherries per pound/kilo?*
- *I'd like 500 grams/half a kilo/a pound of minced beef.*
- *Can I have ten rashers of bacon?*
- *Can I have a litre/pint of milk/a bag of flour/ potatoes/sugar?*
- *a bottle of water/beer/wine*
- *a box of cereal/tissues/washing powder*
- *a carton of cream/juice/milk*
- *a jar of coffee/honey/jam*
- *a packet of biscuits/crisps/spaghetti*
- *a tin/can of beans/peaches/tomatoes*
- *a tube of toothpaste/tomato purée*
- *a bar of soap/chocolate*
- *We had to queue at the checkout.*
- *The till was out of order.*

Services

- *Can I send this letter (by) airmail?*
- *How much is a stamp for the US?*
- *I'd like to send this letter/parcel/package to Paris.*
- *I need to send this first-class/second-class.*

ⓘ Zob. uwagę przy **first-class**[1] o kategoriach znaczków w Wielkiej Brytanii.

- *My watch is broken. Can you mend it?*
- *Could you have a look at my watch?*
- *I need a new strap/battery.*

- *I'd like this film developed in an hour/overnight.*
- *I'd like two sets of colour prints.*
- *Can I have this photo enlarged?*
- *Could you print off the photos on this CD, please?*
- *I need a passport photo.*

- *I'd like a haircut/a trim/a cut and blow-dry.*
- *Can you take about three centimetres off?*
- *I want a completely new style.*
- *I'd like a perm.*
- *I'd like highlights.*
- *A cut and blow-dry, please.*
- *I want my hair coloured.*
- *Do you want conditioner/hairspray/mousse on your hair?*

- *I'd like to report a crime.*
- *I've witnessed a robbery/a mugging/an accident.*
- *I'd like to make a statement.*
- *I've found a wallet and I'd like to hand it in.*
- *I've lost my purse. Has it been handed in here?*
- *The police arrested him for burglary.*
- *She was caught shoplifting.*
- *I was given an on-the-spot fine for a parking offence.*
- *The police patrol the streets at night.*

- *I'd like 100 black-and-white/colour copies, please.*
- *I want this picture enlarged.*
- *I'd like to fax this document to Germany.*
- *Could you do double-sided copies, please?*

- *I have a bank account at ... Bank.*
- *I bank with ... Bank/Building Society.*
- *I have an Internet account.*
- *I'd like to open/close an account.*
- *I want to open a current/deposit/savings account.*
- *I have a joint account with my wife/husband.*
- *I'd like to deposit/withdraw £100, please.*
- *Can you tell me my balance?*
- *I'd like to make a transfer to another account.*
- *I need a new chequebook.*
- *I've lost my debit/credit card.*
- *I'd like a statement, please.*
- *What's the rate of interest on a savings account?*
- *I'd like to arrange a mortgage/loan.*
- *I have an overdraft of £100.*
- *I have to pay back my overdraft.*
- *My account is in credit/is overdrawn.*

Travel

Holidays

- *Every summer I go on holiday with my family/ friends.*
- *The summer holidays start in July and go on till September.*
- *I get fifteen days' holiday a year.*
- *My annual leave is fifteen days.*
- *We usually go abroad/stay in Poland/go to the seaside/go to the mountains.*
- *We go by bus/car/coach/ferry/plane/train.*
- *I like beach/cycling/skiing/walking holidays.*
- *I enjoy camping.*
- *I'd like to go on a cruise.*
- *We usually stay in a hotel/hostel/guest house/ bed and breakfast.*
- *We normally stay at a campsite.*
- *I want to go backpacking around Europe/in the Far East.*

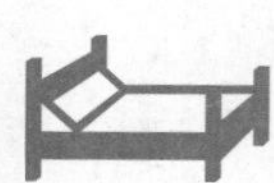

Booking a holiday

- *We normally book our holiday through a travel agent.*
- *I'm looking for a package holiday/an all-inclusive holiday.*
- *I'd like to book a flight to London.*
- *Can you tell me the single/return air fare to Paris?*
- *How much is an adult/child/student ticket?*
- *I'd like an economy/a business/a first-class seat.*
- *a long-haul flight with a stopover in Hong Kong*
- *I'd like to book a sleeper on the overnight train to Istanbul.*
- *Can I confirm my reservation, please?*
- *a one-star/two-star/five-star,* etc. *hotel*
- *I'd like a double/twin/single room with an en suite bathroom.*
- *Does the room have a sea/mountain view?*

Getting there

- *At the airport, first you queue up to check in.*
- *You need your passport and ticket.*
- *I always ask for an aisle/window seat.*
- *You are given a boarding card.*
- *Then you go into the departure lounge.*
- *There you can sometimes buy duty-free goods such as alcohol and perfume.*
- *Next you go to the departure gate and board the plane.*
- *During the flight, there may be in-flight entertainment such as radio, films and TV programmes.*
- *The flight attendants serve you a meal and sell duty-free goods.*
- *If there is turbulence, you have to fasten your seat belt.*
- *When you arrive at your destination, you go through passport control.*
- *Then you collect your luggage from the carousel in the baggage hall and go through customs.*
- *When you get into the arrivals hall, a holiday rep may greet you and take you to your hotel.*
- *At the hotel, you check in at reception.*
- *Then you can go to your room and unpack (your suitcase).*
- *It is a good idea to have travel insurance to cover accidents or lost luggage.*

At your holiday destination

- *Excuse me, can you tell me the way to the tourist office?*
- *I need to change some money.*
- *Can you tell me the exchange rate?*
- *I'd like a street map of the city, please.*
- *Do you have a train timetable?*
- *Can you tell me what time the next bus to the town centre leaves?*
- *Can you give me some information on excursions?*
- *Can you recommend any museums/ monuments/churches/historical sites we could visit?*
- *Where can I hire a car/motorbike/bike?*
- *Do you sell postcards and stamps?*
- *On holiday, I like to relax on the beach/go sightseeing/go swimming/go snorkelling/ visit museums.*

- *I always send postcards to my friends/buy souvenirs/take lots of photos.*
- *It's fun to try the local food/dishes/delicacies.*
- *Some traditional British foods are roast beef and Yorkshire pudding, fish and chips, Cornish pasties, steak and kidney pie, and haggis.*
- *Some traditional American foods are hot dogs, hamburgers and pecan pie.*

Culture

The Arts

- *to go to the cinema/theatre/opera/ballet*
- *to go to see a film/a play/an opera/a ballet*
- *to go to a concert/a show/a musical/an exhibition*
- *There are lots of shows and musicals in the West End of London.*
- *If I go to New York, I'd like to see a show on Broadway.*
- *a theatre/an opera/a ballet company*
- *U2 is/are currently touring the country.*
- *Our band is/are doing a gig at the local pub on Saturday.*
- *Is this film out on DVD yet?*
- *Tickets for the play are available at the box office.*

- *I'd like to book tickets for next Saturday's performance of 'Chicago'.*
- *I'd like to reserve two seats for the 5 o'clock showing of the latest Harry Potter film.*
- *My favourite writer/actor/singer/band/ composer/artist is ...*
- *What kind of music do you like?*
- *I like classical music/jazz/pop/rock.*
- *I read a lot of fiction/non-fiction/historical novels/romances/detective stories/science fiction/poetry/comics.*
- *I play the guitar/violin/saxophone.*
- *I go to dancing/drawing classes.*
- *I write poetry.*
- *I'm a member of the local drama club.*

Festivals and celebrations

In Britain

- **Valentine's Day** *(14th February)* People send cards and gifts to people they love.
- **Shrove Tuesday** *(the last day before Lent)* People eat pancakes.
- **Good Friday** *(March or April)* People eat hot cross buns.
- **Easter** *(March or April)* Christians celebrate Christ's resurrection. People give each other Easter eggs. Some children believe the Easter Bunny brings Easter eggs.

- **April Fool's Day** *(1st April)* Before noon, people play tricks on each other.
- **May Day** *(1st May)* In the past there was a tradition of dancing around a tall pole with ribbons (a May Pole) to celebrate the spring.
- **Halloween** *(31st October)* Children dress up as witches, ghosts, monsters, etc. and go to people's houses and say 'Trick or treat'. If the people do not give them sweets, the children play tricks on them.
- **Bonfire Night** *(5th November)* People light big fires, let off fireworks and burn a model of a man, called a guy, to celebrate the failure of Guy Fawkes to blow up the Houses of Parliament in the 17th century.
- **Christmas** *(25th December)* Christians celebrate the birth of Christ. People give each other gifts and eat a special meal of roast turkey and Christmas pudding.

- **New Year's Eve** *(31st December)* People go to parties with friends and family. In Scotland this day is called **Hogmanay**. Chinese New Year is an important and festive time for the Chinese community. In 2007 it was on 18th February.

In the United States

- **Valentine's Day** jak wyżej
- **Easter** jak wyżej
- **Independence Day** *(4th July)* People celebrate the anniversary of the day in 1776 when America declared itself independent from Britain.
- **Halloween** jak wyżej

- **Thanksgiving** *(4th Thursday in November)* This celebration is associated with the time Europeans first came to North America. They arrived at the beginning of a very hard winter. The original thanksgiving celebration was to thank God and the native Americans for the fact that they had survived. People celebrate with a special meal of roast turkey and pumpkin pie.
- **Christmas** jak wyżej
- **New Year's Eve** jak wyżej

ℹ Zob. też **Ramadan**, **Passover** i **Diwali**.

Strona polsko-angielska

A

a 1 (**A/a**) (*litera*) A, a **2** (**A/a**) (*muz.*) A **3** and, but[1], whereas IDM **~ ty/on itp.?** how/what about…?
abażur lampshade, shade[1]
abdykacja abdication
abdykować abdicate
abecadło ABC
abonament: (*telefoniczny/telewizyjny*) rental
abonent/ka subscriber
aborcj|a abortion; **dokonać ~i** abort
aborygen/ka Aboriginal
abrakadabra abracadabra
absencja absenteeism
absolutnie absolutely IDM **~ nie!** no way
absolutny absolute
absolwent/ka: **~ szkoły średniej** school-leaver; **~ studiów wyższych (licencjackich)** graduate[1]
absorbować/za- absorb, engross, preoccupy, stimulate
abstrahować/wy- digress
abstrakcja abstraction
abstrakcyjn|y abstract[1], theoretical; **pojęcie ~e** abstraction
abstrakt abstract[2]
abstynencj|a abstinence; **praktykujący ~ę** abstinent
abstynent/ka teetotaller; **jest abstynentem** he is teetotal
absurd absurdity, nonsense
absurdalny absurd, ludicrous, nonsensical, preposterous, ridiculous, surreal
aby in order to do sth
ach: **~!** ah
aczkolwiek albeit, although
adaptacja adaptation, dramatization
adapter 1 (*urządzenie*) adaptor **2** (*do odtwarzania płyt*) record player
adaptować/za- adapt, dramatize
adekwatność adequacy
adenoid (*anat.*) adenoids
adept/ka exponent
adidas trainer
adiustator/ka copy editor
adiustować/z- (*tekst do druku*) copy-edit
administracja administration; **~ państwowa** the civil service; (*studia*) **zarządzanie i ~** business studies
administracyjny administrative
administrator/ka (*czyichś pieniędzy, majątku*) trustee
admirał admiral
adnotacj|a annotation, note[1]; **opatrywać ~ami** annotate; **z ~ami** annotated
adopcja adoption
adoptować/za- adopt
adoracja adoration
adrenalina adrenalin
adres address[1]; **~ e-mail** email address[1]; **nowy ~** forwarding address; **na ~ kogoś** c/o
adresat/ka addressee
adresować/za- address[2]
adwent advent
adwokat advocate[2], barrister, counsel[1], lawyer, solicitor; **~ diabła** devil's advocate
aerobik aerobics
aerodynamiczny aerodynamic
aerodynamika aerodynamics
aerozol aerosol
afektacj|a affectation, pose[2]; **bez ~i** unaffected
afektowany affected
afiks affix[1]
afisz placard, poster; **ta sztuka nie schodzi z ~a od ponad dwudziestu lat** that play has had a run of more than twenty years
afiszować się: **czymś** flaunt
aflaston figurehead
aforystyczny aphoristic
aforyzm aphorism
Afroameryka-nin/nka African American
afroamerykański African American adj.
afrodyzjak aphrodisiac
Afrokaraib/ka Afro-Caribbean
afrokaraibski Afro-Caribbean adj.
afront affront, insult[2], snub noun; **robić komuś ~** snub[1]
agat agate
agencja agency
agent/ka agent, tail[1]; **agent sprzedaży nieruchomości** estate agent; **podwójny agent** double agent
agitacja agitation
agitować/za- agitate
agnostyczny agnostic adj.
agnosty-k/czka agnostic
agonia agony
agrafka safety pin
agresja aggression, aggro
agresor aggressor
agrest gooseberry
agresywn|y aggressive, belligerent, offensive[1], violent; **~e zachowanie** aggro; **~y atak** broadside
aha: **~!** aha, oh, oh, I see
AIDS AIDS
Ais/ais A sharp
akademia academy; **~ medyczna** medical school; **~ sztuk pięknych** art college
akademicki academic[1]
akademik hall of residence
akapit paragraph
akcent 1 (*na sylabę*) accent, stress[1] **2** (*znak*) accent, diacritic **3** (*wymowa*) accent; **z obcym ~em** accented **4** (*dodatek*) touch[2]
akcentować/za- accentuate, stress[2]
akcentowany accented
akceptacja acceptance, assent
akceptować/za- accept, come to terms with sth
akcesoria: **wyposażać w dodatkowe ~** accessorize
akcj|a 1 (*działanie*) action, operation; **przeciw czemuś** blitz; **~a odwetowa** reprisal; **~a wojenna** warfare; **film ~i** action movie **2** (*fabuła*) plot[1] **3** (*fin.*) share[2]; **~e nieuprzywilejowane** (*przynoszące dywidendę*) equity
akcjonariusz/ka shareholder
akcyza excise
aklimatyzacja acclimatization
aklimatyzować/za- (się) acclimatize
akompaniament accompaniment
akompaniator/ka accompanist
akompaniować accompany
akord (*muz.*) chord
akordeon accordion
akr acre
akredytacja accreditation
akredytowany accredited
akrobat-a/ka acrobat
akrobatyczny acrobatic
akrobatyka acrobatics
akrylowy acrylic
aksamit velvet
aksamitny 1 (*tkanina*) velvet **2** (*sos itp.*) creamy **3** (*dźwięk*) mellow
aksjomat axiom
akt 1 (*czyn, prawn., teatr*) act[1] **2** (*dokument*) **~ kupna/sprzedaży** bill of sale; **~ własności** deed **3** (*sztuka*) nude[2]
akta file[1] IDM **w ~ch** on file
aktor/ka actor, player; (**aktorka**) actress
aktówka attaché case, briefcase, portfolio
aktualizacja update noun
aktualizować/z- update
aktualnoś|ć (**aktualności**) current affairs
aktualn|y current[1], present[1], up to date, up to the minute; (*wiadomości*) topical; **być ~ym** hold[1]; **~y mistrz świata** the reigning world champion; **czy spotkanie jest nadal ~e?** is the meeting still on?
aktyw hard core
aktywa asset
aktywist-a/ka activist
aktywny active
akumulator battery
akupunktura acupuncture
akustyczn|y acoustic; **warunki ~e** acoustics
akustyka acoustics
akuszerka midwife
akuszerstwo midwifery
akwaforta etching
akwamaryna (*kamień; kolor*) aquamarine
akwarela watercolour
akwarium aquarium
akwedukt aqueduct
alarm alarm[1], alert[3]; **~ bombowy/ ~ o podłożonej bombie** bomb scare; **~ pożarowy** fire alarm; **~ przeciwwłamaniowy** burglar alarm; **próbny ~** drill[1]
alarmist-a/ka alarmist
alarmistyczny alarmist
alarmować/za- alarm[2]
albatros albatross
albedo pith
albinos/ka albino
albo or, or else; **~…, ~** either… or…
album album; (*na wycinki prasowe itp.*) scrapbook
ale anyway, but[1], yet
alegoria allegory
alegoryczny allegorical
aleja avenue, boulevard
alejka lane
alergen allergen
alergia allergy
alergiczny allergic
alfabet ABC, alphabet; **~ łaciński** the Roman alphabet
alfabetyczny alphabetical
alfons pimp, ponce[1]
alga algae
algebra algebra
aliant ally[1]
alias aka, alias[1]
alibi alibi
aligator alligator
alimenty alimony, maintenance
aliteracja alliteration

alkaliczny alkaline
alkohol alcohol, drink[1]; ~ **etylowy** ethanol; ~ **metylowy** methylated spirit; **ma problem z ~em** he's got a drink problem
alkoholi-k/czka alcoholic[2]
alkoholizm alcoholism
alkoholowy alcoholic[1]
alkomat breathalyser
alkowa alcove
Allach (także **Allah**) Allah
aloes aloe vera
alpejski alpine
alpinist-a/ka climber, mountaineer
alpinizm climbing, mountaineering
alt alto
alternatywa alternative[1], option
alternatywn|y alternative[2]; **medycyna ~a** alternative medicine
altówka viola
altruistyczny altruistic, selfless
altruizm altruism
aluminiowy aluminium
aluminium aluminium
aluzj|a allusion, hint[1]; **robić ~ę** hint[2]
amalgamat (*zwł. dentystyczny*) amalgam
amator/ka amateur[1]; **fotograf amator** amateur photographer
amatorski amateur[2]
amazonka horsewoman
ambasada embassy
ambasador/ka ambassador
ambicja 1 (*chęć awansu*) ambition **2** (*duma*) pride[1], self-respect
ambitny ambitious
ambiwalencja ambivalence
ambiwalentny ambivalent
ambona pulpit
ambulans ambulance
ambulatoryjny: **pacjent** ~ outpatient
ameba amoeba
amen amen
Amerykan-in/ka American noun
amerykanizować/z- Americanize
amerykański American
ametyst amethyst
amfetamina amphetamine
amfibiotyczny amphibious
amfila|da: **dwa pokoje w ~dzie** two rooms with a communicating door
amfiteatr amphitheatre
aminokwas amino acid
amnestia amnesty, pardon[2]
amnezja amnesia
amniocenteza amniocentesis
amok IDM **wpaść w ~** run amok
amoniak ammonia
amoralny amoral
amortyzować/z- absorb, cushion[2]
amper amp
amputować amputate
amulet charm[1]
amunicja ammunition, munitions
anabolik anabolic steroid
anachroniczny anachronistic
anachronizm anachronism
anagram anagram
analfabet-a/ka illiterate
analfabetyzm illiteracy
analityczny analytical
analityk analyst; ~ **systemów** systems analyst
analiz|a analysis, breakdown; **robić ~ę** analyse; **przeprowadzić gruntowną ~ę** overhaul
analizować/z-/prze- analyse, examine, survey[2]
analny anal
analogi|a analogy, parallel[2] IDM **przez ~ę** by analogy
analogiczny analogous, corresponding, parallel[1]
analogowy analogue
ananas pineapple
ananasowy pineapple
anarchia anarchy
anarchiczny anarchic
anarchist-a/ka anarchist
anarchizm anarchism
anatomia anatomy
anatomiczny anatomical
anchois anchovy
androgeniczny androgynous
android android
anegdota anecdote
aneksja annexation
anektować/za- annex
anemia anaemia
anemiczny anaemic
anestezjolog anaesthetist
angaż (*artysty/pisarza*) residency
angażować/za- 1 (*wciągać*) engage, involve; **zaangażować się w coś** get into sth **2** (*zatrudniać*) engage sb (as sth)
□ **angażować /za- się: (w coś)** commit yourself (on sth); **nie angażujący się** non-committal
Angielka Englishwoman; → zob. też ANGLIK
angielski 1 English[2]; **język** ~ English[1] **2** (*system miar*) imperial
angielsko- Anglo-
angielszczyć/z- Anglicize
angina tonsillitis
Anglik Englishman; **Anglicy** the English[1]
anglikański Anglican adj.; **Kościół** ~ the Church of England
anglistyka English[1]
anglofon anglophone
anglojęzyczny anglophone
Anglosas/ka Anglo-Saxon
anglosaski Anglo-Saxon adj.
angora (*koza/królik, wełna*) angora
ani neither, nor, or; **~..., ~ (też)...** neither...nor...; ~ **ja** I can't either; ~ **słowa** not a (single) word
IDM **~ trochę** (not) at all, no adv., not a bit, not in the slightest
anielski angelic
animacja: ~ **filmowa** animation
animator/ka (*film*) animator
animowany animated
animozja bad/ill feeling
animusz spirit[1], zest; **dodawać ~u** perk sb/sth up; **odzyskiwać** ~ perk up; **pełen ~u** breezy, bright
anioł angel
aniołek cherub
ankieta survey[1]
anomalia anomaly
anonimowy anon., anonymous, faceless, nameless
anoreksj|a anorexia; **chory na ~ę** anorexic
anorekty-k/czka anorexic
anormalny abnormal
antagonizm antagonism
antagonizować/z- antagonize
antałek keg
antarktyczny Antarctic
Antarktyka Antarctic noun
antena aerial[1]; ~ **satelitarna** satellite dish
antenat/ka ancestor; **(antenaci)** ancestry
antidotum antidote
antologia anthology, collection
antonim antonym, opposite
antrakt interlude, intermission, interval
antropolog anthropologist
antropologia anthropology
antropologiczny anthropological
anty- anti-
antybiotyk antibiotic
antybohater anti-hero
antyczny antique
antyhistamina antihistamine
antyk 1 (*zabytkowy przedmiot*) antique noun **2** (*grecki, rzymski*) antiquity
antykoncepcja contraception
antykoncepcyjny contraceptive adj.
Antyl-czyk/ka West Indian
Antyle the West Indies
antylopa antelope
antylski West Indian adj.
antypatia antipathy
antysemicki anti-Semitic
antysemityzm anti-Semitism
antyseptyczny antiseptic adj.; **środek** ~ antiseptic
antyterrorystyczny counter-terrorist
antyterroryzm counter-terrorism
antyteza antithesis
anulować annul, revoke
anyż (także **anyżek**) aniseed
aorta aorta
aparat instrument; ~ **fotograficzny** camera; ~ **ortodontyczny** brace[1]; ~ **słuchowy** hearing aid
apartament apartment; (*w hotelu*) suite
apaszka scarf
apatia apathy
apatyczny apathetic, listless
apel appeal[1], plea; ~ **w szkole** school assembly
apelacja appeal[1]
apelować/za- appeal[2]
aperitif aperitif
apetyczny appetizing
apetyt appetite
aplauz applause, ovation
aplet applet
aplikator applicator
apodyktyczny authoritarian, bossy, overbearing
apogeum crescendo
apokaliptyczny apocalyptic
apolityczny apolitical
apologet-a/ka apologist
apologetyczny apologetic
apostoł apostle
apostrof apostrophe
aprobat|a approval, endorsement; **z ~ą** approvingly
aprobować/za- approve, condone; (*oficjalnie*) authorize; (*tolerować*) countenance[2]; **nie** ~ disapprove
aprobujący approving
à propos apropos, BTW, incidentally
aprowizacja provision
apteczka: ~ **pierwszej pomocy** first-aid kit
apteka chemist's, pharmacy
apteka-rz/rka chemist
Arab/ka Arab
arabski Arab adj.; **język** ~ Arabic
aranżacja arrangement, orchestration

aranżer/ka (*muz.*) arranger
aranżować/za- 1 (*dla orkiestry*) orchestrate **2** (*organizować*) orchestrate; ~ **w tajemnicy** engineer[2]
arbiter arbiter, judge[1]; (*sport*) referee
arbitralny arbitrary
arbitraż arbitration; **komisja ~u przemysłowego** industrial tribunal
arbuz watermelon
archaiczny archaic
archeolog archaeologist
archeologia archaeology
archeologiczny archaeological
archetypowy archetypal
architekt architect; ~ **krajobrazu** landscape architect; ~ **wnętrz** interior designer
architektoniczny architectural
architektura architecture; ~ **krajobrazu** landscape architecture
archiwaln|y: **materiały ~e** archive material
archiwist-a/ka archivist
archiwizować/z- archive[2]
archiwum archive[1], file[1] IDM **w ~** on file
arcybiskup archbishop
arcydzieło masterpiece
arena 1 arena, ring[1] **2** (*przen.*) scene
areszt custody, detention, remand; ~ **domowy** house arrest
aresztant/ka remand prisoner
aresztować/za- apprehend, arrest[1], nick[2]; **zostać aresztowanym** be under arrest
argument argument, contention, point[1]; (**argumenty**) case
argumentować/za- argue; (*uzasadnić*) rationalize
aria aria
arktyczny Arctic
Arktyka Arctic noun
arkusz (*papieru; blachy itp.*) sheet; (*metalu itp.*) plate; ~ **kalkulacyjny** spreadsheet; ~ **z pytaniami egzaminacyjnymi** question paper
armata cannon
armia army
arogancja arrogance, cockiness
arogancki arrogant, cocky
aromat aroma, fragrance, perfume, scent
aromaterapia aromatherapy
aromatyczny aromatic, fragrant
aromatyzowany scented
arras tapestry
arsenał armoury, arsenal; ~ **broni** stockpile noun
arszenik arsenic
artefakt artefact
artretyczny arthritic
artretyzm arthritis
artykulacja articulation
artykuł 1 item; ~ **żywnościowy** foodstuff; **~y piśmienne** writing materials; **~y spożywcze** grocery **2** (*w gazecie*) article, feature[1], piece[1]; ~ **wstępny** editorial
artykułować: **wyraźnie** ~ enunciate
artyleria artillery
artyst-a/ka artist; ~ **estradow-y/a** artiste, performer
artystyczny artistic; (*często w sposób pretensjonalny*) arty
arystokracja aristocracy, nobility
arystokrata aristocrat, noble[2]
arystokratyczny aristocratic, noble[1]
arytmetyka arithmetic, figure[1]
As/as A flat
as ace
ascetyczny austere
aseksualny asexual
asekuracja insurance, safety net
asekurować/za- się hedge your bets
asfalt asphalt
asfaltować/wy-: ~ **drogę** surface a road with tarmac
asortyment choice[1], selection
aspekt aspect, dimension, facet; **musimy rozważyć ten problem we wszystkich ~ach** we must consider the problem in its entirety
aspiracj|a aspiration; **mieć ~e (do czegoś)** aspire to sth/to do sth
aspiryna aspirin
aspołeczny antisocial
asteroida asteroid
astma asthma
astmatyczny asthmatic adj.
astmaty-k/czka asthmatic
astrolog astrologer
astrologia astrology
astronaut-a/ka astronaut
astronom astronomer
astronomia astronomy
astronomiczny astronomical
astygmatyzm astigmatism
asygnować/wy- allocate, allot; ~ **fundusze** budget[2]; **wyasygnowane fundusze/środki** appropriation
asymetria asymmetry
asymetryczny asymmetric
asymilacja assimilation, osmosis
asymilować/z- (się) assimilate (sb/sth) (into sth)
asystent/ka assistant
atak 1 (*wojsk.*) attack[1], offensive[2], onslaught; (*z użyciem noża itp.*) stabbing[1]; (*zwł. lotniczy*) strike[2]; ~ **na kogoś/coś** attempt[1] (on sb/sth); **szybki** ~ blitz; ~ **z zasadzki/zaskoczenia/znienacka** ambush **2** (*krytyka*) attack[1] **3** (*sport*) attack[1] **4** (*med.*) attack[1], fit[3], seizure; (*drgawek*) fit[3]; (*grypy itp.*) bout, dose; ~ **serca** heart attack
atakować/za- assail, assault verb, attack[2], hit out (at sb/sth), be on the offensive, set on/upon sb, strike[1]; (*insekty, inne szkodniki*) infest; **być atakowanym** be under attack
ateist-a/ka atheist
ateizm atheism
atelier studio
atlas atlas
atłas satin
atłasowy satin
atmosfer|a air[1], ambience, atmosphere, aura, climate, mood, vibes; (*zebrania itp.*) tone[1]; **to miasto ma przyjazną ~ę** the town has a friendly feel
atmosferyczny atmospheric
atom atom
atomowy atomic, nuclear
atonalny atonal
atrakcja attraction
atrakcyjny attractive, desirable, enticing, glamorous, handsome; (*tylko o osobie*) fetching, pretty; (*propozycja itp.*) **mało** ~ unattractive
atrament ink; **czarny jak** ~ inky
atrapa dummy
atrofia atrophy
atut 1 trump **2** (*przen.*) trump card IDM **mieć wszystkie ~y** have a lot going for you
audiencja audience
audiowizualny audio-visual
audycja broadcast noun, edition, programme[1]
audytorium auditorium
aukcja auction[1]
aukcjoner auctioneer
aura 1 weather[1] **2** ~ **tajemniczości** mystique
aureola halo
auspicj|e IDM **pod ~ami kogoś/czegoś** under the auspices of sb/sth
Australazja Australasia
Australia Australia, down under
Australij-czyk/ka Australian, Aussie
australijski Australian, Aussie
aut out[1], out adj.
autentyczny authentic, bona fide, genuine, real[1], true; (*pierwotny*) original[1]
■ **autentycznoś|ć** authenticity; **brak autentyczności** inauthenticity; **potwierdzać autentyczność** authenticate
autentyk the real thing
autobiografia autobiography
autobiograficzny autobiographical
autobus bus; ~ **jednopiętrowy** single-decker; ~ **piętrowy** double-decker; **~em** by bus/road
autograf autograph; **składać** ~ autograph verb
autoimmunologiczny autoimmune
autokar coach[1]
autokracja autocracy
autokrata autocrat
autokratyczny autocratic
automat 1 dispenser; (*z napojami itp.*) vending machine; ~ **na monety** (*do gry, sprzedający napoje itp.*) slot machine; ~ **telefoniczny** payphone, public telephone; ~ **telefoniczny na kartę** cardphone; ~ **z chłodzoną wodą** water cooler **2** (*i osoba*) automaton, robot
automatyczn|y automatic[1], mindless; **urządzenie ~e** automatic[2]; **~a sekretarka** answering machine; **samochód z ~ą skrzynią biegów** automatic[2]
■ **automatycznie** automatically, (all) by itself
automatyzacja automation
automatyzować/z- automate
autonomia autonomy
autonomiczny autonomous
autoportret self-portrait
autopsja autopsy, post-mortem
autor/ka author; **autor tekstów piosenek** lyricist; **autor/ka scenariuszy** scriptwriter
autorski (*film*) art-house
autorstwo authorship
autorytatywny authoritative
■ **autorytatywnie** conclusively
autorytet authority
autostop: **podróżować ~em** hitch[1], hitchhike
autostopowicz/ka hitchhiker
autostrada highway, motorway
autow|y: **linia ~a** sideline
autsajder outsider
autystyczny autistic
autyzm autism
awangarda the avant-garde

awangardowy avant-garde adj. IDM **zbyt** ~ ahead of your time
awans advancement, promotion, rise[1]
awansować 1 (*dostać awans*) rise[2] **2** (*dać awans*) promote sb (from sth) (to sth)
awantur|a 1 (*burda*) row[3], wrangle; **robić (komuś) ~ę** let fly (at sb) **2** (*głośne wyrażanie dezaprobaty/gniewu*) fuss[1], scene; **zrobić ~ę (o coś)** make/kick up a fuss (about/over sth) **3** (*zamieszki*) disturbance, uproar
awanturniczy rowdy, unruly
awanturować się brawl verb, wrangle verb
awaria breakdown, crash[1], emergency, failure, malfunction
awaryjn|y standby adj.; **lądowanie ~e** crash landing
awersja aversion, dislike[2]
awiacja aviation
awokado avocado
azbest asbestos
Azjat-a/ka Asian
azjatycki Asian adj.
azot nitrogen
azyl refuge, retreat[2], sanctuary; ~ **polityczny** (political) asylum; **ubiegając-y/a się o** ~ asylum seeker
aż: **(~) tak** that, this adv.; ~ **po kogoś/coś** down[1] to sb/sth; ~ (*do czasu*) until IDM ~ **do** (*pewnej sumy/liczby*) up to sth, through, until prep.

B

b 1 (**B/b**) (*litera*) B, b **2** (**B/b**) (*muz.*) B flat
baba IDM **~ z wozu, koniom lżej!** good riddance (to sb/sth) | **~-jaga** witch
babcia gran, grandma
babka 1 grandmother, grandparent **2 niezła** ~ chick
babski: ~ **wieczór** hen party
babsztyl cow
babunia gran, grandma
bachor brat
baczki sideburns
bacznoś|ć attention[1]; **stanąć na ~ć** snap to attention; **(mieć się) na ~ci** beware (of sb/sth), look out (for sb/sth), (be) off/on (your) guard, on the alert (for sth); **zawsze mieć się na ~ci** never let your guard drop
baczny intent[1], watchful
baczyć watch[1]; **nie bacząc na deszcz, wyszła na ulicę** she braved the rain and went out into the street
bać się be afraid, get/have cold feet, fear[2], fear for sb/sth, be fearful, be frightened, be scared; ~ **pomyśleć** dread to think
badacz/ka investigator; (*naukowy*) researcher; (*odkrywca*) explorer
badać/z- 1 (*sprawdzić*) enquire into sth, examine, explore, inspect, investigate, look into sth, probe[1] (into sth), survey[2]; (*wzrokiem*) scan; ~ **szczegółowo** scrutinize; **gruntownie zbadać** overhaul; ~ **opinie** canvass, poll[2] **2** (*krew itp.*) test[2]; ~ **sondą** probe[1]
badanie 1 (*sprawdzenie*) examination, exploration, investigation; ~ **drobiazgowe** going-over; ~ **samochodu** road test; ~ **szczegółowe** scrutiny **2** (**badania**) (*naukowe*) research, study[1]; **badania w terenie** fieldwork **3** (*sonda*) survey[1]; ~ **opinii publicznej** poll[1]; ~ **rynku** market research; **dział badań i rozwoju** research and development **4** (*krwi itp.*) test[1]; ~ **lekarskie** check-up, medical[2]; ~ **cytologiczne** (*szyjki macicy*) smear test; ~ **ultrasonograficzne** ultrasound scan, scan noun
badawczy exploratory, investigative; (*pytanie*) probing; (*spojrzenie*) enquiring
badminton badminton
badziewie crap
bagatela trifle
bagatelizować/z- belittle, denigrate
bagaż baggage, luggage; ~ **podręczny** hand luggage; **podróżować bez ciężkiego/dużego ~u** travel light[4]
bagażnik boot[1]; ~ **dachowy** rack, roof rack
bagażowy (*osoba*) porter; (*na lotnisku*) baggage handler
bagietka baguette, French bread
bagnet bayonet
bagnisty boggy, marshy
bagno bog, marsh, swamp[1]
bagrować dredge
bajda tale
bajeczny untold
bajgiel bagel
bajka fairy story/tale; (*Ezopa itp.*) fable
bajt byte
bakalie: **rodzaj farszu bakaliowego** mincemeat; **babeczka z kruchego ciasta z nadzieniem bakaliowym** mince pie
bakałarz: ~ **nauk humanistycznych** BA; ~ **nauk pedagogicznych** BEd; ~ **nauk ścisłych** BSc
bakcyl germ; **zarazili się ~em golfa** they've been bitten by the golf bug
baki sideburns, whiskers
bakier: **na** ~ at an angle
bakłażan aubergine
bakterie bacteria
bal ball, dance[1]
balanga do[3]
balast ballast
baldachim canopy
balerina ballerina
balet ballet
baletka ballet pump
baletnica ballet dancer, dancer
baletowy balletic
balia tub
balkon 1 balcony **2** (*teatr*) circle[1]; **najwyższy** ~ gallery; **pierwszy** ~ dress circle
ballada ballad
balon balloon IDM **robić z kogoś ~a** pull sb's leg
balonik balloon
balow|y: **suknia ~a** ball gown
balsa balsa wood
balsam balm
balsamist-a/ka embalmer
balsamować/za- embalm
balustrada balustrade, banister, handrail, rail
bałagan disorder, mess[1]; **robić** ~ mess sth up; **w twoim pokoju jest okropny** ~ your room's in a terrible muddle
bałaganić/na- mess[2], mess sth up
bałtycki Baltic
bałwan dummy, twit; ~ **śniegowy** snowman
bambus bamboo
bambusowy bamboo
banalny banal, commonplace, tame[1], trite
banał banality, cliché
banan banana
bananowy banana
banda band, gang[1], pack[2], ring[1]
bandana bandanna
bandaż bandage
bandażować/za- bandage verb
bandyta bandit, gangster
bandzior villain
banicj|a: **skazywać na ~ę** banish
banita outlaw[2]
banjo banjo
bank bank[1]; (*pula, zbiórka*) kitty; ~ **specjalizujący się w inwestycjach przemysłowych** merchant bank; ~ **danych** databank; ~ **krwi** blood bank
bankier banker
bankiet banquet, dinner
banknot bill[1], note[1]
bankomat cash machine; (*w banku*) cash dispenser
bankowość banking; ~ **internetowa** e-cash
bankructw|o bankruptcy; **doprowadzać do ~a** bankrupt verb
bankrutować/z- go bankrupt, collapse[1], crash[2], fold[1]
bańka bubble[1]
baptyst-a/ka Baptist; (*Kościół*) **baptystów** Baptist adj.
baptystyczny Baptist adj.
bar bar[1], pub; ~ **hotelowy** lounge bar; ~ **kawowy** coffee bar; ~ **sałatkowy** salad bar; ~ **szybkiej obsługi** fast-food restaurant, snack bar
baran 1 ram[2] **2** (**Baran**) (*znak zodiaku*) Aries IDM (*nosić*) **na ~a** piggyback
baranek lamb; **sztuczny** ~ fleece[1]
barani mutton
baranina mutton
baraszkować frolic, romp
barbaryzm barbarism
barbarzyńca barbarian
barbarzyński barbaric, barbarous
barbarzyństwo barbarism, barbarity
barbituran barbiturate
barczyst|y: **~e ramiona** square shoulders
bardziej more[2] IDM **a tym** ~ let alone | **coraz** ~ more and more
bardzo ever so/ever such (a), most[2], much[2], really, terribly, very, well[1]; (*nieform.*) dead[3], jolly adv., mighty[2], real[2]; (*chcieć, potrzebować itp.*) badly; (*znany itp.*) widely; (*oceniać*) highly; (*kochać itp.*) dearly; (*tęsknić itp.*) sorely; (*rozgrzać itp.*) nicely; (*podekcytowany itp.*) all[2]; (*wściekły itp.*) positively; **nie (tak/za)** ~ not all that…, scarcely; ~ **mocno/ciężko/szybko itp.** like anything
bariera 1 (*płotek*) barrier, crash barrier **2** (*poręcz*) handrail **3** (*przeszkoda; przen.*) barrier (to sth), discouragement
bark shoulder[1]; **brać na swe ~i** (*odpowiedzialność itp.*) shoulder[2]
barka barge[1], canal boat
barman barman
barmanka barmaid
barokowy baroque
barometr barometer
baron baron

baronowa baroness
barszcz: **tani(o) jak ~** dirt cheap
barwa 1 colour[1], hue **2** (*głosu*) timbre
barwić/za- dye[1], tint verb
barwnik colouring, dye[2]
barwny 1 coloured; (*i przen.*) colourful **2** (*opis itp.*) vivid
barykada barricade
barykadować/za- się barricade yourself in
baryłka barrel, keg
baryton baritone
bas bass
baseball baseball
■ **baseballowy**: **mecz ~** ball game
baseballówka baseball cap
basen 1 (*pływacki*) swimming pool; **~ kryty** baths[1], indoor swimming pool, swimming bath **2** (*portowy*) dock[1] **3** (*geogr.*) basin
basowy bass adj.
bastard bastard
bastion bastion, stronghold
baszta tower[1]
baśń (fairy) tale
bat whip[1]
batalion battalion
bateria 1 (*elektr.*) battery **2 kurnik bateryjny** battery
bat micwa (*w religii żydowskiej*) bat mitzvah
baton bar[1]
batut trampoline
batuta baton
bawełna cotton[1]
bawełniany cotton[1]
bawić/za- amuse, keep sb amused, entertain, tickle
□ **bawić/za-/po- się 1** keep yourself amused, have fun, play[1] (with sb/sth); **(z kimś)** play about/around (with sb); **świetnie się bawić** enjoy yourself, have a good/great time, have the time of your life **2 (czymś)** dabble, mess about/around with sth, play about/around (with sth); (*przen.*) mess with sb/sth; **~ (czymś), używając palców** twiddle (with) sth; **~ czymś (bezwiednie)** fiddle[1] (about/around) (with sth), fidget with sth **3 (w coś)** play at sth/being sth, pretend to be sth
bawół buffalo
baz|a 1 (*wojskowa itp.*) base[1]; **~a lotnicza** airbase; **~a wyrzutni rakietowej** pad[1]; **zakładać ~ę** base[2] sb/sth in... **2** (*podstawa*) basis IDM **~a danych** database
bazar bazaar
bazgrać/na- scrawl, scribble
bazgranina scrawl noun, scribble noun
bazgrolić/na- scribble
bazgroły scribble noun
bazylia basil
bażant pheasant
bąb|el 1 bubble[1] **2** (*na skórze*) blister[1]; **pokrywać (się) ~lami** blister[2]
bąbel|ek bubble[1]; **~ki** fizz; **z ~kami** bubbly; (*napój*) fizzy; (*zwł. wino, woda mineralna*) sparkling
bądź IDM **~ co ~** at any rate
bąk top[1]
bąk-ać/nąć/wy- bleat
beatyfikować beatify
beczeć 1 (/za-) (*owca, koza*) bleat **2** (*płakać*) blubber[2]
beczk|a barrel, cask, drum[1]; (*piwo*) **z ~i** draught[2]
beczkowy (*piwo*) draught[2]
beczułka cask
begonia begonia
bejsbolówka baseball cap
bek baa, bleat noun
bek-ać/nąć belch, burp; **głośno beknąć** give a loud belch
bekhend backhand
bekon bacon
bela bale
beletrystyczny fictional
beletrystyka fiction
belka beam[1], timber; **~ główna** girder; **~ stropowa** joist
bełkot babble[1], gibberish, splutter noun
bełkotać/wy- (*mówić szybko i niewyraźnie*) gibber; (*zwł. po wypiciu alkoholu*) slur[1]
bełt plonk[2]
bemol flat[2]; **z ~em** flat[1]
beneficjent/ka beneficiary
benzyna petrol
berbeć tot[1]
beret beret
berło sceptre
bestia beast, brute[1]
bestialski ferocious, inhumane, savage
bestialstwo ferocity, inhumanity, savagery
bestseller best-seller
besztać/z- chide, rap[2], scold
beta: **wersja ~** beta version
beton 1 concrete[2] **2** (*przen.: partia itp.*) monolith
betonować/za- concrete[3]
bez[1] (*spój*) excluding, exclusive[1] of sb/sth, less[3], minus[1], out of, without
bez[2] (*rz.*) lilac; **dziki ~** elder[2]; **kwiat dzikiego bzu** elderflower; **owoc czarnego bzu** elderberry
beza meringue
bezalkoholowy non-alcoholic; **napój ~** soft drink
bezbarwny colourless, drab, insipid, lacklustre, nondescript
■ **bezbarwnie** blandly
bezbłędny faultless, flawless
bezbolesny painless
bezbramkowy goalless
bezbronny defenceless, unarmed
bezcelowy aimless, futile, pointless, senseless, useless
bezcen: **za ~** dirt cheap
bezcenny invaluable, priceless
bezceremonialny offhand[1], point-blank
bezchmurn|y cloudless; **~e niebo** a clear sky
bezcłowy duty-free
bezczelny brazen[1], cheeky, impertinent, impudent, insolent, presumptuous, shameless
■ **bezczelność** cheek, impertinence, impudence, insolence, nerve
bezcześcić/z- defile, desecrate
bezczynnie idly; **stać ~** stand by
bezczynny idle, inactive
■ **bezczynność** idleness, inaction, inactivity
bezdenny 1 (*dziura*) bottomless **2** (*niezmierny*) crass
bezdomny homeless; **bez grosza, ~ i bezrobotny** down and out
■ **bezdomna** (*rz.*) (*nosząca wszędzie ze sobą swoje rzeczy w torbach*) bag lady
bezduszny callous, insensitive, soulless
bezdzietny childless
bezglutenowy gluten-free
bezgraniczny boundless, immense
bezimienny anon., faceless, nameless
bezinteresowny disinterested, selfless, unselfish
bezkarność impunity
bezkofeinow|y: **kawa ~a** decaffeinated coffee
bezkompromisowy uncompromising
bezkres infinity
bezkręgowiec (*biol.*) invertebrate
bezkrwawy bloodless
bezkształtny amorphous, shapeless
bezlitosn|y cold-blooded, cut-throat, hard-hearted, merciless, pitiless, remorseless, ruthless, savage; **~e postępowanie** ruthlessness
bezludn|y uninhabited; **~a wyspa** desert island
bezładny frantic, incoherent
bezmiar immensity
bezmierny wide[1]
bezmyślny (*zwł. osoba*) absent-minded, fatuous, thoughtless, vacuous, witless; (*zwł. czyn*) crass, inane, mindless, unthinking; (*spojrzenie itp.*) absent, vacant
beznadziejn|y 1 abysmal, desperate, dismal, hopeless; **coś ~ego/ktoś ~y** non-starter **2** (*głupi*) dumb, hopeless (at sth) **3** (*bezgraniczny*) abject, crass
beznamiętny clinical, dry, impassive, stolid
bezokolicznik infinitive
bezołowiowy unleaded
bezosobowy impersonal
bezowocny fruitless, futile, vain
bezpestkowy seedless
bezpieczeństw|o safety, soundness; **poczucie ~a** security; **środki ~a** security
bezpiecznik fuse[1]
bezpiecznikow|y: **skrzynka ~a** fuse box
bezpieczn|y all right, safe[1], secure[1], sheltered IDM **w ~-e/ym miejsc-e/u** out of harm's way
bezpłatnie free adv., gratis, for nothing
bezpłatn|y complimentary, free[1], gratis; **~a dostawa** we deliver free of charge; **~a infolinia/numer telefonu** Freephone; **urlop ~y** unpaid leave
bezpłciowy asexual
bezpłodny infertile, sterile
bezpodstawny baseless, groundless, ill-founded, invalid[1], unfounded, unwarranted; (*niesprowokowany*) unprovoked
bezpośredni 1 direct[1]; (*czas: następujący zaraz po czymś*) immediate; (*źródłowy, np. informacja*) first-hand, hands-on; (*relacja wiadomości*) live[2]; (*lot*) non-stop; (*wystrzał*) point-blank **2** (*osoba*) candid, direct[1], outgoing, plain[1]
bezpośrednio 1 direct adv., directly[1], straight[1]; (*patrzeć w twarz kogoś itp.*) square[1]; (*lot, dojazd itp.*) non-stop; (*transmitowany*) live; (*dowiedzieć się*) first-hand **2** (*zaraz*) immediately **3** (*odpowiadać*) candidly, directly[1]; (*coś powiedzieć*) outright
bezprawie illegality, lawlessness
bezprawny illegal, illegitimate, illicit, wrongful
bezpretensjonalny unaffected, unassuming
bezprzedmiotowy moot

bezprzewodowy cordless, wireless
bezradny helpless
bezrobocie joblessness, unemployment
bezrobotny jobless, out of a job, out-of-work, unemployed; **bez grosza, bezdomny i berobotny** down and out
bezruch 1 immobility, stillness; **w ~u** at rest **2** (*przen.*) **stać w ~u** stagnate
bezsenny restless, sleepless
■ **bezsenność** insomnia, sleeplessness
bezsens double Dutch
bezsensowny pointless, senseless
bezsilny impotent, powerless
bezskuteczny of little/no avail, futile, vain
bezsporny indisputable, patent[2], undoubted, unquestionable
bezsprzeczny indisputable, unquestionable
bezstronny disinterested, even-handed, fair-minded, impartial, neutral[1]
■ **bezstronność** impartiality, neutrality, objectivity
bezszelestny noiseless
beztłuszczowy fat-free
beztroski blithe, carefree, complacent, easy-going, happy-go-lucky, unconcerned
bezustannie ceaselessly, continually, incessantly, perpetually, relentlessly; **~ coś robić** keep on (doing sth), keep sth up
bezustanny ceaseless, continual, incessant, perpetual, relentless, unrelenting
bezużyteczn|y good-for-nothing, useless IDM **być ~ym** be no good (doing sth)
bezwartościowy valueless, worthless
bezwarunkowy implicit, unconditional
■ **bezwarunkowo** implicitly, unconditionally, (with) no strings attached, without strings
bezwiedny unwitting
■ **bezwiednie** unwittingly; **ruszać czymś bezwiednie** toy with sth
bezwietrzny calm[1]; **~ wieczór** a still evening
bezwład paralysis
bezwładny inert
bezwłosy hairless
bezwonny odourless
bezwstydny brazen[1], shameless, unashamed
bezwzględny 1 (*osoba; postępowanie*) cut-throat, heartless, ruthless; (*niepotrzebnie używający przemocy*) heavy-handed; (*kara itp.*) draconian **2** (*większość głosów*) absolute, overall **3** (*zaufanie*) implicit
bezzałogowy unmanned
bezzwłocznie forthwith, immediately, instantly, promptly, swiftly
bezzwłoczny immediate, prompt[1], swift
beż beige noun
beżowy beige
bęben 1 (*muz.*) drum[1] **2** (*do nawijania*) reel[1], spool
bębenek 1 (*anat.*) eardrum **2** (*muz.*) **~ (baskijski)** tambourine
bębnić/za- drum[2]; (*na fortepianie itp.*) belt sth out
bęcwał clod
bękart bastard
biada IDM **~ temu, kto** woe betide sb
biadolić gripe verb, whinge
białaczka leukaemia
białawy off-white
białko protein; (*oka; jajka*) white[2]
biał|y white[1]; **kolor ~y** white[2]; **Biały Dom** the White House; **~ej rasy** Caucasian adj.; **~y wiersz** blank verse IDM **(w) ~y dzień** (in) broad daylight
bibelot object[1], ornament, trinket
Biblia the Bible, scripture
biblijny biblical
bibliobus mobile library
bibliografia bibliography
biblioteczka bookcase
biblioteka library; **~ objazdowa** mobile library
biblioteka-rz/rka librarian
bibuła 1 (*do ozdób*) tissue (paper) **2** (*do atramentu*) blotting paper
bibułka tissue (paper)
biceps biceps
bicie beat[2], beating; **~ serca** heartbeat
bicz whip[1]
biczować/u- whip[2]
bić 1 (/po-) kogoś/coś beat[1], beat sb up, clobber, hit out (at sb/sth), thrash, thump; **~ brawo** applaud; **~ młotem** hammer[2] **2 (/wy-)** (*monetę*) mint verb **3 (/po-)** (*rekord*) break[1] **4** (*dzwon, zegar*) peal verb; **biła od niej pewność siebie** she was oozing confidence
□ **bić/po- się** fight[1]
bidet bidet
biec/po- zob. też BIEGAĆ **1** run[1]; **za kimś/czymś** run after sb/sth; **~ drobnymi krokami** scuttle, scurry; **~ susami** bound[2]; **ciężko ~** pound[2] along, down, up, etc. **2** (*droga itp.*) **~ równolegle do czegoś/z czymś** follow
bie|da need[3], poverty; **w ~dzie** needy
bieda-k/czka devil, wretch
biedny deprived, disadvantaged, badly off, penniless, poor, poverty-stricken
biedota poor
biedronka ladybird
bieg 1 run[2]; (*w wyścigu*) race[1]; **~ dla zdrowia** jog[2]; **~ lekkoatletyczny** track event; **~ na orientację** orienteering; **~ przez płotki** hurdle[1]; **~ sztafetowy** relay[2] **2** (*historii itp.*) course; (*wydarzeń*) sequence **3** (*auta*) gear[1]; (*silnika*) motion[1]; **~ wsteczny** reverse[2] **4 ~ próbny** trial run
biegacz/ka runner
biegać zob. też BIEC; run[1]; **codziennie rano przebiegam trzy mile** I go for a three-mile run every morning; **~ dla zdrowia** jog[1]
bieganina bustle[2]
biegle expertly, fluently; **mówić ~ po francusku** be fluent in French
biegł|y (*przym.*) adept, conversant, proficient; (*angielski itp.*) fluent; **~-y/a księgow-y/a** certified/chartered accountant
■ **biegłość** expertise, proficiency, mastery; (*w angielskim itp.*) fluency | **biegł-y/a** (*rz.*) expert; (*prawn. itp.*) assessor
biegun pole; **~ północny** the North Pole; **~ południowy** the South Pole
biegunka diarrhoea
biel white[2]
bielić/po- whiten; **~ wapnem** whitewash[2]
bielizna 1 (*osobista*) underwear; **~ damska** lingerie; **~ ocieplana** thermals[2] **2** (*pościelowa, stołowa*) linen
biern|y 1 inactive, inert, passive; **~e palenie** passive smoking; **~y opór** passive resistance **2** (*gram.*) passive
bierzmować confirm
bies devil
bieżąc|y 1 (*aktualny*) current[1], ongoing, present[1] **2** (*woda*) running[2]
■ **bieżąco** IDM **na ~** clued-up, in/out of touch with sth, up to date | **być na ~** be/keep abreast of sth, keep up (with sth)
bieżnia circuit
bieżnik tread[2]
bigamia bigamy
bigamiczny bigamous
bigamist-a/ka bigamist
bijatyka brawl, fighting, fight[2], punch-up, tussle
bikini bikini
bilans trade-off; **~ płatniczy** balance of payments
bilansować (się) balance[2]
bilard billiards; (*rodzaj gry bilardowej*) pool[1]; (*z użyciem 22 bil o różnych barwach*) snooker
bilateralny bilateral
bilet ticket; **~y na balet** seats for the ballet; **~ w jedną stronę** single[2]; **~ powrotny** return[2]; **~ lotniczy** air ticket; **~ okresowy** pass[2], season ticket; **~ przesiadkowy** transfer[2]
bileter usher[1]
bileterka usherette
billboard hoarding
bim-bom bong
binarny binary; **system ~** binary noun
bingo bingo
biochemia biochemistry
biochemik biochemist
biodegradacj|a: ulegać ~i biodegrade; **ulegający ~i** biodegradable
biodro hip[1]
biodrówki: **spodnie ~** hipsters
biograf biographer
biografia biography, life, life story
biograficzny biographical
biolog biologist
biologia biology
biologiczn|y biological; **wojna ~a** biological warfare
biometryczn|y: informacje ~e biodata
biopsja biopsy
biotechnologia biotechnology
bis encore[1]; **~!** encore[2]
biseksualny bisexual
biskup bishop
bistro bistro
biszkopt sponge cake
bit bit[1]
bitum bitumen
bitwa action, battle[1]
bit|y 1 (*śmietana*) whipped **2 spałem dwanaście ~ych godzin** I slept for twelve solid hours/twelve hours solid
biuletyn bulletin, newsletter
biureta burette
biurko desk
biuro bureau, office; **~ bukmacherskie** bookmaker; **~ matrymonialne** dating agency;

~ **numerów** directory enquiries; ~ **pośrednictwa pracy** employment agency; ~ **podróży** travel agency, travel agent; ~ **rzeczy znalezionych** lost property
biurokracja bureaucracy, red tape
biurokrat-a/ka bureaucrat
biurokratyczny bureaucratic
biurowiec office block
biurowy clerical, white-collar
biust bust²
biustonosz bra
biwakować camp²
biwakowicz/ka camper
biznes business; **wielki** ~ big business; **dla ludzi ~u** executive²
biznesmen businessman; (**biznesmeni**) business people
biznesowy executive²
bizon bison
biżuteria jewellery
blacha brass; ~ **falista** corrugated iron; ~ **do pieczenia** baking sheet
blado: **uśmiechnął się ~ (z powodu zmęczenia)** he gave a weary smile
bladożółty pale yellow
blady pale; (*światło itp.*) watery; (*cera*) ashen, bloodless, green¹, pallid, wan IDM ~ **świt** the crack of dawn
blaknąć/z-/wy- dim², fade, fade away, pale verb
blankiet form¹
blankowanie battlements
blask 1 (*jasność*) blaze², brightness, gleam, glint noun, glitter, glory¹, glow noun, shine²; ~ **księżyca** moonlight; ~ **ognia** firelight **2** (*luksus*) glamour, glitter IDM **wszystko ma swoje ~i i cienie** every cloud has a silver lining
blaszan|y: **instrumenty ~e** brass
blat surface¹; ~ **biurka** desktop; ~ **kuchenny** worktop; ~ **stołu** table top
ble blah adj.; ~, ~, ~ blah
blednąć/z- blanch, pale verb; ~ **ze strachu** go/turn pale with fear
blef bluff²
blefować bluff¹
blezer blazer
blichtr glitz
blisk|i 1 (*w przestrzeni*) close³, handy, near¹, nearby; **z ~a** close up (to sb/sth), at close quarters **2** (*w czasie*) near¹; **(niebezpiecznie) ~i** imminent; **była ~a płaczu** she was on the brink of tears **3** (*zaprzyjaźniony*) close³, intimate; **~i sercu** close/dear/near to sb's heart
blisk|o 1 (*w przestrzeni*) close adv., (close/near) at hand, near², nearby adv.; (*doganiać*) hotly; **~o (do)** up; **z ~a** point-blank adv. **2** (*w czasie*) imminently **3** (*znać kogoś itp.*) intimately IDM **~o (czegoś/zrobienia czegoś)** on the verge of sth/doing sth
bliskość 1 closeness, immediacy, proximity **2** (*duchowa*) affinity, communion
blizn|a scar; **zostawiać ~ę** scar verb
bliźniacz|y sister; **miasto ~e** twin town; **tworzyć ~e miasta** twin verb
bliźnia|k 1 (**bliźnia-k/czka**) twin; **~k/czka dwujajow-y/a** fraternal twin; **~k/czka jednojajow-y/a** identical twin; **~k/czka syjamsk-i/a** Siamese twin **2** (**Bliźnięta**) (*znak zodiaku*) Gemini **3** (**bliźniak**) (*dom*) semi
bloczek book¹
blog blog
blogować blog verb
blok 1 (*budynek*) block¹; ~ **mieszkalny** apartment block **2** (*papieru*) pad¹ **3** (*grupa*) bloc **4** (*nauczania*) module **4** (*kawał skały*) block¹ **5** (*sport*) tackle² **6** (*mechanizm*) pulley
blokad|a 1 blockade **2** (*przeszkoda*) block¹ **3** (*na koła*) clamp²; **nakładać ~ę kół** clamp¹
blokować/za- 1 block² (up), block sth off, blockade verb, box sb/sth in, cut sth off, jam², lock¹ **2** (*sport*) tackle¹ □ **blokować/za- się** lock¹; (*maszyna*) seize up
blond blonde
blondynka blonde noun
blues blues²
bluszcz ivy
bluszczowaty clinging
bluza: **luźna** ~ (*np. dla kobiety w ciąży*) smock; ~ **sportowa** sweatshirt
bluzgać/o- spout², spurt
bluzka blouse
bluźnierczy blasphemous, profane
bluźnierstwo blasphemy
błagać/u-/prze- beg, beseech, entreat, implore, plead
błagalny appealing
błahostka irrelevance, trifle; (**błahostki**) trivia
błahość insignificance, triviality
błahy immaterial, inconsequential, insignificant, petty, trifling, trivial
bławatek cornflower
błazen buffoon, clown¹, hoot²; (*królewski*) jester
błazeński facetious, clownish
błazeństwo (**błazeństwa**) antics
błaznować clown², fool about/around
błaźnić/z- się make a fool of yourself
błąd error, flaw, mistake¹, slip²; ~ **drukarski** misprint; ~ **w sztuce medycznej** medical malpractice; **błędy konstrukcyjne** design faults; **popełniać** ~ err; **popełniać głupi** ~ goof; **wprowadzać w** ~ deceive; **wyprowadzać kogoś z błędu (co do czegoś)** disabuse sb (of sth); **zawierać** ~ (*rachunek*) be out adj.
błądzić (*myśli, wzrok itp.*) wander
błąkać/za- się meander, stray¹; (*uśmiech*) play¹
błędnie 1 erroneously, incorrectly, by mistake, mistakenly, spuriously, wrongly; ~ **interpretować** misinterpret **2** (*nieprzytomnie*) vaguely
błędn|y erroneous, fallacious, false, flawed, incorrect, misguided, mistaken, spurious, unsound, wrong¹; **~e pojęcie/zrozumienie** misconception; **~e przekonanie** fallacy, misapprehension IDM **~e koło** a vicious circle
błękit blue²; (*kolor*) ~ **królewski** royal blue noun
błękitny blue¹
błog|i blessed, blissful; **być w ~iej nieświadomości czegoś** be blithely unaware of sth
błogosławić/po- bless
błogosławieństwo blessing
błogosławiony blessed
błogość bliss
błon|a membrane; **~a bębenkowa** eardrum; **~a filmowa** film¹; **złączony ~ą** (*np. u kaczki*) webbed
błonica diphtheria
błonie (*gminne*) common²; ~ **wiejskie** green²
błonnik cellulose, fibre
błota marsh, swamp¹
błotnik mudguard, wing
błotnisty marshy, muddy
błoto muck¹, mud
błysk flare², flash², gleam, glint noun, spark¹, twinkle noun
błys-kać/nąć/zabłysnąć flash¹, flicker¹, glint □ **błys-kać/nąć się** flash¹
błyskawica flash², flash of lightning; ~ **zygzakowata/płaska** forked/sheet lightning IDM **(szybko) jak** ~ (as) quick as a flash
błyskawiczny lightning², split-second; (*sława*) meteoric; (*odpowiedź*) pat³; (*potrawa*) instant¹ ■ **błyskawicznie** in/like a flash
błyskotka bauble
błyskotliwość snappiness, wit
błyskotliwy 1 bright, brilliant, quick-witted, scintillating, witty; ~ **i zwięzły** snappy **2** (*kariera, sukces*) glittering
błysnąć (się) → BŁYSKAĆ (SIĘ), BŁYSZCZEĆ
błyszcząc|y bright, brilliant, glittering, shiny; (*włosy itp.*) glossy; (*farba itp.*) gloss¹; **na ~ym papierze** glossy
błyszczeć/za-/błysnąć 1 blaze¹, gleam verb, glisten, shine¹; (*oczy*) twinkle **2** (*w nauce itp.*) shine¹
bo cos
boa boa constrictor
boazeria panelling
bobas tot¹
bobek (**bobki**) droppings
bobslej bobsleigh
bochenek loaf
bocian stork
boczek bacon
bocznica siding
boczn|y side¹; (*ruch*) lateral, sideways; (*spojrzenie*) sidelong; **~a droga** byway, side road; **~a ulica** side street; **~y tor** siding; **kierować uwagę/sprawę na ~y tor** sidetrack; **linia autowa/~a** sideline
boczyć się sulk
bo|dziec impetus, impulse, incentive, inducement, spur¹, stimulation, stimulus, urge²; **być ~dźcem (do czegoś)** motivate
bogactw|o luxuriance, means, richness, wealth; (**bogactw-o/a**) riches, treasure¹; **wielkie ~o** opulence; **~a (naturalne)** resources
bogat|y 1 rich, wealthy, well off; (*wnętrze, posiłek itp.*) sumptuous; **bardzo ~y** opulent **2 w coś** rich in sth; **~e źródło** (*np. wiedzy*) fountain
bogini goddess
bohater hero; (**bohaterka**) heroine; (*w filmie/książce itp.*) character, protagonist; ~ **pozytywny** goody
bohaterski heroic
bohaterstwo heroism
boisko 1 (*sport*) field¹, ground¹, pitch¹, playing field; (*baseballowe*) ballpark **2** (*szk.*) playground, yard
boja buoy¹
bojaźliwy cowardly, faint-hearted, fearful, timid
bojkot boycott noun
bojkotować/z- boycott; (*towarzysko*) ostracize
bojler boiler

bojowni-k/czka fighter, militant noun; **(o coś)** champion[1]; ~ **o wolność** freedom fighter

bojowy (*osoba; postawa*) militant; (*dywizja itp.*) operational

bojówka militia

bok side[1]; (*zwierzęcia*) flank[1]; **z ~u** sidelong, sideways; **iść ~iem** sidle up/over (to sb/sth); **na** ~ (*rozchodzić się*) sideways; (*odkładać*) aside; (*spojrzeć*) sidelong IDM (*stać, obserwować itp.*) **z ~u** on the sidelines

bokobrody sideburns, whiskers

boks boxing

bokser/ka boxer, fighter

bokserki boxer shorts, shorts

boksować box[2]

bol|ec: **wtyczka z dwoma ~cami** a two-pin plug

boleć/za- ache[1], hurt[1], pain[2]; (*tylko przen.*) rankle; ~ **strasznie** kill[1]; **strasznie bolą mnie plecy** I've got a terrible pain in my back; **brzuch mnie boli** my stomach is sore

bolesn|y painful, sore[1]; (*słowa*) hurtful; (*wyraz twarzy*) pained; **~a choroba** a distressing illness; **~y cios** sorrow

boleś|ć anguish; **pełen ~ci** agonized

bomba 1 bomb[1]; ~ **atomowa** atomic bomb; **~-pułapka** booby trap **2** (*sensacyjna wiadomość*) bombshell, dynamite

bombardować/z- bomb[2], bombard

bombka (*na choinkę*) bauble

bombonierka a box of chocolates

bombowiec bomber

bombowy smashing, wicked

bon voucher; ~ **towarowy** token[1]; ~ **książkowy** book token

bonifikat|a: **z ~ą** off[1]

bonus bonus

boom (*gospodarczy itp.*) boom[1]

bordo claret; **kolor** ~ claret

bordowy (*kolor*) burgundy adj.

borówka: ~ **amerykańska** blueberry; ~ **czarna** bilberry

borsuk badger

borykać się grapple, struggle[1]

boski divine, heavenly

bosy barefoot

botaniczny botanical

botanik botanist

botanika botany

botek boot[1]

botoks Botox

bożek god, idol

bożnica (*żydowska*) synagogue

boż|y divine; **Boże Narodzenie** Christmas, Xmas; **drugi dzień Świąt Bożego Narodzenia** Boxing Day

bożyszcze cult

bób broad beans

bóbr beaver

bóg (także **Bóg**) god; **Pan Bóg** lord; **mój Boże!** my goodness! IDM **o Boże!** Oh my God!

bójka fight[2], scrap[1], scuffle, tussle; **(bójki)** fighting

ból ache[2], pain[1], soreness; (*zwł. psychiczny*) suffering; (*rozstania itp.*) wrench[2]; **(lekki)** ~ discomfort; **nagły** ~ twinge; ~ **głowy** headache; ~ **ucha** earache; ~ **zęba** toothache; ~ **żołądka** stomach ache; **krzyknąć z ~u** cry out in pain

bóstwo deity

bóść/u- gore[2]

bractwo brotherhood, fraternity

brać/wziąć 1 take; (*lekarstwo*) dose[2] yourself with sth; ~ **narkotyki** be on drugs **2** (*kąpiel itp.*) have, take **3** (*odpowiedzialność itp.*) accept; **coś na siebie** take care of sth, take sth on; ~ **na siebie winę** take the blame for sth **4** ~ **kogoś/coś (za kogoś/coś innego)** mistake[2] A for B, mix sb/sth up (with sb/sth) **5** (*choroba*) ~ **kogoś** come on; **bierze mnie grypa** I'm coming down with flu
□ **brać/wziąć się 1 z czegoś** spring from sth; **skąd się u diabła wziąłeś?** where on earth did you spring from? **2 za coś** take sth up **3 do czegoś** settle (down) to sth; ~ **wspólnie do roboty** get working, pitch in **4 za kogoś/coś** clamp down on sb/sth IDM **(za)brać się do roboty** pull your socks up | **wziąć sie w garść** pull yourself together

Braille: **alfabet ~'a** Braille

brak 1 (*niedostatek*) deficiency, lack[1], scarcity, shortage, shortfall, want[2]; **(braki)** wastage; **z ~u czegoś** for (the) want of sth **2** (*nieobecność*) absence

brakować/zabraknąć fail[1], be lacking, be missing, be/go/run short (of sth), be scarce, be wanting; **brakuje mi pomysłów** I'm running out of ideas; **niczego temu nie brakuje** there's nothing the matter with it

brama gate; ~ **wjazdowa** gate

bramka goal; (*w krykiecie*) wicket; ~ **samobójcza** own goal

bramka-rz/rka (*sport*) goalkeeper; (*przed klubem nocnym*) bouncer

brandy brandy

bransoleta bangle

bransoletka bracelet

branża industry, line[1]

brat brother; **~/siostra** sibling; ~ **cioteczny/stryjeczny** cousin; **bracia** (*relig.*) brethren; (*fin.*) Bros

bratanek nephew

bratanica niece

bratek pansy

braterski brotherly, fraternal

braterstwo brotherhood, comradeship, fraternity

bratni fraternal IDM **~a dusza** after your own heart

bratowa sister-in-law

brawo bravo; **(brawa)** applause IDM **~!** good for you/him/her, etc., hear! hear!, well done!

brawura bravado, bravura

brawurowy rash[2], reckless; ~ **występ** a bravura performance

brąz bronze; **epoka ~u** the Bronze Age; **kolor ~u** bronze, brown noun

brązowawy brownish

brązowieć/z- brown[2]

brązowy bronze adj., brown[1]; ~ **medal** bronze medal

breakdance break-dancing

brednia **(brednie)** drivel

bredzić ramble[1]; **bredzący** delirious

breja 1 mush **2** (*filmy itp.*) slush

brejowaty mushy

breloczek key ring

brevis breve

brew eyebrow

brewiarz breviary

brezent tarpaulin

briefing briefing

brnąć/za-/prze- flounder[1], slog[1] down/up/along, etc., thread your way through sth; (*i przen.*) wade through sth

broda 1 (*włosy*) beard, whiskers **2** (*anat.*) chin

brodaty bearded

brodawka 1 wart **2** ~ **sutkowa** nipple

brodzić paddle[2], wade

brokat 1 (*tkanina*) brocade **2** (*dekoracja karnawałowa*) glitter

broker broker-dealer

brokuły broccoli

bronchit bronchitis

bronić/o- defend, protect; (*sport*) save[1], stick up for sb/sth; **bramkarz wspaniale obronił bramkę** the goalkeeper made a great save
□ **bronić /o- się** fend sb/sth off; ~ **słowami** answer back

broń ammunition, arms, hardware, weapon; ~ **biologiczna** biological weapon; ~ **chemiczna** chemical weapon; ~ **jądrowa** bomb[1], nuke noun; ~ **masowego rażenia** weapon of mass destruction; ~ **nuklearna** bomb[1]; ~ **palna** firearm, gun[1]; ~ **ręczna** handgun

brosza (także **broszka**) brooch

broszura booklet, pamphlet; (*informacyjna*) prospectus; ~ **reklamowa** brochure

broszurow|y (*książka*) **w ~ej okładce** paperback

browar brewer, brewery

bród ford; **w** ~ galore

brud dirt, filth, grime, muck[1]; (*moralny*) sleaze, tawdriness; **(brudy)** (*przen.*) dirt

brudnopis draft[1]

brudny 1 (*nieczysty*) dirty[1]; **bardzo** ~ filthy, grimy, scummy; ~ **i niechlujny** grungy, messy **2** (*kolor*) murky **3** (*nieprzyzwoity; nieuczciwy*) dirty[1], impure, sordid, tawdry
■ **brudno**: **pisać na brudno** draft[2] IDM **na brudno** in rough

brudzić/po-/za- dirty[2], get sth dirty, mess sth up, soil[2]
□ **brudzić/po- się** dirty[2]

brukać/z- defile

brukiew swede

brukować/wy- pave
■ **brukowany** cobbled

brukowiec tabloid

brukow|y: **kostki ~e** cobbles

brukselka Brussels sprout

brunatny bronze adj.

brutal brute[1]

brutalizować brutalize

brutaln|y brutal, ferocious, rough[1], violent; (*siła*) brute[2]; **~a rzeczywistość** stark reality

brutto gross[1]

bruzd|a furrow, rut; **pokryty ~ami** lined

bryczesy breeches; (*do jazdy konnej*) jodhpurs

brydż bridge[1]

brygada brigade, squad

brygadier brigadier

bryk-ać/nąć 1 (*koń*) buck[2] **2** (*w zabawie*) frisk

brylant diamond

brylantow|y: **~e gody/wesele** diamond wedding

bryła lump[1]; (*geom.*) solid[2]
bryłka nugget
bryłowaty lumpy
Brytyj-czyk/ka Brit, Briton; **Brytyjczycy** the British
brytyjski British
brytyjsko- Anglo-
bryz-gać/nąć splash[1]
brzask break of day, the crack of dawn, dawn[1], daybreak
brzdąc tot[1]
brzdąk-ać/nąć strum, twang verb
brzdęk ping; (*struny*) twang
brzeg 1 (*skraj*) border[1], edge[1]; (*strony*) margin; (*filiżanki itp.*) brim[1], lip, rim; **przemieszczać się wzdłuż ~u** skirt[2] **2** (*morza*) coast[1], seashore, shore[1]; ~ **rzeki** bank[1], riverside; **ku ~owi** inshore adv.; **na** ~ ashore
brzemienny 1 (**brzemienna**) pregnant **2** (*w skutki*) fateful, fraught
brzemię burden[1], cross[1]
brzęczeć/za- (*ciężki metal*) clang; (*klucze, łańcuch itp.*) jangle, jingle[2]; (*szkło*) chink[2], clink; (*szkło, lekki metal itp.*) ping; (*pszczoła itp.*) buzz[1], hum; (*dzwonek*) **delikatnie** ~ tinkle
brzęczyk bleeper, buzzer
brzęk (*ciężkiego metalu*) clang noun, clash[2]; (*szkła*) clink, chink[1]; (*kluczy, łańcucha itp.*) jangle noun; (*szkła, lekkiego metalu itp.*) ping
brzmieć/za- 1 go[1], sound[2]; (*bęben*) beat[1]; ~ **znajomo** ring a bell, be vaguely familiar; ~ **prawdopodobnie** have a ring of truth about it **2** (*dzwonek itp.*) ring[2]
brzmienie ring[1] of sth; (*głosu itp.*) tone[1]
brzoskwinia peach
brzoskwiniowy peach adj.
brzoza birch
brzozowy birch
brzuch abdomen, belly, insides[2], stomach[1]; **leżeć na ~u** lie on your front
brzuszny abdominal
brzydki ugly; (*budynek itp.*) grim IDM **~e słowa** bad language | **~e słowo** dirty word
brzydnąć/z-: **(komuś)** pall
brzydota ugliness
brzydzący się squeamish
brzytwa razor
bu (*płacz*) boohoo
bubel dud
bubkowaty snooty
buch-ać/nąć 1 (*dymem*) belch, spew; ~ **płomieniem** blaze[1] **2** (**buchnąć**) (*ukraść*) knock sth off, sneak[1]
buczeć/za- boom[2] (out), drone, hum; (*na znak dezaprobaty*) boo verb; (*klakson*) toot verb
buda shed[1]; **psia** ~ kennel
buddyjski Buddhist adj.
buddyst-a/ka Buddhist
buddyzm Buddhism
budka 1 booth, box[1]; ~ **telefoniczna** phone booth, telephone box **2** (*auta*) hood
budowa 1 (*budowanie*) construction, erection; ~ **okrętów** shipbuilding **2** (*struktura*) composition, constitution, structure[1] **3** (*ciała*) build[2], frame[1], physique
budować/z- build[1]; **coś na czymś** build sth on sth; **na czymś** construct, erect[2]; (*na bazie itp.*) build on sth; (*organizację itp.*) found[2]
budowla construction, edifice, structure[1]
budowlany building
budownictw|o building; **pracować w ~ie** work in the construction industry
budowniczy builder
budujący educational; (*moralnie itp.*) edifying
budulec timber
budyn|ek building; **w/do ~ku** indoors; **w tym samym ~ku** under one roof
budzić/o- awake[2], awaken, get sb up, rouse, wake[1] sb (up), waken; ~ **na nowo** revive; ~ **wstręt** repel
□ **budzić/o- się** awake[2], awaken, get up, wake[1] (up), waken; ~ **na nowo** revive
budzik alarm clock
budżet budget[1]
budżetowy budgetary
bufet buffet[1], cafeteria, snack bar; ~ **z kanapkami** sandwich bar
bufiasty full[1]
bufor buffer
bujać/po- 1 (*kołysać*) swing[1]; (*zwieszać nogi itp.*) dangle **2** (*po świecie itp.*) knock about/around **3** (*kłamać*) fib verb, kid[2]
□ **bujać/po- się** (*na huśtawce*) swing[1]; (*zwisać*) dangle
bujda fib
bujność luxuriance
bujny 1 (*roślina*) lush; (*włosy*) luxuriant **2** (*kobieta*) voluptuous **3** (*przeszłość*) colourful
buk beech
bukiet bouquet, bunch[1]
bukmacher (*na wyścigach itp.*) bookmaker, stakeholder
bukowy beech
buldog bulldog
buldożer bulldozer
bulgot gurgle noun
bulgotać/za- bubble[2], gurgle
bulić/wy-/za-: **(na coś)** cough (sth) up, foot the bill (for sth), fork out (for sth)
bulimia bulimia
bulimiczny bulimic
bulion bouillon
bulwar boulevard
bulwiasty bulbous
bułeczka: **słodka** ~ bun
bułka roll[1]; ~ **paryska** French bread; ~ **tarta** breadcrumbs
bumelować skive
bumerang boomerang
bunkier (*budynek; na polu golfowym*) bunker
bunt defiance, mutiny, rebellion, revolt noun; **wszczynać** ~ riot verb
buntować/z- się mutiny verb, rebel[2], revolt (against sb/sth), rise[2] (up) (against sb/sth)
buntowniczka insurgent, rebel[1]
buntowniczy bolshie, defiant, insurgent adj., rebellious, riotous
buntownik insurgent, rebel[1], rioter
bura reprimand noun
burak 1 beetroot; ~ **cukrowy** sugar beet **2** (*osoba*) country bumpkin, peasant
burbon bourbon
burczeć/za- snarl; (*w brzuchu*) rumble
burd|a brawl, wrangle; (*dopuszczać się wandalizmu*) rampage[2]; **robić ~y** wrangle verb
burdel brothel
burgund (*wino; kolor*) burgundy
■ **burgundzki** burgundy adj.
burka burka
burkliwość gruffness
burkliwy cranky, gruff, monosyllabic
burmistrz mayor
burmistrzowa mayoress
bursztyn amber
bursztynowy amber adj.; **kolor** ~ amber
burt|a (*statku*) **lewa ~a** port; **prawa ~a** starboard; **za ~ą/ę** overboard
burz|a 1 storm[1]; **~a gradowa** hailstorm; **~a piaskowa** sandstorm; **~a z piorunami** thunderstorm; **~a śnieżna** snowstorm **2** (*pomysłów itp.*) flurry; **~a mózgów** brainstorming; **przeprowadzać ~ę mózgów** brainstorm[2] IDM **wywołać ~ę** stir up a hornet's nest
burzliwy 1 (*i przen.*) stormy **2** (*przen.*) tumultuous, turbulent, uproarious, wild[1]; (*życie itp.*) chequered
burzowy stormy
burzyć/z- pull sth down, tear sth down
busola compass
busz bush
but shoe[1]; ~ **z cholewą** boot[1]; ~ **sportowy do biegania** running shoe, trainer
buta (*bezczelność*) insolence; (*duma*) pride[1]
butelka bottle[1]
butelkować/za- bottle[2]
butik boutique
buzi|a face[1], mouth[1]; **zamknąć ~ę** shut up
buziak (**buziaki**) lots of love, luv
buzujący roaring
być 1 be[1,2], shall; **(na/w czymś)** attend; (*znajdować się*) lie[2]; **będzie dobrą nauczycielką** she'll make a good teacher; **był drugi z historii na egzaminie** he came second in the history exam; **Geoff był naszym przywódcą** Geoff acted as our leader; **to ma ~ dobra sztuka** it's supposed to be a good play; **niech będzie** well[3] **2** (*istnieć*) be[1]; **jest kilka osób na zewnątrz** there are some people outside; **nie było odpowiedzi** there was no answer
bydlęcy bovine
bydło cattle
byk 1 bull **2** (**Byk**) (*znak zodiaku*) Taurus **3** (*błąd*) boob
byle any old…; ~ **jak** anyhow, carelessly; ~ **jaki** slapdash; **robić ~ jak** cobble sth together
były ex-, former, one-time
bynajmniej (not) at all, far from sth/doing sth, not in the least (bit), not at all; ~ **(nie)** not nearly; **byjnajmniej nie mądrzejszy** none the wiser
bystro keenly
bystrość: ~ **(umysłu)** penetration, sharpness, wit
bystr|y astute, fast[1], incisive, perceptive, sharp[1], smart[1]; **~y umysł** wit; **o ~ym umyśle** quick-thinking, quick-witted
bystrzyna rapids
byt existence; **zapewniać** ~ provide for sb
bywal-ec/czyni (*zwł. koncertów muzyki klasycznej*) concert-goer
bywały sophisticated
bzdet (**bzdety**) crap

bzdura (także **bzdury**) baloney, drivel, gibberish, a load of rubbish, etc., nonsense, rot noun, rubbish, tosh, tripe
bzdurny 1 (*groteskowy*) cockeyed, preposterous **2** (*bez znaczenia*) piddling, piffling
bzik fixation; **mieć ~a na czyimś/ jakimś punkcie** have a thing about sb/sth; **mający ~a na punkcie kogoś/czegoś** fixated (on sb/sth)
bzy-czeć/knąć buzz[1]
bzyk buzz[2]

C

c 1 (**C/c**) (*litera*) C, c **2** (**C/c**) (*muz.*) C
cal inch[1]
całkiem 1 (*zupełnie*) all[2], altogether; **nie** ~ not quite, not really **2** (*dość*) enough[2], quite; (*duży, długi itp.*) plenty adv.
całkowicie absolutely, altogether, clean[3], completely, dead[3], downright adv., entirely, fully, heartily, to the hilt, just[1], outright, over-, perfectly adv., plain[3], positively, purely, quite, raving adv., stark[2], thoroughly, totally, truly, unreservedly, utterly, well and truly, wholly; (*zakochać się*) head over heels (in love)
całkowitość completeness
całkowity absolute, all out, blind[1], complete[1], dead[1], downright, entire, outright adj., overall adj., perfect[1], pure, raving, total[1], utter[1]
całodobowy round-the-clock
całodzienny nine to five
całościowy global, overall adj.
całoś|ć entirety, lot[3], whole[2]; **w ~ci** completely, in full, at large, overall[1], whole[1], as a whole; **na ~ć** all out adv.
całować/po- kiss
□ **całować/po- się** kiss, snog
całun shroud[1]
całus kiss noun; (**całusy**) (*w liście*) lots of love, luv
cał|y 1 all[1], complete[1], entire, intact, whole[1]; **~y autobus itp.** load[1]; **na/po ~ym** high and low, throughout; **(przez) ~y czas** all along, all the time/ the whole time; **przez ~ą noc** all night long[2]; **~ymi** (*godzinami, dniami itp.*) on end; **spróbować z ~ych sił** try your best/hardest; **~a nuta** semibreve **2** (*osoba*) safe[1]; **~y i zdrowy** in one piece IDM **na ~ego** in full swing, to the full | **iść na ~ego** go the whole hog
car tsar
caryca tsarina
catering catering
cążki: ~ **do paznokci** (a pair of) nail clippers
cebula onion
cebulka 1 (*kwiatu*) bulb **2** (*włosa*) root[1]
cebulowy onion
cech guild
cecha attribute[2], characteristic[2], feature[1], quality, streak[1], trait; **(czegoś)** stamp[1] of sth; ~ **charakterystyczna** hallmark
cedować/s- cede; (*prawn.*) transfer[1]
cedr cedar
cedrow|y: **drewno ~e** cedar
cedzak colander
cedzić/wy-/prze- strain[2] IDM **cedzić słowa** drawl
cegła brick
cekin sequin

cel 1 aim[1], cause[1], direction, end[1], goal, intent[2], object[1], objective[1], purpose, thrust[2]; **mieć coś na ~u** be aimed at sth/doing sth, have, etc. sth in view, look[1] to do sth; **mając na ~u zrobienie czegoś** with a view to doing sth; **dążący do ~u** purposeful; **stawiać sobie jakiś** ~ set out to do sth; **chodzić bez ~u** drift[2], mill about/ around; (*wpłata*) **na jakiś** ~ towards; **na ~e dobroczynne** for charity **2** (*podróży*) destination **3** (*ataku, krytyki itp.*) mark[2], target[1]
cela cell
celebrować celebrate
celibat celibacy
cellulit cellulite
celnik customs officer
celofan Cellophane
celować/wy- 1 aim[2], level sth at sb/ sth, point[2], take aim, zero in on sb/sth **2 w czymś** excel (in/at sth/doing sth)
celownik sight[1] IDM **na ~u** at gunpoint
celowy deliberate[1], intentional, wilful ■ **celowo** deliberately, intentionally, on purpose, purposely, wilfully | **celowość** point[1]
Celsjusz Celsius; **skala ~a** Celsius noun
Celt Celt
celtycki Celtic; (*irlandzki/szkocki*) Gaelic adj.
celująco with flying colours
celujący A, a; ~ **stopień** distinction
celuloza cellulose
cement cement[1]
cementować/za- cement[2]
cen|a 1 cost[1], figure[1], price[1], price tag, rate[1]; **~a biletu** fare[1]; **~a minimalna** bottom line; **~a ofertowa** asking price; **~a produkcji** cost price **2** (*przen.*) penalty, price[1] IDM **za żadną ~ę** not at any price | **za (wysoką) ~ę** at a price | **za wszelką ~ę** at all costs/at any cost, at any price
cenić prize[3], treasure[2], value[2]
cennik price list, tariff
cenny precious, valuable; **jej najcenniejsza własność** her most cherished possession
cent cent; (*US*) penny
centrala (*firmy*) head office; ~ **telefoniczna** switchboard, telephone exchange
centralizacja centralization
centralizować/s- centralize
centraln|y central; **C~a Agencja Wywiadowcza** CIA; **~e ogrzewanie** central heating
centrum 1 (*miasta*) downtown, town; (*kraju, okolicy itp.*) heartland; ~ **fitnessu** fitness centre; ~ **handlowe** shopping centre; **zadaszone** ~ **handlowe** shopping mall; **do/w** ~ **miasta** downtown **2** (*uwagi itp.*) focus[2]; (*działalności*) hub; ~ **uwagi** centre stage, focal point, spotlight; ~ **zainteresowania** the limelight
centryfuga centrifuge
centylitr centilitre
centymetr centimetre; ~ **sześcienny** cc
cenzor censor[1]
cenzura censorship
cenzurować/o- censor[2]
cera complexion
ceramiczn|y ceramic, earthenware; **wyroby ~e** earthenware noun
ceramika ceramic noun, ceramics, earthenware noun

ceregiel|a IDM **bez dalszych ~i** without further/more ado
ceremonia ceremony, rite
ceremonialny ceremonial; **(przesadnie)** ~ ceremonious
cerować/za- darn[1]; **zacerować dziurę** medn a hole
cesarski imperial IDM **~e cięcie** Caesarean
cesarstwo empire
cesarz emperor
cesarzowa empress
cetnar hundredweight
cewka 1 reel[1] **2** ~ **moczowa** urethra
cewnik (*do odprowadzania moczu*) catheter
cętk|a marking; **w ~i** spotted; **lamparty są w ciemne ~i** leopards have dark spots
cętkowany dappled, be dotted with, mottled, spotted
cha: ~, ~, ~! ha[1]
chaber cornflower
chała crap
chałupa cottage, hut, shack
cham bastard, peasant, scumbag
chamieć/s- coarsen
chamski uncouth
chand|ra the blues[2]; **poddawać się ~rze** mope; **mający ~rę** in the doldrums, down in the dumps
Chanuka Hanukkah
chaos chaos, confusion, mayhem, turmoil
chaotyczność incoherence
chaotyczny chaotic, disjointed, disorganized, haphazard, hit-and-miss, incoherent; (*rozmowa*) desultory
chap-ać/nąć snap[1]
charakter character, make-up; (*silny*) grit[1]; **moja praca ma tajny** ~ the nature of my work is secret; **bez ~u** characterless; ~ **pisma** handwriting, writing
charakterystyczny characteristic[1], distinctive, like[1], typical; (*przykład czegoś*) prime[1] IDM **w sposób ~ dla kogoś** true to form
charakteryzacja make-up
charakteryzować/s- characterize
charczeć/za-/wy- wheeze
chart greyhound
charytatywn|y charitable; **organizacja ~a** charity
charyzma charisma
charyzmatyczny charismatic
chaszcze wilderness
chata cabin, cottage, hut
chcieć/ze- please[2], want[1], wish[1], would like[3]; **(bardzo)** ~ be keen that/to do sth, would love[2] sth/to do sth; **bardzo** ~ **czegoś** hanker after/for sth; **~, żeby ktoś coś zrobił** intend sb to do sth; ~ **jak najlepiej** mean well; **jeżeli chcesz** if you like; **kiedy tylko zechcesz** whenever you choose; **to było niechcący** it was an accident; **nie chciała cię obrazić** she didn't mean to offend you; **chcąc nie chcąc** willy-nilly
chciwie greedily, hungrily
chciwość avarice, greed, greediness
chciwy greedy; (*na pieniądze*) avaricious, grasping

cheddar (*gatunek angielskiego sera*) Cheddar
chełpić się boast, gloat
chełpliwy boastful
chemia chemistry
chemiczn|y chemical[1]; **skład ~y** chemistry; **substancja ~a** chemical[2]
chemik chemist
chemikalia chemical[2]
chemioterapia chemotherapy
cherlak weed[1]
cherlawy scrawny, weedy
cherubin (także **cherubinek**) cherub
chęć readiness, willingness; **mieć ~** feel like sth/doing sth; **~ walki** fight[2]
chętnie eagerly, gladly, happily, willingly; (*w odpowiedzi na propozycję kawy itp.*) I wouldn't say no; **~ wziąłbym urlop** I could do with a holiday.
chętniej preferably
chętn|y amenable, eager, happy to do sth, keen, ready to do sth, willing IDM **być ~ym** be prepared to do sth
chichot chuckle noun; (*wydawany wysokim głosem*) giggle noun, titter noun; (*złośliwy*) snigger noun
chichotać/za- chuckle; (*wysokim głosem*) giggle, titter; (*złośliwie*) snigger
chińszczyzna (*coś niezrozumiałego*) double Dutch
chips crisp[2]
chirurg surgeon; **~ plastyczny** plastic surgeon
chirurgia: **~ plastyczna** plastic surgery
chirurgiczny surgical
chlać booze[2]
chlap-ać/nąć splash[1]; **~ trochę farby** slap some paint onto sth
chleb bread
chlew pigsty
chlip-ać/nąć slurp
chlor chlorine
chlorofil chlorophyll
chloroform chloroform
chlorować chlorinate
chlub|a boast noun IDM **przynosić komuś ~ę** do sb credit
chlubny creditable, glorious
chlup-ać/nąć (*nogami*) squelch
chlupotać/za- 1 (*woda, fala itp.*) lap[2], slosh **2** (*błoto itp.*) squelch
chlust gush noun
chlus-tać/nąć gush, spout[2]
chłam crap
chłeptać/wy- lap[2] sth (up)
chłodnica radiator
chłodny 1 (*i przen.*) cold[1], cool[1]; **~ i wietrzny** fresh **2** (*osoba; maniery*) clinical, distant; (*atmosfera itp.*) frigid
chłodziarka fridge
chłodzić/s- (się) chill[2], cool[2] (sth/sb) (down/off)
chłodziwo coolant
chłonąć/w-/po- (*wchłaniać*) imbibe
chłonny receptive
chłop 1 peasant **2** (*facet*) guy
chłopak 1 boy[1], guy, lad **2** (*sympatia*) boyfriend, date[1]
chłopczyca tomboy
chłopczyk baby boy
chłopiec boy[1], lad
chłopięc|y boyish; **~e lata** boyhood
chłopisko: **(wielkie) ~** hunk
chłopka peasant
chłosta beating, flogging
chłostać/wy- cane[2], flog, lash[1], thrash, whip[2]
chłód cool[3], chill[1], coldness, coolness
chmara host, swarm[1] of sth
chmiel hops[2]
chmielina hops[2]
chmur|a cloud[1]; (*pyłu itp.*) shower[1] IDM **pod ~y** sky-high
chochlik goblin, imp, pixie
chociaż albeit, although, even though, though
choć although, though
choćby even if
chodliwy: **~ towar** seller
chodnik pavement
chodzić/iść/pójść 1 (*do szkoły itp.*) go[1]; (*pieszo*) walk[1]; **(często) ~** (*do pewnego teatru itp.*) patronize; **~ ciężkimi krokami/z trudem** trudge; **~ we śnie** sleepwalk; **~ na wędrówkę** ramble[1]; **iść ulicą** walk along/down the street; **(no) chodź/cie!** come on **2 z kimś** date[2]; **~ ze sobą** go out (with sb), go out (together); **chciałbyś pójść z nami na drinka?** would you like to join us for a drink? **3 o coś; gdy/jeśli chodzi o coś/to** when it comes to sth/to doing sth, as/so far as sb/sth is concerned; **jeżeli o mnie/ciebie itp. chodzi** for my, his, their, etc. part; **o co chodzi?** what's up?; **to, o co właśnie chodzi** just the job/ticket **4** (*maszyna itp.*) work[1]; (*silnik*) turn over **5 ta piosenka chodzi mi po głowie cały dzień** I've had that song on my brain all day
choinka Christmas tree
chojrak daredevil
cholera 1 (*med.*) cholera **2** (*przekleństwo*) damn[2], hell
cholerny bloody, damn[1], darn[2], flaming, flipping, a/one hell of a…, raging, rotten, wretched
■ **cholernie** bloody adv., damn adv., darn adv., flipping adv.
cholesterol cholesterol
chomik hamster
chorał chorale
chorągiewka 1 (także **chorągiew**) flag[1]; (**chorągiewki**) bunting **2** (*osoba*) weed[1]
choreograf choreographer
choreografia choreography
chorob|a ailment, condition[1], disease, illness, sickness; (*roślin*) blight[2]; **~a Alzheimera** Alzheimer's disease; **~a Creutzfeldta-Jakoba** CJD; **~a morska** seasickness; **cierpiący na ~ę morską** seasick; **~a weneryczna** STD, venereal disease; **cierpiący na ~ę lokomocyjną** travel-sick; (*podróżujący samolotem*) airsick; (*samochodem*) carsick
chorobliwy morbid, pathological, unhealthy
chorować/za-: **chorować na coś** have[1]; **(za)chorować na coś** get, be/go down with sth; **~ na serce** have a heart condition
chorowity sickly
chor|y (*przym.*) ailing, diseased, grim, ill[1], sick[1]; (*serce itp.*) bad; **osoba ~a** (*na jakąś chorobę*) sufferer; **~y umysłowo** insane
■ **chor-y/a**; **(chorzy)** the sick[2]; **~y na astmę** asthma sufferer
chować/s-/za- 1 hide[1], secrete, tuck sth away; (*na miejsce*) put sth away; (*pod kluczem*) lock[1], lock sth away; (*na później*) hoard[2] (sth) (up), stow sth (away); **kogoś/coś** shut sb/sth away **2** (*zmarłego*) bury IDM **~ do kieszeni** (*np. obrazę*) swallow[1]
□ **chować/s- się** hide[1], lurk
chowan|y: **zabawa w ~ego** hide-and-seek
chód 1 (*osoby*) gait, walk[2] **2** (*maszyny*) motion[1]
chór choir, chorus[1]
chóralny choral; **utwór ~** chorus[1]
chrapać/za- snore
chrapliwy hoarse
chrobotać/za- scrape[1]
chrom chrome
chromatyczny chromatic
chromosom chromosome
chronić/u- conserve, cushion[2], guard[2], preserve, protect, safeguard, save[1], shelter[2] sb/sth (against/from sb/sth), shield[2]; (*przed niebezpieczeństwem/nieprzyjemnością*) ward sb/sth off
□ **chronić/s-/u- się: (przed czymś)** shelter[2] (from sth), take shelter from sth; (*przed niebezpieczeństwem/nieprzyjemnością*) ward sb/sth off
chroniony: **przed czymś** (*prawn. itp.*) immune (from sth)
chronologia chronology
chronologiczny chronological
chronometrażyst-a/ka timer
chropowacieć/s- coarsen
chropowatość roughness
chropowaty coarse, harsh, ragged, rugged, uneven
chrupać/s- chomp, crunch[2], munch
chrupiący crisp[1], crunchy; (*chleb*) crusty
chrust brushwood
chrypiąc|y: **o ~ym głosie** husky-voiced
chrypieć/za- croak
chrypka croak noun
chrypnąć/o-/za-: **ochrypli od krzyku** they shouted themselves hoarse
Chrystus Christ
chryzantema chrysanthemum
chrzan horseradish
chrzanić/s- (*sprawę*) mess sth up, screw (sth) up
chrząk-ać/nąć grunt
chrząstka (*anat.*) cartilage; (*w mięsie*) gristle
chrząstkowaty gristly
chrząszcz beetle; **~ ryjkowiec** weevil
chrzcić/o- baptize, christen
chrzcielnica font
chrzciny christening
chrzest baptism
chrześcijan-in/ka Christian
chrześcijański Christian adj.
chrześcijaństwo Christianity
chrześniaczka godchild, god-daughter
chrześniak godchild, godson
chrzęst (*odgłos chrupania*) crunch[1]
chrzęścić/za- crunch[2]
chuchro weed[1]
chudnąć/s- lose weight
chudy 1 thin[1] **2** (*mięso*) lean[2]
chuligan hooligan, yob
chuliganić/po- rampage[2]
chuliganizm hooliganism
chuligański disorderly; **~e zachowanie** unruliness
chusta shawl; (*na szyję/głowę*) scarf; (*biało nakrapiana*) bandanna
chusteczka (*do nosa*) handkerchief; **~ higieniczna** facecloth, tissue
chustka scarf; **~ do nosa** handkerchief

chwalebny commendable, creditable, praiseworthy

chwalić/po- commend, laud, praise[2]
□ **chwalić/po- się** boast

chwała 1 (*sława*) glory[1] **2** (*szacunek*) praise[1] **3** (*chluba*) boast noun

chwast weed[1]

chwastobójczy: **środek** ~ weedkiller

chwiać/za- wobble
□ **chwiać/za- się** falter, waver, wobble; (*osoba*) **chwiać się na nogach** totter

chwiejność indecision

chwiejn|y 1 rickety, shaky, unstable, wobbly; **na ~ych nogach** groggy; **stać/iść na ~ych nogach** totter **2** (*niezdecydowany*) indecisive

chwil|a instant[2], minute[1], moment, while[2]; **od tej ~i** hence, hereafter IDM **po ~i** after a little | **przez ~ę** for a little | **do tej ~i** up to sth | **w każdej ~i** anytime soon, (at) any minute/moment (now) | **w tej ~i** this minute, at the moment, right now | **za ~ę** in a minute, in a moment

chwileczka a little while
IDM **chwileczkę** just a minute

chwilka tick[2]

chwilowo briefly, in the interim, for the moment/present, momentarily, temporarily, for the time being

chwilowy interim[1], momentary, passing[2], temporary

chwycić/po-/u- zob. też CHWYTAĆ; get, seize; **starać się uchwycić coś** grasp at sth, clutch at sth

chwyt 1 (*rękami*) catch[2]; (*w judo itp.*) hold[2] **2** (*rugby*) tackle[2] **3** (*reklamowy itp.*) come-on, gimmick; ~ **reklamowy** publicity stunt

chwytać/s-/chwycić 1 (*złapać*) catch[1]; ~ **(w sidła)** (*przen.: przestępcę*) trap[2] **2** (*wziąć nagle i gwałtownie*) catch, get, grab, take, etc. hold (of sb/sth), grab, snatch[1]; (*próbować wziąć*) snatch at sth **3** (*mocno trzymać*) grasp[1], grip[2] **4** (**chwycić**) (*przyjąć się*) catch on, take off **5** (*rugby*) tackle[1] **6** (*kurcz*) crick verb

chwytliwy (*hasło*) catchy

chyba arguably, maybe, perhaps, I suppose, surely, well[1]; ~ **nie** hardly, scarcely; ~ **że** unless; ~ **nie pożyczysz mi swego samochodu?** I don't suppose you'd lend me your car?; **„Czy będziesz mógł mi pomóc?" „Chyba tak."** 'Will you be able to help?' 'I expect/suppose so.'

chybi(a)ć miss[1]; **na chybił trafił** haphazardly, hit-and-miss, at random, wild[1]

chybiony (*ocena sytuacji*) wide of the mark

chybotać/za- (się) wobble

chybotliwy rickety, wobbly

chylić się (*ku upadkowi*) decay[2]

chyłkiem: **przemieszczać się** ~ slink

chytrość cunning noun

chytry crafty, cunning, devious, shifty, sly, wily

ciach-ać/nąć slash[1]; ~ **nożyczkami** snip[1] (sth) (off/out/in, etc.)

ciało 1 (*osoby*) body; ~ **zmarłego** corpse **2** (*tkanka*) flesh **3** (*fiz.*) ~ **stałe** solid[2]

ciark|a (**ciarki**) shudder noun; **przechodzą mnie ~i** it gives me the creeps; **~i mnie przechodzą na myśl** I shudder to think; **na samą myśl o tym ~i mi przeszły po plecach** the thought sent a shiver down my spine

ciasno tight adv., tightly

ciasnota narrowness, tightness; ~ **poglądów** insularity

ciasn|y 1 (*obcisły*) tight **2** (*przestrzeń itp.*) poky **3** (*w poglądach*) insular; **o ~ym umyśle** narrow-minded

ciastko cake[1]; (*z ciasta francuskiego*) pastry; **kruche** ~ shortbread

ciasto 1 (*masa*) dough; (*na pierogi itp.*) pastry; ~ **naleśnikowe** batter[2] **2** (*wypiek*) cake[1]

ciąć/po- cut[1], slash[1]; ~ **coś na kawałki** cut sth up; ~ **na plasterki** slice[2]; ~ **na strzępy** shred[1]

ciąg series; (*wydarzeń lub liczbowy itp.*) sequence; (*skarg itp.*) string[1]; (*myśli, zdarzeń*) train[1]; (*czasu*) space[1]; ~ **dalszy** continuation; **cd.** cont.; **w ~u** by, within; **w ~u około godziny** in about an hour IDM **(jednym) ~iem** at a stretch, on the trot

ciągle always, constantly, continually, continuously, endlessly, ever-, forever, permanently, perpetually, persistently, still[1]; (*opisać itp.*) seamlessly; ~ **coś robić** keep[1] doing sth

ciągły 1 constant, continual, continued, continuous, endless, perpetual, persistent, unrelenting; (*walka itp.*) running[2]; (*problem*) perennial; (*opis itp.*) seamless **2** (*gram., czas*) continuous
■ **ciągłoś|ć** continuity; **bez ciągłości** fitfully

ciągnąć/po- drag[1], haul[1], pull[1]; **za kimś/czymś** trail[2]; (*gwałtownie*) wrench[1]; (*z trudem*) heave[1]; (*w górę*) hoist; (*auto itp.*) tow; **wolno** ~ (*coś na kołach*) trundle; **powóz ciągnęło sześć koni** the carriage was drawn by six horses; ~ **kogoś za sobą** with sb in tow; ~ **za coś wielokrotnie** pick at sth IDM **ciągnąć losy** draw lots
□ **ciągnąć się 1** (*sznur itp.*) trail[2], run on **2** (*teren*) spread[1]; (*na dużej przestrzeni*) sprawl **3** (*czas*) go[1], wear on
■ **ciągnący się 1** (*spotkanie itp.*) drawn-out **2** (*cukierek itp.*) chewy, gooey

ciągnik tractor

ciąż|a pregnancy; **okres ~y** gestation, pregnancy; **w ~y** expectant, pregnant
■ **ciążow|y**: **ubranie ~owe** maternity clothes

ciążyć/za-: **ku komuś/czemuś** gravitate to/toward(s) sb/sth

cichaczem surreptitiously

cichnąć/u- die away, die down

cich|o noiselessly, quietly, silently, softly; (*popierać itp.*) tacitly; **~o!** hush[1], be quiet!, sh; **mów ~o!** keep your voice down!; **po ~u** softly; **robiący coś po ~u** secret[1]
IDM **siedzieć ~o** (*przen.*) keep your head down

cichy 1 (*dźwięk*) noiseless, quiet[1], silent, soft **2** (*spokojny*) calm[1], low-key, tranquil **3** (*tajny*) secret[1]; (*zgoda itp. na coś*) tacit

ciec/po- trickle; **ślinka mu ciekła na myśl o milionie dolarów** he was salivating over the thought of the million dollars

ciecierzyca chickpea

ciecz fluid[1], liquid

cieczk|a IDM **mieć ~ę** be on heat

ciekawić/za- interest[2], intrigue[1]

ciekawostka curiosity

ciekawość curiosity

ciekawski curious, inquisitive

ciekawstwo inquisitiveness

ciekaw|y 1 (*nienudny*) exciting, interesting; **~e miejsca** sight[1]; **co ~e** curiously enough, interestingly **2 czegoś** curious, interested; **być ~ym (czegoś)** wonder[1] (about sth)

ciekły liquid; (*metal itp.*) molten

cieknąć/po-/pociec run[1]
■ **cieknący** runny

cielesny 1 bodily[1], carnal, physical **2** (*materialny*) material[2]

cielę calf

cielęcina veal

ciemię crown[1] IDM **nie być w ~ bitym** keep your wits about you

ciemięż-ca/czyni persecutor

ciemnia: ~ **fotograficzna** darkroom

ciemniak dimwit

ciemnieć/ś- dim[2]

ciemno- dark[1]

ciemnogród the dark ages

ciemnoniebieski royal blue

ciemność blackness, dark[2], darkness, gloom

ciemnozielony bottle-green

ciemn|y 1 dark[1]; (*kolor*) deep[1], dull, murky, sombre; **niebo nagle zrobiło się ~e** the sky suddenly darkened **2** (*tępy*) dull-witted **3** (*nieuczciwy*) **~y interes** a dodgy business deal

cieniować/po- shade[2] sth (in)

cienisty shadowy, shady

cienki 1 (*nie gruby/szeroki*) thin[1]; (*włosy, tkanina*) fine[1]; (*tkanina itp.*) flimsy; (*włosy*) wispy; (*złamanie*) **bardzo** ~ hairline[2] **2** (*głos*) high[1] **3** (*słaby z czegoś*) weak (at/in/on sth) **4** (*zupa itp.*) watery; (*wino, kawa*) weak

cienko thin adv., thinly IDM ~ **przędąc** on a shoestring

cie|ń shade[1], shadow[1]; **~ń do powiek** eyeshadow IDM **gabinet ~ni** shadow cabinet | **iść (za kimś) jak ~ń** tag along (behind/with sb) | **kłaść się ~niem** cast a shadow (across/over sth), cast a blight on sth | **pozostać w ~niu** stay in the background, take a back seat

cieplarnia conservatory, greenhouse, hothouse

cieplny thermal[1]

cieplutko: **koło kominka jest** ~ it's nice and warm by the fire

ciepławy lukewarm

ciepło (*rz.*) heat[1], the warm noun, warmth
■ **ciepło** (*przysł.*) warmly; (*ciepło i wygodnie*) snugly; **podskakiwałem, żeby mi było ~ w nogi** I jumped up and down to keep my feet warm

ciepłokrwisty warm-blooded

ciepłota temperature

ciepł|y warm[1]; (*kolor, tony itp.*) mellow; (*bielizna*) thermal[1] IDM **~a posadka** a cushy job

ciernisty prickly, thorny

cierń prickle[2], spine, thorn

cierpieć 1 (**/ś-/u-**) (*przeżywać*) bear[1], endure, go through sth, stick[1], stomach[2], suffer, tolerate;

najbardziej ucierpieć od czegoś/z powodu czegoś bear the brunt of sth; **nie ucierpieć (w wyniku czegoś)** be none the worse (for sth); ~ **z powodu bezrobocia** be hit by unemployment; (*nie znosić*) **nie** ~ can't/couldn't abide sb/sth/doing sth, detest, hate[1] **2 na coś** be afflicted with sth; ~ **ból** be in pain; **często cierpi na ból głowy** he often gets really bad headaches
■ **cierpiący** anguished

cierpienie affliction, pain[1], suffering; (*umysłu*) hurt[3]; (**cierpienia**) anguish, misery, torment; **cierpienia duchowe** anguish IDM **skrócić czyjeś ~** put sb out of his/her misery

cierpki caustic
■ **cierpko** crisply | **cierpkość 1** astringency, sourness **2** (*przen.*) acrimony, astringency

cierpliwość endurance, patience

cierpliwy long-suffering, patient[2]

cierpnąć/ś- go to sleep IDM **sprawiać, że komuś cierpnie skóra** make your flesh creep

cieszyć/u- please[2], tickle; **ucieszyć kogoś** make sb's day
□ **cieszyć się/u- się: (z czegoś)** be delighted, be glad, be happy; **na coś** look forward to sth/doing sth, relish[1]; **czymś** delight in sth/in doing sth; (*z cudzego nieszczęścia*) gloat; **cieszący się złą sławą** notorious (for/as sth)

cieśla carpenter, joiner

cieśnina strait

cietrzew grouse

cięcie 1 cut[2], slash[2]; **głębokie** ~ gash **2** (*w budżecie itp.*) cut[2] (in sth), cutback

cięgi hiding, thrashing

cięt|y scathing; **~a odpowiedź** retort[2] IDM **być ~ym (na kogoś)** have (got) it in for sb

ciężar 1 (*waga*) heaviness, weight[1]; ~ **właściwy** density **2** (*ładunek*) burden[1], load[1] **3** (*obciążenie*) bind[2], burden[1], liability **4** (*treść, istota itp.*) substance IDM **zrzucić ~ z serca** get sth off your chest

ciężar|ek: ćwiczenia z użyciem ~ków weight training

ciężarna pregnant

ciężarowiec (*sport*) weightlifter

ciężarówka lorry

ciężk|i 1 (*waga*) heavy; (*nieporęczny*) unwieldy; (*biżuteria*) chunky **2** (*trudny*) hard[1], stiff[1], tough (on sb); (*praca*) heavy **3** (*stan*) rough[1], severe; (*długi itp.*) crippling; (*pogoda*) oppressive **4** (*mowa, styl pisania*) laboured, ponderous, stodgy **5** (*jedzenie*) rich, stodgy IDM **~i sprzęt** hardware

ciężko 1 heavily **2** (*trudno*) ill[2], rough[4]; **będzie** ~ it'll be hard going; ~ **chodzący/działający** stiff[1]; ~ **mi się czyta tę powieść** I'm finding this novel very heavy going **2** (*pracować*) hard[2] **3** (*poważnie*) ~ **ranny** badly hurt **4** (*mówić, pisać*) ponderously

cii shush

ciołek clod

cios 1 bang[2], blow[2], knock[2]; (*trzęsienia ziemi itp.*) shock[1]; **mocny** ~ bash[2]; ~ **karate** karate chop; ~ **na oślep/na chybił trafił** swipe noun **2** (*emocjonalny*) blow[2]

ciosać/wy- hew

ciota ponce[1], queer noun

ciotka aunt

cis 1 (*bot.*) yew **2** **(Cis/cis)** (*muz.*) C sharp

cis-kać/nąć (*rzucać*) bundle[2], cast[1], chuck, dash[2], fling[1], hurl, slap[1], sling[1], throw IDM **~ gromy na kogoś** harangue

cisnąć 1 **(/przy-)** (*wywierać nacisk*) press[2] **2** (*but itp.*) pinch[1]

cisza hush[2], quietness, quiet[2], silence, stillness; **chwilowa** ~ lull[1]

ciśnienie pressure, stress[1]; ~ **krwi** blood pressure; **utrzymujący odpowiednie dla ludzi ~ atmosferyczne** pressurized

ciuch **(ciuchy)** gear[1], things

ciuciubabka blind man's buff

ciułacz saver

ciżba throng[1]

ckliwość schmaltz

ckliwy mawkish, mushy, schmaltzy, sloppy, slushy, soppy

cł|o duty, tariff; **bez ~a** duty-free adv.

cmentarz cemetery, graveyard

cmentarzysko burial ground

cmok-ać/nąć peck

cnota virtue; (*seksualna*) chastity

cnotliw|y virtuous; (*seksualnie*) chaste; **~e życie** a life of virtue

co 1 what; ~? eh, huh; ~ **(za)?** what, whatever; ~ **będzie, jeżeli** what if…? **2** (*w zdaniu uzupełniającym*) which; **(ten)** ~ who **3** (*jakiś czas*) every, every now and then; ~ **tydzień** weekly[1] IDM **~ do** as for | **~ do kogoś/czegoś** as/so far as sb/sth is concerned | **~ do mnie/ciebie itp.** for my, his, their, etc. part, personally | **a ~ najśmieszniejsze/najdziwniejsze itp., to…** funnily/strangely, etc. enough | **no ~ ty!** come off it | **(i) ~ z tego?** so what?

codziennie daily adv., day in, day out

codzienn|y 1 daily[1], day-to-day; (*życie*) everyday **2** (*ubranie*) casual

cof-ać/nąć/wy- 1 (*auto*) back[4], back sth up, reverse[1] **2** (*to, co się powiedziało*) take sth back, withdraw **3** (*uprawnienia itp.*) revoke **4** (*wskazówki zegara*) put sth back
□ **cof-ać/nąć/wy- się 1** back away (from sb/sth), recede, retreat[1], stand back (from sth); (*szybko, gwałtownie*) flinch (away), pull away, recoil; (*z przerażenia*) shrink **2** (*auto*) back[4], back up **3 do czegoś** retrace IDM **nie ~ przed niczym** stop at nothing

cogodzinny hourly

cokolwiek anything, whatever IDM **czy ~** (*innego itp.*) or whatever

cokół pedestal

comber rump

comiesięczny monthly[1]

conocny nightly

contra versus

coraz and; ~ **(bardziej)** increasingly IDM **~ mniej** less and less

coroczny annual[1], yearly

coś something, stuff[1], thing; (*w pytaniach/przeczeniach*) anything; ~ **innego** something else IDM **~ takiego!** fancy[1], good gracious!

cotygodniowy weekly[1]

country: muzyka ~ country and western

cover (*nowa wersja utworu muzycznego*) cover version

córka daughter, girl

cóż 1 whatever; **a ~ to takiego?** what's that? **2** **(no)** ~ well[3]

cuchnący foul[1], malodorous, smelly; (*zwł. zgnilizną*) putrid

cuchnąć reek, stink

cucić/o- bring sb round, revive

cud 1 (*relig.*) miracle **2** (*przen.*) marvel, miracle, wonder[2]; (*osoba*) prodigy; (*zdążyć na koncert itp.*) **~em** by the skin of your teeth; **jakim ~em…?** how ever…?; **uczynić ~a dla kogoś/czegoś** do wonders for sb/sth, work/perform miracles

cudaczny freakish, quirky, weird

cudo beauty

cudown|y fabulous, gorgeous, magic[2], marvellous, miraculous, wonderful; IDM **~e dziecko** whizz-kid

cudzołożnica adulteress

cudzołożnik adulterer

cudzołóstwo adultery

cudzoziem-iec/ka alien[2], foreigner

cudzoziemski alien[1], foreign

cudzy: żyć na ~ koszt freeload

cudzysłów quotation mark

cugiel bridle[1]

cukier sugar; ~ **kryształ** granulated sugar; ~ **puder** icing sugar

cukierek sweet[2]; ~ **miętowy** mint, peppermint

cukierkowy sugary

cukiernia baker's, bakery

cukiernica sugar bowl

cukierniczy|y: wyroby ~e confectionery

cukinia courgette

cukrzyca diabetes

cukrzycowy diabetic[1]

cukrzyk diabetic[2]; **dla ~ów** diabetic[1]

cumować/za- moor[2]; (*w doku*) dock[2]

c.v. (*życiorys*) CV

cwany shifty, sly

cyberprzestrzeń cyberspace

cybuch blowpipe

cyc tit

cycek (*wymię zwierzęcia*) teat; (*piers*) boob, tit

cydr cider

cyferblat dial[1]

cyfr|a digit, figure[1], numeral; **~y rzymskie** Roman numerals

cyfrow|y digital, numerical; **telewizja ~a** digital television; **zapis ~y** digital recording; **przetwarzać w postać ~ą** digitize

Cygan/ka Gypsy

cyganeri|a: członek ~i bohemian

cyganić/o-/wy- diddle sb (out of sth), wangle

cygaro cigar

cyjanek cyanide

cykada cicada

cykl cycle[1]; ~ **życia** life cycle

cykliczny cyclic, periodic

cyklon cyclone

cykoria chicory

cylinder 1 (*kapelusz*) top hat **2** (*geom.*) cylinder

cylindryczny cylindrical

cymbał prat, twit, wally

cyna tin

cynaderka kidney

cynadra kidney

cynamon cinnamon

cyngiel trigger[1]

cyniczny cynical, jaundiced

cynik cynic

cynizm cynicism

cynk (*metal*) zinc

cynkować/o- galvanize
cypel headland, spit[2]
cyrk **1** circus **2** (*przen.*) carry-on
cyrkiel compass
cyrkulacj|a: **utrzymywać ~ę** circulate
cyrylica: **dot. cyrylicy** Cyrillic
cysta cyst
cysterna **1** (*pojemnik*) tank **2** (*pojazd*) tanker
cytat citation, quotation
cytologiczn|y: **badanie ~e** (*szyjki macicy*) smear test
cytować/za- cite, quote
cytrusowy citrus
cytryna lemon
cytrynowy citric
cywil civilian
cywilizacja civilization
cywilizować/u- civilize
cywilizowany civilized
cywiln|y civil; **stan ~y** marital status; **~e ubranie** plain clothes; **po ~emu** plain-clothes adj.
czador (także **czadra**) chador
czadowy funky
czaić/za- się lurk, prowl, skulk; **(na kogoś)** lie in wait (for sb)
czajniczek teapot
czajnik kettle
czapka cap[1]; **wełniana ~ sportowa** (*w kształcie półpiłki*) beanie
czapla heron
czar allure, magic[1], spell[2]; **(czary)** magic[1], witchcraft
czarno-biały black and white, monochrome
czarnoksiężnik sorcerer, wizard
czarnoskóry black[1]
czarn|y black[1]; **~y jak smoła** pitch-black; **kolor ~y** black[2] IDM **~a dziura** black hole | **~a jagoda** bilberry | **~a magia** black magic | **~a owca** black sheep | **~y charakter** baddy, villain | **~y rynek** black market | **odkładać coś na ~ą godzinę** keep/save sth for a rainy day
■ **czarno** IDM **~ na białym** in black and white
czarodziej wizard, magician
czarodziejka magician
czarodziejski magic[2], magical
czarownica sorceress, witch
czarownik wizard
czart devil
czarter charter[1]
czarterować charter[2]
czarterowy charter[1]; **lot ~** charter flight
czarujący captivating, enchanting, enthralling, fetching
czary-mary abracadabra
czas **1** time[1]; **dużo ~u** for (so) long; **~ trwania** length, running time, standing[2]; **~ letni** summer time; **~ miejscowy** local time; **średni ~ zachodnioeuropejski** GMT; **przez cały ~** all along; **znajdować ~ na coś** get round/around to sth/doing sth; **naprawdę nie mamy ~u** we're really pushed for time **2** (*poświęcony czemuś*) bout; **(określony/proponowany) ~** (*np. spotkania*) timing; **(czasy)** age[1], day(s), time[1]; **w dzisiejszych ~ach** these days; **~y współczesne** the present day; **~ antenowy** slot[1]; **~ wojny** wartime; **~ wolny** leisure; **do ~u czegoś** pending; **do tego ~u** until then, up to sth; **od tego ~u** from now/then on, thereafter; **w ~ie** over, while[1]; **w tym ~ie** meanwhile **3** (*gram.*) tense[2]; **~ ciągły** the continuous tense; **~ dokonany** the perfect tense; **~ przeszły** past[2]; **~ przeszły ciągły** past continuous; **~ przeszły dokonany** past perfect; **~ przeszły dokonany ciągły** past perfect continuous; **~ przeszły niedokonany** the imperfect; **~ przyszły** future; **~ przyszły dokonany** the future perfect; **~ teraźniejszy** the present tense; **~ teraźniejszy dokonany** the present perfect; **~ teraźniejszy prosty** the present simple IDM **na ~ie** timely | **nie na ~ie** dated | **co jakiś ~** (every) now and again/then | **na ~** in good time, in time (for sth/to do sth), on time | **od ~u do ~u** every so often, (every) now and again/then, from time to time, occasionally, off and on, on and off, once in a while | **pod presją ~u** against the clock | **przed ~em** in good time, in time (for sth/to do sth) | **przed ~em/po ~ie** to be ahead of/behind schedule | **w ~ie (czegoś)** in the process of sth/doing sth | **z upływem ~u** in the course of time, as time went by
czasami on occasion(s), occasionally, sometimes, at times, from time to time
czasem sometimes
czasochłonny time-consuming
czasopismo magazine, periodical; (*zwł. monotematyczne*) journal; **~ elektroniczne** e-zine; **~ internetowe** webzine
czasownik verb; **~ frazowy** phrasal verb; **~ modalny** modal; **~ posiłkowy** auxiliary verb; **~ złożony** phrasal verb
czasza: **~ spadochronu** a parachute canopy
czaszka cranium, skull
czaszkowy cranial
czat chat[2]
czatować skulk, watch[1] sb/sth (for sth)
czat|y watch[2]; **stać na ~ach** look out (for sb/sth)
cząsteczka **1** particle **2** (*fiz.*) molecule
cząstka fraction, particle, segment
cząstkowy piecemeal
czcić/u- **1** (*pamięć kogoś/czegoś*) cherish, honour[2], revere, venerate **2** (*obchodzić*) celebrate, commemorate; **dla uczczenia** celebratory **3** (*relig.*) worship
czcigodny honourable, venerable
czcionka font, type[1]
czczy empty[1]
czek cheque; **~ in blanco** blank cheque; **~ podróżny** traveller's cheque
czekać/za-/po- await, hold on, wait[1]; (*przy telefonie*) hold[1]; **~ cierpliwie** bear with sb/sth, wait and see; **~ na coś lepszego** hold out for sth; **~ na swoją kolej** wait your turn; **czeka cię niespodzianka** there's a surprise in store for you
czekolada chocolate; (*nieform.*) choccy; **~ gorzka** dark chocolate; **~ mleczna** milk chocolate
czekoladka chocolate; (*nieform.*) choc, choccy
czekoladowy chocolate adj.; **kolor ~** chocolate
czelność audacity, nerve
czempion/ka champ[2]
czemu why; **~ nie?** why not?
czepek bonnet, cap[1]; **~ kąpielowy** swimming cap
czepiać się: **kogoś** get at sb, have a go at sb
czereda host
czereśnia cherry
czernić/za-/o- blacken
czernieć blacken
czerń black[2], blackness
czerpać/zaczerpnąć derive, get sth out of sth; (*natchnienie itp.*) draw[1]
czerstwieć/s- go stale
czerstwy stale
czerwiec June
czerwienić/za- redden
□ **czerwienić/za- się** flush[1], redden
czerwień red noun
czerwonawy reddish
czerwonka dysentery
czerwon|y red IDM **~a kartka** red card | **~a porzeczka** redcurrant | **~y dywan** the red carpet
czesać/u- comb[2]
□ **czesać/u- się** do your hair, give your hair a comb
czesne (*za studia*) fees, tuition fees
cześć **1** (*szacunek*) homage, honour[1], reverence, veneration; **na ~ kogoś/czegoś** in honour of sb/sth, in sb/sth's honour; **pełen czci** reverent **2** **oddawanie czci boskiej** worship noun
■ **cześć** (*powitanie*) hello, hi, hiya, yo; (*pożegnanie*) bye, cheerio, cheers
często frequently, a lot[2], often, regularly, repeatedly; **bardzo ~** more often than not; **czy ~ chodzisz do kina?** do you go to the cinema much?
częstość frequency
częstotliwoś|ć frequency; **modulacja ~ci** FM
częstować/po- treat[1] sb (to sth); **~ wszystkich** hand sth around/round; **natarczywie ~ kogoś czymś** ply sb with sth
□ **częstować/po- się** help[1], treat[1] yourself (to sth)
częsty frequent[1], repeated; (*powracający*) perennial
częściowo in part, part[3], partially, partly, up to a point
częściowy partial, qualified
częś|ć **1** element, part[1], piece[1], portion, proportion, share[2], unit; **~ć składowa** component, constituent, part[1]; **~ć zapasowa** spare part; **~ci zamienne** spare parts for a car; **~ci garderoby** articles of clothing; **na ~ci** apart; **być ~cią czegoś** go with sth; **stanowić ~ć czegoś** form[2] **2** (*muz.*) movement IDM **~ć mowy** part of speech
czips crisp[2]
czirliderka cheerleader
czk-ać/nąć hiccup
czkawka hiccup
człon-ek/kini **1** insider, member; **członek Kongresu** MC; **członek-założyciel** founder member; **liczba członków** membership **2** **członek męski** penis
członkostwo membership
człowieczy human[1]

człowiek human², individual², man¹, person; ~ **interesu** businessman; **jest tylko ~iem** he's only human
czmych-ać/nąć flee
czołg tank
czołgać się crawl¹, creep¹, grovel
czoł|o 1 (*anat.*) brow, forehead **2** (*pozycja*) head¹, lead²; **na czele** forefront; **być na czele** be/come to the fore, head² IDM **~o fali morskiej** surf¹ | **stawić ~a czemuś/komuś** brave², confront, face², face up to sth, be up against sth/sb
czołobitność sycophancy
czołobitny sycophantic
czołow|y 1 (*główny*) foremost, leading; **~a pozycja** forefront; **na ~ą pozycję** ahead **2** (*atak*) frontal; (*zderzenie*) head-on
■ **czołowo** head-on adv.
czołówka cutting edge, lead²
czop (*osi*) pivot¹
czort devil
czosnek garlic
czółenko pump¹
czterdziesty fortieth
czterdzieści forty
czternasty fourteenth
czternaście fourteen
czterokołowiec quad bike
czterokrotnie: **powiększać (się)** ~ quadruple
cztery four
czubek 1 (*ołówka itp.*) point¹; (*głowy, drzewa*) top¹; (*głowy*) crown¹ **2** (*wariat*) nut
czuci|e feeling, sensation; (*dotyk*) touch²; **bez ~a** numb; **brak ~a** numbness
czuć/po-/wy- feel¹; ~ **instynktownie** sense²; **nadal coś czuje do swojej byłej żony** he still has feelings for his ex-wife; ~ **smak** taste²; ~ **zapach** smell¹; **poczuł zapach jej perfum** he caught a whiff of her perfume IDM **nie czuję nóg** my feet are killing me
□ **czuć/po- się** feel¹; **źle się czuć** not feel yourself
czujka lookout
czujnik: ~ **alarmowy** detector; ~ **pożarowy** smoke alarm
czujność guard¹, vigilance
czujn|y 1 alert¹, vigilant, watchful; **być ~ym** watch¹ sb/sth (for sth); **(nie być/być) ~ym** off/on (your) guard **2** (*sen*) light²
czułek antenna, feeler, tentacle
czułość tenderness
czuł|y 1 (*okazujący czułość*) affectionate, fond, tender¹ **2** (*wrażliwy*) responsive, sensitive; (*słuch itp.*) keen **3** (*fot.*) fast¹ IDM **~e miejsce** a sore point
czuwać: **nad kimś/czymś** keep vigil over sb, watch over sb/sth; ~ **do późna w nocy** stay up
■ **czuwanie** (*przy zwłokach*) wake²; ~ **całonocne** vigil
czwartek Thursday
czwartkowy Thursday
czwarty fourth
czworak|i: **na ~ach** on all fours; **chodzić na ~ach** grovel (around/about) (for sth)
czworobok square²
czworonożny four-footed
czy 1 (*w pytaniach*) might¹, shall **2** (*w pytaniach zależnych*) if, whether **3** ~ **(też)** or; **(bez względu na to)** ~... **czy też nie** whether or not; ~ **coś takiego** or something; ~ **gdzieś tam** or somewhere
czyhać skulk
czyj whose
czyjś one's, your
czyli that is to say…
czyn action, deed; ~ **bohaterski** an act of bravery, brave deed, exploit²; **wprowadzić plan w** ~ put a plan into action
czynel cymbal
czynić/u-/po- do¹
czynieni|e: **mieć z kimś do ~a** have dealings with sb
czynnik factor; ~ **rakotwórczy** carcinogen; **rozkładać coś na ~i** break sth down
czynność activity
czynn|y active; (*gram.*) **w stronie ~ej** active
czynsz rent¹
czyrak (*na skórze itp.*) boil²; (*wrzód*) ulcer
czystk|a purge noun; **~i etniczne** ethnic cleansing
czysto 1 (*śpiewać/grać*) in/out of tune **2 zarabiać/przynosić na** ~ net³
czyst|y 1 (*pozbawiony brudu*) clean¹ **2** (*uporządkowany*) tidy¹ **3** (*bez domieszek*) pure, unadulterated; (*zwł. alkohol*) neat; (*koń itp.*) **~ej krwi** thoroughbred **4** (*woda; niebo*) clear¹ **5** (*papier*) blank¹ **6** (*moralnie*) chaste, pure **7** (*legalny*) above board **8** (*głupota, szaleństwo itp.*) sheer; (*przyjemność itp.*) unadulterated; **przez ~y przypadek** by pure chance **9** (*zysk*) net² **10** (*teoretyczny*) pure
czyścić/wy- clean²; ~ **szczotką** brush², brush sth away, brush sth off (sth); ~ **chemicznie** dry-clean
czyściec purgatory
czytać/prze-/wy- (*książkę itp.; w myślach, oczach*) read¹; (*gazetę itp.*) look at sth; **dużo** ~ do a lot of reading; ~ **dalej** read on; **przeczytałem w gazecie** I saw in the paper; ~ **coś na głos** read sth out; ~ **z ruchu warg** lip-read
czytanie read², reading
czytanka reader
czytelni-k/czka reader; **liczba czytelników** readership
czytelność legibility
czytelny intelligible, legible, readable
czytnik: ~ **kart magnetycznych** card swipe
czyżby indeed, really

Ć

ćma moth
ćpun/ka junkie
ćwiartka quarter
ćwiczeni|e drill¹, exercise¹; (*na instrumencie itp.*) practice; **~a wojskowe** exercise¹; **~a w terenie** fieldwork; **~e sprawdzające rozumienie** comprehension; **robić ~a gimnastyczne** work out
ćwiczyć/prze-/wy- drill², exercise², do exercises; (*na instrumencie itp.*) practise; (*mięśnie itp.*) flex¹; (*piosenkę itp.*) rehearse
ćwiek nail, stud
ćwierć quarter
ćwierćfinał quarter-final
ćwierćnuta crotchet
ćwierkać/za- chirp, twitter

D

d 1 (D/d) (*litera*) D, d **2 (D/d)** (*muz.*) D
dach roof, rooftop; **pod ~em** covered IDM ~ **nad głową** a roof over your head
dachówk|a tile; **~a łupkowa** slate; **pokrywać ~ą** tile verb
daktyl date¹
dal: **w ~i słyszałem płaczące dziecko** I could hear a child crying in the background; **skok w** ~ long jump; **z ~a** clear³ (of sth), from afar; **z ~a od czegoś** away (from sth)
dalej 1 (*w przestrzeni*) along adv., further¹, further adv., onwards, up; **(położony)** ~ beyond adv.; **nie ~ niż** within sth (of sth); **iść/posuwać się** ~ continue **2** (*w czasie*) onwards IDM **no ~!** come on, go on | **i tak ~** and so forth | **i tak ~, i tak ~** blah
daleki distant, far¹, faraway, remote; (*przewozy ludzi/towarów*) long-haul; **Daleki Wschód** the Far East; **~ego zasięgu** long-haul, long-range
daleko far², far afield, out¹; **bardzo ~** way²; **to nie jest ~** it's no distance; **tak ~ jak** as far as; **jeszcze ~ do Świąt Bożego Narodzenia** Christmas is still a long way off; ~ **od celu** wide¹; **strzelić ~ od celu** miss the target by a mile; ~ **od uzyskania/osiągnięcia czegoś** nowhere near IDM **trzymać się z daleka (od kogoś/czegoś)** keep/stay/steer clear (of sb/sth), stay away (from sb/sth) | **trzymający się z daleka (od innych)** aloof | **za ~ się posunąć** go too far
dalekopis telex
dalekosiężny far-reaching
dalekowidz: **jestem ~em** I'm long-sighted
dalekowidzący far-sighted
dalekowzroczn|y 1 long-sighted **2** (*przen.*) far-sighted; (*osoba*) **o ~ych planach** forward-looking
dalmatyńczyk Dalmatian
dalszy 1 (*w przestrzeni*) further¹, onward, outlying **2** (*w czasie*) subsequent; ~ **ciąg** sequel
daltonist-a/ka: **ona jest daltonistką** she's colour-blind
daltonizm: **cierpiący na ~** colour-blind
dama 1 lady; ~ **dworu** courtier **2** (*w kartach*) queen
dane data; (*wprowadzane do komputera*) input¹; (*z komputera*) output; ~ **statystyczne** statistics; **dokładne ~** facts and figures, particulars
danie course, dish¹; **dania gotowe** convenience food
dar (*prezent*) boon; (*talent*) flair; ~ **perswazji** persuasiveness; ~ **niebios** godsend; **szczodry ~** bounty
darczyńca donor
daremność futility
daremny of little/no avail, futile, unsuccessful, vain
■ **daremnie** to little/no avail, vainly, in vain
darmo: **za ~** free adv., for nothing
darmozjad freeloader
dar|ń turf¹; **pokrywać ~nią** turf²
darować/po- 1 (*ofiarować*) give¹, donate, present³ **2** (*winę*) forgive, let sb

off (with sth), pardon **3** (*odpuścić sobie*) skip[1] **4** (*życie*) spare[2]
darowizna donation, endowment
daszek 1 (*czapki*) peak[1], visor **2** (*wózka itp.*) hood **3** (*lampy*) shade[1] **4** (*markiza nad wejściem do sklepu*) canopy
data date[1]; ~ **urodzenia** date of birth, D.O.B.; ~ **ważności** expiry, expiry date
datek donation
datować date[2]
□ **datować się** date back to…, date from…
datownik date stamp
da(wa)ć give[1], offer[1]; **coś (komuś)** give sth in (to sb); (*rezultaty, wyniki itp.*) throw sth up; **(móc)** ~ spare[2]; ~ **dobry przykład** set a good example; ~ **komuś znać** let sb know; **(na)~ (czyjeś/czyjąś) imię/nazwę (po kimś)** name[2] sb/sth (after sb); **pieniądze szczęścia nie dają** money doesn't bring happiness; **ten bilet daje możliwość podróżowania po całym mieście przez jeden dzień** this ticket lets you travel anywhere in the city for a day
□ **da(wa)ć się**: ~ **się we znaki** play (sb) up
daw-ca/czyni donor
dawka dose[1]; (*kofeiny itp.*) fix[2]; (*med.*) ~ **przypominająca** booster; **za duża** ~ overdose
dawkować dose[2]
dawniej formerly
dawn|o long[2]; ~**o tu nie byłem** I haven't been here for a long time; **od ~a** always; ~**o temu** at one time, far back IDM ~**o, ~o temu** once upon a time
dawny former, old, past[1]
dąb oak, oak tree IDM **stawać dęba** bristle[2], buck[2], rear[2] | **sprawiać, że komuś włosy stają dęba** make sb's hair stand on end
dąsać/na- się sulk
dążność drive[2]; **do czegoś** pursuit
dążyć aim[2], aspire, pursue; **dążymy prosto do wyznaczonego celu** so far we're right on target
■ **dążenie 1** (*ambicja*) aspiration **2** (*tendencja*) drift[1]
dbać/za- care[2]; ~ **o kogoś/coś/siebie** cherish, fend for yourself, look after sb/sth/yourself, take care of yourself/ sb/sth; ~ **(szczególnie) o to, żeby** make a point of doing sth
dbałość thoughtfulness
dbały thoughtful
debata debate[1]
debatować debate[2], thrash sth out
debel double[4]
debet debit[1], overdraft; **mieć ~** (*w banku*) be in the red; **z ~em na koncie** overdrawn
debetować debit[2]
debiut debut
debiutować/za- make your debut
dech breath, wind[1]; **bez tchu** breathlessly, puffed; **odczytywać jednym tchem** reel sth off
dech|a: **w ~ę** tremendous
decybel decibel
decydować/z-/za- decide, determine; **ty decyduj** you're the boss
□ **decydować/z- się** choose, go for sb/ sth, make up your mind, opt, plump for sb/sth, settle on sth; **nie móc się zdecydować** vacillate
decydujący conclusive, critical, crucial, decisive; ~ **głos** casting vote
decyzja decision
dedukcja deduction
dedukować/wy- deduce, figure sb/sth out, piece sth together
dedykacja dedication
dedykować/za- dedicate
defekt defect[1], fault[1]
defensyw|a defence; **w ~ie** on the defensive
defensywny defensive[1]
defetyst-a/ka defeatist noun
defetystyczny defeatist
defetyzm defeatism
deficyt deficit, shortage; ~ **bilansu handlowego** trade deficit
defilada parade
defilować/prze- march past
definicja definition
definiować/z- define
definitywny definite
deformacja deformity
deformować/z- deform
defraudacja embezzlement
defraudować/z- defraud, embezzle
degeneracj|a degeneration; **ulegać ~i** degenerate[1]
degenerować/z- degenerate[1]
degradacja 1 (*zniszczenie*) degradation **2** (*ze stanowiska, stopnia itp.*) demotion
degradować/z-: **kogoś** demote
dekadencja decadence
dekadencki decadent
dekiel hubcap
deklamacja declamation
deklamatorski declamatory
deklamować/za- recite
deklaracja declamation, declaration; ~ **celna** declaration; ~ **praw człowieka** bill of rights
deklarować/za-/z- declare
□ **deklarować/z-/za- się** commit yourself (on sth)
deklinacja declension
dekoder decoder
dekolt cleavage
dekonstrukcj|a deconstruction; **przeprowadzać ~ę** deconstruct
dekoracja 1 decoration, ornament **2** (*potrawy*) garnish; (*tortu itp.*) topping **3** (**dekoracje**) (*teatr*) scenery, set[2]
dekoracyjny decorative
dekorator/ka: ~ **wnętrz** decorator, interior decorator
dekorować/u- decorate; (*wstążkami itp.*) festoon; (*potrawę*) garnish; ~ **brzegi** (*np. sukienki, firanki*) trim[1]
dekret decree, edict
dekstroza dextrose
delegacja 1 (*ludzie*) contingent, delegation, deputation **2** (*placówka*) posting
delegat/ka delegate[1]
delegować/od-/wy- 1 (*zlecać komuś coś*) delegate[2] **2** (*posłać*) post[2]
delektować się (*smakiem potrawy/ napoju*) savour
delfin 1 dolphin **2** (*styl pływacki*) butterfly
deliberacja deliberation
deliberować deliberate[2]
delikates 1 delicacy **2** (**delikatesy**) (*sklep*) delicatessen
delikatny 1 (*osoba; przedmiot*) dainty, delicate; (*maniery*) mild; (*przedmiot*) fragile **2** (*w stosunku do innych*) considerate, gentle **3** (*dźwięk; kolor*) soft **4** (*smak; kolor*) subtle **5** (*sprawa*) sensitive, thorny, tricky **6** (*potrawa*) light[2] **7** (*wrażliwy na widok krwi itp.*) squeamish
■ **delikatnie** daintily, delicately, gently, mildly, sensitively, tenderly IDM ~ **mówiąc** to say the least |
delikatnoś|ć delicacy, gentleness, mildness, softness, subtlety; **wymagający delikatności** delicate
delirium delirium
delta delta
demaskować/z- expose, uncover
demencj|a dementia; **cierpiący na ~ę** (*med.*) demented
dementi disclaimer
demilitaryzacja demilitarization
demilitaryzować/z- demilitarize, disarm
demobilizacja demobilization
demobilizować/z- demobilize
demobilizujący demoralizing
demokracja democracy
demokrat-a/ka democrat
demokratyczny democratic
demon demon
demoniczny demonic
demonstracja demonstration, show[2]; ~ **siły** the assertion of power
demonstrant/ka demonstrator
demonstrować/za- demonstrate, display[1], show[1]
demontować/z- disassemble, dismantle
demoralizacja corruption
demoralizować/z- corrupt[2]
denerwować/z- aggravate, make sb angry, annoy, bug[2], disturb, exasperate, faze, grate[2] (on sb), irritate, get on the right/wrong side of sb, upset[1]
□ **denerwować/z- się** flap[2], be in/get into a flap, get worked up about sth, be/get steamed up; **bardzo** ~ be in/get into a state, get yourself into a real state
denerwujący annoying, exasperating, irksome, irritating; **(bardzo)** ~ nerve-racking
denko (*kapelusza*) crown[1]
dentyst-a/ka dentist
dentystyczny dental
dentystyka dentistry
denuncjować/za-: **kogoś** inform on sb
departament department, office; **Departament Stanu** the State Department
depilować/wy- (*woskiem*) wax[2]
deponować/z- deposit[2]
deportacja deportation
deportować deport
depozyt deposit[1]
deprawować/z- pervert[1]
deprecjacja depreciation
deprecjonować/z- cheapen, debase
□ **deprecjonować/z- się** depreciate
depresj|a dejection, depression; **w ~i** depressed
deprymujący discouraging
deptać/z-/po- trample, tread[1] sth (in/ into/down); **nie ~ trawy!** keep off the grass!
deptak pedestrian precinct
dermatolog dermatologist
derywacja derivation

derywat derivative
Des/des D flat
deseń design[1], pattern
deser afters, dessert, pudding, sweet[2]
desk|a board[1], plank; **~a do krojenia** chopping board; **~a do krojenia chleba** breadboard; **~a do pływania** float[2]; **~a do prasowania** ironing board; **~a podłogowa** floorboard; **~a surfingowa** surfboard; **~a windsurfingowa** windsurfer; **pływać na desce** surf[2]; **zabijać ~ami** board sth up IDM (*czytać*) **od ~i do ~i** from cover to cover
deskorolka skateboard
deskorolkowiec skateboarder
desperacja desperation
despot-a/ka autocrat, despot
despotycznie: **rządzić/władać itp.** ~ take a hard line (on sth)
despotyczny authoritarian, autocratic, despotic, domineering
destabilizować/z- destabilize
destrukcyjny corrosive, destructive
destylacja distillation
destylarnia distillery
destylować distil
deszcz rain[1], the wet noun; ~ **monsunowy** monsoon; ~ **ze śniegiem** sleet; ~ **radioaktywny** fallout
deszczowiec raincoat
deszczowy rainy, wet[1]
detaliczn|y: **cena ~a** the retail price; **handel ~y** retail; **przedsiębiorstwo handlu ~ego**; **sprzedawca ~y** retailer
detektyw detective
detektywistyczn|y: **powieść ~a** detective story
detergent detergent
determinacja determination, grit[1], single-mindedness
detoks detox
detonator detonator
detonować/z- detonate, let sth off, set sth off
dewaluacja depreciation, devaluation
dewaluować/z- (*i przen.*) devalue
□ **dewaluować/z- się** depreciate
dewastować/z- ravage; (*budkę telefoniczną itp.*) vandalize
dewiacja aberration, deviance
dewiacyjny deviant
dewiant/ka deviant
dewiza motto
dewizy foreign exchange[1], foreign currency
dezaktywować/z- deactivate
dezaprobat|a censure noun, disapproval; **z ~ą** disapprovingly; **w atmosferze ~y** under a cloud
dezaprobować/z- frown on/upon sth
dezercja desertion
dezerter/ka deserter
dezerterować/z- desert[2]
dezodorant deodorant; ~ **antyperspiracyjny** antiperspirant
dezorganizacja disorganization
dezorganizować/z- upset[1]
dezorientacja disorientation
dezorientować/z- baffle, bewilder, disorientate
dezorientujący bewildering
dezynfekcja disinfection, fumigation
dezynfekować/z- disinfect, fumigate; **środek dezynfekujący** disinfectant
dezynsekcj|a fumigation; **przeprowadzać ~ę** fumigate
dezynsekować/z- fumigate
dębina oak
dębowy oak
dętka: ~ **rowerowa** inner tube of a bicycle tyre
dęt|y: **instrument ~y** wind instrument; **instrumenty ~e** wind[1]; **orkiestra ~a** a brass band; **drewniane instrumenty ~e** woodwind
diabelski devilish IDM ~ **młyn** big wheel
diab|eł 1 demon, devil; **do ~ła!** blow[1], damn[2] **2** (*okrutna osoba*) fiend IDM **gdzie ~eł mówi dobranoc** in the middle of nowhere | **idź do ~ła!** go to hell! | **jak ~li** like hell | (*kto/jak/gdzie/dlaczego itp.*) **u ~ła** hell
diabełek 1 devil, imp **2** (*przen.*) terror
diabety-k/czka diabetic[2]
diaboliczny devilish, fiendish
diagnostyczny diagnostic
diagnoz|a diagnosis; **stawiać ~ę** diagnose
diagram chart[1], diagram, figure[1], graph; ~ **kołowy** pie chart
diakon deacon
diakonisa deaconess
dialekt dialect, vernacular
dializa dialysis
dialog dialogue; ~ **czytany przez lektora** voice-over
diament diamond
diapozytyw slide[2]
diecezja diocese
diesel diesel
diet|a diet[1]; **być na diecie**; **stosować ~ę** be on a diet, diet[2]; **przechodzić na ~ę** go on a diet
dietetyczny dietary
dietety-k/czka dietitian
digitalizować/z- digitize
dinozaur dinosaur
Dis/dis D sharp
diuna dune
dla 1 (*cel*) for[1], for the sake of sth/of doing sth **2** (*z pożytkiem dla kogoś/czegoś*) to
dlaczego what for, why; **(a)** ~ why ever; ~ **nie?** why not?
dlaczegoż: **(a)** ~ why ever
dlatego that's why; ~ **(też)** accordingly, therefore
dławiący stifling, suffocating
dławić 1 kogoś choke[1], strangle, throttle[1] **2** (*naciskać*) squash[1] **3 (/z-)** (*bunt itp.*) crush[1], quash, quell **4 (/z-)** (*inicjatywę itp.*) stifle **5 (/z-)** (*łzy itp.*) choke sth back
□ **dławić /za- się** choke[1]
dło|ń the flat of your hand, palm[1]; **na ~ni** in the palm of his hand
dłub-ać/nąć/po-: **przy czymś** mess about/around with sth, potter[1], tinker; ~ **w nosie/zębach** pick your nose/teeth
dług debt; **mieć** ~ owe IDM **mieć ~ wdzięczności wobec kogoś** be in sb's debt
dług|i lengthy, long[1]; (*przemówienie itp.: i nudny*) tedious; **~a droga** mile
długo far[2], at length; **na** ~ long[2], for (so) long; **(strasznie)** ~ ages[1] IDM **żyli ~ i szczęśliwie** they lived happily ever after
długodystansowy long-distance
długopis ballpoint (pen)
długość length; (*czasu, życia*) span[1]; ~ **fali radiowej** wavelength; ~ **geograficzna** longitude; **średnia ~ życia** life expectancy; **na** ~ lengthways
długoterminowy long-range, long-term
długotrwały ancient, long-lived, long-standing; (*oczekiwanie, pertraktacje itp.*) prolonged, long-drawn-out
długowieczność longevity
długowieczny long-lived
dłuto chisel
dłużnik borrower, debtor
dłużn|y: **być ~ym** owe; **jestem ~y** IOU IDM **nie pozostawać (komuś) ~ym** hit back (at sb)
dmuch-ać/nąć/na- blow[1]; (*wiatr*) bluster, puff[1]
dmuchawa (*do wydmuchiwania szkła*) blowpipe
DNA DNA
dno bottom[1]; (*głębokie dno*) rock bottom; (*morskie itp.*) bed[1], floor[1]; ~ **morskie** the seabed; ~ **oceanu** the ocean floor IDM **iść na** ~ go under
do 1 (*w kierunku*) to, towards; (*w kierunku północnym*) up; (*do domu kogoś*) round[2]; (*na pokład*) aboard; **aż** ~ as far as **2** (*do środka*) into **3** (*cel*) for[1] **4** (*czas*) **(aż)** ~ by, through, until prep. **5 (w stosunku)** ~ to; (*mówić*) ~ **kogoś** to sb; (*krzyczeć itp.*) at sb IDM ~ **tego (jeszcze)** too
dob|a day; **całą ~ę** around/round the clock
do-biegać/biec (*końca itp.*) near[3]
do-bierać/brać się: **do czegoś** tamper with sth
do-bijać/bić destroy IDM ~ **targu (z kimś)** strike a bargain (with sb)
dobitk|a: **i na ~ę** ...and to add to all the drama
dobitny distinct
doborowy select[2]
dobosz/ka drummer
dobór: ~ **słów** wording, vocabulary
dobra OK interj., then
dobrać się → DOBIERAĆ SIĘ
dobranoc goodnight
dobran|y suited; **(dobrze)** ~**y** well matched; **być dobrze ~ym (do czegoś)** match[2]
dobro good[2], right[3]; **czyjeś** welfare, well-being
dobroby|t financial security, prosperity; **w ~cie** prosperous
dobroczynność charity, philanthropy
dobroczynny charitable, philanthropic
dobroczyńca benefactor
dobroć goodness, humanity, virtue; **chodząca** ~ an absolute dear
dobroduszny genial, good-humoured, good-natured
dobrodziejstwo blessing
dobrosąsiedzki neighbourly
dobrotliwy benign, kind-hearted, kindly adj.
dobrowolny optional, unsolicited, voluntary
■ **dobrowolnie** freely, voluntarily, on a voluntary basis; ~ **udzielać informacji** volunteer information
dobruchać/u- appease, humour[2], placate
dobr|y 1 fine, good[1], neat, nice, sound[3]; **w czymś** good[1] at sth; **~y apetyt** a hearty appetite; **~y nastrój** good

humour **2** (*odpowiedni*) right[1]; **~a partia** an eligible young man **3** (*życzliwy*) good-hearted, kind[2], kind-hearted, kindly adj.; **~e serce** goodness; **robić coś z ~ego serca** act out of charity; **~a wola** goodwill; **~ego usposobienia** good-natured
IDM **brać coś za ~ą monetę** take sb/sth at (its, his, etc.) face value | **a to ~e!** I like that! | **~e i złe strony** the pros and cons | **~y wieczór** good evening | **mieć ~ą rękę do (uprawy) roślin** have green fingers, have a green thumb | **na ~e** for good | **na ~e i na złe** through thick and thin | **niezbyt ~y** not much of a…, not up to much | **niezbyt (bardzo) ~y (w czymś)** not much good (at sth)

dobrze 1 well[1]; (*jeść, żyć*) healthily; **(to) ~ (, że…)** it's a good job (that…); **czuję się bardzo ~** I'm very well; **~ coś komuś robić** do you good **2 ~!** all right, OK interj., right[2], right (you are)!, that/this is it IDM **~ (komuś coś robić)** all very well (for sb) | **~ mu/ci itp. tak!** serve sb right | **jak dotąd ~** so far so good | **no ~** well[3]

dobudo(wy)wać build sth onto sth

dobytek effects[1], possessions; **sprzedawać cały ~** sell up

docelowy target

doceni(a)ć appreciate; **doceń ją za to, że próbowała** give her credit for trying; **nie ~ kogoś/czegoś** misjudge, take sb/sth for granted, underestimate, underrate, undervalue

dochodowy commercial[1]

dochodzenie enquiry, investigation; **~ przyczyny zgonu** inquest; **prowadzić ~** investigate

dochodzeniowy investigative

dochodzić/dojść 1 (*wydarzyć się*) come about **2 skądś** emanate from sth **3 do czegoś** get up to sth; (*i przen.*) attain, get, hit[1], reach[1]; (*przen.*) build up (to sth); (*do czegoś złego*) come to sth; **stopniowo ~ do czegoś** work up to sth; **łatwo ~ do czegoś** coast[2]; **dojść do porozumienia** settle a dispute, thrash sth out; **dojść do skutku** go through; **~ do źródła** trace[1] sth (back) (to sth); **dojść do władzy** come/rise to power; **dojść do wniosku** arrive at sth, come to the conclusion; **dojść do szczytu** build up to a climax
IDM **dojść do siebie** come round | **nie ~ do słowa** not get a word in edgeways

dochód income, proceeds, yield[2]; **(dochody)** return[2] (on sth); (*państwa itp.*) revenue

do-ciekać/ciec follow sth up, enquire into sth

dociekliwość inquisitiveness

dociekliwy enquiring, inquisitive, probing

do-cierać/trzeć carry; **~ dokądś** get up to sth, make[1], reach[1]; **~ do świadomości** get through (to sb), penetrate, sink in; **komizm tej sytuacji w ogóle nie dotarł do Johna** the humour of the situation was completely lost on John

docinek dig[2]

doczekać się 1 nie móc się czegoś doczekać can't wait/can hardly wait; **nie mogący się doczekać** impatient, raring to do sth **2** (*komentarza w gazecie itp.*) rate[2]

doczepi(a)ć tack sth on (to sth), tag[2]

doczepk|a: **iść (z kimś) na ~ę** tag along (behind/with sb)

doczesny worldly

dodat|ek 1 addition, insertion, supplement; (*ciąg dalszy programu itp.*) follow-up; (*element wieńczący*) touch[2] **2** (*do słownika itp.*) appendix **3** (*do pensji itp.*) allowance, fringe benefit; (*do podstawowego uposażenia*) perk[1]; **bezpłatny ~ek** giveaway; **odpłatny ~ek** extra[2] **4** (*żywnościowy*) additive; **~ek smakowy** flavouring; **mleko z ~kiem witamin** milk with added vitamins **5** (*do potrawy*) accompaniment **5 (dodatki)** (*do ubrania*) accessories
IDM **na ~ek** into the bargain, to crown it all, too | **w ~ku** on top of sb/sth, what's more

dodatkow|y added, additional, extra[1], further[1], optional, over-, subsidiary[1], supplementary; **~a zaleta** bonus; **~e urządzenia** optional extras

dodatni positive

doda(wa)ć 1 coś do czegoś add, add sth on (to sth), supplement verb; **~ (coś za darmo)** throw sth in **2** (*mat.*) add; **dodać** plus[1] **2 komuś/czemuś czegoś** impart, lend sth (to sth)
IDM **dodający otuchy** uplifting

dodawanie (*mat.*) addition

dodzwonić się: **(do kogoś)** get through (to sb)

dofinansowanie grant[2]

dog Great Dane

dogad(yw)ać: **sobie** bicker
□ **dogad(yw)ać się**: **dogadać się (od razu)** click[1]; **świetnie się ~** get on/along like a house on fire; **mogę dogadać się po hiszpańsku** I can get by in Spanish

do-gadzać/godzić indulge, please[2], spoil

do-ganiać/gonić catch up (with sb), catch sb up, gain on sb/sth

dogląd-ać/nąć oversee

dogłębny poignant
■ **dogłębnie** at length

dogmat dogma

dogmatyczny dogmatic

dogodn|y convenient, expedient, handy, opportune; **być ~ym** suit[2]; **w ~ej chwili** at your leisure

dogodzić → DOGADZAĆ

dogonić → DOGANIAĆ

dogotowany done[2]

dogryw|ka (*w grze*) play-off; **odbyć się w ~ce** go into extra time

doić/wy- (*i przen.*) milk[2]

dojazd 1 accessibility; (*droga*) access road **2 ~ do pracy zajmuje mi 45 minut** the journey to work takes me 45 minutes

do-jeżdżać/jechać get, reach[1]; **~ do pracy** commute

dojrzałość manhood, maturity

dojrzały grown[2], grown-up[1], mature, ripe (for sth)

dojrze(wa)ć grow up, mature verb, ripen

dojrzewani|e: **okres ~a płciowego** puberty; **wiek ~a** adolescence; (*od 13 do 19 lat*) teens

dojście approach[2]

dojść → DOCHODZIĆ

dok dock[1]

dokazywać frisk, play[1], romp

dokąd where

dokądkolwiek wherever

dokądś round[2]

do-kładać/łożyć contribute; (*węgla do ognia itp.*) stoke IDM **~ (wszelkich) starań(, żeby)** be at/take (great) pains to do sth, do/try your best, take (great) pains (with/over sth)
□ **do-kładać/łożyć się** contribute; **~ do czegoś po ileś** chip in (with sth)

dokładnie (*precyzyjnie*) accurately, exactly, precisely; (*według zaleceń itp.*) well[1]; (*zaraz*) directly[1]; (*wyraźnie*) plainly; (*rzeczywiście*) so[1]; (*w sam środek*) bang[3], right[2], slap[2]; (*wykonać jakąś pracę itp.*) painstakingly; (*sprawdzić itp.*) rigorously; (*czytać tekst itp.*) carefully, closely; (*wtedy, gdy*) just[1]; (*punktualnie*) promptly, sharp[2]; (*na wschód itp.*) due[2]; **~ mówiąc** strictly speaking; **~ ta osoba** the very person; **~ tak** just so

dokładn|y 1 (*precyzyjny*) accurate, exact[1], full[1], precise, spot on; (*zgodny z faktami*) authentic **2** (*uważny*) careful, close[3], painstaking, rigorous; (*wiedza*) intimate **3** (*bezpośredni itp.*) direct[1] **4** (*gruntowny*) probing **5** (*szczegółowy*) specific; **~a godzina** the right time; **bardzo ~y** split-second adj. **6** (*rozkaz*) strict

dokoła around

dokonanie accomplishment

dokonany (*gram.*) perfect[1]

dokon(yw)ać accomplish, effect[2], pull sth off; **dokonać wyboru** make a choice; **dokonać prezentacji** make/do the introductions

dokończyć finish[1] (off/up)

dokować/za- dock[2]

dokrewny (*med.*) endocrine

dokrę-cać/cić (*śrubę*) tighten

doktor doctor[1]; (*stopień naukowy*) **dr** PhD

doktorant/ka postgraduate

doktorat doctorate

doktryna doctrine

doku-czać/czyć give sb a hard time, harass, nag, pester, tease

dokuczliw|y trying; **(nic poważnego, ale) ~y** niggling; **rzecz/osoba ~a** nuisance

dokument document; **(dokumenty)** papers

dokumentalny: **film/program ~** documentary

dola 1 (*los*) fate, lot[3] **2** (*udział*) cut[2]

dolar dollar

dolegliwość affliction, ailment, complaint, disorder, trouble[1]

dol(ew)ać top (sth) up; **~ wody** water sth down

dolewka refill

doliczony: **~ czas** (*sport*) injury time

dolina 1 vale, valley; **~ górska** dale, glen; **~ 2** (*przen.*) trough

dolny bottom[2], lower[1]

dołą-czać/czyć accompany, put sth in, put sth on, tack sth on (to sth)
□ **dołą-czać/czyć się** join[1]

dołeczek dimple

doł|ek hole; **pokryć ~kami** pit[2]

dołożyć (się) → DOKŁADAĆ (SIĘ)

dom accommodation, dwelling, home[1], house[1], place[1]; **~ czynszowy** tenement; **~ dziecka** children's home; **~ kultury** community centre; **~ letniskowy** (*zwł. w stylu góralskim*)

chalet; ~ **modlitwy** chapel; ~ **mody** fashion house; ~ **noclegowy** hostel; ~ **parterowy** bungalow; ~ **dziennego pobytu** day centre; ~ **pogrzebowy** funeral parlour; ~ **poprawczy** detention centre; ~ **publiczny** brothel; ~ **spokojnej starości** old people's home; ~ **towarowy** department store, store[1]; **wielki ~ handlowy** (*sprzedający artykuły jednej branży*) superstore; **w ~u** at home; **w/do ~u** home[3], indoors; **ku ~owi** homeward; **od ~u do ~u** house-to-house; **wiodący ku ~owi/ojczyźnie** homeward IDM (*nazwisko panieńskie*) **z ~u** née
domagać się cry out for sth[2], press (for sth/to do sth), demand[2]; (*zwrotu kosztów itp.*) claim[1] for sth; ~ **czegoś podniesionym i/lub rozzłoszczownym głosem** clamour for sth
■ **domaganie się** assertion, insistence
domek cottage; (*zwł. w stylu góralskim*) chalet; (*myśliwski*) lodge[1]; (*dla dzieci*) playhouse
domena domain
domiar IDM **na ~ złego** to cap it all, to crown it all, to make matters/things worse
domieszk|a: **z ~ą czegoś** streaked with sth; **bez ~i** pure
dominacja ascendancy, dominance, domination
dominium dominion
dominować/z- dominate, predominate, rule[2]; (*zamek itp.*) occupy a commanding position
■ **dominujący** dominant, predominant
domknięty shut[2]
domniemanie conjecture noun, guess[2], presumption, supposition
domniemany alleged, implicit
domniem(yw)ać conjecture, presume
domo: **de ~** née
domokrążca door-to-door salesman
domow|y (*obowiązki, zwierzęta*) domestic; (*rodzinny*) home[2]; (*jak w domu*) informal; **~ego wyrobu** home-made; **wojna ~a** civil war IDM **~y sposób** a rule of thumb
domysł conjecture noun; (**domysły**) guesswork
domyś-lać/lić się guess[1]; **czegoś na podstawie/z czegoś** read sth into sth
doniczka flowerpot, pot[1]
doniesienie coverage
doniosłość importance, significance
doniosły important, momentous, weighty
donosiciel/ka informer
do-nosić/nieść 1 o czymś report[1] **2 na kogoś** report sb (to sb) (for sth)[1], inform on sb
donośność resonance
donośny resonant, resounding; ~ **śmiech** a hearty laugh
dookoła around[1,2], round[2,3]
dopasowan|y (*dobrze współdziałający*) compatible with sb/sth; (*rozmiarem*) fitted, fitting[1]; (*kolorem, wzorem*) matching; **być dobrze ~ym** be a snug fit; **klucz jest ~y do zamka** the key fits the lock; **osoba/rzecz ~a (do kogoś innego/czegoś innego)** match[1]
dopaso(wy)wać match[2]; **coś do czegoś** match sth up with sth, match sth against sth; (*rozmiarem*) fit[1]; **ponownie** ~ readjust
■ **dopasow(yw)anie** (*rozmiarem*) fit[3]; (*programem, terminem*) harmonization
do-patrywać/patrzeć się: **czegoś w czymś** read sth into sth
dopełni(a)ć 1 (*program, system*) integrate sth (into sth), A and/with B **2** (*wodą itp.*) top (sth) up
■ **dopełniający** complementary
dopełnianie integration
dopełnienie 1 (*uzupełnienie*) complement[1] **2** (*gram.*) object[1]; ~ **bliższe** direct object; ~ **dalsze** indirect object
dopić drink (sth) up
dopiero just[1]; ~ **co** freshly, just[1], just now, newly, only just
dopilno(wy)wać see, see to sb/sth
dopingować/z- goad sb on, prod, urge sb on; (*zwł. w czasie zawodów sportowych*) cheer sb on, root for sb
dopisek insertion
dopłata premium, surcharge
dopływ flow[1]
dopóki: ~ **(nie)** until
dopracowany polished
do-praszać/prosić się invite
doprawdy just[1], really
doprawi(a)ć season[2]; ~ **solą i pieprzem** season with salt and pepper
doprowa-dzać/dzić 1 (*kierować*) bring, drive[1], lead[1] **2** (*kończyć się czymś*) lead up to sth; **stopniowo ~ do czegoś** work up to sth; **doprowadzać do zwycięstwa** culminate in victory **3** (*do płaczu itp.*) reduce sb/sth (from sth) to sth; **stopniowo ~** (*do złości itp.*) work sb up (into sth) **4** (*do ładu/porządku*) sort[2], straighten sth out, tidy[2]; ~ **coś do końca** go through with sth **5** (*spowodować*) bring; (*przygotować*) set the scene (for sth)
□ **doprowa-dzać/dzić się**: **stopniowo ~** (*do złości itp.*) work yourself up (into sth)
dopust scourge
dopu-szczać/ścić (*pozwalać*) let sb/sth do sth; **być dopuszczonym** pass[1]; **nie ~ do czegoś** keep sb/sth back (from sb/sth), (not) give sb a look-in; **zostać dopuszczonym** (*do sekretu itp.*) be/get in on sth
□ **dopu-szczać/ścić się** (*zbrodni itp.*) perpetrate sth (against/upon/on sb)
dopuszczalność acceptability
dopuszczalny admissible, allowable, permissible
dorad-ca/czyni adviser, aide, consultant, counsellor; **doradca prawny** solicitor
doradczy advisory
dora-dzać/dzić zob. też RADZIĆ; advise, counsel[2]
doradztwo counselling
do-rastać/rosnąć 1 (*stać się dorosłym*) grow up; (*do rozmiaru itp.*) grow into sth **2** (*dorównywać umiejętnościami*) match up (to sb/sth), measure up (to sth)
doraźny ad hoc; (*wyrok itp.*) summary[2]
doręczenie delivery
dorobić się chalk sth up
dorobiony: ~ **klucz** duplicate key
doroczny annual[1], yearly
dorosłość adulthood, maturity
dorosły (*przym.*) adult adj., grown[2], grown-up[1], mature
■ **dorosł-y/a** (*rz.*) adult, grown-up[2]
dorośleć/wy- mature verb
dorówn(yw)ać come up to sth, equal[3], match[2], match up (to sb/sth), rival[2] sb/sth (for/in sth), touch[1]; **(starać się) dorównać komuś** emulate; **nie ~ (komuś/czemuś)** not compare (with/to sb/sth), be no match for sb when it comes to sth
dorsz cod
dorwać: **kogoś** buttonhole[2], collar[2], get/lay your hands on sb
dorywcz|y casual, seasonal; **~e zajęcia/prace** odd jobs; **osoba wykonująca prace ~e** odd-job man
■ **dorywczo** off and on, on and off
dorzu-cać/cić: ~ **coś gratis** throw sth in
□ **dorzu-cać/cić się** ~ **do czegoś po ileś** chip in (with sth)
dosadnie crisply
dosadność neatness
dosadny crisp[1], terse
do-siadać/siąść (*konia itp.*) mount[1]
dosięg-ać/nąć get at sb/sth IDM **nie ~** (*poziomu, celu itp.*) fall short (of sth)
doskonale admirably, excellently, exquisitely, ideally, immaculately, outstandingly, perfectly adv., splendidly, supremely; (*przyjemnie*) lovely and warm, peaceful, fresh, etc.; (*zdać egzamin*) with flying colours
doskonalić/u- perfect[2]
doskonał|y consummate[1], excellent, exquisite, ideal[1], immaculate, outstanding, perfect[1], splendid, sterling[2], top-notch; (*wino*) vintage[2]; **jest ~ym kucharzem** he's an expert cook
dosłownie literally, word for word
dosłowny literal, verbatim
dosłyszeć catch[1]
dosmażony well done
dostar-czać/czyć (*towar*) deliver; (*samolotem*) fly[1]; (*informacji, prowiantu, celu*) provide, serve sth up, supply[2]; (*wody, gazu*) pipe[2]; (*informacji*) feed[1], tell; (*rezultatu, zysku*) yield[1]; (*możliwości*) offer[1] IDM ~ **towar** (*wypełnić zobowiązanie*) come up with/deliver the goods
dostatecznie adequately, enough[2], sufficiently; ~ **dużo** enough[1]
dostateczn|y adequate, passable, reasonable, satisfactory, sufficient; (*wykonanie zadania*) competent; **ocena ~a zaczyna się od 60 punktów** the pass mark is 60 out of 100
dostat|ek affluence; **pod ~kiem** plenty adv.
dostatni affluent
dostawa consignment, delivery, supply[1]
dosta(wa)ć 1 (*otrzymywać*) get, get hold of sth, obtain, receive sth (from sb/sth); **ile dostaniesz za swój samochód?** how much will your car fetch?; ~ **w spadku** inherit sth (from sb) **2** (*wysypki*) break out in sth, come out in sth IDM **dostać kogoś w swoje ręce** get/lay your hands on sb
□ **dosta(wa)ć się** (*dokądś/gdzieś*) get, get into sth IDM ~ **się komuś (za coś)** be (in) for it
dostawca supplier, tradesman
dostęp 1 (*możliwość wejścia gdzieś, możliwość korzystania z czegoś*)

access[1], accessibility, admission to sth; (*swobodny*) the freedom of sth **2** (*droga dojazdowa*) access[1], approach[2]
dostępność accessibility, availability
dostępn|y 1 (*droga, miejsce itp.*) accessible, within (easy) reach of sth; **uczynić coś ~ym** open (sth) up **2** (*towar*) around, available, there; **być ~ym** (*w danym fasonie, kolorze itp.*) come in sth; **jeżeli będzie ~y** subject to availability **3** (*otwarta osoba*) approachable; (*o osobie obecnej w danym miejscu*) available
dostojeństwo dignity
dostosowany attuned to sb/sth
dostosow(yw)ać (*dopasowywać*) adjust
□ **dostosow(yw)ać się** (*do regulaminu, prawa*) conform to sth; (*do innych ludzi/okoliczności*) fit in (with sb/sth)
dostosow(yw)anie adjustment, harmonization
□ **dostosowanie się** (*dopasowanie*) adjustment; (*do regulaminu, prawa*) conformity
dostrojenie adjustment
do-strzegać/strzec discern, distinguish, perceive; (*wzrokiem*) catch sight of sb/sth, sight[2], spot[2], spy[2]; (*poprzez badania itp.*) detect; **~ różnice** discriminate between A and B; **nie ~** miss[1]
dostrzegalny appreciable, discernible, distinguishable, perceptible, visible
dosyć (także **dość**) **1** (*wystarczająco*) enough[1,2]; **~!** that is it; **mieć ~ czegoś** be/get fed up, be sick[1] of sth **2** (*raczej*) fairly, mildly, pretty[1], quite, rather, reasonably
dosztukować → SZTUKOWAĆ
doszuk(iw)ać się: **czegoś w czymś** read sth into sth
doścignąć → ŚCIGAĆ
dośrodkow(yw)ać (*piłkę*) cross[2]
doświad-czać/czyć encounter[1], meet
doświadczeni|e 1 (*przeżycie*) experience[1]; **~e zawodowe** work experience; **brak ~a** inexperience, newness **2** (*eksperyment*) experiment[1], test[1]
doświadczon|y experienced, practised in sth, seasoned; (*w kulturze itp.*) sophisticated; **być ~ym** be an old hand (at sth)
dot. re
dotacja subsidy
dotąd hitherto, so far, yet
dotkliwie acutely, badly, keenly, painfully, soundly
dotkliwość severity
dotkliwy acute, severe; (*przytłaczający*) devastating
dotknąć (się) → DOTYKAĆ (SIĘ)
dotknięcie dab[2], touch[2]
dotknięt|y (*zraniony, przygnębiony*) aggrieved, hurt[2]; **czuć się ~ym** resent, take offence (at sth)
dotować subsidize
dotrzeć → DOCIERAĆ
dotrzym(yw)ać (*umowy*) abide by sth, honour[2]; (*obietnicy, słowa*) keep[1], be true to sth; (*terminu*) meet; **~ kroku** keep up (with sb), keep pace (with sb/sth); **nie ~ prawnego zobowiązania** default[2] on sth; **nie ~** (*obietnicy, słowa*) break[1]
dotychczas to date, so far, hitherto, up to sth, yet, as yet
dotyczyć 1 (*stosować, być ważnym, obejmować*) apply to sb/sth, go for sb/sth, pertain to sth/sb **2** (*być na temat*) concern[1], be concerned with sth, deal with sth, involve; (*form.*) infuse; **dotyczy** (*dokument*) re; **już kogoś nie ~** be well out of sth
■ **dotyczący 1** (*obejmujący*) applicable to sb/sth **2** (*na temat*) concerning, regarding
dotyk 1 (*zmysł*) touch[2] **2** (*dotykanie*) feel[2]; **być w ~u jak coś** feel[1]; **zimny w ~u** cold to the touch
dotykać 1 (*stykać się*) touch[1] **2** (**/dotknąć**) (*sprawdzać dotykiem*) feel[1], handle[1], touch[1]; (*palcami*) finger; (*czule*) fondle[1]; **~ czegoś wielokrotnie** pick at sth **3** (**/dotknąć**) (*mieć wpływ*) affect **4** (**/dotknąć**) (*krzywdzić*) hurt[1], sting[1]; (*choroba, nieszczęście itp.*) afflict **5** (**/dotknąć**) (*tematu, sprawy*) touch on/upon sth
□ **do-tykać/tknąć się** touch[1]
dotykalny tangible
dotykowy tactile
dowcip joke[1]
dowcipkować joke[2]
dowcipniś joker
dowcipny witty
dowiadywać się 1 o kogoś/coś enquire about sb/sth **2** (**/dowiedzieć się**) **o kimś/czymś** find out (sth) (about sth/sb), hear, learn (of/about) sth; **jak się dowiedziałeś?** how did you get to know?; **wiele się dowiedzieć** pick up a lot of information
dowierzać: **nie ~** disbelieve, distrust verb
dowodzić 1 (*wojsk.*) command[2] sb/sth, be in command of sth; (*drużyną*) captain[2] **2** (**/dowieść**) (*słuszności, prawdy*) demonstrate, argue that…, for/against sth; (*niewinności*) vindicate
dowolny unlimited
dowód 1 (*na istnienie czegoś*) demonstration, manifestation, proof, testament (to sth), testimony; (*wdzięczności itp.*) mark[2], token[1]; (*i prawn.*) evidence; (*prawn.*) **~ rzeczowy** exhibit[2] **2** (*dokument*) **~ osobisty** ID card, identity card, identification
dowódca chief[2], commander
dowództwo command[1]
dozgonny lifelong
dozna(wa)ć experience[2], meet with sth; (*obrażeń itp.*) sustain; **doznać szoku** get a shock; **doznać zawodu** draw a blank
dozor-ca/czyni (*w budynku*) caretaker, superintendent; (*na parkingu itp.*) attendant[1]; (*w zoo*) keeper; (*instytucja czuwająca nad bezpieczeństwem itp.*) watch[2]
dozorować watch[1] sb/sth (for sth)
doz|ór: **bez ~oru** unattended
do-zwalać/zwolić let sb/sth do sth
dozwolon|y allowable, permissible; (*prawn.*) legitimate; **być ~ym** pass[1]; **~a ilość** allowance
dożylny intravenous
■ **dożylnie** intravenously; **odżywiać dożylnie** drip-feed
doży(wa)ć live[1]
dożywocie (*kara*) life imprisonment, life sentence; **skazano ją na ~** she was sent to prison for life/she was sentenced to life in prison
dożywotni lifelong; **~e członkostwo** life membership
dół 1 (*spód*) bottom[1], underside, the underneath; (*łóżka*) foot[1]; **na dole**; **w/na ~** down[1], downhill adj., downward, downwards; (*schodami*) downstairs adj.; (*rzeki*) downstream **2** (*dziura*) hole, pit[1] IDM **być opłacanym z dołu** be paid in arrears
drabina (także **drabinka**) ladder; (*składana*) stepladder; (*sznurowa*) a rope ladder
dragować dredge
drak|a bust-up IDM **dla ~i** (just) for the hell of it
drakoński draconian
dramat (*teatr*) theatre; (*i przen.*) drama
dramatopisa-rz/rka playwright
dramaturg dramatist, playwright
dramatyczny dramatic, theatrical
dramatyzacja dramatization
dramatyzować dramatize
drań rogue[2]
drapacz: **~ chmur** skyscraper
drapać 1 (**/po-**) (*paznokciami*) scratch[1] at sth; (*pazurami*) claw[2] (at) sb/sth **2** (*ubranie*) prickle[1] **3** (**/wy-**) (*wydrapać, wyryć*) gouge, scratch[1]
■ **drapiący** (*ubranie*) itchy
drapieżnik (*zwierzę*) hunter, predator
drapieżny (*i przen.*) predatory; **ptak ~** bird of prey
drastyczn|y drastic; **~e szczegóły rozwodu** the gory details of the divorce
drażliwy 1 (*osoba*) edgy, frazzled, irritable, ratty, spiky, touchy **2** (*sytuacja*) explosive[1]; (*temat, problem*) sensitive, touchy; (*sprawa*) thorny
drażniący annoying, exasperating, irritating
drażnić 1 (**/roz-**) (*irytować*) annoy, grate[2] on sb, irk, irritate, jar[2] on sb/sth, niggle (at) sb, rile **2** (**/po-**) (*dokuczać*) tease
drążek bar[1], lever, rod
drążyć/wy- (*otwór*) scoop[2] sth (out/up); **~ tunel** tunnel verb
dredy dreadlocks
drelich 1 (*materiał*) denim **2** (*roboczy*) overalls[2]
drenaż: **~ mózgów** brain drain
dres tracksuit
dreszcz (także **dreszczyk**) (*strachu*) chill[1], shiver noun, shudder noun; (*radosci*) thrill; **przyprawia mnie o ~e** it makes me shudder; **powieść z ~ykiem** thriller
dreszczowiec thriller
drewniak (*but*) clog[2]
drewnian|y wooden IDM **mający ~e ucho** tone-deaf
drewno wood; (*na budowę*) timber; **~ cedrowe** cedar; **~ sosny** pine[1]; **~ na ognisko** logs for the fire; **~ opałowe** firewood
dręczyciel/ka torturer
dręczyć/za- torment verb, torture verb; (*pytaniami itp.*) harass; (*lęk, problem itp.*) assail, do sb's head in, gnaw (away) at sb, prey on sb's mind

□ **dręczyć/za- się** agonize

■ **dręcząc|y 1** (*ból*) agonizing; **~e wątpliwości** niggling doubts **2** (*zapach*) tantalizing

drętwieć/z- (*noga, ręka*) go to sleep, go dead; **~ ze strachu** be numb with fear

drg-ać/nąć/za- 1 (*muskuł*) twitch; (*twarz*) wince **2** (*płomień*) flicker[1] **3** (*struna*) vibrate **4** (*głos*) tremble **5** (*powieki*) flutter[1] **6** (*ruszyć się*) budge; (*szarpnąć*) jerk[1] **7** (*ze strachu itp.*) start[1]

drgawka convulsion

drink drink

drobiazg 1 (*nieistotna sprawa*) trifle **2** (*przedmiot*) novelty; (*w dekoracji*) touch[2]; **~i** bits and pieces, non-essentials, odds and ends

drobiazgowy 1 (*osoba*) fastidious, meticulous, nit-picking adj. **2** (*sprawozdanie*) painstaking, thorough; (*szczegóły*) minute[2]; (*pytania*) searching

drobina molecule

drobiow|y: **mięso ~e** poultry

drobniutki minute[2]

drobnostka trifle

drobnoustrój germ, microbe

drobn|y 1 (*mały*) small, wee[2]; (*form.*) diminutive **2** (*budowa ciała*) petite, slight; (*i słaby*) puny; **mieć ~ą budowę** be slightly built **3** (*nieistotny*) minor[1], petty, trifling **4** (*piasek itp.*) fine[1]

■ **drobne** (*pieniadze*) change[2], small change | **drobno** (*posiekać itp.*) finely

droczyć się tease

dro|ga 1 (*samochodowa*) road; (*aleja*) avenue; (*boczna; wiejska*) lane; **główna ~ga** highway; **~ga pierwszej kategorii** A-road; **~ga drugiej kategorii** B-road; **~ga dwupasmowa** dual carriageway **2** (*dla pieszych/innych pojazdów*) path; (*przez las itp.*) trail[1]; **~ga powietrzna** air[1]; **~ga wodna** waterway; **~gą lądową/morską** by road/sea; **na ~dze** in the way; **z ~gi!** mind out **3** (*właściwa trasa*) the way[1]; **będący w ~dze dokądś** bound[1] for…, destined for…, en route (from…) (to…), (for…); **po ~dze** on the way; **jest mi po ~dze** it's on my way **4** (*możliwa trasa podróży*) route; **wrócić tą samą ~gą** retrace your steps **5** (*odległość*) **długa ~ga** mile; (*i przen.*) **mieć długą ~gę przed sobą** have a long way to go **6** (*do sławy itp.*) gateway IDM (*przen.*) **~ga wolna** the all-clear | **~gą** by means of | (*przen.*) **na dobrej/złej ~dze** on the right/wrong track | **być na ~dze do zwycięstwa** be on course to victory, be on the path to victory | **spytać się o ~gę** ask for directions

drogi 1 (*kochany*) dear[1] to sb, old **2** (*nie tani*) costly, dear[1], expensive, extravagant; (*i modny*) swanky; **za ~** overpriced **3** (*cenny*) valuable; **bardzo ~** precious

drogomierz milometer

drogowskaz signpost

drozd thrush

drożdże yeast

drożeć/po- appreciate

drób fowl, poultry

dróżka lane

drucian|y: **z ~ej siatki** made of wire mesh/netting

drug|i 1 (*w kolejności*) second[1]; **~ie co do wielkości miasto** the second largest city; **byłem ~i** I came second; **nasza drużyna była na ~im miejscu** our team finished second; **po ~ie** secondly **2** (*od pary*) other; (*koniec, strona itp.*) far[1]; (*z dwu wymienionych*) the latter; **w ~iej połowie roku** in the latter half of the year; **co ~i** alternate[2] **3** (*co do jakości*) second best[1]; (*gatunek towaru*) second[2]; **~a klasa** (*w samolocie*) economy class; (*rodzaj listu, dyplomu*) second class; (*podróżować*) **~ą klasą** second-class adv.; **~iej kategorii** second-class IDM **~a natura** second nature (to sb) | **ale z ~iej strony** then/there again | **z ~iej ręki** second-hand, used

drugoplanowy subordinate[1]

drugorzędny 1 (*sprawa itp.*) minor[1], peripheral[1], secondary **2** (*aktor itp.*) second-rate; (*pracownik*) subordinate[1] to sb/sth

druhna bridesmaid

druk 1 (*drukowanie*) printing; **w momencie oddania do ~u** at the time of going to press **2** (*tekst*) print[2] **3** (*formularz*) form[1]; (*promocyjny itp.*) literature on sth

drukarka (*komputerowa*) printer

drukarnia printer

drukarz printer

drukować/wy- print[1]; (*z komputera*) print sth off/out

drut 1 (*pręt*) wire[1]; **~ kolczasty** barbed wire **2** (*do robótek*) needle; **robić na ~ach** knit

drutować/za- wire[2]

druzgocący 1 (*tempo*) blistering **2** (*porażka*) crushing; (*atak*) savage

druzgotać/z- 1 (*rozbić*) smash[1] **2** (*przen.*) devastate, overwhelm

drużba best man

drużyna (*sport*) team[1]; (*w pracy*) squad; (*w podróży*) party; **~ przeciwna** opposition

drwiący derisive, withering; **~ uśmiech** sneer noun

drwić/za- deride, jeer, scoff, sneer

drwina derision, jeer noun; (**drwiny**) mockery

dryblować dribble

dryfować drift[2]

dryg knack of/for doing sth

dryl drill[1]

drzazga chip[1]; (*w kształcie igły*) splinter

drzeć/po- tear[2], tear sth up

■ **drzeć się 1** (**/podrzeć się**) (*na kawałki*) tear[2] **2** (*krzyczeć*) shout at/to sb

drzemać/zdrzemnąć się (*spać lekko*) doze, nap verb; (*być pogrążonym we śnie*) slumber verb

drzemiący (*wulkan*) dormant

drzemk|a (*krótki sen*) doze noun, nap, snooze; (*stan pogrążenia we śnie*) slumber noun; **~a poobiednia** forty winks; **uciąć sobie ~ę** snooze

drzewko sapling, seedling

drzewo 1 tree; **~ herbaciane** tea tree; **~ tekowe** teak **2 ~ genealogiczne** family tree; **wywiodła swoje ~ genealogiczne od** she traced her family tree back to

drzwi 1 (*do budynku itp.*) door; **czy to ktoś puka do ~?** is that someone knocking at the door?; **~ balkonowe** French door, French window; **od ~ do ~** (from) door to door **2** (*otwór, wejście*) doorway **3** (*luk*) hatch[2]; **~ zapadowe** trapdoor

drżący shaky, unsteady; **mówić ~m głosem** quaver[1]

drżeć/za- (*z wrażenia, emocji*) shake[1]; (*ze strachu itp.*) quake, shudder, tremble with sth; (*z zimna itp.*) shiver; (*głos*) quaver; (*lekko: warga, głos*) quiver; (*ręka itp.*) waver; **drżące r** trill

DTP: **technika ~** (*publikacja książek itp.*) desktop publishing

dubbingować/z- dub

dubeltówka shotgun

dubler/ka 1 (*podobna osoba*) double[4] **2** (*teatr*) understudy

dublować/z- 1 duplicate[1] **2** (*sport*) lap[2]

duch 1 (*istota nadprzyrodzona*) ghost, phantom, spirit[1], spook; **Duch Święty** the Holy Spirit **2** (*psychiczny; prawa itp.*) spirit[1]; **w ~u** inwardly; **młody ~em** young at heart; **iść z ~em czasu** keep up (with sth) **3** (*armii, zespołu itp.*) morale; **natchnięty ~em obywatelskim** public-spirited; **~ walki/bojowy** fight[2]; **tracić ~a** your heart sinks; **dodawać ~a** buck (sb/sth) up, hearten; **podnoszący na ~u** heartening IDM **nie było widać ani żywego ~a** there wasn't a soul in sight

duchowieństwo clergy

duchowny (*przym.*) clerical, ecclesiastical

■ **duchowny** (*rz.*) clergyman

duchowy inward adj., spiritual[1]

dudnić/za- rumble

dudy bagpipes

duet duet, duo

dukać/wy- stumble over/through sth

dum|a pride[1]; (*chluba*) boast noun, credit[1] to sb/sth; (*przechwalanie się*) sb's pride and joy; (*wyniosłość*) haughtiness; **powód do ~y** claim to fame

dumać brood[1] on/over/about sth, ponder (on/over) sth

dumnie proudly; **kroczyć ~** strut, swagger; **poruszać się ~** sweep[1]

dumn|y proud; (*wyniosły*) haughty, superior[1]; **jestem z ciebie ~y** I'm proud of you; **być bardzo ~ym z czegoś** take a great pride in sth

dupek git, jerk[2]

duplikat duplicate[2]; (*imitacja*) replica

dur (*muz.*) major[1,2]

dureń fool[1]

durny silly

durszlak colander

dusić 1 (**/u-**) (*ściskać za gardło*) smother sb (with sth), strangle, throttle[1]; (*dym*) asphyxiate, stifle, suffocate **2** (**/z-**) (*w sobie emocje itp.*) bottle sth up, choke sth back **3** (**/z-**) (*inicjatywę itp.*) strangle; **zdusić coś złego w zarodku** nip sth in the bud **4** (**/u-**) (*kulin.*) braise, stew verb

□ **dusić/u- się** (*krztusić się*) choke[1] on sth; (*z braku powietrza*) suffocate; **~ od dymu** be overcome by smoke

dusz|a heart, spirit[1]; (*i relig.*) soul IDM **pragnąć czegoś z całej ~y** set your heart on sth, have your heart set on sth | **w głębi ~y** deep down

duszek elf, fairy

duszny (*pogoda*) close[3], muggy, oppressive, sultry; (*pokój*) airless, stuffy

duszpasterski pastoral
dużo **1** (*wiele, sporo*) a lot of, lot[1,2], many, much[1], plenty; (*pić itp.*) heavily; (*nieform.*) hundreds, lotta; **bardzo** ~ any number of, a good/great many; **dość** ~ quite a few, quite a lot (of); ~ **podróżować** travel extensively/widely **2** (*więcej/bardziej*) far[2], way[2] IDM **już za wiele** a bit much
duż|y **1** big, large **2** (*ruch; deszcz*) heavy **3** **bardzo** ~**y** (*ubranie*) XL; (*łóżko*) king-size **4** (*zysk*) handsome **5** (*litera*) capital[2]; ~**a litera** block capital, capital[1] **6** (*temperatura; cena*) high[1] **7** (*wybór itp.*) wide[1] **8** (*osoba: silna*) hefty
dw|a two; ~**a razy** twice; ~**a razy tyle/więcej** double[2] IDM **na** ~**ie części** in two
dwadzieścia twenty
dwanaście twelve
dwoić się: ~ **komuś w oczach** see double
dworzanin courtier
dworzec (*kolejowy, autobusowy*) station[1]; (*duży*) terminal[1]; (*zajezdnia*) depot; ~ **autobusowy** bus station
dwóchsetlecie bicentenary
dwójka second[2]
dwójkowy binary; **system** ~ binary noun
dwór **1** (*królewski*) court[1] **2** (*szlachecki*) manor, mansion **3** **na dworze** (*przym.*) open-air, outdoor; (*przysł.*) outdoors, out of doors, outside adv.
dwubiegunow|y bipolar; ~**a psychoza afektywna** bipolar disorder
dwuczłonowy binary
dwudziesty twentieth
dwufunkcyjny dual-purpose
dwujęzyczny bilingual
dwukierunkowy two-way
dwukropek colon
dwukrotnie doubly
dwuletni biennial
dwulicowość double-dealing, hypocrisy
dwulicow|y hypocritical, two-faced; ~**a osoba** double-dealer
dwunastnica duodenum
dwunasty twelfth
dwuogniskowy bifocal
dwuosobow|y: **łóżko** ~**e** double bed; **pokój** ~**y** double room
dwupartyjny bipartisan
dwupłat biplane
dwupozycyjny: **wyłącznik** ~ two-way switch
dwuroczny biennial
dwurzędowy (*garnitur*) double-breasted
dwusetn|y: ~**a rocznica** bicentenary
dwusilnikowy twin-engined
dwuskładnikowy binary
dwustronny (*rozmowa, wymiana itp.*) bilateral, two-way
dwutlenek: ~ **węgla** carbon dioxide
dwutygodniowy fortnightly
dwuwymiarowy two-dimensional
dwuznacznik pun
dwuznaczność ambiguity
dwuznaczny ambiguous; (*seksualnie*) suggestive; (*komplement*) backhanded
dychotomia dichotomy
dydaktyczny didactic
dyfrakcj|a diffraction; **poddawać** ~**i** diffract
dyfteryt diphtheria
dyftong diphthong
dyg curtsy
dy-gać/nąć curtsy
■ **dygnięcie** bob[2]
dygotać/za- **1** (*z zimna*) shiver; (*ze strachu*) shudder, tremble **2** (*serce, brzuch*) flutter[1]
dygresj|a digression; **robić** ~**ę** digress, wander
dykcja diction, elocution
dyktando dictation
dyktator dictator
dyktatorski dictatorial
dyktatura dictatorship
dyktować/po- dictate
dylemat dilemma, quandary
dyletancki amateur[2], dilettante
dyletant/ka dilettante
dyliżans coach[1]
dym smoke[1] IDM **pójść z** ~**em** go up in smoke
dymić/za- smoke[2]
dymisj|a resignation; **podawać się do** ~**i** resign
dynamiczny dynamic
dynamika (*i przen.*) dynamics
dynamit dynamite
dynamizm dynamism
dynamo (*maszyna*) dynamo
dynastia dynasty, line[1]
dyndać/za- dangle, swing[1]
dynia pumpkin
dyplom **1** (*szk.*) diploma; (*zawodowy*) credentials; ~ **nauk humanistycznych** arts degree; **otrzymywać** ~ qualify as sth **2** (*w konkursie*) certificate
dyplomacja diplomacy
dyplomat-a/ka diplomat
dyplomatyczn|y (*i przen.*) diplomatic
■ **dyplomatycznie** diplomatically; **postępować** ~ tread carefully
dyplomowany qualified; (*księgowy*) chartered
dyrekcja management
dyrektor/ka (*firmy*) director, head[1], manager; (*stowarzyszenia*) president; (*szkoły*) head[1], headmaster, principal[2]; **dyrektor naczelny/generalny** chief executive officer, executive director of the company, managing director; **dyrektor artystyczny** artistic director
dyrektorka manageress; → zob. też DYREKTOR
dyrektywa directive, instruction
dyrygent conductor
dyrygować **1** (*orkiestrą*) conduct[1] **2** (*przen.*) call the shots/tune
dyscyplina discipline[1]; ~ **wewnętrzna** self-discipline
dyscyplinarny disciplinary
dysertacja dissertation, thesis
dysk **1** (*komput.*) disk; **twardy** ~ hard drive **2** (*kręgosłupa*) disc; **obsunięty** ~ slipped disc **3** (*sport*) discus
dyskdżokej disc jockey, DJ
dyskietka disk, floppy disk
dyskoteka disco
dyskrecja discretion, secrecy
dyskredytować/z- bring sth into disrepute, discredit, disparage
dyskretny **1** (*zachowanie*) discreet, low-key, low-profile **2** (*kolor*) sober[1] **3** (*muzyka*) unobtrusive
dyskryminacja discrimination; ~ **ze względu na czyjąś płeć** sexism
dyskryminować discriminate against sb
■ **dyskryminujący**: ~ **ze względu na płeć** sexist
dyskusj|a airing, debate[1], discussion; **poważna** ~**a** discourse; **możliwy do** ~**i** negotiable; **bez** ~**i** without argument
dyskusyjn|y (*sporny*) arguable, debatable; **kwestia** ~**a** moot point/question; **sprawa** ~**a** matter of opinion
dyskutować/prze- discuss, talk sth over (with sb); (*intensywnie*) brainstorm[2]; **lubiący** ~ argumentative
dyskwalifikacja disqualification
dyskwalifikować/z- disqualify
dysleksja dyslexia
dyslektyczny dyslexic
dyslekty-k/czka dyslexic
dysonans (*muz.*) discord, dissonance
dysonansowy (*muz.*) dissonant
dyspozycj|a IDM **do czyjejś** ~**i** at sb's command, at sb's disposal, there
dyspozytornia control[1]
dysproporcja disparity
dysputa dispute[1]
dystans **1** distance[1]; (*droga*) haul[2]; (*długość basenu itp.*) length **2** (*przen.*) distance[1], perspective; **patrzeć na własne problemy z** ~**u** put your own problems into perspective
dystansować/z- się distance[2] yourself from sb/sth
dystrybucja distribution
dystrybutor **1** (*osoba*) distributor **2** ~ **paliwa** petrol pump
dystyngowany posh, refined; (*kobieta*) ladylike
dystynkcja refinement
dysydencki dissenting
dysydent/ka dissident
dysza nozzle
dyszeć (*po wysiłku*) pant, puff[1]
dyszkant treble[1]
dywan carpet
dywanik mat, rug; ~ **łazienkowy** bath mat
dywidenda dividend
dywizja division
dyzenteria dysentery
dyżu|r duty; **na** ~**rze** on call, on duty; **po** ~**rze** off duty
dyżurny (*przym.: pracownik*) skeleton[2]
■ **dyżurn-y/a** (*rz.*) (*odpowiedzialn-y/a za porządek w klasie*) monitor[1]
dzban (także **dzbanek**) jug, pitcher; ~**ek do kawy** coffee pot
dziać (*na drutach*) knit
dziać się go on; **co się dzieje?** what's up?; **wygląda na to, że coś się dzieje z samochodem** there seems to be something the matter with the car; **coś się musi tam dziać** there must be something on; **nic się nie dzieje** things have been a bit flat
dziadek grandfather, grandparent IDM ~ **do orzechów** nutcracker
dziadzio grandad, grandpa
dział department, desk, division, section; ~ **personalny** personnel; ~ **sprzedaży** sales

działacz/ka activist
działać 1 (*osoba*) act[2], move[1]; **~ w zastępstwie kogoś** deputize for sb **2 (/za-)** (*urządzenie*) function[2], go[1], operate, be in operation, come into operation, perform well/badly/poorly, run[1], work[1]; **nie** ~ be out of action; **źle** ~ malfunction; **czy komputery już działają?** are the computers back up yet?; **dział sprzedaży działa na północy kraju** the sales team covers the north of the country **3 (/za-)** (*pomysł itp.*) do the job/trick, work[1] IDM **~ (komuś) na nerwy** get on sb's nerves, jar[2] on sb/sth
■ **działający** (*urządzenie*) operative, in working order, up and running; **dobrze działający** (as) right as rain; **nie działający** (*komput.*) down[3]
działalność activity; **~ gospodarcza** business, trade[1]
działani|e 1 (*osoby*) action; **~a wojenne** hostilities, warfare; **podczas ~a** in action; **wystawiać kogoś na ~e czegoś** expose sb to sth **2** (*mechanizmu*) mechanics, performance, operation, workings; **gotowy do ~a** operational; **rozpocząć ~e** come into operation
działka 1 (*ziemi*) enclosure, lot[3], plot[1]; (*zwł. ogródek*) allotment **2** (*udział w zysku*) cut[2] **3** (*narkotyków itp.*) fix[2] IDM **dokładnie (czyjaś) ~** (right) up your street
działo cannon
działowy departmental
dzianie (*na drutach*) knitting
dziarski brisk
dziąsło gum
dziczyzna venison
dzida spear
dzieciak kid[1], kiddie
dziecięcy childlike
dziecinka babe
dziecinny (*jak niemowlę*) babyish; (*jak dziecko*) childish; (*niemądry, infantylny*) infantile, juvenile
dzieciństwo childhood
dzieck|o child, kid[1]; (*niemowlę*) baby; **małe ~o** infant; **mieć pierwsze ~o** start a family; **nie bądź ~iem!** oh, grow up!
dziedzic 1 (*majątku; tradycji*) heir to sth **2** (*właściciel majątku ziemskiego*) squire
dziedzictwo (*spadek*) inheritance, legacy; (*narodowe*) heritage; (*rodzinny przedmiot*) heirloom
dziedziczny hereditary IDM **być ~m** run in the family
dziedziczyć/o- inherit
dziedzina area, branch[1], domain, sphere; (*naukowa*) field[1]; (*biznesu*) line[1]
dziedziniec courtyard, quadrangle; (*zwykle betonowy/kamienny*) yard; **~ kościelny** churchyard
dziekan dean
dzielenie division
dzielić 1 (/po-; /roz-) (*na oddzielne części*) break sth up, divide[1], separate sth out, split[1], split sth up; (*na poddziały*) subdivide; (*przegradzać, odgradzać*) partition verb **2 coś z kimś** share[1] **3** (*koszty*) split[1] **4** (*mat.*) divide[1] IDM **~ włos na czworo** split hairs
□ **dzielić/po- się 1** (*na oddzielne części*) divide[1], separate out, split[1]; (*na poddziały*) subdivide **2 czymś z kimś** share[1] **3** (*kosztem*) **~ po połowie** go half and half/go halves with sb **4** (*wiadomościami itp.*) impart sth (to sb)
dzielnica borough, district, quarter, sector
dzielnicowy (*rz.*) bobby
dzielnik factor
dzielność pluck[2]
dzielny brave[1], fearless, gallant, plucky adj., valiant
dzieł|o creation, work[2]; **~o sztuki** artwork, work of art; **~o malarskie** painting; **bezcenne ~a sztuki** the nation's art treasures; **osoba zatrudniona na umowę o ~o** freelance; **pracować na umowę o ~o** freelance IDM **do ~a!** here goes!
dziennik 1 (*gazeta*) daily[2] **2** (*pamiętnik*) diary, journal; (*pokładowy*) log[1]; (*szkolny*) register[2]; **prowadzić ~ szkolny** keep records of the children's progress
dziennikarstwo journalism
dziennika-rz/rka journalist
dzień 1 (*doba, okres dnia*) day; **~ powszedni** weekday; **~ pracy** day, working day; **~ wolny od pracy** (*urlop*) day off; (*wprowadzony ustawowo; święto państwowe*) public holiday; **Dzień Matki** Mother's Day; **Dzień Ojca** Father's Day; **Dzień Wszystkich Świętych** All Saints' Day; **~ Objawienia Pańskiego** Epiphany; **zły ~** off day; **z dnia na ~** day by day, day-to-day, from day to day, from one day to the next; (*nagle*) overnight adv. **2** (*kiedy jest widno*) daytime; **w ~**; **za dnia** by day, in the daytime IDM **~ dobry!** (*po południu*) good afternoon; (*przed południem*) good morning; (*o każdej porze*) hello | **~ po dniu** day in, day out | **~ w ~** day by day | **po ~ dzisiejszy** to date
dzierżaw|a lease, tenancy, leasehold; (*budynek, ziemia*) **na zasadach ~y** leasehold adv.
dzierżaw-ca/czyni (*budynku*) tenant, occupier
dzierżawczy (*gram.*) possessive
dzierżawić/wy- lease verb, rent[2]
dzierżawiony (*budynek, ziemia*) leasehold
dzierżyć wield
dziesiątkować/z- decimate
dziesiąty tenth
dziesiejszy today's
dziesięciolecie decade
dziesięć ten
dziesiętny decimal[1]
dziewczę girl
dziewczęcy girlish; **wiek ~** girlhood
dziewczyna 1 (*osoba*) adolescent, female[2], girl, lass **2** (*sympatia*) date[1], girlfriend
dziewczynka girl; (*niemowlę*) baby girl
dziewiarstwo knitting, knitwear
dziewiąty ninth[1]
dziewica virgin[1]
dziewictwo virginity
dziewiczy virgin[2]
dziewięć nine
dziewięćdziesiąt ninety
dziewięćdziesiąty ninetieth
dziewiętnasty nineteenth
dziewiętnaście nineteen
dzięcioł woodpecker
dziękczynienie: **Święto Dziękczynienia** Thanksgiving (Day)
dzięki 1 (*podziękowanie*) cheers, ta, thanks **2 czemuś/komuś** owing to, thanks to sb/sth, through IDM **~ Bogu!** thank God, goodness, heavens, etc.
dziękować/po- thank
dzik boar
dzik|i 1 (*w przyrodzie*) wild[1]; (*zwł. uciekający z domu/gospodarstwa*) feral; **~a róża** briar **2** (*szalony*) abandoned, frenzied, mad, riotous **3** (*pejzaż*) rugged
■ **dziko** (*szalenie*) crazily, wildly; **mieszkać na ~** squat[1]
dziob-ać/nąć 1 (*ptak*) peck (at) sth **2** (*jedzenie itp.*) pick at sth; **ciągle dziobał kartofel widelcem** he kept jabbing at his potato with his fork
dziobak platypus
dziób 1 (*ptaka*) beak, bill[1] **2** (*samolotu*) nose[1]; (*łodzi, statku*) bow[2], prow **3** (*dzbanka*) spout[1] **4 pokryć dziobami** pit[2]
dzisiaj (także **dziś**) today, the present day; **dziś wieczorem** tonight; **od dziś za tydzień** a week today
dzisiejszy 1 (*gazeta itp.*) today's; **dzisiejsz-y/a wieczór/noc** tonight **2** (*współczesny*) contemporary[1], modern, present-day
dziś → DZISIAJ
dziur|a 1 (*w ubraniu itp.*) hole; (*w płocie itp.*) gap, opening; (*w zębie itp.*) cavity; **robić ~ę** tear[2] **2** (*powietrza*) pocket[1]
dziurawić/prze- perforate, prick[1]; (*oponę*) puncture verb
dziurawy holey
dziurk|a 1 hole; **~a od klucza** keyhole; **~a od guzika** buttonhole[1] **2 (dziurki)** (*w papierze*) perforation IDM **mieć czegoś po ~i w nosie** be cheesed off, be sick to death of sth
dziurkacz punch[2]
dziurkować/po- perforate, punch[1]
dziwactwo eccentricity, idiosyncrasy, peculiarity, quirk
dziwaczność (*niezwykłość*) peculiarity; (*coś dziwnego*) oddity
dziwaczny 1 (*dziwny*) bizarre, cranky, flaky, freakish, freaky, oddball, outlandish, queer, quirky, weird; (*nie pasujący do grupy*) incongruous **2** (*niezwykły*) eccentric, idiosyncratic, peculiar
dziwadło freak[1]
dziwa-k/czka crank, freak[1], oddball, oddity, weirdo; (*ktoś niezwykły*) character, eccentric noun
dziwić/za- astonish, surprise[2]
□ **dziwić/z- się** be astonished/surprised IDM **nie dziwię ci się** I don't blame you
dziwka bitch[2], tart[1], whore
dziwn|y curious, freakish, funny, idiosyncratic, odd, peculiar, queer, strange, surprising; **~e, że** funnily enough; **nic ~ego** no wonder
dzwon (także **dzwonek**) **1** (*urządzenie*) bell; (*do drzwi*) doorbell **2** (*dźwięk*) chime noun, ring[1]; (*melodia do telefonu*) ringtone **3** (*kwiat*) bluebell IDM **od wielkiego ~u** once in a blue moon
dzwonić/za- 1 (*telefonować*) call[1], call sb up, give sb a call, give sb a buzz, phone verb, ring[2], give sb a ring, telephone; (*oddzwonić*) ring (sb) back; (*do telewizji, radia, miejsca swojej pracy*) ring in; **~ bezpośrednio** dial

direct; ~ **pod numer miejscowy** make a local call; ~ **do kogoś na jego koszt** reverse (the) charges **2** (*telefon, dzwon*) ring[2]; (*dzwon, zegar*) chime; (*dzwonek*) jingle[2]; (*naciskając przycisk*) buzz[1]; (*delikatnie*) tinkle **3** (*budzik*) go off
dzwony (*spodnie*) flared jeans/ trousers
dźgać/dźgnąć jab[1], thrust[1]; **kogoś** give sb a jab; (*nożem*) knife[2], stab[1]
dźwięczeć/za- (*metal*) clash[1]
dźwięczny resonant
dźwięk sound[1]
dźwiękoszczelny soundproof
dźwiękowy audio, sonic, sound[1]
dźwig 1 (*budowlany*) crane[1] **2** (*winda*) lift[2]
dźwigać 1 (/dźwignąć; /udźwignąć) (*podnosić*) heave[1], lift[1] **2** (*nosić*) bear[1]
dźwigar girder
dźwigni|a lever; **~a zmiany biegów** gear lever; **siła** ~ leverage
dżdżownica earthworm
dżem jam[1], jelly; ~ **pomarańczowy/ cytrynowy** marmalade
dżentelmen gentleman
dżin gin
dżingiel jingle[1]
dżinn genie
dżinsowy (*materiał*) denim
dżinsy jeans
dżip Jeep
dżojstik joystick
dżokej jockey
dżoker joker
dżudo judo
dżuma plague[1]
dżungla jungle

E

e 1 (E/e) (*litera*) E, e **2 (E/e)** (*muz.*) E
echo echo[1]; **powodować** ~ echo[2]
edukacja education
edukować/wy- educate
edycja edition
edykt edict
edytor: ~ **tekstu** word processor
edytować edit
ee um
efekciarski 1 (*na pokaz*) glitzy **2** (*zachęcający do zakupu*) gimmicky
efekt 1 (*wynik*) effect[1], result[1]; ~ **cieplarniany** the greenhouse effect; ~ **następczy** after-effect **2** (*wrażenie*) effect[1], touch[2]; ~ **dźwiękowy** sound effect; **~y specjalne** special effects
efektowny (*oryginalny*) effective, spectacular; (*auto*) flashy
efektywny effective
efemeryczny ephemeral
egalitarny egalitarian
egocentryczny egocentric, self-centred, selfish
egocentryzm selfishness
egoist-a/ka egoist
egoistyczny egoistic, self-centred, selfish
egoizm egoism, selfishness
egotyst-a/ka egoist; (*skrajny*) egomaniac
egotyzm: **skrajny** ~ egomania
egzamin exam; (*krótszy i mniej ważny*) test[1]; ~ **maturalny** A2 (level); ~ **pisemny** paper; ~ **praktyczny** practical[2]; ~ **ustny** oral[2]; **~y końcowe** final[2]; ~ **na prawo jazdy** driving test
egzaminator/ka examiner
egzaminować/prze- examine, test[2]
egzekucja execution
egzekwować/wy- 1 coś od kogoś exact[2] sth (from sb) **2** (*prawo*) enforce
egzema eczema
egzemplarz (*gazety, płyty, książki*) copy[1]; (*gazety*) number[1]; (*próbka*) specimen; **w dwóch ~ach** in duplicate
egzorcyzmować exorcize
egzotyczny exotic
egzystencja existence; (*przeżycie*) subsistence
egzystencjalizm existentialism
egzystencjalny existential
egzystować: **dzięki czemuś** exist, subsist on sth, get by (on/in/with sth)
ekierka set square
ekipa crew, party
eklektyczny eclectic
eklektyzm eclecticism
eklerka (także **eklerek, ekler**) eclair
ekolog ecologist
ekologia ecology
ekologiczny 1 (*nauka*) ecological **2** (*nieszkodliwy dla otoczenia*) environmentally friendly; (*i polit.*) green[1] **3** (*jedzenie*) organic
ekonomia 1 (*nauka*) economics **2** (*gospodarka*) economy
ekonomiczny (*dot. ekonomii*) economic
ekonomika economics
ekonomista economist
ekosystem ecosystem
ekran screen[1]; ~ **ochronny** shield[1]; ~ **dotykowy** touch screen; ~ **plazmowy** plasma screen; **szeroki** ~ widescreen
ekscelencja: **Wasza Ekselencjo** Your Grace, My Lord, Your Lordship
ekscentryczny eccentric; (*dziwaczny*) cranky; (*i jaskrawy*) jazzy
■ **ekscentryczność** eccentricity
ekscentryk eccentric noun
ekscytujący exhilarating
ekshibicjonist-a/ka exhibitionist
ekskluzywny (*luksusowy*) select[2], upmarket; (*luksusowy, dla wybranej grupy*) exclusive[1]
ekskomunika excommunication
ekskomunikować excommunicate
eksmisja eviction
eksmitować/wy- evict
ekspansja expansion
ekspansjonist-a/ka expansionist
ekspansjonistyczny expansionist
ekspansjonizm expansionism
ekspedient/ka shop assistant
ekspediować/wy- dispatch
ekspedycja expedition
ekspert (*znawca*) expert; (*naukowiec*) scholar
ekspertyz|a survey[1]; **przeprowadzać ~ę** survey[2]
eksperyment experiment[1]
eksperymentalny experimental
eksperymentować experiment[2]; (*z narkotykami itp.*) mess with sb/sth
eksploatacj|a (*maszyny itp.*) usage; **koszty ~i samochodu** the running costs of a car
eksploatować 1 (*maszyny itp.*) run[1], work[1] **2** (*teren itp.*) develop **3** (*ludzi*) exploit[1]
eksplodować detonate, explode, go off
eksploracja exploration
eksploracyjny (*med.*) exploratory
eksplozja explosion
eksponat exhibit[2]
eksport export[2]
eksporter exporter
eksportować/wy- export[1]
eksportowy (*artykuły*) export[2]
ekspozycja array
ekspres 1 (*pociąg*) express[3]; **~em** express adv. **2** (*list*) express letter **2** ~ **do kawy** coffee maker
ekspresja expression
ekspresjonist-a/ka expressionist
ekspresjonistyczny expressionist
ekspresjonizm expressionism
ekspresowy express[2]
ekspresyjny expressive
eksta|za ecstasy, rapture; **w ~zie** ecstatic IDM **wpadać w ~zę** go into raptures
ekstra super
ekstradować extradite
ekstradycja extradition
ekstrapolacja extrapolation
ekstrapolować/z- extrapolate
ekstrawagancja extravagance, flamboyance, indulgence
ekstrawagancki flamboyant
ekstrawertyczny extroverted
ekstrawerty-k/czka extrovert
ekstremalny extreme
ekstremist-a/ka extremist
ekstremizm extremism
ekumeniczny ecumenical
ekwipunek (*sprzęt*) equipment
elastyczność 1 (*tkaniny, przedmiotu itp.*) elasticity, give[2] **2** (*osoby*) flexibility, suppleness **3** (*planu*) flexibility
elastyczny 1 (*tkanina, przedmiot itp.*) elastic, pliable, stretchy; (*ubranie*) elasticated **2** (*osoba*) flexible, supple[2] **3** (*plan itp.*) adaptable, flexible, open-ended
elegancja elegance, snappiness
elegancki (*modny*) chic, dapper, dashing, dressy, fashionable, stylish, smart[1]; (*wytworny*) elegant; (*i drogi*) swanky; (*w manierach*) genteel; (*zwł. mężczyzna: i wytworny*) urbane
elegia elegy
elektorat electorate
elektroda electrode
elektromagnetyczny electromagnetic
elektron electron
elektroniczny e-, electronic; (*zegarek*) digital
elektronika electronics
elektrownia power station
elektryczność electricity; ~ **statyczna** static[2]
elektryczny 1 (*motor; światło; wtyczka*) electric **2** (*usterka; urządzenie; energia*) electrical
elektryfikować/z- electrify
elektryk electrician
elektryzować/z- electrify
■ **elektryzujący** electric
element 1 (*składnik*) constituent, unit; (*zwł. nieuchwytny*) element; (*sukcesu itp.*) ingredient **2** (*chem.*) element **3** (*żywioł*) element
elementarny elementary, rudimentary
elf elf

eliminacj|a elimination; (**eliminacje**) (*w grze/konkursie*) knockout; **etap ~i** heat[1]
eliminować/wy- 1 (*wykluczać możliwość*) eliminate; (*koszty itp.*) cut sth out **2 kogoś/coś z czegoś** filter sb/sth out (of sth); (*z zawodów*) knock sb out (of sth)
elipsa ellipse
eliptyczny (*i przen.*) elliptical
elita cream[1], elite
elitarny elite adj., elitist, select[2]
elitaryzm elitism
elokwencja eloquence
elokwentny eloquent
e-mail email
emalia (*na metalu*) enamel; (*na ceramice*) glaze[2]
emaliować (*ceramikę*) glaze[1]
emancypacja emancipation
emancypować/wy- emancipate
emanować (*i przen.*) radiate; (*pewnością siebie itp.*) emanate, exude
embargo embargo
embrion embryo
embrionalny embryonic
emeryt/ka old-age pensioner
emerytalny retirement
emerytowany retired
emerytu|ra 1 (*stan*) retirement; **na ~rze** retired **2** (*świadczenie pieniężne*) pension
emfatyczny emphatic
emfaza emphasis
emfizema emphysema
emigracja emigration; (*polityczna*) exile
emigrant/ka emigrant, émigré; (*polityczn-y/a*) defector, exile
emigrować/wy- emigrate, go into exile
emisja 1 (*gazu itp.*) emission **2** (*ekon.*) issue[1]; (*akcji*) flotation
emitować/wy- 1 (*gaz itp.*) discharge[1], emit; (*wydzielać*) send sth out **2** (*ekon.*) issue[2] **3** (*program telewizyjny*) televise; (*nagranie*) release[1]
emocj|a emotion, feeling; **bez ~i** clinically
emocjonalny emotional
emocjonujący exhilarating, mind-blowing
□ **emocjonujący się**: **nie ~** stolid
emotikon emoticon
empatia empathy
empiryczny empirical
emulgować (się) emulsify
emulsja 1 (*chem.*) emulsion **2** (*kosmetyczna*) lotion
encyklopedia encyclopedia
endemiczny endemic
endokrynolog endocrinologist
endokrynologia endocrinology
energi|a 1 (*osoby*) drive[2], energy, life, vigour; **bez ~i** lifeless; **pełny/wymagający ~i** energetic; **z (dużą) ~ą** energetically; **dodawać ~i** invigorate **2** (*elektryczna*) power[1]; **~a jądrowa** atomic energy; **~a parowa** steam[1]
energiczny bouncy, breezy, brisk, dynamic, energetic, vigorous
enigma enigma
enigmatyczny enigmatic
enklawa enclave; (*grupa*) pocket[1]
entuzjast-a/ka devotee, enthusiast; **być entuzjastą czegoś** be into sth
entuzjastyczny enthusiastic, rapturous, upbeat, vibrant
entuzjazm enthusiasm, exuberance, keenness; (*i energiczność*) ebullience; **pełen ~u** keen; **bez ~u** coolly, half-hearted, half-heartedly
entuzjazmować/roz- się enthuse, go into raptures
enzym enzyme
epicki epic
epidemia epidemic
epilepsja epilepsy
epileptyczny epileptic adj.
epilepty-k/czka epileptic
epilog epilogue
epitafium epitaph
epizod 1 (*incydent*) episode **2** (*rola w filmie itp.*) bit part
epoka age[1], epoch
epopeja epic noun
era age[1], era; **n.e.** AD; **p.n.e.** BC
erekcj|a erection; **w stanie ~i** erect[1]
ergonomiczny ergonomic
erodować/z- erode
erotyczny blue[1], erotic
erozja erosion
erudycyjny erudite
Es/es E flat
eseist-a/ka essayist
esej essay
esencja essence
eskadra squadron; (*samolotów*) fleet
eskalacja escalation
eskapada escapade
eskapistyczny escapist
eskapizm escapism
Eskimos/ka Eskimo, Inuit
eskimoski Eskimo
eskorta escort[1]
eskortować escort[2]
estet-a/ka aesthete
estetyczny aesthetic[1]
estetyka 1 (*w filozofii*) aesthetics **2** (*idea*) aesthetic[2]
estrada platform, stage[1]
estrogen oestrogen
esy-floresy doodle noun
etanol ethanol
etap phase[1], stage[1]; (*podróży itp.*) lap[1], leg
eta|t: **na ~cie** tenured
eter ether
eteryczny ethereal
etniczny ethnic
etnografia ethnography
etnograficzny ethnographic
etnolog ethnologist
etnologia ethnology
etnologiczny ethnological
etos ethos
etyczny ethical
etyka (*pracy itp.*) ethic
etykieta 1 (*na opakownaiu, ubraniu itp.*) label[1], tag[1] **2** (*reguły zachowania*) etiquette, formality, protocol
etymologia etymology
eufemistyczny euphemistic
eufemizm euphemism
eufori|a euphoria; **stan ~i** high[2]
euforyczny euphoric
eukaliptus eucalyptus, gum tree
euro euro
euroczek Eurocheque
Europa the Continent
europeizować/z- westernize
Europej-czyk/ka European[2]
europejski continental, European[1]
eurosceptyczny Euro-sceptic
eurosceptyk Euro-sceptic
eutanazja euthanasia
ewakuacja evacuation
ewakuacyjn|y: **wyjście ~e** fire escape
ewakuować evacuate
Ewangelia gospel
ewangelicki evangelical
ewentualnie alternatively
ewentualność contingency, option, possibility
ewokacyjny evocative
ewolucja evolution
ewolucyjny evolutionary
ewoluować/wy- evolve
ezoteryczny esoteric

F

f 1 (**F/f**) (*litera*) F, f **2** (**F/f**) (*muz.*) F
fabrycznie: **~ nowy** brand new
fabryka factory, mill[1], plant[1], works[2]
fabrykacja fabrication
fabrykować/s- fabricate
fabularny: **film ~** feature[1]
facet bloke, bod, chap, customer, devil, dude, guy, sort[1]
facetka bod, customer, devil, sort[1]
fach trade[1] IDM **po ~u** by profession
fachowiec professional[2]; **~ od wszystkiego** odd-job man
fachowy competent, professional[1], skilled, technical, workmanlike
■ **fachowość** competence, professionalism, workmanship
fagot bassoon
Fahrenheit Fahrenheit; **skala ~a** Fahrenheit noun
fair fair[1], fair adv. IDM **być nie ~ wobec kogoś** be hard on sb/sth
fajerwerk firework
fajka 1 (*z cybuchem*) pipe[1] **2** (*papieros*) fag **3** (*znak*) tick[2]
fajny (*dobry, ciekawy*) fun[2], neat; (*w porządku*) hunky-dory
fajrant: **robić ~** knock off (sth)
faks fax[1]; **przesyłać ~em**; **wysyłać ~** fax[2]
fakt fact, thing
faktura 1 (*fin.*) invoice **2** (*tkaniny itp.*) texture
fakturowanie billing
faktycznie actually, indeed, as a matter of fact, intrinsically, quite, really, so[1], truly, virtually
faktyczny actual, effective, factual, intrinsic, real[1], tangible, virtual; (*zgodny z faktami*) historical
fal|a 1 (*morska itp.*) wave[1]; **drobna ~a** ripple; **~a pływowa** tidal wave; **~a przybojowa** surf[1]; **~a upałów** heatwave; **~e długie** (*radio*) long wave, LW; **~e krótkie** short wave; **~e średnie** medium wave, MW; **~e radiowe** airwaves **2** (*uczuć itp.*) surge, wave[1]; (*śmiechu itp.*) ripple
falbank|a frill; **z ~ami** frilly
falist|y wavy; **blacha ~a** corrugated iron
falochron breakwater, jetty, pier
falować/za- 1 (*włosy itp.*) flow[2]; (*gałęzie*) wave[2]; (*woda; łan zboża*) ripple; (*zasłona*) billow **2** (*pierś*) **ciężko ~** heave[1] (with sth)
falstart (*sport*) false start
falsyfikat fake[1], forgery
fałda crease[1], fold[2]; (*w spódnicy*) pleat
fałdować/po- crinkle sth (up); (*tkaninę*) gather; (*w zakładki, plisy*) pleat verb
■ **fałdowany** (*karton; metal*) corrugated

□ **fałdować/po- się** crinkle (up)
fałsz deceitfulness, phoniness
fałszerstwo forgery
fałszować/s-/za- 1 (*pieniądze, obraz itp.*) forge[1]; (*podpis*) fake[2]; (*fakty*) fabricate, falsify **2** (*rezultaty ankiety, wyniki wyborów itp.*) doctor[2], fiddle[1], rig[1] **3** (*muz., za wysoko*) be sharp[2]; (*za nisko*) be flat; (*śpiewając*) sing off pitch; (*za nisko*) sing flat; **fałszując** in/out of tune
fałszyw|y 1 (*niezgodny z prawdą*) false, phoney; (*pieniądze, towary*) counterfeit; (*obraz itp.*) fake; (*roszczenie; kontrakt; lekarz itp.*) bogus; (*wbrew pozorom*) spurious; **~e mniemanie** misjudgement; **~a moneta** dud coin; **~y obraz** (*sprawy*) misrepresentation; **dawać ~y obraz** (*sprawy*) misrepresent; **udzielać ~ych informacji** misinform **2** (*postępowanie itp.*) deceitful, underhand IDM **~y alarm** a false alarm, hoax | **~y przyjaciel** (*przen.*) a false friend
fan fan[1]
fanaberia whim
fanatyczny bigoted, fanatical
fanaty-k/czka bigot, fanatic, fiend, maniac, zealot
fanatyzm bigotry, fanaticism
fanfara fanfare
fantastyczny fanciful, fantastic, sensational, smashing
fantastyka: ~ **naukowa** science fiction
fantazja fantasy, whim
fantazjować/po- fantasize, romanticize
fantazyjny dashing
farba paint[1]; (*na włosy itp.*) dye[2]; ~ **emulsyjna** emulsion
farbka colouring
farbować/za-/po- dye[1], tint; (*w praniu*) run[1]
farma farm[1]
farmaceutyczny pharmaceutical
farmacja pharmacy
farmakologia pharmacology
farmakologiczny pharmacological
farsa charade, farce, joke[1], travesty
farsowy farcical
farsz stuffing
fart luck IDM **mieć ~/nie mieć ~u** be in/out of luck
fartuch apron, pinafore; (*z rękawami*) overall[2]; (*lekarski*) gown; (*bluza robocza*) smock
fasada facade
fascynacja fascination
fascynować/za- fascinate, magnetize; ~ **dzieci** capture the children's imagination/interest/attention
■ **fascynujący** fascinating, intriguing; (*wzbudzający zachwyt*) glamorous
faseta facet
fasola bean; ~ **czerwona typu kidney** kidney beans; ~ **wielokwiatowa** runner beans; ~ **zwyczajna** haricot beans
fasolka: ~ **szparagowa** French beans, green beans; ~ **w sosie pomidorowym** baked beans
fason style
fasonować mould[2]
fastrygować/s- tack[2]
faszerować/na- stuff[2]
faszyst-a/ka fascist
faszystowski fascist
faszyzm fascism
fatalistyczny fatalistic
fatalny 1 (*pechowy*) disastrous **2** (*okropny*) abysmal **3** (*błąd, decyzja itp.*) fatal
fatamorgana mirage
fatyga trouble[1]
fatygować trouble[2] sb (for sth)
□ **fatygować/po- się** bother[1] (to do sth/doing sth), (about/with sth)
faul foul[3]
faulować/s- foul[2]
fauna fauna; **dzika ~ i flora** wildlife
faworyt/ka favourite[2]
faworyty whiskers
faworytyzm favouritism
faworyzować favour[2], weight[2]
faworyzowanie favouritism
faza phase[1], stage[1]
febra cold sore
fechtunek fencing
federacja federation
federalny federal
felieton column
felietonist-a/ka columnist
feminist-a/ka feminist
feministyczny feminist
feminizm feminism
fenkuł fennel
fenomen marvel, phenomenon
fenomenalny phenomenal
ferie holiday, recess; ~ **uniwersyteckie** vacation
ferma: ~ **mleczna** dairy farm
ferment ferment[2]
fermentacj|a fermentation; **powodować ~ę** ferment[1]
fermentować/s- ferment[1]
ferwor fervour
festiwal festival
festyn fête
fetor pong, reek noun, stench
fetysz fetish
fetyszyst-a/ka fetishist
fetyszystyczny fetishistic
fetyszyzm fetishism
fetyszyzować/s- make a fetish of sth
feudalizm feudalism
feudalny feudal
fiasko fiasco
figa fig
figi briefs, knickers
fig|iel mischief, practical joke, prank, trick; (*przekręt*) hoax; **spłatać komuś ~la** joke[1]
figlarnie mischievously, whimsically, wickedly
figlarny playful, mischievous; (*uśmiech itp.*) whimsical
figlować/po- frolic
figowiec fig
figura figure[1], shape[1]; (*posąg*) statue; ~ **(szachowa)** piece[1]; ~ **retoryczna** figure of speech; ~ **woskowa** waxwork
figurant/ka figurehead
figurować figure[2] (as sth) (in/among sth); (*w planach*) feature[2] in sth
fikcyjn|y fictitious; **powieść opisywała ~e losy lekarza** the book gave a fictional account of a doctor's life
fiksacj|a: **mający ~ę (na punkcie kogoś/czegoś)** fixated (on sb/sth)
filantrop/ka philanthropist
filantropia philanthropy
filantropijny humanitarian, philanthropic
filar 1 column, pillar **2** (*przen.*) linchpin, pillar
filatelist-a/ka philatelist, stamp collector
filatelistyka stamp collecting
filc felt[2]
filet fillet
filia branch[1], division; (*spółki*) subsidiary[2]
filigranowy dainty; (*tylko osoba*) slight
filiżanka cup[1]; ~ **do herbaty** teacup
film 1 film[1], picture[1]; ~ **akcji** action movie; ~ **animowany** cartoon; ~ **fabularny** feature[1]; ~ **dokumentalny** documentary **2** (*kino*) cinema, screen[1] **3** (*do aparatu*) film[1]
filmować/s- film[2], shoot[1]
filmowy cinematic, cinematographic
filologia philology; ~ **klasyczna** classics[2]
filologiczny philological
filozof/ka philosopher
filozofia philosophy
filozoficzny 1 philosophical **2** (*postawa itp.*) mellow, philosophical (about sth)
filozofować/po- philosophize
filtr filter[1]; ~ **papierowy** filter paper; **krem/mleczko z ~em przeciwsłonecznym** sunblock, suncream, sunscreen
filtrować/prze- filter[2], strain[2]
filunek panel
finalist-a/ka finalist
finalizować/s- finalize
finał (*sport*) final[2] (*muz., teatr*) finale
finanse finance[1]
finansować/s- finance[2]
finansowanie grant[2]
finansowy financial
finisz finish[2]
fioletowy purple, violet adj.; **kolor ~** purple, violet
fiołek violet
fiołkowy violet
fiord fjord
firank|a (**firanki**) lace curtains, net curtains
firma business, company, enterprise, establishment, firm[1], operation, operator, outfit; ~ **kateringowa** caterer; ~ **konsultingowa** consultancy; ~ **macierzysta** parent; ~ **międzynarodowa** multinational[2]
firmowy proprietary
Fis/fis F sharp
fiskalny fiscal
fistaszek peanut
fiszka index card
fizjologia physiology
fizjologiczny physiological
fizjoterapeuta physiotherapist
fizjoterapia physiotherapy
fizyczny physical; (*praca*) manual[1]; (*cielesny*) bodily[1]
fizyk physicist
fizyka physics
flaga flag[1]
flak (*opona*) flat[2], flat tyre
flaki guts[1], tripe
flakon vase
flakowaty flat[1]
flamaster felt-tip pen, marker (pen)
flaming flamingo

flanela flannel
flanka flank[1]
flara flare[2]
flądra flounder[2]
flecist-a/ka flautist
flegma phlegm
flegmatyczny phlegmatic
flejtuch slob, slut
fleksja inflection
flesz flash[2]
flet flute; ~ **dyszkantowy** descant recorder; ~ **prosty** recorder
flipchart flip chart
flirciarski flirtatious
flircia-rz/rka flirt[2]
flirtować/po- flirt[1]
flora flora; **dzika fauna i ~** wildlife
floret foil[1]
flota fleet; ~ **wojenna** navy
flotylla fleet
fluktuacja fluctuation
fluorek fluoride
fluoryzujący fluorescent
fobia phobia
foka seal[2]
folgować/po-: **sobie (w czymś)** indulge (yourself) (in sth)
foli|a: **~a do żywności** cling film; (*aluminiowa itp.*) foil[1]; **~a do rzutnika** transparency; **koperta wzmocniona ~ą bąbelkową** Jiffy bag
folk: **muzyka** ~ folk[1]
folklor folklore
folkloryst-a/ka folklorist
folkow|y folk[2]; **muzyka ~a** folk[1]
fonem phoneme
fonematyczny phonemic
fonetyczny phonetic
fonetyka phonetics
fonia sound[1]
fonolog phonologist
fonologia phonology
fonologiczny phonological
fontanna 1 fountain **2** (*krwi z rany itp.*) spurt noun
forhend forehand
form|a 1 form[1], pattern, shape[1]; **~a sztuki** art form **2** (*szablon*) template **3 ~a odlewnicza** mould[1] **4** (*kondycja fizyczna*) **(dobra) ~a** fitness; **być w ~ie** be on form; **w (dobrej) ~ie** fit[2]; **być nadal w dobrej ~ie** going strong; **znów w dobrej ~ie** (back) on your feet, back to your old self again; **nie być w ~ie** be out of condition, be off form; (*interesy*) **w dobrej ~ie** afloat **5** (*sposób postępowania*) formality
formacja formation
formalizować/s- formalize
formalnie formally, officially; **~ rzecz biorąc** technically
formalnoś|ć formality; **(formalności)** bureaucracy
formalny formal, official[1]; **bardzo ~** stilted
format format[1], size[1]; (*osoby*) stature
formatować/s- format[2]
formować/u- form[2]
formowanie formation
formularz form[1]
formuła formula
formułka drill[1]
formułować/s- compose, draw sth up, formulate, frame[2], phrase[2], put, word[2]; **~ pojęcie** conceptualize sth (as sth); **~ teorie (na temat czegoś)** theorize (about/on sth)
fornir veneer
forsa dough
forsować/s- force[2], push[1]
forsowny strenuous
fort fort
forteca fortress
fortel manoeuvre[1], ploy, ruse
fortepian grand piano, piano; **~ buduarowy** baby grand
fortun|a fortune; **kosztować ~ę** cost you a bomb, cost the earth/a fortune
fortunny fortuitous
fortyfikacja fortification
fortyfikować/u- fortify
forum forum
fory head start, start[2]
fosa moat; **~ orkiestrowa** orchestra pit
fotel armchair, easy chair
fotelik: **~ dziecięcy** (*np. do samochodu*) booster seat
fotka snap[2]
fotogeniczny photogenic
fotograf photographer
fotografia 1 (*technika*) photography **2** (*zdjęcie*) photograph, shot[1]
fotograficzny photographic
fotografik photographer
fotografować/s- photograph verb, shoot[1]
fotokopia photocopy, Xerox
fotokopiarka photocopier
fotokopiować/s- photocopy verb
fotosyntetyzować photosynthesize
fotosynteza photosynthesis
foyer foyer
fracht: **~ morski** shipment
frachtowiec freighter
fragment extract[1], fragment[1], snippet; **najciekawszy ~** highlight[2]
fragmentaryczny bitty, patchy, piecemeal, scrappy, sketchy
frajd|a kick[2]; **szybka jazda samochodem sprawia mu ~ę** he gets a kick out of driving fast
frajer/ka mug[1], sucker
frak tails[1]
frakcja faction
frakcyjny breakaway
frankfurterka frankfurter
frapujący impressive, striking
frazeologia phraseology
frazes platitude
frazesowy platitudinous
fregata frigate
frekwencja attendance, turnout
frenetyczny frenetic
freon (*chem.*) CFC
fretka ferret[1]
freudowski Freudian
frezja freesia
frędz|el tassel; **(frędzle)** fringe[1]
front front[1]; (*technologii*) cutting edge IDM **zmieniać ~** change your tune
frontalny frontal
frontowy front[2]
froterowanie shine[2]
frotka (*do włosów*) scrunchy
frustracja frustration
frustrować/s- frustrate
frustrujący frustrating
fruwać/pofrunąć flit, flutter[1], fly[1]
frytki chip[1]
fryzjer/ka hairdresser, stylist; **fryzjer (męski)** barber
fryzjerski: **salon/zakład ~** hairdresser's
fryzura haircut, hairstyle
fuj: ~! pooh, ugh
fujarka pipe[1]
fuksja fuchsia
fular cravat
funciak quid
fundacja foundation
fundament (fundamenty) foundations
fundamentalist-a/ka fundamentalist
fundamentalistyczny fundamentalist
fundamentalizm fundamentalism
fundamentalny paramount
fundować/za-/u- 1 (*sfinansować*) fund[2], lay sth on; **(sobie/komuś)** treat[1] sb/yourself (to sth); **~ stypendium** endow a scholarship **2** (*zakładać*) found[2]
fundusz 1 fund[1] **2 (fundusze)** finance[1], finances, funds[1]; **gromadzenie ~y** fund-raising
fungicyd fungicide
funkcja facility, function[1], functionality
funkcjonalność functionality
funkcjonalny functional, utilitarian
funkcjonariusz/ka officer
funkcjonować/za- function[2], run[1], work[1]; **źle ~** malfunction
funkowy funky
funky funky
funt pound[1]
fura cart[1], wagon
furgon van
furgonetka van; **~ pocztowa** mail van
furi|a fury; **wpadać w ~ę** fly into a rage; **rzucać się/napadać z ~ą na kogoś/coś** savage verb; **wpadać/wypadać (skądś) z ~ą** storm[2]
furkot whirr
furkotać/za- whirr
furtka 1 gate **2** (*przen.*) loophole
fusy dregs
fuszerować/s- bungle, make a hash of sth, mess sth up
futbol football; **~ amerykański** American football
futerał case, holder; (*na pistolet*) holster
futro fur
futurystyczny futuristic
fuzja fusion; (*przedsiębiorstw*) merger

G

g 1 (G/g) (*litera*) G, g **2 (G/g)** (*muz.*) G
gabinet 1 (*pokój, w domu*) study[1]; **~ dentystyczny** dentist; **~ lekarski** surgery; **~ odnowy biologicznej** fitness centre; **~ figur woskowych** waxworks **2** (*ministrów*) cabinet
gablotka cabinet
gad reptile
gadać/po- chat[1], go on (about sb/sth), natter
gadanina natter noun, talk[2]; **urzędowa (niezrozumiała) ~** gobbledegook
gadatliwy chatty, talkative
gadka tale
gaduła chatterbox, gasbag; **~ i plociuch** big mouth
gadżet gadget
gaf|a blunder[1], boob, faux pas, gaffe; **popełnić ~ę** blunder[2], put your foot in it
gaj grove
gajowy gamekeeper
gala gala, pageantry
galaktyka galaxy
galanteria chivalry
galareta aspic IDM **trząść się jak ~ (ze strachu)** turn to jelly
galaretka jelly

galera galley
galeria gallery
galimatias jumble[2]
galon **1** (*na mundurze itp.*) braid **2** (*miara*) gallon
galop canter noun, gallop noun
galopować/po- canter, charge[2], gallop
galwanizować/z- galvanize
gałązka sprig, twig
gałąź **1** bough, branch[1] **2** (*przen.*) offshoot
gałgan **1** (*szmata*) rag **2** (*osoba*) rascal
gałka **1** ball; (*w drzwiach itp.*) knob; ~ **oczna** eyeball **2** ~ **muszkatołowa** nutmeg
gama **1** the gamut, range[1]; (*artykułów handlowych*) line[1] **2** (*muz.*) scale[1]
gang gang[1]
gangrena gangrene
gangrenowaty gangrenous
gangster gangster
ganić/z- censure, chastise, fault[2], rebuke, tell sb off (for sth/for doing sth)
gap onlooker
gapić/za- się stare, gape, gawp
gar (**gary**) pots and pans
garaż garage
garb hump
garbić/z- się hunch[1], slouch
garbus/ka hunchback
garda hilt
garderob|a **1** wardrobe; **część ~y** garment **2** (*teatr*) dressing room
gardło pharynx, throat; **wąskie ~** bottleneck IDM **na całe ~** at the top of your voice
gardzić/wz-/po- despise, scorn[2], sneer (at sb/sth)
gargulec gargoyle
garncarsk|i: **warsztat ~i** pottery; **wyroby ~e** pottery
garncarstwo pottery
garncarz potter[2]
garnek pot[1]; ~ **żaroodporny** (*z pokrywką*) casserole; ~ **do gotowania na parze** steamer
garnirować garnish, trim[1]
garnirunek (*potrawy*) trimming
garnitur (*męski*) suit[1]
garnizon garrison
garnuszek mug[1]
garstka handful
garść handful IDM **brać się w ~** get your act together, buck your ideas up, get/ keep/take a grip/hold (on yourself), pull yourself together
gasić **1** (**/za-**; **/z-**) (*ogień; papierosa; światło*) extinguish, put sth out; (*światło itp.*) turn sth off, stub sth out; (*światło*) put sth off, turn sth out; (*ogień*) damp[2] sth (down) **2** (**/u-**) ~ **pragnienie** quench your thirst
gasnąć/z- **1** (*światło; ogień*) go out; (*światło itp.*) go off; (*silnik*) peter out, stall[2] **2** (*nadzieja itp.*) fade (away)
gastronomiczny gastronomic
gastryczny gastric
gaśnica fire extinguisher
gatunek **1** (*rodzaj*) sort[1]; (*biol.*) species; (*marka*) brand[1] **2** (*jakość*) quality; **drugi ~** (*towar*) second[2] **3** (*lit.*) genre
gawędziarski chatty
gawędzić/po- chat[1]
gaworzyć/za- **1** (*niemowlę*) gurgle **2** (*cicho; zwł. do dziecka*) coo
gawron rook
gaz **1** (*chem., fiz.*) gas[1]; ~ **biologiczny** biogas; ~ **bojowy** gas[1]; ~ **cieplarniany** greenhouse gas; ~ **łzawiący** tear gas; ~ **trujący** poison gas; **~y spalinowe** exhaust[1] **2** (*w napoju*) fizz
gaza gauze
gazeta newspaper, paper; ~ **wielkoformatowa** broadsheet
gazetka bulletin
gazik swab
gazowany bubbly, fizzy; (*woda*) sparkling
gazownia gasworks
gaźnik carburettor
gąbczasty porous
gąbka **1** (*do mycia itp.*) sponge[1] **2** (*w materacu itp.*) foam[1]
gąsiątko gosling
gąsienica caterpillar
gąsior gander
gbur lout
gburowatość gruffness
gburowaty boorish, churlish, gruff, loutish, surly
gdakać/za- squawk
gderać/na- go/be on (at sb) (about sth), nag (at) sb
gderliwy crusty, disgruntled
gdy **1** (*kiedy*) **(podczas)** ~ as, when, while[1]; ~ **dotrę do domu...** by the time I get home...; ~ **tylko... wówczas/ wtedy...** as soon as, directly[2], no sooner...than **2** (*jeżeli*) **(zawsze)** ~ if
gdyby if, should, suppose; **jak** ~ like[2]; ~ **zaproponowali mi tę pracę, to chyba bym ją przyjął** if they were to offer me the job, I'd probably take it IDM ~ **nie ktoś/coś** but for sb/sth, if it wasn't/weren't for sb/sth
gdyż inasmuch as
gdzie where, whereabouts[2]; ~ **bądź** wherever; ~ **indziej** elsewhere, somewhere; **nie ma ~ się zatrzymać** there's nowhere to stay
gdziekolwiek anywhere, wherever IDM **czy ~** or wherever
gdzieś anywhere, somewhere; ~ **tutaj** hereabouts IDM ~ **około** somewhere around | **mieć kogoś/coś ~** not care/ give a damn (about sb/sth)
gej gay[2]
gejowski gay[1]
gejzer geyser
gem game[1]
gen gene; ~ **uszkodzony** rogue gene
genealogia genealogy, pedigree[1]
genealogiczny genealogical
generacja generation
generalizacja generalization
generalizować generalize
■ **generalizujący** sweeping
generalnie generally
generaln|y general[1], sweeping; **robić ~e porządki** have a clear-out
generał general[2]; ~ **brygady** (*w armii brytyjskiej*) major general; ~ **dywizji** (*w armii amerykańskiej*) major general
generator generator
generować/wy- generate
generyczny generic
genetycznie genetically; ~ **modyfikowany** genetically modified
genetyczny genetic
genetyk geneticist
genetyka genetics
geneza genesis, origin
genialny brilliant; ~ **pomysł** brainwave
genitalia genitals
genitalny genital
geniusz genius, whizz[2]; (*młody*) prodigy
genom genome
geodet-a/ka surveyor
geograf geographer
geografia geography
geograficzny geographical
geolog geologist
geologia geology
geologiczny geological
geometria geometry
geometryczny geometric
geopolityczny geopolitical
geopolityka geopolitics
geotermalny geothermal
gepard cheetah
geranium geranium
geriatria geriatrics
geriatryczny geriatric
germański Germanic
Ges/ges G flat
gest gesture[1]; ~ **teatralny** flourish[2]; **wykonywać ~** gesture[2]
gesti|a: **być w ~i kogoś** be within the remit of sb
gestykulować/wy-/za- gesticulate
getto ghetto
gęb|a: **pięć gąb do wykarmienia** five mouths to feed; **zamykać ~ę (komuś)** shut (sb) up
gęsi: **~e pióro** (*do pisania*) quill IDM **~a skórka** goose pimples | (*iść*) **~ego** in single file | **przechodzić/maszerować ~ego** file[2] in/out/past, etc.
gęstnieć/z- coagulate, thicken; (*zupa itp.*) condense
gęsto densely, thick adv., thickly; ~ **się tłumaczyć** apologize profusely
gęstość consistency, density, thickness
gęsty **1** dense, thick[1]; (*sos*) creamy **2** (*włosy; krzak*) bushy
gęś goose
gibki lithe
gibon gibbon
giełda (*papierów wartościowych*) stock exchange; ~ **walutowa** foreign exchange
giętki flexible, pliable; (*osoba; skóra*) supple; (*tylko o osobie/zwierzęciu*) nimble
giętkość flexibility, suppleness
giga (*skoczny taniec*) jig[1]
gigabajt gigabyte
gigant giant
gigantyczny giant adj., gigantic, mammoth, whopping
gil bullfinch
gilotyna guillotine
gilotynować/z- guillotine verb
gimnasty-k/czka gymnast
gimnastyka exercise[1], gymnastics
gimnastykować/po- się exercise[2], work out
gimnazjum junior high school
ginąć/z- **1** (*umierać*) die, die off, perish; (*w bitwie*) fall[1] **2** (*zanikać*) disappear, go astray; **powoli ~** vanish
ginekolog gynaecologist
ginekologia gynaecology
ginekologiczny gynaecological
ginekolog-położnik obstetrician

gips plaster[1]
gipsować/za- plaster[2]
Gis/gis G sharp
gitara guitar; ~ **basowa** bass
gitarzyst-a/ka guitarist
gladiator gladiator
gleba earth[1], ground[1], soil[1]
ględzić/po- go on (about sb/sth), harp on (about) sth, ramble[1], waffle[2]
glina **1** (*materiał*) clay **2** (*osoba*) cop[1]
gliniany earthenware
gliniarz cop[1]
glista earthworm
globalizacja globalization
globalizować/z- globalize
globaln|y global; **~a wioska** the global village
globtroter globetrotter
globulka globule
globus globe
glukoza glucose
glut bogey; **(glut(y))** snot
gluten gluten
gładk|i **1** (*równy*) even[1], smooth[1]; (*cera*) clear[1] **2** (*tkanina*) plain[1] **3** (*osoba; maniera*) slick[1]; (*odpowiedź, wymówka*) glib **4** (*tok rozmowy*) seamless
■ **gładko** **1** smoothly; ~ **ogolony** clean-shaven **2** (*odpowiedzieć*) glibly **3** (*prowadzić rozmowy*) seamlessly
gładkość **1** smoothness **2** (*mowy*) glibness
gładzić/po- stroke[2]
głaskać/po- pet[2], stroke[2]
głaz boulder
głąb **1** (*kraju itp.*) interior; **w ~/głębi kraju/lądu** inland adv.; **w głębi Australii** in the Australian outback; **w głębi pokoju** at the far side of the room **2** (*kapusty itp.*) stump[1]
głębi|a **1** (*i przen.*) depth; **w ~ serca** at heart, in your heart (of hearts); **z ~ serca** from the (bottom of your) heart, heartfelt, wholehearted **2** (*tonu*) richness
głęboki **1** (*i przen.*) deep[1], profound; **wziąć ~ oddech** take a deep breath **2** (*tonu*) rich
głęboko **1** (*nisko*) deep[2], low[2] **2** (*bardzo*) deeply, intensely, profoundly, strongly IDM **spać ~** be sound asleep, sleep soundly
głębokoś|ć depth; **basen ma metr ~ci** the water is a metre deep
głodny hungry, peckish; ~ **jak wilk** famished, ravenous
głodować go hungry, starve
głodzić/za- (się) starve
głos **1** (*dźwięk*) voice[1]; **nie podnoś ~u** keep your voice down; **przeczytać coś na ~** read sth out loud/aloud; **był głuchy na ~ rozsądku** he just wouldn't listen to reason **2** (*oddany przy głosowaniu*) vote[1]; (*w decyzji*) say[2] (in sth); **prawo ~u** voice[1] (in sth), vote[1]; **oddawać ~** cast a/your vote
głosić profess
głosować/za- vote[2]; **zagłosujmy** let's have a vote/put it to the vote
głosowanie poll[1], vote[1]; (*w wyborach*) polling; ~ **korespondencyjne** postal vote
głosowy vocal
głośnik loudspeaker, speaker; (*zwł. w słuchawce telefonu*) earpiece
głośn|o **1** (*hałaśliwie*) loud adv., loudly, noisily, vociferously; **nastaw ~iej** turn the volume up **2** (*na głos*) aloud, out loud
głośność loudness, volume
głośn|y **1** (*hałaśliwy*) loud, noisy, vociferous; **~e narzekanie** rant **2 przy ~ej kampanii reklamowej** in a blaze of publicity **3** (*osoba*) noted, prominent
głow|a **1** (*anat.*) head[1]; **~ą naprzód** head first, headlong adj.; **nad ~ą** overhead adv.; **zagrać ~ą** head[2]; **dać komuś po ~ie** cuff[2] **2** (*umysł*) brain, head[1], mind[1], nut; **mieć ~ę do czegoś** have a head for sth; **na ~ie** on your hands, on your mind; **mieć coś z ~y** be off your hands, get sth out of your system; **z ~y** ad lib, off the cuff, off the top of your head; **wyleciało mi z ~y** it slipped my memory; **wbić sobie/komuś coś do ~y** get sth into your head, put sth into sb's head; **iść do ~y** go to sb's head; **idący do ~y** heady **3** (*najważniejsza osoba*) head[1]; **~a państwa** head of state IDM **~a do góry** cheer up | **na ~ę** a/per head | **nosić ~ę wysoko** hold your head high, hold up your head | **postawić coś na ~ie** turn sth upside down
głowica (*bojowa*) warhead
głowić/na- się: **nad czymś** puzzle over/about sth, rack your brains
głód **1** hunger[1], starvation; (*klęska*) famine **2 (czegoś)** (*przen.*) hunger[1] (for sth)
głóg hawthorn
główkować/po- (*sport*) head[2]
głównie chiefly, largely, in the main, mainly, predominantly, primarily, principally
główn|y central, chief[1], leading, main[1], major[1], primary[1], prime[1], principal[1], uppermost; (*osoba*) head[1], high[1]; (*argumenty*) salient; (*potrzeby*) bare; (*kara*) capital[2]; **~a atrakcja twojej wycieczki** the high point of your trip; **~a część** body; **~a kwatera** headquarters; **~a rola** lead[2]
głuchnąć go deaf
głuchota deafness
głuch|y **1** deaf **2** (*przen.*) **na coś** deaf to sth, impervious **3** (*dźwięk*) hollow[1]; **~a cisza** a dead silence/calm; **~y odgłos** thud
głupawy dopey, dozy
głup-ek/ia airhead, boob, clod, dimwit, dope[1], dork, nit, prat, twit, wally; **ty głupku!** you dozy thing!
głupi brain-dead, brainless, clueless, daft, dumb, fatuous, foolish, inane, moronic, silly, stupid, thick[1], witless; **beznadziejnie ~** crass
głup|iec fool[1], wally IDM **robić z siebie/kogoś ~ca** make a fool of sb/yourself
głupkowaty dorky, fatuous, goofy
głupol moron
głupota foolishness, lunacy, silliness, stupidity
głupstw|o (także **głupstwa**) nonsense, rot noun, rubbish; **robić ~a** mess about/around
gmach edifice
gmatwać/po-/za- confuse, jumble[1]; **pogmatwać sobie życie** make a mess of your life
gmatwanina jumble[2], mix-up, muddle; (*wełny itp.*) tangle
gmerać/po-: **przy czymś** mess about/around with sth; (*w poszukiwaniu czegoś*) fumble
gnać/po- pelt, race[2], streak[2]
gnębiciel/ka oppressor
gnębić/po-/z- grind sb down, harass, oppress, victimize
■ **gnębiony** oppressed
gniazdko (*elektryczne*) socket
gniazdo nest
gnić/z- decay[2], rot
gnida nit
gnieść/z-/po-/za- **1** (*przyciskać*) crush[1], squash[1]; (*ciasto*) knead **2** (*bluzkę itp.*) crease[2], crumple
□ **gnieść/po- się** (*bluzka itp.*) crease[2], crumple
gniew anger[1]; **wielki ~** wrath; **skory do ~u** bad-tempered, irritable
IDM **wpadać w ~** fly off the handle
gniewać/roz-/z- anger[2], rile
□ **gniewać/roz-/po- się**: **(na kogoś)** be/get angry (with sb), fall out (with sb)
gniewny angry, black[1], cross
gnieździć/za- się **1** (*ptak*) nest verb **2** (*przen.*) nestle
gnojek bugger[1]
gnom gnome
gnój dung, manure, muck[1]
gnuśność indolence
gnuśny indolent
go → JEGO
gobelin tapestry
godło emblem
godnoś|ć (*duma*) decorum, dignity; **~ć osobista** pride[1]; **pełen ~ci** dignified; **poczucie własnej ~ci** self-esteem, self-respect; **pozbawiony ~ci** undignified; **to uwłaczało jej ~ci** it was beneath her
godny **1** (*szanowany, właściwy*) worthy; ~ **pożałowania** regrettable; ~ **uwagi** notable, noteworthy **2** (*moralnie*) decorous
god|y: **miejsce ~ów dzikich zwierząt** breeding ground
godzić **1 (/po-)** reconcile sth (with sth), sb (with sb); **pogodzić wymagania** balance the demands of sth with sth else **2 (/u-) w kogoś/coś** hit[1]
□ **godzić/po- się**: **(z kimś)** make (it) up (with sb), settle your differences, be on speaking terms (with sb); **z czymś** accept that..., come to terms with sth, get over sth/sb, live with sth, reconcile yourself, resign yourself to sth/doing sth, be resigned to sth; (*nieform.*) lump it; ~ **z przeciwnościami losu** take the rough with the smooth
godzin|a hour, o'clock; **która ~a?** what's the time?; **zapytać kogoś o ~ę** ask the time; **powiedzieć, która ~a** tell the time; **co ~a** hourly; **~a lekcyjna** period; **~y nadliczbowe** overtime; **~y odjazdu pociągów do Bristolu** the times of trains to Bristol; **~a policyjna** curfew; **pierwsze ~y po północy** the small hours; **~y przyjęć** surgery; **~y przyjęć lekarza** clinic; **~a szczytu** rush hour; **~y szczytu (dot. zużycia prądu itp.)** peak hours; **~y urzędowania/pracy** business hours; **~y otwarcia** opening hours; **~a zamknięcia** closing time; **~a zero** zero hour IDM **po ~ach** off duty
godzinowy hourly
gofr waffle[1]
gogle goggles
goić/za-/wy- się heal

goj/ka gentile

gokart go-kart

gol goal

golarka electric razor

goleń shin

golf 1 (*sport*) golf **2** (*sweter*) polo neck, polo-neck sweater

golfowy golf

golić/o- shave[1]

□ **golić/o- się** have a shave, shave[1]

gołąb pigeon; ~ **biały** dove[1]

gołoledź black ice

gołosłowny groundless; (*groźby*) empty[1]

goł|y bare, naked IDM **~e oko** (*przen.*) the naked eye | **widoczny ~ym okiem** self-evident

gong gong

gonić/po- chase[1], follow, hunt[1] (for) (sb/sth), race[2]

goniec 1 (*osoba*) courier, messenger **2** (*szachy*) bishop

gonitw|a race[1]; **stawiać/zgłaszać do ~y** race[2]

gorąco (*przysł.*) **1** (*upalnie*) hot; **strasznie** ~ sweltering; **strasznie mi** ~ I'm boiling, I'm really hot; **odczuwać** ~ burn[1] **2** (*serdecznie*) fervently, passionately, warmly; (*zaprzeczać*) hotly; **podziękujmy ~ wszystkim, którzy tak ciężko pracowali** let's have a big thank-you to everybody who worked so hard

■ **gorąco** (*rz.*) heat[1]

gorąc|y 1 (*upalny*) hot[1]; (*powodujący pocenie się*) sweaty; **bardzo ~y** boiling; **być ~ym** burn[1] **2** (*zwolennik itp.*) fervent; (*pocałunek itp.*) passionate **3** (*dyskusja itp.*) heated IDM **~a linia** hotline | **praktyka ~ych biurek** hot-desking | **w ~ej wodzie kąpany** hot-headed

gorączk|a 1 fever; **mieć ~ę** be feverish, have a temperature; **z ~ą** feverish **2** (*zapał*) fervour; (*niecierpliwość itp.*) fever (of sth)

gorączkować be feverish

□ **gorączkować/roz- się** IDM **nie ~** keep your hair on

gorączkowy feverish, frenetic, hectic

gorejący fiery

gorliwość eagerness, fervour, keenness, zeal

gorliwy assiduous, avid, eager, zealous; (*i rel.*) fervent; (*relig.*) devout

gorset corset

gorsz|y inferior, worse; **coś ~ego (z dwóch)** second best[2], worse noun; **~y gatunek** inferiority

gorszyć/z- shock[2], scandalize

gorycz bitterness; **z ~ą** bitterly

goryl gorilla

gorzej worse adv.

gorzelnia distillery

gorzk|i bitter[1]; **~a czekolada** plain chocolate; **czeka cię ~ie rozczarowanie** you're in for a rude shock

gospoda inn

gospodarcz|y economic; **zabudowania ~e** farm buildings

gospodarka economy

gospodarnie economically

gospodarować/za- 1 (*na gospodarstwie rolnym*) farm[2] **2** (*pieniędzmi*) **oszczędnie ~** economize

■ **gospodarowanie 1** (*na roli*) farming **2** (*finansami itp.*) management; (*w domu*) housekeeping

gospodarstw|o 1 (*rolne*) farm[1]; **~o rybne** fish farm; **~o warzywno-owocowe** market garden **2 ~o domowe** household; **zajęcia z ~a domowego** home economics

gospodarz 1 (*rolnik*) farmer **2** (*na przyjęciu; programu*) host **3** (*odnajmujący mieszkanie itp.*) landlord

gospodyni 1 ~ domowa housewife **2** (*na przyjęciu; programu*) hostess **3** (*odnajmująca mieszkanie itp.*) landlady **4** (*rolniczka*) farmer

gosposia housekeeper

gościć/u- host verb, put sb up

gościnność hospitality

gościnny hospitable; **pokój** ~ spare room

■ **gościnnie** (*występować/grać*) away

gość 1 (*ktoś zaproszony*) guest, visitor; (**goście**) company; **nieproszony** ~ intruder **2** (*restauracyjny itp.*) customer, patron; (*restauracyjny*) diner; (*hotelowy*) guest, resident **3** (*facet*) fellow[1], sort[1]

gotować/u- cook[1], do the cooking; (*we wrzątku*) boil[1]; ~ **na wolnym ogniu** simmer; ~ **na parze** steam[2]; ~ **w małej ilości wody/mleka** poach

□ **gotować/u-/za- się** cook[1]; (*we wrzątku*) boil[1]; **woda się gotuje** the kettle's boiling

■ **gotowany** (*jajka*) boiled /poached eggs

gotowanie cooking

gotowoś|ć 1 (*bycie gotowym*) readiness; **stać/być w ~ci** stand by; **w ~ci** on the alert (for sth), on standby; **w ~ci bojowej** an operational squadron **2** (*ochota*) willingness; **z ~cią** willingly; **okazywać ~ć** offer[1] (to do sth)

gotow|y (także **gotów**) **1** (*wykończony*) finished **2** (*przygotowany*) in place, ready, set[3]; **(coś zrobić)** poised; **być ~ym (na coś trudnego/niemiłego)** be prepared for sth; **jedzenie ~e do spożycia** ready-cooked food; **~e rozwiązania** ready-made answers **3** (*z ochotą*) **(coś zrobić)** game[2], willing

gotówk|a cash[1]; **~ą** in cash

gotycki Gothic

goździk 1 (*kwiat*) carnation **2** (*przyprawa*) clove

gó|ra 1 (*geogr.*) mountain; (*w nazwach*) mount[2]; **~ra lodowa** iceberg; **iść do ~ry** climb[1]; **pod ~rę** uphill **2** (*górna część czegoś*) top[1]; **~ra sukienki** bodice; **tą stroną do ~ry** this side up; **do ~ry i na dół** up and down; **iść w ~rę** ascend, go up; **na/w ~rze** on top of sb/sth, overhead; **w ~rę** up, upward; **w ~rę rzeki** upstream; **temperatura poszła szybko w ~rę** his temperature went sky-high **3** (*w domu itp.*) **na ~rę/~rze** upstairs; **na ~rze** in the flat above **4** (*sterta*) mountain (of sth), pile[1]; **nałożył sobie ~rę jedzenia** he heaped food onto his plate IDM **brać ~rę** prevail (against/over sb/sth) | **do ~ry nogami** upside down, upturned, the wrong way up | **patrzeć na kogoś/coś z ~ry** look down on sb/sth, look down your nose at sb/sth | **z ~ry** (*rezerwować*) in advance (of sth); (*płacić*) up front; (*od przełożonych*) from on high | (*zdanie*) **z ~ry wyrobiony** preconceived

górnictwo mining

górnik miner; (*w kopalni węgla*) coal miner

górnolotny bombastic; ~ **styl** bombast

górny high[1]; (*warga itp.*) upper; (*piętro*) upstairs adj.; **na ~m piętrze** upstairs

górować/za- (*i przen.*) tower over/above sb/sth; (*nad miastem*) dominate, be in a dominant position; (*liczbowo*) predominate

■ **górujący** predominant

górski highland

górzysty hilly, mountainous; **teren** ~ upland noun

gówniany crap adj., crappy

gr|a 1 (*zabawa; sport*) game[1]; (*sportowa*) play[2]; **~a w karty** card game; **~a komputerowa** computer game; **~y komputerowe** arcade games; **~a w kręgle** tenpin bowling; **~a planszowa** board game; **~a pozorów** charades; **~a wideo** video game; (*tenis*) **~a podwójna** doubles[4]; **~a pojedyncza** singles[2]; **styl/sposób ~y** game[1]; **~a fair** fair play **2** (*teatr, film*) acting[1]; (*sztuki*) performance **3** (*udawanie*) act[1] **4** (*ukryte motywy postępowania*) game[1] IDM **~a słów** a play on words | **robić dobrą minę do złej ~y** make the best of sth/a bad job | **wchodzić w ~ę** be at stake

grabić 1 (**/z-**) (*trawę itp.*) rake verb **2** (**/za-**) (*rabować*) plunder verb

grabie rake

grabież pillage, plunder

graca hoe

gracj|a grace, gracefulness; **pełen ~i** graceful; **bez ~i** graceless, gracelessly

gracz player; (*hazardzist-a/ka*) gambler; ~ **w golfa** golfer

grać/za- 1 (*w grę sportową/hazardową; muzykę; rolę*) play[1]; ~ **na bębnie** drum[2]; ~ **na wyścigach konnych** have a flutter on the horses; **zagrać głową** head[2] **2** (*teatr, na koncertach*) perform (*teatr, film*) act[2], enact; ~ **główną rolę** star[2]; **sztuka ta była grana przez prawie dwa lata** the play ran for nearly two years; **jego najnowszy film jest grany w miejscowym kinie** his latest film is showing at the local cinema **3** (*na czyichś uczuciach itp.*) play on/upon sth IDM **coś tu nie gra** your story just doesn't add up | **co jest (grane)?** (*o co chodzi?*) what's up?

grad (*i przen.*) hail[2]; (*kamieni itp.*) shower[1]

graffiti graffiti

graficzny graphic, graphical

grafik 1 (*osoba*) designer **2** (*zajęć*) rota

grafika 1 (*dział sztuk plastycznych*) graphic design **2** (*komputerowa itp.*) graphics

grafit 1 (*minerał*) graphite **2** (*w ołówku*) lead[3]

grajek player; ~ **uliczny** busker

gram gram

gramatyczny grammatical

gramatyka grammar

gramofon record player

gramolić/wy- się clamber, climb[1]; (*z łóżka itp.*) tumble

granat 1 (*wojsk.*) grenade **2** (*biol.*) pomegranate
granatowy navy blue
graniastosłup prism
granic|a 1 (*państwa*) border[1], frontier; **za ~ą/ę** abroad **2** (*linia ograniczająca*) boundary, confines, dividing line, division, limit[1], line[1], threshold; (**granice**) bounds; (*wiedzy ludzkiej*) frontier; **~a możliwości** limitation; **~a włosów** hairline[1]; **górna/dolna ~a** (*wieku itp.*) cut-off; **~a wieku** age limit; **~a wytrzymałości** breaking point; **w ~ach** within; **w ~ach rozsądku** within limits, within reason; (*problem itp.*) **przekraczać ~e** transcend
graniczyć 1 back onto sth, border[2] **2** (*przen.*) **z czymś** border on sth, verge on sth
granit granite
granulka granule
grań ridge
grasować: **grasujący** on the prowl
gratisowy complimentary
gratka windfall
gratulacj|a (**gratulacje**) good for you, him, her, etc.; **~e (z okazji czegoś)** congratulations (on sth)
gratulować/po- congratulate
graty junk
grawerować/wy- engrave, inscribe
grawitacja gravity
grawiura engraving
grążel water lily
grejpfrut grapefruit
grill grill[1]
grillować grill[2]
grobl|a dyke, weir; **droga na ~i** causeway
grobowiec tomb
grobow|y: **~a cisza** a stunned silence
groch: **~ włoski** chickpea IDM **jak ~ z kapustą** higgledy-piggledy
grom thunder[1]
gromada flock[1], troop
gromadka cluster[1]
gromadnie: **przemieszczać się ~** troop verb
gromadny social
gromadzić/z-/na- accumulate, gather, mass[3]; (*materiał, fakty*) assemble; (*dużą ilość czegoś*) amass; (*kapitał itp.*) accrue; (*duże zapasy*) hoard[2], stock up (on/with sth), stockpile
□ **gromadzić/z-/na- się** (*ludzie*) assemble, congregate, convene, flock[2], gather, mass[3], meet; (*pył, książki itp.*) accumulate, collect[1], pile up; **(wokół kogoś)** mob[2]; **nad kimś/czymś** cluster around sb/sth
grono cluster[1]
gronostaj stoat
gronostajow|y: **futro ~e** ermine
grosz (**grosze**) peanuts; **nędzne ~e** pittance; **bez ~a** broke[2], penniless, skint; **bez ~a, bezdomny i bezrobotny** down and out; **dla paru ~y** for the sake of a few pence
grosz|ek 1 (*bot.*) pea(s); **~ek śnieżny** mangetout **2** (**groszki**) (*deseń*) **w czarne ~ki** with black dots
grota cave[1]
groteskowy grotesque
groz|a eeriness; **pełen ~y** eerie
grozić/za- menace verb, make threats against sb, threaten; **nic im nie groziło** they thought they were out of danger
■ **grożący** menacing, threatening
groźba menace, threat
groźny dangerous, forbidding, formidable, grave[2], menacing, nasty, threatening, ugly
grób grave[1]
grubiański coarse, crude, gross[1], rough[1], vulgar; (*wyłącznie osoba*) churlish
grubiańskość crudity
grubiaństwo rudeness, vulgarity
gruboskórn|y heavy-handed, thick-skinned IDM **być ~ym** have a thick skin
gruboś|ć thickness; **mieć trzy cale ~ci** be three inches thick
gruboziarnisty coarse
grub|y 1 (*osoba*) fat[1], heavy, stout **2** (*rzecz*) thick[1]; (*sweter itp.*) chunky; **śnieg leżał ~ą warstwą na ziemi** snow lay thick on the ground IDM **~a ryba** a big shot/name | **~a zwierzyna** big game | **z ~sza** crudely
gruchać/za- coo
gruchot banger
gruczoł gland; **~y łzowe** tear ducts
gruczołowy glandular
gruda (*ziemi*) clod
grudka lump[1]
grudkowaty lumpy
grudzień December
grunt earth[1], ground[1], land[1] IDM (*przen.*) **przygotowywać ~ (pod coś)** set the scene (for sth) | (*i przen.*) **tracić ~ pod nogami** be/get out of your depth
gruntownie heartily, to the hilt, radically, thoroughly
gruntowny deep[1], thorough; (*przeobrażenie*) radical[1], sweeping; (*wykształcenie*) well rounded; (*pytanie*) probing; (*wiedza o czymś*) intimate
grupa group[1]; (*zwł. ludzi*) band, body, class[1], huddle[2], lot[3], party, troop; (*zwł. rzeczy*) batch, cluster[1], collection; (*wiekowa, cenowa itp.*) bracket[1]; **~ dyskusyjna** (*komput.*) newsgroup; **~ nacisku** pressure group; **~ użytkownika** user group; **~ krwi** blood group
grupować/po- bracket[2], group[2]
grupow|y collective[1]
■ **grupowo** across the board, collectively
gruszka pear
gruz debris, rubble IDM **w ~ach** in ruin(s)
gruźlica tuberculosis
gryka buckwheat
grymas grimace; **robić ~** grimace verb
grymaśni-k/ca fusspot
grymaśny awkward, choosy, difficult, particular, picky
grypa flu
gryźć 1 (/u-) (*zębami*) bite[1]; (*kość*) gnaw; **~ głośno** champ[1] **2** (*wełna*) be scratchy **3** (*zapach*) be pungent
□ **gryźć się 1** (*obawami*) **on się gryzie, bo…** it bugs him that… **2** (*kolory*) clash[1]
gryz nip noun
gryzący acrid; (*ubranie itp.*) prickly
gryzmolić scrawl, scribble
gryzmoły scrawl noun
gryzoń rodent
grzać/za- (się) heat[2] (sth) (up)
grzałka element
grzanka toast
grzany (*wino*) mulled
grządka patch[1]
grząski slushy
grzbiet 1 (*zwierzęcia*) back[1] **2** (*tylna strona*) back[1] **3** (*łańcucha górskiego*) ridge **4** (*fali*) crest **5** (*książki*) spine
grzbietowy: **styl ~** backstroke
grzebać/po-/za-/wy- 1 (/po-) (*zmarłego*) bury **2 (/wy-)** (*szukać*) fumble, root about/around (for sth), scrabble; **(w czymś)** meddle (in/with sth), poke about/around; **wygrzebywać ze śmieci** (*np. żywność*) scavenge
grzebień 1 (*do włosów*) comb[1] **2** (*koguta; fali*) crest
grzech sin
grzechot rattle[2]
grzechotać/za- rattle[1]
grzechotka rattle[2]
grzecznościow|y: **~a uwaga** pleasantry
grzeczność courtesy, politeness; **robić komuś ~** oblige; **robić coś przez ~** do sth as a favour
grzeczny 1 (*uprzejmy*) courteous, polite **2** (*dobrze wychowany*) good[1]; **bądź ~** keep out of mischief IDM **~ jak aniołek** (as) good as gold
■ **grzecznie** courteously, politely; (*zachowywać się*) nicely
grzejnik heater, radiator; **~ metalowy** stove
grzeszni-k/ca sinner
grzeszny sinful
grzeszyć/z- sin verb IDM **~ nadmiarem czegoś** err on the side of sth
grzęda perch[2], roost
grzęznąć/u- flounder[1], be/get stuck
grzmieć/za- boom[2], rumble, thunder[2]
grzmocić/wy-/grzmotnąć thump, wallop, whack
grzmot clap of thunder, roll[1], rumble noun, thunder[1]; (*armat itp.*) boom[1]
grzyb fungus; **~ jadalny** mushroom[1]; **~ trujący** toadstool; **iść na ~y** go mushroom picking, mushroom[2]
grzybica: **~ stóp** athlete's foot
grzybowy (także **grzybkowy**) fungal; (*zupa itp.*) mushroom[1]
grzywa mane
grzywka fringe[1]
grzywna fine[2], penalty
gubernator governor; **~ generalny** Governor General
gubić/z- lose, mislay; **gubić miejsce** (*w książce, w szydełkowaniu itp.*) lose your place IDM **~ krok** be in/out of step (with sb/sth)
□ **gubić/z- się** go astray, get lost, lose your bearings; (*przen.*) **zgubiłem się** I'm lost; **całkowicie się zgubiłem** (*nie rozumiem, o czym mowa*) you've totally lost me
gulasz stew
gulgot gurgle noun
gulgotać/za- gurgle
gum|a 1 (*materiał*) rubber; **~a arabska** gum; **jak z ~y** rubbery **2** (*do żucia*) chewing gum; **~a balonowa** bubblegum **3** (*przebita opona*) flat[2], puncture; **złapać ~ę** have a blow-out
gumiak wellington
gumka 1 (*do ścierania*) rubber **2** (*w ubraniu*) elastic **3** (*do związania*) rubber band, band[1]
gumowaty rubbery
gumowy rubber
guru guru

gusła witchcraft
gust taste[1]; **w dobrym guście** tasteful; **bez ~u** tasteless; **on zupełnie nie ma ~u w ubiorze** he's got absolutely no dress sense; **w złym guście** naff, tasteless; **(być) w złym guście** (be) in bad, poor, etc. taste; **nie być w czyimś guście** not sb's cup of tea; **zbyt… jak na czyjś ~** too… for your liking
gustowny tasteful
guwernantka governess
guz bump[2], lump[1], tumour
guzdrać/wy- się dawdle, dilly-dally
guzek node
guzik 1 (*na ubraniu*) button **2** (*na aparacie*) knob IDM **zapinać na ostatni ~** sew sth up
guzowaty lumpy, knobbly
gwałciciel/ka rapist
gwałcić/z- 1 (*osobę*) rape[1] **2** (*prawo*) breach[2], infringe, violate
gwałt 1 (*seksualny*) rape[2] **2** (*przemoc*) **na ~** urgently
gwałtown|y 1 (*wybuchowy*) vehement, violent; (*spór*) blazing, flaming; (*jazda*) jerky; **~y charakter** temper **2** (*silny*) dramatic **3** (*nagły*) rapid, sharp[1], rude, steep; **~y napływ** upsurge; **~e pogorszenie (się)**; **~y spadek** nosedive; **~y wzrost** growth spurt
gwar buzz[2]
gwara slang
gwarancj|a 1 (*zwł. fin.*) guarantee[1]; (*na zakupiony towar*) warranty; **mieć trzyletnią ~ę** be guaranteed for three years; **na ~i** under guarantee **2 przeciwko komuś/czemuś** safeguard (against sb/sth), safety net
gwarantować/za- assure, ensure, guarantee[2], safeguard
gwiazda 1 (także **gwiazdka**) star[1]; **spadająca ~** shooting star **2** (*filmowa*) film star, star[1]; **wielka ~** superstar **3** (*sport*) cartwheel
gwiazdka 1 (*znak*) asterisk **2** (*święta*) Christmas zob. też GWIAZDA
gwiazdor heart-throb; (*filmowy*) film star, star[1]
gwiazdorsk|i: **~a obsada** star-studded cast
gwiazdorstwo stardom
gwiazdozbiór constellation
gwiaździsty starry
gwizd toot, whistle[1]; (*pociągu*) hoot[2]
gwizd-ać/nąć/za- zob. też GWIZDNĄĆ; toot verb, whistle[2]
gwizdek whistle[1]
gwizdnąć zob. też GWIZDAĆ; (*ukraść*) nick[2], pinch[1], sneak[1], swipe, whip[2]
gwóźdź nail

H

h 1 (H/h) (*litera*) H, h **2** (*muz.*); **(H/h)** B
ha: **~! (~!)** ha[1]
haczyk catch[2], snag[1]
haczykowaty hooked
hadż (*religia muzułmańska*) hajj
haft embroidery
haftka hook and eye
haftować/wy- embroider
haftowanie embroidery, needlework
haj: **na ~u** high (on sth)[1], stoned
hak hook[1]
haker hacker
hala hall; (*dworcowa itp.*) concourse; **~ odlotów** lounge[1]; **~ tranzytowa** the transit lounge; **~ produkcyjna** shop floor
halka slip[2]
hall lobby[1], lounge[1]
halo 1 (*przywitanie*) hello **2** (*przywołując*) here[2]
halucynacj|a hallucination; **mieć ~e** hallucinate
halucynogenny hallucinogenic
haluks bunion
hałas din, noise, racket, row[3]; **wpadać/wypadać (skądś) z ~em/furią** storm[2]
hałasować bang about/around, bumble around; **nie ~** not make a noise
hałastra mob[1], rabble
hałaśliwie boisterously, noisily, rowdily
hałaśliwość loudness, rowdiness
hałaśliwy boisterous, loud, noisy, rowdy, uproarious
hałda mound; **~ żużlowa** slag heap
hamak hammock
hamburger (*z wołowiny*) hamburger; (*różnych rodzajów*) -burger
hamować/za- 1 (*proces*) hold/keep sth in check, impede; (*wzrost*) stunt[2]; (*żądze, skłonności*) curb[1], inhibit **2** (*auto*) brake[2]; **gwałtownie ~** jam on the brakes/jam the brakes on
hamulec 1 (*auta*) brake[1]; **~ ręczny** handbrake **2** (*przen.*) curb[2] (on sth), inhibition
handel dealing, trade[1], trading; (*zwł. na wielką skalę*) commerce; **~ wymienny** barter noun; **nielegalny ~** traffic (in sth), trafficking
handla-rz/rka dealer, trader; **handlarz narkotykami** pusher; **handlarz nielegalnym towarem** trafficker
handlować/za-: **(czymś)** deal[1], trade[2]; **nielegalnie ~ czymś** traffic in sth; **~ narkotykami** deal[1]; **~ wymiennie** (*np. kupić nowy samochód, pozostawiając w rozliczeniu stary*) trade sth in (for sth); **~ (jako domokrążca)** peddle
handlowiec dealer, merchant
handlowy commercial[1]
handryczyć/po- się squabble
hangar hangar
haniebny dishonourable, ignominious, infamous, shameful
hańba dishonour[1], shame[1]
hańbić/z-/po- defile
harcerka guide[1]
harcerz scout
hardość pride[1]
hardware hardware
hardy (*dumny*) proud; (*bezczelny*) insolent
harem harem
harfa harp[1]
harfist-a/ka (także **harfia-rz/rka**) harpist
harmider commotion, din, hullabaloo, pandemonium, racket, uproar
harmonia 1 harmony **2** (*instrument*) accordion
harmoniczna harmonic noun
harmoniczny 1 (*muz.*) harmonic **2** (*harmonijny*) harmonious
harmonijka: **~ ustna** harmonica
harmonijny harmonious
harmonizować/z- 1 (*muz.*) harmonize; **(nie) ~ z czymś** in/out of tune **2 (z kimś/czymś)** (*przen.*) harmonize, match[2]; **(nie) harmonizujący (z czymś)** in/out of keeping (with sth)
harmonogram schedule[1]; **być zgodnie z ~em** be on schedule
harować be hard at it, slave[2] (away)
harówka drudgery, fag, grind[2]
harpun harpoon
hart (*ducha itp.*) toughness
hartować/za- (się) toughen
hasać/po- frolic
hasło 1 (*zwrot*) slogan **2** (*tajne: do komputera itp.*) password **3** (*w słowniku itp.*) entry, headword
haszysz hashish
hatchback hatchback
hau: **~, ~!** woof
haust gulp[2], swig noun; **wypić coś ~em** swig
hazard: **uprawiać ~** gamble[1]
hazardzist-a/ka gambler
heavy: **~ metal** heavy metal
heban ebony
hebel plane[1]
heblować/wy- plane[2]
hebrajski Hebrew adj.; **język ~** Hebrew
hedonist-a/ka hedonist
hedonistyczny hedonistic
hedonizm hedonism
Heine-Medina: **choroba Heinego-Medina** polio
hej: **~!** here[2], hey
hektar hectare
hel helium
helikopter helicopter
helisa helix
hełm crash helmet, helmet
hemofili|a haemophilia; **osoba chora na ~ę** haemophiliac
hemofilik haemophiliac
hemoglobina haemoglobin
hemoroidy haemorrhoids
henna henna
heraldyka heraldry
herb coat of arms
herbaciarnia cafe, tea room
herbata (także **herbatka**) tea; **~ ziołowa** herbal tea
herbatnik biscuit
herbicyd herbicide
herc Hz
heretycki heretical
herety-k/czka heretic
herezja heresy
hermafrodytyczny androgynous
hermetyczny airtight, hermetic
heroiczny heroic
heroina heroin
herold herald noun
heterogeniczny heterogeneous
heteroseksualist-a/ka heterosexual noun
heteroseksualny heterosexual, straight[2]
hetman (*szachy*) queen
hiacynt hyacinth
hibernacja hibernation
hierarchi|a hierarchy; **na szczycie ~i służbowej** at the top of the chain of command
hierarchiczny hierarchical
hieroglify hieroglyphics
hi-fi hi-fi
higien|a hygiene; **przepisy bezpieczeństwa i ~y pracy** health and safety regulations
higieniczny hygienic, sanitary

higienistka matron
hinduizm Hinduism; **wyznawca ~u** Hindu
hindus/ka Hindu
hinduski Hindu adj.
hip IDM **~, ~ (hura)!** hip, hip, hurray/hurrah
hiperinflacja hyperinflation
hiperłącze hyperlink
hipermarket hypermarket, megastore
hipertekst hypertext
hiperwentylacja hyperventilation
hip hop hip hop
hipis hippie
hipnotyczny hypnotic
hipnotyzer/ka hypnotist
hipnotyzm hypnotism
hipnotyzować/za- hypnotize, mesmerize
hipnoza hypnosis
hipochondry-k/czka hypochondriac
hipokryt-a/ka hypocrite
hipokryzja hypocrisy
hipopotam hippopotamus
hipotek|a mortgage; **mamy ~ę w wysokości 400 tys. funtów** we took out a Ł400000 mortgage
hipotetyczny hypothetical, notional, speculative
hipoteza hypothesis
histerektomia hysterectomy
histeria hysteria, hysterics
histeryczny hysterical
histogram bar chart
histori|a 1 (*przeszłość*) history; **~a życia** life story; **tworzyć ~ę** go down in/make history **2** (*opowiadanie*) saga, story, yarn; **~a miłosna** love story IDM **~a choroby** case history
historyczny 1 (*związany z przeszłością*) historical; **kostium ~** period costume **2** (*ważny*) historic
historyjka story, yarn
historyk historian
hit hit[2]
HIV HIV
hm er, hmm, well[3]
ho: **~ ~!** gee, gosh, wow
hobby hobby, pastime
hochsztapler con man, cowboy
hodometr milometer
hodować/wy- breed[1], keep[1], raise[1], rear[2]
hodowca breeder
hodowl|a 1 (*zool.*) farming; **~a koni** stud; **~a reprodukcyjna** breeding **2** (*bot.*) culture; **własnej ~i** home-grown
hojność bounty, generosity
hojny generous, handsome, lavish[1], liberal, profuse
hokej: **~ na lodzie** ice hockey; **~ na trawie** hockey
hokus: **~ pokus** trick
hol zob. też HALL; tow noun; **brać na ~** tow
holistyczny holistic
Holocaust holocaust
holograf holograph
hologram hologram
holować/wy- haul[1], tow IDM **holując (kogoś za sobą)** with sb in tow
holownik tug[2]
hołd homage, salute, tribute
hołubić pamper
homar lobster
homeopat-a/ka homeopath
homeopatia homeopathy
homeopatyczny homeopathic
homofobia homophobia
homofobiczny homophobic
homofon homophone
homogeniczny homogeneous
homonim homonym
homoseksualista gay[2], homosexual noun
homoseksualizm homosexuality
homoseksualny homosexual; (*slang*) queer
honor honour[1]; **~y wojskowe** salute; **z wszelkimi ~ami** with great ceremony; **zostali podjęci z wszelkimi należnymi im ~ami** they were accorded every respect; **być przyjętym z ~ami** be given the red carpet treatment
honorarium fee
honoris causa honorary
honorować/u- (*paszport itp.*) recognize; (*weksel itp.*) honour[2]
honorowy 1 (*mający poczucie honoru*) honourable **2** (*tytularny*) honorary
hop IDM **nie mów ~, dopóki nie przeskoczysz** don't count your chickens (before they're hatched)
horda horde
hormon hormone
horoskop horoscope
horrendalny horrendous
horror horror film
hortensja hydrangea
horyzont horizon
hospicjum hospice
hospitalizować hospitalize
hot dog hot dog
hotel hotel
hotela-rz/rka hotelier
hrabia count[2], earl
hrabina countess
hrabstwo county
huczący roaring
huczeć/za- crash[2], roar; (*wiatr*) bluster; **w głowie huczało jej od pytań** her head was buzzing with questions
huczny uproarious
huk bang[2], clap[2], crash[1], roar noun, thud; **przejeżdżać itp. z ~iem** thunder[2] IDM **z wielkim ~iem** (*przen.*) with a bang
hukanie (*sowy*) hoot[2]
huknąć say 'boo'
hulajnoga scooter
hulanka binge[1], spree
humanist-a/ka humanist
humanistyczn|y humanistic; **nauki ~e** arts, humanities
humanistyka arts, humanities
humanitarność humanity
humanitarny humane, humanitarian
humanizm humanism
humo|r 1 (*to,co ludzi bawi*) humour[1]; **pełen ~ru** jocular **2** (*nastrój*) frame of mind, mood, temper; **zły ~r** mood, moodiness; **w złym ~rze** moody, sour
humorystyczny humorous
humorzasty moody, stroppy
hura (także **hurra**) hurray
huragan gale, hurricane
hurtownik merchant
hurtowo in bulk, wholesale adv.
hurtowy wholesale
husky husky[2]
huśtać/po- swing[1]
□ **huśtać/po- się** swing[1]; **~ na wodzie** bob up and down in the water
huśtawka (*krzesełkowa*) swing[2]; **~ na długiej desce** see-saw
huta foundry; **~ stali** steel mill, steelworks
hybryd hybrid
hybryda hybrid
hybrydowy hybrid adj.
hycel catcher
hydrant hydrant
hydrauliczny hydraulic
hydrauli-k/czka plumber
hydroelektryczny hydroelectric
hymn anthem, hymn; **~ narodowy** national anthem

I

i 1 (I/i) (*litera*) I, i **2** (*spój.*) and, plus[1]; **~..., ~...** both ... and...
ich (*zaim. dzierżawczy: z rz.*) their; (*bez rz.*) theirs
idea idea
idealist-a/ka idealist
idealistyczny idealistic
idealizm idealism
idealizować/wy- glorify, idealize
idealny ideal[1]
ideał ideal[2]
identycznie alike[2], identically, the same IDM **~ myślący** on the same wavelength
identyczność uniformity
identyczny alike[1], duplicate adj., identical, the same
identyfikacja identification
identyfikować/z- identify
□ **identyfikować się** identify with sb
ideologia ideology
ideologiczny ideological
idiom idiom
idiomatyczn|y idiomatic; **wyrażenie ~e** idiom
idiot-a/ka dork, idiot, prat
idiotycznie idiotically, inanely, stupidly; **wyglądać ~** look absurd
idiotyczny idiotic, inane, stupid
idol idol
idylliczny idyllic
iglast|y coniferous; **drzewo ~e** conifer
iglica spire; (*kościoła*) steeple
igloo igloo
igła (*do szycia*) (*bot.*) needle
ignorancja ignorance
ignorant/ka ignoramus; **być wielkim ignorantem w zakresie czegoś** be very ignorant about sth
ignorować/z- brush sb/sth aside, disregard, ignore
igrać 1 (*z niebezpieczeństwem*) court[2] **2** (*uśmiech na twarzy*) play[1] IDM **~ z losem** push your luck, push it/things
igrzyska: **~ olimpijskie** the Olympic Games
ikona icon
ikra roe
ile how many, how much[1]; **~ masz lat?** How old are you?; **~ to kosztuje?** How much is that?; **~ książek!** What a lot of books! IDM **o ~** as/so far as, as/so long as, if | **o ~ wiem** as far as I know | **o ~ nie** unless
ilekroć whenever
iloczyn product
iloraz: **~ inteligencji** IQ
ilościowy quantitative

iloś|ć amount[1], number[1], quantity, volume; **~ć zdobytych punktów** score[1]; **w dużej ~ci** in quantity
ilu → ILE
iluminacja illumination; (**iluminacje**) illuminations
iluminować/z- illuminate
ilustracja figure[1], illustration
ilustrator/ka illustrator
ilustrować/z- exemplify, illustrate
iluzjonist-a/ka conjuror, magician
iluzoryczny illusory
im: **~...tym...** the... the...
imadło vice
imbecyl imbecile
imbir ginger
imbirowy ginger adj.
imbryczek teapot
imienni-k/czka namesake
imiesłów participle; **~ czasu teraźniejszego** present participle; **~ czasu przeszłego** past participle
imię 1 Christian name, first name, forename; **~ (i nazwisko)** name[1]; **drugie ~** middle name; **nadawać ~** christen; **z imienia/nazwiska** by name **2** (*reputacja*) name[1]; **dobre ~** character IDM **w ~ czegoś** in the interest(s) of sth, in the name of sth | **w imieniu kogoś** on behalf of sb, on sb's behalf, in the name of sb, in sb's name
imigracja immigration
imigrant/ka immigrant
imitacja 1 imitation **2** (*makieta*) mock-up
imitator mimic[2]
imitować/z- imitate
immobilizer immobilizer
immunitet immunity
immunologiczny: **system ~** immune system
impas impasse, stalemate
imperatorski imperial
imperialist-a/ka imperialist
imperializm imperialism
imperialny imperial
imperium empire
impertynencja impertinence
impertynencki impertinent
impet impetus, momentum
implant implant
implikacja implication
implikować imply
implodować implode
implozja implosion
imponujący commanding, grand[1], imposing, impressive
import import[1]
importer importer
importować/za- import[2]
■ **importowany**: **towar importowany** import[1]
impotencj|a impotence; **cierpiący na ~ę** impotent
impregnować/za- impregnate
■ **impregnowany** (*nieprzemakalny*) waterproof
impresjonistyczny Impressionist
impresjonizm Impressionism
impreza bash[2], bunfight, do[3], party; (*charytatywna itp.*) event; **~ sportowa** (*wyznaczona na dany dzień*) fixture
improwizacja improvisation
improwizować/za- ad lib verb, play it by ear, improvise; (*tylko muz.*) jam[2]
■ **improwizowany** ad lib
impuls impulse, spur[1], urge[2]
impulsywność impulsiveness
impulsywny impetuous, impulsive
inaczej 1 (*w inny sposób*) differently; **~ niż** to the contrary, other than **2** (*w przeciwnym razie*) or else, otherwise
inauguracja inauguration, opening
inauguracyjny inaugural
inaugurować/za- inaugurate
incognito incognito
incydent incident
indagować/za- interrogate, question[2]
indeks 1 (*w książce*) index **2** (*ocenzurowanych książek itp.*) blacklist; **umieszczać na ~ie** blacklist verb
Indian-in/ka (*rdzenn-y/a*) Native American noun
indiański Native American
indoeuropejski Indo-European
indoktrynacja indoctrination
indoktrynować/z- indoctrinate
industrializacja industrialization
indygo: **kolor ~** indigo noun; **w kolorze ~** indigo
indyjski Indian
indyk turkey
indywidualist-a/ka individualist, maverick
indywidualistyczny individualistic
indywidualizm individualism
indywidualność 1 (*telewizyjna itp.*) personality **2** (*osobowość*) individuality
indywidualn|y (*osobisty*) personal, private[1]; (*oddzielny*) individual[1], particular; (*zajęcia*) one-to-one; **dla ~ego użytkownika** bespoke
inercja inaction, inertia
infantylny childish, infantile, puerile
infekcja infection
infekcyjny infectious
infiltracja infiltration
infiltrować/z- infiltrate
inflacja inflation
informacj|a 1 (*wiadomość*) feedback, information, pointer; **~e biometryczne** biodata **2** (*miejsce udzielania informacji, np. dla turystów*) information desk; **~a telefoniczna** directory enquiries
informacyjny informative
informator/ka informant; (*o swojej firmie/organizacji*) whistle-blower
informatyka computing, information technology
informować/po- advise, brief[3], inform, let sb know, report[1], tell; **dokładnie kogoś ~** prime[3] sb (for/with sth); **~ na bieżąco** liaise (with sb/sth); **źle ~** misinform
□ **informować się** enquire
■ **informując-y/a się** enquirer
infrastruktura infrastructure
ingerencja interference
ingerować/za- 1 (*zakłócać*) interfere **2** (*interweniować*) intervene
inhalator inhaler
inicjacj|a initiation; **dokonywać czyjejś ~i (w coś)** initiate sb (into sth)
inicjał initial[2]; **podpisywać się ~ami** initial[3]
inicjatyw|a 1 (*pomysł; przedsiębiorczość*) enterprise, initiative; **z ~ą** enterprising; **występować z ~ą** take the initiative; **z własnej ~y** off your own bat, on your own initiative **2** (*wniosek*) motion[1]
inicjować/za- initiate
iniekcja injection
inkasować/za- collect[1]
inklinacja sympathy
inkubacja incubation
inkubator incubator
innowacj|a innovation, novelty; **wprowadzać ~e/zmiany** innovate
innowacyjny innovative
innowator/ka innovator
inn|y alternative[2], the odd man/one out, other; **~y niż ktoś/coś** a contrast to sb/sth, different, other than, unlike adj.; **(jakiś) ~y** another; **coś ~ego** something else; **ktoś ~y** someone else; **nikt ~y** nobody else; **~ego rodzaju** otherwise; **taki lub ~y** some; **w ~y sposób** otherwise IDM **~ymi słowy** in other words, to put it another way
inscenizować/za- stage[2]
insekt bug[1], insect
inspekcja examination, inspection
inspektor/ka (*nadzorca*) warden; (*policji itp.*) inspector
inspicjent/ka stage manager
inspiracja inspiration
inspirować/za- inspire, stimulate
■ **inspirujący** inspiring
instalacja installation; **~ elektryczna** wiring
instalować/za- install; (*mebel*) put sth in
instrukcj|a instruction; (**instrukcje**) (*obsługi*) directions, instructions, manual[2]
instruktor/ka instructor, trainer
instrument 1 (*narzędzie*) implement[2], instrument **2** (*muz.*) instrument; **~ dęty** wind instrument; **~y dęte** wind[1]; **drewniane ~y dęte** woodwind; **~y blaszane** brass; **~y perkusyjne** percussion; **~ strunowy** stringed instrument
instrumentalny (*muz.*) instrumental
instruować/po- brief[3], instruct
instynkt instinct
instynktowny instinctive, instinctual
instytucja institution
instytucjonalizacja institutionalization
instytucjonalizować/z- institutionalize
instytucjonalny institutional
instytut institute[1], school
insulina insulin
insurekcja insurrection, uprising
insygnium insignia
insynuacja innuendo, insinuation
insynuować/za- insinuate
integracja integration
integralny integral
integrować/z- integrate
intelekt intellect
intelektualist-a/ka intellectual[2], thinker
intelektualny intellectual[1]; (*dzieła sztuki*) highbrow
inteligencja 1 (*umysł*) brainpower, intelligence **2** (*grupa społeczna*) intelligentsia
inteligent/ka intellectual[2]
inteligentny bright, intelligent, sharp[1], smart[1], thinking[2]
intencj|a intention; **mieć dobre (najlepsze) ~e wobec kogoś** have/with sb's (best) interests at heart; **mający jak najlepsze ~e** well meaning; **w najlepszej ~i** well meant

intensyfikować/z- raise[1] sth (to sth), step sth up
intensywnie intensely, intensively; ~ **pomyśleć** think hard
intensywność intensity
intensywn|y 1 (*kurs; poszukiwania*) intensive; (*kurs*) crash[3]; (*ćwiczenie*) strenuous; ~**y, dwutygodniowy kurs języka francuskiego** a two-week immersion course in French; ~**a opieka medyczna** intensive care **2** (*kolor; upał*) intense; (*upał*) blistering; (*zapach; światło*) strong
interakcja interaction
interakcyjny interactive
interaktywny interactive; **tablica interaktywna typu whiteboard** interactive whiteboard
interes 1 (*coś korzystnego*) **żywotny, często skrywany** ~ vested interest; **w (czyimś)** ~**ie** in sb's interest(s) **2** (*biznes*) business; (**interesy**) dealing; **dobry** ~ big business; **zrobić dobry** ~ pull off a business deal; **z nimi bardzo łatwo prowadzi się** ~**y** they are very easy to do business with **3** (*transakcja*) deal[2], transaction
interesować/za- interest[2], interest sb in sth
□ **interesować/za- się** be interested in sb/sth; (*jako hobby*) go in for sth/doing sth, take sth up; **zainteresować się czymś** get into sth; **bardziej zainteresować się** take more interest in sth
interesowność self-interest
interesowny mercenary[2]
interesujący interesting; (*pomysł itp.*) attractive
interfejs interface
interkom intercom
internat: **szkoła z** ~**em** boarding school; **mieszkać w internacie** board[2]
internaut-a/ka surfer
internet Internet, the World Wide Web; **przez** ~ electronic, online adv.
internetowy electronic, online
internist-a/ka practitioner
internować intern[1]
interpretacja interpretation, rendition; **zła** ~ misinterpretation
interpretować/z- construe, interpret; **błędnie/źle rozumieć/**~ misconstrue, misinterpret, misread
interpunkcj|a: **stosowanie** ~**i** punctuation
interwencja intercession, intervention
interweniować/za- intercede, intervene, step in
intonacja cadence, intonation
intratność profitability
intratny lucrative, profitable
introligator/ka bookbinder
introligatorstwo bookbinding
intronizacja enthronement
intronizować enthrone
introspekcja introspection
introspektywny introspective
introwertyczny introverted
introwerty-k/czka introvert
intruz intruder; (*na przyjęciu*) gatecrasher IDM **być** ~**em** play gooseberry
intryga intrigue[2], manoeuvre[1]
intrygancki manipulative
intrygować 1 przeciw komuś scheme[2] **2 (/za-)** (*zaciekawiać*) intrigue[1], puzzle[2]
■ **intrygujący** intriguing
intuicja intuition
intuicyjny intuitive
intymny intimate
■ **intymność** sexual intimacy
Inuit/ka Inuit
inwalidztwo disability
inwazj|a invasion; **dokonywać** ~**i** (*i przen.*) invade
inwazyjny invasive
inwektywa invective
inwentaryzacja stocktaking
inwentarz inventory; **żywy** ~ livestock
inwestor/ka investor
inwestować/za- invest
inwestycja investment; ~ **kapitałowa** capital investment
inwigilacja surveillance
inżynier engineer[1]; ~ **chemik** chemical engineer; ~ **elektryk** electrical engineer; ~ **mechanik** mechanical engineer
inżynieria engineering; ~ **genetyczna** genetic engineering; ~ **mechaniczna** mechanical engineering; ~ **wodnolądowa** civil engineering
irlandzki Irish
ironi|a irony; **jak na** ~**ę** ironically, the irony was that
ironiczny ironic
■ **ironicznie** ironically; (*mówić/robić coś*) (with) tongue in cheek
irracjonalność irrationality
irracjonalny irrational
irygacja irrigation
irygować/z- irrigate
irys iris
irytacj|a annoyance, displeasure, impatience; **z** ~**ą** crossly, irritably
irytować/z- annoy, displease, grate[2] (on sb), irritate, niggle, put sb out, ruffle; **(bardzo)** ~ infuriate
irytujący annoying, irritating, maddening; **bardzo** ~ infuriating
iskierka 1 sparkle noun **2** (*przen.*) gleam; ~ **nadziei** a flicker of hope
iskra spark[1], sparkle noun
iskrzyć/za- się glint, shimmer, sparkle, twinkle
islam Islam
islamski Islamic
istnieć/za- be[1], exist, prevail; **czy Bóg istnieje?** is there a god?; **to jest najstarszy istniejący ludzki szkielet** this is the oldest human skeleton in existence
istnienie (*bycie*) being[2], existence
istny veritable
istot|a 1 (*stworzenie*) being[2], creature, entity; ~**a ludzka** human[2] **2** (*podstawowa cecha*) essence; (*sprawy itp.*) complexion, gist, kernel, point[1], thrust[2], relevance; **trafiający w** ~**ę sprawy** to the point; **w istocie** in effect, in (actual) fact
istotn|y essential, intrinsic, relevant; (*dowody*) material[2]; **rzecz niezbędna/**~**a** essential noun
■ **istotnie 1** (*rzeczywiście*) indeed **2** (*niezbędnie*) intrinsically, materially
iść/pójść zob. też CHODZIĆ **1** (*dokądś w określonym celu*) go[1]; (*pieszo*) walk[1]; (*drogą itp.; za kimś/czymś*) follow; (*w kierunku opisanym*) head[2], head for sth; (*wrócić do domu itp.*) get along; **muszę** ~ I must be off; **pójść dokądś i wrócić** be[1] **2 dokądś/na coś** attend, go[1]; **pójść do lekarza** see a doctor; ~ **na drinka** go for a drink; ~ **ulicą** walk along/down the street; **nie poszedłem spać aż do trzeciej** I didn't get to bed until three **3** (*sprawy*) fare[2], go[1]; **jak ci idzie?** how are you getting on?; **jak dobrze pójdzie, to** hopefully **4** (*dotyczyć*) **jeśli o to idzie** for that matter **5** (*fundusze: na jakiś cel*) go towards sth IDM ~ **na całego** go all out for sth, go all out to do sth | ~ **z kimś do łóżka** go to bed with sb
itd. etc.
itp. etc.
izba chamber; (*parlamentu*) house[1]; **Izba Gmin** (*niższa, wybieralna izba parlamentu brytyjskiego*) the House of Commons; **Izba Lordów** (*wyższa, nie wybieralna izba parlamentu brytyjskiego*) the House of Lords; **Izba Reprezentantów** (*niższa izba parlamentu amerykańskiego*) the House of Representatives; **Izba Handlowa** Chamber of Commerce; ~ **przyjęć** accident and emergency
izolacja confinement, insulation, isolation
izolatka ward[1]
izolować/od-/wy- cut sb/sth off (from sb/sth), isolate, insulate
izotop isotope
Izraelit-a/ka Hebrew

J

j (J/j) (*litera*) J, j
ja I; **to** ~! it's me!; **on zarabia znacznie więcej niż** ~ he earns a lot more than I do
jabłecznik cider
jabłko 1 apple **2** (*królewskie*) orb IDM ~ **Adama** Adam's apple
jabłkowy: **napój** ~ cider
jabłoń apple tree
jacht yacht; ~ **motorowy** yacht
jachtowy yacht
jad venom
jadalnia dining room
jadalny edible
jadeit jade
jadłospis menu; (*wybieranie potraw*) **z** ~**u** à la carte
jadowity 1 (*wąż itp.*) poisonous, venomous **2** (*przen.*) scathing, venomous, virulent, vitriolic
jagnię lamb
jagnięcina lamb
jagnięc|y: **mięso** ~**e** lamb
jagoda berry
jaguar jaguar
jajeczkować ovulate
jajecznica scrambled egg
jajko egg[1]; **jajka w koszulkach** poached eggs; ~ **wielkanocne** Easter egg
jajnik ovary
jaj|o (**jaja**) (*bdzura*) bollocks IDM **robić (sobie) żarty/**~**a z kogoś** take the mickey (out of sb)
jajowaty oval
jajowód Fallopian tube
jak (*zaimek przysłowny*) as to, how
■ **jak** (*przyim.*) **1** (*w porównaniach*) like[1]; **tak...jak...** as; **tak,** ~ like[1,2]; **tak samo,** ~ like[1]; ~ **i** as well (as sb/sth); **zarówno...,** ~ **i...** both... and... **2 na kogoś/coś** as people, things, etc. go, for[1] | **jak** (*spój.*) **1** (*w zdaniu*

wtrąconym) as **2** *(wprowadza zdanie czasowe/celowe/przyczynowe)* where **2** ~ **gdyby** as if, as though **3** ~ **tylko** the minute/moment (that) | **jak** *(partykuła)* ~ **najszybciej** as soon as possible IDM ~ **mu tam** so-and-so | **jeszcze** ~ you bet
jakby like[2]
jaki 1 *(pytanie)* what, which; **(a)** ~ whichever; ~ **by nie był** whatever; ~ **tylko chcesz** whichever **2** *(podkreślenie)* how
jakikolwiek any, whatever, whichever
jakiś a, any, certain, one[1], some; ~ **(taki)** a kind of
jakiż: **(a)** ~ whichever
jakkolwiek however
jako as; ~ **członek zarządu/rady** in his guise as chairman; ~ **taki** as such, per se, so-so; ~**, że** since conj.
jakoś 1 *(w jakiś sposób)* somehow **2** *(nieco)* sort of
jakościowy qualitative
jakoś|ć grade[1], quality; **wysoka ~ć** quality; **najwyższej ~ci** de luxe; **niskiej ~ci** downmarket
jałmużna handout
jałowcówka gin
jałowość dryness, infertility
jałowy 1 *(zwierzę; ziemia)* barren, infertile; *(ziemia)* arid, waste[3] **2** *(opatrunek)* sterile **3 bieg** ~ neutral[2]
jama burrow[2], hole
jamnik 1 *(pies)* dachshund **2** *(stół)* coffee table
Jankes/ka Yank
janowiec gorse
jantar amber
japonka *(klapek)* flip-flop
jar canyon, ravine
jard yard
jarmarczność tawdriness
jarmarczny tawdry
jarmark bazaar, market[1]
jarzeniowy fluorescent
jarzębina rowan
jarzmo *(i przen.)* yoke
jarzyć *(rozumieć)* latch on (to sth) □ **jarzyć/za- się** *(błyszczeć)* glow ■ **jarzący** luminous
jarzyna vegetable
jarzynowy vegetable
jaskier buttercup
jaskinia cave[1], cavern IDM ~ **hazardu** gambling den
jaskiniowiec caveman
jaskółka swallow[2]
jaskrawość brightness
jaskrawy bright, vivid; *(kolor)* bold, fluorescent, garish, gaudy, lurid; *(zwł. czerwień)* flaming; *(światło)* glaring; *(ubranie)* flashy; *(krawat itp.)* ~ **i ekscentryczny** jazzy
jasno clearly, explicitly, lucidly; ~ **myślący** clear-sighted IDM **wyrażać się** ~ make yourself clear, make sth clear (to sb)
jasnobrązow|y: **kolor ~y** *(naturalnej skóry)* tan[2]; **koloru ~ego** tan adj.
jasność brightness, brilliance, clarity, lucidity
jasnowidz clairvoyant
jasnowłosy blonde
jasnozielony jade adj.; **kolor** ~ jade
jasn|y 1 *(światło)* bright **2** *(włosy, skóra)* fair[1]; **o ~ych włosach** fair-haired **3** *(oczywisty)* clear[1], distinct, evident, obvious, plain[1]; **~e, że** evidently; **~y jak słońce** crystal clear **3** *(umysł)* clear[1], lucid **4** *(piwo)* light[1] IDM **~e!** sure, sure thing
jastrząb *(zool., polityk)* hawk
jaszczurka lizard
jaśmin jasmine
jaśnieć/za- shine[1]; *(oczy)* twinkle ■ **jaśniejący** shiny
jatk|a massacre; **urządzać ~ę** massacre verb
jaw: **wychodzić na** ~ come to light, emerge, be out adj., get out, unfold
jawn|y blatant, overt, patent[2], public[1]; **spojrzał na niego z ~ą niechęcią** he looked at him with open dislike
jawor sycamore
jazda 1 ride[2]; *(podróż samochodem itp.)* drive[2], driving[1]; ~ **figurowa na lodzie** figure-skating; ~ **na łyżwach** skating; ~ **na deskorolce** skateboarding; ~ **na wrotkach** roller skating; ~ **próbna** trial run **2** *(wojsk.)* cavalry IDM **no to ~!** here goes
jazz jazz[1]
jazzowy jazz[1], jazzy
ją her[1], it
jądro 1 *(orzecha)* kernel **2** *(sprawy; planety)* core **3** *(atomowe)* nucleus **4** *(anat.)* testicle **5** *(ludzie w grupie)* ~ **stowarzyszenia** hard core
jądrowy atomic, nuclear
jąkać/zająknąć się stammer, have a stammer, stumble (over/through sth), stutter
jątrzyć/roz- się fester
jechać/po- go[1]; *(pociągiem itp.)* get, take; *(samochodem)* run[1]; *(w kierunku opisanym)* head[2], head for sth; *(drogą itp.)* follow; **pojechać dokądś i wrócić** be[1]; **jadący dokądś** destined for…
jed|en a, one[1], single[1]; **~en (lub drugi)** either[1]; **~en po drugim** back to back, one by one, one after another/the other; *(w jednej linii)* in single file; **bilet w ~ną stronę** single ticket IDM **wszystko mi ~no** I don't mind
jedenasty eleventh
jedenaście eleven
jednać/po- reconcile
jednak after all, anyway, but[1], however, yet ■ **jednakże** equally, notwithstanding adv.
jednakowość uniformity
jednakowy alike[1], equal[1]
jednocyfrowy: **na poziomie ~m** in single figures
jednoczesny concurrent, simultaneous
jednocześnie 1 concurrently, hand in hand, at the same time, simultaneously, in tandem (with sb/sth), at a time **2** *(jednakże)* equally
jednoczyć/z- rally[2], reunite, unify, unite □ **jednoczyć/z- się** rally[2], rally round/around (sb), reunite, unite; *(zbić się w całość)* coalesce
jednogłośny unanimous
jednojęzyczny monolingual
jednokierunkowy one-way
jednolitość uniformity
jednolity *(w treści)* homogeneous; *(kamień itp.)* solid[1]; *(tkanina; w kolorze)* plain[1]; *(w stylu)* uniform[2]; *(cena)* flat[1]
jednomiejscowy single[1]
jednomyślność consensus
jednomyślny unanimous
jednoosobow|y single[1]; **pokój ~y** single[2]; **dwa ~e łóżka (w jednym pokoju)** twin beds
jednorazow|y *(opłata itp.)* one-off adj., one-time; **~a wypłata** lump sum; **do ~ego użytku** disposable
jednorodny homogeneous
jednorożec unicorn
jednostajność monotony
jednostajny flat[1], monotonous, steady[1], uniform[2]
jednostk|a 1 *(oddzielna część czegoś)* entity, module; **~a miary minimalnej zmiany** point[1] **2** *(osoba)* individual[2] **3 (jednostki)** *(bojowe itp.)* force[1], unit; **~i pływające** shipping
jednostronny one-sided, unilateral
jednosylabowy monosyllabic
jednoszynow|y: **kolej ~a** monorail
jedność unity
jednotorowy blinkered
jednozgłoskowy monosyllabic
jednoznaczny: **z czymś** synonymous (with sth)
jedwab silk
jedwabisty silky
jedwabny silk
jedyna-k/czka an only child
jedynie mere, merely, purely, solely; **odniosła sukces ~ dzięki ciężkiej pracy** her success is due to sheer hard work
jedyn|y exclusive[1], lone, one[1], only, sole[1]; **~a okazja** one-off; **~y (w swoim rodzaju)** one-off, unique
jedzeni|e food; **coś do ~a** a bite to eat
jeep Jeep
jego *(zaim. osobowy: osoba)* him; *(przedmiot)* it ■ **jego** *(zaim. dzierżawczy: osoba)* his[1,2]; *(przedmiotu; zwierzęcia)* its
jej *(zaim. osobowy: osoba)* her[1]; *(przedmiot)* it ■ **jej** *(zaim. dzierżawczy: osoba: z rz.)* her[2]; *(bez rz.)* hers; *(przedmiotu; zwierzęcia)* its
jeleń deer, stag
jelito bowel, gut[1], intestine
jelitowy intestinal
jelonek fawn[2]
jełczeć/z- go/turn rancid
jemioła mistletoe
jemu him
jeniec captive[2]; ~ **wojenny** prisoner of war
jersey: **materiał wełniany typu** ~ jersey
jesienny autumnal
jesień autumn
jesion ash
jesionowy ash
jesiotr sturgeon
jeszcze 1 *(dotychczas)* still[1]; *(w zdaniach przeczących)* yet; *(zostaje/ma itd.)* to go; ~ **do zrobienia itp.** yet to do, etc.; ~ **(teraz)** already, yet; ~ **nie teraz** not just yet **2** *(w dodatku)* again, else; ~ **(jeden)** another, yet another; ~ **raz** again, yet again; **jest miejsce ~ dla trzech osób** there's room for three more people; **pożyje ~ wiele lat** she'll live for years yet **3** *(nawet bardziej itp.)* even[2], still[1];

~ **lepiej, trudniej itp.** all the better, harder, etc. IDM ~ **jak** you bet
jeść/z- eat, feed[1] (on sth); **zjeść coś** have something to eat; ~ **łapczywie i głośno** gobble; ~ **śniadanie/obiad** have breakfast/lunch; ~ **obiad** dine, have dinner; ~ **obiad w restauracji** dine out; ~ **na mieście** eat out; **nie** ~ be off your food
jeśli if; **a** ~ supposing
jezdnia the roadway
jezdny passable
jezioro lake; (*szkockie*) loch
jeździć/po- ride[1]; (*autobusy itp.*) run[1]; ~ **konno** ride[1]; ~ **na łyżwach** skate[1]; ~ **na nartach** ski[1]; ~ **na nartach wodnych** waterski; ~ **na rowerze** cycle[2]; ~ **na rowerze/motorze** ride[1]; ~ **samochodem** drive[1]; ~ **na wrotkach** roller skate
jeździec horseman, rider
jeździecki equestrian
jeździectwo riding
jeż hedgehog
jeżeli if, should, supposing; ~ **nie** unless
jeżyć/z-/na- się bristle[2]; **sprawiający, że włosy jeżą się na głowie** hair-raising
jeżyna blackberry; (*dzika*) bramble
jęczeć/jęknąć 1 groan, moan, wail, whine **2** (*na jakiś temat*) moan
jęczmienny barley
jęczmień 1 barley **2** (*na powiece*) sty
jędrność firmness
jędrny 1 (*twardy*) firm[2] **2** (*język*) pithy
jędza bitch[2], cow
jędzowatość cattiness
jędzowaty bitchy, catty
jęk groan noun, wail noun, whine noun
jęknąć → JĘCZEĆ
języczek 1 (*anat.*) uvula **2** ~ **u wagi** balance of power
język 1 (*anat.*) tongue; **pokazywać** ~ put/stick your tongue out **2** (*polski itp.*) language, tongue; ~ **migowy** sign language; **posługiwać się ~iem migowym** sign[2]; ~ **ojczysty** mother tongue IDM **mieć/znajdować wspólny** ~ relate to sb/sth
językowy language, linguistic
językoznawca linguist
językoznawczy linguistic
językoznawstwo linguistics
jidysz Yiddish
jod iodine
jodła fir
jodyna iodine
joga yoga
jogging: **uprawiać** ~ jog[1]
jogurt yogurt
jo-jo Yo Yo
jowialny genial, hearty, jovial; (*w rezultacie wieku lub doświadczenia*) mellow
Jowisz Jupiter
joystick joystick
jubel do[3]
jubiler jeweller
jubileusz anniversary, jubilee
judaizm Judaism
judo judo
jumbo jet jumbo[1]
junior 1 (**Junior**) (*tytuł*) junior[1] **2 mistrzostwa atletyczne ~ów** the junior athletics championships
junta junta
jurny virile
juror/ka (*konkursu*) adjudicator, judge[1], juror; (*egzaminu*) assessor
jury jury
jurysdykcja jurisdiction
jutr|o tomorrow; **od ~a za tydzień** a week tomorrow
jutrzejszy tomorrow's
już 1 already; ~ **nie** no/not any longer, not any more; ~ **na zawsze** ever after; **od tamtego czasu więcej się ~ nie pokazał** he hadn't been back since **2** (*w pytaniach*) yet

K

k (**K/k**) (*litera*) K, k
kabaczek marrow
kabaret cabaret
kabel 1 cable, flex[2], wire[1] **2** (*osoba*) sneak[2]
kabina booth, cabin, cubicle; ~ **do głosowania** polling booth; ~ **kierowcy/maszynisty** cab; ~ **pilota** cockpit
kabłąkowat|y: ~**e nogi** bow legs; **o ~ych nogach** bow-legged
kabriolet convertible[2]
kabura holster
kac hangover
kaczan: ~ **kukurydzy** corn on the cob
kaczątko duckling
kaczka 1 duck[1] **2** (*kulin.*) duck[1], duckling
kaczor drake
kaczuszka duckling
kadencja 1 term[1]; ~ **prezydenta** presidency **2** (*muz.*) cadence; ~ **wirtuozowska** cadenza
kadet cadet
kadłub hull; ~ **samolotu** fuselage
kadr: ~ **z filmu** still[3]
kadra (**kadry**) **1** personnel **2 dział kadr** human resources
kadzidło incense
kadź tub, vat
kafel tile
kaftan: ~ **bezpieczeństwa** straitjacket
kaganiec muzzle; **próba nałożenia prasie kagańca** an attempt to gag the press
kajak canoe, kayak; **pływać ~iem** canoe verb
kajdanki handcuffs
kajmak fudge[1]
kajuta cabin
kakao chocolate, cocoa
kakofonia cacophony
kakofoniczny cacophonous
kaktus cactus
kalać/s-/po- defile
kalafior cauliflower
kalambur play on words, pun; (**kalambury**) charades
kalanie defilement
kalectwo deformity
kaleczyć/s-/po- 1 hurt[1], injure, maul; (*nożem itp.*) cut[1] **2** (*psychicznie*) screw sb up **3** (*podłogę itp.*) scuff
□ **kaleczyć/s-/po- się** (*nożem itp.*) cut yourself
kalejdoskop kaleidoscope
kaleka cripple[2]
kalendarz calendar
kalendarzyk diary
kalenica ridge
kaliber 1 calibre **2** (*osoby*) stature
kaligraf calligrapher
kaligrafia calligraphy
kalk|a carbon paper; ~**a kreślarska** tracing paper; **kopia przez ~ę** carbon copy
kalklulacja: ~ **kosztów** costing
kalkomania transfer[2]
kalkować/prze-/s- trace[1]
kalkulacj|a reckoning; **przeprowadzać ~ę czegoś** tally verb sth (up)
kalkulator calculator
kalkulować/s- calculate, project[2], work sth out
kaloria calorie
kaloryfer radiator
kalumnia aspersions, smear[2]
kał excrement, faeces
kałamarnica squid
kałdun gut[1]
kałuża puddle; (*krwi itp.*) pool[1] (of sth)
kambuz galley
kamea cameo
kameleon chameleon
kamera: ~ **filmowa** camera; ~**internetowa** webcam; ~**wideo** camcorder
kameraln|y intimate; **muzyka ~a** chamber music; **orkiestra ~a** chamber orchestra
kamerdyner butler
kamerzysta cameraman
kamerzystka camerawoman
kamfora IDM **znikać jak** ~ vanish, etc. into thin air
kamieniarka masonry
kamieniarz mason, stonemason
kamienieć/s- fossilize
kamieniołom quarry[1]; **eksploatować** ~ quarry[2]
kamienisty rocky, stony
kamienny 1 (*zrobiony z kamienia*) stone **2** (*twarz, milczenie itp.*) stony
kamienować stone verb
kamień rock[1], stone; (*osad wapienny*) limescale; ~ **brukowy** paving stone; ~ **do zapalniczki** flint; ~ **milowy** milestone; ~ **nagrobny** gravestone, tombstone; ~ **szlachetny** gem, jewel, precious stone; ~ **węgielny** (*i przen.*) cornerstone; ~ **żółciowy** gallstone IDM **gdy powiedział jej prawdę, spadł mu ~ z serca** telling her the truth took a weight off his mind
kamizelka waistcoat; ~ **kuloodporna** flak jacket; ~ **ratunkowa** life jacket
kampani|a campaign[1], drive[2]; **przeprowadzać ~ę; uczestniczyć w ~i** campaign[2]; **uczestni-k/czka ~i** campaigner
kamuflaż camouflage
kamuflować/za- camouflage verb
kamyk stone, pebble; (**kamyki**) grit[1]
kanalia scumbag, sleaze
kanalik: ~ **łzowy** tear duct
kanalizacja (*rury*) drainage, plumbing; (*system urządzeń sanitarnych*) sanitation; (*kanał ściekowy*) sewer
kanał 1 (*morski*) channel[1]; ~ **La Manche** the Channel[1] **2** (*sztuczny*) canal[1]; (*rów*) ditch[1] **3** (*ściekowy*) sewer **4** (*odprowadzający*) duct, pipe[1], vent **5** (*anat.*) ~ **nosowy** the nasal passages **6** (*TV*) channel[1] **7** ~ **dyskusyjny w czacie** chat room **8** (*dla orkiestry*) orchestra pit
kanapa couch[1], settee, sofa; ~ **rozkładana** sofa bed
kanapka sandwich[1]

kanarek canary
kancelaria: ~ **adwokacka** legal practice
kancerogen carcinogen
kancerogenny carcinogenic
kanciarz con man
kanciasty angular
kanclerz chancellor
kandydat/ka (*na miejsce na uniwersytecie itp.*) applicant, candidate, contender, nominee; (*w konkursie*) entrant; **kandydat/ka odbywając-y/a rozmowę kwalifikacyjną** interviewee
kandydatura candidacy
kandydować run[1] (for sth), stand[1] (for/as sth)
kangur kangaroo
kanibal cannibal
kanibalizm cannibalism
kanion canyon
kanister canister
kanoe canoe
kanonierka gunboat
kanonik canon
kant 1 (*spodni*) crease[1] **2** (*oszustwo*) fiddle[2]; (**kanty**) racket
kantor bureau de change
kantyna cafeteria, canteen
kap-ać/nąć dribble, drip[1], trickle; **kapie z kranu** the tap is dripping
kapeć slipper
kapela band, group[1]
kapelan chaplain
kapelusz hat; ~ **myśliwski** deerstalker; ~ **od słońca** sun hat
kapelusznictwo millinery
kapitalist-a/ka capitalist
kapitalistyczny capitalist
kapitalizm capitalism
kapitalny 1 (*ważny*) **przeprowadzać ~ remont** overhaul **2** (*znakomity*) groovy, smashing, tremendous
kapitał capital[1]
kapitan captain[1] (*na morzu, sport*) skipper
kapitulacja capitulation
kapitulować/s- capitulate, give up
kapka touch[2] (of sth)
kaplica chapel
kapłan/ka priest
kapłaństwo ministry
kapnąć → KAPAĆ
kapral corporal
kaprawy bleary
kapryfolium honeysuckle
kaprys 1 (*osoby*) caprice, whim; (*zwł. wobec jedzenia*) fad **2** (*losu itp.*) freak[1], quirk
kapryśność caprice; (*zwł. przy jedzeniu*) faddiness
kapryśny capricious, moody, whimsical
kapsel cap[1]
kapsuła (także **kapsułka**) capsule
kaptur hood
kapturek (*w ginekologii*) diaphragm
kapusta cabbage; ~ **kiszona** sauerkraut
kar|a fine[2], punishment, sanction[1]; (*sport*) penalty; **~a cielesna** corporal punishment; **~a śmierci** capital punishment, death penalty; **zadawać ~ę** punish; **nakładać (na kogoś) ~ę** (*np. grzywny*) penalize
karabin gun[1], rifle[1]; ~ **maszynowy** machine gun
karać/u- discipline[2]; (*i prawn.*) punish; (*za złamanie przepisu; przen.*) penalize; ~ **grzywną/mandatem** fine verb; ~ **niesprawiedliwie** victimize ■ **karzący** punitive
karafka carafe
karaibski Caribbean adj.
Karaiby the Caribbean
karalny punishable
karaluch cockroach
karambol pile-up
karat carat
karate karate
karawan hearse
karawana caravan
karb nick[1], notch[1]
karbowany corrugated
karcić/s- censure, chasten, rebuke, scold
karczoch artichoke
kardiolog cardiologist
kardiologia cardiology
kardynał cardinal
karencja grace
kareta carriage, coach[1]
karetka: ~ **pogotowia** ambulance
kariera career[1]
karierowicz/ka careerist
karierowiczostwo careerism
kark neck; (*tylna część szyi*) nape IDM **na złamanie ~u** at breakneck speed | (*brać*) **za ~** by the scruff (of the/your neck)
karlica → KARZEŁ
karliczka → KARZEŁ
karłowaty dwarf[1]
karmazyn crimson noun
karmazynowy crimson, magenta
karmel caramel
karmelek caramel
karmić/na- feed[1], nourish; ~ **piersią** breastfeed; **~/być karmionym piersią** nurse[2]; ~ **na siłę** force-feed
karnacj|a colouring, complexion; **ciemnej/jasnej ~i** dark/fair-skinned
karnawał carnival
karnet book[1]
karnisz rail
karny (*kodeks itp.*) criminal[1], penal; (*sankcja itp.*) punitive
karo diamond
karoseria bodywork
karp carp
karpyśny faddy
kart|a 1 card; (**karty**) cards; **gra w ~y** card game; **~a do bankomatu** cash card; **~a bankowa** bank card; **~a czekowa** cheque card; **~a czipowa** chip card; **~a debetowa** bank card; **~a do głosowania** ballot; **~a katalogowa** index card; **~a kredytowa** credit card; (*wydawana przez sklep*) store card; **~a lądowania** landing card; **~a magnetyczna** smart card; (*umożliwiająca wejście do budynku itp.*) swipe card; **~a pamięci** Memory Stick; **~a płatnicza** bank card, debit card; (*stałego klienta*) charge card; **~a pokładowa** boarding card; **~a SIM** SIM card; **~a telefoniczna** phonecard; **płacić ~ą** pay by credit card; (*komórka itp.*) **na ~ę** pay-as-you-go **2** (*dokument*) charter[1] **3** (*dań*) menu IDM **stawiać wszystko na jedną ~ę** put all your eggs in one basket
kartka 1 (*papieru*) piece of paper, sheet; (*mała*) slip[2]; ~ **samoprzylepna** (*do robienia notatek*) Post-it **2** (*w książce*) page[1] **3 do kogoś**; ~ **pocztowa** postcard; ~ **świąteczna** (*z okazji Bożego Narodzenia*) Christmas card
kartkować/prze- leaf through sth, thumb[2]
kartofel potato; (*nieform.*) spud
kartofelkowaty (*nos*) bulbous
kartograf cartographer
kartografia cartography
kartograficzny cartographic
karton 1 (*materiał*) card **2** (*pudełko*) carton
kartote|ka card index, file[1]; **~ki medyczne** medical records IDM **w ~ce** on file
karuzela merry-go-round, roundabout[1]
karygodny criminal[1], culpable; **czyn ~** crime ■ **karygodnie** abominably, criminally
karykatura 1 caricature, travesty **2** cartoon
karykaturzyst-a/ka cartoonist
karzeł/karlica (także **karzełek/karliczka**) dwarf[1], midget
kasa 1 (*żelazna skrzynka*) till[2] **2** (*miejsce: w sklepie*) checkout; (*w supermarkecie*) cash desk; ~ **biletowa** booking office, box office, ticket office; ~ **oszczędnościowa udzielająca pożyczek hipotecznych** building society **3** (*pieniądze*) dough; ~ **podręczna** petty cash; **wspólna ~** kitty
kaseta cartridge, cassette; (*zawierająca nagrania jednego artysty*) album; ~ **magnetofonowa/magnetowidowa/magnetyczna** tape[1]
kaseton panel
kasjer/ka cashier
kask crash helmet, helmet
kaskada cascade[1]
kaskader stuntman
kaskaderka stuntwoman
kaskadowo: **opadać ~** cascade[2]
kasta caste
kastracja castration
kastrować/wy- castrate; (*zwierzę*) neuter[2]
kasyno: ~ **gry** casino
kaszel coughing, cough[2]
kaszleć/za-/kaszlnąć cough[1]
kaszmir cashmere
kasztan (*drzewo; owoc*) chestnut; (*zwyczajny*) horse chestnut
kasztanowiec chestnut; ~ **zwyczajny** horse chestnut
kasztanowy auburn, chestnut adj.
kat executioner, hangman
kataklizm cataclysm
kataklizmowy cataclysmic
katalizator 1 (*i przen.*) catalyst **2** (*w samochodzie*) catalytic converter
katalog catalogue; (*adresów itp.*) directory; ~ **fiszkowy** card index
katalogować/s- catalogue verb, list verb
katapultować się eject
katar cold[2]; ~ **sienny** hay fever; **wyleczyć ~** stop your nose running
katarakta 1 (*na rzece*) rapids **2** (*med.*) cataract
katartyczny cathartic
katastrof|a calamity, catastrophe, disaster; **~a lotnicza** plane crash; **~a morska** shipwreck; **przeczucie ~y** a sense of doom

katastrofalny catastrophic, disastrous
katechizm catechism
katedra 1 (*relig.*) cathedral **2** (*wydział*) faculty **3** (*stanowisko*) chair[1]
kategori|a category; **drugiej ~i** second-class; **w ~ach czegoś** in terms of sth, in… terms
kategoryczny categorical, express[2], flat[1], positive
katering catering
kateter catheter
katharsis catharsis
katolicki Roman Catholic adj.
katolicyzm Roman Catholicism
katoli-k/czka Roman Catholic
katorga fag
katorżniczy back-breaking
katusze torment
kaucj|a 1 (*prawn.*) bail[1]; **zwolnienie za ~ą** bail[1] **2** (*za butelkę itp.*) deposit[1] (on sth)
kawa coffee; **~ rozpuszczalna** instant coffee
kawaler bachelor
kawaleria cavalry
kawalerka: **mieszkanie typu ~** studio
kawalerski: **wieczór ~** stag night
kawalerzysta horseman
kawalkada cavalcade
kawał 1 chunk, hunk **2** (*dowcip*) joke[1] **3 zrobić komuś ~** to play a practical joke IDM **~ czasu** donkey's years
kawał|ek 1 bit[1], chunk, fraction, lump[1], piece[1], scrap[1]; (*pokarmu*) morsel; (*chleba itp.*) slice[1]; (*mięsa*) cut[2]; (*kurczaka itp.*) nugget; (*sznura itp.*) length; **na ~ki** apart, to bits, up; **rozbijać (się) na ~ki** shatter; **rwać na ~ki** tear sth up; **po ~ku** piecemeal adv. **2** (*piosenka itp.*) number[1] IDM **~ek drogi** trek
kawiarenka: **~ internetowa** cybercafe
kawiarnia cafe
kawior caviar
kawon watermelon
kazać/roz-/na- make[1], order[2] sb (to do sth), tell sb to do sth; **kazała dzieciom iść do łóżka** she sent the children to bed; **machnięciem ręki ~ komuś podjechać/podejść lub odjechać/odejść** wave[2] sb/sth away/on/through, etc. IDM **~ komuś (na siebie itp.) czekać** keep sb waiting
kazalnica pulpit
kazani|e sermon; **wygłaszać ~e**; **prawić (komuś) ~a** preach
kazić/s- contaminate, taint verb
kazirodczy incestuous
kazirodztwo incest
kaznodzieja preacher
każd|y all[1], any, each, every; (*osoba*) everybody, anybody; (*bez wyjątku*) every single[1]; (*nieważne który*) whatever, whichever; **~y, kto** whoever; **~emu po** (*np. złotówce*) apiece
kącik nook
kądziel: **po ~i** maternal
kąpać/wy- bath[2]
□ **kąpać/wy- się** (*w wannie*) bath[2]; (*w morzu/rzece itp.*) bathe; **~ w słońcu** lie soaking up the sun
kąpiel bath[1], bathing; **~ parowa** sauna; **szybka ~** (*w morzu itp.*) dip[2]
kąpielówki swimming trunks
kąsek morsel; **smakowity ~** titbit
kąśliwy biting
kąt 1 (*mat.*) angle[1]; **~ ostry** acute angle; **~ prosty** right angle; **~ rozwarty** obtuse angle; **pod (jakimś) ~em** at an angle **2** (*w pokoju itp.*) corner[1] **3** (*widzenia itp.*) angle[1]; **patrząc pod tym ~em** viewed from this angle
kciuk thumb[1] IDM **trzymać ~i** cross your fingers, keep your fingers crossed
kebab kebab
keczup ketchup
kelner waiter
kelnerka waitress
kemping campsite
kempingowanie camping
keyboard keyboard[1]
kędzierzawy frizzy
kępa clump
kępka tuft
kęs bite[2], morsel, mouthful
khaki: **kolor ~** khaki
kibel bog, loo
kibic fan[1], supporter
kibicować support[1]
kibić waist
kibuc kibbutz
kich-ać/nąć sneeze
kici (*wołanie kota*) kitty, puss
kicia kitty
kiciuś kitty
kicz kitsch
kiczowaty kitsch
kiedy as, when, while[1]; **~ (to) możliwe** where possible; **~ (tylko)** once conj.; **~ tylko** whenever; **rzadko ~** hardly ever
■ **kiedyż**: **(a) ~ to** whenever adv.
kiedykolwiek any time, ever, whenever
kiedyś (*w przeszłości*) once, at one time, somewhere along/down the line; (*w przyszłości*) one day, some day, sometime
kielich cup[1], goblet; (*zwł. mszalny*) chalice
kieliszek 1 glass; **~ do jajek** egg cup **2** (*miara*) glassful
kielnia trowel
kieł (*wilka itp.*) fang; (*słonia itp.*) tusk
kiełbasa (także **kiełbaska**) sausage; (*nieform.*) banger
kiełek germ, sprout[2]; **~ fasoli** bean sprouts
kiełkować/wy- germinate, sprout[1]
kiep mug[1]
kiepski 1 bad, dismal, feeble, not much good, low[1], poor, ropy, rotten, second-rate, shoddy, trashy; **żenująco ~** pathetic; **o ~m zdrowiu/samopoczuciu** under the weather; **w ~m stanie** the worse for wear **2 w czymś** (*osoba*) bad (at sth/at doing sth), useless (at sth/at doing sth)
kier heart
kiermasz fête
kierować/po-/s- 1 (*prowadzić*) guide[2]; (*ruchem*) direct[2]; **~ kogoś w określonym kierunku** urge[1] **2** (*odsyłać*) **kogoś** direct[2] sb (to…); **kogoś/coś do kogoś/czegoś** refer sb/sth to sb/sth **3** (*spojrzenie, słowo itp.*) address[2], aim[2] sth at sb/sth, angle[2] sth (at/to/towards sb), direct[2] sth to/towards sb/sth, sth at sb/sth; (*uwagę; spojrzenie*) turn[1]; (*krytykę itp.*) level sth at sb/sth **4** (*sugestia*) guide[2] **5** (*urządzenie itp.*) **zręcznie ~** manipulate; **~ pod kątem** angle[2] **6** (*autem*) drive[1], steer **7** (*być na czele*) head[2], lead[1], run[1]; (*państwem*) govern; (*firmą itp.*) be in control (of sth), manage; **źle ~** mismanage **8 ~ katedrą ekonomii na Uniwersytecie Londyńskim** hold the chair of economics at London University
□ **kierować/s- się 1 dokądś** head for sth, make for sb/sth **2 czymś** go by sth
kierowanie administration, conduct[2] of sth; (*firmą itp.*) running[1]; (*według przepisów*) regulation
kierowca driver, motorist; (*szofer*) chauffeur
kierownic|a (*auta*) steering wheel; (*roweru*) handlebar; **samochody w Australii mają ~ę po lewej stronie** cars in Australia are left-hand drive
kierownictwo (*osoby; działanie*) leadership, management; (*działanie*) direction; **złe ~** mismanagement
kierowniczka manageress; → zob. też KIEROWNIK
kierownicz|y administrative, managerial; **~e stanowisko** a senior managerial position
kierowni-k/czka chief[2]; (*firmy*) director, manager; (*zespołu*) supervisor; (*szkoły*) principal[2]; **kierownik sprzedaży** sales manager; **kierownik sali w restauracji** the head waiter; **kierownik pociągu** guard[1]; **kierowni-k/czka artystyczn-y/a** artistic director; **kierowni-k/czka sceny** stage manager
kierunek 1 bearing, direction, way[1]; **w kierunku** towards **2** (*nurt*) trend **3** (*działania*) line[1]
kierunkowskaz indicator
kieszeń pocket[1]; (*w marynarce itp.*) **~ górna** breast pocket IDM **na każdą ~** budget[3], to suit every pocket | **znać jak własną ~** know sth inside out/like the back of your hand
kieszonkowe pocket money
kieszonkowiec pickpocket
kij stick[2]; (*od miotły*) broomstick; (*baseballowy lub do krykieta*) bat[1]; (*golfowy*) golf club; (*bilardowy*) cue IDM **jakby ~ połknął** bolt upright
kijanka tadpole
kijek stick[2]
kikut stump[1]
kil keel[1]
kilim rug
kilka few, several
kilkadziesiąt dozens (of sth)
kilobajt kilobyte
kilof pick[2]
kilogram kilogram
kiloherc kHz
kilometr kilometre
kilowat kilowatt
kilwater wake[2], wash[2]
kimnąć się conk out
kinematografia cinematography, film[1]
kinematograficzny cinematic, cinematographic
kino 1 (*budynek*) cinema **2** (*film*) cinematography, the pictures[1], screen[1]
kinoman/ka film-goer
kinowy cinematic
kiosk (*budka*) kiosk; (*z książkami*) bookstall
kipieć/za-/wy- 1 bubble[2] **2** (*ze złości itp.*) boil[1], fume, seethe
kisić/za-/skisnąć pickle verb
kiszka bowel, gut[1]
kiszony: **ogórki kiszone** dill pickles
kiść 1 (*winogron itp.*) bunch[1]; (*jagód*) cluster[1] **2** (*nadgarstek*) wrist

kit 1 (*szklarski*) putty **2 do ~u** naff IDM **wciskać (komuś) ~** bullshit[2]
kita: ~ **z piór/materiału** plume
kitel overall[2], smock
kiw-ać/nąć 1 na kogoś motion[2] to sb (to do sth), (for) sb (to do sth); **kiwnąć głową (do kogoś)** nod; **kiwnąć ręką** wave[2] **2** (*kij itp.*) waggle; (*mebel itp.*) wobble IDM **nie kiwnąć palcem** not do a stroke (of work)
□ **kiwać/za- się** jiggle, waggle, wobble
■ **kiwający się** wobbly
kiwi 1 (*zool.*) kiwi **2** (*owoc*) kiwi fruit
klacz mare
klaczka filly
klakson horn
klamerka: ~ **do bielizny** peg[1]
klamka handle[2]
klamr|a 1 (*spinająca*) fastener; (*przy butach itp.*) buckle[2] **2** (*podtrzymująca półkę itp.*) bracket[1] **3** (*blokada na koła itp.*) clamp[2]; **spinać ~ą** clamp[1]
klan clan
klap|a 1 (*u marynarki itp.*) lapel **2** (*niepowodzenie*) flop[2], washout; **zrobić ~ę** flop[1], fold[1]
klapek (*typu japonka*) flip-flop
klapka 1 (*z materiału, przy ubraniu itp.*) flap[1]; **telefon komórkowy z klapką** flip phone **2** (**klapki**) (*na oczy*) blinkers; **z ~mi na oczach** blinkered
klapnąć flop[1] into/onto sth, (down/back), plump (yourself) down
klaps slap noun, smack noun; **dać ~a** smack, spank
klarnet clarinet
klarowność 1 lucidity; ~ **myślenia** clear thinking **2** (*wody itp.*) purity
klarowny clear[1] (to sb), lucid
klas|a 1 (*kategoria*) class[1], league, rank[1], style; **pierwsza ~a** first class[1]; **pierwszej ~y** first class[2]; **druga ~a** second class; **wysoka ~a** quality; **~a robotnicza/pracująca** the working class; **~a średnia** the middle class; **~a wyższa społeczeństwa** the upper class; **~a biznes** business class **2** (*szkolna*) class[1], form[1], grade[1]; **~a profilowana** stream[1] **3** (*pomieszczenie*) classroom IDM **gra w ~y** hopscotch
klaser album; (*na znaczki*) stamp album
klas-kać/nąć applaud, clap[1]
klasyczn|y classic[1], classical; (*wykonanie roli itp.*) vintage[2]; **filologia ~a** Classics[2]; **styl ~y** breaststroke
klasyfikacja classification
klasyfikować/s- categorize, class[2], classify, grade[2]
klasyk|a: **dzieło ~i** classic[2]
klasztor monastery; (*żeński*) convent
klat|ka 1 (*pomieszczenie*) cage; (*dla królików itp.*) hutch; **(trzymany) w ~ce** caged **2** (*kliszy*) exposure **3 ~ka piersiowa** chest, ribcage, thorax **4 ~ka schodowa** staircase, stairway, stairwell
klaustrofobia claustrophobia
klaustrofobiczny claustrophobic
klauzula clause
klawesyn harpsichord
klawesynist-a/ka harpsichordist
klawiatura keyboard[1]
klawisz (*w klawiaturze*) key[1]; ~ **funkcyjny** function key; ~ **zmiany małych liter na wielkie**; ~ **„shift"** shift[2]; ~ **cofający/backspace** backspace
kląć/prze-/za- curse[2], swear
klątw|a curse[1]; **rzucać ~ę** curse[2]
klecić/s- cobble sth together, patch sth up; (*zdanie*) string sth together
kleić/s-/przy- stick[1]; ~ **coś taśmą klejącą** sellotape verb
□ **kleić/s- się** stick[1]
■ **klejąc|y**: **środek klejący** adhesive[1]; **masa klejąca** (*do tapet*) paste[1]
kleistość viscosity
kleisty sticky, tacky; (*konsystencja płynu*) viscous
klej cement[1], glue[1], gum, paste[1]
klejnot gem, jewel; (**klejnoty**) jewellery; **~y koronne** the crown jewels
klekot clack, rattle[2]
klekotać/za- clack, rattle[1]
kleks blot[2], smudge noun; **zrobić ~a** blot[1]
klematis clematis
klementynka clementine
klepać 1 (**/po-/klepnąć**) (*po twarzy, po plecach itp.*) slap[1] **2** (**/wy-**) (*na pamięć itp.*) hammer[2] sth (in/into/onto sth)
klepnięcie pat[2], slap noun
klepsydra: ~ **do jajek** egg timer
kler clergy
klerykalny clerical
kleszcz tick[2]
kleszcz|e 1 (*techn.*) forceps, pincer, pliers **2** (*zool.*) (*skorupiaka*) pincers IDM **w ~ach czegoś** in the grip of sth
klęczk|i IDM **na ~ach** on your knees
klęk-ać/nąć kneel (down)
klęsk|a calamity, defeat[2], disaster, rout noun; **~i żywiołowe** natural disasters IDM **powodzenia i ~i** ups and downs
klient/ka (*w sklepie, restauracji*) customer; (*w sklepie*) shopper; (*który często korzysta z danego sklepu, danej restauracji itp.*) patron; (*usługi*) client; **sklep stracił wielu stałych klientów** the shop lost a lot of custom
klientela clientele
klif cliff
klik click[2]
klika clique
klik-ać/nąć click[1]; (*komput.*) ~ **dwa razy** double-click
klimat 1 climate **2** (*nastrój, posmak itp.*) flavour[1]
klimatyczny climatic
klimatyzacja air conditioning
klimatyzator air conditioner
klimatyzowany air-conditioned
klin wedge[1]
klinga blade
kliniczny clinical
klinika clinic
klinować/za- wedge[2]
klips 1 (*do papieru*) clip[1] **2** (*do uszu*) clip-on earring
kloc 1 (*kamień, beton itp.*) block[1] **2** (*drewno*) log[1]
klocek building block
klomb flower bed
klon 1 (*bot.*) maple **2** (*w genetyce*) clone
klonina maple
klonować/s- clone verb
klonowy maple
klop bog
klown clown[1]
klozet lavatory
klub club[1]; ~ **książki** book club; ~ **młodzieżowy** youth club; ~ **nocny** (night)club[1]
klucz 1 (*i przen.*) key[1]; **pod ~em** under lock and key; **chować/trzymać pod ~em** lock[1], lock sth away; **zamykać kogoś (w pomieszczeniu) na ~** lock sb in/out **2** (*muz.*) clef **3** (*narzędzie*) ~ **płaski** spanner; ~ **do wkrętów z gniazdkiem sześciokątnym** Allen key IDM **lecieć ~em** fly in a V
kluczow|y key[3]; **słowo ~e** keyword
kluczyć weave
kluczyk → KLUCZ(1)
klusk|a: **rodzaj ~i** dumpling
kłacz|ek (**kłaczki**) (*z materiału na ubraniu*) fluff
kładka (*dla pieszych*) footbridge
kłamać/s-/o- lie[1]
kłam-ca/czucha liar
kłamliwie untruthfully
kłamliwy deceitful, untruthful
kłamstewko fib
kłamstwo lie noun, untruth; **niewinne/nieszkodliwe** ~ white lie
kłaniać/ukłonić się (*w pół*) bow[1]; (*głową*) nod IDM **~ (komuś od kogoś)** remember me to sb
kłap-ać/nąć: ~ **zębami** snap[1]
kłaść/położyć get, lay[1], place[2], put, put sth down, set[1]; ~ **coś z powrotem** put sth back; ~ **na miejsce** replace; ~ **dziecko spać** put sth down IDM **położyć czemuś kres** put a stop to sth, stop[1] sb/sth (from) doing sth | ~ **na kimś kreskę** give sb up, give up on sb
□ **kłaść/położyć się** lie[2], lie down; **nie ~** stay up
kłąb cloud[1], puff[2]; **puszczać kłęby** (*dymu*) puff[1]
kłębek curl[2]; **zwijać (się) w ~** coil[1] IDM **~ nerwów** nervous wreck
kłębić/za- się 1 (*dym*) billow **2** (*ludzie*) seethe (with sth)
kłoda log[1]
kłopot (także **kłopoty**) bother[2], difficulty, drag[2], hassle[1], predicament, pressure, problem, trouble[1], woe, worry[2]; **przepraszam za ~** I'm sorry to be a nuisance; **sprawiać ~** inconvenience verb, play (sb) up; **nie chcę ci sprawiać ~u** I don't want you to put yourself out
kłopotać/za- trouble[2]
kłopotliwa: ~ **sytuacja** jam[1]
kłopotliwie embarrassingly, inconveniently
kłopotliw|y awkward, difficult, disconcerting, inconvenient, troublesome; (*sytuacja*) messy, sticky; **~e położenie** mess[1], predicament
kłos ear
kłócić/po- się argue, have an argument, clash[1], fall out (with sb), feud verb, fight[1], have a fight[2], quarrel[2], row verb, have a row[3], wrangle verb; (*o drobiazgi*) bicker
kłódk|a padlock; **zamykać na ~ę** padlock verb
kłótliwy quarrelsome, stroppy
kłótni|a fight[2], quarrel[1], row[3], uproar, wrangle IDM **zaczynać ~ę** come to blows (with sb) (over sth)
kłuć/u- 1 (*igłą itp.*) jab[1], prick[1], stab[1]; (*ubranie itp.*) prickle[1] **2** (*ból*) sting[1]; (*skóra, oczy itp.*) prickle[1]
■ **kłujący** piercing[1], stabbing[2]; ~ **ból** stab of pain, stitch[1]
kłus trot[2]

kłusować 1 (/po-) (*koń*) trot[1] **2** (*polować nielegalnie*) poach
kłusowni-k/czka poacher
kłut|y: **rana ~a** stab wound
kmin cumin
kminek (*ziele*) caraway, cumin
knebel gag[1]
kneblować/za- gag[2]
kned|el: **rodzaj ~la** dumpling
knocić/s- cock sth up
knot wick
knowani|e intrigue[2]; **zbrodnicze ~a** conspiracy
knuć/u- conspire, hatch[1] sth (up), plot[2], scheme[2]
knur boar
knykieć knuckle[1]
koagulacja coagulation
koala: **(miś)** ~ koala
koalicja coalition
koalicyjny coalition
kobalt cobalt
kobaltowy: ~ **błękit** cobalt
kobieciarz womanizer
kobiecość femininity, womanhood
kobiecy feminine, womanly
kobierzec carpet
kobieta female[2], woman; ~ **żołnierz** servicewoman; ~ **interesu** businesswoman
kobieta-burmistrz mayoress
kobra cobra
kobyła mare
kobziarz piper
koc blanket[1]
kochać/po- love[2] IDM **jak Boga kocham!** cross my heart (and hope to die)
□ **kochać/za- się**: **w kimś** be keen on sb; **w sobie** fall in love with each other; **(z kimś)** make love (to sb)
■ **kochający** affectionate, doting, loving
kochanek lover
kochanie darling, dear[3], honey, love[1], luv, sweetheart
kochanka lover, mistress
kochan|y (*przym.*) beloved, dear[1], lovable; **moi ~i** (*zwracając się do grupy znajomych*) folk[1]
■ **kochan-y/a** (*rz.*) love[1]
koci feline IDM **~e oczy** (*przen.*) Catseyes
kociątko kitten
kocioł 1 (*do gotowania*) cauldron **2** (*przemysłowy*) furnace; ~ **parowy** boiler **3** (*muz.*) kettledrum; **(kotły)** timpani **4** ~ **erozyjny** pothole
kocmołuch slut
kocur tomcat
koczowniczy nomadic
koczowni-k/czka nomad
kod code[1]; ~ **bankowy** sort code; ~ **genetyczny** genetic code; ~ **kreskowy** bar code; ~ **pocztowy** postcode
kodeks code[1]; ~ **postępowania zawodowego** code of practice
kodować/za- code[2], encrypt
kodyfikować/s- codify
koedukacyjny co-educational, mixed
koegzystencja coexistence
koegzystować coexist
kofein|a caffeine; **bez ~y** decaffeinated
kognitywny (*psychologia itp.*) cognitive
kogucik cockerel
kogut (*ptak*) cock[1]
koić/u- calm[2], soothe
koja (*w statku*) berth; (*piętrowa*) bunk
kojarzyć/s- 1 (*fakty*) associate[1], connect **2** (*zrozumieć*) latch on (to sth), piece sth together **3** (*ludzi itp.*) match[2]; (*kogoś w pary*) pair sb off (with sb)
kojący restful, soothing, therapeutic
kok bun
kokaina cocaine
kokarda (także **kokardka**) bow[3]
kokieteryjny flirtatious
koklusz whooping cough
kokon cocoon[1]
kokos coconut
koks coke
koksiak brazier
koksownik brazier
koktajl cocktail; ~ **mleczny** milkshake
kolaboracja collaboration
kolaborant/ka collaborator
kolaborować collaborate
kolacja supper, tea; **uroczysta** ~ dinner party
kolan|o 1 (*anat.*) knee; **po ~a** knee-deep adv.; **u mamy na ~ach** on his mother's lap **2** (*rzeki*) twist[2]
kolarz cyclist
kolaż collage
kolba 1 (*wojsk.*) butt[2] **2** ~ **kukurydzy** corn on the cob **3** (*chem.*) flask
kolczasty prickly, spiky, thorny; **drut** ~ barbed wire
kolczyk earring; (*typu kuleczka lub wkrętka*) stud; (*w nosie*) nose stud
kolebać/za- się: **chodzić (drobnymi kroczkami), kolebiąc się** waddle
kolebka (*przen.*) the cradle of sth, the home[1] of sth
kolec 1 (*bot.*) thorn; (*mały*) prickle[2] **2** (*zool.*) spine; (*mały*) prickle[2] **3** (*na ogrodzeniu itp.*) spike
kolega friend, mate[1]; (*z klasy*) classmate; (*z pracy*) colleague, workmate; **koleżanki i koledzy ze studiów** fellow students
kolegium college
koleina rut
kole|j 1 (*szyny; system szyn*) railway **2** (*środek transportu*) rail; **~j jednoszynowa** monorail; **~j podziemna** underground[3] **3** (*w grze itp.*) go[2], rotation, turn[2]; **moje notatki są nie po ~i** my notes are all out of order; **po ~i** consecutively, in turn; **robić coś po ~i** take turns (at sth); **czekać na swoją ~j** wait your turn IDM **w naturalnej ~i rzeczy** in the normal course of events
kolej|ka 1 (*pociąg*) **~ka górska** (*w parku rozrywki*) roller coaster **2** (*w sklepie*) line[1], queue; **stać w ~ce** queue verb, stand in/on line; **ustawiać się w ~ce** line up (for sth), queue verb; **iść bez ~ki** jump the queue **3** (*w grze itp.*) go[2]; (*zamówienie alkoholu itp.*) round[4]; **stracić ~kę** miss a turn IDM (*przen.*) **w ~ce do czegoś** in line for sth
kolejno alternately, consecutively, respectively, in succession; **robić coś** ~ take turns (at sth); **zmieniać** ~ alternate[1] A with B, rotate
kolejnoś|ć sequence; **w dobrej ~ci** the right way round; **w odwrotnej ~ci** the other way round/around; **w pierwszej ~ci** first[2]
kolejn|y alternate[2], consecutive, successive; **~a część** sequel
kolejow|y rail, railway; **sieć ~a** rail, railway
kolekcja collection
kolekcjoner: ~ **znaczków** stamp collector
kolekcjonować collect[1]
kolendra coriander
koleś crony
koleżanka → KOLEGA
koleżeństwo comradeship, fellowship, friendship
kolęda carol
kolędnik carol singer
kolidować clash[1] (with sth), conflict[2] with sth, impinge on/upon sth
kolisty circular[1]
kolizja collision
kolka colic
kolokacja collocation, collocate
kolokwializm colloquialism
kolokwium test[1]
kolonia colony, settlement
kolonializm colonialism
kolonialny colonial
kolonizacja colonization
kolonizator colonist
kolonizować/s- colonize
kolor 1 (*barwa*) colour[1]; (*włosów itp.*) colouring; **(kolory)** (*na twarzy*) colour[1]; ~ **podstawowy** primary colour **2** (*karty*) suit[1]
koloratka dog collar
kolorować/po- colour[2]; (*zwł. ołówkiem*) colour sth in
kolorow|y (*telewizor itp.*) colour[1]; (*barwny*) coloured; (*barwny; i przen.*) colourful; **obrazki są ~e** the pictures are in colour
koloryt colour[1]
koloryzować romanticize
kolosalny colossal, jumbo[2], prodigious
kolumna 1 (*arch.*) column, pillar **2** (*głośnikowa*) speaker **3** (*pojazdów*) fleet
kołatać/za- flutter[1], palpitate
kołatka knocker
kołdra duvet, quilt
kołek 1 (*palik*) stake[1]; (*mały*) pin[1] **2** (*wieszak*) hook[1], peg[1]
kołnierz collar[2], neck
koło (*rz.*) **1** (*mat., geogr.*) circle[1]; ~ **podbiegunowe północne** Arctic noun, the Arctic Circle; ~ **podbiegunowe południowe** the Antarctic Circle; **zataczać** ~ encircle **2** (*obręcz*) hoop, ring[1] **3** (*pojazdu*) wheel[1] IDM ~ **ratunkowe** lifebelt
■ **koło** (*przyim.*) **1** (*w przestrzeni*) by, next to, past[3], past adv. **2** (*w czasie*) towards IDM **lub coś ~ tego** or so
kołować/za- taxi[2]
kołowrotek spinning wheel
kołowrót (*u wejścia*) turnstile
kołowy: **diagram** ~ pie chart
kołtun tangle
kołysać/za-/u- 1 (*w powietrzu*) sway, swing[1]; (*kolebkę itp.*) rock[2]; (*wiatr; na morzu itp.*) toss; **samolot się kołysał** it was a bumpy flight **2 (/u-)** lull[2]
□ **kołysać/za- się** (*na huśtawce*) swing[1]; (*drzewo*) sway, wave[2]; (*w fotelu*) rock[2]; (*na falach*) toss; (*statek, samolot*) pitch[2], roll[2]; (*dziecko*) jiggle
■ **kołyszący się** wiggly
kołysanka lullaby

kołyska cradle[1]
komandor commander
komandos commando
komar gnat, mosquito
kombajn combine harvester
kombatant/ka veteran
kombi estate car
kombinacja combination
kombinator/ka adventurer
kombinezon suit[1]; (*roboczy: z rękawami*) boiler suit, overalls[2]; (*bez rękawów*) dungarees; ~ **kosmonauty** spacesuit
kombinować 1 (*łączyć*) concoct **2** (**/wy-**) (*wymyślać*) contrive, work sth out **3** (*działać nieuczciwie*) get up to sth **4** (**/s-**) (*zdobyć/uzyskać coś z wysiłkiem*) wangle
komedia comedy
komedianctwo histrionics
komenda police station
komendant commandant
komentarz comment[1], commentary; ~ **czytany przez lektora** voice-over; **bez ~a** no comment
komentator/ka commentator; (*w TV/radio*) broadcaster
komentować/s- comment[2]; (*w TV/radio*) commentate
komercjalizacja commercialization
komercjalizm commercialism
komercjalizować/s- commercialize
komercyjny commercial[1]
kometa comet
kometka badminton
komfort comfort[1], convenience
komfortowy comfortable
komiczn|y comic[1], comical, humorous; **opera ~a** comic opera
komik comedian
komiks (*broszura*) comic[2]; (*TV*) cartoon
komin 1 (*arch.*) chimney **2** (*na statku*) funnel
kominek fireplace, hearth, open fire
kominiarz chimney sweep
komisariat police station
komisarz commissioner
komisja commission[1], committee
komitet committee
komiwojażer/ka rep
komizm comedy, humour[1]
komnata chamber
komoda chest of drawers
komora chamber; (*serca; w mózgu*) ventricle; ~ **gazowa** gas chamber
komorne rent[1]
komornik bailiff
komórka 1 (*biol.*) cell; ~ **jajowa** egg[1]; ~ **macierzysta** stem cell **2** (*telefon*) mobile phone
komórkowy (*biol.*) cellular
kompas compass
kompatybilność compatibility
kompatybilny compatible
kompensata compensation
kompensować/s- compensate, recompense, redeem; (*zwł. jakimś czynem*) make up for sth
kompetencj|a (**kompetencje**) remit; **~a władzy; obszar ~i władzy** jurisdiction
kompetentny capable, competent; (*nie marnujący czasu/wysiłków*) efficient; **nie czuję się ~, aby to skomentować** I don't feel qualified to comment
kompilacja compilation
kompilowanie compilation
kompleks 1 (*sklepów itp.*) complex[2]; ~ **sportowy** park[1] **2** (*psych.*) complex[2] (about sth), hang-up; ~ **niższości** inferiority complex
komplement compliment[1]
IDM **prawić komuś ~y** compliment[2], pay sb a compliment, pay a compliment to sb
komplet 1 (*zestaw*) set[2]; (*sportowy itp.*) kit[1] **2** (*stroju*) ensemble **3** (*ludzi na przyjęciu itp.*) complement[1]; (*na posiedzeniu*) quorum
kompletnie clean[3], completely, entirely, plain[3], quite, raving adv., totally, truly, utterly, well and truly, wholly
kompletny complete[1], dead[1], direct[1], out-and-out, raving, right[1], total[1], utter[1]
kompletować/s- complete[2]
komplikować/s- complicate, confuse
komponent component; **egzamin z historii podzielony jest na trzy ~y** the history exam is divided into three papers
komponować/s- 1 (*muz.*) compose, write; (*muzykę do tekstu*) set[1] **2** (*zestaw potraw*) put sth together
kompost compost
kompot compote
kompozycja 1 (*muz.*) composition **2** (*kwiatowa itp.*) arrangement
kompozytor/ka composer; (*piosenek*) songwriter
kompresja compression
kompromis compromise[1], give and take, trade-off; **iść na** ~ compromise[2]; (*w sprawie ceny/płatności*) split the difference
kompromitacja discredit noun, disrepute
kompromitować/s- discredit, disgrace[2]
□ **kompromitować/s- się** compromise[2] yourself, disgrace[2] yourself
kompromitujący compromising, disgraceful
komputer computer; ~ **stacjonarny** desktop computer; ~ **osobisty** PC; **przez** ~ online adv.
komputerowy online
komputeryzacja computerization
komputeryzować/s- computerize
komuna commune
komunalny municipal; ~ **dom mieszkalny** council house
komunał cliché
komunia communion, the sacrament
komunikacja 1 ~ **miejska** public transport **2** (*porozumiewanie się*) communication
komunikat bulletin, communication, communiqué
komunikatywny communicative
komunikować/za- communicate, impart
komunist-a/ka communist
komunistyczny communist
komunizm communism
konar bough, limb
koncentracja concentration; ~ **na jednym celu** single-mindedness
koncentrować/s- concentrate, fix[1], focus[1]
□ **koncentrować/s- się** concentrate, focus[1], focus on sth; (*artykuł itp.*) centre on/around sb/sth; (*na zadaniu, sprawie itp.*) zero in on sb/sth
koncentryczny concentric
koncepcja conception, theory
konceptualizm conceptual art
konceptualizować/s- conceptualize
konceptualn|y: sztuka ~a conceptual art
koncern concern[2]
koncert 1 (*wydarzenie*) concert; ~ **muzyków pop lub jazzowych** gig; ~ **promenadowy** prom **2** (*utwór*) concerto
koncertowy (*płyta, nagranie*) live[2]
koncertyna concertina
koncesj|a concession, franchise; **wydawać ~ę** license[1]
kondensować/s- condense
kondolencje condolence
kondolencyjny: **list** ~ letter of sympathy
konduktor/ka conductor, guard[1]
kondycj|a fitness, form[1], health, shape[1]; **w dobrej ~i** in shape; **być nadal w dobrej ~i** going strong; **w złej/słabej ~i** out of shape, unfit
kondygnacja floor[1], tier; ~ **schodów** flight of stairs
koneksja connection
koneser/ka connoisseur
konewka watering can
konfederacja confederacy, confederation
konfederacki confederate[2]
konfederat confederate[1]
konferansjer compère, entertainer
konferansjerk|a: **prowadzić ~ę** compère verb
konferencja conference, meeting, seminar; ~ **prasowa** briefing, press conference
konfesjonał confessional
konfetti confetti
konfident/ka informer
konfiguracja configuration
konfirmacja confirmation
konfirmować confirm
konfiskata confiscation; (*mienia*) expropriation
konfiskować/s- confiscate; (*mienie*) expropriate
konfitura (także **konfitury**) jam[1]
konflikt clash[2], conflict[1], friction, strife; ~ **pokoleń** the generation gap; **wchodzić w ~ z kimś/czymś** (*po zrobieniu czegoś złego*) fall foul of sb/sth
konformist-a/ka conformist
konfrontacja confrontation; (*w celu rozpoznania przestępcy*) identification parade
konfrontacyjny confrontational
konfrontować/s-: ~ **czyjeś stanowisko** (*w jakiejś sprawie*) tackle[1] sb about sth
konglomeracja conglomeration
konglomerat conglomerate
kongres congress, convention
kongresmen Congressman
kongresmenka Congresswoman
kongresowy congressional
koniak cognac
koniczyna clover; ~ **biała** shamrock
koniec 1 (*w czasie*) close[2], end[1], ending; ~ **roku** the turn of the century/year; ~ **dziewiętnastego**

wieku the late nineteenth century; **bez końca** endless, endlessly, indefinitely, interminably, no end of sth, unending; **w końcu** after all, in the end, eventually, in the long run, finally, ultimately; **na końcu** last; **na samym końcu** lastly; **na** ~ finally; **pod** ~ **posiłku** at the end of the meal; **do końca** up; **od początku do końca** from start to finish; **doprowadzać do końca** finalize; **zbliżać się do końca** draw to a close; **mówili bez końca** the speeches went on and on
2 (*w przestrzeniu*) bottom[1], end[1], extremity; (*książki*) back[1]; (*palca itp.*) tip[1]; **grubszy** ~ (*broni lub narzędzia*) butt[2]; **drugi/trzeci itd. od końca** last/next but one, two, etc. **3** (*śmierć*) death IDM ~! that is it | ~ **końców** at the end of the day | **mieć coś na końcu języka** on the tip of your tongue

koniecznie necessarily, vitally; ~ **coś zrobić** be sure to do sth; ~ **wróć przed jedenastą** make sure you are back home by 11 o'clock
koniecznoś|ć must[2], necessity; **~ć życiowa** a fact of life; **w razie ~ci** at a pinch; **bez ~ci (czegoś)** without recourse (to sth)
konieczny essential, imperative, indispensable, necessary, vital
konik 1 hobby, hobby horse **2** (*zool.*) ~ **polny** grasshopper; ~ **morski** sea horse
koniugacja conjugation
koniugować conjugate
koniunktura situation; **dobra** ~ prosperity
koniuszek extremity, tip[1]; (*ołówka*) stub; ~ **palca** fingertip
konkluzja conclusion
konkret (**konkrety**) the nitty-gritty
konkretny concrete[1], particular; (*dowód*) solid[1]; (*przedstawiający nieprzyjemną rzeczywistość*) gritty
konkretyzować/s- specify
konkubina|t: **żyć w ~cie** cohabit
konkurencja rivalry; (*wydarzenie sportowe*) event
konkurencyjność competitiveness
konkurencyjny competitive
konkurent/ka competitor, opposition, rival[1]; (**konkurent**) (*do ręki młodej damy*) suitor
konkurować compete, be in competition with sb
konkurs competition, contest[1]; ~ **piękności** beauty pageant
konnica cavalry
konno on horseback
konny mounted
konopie hemp
konotacja connotation
konsekracja consecration
konsekrować consecrate
konsekwencj|a 1 (*skutek*) consequence, corollary; **w ~i** consequently **2** (*spójność logiczna itp.*) consistency
konsekwentny consistent
konserwacja conservation, maintenance
konserwatyst-a/ka conservative[2]
konserwatywny conservative[1]
konserwatyzm conservatism
konserwować 1 (**/za-**) (*żywność*) preserve; (*przez solenie/suszenie/wędzenie*) cure[1] **2** (*zabytek*) conserve **3** (*narzędzie*) maintain
konserwowy canned, tinned
konserwujący: **środek** ~ preservative
konserwy convenience food
konsola console[2]
konsolidacja consolidation
konsolidować/s- (się) consolidate
konsorcjum consortium, syndicate
konspiracja conspiracy
konspirować conspire
konsternacja bewilderment, consternation, dismay
konsternować/s- dismay verb, perplex, rattle[1]
konstrukcja construction, design[1], framework
konstruktor/ka: **konstruktor maszyn** machinist
konstruktywny constructive, positive
konstruować/s- construct, structure[2]
konstytucja constitution
konstytucyjny constitutional
konsul consul
konsularny consular
konsulat consulate
konsultacja consultancy, consultation
konsultant/ka consultant; **lekarz konsultant** consultant
konsultować/s- się consult
konsument/ka consumer; (*w restauracji*) diner
konsumować/s- (*żywność*) consume
konsumpcja consumption; ~ **towarów** (*ekon.*) consumerism
konsumpcjonistyczny consumerist
konsumpcjonizm consumerism
konsumpcyjn|y consumerist; **towary ~e** consumer goods
konsylium consultation
konsystencja consistency
kontak|t 1 z kimś communication, contact[1], liaison; (**kontakty**) relationship, relations; **z czymś** exposure; **~ty** (*książka adresowa*) address book; **być w ~cie z kimś/czymś** be in communication with sb/sth, keep track of sb/sth; **tracić ~t z kimś/czymś** lose track of sb/sth; (*być/nie być*) **w ~cie** in/out of touch (with sb); **mieć ~t z czymś** be exposed to sth; **nawiązywać ~t (z kimś)** make contact (with sb) **2** (*elektr.*) connection
kontaktować/s- się communicate, contact[2], reach[1]; **z kimś (w sprawie czegoś)** get on to sb (about sth)
kontaktowy: **sport** ~ contact sport
kontekst context; (*społeczny itp.*) matrix
kontemplacja contemplation
kontemplować contemplate
kontener container; ~ **na butelki do zwrotu** bottle bank
kontinuum continuum
kon|to account[1]; **~to bieżące** current account; **~to depozytowe** deposit account; **mieć ~to w banku** bank[2] (with/at…) IDM **mieć coś na swoim ~cie** have sth to your credit | **na swoim ~cie** under your belt
kontra versus
kontrabas double bass
kontrakt contract[1]
kontraktowy contractual
kontralt contralto
kontrapunkt counterpoint; **wysoki** ~ descant
kontrapunktowy (*muz.*) contrapuntal
kontrast contrast[1]; (*przeciwieństwo*) antithesis (także **kontrasty**) juxtaposition
kontrastować/s- contrast[2], juxtapose
kontrastowy contrasting
kontrasygnować/s- (*czek itp.*) countersign
kontratak counter-attack
kontratakować counter-attack verb; **kogoś** strike back (at/against sb)
kontratenor counter-tenor
kontrnatarcie counter-attack
kontrol|a check[2], inspection, supervision; (*ksiąg rachunkowych*) audit; **~a paszportów** immigration; **~a urodzeń** birth control; **~a zbrojeń** arms control; **punkt ~i** control[1]; **przejąć ~ę nad czymś** take charge of sth; **pod ~ą** under control, in hand; **poza czyjąś ~ą** out of your hands; **pod dokładną ~ą** under close scrutiny
kontroler/ka controller, inspector; ~ **biletów** ticket collector, inspector; ~ **poprawnego parkowania pojazdów** traffic warden; ~ **ruchu powietrznego** air traffic controller
kontrolować/s- 1 (*sprawdzać*) check on sb/sth, check up on sb, inspect, monitor[2], supervise **2** (*zasady, prawa itp.*) regulate
kontrolowany controlled
kontrowersja controversy
kontrowersyjny controversial, divisive
kontrrewolucja counter-revolution
kontuar bar[1], counter[1]
kontur contour, outline[2]
kontynent continent, mainland
kontynentalny continental
kontyngent quota; ~ **wojsk** contingent
kontynuacja continuation, follow-up
kontynuować carry on (with sth/doing sth), carry sth on, continue, continue, get on with sth, go on (doing sth) (with sth), (doing sth), proceed; (*rozmowę*) pursue; **uparcie coś** ~ push ahead/forward (with sth), press ahead/forward/on (with sth)
konurbacja conurbation
konwalia lily of the valley
konwencja convention
konwencjonalny conventional, orthodox
konwersacja conversation
konwersacyjny conversational
konwersować converse[1]
konwojent guard[1]
konwój convoy, escort[1], guard[1]
konwulsj|a convulsion; **przyprawiać o ~e** convulse
konwulsyjny convulsive
koń 1 horse; ~ **wyścigowy** racehorse **2** (*szachy*) knight IDM ~ **mechaniczny** horsepower | **robić kogoś w konia** mess sb about/around, muck sb about/around, pull sb's leg
końcow|y eventual, final[1], ultimate[1]; (*uwagi itp.*) closing; (*z dwóch*) latter; **~a/y stacja/przystanek** terminus; **~y termin** cut-off
końcówka end[1], ending; ~ **fleksyjna** inflection; ~ **meczu** the closing stages of the game
kończyć/s-/u-/za- 1 bring sth to a close/an end, come to an end, close[1], end[2], finish[1], finish (up) with sth, stop[1], terminate; (*działalność czegoś*) wind sth down/up; **z kimś/czymś** be

through (with sb/sth); **gdzieś/w jakiejś sytuacji** finish up…; **szybko** ~ polish sth off; **pomyślnie coś zakończyć** get through (sth); **skończyć pracę** knock off (sth); ~ **szkołę/studia wyższe (licencjackie)** graduate[2]; ~ **list/program** sign off; **kończąc** finally **2 dzisiaj kończy dziesięć lat** he's ten years old today; **skończy 21 lat w czerwcu** he'll be 21 in June □ **kończyć/s-/za- się 1** cease, close[1], come/draw to an end, end[2], finish[1], stop[1], terminate; **czymś** culminate in sth; (*semestr szkoły itp.*) break up; **nie kończący się** endless; **skończyć się tylko na ostrzeżeniu** get off with just a warning **2** (*zapasy, produkty itp.*) dry up, run low (on sth); (*i czas*) run out; **mleko się skończyło** we're out of milk

kończyna limb

kooperacja cooperation

koordynacja coordination

koordynator coordinator

koordynować/s- coordinate[1]

kopać 1 (**/kopnąć**) (*nogą*) kick[1]; (*mocno*) boot[2] **2** (**/wy-**) (*łopatą itp.*) dig[1]; (*norę*) burrow[1]

kopalnia 1 mine[2]; ~ **odkrywkowa** quarry[1]; ~ **węgla** coal mine, colliery; ~ **złota** gold mine **2** (*przen.*) gold mine

koparka excavator

kopcący smoky

koper dill; ~ **włoski** fennel

koperta envelope

kopia copy[1], duplicate[2], replica, reproduction; (*skrót: w liście*) cc; ~ **dokumentacyjna** hard copy; ~ **kserograficzna** Xerox; ~ **przez kalkę** carbon copy

kopiasty (*łyżka*) heaped

kopiec mound

kopiować/s- 1 (*robić odbitkę*) copy[2], duplicate[1], imitate, replicate; ~ **na kserografie** photocopy verb, run sth off, xerox verb **2 nielegalnie** ~ (*nagranie, film*) pirate[2]; (*przepisywać tekst*) lift sth (from sb/sth)

kopnąć → KOPAĆ

kopniak kick[2]

kopnięcie kick[2]

kopnięty wacky

koprodukować co-produce

kopulacja copulation

kopulasty domed

kopulować copulate

kopuł|a dome; **nakryty ~ą** domed

kopyto hoof

kora bark[1]

koral coral

korale beads

koralik bead

koralowy coral

Koran the Koran

korba handle[2]

korcić: **kogoś do czegoś** be bursting to do sth

kordon cordon[1]; **otaczać i zamykać ~em** cordon sth off; **przejść przez ~ pikietujących** cross the picket line

korek 1 (*do butelki*) cork, stopper **2** (*do wanny*) plug[1] **3** (*komun.*) gridlock, jam[1], tailback, traffic jam; **utknąć w korku** get caught in a traffic jam **4** (*w podeszwie buta sportowego*) stud

korekcyjny corrective

korekt|a 1 (*poprawka*) correction, revision; **robić ~ę** proofread **2** (*strony wydrukowane*) proofs

korektor 1 (**korektor/ka**) proofreader **2** (*w płynie*) correction fluid, Tippex

korelacja correlation

korelować/s- correlate

korepetycja tutorial; (**korepetycje**) tuition

korepetytor/ka tutor

korespondencja correspondence, mail, post[1]

korespondencyjn|y: **głosowanie ~e** postal vote

korespondent/ka correspondent; ~ **zagraniczn-y/a** correspondent

korespondować correspond

korkociąg corkscrew

korniszon gherkin

korodować/s- corrode

korona crown[1]

koronacja coronation

koroner coroner

koronka lace[1]

koronkowy 1 (*z koronki*) lace[1] **2** (*jak koronka*) lacy

koronować/u- crown[2]

korowód pageant

korozj|a corrosion; **powodujący ~ę** corrosive

korozyjny corrosive

korporacja corporation

korpus 1 (*w wojsku itp.*) corps; ~ **dyplomatyczny** diplomatic corps **2** (*anat.*) trunk **3** (*tekstów itp.*) corpus

korsarstwo piracy

korsarz pirate[1]

korumpować/s- corrupt[2]

korupcja corruption

korygować/s- correct[2], rectify, revise

korygujący corrective

korytarz corridor, hall, passage; (*powietrzny*) lane

koryto 1 (*naczynie*) trough **2** (*rzeki itp.*) bed[1]

korzeń root[1]

korzystać/s- take advantage of sb/sth, benefit[2], profit[2]; (*z prawa*) exercise[2]; **skorzystać ze sposobności** grab the opportunity of sth, take the opportunity to do sth; **skorzystać (skwapliwie) z czegoś** seize (on/upon) sth; ~ **z sytuacji** cash in (on sth); **skorzystać z czyjejś rady** take sb's advice; **czy mogę skorzystać z twojego telefonu?** could I use your phone?; **możesz swobodnie ~ z parteru** you can have the freedom of the ground floor; **nic nie skorzystam, jeśli zostanę na tej posadzie** I've got nothing to gain by staying in this job

korzystn|y advantageous, beneficial, favourable; (*finansowo*) lucrative, profitable; (*wygląd itp.*) flattering; (*opinia*) high[1]; **być dla kogoś/czegoś ~ym** do sb a/the world of good

korzyść advantage, benefit[1], expediency, gain[2], mileage; **na czyjąś** ~ in sb's favour; **działać na czyjąś** ~ be loaded in favour of sb/sth; **odnosić** ~ gain[1] (by/from sth/doing sth)

kos blackbird

kosa scythe

kosaciec iris

kosiarka (*do trawy*) lawnmower, mower

kosić/s- (*trawę*) mow

kosmaty hairy, shaggy

kosmetyczka 1 (*osoba*) beautician **2** (*torebka*) sponge bag

kosmetyczny cosmetic[2]

kosmetyk cosmetic[1]

kosmiczny cosmic

kosmit-a/ka extraterrestrial

kosmolog cosmologist

kosmologia cosmology

kosmologiczny cosmological

kosmonauta spaceman

kosmonautka spacewoman

kosmopolityczny cosmopolitan

kosmos the cosmos, space[1], the universe

kosmyk wisp

kostium 1 (*damski*) outfit, suit[1]; ~ **kąpielowy** swimsuit; **dwuczęściowy ~ kąpielowy** bikini **2** (*teatr itp.*) costume

kostk|a 1 (*anat.*) (*u ręki*) knuckle[1]; (*u nogi*) ankle **2** (*cukru*) lump[1]; (*mydła*) bar[1]; **~i brukowe** cobbles; **~a lodu** ice cube **3** (*do gry*) dice; **~a do gry w domino** domino **4 ~a do gry na instrumentach muzycznych** plectrum

kostnica morgue, mortuary

kostnieć/s- (*przen.*) fossilize, ossify

kostyczny caustic

kosz basket; ~ **na zakupy** shopping basket; ~ **z pokrywą** hamper[2]; ~ **na śmieci** bin, litter bin, waste-paper basket; ~ **na brudną bieliznę** clothes/laundry basket

IDM ~ **szczęścia** lucky dip

koszara fold[2]

koszary barracks, quarters

koszerny kosher

koszmar nightmare

koszmarny ghastly

koszt (także **koszty**) cost[1], expense(s), price[1]; **~y sądowe** costs[1]; **~y utrzymania** the cost of living, upkeep; **na ~ firmy** on the house

IDM **czyimś ~em** at sb's expense | **~em czegoś** at the expense of sth

kosztorys costing, estimate[1], quotation; **przedstawiać** ~ quote

kosztować 1 cost[2]; **ile kosztował twój bilet?** how much was your ticket?; **ile kosztuje bilet do Leeds?** what's the fare to Leeds? **2** (**/s-**) (*potrawę*) **3** have a taste of sth, sample verb, taste[2], try[1]

kosztowność (**kosztowności**) valuables; (*biżuteria*) jewellery

kosztowny costly, expensive, pricey, valuable

koszula shirt; ~ **nocna** nightdress

koszulka 1 singlet **2** (*przykrycie*) jacket

koszyk basket

koszykówk|a basketball; **rodzaj ~i** netball

kościec skeleton[1]

kościelny ecclesiastical

kościół (także **Kościół**) church; (*Metodystów itp.*) chapel; **Kościół anglikański** the Church of England

kościsty angular, bony; (*kolana*) knobbly

kość bone[1]; ~ **łokciowa** ulna; ~ **ogonowa** coccyx, tailbone; ~ **piszczelowa** tibia; ~ **policzkowa** cheekbone; ~ **promieniowa** radius; ~ **ramienna** humerus; ~ **strzałkowa**

fibula; ~ **szczękowa** jawbone; ~ **udowa** femur, thigh bone; ~ **słoniowa** ivory IDM **dostać od życia parę razy w ~** suffer some hard knocks in your life
koślawy lopsided
kot cat; (*samiec*) tomcat; ~ **perski** Persian
kotara curtain
kotek a little cat
kotka female cat
kotlet (*z kością*) chop[2], cutlet; ~ **mielony** rissole; ~ **mielony wołowy** beefburger; ~ **rybny** fishcake
kotlina hollow[2], valley
kotlist-a/ka timpanist
kotłować/za- się seethe
kotwica anchor[1]
kotwiczyć/za- anchor[2]
kowal 1 (*rzemieślnik*) blacksmith **2** (*kujon*) anorak
kowalność malleability
kowalny malleable
kowboj cowboy
koza goat, nanny goat
kozi: ~**a bródka** goatee
kozioł billy goat, goat IDM ~ **ofiarny** scapegoat | **stół na kozłach** trestle table
koziołek somersault
Koziorożec (*znak zodiaku*) Capricorn
koźlę kid[1]
kożuch 1 (*skóra*) sheepskin; (*płaszcz*) sheepskin coat/jacket **2** (*z brudu*) scum; ~ **żużlowy** dross
kożuszek (*na mleku itp.*) skin[1]
kółk|o 1 circle[1], ring[1]; ~**o do kluczy** key ring; **w ~o** round[2] **2** (*grupa*) ~**o dramatyczne** drama society **3** (*u fotela itp.*) castor IDM ~**o i krzyżyk** noughts and crosses
kpić/za-/o- jeer, mock[1], poke fun at sb/sth, scoff
kpina crack[2], jeer noun; (**kpiny**) farce, mockery, ridicule
krab crab
krach (*fin.*) collapse[2], meltdown, slump[2]; ~ **na giełdzie** crash[1]
kraciasty checked
kradzież theft; ~ **towarów ze sklepu** shoplifting; ~ **z włamaniem** breaking and entering, burglary
kraina: ~ **z bajki** wonderland
kraj 1 country, land[1]; ~ **ojczysty** homeland; **do ~u** homeward; **do/w ~u** home[3]; **po całym ~u** nationally, nationwide adv. **2** (*skraj*) margin
krajać/po- cut[1], slice[2]; (*mięso itp.*) carve
krajobraz country, landscape[1], scenery; ~ **wiejski** the countryside; **tworzyć ~** landscape[2]
krajowiec native[2]
krajowy domestic, home[2], internal
krajoznawcz|y: **wycieczka ~a** ramble[2]
krakers cracker
kraksa smash[2]
kran tap[2]; **woda z ~u** tap water
kranówka (także **kranówa**) tap water
krańcowy extreme, ultimate[1]
krasnal gnome
krasnoludek dwarf[1], elf
krasomów-ca/czyni orator
krasomówstwo elocution
kraść/u-/s-/wy- rob, steal, walk off with sth; (*cudze myśli*) poach
krat|a 1 (*zamknięcie*) bar[1]; (*okratowanie*) grating, grille; ~**a przed kominkiem** fender, fireguard **2** (także **kratka**) (*wzór*) check[2]; **w ~ę** checked, chequered **3** (*diagram*) grid IDM **za ~ami** behind bars
krater crater
kratka 1 (*do kwiatów itp.*) lattice **2** (*wzór*) → KRATA
kratkowany checked
kratownica lattice
kraul crawl[2]
krawat tie[2]
krawcowa dressmaker; (*męski*) tailor[1]
krawę|dź 1 edge[1], margin; ~**dź drogi** verge[1] **2** (*filiżanki, łyżki*) rim; (*filiżanki*) lip **3** (*górska*) ridge IDM **być na ~dzi kłótni** be on a collision course (with sb/sth)
krawężnik kerb
krawiec (*męski*) tailor[1]
krawiectwo dressmaking
krąg 1 circle[1], ring[1] **2** (*światła*) pool[1]
krążek 1 (*płyta CD*) disc **2** (*blok*) pulley **3** ~ **hokejowy** puck
krążenie: ~ **krwi** circulation
krążeniowy cardiovascular
krążownik cruiser
krążyć 1 (*poruszać się wokół*) circle[2]; (*samochód itp.*) cruise[2]; (*osoba: czekać*) hover; ~ **w powietrzu** wheel[2] **2** (*krew; wiadomość itp.*) circulate; **krąży pogłoska, że…** it is rumoured that… **3** (*butelka itp.*) go round/around/about
krech|a black mark IDM **mieć ~ę u kogoś** be in sb's bad books
kreda chalk[1]
kredens dresser, sideboard
kredka pencil[1]; ~ **świecowa** crayon; ~ **do oczu** eyeliner; ~ **do ust** lipstick
kredo creed
kredow|y 1 chalk[1] **2 na ~ym papierze** glossy
kredyt account[1], credit[1], loan; ~ **hipoteczny** mortgage
kredytodawca creditor
krem (*do rąk itp.*) cream[1], lotion; ~ **do rąk** hand cream; ~ **do twarzy** face cream; ~ **nawilżający** moisturizer; ~ **pielęgnacyjny** conditioner; ~ **z filtrem przeciwsłonecznym** suncream, sunscreen; ~ **z filtrem przeciwsłonecznym o najwyższym czynniku ochrony** sunblock; ~ **do golenia** shaving cream/foam
kremacj|a cremation; **poddawać ~i** cremate
krematorium crematorium
kremować/s- cremate
kremowy 1 (*z kremem*) cream[2], creamy **2 kolor** ~ cream noun
Kreol/ka Creole
kreolski: **język** ~ Creole
kreować create
krepa (*tkanina, kauczuk*) crêpe
krepina (*bibuła*) crêpe paper
kres limit[1] IDM **położyć czemuś ~** put an end/a stop to sth, stop[1] | **u ~u sił** on your knees | **u ~u wytrzymałości** at the end of your tether
kresk|a mark[2]; (*piórem itp.*) stroke[1]
kreślarz draughtsman
kreślić/za- (*nanosić na wykres itp.*) plot[2]
kret (*i przen.*) mole
kreton calico
kretowisko molehill
kretyn/ka cretin, moron, nana
kretyński moronic
krew blood; **rozlana/zakrzepła ~** gore[1]; IDM ~ **mnie zalała** I saw red | **mieć coś we krwi** have sth in your blood
krewetka prawn, shrimp
krewn-y/a blood relation, relation, relative[2]; (**krewni**) folk[1], kindred, kinsfolk; **najbliż-szy/si krewn-y/i** next of kin; **krewni żony lub męża** in-laws
kręcenie (się) spin[2], swirl noun; **kręcenie biodrami** wiggle noun
kręcić 1 (**/za-/s-**) (*wokół osi*) swirl, twirl, twist[1], whirl[1], wriggle sth (about/around); **skręcić gwałtownie** wrench[1] sb/sth (away, off, etc.); ~ **palcami** (*np. nerwowo/w roztargnieniu*) twiddle (with) sth **2** (**/po-; /za-**) (*korbą, gałką itp.*) turn[1]; (*korbą itp.*) wind[3] **3** (**/za-; /po-**) (*włosy*) curl[1] **4** (*nie mówić wprost*) beat about/around the bush, fudge[2], hedge[2] **5** (**/na-**) (*film*) shoot[1] IDM ~ **na coś nosem** turn your nose up at sth | ~ **głową** shake your head
□ **kręcić się 1** (**/za-**) (*wokół osi*) swirl, turn[1], twirl, whirl[1] **2** (*chodzić*) **koło kogoś/czegoś** hover; ~ **w pobliżu** stick around; ~ **bez celu** mess about/around, mill about/around **3** (*nie siedzieć spokojnie*) fidget, wriggle; (*nie móc ustać spokojnie*) shuffle[1]; (*z powodu skrępowania/zawstydzenia*) squirm **4** (*rzeka itp.*) twist[1], wind[3] **5** (**/po-; /za-**) (*włosy*) curl[1] IDM ~ **w głowie** spin, swim; (*np. z szoku, nadmiaru wrażeń*) reel[2]
kręcon|y (*włosy*) curly; ~**e schody** spiral staircase
kręg (*med.*) vertebra
kręgarski osteopathic
kręgarstwo osteopathy
kręgarz osteopath
kręg|iel skittle; (**kręgle**) skittles; **gra w ~le** bowling, tenpin bowling
kręgielnia bowling alley
kręgosłup backbone, spine; (*osoba*) **bez ~a** spineless
kręgowiec (*biol.*) vertebrate
kręgowy spinal
krępować/s- constrain, tie sb down
■ **krępujący** awkward
□ **krępować się** tie yourself down IDM **nie ~ (robić czegoś)** feel free (to do sth)
krępulec tourniquet
krępy chunky, stocky
kręty (*ścieżka*) tortuous, winding
krnąbrność insubordination, unruliness
krnąbrny insubordinate, unruly
krochmal starch
krochmalić/wy-/po- starch verb
krocionóg millipede
krocze crotch
kroczyć march[1], pace[2], step[2]
kroić/po-/s- cut[1]
krok 1 (*ruch*) move[2], pace[1], step[1]; ~ **spacerowy** walk[2]; **wielki ~** stride[2]; **stawiać wielkie ~i** stride[1]; **posuwać (się) ~ po ~u** inch[2] forward/past/through, etc. **2** (*miara*) measure[2], step[1] IDM ~ **po ~u** step by step | **o ~ od sławy** on the brink of becoming famous
krokiet croquet
krokiew rafter
krokodyl crocodile
krokus crocus
kromka slice[1]
kronika chronicle; ~ **szkolna** yearbook; ~ **towarzyska** gossip column

kropelka drop[2], globule; (*gęstej cieczy*) blob; (*mleka do kawy itp.*) dash[1]; (*whisky itp.*) tot[1]; (*potu*) bead
kropić/po-/s- sprinkle
krop|ka 1 dot[1], spot[1] **2** (*interpunkcja*) full stop IDM **być w ~ce** be in a quandary | **znaleźć się w ~ce** be at your wits' end
kropkować/wy- dot[2]
kropkowan|y be dotted with; **linia ~a** dotted line
kropla drip[2], drop[2]; (*perfum, farby*) dab[2]; (*potu*) bead; (**krople**) (*med.*) drops[2]; ~ **deszczu** raindrop IDM ~ **w morzu** a drop in the bucket/ocean
kroplomierz dropper
kroplówka drip[2]
krosno loom[2]
krosta pimple, spot[1]
krostowaty spotty
krowa cow
król king; **święto Trzech Króli** Epiphany
królestwo kingdom, realm
królewicz prince
królewsk|i majestic, regal, royal; **Wasza Królewska Mość** Your Majesty, Your Royal Highness; **po ~u** majestically
królica doe
króliczek bunny
królik rabbit IDM ~ **doświadczalny** guinea pig
królowa queen; ~ **matka** the queen mother
krótk|i 1 (*czas*) brief[1], fleeting, short[1]; **~ie spodnie** shorts **2** (*dystans*) little[1], short[1] IDM **~ie spięcie** short circuit
krótko briefly, fleetingly; **na** ~ briefly IDM ~ **mówiąc** in short, the short answer is... | ~ **i węzłowato** in a nutshell
krótkofalowy short wave
krótkoterminowy short-term
krótkotrwałość brevity
krótkotrwały ephemeral, fitful, fleeting, short-lived
krótkowidz: **jestem ~em** I'm short-sighted
krótkowzroczny short-sighted
krówka (*cukierek*) fudge[1]
krtań larynx, voice box
kruchta porch
kruchy (*szkło itp.*) fragile; (*paznokieć itp.*) brittle; (*herbatnik itp.*) crisp[1]; (*ser itp.*) crumbly; (*pieczeń*) tender[1]; (*regał itp.*) flimsy
krucjata crusade
krucyfiks crucifix
kruczek snag[1]
kruczy raven
kruk raven IDM **czarny jak** ~ jet black
kruszyć/po-/roz- (się) crumble
krużganek cloister
krwawić bleed; (*poważnie*) haemorrhage verb
■ **krwawienie** bleeding; ~ **z nosa** nosebleed
krwawy bloodstained, bloody, gory
krwinka corpuscle; ~ **biała** white blood cell; ~ **czerwona** red blood cell
krwiobieg bloodstream
krwiodawca blood donor
krwiożerczy bloodthirsty, ferocious
krwisty (*befsztyk*) rare
krwotok haemorrhage; **mieć** ~ haemorrhage verb
kryć 1 (/u-) (*fakty*) cover sth up **2** (*sport: przeciwnika*) mark[1]
□ **kryć się** lurk; **za czymś** lie behind sth
kryjówka hiding place, lair; (*zwł. przestępcy*) den, hideout; (*broni itp.*) cache[1]; (*dla obserwatorów ptaków itp.*) hide[2]
krykiet cricket
kryminalistyczny forensic
kryminał 1 (*powieść*) detective story, whodunnit **2** (*więzienie*) nick[1]
krypta crypt, vault[1]
krystalicznie: ~ **czysty** crystal clear
krystalizować/s- się (*i przen.*) crystallize
kryształ crystal
kryształow|y crystal; **~a kula** crystal ball
kryterium criterion, gauge[1], standard[1], yardstick
krytyczn|y 1 (*uwaga*) critical, damning, disapproving, judgemental **2** (*ważny; poważny*) critical; **~a sytuacja** emergency; **pacjent w stanie ~ym** a critically ill patient; **nie jest już w stanie ~ym** now he's off the danger list
krytyk critic, reviewer; ~ **filmowy** film critic
krytyka criticism; (*tylko negatywna*) flak; (*pisana*) critique
krytykować/s- criticize, fault[2]; (*nieform.*) bash[1], get at sb, have a go at sb, knock[1], run sb/sth down; (*ostro*) censure; **być ostro krytykowanym** come in for severe criticism
kryzys crisis, depression
krzaczasty bushy
krzak bush; ~ **pomidora** tomato plant
krzątać się bustle[1]
krzem silicon
krzemień flint
krzemowy: ~ **układ scalony** silicon chip
krzepa brawn
krzepki burly, hefty, robust, rugged, sturdy, vigorous
krzepkość sturdiness
krzepnąć/s- (*woda itp.*) solidify; (*galaretka itp.*) set[1]; (*krew itp.*) congeal, coagulate
■ **krzepnięcie** coagulation
krzesać/s-/wy- strike[1]
krzesełko: **wysokie ~ do sadzania małych dzieci przy stole** high chair
krzesiwo flint
krzesło chair[1], place[1]; (**krzesła**) (*ustawione w pewien sposób*) seating; ~ **elektryczne** the electric chair
krzew shrub
krzewiciel apostle
krzewić/za-/roz- promote, propagate
krzta (także **krztyna**) ounce, scrap[1], shred[2], spot[1], touch[2]
krztusić/za- się choke[1]
krzyczący 1 (*potrzeba*) crying **2** (*kolor*) bold, lurid
krzy-czeć/knąć call[1], cry[1] (out), let fly (at sb), roar (at sb), sth (out), scream[1], shout, shout (sth) out
krzyk call[2], cry[2], exclamation, hoot[2], scream[2], shout; (*oburzenia itp.*) outcry; **~i protestu** hue and cry
krzykliwość flamboyance, loudness
krzykliw|y 1 (*głośny*) loud, vociferous **2** (*kolor*) garish, gaudy, lurid **3** (*styl*) flamboyant, flashy; **~a reklama** hype[1]
krzywa curve[1]
krzywd|a harm[1], injustice IDM **doznawać ~y** come to harm
krzywdzący invidious, unfair, wrongful
krzywdzić/s- abuse[2], harm[2], hurt[1], injure, wrong[4]
krzywić/s- się (*z bólu itp.*) wince
krzywo 1 (*nie prosto*) askew, awry **2** (*uśmiechać się itp.*) wryly; ~ **patrzeć na coś** frown on/upon sth
krzywoprzy-sięgać/siąc perjure yourself
krzywoprzysięstwo perjury
krzywy 1 (*nieprosty*) cockeyed, crooked **2** (*uśmiech*) wry
krzyż 1 cross[1] **2** (*anat.*) rump; **ból ~a** backache
krzyżowa rump steak
krzyżować 1 (/s-) (*linie*) intersect **2 (/s-)** (*biol.*) cross[2] sth with sth; (*zool.*) interbreed **2 (/po-)** (*plany*) defeat[1], foil[2], thwart, upset[1]
□ **krzyżować/s- się 1** (*linie*) intersect **2** (*zool.*) interbreed
krzyżowiec crusader
krzyżówka 1 crossword **2** (*biol.*) cross[1]; (*bot.*) hybrid
krzyżyk cross[1]; (*na tarczy telefonu*) hash; (*muz.*) **nuta z ~iem** sharp[3]; **z ~iem** sharp[1]
ksenofobia xenophobia
ksenofobiczny xenophobic
ksero Xerox; **robić** ~ xerox verb
kserograf photocopier
kserograficzn|y: **kopia ~a** Xerox
kserować/s- photocopy verb, xerox verb
ksiądz father[1], priest
książeczka booklet; ~ **z obrazkami** picture book; ~ **do nabożeństwa** prayer book; ~ **czekowa** chequebook
książę duke; (*syna królewski*) prince
książka book[1], volume; ~ **adresowa** address book; ~ **informacyjna** (*np. słownik, encyklopedia*) reference book; ~ **kucharska** cookery book; ~ **telefoniczna** telephone directory
księga volume; **księgi rachunkowe** books[1]
księgarnia bookshop
księgarstwo the book trade
księgarz bookseller
księgowość accountancy, accounting, bookkeeping
księgow-y/a accountant, bookkeeper
księgozbiór library
księżna duchess; (*żona księcia*) princess
księżniczka princess
księżyc (także **Księżyc**) moon
księżycowy lunar; ~ **wieczór** a moonlit evening
ksylofon xylophone
kształcić/wy- educate; (*charakter itp.*) discipline[2]; **podróże kształcą** travel broadens the mind
■ **kształcący** educational, instructive
□ **kształcić/wy- się** (*na lekarza itp.*) train[2]
kształ|t form[1], shape[1]; **nadawać ~t** mould[2]; **w ~cie czegoś** shaped
kształtować/u- form[2], mould[2], shape[2]
kształtujący formative
kto who; (*przypadek zależny od kto/który*) whom; **obojętne** ~ whoever
ktokolwiek anybody, whoever

ktoś anybody, one[2], somebody; ~ **inny** someone else
któr|y (*tylko rzecz*) which; (*rzecz/ osoba*) that; (*tylko osoba*) who; (*przypadek zależny od który*) whom, whose; **~y tylko chcesz** whichever; **~a godzina?** what's the time?/what time is it?; **po ~ym** whereby
którykolwiek any, whichever; (*z dwóch*) either[1]
któr|yś one[1]; **~egoś dnia** some day, sometime
któż: ~ **to** whoever
ku to, towards
kubatura capacity, measurement
kubek 1 mug[1]; ~ **plastikowy/ papierowy** beaker **2** ~ **smakowy** taste bud
kuc-ać/nąć squat[1]
kucha-rz/rka chef, cook[2]
kuchenka cooker, oven; (*elektryczna/ gazowa*) stove; ~ **mikrofalowa** microwave (oven)
kuchnia 1 (*pokój*) kitchen **2** (*sposób przyrządzania potraw*) cookery, cuisine
kucyk 1 (*koń*) pony **2** (**kucyki**) (*włosy*) bunches[1]
kuć/wy- 1 (*metal*) hammer[2], pound[2] **2** (*na egzamin itp.*) cram
kudłaty shaggy
kufel mug[1]
kufer trunk
kuglarz conjuror
kujon swot[1]
kukiełka puppet
kukła effigy
kuksaniec clip[1], clout, poke noun
kukułka cuckoo
kukurydza maize, sweetcorn; **prażona** ~ popcorn
kukuryku (**kukuryku!**) cock-a-doodle-doo
kul|a 1 ball; (*form.*) orb; (*geom.*) sphere; **~a ziemska** globe; **~a śnieżka** snowball[1] **2** (*w pistolecie*) bullet **3** (*podpórka*) crutch **4** (*sprzęt sportowy*) shot[1]; **pchnięcie ~ą** (*sport*) the shot-put IDM **gra w ~e** bowls | **~a u nogi** bind[2]
kulawy lame
kuleć 1 hobble, have (got) a limp, walk with a limp **2** (*gospodarka*) flounder[1]
kulejący 1 lame **2** (*gospodarka*) ailing
kulić/s- się huddle[1]; (*ze strachu*) cower, cringe
kulinarny culinary
kulisa (**kulisy**) wings; **za kulis-y/ami** backstage
kulisty spherical
kulk|a 1 (*płynu*) globule; (*lodów itp.*) dollop, scoop[1]; (*gumowa itp.*) pellet; **~a naftalinowa (przeciw molom)** mothball **2 gra w ~i** marbles
kulminacja crescendo
kulminacyjny climactic; **punkt** ~ culmination
kuloodporny bulletproof
kult cult; **przedmiot ~u** cult
kultura 1 culture; ~ **i sztuka** the arts **2** ~ **osobista** politeness
kulturalny 1 (*centrum itp.*) cultural **2** (*wykształcony*) civilized, cultivated **3** (*grzeczny*) polite
kulturowy cultural
kulturyst-a/ka bodybuilder
kulturystyka bodybuilding
kultywować nourish
kumać: coś cotton on (to sth), latch on (to sth)
kumpel/a buddy, chum, mate[1], pal
kumulacyjny cumulative
kundel mongrel
kunszt craft
kunsztowność intricacy
kunsztowny intricate
kup|a 1 (*sterta*) heap[1], huddle[2], pile[1], stack[1] **2** (*wielka ilość*) a lotta, oodles, piles[1], tons **3** (*kał*) poo; **robić ~ę** poo
kupiec merchant, shopkeeper, tradesman
kupno: ~ **na raty** hire purchase
kupon coupon
ku-pować/pić 1 buy[1], get, invest in sth **2 kogoś** buy sb off IDM ~ **pomysł** be completely sold on the idea of sth
kupując-y/a buyer, purchaser, shopper
kura hen
kuracja course
kurant chime noun
kuratel|a custody; **dziecko znajdujące się pod ~ą** ward[1]
kurator/ka (*czyichś pieniędzy, majątku*) trustee; **kurator/ka sądow-y/a osób, które otrzymały wyrok w zawieszeniu lub zostały zwolnione warunkowo z więzienia** probation officer
kurcz spasm; (*zwł. w szyi*) crick
kurczak chicken[1]
kurczę 1 chicken[1] **2 o ~!** blast[3], blimey, bother[3]
kurczowo: ~ **się trzymać (czegoś)** hang on (to sth)
kurczyć 1 (/s-) constrict, contract[2], narrow[2] **2** (*twarz*) twitch
□ **kurczyć/s- się 1** (*zmniejszać się*) constrict, contract[2], narrow[2], shrink; ~ **do zera** dwindle away to nothing; **skurczyła mi się koszulka (w praniu)** my T-shirt shrank in the wash/I've shrunk my T-shirt **2** (*ze strachu*) cringe
kurek tap[2]
kurier/ka courier, messenger
kuriozum oddity
kurnik: ~ **bateryjny** battery
kuropatwa partridge
kurort resort[1]
kurs 1 (*szk.*) course; ~ **korespondencyjny** correspondence course; ~ **wakacyjny** summer school; ~ **wieczorowy** evening class; ~ **wprowadzający** induction course **2** (*działania*) course, line[1], policy **3** (*fin.*) ~ **wymiany** exchange rate
kursor cursor, pointer
kursować ply, run[1]
kursywa italics
kurtka jacket; ~ **z kapturem** parka; **długa** ~ **przeciwdeszczowa z kapturem** cagoule
kurtuazja courtesy
kurtyna curtain
kurwa slut
kurz dust[1]
kurzajka wart
kusić/s- entice, lure[1], seduce, tempt IDM ~ **los** push your luck, push it/ things
kustosz/ka curator, custodian
kusy scanty, skimpy
kuszący alluring, enticing, seductive, tantalizing, tempting
kuśtykać hobble, limp[2]
kut|y: **~e żelazo** wrought iron; **z ~ego żelaza** wrought-iron
kuzyn/ka cousin; **kuzyn/ka w drugiej linii** second cousin
kuźnia forge[2]
kwadrans a quarter of an hour
kwadrat square[2]; **~y wykładziny dywanowej** carpet tiles; **obraz jest ~em o długości boku wynoszącej 20 cm** the picture is twenty centimetres square; **podniesiony do ~u** squared
kwadratowy square[1]
kwakać/za- quack verb
kwalifikacj|a 1 qualification **2** (**kwalifikacje**) competence, credentials, qualification(s); **~e zawodowe** NVQ; **brak ~i** ineligibility; **dawać/zdobywać ~e** qualify; **nie mający ~i (do czegoś)** ineligible; (*praca*) **wymagający ~i** skilled
kwalifikować/za- certify, fit[1]
□ **kwalifikować/za- się** (*do finału itp.*) qualify (for sth)
kwapić się IDM **nie** ~ be in no hurry (to do sth), not be in any hurry (to do sth)
kwarantanna quarantine
kwarc quartz
kwart|a quart; **pół ~y** pint
kwartalny quarterly
kwartał quarter
kwartet quartet
kwas acid[1]; ~ **solny** hydrochloric acid
kwaskowy tangy
kwasowość acidity
kwaśn|y 1 acid[2], sour; **~a śmietana** sour cream; **~y deszcz** acid rain **2** (*uśmiech itp.*) wry; **~a mina** a long face, a sour expression
kwatera billet; (**kwatery**) quarters; **główna** ~ headquarters
kwaterować/za- house[2]
kwesta fund-raising
kwestarz fund-raiser
kwestia case, issue[1], matter[1], point[1], question[1] IDM ~ **życia lub śmierci** a matter of life and/or death
kwestionariusz questionnaire
kwestionować/za- challenge[2], contest[2], dispute[2], query verb, question[2]
kwestor bursar
kwestować collect[1]
■ **kwestowanie** fund-raising
kwiaciarnia florist
kwiacia-rz/rka florist
kwiat 1 bloom[1], flower[1]; (*drzew owocowych*) blossom[1]; ~ **w butonierce** buttonhole[1] **2** (*wieku*) prime[2]
kwiat|ek: **w ~ki** flowery
kwiatowy floral
kwiczeć/za-: **cicho** ~ squeak verb
kwiecień April
kwiecisty 1 (*w kwiatki*) flowery **2** (*przen.*) flowery, ornate
kwietnik flower bed
kwik: **cichy** ~ squeak
kwilić/za- whimper
kwintesencja substance
kwintet quintet
kwit receipt, voucher
kwita IDM **być** ~ be quits (with sb), be square[1]
kwitek IDM **odprawić kogoś z kwitkiem** give sb the brush-off
kwitnący 1 in bloom **2** (*przen.*) prosperous, thriving; ~ **interes** a going concern

kwitnąć 1 (/za-) (*roślina*) blossom², flower², be in flower; (*kwiat*) bloom² **2 (/roz-)** (*osoba; biznes*) flourish¹, thrive
kwiz quiz¹
kwok-ać/nąć cluck verb
■ **kwocząca** (*kura*) broody
kworum quorum
kwota amount¹, sum¹
kysz: **a ~!** shoo¹

L

l (L/l) (*litera*) L, l
labirynt labyrinth, maze, rabbit warren
laboratorium laboratory; **~ językowe** language laboratory
lać pour; (*deszcz*) pour (down) (with rain); **~ łzy** shed tears IDM **~ wodę** (*przen.*) pad sth out, waffle²
□ **lać się** pour, run¹; (*strumieniami*) stream²
lada bar¹, counter¹ IDM **~ chwila/minuta/dzień** any moment/second/day, etc. (now)
laguna lagoon
laicki lay²
laik layman, layperson
lakier lacquer, paint¹, varnish; **~ do paznokci** nail polish; **~ do włosów** hairspray, lacquer
lakierować/po- varnish verb
lakierowan|y: **skóra ~a** patent leather
lakoniczność curtness
lakoniczny curt, laconic
lakować/za- seal¹
lala bird
lalka doll
lament lament, wail noun
lamentować lament verb, moan, wail
lameta tinsel
laminowany laminated
lamówka binding², trimming
lampa lamp; **~ błyskowa** flash²; **~ jarzeniowa** neon light; **~ kwarcowa** sunlamp; **~ lutownicza** blowlamp; **~ naftowa** oil lamp; **~ olejowa** oil-burning lamp
lampart leopard
lampas stripe
lampion lantern
landrynka boiled sweet
lanie beating, hiding, thrashing
lansować/wy- bring sth out, launch¹, promote; **wylansować nowy kierunek mody** set a/the trend
lan|y: **~e żelazo** cast iron
lapidarny laconic, terse
lapsus faux pas
laptop laptop
larwa grub, larva, maggot
las forest, wood, woodland; **~ deszczowy** rainforest; **tropikalny ~ deszczowy** tropical rainforest
laseczka stick²
laser laser
laska 1 cane¹, walking stick **2** (*dziewczyna*) babe, chick
lasso lasso
latać 1 fly¹ **2 (/polecieć)** (*szybko iść/jechać dokądś*) fly¹, nip
■ **latający** flying; **~ talerz** UFO
latarka: **~ elektryczna** torch
latarnia lamp, lantern; **~ morska** lighthouse; **~ uliczna** street lamp
latawiec kite
lateraln|y: **myślenie ~e** lateral thinking
lato summer, summertime
latynoamerykański Latin American
Latynos/ka Latin American noun
laur 1 laurel **2 (laury)** (*honory*) laurels
lawa lava
lawenda lavender
lawina 1 (*śnieżna itp.*) avalanche; (*kamieni itp.*) shower¹ **2** (*przen.*) flood²
lazur azure noun
lazurowy azure, blue¹
ląd land¹; **~ stały** mainland; **na ~** ashore, on shore; **niedaleko ~u** offshore; **~em** overland adv.
lądować/wy- 1 come down, land², touch down; **spadochroniarz wylądował szczęśliwie** the parachutist dropped safely to the ground **2** (*przen.: gdzieś/w jakiejś sytuacji*) end up (as sth), end up (doing sth), finish up…; **(gdzieś)** land up (in…)
■ **lądowanie** landing, touchdown; **~ awaryjne** crash landing
lądowisko airfield; **~ helikopterów** pad¹
lądowo-morsk|i: **poczta ~a** surface mail
lądow|y overland, terrestrial; **wysłać paczkę pocztą ~ą** send a parcel by surface mail
ląg brood²
lecieć/po- 1 (*ptak itp.*) fly¹ **2** go¹, hurtle, whizz¹; **czymś** get **3 poleciało mi oczko w rajstopach** I've laddered my tights
leczenie therapy, treatment
lecznica infirmary
leczniczy medicated, medicinal, therapeutic
leczyć 1 heal, treat¹ **2 (/wy-)** cure¹; **to lekarstwo powinno wyleczyć cię z kataru** this medicine should stop your nose running
ledwie (także **ledwo**) barely, hardly, immediately conj., just¹, only just, scarcely IDM **ledwo ledwo** by the skin of your teeth, narrowly
legalizacja decriminalization
legalizować/za- decriminalize, legalize, legitimize
legalny above board, lawful, legal
■ **legalność** legality, legitimacy
legar: **~ podłogowy** joist
legat legacy
legenda key¹, legend
legendarny legendary
legia legion
leginsy leggings
legion legion
legitymacja (*potwierdzająca tożsamość*) identification, identity card; (*członkowska*) membership card
legowisko den, lair
lej (*po bombie itp.*) crater
lejce reins
lejek funnel
lek cure², drug¹, medicine
lekarski medical¹
lekarstwo cure², drug¹, medication, medicine, remedy¹
lekarz doctor¹; **~ pierwszego kontaktu** GP; **~ konsultant** consultant; **lek. med.** MD
lekceważący 1 (*bez szacunku*) disdainful, dismissive, disparaging, disrespectful, flippant, irreverent, supercilious **2** (*niedbający*) cavalier, negligent
lekceważenie 1 (*brak szacunku*) disdain, disrespect, irreverence **2** (*niedbałość*) disregard noun, neglect noun
lekceważyć/z- 1 (*nie zwracać uwagi na kogoś/coś*) disregard, ignore, neglect, shrug sth off, override **2** (*przepis*) flout
lekcja 1 class¹, lesson; (*indywidualna lub w małej grupie*) tutorial; **~ mistrzowska** masterclass **2 (lekcje)** school
lekk|i 1 (*nieciężki*) light²; (*garnitur itp.*) lightweight; (*ruchy*) nimble; **wagi ~iej** (*bokser itp.*) lightweight **2** (*łatwy*) light²; (*praca*) cushy **3** (*niegroźny, np. dla zdrowia*) **~a grypa** a touch of flu; **~ie obrażenia** minor injuries
lekkoatlet-a/ka athlete
lekkoatletyczny athletic
lekkoatletyka athletics
lekkomyślność foolishness, frivolity, irresponsibility
lekkomyślny foolish, frivolous, irresponsible, reckless
lekkość lightness
leksykalny lexical
leksykon dictionary, thesaurus
lektor: **komentarz/dialog czytany przez ~a** voice-over
lektura 1 (*czytanie*) read², reading **2** (*szkolna*) text¹, reading matter; **~ obowiązkowa** set text
lemoniada lemonade
len flax
lenieć/wy- moult
lenistwo indolence, laziness
leniuch layabout
leniuchować laze (about/around)
leniwy idle, indolent, lazy; **bardzo ~** bone idle
leopard leopard
lepić/z- (się) stick¹
■ **lepiący się** sticky
lepiej better², preferably
lepki sticky, tacky (*form., fiz.*) viscous; (*nieform.*) cruddy
lepkość viscosity
lepsz|y better¹,³, preferable; (*o wiele*) **~y** superior¹; **być (o wiele) ~ym** outclass; **nie ma nic ~ego niż…** you can't beat…
lesbijka gay², lesbian
lesbijsk|i lesbian adj.; **miłość ~a** lesbianism
lesisty wooded, woodland
leszczyna hazel¹
leszczynowy hazel¹
leśnictwo forestry
leśniczy gamekeeper
leśny woodland
letarg lethargy
letargiczny lethargic
letni 1 (*w czasie lata*) summer, summery **2** (*woda itp.*) lukewarm, tepid
letni-k/czka holidaymaker
lew 1 lion **2 (Lew)** (*znak zodiaku*) Leo IDM **~ morski** sea lion
lewar lever
lewar|ek jack¹; **podnosić coś ~kiem** jack sth up
lewica left⁴, left wing
lewicowiec left-winger
lewicowość leftism

lewicowy leftist, left-wing; (*i politycznie poprawny*) right-on
lewo: **na/w** ~ left[3]; **skręcić w pierwszą ulicę w** ~ take the first turning on the left
leworęczn|y left-handed; **dla ~ych** left-handed
leworęki left-handed
lewoskrzydłowy left-winger
lew|y left[2], left-hand; **~a strona** left[4]; **po ~ej stronie** left-hand, on the left; **z ~ej strony** left-hand; (*w ruchu drogowym w Polsce*) **~y (szybki) pas ruchu** outside lane
leżak deckchair
leżanka couch[1]
leżeć/po- lie[2]; (*list na stole itp.*) sit; **dłużej poleżeć w łóżku** lie in; **śnieg nie poleżał długo** the snow didn't settle for long; **leżący plackiem** (*twarzą ku ziemi*) prostrate IDM **~ na pieniądzach** be rolling in money/in it
lęg brood[2]
lęgowisko breeding ground
lęk angst, anxiety, apprehension, fear[1]; **chorobliwy ~ przestrzeni** agoraphobia; **mieć ~ wysokości** be afraid of heights
lękać się be afraid for sb/sth, dread[1]
lękliwy apprehensive
lgnąć/przy- cling
liberalizacja deregulation, liberalization
liberalizacyjny deregulatory
liberalizm liberalism
liberalizować/z- deregulate, liberalize
liberalny liberal, permissive; **Liberalni Demokraci** (*partia w Wlk. Br.*) the Liberal Democrats
liberał liberal noun
libido libido
licencj|a licence; **wydawać ~ę** charter[2], license[1]
liceum grammar school, senior high school, sixth-form college
lich|o (*rz.*) **do ~a!** heck; **po kiego ~a mi książka o ogrodnictwie?** what earthly use is a gardening book to me?; **u ~a** how/why/where/who etc. on earth, what in the world
■ **licho** (*przysł.*) poorly[1]
lichość mediocrity
lichtarz candlestick
lichwia-rz/rka pawnbroker
lichy **1** (*kiepski*) crummy, low[1], mediocre, pathetic, poor, substandard; (*wymówka itp.*) flimsy **2** (*mały*) paltry
licytacj|a auction[1], bidding; **wystawiać coś na ~ę** auction[2] sth (off)
licytator auctioneer
licytować/z-/prze- bid[1] (sth) (for sth)
■ **licytujący** bidder
liczb|a **1** figure[1], number[1]; (*ofiar itp.*) toll; **~a jednocyfrowa** digit; **~y dwucyfrowe** double figures; **~a mnoga** plural; **w ~ie mnogiej** plural adj.; **~a pojedyncza** singular noun; **w ~ie pojedynczej** singular; **~a ludności** population; **~a urodzeń** birth rate; **~a więźniów wzrosła** the prison population has increased **2** (*obliczanie*) count[2]
liczbowy numerical
liczebnik: **~ główny** cardinal; **~ porządkowy** ordinal

liczenie count[2], figures[1]; **~ w pamięci** mental arithmetic
licznik clock[1], counter[1], dial[1], meter; **~ Geigera** Geiger counter; **~ gazowy** gas meter; **~ do pomiaru przebytej drogi** milometer
liczn|y abundant, myriad, numerous, plentiful, profuse; **odnieść ~e obrażenia** receive multiple injuries
liczyć **1** **(/po-)** count[1], number[2]; **umiejący ~** numerate; **policzyć w pamięci** do sums in your head; **nie licząc kogoś/czegoś** exclusive[1] of sb/sth **2** **na coś** bargain for/on sth, gamble on sth/on doing sth, reckon on sth, be sure of sth; **na kogoś/coś** bank on sb/sth, count on sb/sth, depend on sb/sth, rely; **~ , że** reckon; **nie licz na to!** you'll be lucky
□ **liczyć się** **1** (*mieć znaczenie*) carry weight, count[1], matter[2] **2** **z czymś** (*przywiązywać wagę*) set… store by sth **3** (*darzyć uznaniem*) **z kimś/czymś** reckon with sb/sth
liczydło abacus
lider leader; **~ na rynku** market leader
lifting facelift
liga league; **Pierwsza Liga Piłkarska** the First Division
lignin|a: **chusteczka z ~y** paper handkerchief
lik IDM **bez ~u** no end of sth
likier liqueur
likwidacja liquidation
likwidować/z- liquidate, stamp sth out; (*firmę itp.*) wind sth down, wind sth up; (*ból itp.*) take sth away
lila lilac
lilia lily; **~ wodna** water lily
liliowy lilac adj.
limeryk limerick
limit limit[1]; (*na karcie komórki*) credit[1]
limona (także **limonka**) lime
limuzyna limousine
lin|a cable, line[1], rope[1]; (*w cyrku*) tightrope; **spuszczać się po ~ie** abseil
linczować/z- lynch
linearny linear
lingwist-a/ka linguist
lingwistyczny linguistic
lingwistyka linguistics
lini|a **1** (*geom.*) line[1]; **~a autowa/boczna** sideline; **~a brzegowa** coastline; **~a czasu** timeline; **~a frontu** front[1]; **~a mety** finishing line; **~a włosów** hairline[1]; **w ~e** (*papier itp.*) lined **2** (*komun.*) line[1]; **~a kolejowa** railway; **~a lotnicza** airline; **~a naziemna** (*telekom.*) landline **3** (*postępowania*) line[1], policy; **~a polityczna/partyjna** platform; **iść po ~i** (*np. partyjnej*) toe the (party) line **4** (*produktów/towarów*) line[1]; **~a produkcyjna** production line IDM **być na ~i ognia** be in the firing line | **w ~i powietrznej** as the crow flies | **z ~i matki/ojca** maternal/paternal
linieć/wy- moult
linijka ruler
liniowy linear
link link[1]
linoleum linoleum
lipa (*bot.*) lime
lipcowy July
lipiec July
lipny shoddy, trashy
liryczny **1** (*poetycki*) lyrical **2** (*poezja*) lyric

lis fox
lisica vixen
list letter; **~ pożegnalny (samobójcy)** suicide note; **~ przewodni** covering letter; **~ przewozowy** bill of lading; **~ zapraszający** letter of invitation; **~y uwierzytelniające** credentials
list|a breakdown, list, register[2], roll[1]; (*rzeczy do załatwienia*) checklist; (*dostarczonych towarów, wykonanych prac itp.*) docket; **tworzyć ~ę** list verb; **~a adresowa** mailing list; **~a płac** payroll; **~a przebojów** the charts[1]; **~a rezerwowa** waiting list; **na liście rezerwowej** on standby; **~a życzeń** wish list; **czarna ~a** blacklist
list|ek: **~ki herbaty** tea leaves
listewka slat
listonosz postman
listonoszka postwoman
listopad November
listopadowy November
listowie foliage
listwa strip[2]
liściasty deciduous
liścik note[1]
liść leaf[1]; **~ laurowy** bay leaf
liter|a character, letter; **duże ~y** upper case; **małe ~y** lower case; **~y drukowane** type[1]
literacki literary
literackość writing
literalny literal
literat/ka writer
literatura literature; **~ faktu** non-fiction; **~ piękna** fiction
literować/prze- spell[1]
litościwy merciful, pitying
litość mercy, pity[1]; **budzący ~** pitiful IDM **na ~ boską!** for Christ's/God's/goodness'/Heaven's/pity's sake | **gdzie/dlaczego itp. na ~ boską…?** how/why/where/who etc. on earth
litr litre
liturgia liturgy
lity solid[1]
live live[2]
lizać/po- lick
lizak lollipop
lizus creep[2]
lob lob noun
lobby lobby[1]
lobować lob
loch dungeon
locha sow[2]
lodowaty freezing[1], frosty, glacial, ice-cold, icy; **~ wiatr** bitter wind
lodowcowy glacial
lodowiec glacier
lodowisko skating rink
lodów|ka fridge; **w ~ce** under refrigeration
lody ice cream; **~ na patyku** ice lolly; **~ z owocami, orzechami itp.** sundae
logarytm logarithm
logiczn|y coherent, logical IDM **być ~ym** make sense
logika logic; **~ wewnętrzna** coherence
login login
logistyczny logistic
logistyka logistics
logopeda speech therapist
logopedia speech therapy
logopedyczn|y: **terapia ~a** speech therapy
logować **1** **(/za-)** log in/on; **kogoś** log sb in/on **2** **(/wy-)** log sb off/out
■ **logować/za-/wy- się** log in/on
lojalność faithfulness, loyalty

lojalny faithful, loyal
lok curl[2]
lokal 1 restaurant; ~ **rozrywkowy** hot spot **2** (**lokale**) (*mieszkalne*) housing
lokalizacja location
lokalizować/z- localize, locate
lokalny local[1], provincial; (*zachmurzenie, deszcz itp.*) patchy
lokata (*kapitału*) investment; ~ **terminowa** deposit account
lokator/ka lodger, occupant, occupier, tenant
lokomocj|a: **środek ~i** vehicle
lokomocyjn|y (*osoba podróżująca samochodem*) **cierpiący na chorobę ~ą** carsick
lokomotywa engine, railway engine
lokować/u- 1 (*umieszczać*) locate, plant[2], position[2] **2** (*fin.*) invest
lokówka curler, roller
lont fuse[1]
lora: ~ **kolejowa** truck
lord lord
lordowsk|i: **Wasza Lordowska Mość** Wasza Lordship
lornetka binoculars
los destiny, fate, fortune, lot[3], luck; (**losy**) fortune; **na ~ szczęścia** hit-and-miss; **zdawać się na ~ szczęścia** leave everything to chance IDM **masz ci ~** there you are
losować/wy- draw lots
lot 1 flight; ~ **planowy/według rozkładu** scheduled flight **2** (*droga powietrzna*) air[1] IDM **zdjęcie z ~u ptaka** aerial photograph
loteria lottery; ~ **fantowa** raffle
lotka 1 (*pióro*) feather **2** (*łodzi, szybowca itp.*) fin **3** (*w badmintonie*) shuttlecock
lotnia hang-glider
lotniarstwo hang-gliding
lotnictwo aviation; ~ **wojskowe** air force
lotnicz|y: **poczta ~a** airmail; **drogą ~ą** by air freight
lotnik flyer
lotnisko airfield, airport
lotniskowiec aircraft carrier
lotny volatile
loża box[1]
lód ice[1]; **pokrywać (się) lodem** ice (sth) over/up IDM **przełamywać lody** break the ice
lśniący (*futro, włosy*) sleek
lśnić/za- glisten, glitter verb, shimmer; (*oczy*) twinkle
■ **lśnienie** blaze[2], glitter, shimmer noun, twinkle noun
lub or
lubić/po- be fond of sb/sth, enjoy sth/doing sth, like[3], love[2]; **kogoś** care for sb; **bardzo ~** be very keen on sth; **nie ~** not care for sb/sth, dislike[1]
■ **lubiący** fond
lubieżny lecherous, lustful, randy; ~ **uśmiech** leer noun
lud people
ludność populace, population, public[2]
ludobójstwo genocide
ludow|y folk[2]; **muzyka ~a** folk[1]
ludożerca cannibal
ludożerstwo cannibalism
ludzie folk[1], people, public[2], they
ludzk|i 1 (*dot. człowieka*) human[1]; **istota ~a**; **rodzaj ~i** man[1], mankind; **po ~u** humanly **2** (*humanitarny*) humane; **po ~u** humanely
ludzkość civilization, humanity, humankind, mankind
lufa barrel; **o dwóch ~ch** double-barrelled
luk hatch[2], porthole
luk|a 1 (*puste miejsce*) blank[2], gap; **zapełniać ~ę** bridge a/the gap **2** (*prawn.*) loophole **3** (*przerwa*) break[2]; (*w pamięci itp.*) lapse[1]
lukier glaze[2], icing
lukrecja liquorice
lukrować/po- glaze[1], ice[2]
luksus luxury, self-indulgence
luksusowy de luxe, luxurious
lulać/u- lull[2]
lunapark fair[2]
lunąć pelt (down)
lunch lunch; ~ **roboczy** business/working lunch; **jeść ~**; **iść na ~** lunch verb; **pora ~u** lunchtime
lusterko: ~ **wsteczne** rear-view mirror
lustro mirror
lutnia lute
lutowy February
luty February
luz: **na ~ie** casual, laid-back; (*auto*) in neutral
luzować/po- loosen
luźno loosely; ~ **rozważać** (*możliwość zrobienia czegoś*) toy with sth
luźny 1 loose[1]; (*sweter itp.*) baggy; (*sukienka itp.*) full[1]; (*lina*) slack **2** (*przepis itp.*) lax
lwi IDM **~a część (czegoś)** the lion's share (of sth)
lżejsz|y lightweight; **stawać się ~ym** lighten
lżyć/ze- insult[1]

Ł

łabędziątko cygnet
łabędź swan
łachmany rags
łachy rags
łacina Latin
łaciński Latin adj.
ład order[1]; **bez ~u** randomly, willy-nilly; **doprowadzać coś do ~u** sort[2], straighten sth out
ładnie 1 prettily; ~ **wyglądać** look nice **2 bardzo ~ z twojej strony** it was very considerate/kind of you
ładniutki cute
ładny 1 attractive; (*zwł. kobieta*) pretty[2]; (*chłopak*) handsome **2** (*pogoda*) fine[1]; (*pogoda, wygląd, widok*) nice
ładować 1 (**/za-**) (*na ciężarówkę itp.; broń*) load[2] **2** (**/w-**) **coś w coś** cram sb/sth in (sth), sb/sth into/onto sth **3** (**/na-**) (*baterie itp.*) charge[2]; **ponownie** ~ recharge
□ **ładować /w- się** pile into/out of/off, etc. sth
ładowarka: ~ **do akumulatorów** charger
ładownia (cargo) hold[2], loading bay
ładunek 1 goods, load[1]; (*statku, samolotu*) cargo; **brać** ~ load[2] **2** (*elektr.*) charge[1]
łagodnieć/z- soften, relent
łagodność gentleness, lenience, meekness, mildness
łagodn|y 1 (*charakter*) benign, gentle, good-tempered, lenient, meek, mellow, placid, serene; **~e usposobienie** serenity; **~ego usposobienia** good-natured; **o ~ym głosie** soft-spoken **2** (*smak*) bland; (*smak; pogoda*) mild; (*pogoda*) balmy **3** (*guz*) benign **4** (*kolor; światło*) muted, soft
łagodzić/z-/za- lessen; (*opinię*) qualify; (*kolor; opinię*) mellow, soften, tone sth down; (*umniejszać gniew itp. kogoś*) appease, placate; (*ból itp.*) alleviate, deaden, ease[2], relieve, soothe; (*obawy*) allay; (*problem*) mitigate, patch sth up; (*niedostatki*) offset, redeem
łajać/z- chide, nag (at) sb, rap[2]
łajdak scoundrel
łajno dung
łaknąć hanker; (*pożądać*) lust[2]
łaknienie appetite
łamać/z-/po- 1 (*kość itp.*) break[1]; (*kość*) fracture verb; ~ **z trzaskiem** snap[1] **2** (*prawo; obietnicę; kod*) break[1]; (*obietnicę*) go back on sth; (*zasady itp.*) flout, infringe IDM **~ sobie głowę (nad czymś)** rack your brains | **~ czyjś opór** wear sb/sth down | **~ serce komuś** break sb's heart
■ **łamanie**: ~ **praw człowieka** human rights abuses
□ **łamać/z-/po- się** break[1], give way; ~ **z trzaskiem** snap[1]
■ **łamany** broken[2]
łamigłówka brain-teaser, conundrum, puzzle[1], quiz[1]
łamliwy breakable, brittle, fragile
łania doe
łańcuch 1 chain[1] **2** (*górski*) range[1] IDM **~ pokarmowy** food chain
łańcuchow|y: **reakcja ~a** (*i przen.*) chain reaction
łańcuszek chain[1]
łapa paw[1]
łapacz (*sport*) catcher; (*krykiet itp.*) fielder
łapać/z- 1 (*piłkę; autobus itp.*) catch[1]; (*starać się wydrzeć*) catch, get, grab, take, etc. hold (of sb/sth), grab, snatch (at sth); (*trochę snu itp.*) snatch[1]; ~ **na hak** hook[2] **2** (*osobę, zwierzę*) catch[1], capture[1], get; **ponownie** ~ recapture; ~ **w pułapkę** trap[2] **3** (*rozumieć*) catch[1] IDM **~ kogoś na błędzie/pomyłce** trip sb up | **złapać kogoś na gorącym uczynku** catch sb red-handed | **złapać oddech** catch your breath | **złapać w pułapkę** (*przen.*) entrap, trap[2] | **złapanie powietrza** gulp[2]
łapczywie ravenously, thirstily
łapownictwo bribery
łapówk|a bribe; **dawać ~ę** bribe verb
łapówkarstwo bribery
łasica weasel
łask|a 1 clemency, mercy; **akt ~i** pardon[2]; **prawo ~i** clemency **2** (*dobrodziejstwo*) boon IDM **na łasce kogoś/czegoś** at the mercy of sb/sth | **z ~i** on sufferance
łaskawość benevolence, graciousness
łaskaw|y benevolent, condescending, gracious, merciful; **czy byłbyś ~** would you mind[2]
łaskotać/po- tickle
łaskotk|a: **mający ~i** ticklish
łaskotliwy ticklish
łata marking, patch[1]
łatać/za- patch[2]; (*dach itp.*) patch sth up
łatwizna cinch, doddle, pushover

łatwo easily, readily, simply; ~ **(o coś/ coś się dzieje)** liable to do sth IDM ~ **powiedzieć** easier said than done | **~/dobrze (komuś coś robić)** all very well (for sb)

łatwopalny combustible, flammable, inflammable

łatwoś|ć 1 (*brak trudności*) ease[1]; **z ~cią** easily **2** (*problemu matematycznego itp.*) easiness, simplicity

łatwowierny fond, gullible

łatw|y easy[1], effortless; (*praca*) light[2]; (*do zrozumienia*) straightforward; **~y do zapamiętania** memorable; **~iejsze wyjście** (*z sytuacji*) soft option

ław|a 1 bench; **~a oskarżonych** dock[1]; **~a przysięgłych** the jury box, jury; **sądzenie przez ~ę przysięgłych** trial by jury **2** (*w salonie*) coffee table

ławica 1 (*ryb*) school, shoal **2** (*piasku*) drift[1]

ławka bench; ~ **kościelna** pew; **tylna ~ w Izbie Gmin** (*miejsca, które zajmują zwykli posłowie*) back bench

łazienka bathroom

łazik Jeep

łazikować loiter

łaźnia bath[1]

łączliwość: ~ **wyrazów** collocation

łącznie (all) in one; ~ **z czymś** complete with sth, including, inclusive of sth; **biorąc wszystko** ~ all told

łącznik 1 link[1] **2** (*w piśmie*) hyphen; **pisać z ~iem** hyphenate

łączność 1 communication, liaison; ~ **duchowa** communion; **mieć ~ z kimś/czymś** be in communication with sb/sth **2** (*radio, TV*) telecommunications

łączny (*cena*) all-in

łączyć/z-/po- 1 couple[2], join[1], link[2], link sth up (with sb/sth), piece sth together, unify; **z czymś** connect; **z kimś** (*w pary*) pair sb off (with sb); **w sobie** incorporate; (*w całość*) bind[1], bond[2], combine, integrate, mix[1]; (*myśli, style itp.*) synthesize; (*dwie kategorie*) bracket[2]; (*komputery itp.*) interconnect; (*organizacje*) amalgamate, merge; ~ **ponownie** reunite; ~ **siły (z kimś)** join forces (with sb), team up (with sb); ~ **pokoje/ budynki ze sobą** knock sth together; ~ **przyjemne z pożytecznym** combine business with pleasure **2** (*telefonicznie*) connect; (*z numerem wewnętrznym*) put sb through (to sb), put sb through to an extension □ **łączyć/po-/z- się** connect, join[1], link up (with sb/sth); **z kimś** contact[2]; (*dla jakiejś działalności*) pair off (with sb), team up (with sb); (*w całość*) bond[2], coalesce, combine, fuse[2], mix[1]; (*komputery itp.*) interconnect; (*organizacje*) amalgamate, merge; (*rzeki itp.*) meet; **ze sobą** (*pokoje*) communicate; (*z innym słowem w zdaniu*) take; ~ **ponownie** reunite ■ **łączący** subjunctive adj.

łąka meadow

łeb IDM **na ~ na szyję** headlong | **patrzeć spode łba** scowl verb | **~ w ~** neck and neck (with sb/sth)

łechtaczka clitoris

łkać/za- sob

łobuz scumbag, yob; (*żartobliwie*) rogue[2]

łodyga stalk[1], stem[1]

łoić/z- IDM ~ **skórę pasem** belt[2]

łok|ieć elbow[1]; **trącać ~ciem** nudge

łom crowbar

łomot crash[1], thud

łomotać/za- 1 bang[1], batter[1], pound[2] (at/against/on sth), thud verb **2** (*serce*) pound[2]

łon|o womb IDM **na ~ie czegoś** in the bosom of sth

łonowy pubic

łopata shovel, spade

łopatka 1 (*kuchenna*) spatula; (*do ryb*) fish slice **2** (*anat.*) shoulder blade **3** (*śmigła*) blade **4** (*kulin.*) ~ **barania** shoulder of mutton

łoskot bump[2], clap[2], clatter noun, crash[1]; (*samochodów itp.*) roar noun

łoskotać clatter, crash[2]

łosoś salmon

łoś elk

łot-r/rzyca scoundrel, villain

łowca: ~ **szczurów** rat catcher; ~ **okazji** (*tanich zakupów*) bargain hunter

łowić/z-: ~ **ryby** fish[2] ■ **łowienie**: ~ **ryb** angling, fishing

łowisko (*na terenach wodnych*) fishery

łowy hunt[2], hunting

łożysko 1 (*techn.*) ~ **kulkowe** ball bearing **2** (*w układzie rodnym*) placenta **3** (*gniazdko elektryczne*) socket

łódka dinghy

łódź boat; ~ **motorowa** launch[2], motorboat; ~ **motorowa z kabiną** cruiser; ~ **podwodna** submarine; ~ **ratownicza** lifeboat; ~ **wiosłowa** rowing boat; **(stacjonarna)** ~ **mieszkalna** houseboat

łój suet

łóżeczko: ~ **dziecięce** cot

łóżk|o bed[1]; **~o dwuosobowe** double bed; **~o piętrowe** bunk bed; **~o turystyczne/składane** camp bed IDM **iść z kimś do ~a** go to bed with sb

łucznictwo archery

łuczni-k/czka archer

łudzić delude □ **łudzić się** be under the illusion that…

łuk 1 (*geom.*) arc, curve[1]; **długi** ~ (*np. plaży, drogi*) sweep[2]; **tworzyć** ~ arch[2]; **biec ~iem** curve[2] **2** (*arch.*) arch[1] **3** (*do strzelania*) bow[3]

łukowaty arched

łup booty, haul[2], loot noun, plunder, spoils

łupek 1 slate **2** (*med.*) splint

łupić/z- loot verb, plunder verb

łupież dandruff

łupina (*ziarna*) husk; (*nie dotyczy orzechów*) skin[1]

łuska 1 (*ryby*) scale[1] **2** (*ziarna*) husk

łuskać/wy- shell[2]

łuszczyca psoriasis

łuszczyć/z- się flake[2], peel[1] ■ **łuszczący się** flaky

łyczek sip noun

łydka calf

łyk drop[2], gulp[2], mouthful

łykowaty gristly, tough

łypnięcie: ~ **okiem** wink noun

łysieć/wy- go bald ■ **łysiejący** balding

łysin|a: **mieć ~ę** have a bald patch

łysy bald

łyżeczka: ~ **deserowa** dessertspoon; ~ **do herbaty** teaspoon; **(pełna)** ~ spoonful

łyżka 1 spoon; ~ **do lodów** scoop[1]; ~ **stołowa** tablespoon; ~ **wazowa** ladle[1] **2** (*pełna*) scoop[1], spoonful; (*śmietanki itp.*) dollop

łyżwa skate[2]; **jeździć na ~ch** skate[1]

łyżwiarstwo: ~ **figurowe** figure-skating

łyżwia-rz/rka skater

łyżworolka Rollerblade

łza tear[1]

łzawić water[2] ■ **łzawiący** runny

łzawy tearful

M

m (M/m) (*litera*) M, m

macać/po- finger[2], grope

machać/po-/machnąć 1 (*ręką*) wave[2]; (*nogami*) kick[1]; (*kartą itp.*) flash[1]; ~ **komuś na pożegnanie** wave sb off; ~ **na kogoś/coś** (*w celu zatrzymania kogoś/czegoś*) flag sb/sth down **2** (*ogonem*) wag IDM **~ na coś ręką** wave sth aside/away, shrug sth off

machinacja (machinacje) racket

machinalny mechanical

machlojk|a fiddle[2]; **(machlojki)** monkey business; **~i podatkowe** tax dodge

machnięcie (*ręką*) wave[1]

macho macho

macica uterus

macierz matrix

macierzyński maternal, motherly; (*(po)porodowy*) maternity; **urlop** ~ maternity leave

macierzyństwo motherhood, parenthood

macierzyst|y indigenous IDM **firma ~a** parent | **komórka ~a** stem cell

maciora sow[2]

macka tentacle

macocha stepmother

maczać/za-/po- (*sucharek w herbacie itp.*) dunk IDM ~ **w czymś palce** have a hand in sth

maczeta machete

maczuga club[1]

magazyn 1 (*pokój*) storeroom; (*budynek*) warehouse, depot, store[1]; (*skład towarów*) stock **2** (*czasopismo*) journal; **ilustrowany** ~ colour supplement **3** (*sklep*) store[1]

magazynek storeroom

magazynować/z- store[2]

magia magic[1], mystique

magiczn|y enchanted, magic[2], magical; **sztuczki ~e** conjuring

magik conjuror, magician

magist|er: **stopień ~ra** master's degree; **mgr** MA; **mgr nauk ścisłych** MSc; **mgr zarządzania** MBA

magistrant/ka postgraduate

maglować/wy-: **kogoś** grill[2] sb (about sth)

magnat/ka (*handlow-y/a itp.*) baron, magnate, tycoon

magnes magnet

magnetofon (*bez wzmacniacza*) tape deck; ~ **szpulowy/kasetowy** tape/ cassette recorder

magnetowid video cassette recorder, video recorder

magnetyczny magnetic

magnetyzm magnetism

magnetyzować/na- magnetize

magnez (*chem.*) magnesium

Mahomet Muhammad

mahometanizm Islam

mahometański Islamic

mahoń mahogany

maj May; **Święto 1 Maja** May Day

majaczenie delirium

majaczyć/za- loom[1] (up)
■ **majaczący** delirious

majątek 1 (*ziemski*) estate, manor; (*ruchomy*) possessions; (*bogactwo*) wealth **2** (*dużo pieniędzy*) fortune, packet

majeranek marjoram

majestat grandeur, majesty

majestatyczność grandness

majestatyczny majestic, stately
■ **majestatycznie** majestically; **poruszać się majestatycznie** sweep[1]

majętny wealthy

majonez mayonnaise

major major[2]

majówka picnic

majster: ~ **do wszystkiego** handyman

majsterkować potter[1] (about/around)

majsterkowani|e: **sklep z artykułami do ~a** DIY store

majstrować/z- tinker (with sth); **(z)majstrować przy czymś** muck about/around with sth

majtać/za- dangle, swing[1]

majtki briefs; ~ **damskie** knickers

mak poppy

makabra horror

makabryczny grisly, gruesome, macabre

makaron pasta; (*typu nitki*) noodle; (*typu rurki*) macaroni

makieta design[1], dummy, mock-up

makijaż make-up

makler broker; ~ **giełdowy** broker-dealer, stockbroker

makrela mackerel

makro macro

makroekonomia macroeconomics

makroekonomiczny macroeconomic

maksimum maximum

maksyma adage, maxim

maksymalizować/z- maximize

maksymaln|y maximum adj.
■ **maksymalnie** at the outside; ~ **wykorzystać** exploit to the utmost

makulatur|a scrap paper; **na ~ę** recyclable

makulaturowy: **papier** ~ recycled paper

malaria malaria

malarstwo painting

mala-rz/rka artist; (*artysta; pokojowy*) painter

maleć/z- decline[2], diminish, recede, tail away/off, wane[1]

maleńki minuscule, tiny, wee[2]

maligna delirium

malina raspberry

malinowy raspberry

malkontent/ka whinger

malować 1 (/po-/na-/za-) paint[2]; (*na jakiś kolor*) colour[2]; **pomalować ściany na różowo** paint the walls pink; ~ **i/lub tapetować** decorate; ~ **przez szablon** stencil verb **2 (/u-)** make sb up
□ **malować/po- się** make yourself up, put make-up on

malowanie painting; (*pomalowana powierzchnia*) paintwork

malowidło: ~ **ścienne** mural

malowniczy graphic, picturesque, scenic

maltretować/z- maltreat, mistreat; (*fizycznie*) batter[1], knock sb/sth around

maltretowanie ill-treatment, maltreatment, mistreatment

maluch (*kieliszek mocnego alkoholu*) short[2]

malutki minute[2], tiny

malwersacja embezzlement; **(malwersacje)** malpractice

mała baby

małe (*foki itp.*) pup; → zob. też MŁODE

mało (*z rz. niepolicz.*) little[2,3]; (*z rz. policz.*) few; (*płacić itp.*) modestly; (*zaludniony itp.*) sparsely; ~ **co/kto** hardly; **o ~ co** (*o włos*) narrowly; ~ **znaczący** secondary; **w tej drużynie jest o dwóch zawodników za** ~ the team is two players short[1]

małoletni juvenile

małomiasteczkowy provincial

małomówność reticence

małomówny reticent, retiring

małostkowość narrowness, nit-picking

małostkowy mean[2], nit-picking adj., petty

małość sparseness

małoznaczność triviality

małpa 1 (*zool.*) monkey; (*bezogoniasta*) ape[1] **2** (*kobieta*) bag[1], cow **3** (*komput.*) at

małpka (*wódki*) tot[1]

małpować ape[2]; (*łączyć się dla jakiejś działalności*) climb/jump on the bandwagon

mał|y 1 a bit of a, little[1], mini-, narrow[1], small; (*dziecko*) young[1]; (*wypłata itp.*) modest; (*tłum itp*) sparse; **(śmiesznie) ~y** derisory; **w ~ym rozmiarze** small adv. **2** (*szanse; pojęcie*) remote, slender, slight, slim[1] IDM **mieć coś w ~ym palcu** have sth at your fingertips

małż: ~ **jadalny** clam[1], mussel, scallop

małżeńsk|i conjugal, marital, married, matrimonial; **stan ~i** matrimony; **w stanie ~im** married (to sb)

małżeństw|o (*para*) couple[1], married couple; (*stan cywilny*) marriage, matrimony; **~o kontraktowe** an arranged marriage; **~o mieszane** intermarriage; **~o z rozsądku** marriage of convenience; **są ~em od 50 lat** they've been married for 50 years

małżonek husband, partner, spouse

małżonka wife, partner, spouse

mama mum

mamić/o- beguile sb (into doing sth), entice

mamrotać/wy- mumble, mutter

mamusia mummy

manatki IDM **zbierać** ~ pack up

mandarynk|a mandarin; **rodzaj ~i** satsuma

mandat 1 (*kara*) fine[2], ticket; ~ **za parkowanie w miejscu niedozwolonym** parking ticket **2** (*pełnomocnictwo*) mandate; (*poselski*) seat[1]

manekin dummy, mannequin

manewr manoeuvre[1]

manewrować manoeuvre[2]

mango mango

mangowiec mango

mani|a craze, fixation, fetish; (*i psych.*) mania; **cierpieć na ~ę wielkości** suffer from delusions of grandeur

mania-k/czka crank, fiend, freak[1], maniac; **maniak komputerowy** computer geek

maniakalno-depresyjny bipolar

maniakalny manic

manicure manicure

manier|a mannerism; **(maniery)** manners; **z dobrymi ~ami** well behaved

manieryzm mannerism

manifest manifesto

manifestacja demonstration, rally[1]

manifestant/ka demonstrator

manifestować/za-: **przeciwko czemuś/za czymś** demonstrate (against/for sb/sth)
■ **manifestowanie** (*uczuć*) display[2]

manikiur manicure

maniok cassava

manipulacja manipulation

manipulacyjny manipulative

manipulować 1 manipulate **2** (*sfabrykować, spreparować itp.*) manipulate, fiddle[1], tamper with sth

mankament defect[1]

mankiet cuff[1]

manow|iec IDM **zwieść kogoś na ~ce** lead sb astray

manualn|y: **zdolności ~e** manipulative skills

manuskrypt manuscript

Maorys/ka Maori

maoryski Maori adj.

mapa map[1]; (*ulic*) plan[1]; ~ **morska/nieba** chart[1]; ~ **plastyczna (często dwuwymiarowa)** relief map; ~ **samochodowa/drogowa** road map

mara (*nocna*) nightmare

maraton (*i przen.*) marathon

marcepan marzipan

marchew carrot

margaryna margarine

marginalizacja marginalization

marginalizować/z- marginalize

marginalny peripheral[1]

margines (*strony; bezpieczeństwa itp.*) margin; (*życia politycznego itp.*) periphery; ~ **błędu** margin of error

marginesowy incidental, marginal

marihuana cannabis, marijuana

marionetka marionette, puppet

mark|a 1 (*kawy itp.*) brand[1]; (*samochodu itp.*) make[2]; **dżinsy znanej ~i** designer jeans **2** (*waluta*) **~a niemiecka** mark[2]

marker highlighter

marketing marketing

markiza (*zadaszenie*) awning, canopy

markotność moodiness

markotny glum, moody, morose, withdrawn[2]

markowy branded

marksist-a/ka Marxist

marksistowski Marxist

marksizm Marxism

marmur marble

marmurowy marble

marnieć/z- 1 (*dom*) go to rack and ruin **2** (*osoba*) languish **3** (*roślina*) wilt

marnotrawić/z- dissipate, squander, waste[1]

marnotrawny wasteful

marnotrawstwo wastage

marnować/z- dissipate, waste[1]; (*okazję*) blow[1], foul sth up, lose □ **marnować/z- się** (go) down the drain, go to waste
marny 1 (*pensja itp.*) miserable, paltry **2** (*wymówka*) flimsy **3** (*jakość itp.*) indifferent **4** (*pomieszczenie*) grotty **5** (*osoba*) low[1], ropy, rough[1]
Mars Mars
Marsjan-in/ka Martian
marskość: ~ **wątroby** cirrhosis
marsz march[2] IDM **robić coś z ~u** take sth in your stride
marszałek marshal
marszczyć/z-/po- 1 (*czoło itp.*) wrinkle[2] sth (up); ~ **brwi** frown **2** (*tkaninę itp.*) crease[2]; (*folię aluminiową itp.*) crinkle sth (up) **3** (*powierzchnię wody*) ripple verb □ **marszczyć/z-/po- się 1** (*czoło itp.*) wrinkle[2] (up) **2** (*tkanina itp.*) crease[2], crinkle (up)
marszruta itinerary
martwić/z- bother[1], distress[2], grieve, trouble[2], worry[1] □ **martwić/z- się** be bothered, fret[1], worry[1]; **strasznie się** ~ be worried stiff, get worked up about sth
martwo (*dziecko*) ~ **urodzony** stillborn
martw|y dead[1], inanimate, lifeless IDM **~a natura** still life | **~y punkt** deadlock, stalemate; (*podczas jazdy samochodem*) blind spot
maruda fusspot, straggler
maruder/ka straggler
marudny cranky
marudzić/po-/za- 1 (*dziecko*) go/be on (at sb) (about sth), grizzle **2** (**/za-**) (*zwlekać*) dawdle, dilly-dally, linger
marynark|a 1 (*ubranie*) jacket **2** (także **Marynarka**) **~a handlowa** the merchant navy; **Marynarka Wojenna** navy; **Marynarki Wojennej** naval
marynarz sailor, seaman
marynata marinade, pickle
marynować/za- pickle verb, marinate □ **marynować/za- się** marinate
marzec March
marze|nie dream[1]; (**marzenia**) (*na jawie*) daydream IDM **(być) obiektem ~ń** to die for
marznąć/z-/za- freeze[1]; **zmarznąć na kość** catch your death (of cold)
marzyciel/ka dreamer
marzycielski dreamy
marzyć/po- dream[2]; (*na jawie*) daydream verb, dream[2] (of doing sth/ that...), fantasize; **o czymś** be dying for sth/to do sth; **o jakim każdy marzy** to die for
marża margin, markup
masa 1 (*duża ilość*) bulk, crop[1], heap[1], load[1], mass[1] (of sth) **2** (**masy**) (*społeczeństwa*) the masses[1] **3** (*tworzywo*) substance; ~ **celulozowa** pulp **4** (*fiz.*) mass[1]
masakra massacre, slaughter noun
masakrować/z- massacre verb, mutilate, slaughter
masakrowanie mutilation
masaż massage; **robić komuś** ~ massage verb
masażysta masseur
masażystka masseuse
maska 1 (*na twarz*) mask[1]; ~ **przeciwgazowa** gas mask; **w masce** masked **2** (*samochodu*) bonnet; (*ciemności itp.*) cloak **3** (*zachowanie*) cover[2] (for sth), front[1]
maskarada masquerade
maskonur puffin
maskotka charm[1], mascot
maskować/za- camouflage verb, disguise[1], mask[2]
masło butter[1]; ~ **orzechowe** (*z orzeszków ziemnych*) peanut butter
masochist-a/ka masochist
masochistyczny masochistic
masochizm masochism
mason Freemason
masować/po- massage verb
masow|y mass[2]; (*mord itp.*) indiscriminate; (*fin.*) wholesale; **produkcja ~a** mass production ■ **masowo** en masse; (*fin.*) wholesale adv.; **produkować** ~ mass-produce
mass media mass media, media
mastektomia mastectomy
masturbacja masturbation
masturbować (się) masturbate
masywność solidity
masywny solid[1]
maszerować/po- march[1]
maszkaron gargoyle
maszt mast; ~ **flagowy** flagpole
maszyna machine; ~ **do pisania** typewriter; ~ **do szycia** sewing machine
maszyneria 1 (*mechanizm*) machinery **2** (*działanie*) mechanism
maszynista 1 (*pociągu*) engine driver **2** też; (**maszynistka**) (*stenotypist(k)a*) typist
maszynka: **elektryczna ~ do golenia** shaver
maszynopis manuscript, typing
maszynow|y: **broń ~a** automatic[2]
maść ointment
maślanka buttermilk
mat: **szach i** ~ checkmate
mata mat; ~ **łazienkowa** bath mat
matczyny maternal
matecznik lair
matematyczny mathematical
matematyk mathematician
matematyka mathematics
materac mattress; ~ **nadmuchiwany** air bed, lilo
materia matter[1]
materialist-a/ka materialist
materialistyczny materialistic
materializm materialism
materializować/z- się materialize
materialny material[2], worldly
materiał 1 substance; (*w nauce*) ground[1]; (**materiały**) literature (on sth); **~y do czytania** reading matter; ~ **filmowy** footage; **~y piśmienne** stationery **2** (*tkanina*) cloth, fabric, material[1], textile
matk|a mother[1]; **~a chrzestna** godmother; **~a przełożona** abbess; **~a zastępcza** surrogate mother; **bez ~i** motherless; **ze strony ~i** maternal
matkować mother[2]
matowieć/z- 1 (*lustro, metal itp.*) tarnish **2** (*światło itp.*) dim[2]
matow|y 1 (*farba*) matt; (*włosy itp.*) lacklustre; **czynić ~ym** (*metal*) tarnish **2** (*szkło*) frosted, opaque **3** (*głos*) husky[1]
matrona matron
matryca mould[1], pattern
matrymonialny matrimonial
matura A level
maturzyst-a/ka school leaver
mazać/po- daub, smear[1]
mazak pen
maziowaty gooey
mazisty gungy
maź goo, gunge
maźnięcie smear[2]
mącić/za-/z- cloud[2], fudge[2]; ~ **komuś w głowie** brainwash sb (into doing sth)
mądrala know-all, smart alec
mądrość wisdom
mądr|y (*niegłupi*) intelligent; (*o rozległej wiedzy*) knowledgeable; (*rozsądny*) sensible, wise; (*mający/ zadowalający wyszukane gusty intelektualne*) highbrow IDM **to dla mnie za ~e** be/get out of your depth
mądrzeć grow wiser
mąka flour; ~ **kukurydziana** cornflour; ~ **bez dodatku proszku do pieczenia** plain flour; ~ **zawierająca środek spulchniający** self-raising flour
mąż husband IDM **~ stanu** statesman
mdleć/ze- black out, faint[2], pass out, swoon, go into a swoon
mdlić/ze-: **kogoś** churn; (*od nadmiaru słodyczy itp.*) cloy
mdłości nausea; **mieć** ~ heave[1]; **mający** ~ nauseous, sick[1]; **przyprawiać kogoś o** ~ churn, nauseate; (*i przen.*) gross sb out; **przyprawiający o** ~ nauseating, nauseous, queasy, sickly
mdły 1 (*nijaki*) bland, insipid, tame[1], weak **2** (*nadmiar słodyczy itp: przyprawiający o mdłości*) cloying
meble furniture
meblować/u- furnish
mecenas/ka: **mecenas/ka sztuki** patron
mecenat patronage
mech moss; **porosły mchem** mossy
mechaniczny mechanical
mechanik machinist, mechanic; ~ **samochodowy** motor mechanic
mechanika engineering, mechanics
mechanizacja automation, mechanization
mechanizm machinery, mechanism; (*w komputerze*) unit; ~ **lub część ~u** gear[1]; ~ **zegarowy** clockwork
mechanizować/z- mechanize
mecz game[1], match[1]; ~ **towarzyski** friendly[2]
meczet mosque
medal medal; (*inform.*) gong
medalion locket, medallion
medalist-a/ka medallist, title-holder
media: **studia dot. mediów i kultury ~lnej** media studies
mediacja mediation
mediana median noun
mediator/ka mediator; (*zwł. w sporach*) intermediary; (*pośrednik*) middleman
medium medium[2], psychic
meduza jellyfish
medycyna medicine; ~ **alternatywna/ niekonwencjonalna** alternative medicine
medyczny medical[1]
medytacja contemplation, meditation
medytować/po- meditate
mega mega
megabajt megabyte

megafon loudspeaker, megaphone; **przez ~** over the Tannoy
megagwiazd-a/or megastar
megaherc: **MHz** MHz
megaloman/ka megalomaniac
megalomania megalomania
megalomański megalomaniac
megawat megawatt, MW
Mekka 1 (*miasto w Arabii Saudyjskiej*) Mecca **2** (**mekka**) (*przen.*) Mecca
melancholia melancholy
melancholijny melancholy adj.
melasa treacle
meldować/za- report[1] □ **meldować/za- się** report[1]; (*zgłosić się do odprawy paszportowej*) check in (at…); (*w hotelu*) book in, check into…
meldunek report[2]
melina den
melodia melody, tune[1]
melodramat melodrama
melodramatyczny melodramatic
melodyczny melodic
melodyjny harmonious, lilting, melodious, musical[1], sweet[1], tuneful
meloman/ka music lover
melon melon
melonik (*krykiet*) bowler
membrana membrane
memorandum memo
memoriał memorial
menedżer/ka manager; (*pubu, hotelu itp.*) landlord; (**menedżerka**) landlady
mennica mint
menopauza the menopause
menstruacja menstruation
menstruacyjny menstrual
mentalność mentality
mentor/ka guru, mentor
menu (*kulin.*, *komput.*) menu; **~ rozwijane** (*komput.*) drop-down/ pull-down menu
merdać/za- waggle; (*ogon*) wag
merenga meringue
Merkury Mercury
mesa mess[1]
mesjasz Messiah
meszka midge
met|a finish[2], finishing line; (*baseball*) base[1] IDM **na dłuższą ~ę** in the long run
metaboliczny metabolic
metabolizm metabolism
metafizyczny metaphysical
metafizyka metaphysics
metafora metaphor
metaforyczny figurative, metaphorical
metajęzyk metalanguage
metal metal; **~ szlachetny** precious metal
metaliczny (*dźwięk*) metallic
metalik (*lakier*) metallic
metaloznawstwo metallurgy
metalurgiczny metallurgical
metamorfoza metamorphosis
meteor meteor
meteorolog meteorologist
meteorologia meteorology
meteorologiczny meteorological
meteoryt meteorite
metka label[1], price tag, tag[1], ticket
metkować price[2]
metoda method, way[1]; **~ działania** tactic IDM **~ prób i błędów** trial and error
metodologia methodology
metodologiczny methodological
metodyczny methodical
metodyst-a/ka Methodist
metodystyczny Methodist adj.
metr metre
metraż measurement; **mieszkanie o średnim ~u** a medium-sized flat
metro underground[3]
metropolia metropolis
metryczny metric
metryka certificate
mewa gull
męczarnia agony, ordeal; (*slang*) bugger[1]; (**męczarnie**) torture
męczący exhausting, gruelling, irksome, tiresome, tiring, trying
męczenni-k/ca (*i przen.*) martyr
męczeństwo martyrdom
męczyć/z-/za- 1 (*powodować zmęczenie*) tire[1], wear sb out; (**kogoś**) (**czymś**) keep on (at sb) (about sb/sth) **2** (*torturować*) torture verb □ **męczyć/z- się** tire[1], wear yourself out; **nad czymś** toil
męka torment
męski (*płeć*) male[1]; (*cecha; gram.*) masculine; (*cecha*) manly, virile; **~ szowinizm** chauvinism
męskość manhood, manliness, masculinity, virility
męstwo valour
mętlik: **miała zupełny ~ w głowie** her mind was in (a) turmoil
mętność diffuseness
mętny 1 (*woda*) cloudy **2** (*oczy*) bleary **3** (*mowa*) diffuse, inarticulate, opaque, wishy-washy **4** (*pojęcie*) vague **5** (*interesy itp.*) shady
męty dregs, scum
mężczyzna gentleman, male[2], man[1]
mężny valiant
mgiełka haze, mist[1]
mglić/za- (się) blur[2], cloud[2]
mglistość vagueness
mglist|y 1 (*pogoda*) foggy, hazy, misty **2** (*blady*) watery **3** (*niejasny*) vague; **~e zarysy/wspomnienie** blur[1]
mgł|a fog, mist[1]; **pokrywać (się) ~ą** mist (sth) up/over
mgr → MAGISTER
mi me
miałki fine[1]
mianować 1 (*zatrudniać*) appoint **2** (*wysuwać jako kandydata*) designate, nominate ■ **mianowan|y**: **osoba mianowana** (*na stanowisko, posadę*) appointee
mianowicie namely
miar|a 1 (*temperatury itp.*) measure[2], measurement, yardstick; **wziąć czyjąś ~ę** take sb's measurements; **zrobiony/uszyty na ~ę** made to measure, tailor-made; **wykonujący usługę na ~ę/zamówienie** bespoke **2** (*stopień*) degree IDM **w ~ę** mildly | **w dużej mierze** largely | **żadną ~ą** far from sth/doing sth
miarka dollop
miarodajny authoritative
miarowy steady[1]; **~ oddech** regular breathing
miast|o town; (*wielkie*) city; (*w Wlk Br.: całe miasto lub jego część, posiadająca władze lokalne*) borough; **~o bliźniacze** twin town; **~o portowe** port; **~o rodzinne** hometown; **~o-widmo** ghost town; **do ~a** downtown; **w mieście** downtown; (*bawić się*) (out) on the town
miauczeć/za-/miauknąć miaow verb
miazga pulp
miażdżący 1 (*porażka*) crushing; (*atak*) devastating **2** (*spojrzenie itp.*) withering
miażdżyć/z- annihilate, crush[1], squash[1]
miąć/z- (się) crease[2], crinkle, crumple
miąższ flesh, pulp
miecz sword; **po ~u** paternal
mieć 1 have/has got sth, have[1], hold[1], possess; **przy sobie** carry; (*w programie itp.*) have (got) sth on; **masz!** there you are; **nie ~** lack[2]; **nie ma ich** there aren't any; **nie ma go** he isn't here; **mają przed sobą całe życie** their whole lives lie ahead of them; **~ coś za sobą** get sth over (with); **masz wspaniały widok z tego okna** you get a wonderful view from that window **2** (*wiek*) **ile masz lat?** how old are you?; **Sue ma 18 lat** Sue is 18 **3 coś na sobie** have (got) sth on, wear **4** (*musieć*) **coś zrobić** be[2] to do sth, have (got) sth to do, should, be supposed to do sth; **do pracy masz przychodzić na dziewiątą.** you're meant to get to work at 9 o'clock **5** (*być zamierzonym jako coś*) **to miał być tylko żart** it was only meant as a joke IDM **nie ma za co** (*w odpowiedzi na „thank you"*) you're welcome □ **mieć się** (*dobrze/źle*) go[1]
miednica 1 (*naczynie*) bowl[1] **2** (*anat.*) pelvis
miednicowy pelvic
miedziak copper
miedziany copper
miedź copper
miejsc|e 1 (*wolna przestrzeń*) room, space[1]; **(wolne) ~e** elbow room **2** (*jakiegoś wydarzenia/działalności*) location, place[1], site, spot[1]; (*koncertu itp.*) venue; (*zbrodni itp.*) scene; **~e pracy** workplace; **~e spotkania** meeting place, rendezvous; **~e urodzenia** (*i przen.*) birthplace; **~e zamieszkania** abode, domicile, residence; **katedra była idealnym ~em na ich ślub** the cathedral was the perfect setting for their wedding **3** (*położenie*) position[1], point[1]; **wolne ~e** blank[2]; (*w spisie itp.*) slot[1]; **odpowiednie ~e** niche; **~e przebywania** whereabouts[1]; **~e po przecinku** decimal place; **na (swoim) ~u** in place; **nie na (swoim) ~u** out of place; **w złym/ nieodpowiednim ~u** in the way; **mieć swoje ~e** belong **4** (*siedzące*) seat[1], seating; **~e sypialne** berth; **~e sypialne w pociągu** sleeper; **~e postoju** (*dla statku*) berth **5** (*chwila*) **w tym ~u** here[1] IDM **mieć ~e** take place | **~e internetowe** website | **na czyjeś ~e** in place of sb/ sth, in sb/sth's place | **na ~u** outright, on the spot | **na moim/twoim itp. ~u** if I were you, in my, your, etc. place/ shoes | **nie na ~u** incongruous, out of order, out of place, in the way; (*niestosowny*) not called for, not sb's place to do sth | **pokazać komuś, gdzie jest jego ~e** put sb in his/her place | **w ~e** instead prep. of sb/sth/doing sth | **z ~a** outright, pat adv., on the spot, there and then, then and there

miejscowo: **środek znieczulający** ~ local anaesthetic
miejscowość: ~ **wypoczynkowa** resort[1]
miejscowy local[1]; (*tubylczy*) indigenous; (*sport*) home[2]; **człowiek** ~ native[2]; **czas** ~ local time
miejski civic, metropolitan, municipal, urban
mieli|zna: **na** ~**źnie** aground
mielon|y: **mięso** ~**e** mince
mienić się (*światło itp.*) play[1]; ~ **kolorami** be ablaze with colour, be a blaze of colour
■ **mieniący się** glittering
mienie estate
mierniczy surveyor
miernik gauge[1], standard[1]
mierność mediocrity
miernota 1 (*osoba; rzecz*) nonentity **2** (*o muzyce, sztuce itp.*) tripe
mierny indifferent, mediocre
mierzeja spit[2]
mierzyć/z- 1 gauge[2], measure[1], quantify; ~ **czas** time[2]; ~ **komuś puls** feel/take sb's pulse; ~ **komuś temperaturę** take somebody's temperature **2** ~ **(kogoś) wzrokiem** eye[2] **do kogoś/coś** (*z broni palnej*) zero in on sb/sth
□ **mierzyć/z- się**: **z kimś** glare at each other
miesiąc month; ~ **miodowy** honeymoon; **co** ~ monthly adv.; **na** ~ a/per month
miesiączk|a menstruation, period; **mieć** ~**ę** menstruate
miesiączkować menstruate
miesiączkowy menstrual
miesięcznik monthly[2]
miesięczny monthly[1]
■ **miesięcznie** monthly adv.
mieszać 1 (/za-/po-) (*herbatę itp.*) stir[1] **2 (/wy-/z-)** (*składniki ciasta itp.*) blend[1], mix[1]; ~ **dwa lub więcej składników, aż powstanie coś nowego** mix sth into/to sth **3 (/po-) coś (z czymś)** mingle; (*robić bałagan*) jumble[1] sth (up/together), mix sth up, muddle sth (up) **4 (/w-) kogoś w coś** implicate sb (in sth), involve sb in (doing) sth **5** (*zbić z tropu*) faze, mystify; ~ **komuś w głowie** confuse, muddle sb (up)
□ **mieszać się 1 (/po-/wy-)** merge (with/into sth), (together); (*kolory itp.*) mix[1] **2 (/w-)** (*między ludzi na imprezie itp.*) mingle **3 (/w-) w coś** (*wtrącać się*) interfere, intervene
mieszaniec 1 (*bot.*) hybrid **2** (*kundel*) mongrel
mieszanina medley, mix[2], mixture; (*nieporządek*) jumble[2]; (*połączenie*) amalgam
mieszanka assortment, blend[2], mix[2], mixture; (*zwł. melodii*) medley
mieszan|y assorted, mixed; ~**y debel** mixed doubles; ~**e małżeństwo** intermarriage, mixed marriage; ~**e uczucia** ambivalence; **mieć** ~**e uczucia** have mixed feelings (about sb/sth); **mający** ~**e uczucia** ambivalent
mieszarka mixer
mieszczański bourgeois
mieszczaństwo the bourgeoisie
mieszek follicle
mieszkać/za- 1 dwell, inhabit, live[1]; (*w wynajętym pokoju*) lodge[2]; (*w hotelu itp.*) stay[1]; ~ **byle gdzie** (*zwykle bezdomni*) live/sleep rough **2** (*ptaki*) roost verb
mieszkalny habitable
mieszkanie accommodation, dwelling, home[1], lodging, place[1]; (*w bloku*) flat[2]; (**mieszkania**) housing; ~ **dwupoziomowe** maisonette; **dawać** ~ house[2]
miesz-kaniec/kanka citizen, dweller, inhabitant, local[2], occupant; (**mieszkańcy**) people, population; (**stał-y/a**) ~ resident; **mieszkaniec wsi** countryman; **dla mieszkańców** residential
mieszkaniowy residential; **wydział** ~ the Council's housing department
mieścić/z-: **(w sobie)** fit[1], hold[1], take; (*dom itp.*) accommodate; (*teatr*) seat[2]
□ **mieścić się 1 (/z-)** fit[1], go[1] **2** (*znajdować się*) be housed
mięczak 1 (*zool.*) shellfish **2** (*osoba*) pushover, wimp
mięczakowaty wimpish
między (*dwoma osobami/rzeczami*) between; (*wieloma osobami/rzeczami*) amid, among
międzyczas IDM **w** ~**ie** in the meantime
międzykontynentalny intercontinental
międzymiastowy long-distance
międzynarodow|y international; (*rozmowa telefoniczna*) long-distance; **na arenie** ~**ej** internationally
międzywydziałowy interdepartmental
miękki 1 soft; (*książka*) **w** ~**ej okładce** paperback **2** (*mięso*) tender[1] **3** (*ruch*) floppy **4** (*dźwięk*) mellow **5** (*bojaźliwy*) wet[1] **6** (*jazda itp.*) smooth[1] IDM **o** ~**m sercu** soft-hearted
mięknąć/z- 1 soften **2** (*wzruszyć się*) melt, relent, soften
mięsień muscle
mięsisty meaty, succulent
mięsny meaty
mięso flesh, meat; ~ **drobiowe** poultry; ~ **jagnięce** lamb; ~ **mielone** mince
mięsożerca carnivore
mięsożerny carnivorous
mięśniowy muscular
mięta mint, peppermint; ~ **zielona** spearmint
miętowy mint
miętówka mint
mig: ~**iem** like a shot
migacz indicator
mig-ać/nąć flash[1], flicker[1]
□ **migać/wy- się** (*wykręcać się*) dodge[1]
migawka 1 (*w aparacie fotograficznym itp.*) shutter **2** (**migawki**) (*obrazy z życia itp.*) snapshot
migdał 1 (*orzech*) almond **2** (*anat.*) (także **migdałek**) tonsil; ~**ek gardłowy** adenoids
mignięcie glimpse
migotać/za- blink, flicker[1], glimmer verb, shimmer, twinkle; (*światło itp.*) play[1]
migow|y: **język** ~**y** sign language; **posługiwać się językiem** ~**ym** sign[2]
migracja migration
migracyjny migratory
migrena migraine
migrować migrate
mi-jać/nąć 1 (*przejść obok*) go by, pass[1], pass by (sb/sth) **2** (*czas*) go on, go past, pass[1], tick away/by/past; (*północ*) turn[1] **3** (*słabnąć*) wear off **4** (*kończyć się*) go[1], pass[1]
□ **mijać/roz-/minąć się** pass[1]
IDM ~ **z prawdą** be untruthful
mikrob microbe
mikrobus minibus
mikrofala microwave
mikrofalówka microwave
mikrofilm microfiche
mikrofon microphone; (*noszony przy ustach*) mouthpiece
mikrokomputer microcomputer
mikrokosmos microcosm
mikroprocesor microprocessor
mikroskop microscope
mikroskopijny microscopic, minute[2]
mikroukład microchip
mikser blender, food processor, mixer
miksować/z- 1 (*owoce itp.*) liquidize **2** (*muzykę*) dub, mix[1]
mikstura concoction
mil|a mile; ~ **na godzinę** mph
milczący 1 silent **2** (*porozumienie itp.*) implicit, tacit
milczeni|e silence; **prawo do** ~**a** the right to remain silent; (*siedzieć itp.*) **w** ~**u** without saying anything
mile agreeably; ~ **widziany** desirable, welcome[2]; ~ **wspominać** have fond memories of sb/sth
miliard billion
miliarder/ka billionaire
milicja militia
miligram milligram
mililitr millilitre
milimetr millimetre
milion 1 million **2** (*mnóstwo*) zillion
milioner millionaire
milionow|y millionth noun; **(jedna)** ~**a** millionth[2]
militarny military
militaryst-a/ka militarist
militarystyczny militaristic
militaryzacja militarization
militaryzm militarism
militaryzować/z- militarize
millenium millennium
milord: ~**zie** lord
miło amiably, nicely, pleasantly; **będzie nam** ~ **zobaczyć się z tobą** we'd be glad to see you; ~ **cię/pana/panią/państwa poznać** nice/pleased to meet you, how do you do?; **to bardzo** ~ **z twojej strony** it was very sweet/thoughtful of you (to do sth); **jak to** ~ **z ich strony!** what a kind thought!
miłosierdzie charity, mercy
miłosierny merciful
miłosny amorous
miłoś|ć love[1]; **z** ~**cią** lovingly IDM **na** ~**ć boską!** for Christ's/God's/goodness'/Heaven's/pity's sake
miłośni-k/czka fan[1], lover; (*zwł. opery/win*) buff; (*przesadny*) maniac
IDM **będący miłośnikiem czegoś** keen on sb/sth
miły agreeable, nice, pleasant, pleasing; (*tylko o osobie*) amiable, friendly[1], likeable, lovable; (*dziecko, uśmiech itp.*) cute, sweet[1]; (*wieczór itp.*) enjoyable
mim mime
mimicznie: **grać/wyrażać (coś)** ~ mime verb
mimiczn|y: **gra/ekspresja** ~**a** mime

mimik|a 1 (*pantomima*) mime; **grać/ wyrażać coś ~ą** mime verb **2** (*naśladowanie*) mimicry
mimo (*przyimek: wbrew*) for all IDM **~ to** even so, nevertheless, regardless, still[1], yet | **~ wszystko** all/ just the same, come what may, in any case, regardless | **~ że** although, even though, though
■ **mimo** past adv.
mimochodem parenthetically, in passing
mimowolny inadvertent, involuntary, unwitting
min|a 1 (*wyraz twarzy*) countenance[1]; **robić/stroić ~y** make/pull faces/ a face (at sb/sth) **2** (*bomba*) mine[2]; **~a lądowa** landmine IDM **robić dobrą ~ę do złej gry** make the best of sth/a bad job
minaret minaret
minąć (się) → MIJAĆ (SIĘ)
minerał mineral
mini mini-
miniatura miniature; (*zwierzę lub roślina*) dwarf[1]
miniaturowy miniature
minidysk minidisc
minikamera minicam, Palmcorder
minikomputer minicomputer
minimalistyczny minimalist
minimalizm minimalism
minimalizować/z- minimize; (*problem*) play sth down
minimalny minimal, minimum[1]
minimum minimum adv., minimum[2]; **~ socjalne** breadline
miniony bygone, former, past[1]
minister minister, secretary, Secretary of State; **~ finansów/ skarbu** chancellor; (*w Wlk. Br.*) **Minister Spraw Wewnętrznych** the Home Secretary; **~ spraw zagranicznych** the Foreign Minister, the Foreign Secretary; **~ sprawiedliwości** Attorney General
ministerialny departmental, ministerial
ministerstwo department, ministry, office; **~ skarbu państwa** the Treasury; (*w Wlk. Br.*) **Ministerstwo Spraw Wewnętrznych** the Home Office; (*w Wlk. Br.*) **Ministerstwo Spraw Zagranicznych** the Foreign (and Commonwealth) Office
minorowy minor[1]
minować/za- mine[3]
minus less[3], minus[1,2,3]
minuta minute[1]
minutnik: **~ do jajek** egg timer
miodownik gingerbread
miot litter
miotać buffet[2], hurl, throw
□ **miotać się** be/go on the rampage
miotła brush[1]; (*z kijem*) broom
miód honey
mirabelka wild plum
miraż mirage
miriady myriad
misa basin
miseczka bowl[1]; **~ do zupy** soup bowl
misja mission
misjona-rz/rka missionary
miska bowl[1]
misterność intricacy
misterny elaborate, intricate
mistrz/yni (*w rzemiośle itp.*) master[1]; (*sport*) champion[1]; (*nieform.*) champ[2]; (*duchowy*) guru; **mistrz ceremonii** master of ceremonies, MC, usher[1]; **mistrz murarski** master builder
mistrzostwo 1 (*kunszt*) artistry **2** (*sport*) championship
mistrzowsk|i expert adj.; **lekcja ~a** masterclass; **po ~u** expertly
mistycyzm mysticism
mistyczny mystical
mistyfikacja myth
misty-k/czka mystic
mistyka mystique
miszmasz hotchpotch
mi|ś 1 (*zabawa*) teddy bear; **~ś koala** koala **2** (*tkanina*) **na ~siu** lined with cotton fleece
mit myth
mitologia mythology
mitologiczny mythological
mityczny mythical
mizantrop misanthrope
mizantropia misanthropy
mizantropijny misanthropic
mizerak weed[1]
mizerny 1 (*ilość*) measly, paltry **2** (*jakość*) poor **3** (*osoba; mały*) weedy **4** (*blady*) wan
mizogin misogynist
mizoginia misogyny
mizoginistyczny misogynistic
mknąć/po- speed[2], streak[2]; (*z hałasem*) zoom
mlas-kać/nąć champ[1]
mlecz 1 (*bot.*) dandelion **2** (*zool.*) roe
mleczarnia dairy[1]
mlecza-rz/rka milkman
mleczko 1 (*kokosu itp.*) milk[1] **2** (*do twarzy*) lotion; **~ z filtrem przeciwsłonecznym** sunscreen
mleczn|y 1 (*o dużej zawartości mleka*) milky; **~a czekolada** milk chocolate **2** (*produkt*) dairy[2]
mleć/ze- grind[1], mill[2]
mlek|o milk[1]; **~o odtłuszczone** skimmed milk; **~o matki** breast milk; **kawa z ~iem** white coffee
młode (*rz.*) baby; (*potomstwo*) offspring; (*zwł. zwierząt*) young[2]; (*lisa/niedźwiedzia/lwa/tygrysa/ wilka*) cub; (*słonia itp.*) calf
młodociany juvenile, youthful; **~ przestępca** juvenile delinquent
■ **młodocian-y/a** juvenile noun
młodość youth
młodsz|y (*brat/siostra*) little[1]; (**Młodszy**) (*po nazwisku*) junior[1]; **ona jest od niego dwa lata ~a** she's two years his junior/his junior by two years; **~y rangą** junior[1] (to sb)
mło|dy young[1], youthful; (*zielony*) at a tender age; **dość ~dy** youngish; **~da osoba** youngster, youth; **~dzi (ludzie)** the young[2], youth IDM **~dy duchem** young at heart
młodzieniec adolescent, youth
młodzieńczy youthful
młodzież the young[2], youth
młodzieżowy young[1]
młot (także **młotek**) hammer[1]; **drewniany ~ek** mallet; **~ kowalski** sledgehammer; **~ pneumatyczny** pneumatic drill; (*sport*) **rzut ~em** hammer[1] IDM **znajdować się między ~em a kowadłem** get caught in the crossfire
młyn 1 (*budynek*) mill[1]; **~ wodny** watermill **2** (także **młynek**) (*maszyna*) grinder, mill[1]; **~ek do pieprzu** pepper mill **3** (*sport*) scrum
młyna-rz/rka miller
mniam-mniam yummy
mnich monk
mnie me
mniej zob. też MAŁO **1** (*z rz. niepolicz.; z przym., przysł., cz.*) less[1]; (*z rz. policz.*) fewer; (*znany itp.*) lesser; (*zarabiać itp.*) under **2** (*odejmując*) less[2], minus[1] IDM **~ więcej** about[1], more or less, in the region of sth, thereabouts
mniejszoś|ć minority; **~ć etniczna/ narodowa** ethnic minority, minority; **być w ~ci** be in a/the minority
mniejsz|y zob. też MAŁY; lesser IDM **~a o (to)** neither here nor there | **~e zło** the lesser of two evils
mniemanie: **wysokie ~ o sobie** self-importance
mnogość multitude
mnożyć/po-/roz- multiply A by B
■ **mnożenie** multiplication
mnóstwo a lot of, host, multitude, no end of sth, score[1], wealth; (*po rz.*) galore; (*z rz. policz.*) a good/great many, millions, any number of; (*nieform.*) bags[1], heaps[1], loads[1], masses[1], oodles, stack[1]
mobilizować/z- mobilize
□ **mobilizować/z- się** mobilize; **~ do wyjścia** work up the energy to go out
mobilny: **dom(ek) ~** mobile home
■ **mobilność** mobility
moc 1 (*siła psychiczna/fizyczna*) force[1], power[1]; (*siła fizyczna*) might[2] **2** (*stopień stężenia*) intensity, strength **3** (*chem.*) potency **4** (*fiz.*) energy, power[1] **5** (*prawn.*) **~ prawna** validity; **nabierać ~y** take effect; **nie mieć ~y prawnej** have no legal standing; **w ~y** in effect; **~ą którego** whereby IDM **na ~y czegoś** on the strength of sth, by virtue of sth
mocarstwo power[1]
mocno 1 (*silnie*) strongly; (*trzymać itp.*) fast[2], firmly, tight adv., tightly; (*przymocowany*) securely; **~ zaciśnięty węzeł** a tight knot **2** (*uderzać; padać*) hard[2] **3** (*intensywnie: śnieg itp.: padać*) heavily; (*kochać itp.*) intensely; (*spać*) soundly; (*argumentować itp.*) powerfully **4** (*solidnie*) sturdily **5** (*sporo*) well[1]
mocn|y 1 (*fizycznie; psychicznie*) strong, tough; (*fizycznie*) hefty, mighty[1]; (*uchwyt itp.*) firm[2]; (*uścisk itp.*) tight **2** (*uderzenie; deszcz; sen*) heavy; (*sen*) sound **3** (*ból*) sharp[1] **4** (*kolor, zapach itp.*) rich **5** (*przemówienie itp.*) powerful **6** (*wiatr; nurt*) strong **7** (*rywalizacja*) stiff[1] **8** (*tkanina itp.*) hard-wearing **9** (*idący do głowy*) heady; **~y alkohol** spirit[1] **10** (*chem.*) potent **11** (*solidny; zdrowy*) stout, sturdy IDM **czyjaś ~a strona** forte, strength, sb's strong point
mocować się 1 (*bić się*) grapple (with sb); (*sport*) wrestle **2** (*z zamkiem itp.*) fumble
mocz urine
moczar (także **moczary**) bog, marsh, swamp[1]
moczowy urinary

moczyć (się) 1 (**/z-**) (*zwilżać; stawać się mokrym*) wet[2] **2** (**/za-**; **/na-**) (*naczynia, pranie*) soak

mo|da trend, vogue; (*zwł. styl ubierania się*) fashion; **chwilowa ~da** fad; **być w ~dzie** be in fashion; **wchodzić w ~dę** come into fashion; **wychodzić z ~dy** date[2], go/be out of fashion

modalny modal

model 1 (*rodzaj*) model[1]; (*samochodu itp.*) mark[2] **2** (*miniatura samolotu itp.*) model[1]; **~ w skali** scale model **3** (*wzór*) paradigm **4** (*osoba*) (także **modelka**) model[1]; (*przestarz.*) mannequin; **praca ~a** modelling

modelować/wy- model[2], mould[2]

■ **modelowanie** (*włosów*) blow-dry

modem modem

modernist-a/ka modernist

modernistyczny modernist, modernistic

modernizacja modernization

modernizm modernism

modernizować/z- modernize, update

□ **modernizować/z- się** modernize

modlić/po- się pray, worship

modlitewnik prayer book

modlitw|a (*słowa*) prayer; (*modlenie się*) prayer, worship noun; **~a przed posiłkiem/po posiłku** grace; **uzdrawianie ~ą** faith healing

modniarstwo millinery

modn|y (*zwł. ubranie*) fashionable, trendy; (*nowoczesny*) up to date; (*grupa itp.*) hot[1]; (*kolor; styl; klub itp.*) in[2]; **być ~ym** be in fashion; **nie być ~ym** go/be out of fashion

modrzew larch

modulacja tone[1]; (*głosu*) inflection; **~ amplitudy** AM; **~ częstotliwości** FM

modularny modular

moduł module; (*kurs itp.*) **podzielony na ~y** modular

modułowy modular

modyfikacja modification

modyfikować/z- modify

■ **modyfikowany**: **genetycznie modyfikowany** genetically modified

mogiła grave[1]

moher mohair

moknąć/z- wet[2]

mokry wet[1]; **zupełnie ~** saturated

molekuła molecule

molestować harass; **~ seksualnie** molest

■ **molestowanie**: **~ dzieci** child abuse; **~ seksualne** sexual harassment

moll minor[1]

molo jetty; (*dłuższe*) pier; (*terminal załadunkowy*) quay

momen|t moment, while[2]; (*nieform.*) tick[2]; (*konkretny*) point[1]; **~t zwrotny** watershed; **w tym ~cie** (*wtedy*) at that instant, there; (*teraz*) right now

momentalnie instantaneously, instantly

monarch-a/ini monarch, sovereign[1]

monarchia monarchy

monarszy imperial

moneta coin[1]; (*konkretnej nominacji*) piece[1]; **~ dziesięciocentowa** dime

monetarny monetary

monit reminder

monitor monitor[1]; **~ komputera** VDU

monitoring: **~ wizyjny** closed-circuit television, CCTV

monitorować: **kogoś (na coś)** screen[2] sb (for sth)

monochromatyczny monochrome

monofonia mono noun

monofoniczny mono

monogamia monogamy

monogamiczny monogamous

monolit monolith

monolitowy (także **monolityczny**) monolithic

monolog monologue

mononukleoza: **~ zakaźna** glandular fever

monopol monopoly

monopolizować/z- monopolize; (*nieform.*) hog[2]

monopolowy: **sklep ~** off-licence

monosylaba monosyllable

monotonia monotony

monotonn|y monotonous, repetitive; **mówić ~ym głosem** drone on

monstrualny gross[1], monstrous

■ **monstrualność** monstrosity

monstrum ogre

monsun monsoon

montaż (*składanie: urządzeń*) assembly; (*instalacja*) installation; (*wzniesienie*) erection

montażyst-a/ka editor

montować 1 (**/z-/za-**) (*urządzenie*) assemble, fit[1], mount[1], put sth together; (*instalację*) install; (*nieform*) rig sth up **2** (**/z-**) (*film*) edit

monument monument

monumentalny monumental

mop mop[1]

moped moped

morale morale

moralizatorski didactic, moralistic

moralizować moralize

moralny ethical, moral[1]; **bardzo ~ i potępiający innych** priggish

■ **moralność** morals[2], morality

morał message, moral[2]

moratorium moratorium

mord killing, murder

morda muzzle

morder-ca/czyni killer, murderer; (*oprawca*) butcher[1]; **seryjn-y/a morder-ca/czyni** serial killer

morderczy deadly; (*broń itp.*) lethal; (*maniak itp.*) homicidal, murderous

morderstwo killing, murder

mordęga fag

mordować/za- kill[1], murder; (*nieform.*) bump sb off

morela apricot

morfina morphine

morfologia morphology

morfologiczny morphological

mormorando: **śpiewać ~** hum

mors walrus

morski (*bot., zool.*) marine[1]; (*żegl.*) maritime, nautical; (*wojsk.*) naval; (*ryba itp.*) saltwater

morświn porpoise

morz|e sea; (*literackie*) the deep; **mieszkać nad ~em** live by the sea; **jechać nad ~e** go to the seaside; **na ~u** at sea

mosiądz brass

moskit mosquito

most bridge[1]; **budować ~** bridge[2] IDM **powiedzieć komuś coś prosto z ~u** make no bones about telling sb sth

mostek 1 ~ dla pieszych footbridge **2 ~ kapitański** bridge[1] **3** (*anat.*) breastbone, sternum **4 ~ dentystyczny** bridgework

mostowe toll

mość: **Jej/Jego/Wasza Królewska Mość** Her/His/Your majesty, HM, Her/His/Your Royal Highness, HRH

motać reel sth in

motel motel

motłoch mob[1], rabble

motocykl cycle[1], motorbike

motocyklist-a/ka biker, motorcyclist, rider

motor 1 (*silnik*) engine, motor[1] **2** (*pojazd*) bike motorbike

motorowy motor[2], motorized

motorówka motorboat

motto motto

motyka hoe

motyl butterfly

motylek (*styl pływacki*) butterfly

motyw 1 (*wzór*) motif **2** (*powód*) motive **3** (*muzyczny itp.*) theme

motywacj|a 1 (*zachęta*) motivation; (*chęć*) drive[2]; **dostarczać ~i** motivate **2** (*uzasadnienie*) reasoning

motywować 1 (**/z-**) (*zachęcać*) motivate **2** (**/u-**) (*wyjaśniać*) justify

mow|a 1 (*język*) language, speech; **~a ciała** body language; **~a niezależna** direct speech; **~a zależna** reported speech; **w ~ie** orally **2** (*przemówienie*) speech; **~a pogrzebowa** eulogy IDM **nie ma ~y!** I draw the line at that, it's just not on, no way

mozaika mosaic

mozolić się labour[2] away, plod along/on, slog[1] (away) (at sth), toil

mozolny (*zadanie itp.*) laborious, uphill; **mozolna praca/wędrówka** slog[2]

mozół toil noun

moździerz mortar

może (także **być może**) conceivably, maybe, might[1], perhaps, possibly; **~ i jest bardzo mądry** he may be very clever; **~ by** why not

możliwoś|ć 1 (*zdolność*) capability; (*intelektualne itp.*) power[1] to do sth; (*urządzenia*) facility; **przekraczać czyjeś ~ci** be beyond the capacity of sb **2** (*szansa; sposób*) avenue, means, possibility, prospect of sth/of doing sth, scope for sth/to do sth; (*okazja*) chance[1]; (*zmiany, poprawy itp.*) room for sth; **mieć ~ć czegoś** have the option of sth; **nie ma ~ci czegoś** no question of sth

możliwy possible; (*prawdopodobny*) likely; (*w pytaniach i przeczeniach*) earthly; **~ do przeprowadzenia** practicable; **możliwe, że pojadę do Chin** I may/might be going to China; **jak tylko możliwe** possibly

■ **możliwie** conceivably, perhaps, possibly

można: **robić, co tylko ~** do/try your best

móc 1 (*potrafić*) be able to do sth, can[1] **2** (*w prośbach*) could, may, might[1]; **czy mógłbyś...?** would you mind...? **3** (*wyrażając prawdopodobieństwo*) could, may, might[1]; **~ (coś zrobić)** be likely (to do sth) **4** (*mieć pozwolenie*) be at liberty to do sth, can[1]

mój (*z rz.*) my; (*bez rz.*) mine[1]

mól moth IDM **~ książkowy** bookworm

mór plague[1]

mów-ca/czyni (*osoba zabierająca głos*) speaker; (*dobr-y/a*) orator

mówić 1 (/powiedzieć/po-/wy-) (*wypowiadać się*) **coś komuś** say[1], tell; **z kimś o czymś** speak (to sb) (about sb/sth), talk[1] (to/with sb) (about/of sb/sth); (*wypowiadać słowo/zdanie*) utter[2]; (*mieć na myśli*) mean[1]; **za kogoś** speak for sb; ~ **dalej** continue, go on; ~ **głośniej** speak up; ~ **do rzeczy/z sensem** talk sense; ~ **coś kategorycznie** protest[2]; ~ **przez nos** snuffle; ~ **otwarcie (przeciwko czemuś)** speak out (against sth); ~ **do kogoś protekcjonalnie/z lekceważeniem** talk down to sb; ~ **bez słów** (*ruszać bezgłośnie ustami*) mouth[2]; ~ **szeptem/półgłosem** say sth, speak, etc. under your breath; **nie ~ o czymś nikomu** keep sth to yourself; **źle ~ o kimś/czymś** knock[1]; **powiedzieć, która godzina** tell the time; **wszyscy mówią, że** by all accounts; **mówi się, że…** be reported to be/as sth **2** (*mieć zdolność mowy; po angielsku itp.*) speak **3** (*przepisy itp.*) say[1] sth (to sb); (*odnosić się*) refer to sb/sth (as sth); (*przypominać*) ~ **(komuś) coś** ring a bell IDM **a nie mówiłem?** I told you so | **można powiedzieć, że** it's safe to say that | ~ **samo za siebie** speak for itself | **nie ma o czym** ~ don't mention it | **nie mów już o tym** now give it a rest | **nie mówiąc już o czymś** let alone, not to mention
mównica platform, rostrum
mózg 1 (*anat.*) brain **2** (*planu, akcji itp.*) mastermind IDM **pranie ~u** brainwashing
mózgowy cerebral
mroczny (*ciemny*) dark[1]; (*z powodu braku światła*) dim[1], murky; (*wnętrze, las, niebo itp.*) sombre
mrok 1 (*ciemność*) blackness, dark[2], darkness; (*półmrok*) shadow[1] **2** (*ponurość*) gloom
mrowić się be crawling with sth
mrowie swarm[1]
mrowienie (*na mrozie*) tingle; (*w nodze*) pins and needles; **odczuwać** ~ tingle
mrozić/za- (*jedzenie*) refrigerate IDM **mrożący krew w żyłach** blood-curdling, chilling
mroźny freezing[1], icy; (*i przen.*) frosty
mrożonki convenience food
mrożony (*żywność*) frozen[2]; (*napoje*) iced
mrówka ant
mrówkojad anteater
mrówkowiec tenement
mróz (także **mrozy**) freeze[2], frost[1]; **będzie** ~ it's going to freeze
mruczeć 1 (/mruknąć) (*osoba*) murmur; (*zwł. ze złością*) mutter **2 (/za-)** (*kot*) purr
mrug-ać/nąć (*oczami; światłem*) blink; (*porozumiewawczo oczami*) wink at sb; (*rzęsami*) flutter IDM **(nawet) nie mrugnąć okiem** (*w trudnej sytuacji*) not bat an eyelid, not turn a hair
mrukliwy cranky, grumpy, monosyllabic
mrużyć/z-: ~ **oczy** screw your eyes up IDM **nie zmrużyłem oka** I didn't sleep a wink
msza service[1]; (*katolicka*) mass[1]
mszaln|y: **wino ~e** sacramental wine
mszyca aphid
mścić/po- avenge
□ **mścić/ze- się** avenge, revenge verb yourself on sb, get your revenge, take revenge
mściwy vengeful, vindictive
mu him
mucha fly[2]
muchomor toadstool
muesli muesli
mukowiscydoza cystic fibrosis
mulisty muddy, slimy
multimedialny multimedia
multimilioner/ka multimillionaire
multipleks multiplex
muł 1 (*zool.*) mule **2** (*osad*) mud, sludge, slime; (*na dnie rzeki*) silt
mumia mummy
mundur (także **mundurek**) uniform[1] IDM **ziemniak w ~ku** jacket potato
mur wall
murarz bricklayer
murawa green[2]
Murzyn/ka black[2]
mus mousse
musical musical[2]
musieć have[1], have to, must[1], need[1,2], be obliged to do sth, shall, be supposed to do sth, want[1]; **nie musiał iść do banku** he didn't need to go to the bank
mus-kać/nąć brush[2], skim IDM **musnąć wargami** peck
muskularny brawny, muscular
musować bubble[2]; (*napój bezalkoholowy*) fizz verb
■ **musujący** effervescent, bubbly; (*napój bezalkoholowy*) fizzy; (*woda mineralna, wino*) sparkling
musz|ka 1 (*krawat*) bow tie **2** (*w broni*) **na ~ce** at gunpoint
muszla 1 (także **muszelka**) seashell, shell[1] **2** ~ **klozetowa** toilet
musztarda mustard
musztra drill[1]
musztrować drill[2]
muślin muslin
mutacj|a 1 (*zmiana genów itp.*) mutation **2** (*głos*) **przechodzić ~ę** break[1]
mutant mutant
mutować/z- (się) mutate
muza muse
muzeum museum
muzułman-in/ka Muslim
muzułmański Islamic, Muslim
muzyczny musical[1]
muzy-k/czka musician, player
muzyka music; ~ **country** country and western; ~ **kameralna** chamber music; ~ **ludowa** folk[1]; ~ **poważna** classical music; ~ **soul** soul; ~ **z głośników** (*w supermarkecie*) piped music
muzykalny musical[1]
muzykant musician
muzykologia musicology
muzykolog musicologist
muzykować: ~ **na ulicy** busk
my we
myć/u-/z- wash[1]; (*zęby*) clean[2]; ~ **szamponem** shampoo verb; ~ **podłogę mopem** mop[2]; ~ **gąbką** sponge[2]
□ **myć/u- się** wash[1]
mydlany soapy
mydliny lather, suds
mydło soap
myjnia: ~ **samochodowa** car wash
mylący confusing, deceptive
mylić/po-: **kogoś/coś (z kimś/czymś)** confuse A and/with B, mix sb/sth up (with sb/sth)
□ **mylić/po- się** (*popełnić błąd*) be mistaken, slip up, go wrong; (*w rachunkach*) be out adj.; **o ile się nie mylę** I suppose
mylny erroneous, incorrect, mistaken; (*opinia*) misguided; ~ **osąd** an error of judgement
■ **mylnie** erroneously, by mistake, mistakenly, wrongly
mysi mousy
mysz mouse
myszkować: **(po/w czymś)** (*w poszukiwaniu czegoś*) ferret[2] (about/around) (for sth); (*w torbie itp.*) burrow[1]; (*zwł. w poszukiwaniu poufnych informacji*) nose about/around, poke about/around, snoop around
myszołów buzzard
myśl idea, inspiration; **mieć coś na ~i** be on about sth, mean[1], refer to sb/sth (as sth)
myśleć/po- figure[2] (that), reckon, say to yourself, think; **o czymś/kimś** make sth of sb/sth, think about/of sb; (*o kimś chorym itp.*) spare a thought for sb; ~ **sobie (nie całkiem serio)** toy with sth; **tak właśnie myślałem** it/that figures; **zawsze o tobie myślę** you are always in my thoughts
■ **myśleni|e** thinking[1], thought[2]; **sposób myślenia** mentality, mindset
myśliciel/ka thinker
myśliwiec fighter
myśliwski: **kapelusz** ~ deerstalker
myśliwy hunter
myślnik dash[1]
myślowy intellectual[1], inward adj., notional
myto toll
mżawka drizzle
mżyć drizzle verb

N

n (N/n) (*litera*) N, n
na 1 (*położenie*) on, over; (*ulicy itp.*) along **2** (*kierunek*) onto, to, towards; ~ **zachód od czegoś** to the west of sth **3** (*jakąś ilość*) a, per, the; (*osobę itp.*) apiece; **jedzenie ~ dwa dni** two days' worth of food **4** (*czas*) for[1]; (*godzinę itp.*) by **5** (*czynność, zajęcie*) for[1] **6** (*wpłata*) ~ **jakiś cel** towards **7** (*koncercie itp.*) at **8** (*jakąś chorobę*) of **9** (*niż*) to **10** (*wymieniać*) for[1]; (*przebierać; tłumaczyć; dzielić*) into **11** (*ciepły, tani itp.*) **(jak)** ~ for[1] **12** (*ubrany: na czarno itp.*) in[1]; (*mieć*) ~ **sobie** on IDM ~ **co** what for?; (*po czym*) whereupon | **co ty ~ to?** what do you say?
nabałaganić → BAŁAGANIĆ
nabawi(a)ć się (*choroby*) catch[1], contract[2]
nabazgrać → BAZGRAĆ
nabazgrolić → BAZGROLIĆ
nabiał dairy products/produce; **sklep z ~em** dairy[1]
nabiegły: ~ **krwią** bloodshot
nab(ie)rać 1 (*przyzwyczajenia, nawyków*) develop, get into the habit of, take to sth/doing sth; ~ **pewności siebie** grow in confidence

2 (*doświadczenia*) gain[1]; (*wprawy*) get into your stride, master[2]; ~ **otuchy** take heart (from sth) **3** ~ **szybkości** gather speed, pick up speed **4 kogoś** con[2] sb (into doing sth/out of sth), have sb on, fool[2] sb (into doing sth), kid[2], string sb along, take sb in, take sb for a ride **5** (*brać dużo*) take; (*podnosić*) scoop[2] sb/sth (up)
□ **nab(ie)rać się** fall for sth
nabi(ja)ć 1 nabić sobie siniaka bruise verb **2** (*na liczniku*) clock sth up
■ **nabijany czymś** studded | **nabity** (*przestrzeń itp.*) tight
□ **nabijać się: z kogoś/czegoś** mock[1]
nabożeństwo service[1], worship noun
nabój cartridge, refill; (*w broni palnej*) round[4]
nabór intake
nabrać (się) → NABIERAĆ (SIĘ)
nabrzeż|e (*murowane, z ziemi*) embankment; (*murowane: gdzie cumują łodzie*) quay; (*i drewniane*) jetty; (*gdzie rozładowują statki*) wharf; **teren koło ~a** quayside
nabrzmie(wa)ć fester
naburmuszeni|e grumpiness; **z ~em** huffily
naburmuszon|y grumpy, huffy, sulky; **z ~ą miną** sulkily
nabyci|e: możliwy do ~a obtainable
IDM **do ~a w promocyjnej cenie** on offer
nabytek 1 (*zakup*) acquisition, purchase **2** (*ktoś ceniony; coś cennego*) **cenny** ~ asset (to sb/sth)
naby(wa)ć acquire; (*zwł. z trudnością*) get hold of sth verb, procure sth (for sb); (*kupować*) purchase
nabyw-ca/czyni purchaser; ~ **domu/mieszkania** homebuyer
nabzdyczony grumpy
nachy-lać/lić (się) dip[1], slant[1], tilt; (*teren*) slope verb[1], incline[1] towards sth
■ **nachyleni|e** slant[2], tilt noun; (*góry*) incline[2]; **stopień nachylenia** gradient
naciąć → NACINAĆ
naciągacz cowboy
naciąg-ać/nąć 1 (*mięśnie*) pull[1], strain[2] **3 kogoś na coś** scrounge sth (from/off sb), trick verb, trick sb into sth/doing sth **4** (*wyniki*) tweak **5** (*herbata itp.*) brew, infuse
■ **naciąganie kogoś na coś** con[1], imposition, trickery | **naciągany** (*nierzetelny*) far-fetched
na-cierać/trzeć: na kogoś/coś charge[2]
■ **nacieranie** (*kremem*) rub noun
nacięcie incision; (*zwł. przez pomyłkę*) nick[1]
na-cinać/ciąć (*długim, wąskim nacięciem*) slit[2]; (*zwł. przez pomyłkę*) nick[2]
nacisk 1 (*fizyczny; moralny*) push[2]; **grupa ~u** pressure group; **wywierać** ~ push[1] sb (to do sth /into doing sth) **2** (*na słowo/fakt*) accent, emphasis, stress[1]; **kłaść ~ na coś** emphasize, lay emphasis on sth, stress[2]
naciskać 1 (/nacisnąć) (*przycisk*) press[2], push[1]; (*form.*) depress; ~ **klakson** sound the horn of your car; ~ **sprzęgło** engage the clutch **2 na kogoś/coś** bear down (on sb/sth), press[2] sb (for sth/to do sth), push[1] sb (to do sth /into doing sth)
nacja people
nacjonalist-a/ka nationalist
nacjonalistyczny nationalistic
nacjonalizacja nationalization
nacjonalizm nationalism
nacjonalizować/z- nationalize
naczelnik chief[2]; ~ **więzienia** warden
naczelny (*przym.*) chief[1], general[1], prime[1], supreme; **ssak** ~ primate
■ **naczelny** (*rz.*) head[1]
naczyni|e 1 (*kuchenne*) dish[1]; (*form.*) receptacle; (**naczynia**) crockery
2 (*anat.*) vessel; **~e krwionośne** blood vessel; **~e włoskowate** capillary
naćpany high[1] on sth, spaced out, stoned, zonked out
nad 1 (*powyżej*) above, over; ~ **rzeką/morzem** on the river/seafront
2 (*bardziej*) before[1] IDM **~e wszystko** first and foremost
nadać (się) → NADAWAĆ (SIĘ)
nadający się eligible, fit[2] for sb/sth, to do sth
nadajnik transmitter
nadal still[1]
nadaremnie: ~ próbując ukryć łzy in a vain attempt to hide her tears
nada(wa)ć 1 (*radio, TV*) be on (the) air, broadcast; ~ **przez radio** radio verb; ~ **w telewizji** telecast, televise; ~ **błyskawicznie** flash[1] **2** (*dać: nagrodę itp.*) bestow sth (on/upon sb), confer sth (on sb); ~ **imię** (*w ceremonii chrześcijańskiej*) christen; ~ **przezwisko** nickname verb; ~ **komuś prawo wyborcze** enfranchise **3** ~ **ważność** validate **4** (*styl; tempo*) set
□ **nada(wa)ć się: do czegoś** lend itself to sth; (*osoba*) be cut out for sth, be cut out to be sth; **czy ta woda nadaje się do picia?** is it safe to drink the water here?; **nadawałby się do tej pracy** he would be a good person for the job
nadawca sender
nadawczo-odbiorczy two-way
nadąć (się) → NADYMAĆ (SIĘ)
nadąsać się → DĄSAĆ SIĘ
nadąsany sulky
nadą-żać/żyć 1 (*iść itp. równie szybko; przen.*) keep pace (with sb/sth), keep up (with sth/sb) **2** (*w rozumieniu tego, co ktoś mówi*) be with sb **3** (*za modą*) follow
nadbagaż excess baggage
nad-chodzić/ejść (*dzień; wydarzenie*) arrive, come, come round; (*wiadomość itp.*) come, come in, come through; **nadchodzi przypływ** the tide is coming in
■ **nadchodzący** coming adj., forthcoming, incoming, oncoming
nadciągający imminent
nadciśnienie hypertension
naddźwiękowy supersonic
nadejście coming; (*zimy itp.*) onset
nadepnąć: nadepnął komuś na palec tread on sb's toe
nader sadly
nadęty pompous, snooty
nadfioletowy ultraviolet
nadgarstek wrist
nadgodziny overtime
nadgorliwy officious
nadinspektor superintendent
nadjeżdżający oncoming
nadliczbow|y: godziny ~e overtime; **w godzinach ~ych** overtime adv.
nadludzki superhuman
nadmia|r excess[1], glut, plethora, surfeit, surplus; **w ~rze** ample, to spare
nadmieni(a)ć mention
nadmierny excess[2], excessive, extravagant, inordinate, superfluous, surplus adj., undue, unreasonable; (*za drogi*) exorbitant
nadmuch(iw)ać zob. też DMUCHAĆ; blow sth up, puff sth out/up
■ **nadmuchiwany** inflatable
nadobowiązkowy optional
nadpobudliwy hyperactive, irritable
nadprodukcja surplus
nadprogramowo overtime adv.
nadprzyrodzony miraculous; (*tajemny*) occult, supernatural
nad-rabiać/robić: ~ zaległości catch up on sth
nadrukować (*wzór, logo*) imprint[2]
nadrzędny overriding
nadskakiwać: komuś court[2]
nadsłuchiwać: czegoś listen (out) for sth
nadstawi(a)ć IDM **~ usz-y/u** prick up your ears
nadszarp-ywać/nąć (*autorytet itp.*) undermine
nadto: aż ~ ample
nadużycie (*przestępstwo*) malpractice; ~ **zaufania** a breach of confidence
nadużyć(wa)ć (*władzy itp.*) abuse[2]; (*czyjegoś czasu*) encroach on/upon sth; (*cierpliwości*) try sb's patience
nadwag|a: z ~ą overweight
nadwąt-lać/lić sap[2] (sb of) sth
nadwerę-żać/żyć (także **nadwyrężać**) **1** (*mięśnie*) strain[2] **2** (*stosunki*) strain[2] **3** (*autorytet itp.*) undermine; (*poważnie: gospodarkę*) cripple[1] **4** (*wiarę itp.*) shake[1]
nadwozie bodywork
nadwrażliwoś|ć: zespół ~ci jelita grubego irritable bowel syndrome
nadwrażliwy hypersensitive
nadwyżka surplus
nadwyżkowy surplus adj.
na-dymać/dąć (się) inflate
nadziać się → NADZIEWAĆ SIĘ
nadziany (*bogaty*) loaded
nadziej|a hope[2]; (*oczekiwanie*) expectancy, expectation; (*oznaki, że ktoś/coś będzie mieć powodzenie itp.*) promise[2]; **mieć ~ę** hope[1]; **mam/y ~ę, że** hopefully; **pełen nadziei** expectant, hopeful; **z ~ą** expectantly, hopefully; **w nadziei na coś/że** in the hope of sth/that...; **rokujący ~ę** hopeful
nadziemn|y: kolej ~a an elevated railway
nadzienie (*w cieście, czekoladzie*) filling[1]; (*w mięsie*) stuffing
nadzi(ew)ać 1 (*mięso*) stuff[2] sth (with sth) **2** (*na szpikulec*) impale sb/sth (on sth)
nadzor-ca/czyni supervisor, warden
nadzorować be in charge[1], supervise; (*projekt itp.*) oversee; (*seminar itp.*) preside over sth; **źle ~** mismanage
nadzór control[1] (on/over sth), supervision; (*policyjny*) surveillance; **sprawować ~** be in charge, oversee
nadzwyczajn|y extraordinary, unusual; **środki ~e** emergency measures

■ **nadzwyczajnie** exceedingly, greatly, immensely, remarkably, unusually; (*zwł. przystojny*) devastatingly
naelektryzowany electric
nafaszerować → FASZEROWAĆ
nafta paraffin
nagab-ywać/nąć pester; (*prostytutka*) solicit
nagan|a chastisement, lecture noun, rebuke, reprimand noun; **udzielać ~y** reprimand sb (for sth)
naganny reprehensible
nagderać → GDERAĆ
nag|i 1 (*część ciała*) bare; (*całe ciało*) naked, nude[1], in the nude **2** (*ściana*) bare; (*krajobraz itp.*) stark[1] IDM **~a prawda** the bald truth
■ **nago** in the nude
nagietek marigold
na-ginać/giąć 1 (*pod kątem*) slant[1] **2 ~ przepisy** bend the rules
naglący imperative, urgent; (*potrzeba*) crying
nagle all at once, all of a sudden, suddenly; (*niespodziewanie*) unexpectedly; (*gwałtownie*) abruptly; (*w krótkim czasie*) overnight, short adv.
naglić: **czas mnie nagli** I'm pressed for time
nagłaśniający: **system ~** Tannoy
nagłowić się → GŁOWIĆ SIĘ
nagłów|ek (*artykułu itp.*) heading; (*w gazecie itp.*) headline; **nagłowek listu** (*na papierze firmowym*) letterhead; **w ~ku** at the head of the paper
nagł|y (*zmiana itp.*) sudden; (*śmierć itp.*) unexpected; (*wzrost/spadek cen*) sharp[1], steep; (*gwałtowny*) abrupt, dramatic; (*natychmiastowy*) immediate, instant[1], overnight; (*pilny*) urgent; (*ruch itp.*) jerky; **~y ból** twinge; **~y popyt** rush[2] (on sth); **~e uczucie** (*czegoś nieprzyjemnego*) twinge (of sth); **~y wzrost** upsurge (in sth)
nagminny rife
nagniotek corn
nagolennik shin guard
nagrać → NAGRYWAĆ
na-gradzać/grodzić reward[2]
nagranie recording; **~ cyfrowe** digital recording; **~ na taśmę** tape recording
nagrobek gravestone; (*tylko pionowy*) headstone
nagroda prize[1]; (*często tylko uznania*) award[1]; (*za ujawnienie informacji itp.*) reward[1] for sth/for doing sth; (*za całokształt kariery/dobrze wykonaną pracę*) gong; **~ pieniężna** bounty; **~ pocieszenia** booby prize; **pierwsza ~** blue riband
nagrodzon|y prize[2]; **~a powieść** a prize-winning novel
nagromadzenie (się) accumulation
nagromadzić (się) → GROMADZIC (SIĘ)
nagr(yw)ać record[2]; **~ na taśmę** tape[2]; **~ na wideo** video verb; **~ na CD/DVD** burn[1]
naiwnia-k/czka mug[1], sucker
naiwn|y gullible, ingenuous, innocent, naive; **była na tyle ~a, żeby...** she was fool enough to...
najazd 1 invasion; (*zwł. przez policję*) raid **2 robić ~ kamerą** zoom in
nająć → NAJMOWAĆ
najbardziej best[2], most[2] IDM **jak ~!** by all means
najbliższ|y (*następny*) immediate, next[1]; (*nadchodzący*) coming adj.; **najbliż-szy/si krewn-y/i** next of kin
najczęściej mostly
najdalej at the longest
najdalszy furthermost; (*od centrum*) outermost
najechać → NAJEŻDŻAĆ
najedzony full[1] up
naj|em (*wynajęcie*) hire[2]; (*mieszkania itp.*) tenancy; (*budynek, ziemia*) **na zasadach ~mu** leasehold
najem-ca/czyni tenant
najemnik mercenary[1]
najeźdźca invader
na-jeżdżać/jechać 1 koło najechało na chodnik my wheel clipped the pavement **2** (*armia*) invade
najeżon|y: **być ~ym czymś** bristle with sth
najeżyć (się) → JEŻYĆ (SIĘ)
najgłębszy (*uczucia; marzenia*) innermost
najgorsz|y (*przym.*) worst[1,2], worst-case; **nie ~y** not too bad IDM **w ~ym razie/wypadku** (as) a last resort, in the last resort, at (the) worst, if the worst comes to the worst
■ **najgorsze** (*rz.*) **~ już ma za sobą** he's out of danger
najgorzej worst adv.
najlepiej best[2]; **jak ~** as best you can; **jak ~ dojechać do...?** what's the best way to get to...?; **nie czuję się ~** I'm not in the best of health
najlepsz|y (*przym.*) best[1,3], foremost, only, premier[1], top[2]; **~ eoceny** full marks; **wyzwolić to, co w ludziach ~e** bring out the best in people IDM **w ~ym razie/wypadku** at (the) most, at best | **wszystkiego ~ego!** all the best
■ **najlepsze** (*rz.*) **~ w mojej pracy jest to, że...** the best thing about my job is... IDM **~, co można zrobić to...** your best bet is...
najmniej least adv. IDM **co ~** at least, at the (very) least
najmniejsz|y least; **(nawet) ~y** the merest IDM **to nie ma ~ego znaczenia** it doesn't matter in the least | **nie mieć ~ego (pojęcia)** not have the faintest/foggiest (idea), not have the slightest idea | **w ~ym stopniu** not in the least (bit)
najmować/nająć/wynająć (*do pracy*) engage sb (as sth), hire[1]
najniższ|y: **~a płaca** minimum wage; **~y poziom** rock bottom
najnowocześniejszy: **~ system** a state-of-the-art system
najnowszy latest
najpierw to begin with, first[2], first of all, first off
najpóźniej at the latest
najprędzej at the earliest
najskrytszy innermost, intimate
najszybciej: **jak ~** asap
najważniejsz|y main[1], paramount, primary[1], prime[1], principal[1], uppermost; **być ~ym** come first
najwcześniej at the earliest; **jak ~** as soon as possible
najwidoczniej apparently
najwięcej most[1,2]
największ|y: **w ~ym stopniu** most[2]; **z ~ą szybkością** at the top speed
najwyraźniej apparently, evidently, patently
najwyżej at the longest, at (the) most; **co ~** at the outside
najwyższ|y 1 (*położony wysoko*) top[2], topmost, uppermost; **dyskusje na ~ym szczeblu** top-level discussions **2** (*najlepszy*) prime[1]; **~ej klasy** top-class **3** (*intensywny*) extreme[1] **4** (*znaczenie itp.*) utmost[1] **5** (*władca*) sovereign[2]; (*sąd*) supreme; (*wymiar kary*) capital[2] **6** (*oceny*) full IDM **~y czas** (and) about time (too), it's about/high time, (and) not before time
nakarmić → KARMIĆ
nakaz warrant[1]; **~ rewizji** search warrant; **~ sądowy** injunction, writ; **~ stawiennictwa** summons
nakaz(yw)ać zob. też KAZAĆ; impose sth (on/upon sb/sth), prescribe
nakierow(yw)ać guide[2]; (*jakimś medium*) channel[2]; **na kogoś/coś** point[2] sth (at/towards sb/sth)
na-klejać/kleić affix[2] sth (to sth); **~ znaczek** stamp[2]
nakład 1 (nakłady) (*pieniędzy*) spending, outlay (on sth); (*i energii*) input[1] (of sth) (into/to sth) **2** (*gazety*) circulation; (*książki*) print run **3** (*wydanie*) edition
na-kładać/łożyć 1 (*kłaść: jedno na drugie*) superimpose sth (on sth); **~ potrawy na talerze** dish sth up; **szybko ~** clap[1] **2** (*ubranie*) get sth on, put sth on; **~ kaganiec** muzzle verb **3** (*podatek itp.*) impose sth (on/upon sb/sth); (*podatek*) levy sth (on sb); (*dodatkowe opłaty*) put sth on sth; (*karę itp.*) inflict sth (on sb)
□ **na-kładać/łożyć się**: **na siebie** clash[1] with sth
na-kłaniać/kłonić coax sb (into sth/doing sth), dare[1] sb (to do sth), get sb/sth to do sth, prompt[2], urge[1] sb (to do sth), sth
nakłucie prick[2]
nakrapiany dappled, speckled, spotted
nakreś-lać/lić (*sformułować*) outline[1] sth (to sb)
nakrę-cać/cić zob. też KRĘCIĆ **1** (*śrubę*) screw[2]; **~ zegarek** wind up/set your watch **2** (*film*) make a tape of sth, tape[2]
□ **nakrę-cać/cić się** screw[2]
nakrętka 1 (*na śrubę*) nut **2** (*przykrywka*) cap[1]
nakry(wa)ć 1 (*przewyższać*) top[3] sth (with sth) **2 ~ do stołu** lay the table, set the table
nalać → NALEWAĆ
nalany puffy
naleciałość suggestion
nalegać insist on sth/doing sth, press[2] (for sth/to do sth); **bardzo ~** be very/most insistent
nalepka sticker; (*na tylnym zderzaku*) bumper sticker
naleśnik pancake; **cienki ~** crêpe; **gruby ~** flapjack
nal(ew)ać (*soku itp.*) pour sth (out); (*wody na kąpiel itp.*) run[1]; **~ do pełna** fill sth (with sth)
należeć (*być częścią; do tej samej grupy*) belong to sth, go together; (*do tej samej kategorii*) come under sth, fall[1]; **do kogoś** belong to sb
□ **należeć się**: **komuś** due[1] for sth; **ile ci się jeszcze należy?** how much is

still owing to you?; **więcej niż/tyle ile się komuś należy** (more than) your fair share of sth
należność charge[1]
należny due[1], owing to sb
należyty due[1]
■ **należycie** duly, properly
naliczyć clock sth up
nalot (*zwł. bombowy*) blitz; (*policyjny*) bust[2], raid; (*powietrzny*) air raid; **robić ~** (*zwł. policyjny*) raid verb, swoop
naładować (się) → ŁADOWAĆ SIĘ
naładowan|y (*pistolet itp.*) loaded
IDM **być ~ym** (*złością*) be/get steamed up
nałogowiec addict
nałogow|y compulsive, habitual; **~y palacz** a chain/heavy smoker; **~y pijak** a heavy drinker; **jest ~ym fanem piłki nożnej** he's addicted to football
nałożyć (się) → NAKŁADAĆ (SIĘ)
nał|óg 1 (*wada*) vice **2** (*uzależnienie*) addiction; **zerwać z ~ogiem** break the habit
namacalny tangible; (*dowód*) empirical
namagnetyzować → MAGNETYZOWAĆ
namalować → MALOWAĆ
namaszczony solemn
na-mawiać/mówić: **kogoś do czegoś** egg sb on (to do sth), persuade sb (to do sth), talk sb into/out of doing sth, urge sb on, urge[1] sb (to do sth)
■ **namawianie** persuasion, prodding
namiastka substitute, surrogate
namie-rzać/rzyć: **kogoś/coś** home in on sb/sth; **namierzyć numer telefonu** trace the call
■ **namierzony** intended
namiętn|y passionate; **~e zainteresowanie (czymś)** bug[1]
■ **namiętność** lust[1], passion
namiot tent; **duży ~** (*na festyny, wesela*) marquee; **rozbijać ~** pitch a tent
namoczyć → MOCZYĆ
namowa instigation, prompting
namysł afterthought, consideration, reflection, second thoughts, thought[2]; **bez ~u** glibly, head first, headlong, pat[3], on the spur of the moment, off the top of your head; **po namyśle** on second thoughts, on balance, on reflection
namyś-lać/lić się reflect on/upon sth
nanizać → NIZAĆ
nanometr nanometre
na-nosić/nieść 1 muł naniesiony przez powódź mud deposited by a flood **2** (*wykres*) plot[2]
nanotechnologia nanotechnology
naokoło round[2]
naoleić → OLEIĆ
naoliwić → OLIWIĆ
naostrzyć → OSTRZYĆ
napad 1 (*med.*) attack[1], fit[3], seizure **2** (*złości, śmiechu*) fit[3]; **~ złości** tantrum **3** (*na bank itp.*) raid on sth, robbery; **~ z nożem** stabbing[1]; **zbrojny ~** hold-up
na-padać/paść: **na kogoś/coś** assail, assault verb, hit out (at sb/sth), set on/upon sb; **ostro ~ (na kogoś/coś)** lash out (at/against sb/sth); **~ na coś zbrojnie** hold up sth; **~ z zasadzki** ambush verb; **napaść i obrabować** mug[2]

napa-lać/lić się be/get hooked (on sth)
napar infusion
naparstek thimble
napaskudzić → PASKUDZIĆ
napastliwy combative, hectoring
napastni-k/czka 1 (*wróg*) aggressor, assailant, attacker **2** (*sport*) forward[4], striker
napastować hector, molest
napaść[1] (*cz.*) → NAPADAĆ
napaść[2] (*rz.*) **na kogoś/coś** assault, onslaught, swoop noun (on sb/sth); (*na kraj itp.*) invasion; **~ uliczna** mugging
napaść się → PAŚĆ SIĘ
napawać: **~ wstrętem** disgust[2]
□ **napawać się**: **czymś** gloat about/over sth
napchany crammed
napełni(a)ć 1 (*płynem*) fill sth (with sth); **~ ponownie** refill **2** (*uczucie*) pervade
□ **napełni(a)ć się** brim[2] with sth, fill (with sth)
napęd 1 (*samochodu*) drive[2], transmission; **~ na cztery koła** four-wheel drive **2** (*dysku*) drive[2]
napędowy driving[2]
napę-dzać/dzić drive[1], power[2], propel
IDM **~ komuś strachu** freak[2] sb (out)
napiąć → NAPINAĆ
napić się zob. też PIĆ; have a drink; **~ filiżankę kawy** have a cup of coffee
na-pierać/przeć: **na coś** press[2] across/against/around, etc. (sth)
napięci|e 1 (*naprężenie; emocjonalne*) pressure, strain[1], tension, tightness; (*oczekiwanie*) suspense; **pełen ~a** electric **2** (*elektr.*) voltage; **pod ~em** live[2]
napiętnować → PIĘTNOWAĆ
napiętnowanie stigmatization
napięty 1 (*atmosfera; stosunki itp.*) fraught, strained **2** (*mięsień*) strained, taut, tense[1] **3** (*lina; harmonogram*) tight
na-pinać/piąć (*stosunki; mięsień itp.*) strain[2]
napis 1 (*znak*) sign[1], writing; (*wypisany lub wyryty*) inscription **2** (**napisy**) (*na filmie*) subtitles; (*po zakończeniu filmu*) credits[1]
napisać zob. też PISAĆ; **szybko coś ~** dash sth off; **~ parę słów do kogoś** drop sb a line
■ **napisan|y**: **~y na maszynie lub komputerze** typewritten; (*poinformować*) **być napisanym** say[1]
napiwek gratuity, tip[1]; **dawać ~** tip[2]
napletek foreskin
napływ (*informacji itp.*) flow[1]; (*gotówki; imigrantów itp.*) influx; (*nowych studentów itp.*) intake; (*problemów itp.*) spate; (*gwałtowny*) upsurge
napły-wać/nąć 1 (*woda*) flood[1]; **ślinka napłynęła mi do ust** my mouth watered **2** (*listy itp.; ludzie*) flood[1] in/into/out of sth, pour, roll in, surge; (*powoli*) trickle
napomknięcie allusion, hint[1]
napomnieni|e: **udzielać ~a** caution[2]
napompow(yw)ać zob. też POMPOWAĆ; inflate, pump sth up
napomykać allude to sb/sth
napot(y)kać come across sb/sth; (*zwł. coś niezwykłego/nowego*) encounter[1]
napowietrzny overhead
napój beverage, drink[1]; **napoje alkoholowe** alcohol, liquor; **~ bezalkoholowy** soft drink; **~ gazowany** fizzy drink, pop[1]; **~ cytrynowy** lemonade; **~ pomarańczowy** orange squash
napór pressure
napraw|a repair[2]; **oddać samochód do ~y** get the car repaired; **nie do ~y** beyond repair
naprawdę actually, honestly, indeed, really, seriously, truly; **tak ~** in (actual) fact, really; **~?** indeed, really; **~!** honestly; **~ być wartą przeczytania** be well worth reading
naprawi(a)ć 1 (*coś małego*) fix[1]; (*ubranie*) mend[1]; (*samochód itp.*) repair[1] **2** (*błąd*) put/set sth right, rectify **3** (*straty*) remedy[2]; (*zło*) undo; (*stosunki*) heal, repair[1]; **naprawić krzywdę** right a wrong
■ **naprawieni|e**: **nie do naprawienia** irreparable
naprę-żać/żyć (*mięśnień*) tense[3] sth (up)
■ **naprężenie** stress[1], strain[1], tension | **naprężony 1** (*mięśnień*) taut, tense[1] **2** (*atmosfera itp.*) tense[1] **3** (*harmonogram itp.*) tight
napromieniow(yw)ać irradiate; **zostać napromieniowanym** be exposed to radiation
naprowadzający (*pytanie*) leading
naprzeciw (także **naprzeciwko**) opposite; **znajdować się ~ kogoś/czegoś** face[2]
naprzeć → NAPIERAĆ
naprzód ahead of sb/sth, along adv., forward[1], onwards; **głową ~** head first, headlong adj.; **posuwać się ~** advance[2]
naprzykrzać się be onto sb, bother[1], hassle[2], make a nuisance of yourself
napsioczyć → PSIOCZYĆ
na-puszczać/puścić: **kogoś przeciw komuś** play A off against B
napuszony pompous
nap(y)chać (*torbę itp.*) cram, stuff[2] sth (with sth); (*salę koncertową itp.*) pack sth out; (*program dnia itp.*) pack sth in/into sth
napytać IDM **~ sobie biedy** get into trouble
narada consultation
nara-dzać/dzić się (*przed podjęciem decyzji*) confer (with sb) (on/about sth), consult with sb; (*form.*) deliberate[2]; **wspólnie się naradzać** put/get your heads together
na-rastać/rosnąć (*odsetki itp.*) accrue (to sb) (from sth); (*długi itp.*) mount up
■ **narastający** (*liczba itp.*) growing; (*ilość, stopień itp.*) cumulative; (*koszt, dodatki do pensji itp.*) incremental; (*bezrobocie; agresja, niezadowolenie itp.*) mounting; **według narastającego stopnia trudności** in ascending order of difficulty | **narastanie** build-up
naraz 1 (*nagle*) all at once **2** (*jednocześnie*) (all) at once
nara-żać/zić 1 (*życie, zdrowie itp.*) endanger, risk[2]; (*karierę itp.*) jeopardize **2** (*na niebezpieczeństwo itp.*) expose sb/sth to sth, subject sb/sth to sth; **nie narażać kogoś na coś** keep sb out of sth; **narażając (się) na coś** at the risk of sth/doing sth
■ **narażony** (*na katastrofy itp.*) liable to sth; (*i na choroby*) subject[2] to sth
□ **nara-żać/zić się 1** (*na katastrofę itp.*) court[2], go out on a limb **2** (*na wydatek/stratę*) incur
narciarski ski adj.

narciarstwo skiing
nar-ciarz/ciarka skier; (*skoczek*) ski jumper
narcystyczny narcissistic
narcyzm narcissism
nareszcie 1 (*wreszcie*) at (long) last **2 ~!** (*ciesząc się, że ktoś odszedł/coś minęło*) good riddance (to sb/sth)
naręcze armful
narkoman/ka drug addict
narkomania drug addiction
narkotyczny narcotic adj.
narkotyk drug[1], narcotic; (*nieform.*) dope[1]; **twardy ~** hard drug
narkoz|a anaesthetic, sedation; **stosować ~ę** anaesthetize
narobić: **~ sobie biedy** invite trouble
narodowość nationality
narodow|y national[1]; **mniejszości ~e** ethnic minorities
narodzenie: **~ Chrystusa** nativity
narodziny birth
narodzony: **nowo ~** newborn
narosnąć → NARASTAĆ
narośl growth
narowisty handful
narozkoszować się → ROZKOSZOWAĆ SIĘ
naród nation, people
narracja narrative
narrator narrator
narta ski[2]; **~ wodna** waterski noun; **jeździć na ~ch** ski[1]
nartostrada ski run
naru-szać/szyć 1 (*prawo*) breach[2], break[1], contravene, infringe, offend; (*i umowę*) breach[2]; (*umowę itp.*) violate **2** (*prywatność; prawa*) encroach on/upon sth, infringe on/upon sth, violate **3** (*zwyczaj*) offend **4** (*towary do sprzedaży itp.*) tamper with sth
■ **naru-szanie/szenie 1** (*prawa*) contravention, infringement; (*i umowy*) breach[1] of sth; **naruszanie praw człowieka** human rights abuses **2** (*prywatności; praw*) infringement, intrusion, invasion, violation
narysować → RYSOWAĆ
narząd organ; **zewnętrzne ~y płciowe** genitals
narzeczeństwo engagement; (*przestarz.*) courtship
narzeczona fiancée; (*przestarz.*) betrothed noun
narzeczony fiancé; (*przestarz.*) betrothed noun
narzekać/po- complain (to sb) (about sth/that...); (*pod nosem*) grumble; **głośno ~ (na coś)** rant (on) (about sth)
narzędzi|e (*młotek itp.*) tool; (*rolnicze itp.*) implement[2]; (*kuchenne*) utensil; (*do pracy w domu i ogrodzie*) hardware; (*do pracy precyzyjnej; przen.*) instrument; **~a ogrodnicze** gardening tools; **~e zbrodni** the murder weapon
narzu-cać/cić 1 (*ubranie*) slip[1] sth on **2** (*warunki*) enforce, foist sth on/upon sb, impose, thrust sb/sth upon sb; (*swoje poglądy*) inflict sth (on sb); **~ swoją wolę** boss[2] sb (about/around)
□ **narzu-cać/cić się** impose, intrude on/upon sb/sth
narzuta bedspread
nasadka 1 cap[1] **2 ~ na wtyczkę umożliwiająca połączenie elektryczne różnych standardów** adaptor
nasą-czać/czyć: **coś (czymś)** impregnate sth (with sth)
nasenn|y narcotic adj.; **pigułka ~a** sleeping pill; **środek ~y** narcotic, sedative
nasiąknięty: **~ wodą** waterlogged
nasienie 1 (*bot.*) seed; **nasiona jadalnenie których roślin strączkowych** pulse[1] **2** (*męskie*) semen, sperm
nasi-lać/lić się intensify; (*dźwięk*) swell[1]
naskoczyć → SKAKAĆ
nasłoneczniony sunlit, sunny
nasłuch: **prowadzić ~** (*zagranicznego radia i TV*) monitor[2]
nasłuchiwać prick up your ears
nasta(wa)ć (*nadejść*) set in
■ **nastanie** advent, coming
nastawi(a)ć 1 (*w jakimś kierunku; urządzenie itp.*) regulate, set[1]; **~ zegarek** wind up/set your watch; **~ radio/telewizor na daną stację/kanał** tune[2] sth (in) (to sth), tune in (to sth); **głośniej ~** (*np. radio*) turn sth up; **~ ostrość** focus[1] sth (on sth) **2 na coś** gear sth to/towards sb/sth **3** (*złamaną kość*) set[1] **4** (*uszy*) cock[2] **5 przychylnie/nieprzychylnie ~ kogoś** bias[2]; **~ kogoś uprzedzająco** prejudice[2] sb (against sb/sth)
■ **nastawiony na coś** minded, poised to do sth
□ **nastawi(a)ć się**: **na coś** psych yourself up (for sth), steel[2] yourself
nastawienie 1 (*stanowisko*) attitude, position[1]; (*polityczne itp.*) slant[2]; (*przychylne lub nieprzychylne*) bias[1]; **powszechne ~** public feeling **2** (*nastrój*) spirit[1] **3** (*urządzenia*) setting
następ-ca/czyni successor; **następ-ca/czyni tronu** Crown prince/princess, the heir to the throne
następny next[1]; (*kolejny*) following[1]
■ **następnie** subsequently, then
na-stępować/stąpić 1 (*nadejść*) come, follow (on) (from sth); (*wynikać*) ensue; **jak następuje** as follows; (*skutek*) **~ po czymś** knock-on; **mieć nastąpić w przyszłości** be in store (for sb/ sth) **2** (*król itp.*) succeed
■ **następujący** following[1], next[1]; (*wynikający*) consequent
następstw|o 1 (*skutek*) consequence, corollary, sequel; (*nieprzyjemny*) aftermath, after-effect, repercussion; **być ~em czegoś** ensue; **w ~ie** following[3] **2** (*tronu*) succession
nastolat-ek/ka adolescent, teenager; **dla nastolatków** adolescent adj., teenage
nastoletni adolescent adj., teenage
na-strajać/stroić zob. też STROIĆ; **~ na daną stację/kanał** tune[2] sth (in) (to sth)
□ **na-strajać/stroić się** psych yourself up (for sth)
nastrojowy ambient, atmospheric
nastroszyć → STROSZYĆ
nastr|ój 1 (*osoby*) frame of mind, mood, spirits[1]; **w ponurym ~oju** moody **2** (*sytuacji*) air[1] (of sth), atmosphere; (*miejsca*) ambience; (*zebrania itp.*) tone[1]; (*przyjęcia itp.*) spirit[1]; (*dyskusji itp.*) vein; (*społeczny, polityczny itp.*) climate
nasy-cać/cić (*rynek itp.*) saturate
■ **nasycony** steeped in sth; (*i rynek itp.*) saturated
nasyceni|e: **punkt ~a** saturation point
nasyp bank[1], embankment
nasz (*z rz.*) our; (*bez rz.*) ours
naszkicować zob. też SZKICOWAĆ; **szybko coś ~** dash sth off
naszpikowan|y: **być ~ym czymś** be heavily dosed with sth
naszyjnik necklace
naszykować → SZYKOWAĆ
naście: **„naście" lat** teens
naśladować 1 (*wzorować się*) follow suit, model yourself on sb/sth, take your cue from sb/sth; (*coś modnego*) climb/jump on the bandwagon **2** (*udawać*) copy[2], imitate; (*parodiować*) mimic[1], send sb/sth up, take sb off
■ **naśladujący** (*nieprawdziwy*) mock[2]; (*imitujący*) copycat adj.
naśladowca mimic[2]
naśmiecić → ŚMIECIĆ
naśmiewać się deride, taunt
naświet-lać/lić 1 (*promieniami*) irradiate **2** (*kwestię itp.*) elucidate
natarcie 1 (*przemieszczanie się*) advance[1] **2** (*atak*) onslaught
natarczywy (*pytania itp.*) aggressive; (*żądania itp.*) insistent
natchnąć inspire
natchnieni|e 1 (*czynu itp.*) inspiration; **być ~em; stanowić ~e (dla kogoś)** inspire sth, sb (to do sth); **będący źródłem ~a** inspiring **2** (*genialny pomysł*) brainwave
natę-żać/żyć strain[2]
■ **natężenie** (*dźwięku*) volume
□ **natę-żać/żyć się 1** (*osoba; mięsień*) strain[2] **2** (*dźwięk*) swell[1]
natka parsley
natknąć się → NATYKAĆ SIĘ
natłok spate
natłuszczony oily
natomiast whereas, while[1]
natrafi(a)ć 1 (*znaleźć*) come across sth; (*złoża złota, ropy*) strike[1] **1** (*trudności*) come up against sb/sth, hit[1], run into sth
natrzeć → NACIERAĆ
natu|ra nature, self; **druga ~ra** second nature (to sb); **~ra ludzka** human nature; **leżeć w czyjejś ~rze** come naturally to sb; **wbrew ~rze** unnatural, unnaturally; **z ~ry** inherently adv., naturally
naturalist-a/ka naturalist
naturalizacja naturalization
naturalizować naturalize
naturalnie certainly, naturally, of course
naturaln|y natural; (*szczery; nie sztuczny*) genuine[1]; (*zachowanie*) unaffected; (*żywność*) organic; **wielkości ~ej** full-scale; **~e otoczenie/środowisko** the wilds[2]; **rzecz ~a** a matter of course; **to zupełnie ~e** it's quite normal
■ **naturalność** simplicity
naturyst-a/ka nudist
naturyzm nudism
natychmiast right/straight away, at the drop of a hat, immediately, instantly, this minute, at once, promptly, right[2], on the spot

natychmiastow|y immediate, instant[1], instantaneous, prompt[1]; **przejść ~ą operację** undergo emergency surgery
na-tykać/tknąć się 1 (*przypadkiem*) come across sb/sth, run into sb, stumble across/on/upon sb/sth **2** (*na trudność*) encounter[1] hit[1]
nau-czać/czyć zob. też UCZYĆ (SIĘ); teach, instruct sb (in sth)
■ **nauczanie** teaching; (*zwł. indywidualne lub w małej grupie*) tuition in sth
nauczk|a lesson; **dawać komuś ~ę** teach sb a lesson
nauczyciel school teacher, teacher[1]; (*uniwersytecki*) professor; (*przestarz.*) master[1]; **zawód ~a** teaching
nauczycielka zob. też NAUCZYCIEL; (*przestarz.*) mistress
nauk|a 1 (*uczenie się: w ogóle*) learning; (*na uniwersytecie*) study[1]; (*w szkole*) schooling **2** (*dziedzina wiedzy*) scholarship; **~a ścisła** science; **~i społeczne** social science; **~a o środowisku** environmental science **3** (**nauki**) (*kościoła, filozofa itp.*) teaching **4** (*wniosek*) moral[2] **5** **~a jazdy** L-plate
naukowiec (*specjalista nauk ścisłych*) scientist
naukowy academic[1]; (*czasopismo itp.*) learned, scholarly; (*dot. nauk ścisłych*) scientific
na-wadniać/wodnić irrigate
nawa-lać/lić (*urządzenie*) conk out; (*komput.*) crash[2]
■ **nawalony** stoned, zonked out
nawa|ł 1 (*duża liczba*) spate; (*pytań itp.*) barrage **2** (*nacisk*) pressure
nawałnica (*burza, ulewa itp.*) hurricane, squall
nawet even[2]; **~ bardziej/ więcej itp.** still[1]; **~ gdyby/jeśli** even if
nawiać → NAWIEWAĆ
nawias bracket[1]; **~ trójkątny** angle bracket; **brać w ~** bracket[2]; **w ~ie** in parenthesis IDM **być/czuć się poza ~em** be/feel out of it | **~em mówiąc** by the way, incidentally
nawiązk|a: **z ~ą** with a vengeance
nawiąz(yw)ać 1 (*stosunki*) forge[1]; **nawiązać kontakt (z kimś)** make contact, get hold of sb **2** (*rozmowę itp.*) strike up sth (with sb) **3** (*odnosić się*) refer to sb/sth
■ **nawiązani|e**: **w nawiązaniu do kogoś/czegoś** with reference to sb/sth, with respect to sth; (*w korespondencji*) further to
nawie-dzać/dzić haunt[1]
nawierzchnia surface[1]
nawi(ew)ać: **nawiało prawie dwa metry śniegu** the snow drifted up to two metres deep
nawieźć → NAWOZIĆ
nawigacja navigation
nawigator navigator
nawigować navigate
nawi-jać/nąć (*nici itp.*) wind[3]; (*za pomocą kołowrotka*) reel sth in
nawilżacz: **~ powietrza** humidifier
nawil-żać/żyć moisturize
■ **nawilżający**: **krem nawilżający** moisturizer
na-wlekać/wlec thread[2]
nawodnić → NAWADNIAĆ
na-wozić/wieźć (*ziemię*) fertilize
nawóz fertilizer; **~ naturalny** dung, manure, muck[1]
na-wracać/wrócić (się) (*relig.*) convert[1] (sb) (from sth) (to sth)
nawrót (*powtórzenie się*) recurrence; **~ choroby** relapse noun
nawyk habit, way[1] (of doing sth); **mieć ustalone ~i** be set in your ways
nawykły: **do (robienia) czegoś** used to sth/to doing sth
nawzajem each other IDM **~!** (the) same to you
naziemny terrestrial
nazwa name[1]; **~ handlowa** trade name; **~ firmowa** brand name; **~ pliku** filename; **~ użytkownika** username; **~ miasta itp.** place name; **~ własna** (*np. „Africa", „Jane"*) proper noun
nazwisk|o family name, surname; **imię i ~o** name[1]; **~o panieńskie** maiden name; **powszechnie znane ~o** household name; **znać kogoś z ~a** know sb by name IDM **na czyjeś ~o** in the name of sb, in sb's name
naz(y)wać call[1]; **po kimś** name[2] sb/sth (after sb); (*przezywać*) dub; (*określać*) term[2]
□ **nazywać się** be called
nefryt jade
negatyw (*fot.*) negative[2]; **~ główny** master[1]
negatywn|y negative[1]; **~a strona** downside
negocjacj|a (**negocjacje**) negotiations; (*cena*) **do ~i** or near(est) offer, ono
negocjator/ka negotiator
negocjować/wy- negotiate
nekrolog obituary
nektar nectar
nektarynka nectarine
nenufar water lily
neofit-a/ka convert[2]
neon neon
nepotyzm nepotism
Neptun Neptune
nerka (*anat.*) kidney
nerw 1 nerve **2** (**nerwy**) nerves
nerwic|a neurosis; **cierpiący na ~ę** neurotic
nerwowy 1 (*osoba*) highly strung, irritable, jumpy, nervous, prickly, restless **2** (*atmosfera itp.*) frantic **3** (*med.*) nervous; (*nerwicowy*) neurotic
neska (*kawa*) instant coffee
netto net[2] of sth
neurochirurg brain surgeon
neurolog neurologist
neurologia neurology
neurologiczny neurological
neuron neuron
neurotyczny neurotic
neutralizować/z- neutralize; (*przeciwdziałać*) counteract
neutralny neutral[1]
■ **neutralność** neutrality
neutron neutron
nęcić/z-/za- entice, lure[1], tempt; (*seksualnie*) seduce
■ **nęcący** inviting, seductive
nędz|a (*ubóstwo materialne*) destitution; (*niechlujne warunki*) squalor; **w ~y** destitute; **żyć na granicy ~y** live on the breadline
nędzny 1 (*wygląd, życie itp.*) abject, wretched **2** (*zbyt mały: płaca itp*) derisory, measly, paltry; (*i złej jakości*) miserable **3** (*niechlujny*) sordid, squalid
■ **nędznie** (*ubrany itp.*) shabbily
nękać 1 (*osobę; dręczyć*) harass, hassle[2]; **nękany kłopotami** beleaguered **2** (*karierę itp.*) blight[1] **3** (*wątpliwość; ból*) nag, niggle (at) sb; (*problem itp.*) assail **4** (*wiatr itp.*) batter[1]
niania nanny; (*opiekunka*) childminder
niańczyć (*trzymać w ramionach/na ręku*) cradle[2]
niby of a kind
ni|c none[1] of sb/sth, nothing; (*zero*) nil; **zupełnie ~c** anything; **prawie (tyle co) ~c** next to nothing; **~c tylko** nothing but; **być do ~czego** be useless; **do ~czego** dismal, failure; **na ~c** for nothing
niczyj: **ziemia ~a** no-man's-land
niczym (*jak*) like[1]
nić 1 (*tkaniny*) cotton[1], thread[1]; (*pojedynczy kawałek*) strand **2** **~ dentystyczna** dental floss
nie (*partykuła*) no[1,2]; (*nieform.*) nope; **(no) ~?** eh IDM **jak ~, to ~** too bad
■ **nie** (*z cz., przysł. itp.*) not; **mam nadzieję, że ~** I hope not; **~ (wolno)** no[2]
nieaktualny out of date
nieaktywny (*wulkan itp.*) dormant
niealterowany (*nuta*) natural[1]
nieatrakcyjny unattractive; (*odpychający*) off-putting; (*zwł. dziewczyna/kobieta*) homely, plain[1]
nieautentyczny inauthentic
niebawem presently, shortly, soon
niebezpieczeństwo danger, hazard[1], menace; (*ryzyko*) risk[1]; (*wymagające natychmiastowej pomocy*) distress[1]; **wielkie ~** peril; **wystawiać na ~** jeopardize; **w niebezpieczeństwie** in jeopardy
niebezpieczny 1 (*stwarzający zagrożenie*) dangerous; (*sytuacja*) ugly; (*nieform.*) hot[1]; (*zwierzę*) vicious; (*osoba: agresywny*) nasty; (*drabina itp.*) precarious; (*dzielnica; morze*) rough[1]; **bardzo ~** perilous **2** (*ryzykowny*) hazardous, risky
niebiański heavenly
niebieskawozielony aquamarine adj.
niebieskawy bluish
niebieski 1 blue[1]; **kolor ~** blue[2] **2** **ciała ~e** heavenly bodies
niebios|a 1 the heavens **2** (*raj*) heaven; **w ~ach** on high
niebo 1 (*przestrzeń nad nami*) sky; (*przestarz.*) ether; **do samego nieba** sky-high **2** (*raj*) heaven; **na niebie** in the heavens IDM **o ~ lepszy** streets ahead (of sb/sth) | **wielkie nieba!** (good) heavens!
niebosiężny: **~ szczyt** dizzy heights
nieboszczyk corpse
niebywał|y untold; **to rzecz ~a** it's without parallel
niecałkowity incomplete
niech let, may IDM **a ~ to...!** bother[3]
niechcący unwittingly
niechceni|e: **robić coś od ~a** play at sth/being sth; (*uśmiechać się*) **od ~a** faint[1]
niechciany unwanted
niechęć: **do kogoś/czegoś** antipathy, aversion, dislike[2], distaste; (*wrogość*) animosity; (*podjęcia działania*) reluctance; **czuć ~ do czegoś** dislike[1] (doing) sth; **poczuć ~ do kogoś/czegoś** take a dislike to sb/sth

niechętny loath to do sth, reluctant to do sth, unwilling; (*do rozmowy itp.*) coy; (*podziękowania itp.*) grudging; **raczej ~** lukewarm about sb/sth
■ **niechętnie** grudgingly, reluctantly, unwillingly; (*rozmawiać itp.*) coyly; **~ przyznał się do błędu** he was loath to admit his mistake; **~ rozmawia o swojej pracy** she isn't very forthcoming about her job
niechlujny (*osoba; praca*) sloppy, slovenly; (*ubranie; wygląd*) scruffy; (*pokój itp.*) messy, squalid, untidy; **brudny i ~** grungy
niechroniony (*niestrzeżony*) unguarded
niechwiejny (*zdecydowany*) single-minded
niechybny inevitable, unavoidable
niechże → NIECH
nieciągły (*przerywany*) fitful
nieciekawy unattractive; (*tekst itp.*) dry[1]; (*w kolorach*) drab; (*małżeństwo itp.*) **już ~** stale
niecierpliwić/z- się champ at the bit
niecierpliwy impatient
niecka trough
niecny (*osoba; metoda*) disreputable; (*zamiar itp.*) suspect[3]; (*przeszłość itp.*) sordid
nieco 1 (*z przym./przsł.*) mildly, slightly, somewhat, a trifle, vaguely; (*za duży/mały/wysoki itp.*) on the big, small, high, etc. side **2** (*z rz.*) some
niecodzienny out of the ordinary, unusual; **~ wypadek** a freak accident
nieczęsty infrequent
nieczuły 1 (*bezduszny*) callous, cold-hearted, hard-hearted, heartless; (*i na zimno, ból itp.*) insensitive to sth **2** (*na krytykę itp.*) impervious to sth
nieczynny (*urządzenie*) out of action; (*wulkan itp.*) inactive
nieczystość 1 (**nieczystości**) filth **2** (*moralna*) impurity
nieczyst|y 1 (*brudny*) dirty **2** (*myśli itp.*) impure **3** (*interesy itp.*) shady **4** (*gra*) unfair **5 ~e sumienie** a guilty conscience
■ **nieczysto 1** (*niezgodnie z regułami*) **grać ~** play dirty **2** (*śpiewać/grać*) out of tune
nieczytelny 1 (*podpis itp.*) illegible **2** (*trudny do zrozumienia*) unintelligible
niedaleki near[1]
■ **niedaleko** near[2], nearby adv.
niedawn|o lately, recently, the other day, morning, week, etc.; (*dopiero co*) only just; (*świeżo: upieczony chleb itp.*) freshly; (*mianowany, poślubiony*) newly; **jestem tu od ~a** I haven't been here long
niedawny recent
niedbały (*niestaranny*) careless, slapdash; (*i ubranie*) sloppy; (*w wykonywaniu pracy itp.*) remiss (of sb) (to do sth), in sth/in doing sth, slack; (*nonszalancki*) casual, negligent
niedelikatny indelicate
niedługo soon
niedobór dearth, scarcity, shortage; (*witamin itp.*) deficiency in/of sth
niedobry 1 (*zły, kiepski*) bad; (*moralnie*) wrong[1] to do sth **2** (*nieprawidłowy*) wrong[1]
niedobrze 1 (*niepoprawnie*) wrong[2], wrongly **2** (*czuć się*) unwell; **robi mi się od niego ~** it makes me feel ill; **zrobiło mi się ~** I feel a bit funny **3** (*nieodpowiednio; kiepsko*) badly
IDM **i tak źle, i tak ~** you can't win
niedocenianie underestimate noun
niedociągnięcie shortcoming
niedogodny awkward
■ **niedogodność** nuisance
niedojrzały juvenile, at a tender age; (*i ciało*) immature
niedokładny imprecise, inaccurate, inexact
niedokończony undone, unfinished
niedola woe
niedołężnieć/z- go senile
niedołężny decrepit, infirm
niedopałek butt[2], stub; **~ papierosa** a cigarette end
niedopatrzenie oversight
niedopracowany (*pomysł, plan*) half-baked
niedopuszczalny (*prawn.*) inadmissible
niedorosły immature
niedorozwinięty: **~ umysłowo** subnormal
niedorzeczny absurd, nonsensical; (*niepraktyczny*) airy-fairy; (*śmieszny*) ludicrous, preposterous; (*nierozsądny*) unreasonable
niedoskonały 1 (*niecałkowity*) deficient, incomplete, wanting in sth **2** (*wadliwy*) imperfect
niedosmażony rare
niedostateczny inadequate, insufficient
■ **niedostatecznie** inadequately, scantily
niedostat|ek 1 (*brak*) deficiency, lack[1], need[3] of sth, scarcity, want[2] of sth **2** (*ubóstwo*) deprivation; **w ~ku** needy
niedostępny 1 (*miejsce*) impenetrable, inaccessible **2** (*nieosiągalny: posada itp.*) beyond/out of (sb's) reach, inaccessible **3** (*cena*) prohibitive
niedostrzegalny imperceptible
niedoszły would-be
niedościgniony (*mistrz; wiedza*) unrivalled
niedoświadczony inexperienced
niedotknięty (*bez zmiany*) unaffected
niedotrzymany (*obietnica, umowa*) broken[2]
niedouczony illiterate
niedowag|a (*osoba*) **z ~ą** underweight
niedowierzani|e disbelief, distrust, incredulity; **pełen ~a** incredulous
niedozwolony (*zakazany*) illicit
niedożywienie malnutrition
niedożywiony malnourished
niedrogi (*produkty*) affordable, inexpensive
nieduży little[1]
niedwuznaczny (*jasny*) explicit; (*prosty*) straightforward
■ **niedwuznacznie** (*uszczypliwie*) pointedly
niedyskretny indiscreet
niedysponowany unwell; (*nieform.*) under the weather
niedziela Sunday IDM **Niedziela Palmowa** Palm Sunday
niedzielny Sunday
niedźwiedź bear[2]; **~ polarny** polar bear
nieefektywny (*nieskuteczny*) ineffective; (*niewydajny*) inefficient
nieekonomiczny uneconomical
nieelastyczny inflexible
nieelegancki inelegant
nieelokwentny inarticulate
nieetyczny immoral
niefachowy inexpert
nieformalny informal
niefortunny unfortunate; (*godzina na coś*) inopportune; (*wydarzenie*) untoward
■ **niefortunnie** unhappily
niefrasobliwy (*osoba*) easy-going, happy-go-lucky, light-hearted, unconcerned about/by/with sth; (*podejście do czegoś*) cavalier; (*poczucie humoru*) whimsical
niegazowany (*woda*) still[2]
niegodziwy (*moralnie zły*) wicked; (*metody itp.*) disreputable, unscrupulous; (*sposób traktowania kogoś*) shabby
■ **niegodziwość** infamy, wickedness
niegościnny inhospitable
niegramatyczny (*tekst*) illiterate
niegrzeczny 1 (*zachowanie dziecka*) naughty **2** (*nieuprzejmy*) impolite, offhand[1], rude; (*nieokrzesany*) uncouth **3** (*nieżyczliwy*) unfriendly, unkind, unpleasant
niegustowny tasteless
nieharmonijny discordant
niehigieniczny insanitary
niehumanitarny inhumane
nieinteligentny unintelligent
nieinteresujący unattractive
nieistniejący non-existent
nieistotn|y 1 (*nieważny*) insignificant, non-essential, unimportant; (*różnica itp.*) immaterial, negligible, slight; (*powiązanie*) tenuous; (*argument*) academic[1]; **~e sprawy/rzeczy** non-essentials **2** (*niezwiązany z tematem*) extraneous, incidental; **rzecz ~a** irrelevance
niejadalny inedible
niejako as it were
niejasny (*mylący*) confusing; (*mętny*) diffuse, opaque; (*powód*) obscure[1]; (*wątpliwy*) questionable; (*poczucie*) vague; (*wspomnienie itp.*) indistinct, hazy
niejeden (*wielu/wiele*) many
niejednakowy (*nierówny*) unequal, uneven
niejednoczesny (*rozłożony w czasie*) staggered
niejednolity 1 (*wiedza: fragmentaryczny*) patchy **2** (*chropowaty; nierówny*) uneven
niekiedy at times
niekłamany wholehearted
niekompatybilny incompatible
niekompetentny (*bez niezbędnych kwalifikacji*) unqualified; (*niezdolny*) incompetent
niekompletny deficient
niekonieczny (*zbędny*) dispensable; (*niepotrzebny*) unnecessary
■ **niekoniecznie** not necessarily, unnecessarily
niekonsekwentny inconsistent
niekontaktowy: **sport ~** non-contact sport
niekontrolowany (*rozwój itp.*) uncontrolled; (*ogień; przestępczość*)

unchecked; (*śmiech itp.*) uncontrollable
niekonwencjonalny unorthodox; (*medycyna*) alternative[2]
niekończący się interminable, unending
niekorzystn|y disadvantageous, unfavourable; (*warunki pogody itp.*) adverse; **stawiać kogoś/być w ~ej sytuacji** put sb/be at a disadvantage
niekorzyść: **działać na czyjąś ~** be loaded against sb, put sb at a disadvantage, be weighted against sb; **na czyjąś ~** to sb's disadvantage
niektóry certain pron., a few, some
niekulturalny uncouth
niekwestionowany indisputable, outright adj.
nielegalny illegal, illicit; (*metoda itp.*) improper; (*nagranie itp.*) bootleg[1]; **~ handel** trafficking; **~ produkt** bootleg noun
nieletni (*przym.*) under age; (*prawn.*) juvenile **~/a przestęp-ca/czyni** delinquent, young offender noun
■ **nieletni/a** (*rz., prawn.*) juvenile noun, minor[2]
nieliczenie się (*z czyimiś potrzebami, uczuciami itp.*) inconsiderateness
nieliczny scant, sparse; **(tylko/bardzo) nieliczn-i/e** few
nielogiczny illogical, inconsistent
nielojalny disloyal
nieludzki inhuman; (*niehumanitarny*) inhumane; **~ czyn** atrocity
nieła|d (*w pokoju itp.*) mess[1], clutter[2], untidiness; (*i w interesach*) disorder; (*w planowaniu*) disorganization; **w ~dzie** disordered, higgledy-piggledy; (*włosy itp.*) awry adj.; **doprowadzić coś do ~du** turn sth upside down
nieładny 1 (*wygląd*) unattractive; (*zwł. kobieta, dziecko*) plain[1] **2** (*nieuprzejmy*) wrong[1] to do sth
■ **nieładnie**: **to nieładnie z naszej strony** it was wrong of us
niełask|a: **popaść w ~ę** fall from favour
niemal (także **niemalże**) almost, as good as, close on, practically; **~ nic** next to nothing
niemało quite a few, quite a lot (of)
niemały considerable; (*pensja itp.*) respectable
niemądr|y foolish, silly, unwise; **nie być tak ~ym, żeby** know better (than that/than to do sth)
niemile disagreeably; **~ widziany** unpopular with sb
niemiłosierny hard-hearted, merciless, pitiless
niemiły disagreeable, nasty, unpleasant; (*osoba*) mean[2] to sb; (*słowo, otoczenie*) harsh
niemniej: **~ jednak** nevertheless, nonetheless, notwithstanding adv., still[1], though; **~, dziękuję** but thanks anyway; **tym ~** nonetheless
niemoc infirmity
niemodny dated, outmoded, unfashionable; (*osoba; ubranie*) dowdy, frumpy; (*ubranie itp.*) naff, out[1]; **~ i nudny** nerdy
niemoralny immoral
niemowa mute
niemowlę baby, infant; (*przestarz.*) babe
niemowlęcy: **wiek ~** infancy
niemożliwy 1 impossible; **niemożliwe!** never!, not likely! **2** (*przeklęty*) blessed
niemożność inability to do sth
niemrawy 1 (*interesy itp.*) slow[1], sluggish **2** (*osoba*) wet[1]
niemy 1 (*osoba*) dumb, mute **2** (*protest; litera*) silent
nienadający się inadequate, unfit, useless
nienaganny faultless; (*osoba i jej zachowanie*) irreproachable
nienależyty inadequate
nienamacalny intangible
nienarodzony unborn
nienaruszalny sacred
■ **nienaruszalność** sanctity
nienaruszon|y intact; **w ~ym stanie** pristine
nienasycony insatiable, voracious
nienaturalny unnatural
nienawidzić/z- can/could not bear, hate[1], detest, take a dislike to sb/sth, loathe; **to coś, czego nienawidzę** it's (an) anathema to me
nienawistny hateful
nienawiść hate[2], hatred, loathing; (*wobec wroga*) enmity
nienawykły unused to sth/doing sth
nienormalny abnormal
nieobecn|y (*przym.*) **1** absent, gone[2]; (*w pracy*) off[1]; (*poza miastem, krajem*) away from sth **2 patrzyła ~ym wzrokiem** she had a distant look in her eyes
■ **nie obecn-y/a** (*rz.*) absentee | **nieobecność** absence
nieobeznany unfamiliar with sb/sth
nieobfity insubstantial
nieobliczalny incalculable
nieobrobiony raw
nieobyty gauche
nieoceniony invaluable; (*bezcenny*) priceless
nieoczekiwan|y unexpected; **~e szczęście/powodzenie** windfall
■ **nieoczekiwanie** unawares, unexpectedly, out of the blue
nieoczyszczony crude
nieodległy near[1]
nieodłączny (*część*) inherent in sb/sth; (*przyjaciel*) inseparable
nieodnawialny (*źródła energii*) non-renewable
nieodparty 1 (*humor, nastrój*) irrepressible **2** (*chęć; wdzięk*) irresistible
nieodpowiedni inappropriate, unsuitable, wrong[1]; (*pora*) bad, inopportune; (*zachowanie*) improper; (*niewystarczający*) inadequate, insufficient; (*rozmiarem itp.*) incongruous
nieodpowiedzialny irresponsible
nieodstępny inseparable
nieodwołalny irreversible
■ **nieodwołalność** finality
nieodwracalny 1 (*decyzja itp.*) irreversible **2** (*strata itp.*) irredeemable, irretrievable
nieodzowny indispensable, necessary
nieoficjalny 1 (*nieformalny*) informal; (*wypowiedź*) off the record **2** (*bezprawny*) unofficial
nieograniczony unlimited; (*nieokreślony*) open-ended; (*możliwości itp.*) endless; (*cierpliwość itp.*) infinite; (*wsparcie*) unreserved; (*władza itp.*) sovereign[2]; (*zasoby energetyczne itp.*) boundless, inexhaustible
nieokiełznany (*gwałtowny*) violent; (*niekontrolowany*) rampant
nieokreślony 1 (*niesprecyzowany*) indefinite, vague; **umowa na czas ~** an open-ended contract **2** (*nie do określenia*) indefinable; (*kolor, wiek*) indeterminate **3** (*bezbarwny*) nondescript **4** (*przyszłość*) uncertain
nieokrzesany crude, uncouth; (*zwł. młody mężczyzna*) loutish
nieomylny infallible
nieopanowany 1 (*gniew itp.*) uncontrollable; (*śmiech itp.*) uncontrolled **2** (*tłum*) unruly
nieopatrzny unguarded
nieopisany indescribable
nieopłacalny uneconomic
nieopłacany unpaid
nieoprocentowany interest-free
nieorganiczny inorganic
nieosiągalny beyond/out of (sb's) reach
nieosłonięty exposed
nieostrożność carelessness; (*w zachowaniu/rozmowie*) indiscretion
nieostrożny careless
nieostry 1 (*kulin.*) mild **2** (*zdjęcie*) out of focus
nieoszczędny uneconomical
nieoświetlony: **zupełnie ~** pitch-black
nieożywiony inanimate
niepalący (*przym.*) non-smoking
■ **niepalą|c-y/a** (*rz.*) non-smoker; **przedział dla niepalą cych** a non-smoking compartment
niepalny non-flammable
nieparzysty odd
niepasujący the odd man/one out
niepełnoletni under age
niepełnosprawn|y disabled; (*eufemistycznie*) challenged; **osoba ~a** invalid[2]; **czynić ~ym** disable
niepełn|y (*praca*) **w ~ym wymiarze godzin** part-time
niepewny 1 czegoś doubtful, dubious, hesitant, tentative, uncertain, undecided, unsure **2 siebie** diffident, faint-hearted, uneasy, insecure, mixed-up, unsure of yourself **3** (*nieokreślony*) uncertain **4** (*dyskusyjny*) arguable, debatable **4** (*urządzenie itp.; przyszłość*) insecure, shaky, unstable; (*niesolidny*) unsound; (*czasy; pogoda*) unsettled **5** (*rezultat*) undecided; (*szczegóły*) hazy **6** (*krok itp.*) unsteady
niepiśmienny illiterate
niepłatny unpaid
niepobity (*rekord itp.*) unbeaten, unbroken
niepociągający off-putting
niepocieszony disconsolate, inconsolable
niepodatny (*na krytykę itp.*) immune to sth
niepodlegający (*prawu itp.*) immune from sth
niepodległy independent
■ **niepodległość** independence
niepodobny dissimilar, unlike
niepodważalny incontrovertible
niepodzielny indivisible
niepohamowany 1 (*nałogowy*) compulsive **2** (*uczucie*)

uncontrollable; (*pełen energii*) irrepressible; (*gwałtowny*) violent **3** (*pożar itp.*) unchecked
niepojętny dull-witted, slow[1]
niepojęt|y (*niezrozumiały*) incomprehensible, inconceivable, mind-boggling; (*nieuchwytny*) intangible; **rzecz ~a** marvel
niepokoić/za- 1 (*zasmucać*) upset[1]; (*martwić*) concern[1], daunt, disconcert, disturb, perturb, trouble[2], unsettle, worry[1] **2** (*nie dawać spokoju*) bother[1], pester
□ **niepokoić/za- się** (*martwić się*) fret[1], worry[1]
niepokojący disconcerting, disquieting, disturbing, unsettling, worrying; (*cecha*) dark[1]
niepokonany invincible, unbeatable; (*rekord itp.*) unbeaten
niepokój 1 (*osoby*) anxiety; (*i zażenowanie*) discomfort; (*podenerwowanie*) flutter[2], nervousness; (*emocjonalny itp.*) upset[3] **2** (*społeczny*) unrest; (*sytuacja polityczna*) turbulence
niepoliczalny uncountable
niepomny: **czegoś** oblivious to/of sb/sth
niepomyśln|y unfavourable; **być ~ym dla kogoś** go against sb
niepopłatny uneconomic
niepoprawny 1 (*błędny*) incorrect **2** (*kłamca itp.*) incorrigible
niepopularny unpopular
nieporadny gauche
nieporęczny bulky, cumbersome, unwieldy
nieporozumienie 1 (*pomyłka*) misunderstanding; (*zamieszanie*) confusion **2** (*sprzeczka*) difference, misunderstanding
nieporównywalny 1 (*nie do porównania*) incomparable **2** (*różny*) disparate
nieporządek disorder, mess[1], untidiness
nieporządny disorderly, messy, untidy
nieposkromion|y uncontrollable; **~a duma** hubris
nieposłuszeństwo disobedience, insubordination; (*bunt*) defiance; (*zwł. dziecka*) naughtiness; **~ obywatelskie** civil disobedience
nieposłuszny disobedient, insubordinate; (*niezdyscyplinowany*) unruly; (*zwł. dziecko*) a handful, naughty
nieposzlakowany unblemished
niepotrzebny needless, redundant, superfluous, unnecessary, unwanted, useless
■ **niepotrzebnie** needlessly, unnecessarily; (*bez uzasadnienia*) gratuitously; **~ zapakowaliśmy ciepłe ubrania** we needn't have packed our warm clothes
niepotwierdzony (*urzędowo*) unofficial
niepoważny frivolous
niepowetowany irreparable
niepowiązany disjointed
niepowodzeni|e defeat[2], failure; (*rozmów itp.*) breakdown; (*rozmowy itp.*) **kończyć się ~em** break down; **skazany na ~e** doomed
niepowstrzymany irrepressible; (*przestępczość, przemoc itp.*) unchecked
niepowtarzalny inimitable, unique
niepozorny inconspicuous
niepożądany undesirable, unwanted
niepraktyczny impractical
nieprawda untruth
nieprawdopodobny 1 (*niezbyt wiarygodny*) improbable, unlikely **2** (*niesamowity*) incredible, unbelievable
■ **nieprawdopodobnie 1** improbably **2** beyond belief, impossibly, incredibly, unbelievably
nieprawdziwy 1 (*niezgodny z prawdą*) false, untrue **2** (*nierzeczywisty*) phoney, unreal
nieprawidłowy 1 (*niewłaściwy*) incorrect, wrong[1]; (*odbiegający od normy*) abnormal, anomalous **2** (*zachowanie*) improper **3** (*polecenie w komputerze itp.*) invalid[1] **4** (*niesprawny*) wrong[1] with sb/sth
nieprawomocny invalid[1]
nieprawość illegitimacy
nieprecyzyjny imprecise, vague; (*interpretacja itp.*) loose[1]
nieprofesjonalny amateur[2]
nieproporcjonalny disproportionate, out of proportion (to sth)
■ **nieproporcjonalnie** disproportionately; **~ dużo czasu** an inordinate amount of time
nieproszony 1 (*narzucający się*) intrusive **2** (*rada itp.*) unasked-for
nieprzechodni (*gram.*) intransitive
nieprzejednany implacable, irreconcilable, intransigent
nieprzejezdny impassable
nieprzejrzysty opaque
nieprzekonujący (*powód, argument itp.*) implausible, lame; (*dowód itp.*) inconclusive
nieprzekraczaln|y: **~a granica/data (czegoś)** deadline
nieprzekupny incorruptible
nieprzemakalny rainproof, waterproof; **płaszcz ~** mac
nieprzemyślany 1 (*argument itp.*) facile; **~ do końca** half-baked **2** (*bezmyślny*) rash[2], thoughtless
nieprzenikliwy (*techn.*) impervious to sth
nieprzeparty irresistible, overwhelming
nieprzepisow|y: (*sport*) **~e zagranie** foul play
nieprzepuszczalny (*techn.*) impervious to sth
nieprzerwany ceaseless, continued, continuous, non-stop, unbroken; (*zwł. coś irytującego*) incessant; (*rozwój itp.*) seamless
nieprzewidywalny unpredictable; (*zwł. zachowanie*) erratic
nieprzewidziany unforeseen
nieprzezroczysty opaque
nieprzezwyciężony (*zwł. problem*) insuperable, insurmountable
nieprzychylny disapproving, unfavourable; (*nieprzyjazny*) inimical
nieprzygotowany impromptu
nieprzyjaciel enemy, foe
nieprzyjazny 1 (*nieżyczliwy*) unfriendly; (*nieform.*) off[2] **2** (*wrogi*) antagonistic, hostile **3** (*rejon itp.*) inhospitable
nieprzyjemny disagreeable, nasty, objectionable, undesirable, unpleasant; (*nieżyczliwy*) mean[2] to sb; (*sytuacja; wiadomość itp.*) grim; (*niszczący harmonię*) discordant; (*zwł. moralnie*) unsavoury
nieprzystający the odd man/one out
nieprzystępny 1 (*książka itp.*) inaccessible **2** (*osoba*) remote
nieprzystosowany (*społecznie*) maladjusted
nieprzytomny 1 (*rozkojarzony*) dazed, in a daze; (*wzrok*) faraway **2** (*w stanie omdlenia*) senseless, unconscious
■ **nieprzytomnoś|ć** unconsciousness; **pijany do nieprzytomności** in a drunken stupor
nieprzyzwoit|y improper, indecent, obscene, offensive[1]; (*język itp.*) dirty[1], filthy; **~-e/y słowo/czyn** obscenity; **~y wyraz** four-letter word; **sprośne/~e słowa/zdjęcia itp.** filth
nieprzyzwyczajony unused to sth/doing sth
nieracjonalny irrational, unreasonable
nierafinowany: **cukier ~** raw sugar
nieraz repeatedly
nierdzewn|y rustproof; **stal ~a** stainless steel
nierealistyczny unrealistic
nierealny unreal; (*wymyślony*) fictitious; (*marzenie itp.*) fond, unrealistic
niereformowalny irredeemable
nieregularny irregular; (*występujący zrywami*) fitful, spasmodic; (*opady itp.*) patchy
nierentowny uneconomic
nierozcieńczony unadulterated; (*alkohol*) neat
nierozdzielny inseparable
nierozgarnięty dopey, dull-witted, slow-witted
nierozłączny inseparable
nierozpuszczalny insoluble
nierozsądek irrationality
nierozsądny unreasonable; (*niewskazany*) ill-advised, imprudent, inadvisable; (*głupi*) silly
nierozstrzygający inconclusive
nierozstrzygnięty 1 (*spór itp.*) open[1], pending adj., unsettled **2 ~ bieg** dead heat
nieroztropny inadvisable; (*wypowiedź itp.*) indiscreet; (*decyzja itp.*) rash[2]
nierozumny irrational
nierozważny 1 (*nieostrożny*) careless, unguarded; (*bezmyślny*) thoughtless **2** (*pochopny*) hasty, rash[2]
■ **nierozważnie** headlong, recklessly, thoughtlessly
nierozwiązalny insoluble
nierozwiązywalny insuperable, insurmountable
nierozwinięty immature
nieróб layabout
nierównomierny irregular; (*wzrost itp.*) patchy
nierównowaga imbalance
nierówny 1 (*nieregularny*) irregular; (*zmienny*) uneven **2** (*chropowaty*) rough[1], uneven **3** (*droga itp.*) bumpy;

(*brzeg itp.*) ragged **4** (*ilością*) unequal, patchy **5** (*ruch ręki itp.*) unsteady
■ **nierówność 1** (*nieregularność*) irregularity **2** (*różnica*) disparity; (*społeczna*) inequality
nieruchomy 1 (*nieporuszający się*) immobile, motionless, still[2]; (*zwł. pojazd*) at rest, stationary **2** (*ceny itp.*) static[1]
■ **nieruchomość 1** (*brak ruchu*) immobility **2** (**nieruchomości**) (*domy itp.*) real estate, property
nierzeczywisty unreal
niesamodzielny (*zwł. dziecko*) clinging
niesamowity 1 (*niezwykły*) fantastic, mind-blowing, staggering **2** (*dziwny*) funny, uncanny, unearthly, weird, wacky; (*przerażający*) creepy
■ **niesamowicie** staggeringly, tremendously, fantastically
niesforny 1 (*niespokojny*) restless **2** (*włosy*) **cienki i** ~ wispy
nieskalany unblemished
nieskazitelny|y 1 (*doskonały*) immaculate, impeccable, irreproachable **2** (*bez plam*) spotless, unblemished; **~ie czysty** pristine
nieskażony unadulterated
nieskłonny unwilling
nieskomplikowany light[2], simple
nieskończon|y 1 (*czas*) everlasting **2** (*niedokończony*) unfinished **3** (*mat.*) infinite
■ **nieskończoność 1** (*czas*) eternity **2** (*mat.*) infinity
nieskory coy
nieskromny immodest
nieskrywany open[1]
nieskuteczny fruitless, ineffective, ineffectual; (*niewydajny*) inefficient
niesława infamy
niesławny infamous
niesłychany extreme, stupendous, unheard-of, unprecedented, untold; (*okrucieństwo itp.*) nameless
■ **niesłychanie** devastatingly
niesłyszalny inaudible
niesmaczny 1 (*jedzenie*) distasteful, tasteless **2** (*przen.*) tasteless
niesmak distaste
niesnaski strife
niesolidny unreliable, unsound
niespełna: **w** ~ inside[1]
niespieszny 1 (*powolny*) leisurely **2** (*rozważny*) deliberate[1]
niespodzianka surprise[1]; **ale ~!** fancy[1]
niespodziewan|y 1 (*nagły*) sudden **2** (*nieoczekiwany*) unexpected; **~a korzyść** a blessing in disguise
■ **niespodziewanie 1** (*nagle*) suddenly **2** (*nieoczekiwanie*) unawares, unexpectedly
niespokojny 1 o kogoś/coś anxious, uneasy, nervous, upset[2] **2** (*w ruchu*) fidgety, restless **3** (*sytuacja itp.*) unsettled, turbulent
niespotykany unheard-of, unprecedented
niesprawiedliw|y unfair, wrongful
IDM **być ~ym dla kogoś/w stosunku do czegoś** be hard on sb/sth
■ **niesprawiedliwość 1** unfairness **2** (*krzywda*) injustice, wrong[3]
niesprawny wrong[1] with sth; (*komput.*) down[3]; ~ **(fizycznie)** unfit
niesprecyzowany indefinite
nieprzyjający adverse, unfavourable
niestabilny unstable; (*osoba; sytuacja*) volatile
■ **niestabilność** instability
niestały 1 (*skłonny do zmiany*) variable **2** (*plan itp.*) fluid[2] **3** (*ruchomy; zmieniający miejsce*) floating **4** (*osoba: w decyzjach; zamiarach*) fickle; (*zwł. kobieta*) flighty
■ **niestałość** instability, variability
niestety (*na nieszczęście*) unfortunately, unhappily, unluckily; (*wyrażając żal*) alas, regrettably, sadly
niestosowny 1 (*niepasujący; niestosowny*) inappropriate; (*i sprośny*) improper; (*wypowiedź; czyn*) uncalled for **2** (*błędny*) incorrect **3** (*w niewłaściwym miejscu*) out of place; (*i dziwny*) incongruous
niestrawn|y indigestible
■ **niestrawność** indigestion
niestrudzony tireless
niestrzeżony unguarded
niesubordynacja insubordination
niesubordynowany insubordinate
nieswojo: **czuć się** ~ (*niewygodnie*) not feel comfortable; (*niezdrowo*) not feel yourself, be/feel off colour
niesymetryczny asymmetric; (*o różnym rozmiarze itp.*) unequal
nieszablonowy maverick, unorthodox
nieszczelny leaky
■ **nieszczelność** leak[2]
nieszczery insincere; (*zwł. udając, że się czegoś nie wie*) disingenuous; (*słowa*) hollow[1]
nieszczęsny wretched
nieszczęści|e 1 (*pech*) misfortune; (*katastrofa*) disaster; **doznawać ~a** come to harm; **mieć ~e** have bad luck **2** (*brak radości*) unhappiness, woe **3** (*cierpienie*) misery; (*zwł. choroba*) affliction IDM **na ~e 1** (*pechowo*) unfortunately, unluckily, worse luck **2** (*w smutny sposób*) unhappily
nieszczęśliwy 1 (*smutny*) joyless, miserable, unhappy, wretched **2** (*pechowy*) unfortunate, unlucky **3** (*biedny*) poor
nieszczęś-nik/nica wretch
nieszkodliwy 1 (*niewinny*) harmless, innocent, inoffensive **2** (*substancja itp.*) harmless, innocuous
nieściągalny: ~ **dług** bad debt
nieścieralny indelible
nieścisły inaccurate
nieść/u-/wz- zob. też NOSIĆ; (*w powietrzu*) waft
nieślubn|y (*dziecko*) illegitimate; **~e pochodzenie** illegitimacy
nieśmiały bashful, diffident, mousy, retiring, sheepish, shy[1], timid; **(pozornie)** ~ coy
■ **nieśmiało** sheepishly, shyly, timidly; (*z zażenowaniem*) self-consciously; (*kokieteryjnie*) coyly; **zaprotestować nieśmiało** make a faint protest
nieśmiertelny immortal
■ **nieśmiertelność** immortality
nieświadomy 1 (*bez wiedzy*) ignorant **2** (*niezdający sobie sprawy*) unaware, unconscious, unwitting
■ **nieświadomoś|ć 1** (*zwł. sen; omdlenie*) oblivion **2** (*niewiedza*) **pozostać w zupełnej nieświadomości czegoś** be in complete ignorance of sth; **trzymać kogoś w nieświadomości** (be/keep sb) in the dark (about sth) **3** (*brak jasności*) vagueness
nieświeży (*mleko, masło, mięso*) off[2]; (*chleb*) stale
nietakt bluntness, clumsiness
nietaktowny tactless; (*bez ogródek*) clumsy; (*niezręczny*) gauche; (*gruboskórny*) heavy-handed; (*nieczuły*) indiscreet, insensitive to sth
nietknięty intact
nietolerancja intolerance
nietolerancyjny bigoted, illiberal, intolerant
nietoperz bat[1]
nietowarzyski antisocial
nietrwały insubstantial
nietrzeźwy drunken, inebriated; **stan** ~ intoxication; **w stanie ~m** intoxicated
nietykalność immunity
nietypowy atypical, out of character, uncharacteristic, untypical
nieuchronn|y inescapable, inevitable, unavoidable; **rzecz ~a** the inevitable noun
nieuchwytny 1 (*niedający się określić*) elusive; (*i zmierzyć*) intangible **2** (*nieokreślony*) indefinable **3** (*dla oka*) imperceptible
nieuczciw|y dishonest; (*praktyka*) fraudulent; (*inform.*) bent[2], crooked; (*rywalizacja; gra*) dirty[1], unfair
nieudany abortive, unsuccessful
nieudoln|y 1 (*niekompetentny*) incapable, incompetent, inept; (*nieskuteczny; niewydajny*) inefficient; **osoba ~a** incompetent noun **2** (*w zachowaniu*) bumbling
■ **nieudolność** impotence, inadequacy, incompetence, inefficiency
nieufn|y 1 (*bez zaufania*) distrustful **2** (*podejrzliwy*) suspicious
■ **nieufnoś|ć** distrust, mistrust noun; **wotum ~ci** a vote of censure in parliament
nieugięty inflexible; (*i nieustanny*) adamant, relentless; **pozostaje** ~ nothing will budge him
nieukojony inconsolable
nieuleczalny (*choroba*) terminal[2]; (*i uczucie*) incurable
nieumiarkowany immoderate
nieumyślny (*czyn; przestępstwo*) inadvertent; (*odruchowy*) involuntary
■ **nieumyślnie** (*przypadkowo*) accidentally, inadvertently; (*odruchowo*) involuntarily
nieuniknion|y inescapable, inevitable, unavoidable
nieupoważniony unauthorized
nieuprawny waste[3]
nieuprzejmy discourteous, impolite, rude; (*trudny klient itp.*) difficult; (*niewrażliwy*) inconsiderate; ~ **i szorstki** short[1] with sb
■ **nieuprzejmość** inconsiderateness, meanness, nastiness, rudeness, unkindness
nieuprzywilejowany disadvantaged
nieuregulowany (*rachunek*) unsettled
nieurodzaj crop failure
nieurodzajny 1 (*ziemia*) barren, infertile **2** (*rok*) lean[2]
nieurzędowy informal
nieusprawiedliwiony (*niestosowny*) uncalled for, unwarranted; (*wandalizm itp.*) wanton
nieustający (także **nieustanny**) (*ciągły*) ceaseless, constant, endless; (*atak*)

remorseless; (*wsparcie itp.*) unfailing; (*walka*) running[2]; (*zwł. coś irytującego*) incessant; (*bezwzględny*) relentless
nieustępliwy 1 (*uparty*) headstrong, obstinate, stubborn **2** (*wróg*) implacable; (*walka*) relentless **3** (*wytrwały; zdeterminowany*) tenacious **4** (*niezmienny*) unrelenting
nieustraszony fearless, intrepid
nieusuwalny (*atrament itp.*) indelible
nieuwag|a inattention; **chwilowa ~a** a temporary lapse in concentration; **w chwili ~i** in an unguarded moment
nieuważny 1 (*roztargniony; niesłuchający*) inattentive **2** (*czyn*) inadvertent
nieuwiązany loose[1]
nieuzasadniony 1 (*nielogiczny*) illogical **2** (*bez poparcia faktami*) baseless, unfounded **3** (*przemoc*) gratuitous
nieuzbrojony unarmed
nieużytki waste[2], waste ground, wasteland
nieużywany brand new, disused; **jeszcze ~** unused[1]
nieważkoś|ć weightlessness; **w stanie ~ci** weightless
nieważny 1 (*nieistotny*) immaterial, petty, unimportant; **to naprawdę nieważne** it really doesn't matter **2** (*paszport; bilet*) invalid[1], out of date; (*i umowa*) null and void, void[2]
IDM **nieważne** never mind, not to worry
niewątpliwy undoubted, unmistakable, unquestionable
■ **niewątpliwie** no doubt, without (a) doubt, doubtless, surely, undoubtedly, unmistakably, unquestionably
niewdzięczn|y thankless, ungrateful; **być w ~ej sytuacji...** be in the invidious position of having to do sth
■ **niewdzięczność** ingratitude
niewesoły (*sytuacja*) bleak
niewiadom|y unknown[1] to sb
IDM **wielka ~a** anybody's/anyone's guess
niewiarygodny 1 (*nieprawdopodobny*) unbelievable, incredible; (*niesamowity*) staggering **2** (*nieprzekonujący*) implausible
niewiasta woman
niewidoczny invisible; (*za mały*) imperceptible
niewidomy (*osoba*) blind[1]; **być ~m** be visually handicapped
niewidzialny invisible
niewiel|e (także **niewielu**) (*z rz. niepolicz.*) little[3]; (*z rz. policz.*) few
IDM **~e wart** not up to much
niewielk|i 1 (*mały*) small; (*drobniutki*) diminutive; (*za mały: pensja itp.*) meagre **2** (*nadzieja; pieniądze*) little[1]; (*problem itp.*) a bit of a; **~a ilość** a little det., pron. **3** (*wiatr; śniadanie*) light[2]
niewierny 1 (*mąż/żona*) unfaithful to sb/sth **2** (*przyjaciel; obywatel*) disloyal to sb/sth
■ **niewierność** disloyalty, infidelity, unfaithfulness
niewieści womanly
niewietrzony (*pokój*) airless, stuffy
niewinn|y 1 (*bez winy*) blameless, innocent; **~e kłamstwo** a white lie **2** (*seksualnie*) chaste, innocent, pure **3** (*nieszkodliwy*) harmless, inoffensive; (*pytanie*) innocent; (*uwaga itp.*) innocuous
■ **niewinność** innocence
niewłaściw|y (*nieodpowiedni*) inappropriate; (*i sprośny*) improper; **~e używanie** misuse noun; **~e zachowanie** misbehaviour
■ **niewłaściwość** impropriety
niewol|a bondage, captivity; (*niewolnictwo*) slavery; **brać kogoś do ~i** capture, take sb captive/prisoner
niewolnictwo slavery
niewolni-k/ca slave[1]; **czynić kogoś niewolnikiem** enslave; **pracować jak niewolnik** slave[2] (away)
niewprawny inexpert
niewrażliwy 1 na coś insensitive, stolid **2** (*nieuprzejmy*) inconsiderate
niewskazany inadvisable
niewspółmierny disproportionate, out of proportion (to sth)
niewybaczalny inexcusable
niewybredny indiscriminate
niewyczerpany inexhaustible, infinite; (*optymizm itp.*) unfailing
niewydajność inefficiency
niewydajny 1 (*pracownik; system*) inefficient **2** (*uprawy*) lean[2]
niewydarzony bumbling
niewydolność malfunction; **umrzeć na ~ serca** die of heart failure
niewygod|a discomfort, inconvenience, trouble[1]; **duża ~a** hardship; **powodować ~ę** inconvenience verb
niewygodny 1 (*fotel itp.*) uncomfortable; (*do niesienia itp.*) cumbersome **2** (*fakt*) inconvenient; (*prawda*) awkward; (*moment*) bad; (*pytanie*) vexed
niewygórowany (*ceny*) affordable, reasonable
niewyjaśniony inexplicable; (*dziwny*) uncanny
niewykluczon|y: **~e, że ona mówi prawdę** she might just conceivably be telling the truth
niewykonalność impossibility
niewykonaln|y impossible, impracticable; **rzecz ~a** the impossible
niewykonany undone
niewykorzystany: **~ teren** waste ground
niewykształcony uneducated; (*prostacki*) vulgar
niewykwalifikowany unqualified, unskilled
niewymagający cushy
niewymuszenie naturally
niewyobrażalny inconceivable, mind-boggling
niewypał 1 (*bomba*) live bomb **2** (*niepowodzenie*) disappointment, fiasco, flop[2], non-event; **być ~em** fall flat, flop[1]
niewyparzon|y: **o ~ej gębie** loud-mouthed
niewypłacalność insolvency
niewypłacalny insolvent
niewypowiedziany tacit, untold
niewyraźny imprecise, indistinct, vague; (*światło*) dim[1]; (*zarysy*) fuzzy, shadowy; (*zdjęcie*) out of focus; (*mowa*) inarticulate
niewyrobiony (*towarzysko*) immature
niewysłuchany unheard
niewysoki low[1]; (*osoba*) short[1]
niewystarczający inadequate, insufficient, scarce, short[1] (of/on sth); (*informacje itp.*) scanty; (*zainteresowanie itp.*) scant
niewystawny low-key
niewyszukany homely, plain[1], simple
niewytłumaczalny inexplicable
niewyważony unbalanced
niewzruszony 1 (*spokojny*) impassive, imperturbable, unmoved **2** (*w poglądach*) adamant, confirmed
niezaangażowany (*kraj itp.*) non-aligned
niezabezpieczony insecure, vulnerable (to sb/sth)
niezachwiany (*wiara itp.*) invincible
niezadowalający disappointing
niezadowolenie discontent, displeasure, dissatisfaction; **~ społeczne** social unrest; **wywoływać ~** displease; **z ~m** sulkily
niezadowolony discontented, disgruntled, displeased, dissatisfied, unhappy
niezagospodarowany: **teren ~** wasteland
niezależnie independently; **od czegoś** irrespective of; **~ od kogoś/czegoś** regardless of sb/sth
niezależn|y free[1], independent, self-reliant; (*partia polityczna itp.*) unattached; (*muzyka, wydawnictwo itp.*) indie; (*zwł. komput.*) stand-alone; **~y dziennikarz** freelance journalist; **osoba ~a** free agent
■ **niezależność** independence
niezamężna single[1], unattached, unmarried; **kobieta ~** maiden
niezamierzony (*żart*) unconscious
niezamieszkały uninhabited
niezapłacony unpaid, unsettled
niezapominajka forget-me-not
niezapomniany memorable, unforgettable
niezaprzeczalny incontestable, undeniable
niezarezerwowany unreserved
niezasłużony unwarranted
niezaspokojony insatiable
niezastąpiony irreplaceable
niezatarty (*i przen.*) indelible
niezauważalny imperceptible, inconspicuous
niezauważony lost[2] on sb, unnoticed; **przejść ~m** go unheard
niezawodność infallibility, reliability
niezawodny dependable, foolproof, infallible, sure; (*wsparcie itp.*) unfailing
■ **niezawodnie** without fail, reliably, unfailingly
niezbędność necessity
niezbędn|y crucial, essential, imperative, indispensable, necessary, vital; (*personel*) skeleton[2]; **rzecz ~a** essential noun
niezbity irrefutable, watertight
niezbyt not all that...; **~ ją lubię** I don't like her very much. IDM **~ szczęśliwy/czysty/zadowolony itp.** none too happy/clean/pleased, etc.
niezbywalny (*czek itp.*) non-negotiable
niezdara butterfingers
niezdarność awkwardness, clumsiness

niezdarny awkward, clumsy, ungainly; ~ **wizerunek czegoś** crude representations of sth
niezdatny unfit
niezdecydowanie (*rz.*) hesitancy, hesitation, indecision, uncertainty, vacillation
niezdecydowany hesitant, indecisive, uncertain, undecided; **być ~m** dither, be in two minds (about sth/doing sth), waver
niezdolność inability; (*do jakiejś pracy itp.*) disqualification
niezdoln|y incapable, unable; (*do wykonania czegoś specyficznego*) powerless; **uczynić ~ym (do czegoś)** incapacitate; **uznać kogoś za ~ego (do czegoś)** disqualify sb (from sth/doing sth)
niezdrowy 1 (także **niezdrów**) unhealthy, unwell **2** (*zainteresowanie itp.*) morbid, sick[1]
niezdyscyplinowany unruly
niezepsuty not broken
niezgłębiony bottomless
niezgoda discord, dissidence, friction; **w niezgodzie (z kimś)** at loggerheads (with sb)
niezgodnie inconsistently, out of keeping (with sth); ~ **z przepisami** irregularly
niezgodność 1 (*niekonsekwencja*) incongruity, inconsistency; (*pojęć itp.*) incompatibility; ~ **z przepisami/zasadami** irregularity **2** (*poglądów itp.*) disagreement, dissonance; (*usposobień*) incompatibility; ~ **charakterów** personality clash
niezgodny (*poglądy itp.*) dissonant, incompatible; (*niekonsekwentny*) inconsistent; (*z przepisami/zasadami*) irregular; **być ~m z czymś** go against sb/sth, be out of keeping with sth
niezgrabność clumsiness
niezgrabny awkward, clumsy, ungainly
niezidentyfikowany unidentified
nieziemski 1 (*dotyczący duchów itp.*) ghostly **2** (*wspaniały*) sublime
niezliczon|y countless, innumerable, untold; **~a ilość razy** umpteen
niezłączony unattached
niezły not bad, decent
niezmącony (*spokój itp.*) tranquil; (*woda itp.*) still[2]
niezmieniony unchanged
niezmienność permanence
niezmienny constant, firm[2], fixed, invariable, permanent, settled, standing[1], static[1], steady[1]; ~ **z upływem czasu** timeless
niezmiernie exceedingly, extremely, immeasurably, immensely, vastly; ~ **uradowany** overjoyed
niezmierny immeasurable, immense
niezmordowany tireless; **człowiek** ~ glutton for sth
nieznaczny insignificant, insubstantial, marginal, small; (*suma itp.*) modest; (*zwycięstwo itp.*) narrow[1]; (*szansa itp.*) outside[2]
nieznajomość ignorance
nieznajom-y/a stranger, unknown[2]
nieznany nameless, obscure[1], unfamiliar, unknown[1]
niezniszczalność incorruptibility
niezniszczalny incorruptible, indestructible
nieznośny horrid, impossible, insufferable, intolerable, tiresome, unbearable; ~ **upał** blazing heat
niezręczność gaucheness
niezręczny awkward, clumsy; (*w zachowaniu*) gauche
niezrobiony undone
niezrozumiały incomprehensible, inconceivable, lost[2] on sb, obscure[1], unintelligible
niezrozumienie incomprehension, misunderstanding
niezrównany incomparable, inimitable, unrivalled
niezrównoważony unbalanced, unequal; (*zachowanie itp.*) erratic
niezupełnie 1 (*źle*) incompletely **2** (*zgadzać się itp.*) not exactly, not quite
niezupełny incomplete
niezważający (*na czyjeś potrzeby, uczucia itp.*) inconsiderate
niezwiązany 1 unattached; (*włosy*) loose[1] **2** (*nie na temat*) extraneous
niezwracający: ~ **na siebie uwagi** inconspicuous
niezwyciężony impregnable, invincible
niezwykle abnormally, curiously, extraordinarily, phenomenally, singularly, strangely, supremely
niezwykłość oddness, oddity, originality, rarity, strangeness
niezwykły curious, extraordinary, out of the ordinary, original[1], phenomenal, rare, remarkable, singular, strange, uncommon, unique, unusual
nieźle: **brzmi** ~ it sounds fun
nieżonaty single[1], unattached, unmarried
nieżyczliwość unkindness
nieżyczliwy unfriendly, unkind
nieżywy lifeless
nigdy never IDM **na święty** ~ once in a blue moon
nigdzie anywhere, nowhere
nijaki 1 (*bez charakterystycznych cech*) neutral[1]; (*smak, styl*) bland, insipid; (*krajobraz itp.*) featureless; (*włosy*) lacklustre; (*osobowość, impreza itp.*) tame[1] **2** (*gram.*) neuter[1]
nikczemnik villain
nikczemny despicable, dishonourable, ignoble, mean[2], shoddy, sordid, wicked
nikiel nickel
niklowy nickel
nikły measly; (*szansa itp.*) faint[1], outside[2]
niknąć wear off
nikotyna nicotine
nikt anybody, nobody[1,2], none[1]
nim him
nimfa nymph
niniejszy present[1]
nisk|i 1 low[1]; **~i poziom** low[3]; **zbyt ~a ocena** underestimate noun **2** (*osoba*) short[1] **3** (*dźwięk, głos*) deep[1], low[1]; (*nuta*) **za ~i** flat[1] **4** (*niegodny*) low[1], tawdry
■ **nisko 1** low[2]; ~ **płatny** low-paid; **za ~ szacować** underestimate; **zbyt ~ oceniać** undervalue **2** (*śpiewać/grać*) **za** ~ flat adv.
nisza niche
niszczeć decay[2]
niszczyciel 1 (także **niszczycielka**) destroyer **2** (*okręt*) destroyer
niszczycielski destructive, devastating
niszczyć/z- 1 (*doszczętnie*) annihilate, destroy, devastate, kill sth off, obliterate, ruin[1], tear sth apart, wipe sth out, wreak havoc, wreck; (*budkę telefoniczną itp.*) vandalize; (*karierę itp.*) blight[1]; (*przez częste używanie*) wear sth away **2** (*psychicznie*) sap[2] sb of sth, shatter, traumatize, walk (all) over sb **3** (*plany itp.*) squash[1]
nit rivet[1]
nitka thread[1]
niuans nuance
niweczyć/z- kill[1], negate, put paid to sth; (*nadzieje*) dash sb's hopes (of sth/of doing sth), shatter; (*i plany, zamiary itp.*) squash[1]; ~ **czyjeś plany** play havoc with sb's plans
niwelować level[3]
nizać/na- thread[2]
nizina lowland
nizinny low-lying
niż before[2], than
niższoś|ć inferiority; **kompleks ~ci** inferiority complex
niższ|y down[3], lower[1]; **~a pozycja** (*np. społeczna*) inferiority; **~y rangą** inferior, junior[1]
no now; ~ **co ty!** come off it; ~, ~! well[3]
noc night, night-time; **(powtarzający się) co** ~ nightly; **na/przez** ~ overnight adv.
nocleg accommodation; **przyjąć kogoś na** ~ put sb up IDM **(mały hotel, który oferuje) ~ ze śniadaniem** bed and breakfast, B and B, B & B
nocnik potty[2]
nocn|y nightly; (*pobyt*) overnight; **~a pora** night-time; **~e życie** nightlife
nocować/prze-: **u kogoś** sleep over; **kogoś** put sb up; **apartament, w którym mogą przenocować cztery osoby** an apartment that sleeps four people
nog|a 1 (*anat.*) leg; (*stopa*) foot[1] **2** (*stołu itp.*) leg; **w ~ach łóżka** at the foot of the bed IDM **dawać ~ę** do a bunk | **być jedną ~ą w grobie** have one foot in the grave | **być na ~ach** be on the go | (*i przen.*) **pod ~ami** under your feet
nogawka leg
nokaut knockout
nokautować/z-: **kogoś** knock sb out, knock sb unconscious
nomada nomad
nomenklatura (*prawna, medyczna itp.*) terminology
nominacja nomination
nominaln|y nominal; **wartość ~a** face value
nominować nominate
nominowan-y/a nominee
nonkonformist-a/ka nonconformist
nonkonformistyczny nonconformist adj.
nonsens nonsense
nonsensowny ludicrous
nonszalancja nonchalance
nonszalancki casual, cavalier, negligent, nonchalant
nora 1 burrow[2], den, hole, nest **2** (*przen.*) dump[2], hovel
nordyjski: **język** ~ Norse
norka mink
norm|a norm, normal[2], the ordinary/average, etc. run of sth; (*ilość standardowa/określona przepisami*) quota; (*golf*) par[1]; **~a zachowania** standard[1]; **odbiegający od ~y** abnormal, anomalous

normalizacja standardization
normalizować/z- normalize, standardize
□ **normalizować/z- się** normalize
normalność normality
normalny natural[1], normal[1], ordinary, regular[1], right[1]; (*osoba*) sane
normować/u- (się) normalize
nos nose[1]
nosek (*buta*) toe[1]
nosiciel carrier
nosić 1 (*dźwigać*) carry, cart[2] **2** (*ubranie, biżuterię itp.*) wear[1] **3** (*ślad*) bear[1] **4** (*rozmiar ubrania*) take
□ **nosić się 1** (*ubierać się*) wear[1] **2** ~ **z zamiarem czegoś** think of/ about doing sth
nosidełko carrycot
nosorożec rhinoceros
nosowy nasal
nostalgia nostalgia
nostalgiczny nostalgic
nosze stretcher
nośnik vehicle
nota: ~ **prasowa** press release IDM **zła** ~ black mark
notabene incidentally, NB
notacja notation
notariusz solicitor
notatk|a note[1], record[1]; (*służbowa*) memo; **robić ~i** take notes
notatnik notebook, notepad, pocketbook
notebook notebook
notes notebook, pocketbook; ~ **na adresy** address book
notoryczny notorious
notować/za- chart[2], get sth down, note sth down, put, take sth down; ~ **coś w pamięci** register[1]; ~ **nazwisko** (*za karę*) book[2]
■ **notowany 1 wysoko notowany** top-ranking **2 być notowanym** have a criminal record
notowa|nie (**notowania**) showing; **według obecnych ~ń** on its present showing
nowator/ka pioneer
nowatorski innovative, novel[2]
nowatorstwo novelty
nowela short story
nowicjusz/ka novice; (*w armii itp.*) recruit[2]
nowiny news
nowiutki brand new
now|o newly; **od ~a** afresh; **~o wybrany** incoming
nowoczesność modernity
nowoczesny modern, up to date; (*sytuacja*) enlightened
nowomodny newfangled
nowomowa gobbledegook
noworodek infant
nowość 1 (*cecha rzeczy nowej*) newness **2** (*niezwykłość, nowinka itp.*) innovation, novelty, strangeness **3** (*przedmiot*) the latest
nowotworowy cancerous
nowotwór cancer, growth, tumour
nowożeńc|y: **apartament dla ~ów** the bridal suite in a hotel
nowożytn|y modern; **języki ~e** modern languages
now|y new, unused[1]; (*rząd itp.*) incoming; (*idee itp.*) fresh; (*banknot*) crisp[1]; **fabrycznie ~y** brand new; **coś ~ego** novelty; **na ~o**; **od ~a** anew; **Nowy Rok** New Year's Day
nozdrze nostril
nożny foot[1]
nożyce cutters, scissors; ~ **ogrodnicze** shears
nożyczki scissors; ~ **do paznokci** nail scissors
nożyki (*zwł. do paznokci*) clippers
nów new moon
nóż knife[1]; ~ **do krajania mięsa** carving knife; ~ **sprężynowy** flick knife
nóżka 1 (*pieczonego kurczaka*) drumstick **2** (*kieliszka*) stem[1]
nucić/za- croon, hum
nuda bore[2], boredom, drag[2], dullness
nudności nausea, sickness; **mieć** ~ heave[1]; **mający** ~ sick[1]
nudny boring, colourless, dreary, dry[1], dull, flat[1], grey[1], heavy, pedestrian[2], tame[1], tedious; (*nieform.*) blah; (*osoba*) stuffy; **niemodny i** ~ nerdy; **śmiertelnie** ~ deadly; (*praca/ zadanie*) soul-destroying
nudyst-a/ka nudist
nudyzm nudism
nudzia-rz/ra bore[2]
nudzić/za-/z- bore[1]
□ **nudzić/za-/z- się** get bored, pall (on sb), be sick[1] of sb/sth, tire of sth/sb
nugat nougat
nuklearny nuclear
numer 1 code[1], number[1]; ~ **kierunkowy** (area) code, dialling code; ~ **rejestracyjny samochodu** registration number; ~ **serii/ seryjny** serial number; ~ **sprawy** reference; ~ **wewnętrzny** extension; **mieszkać pod ~em 5** live at number 5 **2** (*czasopisma*) issue[1] **3** (*w kabarecie itp.*) act[1]
numerek (*seks*) bonk
numerować/po- number[2]
numerowy porter
nur: **dawać ~a** dive[1]
nurek diver
nurkować/za- (*w wodzie*) dive[1], plunge in, plunge into sth/in
nurkowanie 1 dive[2], diving, plunge[2]; (*ze sprzętem do nurkowania*) scuba-diving; ~ **bez kombinezonu** skin-diving; ~ **z rurką** snorkelling **2** (*samolotu*) nosedive
nurt current[2]; **główny** ~ mainstream
nurzać się wallow
nuta 1 (*muz.*) note[1] **2** (**nuty**) (*zapis utworu*) music, score[1] **3** (*w nastroju itp.*) note[1], undercurrent
nużący tedious, tiresome, tiring, trying
nużyć/z- (się) tire[1]
nylon nylon

O

o 1 (*temat*) about[2], on, over; ~ **rety!** **2** (*opierać, rzucać itp.*) against **3** (*czas*) **4** (*z liczbą*) by **5** (*cel*) for[1]
■ **o**; (**O/o**) (*litera*) O, o
oaza oasis
oba (także **obaj, obie, oboje**) both, either[1]
oba-lać/lić 1 (*władzę itp.*) bring sb/sth down, overthrow, topple; (*system*) subvert **2** (*decyzję*) overturn **3** (*teorię itp.*) demolish, kill[1], rebut, refute, disprove, invalidate
obar-czać/czyć burden[2] sb (with sth), encumber, land sb with sb/sth, lumber[2] sb (with sb/sth), saddle sb with sth; (*winą*) place[2]
□ **obarczać/czyć się** burden[2] yourself (with sth)
obaw|a 1 o kogoś/coś concern[2] **2 przed kimś/czymś** anxiety, apprehension, fear[1], fearfulness, misgiving; **pełen** ~ apprehensive; **z ~ą** anxiously, fearfully, warily IDM **bez** ~ never fear! | **nie ma ~y** no fear
obawiać się be afraid, be/feel apprehensive (about sth), fear[2], shy away from sth/from doing sth, be wary IDM **obawiam się (że)** I'm afraid (that…)
obcas heel[1]
obcesowy abrupt, blunt, brusque, point-blank
obcęgi pincers, pliers
obchody celebration
obchodzenie się treatment; **złe** ~ mistreatment
obchodzić/obejść 1 (*wokół*) circumvent **2** (*uroczyście*) celebrate, commemorate, mark[1] **3** (*interesować*) **kogo to obchodzi?** who cares?; **nic mnie itp. to nie obchodzi** I, etc. couldn't care less
□ **obchodzić/obejść się**: **źle ~ z czymś** mistreat, misuse
obchód 1 (*strażnika itp.*) round[4]; **robić** ~ patrol[1] **2** (**obchody**) commemoration, festivity
ob-ciążać/ciążyć encumber, load[2]; **coś** weight[2] sth (down) (with sth); **kogoś** burden[2], weigh sb down; ~ **zarzutami** incriminate; **być obciążonym długami** be encumbered with debt
□ **ob-ciążać/ciążyć się** burden[2] yourself (with sth)
■ **obciążony** heavy, laden, loaded
obciążenie 1 (*ciężar; emocjalne*) stress[1], strain[1] **2** (*przy balonie, w łodzi itp.*) ballast **3** (*obowiązek*) demand[1] **4** (*finansowe*) drain on sb/sth
obcierać/obetrzeć 1 (*pot itp.*) wipe[1] **2** (*ubranie (o skórę) itp.*) dig (sth) in, dig sth into sb/sth; (*kołnierz itp.*) chafe, rub (on/against sth)
obcinać/obciąć 1 coś (z czegoś) cut[1], cut sth off (sth), lop sth off (sth); **muszę obciąć włosy** I have to get my hair cut; ~ **bardzo krótko** crop[2] **2** (*wydatki*) axe[2], cut sth back, cut back (on sth) **3** (*zarobki*) dock[2]
obcisły clinging, close-fitting, skintight, tight-fitting
obcokrajowiec alien[2], foreigner
obcować associate[1] with sb; (*towarzysko*) mix[1] (with sb)
■ **obcowanie**: ~ **z innymi kulturami** exposure to other cultures
obc|y alien[1], foreign, strange, unfamiliar; (*ufo itp.*) extraterrestrial; **~y sobie** estranged (from sb); **osoba ~a** stranger, outsider
obdarty ragged, shabby
obda-rzać/rzyć (*zaufaniem*) place[2]; **hojnie** ~ lavish sth on sb/sth
■ **obdarzony**: **być obdarzonym** (*np. talentem*) be blessed with sth/sb, be endowed with sth
obdzie-lać/lić dole sth out
obdzierać/obedrzeć: ~ **ze skóry** skin[2]
obecnie at present, currently, now, nowadays, presently

obecność attendance, presence
obecn|y about[1], around, present[1]; **tu ~y** here[1]; (*ustawa itp.*) **w ~ej formie** as it stands
obejmować/objąć 1 (*przytulać*) hug; (*form.*) embrace **2** (*zawierać*) include; (*okres*) span[2]; (*teren*) cover[1]; **~ dwie części/połowy czegoś** straddle; **rozmowa obejmowała wiele tematów** the conversation ranged widely **3** (*stanowisko, władzę*) assume; **~ prowadzenie** go into the lead **4** (*umysłem itp.*) take sth in
■ **obejmujący** inclusive; **wszystko obejmujący** all-encompassing; **~ szeroki zakres** (*np. zagadnień*) wide-ranging
obejrzeć (się) → OGLĄDAĆ (SIĘ)
obejście 1 (*przeszkody itp.*) circumvention **2** (*podwórze gospodarskie*) farmyard
obejść (się) → OBCHODZIĆ (SIĘ)
obelga (**obelgi**) abuse[1]; **obrzucać się ~mi** yell insults (at sb)
obelżywy abusive, scurrilous
oberwanie: **~ chmury** cloudburst, deluge[1]
oberżyna aubergine
obetrzeć → OBCIERAĆ
obeznanie familiarity
obeznany attuned (to sb/sth), au fait, clued-up, conversant with sth, familiar with sth; (*z komputerem itp.*) literate
obezwładni(a)ć overwhelm
■ **obezwładniający** overpowering
obfitować abound with sth, teem with sth
obfity abundant, bountiful, copious, generous, hearty, lavish[1], liberal, plentiful, profuse
■ **obfitość** abundance, profusion, a wealth of sth
obgad(yw)ać knock[1]; **kogoś** slag sb off
■ **obgadywanie**: **~ kogoś za jego plecami** backbiting, back-stabbing
obgotow(yw)ać blanch
ob-gryzać/gryźć chew (on) sth; **pies obgryzł kości z mięsa** the dog picked the bones clean
obiad dinner, lunch; **jeść ~**; **iść na ~** lunch verb; **pora ~u** lunchtime
obibok slob
obicie upholstery; (*drzwi itp.*) padding
obić (się) → OBIJAĆ (SIĘ)
obie → OBA
obiecujący budding, hopeful, promising; **był ~m muzykiem** he showed great promise as a musician
obiec(yw)ać promise[1]; **wiele sobie ~ po czymś** have high hopes for sth
obieg 1 (*samochodem itp.*) circuit **2** (*wody itp.; czasopisma itp.*) circulation; (*idei itp.*) currency; **puszczać w ~** (*akcje*) float[1]; **puść zdjęcia ~iem** pass the photographs round
o-biegać/biec circulate; (*wieść o tragedii itp.*) resound
obiegowy current[1]
obiekcja objection
obiekt object[1] IDM **być ~em ataków** be in the firing line
obiektyw lens; **~ szerokokątny** wide-angle lens; **~ ze zmienną ogniskową** zoom lens
obiektywność objectivity
obiektywny disinterested, dispassionate, objective[2]
obierać/obrać 1 (*ze skórki*) pare, peel[1]; **~ mięso z kości/rybę z ości** bone[2] **2** (*zawód*) enter, go into sth **3 kogoś na kogoś** appoint **4 ~ kogoś/coś za cel** (*działania, ataku itp.*) target[2]
obietnica promise[2], undertaking
obieżyświat globetrotter
obi(ja)ć 1 (*uderzyć*) bruise verb; **~ sobie plecy** jar your back **2** (*meble*) pad[2]
□ **obi(ja)ć się 1** (**/obić się**) (*uderzyć się*) bruise verb **2** (*leniuchować*) doss about/around, faff about/around, goof off, hang about/around, mess about/around, ponce about/around, veg out
obity upholstered
objadać /objeść się binge[2] (on sth), gorge[2] (yourself) (on/with sth), pig[2] yourself
objaśni(a)ć elucidate, enlighten, explain, explain yourself, interpret
■ **objaśniający** explanatory
objaśnienie elucidation, explanation, interpretation; (*do diagramu itp.*) key[1]; (*w podręczniku itp.*) rubric; **szczegółowe ~** delineation
objaw (*choroby*) symptom
objawiać się: **czymś** manifest (in/as sth)
objawienie eye-opener, revelation, vision
objazd 1 (*okrężna droga*) round[4] **2** (*z powodu robót drogowych itp.*) detour, diversion; **cały ruch jest skierowany na ~** all traffic is being diverted **3** (*z występami*) tour
objazdow|y itinerant; **biblioteka ~a** mobile library
objąć → OBEJMOWAĆ; (*stanowisko*) accede (to sth); **~ coś siłą** (*np. władzę*) seize
objeść się → OBJADAĆ SIĘ
ob-jeżdżać/jechać 1 bypass[2], drive round sth; (*z występami*) tour verb **2** (*besztać*) **kogoś** tick sb off
objęcie 1 (*osoby*) embrace noun, hug noun **2** (*urzędu*) accession, assumption
objętość volume; (*książki itp.*) length
oblać zob. też OBLEWAĆ; (*egzamin; kogoś*) fail[1]
oblamować edge[2] sth (with sth)
oblanie: **~ egzaminu** fail[2]
oblany: **czymś** run with sth; **~ potem** sweaty
ob-legać/lec besiege
oblepi(a)ć cake[2], plaster[2]
ob-lewać/lać 1 (*płynem*) douse, wash[1]; **oblał ciastko śmietaną** he smothered his cake with cream; **oblał go zimny pot** he broke out in a cold sweat **2** (*studenta, egzamin itp.*) fail[1]
■ **oblewanie**: **~ nowego mieszkania/domu** house-warming
oblężony beleaguered; **był ~m** be under siege
obli-czać/czyć calculate, compute, estimate[2], project[2], quantify, tally verb, work sth out; **źle ~** miscalculate
■ **obli-czanie/czenie** (*wymiarów*) calculation, measurement, reckoning, sum[1]
oblicze countenance[1]
obligacja bond[1], stock[1]
oblodzenie frost[1]
oblodzić (się) ice (sth) over/up
■ **oblodzony** icy
obluzgać → BLUZGAĆ
obluzowany loose[1]
obluzow(yw)ać (się) slacken
obładow(yw)ać: **kogoś/coś (czymś)** load sb/sth down (with sth)
■ **obładowany** laden
obłaskawi(a)ć tame[2]
obław|a raid; **robić ~ę** raid verb
obłąkanie insanity, madness, wildness
obłąkaniec madman; (*kobieta*) madwoman
obłąkany (*przym.*) deranged, insane, mad
■ **obłąkan-y/a** (*rz.*) crackpot, lunatic[1], maniac
obłęd insanity, lunacy, madness; **bliski ~u** demented
obłok cloud[1]
obłowić się make a killing
obłuda hypocrisy
obłudni-k/ca hypocrite
obłudny false, hypocritical
obmurowanie brickwork
ob-myślać/myślić devise, think sth out
obmy(wa)ć wash[1]
obnażony naked
obni-żać/żyć bring sth down, depress, drop[1], lessen, lower[2], reduce; (*cenę*) knock sth off, mark sth down/up; (*znacznie*) slash[1]; (*cenę/wartość*) cheapen; (*wartość*) debase; (*rangę, kategorię*) downgrade; (*jakość oferowanych usług*) go downmarket
■ **obniżanie**: **~ kosztów** cost-cutting | **obniżenie (się) 1** (*cen itp.*) dip[2], reduction; **obniżenie się stopy życiowej** comedown **2** (*lotu*) descent **3** (*wgłębienie*) depression | **obniżony** (*ogród itp.*) sunken
□ **obni-żać/żyć się** descend, dip[1], go down, drop[1], sink[1]; (*gwałtownie*) plummet; (*ceny*) come down
obniżka drop[2], fall[2], reduction; **~ kosztów** cost-cutting
obnosić się: **z czymś** flaunt
obojczyk collarbone
oboje → OBA
obojętnie impassively, indifferently, listlessly, nonchalantly; (*patrzeć itp.*) blankly; **~ co** anything, whatever; **~ gdzie** anywhere; **~ który/jaki** whichever; **~ kto/co/gdzie itp.** no matter who/what/where, etc.
obojętność detachment, indifference, nonchalance
obojętny 1 (*osoba; uwaga*) casual, cool[1], detached, impassive, indifferent, matter-of-fact, stolid, nonchalant, unconcerned, uninterested, unsympathetic; (*wyraz twarzy itp.*) bland, blank[1]; **być komuś ~m** not be bothered (about sth) **2** (*chem.*) neutral[1]
obok 1 (*w pobliżu*) alongside, beside, by, next[1], next to; (*zza ściany/płotu itp.*) next door (to sb/sth); **tuż ~ (kogoś/czegoś)** close by (sb/sth); **~ siebie** side by side; **dom ~** the next-door house **2** (*mimo*) past[3], past adv.
obolały sore[1]
obopólny mutual, reciprocal
obora barn
obornik manure
obowiązek duty, obligation, onus; (*zawodowy*) brief[2]
obowiązkow|y 1 (*przymusowy*) compulsory, mandatory, obligatory; (*lektura itp.*) set[3]; **przedmioty ~e** core curriculum **2** (*osoba*) dutiful
obowiązywać be in force, hold[1]

■ **obowiązujący 1** (*prawnie ważny*) in effect, operative, valid **2** (*konieczny*) binding[1], obligatory
obój oboe
obóz camp[1]; (*zwł. dla nielegalnych imigrantów*) detention centre; ~ **wakacyjny** holiday camp; ~ **wędrowny** walking holiday; ~ **koncentracyjny** concentration camp
obrabiać/obrobić: **(kogoś/coś)** bitch[1] (about sb/sth)
obrabować → RABOWAĆ
obrabow(yw)ać: **napaść i obrabować** mug[2]
o-bracać/brócić rotate, spin[1], turn[1], turn sb/sth around/round, twist[1]; (*na osi itp.*) swivel; (*sukienką w tańcu itp.*) swirl; ~ **palcami** (*np. nerwowo/w roztargnieniu*) twiddle (with) sth IDM ~ **coś na swoją korzyść** make capital (out) of sth
□ **o-bracać/brócić się** pivot[2], revolve (around/round sb/sth), rotate, spin[1], turn[1], turn around/round; (*coś na kołach*) wheel[2]; (*na osi itp.*) swivel; (*na pięcie itp.*) swing[1]; (*sukienka itp.*) swirl
obrać → OBIERAĆ
obradować debate[2], sit; (*sąd itp.*) be in session
obrady debate[1], proceedings
o-bradzać/brodzić (*pola uprawne*) **nie obradzać** fail[1]
obramowanie border[1]
obramowany IDM **być ~m czymś** be fringed with sth
obrany (*cel itp.*) avowed
obraz (*w ogóle*) picture[1]; (*sztuka*) painting; (*w głowie*) image; ~ **olejny** oil painting; **dawać** ~ depict
obraza affront, insult[2], offence, outrage; ~ **sądu** contempt of court
obrazoburczy iconoclastic
obrazoburstwo iconoclasm
obrazowość imagery
obrazowy graphic, pictorial, visual
obraźliwy 1 (*słowo*) crude, hurtful, insulting, offensive[1]; ~ **termin** dirty word **2** (*osoba*) touchy
ob-rażać/razić hurt[1], insult[1], offend; **nie chciałem cię obrazić** I didn't mean to cause you any offence, I didn't mean it personally
■ **obrażony** hurt[2]
□ **ob-rażać/razić się** be offended, take offence (at sth)
obrączka ring[1]; ~ **ślubna** wedding ring
obręb confines; **w ~ie** within
obrębi(a)ć hem[2]
obręcz hoop, ring[1]
obrobić → OBRABIAĆ
obrodzić → OBRADZAĆ
obrok fodder
obron|a 1 (*przed atakiem itp.*) defence, protection; **system ~y** defence; **występować w ~ie** defend; **brać kogoś/coś w ~ę** stick up for yourself/ sb/sth; **w ~ie własnej** in self-defence; **nie do ~y** indefensible **2** (*prawn.*) the defence
obronić (się) → BRONIĆ (SIĘ)
obronny defensive[1]
obroń-ca/czyni defender, guardian, protector; (*sport*) sweeper; **(obrońcy)** defence
obrotowy revolving, rotary; **ruch** ~ rotation
obroża collar[1]
obrócić (się) → OBRACAĆ (SIĘ)
obrót 1 (*dookoła osi*) rotation, revolution, turn[2]; (*nieform.: silnika*) rev[2] **2** (*spraw itp.*) turn[2] **3** (także **obroty**) (*handlowy*) sales, turnover; ~ **akcjami** share dealing IDM **chodzić na zwolnionych obrotach** tick over
obrus tablecloth
o-bruszać/bruszyć się: **(na coś)** bridle[2] (at sth)
obryzg(iw)ać spatter, splatter
obrządek religion, rite
ob-rządzać/rządzić (*konia*) groom[1]
obrzez(yw)ać circumcise
obrzeże 1 rim **2** (**obrzeża**) fringe[1]; (*miasta*) outskirts
obrzęd rite
obrzęk swelling
obrzmiały swollen[2]
obrzmienie soreness, swelling
obrzu-cać/cić pelt; (*gradem czegoś*) pepper[2] sb/sth with sth; ~ **kogoś obelgami** abuse[2]; ~ **kogoś oszczerstwami** cast aspersions on sb
□ **obrzu-cać/cić się**: ~ **obelgami** yell insults at each other
obrzydliwie disgustingly; ~ **brudny** filthy dirty; ~ **duży** obscene; ~ **bogaty** filthy rich
obrzydliwość eyesore
obrzydliw|y 1 (*budzący wstręt*) abominable, foul[1], loathsome; (*zapach, smak*) nauseating, sickening; (*brudny*) cruddy; **~e szczegóły ich romansu** the sordid details of their affair **2** (*brzydzący się krwią itp.*) squeamish
obrzydzenie: **wywoływać** ~ sicken
obsa|da cast[2] IDM **w pełnej ~dzie** at full strength | **nie w pełnej ~dzie** below strength
ob-sadzać/sadzić 1 (*roślinami*) plant[2] **2** (*posadę*) fill; (*personelem*) man[2], staff; (*w roli*) cast[1]; ~ **w głównej roli** star[2] **3** (*brylantami itp.*) set[1]
■ **obsadzony 1** (*drzewami itp.*) bordered with sth **2** (*stanowiska pracy itp.*) **nie w pełni obsadzony** short-staffed
obserwacj|a 1 (*uważne przyglądanie się*) observation, watch[2]; **być pod ~ą** be (kept) under observation **2** (*uwaga*) remark noun
obserwator/ka lookout, observer, onlooker
obserwatorium observatory
obserwować/za- 1 (*przyglądać się*) have (got) your eye on sb, observe, regard[1], spy on sb/sth, survey[2], watch[1]; (*z ukrycia*) stake sth out; **dobrze** ~ keep a close watch on sth **2** (*zrobić uwagę*) remark
■ **obserwowanie**: ~ **ptaków** birdwatching
obsesj|a fixation, mania, obsession; (*zwł. seksualna*) fetish; **mieć ~ę na punkcie punktualności** be fixated (on sb/sth), be obsessed (about/with sb/sth), be obsessive about sth
obsesyjn|y obsessive
■ **obsesyjnie**: **myśleć o czymś** ~ be/ get hung up (about/on sb/sth)
ob-siewać/siać (*roślinami*) plant[2]; ~ **pole pszenicą** sow a field with wheat
obskurny dingy, sleazy, sordid
obsług|a service[1]; **~a kelnerska do pokojów** room service; **~a komputera** computing; **członek ~i** attendant[1]
ob-sługiwać/służyć 1 man[2], operate, work[1] **2** (*podać jedzenie*) serve
□ **ob-sługiwać/służyć się** help[1] yourself (to sth)
obstawać: **przy czymś** insist, persist (in sth/doing sth), press[2]
obstrzał: **pod ~em** under fire; **pod ~em krytyki** beleaguered
ob-suwać/sunąć się subside
■ **obsunięcie się** (*budynku itp.*) subsidence; ~ **ziemi** landslide
obsyp(yw)ać 1 czymś rain[2] sth (down) (on sb/sth); (*gradem czegoś*) pepper[2] sb/sth with sth **2** (*pochwałami itp.*) heap[2] B with A, shower[2]
obszar 1 area, expanse, extent, region, space[1], stretch[2], terrain, territory, zone; **mały** ~ pocket[1]; ~ **administracyjny** parish; ~ **podzwrotnikowy** tropic **2** (*zagadnień*) ground[1]
obszarpany ragged
obszerność spaciousness
obszerny 1 (*mieszkanie*) spacious; (*przestrzeń itp.*) extensive; (*parking itp.*) ample; (*płaszcz itp.*) loose[1], voluminous **2** (*artykuł*) wide-ranging
obszycie binding[2]
obszy(wa)ć edge[2]
obtarty raw
obudować build sth in/on, build sth into/onto sth
obudzić (się) → BUDZIĆ (SIĘ)
oburęczny ambidextrous
o-burzać/burzyć disgust[2], outrage verb, scandalize, shock[2]
oburzając|y outrageous, scandalous, shocking; **rzecz ~a** outrage
oburzenie disgust[1], indignation, outrage; **z ~m** indignantly
oburzony disgusted, indignant
obustronny bilateral, mutual, reciprocal, two-way
obuwie footwear, shoes[1]; ~ **sportowe** plimsolls
obwarowany: ~ **murem** walled
ob-wieszczać/wieścić proclaim, publish
obwieszczenie edict, proclamation, publication
ob-wijać/winąć: **coś czymś** fold[1] A in B, B round/over A
obwini(a)ć blame[1], put the blame on sb
ob-wisać/wisnąć sag
obwisły drooping, flabby, slack
obwodnica bypass[1], orbital noun, ring road
obwodowy peripheral[1]
obwoluta wrapper
obwód 1 (*okręgu*) circumference; (*terenu*) perimeter; (*osoby w talii/ pasie, drzewa itp.*) girth **2** (*elektr.*) circuit **3** (*obszar*) district
obwódka rim
obyci|e: **brak ~a** gaucheness
obyczaj convention, custom; **(obyczaje)** morals[2]
obyczajność decorum
obyty: ~ **w świecie** urbane
o-bywać/być się: ~ **bez kogoś/czegoś** dispense with sb/sth, do/go without (sth), forgo
obywatel/ka citizen, national[2]
obywatelski 1 (*obowiązek itp.*) civic; **natchnięty duchem ~m** public-

spirited **2** (*prawo itp.*) civil; **prawa ~e** civil rights
obywatelstwo citizenship, nationality
obżarstwo binge[1], gluttony
obżartuch pig[1], a voracious eater
obżerać się pig[2] yourself, pig out (on sth), stuff[2] yourself (with sth)
o-calać/calić save[1]
ocalał|y (*przym.*) **~e dobro/mienie** salvage[1]
■ **ocalał-y/a** (*rz., z wypadku itp.*) survivor
ocean ocean; (*literackie*) the deep; **za ~** overseas adv.
oceaniczny oceanic
ocena 1 (*osąd*) appraisal, assessment, evaluation, rating; **ponowna ~** reappraisal; **zła ~** misjudgement **2** (*szacowanie*) estimation; **zbyt niska ~** underestimate noun **3** (*szk.*) mark[2], grade[1], result[1]
oceni(a)ć 1 (*wydać opinię*) appraise, evaluate, find[1], gauge[2], judge[2], measure[1] sth (against sth), rate[2], size sb/sth up, sum sb/sth up, weigh sb/sth up; **błędnie ~** misjudge **2** (*szacować*) estimate[2]; **zbyt nisko ~** underestimate, undervalue **3** (*pracę uczniów*) mark[1]
ocenzurować → CENZUROWAĆ
ocet vinegar
och oh
ochlap(yw)ać splatter
ochłodzić (się) → CHŁODZIĆ (SIĘ)
ochłonąć cool[2]
ochmistrz (*na statku*) purser
ochoczy eager, game[2], willing
■ **ochoczo** eagerly, gladly, willingly
ochot|a willingness; **wielka ~a** craving; **mieć ~ę (na coś)** would you care for.../to do sth, fancy[1], feel like sth/doing sth, like[3]; **mieć wielką ~ę na coś** be up for sth; **mający ~ę (coś zrobić)** inclined (to do sth); **jeśli masz na to ~ę** if you like; **nie mieć zbytniej ~y na coś** not be too keen on (doing) sth
ochotniczy voluntary
■ **ochotniczo**: **~ wstępować do wojska** volunteer[2] (for sth)
ochotni-k/czka (*i do wojska*) volunteer[1]; **zgłaszać się na ochotnika** volunteer verb
ochr|a: **kolor ~y** ochre
ochraniacz guard[1]; **~e na golenie** shin pads
ochron|a 1 czegoś/przed czymś protection; (*zabytków itp.*) conservation, preservation, treatment; **~a danych** data protection; **~a środowiska** conservation; **zwolenni-k/czka ~y środowiska** conservationist **2** (*grupa ochroniarzy*) bodyguard; (*organizacja*) security; **uzbrojona ~a** armed guard; **służba ~y wybrzeża** coastguard
ochroniarz bodyguard, guard[1]
ochronić (się) → CHRONIĆ (SIĘ)
ochronny protective
ochrypły hoarse, husky[1], raucous
ochrypnąć → CHRYPNĄĆ
o-chrzaniać/chrzanić rap[2]
ochrzcić → CHRZCIĆ
ociągać się dawdle, dilly-dally, hang back
■ **ociągający się** reluctant
o-cieplać/cieplić (się) warm[2] (sb/sth) (up)
ocieplan|y thermal[1]; **bielizna ~a**; **ubranie ~e** thermals[2]
ocieplenie: **globalne ~** global warming
o-cierać/trzeć 1 (*łzy z oczu itp.*) wipe[1]; (*oczy*) rub **2** (*kaleczyć*) graze[1]
□ **o-cierać /trzeć się 1** rub **2 o coś** graze[1]; (*lekko*) brush[2] IDM **~ o kogoś** rub shoulders with sb
ociężały ponderous
■ **ociężale** ponderously; **chodzić ociężale** lumber[2]
ocucić → CUCIĆ
ocukrzony: **obficie ~** sugary
ocyganić → CYGANIĆ
ocynkować → CYNKOWAĆ
oczarowany enchanted
oczarow(yw)ać beguile, bewitch, captivate, charm[2], dazzle, enchant, enrapture, enthral
oczekiwać 1 (*czekać*) await; (*na dworcu itp.*) meet **2** (*spodziewać się*) anticipate, bargain for/on sth, expect, hope[1], reckon, reckon on sth, think; **~, że ktoś coś zrobi/czegoś od kogoś** expect sth (from sb), sb to do sth, look to sb for sth, look to sb to do sth; **~ czegoś z radością** look forward to sth/doing sth
oczekiwani|e 1 (*czekanie*) wait[2] **2** (*spodziewanie się*) anticipation, expectancy, expectation; **w ~u czegoś/że** in the hope of sth/that...; **wbrew wszelkim ~om** against/contrary to (all) expectation(s)
oczekujący: **lista ~ch** waiting list
oczerni(a)ć blacken, denigrate
oczko 1 → EYE **2** (*w robótkach ręcznych*) stitch[1]; **prawe ~** plain[2]; **lewe ~** purl **3** (*w rajstopach itp.*) ladder
oczodół eye socket
o-czyszczać/czyścić 1 (*usunąć brud*) cleanse **2** (*wodę itp.*) purify, refine **3** (*z zarzutów itp.*) absolve, clear[2], exonerate **4** (*pozbyć się czegoś*) rid yourself/sb/sth of sb/sth IDM **oczyścić atmosferę** clear the air
■ **oczyszczanie** treatment; **zabieg oczyszczania twarzy** facial[2] | **oczyszczenie** clearance | **oczyszczony** (*surowce*) refined
oczytany well read
oczywist|y apparent, clear[1], evident, manifest adj., obvious, plain[1]; (*fakt itp.*) self-evident; (*różnica itp.*) clear-cut; (*nieprawda itp.*) patent[2]; **w ~y sposób** manifestly; **to jest ~e** that goes without saying
oczywiście absolutely, certainly, clearly, of course, naturally, obviously
od 1 (*kierunek; wskazuje np. na ofiarodawcę*) from, out of; **na północ ~ Leeds** five miles north of Leeds **2** (*czas: od kiedyś*) as from, as of, ever since..., from... on, since; **siedzi w więzieniu ~ 20 lat** he has been in prison for 20 years **3** (*porównanie*) than, to **4** (*przy podziale jakiejś kwoty: na osobę itp.*) per
oda ode
odbarwi(a)ć (się) discolour
odbicie 1 (*obraz*) image, impression; (*w lustrze*) reflection **2** (*światła*) deflection **3** (*piłki*) bounce noun, rebound noun, return[2] **3** (*kopia*) imprint[1], print[2] **4** (*komput.*) return[2] **5** (*przen.*) reflection on/upon sb/sth
□ **odbicie się 1** (*piłki*) bounce noun **2** (*po jedzeniu*) burp noun
od-biegać/biec (*od normy itp.*) deviate; **~ od tematu** wander; **odbiegający od normy itp.** deviant, unorthodox
odbierać/odebrać 1 (*usuwać*) **kogoś/coś komuś** take sb/sth away (from sb) **2** (*wziąć*) collect[1], pick sth up **3** (*zabrać z powrotem*) reclaim **4** (*wiadomości*) receive; (*program telewizyjny*) pick sth up **5** (*rozumieć*) perceive; **być odbieranym jako...** be construed as... **6** (*telefon*) answer[2] **7** (*prawo itp.*) revoke **8** (*poród*) deliver IDM **~ sobie życie** take your (own) life
od-bijać/bić 1 (*coś w lustrze*) reflect; **~ obraz** mirror verb **2** (*światło itp.*) deflect **3** (*piłkę*) bounce; (*do przeciwnika*) return[1] **4** (*dźwięk*) echo[2] **5** (*na ksero itp.*) run sth off **6** (*miasto itp.*) recapture IDM **odbiło mu!** he's off his head!
□ **od-bijać/bić się 1** (*światło*) deflect **2** (*piłka*) bounce, rebound; **dobrze odbijający się** bouncy **3** (*dźwięk*) echo[2], reverberate **4 komuś** belch, burp
odbior-ca/czyni recipient; (*jakiejś kwoty*) payee
odbiornik receiver, set[2]; **cyfrowy ~ telewizyjny** digital television
odbiór 1 (*radio, TV*) reception **2** (*odebranie*) collection, receipt; (*bagażu itp.*) reclamation; **~ bagażu** (*na lotnisku*) baggage reclaim; **potwierdzać ~** acknowledge
odbitk|a print[2]; **~a kserograficzna** photocopy; **robić ~ę fotograficzną** print[1]
odblask gleam
odblaskow|y fluorescent, reflective; **światło ~e** reflector
odbudowa 1 reconstruction, restoration **2** (*narkomana itp.*) rehabilitation
odbudow(yw)ać rebuild, reconstruct
od-burkiwać/burknąć snap[1] (sth) (at sb)
odbyt anus
odbytnica rectum
odbytniczy anal
odby(wa)ć się go off, be held, take place; (*zgodnie z planem*) follow, go ahead
od-cedzać/cedzić 1 filter[2]; (*makaron itp.*) drain **2** (*przen.*) **coś z czegoś** filter sb/sth out (of sth)
odchody droppings, excrement
odchodzić/odejść 1 (*oddalić się*) go away, leave[1], slip away, walk away/off; (*pociąg itp.*) depart; (*z określonymi wrażeniami itp.*) come away with sth; **o której odchodzi pociąg?** what time does the train go? **2** (*ze stanowiska itp.*) quit (as sth); **~ na emeryturę** retire **3** (*umrzeć*) pass away **4** (*odrywać się*) **~ płatami** peel[1] (off/away/back) IDM **~ z czyimś mężem/czyjąś żoną** go with sb's husband/wife | **~ w zapomnienie** fade into oblivion
■ **odchodzenie** movement
od-chrząkiwać/chrząknąć clear your throat
od-chudzać/chudzić się be/go on a diet, diet[2], slim[2]
od-chwaszczać/chwaścić weed[2]
od-chylać/chylić deflect
□ **od-chylać/chylić się** deflect, deviate, diverge, oscillate

■ **odchylenie** deflection, deviation; ~ **od normy** aberration, deviance
od-ciążać/ciążyć lighten
odcie|ń hue, nuance, shade[1], tinge, tint, tone[1]; **z ~niem** tinged (with sth)
od-cinać/ciąć chop sth off (sth), cut sth off (sth), lop sth off (sth), trim[1]; **kogoś/coś (od kogoś/czegoś)** cut sb/sth off (from sb/sth), shut sb/sth off (from sth); (*dostęp*) seal sth off; (*dopływ gazu itp.*) disconnect
□ **od-cinać/ciąć się** dissociate yourself (from sth), shut yourself off (from sth)
odcin|ek section, segment, part[1]; (*czeku*) counterfoil; (*drogi*) stretch[2]; (*podróży*) leg; (*zagadnienia itp.*) strand; (*książki*) instalment; (*serialu*) episode; **wydawać w ~kach** serialize
odcisk 1 (*odbicie*) impression, imprint, print[2]; ~ **palca** fingerprint; **genetyczny ~ palca** (*przen.*) genetic fingerprint **2** (*na palcu*) corn
odcyfrow(yw)ać decipher, make sb/sth out, puzzle sth out
odczepi(a)ć 1 (*uwolnić kogoś/coś od czegoś*) disengage **2** (*haftkę itp.*) unfasten
□ **odczepi(a)ć się 1** (*odsunąć się itp.*) disengage yourself (from sb/sth) **2 od kogoś** lay off (sb)
odczepn|y: **na ~ego** offhandedly
od-człowieczać/człowieczyć brutalize
odczucie feeling
odczu(wa)ć feel[1], perceive IDM ~ **swój wiek** feel your age
odczuwaln|y perceptible
■ **odczuwalnie** perceptibly, perceptively
odczyt reading; **dane nadające się do automatycznego ~u** machine-readable data
odczyt(yw)ać make sb/sth out, read[1]; **nie mogę odczytać godziny na zegarze** I can't read the clock
oddać (się) → ODDAWAĆ (SIĘ)
od-dalać/dalić 1 (*odsunąć*) distance[2] sb (from sb/sth); (*obawy itp.*) neutralize; ~ **na jakiś czas** (*niebezpieczeństwo, choroby itp.*) stave sth off **2** (*skargę itp.*) reject[1] **3** (*prawn.*) dismiss
□ **od-dalać/dalić się 1** recede **2** (*przen.*) **od kogoś** grow apart (from sb); **od siebie** drift apart
oddaleni|e 1 distance[1], remoteness **2** (*skargi itp.*) rejection
oddalony apart, outlying, removed; **najbardziej** ~ furthermost
oddanie dedication, devotion; **z ~m** lovingly, faithfully
oddany committed, dedicated, devoted, stalwart, staunch, supportive; **komuś** loving; **czemuś** intent[1] on/upon sth/doing sth; **być ~m komuś** stand by sb
odda(wa)ć 1 (*dać*) give sth away; (*w czyjeś ręce*) give sb up (to sb), give sth up (to sb), hand sth in (to sb), hand (sb) over to sb, hand sb/sth over (to sb); (*do depozytu*) deposit[2]; **nie ~ czegoś** hold on to sth, hold onto sth; **oddać broń** surrender your weapons **2** (*zwracać*) bring/give/take sth back, restore sth to sb, return[1] **3** ~ **głos** (*w wyborach*) vote[2] **4** (*władzę*) yield[1] **5** (*przedstawić*) capture[1], recapture **6** (*w bójce*) fight back (against sb/sth) IDM ~ **cześć boską** worship | ~ **komuś/czemuś hołd** pay tribute to sb/sth | ~ **honory wojskowe** salute verb | ~ **kał** defecate, excrete | ~ **mocz** pass water, urinate | ~ **komuś dobrą przysługę** (do sb) a good turn | ~ **komuś ostatnią posługę** pay your last respects to sb | ~ **komuś sprawiedliwość** do justice to sb/sth, do sb/sth justice
□ **odda(wa)ć się 1** (*w czyjeś ręce*) give yourself up (to sb) **2 czemuś** indulge (yourself) (in sth)
oddech breath, breathing, wind[1] IDM **wstrzymywać ~** hold your breath
oddechowy respiratory
oddelegować → DELEGOWAĆ
oddelegowanie (*do pracy w innym kraju*) posting
oddychać/odetchnąć breathe; **ciężko ~** wheeze
oddychanie breathing, respiration
oddział branch[1], party, squad, troop, unit; ~ **szpitalny** ward[1]; ~ **intensywnej opieki medycznej** intensive care; ~ **położniczy** maternity ward
oddział(yw)ać affect, influence[2]; (*wzajemnie na siebie*) interact (with sb)
od-dzielać/dzielić dissociate, divorce[2], segregate, separate[2], separate sth out; ~ **coś zasłoną** curtain sth off; ~ **prawdę od kłamstw** disentangle the truth from the lies
□ **od-dzielać /dzielić się** separate[2], separate out
oddzielny discrete, distinct, isolated, separate[1]
oddzielony isolated
oddzwonić phone sb back, return sb's call
oddźwięk response; **wywoływać ~** get sth across (to sb)
odebrać → ODBIERAĆ
odebrany: **zostać (dobrze/źle) ~m (przez kogoś)** go down (with sb)
odegłość distance[1]
odegrać (się) → ODGRYWAĆ (SIĘ)
odegranie portrayal
□ **odegranie się**: **(na kimś)** vengeance (on sb)
odejmować/odjąć deduct, subtract
odejmowani|e subtraction; **znak ~a** minus[2]
odejście 1 departure, going[1] **2** (*od norm*) departure; (*od stylu, przyzwyczajeń itp.*) breakaway noun
odejść → ODCHODZIĆ
odepchnąć → ODPYCHAĆ
odeprzeć → ODPIERAĆ
oderwać (się) → ODRYWAĆ (SIĘ)
oderwanie detachment
oderwan|y 1 (*dom*) detached; **~y od życia** divorced from everyday life; **rzecz ~a od tematu** irrelevance **2** (*frakcja polityczna itp.*) breakaway
odesłać → ODSYŁAĆ
odesłanie: ~ **z kwitkiem** rebuff
odetchnąć → ODDYCHAĆ
odfajkow(yw)ać tick[1]
odfiltrować: **coś z czegoś** filter sth out (of sth)
od-gadywać/gadnąć figure[2] (that)
odgałęzieni|e: **o (kilku) ~ach** -pronged
od-ganiać/gonić banish, shoo[2] sb/sth away/off/out, etc.
odgłos reverberation, sound[1]; ~ **kroków** footstep, tread[2]
od-gradzać/grodzić fence sb/sth in, fence sth off, rope sth off
odgrażać się menace verb
■ **odgrażanie się** bluster noun
odgrywać/odegrać (*rolę*) enact, feature[2], impersonate, play[1], have/play a part (in sth), portray; **w jego powieściach kobiety nie odgrywają dużej roli** women don't figure much in his novels
□ **od-grywać/egrać się**: **na kimś** get back at sb, strike back (at/against sb)
■ **odgrywanie** (*roli*) impersonation; ~ **scenki** role-play
od-gryzać/gryźć się: **komuś** hit back (at sb)
odgrzeb(yw)ać (*żenujące fakty itp.*) rake sth up; (*stare pomysły*) trot sth out
odha-czać/czyć (*na liście*) tick[1], tick sb/sth off
odizolować zob. też IZOLOWAĆ; shut sb/sth off (from sth)
odizolowany isolated, marooned
odjazd 1 departure, going[1] **2 robić ~ kamerą** zoom out
odjazdowy cool[1], funky, tremendous, wicked
odjąć → ODEJMOWAĆ
odjechany funky
odjeżdżać/odjechać depart, drive off, move off, pull away (from sb/sth); (*ze stacji*) draw[1], pull out (of sth); (*z określonymi wrażeniami*) come away with sth
■ **odjeżdżający** outward
odjęcie deduction
odkaszlnąć cough[1] (up) sth
odka-żać/zić disinfect, fumigate
■ **odkażający**: **środek odkażający** disinfectant | **odka-żanie/żenie** disinfection, fumigation
odkąd ever since…, since conj.
od-klejać/kleić się come unstuck, peel[1] (off/away/back)
odklejony unstuck
od-kładać/łożyć 1 (*położyć na swoje miejsce*) pack sth away, put sth back, tidy sth away **2** (*odsunąć na bok*) leave sth on one side, put sth aside, put sth on/to one side, set sth aside **3** (*pieniądze*) put sth away/by/aside, save[1] (sth) (up) (for sth); ~ **coś na czarną godzinę** keep/save sth for a rainy day; (*pieniądze*) **być odłożonym** go towards sth **3** (*spotkanie itp.*) defer, delay[2], postpone, put sth off, put off doing sth **4** (*słuchawkę*) replace; **nie ~ słuchawki** hold[1] **5** (*nie nadawać sprawie dalszego biegu*) ~ **coś na półkę** shelve
od-kłaniać /kłonić się acknowledge
odkodow(yw)ać decode
odkomenderowany: ~ **oddział** detachment
odkop(yw)ać dig sth up; **coś (z czegoś)** dig sth out (of sth); (*coś w czasie prac wykopaliskowych*) excavate
od-krawać/kroić cut[1] sth (from sth)
odkrę-cać/cić twist sth off, unscrew; ~ **kurek z wodą** run a tap; ~ **śruby** unscrew
odkryci|e discovery, find[2], revelation; **dokonywać ~a** break fresh/new ground

odkryty (*nieochroniony, niepokryty*) exposed; (*płomień itp.*) naked; (*basen itp.*) open-air
odkry(wa)ć discover, find[1]; (*tajemnicę itp.*) uncover
odkryw-ca/czyni (*penicyliny itp.*) discoverer; (*nowego lądu*) explorer
odkrywczy investigative, revealing
odkupić redeem yourself
■ **odkupieni|e** redemption; **nie do odkupienia** beyond redemption
odkurzacz vacuum cleaner
od-kurzać/kurzyć/po- hoover, hoover sth up, vacuum[2]; **poodkurzać pokój** give a room a quick vacuum
od-latywać/lecieć 1 (*samolot*) depart **2** (*balonik*) blow away **3** (*guzik*) come off (sth)
odległoś|ć distance[1], haul[2], length, way[1]; **~ć między falami dźwiękowymi** wavelength; **w ~ci** away (from sth), within sth (of sth); **w pewnej ~ci** off[1]; (*wystrzał*) **z bliskiej ~ci** point-blank
odległy distant, far[1], faraway, remote
odlew: **robić ~** cast[1] sth (in sth)
odl(ew)ać cast[1], mould[2]
odlewnia foundry
odli-czać/czyć count sth out; **odliczany od podatku** tax-deductible
■ **odli-czanie/czenie 1** deduction **2** (*czasu itp.*) count-down; **końcowe odliczanie** (*przed ważnym wydarzeniem*) build-up
odlot 1 (*samolotu*) departure **2** (*podniecenie*) buzz[2]
odlotowy smashing
■ **odlotowo** (*ładny*) drop-dead
odludek recluse
odludny lonely, solitary
odludzie the outback, the wilds[2]
odłam faction
odłamek chip[1], splinter; (**odłamki**) (*bomby*) shrapnel
odłam(yw)ać (się) break (sth) off
od-łączać/łączyć detach, disconnect, separate[2], sever; (*od organizacji*) disaffiliate
□ **od-łączać/łączyć się** separate[2]; (*od organizacji itp.*) break away (from sb/sth), disaffiliate; (*od innego kraju/organizacji itp.*) secede
odłączny separable
odłogowy fallow
odłożenie postponement
odłożyć → ODKŁADAĆ
odł|óg (**odłogi**) waste[2]; **leżeć ~ogiem** lie fallow, lie waste[3]
odłup(yw)ać (się) chip[2]
od-mawiać/mówić 1 decline[2], deny, refuse[1], reject[1], repudiate; **komuś/czegoś** turn sb/sth down; (*udzielenia, wydania*) withhold; **~ komuś wstępu** turn sb away **2 ~ pacierz/modlitwę** pray
odmian|a 1 (*zmiana*) contrast[1], transformation; **dla ~y** for a change; **stanowić miłą ~ę** make a change **2** (*rośliny, zwierzęcia, choroby*) strain[1], variety **3** (*pisowni*) variant **4** (*gram.*) form[1], inflection; (*czasownika*) conjugation; (*rzeczownika, przymiotnika*) declension
odmieni(a)ć 1 (*przeobrazić*) alter, transform **2** (*czasownik*) conjugate
□ **odmieni(a)ć się** alter
odmieniec weirdo
odmienny (*odrębny*) distinctive, diverse, opposing, opposite, removed
odmie-rzać/rzyć measure sth out
od-mładzać/młodzić rejuvenate
odmowa denial, refusal, rejection; (*nieform.*) brush-off
odmówić → ODMAWIAĆ
od-mrażać/mrozić defrost, de-ice
odmrożenie frostbite; **lekkie ~** (*palców rąk i nóg*) chilblain
odmrożony (*część ciała*) frostbitten
odmruknąć grunt
od-najdować/naleźć find[1], retrieve
odnajdywać retrieve
od-nawiać/nowić 1 (*kontakty; umowę itp.*) renew **2** (*dom, pokój*) do sth up, refurbish, renovate **3** (*obraz*) restore
odnawialny renewable
odniesieni|e reference; **w ~u do kogoś/czegoś** with reference to sb/sth, as regards sb/sth, in this/that/one regard, in/with regard to sb/sth, in/with relation to sb/sth, towards
odnoga fork[1]; **o (kilku) ~ch** -pronged
od-nosić/nieść 1 (*zanieść coś z powrotem*) take sth back **2** (*wrażenie itp.*) form[2] **3** (*osiągnąć coś*) **~ korzyści/pożytek (z czegoś)** profit[2] (from/by sth); **~ sukces** do well, make the grade, make it, succeed; **~ zwycięstwo** triumph[2]; **odnieść łatwe zwycięstwo** walk off with sth **4** (*obrażenia itp.*) sustain
□ **odnosić się 1** (*dotyczyć*) be applicable to sb/sth, apply, concern[1], refer to sb/sth, relate to sb/sth; **odnoszący się do kogoś/czegoś** applicable, pertinent, regarding **2** (**/odnieść się**) (*traktować*) treat[1] sb/sth (with/as/like sth)
odnośnie: **~ do kogoś/czegoś** concerning, as regards sb/sth, in/with relation to sb/sth, with respect to sth
odnośnik cross reference, footnote, reference
odnotow(yw)ać enter sth (in/into/on/onto sth), log[2]
odnowa 1 (*kontaktów,umowy itp.*) renewal **2** (*domu, pokoju*) refurbishment
odnowić → ODNAWIAĆ
odnóże leg
odosabni(a)ć isolate
■ **odosobnienie** confinement, isolation
odosobniony isolated, outlying, secluded
odór odour, stench; **~ potu** body odour
od-padać/paść 1 (*guzik itp.*) come off (sth); (*tapeta itp.*) come away (from sth) **2** (*z zawodów itp.*) drop out (of sth)
■ **odpadający** flaky
odpadki litter, refuse[2], wastage, waste[2], waste matter
odpadkowy (także **odpadowy**) waste[3]
odpady waste[2]; (*z maszyn itp.*) scrap[1]; (*zwł. żużlowe*) dross
odpa-lać/lić 1 (*ładunek wybuchowy*) detonate, let sth off **2** (*rakietę*) blast off
■ **odpalenie** blast-off
odparow(yw)ać counter[2], retort
odpaść → ODPADAĆ
odpę-dzać/dzić keep sth off (sb/sth), ward sb/sth off; (*myśli*) banish; (*bolesne wspomnienia itp.*) exorcize
odpierać/odeprzeć 1 (*atak itp.*) beat sb/sth off, fend sb/sth off, fight sb/sth off, repel **2** (*wywody itp.*) disprove
odpis(yw)ać 1 (*przepisywać*) copy[2], crib[2] **2** (*odpowiadać na list*) reply, write back (to sb)
■ **odpisanie** (*od dochodu/podatku*) deduction
odplamiacz remover
odpła-cać/cić (się) get back at sb, be/get even (with sb), pay sb back (for sth), repay sb (for sth), strike back (at/against sb) IDM **odpłacić pięknym za nadobne** get/have your own back (on sb)
□ **odpłacanie (się)** IDM **odpłacanie (się) pięknym za nadobne** tit for tat
odpłatny: **~ dodatek** extra[2]
odpływ 1 (*na wodę itp.*) outlet; (*wanny*) plughole **2** (*morze*) the ebb, low tide, tide[1]; **jest ~** the tide is (going) out; **dotyczący ~u** tidal
odpły-wać/nąć 1 (*łódź*) depart, sail[1] **2** (*woda*) drain[1] **3** (*morze*) ebb
odpoczynek refreshment, relaxation, rest[2]
odpo-czywać/cząć put your feet up, lie about/around, relax, rest[1], get some rest, have a rest, sit back; **dawać odpocząć** give sth a rest; **muszę odpocząć** I need a rest
odpokutować (*winę*) redeem yourself
■ **odpokutowani|e**: **nie do odpokutowania** beyond redemption
odpornościowy: **system ~** immune system
odporność resilience; (*organizmu*) resistance; (*na chorobę*) immunity
odporny 1 (*nie słaby*) resilient, tough; (*roślina*) hardy; (*na korozję itp.*) -proof, resistant **2** (*na chorobę*) immune **3** (*osoba: na zmianę*) resistant
odpo-wiadać/wiedzieć 1 answer[2], reply, respond; **niegrzecznie ~ (komuś)** talk back (to sb) **2 przed kimś (za coś/kogoś)** answer for sb/sth, answer to sb (for sth) **3 czemuś** correspond, represent; (*np. normom, wymaganiom*) conform, meet; **Jo doskonale odpowiada temu opisowi** the description fits Jo perfectly **4** (*podobać się*) **komuś** be to your liking, suit[2]; **nie ~ komuś** not sb's cup of tea
■ **odpowiadający** equivalent (to sth)
odpowiedni appropriate[1], fit[2], fitting[1], suitable; (*kandydat*) eligible; (*mąż itp.*) suited; (*kwalifikacje*) adequate; (*formularz itp.*) corresponding, relevant; (*odpowiedź, procedura itp.*) correct[1], right[1]; (*rozważenie sprawy itp.*) due[1]; (*zachowanie*) respectable; **bardziej ~** preferable; **być/czynić ~m** fit[1]
odpowiedni-k/czka counterpart, equivalent noun, your opposite number
odpowiedzialnoś|ć 1 accountability, responsibility; **ponosić ~ć** be to blame (for sth); **przejąć ~ć** be in charge[1] (of sb/sth); **z poczuciem ~ci** responsibly **2** (*prawn.*) liability
odpowiedzialn|y 1 accountable, answerable, responsible; (*za biuro itp.*) in charge of sth; (*obywatel itp.*) upright; (*nauczyciel itp.*) **mieć moralnie ~e stanowisko** be in a position of trust **2** (*prawn.*) liable
odpowie|dź 1 answer[1], reply noun, response; **~dź twierdząca** yes noun; **w ~dzi na** (*w korespondencji*) in answer (to sth), further to

2 (*rozwiązanie*) solution; (**odpowiedzi**) key[1]
odpowietrznik vent
odpraw|a 1 (*ostra odpowiedź*) brush-off, rebuff **2** (*wynagrodzenie*) **~a przy zwolnieniu z pracy** redundancy pay; **dać komuś ~ę i zwolnić z pracy** pay sb off **3 ~a celna** customs **4** (*na lotnisku itp.*) check-in; **stanowisko ~y pasażerów** check-in (desk); **przechodzić ~ę** check in (at…), check into…
odprawi(a)ć 1 kogoś (z niczym) give sb the brush-off, rebuff verb, turn sb away **2** (*pracownika*) dismiss **3** (*mszę*) celebrate
odprę-żać/żyć loosen sb/sth up
□ **odprę-żać/żyć się** let your hair down, loosen up, relax, rest[1], sit back, unwind, wind down
■ **odprężenie** (*polit.*) détente | **odprężony** relaxed
odprowa-dzać/dzić 1 (*osobę*) escort[2], see, see sb off, walk[1] **2** (*pieniądze, niezgodnie z przeznaczeniem*) siphon sth off, sth (from/out of sb/sth)
odprys-kiwać/nąć blister[2]
odpukać (*w niemalowane drewno*) touch wood
odpust church fête
odpu-szczać/ścić: **sobie** give sth a miss
■ **odpuszczenie** (*grzechu*) forgiveness
odpychać/odepchnąć drive sb/sth off; **odepchnąć kogoś z drogi** elbow sb out of the way
odpychający forbidding, odious, repellent[1]
odpys-kiwać/kować: **komuś** bite sb's head off
odra measles
od-rabiać/robić 1 (*zaległości itp.*) retrieve **2** (*lekcje*) do your homework
od-raczać/roczyć defer, postpone, put sth off, put off doing sth, suspend; (*formalne spotkanie*) adjourn; **~ wykonanie kary śmierci** reprieve
odra-dzać/dzić discourage; (*form.*) counsel sb against doing sth
od-rastać/rosnąć grow back
odraz|a abhorrence, aversion, horror, repulsion, revulsion; **czuć ~ę** abhor, loathe; **żywić ~ę** revolt
odrażający abhorrent, disgusting, hideous, repellent[1], repulsive, revolting, tawdry
odrąbać → RĄBAĆ
odrąb(yw)ać chop sth off (sth)
odrestaurować → RESTAUROWAĆ
odrębność discreteness
odrębny discrete, distinct
odręczn|y freehand; **pismo ~e** longhand
odrętwieni|e numbness, stupor; **wprowadzać w stan ~a** numb verb
odrobić → ODRABIAĆ
odrobin|a 1 (*cząsteczka*) particle **2** (*mała ilość*) a bit[1], spot[1], touch[2]; (*pokarmu*) morsel, taste[1]; (*soli itp.; ludzi*) sprinkling; (*farby itp.*) dab[2]; (*wątpienia*) shadow[1]; (*prawdy*) atom, scrap[1]; (*rozumu itp.*) ounce; (*akcentu itp.*) suggestion; (*smutku itp.*) hint[1]; (*koloru; smutku itp.*) tinge
■ **odrobinę** (*przysł.*) a bit[1], a little det., fractionally, a shade[1], a trifle, a wee bit
odroczenie adjournment, postponement
odrodzenie 1 (także **odrodzenie się**) resurgence **2** (*okres historyczny*) the Renaissance
odrodzony born-again
odrosnąć → ODRASTAĆ
odrost shoot[2]; **~ korzeniowy** sucker
odróżni(a)ć differentiate, distinguish, draw a distinction between sth and sth, tell A and B apart, tell the difference between A and B
□ **odróżniać się**: **(silnie) ~** contrast[2]
odróżnieni|e contrast[1], distinction; **w ~u od kogoś/czegoś** as distinct from sth, unlike; **nie do ~a** indistinguishable
odruch instinct, reaction; **~ warunkowy** reflex; **mieć ~ wymiotny** retch
odruchowy gut[3], involuntary, knee-jerk
odrywać/oderwać detach, split sth away/off (from sth); **nie odrywaj wzroku od drogi** keep your eyes firmly fixed on the road; **oderwany od tematu** irrelevant
□ **odrywać/oderwać się 1** come away (from sth), split away/off (from sth) **2** (*od rozmowy itp.*) tear yourself away (from sb/sth); **nie można się oderwać od tej książki** this book makes compulsive reading; **trudno było się oderwać** I could hardly wrench myself away
odrzu-cać/cić 1 (*głowę do tyłu*) throw back your head, toss **2** (*wniosek itp.*) disallow, overrule; (*prośbę itp.*) refuse[1], turn sth down; (*kandydata*) knock sb back, reject[1], turn sb down; (*propozycję*) dismiss, refute, reject[1], repudiate, throw sth out; **~ z pogardą** spurn **3** (*pozbyć się*) cast sb/sth off; (*odpędzić*) repel
odrzut reject[2], second[2]
odrzutowiec jet[1]; **wielki pasażerski ~** jumbo[1]
odrzutowy: **silnik ~** jet engine
odsapnąć get your breath (again/back)
od-sączać/sączyć filter[2]
odseparować → SEPAROWAĆ
odseparow(yw)ać isolate
odset|ek 1 percentage **2 ~ki proste/składane** simple/compound interest
od-siadywać/siedzieć sit sth out; (*wyrok*) serve, serve sth out
od-skakiwać/skoczyć (*piłka*) bounce, rebound; (*osoba*) leap back
odskocznia 1 launch pad **2** (*przen.*) springboard, stepping stone
od-słaniać/słonić 1 reveal, uncover; (*część ciała*) expose; (*pomnik*) unveil **2** (*tajemnicę itp.*) expose, uncover **3** (*zasłony*) draw[1]
odsprzed(aw)ać sell
odstawać (*nie przylegać*) protrude, stick (sth) out (of sth); **ona ma odstające uszy** her ears stick out
odstawi(a)ć 1 (*na dalsze miejsce*) stick sth out (of sth) **2** (*upiększać*) tart sb/sth up
□ **odstawi(a)ć się** tart yourself up
odstęp interval IDM **w ~ach** at intervals
od-stępować/stąpić 1 cede, waive; **nie ~ od czegoś** keep to sth **2** (*od religii itp.*) dissent[2]
odstępstwo 1 (*od religii itp.*) dissent[1] **2** (*od reguły itp.*) departure, exception
od-straszać/straszyć deter sb (from doing sth), scare sb/sth away/off; **środek odstraszający** deterrent
■ **odstraszanie** discouragement
odstrzał: **~ selektywny** cull[2]
odstrzeli(wa)ć: **~ (selektywnie)** cull[1]
odsu-wać/nąć 1 (*oddalić*) distance[2] sb (from sb/sth) **2 kogoś/coś od siebie** dismiss sb/sth (as sth), shut sb/sth out; **~ na bok** brush sb/sth aside, leave sth on one side, put sth on/to one side, sweep sb/sth aside **3 ~ na jakiś czas** (*niebezpieczeństwo itp.*) stave sth off **4** (*od władzy itp.*) oust
□ **od-suwać/sunąć się 1 (skądś) do tyłu** stand back (from sth); **~ na bok** stand aside; **~ od drzwi** stand clear of the doors **2** (*przen.*) distance[2] yourself from sb/sth
odsyłacz 1 (*notatka*) cross reference **2** (*symbol*) asterisk
odsyłać/odesłać 1 (*przesyłać*) consign, send **2** (*kierować*) refer sb/sth to sb/sth **3** (*zwracać*) return[1] **4** (*z boiska*) send sb off IDM **~ kogoś z kwitkiem** rebuff verb
odszczek(iw)ać take sth back
odszczepieniec dropout
odszkodowanie award[1], compensation, damages[1], indemnification, indemnity, recompense noun; **wypłacać komuś ~ (za coś)** indemnify sb (for sth)
odszuk(iw)ać hunt sth down/out, trace[1] sb/sth (to sth)
odszumować → SZUMOWAĆ
odszyfrow(yw)ać decipher, decode
od-śnieżać/śnieżyć: **~ drogi** clear the roads of snow/clear snow from the roads
odśrodkowy outward
odśrubow(yw)ać unscrew
odświeżacz: **~ powietrza** air freshener
odświe-żać/żyć 1 (*czynić świeżym*) freshen sth (up), refresh **2** (*znajomość*) renew **3** (*wiedzę*) brush sth up/brush up on sth; **odświeżyć czyjąś pamięć** jog sb's memory, refresh your memory (about sb/sth)
□ **odświe-żać/żyć się** freshen (yourself) up
odtajni(a)ć declassify
odtąd from… on, henceforth, since
od-trącać/trącić: **~ z pogardą** spurn
odtrutka antidote
odtruwanie (*organizmu*) detox
odtwarzacz player; **~ MP3** MP3 player; **~ płyt kompaktowych** CD player
od-twarzać/tworzyć 1 (*po zniszczeniu*) reconstruct, reproduce **2** (*poszczególne etapy procesu itp.*) retrace **3** (*wiernie przedstawiać*) impersonate, portray **4** (*za pomocą urządzenia: film itp.*) play sth back (to sb)
odtwórca impersonator
o-durzać/durzyć: **~ (podstępnie)** dope[2]
■ **odurzający** heady | **odurzenie**: **odurzenie alkoholowe** intoxication | **odurzony** heady; (*narkotykami itp.*) dopey, intoxicated
od-wadniać/wodnić (się) 1 drain[1] **2** (*osoba*) dehydrate

odwag|a bravery, courage, daring noun, fearlessness, nerve, pluck[2], valour; (*zwł. w bitwie*) gallantry; (*nieform.*) balls[1], grit[1], guts[1]; **nie mieć ~i czegoś zrobić** shy away from sth/from doing sth; **dodawać ~i** hearten
odwa-lać/lić (*kawał roboty*) get through sth
odwar stock[1]
od-ważać/ważyć się dare[1]; **odważył się wyjść w czasie burzy** he ventured out into the storm
odważnik weight[1]
odważny brave[1], courageous, daring, plucky adj., valiant; (*krytyka itp.*) hard-hitting
odważyć się → WAŻYĆ SIĘ
odwdzię-czać/czyć się: **komuś** make it up to sb
odwet reprisal, retaliation
odwetow|y: **akcja ~a** reprisal
odwieczny perennial
od-wiedzać/wiedzić pay a call on sb, visit; (*często: bar itp.*) frequent[2]
■ **odwiedzając -y/a** (*rz.*) caller
odwiedziny visit noun
odwiert: ~ **naftowy** oil well
odwieść → ODWODZIĆ
odwieźć → ODWOZIĆ
od-wijać/winąć 1 (*linę itp.*) reel sth out, unwind **2** (*rękawy itp.*) roll sth down
□ **od-wijać/winąć się** unwind
odwilż thaw noun; **zaczyna się ~** it's starting to thaw
odwirow(yw)ać zob. też WIROWAĆ; spin[1]
od-wlekać/wlec defer
odwodnić (się) → ODWADNIAĆ (SIĘ)
odwodnienie dehydration
odwodniony dehydrated
od-wodzić/wieść (*odwracać uwagę*) deflect; **od zrobienia czegoś** dissuade
odwołani|e appeal[1], cancellation; **muzeum jest zamknięte do ~a** the museum is closed until further notice
odwołany off[1]
odwoł(yw)ać 1 (*czyjąś wizytę itp.*) call sth off, cancel, put sb off (doing sth) **2** (*z posady*) recall, remove, withdraw
□ **odwoł(yw)ać się**: **do czegoś** appeal[2] to sth; (*do sądu itp.*) appeal[2] (against/for sth); (*do kogoś o pomoc itp.*) appeal[2] to sb (for sth)
■ **odwoływanie się** reference (to sb/sth)
od-wozić/wieźć (*na policję itp.*) cart sb off
od-wracać/wrócić 1 (*zmienić położenie/pozycję*) invert, reverse[1], turn[1], turn sb/sth around/round; (*kartkę itp.*) turn sth over; (*szybkim ruchem*) flip; ~ **krzesło** moved your chair round; ~ **znaki** switch the signs round; ~ **kierunek** divert; ~ **głowę** turn away; ~ **oczy** turn away; ~ **wzrok** look away; **~e odbicie** an inverted image **2** (*uwagę*) deflect, distract sb (from sth)
■ **odwrócon|y** reverse[1]; **była odwrócona do mnie tyłem** she had her back towards me
□ **od-wracać/wrócić się** turn[1]; (*szybkim ruchem*) flip; (*osoba*) look round, turn away, turn around/round, turn your back on sb/sth
odwrotnie backwards, to the contrary, conversely, inversely, the other way round/around; **(i)** ~ vice versa
odwrotność converse[2], the inverse, reversal
odwrotn|y (*od zamierzonego, przewidywanego itp.*) reverse[3]; (*efekt*) converse; (*w proporcjach*) inverse; **w kierunku ~ym** counter[3] to sth; **w ~ej kolejności** in reverse, in/into reverse order, the other way round/around IDM **pocztą ~ą** by return (of post)
odwrót 1 (*wojsk.*) retreat[2]; **dokonywać odwrotu** retreat[1]; (*przen.*) **nie ma odwrotu** there can be no turning back **2** (*tylna strona*) **na ~** back to front; **na odwrocie strony** overleaf
odwyk withdrawal
odwykowy withdrawal
odwzajemni(a)ć reciprocate, repay, return[1]
□ **odwzajemni(a)ć się** reciprocate, repay; ~ **(czymś nieprzyjemnym)** retaliate
odzew response
odziany attired, clad, clothed
odziedziczyć → DZIEDZICZYĆ
odziewać → ODZIANY
odzież clothes, clothing, things, wardrobe; ~ **męska** menswear
odznaka badge, shield[1]
od-zwierciedlać/zwierciedlić (*i przen.*) mirror verb, reflect; (*poglądy itp.*) echo[2]
od-zwyczajać/zwyczaić: **kogoś od czegoś** wean sb off/from sth
odzysk (*terenu*) reclamation; **nadający się do ~u** recycling
odzysk(iw)ać 1 (*zdobyć znowu*) recapture, get sth back, reclaim, recover, regain; (*i dane z komputera*) retrieve **2** (*surowce*) recycle; (*teren poprzez osuszanie*) reclaim **3** ~ **zdrowie** pick up, recover, recuperate; ~ **przytomność** recover; **odzyskać siły** build up your strength; ~ **równowagę** steady[2]
odzyskiwalny recyclable
odźwierny doorman, porter
odżegn(yw)ać się distance[2] yourself from sb/sth
odży(wa)ć rejuvenate
odżywczy nutritional, nutritious
odżywi(a)ć nourish; ~ **dożylnie/pozajelitowo** drip-feed
□ **odżywi(a)ć się** live on a diet of sth
■ **odżywianie** nutrition; **złe odżywianie** malnutrition |
odżywiony: **dobrze odżywiony** well fed
odżywka conditioner
ofensyw|a offensive[2]; **być w ~ie** be on the offensive; **przechodzić do ~y** take the offensive
ofensywny offensive[1]
oferować/za- offer[1], serve sth up; **zaoferować swoje usługi** volunteer your services
ofert|a approach[2], offer[2], offering, proposition; (*przetargowa*) bid[3], offer[2], tender; **składać ~ę** bid[1]
ofiar|a 1 (*osoba*) victim; (*wypadku itp.*) casualty, fatality, injured; (*życiowa*) loser; **~a nagonki** quarry[1]; **~a żartu primaaprilisowego** April Fool; **bez ~ w ludziach** without loss of life; **być ~ą** (*np. żartu*) be the butt of sth **2** (*relig.*) sacrifice[1]; **składać w ofierze** sacrifice[2]
ofiarodaw-ca/czyni benefactor, donor
ofiarow(yw)ać offer[1], present[3]; (*zwł. pieniądze*) donate
oficer officer; ~ **okrętowy** mate[1]
oficjalny formal, official[1]; (*wizyta itp.*) state[2]
oficjele officialdom
oficyna annexe
ofoliowany shrink-wrapped
ofrankowanie postage
ofsajd offside
ofsajdowy (*część samochodu*) offside
ogar hound[1]
ogar-niać/nąć 1 (*uczucie*) come over sb, engulf, sweep over sb; (*zwł. coś negatywnego*) overcome **2** (*teren*) spread[1], sweep[1]
ogień 1 (*płomień*) fire[1] **2** (*żar*) heat[1] **3** (*do papierosa*) light[1] **4** (*broni palnej*) **ognia!** fire!; ~ **krzyżowy** crossfire; ~ **zaporowy** barrage; **otwierać ~** open fire (at/on sb/sth) **5** (*pytań*) barrage; **brać w krzyżowy ~ pytań** cross-examine
ogier stallion
oglądać/obejrzeć behold, see, view[2]; (*telewizję*) watch[1]; (*towar*) browse; (*dużo rzeczy w sklepie*) look round (sth); **za kimś/za czymś** look past sb/sth; (*w sklepie itp.*) **tylko oglądam** I'm just looking (around)
□ **oglądać/obejrzeć się**: **dokoła** look round; **obejrzyj się!** look behind you!
■ **oglądanie**: ~ **wystaw sklepowych** window-shopping
ogład|a: **z ~ą** suavely
o-głaszać/głosić announce, call[1], declare, post[2], proclaim, promulgate, publish, put sth out; **kogoś/coś kimś/czymś** hail[1], vote[2]; (*w reklamie; że się poszukuje*) advertise
ogłoszenie 1 (*podanie do publicznej wiadomości; wiadomość*) announcement, notice[1], proclamation, promulgation, publication **2** (*że się poszukuje*) advertisement; ~ **drobne** classified advertisement
ogłoszeniodawca advertiser
ogłupi(a)ć 1 (*zbić z tropu*) floor[2] **2** (*propaganda itp.*) brainwash
ogłupiały brain-dead; (*z miłości*) besotted
ogłu-szać/szyć 1 deafen **2** (*przen.*) stun
ogniotrwał|y: **drzwi ~e** fireproof door
ognisko 1 (*ogień*) bonfire, camp fire **2** (*promieni*) focus[2]
ogniskować focus[1]
ognisty 1 (*kolor itp.*) fiery, flaming **2** (*przemówienie itp.*) sparkling
ogniwo link[1]
ogolić (się) → GOLIĆ (SIĘ)
ogolony shaven
ogon 1 tail[1] **2** (*tajniak*) tail[1]
IDM **koński ~** ponytail | **mysi ~ek** pigtail
ogorzały weather-beaten
ogólnie broadly, generally, generically, globally, popularly, on/from all sides, on/from every side, substantially
IDM **~ mówiąc** altogether, by and large, overall[1]
ogólnikowy broad
ogólnokrajowy nationwide
ogólnokształcący: ~ comprehensive[1]
ogólnonarodowy nationwide
ogólnopaństwowy nationwide

ogólnoświatowy global, worldwide
ogólnoustrojowy systemic
ogóln|y broad, general[1], generic, overall adj., prevailing, prevalent; **~a suma** total[2]
ogół 1 ~ społeczeństwa the general public, society at large **2 ~ transakcji** sale IDM **na ~; w ogóle** by and large, in general, in the main, on the whole | **na ~ coś robić** tend to do sth | **~em (biorąc)** in all, altogether | **w ogóle (żaden)** anything like sb/sth, (not) at all, whatever
ogór|ek cucumber; **~ki kiszone** dill pickles
o-gradzać/grodzić enclose, fence[2]
ograni-czać/czyć 1 (*używanie/robienie czegoś*) confine sb/sth to sth, constrain, constrict, control[2], curb[1], infringe on/upon sth, restrict, tie[1] sb (to sth/to doing sth), tie sb down; (*ilość/sumę czegoś*) cut sth down, cut down (on sth); (*wydatki*) cap[2]; (*i prędkość*) limit[2] **2** (*granica*) confine, fence sb/sth in
□ **ograni-czać/czyć się** confine yourself to sth, tie yourself down
ograniczenie constraint, constriction, curb[2], limit[1], limitation, restraint, restriction; **~ prędkości** speed limit; **~ wieku** age limit; **~ wydatków rządowych** a government squeeze on spending
ograniczoność narrowness
ograniczon|y 1 limited, restricted; (*wiedza itp.*) scanty; (*miejsce*) confined; (*aprobata itp.*) qualified; **spółka z ~ą odpowiedzialnością** limited company **2** (*mat.*) finite **3** (*osoba*) insular, narrow-minded, simple-minded
ogrodnictwo gardening, horticulture
ogrodnicz|y horticultural; **narzędzia/rękawice ~e** gardening tools/gloves
ogrodni-k/czka gardener
ogrodow|y: **meble ~e** outdoor furniture
ogrodzenie fence[1], railing
ogrom enormity, immensity, magnitude; **~ jego wiedzy** the extent of his knowledge
ogromn|y enormous, formidable, great[1], huge, immeasurable, immense, incredible, infinite, massive, monstrous, monumental, mountainous, stupendous, tremendous, vast; (*nieform.*) jumbo[2]; (*wiedza itp.*) prodigious; (*sukces*) resounding, roaring; (*bogactwo itp.*) fabulous; **w ~-ym/ej stopniu/mierze** vastly
ogród garden[1]; **Ogród Botaniczny** the Botanical Gardens; **~ zoologiczny** zoo; **~ z tyłu domu** backyard
ogródek: **~ działkowy** allotment
ogródka: **bez ogródek** baldly, bluntly, outright, point-blank, straight out; **mówić ~mi** beat about/around the bush; **mówiący bez ogródek** outspoken; **powiedz mi bez ogródek** don't be coy
o-gryzać/gryźć gnaw, nibble
ogryzek core
ogrz(ew)ać się warm[2] (up)
ogrzewanie heating; **centralne ~** central heating
ohydny abominable, atrocious, disgusting, hideous, lousy, monstrous, obnoxious, odious, vile; (*przestępstwo*) heinous
oj ouch
ojciec father[1]; **~ chrzestny** godparent; **bez ojca** fatherless; **po ojcu** paternal IDM **Ojcze nasz!** (*modlitwa*) the Lord's Prayer
ojcostwo fatherhood, parenthood, paternity
ojcowski fatherly, paternal
ojczym stepfather
ojczysty native[1]; **język ~** mother tongue
ojczyzna homeland, mother country, motherland; (*zwł. o Niemczech*) fatherland
ojej: **~!** boy[2], dear[2], gee, golly, good grief, gosh, oh
okalany IDM **być ~m czymś** be fringed with sth
okale-czać/czyć cripple[1], maim, mutilate
okantowany had
okap eaves
okaz exhibit[2], specimen
okazać (się) → OKAZYWAĆ (SIĘ)
okazałość grandness, grandeur, splendour
okazały grand[1], imposing, spectacular, splendid, sumptuous; (*ostentacyjny*) ostentatious
okazanie IDM **za ~m czegoś** on production of sth
okaziciel/ka bearer, holder
okazj|a 1 (*szansa*) break[2], chance[1], occasion, offer[2], opening, opportunity; **mieć ~ę** get to do sth; **z ~i** celebratory, for[1] **2** (*korzystny zakup*) bargain[1], offer[2]; **wyjątkowa ~a** snip[2] IDM **przy ~i** by the way, in passing
okaz(yw)ać display[1], exhibit[1], manifest, produce[1]; (*uprzejmość*) extend; (*życzliwość itp.*) show[1]; (*pomoc*) render; **~ dezaprobatę** signal your disapproval
□ **okaz(yw)ać się** emerge, manifest (itself) (in/as sth), prove, turn out (to be sth); **jeszcze się okaże, czy…** it remains to be seen whether…
okej OK interj., okey-doke
okiełznywać tame[2]
okienko 1 (*okno*) hatch[2] **2** (*w harmonogramie itp.*) slot[1]; (*w harmonogramie*) window
okiennica shutter
oklapnąć flag[2], run out of steam
oklask|i applause, clap[2]; **nagradzać kogoś gromkimi ~ami** give sb a big hand
oklask(iw)ać applaud
oklep: **na ~** bareback
oklepany stale
okład: **z ~em** odd
okładka cover[2]; (*płyty gramofonowej*) sleeve
okładzina lining
okłam(yw)ać (się) deceive sb/yourself (into doing sth)
okno (*i komput.*) window; **~ wykuszowe** bay window; (*komput.*) **~ dialogowe** dialog box
ok|o eye[1]; **nie widzi na jedno ~o** he is blind in one eye; **zawiązać komuś oczy** blindfold verb IDM **jak ~iem sięgnąć** as far as the eye can see | **mając oczy otwarte** with your eyes open | **mieć kogoś/coś na ~u** keep tabs on sb/sth | **na czyichś oczach** before sb's very eyes, in full view of sb | **na ~o** at a guess | **~o w ~o** face to face (with sb/sth) | **~o za ~o, ząb za ząb** an eye for an eye | **w czyichś oczach** in the eyes of sb/in sb's eyes
okolic|a 1 (*otoczenie*) environs; (*sąsiedztwo*) neighbourhood; (*wieś*) the countryside; **w ~y** round[3], round about; **w najbliższej ~y** locally **2** (*obszar*) area, part[1], region
okolicznoś|ć circumstance, consideration; (**okoliczności**) things; **w tych ~ciach** in/under the circumstances; **zależnie od ~ci** as the case may be
okoliczny surrounding
około about[1], approximately, around, circa, in the region of sth, round about sth, or so; **coś ~** something like; **gdzieś ~** somewhere around
okoń perch[2]
okop trench
okólnik circular[2]
okółko(wy)wać ring[2]
okpić → KPIĆ
okpi(wa)ć fool[2]
o-kradać/kraść burgle, rob; **~ firmę na miliony** defraud the company of millions
okrakiem astride; **stać/siedzieć ~** straddle
okratowanie grating
okrągły circular[1], round[1]; (*sylwetka*) full[1]
okrą-żać/żyć 1 (*przeszkodę*) round[5] **2** (*stanąć w koło*) encircle, surround
okrążenie (*bieżni*) circuit, lap[1]
okres 1 (*czas trwania*) period, phase[1], season[1], span[1], term[1]; (*przerwa*) interlude, lapse[1], space[1]; (*życia, pracy itp.*) lifespan; **krótki ~** interval, spell[2]; **~ ostatnich przygotowań** run-up; **~ próbny** trial period; (*na nowym stanowisku itp.*) probation; **~ wojenny** wartime; **~ zimowy** wintertime **2** (*cykl*) cycle[1] **3** (*miesiączka*) menstruation, period; **mieć ~** menstruate IDM **w dłuższym/krótszym ~ie** in the long/short term
okresowy cyclic, periodic; **bilet ~** season ticket; **~ bilet autobusowy** bus pass
okreś-lać/lić 1 (*opisywać*) describe **2** (*kogoś mianem*) label[2] sb/sth (as) sth **3** (*znaczenie czegoś*) define, term[2]; (*prawo, autorytet*) prescribe; **szczegółowo/dokładnie ~** delineate; **4** (*wiek itp.*) determine, establish; (*rozpoznawać*) place[2]; **~ cenę** price[2]; **~ z góry** predetermine **5** (*oznaczać*) mark[1]
■ **określeni|e 1** (*przen.: etykietka*) label[1], term[1]; **nie do ~a** indefinable **2** (*polityki itp.*) determination | **określony**: **na czas nie~** indefinitely; **ściśle ~** precise
określnik determiner
okrę-cać/cić twist[1]
□ **okrę-cać/cić się** coil[1], twist[1]
okręg district, sector; **~ wyborczy** constituency, ward[1]
okręt ship[1], vessel; **~ wojenny** warship
okrętować/za- się embark
okrętownictwo shipbuilding
okrętowy naval

okrężnica colon
okrężn|y 1 (*droga, ruch*) circular[1]; (*trasa*) circuitous **2** (*sposób*) indirect, roundabout[2]; **~ą drogą** indirectly
okroić → OKRAWAĆ
okropność cruelty, horror
okropny atrocious, awful, beastly, dreadful, frightful, ghastly, gruesome, hateful, horrible, horrific, objectionable, odious, shocking, terrible, yucky IDM **być ~m** be the pits
okruch fragment[1]; (*chleba itp.*) crumb
okrucieństwo cruelty, ferocity, inhumanity, savagery; (*zwł. wojenne*) atrocity
okruszyna (*chleba itp.*) crumb
okrutnik fiend
okrutny cruel, ferocious, fiendish, inhuman, inhumane, savage, sick[1], unkind, vicious
okry(wa)ć cover[1], envelop, shroud[2]; **~ hańbą** dishonour[2]
okrzyk chant[1]; (*pojedyncze słowo*) ejaculation, exclamation, interjection, shout noun; **wznosić ~i** cheer[2]
o-krzykiwać/krzyknąć: **kogoś/coś kimś/czymś** hail[1] sb/sth as sth
oktagon octagon
oktagonalny octagonal
oktan octane
oktawa octave
okular eyepiece
okulary glasses; **~ do czytania** reading glasses; **~ dwuogniskowe** bifocals; **~ ochronne** goggles; **~ przeciwsłoneczne** dark glasses, sunglasses
okultyzm occult
okup ransom
okupacja occupation
okupować invade, occupy
okupowany occupied
olbrzym 1 (*osoba*) giant; **zły ~** ogre **2** (*coś olbrzymiego*) whopper
olbrzymi colossal, enormous, fantastic, giant adj., gigantic, huge, king-size, mammoth, monstrous, monumental, mountainous, supreme, tremendous; (*sukces*) runaway[1]; (*bogactwo itp.*) untold
oleić/na- oil verb
oleisty oily
olej oil; **~ lniany** linseed oil; **~ napędowy** diesel; **~ skalny** petroleum
olejek: **~ do opalania** suntan oil
olejny: **obraz ~** oil painting
olejowy oily
olimpiada the Olympic Games
olimpijski Olympic
oliwa lubricant, oil; **~ z oliwek** olive oil
oliwić/na- lubricate, oil verb
oliwienie lubrication
oliwka olive
oliwkowy olive adj.; **kolor ~** olive
olstro holster
o-lśniewać/lśnić dazzle; **olśniło mnie** it hit me
olśniewający brilliant, dazzling, glamorous, stunning
ołów lead[3]
ołów|ek pencil[1]; **pisać/rysować ~kiem** pencil[2]
ołtarz altar

omacek: **szukać po omacku** feel[1] (about) (for sb/sth), grope (about/around) (for sth)
omami(a)ć zob. też MAMIĆ; **kogoś** mess sb about/around, muck sb about/around
o-mawiać/mówić discuss, go over sth, go through sth, run through sth, talk sth over (with sb), talk sth through; (*książka itp.*) treat[1]; **~ coś szczegółowo** elaborate[2] (on sth); **~ sprawy** talk things over; **omówić wszystko** cover everything
omdlały faint[1]
omdlenie swoon
omdle(wa)ć droop; **~ z zachwytu na widok kogoś/czegoś** drool (over sb/sth)
omen omen
o-mijać/minąć bypass[2]; (*prawo itp.*) circumvent, get round/around sth; (*temat itp.*) skirt round sth; **~ kogoś/coś z daleka** keep away from sb/sth
omlet omelette
omówić → OMAWIAĆ
omówienie airing, overview; (*w gazecie itp.*) write-up; **szczegółowe ~** coverage
omszały mossy
omylny fallible
on he[1,2]; (*przedmiot; zwierzę*) it
ona she; (*przedmiot; zwierzę*) it
onanizm masturbation
onanizować się masturbate
ondulacja wave[1]
one they
oni they
oniemiały 1 dumb, mute **2** (*z wrażenia*) dumbfounded, gobsmacked, speechless, tongue-tied
o-nieśmielać/nieśmielić intimidate, overawe
online on line
ono it
opactwo abbey
opacznie: **~ kogoś zrozumieć** get sb wrong; **~ coś zrozumieć** get (hold of) the wrong end of the stick
opad fall[2]; **~ radioaktywny** fallout; **~ śniegu** snowfall; **~y przelotne** shower[1]; **wysokość ~ów deszczu** rainfall
o-padać/paść 1 (*obniżać się*) drop[1], go down, sink[1], slump[1], spiral; (*i liście*) fall[1]; (*mgła, dym itp.*) clear[2]; (*woda morska podczas odpływu*) ebb; (*teren*) shelve; **nieco ~** slip[1] **2** (*skarpetki itp.*) slip down **3 jej włosy opadały na plecy** her hair hung down her back **4** (*gorączka; gniew*) subside **5** (*kwiat*) droop
opak: **na ~** awry
opakowanie 1 (*tekturowe itp.*) packaging; (*miękki materiał ochronny*) packing; (*czekolady itp.*) wrapper, wrapping **2** (*razem z zawartością*) container, pack[2]; (*orzechów itp.*) bag[1], packet; (*mleka itp.*) carton; (*proszku itp.*) sachet
o-palać/palić 1 (*nad ogniem*) singe; (*trawę itp.*) brown[2] **2** (*sobie nogi itp.*) tan[1]
□ **o-palać/palić się 1** sun[2] yourself, sunbathe, tan[1]; (**opalić się**) catch the sun **2** (*trawa itp.*) brown[2]
opalenizna suntan
opalizacja iridescence
opalizujący iridescent
opalony bronzed, brown[1], suntanned, tanned

opał fuel[1]
opamiętani|e: **bez ~a** hectically
opamięt(yw)ać się come to your senses
opancerzony armoured
opanowanie composure, grip[1], nerve, poise, restraint; **z ~m** coolly
opanowany 1 (*spokojny*) calm[1], collected, composed, controlled, cool[1], good-tempered, poised **2** (*przez owady itp.*) infested
opanow(yw)ać 1 (*miasto*) invade, overrun **2** (*sytuację: ogień itp.*) bring sth under control, come/get to grips with sth; (*rynek*) corner[2]; **~ pożar** tackle the blaze **3** (*osobę*) cool sb down/off; (*nerwy, drżenie głosu*) steady[2]; (*zebrać myśli*) collect[1] **4** (*strach*) grip[2], overcome, overpower **5** (*wiedzę, technikę*) master[2]
□ **opanow(yw)ać się** collect[1] yourself, compose yourself, cool down/off, pull yourself together
opar vapour
oparci|e 1 (*krzesła*) back[1], backrest; **punkt ~a** hold[2]; **~e dla nóg** foothold, footing; **~e na rękę** armrest **2** (*zależność*) reliance; **w ~u o coś** on the strength of sth **3** (*ostoja*) mainstay
oparzenie burn[2], scald noun; **~ słoneczne** sunburn
oparzyć → PARZYĆ
oparzyć (się) → PARZYĆ SIĘ
opasać → OPASYWAĆ
opaska 1 (*taśma; pasek materiału*) band; **~ na głowę** headband; **~ na oczy** blindfold; **~ przeciwpotowa** sweatband; **~ na rękę** armband; **~ na włosy** hairband **2 ~ uciskowa** (*med.*) tourniquet **3** (*opakowanie*) wrapper
opasły gross[1]
opas(yw)ać encircle
opaść → OPADAĆ
opat abbot
opatentować → PATENTOWAĆ
opatrunek dressing
o-patrywać/patrzeć dress[2]
opatu-lać/lić (się) wrap (sb/yourself) up
opchnąć → OPYCHAĆ
opcja option
opera 1 (*utwór*) opera **2** (*budynek*) opera house
operacja 1 (*wojsk., komput.*) operation **2** (*med.*) operation, surgery; **liftingująca ~ plastyczna** facelift; **~ plastyczna** plastic surgery **3** (*handl.*) transaction
operacyjny 1 operational, operative **2** (*med.*) surgical
operator/ka operator; **operator/ka maszyny** machinist
operować/z- operate
operowy operatic
opętany obsessed (about/with sb/sth)
opęt(yw)ać: **kogoś (czymś)** possess
opić się → OPIJAĆ SIĘ
opiek|a 1 attention[1], care[1]; **~a medyczna** health care, medical treatment/care; **~a nad dziećmi** childcare; **~a społeczna** social security, welfare; **~a dzienna** day care; **pod czyjąś ~ą** in your hands, in the hands of sb; **pod ~ą osoby dorosłej** accompanied by an adult; **bez ~i** (all) by themselves, unaccompanied, unattended, without supervision **2** (*prawn., nad dziećmi*) custody
opiekować/za- się care for sb, have[1], look after sb/sth/yourself, nurse[2], take

care of yourself/sb/sth, take sb under your wing, tend; ~ **się dzieckiem** babysit
opiekun/ka carer, guardian, minder, protector; (*grupy (studentów)*) tutor; (*przyzwoitka*) chaperone; (*muzeum itp.*) custodian, keeper; **opiekun/ka do dziecka** childminder; **(dochodząca) opiekunka do dziecka** babysitter; **opiekun sądowy osób, które otrzymały wyrok w zawieszeniu lub zostały zwolnione warunkowo z więzienia** probation officer
opiekuńcz|y caring, protective; **państwo ~e** welfare state
o-pierać/przeć 1 coś o coś lean[1], prop[2], rest[1] **2** (*na faktach itp.*) base sth on sth, found[2], predicate[2]
□ **o-pierać /przeć się 1 o coś** lean[1], rest[1] **2** (*na faktach*) go by sth, go on sth, rest on sb/sth **3 komuś/czemuś** react against sb/sth, resist, withstand; **taki, że nie można się oprzeć** irresistible **4 na kimś** fall back on sb
opierdzielać się fart around
opieszałość inertia
opieszały 1 (*ociężały*) inert **2** (*niedbały*) negligent
opi(ja)ć się binge[2]
opiłow(yw)ać file[2] (away/down, etc.)
opini|a 1 (*pogląd*) belief, estimation, feeling, judgement, opinion, perception, sentiment, thinking[1], thought[2], view[1]; (*nieform.*) bet[2]; (*zebrane informacje o poglądach pewnej grupy ludzi*) feedback; **~a publiczna** tide[1] **2** (*zawodowa*) reference **3** (*o postępach w nauce*) report[2]; (*reputacja*) name[1], reputation; **mieć złą ~ę w sprawach bezpieczeństwa** have a bad safety record; **cieszący się dobrą ~ą** reputable
opis 1 (*określenie*) description; ~ **zawartości** (*np. przesyłki*) docket; **szczegółowy** ~ delineation **2** (*relacja*) account[1] **3** (*techniczny*) specification
opisowy descriptive
opis(yw)ać characterize, depict, describe, portray, represent; **nie do opisania** indescribable
opium opium
o-platać/pleść entwine
opluć → PLUĆ
opła-cać/cić się pay[1], pay off
■ **opłacający się** worthwhile
opłacalny commercially viable, cost-effective IDM **ponosić w pełni ~ wydatek** get your money's worth
opłakany sorry[1]; **w ~m stanie** dilapidated
opłak(iw)ać lament verb, mourn
opłata charge[1], fare[1], fee, payment, rate[1]; ~ **dodatkowa** surcharge; ~ **pocztowa** postage; ~ **skarbowa** (*stosowana przy wydawaniu dokumentów sądowych*) stamp duty; ~ **targowa** toll; ~ **za obsługę** service charge; ~ **za przejazd** (*np. przez most*) toll; ~ **za wstęp** cover charge; ~ **za wypożyczenie** rental
opłatek wafer
opłuk(iw)ać rinse sth out
opływow|y sleek, streamlined; **nadawać kształt/linię ~-y/ą** streamline
opodatkowani|e taxation; **podlegający ~u** taxable
opodatkow(yw)ać tax verb
opona tyre
oponent/ka opponent
oponować/za- oppose, protest[2] about/against/at sth
oporny disobedient, resistant (to sth)
oportunist-a/ka opportunist
oportunistyczny expedient, opportunist, opportunistic
oportunizm opportunism
opo-wiadać/wiedzieć narrate, recount, relate, tell; ~ **dowcipy/kawał** joke[2], tell/crack jokes; ~ **wspomnienia** reminisce
□ **opo-wiadać/wiedzieć się: za czymś** espouse, opt to do sth
opowiadający narrator
opowiadanie narration, narrative, short story, story, yarn
opowiastka tale
opowieść story, tale
opozycj|a dissidence, opposition; **w ~i do czegoś** versus
opozycjonist-a/ka dissident
opór defiance, opposition, reaction (against sb/sth), resistance, stand[2] (against sth); **stawiać komuś/czemuś** ~ fight back (against sb/sth), resist
opóźni(a)ć: kogoś/coś delay[2], hold off (sth/doing sth), hold sb/sth up, set sb/sth back; **kogoś** keep[1]
opóźnienie delay[1], hold-up, lag[2]; **mieć** ~ run behind schedule; **jechać itp. z ~m** be running late
opóźniony (*z wykonaniem pracy, zapłaceniem czynszu itp.*) behind (with/in sth); **być ~m** (*w stosunku do czegoś*) lag[1]; (*autobusy itp.*) be running late; ~ **w rozwoju** retarded, stunted, subnormal
opraco(wy)wać develop, formulate, map sth out, work sth out; (*publikację*) compile
oprawa 1 (*książki*) binding[2] **2** ~ **plastyczna** (*książki itp.*) artwork **3** (także **oprawka**) (*okularów; obrazu*) frame[1]; **ze srebrną oprawką** with silver rims
oprawi(a)ć (*książkę*) bind[1]; ~ **w ramę** frame[2]
oprocentowani|e interest[1]; **kredyt bez ~a** interest-free credit
oprogramowanie software
o-prowa-dzać/prowadzić conduct[1], show sb around/round (sth)
oprócz 1 (*w dodatku do czegoś*) besides, beyond, other than; (*mnie itp.*) else **2** (*z wyjątkiem czegoś*) apart from, bar[3], barring, but[2], except[1], short of sth/doing sth
opróżni(a)ć (się) empty[2]
■ **opróżnianie** clear-out | **opróżnienie: nie zdążę przed opróżnieniem skrzynki** I'll miss the post
oprysk(iw)ać spatter
opryskliwość gruffness, snappiness
opryskliw|y abrasive, brusque, gruff, snappy, surly; **~e odzywanie się** snarl noun
opryszczka herpes; (*na wardze*) cold sore
opryszek thug
oprzeć (się) → OPIERAĆ (SIĘ)
optować opt
optyczny optical
optyk optician
optymalizować/z- 1 optimize **2** (*produkcję itp.*) streamline
optymalny optimum
optymist-a/ka optimist
optymistyczny bullish, optimistic, sanguine, upbeat
optymizm optimism
opublikować → PUBLIKOWAĆ
opublikowany in print
opuchlizna swelling
opuchnięty bloated
opustoszały derelict, desolate, empty[1]
opustoszeć → PUSTOSZEĆ
opu-szczać/ścić 1 (*rolety itp.*) roll sth down; ~ **szybę** wind a car window down **2** (*fragment tekstu itp.*) cut sth out, leave sb/sth out (of sth), miss sb/sth out, omit **3** (*kraj, dom; rodzinę*) abandon, desert[2], forsake, neglect, quit (as sth); **kogoś** walk out on sb; **nie ~ kogoś** (*w kłopotach*) stick by sb **4** (*lekcje*) skip[1]
■ **opuszczany** (*łóżko itp.*) pull-down | **opuszczon|y** abandoned, deserted, desolate; (*osoba*) forlorn, friendless; **opuszczona linia kolejowa** a disused railway line
opychać/opchnąć (*sprzedać*) flog
□ **opychać się** guzzle, stuff[2] yourself (with sth)
opy-lać/lić flog
orać/za- plough verb
orangutan orang-utan
oranżeria hothouse
orator/ka orator
oraz plus[1]
orbi|ta orbit; **krążyć po ~cie** orbit verb
orbitalny orbital
orbitować/za- orbit verb
orchidea orchid
ordynarność crudity
ordynarn|y foul[1], foul-mouthed, loutish, uncouth, vulgar; **~e słowo** swear word; **stawać się ~ym** coarsen
ordynus lout
orędowni-k/czka champion[1]
organ organ, vehicle
organiczny organic
organist-a/ka organist
organizacja organization, outfit; ~ **pozarządowa** NGO; **Organizacja Narodów Zjednoczonych** the United Nations; **Organizacja Współpracy Gospodarczej i Rozwoju** OECD
organizacyjny organizational
organizator 1 (także **organizatorka**) arranger, organizer; (*osoba/firma*) ~ **wycieczki** tour operator **2** (*książka; program komputerowy*) planner
organizm 1 organism **2** (*osoby*) constitution, system
organizować/z- arrange, organize, line sth up; (*wprowadzać zmiany*) orchestrate; (*grupę itp.*) form[2], set (sth) up; (*przyjęcie itp.*) hold[1]; (*bankiet itp.*) lay sth on; (*przedstawienie itp.*) put sth on, stage[2]; (*wystawę*) mount[1]
organki harmonica
organowy organ
organy organ
orgazm orgasm
orgia orgy
orientacj|a 1 ~a w terenie sense of direction; (*w opcji ustawienia strony pliku*) **~a pionowa** portrait;

~**a pozioma** landscape[1]; **nabierać ~i** get/find your bearings; **tracić ~ę** lose your bearings **2 ~a seksualna** sexuality
orientalny oriental
orientować/z- się 1 (*w temacie itp.*) get the hang of (doing) sth, tell, understand; **dobrze ~** know what's what; **o ile się orientuję** as far as I can see **2** (*w terenie*) orient yourself
orkiestra orchestra; ~ **dęta** brass band; ~ **kameralna** chamber orchestra
orkiestrowy orchestral
orlica (*paproć*) bracken
ornamentalny ornamental
ornitolog ornithologist
ornitologia ornithology
orny arable
ortodoksyjny orthodox
ortodontyczny: **aparat** ~ brace[1]
ortografia orthography, spelling
ortograficzny orthographic; **test** ~ spelling test
ortopedia orthopaedics
ortopedyczny orthopaedic
oryginalność originality
oryginalny novel[2], original[1], quaint
oryginał master[1], master copy, original[2]
orzec → ORZEKAĆ
orzech nut; ~ **brazylijski** brazil; ~ **kokosowy** coconut; ~ **laskowy** hazelnut; ~ **nerkowca** cashew; ~ **pistacjowy** pistachio; ~ **włoski** walnut; **z ~ami** nutty
orzechowy nutty
orzeczenie 1 (*sądu itp.*) judgement, ruling[2] **2** (*gram.*) predicate[1]
orzecznikowy predicative
o-rzekać/orzec adjudicate, rule[2], vote[2]
orzeł eagle IDM **grać w orła i reszkę** toss (up) (for sth) | ~ **czy reszka?** heads or tails?
orzeszek: ~ **ziemny** peanut
orzeźwi(a)ć invigorate
orzeźwiający bracing, invigorating, refreshing
orzeźwienie refreshment
osa wasp
osa-czać/czyć corner[2], hem sb in
osad deposit[1], residue, sediment; (*fusy*) dregs; ~ **nazębny** plaque; **pozostawiać coś jako** ~ deposit[2]
osada hamlet, settlement
osadni-k/czka settler
osa-dzać/dzić 1 (*wcisnąć, nacisnąć*) bed[2], embed **2 zostać osadzonym** (*na wyspie itp.*) be marooned **3** (*akcję filmu itp.*) set[1]
□ **o-sadzać/sadzić się** settle
osadzenie: ~ **w separatce** solitary confinement
osamotnieni|e loneliness, solitude; **powodujący uczucie ~a** lonesome
osamotniony bereft, isolated
osąd estimation
osą-dzać/dzić find[1], judge[2]; **źle** ~ misjudge
oschłość briskness
oschły brisk, crisp[1], dour, stiff[1]
oscylacja oscillation
oscylować alternate[1] between A and B, fluctuate, oscillate
oset thistle
o-siadać/siąść 1 (*osoba; pył*) settle **2** (*teren, budynek*) subside IDM ~ **na mieliźnie** run/go aground
o-siągać/siągnąć accomplish, achieve, attain, hit[1], notch sth up, reach[1]; ~ **z trudem** (*zgodę itp.*) hammer sth out; ~ **cenę** fetch; ~ **zysk** make money; ~ **(oczekiwany) poziom** make the grade; **osiągnąć podwójny cel** kill two birds with one stone; (*trzęsienie ziemi*) **osiągnąć siłę 6.4 w skali Richtera** register 6.4 on the Richter scale
osiągalny attainable, available
osiągnięci|e accomplishment, achievement, attainment, performance; (*odkrycie*) discovery; ~**a w pracy jednostki/organizacji** track record; **pomagać w ~u czegoś** make for sth
osiąść → SIADAĆ
osied-lać/lić się settle
osiedle estate; ~ **mieszkaniowe** housing development/estate; ~ **przemysłowe** industrial estate
osiem eight
osiemdziesiąt eighty
osiemdziesiąty eightieth
osiemnasty eighteenth
osiemnaście eighteen
osiero-cać/cić orphan verb
osierocony fatherless, motherless
osiodłać → SIODŁAĆ
osioł ass, donkey
oskard pick[2]
oskar-żać/żyć accuse, charge[2], incriminate, indict
oskarżeni|e accusation, charge[1], indictment; **wzajemne ~a** recrimination; **świadek ~a** witness for the prosecution
oskarżon-y/a (*rz.*) the accused, defendant
oskarżyciel/ka accuser, the prosecution, prosecutor; **oskarżyciel publiczny** public prosecutor
oskarżycielski accusing
oskarżyć → SKARŻYĆ
oskrobać shave sth off (sth)
oskub(yw)ać zob. też SKUBAĆ; **kogoś** fleece[2], rip sb off
osłabi(a)ć/osłabnąć debilitate, drain[1], impair, shake[1], weaken, wear sb/sth down; (*ból itp.*) alleviate; (*rozwój biznesu*) depress; (*odporność itp.*) lower[2]; (*wypowiedź*) qualify, water sth down; (*zaufanie itp.*) undermine
■ **osłabiony** (*osoba*) run-down
osłabnąć → SŁABNĄĆ
o-słaniać/słonić 1 (*ochraniać*) protect; (*przykrywać*) cover[1], shroud[2]; (*od wiatru itp.,*) shelter[2]; (*od słońca itp.*) shield[2]; (*przed światłem itp.*) shade[2]; (*od ciosów*) cushion[2] **2** (*kryć kogoś przed karą*) cover up for sb
osłon|a (*zabezpieczenie*) protection; (*przykrywka*) casing, cloak, cover[2], jacket; (*przed słońcem itp.*) shield[1]; (*dająca cień*) canopy; (*przen.*) cocoon[1]; ~**a przeciwsłoneczna** (*w samochodzie*) visor; **pod ~ą czegoś** under (the) cover of sth
osłonięty sheltered
osłupiały amazed, dumbfounded
osłupienie amazement, bewilderment; **wprawiać w** ~ stupefy
osmagany (*wiatrem*) weather-beaten
osma-lać/lić singe
osmoza osmosis
osnu(wa)ć envelop
osob|a figure[1], individual[2], person; **trzy ~y zginęły** three lives were lost; **pierwsza ~a** (*gram.*) (*narracji*) the first person IDM **we własnej ~ie** in the flesh
osobistość celebrity, figure[1], name[1], personality
osobisty individual[1], particular, personal, private[1]
osobiście herself, himself, myself, in person, personally, privately, themselves, yourself
osobliwość curiosity, oddness, oddity, peculiarity, rarity
osobliwy curious, odd, peculiar, quaint, singular
osobnik character, individual[2]
osobn|o apart, independently, separately; (*kwestia itp.*) **z ~a** in isolation
osobnoś|ć IDM **na ~ci** in private
osobny independent, individual[1], separate[1]
osobowość personality, self
osocze plasma
ospa smallpox; ~ **wietrzna** chickenpox
ospałość drowsiness, dullness, lethargy
ospał|y lethargic, slow[1], sluggish; ~**e popołudnie** a languid afternoon
osprzęt fixture
ostatecznie after all, definitively, eventually, finally, ultimately
ostatecznoś|ć extremity, finality IDM **w ~ci** in the last resort, (as) a last resort
ostateczny definite, definitive, eventual, final[1], ultimate[1]; ~ **termin** cut-off, deadline IDM **w ~m rachunku** at the end of the day
ostatki 1 (*resztki*) the last noun **2** (*wtorek przed Środą Popielcową*) Pancake Day, Shrove Tuesday
ostatni final[1], last[1], latest, past[1], recent, ultimate[1]; (*wiadomości itp.*) up to the minute; ~**e miejsce** (*z tyłu autobusu itp.*) the end seat; **mieszkam w ~m domu** I live in the end house IDM ~**a chwila** the last minute/moment | ~**e słowo** (*w jakiejś sprawie*) the last/final word (on sth)
ostatnio last[2], lately, latterly, newly, recently
ostemplować → STEMPLOWAĆ
ostentacja show[2]
ostentacyjny ostentatious
osteoporoza osteoporosis
ostoja backbone, mainstay; (*komuś w kryzysie*) comfort[1] (to sb)
ostroga spur[1]
ostrokrzew holly
ostrosłup pyramid
ostrość harshness, sharpness; **nastawiać** ~ focus[1]
ostrożny careful, cautious, circumspect, guarded, wary; (*ocena*) conservative[1]; (*kierowca itp.*) safe[1]; **być ~m** watch[1]
■ **ostrożnie** carefully, cautiously, delicately, gingerly, guardedly, warily; (*zgadywać itp.*) conservatively; (*na przesyłce itp.*) ~! handle with care! |
ostrożnoś|ć care[1], carefulness, caution[1], precaution; **środek ostrożności** precautionary measure
ostry 1 (*nóż itp.*) pointed, sharp[1] **2** (*ból*) acute **3** (*zapach*) acrid, pungent; (*jedzenie*) hot[1], spicy; ~ **smak** sharpness **4** (*dźwięk*) shrill **5** (*ścierny*)

abrasive **6** (*krytyka, uwaga*) cutting[2], fierce, harsh, scathing, sharp[1], strident; (*opis*) gritty; ~ **atak** broadside **7** (*wzrost*) drastic, steep **8** (*broń*) live[2]
ostryga oyster
ostrzał bombardment IDM **znaleźć się/być pod ~em krytyki** be in the firing line, come/be under fire
ostrzałka sharpener
ostrz|e 1 (*noża itp.*) blade, edge[1], knife[1]; (*szpikulec itp.*) spike **2** (*ataku itp.*) prong IDM **być na ~u noża** come to a head
o-strzegać/strzec alert[2], caution[2], warn; (*zawczasu*) forewarn
ostrzegawczy cautionary
ostrzel(iw)ać bombard; (*pociskami*) shell[2]
ostrzeżenie caution[1], notice[1], warning; (*zawczasu*) advance warning, forewarning
ostrzyc (się) → STRZYC (SIĘ)
ostrzyć/na-/za- grind[1], hone, sharpen
ostudzić → STUDZIĆ
ostygnąć → STYGNĄĆ
o-suszać/suszyć (*bibułą*) blot[1]
■ **osuszanie** (*terenów podmokłych*) reclamation
o-suwać/sunąć się give[1]
o-swajać/swoić tame[2]
oswo-badzać/bodzić free[2], liberate, release[1]
oswobodzenie freedom, liberation, rescue noun
oswobodziciel/ka liberator
oswojony domesticated, tame[1]
oszacowanie appraisal, assessment; (*w przybliżeniu*) estimate[1]; (*wartości*) valuation
oszacow(yw)ać zob. też SZACOWAĆ; appraise, gauge[2], value[2]; (*w przybliżeniu*) estimate[2]
oszalały crazy, demented, frantic, mad; (*z powodu narkotyków, alkoholu itp.*) out of/off your head
oszaleć zob. też SZALEĆ; go mad; ~ **z zachwytu** go into ecstasies, go wild with excitement
o-szałamiać/szołomić bewilder, stun, stupefy
oszczep javelin
oszczerczy defamatory, slanderous
oszczerstw|o aspersions, scandal; (*werbalne*) slander; **obrzucać ~ami** defame
oszczędność 1 (*oszczędne używanie*) cut[2], cutback, economy, saving; ~ **energii** the conservation of energy **2** (*cecha osoby*) frugality, thrift **3** (**oszczędności**) savings
oszczędny 1 (*urządzenie itp.*) economical **2** (*osoba itp.*) frugal, sparing, thrifty
oszczę-dzać/dzić 1 (*pieniądze, czas, gaz itp.*) save[1]; (*energię*) conserve; (*ograniczyć wydatki/używanie czegoś*) economize; (*wysiłki, wydatki itp.*) spare[2] no effort, expense, etc.; **oszczędzający pracę** labour-saving **2 komuś czegoś** spare[2] sb (from) sth/doing sth, sb/sth (from sth)
oszkalować → SZKALOWAĆ
oszklić → SZKLIĆ
oszołomić → OSZAŁAMIAĆ
oszołomieni|e bewilderment; **w ~u** in a daze/dream
oszołomiony bewildered, dazed, flabbergasted, staggered, stunned; **całkowicie** ~ in a complete daze
oszpe-cać/cić deface
oszroniony frosty
oszukańczy deceitful, fraudulent, underhand
oszukaństwo trickery
oszuk(iw)ać 1 cheat[1] (at sth); ~ **na cenie** overcharge **2 kogoś** cheat[1], deceive, delude, kid[2], trick verb; **na coś** defraud, diddle sb (out of sth); (*wciskać tandetę*) fob sb off (with sth); ~ **samego siebie** flatter yourself (that)
IDM **oszukać głód** stave off hunger
oszust/ka cheat[2], con man, crook, fake[1], fraud, rogue[2], swindler; (*w zamkniętej organizacji itp.*) impostor
oszustwo con[1], deceit, deception, dishonesty, fraud; (**oszustwa**) (*komercyjne*) racket, scam; (*sprzedaż za wygórowaną cenę*) rip-off; (*w księgach rachunkowych*) fiddle[2]; ~ **podatkowe** a tax swindle
oszwindlować → SZWINDLOWAĆ
oś 1 axis, pivot[1] **2** (*w samochodzie*) axle
ościenny neighbouring
oścież: **otwarty na** ~ wide open
ość bone[1]
oślep (*przeprowadzany*) **na** ~ indiscriminate
oślepi(a)ć (*i przen.*) blind[2]; (*światłem*) dazzle
oślepiający blinding, dazzling, glaring; ~ **blask** glare[2]
ośli: **z ~mi uszami** dog-eared
o-śmielać/śmielić się: **nie ośmielić się czegoś zrobić** not have the confidence to do sth
o-śmieszać/śmieszyć make a mockery of sth; (*zwł. w sztuce itp.*) satirize; **kogoś** put sb down
■ **ośmieszający** (*spojrzenie, krytyka itp.*) withering
ośmioboczny octagonal
ośmiobok octagon
ośmiokąt octagon
ośmiokątny octagonal
ośmiornica octopus
ośrodek 1 centre[1]; ~ **kultury** community centre; ~ **sportowy** sports centre **2** (*zainteresowania*) focus[2]
oświad-czać/czyć affirm, profess, pronounce (on sth), state[3]
□ **oświad-czać/czyć się** propose (to sb)
oświadczenie affirmation, declaration, statement; ~ **dla prasy** press release
oświadczyny proposal
oświata education
oświe-cać/cić enlighten
oświecony enlightened
oświet-lać/lić illuminate, light[3], light sth up, shine[1]
oświetlenie illumination, light[1], lighting
o-taczać/toczyć encircle, engulf, ring[2], surround; (*ogrodzeniem*) enclose; **park jest otoczony murem** the park has a wall all around
■ **otaczający** ambient, surrounding
otaksow(yw)ać value[2] sth (at sth)
■ **otaksowanie** valuation
otarcie 1 (*na skórze*) graze[2] **2** (*łez itp.*) dab[2]
otchłań abyss
otępi(a)ć stupefy
■ **otępiający** mind-numbing | **otępienie** dullness, stupor; **otępienie umysłowe** dementia
oto here[1]; (*na coś blisko mówcy*) this is; (*na coś dalej od mówcy*) that is; **a ~ nazwiska zwycięzców zawodów** the following are the winners of the competition
otoczak pebble
otoczenie 1 (*naturalne, ludzkie itp.*) atmosphere, environment, scene, surroundings; ~ **społeczne** social setting **2** (*przestępcy przez policję w jakimś budynku itp.*) siege
otoczyć → OTACZAĆ
otóż well[3]
otręby roughage; (*pszenne itp.*) bran
otrucie poisoning
otruć → TRUĆ
o-trząsać/trząsnąć się: **(z czegoś)** shake sb/sth off
otrzeć (się) → OCIERAĆ (SIĘ)
otrzeźwi(a)ć (się) sober (sb) up
■ **otrzeźwiający** sobering
otrzeźwieć sober up
otrzymanie receipt
otrzym(yw)ać get, obtain, receive; (*form.*) acquire; ~ **wiadomość (od kogoś)** hear (sth) from sb
■ **otrzymany** forthcoming
otuch|a comfort[1]; **dodawać ~y** cheer[2], comfort[2], perk sb up; **dodający ~y** uplifting; **nabierać ~y** buck up; **nabraliśmy ~y** our spirits lifted; **tracić ~ę** your heart sinks
otu-lać/lić wrap sth round/around sb/sth; (*pierzyną w łóżku*) tuck sb in/up; (*dla ochrony*) cocoon[2] sb/sth (in sth)
otulina jacket
otumanienie haze
otwartość bluntness, candour, frankness, openness, outspokenness
otwart|y 1 (*niezamknięty; niezakończony*) open[1]; (*dyskusja*) open-ended **2** **~a przestrzeń** wide open spaces **3** (*szczery*) candid, demonstrative, forthcoming, forthright, frank, open[1], plain[1]; (*zwolennik*) avowed, overt; (*krytyka itp.*) hard-hitting **4** (*toleracyjny*) **(na coś)** receptive, open to sth; **o ~ym umyśle** open-minded IDM **dzień ~ych drzwi** open day | **z ~ymi ramionami** with open arms
otwieracz opener; ~ **do butelek** bottle-opener; ~ **do konserw** tin-opener
o-twierać/tworzyć open[2]; (*interes, sklep itp.*) open sth up; (*plik komputerowy*) access[2]; (*przez opuszczenie*) roll sth down; ~ **okno** (*w samochodzie*) wind sth down; **gwałtownie otworzyć** burst sth open; ~ **drzwi** open up; **otworzyć drzwi (w odpowiedzi na pukanie lub dzwonek)** answer the door; ~ **kluczem** unlock; ~ **książkę na danej stronie** turn to sth; ~ **parasol** put an umbrella up IDM ~ **ogień** open fire (at/on sb/sth)
□ **o-twierać/tworzyć się** open[2], open up; **gwałtownie się otworzyć** burst open

otwór gap, hole, opening, slot[1]; ~ **w ścianie** hatch[2]; ~ **wentylacyjny** vent
otyłość obesity
otyły obese, stout
otynkować → TYNKOWAĆ
outing: **dokonywać ~u (na kimś)** out[2]
owacja ovation
owad insect
owadobójczy: **środek** ~ insecticide
owak: **tak czy** ~ anyway
owaki: **taki** ~ so-and-so
owalny oval
owc|a sheep; **samica ~y** ewe
owczarek sheepdog; ~ **niemiecki** Alsatian; ~ **szkocki** collie
owczarnia fold[2]
owcz|y: **~a skóra** sheepskin
owdowiał-y/a widowed
owerol overall[2]
owies oats
o-wijać/winąć wind[3]; **(wokół czegoś)** twist[1] (sth) (round/around sth); **kogoś/coś (w coś)** drape sth round/over sth, swathe verb sb/sth (in sth), tuck sth in/under/round, etc. (sth), wrap sth round/around sb/sth IDM ~ **w bawełnę** beat about/around the bush
□ **o-wijać /winąć się**: **(wokół czegoś)** twist[1] (round/around sth)
owładnięty: ~ **panicznym lękiem** panic-stricken
owłosiony hairy
owo IDM **to i** ~ this and that, this, that and the other
owoc 1 fruit **2** (**owoce**) (*pracy*) the fruits (of sth) IDM **~e morza** seafood
owocny fruitful, productive
owrzodzenie 1 (*stan owrzodzenia, zaczerwienienie*) soreness **2** (*owrzodzone miejsce na ciele*) sore[2]
owsianka porridge
owszem yes
owulacja ovulation
ozdabi(a)ć adorn, decorate, embellish; ~ **brzegi** trim[1]
ozdoba adornment, decoration, frill, ornament
ozdobny decorative, fancy[3], ornamental, ornate
oziębłość coldness
oziębły 1 chilly, cold[1], cool[1] **2** (*płciowo*) frigid
oznaczać 1 (**/oznaczyć**) (*pokazywać znakiem*) mark[1], mark sth out; (*własnym inicjałem/imieniem/znakiem itp.*) personalize; (*naszywką, etykietką itp.*) label[2] **2** (*znaczyć*) amount[2] to sth, denote, indicative (of sth), mean[1], represent, signify, stand for sth, symbolize; **co oznacza „C"w (skrócie) BBC?** what's the 'C' for in 'BBC'?
oznaczenie marking; ~ **tonacji** key signature
oznajmi(a)ć state[3]; (*podniesionym głosem*) announce
oznak|a indication, mark[2], sign[1], stamp[1]; (*urzędu, zamożności itp.*) trappings; (*jakiegoś uczucia*) stirring; **być ~ą czegoś** indicate, be indicative of sth
oznakow(yw)ać mark[1]
ozon ozone
ozonow|y: **warstwa ~a** the ozone layer
ozorek tongue
ozór (*potrawa*) tongue
ożenić się → ŻENIĆ SIĘ
oży(wa)ć comes alive
ożywczy bracing, inspiring
ożywi(a)ć enliven, exhilarate, jazz sth up, liven sb/sth up, pep sb/sth up, revive, stimulate
□ **ożywi(a)ć się** come to life, liven up, perk up; (*twarz*) light up
ożywiający exhilarating, refreshing
ożywienie 1 (*reanimacja*) resuscitation **2** (*podniecenie*) activity, animation, effervescence, lift[2]; **radosne** ~ exhilaration **3** (*zainteresowania; ekonomiczne itp.*) revival; ~ **gospodarcze** economic recovery
ożywiony alive, lively; (*tempo*) brisk; (*osoba; rozmowa itp.*) animated; (*osoba*) bright, bubbly, effervescent; (*zwł. dziecko, zwierzę*) frisky; (*rozmowa itp.*) heated, spirited

Ó

ósemka 1 figure of eight **2** (*muz.*) quaver[2]
ósmy eighth
ówczesny contemporary[1]
ówdzie IDM **tu i** ~ here and there

P

p (**P/p**) P, p
pa: **~!** bye
pacha 1 (*anat.*) armpit, underarm **2** (*koszuli*) armhole
pachnący fragrant, scented
pachnieć/za- 1 smell[1] (of sth) **2** (*przen.: czymś nieprzyjemnym*) smack of sth
pachołek cone
pachwina groin
pacierz prayer; **mówić** ~ say your prayers
pacierzowy spinal
pacior|ek bead; (*oczy*) **jak ~ki** beady
pacjent/ka patient[1]; ~ **ambulatoryjn-y/a** outpatient
packa trowel
pacnąć (*czymś płaskim*) swat
pacyfist-a/ka conscientious objector, pacifist
pacyfizm pacifism
paczk|a 1 (*pocztowa*) pack[2], package, parcel; **robić ~ę** parcel sth up **2** (*ludzi*) bunch[1], crowd[1]; (*przyjaciół*) gang[1]
paczkować (*towar*) parcel sth up
paczuszka pack[2], packet
paczyć/wy- (się) 1 (*drewno*) warp **2** (*przen.*) distort, pervert[1], twist[1], warp
paćkać/za- mess[2], mess sth up, smear[1], smudge
padaczka epilepsy
pa-dać/ść 1 fall[1]; (*z wyczerpania*) collapse[1], flake out, flop[1] **2** (**/spaść**) (*deszcz*) rain[2]; (*śnieg*) snow[2]; (*grad*) hail[1] **3** (*światło*) shine[1] IDM **paść trupem** drop dead
padlina carcass
padlinożerca scavenger
padnięty zonked
padok paddock
pager bleeper, pager
pagórek hill
pagórkowaty hilly
pajacyk (*ubranie*) Babygro
pająk spider
pajda hunk, slab
pajęczyna cobweb, web
paka crate
pakiet package; ~ **informacyjny** information pack
pakowacz/ka packer
pakować/za- pack[1]; (*do wysyłki*) package; (*owijać*) wrap; ~ **do pudełka** box[2]; ~ **coś przed odjazdem** pack up, pack sth up
□ **pakować/za- się** pack[1]; ~ **przed odjazdem** pack up IDM ~ **się w tarapaty** stay out of trouble
pakowy: **papier** ~ wrapping paper
pakt pact
pakunek pack[2], package, parcel
pal pole; (*podpórka*) prop[1]; (*konstrukcyjny*) stilt
palacz/ka (*papierosów*) smoker
palant jerk[2]
palący 1 (*problem itp.*) burning **2** (*jedzenie*) hot[1]
pal|ec 1 (*u ręki*) finger[1]; **~ec wskazujący** the forefinger/index finger; **~ec środkowy** middle finger; **duży ~ec** thumb **2** (*u nogi*) toe[1]; **wielki ~ec u nogi** big toe; **chodzić na ~cach** tiptoe[2]; **na ~cach** (*stawać/chodzić*) on tiptoe IDM **patrzeć przez ~ce** connive at sth, overlook
palenie 1 (*tytoniu*) smoking; (*papierosa*) smoke[1] **2** (*ból*) sting[2]
palenisko fireplace, grate[1], hearth
paleta palette
palić 1 (**/s-**) burn[1]; ~ **w piecu** stoke a furnace **2** (**/wy-**) (*tytoń*) smoke[2]; (*papieros*) puff on sth; (*fajkę*) puff[1]; **nie** ~ no smoking; ~ **nałogowo** (*jednego papierosa za drugim*) chain-smoke **3** (*zakłuć*) sting[1] IDM **palą kogoś uszy** sb's ears are burning | **spalić na panewce** come unstuck
□ **palić/za- się 1** burn[1], be on fire **2** (*światło itp.*) be on, burn[1] **3 do czegoś** be bursting to do sth; **palący się do czegoś** anxious to do sth; **nie za bardzo palący się do jakiegoś pomysłu** not be very keen on the idea of doing sth
palik stake[1]
palikować stake sth out
paliwo fuel[1]; (*płynne*) petrol; ~ **stałe** solid fuel; ~ **pochodzenia organicznego** fossil fuel
palma palm[1]
palmtop palmtop
palnik ring[1]; ~ **Bunsena** Bunsen burner
paln|y inflammable; **broń ~a** gun[1]
palto coat[1], overcoat
paluszek (*słony, kruchy itp.*) breadstick; ~ **rybny** fish finger
pała nut
pałac mansion, palace
pałąkowat|y: **~e nogi** bow legs; **o ~ych nogach** bow-legged
pałeczka 1 stick; ~ **sztafetowa** baton **2** (*do perkusji*) drumstick **3** (*do jedzenia*) chopstick
pałka club[1]; ~ **policyjna** truncheon; ~ **wodna** bulrush
pamflet satire
pamiątka memento, reminder; (*historyczna*) relic; (*z wakacji*) souvenir; (*pamiątkowy drobiazg*) novelty; (**pamiątki**) (*z danego okresu, środowiska itp.*) memorabilia; ~ **rodzinna** heirloom
pamiątkowy commemorative
pamię|ć recollection; (*i komputerowa*) memory; **na ~ć** by heart; **uczyć się na**

~**ć** memorize; **uczenie się na** ~**ć** rote; **ku** ~**ci kogoś** in memory/ remembrance of sb; (*zsumować*) **w** ~**ci** in your head; ~**ć ROM** ROM; ~**ć podręczna** (*komput.*) cache[1]; **zapisywać w** ~**ci podręcznej/cache** cache[2]; ~**ć przenośna** USB; **uczczenie** ~**ci** remembrance; **wymazać coś z** ~**ci** block sth out IDM (*zakochać się*) **bez** ~**ci** head over heels (in love)
pamiętać/za- recollect, remember; **że/o czymś** bear in mind (that), bear/ keep sb/sth in mind; **nie** ~ forget; **pamiętający o czymś** mindful of sb/ sth, that...
pamiętnik diary, journal; (**pamiętniki**) memoirs
pamiętny memorable
pan 1 (*mężczyzna*) gentleman; **wielki** ~ lord, noble[2]; ~ **młody** bridegroom **2** (**Pan**) (*tytuł*) Mr; (**Panowie**) Messrs **3** (*przy zwracaniu się do nieznanego mężczyzny*) you; (*form.*) sir; (*zwrot grzecznościowy w liście do mężczyzny lub mężczyzn*) sir **4** (*właściciel*) master[1]
pana 1 (*z rz.*) your **2** (*bez rz.*) yours
panaceum panacea
pancernik 1 (*zool.*) armadillo **2** (*okręt*) battleship
pancerz (*żółwia*) shell[1]
panda panda
panegiryk eulogy
panel panel
panew|ka IDM **spalić na** ~**ce** come unstuck
pani (*rz.*) **1** (*kobieta*) lady; **wielka** ~ noble[2] **2** (**Pani**) (*tytuł*) Ms; (*zamężna*) Mrs **3** (*przy zwracaniu się do nieznanej kobiety*) you; (*form.*) madam; (*zwrot grzecznościowy w liście do kobiety lub kobiet*) madam **4** (*właścicielka*) mistress
■ **pani 1** (*określnik*) you **2** (*zaimek*) yours
panicz master[1]
paniczny: ~ **strach** terror
panienka girl, lass
panieński: **nazwisko** ~**e** maiden name; ~ **wieczór** hen party
panierka coating
panierowany breaded
panik|a panic, scare[2]; **sianie** ~**i** scaremongering
panikarski alarmist
panika-rz/ra alarmist, scaremonger
panikować/s- freak[2] (out), panic verb
panna 1 (*dziewczyna*) maiden; ~ **młoda** bride; **stara** ~ spinster **2** (*tytuł*) Miss **3** (**Panna**) (*znak zodiaku*) Virgo
panorama panorama; (*miasta itp.*) skyline; **piękna** ~ vista
panoramiczny panoramic
panować 1 (*król itp.*) reign, rule[2] **2** (**/za-**) **nad kimś/czymś** control[2], master[2]; **zapanować nad sytuacją** take command of a situation; ~ **nad klasą** keep control of your class, keep a firm grip on a class; ~ **nad swoimi uczuciami** keep your feelings under control; ~ **nad sobą** control your temper, exercise self-restraint **3** (**/za-**) (*istnieć*) be **4** (**/za-**) (*mieć przewagę*) predominate, prevail; (*aktor itp.*) ~ **niepodzielnie** reign supreme
pantera panther
pantof|el slipper; ~**le domowe** indoor shoes IDM **pod czyimś** ~**lem** henpecked, under sb's thumb
pantoflarz: **być** ~**em** be henpecked
pantomima mime
pański 1 (*z rz.*) your **2** (*bez rz.*) yours
państwa 1 (*z rz.*) your **2** (*bez rz.*) yours
państwo 1 (*polit.*) nation, state[1]; ~ **opiekuńcze** welfare state; ~ **policyjne** police state **2** (*osoby*) you
państwowy national[1], state[1,2]
papa pop[1]
papaja papaya
papcio pop[1]
papier 1 paper; ~ **listowy** notepaper, writing paper; ~ **milimetrowy** graph paper; ~ **pakowy** brown paper, wrapping paper; ~ **ścierny** sandpaper; ~ **toaletowy** toilet paper; ~ **woskowany** greaseproof/wax paper **2** (**papiery**) (*dokumenty*) papers, paperwork
papierki (*nudne dokumenty, reklama itp.*) bumf
papiernia paper mill
papierniczy: **sklep** ~ stationer's
papieroch fag
papieros cigarette; **wyjść na** ~**a** go outside for a smoke
papież pope
papilot curler
papka mush, pulp
papkowaty gooey
papla blabbermouth, chatterbox
paplać babble[2], blabber, chatter, natter, prattle
paplanina babble[1], chatter noun, natter noun, prattle
paproć (także **paprotka**) fern
papryka 1 (*warzywo*) pepper[1]; ~ **chilli** chilli **2** (*przyprawa*) paprika
papuga 1 parrot **2** (*przen.*) copycat; **jak** ~ parrot-fashion
papużka: ~ **falista** budgerigar
par peer[1]; **godność** ~**a**; **zgromadzenie** ~**ów** peerage
pa|ra 1 (*dwie osoby/rzeczy*) a couple of people/things, etc., pair[1]; ~**rami**; **w** ~**rach** in pairs; **w** ~**rze (z kimś/ czymś)** hand in hand, in tandem (with sb/sth); **nie do** ~**ry** odd; **dobierać do** ~**ry** pair (sb) off (with sb) **2** (*małżonków, narzeczonych itp.*) couple[1] **3** (*wodna*) steam[1], vapour; **gotować na** ~**rze** steam[2]; **garnek do gotowania na** ~**rze** steamer IDM **nie puszczać** ~**ry z ust** (not) breathe a word (of/about sth) (to sb) | **pełną** ~**rą** at full stretch
parabola parabola
parać się: ~ **(czymś)** dabble
parada pageantry, parade, pomp
paradoks irony, paradox
paradoksalny ironic, paradoxical
paradować swagger
paradygmat paradigm
paradygmatyczny paradigmatic
parafia parish
parafialny parochial
parafian-in/ka parishioner; (**parafianie**) congregation, parish
parafować initial[3]
parafraza paraphrase noun
parafrazować/s- paraphrase
paragon receipt
paragraf clause
paraliż 1 (*med.*) paralysis; ~ **dziecięcy** polio **2** ~ **komunikacyjny** gridlock
paraliżować/s- 1 cripple[1], paralyse **2** (*przen.*) numb verb
paralotniarstwo paragliding
paramilitarny paramilitary
paranoiczny paranoid
paranoidalny paranoid
paranoja paranoia
parapet ledge, sill; ~ **okienny** windowsill
parapetówka house-warming (party)
parasol (także **parasolka**) (*od deszczu*) umbrella; (*od słońca*) parasol
parawan cover[2], screen[1]
parcela lot[3], plot[1]
parcelować/roz- partition verb
parch mange
parcie pressure
parecznik (*Chilopoda*) centipede
parę a couple of people/things, etc., a few, several
parias pariah
pariodować/s- take sb off
park gardens[1], grounds[1], park[1]; ~ **narodowy** national park; ~ **rozrywki** amusement park; (*oparty na jednym pomyśle/temacie*) theme park
parkan fence[1]
parkiet parquet
parking car park
parkingowy (*osoba*) car park attendant
parkomat parking meter
parkometr parking meter
parkować/za- park[2]; ~ **na drugiego** double-park
parkowanie parking; ~ **zabronione** No Parking
parlament parliament
parlamentarny parliamentary
parlamentarzyst-a/ka parliamentarian
parny muggy, sultry, sweaty
parodi|a 1 parody; (*filmu, powieści itp.*) spoof; (*jakiejś postaci*) impression; **robić** ~**ę z czegoś** make a mockery of sth **2** (*sprawiedliwości itp.*) travesty
parodiować imitate, parody verb, send sb/sth up
■ **parodiowanie** impression, mimicry
parować 1 (**/wy-**) evaporate **2** (**/za-**) steam[2]; **okna są zaparowane** the windows are covered in condensation
parowiec steamer
parowóz engine
parów ravine
parówka frankfurter, sausage
pars-kać/nąć snort; **parsknąć śmiechem** crack up, hoot[1]
parszywy lousy, vile
partacz cowboy
partaczyć/s- botch sth (up), bungle, cock sth up, make a hash of sth, mess sth up, muck sth up
partanina cock-up
parte|r ground/bottom floor; (*teatr*) **miejsca na** ~**rze** the stalls[1]
partia 1 (*polit.*) party; **Partia Demokratyczna** the Democratic Party; **Partia Konserwatywna** the Conservative Party; **Partia Pracy** the Labour Party; **Partia Republikańska** the Republican Party **2** (*szachów, w grze w karty itp.*)

game[1]; (*golfa, brydża itp.*) round[4] **3** (*rzeczy*) batch, lot[3]
partner/ka partner; **być partner-em/ką** partner verb
partnerski (*zwł. mężczyzna*) domesticated
partnerstwo partnership
partycypować participate
partykuła particle
partytura score[1]
partyzantka 1 (także **partyzant**) guerrilla, partisan[2] **2** (**partyzantka**) guerrilla warfare
parytet parity
parzyć 1 (**/o-**) (*kaleczyć: słońce*) burn[1]; (*gorąca woda*) scald **2** (**/za-**) (*herbata itp.*) infuse **3** (**/o-/po-**) (*pokrzywa*) sting[1] **4** (*zool.*) mate[2]
□ **parzyć/o-/s- się 1** burn[1] **2** (*zool.*) mate[2]
parzysty (*liczba*) even[1]
pas 1 (*do spodni itp.*) belt[1]; **~ do pończoch** suspender belt; **~ wyszczuplający** girdle; **~ bezpieczeństwa** seat belt; **~ ratunkowy** lifebelt **2** (*talia*) middle[1], waist, waistline **3** (*smuga koloru itp.*) band **4** (*fragment drogi*) **~ ruchu** carriageway, lane; **~ drogi przeznaczony dla wolniejszego ruchu** inside lane; **~ jezdni dla ruchu rowerowego** cycle lane; **~ startowy/do lądowania** airstrip; **~ startowy** runway **5** (**pasy**) (*na ulicy*) zebra crossing **6** (*obszar*) belt[1]; **~ ziemi** (*zwł. zebranych plonów/ściętych roślin*) swathe IDM **poniżej ~a** below the belt
pasaż: **~ handlowy** arcade; **wąski, odkryty ~** (*między budynkami*) alley
pasażer/ka passenger; **~ na gapę** stowaway
Pasch|a: **święto ~y** (*w religii żydowskiej*) Passover
pasek 1 (*do spodni itp.*) belt[1], strap; (*wszyty*) waistband; **~ do zegarka** watch strap **2** (*koloru itp.*) band, streak[1], strip[2], stripe; **w paski** striped IDM **~ klinowy** fan belt | **~ menu** menu bar | **~ narzędzi** toolbar | **~ do przewijania** scroll bar
pasemko (**pasemka**) (*na włosach*) highlights[2]
pasiasty striped
pasierb stepson
pasierbica stepdaughter
pasikonik grasshopper
pasja 1 (*zamiłowanie*) passion **2** (*gniew*) violence
pasjans patience
pasjonat fiend
pasjonować absorb
pasjonujący absorbing, compulsive, consuming, gripping, mind-blowing, stirring adj., thrilling
paskudny foul[1], horrible, horrific, nasty, ugly, wretched; (*nieform.*) cruddy, rotten, yucky IDM **być ~m** be the pits
paskudzić/na- mess[2]
pasmanteria haberdashery
pasmo 1 (*koloru itp.*) strip[2] **2** (*ruchu*) lane **3** (*radio*) bandwidth
pasować 1 (*być odpowiednim*) belong, blend (in) with sth, go[1], go together, go with sth, hang together, harmonize, be in line with sth, match[2], match up (with sth), suit[2]; **Bill i Sam dobrze pasują do siebie** Bill and Sam are a good match; **nie ~ (do czegoś)** clash[1], be at odds (with sth); **zupełnie do siebie nie pasują** they're completely incompatible; **pasujący (do siebie)** matching; **(nie)pasujący (do czegoś)** in/out of keeping (with sth) **2** (*być odpowiedniego wymiaru/kształtu*) fit[1], slot[2]
pasożyt freeloader, parasite
pasożytować: (na kimś) freeload, sponge off sb
pass|a (*dobra/zła*) streak[1]; **dobra ~a** boom[1]; **mieć złą ~ę** go through a bad patch, have a run of bad luck
pasta (*spożywcza*) paste[1]; **~ do polerowania** polish[1]; **~ do zębów** toothpaste
pastelowy delicate, muted, pastel
pasternak parsnip
pasteryzowany pasteurized
paste-rz/rka shepherd[1]
pastor minister; **kobieta ~** clergywoman
pastoralny pastoral
pastuch cowboy
pastw|a IDM **zostawić kogoś na ~ę losu** leave sb in the lurch
pastwisko pasture
pastylka tablet; **~ do ssania** lozenge
pasywny passive
pasza fodder
paszcza jaw
paszkwil libel; **napisać ~** libel verb
paszport passport
pasztecik pastry, pasty, pie; **~ z nadzieniem z farszu kiełbasianego** sausage roll
pasztet pâté
pasztetowa liver sausage
paść → PADAĆ
paść/na- się graze[1]
pat stalemate
patchwork patchwork
patelnia frying pan
patent patent[1]; **uzyskać ~** patent verb
patentować/o- patent verb
patentowy proprietary
patio patio
patolog pathologist
patologia pathology
patologiczny pathological
patos (*negatywnie*) bombast
patow|y: **sytuacja ~a** stalemate
patriot-a/ka patriot
patriotyczny patriotic
patriotyzm patriotism
patrol patrol[2]
patrolować/s- patrol[1], police[2]
patron/ka: **~ honorow-y/a** patron
patronat patronage; **pod ~em kogoś/czegoś** under the auspices of sb/sth
patroszyć/wy- gut[2]
patrzeć/spojrzeć look[1] (at sth), view[2], watch[1]; **~ w górę** look up; **~ uporczywie** stare; **~ uważnie** follow; **~ na kogoś/coś** (*np. ze złością, z radością*) look on sb/sth with sth; **~ ze złością na kogoś** glare[1] (at sb/sth); **~ komuś prosto w oczy** look sb in the eye; **~ w przyszłość** look ahead (to sth) IDM **~ na kogoś/coś z góry** look down your nose at sb/sth, look down on sb/sth | **~ przez palce** connive at sth, overlook | **~ wilkiem** scowl verb
patyk 1 stick[2] **2** (*pieniądze*) grand[2]
pauza 1 pause[2] **2** (*szk.*) playtime, recess **3** (*interpunkcja*) dash[1] **4** (*przycisk*) pause[2] **5** (*muz.*) rest[2]
paw peacock
pawian baboon
pawilon annexe
paznokieć nail; (*u palca*) fingernail; (*u nogi*) toenail
pazur claw[1], talon
pa|ź (*fryzura*) bob[2]; **ostrzyżony na ~zia** bobbed
październik October
pączek doughnut
pączkować bud
pąk bud
pchać/pchnąć 1 push[1], shove, thrust[1]; **~ do przodu** propel **2** (*nożem*) knife[2], stab[1] IDM **~ kulą** put the shot
□ **pchać się** shoulder[2], shove
pchli: **~ targ** flea market
pchła flea
PCW PVC
pech jinx, misfortune, a stroke of bad luck; **a to ~!** bad/hard luck!, that's tough!; **mieć ~a** be unlucky; **przynosić ~a** jinx verb; **mający ~a** jinxed adj.; **rzecz/osoba przynosząca ~a** jinx
pechowiec unfortunate person
pechowy jinxed adj., tough (on sb), unfortunate, unlucky; **~ dzień** bad hair day, off day
pedagogiczny pedagogic
pedał 1 pedal; **~ gazu** accelerator **2** (*osoba*) ponce[1], queer noun
pedałować pedal verb; **~ do tyłu** back-pedal
pedant/ka pedant
pedanteryjny anal
pedantyczny anal, pedantic
pediatra paediatrician
pediatria paediatrics
pediatryczny paediatric
pedikiur pedicure
pedofil paedophile
pejoratywny pejorative
pejzaż landscape[1]
pekan (*orzech*) pecan
pelargonia geranium
peleryna cloak; (*krótsza*) cape
pelikan pelican
pełen → PEŁNY
pełni|a 1 (*księżyca*) full moon; **w ~** fully, richly, wholeheartedly **2** (*największe nasilenie czegoś: życia itp.*) prime[2]; **~a lata** the height of summer; **w ~ zimy** in the depths of winter
pełnić/s-: **~ funkcję** act[2] as sth; **~ czyjąś funkcję** substitute verb for sb/sth; **pełniący obowiązki** acting[2]
pełnoetatowy full-time
pełnoletność (*prawna do rozpoczęcia współżycia seksualnego*) the age of consent; **osiągnąć ~** come of age
pełnometrażowy full-length
pełnomocnictwo proxy; (**pełnomocnictwa**) plenipotentiary powers; **dawać ~** empower
pełnomocni-k/czka plenipotentiary; (*rządu itp.*) commissioner
pełnomocny plenipotentiary
pełnoprawny (*członek*) paid-up
pełnowartościow|y: **~a dieta** balanced diet
pełnoziarnisty wholegrain
pełn|y (także **pełen**) complete[1], full[1], whole[1]; (*miasto itp.*) crowded; (*gwiazd itp.*) studded (with sth), thick (with sth); (*błędów itp.*) riddled with sth; (*poczucia winy*) ridden[2];

(*niebezpieczeństw*) fraught with sth; (*sukces*) unqualified; ~**e poparcie** wholehearted support; **sala ~a po brzegi** a full house; **na ~y etat** full-time adv.; **na ~ym morzu** out in the open sea
■ **pełn|o**: **do ~a** fill up the tank; **w mieście było ~o plotek** the city was awash with rumours
pełz-ać/nąć **1** crawl[1], creep[1]; (*żmija*) slither **2** **przed kimś** grovel
pełznąć/s- IDM **spełznąć na niczym** come to nothing, not come to anything
penicylina penicillin
penis penis
pens penny
pensja salary; ~ **tygodniowa** wage[1]
pensjonariusz/ka guest, inmate
pensjonat boarding house, guest house
pentagon pentagon
peonia peony
percepcja perception
perfekcja perfection
perfekcjonist-a/ka perfectionist
perfidia treachery
perfidny treacherous
perforacja perforation
perforować perforate
perfumować/wy- scent verb
perfumy perfume
pergamin parchment
periodyczny periodic
periodyk periodical
perkal calico, chintz
perkaty snub[2]
perkusist-a/ka drummer
perkusj|a percussion; **grać na ~i** play the drums
perła pearl
perłowy pearl
permanentny permanent
peron platform
perorować pontificate
Pers/janka Persian
perski Persian adj.; **język** ~ Persian IDM ~**e oko** wink noun
personalny: **dział** ~ personnel
personel personnel, staff, workforce
personifikacja personification
personifikować personify
perspektyw|a **1** (*w rysunku itp.*) perspective **2** (*to, co może być w przyszłości*); (**perspektywy**) (**na coś**) outlook, prospect; **praca bez** ~ dead-end job; **w ~ie** on the horizon IDM **z ~y czasu** in retrospect
perswazja persuasion
pertraktacj|a (także **pertraktacje**) negotiation(s)
pertraktować negotiate
peruka wig
perwersja perversion
perwersyjność perversity
perwersyjny kinky, perverse
peryferie fringe[1], periphery; (*miasta*) outskirts, the suburbs
peryferyjn|y outer, peripheral[1]; (*dot. miasta*) suburban; **urządzenie ~e** (*komput.*) peripheral[2]
perymetr perimeter
pestka **1** (*śliwki itp.*) stone; (*jabłka itp.*) pip; (*migdałów itp.*) kernel **2** (*coś łatwego*) cinch, a piece of cake, pushover
pestycyd pesticide
pesymist-a/ka pessimist
pesymistyczn|y downbeat, pessimistic; ~**e spojrzenie na życie** a jaundiced view of life
pesymizm pessimism
peszyć/s- overawe
pet end[1], stub
petarda banger
petunia petunia
petycja petition
pewien certain, certain pron., one[1]; ~ **siebie** self-confident
pewniak cert, winner
pewnie as likely as not, most/very likely, reliably; (*zachowywać się*) confidently; (*zamknięty itp.*) fast[2]; **iść** ~ stride[1]; ~ **że tak** surely; ~! you bet, sure, sure thing
pewnik certainty
pewno: **na** ~ absolutely, for certain, certainly, definitely, for sure; **na ~ nie!** not likely!; **na** ~ (**coś się zdarzy itp.**) it is certain that…; **na** ~ **zapłaciłam rachunek** I'm sure I did pay the bill; **na** ~ **będą problemy** there are bound to be problems; **na** ~ **zdasz** you're bound to pass the exam, you are sure to pass
pewnoś|ć **1** certainty, certitude, confidence, reliability; **z** (**całą**) ~**cią** bound[1] to do sth, certainly, for certain, easily the best, worst, nicest, etc., God/goodness/Heaven, etc. knows, for sure, surely; **z ~cią jesteś głodny** you must be hungry; **mieć ~ć, że…** make certain of sth; **wiedzieć z całą ~cią** know for a fact **2** ~**ć siebie** assertiveness, assurance, confidence, self-confidence; **nadmierna ~ć siebie** cockiness; **brak ~ci siebie** diffidence, insecurity; **zachowywać się z ~cią siebie** assert; **jej nowa fryzura naprawdę dodała jej ~ci siebie** her new hairstyle is a real confidence booster
pewny **1** certain, clear[1] (about/on sth), confident (of sth/that…), positive (about sth/that…), sure; (*determinacja itp.*) single-minded; (*inwestycja*) sound[3] **2** ~ **siebie** assured, confident, secure[1], sure of yourself; **bardzo** ~ **siebie** self-important; **zbyt** ~ **siebie** cocky **3** (*godny zaufania*) dependable, reliable, trustworthy **4** (*ręka itp.*) steady[1]
pęcherz blister[1] IDM ~ **moczowy** bladder
pęcherzyk: ~ **żółciowy** gall bladder
pęd **1** (*pośpiech*) dash[1], rush[2]; **masowy** ~ (**na oślep**) stampede; **biec ~em** dash[2] **2** (*bot.*) shoot[2], sprout[2]
pędzel paintbrush
pędzić/za- career[2], chase[1], hurtle, nip, pelt, race[2], rush[1], scamper, scurry, scuttle, speed[2], streak[2], tear[2] along/up/down/past, etc., whizz[1]; (*grupę ludzi/zwierząt*) herd[2]; ~ **na oślep** stampede verb
pęk (*kluczy*) bunch[1]
pęk-ać/nąć **1** break[1]; (*balon itp.*) burst[1], puncture; (*pęcherz itp.*) rupture; (*sufit itp.*) crack[1]; (*rura itp.*) fracture; (*szew*) split[1]; ~ **z trzaskiem** pop[2] **2** (*jajko*) hatch[1] **3** (**od/z czegoś**) be bursting (with sth); ~ **ze śmiechu** laugh/scream, etc. your head off, be in stitches IDM **głowa pęka mi z bólu** I've got a pounding headache | **nagle coś we mnie po prostu pękło** suddenly something just snapped
pękaty squat[2]
pępek navel
pępowina umbilical cord
pęseta (a pair of) tweezers
pętać/s- tether[1]
pętl|a loop, noose; **tworzyć/zawiązywać ~ę** loop verb
pH pH
phi: ~! phew
piach sand
piać/za- crow[2]
pian|a foam[1], froth[1]; (*z mydła*) lather; **pokrywać się ~ą** froth[2]; **pies toczył ~ę z pyska** the dog was foaming at the mouth
pianino piano, upright piano
pianist-a/ka pianist
pianka foam[1], froth[1]; ~ **do golenia** shaving cream/foam; ~ **do włosów** mousse
pias|ek (także **piaski**) sand
piasta hub
piastować cradle[2]
piastowanie (*urzędu*) tenure
piastunka nanny
piaszczysty sandy
piąć/ws- się **1** trail[2] **2** ~ **po szczeblach kariery** rise through the ranks to become sth
piątek Friday
piątka (*ocena*) A, a
piąt|y fifth IDM ~**e koło u wozu** white elephant
picer bullshitter
pichcić/u- concoct, knock sth up, whip sth up
pici|e (*alkoholu*) drinking; **czy mogę prosić o coś do ~a?** can I have a drink, please?
pić/wy- **1** drink[2] **2** (*alkohol*) drink[2], imbibe; ~ **dużo** drink heavily; ~ **czyjeś zdrowie** drink to sb/sth; **wypijmy za twoje szczęście!** here's to your happiness!
piec[1] (*rz.*) fire[1]; (*do gotowania*) cooker; (*w stalowni itp.*) furnace; (*do wypalania, suszenia i prażenia*) kiln; ~ **metalowy** stove; ~ **do spalania nieczystości** incinerator
piec/u-[2] (*cz.*) **1** (*z dodatkiem tłuszczu*) roast[1]; ~ **na sucho** bake; ~ **na grillu** grill[2]; ~ **grzanki** toast verb **2** (*oczy itp.*) smart[2]
piechot|a **1** infantry **2** **czy do sklepów można dojść na ~ę?** are the shops within walking distance?; **iść ~ą** walk[1]
piechur/ka walker
piecyk fire[1]; ~ **gazowy** geyser; ~ **metalowy** stove
piecz|a custody; **sprawować nad kimś/czymś ~ę** watch over sb/sth
pieczara cavern
pieczarka mushroom[1]
pieczątka rubber stamp, stamp[1]
pieczeń joint[2], roast[2]
pieczęć **1** (*pieczątka*) stamp[1] **2** (*znak na wosku/laku*) seal[2]
pieczętować **1** (*pieczątką*) stamp[2] **2** (**/za-**) (*znakiem na wosku/laku*) seal[1]
pieczywo: ~ **chrupkie** crispbread
pieg freckle
piegowaty freckled

piekarnia baker's, bakery
piekarnik oven
piekarz baker
piekieln|y (*straszny*) blasted, devilish, a/one hell of a…, hellish; (*ból głowy*) raging; (*żar*) baking
■ **piekielnie** fiendishly; (*znudzony, przemarznięty, wystraszony itp.*) stiff[2]
pieklić się rave[1]
piekło hell IDM **robić komuś ~** give sb hell
pielęgniarstwo nursing
pielęgnia-rz/rka nurse[1]; **~ środowiskow-y/a** district nurse, health visitor; **pielęgniarka szkolna** matron
pielęgnować 1 (*osoby*) nurture; (*zwł. chorego*) nurse[2], tend **2** (**/wy-**) (*rośliny*) cultivate, nurture **3** (*związki, talent itp.*) nurture **4** (*pamięć itp.*) cherish
pielgrzym pilgrim
pielgrzymka pilgrimage
pielić/wy- weed[2]
pieluszka nappy
pieniactw|o: **skłonny do ~a** litigious
pieniądze cash[1], money
pienić/za- się 1 foam[2], froth[2] **2** (*osoba*) bristle[2] (with sth) (at sb/sth), snap[1] (sth) (at sb)
pieniek IDM **mieć z kimś na pieńku** have a bone to pick with sb
pieniężny monetary
pienisty frothy
pień trunk IDM **głuchy jak ~** stone deaf
pieprz pepper[1]; **~ mielony** ground pepper
pieprzyć 1 (**/po-**) (*pieprzem*) pepper[2] **2** (*mówić głupoty*) talking a load of crap **3** (**/s-**) (*partaczyć*) bugger[2], bugger sth up IDM **pieprzmy koszty** bugger the cost
pieprzyk beauty spot, mole
piercing piercing[2]
pierdoły bollocks, crap
pier-dzieć/dnąć fart
pierniczek gingerbread
piernik: **rodzaj ~a** gingerbread
piersiast|y (*kobieta*) **atrakcyjna i ~a** buxom
pierś 1 chest **2** (*kobieca*) breast; (*piersi*) bosom
pierścień ring[1]
pierścionek ring[1]; **~ zaręczynowy** engagement ring
pierwiastek 1 (*chem.*) element **2** (*mat.*) **~ kwadratowy** square root; **~ trzeciego stopnia** cube root
pierwiosnek (*Primula veris*) cowslip; (*Primula vulgaris*) primrose
pierworództw|o: **prawo ~a** birthright
pierwotny 1 (*kultura itp.*) primitive **2** (*las itp.*) primeval **3** (*pierwszy*) original[1]
pierwszeństw|o: **(przed kimś/czymś)** precedence, preference, priority; **mieć ~o** come before sb/sth, override; **dawać ~o komuś/czemuś** give (a) preference to sb/sth; **dawać ~o przejazdu** give way (to sb/sth), yield[1] (to sb/sth); **prawo ~a** right of way
pierwszoroczniak fresher, freshman
pierwszorzędny first-class, first-rate, high-class, prime[1], super; (*żołnierz; sportowiec*) crack[3]
pierwsz|y first[1,2,3]; (*liga; szef kuchni itp.*) premier[1]; **~y (z dwóch)** the former; **~e, co robię** the first thing I do; **~a klasa** first class; **~ej klasy** first-class; **~y dzień Świąt** Christmas; **po raz ~y** first[2]; **z ~ej ręki** first-hand adv.; **z ~ej strony** (*gazety*) front-page IDM **kto ~y, ten lepszy** first come, first served | **~a pomoc** first aid | **po ~e** to begin with, first[2], firstly, in the first place, for one thing, for a start, to start (off) with
pierzasty (*chmury*) wispy
pierzchnąć scamper
pierzyć się moult
pierzyna duvet, eiderdown
pies dog[1]; **~ łańcuchowy (podwórzowy)** guard dog; **~ eskimoski** husky[2]; **~ gończy** hound[1]; **~ przewodnik** guide dog IDM **schodzić na psy** go to rack and ruin
piesek (*styl pływacki*) dog-paddle
pieszczoch pet[1]
pieszczota caress noun
piesz|y pedestrian[1]; **dla ~ych** pedestrian[2]; **~a wycieczka** hike; **~e wycieczki** walking; **robić ~e wycieczki** walk[1]
pieścić caress, fondle; (*seksualnie*) pet[2]
□ **pieścić się** pet[2]
pieśń chant[1], song; **~ żałobna** lament; **~ religijna** hymn
pietruszka parsley
piewik cicada
pięciobok pentagon
pięciobój pentathlon
pięciocentówka nickel
pięciokąt pentagon
pięciolinia (*muz.*) stave[1]
pięć five IDM **ni w ~ ni w dziewięć** irrelevantly
pięćdziesiąt fifty
pięćdziesiąty fiftieth
piękno beauty
piękność beauty
piękny beautiful, fine[1]; (*zwł. dziewczyn(k)a*) bonny; (*zwł. mężczyzna*) handsome
pięś|ć fist; **uderzać ~cią** punch[1]
pięta heel[1] IDM **~ Achillesa** Achilles heel
piętnasty fifteenth
piętnaście fifteen
piętno mark[2], stamp[1] of sth, stigma
piętnować/na- 1 brand[2] **2** (*przen.*) brand[2], stigmatize
piętro floor[1], level[1], storey; (*autobusu*) deck
piętrow|y storey; **autobus ~y** double-decker; **~e łóżka** bunk beds
pif-paf: **~!** bang[4]
pigment pigment
pigułka pill; **~ antykoncepcyjna** the Pill
pijacki drunken
pija-k/czka drinker; **~ (nałogow-y/a)** drunk
pijan|y 1 drunk[1], drunken, inebriated; **~y kierowca** drink-driver; **jazda samochodem po ~emu** drink-driving **2** (*szczęściem itp.*) elated
pijaństwo alcoholism, drinking, drunkenness, inebriation
pijatyka binge[1]
pijawka leech
pik spade
pika spear
pikanteri|a earthiness, spice[1]; **nadawać ~i** spice[2] sth (up)
pikantny 1 (*smak jedzenia*) savoury, sharp[1], spicy **2** (*dowcip, komentarz itp.*) earthy; (*plotka itp.*) juicy; (*powieść itp.*) racy
pikieta picket
pikietować picket verb
pikle pickle
piknik picnic, picnic lunch
pikolo (*muz.*) piccolo
pikować/za- dive[1], nosedive verb
pikowany quilted
piksel pixel
piktogram icon
pilnik file[1]; **~ do paznokci** nail file
pilnować keep a close watch on sb/sth, keep an eye on sb/sth, guard[2], have (got) your eye on sb, mind[2], watch[1] sb/sth (for sth); (*interesów*) look after sb/sth/yourself; (*podczas egzaminu*) invigilate IDM **~ własnego nosa** mind your own business
□ **pilnować się** watch[1]
pilny 1 (*sprawa*) crying, immediate, pressing, urgent **2** (*osoba*) diligent, studious
pilot 1 (także **pilotka**) (*osoba*) flyer, pilot[1]; **~/ka wycieczki** courier **2** (*do telewizora itp.*) remote control
pilotażowy pilot[3]
pilotować navigate, pilot[2], shepherd[2]
pilśń felt[2]
piła saw[2]; **~ łańcuchowa** (electric) chainsaw
piłka ball; **~ futbolowa**; **~ nożna** football
piłkarz footballer
piłować/u-/prze- saw verb
pinakl pinnacle
pinceta tweezers
pinezka drawing pin, tack[1]
ping-pong table tennis
pingwin penguin
pionek 1 (*w warcabach itp.*) counter[1], piece[1]; (*w szachach*) pawn[1] **2** (*przen.: w czyichś rękach*) pawn[1]
pionier/ka pioneer, trailblazer, settler
pionierski pioneering, trailblazing
pionow|y perpendicular, upright, vertical; **orientacja ~a** (*ustawienia strony dokumentu do wydruku*) portrait
piorun lightning[1]; **~ liniowy** forked lightning IDM **~em** like a shot
piorunochron lightning conductor
piorunujący (*błyskawiczny*) lightning[2] IDM **~ wzrok** glaring eyes
piosenka song
piosenka-rz/rka singer
piórko (*do gry na instrumentach muzycznych*) plectrum
piórnik pencil case
pióro 1 (*ptaka*) feather, quill; (*duże i często kolorowe*) plume **2** (*do pisania*) pen; **wieczne ~** fountain pen
pióropusz plume
pipeta (także **pipetka**) pipette
pi-pip: **~!** peep[2]
piracki (*kaseta itp.*) bootleg[1]
piractwo piracy; **uprawiać ~ komputerowe** hack (into) (sth)
piramida pyramid
pirat pirate[1]; **~ komputerowy** hacker
pisać/na-/za- write; (*wyraźnie, każdą literę osobno*) print[1]; **napisać coś w całości** write sth out; **~ na czysto** write sth up; **~ na maszynie/komputerze itp.** type[2]; **~ w pośpiechu i niestarannie** scribble
■ **pisany** IDM **~ jest jej sukces** she is destined for success

□ **pisać się** spell[1]
pisanka Easter egg
pisarstwo writing
pisa-rz/rka writer
pisemn|y written[2]
■ **pisemnie** in writing
pisk screech noun, shriek noun, squeal noun; **cichy** ~ squeak
pisklę chick
piskliwy shrill, squeaky
pism|o script; **charakter ~a** writing; **~o drukarskie** type[1]; **na piśmie** in black and white, on paper, in writing, written[2] IDM **Pismo Święte** scripture
pisnąć → PISZCZEĆ
pisownia spelling
pistacja pistachio
pistacjowy: **orzech** ~ pistachio
pistolet gun[1], pistol; ~ **natryskowy** airbrush
pisuar urinal
pisywać (*artykuły do pisma itp.*) contribute
piszczałka pipe[1]
piszczeć/pisnąć screech, shriek, squeal; **cicho** ~ peep[1], squeak verb, whimper IDM **nie piśnij ani słowa** don't breathe a word of this
piśmienn|y literate; **artykuły ~e** stationery
pitn|y: **woda ~a** drinking water
piwnica basement, cellar
piwny (*oczy*) brownish, hazel[2]
piwo ale, beer; ~ **ciemne** (*o gorzkim smaku*) bitter[2]; ~ **jasne leżakowane** lager
piwonia peony
piwowar brewer
pizza pizza
piżama pyjamas
piżmo musk
piżmowy musky
plac field[1], square[2]; (*zabaw itp.*) ground[1]; (*przed budynkiem*) forecourt; ~ **budowy** building/ construction site; ~ **gier** playing field; ~ **targowy** marketplace; ~ **zabaw** playground
placebo placebo
placek cake[1], flan; ~ **z owocami** tart[1]; **nadziewany** ~ pie
■ **plackiem** (*padać*) flat adv.
placówka outpost; ~ **oświatowa** educational establishment
plaga (*mrówek itp.*) infestation, pest, plague[1]; (*bezrobocia itp.*) blight[2], scourge
plagiat plagiarism; **dokonywać ~u** plagiarize
plagiatorstwo plagiarism
plajtować/s- go bust, go under
plakat broadsheet, placard, poster
plam|a 1 (*tłusta itp.*) blemish, blotch, mark[2], smear[2], smudge noun, splash[2], spot[1], stain noun, taint; **~a ropy** oil slick **2** (*przen.*) blemish, blot[2] **3** (*mała część powierzchni*) patch[1]; (*światła*) pool[1] **4** (**plamy**) marking IDM **dawać ~ę** put your foot in it
plamić/po- 1 mark[1], smudge, soil[2], stain, taint verb **2** (*reputację*) tarnish
□ **plamić/po- się** stain
plamka fleck, mark[2], speck, spot[1]
plan 1 (*zamiar; schemat*) plan[1], programme[1], project[1], schedule[1], scheme[1]; (*rządowy*) blueprint; ~ **lekcji** timetable; ~ **podróży** itinerary; **mieć** ~ have sth in mind **2** (*miasta*) map[1], street map **3** (*na obrazie itp.*) **dalszy** ~ background; **przedni** ~ foreground
planeta planet
planetarium planetarium
planist-a/ka planner
plankton plankton
planować/za- arrange, design[2], figure on sth/on doing sth, line sth up, organize, plan[2], programme[2], project[2], propose, schedule[2], have, etc. sth in view, work sth out
■ **planowanie** organization, planning; ~ **rodziny** family planning
plansza board[1], plate
planszow|y: **gra ~a** board game
plantacja plantation
plaster 1 (*med.*) adhesive[1], plaster[1] **2** (*szynki itp.*) slice[1]; ~ **miodu** honeycomb
plasterek sliver; (*bekonu*) rasher
plastyczność malleability
plastyczn|y 1 (*giętki*) malleable **2 zajęcia ~e** art class **3** (*opis*) vivid **4 chirurgia/operacja ~a** plastic surgery **5 mapa ~a** (*często dwuwymiarowa*) relief map
plastyk plastic[1]
plastykowy plastic[2]
platan sycamore
platform|a 1 ~a kolejowa truck, wagon **2 ~a wiertnicza** oil rig **3** (*wyborcza*) platform IDM **buty na ~ach** platform shoes
platoniczny platonic
platyna platinum
platynowy platinum
plazma plasma
plaża beach
plądrować/s- loot verb, pillage, plunder verb; (*w poszukiwaniu czegoś*) ransack
plątać/po-/za- mix sth up, muddle sth (up)
□ **plątać/za- się 1** (*w zeznaniach itp.*) flounder[1] **2** (*pod nogami, po podłodze itp.*) knock about/around
plątanina mix-up, muddle noun, tangle
plebania vicarage
plecak backpack[1], pack[2], rucksack
plecionka plait noun
pleciuch: **gaduła i pleciuch** big mouth
plec|y 1 (*anat.*) back[1]; **ból ~ów** backache; **siedzieć ~ami do siebie** sit back to back **2** (*przen.: poparcie jakiejś osoby*) favouritism IDM **za czyimiś ~ami** behind sb's back
pled rug
plektron plectrum
plemienny tribal
plemię tribe
plemnik sperm
plenarny plenary
plene|r: **w ~rze** on location
pleść 1 (**/za-/u-**) (*warkocz*) plait **2** (*mówić*) ~ **bzdury** gabble nonsense
pleśń mildew, mould[1]
plewić/wy- weed[2]
plik 1 (*papierów*) bundle[1]; (*banknotów*) wad, sheaf **2** (*komput.*) file[1], folder
plisa (*ozdobna*) frill; (*fałda*) pleat
plisować (*fałdować*) pleat verb
■ **plisowany** (*ozdobiony, zwł. falbankami*) frilly
plomba 1 (*na paczce itp.*) seal[2] **2** (*w zębie*) filling[1]
plon crop[1], yield[2]; (**plony**) harvest; **dawać ~y** crop[2]
plotka gossip, rumour; (**plotki**) scandal
plotkarstwo gossip
plotka-rz/rka gossip
plotkować gossip verb, have a gossip, talk[1]
pluć/o- spit[1] (sth) (out); ~ **krwią** cough (up) blood
plugastwo filth
plugawić/s- defile, taint verb
plugawy filthy, squalid
pluralistyczny pluralist
plus plus[1,2]; **z ~em** plus[3] IDM **mieć ~ u kogoś** be in sb's good books | **~ minus** give or take
plusk plop[1], splash[2]
plus-kać/nąć dabble, lap[2]; (**plusnąć**) plop[2]
pluskiewka drawing pin, tack[1]
pluskw|a 1 (*zool.*) bug[1] **2** (*mikrofon*) bug[1]; **podłożyć ~ę** bug[2]
pluton 1 (*chem.*) plutonium **2** (*wojsk.*) platoon; ~ **egzekucyjny** firing squad **3** (**Pluton**) (*planeta*) Pluto
plwocina spit[2]
płaca pay[2]; **najniższa** ~ minimum wage
płacić 1 (**/za-**) give[1], pay[1]; **za mało** ~ underpay; ~ **rachunek** foot the bill (for sth); **do zapłacenia** payable; ~ **komuś za milczenie** pay sb off **2** (**/s-**) (*odszkodowanie*) settle; (*dług*) settle, settle up (with sb) **3** (*za wyrządzoną krzywdę itp.*) pay[1]
płacz cry[2]
płaczliwy 1 plaintive, tearful **2** (*zbyt ckliwy itp.*) slushy
płakać/za- cry[1], weep
płaski even[1], flat[1], level[2]
płaskorzeźba carving
płaskowyż plateau
płastuga plaice
płaszcz coat[1], jacket, overcoat; ~ **nieprzemakalny** mac, raincoat
płaszczka skate[2]
płaszczyć się: (**przed kimś**) crawl[1] (to sb), grovel
płaszczyk: **pod ~iem czegoś** under the guise of sth
płaszczyzna plane[1]
płat 1 (*tkaniny itp.*) patch[1]; **odpadać ~ami** flake[2] (off) **2** (*mięsa itp.*) cut[2], steak **3** (*anat.*) lobe
płat|ek 1 (*róży itp.*) petal **2** (*cienki kawałek czegoś*) flake[1]; **~ki zbożowe** cereal; **~ki kukurydziane** cornflakes; **~ek śniegu** snowflake **3** (*ucha*) ear lobe
płatn|y due[1], payable; **dobrze ~y** well paid; **~y morderca** hit man; **banda ~ych zabójców** hit squad
pławić się: (**w czymś**) bask, revel in sth/doing sth, wallow
pławik buoyancy aid
płaz amphibian
płciowy sexual; (*narząd*) genital
płeć gender, sex; **płci żeńskiej** female[1]; **płci męskiej** male[1]
płetwa 1 (*ryby*) fin **2** (*foki itp.*) flipper
płetwonurek frogman, skin-diver
płetwonurkowanie skin-diving
płochliwość shyness
płochliwy shy[1]
płodność fertility
płodny 1 fertile **2** (*pisarz itp.*) prolific, productive

płody → PŁÓD
płodzić/s- procreate; (*dziecko*) father[2]
płomienny fiery, impassioned, passionate
płomie|ń blaze[2], flame(s), flare[2]; **w ~niach** ablaze; **stanąć w ~niach** burst into flames
płonąć 1 (/s-; /za-) (*ogień*) blaze[1], burn[1], be in flames **2 (/za-)** (*uczuciem*) burn[1] with sth
■ **płonący** ablaze, alight[1], flaming
płonny vain
płoszyć/s- frighten sb/sth away/off, scare sb/sth away/off, shoo[2] sb/sth away/off/out, etc.
□ **płoszyć/s- się** shy[2]
płot fence[1]
płotek (*sport*) hurdle[1]
płowieć/s-/wy- fade
płowy (*kolor*) fawn[1]
płócienny: ~ **but** (*z gumowymi podeszwami*) plimsoll
płód 1 (*ludzki itp.*) foetus **2 (płody)** (*rolne*) produce[2]
płótno 1 ~ **lniane** linen **2** (*w malarstwie*) canvas **3** (*obraz*) painting
płucny pulmonary
płuco lung
pług plough; ~ **śnieżny** snowplough
płukać/wy-/prze- rinse, swill sth (out/down); ~ **gardło** gargle; **płyn do płukania tkanin** conditioner
płukanka: ~ **do włosów** rinse noun
płycina panel
płyn fluid[1], liquid; ~ **do kąpieli** bubble bath; ~ **do płukania ust** mouthwash; ~ **po goleniu** aftershave; ~ **do zmywania twarzy** cleanser; ~ **do zmywania naczyń** washing-up liquid; ~ **do polerowania** polish[1]; ~ **owodniowy** amniotic fluid
płynąć/po- zob. też PŁYWAĆ; (*w kierunku opisanym*) head[2]
płynność fluency
płynny 1 (*ciekły*) liquid; (*metal*) molten **2** (*ruch; plany*) fluid[2] **3** (*język, styl*) fluent; (*tok rozmowy itp.*) seamless
płyta 1 (*metalowa*) plate; (*z kamieni, betonowa*) slab; (*szklana itp.*) sheet; ~ **gipsowa** plasterboard; ~ **wiórowa** chipboard; ~ **nagrobna** gravestone; ~ **pamiątkowa** plaque; ~ **dentystyczna** (*ze sztucznymi zębami*) plate **2** (*kuchenna*) hob **3** (*muz.*) (*zawierająca nagrania jednego artysty*) album; ~ **kompaktowa** CD; ~ **gramofonowa** record[1]; **ostatnia** ~ **zespołu** a band's latest release
płytka 1 (*powlekana złotem/srebrem*) plate; (*ceramiczna*) tile **2** (*kuchenna*) hob, ring[1] IDM ~ **Petriego** Petri dish
płytki 1 (*płaski*) flat[1], two-dimensional; (*woda; naczynie*) shallow **2** (*osoba itp.*) superficial
płytkość shallowness
pływ-ać/nąć 1 (płynąć) (*woda*) flow[2] **2** (*osoba, zwierzę*) swim; ~ **na desce surfingowej** surf[2] **3** (*statek itp.*) sail[1] **4** (*unosić się na powierzchni wody*) float[1] **5** (*w długach itp.*) be swimming (in/with sth)
■ **pływający** (*unoszący się na powierzchni wody*) buoyant
pływak 1 (także **pływaczka**) swimmer **2** (*u wędki*) float[2]
pływalnia baths[1], swimming bath(s)
pływalność buoyancy
pływowy tidal
pnącze creeper
pneumatyczny inflatable, pneumatic
pniak stump[1]
po 1 (*przestrzeń*) about[1], around[2]; (*ulicy itp.*) along[2]; ~ **drugiej stronie** on the other side **2** (*kolejność, zwł. w czasie*) following[3], on; (*danej godzinie itp.*) gone[3], past[3]; ~ **kimś** after; ~ **czym** since, thereupon, whereupon; **zaraz ~ Paryżu to Kraków jest moim ulubionym miastem** next to Paris my favourite city is Kraków **3** (*granice w czasie*) to **4 każdemu** ~ (*np. złotówce*) apiece, at **5** (*mówić*) in[1]; **jak jest ~ włosku „window"?** what's the Italian for 'window'? **6** (*sposób*) like[1] **7** (*cel*) for; ~ **co** what for; ~ **co próbować?** what's the use of trying?; **kłócicie się tylko ~ to, żeby się kłócić** you're just arguing for the sake of it IDM **i już** ~ bang goes sth
pobawić się → BAWIĆ SIĘ
pobici|e 1 (*użycie przemocy*) battery **2** (*cena itp.*) **nie do ~a** unbeatable
pobić (się) → BIĆ (SIĘ)
pobiec → BIEC
pobie-lać/lić zob. też BIELIĆ; whiten
pobielić
pob(ie)rać 1 pick sth up; ~ **wymaz z gardła** take a throat swab **2** (*opłatę*) charge[2], collect[1], levy; ~ **małą opłatę** make a small charge, charge a small fee
□ **pob(ie)rać się** get married, marry, wed
pobieżność superficiality
pobieżn|y cursory, superficial
■ **pobieżnie** superficially; ~ **czytać** skim (through/over) sth
pobliski nearby, neighbouring
pobliż|e: **w ~u (czegoś)** around, thereabouts, round[3], in the vicinity (of sth); (*tylko przestrzeń*) within (sb's) reach, within walking distance
pobłażać indulge; (*pozwalać na coś złego*) connive at sth
■ **pobłażający sobie** self-indulgent
pobłażliwość lenience
pobłażliwy forgiving, indulgent, lenient, permissive
pobłogosławić → BŁOGOSŁAWIĆ
pobocze hard shoulder, roadside, the side of the road, verge[1]
poboczny extraneous
poborca: ~ **podatkowy/czynszu** tax/rent collector
poborowy (*rz.*) conscript[2]
pobory (*płaca*) pay[2], salary
pobożność devotion, piety
pobożn|y devout, pious, religious IDM **~e życzenia** wishful thinking
pobór 1 (*do wojska*) conscription, recruitment; **przeprowadzać** ~ (*do wojska*) draft[2] **2** (*powietrza itp.*) intake
pobrać się → POBIERAĆ SIĘ
pobrudzić (się) → BRUDZIĆ (SIĘ)
pobrzękiwać (*ciężki metal*) clank; (*o naczyniach itp.*) clatter; (*klucze, łańcuch itp.*) jangle, jingle[2]; (*szkło*) chink[2], clink verb
pobud|ka motive, urge[2]; **dostarczać ~ek** motivate
pobudliwy excitable, prickly
pobu-dzać/dzić arouse, excite, rouse; **kogoś do zrobienia czegoś** galvanize sb (into sth/into doing sth), goad sb/sth (into sth/doing sth), prompt[2], spur[2] sb/sth (on/onto sth); (*napój itp.*) energize; (*uczucie*) stir[1]; (*apetyt*) whet; (*czyjąś pamięć*) jog[1]; (*wyobraźnię itp.*) stimulate; **pobudź swą wyobraźnię!** use your imagination!
■ **pobudzający** stimulating; **środek pobudzający** stimulant
pobujać (się) → BUJAĆ (SIĘ)
pobyt residence, stay[2]
pocałować (się) → CAŁOWAĆ (SIĘ)
pocałunek kiss noun
pochlebca sycophant; (*w stosunku do kogoś bogatego/ważnego*) hanger-on
pochlebi(a)ć flatter
pochlebny complimentary, flattering, glowing
pochlebstwo flattery
pochlipywać snivel
po-chłaniać/chłonąć zob. też CHŁONĄĆ **1** (*wodę itp.*) absorb; (*odkurzacz*) suck sth up **2** (*czas; koszty*) take; (*czas, energię itp.*) take up sth; (*oszczędności itp.*) swallow[1] sth (up) **3** (*ofiary*) claim[1] **4** (*uwagę*) engross, enthral, preoccupy **5** (*jeść/pić łapczywie; książki itp.*) devour; (*pigułkę itp.*) swallow[1] **6** (*komplementy itp.*) lap sth up
pochłonięt|y: **czymś** absorbed, engrossed, full[1] of sb/sth, preoccupied, rapt, in the thick of sth; **być ~ym** (*np. żądzą zemsty*) be consumed by sth; **była ~a lekturą** she was buried in a book; **była tak ~a pracą, że nie usłyszała, jak wszedłem** she was so intent upon her work that she didn't hear me come in
pochmurny cloudy, dull
pochodnia torch
pochodzeni|e 1 descent, extraction, origin; (*społeczne*) background; (*osoby, zwierzęcia*) pedigree[1]; **jest z ~a Irlandczykiem** he is of Irish ancestry **2** (*słowa*) derivation, etymology
pochodzić 1 skądś come from…, emanate from sth; **od kogoś** be descended from sb; (*wynikać*) result[2] (from sth), stem from sth; **skąd pochodzisz?** where do you come from?; **koala pochodzi z Australii** the koala is a native of Australia **2** (*słowo*) derive; **nazwa miasta pochodzi od rzeki** the town derives its name from the river **3** (*przedmiot: z danego okresu*) date back to…, date from…, go back (to sth)
pochopny hasty, premature, rash[2]; (*uwaga itp.*) facile
■ **pochopnie** hastily, rashly; ~ **decydować się na coś** rush[1] (into sth/into doing sth)
poch|ód march[2], procession; (*kolorowy*) pageant; **iść w ~odzie** march[1]
pochuliganić → CHULIGANIĆ
pochwa 1 (*anat.*) vagina **2** (*na broń*) holster, sheath
pochwa-lać/lić approve, commend
pochwalić (się) → CHWALIĆ (SIĘ)
pochwalny appreciative
pochwał|a approval, praise[1]; (*nieform.*) a pat/slap on the back (for sth/doing sth); **oficjalna ~a** citation; **godny ~y** laudable, praiseworthy
pochwycić → CHWYCIĆ
pochy-lać/lić się bend[1], lean[1], slope verb
pochyłość incline[2], slope

pochył|y slanting; **być ~ym** slant[1]; **pismo ~e** italic handwriting, italics
pociąć → CIĄĆ
pociąg 1 train[1]; **~ ekspresowy** express train; **~ osobowy** passenger/stopping/slow train; **~ pospieszny** express[3], fast train; **~ towarowy** goods/freight train; **~ z wagonami sypialnymi** sleeper **2 do kogoś/czegoś** appeal[1], attraction
pociągać zob. też CIĄGNĄĆ **1 (pociągnąć)** (*przesunąć*) pull[1], tweak **2** (*być atrakcyjnym*) draw[1], magnetize **3 (pociągnąć) za sobą** entail, involve IDM **~ nosem** sniff | **~ za sznurki** (*używać wpływów/protekcji*) pull strings
■ **pociągnięci|e 1** pull[2], tweak noun **2** (*pióra, pędzla itp.*) stroke[1]
IDM **jednym pociągnięciem** at a/one stroke
pociągający appealing, inviting, tantalizing
pocić /s- się 1 perspire, sweat **2 (nad czymś)** sweat (over sth)
pociec → CIEC, CIEKNĄĆ
pociecha comfort[1], consolation
pociekną ć → CIEKNĄĆ
pocieniować → CIENIOWAĆ
po-cierać/trzeć rub; **~ zapałkę** light/strike a match
pocie-szać/szyć cheer[2], comfort[2], console[1], hold sb's hand
■ **pocieszający** heartening
pocieszenie consolation, solace
pocisk missile; (*z pistoletu*) bullet; **~ artyleryjski** shell[1]; **~ balistyczny** ballistic missile; **~ kierowany** guided missile
począć (*dziecko*) conceive
począt|ek appearance, beginning, birth, opening, start[2]; (*choroby itp.*) onset; **na ~ku** first[2]; **od ~ku** anew, all along, from scratch; **od (samego) ~ku** from the (very) first, at/from the outset (of sth); **od ~ku do końca** through; **znowu od ~ku** all over again; **zaczynać wszystko od ~ku** make a fresh start; **z ~ku** at first, to begin with; **na/z ~ku** early on; **na ~ku** to start (off) with; **na (samym) ~ku** at/from the outset (of sth)
początkowy early, incipient, initial[1], opening adj.
początkując-y/a (*rz.*) beginner, learner; (*w zawodzie*) entrant
poczekać → CZEKAĆ
poczekalnia waiting room
poczekani|e (*wymyślеć*) **na ~u** off the top of your head
poczęcie conception
poczęstować (się) → CZĘSTOWAĆ (SIĘ)
poczęstunek treat[2]
poczt|a 1 (*listy*) mail, post[1]; (*doręczenie*) delivery; **~a elektroniczna** email; **~a głosowa** voicemail; **~a lądowo-morska** surface mail; **~a lotnicza** airmail; **~ą odwrotną** by return (of post) **2** (*budynek*) post office IDM **~a pantoflowa** the grapevine
pocztowy postal
pocztówka card, postcard
poczucie feeling, sense[1]; **~ humoru** humour[1]; **~ własnej wartości** ego
poczuć (się) → CZUĆ (SIĘ)
poczwara monster, ogre
poczwarka chrysalis
poczynić → CZYNIĆ
poczyt(yw)ać 1 za coś deem **2 (poczytać)** (*na jakiś temat*) read up on sth
pod 1 (*poniżej*) below, beneath, under, underneath; **~ wodą** under adv. **2** (*miastem itp.*) outside[3] **3** (*kierunek*) **~ wiatr** against the wind **4** (*wieczór*) towards **5** (*pseudonimem itp.*) under
podać (się) → PODAWAĆ (SIĘ)
podanie 1 (*o pracę itp.*) application **2** (*piłki*) pass[2]
podaniowy (*formularz, wniosek o coś itp.*) application
podarować → DAROWAĆ
podarty tattered
podarunek gift, present[2]
podat|ek tax; **~ek akcyzowy** excise; **~ek dochodowy** income tax; **~ek drogowy** road tax; **~ek komunalny** council tax; **wolny od ~ku** tax-free
podatnik taxpayer
podatność vulnerability; **~ na czyjś wpływ** malleability
podatn|y 1 (*ulegający czemuś*) liable to do sth; (*na chorobę*) vulnerable; (*na wpływy*) impressionable, malleable, pliable, receptive, susceptible; **uczynić ~ym kogoś na coś** predispose sb to sth **2** (*łatwy do prowadzenia/zarządzania*) manageable
poda(wa)ć 1 give[1], hand[2], hand sth around/round, hold sth out, pass[1]; **~ do stołu** serve, serve sth up; (*zwykle w restauracji*) wait on sb; **~ komuś rękę** shake sb's hand/shake hands (with sb)/shake sb by the hand **2** (*lekarstwo*) administer, dose[2] **3** (*piłkę zawodnikowi*) pass[1] (sth) (to sb) **4 (za kogoś/coś)** pass sb/sth off (as sb/sth), purport **5 ~ kogoś do sądu** sue (sb) (for sth) IDM **~ czas** tell the time
□ **poda(wa)ć się: (za kogoś/coś)** make yourself out to be sth, masquerade as sth, pass yourself off (as sb/sth); **za kogoś innego** impersonate
podaż: **~ i popyt** supply and demand
podbicie 1 (*anat.*) arch[1] **2** (*palta itp.*) lining, padding
pod-biegać/biec run up to sb/sth
podbiegunowy polar
pod-bierać/ebrać siphon sth off
podbi(ja)ć conquer IDM **~ czyjeś serce itp.** make a hit (with sb)
podbit|y: **~y obszar** conquest; **~e oko** black eye
podb|ój conquest; **~oje sercowe** romantic conquests
podbródek chin
podbu-rzać/rzyć incite
podchmielony merry, tipsy
podchodzić/podejść 1 approach[1], walk up (to sb/sth); **podejdź tu** come (over) here **2** (*zwierzynę*) stalk[2] **3** (*do problemu itp.*) approach[1]
podchwytliw|y loaded; **~e pytanie** trick question
pod-cinać/ciąć 1 (*nożem itp.*) slice[2], trim; **podciął sobie żyły** he slit his wrists **2** (*działalność konkurencji metodą wojny cenowej*) undercut
IDM **~ komuś nogę** trip[2] sb (up)
podczas during, over; **~ gdy** when, whereas, while[1], with
podczerwony infrared
poddan|y 1 być ~ym czemuś come in for sth **2** (*także* **poddana**) subject[1]
poddasz|e attic, loft; **na ~u** in the roof
podda(wa)ć: kogoś czemuś subject sb to sth; **~ komuś myśl** put it to sb that…; **~ pod dyskusję** moot verb; **~ próbie** try sb/sth out (on sb)
□ **podda(wa)ć się** give up, submit, surrender; (*w sporze itp.*) cave in; **czemuś** undergo; (*presji itp.*) yield[1]; **komuś/czemuś** give in (to sb/sth), give way (to sb/sth), knuckle under (to sb/sth); **nie ~** bear up; **nie ~ (czemuś)** hold your own (against sb/sth)
poddzierżawi(a)ć sublet
podebrać → PODBIERAĆ
pod-ejmować/jąć 1 (*podnosić*) pick sth up **2** (*pieniądze z banku*) draw sth out, withdraw **3** (*pracę*) take/get a job as a sth; (*hobby itp.*) take sth up; **~ na nowo** resume **4** (*decyzję*) arrive at a decision, make/reach/take a decision; (*środki, kroki*) take; **podjąć działania** take action; **podjąć stanowczy krok** (*po długim namyśle*) take the plunge; **~ akcję strajkową** take strike action **5 ~ gości** entertain
□ **pod-ejmować/jąć się** (*wykonania czegoś*) undertake
podejrzan|y (*przym.*) disreputable, dodgy, dubious, fishy, seedy, shady, sleazy, suspect[3], suspicious, unsavoury; **o coś** under suspicion of sth
■ **podejrzan-y/a** (*rz.*) suspect[2]
podejrzeni|e hunch[2], suspicion; **wzbudzić czyjeś ~a** make sb suspicious
podejrzewać suspect[1]; **niczego nie podejrzewający** unsuspecting
podejrzliwość suspicion
podejrzliwy distrustful, suspicious
podejście approach[2]; (*do egzaminu itp.*) attempt[1], go[2]
podenerwowanie flutter[2]
podeprzeć → PODPIERAĆ
podeptać → DEPTAĆ
poderwać → PODRYWAĆ
podest 1 (*podium*) dais **2** (*schodów*) landing
podeszły: **w ~m wieku** the elderly
podeszwa sole[2]
pod-garniać/garnąć tuck sth in/under/round, etc. (sth)
podglądacz/ka voyeur
podgląd-ać/nąć spy on sb/sth
■ **podglądanie** voyeurism
podgórze foothill
podgrupa subset
podgrz(ew)ać heat sth up, warm[2] sb/sth (up)
podiatra chiropodist
podiatria chiropody
podirytowany irritated
podium dais, platform, podium
podjazd drive[2]
podjąć → PODEJMOWAĆ
pod-jeżdżać/jechać (*auto itp.*) draw up; **po kogoś** pick sb up
podju-dzać/dzić incite, instigate; (*nieform.*) egg sb on (to do sth)
podkład 1 (*z waty itp.*) wad **2** (*podszewka itp.*) lining **3** (*kosmetyczny*) foundation
pod-kładać/łożyć 1 (*bombę itp.*) plant[2] **2** (*głos, muzykę itp.*) dub
podkładka 1 pod coś mat; **~ pod mysz komputerową** mouse mat

2 (*ochronna*) pad[1] **3** (*pod nakretkę itp.*) washer
podkochiwać się: **w kimś** have a huge crush on sb
podkop(yw)ać (*autorytet itp.*) undermine; (*znaczenie czegoś itp.*) erode
podkoszulek singlet, vest
podkowa horseshoe
pod-kradać/kraść pilfer, siphon sth off
□ **pod-kradać/kraść się** sneak[1] into/ out of/past, etc. sth, in/out/away, etc., sneak up (on sb/sth); (*do zwierzyny*) stalk[2]
podkreś-lać/lić accentuate, emphasize, highlight[1], set sth off, stress[2], underline
■ **podkreślenie** (*symbol*) underscore[2]
podkrę-cać/cić **1** (*ogrzewanie itp.*) turn sth up **2** ~ **piłkę** put some spin on a ball
podku(wa)ć shoe[2]
podlegać be bound by sth; (*w pracy*) ~ **bezpośrednio komuś** report to sb
■ **podlegający** subject[2] to sth; ~ **opodatkowaniu** taxable
podległy subject[2] to sth
podl(ew)ać water[2]
podli-czać/czyć add sth up, tot sth up
podliz(yw)ać się: **(komuś)** crawl[1] (to sb), pander to sb, suck up (to sb)
■ **podlizujący się** slimy
podłą-czać/czyć connect, hook sb/sth up (to sth), install
□ **podłą-czać/czyć się** hook up (to sth)
podłoga floor[1]
podłogow|y: **kafle ~e** (ceramic) floor tiles
podłoż|e base[1]; **być ~em czegoś** underlie; **morderstwo o ~u politycznym** a politically inspired killing
podłożyć → PODKŁADAĆ
podłubać → DŁUBAĆ
podłu-żać/żyć (*sukienkę itp.*) let sth down
podłużny oblong adj.
podły **1** (*osoba; zachowanie*) dishonourable, foul[1], low[1], mean[2], shabby, shoddy **2** (*miejsce itp.*) grotty, sleazy, sordid
podmiejski suburban
podmiot subject[1]
podmuch (*powietrza/wiatru*) blast[1], gust
podmy(wa)ć eat sth away/eat away at sth, wear sth away
podnaj-mować/ąć sublet
podniebienie palate
podnie-cać/cić excite, rouse, stir[1]; (*ciekawość itp.*) stimulate; (*zwł. seksualnie*) titillate, turn sb on; (*zdenerwować*) fluster
□ **podnie-cać/cić się** flip (out); **czymś** get off on sth; **zbytnio się podniecać** go overboard (on/about/for sb/sth)
podniecający exciting, rousing; (*zmysłowy*) sensuous; (*zwł. seksualnie*) provocative
podnieceni|e excitement; (*radosne*) elation; (*zdenerwowanie*) fluster noun; **(ogólne) ~e** drama, stir[2]; **z ~em** excitedly
podniecony excited; (*radosny*) elated
podniesiony (*głowa itp.*) erect[1]
podnieta impulse, stimulation, stimulus
podniosły sublime
podniszczony the worse for wear
pod-nosić/nieść **1** (*w górę*) lift[1] sb/sth (up), pick sb/sth up, raise[1], scoop[2] sb/ sth (up); (*z trudem*) heave[1], hoist; ~ **jednym końcem w górę** tip[2] sth (up/ over); **podnieście ręce** hands up **2** (*cenę*) put sth up, mark sth up, raise[1] **3** (*ilość, prędkość itp.*) step sth up **4** (*głos; kwestię; alarm*) raise[1] **5** (*do rangi*) elevate **6** ~ **do trzeciej potęgi** cube[2] IDM ~ **kogoś na duchu** comfort[2], lift[1] | **podnoszący na duchu** inspiring, uplifting
■ **podnoszenie**: ~ **ciężarów** weightlifting
□ **pod-nosić/nieść się** **1** (*w górę; przen.*) rise[2]; (*ilość czegoś itp., napięcie*) mount[1]; (*cena itp.*) climb[1]; (*mgła itp.*) lift[1]; ~ **jednym końcem w górę** tip[2] (up/over) **2** (*z krzesła itp.*) get up, sit up, stand[1] (up)
podnośnik jack[1]; ~ **widłowy** fork-lift truck
podobać/s- się appeal[2] (to sb), enjoy, like[3], be to your liking; (*to co zobaczono/usłyszano*) like the look/ sound of sb/sth; **spodobać się komuś** take sb's fancy; **chyba mu się podobasz** I think he fancies you; **nie podoba mi się ten kolor** I don't care for that colour; **jak ci się podobał film?** what did you think of the film?
podobieństwo affinity, likeness, resemblance, similarity
podobizna likeness
podobnie likewise, similarly; **do kogoś/czegoś** like[1]
podobno apparently, reportedly, supposedly; **to ~ jest...** this is supposed to be...; **on ~ zarabia £100000 na rok** he is reputed to earn £100000 a year
podobn|y: **(do kogoś/czegoś)** akin to sth, alike[1], comparable, like[1,5], reminiscent, similar; (*w poglądach*) on the same wavelength; **być ~ym** resemble; **być ~ym do kogoś w rodzinie** take after sb; **być (bardzo) ~ym do kogoś** bear a (strong) resemblance to sb, be the spitting image of sb; **o ~ych zapatrywaniach/ zainteresowaniach** like-minded IDM **bardzo ~y** of a kind, much the same | **coś ~ego!** good gracious, good grief, good heavens, etc., indeed | **i tym ~e** and so forth
podoficer junior officer
podołać cope
podołek lap[1]
podorędzi|e: **na ~u** ready
podpalacz/ka arsonist
podpa-lać/lić set fire/light to sth, set sth on fire
■ **podpalenie** (*prawn.*) arson
podpałka tinder
podparcie reinforcement, support[2]
podpaska sanitary towel
podpa-trywać/trzeć peep[1] (at sth)
pod-pierać/eprzeć keep sth up, prop[2], prop sth up, shore sth up; (*i osobę*) bolster, support[1]
podpis **1** (*osobisty*) signature **2** (*pod rysunkiem/fotografią*) caption
podpis(yw)ać **1** (*list itp.*) sign[2]; (*własne dzieło*) autograph verb **2** (*ręcznik itp.*) personalize
□ **podpis(yw)ać się** **1** (*nazwiskiem*) sign[2]; ~**inicjałami** initial[3] **2** **pod czymś i popierać** subscribe to sth
podpity merry
podpora pillar, support[2]
podporządkow(yw)ać subjugate, subordinate[2]
podpo-wiadać/wiedzieć prompt[2]
podpowiedź prompt[3]
podpórka post[1], prop[1]; (*pod półkę itp.*) bracket[1]
podprogowy subliminal
podprowadzić (*ukraść*) swipe
podpuchnięty puffy
podpunkt subsection
pod-rabiać/robić fake[2], forge[1]
podrapać zob. też DRAPAĆ; scratch[1]
podrażni(a)ć zob. też DRAŻNIĆ; irritate
podręcznik handbook, manual[2]; (*na kurs*) coursebook, textbook, workbook
podręczny: **dział** ~ reference section
podrobić → PODRABIAĆ
podrobiony bogus, counterfeit, dummy adj., fake adj.; ~ **obraz/ dokument/podpis** forgery
podroby offal; (*z kury itp.*) giblets
podrożeć → DROŻEĆ
podróbka fake[1], imitation
podróż journey, trip[1]; (*morska; w kosmos*) voyage; (*morska*) crossing, passage; (**podróże**) travel[2]; ~ **w obie strony** round trip; ~ **służbowa** business trip; **być w ~y służbowej** be away on business; **biuro ~y** tour operator; **plan ~y** itinerary; **w ~y** on the road
podróżniczy travel[2]
podróżni-k/czka traveller, voyager
podróżny travel[2]
podróżować be on the road, travel[1]; **dużo** ~ get around
pod-rywać/erwać **1** **kogoś** (*w klubie nocnym itp.*) pick sb up; ~ **kogoś przez zagadywanie** chat sb up **2** (*autorytet itp.*) undermine
podrzeć (się) → DRZEĆ (SIĘ)
podrzędn|y inferior, lowly, substandard; (*hotel itp.*) seedy; **coś ~ego** second best[2] IDM **zdanie ~e** subordinate clause
podrzu-cać/cić **1** (*kłaść*) pop[2] sth in/ into, etc. sth **2** (*monetę itp.*) flip, toss **3** (*pasażerów na wybojach itp.*) jolt[1] **4** (*przesyłkę itp.*) drop[1] sb/sth (off) **5** (*pozbyć się*) dump[1]
podsekretarz: ~ **stanu** the minister's under-secretary
pod-skakiwać/skoczyć **1** (*osoba*) bounce, dance[2], jig[2] about/around, leap up and down, prance, skip[1]; (*ze strachu itp.*) jump[1]; (*jak korek*) bob[1]; (*auto itp.*) jolt[1]; (*serce*) give a leap **2** (*cena itp.*) jump[1] (from sth) to sth, shoot up
podskoczyć → SKAKAĆ
podskok jump[2], leap[2], skip[2]; ~ **na jednej nodze** hop[2]
podskórny hypodermic
podsłuch tap[2]; (*radiowy, telefoniczny*) interception; **ten pokój jest na ~u** this room is bugged; **zakładać ~ telefoniczny** tap[1]
podsłuch(iw)ać (*czyjąś rozmowę*) eavesdrop, listen in (on/to sth)
podstarzały ageing adj.
podstaw|a **1** (*budynku itp.*) base[1], foundations; (*mebla*) stand[2] **2** (*działań, teorii*) basis, core, cornerstone, framework, grounds[1],

principle; (**podstawy**) ABC, building blocks, fundamentals, ground rules, rudiments; (*fizyki itp.*) grounding; **leżeć u ~ czegoś** underlie; **na ~ie czegoś** on the strength of sth; **bez ~y** without substance IDM **być ~ą czyjegoś powodzenia** be the making of sb
podstawi(a)ć: ~ **komuś nogę** trip[2] sb (up)
podstawka mat
podstawow|y basic, elementary, fundamental, principal[1], rudimentary, standard[2]; (*potrzeby itp.*) bare, vital; (*wykształcenie itp.*) primary[1]; (*znaczenie słowa*) literal; **kolor ~y** primary colour; **~e produkty/zasady itp.** basics
podstęp artifice, deception, manoeuvre[1], ruse, trap[1], trick; **~em** on/under false pretences; **~em pozbawiać kogoś czegoś** trick sb out of sth
podstępny deceitful, devious, insidious, underhand, wily
podstrzyganie trim noun
podsumow(yw)ać encapsulate, recap, sum (sth) up
IDM **podsumowując** in conclusion
■ **podsumowanie** precis, summing-up
podsy-cać/cić 1 (*ogień*) fan[2] **2** (*przen.*) foster, fuel[2], stoke sth (up)
podszept instigation
podszewk|a lining IDM **~ą na zewnątrz** inside out
podszycie 1 (*palta itp.*) padding **2** (*lasu*) undergrowth
podszy(wa)ć line[2]
□ **podszy(wa)ć się**: **(pod kogoś/coś)** pass yourself off (as sb/sth)
podświadomoś|ć subconscious; **w ~ci** at/in the back of your mind
podświadomy subconscious adj.
podtekst overtone, subtext, undertone
podtrzym(yw)ać 1 (*podpierać*) buoy[2] sb/sth (up), shore sth up, support[1], sustain; (*wniosek*) carry **2** (*wysoki poziom itp.*) keep sth up, maintain **3** (*decyzję*) uphold
podtytuł subheading
podupa-dać/ść decay[2], languish, go to rack and ruin; (*na zdrowiu*) fail[1]
podupadły derelict
poduszczenie instigation
poduszeczka cushion[1]
poduszka 1 (*na łóżku*) pillow; (*w salonie*) cushion[1]; ~ **powietrzna** airbag **2** (*łapy kota itp.; usztywniająca ramiona marynarki itp.*) pad[1] **3** ~ **powietrzna** a cushion of air
poduszkowiec hovercraft
po-dwajać/dwoić (się) double[5]
podwaliny groundwork
podwa-żać/żyć 1 (*łomem itp.*) lever verb, prise **2** (*autorytet itp.*) challenge[2], shake[1], undermine
podwędzić swipe
podwiązka suspender
podwieczorek afternoon tea, tea
podwiezienie lift[2]; **prosić o** ~ hitch[1]
podwi-jać/nąć tuck sth in/under/round, etc. (sth)
podwładn-y/a inferior noun, subordinate noun
podwodny underwater
podwoić (się) → PODWAJAĆ (SIĘ)
pod-wozić/wieźć drive[1], give sb a lift
podwozie chassis; (*samolotu*) undercarriage
podwójnie double[3], doubly, twice
podwójn|y double[1], dual; **~a stawka/kwota** double[4]; **~a porcja** (*alkoholu*) double[4]; **~e szyby w oknach** double glazing; (*okno itp.*) **z ~ą szybą** double-glazed; **~y podbródek** double chin; **~e obywatelstwo** dual nationality; (*nazwisko*) **~e** double-barrelled; (*w tenisie*) **gra ~a** doubles[4]; **~e dno** false bottom; **~y agent** double agent; **~a gra** double-dealing IDM **z ~ą siłą** with a vengeance
podwórko (*za domem*) backyard, ground[1]
podwórze courtyard, yard; ~ **gospodarskie** barnyard, farmyard
podwyżk|a (także **podwyżki**) increase[2], rise[1], wage increase; **(automatyczna) ~a** increment
podwyż-szać/szyć raise[1] sth (to sth), step sth up
■ **podwyższony** (*nuta*) sharp[1]
podyktować → DYKTOWAĆ
podyplomow|y postgraduate; **student/ka ~-y/a** (*zwł. na studiach magisterskich*) graduate student
podział divide[2], division, segregation, split[2]; (*na mniejsze części/jednostki*) subdivision; (*państwa*) partition; **powodujący ~y** divisive
podziałka (*na termometrze itp.*) scale[1]
podzielać (*czyjeś poglądy itp.*) concur, sympathize, be in sympathy (with sb/sth); **(nie)** ~ (*np. czyichś poglądów*) be in/out of tune
podzielić (się) → DZIELIĆ (SIĘ)
podzielny divisible
podziemie (*przen.*) **w** ~ underground[2]
podziemny 1 (*pod ziemią*) subterranean, underground[1] **2** (*przen.*) clandestine, underground[1]
podziękować → DZIĘKOWAĆ
podziękowani|e (także **podziękowania**) acknowledgement, thanks, thank you
podziobać: ~ **widelcem w jedzeniu** toy with your food
podziurkować → DZIURKOWAĆ
podziw admiration, wonder[2]; **godny ~u** admirable; **pełen ~u** admiring; **być pełnym ~u dla kogoś/czegoś** be in awe of sb/sth; **wprawiać kogoś w** ~ bowl sb over; **z ~em** admiringly
podziwiać admire, marvel verb (at sth), wonder[1] (at sth)
podzwaniać jangle, jingle[2]
podzwrotnikowy tropical; **obszar** ~ the tropics
podżegać incite
poemat poem
poet-a/ka poet
poetycki poetic
poetyczny poetic
poezj|a poetry; **pełen ~i** poetic
pofałdować (się) → FAŁDOWAĆ (SIĘ)
pofałdowany crinkly
pofantazjować → FANTAZJOWAĆ
pofarbować → FARBOWAĆ
pofatygować się → FATYGOWAĆ SIĘ
pofiglować → FIGLOWAĆ
pofilozofować → FILOZOFOWAĆ
poflirtować → FLIRTOWAĆ
pofolgować → FOLGOWAĆ
pofrunąć → FRUWAĆ
pogadać → GADAĆ
pogaduszk|a chat[2]; (**pogaduszki**) chit-chat
pogalopować → GALOPOWAĆ
pogan-in/ka heathen, pagan noun
pogański pagan
pogard|a contempt, disdain, scorn[1]; **odnosić się z ~ą do czegoś** be contemptuous of sth; **odrzucać z ~ą** scorn[2]; **godny ~y** contemptible, despicable
pogardliwy contemptuous, derogatory, disdainful, dismissive (of sb/sth), scornful
pogardzać despise
pogardzić → GARDZIĆ
po-garszać/gorszyć aggravate, compound[2], exacerbate, make sth worse, get worse, worsen
□ **po-garszać/gorszyć się** decline[2], deteriorate, go downhill, suffer, get worse, worsen; (*nieform.*) go off; (*zdrowie*) fail[1], take a turn for the worse; **znacznie się pogorszyć** go from bad to worse; **jej nastrój gwałtownie się pogorszył** her spirits plummeted
pogawędka chat[2], chit-chat
pogawędzić → GAWĘDZIĆ
pogimnastykować się → GIMNASTYKOWAĆ SIĘ
pogląd persuasion, view[1]; ~ **na świat** outlook (on sth); **~y polityczne** politics
poględzić → GLĘDZIĆ
pogładzić → GŁADZIĆ
pogłaskać → GŁASKAĆ
po-głaśniać/głośnić turn the volume up
pogłębi(a)ć (się) deepen; (*tylko przen.*) intensify
pogłębiark|a dredger
pogłos resonance, reverberation
pogłoska hearsay, rumour, tale
pogłówkować → GŁÓWKOWAĆ
pogmatwać → GMATWAĆ
pogmatwany confused, muddled; (*historia*) garbled; (*tekst*) involved, rambling
pogmerać → GMERAĆ
pognać → GNAĆ
pognębi(a)ć zob. też GNĘBIĆ; **kogoś** get on top of sb
pogniecion|y: **twoja koszula jest cała ~a** your shirt is full of creases
pognieść (się) → GNIEŚĆ (SIĘ)
pogniewać się → GNIEWAĆ SIĘ
pogoda weather[1] IDM ~ **ducha** buoyancy, cheerfulness, good humour, serenity
pogodny 1 (*dzień*) fair[1] **2** (*osoba; uśmiech itp.*) cheerful, good-humoured, happy, placid, serene
pogodzeni|e conciliation; **nie do ~a** irreconcilable
□ **pogodzenie się** acceptance; (*zwł. niechętnie*) resignation
pogodzić (się) → GODZIĆ (SIĘ)
pogonić → GONIĆ
pogo|ń chase[2], pursuit; **być w ~ni** (*np. za sukcesem*) be out for sth, be out to do sth, be in pursuit (of sb/sth); **ruszać w ~ń** (*za osobą*) give chase, go after sb/sth
pogorszenie aggravation, decline[1], deterioration, exacerbation; (*sytuacji*) comedown
□ **pogorszenie się** deterioration

pogorszyć (się) → POGARSZAĆ (SIĘ)

pogotowi|e 1 (*alarm*) alert[3]; **w ~u** on call, ready **2** (*ratunkowe*) ambulance

pogranicz|e borderline; **on jest na ~u** he's a borderline case

pogratulować → GRATULOWAĆ

pogrą-żać/żyć: **kogoś/coś w czymś** plunge sb/sth into sth
□ **pogrą-żać/żyć się 1** (*w błocie itp.*) sink[1] **2** (*w lekturze itp.*) immerse yourself (in sth); **~ w czarnych myślach** mope (about/around)

pogrążon|y rapt; **w czymś** be wrapped up in sth; **być ~ym** (*np. w smutku*) be overcome; **~y w myślach/rozmowie** deep in thought/conversation

pogrom rout noun

pogróżka threat

pogrupować → GRUPOWAĆ

pogrzeb burial, funeral

pogrzebacz poker

pogrzebać → GRZEBAĆ

pogrzebowy funereal

pogwałcenie (*praw, zasad itp.*) infringement, violation

pohandryczyć się → HANDRYCZYĆ SIĘ

pohańbić → HAŃBIĆ

pohasać → HASAĆ

pohuśtać (się) → HUŚTAĆ (SIĘ)

poinformować → INFORMOWAĆ

poinformowany informed; **dobrze ~** well informed

poinstruować → INSTRUOWAĆ

pointa punchline

poirytowany in a huff

pojawi(a)ć się appear, come along, creep in, emerge, figure[2], show up, turn up; (*na scenie/boisku itp.*) come on; (*tylko problemy itp.*) arise, eventuate, originate; (*idea*) be born; (*trudności itp.*) crop up; **gdzieś** (*osoba*) turn out (for sth); **skądś** spring from sth; (*znienacka*) poke out of/through sth; poke out/through/up, pop up; **ponownie się pojawiać** reappear

pojazd vehicle; **~ kosmiczny** spacecraft; **~ terenowy** ATV; **~ wielozadaniowy** MPV; **ciężki ~ ciężarowy** HGV

pojąć → POJMOWAĆ

pojechać → JECHAĆ

pojednać → JEDNAĆ

pojednanie conciliation, reconciliation

pojednawczy conciliatory, peaceful

pojedyncz|y 1 individual[1], odd, single[1], solitary; **dwa ~e łóżka** (*w jednym pokoju*) twin beds; **pokój ~y** single[2] **2** (*gram.*) singular
IDM **w pojedynkę** alone, single-handed, solo[1]
■ **pojedynczo** individually, one at a time, one by one, singly

pojedynek duel

pojemnik container, holder; **~ na pieczywo** bread bin; **~ na śmieci** (*na kółkach*) wheelie bin

pojemny voluminous
■ **pojemność** capacity, volume

pojeździć → JEŹDZIĆ

pojęci|e 1 (*w nauce/teorii*) concept, idea **2** (*rozumienie*) appreciation, glimpse (into/of sth), grasp[2], idea, notion; **nie mieć ~a** not have a clue, be clueless about sth; **nie mam ~a** (it) beats me, your guess is as good as mine; **być nie do ~a** be beyond sb

pojęciowy conceptual, notional

pojętny intelligent

pojmać capture[1]

pojmować/pojąć appreciate, catch on, comprehend, fathom, grasp[1], get the idea, make sense of sth, take sb's point, understand; **nie pojmujący** vague

pokalać → KALAĆ

pokaleczyć (się) → KALECZYĆ (SIĘ)

pokarm feed[2], food, nourishment; **~ stały** solids

pokarmowy: **składnik ~** nutrient

pokaz demonstration, display[2], exhibition, show[2], showing; **~ mody** fashion parade/show; **na ~** for effect, token[2]; **jego odwaga jest na ~** his bravery is all show

pokaz(yw)ać indicate, manifest, produce[1], show[1], show sth up; (*przyrząd pomiarowy*) register[1]; (*mapa itp.*) say[1]; (*w telewizji itp.*) screen[2]; **~ drogę** show sb the way
IDM **niczego po sobie nie pokazać** not turn a hair
□ **pokaz(yw)ać się** appear, manifest (itself) (in/as sth); **pokazać się publicznie** show your face

pokaźny appreciable, fair[1], respectable, substantial

poker poker

pokiereszować scar verb

pokierować → KIEROWAĆ

poklask: **uzyskać ~** be applauded by sb

poklep(yw)ać zob. też KLEPAĆ; pat[1]

pokła|d 1 (*na statku*) deck; **na ~d/~dzie** aboard, on board, on deck; **weszliśmy na ~d statku** we went aboard the boat **2** (*warstwa*) seam

pokładać (*zaufanie itp.*) place[2]; **~ w kimś swoje zaufanie** trust[2] sb (with sth); **~ (całą) nadzieję w kimś/czymś** pin (all) your hopes on sb/sth
□ **pokładać się** IDM **pokładający się ze śmiechu** in stitches

pokłócić się → KŁÓCIĆ SIĘ

pokłusować → KŁUSOWAĆ

pokochać → KOCHAĆ

pokojowość peacefulness

pokojow|y non-violent, peaceful; **siły ~e Narodów Zjednoczonych** a United Nations peacekeeping force; **podjąć ~e kroki w stosunku do szefa** make some peace overtures to the boss

pokojówka chambermaid, maid

pokole|nie generation; **konflikt ~ń** the generation gap

pokolorować → KOLOROWAĆ

pokonani|e: **do ~a (drogą negocjacji/dyskusji)** negotiable; **nie do ~a** insuperable, insurmountable

pokon(yw)ać 1 (*armię wroga*) conquer, defeat[1]; (*rywala*) beat[1], overpower, thrash, trounce **2** (*przeszkodę itp.*) negotiate, overcome, surmount; **~ przeszkodę** clear a hurdle **3** (*odległość*) cover[1], do[1]

pokora humility, submission

pokorny humble[1], submissive

pokost varnish

pokostować varnish verb

pok|ój 1 (*w mieszkaniu itp.*) room; (*w czacie*) chat room; **~ój dzienny** living room; **~ój stołowy** dining room; **~ój nauczycielski** staffroom; **~ój jednoosobowy/pojedynczy** single (room); **~ój dwuosobowy** double (room); **wolny ~ój** (*np. w hotelu*) vacancy; **~oje do wynajęcia** lodgings, rooms to let **2** (*polit.*) peace; **okres ~oju** peacetime

pokrajać → KRAJAĆ

pokrewieństwo relationship; (*form.*) kindred

pokrewny allied (to sth), akin to sth, kindred adj.

pokręcić (się) → KRĘCIĆ (SIĘ)

pokrętło knob

pokrętny (*komentarz, aluzja itp.*) oblique

pokroić → KROIĆ

pokropić → KROPIĆ

pokrowiec casing

pokrój mould[1]

pokrótce in short

pokruszyć (się) → KRUSZYĆ (SIĘ)

pokryci|e: **czek bez ~a** dud cheque

pokrywa cover[2], covering; (*śniegu itp.*) blanket[1], carpet

pokry(wa)ć 1 cover[1]; (*nawierzchnię*) surface[2]; (*śniegiem, zwł. góry*) cap[2]; (*pnącze itp.: zarosnąć*) overrun **2** (*czekoladą itp.*) coat[2] sth (with/in sth), cover[1] sb/sth in/with sth, smother sth/sb in/with sth; **~ coś (grubą) warstwą** plaster[2] sb/sth (in/with sth) **3 ~ koszt (czegoś)** cover the cost (of sth)
□ **pokry(wa)ć się 1 czymś** (*skóra, twarz itp.*) break out in sth **2 ~ częściowo** (*zachodzić na siebie*) overlap

pokrywka lid

pokrzepiający refreshing

pokrzywa nettle

pokrzywdzon-y/a loser

pokrzyżować → KRZYŻOWAĆ

pokupny: **~ towar** seller

pokusa 1 (*chęć zrobienia czegoś*) compulsion, temptation **2** (*uwodzenie*) seduction **3** (*coś, co pociąga*) bait, enticement, lure[2]

pokuszenie się: **(o coś)** bid[3] (for sth)

pokuta penance

pokwitanie puberty

pokwitowanie receipt

polać → POLEWAĆ

polakierować → LAKIEROWAĆ

polana clearing, glade

polano log[1]

polar fleece[1]

polarny polar

polaryzować/s- polarize

pole 1 (*roln.*) field[1]; **~ ryżowe** paddy **2** (*teren*) **~ bitwy** battlefield; **~ karne** the penalty area; **~ minowe** minefield; **~ naftowe** oilfield **2** (*sport*) course **3 ~ widzenia** field/line of vision, view[1] **4 ~ manewru** room for manoeuvre **5** (*komput.*) **~ wyboru** checkbox **6** (*na szachownicy*) square[2]
IDM **na polu** out of doors

polec fall[1]

pole-cać/cić 1 (*kazać*) direct[2], instruct **2** (*zachęcać*) interest sb in sth, recommend

poleceni|e 1 (*instrukcja*) bidding, instruction; **~e zapłaty** (*z konta*) direct debit **2** (*rekomendacja*) recommendation; **godny ~a** commendable **3** (*komput.*) keyword

polecieć → LATAĆ, LECIEĆ

polecon|y: **przesyłka ~a** registered mail

polegać 1 (*zasadzać się na czymś*) consist in sth, lie[2] (in sth) **2** (*liczyć na kogoś/coś*) count on sb/sth, depend on

sb/sth (for sth), rely on/upon sb/sth (to do sth); **polegający na sobie samym** self-reliant; **nie polegaj za bardzo na jej obietnicach** don't place too much reliance on her promises
polemiczny polemical
polep-szać/szyć ameliorate, enhance, improve, raise[1] sth (to sth); (*jakość itp.*) enrich
□ **polep-szać/szyć się** improve, look up; (*zdrowie*) be on the mend
polepszenie amelioration, improvement
polerować/wy- polish[2], rub, shine[1]
polewa coating, glaze[2]
po-lewać/lać pour; **kalafior polany sosem serowym** cauliflower topped with cheese sauce
poleżeć → LEŻEĆ
polędwica: ~ **wołowa** sirloin
poliandria polygamy
policja the police[1], the police force; (*danego okręgu*) constabulary
policjant/ka police officer; (*przestarz.*) bobby; (**policjant**) policeman; (**policjantka**) policewoman
policyjn|y: **godzina ~a** curfew
policzalny countable
policzek cheek; **wymierzyć komuś ~** give sb a slap across the face
policzkować/s- slap[1]
policzyć zob. też LICZYĆ; **(komuś) za coś** charge[2] (sb/sth) for sth
poliester polyester
polietylen polythene
poligamia polygamy
poligamiczny polygamous
poligamist-a/ka polygamist
polio polio
polisa policy; ~ **ubezpieczeniowa** insurance policy
polistyren polystyrene
politologia politics
politowani|e pity[1]; **godny ~a** pitiful, sad
polityczn|y political; **~a poprawność** political correctness
polityk politician
polityk|a 1 (*działalność publiczna*) politics; **interesujący się ~ą** political **2** (*zasada postępowania*) policy
polizać → LIZAĆ
polo polo
polor refinement
polot bravura, flair, panache, spark[1]
polować 1 (/za-) (*myślistwo, ściganie*) hunt[1], prey on sth, shoot[1] **2** (*szukać*) hunt[1] (for) (sb/sth) **3 (/u-)** (*starać się uzyskać*) angle for sth, fish for sth
polowanie blood sport, hunt[2], hunting, shooting; ~ **na lisa** fox-hunting; ~ **na czarownice** witch-hunt
polow|y: **łóżko ~e** folding bed
polubić zob. też LUBIĆ; take to sb/sth, take a liking to sb, warm to/towards sb, warm to sth; **dawać się ~** grow on sb
□ **polubić się** hit it off (with sb)
polubowny amicable
polukrować → LUKROWAĆ
poluzować → LUZOWAĆ
poła flap[1]
połać swathe
połamać (się) → ŁAMAĆ (SIĘ)
połapać się: **w czymś** get the hang of (doing) sth, suss (sth) (out)
połaskotać → ŁASKOTAĆ
poławiać trawl (for sth)
połączeni|e 1 (*kombinacja*) amalgam, combination, composite noun, integration, link-up **2** (*organizacji itp.*) amalgamation; (*zwł. firm*) merger **3** (*komun., telefon*) connection, link[1]; **mieć ~e** connect (with sth); **regularne ~e autobusowe** a regular bus service; **nowe ~e międzynarodowe** a new international service; (*komput.*) **~e typu broadband/ szerokopasmowe** broadband **4** (*skojarzenie*) association, connection between A and B, with/to sth; **w ~u z czymś** in conjunction with sth **5 ponowne ~e** (*ludzi*) reunion
połączony 1 (*w całość*) combined; (*z łazienką itp.*) en suite **2** (*umową itp.*) allied **3** (*powiązany*) associated
połączyć (się) → ŁĄCZYĆ (SIĘ)
połknąć → POŁYKAĆ
połknięcie gulp[2]
połow|a 1 (½) half[1]; **do ~y**; **w ~ie** half[2]; **po ~ie** fifty-fifty adv.; **podzielić kraj na ~ę** split a country down the middle **2** (*czasu, dystansu itp.*) middle[1]; **w ~ie** mid; **~a tygodnia** midweek; **~a czerwca** mid June; **w ~ie drogi między dwoma miastami** midway between two towns; **w ~ie Hope Street** halfway along Hope Street; **w ~ie książki** halfway through the book **3** (*meczu*) half-time
połowiczn|y: **okres ~ego rozpadu** half-life
położenie 1 (*miejsce*) location, position[1] **2** (*sytuacja*) circumstances, situation; **trudne ~** plight **3** (*według kompasu*) bearing
położna midwife
położnictwo obstetrics
położniczy maternity; **oddział ~** the hospital's maternity ward
położyć (się) → KŁAŚĆ (SIĘ)
połów catch[2], haul[2]
południ|e 1 (*czas*) midday, noon; **po ~u** p.m.; **przed ~em** a.m. **2** (*kierunek*) south[1]; **na ~e** southwards; **na południe/niu** down[1], south adv.; **z ~a** south[2], southerly
południk meridian
południowo-wschodni south-east[2], south-easterly, south-eastern
południowo-zachodni south-west[2], south-westerly, south-western
południowy south[2], southerly, southern, southward; ~ **wschód** south-east[1]; ~ **zachód** south-west[1]
po-łykać/łknąć swallow[1]; (*w pośpiechu*) gulp[1]; (*zwł. z trudem*) get sth down
połysk gloss[1], sheen, shine[2]; **nadawać ~** polish[2]
połyskiwać gleam verb
połyskliwy glossy
pomacać → MACAĆ
pomachać → MACHAĆ
pomaczać → MACZAĆ
pomadka: ~ **do ust** lipstick
po-magać/móc aid[2], assist, hold sb's hand, help[1], help (sb) out, lend (sb) a hand/lend a hand (to sb)
pomalować (się) → MALOWAĆ (SIĘ)
pomarańcza orange[1]
pomarańczowy 1 (*sok, napój*) orange[1] **2** (*kolor*) orange[2]; **kolor ~** orange[1]
pomarszczony (*twarz itp.*) lined, wrinkled
pomarszczyć (się) → MARSZCZYĆ (SIĘ)
pomarudzić → MARUDZIĆ
pomarzyć → MARZYĆ
pomasować → MASOWAĆ
pomaszerować → MASZEROWAĆ
pomaturalny tertiary
pomazać → MAZAĆ
pomedytować → MEDYTOWAĆ
pomiar (także **pomiary**) measurement; **~y terenu i sporządzenie mapy** survey[1]; **dokonywać ~ów** gauge[2]
pomiatać: **kimś** kick sb around, push sb about/around
pomidor tomato
pomidorowy tomato
pomieszać (się) → MIESZAĆ (SIĘ)
pomieścić zob. też MIEŚCIĆ; (*apartament itp.*) sleep[1]
pomiędzy amid, among, between
pomięty: **w ~m ubraniu** dishevelled
po-mijać/minąć 1 (*nie uwzględnić*) miss sb/sth out, omit, overlook, skip[1]; (*w spisie itp.*) leave sb/sth off (sth), leave sb/sth out (of sth); **na liście pominięto kilka nazwisk** there were several omissions on the list of names **2** (*nie brać pod uwagę*) discount[2], disregard, drop[1], put sth aside; ~ **milczeniem** brush sb/sth aside; **pomijając inne sprawy** apart from anything else
pomimo despite, for all, notwithstanding, in spite of; ~ **to** still[1], yet
pomknąć → MKNĄĆ
po-mnażać/mnożyć multiply; (*kapitał itp.*) accrue
□ **po-mnażać/mnożyć się** multiply
po-mniejszać/mniejszyć diminish, lessen; (*budynki itp. przytłaczać*) dwarf[2]; (*fakty itp.*) understate; (*znaczenie, zasługi itp.*) denigrate
■ **pomniejszający** (*uwagi*) disparaging
□ **po-mniejszać/mniejszyć się** diminish
pomniejszy lesser; (*nieważny*) petty
pomnik memorial, monument
pomnożyć → MNOŻYĆ
pomoc aid[1], assistance, backup, hand[1], help[2], helpfulness, relief; **~y!** help![1]; **pierwsza ~** first aid; ~ **wizualna** visual aid; **do ~y** on hand; **za ~ą** by means of, via, whereby; **bez (niczyjej) ~y** (all) by oneself/ themselves, (all) on your, etc. own, unaided; (*sam przeciw wszystkim itp.*) out on a limb; **przychodzić z ~ą** come forward; **przychodzić komuś z ~ą** come to sb's rescue, go to the aid of sb; **pośpieszyć komuś z ~ą** leap to sb's defence; **pośpieszyć komuś na ratunek** come to sb's rescue; **służyć za ~** pilot[2]
pomocni-/k/ca/czka aid[1], helper
pomocniczy 1 (*pracownik itp.*) assistant adj., auxiliary, subservient **2** (*mniej ważny, drugoplanowy*) subsidiary[1]
pomocn|y helpful, useful; (*tylko osoba*) cooperative[1], supportive; **rozmowny i ~y** forthcoming IDM **~a dłoń** helping hand
pomodlić się → MODLIĆ SIĘ

pomóc → POMAGAĆ
pomór plague[1]
pomówić → MÓWIĆ
pomp|a 1 (*techn.*) (także **pompka**) pump[1]; **na ~(k)ę** pump-action **2** (*ceremonia*) pomp; **z wielką ~ą** with a bang
pompatyczny bombastic, pompous; **~ styl** bombast
pompka zob. też POMPA; (*ćwiczenie*) press-up
pompon bobble, pompom
pompować 1 (**/na-**) pump[2] **2** (**/w-**) (*pieniądze w biznes*) inject
pomruk hum noun, murmur noun
pomrukiwać murmur
pomścić → MŚCIĆ
pomyleniec crackpot, loony, nut
pomylić (się) → MYLIĆ (SIĘ)
pomylony deranged, loony adj., mad, nutty
pomyłk|a error, mistake[1], slip[2]; (*przy odbiorze bagażu itp.*) confusion; **~a lekarska** malpractice; **~a sądowa** a miscarriage of justice; **~a telefoniczna** wrong number; (*nieform.*) **popełniać ~ę** goof; **przez ~ę** by mistake, mistakenly
pomyłkowo mistakenly
pomysł idea, thought[2]; **genialny ~** brainchild; **nagły/dobry ~** inspiration; **mieć ~** conceive; **pełen ~ów** inventive
pomysłowość cleverness, creativity, ingenuity, initiative, inventiveness
pomysłowy artful, clever, creative, ingenious, inventive, resourceful
pomyśleć zob. też MYŚLEĆ IDM **niech pomyślę** let me see, let's see
pomyśleni|e: **nie do ~a** unthinkable
pomyślnoś|ć fortune, welfare, well-being IDM **wiele lat ~ci!** many happy returns (of the day)
pomyślny 1 (*korzystny*) auspicious, bright, opportune **2** (*dobry*) successful, well[2]
ponad 1 (*wyżej niż*) above, over **2** (*z ilością*) above, in excess of, odd, over, plus[3], upwards of **3** (*osoba*) above sth **4** (*przewyższający wyobrażenia/siły itp.*) beyond sb/sth
ponaddźwiękowy supersonic
ponadto in addition (to sth), additionally, besides adv., either[2], furthermore, moreover
ponadwymiarowy outsize
po-naglać/naglić rush[1]
ponarzekać → NARZEKAĆ
po-nawiać/nowić renew
poncz punch[2]
ponętny alluring, enticing, inviting, seductive, tempting; (*kobieta*) sultry, voluptuous
poniedział|ek Monday; **w ~ki** on Mondays/on a Monday
ponieść → PONOSIĆ
ponieważ as, because, for[2], seeing, since; (*form.*) inasmuch as
poniewczasie belatedly
poniewierać/s- 1 (*maltretować*) knock sb/sth around, maltreat, walk (all) over sb **2** (*wiatr itp.*) buffet[2]
□ **poniewierać się** (*po podłodze itp.*) lie around/about
po-niżać/niżyć cheapen, degrade, demean
■ **poniżający** degrading, derogatory
□ **po-niżać/niżyć się** demean yourself; **~ do tego stopnia, aby coś zrobić** stoop to sth/doing sth
poniżej 1 (*niżej niż*) below; (*wiek, zarobki itp.*) under; **~ normy** subnormal **2** (*poziomu; oczekiwań itp.*) beneath
poniżenie degradation, indignity
po-nosić/nieść 1 (*koszty itp.*) bear[1], incur **2 ~ odpowiedzialność za coś** be (held) responsible (for sth); **~ winę za coś** be to blame for sth **3** (*klęskę itp.*) sustain **4 dawać się ponieść** (*uczuciom*) be/get carried away, let yourself go
ponowić → PONAWIAĆ
ponownie: **~ dopasowywać/regulować** readjust; **~ się ukazywać/pojawiać** reappear; **~ wykorzystywać** recycle; **załadowywać ~** reload
ponown|y: **~a ocena** reappraisal
ponton raft
ponumerować → NUMEROWAĆ
ponurość bleakness
ponury brooding, gloomy, sombre; (*zwł. osoba, wyraz twarzy itp.*) black[1], glum, morose, mournful, sullen; (*pogoda*) dreary, grey[1]; (*przyszłość itp.*) bleak, dim[1], dismal, grim
pończocha stocking
poodkurzać → ODKURZAĆ
poorany: **~ bruzdami/zmarszczkami** lined
pop (*muz.*) pop[1]
po-padać/paść 1 w coś get into sth; (*w długi itp.*) slide[1]; **popaść w długi** get into debt; **~ w atrofię** atrophy verb; **~ w złe nawyki** lapse into sth **2** (*w sentimentalizm itp.*) wax[2].
poparcie backing, backup, encouragement, espousal of sth, favour[1] (with sb), following[2], support[2]
poparzenie burn[2]
poparzony (*po intensywnym opalaniu*) sunburned
poparzyć (się) → PARZYĆ (SIĘ)
popaść → POPADAĆ
popatrzeć zob. też PATRZEĆ; **na coś** check sb/sth out, have a look at sth
popchnąć → POPYCHAĆ
popełni(a)ć (*zbrodnię itp.*) commit, perpetrate; **~ przestępstwo** offend; **~ błąd/pomyłkę** trip up; **~ grzech** sin verb
popędliwy fiery, impetuous, impulsive
popę-dzać/dzić bustle[1], dart[2], hurry[1] sb (into sth/doing sth), prod
popękany (*wargi*) chapped
popić → POPIJAĆ
popielniczka ashtray
popieprzyć → PIEPRZYĆ
po-pierać/przeć back[4], back sb/sth up, believe in sb/sth, be in favour of sb/sth, encourage, espouse, promote, support[1], be in sympathy (with sb/sth); (*propozycję itp.*) agree with sth, believe in doing sth, stand for sth; (*form.*) countenance[2]; (*oficjalnie*) endorse; (*wniosek itp.*) second[3]; (*rozwój zwł. relacji międzyludzkich/idei itp.*) foster
popiersie bust[2]
po-pijać/pić drink[2]; (*małymi łykami*) sip
popijawa booze-up
popilnować → PILNOWAĆ
popiół ash, cinder
popis display[2]; (**popisy**) antics
popis(yw)ać się show (sth) off
poplamić się) → PLAMIĆ (SIĘ)
poplamiony (*zwł. o skórze*) blotchy
poplątać → PLĄTAĆ
poplątany 1 (*historia itp.*) confused, muddled **2** (*wełna itp.*) tangled
popleczni-k/czka supporter; (*przestępcy itp.*) henchman
popłoch panic; **wpadać w ~** panic verb
popłynąć → PŁYNĄĆ
popołudnie afternoon
■ **popołudniowy** afternoon
poporodowy post-natal
poprawa amelioration, improvement; (*zdrowia; warunków finansowych itp.*) recovery (from sth); (*sytuacji w biznesie itp.*) upturn
poprawczak detention centre
poprawczy corrective
poprawi(a)ć 1 (*polepszać*) ameliorate, improve, improve on/upon sth; (*program komputerowy itp.*) upgrade; (*książkę itp.*) revise; (*sytuację itp.*) retrieve; **poprawić apetyt** give sb an appetite **2** (*błędy*) correct[2], rectify **3 ~ krawat** straighten your tie
□ **poprawi(a)ć się** improve, look up, pick up; (*zdrowie*) do well; (*osoba*) reform, shape up
poprawk|a 1 (*usunięcie błędu*) correction **2** (*zmiana*) adjustment; (*mała*) tweak; (*i prawn.*) amendment; (*korekta książki itp.*) revision; **wnosić ~i** amend
poprawny 1 (*odpowiedź itp.*) correct[1], right[1] **2** (*osoba; zachowanie*) civil; **bardzo ~** prim
■ **poprawność** correctness; (*zachowania itp.*) formality
poprosić → PROSIĆ
poprowadzić → PROWADZIĆ
poprzeczka crossbar
poprzeć → POPIERAĆ
poprzedni the former, prior; (*miejsce pracy, szkoła itp.*) old; **~ego dnia** the day before
poprzedni-k/czka predecessor
poprzednio already, previously
po-przedzać/przedzić go before, head[2], precede
■ **poprzedzający** previous, prior
poprzek: **w ~** over
poprzesta(wa)ć: **na czymś** confine sb/sth/yourself to sth
poprzestawiać rearrange
poprzez through, via
popsuć (się) → PSUĆ (SIĘ)
popudrować → PUDROWAĆ
populacja population
popularnoś|ć popularity; **brak/utrata ~ci** unpopularity
popularny fashionable, hot[1], popular
popularyzować/s- popularize
po-puszczać/puścić: **komuś** ease off
po-pychać/pchnąć poke, prod, push[2], thrust[1]; (*ludzi, zwł. w tłumie*) hustle, jostle
popychadło dogsbody, doormat
popyt demand[1], market[1]; **nagły i masowy ~** a run[2] on sth; **cieszący się olbrzymim ~em** best-selling
por 1 (*anat.*) pore[1] **2** (*warzywo*) leek
po|ra time[1]; **~ra roku** season[1]; **~ra snu** bedtime; **~ra deszczowa** rains[1]; **do tej ~ry** to date, up to sth, yet; **w ~rę** opportune; **nie w ~rę** inopportune; **o każdej ~rze** any time; **od tamtej ~ry**

since then; **w samą ~rę** in the nick of time; **zachodzący w samą ~rę** timely
porachować → RACHOWAĆ
porada advice, consultation, counsel[1], counselling, guidance; (*wskazówka*) hint[1], pointer, suggestion
poradnia clinic
poradnictwo guidance; (*zwł. terapeutyczne*) counselling; **fachowe ~** mentoring
poradnik handbook
poradzić (się) → RADZIĆ (SIĘ)
poranek morning
porazić → RAZIĆ
po-rażać/razić paralyse
porażenie paralysis; **~ mózgowe** cerebral palsy; **~ prądem** electric shock[1]; **(śmiertelne) ~ prądem elektrycznym** electrocution; **~ słoneczne** sunstroke
porażka beating, defeat[2]
porąbać → RĄBAĆ
porcelana 1 (*materiał*) china, porcelain **2** (*stołowa i kuchenna*) crockery
porcelanow|y china, porcelain; **wyroby ~e** china
porcja helping, portion; **to ~ dla czworga** this recipe serves four
poręba glade
poręcz 1 (*na balkonie*) handrail, rail; (*przy schodach*) banister **2** (*fotela*) arm[1]
poręczenie guarantee[1]
poręczny handy
poręczyć → RĘCZYĆ
pornografia pornography
pornograficzny pornographic
porodówka the hospital's maternity ward
poronić miscarry
porost (*bot.*) lichen
porowaty porous
porowkować → ROWKOWAĆ
porozkoszować się → ROZKOSZOWAĆ SIĘ
porozmawiać → ROZMAWIAĆ
porozumienie 1 (*wzajemne zrozumienie*) rapport, understanding[1] **2** (*zgoda*) agreement, consensus; (*oficjalne*) accord[1], settlement
porozumie(wa)ć się communicate; (*w obcym języku itp.*) make yourself understood
porozumiewawczy meaningful
porozwiewać: **po czymś** blow[1] sth (all over sth)
poroże a pair of antlers
por|ód birth, childbirth, delivery, labour[1]; **~ód pośladkowy** breech birth; **przy ~odzie** in childbirth
porównani|e comparison, contrast[1], parallel[2]; **~e literackie** simile; **w ~u z kimś/czymś** compared to/with sb/sth, by/in comparison (with sb/sth), in/with relation to sb/sth; (*z ubiegłym rokiem itp.*) on IDM **bez ~a** by far
porównawczy comparative[1]
porówn(yw)ać zob. też RÓWNAĆ; compare, draw a comparison/a parallel, liken, weigh sth (against sb/sth)
porównywalny analagous, comparable
poróżnić divide[1]; **kogoś z kimś** come between sb and sb
port harbour[1], port
portal: **~ internetowy** portal
portfel 1 (*na pieniądze*) wallet **2** (*dossier*) portfolio
portier/ka porter; (*w hotelu itp.*) receptionist
portiernia lodge[1], reception
portmonetka purse[1]
porto port
portret portrait; **~ pamięciowy** mental picture
portretować/s- portray
portwajn port
porucznik lieutenant
poru-szać/szyć 1 (*temat*) bring sth up, raise the subject of sth, touch on/upon sth; (*delikatny temat*) broach; **z kimś** take sth up with sb; **nie poruszać dalej** (*np. tematu*) let sth rest **2 kogoś** affect, move[1], stir[1], touch[1]
■ **poruszający** emotional, impressive, moving; (*przemowa itp.*) stirring
□ **poru-szać/szyć się**: **w kierunku kogoś/czegoś** make for sb/sth
porwać → PORYWAĆ
porwać się → RWAĆ SIĘ
poryw: **~ wiatru** gust
porywacz/ka captor; (*ubiegający się o okup*) kidnapper; (*samolotu itp.*) hijacker
por(y)wać 1 (*chwytać*) grab, make off (with sth) **2** (*dla okupu*) hold sb to ransom, kidnap; (*samolot itp.*) hijack **3** (*woda*) wash[1], wash sb/sth away; (*wiatr*) sweep[1] **4** (*wzbudzić zachwyt*) magnetize, rivet[2]
porywający irresistible, magnetic, riveting, thrilling; (*przemowa, muzyka itp.*) rousing, stirring; (*debata itp.*) spirited
porywczość short temper
porywczy fiery, hot-blooded, hot-tempered, impetuous, passionate, quick-tempered, short-tempered, vehement, violent
porząd|ek 1 (*kolejność*) order[1], sequence; **ustalony ~ek** (*zajęć*) routine[1] **2** (*ład*) neatness; **doprowadzać coś do ~ku** straighten sth out; **robić ~ek** tidy[2] (sb/sth/yourself) (up) IDM **~ek dzienny** agenda | **w ~ku** all right, fair enough, OK[1], very well | **nie w ~ku** amiss, wrong[1] | (*u kogoś*) **wszystko w ~ku** all is well (with sb)
porządkować/u- neaten, sort[2], sort sth out, tidy[2] sb/sth/yourself (up); (*dokumenty itp.*) sort through sth (for sth); (*myśli*) compose; **uporządkować swoje notatki** put my notes in order; **uporządkować sprawy domowe** sort things out at home; **zbierać i ~** (*informacje*) compile
porządkowy: **liczebnik ~** ordinal
porządny 1 (*utrzymujący porządek*) neat, tidy **2** (*moralny*) proper
porzeczka currant; **czarna ~** blackcurrant
porzu-cać/cić leave sb/sth behind, turn your back on sb/sth; (*bardziej form.*) abandon, cast sb/sth off, desert[2], forsake; (*nieform.*) ditch[2], dump[1]; (*żonę/męża*) leave[1]; **~ pracę** quit (as sth)
■ **porzucon|y** abandoned; (*na wyspie itp.*) marooned; **~e dziecko** waif
posada appointment, office, position[1], post[1]; **wolna ~** vacancy
posadzić → SADZAĆ
posag dowry
posapywać: **toczyć się, posapując** chug
posąg statue; (*przedstawiający osobę zazw. w pozycji leżącej*) effigy
posegregować → SEGREGOWAĆ
poselstwo deputation
pos-eł/łanka Member of Parliament; **szeregow-y/a pos-eł/łanka** backbencher
posępność gloominess
posępny dismal, funereal, morose, sombre, sullen
posiadacz/ka holder, possessor, proprietor
po-siadać/siąść hold[1], possess; (*cechy*) embody
□ **posiadać się**: **z czegoś** be beside yourself with sth; **nie posiadać się ze szczęścia** be bursting with happiness; **nie posiadający się z radości** overjoyed, over the moon
posiadani|e ownership, possession; **tytuł prawny ~a** (*nieruchomości*) tenure
posiadłość estate, property
posiedzenie meeting, session, sitting
posiekać → SIEKAĆ
posił|ek 1 meal; **pora ~ku** mealtime **2 (posiłki)** (*wojsk.*) reinforcements
posiniaczony black and blue
posiniaczyć bruise verb
posiwieć → SIWIEĆ
poskarżyć (się) → SKARŻYĆ (SIĘ)
poskąpić → SKĄPIĆ
po-skramiać/skromić repress, subdue, suppress
poskręcany twisted
poskutkować → SKUTKOWAĆ
posłać → POSYŁAĆ
posłanie message
posłaniec courier, go-between, messenger
posłanka → POSEŁ
posłannictwo mission
posłanni-k/czka messenger
posłodzić → SŁODZIĆ
posłuch clout
posłuchać → SŁUCHAĆ
posług|a: **oddać komuś ostatnią ~ę** pay your last respects to sb
po-sługiwać /służyć się make use of sth/sb, use[1]
posłuszeństwo obedience, submission; (*królowi itp.*) allegiance
posłuszny amenable, dutiful, obedient; (*zwł. przesadnie*) docile, submissive; **być ~m** obey
posłużyć → SŁUŻYĆ
posłużyć się → POSŁUGIWAĆ SIĘ
posma|k 1 flavour[1], tang; (*w ustach po wypiciu/jedzeniu*) aftertaste **2** (*uczucia*) tinge; **z ~kiem czegoś** tinged (with sth) **3** (*przen.*) **mieć ~k czegoś** smack of sth
posmakować → SMAKOWAĆ
posmarować → SMAROWAĆ
posoka gore[1]
posolić → SOLIĆ
pospacerować → SPACEROWAĆ
pospie-szać/szyć → POŚPIESZAĆ
pospolity common[1], homely, mundane
posprzątać → SPRZĄTAĆ
posprzeczać się → SPRZECZAĆ SIĘ
post fast; **Wielki Post** Lent

postać 1 (*forma*) form[1] **2** (*osoby*) character, figure[1] **3 główna** ~ (*np. w filmie/książce*) hero, heroine, protagonist
po-stanawiać/stanowić 1 coś zrobić determine, resolve, elect to do sth, make it your business to do sth, set out to do sth **2** (*sąd*) rule[2]
postanowienie decision, resolution, ruling[2]
postarać się → STARAĆ SIĘ
po-starzać/starzyć age[2]
postawa bearing, demeanour, posture
postawić → STAWIAĆ
posterunek post[1]; ~ **policji** police station
posterunkowy constable, police constable
postęp (także **postępy**) advance[1], advancement, development, improvement, progress[1], progression; **robić ~y** gain ground, get ahead, get on/along, progress[2], shape up; **robić (z trudem) ~y** make headway; **robić wielkie ~y** make great strides
po-stępować/stąpić 1 (*rozwijać się*) come on, go along **2 z kimś** behave well/badly, etc. (towards sb), deal with sb **3** ~ **zgodnie z czyjąś decyzją** go along with sb/sth
postępowani|e 1 (*zachowanie*) demeanour; **złe/nieprofesjonalne ~e** misconduct **2** (*procedura*) process[1]; **~e prawne** proceedings; **sposób ~a** procedure
postępowy forward-looking, progressive
postmodernist-a/ka postmodernist
postmodernistyczny postmodern, postmodernist
postmodernizm postmodernism
postój halt, stop[2]; ~ **taksówek** taxi rank
postrach terror; (*dla dzieci*) bogeyman
postradać forfeit IDM ~ **zmysły** be/go out of your mind
postronek halter
postronn|y: **osoba ~a** third party
postrzegać: **kogoś/coś jako kogoś/coś** conceive (of) sb/sth (as sth), look on sb/sth as sth, perceive, see
postrzelić gun sb down, shoot[1]
postrzelony (*zwariowany*) potty[1]
postrzępić (się) → STRZĘPIĆ (SIĘ)
postrzępiony 1 (*broda itp.*) scraggly; (*włosy*) **rzadki i** ~ wispy **2** (*ubranie*) ragged **3** (*kamienie*) jagged
postument (*kolumny, pomnika itp.*) pedestal
postura frame[1], posture
posu-wać/nąć 1 (*ukradkiem*) slide[1] **2** ~ **naprzód** (*wskazówki zegara*) put sth forward **3** (*sprawę itp. do przodu*) advance[2], forward[3], further[2], get sth moving
□ **po-suwać /sunąć się 1** (*ukradkiem*) slide[1]; **powoli** ~ **naprzód** creep[1], nose[2]; ~ **krok po kroku** inch[2] forward/past/through, etc., edge[2] across/along/away/back, etc.; ~ **z trudem** labour[2] **2** (*robić postępy*) advance[2], come on, get somewhere (with sb/sth), go along, move[1] (on/ahead), progress[2], push ahead/forward (with sth); ~ **z trudem naprzód** make headway; (*w rozmowie itp.*) ~ **dalej/naprzód** move on (to sth) **3** ~ **w latach** get on IDM ~ **się za daleko** go too far, overstep the mark/line
pos(y)łać send; **po kogoś/coś** send for sb/sth; ~ **(towary) morzem** ship[2]; ~ **do jakiejś instytucji** (*np. swoje postulaty*) write in (to sb/sth) (for sth) IDM **posłać (komuś) całusa** blow (somebody) a kiss | **posłać piłkę** drive a ball into sth
posyp(yw)ać sprinkle
poszanowanie 1 (*szacunek*) respect[1] **2** (*honorowanie, przestrzeganie obyczajów itp.*) observance (of sth)
poszarpać → SZARPAĆ
poszarpany ragged, rugged
poszarzały ashen
poszatkować → SZATKOWAĆ
poszczególny individual[1], respective
posze-rzać/rzyć broaden sth (out), widen; (*spódniczkę itp.*) let sth out; ~ **działalność** branch out (into sth)
□ **posze-rzać/rzyć się** broaden (out), open out, widen
poszewka (*na poduszkę*) pillowcase
poszkodowany injured
■ **poszkodowan-y/a** (*rz.*) loser
poszlakowy circumstantial
poszperać → SZPERAĆ
poszukać → SZUKAĆ
poszukiwacz/ka searcher, seeker; **poszukiwacz/ka przygód** adventurer
poszukiwać be after sb/sth, be on the lookout for sb/sth, keep a lookout for sb/sth, search, seek; ~ **kogoś do pracy** advertise (for sb/sth); **być poszukiwanym przez policję** be wanted by the police
poszukiwani|e (także **poszukiwania**) exploration, hunt[2], quest, search noun
poszukiwawcz|y: **wyprawa ~a** search party
poszwa (*na kołdrę*) duvet cover
poszybować → SZYBOWAĆ
pościć fast[3]
pościel bedclothes; (*często z materacem i poduszką*) bedding; **zmieniać** ~ change the bed
pościg chase[2]
pośladek buttock; **(pośladki)** (*razem z tylną częścią ud*) haunches
pośledni inferior
poślizg skid noun
pośliz-nąć/gnąć się slide[1], slip (over), slip (on sth), slip[1]
poślubi(a)ć wed
poślubiony: **świeżo** ~ newly-wed
pośmiać się → ŚMIAĆ SIĘ
pośmiertny posthumous
pośmiewis|ko joke[1], laughing stock; **być ~kiem** be the butt of sth; **wystawiać coś na ~ko** make a mockery of sth
pośpiech haste, hurry[2], rush[2]; **robić coś bez ~u** linger; **w wielkim ~u** against the clock
pośpie-szać/szyć (się) zob. też ŚPIESZYĆ SIĘ; hasten
pośpieszny fast[1], hasty, hurried, swift; (*decyzja itp.*) snap[3]
pośredni 1 (*niebezpośredni*) indirect **2** (*etap itp.*) intermediate, transitional
pośrednictw|o 1 (*w rozwiązywaniu sporu itp.*) mediation **2** (*handl.*) agency; **biuro ~a pracy** jobcentre IDM **za ~em czegoś** by means of, through, via
pośredniczyć 1 (*w rozwiązywaniu sporu*) mediate **2 pośredniczący w czymś** instrumental in doing sth
pośredni-k/czka agent, go-between, intermediary; (*w rozwiązywaniu sporu*) mediator; (*w handlu*) middleman; (*w obrocie akcjami na giełdzie itp.*) broker
pośrodku between adv.
pośród amid, among
po-świadczać/świadczyć zob. też ŚWIADCZYĆ; certify, corroborate, witness[2]
poświadczyć
po-święcać/święcić zob. też ŚWIĘCIĆ **1** (*czas, energię*) commit, devote, expend, give[1], sacrifice[2], spare[2] **2** (*książkę itp.*) dedicate **3** (*relig.*) consecrate
□ **po-święcać/święcić się** devote yourself to sb/sth
pot perspiration, sweat noun
IDM **oblany zimnym ~em** in a cold sweat
potajemn|y clandestine, furtive, secret, stealthy, surreptitious, underhand; **~e działanie** stealth
■ **potajemnie** furtively, on the quiet, stealthily
potańcówka dance[1]; (*zabawa organizowana na koniec roku szkolnego*) prom
potargać → TARGAĆ
potargany tousled; (*na wietrze*) windswept
potargować się → TARGOWAĆ SIĘ
potas potassium
potasować → TASOWAĆ
potem after[3], afterwards, later on, next[2], then
potencja potency
potencjalny potential[1], would-be
potencjał potential[2]
potentat/ka magnate, tycoon
potęga 1 force[1], might[2], potency, power[1], strength **2** (*mat.*) **trzecia** ~ cube[1]
potęgować/s- fester
potępi(a)ć condemn, damn[2], denounce, deplore, deprecate, frown on/upon sth
potężny almighty, mighty[1], powerful
potknąć się → POTYKAĆ SIĘ
potknięcie (*drobne*) blip, hiccup
potłuczony broken[2]
potoczny colloquial, conversational
potoczyć (się) → TOCZYĆ (SIĘ)
potok 1 (*wody*) gush noun, stream[1], torrent **2 w ~ach** (*światła*) bathed in sth **3** (*ludzi, samochodów itp.*) stream[1]; (*słów itp.*) flow[1]; (*przekleństw itp.*) hail[2], torrent, volley
potomek descendant, offspring
potomność posterity
potomstwo offspring
potop (*i przen.*) deluge[1]
potrafić can[1], know[1] how to do sth, manage
po-trajać/troić (się) treble[2], triple verb
potraktować → TRAKTOWAĆ
potrawka casserole
potrą-cać/cić 1 (*uderzyć*) knock sb down **2** (*podatki*) deduct
■ **potrącenie** deduction; **przed potrąceniem** gross[1]
potrójny treble det., triple
potruchtać → TRUCHTAĆ
potrzask trap[1]

potrząs-ać/nąć shake[1]; (*kluczami itp.*) jiggle; (*bronią*) brandish IDM **~ głową** shake/toss your head
potrzeb|a necessity, need[3], requirement, want[2]; **(potrzeby)** purposes; **nagła ~a** urgency; **artykuł pierwszej ~y** necessity; **~a było trzech ludzi, aby przesunąć pianino** it took three people to move the piano IDM **w razie ~y** at a pinch
potrzebny necessary
potrzebować must[1], need[1,2], require, want[1]
potrzebujący deprived, needy
potrzeć → POCIERAĆ, TRZEĆ
potulność meekness
potulny meek
potwarz aspersions, slander, smear[2]
potwier-dzać/dzić affirm, approve, attest, back sth up, confirm, corroborate, support[1], verify; (*teorię itp.*) validate; (*sprawozdanie*) give substance to sth; ~ **autentyczność** authenticate; ~ **czyjeś słowa/zdanie** bear sth out; ~ **słuszność** vindicate
■ **potwierdzenie** affirmation, confirmation, corroboration, endorsement, validation, verification
potworność monstrosity; (*zbrodni itp.*) enormity
potworny ghastly, gruesome, monstrous
potwór monster, ogre
potyczka skirmish
po-tykać/tknąć się stumble, trip[2]
po-uczać/uczyć **1** (*wtajemniczać*) show sb/know/learn the ropes **2** (*wygłaszać kazanie*) preach
pouczający didactic, edifying, informative, instructive
pouczeni|e: **udzielać ~a** caution[2]
poufałość familiarity
poufały familiar, intimate
poufność confidentiality
poufn|y confidential; (*prywatny*) personal, private[1]; (*informacje firmy itp.*) inside adj.; **~a informacja** tip-off, the low-down (on sb/sth)
powab allure, attraction, enticement, lure[2]
powabny enticing; (*zwł. kobieta*) sultry
powachlować → WACHLOWAĆ
powag|a seriousness; (*sytuacji*) enormity, gravity, severity, solemnity; (*dostojność*) dignity; **z ~ą** solemnly; **brak ~i** frivolity
powałęsać się → WAŁĘSAĆ SIĘ
powałkonić się → WAŁKONIĆ SIĘ
poważać respect[2]
poważanie deference, respect[1]; **z ~m** respectfully; (*w liście*) yours
poważany respectable
poważnie **1** (*mówić, myśleć itp.*) earnestly, in earnest, seriously; **mówić ~** mean[1]; **czy mówisz ~?** are you serious (about sth)?; **traktować ~** take sb/sth seriously **2** (*ranny itp.*) badly, critically, gravely, severely
poważn|y **1** (*pełen powagi*) dire, grave[2], serious; (*okazja itp.*) solemn; (*wypadek itp.*) bad, nasty, severe; (*zainteresowanie itp.*) intense; **~e trudności** considerable difficulty **2** (*osoba; rozmowa itp.*) earnest, grim, serious, sober[1]; **z ~ą miną** straight-faced; **opowiadać dowcipy z ~ą miną** have a dry sense of humour **3** (*ważny*) important, major[1] **4** (*oferta*) firm[2] **5** (*muz.*) classical
powąchać → WĄCHAĆ
powątpiewanie doubt[1]; **z ~m** dubiously
powędrować → WĘDROWAĆ
powiać → WIAĆ
powia-damiać/domić inform, notify
■ **powiadamiani|e** (*w internecie*) **system szybkiego powiadamiania w internecie** (*np. gadu-gadu*) instant messaging
powiastka tale
powiązani|e link[1], relation; (*organizacji*) affiliation; **bez ~a** disjointedly
powiązany associated, interrelated, related
powiąz(yw)ać zob. też WIĄZAĆ; relate; ~ **wzajemnie** interrelate
powiedzeni|e **1** (*przysłowie*) adage, saying **2** (*slogan*) byword, catchphrase **3** (*mieć*) **coś do ~a** (a) say[2] (in sth)
powiedzieć zob. też MÓWIĆ; say[1], tell; **nigdzie nie jest powiedziane, że...** it doesn't follow that...; **to za mało powiedziane** that's an understatement IDM **chcieć ~** mean[1] | **że tak powiem** so to speak | **powiedzmy** let us, let's say
powiedzonko saying
powieka eyelid
po-wielać/wielić duplicate[1], replicate, reproduce
powiernictwo trust[1]
powierni-k/czka trustee
po-wierzać/wierzyć entrust, trust[2]; ~ **komuś kierownictwo** place/put sb in charge
powierzchnia area, surface[1]
powierzchowność **1** (*zewnętrzna strona*) exterior[1], surface[1] **2** (*zainteresowań itp.*) shallowness, superficiality
powierzchown|y **1** (*woda*) shallow **2** (*wiedza itp.*) superficial; (*uczucie, pogląd*) skin-deep; (*czytanie*) cursory, perfunctory; **~a znajomość (czegoś)** smattering (of sth) **3** (*zmiana*) cosmetic[2], superficial **4** (*niepogłębiony: postacie w książce itp.*) two-dimensional
powiesić → WIESZAĆ
powieszenie (*kara śmierci*) hanging
powieściopisa-rz/rka novelist
powieściowy fictional
powieść[1] novel[1]; ~ **detektywistyczna** detective story
powieść[2] → WODZIĆ
powieść się → POWODZIĆ SIĘ, WIEŚĆ SIĘ
powietrz|e air[1]; (*wyraz literacki*) ether; **(unoszący się) w ~u** airborne; **na świeżym ~u** in the open air, outdoor; **na wolnym ~u** open-air IDM **wisieć w ~u** be in the air | **świeże ~e** a breath of fresh air
powietrzny aerial[2]
powiew (*zwycięstwa itp.*) scent IDM **~ świeżego powietrza** a breath of fresh air
powiewać (*sukienka, włosy*) flow[2]; (*flaga*) flutter[1], fly[1]
powięk-szać/szyć augment, enlarge, magnify; (*terytorium*) expand; (*budynek itp.*) extend; (*fotografię*) blow sth up; (*efekt*) heighten; (*koszty, napięcie itp.*) escalate sth (into sth)
□ **powięk-szać/szyć się** enlarge; (*terytorium*) expand; (*tłum itp.*) swell[1]; (*efekt*) heighten; (*koszty, napięcie itp*) escalate (into sth); (*nastrój*) deepen; **powiększyła im się rodzina** they've got a new addition to the family
powijak|i: **w ~ach** in its infancy
powikłać → WIKŁAĆ
powikłanie complication
powinien you, etc. had better, ought to, should; ~ **bardziej uważać na to...** he wants to be more careful about...
powinność duty
powinowat-y/a relation, relative[2]
powitać → WITAĆ
powitanie greeting, welcome noun
po-wlekać/wlec coat[2]
□ **powlec się** → WLEC SIĘ
powłoczka pillowcase
powłoka coating; **cienka ~** film[1]
powłóczyć (się) → WŁÓCZYĆ (SIĘ)
powodować/s- bring, bring sth about, bring sth on, cause[2], create, engender, generate, give[1], induce, make[1], produce[1], provoke, be responsible (for sth), send, set sth off; (*decyzję*) motivate; (*szkodę itp.*) wreak; (*wrogość itp.*) breed[1]; ~ **następowanie/uruchomienie czegoś** trigger[2] sth (off); **przez przypadek poruszyłem stół i spowodowałem, że wszystkie szklanki i kieliszki znalazły się w powietrzu** I accidentally pushed the table and sent all the drinks flying
powodzeni|e joy, luck, success, well-being; **~e materialne** prosperity; **bez ~a** unsuccessfully; **osiągać ~e** get on; **z mniejszym lub większym ~em** with varying degrees of success IDM **~a!** good luck (to sb) | **~a i klęski** ups and downs
po-wodzić/wieść się get on/along, make a go of it, succeed; **nie powieść się** come unstuck, not meet with much success; **dobrze się powodzić** prosper; **dobrze/źle się komuś powodzi** be well/badly off
powojenny post-war
powojnik clematis
powoli slow adv., slowly
powolność slowness
powolny **1** slow[1], sluggish **2** (*dzień itp.*) lazy, leisurely; (*nudny*) flat[1]
powołanie **1** (*do jakiegoś zawodu itp.*) calling, vocation **2** ~ **czegoś do życia** creation
powoł(yw)ać ~ **kogoś do wojska** call sb up, conscript[1]; **zostać powołanym do wojska** be drafted into the army
□ **powoł(yw)ać się** refer to sb/sth
powonienie smell[2]
powód[1] (*przyczyna*) call[2] for sth, cause[1], reason[1], trigger[1]; **racjonalne powody** rationale; **nie ma najmniejszego powodu, dla którego...** there's no earthly reason why...; **powodem ataku była nienawiść rasowa** the attack was inspired by racial hatred; **z powodu czegoś/kogoś** because of, on account of sth, due[1] to sb/sth, for[1], owing to, through, in view of sth, by virtue of sth; (*umierać z jakiejś przyczyny*) of
powód/ka[2] (*prawn.*) plaintiff, the prosecution

powództwo action
powódź flood[2]
powóz carriage
po-wracać/wrócić recur, return[1]; (*do poprzedniego stanu/właściciela*) regress, revert; ~ **do zdrowia** (*np. w sanatorium*) convalesce; ~ **do poprzedniego stanu po okresie poprawy** relapse
■ **powracający** recurrent; (*problem*) **stale powracający** vexed
powrotny homeward, return[2]; **bilet** ~ return[2], return ticket, round-trip ticket
powrót 1 (*z jakiegoś miejsca*) return[2]; (*na scenę itp.*) comeback; (*do dzieciństwa itp.*) retreat[2]; ~ **do domu/ojczyzny** homecoming; **przynosić/przywozić kogoś/coś z powrotem** bring sb/sth back; **dostawać coś z powrotem** get sth back; **nikt nie chce powrotu do czasów pracy dzieci** nobody wants to bring back the days of child labour **2** (*problemu itp.*) recurrence **3** ~ **do zdrowia** recovery, recuperation IDM **tam i z powrotem** back and forth, backward(s) and forward(s), to and fro
powróżyć zob. też WRÓŻYĆ; **komuś** tell your fortune
powsta(wa)ć 1 (*pojawiać się*) come into existence, emerge, originate, spring from sth **2** (*wstawać*) get to your feet, stand[1], stand up **3 przeciw komuś/czemuś** rebel[2] (against sb/sth)
■ **powstanie 1** (*wyzwoleńcze itp.*) insurrection, rising[2], uprising **2** (*rozpoczęcie*) inception
powstrzym(yw)ać 1 kogoś/coś check[1], hold sb/sth back, hold/keep sth in check, stop[1]; (*inflację itp.*) contain; (*protest itp.*) stem[2]; (*rozwój itp.*) hinder; (*wzrost*) stunt[2]; **kogoś/coś (od czegoś)** deter, hold sb back (from doing sth), keep sb/sth back (from sb/sth), restrain, stop[1] sb/sth (from) doing sth; ~ **kogoś (przed czymś)** inhibit sb (from sth/from doing sth); ~ **kogoś przed czymś** keep sb from sth/from doing sth **2** (*łzy itp.*) hold sth back; (*gniew itp.*) repress; (*ziewnięcie*) suppress
■ **powstrzymywany** (*uczucie*) pent-up
□ **powstrzym(yw)ać się** abstain, hold back (from doing sth), refrain[1], resist, stop[1]; ~ **od czegoś w ostatniej chwili** stop short of sth/doing sth; **nie mogłem się powstrzymać od śmiechu** I couldn't help laughing
powszechn|y broad, broad-based, common[1], general[1], popular, prevailing, universal; **~y użytek** currency; **na ~e żądanie kogoś** by popular demand
■ **powszechnie** commonly, popularly, universally; ~ **używany** current[1], ubiquitous; **być rzeczą ~ie znaną** be common/public knowledge; **kamery są ~ zainstalowane w sklepach** it is common practice to have security cameras in shops
powszedni daily[1], everyday; **dzień** ~ weekday
powszednieć/s- become commonplace
powściągliwość deliberation, moderation, reserve[2], restraint, reticence
powściągliwy circumspect, restrained; (*w wyrażaniu poglądów*) reticent; (*w okazywaniu uczuć*) downbeat, reserved, stolid; (*reakcja itp.*) muted
po-wtarzać/wtórzyć 1 (*słowa*) repeat[1], say sth again; (*jak echo*) echo[2]; (*zwł. z naciskiem*) reiterate; (*tekst*) duplicate[1], replicate; **bezmyślnie** ~ regurgitate **2** (*materiał do egzaminu*) revise (for sth)
□ **po-wtarzać/wtórzyć się** (*problem itp.*) recur
■ **powtarzający się** recurrent, repeated, repetitive
powtórka 1 repeat[2], repetition; (*z meczu*) action replay **2** (*do egzaminu*) revision
powtórze|nie repetition; **pełen ~ń** repetitious
powyciągać się go out of shape
powyciągany shapeless
powyżej 1 (*wyżej*) above, overhead adv.; ~ **tonacji** sharp[2] **2** (*ponad*) over, in excess of IDM **mieć ~ uszu** be sick and tired of sth
poza[1] (*przym.*) **1** (*dalej*) beyond, outside[3] **2** (*domem/pracą*) away, out[1], out of **3** (*oprócz*) besides, except[1]; ~ **tym** besides adv., moreover, other than that, otherwise **4** (*czasem/wiekiem na robienie czegoś*) past[3]
poza[2] (*rz.*) front[1], pose[2]
pozagrobow|y: **życie ~e** afterlife
pozajelitowo: **odżywiać** ~ drip-feed
pozalekcyjny extra-curricular
pozamałżeński adulterous, extramarital
pozarządow|y: **organizacja ~a** NGO
pozasądowy extrajudicial
pozaszkolny extra-curricular
pozazadroszczeni|e: **godny pozazdroszczenia** enviable
pozaziemsk|i 1 extraterrestrial adj.; **istota ~a** extraterrestrial **2** (*nadzwyczajny*) ethereal
pozbawi(a)ć deprive, do sb out of sth; (*prawn.*) strip[1] sb/sth (of sth); (*snu*) rob sb/sth (of sth); **podstępem ~ kogoś czegoś** trick sb out of sth; ~ **sił** debilitate; ~ **tchu** wind[2]
pozbawiony: **czegoś** bereft of sth, devoid of sth, void[2] of sth
pozbierać: ~ **myśli** collect your thoughts
□ **pozbierać się** bounce back, recover
■ **pozbierany** (*zorganizowany*) together[2]
pozby(wa)ć się dispense with sb/sth, dispose of sb/sth, do away with sb/sth, dump[1], offload, get rid of sb/sth, be off your hands, shake sb/sth off, scrap[2]; (*odpowiedzialności*) shed[2]; **nie** ~ hang on to sth; ~ **swoich zahamowań** lose your inhibitions; **pozbywanie się czegoś** clear-out
po-zdrawiać/zdrowić acknowledge, greet, give/send sb your love
pozdrowieni|e greeting; (**pozdrowienia**) greetings, regards[2]; (*w liście*) (lots of) love (from); **przesyłać ~a** give/send sb your love
pozer/ka show-off
poziom 1 (*wysokość*) level[1]; (*płaszczyzna*) plane[1], tier; **wysoki** ~ high[2]; ~ **morza** sea level; **być na określonym ~ie** be running at; **pozostawać na stałym ~ie** level out; **na tym samym ~ie z kimś/czymś** level[2] with sb/sth; **na ~ie oczu** eye level **2** (*pułap*) mark[2]; (*o jakości*) notch[1] **3** (*jakość*) standard[1]; ~ **życia** standard of living; **wysoki** ~ quality; **na wysokim ~ie** polished; **(być) na ~ie** (be/come) up to scratch; **na tym samym ~ie z kimś/czymś** on a par with sb/sth; **na najwyższym/najniższym odnotowanym dotąd ~ie** at an all-time high/low; **poniżej ~u** substandard
poziomka wild strawberry
poziomnica spirit level
poziomować/wy- level[3]
poziom|y horizontal; (*i równy*) level[2] (*ustawienie strony pliku*) **orientacja ~a** landscape[1]
po-złacać/złocić zob. też ZŁOCIĆ; gild
pozłota gilt
pozmieniać rearrange
pozmywać → ZMYWAĆ
pozna(wa)ć 1 (*zacząć znajomość*) meet; (*dobrze znać*) get to know sb **2** (*rozpoznać*) recognize
poznawczy (*psych.*) cognitive
pozorny apparent, seeming; (*na pokaz*) token[2]
pozorować/u- pretend
pozostałość remnant, vestige; (*form.*) residue; (**pozostałości**) remains; (*mała ilość*) trace[2]
pozostały (*przym.*) other, remaining; (*kawałki drewna itp.*) odd; (*form.*) residual
■ **pozostali** (*rz.*) remainder
pozosta(wa)ć 1 (*nie opuszczać miejsca*) remain, stay[1]; (*np. dłużej, w tyle*) stay behind; ~ **w tyle** drop back, drop behind (sb); (*zwł. na wyścigach*) trail[2] by/in sth; ~ **(do późna) poza domem** stay out; **pozostać na stanowisku dyrektora szkoły** continue as head teacher **2** (*nadal być w jakimś stanie: ciepłym, nieruchomym itp.*) keep[1]; (*najwyższym; niepobitym (rekordzie) itp.*) stand[1] (at) sth; (*niezauważonym itp.*) go[1]; ~ **bez zmian** stand[1]; ~ **komuś wiernym** stick by sb **3 do zrobienia** remain; **nie pozostaje nic innego, jak** there is nothing (else) for it (but to do sth)
pozostawi(a)ć leave sb/sth (behind)
■ **pozostawiony** (*na lodzie itp.*) stranded
pozować pose[1]
pozór facade, pretence, semblance; (**pozory**) make-believe; **na** ~ apparently, outwardly; **pod pozorem czegoś** under the guise of sth IDM **pod żadnym pozorem** not on any account, on no account, on no condition
pozwać → POZYWAĆ
po-zwalać/zwolić 1 (*udzielać zgody*) allow, consent[1] to sth, let, permit[1], sanction[2], tolerate; **czy pozwolisz, że zapalę?** do you mind if I smoke? **2** (*umożliwiać*) allow, enable, let **3 sobie na coś** (*finansowo*) afford; (*folgować sobie*) indulge (yourself) (in sth) **4** ~ **sobie skłamać** not to be above telling a few lies IDM **za dużo sobie ~** go too far
pozwan|y defendant; **strona ~a** the defence
pozwoleni|e 1 (*zgoda*) consent[2], OK[2], permission, sanction[1]; **~e, żeby coś**

zacząć go-ahead[1]; **bez ~a** unauthorized **2** (*dokument*) licence, permit[2]; **~e na pracę** work permit; **wydawać ~e** license[1]
pozycja 1 (*położenie, miejsce*) place[1], position[1]; (*sport*) **~ gry** position[1], stance **2** (*ważna/wysoka*) standing[2], stature **3** (*posterunek*) post[1]; (*stanowisko dyrektora itp.*) capacity **4** (*w spisie*) item; (*zwł. na aukcji*) lot[3]; (*w konkursie*) entry
pozysk(iw)ać 1 kogoś (do czegoś) win sb over/around/round (to sth); (*kupić kogoś*) buy sb off **2 sobie** endear yourself to sb
pozytywny positive; (*pochlebny itp.*) glowing
poz(y)wać: **pozwać kogoś do sądu** take sb to court
pożałować → ŻAŁOWAĆ
pożałowani|e: **~a godny** unfortunate, untoward
pożar fire[1]; (*olbrzymi*) blaze[2]
pożądać covet, crave, desire[2], hunger for/after sth, lust[2] after sb, after/for sth
pożądany desirable, welcome[2]; (*mężczyzna/kobieta, jako partner (ka)*) eligible; **bardziej ~** preferable to sth/doing sth; **najmniej ~** last[1]
pożądliwy lustful, randy
pożeglować → ŻEGLOWAĆ
pożegnać się → ŻEGNAĆ SIĘ
pożegnaln|y valedictory; **~a impreza** farewell party
pożegnanie goodbye noun, farewell noun, parting
po-żerać/żreć devour, gobble sth (up/down) IDM **~ kogoś/coś wzrokiem** drool over sb/sth
pożyci|e: **łatwy w ~u** easy-going
po-życzać/życzyć 1 (komuś) lend, loan verb **2 (od kogoś)** borrow
pożyczający 1 (komuś) lender **2 (od kogoś)** borrower
pożyczka borrowing, loan; (*z banku itp.*) credit[1]
pożyczkodawca lender
pożyczyć → POŻYCZAĆ, ŻYCZYĆ
pożyteczny profitable, useful
pożytek benefit[1], good[2], use[2], usefulness; (*form.*) utility; (*nieform.*) mileage
pożywić się → ŻYWIĆ SIĘ
pożywienie food, nourishment
pożywny nutritious
pójść → IŚĆ, CHODZIĆ
pół half[1]; **dzielić na ~** halve; **podzielić kraj na ~** split the country down the middle IDM **~ na ~** fifty-fifty adv.
półdiablę devil
półfinalist-a/ka semi-finalist
półfinał semi-final
półgłos undertone; **~em** in an undertone, in undertones; **mówić ~em** murmur, say sth, speak, etc. under your breath; **śpiewać ~em** croon
półka (*drewniana itp.*) shelf; (*z prętów*) rack[1]; **~ na bagaż** luggage rack; **~ na książki** bookshelf; **~ nad kominkiem** mantelpiece
półkole semicircle
półkula (*i ziemska*) hemisphere
półmisek dish[1]
półmrok shadow[1]
północ 1 (*czas*) midnight **2** (*kierunek*) north[1]; (*jadący/idący itp.*) **na ~** northbound, northwards; **na ~/y** north adv.; **z ~y** north[2], northerly
północno-wschodni north-east[2], north-easterly, north-eastern
północno-zachodni north-west[2], north-westerly, north-western
północny north[2], northerly, northern, northward adj.; **~ wschód** north-east[1]; **~ zachód** north-west[1]
półnuta minim
półpiętro landing
półprzezroczysty translucent
półprzytomny spaced out
półszept undertone; **~em** in an undertone, in undertones
półton semitone
półtor|a half[1]; **~ej godziny** an hour and a half
półwysep peninsula
później afterwards, later on, next[2], onwards, subsequently; (*form.*) thereafter
późniejszy latter, subsequent
późn|y late; **dość ~y** latish; **do ~ych godzin** at/till all hours
■ **późn|o** late[2]; **za ~o** (*poniewczasie*) belatedly; **jak najpóźniej** last thing; **do ~a** late; **do ~a w nocy** far into the night; **robić się ~o** get on; **~o już** it's late
pra- (*-dziadek itp.*) great[1]
prac|a 1 (*zawodowa; artystyczna*) job, work[2]; (*wykonywane zajęcie*) business; (*zwł. fizyczna*) labour[1]; **~a biurowa** desk job; **~a domowa** (*szk.*) homework; (*pisemna analiza*) project[1]; **~e domowe** household chores, housework; **~a społeczna** (*wykonywana odpłatnie*) social work; (*wykonywana dobrowolnie lub nakazana wyrokiem sądowym*) community service; **~e remontowe** restorations; (*ziemne itp.*) works[2]; **~a dodatkowa** sideline; **~a przygotowawcza** groundwork; **~a zespołowa** teamwork; **bez ~y** unemployed; **Praca/Dam ~ę.** (*rubryka ogłoszeń w gazecie*) Situations Vacant; **urząd ~y** jobcentre **2** (*naukowa*) research, study[1]; (*magisterska itp.*) dissertation, thesis **3** (**prace**) (*komisji itp.*) proceedings **4** (*komputera, maszyny*) operation
pracodaw-ca/czyni employer
pracoholi-k/czka workaholic
pracować work[1]; **ciężko ~** labour[2] away; **~ nadal/wytrwale nad czymś** keep at it/sth; **~ w systemie zmianowym** work in shifts; **czy siostra Peters pracuje dziś?** is Nurse Peters on today?
pracowity (*osoba*) busy, diligent, hard-working, industrious; (*form.*) assiduous; (*dzień*) busy
pracownia study[1]; (*artystyczna*) studio
pracowniczy working
pracow-nik/nica/niczka employee, worker; **pracownik fizyczny** workman; **pracownik naukowy** academic[2]; **pracownik socjalny** social worker
prać/wy- 1 (*ubrania*) wash[1]; (*form.*) launder **2** (*brudne pieniądze*) launder **3** (*bić*) wallop
□ **prać/wy- się** wash[1]
pradawny primeval
pragmatyczny pragmatic
pragnąć/za- crave (for) sth, desire[2], long[3] for sth, (for sb) to do sth, lust[2] (after sb), (after/for sth), wish[1] to do sth **kogoś** (*seksualnie*) want[1]; **bardzo czegoś ~** be dying for sth/to do sth, hunger for/after sth; **ona może kupić wszystko, czego zapragnie** she can buy anything she pleases
pragnienie 1 (*chęć napicia się*) thirst **2** (*wielka chęć*) craving, desire[1], hunger[1] for sth, longing, wish[2], yearning; (*wiedzy*) thirst for sth; **(być) obiektem pragnień** to die for
praktyczn|y functional, practical[1], utilitarian; (*przyrząd*) nifty; (*wiedza*) non-academic; (*osoba*) businesslike, down to earth; **~a znajomość francuskiego** a working knowledge of French; **strona ~a** practicality; **~a zasada** a rule of thumb
praktyk (*lekarz, adwokat itp.*) practitioner
praktyk|a 1 (*doświadczenie*) experience[1], practice; **odbywać ~ę zawodową** do work experience **2** (*praca lekarza/adwokata*) practice
praktykować practise; **~ w przychodni** be in general practice
■ **praktykujący 1 ~ lekarz/adwokat** practitioner **2** (*relig.*) **osoba praktykująca** churchgoer
pralka (*automatyczna*) washing machine
pralnia laundry; **~ chemiczna** dry-cleaner's; **~ samoobsługowa** launderette
prani|e 1 (*czynność prania*) wash[2], washing; **w ~u** in the wash **1** (*brudna bielizna*) laundry, washing IDM **~e mózgu** brainwashing
prapremiera preview
prasa press[1]; **~ drukarska** printing press
prasować/wy- iron[2], do the ironing, press[2]
prasowy press[1]
prastary primeval
praw|da truth; **to ~da** granted; **~da jest taka, że** the fact (of the matter) is (that)… IDM **~dę mówiąc** actually, as a matter of fact | **spojrzeć ~dzie w oczy** face facts
prawdomówny truthful
prawdopodobieństwo likelihood, the odds (on sth/sb), probability; **duże ~ czegoś** a good chance that…
prawdopodobny arguable, on the cards, likely adj., possible, probable; **mało ~** unlikely
prawdziwy authentic, bona fide, genuine, proper, real[1], true, veritable; (*nieform.*) quite a, for real, right[1]; (*zgodny z faktami*) realistic; (*sportowiec, władca itp.*) born[2]; **na dworze jest ~ mróz!** it's absolutely freezing outside!
prawica right[3]
prawicowiec right-winger
prawicowy rightist, right-wing
prawiczek virgin[1]
prawidłowy 1 (*odpowiedź itp.*) correct[1]; (*stwierdzenie*) truthful **2** (*stosowny*) proper
prawie about[1], as good as, near[1], nearly, practically, pretty much/nearly/well, virtually; **(już) ~** just

about; ~ **(tyle co) nic** next to nothing; ~ **(nie/nigdy/nikt itp.)** hardly; ~ **wcale nie chodzimy teraz do teatru** we hardly ever go to the theatre nowadays; ~ **uwierzyłem, że może przyjść** I half thought he might come; **mieszkają tutaj już ~ od czterdziestu lat** they've lived here for the best part of forty years
prawnicz|y legal; **firma ~a** law firm
prawni-k/czka lawyer; **(prawnicy)** the legal profession
prawn|y legal; (*właściel itp.*) rightful; **nie mający mocy ~ej** null and void, void[2]
praw|o 1 (*przepisy*) law, legislation, statute; **~o autorskie** copyright; **~o cywilne** civil law; **~o zwyczajowe** common law; **~o łaski** clemency; **w granicach ~a** legitimately **2** (*uprawnienie*) authority, power[1], right[3]; **do czegoś** claim[2], entitlement; **~a człowieka** human rights; **~a obywatelskie** civil rights; **~a zwierząt** animal rights; **~o głosu** a voice[1] (in sth); **~o jazdy** driving licence; **~o do opieki** custody; **~o pierworództwa** birthright of the eldest child; **~o wyborcze** franchise; **mieć ~o (coś robić)** be within your rights (to do sth); **mieć ~o do czegoś** be entitled to sth; **nie mający ~a (do czegoś)** ineligible (for/to do sth); **nie mieć ~a czegoś zrobić** have no business to do sth/doing sth; **nadawać ~a; otrzymywać ~a** qualify (sb) (for sth/to do sth); **na równych ~ach** be on equal terms (with sb); **odmówiono im ~a wstępu** they were refused entrance to the disco **3** (*reguły fizyki itp.*) law, principle **4** (*kierunek*) **w ~o** right[2]
prawodawstwo legislation
prawomyślny law-abiding
praworęczny right-handed
praworządność law and order
praworządny law-abiding
prawoskrzydłowy right-winger
prawosławny: **kościół** ~ the (Eastern) Orthodox Church
prawostronny right-hand
prawość honesty, integrity, rightness, virtue
prawowierny orthodox
prawowity lawful, legitimate, rightful ■ **prawowitość** legitimacy
prawoznawstwo jurisprudence
praw|y 1 (*nie lewy*) right[1]; **~a strona** right[3]; **po ~ej stronie** on the right-hand side **2** (*szlachetny*) honest, righteous, straightforward, upright, virtuous IDM (*przen.*) **~a ręka** right-hand man
prażyć 1 (*w kuchni*) roast[1] **2** (*ziemię itp.*) bake
prącie penis
prąd 1 (*elektryczny*) current[2], electricity; ~ **stały** DC; ~ **zmienny** AC **2** (*rzeki*) current[2]; (*i przen.*) **pod** ~ upstream; **z ~em** downstream; **płynąć z ~em rzeki** sail down the river **3** ~ **termiczny** thermal[2]
prądnica dynamo, generator
prążek stripe
prążkowany striped
preambuła preamble
precedens precedent; **bez ~u** unprecedented; **stwarzać** ~ set a precedent
precjoza valuables
precyzj|a exactness, precision; **wymagający ~i** delicate
precyzować/s- get sth straight, pin sth down, pinpoint, specify
precyzyjny 1 precise, spot on; (*rozkaz; interpretacja prawa itp.*) strict **2** (*przyrząd*) sensitive
predysponować: **kogoś do czegoś** predispose sb to sth/to do sth
prefabrykat: **budynek z ~ów** prefab
preferencja preference
preferencyjny preferential; **w porządku ~m** in order of preference
preferować prefer
prehistoryczny prehistoric
prekursor forerunner
prelekcja talk[2]
preludium prelude
premedytacj|a: **(dokonany) z ~ą** premeditated, wilful
premia bonus
premier premier[2], prime minister
premier|a (*przedstawienie itp.*) opening, opening night, premiere; **mieć ~ę** (*filmu/sztuki*) premiere verb
prenatalny antenatal
prenumerata subscription
prenumerator/ka subscriber
prenumerować/za- subscribe
preparować/s- cook sth up, doctor[2]
preria prairie
prerogatywa prerogative
presj|a pressure; **pod ~ą** strained, under pressure; **być pod ~ą** (*np. terminów*) be pressed for sth; **wywierać na kimś ~ę** put pressure on sb (to do sth)
prestiż prestige
prestiżowy prestige, prestigious
pretekst pretext
pretendent/ka (*do stanowiska*) challenger, contender
pretendowanie: **do robienia czegoś** pretension
pretensj|a pretension IDM **mieć ~e do całego świata** have a chip on your shoulder (about sth)
pretensjonalny pretentious, showy
prewencj|a: **policyjne siły ~i** riot police
prewencyjny preventive
prezencj|a: **mający dobrą ~ę** presentable
prezent gift, present[2]; **(prezenty)** (*nieform.*) goodies
prezentacj|a presentation; **dokonać ~i** make/do the introductions
prezenter/ka announcer, presenter; **prezenter/ka wiadomości radiowych/telewizyjnych** newsreader; **prezenter/ka telewizyjn-y/a lub radiow-y/a** anchorman, anchorwoman
prezentować/za- present[3]; (*strój na pokazie mody*) model[2]
prezerwatywa condom
prezes/ka chairman, chairperson, president; **(prezeska)** chairwoman; (*banku itp.*) governor
prezesura chairmanship
prezydencki presidential
prezydent president
prezydentura presidency
prędki quick[1], rapid, speedy, swift; (*w podejmowaniu decyzji itp.*) incisive
prędkość rapidity, speediness, velocity; (*i samochodu*) speed[1]
pręg|a stripe; **w ~i** striped; **pokryty ~ami** streaked
pręgowany streaked, striped; **szary ~ kot** tabby
pręt rod
prężność buoyancy, resilience, suppleness; ~ (*działania*) dynamism
prężny 1 (*odporny*) resilient **2** (*ciało*) supple **3** (*organizacja, kraj*) dynamic; (*gospodarka*) buoyant
prima: ~ **aprilis** April Fool's Day
priorytet priority
priorytetowy (*przesyłka itp.*) first-class ■ **priorytetowo**: **traktować priorytetowo** prioritize
proaktywny proactive
probierz yardstick
problem 1 (*kłopot*) liability, the matter[1] (with sb/sth), problem; (*nieform.*) bug[1], bugbear; **stwarzać ~y** rock the boat; **nie stanowić ~u** money, etc. is no object; **miał ~y ze zdaniem egzaminu na prawo jazdy** he found it difficult/it was difficult for him to pass the driving test **2** (*kwestia*) question[1]
problematyczny problematic
proboszcz rector, vicar
probówk|a test tube; **dziecko z ~i** test-tube baby
proca catapult[1]
procedura (*sądowa itp.*) procedure
procent 1 (*ze stu*) per cent noun, percentage **2** (*od kapitału*) interest[1] (on sth)
procentow|y per cent; **stopa ~a** interest rate
proces 1 (*przebieg*) process[1] **2** ~ **sądowy** court case, lawsuit, trial
procesja procession
procesować się litigate, sue
proch (prochy) ashes; ~ **strzelniczy** gunpowder
producent/ka maker, manufacturer, producer; **producent/ka filmow-y/a** film producer
produkcja generation, output; (*i filmu*) production; (*przemysłowa*) manufacture noun, manufacturing
produkować/wy- fabricate, make[1]; (*i film/sztukę*) produce[1]; (*maszynowo*) manufacture; ~ **coś szybko i w dużych ilościach** churn sth out, grind sth out
produkt product; ~ **końcowy** end product; ~ **uboczny** by-product; ~ **odpadowy** waste product; ~ **krajowy brutto** GDP; ~ **narodowy brutto** GNP; ~ **wiodący** market leader
produktywność productivity
produktywny productive
profanować/s- defile
profesjonalist-a/ka professional[2]
profesjonalizm professionalism
profesjonalny professional[1]
profesor/ka professor
profesura chair[1]
profil 1 (*twarzy*) profile **2** (*rynku itp.*) profile **3** (*przekrój*) section
profilaktyczny preventive, prophylactic
profilaktyka prevention
profilowan|y: **klasa ~a** stream[1]
progesteron progesterone
prognoza forecast noun, prognosis, projection; ~ **pogody** weather forecast
prognozować forecast ■ **prognozowanie** projection

program 1 (*działania*) programme[1], scheme[1]; ~ **nauczania** curriculum, syllabus **2** (*radio, TV*) broadcast noun, programme[1]; ~ **telewizyjny** (*film itp.*) telecast; (*spis programów*) TV guide; ~ **dokumentalny** documentary **3** (*teatr*) bill[1], programme[1]; ~ **rozrywkowy** a variety show **4** (*komput.*) feature[1] (on sth), program[1]; ~ **użytkowy** application, utility
programist-a/ka programmer
programować/za- programme[2]
prohibicj|a: **przestrzegający ~i** dry[1]
projekcja showing
projekt 1 (*podróży itp.*) plan[1]; (*plan, zamierzenie*) project[1], proposal, scheme[1] **2** (*szkic*) design[1] **3** (*wstępny*) draft[1]; ~ **ustawy** bill[1]
projektant/ka designer; **projektant/ka mody** fashion designer; **projektant/ka wnętrz** interior designer
projektor projector
projektować/za- design[2], lay sth out, plan[2], project[2]; (*krajobraz*) landscape[2]; ~ **coś na specjalne zamówienie** tailor[2]
■ **projektowanie** design[1]; ~ **wnętrz** interior design
proklamacja proclamation
proklamować proclaim
prokreacja procreation
prokurator prosecutor, public prosecutor; **Prokurator Generalny** the Director of Public Prosecutions
proliferacja proliferation
prolog prologue
prolongata extension; ~ **terminu płatności** grace
prom boat, ferry[1]; ~ **kosmiczny** space shuttle; **przewozić ~em** ferry[2]
promenada (*nadmorska*) promenade; (*nadmorska z desek*) boardwalk
promienieć shine[1]
■ **promieniejący** radiant
promieniotwórczość radioactivity
promieniotwórczy radioactive
promieniować 1 radiate; (*słońce, światło*) beam[2] **2** (*przen.*) beam[2] (at sb/sth); **czymś** exude, glow (with sth), radiate
promieniowanie radiation, radioactivity; ~ **rentgenowskie** X-ray
promieniście: **rozchodzić się ~** radiate
promienny radiant
promie|ń 1 (*słońca itp.*) ray, shaft; **~ń słońca** sunbeam; **~nie słoneczne** sun[1]; **wysyłać ~nie** beam[2]; **naświetlać ~niami** irradiate **2** (*okręgu itp.*) radius
promocja plug[1], promotion
promocyjny (*cena itp.*) introductory
promotor/ka supervisor
promować/wy- promote; (*nieform.*) plug[2]
promyk IDM ~ **nadziei** ray of hope
propaganda propaganda
propagator/ka exponent
propagować/roz- popularize, propagate
proponować/za- offer[1], propose, suggest; **komuś coś** put sth to sb
proporcj|a proportion; **spróbuj widzieć te sprawy we właściwych ~ach** try to keep these issues in perspective; **zmieszać płyn do sprzątania z wodą w ~i jeden do dziesięciu** use one part cleaning fluid to ten parts water IDM **we właściwej ~i** in proportion
proporcjonalny proportional, pro rata; **(do czegoś)** proportionate; **system** ~ (*polit.*) proportional representation
propozycja approach, offer[2], offering, proposal, proposition, suggestion
proroctwo prophecy
proroczy prophetic
prorok/ini prophet
prorokować/wy- predict, prophesy
prosiak (także **prosiaczek, prosiątko**) piglet
prosić/po- 1 kogoś, o coś ask, request; ~ **kogoś o przysługę** beg/ask a favour of sb; ~ **listownie o coś** write in (to sb/sth) (for sth), write off/away (to sb/sth) (for sth); **usilnie** ~ entreat **2** (**proszę**) (*rozkaz; zaproszenie*) please[1]; **oczywiście, proszę bardzo** sure, go ahead; **proszę pan-a/i!** here[2] **3** (**proszę**) (*podając coś*) here you are, there you are **4** (**proszę**) (*w odpowiedzi na ofertę*) **tak, proszę** yes, please **5** (**proszę**) (*odpowiedź na czyjeś podziękowanie*) **proszę (bardzo)** that is (quite) all right, be my guest, don't mention it, not at all, you're welcome **6** (**proszę**) (*przepuszczając kogoś, np. w drzwiach*) after you IDM **no i proszę** there you are
□ **prosić się**: **(aż) się prosić o coś** cry out for sth
proso millet
prospekt brochure, handout, pamphlet, prospectus
prosperować prosper; **dobrze ~** boom[2], thrive
■ **prosperujący**: **dobrze prosperujący** successful
prostacki coarse, common[1], gross[1], ignorant, indelicate, vulgar
prostactwo indelicacy, vulgarity
prosta-k/czka peasant, pleb
prosto 1 (*nie skręcając*) direct adv.; (*nie zbaczając*) straight[1]; **ruszyć ~ do czegoś** make a beeline for sth; **iść** ~ go straight on; **iść ~ przed siebie** follow your nose **2** (*w coś uderzyć itp.*) full[2] in/on (sth), slap[2], square[1] **3** (*pionowo*) straight[1], upright adv.; **stawać** ~ straighten up **4** (*zwyczajnie*) plainly, simply IDM **~ z mostu**; **~ w oczy** to sb's face, point-blank, straight out | **mówiący ~ w oczy/z mostu** outspoken | **powiedzieć komuś coś ~ z mostu** make no bones about telling sb sth
prostoduszność naivety
prostoduszny ingenuous, innocent, naive
prostokąt oblong, rectangle
prostokątny oblong, rectangular; **trójkąt** ~ right-angled triangle
prostolinijność earthiness
prostolinijny forthright, straight[2], straightforward
prostopadły perpendicular
prostota simplicity; (*stylu życia itp.*) austerity
prostować/wy-/s- align, straighten sth (up/out) IDM ~ **fakty** put/set the record straight
□ **prostować/wy- się** straighten (up/out)
prosty 1 (*nie zgięty*) straight[2]; (*stojący*) erect[1] **2** (*bezpośredni*) direct[1] **3** (*łatwy*) simple, straightforward **4** (*zwyczajny*) homely, plain[1], primitive, simple **5** (*styl życia itp.*) austere **6** (*słowa; prawda*) bald; (*uczciwy*) straight[2] **7** (*niewykształcony*) simple; **pochodzi z prostej rodziny** she comes from a humble background IDM **po prostu** merely, sheer, simply
prostytucja prostitution
prostytutka prostitute
prosz|ek powder; (*na ciasto itp.*) mix[2]; **~ek do pieczenia** baking powder; **~ek do prania** soap powder, washing powder; (*mleko itp.*) **w ~ku** dried[2], powdered
proszę → PROSIĆ
proszkować/s- pulverize
proszon|y: **~a kolacja** dinner party
prośb|a request[1]; **~a o informację** enquiry; **pisemna ~a** petition; **usilna ~a** plea; **pisać do kogoś z ~ą o coś** send away (to sb) (for sth), send off (for sth)
protagonista protagonist
proteina protein
protekcja favouritism
protekcjonalność condescension
protekcjonalny condescending, patronizing
protektor 1 (także **protektorka**) protector; (*organizacji charytatywnej itp.*) patron **2** (*u opony*) tread[2]
protest protest[1], revolt noun
protestancki Protestant adj.
protestant/ka Protestant
protestować/za- object[2], protest[2]
■ **protestując-y/a** (*rz.*) objector, protester
protokół 1 (*spotkania*) minutes[1], record[1] **2** (*dyplomatyczny itp.*) protocol
proton proton
prototyp prototype
prowadząc-y/a (*rz.*) coordinator
prowadzić 1 (*wieść; droga*) go[1], lead[1] **2** (**/za-/prze-/po-**) (*kierować*) guide[2], pass[1] sth along/down/through, etc. (sth); (*ludzi*) show[1], shepherd[2] **3** (**/do-**) (*do jakiegoś stanu*) lead[1] to sth **4** (*samochód itp.*) drive[1]; ~ **rower na wzgórze** wheel your bicycle up the hill **5** ~ **(coś) dalej** carry on sth, continue (with sth), follow sth up, proceed (with sth), pursue **6** (**/prze-**) (*realizować*) ~ **prace badawcze/naukowe** research verb (into/in/on) (sth); ~ **dochodzenie** investigate **7** (*firmę itp.*) manage, run[1]; (*sklep, restaurację itp.*) keep[1]; (*interesy, usługi itp.*) operate; ~ **interesy (z kimś)** deal[1] (with sb) **8** ~ **sprawę sądową** prosecute; ~ **czyjąś sprawę** plead (sth) (for sb/sth) **9** (*wojnę*) wage[2] sth (against/on sb/sth); (*w zapasach*) ~ **walkę** wrestle **10** (**/prze-**) (*rozmowę*) hold[1] **11** (*zapiski*) keep[1]; ~ **swoje rachunki** keep your own accounts **12** (*pewien tryb życia*) lead[1] **13** (*wyprzedzać*) lead[1] **14** ~ **rachunek czegoś** keep/lose count (of sth)
■ **prowadząc-y/a** (*rz.*) **prowadząc-y/a program** host, hostess

□ **prowadzić się** conduct[1] yourself well, badly, etc.
prowicjonalny provincial
prowincja 1 (*wieś*) the country, the provinces **2** (*jednostka administracyjna*) province
prowincjonalizm parochialism
prowincjonalny parochial, provincial
prowizja commission[1]
prowizoryczny makeshift, provisional, temporary; (*plany*) tentative
prowokacja instigation, provocation
prowokacyjny provocative; (*nieform.*) bolshie
prowokować/s- 1 kogoś goad, provoke; (*bunt itp.*) instigate, invite; ~ **bijatykę/kłótnię (z kimś)** pick a fight (with sb) **2** (*sprowadzić: sen itp.*) induce
proza prose
prozaiczny commonplace, mundane, pedestrian[2], prosaic
prozai-k/czka prose writer
prób|a 1 (*badanie*) test[1], trial, trial run **2** (*wysiłek*) attempt[1], endeavour noun, go[2], shot[1], try[2]; **~a (zdobycia)** bid[3] (for sth); **wystawiający na ~ę** taxing **3 ~a zamachu na życie prezydenta** an attempt on the President's life **4** (*teatr*) rehearsal; (*i przen.*) **~a generalna** dress rehearsal; **odbywać ~ę** rehearse **5** (*metali*) hallmark IDM **metoda ~ i błędów** trial and error | **poddawać kogoś/coś ~ie** put sb/sth to the test
próbka sample, specimen
próbny pilot[3]; **okres ~** probation; **~ egzamin** mock[3], mock exam
próbować/s- 1 (*podjąć próbę*) attempt[2], endeavour, seek (to do sth), try[1], give sth a try, try your hand at sth; (*nieform.*) have a bash (at sth/at doing sth), have a shot at sth, have a stab at sth/doing sth, give sth a whirl; **spróbować swoich sił (w czymś)** have a crack (at sth/at doing sth) **2** (*sprawdzić*) test[2] **3** (*potrawę, napój*) have a taste of sth, sample verb, taste[2], try[1] **4** (*teatr*) rehearse
próchnica rot noun
próg 1 (*w drzwiach*) doorstep, threshold **2 (progi)** (*na rzece*) rapids **3** (*w gitarze*) fret[2] **4** (*granica*) threshold IDM (*przen.*) **tuż za progiem** on your/the doorstep | **u progu** on the verge of sth/doing sth
prószyć (*śnieg*) snow[2]
próżnia void[1]; (*i fiz.*) vacuum[1]
próżniactwo laziness
próżniaczy lazy
próżniak bum
próżno IDM **na ~** in vain
próżność vanity
próżnować fart around, lie back
próżny 1 (*osoba; zachowanie*) vain **2** (*wysiłek itp.*) vain **3** (*obietnica itp.*) idle **4** (*pusty*) void[2]
pruć/roz- belt[2] along, down, up, etc., bomb[2], rip through sth
□ **pruć/roz- się** come apart, unravel
pruderyjność prudishness
pruderyjny prissy, prudish
prych-ać/nąć snort, splutter; **pogardliwie ~** blow a raspberry
prym lead[2]
prymat pre-eminence
prymitywność crudity
prymitywny crude, primitive
prys-kać/nąć splash[1], spray[2]
pryszcz pimple; (*zwł. na twarzy*) spot[1], zit
pryszczaty spotty
prysznic shower[1]; **brać ~** have a shower, shower[2]
pryta plonk[2]
prywatka get-together, party
prywatność privacy
prywatn|y personal, private[1]; **szkoła ~a** (*dla dzieci w wieku od 13 do 18 lat, często z internatem*) public school; **~a szkoła podstawowa** preparatory school; **przedsiębiorczość ~a** private enterprise
■ **prywatnie** personally, privately, in private; (*poinformować itp.*) informally
prywatyzacja privatization
prywatyzować/s- privatize
pryzmat prism
prząść/u- spin[1]
przeanalizować → ANALIZOWAĆ
przeba-czać/czyć forgive, pardon verb
przebarwi(a)ć (się) discolour
przebici|e (*opony, dętki*) blowout, puncture; **nie do ~a** impenetrable
przebić (się) → PRZEBIJAĆ (SIĘ)
przebieg (*samochód*) **mieć mały ~** have a low mileage
prze-biegać/biec 1 (*dziać się*) proceed **2 przez coś** (*badać*) run through sth; **~ wzrokiem po czymś** scan; **przebiec palcem** run your finger down sth
przebiegłość cunning noun, guile
przebiegły artful, crafty, cunning, devious, sly, wily; (*plan itp.*) fiendish; (*decyzja itp.*) tactical; (*wypowiedź polityka itp.*) slick[1]
prze-bierać/brać 1 kogoś/coś (za kogoś/coś) disguise[1] sb/sth (as sb/sth) **2** (*grymasić*) pick and choose
□ **prze-bierać/brać się 1 w coś** change[1] (into sth) **2 za kogoś/coś** be disguised as sb/sth, dress up
■ **przebieranie się**: **~ za kobietę** drag[2]
przebieralnia changing room
przebi(ja)ć penetrate, pierce; (*zwł. oponę*) puncture; (*balonik*) pop[2]; (*dziurkaczem*) punch[1]
□ **przebi(ja)ć się** penetrate
przebijak punch[2]
przebiśnieg snowdrop
przebitka carbon copy
przebłagać → BŁAGAĆ
przebłysk 1 (*światła*) gleam, glimmer **2** (*uczucia*) flicker[2]; (*talentu*) spark[1]; **~ nadziei** a glimmer/ray of hope; **~ geniuszu** a stroke of genius
przebojowy feisty, pushy
przeboleć get over sth
przeb|ój blockbuster, hit[2], smash[2]; **lista ~ojów** the charts[1]
przebrać (się) → PRZEBIERAĆ (SIĘ)
przebranie disguise[2]; (*na bal maskowy itp.*) fancy dress
przebrnąć zob. też BRNĄĆ **1** (*przez książkę itp.*) plough through sth, wade through sth **2** (*przez egzamin itp.*) scrape through (sth)
przebrzmiał|y: **~a sława** has-been
przebudowa redevelopment
przebudo(wy)wać convert[1], redevelop
przebudzenie awakening
przebyci|e: **(możliwy) do ~a** passable; **nie do ~a** impassable
przebywać 1 (*mieszkać*) reside; (*w jakimś miejscu*) sit **2 (/przebyć)** (*przejść, przejechać*) cover[1], travel[1]
przecedzić → CEDZIĆ
przecena sale
przeceni(a)ć 1 (*za wysoko ocenić jakość*) overrate **2** (*ilość itp.*) overestimate
przeceniony cut-price, on sale
przechadzać /przejść się saunter, stroll verb, walk[1]
przechadzka stroll, walk[2], wander noun
przechodni transitive
przechodzący passing[2]
prze-chodzić/jść 1 przez coś cross[2] (over) (from sth/to sth), get across sth **2 obok kogoś/czegoś** go by, pass[1], pass by (sb/sth); **przejść tuż koło kogoś** walk straight by sb **3** (*doświadczyć, przebyć*) get through (sth), go through sth, undergo; **~ badanie wzroku** have your eyes tested; **pomagać komuś przejść przez coś** get (sb) through (sth); **~ zły okres w życiu** go through a bad patch **4** (*choroba*) clear up, go[1]; (*ból*) wear off; (*gniew itp.*) drain[1] **5 do czegoś/na coś innego** get on to sth, go on to sth, go over to sth, get through (to sth), proceed to do sth; (*do nowego tematu*) move on (to sth); **~ nad czymś do porządku dziennego** gloss over sth; **~ na wyższy poziom** graduate[2] (from sth) to sth; **łatwo przejść** have an easy passage to sth **6 (z czegoś) (na coś)** (*zmieniać*) change over (from sth) (to sth) **7** (*na inną wiarę*) convert[1] **8 samego siebie** excel yourself **9** (*o ustawie*) go through **10 (na kogoś/coś)** (*zwł. jako spadek*) devolve on/upon sb/sth; (*cechy, nastrój itp.*) rub off (on/onto sb) IDM **~ wszelkie/czyjeś pojęcie/wyobrażenie** be beyond sb | **~ z rąk do rąk** change hands | **na samą myśl o tym przechodzą mnie ciarki** the mere thought of it gives me the creeps
przechodzień passer-by
przechowalnia 1 (*magazyn*) storeroom **2** (*bagażu*) left-luggage office
przechow(yw)ać keep[1]; (*w komputerze, magazynie itp.*) store[2]
przechrzta convert[2]
przechwalać się brag, crow[2]
przechwałka boast noun
prze-chwytywać/chwycić 1 (*informacje*) intercept **2** (*władzę*) seize
prze-chylać/chylić (*jednym końcem w górę*) tilt, tip[2] sth (up/over); **~ szalę na (czyjąś) stronę** sway
□ **prze-chylać/chylić się** (*jednym końcem w górę*) tilt, tip[2] (up/over); (*łódź itp.*) lurch verb, pitch[2]
przechył lurch
przechytrzyć double-cross, outwit
przeciąć (się) → PRZECINAĆ (SIĘ)
przeciąg 1 (*wiatr*) draught[1]; **z ~ami** draughty **2** (*czasu*) **w ~u** within
prze-ciągać/ciągnąć 1 coś przez coś hook[2] **2 przeciągnąć ręką po twarzy** rub your hand across your face **3** (*ciężki worek itp.*) drag[1] **4** (*rozmowę itp.*) drag sth out, string sth out; **~ posiłek** linger over a meal
IDM **~ strunę** overstep the mark/line, push your luck, push it/things

□ **prze-ciągać/ciągnąć się 1** (*osoba*) have a stretch, stretch[1] (out) **2** (*spotkanie itp.*) drag[1] (on), extend ■ **przeciągający się** drawn-out, long-drawn-out
przecią-żać/żyć 1 (*linię elektryczną*) overload **2** (*osobę obowiązkami*) overload, overwork ■ **przeciążenie 1** (*w ruchu drogowym itp.*) congestion **2** ~ **pracą** overwork noun | **przeciążony 1** (*zatłoczony, np. samochodami*) congested; **przeciążony u góry** top-heavy **2** (*pracą*) overworked
przeciek (*informacji*) leak[2]; **powodować** ~ (*informacji*) leak[1] sth (to sb)
prze-ciekać/ciec escape[1], filter[2] out, through, etc., leak[1]; (*woda itp.*) drip down through sth, seep; (*tajne informacje*) leak out ■ **przeciekający** leaky
przecier purée
prze-cierać/trzeć: **lekko ~ oczy** dab[1], give your eyes a dab (with sth) IDM **~ szlak (w jakiejś dziedzinie)** break fresh/new ground □ **prze-cierać/trzeć się** clear[2], clear up
przecież mind you; **ale** ~ then/there again; **„Dlaczego nie kupiłeś mleka?" „Przecież kupiłem."** 'Why didn't you buy any milk?' 'I did buy some.' IDM
przecięci|e się: **punkt ~a się** intersection
przeciętn|y average[1]; (*nieform.*) bog-standard; **osoba/rzecz ~a** lightweight noun, the ordinary, average, etc. run of sth; **ich muzyka jest skierowana do ~ego słuchacza** their music is very middle-of-the-road
prze-cinać/ciąć 1 (*nożem*) cut[1], slash[1]; (*linę*) cut through sth **2** (*na plastry*) slice[2] **3** (*drogę, linię*) cut across, along, through, etc. (sth), intersect; **wielokrotnie** ~ criss-cross verb □ **prze-cinać/ciąć się** (*droga, linia*) cross[2], intersect; **wielokrotnie** ~ criss-cross verb
przecinak cutters
przecinek comma; ~ **dziesiętny** decimal point, point[1]
prze-ciskać/cisnąć squeeze[1] sb/sth into, through, etc. sth, sb/sth through, in, past, etc. □ **przecis-kać/nąć się** squeeze[1] into, through, etc. sth, through, in, past, etc.; ~ **powoli w jakimś kierunku** worm[2] your way/yourself along, through, etc.
przeciw against, anti, versus IDM **za i** ~ the pros and cons
przeciwbólowy: **środek** ~ analgesic, painkiller
przeciwciało antibody
przeciwdepresyjny: **lek** ~ antidepressant
przeciwdziałać counteract
przeciwieństw|o antithesis, contradiction, contrast[1], opposite; **w ~ie do czegoś** contrary[1], as opposed to, unlike
przeciwko against, averse to sth; **mieć coś** ~ mind[2]; **mieć coś ~ komuś** have (got) sth against sb/sth; **nie mam nic ~ temu** that's fine by me
przeciwległy opposite
przeciwnie conversely; **do czegoś** counter[3] to sth; **wprost** ~ on the contrary
przeciwni-k/czka adversary, competitor, enemy, opponent
przeciwnoś|ć (*losu*) adversity; **(po) mimo wszystkich ~ci** against (all) the odds IDM **pogodzić się z ~ciami losu** take the rough with the smooth
przeciwny 1 (*strona*) opposite **2** (*różny*) contrary[1], converse, opposite, reverse[2,3]; **w ~m razie** failing[2], or, or else, otherwise conj.; ~ **czyjejś naturze/usposobieniu** (be/go) against the grain **3** (*nie w zgodzie*) opposed; **być ~m komuś/czemuś** object[2] (to sb/sth), be set against sth/doing sth **4** (*drużyna, armia itp.*) opposing
przeciwprostokątna hypotenuse
przeciwsłoneczn|y: **osłona ~a** (*w samochodzie*) visor
przeciwstawi(a)ć contrast[2], pit A against B □ **przeciwstawi(a)ć się** (*osoba*) defy, oppose
przeciwstawny opposing
przeciwuderzenie counter-attack
przeciwutleniacz antioxidant
przeciwwiatrowy windproof
przeczący negative[1]
przeczenie negative[2]
przeczes(yw)ać comb[2] sth (for sb/sth), sweep[1] sth (for sb/sth)
przecznica turn[2], turning
przeczucie feeling, hunch[1], inkling, intuition, presentiment; **złe** ~ foreboding, premonition; **pełen złych przeczuć** full of doom and gloom
przeczulony: **być ~m na punkcie czegoś** be/get hung up (about/on sb/sth)
przeczyszczający (*lek itp.*) laxative adj.; **środek** ~ laxative
przeczytać zob. też CZYTAĆ; read sth through; **źle** ~ misread
przećwiczyć → ĆWICZYĆ
przed 1 (*miejsce*) in front of sb/sth; (*drzwiami*) outside[3]; (*na ulicy itp.*) past[3] **2** (*do przodu*) ahead **3** (*wcześniej*) before[1], prior to; **nie możemy stąd wyjść ~ dziesiątą** we can't leave until 10 o'clock; **~ wyjściem wyłącz światło** turn the lights off before you leave **4** (*deszczem itp.*) from; (*chorobą, zimnem*) against IDM **~e wszystkim** above all
przedawkować take an overdose
przeddzień eve
przedefilować → DEFILOWAĆ
przedhistoryczny prehistoric
przedimek article; ~ **nieokreślony** the indefinite article; ~ **określony** the definite article
przed-kładać/łożyć 1 kogoś/coś nad kogoś/coś put sb/sth before/above sb/sth **2** (*złożyć pracę roczną/projekt itp.*) submit; (*ofertę*) tender[2]
przedłożenie submission
przedłużacz (*elektr.*) extension lead
prze-dłużać/dłużyć drag sth out, prolong, spin sth out; (*wizę itp.*) extend; (*prenumeratę, umowę itp.*) renew; ~ **pobyt (gdzieś)** stay on (at…) □ **prze-dłużać/dłużyć się** extend, run on
przedłużeni|e continuation; (*wizy itp.*) extension; (*prenumeraty, umowy itp.*) renewal; **do ~a** renewable
przedmieści|e suburb; **~a** suburbia
przedmiot 1 (*rzecz*) article, object[1], thing **2** (*nauki; rozmowy*) subject[1], subject matter; ~ **ścisły** science; ~ **kierunkowy** major[2] **3** (*pożądania itp.*) the object[1] of sth
przedmowa foreword, introduction, preface
przedn|i forward[2], front[2]; **~ia część** front[1]; **~ia noga/łapa zwierząt** foreleg
przedostatni last/next but one, penultimate; ~ **tydzień** the week before last
przedosta(wa)ć się work its way; **(do czegoś)** penetrate; **przez coś** thread your way through sth
przedpłata down payment
przedpokój hall
przedpołudnie morning
przedpołudniowy morning
przedramię forearm
przedrostek prefix
przedrzeć (się) → PRZEDZIERAĆ (SIĘ)
przedsiębiorca entrepreneur
przedsiębiorczość enterprise, initiative; ~ **prywatna** private enterprise
przedsiębiorczy enterprising, entrepreneurial, go-ahead[2]
przedsiębiorstwo company, corporation, enterprise, firm[1]; ~ **handlu detalicznego** retailer
przedsięwzięcie enterprise, proposition, task, undertaking; (*nowe, często ryzykowne*) venture[1]
przedsionek porch, threshold
przedsmak foretaste
przedstawi(a)ć 1 kogoś komuś introduce sb (to sb), present[3] sb (to sb) **2** (*sztukę itp.*) perform, produce[1] (*radio, TV*) present[3] **3** (*pokazać*) present[3], show[1]; (*na rysunku/fotografii*) picture[2]; (*film, sztuka itp.*) feature[2]; ~ **komuś dowody** confront sb with the evidence **4** (*wyjaśniać*) depict, present[3], represent; ~ **w ogólnym zarysie** outline[1]; **fałszywie** ~ misrepresent; **co ten obraz ma ~?** what is this picture meant to be? **5** (*propozycję, opinię itp.*) bring sth forward, present[3], put sth forward, set sth forth, stake sth out, submit; **przedstawić propozycję** make a suggestion; **przedstawić komuś swoją sugestię** put a suggestion to sb; **przedstawić szczodrą ofertę** make a generous offer **6** (*kandydaturę*) put yourself/sb forward □ **przedstawi(a)ć się** introduce yourself (to sb)
przedstawiciel/ka agent, representative[1], rep; **przedstawiciel/ka handlow-y/a** sales representative; **być przedstawicielem** represent
przedstawicielstwo 1 (*w parlamencie itp.*) representation **2** (*filia przedsiębiorstwa itp.*) subsidiary[2]
przedstawienie 1 (*faktów itp.*) presentation; **złe** ~ misrepresentation **2** (*interpretacja*) representation **3** (*widowisko*) show[2]; (*sztuki*) performance, play[2] (*radio, TV*) drama; (*taneczne itp.*) exhibition;

(*opis/odtworzenie postaci*) portrayal **4 kogoś komuś** introduction

przedszkole kindergarten, nursery school

przedtem before[3], beforehand, formerly

przedwczesny premature ■ **przedwcześnie** prematurely; (*talent itp.*) ~ **rozwinięty** precocious; **robić coś przedwcześnie** jump the gun

przedwczoraj the day before yesterday

przedwyborczy: **okres** ~ the run-up to the election

przedyskutować → DYSKUTOWAĆ

przedział 1 (*w pociągu*) compartment **2** ~ **czasu** slot[1]; ~ **wiekowy 30-40 lat** the 30-40 age bracket

przedział|ek parting; **czesać się z ~kiem** part[2]

prze-dzielać/dzielić partition sth off

prze-dzierać/drzeć się break through (sth); (*nagle*) burst[1] into sth; (*w pośpiechu*) scramble; (*z mozołem*) thread your way through sth

przedziurawi(a)ć pierce

przedziurawić → DZIURAWIĆ

przedziwny extraordinary, weird

przeegzaminować → EGZAMINOWAĆ

przefiltrować → FILTROWAĆ

przegapić miss[1]

przegięcie IDM ~ **pały** over the top, OTT

przegląd 1 overview, survey[1], review[1]; **robić** ~ (*np. prasy*) review[2] **2** (*techniczny*) service[1]; **dokładny** ~ a good going-over; **robić** ~ (*np. samochodu*) service[2]

prze-glądać/jrzeć 1 (*sprawdzać*) browse, go over sth, go through sth, look through sth, peruse, sort through sth (for sth); (*dane w komputerze*) call sth up **2** (*przejrzeć kogoś/coś na wylot*) see through sb/sth

przeglądarka browser

przegotow(yw)ać overdo

przegran|y (*przym.*) ~**a bitwa** a losing battle; ~**a sprawa** a lost cause; ~-**y/a facet/kobieta** underdog ■ **przegran-y/a** (*rz.*) loser

przegroda partition

przegródka compartment; (*na listy*) pigeonhole

przegr(yw)ać lose, trail[2]

przegrywając-y/a (*rz.*) loser

przegub joint[2]; (*ręki*) wrist

przegubowy articulated

przehandlow(yw)ać trade[2]

przeholować go too far

przeina-czać/czyć put a wrong interpretation on sth

prze-jadać/jeść się 1 (*za dużo jeść*) overeat **2 komuś** (*znudzić się*) pall

przejaśnienie a sunny interval

przejaw (**przejawy**) (*piastowania urzędu, zamożności itp.*) trappings

przejawiać się manifest (itself), (in/as sth)

przejazd 1 (*kolejowy itp.*) crossing; ~ **kolejowy** level crossing; ~ **podziemny** underpass **2** (*miejsce*) clearance

przejażdżk|a drive[2], ride[2], run[2]; (*nieform.*) jaunt; ~**a łodzią** (*żaglówką*) sail[2]; ~**a łódką wiosłową** row noun IDM **jechać/zabierać kogoś na ~ę** go/take sb for a spin

przejąć (się) → PRZEJMOWAĆ (SIĘ)

przejeść się → PRZEJADAĆ SIĘ

przejezdny (*droga*) open to traffic

prze-jeżdżać/jechać 1 przez coś cross[2]; **obok** pass[1] **2 kogoś/coś** (*samochodem*) run sb/sth down, run sb/sth over **3** (*ilość kilometrów*) clock sth up

przejęcie 1 (*sądowe itp.*) seizure, takeover **2** (*emocje*) **z ~m** intently

przejęty earnest

przejęzyczenie się a slip of the tongue

przej-mować/ąć seize; (*mienie prywatne*) expropriate; (*przestępcę itp.*) intercept; (*kontrolę, firmę itp.*) take sth over (from sb); ~ **po kimś obowiązki, władzę** succeed, take (sth) over from sb □ **przej-mować/ąć się** flap[2]; **zbytnio** ~ fuss[2]; ~ **drobiazgami** fuss[2]; **nie** ~ take it/things easy; **nie przejmuj się kosztami** never mind about the cost; **nie przejmuj się tym** forget it

przejmujący 1 (*wiatr itp.*) cutting[2]; (*ból*) sharp[1] **2** (*wspomnienie itp.*) poignant

przejrzeć → PRZEGLĄDAĆ

przejrzystość clarity, lucidity

przejrzysty clear[1], lucid

przejści|e 1 (*graniczne itp.*) crossing **2** (*droga*) gangway, passage; **wąskie** ~**e** alley; ~**e dla pieszych** pedestrian crossing; ~**e podziemne** subway, underpass; ~**e między rzędami krzeseł/ławek** aisle **3** (*zmiana*) transition **4 ciężkie** ~**a** ordeal

przejściow|y interim[1], passing[2], transitional; **opady** ~**e** intermittent showers

przejść (się) → PRZECHODZIĆ, PRZECHADZAĆ SIĘ

przekalko(wy)wać zob. też KALKOWAĆ; trace[1]

przekartkować → KARTKOWAĆ

przekaz: ~ **pocztowy** postal order; **środek** ~**u** medium[2]; **środki masowego** ~**u** media

przekaz(yw)ać 1 kogoś/coś komuś convey, hand sth on (to sb), hand (sth) over (to sb), hand (sb) over to sb, pass sth on (to sb); (*dokument itp.*) give out sth; (*wiadomości*) communicate, relay[1]; (*i wiedzę*) impart; (*władzę itp.*) devolve sth to/on/upon sb; (*piłkę*) foward[3]; ~ **pozdrowienia** remember me to sb **2** (*radio, TV*) relay[1], transmit **3** (*w spadku*) hand sth down (to sb), pass sth down ■ **przekazanie**: ~ (*np. książki*) transmission; ~ **władzy** (*samorządom lokalnym*) devolution; ~ **uprawnień** delegation

przekąsić snack verb on sth

przekąska hors d'oeuvre, snack

przekątn|a: **po** ~**ej** diagonally

przekątny diagonal

przekimać doss down

przekląć → KLĄĆ, PRZEKLINAĆ

przekleństwo 1 (*wulgarny wyraz*) expletive, swear word; (**przekleństwa**) bad language, swearing **2** (*klątwa*) bane, curse[1]

przeklęty 1 (*cholerny*) blasted, blessed, damn[1], darn[2], flaming, flipping, rotten **2 pod klątwą** under a curse

prze-klinać/kląć 1 (*wulgarnie*) curse[2], swear **2** (*rzucić klątwę*) curse[2] (sb/sth) (for sth)

przekład translation

prze-kładać/łożyć 1 (*inaczej układać, ustawiać*) disturb, rearrange **2 coś przez coś** hook[2] **3** ~ **coś na wcześniejszy termin** bring sth forward **4** (*tłumaczyć*) translate

przekładnia gear[1]

przekłut|y: ~**a opona/dętka** puncture

przekłu(wa)ć perforate, pierce ■ **przekłuwanie** perforation; ~ **uszu** ear-piercing[2]

przekomarzać się banter verb

przekonani|e 1 (także **przekonania**) belief, persuasion **2** (*pewność siebie*) conviction

przekonan|y certain, convinced, positive, sure; **jestem** ~**y, że…** it's my belief that…; **jest** ~**a, że zda egzamin** she feels confident of passing/that she can pass the exam

przekonujący compelling, convincing, forcible, persuasive

przekon(yw)ać (**przekonać**) bring sb round (to sth), bring sth home to sb, convince, get round/around sb, persuade, satisfy sb (that…); **kogoś, aby coś zrobił** get sb to do sth; **usilnie** ~ **kogoś do czegoś** urge[1] sb (to do sth) □ **przekon(yw)ać się**: **przekonać się (do czegoś)** come round (to sth)

przekora perversity

przekorny perverse

przekór: **na** ~ **czemuś** in defiance of sth

prze-kraczać/kroczyć 1 (*granicę itp.*) cross[2]; (*problem, epidemia itp.*) ~ **granice** transcend; ~ **próg** set foot in/on sth **2** (*kategorie*) cut across sth, transcend **2** (*przewyższać*) go beyond sth, exceed, pass[1]; ~ **wyznaczony czas** overrun; **przekroczyć już wiek, kiedy…** be past the age when…; **inflacja przekroczyła wskaźnik 10%** inflation has topped the 10% mark; **jego sukces przekroczył wszelkie nasze oczekiwania** his success was beyond all our expectations. **3** (*przepis*) break[1], contravene; (*uprawnienia, granice itp.*) overstep; ~ **dozwoloną przepisami szybkość** speed[2] ■ **przekraczanie**: ~ **stanu konta bankowego** overdraft

prze-kradać/kraść się sneak[1] into, out of, past, etc. sth, in, out, away, etc.

przekreś-lać/lić 1 (*tekst*) cross sth out **2** (*szansę*) compromise[2]

przekrę-cać/cić 1 (*zmienić położenie*) roll[2] sth (over), turn[1] **2** (*znaczenie*) distort, pervert[1], twist[1] □ **przekrę-cać/cić się** roll[2] (over)

przekroczeni|e 1 (*granic itp.*) **po** ~**u** beyond **2** (*przepisu*) contravention; ~**e prawa** guilt

przekroczyć → PRZEKRACZAĆ

przekrój section; (*poprzeczny; przen.*) cross section

przekrzywiony askew, cockeyed

przekształ-cać/cić transform □ **przekształ-cać/cić się**: **(w coś)** degenerate[1], mutate (into sth)

przekupny corrupt[1]

przekupstwo corruption

prze-kupywać/kupić: **kogoś** bribe verb, buy sb off

prze-latywać/lecieć 1 fly[1]; ~ **przez Atlantyk** fly the Atlantic **2** ~ **przez kierownicę** pitch forwards over the handlebars

przelew draft[1]; ~ **bankowy** bank draft

przel(ew)ać 1 ~ **syfonem/rurką** siphon **2** (*pieniądze*) transfer[1] IDM ~ **krew** shed blood

□ **przel(ew)ać się** overflow, slop
przelicytować → LICYTOWAĆ
przeli-czać/czyć 1 (*rzeczy*) count[1], count sb/sth out **2** (*cale na centymetry itp.*) convert[1]
□ **przeliczyć się** miscalculate
przeliczeniow|y: **tabela ~a na system metryczny** metric conversion table
przeliterow(yw)ać zob. też LITEROWAĆ; spell sth out
przelot flight
przelotn|y fleeting, short-lived; **~e spojrzenie** glimpse; **~e opady** scattered showers; **złożył nam ~ą wizytę** we had a flying visit from him
przeludniony crowded
przeładowany fussy
przeładow(yw)ać 1 overload **2** (*przen.*) overload sb (with sth); (*pracą*) overwork
przełaj: **na ~** cross-country adv.
przełajowy cross-country
przełam(yw)ać break[1]
przełą-czać/czyć switch sth over; **przełączyć na światła mijania** dip your headlights
□ **przełą-czać/czyć się**: **(na coś)** turn over (to sth)
przełącznik switch[1]
przełęcz pass[2]
przełknąć → PRZEŁYKAĆ
przełom 1 (*moment zwrotny*) breakthrough **2** (*rzeki*) gorge[1] **3** (*med.*) crisis IDM **~ wieku** the turn of the century/year
przełomow|y crucial, groundbreaking; **wydarzenie ~e** watershed
przełożon-y/a (*rz.*) superior[2]; (**przełożona**) (*pielęgniarek*) matron
przełożyć → PRZEKŁADAĆ
przełyk gullet, oesophagus
prze-łykać/łknąć 1 (*jedzenie*) swallow[1] **2 ~ (ślinę)** (*z emocji*) gulp[1] **3** (*gorzką pigułkę itp.*) swallow[1]
prze-maczać/moczyć drench, saturate
przemarznięty frozen[2]
prze-mawiać/mówić 1 (*wygłosić mowę*) speak (on/about sth), talk[1] (to/with sb) (about/of sb/sth) **2** (*powiedzieć coś*) **~ komuś do rozsądku** make sb see reason, reason with sb **3 za czymś** support[1]; **kilka czynników przemawiało na naszą korzyść** several factors were operating to our advantage **4 (do kogoś)** (*pomysł*) appeal[2] (to sb); (*do czyjegoś poczucia honoru itp.*) appeal[2] to sth
przemądrzały big-headed
przemę-czać/czyć się overdo it/things, tire yourself out
■ **przemęczenie** burnout, exhaustion | **przemęczony** burnt-out
przemian|a 1 (*jakościowa*) conversion, metamorphosis, transformation **2** (*przejście z jednego stanu w drugi itp.*) transition **3 robić coś na ~** alternate[1] A with B, take turns (at sth); **występować itp. na ~** alternate[1] with sth, between A and B IDM **~a materii** metabolism
przemieni(a)ć change[1], convert[1], transform, turn sb/sth (from sth) into sth
□ **przemieni(a)ć się** change[1], convert[1]
przemienny alternate[2]
przemie-rzać/rzyć (*chodzić: po pokoju itp.*) pace[2], tread[1]; (*pewien dystans*) cover[1]
prze-mieszczać/mieścić displace, move[1]; (*kogoś z miejsca na miejsce*) shunt; (*kość przy złamaniu*) dislocate
□ **prze-mieszczać/mieścić się** move[1], pass[1] along, down, through, etc. (sth), work its way
prze-mijać/minąć 1 (*czas*) fly[1] **2** (*kłopoty itp.*) blow over
przemijający ephemeral, passing[2], short-lived
przemil-czać/czeć suppress
przemiły sweet[1]
przemknąć zob. też PRZEMYKAĆ (SIĘ); dart[2], flash[1], shoot[1]
przemoc violence; **~ w rodzinie** domestic violence; **dokonany ~ą** forcible; **niestosujący ~y** non-violent
przemoczony saturated, soaked, soggy IDM **~ do suchej nitki** soaking, wet through
przemoczyć → PRZEMACZAĆ
przemoknąć get drenched
przemożny 1 (*argument itp.*) compelling **2** (*zapach itp.*) overpowering
przemówić → PRZEMAWIAĆ
przemówienie address[1], speech; **wygłoszać ~** address[2]
przemy-cać/cić smuggle; **przemycany towar** contraband; **przemycić komuś wiadomość do więzienia** sneak a note to sb/sneak sb a note in prison
przemyć → PRZEMYWAĆ
prze-mykać/mknąć 1 (*osoba*) breeze[2] along, in, out, etc. **2** (*uśmiech; pomysł*) flicker[1] **3** (*z miejsca na miejsce*) flit (from A to B), (between A and B)
□ **prze-mykać/mknąć się** flit (from A to B), (between A and B)
przemysł industry; **gałąź ~u** industry; **~ ciężki** heavy industry; **~ rozrywkowy** show business; **~ stoczniowy** shipbuilding; **~ surowcowy** primary industry
przemysłowiec industrialist
przemysłowy industrial
przemyślany premeditated; **~ wybór** an informed choice
prze-myśliwać/myśleć: **coś** mull sth over, ponder (on/over) sth, have a think about sth, think sth out, think sth over, think sth through, put some thought into sth, turn sth over; **nad czymś** toy with sth; **przemyśleć ponownie** rethink
przemyt smuggling
przemytni-k/czka smuggler; (*zwł. narkotyków*) runner
przemy(wa)ć bathe
przeniesienie displacement, transfer[2]; (*w pracy*) **~ tymczasowe** secondment
przenieść (się) → PRZENOSIĆ (SIĘ)
przenik-ać/nąć filter[2] in, through, etc., infiltrate, penetrate, percolate, permeate, pervade
przenikliwość acumen, penetration
przenikliwy 1 (*dźwięk*) ear-piercing[1], shrill **2** (*wiatr*) biting **3** (*spojrzenie itp.*) piercing[1], searching **4** (*komentarz itp.*) incisive, penetrating, shrewd
przenocować → NOCOWAĆ
prze-nosić/nieść 1 (*z miejsca na miejsce*) get, move[1], shift[1], transfer[1]; (*bagaż itp.*) carry; (*na inny termin*) switch[2] **2** (*na inne stanowisko, do innego działu*) second[4]; (*na wyższe stanowisko*) promote; (*na niższe miejsce/stanowisko*) relegate **3 na kogoś** devolve sth to/on/upon sb, hand (sth) over (to sb) **4** (*chorobę*) communicate, transmit **5** (*tekst*) lift[1]
□ **prze-nosić/nieść się** move[1], transfer[1]
przenośni|a figure of speech, metaphor; **w ~** metaphorically
przenośn|y 1 (*ruchomy*) portable; **dom(ek) ~y** mobile home **2** (*język*) figurative; **w znaczeniu ~ym** figuratively
przeobra-żać/zić transform
■ **przeobrażenie** transformation | **przeobrażanie się** transition
przeoczyć miss[1], omit, overlook
■ **przeoczenie** omission, oversight
przeogromny almighty
przepadać 1 (/przepaść) (*na wojnie itp.*) perish **2 (za kimś/czymś)** be wild[1] (about sb/sth); **nie ~ za czymś** no be a great fan of sth
prze-pajać/poić imbue sb/sth (with sth)
przepa-lać/lić blow[1], fuse[2]
□ **przepa-lać/lić się** blow[1], fuse[2]; **żarówka się przepaliła** the bulb's gone
przepaska patch[1]
przepaść[1] → PRZEPADAĆ
przepaść[2] **1** (*geogr.*) abyss, chasm, precipice **2** (*przen.*) divide[2], gulf, rift; (*dzieląca poglądy itp.*) gap; **~ międzypokoleniowa** the generation gap
przepchnąć (się) → PRZEPYCHAĆ (SIĘ)
przepełni(a)ć 1 (*ludzie*) crowd[2] **2** (*przen.*) imbue, infuse, saturate
□ **przepełni(a)ć się** brim over (with sth)
przepełniony chock-a-block; (*zwł. ludźmi*) overcrowded; (*wodą itp.*) saturated
przepę-dzać/dzić fight sb/sth off; (*bolesne wspomnienia itp.*) exorcize
przepić → PRZEPIJAĆ
prze-piekać/piec overdo
przepierzenie partition
przepiękny exquisite, gorgeous, ravishing
przepi(ja)ć: **do kogoś** toast verb
przepiłow(yw)ać zob. też PIŁOWAĆ; file[2] sth (away, down, etc.)
przepiórka quail
przepis 1 (*kulinarny*) recipe **2** (*polecenie*) instruction; (*chemia: receptura*) formula **3** (*na sukces itp.*) formula for (doing) sth **4** (*prawny*) regulation, rule[1]
przepis(yw)ać 1 (*tekst, np. z tablicy*) copy[2] sth (down/out), write sth out; (*tekst mówiony na pisany itp.*) transcribe sth (into sth) **2** (*odpisywać od kogoś/z czegoś*) lift sth from sb/sth **3** (*ponownie*) rewrite **4** (*lek*) prescribe
prze-platać/pleść intersperse
prze-płacać/płacić overpay
prze-płaszać/płoszyć: **kogoś/coś** frighten sb/sth away/off
przepłukać → PŁUKAĆ
przepływ flow[1]; (*wody, gazu itp.*) stream[1]; **~ gotówki** cash flow

prze-pływać/płynąć 1 (*rzeka itp.*) flow[2] **2** (*przen.*) stream[2] **3** (*łódź itp.*) sail by; (*osoba*) swim by; **przepłynąłem 25 długości basenu** I swam 25 lengths of the pool
przepoić → PRZEPAJAĆ
przepojony: ~ **wodą** waterlogged
przepo-ławiać/łowić bisect, halve
przepona diaphragm; ~ **brzuszna** midriff
przepo-wiadać/wiedzieć forecast, foretell, prophesy
przepracowany overworked
prze-praszać/prosić be apologetic, apologize, say sorry; **przepraszam!** (*za przewinienie*) pardon[1], I beg your pardon, sorry[2], I'm sorry; (*w poważniejszych sytuacjach*) forgive me; (*chcąc przyciągnąć czyjąć uwagę*) excuse me; **przepraszam, że przeszkadzam…** I hate to bother you but…
przepraszający apologetic
przeprawa 1 crossing **2** (*przen.*) ordeal
przeprawi(a)ć ferry[2]; ~ **kogoś łódką** row[2]
przeprosiny apology
prze-prowadzać/prowadzić zob. też PROWADZIĆ **1 kogoś/coś przez coś** pilot[2], see sb across sth **2** (*badania, wywiad itp.*) conduct[1]; (*program itp.*) execute, undertake; **przeprowadzić test/kontrolę** run[1] a test/check (on sth); ~ **rozmowę kwalifikacyjną/wywiad** interview[2] sb (for sth); ~ **głosowanie** take a vote; ~ **paralelę** draw a parallel; ~ **syntezę** synthesize; ~ **z ukrycia** (*np. akcję*) engineer[2]
■ **przeprowadzeni|e** (*programu itp.*) execution; **do przeprowadzenia** practicable; **możliwość przeprowadzenia** practicality; **nie do przeprowadzenia** impracticable
□ **prze-prowadzać/prowadzić się** move[1]
przeprowadzka move[2], removal
przepuklina hernia
przepustka 1 pass[2], permit[2] **2** (*do sławy itp.*) passport to sth
przepustnica throttle[2]
przepustowość: ~ **łącza** bandwidth
przepuszczać 1 (**/przepuścić**) (*pozwolić/umożliwiać przejście*) let sb/sth through, let sb/sth get by; (*w ruchu drogowym*) give way (to sb/sth); (*dać pozwolenie na odlot itp.*) clear[2]; (*studenta na egzaminie*) pass[1]; ~ **przez maszynkę** (*mięso*) mince verb **2** (*gaz itp.*) leak[1] **3** (**/przepuścić**) (*okazję itp.*) lose, throw sth away **4** (**/przepuścić**) (*pieniądze*) blow[1] sth (on sth)
przepuszczalny permeable, porous
przepych luxury, pomp, splendour; **zdobiony itp. z ~em** sumptuous
przepychacz (*do zlewu itp.*) plunger
prze-pychać/pchnąć (*decyzję, ustawę itp. przez coś*) railroad verb sth (through/through sth)
□ **prze-pychać/pchnąć się** barge[2], jostle, push[1], push and shove
przepyt(yw)ać grill[2] sb (about sth), quiz[2]
■ **przepytywanie** inquisition
prze-rabiać/robić: **coś na coś** make sth of sth; (*ubranie*) alter; (*pokój itp.*) revamp; (*tekst*) rewrite; (*książkę itp.*) adapt sth (for sth); (*utwory literackie/filmowe/muzyczne*) rehash; (*ser itp.*) process[2]; **przerobić ten pokój na sypialnię** make this room into a bedroom
prze-radzać/rodzić się: **w coś** deteriorate into sth, develop
prze-rastać/rosnąć top[3]
przeraźliwy 1 (*budzający strach*) eerie, fearful **2** (*dźwięk*) ear-piercing[1], shrill, strident
prze-rażać/razić alarm[2], appal, daunt, dismay verb, horrify, intimidate sb (into sth/doing sth), make sb's hair stand on end, rattle[1], terrify
przerażający alarming, appalling, daunting, fearsome, frightening, horrible, horrific, horrifying, intimidating, scary, terrifying; (*przeżycie*) harrowing; (*niesamowity*) creepy; (*makabryczny*) ghastly, grisly; (*zatrważający*) hairy
przerażenie alarm[1], dismay, fright, horror, terror
przerażony aghast, alarmed, appalled, dismayed, frightened, horrified, petrified, terrified
przerobić → PRZERABIAĆ
przerodzić się → PRZERADZAĆ SIĘ
przerosnąć → PRZERASTAĆ
przeróbka (*utworu literackiego itp.*) rehash; (*w mieszkaniu itp.*) revamp
przerw|a break[2], cessation, gap, pause[2]; (*po dużej pracy itp.*) breather; (*teatr*) interval, intermission; (*między lekcjami; w trakcie procesu sądowego*) recess; (*w szkole*) playtime; (*między wydarzeniami*) interlude; **~a na kawę** coffee break; **~a obiadowa** lunch hour; **~a w pracy** (*zwł. z powodu strajku*) stoppage; **~a w podróży** stopover; **~a w dopływie prądu** power cut; **robić sobie ~ę** break[1], interrupt; **robić (krótką) ~ę** pause[1] (for sth); **robić ~ę w podróży** stop off (at/in…); **wywoływać ~ę** disrupt; **z ~ami** intermittently, at intervals IDM **bez ~y** continuously, flat out, incessantly, without interruption, solidly, at a stretch, on the trot
przerysow(yw)ać copy[2]
przer(y)wać (*rozerwać*) break[1], sever; (*nie skończyć*) disrupt, interrupt; **czymś** punctuate sth (with sth); (*na krótką chwilę*) pause; (*pracę itp.*) stop[1] (for sth), (and do/to do sth); (*studia*) discontinue; (*karierę itp.*) cut sth short; (*bójkę itp.*) break sth up, intervene; **(komuś)** cut in (on sb/sth), cut sb off, cut sb short, interrupt (sb) (with sth); (*rozmowę itp.*) chip in (with sth); ~ **ciążę** abort; ~ **(komuś) dostawę czegoś** cut sb/sth off; ~ **mówcy niegrzecznymi pytaniami/uwagami** heckle; ~ **podróż gdzieś** stop off (at/in…)
□ **przer(y)wać się** rupture verb
przerywany broken[2], intermittent
prze-rzedzać/rzedzić się thin[2] (out)
prze-rzucać/rzucić 1 ~ **łopatą/szuflą** shovel verb **2** (*papiery itp.*) search through sth **3** (*strony*) skim (through/over) sth; ~ **kartki czegoś** flick/flip through sth; ~ **(szybko) kartki** thumb[2] (through) sth IDM ~ **na kogoś odpowiedzialność** shift the blame/responsibility (for sth) (onto sb)
□ **prze-rzucać/rzucić się**: **(z czegoś na coś)** switch[2] (over) (from sth) (to sth), (between A and B)
przesada 1 exaggeration **2** (*nadmiar*) excess[1]
przesadny excessive, extravagant, inordinate, undue
prze-sadzać/sadzić 1 (*roślinę*) transplant[1] **2** (*przebrać miarę*) make heavy weather of sth; (*z pochwałami, solą itp.*) overdo; (*z pracą itp.*) overdo it/things; **nie ~ z czymś** go easy on sb/on/with sth **3** (*znaczenie*) exaggerate, magnify, overstate; **nie przesadzaj!** come off it!
przesadzony exaggerated, far-fetched
przesączyć się → SĄCZYĆ SIĘ
przesąd superstition
przesądny superstitious
przesą-dzać/dzić decide; ~ **, że ktoś jest…** mark sb down as sth
przesądzon|y doomed; **sprawa z góry ~a** a foregone conclusion
przesiać → PRZESIEWAĆ
prze-siadać/siąść się change[1]
■ **przesiadanie się** transfer[2]
przesiadk|a: **mieć ~ę** have to change trains; **z ~ą** indirect
przesiadkowy: **bilet** ~ transfer[2]
przesiadywać hang out, sit about/around
przesią-kać/knąć permeate, saturate, soak into/through sth, in
przesiąknięty saturated, steeped in sth
przesiąść się → PRZESIADAĆ SIĘ
przesiedlać: ~ **do kraju** repatriate
przesi(ew)ać 1 (*mąkę itp.*) sieve verb, sift **2** (*kandydatów*) weed sth/sb out **3** (*fakty itp.*) sift (through) sth
przesilenie (*letnie/zimowe*) solstice
prze-skakiwać/skoczyć 1 (*z miejsca na miejsce*) jump[1], leap[1]; (*przez płot itp.*) clear[2] **2** (*z jednego zajęcia na drugie*) hop[1] (from sth to sth)
■ **przeskakiwanie**: ~ **po kanałach telewizji** surfing
przeskok jump[2]
przesłać → PRZESYŁAĆ
przesłanie message
przesłank|a reason[1]; **racjonalne ~i** rationale
przesłodzony cloying, sugary
przesłona (*fot.*) aperture
przesłuchani|e 1 (*oskarżonego itp.*) interrogation, inquisition; (*biorąc kogoś w krzyżowy ogień pytań*) cross-examination **2** (*śpiewaka, aktora*) audition[1]; **przeprowadzać ~e**; **uczestniczyć w ~u** audition[2] (sb) (for sth)
przesłuch(iw)ać interview[2]; (*oskarżonego itp.*) interrogate; (*intensywnie*) cross-examine
przesma-żać/żyć overdo
przesmyk inlet
przesolony too salty
przesortować → SORTOWAĆ
przespać zob. też SPAĆ; oversleep
□ **przespać się**: ~ **gdzieś** bed down
przestankowy intermittent
przestarzały antiquated, archaic, out of date, dated, obsolete, outdated, outmoded
przestawać 1 (**/przestać**; **/za-**) cease, cut sth out, stop[1]; (*na krótką chwilę*) pause; **przestać pracować** give out; **nie ~ czegoś robić** keep at it/sth, keep on (doing sth), keep sth up; **przestać o tym mówić** let the subject rest

2 z kimś (*utrzymywać stosunki towarzyskie*) go round/around/about with sb
przestawi(a)ć 1 move[1]; ~ **zegar(y) o godzinę do przodu/tyłu** put the clock/clocks forward/back **2** (*zwł. słowa lub litery w wyrazie*) transpose
przestęp-ca/czyni criminal[2], crook, lawbreaker, offender; **(nieletni/a)** ~ delinquent noun
przestępczość (*młodocianych*) delinquency
przestępczy criminal[1], delinquent; **świat** ~ the underworld
przestępny: **rok** ~ leap year
przestępstwo crime, offence
przestój: ~ **w pracy** (*zwł. z powodu strajku*) stoppage
przestraszony frightened, scared, startled adj., terrified
przestraszyć give sb a fright, frighten, scare[1], give sb a scare, startle
□ **przestraszyć się** scare[1]
przestroga caution[1]
przestronny ample, roomy, spacious
przestrzegać 1 (/przestrzec) kogoś (przed kimś/czymś) caution[2] (sb) against sth **2** (*prawa itp.*) abide by sth, comply (with sth), follow, observe
przestrzenny spatial
przestrzeń space[1]; (*ziemi, drogi, wody*) stretch[2]; (*do pracy itp.*) elbow room; **duża** ~ spaciousness; **czegoś** expanse; ~ **internetowa/wirtualna** cyberspace; ~ **kosmiczna** space[1]; ~ **powietrzna** airspace
przestudiować → STUDIOWAĆ
przestudzić → STUDZIĆ
przestygnąć → STYGNĄĆ
przesunięcie (*w czasie*) postponement
przesuszony desiccated
prze-suwać/sunąć 1 (*zmienić położenie*) budge, move[1], shift[1]; **przez coś** pass[1] sth along, down, through, etc. (sth); (*palcem itp. wzdłuż czegoś*) run[1]; ~ **ostrożnie** ease[2] **2** (*w czasie*) postpone, put sth off, put off doing sth, rearrange (for another time)
□ **przesu-wać/nąć się** budge, move[1]; (*dalej itp.*) move[1] along, down, over, up, etc.; ~ **się powoli w jakimś kierunku** worm[2] your way/yourself along, through, etc.
przesy-cać/cić: kogoś/coś (czymś) suffuse sb/sth (with sth)
przes(y)łać (*pozdrowienia itp.*) send; (*zgłoszenia, podanie*) send sth in; ~ **pocztą elektroniczną** email verb; ~ **na inny/nowy adres** forward[3]
przesyłka consignment, parcel; ~ **towarów drogą morską** shipment; ~ **na koszt adresata** Freepost
przesyt glut, surfeit
przeszczep transplant[2]; (*skóry*) graft; **dokonywać ~u** transplant[1]
przeszczepi(a)ć transplant[1]; (*skórę*) graft verb sth onto sth
prze-szkadzać/szkodzić 1 komuś disturb, interrupt sb (with sth), intrude on/upon sb **2 w czymś** interfere (with sth) **3 w zrobieniu czegoś** hamper[1], handicap[2], hinder, impede, prevent sb/sth (from) (doing sth) **4** (*w przejściu itp.*) encumber sb/sth (with sth)
przeszkod|a (*przedmiot; przen.*) bar[1] (to sth), block[1], disturbance, handicap[1], hindrance, hitch[2], hurdle[1], impediment, obstacle, stumbling block; (*argumenty przeciw czemuś*) objection; (*coś co przeszkadza w posuwaniu się do przodu*) setback; **~a do przeskoczenia** jump[2]; **stawać na ~zie** prevent sb/sth (from) (doing sth); **na ~zie** in the way
przeszkolić (się) → SZKOLIĆ (SIĘ)
przeszłoś|ć past[2]; **w ~ci** back[3], formerly; **należący do ~ci** over and done with; **podróż w ~ć** a journey backwards through time; **spoglądać/patrzeć w ~ć** look back (on sth)
przeszły past[1]
przeszmuglować → SZMUGLOWAĆ
przeszuk(iw)ać examine, scour, search, go through sth
przeszy(wa)ć (*dźwięk; ból*) pierce (through/into) sth; (*ból*) shoot[1]; ~ **(kogoś) wzrokiem** glare[1] (at sb/sth)
■ **przeszywający** (*dźwięk*) penetrating; (*dźwięk; ból*) piercing[1]; (*ból*) sharp[1]
prześcieradło sheet
prze-ścigać/ścignąć: kogoś/coś surpass; **kogoś** outdo, be way ahead of sb; **coś** improve on/upon sth; **(starać się) prześcignąć kogoś** emulate
prześladować 1 (*politycznie, religijnie itp.*) persecute **2** (*nieszczęścia*) beset **3** (*telefonami itp.*) harass **4** (*myśl itp.*) be obsessed (about/with sb/sth); (*wspomnienia, sen itp.*) haunt[1]
prześladow-ca/czyni persecutor
prześledzić zob. też ŚLEDZIĆ; chart[2]
prześmieszny hilarious
przeświadczenie confidence, conviction
przeświadczony convinced, positive
prze-świetlać/świetlić 1 (*kliszę*) expose **2** ~ **promieniami Roentgena** X-ray verb **3** (*walizkę, osobę*) scan
prześwit clearance
prześwitujący see-through
prze-taczać/toczyć (*wagony*) shunt
przetak sieve
prze-tapiać/topić melt sth down
przetarg: **brać udział w ~u** tender[2]
przetasowanie shake-up
przeterminowany out of date
przetestować → TESTOWAĆ
przetłumaczyć → TŁUMACZYĆ
przetoczyć → PRZETACZAĆ
przetopić → PRZETAPIAĆ
przetransportować → TRANSPORTOWAĆ
przetrawi(a)ć (*przen.*) digest
przetrwać zob. też TRWAĆ **1** (*trwać*) last[4] **kogoś** (*płaszcz itp.*) see sb out **2** (*wytrzymać*) stand[1] **3** (*dalej żyć*) live on, outlast, pull through (sth); (*wypadek itp.*) survive; ~ **burzę/trudny okres** weather[2]
■ **przetrwanie** survival; (*utrzymanie się przy życiu*) subsistence
przetrząs-ać/nąć (*w poszukiwaniu czegoś*) ransack sth (for sth), rifle[2] (through) sth, rummage, scour
przetrzeć (się) → PRZECIERAĆ (SIĘ)
przetrzym(yw)ać 1 (*ból itp.*) endure **2** (*w areszcie*) detain
■ **przetrzymanie**: **gra na przetrzymanie** (*polit.*) brinkmanship
przetwarzacz processor
prze-twarzać/tworzyć (*i dane*) process[2]
■ **przetwarzanie**: ~ **danych** data processing; **komputerowe przetwarzanie tekstu** word processing
przewag|a advantage, ascendancy, cutting edge, an/the edge on/over sb/sth, the initiative, lead[2], margin, predominance, superiority, supremacy; (*w głosowaniu/wyborach*) majority (over sb); (*fory*) start[2]; **dać komuś ~ę** be weighted in favour of sb; **mieć ~ę liczebną** outnumber; **z niewielką ~ą** close[3]
przewa-żać/żyć 1 (*ławka, deska itp.*) tip[2] (up/over) **2** (*być za ciężkim; przen.*) outweigh **3** (*stanowić większość*) predominate **4** (*zwyciężać*) prevail IDM ~ **szalę na (czyjąś) stronę** sway
■ **przeważając|y** predominant, preponderant, prevailing, prevalent; **~a część** the best/better part of sth, most[1]; **w przeważającej części** mostly
przeważnie in the main, mainly, for the most part, mostly, predominantly, principally, substantially
przewentylować (się) → WENTYLOWAĆ (SIĘ)
przewertować → WERTOWAĆ
przewidując|y far-sighted; **być ~ym i coś zrobić** have the foresight to do sth
prze-widywać/widzieć 1 (*przyszłość*) foresee, foretell, predict; (*pogodę itp.*) forecast; **możliwy do przewidzenia** foreseeable; **łatwy do przewidzenia** predictable; **mało przewidujący** short-sighted; ~ **coś (na podstawie czegoś)** extrapolate (sth) (from/to sth) **2** (*zaplanować*) anticipate; ~ **wydatki** budget[2] (sth) (for sth) **3** (*w umowie itp.*) stipulate
przewidywalny foreseeable, predictable
przewiercień: **(wiciokrzew)** ~ honeysuckle
przewiesić sling[1]
przewietrzenie ventilation
przewietrzyć się zob. też WIETRZYĆ (SIĘ); **muszę się przewietrzyć** I need a breath of fresh air
przewiewny airy
przewieźć → PRZEWOZIĆ
prze-wijać/winąć 1 (*taśmę itp.*) wind[3]; **szybko ~ (taśmę) do przodu** fast forward; **szybko ~ (taśmę) do tyłu** rewind **2** (*na komputurze*) scroll[2] (up/down) **3** (*dziecko*) change[1]
□ **prze-wijać/winąć się** (*kluczyć*) weave
przewinienie offence
prze-wlekać/wlec 1 coś przez coś thread[2] **2** ~ **pobyt** linger
przewlekły drawn-out, long-drawn-out; (*choroba; stan*) chronic
przewodnictwo leadership; (*zebrania*) chairmanship
przewodnicząc-y/a (*rz.*) head[1], leader; (*stowarzyszenia*) president; (*banku itp.*) governor; (*zebrania*) chair[1], chairperson; (**przewodniczący**) chairman; (**przewodnicząca**) chairwoman
przewodniczyć preside, chair[2]; ~ **czemuś** preside over sth
przewodnik 1 (*także* **przewodniczka**) guide[1]; **służyć za ~a** pilot[2];

zwiedzanie z ~iem conducted/guided tour **2** (*elektr.*) conductor
przewodzić 1 (*prowadzić*) lead[1]; (*kierować organizacją*) head[2]; (*akcji, atakowi itp.*) spearhead verb **2** (*elektr.*) conduct[1]
prze-wozić/wieźć carry, convey, transport; (*samolotem*) fly[1]; ~ **kogoś/coś błyskawicznie** whisk[1]
przewozić → WOZIĆ
przewoźnik carrier
przewód 1 (*elektryczny*) line[1], wire[1]; ~ **elektryczny** flex[2], lead[2]; **główny ~ elektryczny** main[2] **2** (*kanalizacyjny itp.*) pipe[1]; ~ **kominowy** flue; ~ **wentylacyjny** air duct **3** (*anat.*) canal, duct, passage
przewóz carriage, transit, transport; (*towarów*) freight; (*samochodowy/kolejowy*) haulage; **koszt przewozu** haulage
prze-wracać/wrócić 1 (*stronę*) turn[1] **2** (*do góry nogami*) overturn, roll[2] sth (over), turn sth over, turn sth upside down; (*na ziemię*) bowl sb over, knock sb down, knock sb/sth over, push sb/sth over, upset[1]
□ **prze-wracać/wrócić się 1** (*spaść*) come a cropper, fall[1] (down/over), keel over, topple (over); (*z hukiem*) tumble down **2** (*na drugi bok*) roll[2] (over), turn over
przewrażliwiony highly strung, hypersensitive, prickly, self-conscious, touchy
przewrotność perversity
przewrotny perverse
przewrócić (się) → PRZEWRACAĆ (SIĘ)
przewrót coup, overthrow noun, subversion, upheaval; ~ **wojskowy** military takeover
prze-wyższać/wyższyć 1 (*być wyższym*) tower over/above sb/sth **2** (*być większym*) exceed, top[3]; (*problem; osiągnięcia itp,*) transcend; ~ **liczebnie** outnumber **3** (*być lepszym*) get the better of sb/sth, improve on/upon sth, outdo, tower over/above sb/sth, surpass; ~ **o klasę** outclass
przez 1 (*na drugą stronę*) across; (*miasto itp.*) through **2** (*ponad; mijając preszkodę*) over **3** (*poprzez*) through; (*wymienioną miejscowość*) via **4** (*czas*) for[1]; ~ **cały czas** throughout adv. **5** (*zimę itp.*) through **6** (*za pomocą; w konstrukcjach strony biernej*) by **7** (*mat.*) into
przeziębi(a)ć się catch a chill, catch cold, get a cold
przeziębienie chill[1], cold[2]
prze-znaczać/znaczyć designate sth (as) sth, earmark sb/sth (for sth/sb), intend sth for sb/sth, mark sth down for sth; (*czas, środki*) allow sth (for sb/sth), commit; (*do rozbiórki itp.*) condemn sth (as sth)
przeznaczeni|e 1 (*los*) destiny, doom, fate **2** (*wyasygnowanie*) appropriation **3 miejsce ~a** destination
przeznaczony destined, intended, predestined
przezorność foresight, forethought
przezorny: **być zbyt ~m** err on the side of caution
przezroczysty transparent; (*szklisty*) glassy
przezwisko nickname
prze-zwyciężać/zwyciężyć overcome, surmount
przez(y)wać dub
przeźrocze slide[2], transparency
przeżegnać się cross[2] yourself
przeżu(wa)ć chew
przeżycie 1 (*doświadczenie*) experience[1]; **bolesne** ~ heartbreak **2** (*przetrwanie*) survival
przeżytek anachronism, survival
przeży(wa)ć 1 (*pozostać przy życiu*) survive; (*żyć dłużej niż ktoś/coś*) outlive, survive; (*o jakiś czas*) outlast; (*ostatnie lata życia*) live out sth; **nie przeżyć** not make it; ~ **na nowo** relive; **bardzo trudno jest przeżyć z tak niskiej pensji** it's very hard to get by on such a low income **2** (*doświadczać*) experience[2], go through sth, live through sth
przędza yarn
przędzalnia: ~ **bawełny** cotton mill
przodek ancestor, forebear; (**przodkowie**) ancestry
przód 1 front[1]; (*budynku itp.*) face[1]; (*pochodu itp.*) head[1]; **w ~/do przodu** forward[1]; **z/do przodu** ahead (of sb/sth); **iść/jechać przodem** go ahead **2** (*buta*) toe[1]
prztyczek clip[1], flick noun
przty-kać/knąć flick sth (away, off, out, etc.)
przy 1 (*obok*) by; (*ścianie itp.*) against; (*kuchni itp.*) off[1]; (*dotykając*) to; ~ **łóżku** at the side of his bed/at his bedside **2** (*podczas*) at **3** (*wzdłuż*) along, alongside **4** (*w obecności kogoś*) in front of sb/sth **5** ~ **(sobie)** on **6** (*pomocy kogoś*) with IDM ~ **tym** moreover
przybiec come running
przyb(ie)rać 1 ~ **kształt** take shape; ~ **na sile** intensify; ~ **na wadze** fill out, put sth on; ~ **dużo na wadze** gain a lot of weight **2** (*rzeka*) swell[1] (up) **3** (*nazwisko, tożsamość itp.*) assume **4** ~ **brzegi** (*np. sukienki, firanki*) trim[1] sth (with sth)
przybi(ja)ć: ~ **gwoździem** nail verb
przybity despondent, downbeat, downcast, downhearted, low[1], shattered
przy-bliżać/bliżyć bring sth forward
przybliżeni|e: **w ~u** approximately, roughly
przybliżon|y approximate, rough[1]; **~a liczba/odpowiedź itp.** approximation
przybory paraphernalia; ~ **piśmienne** stationery; ~ **toaletowe** toiletries
przybrać → PRZYBIERAĆ
przybranie garnish noun, trimming; (*tortu, pizzy itp.*) topping; ~ **głowy** headdress
przybran|y (*rodzice*) adoptive; **~a matka** foster mother; **~y ojciec** foster father; **~a matka/~y ojciec** foster parent; **~e dziecko** foster child; **~e nazwisko** assumed name
przybrzeżny (*tylko o brzegu morza*) coastal, inshore, offshore
przybudówka annexe, extension
przybycie 1 appearance, arrival **2** (*przen.*) advent
przybyły (*przym.*) **świeżo/niedawno** ~ new (to sth)
■ **przybył-y/a** (*rz.*) **nowo** ~ arrival; (*tylko osoba*) newcomer
przybysz arrival; ~ **z kosmosu** extraterrestrial
przyby(wa)ć arrive (at/in…), make it, reach[1], turn up; (*księżyc*) wax[2]
■ **przybywający** (*list itp.*) incoming
przychodnia health centre; ~ **lekarska** doctor's[1], practice
przychodzić/przyjść 1 arrive (at/in…), come, get in, turn up; (*z wizytą*) come round (to…); **po kogoś** call for sb; (*wiadomości*) come in; **przychodzące rozmowy telefoniczne** incoming telephone calls; ~ **na świat** arrive **2** (*następować*) come **3 do siebie** come round, recover (from sth); **do siebie po czymś** get over sth/sb IDM **jak przyjdzie co do czego** if/when it comes to the crunch, if/when the crunch comes | **łatwo ~ (komuś)** come easily, naturally, etc. to sb | ~ **do głowy/na myśl** cross your mind, occur to sb | **(nagle) ~ do głowy/na myśl** come/spring to mind | **nigdy nie przyszłoby mi do głowy** I wouldn't dream of doing sth
przychód proceeds
przychylność favour[1] (with sb)
przychylny favourable
przy-ciągać/ciągnąć attract, draw[1]
■ **przyciągający** magnetic
przyciąganie pull[2]; ~ **ziemskie** gravity
przyciemni(a)ć darken, dim[2]
przycięcie clip[1]
przy-cinać/ciąć 1 (*paznokcie, gałęzie itp.*) clip[2]; (*brodę, włosy; kartkę*) trim[1]; (*żywopłot*) prune[2]; ~ **czymś** (*np. sobie palec*) shut sth in sth; **przyciąć sobie palec (czymś)** catch your finger (in sth) **2** (*palik na końcu itp.*) truncate
przycisk button; ~ **głośności** volume control/dial
przy-ciskać/cisnąć 1 (*przygniatać*) depress, press[2], push[1] **2** (*przytulać*) hug **3** (*zmuszać*) push[1] sb (to do sth / into doing sth), twist sb's arm
przy-ciszać/ciszyć (*radio itp.*) turn sth down
■ **przyciszony** soft
przycumo(wy)wać lash[1] A to B, A and B together, make sth fast
przycupnąć crouch (down); (*na brzegu krzesła itp.*) perch[1]
przyczepa trailer; ~ **kempingowa** caravan
przyczepi(a)ć hitch[1], link[2]; (*szpilką*) pin[2]; (*szufladę, półkę itp.*) anchor[2]; ~ **klamerkami** (*np. pranie*) peg[2] sth (out)
□ **przyczepi(a)ć się**: **do kogoś** pick on sb
przyczyn|a cause[1], grounds[1], reason[1], root[1]; **być ~ą czegoś** be at the bottom of sth; **z jakiejś ~y** somehow; **z niewiadomych** ~ for some reason or another
przyczyni(a)ć się contribute (sth) (to/towards sth), make for sth; **przyczyniający się (do zrobienia czegoś)** contributory, instrumental in doing sth
przyćmienie eclipse[1]
przyćmi(ewa)ć 1 (*w czasie zaćmienia*) eclipse[2] **3** (*przen.: obchody itp.*) overshadow; **kogoś** eclipse[2]

przyćmiony 1 (*światło*) dim[1] **2** (*osoba*) subdued
przydarzyć się: **każdemu może ~ wypadek, kiedy…** we're all liable to have accidents when…
przydatnoś|ć fitness, usefulness; **termin ~ci do spożycia** best-before date, expiry date
przydatny helpful, useful; **okazać się ~m** come in handy
przyda(wa)ć impart sth (to sth) □ **przyda(wa)ć się** not come/go amiss, come in handy, come into your own, come in useful
przydawkowy attributive
przy-deptać/depnąć tread[1] sth (in/into/down)
przydługi long-winded
przydomek nickname
przydrożn|y: **~a restauracja** roadside café
przydział allocation, allowance, issue[1], ration
przy-dzielać/dzielić 1 (*czas, pieniądze itp.*) allocate, allot, allow sth (for sb/sth); (*mundur itp.*) issue[2] **2** (*osobę do czegoś*) assign sb to sth, attach sb to sb/sth
przygarbienie stoop noun
przygarbiony bent[2]
przygasić deflate ■ **przygaszony** downbeat, subdued
przy-glądać/glądnąć się gaze, look at sth, watch[1]; **bacznie/badawczo ~ (komuś/czemuś)** peer[2] (at sb/sth)
przygłup airhead, dimwit
przygnębi(a)ć depress, get sb down, get on top of sb
przygnębiając|y black[1], depressing, disheartening, gloomy, melancholy adj.
przygnębieni|e dejection, depression, despondency, gloom, gloominess, glumness, melancholy; **z ~em** dejectedly
przygnębiony crestfallen, dejected, depressed, despondent, disheartened, dispirited, in the doldrums, down in the dumps, down[3], downhearted, gloomy, low[1], in low spirits, miserable, shattered, subdued, unhappy
przy-gniatać/gnieść 1 (*popularnością itp.*) overwhelm **2 przygnieciony drzewem, które się zawaliło** pinned under the fallen tree
przygniatający overwhelming
przygoda adventure, experience[1]; **pełen przygód** adventurous
przygotowani|e arrangement, groundwork, preparation, readiness (for sth); **(przygotowania)** build-up, preparations; **~e zawodowe** credentials; **bez ~a** ad lib, impromptu adv., off the cuff, off the top of your head; **w trakcie przygotowań** in the pipeline
przygotowany poised (to do sth); **być ~m (dla kogoś)** be in store (for sb); **być ~m (na coś trudnego/niemiłego)** be prepared for sth
przygotowawcz|y exploratory, preparatory; **praca ~a** groundwork
przygotow(yw)ać (*obiad itp.*) fix[1] sth (for sb), fix sth (up), get (sb) sth, sth (for sb), get sth ready, prepare; (*plany*) lay[1]; (*zwł. do czegoś ciekawego, wymagającego wysiłku*) gear sb/sth up (for sb/sth); **~ coś naprędce (dla kogoś)** rustle sth up (for sb); **~ się/kogoś/coś (do kogoś/czegoś)** gear up (for sb/sth) IDM **~ grunt (pod coś)** (*przen.*) set the scene (for sth) □ **przygotow(yw)ać się** get ready, prepare; (*zwł. do czegoś ciekawego, wymagającego wysiłku*) gear up (for sb/sth); (*na coś trudnego*) brace[2] yourself (for sth)
przy-gważdżać/gwoździć (*do ściany itp.*) pin[2] sb/sth against, to, under, etc. sth; **~ kogoś do muru** pin sb down
przyhamować ease up
przyimek preposition
przyjaciel 1 friend, pal; (*sympatia*) boyfriend; **serdeczny ~** bosom friend; **~ korespondencyjny** penfriend **2** (*członek stowarzyszenia*) friend of/to sth
przyjaciółka friend, pal; (*przyjaciółki*) girls; (*sympatia*) girlfriend; **~ korespondencyjna** penfriend
przyjazd arrival
przyjazny 1 affable, amicable, friendly[1], neighbourly **2** (*program komputerowy itp.*) intuitive, user-friendly; **~ środowisku** eco-friendly, environmentally friendly
przyjaźnić/za- się be/make friends (with sb)
przyjaźń 1 (*więź z kimś*) friendship **2** (*życzliwość*) friendliness
przyjąć (się) → PRZYJMOWAĆ (SIĘ)
przyjemnoś|ć enjoyment, fun[1], pleasure; (*czekolada itp.*) indulgence; **duża ~ć** treat[2]; **wielka ~ć** kick[2]; **uczenie tej klasy to prawdziwa ~ć** that class is a joy to teach; **znajdować ~ć** enjoy; **(nie) znajdować ~ć/ci w czymś** take (no) pleasure in sth/doing sth; **znajdowanie (w czymś) ~ci** appreciation; **sprawiać ~ć** gratify, please[2]; **przyjmuję z ~cią** I am happy to accept, I'd be pleased to accept; **z ~cią** I'd be delighted to, I'd love to, with pleasure; **cała ~ć po mojej stronie** you're welcome; **dla ~ci** (just) for fun/for the fun of it
przyjemny enjoyable, likeable, nice, pleasant, pleasing, pleasurable; (*towarzystwo itp.*) congenial, friendly[1]; (*wygodny*) comfortable; (*zapach; kolor; dźwięk*) rich
przyjezdny visitor
przy-jeżdżać/jechać arrive (at/in…), come; (*pociąg itp.*) draw[1] in, into sth, get in; **(dokądś) (skądś)** come over (to…) (from…); **po kogoś** call for sb; **kiedy przyjeżdża następny pociąg/autobus?** what time is the next train/bus due (in)?
przyjęci|e 1 (*akceptacja*) acceptance; (*roli itp.*) assumption; (*systemu miar, waluty itp.*) adoption; **możliwy do ~a** acceptable, admissible, palatable (to sb); (*informacja itp.*) plausible; **nie do ~a** inadmissible, unacceptable, intolerable, not on **2** (*impreza*) dinner party, party, reception; (*nieform.*) bunfight; **wielkie ~e** blowout; **~e pożegnalne** farewell party **3** (*oddźwięk*) reception **4 godziny przyjęć** surgery
przyjęty customary; **ogólnie ~** orthodox
przyjmować/przyjąć 1 (*akceptować*) accept; (*kartę kredytową itp.*) take **2** (*wiadomość itp.*) take; **~ do wiadomości** accept sth (as sth), that… **3 (na siebie)** (*odpowiedzialność itp.*) accept, take **4** (*wniosek, propozycję itp.*) adopt, pass[1]; (*w głosowaniu*) carry **5** (*gości itp.*) receive **6** (*do pracy itp.*) take sb on; (*na uniwersytet/kurs*) admit sb/sth (into/to sth) **7** (*odebrać*) greet sb/sth (as/with sth); (*chrześcijaństwo itp.*) embrace; **~ z radością** welcome[1]; **krytycy dobrze przyjęli ten film** the film went down well with the critics **8** (*zakładać*) **przyjmując (że)** assuming (that…) **9 przyjąć zamówienie** take sb's order **10** (*poród*) deliver □ **przyjmować/przyjąć się** (*idea itp.*) catch on, gain currency; (*moda itp.*) come in
przyjście coming
przyjść → PRZYCHODZIĆ
przykazanie commandment
przy-klaskiwać/klasnąć applaud
przy-klejać/kleić zob. też KLEIĆ (SIĘ); glue[2], paste[2]; (*taśmą klejącą*) sellotape verb
przyklejony (*do telewizji itp.*) glued to sth IDM **uśmiech ~ do twarzy** a fixed smile
przykład example, illustration, instance; (*zwł. przykrego stanu czegoś*) commentary on sth; **na ~** for example, for instance, e.g.; **jak na ~** such as; **być ~em** exemplify; **być typowym ~em** typify IDM **brać ~ z kogoś/czegoś** take your cue from sb/sth | **dawać (komuś) (dobry/zły) ~** set a(n) (good/bad) example (to sb) | **iść za czyimś ~em itp.** follow sb's example/lead
przy-kładać/łożyć apply sth (to sth) □ **przy-kładać/łożyć się** address[2] (yourself to) sth, apply yourself (to sth/doing sth)
przy-kręcać/kręcić bolt[2], screw[2] □ **przy-kręcać/kręcić się** screw[2]
przykro: **~ mi** I'm sorry; **bardzo mi ~, że…** I'm very sad that…
przykroś|ć 1 (*nieprzyjemność*) offence (to sb/sth); (*gorycz*) bitterness; **sprawiać komuś ~ć** pain[2] **2** (*żal*) regret[2]; **z ~cią coś zrobić** regret[1]
przykry unpleasant; (*sytuacja itp.*) distressing, miserable, trying; (*gorzki*) bitter[1]; (*wspomnienie itp.*) painful, troublesome; (*uwaga itp.*) distasteful; (*rozwód itp.*) messy
przykrycie cover[2]
przykry(wa)ć cover[1] sb/sth (up/over) (with sth); (*tkaniną itp.*) drape sb/sth (in/with sth); (*liśćmi itp.*) bury; (*śniegiem itp.*) blanket sth (in/with sth)
przy-kucać/kucnąć crouch (down)
przyku(wa)ć 1 ~ łańcuchem chain[2] **2** (*uwagę*) engage, rivet[2] **3 ~ (do łóżka)** confine sb/sth (in/to sth) ■ **przykuty**: **~ do łóżka** bedridden
przy-latywać/lecieć be due (in)
przylądek cape, headland
przy-legać/lec 1 (*dotykać*) adhere (to sth); (*ubranie itp.*) cling to sb/sth **2** (*wtulić się*) nestle ■ **przylegający** (*ubranie itp.*) clinging
przyległy adjoining
przylepi(a)ć: **~ komuś etykietkę** label[2] sb (as) sth

przylepiec 1 adhesive[1] **2** (*med.*) plaster[1]
przylepny adhesive[2]
przylgnąć → LGNĄĆ
przylot arrival
przyłapać: **kogoś (na czymś)** find sb out
przyłą-czać/czyć annex, attach
□ **przyłą-czać/czyć się** associate[1] yourself with sth, join[1], join in (sth/doing sth)
przyłbica visor
przyłożyć (się) → PRZYKŁADAĆ (SIĘ)
przy-mierzać/mierzyć try sth on
□ **przy-mierzać/mierzyć się**: **(do robienia czegoś)** have a crack (at sth/at doing sth)
przymierzalnia (*w sklepie*) fitting room
przymierze alliance, league
przymi-lać/lić się ingratiate yourself (with sb)
przymilny ingratiating
przymiot quality
przymiotnik adjective
przymiotnikowy adjectival
przymknąć → PRZYMYKAĆ
przymoco(wy)wać affix[2], attach, fasten, fix[1]; (*szpilką*) pin[2], put, secure[2]; (*pasem*) strap; (*metkę, etykietkę*) tag[2]; (*taśmą klejącą*) tape[2] sth (up)
przymroz|ek: **przygruntowe ~ki** ground frost
przymrużenie IDM **traktować coś z ~m oka** take sth with a pinch of salt
przymulony spaced out
przymus coercion, compulsion, duress; **bez ~u** freely; **pod ~em** under protest
przymusowy enforced
przy-muszać/musić coerce, constrain
przy-mykać/mknąć (*aresztować*) bust[1] IDM **~ oczy** turn a blind eye (to sth)
przy-naglać/naglić hurry[1], spur[2]
przynajmniej anyway, at least, at any rate
przynależność membership; **~ etniczna/rasowa** ethnicity; **~ państwowa** nationality
przynęta bait, decoy, enticement, lure[2]
przy-nosić/nieść 1 bring, get; **pójść i przynieść** fetch; **~ korzyść (z czegoś)** benefit[2], profit[2] (from/by sth); **~ ulgę** relieve; **~ owoce** bear fruit **2** (*skutki*) throw sth up; **~ w rezultacie** result in sth **3** (*dochód itp.*) fetch, generate; (*procent, zysk itp.*) earn; **przynoszący zysk** economic
przyozdabi(a)ć festoon
przy-padać/paść fall[1] **na kogoś/coś** (*obowiązek itp.*) devolve on/upon sb/sth IDM **~ (sobie) do gustu** hit it off (with sb)
przypad|ek 1 (*zdarzenie nieplanowane*) chance[1] **2** (*przykład*) instance; (*i med.*) case; **w wielu ~kach** often **3** (*gram.*) case
■ **przypadkiem** by accident, by any chance
przypadkowo by accident, accidentally, by any chance, coincidentally, haphazardly, randomly; **~ coś zrobić** happen to do sth
przypadkowy accidental, chance[3], coincidental; (*zdarzający się nieregularnie*) occasional, odd, haphazard, random; (*świadek*) innocent; **~ świadek** bystander
przypadłość affliction
przypa-lać/lić scorch
□ **przypa-lać/lić się** burn[1]
przy-patrywać/patrzeć się contemplate, gaze, regard[1]; **przypatrywać się biernie** look on
przypiąć → PRZYPINAĆ
przypieczętować seal[1]
przy-piekać/piec scorch
□ **przy-piekać /piec się** (*kromka chleba itp.*) toast verb
przy-pierać/przeć: **kogoś do czegoś** pin[2] sb/sth against, to, under, etc. sth; **~ kogoś do muru** corner[2], pin sb down
przy-pinać/piąć fasten; (*spinaczem*) clip[2]; (*szpilką*) pin[2]
■ **przypinany** (*muszka itp.*) clip-on
przypis annotation, footnote, note[1]; **opatrywać ~ami** annotate
przypisek note[1]
przypis(yw)ać ascribe sth to sb/sth, attribute[1] sth to sb/sth, put sth down to sth; (*komuś/czemuś coś dobrego*) credit[2] sb/sth with sth, sth to sb/sth; **przypisać komuś winę** lay the blame on sb
przypływ 1 (*zwł. ludzi, pieniędzy*) influx; (*gniewu itp.*) fit[3]; (*natchnienia itp.; gniewu*) flash[2]; (*emocji*) flurry, stirring; (*sił itp.*) burst[2]; **nagły ~** surge **2** (*morski*) high tide; **nadchodzi ~** the tide's coming in
przypodob(yw)ać się: **komuś** ingratiate yourself (with sb), pander to sb
przypominać 1 kogoś/coś resemble; **(komuś coś)** resonate (with sb/sth); **bardzo coś ~** be very reminiscent of sth; **trochę coś ~** be not unlike sth **2 (/przypomnieć) komuś (o czymś)** bring sth back, remind **3 (/przypomnieć) sobie coś** bring/call sb/sth to mind, recall, recollect, remember, think; **nie ~ sobie czegoś** have no recollection of sth; **nie mogę sobie przypomnieć, jak się nazywa** his name eludes me
□ **przypom-inać/nieć się** come back (to sb)
przypomnienie reminder
przypora buttress[1]
przypowieść parable
przyprawa condiment, flavouring, seasoning; (*korzenna*) spice[1]
przyprawi(a)ć 1 (*jedzenie*) flavour[2] **2 kogoś o coś** give[1]; **~ mnie o ból głowy** give sb a headache; **przyprawiający o mdłości** sickly
przy-prowadzać/prowadzić bring, fetch, get
przyprzeć → PRZYPIERAĆ
przy-puszczać/puścić assume, believe, conjecture, expect, guess[1], imagine, presume, reckon, suppose; **przypuszczam, że...** I dare say, my guess is that..., I take it (that...); **przypuśćmy(, że)** say[1], suppose
przypuszczaln|y alleged, hypothetical
■ **przypuszczalnie** allegedly, presumably
przypuszczenie assumption, conjecture noun, guess[2], hypothesis, inkling, presumption, supposition
przyroda nature
przyrodn|i: **~i/a brat/siostra** (*z którym ma się wspólnego rodzica*) half-brother, half-sister; (*dziecko ojczyma/macochy*) stepbrother, stepsister
przyrodnicz|y: **nauki ~e** science
przyrodni-k/czka naturalist
przyrodoznawstwo natural history
przyrodzony natural[1]
przyrost accrual, growth, increase[2]; (*zwł. płacy*) increment
przyrostek suffix
przyrostowy incremental
przyrównywać compare
przyrumienić (się) → RUMIENIĆ (SIĘ)
przyrząd appliance, device, implement[2], instrument; **~ pomiarowy** gauge[1], instrument; **~ do przymocowania** attachment
przyrzeczenie pledge, promise[2], undertaking
przy-rzekać/rzec promise[1], vow verb
przysadka: **~ mózgowa** pituitary
przysadzisty chunky, dumpy, squat[2]
przy-siadać/siąść IDM **przysiąść fałdów** pull your socks up
przysięg|a oath, vow; **zeznawać pod ~ą** be on/under oath
przy-sięgać/siąc swear
przy-słaniać/słonić obscure[2]
przysłowi|e adage, proverb, saying; **według ~a** proverbially
przysłowiowy proverbial
przysłówek adverb
przysłówkowy adverbial
przysług|a favour[1], kindness; **oddać komuś ~ę** do sb a favour; **poprosić kogoś o ~ę** ask sb a favour
przy-sługiwać/służyć się: **dobrze przysługiwać się komuś** do sb a good turn; **źle się komuś przysłużyć** do sb a disservice
przysmak delicacy
przysnąć → PRZYSYPIAĆ
przy-sparzać/sporzyć pose[1]; **~ komuś kłopotu** put sb out
przysposobienie preparation
przyssanie się suction
przyssawka suction pad
przystanek stop[2]; **~ autobusowy** bus stop
przystań harbour[1], pier, port; **~ jachtowa** marina
przysta(wa)ć 1 (*zatrzymywać się*) halt verb, pause[1] **2 na kogoś/coś** (*być odpowiednim, np. okazji*) befit **3 (na coś)** (*zgadzać się*) accede (to sth)
przystaw|ka hors d'oeuvre, starter; **zestaw ~ek** a selection of side dishes
przystępność accessibility
przystępny 1 (*dla laików itp.*) accessible, popular **2** (*osoba*) approachable, forthcoming
przy-stępować/stąpić 1 do (zrobienia) czegoś (*zaczynać*) proceed to do sth; (*do negocjacji (z kimś)*) enter into sth (with sb); **~ do czynu/działania** go/spring into action, move[1]; **~ do ataku** go on the attack, take the offensive **2** (*do egzaminu*) enter (for) sth, sb (in/for sth), sit; (*do zawodów, konkurencji itp.*) go in for sth **3 do czegoś** (*przyłączać się*) join[1]
przystojniak hunk
przystojny attractive, good-looking, handsome
przystoso(wy)wać adapt, adjust, gear sth to/towards sb/sth, tailor[2] sth to/for sb/sth; **specjalnie przystosowany/wybudowany** purpose-built

□ **przystoso(wy)wać się** adapt, adjust, conform; (*do nowych warunków itp.*) settle in/into sth; **ponownie ~** readjust (to sth); **coraz trudniej przystosowuje się do nowych warunków** he's getting more and more set in his ways
przy-strzygać/strzyc zob. też STRZYC; (*brodę itp.*) trim[1]
przy-suwać/sunąć: **przysuń swoje krzesło do ognia itp.** draw your chair up to the fire, pull your chair a bit nearer to the fire
przy-swajać/swoić: **sobie** absorb, assimilate
przy-sypiać/snąć nod off
przyszłościowy forward[2]
przyszłoś|ć 1 future; **w ~ci** away, hereafter, to come, in future; **na ~ć** henceforth; (*naprzód*) **w ~ć** forward[1] **2** (*los*) fortune
przyszły -to-be, future adj., next[1]; **czas ~** future; **czas ~ dokonany** the future perfect
przyszykować → SZYKOWAĆ
przyszy(wa)ć sew sth (on); **~ guzik do czegoś** put a button on sth
przy-śpieszać/śpieszyć accelerate, hasten, increase your speed, quicken, speed sth up
przyśrubow(yw)ać screw[2] sth (on, down, etc.)
przy-taczać/toczyć cite, quote; **~ coś na usprawiedliwienie** plead sth (for sth)
przytępiony: **o ~m słuchu** hard of hearing
przy-tłaczać/tłoczyć 1 (*przygnębić*) overcome, overwhelm, weigh sb down, weigh on sb/sth **2** (*ciężar*) weigh sb/sth down **3** (*drapacz chmur itp.*) dwarf[2]
przytłaczający 1 oppressive, overpowering, overwhelming **2** (*zwycięstwo*) landslide
przytłumi(a)ć offset
przytłumiony dull, muffled, muted
przytoczyć → PRZYTACZAĆ
przytomnoś|ć consciousness; **brak ~ci** unconsciousness; **stracić ~ć** black out, have a black out, pass out; **odzyskiwać ~ć** come round; **przywracać kogoś do ~ci** bring sb round
przytomny conscious
przytrafi(a)ć się become of sb/sth, befall, happen to sb/sth
przy-trzaskiwać/trzasnąć: **coś czymś** shut sth in sth; **~ sobie palce drzwiami** get your fingers caught in the door
przytrzymać się → TRZYMAĆ SIĘ
przytrzym(yw)ać 1 (*gwoździem itp.*) hold sth on **2** (*złodzieja itp.*) tackle[1]
przy-tulać/tulić give sb a cuddle, hug; **przytuliłem ją do siebie** I held her close
□ **przy-tulać/tulić się** cuddle; **do siebie** cling together, snuggle (up to sb), (up/down)
przytulny cosy, homely, intimate, snug
przytułek hostel
przy-twierdzać/twierdzić clamp[1] A and B (together), A to B, fasten sth (on/to sth), A and B (together), put, secure[2] sth (to sth)
przytyk dig[2]

przywiązanie: **do kogoś/czegoś** affection, attachment, devotion; **czujący ~ do kogoś/czegoś** fond
przywiązany: **do kogoś/czegoś** attached to sb/sth; **być głęboko ~m do czegoś** feel a strong attachment to sth
przywiąz(yw)ać 1 (*przymocować*) bind[1], tether[1], tie[1], tie sb/sth up **2** (*wagę itp.*) attach sth to sb/sth; **~ dużą wagę do czegoś** set... store by sth, treasure[2], value[2] sb/sth (as sth)
przy-wierać/wrzeć cling (on) to sb/sth, together
przywilej prerogative, privilege
przy-właszczać/właszczyć: **sobie** appropriate[2]; (*sobie pieniądze*) pocket, 2; (*sobie cudzą własność*) expropriate
przy-wodzić/wieść IDM **~ kogoś/coś na myśl** bring sth back, bring/call sb/sth to mind
przywoł(yw)ać 1 hail[1]; (*urządzenie elektroniczne*) **~ kogoś za pomocą brzęczyka** bleep[2] **2** (*wspomnienie*) evoke
przy-wozić/wieźć bring, get; (*towary*) import[2] sth (from...); **pojechać i przywieźć** fetch; **pierwsze króliki zostały przywiezione do Australii w XVIII wieku** rabbits were first introduced to Australia in the 18th century
przywód-ca/czyni leader; (*organizacji przestępczej itp.*) ringleader; (*w akcji politycznej itp.*) protagonist
przywództwo leadership
przywóz import[1]
przy-wracać/wrócić 1 bring sth back, restore sb/sth (to sb/sth); (*przepisy itp.*) reinstate **2** (*do pracy/na stanowisko*) reinstate sb (in/as sth)
przywrzeć → PRZYWIERAĆ
przywykły: **do czegoś/do robienia czegoś** used to sth/to doing sth
przyziemny mundane, pedestrian[2]
przyzna(wa)ć 1 (*rację*) acknowledge, concede; **~ rację** grant[1]; **~, że** admit, recognize; **trzeba przyznać, że** admittedly; **firma, trzeba jej to przyznać,...** the company, to its credit,... **2** (*prawo do czegoś*) allow sb sth, sth (for sb/sth), concede sth (to sb); **~ komuś prawa wyborcze** enfranchise **3** (*nagrodę itp.*) award[2], confer, grant[1]
□ **przyzna(wa)ć się**: **(do czegoś)** admit to sth/doing sth, come clean (with sb) (about sth), confess (to sth/to doing sth), own up (to sth); **~ do błędu** climb down (over sth); **(nie) przyznała się do winy** she pleaded (not) guilty to the crime; **nikt nie przyznał się do dokonania ataku bombowego** no one has claimed responsibility for the bomb attack
przyzwalać: **na coś** connive at sth
przyzwoitka chaperone; **towarzyszyć jako ~** chaperone verb
przyzwoitoś|ć decency, decorum; **mieć na tyle ~ci, żeby** have the grace to do sth
przyzwoity decent, proper; (*żart itp.*) clean[1]; **być na tyle ~m, żeby** have the grace to do sth
przyzwolenie acquiescence
przy-zwyczajać/zwyczaić accustom sb/sth to sth

■ **przyzwyczajenie** habit | **przyzwyczajony** accustomed to sth, used to sth/to doing sth
□ **przy-zwyczajać/zwyczaić się** accustom yourself to sth, adjust (to sth), get accustomed to sb/sth, get used to sb/sth; **do robienia czegoś** get into the habit of doing sth, take to sth/doing sth
P.S. PS
pseudonim alias[2], pseudonym
psi canine; **za ~e pieniądze/~ grosz** dirt cheap
psik: **a ~!** atishoo
psikus hoax, practical joke, prank, trick
psioczyć/na- bitch[1] (about sb/sth)
psota mischief, trick
psotny mischievous
pstrąg trout
pstryczek flick noun
pstryk click[2]
pstryk-ać/nąć 1 (*wydać odgłos*) click[1]; (*palcami*) snap your fingers **2 czymś** (*przycisk, kontakt itp.*) flick sth (off, etc.) **3** (*zdjęcia*) snap[1]
psuć/ze-/po- 1 (*niszczyć*) break[1], damage[2]; (*zęby itp.*) rot **2** (*zabawę itp.*) mar, mess sth up, spoil, upset[1]; (*humor itp.*) cloud[2]; (*stosunki itp.*) sour verb; (*reputację itp.*) blemish verb, taint verb; (*plany itp.*) foul sth up; **~ szyki** thwart sth **3** (*zwł. dziecko*) spoil **4** (*charakter itp.*) pervert[1]
□ **psuć/ze-/po- się 1** (*niszczyć się*) break[1]; (*maszyna*) break down; (*komputer itp.*) crash[2], go wrong; (*hamulec itp.*) fail[1], go[1]; **zepsuć się całkowicie** have had it; **silnik samochodu się popsuł** the car developed engine trouble **2** (*stosunki itp.*) go/turn sour **3** (*żywność*) go off; **nie ~** keep[1]; **łatwo psujący się** perishable **4** (*ząb itp.*) decay[2] **5** (*zespół muzyczny itp.*) go off
psychiatra psychiatrist
psychiatria psychiatry
psychiatryczny psychiatric
psychiczny mental
psychika psyche
psychoanality-k/czka psychoanalyst
psychoanaliz|a psychoanalysis; **przeprowadzać ~ę** psychoanalyse
psychodeliczny psychedelic
psycholog psychologist
psychologia psychology
psychologiczny psychological
psychometryczny psychometric
psychopat-a/ka psychopath
psychoterapeut-a/ka psychotherapist
psychoterapia psychotherapy
psychotyczny psychotic
psychoza psychosis; **~ maniakalno-depresyjna** bipolar disorder
pszczelarstwo bee-keeping
pszczelarz bee-keeper
pszczoła bee
pszenica wheat
ptak bird, fowl; **~ drapieżny** bird of prey
ptasi: **~a grypa** bird flu
ptaszarnia aviary
ptaszek 1 (*znaczek*) tick[2]; **stawiać ~** tick[1] **2** (*anat.*) willy

pub pub, public house; (*nieform.*) boozer; **lokalny** ~ local[2]
publiczność audience; ~ **mimo woli** a captive audience
publiczn|y public[1]; **szkoła ~a** public school; **podany do ~ej wiadomości** in the public domain. IDM **być ~ą tajemnicą** be common/public knowledge
■ **publicznie** publicly, in public
publikacja publication
publikować/o- publish; (*serię artykułów itp.*) run[1]
puch down[4], fluff
puchar cup[1]
puchaty fluffy
puchnąć/s- puff up, swell[1] (up)
pucołowaty chubby
pucować/wy-: **wypucować sobie buty** give your shoes a shine
pucowanie shine[2]
pudding pudding
pudel poodle
pudełk|o box[1], pack[2], packet; (*duże*) case; **plastikowe ~o z przykrywką** tub; **~o (od) zapałek** matchbox; **~o z farbami** paintbox; (*zestaw*) **w ~u** boxed
puder powder
pud|ło 1 (*pudełko*) box[1] **2** (*więzienie*) nick[1]; **w ~le** inside[1] **3** (*chybiony strzał*) miss[2]
pudrować/po- powder verb
pukać/za-/puknąć knock[1], rap[2]; **lekko** ~ tap[1]
pukiel curl[2]
pula 1 (*stawka w grze*) pool[1], stake[1] **2** (*w loterii itp.: skumulowana*) the jackpot **3 wspólna** ~ kitty IDM ~ **genów** gene pool
pulchny chubby, plump[1]
pulower pullover
pulpet meatball
pulpit 1 (*ekran monitora*) desktop **2** (*do nut*) music stand
puls pulse[1]
pulsować pulsate, throb
pułap 1 (*poziom*) mark[2]; (*emocji, podniecenia itp.*) pitch[1] **2** (*cen itp.*) ceiling
pułapk|a 1 trap[1]; **łapać w ~ę** trap[2] **2** (*przen.*) catch[2], pitfall, trap[1]; **złapać w ~ę** entrap; **zapędzać w ~ę** trap[2] sb (into sth/into doing sth)
pułk regiment
pułkownik colonel
pułkowy regimental
punk punk
punkcik speck, spot[1]
punkcja: ~ **owodni** amniocentesis
punkowy punk
punkt 1 (*w czasie*) juncture, point[1]; ~ **kulminacyjny** climax, culmination; **osiągać ~ kulminacyjny** climax verb **2** (*miejsce*) point[1]; ~ **kontrolny** checkpoint; ~ **obserwacyjny** lookout, vantage point; ~ **charakterystyczny/orientacyjny** (*w terenie*) landmark; ~ **zaczepienia** foothold **3** (*sprzedaży detalicznej*) outlet; ~ **bukmacherski** bookmaker **4** (*poziom*) point[1] **5** (*kropka*) dot[1]; ~ **w tekście** (*kolejny*) bullet point **6** (*programu*) act[1], event, item **7** (*w grach itp.*) **zdobywać ~y** score[2]; **prawo jazdy bez ~ów karnych** a clean driving licence **8** ~ **dziewiąta** 9 o'clock on the dot IDM **martwy** ~ standstill | ~ **zapalny** hot spot | ~ **widzenia** angle[1], perspective, point[1], point of view, standpoint, vantage point, view[1], viewpoint | ~ **wyjścia** starting point (for sth) | ~ **zwrotny** turning point; (*w historii itp.*) landmark
punktor bullet point
punktować mark[1]
punktualność punctuality
punktualn|y punctual
■ **punktualnie** on the dot, punctually, sharp[2]; **wszyscy zebrali się ~ o 7.30 jak ustalono** we all duly assembled at 7.30 as agreed
pupa bum, rear[1]
purée (*ziemniaczane itp.*) purée
purpurowy magenta, purple
puryst-a/ka purist
purytan-in/ka puritan
purytański puritan, strait-laced
puryzm purism
pustak breeze block
pustelniczy reclusive
pustelni-k/ca hermit, recluse
pustk|a desolation, emptiness, void[1]; **poczucie ~i** vacuum[1]
pustkowie desolation, the outback, wilderness
pustoszeć/o- empty[2]
pustoszyć/s- devastate, ravage
pust|y 1 (*szklanka itp.*) empty[1], void[2]; (*kłoda itp.*) hollow[1]; (*ściana*) bare; (*karta; taśma*) blank[1] **2** (*słowa*) idle; (*dyskusja itp.*) sterile; (*wzrok*) vacant; (*osoba*) vain IDM (*wrócić skądś*) **z ~ymi rękami** empty-handed
pustynia 1 desert[1], wilderness **2** (*przen.*) wasteland
puszcza wilderness
pu-szczać/ścić 1 (*wypuścić*) let sb/sth go, let go of sb/sth, leave go (of sth), release[1]; **nie ~ kogoś/czegoś (gdzieś/do siebie)** shut sb/sth out **2** (*latawca itp.*) fly[1] **3** ~ **pędy** sprout[1] **4** (*kasetę, płytę itp.*) play[1], play sth back (to sb), put sth on **5** ~ **w obieg** circulate; ~ **coś obiegiem** pass sth around/round **6** ~ **bańki/kółka z dymu** blow bubbles/smoke rings IDM ~ **farbę** spill the beans
pusz|ka (*napoju itp.*) can[2], tin; (*farby itp.*) pot[1]; (*na mąkę itp.*) canister
puszkować/za- can[3]
puszysty 1 (*kot*) fluffy, furry **2** (*osoba*) plump[1]
puścić → PUSZCZAĆ
puzon trombone
puzzle jigsaw
pycha haughtiness, pride[1], vanity
pyk-ać/nąć puff[1]
pył dust[1]; ~ **wodny** spray[1]
pyłek 1 (*drobina czegoś*) speck; (*kurz itp.*) fleck **2** (*kwiatowy*) pollen
pysk muzzle, snout
pyskówka uproar
pysznić się pride yourself on sth/doing sth
pyszny 1 (*wyniosły*) haughty, proud **2** (*jedzenie*) delicious, scrumptious, yummy **3** (*piękny*) gorgeous
pytać/za-/s- ask, question, enquire[2]; **o kogoś** ask after sb; ~ **o czyjeś zdrowie** enquire after sb
□ **pytać/za-/s- się** enquire; **spytać się o drogę** ask for directions; ~ **o czyjeś zdrowie** enquire after sb
pytając|y (*przym.*) interrogative[1], quizzical
■ **pytający/a** (*rz.*) enquirer
pytajnik question mark
pytajny (*przysłówek itp.*) interrogative[1]
pytani|e query, question[1]; **~e retoryczne** rhetorical question; **zadać ~e** query verb, question[2]; **brać bez ~a** help[1] yourself to sth
pyton python
pyzaty chubby

Q

q (**Q/q**) (*litera*) Q, q
quiz: ~ **telewizyjny** panel game

R

r (**R/r**) (*litera*) R, r
rabarbar rhubarb
rabat discount[1]
rabin rabbi
rabować/ob-/z-: **coś komuś/czemuś** rob sb/sth (of sth)
rabunek: ~ **uliczny** mugging
rabuś: ~ **uliczny** mugger
rachować/po- count[1] sth
rachub|a: **nie brać kogoś/czegoś w ~ę** count sb/sth out, discount[2]; **nie wchodzić w ~ę** out adj.; **nie wchodzący w ~ę** out of the question; **stracić ~ę czasu** lose (all) track of time
rachun|ek 1 (*działanie matematyczne*); (**rachunki**) arithmetic, sums; (*obliczanie*) count[2]; **~ek pamięciowy** mental arithmetic; **nie jestem dobry w ~kach** I don't have a head for figures **2** (*konto*) account[1]; **~ek oszczędnościowy** savings account **3** (*należność*) bill[1], tab; **na (czyjś) ~ek** at sb's expense; **na ~ek firmy** on the house IDM **wyrównać ~ki** settle matters
rachunkowość accountancy, accounting, bookkeeping
racica hoof
racj|a 1 (*słuszność*) **mieć ~ę** be in the right; **masz całkowitą ~ę** you're quite right; **~a!** hear! hear!, quite **2** (*powód; argument*) reason[1], point[1]; **z ~i czegoś** by virtue of sth **3** (*żywnościowa*) ration
racjonalizacja rationalization
racjonalizować/z- rationalize
racjonalny rational, reasonable, sane
racjonować ration verb
raczej 1 (*dość*) pretty[1], rather; ~ **(nie)** hardly **2** (*chętniej*) preferably; **a ~** or rather
raczyć bother to do sth, condescend (to do sth), deign to do sth
rad|a 1 (*porada*) advice, a piece of advice, counsel[1]; **dobra ~a** tip[1]; **jakoś dawać sobie ~ę** muddle through **2** (*miejska/państwowa*) council; **~a miejska** town council; **~a ministrów** cabinet; **~a nadzorcza** board of directors **3 dawać sobie ~ę** fend for yourself, get on/along, manage, stand on your own (two) feet
radar radar
radca counsellor
radiacja radiation
radio radio
radioaktywność radioactivity
radioaktywny radioactive
radiolog radiographer, radiologist
radiologia radiology
radiolokator radar
radioodbiornik radio
radiostacja radio
radiowy radio, wireless

radn-y/a councillor
radosny bubbly, glad, gleeful, happy, jolly, joyful, joyous
radoś|ć delight[1], gladness, glee, joy, joyfulness, merriment, rejoicing; (*z powodzenia, zwycięstwa itp.*) triumph[1]; **(wielka) ~ć z robienia czegoś** relish[2]; **pełen ~ci** exalted; **nie posiadający się z ~ci** delirious, jubilant; **przyjmować z ~cią** welcome[1]
radować/u- delight[2], exhilarate, please[2]
□ **radować/u- się** rejoice (at/over sth)
■ **radowanie się** jubilation
radykalist-a/ka radical[2]
radykalizować/z- radicalize
radykalny dramatic, radical[1]
radykał radical[2]
radzić/po-/do- 1 komuś advise, counsel[2], recommend, tell sb to do sth; (*nachalnie*) preach **2 sobie (z czymś)** bear up, cope (with sb/sth), deal with sth, get on/along with sth, get by (on/in/with sth), manage (with sb/sth), (on sth); (*w szkole itp.*) do[1], get on/along; (*z trudnym zadaniem*) contrive; (*z łatwością*) take sth in your stride; **z kimś** deal with sb; **bez czegoś** do without (sth); **poradzić sobie z wyzwaniem** meet the challenge; **łatwo sobie (z czymś) radzić** sail through (sth); **nie mogłem nic na to poradzić - musiałem się roześmiać** I just couldn't help myself - I had to laugh
□ **radzić/po- się** consult sb/sth (about sth), refer to sb/sth
radziecki Soviet
rafa reef
rafineria refinery
rafinować purify, refine
rafinowany refined
raj heaven, paradise
rajd rally[1]; **~ konny** pony-trekking
rajfur pimp
rajski heavenly
rajstopy tights
rak 1 (*med.*) cancer **2** (**Rak**) (*znak zodiaku*) Cancer
rakieta 1 (*statek kosmiczny*) rocket[1]; **~ nośna** booster **2** (*sygnał*) **~ świetlna** flare[2] **3** (*sport*) racket
rakietka (*do tenisa stołowego*) bat[1]
rakotwórczy carcinogenic; **czynnik ~** carcinogen
rakowy cancerous
rama 1 frame[1] **2** (*roweru*) crossbar
ramiącz|ko: **bez ~ek** strapless
rami|ę (*ręka*) arm[1]; (*bark*) shoulder[1]; **do ~on** shoulder-length; **~ę w ~ę** abreast (of sb/sth), side by side
ramka (*w tekście, w formularzu na podpis*) box[1]; (*zawierająca dodatkową informację, np. mapkę*) inset
rampa ramp
ran|a injury, wound[1]; **głęboka ~a** gash; **~a cięta** cut[2]; **~a otwarta** sore[2]
IDM **jątrzyć czyjeś ~y** rub salt into the wound/sb's wounds | **o ~y!** golly, good gracious!, good grief, wow | **~y boskie!** gosh
rancho ranch
ranczo ranch
randka date[1]; **~ w ciemno** blind date
ranek morning
rang|a league, rank[1]; **wysokiej ~i** top-ranking; **osoba równa komuś ~ą** peer[1]
ranić/z- 1 cut[1], hurt[1], injure, wound[2] **2** (*uczucia*) hurt[1]; (*krytyką itp.*) sting[1], wound[2]
ranking league table
ranny 1 (*poranny*) morning **2** (*zraniony*) hurt[2], injured, wounded
IDM **~ ptaszek** an early riser
rano morning
rap: **muzyka/utwór w stylu ~** rap[1]; **wokalizować w stylu muzyki ~** rap[2]
raper/ka MC, rapper
raport report[2]; **składać ~** report back (on sth) (to sb)
raptem (*nagle*) all of a sudden
raptowność suddenness
raptowny heady
rasa 1 (*ludzi*) colour[1], race[1]; **~ ludzka** the human race **2** (*zwierząt*) breed[2]
rasist-a/ka racist
rasistowski racist
rasizm racism
rasow|y 1 (*dyskryminacja itp.*) racial; **stosunki ~e** race relations **2** (*pies itp.*) pedigree[2]
rata instalment; **pierwsza ~** down payment
ratować/u- 1 kogoś/coś help[1], rescue, save[1]; **ratujący życie** life-saving **2** (*sytuację itp.; rzeczy z pożaru itp.*) retrieve, salvage[2]
ratownictw|o life-saving noun; **oddział ~a medycznego** accident and emergency
ratowni-k/czka rescuer; (*na basenie, nad morzem*) lifeguard; **~ medyczn-y/a** paramedic
ratun|ek (*pomaganie komuś*) help[2] (with sth), rescue noun, salvation; **~ku!** help[1]; **pośpieszyć komuś na ~ek** come to sb's rescue
ratunkow|y: **operacja ~a** salvage operation
ratusz town hall
ratyfikacja ratification
ratyfikować ratify
rausz high[2]
raut bash[2]
ra|z 1 (*chwila*) time[1]; (*jeden raz*) once; **jeszcze ~z** anew, once again/more, once more; **po ~z pierwszy** first[2]; **na ~z** at a time, together[1]; **na ~zie** for the time being, for the moment/present, meanwhile; **od ~zu** offhand[2], at once, outright, pat adv.; **tylko ten (jeden) ~z** just this once, (just) for once **2** (**razy**) (*licząc*) times[2]; **trzy ~zy droższy** three times as/more expensive; **wiele ~zy** repeatedly; **x ~zy** umpteen times **3** (*przypadek*) **w ~zie czegoś** in the event of sth, in case of sth, (just) in case; **w takim ~zie** in that case, then; **w każdym ~zie** anyway, in any case, at any rate, all/just the same IDM **na ~zie** (*cześć!*) see you (later) | **~z jest, ~z go nie ma** it comes and goes | **~z kozie śmierć!** here goes | **~z na zawsze** once and for all | **~z po ~z**; **~z za ~zem** in succession, time after time, time and (time) again | **w sam ~z** tailor-made
razem altogether, (all) in one, together[1]; **z kimś/czymś** along with sb/sth, in common with sb/sth, in concert (with sb/sth), in conjunction with sb/sth, together[1], together with sb/sth; **biorąc wszystko ~** altogether, put together, all told
razić/po-: **~ (śmiertelnie) prądem elektrycznym** electrocute
razowy wholemeal
rażący 1 (*blaskiem*) glaring **2** (*uchybienie, błąd itp.*) flagrant, gross[1], glaring
rąbać 1 (**/od-/po-**) chop[1] sth (up) (into sth), hack (away) (at) sth; (*form.*) hew **2** (**/rąbnąć**) smash[1] sth against, into, through, etc.
□ **rąbnąć się** smash[1] against, into, through, etc.
rąbek hem[1]
rąbnięty wacky
rączka handle[2]
rdz|a rust; **poddawać coś działaniu ~y** rust verb
rdzeniowy spinal
rdzeń core IDM **~ kręgowy** spinal cord
rdzewieć/za- rust verb
reagować/za- react, respond; **~ za mocno/emocjonalnie** overreact
reakcja reaction, response; **gwałtowna ~** backlash; **za mocna ~** overreaction; **~ łańcuchowa** chain reaction
reakcjonist-a/ka reactionary
reakcyjny reactionary adj.
reaktor: **~ jądrowy** nuclear reactor
realist-a/ka realist; **być realist-ą/ką** be realistic
realistyczny realistic
realizacja realization
realizator/ka producer
realizm realism
realizować/z- 1 fulfil, go through with sth, live out sth, realize; **realizować jakąś politykę** pursue a policy of sth **2** (*czek*) cash[2]; **być zrealizowanym** clear[2]
□ **realizować/z- się** fulfil yourself
realn|y workable
■ **realnie**: **~ myślący** practical[1]
reanimacja resuscitation
reanimować/z- resuscitate
reasumować/z- recap, sum sth up
rebelia rebellion
rebeliancki insurgent adj.
rebeliant/ka insurgent, rebel[1]
rebus puzzle[1]
recenzja critique, write-up
recenzować/z- review[2]
recepcja reception
recepcjonist-a/ka receptionist
recepta 1 (*lekarska*) prescription **2** (*na sukces itp.*) formula for (doing) sth, recipe for sth
receptura formula
recesja depression, recession
rechot 1 (*śmiech*) cackle noun, chortle noun **2** (*żaby*) croak noun
rechotać/za- (*śmiać się*) cackle, chortle
■ **rechotanie** chortle
recital recital
recyklizacja recycling
recytować/wy- recite, reel sth off
redagować/z- edit; (*sformułować*) word[2]
■ **redagowanie**: **komputerowe redagowanie tekstu** word processing
redakcja (*tekstu*) wording
redaktor/ka editor; **redaktor kroniki/rubryki towarzyskiej** gossip columnist
redukcja cut[2] (in sth), cutback, reduction; **~ kosztów** cost-cutting; **~ zatrudnienia** downsizing

redukować/z- cut sth back, cut back (on sth), cut sth down, cut down (on sth), reduce; (*wydatki, pracowników itp.*) axe^2, cut^1, pare sth (back/down); (*pracownika itp.*) shed^2; ~ **zatrudnienie** make cutbacks in staff, downsize
redystrybucja redistribution
reedukować (*społecznie*) reform
refektarz refectory
referat paper
referencje 1 (*list polecający*) reference **2** (*dyplom potwierdzający czyjeś kwalifikacje itp.*) credentials
referendum referendum
referować/z- relate sth (to sb)
refleks reflex
refleksj|a afterthought, second thoughts; **skłaniający do ~i** thought-provoking
refleksyjny reflective
reflektor 1 floodlight; (*do poszukiwań*) searchlight; (*w samochodzie*) headlight; ~ **punktowy (wąskostrumieniowy)** spotlight; **oświetlony ~ami** floodlit **2** (*przy rowerze, ubraniu*) reflector
reforma reform noun, reformation; **gruntowna** ~ overhaul noun
reformacja reformation
reformator/ka reformer
reformować/z- reform
refren chorus^1, refrain^2
regał shelving; (*tylko na książki*) bookcase
regaty regatta; ~ **jachtowe** yacht race
regenerować/z- (*surowce*) reclaim, recycle
reggae: **muzyka** ~ reggae
region region
regionalny provincial, regional
regres: **ulegać ~owi** regress
regulacja control^1
regulamin regulation; **zgodnie z ~em** by the book; **niezgodny z ~em** against the rules
regulaminowo fair play
regularność regularity
regularny regular^1
regulować 1 (/wy-) adjust, regulate, tune^2; **ponownie** ~ readjust **2** (*ruch drogowy itp.*) control^2 **3 (/u-)** (*rachunek*) settle
■ **regulowanie** (*urządzenia*) setting
reguł|a norm, principle, rule^1; **~y dobrego zachowania** code of conduct; **z ~y** as a general rule, substantially
rehabilitacja rehabilitation
rehabilitować/z- rehabilitate
reinkarnacja reincarnation
rejest|r record^1, register^2; **prowadzić ~r czegoś** keep a tally of sth; **być w ~rze** (*organizacji*) be on sb's books
rejestracja recording, registration; ~ **samochodu** registration number
rejestrować/za- 1 (*zapisywać*) log^2, record^2, register^1; (*organizację*) charter^2; ~ **na wideo** video verb; ~ **godzinę przyjścia do/wyjścia z pracy** clock in/on, clock off **2** (*przyrządem pomiarowym*) register^1
□ **rejestrować/za- się** register^1
rejon area; (*szkolny itp.*) catchment area
rejonow|y: **pielęgniarka ~a** community/district nurse
rejs sailing; (*wycieczkowy*) cruise^1; **dziewiczy** ~ maiden voyage
rekin shark
reklama 1 (*plakat itp.*) advertisement, commercial^2 **2** (*działalność*) advertising, promotion, publicity
reklamować/za- advertise, bill^2 sb/sth as sth, plug^2, publicize
reklamowy advertising
reklamówka carrier bag
rekolekcje religious retreat
rekomendacja recommendation
rekomendować/za- interest sb in sth, recommend
rekompensata compensation, recompense noun
rekompensować/z- offset
rekonesans reconnaissance
rekonstrukcja reconstruction
rekonstruować/z- reconstruct
rekonwalescencja convalescence, recuperation
rekonwalescent/ka convalescent
rekord record^1; **pobić** ~ break^1
rekordowy bumper^2, record^1, record-breaking
rekordzist-a/ka title-holder
rekreacja recreation
rekreacyjny: **ośrodek** ~ leisure centre
rekrut/ka conscript^2, recruit^2
rekrutacja recruitment
rekrutować/z- recruit^1
rektor president
rekwirować/za- commandeer
rekwizyt prop^1
relacja 1 (*sprawozdanie*) account^1, coverage, report^2; (*prasowa itp.*) story **2** (*stosunek*) relation (between sth and sth), (to sth)
relacjonować/z- report^1 (on) sth, report back (on sth) (to sb); (*gazeta itp.*) cover^1
relaks relaxation
relaksować/z- się chill^2, chill out, put your feet up, relax, rest^1, sit back
■ **relaksujący** relaxing
religia faith, religion
religijny religious
relikt relic, survival
remanent stocktaking
remedium remedy^1
remis draw^2, tie^2; **mecz zakończył się ~em** the match was drawn
remisja remission
remisować/z-: **(z kimś)** draw^1, equalize, tie^1 (with sb) (for sth)
remisowy (*wynik*) square^1
remiza depot; ~ **strażacka** fire station
remont decoration, refurbishment, renovation, repair^2; **kapitalny** ~ overhaul noun
remontować/wy- decorate, refurbish, renovate
remontow|y: **prace ~e** restorations
renegat renegade
renesans the Renaissance
renesansowy (*sztuka itp.*) Renaissance
renifer reindeer
renkloda greengage
renoma repute
renowacj|a refurbishment, renovation; **przeprowadzać ~ę** renovate
renta pension; ~ **starcza** old-age pension; **dożywotnia roczna** ~ annuity
rentgen (*zdjęcie rentgenowskie*) X-ray
rentgenogram X-ray
rentgenolog radiographer
rentowność efficiency, profitability
rentowny economic, productive, profitable
reorganizacja reorganization
reorganizować/z- reorganize
repatriacja repatriation
repatriować repatriate
reperkusje repercussions
reperować/z- mend^1, repair^1
repertuar repertoire
replay action replay
replika carbon copy, replica
reporter/ka reporter
represj|a repression; **stosować ~e** victimize
represjonować repress
■ **represjonowanie** victimization
represyjny repressive
reprezentacj|a representation; **ona gra w ~i hokejowej Anglii** she plays hockey for England; **wybierać do ~i narodowej** cap^2
reprezentatywn|y: **~a grupa** (*do badań*) sample
reprezentować represent
reprodukcja reproduction
reprodukować reproduce
reproduktor: **trzymać w stadninie ogiera ~a** keep a stallion at stud
reprymend|a chastisement, rebuke noun, reprimand noun; **udzielać ~y** reprimand, tell sb off (for sth/for doing sth); **udzielać surowej ~y** chastise
republika republic
republikan-in/ka republican
republikańsk|i republican adj.; **Partia Republikańska** the Republican Party
reputacja character, name^1, reputation, repute; **zła** ~ disrepute
resory suspension
respekt respect^1; **budzący** ~ formidable
respektować respect^2
respirator life-support machine, ventilator
restauracj|a restaurant; **pójść do ~i** eat out
restaurować/od- do sth up, restore
restrykcja restraint, restriction
reszka tail^1; **orzeł czy** ~ heads or tails?
reszt|a 1 balance^1, everything else, remainder, remnant, residue, rest^2; **zapłacić ~ę** pay the difference **2** (*pieniędzy*) change^2
resztk|a end^1, last^3, remnant, scrap^1, trace^2 (of sth); (*ołówka*) stub; **(resztki)** oddments, remainder, remains; (*jedzenia*) leftovers
retorta flask, retort^3
retoryczny rhetorical
retoryka rhetoric
retrospekcja (*film, teatr*) flashback
retrospektywny retrospective
rety: **o** ~! good gracious!, whoops
reumatyzm rheumatism
rewanżować/z- się: **z kimś** be/get even (with sb)
rewanżowy: **mecz** ~ return match
rewelacja eye-opener, revelation, sensation
rewelacyjny sensational
rewers: ~ **dłużny** IOU
rewident auditor
rewidować/z- 1 (*przeszukiwać*) frisk, search **2** (*zmieniać*) reconsider, revise
rewir: ~ **policyjny** beat^2

rewizj|a 1 (*przeszukanie*) search noun; **nakaz ~i** search warrant **2** (*zmiana*) review[1]; **poddawać ~i** (*np. pogląd*) reconsider; **poddawać ~i** review[2] **3** (*ksiąg podatkowych*) audit
rewizyt|a: **zapraszać na ~ę** invite sb back
rewolta mutiny, revolt noun
rewolucja revolution
rewolucjonist-a/ka revolutionary[2]
rewolucjonizować/z- revolutionize
rewolucyjny revolutionary[1]
rewolwer revolver
rezerw|a 1 (*towar*) stock[1]; (*zapas; osoba*) standby; (*w zespole sportowym*) reserve[2]; **w ~ie** in reserve **2** (*powściągliwość*) coolness, reserve[2]; **odnoszący się z ~ą** aloof, distant
rezerwacja booking, reservation; **~ biletów** advance bookings
rezerwat reserve[2]; (*przyrody*) sanctuary; (*dla Indian amerykańskich*) reservation
rezerwować/za- book[2], reserve[1] sth (for sb/sth), set sth aside; **~ komuś pokój** book sb in; **~ z wyprzedzeniem** pre-book
rezerwow|y (*przym.*) spare[1], standby adj.; **gracz/zawodnik ~y** substitute; **lista ~a** waiting list
■ **rezerwow-y/a** (*rz.*) **~-y/a (zawodnik/czka)** reserve[2]
rezerwuar reservoir; **~ klozetowy** cistern
rezolucja resolution
rezonans resonance
rezonować (*instrument*) resonate
rezulta|t consequence, effect[1], outcome, product of sth, result[1], upshot; **(rezultaty)** findings; **być ~tem czegoś** come from (doing) sth; **w ~cie** consequently, effectively
rezydencj|a mansion, residence, residency; **~a wiejska** country house; **mieć ~ę** reside (in/at…)
rezydować dwell, reside (in/at…)
rezygnacja 1 (*dymisja*) renunciation, resignation (from sth) **2** (*pogodzenie się*) resignation
rezygnować/z-: **z czegoś** abandon, renounce, surrender sth (to sb); (*z honorarium itp.*) waive; (*z okazji, aby coś zrobić*) bow out (of sth/as sth), drop out (of sth), give up, opt out (of sth), resign (from/as) (sth), throw sth up
reżim regime
reżyser director; **~ filmowy** film director
reżyseria direction
reżyserować/wy- direct[2]
ręcznik towel
ręczn|y manual[1]; **~ej roboty** handmade
■ **ręcznie** by hand, manually; **pisany ~** handwritten
ręczyć/po- guarantee[2], pledge verb sth (to sb/sth); **(za kogoś/coś)** answer for sb/sth, vouch for sb/sth
ręk|a arm[1]; (*dłoń*) hand[1] IDM **brać się/kogoś za ręce** link arms; **do rąk własnych** (*na liście*) personal | **gołymi ~ami** with your bare hands | **mieć pełne ręce roboty** be rushed/run off your feet | **mieć związane ręce** your hands are tied | **na własną ~ę** off your own bat, single-handed | **od ~i** there and then, then and there | **pod ~ą** handy, on hand, ready, to hand | **pod ~ę** arm in arm | **ręce do góry!** hands up | **ręce przy sobie!** hands off (sb/sth) | **trzymać ~ę na pulsie** be/keep abreast of sth | **trzymając się za ręce** hand in hand | **w czyichś ~ach** in your hands, in the hands of sb | **w dobrych ~ach** in capable hands, in safe hands | **w zasięgu ~i** to hand | **z drugiej ~i** second-hand, used | **z pierwszej ~i** (*informacja*) (at) first hand, first-hand adv.
rękaw arm[1], sleeve; **bez ~ów** sleeveless
rękawek: **nadmuchiwany ~** armband
rękawic|a glove; **~a z jednym palcem** mitten; **~e ogrodnicze** gardening gloves
rękawiczka glove
rękoczyn IDM **posunąć się do ~ów** come to blows
rękodzieło handicraft
rękojeść handle[2]; (*miecza, noża*) hilt
rękopis manuscript
ring ring[1]
riposta retort[2]
ripostować/z-/za- retort[1]
robak worm[1]
robić/z- do[1], make[1], produce[1]; (*kurs*) do[1]; **kogoś/coś z kogoś/czegoś** make sb/sth into sb/sth; **robić coś dalej** get on with sth, proceed (with sth); **dobrze robić coś dalej** keep it up; **nie zrobić czegoś** give sth a miss; **nic nie robić** lie about/around; **robić zdjęcie** take a photo(graph); **robić na drutach** knit; **zrobić złe wrażenie** create a bad impression; **robić coś na poczekaniu** improvise; **urlop dobrze ci zrobi** a holiday will do you good IDM **robić swoje** do your own thing
□ **robić /z- się** get, go[1]
robot 1 (*maszyna*) robot **2** (*osoba*) automaton, robot IDM **~ kuchenny** food processor
robot|a chore, job, labour; (*przen., zwł. o czymś złym*) handiwork[1]; **~y drogowe** roadworks; **papierkowa ~a** paperwork; **(za)brać się do ~y** pull your socks up
robotnicz|y: **klasa ~a** the working class
robotni-k/ca hand[1], labourer, worker, workman; **robotnik rolny** farmhand
robótka: **~ szydełkowa** crochet
rock rock[1]; **~ and roll** rock and roll
rockowy rock[1]
rocznica anniversary; **dwusetna ~** bicentenary
rocznik 1 (*książka*) annual[2], yearbook **2** (*wina*) vintage[1]
roczny annual[1], yearly
roda-k/czka compatriot, countryman
rodeo rodeo
rodowód genealogy, pedigree[1]
rodzaj 1 (*odmiana, gatunek*) form[1], kind[1], sort[1], type[1]; (*humoru itp.*) brand[1]; **pewnego ~u** of some description; **tego rozdaju** of that ilk/nature; **tego samego ~u** of a kind; **coś w ~u (czegoś)** a kind of, of a kind, something like, a sort of sth; **coś w tym ~u** or something; **wszelkiego ~u** all manner of… **2** (*biol., zool.*) genus, species **3** (*w sztuce*) genre; **~ sztuki** art form **4** (*gram.*) gender
rodzajnik: **~ nieokreślony** the indefinite article; **~ określony** the definite article
rodzeństwo brothers and sisters, siblings
rodzic parent; **~ chrzestny** godparent
rodzice parents; (*nieform.*) folks[1]
rodzicielski parental; **stan ~** parenthood
rodzić/u- bear[1], give birth (to sb), engender, produce[1]; (*wydawać na świat*) be in labour; **zacząć rodzić** go into labour
□ **rodzić /u- się** be born
rodzimy natural[1], native[1]; **~ mieszkaniec itp.** native[2]
rodzin|a family; **~a niepełna** one-parent family; **~a wielopokoleniowa** extended family IDM **własna ~a** your (own) flesh and blood
rodzinn|y domestic, family adj., home[2]; (*miasto itp.*) native[1]; **miasto ~e** home town
rodzyn|ek 1 (także **rodzynka**) (*bakalie*) currant, raisin; **~ka sułtańska** sultana **2** (*interesująca wiadomość*) titbit
rogalik croissant
rogatkowe toll
rogówka cornea
roić/za- się bustle[1] (with sth), be crawling with sth, be overrun by sth, seethe (with sth), swarm with sb/sth, teem with sth; **rojący się (od czegoś)** infested (with sth); **wody rojące się od rekinów** shark-infested waters
rok year; **~ finansowy** financial year; **~ przestępny** leap year; **~ świetlny** light year; **~u Pańskiego** AD; **w przyszłym ~u** next year; **przez cały ~** all year round; **co ~u** annually; **~ po ~u**; **~ za ~iem** year after year, year in year out; **na ~** p.a.; **raz do ~u**; **raz na ~** yearly adv. IDM **lata całe** yonks
rokowanie prognosis
rokrocznie annually, yearly adv.
rol|a 1 (*funkcja*) function[1], role, part[1]; **pieniądze itp. nie odgrywają żadnej ~i** money, etc. is no object **2** (*aktora*) role, part[1], lines[1] **3** (*uprawna*) **praca na ~i** farming; **pracować na ~i** work on a farm
roleta blind[3], roller blind; (*zewnętrzna*) shutter
rolka reel[1], roll[1]; **~ papieru toaletowego** toilet roll
rolnictwo agriculture
rolniczy agricultural; **obszar ~** farming areas
rolni-k/czka farmer
Rom/ka Gypsy, Romany
romani: **język ~** Romany
romans 1 (*związek*) affair, liaison, relationship, romance, love affair; **zacząć z kimś ~** get off with sb **2** (*powieść*) love story
romansować court[2]
romantyczność romance
romantyczny romantic[1]
romanty-k/czka romantic[2]
romański 1 (*język*) Latin adj., Romance **2** (*arch.*) Romanesque
romb diamond
Romka → ROM
romski Romany
rondel pan[1], saucepan
rondo 1 (*drogowe*) roundabout[1] **2** (*kapelusza*) brim[1]

ropa 1 ~ **naftowa** crude oil, oil, petroleum **2** (*w ranie*) pus
ropieć/za-/z- fester
ropień abscess, ulcer
ropucha toad
rosa dew
rosé (*wino*) rosé
rosnąć 1 (**/u-/wy-**) (*roślina*) grow; ~ **dziko** straggle **2** (**/u-**) (*dziecko*) grow up **3** (**/wz-**) grow (in sth), pile up; ~ **lawinowo** snowball[2]; ~ **w siłę** rally[2]
■ **rosnący** growing
rosół chicken broth, chicken soup
roszczeni|e claim[2] (to sth), (for sth); **osoba zgłaszająca ~a** claimant
rościć: ~ **sobie prawo do czegoś** stake a/your claim (to sth)
roślina plant[1]; ~ **doniczkowa** pot plant
roślinność flora, vegetation
roślinożern|y herbivorous; **zwierzę ~e** herbivore
rotacja rotation; ~ **pracowników** turnover (of sth)
rotacyjny rotary
rotor rotor
rottweiler: **pies rasy** ~ Rottweiler
rowek groove, nick[1], slit[1]
rower bicycle, bike, cycle[1]; ~ **górski** mountain bike; ~ **na trzech kołach** tricycle; ~ **treningowy** exercise bike; ~**em** by bike
rowerzyst-a/ka biker, cyclist, rider
rowkować/po- nick[2]
rozbawi(a)ć amuse
rozbawieni|e amusement; **ku wielkiemu ~u uczniów** much to the pupils' amusement
rozbicie breakage; ~ **statku** shipwreck
rozbić (się) zob. też ROZBIJAĆ (SIĘ)
IDM **rozbić obóz** set up camp
rozbie-gać/c się diverge (from sth), scatter
roz-bierać/ebrać 1 (*zdejmować ubranie*) strip[1] sth (off), undress **2** (*budynek itp.*) demolish, dismantle, knock sth down/over, pull sth down, take sth down; (*na części*) disassemble
□ **roz-bierać/ebrać się** strip[1] (off), undress
rozbieżność discrepancy; ~ **zdań** disagreement, dissent[1]
rozbieżny disparate, dissonant
rozbi(ja)ć break[1], crack[1], crash[2], smash[1], wreck; (*samochód itp.*) smash[1] sth (up); ~ **na kawałki** shatter; **rozbiła sobie głowę** she cut her head open; **rozbić międzynarodową szajkę handlarzy narkotyków** crack an international drug-smuggling ring
□ **rozbi(ja)ć się** break up, break[1], smash[1]; ~ **na kawałki** shatter
rozbiór 1 (*państwa*) partition **2** (*problemu itp.*) analysis
rozbiórka demolition
rozbitek 1 wreck, shipwrecked sailor; ~ **życiowy** down-and-out **2** (*ze statku*) castaway
rozbit|y 1 (*waza itp.*) broken[2] **2** (*związek*) on the rocks; **~y dom** broken home; **~e małżeństwo** broken marriage
roz-brajać/broić 1 (*kraj itp.*) disarm; (*bomba itp.*) deactivate, defuse **2** (*przen.*) disarm
■ **rozbrojenie** disarmament
□ **roz-brajać/broić się** (*kraj itp.*) disarm

rozbrykany frisky
rozbrzmi(ewa)ć 1 (*głos*) resonate, resound (through sth), reverberate, ring[2] (with sth), ring out; (*śmiechem itp.*) echo[2]; (*dzwony*) peal verb; **dzwon rozbrzmiał** the bell went **2** (*przen.*) **czymś** resonate (with sth), resound (with/to sth)
rozbudow(yw)ać extend
rozbu-dzać/dzić 1 (*ze snu*) awaken, wake sb up **2** (*uczucie*) kindle; ~ **czyjś entuzjazm** energize; ~ **w kimś** (*np. zapał*) fire sb up; ~ **(na nowo)** revive
■ **rozbudzenie**: **kawa na rozbudzenie** coffee to wake me up
rozbudzony: **zupełnie** ~ wide awake
rozcapie-rzać/rzyć splay sth (out)
rozchlap(yw)ać slosh
rozchmu-rzać/rzyć się buck up, cheer up
rozchodzić/rozejść się 1 (*tłum itp.*) disassemble, disperse[2] **2** (**z kimś**) separate, split up (with sb) **3** (*droga itp.*) diverge (from sth) **4** (*wiadomości itp.*) percolate; (*plotki itp.*) get about/around/round; **wiadomości szybko się rozchodzą** news travels fast
rozchorować się: **poważnie się rozchorować** get/finish up seriously ill
rozchód outgoings
rozchwiany loose[1]
rozchwytywany in demand
rozciąć → ROZCINAĆ
rozciąg-ać/nąć 1 (*materiał*) stretch[1] **2** (*wydłużać trwanie czegoś; powodować, że coś wystarcza na dłuższy czas*) eke sth out, spin sth out
□ **rozciąg-ać/nąć się** extend, range[2] between A and B, from A to B, span[2], stretch[1]; (*zabudowania itp.*) sprawl
rozciągliwy stretchy
rozciągnięty sprawling
rozcień-czać/czyć dilute sth (with sth); **rozcieńczać wodą** water sth down
rozcieńczony dilute adj.
rozcięcie slash[2], slit[1]
roz-cinać/ciąć cut[1] sth (in/into sth), cut sth open, slash[1] (at) sb/sth, slit[2]; **głęboko rozcinać** gash verb
rozczapie-rzać/rzyć → ROZCAPIERZAĆ
rozczarowanie disaffection, disappointment, discontent; (*pozbycie się złudzeń*) disillusion; (*po początkowym zachwycie*) anticlimax, disenchantment, let-down; **gorzkie** ~ a rude awakening; **przynoszący** ~ disappointing
rozczarowany bitter[1] (about sth), disaffected, disappointed, disenchanted, disillusioned
rozczarow(yw)ać disappoint; (*pozbawić złudzeń*) disillusion
rozczłonkow(yw)ać 1 (*odcinać członki*) dismember **2** (*kraj*) partition verb
rozczochran|y straggly, unkempt, untidy; (*na wietrze*) windswept
rozczul-ać/ić się melt
■ **rozczulanie się**: ~ **nad sobą** self-pity
rozczulający moving
rozdając-y/a dealer
rozdanie (*kart*) deal[2], hand[1]
rozdarcie rip[2], split[2], tear noun
rozda(wa)ć deal[1] (sth) (out), (sth) (to sb), deal sth out, dish sth out, dispense, distribute, give sth out; (*coś już niepotrzebnego*) give sth away; (*karty*) deal[1] (sth out)

rozdmuchany grandiose
rozdmuch(iw)ać build sth up
roz-drabniać/drobnić (się) fragment[2]
rozdrażni(a)ć zob. też DRAŻNIĆ; exasperate
rozdrażnienie annoyance, exasperation
rozdrażniony annoyed, cranky, on edge, edgy, exasperated, fraught, het up, in a huff, irritated, peeved
rozdrobnić (się) → ROZDRABNIAĆ (SIĘ)
rozdroże fork[1]
rozdział 1 (*przydział czegoś*) allocation; **ponowny** ~ redistribution **2** (*książki*) chapter
rozdziel-ać/ić zob. też DZIELIĆ **1** (*pieniądze itp.*) allocate, allot, distribute, dole sth out, parcel sth out; (*między ludźmi*) divide[1] sth (out/up) (between/among sb), sth (between A and B); **rozdzielać ponownie** redistribute **2** (*na części*) divide[1] sth (up) (into sth); (*grupę ludzi*) split[1] sb (up) (into sth) **3** (*jedną grupę od drugiej itp.*) segregate sb/sth (from sb/sth), separate[2] sb/sth (from sb/sth); (*odciąć kogoś/coś od czegoś itp.*) divorce[2] sb/sth from sth; (*zasłony itp.*) part[2], **dający się rozdzielić** separable
□ **rozdziel-ać/ić się** zob. też DZIELIĆ SIĘ **1** (*na części*) divide[1] (up) (into sth), (from sb/sth), split[1] (up) (into sth) **2** (*zasłony itp.*) part[2], separate[2] **3** (*drogi itp.*) diverge (from sth), fork[2]
rozdzielczoś|ć: **o niskiej ~ci** low-resolution; **o wysokiej ~ci** high-resolution
rozdzielcz|y: **tablica ~a** panel
roz-dzierać/edrzeć rip[1], split[1] sth (open), tear sth apart; (*na wystającym gwoździu itp.*) snag[2]
■ **rozdzierający** (*bolesny*) agonizing, excruciating, piercing[1]; (*dźwięk*) ear-piercing[1]; ~ **serce** heartbreaking, heart-rending
□ **roz-dzierać/edrzeć się** rip[1], split[1] (open)
rozdźwięk dichotomy, discord, dissonance
rozebrać (się) → ROZBIERAĆ (SIĘ)
rozebrany undressed
rozedma: ~ **płuc** emphysema
rozedrzeć (się) → ROZDZIERAĆ (SIĘ)
rozegrać się → ROZGRYWAĆ SIĘ
rozejrzeć się → ROZGLĄDAĆ SIĘ
rozejść się → ROZCHODZIĆ SIĘ
rozentuzjazmować się → ENTUZJAZMOWAĆ SIĘ
rozeprzeć się → ROZPIERAĆ SIĘ
rozerwać (się) → ROZRYWAĆ (SIĘ), RWAĆ (SIĘ)
rozesłać → ROZSYŁAĆ
roześmiać się laugh[1]
rozeta (także **rozetka**) rosette
rozeznanie discrimination
rozgadać się: **kiedy Charlie się rozgada...** once Charlie's in full flow...
rozgałęziacz adaptor
rozgałęzi(a)ć się branch off, fork[2]
rozgardiasz 1 (*bałagan*) clutter[2], mess[1]; **robić** ~ mess sth up **2** (*harmider*) pandemonium
rozgarnięty brainy
roz-gaszczać/gościć się make yourself comfortable
roz-glądać/ejrzeć się look around/round, look round; (*w sklepie*) browse; **za czymś** look around/round for sth; **za kimś/czymś** look out for sb/sth

rozgłaszać: ~ **plotki** spread scandal
rozgłos fame, prominence, publicity; **bez ~u** low-key; **nadawać ~** publicize; **nabierający ~u** rising[1]; **nadając czemuś nadmierny ~** sensationally
rozgłośnia station[1]
roz-gniatać/gnieść crush[1] sth (up)
rozgniewać → GNIEWAĆ
rozgniewany irate
rozgorączkować się → GORĄCZKOWAĆ SIĘ
rozgorączkowanie fever (of sth)
rozgorączkowany feverish
rozgoryczenie glumness
rozgoryczony discontented, embittered
rozgościć się → ROZGASZCZAĆ SIĘ
roz-gramiać/gromić (*przeciwnika*) rout, thrash
roz-grywać/egrać się (*scena, akcja itp.*) be enacted, be set[1]
rozgrywk|a (**rozgrywki**) games[1]; **~i sportowe** tournament; **ostateczna ~a** (*w długim sporze*) showdown
rozgryźć crack[1], figure sb/sth out, suss sb/sth (out)
rozgrze-szać/szyć absolve sb (from/of sth)
rozgrz(ew)ać (*emocje itp.*) whip sth up; **ćwiczenia rozgrzewające** warm-up exercises
□ **rozgrz(ew)ać się** hot up, warm up
rozgrzewk|a warm-up; **robić ~ę** warm up
rozgwiazda starfish
rozjaśni(a)ć 1 (*dać więcej światła*) lighten sth (up); (*dać więcej koloru*) brighten, freshen **2** (*włosy*) bleach[1]
□ **rozjaśni(a)ć się 1** (*mocniej nasycić światłem/kolorem*) brighten (up); (*mocniej nasycić światłem*) lighten **2** (*niebo*) clear[2], clear up **3** (*twarz itp.*) light up
rozjazd: **być w ~ach** be on the move
rozjątrzyć (się) → JĄTRZYĆ (SIĘ)
rozjem-ca/czyni arbitrator; **między A i B** intermediary (between A and B)
rozjemczy conciliatory
rozjusz-ać/yć inflame
rozjuszon|y: **być ~ym** be up in arms
rozkaz command[1], instruction, order[1]; **na czyjś ~** at/by sb's command
rozkazujący 1 authoritative **2** (*gram.*) **tryb ~** the imperative
rozkaz(yw)ać zob. też KAZAĆ; command[2], instruct, order[2], order sb about/around
rozklekotany beat-up, ramshackle, rickety, shaky
rozkład 1 (*plan: zajęć, jazdy*) timetable; (*zajęć*) rota; **według ~u pociąg powinien przyjechać o 10.07** the train was scheduled to arrive at 10.07 **2** (*dystrybucja*) distribution **3** (*listu itp.*) layout **4** (*upadek*) disintegration; (*biol.*) decomposition, rot noun
roz-kładać/łożyć 1 (*przedmioty*) lay sth out, space[2] sth (out), spread[1] sth (out) (on/over sth); (*mapę itp.*) unfold **2** (*rozdzielać*) distribute; (*spłatę czegoś itp.*) spread[1] sth (out) (over sth) **3 ~ na części** dismantle, pull sth apart, take sth apart; **~ coś na czynniki** break sth down **4 hiszpański upał całkowicie ich rozłożył** they were completely incapacitated by the heat in Spain
□ **rozkładać się 1** (*krzesło itp.*) unfold **2** (*materiał*) decompose, rot
rozkładan|y convertible[1]; (*siedzenie, fotel*) reclining; **~a suszarka do ubrań** clothes horse
rozkładówka centrefold, spread[2]
rozkojarzony muddle-headed
rozkop(yw)ać (*ulicę itp.*) dig sth up
rozkosz bliss, relish[2]
rozkoszny adorable, sweet[1]
rozkoszować/po-/na- się delight in sth/in doing sth, relish[1], glory in sth, revel in sth/doing sth, savour; (*zwł. sławą*) bask (in sth); (*pysznić się*) gloat (about/over sth)
rozkrę-cać/cić się hot up
rozkruszyć (się) → KRUSZYĆ (SIĘ)
rozkrzewić → KRZEWIĆ
rozkwiecony in blossom
rozkwit-ać/nąć 1 (*kwiat*) be out adj. **2** (*przen.*) blossom[2] (into sth)
rozlać (się) → ROZLEWAĆ (SIĘ)
roz-latywać/lecieć się disintegrate, fall apart, fall to pieces
■ **rozlatujący się** broken-down
roz-legać/lec się ring out
rozległość spaciousness
rozległy vast; (*wybór itp. czegoś*) wide[1]; (*zniszczenia itp.*) widespread; (*plany itp.*) extensive
rozleniwiony languorous
rozlew: ~ **krwi** bloodbath, bloodshed
rozl(ew)ać pour sth (out); (*niechcący*) slop, spill; ~ **do butelek** bottle[2]
□ **rozl(ew)ać się** run[1]; (*przez przypadek*) slop, spill
rozli-czać/czyć (*czek*) clear[2]
□ **rozli-czać/czyć się**: **(z kimś)** square up (with sb)
rozluźni(a)ć 1 (*mięsień*) relax; (*osobę*) loosen sb up **2** (*linę itp.*) loosen, slacken
□ **rozluźni(a)ć się 1** (*osoba*) relax, let your hair down, loosen up, unwind **2** (*lina itp.*) loosen, slacken
rozluźniony (*dyscyplina itp.*) lax, slack
rozładow(yw)ać 1 (*towary*) unload **2** (*sytuację*) defuse
rozłam break-up; (*w partii itp.*) split[2], rupture
rozłą-czać/czyć: **kogoś/coś (od kogoś/czegoś)** disengage sth/sb (from sth/sb); **kogoś (z kimś)** part[2] sb (from sb); (*w rozmowie telefonicznej*) cut sb off
□ **rozłą-czać/czyć się**: **(od kogoś/czegoś)** disengage (yourself) (from sth/sb); **proszę się nie rozłączać** can you hold the line?
rozłączny separable
rozłąka separation
rozłożyć → ROZKŁADAĆ
rozłożyć się settle down
rozłup(yw)ać (się) crack[1], split[1] (sth) (open), splinter verb
rozmach panache; **z ~em** big adv., grandly
rozmaitość variety
rozmaity diverse, miscellaneous, sundry, various
rozmamłany sloppy; ~ **psychicznie** blah adj.
rozmaryn rosemary
rozmarzony (*wzrok*) faraway
rozmawiać/po- chat[1], converse[1], speak, talk[1], have a talk/chat; ~ **przez telefon** be on the phone/telephone; ~ **szczerze** open up; ~ **o sprawach zawodowych (poza pracą)** talk shop
rozmaz(yw)ać się smudge
rozmiar dimension, measurement; (*skala*) scale[1]; (*i ubrania*) size[1]; (*ubrania*) fit[3]; (**rozmiary**) proportions; (*problemu itp.*) extent of sth; (*epidemii itp.*) incidence of sth; **~u** size[1]; **duży ~** bulk; **dużych ~ów** large-scale; **sporych ~ów** sizeable; **mieć ~** measure[1]
rozmieni(a)ć change[1]
rozmie-szczać/ścić distribute
■ **rozmieszczeni|e**: **plan rozmieszczenia gości przy stole** seating plan
rozmi-jać/nąć się 1 (*drogi*) cross[2] **2 z kimś** miss[1]
rozmiłowany: ~ **w nauce** studious
rozminąć (się) → MIJAĆ (SIĘ), ROZMIJAĆ SIĘ
roz-mnażać/mnożyć (*rośliny*) propagate
□ **roz-mnażać/mnożyć się 1** (*zool.*) breed[1], procreate, reproduce; (*bot.*) propagate **2** (*zwielokrotnić*) multiply, proliferate
rozmokły dank, soggy; (*teren*) waterlogged
rozmontow(yw)ać take sth apart
rozmow|a conversation, discussion, talk[2]; (**rozmowy**) (*handlowe, polityczne itp.*) negotiations, talks[2]; **~a kwalifikacyjna/o pracę** interview[1]; **~a towarzyska** small talk; **~a zamiejscowa/międzynarodowa** long-distance call
rozmowny affable, communicative, talkative; ~ **i pomocny** forthcoming
rozmówki: ~ **obcojęzyczne** phrase book
roz-mrażać/mrozić (się) defrost, thaw (sth) (out)
rozmysł: **z ~em** advisedly
rozmyślać meditate (on/upon sth), muse verb (about/on/over/upon sth), ponder (on/over) sth, think (about sth); (*martwiąc się*) brood[1] (on/over/about sth)
□ **rozmyślić się** think better of (doing) sth
rozmyślani|e contemplation, meditation
rozmyślny deliberate[1], premeditated, wilful
rozmyty (*kolor*) wishy-washy
rozneglizowany undressed
roznie-cać/cić fan[2]
roznosiciel paper boy
roznosicielka paper girl
roz-nosić/nieść distribute; (*pocztę*) deliver
□ **roz-nosić/nieść się** spread[1]; (*wiadomości itp.*) percolate; (*dźwięk*) reverberate
rozogniony heated
rozpacz despair[1], desperation, distress[1]; **doprowadzać do ~y** distress[2]; **doprowadzony do ~y** desperate; **szaleć z ~y** go frantic
rozpaczać 1 po kimś/po czymś grieve (for sb) **2** (*tracić nadzieję*) despair[2] (of sb/sth)
rozpaczliwy 1 (*głos itp.*) despairing **2** (*sytuacja*) desperate, distressing

rozpad break-up, disintegration; (*biol.*) decomposition
roz-padać/paść się come apart, disintegrate, fall apart; (*małżeństwo itp.*) break up; (*ser itp.*) crumble (up)
■ **rozpadający się** decrepit, dilapidated; (*ser itp.*) crumbly
rozpadlina chasm
rozpakow(yw)ać 1 (*walizkę*) unpack **2** (*prezent itp.*) unwrap
□ **rozpakow(yw)ać się** unpack
rozpal-ać/ić 1 (*ogień*) kindle **2** (*uczucia*) inflame
rozpalony: ~ **do czerwoności** red-hot
rozparcelować → PARCELOWAĆ
rozpasany rampant
rozpaść się → ROZPADAĆ SIĘ
roz-patrywać/patrzyć hear
rozpatrywany in hand, in question
rozpęd impetus, momentum
rozpę-dzać/dzić disperse
rozpęt(yw)ać (*burzę emocji itp.*) unleash
□ **rozpęt(yw)ać się** IDM **rozpętało się piekło** all hell broke loose
rozpiąć (się) → ROZPINAĆ (SIĘ)
roz-pierać /eprzeć się lounge[2] (about/around)
rozpie-szczać/ścić pamper, spoil
rozpiętość range[1], span[1]; ~ **skrzydeł** the wingspan of a bird; **mała ~ uwagi** a short attention span
rozpięty open[1], undone
roz-pinać/piąć undo, unfasten; (*guziki*) unbutton; (*zamek błyskawiczny*) unzip
□ **roz-pinać/piąć się**: **rozpięła ci się bluzka** your blouse has come undone
rozplanow(yw)ać lay sth out
rozpląt(yw)ać unravel, untangle; (*i przen.*) disentangle
□ **rozpląt(yw)ać się** unravel
rozpłat(yw)ać (*rozdzielać*) split[1] sth (open); (*materiał, ciało itp.*) gash verb
rozpły-wać/nąć się: **(nad kimś/czymś)** enthuse (about/over sth/sb), gush, wax (on sth)
rozpoczęci|e commencement, start[2]; **miejsce ~a** starting point
rozpo-czynać/cząć commence, embark on sth, go ahead (with sth), launch[1], start[1] sth (up); (*spotkanie itp.*) open[2]; (*karierę itp.*) start out; **(z kimś)** enter into sth (with sb); **rozpoczynać działalność** enter
□ **rozpo-czynać/cząć się** start[1] (up); (*spotkanie itp.*) open[2]; **dobrze/źle się rozpoczynać** get off to a good, bad, etc. start; **rozpoczyna się właśnie nowa pokojowa era** a new era of peace is dawning
rozpoczynając-y/a: **rozpoczynający/a studia** entrant
rozpolitykowany political
rozporek fly[2]
rozporzą-dzać/dzić decree verb
rozporządzenie decree, edict
rozpostarty (*ręce itp.*) outstretched
rozpowszechni(a)ć disseminate, promulgate; (*plotki itp.*) peddle
rozpowszechnion|y pervasive, rife; (*wiadomość*) **zostawać ~ym** break[1]
rozpoznanie reconnaissance; (*choroby, sytuacji itp.*) diagnosis
rozpozna(wa)ć 1 (*osobę, przedmiot*) distinguish, make sb/sth out, place[2], recognize; **kogoś/coś (wsród kogoś/czegoś)** pick sb/sth out; **kogoś jako/z czegoś** know[1] sb as sth, sb for sth, sb to be sth; ~ **smak** taste[2]; **nic nie wskazywało, że mnie rozpoznał** he showed no sign of recognition **2** (*chorobę*) diagnose
rozpoznawalny distinguishable, identifiable, recognizable
rozpoznawczy exploratory
rozpracow(yw)ać thrash sth out
roz-praszać/proszyć 1 (*tłum itp.*) break sth up, disperse **2** (*obawy*) remove; (*gniew itp.*) dispel, dissipate **3** (*czyjąś uwagę*) disrupt, distract sb (from sth), put sb off (sb/sth/doing sth)
□ **roz-praszać/proszyć się 1** (*tłum itp.*) disperse, scatter, spread (yourself) out **2** (*gniew itp.*) dissipate
rozprawa 1 ~ **sądowa** hearing, trial **2** (*naukowa*) dissertation, paper, thesis
rozprawi(a)ć się z kimś/czymś crack down (on sb/sth), tackle[1]
rozpromieni(a)ć (się) brighten (sth) (up)
rozpromieniony beaming with pleasure, radiant
rozpropagować → PROPAGOWAĆ
rozprostow(yw)ać IDM ~ **nogi** stretch your legs
rozproszenie 1 (*tłumu itp.*) dispersal **2** (*rozprzestrzenienie się*) diffuseness
rozproszony 1 (*ludzie, przedmioty*) scattered **2** (*uwaga*) distracted **3** (*rozległy*) diffuse
rozproszyć (się) → ROZPRASZAĆ (SIĘ)
rozprowa-dzać/dzić distribute
rozpruć (się) → PRUĆ (SIĘ)
rozprys-kiwać/nąć/kać slosh
rozpryskow|y: **~a bomba kasetowa** cluster bomb
rozprzestrzeni(a)ć spread[1]
□ **rozprzestrzeni(a)ć się** spread[1], sweep[1]; (*informacje*) percolate
rozprzestrzeniony diffuse
rozpusta debauchery, vice
rozpustny debauched
rozpu-szczać/ścić (się) dissolve, melt
rozpuszczalnik solvent
rozpuszczaln|y soluble; **kawa ~a** instant coffee
rozpychać się jostle, shoulder[2]; ~ **łokciami** elbow[2] IDM **rozpychający się łokciami** pushy
rozpy-lać/lić (się) spray[2]
rozradowany overjoyed
rozrodczy reproductive; **okres ~** breeding season
rozróba trouble[1]
rozróżni(a)ć differentiate, discriminate, distinguish
rozróżnieni|e distinction; (*dokonany*) **bez ~a** indiscriminate; **umiejętność ~a między dobrem a złem** discrimination between right and wrong
rozruchy disorder, riot
rozruszać (*silnik*) rev[1] sth (up)
rozrusznik pacemaker
roz-rywać/erwać 1 (*zniszczyć*) rip[1]; (*torbę papierową itp.*) burst[1]; (*na kawałki*) dismember, tear sth apart **2** (*zabawić*) amuse
□ **roz-rywać/erwać się** (*sukienka itp.*) rip[1]; (*balonik*) burst[1]
rozrywka amusement, distraction, entertainment, pastime, play[2], pursuit, recreation
rozrywkowy entertaining, light-hearted
rozrze-dzać/dzić thin[2] sth (out)
rozrzedzony thin[1], watery
rozrzewniający moving, pathetic, touching
rozrzu-cać/cić scatter
rozrzucony diffuse, scattered
rozrzutni-k/ca spendthrift
rozrzutność extravagance, profligacy
rozrzutny extravagant, lavish[1], profligate, spendthrift, wasteful
rozsa-dzać/dzić burst[1]
■ **rozsadzający**: ~ **ból głowy** a splitting headache
rozsąd|ek judgement, prudence, reason[1]; **(zdrowy) ~ek** sanity; **brak ~ku** silliness
rozsądn|y advisable, judicious, logical, prudent, rational, reasonable, sane, sensible, sound[3]; (*osoba*) down to earth; (*sprawiedliwy*) just[2]; **wątpię, czy ~e jest zbyt wczesne podejmowanie decyzji** I doubt the wisdom of taking a decision too early
rozsą-dzać/dzić arbitrate
rozsiany dotted about/around
rozsiewanie (*ziarna*) dispersal
rozsmaro(wy)wać → SMAROWAĆ; spread[1]
rozstać się → ROZSTAWAĆ SIĘ
rozstaje fork[1]
rozstajn|y: **~e drogi** crossroads
rozstanie parting
rozstaw gauge[1]
rozsta(wa)ć się part[2] (from sb), part with sth, part company (with sb/sth); (*nieform.*) give sb the push
rozstawi(a)ć 1 (*ustawiać*) deploy, lay sth out, space[2] sth (out); (*kogoś/coś z odstępami w rzędzie*) string sb/sth out **2** (*wojsko; broń*) deploy; (*wojsko*) station[2]
roz-strajać/stroić (*kogoś; żołądek*) upset[1]
■ **rozstrojony** upset[2]
rozstrój: ~ **żołądka** upset[3]
rozstrzygać zob. też ROZSTRZYGNĄĆ; adjudicate, arbitrate
rozstrzygając|y conclusive, final[1]
rozstrzygnąć zob. też ROZSTRZYGAĆ; (*spór*) clinch, settle
rozstrzygnięty: **nie** ~ open[1], pending adj.
rozsunąć → ROZSUWAĆ
rozsunięty open[1]
rozsupł(yw)ać 1 (*rozwiązać*) undo, untie **2** (*rozwikłać*) disentangle
rozsu-wać/nąć (się) open[2], part[2]
rozsuwan|y: **drzwi ~e** sliding door
roz-syłać/esłać send sth out
rozsyp(yw)ać scatter
□ **rozsyp(yw)ać się** (*tkanina itp.*) fall/come apart; (*ser itp.: kruszyć się*) have a crumbly texture
rozszaleć się 1 (*burza itp.*) blow up **2** (*tłum*) run riot
rozszarp(yw)ać tear sth apart
rozszczep: ~ **kręgosłupa** spina bifida; ~ **podniebienia** cleft palate; ~ **wargi** cleft lip
rozszczepi(a)ć (się) splinter verb, split[1] (sth) (open)
■ **rozszczepienie**: ~ **jądra atomu** fission, nuclear fission

rozsze-rzać/rzyć 1 enlarge, expand, splay sth (out), widen; (*źrenice itp.*) dilate **2** (*działalność itp.*) diversify, expand
■ **rozszerzany**: (*spodnie*) ~ **dołem** flared
□ **rozsze-rzać/rzyć się** enlarge, expand, widen; (*źrenice itp.*) dilate

rozszyfrowani|e: **nie do ~a** indecipherable

rozśmie-szać/szyć amuse, make sb laugh, kill[1] sb, set sb off laughing

roz-taczać/toczyć 1 ~ **opiekę nad kimś/czymś** watch over sb/sth **2** (*zapach itp.*) exude
□ **roz-taczać/toczyć się** (*zapach itp.*) exude

roztargnieni|e absent-mindedness; **w ~u** absent-mindedly

roztargniony absent-minded, dozy, flaky, scatty

rozter|ka: **być w ~ce między jednym a drugim** be torn between A and B

roztop a slushy road

roztropność prudence

roztropny clear-headed, prudent, wise

roztrwonić → TRWONIĆ

roztrwoniony misspent

roztrzask(iw)ać (się) shatter, smash[1]

roztrzepaniec scatterbrain

roztrzepany scatterbrained, scatty

roztrzęsion|y: **na samą myśl o egzaminie jestem cała ~a!** thinking about the exam gives me the jitters!

roztwór solution

rozum brain, intellect, judgement, mind[1], reason[1], sense[1], wit IDM **mieć więcej ~u w głowie** know better (than that/than to do sth)

rozumieć/z- catch[1], comprehend, figure sb/sth out, follow, gather, get, grasp[1], get the idea, interpret, learn, make sb/sth out, make head or tail of sth, make sense of sth, get the message, take sth in, take sb's point, see, understand; **kogoś** work sb out; **coś jako coś** construe sth (as sth); **(przez coś)** mean[1]; (*wierzyć*) credit[2]; **nie** ~ miss[1], not be in tune with what sb is thinking; **błędnie/źle** ~ misconstrue, misinterpret, mistake[2], misunderstand; **rozumiem, o co ci chodzi** I see your point; **rozumie-sz/cie** you know, you see
□ **rozumieć się** talk at cross purposes IDM **to się rozumie (samo przez się)** it goes without saying, it stands to reason

rozumienie reading, insight; **złe** ~ misinterpretation

rozumny intelligent, judicious, rational

rozumować reason[2]

rozumowy intellectual[1]

roz-wadniać/wodnić dilute, water sth down

rozwag|a carefulness, caution[1], consideration, deliberation, poise, prudence; **powinno się obchodzić z elektrycznością z ~ą** electricity should be treated with respect; **brak ~i** carelessness, imprudence, thoughtlessness

rozwal-ać/ić bust[1], smash[1]
□ **rozwal-ać /ić się 1** (*rozlecieć się*) smash[1] **2** (*na krześle itp.*) lounge[2] (about/around), sprawl
■ **rozwalający się** beat-up

rozwalcować roll[2] sth (out)

rozwałkować roll[2] sth (out)

rozwarstwi(a)ć (*społeczeństwo itp.*) stratify

rozwarty: **kąt** ~ obtuse angle

rozwa-żać/żyć balance[2] sth against sth, consider, contemplate, debate[2], mull sth over, ponder (on/over) sth, weigh sth (up); **luźno rozważać** (*możliwość zrobienia czegoś*) toy with sth
■ **rozważany** afoot, in question

rozważny clear-headed, deliberate[1], prudent

rozwesel-ać/ić amuse, cheer sb/sth up
□ **rozwesel-ać/ić się** cheer up
■ **rozweselony** amused

rozwiać (się) → ROZWIEWAĆ (SIĘ)

rozwiązani|e answer[1], course (of action), fix[2], resolution, solution, termination; **~e akcji** denouement; **nie do ~a** insoluble

rozwiązłość debauchery, licentiousness

rozwiązły debauched, licentious

rozwiąz(yw)ać 1 (*węzeł*) undo, untie **2** (*problemy itp.*) clear sth up, get over sth, iron sth out, solve, work sth out; (*zagadkę itp.*) puzzle sth out; (*zadanie, zagadkę, krzyżówkę itp.*) do[1]; (*problem techniczny itp.*) cure **3** (*sytuację*) resolve, settle **4** (*umowę*) terminate **5** (*stowarzyszenie itp.*) disband; (*firmę itp.*) liquidate
□ **rozwiąz(yw)ać się 1** (*węzeł*) come untied **2** (*stowarzyszenie itp.*) disband

rozwiązywalny soluble

rozwichrzon|y: **z ~ymi włosami** dishevelled

rozwi-dlać/dlić się branch off, fork[2]

rozwidlony forked

rozwiedziony divorced

rozwie-szać/sić string[2] sth (up)

rozwieść się → ROZWODZIĆ SIĘ

rozwi(ew)ać (*obawy itp.*) dispel, dissipate; (*nadzieje*) dash sb's hopes (of sth/of doing sth)
□ **rozwi(ew)ać się 1** (*dym itp.*) clear[2]; (*mgła itp.*) lift[1] **2** (*obawy itp.*) dissipate

rozwi-jać/nąć 1 (*coś zwiniętego*) unroll, unwind; (*wydobywać coś z papieru itp.*) unwrap; (*nawijać*) reel sth in/out **2** (*talent itp.*) build[1], develop, evolve; (*siłę itp.*) build sth up; (*fabuła itp.*) unfold; (*biznes*) expand **3** (*temat, myśl*) develop, enlarge on sth, expand on sth; (*komentarz itp.*) amplify
□ **rozwi-jać/nąć się 1** (*coś zwiniętego*) unroll, unwind **2** (*talent itp.*) develop, evolve, progress[2], shape up; (*fabuła itp.*) unfold; (*biznes itp.*) expand; **dobrze się rozwijać** flourish[1], get ahead, thrive; (*biznes itp.*) boom[2]; **szybko się rozwijać** burgeon

rozwijan|y: **menu ~e** (*komput.*) pull-down

rozwikł(yw)ać (się) unravel, untangle

rozwinięty advanced, developed, mature; (*choroba*) full-blown; **nad wiek** ~ forward[2]; (*kraj*) **słabo** ~ underdeveloped; **w pełni** ~ fully fledged

rozwle-kać/c (*tekst*) pad sth out

rozwlekłość diffuseness

rozwlekły diffuse, lengthy, long-winded

rozwodnić → ROZWADNIAĆ

rozwodnik divorcé, divorcee

rozwodniony dilute adj.

rozwodzić się 1 (**/rozwieść się**) **(z kimś)** get a divorce, divorce[2], get divorced **2 nad czymś** dwell on/upon sth, go into sth

rozwolnienie diarrhoea

rozwód divorce[1]; **wziąć** ~ divorce[2]

rozwódka divorcee, divorcée

rozw|ój (*technologii itp.*) advancement, evolution; (*talentu itp.*) development; (*biznesu itp.*) expansion, growth; **brak logicznego ~oju myśli** no logical progression in your thoughts; **nowy ~ój wypadków** a number of new developments; **w miarę ~oju akcji…** as the story unfolded…

rozwście-czać/czyć enrage, infuriate, make sb sick

rozzłoszczony angry, in a temper

rozzłościć (się) → ZŁOŚCIĆ (SIĘ)

rozżalony embittered, resentful

rozżarzyć się → ŻARZYĆ SIĘ

rożek crescent

rożen 1 (*szpikulec*) spit[2] **2** (*grill*) barbecue, grill[1]

ród ancestry, birth, family, line[1]

róg 1 (*ulicy itp.*) corner[1]; **(tuż) za rogiem** (just) round the corner **2** (*byka itp.*) horn; (*jelenia*) antler **3** (*muz.*) horn; (*waltornia*) French horn

rój swarm[1]

róść → ROSNĄĆ

rów channel[1], ditch[1], trench; ~ **odwadniający** dyke

rówieśni-k/czka contemporary[2]

rówieśnik peer[1]

równać/wy-/z-: ~ **spychaczem** bulldoze
□ **równać się 1** (*mat.*) equal[3], make[1] **2 czemuś** amount[2] to sth, represent **3 (/po-) z kimś/czymś** (*dorównywać*) compare (with/to sb/sth) **4 (/z-) jakiś samochód zrównał się z moim** a car drew level with mine

równanie (*mat.*) equation

równia: **na równi z kimś/czymś** on a par with sb/sth

równie: ~ **dobrze** may/might (just) as well

również also

równik the equator

równikowy equatorial

równina plain[2]

równo 1 equally, evenly, fifty-fifty adv. **2** (*przeciąć*) cleanly **3** (*czas, godzina*) promptly

równoczesny simultaneous
■ **równocześnie** all at once, at once, simultaneously

równoległobok parallelogram

równoległ|y parallel[1]; **~a linia** parallel[2]

równomierny even[1], steady[1]

równonoc equinox

równorzędny equal[1], equivalent

równość equality, parity

równouprawnienie equality; ~ **pod względem płci** sexual equality

równowag|a 1 (*i przen.*) balance[1], equilibrium; (*tylko osoby*) footing; **brak ~i** imbalance; **~a sił** balance of power; **utrzymywać ~ę/coś w równowadze** balance[2];

wyprowadzać kogoś z ~i put sb out **2** (*tenis*) deuce
równowartość worth[2]
równoważny equivalent
równoważyć/z- balance[2] sth (out) (with sth), compensate (for sth), offset
równoznacznik equivalent noun
równoznaczn|y: **z czymś** tantamount to sth; **być ~ym z czymś** amount[2] to sth, spell[1]
równ|y 1 (*płaski*) even[1], flat[1], level[2] **2** (*tej samej ilości/jakości*) equal[1], fifty-fifty; **~y/a sobie** equal[2]; **na ~ej stopie z kimś** on an equal footing with sb **3** (*kształt*) regular[1] **4 ~y facet**; **~a dziewczyna** sport; **~y chłop** a tough old bugger
róż 1 (*kolor*) pink noun **2** (*kosmetyk*) blusher, rouge
róża rose[2]
różaniec rosary
różdżka wand
różnic|a difference, distinction, variation; (*punktów, głosów itp.*) margin; **zasadnicza ~a** contrast[1]; **~a zdań** dissent[1]; **nie robić ~y** make no difference (to sb/sth), not make any difference; **sprawiać/stanowić ~ę** make a, some, etc. difference (to sb/sth)
różnicować/z- (się) polarize
różnić się differ, diverge, vary; **bardzo się różnić** be very different from sth, be far removed from sth; **~ w zapatrywaniach** dissent[2] (from sth); **nie ~** be not dissimilar to sth
różnorodność diversity, variety; **~ w przyrodzie** biodiversity
różnorodny assorted, disparate, heterogeneous, miscellaneous, sundry, varied, various
różn|y 1 (*rozmaity*) miscellaneous, sundry, various; **~e przedmioty** a variety of subjects **2** (*odmienny*) different, dissimilar, distinct IDM **o ~ych porach** at/till all hours
różowawy pinkish
różowy pink, rosy
różyczka German measles
rtęć mercury
rubaszność earthiness
rubaszny earthy, hearty
rubin ruby
rubinowy ruby
rubryka column
ruch 1 (*zmiana miejsca, poruszanie się*) motion[1], move[2], movement; **(ruchy)** (*ręką, ciałem*) gesture[1]; **~ obrotowy** rotation; **bez ~u** motionless, still[2]; **wykonywać ~** move[1] **2** (*ćwiczenie fizyczne*) exercise[1]; (*rąk w pływaniu*) stroke[1] **3** (*przestępcy itp.*) movements **4** (*drogowy itp.*) traffic; **w centrum miasta był duży ~** the town centre was very busy **5** (*na ulicy, w domu itp.*) activity **6** (*polit.*) movement **7** (*w szachach itp.*) move[2] IDM (*osoba*) **być w ~u** be on the go | **mieć ~ w interesie** have a field day | **~ w interesie** business
ruchliwość mobility
ruchliwy 1 (*osoba*) agile; (*dziecko*) fidgety **2** (*ulica itp.*) busy[1]
ruchomości belongings, effects[1], property
ruchom|y 1 (*w ruchu*) floating, mobile[1], moving **2** (*dający się poruszyć*) adjustable, movable; **być ~ym** come off; **~y czas pracy** flexible working hours, flexitime IDM **~e piaski** quicksand | **~e schody** escalator
ruda ore
rudawobrązowy maroon; (*włosy*) auburn
rudera dump[2], hovel, ruin[2]
rudy ginger adj., red; **kolor ~** ginger
rudyment: **~y czegoś** rudiments (of sth)
rudzielec redhead
rudzik robin
rufa stern[2]
rugać/wy-: **kogoś** tick sb off
rugby rugby
rugować supercede
ruin|a destruction, dilapidation, downfall, ruin[2], wreck; **doprowadzać do ~y** ruin[1]; **w ~ie** in a state of ruin
ru|ja IDM **być w okresie ~i** be on heat | **w ~i** in season
rujnować/z- ruin[1], wreck; (*plany itp.*) squash[1]
rukiew: **~ wodna** watercress
ruletka roulette
rulon roll[1]
rum rum
rumb point[1]
rumianek chamomile
rumiankowy chamomile
rumienić/z-/przy- (*kotlety itp.*) brown[2] □ **rumienić się 1 (/za-)** (*osoba*) blush, flush[1], glow (with sth) **2 (/przy-)** (*kotlety itp.*) brown[2]
rumieniec blush noun, flush[2], glow noun; **(rumieńce)** colour[1] IDM **nabierać rumieńców** take shape
rumowisko debris
runąć 1 (*upaść*) collapse[1], come down, tumble, tumble down **2** (*pikować: ptak*) swoop
runda round[4]
runo fleece[1]
rupiecie junk, odds and ends
rura pipe[1], tube; **(rury)** tubing; **główna ~ wodociągowa/kanalizacyjna/gazowa** main[2]; **~ spalinowa** flue; **~ spustowa** spout[1]; **~ wydechowa** exhaust[1]
rurka tube; **(rurki)** tubing; **~ do picia** straw; **~ do nurkowania** snorkel
rurociąg pipeline
rustykalny rustic
ru-szać/szyć dislodge, move[1], touch[1]; (*lekko*) stir[1] IDM **rusz głową!** use your head! | **~ z miejsca** get off the ground □ **ru-szać/szyć się 1** move[1]; (*lekko*) stir[1]; **ruszający się ząb** a loose tooth **2** (*z miejsca*) get cracking, get moving, make a move, move[1] (on/ahead); **szybciej się ruszać** get a move on
ruszt grate[1]; **~ w piecyku** grill[1]
rusztowanie scaffolding
rutyn|a routine[1] IDM **popaść w ~ę** be in a rut
rutynowy routine[2]
rwać 1 (/roze-) (*rozrywać*) tear[2] **2** (*kupować*) snap sth up ■ **rwący** (*rzeka*) turbulent; **czuła rwący ból w palcu** her finger throbbed with pain □ **rwać się 1 (/po-/roze-)** (*papier itp.*) tear[2] **2 do czegoś** snatch at sth ■ **rwący się (do czegoś)** impatient, keen on sb/sth, raring to do sth
rwetes pandemonium
ryba 1 fish[1]; **~ z wody** poached fish **2** (**Ryby**) (*znak zodiaku*) Pisces
rybak fisherman
rybi 1 (*potrawa itp.*) fish[1] **2** (*zapach itp.*) fishy
rybik silverfish
rybitwa gull
rybny fish[1]; **sklep ~** fishmonger
rybołówstwo fishing
rycerski chivalrous, gallant
rycerskość chivalry, gallantry
rycerz knight
rychły prompt[1], quick[1], speedy, swift
rycina engraving, print[2]
ryczeć 1 (/za-) (*krowa*) moo; (*byk*) bellow; (*niedźwiedź*) growl; (*lew*) roar; (*osioł*) bray **2 (/ryknąć)** (*osoba*) bellow, yell; (*ze śmiechu itp.*) bray, hoot[1] **3** (*muzyka itp.*) belt sth out
ryć 1 (/z-) (*kopać*) burrow[1] **2 (/wy-)** (*napis*) engrave, etch, inscribe
rydelek: **~ ogrodniczy** trowel
rydwan chariot
rygiel bolt[1]
ryglować/za- bolt[2]
rygor rigorousness, rigour
rygorystycznie rigidly, rigorously
ryj muzzle, snout
ryk 1 (*byka*) bellow noun; (*niedźwiedzia*) growl noun; (*lwa*) roar noun **2** (*osoby*) howl noun, yell noun
ryknąć → RYCZEĆ
rykoszet: **odbić się ~em** glance off (sth), ricochet (off sth)
rykowisko breeding ground
rym rhyme[1]
rymować (się) rhyme[2]
rynek 1 (*targowisko*) market[1] **2** (*główny plac*) marketplace, market square **3** (*fin.*) market[1], marketplace; **~ wewnętrzny/zagraniczny** the home/overseas market; **~ papierów wartościowych** stock exchange; **~ zniżkujący** (*giełda*) bear market; **~ zwyżkujący** (*giełda*) bull market; **wprowadzać na ~** (*za pomocą reklamy*) market[2]
rynna chute; (*koryto wzdłuż okapu*) gutter; **~ odpływowa** drainpipe
rynsztok ditch[1], gutter
rynsztunek kit[1]
rys feature[1]; **~ charakteru** trait
rys|a crack[2], flaw, scratch[2], split[2]; **zrobić ~ę** gouge
rysować 1 (/na-) (*rysunek*) draw[1] **2** (*opisać*) **szczegółowo/dokładnie ~** delineate **3 (/za-)** (*wyżłobić*) gouge ■ **rysujący się** silhouetted
rysownik cartoonist
rysunek 1 (*obraz*) drawing, picture[1] **2** (*zabawny*) cartoon **3** (*schemat*) diagram, figure[1] **4** (*opis*) **szczegółowy ~** delineation
rysunkowy animated
rytm rhythm
rytmiczność regularity
rytmiczny regular[1], rhythmic
rytualny ritual adj.
rytuał rite, ritual
rywal challenger, competitor, opposition; **największy ~** archrival
rywal/ka rival[1]
rywalizacj|a competition, rivalry; **oparty na ~i**; **skory do ~i** competitive
rywalizować contend (for sth), be in contention (for sth), emulate, vie (with sb) (for sth); (*sport*) compete
ryzykancki foolhardy
ryzykant/ka daredevil, gambler
ryzyko chance[1], gamble[2], hazard[1], risk[1]; **lubiący ~** adventurous; **ponosić**

~ venture[2]; **na własne** ~ at your own risk

ryzykować/za- chance[2], hazard[2], risk[2], take a risk, run the risk of sth, stake[2] sth (on sth), take a chance on sth, venture into sth

ryzykowny dodgy, hazardous, perilous, precarious, risky; (*sytuacja*) hot[1]

ryż rice

ryży ginger adj., red; **kolor** ~ ginger

rzadki 1 (*nieczęsty*) infrequent, rare, sporadic, uncommon, unusual; **bardzo** ~ few and far between **2** (*włosy itp.*) sparse; ~ **i postrzępiony** wispy **3** (*dym itp.; zaludnienie*) thin[1] **4** (*konsystencja*) runny; (*zupa itp.*) thin[1], watery; (*sos itp.*) smooth[1]

rzadk|o 1 (*nie często*) infrequently, rarely, seldom, sporadically; ~**o kiedy** hardly ever; ~**o spotykany** rare, thin on the ground; **z** ~**a** once in a while **2** (*zaludniony itp.*) sparsely, thinly

rzadkość 1 (*niezwykłość*) rarity **2** (*brak gęstości*) sparseness

rząd 1 rank[1], row[1]; (*krzeseł zwł. powyżej poprzedniego*) tier; **w jednym rzędzie** abreast (of sb/sth); **ustawiać w rzędzie** align sth (with sth); **przechodzić/maszerować rzędem** file[2] in, out, past, etc. **2** (*zespół rządzący*) the Administration, government **3** (**rządy**) (*administracja*) government, regime; ~**y prawa** the rule of law IDM **pod** ~ in a row, running[2], in succession | **z rzędu** consecutive, in a row, running[2]

rządowy governmental

rządzić 1 (*król itp.*) govern **2 kimś/czymś** boss[2] sb (about/around), order sb about/around

■ **rządzący** ruling[1]

rzecz item, object[1], thing; (*sprawa*) matter[1]; (**rzeczy**) stuff[1], things; (*osobiste*) belongings, property; ~**y używane** (*przeznaczone do wyprzedaży dobroczynnej*) jumble[2] IDM **do** ~**y** to the point | **na** ~ **kogoś/czegoś** in aid of sb/sth, on behalf of sb, on sb's behalf | **od** ~**y** irrelevant(ly) | **(praktycznie)** ~ **biorąc** altogether, to/for all intents and purposes | ~ **pewna** certainty

rzeczni-k/czka advocate[2], mouthpiece, spokesman, spokesperson; (**rzeczniczka**) spokeswoman; **rzecznik praw obywatelskich** ombudsman

rzeczownik noun; ~ **abstrakcyjny** abstract noun; ~ **odczasownikowy** gerund; ~ **pospolity** common noun; ~ **własny** proper noun; ~ **zbiorowy** collective noun

rzeczowy businesslike, hard-headed, matter-of-fact

rzeczoznawca assessor; (*zwł. powołany przez rząd i odpowiedzialny za istotne sprawy*) tsar; ~ **budowlany** surveyor

rzeczywistoś|ć fact, hard facts, reality; **w** ~**ci** in (actual) fact, effectively, in effect, as a matter of fact, in reality; **z poczuciem** ~**ci** realistically

rzeczywisty actual, factual, intrinsic, real[1], tangible, truthful

rzeczywiście actually, indeed, intrinsically, quite, really, so[1], sure enough, truly

rzednąć/z- thin[2] (out); (*męskie włosy*) recede

rzeka 1 river, stream[1]; ~ **dopływowa** tributary **2** (*ludzi itp.*) stream[1]

rzekom|y ostensible, reputed

■ **rzekomo** ostensibly, reputedly, supposedly

rzemieślnik artisan, craftsman

rzemiosło 1 (*działalność*) craft, handicraft, trade[1] **2** (*umiejętność*) craftsmanship

rzemyk strap

rzep (*rodzaj zapięcia*) Velcro

rzepa turnip

rzepka (*anat.*) kneecap

rzesze the masses[1]

rzeszoto sieve

rześki crisp[1], fresh, nippy

rzetelny 1 (*rozwiązanie*) credible **2** (*praca*) sterling[2]

rzewny sloppy

rze|ź butchery, carnage, massacre, slaughter noun; **dokonać** ~**zi** butcher[2], massacre verb, slaughter

rzeźba carving, sculpture

rzeźbiarstwo sculpture

rzeźbia-rz/rka sculptor

rzeźbić/wy- carve

rzeźnia slaughterhouse

rzeźnik butcher[1]

rzeżucha cress

rzęsa 1 (*anat.*) eyelash **2** (*na stawie itp.*) weed[1]

rzęsisty: ~ **deszcz** heavy rain

rzodkiewka radish

rzu-cać/cić 1 (*ciskać*) fling[1], slap[1], sling[1], pitch[2]; (*piłką itp.*) throw; (*lekko*) toss; (*niedbale*) dump[1], stick[1]; (*z trzaskiem*) slam; (*coś ciężkiego*) heave[1]; (*z wieży, do morza itp.*) plunge[1] **2** (*eliminować*) cut sth out, drop[1], give sth up, give up doing sth, quit; (*nałóg*) kick the habit **3** (*pracę itp.*) chuck sth in, ditch[2], jack sth in, pack sth in; **rzucić szkołę** drop out of college **3 kogoś** dump[1], walk out on sb; (*kogoś z pracy*) throw **4** (*światło, cień*) throw; (*światło*) project[2] sth (on/onto sth) **5** (*spojrzenie, uśmiech itp.*) cast[1], dart[2], flash[1], shoot[1] IDM (*przen.*) **rzucać cień** cast a shadow (across/over sth) | **rzucać kotwicę** anchor[2] | **rzucać okiem** cast an eye/your eye(s) over sb/sth | **rzucać urok (na kogoś/coś)** cast a spell (on sb/sth), enchant | (*przen.*) **rzucać światło na coś** illuminate, shed light on sth | **rzucać (nowe) światło na coś** cast light on sth □ **rzu-cać/cić się 1** (*śpieszyć się*) dart[2], dive[1], rush to do sth, scramble (for sth/to do sth); (*na pomoc itp.*) spring[2]; ~ **do przodu** lunge verb; **rzucić się do ucieczki** try to make a run for it; **wszyscy rzucili się do wyjścia** there was a rush for the exits; **rzucić się tłumnie na kogoś** mob[2] **2** (*miotać się*) flail, thrash (sth) (about/around); (*z boku na bok*) toss **3 na kogoś/coś** (*żeby złapać*) grab at/for sth, pounce (on sb/sth), snatch at sth, swoop; **ludzie rzucili sie na siedzenia** there was a mad dash for the seats **4 na kogoś** (*rozzłościć się*) go for sb, let fly (at sb) IDM **rzucać się w oczy** stand out (from/against sth) | **rzucający się w oczy** conspicuous | **nie rzucający się w oczy** unobtrusive | **rzucać się w wir czegoś** throw yourself/sth into sth

rzut ball, throw noun, return[2]; ~ **dyskiem** discus; ~ **młotem** hammer[1]; ~ **rożny** corner[1]; ~ **wolny** free kick; ~ **kostką** roll of the dice; ~**y karne** penalty shoot-out IDM ~ **oka** glance[2], peep[2] | **na pierwszy** ~ **oka** at first glance/sight, at a (single) glance

rzutki go-ahead[2]

rzutnik: ~ **pisma** OHP, overhead projector

rzygacz gargoyle

rzygać/wy- barf, puke, spew (sth) (up)

rzygowiny barf noun, puke noun, sick[2]

Rzymian-in/ka Roman noun

rzymski Roman

rzymskokatolicki Roman Catholic adj.

rżeć/za- neigh verb

rżnąć/u- (*piłą*) saw verb

S

s (**S/s**) (*litera*) S, s

sabotaż sabotage; **dokonywać** ~**u** sabotage verb

sabotować sabotage verb

sacharyna saccharin

sad orchard

sadomasochist-a/ka sadomasochist

sadomasochistyczny sadomasochistic

sadomasochizm sadomasochism

sadowić/u- (się) settle

sadyst-a/ka sadist

sadystyczny sadistic

sadyzm sadism

sadza soot

sadzać/posadzić seat[2], sit sb (down)

sadzawka pool[1]

sadzić 1 (/po-) (*kwiaty*) plant[2]; ~ **w doniczce** pot[2] **2** (*iść wielkimi krokami*) stride

sadzonka cutting[1], plant[1], seedling

safari safari

saga saga

sakiewka pouch

sakralny (*muzyka*) sacred

sakrament sacrament

sakramentalny sacramental

saksofon saxophone

saksofonist-a/ka saxophonist

sala chamber, hall; ~ **balowa** ballroom; ~ **gimnastyczna** gym; ~ **klubowa** lounge bar; ~ **konferencyjna** boardroom; ~ **operacyjna** operating theatre; ~ **rozpraw** courtroom; ~ **sądowa** courtroom; ~ **sypialna** dormitory; ~ **szkolna** classroom; ~ **wykładowa** lecture theatre

salaterka salad bowl

saldo balance[1]; ~ **dodatnie/kredytowe** credit[1]

salmonella salmonella

salon 1 (*fryzjerski itp.*) salon; ~ **fryzjerski** hairdresser's; ~ **kosmetyczny** beauty salon (*samochodowy, sprzętu grającego itp.*) showroom; ~ **gier** arcade **2** (*w hotelu itp.*) lounge[1]; (*w mieszkaniu*) drawing room, living room

salto somersault

salutować/za- salute verb, give a salute

salwa 1 (*wystrzał*) volley **2** (*śmiechu*) peal

sałata lettuce

sałatka salad

sam 1 (*samotny, w pojedynkę*) alone, unattached **2** (*samodzielnie; przez ważną osobę*) herself, himself, itself, myself, oneself, ourselves, themselves, yourself, (all) by itself/herself/himself/itself/myself/oneself/ourselves/themselves/yourself/yourselves, (all) on your, etc. own, in your own right; **~emu** personally **3 taki** ~ alike[1], like[5]; **tak ~o** the same thing; **ten** ~ identical, one[1], the same; **to ~o** ditto, the same pron., (the) same again **4 (już)** ~ mere, the merest; **z ~ego rana** first thing tomorrow morning; ~ **środek tarczy** the dead centre of the target; **na** ~ **szczyt** to the very top of the mountain **5 mamy ~e kłopoty** we've had nothing but trouble; **do ~ego końca** right to the end IDM ~ **w sobie** as such | **tym ~ym** thereby | **w** ~ **raz** just right
samczy male[1]
samica female[2], mate[1]; (*ptaków*) hen; (*niektórych zwierząt*) cow; ~ **jelenia/królika/zająca** doe; ~ **owcy** ewe
samiczy female[1]
samiec male[2], mate[1]; (*ptaki*) cock[1]; (*wieloryba/słonia*) bull; ~ **jelenia/królika** buck[1]; ~ **psa/lisa** dog[1]
samobójczy self-destructive, suicidal
samobójstwo suicide, self-destruction
samochodowy motor[2], motoring
samochodzik toy car
samochód car; ~ **kempingowy** camper; ~ **kombi** estate car; ~ **pomocy drogowej** breakdown truck; ~ **terenowy** Jeep; **sportowy** ~ sports car; ~ **typu pickup** pickup; ~ **typu sedan** saloon; **samochodem** by car, by road
samochwała braggart
samodzielnie (all) by itself/herself/himself/itself/myself/oneself/ourselves/themselves/yourself/yourselves
samogłoska vowel
samokontrola self-control
samolot aeroplane, aircraft, craft; ~ **myśliwski** fighter; ~ **pasażerski** airliner; **~em** by air, by plane
samolubny egocentric, egoistic, self-centred, selfish
samolubstwo selfishness
samoobrona self-defence
samoobsługowy self-service
samorealizacja fulfilment
samorząd: ~ **lokalny** local goverment
samorzutnie voluntarily
samosąd: **dokonywać ~u** lynch
samostanowienie self-determination
samotniczy reclusive, solitary
samotnie alone, (all) by itself/herself/himself/itself/myself/oneself/ourselves/themselves/yourself/yourselves, (all) on your, etc. own
samotnik 1 (także **samotniczka**) loner, recluse; **regaty ~ów** single-handed yacht race **2** (*gra planszowa*) solitaire
samotność loneliness, solitude
samotn|y 1 (*bez towarzystwa*) friendless, lonely, lonesome **2** (*odosobniony*) lone, (all) by itself **3** (*robiony w pojedynkę*) solitary **4** (*stanu wolnego*) single[1]; **~a matka** single mother; **~y rodzic** single parent
samouk: **jest ~iem** he's self-taught
samounicestwienie self-destruction
samowładztwo autocracy
samowolny wilful
samowystarczalny self-sufficient
samozadowolenie smugness; **z ~m** smugly
samozniszczenie self-destruction
sample (*muz.*) sample
sanatorium sanatorium
sandałek sandal
saneczki toboggan
sanie sledge, sleigh
sanitariusz/ka orderly[2]
sanitarny sanitary
sankcj|a (sankcje) crackdown, sanctions[1]; **~a karna** penalty; **stosować ~e** crack down (on sb/sth)
sankcjonować/u- legitimize
sank|i sledge; **zjeżdżać na ~ach** sledge verb
sanktuarium sanctuary, shrine
sapać/za-/sapnąć 1 (*osoba*) gasp, pant, puff[1], wheeze; **posapujący** breathy **2** (*pociąg itp.*) chug
sapliwy breathy
sardela pilchard
sardoniczny sardonic
sardynka sardine
sari sari
sarkastyczny pointed, sarcastic
sarkazm sarcasm
saszetka sachet
satelita satellite
satelitarny satellite
satsuma satsuma
Saturn Saturn
satyna satin
satynowy satin
satyr|a satire; **napisać (na coś) ~ę** satirize
satyryczny satirical
satyryk satirist
satysfakcja fulfilment, reward[1], satisfaction
satysfakcjonować/u- satisfy
satysfakcjonujący fulfilling, rewarding, satisfying
sauna sauna
sączyć 1 (*ślinę*) dribble **2** (*zapach itp.*) exude
□ **sączyć/prze- się** drip[1], ooze, seep, trickle; (*ślina*) dribble; (*woda itp.*) percolate; (*zapach itp.*) exude
sąd 1 (*miejsce*) courthouse; (*miejsce instytucja*) court[1]; ~ **trybunalski** tribunal; ~ **konkursowy** jury; ~ **najwyższy** High Court; ~ **wojskowy** court martial **2** (*opinia*) verdict; **wydawać** ~ judge[2]
sądowy forensic, judicial
sądzić 1 (*prawn.*) judge[2], try[1] sb (for sth) **2 (/o-)** (*oceniać*) judge[2] **3** (*myśleć*) consider, make sth of sb/sth, reckon, suppose, think; **co sądzisz na ten temat?** what are your feelings on this matter?
□ **sądzić się**: **sądzi się, że zbieg przebywa w tej okolicy** the escaped prisoner is believed to be in this area
sąsiad/ka neighbour
sąsiadować (*tyły budynku itp.*) back[4] onto sth
sąsiedni adjacent; (*pobliski*) nearby; (*dom, pokój itp.*) next[1]; (*kraj itp.*) neighbouring; (*teren itp.*) surrounding
sąsiedzk|i next door adj.; **po ~u z kimś** next door (to sb)
sąsiedztw|o proximity; (*mieszkań, domów*) neighbourhood; **w ~ie (czegoś)** in the vicinity (of sth), nearby adv.
scal-ać/ić integrate, merge
scedować → CEDOWAĆ
scena 1 (*miejsce w teatrze itp.*) stage[1] **2** (*w sztuce, filmie itp.*) scene **3** (*polityczna itp.*) arena, scene
scenariusz scenario, screenplay, script
scenarzyst-a/ka screenwriter, scriptwriter
sceneria scenery, setting
scentralizować → CENTRALIZOWAĆ
sceptycyzm scepticism
sceptyczny sceptical
scepty-k/czka sceptic
schamieć → CHAMIEĆ
scharakteryzować → CHARAKTERYZOWAĆ
scheda heirloom, inheritance
schemat 1 (*projekt*) plan[1]; ~ **działania** flow chart **2** (*forma*) pattern
schematyczny schematic
schizma schism
schizofrenia schizophrenia
schizofreniczny schizophrenic
schizofreni-k/czka schizophrenic
schlebi(a)ć: **komuś** flatter, get on the right side of sb; **sobie** flatter yourself (that...); **(fałszywie)** ~ **komuś** pander to sb/sth
■ **schlebianie** adulation, flattery
schludność neatness, tidiness
schludny neat, tidy[1], trim[2]
schłodzić (się) → CHŁODZIĆ (SIĘ)
schodek stair, step[1]
schodnia gangway
schod|y stairs; **~y ruchome** escalator; **~y zewnętrzne** stairway; **ze ~ów** downstairs
schodzić/zejść 1 (*na dół*) descend **2** (*drogi*) meet **3** (*z pokładu*) disembark **4** (*plama itp.*) come out (of sth) **5** (*z tematu*) wander **6** (*przen.: odczepić się od kogoś/czegoś*) get off (sb/sth) IDM **schodzić na psy** go to rack and ruin
□ **schodzić/zejść się 1** (*gromadzić się*) meet **2** (*odbywać się w tym samym czasie*) coincide (with sth)
schować (się) → CHOWAĆ (SIĘ)
schowek compartment, locker; (*w samochodzie*) glove compartment
schron: ~ **przeciwlotniczy** air-raid shelter
schronić (się) → CHRONIĆ (SIĘ)
schronienie cover[2], haven, refuge, retreat[2], shelter[1]; **zapewniać** ~ house[2]; **dawać** ~ (*np. przestępcy, zbiegowi*) harbour[2]
schronisko shelter[1]; (*młodzieżowe; dla bezdomnych itp.*) hostel; ~ **młodzieżowe** youth hostel
schropowacieć → CHROPOWACIEĆ
schrupać → CHRUPAĆ
schrzanić → CHRZANIĆ
schudnąć → CHUDNĄĆ
schwytać → CHWYTAĆ
schy-lać/lić (*głowę*) incline[1]
□ **schy-lać/lić się** stoop
schyłek 1 (*upadek*) fall[2] of sth **2** (*zwł. upadek moralny*) decadence
IDM ~ **wieku** the turn of the century
schyłkowy decadent
scyzoryk penknife, pocket knife; **duży** ~ jackknife noun
sczepi(a)ć piece sth together
sczerstwieć → CZERSTWIEĆ
seans 1 (*sesja*) session **2** ~ **spirytystyczny** seance

secesja 1 (*regionu od kraju itp.*) secession (from sth) **2** (*sztuka*) art nouveau
sedes lavatory, toilet
sedn|o crux, heart, kernel, root[1], substance; **~o sprawy** the core issue, the nitty-gritty, point[1]; (*przy negocjacjach, rozstrzyganiu o czymś*) the bottom line; **dochodzić do ~a sprawy** get to the bottom of sth; **trafiający w ~o sprawy** to the point
segment section, segment
segregacja 1 (*rasowa itp.*) segregation **2** (*informacji itp.*) collation
segregator binder, file[1], ring binder
segregować/po- 1 (*dzielić na grupy itp.*) grade[2], group[2], sort[2] **2** (*informacje itp.*) collate **3** (*rozdzielać*) segregate
sejf safe[2]
sejsmiczny seismic
sekator secateurs
sekciarski sectarian
sekcj|a 1 (*w ministerstwie itp.*) desk, section **2** (*rośliny,zwierzęcia itp.*) dissection; **robić ~ę** dissect; **~a zwłok** autopsy, post-mortem
sekre|t 1 (*tajne informacje*) secret[2] **2** (*stan tajemnicy*) secrecy; **w ~cie** confidentially
sekretariat secretariat
sekretarka PA, secretary
sekretarz PA, secretary; **~ stanu** Secretary of State
sekretarzyk bureau
sekretny (*motyw itp.*) ulterior
seks sex; **pełen ~u** sexy
seksapil sex appeal
seksizm sexism
seksown|y sexy, slinky
□ **seksownie** voluptuously
seksualność sexuality
seksualny sexual
sekta sect
sektor sector
sekunda second[2]; (*krótka chwila*) while[2]
sekundnik the second hand
selekcja pick[2], selection
selekcjonować/wy- pick[1], select[1]; (*najlepsz-ych/e*) cream sb/sth off
selektywny selective
seler celery
semantyczny semantic
semestr semester, term[1]
seminarium 1 (*na uniwersytecie*) seminar **2 ~ duchowne** seminary
sen 1 (*stan fizjologiczny*) sleep[2]; (*drzemka*) kip noun; **spokojny ~** slumber; **~ zimowy** hibernation; **pora snu** bedtime; **we śnie** asleep; **widziałem go tuż przed snem w piątek wieczorem** I saw him last thing on Friday evening **2** (*marzenie senne*) dream[1]
senacki senate
senat senate
senator senator
senior veteran; (*po nazwisku*) senior[1]
senność drowsiness
senny 1 drowsy, lazy, sleepy **2** (*przen.*) dead[1], sleepy
sens meaning, point[1], sense[1], substance; **ogólny ~** drift[1], gist; **mieć ~** make sense; **bez ~u** meaningless; **nie ma ~u uczyć się do egzaminu w ostatniej chwili** it's no use studying for an exam at the last minute; **nie uważam, aby ten plan miał ~** I don't see the wisdom of this plan IDM **w pewnym ~ie** in a sense, in a/one/any way, in some ways | **w tym ~ie** to this/that effect
sensacj|a hit[2], sensation; **pogoń za ~ą** sensationalism
sensacyjn|y sensational; **~a wiadomość** (*podana wcześniej niż w konkurencyjnych gazetach*) scoop[1]
sensown|y logical, rational, reasonable, sensible; **być ~ym** make sense
sentencja maxim
sentyment affinity, sentiment; **mający ~ do kogoś/czegoś** partial to sb/sth; **z ~em** sentimentally
sentymentalizm sentimentality
sentymentalność sentimentality
sentymentalny sentimental, soppy
separacj|a separation; **żyjący w ~i** estranged; (*być*) **w ~i** separated
separować/od- separate[2]
seplenić/za- lisp verb; **lekko sepleni** he speaks with a slight lisp
septyczny septic
ser cheese
serc|e heart; IDM **bez ~a** heartless | **brać sobie coś do ~a** take sth to heart | **całym ~em** with all your heart, with your whole heart, wholeheartedly | **w głębi ~a** deep down | **mieć złote ~e** have a heart of gold | **nie mieć ~a (do robienia czegoś)** not have the heart (to do sth), your heart is not in sth | **otworzyć ~e (przed kimś)** pour your heart out (to sb)
sercowo-naczyniowy cardiovascular
sercowy cardiac
sercówka: **~ jadalna** (*mięczak*) cockle
serdeczność warmth
serdeczny cordial[1], friendly[1], good-hearted, hearty, intimate, warm-hearted, wholehearted, warm[1]; **~ przyjaciel** bosom friend
serdelek sausage
serduszko heart
serek: **~ topiony** cheese spread; **~ wiejski** cottage cheese
seria 1 (*sekwencja*) catalogue, run[2], series, set[2], succession; (*przykrych zdarzeń*) rash[1]; **~ włamań w tej okolicy** a spate of burglaries in the area **2** (*TV itp.*) series **3** (*tabletek itp.*) course (of sth) **4** (*rozmów; z broni*) round[4] **5** (*rozgrywek sportowych itp.*) circuit IDM **numer serii** serial number
serial serial
serio: **(na) ~** in earnest, for real, serious, seriously; **mówić ~** mean[1]; **traktować kogoś/coś ~** take sb/sth seriously
sernik cheesecake
serpentyna 1 (*drogi*) hairpin bend **2** (*papierowa*) streamer
serwatka whey
serwer server
serwetka napkin, serviette
serwis 1 service[1]; **~ gwarancyjny** service[1] **2 ~ informacyjny** bulletin
serwować/za- 1 (*posiłki/napoje*) serve, serve sth out, serve sth up **2** (*w krykecie itp.*) bowl[2]; (*w tenisie*) serve
seryjn|y: **~y morderca** serial killer; **produkcja ~a** mass production
■ **seryjnie**: **produkować ~** mass-produce
sesja session, sitting
set set[2]
seter setter
setk|a: **~i funtów** hundreds of pounds
setny hundredth; (*po raz*) umpteenth; **setna rocznica** centenary
sezon season[1]; **~ letni** summertime; **po ~ie; poza ~em** out of season; **pomidory są najtańsze kiedy jest na nie ~** tomatoes are cheapest when they are in season IDM **~ ogórkowy** the low season
sezonować (*drewno*) weather[2]
sezonowy (*praca itp.*) casual, seasonal
sędzia 1 (także **sędzina**) (*prawn.*) judge[1]; (**sędziowie**) the judiciary; (*tytuł*) justice; **~ pokoju** Justice of the Peace **2** (*w zawodach sportowych itp.*) adjudicator; **~ sportowy** judge[1], referee, umpire; **~ liniowy** linesman
sędziować judge[2], referee verb; (*w tenisie/krykiecie itp.*) umpire verb
sędziowski judicial
sękaty gnarled
sęp vulture; (*z rodziny Cathartidae*) buzzard
sfabrykować → FABRYKOWAĆ
sfałszować → FAŁSZOWAĆ
sfałszowany: **wynik ~** fix[2]
sfastrygować → FASTRYGOWAĆ
sfatygowany shabby, tatty
sfaulować → FAULOWAĆ
sfer|a quarter, sphere; **~y urzędowe** officialdom; **wyższe ~y** the upper class
sfermentować → FERMENTOWAĆ
sferyczny spherical
sfetyszyzować → FETYSZYZOWAĆ
sfilmować → FILMOWAĆ
sfinalizować → FINALIZOWAĆ
sfinansować → FINANSOWAĆ
sfingowany: **wynik ~** fix[2]
sflaczały (*brzuch itp.*) flabby; (*kapelusz itp.*) floppy
sformalizować → FORMALIZOWAĆ
sformalizowanie formalization
sformatować → FORMATOWAĆ
sformułować → FORMUŁOWAĆ
sformułowanie (*wypowiedzi*) wording; (*teorii itp.*) articulation
sforsować → FORSOWAĆ
sfotografować → FOTOGRAFOWAĆ
sfotokopiować → FOTOKOPIOWAĆ
sfrustrować → FRUSTROWAĆ
sfrustrowany frustrated
sfuszerować → FUSZEROWAĆ
sherry sherry
showman showman
siać 1 (**/za-**) plant[2], sow[1] **2 ~ postrach** terrorize
■ **sianie**: **~ paniki** scaremongering
siadać 1 (**/usiąść**) seat[2], sit down; (*na rower itp.*) mount[1]; **proszę usiąść** please be seated, please take a seat; **~ wygodnie** settle down **2** (**/o-**) settle **3** (**/usiąść**) (*ptak*) land[2], perch[1]
siak: **tak czy ~** at all events/in any event
siano hay
siarka sulphur
siatk|a 1 (*tworzywo*) mesh, netting; **ogrodzenie z ~i metalowej** wire fence **2** (*ulic itp.*) grid; **~a geograficzna** grid **3** (*sport*) net[1]; **trafiać w ~ę** (*np. piłką*) net[3] **4** (*zabezpieczająca przed upadkiem*

na ziemię) safety net **5** (*na zakupy*) string bag
siatkówka 1 (*anat.*) retina **2** (*sport*) volleyball
siąk-ać/nąć: **siąkać nosem** sniffle
sidła 1 snare, trap[1]; **łapać w** ~ trap[2] **2** (*przen.*) **zapędzać w** ~ trap[2] sb (into sth/into doing sth)
siebie each other, herself, himself, itself, myself, oneself, ourselves, themselves, yourself; ~ **(wzajemnie)** one another; **od** ~ apart IDM **być sobą** be yourself | **na sobie** to your cost | **nie bierz tego do** ~ don't take it personally | **poczuć się u** ~ feel you belong
sieć 1 (*rybacka*) net[1]; **łapać w** ~ net[3] **2** (*druciana itp.*) mesh, netting **3** (*sklepów itp.*) chain[1]; (*przedsiębiorstw itp.*) network **4** (*kolejowa itp.*) matrix, network; (*kanalizacyjna, elektryczna itp.*) the mains[2]; ~ **energetyczna**; ~ **wysokiego napięcia** grid **5** (*komput.*) network; **wewnętrzna** ~ **komputerowa** intranet; **światowa** ~ **komputerowa** the World Wide Web; **podłączony do sieci komputerowej** on line **6** ~ **telewizyjna/radiowa** network
siedem seven
siedemdziesiąt seventy
siedemdziesiąty seventieth
siedemnasty seventeenth
siedemnaście seventeen
siedlisko breeding ground; ~ **królików** rabbit warren
siedzący sedentary
siedzenie 1 (*krzesło*) place[1], seat[1] **2** (*osoby*) backside, bottom[1]
siedziba residence; ~ **główna** head office
siedzieć sit; ~ **sobie** sit about/around; ~ **dalej** (*np. przy pracy*) stick at sth; ~ **do późna w nocy** sit up, stay up late IDM ~ **w długach** be in/out of debt
siekać/po- chop[1] sth (up) (into sth), cut sth up, hack (away) (at) sth; **siekać przez maszynkę** (*mięso*) mince verb
siekiera axe[1]
siekierka chopper, hatchet
sielankowy idyllic, pastoral
sielski pastoral, rural
siema hiya
sierociniec orphanage
sierota orphan
sierp sickle IDM ~ **księżyca** crescent
sierpień August
sierpniowy August
sierpowy: **cios** ~ hook[1]
sierść coat[1], fur
sierżant sergeant
się each other, herself, himself, itself, myself, one another, oneself, ourselves, themselves, yourself
sięgać 1 (*dotknąć; do pewnego poziomu/wysokości*) reach[1], stretch[1] (out); **włosy sięgają jej do pasa** her hair comes down to her waist **2 (/sięgnąć) po coś** grasp at sth, reach[1] (out) (for sb/sth); (*do kieszeni itp.*) delve, dip into sth, dive into sth **3 wstecz (do czegoś)** go back (to sth); ~ **myślą wstecz** think back to sth **4** (*mieć zasięg/osiągać rozpiętość*) range[2] between A and B, from A to B

sikacz plonk[2]
sik-ać/nąć spout[2], spurt, squirt
Sikh Sikh
Sikhizm Sikhism
sikorka tit
silnik engine, motor[1]; ~ **odrzutowy** jet engine; ~ **parowy** steam engine; ~ **spalinowy** internal combustion engine; ~ **zewnętrzny/(znajdujący się) za burtą** outboard motor
siln|y powerful, strong; (*zauważalny: akcent itp.*) broad, thick[1]; (*osobowość*) forceful; (*kopniak itp.*) hefty; (*uczucie*) intense; (*władca itp.*) mighty[1]; (*lekarstwo itp.*) potent; (*wytrzymały*) resilient; (*materiał itp.*) stiff[1]; (*ból*) acute; (*trucizna; wirus itp.*) **bardzo ~y** virulent; **~a ręka** hold[2] (on/over sb/sth); **~e wiatry** high winds; **~y mróz** hard frost; **~y ból głowy** a bad headache
■ **silnie** powerfully, strongly; (*z wysiłkiem*) hard[2]; (*padać itp.*) heavily
sił|a 1 strength; (*i polit.*) might[2], power[1]; (*energia*) energy; (*uczucia*) poignancy; **brak** ~ weakness; **nie mam ~y na kolejną awanturę** I can't face another argument; **przybierać na sile** (*muz.*) swell[1]; **w sile** strong **2** (*fiz.*) (*wiatru*) force[1] **4** (*przemoc*) **użycie ~y** violence; **będziesz musiał użyć ~y, żeby otworzyć to okno** you'll have to use brute force to get this window open **5 (siły)** (*zbrojne*) forces[1]; **~y zbrojne** the armed forces, the services[1]; **~y bezpieczeństwa** the security forces **6 ~y nadprzyrodzone** the supernatural **5** (*natężenie*) intensity, potency IDM **łączyć ~y** join forces (with sb) | **na ~ę** forcibly; (*przen.*) at a pinch, at a push | **na ~ach, aby coś zrobić** up to sth | **~a napędowa** driving force | **~a nawyku** force of habit | **~a negocjacji** bargaining power | **~a przekonywania** persuasiveness | **~a robocza** labour[1], labour force, manpower, workforce | **~a woli** willpower
siłować się grapple (with sb)
siłownia 1 (*zakład energetyczny*) power station **2** (*sala ćwiczeń*) gym
siniak bruise
sin|y livid; **ręce ~e z zimna** hands blue with cold
sio: **a ~!** shoo[1]
siodełko saddle[1]; **tylne ~ motocykla** pillion
siodłać/o- saddle[2]
siodło saddle[1]; **wakacje w siodle** pony-trekking
siorb-ać/nąć slurp
siostra sister; (*nieform.*) sis; **brat/~** sibling; **~ cioteczna**; **~ stryjeczna** cousin; **~ przełożona** sister; (*główna pielęgniarka*) matron; **~ zakonna** sister
siostrzany sisterly
siostrzenica niece
siostrzeniec nephew
siódmy seventh
sito sieve
sitowie bulrush, rush[2]
siusiać/wy- pee, piddle, wee verb
siusiak willy
siusiu wee[1]; **robić** ~ have a pee, pee
siwieć/po- go grey
siwy grey[1]
sjesta siesta
skafander anorak

skakać 1 (/skoczyć/podskoczyć) (*na dwóch nogach*) jump[1], leap[1], spring[2]; (*na jednej nodze*) hop; (*po łóżku itp.*) bounce; (*z podparciem rąk lub tyczki*) vault[2] (over) sth; (*z podniecenia itp.*) dance[2]; **~ z radości** jump for joy; **~ lekko**; **~ przez skakankę** skip[1]; **~ do wody** dive[1]; **~ przez płotki** hurdle[2] (over sth); **~ z samolotu ze spadochronem** parachute verb **2 (/naskoczyć) (na kogoś/coś)** pounce (on sb/sth) **3 (/wskoczyć)** (*do sklepu itp.*) hop[1], nip[1], pop[2] across, down, out, etc. IDM **~ koło kogoś/czegoś** make a fuss of/over sb/sth | **~ z (tematu) na (temat)** jump[1] (from sth) to sth
skakanka rope[1], skipping rope
skal|a the gamut, range[1], scale[1] IDM **na dużą/wielką ~ę** big adv., in a big way, full-scale, large-scale | **na małą ~ę** small-scale, in a small way
skalać → KALAĆ
skalanie defilement
skaleczon|y: **~e miejsce** wound[1]
skaleczyć (się) → KALECZYĆ (SIĘ)
skalisty craggy, rugged
skalkować → KALKOWAĆ
skalkulować → KALKULOWAĆ
skalp scalp
skalpel scalpel
skała rock[1]
skamielin|a fossil; **tworzyć ~ę** fossilize
skamieniały: **~ (ze strachu)** petrified
skamienieć → KAMIENIEĆ
skamleć/za- yelp
skandal crime, disgrace[1], scandal
skandaliczny disgraceful, outrageous, scandalous, shameful, shocking; (*zaniedbanie itp.*) criminal[1], gross[1]; (*lekceważenie itp.*) flagrant
skandować/za-/wy- chant[2]
Skandynawia Scandinavia
skandynawski Scandinavian
skaner scanner
skanować 1 (/ze-) scan **2 (/w-) do czegoś** scan sth into sth, scan sth in
skansen a museum of rural life
skapitulować → KAPITULOWAĆ
skapować cotton on (to sth), get the hang of (doing) sth, latch on (to sth)
skarb 1 (*klejnoty, złoto itp.*) hoard of treasure, treasure[1] **2 ministerstwo ~u państwa** the Treasury **3** (*przedmiot/osoba*) find[2], gem **4 (skarbie)** dear[3], honey, sweetheart
skarbiec vault[1]
skarbni-k/czka treasurer
skarbonka money box, piggy bank
skarcić → KARCIĆ
skarg|a complaint; (*form.*) grievance; **składać ~ę** report[1] sb (to sb) (for sth)
skarłowaciał|y: **~e drzewa** stunted trees
skarpa slope
skarpeta sock
skarżyć/o-/za- complain; **na kogoś** tell on sb; **(kogoś) (o coś)** sue (sb) (for sth) □ **skarżyć/po- się** complain (to sb) (about sth/that…), moan; (*na ból itp.*) complain of sth
skatalogować → KATALOGOWAĆ
skaut Boy Scout, cub, scout; **członkini ~owskiej drużyny dla dziewcząt** brownie; **organizacja ~owska dla młodszych chłopców** (*podobna do zuchów*) cubs
skaz|a blemish, defect[1], flaw; (*korupcji itp.*) taint; **bez ~y** flawless,

immaculate; (*skóra*) clear[1]; **ze ~ą** flawed
skazać → SKAZYWAĆ
skazanie conviction
skazaniec convict[2]
skazan-y/a convict[2]
skazić → KAZIĆ, SKAŻAĆ
skaz(yw)ać: **(na coś)** condemn sb (to sth/to do sth); (*prawn.*) convict[1] sb (of sth), sentence[2] sb (to sth); **~ na wygnanie** exile verb
ska-żać/zić 1 (*wodę itp.*) adulterate sth (with sth), poison[2] **2** (*muzykę itp.*) bastardize
■ **skażenie** adulteration, contamination
skąd whence IDM **ależ ~?** not at all
skądkolwiek: **czy ~** or wherever
skąpany bathed in sth
skąpić/po- skimp (on sth)
skąpiec miser
skąpstwo meanness, stinginess
skąpy 1 (*osoba*) grudging, mean[2], miserly, stingy **2** (*mały*) meagre, scant, scanty, skimpy
skecz sketch
skiero(wy)wać zob. też KIEROWAĆ (SIĘ); divert
■ **skierowany do kogoś/czegoś** oriented
skin skinhead
skinąć: **(na kogoś)** beckon; (*głową*) nod
skinienie sign[1]; (*głowy*) bob of the head, nod noun IDM **na każde ~** at sb's beck and call
skisnąć → KISIĆ
sklasyfikować → KLASYFIKOWAĆ
skle-cać/cić zob. też KLECIĆ; knock sth together, rig sth up
skle-jać/ić → KLEIĆ (SIĘ); cement[2], glue[2]
sklejka plywood
sklep shop[1]; **(mały) ~ spożywczy** grocer's, grocery; **~ ogólnospożywczy** (*często całodobowy*) convenience store; **~ z antykami** antique shop; **~ internetowy** dot-com; **~ jubilerski** jeweller's; **~ mięsny** butcher's[1]; **~ papierniczy** stationer's; **~ rybny** fishmonger's; **~ zoologiczny** pet shop; **~ danej sieci** chain store; **~ warzywny** greengrocer's; **~ wielobranżowy** general store; **~ prowadzący sprzedaż towarów określonej firmy** stockist
sklepienie vault[1]
sklepik a little shop
sklepika-rz/rka shopkeeper
sklepion|y: **~e przejście** archway
sklonować → KLONOWAĆ
skład 1 (*struktura*) composition, constitution **2** (*budynek*) depot, store[1], storeroom, warehouse; **~ wojskowy** depot; **na ~zie (towaru)** in stock
składać 1 (/złożyć) (*budować*) assemble, fit sth together, put sth together; (*scalać*) integrate sth (into sth), A and B/integrate A with B; **~ do kupy** patch sth up **2** (*pieniądze*) deposit[2] **3 (/złożyć)** (*zamówienie*) place[2]; (*podanie itp.*) submit sth (to sb/sth); (*rezygnację*) tender[2] sth (to sb); **~ ofertę** bid[1] (sth) (for sth); **~ petycję** petition verb; **~ podanie** apply (to sb) (for sth); **~ prośbę** request[2] sth (from/of sb); **~ skargę (u kogoś)** report[1] sb (to sb) (for sth), take sth up with sb; **~ wniosek o pożyczkę** request a loan from the bank; **~ rezygnację/urząd** hand in your resignation, resign (from/as) (sth); **~ listownie zamówienie** (*na towary*) write off/away (to sb/sth) (for sth); **~ zeznania** give evidence; **~ życzenia** wish[1] **4 ~ komuś wizytę** pay sb a visit, visit; **~ (komuś) kurtuazyjną wizytę** pay your respects (to sb) **4 (/złożyć)** (*papier itp.*) fold[1] sth (up) **5 (na coś)** pool[2]; **~ się na coś** put sth towards sth
■ **składany 1** (*krzesło itp.*) collapsible, folding **2 odsetki składane** compound interest
□ **składać się 1 (/złożyć się)** (*krzesło itp.*) collapse[1], fold[1] (up) **2 z czegoś** be composed of sth, comprise, consist of sth **3 (/złożyć się)** (*na kupno czegoś*) club together (to do sth) IDM **tak się składa/złożyło, że** as it happens/happened
składanka compilation; (*muz.*) medley
składka collection; **~ członkowska** fee; **~ ubezpieczeniowa** insurance premium
składnia syntax
składnica store[1], storeroom
składnik constituent (*kulin., przen.*) ingredient; **~ pokarmowy** nutrient
składować store[2]
■ **składowanie** storage
składowy (*część itp.*) component adj., constituent adj.
składzik storeroom
skłamać → KŁAMAĆ
skłaniać/skłonić 1 (*zachęcać*) decide, induce, prompt[2]; **skłonić kogoś do zrobienia czegoś poprzez zawstydzenie** shame sb into doing sth **2** (*głowę*) bow[1] (sth) (to sb)
□ **skłaniać/skłonić się**: **ku czemuś** incline[1] to/towards sth, tend
skłonny amenable, apt to do sth, inclined (to do sth), prone to sth/to do sth, willing (to do sth)
■ **skłonność** disposition, inclination, propensity, tendency, willingness; **mieć skłonność do czegoś** tend to do sth; **mający skłonność do czegoś** liable to sth, inclined to do sth, prone to sth/to do sth
skłó-cać/cić: **skłócać kogoś z kimś** (*szczególnie gdy samemu z tego wynosi się korzyść*) play A off against B
sknera miser
sknocić → KNOCIĆ
skoczek 1 (*osoba*) jumper; (*do wody*) diver; **~ narciarski** skier **2** (*szachy*) knight
skocznia diving board; **~ narciarska** ski jump
skoczyć → SKAKAĆ
skodyfikować → KODYFIKOWAĆ
skojarzenie association
skojarzyć → KOJARZYĆ
skok 1 bound noun, jump[2], leap[2], spring[1]; (*w przepaść, wodę itp.*) plunge[2]; **lekki ~** skip[2]; **~ całym ciałem naprzód** lunge (at sb), (for sb/sth); **~ do wody** dive[2]; **~ w dal** long jump; **~ wzwyż** high jump; **~ o tyczce** the pole vault; **~i na bungee** bungee jumping; **~i narciarskie** ski jumping **2** (*zmiana: cen/wartości*) jump[2] (in sth); **nagły ~** surge
skolonizować → KOLONIZOWAĆ
skołtuniony tangled
skombinować → KOMBINOWAĆ
skomentować → KOMENTOWAĆ
skomercjalizować → KOMERCJALIZOWAĆ
skomleć/za- whimper, whine
skompensować → KOMPENSOWAĆ
skompletować → KOMPLETOWAĆ
skomplikować → KOMPLIKOWAĆ
skomplikowany complex[1], complicated, elaborate[1], sophisticated; (*trudny: temat itp.*) hot[1]
skomponować → KOMPONOWAĆ
skompromitować (się) → KOMPROMITOWAĆ (SIĘ)
skompromitowany in disgrace
skomputeryzować → KOMPUTERYZOWAĆ
skomputeryzowany (*podłączony do sieci komputerów*) wired; (*techn.: nowoczesny*) high-tech
skonany fagged, frazzled, washed out
skoncentrować (się) → KONCENTROWAĆ (SIĘ)
skoncentrowany concentrated
skonceptualizować → KONCEPTUALIZOWAĆ
skondensować → KONDENSOWAĆ
skonfiskować → KONFISKOWAĆ
skonfrontować → KONFRONTOWAĆ
skonkretyzować → KONKRETYZOWAĆ
skonsolidować (się) → KONSOLIDOWAĆ (SIĘ)
skonsternować → KONSTERNOWAĆ
skonstruować → KONSTRUOWAĆ
skonsultować się → KONSULTOWAĆ SIĘ
skonsumować zob. też KONSUMOWAĆ; (*małżeństwo*) consummate[2]
skontaktować się → KONTAKTOWAĆ SIĘ
skontrastować → KONTRASTOWAĆ
skontrasygnować → KONTRASYGNOWAĆ
skontrolować → KONTROLOWAĆ
skończony 1 done[2], at an end, finished, over adj., over and done with **2** (*mat.*) finite
skończyć zob. też KOŃCZYĆ (SIĘ) **1 z kimś/czymś** finish[1] sth (off/up), finish with sb/sth, be finished (with sb/sth); **(na czymś/jako coś)** end up (as sth), end up (doing sth); **przerwać pisanie, czas się skończył** stop writing – your time's up **2** (*ileś lat*) turn[1]; **mój syn za miesiąc skończy sześć lat** my son is six (years old) next month
skoordynować → KOORDYNOWAĆ
skopiować → KOPIOWAĆ
skorelować → KORELOWAĆ
skoro 1 (*ponieważ*) inasmuch as, now conj., seeing, since conj. **2** (*gdy tylko*) directly[2]
skorodować → KORODOWAĆ
skoroszyt file[1], folder
skorowidz index
skorpion 1 (*zool.*) scorpion **2 (Skorpion)** (*znak zodiaku*) Scorpio
skorumpować → KORUMPOWAĆ
skorumpowanie corruption
skorumpowany corrupt[1]
skorupa 1 (*pancerz skorupiaka*) shell[1] **2** (*ziemska*) crust
skorupiak shellfish
skorupka: **~ jajka** eggshell
skory prompt[1] (in doing sth/to do sth); **~ do gniewu** bad-tempered
skorygować → KORYGOWAĆ

skorygowanie correction
skorzystać → KORZYSTAĆ
skos bias[1], slant[2]; **po ~ie** obliquely
skosić → KOSIĆ
skostniały numb
skostnieć → KOSTNIEĆ
skostnienie ossification
skosztować → KOSZTOWAĆ
skośny oblique, slanting
skowronek lark
skowyczeć/za- whine, yelp
skowyt whine noun, yelp noun
skó|ra 1 (*anat.*) skin[1]; **~ra głowy** scalp **2** (*na buty itp.*) hide[2], leather; **~ra lakierowana** patent leather; **z (określonej) ~ry** skin[1] IDM **jest podobna do swojej matki jakby ~rę zdjął** she's the spitting image of her mother | **na własnej ~rze** to your cost
skórka 1 (*wokół paznokcia*) cuticle **2** (*owocu*) skin[1], peel[2]; (*pomarańczy, sera itp.*) rind **3** (*chleba*) crust
skórzany leather
skra sparkle noun
s-kracać/krócić (*zmniejszyć*) lessen, wear sth down; (*trwanie czegoś*) curtail, shorten; (*słowo*) abbreviate, contract[2], truncate; (*tekst*) abridge, condense sth (into sth), cut sth down, shorten; (*przerwać komuś*) cut sb short; (*ubranie*) take sth up; **skracać sobie czas** while sth away
□ **s-kracać/krócić się** (*odległość; długość*) shorten; (*z zużycia*) wear down; (*dzień*) draw in
skradać/zakraść się creep[1], prowl (about/around), slink
skraj edge[1], margin, periphery; (*przepaści itp.*) brink; **~ drogi** verge[1]; **ciągnąć się ~em** skirt[2] IDM **na ~u czegoś** on the verge of sth/doing sth | **na ~u przepaści** on the rocks
skrajność extreme noun, extremity
skrajn|y extreme, far[1], radical[1]; **~a bieda** abject poverty, dire poverty; **w ~ej rozpaczy** in the depths of despair
s-kraplać/kroplić (się) condense
skraść → KRAŚĆ
skrawek snippet
skremować → KREMOWAĆ
skreś-lać/lić 1 (*wyeliminować skreśleniem*) cross sth out, delete; **coś z czegoś** cross sth off (sth) **2** (*nie liczyć*) count sb/sth out
skrę-cać/cić zob. też KRĘCIĆ **1** (*drut itp.*) bend[1]; **skręcać w bok** deflect **2** (*samochód itp.*) bear[1], fork[2], turn[1]; **(z czegoś)** turn off (sth); **skręć w następną ulicę** take the next turn on the left; **skręć w trzecią ulicę** take the third turning on the right; **skręć za rogiem** go around the corner; **nagle/gwałtownie skręcić** (*np. z drogi*) swerve **4** (*część ciała*) sprain, wrench[1]; (*lekko*) twist[1]
□ **skrę-cać/cić się** twist[1]; (*tylko osoba, zwierzę*) writhe
skrępować → KRĘPOWAĆ
skrępowanie awkwardness, constraint, discomfort, tie[2], unease
skrępowany awkward, inhibited, self-conscious, uncomfortable
skręt 1 (*samochodu itp.*) turn[2] **2** (*drogi itp.*) twist[2] **3** (*na drucie itp.*) kink **4** (*papieros*) joint[2]

skrobać 1 (/ze-/wy-) (*patelnię, błoto itp.*) scrape[1] sth (down/out/off) **2 (/wy-)** (*zebrać z trudem pieniądze itp.*) scrape sth together/up
skrobia starch
skroić → KROIĆ
skromność 1 (*cecha charakteru*) humility, modesty **2** (*posiłku, środków itp.*) frugality
skromn|y 1 (*osoba; dom itp.*) modest, homely, humble[1]; (*maniery*) unassuming; (*zwł. dziewczyna: w manierach/ubraniu itp.*) demure **2** (*oszacowanie*) conservative[1] **3** (*jedzenie itp.*) frugal, meagre
■ **skromnie**: **~ mówiąc** to say the least
skroń temple
skropić → KROPIĆ
skroplenie condensation
skroplić (się) → SKRAPLAĆ (SIĘ)
skrócić (się) → SKRACAĆ (SIĘ)
skrót 1 (*tekstu itp.*) abbreviation, contraction, summary[1]; **~ najważniejszych wiadomości** headline; **być ~em od czegoś** be short[1] for sth, stand for sth; **w skrócie** in brief **2** (*droga itp.*) short cut; **iść na ~y (przez coś)** cut across, along, through, etc. (sth), take a short cut
skrótowiec acronym
skrótowo for short
skruch|a contrition, remorse, repentance; **pełen ~y** remorseful; **okazywać ~ę** repent (of sth); **ze ~ą** apologetically, remorsefully
skrupi(a)ć się: **na czymś** bear the brunt of sth
skrupulatność rigour
skrupulatn|y 1 (*sumienny*) conscientious, scrupulous **2** (*pracujący precyzyjnie*) meticulous, precise; **jest ~a** she has an eye for detail
skrupuł|y qualms, scruples; **bez ~ów** unscrupulous
skruszony apologetic, contrite, penitent, remorseful, repentant
skryć → SKRYWAĆ
skrypt: **~ dłużny** IOU
skrystalizować się → KRYSTALIZOWAĆ SIĘ
skrytka safe[2]; **~ pocztowa** PO box
skrytość reserve[2], secretiveness
skryty (*prywatny; strzegący swej prywatności*) private[1], reserved; (*tajemniczy*) mysterious, secretive, underhand; (*uczucia itp.*) inner, inward; (*motyw itp.*) ulterior
skrytykować → KRYTYKOWAĆ
skry(wa)ć conceal, hide[1]; (*uczucia itp.*) harbour[2]
skrywany (*uczucie, wrażenie itp.*) sneaking; **wiele ~ch napięć** a lot of tensions below/beneath the surface
skrzący się glittering
skrzeczeć/za- screech, squawk
skrzek 1 (*ptaka*) screech noun, squawk noun **2 żabi ~** frogspawn
skrzele gill
skrzep clot[1]
skrzepnąć → KRZEPNĄĆ
skrzepnięcie: **powodować ~** clot[2]
skrzesać → KRZESAĆ
skrzętnie busily
skrzyczeć scold
skrzyć/za- się glitter verb, glint, sparkle
skrzydełko flap[1]
skrzydł|o 1 (*ptaka; samolotu*) wing **2** (*budynku*) wing; **nowe ~o szpitala** an extension on the hospital **3** (*oddziału wojska*) flank[1] **4 lewe ~o** (*boiska*) left wing **5** (*polit.*) wing IDM **wziąć kogoś pod swoje ~a** take sb under your wing
skrzydłow-y/a wing
skrzynia chest, crate IDM **~ biegów** gearbox
skrzynka box[1], case, crate; **~ bezpiecznikowa** fuse box; **~ odbiorcza** inbox; **~ pocztowa** letter box, mailbox, pillar box, postbox
skrzyp creak noun
skrzypce violin
skrzy-pek/paczka violinist; (*nieform.*) fiddler
skrzypiący creaky, squeaky
skrzypieć/za- creak, crunch[2]
skrzywdzić → KRZYWDZIĆ
skrzywi(a)ć contort
■ **skrzywienie** kink | **skrzywiony 1** (*uśmiech itp.*) lopsided **2** (*psychika itp.*) twisted
skrzywić się → KRZYWIĆ SIĘ
skrzyżować (się) → KRZYŻOWAĆ (SIĘ)
skrzyżowani|e 1 (*dróg*) crossing, crossroads, intersection, (road) junction; **~e dwóch dróg w kształcie litery T** T-junction **2** (*gatunek*) cross[1], hybrid
skserować → KSEROWAĆ
skubać 1 (/wy-/o-) (*drób; brwi*) pluck[1] **2 (/skubnąć)** (*wyrywać*) pluck[1] sth/sb (from sth/out) **3 (/skubnąć)** (*jeść małymi kęsami/nadgryźć*) nibble
skudłacony (*zwł. z wilgoci, brudu itp.*) matted
skuknięty: **zupełnie stuknięty** as nutty as a fruitcake
skulić się → KULIĆ SIĘ
skulony: **~ z zimna** hunched up with the cold
skundlić (*muzykę itp.*) bastardize
skupi(a)ć 1 (*uwagę na czymś*) concentrate, focus[1] sth (on sth); **~ czyjąś uwagę** hold sb's attention **2** (*wzrok*) focus[1] sth (on sth) **3** (*zebrać w całość*) compress sth (into sth)
□ **skupi(a)ć się 1** (*uwaga*) centre on/around sb/sth, concentrate (on sth/doing sth), focus[1] (on sth), keep your mind on sth, zero in on sb/sth; **nad czymś** apply yourself/sth (to sth/doing sth) **2** (*i przen.: schodzić się; spotykać się*) converge (on sb/sth) **3** (*zbić się w grupę*) bunch[2] (up/together)
skupiony collected
skupisko concentration
skurcz cramp, spasm, twitch noun; **~ porodowy** contraction
skurczenie constriction
skurczyć (się) → KURCZYĆ (SIĘ)
skusić → KUSIĆ
skuteczność effectiveness, efficiency
skuteczny effective, efficient, telling; **bardzo ~** powerful
skut|ek consequence, effect[1], result[1]; **~ek uboczny** by-product, side effect; **~kiem tego** as a result; **być ~kiem czegoś** eventuate; **dochodzić do ~ku** materialize; **nie dojść do ~ku** fall through; **odnosić coraz mniejszy ~ek** wear thin
skuter scooter; **~ wodny** Jet Ski
skutkować/po- take effect
skuwka top[1]
skwapliwie: **~ coś zrobić** hasten to do sth; **~ korzystać** snatch at sth; **~ przyjąć coś** leap at sth
skwarny scorching, sweltering
skwaśniały sour

skwer square[2]

skwierczeć/za- sizzle

slajd slide[2], transparency

slalom slalom

slang slang

slipy (także **slipki**) briefs; (*z frontem uformowanym w kształcie litery Y*) Y-fronts; ~ **męskie** underpants

slogan catchphrase, slogan

slumsy shanty town, slum

słabeusz wimp

słabnąć/o-/za- abate, die down, dwindle (away), ebb (away), moderate[2], recede, slacken (sth) (off), tail away/off, wane[1], weaken, wear off

słabo faintly, feebly, lightly, poorly[1], shakily, weakly; (*czuć się*) ~ poorly[2]; ~ **mi** I feel faint/giddy/a bit funny ■ **słabiej** (*gorzej*) worse adv.

słabość 1 (*brak siły*) weakness **2** (*wada*) failing[1], weakness **3** (*fizyczna*) frailty, infirmity **4** (*upodobanie*) **(do czegoś/kogoś)** weakness for sth/sb; **mieć ~ do kogoś/czegoś** be attracted to sb/sth, have a soft spot for sb/sth; **mający ~ do czegoś** partial to sb/sth

słabowity puny, sickly, wimpish

słab|y 1 (*bez siły*) weak; (*stara osoba itp.*) feeble, frail, shaky; (*chory*) infirm; (*tymczasowo*) funny; **~ego charakteru** weedy **2** (*niesolidny*) flimsy, weak **3** (*światło słońca*) watery **4** (*zapach, dźwięk itp.*) faint[1] **5** (*argument itp.*) feeble, flimsy, lame **6** (*okres w interesach itp.*) slack **7** (*jakość*) poor, not up to much **8** (*w rachunkach itp.*) weak (at/in/on sth) **9** (*możliwości*) slender, slim[1] **10** (*związek/więzy z czymś*) tenuous IDM (*fonetyka*) **~a forma** weak form | **~y punkt** flaw | **~a strona** disadvantage, shortcoming, weakness | **o ~ym słuchu** hard of hearing

słać: ~ **łóżko** make the bed □ **słać się** (*roślina, np. po ziemi*) trail[2]

słaniać się stagger ■ **słaniający się** groggy

sław|a the big time, celebrity, fame, glory[1], name[1], renown, repute; (*znana osoba*) name[1]; **osiągnąć ~ę** shoot to stardom

sławić praise[2]

sławn|y celebrated, famed, famous, glorious, illustrious, notable, prominent, renowned, well known; **ten ~y** the; **stawać się ~ym** make a name for yourself, make your name

słodki 1 (*napój itp.*) sweet[1] **2** (*osobowość*) sweet[1]; (*zwł. mężczyzna: podejrzanie układny/miły*) smooth[1] **3** (*woda*) fresh

słodkowodny freshwater

słodycz sweetness

słodycze confectionery; **lubić** ~ have a sweet tooth

słodzić/po- sweeten; **czy słodzisz herbatę?** do you take sugar in (your) tea?

słodzik sweetener

słoik jar[1]; ~ **do dżemu** jam jar

słoma straw

słomiany straw

słomka straw

słonawy (*woda*) brackish

słonecznik sunflower

słoneczny 1 (*pogoda*) sunny **2** (*energia itp.*) solar

słonica cow

słono dearly IDM **~ (za coś) policzyć/płacić** charge/pay the earth

słonowodny saltwater

słony 1 (*woda*) salt adj. **2** (*jedzenie*) salty **3** ~ **dowcip** crude joke

słoń elephant

słońce 1 sun[1] **2** (*światło*) sunshine IDM **jasny jak** ~ crystal clear

słotny wet[1]

Słowian-in/ka Slav

słowiański Slavic

słowik nightingale

słownictwo vocabulary

słowniczek glossary

słownik dictionary; (*na końcu książki*) glossary; ~ **synonimów** thesaurus

słowny verbal

słow|o word[1]; **(słowa)** (*piosenki*) lyrics; **~o kluczowe** keyword; **~o wstępne** foreword; **wolność ~a** freedom of expression/speech; **puste ~a** talk[2]; **bez ~a** dumbly; **parę słów** note[1], word[1]; **~o w ~o** verbatim adv., word for word; **nie mam słów!** words fail me!; **nie znajdować słów** be lost for words; **wyszła bez ~a** she left without uttering a word IDM **innymi ~y** to put it another way

słód malt

słój 1 (*pojemnik*) jar[1] **2** (*w drewnie*) grain

słuch hearing; (*do języków; muzyczny*) an ear (for sth); **nie mający ~u muzycznego** tone-deaf IDM **(być) poza zasięgiem/w zasięgu ~u** (be) out of/within earshot | **grać ze ~u** play (sth) by ear

słuchacz/ka listener

słuchać 1 (/wy-) listen (to sb/sth); ~ **uważnie** follow; **potrafi** ~ he's a good listener **2 (/posłuchać)** obey; **nie** ~ disobey IDM **posłuchaj/cie** (I'll) tell you what, look interj. | **ale posłuchaj!** look here | **słucham!** hello | **słucham?** pardon[1], I beg your pardon, sorry[2]

słuchawk|a 1 (*telefonu*) receiver; **odkładać ~ę** hang up; **telefon komórkowy ze ~ami itp.** hands-free **2** (*zwł. wkładana do ucha*) earpiece; **(słuchawki)** earphones, headphones **3 ~a lekarska** stethoscope

słuchawkowy: **zestaw** ~ headset

słuchowy auditory, aural

sługus creep[2]

słup column, pole, post[1]; (*sieci elektrycznej*) pylon; ~ **latarni** lamp post; ~ **telegraficzny** telegraph pole

słupek pole, post[1], stake[1]; ~ **bramki** goalpost; ~ **drogowy** bollard; ~ **milowy** milestone

słusznoś|ć justice, rightness, validity; **dowodzić ~ci** vindicate IDM **mieć ~ć** be in the right

słuszny 1 (*właściwy*) correct[1], right[1]; (*sprawiedliwy*) fair[1], just[2], rightful **2** (*wnioski itp.*) valid **3** (*pretensje*) legitimate **4** (*nagroda*) well earned ■ **słusznie** (*trafnie*) correctly, rightly; (*sprawiedliwie*) fairly, justly, rightfully; (*zgodnie z prawem*) legitimately; (*zasłużenie*) deservedly IDM **~!** hear! hear!

służalczość subservience

służalczy abject, obsequious, servile, subservient

służąca maid, servant

służący servant

służb|a 1 (*odpowiedzialność*) duty, office, service[1]; **~a wojskowa** military service; **zasadnicza ~a wojskowa** national service; **na ~ie** on duty **2** (*instytucja*) service[1]; **~a cywilna** the civil service; **~a zdrowia** the health service; **~y bezpieczeństwa** the secret service; **~y ratownicze** emergency services; **~y specjalne** Security Service

służyć 1 (*pomagać*) oblige, serve; **czym mogę ~ ?** can I be of any assistance?, are you being served? **2 (/po-) (za/jako coś)** serve

słychać: **co ~?** how are things?; **a co ~ u…?** how/what about…?

słynąć/za-: **z czegoś** be notable for sth, be noted for sth; (*z czegoś złego*) be notorious for sth

słynny big time[2], famous, noted (for/as sth), well known; ~ **na cały świat** world-famous; **ten** ~ your

słyszalny audible

słyszeć/u- get, hear; **o kimś/czymś** hear (sth) of sb/sth; **nie** ~ miss[1] IDM **nie chcieć ~ (o czymś)** won't/wouldn't hear of sth | **z tego co słyszę** by the sound of it/things

smaczn|y delicious, luscious, palatable, tasty IDM **~ego!** bon appétit

smagać/wy- (*deszcz itp.*) lash[1]

smak 1 flavour[1], savour noun, taste[1]; **wyrazisty** ~ tang; **bez ~u** bland; **mieć ~ (czegoś)** taste[2] (of sth); **napój mleczny o ~u truskawkowym** strawberry-flavoured milkshake **2** (*przen.: życia itp.*) savour noun; (*sukcesu itp.*) taste[1] **3** (*gust*) taste[1] (for sth)

smakołyki goodies

smakosz/ka epicure, foodie, gourmet

smakować 1 (/po-) taste[2] (of sth); (*być smacznym*) be to your liking **2 (/za-)** enjoy sth/doing sth

smakowity appetizing, delicious, luscious, mouth-watering, tasty

smalec lard

smar grease[1], lubricant

smark bogey; **(smark/i)** snot

smarować 1 (/po-) apply sth (to sth), smear[1] sth on/over sth, spread[1] A on/over B, B with A; (*olejem itp.*) lubricate; (*tłuszczem*) grease[2]; (*olejem*) oil verb **2** (*poruszać się szybko*) bomb[2] along, down, up, etc.

smażyć/u- (się) fry[1]; **smażyć metodą stir-fry** stir-fry

smecz smash[2]

smeczować smash[1]

smętny dismal

smoczek 1 (*do karmienia butelką*) teat **2** (*do uspokajania dzieci*) dummy

smog smog

smok dragon

smoking dinner jacket

smolist|y: **substancja ~a** (*w papierosie*) tar

smoła tar IDM **czarny jak** ~ jet black

smród pong, reek noun, stink noun

SMS SMS, text message ■ **SMS-owanie** text-messaging

smucić/za- grieve

smuga (*koloru itp.*) streak[1]; ~ **brudu** smudge noun; **pokryty ~mi** streaked

smukły slender

smut|ek heartache, melancholy, pathos, sadness, sorrow; **pełen ~ku** mournful, regretful(ly), sadly, sorrowfully
smutn|y blue[1], doleful, down[3], melancholy adj., rueful, sad IDM **~a mina** a long face
smycz lead[2]
smyczek 1 (*do grania na wiolonczeli itp.*) bow[3] **2** (**smyczki**) strings[1]
smyczkow|y: **instrumenty ~e** strings[1]
smykałk|a: **~a do interesów** good business sense IDM **mieć ~ę do ogrodnictwa** have green fingers
snajper marksman, sniper
snob/ka snob
snobistyczny snobbish
snobizm snobbery
snobowanie się snobbishness
snop 1 (*papierów itp.*) sheaf **2** (*światła*) beam[1], shaft
snowboard snowboard
snowboarding snowboarding
snowboardzist-a/ka snowboarder
snuć: ~ **domysły (na temat czegoś)** conjecture, speculate
sobie itself; ~ **(nawzajem)** each other IDM **tak** ~ so-so
sobkostwo selfishness
sobota Saturday; ~ **i niedziela** weekend
sobotni Saturday
sobowtór double[4], lookalike
soból sable
socha plough
socjalist-a/ka socialist
socjalistyczny socialist
socjalizm socialism
socjalny social
socjolog sociologist
socjologia sociology
socjologiczny sociological
soczewica lentil
soczewka lens; ~ **kontaktowa** contact lens
soczystość richness
soczysty 1 (*mięso, owoce itp.*) juicy, succulent **2** (*kolor*) mellow, rich
sofa settee, sofa
soja soya, soya bean(s)
sojowy soya
sojusz alliance
sojusznik ally[1]
sok 1 (*owocowy, warzywny*) juice; ~ **pomarańczowy** orange[1] **2** ~ **trawienny** juice **3** (*drzewa*) sap[1]
sokół falcon
sola (*ryba*) sole[2]
solanka brine
solić/po- salt[2]
solidarność solidarity
solidaryzować się: **(z kimś/czymś)** sympathize, be in sympathy (with sb/sth)
solidność reliability, solidity, sturdiness, toughness
solidn|y 1 (*ściana itp.*) solid[1], strong **2** (*ubranie*) sturdy; (*buty*) stout, tough; (*biżuteria itp.*) chunky **3** (*duży*) substantial; **~y posiłek** a square meal **4** (*osoba; firma*) reliable; (*podejście/stosunek do czegoś*) businesslike **5** **~a znajomość gramatyki** a firm grasp of grammar
■ **solidnie 1** (*zbudowany*) solidly **2** (*przymocowany*) securely
solist-a/ka soloist
solo solo[2]
solony salted
solowy solo[1]
solówka solo[2]
sonata sonata
sond|a 1 (*badanie*) probe[2] **2** (*instrument medyczny*) probe[2]; **badać ~ą** probe[1]
sondaż: **nieoficjalny** ~ straw poll
sondować/wy- (*opinię itp.*) probe[1] (into sth); **kogoś** sound sb out (about sth)
sonet sonnet
sopel: ~ **lodu** icicle
sopran soprano
sortować/prze- grade[2], sort[2]; (*wybrać*) pick[1]
sos sauce, dressing; (*zwł. US*) condiment; **gęsty** ~ dip[2]; ~ **pomidorowy** ketchup; ~ **sałatkowy** dressing; ~ **sojowy** soy sauce; ~ **własny** (*z mięsa*) jiuce
sosna pine[1]
sosnowy pine[1]
sośnina pine[1]
soul: **muzyka** ~ soul
soulowy soul
sowa owl
sowiecki Soviet
sód sodium
sójka (*uderzenie*) poke noun
sól salt[1]
spa spa
spacer walk[2], stroll, wander noun; **iść na** ~ go for a walk
spacerować/po- walk[1], stroll verb
spacerowicz/ka walker
spacj|a: **klawisz ~i** space bar
spać/prze- (się) be asleep, sleep[1]; (*krótko*) kip; **iść spać** go to sleep; **nie spać** be/keep/stay awake[1]; **spać głęboko** be sound asleep; **przespałem się godzinę** I grabbed an hour's sleep; **spać pod namiotem** camp[2] (out); (*zwykle bezdomni*) **spać byle gdzie** sleep rough
spa-dać/ść 1 (*osoba; przedmiot*) fall[1]; **(z czegoś)** come off (sth), fall off (sth); **spadać powoli** slide[1]; **West Ham spadł do drugiej ligi** West Ham were relegated to the Second Division **2** (*cena itp.*) decrease[1], drop[1], go down, plunge[1]; **gwałtownie spadać** nosedive verb, sink[1], plummet, slump[1], tumble **3** (*odpowiedzialność itp.*) **po śmierci ojca na mnie spadł obowiązek zajęcia się sprawami rodziny** when my father died it was down to me to look after the family's affairs IDM **spadać na cztery łapy** fall/land on your feet | **spadaj!** hop it!
spadek 1 (*cen itp.*) decrease[2], dip[2], drop[2], fall[2]; (*w biznesie: wartości akcji/zysków*) decline[1], downturn; **gwałtowny** ~ plunge, slump[2] **2** (*lawiny itp.*) fall[2] **3** (*terenu itp.*) dip[2], drop[2], slope **4** (*dziedzictwo*) bequest, inheritance, legacy
spadkobier-ca/czyni beneficiary, heir, successor
spadkow|y 1 tendencja ~a downward trend **2 podatek ~y** inheritance tax
spadochron parachute
spadochronia-rz/rka (*wykonując-y/a akrobatyczne skoki*) skydiver
spadzist|y (*dach*) sloping
s-pajać/poić bond[2], cement[2], join[1], piece sth together
■ **spajający** cohesive
□ **s-pajać/poić się** bond[2]
spa-lać/lić zob. też PALIĆ **1** (*paliwo*) burn[1] **2** (*zniszczyć za pomocą ognia*) burn sth off, burn sth out, incinerate; **spalać doszczętnie** burn sth down, burn sth up **3** (*na słońcu itp.*) bake IDM **spalić na panewce** fall flat
■ **spalanie** combustion
□ **spa-lać/lić się 1** (*ulegać zniszczeniu za pomocą ognia*) burn off; **spalić się doszczętnie** burn down **2** (*na słońcu itp.*) bake
spalinowy: **silnik** ~ internal combustion engine
spaliny exhaust[1], fumes
spalon|y 1 burnt-out; **~a słońcem pustynia Arizony** the scorched landscape of the Arizona desert **2** (*sport*) **zasada ~ego** the offside rule; **na ~ym** offside
spam spam
spaniel spaniel
spanikować → PANIKOWAĆ
sparafrazować → PARAFRAZOWAĆ
sparaliżować → PARALIŻOWAĆ
sparaliżowany (*ze strachu*) petrified
spartaczyć → PARTACZYĆ
spartański spartan IDM **żyć w warunkach ~ch** rough it
sparzyć się → PARZYĆ SIĘ
spaść → PADAĆ, SPADAĆ
spatrolować → PATROLOWAĆ
spawać/ze- weld
spazm spasm
spazmatyczny convulsive, spasmodic
specjalist-a/ka expert, specialist; (*nieform.*) boffin
specjalistyczn|y technical; **udzielić ~ej porady** give specialist advice
specjalizacja major[2], specialism, speciality, specialization
specjalizować/wy- się major in sth, specialize (in sth)
specjalnie especially, expressly, peculiarly, specially, specifically; ~ **dla kogoś** for sb's benefit
specjalność speciality
specjaln|y particular, special[1]; **szkoła ~a** special school; **więzienie pod ~ym nadzorem** maximum security prison IDM **nic ~ego** nothing much
specyficzność peculiarity
specyficzny idiosyncratic, individual[1], particular, peculiar, specific; (*dla kogoś/jakiegoś miejsca*) peculiar to sb/sth
specyfikacja specification
spektakularny runaway[1]
spektrum spectrum
spekulacja speculation
spekulacyjny speculative
spekulant/ka adventurer, speculator
spekulatywny speculative
spekulować (*domyśliwać; fin.*) speculate
speleologia potholing
spelunka a seedy nightclub
spełni(a)ć zob. też PEŁNIĆ; (*zadanie*) discharge[1], fulfil, perform; (*rozkaz*) comply (with sth); (*wymagania*) satisfy; (*czyjeś potrzeby*) accommodate; (*ambicję itp.*) realize; (*obietnice*) deliver (on sth); **spełnić groźbę** carry out a threat; ~ **czyjeś zachcianki** humour[2]; ~ **czyjeś oczekiwania** live up to sth
□ **spełni(a)ć się 1** (*życzenie*) come true **2** (*zawodowo itp.*) fulfil yourself

spełnienie fruition, fulfilment, realization; ~ **marzeń** a dream come true
spełznąć zob. też PEŁZNĄĆ IDM ~ **na niczym** misfire, go up in smoke
sperma semen, sperm
speszony mixed-up
speszyć → PESZYĆ
spę-dzać/dzić 1 (*czas*) spend; **miło ~ czas** enjoy yourself **2** (*zgromadzić w jednym miejscu*) round sb/sth up
spętać → PĘTAĆ
spiąć (się) → SPINAĆ (SIĘ)
spichlerz granary
spiczasty pointed
spiec się (*na słońcu*) catch the sun
spieczony parched
spienię-żać/żyć cash[2]
spieprzyć → PIEPRZYĆ
spierać się argue, quarrel[2]; (*o szczegóły/coś nieważnego*) quibble ■ **spieranie się** hassle[1]
spierzchnięty chapped
spieszyć się → ŚPIESZYĆ SIĘ
spięcie: **krótkie** ~ short circuit
spięt|y fraught, het up, tense[1], uptight; (*zamknięty w sobie*) inhibited; **stawać się ~ym** tense[3] (up)
spiker/ka announcer
spinacz paper clip; **duży** ~ (*o walcowatym grzbiecie z dwiema metalowymi wypustkami*) Bulldog clip
spi-nać/ąć 1 (*spinaczem*) clip[2]; (*klamrą*) buckle[1]; (*szpilką*) pin[2] **2 ~ na krótko** short-circuit verb **3 ~ ostrogami** (*konia*) spur[2] sth (on/ onto sth)
□ **spi-nać/ąć się** (*spinaczem*) clip[2]; (*klamrą*) buckle[1]
spinka (*do kołnierzyka*) stud; ~ **do mankietów** cufflink; ~ **do włosów** hair clip, hairgrip, hairpin
spirala curl[2], spiral
spiralny spiral adj.
spirytus: ~ **metylowy** methylated spirit
spirytusowy alcoholic[1]
spirytyst-a/ka spiritualist
spirytyzm spiritualism
spis list, register[2], table; (*instytucji itp.*) directory; (*dostarczonych towarów; wykonanych prac itp.*) docket; ~ **alfabetyczny** index; ~ **kontrolny** checklist; ~ **ludności** census; ~ **treści** table of contents; ~ **wyborców** electoral register/roll; **tworzyć** ~ list verb
spisek conspiracy, plot[1]
spiskować conspire, plot[2], scheme[2]
spiskowiec conspirator
spis(yw)ać 1 (*tworzyć listę*) list verb; ~ **protokół** take the minutes **2 ~ nazwisko** book[2] **3 ~ coś na straty** write sth off; ~ **kogoś/coś na straty (jako coś)** write sb/sth off (as sth)
□ **spis(yw)ać się** acquit yourself…; **dobrze się** ~ carry it/sth off
spity plastered
spiżarnia larder, pantry
splajtować → PLAJTOWAĆ
s-platać/pleść entwine, intertwine; (*włosy, sznur itp.*) plait
□ **s-platać/pleść się** intertwine
splądrować → PLĄDROWAĆ
splecion|y entwined; **być ~ym** (*np. w uścisku*) be locked together/in sth
spleśniały mouldy, musty
splot 1 tangle, twist[2] **2** (*zagadnień itp.*) strand; ~ **wydarzeń** the complex chain of events
splugawić → PLUGAWIĆ
spła-cać/cić (*dług itp.*) pay sth back (to sb), pay sth off, pay up, repay, settle up (with sb), square up (with sb); (*u lichwiarza itp.*) redeem; (*udziały partnera w firmie itp.*) buy sb out
spłasz-czać/czyć (się) flatten
spłata payment, repayment
spłatać zob. też PŁATAĆ IDM ~ **komuś figla** play a joke/a trick/tricks on sb
spławny navigable
spłodzić → PŁODZIĆ
spłonąć → PŁONĄĆ
spłoszyć (się) → PŁOSZYĆ (SIĘ)
spłowieć → PŁOWIEĆ
spłukan|y broke[2], penniless, skint IDM **być ~ym** be hard up (for sth)
spłuk(iw)ać 1 (*do kanalizacji*) flush[1] sth away, down, etc.; ~ **toaletę** flush[1] **2** (*naczynia*) rinse
□ **spłuk(iw)ać się** (*toaleta*) flush[1]
spły-cać/cić (*zagadnienie itp.*) oversimplify
spływ: ~ **górski** white-water rafting
spły-wać/nąć 1 (*woda*) pour; **po czymś** run down sth; **czymś** run with sth; ~ **miękko** flow[2]; **łzy spływały jej po policzkach** tears were pouring down her cheeks **2** (*ludzie, rzeczy*) ~ **obficie** stream[2] **3** (*zniknąć*) clear off, get lost
spocić się → POCIĆ SIĘ
spocony sweaty; **obudził się cały** ~ he woke up in a sweat
spoczynek: **udawać się na** ~ retire
spodek saucer
spodnie trousers, slacks; (*pidżamy itp.*) bottoms[1]; **krótkie** ~ shorts; ~ **ogrodniczki** dungarees
spodobać się → PODOBAĆ SIĘ
spodziewać się 1 (*sądzić*) expect, hope[1], think; **nie spodziewający się niczego złego** unsuspecting; ~ **czegoś** gamble on sth/on doing sth **2** (*mieć coś robić*) be due (to do sth)[1]; **należy się spodziewać** be likely (to do sth)
spodziewany in the offing, prospective
spoglądać/spojrzeć 1 ~ w górę look up **2 ~ w przyszłość** look ahead (to sth)
spoić (się) → SPAJAĆ (SIĘ)
spojrzeć zob. też PATRZEĆ; glance[1]; ~ **prosto w twarz** face[2] IDM **spójrzmy prawdzie w oczy** let's face it
spojrzenie look[2], peep[2]; ~ **pełne gniewu/nienawiści itp.** glare[2]; ~ **na świat** outlook
spokojny calm[1], controlled, cool[1], easy[1], imperturbable, mellow, orderly[1], peaceful, phlegmatic, placid, poised, quiet[1], sedate[1], tranquil; (*woda itp.*) still[2]; **być/czuć się ~m** be/ feel at (your) ease; **bądź (o to)** ~ no fear
spokój calmness, calm[3], composure, coolness, peace, peacefulness, poise, quietness, quiet[2], stillness; **zachowywać/tracić** ~ keep/lose your cool; **dawać komuś** ~ get off sb's back; **nie dawać komuś spokoju** keep on (at sb) (about sb/sth), nag, persecute; **nie dający komuś spokoju** haunting; **dać sobie z kimś** ~ give sb up, give up on sb; **daj ~!** come off it
spokrewniony related
spolaryzować → POLARYZOWAĆ
spoliczkować → POLICZKOWAĆ
społeczeństwo society
społeczność community; ~ **miejscowa** the local population
społeczn|y civil, social; **praca ~a** community service
sponiewierać → PONIEWIERAĆ
sponiewierany downtrodden
sponsor/ka backer, sponsor; (*organizacji charytatywnej itp.*) patron
sponsorować/za- sponsor verb
sponsorowanie sponsorship
spontanicznie on (an) impulse, spontaneously, on the spur of the moment
spontaniczność spontaneity
spontaniczny spontaneous, unsolicited
spopiel-ać/ić incinerate
spopularyzować → POPULARYZOWAĆ
sporadyczny few and far between, intermittent, occasional, sporadic
sporn|y arguable, contentious, debatable; **kwestia/sprawa ~a** a matter of opinion
sporo a bit[1], a good/great deal (of sth), a good few, quite a few, many, much[1], quite a lot (of)
sport game[1], sport; ~ **ekstremalny** extreme sport; ~ **widowiskowy** spectator sport; **~y wodne** water sports; **~y zimowe** winter sports
sportow|iec athlete, sportsman; (**sportowcy**) sports people
sportowy athletic, sporting; **sprzęt** ~ (*zwł. wędkarski*) tackle[2]
sportretować → PORTRETOWAĆ
sportsmenka athlete, sportswoman
spory considerable, fair[1]
sporzą-dzać/dzić 1 (*coś z wielu składników itp.*) concoct **2** (*lekarstwa*) dispense **3** (*schemat, mapę itp.*) draw sth up; (*czek itp.*) make sth out; ~ **mapę/plan** map[2]; ~ **rozkład** schedule[2] sth (for sth); ~ **indeks/ skorowidz** index verb
sposobność occasion, opening, opportunity, place[1], scope
sposób approach[2], fashion, manner, means, method, mode, plan[1], route, technique, way[1]; **w ten** ~ so[1], thereby, thus; **w ten sam** ~ like[1]; **w inny** ~ otherwise IDM **w żaden** ~ by no means, not by any means
spostrze-gać/c spot[2]
spostrzegawczość observation
spostrzegawczy observant, perceptive
spostrzeżenie observation, remark noun
spośród out of
spotęgować → POTĘGOWAĆ
spotkać (się) → SPOTYKAĆ (SIĘ)
spotkanie get-together, meeting; **nieoczekiwanie i nieprzyjemne** ~ encounter[2]; **umówione** ~ appointment, date[1], engagement, rendezvous; ~ **towarzyskie** party
spot(y)kać meet; (*niespodziewanie*) encounter[1]

□ **spot(y)kać się 1 z kimś** get together (with sb), meet, meet up (with sb), meet with sb; (*na randce*) date[2], go out (together), go out (with sb) **2 z czymś** encounter[1], meet with sth **3** (*z ostrą krytyką itp.*) come in for sth
spowalni(a)ć slow sb/sth down/up
spowiadać/wy- się confess
spowiedź confession
spowi(j)ać envelop; **wioskę spowijała poranna mgła** the village was swathed in early morning mist
spowinowacony related by marriage
spowodować → POWODOWAĆ
spowodowany: **czymś/przez kogoś** due[1] to sb/sth
spowszednieć → POWSZEDNIEĆ
spożycie consumption, intake
spożytkować utilize
spoży(wa)ć consume
■ **spożywanie** intake
spożywcz|y: **artykuły ~e** groceries; **sklep ~y** grocery
spód 1 bottom[1], the underneath, underside **2** (*podnóże; dół, np. strony*) foot[1]
spódnica skirt[1]
spódniczka skirt[1]; **uganianie się za ~mi** womanizing
spójnik conjunction
spójność coherence, cohesion
spójny coherent, cohesive
spółdzielczy cooperative[1]
spółdzielnia collective[2], cooperative[2]
spółk|a corporation, partnership; **~a akcyjna** public company; **~a typu joint venture** joint venture; **~a z ograniczoną odpowiedzialnością** limited company; **zawiązać ~ę** go into partnership (with sb) IDM **do ~i** between
spółkować copulate
spór argument, contention, debate[1], dispute[1], strife; (*między rodzinami itp.*) feud; **~ prawny** legal wrangle; **~ sądowy** litigation; **toczyć ~** feud verb; **być przedmiotem sporu**; **być w trakcie sporu** be in dispute
spóźni(a)ć się zob. też PÓŹNIĆ SIĘ; **na coś** miss[1]; **~ o dziesięć minut** be ten minutes late (for sth); **pociąg spóźnia się o dwadzieścia minut** the train is twenty minutes behind schedule; **~ z czynszem** be late with the rent; **ten zegar spóźnia się pięć minut** that clock is five minutes slow; **mój zegarek trochę się spóźnia** my watch is a bit slow
spóźnialsk-i/a latecomer
spóźnienie hold-up; **przepraszam za ~** I'm sorry I'm late
spóźnion-y/a latecomer
spóźnion|y belated, late, overdue
sprać się wash out
spragnion|y 1 thirsty; **bardzo ~y** parched **2 wiedzy itp.** avid for sth, desperate (for sth/to do sth), hungry for sth; **być ~ym czegoś** be starved of sth, hunger for/after sth
spraw|a 1 (*problem*) issue[1], matter[1], proposition, question[1]; (*trudna sytuacja*) affair, business; **w ~ie czegoś** into; **robić z czegoś dużą ~ę** make an issue (out) of sth; **~a życia lub śmierci** a matter of life and/or death; **w ~ie kogoś/czegoś** in connection with sb/sth, in this/that/one regard, in/with regard to sb/sth, in/with relation to sb/sth **2** (**czyjaś**) affair, business, concern[2], job; **nie twoja ~a** it's nothing to do with you **3** (**sprawy**) affairs, business; **Minister Spraw Wewnętrznych** the Home Secretary; **Minister Spraw Zagranicznych Francji** the French Foreign Minister **4** (*rzecz istotna, przedmiot zainteresowania*) cause[1] **5** (*prawn.*) case; **~a sądowa** prosecution, proceedings; **wnosić ~ę do sądu** file a lawsuit IDM **nie ma ~y** fair enough, no problem
spraw-dzać/dzić 1 check[1], check on sb/sth, check sb/sth out, check up on sth, examine sb/sth (for sth), go over sth, inspect, test[2], try[1] (doing) sth, verify; (*med. itp.*) screen[2] sb (for sth); (*egzaminować*) examine sb (in/on sth); **czy** make sure; **~ ponownie/dokładnie** double-check; **sprawdzić nasze pomysły w praktyce** put our ideas into practice **2 kogoś** (*np. czy nie blefuje*) call sb's bluff **3** (*w słowniku itp.*) consult sth (about sth), look sth up
□ **spraw-dzać/dzić się**
1 (*przepowiednia itp.*) come true
2 (*mieć zadatki na coś*) come into your own, make[1] **3** (*potwierdzić swoją przydatność/skuteczność w działaniu*) prove yourself (to sb)
sprawdzian test[1]
sprawi(a)ć 1 cause[2], have[1], give[1] sb sth, sth to sb; **uczenie sprawia jej dużo przyjemności** she gets a lot of enjoyment from teaching; **wnuki sprawiają mu wiele radości** he takes great pleasure in his grandchildren **2** (*ryby itp.*) gut[2]
sprawiedliwoś|ć fairness, justice; **minister ~ci** Attorney General IDM **oddawać komuś ~ć** give sb his/her due | **po ~ci** by rights
sprawiedliw|y balanced, equitable, even-handed, fair[1], fair-minded, just[2], righteous; **~y i uczciwy** square[1]
■ **sprawiedliwie** deservedly, equitably, fairly, justly
sprawny 1 (*urządzenie*) efficient, functional, operational, in working order; **~ manualnie** practical[1] **2** (*osoba*) capable, efficient, proficient; (*w ruchach*) agile
sprawować: **~ nadzór nad czymś** preside over sth; **~ nad kimś/czymś pieczę** watch over sb/sth
sprawowanie conduct[2]; **złe ~** misdemeanour
sprawozdanie commentary, report[2]; **szczegółowe ~** a blow-by-blow account/description, etc. (of sth); **zdawać ~** report back (on sth) (to sb)
sprawozdaw-ca/czyni commentator, reporter
sprawunki shopping
spray spray[1]; **farba w ~u** spray paint; **pojemnik ze ~em** spray can
sprecyzować → PRECYZOWAĆ
sprecyzowany precise
spreparować → PREPAROWAĆ
sprężenie compression
sprężyna spring[1]
sprężystość elasticity
sprężysty springy; (*krok itp.*) lithe, nimble
sprint sprint noun; **biec ~em** sprint
sprofanować → PROFANOWAĆ
sprostać: **czemuś** meet; **czułem, że całkowicie nie umiem ~ wymaganiom** I felt totally inadequate
sprostować → PROSTOWAĆ
sproszkować → PROSZKOWAĆ
sproszkowany powdered
sprośność lewdness, obscenity
sprośn|y bawdy, dirty[1], filthy, foul[1], lewd, obscene, rude; **~e słowa/zdjęcia itp.** filth
sprowa-dzać/dzić bring; (*z innego kraju*) import[2]; (*na inny temat itp.*) steer; **kogoś** bring sb in; **sprowadzić na kogoś nieszczęście** plague[2]
□ **sprowa-dzać/dzić się**: **do czegoś** boil down to sth, come down to sth/to doing sth; **sprowadzający się do czegoś** tantamount to sth
sprowokować → PROWOKOWAĆ
sprowokowany: **niczym nie ~** unprovoked
spróbować → PRÓBOWAĆ
spróchniał|y rotten; **deski podłogi są ~e** the floorboards have got rot in them
sprysk(iw)ać się be treated with insecticide
spryt cunning noun
sprytny crafty, sharp[1]
■ **sprytnie** craftily, cunningly
sprywatyzować → PRYWATYZOWAĆ
sprzączka buckle[2]
sprzątacz cleaner
sprzątaczka cleaner, cleaning lady
sprzątać/po-/sprzątnąć clean (sth) up, do the cleaning, clear (sth) up, tidy[2] (sb/sth/yourself) (up); **sprzątnąć naczynia ze stołu** clear the dishes away; **posprzątać ze stołu** clear the table
sprzątnąć zob. też SPRZĄTAĆ; **kogoś** zap
sprzeciw objection, opposition, protest[1], reaction (against sb/sth), resistance; (*na forum ONZ itp.*) veto noun; **ostry ~** backlash; **głośny ~** outcry
sprzeciwi(a)ć się baulk (at sth), contradict, defy, disobey, go against sb/sth, object[2], oppose, protest[2], react against sb/sth; **~ komuś** cross[2]; **stanowczo ~** strongly disagree with sth
■ **sprzeciwiając|y się** resistant (to sth); **osoba sprzeciwiająca się** objector
sprzeczać/po- się argue, have an argument (with sb), disagree, quarrel[2]
sprzeczka argument, contention, difference, disagreement, quarrel[1]; (*głośna*) row[3]; (*nieform.*) bunfight, tiff
sprzeczność clash[2], conflict[1], contradiction, discrepancy
sprzeczny contradictory, dissonant, inconsistent; **być ~m** conflict[2], contradict, disagree, go against sb/sth; **nie być ze sobą ~m** not be mutually exclusive
sprzedajny crooked
sprzeda(wa)ć 1 sell; (*nieform.*) flog; **~ po cenie niższej niż konkurencja** undercut **2** (**sprzedać**) (*mecz, wyścig itp.*) fix[1]
□ **sprzeda(wa)ć się** sell
sprzedaw-ca/czyni salesperson, seller, vendor; (**sprzedawca**) salesman; (**sprzedawczyni**) saleswoman; (*w sklepie*) shop assistant; **sprzedawca (detaliczny)** retailer
sprzedaż sale; **~ wysyłkowa** mail order; **prowadzić ~** sell; **być na ~** be up

for sale; **na** ~ for sale, available; **w ~y** on the market, on sale; **możliwy do ~y** marketable
sprze-niewierzać/niewierzyć embezzle, misappropriate
sprzęgło clutch[2]
sprzęt apparatus, gear[1], hardware, implements[2], kit[1], paraphernalia, utensils; ~ **komputerowy** hardware; ~ **sportowy** (*zwł. wędkarski*) tackle[2]
sprzyjać promote; **sprzyjający (czemuś/komuś)** propitious (for sth/sb); **niesprzyjający czemuś** inimical to sth; **ten upał nie sprzyja ciężkiej pracy** this hot weather is not conducive to hard work
sprzyjający conducive (to sth), favourable; (*zbieg okoliczności itp.*) happy
sprzykrzyć się pall
sprzy-mierzać/mierzyć się: **z kimś/czymś** ally[2] (yourself) with sb/sth
sprzymierzeniec ally[1]
sprzymierzony allied
sprzy-sięgać/siąc się: **(przeciwko komuś/czemuś)** conspire (against sb/sth)
sprzysiężeni|e: **w ~u z kimś** in league (with sb)
spuchnąć → PUCHNĄĆ
spuchnięty swollen[2]
spust trigger[1]
spustoszenie desolation, devastation, havoc
spustoszyć → PUSTOSZYĆ
s-puszczać/puścić let sth down, lower[2]; ~ **powietrze** (*np. z balonika*) let sth down; ~ **wodę** (*w toalecie*) flush the toilet; **spuścić psa ze smyczy** let a dog loose; ~ **z tonu** moderate[2] IDM **nie ~ kogoś/czegoś z oka** keep a close watch on sb/sth
□ **s-puszczać/puścić się**: ~ **się po linie** abseil (down, off, etc. sth)
spuszczony downcast
spuścizna heritage, inheritance
spychacz bulldozer
spytać → PYTAĆ
squash squash[2]
srebrn|y 1 (*ze srebra*) silver[2]; **~a moneta/pieniądz** silver[1]; **~y medal** silver medal; **~-y/a medalist-a/ka** silver medallist **2** (*przypominający srebro*) silvery **3** (*dwudziestopięciolecie*) silver[2]
srebro silver[1]; ~ **stołowe** silverware
srebrzysty silvery
srogi 1 (*osoba*) cruel, severe, stern[1], strict **2** (*mróz*) hard[1], severe IDM **~e brytany** fierce dogs
sroka magpie
srom vulva
sromotn|y ignominious; **~a klęska** hammering; **jako aktor poniósł ~ą klęskę** he failed miserably as an actor
ssać/wy- suck
ssak mammal; ~ **naczelny** primate
ssanie 1 (*fiz.*) suction **2** (*w samochodzie*) choke[2] **3** ~ **w żołądku** hunger pangs
ssawka (*owada itp.*) sucker
stabilizacja stability
stabilizować/u- stabilize
stabilność stability
stabilny secure[1], stable[1]
stacja 1 (*autobusowa itp.*) stop[2]; ~ **kolejowa** station[1] **2** (*radio*) station[1]; (*TV*) channel[1] **3** ~ **benzynowa** petrol station; ~ **obsługi** garage; ~ **obsługi przy autostradzie** motorway service station **4** (*dysków*) disk drive, drive[2]
stacjonarny stationary; **komputer** ~ desktop computer
stacjonować station[2]
sta-ć/nąć 1 (*być w pozycji pionowej*) stand[1]; **sobie** stand around; (*waza itp.: na stałym miejscu*) go[1]; ~ **w kolejce** line up (for sth); (*przen.*) **przedsiębiorstwo stoi teraz mocno na nogach** the company is now on a firm footing **2** (*znieruchomieć*) come to a halt, hold on; **stój!** hold it!; **ceny stanęły w miejscu na 89p** share prices languished at 89p **2 kogoś na coś** afford sth/to do sth **3** (*umowa*) **stoi!** done[3]; **w końcu stanęło na tym, że poszliśmy** we ended up going out for a meal **4** (*w jakiejś sprawie*) stand[1] IDM **stać między kimś/czymś a czymś** stand between sb/sth and sth | (*przen.*) **stanąć na nogi** find your feet | **stać na stanowisku** stand[1] (on sth) | **~ przy kimś** stand by sb | **~ przed czymś** be faced with sth | (*przen.*) **~ w miejscu** get nowhere (with sb/sth) | **~ za czymś** be at the bottom of sth
stać się → STAWAĆ SIĘ
stadion stadium
stadium phase[1], stage[1]
stadnina stud
stadny social
stado (*bydła*) herd[1]; (*wilków itp.*) pack[2]; (*ptaków*) flock[1]; (*ryb*) school
stagnacj|a depression, plateau, stagnation; **być w ~i** stagnate
stagnacyjny stagnant
stajać → TAJAĆ
stajenny groom[2]
stajnia barn, stable[2]
stal steel[1]; ~ **nierdzewna** stainless steel
stale always, constantly, forever, habitually, permanently, perpetually, persistently
stalówka nib
stałocieplny warm-blooded
stałość permanence, persistence
stał|y 1 (*uczucie; problem itp.*) constant, enduring, persistent; (*problem*) chronic **2** (*adres; praca*) permanent; (*praca*) steady[1], tenured; **prawo ~ego pobytu** the right of abode, residency; **bez ~ego miejsca zamieszkania** (of) no fixed abode/address **3** (*klient; dochód*) regular[1]; **~-y/a klient/ka itp.** regular[2]; **stracić wielu ~ych klientów** lose a lot of custom **4** (*oprocentowanie, cena*) fixed **5** (*umowa itp.*) standing[1] **6** (*ciało; paliwo*) solid[1]; **dziecko nie przeszło jeszcze na pokarm ~y** the baby is not yet on solids; **~y ląd** dry land
stamtąd thence
stan 1 (*sytuacji; emocji; zdrowia*) shape[1], state[1], condition[1]; (*sytuacja*) circumstance; (*zdrowia*) health; **w dobrym ~ie** sound[3]; **w złym ~ie** out of condition; **w dobrym/złym itp. ~ie** in good, bad, etc. repair, in good/bad nick; **ciężki** ~ plight; ~ **faktyczny** case; ~ **rzeczy** showing, state of affairs; **istniejący** ~ **rzeczy** the status quo; ~ **umysłu** state of mind; **(nie) być w ~ie coś/czegoś zrobić** be able/unable to do sth, (not) be in a position to do sth, (not) be up to sth; **będący w ~ie coś zrobić** capable of (doing) sth **2** (*status*) ~ **cywilny** status; ~ **duchowny** ministry; ~ **małżeński** marriage; ~ **wojenny** martial law; **w ~ie wojny** at war; ~ **wyjątkowy** a state of emergency **3** (*polit.*) state[1] **4** (*sukienki itp.*) waist, waistline
stanąć zob. też STAĆ, STAWAĆ; ~ **w płomieniach** burst into flames, go up in flames
standard benchmark, norm, standard[1]
standardowy standard[2]
standaryzacja standardization
standaryzować/u- standardize
stanie: ~ **w miejscu** standstill; ~ **na rękach** handstand
stanik bra; (*u sukienki*) bodice; **bez ~a** topless; **w stroju kąpielowym bez ~a** sunbathe topless
stanowczo assertively, categorically, decisively, definitively, emphatically, firmly, flatly, insistently, resolutely; (*przekonany itp.*) positively; ~ **nie** by no means, not by any means
stanowczość assertiveness, decision, decisiveness, firmness, resolution
stanowczy assertive, categorical, decisive, emphatic, firm[2], flat[1], insistent, resolute, strong; (*działanie itp.*) positive
stanowić account for sth, comprise, constitute, qualify (as sth); (*ryzyko itp.*) pose[1]
stanowisko 1 (*posada*) appointment, capacity, office, post[1], position[1] **2** (*zdanie*) position[1], stance, stand[2] (on/against sth), standing[2], standpoint; **zajmować ~ w sprawie** commit yourself (on sth) **3** ~ **komputerowe** workstation
stanowy state[2]
s-tapiać/topić fuse[2]
starać/po- się endeavour, seek (to do sth), try[1]; **o coś** solicit, try for sth; (*o pracę*) look for/apply for /find a job; **bardzo się** ~ go all out for sth, go all out to do sth, go out of your way (to do sth), go to great lengths, take trouble over/with sth, take trouble to do sth/doing sth
stara|nie effort, endeavour noun; **dokładać wszelkich ~ń (, żeby)** do/try your best, be at/take (great) pains to do sth, take (great) pains (with/over sth)
starannoś|ć care[1] (over sth/in doing sth), neatness, tidiness; **brak ~ci** negligence
staranny assiduous, careful, neat, painstaking, tidy[1]
staranować → TARANOWAĆ
starcie 1 (*szmatą itp.*) wipe[2] **2** (*sprzeczka*) clash[2]
starczy senile
starczyć/wy-: **(komuś) na coś** last[4]
staroangielski Anglo-Saxon
starocie bric-a-brac
starodawny ancient, old
staromodny old-fashioned, old hat
starość age[1], old age; (*zabytku, mebla itp.*) antiquity
staroświecki old-fashioned, old hat, quaint, stuffy
starożytność antiquity
starożytny ancient
starszeństwo seniority

star|szy 1 senior[1]; *(brat/siostra)* big, elder[1]; **~si ludzie** the aged, the old **2** *(rangą)* senior[1] (to sb)
■ **starsz-y/a** elder[2]
start start[2]; *(samolotu)* take-off; *(rakiety)* lift-off IDM **do ~u, gotowi, hop!** on your marks, get set, go!
startować/wy- take off; *(rakieta)* lift off
staruszkowie the old
star|y old; **bardzo ~y** ancient; **~ej daty** old-fashioned; **ludzie ~si** the elderly, the old
■ **stary** *(rz., nieform.: mówiąc do mężczyzny)* mate[1] | **staro: wygląda bardzo ~!** he looks ancient!
starzeć/ze- się age[2], get on, grow older; *(tylko przedmioty)* date[2]
starzyzna junk
statecznik fin; ~ **poziomy** tailplane
stateczny sedate[1], staid
statek boat, craft, ship[1], vessel; ~ **dalekomorski** liner; ~ **rybacki** trawler; ~ **towarowy** cargo ship; ~ **kosmiczny** spaceship
statua statue
status: ~ **społeczny** status
statut charter[1], statute
statyczny static[1]
statyst-a/ka extra[2]
statystyczny statistical
statystyk statistician
statystyka statistics
statyw tripod
staw 1 *(wodny)* pond **2** *(anat.)* joint[2], socket; *(palca)* knuckle[1]
sta-wać/nąć 1 *(zatrzymać się)* stop[1]; *(pociąg itp.)* call[1] at…; *(urządzenie)* conk out, give out; *(samochód)* stall[2] *(silnik)* **stanąć na baczność** snap to attention **2** ~ **prosto** straighten up **3 przed kimś/jakimś zadaniem** confront sth **4** ~ **w obronie kogoś/czegoś** stand up for sb/sth; ~ **po czyjejś stronie (przeciw komuś)** side with sb (against sb), take sides (with sb) **5** ~ **na czele** spearhead verb **6** *(do konkursu itp.)* go in for/enter a competition IDM ~ **dęba** *(koń)* rear[2] (up); *(jeżyć się)* bristle[2] | ~ **na (własne) nogi** stand on your own (two) feet | **stanąć na nogi o własnych siłach** pull/drag yourself up by your (own) bootstraps
□ **sta(wa)ć się 1** *(robić się)* become, get, go[1], grow, make[1], turn[1] **2** *(zdarzyć się)* become of sb/sth, happen to sb/sth; **co jej się stało?** what's the matter with her?; **co się stało z samochodem?** what's wrong with the car?; **jak to się stało, że…?** how come…?; **jak to się stało, że zgubiłeś swój paszport?** how did you come to lose your passport?; **sprawdzić, czy nikomu nic się nie stało** check that all the passengers are safe; **czy coś się stanie, jeśli się trochę spóźnimy?** does it matter if we are a little bit late? **3 komuś** get into sb IDM **nic się nie stało!** no harm done, it doesn't matter
stawiać/postawić 1 *(umieszczać)* put[1], place[2], stand[1]; *(ogrodzenie itp.)* put sth up; *(pomnik itp.)* erect[2]; *(na miejsce)* replace; **gdzie postawić tę wazę?** where does this vase go? **2** *(na straży itp.)* post[2]; ~ **kogoś w jakimś położeniu** put sb in/into sth **3** *(pytanie)* pose[1] **4** *(pieniądze)* back[4]; *(hazard)* bet, gamble[1], put sth on sth, put money on sth, wager verb **5** *(opór)* put up sth; ~ **opór** take/make a stand against sth **6** ~ **czoło komuś/czemuś** brave[2], confront, stand up to sb/sth **7** ~ **kogoś/coś w złym/dobrym świetle** project[2] IDM **ja stawiam!** *(drinki)* the drinks are on me!, it's my round, my treat | **postawić na swoim** get/have your own way, put your foot down | ~ **kogoś na nogi** set sb up
□ **stawiać/postawić się** IDM **postawić się na czyimś miejscu** put yourself in sb's place
stawienie się presence
stawiennictw|o: nakaz ~a summons
stawka 1 *(w grze)* stake[1] **2** *(godzinowa)* rate[1]
staż residency, work experience; *(w szpitalu)* internship; **lekarz pracujący w szpitalu na ~u** house officer, intern[2]
stąd away (from sth), hence
stąpać pace[2], step[2], tread[1]; *(sztywno)* stump[2]; **ciężko** ~ plod, stamp[2], stomp, tramp[2]
stchórzyć → TCHÓRZYĆ
stek 1 *(mięso)* steak **2** *(kłamstw itp.)* crop[1]; *(przekleństw itp.)* volley; ~ **bzdur** a pack of lies
stempel rubber stamp, stamp[1]; ~ **pocztowy** postmark
stemplować/o- stamp[2]
stenografia shorthand
stenografować write in shorthand
stenotypist-a/ka shorthand typist
step 1 *(zwł. północnoamerykański)* prairie **2** *(taniec)* tap dance
stepować tap dance
ster 1 *(koło sterowe itp.)* helm **2** *(z tyłu łodzi)* rudder IDM **być u ~u (czegoś)** be in control (of sth), be at the helm
sterany jaded
sterburta starboard
sterczący spiky
sterczeć jut (out), overhang, project[2], protrude, stick out; ~ **do góry** stick up
sterczyna pinnacle
stereo (także **stereofonia**) stereo; **zestaw** ~ stereo
stereofoniczny stereo adj.; **zestaw** ~ stereo
stereotyp stereotype
stereotypowy conventional, stereotypical
steroid: ~ **anaboliczny** anabolic steroid
sterować 1 steer; *(samolotem)* fly[1]; *(statkiem)* navigate; **systemy sterowane komputerowo** computer-controlled systems **2** ~ **z ukrycia** *(sprawami)* engineer[2]
sterownia control[1]
sterownicz|y: urządzenie ~e controls[1]
sterroryzować → TERRORYZOWAĆ
sterta heap[1], mound, mountain
steryd steroid; ~ **anaboliczny** anabolic steroid
sterylizacja sterilization
sterylizować/wy- sterilize
sterylny sterile
stetoskop stethoscope
steward steward, flight attendant
stewardesa air hostess, flight attendant, stewardess
stęchły mouldy, musty, stale
stępi(a)ć blunt verb
stępka keel[1]
stęskniony: ~ **za domem/ojczyzną** homesick (for sth)
stężeć → TĘŻEĆ
stężenie concentration
stężony concentrated
stiuk stucco
s-tłaczać/tłoczyć jam[2] sb/sth in, under, between, etc. sth
□ **s-tłaczać/tłoczyć się** huddle[1] (up) (together)
stłoczony on top of sb/sth
stłuc (się) → TŁUC (SIĘ)
stłuczenie break[2]
stłuczka breakage
stłumić → TŁUMIĆ
stłumienie suppression
stłumiony *(dźwięk)* muffled, muted
sto hundred IDM ~ **lat!** *(w życzeniach urodzinowych)* many happy returns (of the day)
stocznia dock[1], shipyard; *(firma budująca statki)* shipbuilder
stoczniowiec shipbuilder
stoczyć (się) → TOCZYĆ (SIĘ)
stodoła barn
stoicki stoic
stoicyzm stoicism
stoisko stall[1], stand[2]
stojak prop[1], stand[2]
stojący 1 upright **2** *(woda)* stagnant
stok hillside; ~ **górski** mountainside
stokrotka daisy
stolarka carpentry, joinery, woodwork
stolarstwo woodwork
stolarz carpenter; ~ **budowlany** joiner
stolec faeces
stolica capital[1]
stolik table; ~ **do kawy** coffee table; ~ **na kółkach** *(z którego podaje się jedzenie lub napoje)* trolley
stołek stool
stołówka cafeteria, canteen; ~ **wojskowa** mess[1]
stomatolog dentist
stomatologia dentistry
stomatologiczny dental
stonować → TONOWAĆ
stonowany soft, subdued; *(oświadczenie)* sober[1]
stop alloy
stop|a 1 *(anat.)* foot[1]; *(spodnia część stopy/buta)* sole[2]; **pod ~ami** underfoot; **specjalist-a/ka od chorób stóp** chiropodist; **pielęgnacja stóp** chiropody **2** *(procentowa, podatkowa)* rate[1]; **~a inflacji** the inflation rate/rate of inflation **3 na ~ie towarzyskiej** socially
stoper 1 *(sport)* stopwatch **2** *(do ucha)* earplug
stopić (się) → STAPIAĆ, TOPIĆ (SIĘ)
stop|ień 1 *(miary)* degree, grade[1], measure[2], notch[1]; **~ień podziałki** gradation; **do pewnego ~nia** as it were, to a certain/to some extent, up to a point, in a sense; **do jakiego ~nia** to what extent; **w większym ~niu** further adv.; **w wysokim ~niu** remarkably; **w najmniejszym ~niu** remotely **2** *(w hierarchii)* rung[1]; *(wojskowy)* rank[1] **3 ~ień naukowy** degree **4** *(szk.: ocena)* grade[1], mark[2], result[1]; **~ień końcowy na studiach** class[1] **5** *(gram.)* **~ień wyższy** comparative[2]; **~ień najwyższy** superlative
stopnieć → TOPNIEĆ
stopniowanie gradation

stopniowy gradual, progressive
■ **stopniowo** bit by bit, gradually, little by little, progressively, step by step
storczyk orchid
stos collection, heap[1], mountain, pile[1], stack[1]; (*duża ilość*) crop[1]
stosować/za- apply, employ, use[1]
□ **stosować/za- się**: **do czegoś** adhere to sth, follow, keep to sth
stosowność adequacy, suitability
stosown|y appropriate[1], expedient, fitting[1], proper, suitable, suited; (*zachowanie*) decorous
■ **stosownie** accordingly, appropriately, properly, suitably; (*do prawa itp.*) under; (*zachowywać się*) decorously; **do czegoś** according to sth
stosun|ek 1 (*związek*) relation; (**stosunki**) relations, relationship; (*zażyłe, przyjacielskie itp.*) footing; **~ek płciowy** sex; **~ki między daną organizacją a ludnością** public relations; **w ~ku do kogoś/czegoś** compared to/with sb/sth, by/in comparison (with sb/sth), on, as regards sb/sth, in/with relation to sb/sth, towards; **mieć dobre/przyjazne ~ki z kimś** be on good, friendly, etc. terms (with sb), get on/along with sb, get on/along (together) **2** (*proporcja*) proportion, rate[1], ratio; **w ~ku do czegoś** in proportion to sth **3** (*nastawienie*) **do kogoś/czegoś** attitude
stosunkow|y relative[1] (to sth)
■ **stosunkowo** comparatively, relatively
sto-warzyszać/warzyszyć affiliate
stowarzyszenie association, guild
stowarzyszony affiliated, associated
stożek cone
stożkowaty conical
stożkowy conical
stół table; ~ **do bilarda** billiard table; ~ **kuchenny** kitchen table; ~ **montażowy/laboratoryjny** bench; ~ **operacyjny** operating table; ~ **w jadalni** dining table; ~ **warsztatowy** workbench; **przy stole** at the table
stracenie: **(kogoś)** execution
strach alarm[1], dread[2], fear[1], fearfulness, fright, scare[2]; ~ **pomyśleć** it doesn't bear thinking about IDM ~ **na wróble** scarecrow
stracić zob. też TRACIĆ; **kogoś** execute sb (for sth)
stracon|y wasted; **bezpowrotnie ~y** irretrievable IDM **~a sprawa** a lost cause
stragan stall[1], stand[2]
strajk industrial action, strike[2]; ~ **głodowy** hunger strike; ~ **włoski** work to rule; **zaczynać** ~ strike[1]
strajkować/za- be on strike
strajkowy strike[2]
strapić się → TRAPIĆ SIĘ
strapienie dejection, desolation, heartache, worry[2]; **ze ~m** dejectedly
strapiony 1 (*smutny*) crestfallen, dejected **2** (*zmartwiony*) worried
straszliwy fearful, horrendous, horrific
straszn|y 1 (*przerażający*) dreaded, eerie, fearsome, horrific, scary, spooky **2** (*złej jakości*) awful, dire, frightful, horrible, horrid, monstrous, terrible; **być ~ym** be the pits
■ **strasznie**: ~ **nam się śpieszy** we're in a frightful rush
straszyć/wy-/prze- frighten sb/sth away/off, spook verb, terrify, threaten; (*duchy*) haunt[1]; **nie chciałem cię wystraszyć** I didn't mean to shock you
straszydło bogey
strat|a 1 (*materialna; przegrana*) loss; **~a całkowita** bottom line; **~y w ludziach** casualties; **ponosić ~y** lose; **przedmiot spisany na ~y** write-off **2** (*czasu, pieniędzy*) waste[2]; (**straty**) wastage
strateg strategist
strategia strategy; ~ **postępowania** policy
strategiczny strategic
stratować → TRATOWAĆ
strawić → TRAWIĆ
straż guard[1], watch[2]; (*konwój*) escort[1]; ~ **pożarna** fire brigade
straża-k/czka firefighter; (**strażak**) fireman
strażni-k/czka guard[1]; ~ **więzienn-y/a** jailer, prison warder/officer, warder
s-trącać/trącić knock sth onto the floor, etc.
strąk pod
strefa area, belt[1], sphere, territory, zone; ~ **czasu** time zone
stremowany jittery, nervous
stres strain[1], stress[1]; **~y miejskiego życia** the pressures of city life
stresować/ze- unsettle
■ **stresujący** stressful, unsettling
s-treszczać/treścić compress, encapsulate, summarize; (*powtórzyć główne punkty*) recap
streszczenie 1 (*tekst*) abstract[2], precis, summary[1], synopsis **2** (*skracanie*) compression
striptiz (także **striptease**) striptease
striptizer/ka stripper
strofa stanza, verse
strofować admonish, chasten, chide, rebuke
stroiciel/ka tuner
stroić 1 (**/wy-**) (*ozdobić*) festoon sb/sth (with sth) **2** (**/na-**) (*instrument*) tune[2] sth up
□ **stroić/wy- się** dress up, smarten (yourself) up
stroik reed
strojn|y dressy; **zbyt ~e** prissy
stromość steepness
stromy sheer, steep
stron|a 1 side[1], face[1], facet; **po drugiej ~ie** across, over, round[3]; (*jechać*) **po lewej ~ie** on the left; **ze wszystkich ~** on/from all sides, on/from every side **2** (*kierunek*) direction; **w ~ę** towards; **na ~ę** aside; **w jedną ~ę** one-way, single[1] **3** (*cecha*) aspect, point[1]; **czyjaś słaba ~a** blind spot; **dobre ~y** (*stanowiące przeciwwagę dla złych*) compensations; **dobre i złe ~y** the pros and cons; **mieć dobre ~y** have your, etc. (good) points **4** (*uczestnik sporu/procesu/umowy itp.*) party, quarter; **z czyjejś ~y** on the part of sb/on sb's part; **~a pozwana** the defence **5** (*książki itp.*) page[1]; **z pierwszej ~y** (*gazety*) front-page **6** (*internetowa*) **~a internetowa** web page; **~a domowa (internetowa)** home page **7** (*gram.*) (*bierna/czynna*) voice[1] **8** (**strony**) (*okolica*) parts[1] IDM **na lewą ~ę** inside out | **w tę czy w tamtą ~ę** give or take | **z drugiej ~y** at the same time | **z jednej ~y…z drugiej ~y** on the one hand… on the other (hand) | **ze ~y ojca** paternal
stronica page[1]
stronniczość bias[1], partiality
stronniczy biased, one-sided, partisan[1], unbalanced
stronni-k/czka adherent, follower, supporter, sympathizer
strop roof
stroszyć/na- ruffle sth (up)
strój attire, costume, ensemble, wear[2]; ~ **narodowy** national dress; ~ **nurka** wetsuit; ~ **wieczorowy** evening dress
stróż/ka guardian, keeper, watch[2]; **stróż/ka nocn-y/a** nightwatchman
stróżować keep a close watch on sb/sth, watch[1] sb/sth (for sth)
stróżówka lodge[1]
strug plane[1]
struga spurt noun; **wąska** ~ trickle noun
strugać/ze- plane[2], shave sth off (sth)
struktura 1 (*skład*) fabric, framework, structure[1] **2** (*budynek itp.*) structure[1]
strukturalny structural
strumie|ń 1 (*rzeka*) stream[1]; **~ń dopływowy** tributary **2** (*wody*) jet[1], stream[1]; **deszcz lał się ~niami** the rain was coming down in torrents; **zalew uchodźców ograniczono do małego ~nia** the flood of refugees had been reduced to a trickle
strumyk brook[1], creek
strun|a string[1] IDM **~y głosowe** vocal cords
strunowy: **instrument** ~ stringed instrument
strup scab
struś ostrich
strwożyć → TRWOŻYĆ
strych loft; **przechowywać rzeczy na ~u** store things in the roof
stryczek noose
stryj (także **stryjek**) uncle
strywializować → TRYWIALIZOWAĆ
strzał 1 (*z pistoletu itp.*) gunshot, shot[1]; ~ **w dziesiątkę** bullseye **2** (*do bramki*) shot[1]
strzała arrow
strzałka arrow, dart[1]
s-trząsać/trząsnąć shake sth off
strzec/u- guard[2]; **przed czymś** guard against sth
□ **strzec/u- się**: **kogoś/czegoś** beware (of sb/sth), watch out for sb/sth
strzech|a: **pokryty ~ą** thatched
strze-lać/lić 1 (*z pistoletu itp.*) fire[2], shoot[1]; **strzelić do tarczy** take a shot at the target **2** (*gaźnik*) backfire **3** (*gola itp.*) shoot[1]; ~ **bramkę** score[2] **3 balon strzelił** the balloon went pop IDM **strzelać palcami** snap your fingers
■ **strzelanie** gunfire
strzelanin|a shooting; **podczas ~y zabito dziennikarza** the journalist was killed in crossfire
strzelba gun[1]
strzelec 1 dobry ~ marksman; ~ **doborowy** crack shot; ~ **wyborowy** marksman, sniper **2** (**Strzelec**) (*znak zodiaku*) Sagittarius IDM **wolny** ~ freelance

strzelić zob. też STRZELAĆ; ~ **byka** boob verb

strzelisty lofty

strzemiączko strap

strzemię stirrup

strzep-ywać/nąć brush sth away, brush sth off (sth), flick sth (away, off, onto, etc.)

strzęp 1 shred[2]; **rwać na ~y** rip sth up; **na ~y** to bits; **w ~ach** in tatters, tattered **2** (*wiadomości itp.*) snippet; (*słów z rozmowy itp.; melodii*) snatch[2]

strzępiasty (*chmura itp.*) wispy

strzępić/po-/wy- (się) (*ubranie, materiał*) fray

strzyc/o-/przy- clip[2], cut[1]; (*trawę*) mow; (*owcę itp.*) shear; ~ **na krótko** crop[2]
□ **strzyc/o- się**: ~ **się u fryzjera** have your hair cut; **musisz się ostrzyc** you need (to have) a haircut

strzykanie: ~ **w kościach/stawach** twinge

strzykawka syringe

strzyżeni|e clip[1], cut[2]; (*włosów*) haircut; **maszynka do ~a** clippers; **maszyna do ~a trawy** mower

student/ka student, undergraduate; **student/ka ostatniego roku studiów** senior[2]

studio studio

studiować 1 (*na uniwersytecie itp.*) do[1], read[1], study[2] **2** (**/prze-**) (*wzrokiem*) study[2]

studi|um study[1]; (**studia**) studies[1]; **~a wyższe** higher education; **~um przypadku** case study

studnia well[4]

studyjny art-house

studzić/o-/prze-/wy- cool[2] sth/sb (down/off); (*emocje*) damp[2] sth (down), dampen

studzienka manhole

stuk clack

stuk-ać/nąć clack, hammer[2], hit[1]; (*zwł. w drzwi*) knock[1], rap[2]; (*silnik itp.*) chug; **lekko** ~ patter verb, tap[1]

stuknięty barking mad, batty, crackers, daft, potty[1], wacky

stukot clack, clatter noun, rattle[2]; (*lekko*) patter, tap[2]

stukotać/za- clack, clatter, rattle[1]

stulecie 1 (*wiek*) century **2** (*rocznica*) centenary

stulić: **stul pysk** shut up

stwardnieć → TWARDNIEĆ

stwardnienie: ~ **rozsiane** multiple sclerosis

s-twarzać/tworzyć pose[1], present[3]

stwier-dzać/dzić zob. też TWIERDZIĆ; affirm, ascertain, certify, determine IDM **muszę stwierdzić** I must say

stwierdzenie: **(stanowcze)** ~ assertion

stworzenie 1 (*akt twórczy*) creation; ~ **świata** creation **2** (*żyjące*) being[2], creature

stworzony: **być ~m dla kogoś/do czegoś** be cut out for sth, be cut out to be sth, be made for sb/each other

stworzyć → STWARZAĆ, TWORZYĆ

stwór: ~ **z innej planety** alien[2]

stwórca creator

styczeń January

styczna tangent

styczniowy January

styczność contact[1]

stygnąć/o-/prze-/wy- cool[2] (down/off), get cold

styk joint[2] IDM **na ~** end to end

stykać/zetknąć touch[1]
□ **stykać/zetknąć się** touch[1]; (*przewody itp.*) come into contact with each other; **z czymś** border on sth

styl 1 style, trend; (*mody*) chic noun, fashion, look[2]; (*język*) register[2]; **(dobry)** ~ style; **nie w czyimś ~u** unlike **2** (*pływania*) stroke; ~ **grzbietowy** backstroke[1]; ~ **klasyczny** breaststroke; ~ **motylkowy** butterfly IDM **~ życia** lifestyle, a/sb's way of life

stylist-a/ka hairstylist, stylist

stylistyczny stylistic

stylowy elegant, stylish

stymulacja stimulation

stymulator: ~ **serca** pacemaker

stymulować stimulate

stypendium bursary, fellowship, grant[2]; ~ **naukowe** scholarship

stypendyst-a/ka fellow[1], scholar

styranizować → TYRANIZOWAĆ

subiektywny subjective

subkontynent subcontinent

subkultura subculture

sublimacja sublimation

sublimować/wy- sublimate

sublokator/ka boarder

subskrypcja subscription

substancja matter[1], substance

subsydiować/za- subsidize

subtelność delicacy, subtlety

subteln|y delicate, fine[1], subtle; **~a różnica** a fine line between A and B

subwencja grant[2], subsidy

suchość dryness

such|y dry[1]; (*teren*) arid IDM **~e fakty** the bare facts | **~y jak pieprz** bone dry
■ **sucho** (*sposób mówienia*) shortly IDM **uchodzić komuś na ~** get away with sth/doing sth

sufit ceiling

suflerować prompt[2]

suflet soufflé

suflować prompt[2]

sugerować/za- (*mieć na myśli*) get at sth, indicate, insinuate, point[2] to sth, suggest; **komuś coś** put sth to sb, suggest; **przedstawić komuś swoją sugestię** put a suggestion to sb

sugestia suggestion

sugestywny expressive, suggestive

suka bitch[2]

sukces success, triumph[1]; **wielki** ~ the big time; **poczucie ~u** sense of achievement; **odnosić ~y** get on/along

sukcesja succession

sukienka dress[1], frock

sukinsyn bastard

suknia dress[1], gown; ~ **wieczorowa** evening dress

sułtan sultan

sum|a amount[1], sum[1]; **~a ogólna** grand total IDM **w ~ie** on aggregate, in all, on balance, overall[1], all told, in total

sumiast|y: **~e wąsy** a straggling moustache

sumieni|e conscience IDM **mieć coś na ~u** have sth on your conscience

sumienność thoroughness

sumienny assiduous, conscientious, dutiful, scrupulous, thorough; **jest ~m pracownikiem** he's a hard worker

sumować/z- total verb, pool[2]
■ **sumowanie** addition

sunąć glide, slide[1]

supeł knot[1]

super awesome, cool[1], super, wicked

superata surplus

superlatywa (*mówić, pisać*) **w samych ~ch** glowingly

supermarket supermarket

supermocarstwo superpower

supermodel/ka supermodel

supernowoczesny high-tech

supersam supermarket

suplement supplement

surfer: ~ **po internecie** surfer

surfing surfing; **uprawiać** ~ surf[2]

surfować IDM **~ po internecie** surf the net

surogat surrogate

surowcowy: **przemysł** ~ primary industry

surowiec material[1]; (**surowce**) raw materials

surowy 1 (*warunki*) hard[1], oppressive, severe, tough; (*wymagający*) strict; **być ~m dla kogoś/czegoś** be hard on sb/sth **2** (*prawo itp.*) draconian, rigid, stringent **3** (*wyraz twarzy*) dour, stern[1] **4** (*klimat*) harsh; (*rejon itp.*) inhospitable **5** (*skromny, prosty*) austere, stark[1] **6** (*żywność*) raw **7** (*surowce*) crude

surówka 1 (*potrawa*) salad **2** ~ **bawełniana** calico

surrealistyczny surreal

sus bound noun, jump[2], leap[2]; **biec ~ami** bound[2]; **dawać ~a** dash[2]

susza drought

suszarka dryer; **rozkładana ~ do ubrań** clothes horse; ~ **do bielizny** tumble dryer; ~ **do naczyń** draining board; ~ **do włosów** hairdryer

suszon|y desiccated, dried[2]; **~e warzywa** dehydrated vegetables

suszyć/wy- (się) dry[2], dry (sth) out; **wietrzyć i ~ (się)** air[2]

sutek nipple

suterena basement

suty generous, lavish[1]

suwenir souvenir

suwerenność sovereignty

suwerenny independent, sovereign[2]

swatać/ze- match[2]

swawolny frisky, playful

sweter (*wkładany przez głowę*) jumper, sweater; ~ **wełniany** jersey; ~ **rozpinany** cardigan

swędzić (także **swędzieć/za-**) itch verb, tickle; **swędzi mnie gardło** I've got a tickle in my throat
■ **swędzący** itchy | **swędzenie** itch, tickle noun

swobod|a freedom, liberty; **~y obywatelskie** civil liberties

swobodny free[1], free and easy, loose[1]
■ **swobodnie** free adv., freely, loosely, naturally

swoisty individualistic

swojski homely

sworzeń 1 (*śruba*) bolt[1] **2** (*obrotowy*) pivot[1]

swój her[2], hers, his[1,2], its, own[1], their; (*sport*) home[2] IDM **postawić na swoim**; **robić po swojemu** get/have your own way

sycący filling[2]

syczeć/za- hiss

syfilis syphilis

syfon: **przelewać ~em** siphon

sygnalizować/za- indicate, point sth out (to sb), signal verb
■ **sygnalizujący** telltale

sygnał indication, signal, cue; (*słyszalny po podniesieniu słuchawki telefonu*) dialling tone; ~ **ostrzegawczy** alarm[1]; ~ **programu** signature tune; ~ **radiowy** signal; ~ **świetlny** flare[2]; ~ **telefoniczny** tone[1]; **dawać** ~ signal verb
sygnatariusz/ka signatory
syk hiss noun
sylaba syllable
Sylwester New Year's Eve
sylwestrow|y: **zabawa ~a** Hogmanay
sylweta silhouette
sylwetka 1 (*kształt*) silhouette; (*miasta itp.*) skyline **2** (*budowa ciała*) figure[1]
symbiotyczny symbiotic
symbioza symbiosis
symbol emblem, icon, symbol; **czegoś** byword; ~ **seksu** sex symbol
symboliczny iconic, nominal, symbolic; (*przekazanie władzy itp.*) token[2]
symbolizm symbolism
symbolizować symbolize
symetria symmetry
symetryczny symmetrical
symfonia symphony
symfoniczn|y: **orkiestra ~a** symphony orchestra
sympati|a 1 (*uczucie*) feeling; **czujący ~ę do kogoś/czegoś** fond; **zdobywać ~ę** endear sb/yourself to sb **2** (*osoba*) sweetheart, boyfriend
sympatyczny agreeable, amiable, congenial, kind[2], likeable, lovable, nice, pleasant
sympaty-k/czka sympathizer; ~ **partii politycznej** (*zwł. komunistycznej*) fellow-traveller
sympatyzować sympathize
symptom symptom
symptomatyczny symptomatic
symulacja mock-up, simulation
symulować/za- feign, pretend, simulate
syn son
synagoga synagogue
synchronizować/z- synchronize; **synchronizować czas** (*jakiegoś wydarzenia z czymś*) time[2]
syndrom syndrome
syndykat syndicate
synergia synergy
syngiel 1 (*płyta*) single[2] **2** (*tenis itp.*) singles[2]
synkopa syncopation
synkopowy syncopated
synonim 1 (*nie antonim*) synonym **2** (*hasło*) byword
synonimiczny synonymous
synowa daughter-in-law
syntetyczny man-made, synthetic
syntetyzator keyboard[1], synthesizer
syntetyzować/z- synthesize
syntez|a synthesis; **~a jądrowa** nuclear fusion; **przeprowadzać ~ę** synthesize
syp-ać/nąć (*śnieg*) snow[2]; ~ **dowcipami** crack jokes IDM **~ jak z rękawa** reel sth off
□ **syp-ać/nąć się**: **na kogoś/coś** rain[2] (down) (on sb/sth)
sypiać: **z kimś** sleep together, sleep with sb
sypialnia bedroom
syrena 1 (*alarmowa*) siren **2** (*nimfa*) mermaid
syrop syrup; ~ **na kaszel** cough mixture; ~ **owocowy** cordial[2]
system system; ~ **binarny** binary noun; ~ **dwójkowy** binary noun; ~ **immunologiczny/odpornościowy** immune system; ~ **operacyjny** operating system; ~ **proporcjonalny** (*polit.*) proportional representation
systematyczność neatness
systematyczny methodical, neat, orderly[1], systematic
systematyzować/u- systematize
systemiczny systemic
sytuacja matter[1], position[1], situation, thing; **trudna/przykra** ~ plight; **nowa** ~ a (whole) new/different ball game
sytuować/u- set[1]
sytuowany: **dobrze** ~ better off, well-to-do
syty full[1] (up)
sza: **~!** hush[1], sh, shush
szabas sabbath
szablon pattern, template; (*do rysowania*) stencil
szablonowość triteness
szablonowy stock[3]
szach check[2]
szachownic|a chessboard; (*wzór*) **w ~ę** chequered
szachraj/ka swindler
szachrajstwo swindle noun
szachy chess
szacować/o- assess, rate[2], weigh sth (up); ~ **koszt** cost[2]; **za nisko** ~ underestimate
■ **szacowanie** projection
szacun|ek 1 (*poszanowanie*) deference, esteem, regard[2], respect[1]; **powszechny ~ek** respectability; **~ek połączony z lękiem lub podziwem** awe; **pełen ~ku** respectful; **bez ~ku** disrespectful, irreverent; **brak ~ku** disrespect, irreverence; **domagać się należnego ~ku** assert your authority; **przez ~ek dla kogoś/czegoś** in deference to sb/sth; **utrata ~ku** sb's fall from grace **2** (*oszacowanie*) reckoning
szacunkow|y: **~e obliczenie** guesstimate
szafa cupboard; (*na ubrania*) wardrobe; ~ **w ścianie** closet; ~ **na dokumenty** filing cabinet; ~ **grająca** jukebox
szafir sapphire
szafirowy (*kolor*) royal blue, sapphire
szafka cabinet, cupboard, locker; ~ **do wietrzenia i suszenia odzieży** airing cupboard; ~ **nocna** bedside table
szafot scaffold
szafran saffron
szajbnięty bonkers
szajka gang[1], ring[1]
szal shawl
szaleć/o-/za- 1 (*wariować*) go crazy, go mad; **na czyimś punkcie, na punkcie czegoś** rave[1] (about sb/sth); **(za kimś/czymś)** be wild[1] (about sb/sth); **oszaleć z rozpaczy** go frantic; **zaszaleć, np. z zakupami** go to town (on sth) **2** (*nastroje itp.*) run high; (*wyobraźnia itp.*) run riot; (*bitwa itp.*) rage[2] IDM **zaszalej sobie!** be a devil
szalenie extremely; (*ruszać się*) frenetically, hectically; (*kochać itp.*) madly; (*piękny itp.*) raving adv.
szaleniec crackpot, lunatic[1], madman, madwoman, maniac
szaleńcz|y lunatic[2], manic
■ **szaleńczo** crazily, dementedly, insanely, wildly
szaleństw|o 1 (*obłąkanie*) craziness, insanity, lunacy, madness; **(na punkcie czegoś)** craze; (*nierozsądne pomysły/działania*) folly, nonsense; **doprowadzać kogoś do ~a** drive sb round the bend; (*przen.*) **do ~a** to distraction **2** (*szał*) frenzy, wildness; (*zakupy; pijaństwo itp.*) spree
szalik scarf
szalon|y 1 (*obłąkany*) cockeyed, crackers, crackpot, crazy, dippy, insane, mad, nutty, raving, round the bend **2** (*pomysły itp.*) foolhardy; **~e dni jej młodości** the heady days of her youth **3** (*ruchy itp.*) abandoned, wild[1] **4** (*pośpiech itp.*) frenetic, frenzied, hectic
szalotka shallot
szalupa dinghy
szał frenzy, mania, wildness; **(na punkcie czegoś)** craze; **wpaść w** ~ go berserk; **doprowadzać kogoś do ~u** drive sb crackers/mad/nuts/up the wall; **doprowadzający do ~u** infuriating
szałas hut, shack
szałwia sage
szambo cesspit
szamotać/za- się struggle[1] (with sb/sth), (against sth)
szamotanina tussle
szampan champagne
szampon shampoo
szanować/u- respect[2], look up to sb
■ **szanujący się** self-respecting
szanowany worthy
szanowny dear[1]; **szanowni państwo!** ladies and gentlemen!
szans|a 1 (*możliwość zrobienia czegoś*) break[2], chance[1], opportunity **2** (*prawdopodobieństwo, że wygrasz itp.*) the odds, possibility, probability, prospect; **małe ~e na coś** very little likelihood of sth; **mieć ~e (na coś)** bein/out of the running (for sth); **mieć ~e wygrania/coś do stracenia** stand[1] to do sth; **mieć wszelkie ~e** have a lot going for you; **mający duże ~e** strong; **nie mieć ~ (na coś)** be in/out of the running (for sth); **coś/ktoś bez ~ (na powodzenie)** non-starter IDM **wyrównane ~e** a level playing field
szantaż blackmail, extortion
szantażować/za- blackmail verb
szantażyst-a/ka blackmailer
szarańcza locust
szarawy greyish
szarfa sash
szargać/za- (*reputację*) tarnish
szarlatan charlatan
szarmancki chivalrous, suave
szarość dullness
szarpać 1 (/szarpnąć) (*nagłym/gwałtownym ruchem*) jerk[1], jolt[1] **2 (/szarpnąć) za coś** pluck at sth, pull[1], tug[1], yank **3 (/szarpnąć)** (*struny*) pluck[1] **4 (/po-)** mangle, maul
IDM **szarpiący nerwy** nerve-racking

□ **szarp-ać/nąć się 1** (*walczyć*) struggle[1] **2** (**szarpnąć się**) (**na coś**) splash out (on sth)
szarpanina scramble noun
szarpany jerky
szary 1 (*kolor*) grey[1] **2** (*nieciekawy*) bland, dull IDM **~ człowiek** the man in the street
szarża charge[1]
szarżować/za- 1 (*pistolet itp.*) charge[2] **2** (*przesadzić*) overdo it/things
szastać: **~ pieniędzmi** splurge verb (sth) (on sth)
szaszłyk kebab
szata robe
szatan 1 (*diabeł*) devil, Satan **2** (*zły człowiek*) fiend
szatański demonic, fiendish
szatkować/po- shred[1]
szatnia 1 (*przechowalnia*) cloakroom **2** (*przebieralnia*) changing room
szatynka brunette
szczątek fragment[1]; (**szczątki**) debris, remains, wreckage
szczeb|el 1 (*skali*) notch[1] **2** (*ranga*) echelon; **dyskusje na najwyższym ~lu** top-level discussions **3** (*drabiny*) rung[1]
szczebiot chirp noun
szczebiotać/za- chirp, trill verb, twitter, warble
szczebiotka chatterbox
szczecin|a (*na brodzie*) stubble; **pokryty ~ą** bristly
szczególnie especially, notably, in particular, particularly, peculiarly, singularly, specially
szczególnoś|ć: **w ~ci** in particular
szczególn|y especial, particular, special[1]; **znaki ~e** distinguishing features
szczegół complexity, detail[1]; (**szczegóły**) the ins and outs (of sth), particulars; **~ techniczny/fachowy** technicality; **podawać ~y** detail[2] IDM **wdawać się w ~y** go into detail(s)
szczegółowość rigorousness
szczegółow|y in depth, descriptive, detailed, fine[1], minute[2], rigorous, specific (about sth); **~e badanie przyczyn** a scrupulous investigation into the causes
■ **szczegółowo** in depth, in detail, at length, rigorously
szczekać/za- bark[2]; **~ piskliwie** yap
szczelina chasm, chink[1], cranny, crevice, fissure, leak[2], rift, slit[1], slot[1], split[2]; (*w grubej warstwie lodu*) crevasse
szczeln|y airtight, -proof, tight; **~e zamknięcie** seal[2]
szczeniak puppy
szczenię pup, puppy
szczep 1 (*zraz*) graft **2** (*odmiana rośliny itp.*) strain[1] **3** (*plemię*) tribe
szczepić/za- 1 kogoś/coś immunize, inoculate, vaccinate **2** (*część rośliny; skórę*) graft verb sth onto sth
szczepionka vaccine
szczepowy tribal
szczerba chip[1], nick[1]
szcze|ry direct[1], forthright, frank, genuine, heartfelt, hearty, honest, open[1], plain[1], sincere, straight[2], truthful; (*aż do bólu*) outspoken
■ **szczerość** frankness, openness, outspokenness, sincerity | **szczerze**: **~ mówiąc** (quite) frankly
szcześciar|a: **jestem szczęściarą** I'm very lucky
szczędzić: **nie ~ wydatków** spare no expense in doing sth; **nie ~ wysiłków** pull your weight
szczęk clank noun
szczęka jaw
szczękać/za-/szczęknąć clang, clank; (*zębami*) chatter
szczęknąć → ZASZCZĘKAĆ
szczęściarz: **~!** what a lucky bastard!; **jestem ~em** I'm very lucky
szczęści|e 1 (*powodzenie*) blessing, fortune, luck, good luck (to sb); **mieć ~e** have good luck, be in luck; **mający ~e** lucky; **na ~e** it was fortunate..., fortunately, be a good thing (that), happily, it's lucky..., luckily, mercifully, thankfully; **szukać ~a** seek your fortune **2** (*radość*) gladness, happiness IDM **wiele lat ~a!** many happy returns (of the day) | **całe ~e, że** it's a good job, it is just as well (that...)
szczęśliw|y 1 (*pomyślny*) blessed, fortunate, happy, lucky; **~ym przypadkiem** fortuitous **2** (*radosny*) happy; **bardzo ~y** chuffed (about sth) IDM **Szczęśliwego Nowego Roku!** Happy New Year!
■ **szczęśliwie 1** (*pomyślnie*) fortunately, luckily, successfully **2** (*radośnie*) happily
szczodrość generosity
szczodry bountiful, generous; (*wpłata itp.*) handsome
szczoteczka: **~ do paznokci** nail brush; **~ do zębów** toothbrush
szczotk|a brush[1]; **~a do włosów** hairbrush; **~a do dywanów** carpet sweeper; **~a do wykładzin** carpet sweeper; **~a do zmywania podłogi** mop[1]; **czyszczenie ~ą** brush[1]
szczotkować/wy- brush[2]; (*psa itp.*) groom[1]
szczudło stilt
szczupak pike
szczupły lean[2], slender, slim[1], trim[2]
szczur rat
szczwany sly
szczycić się: **czymś** boast, pride yourself on sth/doing sth; **szczycimy się tym, że oferujemy najlepsze usługi w mieście** we take great pride in offering the best service in town
szczypać 1 (**/u-/uszczypnąć**) pinch[1] **2** (*skóra itp.*) prickle[1], sting[1]; (*oczy*) smart[2] (*mróz itp.*) nip, tingle
szczypce 1 (*narzędzie*) pincers, pliers, tongs **2** (*zool.*) claws[1]
szczypiorek chive
szczypta dash[1], grain, pinch[2], sprinkling
szczy|t 1 (*wierzchołek*) top[1]; (*góry*) brow, crest, crown[1], hilltop, summit, top[1], pinnacle, peak[1]; (*dachu itp.*) apex; (*dachu*) gable **2** (*góra*) mount[2] **3 siedzieć u ~tu stołu** sit at the head of the table **4** (*zysków itp.*) high[2] **5** (*przen.*) zenith; (*kariery*) heyday, peak[1]; (*kariery, powodzenia itp.*) prime[2]; (*mody itp.*) height; (*wygody itp.*) ultimate[2]; **~t sezonu** the high season; (*rozmowy itp.*) **na ~cie** high-level; **znajdować się na ~cie** (*np. listy przebojów*) top[3]; **osiągać ~t (w czymś)** climax verb, culminate in sth, peak[2]; **u ~tu formy** at its/your best **6 godzina ~tu** the rush hour; **poza godzinami ~tu** off-peak
szczytny noble[1]
szczytować climax verb
szczytowy 1 (*godziny itp.*) peak[3] **2** (*osiągnięcie*) crowning; (*wykonanie utworu itp.*) definitive; (*kulminacyjny*) climactic
szef/owa boss[1], chief[2], head[1], supervisor; **szef kuchni** chef
szejk sheikh
szelest rustle noun
szeleścić/za- rustle
szelki braces[1]; **~ (zabezpieczające)** harness[1]
szelma rascal, rogue[2]
szemrać/za- babble[2]
■ **szemranie** murmur noun
szept whisper noun; **~em** softly IDM **mówić ~em** say sth, speak, etc. under your breath
szeptać/za-/wy-/szepnąć 1 (*cicho mówić*) whisper **2** (*wiatr itp.*) sigh IDM **szepnąć słówko za kimś** put in a (good) word for sb
szereg chain[1], line[1], rank[1], row[1], series, succession; (*stopni*) flight; **ustawiać w ~u** align sth (with sth)
szeregowiec private[2]
szeregow|y[1] (*przym.*) **1** (*tytuł*) associate[3] **2** (*dom*) terraced
szeregow|y[2] (*rz., żołnierz*) man[1], the rank and file, private[2] (*żołnierze, członkowie*) **~i** the ranks[1]
szermierk|a fencing; **uprawiać ~ę** fence[2]
szeroki broad, wide[1]; (*teren*) open[1]; (*poparcie itp.*) broad-based; **~ zamaszysty ruch** sweep[2] IDM **~ej drogi** bon voyage
■ **szeroko** (*rozpowszechniony itp.*) globally, widely; **otwórz szeroko usta** open your mouth wide
szerokoś|ć breadth, width; (*między torami kolejowymi*) gauge[1]; **~ć geograficzna** latitude; **~ć pasma** bandwidth; **mający (x m itd.) ~ci** wide[1]
szerszeń hornet
szeryf sheriff
szerzyć disseminate, propagate
□ **szerzyć się** pervade; **w mieście szerzą się kradzieże samochodów** car theft is rampant in this town
■ **szerzący się** pervasive
szesnastka semiquaver
szesnasty sixteenth
szesnaście sixteen
sześcian (*geom., mat.*) cube[1]
sześcienny cubic
sześciokąt hexagon
sześciokątny hexagonal
sześć six
sześćdziesiąt sixty
sześćdziesiąt|y sixtieth; **lata ~e** the sixties
szew seam; **~ chirurgiczny** stitch[1]
szewc cobbler
szkalować/o- defame, malign
szkaradność ugliness
szkaradny ugly, unsightly
szkaradzieństwo eyesore
szkarłat scarlet noun
szkarłatny scarlet
szkic sketch; (*zwł. tekstu*) draft[1]
szkicować/na- design[2], draw[1], sketch verb; **~ w ogólnym zarysie** outline[1]
szkicowy sketchy

■ **szkicowo** in rough
szkielet 1 (*anat.*) skeleton[1]; (*postura*) frame[1] **2** (*budynku itp.*) framework, shell[1]
szkiełko: ~ **mikroskopowe** slide[2]
szklaneczka (*whisky itp.*) tot[1]
szklanka 1 glass, tumbler **2** (*zawartość*) glassful
szklany 1 (*ze szkła*) glass **2** (*jak szkło*) glassy
szklarnia conservatory, glasshouse, greenhouse
szklarz glazier
szklić/o- glaze[1]
szklisty 1 (*jak szkło*) glassy **2** (*oczy*) glassy, glazed; **stawać się ~m** glaze over
szkliwo enamel
szkło 1 (*materiał*) glass **2** (*szklanki itp.*) glass, glassware **3** (*w okularach*) lens IDM **~ powiększające** magnifying glass
szkocki Scots, Scottish
szkod|a 1 (*krzywda*) damage[1], harm[1], wrong[3]; **wyrządzać ~ę** do sb a disservice; **ze ~ą dla kogoś/czegoś** to the detriment of sb/sth **2** (*przykrość*) pity[1], shame[1]; **wielka ~a** a crying shame; **wielka ~a!** too bad!; **wielka to ~a** it's rather a pity; **jaka ~a** sorry[1] (to see, hear, etc.) that...
szkodliwy bad for sb/sth, damaging, detrimental, harmful, ill[1], noxious; ~ **dla zdrowia** unhealthy
szkodnik pest; (**szkodniki**) vermin
szkodzić/za- prejudice[2]; **(nic) nie szkodzi** it doesn't matter, never mind, that's all right; **nie zaszkodzi (coś zrobić)** there is no harm in doing sth, it does no harm (for sb) to do sth, it won't/wouldn't hurt (sb/sth) (to do sth); **nie zaszkodziłoby** be (just) as well (to do sth); **ostatni skandal zaszkodzi reputacji rządu** this latest scandal will do nothing for this government's reputation
szkolenie instruction (in sth), training; ~ **zawodowe** vocational training
□ **szkolenie się** instruction (in sth)
szkolić/wy-/prze- (się) train[2]
szkoln|y school; **lata ~e** your schooldays; **w wieku ~ym** of school age
szkoła school; ~ **podstawowa** elementary school, primary school; (*dla dzieci w wieku od 9 do 13 lat*) middle school; ~ **dla dzieci w wieku od 7 do 11 lat** junior school; ~ **średnia** high school, junior high school, secondary school, senior high school; ~ **średnia ogólnokształcąca** comprehensive[2]; ~ **wyższa** academy, college, school; ~ **zawodowa** vocational school; ~ **policealna dla dorosłych** college of further education; ~ **publiczna** public school; ~ **prywatna** (*dla dzieci w wieku od 13 do 18 lat, często z internatem*) public school; ~ **biznesu** business school; ~ **jazdy** driving school; ~ **specjalna** special school; ~ **z internatem** boarding school IDM **~ naukowa** a school of thought
szkopuł hitch[2], stumbling block
Szkot/ka Scot
szkółka (*ogrodnicza*) nursery
szkrab kiddie
szkwał squall
szlachcic noble[2]
szlachecki noble[1]; **~e urodzenie** gentility; **tytuł/stan** ~ knighthood
szlachetność nobility
szlachetny noble[1] IDM **metal ~** precious metal | **być (zorganizowanym itp.) w ~m celu** be for/in a good cause
szlachta gentry, nobility
szlaczek strip[2]
szlafrok dressing gown
szlag: **telewizor ~ trafił** this television has had it; **a niech to ~!** bugger (it)!
szlak track[1], trail[1], way[1]; (*wodny*) lane
szlaka dross
szlam mud, silt, slime, sludge
szlamować dredge
szlamowaty slimy
szlauch hose
szlem: **wielki** ~ grand slam
szlifierka grinder
szlifować/wy- grind[1], polish[2]
szloch sob noun
szlochać/za- sob
szmal IDM **zarabiać mnóstwo ~u** rake sth in
szmaragd emerald
szmaragdowy emerald
szmata rag
szminka: ~ **do ust** lipstick
szmugiel smuggling
szmuglować/prze- smuggle
sznur 1 (*lina*) cord, rope[1]; ~ **do suszenia bielizny** clothes line **2** (*pereł itp.*) string[1] of sth **3** (*ciąg*) string[1] of sth
sznurek line[1], string[1]; ~ **do ściągania** drawstring
sznurować/za- (*buty*) do sth up, lace[2] sth (up)
□ **sznurować/za- się** lace[2] (up)
sznurowadło shoelace
sznurowany lace-up
sznurow|y: **drabinka ~a** rope ladder
sznurówka lace[1]
szofer chauffeur
szoferka cab
szok jolt[2], shock[1]; ~ **kulturowy** culture shock
szokować/z- appal, freak[2] sb (out), shock[2]
szokujący appalling, shocking
szopa shed[1]
szopka 1 (*niepoważn-a/e sytuacja/zachowanie*) carry-on **2** (*bożonarodzeniowa*) nativity
szorować/wy- scour, scrub[1]; **wyszorować patelnię do czysta** scrape a pan clean
szorstk|i 1 (*tkanina itp.*) rough[1], scratchy; (*włosy itp.*) coarse; **stawać się ~im** coarsen, roughen **2** (*osoba; maniery*) abrasive, abrupt, crisp[1], curt, graceless; **nieuprzejmy i ~i** short[1] (with sb)
szorstkość curtness, roughness
szorty shorts
szosa road; **główna** ~ highway; ~ **szybkiego ruchu** dual carriageway
szowinist-a/ka chauvinist
szowinistyczny chauvinistic
szowinizm chauvinism
szósty sixth IDM **~ zmysł** sixth sense
szpachelka spatula
szpada sword
szpak starling
szpakowaty (*włosy*) greyish
szpalta column
szpanerski (*luksusowy*) posh; (*modny*) funky
szpanerstwo pose[2]
szpanować/za- pose[1]
szpara chink[1], crack[2], cranny, crevice, fissure, rift, slit[1]
szparag asparagus
szpecić/ze- blemish verb
szperacz searchlight
szperać/po-: **(po/w czymś) (za czymś)** ferret[2] (about/around) (for sth), poke about/around, rummage, snoop (around); (*wertować książki itp.*) browse; ~ **po internecie** surf the net
szpetny ugly, unsightly
szpetota ugliness
szpic point[1], spike; (*buta*) toe[1]; **sweter z wycięciem w** ~ V-neck sweater
szpicel tail[1]
szpiczasty pointed
szpieg spook, spy[1]
szpiegostwo espionage
szpiegować spy[2], spy on sb/sth
szpik: ~ **kostny** bone marrow IDM **do ~u kości** to the core
szpikulec (*do szaszłyków itp.*) skewer
szpilka 1 pin[1] **2** (*but; obcas*) stiletto
szpilkowy coniferous
szpinak spinach
szpital hospital, infirmary; ~ **dla psychicznie/umysłowo chorych** mental hospital
szpon 1 claw[1], talon **2** (**szpony**) (*przen.*) clutches[2]; **być w ~ach (czegoś)** be/get hooked (on sth)
szprycha spoke[1]
szpula (także **szpulka**) bobbin, reel[1], spool
szpunt bung[2]
szrama scar
szrapnel shrapnel
szron frost[1]; **pokrywać się ~em** frost over/up
sztab: ~ **ekspertów** think tank
sztab|a bar[1]; **~y złota/srebra** bullion
sztafeta relay[2]
sztaluga easel
sztandar banner
szterling sterling[1]
sztruks corduroy
sztruksow|y corduroy; **spodnie ~e** cords
sztuczk|a 1 (*fortel*) artifice, gimmick, stunt[1]; (*w celu osiągnięcia czegoś*) ploy; (**sztuczki**) sleight of hand **2** (*magiczna*) trick; **~i magiczne** magic[1]; **robić ~i magiczne** conjure
sztuczność affectation
sztuczn|y 1 (*materiał itp.*) artificial, dummy adj., false, man-made, mock[2], synthetic; **~a skóra** imitation leather; **~a szczęka** false teeth, plate; **~e tworzywo** plastic[1]; **~a inteligencja** artificial intelligence; **~e oddychanie** resuscitation; **~e zapłodnienie** artificial insemination **2** (*osoba; zachowanie*) affected, contrived IDM **~y ogień** firework
sztućce cutlery
sztuk|a 1 (*twórczość artystyczna*) art, craft; **~a konceptualna** conceptual art; **~a kulinarna** cookery; **wschodnie ~i walki** martial arts;

kultura i ~a arts; **~i piękne** fine art(s); (*przen.*) **forma ~i** art form
2 (*umiejętność*) artistry; **(robienia czegoś)** trick; **~a aktorska** acting[1]
3 (*teatr*) drama, piece[1], play[2]
4 (*kawałek: materiału itp.*) length; **~a odzieży** item of clothing; **na ~i** singly
sztukator plasterer
sztukatorstwo plasterwork
sztukmistrz conjuror
sztukmistrzostwo magic[1]
sztukować/do- eke sth out
szturch-ać/nąć hustle, jostle; (*czymś spiczastym*) jab[1], jog[1], poke, prod
szturchaniec clip[1], cuff[1]; (*czymś spiczastym*) poke noun
szturchnięcie (*czymś spiczastym*) dig[2], jab[2], jog[2], prod noun
szturm attack[1]; **brać ~em** storm[2]
szturmować/za- storm[2]
sztych engraving, etching, print[2]
sztyft pin[1]
sztylet dagger
sztyletować/za- stab[1]
sztywnieć/ze- stiffen
sztywność inflexibility, rigidity, stiffness
sztywn|y 1 (*materiał itp.*) inflexible, rigid, stiff[1]; **ubij białko na ~ą pianę** beat the egg whites until they are stiff **2** (*osoba*) inflexible, rigid, set in your ways; (*poważny w sprawach seksu itp.*) prim, stiff[1], straight[2]; (*wypowiedź, tekst*) stilted
szubienica gallows
szufelka scoop[1]; (*do szczotki*) dustpan
szufla shovel
szuflada drawer
szufladkować/za- typecast sb (as sth)
szuflować/za- shovel verb
szukać/po- cast around/about for sth, hunt[1] (for) (sb/sth), keep an eye open/out (for sb/sth), look[1] (for sb/sth), seek; (*w torbie itp.*) burrow[1]; (*pożywienia*) forage (for sth); **~ po omacku** feel[1] (about) (for sb/sth); **poszukam tej książki później** I'll have a good look for that book later; **długo byś szukał lepszej kucharki niż Mary** Mary's cooking takes some beating
IDM **szukać dziury w całym** find fault (with sb/sth) | **szukać nieszczęścia** ask for trouble/it
■ **szukanie** IDM **~ dziury w całym** nit-picking | **~ wiatru w polu** wild goose chase
szum 1 hum noun, whoosh **2** (*medialny itp.*) hype[1]; **robić ~ (wokół czegoś)** hype[2] sth (up)
szumować/od- skim sth (off/from sth)
szumowin|a (szumowiny) scum; **pokryty ~ą** scummy; **~y, które śmiecą** scummy people dropping litter
szurać/za- scrape[1]; **~ nogami** shuffle[1]
szust whoosh
szwadron squadron
szwagier brother-in-law
szwagierka sister-in-law
szwajcar doorman, porter
szwank: **bez ~u** intact, unscathed
szwindel fiddle[2], swindle noun
szyb (*kopalni, windy itp.*) shaft; **~ naftowy** oil well
szyb|a pane, sheet/pane of glass, window, windowpane; **podwójne ~y w oknach** double glazing; **przednia ~a** (*w samochodzie*) windscreen
szybk|i fast[1], prompt[1], quick[1], rapid, snappy, speedy, swift; **wyruszać w ~im tempie** set off at a smart pace
■ **szybko** fast[2], quick[2], quickly, rapidly, snappily, soon, speedily, swiftly; **nie jedz tak ~o** don't rush your food; **~ wyzdrowieć** make a speedy recovery from an illness
szybkościomierz speedometer
szybkość pace[1], rapidity, speed[1], speediness, velocity
szybkowar pressure cooker
szybować/po- float[1], flutter[1], glide, soar, sail (over, etc. sth)
szybowiec glider
szybownictwo gliding
szychta shift[2]
szycie needlework, sewing
szyć/u- sew, stitch[2]; (*szybko np. całą sukienkę*) run sth up; **szyć ubrania** tailor[2]; **szyty na miarę** bespoke
szydełk|o: **robić na ~u** crochet
szydełkować crochet verb
szydełkow|y: **robótka ~a** crochet
szyderczy derisive; **~ uśmiech** sneer noun
szyderstwo jeer noun, ridicule, sneer noun, taunt noun
szydzić/wy- scoff, sneer, taunt
szyfon chiffon
szyfr code[1]
szyfrować/za- encrypt
szyj|a neck IDM **po ~ę w czymś** up to your neck in sth
szyjka 1 (*butelki itp.*) neck **2 ~ macicy** cervix
szyjkowy (także **szyjny**) (*anat.*) cervical
szyk chic noun, elegance, style; **dodawać ~u** smarten yourself/sb/sth up
szykana speed hump
szykanować harass, persecute; (*jako innego*) discriminate (against sb)
szykować 1 (/na-/przy-) line sth up **2 co te dzieci nam szykują?** what are the children up to?
szykowny (*modny*) chic, smart[1], stylish; (*osoba; ubranie*) dapper, dressy, snappy; (*hotel*) plush
szyld sign[1]
szyling shilling
szympans chimpanzee
szyna 1 ~ kolejowa rail **2 ~ chirurgiczna** splint
szynk tavern
szynka gammon, ham
szyszka cone; **~ jodły** fir cone

Ś

ścian|a 1 (*budynku*) wall; **od ~y do ~y** wall-to-wall **2** (*góry*) face[1]; **~a skalna** cliff
ścianka 1 (*działowa*) partition **2** (*szlachetnego kamienia itp.*) facet
ściąć (się) → ŚCINAĆ (SIĘ)
ściąg-ać/nąć 1 (*odpisywać*) copy[2]; **(od kogoś)** crib[2] sth (from/off sb) **2** (*komput.*) download, upload **3** (*podatki itp.*) levy sth (on sb) **4 ściągać na siebie czyjś gniew** incur sb's anger **5 ściągać śmietankę (towarzyską itp.)** cream sb/sth off
ściągający (*krem itp.*) astringent
ściągnięty pinched
ścieg stitch[1]; **zwykły ~** plain[2]
ściek 1 (*studzienka ściekowa*) drain[2]; (*rynsztok*) gutter; (*kanalizacja*) sewer **2 (ścieki)** effluent, sewage
ściemni(a)ć darken; **~ oświetlenie** turn the lights down
□ **ściemni(a)ć się** darken; **ściemnia się** it's getting dark
ściemnieć → CIEMNIEĆ
ścierać/zetrzeć 1 (*z powierzchni*) rub sth off (sth), wipe[1]; (*kurze*) dust[2]; (*zwł. szczotką*) scrub[1] **2** (*zwł. gumką*) rub sth out **3** (*na tarce*) grate[2]
□ **ścierać/ze- się** (*w walce*) clash[1] (with sb) (over sth)
ściereczka: **~ czyszcząca** (*nasączona płynem/mleczkiem do czyszczenia*) wipe[2]
ścierka cloth; **~ do kurzu** duster; **~ do mycia naczyń** dishcloth; **~ do naczyń** (*do osuszania naczyń*) tea towel
ściernisko stubble
ścierny abrasive; **papier ~** sandpaper
ścierń stubble
ścierpieć → CIERPIEĆ
ścierpnąć → CIERPNĄĆ
ścierpnięty dead[1]
ścieśni(a)ć (się) constrict, narrow[2]
■ **ścieśniony** confined
ścieśni(a)ć się bunch[2] (up/together)
ścież|ka 1 avenue; (*spacerowa lub do jazdy konnej*) bridle path, footpath, path **2 ~ka dźwiękowa** soundtrack
IDM **być na ~ce wojennej; wchodzić na ~kę wojenną** (be/go) on the warpath
ścięgno sinew, tendon; **~ podkolanowe** hamstring; **~ stawu kolanowego** hamstring
ścięty stiff[1]
ścigać 1 (/doścignąć) be after sb/sth, chase[1] (after) sb/sth, follow, hunt[1] (for) (sb/sth), pursue **2** (*prawn.*) prosecute sb (for sth)
□ **ścigać się** race[2] (against/with) (sb/sth)
ści-nać/ąć 1 (*drzewo itp.*) chop sth down, cut sth down, fell[2]; **ścinać głowę** behead, decapitate; **ścinać na gilotynie** guillotine verb **2** (*skrzepnąć*) congeal; IDM **krzyk ściął jej krew w żyłach** the scream made her blood curdle
□ **ści-nać/ąć się** congeal, clot[2], set[1]
ścinek snippet
ścisk crush[2], squash[2], squeeze[2]
ścis-kać/snąć clamp[1], clasp[1], clutch[1], compress sth (into sth), grip[2], jam[2] sb/sth in, under, between, etc. sth, press[2], squash[1], squeeze[1] IDM **ściskać komuś dłoń** shake sb's hand/shake hands (with sb)/shake sb by the hand
□ **ścis-kać/nąć się** squash[1]
ścisł|y 1 (*dokładny*) exact[1], precise, specific, strict; **nauki ~e** science **2** (*przepis itp.*) strict, stringent
■ **ściśle** precisely, strictly; **~ kontrolowany** tight; **~ mówiąc** to be exact/precise, strictly speaking; **~ tajne** top secret | **ścisłość** precision
ści-szać/szyć: **~ radio** turn the radio down, turn the volume down
■ **ściszony**: **mówić ściszonym głosem** speak in low voices
ściśnięt|y IDM **mieć ~e gardło** have/feel a lump in your throat
ślad 1 (*trop*) mark[2], sign[1], track[1], trail[1]; (*szrama*) scar; (*stopy*) footprint, footstep; (*naprowadzający do wyjaśnienia zbrodni*) lead[2]; (*korupcji itp.*) taint; **~ palca** fingermark;

~ **wodny statku** wash[2]; **iść w czyjeś ~y** follow in sb's footsteps; **iść ~em** trace[1] sth (back) (to sth); **~em kogoś/czegoś** in the wake of sb/sth; **nie było ~u karetki** there was no ambulance in evidence **2** zwykle; (**ślady**) (*pozostałości*) traces[2], vestige **3** (*doświadczenia*) imprint; **nosić ~ czegoś** bear[1] IDM **tracić** ~ lose track of sb/sth
ślamazarny slow[1]
ślęczeć: **nad czymś** plod along/on
śledcz|y: **dziennikarstwo ~e** investigative journalism
śledzić 1 follow, track[2]; (*krok po kroku*) dog[2], shadow[2], tail[2]; (*szpiegować*) spy on sb/sth; (*obsesyjnie: zwł. kobietę*) stalk[2]; **śledzi go policja** the police have put a tail on him **2** (**/wy-**) (*starać się znaleć/złapać*) get hold of sb, trace[1] sb/sth (to sth), track sb/sth down **3** (**/prze-**) (*czyjeś losy itp.*) follow, keep track of sb/sth
śledztwo enquiry, investigation; **prowadzić** ~ investigate
śledź 1 (*ryba*) herring **2** (*do namiotu*) peg[1]
ślepota blindness
ślep|y 1 (*niewidomy*) blind[1] **2** (*przen.*) blind[1] (to sth) **3 ~e naboje** dummy bullets IDM **~a uliczka/zaułek** cul-de-sac; (*i przen.*) a dead end; (*przen.*) corner[1]
■ **ślepo**: **(na) ~o** blindly, wild[1]; ~ **ufać komuś** take sb/sth at (its, his, etc.) face value
ślęczeć: **nad czymś** pore over sth, slog[1] (away) (at sth)
ślicznotka beauty
śliczny cute, lovely
ślimak snail; ~ **nagi** slug
ślina saliva, spit[2]
śliniak bib
ślinić/za- się dribble, drool, salivate, water[2]
ślinka: ~ **napłynęła mi do ust** it made my mouth water; **powodujący, że ~ komuś cieknie** mouth-watering
śliski slippery
śliwka plum; **suszona** ~ prune[1]
ślizgacz speedboat
ślizgać się glide, slide[1]; (*po wodzie itp.*) skim; (*z trudem łapiąc równowagę*) slither
ślub marriage, wedding; ~ **cywilny** civil marriage; **brać** ~; **dawać** ~ marry
ślubn|y 1 (*sukienka; apartament*) bridal; (*goście; przyjęcie*) wedding **2** (*dziecko*) legitimate; **jego ~a żona** his lawful wife
ślubować vow verb
ślusarz locksmith
śluz 1 (*szlam*) slime **2** (*anat.*) mucus
śluza lock[2]
śluzowaty slimy
śluzowy mucous
śmiać/u-/po- się laugh[1]; **z kogoś/czegoś** laugh at sb/sth; **dobrze się uśmiać** have a good laugh IDM **śmiać się do rozpuku** laugh, scream, etc. your head off | **śmiać się ostatni** have the last laugh
śmiałek daredevil
śmiałość audacity, boldness, daring noun, guts[1], pluck[2]
śmiał|y adventurous, audacious, bold, daring, plucky adj.; **~e sceny miłosne** explicit sex scenes
■ **śmiało** audaciously, boldly; **dzwoń ~o** don't hesitate to phone
śmiech laugh[2], laughter; **głośny ~** hilarity; **histeryczny** ~ hysterics; **~u wart** laughable IDM **dla ~u** for a laugh
śmieciarka dustcart
śmieciarz dustman
śmiecić/na- litter verb
śmieć[1] (*cz.*) dare[1]; **jak śmiesz?** how dare you?
śmie|ć[2] (*rz.*) (także **śmieci**) **1** landfill, refuse[2], rubbish; (*papierowe*) litter; **pojemnik na ~ci** bin **2** (*przen.*) dross; **traktować kogoś jak ~ć** treat sb like dirt
śmiercionośny murderous
śmier|ć death, demise; **na ~ć i życie** life-and-death (*obrazić się itp.*); **na ~ć** mortally; **~ć z głodu** starvation; **nieumyślne spowodowanie ~ci** (*prawn.*) manslaughter; **w stanie ~ci mózgowej** brain-dead
śmierdzący 1 smelly, stinky **2** (*interes itp.*) stinky
śmierdzieć 1 pong verb, reek, smell[1], stink **2** (*przen.*) (**czymś**) stink (of sth)
śmiertelni-k/czka mortal[2]
śmiertelność mortality
śmierteln|y deadly, deathly, fatal, incurable, lethal, mortal[1], terminal[2]; **~a choroba** killer disease; **~a pułapka** death trap; **~y wróg** arch-enemy
■ **śmiertelnie** deadly adv., fatally, incurably, lethally, mortally, terminally IDM **być ~ie przerażonym** be scared witless | ~ **się nudzić** be bored stiff/witless
śmieszn|y amusing, comic[1], comical, funny, humorous, laughable, ludicrous, preposterous, ridiculous; **bardzo ~y** hysterical; **coś ~ego**; **~a osoba** scream[2]; **nie bądź ~y!** don't be absurd!
■ **śmiesznie** comically, funnily, humorously, ludicrously, ridiculously; ~ **mały** derisory
śmietana cream[1]
śmietanka 1 cream[1] **2** ~ **towarzyska** cream[1]
śmietanowy (także **śmietankowy**) creamy
śmietniczka dustpan
śmietnik 1 (*pojemnik*) dustbin **2** (*przen.: mieszkanie itp.*) tip[1]
śmietnisko tip[1]
śmiga sail[2]
śmigło propeller
śniadanie breakfast; **drugie** ~ (*zapakowane w specjalny pojemnik*) box lunch; **drugie ~ do zjedzenia poza domem** bag lunch, packed lunch; **tradycyjne angielskie** ~ English breakfast
śniady swarthy
śnić: **o zrobieniu czegoś** dream[2]; (*na jawie*) daydream verb
□ **śnić się** dream[2] about sb/sth
śnieg snow[1]
śniegowy snowy
śnieżny snowy
śnieżyca: **nagła, krótkotrwała** ~ flurry
śnieżyczka snowdrop
śnieżyć snow[2]
śpiący dozy, drowsy, sleepy IDM ~ **jak zabity** comatose
śpiączk|a coma; **w stanie ~i** comatose
śpieszyć się 1 (**/po-**) hurry[1], hurry up (with sth), be in a hurry (to do sth), get a move on, put on a spurt, rush[1]; **strasznie się śpieszę** I'm in a terrible rush; **nie** ~ be in no hurry (to do sth), not be in any hurry (to do sth), take your time; **pośpiesz/cie się** make it snappy; **lepiej pośpieszmy się** we'd better get going **2** (*zegarek, zegar*) be fast[1]; (*przyśpieszać*) gain[1]
śpiew 1 (*lekcja*) singing, song **2** (*ptaków*) call[2], song
śpiewać/za- sing; **śpiewać rytmicznie** chant[2]
śpiewa-k/czka singer
śpiewn|y lilting; **~a intonacja** lilt
śpiwór sleeping bag
średn|i 1 average[1], mean[2], median, medium[1], mid, moderate[1]; **~i poziom** mediocrity; **~i wiek** middle age; **w ~im wieku** middle-aged; **klasa ~ia** the middle class; **~iej wielkości** medium-sized **2** (*jakość*) mediocre
■ **średnio** moderately; **osiągać ~io** average[3]; **wynosić ~io** average out (at sth); ~ **zaawansowany** intermediate
średnia average[2]
średnica diameter
średnik semicolon
średniofalowy medium wave
Średniowiecze the Middle Ages; (*i przen.*) the dark ages
średniowieczny medieval
środa Wednesday; **Środa Popielcowa** Ash Wednesday
środ|ek 1 (*punkt centralny*) centre[1], interior, middle[1]; (*form.*) midst; (*lasu itp.*) heart; (*miasta itp.*) hub; **~ek owocu** core; **~ek lata** midsummer; **~ek zimy** midwinter; **w ~ku** between adv., inside[1], within; **w ~ku nocy** in/at the dead of night, in the deep of the night; **telefon zadzwonił w samym ~ku mojego ulubionego programu** the phone rang slap bang in the middle of my favourite programme; **do ~ka** inside[1]; **w ~ku pienił się ze złości** there was a lot of anger beneath the surface **2** (*sposób działania*) instrument, means, mode; (**środki**) measures[2]; **~ek ostrożności** precaution; **~ki bezpieczeństwa** security; **~ek do osiągnięcia celu** a means to an end **3** (**środki**) resources; (*pieniądze*) funds[1]; (*do życia*) means; **małymi ~kami** on a shoestring **4** (*komunikacji itp.*) medium[2]; **~ki masowego przekazu** mass media, media **5 ~ek transportu** transport **6** (*lek itp.*) remedy[1]; **~ek antykoncepcyjny** contraceptive; **~ek nasenny** sedative; **~ek pobudzający** stimulant; **~ek przeciwbólowy** analgesic, painkiller; **~ek przeczyszczający** laxative; **~ek przeciwdepresyjny** antidepressant; **~ek uspokajający/usypiający** sedative, tranquillizer; **~ek zapobiegawczy** prophylactic noun; **~ek znieczulający** anaesthetic **7** (*chemiczny*) **~ek czyszczący** detergent; **~ek chwastobójczy** weedkiller; **~ek grzybobójczy** fungicide; **~ek konserwujący** preservative; **~ek odstraszający** repellent[2]; **~ek owadobójczy**

insecticide; **~ek tonizujący** (*np. wzmacniający/ożywiający*) tonic; **~ek mocujący** fixative; **~ek utrwalający** (*zwł. do kolorów i zapachów*) fixative IDM **~ek ciężkości** centre of gravity | (*przen.*) **w samym ~ku czegoś** in the thick of sth
środkow|y central, intermediate, median, mid, middle[2], midway adj.; **Środkowy Wschód** the Middle East; **Środkowy Zachód** the Midwest; **ucho ~e** inner ear
środowisk|o environment, setting, surroundings; (*społeczność*) community; (*ważny, szkodliwy itp.*) **dla ~a** environmentally; **~o akademickie** academia; **~o naturalne** environment; (*roślin i zwierząt*) habitat; (*ważny, szkodliwy itp.*) **dla ~a** environmentally
środowiskow|y environmental; **pielęgniarka ~a** community/district nurse
śródlądowy inland
śródmiejski downtown
śródmieści|e downtown; **do/w ~-a/u** downtown; (*mieszkanie itp.*) **w ~u** central
śródziemnomorski Mediterranean adj.; **kraje ~e** the Mediterranean
śruba 1 (*wkręt itp.*) screw[1] **2** (*okrętowa*) propeller
śrubokręt screwdriver
śrucina pellet
śrut pellet
śrutówka shotgun
świadczeni|e benefit[1]; **~a socjalne** social services
świadczyć/za-/po- testify; **(o czymś)** bear witness (to sth), be a reflection on sth, be a testament to sth; **(dobrze/źle itp.) o kimś/czymś świadczyć** reflect (well, badly, etc.) on sb/sth
świadectw|o 1 (*dokument*) certificate; **~o pracy** reference; **~o urodzenia** birth certificate **2** (*dowód*) credentials, evidence, testament, testimony; **być ~em (czegoś)** bear witness (to sth)
świad|ek witness[1]; **~ek obrony/oskarżenia** witness for the defence/prosecution; **być ~kiem (czegoś)** see, witness[2]
świadomoś|ć awareness, consciousness; **z pełną ~cią** with your eyes open
świadom|y aware, conscious, mindful; (*kontrolowany: ruchy ciała*) voluntary
■ **świadomie** advisedly, consciously, knowingly
świat the universe, world; **na całym świecie** the world over, worldwide adv.; **~ mody** the fashion scene; **~ przestępczy** the underworld; **~ zewnętrzny** the outside world IDM **kiedy cię jeszcze na świecie nie było** before your time | **~a poza kimś nie widzieć** think the world of sb/sth
świat|ło light[1]; (*zatopione w asfalcie na szosie*) Catseye; **~ło dzienne** daylight; **~ło gwiazd** starlight; **~ło księżyca** moonlight; **~ło odblaskowe** reflector; **~ło ostrzegawcze** beacon; **~ło słoneczne** sunlight, sunshine; **~ło stopu** brake light; **~ło sygnalizacyjne** (*na skrzyżowaniu*) traffic light; **~ło świec** candlelight IDM **w dobrym/złym świetle** in a good, bad, etc. light | **w nowym świetle** in a new perspective | **stawiać kogoś/coś w innym świetle** put a different complexion on sb/sth | **w świetle** (*np. pewnych informacji*) in the light of sth | **wychodzić na ~ło dzienne** come to light | **wyciągać coś na ~ło dzienne** bring sth to light | **wydobywać na ~ło dzienne** unearth
światłowodow|y fibre-optic; **technika ~a** fibre optics
światłowód (*włókno*) optical fibre
światł|y cultured, enlightened; **~-y/a mężczyzna/kobieta** a man/woman of culture
światow|y 1 (*wydarzenie*) world; (*trend itp.*) global, worldwide; **~ej klasy** world-class; **~ej sławy** world-famous **2** (*osoba: obyty*) worldly; **~a młoda dama** a very sophisticated young woman
świąteczny festive
świątobliwy saintly
świątynia temple
świdrować bore[1]
■ **świdrujący** piercing[1]
świeca 1 (*z wosku*) candle **2 ~ zapłonowa** spark plug
świecący (się) luminous, shiny
świecić/za- (*światło itp.*) burn[1]; (*oślepiającym blaskiem*) glare[1], flash[1], shine[1]
□ **świecić/za- się** flash[1], shine[1]
świecidełko trinket
świeck|i 1 (*instytucja*) secular; (*pieśni itp.*) profane **2** (*osoba*) lay[2]; **kobieta ~a** laywoman; **osoba ~a** layman
świeczka candle
świecznik candlestick
świergotać/za- twitter, warble
świerk spruce[2]
świerszcz cricket
świerzb mange
świerzbić/za- tingle
świetlany bright
świetlica (*dla studentów/uczniów*) common room
świetlik 1 (*statku*) porthole **2** (*okienko w dachu*) skylight
świetln|y: **ozdoby ~e** illuminations
świetność 1 excellence **2** (*blask*) magnificence, splendour, glitter
świetn|y brilliant, excellent, fantastic, fine[1], great[1], lovely, magnificent, splendid, terrific; (*żołnierz; sportowiec*) crack[3]; **~y pomysł** a bright idea
■ **świetnie** excellently, magnificently; (*bawić się z kimś*) famously; **~!** nice one!
świeżość freshness
śwież|y 1 (*jedzenie; kwiaty; powietrze*) fresh; (*sałata, herbatnik itp.*) crisp[1]; **~e powietrze** the open; **na ~ym powietrzu** in the open, in the open air, out of doors **2** (*niedawny*) recent **3** (*zimne powietrze itp.*) crisp[1] IDM (*przen.*) **~e powietrze** a breath of fresh air
■ **świeżo** freshly; **~ przybyły skądś** fresh from/out of sth; **~ malowane!** wet paint!
święceni|e: **~a kapłańskie** holy orders, ordination
święcić/po-/u- 1 (*relig.*) consecrate **2 nowy program święcił tryumf wśród publiczności** the new programme was a triumph with the public
święt|o festival, holiday; **Święta Bożego Narodzenia** Christmas, the festive season; **~o Trzech Króli** Epiphany; (*hinduizm*) **~o ognia** Diwali
świętokradczy sacrilegious
świętokradztwo sacrilege
świętosz-ek/ka goody-goody; (*unikający tematu seksu*) prude; (*potępiający innych*) prig
świętoszkowaty sanctimonious
świętość holiness, sanctity (of sth), sanctity
świętować celebrate
■ **świętowanie** celebration, festivity
święt|y (*przym.*) blessed, holy, sacred; **~-y/a patron/ka** patron saint; **Święty Mikołaj** Father Christmas; **Dzień Wszystkich Świętych** All Saints' Day IDM **~a prawda** gospel | **~ej pamięci** late
■ **święt-y/a** (*rz.*) saint
świni|a 1 pig[1]; (*przestarz.*) **~e** swine **2** (*osoba*) pig[1], swine
świnka 1 (*med.*) mumps **2 ~ morska** guinea pig
świński: **~ dowcip** dirty joke
świr crackpot
świrnięty bonkers, nutty
świsnąć (*ukraść*) go off with sth, pinch[1]
świst whoosh; **przemieszczać się ze ~em** whoosh verb; **przelecieć ze ~em** go whizzing by
świstek slip[2]
świt break of day, dawn[1], daybreak, sunrise
świtać/za- dawn[2]; **świtało** dawn was breaking

T

t (T/t) (*litera*) T, t
tabaka tobacco; (*wciągana do nosa*) snuff
tabel|a scale[1], table; **~a ligi** league table; **zestawiać w formie ~i** tabulate
tabletka lozenge, pill, tablet; **~ nasenna** sleeping pill
tablica board[1], plate; **duża ~ reklamowa** hoarding; **~ informacyjna** indicator board; **~ ogłoszeń** noticeboard; (*komput.*) bulletin board; **internetowa ~ ogłoszeń** message board; **~ oznaczająca, że kierujący pojazdem uczy się jeździć** L-plate; **~ rejestracyjna** number plate; **~ rozdzielcza** dashboard, instrument panel, panel; **~ szkolna** blackboard; (*typu whiteboard: biała, na której pisze się specjalnymi łatwo ścieralnymi markerami*) whiteboard; **~ wyników** scoreboard
tabliczka 1 bar[1] **2 ~ mnożenia** multiplication table
taboret stool
tabu taboo
tabulacj|a: **klawisz ~i** tab key
taca tray
tacka: **~ na korespondencję przychodzącą** in tray
taczka wheelbarrow
tafla 1 plate, sheet **2** (*jeziora itp.*) surface[1]
taić/za- suppress
tajać/s- thaw (out)
tajemnic|a mystery, secrecy, secret[2]; **w ~y** on the quiet, in secret, secretly, secretively, surreptitiously; **w największej ~y** the information

was given to me in strict confidence IDM **trzymać coś w ~y (przed kimś)** keep it/sth dark (from sb), keep quiet about sth, keep sth quiet
tajemniczość mystery, secretiveness
tajemniczy cryptic, mysterious, shadowy, secretive; (*niepokojący*) uncanny
tajemny 1 (*motyw itp.*) ulterior **2** (*związany z magią*) occult
tajfun typhoon
tajniak tail[1]
tajnik (**tajniki**) the ins and outs (of sth)
tajn|y classified, confidential, covert, cryptic, hush-hush, secret[1]; (*dokument itp.*) classified, confidential; (*agent*) undercover; **~y agent** secret agent; **ściśle ~y** top secret; **~a policja** secret police; **~e głosowanie** ballot; **~e służby** the secret service
tak (*wykrzyk.; rz.*) yes; (*nieform.*) yeah, yep, OK; **~, oczywiście** surely; **~, czy nie** true or false?
■ **tak** (*przyszł.*) **1** (*w taki sposób*) thus; **zrób to** ~ do it like this; **~, żeby** so as to do sth, so[2] (that); **~ samo** alike[2], identically, likewise, the same; **nie** ~ amiss; **~ jak** as, so[1]; **~...jak...** as; **(nie) ~ (...jak)** so[1]; **~ czy owak**; **~ czy inaczej** anyway, at all events, in any event **2** (*bardzo*) so[1]; **(aż)** ~ that, this adv. IDM **~ czy siak** at all events/in any event | **i ~ dalej** and so on (and so forth) | **~ jest!** that/this is it, that is so, very well, yes | **~ sobie** so-so
taki 1 (*rodzaj*) such; **~ jak** like[1], such as; **~ lub inny** some; **~ sam** alike[1], identical, same; **~ a ~** so-and-so; **~ owaki** so-and-so **2** (*wzmocnienie*) such; **jest ~m dobrym mężczyzną** he's ever such a kind man IDM **coś ~ego!** good gracious, good grief, good heavens, etc. | **~ sobie** not much good
takielunek rigging
taksator assessor
taksówka taxi[1]
takt 1 (*maniery*) diplomacy, tact; **brak ~u** gaucheness, insensitivity **2** (*muz.*) bar[1], beat[2]; **iść w** ~ be in/out of step (with sb/sth)
taktowny tactful
taktyczny tactical
taktyka tack[1]; (*wojskowa itp.*) tactic
także also, too, as well (as sb/sth); **~ nie** either[2]
talent accomplishment, bent[3] for sth/doing sth, flair, genius, gift (for sth/doing sth), knack (of/for doing sth), talent; **wielki** ~ genius
talerz 1 dish[1], plate; **pełny ~ (czegoś)** plateful **2** (*perkusyjny*) cymbal IDM **latający** ~ flying saucer | **~ obrotowy** turntable
talia 1 (*anat.*) middle[1], midriff, waist; **rozmiar w talii** waistline **2** (*kart*) pack[2]
talizman charm[1]
talk: **~ kosmetyczny** talcum powder
talk show (także **talk**) chat show, talk show
talon coupon
tam (over) there; **~ i z powrotem** about[1], back and forth, backward(s) and forward(s), to and fro, up and down; **tu i** ~ about[1]
tam|a dam, dyke, weir; **budować ~ę** dam verb
tamburyn tambourine
tamować/za- 1 (*rzekę*) dam verb **2** (*krwotok*) stop[1] **3** (*dziurę*) plug[2] **4** (*powstrzymywać*) interfere (with sb/sth), obstruct, stem[2]
tampon 1 (*higieniczny*) tampon **2** (*gazik*) pad[1], swab; (*do oczyszczania ran*) wad
tamten (*wskazując na coś*) that
tance-rz/rka dancer; **~ baletu** ballet dancer
tandem (*rower*) tandem
tandeta dud
tandetność tawdriness
tandetny cheap[1], crummy, shoddy, tacky, tawdry; (*piosenka itp.*) cheesy
tani cheap[1], inexpensive; **~ chwyt** a gimmicky idea
taniec dance[1]; (**tańce**) dance[1], dancing; **tradycyjne tańce towarzyskie** ballroom dancing
tankowiec tanker
tantiema royalty
tańczyć/za- dance[2]; **~ tango** tango verb; **~ walca** waltz[2]
tapczan divan
tapeta (*i komput.*) wallpaper
tapetować/wy- wallpaper verb; **malować i tapetować** decorate
tapicerka upholstery
tapicerowany upholstered
taplać dabble
taranować/s- batter[1], ram[1]
tarapat|y scrape[2], trouble[1]; **w finansowych ~ach** in a financial mess; **być w ~ach** be in difficulty, be in dire straits; **wpadać w ~y** get into trouble; **w finansowych ~ach** in a financial mess; **wyciągać kogoś/wyjść z ~ów** get/let sb off the hook
taras terrace
tarasować/za- obstruct
tarasowaty (także **tarasowy**) terraced
tarci|e 1 (*fiz.*) friction **2** (**tarcia**) (*sprzeczność*) friction (between A and B)
tarcz|a 1 (*rycerska, herbowa itp.*) shield[1] **2** (*zegara itp.*) dial[1]; **~a zegara** clock face **3** (*strzelnicza*) target[1]; **środek ~y** bullseye **4** (*zwł. podająca tożsamość*) disc
tarczyca thyroid
targ market[1], marketplace; (**targi**) fair[2]
targać/po- 1 kimś gnaw (away) at sb **2 ~ na strzępy** shred[1]
targować/po- się bargain[2], haggle
targowy market[1]
tarka grater
tarta flan; **słona ~ z serem itp.** quiche
taryfa tariff
tarzać/wy- się roll[2]
tasak chopper; **~ kuchenny** cleaver
tasiemka tape[1]; **~ do ściągania** drawstring
tasować/po- shuffle[1]
taszczyć/wy- cart[2], lug
taśm|a 1 (*opaska, wstążka*) band, tape[1]; **(przezroczysta) ~a klejąca** Sellotape; **~a magnetofonowa/magnetowidowa/magnetyczna** tape[1]; **~a miernicza** tape measure **2** (*pas*) belt[1]; **~a montażowa** assembly line; **~a do bagaży** carousel
taśma-matka master[1]
tata: **tat-a/o** dad
tatuaż tattoo
tatuować/wy- tattoo verb
tatuś daddy, pop[1]
tawerna tavern
tchawica trachea, windpipe
tchórz coward
tchórzliwy cowardly
tchórzostwo cowardice
tchórzyć/s-: **(przed czymś)** chicken out (of sth)
teatr playhouse, theatre; (*w budynku, gdzie jest więcej niż jedna scena*) stage[1]; **~ awangardowy/niekomercyjny** fringe theatre; **~ rozrywki** variety theatre; **~ stały** repertory
teatralny 1 (*teatr*) theatre, theatrical **2** (*zachowanie*) histrionic
teatroman/ka theatregoer
techniczny technical, technological; (*przedmioty*) non-academic; **zmysł ~** a mechanical mind
technik engineer[1], technician
technika 1 (*metoda*) technique; **~ malarska** brushwork **2** (*wiedza na temat technologii, przemysłu itp.*) technology **3** (*praca inżyniera*) engineering
technolog technologist
technologia technology
technologiczny technological
teczka 1 (*(na) dokumenty*) file[1], holder, portfolio; **~ do akt** folder **2** (*torba*) briefcase; **~ szkolna** satchel
teflonowy non-stick
tek teak
teka portfolio
tekst script, text[1]; **~ piosenki** lyrics
tekstylny textile
tektura cardboard
tekturowy cardboard
telefon 1 (*narzędzie*) telephone; **~ komórkowy** mobile phone; **~ komórkowy w samochodzie** car phone; **~ wewnętrzny** intercom; **rozmawiać przez** ~ be (talking) on the phone **2** (*rozmowa*) call[2]; **dziękuję za** ~ thank you for calling
telefoniczny telephone
telefonist-a/ka operator
telefonować/za- phone verb, ring[2], give sb a ring, telephone
telefonując-y/a caller
telegazeta teletext
telegraf telegraph
telegram telegram
telekomunikacja telecommunications
teleks telex
teleman (także **telemaniak**) couch potato
telenowela soap opera
teleobiektyw telephoto lens
telepać/za- jiggle
□ **telepać/za- się** jerk[1], jolt[1]
telepatia telepathy
teleprompter Autocue
teleskop telescope
teletekst teletext
teleturniej game show, quiz programme
telewidz viewer
telewizja television; (*nieform.*) box[1]; **~ cyfrowa** digital television; **~ kablowa** cable television; **~ satelitarna** satellite television; **w telewizji** on television
telewizor television; **~ plazmowy** plasma TV
telezakupy teleshopping
temat 1 (*główna myśl*) matter[1], subject[1], subject matter, topic; **~ dnia**

lead story; **na ~** on, over; **nie na ~** beside the point; **odchodzić od ~u** digress **2** (*lit., muz. itp.*) theme **3** (*wyrazu*) stem[1]
tematyczny thematic
tematyka theme
temblak sling[2]
temperament temperament
temperatura temperature; **~ topnienia** melting point; **~ wrzenia wody** boiling point; **~ zamarzania wody** freezing point; **wysoka ~** (*ciała*) fever
temperówka pencil sharpener, sharpener
temp|o pace[1], rate[1], tempo; **nabierać ~a** hot up
temu (*okoliczniki czasu*) ago, back[3]
ten the one[2]; (*blisko mówcy*) this; (*daleko od mówcy*) that; **właśnie ~** one[1]; **~ (sławny)** the IDM **~ a ~** so-and-so
tendencj|a drift[1], tendency, trend; **~e rynkowe** market forces; **nieczytelna od razu ~a** undercurrent; **mieć ~ę do czegoś** tend to do sth; **mający ~ę** (*np. do zapominania*) apt to do sth
tendencyjność tendentiousness
tendencyjny partisan[1], tendentious
tenis tennis; **~ stołowy** table tennis
tenisówka plimsoll
tenor tenor
tenorowy tenor adj.
teolog theologian
teologia theology
teologiczny theological
teoremat theorem
teoretyczn|y abstract[1], theoretical; **(czysto) ~y** academic[1]
■ **teoretycznie** in the abstract, theoretically, in theory
teoretyk theorist
teoretyzować theorize
teoria a school of thought, theory
terakota terracotta
terakotowy terracotta
terapeut-a/ka therapist; **~ zajęciow-y/a** occupational therapist
terapeutyczny therapeutic
terapia therapy; **~ genowa** gene therapy; **~ logopedyczna** speech therapy; **~ zajęciowa** occupational therapy; **zastępcza ~ hormonalna** HRT
terasa terrace
teraz now, at present, presently, today; (*tymczasem*) meanwhile; **~, gdy** now conj.; **właśnie ~** just now
teraźniejszość present[2]
teraźniejszy present[1]
teren 1 (*obszar ziemi i jej cechy*) area, country, terrain **2** (*przeznaczony do pewnych celów*) land[1]; (*bitwy itp.*) field[1]; **~ zabudowany/pod zabudowę** development, site; **~ przemysłowy** industrial estate **3** (*około budynku*) grounds[1]; **~ z tyłu domu** backyard; **~ uczelni** campus **4** (*działania itp.*) territory IDM **w ~ie** away
terier terrier
terkot clack
terkotać/za- clack
terma boiler; **~ gazowa** geyser
termiczny thermal[1]; **prąd ~** thermal[2]
termin (*czas*) term[1]; (*nauka rzemiosła*) apprenticeship; (*data*) date[1]; **określony ~** time limit; **ostateczny ~** the cut-off date, deadline; **~ przydatności do spożycia** best-before date, expiry date; **~ ważności** expiry date; **~, do kiedy towar może być wystawiony do sprzedaży** sell-by date; **w krótkim ~ie** at short notice
terminal (*na lotnisku, komput.*) terminal[1]
terminarz diary, planner
terminator/ka apprentice
terminologia terminology
termit termite
termofor hot-water bottle
termometr thermometer
termos Thermos, vacuum flask; **~ bufetowy** urn
termostat thermostat
terpentyna turpentine
terror terror
terroryst-a/ka bomber, terrorist noun
terrorystyczny terrorist; **kampania terrorystyczna** terror campaign
terroryzm terrorism
terroryzować/z- terrorize
terytorialny territorial
terytorium territory
test test[1]; **~ rozumienia ze słuchu** aural comprehension test
testament 1 (*akt*) will[3] **2 Stary/NowyTestament** the Old/New Testament
testosteron testosterone
testować/prze- experiment[2], test[2]; **kogoś** test[2] sb (on sth)
teściowa mother-in-law
teść father-in-law; **(teściowie)** in-laws
teza a line of argument, thesis
tezaurus thesaurus
też also, so[1], too, as well (as sb/sth); **~ nie** either[2], neither, nor; **ani..., ani ~...** neither; **i ja ~** same here
tęcza rainbow
tęczówka iris
tęg|i burly, stout IDM **~a głowa** brain, brainbox
tępak dimwit, dope[1]
tępić/wy- eradicate, exterminate, kill sth off
tępota obtuseness
tęp|y 1 (*nóż itp.*) blunt **2** (*osoba*) dense, dim[1], dim-witted, dull, dull-witted, gormless, obtuse, slow[1], thick[1]; **o ~ym umyśle** slow-witted
tęsknić/za- long[3] for sth, miss[1], yearn; **~ za domem** be homesick
tęsknot|a longing, nostalgia, yearning; **~a za domem/ojczyzną** homesickness; **pełen ~y** wistful
tęskny wistful
tętniący: **~ życiem** vibrant
tętnica artery
tętnić/za- 1 (*krew itp.*) pulsate, throb **2** (*głośny dźwięk w uszach*) ring[2] (with sth) **3** (*życiem*) bustle[1] (with sth), buzz[1] (with sth)
tężec tetanus
tężeć/s- solidify
tężyzna brawn
tik tic
tkać/u- weave
tkanina cloth, fabric, fibre, material[1], textile
tkanka tissue
tkwić/u- 1 w czymś lodge[2], stick[1] (in sth); **miał utkwiony we mnie wzrok** his eyes were fastened on me **2** (*osoba: w jakiejś sytuacji*) linger; **tkwić gdzieś bez celu** loiter **3** (*problem*) **w czymś** lie[2] (in sth)
tlen oxygen
tlenek: **~ węgla** carbon monoxide
tlić/za- się smoulder
tło background, setting
tłoczyć press[2], squash[1]
□ **tłoczyć się 1** squash[1] **2 (/s-) (wokół kogoś)** crowd around/round (sb), mob[2], throng[2] **3 (/w-) do czegoś/w coś** crush (sb/sth) into, past, through, etc. sth, press[2] across/against/around, etc. (sth)
tłok 1 crush[2], rush[2], squash[2], squeeze[2], throng[1] **2** (*techn.*) piston; (*w strzykawce itp.*) plunger
tłu|c 1 (/s-/u-) (*rozbijać*) break[1], mash, pound[2], smash[1]; **ziemniaki ~czone** mashed potato **2 (/s-) kogoś** bludgeon, clobber, strike[1] **3** (*łomotać*) bang[1], hammer[2], pound[2] (at/against/on sth) **4 (/s-)** (*kolano itp.*) jar[2]
□ **tłuc/s- się** break[1], smash[1]; **łatwo ~kący się** breakable
tłuczek (*do moździerza*) pestle
tłum crowd[1], flock[1], horde, host
tłumacz/ka translator; **~ ustn-y/a** interpreter
tłumaczenie translation; (*ustne*) interpretation
tłumaczyć 1 (/prze-) (*z jednego języka na drugi*) translate; (*ustnie*) interpret **2 (/wy-)** (*wyjaśniać*) account for sth, explain, justify; **czymś** credit[2] sb/sth with sth; **źle ~ sobie** misunderstand; **~ język oprogramowania** disassemble; **czy mógłby mi pan wytłumaczyć, jak dojść do dworca?** can you tell me the way to the station?
□ **tłumaczyć/wy- się** explain yourself
tłumiący (*namiętności itp.*) repressed
tłumić/s- 1 (*dźwięk*) keep sth down, muffle **2** (*bunt itp.*) crush[1], put sth down, quash, quell, repress, suppress; (*inicjatywę itp.*) stifle, strangle **3** (*uczucie itp.*) dampen, deaden, repress, shut sth out, smother, suppress; (*czyjeś oczekiwania itp.*) damp[2] sth (down); **tłumić w sobie** bottle sth up **4** (*płomień*) smother IDM **stłumić coś złego w zarodku** nip sth in the bud
tłumik silencer
tłumiony (*uczucie*) pent-up, repressed
tłumnie: **schodzić się ~** flock[2]; **ludzie ~ wychodzili ze stacji** people were pouring out of the station
tłumok pack[2]
tłusty 1 (*jedzenie*) fatty, rich **2** (*garnek itp.; włosy*) greasy **3** (*osoba*) podgy **4** (*druk*) bold
tłuszcz fat[2]; (*wielorybi itp.*) blubber[1]; (*w garnku itp.; na włosach*) grease[1]; **~ nasycony** saturated fat; (*mięso*) **bez ~u** lean[2]
tłuszcza horde
tłuściutki plump[1]
to zob. też TEN; **~ (jest)** it; **(wszystko) ~, co** what; **(właśnie) ~** just the thing, the real thing; **tj.** that is (to say), i.e., viz.; **z tym, że** provided (that) IDM **~ i owo** this and that, this, that and the other
toaleta lavatory, toilet; (*nieform.*) loo; **~ damska** the Ladies; **~ publiczna** (public) convenience, restroom
toaletka dresser, dressing table
toast toast
tobogan toboggan

tobół pack[2]

toczący się ongoing

toczyć 1 (/po-) (*beczkę itp.*) roll[2]; (*coś na kółkach*) wheel[2] **2 (/s-)** (*wojnę*) fight[1], wage[2] sth (against/on sb/sth) □ **toczyć/po- się 1** (*beczka itp.*) roll[2], trundle; **stoczyć się ze schodów** tumble all the way down the steps **2** (*sprawy; życie*) proceed, run[1]; (*rozmowa itp.*) ~ **się długo i z wieloma dygresjami** meander; **stoczył się na samo dno** he hit rock bottom

toffi toffee

toga gown, robe

tok process[1]; **w ~u** afoot, in progress, pending adj., under way; **normalny ~ postępowania** a matter of course

tokarka lathe

tokować crow[2]

toksyczny poisonous, toxic

toksyna toxin

tolerancja tolerance

tolerancyjny broad-minded, tolerant

tolerować connive at sth, stomach[2], tolerate; **nie ~** not brook sth/brook no…

tom volume

ton 1 tone[1] **2** (*nuta*) note[1] IDM **nadawać ~** call the shots/tune

tona (*metryczna*) tonne; (= *2200 funtów ang.*) ton

tonacja 1 (*muz.*) key[1], tonality **2 ~ kolorystyczna** colour scheme

tonalny tonal

tonąć/za-/u- go down, drown, sink[1], go under IDM **tonąć we łzach** be in floods of tears

toner toner

tonik 1 (*napój*) tonic **2** (*kosmetyk*) toner

tonizujący: **środek ~** (*np. wzmacniający/ożywiający*) tonic

tonować/s- (*oświadczenie, raport itp.*) tone sth down, water sth down

tonowy tonal

top (*bez ramiączek*) boob tube

topić 1 (/u-) (*osobę*) drown **2 (/s-)** (*śnieg itp.*) melt □ **topić się 1 (/u-)** (*osoba*) drown **2 (/s-)** (*śnieg itp.*) melt, thaw

tople|s (także **topless**) (*bez stanika*) topless; **w ~ssie** topless adv.

topnieć/s- melt, thaw

topnieni|e: **temperatura ~a** melting point; (*rdzenia reaktora nuklearnego*) meltdown

topola poplar

toporek hatchet

toporność crudity

toporny crude

topór: **~ rzeźniczy** cleaver

tor path; (*na bieżni*) circuit, lane; (*kolejowy, tramwajowy*) line[1], rail, track[1]; **~ ziemny** dirt track; **~ wyścigowy** course, track[1]; **~ wyścigów konnych** racecourse

Tora the Torah

torba 1 bag[1]; **~ na ramię** shoulder bag; **~ podróżna** holdall; **~ kabinowa** carry-on; **~-reklamówka** carrier bag **2** (*kangura itp.*) pouch

torbacz marsupial

torbiel cyst

toreador bullfighter

torebka bag[1], pack[2], packet; **~ damska** handbag; **~ herbaty** tea bag

torf peat

tornado tornado

tornister satchel

torować/u- 1 ~ sobie drogę nose[2] **2** (*przen.*) **torować drogę** pioneer verb

torpeda torpedo

tors torso, trunk

tort gateau

torturować torture verb

tortury torture

torys Tory

tost toast; **robić ~y** toast verb

toster toaster

totalitarny totalitarian

totalitaryzm totalitarianism

totalny out-and-out, total[1]

tournée tour

towar (*fin.*) commodity, merchandise, stock[1]; (**towary**) goods, wares; (*ładunek na statku/w pociągu itp.*) freight; **~y konsumpcyjne** consumer goods; **sklep z ~ami żelaznymi** (*np. narzędziami*) hardware shop

towarowy (*pociąg*) freight

towarzysk|i (*okazja*) social; (*atmosfera, znajomi*) convivial, genial; (*osoba*) gregarious, outgoing, sociable; (*mecz itp.*) friendly[1]; **atmosfera spotkania ~iego** an atmosphere of informality

towarzystw|o 1 (*ludzi*) companionship, company, fellowship; **bez ~a** unaccompanied; **dotrzymywać komuś ~a** keep sb company **2** (*naukowe itp.*) society

towarzysz/ka companion; (*broni; w partii politycznej*) comrade; **~ podróży** fellow-traveller; **~ zabaw** playmate; **~ życia** partner; **towarzysze oficerowie** brother officers

towarzyszyć accompany, go with sth; (*tylko osobę*) escort[2]; (*trudności*) dog[2] ■ **towarzyszący** attendant[2]

towotnica grease gun

tożsamość identity

tożsamy: **z czymś** synonymous (with sth)

tracić 1 (/s-) (*już dłużej nie mieć*) lose; (*okazję itp.*) forfeit; (*drzewo: liście itp.*) shed[2]; **~ kontakt (z kimś/czymś)** lose touch (with sb/sth); **stracić miejsce** lose your place; **~ nadzieję** despair[2], give up hope; **~ panowanie nad sobą** go to pieces; **~ przytomność** have a blackout; **~ równowagę** lose your balance, overbalance; **~ siły** flag[2]; **~ na gwałtowności/sile** moderate[2]; **~ na wadze** lose weight; (*paszport itp.*) **~ ważność** lapse[2], run out; **~ na wartości** depreciate; **funt traci na wartości względem dolara** the pound is sliding against the dollar; **~ wzrok** go blind; **stracił wzrok/głos/pamięć** his sight/voice/mind has gone; **~ życie** lose your life, perish **2 (/s-) (na czymś)** lose out (on sth/to sb) **3 (/s-)** (*czas; pieniądze*) waste[1] **4 (/s-)** (*sposobność, okazję*) miss out (on sth) **5 (/u-)** (*prawa, depozyt itp.*) forfeit IDM (*mieć*) **do stracenia** to spare | **nic nie ~ (na czymś)** be none the worse (for sth) | **~ ducha** your heart sinks | **~ głowę** get flustered, lose your head | **nie ~ głowy** keep your head | **~ otuchę** your heart sinks | **~ kogoś/coś z oczu/z pola widzenia** lose sight of sb/sth | **~ pozycję (w stosunku do kogoś)** give/lose ground (to sb/sth) | **~ rachubę** keep/lose count (of sth) | **~ serce (do czegoś)** lose heart | **~ twarz** lose face | **~ (specjalną) umiejętność** lose your touch | **~ na znaczeniu** wear thin

tradycja tradition

tradycyjny classic[1], conventional, traditional

traf chance[1], luck; **szczęśliwy ~** fluke

trafi(a)ć 1 (*w cel*) hit[1]; **nie ~** miss[1] **2** (*na jakieś wydarzenie/okazję*) **~ gdzieś** find[1], find your way somewhere, land up (in…); **wytłumaczę ci, jak trafić do mojego domu** I'll give you directions to my house **3** (*dostać czymś itp.*) catch[1] IDM **~ w (samo) sedno rzeczy** hit the nail on the head

trafność relevance

trafny (*uwaga*) apt, opportune, pertinent, to the point, shrewd; (*argument itp.*) neat, valid

tragarz porter

tragedia tragedy

tragiczny tragic

tragizm pathos

trajkot gabble noun

trajkotać/za- chatter, gabble

trakt 1 (być) w trakcie (czegoś) in the act (of doing sth), in the course of sth, be in the middle of sth/doing sth, in the midst of sth, in the process (of sth/doing sth); **w trakcie budowy** under construction **2** (*droga*) way[1]

traktat treaty

traktor tractor

traktować 1 (/po-) kogoś/coś jak(o) kogoś/coś look on sb/sth as sth, regard[1], treat[1]; **~ poważnie** take sb/sth seriously; **źle ~** ill-treat; **być źle traktowanym** get a raw deal; **nie ~ kogoś/czegoś odpowiednio** mess with sb/sth **2 o czymś** deal with sth

tramp tramp[1]

trampolina diving board, springboard

tramwaj tram

trans trance

transakcja deal[2], transaction; (*sprzedaż*) sale

transatlantycki transatlantic

transatlantyk liner

transeksualist-a/ka transsexual

transfer transfer[2]

transferować transfer[1]

transformator transformer

transfuzja: **~ krwi** (blood) transfusion

transkrybować transcribe

transmisja transmission

transmitować beam[2], broadcast, transmit; **~ w telewizji** telecast, televise

transparent banner

transplantacja transplant[2]

transplantować transplant[1]

transponować transpose

transport carriage, haulage, transport; **~ wodny** shipping

transporter 1 ~ taśmowy conveyor belt **2** (*pojazd*) freighter

transportować/prze- transport verb

transportowiec carrier

transpozycja transposition

transwestyt-a/ka transvestite

tranzystor transistor

tranzyt transit

trap gangway

trapez trapeze

trapić torment verb, torture verb □ **trapić/s- się** agonize, worry[1]

trasa route, way[1]; **~ spacerowa** walk[2]

tratować/s- trample
tratwa raft
trauma trauma
traumatyczny traumatic
trawa grass
trawiasty grassy
trawić 1 (/s-) (*pokarm*) digest **2 (/s-)** (*ogień*) consume **3** (*zmartwienie*) **kogoś** consume
trawienie digestion
trawka dope[1]
trawler trawler
trawnik lawn
trawożern|y herbivorous; **zwierzę roślinożerne** herbivore
trąba IDM **~ powietrzna** whirlwind | **~ słonia** trunk
trąbić/za- (*klaksonem*) beep verb, blow your horn, honk, hoot[1], peep[1], toot verb
trąbka trumpet; (*sygnałówka*) bugle
trą-cać/cić clip[2], jog[1]; **~ łapą** paw[2] (at) sth; **~ łokciem** nudge, give sb a nudge
trąd leprosy
trądzik acne
trefl club[1]
trejaż trellis
trel trill; **wywodzić ~e** warble
treliaż trellis
trem|a the jitters, nervousness, stage fright; **mieć ~ę** have butterflies (in your stomach)
tren: **włosy powiewały za nią jak ~ na wietrze** her long hair trailed behind her in the wind
trend: **~ mody** trend
trener/ka coach[1], trainer; **~ osobist-y/a** personal trainer; **trener rozwoju osobistego** life coach
trening training; (*zwł. fizyczny*) workout
trenować 1 (*ćwiczyć*) practise, train[2] (for sth), be in training for sth **2 (/wy-)** (*osobę, ekipę*) coach[2], train[2]
treser/ka trainer
tresować/wy- 1 (*ćwiczyć*) train[2] (for sth) **2** (*osobę, ekipę*) train[2] sb (as sth/to do sth)
treściwy concise, meaningful, meaty, pithy, succinct
treś|ć 1 (*książki*) content[1], matter[1]; **mało ~ci** little substance **2** (*znaczenie*) meaning; **ogólna ~ć** gist; **o podobnej ~ci** to this/that effect
trędowat-y/a leper
triangel (także **triangiel**) triangle
trik stunt[1], trick
trio trio
triumf triumph[1]; **pełen ~u** jubilant
triumfalny triumphant
triumfować/za- triumph[2], prevail
■ **triumfowanie** jubilation, triumph[1]
troch|ę a little det., pron., a bit[1] (of sth), kind of, slightly, some, sort of, a trifle; **ani ~ę** (not) at all, remotely; **po ~u** bit by bit, little by little
trociny sawdust
trofeum trophy
trojaczek triplet
trojaki triple
trojkołowiec tricycle
trolejbus trolleybus
tron throne
trop 1 (*zwierzęcia*) scent, track[1] **2** (*przen.*) clue, lead[2], trail[1]; **na ~ie (kogoś/czegoś)** in pursuit (of sb/sth); **być na czyimś ~ie** be onto sb; **na dobrym/złym ~ie** on the right/wrong track
tropić/wy- (*znaleźć*) hunt sb down, trace[1], track sb/sth down; (*śledzić*) dog[2], hound[2], pursue; **tropić (kogoś) niezmordowanie** be in hot pursuit
tropik the tropics
tropikalny tropical
troska care[1], regard[2] to/for sb/sth; **nieustająca ~** preoccupation
troskliwość thoughtfulness
troskliwy attentive, caring, considerate, friendly[1], thoughtful
troszczyć/za- się: **o kogoś/coś** care[2], care for sb, cater for sb/sth, cherish, concern[1] yourself with sth, think about/of sb; **o siebie** fend for yourself
troszeczkę a trifle
troszkę a shade
trotuar pavement
trotyl TNT
trójca: **Trójca Święta** the Trinity
trójkąt (*i muz.*) triangle
trójkątny triangular
trójnóg tripod
trójskok the triple jump
trójwymiarowy three-dimensional
trucht: **biec ~em** trot[1]
truchtać/po- trot[1]
trucizn|a poison[1]; **dodawać do czegoś ~ę** poison[2]
truć/o- poison[2]
trud (*wysiłek*) bother[2], effort, toil, trouble[1]; (**trudy**) rigour; **z ~em** ill[2], just[1]; **zrobić coś z ~em** scrape[1]; **z ~em dalej coś robić** struggle along/on; **zadawać sobie ~, żeby** be at/take (great) pains to do sth, take (great) pains (with/over sth); **zadawać sobie ~ (dla kogoś)** put yourself out (for sb); **zadawać sobie wiele ~u** go to a lot of trouble (to do sth)
trudno 1 (*niełatwo*) hard; **~ komuś coś zrobić** find it difficult to do sth **2** (*spodziewać się, uwierzyć, zrobić itp.*) hardly
trudność difficulty, hardship, hitch[2], setback, stumbling block, toughness; (**trudności**) pressure
trudn|y (*pytanie itp.; sytuacja*) difficult, hard[1], tricky; (*decyzja itp.*) tough (on sb); (*niezręczny: sytuacja itp.*) awkward; (*osoba*) bolshie, difficult; (*otoczenie itp.*) harsh; (*książka, rozmowa itp.*) heavy; (*konkurencja*) stiff[1]; (*sytuacja finansowa*) straitened; **~y do zrozumienia/rozwiązania** baffling; **~y do uchwycenia** fiddly; (*problem itp.*) **być zbyt ~ym** defeat[1]; **nic ~ego** a piece of cake
trudzić się toil
trujący noxious, poisonous, toxic
trumna coffin
trunek drink[1], liquor
trup dead body
trupa troupe; **~ teatralna** company
truskawka strawberry
truskawkowy strawberry
trutka: **~ na szczury** rat poison
trwać 1 (*przez jakiś czas*) continue, endure, go on, hold[1], keep it up, last[4], be ongoing, remain; **przy/w czymś** persist; **jak długo trwała podróż?** how long did the journey take?; **trwający od dawna** long-standing **2 (/wy-)** (*nie zmieniać*) **(przy czymś/w robieniu czegoś)** cling (on) to sth, persist (in sth/doing sth), persevere (at/in/with sth) **3 (/prze-)** (*przeżyć*) subsist (on sth)
trwałość durability, permanence, persistence
trwał|y 1 (*długo trwający; niezmienny*) abiding, enduring, lasting, permanent, persistent, stable[1] **2** (*odporny*) durable, hardy, heavy-duty, tough; (*meble itp.*) substantial; (*pamięć itp.*) indelible **3** (*kolor*) fast[1] IDM **~a (ondulacja)** perm
trwani|e persistence; **czas ~a (czegoś)** duration; **powodować dalsze ~e czegoś** perpetuate; **w trakcie ~a** in progress
trwonić/roz- dissipate, fritter sth away (on sth), squander, waste[1]
trwożyć/za-/s- alarm[2], perturb
tryb 1 (*pracy itp.*) mode; **~ życia** lifestyle **2** (*gram.*) **~ łączący** subjunctive; **~ rozkazujący** the imperative **3** (*wydarzeń itp.*) course **4** (*techn.*) cog
trybun|a platform, stand[2]; (**trybuny**) (*z miejscami stojącymi*) terraces; **kryte ~y** grandstand
trybunał tribunal
trycykl tricycle
tryk ram[2]
trykot leotard
tryktrak backgammon
tryl trill
trylion trillion
trylogia trilogy
trylować trill verb
trymestr term[1]
trys-kać 1 (/trysnąć) (*woda itp.*) gush, spout[2], spurt, squirt; (*krew itp.*) pump[2] **2** (*entuzjazmem, radością itp.*) brim over (with sth), bubble[2] (over) (with sth), be bursting (with sth); (*zdrowiem, radością itp.*) exude; **tryskający radością/energią** effervescent, exuberant
tryumf → TRIUMF
tryumfalny → TRIUMFALNY
tryumfować → TRIUMFOWAĆ
trywializować/s- trivialize
trywialność triviality
trywialny trivial
trzask clap[2], crack[2], crash[1]; (*gałęzi itp.*) snap[2]; (*cichy*) click[2], pop[1]; **zwalać się/przebijać się z ~iem** crash[2]
trzas-kać/nąć 1 (*uderzać*) whack; (*pięścią*) bang[1]; (*w drzwi itp.*) rap[2]; (*czymś płaskim: np. muchę łapką*) swat; **trzasnąć z bicza** crack a whip **2** (*trzeszczeć*) crack[1]; (*gałąź itp.*) snap[1]; (*drzwiami*) bang[1], slam; **lekko trzaskać** click[1], pop[2]
trząść/za- shake[1], waggle
□ **trząść/za- się** jerk[1], quiver, shake[1], waggle; (*tylko osoba*) shiver, quake, tremble
trzcina cane[1], reed; **~ cukrowa** sugar cane
trzeba: **~ koniecznie...** it's imperative that...; **~ uprać ten sweter** this jumper needs washing/to be washed; **to ~ uczcić!** this calls for a celebration!
trzeci third[1]; **ktoś/osoba ~/a** third party; **~ świat** the Third World; **dyplom ~ej kategorii** third[2]; **po ~e** thirdly
trzeć 1 (/po-) (*pocierać*) rub **2 (/u-)** (*marchew itp.*) grate[2]; (*ziemniaki itp.*) mash
trzepaczka (*do piany itp.*) whisk[2]
trzepnięcie cuff[1]
trzepotać/za- flap[2], flutter[1]; (*skrzydłami*) beat[1]

□ **trzepotać się** (*flaga*) flap[2]
trzeszczeć/za- crackle
■ **trzeszczący** creaky; (*pióro; płyta*) scratchy
trzeźwieć/wy- sober up
trzeźw|y 1 (*nie pijany*) sober[1] **2** (*przen.*) dispassionate, lucid
■ **trzeźwo** (*przen.*) dispassionately; ~ **myślący** clear-sighted, practical[1]
trzęsący się shaky
trzęsienie: ~ **ziemi** earthquake
trzmiel bumblebee
trzoda herd[1]
trzonowy: **ząb** ~ molar
trzpień pin[1], pivot[1]
trzustka pancreas
trzy three
trzydziestodwójka (*muz.*) demisemiquaver
trzydziesty thirtieth
trzydzieści thirty
trzykrotny treble det., triple
trzymać 1 (*w rękach itp.*) hold[1]; **mocno** ~ grasp[1]; ~ **kurczowo** clutch[1]; (*i przen.*) ~ **coś dobrze** hold sth together **2 (/za-)** (*przechować; nie wyrzucać*) have[1], keep[1]; ~ **pod kluczem** lock sth away **3 (/za-)** (*pozostawiać*) keep[1]; **zatrzymany** (*w powietrzu*) poised **4 (/za-)** (*w areszcie*) ~ **kogoś w niewoli** hold sb captive/prisoner; **trzymany w klatce/na uwięzi** captive[1] IDM ~ **kogoś/coś z dala (od kogoś/czegoś)** hold/keep sb/sth at bay, keep sth off (sb/sth) | ~ **język za zębami** keep your mouth shut | ~ **kogoś za słowo** take sb up on sth
□ **trzymać się 1 (/przy-)** (*rękami itp.*) hold on (to sb/sth), hold onto sb/sth; ~ **za ręce** hold hands (with sb); **kurczowo** ~ **czegoś** cling (on) to sth **2** (*być zamocowanym*) (*rzecz; argument itp.*) ~ **dobrze** hold together **3** (*pozostawać*) keep[1]; (*droga; samochód itp.*) **(blisko)** ~ **(czegoś)** hug; ~ **lewej strony jezdni** keep left **4** (*przepisu itp.*) adhere to sth, keep to sth, stand by sth, stick to sth; (*planu itp.*) stick with sth **5** (*ludzie*) stick with sb; ~ **razem** hold together, stick together IDM ~ **z dala (od kogoś/czegoś)** be aloof, keep away from sb/sth, keep back (from sb/sth), keep off sth, keep out (of sth), keep (yourself) to yourself | ~ **od czegoś z daleka** keep your distance, stay out of sth | **trzymaj się!** hang (on) in there!, take care!
trzynasty thirteenth
trzynaście thirteen
tu here[1]; ~ **i tam** about[1], around, here and there
tuba 1 (*instrument muzyczny*) tuba **2** (*amplifikująca dźwięk*) megaphone
tubka tube
tubylczy aboriginal adj., indigenous, native[1]
tubylec native[2]
tuczyć/u- fatten sb/sth (up)
tulić/u- nurse[2]
□ **tulić/w- się** nestle
tulipan tulip
tułaczka migration
tułać się wander
tułów body, torso, trunk; (*owada*) thorax
tuman 1 (*kurzu itp.*) cloud[1] **2** (*tępak*) airhead
tunel tunnel; ~ **pod kanałem La Manche** the Channel Tunnel
tuner tuner
tunika tunic
tuńczyk tuna
tup-ać/nąć stamp[2]
tupecik toupee
tupet cheek, cockiness, nerve, self-confidence; **z ~em** (*przym.*) forward[2], self-confident; (*przysł.*) impertinently
tupot patter
turban turban
turbina propeller, turbine
turbulencja (*podczas lotu samolotem*) turbulence
turbulentny (*woda; powietrze*) turbulent
tureck|i (*siedzieć*) **po ~u** cross-legged
turkot rattle[2]
turkotać/za- rattle[1]
turkus (*geol., kolor*) turquoise
turkusowy turquoise adj.
turnia crag
turniej quiz[1]
turyst-a/ka tourist, tripper; (*piesz-y/a*) hiker, rambler; (*uprawiając-y/a wędrówkę z plecakiem*) backpacker
turystyczny tourist
turystyk|a tourism, tourist trade; **uprawiać ~ę pieszą z plecakiem** backpack[2]
tusz ink IDM ~ **do kresek** eyeliner | ~ **do rzęs** mascara
tuszować/za- 1 (*czyjś błąd*) gloss over sth **2** (*uciszyć sprawę itp.*) hush sth up
tutaj here[1]
tuzin dozen
tuż immediately; ~ **przed** just before; ~ **przy** off[1] IDM ~ ~ on your doorstep
twardnieć/s- 1 (*cement itp.*) harden **2** (*osoba*) coarsen
twardość firmness, hardness, toughness
tward|y 1 hard[1]; (*materac itp.*) firm[2]; (*buty itp.*) rugged, stiff[1]; (*mięso; buty itp.*) tough; **książka w ~ej oprawie** hardback; **ugotowany na ~o** hard-boiled **2** (*osoba; zachowanie*) hard[1], hard-headed, tough-minded; **~e rozmowy** long, hard talks **3** (*reguła itp.*) hard and fast; **~e stanowisko** hard line IDM **~y dysk** hard disk, hard drive | **~y narkotyk** hard drug | **~a ręka** a firm hand | **rządzić/władać itp. ~ą ręką** take a hard line (on sth) | **~a waluta** hard currency
■ **twardo** firmly IDM **spać ~o (jak zabity)** be sound/fast asleep
twarz face[1]; **wyraz ~y** countenance[1]; **na ~y** facial[1] IDM **stawać ~ą w ~ (z kimś/czymś)** confront | **~ą w ~ (z kimś/czymś)** face to face (with sb/sth) | **być do ~y** suit[2]
twarzowy 1 facial[1] **2** (*ubranie*) fetching, flattering
twierdza bastion, fortress
twierdzenie claim[2], contention; (*że ktoś popełnił zbrodnię itp.*) allegation; (*zwł. matematyczne*) theorem
twierdzić/s- affirm, assert, claim[1], contend, maintain, profess, purport; (*popełnienie zbrodni itp.*) allege; ~ **(coś) kategorycznie** protest[2]; **twierdził, że...** his argument was...
■ **twierdzący** affirmative; **odpowiedź twierdząca** yes noun
tworzyć/s- create, establish, form[2], found[2], make sth up, produce[1], set sth up; ~ **całość** compose, go together
□ **tworzyć/u- się** form[2]
tworzywo substance
twój 1 (*z rz.*) your **2** (*bez rz.*) yours
twór creation
twór-ca/czyni artist, creator; **twórca piosenek** songwriter
twórczość: ~ **literacka** writing
twórczy constructive, creative, formative
ty you, yourself
tyci wee[2]
tycz|ka perch[2], pole IDM **skok o ~ce** the pole vault
tyczkowaty lanky
tyczyć się: **co się tyczy** as for
tyć/u- get fat, put on weight
tydzień week; **każdego tygodnia** weekly[1]; **dwa tygodnie** fortnight; **raz na dwa tygodnie** fortnightly; ~ **przed** (*licząc od wczoraj, zeszłego poniedziałku itp.*) a week yesterday, last Monday, etc.; **za** ~ (*np. od dziś, jutra*) today/tomorrow/Monday, etc. week IDM ~ **za tygodniem** week in, week out
tyfus typhoid
tygiel 1 crucible **2** (*przen.*) melting pot
tygodnik weekly[2], weekly paper
tygodniowy weekly[1]
tygrys tiger
tykać tick[1]
tykwa gourd
tyle (*z rz. policz.*) so many; (*z rz. niepolicz.*) so much; **~...co...** as...as; **~, ile** as much as; **o ~ (że)** inasmuch as IDM **i ~!** so much for...!, and that's that! | **to ~ (na razie)** that's that
tylko just[1], mere, merely, only adv., conj., simply; ~ **(sam)** alone; **gdy** ~ as soon as; **jak** ~ immediately; **nie ~...ale także** not only... (but) also
tyln|y back[2], rear; (*kończyny zwierzęcia*) hind; **~e drzwi** back door
tył back[1], rear[1]; **w** ~ backward, backwards; **do ~u** backwards; ~ **na przód** back to front; **~em do siebie** back to back; **pozostawać w tyle** drop back, drop behind (sb)
tyłek backside, behind[3], butt[2], rear[1]
tymczasem in the interim, in the meantime, meanwhile
tymczasowy interim[1], provisional, temporary; (*plan itp.*) tentative
tymianek thyme
tynk plaster[1]
tynkarz plasterer
tynkować/o- plaster[2]
typ 1 sort[1], type[1], variety; (*nauczyciela, biznesmena itp.*) mould[1] **2** (*osoba*) chap, type[1]
typować/wy- tip[2] sb/sth (as sth/to do sth)
typow|y in character, like[1], normal[1], quintessential, representative[2], standard[2], typical; (*przykład czegoś*) prime[1]
■ **typowo** peculiarly, typically; **dla kogoś** true to form
tyrać slave[2] (away)
tyrada tirade
tyraliera: **rozwijać tyralierę** spread (yourself) out
tyran tyrant; (*w pracy itp.*) bully[1]
tyrania tyranny
tyranizować/s- tyrannize
tyrański tyrannical

tysiąc thousand
tysiąclecie millennium
tysięczny thousandth; **(po raz) ~** umpteenth
tytan: **~ pracy** a glutton for hard work
tytoń tobacco
tytuł title; (*rozdziału w podręczniku itp.*) rubric; **pod ~em** entitled IDM **~em próby** tentatively
tytułować/za- address[2]; (*artykuł itp.*) head[2]
tytułow|y: **~a rola** title role

U

u[1]; **(U/u)** (*litera*) U, u
u[2] (*przyimek*) **~ kogoś** (*w domu/gościach*) at; (*pod czyjąś opieką*) with
uaktualni(a)ć update; (*komputer itp.*) upgrade
uatrakcyjni(a)ć glamorize
ubarwi(a)ć embellish
ubaw hoot[2]
u-bezpieczać/bezpieczyć cover[1] sb/sth against/for sth, insure sth (against/for sth)
□ **u-bezpieczać/bezpieczyć się**: **(od czegoś)** insure yourself (against/for sth), take out insurance against sth
ubezpieczenie cover[2], indemnity, insurance
ubiczować → BICZOWAĆ
ubić → BIĆ, UBIJAĆ
ubiegać 1 (/ubiec) kogoś w czymś forestall **2 kogoś** beat sb to sth
□ **ubiegać się**: **(o coś)** claim[1] (for sth), contest[2], try out for sth, vie (for sth); **móc ~ o emeryturę** qualify for a pension; **ubiegając-y/a się o azyl** asylum seeker
ubiegły last[1], past[1]
ub(ie)rać clothe, dress[2]; **~ w słowa** couch[2]
□ **ub(ie)rać się** dress[2], dressed, get sth on; **~ się ciepło** wrap (yourself) up
ubi(ja)ć 1 (*jajka*) beat[1], whisk[1]; (*śmietanę*) whip[2]; (*masło*) churn; (*ziemniaki itp.*) mash **2** (*interes*) clinch; **ubić interes** do a deal
ubikacja bathroom, lavatory, loo, toilet, washroom; **~ dla panów** the gents; **~ dla pań** the ladies
ubiór attire, costume, dress[1]
u-bliżać/bliżyć insult[1]
ubłagać → BŁAGAĆ
ubocz|e IDM **na ~u** off the beaten track
uboczny extraneous, incidental; **produkt ~** by-product; **skutek ~** by-product, side effect
ubogi deprived, poor, poverty-stricken
ubolewać regret[1]
■ **ubolewający** regretful
ubolewani|e regret[2]; **godny ~a** deplorable; **wyrażać ~e** deplore; **z ~em** regretfully
ubój: **~ selektywny** cull[2]
ubóstwiać idolize
ubóstwo deprivation, need[3], poverty
ubóść → BÓŚĆ
ubrać (się) → UBIERAĆ (SIĘ)
ubranie clothes, clothing, dress[1], garment, outfit; (*określonego rodzaju*) wear[2]; **~ ciążowe** maternity clothes
ubran|y clothed, dressed in sth; **w co była ~a?** what did she have on?; (*żartobliwie*) **nie jestem ~y** I'm not decent
ubytek 1 (*zmniejszenie ilości*) loss, shortfall **2** (*w zębie*) cavity
uby(wa)ć wane[1]
ubzdurać: **coś sobie** get sth into your head
uch|o 1 (*anat.*) ear; **(muzykalne) ~o** an ear (for sth); (*uśmiechnąć się*) **od ~a do ~a** broadly; (*melodia itp.*) **wpadający w ~o** catchy **2** (*dzbanka itp.*) handle[2] **3** (*igły*) eye[1] IDM **dać komuś w ~o** cuff | **mieć kogoś/czegoś powyżej uszu** be/get/look fed up (with/of sb/sth/doing sth), be sick and tired of sth | **tkwić w czymś po uszy** be up to your eyes in sth
uchodzić 1 (/ujść) (*wydostać się*) elude, escape[1]; **~ (komuś) na sucho** get away with sth/doing sth **2 (/ujść)** (*uwadze*) escape[1] **3 za kogoś/coś** pass for/as sb/sth **4 z balonu uszło powietrze** the balloon slowly deflated
uchodźca émigré, exile, refugee
uchodźstw|o: **żyć na ~ie** live in exile; **Rząd Polski na Uchodźstwie** the Polish Government-in-Exile
uchronić (się) → CHRONIĆ (SIĘ)
uchwa-lać/lić (*ustawę itp.*) enact, legislate (for/against sth), pass[1]
uchwała resolution
uchwycić → CHWYCIĆ
uchwyt 1 (*ręką*) grip[1], grasp[2] **2** (*torby itp.*) handle[2], strap **3** (*do otwierania puszek/konserw*) ring-pull, tab
uchwytny: **nieuchwytny dla ucha** inaudible
uchybiający irreverent
uchy-lać/lić (*prawo*) repeal; (*zakaz, ograniczenie*) lift[1]; (*przepis itp.*) waive; (*umowę itp.*) rescind; (*decyzję*) overrule, revoke
□ **uchy-lać/lić się 1** (*przed kamieniami itp.*) dodge[1] **2** (*od płacenia podatków itp.*) evade; (*od odpowiedzialności*) shirk; (*od zrobienia czegoś nieprzyjemnego*) flinch from sth/doing sth
■ **uchylanie się** evasion; **~ od płacenia podatków** tax evasion
uchylony (*drzwi*) ajar
uciąć → UCINAĆ
uciążliwość nuisance
uciążliw|y arduous, burdensome, cumbersome, inconvenient, onerous; **~e zmagania/zadanie** an uphill battle/struggle; **rzecz/osoba ~a** nuisance; **coś ~ego** bugger[1]
u-cichać/cichnąć zob. też CICHNĄĆ; **powoli ~** die away
uciech|a enjoyment, joy, joyfulness, merriment, rejoicing; (*krótki okres uciechy*) fling[2]; **z ~ą** gleefully, joyfully
ucieczka escape[2], flight, getaway
u-ciekać/ciec 1 break away (from sb/sth), break out (of sth), escape[1], flee, get away (from…), get out (of sth), make off, be on the run, run away; **szybko uciec** make a quick getaway, run for it; **~ z kraju** (*z powodów politycznych*) defect[2]; **nie uciekaj – chcę z tobą porozmawiać** don't rush off – I want to talk to you **2** (*z pieniędzmi itp.*) abscond (from sth) (with sth), run off with sth
□ **u-ciekać/ciec się** fall back on sb/sth, resort[2] to sth/doing sth
uciekinier/ka fugitive, runaway[2]; **~ polityczn-y/a** defector
ucieleśni(a)ć embody, personify
u-cierać/trzeć IDM **~ komuś nosa** snub[1]
ucierpieć → CIERPIEĆ
ucieszony gleeful, joyful, pleased
ucieszyć (się) → CIESZYĆ (SIĘ)
ucięcie curtailment
u-cinać/ciąć curtail; (*wejść komuś w słowo*) cut sb short; (*rozmowę*) kill[1]
ucisk oppression, pressure
uciskać 1 (/ucisnąć) na coś apply pressure **2 kogoś** oppress
u-ciszać/ciszyć lull[2], quieten sb/sth (down), shush verb, silence verb
□ **u-ciszać/ciszyć się** quieten down; (*burza itp.*) subside
ucywilizować → CYWILIZOWAĆ
uczący-y/a się learner
uczcić → CZCIĆ
uczciwość honesty, integrity
uczciw|y fair, honest, honourable, noble, upright; **sprawiedliwy i ~y** square[1] IDM **wstępować na ~ą drogę** go straight
uczczenie celebration, commemoration
uczelnia college, school; **~ techniczna** technical college
uczenie się learning, study[1]
ucze-ń/nnica (*szkoły podstawowej*) pupil, schoolchild; (*szkoły średniej*) student; (*w zawodzie*) apprentice; (*mistrza; pewnej szkoły myślenia*) disciple, follower; **ucze-ń/nnica z wyższej klasy** senior[2]; **starsz-y/a ucze-ń/nnica** (*często odpowiedzialn-y/a za zachowanie młodszych*) prefect
uczesać (się) → CZESAĆ (SIĘ)
uczestnictwo participation
uczestniczyć take part (in sth), participate
uczestni-k/czka participant; (*w konkursie*) entrant
uczęszczać frequent[2]
■ **uczęszczany** (*droga*) well travelled
uczoność scholarship
uczony (*przym.*) erudite, learned, scholarly
■ **uczon-y/a** scholar, scientist
uczta feast
ucztować feast verb
uczuci|e affection, emotion, feeling, sensation, sense[1], soul; **nagłe ~e** (*czegoś nieprzyjemnego*) twinge; **ostre, nagłe ~e** (*np. bólu, głodu, winy*) pang; **mieszane ~a** ambivalence; **~a religijne** religious sensibilities; **pełen ~a** soulful; **z ~em** sentimentally
uczuciowość sentimentality
uczuciowy emotional, sentimental
uczu-lać/lić alert[2] sb (to sth), sensitize
uczulenie (*na pyłki itp.*) allergy (to sth)
uczuleniowy allergic
uczulony sensitive (to sth); (*na pyłki itp.*) allergic (to sth)
uczyć teach; **kto cię uczy historii?** who takes you for History?
□ **uczyć/na- się** do[1], learn, study[2]; **(/na-)** get the knack of sth, pick sth up; **~ na własnych błędach** learn from your mistakes
uczyn|ek act[1] IDM **na gorącym ~ku** in the act (of doing sth)
uczynić → CZYNIĆ
udany happy, successful
udar: **~ słoneczny** sunstroke
udaremni(a)ć defeat[1], foil[2], frustrate, pre-empt, thwart, upset[1]
uda(wa)ć act[2], put on an act; **(coś)** fake[2], feign, pretend, put sth on; **kogoś** make yourself out to be sth, pose[1] as sb/sth; **nie udawaj głupiego** don't act like

a fool; ~, **że** make out that…; **styl udający styl georgiański** a mock Georgian style
■ **udawanie** act[1], make-believe, phoniness | **udawany** mock[2], phoney
□ **uda(wa)ć się**: **komuś** come off, get to do sth, make a go of sth, succeed in doing sth; **nie udać się** come to nothing, not come to anything, miscarry; **nie ~ się (komuś)** fail[1]; **(móc) się udać (gdzieś)** make[1]; **drużynie udało się odnieść zdumiewające zwycięstwo** the team brought off an amazing victory
IDM **~ się na spoczynek** retire
udekorować → DEKOROWAĆ
ude-rzać/rzyć 1 beat[1], cuff[2], hit[1], strike[1]; *(pięścią: kogoś)* punch[1] sb; *(pięścią: w stół)* thump; **w/o coś** bang[1], bonk verb, knock[1] sth (on/against sth); *(z głuchym odgłosem)* thud verb; **czymś w kogoś/coś** jab[1] sth into sb/sth; **czymś o coś** bump[1] sth (against/on sth); *(gałąż itp.)* catch[1]; **mocno kogoś ~** deal sb/sth a blow, deal a blow to sb/sth; ~ **lekko** bop[2]; ~ **batem** whip[2]; ~ **batem/rzemieniem** lash[1]; ~ **młotem** hammer sth (in/into/onto sth); ~ **głową** butt[1] **2** *(wywierać wrażenie)* strike[1] sb (as sth)
IDM **~ komuś do głowy** go to sb's head | **uderzyć w czyjąś czułą/właściwą strunę** strike a chord (with sb)
□ **ude-rzać/rzyć się** bump[1] against/into sb/sth; *(w głowę itp.)* bonk verb, hit[1] your head, etc.(on/against sth), knock[1] your head, etc. (on/against sth); *(w palec u nogi)* stub verb
uderzający blatant, striking
uderzeni|e 1 hit[2]; **w/o coś** bang[2], bonk, bump[2], knock[2]; *(pięścią)* thump noun; *(batem/biczem)* crack[2], lash[2] (on sb/sth); *(zwł. szybkie w karate itp.)* chop[2]; **siła ~a** impact, shock[1] **2** *(miltarne, zwł. lotnicze)* strike[2], swoop noun **3** *(wiosłem; rakietą itp.)* stroke[1] **4** *(w bęben/serca)* beat[2]; **~e serca** heartbeat
udko thigh
udo thigh; ~ **barani-e/a** leg of mutton
udobruchać → DOBRUCHAĆ
udobruchanie appeasement
u-dogadniać/dogodnić facilitate
udogodnienie convenience; (**udogodnienia**) amenities, facilities
udomowiony domesticated
u-doskonalać/doskonalić zob. też DOSKONALIĆ (SIĘ); enhance, hone, improve, refine, reform
□ **u-doskonalać/doskonalić się** improve
u-dowadniać/dowodnić prove
udręczony anguished
udręka agony, anguish, torment; *(nieform.)* a pain (in the neck), a pain in the arse
udusić (się) → DUSIĆ (SIĘ)
uduszenie (się) asphyxiation, suffocation
udział 1 *(uczestnictwo)* part[1] (in sth), participation; *(w pomocy; finansowy)* contribution; **brać ~ (w czymś)** engage in sth, participate, take part (in sth), be/get in on sth; **mieć w czymś ~** have a hand in sth; **nie brać czynnego ~u w czymś** not take an active part in sth **2** *(część)* portion, proportion, slice[1] **3** *(fin.)* stock[1]; (**udziały**) shares[2] (in sth); *(w firmie)* interest[1], stake[1]
udziałowiec shareholder, stakeholder
udziec joint[2]
u-dzielać/dzielić accord[2], allow sb sth, give[1], grant[1]; *(rady itp.)* lend; **nie ~** withhold; ~ **informacji** tell sb sth/that…; ~ **wyczerpujących informacji** prime[3] sb (for/with sth); ~ **odpowiedzi** respond; ~ **wywiadu** give an interview; ~ **komuś lekcji gotowania** give sb a cooking lesson; ~ **nagany** lecture verb; ~ **schronienia** shelter[2] sb/sth (from sb/sth); ~ **ślubu** marry
□ **udzielać się 1 (/udzielić się) komuś** infect, rub off (on/onto sb) **2** ~ **towarzysko** socialize
udźwignąć → DŹWIGAĆ
uelastyczni(a)ć tone[2] sth (up)
uf: ~! phew
ufać 1 (/za-) trust[2], trust in sb/sth, place/put your trust in sb; **nie ~** distrust verb, mistrust **2** ~, **że** hope[1] that…
ufnoś|ć confidence; **z ~cią** confidently
ufny 1 *(ufający komuś)* trusting **2** *(pełen nadziei na coś)* ~, **że** hopeful that…
uformować → FORMOWAĆ
ufortyfikować → FORTYFIKOWAĆ
ufundować → FUNDOWAĆ
ufundowanie foundation
u-gaszać/gasić zob. też GASIĆ; douse
u-gaszczać/gościć entertain
ugięcie *(fiz.)* diffraction
u-ginać/giąć *(fiz.)* diffract
□ **u-ginać/giąć się 1** *(pod ciężarem kogoś/czegoś)* be weighed down; *(nogi/kolana)* **ugiąć się (pod kimś)** turn to jelly **2** *(przen.)* **uginający się pod ciężarem** *(np. winy, trosk)* laden (with sth) **3 przed kimś/czymś** bow to sb/sth
u-gniatać/gnieść knead
ugoda agreement, settlement
ugorowy fallow
ugościć → GOŚCIĆ, UGASZCZAĆ
ugotować (się) zob. też GOTOWAĆ (SIĘ); **można się tu ugotować** it's boiling hot in here
ugrupowanie group[1]
ugryzienie *(i ślad po nim)* bite[2]
ugryźć → GRYŹĆ
ugrzęzły bogged down
ugrzęznąć → GRZĘZNĄĆ
uhonorować zob. też HONOROWAĆ
ujarzmi(a)ć subdue, subjugate
ujawni(a)ć expose, reveal, show[1]; *(informacje)* bring sth to light, bring sth out into the open, disclose, release[1]; *(tajemnicę)* give sth away, leak[1] sth (to sb), let sth out
□ **ujawni(a)ć się** *(wady, usterki itp.)* come out into the open, develop
ująć (się) → UJMOWAĆ (SIĘ)
ujedno-licać/licić standardize
ujemn|y minus[3], negative[1]; **~a strona** disadvantage
ujęcie shot[1]
ujędrni(a)ć tone[2] sth (up)
ujma disgrace[1], reflection on/upon sb/sth
uj-mować/ąć 1 *(sprawiać, że coś wydaje sie gorsze/mniej ważne)* detract from sth **2** *(w dłoń)* cup[2] **3** *(złapać)* apprehend **4** ~ **zwięźle** *(słowami)* encapsulate sth (in sth) **5 sobie (kogoś)** ingratiate yourself (with sb)
□ **uj-mować/ąć się**: **za kimś/czymś** stand up for sb/sth, stick up for yourself/sb/sth
ujmujący endearing
ujrzeć behold, set eyes on sb/sth, spy[2]
ujście 1 *(rynny)* outlet **2** *(rzeki)* estuary, mouth[1] **3** *(agresji itp.)* outlet (for sth)
ujść → UCHODZIĆ
ukamieniować → KAMIENIOWAĆ
ukarać → KARAĆ
ukaranie punishment
ukartow(yw)ać rig[1]
ukatrupić: **kogoś** bump sb off
ukaz(yw)ać IDM **~ czyjeś zalety** do justice to sb/sth, do sb/sth justice
□ **ukazywać się 1** *(pojawić się)* appear, show[1]; **ponownie się ~** reappear **2** *(słońce; książka itp.)* be out adj., come out; **wiadomość ukazała się w gazetach** the story broke in the newspapers
ukąszenie bite[2]
ukierunkowany: **(przesadnie) ~ (na kogoś/coś)** skewed (towards sb/sth)
układ 1 *(system; schemat)* system; *(społeczny itp.)* order[1]; *(dnia)* routine[1]; *(skład)* constitution; *(mechaniczny)* gear[1]; ~ **kierowniczy** steering; ~ **nerwowy** the nervous system; ~ **pokarmowy** digestive system; ~ **słoneczny** the solar system **2** *(polit.)* convention, treaty **3** ~ **graficzny** page layout
IDM **~ odniesienia** frame of reference | **~ okresowy pierwiastków** the periodic table | **~ scalony** microchip
u-kładać/łożyć 1 *(porządkować)* arrange; *(włosy)* set[1]; *(układankę)* fit sth together **2** *(kłaść)* lay[1]; *(w stos)* heap[2] **3** *(tworzyć: przemówienie, list itp.)* phrase[2]; ~ **choreografię** choreograph **4** *(składać)* collate
□ **u-kładać/łożyć się 1** ~ **wygodnie** snuggle (up to sb), (up/down) **2** *(warunki)* negotiate (with sb) (for/about sth) **3** *(przebiegać)* pan out
IDM **ułożyć się w głowie** fall/slot into place
układanka jigsaw, jigsaw puzzle, puzzle[1]
ukłon bow[2], nod noun; **głęboki ~ dworski** curtsy
ukłonić się → KŁANIAĆ SIĘ
ukłucie jab[2], prick[2], stab[2]
ukłuć → KŁUĆ
uknuć → KNUĆ
ukochan-y/a beloved, darling, sweetheart
ukoić → KOIĆ
ukojenie solace
ukokosić się → KOKOSIĆ SIĘ
ukołysać → KOŁYSAĆ
ukończenie: ~ **studiów wyższych** graduation
ukończyć → KOŃCZYĆ
ukoronować → KORONOWAĆ
ukos: **na ~** obliquely; **patrzeć na niego z ~a** give sb a sideways look
ukośnik slash[2]; *(prawy)* forward slash; *(komput.)* **lewy ~** backslash
ukośny diagonal, oblique, slanting
u-kracać/krócić put a stop to sth

ukradkiem by/through the back door, covertly, surreptitiously; **robić coś ~** sneak[1]; **robiący coś ~** secret[1]; **~ spojrzeć na kogoś/coś** steal a glance at ab/sth
ukradkowy furtive, stealthy, surreptitious
ukraść → KRAŚĆ
ukryci|e hiding; **~e prawdy** cover-up; **w ~u** on the quiet
□ **ukrycie się** hiding
ukryt|y implicit, latent, sneaking, underlying, ulterior, repressed; (*komentarz, aluzja itp.*) oblique; **~e znaczenie** implication; **~y zapas** stash noun
ukry(wa)ć cache[2], conceal, hide[1], secrete, stash, suppress, shut sb/sth away, tuck sth away; (*przestępcę, zbiega itp.*) harbour[2]; (*informację*) cover sth up, hold sth back; (*wstyd itp.*) cover
■ **ukrywający** (*namiętności itp.*) repressed
□ **ukry(wa)ć się** hide[1], be in/go into hiding
ukrzyżować crucify
■ **ukrzyżowanie** crucifixion
ukształtować → KSZTAŁTOWAĆ
ukuć (*wyrażenie itp.*) coin[2]
ul beehive
ulać: **jak ulał** snugly
u-latniać/lotnić się (*gaz itp.*) escape[1], leak[1]; (*tłum itp.*) melt away
■ **ulatniający się** (*perfumy itp.*) volatile
uleczalny curable
u-legać/lec 1 komuś/czemuś relent, submit, weaken, yield[1]; (*życzeniom itp.*) indulge, pander to sb/sth; **łatwo ulega wpływom** he's too easily led **2** (*pokusie itp.*) succumb; (*uczuciom, emocjom itp.*) indulge (yourself) (in sth) **3** (*zniszczeniu*) sustain
■ **ulegający**: **łatwo ulegający** indulgent; **~ nastrojom** temperamental
uległość submission
uległy amenable, docile, pliable, submissive
u-lepszać/lepszyć (*nieznacznie*) tweak, upgrade
ulepszenie improvement, refinement, reformation, upgrade noun
ulewa cloudburst, downpour, deluge; **nagła, krótkotrwała ~** flurry
ulewny torrential
ulg|a 1 (*od bólu itp.*) alleviation, relief; (*od stresu*) release[2]; **sprawiać ~ę** (*w bólu itp.*) ease[2]; **doznać ~i słysząc coś** be very relieved to hear sth **2** (*zniżka*) exemption; **~a podatkowa** relief
ulgowy concessionary
ulica avenue, drive[2], lane, road, street, street; **główna ~** high street
uliczka: **wąska ~** alley
ulistniony: **bogato ~** leafy
ulokować → LOKOWAĆ
ulokowany situated; **źle ~** misplaced
ulotka circular[2], flyer, handout, leaflet
ulotnić się → ULATNIAĆ SIĘ
ulotny ephemeral; **~ zapach** whiff
ultimatum ultimatum
ultradźwięk ultrasound
ultradźwiękowy supersonic
ultrafioletowy ultraviolet
ultranowoczesny ultra-modern
ultrasonograf scanner
ultrasonografia ultrasound
ultrasonograficzn|y: **badanie ~e** scan noun, ultrasound scan
ulubie-niec/nica favourite[2], pet[1]
ulubion|y favourite[1]; (*temat itp.*) (right) up your street; **~y temat** pet subject; **coś ~ego** favourite[2]
ululać → LULAĆ
ulżyć relieve, alleviate
ułamek fraction; **~ dziesiętny** decimal[2]; **~ sekundy** split second; **o ~ sekundy** fractionally
ułatwi(a)ć 1 (*czynić łatwiejszym/prostszym*) simplify **2 komuś coś** encourage, facilitate, promote
ułomność disability
ułożyć (się) → UKŁADAĆ (SIĘ)
ułuda delusion
u-macniać/mocnić fortify; **~ sworzniem** bolt[2]
□ **u-macniać/mocnić się** rally[2]
umalowany made-up
u-mawiać/mówić się agree, make a deal to do sth; **umówić się na spotkanie z kimś** make an appointment to see sb; **umówić się na wizytę do lekarza** make an appointment to see the doctor; **umówić się z kimś na randkę** ask sb out; **umówić się na lunch** make a date to have lunch together
umeblować → MEBLOWAĆ
umeblowany furnished
umęczony harassed; **~ i drażliwy** frazzled
umiar moderation; **brać coś z ~em** take sth in moderation; **zachowujący ~ w czymś** abstemious
umiarkowany mild, moderate[1], reasonable; (*klimat*) temperate; (*reakcja*) muted, restrained; (*gusty itp.*) middle-of-the-road
umieć can[1], know[1] how to do sth
umiejętnoś|ć ability, capability, competence, power[1], skill; (*sztuka*) art; **cenna ~ć** asset; **wrodzona ~ć** gift (for sth/doing sth); **~ć czytania i pisania** literacy; **wymagający ~ci** skilled; **mieć ~ć wykonywania czegoś** turn your hand to sth
umiejętny skilful
u-miejscawiać/miejscowić localize, locate, site verb
umiejscowiony situated
u-mierać/mrzeć die, pass away; (*na skutek choroby*) succumb to an illness IDM **~ z głodu** be absolutely famished, be ravenous, be starving, starve to death | **~ z gorąca** swelter | **~ z ciekawości** be on tenterhooks | **~ ze śmiechu** die laughing, kill yourself laughing
u-mieszczać/mieścić 1 deposit[2], insert, locate, place[2], put, set[1], position[2], place[2]; (*kogoś na stanowisku*) install sb (as sth); (*w budynku*) house[2]; **~ obok siebie** juxtapose; **~ w kontekście** contextualize; **~ na liście/w spisie** list verb, register[1] **2** (*w szpitalu psychiatrycznym itp.*) commit sb to sth; **~ kogoś w zakładzie** institutionalize
□ **u-mieszczać/mieścić się**: **~ w spisie** register[1]
umięśniony beefy, muscular
umiłowany precious
umknąć → UMYKAĆ
u-mniejszać/mniejszyć belittle, denigrate, detract from sth, minimize
■ **umniejszający** derogatory |
umniejszanie (*faktów itp.*) understatement
umocnić (się) → UMACNIAĆ (SIĘ)
umocnienie fortification; (**umocnienia**) defence
umoco(wy)wać anchor[2], fix[1]
■ **umocowany** fast[1]; **dobrze umocowany** secure[1]
u-moralniać/moralnić moralize
■ **umoralniający** elevating
umorusany grubby, mucky
umotywować → MOTYWOWAĆ
umow|a 1 (*ugoda*) agreement, arrangement, bargain[1] **2** (*kontrakt*) contract[1]; **(pracujący) na ~ę o dzieło/zlecenie itp.** freelance **3** (*międzynarodowa*) treaty
umowny symbolic
u-możliwiać/możliwić empower, enable, facilitate, permit[1]
umówić się → UMAWIAĆ SIĘ
umówion|y prearranged; **tylko ~e wizyty** visits are by appointment only
umrzeć → UMIERAĆ
umundurowany uniformed
umyć (się) → MYĆ (SIĘ), UMYWAĆ (SIĘ)
u-mykać/mknąć: **~ z pamięci** elude
umysł brain, intellect, mind[1]; **mieć otwarty ~** have/keep an open mind (about/on sth)
umysłowość psychology
umysłow|y intellectual[1], mental
■ **umysłowo**: **człowiek ~o chory** lunatic[1]
umyśln|y intentional, wilful
■ **umyślnie** intentionally, knowingly, on purpose, purposely
umy(wa)ć IDM **~ ręce od kogoś/czegoś** wash your hands of sb/sth
□ **umywać się** IDM **nie ~ się do kogoś/czegoś** not be a patch on sb/sth
umywalka basin, washbasin
uncja ounce; **~ płynu** fluid ounce
unia: **Unia Europejska** the European Union; **Unia Ekonomiczna i Monetarna** EMU
unicestwi(a)ć annihilate, exterminate, squash
unie-możliwiać/możliwić block[2], preclude, prevent
unie-ruchamiać/ruchomić ground[2], immobilize
■ **unieruchomienie** standstill
uniesienie elation, heat[1], high[2], rapture; **wpadać w ~ (z powodu kogoś)** swoon (over sb)
unieszczęśliwi(a)ć distress[2]
unieszkodliwianie: **unieszkodliwianie i usuwanie wybuchów** bomb disposal
unieszkodliwi(a)ć neutralize
unieść → NIEŚĆ, UNOSIĆ (SIĘ)
□ **unieść się** IDM **~ (gniewem)** fly off the handle
unieśmiertelni(a)ć immortalize
unieważni(a)ć disallow, overrule, quash, revoke, undo; (*zamówienie*) cancel; (*kontrakt itp.*) annul, invalidate
unieważniony void[2]
uniewinni(a)ć acquit sb (of sth)
unik cop-out, dodge[2], evasion; **robić ~** duck[2]
unik-ać/nąć avert, dodge[1], escape[1], evade, keep out of sth, keep sb out of sth, miss[1], shun, be shy[1] (of/about sth/doing sth), stay out of sth; **nie można było uniknąć wypadku** the accident

couldn't be helped; **pomóc komuś uniknąć kary** get sb off (with sth)
■ **unikanie** avoidance; ~ **płacenia podatku** tax avoidance
unikatowy one-off adj., unique
uniknięci|e escape[2]; **możliwy do ~a** avoidable, preventable
unisono in unison
uniwersalny 1 universal **2** (*do różnorodnego użycia*) versatile
uniwersytecki university
uniwersytet school, university; ~ **otwarty** the Open University
uniżenie humbly
uniżoność humility
unormować (się) → NORMOWAĆ (SIĘ)
u-nosić/nieść: **być unoszonym z prądem** drift[2] IDM ~ **brwi** raise your eyebrows
■ **unoszony**: ~ **na fali** adrift
□ **u-nosić/nieść się 1** (*w powietrzu*) hover, waft; ~ **na wodzie** float[1] (in/on sth); (*zapach*) **długo się unosić** linger (on); **helikopter uniósł się w powietrze** the helicopter rose into the air **2** (*rozgniewać się*) boil over
unowocześni(a)ć modernize, update
□ **unowocześni(a)ć się** modernize
uodparni(a)ć immunize
uodporniony immune
uogólni(a)ć generalize
■ **uogólniający** (*zmiany itp.*) sweeping
u-osabiać/osobić embody, personify
u-padać/paść 1 (*przewrócić się*) collapse[1], come a cropper, fall[1] (down/over), keel over, sink[1]; (*głową naprzód*) pitch[2]; (*z hukiem*) tumble down; **upadł na plecy** he fell and landed on his back **2** (*zbankrutować*) crash[2], go under; (*doznać klęski*) implode IDM **nie ~ na duchu** bear up | **upadł na duchu** his spirits fell
upad|ek 1 (*przewrócenie się*) collapse[2], fall[2]; **gwałtowny ~ek** tumble noun **2** (*zepsucie*) decay[1], ruin[2]; (*śmierć*) death **3** (*klęska*) comedown, decadence, decline[1], demise, downfall, fall[2], implosion, overthrow noun IDM **wzloty i ~ki** ups and downs
upadłoś|ć bankruptcy; **być na skraju ~ci** flounder[1]
upajać się go into raptures (about/over sb/sth), revel in sth/doing sth
upalny blazing, scorching, sweltering
upał heat[1]; (**upały**) heatwave
upamiętni(a)ć commemorate, record[2]; **nabożeństwo w intencji upamiętniającej** memorial service
u-państwawiać/państwowić nationalize
upaprany mess[1]
uparty dogged, headstrong, obstinate, pig-headed, stubborn, wilful
upaść → UPADAĆ
u-patrywać/patrzyć IDM **upatrzyć sobie coś do kupienia** have (got) your eye on sth
upchnąć → UPYCHAĆ
upewni(a)ć się ensure, make certain (that...), make sure; **co do czegoś** ascertain
upiąć → UPINAĆ
upichcić → PICHCIĆ
upiec (się) zob. też PIEC (SIĘ) IDM **upiec dwie pieczenie przy jednym ogniu** kill two birds with one stone | ~ **komuś** get away with sth/doing sth
u-pierać/przeć się: **przy czymś** be bent on sth/on doing sth, insist (on sth/doing sth), persist (in sth/doing sth), be set on sth/doing sth
upierzenie plumage
u-piększać/piększyć beautify, embellish; (*opowiadanie itp.*) embroider
■ **upiększenie** frill | **upiększony** glorified
upi(ja)ć się get drunk
upiłować → PIŁOWAĆ
u-pinać/piąć twist[1]
upiorny ghostly
upiór phantom, spectre
upleść → PLEŚĆ
upłynni(a)ć: ~ **kurs waluty** (*ekon.*) float[1]
upływ passing[1], lapse[1]; ~ **krwi** loss of blood; **w miarę ~u czasu** as time went by/on, as you go along; **z ~em czasu** in the course of time, with the passage of time; **przed ~em** within
u-pływać/płynąć (*czas*) go by, go on, elapse; (*czas między dwoma okresami*) intervene; **wolno** ~ wear on; **pod koniec tego roku upłynie pięć lat, odkąd tutaj pracuję** at the end of this year, I shall have been working here for five years
upodobać: **sobie kogoś/coś** take a fancy to sb/sth
upodobanie liking, predilection, preference; (**upodobania**) likes[4]
upojenie rapture; ~ **alkoholowe** inebriation
upojony intoxicated
u-pokarzać/pokorzyć humble[2], humiliate, put sb down
■ **upokarzający** degrading, humiliating | **upokorzenie** humiliation, indignity
upolityczni(a)ć politicize
upolować → POLOWAĆ
u-pominać/pomnieć lecture verb
upominek gift, present[2]
upomnienie lecture, reminder
uporać się handle[1], get through (sth)
uporczywość persistence
uporczywy constant, insistent, obstinate, persistent, unrelenting; (*ból, zmartwienie itp.*) niggling
uporządkować → PORZĄDKOWAĆ
uporządkowany orderly[1], tidy[1], trim[2]
uposażenie (*zwł. osoby duchownej*) stipend
upośledzony disabled; (*warstwa społeczna itp.*) underprivileged
upoważni(a)ć authorize, empower, entitle sb (to sth)
upoważnienie authority, authorization, empowerment, power[1], warrant[1]; (*dla kogoś, aby działał dla ciebie*) proxy
upozorować → POZOROWAĆ
upór obstinacy, stubbornness
upragnienie: **z ~m** longingly
upraszać entreat, request[2]
u-praszczać/prościć simplify; **nadmiernie** ~ oversimplify
uprawa cultivation, culture, production
uprawiać 1 (*ziemię*) cultivate, farm[2], grow; ~ **ogród** garden[2] **2** (*sport itp.*) practise; (*hobby itp.*) pursue; ~ **jogging** jog[1]; ~ **judo/aerobik/windsurfing** do judo/aerobics/windsurfing; ~ **surfing** surf[2]; ~ **wspinaczkę** go climbing IDM ~ **seks** make love (to sb)
uprawni(a)ć empower, entitle sb (to sth)
■ **uprawnie|nie** entitlement; **dać komuś uprawnienia coś robić** qualify sb to do sth; **nie mający uprawnień (do czegoś)** ineligible (for/to do sth) | **uprawniony do czegoś** eligible (for sth/to do sth)
uprawny cultivated
uprawomocni(a)ć validate
uproszczenie simplification
uproszczony simplistic
u-prowadzać/prowadzić abduct; (*dla okupu*) kidnap
■ **uprowadzenie** abduction; (*dla okupu*) kidnapping; (*samolot*) hijack noun
uprząść → PRZĄŚĆ
u-przątać/przątnąć clear[2], put sth away
uprząż harness[1]; **nakładać** ~ harness[2]
uprzeć się → UPIERAĆ SIĘ
uprzedni previous
uprzednio already, before[2,3], beforehand, formerly, once, previously, ready adv.
u-przedzać/przedzić: **kogoś (o czymś)** forestall, forewarn; (*czyjeś pytanie itp.*) pre-empt
uprzedze|nie 1 (przed czymś) forewarning, warning **2** (*w stosunku do czegoś/kogoś*) bias[1], preconception, prejudice[1]; **bez ~ń** open-minded
uprzedzony prejudiced
uprzejmoś|ć courtesy, kindness, niceness, politeness; **wyświadczona ~ć** kindness; **wymiana zwykłych ~ci** exchanging the usual pleasantries; **dzięki ~ci** (by) courtesy of sb
uprzejmy accommodating, amiable, civil, considerate, courteous, kind[2], nice, obliging, polite
uprzemysławi(a)ć (się) industrialize
uprzemysłowiony industrial
u-przytamniać/przytomnić: **sobie coś** realize, wake up to sth
uprzywilejowany advantaged, preferential, privileged
upstrzony be dotted with
u-puszczać/puścić drop[1]
u-pychać/pchnąć jam[1]
uradować (się) → RADOWAĆ (SIĘ)
uradowany joyful, pleased
Uran Uranus
uran uranium
uratować → RATOWAĆ
uraz injury (to sb/sth); (*psychiczny*) trauma; **powodować ~ psychiczny** traumatize
uraz|a animosity, bad/ill feeling, grudge[1], hurt[3], offence, resentment; **z ~ą** resentfully; **bez ~y** no hard feelings
urazowy traumatic
u-rażać/razić 1 (*ranić*) hurt[1], wound[2] **2** (*obrażać*) displease, hurt[1], spite verb, wound[2]
■ **urażony** resentful; (*dosłownie i przen.*) hurt[2], injured; **czuć się urażonym** resent
urbanist-a/ka planner
urbanistyka town planning
urdu: **język** ~ Urdu
uregulować → REGULOWAĆ

urlop holiday, leave[2]; **brać ~** take sth off; **~ macierzyński** maternity leave; **~ okolicznościowy** (*np. z powodu śmierci bliskiej osoby*) compassionate leave
urlopowicz/ka holidaymaker
urna urn; **~ wyborcza** ballot box
uroczy adorable, charming, endearing, fetching, lovely
uroczystość celebration, ceremony, festivity, function[1], gala
uroczysty ceremonial, solemn
uroda beauty, good looks, looks[2], prettiness
urodzajność fertility
urodzajny fertile
urodzenie birth
urodzić (się) → RODZIĆ (SIĘ)
urodziny birthday
urodzony born[1,2]; **być ~m** (*np. artystą*) be cut out for sth/to be sth
urojony imaginary
urok 1 (*uroda*) allure, appeal[1], charm[1], loveliness; **dodawać ~u** glamorize **2** (*magiczny*) curse[1], spell[2]
urosnąć → ROSNĄĆ
u-rozmaicać/rozmaicić intersperse, vary
urozmaicenie diversity, variety; (*w gamie produktów itp.*) diversification
■ **urozmaicony** varied; (*bogaty w wydarzenia*) eventful
urość → ROSNĄĆ
u-ruchamiać/ruchomić (*samochód; firmę*) run[1], start[1] sth (up); (*proces*) activate, initiate; (*urządzenie*) activate, trigger[2] sth (off); (*komput.*) boot[2] sth (up); **ponownie ~** reactivate; (*komput.*) **~ ponownie** reboot
□ **uruchamiać się** start[1] (up); (*komput.*) boot[2] (up)
urwis rascal
urwisko cliff, precipice
urwisty craggy
ur(y)wać snap[1]
urywany jerky
urywek fragment[1], nugget, snatch[2], snippet
urywkowy piecemeal
urząd agency, office; **~ pocztowy** post office; **~ pracy** employment agency; **~ skarbowy** Inland Revenue, the tax office; **~ stanu cywilnego** registry office; **~ zajmujący się sporządzaniem rejestrów** registry
IDM **składać ~** resign (from/as) (sth)
u-rządzać/rządzić: **inaczej ~** rearrange
urządzenie 1 appliance, device; **nietypowe ~** contraption; **~ alarmowe** alarm[1]; **~ kontrolne** monitor[1]; (*komput.*) **~ peryferyjne** peripheral[2]; **~ sterownicze** control[1] **2** (**urządzenia**) fitting[2]
urzeczenie fascination
urzeczony thrilled
urzeczywistni(a)ć (*marzenia itp.*) live out sth, realize
■ **urzeczywistnienie** fruition, realization
□ **urzeczywistni(a)ć się** materialize, come true
u-rzekać/rzec beguile, charm[2], fascinate, thrill verb
■ **urzekający** alluring, fascinating, spellbinding, stunning
urzędniczy clerical
urzędni-k/czka clerk, office worker; **~ państwow-y/a** civil servant; **(wyższ-y/a) ~** (*np. państwowy, kościelny*) officer, official[2]; **~ stanu cywilnego** registrar
urzędowani|e: **godziny ~a** office hours
urzędowy bureaucratic, formal, official[1]
urżnąć → RŻNĄĆ
usadawi(a)ć plant[2]; **wygodnie się ~** nestle
□ **usadawiać się** install yourself
usadowić (się) → SADOWIĆ (SIĘ)
usamodzielni(a)ć emancipate
usankcjonować → SANKCJONOWAĆ
usatysfakcjonować → SATYSFAKCJONOWAĆ
usatysfakcjonowany satisfied
usiany: **~ gwiazdami** starry, studded with stars
usiąść → SIADAĆ
u-sidlać/sidlić 1 trap[2] **2** (*przen.*) entrap, trap[2] sb (into sth/into doing sth)
usiln|y: **~e starania** a strenuous effort
■ **usilnie** really
usiłować attempt[2], endeavour, strive
■ **usiłowanie** attempt[1], bid[3], endeavour noun; **~ gwałtu/morderstwa/włamania** attempted rape/murder/robbery
uskuteczni(a)ć effect[2]
usług|a (**usługi**) service[1]; **~i pocztowe** mail
usługiwać: **~ przy stole** wait on sb
usłużny accommodating, obliging
usłyszeć → SŁYSZEĆ
usmażyć (się) → SMAŻYĆ (SIĘ)
u-spokajać/spokoić allay, calm[2] sb/sth (down), cool sb down/off, ease sb's mind, moderate[2], pacify, placate, put/set sb's mind at rest, quieten, quieten sb/sth down, reassure, settle, soothe, silence verb
□ **u-spakajać/spokoić się** calm[2] (down), cool down/off, hush[1], moderate[2], quieten down, put/set your mind at rest, relax, settle, settle down; (*nerwy, drżenie serca*) steady[2]
uspokajający reassuring, soothing; **środek ~** sedative, tranquillizer; **podawać komuś środek ~** sedate[2], put sb under sedation
uspokojenie appeasement
uspokojony relieved
usposabi(a)ć się psych yourself up (for sth)
usposobienie disposition, frame of mind, mood, nature, temperament, vein; **zmienne ~** moodiness
usprawiedliwi(a)ć excuse[2], exonerate, justify, rationalize; (*decyzję itp.*) vindicate
■ **usprawiedliwieni|e** excuse[1], justification; **nie do usprawiedliwienia** indefensible | **usprawiedliwiony** justifiable
□ **usprawiedliwi(a)ć się** explain sth away
usprawni(a)ć rationalize, reform, streamline
■ **usprawniający**: **~ pracę** labour-saving
usta mouth[1]; **pocałować kogoś w ~** kiss sb on the lips
ustabilizować → STABILIZOWAĆ
ustabilizowany settled, steady[1]
ustać (się) → USTAWAĆ (SIĘ)
u-stalać/stalić 1 (*potwierdzić*) determine, establish; (*tożsamość*) identify sb/sth (as sb/sth); (*zasady itp.*) establish; **~ wiek czegoś** date[2]; **~ na pewnym poziomie** (*np. cenę*) peg[2] sth (at/to sth) **2** (*zaplanować*) arrange; (*datę itp.*) appoint, fix[1] sth (up), set[1]
■ **ustalony** cut and dried, fixed, set[3], settled; **mieć ustalone nawyki** be set in your ways
□ **ustalać się** set in
u-stanawiać/stanowić establish, put, set[1]; (*przepis*) lay sth down; **(kogoś czymś)** (*prawo*) legislate (for/against sth), appoint sb (to sth)
ustandaryzować → STANDARYZOWAĆ
ustanowienie establishment
ustatkować się settle down
ustawa act[1], law, statute; (**ustawy**) legislation
u-stawać/stać cease, subside; **nie ~** persevere, persist
□ **u-stawać/stać się** settle
ustawi(a)ć 1 arrange, deploy, position[2]; (*automat itp.*) programme[2], set[1]; (*wynik meczu*) fix[1]; **~ w kolejności** rank[2] sb/sth (as sth); **~ w rzędzie/szeregu** align sth (with sth), line sth up; **~ pod kątem** angle[2] **2 kogoś** set sb up
□ **ustawi(a)ć się** position[2]; **~ się według parametrów standardowych** (*komputer*) default[2] (to sth)
ustawiczny continual, incessant
ustawienie deployment; **~ w linii/rzędzie/szeregu** alignment; (*komput.*) **~ standardowe** default[1]
ustawodawcz|y legislative; **ciało/władza ~e** legislature
ustawodawstwo legislation
ustawowy statutory
ustąpienie resignation (from sth)
usterka fault[1], glitch; **~ techniczna** technical hitch
ustęp excerpt, passage
ustępliwy flexible
u-stępować/stąpić 1 (*ulegać*) budge, concede sth (to sb), relent, yield[1] (to sb/sth); (*miejsca itp.*) give sth up (to sb); (*komuś dla świętego spokoju*) humour[2]; **~ pod naciskiem** give[1]; **~ komuś pola w jakiejś sprawie** give/lose ground (to sb/sth) **2** (*ze stanowiska*) stand down (as sth), step aside/down **3** (*ból itp.*) ease[2]
ustępstwo concession; **polityka ustępstw** a policy of appeasement; **robić ~** stretch a point; **nie godzić się na ustępstwa** hold/keep/stand your ground
ustępujący outgoing
ustnik mouthpiece
ustny oral[1], verbal
ustronie seclusion
ustronny secluded
ustrój system
ustrzec (się) → STRZEC (SIĘ)
usunięcie clearance, disposal, elimination, extraction, removal; (*tekstu*) deletion; **~ w cień** eclipse[1]
u-suwać/sunąć 1 (*z miejsca*) clear[2], dislodge, dispose of sb/sth, drop[1], eliminate, exclude, extract[2], remove, take sth away; (*z rejestru itp.*) strike sb/sth off (sth); (*tekst*) delete; **~ błędy w oprogramowaniu** (*komput.*) debug;

~ **stopniowo** phase sth out **2** (*ze stanowiska*) eject sb (from sth), oust; (*ze stanowiska, z tronu*) depose **3** (*ząb, wyrostek robaczkowy itp.*) have sth out, take sth out; IDM **~ kogoś w cień** overshadow | **~ na dalszy plan** marginalize

u-sychać/schnąć 1 shrivel (up), wither (away) **2 ~ z tęsknoty** pine[2] (for sb/sth)

u-sypiać/śpić 1 (*kłaść dziecko itp. spać*) get sb off to sleep; (*muzyka itp.*) send sb to sleep **2** (*do operacji itp.*) anaesthetize, drug[2] **3** (*czujność itp.*) lull[2] sb into sth **4** (*zwierzę*) put sth down, put sth out of its misery, put (an animal) to sleep

■ **usypiający**: **środek usypiający** sedative; **podawać komuś środek usypiający** sedate[2], put sb under sedation

usyp(yw)ać (*w kopiec*) heap[2] sth (up), pile[2] sth (up)

usystematyzować → SYSTEMATYZOWAĆ

usystematyzowanie systematization

usytuować → SYTUOWAĆ

usytuowany situated

uszanować → SZANOWAĆ

uszczelka seal[2], washer

uszczelni(a)ć insulate, seal[1] sth (up)

uszczerb|ek: **przynosić ~ek** prejudice[2]; **z ~kiem dla kogoś/czegoś** to the detriment of sb/sth; **bez ~ku** unscathed

uszczęśliwi(a)ć (*kogoś prezentem itp., który nam nie odpowiada*) offload sth (on/onto sb)

uszczęśliwiony delirious, as happy, quick, etc. as anything, over the moon

u-szczuplać/szczuplić deplete

uszczypać → SZCZYPAĆ

uszczypliwość acrimony, astringency, cattiness, sharpness

uszczypliwy catty, cutting[2], pointed, sharp[1], snide

uszczypnąć → SZCZYPAĆ

uszczypnięcie nip noun, pinch[2]

u-szkadzać/szkodzić damage[2], impair

uszko (*do otwierania puszek/konserw*) ring-pull, tab

uszkodzenie damage[1]; ~ **mózgu** brain damage; ~ **przeciążeniowe** RSI

uszkodzić → SZKODZIĆ

uszkodzony out of action, broken-down

usztywni(a)ć 1 (*czynić sztywnym*) stiffen **2** (*stanowisko*) harden

□ **usztywni(a)ć się** harden

uszy → UCHO

uszyć → SZYĆ

uścisk embrace noun, grip[1], hug noun, squeeze[2]; ~ **dłoni** handshake IDM **(serdeczne) ~i** (lots of) love (from)

u-ściskać/ścisnąć hug

uśmiać się → ŚMIAĆ SIĘ

uśmiech smile[2]; **promienny** ~ beam[1]; **szeroki** ~ grin noun; **wyrażać coś ~em** smile[1]; **z ~em na twarzy** with good grace, gracefully IDM **~ losu** a stroke of luck

u-śmiechać/śmiechnąć się smile[1]; (*z samozadowoleniem*) smirk verb; ~ **szeroko** grin (at sb)

u-śmiercać/śmiercić kill[1], put sb to death, slay

u-śmierzać/śmierzyć ease[2], mitigate, soothe

uśmierzenie relief

uśmieszek: ~ **samozadowolenia** smirk

uśpić → USYPIAĆ

uśpiony dormant

uświa-damiać/domić: **komuś, że** awaken sb to sth; **sobie coś** perceive, realize, wake up to sth

■ **uświadomienie**: ~ **sobie** realization

u-święcać/święcić sanctify

uświęcić → ŚWIĘCIĆ, UŚWIĘCAĆ

utajony latent, sneaking

utalentowany able, accomplished, clever, gifted, talented

utarczk|a scrap[1], scuffle, skirmish; **mieć ~ę z kimś** (have) a brush with sb/sth

utarty: ~ **zwrot** cliché

utkać → TKAĆ

utknąć get stuck[2]; (*w rozmowie itp.*) get bogged down in sth; ~ **w korku** get caught in the traffic; ~ **w martwym punkcie** grind to a halt/standstill

utkwić → TKWIĆ

u-tleniać/tlenić oxidize

utłuc → TŁUC

utonąć → TONĄĆ

utopia utopia

utopić (się) → TOPIĆ (SIĘ)

utopijny utopian

utorować → TOROWAĆ

utożsami(a)ć identify sth with sth

□ **utożsami(a)ć się** empathize (with sb/sth), identify with sb

utracić → TRACIĆ

utrapienie annoyance, cross[1], headache, menace, a pain (in the neck), a pain in the arse, pest, scourge

utrat|a loss; (*praw itp.*) forfeit noun; **chwilowa ~a** lapse[1]; **~a bliskiej osoby** bereavement; **~a pamięci** amnesia; **~a wartości** depreciation; **pomimo ~y dwóch goli, wciąż prowadzili** despite conceding two late goals, they still won

utrudni(a)ć encumber, handicap[2], impede

utrwalacz (*zwł. do kolorów i zapachów*) fixative

u-trwalać/trwalić cement[2], consolidate, perpetuate, record[2]

□ **u-trwalać/trwalić się** consolidate

utrzeć → TRZEĆ, UCIERAĆ

utrzymani|e keep[2], living[2], support[2], upkeep; **być na czyimś ~u kogoś** depend on sb (for sth), be dependent (on sb); **mieć na ~u** (*np. dziecko*) maintain; **osoba będąca na czyimś ~u** dependant; **mieć u kogoś ~e** board[2]; **dawać na czyjeś ~e** keep[1]; **koszty ~a** the cost of living; **środki ~a** livelihood

utrzymany: **dobrze** ~ well kept

utrzym(yw)ać 1 (*porządek, stan rzeczy*) maintain; ~ **w dobrym stanie** condition[2], maintain; ~ **na pewnym poziomie** keep sth to/at sth; (*np. cenę*) peg[2] sth (at/to sth); ~ **coś na wysokim poziomie** keep sth up; ~ **na niskim poziomie** hold sth down, keep sth down; ~ **z kimś kontakt** keep in touch with sb, keep up with sb; ~ **w mocy** (*np. decyzję*) uphold **2** (*ciężar*) bear[1] **3** (*rodzinę*) keep[1], provide for sb, raise[1], support[1] **4** (*samochód itp.*) maintain, run[1] **5** (*twierdzić*) claim[1], hold[1], insist, maintain, profess, purport; **utrzymywał, że jest niewinny** he protested his innocence

□ **utrzymywać się 1** (*trwać*) hold[1], last[4]; **(w czymś)** persist (in sth/doing sth) **2 (z czegoś)** earn; ~ **się (przy życiu)** exist (on sth), subsist (on sth)

utrzymywanie preservation, retention; ~ **w dobrym stanie** maintenance

□ **utrzymywanie się**: ~ **się przy życiu** subsistence

utuczyć → TUCZYĆ

utulić → TULIĆ

u-twardzać/twardzić harden, toughen sb/sth (up)

□ **u-twardzać/twardzić się** toughen (up)

utworzenie creation

utworzyć się → TWORZYĆ SIĘ

utwór 1 (*muzyczny itp.*) composition, number[1], piece[1], work[2]; **jeden ~ muzyczny** (*na płycie*) track[1] **2** (*geol.*) formation

utyć → TYĆ

utykać (*na nogę*) hobble, limp[2]; **mocno** ~ walk with a bad limp

utylizacja recycling

utyskiwać grumble

utytłany grubby

utytułowany (*arystokrata*) titled

uwag|a 1 (*skupienie się na czymś*) attention[1], consideration, notice[1], regard[2] to/for sb/sth; **brać coś pod ~ę** balance[2], consider, make allowances for sb/sth, note[2], take account of sth, take sth into account, take sth into consideration, take note (of sth); **brać kogoś pod ~ę** (*np. przy wyborze na stanowisko*) have sb in mind (for sth); **biorąc pod ~ę** (*okoliczności*) considering, given[3], in view of sth; **wziąwszy wszystko pod ~ę** on balance; **nie brać kogoś/czegoś pod ~ę** count sb/sth out; **nie zwracać ~i** overlook; **nie zwracający ~i** oblivious (to/of sb/sth); **odwrócić ~ę od czegoś** divert attention away from sth; **odwracać czyjąś ~ę od czegoś** take sb's mind off sth; **poświęcać (komuś/czemuś) całkowitą ~ę** give your undivided attention (to sb/sth); **skupiać na sobie czyjąś całkowitą ~ę** have sb's undivided attention; **mający kogoś/coś na uwadze** minded, mindful; **godny ~i** remarkable; **brak ~i** negligence; **w centrum ~i** the centre of attention **2** (*komentarz*) comment[1], observation, remark noun; **dobra ~a** point[1]; **~a na stronie** aside noun; **robić ~ę** observe, remark **3** (*upomnienie*) caution[1] **4** (**uwaga!**) attention[2], danger!, watch out!; **~a! już!** here goes!; **~a! stopień!** mind that step!; **~a, zły pies!** beware of the dog!

uwalić się plonk[1] (yourself) (down)

u-walniać/wolnić: **(od kogoś/czegoś)** disengage, free[2], set sb free, liberate, release[1], rid sb/sth of sb/sth; **(do/dla czegoś)** free[2] sb/sth (up) for sth, sb/sth (up) to do sth; (*z więzów*) untie; (*ceny itp.*) deregulate

□ **u-walniać/wolnić się** disengage yourself (from sb/sth), get away (from…)

uwarstwi(a)ć stratify

uwarunkować → WARUNKOWAĆ

uwarunkowany: **czymś** subject[2] to sth

uwarzyć → WARZYĆ
uważać 1 kogoś/coś za coś count[1], deem, find[1], hold[1], be of the opinion that..., reckon, regard[1], view[2]; **uważam** I should imagine, say, think, etc. **2 na siebie/kogoś/coś** (*dbać*) take care of yourself/sb/sth **3** (*być ostrożnym*) beware (of sb/sth), heed[1], take heed (of sb/sth), mind[2], look out (for sb/sth), be on the lookout for sb/sth, keep a lookout for sb/sth, pay attention (to sb/sth), pay heed (to sb/sth), take care (that.../to do sth), watch[1], watch out, watch out for sb/sth; **uważaj, żebyś nie spadł** be careful you don't fall; **uważałem, żeby niczego nie powiedzieć** I was careful not to say anything; ~ **co się robi**; ~ **jak się idzie** watch your step
□ **uważać się**: **za kogoś** fancy[1] yourself (as) sth; **uważa się ją za jedną z najlepszych zawodniczek na świecie** she's ranked as one of the world's top players
uważający considerate
uważn|y attentive, careful, cautious, intent[1] (on/upon sth), observant, watchful
■ **uważnie** attentively, carefully, cautiously, closely, gingerly, intently; **bardzo ~ie przyglądać się komuś/czemuś** look hard at sb/sth
uwertura overture
uwiąd: ~ **starczy** senility
uwiązać (się) → UWIĄZYWAĆ (SIĘ), WIĄZAĆ (SIĘ)
uwiąz(yw)ać 1 lash[1] A to B, A and B together, tie sb/sth up **2 kogoś** tie sb down
□ **uwiąz(yw)ać się** tie yourself down
u-widaczniać/widocznić show sth up
uwieczni(a)ć immortalize
uwiedzenie seduction
uwielbiać adore, love[2], worship; **coś robić** delight in sth/in doing sth
uwielbienie adoration; **z ~m** lovingly
uwieńczyć → WIEŃCZYĆ
uwierać pinch[1]
uwierzyć → WIERZYĆ
uwieść → UWODZIĆ
uwięzić zob. też WIĘZIĆ; commit sb to sth, imprison
■ **uwięzienie** imprisonment, incarceration | **uwięziony 1** (*w więzieniu*) captive[1] **2** (*w nudnej pracy itp.*) trapped
u-wijać/winąć się bustle[1]
uwikłać (się) → WIKŁAĆ (SIĘ)
uwikłany entangled
u-właczać/włączyć: ~ **czyjejś godności** be beneath sb
■ **uwłaczający** derogatory
uwodziciel/ka seducer
uwodzicielski seductive
u-wodzić/wieść lure[1]; (*zwł. kobietę/mężczyznę*) seduce
uwolnić (się) → UWALNIAĆ (SIĘ)
uwolnienie freedom, liberation; (*z więzienia*) release[2]; (*od zobowiązań itp.*) disengagement
□ **uwolnienie się** disengagement
uwrażliwi(a)ć sensitize
uwspółcześni(a)ć update
uwydatni(a)ć emphasize (that...), heighten; (*wzmocnić, upiększyć*) enhance
□ **uwydatni(a)ć się** heighten
uwypuk-lać/lić accentuate; (*wzmocnić, upiększyć*) enhance
uwzględni(a)ć allow for sb/sth, cover[1]; (*brak doświadczenia itp.*) make allowances for sb/sth; **nie** ~ exclude
uwziąć się: **(na kogoś)** pick on sb
uzależni(a)ć subordinate[2]
uzależnienie dependency, reliance on sb/sth; **powodujący** ~ addictive
uzależniony dependent on sb/sth, governed by sth, reliant on sb/sth; (*od narkotyków itp.*) addicted (to sth)
uzasadni(a)ć justify, rationalize, warrant[2]; (*teorię itp.*) validate
■ **uzasadnienie** justification, validation; **racjonalne uzasadnienie** rationale | **uzasadniony** justifiable, valid; **prawnie uzasadniony** legitimate
u-zbrajać/zbroić się
IDM ~ **w cierpliwość** bide your time
uzbroić (się) → UZBRAJAĆ SIĘ, ZBROIĆ (SIĘ)
uzbrojenie armaments, munitions
uzbrojony 1 armed; ~ **bandyta** gunman **2** (*mina itp.*) live[2]
uzd|a bridle[1]; **zakładać ~ę** bridle[2]
uzdatni(a)ć purify
uzdolnienie (*talent*) accomplishment, aptitude (for sth/for doing sth)
uzdolniony talented; (*muzycznie itp.*) inclined; ~ **artystycznie** artistic
u-zdrawiać/zdrowić 1 cure[1] **2** (*przen.*) repair[1]
■ **uzdrawianie**: ~ **modlitwą** faith healing
uzdrowiciel/ka faith healer, healer
uzdrowienie cure[2], rehabilitation
uzdrowisko spa
u-zgadniać/zgodnić: **że** make an arrangement to do sth; ~ **werdykt** reach a verdict
uzgodnienie arrangement
uzgodniony cut and dried
uziemi(a)ć earth[2]
u-zmysławiać/zmysłowić: **coś sobie/komuś** bring sth home to sb, hit[1], realize, visualize
uznać → UZNAWAĆ
uznani|e 1 (*zasług itp.*) acknowledgement, acceptance, recognition; **wyrażać ~e za coś** acknowledge **2** (*poważanie*) credit[1], salute; (*krytyki*) acclaim noun; **dowód/wyrazy ~a** accolade; **wyrazy mojego ~a dla szefa kuchni!** my compliments to the chef!; **przyjmować z ~em** acclaim sb/sth (as sth) **3** (*decyzja*) **postępuj według swojego ~a** use your discretion; **według czyjegoś ~a** at sb's discretion
uznany accredited, celebrated
uzna(wa)ć acknowledge, concede, recognize, vote[2]; **za kogoś/coś** identify sb with sth, pronounce, rate[2] sb/sth (as) sth, as sth; ~ **prawnie** legitimize; **nie** ~ repudiate; **rada przysięgłych uznała oskarżonego za niewinnego** the jury found the accused not guilty; **wszyscy uznali imprezę za wielki sukces** hhe party was judged a great success by everybody; **zaginieni żołnierze zostali uznani za zmarłych** the soldiers were missing, presumed dead
uznawany: **być ~m za ważne** count[1] (as sth); **być ~m na czyjąś niekorzyść** count against sb
uzupełni(a)ć 1 (*zapasy itp.*) make sth up, replenish, supplement verb **2** (*jako kolejny krok*) follow sth up
■ **uzupełniający** subsidiary[1], supplementary | **uzupełnienie** complement[1]
□ **uzupełniać się** complement[2]
■ **uzupełniający się** complementary
uzurpator/ka usurper
uzurpować: **sobie** usurp
uzysk(iw)ać 1 (*dostać*) draw[1] sth (from sb/sth), obtain; (*zarabiać*) make[1]; (*fundusze itp.*) raise[1]; (*pożyczkę itp.*) take sth out; (*informacje itp.*) pick sth up; (*pomoc itp.*) enlist **2** (*kontrakt itp.*) secure[2]
■ **uzyskani|e**: **(możliwy) do uzyskania** obtainable
uża-lać/lić się: **nad kimś** be/feel sorry for sb
użądlenie sting[2]
użądlić → ŻĄDLIĆ
użyci|e employment, use[2]; ~**e siły** violence; **w ~u** functional; **wychodzić z ~a** fall into disuse, go out of use
użyć → UŻYWAĆ
użytecznoś|ć helpfulness, usefulness, utility; **zakład ~ci publicznej** utility
użyteczny helpful, useful
użytek application
użytkować/z- utilize
użytkowni-k/czka user; **grupa użytkownika** user group
uży(wa)ć employ, make use of sth/sb, use[1]; (*farb olejnych itp.*) work[1]; **zacząć być używanym** come into out of use
IDM ~ **sobie** live it up
używalny usable
używanie usage, use[2]
używany second-hand, used
użyźni(a)ć fertilize

V

v **(V/v)** (*litera*) V, v
VAT: **podatek** ~ value added tax
vel aka
verte PTO
vitro: **in** ~ in vitro
voyerystyczny voyeuristic
voyeuryzm voyeurism

W

w[1]; **(W/w)** (*litera*) W, w
w[2] (*przyimek*) **1** (*wewnątrz*) ~ **czymś** in[1], inside; (*autobus itp.*) aboard; ~ **domu/pracy** in[1]; ~ **tym/nim itp.** therein **2** (*kierunek*) ~ **coś** into **3** (*czas: rok, miesiąc*) in[1]; (*dni tygodnia*) on **4** (*w przeciągu czasu*) during; ~ **dzień** by day; ~ **weekend** at the weekend **5** (*kierunek, lewo/prawo*) to **6** (*spośród; forma, wzór; ubranie; opakowanie; stan*) in[1] **7** (*telewizja, radio*) on **8** (*tempo*) at **9** (*uderzyć*) ~ **głowę** on the head **10** (*tydzień*) a
wabić/z- attract, decoy verb, entice, lure[1]; ~ **do pracy** (*ludzi z innej firmy*) poach
wabik come-on, decoy, gimmick, lure[2], ploy
wachlarz 1 (*przedmiot*) fan[1] **2** (*gama*) range[1] (of sth) IDM **rozstawiać się ~em** fan out
wachlować/po- fan[2]
wacik swab; **oczyszczać ~iem** swab verb
wada defect[1], deficiency, disadvantage, drawback, failing[1], fault[1], flaw, imperfection, shortcoming, vice;

(*med.*) failure; (*skaza*) taint; ~ **wymowy** impediment, speech defect
wadliwość defectiveness
wadliwy defective, faulty, flawed, imperfect, unsound
wafel (*w kształcie stożka*) ice cream cone; **cienki** ~ wafer
wag|a 1 (*ciężar*) weight[1]; **tracić na wadze** lose weight; (*boks*) **~a ciężka** heavyweight; (*bokser itp.*) **~i lekkiej** lightweight **2** (*przyrząd*) balance[1], scales[1] **3** (*znaczenie*) substance; **przywiązywać dużą ~ę do czegoś** value[2] sth (as sth); **przywiązywać dużą ~ę do mody** be very fashion-conscious **4** (**Waga**) (*znak zodiaku*) Libra
wagarowicz/ka truant
wagary: **chodzić na** ~ play truant
wagon car, carriage; ~ **restauracyjny** buffet car; **luksusowy** ~ **restauracyjny** club car; ~ **towarowy** wagon; **odkryty** ~ **kolejowy** truck
wagonik: ~ **kolejki linowej** cable car
wahać się 1 (**/za-**) (*osoba*) dither, falter, hesitate, oscillate, vacillate, waver, swing[1]; (*przed czymś*) baulk (at sth) **2** (*temperatura itp.*) fluctuate; (*następować w regularnych odstępach z czymś innym*) alternate[1]
wahadło pendulum
wahadłowiec shuttle
wakacje holiday, vacation
wakat opening, vacancy
wakujący vacant
walący się decrepit, ramshackle
walc waltz[1]
walcowaty cylindrical
walczyć 1 (**/za-**) (**przeciw komuś/ czemuś**); (**z kimś/czymś**) fight[1] (against sb/sth); **osoba walcząca** combatant **2** (**/za-**) **o coś** battle[2] (with/ against sb/sth) (for sth), combat[2], contend with/against sb/sth, contest[2], fight[1] (for sth/to do sth), scramble (for sth/to do sth)
walczyk waltz[1]
walec 1 (*figura geometryczna*) cylinder **2** (*maszyny*) roller **3** ~ **drogowy** steamroller
waleczność valour
walenie hammering
walentynka valentine
walet jack[1]
wal-ić/nąć bang[1], bash[1], batter[1], crack[1], dash[2], hammer[2], pound[2] (at/ against/on sth), smash[1] sth against, into, through, etc., strike[1], thump, wallop, whack; (*serce itp.*) pound[2]; ~ **ciężkim przedmiotem** club[2]; **(próbować)** ~ **w kogoś/coś na oślep** swipe (at) sb/sth
□ **walić/z-/za- się** come down, tumble down; **walnąć (się)** (*np. w coś/o coś*) smash[1] against, into, through, etc.
walijski 1 Welsh **2** ~ **(język)** Welsh noun
waliza suitcase
walizka suitcase; ~ **kabinowa** carry-on
walk|a 1 (*zwł. na wojnie*) battle[1], conflict[1], fight[2], war; (*na ulicy itp.*) strife; (*w sporcie*) contest; (*akcja: na wojnie*) action, combat[1]; (**walki**) fighting; **chęć/duch ~i** fight[2]; **~a byków** bullfight **2** (*w celu osiągnięcia czegoś*) battle[1], fight[2], struggle[2], war (against/on sb/sth)
walkie-talkie walkie-talkie
walkman personal stereo
walkower: **~em** by default
walnąć (się) → WALIĆ (SIĘ)
walnięcie thump noun
waltornia French horn
waluta currency, money; ~ **obca** exchange[1]; **kantor wymiany walut** bureau de change
walutowy monetary
wał 1 (*nasyp itp.*) bank[1]; ~ **obronny** bulwark, ramparts **2** (*w mechanice*) shaft
wałek 1 (*do rozprowadzania farby itp.*) roller; ~ **do ciasta** rolling pin **2** (*w mechanice*) shaft **3** (*do włosów*); (**wałki**) rollers
wałęsać/po- się gad about/around, hang about/around, loiter, mooch
wałkonić/po- się lounge about, muck about/around
wałkoń good-for-nothing, slob
wampi-r/rzyca vampire
wandal vandal
wandalizm vandalism
wanienka tub
wanilia vanilla
waniliowy vanilla
wanna bath[1]; ~ **z masażem wodnym** Jacuzzi
wapień limestone
wapno 1 (*lekarstwo*) calcium **2** (*budowlane*) lime **3** (*malarskie*) whitewash[1]
warcaby draughts[1]
war-czeć/knąć drone, growl, snap[1] (sth) (at sb), snarl
warga lip
wariacja variation
wariacki loony adj., lunatic[2]
wariactwo 1 craziness **2** (**wariactwa**) nonsense
wariant variant, variation
wariat/ka loony, lunatic[1], madman, madwoman, nutcase; **jeździć jak wariat** drive like a maniac
wariograf lie detector
wariować/z- go crazy, be/go haywire, lose it, be/go out of your mind
warknąć → WARCZEĆ
warkocz braid, plait noun
warkoczyk pigtail
warkot drone noun, throb noun, whirr
warkotać/za- whirr
warstewka 1 (*oleju itp.*) film[1] **2** (*ogłady, grzeczności itp.*) veneer
warstwa coating, covering, layer, coat[1]; (*ciasta itp.*) tier; (*kremu, bitej śmietany itp.*) filling[1] IDM ~ **ozonowa** the ozone layer | ~ **społeczna** a walk of life
warstwica contour
warsztat 1 (*fabryka*) workshop; ~ **garncarski** pottery; ~ **tkacki** loom[2] **2** (**warsztaty**) (*seminarium dyskusyjne*) workshop
wart (także **warto**) **1** (*sumy pieniędzy*) worth[1]; **nic nie** ~ worthless; **niewiele** ~ not up to much **2 coś robić** worth[1] doing, etc.; (*czyjegoś czasu itp.*) worth sb's while, worthwhile; **nie ~o (czegoś robić)** be no good (doing sth), it isn't worth it; **nie ~o już iść na zakupy** it's not worth going shopping now **3** (*zaufania itp.*) worthy of sth/to do sth
wart|a guard[1]; **~a honorowa** guard of honour; **trzymać ~ę** watch[1] sb/sth (for sth)
wartki: (*film*) **o ~ej akcji** action-packed
wartko: **toczyć się** ~ flow[2]
warto → WART
wartościowy precious, valuable
wartoś|ć merit[1], value[1], worth[2]; **~ć nominalna** face value; **poczucie własnej ~ci** ego, self-esteem
wartowni-k/czka sentry
warun|ek 1 (*umowy itp.; wymaganie*) condition[1], requirement; (**warunki**) terms[1]; **~ek wstępny** precondition, prerequisite; **pod ~kiem, że** as/so long as, on condition (that…), provided /providing (that), on the understanding that…; **nie stawiając ~ków** (with) no strings attached, without strings **2** (*życia, pracy itp.*) **~ki pracy** working conditions **3** (**warunki**) (*w szkole itp.*) facilities
warunkować/u- condition[2]
warunkow|y conditional; **zwolnienie ~e z więzienia** probation
warzyć/u- (*piwo*) brew
□ **warzyć/z- się** curdle
warzywniak greengrocer
warzyw|o vegetable; **~a zielone** (*np. kapusta, groszek*) greens[2]
wasz (*zaim. osobowy*) your; (*zaim. dzierżawczy*) yours; (*w tytułach*) **~a** (*wysokość itp.*) your
waśnić/z- się feud verb
waśń feud
wat watt
wat|a cotton wool IDM **~a cukrowa** candyfloss | **być jak z ~y** turn to jelly
watować pad[2]
wawrzyn laurel
wazon vase
ważka dragonfly
ważki weighty
ważniak big-head
ważnoś|ć 1 (*znaczenie*) importance, magnitude, significance **2** (*moc prawna*) validity; **data ~ci** expiry
ważn|y 1 (*istotny*) important, material[2], meaningful, momentous, significant; (*przyczyna itp.*) good[1]; (*imponujący*) big, grand[1]; (*polityk itp.*) high-powered; (*aktor itp.*) big time[2]; **być ~iejszym od czegoś** come before sb/sth **2** (*arogancki*) big-headed, full[1] of yourself **3** (*mający moc prawną*) valid; **być ~ym** be in force; **bilet jest ~y przez następne trzy dni** this ticket's good for another three days; **moja umowa jest jeszcze ~a przez dwa miesiące** my contract has two months left to run
ważyć/z- weigh; **nic nie ważący** weightless
□ **ważyć się 1** (*losy*) be, etc. in the balance **2** (**/od-**) (*ośmielać się*) dare[1]
wąchać/po- smell[1], have a smell of sth, sniff (at) sth
wągier blackhead
wąglik anthrax
wąs 1 (także **wąsy**) (*mężczyzny*) moustache **2** (*kota itp.*) whisker
wąski 1 (*nie szeroki*) narrow[1] **2** (*obcisły*) tight
wąskość narrowness

wąskotorow|y: **kolej ~a** a narrow-gauge railway
wątek 1 (*powieści*) plot[1] **2** (*myśli*) strand, thread[1]; (*główny sens wypowiedzi*) drift[1]
wątły 1 (*dziecko itp.*) delicate, frail **2** (*związek*) tenuous
wątpić/z- doubt[2]
wątpieni|e doubt[1]; **bez ~a** easily the best, worst, nicest, etc.
wątpliwoś|ć doubt[1], question[1]; **mający ~ci** in doubt, unsure; **mieć poważne ~ci co do czegoś** be very dubious about sth; **poddawać w ~ć** cast doubt on sth, question[2]; **ponad wszelką ~ć** beyond (any) doubt
wątpliwy in doubt, doubtful, questionable; (*kompromis itp.*) uneasy
wątroba liver
wątrobianka liver sausage
wątróbka liver
wąwóz ravine
wąż 1 (*zool.*) serpent, snake[1] **2** (*rura*) tube; (*zwł. do polewania ogrodu*) hose
wbi(ja)ć (*kij itp.*) dig sth in, dig sth into sb/sth, embed, stick[1] sth in/into (sth); (*gwóźdź itp.*) drive[1]; (*nóż itp.*) plunge sth into sth, plunge sth in; **~ klin** wedge[2] IDM **~ (komuś) coś do głowy** drive sth home (to sb), drum sth into sb, hammer sth into sb
□ **wbi(ja)ć się** dig in
wbrew against, contrary[1], despite, in spite of; **postępować ~ czemuś** compromise[2] sth
wbudow(yw)ać build sth in/on, build sth into/onto sth
wcale (*bynajmniej, zupełnie*) **~ nie** any, anything but, anything like sb/sth[2], not at all, not a bit, not…either, not nearly, not in the slightest, nothing like, whatever; **prawie ~ (nie)** scarcely; **~ nie jestem mądrzejszy** I'm still none the wiser
w-chłaniać/chłonąć absorb, soak sth up
■ **wchłaniający: (dobrze) wchłaniający płyn** absorbent
wchłonąć → CHŁONĄĆ, WCHŁANIAĆ
w-chodzić/ejść 1 (*do pomieszczenia*) enter, go into sth; (*do pokoju itp.*) come in, go in; **~ na hiszpański rynek** penetrate the Spanish market **2** (*na drzewo/górę*) climb[1] (up) (sth), mount[1], scale[2] **3 ~ na ekrany** be/go on release **4 w coś** (*zagłębiać się*) enter into sth **5 ~ w życie** (*ustawa, prawo itp.*) come into effect, come into force, take effect IDM **~ komuś na głowę** get on top of sb, walk (all) over sb
wciąć → WCINAĆ
wciąg-ać/nąć 1 (*flagę itp.*) hoist, winch verb **2** (*sweter itp.*) pull sth on; (*spodnie itp.*) pull sth up **3** (*w działalność*) involve sb/sth in (doing) sth, rope sb in (to do sth); (*w zbrodnię*) implicate sb (in sth)
■ **wciągający** absorbing
□ **wciąg-ać/nąć się** (*w normalny tok pracy*) get into your stride
wciągarka winch
wciąż always, still[1]; **~ coś robić** keep[1] doing sth
wcie-lać/lić incorporate
wcielenie incarnation; **ponowne ~** reincarnation
w-cierać/etrzeć grind[1] sth in/into sth, rub sth in (to sth)
wcięcie: **robić ~ akapitowe** indent
w-cinać/ciąć 1 (*jedzenie*) tuck in, tuck into sth **2** (*akapit*) indent
wcis-kać/nąć 1 coś/kogoś (w coś) cram sb/sth in (sth), sb/sth into sth, crush sb/sth into sth, fit sb/sth in, fit sb/sth in/into sth, jam[2] sb/sth in sth, slot sb/sth in, squeeze[1] sb/sth into sth, wedge[2]; **(pomiędzy kogoś/coś)** sandwich sb/sth (between sb/sth); (*zwł. ludzi*) crowd sb/sth into sth, crowd sb/sth in **2** (*niedopałek itp.*) grind[1] sth in/into sth **3** (*nóż itp.*) plunge sth into sth, plunge sth in **3 coś (komuś)** palm sb off (with sth), palm sth off (on sb); (*tandetny towar itp.*) fob sb off (with sth)
□ **wcis-kać/nąć się 1 gdzieś** penetrate, squeeze[1] into sth, in; (*zwł. ludzie*) crowd into sth, crowd in **2** (*w ubranie*) get into sth
wcze|sny early[1]; **obowiązywać z ~śniejszą datą** backdate
■ **wcześnie**: **(za) ~** early[2]; **jest za ~** (*by coś wiedzieć itp.*) it's early days (yet); (*talent itp.*) **~ rozwinięty** precocious | **wcześniej** previously; **jak najwcześniej** first thing IDM **~j czy później** sooner or later | **wcześniejszy** earlier; (*uprzedni*) advance[3], previous, prior
wcześniak premature baby
wczołgać się → CZOŁGAĆ SIĘ
wczoraj yesterday
wczorajsz|y: **~y dzień** yesterday; **~a gazeta** yesterday's paper
wczu(wa)ć się (*w czyjąś sytuację*) empathize (with sb)
wczyt(yw)ać swipe
wda(wa)ć się: **w coś** get into sth, get yourself into sth
wdech breath; **gwałtowny ~** a sharp intake of breath; **na ~u podnosimy ciężar** breathe out as you lift the weight
wdeptać tread[1] sth (in/into)
wdowa widow
wdowiec widower
wdrap(yw)ać się clamber up, climb[1], scramble
w-drażać/drożyć implement[1], institute[2]
wdrożenie implementation, institution
wdychać inhale
w-dzierać/edrzeć się: **(gdzieś)** penetrate; (*nagle*) burst[1] into (sth)
wdzięcznoś|ć appreciation, debt, gratitude; **z ~cią** gratefully, thankfully
wdzięczny appreciative, glad (of sth), grateful, indebted, thankful
wdzięczyć się ponce about/around
wdzięk charm[1], grace, loveliness, gracefulness; **pełen ~u** graceful; **bez ~u** graceless
webcam webcam
według in accordance with sth, according to, by, to, under
wedrzeć się → WDZIERAĆ SIĘ
weekend weekend
wegan-in/ka vegan
wegański vegan adj.
wegetacja vegetation
wegetarian-in/ka vegetarian
wegetariański vegetarian adj., veggie adj.
wehikuł: **~ czasu** time machine
wejrzeni|e: **miłość od pierwszego ~a** love at first sight
wejście 1 (*drzwi; wchodzenie*) access[1] (to sth), doorway, entrance, the way in somewhere; **~ na statek** embarkation **2** (*wstęp*) entrance (into/onto sth), entry **3** (*elektr.*) socket
wejść → WCHODZIĆ
wekować/za- preserve
weksel bill of exchange
welon veil
welur velour
welwet velvet
wełna 1 (*włókno*) wool **2** (*runo*) fleece[1]
wełniany woollen
wełnisty woolly
wendeta vendetta
weneryczn|y: **choroba ~a** venereal disease
wenta bazaar; **~ dobroczynna** jumble sale
wentyl valve
wentylacja ventilation
wentylator fan[1], ventilator
wentylować/prze- 1 air[2], ventilate **2** (*kwestię itp.*) air[2]
□ **wentylować/prze- się** air[2]
wentylowany: **dobrze ~** airy
Wenus Venus
wepchnąć (się) → WPYCHAĆ (SIĘ)
weranda veranda
werbalny verbal
werbel roll[1]
werbować/z- enlist, recruit[1]
werbunek recruitment
werdykt verdict
werniks varnish
werniksować varnish verb
wernisaż private view
wersalka sofa bed
wersja version; (*wydarzeń*) story, side of the story; **~ ostateczna** the definitive version
wertować/prze- (*książkę itp.*) browse through sth, dip into sth
werw|a drive[2], spirit[1], verve, zest; **z ~ą** with gusto, heartily; **pełen ~y** bouncy, breezy, bright, sparkling; **odzyskiwać ~ę** buck up; **grupa pełnych ~y nastolatków** a group of high-spirited teenagers
weryfikacja verification
weryfikować/z- verify
wesele wedding
weselny bridal
wesołek laugh[2]
wesołość cheerfulness, chirpiness, gaiety, glee, hilarity, merriment, mirth
wesoł|y buoyant, cheerful, cheery, convivial, festive, fun[2], gay[1], good-humoured, happy, jolly, light-hearted, merry, playful; (*tylko osoba*) chirpy IDM **Wesołych Świąt (Bożego Narodzenia)!** Happy Christmas! | **Wesołych Świąt (Wielkanocnych)!** Happy Easter! | **~e miasteczko** fair[2]
wesprzeć (się) → WSPIERAĆ (SIĘ)
wessać → WSYSAĆ
westchnąć → WZDYCHAĆ
wesz louse
wet: **~ za ~** tit for tat; **oddawać ~ za ~** retaliate (against sb/sth)
weteran/ka (*wojny itp.*) veteran
weterynaryjny veterinary
weterynarz vet[1], veterinary surgeon
wetknąć → WTYKAĆ
weto veto noun
wetować/za- veto
wetrzeć → WCIERAĆ

wewnątrz within; **(do)** ~ inside[1]
wewnątrzwydzielniczy endocrine
wewnętrzn|y inside adj., interior adj., internal, inward adj.; (*i przen.*) inner; (*krajowy*) home[2]; **~a strona** inside[2]; **sprawy ~e** (*kraju*) the Interior
wezbrać → WZBIERAĆ
wezwać → WZYWAĆ
wezwanie appeal[1], summons
węch smell[2]
wędka fishing rod
wędkarstwo angling, fishing
wędkarz (także **wędkarka**) angler, fisherman
wędkować fish[2]
wędrować 1 (/po-) (*pieszo*) hike verb, ramble[1], roam, trek verb, wander **2 (/wy-)** (*migrować*) migrate
wędrowiec hiker, traveller, rambler
wędrowni-k/czka rambler
wędrown|y itinerant, migratory, nomadic
wędrówka 1 (*piesza*) hike, ramble[2], walking; **długa piesza** ~ trek **2** (*migracja*) migration
wędzidło bit[1]
wędzony 1 (*ryba, ser itp.*) smoked **2** (*smak*) smoky
węgiel 1 coal; ~ **drzewny** charcoal; **żarzące się węgle** coals **2** (*pierwiastek chemiczny*) carbon IDM **czarny jak** ~ jet black
węglowodan carbohydrate
węgorz eel
węszyć 1 (/z-/wy-) (*pies itp. szukając*) sniff (at) sth, snuffle; (*wyczuć węchem*) scent verb **2 (/z-)** (*osoba: starać się coś znaleźć*) nose about/around
węzeł 1 (*na sznurku itp.*) knot[1] **2** ~ **chłonny** gland **3** (*bot.*) node **4** (*dwóch linii/systemów*) ~ **kolejowy** junction **5** (*żegl.*) knot[1]
węzłowato: **(mówiąc) krótko i** ~ in a nutshell
wężyk tube
WF PE
w-ginać/giąć dent[1]
wgląd: **(w coś)** insight; **mieć** ~ **do czegoś** get/have a look-in; **nie mieć ~u do czegoś** not get/have a look-in
wgłębienie depression
wgr(yw)ać (*program komputerowy*) load[2]
whisky whisky; (*szkocka*) Scotch
wiać/po-/za- blow[1]; ~ **porywiście** gust verb
wiadomo: **nie** ~ God, goodness, Heaven, etc. knows; **nigdy nie** ~ you never know; **nigdy nie** ~**, co…** there's no telling what…
wiadomoś|ć communication, information, item, message, piece of news; (**wiadomości**) news; **wydanie ~ci** news bulletin; **podawać do (publicznej) ~ci** disclose; **przyjmować do ~ci** accept (that…); **do ~ci kogoś** (*bez potrzeby podejmowania działania*) FYI; (*kiedy należy podjąć jakieś działanie*) fao
wiadro bucket
wiadukt viaduct; (*na autostradzie*) flyover
wiar|a 1 (*relig.*) belief, faith **2 w kogoś/coś** faith (in sb/sth); **dawać ~ę** swallow[1]; **dawać komuś ~ę** take it from me; **(zrobiony itp.) w dobrej wierze** in good faith, innocent
wiarygodność credibility, reliability
wiarygodny authoritative, believable, credible, plausible, reliable
wiata: ~ **autobusowa** bus shelter
wiatr wind[1]; **pod** ~ against the wind
wiatraczek fan[1]
wiatrak windmill
wiatrochron windbreak
wiąz elm, elm tree
wiązać 1 (/z-/po-) (*łączyć węzłem*) bind[1], bunch[2] sth/sb (up/together), connect, hitch[1], join[1], rope[2] A to B, A and B together; **ze sobą** couple[2]; (*fakty itp.*) interrelate; ~ **sznurówki** do up your laces **2** (*ograniczać kogoś*) tie sb down IDM **(ledwo) ~ koniec z końcem** eke out a living, keep your head above water, make ends meet, scrape by
■ **wiążący** (*obowiązujący*) binding[1], valid (for sth)
□ **wiązać się 1 (/z-)** bond[2] **2 (/z-)** (*ludzie*) **nie chciała się z nim ~ emocjonalnie** she didn't want to get emotionally entangled with him **3** (*mieć związek*) interrelate, relate to sb/sth, tie in (with sth) **4 (/u-)** (*ograniczać się*) tie yourself down
wiązadło ligament
wiązanie (*naciarskie*) binding[2]
wiązanka 1 (*kwiatów*) bouquet **2** (*muz.*) medley
wiązka 1 (*drzewa na opał itp.*) bundle[1] **2** (*promieni*) beam[1]
wibracja vibration
wibrować vibrate
wicehrabia viscount
wicher gale
wić się 1 (*droga itp.*) meander, snake[2], twist[1], wind[3] **2** (*osoba*) writhe, thrash (sth) (about/around) **3** (*włosy*) curl[1]
■ **wijący się 1** (*droga itp.*) winding **2** (*ruch*) sinuous **3** (*włosy*) curly
widać: **nie ~ tego** it doesn't show; **na tych brązowych spodniach nie ~ brudu** these brown trousers don't show the dirt; **było po niej ~ oznaki stresu** she was showing signs of stress IDM **nie tylko to, co ~** there is more to sb/sth than meets the eye
widelec fork[1]
wideo video
wideokaseta video
wideokonferencja videoconferencing
widlasty forked
widły fork[1], pitchfork
widmo 1 (*duch*) apparition, ghost, phantom, spectre **2** (*fizyczne*) spectrum
widmowy ghostly
widocznoś|ć prominence, visibility; **z ograniczoną ~cią** blind[1]
widoczny apparent, conspicuous, noticeable, prominent, seeming, visible; (*zewnętrzny*) outward; **(być) ~m** (to be) in evidence; **~ z budynku** in full view of the house; **mój wiek zaczyna być ~!** my age is beginning to tell!
widok 1 (*z okna itp.*) view[1]; **piękny** ~ vista; (*okno itp.*) **z ~iem na coś** overlook; **pokój z ~iem na morze** a room with a sea view **2** (*bycie widocznym*) sight[1]; **na ~u (kogoś/czegoś)** in full view (of sb/sth), in sight; (*strzelić itp.*) **na** ~ on sight **3 (widoki)** (*na pracę itp.*) outlook (for sth), probability, prospects; (*na spadek itp.*) expectations; **mieć ~i (na coś)** be in the running (for sth); **nie mieć ~ów (na coś)** be out of the running (for sth)
widomy blatant
widowisko exhibition, show[2], spectacle; ~ **w plenerze** pageant
widowiskowy spectacular; **sport** ~ spectator sport
widownia 1 (*ludzie*) audience **2** (*miejsce*) auditorium, house[1]
widywać się: **często ~ z kimś** see a lot of sb
widz spectator
widzeni|e 1 (*zmysł*) **znać kogoś z ~a** know sb by sight **2** (*z dziećmi itp.*) access[1] (to sb) IDM **do ~a** goodbye
widzialny visible
widzieć/zobaczyć 1 catch sight of sb/sth, look at sth, see, sight[2]; **zobaczyć (przelotnie)** glimpse verb; **po raz pierwszy coś zobaczyć** have your first sight of sb/sth **2 ~ we śnie** dream[2] (about sb/sth) IDM **nie widzieć świata poza kimś** dote on sb/sth
■ **widziany** IDM **mile widziany** welcome[2]
□ **widzieć/zobaczyć się**: **z kimś** see sb
wiec mass meeting
wieczność eternity, infinity
wieczn|y ageless, eternal, everlasting, perpetual, timeless IDM **~e pióro** fountain pen
■ **wiecznie** eternally, ever-, forever
wieczorowy nightly
wieczór evening, night; **dziś wieczorem** this evening; **(powtarzający się) co** ~ nightly IDM ~ **kawalerski** stag night
wiedz|a 1 knowledge; (*naukowa*) learning, scholarship; **~a ogólna** general knowledge; (*dot. nieważnych faktów*) trivia; **~a tajemna** occult; **o dużej ~y** learned; **kobiety i mężczyźni wielkiej ~y** men and women of learning **2 bez ~y szefa** unknown to the boss
wiedzieć know[1], know of sb/sth, tell; **nic nie ~ (o czymś)** be in the dark (about sth); **o ile wiem** to my knowledge; **wiem tyle, co ty** your guess is as good as mine IDM **kto wie** God, goodness, Heaven, etc. knows | **no wiesz!** come on, you know | **powinienem/nam ~, że** I might have known | **~, co i jak** know what's what | **wiesz co** (I'll) tell you what
wiedźma hag, witch
wiejski pastoral, rural, rustic, village; (*jajka, drób*) free-range
wiek 1 (*zwł. osoby*) age[1]; (*organizacji itp.*) year; **w ~u** aged; **w ~u szkolnym** children of school age; **w ~u między 60 i 69 lat** in your sixties; **~ dziewczęcy** girlhood; ~ **męski** manhood; **przedział ~u** age group **2** (*sto lat*) century **3 (wieki)** (*bardzo długo/dawno*) yonks; **~i całe** donkey's years; **na ~i** eternally
wieko lid
wiekopomność immortality
wiekopomny immortal
wiekow|y: **grupa ~a** age group

wielbiciel/ka 1 (*miłośnik*) devotee, enthusiast, fan[1]; (*zwł. opery, win*) buff **2** (*admirator*) admirer
wielbić worship
wielbłąd camel
wielce enormously, much[2], remarkably, sadly, sorely
wiele: **czegoś** a good/great deal (of sth), lot[1]; (*tylko z rz. policz.*) hundreds, many, miles, various; (*tylko z rz. niepolicz.*) much[1]; **o ~** far[2], infinitely, lot[2], much[2] IDM **tego już za ~** it's a bit much
wielebny reverend
Wielkanoc Easter
wielkanocny Easter
wielki 1 (*duży*) big, large, massive; (*bałagan itp.*) terrible **2** (*liczny; intensywny; ważny*) grand[1], great[1], profound; (*uczucie*) intense IDM **nic ~ego** nothing much | **~ Boże!** (Good) Lord! | **Wielka Brytania** Great Britain | **Wielki Czwartek** Maundy Thursday | **Wielki Piątek** Good Friday | **Wielki Tydzień** Holy Week | **Wielki Wybuch** big bang
wielkoduszność generosity
wielkoduszny generous, magnanimous, noble[1]
wielkolud giant, ogre
wielkomiejski metropolitan, urban
wielkopańsko grandly
wielkoś|ć 1 (*rozmiar*) magnitude, scale[1], size[1], volume; **sporej ~ci** sizeable **2** (*znaczenie*) greatness; (*wspaniałność*) grandeur
wielmożny: **odpowiednik JWP** Esq.
wielobranżowy: **sklep ~** general store
wielofunkcyjny multi-purpose
wielokąt polygon
wielokrotność multiple[2]
wielokrotny multiple[1], repeated
■ **wielokrotnie** again and again, repeatedly
wielokulturowy multicultural
wieloletni: **~ problem** a problem of many years' standing
wielomęstwo polygamy
wielonarodowy cosmopolitan, multinational[1]
wielonienasycony polyunsaturated
wielopaństwowy multinational[1]
wielopiętrowy high-rise
wielopoziomowy: **parking ~** multi-storey car park
wielorasowy multiracial
wieloryb whale
wielorybnictwo whaling
wieloskładnikowy (*dieta*) omnivorous
wielostronny multilateral
wielościan a many-sided shape
wielowarstwowy laminated
wielozadaniowość multitasking
wieloznaczność ambiguity
wieloznaczny ambiguous
wielożeństwo polygamy
wielu → WIELE
wieniec wreath
wieńcowy coronary[1]
wieńczyć/z-/u- cap[2], crown[2], top[3]
wieprz hog[1]
wieprzowina pork
wiercić/wy- bore[1], drill[2]
□ **wiercić się** fidget (with sth), jig[2] about/around, shuffle[1], squirm, wriggle (sth) (about /around)
wiernopoddańczość subservience
wierność allegiance, faithfulness, fidelity, loyalty
wiern|y (*przym.*) **1** (*przyjaciel itp.*) faithful, loyal, stalwart; **być ~ym komuś** stand by sb **2 ~a kopia** facsimile
■ **wiern-y/a** (*rz.*) worshipper; (**wierni**) congregation
wiersz 1 (*utwór*) poem, verse; **poezja pisana ~em** poetry written in rhyme **2** (*linijka*) line[1]
wierszyk rhyme[1]; **~ dla dzieci** nursery rhyme
wiertarka drill[1]
wiertło drill[1]
wierutn|y: **~e kłamstwo** whopper
wierząc|y: **osoba ~a** believer
wierzba willow; **~ płacząca** weeping willow
wierzch 1 (*górna część*) top[1]; (*kłaść/leżeć itp.*) **na ~/u** on top **2** (*pizzy itp.*) topping
wierzchołek apex, peak[1], top[1] IDM **~ góry lodowej** the tip of the iceberg
wierzg-ać/nąć kick[1]
wierzyciel creditor
wierzyć/u- accept, believe, credit[2]; **głęboko/święcie ~ w kogoś/coś** have every confidence in sth, swear by sb/sth; **nie ~** disbelieve; **uwierz/cie mi** take it from me; **choć trudno w to uwierzyć** believe it or not; **nie mogę uwierzyć, że ktoś mógłby być tak głupi!** it amazes me that anyone could be so stupid!; **wierzę, że świetnie poradzisz sobie z tym zadaniem** I've got great faith in your ability to do the job IDM **~ komuś na słowo** take sth on trust, take sb's word for it
wieszać 1 (**/zawiesić**) hang[1], hang sth up; (*ogłoszenie itp.*) put sth up; (*pranie*) hang sth out **2** (**/powiesić**) **~ (kogoś)** hang[1]
wieszak hanger, peg[1]; **poziomy ~** (*np. na ręczniki*) rail; **~ stojący** coat stand
wieś country; (*wioska*) village
wieść[1] (*cz., ciężkie itp. życie*) lead[1]
□ **wieść/po- się** fare[2]
wieść[2] (*rz.*) hearsay, lead[1]; (**wieści**) news
wieśnia-k/czka peasant; (**wieśniacy**) country folk
wietrzeć/z- (*skały*) weather[2]
wietrznik ventilator
wietrzny breezy, windswept, windy; **bardzo ~** blustery; **chłodny i ~** fresh
wietrzyć/prze-/wy- 1 (*pokój itp.*) air[2], ventilate **2** (*węszyć*) scent verb
□ **wietrzyć/prze-/wy- się** air[2]
wietrzyk breeze[1]
wiewiórka squirrel
wieża 1 (*budowla*) tower[1]; (*szpiczasty dach*) spire; **strzelista ~** steeple; **~ kontrolna** control tower; **~ obserwacyjna** watchtower **2** (*stereofoniczna*) hi-fi **3** (*szachy*) castle
wieżowiec tower block
wieżyczka pinnacle, turret
więc: **(a) ~** hence, so[2], then, therefore, well[3]; **tak ~** so[2], thus
więcej extra[1], further adv., more[1,2], over, plus[3]; **co ~** moreover, what's more; **nic ~** nothing else; **coraz ~** more and more; **nigdy ~ tego nie rób!** don't ever do it again! IDM **mniej ~** more or less
więdnąć/z- droop, wilt, wither (away)
większoś|ć majority, most[1]; **ogromna ~ć** the bulk; **bezwzględna ~ć** an overall majority; **w ~ci** mainly, mostly; **być w ~ci; stanowić ~ć** be in the/a majority
większy major[1]
więzić/u- incarcerate
więzieni|e jail[1], prison, penitentiary; **została skazana na karę pięciu lat ~a** she was sentenced to five years' imprisonment
wię-zień/źniarka convict[2], inmate, prisoner; **~ sumienia** prisoner of conscience
więź bond[1], link[1], tie[2]; **tworzyć emocjonalną ~** bond[2] (with sb)
wigilia 1 eve **2** (**Wigilia**) Christmas Eve
wigor pep noun, stamina, vigour; **pełen ~u** vigorous; **mój dziadek jest pełen ~u jak na swoje lata** my grandfather is very active for his age; **z ~em** vigorously
wikary curate
wiking Viking
wiklina rush[2], wicker
wiklinowy wicker
wikłać 1 (**/u-**) **kogoś (w coś)** embroil sb (in sth), involve sb in (doing) sth **2** (**/po-**) **coś** confuse
□ **wikłać/u- się** embroil yourself (in sth), get yourself entangled in sth; **uwikłać się w kłopoty** get into trouble
wiktoriański Victorian
wilczur Alsatian
wilczy: **~ apetyt** a voracious appetite
wilgoć damp noun, humidity, moisture
wilgotność humidity
wilgotny damp[1], humid, moist, wet[1]; (*w nieprzyjemny sposób*) clammy
wilk wolf; **patrzeć ~iem** scowl verb IDM **i ~ syty, i owca cała** have your cake and eat it | **o ~u mowa (a ~ tuż)** speak/talk of the devil
win|a blame[2], fault[1], guilt; **z poczuciem ~y** guiltily; **ponosić ~ę za coś** be at fault
winda lift[2]
windsurfing windsurfing; **uprawiać ~** windsurf
winiarnia wine bar
winić blame[1], reproach
winnica vineyard
winny (także **winien**) **1** (*odpowiedzialny*) culpable, guilty, in the wrong; **być ~m** be to blame (for sth), be at fault **2** (*dłużny*) **być komuś coś ~m** owe
wino wine; **~ różowe** rosé; **~ firmowe** house wine; **~ marki ~** plonk[2]
winogrono grape
winorośl vine
winowaj-ca/czyni culprit, offender
winyl vinyl
wiolonczela cello
wiolonczelist-a/ka cellist
wiosenn|y spring[1]; **robić ~e porządki** spring-clean
wioska hamlet
wiosło oar; **krótkie ~ o szerokim piórze** paddle[1]
wiosłować row[2]; (*krótkim wiosłem*) paddle[2]
wiosna spring[1], springtime
wiórkować shave sth off (sth)
wiórow|y: **płyta ~a** chipboard
wi|r 1 (*wodny*) eddy, whirlpool **2** (*zdarzeń*) whirl[2]; **rzucać się w ~r czegoś** plunge into sth/in, throw yourself/sth into sth; **w ~rze (czegoś)**

in the thick of sth **3** (*w głowie itp.*) whirl[2]
wirnik rotor
wirować **1** (**/za-**) (*kręcić*) spin[1], swirl, twirl, whirl[1] **2** (**/od-**) (*pralka*) spin-dry **3** (**/za-**) (*przed oczami*) reel[2], swim
wirówka **1** (*na bieliznę*) spin dryer **2** (*techn.*) centrifuge
wirtualn|y virtual; **~a rzeczywistość** virtual reality
wirtuoz/ka virtuoso
wirus **1** (*med.*) bug[1], virus **2** ~ **komputerowy** virus
wirusowy viral
wisieć/zawisnąć **1** (*zwisać*) hang[1] (above/over sb/sth); ~ **w powietrzu** hover **2** (*przen.*) loom[1] (up); **nad kimś** hang over sb; ~ **w powietrzu** be brewing, be in the offing; **wiszący w powietrzu** impending
wisielczy: **być w ~m nastroju** be in a black mood
wisiel|ec: **gra w ~ca** hangman
wisior (także **wisiorek**) pendant
wiśnia cherry
witać/po- greet, welcome[1]; **serdecznie powitać** extend a warm welcome to sb, make sb welcome; **witaj/cie!** hi, welcome interj.
witalny vital
■ **witalność** vitality
witamina vitamin
witaminowy vitamin
witraż stained glass
witryna: ~ **internetowa** website
wiwat cheer[1]
wiwatować/za- cheer[2], give a cheer
wiwisekcja vivisection
wiza visa
wizerunek image
wizja vision
wizjer spyhole
wizjoner/ka visionary noun
wizjonerski visionary
wizualny visual
wizyt|a call[2], visit; (*u lekarza itp.*) consultation; **krótka ~a** flying visit; **premier pojechał z ~ą do Niemiec** the Prime Minister is on a visit to Germany
wizytówka business card
wjazd entrance, entry, slip road, the way in somewhere
w-jeżdżać/jechać **1** **wjeżdżać na stację** pull in (to sth) **2** **na/w kogoś/coś** (*powodować wypadek*) crash[2], go into sth, run (sth) into sb/sth
w-klejać/kleić paste[2]
wklepywać (*perfumy w skórę itp.*) dab sth on/off (sth)
wklęsły concave, hollow[1]
wklęśnięcie dent[2]
wkład **1** (*udział*) contribution, input[1] **2** (*do długopisu itp.*) cartridge, refill noun; **wymienny** ~ (*chroniący pojemnik, wnętrze czegoś*) liner
w-kładać/łożyć **1** **coś do czegoś** put; (*monetę, dyskietkę itp.*) insert; (*film, nabój*) load[2]; ~ **do kieszeni** pocket[2]; **włóż koszulę w spodnie** tuck your shirt in; **nie mogę nic więcej włożyć** I can't get any more in **2** (*czas/energię w coś*) put sth in, put sth into sth/into doing sth; (*czas, energię; kapitał*) invest (sth) (in sth) **3** (*ubranie*) get sth on, put sth on
wkładka: ~ **wewnątrzmaciczna** IUD
wkoło → WOKOŁO
w-kraczać/kroczyć **1** (*wejść*) enter, march in, step in **2** (*bez pozwolenia na czyjś grunt*) trespass **3** (*w czyjeś prawa itp.*) impinge on/upon sth **4** (*w nowy etap itp.*) enter
w-kradać/kraść się creep in, steal in IDM ~ **w czyjeś łaski** ingratiate yourself (with sb), worm your way/yourself into sth
w-kręcać/kręcić się wriggle
wkręt (*z sześciokątnym gniazdkiem*) Allen screw
wkroczenie entry
wkroczyć → WKRACZAĆ
wkrótce directly[1], in the not too distant future, presently, shortly, soon
wku-rzać/rzyć się flip (out)
wkurzony brassed off
wku(wa)ć (*do egzaminu itp.*) cram, swot[2]
w-latywać/lecieć: ~ **tłumnie/gromadnie** swarm[2]; ~ **przez okno** come flying through the window
wlec/za- drag[1], haul[1], lug, trail[2]; **wlekąc (kogoś za sobą)** with sb in tow
□ **wlec się** **1** (**/po-/za-**) (*iść*) crawl[1], plod (along/on), slog[1] down, up, along, etc., traipse; **za kimś/czymś** lag[1] (behind) (sb/sth), straggle, trail[2] **2** (*czas*) drag[1] (on), wear on; ~ **w nieskończoność** run on
wl(ew)ać pour
wli-czać/czyć count[1], include; **nie** ~ exclude; **w cenę wczasów wliczone jest…** the price of the holiday includes…; **10% zostanie wliczone do waszego rachunku jako opłata za obsługę** 10% will be added on to your bill as a service charge
wlot (*techn.*) inlet
wlotowy: **otwór** ~ inlet
władać **1** (*rządzić*) rule[2] (over sb/sth) **2** (*językiem*) **ona dobrze włada francuskim** she has a good command of French **3** (*szablą itp.*) wield
■ **władanie** **1** (*króla itp.*) reign noun **2** (*językiem itp.*) command[1] IDM **we władaniu** in your hands, in the hands of sb
wład-ca/czyni ruler
władczy bossy, domineering, imperious, overbearing; (*wskazujący, że ktoś/coś należy do kogoś*) proprietorial; (*głos itp.*) commanding
władować zob. też ŁADOWAĆ; (*przen.*) pump sth into sth/sb
władz|a **1** (*polit.*) authorities; **~a ustawodawcza** legislature; **~e lokalne** authority; **~e samorządowe** local authority; **~a wykonawcza** executive[1]; **dojść do ~y** rise to power; **u ~y** in government **2** (*oddziaływanie*) **(nad kimś/czymś)** authority, control[1], mastery (of/over sb/sth), hold[2] (on/over sb/sth), leadership, power[1]; **mieć ~ę** have/wield power **3** **stracić ~ę w ręce** lose the use of your hand
włamanie break-in; **kradzież z ~m** breaking and entering, burglary
włamywacz/ka burglar
włam(yw)ać się break in, break into sth, burgle, force entry
własnoręczn|y: **~e dzieło** handiwork
■ **własnoręcznie** (all) by yourself, etc., yourself
własnościowy proprietorial
własnoś|ć **1** (*dom itp.*) ownership, property; **~ć intelektualna** intellectual property; **~ć ziemi** landownership; **prawo ~ci** freehold; **mieć na ~ć** own[2]; **na ~ć** for keeps **2** (*cecha*) quality
własn|y own[1], personal; **we ~ej osobie** myself; **z ~ej woli** of your own free will, of your own accord, of their own volition; **~ego wyrobu** home-made; **pracujący na ~e konto** self-employed; **znam ten problem z ~ego doświadczenia** I've experienced the problem first-hand
właściciel owner, possessor, proprietor; (*małego hotelu, domu czynszowego, pubu*) landlord; (*paszportu itp.*) bearer, holder; (*rezydencji; psa itp.*) master[1]; **~/ka domu/mieszkania** homeowner; **~/ka ziemsk-i/a** landowner; **być ~em (czegoś)** own[2]
właścicielka zob. też WŁAŚCICIEL; (*małego hotelu, domu czynszowego, pubu*) landlady; (*rezydencji; psa itp.*) mistress
właściw|y **1** (*odpowiedni*) appropriate[1], correct[1], proper, right[1]; (*według prawa*) legitimate **2** **(komuś/czemuś)** inherent (in sb/sth), peculiar to sb/sth, unique to sb/sth IDM **we ~ym czasie** in due course
■ **właściwie** **1** (*w rzeczywistości*) actually, in (actual) fact **2** (*odpowiednio*) correctly, properly, suitably | **właściwość** **1** correctness, suitability **2** feature[1], peculiarity, property
właśnie exactly, just[1], just about, just so, precisely; (*nieform.*) bang[3]; ~ **tak; no,** ~ precisely, so[1], quite; **w tym ~ czasie** at that particular time; ~ **mieć zamiar coś zrobić** be about to do sth
właz hatch[2]; ~ **kanalizacyjny** manhole
włą-czać/czyć **1** (*światło itp.*) switch (sth) off/on, pop sth on, put sth on, turn sth on; (*alarm*) set sth off **2** (*jako część czegoś*) include; (*tekst itp.*) incorporate; ~ **do akt/kartoteki/archiwum** file[2] sth (away)
□ **włą-czać/czyć się** **1** (*do dyskusji itp.*) get in on sth, join in (sth/doing sth) **2** (*urządzenie*) go on; (*alarm*) go off; ~ **do ruchu** pull out **3** ~ **do sieci komputerowej** log in/on
włącznie: **od…do** inclusive; **z kimś/czymś** down[1] to sb/sth
włączony on
włochaty hairy, shaggy; (*dywan*) shag
włos (strand) of hair; (*bot.*) hair; (**włosy**) hair; **o** ~ narrowly
IDM **uniknięcie czegoś o** ~ a near miss | **uniknięcie nieszczęścia o mały** ~ a close shave/thing, a narrow/lucky escape | **być o** ~ **(od czegoś)** come close (to sth/to doing sth)
włosek **1** (*zwierzęcia*) bristle[1] **2** (*bot.*) hair
włosie bristle[1]
włoszczyzna greens[2]
włożyć → WKŁADAĆ
włóczęga bum, nomad, tramp[1], vagabond, vagrant
włócznia spear

włóczyć/po-: ~ **nogami** shuffle[1] ◻ **włóczyć się 1** (*wędrować*) roam, rove, wander **2** (*bez wyraźnego celu*) gad about/around, hang about/around, loiter
włókno 1 fibre; (*szklane itp.*) filament; ~ **lniane** flax; ~ **szklane** fibreglass **2** (*elektr.*) filament
wmanewrować → MANEWROWAĆ
w-mawiać/mówić 1 (*łagodną perswazją*) coax sb (into/out of sth/doing sth) **2 (coś) komuś** palm sb off (with sth)
wmieszać → MIESZAĆ(SIĘ); ~ **kogoś w coś wbrew jego woli** dupe ◻ **wmieszać się 1** (*w tłum itp.*) mingle **2** (*w zbrodnię itp.*) be/get mixed up in sth
wmonto(wy)wać build sth in/on, build sth into/onto sth
wmurować build sth in/on, build sth into/onto sth
wmuro(wy)wać embed
wnerwiony brassed off
wnęka bay, recess; (*zwykle z półką*) niche
wnętrz|e inside[2], interior; **we ~u** within adv.
wnętrzności guts[1]; (*jako jedzenie*) offal
wniebogłosy at the top of your voice
Wniebowstąpienie Ascension Day
wniebowzięty exalted
wni-kać/knąć: **w coś** enquire into sth, delve into sth
wnikliwy acute, astute, in depth, discerning, enquiring, penetrating; **po długim i ~m namyśle** after much soul-searching
wnios|ek 1 (*wynik*) conclusion, deduction, inference **2** (*propozycja*) motion[1], proposition; **wolne ~ki** AOB
wnioskować/wy- conclude, deduce, gather, infer, piece sth together, presume, understand
w-nosić/nieść 1 (*walizkę itp.*) bring; **wnieść coś do domu/środka** get sth in **2** ~ **wkład do czegoś** contribute (sth) (to/towards sth) **3** (*podanie itp.*) lodge[2]; ~ **apelację** appeal[2]; ~ **oskarżenie** bring/press charges (against sb); ~ **petycję** petition verb; ~ **prośbę** put sth in **4 (z czegoś, że)** infer sth (from sth)
wnuczka grandchild, granddaughter
wnuk grandchild, grandson
woalka veil
wobec with; ~ **tego, że** since conj.; ~ **tego** then
wo|da water[1] (*unosić się*) **na ~dzie** afloat; **pod ~dą** underwater adv.; **~da kolońska** eau de cologne; **~da mineralna** mineral water; **~da morska** salt water; **~da pitna** drinking water; **~da sodowa** soda; **~da z kranu** tap water; **~dy (terytorialne)** waters[1]; **~dy morskie** sea; **~dy słone** salt water
wodewil variety
Wodnik (*znak zodiaku*) Aquarius
wodnisty thin[1], watery, weak
wodno-lądowy amphibious
wodny aquatic; **transport** ~ shipping
wodolot hovercraft
wodoodporn|y: **kurtka ~a** waterproof jacket
wodorost algae; **(wodorosty)** seaweed
wodorowęglan: ~ **sodowy** sodium bicarbonate
wodospad cascade[1], fall[2], waterfall
wodoszczelny waterproof, watertight
wodotrysk fountain
wodować/z- (*statek*) launch[1]
wodór hydrogen
wodza rein
wodzić/powieść: ~ **wzrokiem** rove; **powiódł szybko wzrokiem po stronie** his eyes swept quickly over the page
wojenny martial; **okres** ~ wartime
wojewoda governor
województwo province
wojn|a war; **~a biologiczna** biological warfare; **~a domowa** civil war; **~a jądrowa** nuclear warfare; **~a krzyżowa** crusade; **~a partyzancka** guerrilla warfare; **~a światowa** world war; **czas ~y** wartime; (*państwo*) **w stanie ~y** at war; **został zabity na ~ie** he was killed in the war
wojowniczy belligerent, combative, militant, warlike
wojownik warrior
wojsk|o army, troop; **~a spadochronowe** paratroops
wojskowy military; (*osoba*) **były** ~ ex-serviceman
wojując|y: **osoba ~a** combatant
wok wok
wokalist-a/ka vocalist
wokalny vocal
wokoło (także **wokół**, **wkoło**) around[1,2], round[2,3]
wol|a volition, will[3]; **wolna ~a** self-determination; **z własnej ~i** willingly; **osoba o silnej/słabej ~i** a strong-willed/weak-willed person
woleć choose (to do sth), favour[2], prefer, have a preference for sth, would rather… (than)
wolej volley; **uderzać piłkę z ~a** volley verb
woln|o 1 (*powoli*) slow adv., slowly; **z ~a** languidly **2** (*można*) free adv.; (*pozwolenie*) **~o (ci/mi itp.)** at liberty (to do sth); **nie ~o** you mustn't do sth; **nie ~o fotografować** photography is not allowed, you may not take photographs; **~o mi wychodzić tylko w soboty** I'm only allowed out on Saturday nights **3** (*nieprecyzyjnie: tłumaczyć itp.*) loosely
wolnocłowy duty-free
wolnomularz Freemason
wolnoś|ć freedom, liberty; **~ć informacji** freedom of information; **~ć słowa** free speech; **~ć zgromadzeń** freedom of assembly; **~ć zrzeszania się** freedom of association; **na ~ci** free[1], in the wild; (*więzień*) at large, on the run
woln|y 1 (*swobodny: dzień*) off[1]; **dzień ~y** (*od pracy*) holiday; **w ~ej chwili** at your leisure; **w ~ych chwilach** at odd moments **2 od czegoś** clear[1] (of sth), free[1] (to do sth), from/of sth; (*od oskarżenia itp.*) immune (from sth); **~e miejsce** blank[2]; **~y od podatku** tax-free; (*świadek w sądzie*) **być ~ym** stand down **3** (*nieskrępowany: pies itp.*) loose[1] **4** (*pokój w hotelu*) free[1], vacant; (*bilet itp.*) spare[1]; **~y pokój**; **~a posada** vacancy; **(mieć coś) ~ego** (have sth) to spare **5** (*tempo*) slow[1] IDM **mieć ~ą rękę** get, have, etc. a free hand | **na ~ym powietrzu** in the open air | **~a inicjatywa** free enterprise | **~y przekład** a loose translation | **~y strzelec** freelance | **~a przestrzeń** open country
wolontariusz/ka volunteer[1]
wolt volt
woltaż voltage
wołać/za- call[1], hail[1] ■ **wołanie** call[2]; **~o pomoc** a cry for help
wołowina beef
wołowy bovine; (*mięso*) beef
woń odour, perfume, smell[2]; **mieć** ~ smell[1] (of sth)
wor|ek bag[1], pouch, sack[1]; **~ek do pojemnika na śmieci** bin liner, dustbin liner IDM **~ki pod oczami** bags[1]
workowaty baggy
workowiec marsupial
wosk wax; ~ **do polerowania** polish[1]; ~ **pszczeli** beeswax
woskować wax[2]
woskowina wax
wotum: ~ **nieufności** vote of censure in parliament, vote of no confidence
wozić/prze- drive[1]; (*wózek*) wheel[2]; ~ **zawodowo samochodem** chauffeur verb
wóda booze[1]
wódka vodka
wódz (*plemienia*) chief[2], chieftain
wół bullock, ox
wówczas then, at the time; **gdy tylko… wówczas…** no sooner…than…
wóz cart[1], wagon; ~ **strażacki** fire engine
wózek trolley; (*handlarza*) barrow; ~ **dziecinny** pram; **składany ~ dziecinny** pushchair; ~ **inwalidzki** wheelchair; ~ **widłowy** forklift truck
w-padać/paść 1 dokądś burst in on sb/sth, breeze[2] along, in, out, etc., pop[2] across, down, out, etc.; **do kogoś** drop by, drop in (on sb), call by, come round to see sb, go round (to…), pop in; ~ **tłumnie/gromadnie** swarm[2] **2 na kogoś/coś** bang[1], bash[1], bump into sb, collide, walk slap into sb; ~ **na kogoś/coś przypadkiem** run across sb/sth **3** (*do oczu itp.*) flop[1] around, back, down, etc. **4** (*na rozwiązanie itp.*) hit on/upon sth; ~ **do głowy** strike[1] IDM **~ jednym uchem, wypadać drugim** go in one ear and out the other | ~ **w furię/szał** do your nut, be in a rage, fly into a rage, rage[2] | **wpaść komuś w oko** take a fancy to sb | ~ **w poślizg** skid | ~ **w tarapaty** get into trouble
w-pajać/poić: **coż komuś** drum sth into sb, impress sth on/upon sb, inculcate sth (in/into sb), sb with sth, instil sth (in/into sb)
wpakow(yw)ać się IDM **wpakować się w kabałę** get into trouble
wpasow(yw)ać blend (into sth); (*w wolne miejsce itp.*) slot in
wpa-trywać/trzeć się: **(w kogoś/coś)** peer[2], stare, study[2]
wpatrzony: **w siebie** introverted
wpis entry
wpis(yw)ać inscribe, put sth in; (*do rejestru/komputera itp.*) enter sth (in/into/on/onto sth); (*do komputera*) key[2] sth (in); ~ **informacje do komputera** feed information into a computer; ~ **do rejestru** register[1]; ~ **kogoś/coś wstępnie** pencil sth/sb in

□ **wpis(yw)ać się** sign in; ~ **się do rejestru** register[1]
wpląt(yw)ać: **kogoś (w coś)** embroil sb (in sth), get sb into sth, implicate sb (in sth)
■ **wplątany**: **być wplątanym w coś** be concerned in sth
□ **wpląt(yw)ać się**: **(w coś)** embroil yourself (in sth), get yourself entangled (in sth), get into sth, get yourself into sth, be/get mixed up in sth
wpła-cać/cić credit[2], pay sth in, pay sth into sth; (*część należnej kwoty*) put sth down; (*na konto*) deposit[2]
wpłata credit[1]
wpływ 1 control[1], hold[2], impact, influence[1], pull[2]; **wywierać** ~ influence[2], infuse **2** (**wpływy**) income, revenue; **~y kasowe** takings
wpły-wać/nąć 1 (*oddziaływać*) affect, colour[2], govern, impinge on/upon sth, influence[2], make a difference; **doskonale ~ na kogoś/coś** do wonders (for sb/sth) **2** (*listy itp.*) pour in **3** (*statek*) ~ **do portu** dock[2] **4** (*pieniądze*) ~ **na konto** be credited to an account
wpływowy forceful, influential, powerful
wpoić → WPAJAĆ
wpompować → POMPOWAĆ
wpół (*do danej godziny*) half past...
w-praszać/prosić się intrude on/upon sb/sth
wpraw|a knack (of/for doing sth), mastery, practice, skill; **wyjść z ~y** be/get out of practice; **nie wychodzić z ~y** keep your hand in; **mający ~ę (w czymś/w robieniu czegoś)** used to sth/to doing sth
wprawi(a)ć (*kogoś w jakiś stan*) render, send sb (to/into sth); ~ **kogoś w zakłopotanie** disconcert, show sb up
wprawny familiar with sth, practised (in sth), skilful, skilled
wprosić się → WPRASZAĆ SIĘ
wprost direct adv., point-blank adv., square[1], straight[1]; (*komentarz, aluzja itp.*) **nie** ~ oblique IDM ~ **przeciwnie** far from it
wprowa-dzać/dzić 1 (*do pomieszczenia*) usher[2] **2** (*zapoznać itp.*) **w coś** introduce sb to sth, put sb in/into sth; (*w arkana czegoś*) initiate sb (into sth); ~ **na urząd** install sb (as sth); ~ **uroczyście na stanowisko** inaugurate; ~ **kogoś (w jakiś temat)** fill sb in (on sth); **dzień wprowadzający** an induction day for new students **3** (*ustawę itp.*) bring sth in, implement[1], institute[2], introduce, pioneer verb; ~ **coś w życie** bring sth into force, bring/put sth into effect; ~ **stopniowo** phase sth in; ~ **coś nowego** bring sth out; ~ **zmiany** vary; ~ **do rozkładu dodatkowe pociągi** put on extra trains **4** (*komput.*) (*dane do komputera*) feed[1] A (with B), B into/to/through A, keyboard[2], input[2] IDM ~ **w błąd** mislead
■ **wprowadzający** (*kurs itp.*) introductory | **wprowa-dzanie/dzenie 1** implementation, introduction; **wprowadzanie w życie** enforcement, institution; **wprowadzenie na urząd** installation **2** (*podstawa*) grounding **3** (*spotkanie orientacyjne dla nowych studentów itp.*) induction, initiation
□ **wprowa-dzać/dzić się**: **(do czegoś)** move in, move into sth
w-przęgać/prząc harness[2]
wpu-szczać/ścić admit, let
■ **wpuszczony** (*w podłogę itp.*) sunken
w-pychać/epchnąć bundle[2], cram, crowd sb/sth into sth, crowd sb/sth in, shove, stuff[2], thrust[1]; (*coś spiczastego*) jab[1] sth into sb/sth, plunge sth into sth/in; **demonstranci zostali wepchnięci do furgonetek policyjnych** the demonstrators were hustled into police vans
□ **w-pychać/epchnąć się** crowd into sth, crowd in, shove; ~ **bez kolejki** push in
w-rabiać/robić: **(kogoś w coś)** frame, set sb up[2]
wracać/wrócić 1 be back, come back, get back, go back, return[1]; **do kogoś** come back (to sb); ~ **do domu** come back home, get home; **wracaj do pracy!** get on with your work!; **wrócić do pracy** (*np. po urlopie macierzynskim*) resume your career; ~ **tą samą drogą** backtrack **2** ~ **do zdrowia** recover, recuperate; ~ **do formy** make a return to form **3** (*do tematu itp.*) get back to sth, go back (to sth), pick up on sth
wrak a shipwrecked vessel, wreck, wreckage; (*samochód nie nadający się do naprawy*) write-off
wraz: ~ **z kimś/czymś** along with sb/sth, together with sb/sth, with; ~ **z tym** herewith
wrażenie 1 (*doznanie*) air[1], effect[1], impact, impression, sensation; **mocne** ~ thrill; ~ **w dotyku** texture; **pod ~m (kogoś/czegoś)** impressed (by/with sb/sth); **sprawiać** ~ come across/over (as sth); **wywierający** ~ impressive **2** (*opinia*) **mieć/odnosić** ~ fancy[1] (that), get the feeling that, get the idea that..., have an idea that...
wrażliwoś|ć sensibility, sensitivity, tenderness; **~ć uczuć** sensibility; **~ć na muzykę** a feeling for music; **grała z wielką ~cią** she played with great delicacy
wrażliwy 1 sensitive, susceptible, tender[1]; (*np. na widok krwi*) squeamish **2** (*słuch itp.*) keen
wrąb nick[1]
wredny catty
wreszcie finally, at (long) last
wręcz: **walka** ~ unarmed combat IDM ~ **przeciwnie** far from it, quite the reverse
wrę-czać/czyć: **coś (komuś)** give sth in (to sb), hand[2] sb sth, sth to sb, hand sth in (to sb), hand sth over (to sb), present[3]
wrobić → WRABIAĆ
wrodzony innate, intrinsic, natural[1]; (*genetyczy*) congenital
wrogi antagonistic, hostile, malevolent
wrogość enmity, hostility, malevolence
wrona crow[1]
wrotka-rz/rka skater
wróbel sparrow
wrócić → WRACAĆ
wróg enemy, foe
wróżb|a IDM **być dobrą/złą ~ą** augur well/ill for sb/sth
wróżbit-a/ka fortune-teller
wróżka fairy, fortune-teller; **dobra** ~ fairy godmother
wróżyć/wy- foretell; ~ **dobrze/źle** bode well/ill (for sb/sth); **wyraz jej twarzy nie wróżył nic dobrego** her expression was rather ominous
wryć się imprint A in/on B, imprint B with A; (*w pamięć/serce/duszę*) imprint[2]
wrzask bellow noun, clamour, cry[2], scream[2], shout noun, shriek noun, yell noun
wrzaskliwy brassy, tumultuous, uproarious, raucous
wrzasnąć = WRZESZCZEĆ
wrzawa clamour, furore, hubbub, hue and cry, hullabaloo, racket, turmoil, uproar
wrzeć/za- 1 boil[1] **2** (*przen.*) **wrzeć jak w ulu** buzz (with sth); **w klasie wrzała praca** the classroom was humming with activity; **w Iraku wrze** Iraq is in ferment
■ **wrzący 1** scalding **2** (*sytuacja itp.*) turbulent
wrzeni|e: **doprowadzić do ~a** bring the soup to the boil; **temperatura ~a** boiling point
wrzesień September
wrzeszczeć/wrzasnąć bawl, bellow, bluster, rave[1], roar, scream[1], shout, shriek, yell
wrześniowy September
wrzos heather
wrzosowisko heath, moor[1]
wrzód abscess, ulcer
wrzu-cać/cić 1 bung[1] **2 coś na siebie** pop sth on **3** ~ **do jednego worka** lump[2] A and B together, A (in) with B
wsa-dzać/dzić 1 poke sth into, through sth; ~ **do kieszeni** pocket[2]; **wsadź to tam** shove it over there **2** ~ **kogoś do więzienia** jail[2], nick[2], put sb away, send sb to prison
wschodni east[2], easterly, eastern, eastward adj.
wschodzić/wzejść 1 (*słońce/księżyc*) come up, rise[2] **2** (*roślina*) come up, germinate
wsch|ód 1 (*geogr.*) east[1]; **na ~ód** eastwards; **na ~ód/~odzie** east adv.; **ze ~odu** east[2], easterly **2** (**Wschód**) (*Azja*) the East[1]; **Daleki Wschód** the Orient, the Far East **3** (*słońca*) sunrise
w-siadać/siąść (*do autobusu itp.*) board[2], get on/onto sth; (*do samochodu itp.*) get in, get into sth; ~ **na statek** embark
wsiąk-ać/nąć 1 (*płyn*) soak sth up **2 (w coś)** sink in, sink into sth
w-skakiwać/skoczyć: **(do/z czegoś)** hop in/into sth, hop on/onto sth, jump in/into sth
wskanować → SKANOWAĆ
wskazanie indication; (**wskazania**) (*przyrządu pomiarowego itp.*) reading
wskazan|y advisable; **~e byłoby** be (just) as well (to do sth)
wskazówka 1 (*wskaźnik*) pointer **2** (*zegara*) hand[1]; ~ **minutowa** minute hand **3** (*rada*) clue, guide[1], guideline, hint[1], tip[1]; (**wskazówki**) directions
wskaz(yw)ać 1 na kogoś/coś (*zwł. ręką*) gesture[2], indicate, point[2] (at/to

sb/sth) **2 coś komuś** indicate, point sth out (to sb); **wszystko wskazuje na to, że** there is every indication that **3** (*znak*) read[1] **4** (*wyznaczyć*) designate
wskaźnik gauge[1], index, indicator, pointer, rate[1], rating; ~ **urodzeń** birth rate
wskoczyć → SKAKAĆ, WSKAKIWAĆ
wskórać: **przeprosinami nic u mnie nie wskórał** his excuses cut no ice with me
wskroś: **na** ~ throughout
wskrze-szać/sić revive, resurrect
wskutek: **(czegoś)** consequently, owing to; ~ **tego** thereupon
wspaniałomyślny generous, magnanimous
wspaniałość glory[1], grandness, grandeur, magnificence, splendour
wspaniały admirable, delightful, fine[1], glorious, gorgeous, grand[1], great[1], heavenly, imposing, lovely, magnificent, splendid, sumptuous, super, superb, terrific
wsparcie backing, espousal, support[2]; ~ **duchowe** moral support; ~ **moralne** morale booster
wspiąć się → PIĄĆ SIĘ
w-spierać/esprzeć back[4], buttress[2], espouse, further[2], reinforce, prop sth up, be supportive
□ **wspierać/wesprzeć się** lean[1]
wspinaczka ascent, climb[2], climbing; ~ **górska** mountaineering; ~ **wysokogórska** rock climbing
ws-pinać/piąć się ascend, climb[1] (up) (sth), mount[1], scale[2]; (*sport*) climb[1]
wspomagający auxiliary
wspomaganie: ~ **kierownicy** power steering
wspo-minać/mnieć 1 cast your mind back, look back (on sth), reminisce **2 o kimś/czymś** mention, note[2]; **nie** ~ **czegoś** remain silent on sth
■ **wspomniany**: **wyżej wspomniany** above-mentioned, aforementioned
wspomnieni|e memory, recollection; **powracać ~ami do czegoś** look back (on sth)
wspólni-k/czka confederate, partner
wspólnota 1 (*organizacja*) community; **Wspólnota Brytyjska** the Commonwealth; **Wspólnota Niepodległych Państw** CIS **2** (*rodzinna itp.*) communion, togetherness
wspóln|y common[1] (to sb/sth), mutual; (*wysiłki itp.*) concerted, cooperative[1], joint[1]; (*pomieszczenie itp.*) communal; **~e zainteresowania/poglądy itp.** common ground; **~e przedsięwzięcie** joint venture IDM **mieć coś ~ego (z kimś/czymś)** have sth in common (with sb/sth), be/have to do with sb/sth | **nie mieć nic ~ego z kimś/czymś** be/have nothing to do with sb/sth
■ **wspólnie** collectively, in common with sb/sth, jointly, together[1]
współczesny (*przym.*) contemporary[1], modern, present-day
■ **współczesn-y/a** (*rz.*) contemporary[2]
współczuci|e compassion, pity[1], sympathy; **budzący ~e** pitiful; **wyrażać ~e** commiserate; **wyrazy ~a** commiseration, condolences
współczuć: **komuś** feel for sb, pity[2], be/feel sorry for sb, sympathize
■ **współczujący** compassionate, pitying, sympathetic
współczynnik ratio (of A to B); ~ **umieralności** mortality
współdziałać associate[1] yourself with sth, cooperate (with sb/sth), pull together; (*w zbrodni itp.*) connive (with sb) (to do sth)
■ **współdziałanie** coordination, interaction (between/with sb/sth)
współgrać blend (in) with sth
współistnieć coexist
współlokator/ka flatmate, housemate, room-mate
współmierny proportional (to sth)
współosiowy concentric
współpraca association, collaboration, cooperation, teamwork
współpracować collaborate, cooperate, team up (with sb), work in association with sb/sth
współpracowni-k/czka associate[2], collaborator; (*pisma itp.*) contributor
współrzędna coordinate[2]
współśrodkowy concentric
współuczestniczyć (*w przestępstwie*) aid and abet
współudział partnership, complicity
współwię-zień/źniarka cellmate
współwinny (*przym.*) complicit (in/with sb/sth)
■ **współwinn-y/a** (*rz.*) accessory (to sth), accomplice
współzależny interdependent; **być ~m** correlate
współzawodnictwo rivalry
współzawodniczyć compete, contend (for sth), emulate, race[2] (against/with) (sb/sth)
współzawodni-k/czka competitor
wsta(wa)ć 1 (*obudzić się*) get up; **późno wstać** sleep in; **czy już wstał (z łóżka)?** is he up yet? **2** (*do pozycji stojącej*) rise (to your feet), stand[1] (up) **3** (*słońce*) rise[2]
wstawi(a)ć put sth in; (*szybę itp.*) inset verb A (with B), B (into A); **coś (do czegoś)** inset verb sth (into sth), interpolate sth (into sth), poke sth into sth; (*dodatkowy tekst itp.*) insert; ~ **nowe okna** fit new windows
□ **wstawi(a)ć się** IDM ~ **się za kimś** put in a (good) word for sb
wstawka insertion, inset
wstąpić → WSTĘPOWAĆ
wstążeczka tape[1]
wstążka band, ribbon
wstecz backward, backwards; **działający** ~ retrospective IDM **patrząc** ~ in retrospect
wsteczny: **bieg** ~ reverse[2]
wstęga (*dymu*) wisp
wstęp 1 (*początek; w książce*) introduction, preliminary[2], prelude (to sth); (*nieform.*) intro; (*w książce*) preface; **bez zbędnych ~ów** without preamble **2** (*wejście*) admission, admittance, entrance, entry; **bilet ~u** admission; **nie mieć ~u do czegoś** be excluded from sth; ~ **wzbroniony** danger - keep out!, no admittance, no entry
wstępniak editorial
wstępn|y initial[1], introductory, opening adj., preliminary[1]; **słowo ~e** foreword; **warunek ~y** prerequisite
w-stępować/stąpić 1 (*zapisywać się*) enter, join[1]; ~ **do wojska** enlist, join the army, join up **2** (*odwiedzać*) stop by (sth) **3 wstąpić na tron** accede to the throne IDM ~ **na uczciwą drogę** go straight
wstręt abhorrence, disgust[1], horror, loathing, repulsion, revulsion; **żywić** ~ abhor, loathe; **budzić** ~ revolt
wstrętny beastly, disgusting, foul[1], hateful, horrid, loathsome, lousy, nasty, obnoxious, odious, repellent[1], repulsive, revolting, rotten, shocking, sickly, vile, yucky
wstrząs 1 (*psychiczny*) shock[1], upheaval; **wywoływać** ~ shock[2] **2** (*med.*) ~ **mózgu** concussion; **powodować** ~ **mózgu** concuss **3** (*fizyczny*) impact, jolt[2]; **lekki** ~ **ziemi** earth tremor
wstrzą-sać/snąć 1 (*fizycznie*) jar[2], jolt[1], rock[2]; (*butelkę itp.*) shake[1]; (*klucze itp.*) jiggle; (*osobą*) convulse **2** (*zszokować*) appal, rattle[1], shock[2], give sb a shock
□ **wstrzą-sać/snąć się** convulse
wstrząsający appalling, devastating, distressing, harrowing, shocking, startling
wstrząśnienie: ~ **mózgu** concussion; **powodować** ~ **mózgu** concuss
wstrząśnięty appalled, devastated, flabbergasted, staggered, startled adj.
wstrzemięźliwy moderate[1], sparing; (*zwł. w jedzeniu i piciu*) abstemious; (*zwł. niepijący alkoholu*) abstinent
wstrzy-kiwać/knąć (*i przen.*) inject
wstrzym(yw)ać hold off sth/doing sth, impede, inhibit, suspend, withhold; (*wypłatę itp.*) stop[1]; (*praca w fabryce itp.*) **zostać wstrzymanym** come to a halt
□ **wstrzym(yw)ać się** hold off; (*od głosu*) abstain
wstyd disgrace[1], mortification, shame[1]
wstydliw|y bashful, coy, diffident
■ **wstydliwie** coyly
wstydzić/za- się be ashamed
wsu-wać/nąć 1 poke sth into sth, pop[2] sth in, into, etc. sth; **komuś** slip[1] sth (to sb), (sb) sth; **ostrożnie wsunąć klucz do zamka** ease a key into a lock; **wsunęła dłoń do kieszeni** she slid her hand into her pocket **2** (*jedzenie*) scoff, tuck in, tuck into sth
wsuwka: ~ **do włosów** a hairpin
w-sysać/essać suck
■ **wysysanie** suction
wszczepi(a)ć: **coś komuś** inculcate sth (in/into sb), sb with sth
w-szczynać/szcząć: ~ **bunt** rebel[2] (against sb/sth); ~ **rewoltę** mutiny verb
wszech: ~ **czasów** all-time
wszechmocny almighty
wszechmogący almighty
wszechobecny omnipresent, pervasive, ubiquitous
wszechogarniający all-encompassing
wszechstronny all-round, comprehensive[1]; (*do różnorodnego użycia*) versatile; (*wykształcenie itp.*) rounded, well rounded; (*zainteresowania*) catholic
wszechświat the cosmos, the universe
wszelki every IDM **na ~ wypadek** on the safe side; (*nie spodziewając się, że się uda*) on the off chance
wszerz IDM **wzdłuż i ~** the length and breadth of sth
wszędobylsk-i/a (*rz.*) busybody

wszędzie everywhere, high and low, over, all over the place, throughout adv.; ~ **tam, gdzie** wherever

wszyst|ek (**wszystkie**) all[1] IDM **~kiego dobrego!** (*formuła kończąca list*) Best Wishes | **~kiego najlepszego!** all the best | **~kiego najlepszego z okazji urodzin!** Happy Birthday!, many happy returns (of the day) ■ **wszyscy** all[1], everybody; ~ **razem** the lot[3]; ~ **bez wyjątku** all and sundry

wszystk|o all[1], everything; **~o (to) co** whatever; **~o razem** the lot[3]; **~o układa się pomyślnie** things are going very well IDM **nade ~o** first and foremost | **przede ~im** basically, primarily | **~o jedno gdzie itp.** no matter who, what, where, etc. | **~o mi jedno** I'm easy, I'm not fussed | **być komuś ~o jedno** not be bothered (about sth)

wszystkożern|y omnivorous; **zwierzę ~e** omnivore

wścibiać: ~ **nos w nie swoje sprawy** meddle, pry

wścibski (*przym.*) inquisitive, interfering, nosy ■ **wścibsk-i/a** (*rz.*) busybody

wście-kać/c się go ballistic, go crazy, hit the roof, rage[2] (at/against/about sb/sth), see red, rave[1], be/get steamed up, go up the wall

wścieklizna rabies

wściekły 1 (*osoba*) berserk, crazy, furious, glaring, hacked off, incensed, irate, livid, mad, rabid, sick[1] (at/about sth), up the wall **2** (*pies*) rabid ■ **wściekłoś|ć** fury, rage[1]; **doprowadzać do wściekłości** enrage; **doprowadzający do wściekłości** infuriating

wśród amid, among; **jest ~ nich wróg** there's an enemy in their midst

wtajemni-czać/czyć: **kogoś** show sb the ropes ■ **wtajemniczenie** initiation | **wtajemniczon|y** in the know; **osoba ~a** insider

wtargnąć burst in on sb/sth, intrude on/upon sb/sth; (*na czyjąś ziemię*) encroach (on/upon sth); (*do kraju*) invade |

wtedy then, at the time IDM **gdy tylko... ~...** no sooner...than

w-tłaczać/tłoczyć pack sth in/into sth; **kogoś/coś (pomiędzy kogoś/coś)** sandwich sb/sth (between sb/sth) □ **w-tłaczać/tłoczyć się** cram in (sth), into/onto sth, pile into sth

wtorek Tuesday

wtó|r: **przy ~rze czegoś** to the accompaniment of sth

wtórny secondary

wtrą-cać/cić 1 (*słowo*) chip in (with sth), get sth in, interject, interpolate, intervene, put sth in **2** ~ **do więzienia** imprison, lock sb up ■ **wtrącony**: ~ **mimochodem** parenthetical □ **wtrą-cać/cić się 1** (*w czyjeś sprawy; do czegoś*) interfere, meddle, mess with sb/sth, pry; **nie** ~ mind your own business **2** (*do rozmowy*) chime in (with sth), chip in (with sth), cut in (on sb/sth); (*np. do rozmowy*) break in (on sth), butt in (on sb/sth)

wtryni(a)ć: **coś (komuś)** palm sth off (on sb)

wtrysk injection

wtulić się → TULIĆ SIĘ

wtulon|y: **wioska ~a w piękną dolinę rzeczną** a village nestling in a beautiful river valley

wtyczk|a 1 plug[1]; **nasadka na ~ę, umożliwiająca połączenie elektryczne różnych standardów** adaptor **2** (*szpieg*) mole

wtykać/wetknąć poke sth into sth, pop[2] sth in, into, etc. sth, stick[1] sth in/into (sth); (*chować*) tuck sth (away) IDM **~ nos w nieswoje sprawy** poke/stick your nose into sth

wuj (także **wujek**) uncle

wulgarn|y foul-mouthed, rude, vulgar ■ **wulgarnie** rudely; **wyraża się** ~ he's got a foul mouth | **wulgarność** crudity, vulgarity

wulkan volcano

wulkaniczny volcanic

wwier-cać/cić się wriggle

wy you, yourself

wyabstrahować → ABSTRAHOWAĆ

wyartykułować → ARTYKUŁOWAĆ

wyasfaltować → ASFALTOWAĆ

wyasygnować → ASYGNOWAĆ

wyasygnowanie appropriation

wy-baczać/baczyć excuse[2], forgive, pardon verb

wybaczalny excusable, forgivable, pardonable

wybadać sound sb out (about sth)

wybaw-ca/czyni rescuer

wybawi(a)ć rescue; ~ **kogoś z kłopotu** bail sb out

wybawiciel saviour

wybawienie lifeline, lifesaver

wybąkać → BĄKAĆ

wybełkotać → BEŁKOTAĆ

wybić → BIĆ, WYBIJAĆ

wybieg 1 (*podstęp*) device **2** (*dla koni*) paddock; (*dla świń/owiec*) pen **3** (*dla modelek*) catwalk

wy-biegać/biec (*biec*) rush out (of sth)

wybielacz bleach[2]

wy-bielać/bielić 1 bleach[1] **2** (*przen.: osobę itp.*) whitewash[2]

wyb(ie)rać 1 choose, go for sb/sth, opt to do sth/for sth, pick[1], plump for sb/sth, select[1], take; (*na prezydenta itp.*) elect, make[1]; **kogoś/coś (za coś)** single sb/sth out (for sth); **coś z czegoś/skądś** cull sth from sth; ~ **czas** time[2] **2** (*wydłubywać*) scoop[2] sth (out/up)

wybieralny (*w wyborach*) eligible

wybi(ja)ć 1 (*piłkę*) bat[2]; ~ **piłkę do góry** chip[2] **2** ~ **godziny** chime, strike[1] **3** (*takt*) beat time (to sth) **4** (*zabijać*) kill sb/sth off

wybiórczy selective

wybitny distinguished, eminent, leading, outstanding, pre-eminent, prominent; (*cecha*) salient; ~ **skrzypek** a violinist of distinction ■ **wybitność** distinction

wybit|y: **na monetach jest ~a głowa Królowej** the coins bear the Queen's head on them

wyblakły dim[1]

wyblaknąć → BLAKNĄĆ

wyboisty (*droga*) bumpy

wybor-ca/czyni constituent, elector, voter

wyborczy electoral

wyborowy choice[2], prime[1]

wybory ballot box, election, polling; ~ **dodatkowe** by-election; ~ **powszechne** general election; ~ **głównego kandydat-a/ki partii politycznej** (*np. na prezydenta*) primary[2]

wybój bump[2], pothole

wyb|ór 1 choice[1], option, pick[2]; **~ór na stanowisko** appointment (to sth); **z (własnego) ~oru** out of/from choice; **nie mamy innego ~oru, jak tylko odwołać naszą wycieczkę** we have no choice but to cancel our trip **2** (*zbiór różnych rzeczy*) assortment, collection, selection

wybrać → WYBIERAĆ

wybrakowany defective; ~ **towar** faulty goods, reject[2]

wybrany select[2]; **być ~m** get in, get into sth

wybredn|y choosy, fastidious, finicky, fussy, particular, picky; (*zwł. w jedzeniu*) faddy; (*mający dobry gust*) discerning; **jest ~a w jedzeniu** she's a fussy eater

wybredzać pick and choose

wybrnąć: **starać się ~ z trudnej sytuacji** make the best of sth/a bad job

wybrukować → BRUKOWAĆ

wybryk (*natury*) freak[1]

wybrzeże coast[1], seashore, seaside, shore[1]

wy-brzuszać/brzuszyć się bulge[1] ■ **wybrzuszony** bulging

wybuch 1 (*bomby*) blast[1], explosion **2** (*wulkanu*) eruption **3** (*epidemii; wojny*) outbreak **4** (*entuzjazmu itp.*) burst[2]; (*gniewu; śmiechu*) outburst; **~y złości** temper

wybu-chać/chnąć 1 (*bomba*) blow up, detonate, explode, go off; ~ **płomieniem** flare up **2** (*wulkan*) erupt **3** (*wojna itp.*) break out **4** (*gniewem itp.*) blow up; (*śmiechem itp.*) burst out; (*płaczem itp.*) burst into sth; ~ **gniewem** blow up (at sb), flare up

wybuchowy 1 (*substancja*) explosive[1]; **materiał ~** explosive[2] **2** (*osoba*) bad-tempered, quick-tempered, spiky, vehement, temperamental; ~ **charakter** a violent temper

wybujać run riot

wybulić → BULIĆ

wybu-rzać/rzyć demolish, knock sth down/over

wycedzić → CEDZIĆ

wycelować zob. też CELOWAĆ; train[2] sth (at/on sb/sth)

wycena valuation

wyceni(a)ć cost[2], price[2], value[2]

wycharczeć → CHARCZEĆ

wychlać → CHLAĆ

wychłeptać → CHŁEPTAĆ

wychłostać → CHŁOSTAĆ

wychodnia (*geol.*) outcrop

wychodzić/wyjść 1 skądś (*i z programu komputerowego*) exit[2], get out (of sth); (*z domu/pracy itp.*) leave[1]; (*na zewnątrz itp.*) step[2]; (*głos z innego pokoju itp.*) issue from sth; ~ **z pracy** get off (sth); ~ **z domu** leave home; ~ **ostentacyjnie** walk out (of sth); ~ **pośpiesznie** make off; **moja babcia nie wychodzi często z domu** my grandmother doesn't get out of the house much **2** (*na scenę*) come on

3 (*okno, pokój itp.*) face[2], look[1], open into/onto sth, overlook **4** (*zabawiać się*) go out; **(z kimś)** go off (with sb); ~ **na spotkanie** meet **5** (*z wypadku itp.*) ~ **cało z czegoś** come through (sth) (*z opresji itp.*) emerge (from sth); ~ **cało z opresji** fall/land on your feet **6** (*pomysł*) work[1] **na czymś** (*dobrze lub źle*) come off; **dobrze komuś wyjść** work out; **nic z tego nie wyszło** nothing has come of it; **nie wyjść** fall through **7** (*zdjęcie; drukiem; zza chmur*) come out; **czy to wyszło już na DVD?** is it out on DVD yet? IDM ~ **na jaw** come to light, come out, be out adj., unfold | ~ **za mąż** marry | ~ **z mody** be out, be on the way out, go out | ~ **na światło dzienne** come to light | ~ **z użycia** fall into disuse, go out | **wyjść na zero/czysto** break even

wychodźstwo exile

wychowan-ek/ka 1 (*student*) pupil **2** (*sądownie*) ward[1]

wychowanie 1 nurture noun, upbringing; **dobre** ~ breeding, politeness, urbanity; **złe** ~ bad manners **2** ~ **fizyczne** PE

wychowany: **dobrze** ~ polite, well brought up, well behaved, well mannered; **źle** ~ ill-mannered

wychowaw-ca/czyni tutor

wychowawczy educational

wychow(yw)ać bring sb up, nurture, raise[1], rear[2]; ~ **przybrane dziecko** foster

wychrypieć → CHRYPIEĆ

wychudły scrawny

wychudzony emaciated, gaunt, scrawny, skinny, wasted, weedy

wychwalać praise sb/sth (for sth)

wychwy-tywać/cić pick up on sth

wychy-lać/lić się lean[1], lean over; ~ **się z okna** hang out of

wyciąć → WYCINAĆ

wyciąg 1 (*wywar*) essence, infusion **2** ~ **krzesełkowy** chairlift; ~ **narciarski** ski lift **3** ~ **z konta** bank statement

wycią-gać/gnąć 1 (*wydostać*) draw[1] sth (from sth/out of sth), fish sth out (of sth), pull sth out; **błyskawicznie coś wyciągnąć** whip sth out **2** (*prostować ręce/nogi; rozciągnąć*) stretch[1] sth (out) **3** (*rękę*) extend, reach[1] (out) (for sb/sth); ~ **szyję** crane[2] **4** (*za pomocą wyciągarki*) winch verb **5 coś od kogoś** drag sth out (of sb), get sth out of sb/sth; (*wyłudzać pieniądze itp.*) scrounge (sth) (from/off sb); (*fakty itp.*) nail sb down (to sth); ~ **coś przykrego z przeszłości** dredge sth up **6** ~ **wnioski** draw some conclusions, reach conclusions, reason[2] IDM **wyciągnąć asa z rękawa** play your trump card | ~ **coś na światło dzienne** bring sth to light | ~ **z czegoś jak najwięcej** make the most of sth

□ **wycią-gać/gnąć się** stretch[1] (out)

wyciągarka winch

wyciągnięty outstretched

wycie blare noun, howl noun, wail noun; (*syreny statku*) hoot[2]; (*z bólu itp.*) yell noun

wycieczk|a excursion, outing, trip[1], tour; **mała** ~**a** run[2]; **piesza** ~**a** walk[2]; ~**a krajoznawcza** ramble[2]; ~**a morska** cruise[1]; ~**a naukowa/badawcza w terenie** field trip; ~**a objazdowa** tour; ~**a turystyczno-krajoznawcza** tour; **iść na** ~**ę** hike verb; **jechać na** ~**ę objazdową** tour verb IDM (*przen.*) **robić osobiste** ~**i** get personal

wycieczkowicz/ka tripper

wyciek escape[2] (from sth), leak[2], leakage, spill; (*i z rany*) discharge[2]

wy-ciekać/ciec leak[1], ooze from/out of sth

wycień-czać/czyć debilitate, wear sb out

■ **wycieńczony** frazzled, gaunt

wycieraczka: ~ **przed drzwiami** doormat; ~ **szyby samochodowej** windscreen wiper

wy-cierać/trzeć 1 (*buty*) wipe[1]; ~ **coś na mokro** mop[2], mop sth up, wipe sth down; ~ **gąbką** sponge[2]; ~ **z kurzu** dust[2] **2** (*ręce itp.*) dry[2]; (*naczynia*) dry sth up; **wytrzeć włosy do sucha** rub your hair dry IDM ~ **nos** blow your nose, give your nose a blow

□ **wy-cierać/trzeć się** fray

wycięcie: ~ **nasieniowodu** vasectomy

wycięty: **głęboko** ~ revealing

wy-cinać/ciąć 1 coś (z czegoś) cut sth out; (*i komput.*) cut[1] **2** (*rzeźbić*) carve (sth) (out of sth) **3** (*wyrostek robaczkowy itp.*) take sth out

■ **wycinanie**: ~ **lasów** deforestation

wycinek segment; (*prasowy*) cutting[1]

wyciosać → CIOSAĆ

wycisk (*przen.*) going-over

wyciskacz: ~ **łez** tear jerker; ~ **do cytryn** lemon squeezer

wycis-kać/nąć press[2], squeeze[1]

wyciszony soundproof

wycof(yw)ać zob. też COFAĆ (SIĘ); **kogoś/coś (skądś)** pull sb/sth out (of sth), withdraw sb/sth (from sth); (*ze sprzedaży itp.*) recall, withdraw; (*pieniądze*) withdraw; (*skargę itp.*) retract

□ **wycof(yw)ać się** back out (of sth), back-pedal, backtrack (on sth), pull out (of sth), retreat[1], retire (from sth), withdraw; (*w kłótni itp.*) back down

wycyganić → CYGANIĆ

wyczarow(yw)ać conjure sth up, conjure sth (up) from/out of sth

wyczekujący expectant

wyczerpanie depletion, exhaustion

wyczerpan|y 1 (*osoba*) drawn[2], exhausted, run-down, wan, worn out **2** (*zapasy*) exhausted **3** (*bateria*) dead, flat[1]; **naładować** ~**ą baterię** recharge a flat battery **4** (*nakład książki*) out of print, out of stock

wyczerpujący 1 (*męczący*) exhausting, gruelling, punishing, taxing **2** (*informacje*) comprehensive[1], exhaustive, profound

wyczerp(yw)ać 1 (*osobę*) exhaust[2], tire sb out, take a lot out of sb, wear sb out **2** (*zapasy*) deplete, exhaust[2], stretch[1], use sth up **3** (*akumulator*) run sth down

□ **wyczerp(yw)ać się 1** (*osoba*) wear yourself out **2** (*zapasy itp.*) dry up, peter out **3** (*akumulator*) run down

wyczołgać się → CZOŁGAĆ SIĘ

wyczuci|e 1 feel[2], sense[1], sensitivity; **z** ~**em** sensitively, tactfully **2** (*gust*) taste[1]; **bez** ~**a** tasteless

wyczuć → CZUĆ

wyczulony acute; **(na coś)** alert[1] (to sth); **być zorientowanym i** ~**m na nowości** be on the ball

wyczu(wa)ć 1 (*rozumieć*) sense[2] **2** (*węchem*) scent verb

wyczyn coup, exploit[2], feat; ~ **kaskaderski** stunt[1]

wyczynowo competitively

wyczyścić zob. też CZYŚCIĆ; clean sth up; (*wnętrze czegoś*) clean sth out

wyczytać → CZYTAĆ

wyć/za- (*syrena*) blare sth (out), wail; (*z bólu itp.*) yell (out) (sth); (*z rozpaczy itp.*) howl, wail

wyćwiczony (*ciało*) honed to perfection

wyćwiczyć → ĆWICZYĆ

wydać (się) → WYDAWAĆ SIĘ

wydajny cost-effective, efficient, productive

wyda-lać/lić expel; (*z kraju*) deport

■ **wydalanie**: ~ **dwutlenku węgla do atmosfery** the release of carbon dioxide into the atmosphere

wydanie 1 (*książki, gazety*) edition; (*czasopisma*) issue[1] **2** (*przestępcy itp.*) extradition

wydany out adj.

wydart|y: ~**a dziura** tear noun

wyda-rzać/rzyć się intervene, occur

wydarzeni|e affair, event, happening, incident, occasion, occurrence; **nowe** ~**e** development; **moralnie podejrzane** ~**a** goings-on; ~**a bieżące** current affairs; ~**e przełomowe** landmark; **bogaty w** ~**a** eventful IDM **wielkie/małe** ~**e** a big deal/no big deal

wydatek expense, outlay (on sth); (**wydatki**) expenditure, expenses, spending; **wydatki na podróż** travelling expenses

wydatkować expend sth (on sth)

wydatny salient

wyda(wa)ć 1 (*pieniądze*) expend sth (on sth), spend (sth) (on sth); (*dużo pieniędzy*) get through sth **2** (*przyjęcie; polecenie; resztę; opinię; okrzyk*) give[1]; (*przyjęcie itp.*) hold[1]; (*napoje itp.*) dispense, hand sth out (to sb); (*okrzyk itp.*) let sth out; ~ **głos** utter[2]; **wydać oświadczenie** make a statement; **wydać rozkaz** give an order; ~ **ustawy** legislate (for/against sth) **3** (*potwierdzenie, dekret itp.*) issue[2] **4** (*gaz itp.*) emit, let sth out **5** (*wyrok*) pass[1] sth (on sb); **wydać werdykt „niewinny"** return a verdict of 'not guilty' **6** (*tajemnicę; współtowarzyszy*) give sth/sb away **7** (*drukiem*) bring sth out, publish; ~ **szybko** (*np. książkę, płytę*) rush sth out **8** (*przestępcę innemu państwu*) extradite **9** (*plony itp.*) produce[1] **10** ~ **na świat** bear[1]; (*zwierzęta*) produce[1]

□ **wyda(wa)ć się 1 komuś** believe, feel[1], get the idea that…, have an idea that…, imagine, seem, think **2** (*informacja*) leak out; (*tajemnica*) get out IDM **jest więcej, niż się wydaje** there is more to sb/sth than meets the eye

wydawca editor, publisher

wydawnictw|o 1 press[1], publisher, publishing house **2** (**wydawnictwa**) (*literatura*) literature (on sth)

wydąć (się) → WYDYMAĆ (SIĘ)

wydech breath, exhalation; **na** ~**u podnosimy ciężar, a na wdechu**

obniżamy go breathe out as you lift the weight and breathe in as you lower it
wydedukować → DEDUKOWAĆ
wydekoltowany revealing
wydelegować → DELEGOWAĆ
wydepilować → DEPILOWAĆ
wydept(yw)ać (*ścieżkę*) wear[1]
wydębić: **próbować coś** ~ fish for sth
wydęcie: ~ **ust** pout noun
wydłub(yw)ać gouge sth out, scoop[2] sth (out/up)
wydłu-żać/żyć 1 (*czynić dłuższym*) elongate, lengthen **2** (*pobyt*) lengthen, prolong
□ **wydłu-żać/żyć się 1** (*robić się dłuższym*) lengthen, elongate **2** (*pobyt*) draw out, lengthen
wydma dune
wydmuch(iw)ać blow[1]
wydobycie mining, production
wydoby(wa)ć 1 coś (skądś) fish sth out (of sth), get sth out (of sth); (*spod ziemi*) excavate, extract[2]; (*węgiel itp.*) mine[3]; ~ **z kopalni odkrywkowej** quarry[2]; ~ **na światło dzienne** unearth **2 coś z kogoś** elicit sth (from sb), get sth out of sb
□ **wydobywać się** issue from sth
wydoić → DOIĆ
wydorośleć → DOROŚLEĆ
wydosta(wa)ć disentangle, get sth out (of sth)
wydra otter
wydrapać → DRAPAĆ
wydrą-żać/żyć zob. też DRĄŻYĆ; hollow sth out
■ **wydrążenie** cavity | **wydrążony** hollow[1]
wydruk: ~ **komputerowy** hard copy, printout
wydrukować → DRUKOWAĆ
wydrzeć (się) zob. też WYDZIERAĆ (SIĘ); ~ **kartkę** tear a page out of sth
wydukać → DUKAĆ
wydumany airy-fairy
wydusić: **(z siebie)** cough (sth) up
wydychać exhale
wy-dymać/dąć: ~ **usta** pout
□ **wy-dymać/dąć się** billow
wydział department, faculty, school; ~ **humanistyczny** the arts faculty
wydziałowy departmental
wydziedzi-czać/czyć disinherit
wydzie-lać/lić discharge[1], give off sth, give out sth, secrete, send sth out; (*zapach itp.*) exude
■ **wydzielanie** emission, secretion
□ **wy-dzielać/dzielić się** (*zapach itp.*) exude
wydzielina discharge[2], secretion; ~ **z nosa** (*spowodowana katarem*) catarrh
wy-dzierać/drzeć 1 (*dziurę*) tear[2]; (*dziurę w skarpetce itp.*) wear[1] **2 (coś komuś)** extort sth (from sb) **3 sobie coś** scramble (for sth/to do sth)
□ **wy-dzierać/drzeć się** bellow, blare (out), laugh, scream, etc. your head off
wydzierżawić → DZIERŻAWIĆ
wydzierżawiony rented
wyedukować → EDUKOWAĆ
wyegzekwować → EGZEKWOWAĆ
wyeksmitować → EKSMITOWAĆ
wyekspediować → EKSPEDIOWAĆ
wyeksportować → EKSPORTOWAĆ
wyelegantować (się) spruce (sb/yourself) up
wyeliminować → ELIMINOWAĆ
wyemancypować → EMANCYPOWAĆ
wyemigrować → EMIGROWAĆ
wyemitować → EMITOWAĆ
wyewoluować → EWOLUOWAĆ
wyfroterowany polished
wyga IDM **stary** ~ an old hand (at sth)
wygadać się 1 (*zdradzić się*) blab, blurt sth out, let sth slip, spill the beans **2** (*zwierzyć się*) get sth off your chest, pour sth out
wygadany glib
wy-ganiać/gonić banish
wygarnąć IDM ~ **komuś prawdę w oczy** give sb a piece of your mind
wygas-ać/nąć 1 (*świeca itp.*) go out **2** (*bilet itp.*) expire, lapse[2]
wygasły (*wulkan*) extinct
wygaszacz: ~ **ekranu** screen saver
wygenerować → GENEROWAĆ
wygestykulować → GESTYKULOWAĆ
wygięcie dent[2]
wygięty curved
wy-ginać/giąć crumple sth (up), dent[1], mangle, warp; (*w łuk*) arch[2], curve[2]
□ **wy-ginać/giąć się** crumple (up), give[1]; (*w łuk*) curve[2]
wyginięcie extinction
wygląd appearance, look[2], presentation; ~ **zewnętrzny** exterior[1], surface[1], semblance; **atrakcyjny** ~ good looks
wyglądać 1 (*zdawać się*) look[1] (like sb/sth) (to sb), (to sb) as if.../as though..., seem; **wygląda na to, że** the chances are (that)..., evidently, by the sound of it/things; **nie wygląda na to, że jest on bardzo godny zaufania** it doesn't sound as if/though he's very reliable **2** (*mieć wygląd*) ~ **dobrze** look good; ~ **normalnie** look yourself; ~ **nieswojo** (not) look yourself **3 (skądś/zza czegoś)** peep[1]; ~ **przez okno** look out of the window
wygła-dzać/dzić smooth[2] sth (away/back/down/out, etc.)
wy-głaszać/głosić (*prelekcję itp.*) deliver; **wygłosić komentarz** make a comment; **wygłosić mowę** make a speech
wygłodniały famished, ravenous
wygłodzenie starvation
wygłupi(a)ć się fool about/around, goof, goof around, mess about/around, muck about/around
wygnanie exile
wygoda comfort[1], convenience, expediency; **pokoje bez wygód** very basic rooms
wygodny comfortable, convenient, snug; ~ **w użyciu** handy
■ **wygodnie** comfortably, conveniently, snugly; **mieszkać wygodnie** live in comfort; **podróżować wygodnie** travel in comfort
wygoić się → GOIĆ SIĘ
wygon pasture
wygonić → WYGANIAĆ
wygórowany excessive, inordinate, unreasonable; (*koszt itp.*) exorbitant, extortionate, prohibitive, steep
wygrać → WYGRYWAĆ
wygramolić się → GRAMOLIĆ SIĘ
wygran|a 1 (*zwycięstwo*) victory, win noun; **łatwa ~a** walkover; **całkowita ~a** a clean sweep; **dawać za ~ą** give up **2** (*nagroda*) prize[1], winnings; **największa ~a w grze** the jackpot
wygrany victorious
wygrawerować → GRAWEROWAĆ
wygrażać bluster
wygr(yw)ać get the better of sb/sth, win
wygrzeb(yw)ać zob. też GRZEBAĆ; dig sth up, dig sb/sth out (of sth), unearth; (*wydłubywać*) scoop[2] sth (out/up)
wygrzmocić → GRZMOTNĄĆ
wyguzdrać się → GUZDRAĆ SIĘ
wygwizd(yw)ać hiss
wyhaftować → HAFTOWAĆ
wyheblować → HEBLOWAĆ
wyhodować → HODOWAĆ
wyholować → HOLOWAĆ
wyidealizować → IDEALIZOWAĆ
wyidealizowany glorified
wyimaginowany imaginary, unreal
wyizolować → IZOLOWAĆ
wyjadacz: **być starym ~em** be an old hand (at sth)
wyja-ławiać/łowić sterilize
wyjaśni(a)ć account for sth, clarify, clear sth up, elucidate, explain, explain yourself, get sth straight, illuminate, spell sth out, straighten sth out, unravel; ~ **nieporozumienie** put/set the record straight
□ **wyjaśni(a)ć się** fall/slot into place, unravel
wyjaśnienie clarification, elucidation, explanation
wyjawi(a)ć bring sth out into the open, divulge, expose, reveal; **nie ~ czegoś (komuś)** keep sth back (from sb), keep sth from sb
□ **wyjawi(a)ć się** come out into the open
wyjazd the way out of somewhere; **grać na wyjeździe** play away (from home)
wyjazdow|y (*mecz*) away adj.; **wiza ~a** exit visa
wyjąć → WYJMOWAĆ
wyjąk(iw)ać stammer
wyjąt|ek 1 (*odstępstwo*) exception; **z ~kiem czegoś** bar[3], barring, excluding, with the exception of, short of sth/doing sth; **bez ~ku** without exception; **robić ~ek** stretch a point; **zrobić (dla kogoś) ~ek** make an exception (of sb) **2** (*z dzieła*) excerpt
wyjątkow|y especial, exceptional, special[1], unusual; **być ~ym** take a lot of/some beating
wy-jeżdżać/jechać be off, go away, leave[1], quit; **wyjechać na urlop** get away
wyj-mować/ąć get sth out (of sth), pick[1], take sth out (of sth)
wyjrzeć → WYGLĄDNĄĆ
wyjści|e 1 (*drzwi itp.*) exit[1], the way out (of somewhere); (*do samolotu*) gate; **~e awaryjne** an emergency exit; **~e ewakuacyjne** fire escape **2** (*z sytuacji*) course; **sytuacja bez ~a** corner[1]; **nie mieć innego ~a** have no option; **bez ~a** no-win **3** (*w dyskusji*) **punkt ~a** starting point (for sth) **4** (*z partii itp.*) breakaway noun
wyjść zob. też WYCHODZIĆ IDM **~ na dobre** be (all) for the best
wykałaczka toothpick
wy-kańczać/kończyć 1 (*skończyć*) put the finishing touches to sth; (*zaprzestać*) put paid to sth

2 (*zamęczyć*) debilitate, finish sb/sth off, wear sb out
□ **wy-kańczać/kończyć się** wear yourself out
wykastrować → KASTROWAĆ
wykaz index, list, register[2]
wykaz(yw)ać show[1], demonstrate
wykąpać (się) → KĄPAĆ (SIĘ)
wykiełkować → KIEŁKOWAĆ
wykipieć zob. też KIPIEĆ; boil over
wykitować drop dead
wyklep(yw)ać zob. też KLEPAĆ **1** (*metal*) hammer sth out **2** (**wyklepać**) (*listę imion itp.*) rattle sth off, reel sth off
wyklu-czać/czyć 1 (*eliminować*) eliminate, except[2], exclude sb/sth (from sth) **2** (*możliwość itp.*) draw the line at sth/doing sth, preclude, rule sb/sth out
■ **wykluczon|y** out of the question IDM **~e!** certainly not, no chance, no way
wyklu(wa)ć się hatch[1] (out)
wykład lecture, talk[2]
wykładać 1 (/wyłożyć) coś czymś line[2]; (*podłogę kafelkami itp.*) surface[2]; (*ścieżkę itp.*) pave sth (with sth); **~ kafelkami** tile verb; **wyłożony dywanami** carpeted; **ściany były wyłożone książkami** the walls were lined with books **2** (*prowadzić wykłady*) lecture verb
wykładnik: **~ potęgi** (*mat.*) exponent
wykładow-ca/czyni lecturer, professor
wykładzina: **~ dywanowa** (*położona w pomieszczeniu*) a fitted carpet
wykłó-cać/cić się fight[1] (with sb) (about/over sth)
wykole-jać/ić derail
wykombinować → KOMBINOWAĆ
wykonać → WYKONYWAĆ
wykonalny feasible, manageable, practicable, practical[1], workable
wykonani|e execution; (*piosenki itp.*) rendition; **możliwość ~a** practicality
wykonaw-ca/czyni contractor; (*muzyk itp.*) performer
wykonawcz|y executive[2]; **władza ~a** executive[1]
wykon(yw)ać carry sth out, do[1], execute, get through sth, perform, undertake; (*piosenkę itp.*) perform; (*wyrok sądu itp.*) enforce; (*receptę*) dispense; **wykonać na kimś wyrok** execute sb (for sth)
wykończenie finish[2]
wykończony (*osoba*) fagged, knackered, pooped, shattered
wykończyć → WYKAŃCZAĆ
wykop ball
wykopalisk|o (także **wykopaliska**) dig[2]; **prowadzić ~a** excavate
wykopaliskow|y: **prace ~e** excavation
wykop(yw)ać zob. też KOPAĆ **1 kogoś/coś (z czegoś)** dig sb/sth out (of sth), dig sth up, unearth **2** (*wyrzucać*) boot sb/sth out (of sth), kick sb out (of sth), turf sb out (of sth)
wykorzeni(a)ć eradicate, root sth out, stamp sth out, uproot; **nie dawać się łatwo wykorzenić** die hard
wykorzyst(yw)ać use[1], make use of sth/sb, utilize; (*źródła energii itp.*) exploit[1], harness[2]; (*zasoby*) tap[1] (into sth); (*pieniądze z firmy itp.*) milk[2]; (*do własnych celów*) capitalize on sth; **wykorzystać szansę/okazję** seize a chance/an opportunity; **~, jak się tylko da** make the most of sth
■ **wykorzystywanie** exploitation; **~ seksualnie** sexual abuse
wykosić: **kogoś** mow sb down
wykosztować się splash out (on sth)
wykpi(wa)ć satirize
wy-kraczać/kroczyć: **szczegółowe omówienie tych spraw wykracza poza zakres tej książki** it's not within the scope of this book to discuss these matters in detail
wykraść → KRAŚĆ
wy-krawać/kroić: **coś (z czegoś)** cut sth out
wykres chart[1], diagram, figure[1], graph; **~ kolumnowy** bar chart
wykreś-lać/lić cross sth off (sth)
wykrę-cać/cić 1 (*rękę*) twist[1]; (*ucho, nos*) tweak **2** (*bieliznę*) wring sth (out) **3** (*numer telefoniczny*) dial[2] **4** (*znaczenie*) twist[1]
□ **wykrę-cać/cić się 1** (*ręka itp.*) twist[1] **2 od/z czegoś** back out (of sth), cop out (of sth), dodge[1], duck[2] (out of) sth, flinch from sth/doing sth, get out of sth/doing sth, wriggle out of sth/doing sth; (*od odpowiedzialności*) shirk
wykręt (*wybieg*) device; (*unik*) dodge[2], evasion
wykrochmalony starched
wykroczenie offence; **drobne ~** misdemeanour; **popełnić ~ drogowe** commit a motoring offence
wykroczyć → WYKRACZAĆ
wykroić → WYKRAWAĆ
wykropkować → KROPKOWAĆ
wykrój pattern
wykrywacz detector; **~ kłamstw** lie detector
wykry(wa)ć detect
■ **wykryty**: **nie zostać ~m** escape detection
wykrzesać → KRZESAĆ
wykrzes(yw)ać muster
wykrztusić zob. też KRZTUSIĆ; splutter
wykrzyczeć się let off steam
wykrzyki-wać/knąć bark[2] (sth) (out) (at sb), bawl, burst out, ejaculate, exclaim, rant and rave, shout sth (at/to sb)
wykrzyknik exclamation mark, interjection
wykrzywi(a)ć buckle[1], contort, curve[2], distort, twist[1], warp; **~ usta** curl your lips; **~ twarz** screw your eyes, face, etc. up; (*z bólu itp.*) grimace verb
■ **wykrzywiony** (*wiekiem, ciężką pracą itp.*) gnarled
□ **wykrzywi(a)ć się 1** buckle[1], contort, curve[2], twist[1] **2** (*twarz*) make/pull faces/a face (at sb/sth)
wyksięgować write sth off
wykształceni|e education, schooling; **bez ~a** uneducated; **jest z ~a lekarzem** he's a doctor by profession
wykształcić (się) → KSZTAŁCIĆ (SIĘ)
wykształcony educated, literate
wykuć → KUĆ
wykup (*akcji przedsiębiorstwa*) buyout; **masowy ~** (*towarów*) rush[2] (on sth)
wykup-ywać/ić redeem
■ **wykupiony** gone[2]
wykwalifikowany certified, qualified, skilled
wykwintny 1 (*maniery itp.*) dainty, gracious **2** (*dom itp.*) opulent, plush, posh
wylać (się) → WYLEWAĆ (SIĘ)
wylansować → LANSOWAĆ
wylansowanie launch[2]
wy-latywać/lecieć: **to spotkanie wyleciało mi z głowy** the appointment completely slipped my memory; **jego imię wyleciało mi z głowy** I couldn't remember his name – my mind was a complete blank
wylądować → LĄDOWAĆ
wyląg brood[2]
wylec → WYLEGAĆ
wyleczenie cure[2]
wyleczyć → LECZYĆ
wy-legać/lec swarm[2]; (*na ulice itp.*) turn out (for sth)
wylegiwać się lounge[2] (about/around); (*na słońcu*) bask (in sth)
wylenieć → LENIEĆ
wylew: **~ krwi do mózgu** cerebral haemorrhage, stroke[1]
wyl(ew)ać 1 coś (z czegoś na coś) empty[2] sth (out/out of sth), pour, tip[2] **2** (*przelewać się*) flood[1]; (*rzeka*) burst its banks; **~ potoki czegoś** gush **3 (przed kimś)** (*żale itp.*) pour sth out; **~ łzy** shed tears **4** (*z pracy*) fire[2], sack[2]
□ **wyl(ew)ać się 1** (*rzeka itp.*) flood[1], overflow (into sth) **2** (*ludzie, rzeczy*) spill out, over, into, etc.
wylewny demonstrative, effusive, expansive, exuberant
wyleźć → WYŁAZIĆ
wylęg: **przechodzić/poddawać proces/owi ~u** incubate
wylęgani|e incubation; **okres ~a** incubation
wylęgarka incubator
wylęgarnia breeding ground
wyli-czać/czyć enumerate
□ **wyli-czać/czyć się**: **wyliczyć się z pieniędzy** account for all the money spent
wyliniały mangy
wylinieć → LINIEĆ
wylogo(wy)wać zob. też LOGOWAĆ; log off/out; **kogoś** log sb off/out
wylosować → LOSOWAĆ
wylot outlet, vent; **~ lufy** muzzle; **~ rury** nozzle IDM **znać na ~** know inside out/like the back of your hand
wyludniony desolate
wyluzować się chill out
wyładow(yw)ać unload (sth) (from sth); (*ze statku*) land[2]
□ **wyładow(yw)ać się** let off steam; **(na kimś)** take it/sth out on sb
wyłam(yw)ać break sth down
□ **wyłam(yw)ać się** break away (from sb/sth)
wy-łaniać/łonić się emerge, surface[2]
wyłapywacz catcher
wy-ławiać/łowić: **kogoś/coś (skądś/spośród kogoś/czegoś)** pick sb/sth out; **~ ciało z kanału** retrieve a body from a canal
wy-łazić/leźć IDM **~ bokiem komuś** be sick[1] of sb
wyłą-czać/czyć 1 (*światło itp.*) switch sth off/on, turn sth off; (*światło*) turn sth out; (*prąd, telefon itp.*) cut sb/sth off, disconnect; (*wtyczkę z kontaktu, drukarkę itp.*) unplug **2** (*ze spisu*) except[2] sb/sth (from sth)
■ **wyłączenie** exclusion; **~ prądu** power cut | **wyłączony** (*światło itp.*) off[1]

□ **wyłą-czać/czyć się** go off; ~ **z sieci komputerowej** log off/out
wyłączn|y exclusive[1], sole[1]
■ **wyłącznie** exclusively, nothing but, purely, solely
wyłom breach[1], break[2]; **robić ~** breach[2]
wyłonić się → WYŁANIAĆ SIĘ
wyłowić → WYŁAWIAĆ
wyłożyć (się) → WYKŁADAĆ (SIĘ)
wyłu-dzać/dzić trick verb; **coś od kogoś** cheat sb (out) of sth, coax sb out of sth, sth out of/from sb, swindle sb/sth (out of sth), trick sb out of sth, wangle
wyłupiast|y (*oczy*) bulging; **o ~ych oczach** pop-eyed
wyłuskać → ŁUSKAĆ
wyłysieć → ŁYSIEĆ
wymacać → MACAĆ
wymachiwać: **czymś** brandish, flourish[1], wave[2]; (*rękami, nogami*) flail; (*nogami itp.*) dangle
wymagać 1 (*sytuacja itp.*) call for sth, demand[2], entail, involve, necessitate, need[1], require, want[1], take; ~ **dużo pracy/wysiłku** take a lot of/some doing **2** (*prosić*) ask (sb) for sth, exact[2] sth (from sb), expect sth (from sb); **zawsze wymaga tego, co najlepsze** he always insists on the best
■ **wymagający** (*praca itp.*) challenging, demanding; (*osoba*) demanding, exacting, fastidious, particular (about/over sth); (*wybredny*) selective | **wymaganie** requisite noun, want[2]; (**wymagania**) demands[1], needs[3], purposes
wymaglować → MAGLOWAĆ
wymamrotać → MAMROTAĆ
wymanewrować → MANEWROWAĆ
wymarcie extinction
wymarły dead[1], extinct
wy-mawiać/mówić pronounce; **wyraźnie** ~ articulate[1], enunciate; **niepoprawnie** ~ mispronounce
wymaz swab; **pobieranie ~u z szyjki macicy** smear test
wymaz(yw)ać blot sth out, wipe[1] sth (off) (sth); (*zwł. gumką*) erase, rub sth out; ~ **z pamięci** block sth out; (*winę, ośmieszenie itp.*) not live sth down
wymęczony washed out
wymian|a 1 exchange[1], replacement, swap noun; **(ostra) ~a zdań** exchange[1] **2** (*fin.*) exchange[1]; **system ~y walut** foreign exchange; **kantor ~y walut** bureau de change
wymiar dimension
wymiarowy -dimensional
wymieni(a)ć 1 coś na coś innego barter sth (for sth), change[1] sth (for/into sth), exchange[2] A for B, replace sth (with/by sb/sth), swap A for B **2** (*wyliczać*) enumerate, specify; (*w sposób nieformalny*) bandy sth about/around; (*poglądy itp.*) compare notes (with sb); ~ **imię/nazwisko/nazwę** name[2]; ~ **kogoś** (*w testamencie*) remember
□ **wymieni(a)ć się** change[1] sth (with sb)
wymienialny convertible[1]
wymieniony: **wyżej** ~ above-mentioned, aforementioned
wymienny interchangeable
■ **wymiennie** interchangeably; **handlować wymiennie** (*np. kupić nowy samochód, pozostawiając w rozliczeniu stary*) trade sth in (for sth)
wy-mierać/mrzeć die, die off, die out, disappear
wymie-rzać/rzyć (*karę itp.*) mete sth out (to sb); (*sprawiedliwość*) wreak sth (on sb/sth) IDM ~ **komuś cios** deal sb/sth a blow, deal a blow to sb/sth
wymieszać (się) → MIESZAĆ (SIĘ)
wymieść → WYMIATAĆ
wymię udder
wymiętoszony: **brudny i/albo ~, i/albo rozczochrany** mess[1]
wymig(iw)ać się zob. też MIGAĆ SIĘ; shirk; **od czegoś** flinch from sth/doing sth, get out of sth/doing sth
wymijając|y evasive; (*odpowiedź itp.*) indirect, non-committal; (*komentarz, aluzja itp.*) oblique
■ **wymijająco** indirectly, obliquely; **działać/odpowiadać ~o** stall[2]
wymiociny vomit noun
wymiotować/z- bring sth up, be sick, throw (sth) up, vomit
wymioty sick[2]; **zbierać się komuś na ~** nauseate sb
wymizerowany haggard, wasted
wymknąć się → WYMYKAĆ SIĘ
wymodelować → MODELOWAĆ
wymowa articulation, pronunciation; **zła ~** mispronunciation
wymowny 1 (*potrafiący pięknie mówić*) eloquent **2** (*w wyrażaniu swojego zdania*) vocal **3** (*milczenie itp.*) telling
wym|óg need[3], qualification, requirement, requisite noun, stipulation; **spełniać ~ogi** be/come up to scratch
wymówić → MÓWIĆ, WYMAWIAĆ
wymówienie notice[1]
wymówk|a 1 (*pretekst*) evasion, excuse[1] **2** (*wyrzut*) reproach noun, reproof; **robić ~i** reproach sb (for/with sth)
wymrzeć → WYMIERAĆ
wymuskać się spruce yourself up
wymu-szać/sić enforce, force[2]; **coś na kimś** extort sth (from sb), extract[2]; (*zwł. kłótnią*) bludgeon sb (into sth/doing sth), browbeat sb (into doing sth); (*przymilaniem się*) coax sb (into/out of sth/doing sth), sth out of/from sb
■ **wymuszenie** coercion | **wymuszony** enforced; (*uśmiech itp.*) half-hearted
wy-mykać/mknąć się 1 (*uciekać skądś*) elude, sneak[1] out of sth, out, away, etc., steal away, out, etc.; **komuś/czemuś** dodge[1], give sb the slip **2** (*uwaga itp.*) slip out **3 ~ spod kontroli** be/get out of control; **wymykający się spod kontroli** runaway[1]; ~ **z rąk** get/be out of hand
wymysł concoction, invention, make-believe
wymyś-lać/lić 1 concoct, contrive, devise, invent, dream sth up, think of sth, think sth up **2 (komuś)** rant (at sb); **(komuś za coś)** berate **3** (*obrzucać wyzwiskami*) call sb names
wymyśln|y fancy[3]; **prosty posiłek bez żadnych ~ych potraw** a plain simple meal - no frills
■ **wymyślnie 1** (*starannie i wykwintnie*) elaborately **2** (*specjalnie*) wilfully
wymyślony contrived, fanciful, fictitious, made-up
wyna-gradzać/grodzić 1 (*kompensować*) remedy[2]; (*stratę*) compensate (sb) (for sth), recompense; (*komuś krzywdę, czas itp.*) make it up to sb; ~ **szkodę** make amends **2** (*nagradzać*) reward[2] **3** (*płacić*) **źle ~** underpay
■ **wynagrodzenie 1** (*strat itp.*) compensation **2** (*nagroda*) reward[1] **3** (*płaca*) pay[2], remuneration
wynająć → NAJMOWAĆ, WYNAJMOWAĆ
wy-najdować/naleźć devise, discover, invent
wynajęci|e hire[2]; (*mieszkanie itp.*) **do ~a** available
wynaj-mować/ąć 1 (*samochód itp.*) hire[1]; (*mieszkanie itp.*) rent[2] **2 kogoś** hire[1]; (*na podstawie umowy*) contract[2]
wynalaz-ca/czyni inventor
wynalazczy inventive
wynalazek brainchild, discovery, invention
wynaleźć → WYNAJDOWAĆ
wynegocjować → NEGOCJOWAĆ
wynegocjowani|e: **(możliwy) do ~a** negotiable
wynędzniały pinched
wyniesienie elevation
wynieść (się) → WYNOSIĆ (SIĘ)
wynik (*pewnego wydarzenia itp.*) outcome, result[1], upshot; (*egzaminu itp.*) result[1]; (*sport*) score[1], tally; (*mat.*) sum[1] (of sth), product of sth; **(wyniki)** (*badań*) findings; (*pracy itp.*) performance; **być ~iem czegoś** result[2] (from sth) IDM **w ~u czegoś** in view of sth
wynik-ać/nąć: **z czegoś** come from (doing) sth, come of sth/of doing sth, eventuate, follow (on) (from sth), spring from sth; (*trudności itp.*) develop, ensue
■ **wynikający** consequent
wyniosły haughty, lofty, proud, supercilious, superior[1]
wynos: **potrawy na ~**; **restauracja oferująca potrawy na ~** takeaway
wy-nosić/nieść 1 (*na zewnątrz*) put sth out **2** (*na wyższe stanowisko*) elevate; (*na wysoką pozycję, np. gwiazdy filmowej*) catapult[2] **3** (*suma itp.*) add up to sth, amount[2] to sth, come to sth, make[1], total verb, work out (at sth) **4** (*rekord, inflacja itp.*) stand at sth
□ **wy-nosić/nieść się** get out (of sth); ~ **ukradkiem** steal away, in, out, etc.; **wynoś się stąd!** get out!/get out of here!, hop it!
wynu-rzać/rzyć się surface[2]
wyobcow(yw)ać alienate sb (from sb/sth)
wyobraźni|a fantasy, imagination, vision; **obdarzony ~ą** imaginative; **pełen ~** imaginative
wyobra-żać/zić: **sobie** conceive, envisage, imagine, picture[2] sb/sth (as sth), see, think, have visions of sth, visualize; **sobie siebie jako kogoś** fancy[1] yourself (as) sth; **czy tak sobie**

wyobrażasz żarty? is that your idea of a joke?
wyobrażalny conceivable, imaginable
wyobrażeni|e 1 (*myśl*) idea, notion; **być nie do ~a** be beyond sb **2** (*wizerunek*) image, picture[1], representation, vision
wyodrębni(a)ć isolate
wyolbrzymi(a)ć exaggerate, magnify, overstate, get sth out of proportion; (*zadanie, pracę*) make heavy weather of sth
■ **wyolbrzymiony** exaggerated, grandiose
wypaczony skewed, warped
wypaczyć (się) → PACZYĆ (SIĘ)
wypad outing
wypa-dać/ść 1 (*przez okno, z ręki itp.*) fall[1], fall out **2** ~ **z gry** be/go out **3** (*z pamięci*) escape[1]; ~ **komuś z głowy** go clean out of your mind, slip your mind **4** (*udać się dobrze/źle itp.*) fare[2], go off; **dobrze** ~ carry it/sth off; ~ **korzystnie w porównaniu z czymś** compare favourably with sth; **kiepsko wypada na egzaminach** she's a poor performer in exams **5** (*zdarzyć się*) pop up **6** (*wybiec, np. z pokoju*) breeze[2] out
wypad|ek 1 (*kolizja*) accident; **~ek samochodowy** car crash; **nagły ~ek** emergency; **nieprzewidziany ~ek** contingency **2** (*przypadek*) instance IDM **na wszelki ~ek** (just) in case, at all events/in any event | **na ~ek czegoś** (just) in case | **w najgorszym ~ku** if the worst comes to the worst | **w najlepszym ~ku** at best | **w ~ku czegoś** in case of sth | **w żadnym ~ku** in/under no circumstances
wypa-lać/lić zob. też PALIĆ; (*dziurę itp.*) burn[1]; (*samochód itp.*) burn sth out; (*spalać*) burn sth off
□ **wypa-lać/lić się 1** (*spalać się*) burn off **2** (*przen.: osoba*) burn (yourself) out
wypaplać blurt sth out
wyparcie się denial, disavowal
wyparować → PAROWAĆ
wyparowanie evaporation
wypaść → WYPADAĆ
wypatroszyć → PATROSZYĆ
wypa-trywać/trzeć be on the lookout for sb/sth, keep an eye open/out (for sb/sth), keep a lookout for sb/sth, keep watch for sb/sth; ~ **oczy** keep your eyes peeled/skinned (for sb/sth)
wypchan|y: **być porządnie ~ym czymś** bulge[1] (with sth), be packed solid with sth
wypchnąć → WYPYCHAĆ
wypełni(a)ć 1 (*napełniać*) choke[1] sth (up) (with sth), crowd[2], fill sth up (with sth), pack[1]; (*teatr itp.*) pack sth out **2** (*formularz itp.*) complete[2], fill sth in **3** (*obowiązek, badanie itp.*) carry sth out, fulfil
■ **wypełnienie** filling[1], stuffing | **wypełniony** IDM **wypełniony po brzegi** chock-full (of sth/sb), jammed full of sth, jam-packed (with sb/sth)
□ **wypełni(a)ć się** (*całkowicie czymś*) fill up (with sth)
wyperfumować → PERFUMOWAĆ
wyperswadow(yw)ać: **coś komuś** dissuade, persuade sb not to do sth, talk sb out of doing sth
wypę-dzać/dzić banish
wypić zob. też PIĆ; drink (sth) up; ~ **do dna** down[2], drain[1]
wypieczony: **dobrze** ~ well done; **średnio** ~ medium[1]
wypie-kać/c (się) bake
wypiek|i flush[2]; **z ~ami na twarzy** flushed
wypielęgnować → PIELĘGNOWAĆ
wypielić → PIELIĆ
wy-pierać/przeć displace, supersede; **mniejsze przedsiębiorstwa są wypierane z rynku** smaller companies are being crowded out of the market
□ **wy-pierać/przeć się** deny, disavow, disclaim, disown
wypis 1 (*część tekstu*) extract[1] **2** (**wypisy**) (*książka*) reader
wypis(yw)ać 1 (*czek itp.*) make sth out, write sth (out) (for sb); **wypisać czek na kogoś** make a cheque out to sb, make a cheque payable to sb **2** (*receptę*) make sth out **3** (*ze szpitala itp.*) discharge[1]
□ **wypis(yw)ać się** (*z organizacji*) sign out
wypląt(yw)ać 1 disentangle **2** (*przen.*) extricate, disengage sth/sb (from sth/sb)
□ **wypląt(yw)ać się** disengage yourself (from sb/sth), extricate yourself
wyplewić → PLEWIĆ
wyplu(wa)ć (*z siebie dym itp.*) spew, spout[2]
wypła-cać/cić (*pensję itp.*) pay (sb) (for sth); (*pieniądze z banku*) take some money out of the bank, withdraw
wypłak(iw)ać IDM ~ **oczy** cry your eyes out
□ **wypłakać się** have a good cry
wypłat|a 1 (*pensja*) pay[2], wage(s)[1]; **dzień ~y** payday; **~y z tytułu zatrudnienia** payroll **2** (*z banku*) withdrawal
wypłowieć → PŁOWIEĆ
wypłuk(iw)ać zob. też PŁUKAĆ; rinse, wash sth out
wypły-wać/nąć 1 (*woda itp.*) well[5] (out/up); (*z dużą szybkością*) spew; ~ **na powierzchnię** surface[2] **2** (*w dyskusji itp.*) come up
wypoczęty fresh
wypoczynek recreation
wypolerować → POLEROWAĆ
wypolerowany polished
wypo-minać/mnieć: **coś komuś** rub it/sth in
wyposa-żać/żyć equip, fit[1], kit sb out/up (in/with sth); ~ **w dodatkowe akcesoria** accessorize
□ **wyposa-żać/żyć się** kit yourself out/up (in/with sth)
wyposażenie equipment; ~ **ruchome** fitting[2]; ~ **stałe** fixture; ~ **wnętrza** furnishings; **kuchnia z pełnym ~m** a fully-equipped kitchen
wypo-wiadać/wiedzieć articulate[2], express[1], formulate; (*słowa*) utter[2]; (*publicznie*) air[2]; ~ **swoje zdanie** have your say; (*bez ogródek*) speak your mind IDM ~ **wojnę** declare war on another country
□ **wypo-wiadać/wiedzieć się** express[1] yourself, pronounce; **przeciw czemuś** come out against sth
wypowiedź utterance
wypoziomować → POZIOMOWAĆ
wypoży-czać/czyć: **coś (komuś)** hire sth (out) (to sb), loan verb sth (to sb); **coś (od kogoś)** borrow (sth) (from/off sb/sth), hire[1] sth (from sb), rent[2] sth (from sb)
wypożyczalnia: ~ **kaset wideo** video (rental) shop
wypożyczony on loan, rented
wypracowanie composition, essay
wypracowany elaborate[1]
wypracow(yw)ać hammer sth out, thrash sth out, work sth up
wyprać (się) → PRAĆ (SIĘ); wash sth out
wyprasować → PRASOWAĆ
wypraw|a 1 expedition; **~a poszukiwawcza** search party **2** (**wyprawy**) travel[2]
wyprawiać: **co dzieci wyprawiają?** what are the children getting up to ?
wyprodukować → PRODUKOWAĆ
wypromować → PROMOWAĆ
wyprorokować → PROROKOWAĆ
wyprostowany straight[2]
wyprosto(wy)wać (się) zob. też PROSTOWAĆ (SIĘ); right[4]
wyprowa-dzać/dzić 1 (*psa na spacer*) walk[1] **2** (*pieniądze*) siphon sth off, sth (from/out of sb/sth)
□ **wyprowa-dzać/dzić się** move out, vacate; ~ **z domu** leave home
wypróbow(yw)ać test[2] sth (on sb/sth), try sb/sth out (on sb)
■ **wypróbowany** practised (in sth)
wypru(wa)ć IDM ~ **z siebie flaki** work/sweat your guts out
wyprysk (*na skórze*) blemish, spot[1], zit
wyprzeć (się) → WYPIERAĆ (SIĘ)
wyprzeda(wa)ć (*cały zapas czegoś*) sell sth off, sell out (of sth), be sold out (of sth); **zostać wyprzedanym** sell out, be sold out
□ **wyprzeda(wa)ć się** sell up
wyprzedaż sale; ~ **rzeczy używanych we własnym garażu** garage sale
wyprze-dzać/dzić lead[1], overtake; **kogoś** beat sb to sth; ~ **przeciwnika o całe okrążenie toru** lap[2]
■ **wyprzedzenie**: **zastanowić się i zaplanować z wyprzedzeniem** think ahead | **wyprzedzający** pre-emptive; **wyprzedzający swoją epokę** ahead of your time
wypsnąć się let sth slip
wypucować → PUCOWAĆ
wypukłość bulge[2], protrusion
wypukł|y convex; (*wystający*) bulging; **~e czoło** a domed forehead
wy-puszczać/puścić 1 (*na wolność*) let sb/sth out of sth, release[1]; (*kogoś, zwł. z lekką karą*) let sb off (with sth) **2** (*gaz itp.*) discharge[1]; ~ **powietrze** deflate **3** (*płytę itp.*) release[1]
wy-pychać/pchnąć 1 (*napychać*) stuff[2] sth (with sth) **2** (*pchać na zewnątrz*) bundle[2] out of sth
wypyt(yw)ać question[2] sb (about/on sth)
wy-rabiać/robić make[1]; (*opinię, pogląd*) form[2]; ~ **w kimś posłuszeństwo, charakter itp.** discipline[2]; **wyrobić pozycję** establish sb/sth (as sth); **wyrobić sobie opinię człowieka, który...** acquire a reputation for being...
IDM ~ **sobie (dobre) imię** make a name for yourself, make your name
□ **wy-rabiać/robić się** (*śruba itp.*) work loose
wyrachowanie calculation
wyrachowany calculating; (*oczekujący zysku*) mercenary[2]

wyrafinowanie sophistication, subtlety
wyrafinowany 1 (*argument itp.*) subtle **2** (*wykształcony*) cultured
wy-rajać/roić się swarm[2]
wy-rastać/rosnąć 1 (*roślina*) come up; ~ **jak grzyby po deszczu** mushroom[2] **2 z czegoś** grow out of sth, outgrow **3 na kogoś/coś** grow into sth **4** (*przen.: budynki itp.*) go up **5** (*wznosić się: góra itp.*) rise[2] **6** (*przen.: z nawyku itp.*) grow out of sth
wyraz 1 (*twarzy*) facial expression, look[2]; **bez ~u** blankly, deadpan, featureless; **pełen ~u** soulful **2** (*słowo*) expression, word[1]; (*wdzięczności itp.*) token[1]; ~ **pochodny** derivative; ~ **złożony** compound[1] **3 ~y szacunku** regards[2]; **~y szacunku/pozdrowienia** (*np. przy przesyłaniu/darowaniu czegoś w upominku*) compliments[1]; **Z ~ami szacunku** (*zwrot grzecznościowy stosowany na zakończenie listu*) Yours (sincerely),
wyraziciel/ka mouthpiece
wyrazisty expressive, forcible, incisive
wyraźn|y 1 (*dźwięk itp.*) distinct, resonant; (*akcent*) broad; (*kolor*) bold; (*zdjęcie*) in focus; **~a wymowa** enunciation **2** (*kontrast*) sharp[1]; (*zmiana itp.*) definite; (*różnica itp.*) marked, palpable, pronounced, tangible; (*błąd itp.*) clear[1]; (*niepowodzenie itp.*) manifest; (*rozkaz*) strict; (*polecenia itp.*) explicit, express[2]; (*entuzjazm itp.*) seeming
wyra-żać/zić express[1], mean[1], say[1], signify; (*słowami*) formulate, phrase[2], put, verbalize; (*pogląd*) register[1], voice[2]; (*podziękowania*) extend; ~ **jasno** put sth across/over (to sb); ~ **coś w inny sposób** rephrase
IDM ~ **komuś uznanie** pay tribute to sb/sth
□ **wyra-żać/zić się**: ~ **jasno** make yourself understood, put yourself across/over (to sb)
wyrażenie expression, figure of speech, phrase[1], utterance
wyrąb(yw)ać (*las itp.*) fell[2]
wyrecytować → RECYTOWAĆ
wyregulować → REGULOWAĆ
wyremontować → REMONTOWAĆ
wyreżyserować → REŻYSEROWAĆ
wyręka: **chwilowa** ~ stopgap
wyrobić (się) → WYRABIAĆ (SIĘ)
wyrobienie sophistication
wyrobiony sophisticated; (*publiczność itp.*) discriminating
wyrocznia oracle
wyroić się → WYRAJAĆ SIĘ
wyrok conviction, judgement, sentence[1]; ~ **w zawieszeniu** probation, suspended sentence
wyrosnąć → WYRASTAĆ
wyrostek: ~ **robaczkowy** appendix
wyrozumiał|y forgiving (of sth), tolerant, understanding[2]; **bądź dla niego ~y** go easy on him; **być ~ym dla kogoś** make allowances for sb/sth
wyr|ób manufacture noun; (**wyroby**) ware; **~oby cukiernicze** confectionery
wyrównanie 1 (*doprowadzenie do stanu równości*) alignment **2** (*sport*) ~ **szans** handicap[1]
wyrównany even[1]
wyrównawczy (*lekcje*) remedial
wyrówn(yw)ać zob. też RÓWNAĆ **1** (*rachunek*) pay up, settle; (*długi, liczbę itp.*) cancel sth out; (*braki itp.*) redeem **2** (*wygładzać*) flatten sth (out), level[3], smooth[2] sth (down, out, etc.); (*robić jednolitym*) even sth out **3** (*linie itp.*) align sth (with sth)
■ **wyrównywanie** (*włosów*) trim noun
□ **wyrówn(yw)ać się 1** (*stać się jednolitym*) flatten (out), even out, level off/out **2** (*długi, liczby itp.*) cancel out
wyróżni(a)ć 1 differentiate, distinguish A (from B) **2 kogoś/coś (za coś)** single sb/sth out (for sth)
□ **wyróżni(a)ć się** distinguish yourself; **(od czegoś)** stand out (from/against sth)
■ **wyróżniający się** distinctive
wyróżnieni|e 1 (*zaszczyt*) privilege **2** (*wybitność*) distinction; (*dyplom uczelni*) **z ~em** first-class; **dyplom ukończenia studiów z ~em** first[3] (in sth)
wyróżniony (*uprzywilejowany*) privileged
wyrug(ow)ać → RUGAĆ
wyru-szać/szyć (*w podróż*) set forth, set off, set out, start[1]; (*po krótkim postoju*) draw out; ~ **w rejs** sail[1], set sail
wyrw|a breach[1]; **robić ~ę** breach[2]
wyr(y)wać zob. też RYĆ **1** (*ząb*) extract[2], have sth out, take sth out **2** (*wyszarpać*) grab sth (from sb), pluck[1] sth/sb (from sth/out), pull sth away, back, etc., snatch[1], tear[2]; ~ **z korzeniami** uproot; **wyrwać drzwi** wrench the door off (sth)
□ **wyr(y)wać się 1** (*na wolność*) bolt[2]; (*z zebrania, pracy itp.*) extricate yourself from sth, get away (from…), get out (of sth) **2** (*cofać się*) pull[1] away, back, etc. **3** (*z historyjkami itp.*) come out with sth
wyrywkow|y random; **~a kontrola** spot check
wyrzą-dzać/dzić: ~ **komuś krzywdę** do sb an injustice, wrong[4] sb; ~ **szkodę** harm[2]; **wyrządzić wiele szkód** do a lot of damage
wyrzeczenie sacrifice[1], self-sacrifice
wyrze-kać/c się (*pieniędzy itp.*) forgo; (*rodziny itp.*) disown; ~ **związku z czymś** dissociate yourself (from sth)
■ **wyrzekanie się** renunciation
wyrzeźbić → RZEŹBIĆ
wyrzu-cać/cić 1 discard, dump[1], empty[2] sth (out/out of sth), scrap[2], tip[2]; (*do kosza*) consign sth to sth, chuck sth (away/out), throw sth away; **gwałtownie** ~ catapult[2]; ~ **potoki czegoś** gush **2 kogoś/coś (z czegoś)** boot sb/sth out (of sth), drop[1] sb/sth (from sth); **kogoś (skądś)** chuck sb out (of sth), eject sb (from sth), kick sb out (of sth), throw sb out (of…); ~ **kogoś z pracy** fire[2], sack[2], give sb the sack **2 coś z siebie** (*wygadać się*) spout[2]; (*dot. przestępstwa itp.*) come clean (with sb) (about sth)
wyrzut reproof; **pełen ~u** reproachful; ~ **sumienia** remorse (for sth/doing sth); **~y sumienia** qualms; **w jej głosie brzmiał** ~ there was a note of accusation in her voice
wyrzutek outcast
wyrzutnia: ~ **rakietowa** launch pad
wyrzygać (się) → RZYGAĆ
wy-rzynać/rżnąć massacre verb
wysa-dzać/dzić 1 (*w powietrze*) blast[2], blow sth up, explode **2** (*kogoś z samochodu*) drop[1] sb/sth (off) **3** (*drogę drzewami itp.*) edge[2] sth (with sth)
■ **wysadzany** (*ćwiekami itp.*) studded; (*drzewami itp.*) fringed with sth
wysap(yw)ać gasp
wyschnąć → WYSYCHAĆ
wyselekcjonować → SELEKCJONOWAĆ
wyselekcjonowany hand-picked
wysepka: ~ **uliczna** traffic island
wysforow(yw)ać się forge ahead
wy-siadać/siąść 1 (*z autobusu itp.*) get off (sth); (*ze statku, samolotu*) disembark; (*form.*) alight[2] (from sth), exit[2]; ~ **z samochodu** step out of a car **2** (*urządzenie*) conk out, go[1]
wysiadywać 1 (**wysiedzieć**) (*jaja*) brood[1]; (*pisklęta*) hatch[1], incubate **2** (*przesiadywać*) sit sth out, sit through sth
wysied-lać/lić displace, evict
wysi-lać/lić się exert yourself, go out of your way (to do sth), pull out all the stops, strain[2], take trouble over/with sth, take trouble to do sth/doing sth; **nie** ~ take it/things easy
wysił|ek effort, endeavour noun, exertion, struggle[2]; (**wysiłki**) energy; **pełen ~ku** strenuous; **wymagający wiele ~ku** formidable; **z ~kiem** hard[2], laboured, strenuously; **zrobić coś z ~kiem** scrape[1]
wysiudać: **kogoś (skądś)** turf sb out (of sth)
wysiusiać → SIUSIAĆ
wy-skakiwać/skoczyć 1 skądś jump out of sth, leap out of sth **2** (*z autobusu itp.*) hop off sth, hop out (of sth) **3** (*jak diabeł z pudełka*) poke out of/through (sth), pop out, spring from…; (*jak grzyby po deszczu*) spring up
wyskandować → SKANDOWAĆ
wysklepiony domed
wyskokowy alcoholic[1]
wyskrobać zob. też SKROBAĆ; (*zebrać*) scrape sth together/up
wyskubać → SKUBAĆ
wysłać → WYSYŁAĆ
wysłanni-k/czka envoy
wysławiać praise[2] sb/sth (for sth)
□ **wy-sławiać/słowić się** express[1] yourself; **umiejący dobrze się** ~ articulate[2], eloquent
wysłuchać → SŁUCHAĆ
wysłuchanie hearing
wysmagać → SMAGAĆ
wysmażony: **dobrze** ~ well done; **średnio** ~ (*kulin.*) medium[1]
wysok|i 1 (*zwł. osoba; drzewo*) tall; (*zwł. góra*) high[1] **2** (*dźwięk*) high[1], high-pitched **3** (*jakość*) high[1] **4 ~ą pensję** a hefty salary **5** (*władza*) high[1]; **~iej mocy** high-powered
IDM **w ~im stopniu** highly
■ **wyższy 1** (*wyżej położony; bardziej zaawansowany*) higher; **studia wyższe** higher education; **klasa wyższa społeczeństwa** the upper

class **2** (*rangą*) superior[1] (to sb) **3** (*osoba*) taller **4** (*gram.*, *stopień*) comparative[1]

wysoko **1** ~ **położony** high[1] **2** (*śpiewać itp.*) high[3] **3** (*bardzo*) highly **4** (*osoba; stanowisko*) ~ **postawiony** exalted

wysokogórski alpine

wysokoprężny: **pojazd** ~ diesel

wysokościowiec tower block

wysokoś|ć **1** (*miara; odległość*) height; (*nad poziomem morza*) elevation; (*nad ziemią*) altitude; **mający x metrów ~ci** to be x meters high[1]; **na dużych ~ciach** at high altitudes **2** **~ć tonu** pitch[1] **3** (*tytuł*) **Jego/Jej Wysokość** His/Her Grace/Highness/Lordship IDM **na ~ci** on high | **stawać na ~ci zadania** rise to the occasion, challenge, task, etc.

wysondować → SONDOWAĆ

wysp|a island, isle; **Wyspy Brytyjskie** the British Isles

wyspecjalizować się → SPECJALIZOWAĆ SIĘ

wyspecjalizowany specialized

wyspiarski insular

wyspia-rz/rka islander

wysportowany athletic, sporty

wyspowiadać się → SPOWIADAĆ SIĘ

wysprzątać clear sth out

■ **wysprzątany** trim[2]

wyssać → SSAĆ, WYSYSAĆ

wystający prominent

wystar-czać/czyć do[1], go far, suffice; (*zapas wody itp.*) hold out; **komuś** serve sb's purpose; (*dla określonej liczby osób*) serve; (*dla wszystkich/na wszystko*) go round; ~ **na długo** go a long way; **wystarczyć na zaspokojenie podstawowych potrzeb** be enough to meet our basic needs; **wystarczy mi kanapka** a sandwich will be fine (for me) IDM **wystarczy na dzisiaj** let's call it a day

wystarczając|y adequate, ample, fine[1], sufficient; **~a ilość/liczba** enough[1]

wystarczyć → STARCZYĆ, WYSTARCZAĆ

wystartować → STARTOWAĆ

wystaw|a **1** (*w muzeum*) exhibition **2** (*pokaz*) show[2] **3** (*różnych rzeczy*) array, display[2]; **~a sklepowa** shop window; **na ~ie** on display

wystawać jut (out) (from/into/over sth), overhang, project[2], protrude, stick out (of sth), stick up; (*brzuch itp.*) bulge[1]; **wystające górne zęby** buck teeth

wystaw-ca/czyni exhibitor

wystawi(a)ć **1** (*na zewnątrz*) put sth out; (*głowę, język*) stick sth out (of sth); ~ **głowę przez okno** poke your head out of the window **3** ~ **na pokaz** display[1], expose, flaunt **4** (*w muzeum*) exhibit[1] **5** (*w teatrze*) present[3], produce[1], put sth on, stage[2] **6** ~ **na niebezpieczeństwo** jeopardize, subject sb/sth to sth **7** ~ **stopień/ocenę** mark[1] **8** ~ **komuś/czemuś wyśmienite świadectwo** be a tribute to sb/sth **9** **wystawić swój dom na sprzedaż** put your house up for sale; ~ **akcje na sprzedaż** go public **10** (*drużynę*) field[2] **11** ~ **fakturę** put in an invoice; ~ **komuś rachunek** bill sb (for sth) IDM ~ **kogoś do wiatru** stand sb up

■ **wystawiający**: ~ **na próbę** taxing | **wystawiony**: **wystawiony na działanie czynników zewnętrznych** exposed; **wystawiony na wiatr** windswept

wystawny ostentatious, sumptuous

wystąpić → WYSTĘPOWAĆ

wystąpienie **1** (*referat itp.*) presentation **2** **o coś** claim[2] (for sth)

wysterylizować → STERYLIZOWAĆ

występ **1** (*pojawienie się*) appearance **2** (*w filmie/na koncercie itp.*) performance; (*muzyków pop lub jazzowych*) gig **3** (*skalny itp.*) ledge, protrusion

występek vice

wy-stępować/stąpić **1** (*znajdować się*) be found, occur; (*pokazać się*) appear **2** (*w filmie*) feature[2], star[2] **3** (*z innym słowem w zdaniu*) take; (*wyrazy*) ~ **razem** collocate **4** **o coś** apply (to sb) (for sth), claim[1] (for sth); ~ **o bankructwo** file for bankruptcy **5** (*wystawać*) jut (out) (from/into/over sth) **6** (*rzeka*) ~ **z brzegów** overflow its banks **7** (*ze stowarzyszenia itp.*) disaffiliate (from sth) **8** ~ **w czyjejś obronie** speak out in sb's defence **9** (*stawać się komuś*) get into sb

■ **występowanie** incidence of sth; **powszechne występowanie** prevalence

wystraszyć → STRASZYĆ

wystroić (się) → STROIĆ (SIĘ)

wystrój decor, decoration; ~ **wnętrz** interior decoration

wystrzał gunfire, gunshot, pop[1], shot[1]

wystrzegać się beware (of sb/sth), shun, be wary of sth

wystrzeli(wa)ć **1** (*z broni*) fire sth off **2** (*rakietę*) launch[1]

wystrzępić (się) → STRZĘPIĆ (SIĘ)

wystudiowany (*gest, uśmiech itp.*) studied

wystudzić → STUDZIĆ

wystygnąć → STYGNĄĆ

wysublimować → SUBLIMOWAĆ

wysubtelni(a)ć refine

wysu-szać/szyć (się) zob. też SUSZYĆ (SIĘ); dry (sth) up, shrivel (sth) (up)

■ **wysuszony** desiccated; ~ **na pieprz** parched

wysu-wać/nąć **1** (*wystawiać*) poke sth out of sth, protrude (from sth) **2** (*kasetę*) eject **3** (*wniosek*) put sth forward, propose; (*czyjąś kandydaturę itp.*) propose sb for/as sth, put sb forward

□ **wysu-wać/nąć się** **1** (*w meczu itp.*) be/get ahead (of sb/sth); ~ **naprzód** forge ahead; ~ **na pierwszy plan** be/come to the fore **2** (*kaseta*) eject

wy-sychać/schnąć dry out, dry up; (*rzeka itp.*) run dry

wys(y)łać **1** (*pocztą*) dispatch, mail verb, post[2], send, send sth in, send sth off, send sth out; ~ **przez radio** radio verb **2** (*światło, ciepło itp.*) send sth out

wysyłka (*towaru*) consignment; ~ **towarów drogą morską** shipment

wysypisko (*śmieci*) dump[2], landfill, tip[1]

wysypka rash[1]

wysyp(yw)ać tip[2]

□ **wysyp(yw)ać się** **1** tumble, pile out of sth **2** (*przen.*) spill out

wy-sysać/ssać **1** suck **2** (*przelewać syfonem*) siphon sth out of sth, sth off/out

wyszaleć się run wild

wyszarp(yw)ać pull sth out

wyszczególni(a)ć **1** (*podać szczegóły*) detail[2], itemize **2** (*wskazać*) point sth out (to sb)

wyszczerbi(a)ć chip[2], nick[2]

■ **wyszczerbion|y** jagged; **być wyszczerbionym** have a chip in it

□ **wyszczerbi(a)ć się** chip[2]

wyszcze-rzać/rzyć: ~ **zęby w uśmiechu** grin (at sb)

wyszczotkować → SZCZOTKOWAĆ

wyszczup-lać/lić: ~ **kogoś** make sb look thin

wyszeptać → SZEPTAĆ

wyszkolić (się) → SZKOLIĆ (SIĘ)

wyszlifować → SZLIFOWAĆ

wyszlifowany polished

wyszorować → SZOROWAĆ

wyszperać dig sth out (of sth), ferret sth out

wyszukany (*nie prosty*) fancy[3]; (*gusty itp.*) cultured

wyszuk(iw)ać browse; (*przez internet*) google; (*w pamięci komputera*) retrieve

■ **wyszukiwanie**: ~ **danych** data capture/retrieval; (*komput.*) **oparty na wyszukiwaniu** searchable

wyszukiwarka search engine, searcher

wyszumieć się let off steam

wyszy-dzać/dzić zob. też SZYDZIĆ; jeer (at) sb/sth; (*w sztuce itp.*) satirize

wyszywanka embroidery

wyście-lać/lić pad[2] sth (with sth)

■ **wyściełany** (*fotel itp.*) upholstered

wyścig race[1], run[2]; (**wyścigi**) racing; **~i konne** the horses, horse racing, the races[1]; **~i samochodowe** motor racing; **stawiać/zgłaszać do ~u** race[2] IDM ~ **z czasem** a race against the clock | ~ **o karierę/szczurów** the rat race | ~ **zbrojeń** arms race

wyściółka **1** (*poduszka usztywniająca, np. ramiona marynarki*) pad[1] **2** (*poduszki, kołdry itp.*) padding, stuffing

wyśledzenie detection

wyśledzić → ŚLEDZIĆ

wyśliz-giwać/gnąć/nąć się slip[1]; **wyślizgnąć się z pokoju** slide out of the room

wyśmienity exquisite, fabulous, luscious

wyśmi(ew)ać (się) deride, make fun of sb/sth, jeer (at) sb/sth, laugh at sb/sth, mock[1], ridicule verb, scoff (at sb/sth), taunt; (*w sztuce itp.*) satirize

wyświad-czać/czyć (*przysługę*) render; ~ **komuś przysługę** do sb a good turn

wyświechtany **1** (*ubranie*) shabby, threadbare **2** (*dowcip itp.*) corny, trite

wyświetlacz display[2]

wyświet-lać/lić (*film*) screen[2]; (*slajdy itp.*) project[2] sth (on/onto sth)

wyświę-cać/cić ordain

wy-taczać/toczyć: **wytoczyć proces** take legal action (against sb/sth)

wytapetować → TAPETOWAĆ

wytart|y **1** (*ubranie*) threadbare; (*osoba*) **w ~ym ubraniu** shabby **2** (*dowcip*) corny; **~y frazes** cliché

wytarzać się → TARZAĆ SIĘ

wytaszczyć → TASZCZYĆ

wytatuować → TATUOWAĆ

wytchnąć get your breath (again/back)

wytchnieni|e respite; **chwila ~a** breather, breathing space IDM **bez ~a** on the trot

wytępić → TĘPIĆ

wytępienie eradication

wytę-żać/żyć strain[2]; ~ **słuch** prick up your ears, strain your ears □ **wytę-żać/żyć się** exert yourself

wytężony 1 (*wysiłek itp.*) exacting, strenuous **2** (*zaabsorbowany*) rapt

wy-tłaczać/tłoczyć: ~ **wzór** emboss A with B, B on A

wytłumaczalny explicable

wytłumaczeni|e explanation; **nie do ~a** inexplicably

wytłumaczyć zob. też TŁUMACZYĆ (SIĘ); explain sth away □ **wytłumaczyć się** excuse[2]

wytoczyć → WYTACZAĆ

wytrajkotać rattle sth off

wytrawi(a)ć etch A (with B), B (in/into/on A)

wytrawny 1 (*specjalista itp.*) practised (in sth); (*wyrafinowany*) discerning **2** (*wino*) dry[1]

wytrą-cać/cić: ~ **kogoś z równowagi** unnerve, upset[1]

wytrenować → TRENOWAĆ

wytresować → TRESOWAĆ

wytropić → TROPIĆ

wytrwać → TRWAĆ

wytrwa|ły dogged, persistent, tenacious ■ **wytrwale** persistently; ~ **znoszący coś** long-suffering; ~ **coś robić** keep sth up; ~ **dalej coś robić** stick at sth | **wytrwałość** perseverance, persistence, stamina, tenacity

wytrych: **otwierać zamek ~em** pick a lock

wytrysk jet[1], squirt; (*nasienia*) ejaculation; **mieć** ~ (*nasienia*) ejaculate

wytrys-kiwać/nąć spout[2]

wytrzeć (się) → WYCIERAĆ (SIĘ)

wytrze-szczać/szczyć (*oczy*) pop out ■ **wytrzeszczony**: **o wytrzeszczonych oczach** pop-eyed

wytrzeźwieć → TRZEŹWIEĆ

wytrzymałość durability, endurance, soundness, stamina, sturdiness, toughness, strength

wytrzymały 1 (*osoba*) strong, tough **2** (*materiał*) durable, sturdy, hard-wearing, tough; (*urządzenie*) heavy-duty **3** (*roślina*) hardy

wytrzym(yw)ać put up with sb/sth, stand[1], withstand; (*poczekać, np. z podjęciem decyzji*) hold on; ~ **do końca** stick it/sth out; **te dane nie wytrzymają dokładnej analizy** these figures won't bear close examination ■ **wytrzymani|e**: **nie do wytrzymania** unbearable

wy-twarzać/tworzyć fabricate, generate, make[1], produce[1]; (*maszynowo*) manufacture

wytworny classy, refined, smart[1], sophisticated; (*modny*) fashionable; (*kobieta: w manierach*) ladylike; (*maniery*) **(przesadnie)** ~ genteel; (*mężczyzna*) ~ **i elegancki** dapper, dashing, urbane

wytworzyć → WYTWARZAĆ

wytwór creation, product; ~ **wyobraźni** a figment of sb's imagination

wytwór-ca/czyni maker, manufacturer

wytwórczość output

wytwórnia: ~ **filmowa** studio; ~ **płyt** label[1]

wyty-czać/czyć (*granicę itp.*) demarcate, mark sth out, stake sth out

wytyczna guideline, line[1]

wytypować → TYPOWAĆ

wyuczony: **doskonale ~ na pamięć** word-perfect

wyuzdany debauched

wywabi(a)ć coax sth (out of sth)

wywa-lać/lić 1 empty[2] sth (out/out of sth), tip[2] **2 (kogoś skądś)** turf sb out (of sth); (*z posady*) give sb the push □ **wywa-lać/lić się** (*upaść*) tumble

wywar stock[1]

wywa-żać/żyć (*otworzyć siłą itp.*) prise sth off, apart, open, etc.

wyważony balanced; **dobrze** ~ well balanced

wywędrować → WĘDROWAĆ

wywęszyć zob. też WĘSZYĆ; ferret sb/sth out, get wind of sth

wywiad 1 (*szpiegowski itp.*) intelligence **2** ~ **dziennikarski** interview[1]

wywiąz(yw)ać: **nie ~ się z płatności** default[2] (on sth) □ **wywiąz(yw)ać się**: **z czegoś** carry sth out, deliver (on sth), discharge[1]; **źle/dobrze ~ się z czegoś** make a bad, good, etc. job of sth; ~ **się doskonale** (*np. z pracy*) do nothing/not do anything by halves ■ **wywiązywanie się** performance

wy-wierać/wrzeć 1 (*wpływ itp.*) exert; ~ **wpływ na kogoś** sway; ~ **negatywny wpływ na kimś** get to sb; ~ **wrażenie** impress sb (with sth); ~ **pewien efekt** do[1]; ~ **presję na kimś** put pressure on sb, pressurize sb (into sth/doing sth) **2** (*zemstę itp. na kimś*) wreak sth (on sb/sth)

wywiercić → WIERCIĆ

wywie-szać/sić hang[1]; (*na tablicy ogłoszeń itp.*) stick sth on sth; (*plakaty itp.*) display[1]; (*wyniki egzaminów itp.*) post[2]

wywieszka notice[1]

wywieść → WYWODZIĆ

wywietrznik ventilator

wywietrzyć (się) → WIETRZYĆ (SIĘ)

wywieźć → WYWOZIĆ

wywi-jać/nąć lash[1] □ **wywi-jać/nąć się**: **z czegoś** wriggle out of sth/doing sth; (**wywinąć się**) get off (with sth)

wywikłać extricate

wywle-kać/c: ~ **brudy na temat kogoś/czegoś** dig up dirt on sb/sth

wywła-szczać/szczyć expropriate; **kogoś (z czegoś)** dispossess sb (of sth)

wywnioskować → WNIOSKOWAĆ

wy-wodzić/wieść IDM ~ **trele** warble | ~ **kogoś w pole** outwit □ **wywodzić się** derive, stem from sth

wywoł(yw)ać 1 (*ogłaszać, np. zwycięzców*) call sth out **2** (*powodować*) bring sth about, conjure sth up, induce, instigate, make[1], produce[1], provoke, give rise to sth, set sth off, spark sth off; (*zainteresowanie itp.*) evoke; (*brak zaufania itp.*) breed[1]; (*burzę emocji itp.*) unleash sth (on/upon sb/sth); **wywołać pożar** start a fire; **wywołać szok** deal sb/sth a blow, deal a blow to sb/sth; **wywołać podwyżkę cen** send prices up; **ta wiadomość wywołała wśród nas zamieszanie** we were thrown into confusion by the news **3** (*fot.*) develop, process[2]

wy-wozić/wieźć: **błyskawicznie wywieźć kogoś** whisk sb away; ~ **kogoś/coś po kryjomu** spirit sb/sth away/off ■ **wywożenie**: ~ **śmieci** refuse collection, rubbish collections

wy-wracać/wrócić subvert, tip sth up/over, upset[1]; (*łódź*) capsize ■ **wywrócony** upturned □ **wy-wracać/wrócić się** tip up/over; (*łódź*) capsize

wywrotka dumper truck

wywrotowiec subversive noun

wywrotowy subversive

wywróżyć → WRÓŻYĆ

wyzby(wa)ć się discard

wyzdrowieć → ZDROWIEĆ

wyzdrowienie recovery

wy-zierać/jrzeć: **(skądś/zza czegoś)** peep[1]

wyziewy fumes

wyziębienie exposure

wyzna-czać/czyć 1 (*zadanie, cel itp.*) set[1]; (*dzień, cenę*) appoint sth (for sth), make[1], name[2], set[1]; (*zadanie, fundusze itp.*) assign sth to sb/sth, earmark sth (for sth); (*granicę*) demarcate **2** (*kogoś na stanowisko*) assign sb to sth, designate sb (as) sth, earmark sb (for sth/sb), nominate sb (for/as sth) **3** (*oznacznać*) denote

wyznacznik gauge[1] (of sth), measure[2]

wyznanie (*zwł. religijne*) confession, denomination, creed, religion, persuasion

wyzna(wa)ć (*winę*) confess, own up (to sth)

wyznaw-ca/czyni follower

wyzwać → WYZYWAĆ

wy-zwalać/zwolić emancipate, liberate IDM ~ **najlepsze/najgorsze w kimś** bring out the best/worst in sb □ **wy-zwalać/zwolić się** break away (from sb/sth)

wyzwanie challenge[1], dare[2]; **rzucać** ~ challenge[2] sb (to sth/to do sth)

wyzwisk|o: **obrzucać kogoś ~ami** call sb names

wyzwolenie emancipation, liberation

wyzwoliciel/ka liberator

wyzwolić (się) → WYZWALAĆ (SIĘ)

wyzysk exploitation

wyzysk(iw)ać exploit[1]

wyz(y)wać 1 (do zrobienia czegoś) challenge[2], dare[1], defy sb to do sth **2** (*ubliżać*) call sb names ■ **wyzywający 1** (*buntowniczy*) defiant, provocative **2** (*wygląd; zachowanie*) brassy, flamboyant

wyż high[2]; ~ **demograficzny** baby boom, the population explosion

wyżąć → WYŻYMAĆ

wyżebrać → ŻEBRAĆ

wy-żerać/żreć eat sth away/eat away at sth, erode

wyżerka blowout, a slap-up meal

wy-żłabiać/żłobić gouge sth out, hollow sth out ■ **wyżłobienie** groove

wyższoś|ć predominance, superiority; **poczucie ~ci** self-righteousness

wyższ|y → WYSOKI

wy-żymać/żąć wring sth (out)

wyżyn|a 1 (*geogr.*) upland noun; (**wyżyny**) downs **2 ~y swojej kariery** the high point of his career
■ **wyżynny** upland
wyży(wa)ć się let off steam
wyżywieni|e 1 (*dieta*) diet[1] **2** (*posiłki na wczasach itp.*) board[1]; **z częściowym ~em** half board; **z pełnym ~em** full board; **bez ~a** self-catering
wzajemn|y mutual, reciprocal; **~e ustępstwa** give and take
■ **wzajemnie 1** (*nawzajem*) mutually **2 znosić się ~** cancel out
wzbierać/wezbrać 1 (*wzrastać*) surge; (*uczucie*) swell[1] **2** (*rzeka*) swell[1] (up)
wzbi(ja)ć się soar
wzboga-cać/cić 1 enrich **2** (*przen.*) enhance, enrich
wz-braniać/bronić prohibit
■ **wzbronion|y**: (*w zakazach*) **~e** no[2]
□ **wz-braniać/bronić się**: **przed czymś** shrink from sth/doing sth
wzbu-dzać/dzić arouse, awake[2], awaken, excite, inspire, stir sth up; (*nadzieję itp.*) raise[1]; (*silne emocje w kimś*) fire[2] sb with sth; (*szacunek*) command[2]; (*zainteresowanie*) stimulate
wzbu-rzać/rzyć 1 kogoś fluster; (*gniewać*) infuriate **2 coś** churn sth (up)
■ **wzburzenie** ferment[2] | **wzburzony** (*morze*) rough[1], stormy; **lekko ~** choppy; **na ~m morzu** in heavy seas
□ **wzbu-rzać/rzyć się 1** (*uczucia, nastroje itp.*) run high **2** (*woda itp.*) churn sth (up)
wzdęcie wind[1]
wzdłuż 1 (*znajdować się*) alongside; (*ulicy itp.*) along, down[1] **2** (*ciąć*) lengthways IDM **~ i wszerz** the length and breadth of sth
wzdragać się shrink from sth/doing sth
wzdryg-ać/nąć się flinch, shudder, start[1]
wzdychać/westchnąć 1 (*oddychać*) sigh, give a sigh; **~ głęboko** heave a sigh **2 (za kimś/czymś)** pine[2], yearn
wzejść → WSCHODZIĆ
wzgardliwy contemptuous
wzgar-dzać/dzić zob. też GARDZIĆ; scorn[2], spurn
wzgl|ąd 1 (*szacunek*) respect[1]; (*na czyjeś uczucia itp.*) consideration (for sb/sth) **2** (*powód*) consideration, regard[2] to/for sb/sth; **bez ~ędu (na kogoś/coś)** however, irrespective of, no matter who, what, where, etc., regardless prep. of sb/sth; **bez ~ędu na to, co** whatever; **mieć ~ąd na coś** consider; **mający kogoś/coś na ~ędzie** mindful of sb/sth; **pod pewnym ~ędem** in a/one/any way, in some ways; **pod (tym) ~ędem** in/with regard to sb/sth, in this/that/one regard, on that score; **pod każdym ~ędem** on all counts; **pod ~ędem wielkości** in terms of size; **przez ~ąd na kogoś/coś** for the sake of sb/sth, for sb's/sth's sake; **ze ~ędu na kogoś/coś** in view of sth, with; **ze ~ędu na mnie** for my sake; **ze ~ędu** (*np. na bezpieczeństwo*) in the interest(s) of sth
względnoś|ć relativity; **teoria ~ci** relativity
względny comparative[1], relative[1]
wzgórze hill, hilltop
wziąć (się) → BRAĆ (SIĘ)
wzięcie (*powodzenie*) vogue
wzięty in demand, sought after; **~ aktor** a successful actor
wzlot IDM **~y i upadki** the ebb and flow (of sth), ups and downs; (*kariery*) the highs and lows of her career
wzmacniacz amplifier, booster
wz-macniać/mocnić bolster sb/sth (up), build sth up, buttress[2], reinforce, strengthen; (*dźwięk*) amplify, raise[1] sth (to sth); (*mięsień*) tone[2] sth (up); (*kogoś*) toughen sb (up); (*intensyfikować itp.*) consolidate, intensify; (*dodawać energii*) energize, invigorate
■ **wzmacniający** invigorating, refreshing
□ **wz-macniać/mocnić się** strengthen; (*narastać: dźwięk, uczucie itp.*) swell[1]; (*wracać do zdrowia*) rally[2]; (*poprzez ciężkie warunki*) toughen (up); (*zintensyfikować się*) consolidate, intensify
wz-magać/móc escalate sth (into sth), heighten, intensify
□ **wz-magać/móc się**: **do czegoś** build up (to sth), escalate (into sth); (*uczucie*) heighten, intensify, swell[1]
wzmianka mention noun, reference
wzmiankować mention, touch on/upon sth
wzmocnić (się) → WZMACNIAĆ (SIĘ)
wzmocnienie boost[2], consolidation, reinforcement; (*dźwięku*) amplification
wzmożony intensive; **~ akcent** emphasis (on sth)
wzmóc (się) → WZMAGAĆ (SIĘ)
wz-nawiać/nowić (*kontrakt itp.*) renew; (*pracę itp.*) resume; (*wskrzesić*) resurrect, revive
wznie-cać/cić give rise to sth; (*uczucia*) excite, fire[2] sb with sth, stir sth up
wzniesienie 1 (*terenu*) ascent, elevation, slope **2** (*na stanowisko prezydenta itp.*) elevation
wzniosły high[1], lofty, noble[1], sublime
■ **wzniosłość** elevation, loftiness
wz-nosić/nieść zob. też NIEŚĆ **1** (*budować*) erect[2] **2 ~ toast (za kogoś/coś)** drink to sb/sth, toast verb
□ **wz-nosić/nieść się** ascend, rise[2]; (*samolot itp.*) spiral verb
wznowić → WZNAWIAĆ
wznowienie renewal, resumption, revival
wzorcowy standard[2]
wzorować: **coś/kogoś na kimś/czymś** model sth/yourself on sb/sth
□ **wzorować się** imitate
wzorowy exemplary
wzorzec model[1]
wzorzysty patterned
wzór 1 (*przykład, wzorzec itp.*) benchmark, design[1], example (to sb), ideal[2] (of sth), model[1], sample; **być typowym wzorem** typify **2** (*deseń*) design[1], motif, pattern **3** (*chem.*) formula
wz-rastać/rosnąć build up (to sth), escalate (into sth), go up, grow (in sth), increase[1], be on the increase; **nagle wzrosnąć** surge verb; **~ gwałtownie** rocket[2]
■ **wzrastając|y** rising[1]; (*stopniowo*) progressive; (*popyt, podaż itp.*) buoyant
wzrok eye[1], eyesight, sight[1], vision; **nieruchomy ~** gaze noun; **badanie ~u** eye test; **utrata ~u** blindness; **przyciągający ~** eye-catching; **popatrzeć na kogoś obojętnym ~iem** give sb a blank stare
wzrokowy optic, optical, visual; **nawiązać z kimś kontakt ~** make eye contact with sb
wzrosnąć → ROSNĄĆ, WZRASTAĆ
wzrost 1 (*rośliny, osoby itp.*) growth **2** (*wysokość osoby*) height, stature; **ma pięć stóp ~u** she's five feet tall; **jakiego jesteś ~u?** how tall are you? **3** (*cen itp.*) gain[2], increase[2], leap[2], rise[1]; (*kapitału*) accrual; (*wzmocnienie*) boost[2], escalation; **gwałtowny ~** explosion; **nagły ~** surge, upsurge; **~ wartości** appreciation
wzru-szać/szyć 1 move[1], touch[1], thrill verb; **wzruszyć kogoś do łez** make sb cry **2** (*ramionami*) shrug
■ **wzruszając|y** emotive, moving, full of pathos, poignant, stirring adj., touching
□ **wzru-szać/szyć się** be overcome (with sth); **bardzo się wzruszać** get very emotional
wzwyż up
w-zywać/ezwać call[1], call for sth, send for sb/sth, summon; (*fachowca itp.*) call sb out, get sb in; **kogoś do zrobienia czegoś** appeal[2] to sb (for sth)

X

x (X/x) (*litera*) X, x

Y

y (Y/y) (*litera*) Y, y
yuppie yuppie

Z

z[1] (Z/z) (*litera*) Z, z
z[2] 1 (*z miejsca/czasu*) from; (*wysiąść z autobusu itp.*) off[1] **2** (*spośród*) out of; **~ (większej liczby)** of; **jeden ~ moich przyjaciół** a friend of mine **3** (*zakresu, tematu*) on **4** (*razem z; posiadający coś*) with; **(razem) ~ (kimś)** (*iść*) along; (*pracować itp.*) alongside **5** (*z powodu*) at, out of; (*przerażeniem, rozbawieniem itp.*) in[1] **6** (*przeciwko*) against, with **7** (*zrobiony itp.*) of, out of **8** (*prędkością*) at **9** (*fizyki itp.*) at
za[1] (*przyim.*) **1** (*miejsce*) behind[1,2], beyond; **~ rogiem** round the corner; **wejść ~ kimś** enter after sb **2** (*cel; z powodu*) for[1] **3** (*w przyszłości*) in[1]; **~ trzy tygodnie** three weeks away **4** (*godzina*) to **5** (*podczas*) during, in[1] **6** (*rękę itp.*) by **7** (*funkcja*) as **8** (*na dzień itp.*) a, the **9** (*wznosząc toast*) here's to sb/sth **10** (*głosować itp.*) for[1], in favour of sb/sth **11** (*wymiana*) for[1] **12** (*pomocą czegoś*) with IDM **nie ma ~ co** not at all | **~ i przeciw** the pros and cons
za[2] (*przysł.*) too
zaabsorbować → ABSORBOWAĆ
zaabsorbowanie preoccupation (with sth)
zaabsorbowany absorbed, engrossed, preoccupied, rapt
zaadaptować → ADAPTOWAĆ
zaadiustować → ADIUSTOWAĆ

zaadoptować → ADOPTOWAĆ

zaadresować → ADRESOWAĆ

zaagitować → AGITOWAĆ

zaakcentować → AKCENTOWAĆ

zaakceptować → AKCEPTOWAĆ

zaakceptowan|y accepted; **zostać ~ym** gain/achieve acceptability

zaaklimatyzować (się) → AKLIMATYZOWAĆ (SIĘ)

zaaklimatyzowany acclimatized

zaalarmować → ALARMOWAĆ

zaanektować → ANEKTOWAĆ

zaangażować (się) → ANGAŻOWAĆ (SIĘ)

zaangażowanie commitment, dedication, involvement

zaangażowany committed, dedicated, involved (in sth); (*uczuciowo itp.*) involved (with sb); **~ politycznie** political

zaapelować → APELOWAĆ

zaaprobować → APROBOWAĆ

zaaranżować → ARANŻOWAĆ

zaaresztować → ARESZTOWAĆ

zaargumentować → ARGUMENTOWAĆ

zaasekurować się → ASEKUROWAĆ SIĘ

zaatakować → ATAKOWAĆ

zaawansowany advanced

zabalsamować → BALSAMOWAĆ

zabandażować → BANDAŻOWAĆ

zabarwić → BARWIĆ

zabarwienie 1 (*kolor*) tinge, tint **2** (*słowa*) connotation, undertone

zabarwiony tinged (with sth)

zabarykadować (się) → BARYKADOWAĆ (SIĘ)

zabaw|a 1 (*impreza*) party; (*taneczna*) dance[1] **2** (*gra*) game[1] **3** (*przyjemne spędzenie czasu*) amusement, fun[1], merriment, fling[2], play[2]; (*świąteczna itp.*) festivity; **dla ~y** (just) for fun/for the fun of it, for the heck of it, for a laugh; **robić sobie ~ę z czegoś** play at sth/being sth

zabawi(a)ć zob. też BAWIĆ (SIĘ); amuse, entertain

□ **zabawi(a)ć się**: **(z kimś)** play about/around (with sb)

zabawka plaything, toy[1]

zabawn|y 1 (*śmieszny*) amusing, comic[1], comical, funny, humorous; **bardzo ~y** hysterical; **~a osoba/rzecz** laugh[2] **2** (*rozrywkowy*) entertaining, fun[2], light-hearted

zabeczeć → BECZEĆ

zabetonować → BETONOWAĆ

zabezpie-czać/czyć 1 kogoś/coś (przed kimś/czymś) guard[2], guard against sth, protect, safeguard, secure[2] sth (against/from sth); (*przed stratą finansową*) indemnify sb (against sth); (*upewniać się*) ensure; (*pokój itp.*) preserve; **zabezpieczyć kogoś finansowo** make provision for sb **2** (*środkiem chemicznym*) treat[1] sth (with sth)

■ **zabezpieczanie** prevention | **zabezpieczeni|e** protection (against/from sth), safeguard, safety net, security; (*przed stratą finansową itp.*) indemnification, insurance (against sth); **brak zabiezpieczenia** vulnerability; **zabezpieczenie spłaty długu** collateral

□ **zabezpie-czać/czyć się** provide for sth

zabezpieczony -proof, safe[1], secure[1]

zabębnić → BĘBNIĆ

zabici|e kill[2] IDM **robić coś dla ~a czasu** kill time

zabieg 1 ~ chirurgiczny surgery **2** (**zabiegi**) endeavour

zabiegać: **o coś** solicit; (*usilnie*) push for sth; (*o czyjeś względy*) court[2]; (*o głosy wyborców*) canvass (sb) (for sth)

■ **zabieganie** (*o czyjeś względy*) overture

za-bierać/brać 1 (*przynieść, przyprowadzić*) **ze sobą** bring; **coś (komuś)** take, take sth away (from sb); (*na przyjęcie itp.*) take sb out; (*autobus itp.*) take sth/sb on; (*samochodem itp.*) pick sb up; **~ kogoś/coś pośpiesznie dokądś** rush[1]; **~ kogoś/coś po kryjomu** spirit sb/sth away/off **2** (*bez pozwolenia*) go off with sth, take **3** (*czas*) take (*czyjś czas, energię itp.*) encroach (on/upon sth)

□ **za-bierać/brać się**: **do robienia czegoś** (*zaczynać*) get down to sth/doing sth, get round/around to sth/doing sth, be on the point of doing sth, set about sth, take sth up; (*do czegoś nowego*) launch out; (*do czegoś trudnego*) go about sth/doing sth; (*z entuzjazmem*) launch into sth, launch yourself into sth; (*energicznie*) throw yourself/sth into sth; (*poważnie*) knuckle down (to sth); **~ do pracy/roboty** get down to business, get busy, get/go/set to work (on sth); **muszę się zabrać do roboty** I'd better get cracking; **ostro zabrałem się do pracy w ogrodzie** I had a blitz on the garden

zabi(ja)ć 1 (*uśmiercać*) destroy, finish sb/sth off, kill[1], liquidate, slay **2** (*coś deskami*) board sth up IDM **~ czas** pass[1], while sth away

zablokować (się) → BLOKOWAĆ (SIĘ)

zablokowany bunged up

zabłąkać się → BŁĄKAĆ SIĘ

zabłąkany stray adj.

zabłocony muddy

zabłysnąć → BŁYSKAĆ, BŁYSZCZEĆ, ZABŁYSNĄĆ

zabłyszczeć → BŁYSZCZEĆ

zaboleć → BOLEĆ

zaborczy possessive (of/about sb/sth)

zabój-ca/czyni killer

zabójczy homicidal

zabójstwo homicide, killing

zabór annexation, partition

zabrać (się) → ZABIERAĆ (SIĘ)

zabraknąć → BRAKOWAĆ

za-braniać/bronić bar[2], forbid, prohibit

□ **za-braniać/bronić się**: **zabrania się wprowadzania psów** no dogs allowed; **zabrania się wstępu na ten teren wszystkim pracownikom** this area is out of bounds to all staff

zabrnąć → BRNĄĆ

zabroniony out of bounds

zabrudzić → BRUDZIĆ

zabrzęczeć → BRZĘCZEĆ

zabrzmieć → BRZMIEĆ

zabuczeć → BUCZEĆ

zabudować zob. też BUDOWAĆ; build sth in/on, build sth into/onto sth

■ **zabudowywanie**: **~ terenu** development

zabudowany 1 (*szafka itp.*) fitted **2** (*obszar*) built-up

zabulgotać → BULGOTAĆ

zabulić → BULIĆ

zaburczeć → BURCZEĆ

zabu-rzać/rzyć 1 (*porządek*) disturb **2** (*czyjąś ocenę/pamięć itp.*) cloud[2]

■ **zaburzeni|e** disorder; **~e emocjonalne** emotional disturbance; **z zaburzeniami (psychicznymi)** disturbed

zabutelkować → BUTELKOWAĆ

zabytek relic

zabytkowy antique

zacementować → CEMENTOWAĆ

zacerować → CEROWAĆ

zacharcheć → CHARCZEĆ

zachciank|a whim; **mieć ~i na coś** have cravings for sth; **spełniać czyjeś ~i** humour[2]

zachę-cać/cić cheer sb on, encourage, invite, promote, urge sb on

■ **zachęcający** encouraging; (*wygląd*) **być zachęcającym** look good

zachęta encouragement, incentive, inducement, prompting, spur[1]; (*nieform.*) carrot

zachichotać → CHICHOTAĆ

zachlupotać → CHLUPOTAĆ

zachłanny grasping, greedy (for sth)

■ **zachłannie** greedily, voraciously | **zachłanność** greed, greediness

zachmurzony cloudy, overcast

zachmurzyć się cloud over

zachodni west[2], westerly, western[1], westward

za-chodzić/jść 1 (*słońce*) go down, set[1]; **~ za chmurę** go in **2 do kogoś** (*odwiedzać*) come round (to…), go round (to…) **3** (*jedno na drugie*) overlap **4 w ubiegłym roku zaszły olbrzymie zmiany** last year saw huge changes in the education system

IDM **zajść w ciążę** conceive, get pregnant | (*przen.*) **zajść daleko** go far

■ **zachodzący (między czymś)** intervening

zachorować zob. też CHOROWAĆ; **(na coś)** develop, come down with sth, go down with sth, be taken ill

zachowani|e behaviour, conduct[2]; **złe ~e** misbehaviour; **sposób ~a** manner; **dla ~a twarzy** face-saving

□ **zachowanie się** conduct[2], demeanour; **odpowiednie ~e się przy stole** table manners

zachow(yw)ać zob. też CHOWAĆ **1** (*utrzymywać*) keep[1], maintain; (*dietę itp.*) observe; **~ w pamięci/sercu** treasure[2]; **~ świeżość** keep[1] **2** (*bilet itp.*) retain, save[1]; **coś dla siebie** hold sth back, keep sth to yourself; **zachować resztę** keep the change **3** (*tradycje*) preserve

IDM **~ powagę** keep a straight face | **~ spokój** keep/lose your temper | **zachować twarz** save face

□ **zachow(yw)ać się** act[2], behave, conduct[1] yourself well, badly, etc.; **źle się ~** misbehave; **~ się naturalnie** be yourself; **nie potrafiać się zachować** have no manners

zach|ód 1 (*geogr.*) west[1]; **na ~ód** westwards; **na ~ód/~odzie** west adv.; **z ~odu** west[2], westerly **2** (**Zachód**) (*Zachodnia Europa i Stany*) the West[1] **3** (*słońca*) sunset; **przed ~odem/po ~odzie słońca** before/after dark

zachrapać → CHRAPAĆ

zachrobotać → CHROBOTAĆ

zachrypieć → CHRYPIEĆ

zachrypnąć → CHRYPNĄĆ

zachrzęścić → CHRZĘŚCIĆ

zachwalać praise sb/sth (for sth)

zachwiać (się) → CHWIAĆ (SIĘ)

zachwy-cać/cić charm[2], delight[2], enchant, enrapture, fascinate, thrill verb; **coś, co zachwyca** delight[1] □ **zachwy-cać/cić się** enthuse (about/over sth/sb), go into raptures (about/over sb/sth), rave[1] (about sb/sth), swoon (over sb)

zachwycający delightful, enchanting, fascinating, ravishing

zachwycony delighted, enchanted, thrilled

zachwyt delight[1], ecstasy, fascination, rapture; **pełen ~u** ecstatic; **wpadać w ~** go into raptures (about/over sb/sth)

zachybotać (się) → CHYBOTAĆ (SIĘ)

zaciąć (się) → ZACINAĆ (SIĘ)

zaciąg-ać/nąć 1 (*dług*) incur; (*znaczne długi*) run sth up **2** (*przy wymawianiu*) drawl □ **zaciąg-ać/nąć się**: **mocno zaciągnąć się papierosem** take a long drag/pull on a cigarette

zaciążyć → CIĄŻYĆ

zaciekawić → CIEKAWIĆ

zaciekawienie curiosity

zaciekawiony curious, interested

zaciekły furious, rabid; **~ sprzeciw wobec planu** stiff opposition to the plan

zaciemni(a)ć 1 (*pomieszczenie*) darken **2** (*sens*) obscure[2] ■ **zaciemnienie** (*podczas wojny*) blackout

zacieniony shady

zacieniować → CIENIOWAĆ

za-cierać/trzeć 1 ~ ręce rub your hands together **2** (*ślady itp.*) obliterate

zacieśni(a)ć tighten sth (up)

zacięci|e: **z ~em** competitively, gritty

zacięty competitive

za-cinać/ciąć lash[1]; (*zwł. konia*) whip[2] □ **zacinać się 1 (/zaciąć się)** (*urządzenie*) jam[2] (up), stick[1], be/get stuck[2]; (*silnik itp.*) pack up, seize up **2** (*jąkać się*) stammer

zacisk 1 (*narzędzie*) vice **2** (*zatrzask*) catch[2]

zacis-kać/nąć clamp[1], tighten sth (up); (*zęby, pięści*) clench; (*i przen.*) **~ zęby** grit your teeth; **~ usta** purse your lips IDM (*przen.*) **zacisnąć pasa** tighten your belt

zacisze seclusion; (*schronienie*) retreat[2]

zaciszny secluded

zaciśnięty: **mocno ~ węzeł** a tight knot

zacny respectable, virtuous, worthy

zacofany backward, behind the times

zacumować → CUMOWAĆ

zacytować → CYTOWAĆ

zaczaić się → CZAIĆ SIĘ

zaczarować charm[2] ■ **zaczarowany** enchanted; (*magiczny*) magic[2], magical

zacząć (się) → ZACZYNAĆ (SIĘ)

zaczątek nucleus

zaczekać → CZEKAĆ

zaczepi(a)ć 1 coś catch[1], hook[2] **2 kogoś** accost ■ **zaczepieni|e**: **punkt zaczepienia** foothold □ **zaczepi(a)ć się** hook[2]

zaczepny offensive[1]

zaczernić → CZERNIĆ

zaczerpnąć → CZERPAĆ

zaczerwienić (się) → CZERWIENIĆ (SIĘ)

zaczerwienienie soreness

zaczerwieniony red

za-czynać/cząć begin, start[1]; **coś robić** get into sth, go ahead (with sth), start on sth, take to sth/doing sth; **od czegoś** make a start on sth, start off; (*w dyskusji itp.*) set/start the ball rolling; **zacząć od nowa** make a fresh start, start over IDM **na twoim miejscu nie zaczynałbym z nim!** I wouldn't mess with him if I were you! □ **za-czynać /cząć się** begin, start[1]

zaćma cataract

zaćmieni|e 1 (*astr.*) eclipse[1] **2 ~e umysłu** brainstorm[1]; **doznać ~a pamięci/umysłu** have a block (about sth); **poczułem ~e umysłu** my mind went blank

zaćmi(ewa)ć 1 (*astr.*) eclipse[2] **2** (*przen.*) eclipse[2], overshadow

zaćwierkać → ĆWIERKAĆ

zad (*koński itp.*) rump; (*ludzki*) haunches

zadać → ZADAWAĆ

za-damawiać/domowić się (*ptak*) **~ na czyimś dachu** roost in sb's roof

zadanie assignment, job, project[1], task, work[2]; (*szkolne*) exercise[1]; (*arytmetyczne*) sum; (*algebraiczne itp.*) problem; (*zarządu itp.*) function[1]; (*urzędowe*) brief[2]; (*wymagające wysiłku*) challenge[1]; **skomplikowane ~** conundrum; **~ domowe** homework; **~ specjalne** mission

zadart|y snub[2], upturned; **z ~ym nosem** snub-nosed

zadaszenie canopy

zadaszony covered

zadat|ek (*pieniądze*) deposit[1] IDM **mieć ~ki na coś** have the makings of sth, make[1]

zada(wa)ć 1 (*pracę*) assign, set[1] **2** (*pytanie*) put sth to sb **3** (*ból*) inflict; **~ rany** wound[2]; **~ komuś/czemuś cios** deal sb/sth a blow, deal a blow to sb/sth IDM **~ kłam** belie | **~ sobie trud, żeby** be at/take (great) pains to do sth, take (great) pains (with/over sth), take the trouble to do sth □ **zadawać się**: **z kimś** go round/around/about with sb

zadbać → DBAĆ

zadebiutować → DEBIUTOWAĆ

zadecydować → DECYDOWAĆ

zadedykować → DEDYKOWAĆ

zadeklamować → DEKLAMOWAĆ

zadeklarować (się) → DEKLAROWAĆ(SIĘ)

zadekretować decree verb

zademonstrować → DEMONSTROWAĆ

zadenuncjować → DENUNCJOWAĆ

zadeptać tread[1] sth (in/into/down)

zadęcie blast[1]

zadławić (się) → DŁAWIĆ (SIĘ)

zadłużenie debt

zadłużon|y: **(nie) być ~ym** be in/out of debt

zadokować → DOKOWAĆ

zadomowić się → ZADAMAWIAĆ SIĘ

zadośćuczynić: **czemuś** meet ■ **zadośćuczynienie** retribution (for sth); (*zwł. finansowe*) compensation; **jako zadośćuczynienie** in return (for sth)

zado-walać/wolić gratify, please[2], satisfy; (*gusta*) cater for sb/sth, to sth ■ **zadowalając|y** fine[1], gratifying, passable, pleasing, satisfactory, satisfying, well[2]; **być na zadowalającym poziomie** be of a reasonable standard | **zadowolony** content[2], contented, fine[1], glad, happy, pleased, satisfied; (*z powodu spełnienia marzeń itp.*) fulfilled; (*z siebie lub sytuacji*) complacent, smug □ **za-dowalać/dowolić się**: **czymś** content[3] yourself with sth, make do with sth, settle for sth

zadowoleni|e contentment, enjoyment, pleasure, satisfaction; **~e z siebie** complacency; **z ~em** contentedly; **z (bezpodstawnym) ~em** complacently; **z ~em dowiedziałem się, że...** I was gratified to hear that...

zadrapać graze[1], scrape[1], scratch[1]

zadrasnąć graze[1]

zadręczyć (się) → DRĘCZYĆ (SIĘ)

zadrgać → DRGAĆ

zadrutować → DRUTOWAĆ

zadrwić → DRWIĆ

zadrżeć → DRŻEĆ

zadudnić → DUDNIĆ

zadufany: **w sobie** full[1] of yourself, opinionated, self-important; (*we własne siły*) complacent ■ **zadufanie** complacency

zadumany thoughtful

zadurzony infatuated ■ **zadurzenie** infatuation

Zaduszki All Souls' Day

zadygotać → DYGOTAĆ

zadymić → DYMIĆ

zadymiony smoky

zadyndać → DYNDAĆ

zadyszany breathless, out of/short of breath

zadyszk|a pant noun; **mieć ~ę** be out of breath; **dostać ~i** get out of breath; **z ~ą** breathlessly

zadziałać zob. też DZIAŁAĆ; take effect; (*pomysł przedsięwzięciu itp.*) do the job/trick

zadziorny feisty

zadziwi(a)ć zob. też DZIWIĆ; astonish, bowl sb over ■ **zadziwiając|y** astonishing, extraordinary, mind-blowing, surprising; **~e, że** it's a wonder (that)...

zadzwonić → DZWONIĆ

zadźwięczeć → DŹWIĘCZEĆ

zafalować → FALOWAĆ

zafałszować → FAŁSZOWAĆ

zafarbować → FARBOWAĆ

zafascynować → FASCYNOWAĆ

zafundować → FUNDOWAĆ

zafunkcjonować → FUNKCJONOWAĆ

zafurkotać → FURKOTAĆ

zagadać → ZAGADYWAĆ

zagadka conundrum, enigma, problem, puzzle[1], riddle

zagadkow|y cryptic, enigmatic, mysterious; (*podobieństwo itp.*) uncanny; (*postać*) shadowy; **~a osoba/sprawa** riddle

zagadnienie issue[1]

zagad(yw)ać blag; **podrywać kogoś przez zagadywanie** chat sb up

zagajnik copse, grove, shrubbery

za-ganiać/gonić drive[1]

zagapić się → GAPIĆ SIĆ

zagar-niać/nąć scoop[2] sb/sth (up)

zagasić → GASIĆ

zagaworzyć → GAWORZYĆ

zagazo(wy)wać gas[2]

zagdakać → GDAKAĆ

zagestykulować → GESTYKULOWAĆ
zagęszczacz thickener
zagę-szczać/ścić (się) condense, thicken
■ **zagęszczenie**: **duże zagęszczenie** (*np. ludności*) a high density of sth
zagięcie 1 (*materiału, kartki*) fold[2]; (*zwł. na materiale*) crease[1] **2** (*druta*) kink
zagięty crooked
za-ginać/giąć: **kogoś** catch sb out
zaginięcie disappearance
zaginiony lost[2], missing
zagipsować → GIPSOWAĆ
za-glądać/jrzeć 1 (*patrzeć (potajemnie)*) peek, peep[1] **2 do kogoś** call[1] (in/round) (on sb/at…), call by **2** (*do książki itp.*) consult sth (about sth), dip into sth, refer to sth
zagłada extermination; (*zwł. podczas drugiej wojny światowej*) holocaust
zagłębi(a)ć się delve into sth, enter into sth, immerse yourself (in sth), pore over sth
zagłębie field[1]
zagłębienie (*terenu*) dip[2], hollow[2], trough
zagłodzić się → GŁODZIĆ SIĘ
zagłosować → GŁOSOWAĆ
zagłówek headrest
zagłu-szać/szyć deafen, drown sb/sth (out); (*fale radiowe itp.*) jam[2]
zagmatwać → GMATWAĆ
zagmatwani|e: **w stanie ~a** confusedly
zagmatwany convoluted, tangled
zagnieść → GNIEŚĆ
zagniewać (się) → GNIEWAĆ (SIĘ)
zagnieździć się → GNIEŹDZIĆ SIĘ
zagoić się → GOIĆ SIĘ
zagon patch[1]
zagonić → ZAGANIAĆ
zagorzalec fanatic
zagorzał|y fanatical, fervent, fervid, staunch, zealous; **być ~-ym/ą zwolenni-kiem/czką kogoś/czegoś** swear by sb/sth
zagospodarow(yw)ać zob. też GOSPODAROWAĆ; (*teren*) develop
zagościć: **na jej widok uśmiech zagościł na jego twarzy** the sight of her brought a smile to his face
zagotować (się) zob. też GOTOWAĆ (SIĘ); come to the boil
zagórować → GÓROWAĆ
zagrabić → GRABIĆ
zagrać → GRAĆ
za-gradzać/grodzić (*drogę*) bar[2], block sth off, obstruct
zagranic|a: **za granic-ę/ą** overseas adv.
zagraniczn|y alien[1], foreign, overseas; **minister spraw ~ych** the Foreign Secretary
za-grażać/grozić zob. też GROZIĆ; endanger, threaten; **~ czyjemuś życiu** put sb's life in peril; **~ życiu** life-threatening
■ **zagrażający** impending, menacing
zagroda 1 (*dla bydła*) enclosure, pen **2** (*gospodarstwo*) farmhouse
zagrodzić → ZAGRADZAĆ
zagrożenie danger, distress[1], menace, risk[1], threat; **wielkie ~** peril
zagrożon|y at stake, at risk; **~y wyginięciem** endangered
zagruchać → GRUCHAĆ
zagrywka service[1]
zagrzać (się) → GRZAĆ (SIĘ), ZAGRZEWAĆ
zagrzebać → GRZEBAĆ
zagrzechotać → GRZECHOTAĆ
zagrz(ew)ać: **kogoś (do czegoś)** spur[2] sb/sth (on/onto sth)
zagrzmieć → GRZMIEĆ
zagubion|y 1 lost[2]; **rzeczy ~e** lost property **2** (*przen.*) at sea
zagulgotać → GULGOTAĆ
zagwarantować → GWARANTOWAĆ
zagwizdać → GWIZDAĆ
zaha-czać/czyć catch[1], hook[2]
□ **zaha-czać/czyć się** hook[2]
zahamowa|nie inhibition; **bez ~ń** uninhibited
zahamow(yw)ać zob. też HAMOWAĆ; hold sb/sth back, pull up
zahandlować → HANDLOWAĆ
zahartować (się) → HARTOWAĆ (SIĘ)
zahipnotyzować → HIPNOTYZOWAĆ
zahuczeć → HUCZEĆ
zaimek pronoun; **~ osobowy** personal pronoun; **~ pytajny** interrogative[2]
zaimportować → IMPORTOWAĆ
zaimpregnować → IMPREGNOWAĆ
zaimprowizować → IMPROWIZOWAĆ
zaimprowizowany ad lib, impromptu
zainaugurować → INAUGUROWAĆ
zaindagować → INDAGOWAĆ
zainicjować → INICJOWAĆ
zainicjowanie initiation
zainkasować → INKASOWAĆ
zainscenizować → INSCENIZOWAĆ
zainspirować → INSPIROWAĆ
zainstalować → INSTALOWAĆ
zainsynuować → INSYNUOWAĆ
zainteresować (się) → INTERESOWAĆ (SIĘ)
zainteresowani|e interest[1]; **bez ~a** flatly, offhandedly; **wzbudzać czyjeś ~e** interest sb in sth
zainteresowan|y interested; **być ~ym (kimś/czymś)** be taken with sb/sth; **bardzo ~y kimś/czymś** keen on sb/sth; **nie ~y** uninterested (in sb/sth); **dla wszystkich ~ych** for/to all concerned
zainterweniować → INTERWENIOWAĆ
zaintrygować → INTRYGOWAĆ
zainwestować → INWESTOWAĆ
zaiskrzyć (się) → ISKRZYĆ (SIĘ), SKRZYĆ SIĘ
zaistnieć → ISTNIEĆ
zaizolowanie insulation
zajadać tuck in, tuck into sth
zajarzyć się → JARZYĆ SIĘ
zajaśnieć → JAŚNIEĆ
zajazd inn
zając hare
zająć (się) → ZAJMOWAĆ (SIĘ)
zająknąć się → JĄKAĆ SIĘ
zajezdnia depot, terminus
zajęci|e 1 (*praca*) engagement, job, occupation **2** (*zwł. rekreacyjne*) activity, pursuit; **~a na świeżym powietrzu** outdoor activities **3** (**zajęcia**) (*szkolne*) class[1], lesson
zajęcz|y: **~a warga** harelip
zajęczyca doe
zajęt|y 1 (*osoba*) busy[1], engaged (in/on sth), engrossed (in/with sth), occupied (at/with sth); **być (bardzo) ~ym** have your hands full, be tied up; **są bardzo zajęci** they lead a busy life **2** (*telefon*) busy[1], engaged
zajmować/zająć 1 (*czas; miejsce*) fill sth (up), occupy, take up sth; (*miejsce*) cover[1]; **~ czyjeś/czegoś miejsce** displace, take sb's/sth's place, take the place of sb/sth; **~ pozycję** rank[2] (as sth), position yourself **2** (*kraj itp.*) occupy **3** (*czyjąś uwagę*) engage **4 ~ stanowisko** (*w jakiejś sprawie*) commit yourself (on sth), stand[1] (on sth)
□ **zajmować/zająć się** busy[2] yourself with sth, yourself doing sth, concern[1] yourself with sth, engage in sth, go into sth, occupy yourself; (*zwł. problemem*) attend to sth, deal with sth, handle[1], see about sth/doing sth, see to sb/sth, take care of sth; (*czymś, co zwykle robimy*) go about sth; (*opiekować się*) attend to sb, have[1], take care of sb
zajmujący compelling, enthralling, interesting
zajrzeć → ZAGLĄDAĆ
zajście incident
zajść → ZACHODZIĆ
zakamarek nook, recess IDM (*przeczesać*) **każdy ~** every nook and cranny
zakamuflować → KAMUFLOWAĆ
za-kańczać/kończyć bring something to a conclusion/an end, complete[2], conclude, cut[1], round sth off (with sth)
zakaszleć → KASZLEĆ
zakatarzony runny-nosed
zakaz ban noun, prohibition; (*importu, wywozu*) embargo; (*w zakazach*) no[2]; **~ sądowy** injunction; **z ~em wstępu** off limits
zakaz(yw)ać ban, bar[2], forbid, outlaw[1], prohibit
■ **zakazany** illicit, taboo adj.
zakaźny contagious, infectious, septic
za-każać/kazić infect
■ **zakażenie** contagion, infection
zakątek corner[1]; **uroczy ~** beauty spot; **cichy ~** backwater
zakipieć → KIPIEĆ
zakisić → KISIĆ
zakląć → KLĄĆ
za-klejać/kleić seal[1] sth (up/down)
zaklekotać → KLEKOTAĆ
zaklep(yw)ać bag[2]
zaklęcie spell[2]
zaklinować → KLINOWAĆ
zaklinow(yw)ać się stuck[2]
zakład 1 (*przedsiębiorstwo: produkcyjny*) mill[1], plant[1], works[2]; (*produkcyjny; remontowy*) workshop; **~ fryzjerski** hairdresser's; **~ fryzjerski męski** barber's; **~ optyczny** optician's; **~ pogrzebowy** funeral parlour; **~ użyteczności publicznej** utility **2** (*karny, wychowawczy, zdrowotny itp.*) establishment, institution; **~ dla nieuleczalnie chorych** hospice; **~ dla psychicznie chorych** asylum, mental institution **3** (*naukowy*) institute[1] **4 o coś (, że)** bet[2], wager; **~y ligi piłkarskiej** football pools
za-kładać/łożyć 1 (*ubranie*) put sth on **2** (*rury itp.*) lay[1], put **3** (*instytucję, organizację*) establish, found[2], set sth up **4 założyć ręce** cross/fold your arms **5** (*przypuszczać*) assume, figure on sth/on doing sth, presume; **zakładam, że** I take it (that…); **~ z góry** take sth for granted; **~ z góry istnienie czegoś** presuppose
IDM **zakładać weto** veto

□ **za-kładać/łożyć się** bet[1], wager verb
zakładka (*i komput*) bookmark
zakładni-k/czka hostage
zakładowy institutional
zakłębić się → KŁĘBIĆ SIĘ
zakłopotać → KŁOPOTAĆ
zakłopotani|e (*zmieszanie*) bewilderment, confusion; (*zawstydzenie*) embarrassment, self-consciousness; **wprawiać w ~e** baffle, disconcert, embarrass, perplex, puzzle[2]; **z ~em** sheepishly, uneasily
zakłopotany baffled, bemused, confused, nonplussed, perplexed, puzzled, sheepish; (*zawstydzony*) embarrassed
zakłó-cać/cić (*spokój itp.*) disrupt, disturb, violate; (*spotkanie itp.*) hijack ■ **zakłóceni|e** disruption, disturbance; **~e porządku publicznego** disturbance; (*w radiu/TV*) **~a atmosferyczne** interference, static[2]
zakneblować → KNEBLOWAĆ
zakochanie (się) crush[2], infatuation
zakochany in love (with sb), infatuated (with sb/sth); **szalenie ~** madly in love (with sb); **~ do szaleństwa** crazy about sb/sth, nuts about sb/sth
zakoch(iw)ać się zob. też KOCHAĆ SIĘ; **w kimś** fall for sb, fall in love with sb
zakodować → KODOWAĆ
zakole: **tworzyć ~** loop verb
zakolebać się → KOLEBAĆ SIĘ
zakołatać → KOŁATAĆ
zakołować → KOŁOWAĆ
zakołysać (się) → KOŁYSAĆ (SIĘ)
zakomunikować → KOMUNIKOWAĆ
zakonnica nun
zakonserwować → KONSERWOWAĆ
zakończenie 1 (*czynności*) completion, conclusion, ending, termination; **na ~** in conclusion, to finish with,..., lastly; **na ~ chciałbym podziękować** may I conclude by... **2** (*palca itp.*) tip[1]; **szpiczaste ~** point[1]
zakończony complete[1], up
zakończyć (się) → KOŃCZYĆ (SIĘ), ZAKAŃCZAĆ
zakopcony smoky
zakop(yw)ać bury
zakorkowany gridlocked
zakorzeniony: **gdzieś** settled; (*nawyk itp.*) ingrained (in sb/sth); (*problem itp.*) **głęboko ~** deep-rooted
zakotłować się → KOTŁOWAĆ SIĘ
zakotwiczyć → KOTWICZYĆ
zakpić → KPIĆ
za-kradać/kraść się zob. też SKRADAĆ SIĘ; creep[1], sneak[1] into, etc. sth, in, etc.
zakraplacz dropper
zakres 1 (*wyboru itp.*) domain, extent, field[1], gamut, range[1], scope, sphere, territory; **~ obowiązków** job description **2 ~ fal radiowych** waveband IDM **w małym/dużym ~ie** in a big/small way
zakreślacz highlighter
zakreś-lać/lić zob. też KREŚLIĆ; check sth off; (*kółkiem*) circle[2], ring[2]
zakrę-cać/cić (się) zob. też KRĘCIĆ (SIĘ) **1** (*wieczko itp.*) screw[2] **2** (*rzeka itp.*) loop verb
zakręt bend[2], turn[2], turning, twist[2]; **wziąć ~** go round the corner
zakrętas squiggle
zakrętka top[1]
zakrwawiony bloodstained, bloody
zakry(wa)ć blot sth out, cover sth up
zakrzepica thrombosis; **~ żył głębokich** deep vein thrombosis
zakrzewić → KRZEWIĆ
zakrztusić się zob. też KRZTUSIĆ SIĘ; (*silnik*) falter
zakrzyczeć shout sb down
zakrzywiony curved, hooked
zaktualizować → AKTUALIZOWAĆ
zakulisowy inside adj.
zakup buy[2], purchase; **dokonywać ~u** purchase verb; **robić ~y** shop[2] (for sth)
zakupoholi-k/czka shopaholic
zakupy shopping; **chodzić na ~** go shopping
zakup-ywać/ić purchase verb
zakurzony dusty
zakutać wrap sth round/around sb/sth
zakwakać → KWAKAĆ
zakwalifikować (się) → KWALIFIKOWAĆ (SIĘ)
zakwaterow(yw)ać zob. też KWATEROWAĆ; accommodate, billet verb, house[2]
■ **zakwaterowanie** accommodation, lodging
zakwestionować → KWESTIONOWAĆ
zakwiczeć → KWICZEĆ
zakwilić → KWILIĆ
zalać → ZALEWAĆ
zalakować → LAKOWAĆ
zalan|y 1 ~y wodą awash (with sth); **~ych zostało kilka pól** several fields were under water **2** (*światłem*) bathed in sth; **~y słońcem** sunlit **3** (*pijany*) plastered, sloshed; **~y w trupa** comatose; **~y w pestkę** stoned
zalążek (*przen.*) seed
zale-cać/cić advocate[1], direct[2], preach, recommend, urge[1]
■ **zalecenie** guideline, recommendation; **według zaleceń** as directed IDM **zalecenia i przestrogi** (*co należy robić, a czego unikać*) dos and don'ts
□ **zalecać się** court[2]
zaledwie just[1], mere, scarcely
zalegać: **z czymś** fall behind with sth, be/get behind (with sth)
zalegalizować → LEGALIZOWAĆ
zaległości arrears, backlog; **mieć ~ w czymś** fall behind with sth; (*w spłatach*) be in arrears, fall/get into arrears
zaległ|y back[2], outstanding; **~a wypłata** arrears
zalesiony wooded
zalet|a advantage, merit[1], virtue; **mieć ~y** have your, etc. (good) points
zalew deluge[1]
zalewa: **~ solna** brine
zal(ew)ać 1 deluge[2], flood[1], inundate, submerge, swamp[2] **2** (*przen.*) engulf, inundate, swamp[2] sb/sth (with sth); (*rozprzestrzeniać się*) sweep[1]; **kogoś/coś (czymś)** suffuse sb/sth (with sth); **~ potokiem słów** spout[2] (on/off) (about sth)
zależeć: **od czegoś** depend on sth, hang on sth, hinge on sth; **od kogoś** be down to sb, be up to sb; **~ od swego otoczenia** be conditioned by your environment; **policji bardzo zależy na odnalezieniu tego człowieka** police are anxious to find the man; **bardzo mi na tym domu zależało** my heart was set on that house IDM **to zależy** that depends, it (all) depends
zależność dependence on sb/sth
zależn|y dependent (on sb/sth); **od czegoś** conditional (on/upon sth); **być ~ym od kogoś/czegoś** depend on sb/sth (for sth), rely on sb/sth
zali-czać/czyć rank[2], rate[2] sb/sth (as sth); **zaliczyłbym go do moich pięciu ulubionych pisarzy** I'd put him in my top five favourite writers
□ **zaliczać się** rank[2] (as sth)
zaliczka advance[1], deposit[1], down payment
zalogować (się) → LOGOWAĆ
zalotny flirtatious
zaloty courtship
zalśnić → LŚNIĆ
zaludni(a)ć populate
załadować → ŁADOWAĆ
załadowany loaded (with sth)
załagodzić → ŁAGODZIĆ
załam(yw)ać: **kogoś** devastate; (*psychicznie*) mess sb up
■ **załamanie** (*fizyczne lub nerwowe*) collapse[2]; **~ nerwowe** nervous breakdown | **załamany** crestfallen, desolate
□ **załam(yw)ać się 1** (*gałąź itp.*) yield[1] **2** (*osoba*) break down, crack up, go to pieces; (*głos*) crack[1] **3** (*gospodarka itp.*) falter, slump[1]
■ **załamanie się** breakdown
załap(yw)ać get the hang of (doing) sth, get the message
załatać → ŁATAĆ
załatwi(a)ć 1 (*sprawy*) deal with sth, handle[1], see about sth/doing sth, settle; (*z trudem, zwł. coś nielegalnego*) wangle; **coś dla kogoś** fix sb up (with sth); **~ czyjeś/swoje sprawy** sort sth/sb/yourself out; **załatwić coś gadaniem** blag **2** (*zabić*) bump sb off, zap
■ **załatwianie**: **~ spraw (dla kogoś)** (*np. zakupów*) errand | **załatwion|y**: **załatwione!** OK, it's a deal!
załą-czać/czyć accompany
■ **załączeni|e**: **przesyłać w załączeniu** enclose; **w załączeniu** herewith
załącznik (*komput.*) attachment, enclosure; **w ~u** encl.
załkać → ŁKAĆ
załoga crew, workforce; (*fabryki*) shop floor; **~ samolotu** cabin crew; **~ naziemna** ground crew
załomotać → ŁOMOTAĆ
załopotać → ŁOPOTAĆ
założeni|e 1 (*instytucji itp.*) foundation, establishment **2** (*domniemanie*) presumption; **być czymś z ~a** be meant to be sth
założyciel founder; **członek-założyciel** founder member
założyć (się) → ZAKŁADAĆ (SIĘ)
zamach assassination; **~ bombowy** bombing; **~ stanu** coup; **próba ~u na życie prezydenta** an attempt on the President's life; **dokonywać ~u (na kogoś)** assassinate IDM **za jednym ~em** at a/one stroke
zamachnąć się: **~ ręką (na kogoś/coś)** swing[1] (at sb/sth)
zamachowiec assassin
zamaczać → MACZAĆ
zamajaczyć → MAJACZYĆ
zamajtać → MAJTAĆ
zamalować → MALOWAĆ

zamanifestować → MANIFESTOWAĆ
zamarudzić → MARUDZIĆ
zamarynować → MARYNOWAĆ
za-marzać/marznąć zob. też MARZNĄĆ; congeal, freeze[1], freeze over, frost over/up, ice (sth) over/up; **zamarznąć na dobre** freeze solid IDM (*przen.*) **zamarznąć na śmierć** catch your death (of cold)
■ **zamarzanie**: **temperatura zamarzania wody** the freezing point of water | **zamarznięty** frozen[2]
zamaskować → MASKOWAĆ
zamaskowany 1 (*w masce*) masked **2** (*ukryty*) covert
zamaszysty: **szeroki ~ ruch** sweep[2]
■ **zamaszyście**: **iść zamaszyście** stride[1]
za-mawiać/mówić commission[2], order[2]; **być zamówionym** be on order; **idę pierwszy! zamawiam!** bags I go first!
zamaz(yw)ać (się) blur[2]
■ **zamazany** blurred, fuzzy
zamącić → MĄCIĆ
zameczek clasp[2]
zamek 1 (*budowla*) castle; **~ z piasku** sandcastle **2** (*w drzwiach itp.*) catch[2], lock[2]; **~ szyfrowy** combination lock **3 ~ błyskawiczny** zip, zip fastener
zameldować (się) → MELDOWAĆ (SIĘ)
zamerdać → MERDAĆ
zamerykanizować → AMERYKANIZOWAĆ
zamę-czać/czyć zob. też MĘCZYĆ; drive[1], torment verb
zamęt mayhem, muddle noun; **miał ~ w myślach** his mind was in a fog
zamężna married (to sb)
zamglić (się) → MGLIĆ (SIĘ)
zamglony 1 (*wzrok, oczy*) blurred **2** (*obraz*) blurred, shadowy **3** (*niebo*) misty
zamian: **w ~ za coś** in exchange for sth, in return (for sth)
zamiana conversion, exchange[1], swap noun; **~ ról** reversal of roles
zamiar intent[2], intention, plan[1], purpose; **mieć ~** intend, mean[1] (sb) to do sth; **mając ~ coś zrobić** with a view to doing sth; **w najlepszych ~ach** well meant
zamiast instead (of sb/sth/doing sth), in lieu (of sth), in place of sb/sth, in sb/sth's place, rather than
zamiatacz/ka sweeper
za-miatać/mieść sweep[1], sweep sth out, sweep sth up
zamiatarka sweeper
zamiauczeć → MIAUCZEĆ
zamieć blizzard
zamiejscowy (*rozmowa itp.*) long-distance
zamieni(a)ć change[1] sth (with sb), exchange[2] A for B, sth (with sb), swap (sth) (with sb), A for B; **coś/kogoś w kogoś/coś** convert[1], turn[1]
□ **zamieni(a)ć się**: **czymś** reverse[1], swap (with sb), A for B, switch[2] (with sb/sth), (over/round); **w coś** convert[1], turn[1]; **(z czegoś) (na coś)** change over (from sth) (to sth); **~ się miejscami** change/swap places (with sb)
zamienn|y interchangeable; **części ~e** spare parts
za-mierać/mrzeć tail away/off IDM **serce zamiera** your heart sinks
zamie-rzać/rzyć aim[2], be going to do sth, intend, mean[1], plan[2], propose, think of/about doing sth
■ **zamierzenie** intention | **zamierzony** intended, intentional, wilful; **być zamierzonym, żeby coś wywołać** be calculated to do sth
zamieszać (się) → MIESZAĆ (SIĘ)
zamieszanie 1 (*bałagan*) confusion, muddle noun; (*gniewna reakcja*) aggro, commotion, furore; **jego oświadczenie wywołało ~ w sądzie** his statement threw the court into turmoil **2** (*kłopot*) faff noun, fuss[1] **3 (w coś)** implication (in sth)
zamieszany: **w coś** complicit (in/with sb/sth); **być/zostać ~m w coś** be/get caught up in sth, be connected with sth
zamieszczać: **~ ofertę** advertise (for sb/sth)
zamieszkani|e habitation; **miejsce ~a** abode, residence; **nie nadający się do ~a** uninhabitable
zamiesz|ki disorder, disturbance, riot, turbulence, unrest; **wszczynać ~ki** riot verb; **uczestnik ~ek** rioter
zamieszk(iw)ać zob. też MIESZKAĆ; inhabit, occupy, make your home somewhere, take up residence somewhere
■ **zamieszkiwanie** habitation; (*w domu itp.*) occupation | **zamieszkujący** resident adj.
zamieść → ZAMIATAĆ
zamigotać → MIGOTAĆ
zamiłowanie fondness, love[1], love affair
zaminować → MINOWAĆ
zamknąć (się) → ZAMYKAĆ (SIĘ)
zamknięcie closing noun, closure
zamknięt|y 1 (*drzwi itp.*) closed, shut[2]; (*w pudełku itp.*) enclosed; **w ~ej przestrzeni** in enclosed spaces; **~y jak w więzieniu** cooped up **2 w sobie** introverted, private[1], repressed, withdrawn[2] **3** (*grupa ludzi*) incestuous
zamocować fix[1]
zamoczyć (się) → MOCZYĆ (SIĘ)
zamontować → MONTOWAĆ
zamontowan|y: **~e szafki** fitted cupboards; **kuchnia z ~ym wyposażeniem** fitted kitchen
zamordować → MORDOWAĆ
zamorski overseas
zamortyzować → AMORTYZOWAĆ
zamożność affluence, means, wealth
zamożny affluent, well off, wealthy, well-to-do
zamówić → ZAMAWIAĆ
zamówienie (*w restauracji itp.*) order[1]; (*handlowe*) commission[1]; **robiony na ~** made to order; **wykonany na indywidualne ~** bespoke
za-mrażać/mrozić freeze[1]
zamrażalnik freezer
zamrażarka freezer
zamroczenie stupor
zamrozić → MROZIĆ, ZAMRAŻAĆ
zamrożenie freeze[2]
zamrożony frozen[2]
zamruczeć → MRUCZEĆ
zamrzeć → ZAMIERAĆ
zamsz suede
zamurowany (*zaskoczony*) tongue-tied
za-mykać/mknąć 1 (*drzwi itp.*) close[1], shut[1]; (*na klucz*) lock[1], lock sth up; (*hermetycznie*) seal[1] sth (up/down); (*dojazd/wejście*) close sth off; **w czymś** confine sb/sth (in/to sth), enclose sth (in sth), shut sb/sth up (in sth); (*w szpitalu psychiatrycznym itp.*) commit sb to sth; **~ kogoś (w pomieszczeniu) na klucz** lock sb in/out; **~ szczelnie/mocno** fasten; **~ parasol** put an umbrella down **2** (*fabrykę itp.*) close sth down, shut sth down, wind sth up **3 ~ gębę komuś** shut sb up **4 ~ program komputerowy** exit[2], quit IDM **~ pochód** bring up the rear
□ **za-mykać/mknąć się 1** (*drzwi itp.*) close[1], shut[1]; **w czymś** shut yourself in (sth) **2** (*fabryka itp.*) close down, shut down **3** (*osoba*) shut up; **w sobie** clam up (on sb), go, retreat, etc. into your shell
zamysł idea
zamyślać intend, plan[2]
■ **zamyśleni|e**: **w zamyśleniu** thoughtfully
zamyślony distant, thoughtful, reflective, sober[1]
zanadto too
zanalizować → ANALIZOWAĆ
zanęcić → NĘCIĆ
zangielszczyć → ANGIELSZCZYĆ
zaniechać abandon, abort, relinquish
zanieczy-szczać/ścić contaminate, dirty[2], foul[2], pollute; (*wodę itp.*) adulterate
■ **zanieczyszczając|y**: **substancja zanieczyszczająca** pollutant | **zanieczyszczenie** adulteration, contamination, impurity, pollution | **zanieczyszczony** impure; (*specjalnie*) poisoned
zaniedbanie inattention, neglect noun, negligence; (*domu, maszyny itp.*) disrepair; **to było wyraźne ~ jej obowiązków** she had clearly been remiss in her duty
zaniedbany neglected; (*dom, samochód itp.*) run-down; (*pozostawiony w nieporządku*) untidy; (*wygląd osoby*) unkempt; (*pokryty rdzą*) rusty
zaniedb(yw)ać fail[1] to do sth, neglect
■ **zaniedbujący się**: **~ w czymś** negligent
□ **zaniedb(yw)ać się** let yourself go
zaniemówić dry up, be rendered speechless, be struck dumb; (*ze zdumienia*) catch your breath
zaniepokoić (się) → NIEPOKOIĆ (SIĘ)
zaniepokojeni|e unease, upset[3], worry[2]; **z ~em** anxiously
zaniepokojony anxious, concerned, perturbed, uneasy, upset[2], worried
zanieść → ZANOSIĆ
zanik (*mięśni; wartości itp.*) atrophy; **w ~u** on the wane
zanik-ać/nąć 1 (*dźwięk itp.*) die away, fade (away), trail away/off **2** (*tradycja itp.*) die out, wither (away), vanish **3** (*przepływ, napływ czegoś*) peter out **4** (*mięśnie itp.*) atrophy verb
■ **zanikający** (*przestarzały; prawie nieistniejący*) obsolescent
zanim before[2]
zani-żać/żyć understate
za-nosić/nieść get

□ **zanosić się 1 na coś** be in the air, be brewing; **zanosi się na deszcz** it looks like rain; **zanosi się na śnieg** it feels as if it is going to snow soon; **nie zanosi się na to, żeby wyzdrowiał** he is unlikely to recover **2 (/zanieść się)** (*śmiechem*) peal verb; ~ **od śmiechu** be in hysterics, laugh, scream, etc. your head off
zanotow(yw)ać zob. też NOTOWAĆ; jot sth down, write sth down
zantagonizować → ANTAGONIZOWAĆ
zanucić → NUCIĆ
zanu-dzać/dzić zob. też NUDZIĆ (SIĘ); **(kogoś) (czymś)** keep on (at sb) (about sb/sth)
■ **zanudzony**: ~ **na śmierć** sick to death of sb/sth
zanurkować → NURKOWAĆ
zanu-rzać/rzyć dip¹, duck², dunk, immerse, sink¹, submerge
□ **zanu-rzać/rzyć się** submerge
zaobserwować → OBSERWOWAĆ
zaobserwowanie sighting
zaoferować → OFEROWAĆ
zaoferowani|e: **do ~a** on offer
zaoferowany forthcoming
zaogni(a)ć inflame
□ **zaogni(a)ć się** fester
zaokrąg-lać/lić (*w górę/ w dół*) round sth up/down
■ **zaokrągleni|e**: **w zaokrągleniu** in round figures/numbers | **zaokrąglony** rounded, well rounded
□ **zaokrąg-lać/lić się** fill out
zaokrętować się → OKRĘTOWAĆ SIĘ
zaokrętowanie się embarkation
zaopa-trywać/trzyć stock², supply²; (*w sprzęt*) equip sb/sth (with sth), kit sb out/up (in/with sth)
■ **zaopatrzenie 1** (*dostarczanie; dostawa*) provision **2** (*wojenne: broń*) munitions
□ **zaopa-trywać/trzyć się** kit yourself out/up (in/with sth)
■ **zaopatrywanie się**: **stałe zaopatrywanie się w danym sklepie** custom
zaopiekować się → OPIEKOWAĆ SIĘ
zaoponować → OPONOWAĆ
zaorać → ORAĆ
zaorbitować → ORBITOWAĆ
za-ostrzać/ostrzyć zob. też OSTRZYĆ **1** (*pogarszać*) exacerbate **2** (*restrykcje itp.*) tighten up (on) sth **3** (*słuch, wzrok itp.*) sharpen IDM ~ **apetyt** whet sb's appetite
□ **za-ostrzać/ostrzyć się** (*pogarszać się*) fester
zaoszczę-dzać/dzić save¹ sb sth/doing sth
zapach aroma, fragrance, odour, perfume, savour noun, scent, smell²; **ulotny** ~ whiff; **mieć** ~ smell¹ (of sth); **nadawać** ~ scent verb sth (with sth)
zapachnieć → PACHNIEĆ
zapaćkać → PAĆKAĆ
za-padać/paść 1 w zapadającej ciemności in the gathering darkness **2 w coś** lapse into sth **3 zapaść w sen** go to sleep; ~ **w sen zimowy** hibernate **4** (*na chorobę*) catch¹
□ **za-padać/paść się** cave in, sag, sink¹
zapadł|y godforsaken; **na ~ej prowincji** in the depths of the country
zapadnia trapdoor
zapadnięcie się (*terenu, domu itp.*) subsidence
zapadnięty hollow¹, sunken
zapakować (się) → PAKOWAĆ (SIĘ)
zapa-lać/lić zob. też PALIĆ (SIĘ) **1** (*rozniecić ogień*) ignite, light³, set sth alight, set light to sth; ~ **zapałkę** light/ strike a match **2** (*światło*) put sth on, turn sth on **3** (*papierosa*) light sth up; **zapalić papierosa** have a cigarette **4** (*silnik*) turn over; **samochód nie chce zapalić** the car won't start **5 kogoś (do czegoś)** fire sb up
■ **zapalający** (*mechanizm itp.*) incendiary | **zapalanie** (*w samochodzie*) ignition
□ **zapa-lać/lić się 1** (*drzewo itp.*) catch fire, light³ **2** (*światło itp.*) go on **3** (*oczy*) light up
zapalczywy fierce, fiery, impetuous, passionate
zapalenie inflammation; ~ **krtani** laryngitis; ~ **migdałków** tonsillitis; ~ **mózgu i rdzenia z mialgią** ME; ~ **opon mózgowych** meningitis; ~ **oskrzeli** bronchitis; ~ **płuc** pneumonia; ~ **skóry** dermatitis; ~ **wątroby** hepatitis; ~ **wyrostka robaczkowego** appendicitis
zapaleniec freak¹
zapalniczka cigarette lighter
zapalnik fuse¹
zapaln|y 1 (*med.*) **stan ~y** inflammation; **w stanie ~ym** inflamed **2** (*przen.*) **punkt ~y** hot spot, trouble spot
zapalony 1 (*w płomieniach*) alight¹ **2** (*osoba*) avid, keen, zealous
zapał drive², eagerness, enthusiasm, fervour, keenness, spirit¹, zeal, zest; **pełen ~u** enthusiastic; **z ~em** avidly, enthusiastically, with gusto, zealously; **z wielkim ~em** heart and soul; **bez ~u** lukewarm (about sb/sth)
zapałka light¹, match¹, matchstick
zapamiętani|e: **łatwy do ~a** memorable
zapamięt(yw)ać zob. też PAMIĘTAĆ; memorize
zapanować → PANOWAĆ
zaparcie constipation
zaparkować → ZAPARKOWAĆ
zaparować zob. też PAROWAĆ; (*szyby, okulary*) mist sth up/over, steam sth up
zapart|y IDM **z ~ym tchem** with bated breath
zapa-rzać/rzyć zob. też PARZYĆ (SIĘ); brew, infuse; (*kawę w ekspresie*) percolate
zapas hoard¹, reserve², standby, store¹, supply¹; (*towaru*) stock¹; **~y żywności** provisions; **duże ~y** stockpile noun; **robić ~y** hoard² sth (up); **w ~ie** in hand, in reserve; **na** ~ for good measure
zapaskudzony messy
zapasow|y spare¹, standby adj.; **część ~a** spare part; **kopia ~a pliku** backup; **~y bezpiecznik** spare noun
zapasy (*sport*) wrestling
zapaść (się) → ZAPADAĆ (SIĘ)
zapaśni-k/czka wrestler
zapatrywani|e slant², view¹ (about/on sth); **~a polityczne** politics
zapatrzon|y 1 (*wzrok*) distant **2 być ~ym w kogoś/ coś** be wrapped up in sb/sth
zapchać (się) → ZAPYCHAĆ (SIĘ)
zapchany: **(czymś)** crammed, jam-packed (with sb/sth), thick¹ (with sth)
zapełni(a)ć (*ulicę itp.*) throng²; (*kawiarnię itp.*) crowd sth out IDM ~ **lukę** bridge a/the gap
■ **zapełniony** full¹ of sb/sth
zapewni(a)ć assure, ensure, reassure; **(sobie)** make certain (that...); **(o czymś)** assert, profess; ~ **byt** provide for sb; (*inwestycja itp.*) **zapewniający zysk** blue-chip; **dzisiejsze zwycięstwo drużyny zapewniło im miejsce w finale** the team's victory today has earned them a place in the final
zapę-dzać/dzić zob. też PĘDZIĆ IDM ~ **w kozi róg** stump² | ~ **w pułapkę/ sidła** trap² sb (into sth/into doing sth)
zapęt-lać/lić loop verb
zapiać → PIAĆ
zapiąć (się) → ZAPINAĆ (SIĘ)
zapieczętować → PIECZĘTOWAĆ
zapienić się → PIENIĆ SIĘ
za-pierać/przeć: ~ **dech w piersiach** catch your breath, take your breath away; **zapierający dech w piersiach** breathtaking; **dech jej zaparło ze zdumienia** she gave a gasp of surprise
□ **za-pierać/przeć się** (*nogami itp.*) brace² sth/yourself (for sth)
zapięcie fastener
zapikować → PIKOWAĆ
za-pinać/piąć (*na guziki itp.*) do sth up; (*na klamerkę*) buckle¹; (*na zamek błyskawiczny*) zip verb; ~ **pasy** belt up IDM ~ **na ostatni guzik** sew sth up
□ **za-pinać/piąć** fasten; (*klamerką itp.*) buckle¹
zapinka buckle², clasp², fastener
zapis 1 (*system znaków umożliwiający zapis czegoś*) notation; (*notatka*) entry **2** (*rozmowy*) transcript; ~ **cyfrowy** digital recording **3** (*w testamencie*) bequest; ~ **darowizny** endowment **4 (zapisy)** (*do szkoły itp.*) enrolment, registration
zapis|ek (zapiski) record¹
zapis(yw)ać zob. też PISAĆ **1** get sth down, jot sth down, keep a note of sth, note sth down, put sth down, record², register¹, stick sth down, take sth down, write sth down; (*policjant: nazwisko itp.*) take; **proszę to zapisać na mój rachunek** could you charge that to my account?; **zapisz te daty w kalendarzu** put these dates down in your diary; ~ **coś w dzienniku okrętowym/ pokładowym** log² **2** (*komput.*) enter sth (in/into/on/onto sth); ~ **automatycznie** autosave **3** (*w testamencie*) bequeath sth (to sb), leave a bequest to sb; ~ **darowiznę na rzecz instytucji edukacyjnej** endow **4** (*do szkoły itp.*) enrol, register¹
□ **zapis(yw)ać się** (*do szkoły itp.*) enrol; (*do wojska itp.*) register¹, join¹, sign up (for sth)
zaplanować → PLANOWAĆ
zaplanowan|y: **nie mamy nic ~ego** we haven't got anything on
za-platać/pleść zob. też PLEŚĆ; plait
zaplątan|y entangled; **być ~ym** (*np. w kłótnię*) be locked in sth
zapleśniały mouldy
zapłacenie payment
zapłacić → PŁACIĆ
za-pładniać/płodnić fertilize, impregnate
zapłakać → PŁAKAĆ
zapłakany tearful

zapłata payment (for sth); ~ **tygodniowa** wage[1]
zapłodnienie fertilization, impregnation
zapłon ignition
zapłonąć zob. też PŁONĄĆ; flare[1]
zapo-biegać/biec avert, prevent
■ **zapobieganie** prevention; ~ **ciąży** family planning
zapobiegawczy deterrent adj., preventive, protective, prophylactic
zapobiegliwość foresight, forethought
zapoczątkow(yw)ać inaugurate, initiate, pioneer; (*okres pokoju itp.*) enter, usher sth in
zapo-dziewać/dziać mislay
zapolować → POLOWAĆ
zapo-minać/mniec forget; (*bilet itp.*) leave[1] sth (behind), lose sight of sb/sth; (*celowo lub nie*) omit to do sth; ~ **o różnych rzeczach** be a bit forgetful; ~ **o czymś przykrym** put sth behind you
□ **zapo-minać/mniec się** forget yourself
zapominalski forgetful
zapomnienie oblivion, obscurity
□ **zapomnienie się**: **(chwilowe)** ~ lapse[1]
zapomoga relief
zapora 1 ~ **drogowa** roadblock; ~ **wodna** dam, dyke **2** (*przen.*) **(przed czymś)** bulwark (against sth) **3** (*komput.*) ~ **sieciowa** firewall
zapotrzebowanie demand[1]
zapo-wiadać/wiedzieć foreshadow; (*czyjś występ*) introduce
□ **zapowiadać się** promise[1]
■ **zapowiadający się**: **dobrze się zapowiadający** budding, promising
zapowiedziany prospective
zapowiedź omen
zapozna(wa)ć introduce
■ **zapoznany** acquainted with sth
□ **zapozna(wa)ć się**: **z kimś** meet; **z czymś** familiarize yourself (with sth), know/learn the ropes
zapoży-czać/czyć borrow sth (from/off sb/sth)
zapracowany: **być bardzo ~m** have your hands full
zapragnąć → PRAGNĄĆ
za-praszać/prosić ask sb (to sth), invite sb (to/for sth); ~ **kogoś do siebie do domu** invite sb over/round; ~ **kogoś do swojego domu po wspólnym pobycie gdzieś** invite sb back; ~ **kogoś do środka** (*do siebie do domu*) invite sb in; ~ **kogoś na wspólne wyjście** ask sb out, invite sb out
zaprawa 1 ~ **fizyczna** workout **2** ~ **murarska** mortar
zaprawi(a)ć 1 (*potrawę*) spice[2] sth (up) (with sth); ~ **coś trucizną** poison[2] **2** (*żartem itp.*) spice[2] sth (up) (with sth)
zaprenumerować → PRENUMEROWAĆ
zaprezentować → PREZENTOWAĆ
zaprogramować → PROGRAMOWAĆ
zaprojektować → PROJEKTOWAĆ
zaproponować → PROPONOWAĆ
zaprosić → ZAPRASZAĆ
zaproszenie invitation
zaprotestować → PROTESTOWAĆ
zaprowa-dzać/dzić zob. też PROWADZIĆ; walk[1]
zaprowiantowanie provision
zaprząc → ZAPRZĘGAĆ
zaprze-czać/czyć contradict, deny, disavow, disclaim, negate, quarrel[2] with sth
■ **zaprzeczeni|e** contradiction, denial; **jej działanie było dokładnym zaprzeczeniem moich poleceń** what she did was in direct opposition to my orders
zaprzeć (się) → ZAPIERAĆ (SIĘ)
zaprzepa-szczać/ścić muck sth up
zaprzesta(wa)ć zob. też PRZESTAWAĆ; abandon, cease, cut sth out, give sth up, relinquish; (*produkcji czegoś itp.*) discontinue; **coś robić** give up doing sth; (*wojsk.*) ~ **walki** disengage
za-przęgać/prząc harness[2] sth (to sth)
zaprzyjaźni(a)ć się zob. też PRZYJAŹNIĆ SIĘ; **(z kimś)** befriend, be/become/make friends (with sb), form a friendship; **zaprzyjaźnić się szybko** click[1]
■ **zaprzyjaźniony z kimś** friendly[1] with sb
za-przysięgać/przysiąc: **kogoś** swear sb in
zaprzysięgły confirmed
zapukać → PUKAĆ
za-puszczać/puścić (*włosy itp.*) grow; (*włosy*) grow (sth) out
zapuszczony 1 (*zaniedbany: budynek; miejsce*) run-down **2** (*pusty: teren*) waste[3]
zapuszkować → PUSZKOWAĆ
zap(y)chać block[2], clog[1], jam[2]
■ **zapychający** (*jedzenie*) stodgy
□ **zap(y)chać się** clog[1] (up)
zapy-lać/lić fertilize, pollinate
zapytać → PYTAĆ
zapytanie enquiry
zapyziały manky
za-rabiać/robić be on, earn, make[1], make money; ~ **na życie** earn a living
zaradczy remedial
zaradny resourceful
zaranie dawn[1]
za-rastać/rosnąć (*fryzura itp.*) grow out; (*rosnąć dziko*) straggle
zaraz right/straight away, directly[1], immediately, just[1], now, at once, presently, right[2], shortly, soon; ~ **będzie padać** it's going to rain soon
IDM ~, ~ let me see, let's see, now
zaraza (*choroba*) blight[2], bug[1], contagion, plague[1]
zaraz|ek germ; **pełen ~ków** septic
zarazem at the same time
zaraźliwy catching, contagious, infectious
zara-żać/zić 1 give sth to sb, infect **2** (*przen.*) infect; ~ **kogoś entuzjazmem** enthuse sb (with sth)
■ **zarażenie** infection | **zarażony**: **być zarażonym entuzjazmem** be inspired with enthusiasm
□ **zara-żać/zić się** catch[1], contract[2]
zarchiwizować → ARCHIWIZOWAĆ
zardzewiały (*i przen.*) rusty
zardzewieć → RDZEWIEĆ
zareagować → REAGOWAĆ
zarechotać → RECHOTAĆ
zarejestrować (się) → REJESTROWAĆ (SIĘ)
zarejestrowany (*towarzystwo, firma*) incorporated
zareklamować → REKLAMOWAĆ
zarekomendować → REKOMENDOWAĆ
zarekwirować → REKWIROWAĆ
zarezerwować → REZERWOWAĆ
zarę-czać/czyć: **zaręczyć, że** give an undertaking that
□ **zaręcz-ać/yć się** get engaged
zaręczony betrothed, engaged (to sb)
zaręczyny engagement
zaripostować → RIPOSTOWAĆ
zarobić → ZARABIAĆ
zarobki earnings
zarodek 1 embryo, foetus **2** (*przen.*) germ of sth, seed
zarodkowy (*i przen.*) embryonic
zaroić się → ROIĆ SIĘ
zaropieć → ROPIEĆ
zarosnąć → ZARASTAĆ
zarost: **kilkudniowy** ~ several days' growth of beard
zarośla scrub[2], shrubbery
zarośnięty (*trawnik itp.*) overgrown
zarozumiały cocky, conceited, haughty, immodest, self-important, self-righteous, superior[1]
zarówno: ~**..., jak i...** both ... and...
zaróżowiony rosy
zarumienić się → RUMIENIĆ SIĘ
zarumieniony flushed
zaryczeć → RYCZEĆ
zaryglować → RYGLOWAĆ
zary|s 1 (*linia; rysunek czegoś*) contour, outline[2]; (*głowy*) profile **2** (*streszczenie*) outline[2], overview **3** (*brudnopis*) draft[1], sketch; **w ~sie** in rough; **w ogólnym ~sie** sketchy
zarysow(yw)ać zob. też RYSOWAĆ; scrape[1] sth (against/along/on sth)
zaryzykować → RYZYKOWAĆ
zarząd administration, authority, board[1], committee, council, management; **centralny** ~ headquarters; ~ **miasta** corporation
zarząd-ca/czyni administrator, manager; (*prowincji itp.*) governor
zarzą-dzać/dzić administer, govern, manage
■ **zarządzający** controller | **zarządzan|y**: **zarządzane przez kogoś** (*w czyjejś gestii*) in your hands, in the hands of sb | **zarządzani|e** administration, management; (*studia*) **zarządzanie i administracja** business administration, business studies
IDM **zarządzane przez kogoś** (*w czyjejś gestii*) in your hands, in the hands of sb | **zarządzenie** directive, edict
zarzu-cać/cić 1 coś komuś allege, reproach sb (for/with sth); ~ **kogoś pytaniami** fire questions at sb **2** (*rzucać*) drop[1] **3** (*wędkę*) cast[1]
■ **zarzuceni|e**: **coś do zarzucenia komuś** quarrel[1] | **zarzucony**: **rynek jest zarzucony tanimi towarami z importu** the market is saturated with cheap imports
zarzut accusation, allegation, charge[1], reproach noun, reproof; **bez ~u** faultless, impeccable, beyond reproach; **główny** ~ main criticism; **mały** ~ quibble noun; **pod ~em morderstwa** on suspicion of murder
za-rzynać/rżnąć (*zwierzęta*) slaughter
zarżeć → RŻEĆ
zarżnąć → RŻNĄĆ
zarżnięty knackered
zasa|da 1 (*reguła, zasadnicza idea*) concept, law, principle, rule[1]; **(zasady)**

fundamentals, ground rules; ~**dy postępowania** policy (on sth); ~**dy zachowania się** manners; ~**dy etyczne** ethics **2** (*podstawa*) basis; **w ~dzie** basically, in principle, ultimately **3** (*chem.*) alkali
zasadnicz|y 1 (*podstawowy*) basic, fundamental, integral, intrinsic, primary[1]; (*podejście, styl itp.*) no-nonsense; **sprawy ~e** the nitty-gritty **2** (*zmiana*) pivotal, radical[1]
zasadność (*prawa*) legitimacy
zasadowy alkaline
zasadzka booby trap
zasalutować → SALUTOWAĆ
zasapać → SAPAĆ
zasą-dzać/dzić convict[1] sb (of sth)
zaseplenić → SEPLENIĆ
zaserwować → SERWOWAĆ
za-siadać/siąść serve on sth
zasi(ew)ać zob. też SIAĆ; **zasiać ziarno wątpliwości** planted the seeds of doubt (in sb's mind)
zasięg range[1], reach[2]; (*w geografii itp.*) radius; (*szerokość*) breadth; (*epidemii itp.*) incidence of sth; ~ **wzroku** sight[1]; **w ~u słuchu** in/within sb's hearing; **dalekiego ~u** long-range; **poza ~iem** beyond/out of (sb's) reach; **w ~u ręki/strzału itp.** within sb's grasp[2], within (sb's) reach, within striking distance
za-sięgać/sięgnąć: ~ **informacji na temat czegoś** make some enquiries into sth
■ **zasięganie**: ~ **informacji** enquiry (about/concerning/into sb/sth)
zasi-lać/lić boost[1], power[2]; **zasilić szeregi bezrobotnych** join the ranks of the unemployed
zasiłek allowance, benefit[1]; ~ **dla bezrobotnych** the dole, unemployment benefit; ~ **na dziecko** child benefit
za-skakiwać/skoczyć amaze, knock sb back, surprise[2], take sb aback, take sb by surprise; **(czymś kogoś)** spring sth on sb; (*tak, że aż drgnie*) startle
■ **zaskakujący** amazing, mind-blowing, surprising
zaskamleć → SKAMLEĆ
zaskandować → SKANDOWAĆ
zaskarbi(a)ć: **sobie** (*czyjeś względy*) cultivate
zaskar-żać/żyć (*wyrok, orzeczenie sądu*) prosecute; **zaskarżać do sądu** litigate, prosecute sb (for sth)
zaskoczeni|e amazement; **z ~a** unawares
zaskoczon|y amazed, surprised; (*nieprzygotowany*) off (your) guard; **zostać ~ym** get a surprise; **zostać całkowicie ~ym** be taken completely unawares (by sth)
zaskoczyć zob. też ZASKAKIWAĆ; (*zrozumieć*) click[1]
zaskomleć → SKOMLEĆ
zaskowyczeć → SKOWYCZEĆ
zaskórnik blackhead
zaskrzeczeć → SKRZECZEĆ
zaskrzypieć → SKRZYPIEĆ
zaskwierczeć → SKWIERCZEĆ
zasłabnąć → SŁABNĄĆ
za-słaniać/słonić block[2], screen[2], shield[2]; (*przed słońcem*) shade[2]; (*maskować*) shroud[2]; (*okna zasłonami*) draw the curtains[1]

zasłona 1 (*w oknie*) curtain; (*teatr*) ~ **dekoracyjna w głębi sceny** backdrop **2** (*parawan*) screen[1] **3** (*abażur*) shade[1] **4** (*przen.*) curtain
zasługa 1 credit[1], merit[1], worth[2] **2** (**zasługi**) service[1]
za-sługiwać/służyć: **na coś** deserve, earn, merit[2], rate[2], warrant[2]
■ **zasługujący na coś** worthy of sth/to do sth | **zasłużony** (*nagroda itp.*) well earned
zasłynąć → SŁYNĄĆ
zasmakować → SMAKOWAĆ
zasmu-cać/cić zob. też SMUCIĆ; grieve, pain[2], sadden
■ **zasmucony** pained, sorrowful
zasnąć → ZASYPIAĆ
zasobny prosperous
zasób stock[1], supply[1]; **(zasoby)** resources; **zasoby finansowe** means; ~ **słów** vocabulary; ~ **wyrazów danego języka** wordpower
zaspa bank[1], drift[1]; ~ **śnieżna** snowdrift
zaspać oversleep
zaspo-kajać/koić satisfy; (*potrzeby*) fulfil; (*czyjeś potrzeby*) accommodate; (*potrzeby itp.*) cater for sb/sth, to sth
zasponsorować → SPONSOROWAĆ
zassać → ZASYSAĆ
zastać → ZASTAWAĆ
zasta-nawiać/nowić się: **(nad czymś)** contemplate, consider doing sth, debate[2], give sth some thought, look at sth, muse, ponder (on/over) sth verb, reflect (on/upon sth), take stock (of sth), wonder[1] (about sth); (*ale nie całkiem poważnie*) flirt with sth
■ **zastanawianie się**: **głębokie zastanawianie się** soul-searching | **zastanowienie** afterthought, deliberation, thought[2]; **bez zastanowienia** at the drop of a hat, offhand[2] | **zastanowienie się** deliberation, reflection IDM **po zastanowieniu się** on reflection
zastaw deposit[1]; (*coś co dajemy pod zastaw spłaty długu*) collateral, security; **osoba pożyczająca pieniądze pod** ~ pawnbroker
zastawa: ~ **obiadowa** dinner service
zasta(wa)ć: **poszedłem do tego domu, ale nikogo tam nie zastałem** I went to the house but there was nobody around
zastawi(a)ć 1 (*w lombardzie*) pawn[2] **2** (*pułapkę itp.*) lay[1]; ~ **sidła** snare verb
zastąpić → ZASTĘPOWAĆ
zastąpieni|e: **możliwy do ~a** replaceable
zastęp-ca/czyni substitute, surrogate; (*w zarządzie itp.*) deputy; ~ **dyrektora** assistant manager; **zastępca kapitana** mate[1]
zastępcz|y: **matka ~a** surrogate mother
za-stępować/stąpić replace, supersede, take sb's/sth's place, take the place of sb/sth; **kogoś/coś (kimś/czymś innym)** substitute verb sb/sth (for sb/sth), for sb/sth; (*na stanowisku itp.*) deputize (for sb); ~ **(kogoś) w pracy** cover[1] (for sb), fill in (for sb); ~ **(kogoś) czasowo** stand in (for sb)
zastępstw|o: **za kogoś** cover[2], substitution
zastępujący assistant adj.
zastosowanie application, employment, implementation, introduction, practice, use[2]; **mieć** ~ pertain; **znajdować** ~ operate
zastoso(wy)wać zob. też STOSOWAĆ (SIĘ); implement[1]
□ **zastoso(wy)wać się**: **do kogoś/czegoś** defer to sb/sth
zastój plateau; (*gospodarczy*) recession, slump[2], stagnation; **być w zastoju** stagnate; **jest ~ w handlu** trade is very slack; **w zastoju** stagnant, in the doldrums
zastrajkować → STRAJKOWAĆ
zastra-szać/szyć browbeat, intimidate
za-strzegać/strzec stipulate
zastrzelić 1 (*z pistoletu itp.*) gun sb down, shoot[1], shoot sb/sth down **2** (*wiadomością itp.*) spring sth on sb
zastrzeże|nie 1 (*ograniczenie*) limitation, qualification, stipulation; **bez ~ń** unconditionally, unreservedly; **z ~niem, że** provided/providing (that) **2** (*wątpliwość*) question[1], reservation; **drobne ~nie** quibble noun
zastrzeżony classified; (*numer telefonu*) ex-directory
zastrzyk 1 (*med.*) injection, jab[2], shot[1]; **dawać** ~ inject **2** (*przen.*) infusion, injection; **dawać ~ (czegoś)** inject sth (into sth)
zastukotać → STUKOTAĆ
zastyg-ać/nąć freeze[1]
zasubsydiować → SUBSYDIOWAĆ
zasugerować → SUGEROWAĆ
zasuszony desiccated
zasuw|a bolt[1]; **zamykać na ~ę** bar[2]
zasu-wać/nąć (*zasłony*) draw[1] IDM **zasunąć bombę** drop a bombshell
zasuwka latch[1]
zaswędzieć → SWĘDZIEĆ
zasyczeć → SYCZEĆ
zasygnalizować → SYGNALIZOWAĆ
zasymilować → ASYMILOWAĆ
zasymulować → SYMULOWAĆ
za-sypiać/snąć fall asleep, get to sleep, go to sleep
zasyp(yw)ać deluge[2], inundate, overwhelm, shower[2], swamp[2]; **zasypany śniegiem** snowed in; ~ **kogoś pytaniami** ply sb with sth
za-sysać/ssać siphon sth into sth
zaszaleć → SZALEĆ
zaszamotać się → SZAMOTAĆ SIĘ
zaszantażować → SZANTAŻOWAĆ
zaszargać → SZARGAĆ
zaszarżować → SZARŻOWAĆ
zaszczebiotać → SZCZEBIOTAĆ
zaszczekać → SZCZEKAĆ
zaszczepi(a)ć zob. też SZCZEPIĆ; **(coś komuś)** impress sth on/upon sb
□ **zaszczepi(a)ć się**: **zaszczepić się przeciwko grypie** have a flu jab
zaszczękać → SZCZĘKAĆ
zaszczy-cać/cić flatter, honour[2] sb/sth (with sth)
■ **zaszczycony** privileged
zaszczyt honour[1], privilege; **przynosić komuś** ~ do sb credit
zaszczytn|y creditable
■ **zaszczytnie** with flying colours
zaszeleścić → SZELEŚCIĆ
zaszemrać → SZEMRAĆ
zaszeptać → SZEPTAĆ
zaszkodzić zob. też SZKODZIĆ; (*jedzenie*) not agree with sb, disagree with sb; **zbyt dużo słodyczy może ci** ~ too many sweets are bad for you
zaszlochać → SZLOCHAĆ
zasznurować (się) → SZNUROWAĆ (SIĘ)
zaszokowany shocked, staggered

zaszpanować → SZPANOWAĆ
zaszturmować → SZTURMOWAĆ
zasztyletować → SZTYLETOWAĆ
zaszufladkować → SZUFLADKOWAĆ; typecast sb (as sth)
zaszuflować → SZUFLOWAĆ
zaszumieć → SZUMIEĆ
zaszurać → SZURAĆ
zaszyfrować → SZYFROWAĆ
zaszy(wa)ć sew sth up; **zaszyć dziurę** mend a hole (in sth)
zaś whereas
zaścianek backwater
zaściankowy insular, provincial
zaślinić się → ŚLINIĆ SIĘ
zaśmie-cać/cić clutter[1] sth (up)
zaśmi(ew)ać się kill[1] yourself
zaśpiewać zob. też ŚPIEWAĆ; burst/ break into song
zaświad-czać/czyć zob. też ŚWIADCZYĆ; pronounce (on sth)
zaświadczenie certificate
zaświecić (się) → ŚWIECIĆ (SIĘ)
zaświergotać → ŚWIERGOTAĆ
zaświerzbić → ŚWIERZBIĆ
zaświtać zob. też ŚWITAĆ; ~ **(komuś) w głowie** dawn[2] (on sb)
za-taczać/toczyć: ~ **koła w powietrzu** wheel[2]
□ **za-taczać/toczyć się** reel[2], stagger
za-tajać/taić zob. też TAIĆ; **coś (przed kimś)** keep sth back (from sb), keep sth from sb, neglect to mention sth
■ **zatajenie** cover-up, suppression
zatamować → TAMOWAĆ
zatańczyć → TAŃCZYĆ
za-tapiać/topić 1 bury, immerse sth (in sth), sink[1]; **zatopić nóż w czymś** plunge a knife into sth; **nie wolno zatapiać odpadów nuklearnych w morzu** nuclear waste should not be dumped in the sea **2** (*przen.*) engulf
zatarasować → TARASOWAĆ
zatelefonować → TELEFONOWAĆ
zatelepać (się) → TELEPAĆ (SIĘ)
zatem accordingly, therefore, well[3]; **a ~** thus
zaterkotać → TERKOTAĆ
zatęchły high[1]
zatęsknić → TĘSKNIĆ
zatętnić → TĘTNIĆ
zatkać → ZATYKAĆ
zatkajdziura stopgap
zatkanie blockage
zatlić się → TLIĆ SIĘ
zatłoczenie congestion
zatłoczony congested, cramped, crowded, overcrowded
zatłuc zob. też TŁUC; club sb to death
zatoczka 1 (*morska*) cove, inlet; **wąska** ~ creek **2** (*na szosie*) lay-by
zatoczyć (się) → ZATACZAĆ (SIĘ)
zatoka 1 (*morska*) bay, gulf **2** (*na szosie*) lay-by **3** (*czołowa, szczękowa*) sinus
zatonąć → TONĄĆ
zatopić → ZATAPIAĆ
zatopiony 1 sunken
2 ~ **w marzeniach** lost in a daydream
zator blockage, jam[1], obstruction; (*korek*) traffic jam
zatracenie doom
zatrajkotać → TRAJKOTAĆ
zatrąbić → TRĄBIĆ
zatriumfować → TRIUMFOWAĆ
zatroskany concerned
zatroszczyć się → TROSZCZYĆ SIĘ
zatrucie poisoning; ~ **pokarmowe** food poisoning
zatruć → ZATRUWAĆ
zatrudni(a)ć bring sb in, employ, engage, take sb on
■ **zatrudnienie** employment, occupation | **zatrudniony** working
zatru(wa)ć poison[2]
zatrważający alarming, hairy
zatrwożony alarmed
zatrwożyć → TRWOŻYĆ
zatrzask catch[2], clasp[2], latch[1], lock[2], popper
zatrzas-kiwać/nąć (się) slam
zatrzaśnięty (*drzwi: a nie zamknięty na klucz*) on the latch
zatrząść (się) → TRZĄŚĆ (SIĘ)
zatrzeć → ZACIERAĆ
zatrzepotać → TRZEPOTAĆ
zatrzeszczeć → TRZESZCZEĆ
zatrzymanie 1 (*aresztowanie*) detention; ~ **w areszcie** remand **2** ~ **pracy serca** cardiac arrest
□ **zatrzymanie się** halt, stop[2]
zatrzyman-y/a (*zazw. więzień polityczny*) detainee
zatrzym(yw)ać zob. też TRZYMAĆ (SIĘ) **1** (*przerwać*) halt verb, bring sth to a halt, hold[1], immobilize, stop[1], trap[2]; (*krwotok itp.*) check[1]; **zatrzymać pojazd** pull up; ~ **samochód (prosząc o podwiezienie)** thumb a lift **2** (*zachowywać*) hang on to sth, keep[1]; (*ciepło itp.*) retain; ~ **coś (dla siebie)** hold on to sth, hold onto sth **3** (*policja*) apprehend, detain, hold sb up, pick sb up **4** (*powstrzymywać*) hold sb/sth back; ~ **dłużej wzrok/myśli na kimś/czymś** linger (on sb/sth); ~ **kogoś/coś (przed czymś)** keep sb/ sth back (from sb/sth); ~ **kogoś na rozmowę** buttonhole[2] **5** (**zatrzymać**) (*chwycić*) get
□ **zatrzym(yw)ać się 1** (*przestać się przemieszczać*) come to rest, come to a stop, stop[1]; (*autobus itp.*) draw in; (*w jakimś miejscu/na jakiejś stacji*) call[1] at…; (*na krótki postój*) lay over (at/in…), stop off (at/in…), stop over (at/in…); **zjechać na pobocze** pull in (to sth) **2** (*u kogoś na noc*) stay[1], stay over **3** (*nagle w połowie zdania*) break off, stop short
zaturkotać → TURKOTAĆ
zatuszować → TUSZOWAĆ
zatwardzenie constipation
zatwardziały bloody-minded, confirmed, incorrigible, irredeemable, obstinate
zatwier-dzać/dzić approve, pass[1], validate; ~ **coś bez zastanowienia się nad tym** rubber-stamp verb
zatyczka bung[2], pin[1], plug[1], stopper, top[1]; ~ **do ucha** earplug
zat(y)kać choke[1], jam[2] sth (up) (with sb/sth), plug[2]; **zatkał uszy rękami** he put his hands to his ears
zatytułować → TYTUŁOWAĆ
zatytułowany entitled
zaufać → UFAĆ
zaufani|e confidence (in sb/sth), credibility, faith (in sb/sth), reliance on sb/sth, trust[1] (in sb/sth); **mieć ~e do kogoś/czegoś** rely on/upon sb/sth (to do sth); **godny ~a** trustworthy; **brak ~a** distrust, mistrust noun; **nadużycie ~a** a breach of confidence; **w ~u** confidentially; **powiedzieć komuś coś w ~u** take sb into your confidence; **z pełnym ~em** confidently
zaufany trustworthy
zaułek lane
zauroczon|y: **być ~ym (kimś/czymś)** be taken with sb/sth
zauroczyć enchant
zautomatyzować → AUTOMATYZOWAĆ
zautomatyzowany high-tech
zauwa-żać/żyć 1 (*spostrzec*) discern, distinguish, note[2], notice[2], observe, perceive, spot[2]; **nie** ~ overlook; **zauważyć brak** miss[1]; **nie można tego nie zauważyć!** you can't miss it! **2** (*powiedzieć*) remark (on/upon sb/ sth)
zauważalny appreciable, noticeable, perceptible
zawada handicap[1], hindrance, impediment, obstruction
zawadzać encumber, obstruct; **czułem, że zawadzam na przyjęciu mojej córki** I felt rather in the way at my daughter's party
zawahać się → WAHAĆ SIĘ
zawa-lać/lić 1 czymś inundate sb (with sth) **2** (*sprawę*) screw sth up
■ **zawalony** (*pracą itp.*) snowed under
□ **zawalić się** zob. też WALIĆ SIĘ; collapse[1]
zawalczyć → WALCZYĆ
zawał: ~ **serca** coronary[2], heart attack
zawarcie (*umowy itp.*) conclusion
zawarkotać → WARKOTAĆ
zawarow(yw)ać stipulate
zawartoś|ć content[1]; **o niskiej ~ci** (*np. soli, alkoholu*) low[1]
zaważyć: **na czymś** weigh against (sb/ sth)
zawdzięczać owe sth (to sb/sth); **zawdzięczający wszystko samemu sobie** self-made
zawekować → WEKOWAĆ
zawetować → WETOWAĆ
zawę-żać/zić narrow sth down
■ **zawężony** narrow[1]
zawiać → WIAĆ
zawia-damiać/domić inform, notify, report[1]; (*zwł. o czymś przykrym*) break the news (to sb)
■ **zawiadomienie** announcement, notice[1], notification
zawias hinge[1]
zawiązek germ of sth
zawiąz(yw)ać bundle sth (up), do sth up, knot[2]; **zawiązać oczy** blindfold verb
zawiedziony disappointed
za-wierać/wrzeć 1 (*obejmować części*) contain, hold[1], include, incorporate sth (in/into/within sth); (*zwł. coś pojęciowego*) embody, embrace **2** ~ **(z kimś) znajomość** strike up sth (with sb) **3** (*umowę itp.*) conclude sth (with sb); ~ **kontrakt z kimś** sign[2] sb (up)
■ **zawierający** inclusive (of sth)
zawiesić → WIESZAĆ
zawiesina slime
zawie-szać/sić suspend; ~ **wykonanie kary śmierci** reprieve
zawieszeni|e suspension; **~e broni** armistice, ceasefire, truce; **stan ~a** limbo; **wyrok w ~u** probation, suspended sentence; **będący w ~u** dormant
zawieść → ZAWODZIĆ
zawieźć → ZAWOZIĆ

zawi-jać/nąć 1 (*prezent itp.*) wrap sth (up) (in sth), sth round/around sb/sth; (*meble materiałem itp.*) drape sth round/over sth **2** (*włosy*) curl[1] **3** (*zagiąć*) **coś w coś** fold[1]
□ **zawi-jać/nąć się** curl[1]

zawilgocony dank

zawiły intricate, involved, tricky; (*wyjaśnianie itp.*) convoluted, rambling, tortuous
■ **zawiłość** the intricacies of sth

zawiniątko pack[2], parcel

zawirować → WIROWAĆ

zawirowanie 1 (*wody itp.*) eddy **2** (*zamieszanie*) upset[3]

zawisnąć → WISIEĆ

zawistny envious, jealous
■ **zawiść** envy[1], jealousy

zawlec (się) → WLEC (SIĘ)

zawładnąć 1 czymś catch, get, grab, take, etc. hold (of sb/sth), seize **2** (*terenem, regionem*) annex **3** (*umysłem, wyobraźnią*) grip[2]

zawodni-k/czka contender, contestant, player

zawodny fallible, unreliable

zawodow|iec professional[2]; **zostać ~cem** turn professional

zawodow|y occupational, professional[1], vocational, working; **żołnierz ~y/armia ~a** regular soldier/army

zawody contest[1]; **~ eliminacyjne** knockout; **~ halowe** indoor games; **~ sportowe** games[1], tournament; **iść w ~** race[2] (against/with) (sb/sth)

zawodzić 1 (**zawieść**) (*rozczarować*) disappoint, let sb/sth down; **~ (czyjeś) oczekiwania** not come up to (sb's) expectations; **~ czyjeś zaufanie itp.** fall short (of sth) **2** (**zawieść**) (*pamięć itp.*) fail[1], lapse[2]; (*nerwy itp.*) fray **3** (*jęczeć*) wail

zawojow(yw)ać (*przen.*) **(kogoś)** make a hit (with sb)

zawołać → WOŁAĆ

zawołanie IDM **jak na ~** (right) on cue | **na każde ~** at sb's beck and call

za-wozić/wieźć drive[1]

zawód 1 (*fach*) calling, career[1], occupation, profession; **jaki masz ~?** what do you do?; **z zawodu** by profession **2** (*rozczarowanie*) anticlimax, disappointment; **przynoszący ~** disappointing

zawór valve; **~ bezpieczeństwa** safety valve

za-wracać/wrócić 1 (*z drogi*) turn (sb/sth) around/round, turn (sb/sth) back; (*auto*) do/make a U-turn; (*rzeka itp.*) loop verb **2 ~ komuś głowę** bother[1], hassle[2], worry[1]; **nie chcieć ~ sobie czymś głowy** can't be bothered (to do sth)

zawrotn|y 1 (*prędkość*) breakneck, dizzy; **w ~ym tempie** at a blistering pace **2** (*wysokość*) mountainous

zawrót: **~ głowy** dizziness; (*spowodowane lękiem wysokości*) vertigo; **cierpiący na zawroty głowy** dizzy, giddy, light-headed

zawrzeć → WRZEĆ, ZAWIERAĆ

zawsty-dzać/dzić mortify, shame[2], show sb up

zawstydzić się → WSTYDZIĆ SIĘ

zawstydzony abashed, sheepish

zawsze always, invariably; **na ~** forever, for keeps, for good

zawyć → WYĆ

zawziąć się put your foot down

zawzię|ty bitter[1], fierce; **(w robieniu czegoś)** intent[1] on/upon sth/doing sth, obstinate
■ **zawzięcie** fiercely; **pracować ~** work away for five hours, etc. |
zawziętość obstinacy

zazdrosny envious, jealous
■ **zazdrość** jealousy, envy[1]

zazdrościć envy[2]

zazębiać się engage with sth

zazna-czać/czyć (*pozycje w spisie*) check sth off, tick[1]; **~ markerem** highlight[1]

zazna-jamiać/jomić: **(kogoś z kimś)** introduce sb (to sb); **kogoś z czymś** take sb through sth
■ **zaznajomiony (z kimś)** acquainted (with sb); **(z czymś)** au fait (with sth); **(z kimś/czymś)** attuned (to sb/sth)
□ **zazna-jamiać/jomić się** familiarize yourself (with sth), know/learn the ropes

zazna(wa)ć know[1]

zazwyczaj in general, mostly, normally, more often than not, ordinarily, usually

zażalenie complaint, grievance

zażarcie: **~ protestować** be up in arms

zażartować → ŻARTOWAĆ

zażarty bitter[1]

zażądać → ŻĄDAĆ

zażegn(yw)ać: **~ na jakiś czas** (*np. niebezpieczeństwo*) stave sth off

zażenować → ŻENOWAĆ

zażenowanie embarrassment, mortification, self-consciousness; **odczuwać ~** cringe; **z ~m** self-consciously, sheepishly, uneasily

zażenowany embarrassed, self-conscious, sheepish, uncomfortable

zażerać się guzzle

zażyły intimate, close(ly)/tightly-knit; **zbyt ~** incestuous

zaży(wa)ć: **~ ruchu** exercise[2]

ząb 1 (*anat.*) tooth; **~ jadowy** fang; **~ mądrości** wisdom tooth; **~ trzonowy** molar **2** (*koła, kółka*) cog; (*widelca, wideł*) prong; (*grzebienia*) tooth IDM **coś na ~** something to eat

ząbek: **~ czosnku** clove of garlic

ząbkować teethe

ząbkowany jagged, serrated

z-baczać/boczyć (*piłka z toru itp.*) deflect; **~ z tematu itp.** deviate (from sth), stray[1]; **~ z właściwej drogi** stray[1], wander (away/off) (from sb/sth)

zbadać → BADAĆ

zbadani|e examination; **przy bliższym ~u** on inspection

zbagatelizować → BAGATELIZOWAĆ

zbankrutować → BANKRUTOWAĆ

zbankrutowany bankrupt

zbaranieć: **zbaraniałem przy pytaniu numer 14** I was completely stumped by question 14

zbawca saviour

Zbawiciel saviour

zbawienie redemption, salvation; (*ratunek w trudnej sytuacji*) lifeline

zbesztać → BESZTAĆ

zbezczeszczenie defilement, desecration

zbezcześcić → BEZCZEŚCIĆ

zbędny dispensable, expendable, needless, redundant, unwanted

zbić zob. też ZBIJAĆ; **~ z tropu** mystify, stump[2], throw; (*wywołać u kogoś spadek entuzjazmu itp.*) deflate
□ **zbić się** → ZBIJAĆ SIĘ

zbiec (się) → ZBIEGAĆ (SIĘ)

zbieg deserter, fugitive, runaway[2] IDM **~ okoliczności** coincidence

zbie-gać/c flee; (*skądś unosząc ze sobą coś*) abscond (from sth) (with sth)
□ **zbie-gać/c się 1** (*zgromadzić się*) **na ich krzyki zbiegli się ludzie** their screams brought people running **2** (*ulice itp.*) converge (on sb/sth) **3 ~ (w czasie z czymś)** coincide (with sth) **4** (*ubranie*) shrink

zbiegły escaped, on the run, runaway[1]; **~ i niebezpieczny** on the loose

zbieleć → BIELEĆ

zbieracz collector

zbierać/zebrać 1 assemble, collect[1], gather, get sb/sth together, round sb/sth up **2** (*kwiaty itp.*) pick[1]; (*plony z pól*) harvest; (*plony, korzyści itp.*) reap; **~ grzyby** mushroom[2]; **~ z powierzchni** skim sth (off/from sth); **zebrać wodę ścierką** soak water up with a cloth; **zebrać mocne argumenty** put together a very strong case **3** (*siły itp.*) muster sth (up), summon sth (up) **4** (*dane itp.*) glean sth (from sb/sth); **coś z czegoś/skądś** cull sth from sth; **~ i porządkować** (*informacje*) compile **5** (*pieniądze, dowody poparcia itp.*) raise **6** (*duże zapasy*) hoard[2] (sth) (up) IDM **~ manatki** pack up | **~ obfite żniwo (czegoś)** take a heavy toll/take its toll (on sth)
■ **zbieranie**: **~ danych** data capture/retrieval
□ **zbierać/zebrać się 1** (*zgromadzić się*) assemble, congregate, gather, meet; (*żołnierze itp.*) muster; (*sąd*) sit; (*długi itp.*) accumulate **2 w sobie** brace[2] sth/yourself (for sth); **~ na odwagę** pluck up courage **3** (*iść*) get along

zbieranin|a: **stanowiący ~ę** motley

zbieżność 1 (*analogia*) correspondence; **~ stanowisk** alignment **2** (*kół*) alignment; **ustawiać ~ kół samochodu** align the wheels of a car

zbieżn|y concurrent; **być ~ym** coincide (with sth)

zbijać: **~ bąki** fart around, laze (about/around)
□ **zbi(ja)ć się**: **~ w grupę/kupę** huddle[1] (up) (together)

zbiornik container, holder, receptacle; (*na benzynę itp.*) tank; (*na wodę*) reservoir; (*na wodę z toalety*) cistern

zbiornikowiec tanker

zbiorowy collective[1], concerted, corporate

zbiór 1 (*kolekcja*) collection, conglomeration; (*dużych zapasów*) hoard[1]; **dokument był zbiorem informacji pochodzących z różnych źródeł** the document was a composite of information from various sources **2** (*komput.*) folder; (*dzieł*) corpus **3** (*warzyw itp.*) crop[1] **4** (także **zbiory**) (*zbieranie plonów*) harvest

zbiórka assembly; **~ pieniędzy** collection

zbir thug, villain

zbiurokratyzowany bureaucratic

zblaknąć → BLAKNĄĆ
zblazowany blasé
zblednąć → BLEDNĄĆ
zbli-żać/żyć bridge a/the gap
■ **zbliżenie 1 (z kimś/między A i B)** rapprochement (with sb), (between A and B) **2** (*fot.*) close-up
□ **zbli-żać/żyć się 1** approach[1], come up, draw nearer, gain on sb/sth, near[2], walk up (to sb/sth); (*ulicą itp.*) come along; (*coś strasznego*) bear down (on sb/sth); (*zwł. aby zaatakować*) close in (on sb/sth); **nie ~ do czegoś** keep off sth **2 do czegoś** (*czas*) get on for sth; **zbliża się północ** it's close to midnight; **zbliża się do sześćdziesiątki** he's in his late fifties **3 do czegoś** (*graniczyć się z czymś*) verge on sth IDM **(nawet) nie zbliżając się do (uzyskania/osiągnięcia) czegoś** nowhere near
■ **zbliżający się** forthcoming, impending
zbliżony approximate
zbłaźnić się → BŁAŹNIĆ SIĘ
zbocze hillside, slope; (*drogi itp.*) incline[2]
zboczenie 1 (*z drogi*) deflection, deviation **2** (*patologia, zwł. seksualna*) perversion
zboczeniec pervert[2]
zboczyć → ZBACZAĆ
zbojkotować → BOJKOTOWAĆ
zbombardować → BOMBARDOWAĆ
zboże cereal, corn, grain
zbożow|y: **produkty ~e** grain
zbrązowiały (*od słońca/wiatru*) weather-beaten
zbrązowieć → BRĄZOWIEĆ
zbrodni|a crime, felony; **~a wojenna** war crime; **narzędzie ~** the murder weapon
zbrodnia-rz/rka criminal[2], felon
zbroić/u- (się) arm[2]
zbroja armour, suit of armour
zbrojenie 1 armament **2** (**zbrojenia**) armaments
zbrojny armed; **konflikt ~** armed conflict
zbrojownia armoury
zbrukać → BRUKAĆ
zbrzydnąć → BRZYDNĄĆ
zbudować → BUDOWAĆ
zbudowany built[1]; (*osoba*) **dobrze ~** athletic, beefy
zbulwersowany indignant
zbuntować się → BUNTOWAĆ SIĘ
zbuntowany rebellious
zburzyć comparative of BURZYĆ
zbutwiały musty
zbyci|e: **możliwy do ~a** marketable IDM (*mieć*) **na ~u** to spare
zbyć → ZBYWAĆ
zbyt[1] (*przysł.*) too
zbyt[2] (*rz.*) market[1]; **mieć (duży/mały) ~** sell
zbyteczn|y expendable, needless, redundant, superfluous, surplus adj., unwanted, useless; **~e wydatki** avoidable expense
zbytek luxury
zbytkowny luxurious; (*styl życia itp.*) gracious
zby(wa)ć 1 (*odstręczyć kogoś*) put sb off (sb/sth/doing sth) **2 kogoś (czymś)** fob sb off (with sth); **~ coś śmiechem** laugh sth off
■ **zbywający** odd, spare[1]
zbzikowany barmy, batty, loony adj., nutty, potty[1]
zcierać/zetrzeć (*przen.*) **~ na proch** pulverize
zci-szać/szyć: **zciszyć głos** lower your voice
zdać zob. też ZDAWAĆ (SIĘ); (*egzamin*) pass[1]; **nie ~** fail[1]
zdaln|y: **~e sterowanie** remote control
zdani|e 1 (*opinia*) judgement, opinion, thinking[1], thought[2], view[1]; **moim ~em** as far as I'm concerned, if you ask me, my bet is that…, my own feeling is that…, to my mind, in my opinion, I should imagine, say, think, etc., in my view; **być ~a, że** be of the opinion that…; **twoim ~em** in your judgement; **co, twoim ~em, mogło się zdarzyć?** what do you suppose could have happened?; **jak, twoim ~em, rozwinie się sytuacja?** how do you see the situation developing?; **być innego ~a** differ (with sb) (about/on sth), disagree (with sb/sth) (about/on sth), dissent[2] (from sth); **zmieniać czyjeś ~e** budge; **mieć o kimś/czymś dobre/złe itp. ~e** have a good, high, etc. opinion of sb/sth, have a bad, low, poor, etc. opinion of sb/sth, think highly, a lot, not much, etc. of sb/sth **2** (*gram.*) clause, sentence[1]; **~e podrzędne** subordinate clause
zdany: **na siebie** unaided
zdarcie wear[2]
zdarty worn out
zda-rzać/rzyć się come about, come up, happen, take place; **zdarzało się, że śnieg padał w czerwcu** it's been known to snow in June
zdarzenie happening, incident
zdatny serviceable, useful
■ **zdatność** fitness
zda(wa)ć 1 ~ egzamin do/take/sit an exam; **zdać egzamin** pass an exam **2** (*z czegoś sprawę itp.*) relate **3 ~ sobie sprawę (z czegoś)** appreciate, realize, wake up to sth; **nie zdający sobie z czegoś sprawy** unconscious of sb/sth
□ **zda(wa)ć się** appear, fancy[1] (that), seem
zdawkowy bland, perfunctory
zdą-żać/żyć 1 (*na czas itp.*) catch[1]; **~ gdzieś na czas** make it **2** (*w kierunku opisanym*) head[2]
zdechły dead[1]
zdecydować (się) → DECYDOWAĆ (SIĘ)
zdecydowanie[2] (*przysł.*) certainly, convincingly, decidedly, decisively, definitely, by far, positively, purposefully, resolutely; **iść ~** stride[1]
zdecydowani|e[1] (*rz.*) decision, decisiveness, resolution; **brak ~a** uncertainty
zdecydowany 1 (*wynik itp.*) definite; (*zwycięstwo*) convincing; (*zmiana itp.*) decided, pronounced **2** (*osoba; postępowanie*) decisive, determined, purposeful, resolute, set[3] (for sth), (to do sth), strong; **o ~ch poglądach** strong-minded
zdefiniować → DEFINIOWAĆ
zdeformować → DEFORMOWAĆ
zdeformowany deformed, gnarled, out of shape, stunted
zdefraudować → DEFRAUDOWAĆ
zdegenerować → DEGENEROWAĆ
zdegenerowany degenerate[2]
zdegradować → DEGRADOWAĆ
zdegustowan|y sick[1] (at/about sth); **wyjść ~ym** walk out in disgust
zdejmować/zdjąć 1 coś (z czegoś) get sth off (sth), remove sb/sth (from sth); (*farbę, warstwę itp.*) strip[1] sth (off) **2** (*ubranie*) take sth off; **zdjąć buta** get your shoe off **3 ~ odciski palców** take sb's fingerprints **4** (*z półki itp.*) bring/lift sth down/off sth
zdeklarować (się) → DEKLAROWAĆ (SIĘ)
zdeklarowany (*zwolennik itp.*) avowed
zdemaskować → DEMASKOWAĆ
zdemilitaryzować → DEMILITARYZOWAĆ
zdemobilizować → DEMOBILIZOWAĆ
zdemontować → DEMONTOWAĆ
zdemoralizować → DEMORALIZOWAĆ
zdenerwować (się) → DENERWOWAĆ (SIĘ)
zdenerwowanie agitation, annoyance, exasperation, excitement, the jitters, nervousness
zdenerwowan|y agitated, on edge, edgy, het up, irritated, jittery, nervous, upset[2], uptight, worked up; **być ~ym** be in/get into a flap
zdeponować → DEPONOWAĆ
zdeprawować → DEPRAWOWAĆ
zdeprawowanie depravity
zdeprawowany depraved
zdeprecjonować (się) → DEPRECJONOWAĆ (SIĘ)
zdeptać → DEPTAĆ
zde-rzać/rzyć clash[1]
□ **zde-rzać/rzyć się 1** bash[1], bump[1], crash[2], collide **2** (*nie zgadzać się*) clash[1] (with sb/sth)
zderzak buffer, bumper[1]
zderzenie collision, crash[1]; **~ czołowe** head-on collision
zdesperowany desolate
zdestabilizować → DESTABILIZOWAĆ
zdeterminowan|y determined, intent[1], set[3] (to do sth)
zdetonować → DETONOWAĆ
zdewaluować (się) → DEWALUOWAĆ (SIĘ)
zdewastować → DEWASTOWAĆ
zdewastowany devastated
zdezaktualizowany obsolete
zdezaktywować → DEZAKTYWOWAĆ
zdezaprobować → DEZAPROBOWAĆ
zdezelowany ramshackle
zdezerterować → DEZERTEROWAĆ
zdezorganizować → DEZORGANIZOWAĆ
zdezorganizowany disorganized
zdezorientować → DEZORIENTOWAĆ
zdezorientowan|y bewildered; **być ~ym** bumble
zdezynfekować → DEZYNFEKOWAĆ
zdezynsekować → DEZYNSEKOWAĆ
zdigitalizować → DIGITALIZOWAĆ
zdjąć → ZDEJMOWAĆ
zdjęci|e photograph, picture[1], shot[1]; (*naświetlona klatka*) exposure; **robić ~e** photograph verb, take a photo (graph); **robić ~e rentgenowskie** X-ray verb; **~a trikowe** special effects
zdławić → DŁAWIĆ
zd-muchiwać/muchnąć blow (sth) out
zdobyci|e 1 capture[2]; **nie do ~a** impregnable **2** (*osiągnięcie*) achievement

zdobycz 1 (*łup*) haul[2], plunder, spoils **2** (*zwierzęcia*) the kill, prey[1] **3** (*nauki itp.*) triumph[1] **4** (*nabycie czegoś*) acquisition
zdobyt|y: **ledwo ~e zwycięstwo** a narrow victory
zdoby(wa)ć 1 (*otrzymać*) acquire, come by sth, get hold of sth; (*dostęp do czegoś; sławę*) gain[1]; (*poparcie itp.*) muster sth (up); (*kontrakt, pracę itp.*) land[2] **2** (*miasto itp.*) capture[1], conquer, take possession of sth; **~ przewagę/kontrolę** get, have, etc. the upper hand **3** (*osiągnąć*) chalk sth up, notch sth up; (*nagrodę*) win
□ **zdoby(wa)ć się**: **~ na odwagę** pluck up courage; **nie mógł się zdobyć na pójście do pracy** he couldn't face going to work yesterday
zdobyw-ca/czyni captor, conqueror
zdolność 1 ability, capacity, capability, power[1], talent; (*myślenia, odczuwania itp.*) faculty; (**zdolności**) flair; **wybitna ~** (*do robienia czegoś*) prowess **2 ~ kredytowa** creditworthiness
zdolny able adj., capable, clever, talented, together[2] IDM **uważać, że ktoś jest ~ do zrobienia czegoś złego** not put it past sb (to do sth)
zdołać: **coś zrobić** bring sth off, manage
zdominować → DOMINOWAĆ
zdopingować → DOPINGOWAĆ
zdrada betrayal, treason; **~ małżeńska** infidelity
zdradliwość treachery
zdradliwy insidious, treacherous
zdra-dzać/dzić 1 (*oszukać*) betray; (*męża/żonę*) cheat[1] (on sb), be unfaithful (to sb) **2** (*tajemnicę itp.*) give sth/sb away, let on (about sth) (to sb), tell; **~ tajemnicę** give the game away; **zdradził ją wyraz twarzy** her face was a dead giveaway
■ **zdradzający** telltale
zdradziecki insidious, treacherous
zdraj-ca/czyni renegade, traitor
zdrapka scratch card
zdrap(yw)ać scratch[1]; (*farbę itp.*) chip
zdrętwiały dead[1], numb
zdrętwieć → DRĘTWIEĆ
zdrętwienie crick
zdrobnieni|e: **w ~u** for short
zdrowie health; **~ psychiczne** sanity IDM **na ~!** cheers; (*w odpowiedzi na kichnięcie*) bless you!
zdrowieć/wy- be/get better, be on the mend, pull through (sth), recover, recuperate
zdrowotn|y: **ubezpieczenie ~e** health insurance
zdrowszy better[1]
zdrow|y 1 (*nie chory*) all right, fit[2] (for sth/to do sth), fine[1], healthy, (as) right as rain, well[2], yourself, etc.; (*po chorobie*) (back) on your feet; (*po wypadku*) safe[1]; **~y (fizycznie)** able-bodied **2** (*żywność, styl życia itp.*) good[1] (for sb/sth), healthy, wholesome; **~a żywność** health food, wholefood; **pieczywo pełnoziarniste jest ~sze od białego** wholemeal bread has more goodness in it than white **4** (*moralność itp.*) wholesome IDM **przy ~ych zmysłach** sane | **~y rozsądek** common sense, good sense, sense[1]

zdruzgotać → DRUZGOTAĆ
zdruzgotanie devastation
zdrzemnąć zob. też DRZEMAĆ; conk out, doze off, drop off, snooze
zdubbingować → DUBBINGOWAĆ
zdublować → DUBLOWAĆ
zdumienie amazement, astonishment, wonder[2]
zdumie(wa)ć amaze, astound, boggle the mind, floor[2], take sb aback
□ **zdumie(wa)ć się** the mind boggles, marvel verb (at sth), wonder[1] (at sth)
zdumiewając|y amazing, astounding, marvellous, stupendous; **~e!** the mind boggles!; **~e, że** it's a wonder (that)…
zdumiony amazed, astounded
zdusić → DUSIĆ
zduszony: **~ śmiech** chuckle noun
zdyskredytować → DYSKREDYTOWAĆ
zdyskredytowanie discredit noun
zdyskwalifikować → DYSKWALIFIKOWAĆ
zdystansować się → DYSTANSOWAĆ SIĘ
zdziczały 1 (*kot itp.*) feral **2** (*zachowanie itp.*) abandoned
zdziecinniały senile
zdziecinnienie senility
zdzielić: **kogoś** catch[1]
zdzierać/zedrzeć 1 (*zużywać*) wear sth away, wear sth down, wear sth out; (*buty*) scuff **2** (*zrywać*) strip[1] sth (off)
□ **zdzierać/zedrzeć się** wear[1], wear away, wear down, wear out
zdzierstwo: **to ~!** that's extortionate!
zdziesiątkować → DZIESIĄTKOWAĆ
zdzira slut
zdziwić się → DZIWIĆ SIĘ
zdziwienie astonishment, surprise[1], wonder[2]
zdziwiony astonished, surprised
zebra 1 (*zool.*) zebra **2** (*przejście dla pieszych*) zebra crossing
zebrać (się) → ZBIERAĆ (SIĘ)
zebranie gathering, meeting
zechcieć → CHCIEĆ
zedrzeć (się) → ZDZIERAĆ (SIĘ)
zegar clock[1]; **~ słoneczny** sundial; **~ stojący** grandfather clock
zegar|ek watch[2]; **~ek na rękę** wristwatch IDM **iść jak w ~ku** go like clockwork
zejście descent; (*ze statku*) disembarkation
zejść (się) → SCHODZIĆ (SIĘ)
zekstrapolować → EKSTRAPOLOWAĆ
zelektryfikować → ELEKTRYFIKOWAĆ
zelektryzować → ELEKTRYZOWAĆ
zelówka sole[2]
zelżyć → LŻYĆ
zelżeć ease[2], ease off
zemdleć → MDLEĆ
zemleć → MLEĆ
zemsta revenge, vengeance
zemścić (się) → MŚCIĆ (SIĘ)
zenit 1 (*astr.*) zenith **2** (*przen.*) height, zenith
zepsuci|e: **nie do ~a** foolproof
zepsuć (się) → PSUĆ (SIĘ)
zepsuty 1 (*urządzenie*) broken[2], broken-down, bust[3], out of order; (*linia telefoniczna*) dead[1] **2** (*żywność*) bad, off[2] **3** (*osoba*) corrupt[1] **4** (*ząb*) decayed
zerk-ać/nąć glance[1], peek, peep[1]; **zerknij na ten artykuł** take a look at this article
zer|o 1 nought, zero[1]; (*zwł. w wynikach sportowych*) nil; **poniżej ~a** minus[1]; **~o tolerancji** zero tolerance **2** (*w tenisie*) love[1] **3** (*osoba*) nobody[2] **4** (*temperatura*) freezing[2]; **spadać poniżej ~a** freeze[1] IDM (*zacząć itp.*) **od ~a** from scratch
zerodować → ERODOWAĆ
zerowy 1 zero[1] **2** (*elektr.*) neutral[1]
zerwać (się) → ZRYWAĆ (SIĘ)
zerwanie break[2], rupture; **~ stosunków** breach[1], rupture
zeschnąć się → ZSYCHAĆ SIĘ
zeskanować → SKANOWAĆ
zeskrob(yw)ać zob. też SKROBAĆ; scrape[1] sth (down/out/off)
zesłać → ZSYŁAĆ
ze-spalać/spolić join[1]
□ **ze-spalać/spolić się** coalesce (into/with sth), join[1] (up)
zespawać → SPAWAĆ
zespołow|y corporate; **praca ~a** teamwork
zespół 1 crew, party, team[1], unit; (*specjalistów itp.*) panel; **~ muzyczny** band, group[1]; **~ muzyczny/taneczny/aktorski** ensemble **2** (*med.*) **~ Downa** Down's syndrome; **~ napięcia przedmiesiączkowego** PMS
zestarzeć się → STARZEĆ SIĘ
zestaw collection, kit[1], package, set[2]; **~ dnia** the set menu; **~ stereo (foniczny)** stereo; **~ wypoczynkowy** suite
zestawi(a)ć 1 (*dane itp.*) collate; **~ w formie tabeli** tabulate **2 coś z czymś** (*przedstawiać kontrast*) juxtapose **3** (*drużynę*) field[2]
■ **zestawienie** (*danych itp.*) collation; **~ bilansowe** balance sheet
ze-strajać/stroić się tune sth up
zestrajanie harmonization
zestresować → STRESOWAĆ
zestresowany strained, stressed
zestrugać → STRUGAĆ
zestrzelić shoot sb/sth down
zeswatać → SWATAĆ
zeszły last[1], past[1]
zeszpecić → SZPECIĆ
zesztywniały stiff[1]
zesztywnieć → SZTYWNIEĆ
zesztywnienie stiffness
zeszyt book[1]; (*do ćwiczeń*) exercise book
ześlizgnąć się glance off (sth)
ześrodkow(yw)ać (się) focus[1] (sth) (on sth)
zetknąć (się) → STYKAĆ (SIĘ)
zetknięcie się encounter[2]
zetrzeć (się) → ŚCIERAĆ (SIĘ), ZCIERAĆ
zeuropeizować → EUROPEIZOWAĆ
zewnątrz (*na/z*) outside[1]; **na ~** out adj., outdoors, out of doors, outside[3], outside adv., outwards; **osoba z ~** outsider; **z ~** external, externally
zewnętrzn|y 1 exterior[2], outer, outside[2]; (*ściana itp.*) external; (*techn.*) peripheral[1]; **~a strona** exterior[1], outside[1]; **~a warstwa** surface[1] **2** (*oznaki; objawy itp.*) outward; **cechy ~e** physical attributes; **hałasy ~e** extraneous noises; **wygląd ~y** exterior[1]
zewrzeć → ZWIERAĆ
zez squint noun
zeznanie testimony; **~ podatkowe** tax return
zezna(wa)ć testify
zezować squint
zezowaty cross-eyed

ze-zwalać/zwolić allow, clear[2], grant[1], grant sb permission to do sth, permit[1], sanction[2]
zezwolenie clearance, licence (to do sth), permission, permit[2], sanction[1]; **wydawać ~** license[1]
zębaty serrated
zga-dywać/dnąć guess[1], make a guess, hazard[2]
zgadywanie guesswork
z-gadzać/godzić się 1 (*być takiego samego zdania*) agree (with sb/sth), (that…), go along with sb/sth, see eye to eye (with sb), subscribe to sth; **nie ~ (z czymś)** disagree, quarrel[2] with sth; **nie ~ z kimś (co do czegoś)** be at odds (with sb) (over sth); **wszyscy zgadzają się z nami** we've got everybody with us on this issue **2 na coś** (*pozwalać*) accede (to sth), acquiesce in/to sth, agree (to do sth), (on) sth, be agreeable (to sth), concur, consent[1] (to sth), grant[1]; **nie ~ na coś/ zrobienie czegoś** be set against sth/ doing sth, won't/wouldn't hear of sth; **pozornie się zgadzać (na coś) (z kimś)** play along (with sb/sth); **zgadza się?** OK interj.; **no zgódź się!** go on **3** (*fakty, wyniki itp.*) accord[2] (with sth), add up, correspond (to/with sth), square[3] (sth) with sb/sth, tally verb (with sth); **zgadza się!** that is so; **nie ~** disagree
zgaga heartburn
zgalwanizować → GALWANIZOWAĆ
zganić → GANIĆ
zgarbić się → GARBIĆ SIĘ
zgarbion|y: **~e plecy** stoop noun
zgar-niać/nąć 1 (*w jedno miejsce*) scoop[2], sweep[1]; (*co najlepsze*) cream sth off **2** (*wygraną itp.*) pocket[2]
zgasić → GASIĆ
zgasnąć → GASNĄĆ
zgaszony out adj.
zgęstnieć → GĘSTNIEĆ
zgiąć → ZGINAĆ
zgiełk bustle[2], commotion, hubbub, hullabaloo, noise, row[3], turmoil, uproar; **pełen ~u** bustling (with sth)
zgiełkliwy tumultuous
zgięcie: **~ w łokciu** the crook of your arm
zgilotynować → GILOTYNOWAĆ
z-ginać/giąć bend[1], flex[1]; **kogoś** double sb up/over
□ **z-ginać/giąć się** double up/over
zginąć → GINĄĆ
zglobalizować → GLOBALIZOWAĆ
z-głaszać/głosić report[1]; **~ do oclenia** declare; **~ udział** enter (for) sth, sb (in/for sth)
□ **z-głaszać/głosić się 1** report[1] (to sb/ sth) for sth **2 po coś** claim[1]
z-głaśniać/głośnić turn the sound up
zgłębi(a)ć fathom, follow sth up; (*tajniki czegoś itp.*) penetrate
zgłodniały famished
zgłodnieć get hungry
zgłoszenie (*na kurs, do klubu itp.*) enrolment; (*na konkurs*) entry
zgnębić → GNĘBIĆ
zgnębiony harassed
z-gniatać/gnieść zob. też GNIEŚĆ; squeeze[1] sth (out), sth (from/out of sth); **~ w kulkę** screw[2] sth (up) (into sth)
zgnić → GNIĆ
zgniły decayed, rotten
zgod|a 1 (*porozumienie*) agreement, consensus **2** (*stan pokoju*) harmony, reconciliation, unity; **(nie) w ~zie z kimś/czymś** in/out of tune; **prezent na ~ę** a peace offering **3** (*zezwolenie*) acquiescence, approval, assent, consent[2], OK[2], okey-doke; **wyrażać ~ę** agree, assent verb (to sth); **za ~ą kogoś** (by) courtesy of sb **4** (*fakty itp.*) **być w ~zie** square[3] with sb/ sth **4** (*gram.*) agreement IDM **~a!** all right, done[3], OK interj., right (you are)!, very well
zgodnie 1 (*rozprawiać o czymś itp.*) harmoniously; (*grupa ludzi*) unanimously, in unison **2 z czymś** in accord, in accordance with sth, according to, in keeping (with sth), under; **~ z prawdą** truthfully; **~ z tradycją** by tradition
zgodn|y 1 (*wnioski itp.*) harmonious; (*grupa ludzi*) unanimous **2 z czymś** in accord, in accordance with sth, compatible, consistent (with sth); (*z przepisami itp.*) compliant (with sth), in keeping (with sth); **~y z oczekiwaniami** true (to sb/sth); **~y z prawdą** true, truthful; **być ~ym z czymś** accord with sth, be in line with sth, resonate (with sth)
zgodzić (się) → ZGADZAĆ (SIĘ)
zgon death, demise
zgorszyć → GORSZYĆ
zgorzel gangrene
zgorzelinowy gangrenous
zgorzkniały bitter[1] (about sth), embittered
■ **zgorzkniale** sourly
zgotować 1 (*udzielić*) accord[2]; **~ serdeczne przyjęcie** make sb welcome **2** (*klęskę*) put sb through sth
zgrabny 1 (*osoba*) dainty, graceful **2** (*rozwiązanie, wypowiedź itp.,*) neat; (*występ itp.*) slick[1] **3** (*pojazd: opływowy*) sleek
zgranie[1] (*rz.*) cohesion
zgranie[2] (*przysł.*) harmoniously
zgromadzenie assembly, gathering
zgromadzić (się) → GROMADZIĆ (SIĘ)
zgrubienie node
zgryzota unhappiness
zgryźliwy pointed
zgrzeszyć → GRZESZYĆ
zgrzybiały decrepit
zgrzyt creak noun, scrape[2]
zgrzyt-ać/nąć creak, grate[2] (against/ on sth), grind[1], scrape[1] (sth) against/ along/on sth IDM **~ zębami** gnash your teeth
zgrzytliwy discordant
zguba loss
zgubić (się) → GUBIĆ (SIĘ)
zgubiony lost[2], missing
zgubny (*błąd*) fatal; (*wpływ itp.*) malign; (*decyzja finansowa itp.*) ruinous
zgwałcić → GWAŁCIĆ
zhańbić → HAŃBIĆ
zharmonizować → HARMONIZOWAĆ
ziać (*otwór*) gape (open)
ziarenko grain, granule
ziarnisty grainy
ziarnko bean; **~ gradu** hailstone IDM **~ prawdy** element of truth
ziarno corn, grain, seed; **ziarna kawy** coffee beans IDM **~ prawdy** a grain/ kernel of truth
zidentyfikować → IDENTYFIKOWAĆ
ziela-rz/rka herbalist
zieleniak (*sklep*) greengrocer's
ziele|ń 1 (*kolor*) green[2]; **~ń butelkowa** bottle-green noun **2** (*rośliny*) greenery; **pas/strefa ~ni** green belt
zielonkawy greenish
zielon|y 1 (*kolor*) green; (*drzewo*) **wiecznie ~y** evergreen; **~a karta** green card **2** (*niedoświadczony*) clueless, green[1] **3** (*dolar*) buck[1] **4** (*dzielnica, ulica itp.*) leafy IDM **nie mieć ~ego (pojęcia)** not have the faintest/foggiest (idea) | **zapalać/ dostać ~e światło** give sb/get the green light/the all-clear, get/be given the thumbs down | **Zielone Świątki** Whitsun
■ **Zieloni** (*rz., polit.*) the Greens[2]
zielsko weed[1]
ziemi|a 1 (*grunt*) ground[1]; **nad/pod ~ą** above/below ground; **pod ~ą** underground[2] **2** (*do sprzedaży itp.*) land[1]; **~a niczyja** no-man's-land **3** (*gleba*) dirt, earth[1], soil[1] **4** (**Ziemia**) earth[1], planet, world **5** (*suknia itp.*) **do ~** full-length IDM (*przen.*) **nie z tej ~** out of this world, unearthly | **~a ojczysta** your native land
ziemiański landowning
ziemiaństwo the landed gentry
ziemisty earthy
ziemniak potato; (*nieform.*) spud; **~ w mundurku** jacket potato
ziemski earthly, worldly
ziew-ać/nąć yawn
zięba finch
zięć son-in-law
zignorować → IGNOROWAĆ
ziluminować → ILUMINOWAĆ
zilustrować → ILUSTROWAĆ
zima winter, wintertime
zimitować → IMITOWAĆ
zimnica malaria
zimno (*przysł.*) **na dworze jest ~** it's cold outside; **jest mi ~** I'm cold; **strasznie mi ~** I'm freezing
■ **zimno** (*rz.*) **1** cold[2], the cool[3] **2** (*med.*) cold sore
zimnokrwisty cold-blooded
zimn|y 1 chilly, cold[1] **2** (*osoba*) cold-hearted; (*uczucia, atmosfera*) impersonal; **bardzo ~y** freezing[1] IDM **~a krew** nerve | **z ~ą krwią** in cold blood
zimowy winter, wintry
zimozielony evergreen
zindoktrynować → INDOKTRYNOWAĆ
zindustrializować (się) → INDUSTRIALIZOWAĆ (SIĘ)
zinfiltrować → INFILTROWAĆ
zinstytucjonalizować → INSTYTUCJONALIZOWAĆ
zintegrować → INTEGROWAĆ
zintensyfikować → INTENSYFIKOWAĆ
zinterpretować → INTERPRETOWAĆ
zioło herb
ziołolecznictwo herbalism
ziołowy herbal
zionąć yawn
zirygować → IRYGOWAĆ
zirytować → IRYTOWAĆ
zirytowany annoyed, impatient, peeved
z-jadać/jeść swallow[1]; **zjedz wszystko** eat (your dinner) up

zjadliwy acrimonious, catty, caustic, pointed, scathing, vicious, vitriolic
zjawa apparition, ghost, phantom
zjawi(a)ć się appear, roll up, show up, turn up
zjawisk|o occurrence, phenomenon; **~a nadprzyrodzone** the supernatural
zjazd 1 (*spotkanie*) conference, congress, convention; (*szkolny itp.*) reunion **2** (*droga*) exit[1], slip road; **~ z głównej drogi** turn-off
zjazdow|y: **narciarstwo ~e** downhill skiing
zjednoczenie unification, union
zjednoczony bound together, knit, united; **Zjednoczone Królestwo** the United Kingdom
zjednoczyć (się) → JEDNOCZYĆ (SIĘ)
zjedn(yw)ać (*poparcie*) enlist; (*klientów itp.*) drum sth up
zjełczały rancid
zjełczeć → JEŁCZEĆ
zjeść → JEŚĆ, ZJADAĆ
z-jeżdżać/jechać 1 (*z drogi*) pull off (sth), turn off (sth); **~ na bok** pull over **2** (*na wolnym biegu*) coast[2]; **~ na sankach** sledge verb **3** (*zniknąć*) clear off; **zjeżdżaj!** hop it! **4** (**zjechać**) (*krytykować*) blast[2]
zjeżdżalnia slide[2]; (*na basenie*) water chute
zjeżyć (się) → JEŻYĆ (SIĘ)
zlać się → ZLEWAĆ SIĘ
zle-cać/cić (*pracę na zewnątrz*) commission[2], contract sth out (to sb), delegate[2], instruct sb (to do sth)
zleceni|e 1 commission[1]; **na umowę ~a** freelance; **osoba zatrudniona na umowę ~a** freelance; **pracować na umowę ~a** freelance verb **2 ~e stałe** standing order
zlekceważony neglected
zlekceważyć → LEKCEWAŻYĆ
zlepek amalgam, conglomeration
zlepić (się) → LEPIĆ (SIĘ)
zlew sink[2]
zl(ew)ać się coalesce (into/with sth); **rzeki zlewają się w Oksfordzie** the rivers meet in Oxford; **~ w jedno** blend (into sth), fuse, merge (with sth)
zlewka beaker
zlewozmywak sink[2]
zliberalizować → LIBERALIZOWAĆ
zlicytować → LICYTOWAĆ
zli-czać/czyć reckon (sth) up, tot (sth) up
zlikwidować → LIKWIDOWAĆ
zlikwidowanie closing noun
zlikwidowany defunct
zlinczować → LINCZOWAĆ
zlokalizować → LOKALIZOWAĆ
zlokalizowanie location
złachany ratty
złachmaniony ragged
zła-gadzać/godzić zob. też ŁAGODZIĆ; relax
złagodnieć → ŁAGODNIEĆ
złagodzenie relief
złajać → ŁAJAĆ
złamać (się) → ŁAMAĆ (SIĘ)
złamanie 1 break[2], fracture **2** (*prawa itp.*) infringement IDM **na ~ karku** at breakneck speed
złamany broken[2]
złapać → ŁAPAĆ
złapanie catch[2]
złącze 1 (*techn.*) connection, join[2], joint[2] **2 między A i B** (*i komput.*) interface (between A and B)
złączeni|e: **miejsce ~a** join[2]
złączon|y: **stań ze ~ymi stopami** stand with your feet together
złączyć (się) → ŁĄCZYĆ (SIĘ)
zło badness, evil[2], wickedness, wrong[3]
złocenie gilt
złocić/po- gild
złocień chrysanthemum
złocisty golden
złoczyńca offender
złodziej/ka burglar, robber, thief
złodziejstwo rip-off, theft
złoić → ŁOIĆ
złom scrap[1]
złomowisko scrap heap
złościć/roz- anger[2], enrage, wind sb up □ **złościć/roz- się** get angry, lose your temper, get cross[3] (with sb) (about sth)
złoś|ć acrimony, anger[1]; **ze ~cią** angrily, crossly; **powiedzieć coś na ~ć** say sth to spite sb
złośliwy 1 (*osoba*) bitchy, catty, malicious, mean[2], nasty, sharp[1], spiteful, venomous, vicious, vindictive **2** (*wandalizm itp.*) wanton **3** (*odmiana choroby*) virulent; (*nowotwór itp.*) malignant
złośni-k/ca grump
złotnik jeweller
złoto gold
złot|y 1 (*ze złota*) gold adj.; **~-y/a medalist-a/ka** gold medallist; **~y medal** gold medal **2** golden (*kolor*) IDM **~a rybka** goldfish | **~a rączka** handyman | **~a zasada** the golden rule (of sth) | **znajdować ~y środek** strike a balance (between A and B)
złowić → ŁOWIĆ
złowieszczy ominous, sinister
■ **złowieszczo** darkly
złowrog|i malevolent, sinister; **~a cisza** a brooding silence
■ **złowrogo** darkly, malevolently
złowróżbny inauspicious, ominous, sinister
złoże field[1]
złożenie submission
złożonoś|ć complexity, intricacies; **przedyskutować problem w całej jego ~ci** discuss a problem in depth
złożony 1 (*skomplikowany*) complex[1], intricate **2** (*składający się z czegoś*) composite **3** (*różnoraki*) multiple[1]; **czasownik ~** phrasal verb
złożyć (się) → SKŁADAĆ (SIĘ)
złuda fallacy, illusion
złudny illusory
złudzenie delusion, illusion, mirage, phantom; **~ optyczne** optical illusion
złupić → ŁUPIĆ
złuszczyć (się) → ŁUSZCZYĆ (SIĘ)
zł|y 1 (*niedobry*) bad; (*niepoprawny, nieodpowiedni*) wrong[1]; (*nielegalny/przestępczy*) wrong[1] (to do sth) **2** (*szkodliwy*) ill[1] **3** (*zepsuty*) bad; (*bardzo zepsuty*) evil[1], wicked **4 na kogoś/coś** angry, annoyed, cross[3], grumpy; **bardzo ~y** in a temper; **w ~ym humorze** sour **5** (*pies*) fierce **6** (*marny*) rough[1]; **w ~ym stanie** out of condition **7 mieć coś komuś za ~e** bear a grudge against sb, hold sth against sb, resent; **nie mieć komuś za ~e** I don't blame you/her, etc. (for doing sth); **jestem pewna, że Simon nie będzie miał ci tego za ~e, jeśli go nie zaprosisz** I'm sure Simon won't mind if you don't invite him IDM **cieszący się ~ą sławą** infamous (for sth) | **brać za ~e** take sth amiss | **być ~ym na siebie** kick yourself | **dobre i ~e strony** the pros and cons | **na dobre i na ~e** through thick and thin | **patrzeć na kogoś/coś ~ym okiem** look on sb/sth with a jaundiced eye | **~a sława** notoriety | **~a strona** downside
zmagać się fight sb/sth off, struggle[1] (with sth/for sth/to do sth), wrestle (with sth); (*w wodzie itp.*) flounder[1]
zmaganie struggle[2], war; **(zmagania)** strife
□ **zmaganie się** struggle[2]
zmagazynować → MAGAZYNOWAĆ
zmajstrować → MAJSTROWAĆ
zmaksymalizować → MAKSYMALIZOWAĆ
zmaleć → MALEĆ
zmaltretować → MALTRETOWAĆ
zmarginalizować → MARGINALIZOWAĆ
zmarły (*przym.*) dead[1], deceased adj., late
■ **zmarł-y/a** the deceased
zmarniały (*osoba*) wan
zmarnieć → MARNIEĆ
zmarnotrawić → MARNOTRAWIĆ
zmarnotrawiony wasted
zmarnować (się) → MARNOWAĆ (SIĘ)
zmarnowanie waste[2]
zmarnowany wasted
zmarszczenie: **~ brwi** frown noun
zmarszczk|a crease[1], furrow, wrinkle[1], line; **pokryty ~ami** lined
zmarszczony wrinkled
zmarszczyć (się) → MARSZCZYĆ (SIĘ)
zmartwić (się) → MARTWIĆ (SIĘ)
zmartwie|nie trouble[1], upset[3], worry[2]; **wydaje się nie mieć żadnych ~ń** he doesn't seem to have a care in the world; **pełen ~nia** agonized; **sprawiać komuś ~nia** play sb up
zmartwiony bothered, distraught, unhappy, worked up, worried
Zmartwychwstanie the Resurrection
zmarznąć → MARZNĄĆ
zmarznięty frozen[2]
zmasakrować → MASAKROWAĆ
zmaterializować się → MATERIALIZOWAĆ SIĘ
zmatowieć → MATOWIEĆ
z-mawiać/mówić się conspire, gang up on sb
zmaz(yw)ać wipe[1] sth (off) (sth)
zmącić → MĄCIĆ
zmechanizować → MECHANIZOWAĆ
zmęczenie 1 fatigue, tiredness, weariness; **ze ~m** wearily **2** (*materiału*) fatigue
zmęczony exhausted, tired, weary
zmęczyć → MĘCZYĆ
zmian|a 1 change[2]; (*kierunku, położenia itp.*) shift[2]; **~a zdania** climbdown; **~a kierunku** reversal; **~a na lepsze** upturn; **~a na lepsze/gorsze** a change for the better/worse; **~a pracy** move[2]; **~a w sposobie myślenia/patrzenia** a change of heart; **drobna ~a** alteration, modification; **nagła ~a** switch[1]; **ciągłe ~y** flux; **(nieoczekiwana) ~a w wydarzeniach/sprawach** twist[2]; **operacja ~y płci** sex change; **wprowadzać ~y** innovate **2 czegoś na coś** changeover **3** (*środka lokomocji*) transfer[2] **4** (*w pracy*) shift[2]; **pracować na ~y** do shift work **5** (*kolej*) rotation, turn[2]; **robić coś na ~ę** take

turns (at sth); **na ~y** in relays **6** (*w stołówce*) sitting
zmiatać/zmieść sweep sth off sth; (*z powierzchni ziemi itp.*) wipe sth out IDM **~ jedzenie z talerza** gobble sth (up/down)
zmiażdżyć → MIAŻDŻYĆ
zmiąć (się) → MIĄĆ (SIĘ)
zmieni(a)ć alter, change[1], rearrange; (*głos, charakter pisma itp.*) disguise[1] sb/sth (as sb/sth); **w coś** form[2]; **kogoś/coś (z czegoś) w coś** turn sb/sth (from sth) into sth; (*kolejno*) alternate[1] A with B, rotate; **~ temat** change the subject; **nagle ~** (*np. temat*) go off at a tangent; **~ zdanie** change your mind, climb down (over sth), think better of (doing) sth, have second thoughts (about sth); **~ zdanie/decyzję** backtrack (on sth), reverse[1]; **~ czyjeś zdanie** budge; **~ położenie/kierunek** shift[1]; **~ wygląd pod wpływem warunków atmosferycznych** weather[2] IDM **~ front** change your tune
□ **zmieni(a)ć się 1** alter, change[1], shift[1]; **w coś** grow into sth; **prawie się nie zmienić** remain almost unchanged; **zmienić się na lepsze** change your ways **2 z A na B** fluctuate (between A and B), vary (from… to…); (*kolejno*) rotate, take turns
zmienn|y 1 changeable, fitful, uneven, unsettled, unstable, variable, volatile; (*plany itp.*) fluid[2]; (*koleje losu itp.*) chequered **2** (*osoba*) fickle, unsettled, unstable, volatile; (*zwł. kobieta*) flighty; (*niezdecydowany przy głosowaniu itp.*) floating
zmierzać zob. też MIERZYĆ (SIĘ) **1** (*jechać*) head for sth **2** (*sugerować*) be driving at sth, get at sth **3 kogoś/coś z kimś/czymś** match sb/sth against/with sb/sth IDM **zmierzający do celu po trupach** cut-throat
□ **zmierzyć się**: **zdolny ~** (*np. z zadaniem*) equal[1] to sth
zmierzch dusk, twilight
zmierzwiony matted, shaggy
zmieszać → MIESZAĆ
zmieszany bemused, confused, mixed-up, perplexed
zmieścić (się) → MIEŚCIĆ (SIĘ)
zmieść → ZMIATAĆ
zmięk-czać/czyć soften
zmięknąć → MIĘKNĄĆ
zmiksować → MIKSOWAĆ
zmilitaryzować → MILITARYZOWAĆ
zminimalizować → MINIMALIZOWAĆ
zmizerniały haggard
zmizerowany haggard
zmniej-szać/szyć cut sth down, cut down (on sth), decrease[1], diminish, lessen; (*temperaturę itp.*) lower[2], reduce; (*ogrzewanie itp.*) turn sth down; (*ból itp.*) alleviate; (*strach itp.*) allay; (*złe wskutki itp.*) minimize, mitigate; (*prędkość itp.*) slacken sth (off); (*rozmiar*) contract[2], shrink; (*przez zużycie*) wear sth down; **(proporcjonalnie) ~** scale sth down; **zmniejszyć przeludnienia** relieve overcrowding; **~ ciężar** lighten
□ **zmniej-szać/szyć się** decline[2], decrease[1], diminish, fall[1], lessen; (*fundusze itp.*) dwindle (away); (*entuzjazm itp.*) wane[1]; (*prędkość*) slacken (off); (*rozmiar*) contract[2], shrink; (*przez zużycie*) wear down; (*księżyc*) wane[1]; **nieco zmniejszać się** slip[1]
■ **zmniejszenie (się)** decrease[2], reduction; (*obrotów handlowych*) downturn; **~ się** the depletion of the ozone layer
zmobilizować (się) → MOBILIZOWAĆ (SIĘ)
zmoczony wet[1]
zmoczyć (się) → MOCZYĆ (SIĘ)
zmodernizować (się) → MODERNIZOWAĆ (SIĘ)
zmodyfikować → MODYFIKOWAĆ
zmoknąć → MOKNĄĆ
zmoknięty soaked
zmonopolizować → MONOPOLIZOWAĆ
zmontować → MONTOWAĆ
zmora the bane of sb/sth, menace, nightmare; **~ nocna** nightmare
zmordowany fagged, frazzled
zmotoryzowany (*przym.*) motorized
■ **zmotoryzowany** (*rz.*) motorist
zmotywować → MOTYWOWAĆ
zmow|a collusion, conspiracy, plot[1]; **działać z kimś w ~ie** collude (with sb) (in sth/in doing sth), (with sb) (to do sth); **w ~ie z kimś** in league (with sb)
zmówić się → ZMAWIAĆ SIĘ
zmrok nightfall, twilight IDM **przed ~iem/po ~u** before/after dark
zmrużyć → MRUŻYĆ
zmu-szać/sić bully[2] sb (into doing sth), coerce, compel, force[2], make[1], oblige, railroad verb sb (into sth/into doing sth); (*do dyscypliny itp.*) enforce; **~ kogoś do myślenia** set sb thinking
□ **zmu-szać/sić się** bring yourself to do sth; **~ siłą woli** will[2]
zmuszony bound[1] (by sth) (to do sth)
zmutować (się) → MUTOWAĆ (SIĘ)
zmyć (się) → MYĆ, ZMYWAĆ (SIĘ)
zmykać scuttle
zmylić belie
zmysł acumen, faculty, sense[1]; **~ smaku** taste[1]
zmysłowość sensuality, sensuousness
zmysłowy lustful, sensual, sensuous, slinky, voluptuous
zmyś-lać/lić cook sth up, fabricate, fib verb, make sth up
■ **zmyślenie** make-believe
zmyślony fanciful, far-fetched, fictitious, imaginary, unreal
zmywacz remover
zmy(wa)ć/po- wash[1]; (*płukać*) swill sth (out/down); **(skądś)** wash sth off (sth); (*naczynia*) wash sth up
■ **zmywanie** wash[2]; **~ naczyń** washing-up
□ **zmy(wa)ć się** wash off (sth)
zmywarka: **~ do naczyń** dishwasher
znacjonalizować → NACJONALIZOWAĆ
znaczący meaningful, noteworthy, significant, telling; **w ~ sposób** importantly
znaczek badge; **~ pocztowy** stamp[1]
znaczeni|e 1 (*sens*) meaning, sense[1]; **bez ~a** meaningless **2** (*waga*) consequence, importance, significance, substance, value[1]; **mieć ~e** carry weight, matter[2] (to sb); **mieć (duże) ~e** mean[1] sth (to sb); **mieć większe ~e** outweigh; **przywiązywać duże ~e** value[2] sb/sth (as sth); **bez ~a** immaterial, negligible; **nie mieć ~a** make no difference (to sb/sth), not make any difference **3** (*splendor*) grandeur
znacznik 1 (*pióro*) marker **2** (**znaczniki**) (*w korektach*) markup
znaczn|y appreciable, considerable, marked, significant, substantial
■ **znacznie** considerably, far[2], a lot[2], markedly, much[2], significantly, substantially, widely; (*nieform.*) miles; **~ lepiej itp.** heaps better, more, older, etc.
znaczyć 1 (*oznaczać*) mean[1], signify, spell[1]; **to znaczy** that is (to say); **tzn.** i. e., viz. **2** (*być ważnym*) matter[2] (to sb); **~ (coś ważnego)** mean[1] sth (to sb); **mało znaczący** negligible, secondary
znać/po- know[1]
□ **znać/po- się**: **z kimś** know[1] sb; **na czymś** know what you are talking about; **dobrze ~ na czymś** be hot at/on sth; **znający się na rzeczy** knowledgeable
znajdować/znaleźć find[1], get/lay your hands on sth, pick sth up, track sb/sth down; (*drogę dokądś*) hit[1]; **~ sposób na coś** come up with sth, get round/around sth, work sth out
□ **znajdować/znaleźć się** lie[2], be located, be situated; **znaleźć się gdzieś/w pewnej sytuacji** turn up, wind up; **~ na szczycie** (*np. listy przebojów*) top[3]
znajomość 1 (*towarzystwo*) **~ powierzchowna** acquaintance with sb **2** (*w biznesie itp.*) connection, contact[1] **3** (*wiedza*) familiarity (with sth), knowledge, understanding[1]; (*języka obcego itp.*) command[1]; **~ powierzchowna** acquaintance with sth; **~ rzeczy** know-how
znajom|y familiar (to sb)
■ **znajom-y/a** (*rz.*) acquaintance, friend
znak 1 (*drogowy itp.*) marking, sign[1]; (*świetlny; ręki itp.*) signal; (*znacznik*) marker; (*ślad*) mark[2], trace[2], vestige; (*czegoś złego*) omen; **~ zodiaku** star sign; **być ~iem czegoś** indicate; **być typowym ~iem** typify; **dawać ~** motion[2] to sb (to do sth), signal verb **2** (*symbol*) sign[1], symbol; (*wdzięczności, przyjaźni itp.*) token[1] **3** (*litera itp.*) character; **~ diakrytyczny** accent, diacritic; **~ dodawania** plus[2]; **~ dziesiętny** point[1]; **~ metryczny** (*muz.*) time signature; **~ zapytania** question mark; **~ zgłoszenia systemu komputerowego** prompt[3]; **stawianie ~ów przestankowych** punctuation **3 ~ firmowy** brand[1], logo; **chroniony ~ firmowy/handlowy** trademark IDM **stawiać pod ~iem zapytania** question[2] | **dawać się komuś we ~i** bite[1], get on top of sb
znakomity accomplished, brilliant, distinguished, excellent, fabulous, fine[1], first-class, glorious, grand[1], high-class, illustrious, outstanding, remarkable, splendid, superb
znalazca finder
znalezienie discovery
znaleźć (się) → ZNAJDOWAĆ (SIĘ)
znamienny symptomatic
znamię mark[2]; (*na skórze*) birthmark
znamionować distinguish A (from B)
znan|y familiar (to sb), famed (for sth), noted (for/as sth), your; **być ~ym jako**

know[1] sb/sth as sth; **powszechnie ~y** well known; **~y też jako/pod pseudonimem** alias[1]
znaw-ca/czyni connoisseur, expert, judge[1] of sth
znawstw|o expertise; **ze ~em** knowledgeably
zneutralizować → NEUTRALIZOWAĆ
znęcać się ill-treat, mistreat; **~ nad słabszym** bully[2] sb (into doing sth); **osoba znęcająca się nad słabszymi** bully[1]
■ **znęcanie się** abuse[1], ill-treatment, mistreatment; **~ nad dziećmi** child abuse; **~ nad słabszymi** bullying
znęcić → NĘCIĆ
znękany harassed
zniechę-cać/cić 1 kogoś (do zrobienia czegoś) discourage, dishearten; (*zwolenników itp.*) alienate; **~ do dalszego działania** demoralize; **coś, co zniechęca** disincentive **2 kogoś (do kogoś)** put sb off (sb)
zniechęceni|e dejection, despondency, disaffection; **ze ~em** dejectedly
zniechęcony dejected, despondent, disaffected, discouraged, disheartened, dispirited
zniecierpliwić się → NIECIERPLIWIĆ SIĘ
zniecierpliwienie impatience
zniecierpliwiony impatient
znieczu-lać/lić 1 anaesthetize; **środek znieczulający stosowany w znieczuleniu ogólnym** general anaesthetic **2 na coś** harden sb (to sth/doing sth)
□ **znieczul-ać/ić się**: **na coś** harden yourself to sth
znieczulenie anaesthetic
zniedołężnieć → NIEDOŁĘŻNIEĆ
zniekształ-cać/cić deform, disfigure, distort
zniekształcony deformed, out of shape; (*kapelusz itp.*) battered
znienacka out of the blue, unawares; **zostać ~ zaskoczonym** be caught unawares
znienawidzić → NIENAWIDZIĆ
znieruchomiały immobile
zniesieni|e 1 (*ustawy itp.*) abolition **2 nie do ~a** (*przykry*) insufferable, intolerable
zniesławi(a)ć defame, slander verb; (*na piśmie*) libel verb
■ **zniesławiający** defamatory, scurrilous
zniesławienie defamation, slander; (*na piśmie*) libel
znieść → ZNOSIĆ
zniewaga affront, insult[2], outrage, slur[2]
z-niewalać/niewolić enslave; **zniewalający uśmiech** a devastating smile
zniewa-żać/żyć insult[1]
znieważenie: **czynne ~ policjanta** assaulting a police officer
zniewieściały effeminate
zniewolenie enslavement
zniewolić → ZNIEWALAĆ
znik-ać/nąć disappear, evaporate, go away, melt away, slip away, vanish
znikom|y 1 (*nieznaczny*) insignificant, trifling; **~e znaczenie** insignificance **2** (*szanse*) outside[2], slender; **~a szansa** off chance
zniszczeni|e annihilation, damage[1], destruction, devastation, dilapidation, ruin[2]; **stan ~a** disrepair
zniszczony decrepit, dilapidated, ruined, in ruin(s), tatty; (*kapelusz itp.*) battered
zniszczyć → NISZCZYĆ
zniweczenie annihilation
zniweczyć → NIWECZYĆ
zniwelować → NIWELOWAĆ
zni-żać/żyć dip[1], drop[1], lower[2]
□ **zni-żać/żyć się** dip[1], drop[1], stoop to sth/doing sth; (*do czyjegoś poziomu*) condescend (to sb); (*głos*) **zniżyć się do szeptu** fall to a whisper
zniżka concession, discount[1]
zniżkować sink[1], slide[1]
zniżkowy concessionary
znokautować → NOKAUTOWAĆ
znormalizować (się) → NORMALIZOWAĆ (SIĘ)
z-nosić/nieść 1 (*prąd rzeki, powietrze*) wash sb/sth away; (*z pokładu itp.*) sweep[1] **2** (*tolerować*) **kogoś/coś** bear[1], endure, put up with sb/sth, stand[1], stick[1], stomach[2], take, tolerate, withstand; **nie ~** not brook[2] sth, hate[1]; **~ do końca** stick it/sth out **3** (*ustawę itp.*) abolish, lift[1], repeal; (*nieform.*) do away with sth; **~ kontrolę** deregulate **4** (*jaja*) lay[1]
znoszenie (*ubrania*) wear[2]
znoszony ratty, worn out
znośny bearable, tolerable
znowu again, anew, once again/more, yet again
znój drudgery, toil noun
znudzeni|e: **do ~a** ad nauseam
znudzić się → NUDZIĆ SIĘ
znudzony bored; (*brakiem zajęcia*) at a loose end
znużony jaded, tired, weary
znużyć (się) → NUŻYĆ (SIĘ)
zobaczeni|e IDM **do ~a** see you around
zobaczyć zob. też WIDZIEĆ IDM **~, czy** see if… | **zobaczysz!** (just) you wait
zobojętni(a)ć neutralize
zobojętniały listless
zobowiązani|e commitment, debt, obligation, pledge, undertaking; **mam inne ~a** I'm otherwise engaged; **bez żadnych zobowiązań** (with) no strings attached, without strings
zobowiązany bound[1] (by sth) (to do sth), indebted (to sb) (for sth), obliged
zobowiąz(yw)ać bind[1], oblige
□ **zobowiąz(yw)ać się** commit yourself (to sth/to doing sth), pledge verb sth (to sb/sth), undertake
zoczyć spy[2]
zodiak the zodiac
zombi zombie
zona zone
zoo zoo
zoolog zoologist
zoologia zoology
zoologiczny zoological; **sklep ~** pet shop
zoperować → OPEROWAĆ
zoptymalizować → OPTYMALIZOWAĆ
zorganizować → ORGANIZOWAĆ
zorganizowany organized
zorientować się → ORIENTOWAĆ SIĘ
zorientowan|y aware, clued-up (on sth); **być dobrze ~ym** be hot at/on sth; **być ~ym i wyczulonym na nowości** be on the ball
zosta(wa)ć 1 (*pozostać*) remain, stay[1]; (*na noc/obiad itp.*) stay[1]; (*gdzieś po odejściu innych*) wait behind; **~ na miejscu** stay put; **~ w domu** stay in; (*w oczekiwaniu na coś*) wait in; **~ w tyle (za kimś/czymś)** fall behind (sb/sth), lag[1] (behind) (sb/sth) **2** (*być: zazw. w stronie biernej*) be[2] **3** (*stać się kimś*) become[2], make[1] **4** (*reszta jedzenia itp.*) be left (over), remain; **została jeszcze tylko minuta** there's only one minute left to go; **zostało nam jeszcze 50 mil.** we've still got 50 miles to go
zostawi(a)ć leave[1], leave[1] sth (behind); **najwyższy czas, byś pozostawiła już swoje problemy za sobą** it's time you put your problems behind you; **~ (komuś coś do zrobienia)** leave[1]; **~ kogoś/coś w tyle** leave sb/sth behind IDM **~ kogoś/coś (w spokoju)** leave sb/sth alone | **~ kogoś w spokoju** give sb a break
zozdrażnieni|e: **z rozdrażnieniem** irritably
zrabować → RABOWAĆ
zracjonalizować → RACJONALIZOWAĆ
zradykalizować → RADYKALIZOWAĆ
zranić → RANIĆ
zraniony (*i przen.*) hurt[2], injured
z-rastać/rosnąć się (*kości*) fuse together
zraszacz sprinkler
z-raszać/rosić sprinkle A (on/onto/over B), B (with A)
z-rażać/razić alienate, antagonize; **(kogoś do kogoś/czegoś)** prejudice[2] sb (against sb/sth)
■ **zrażający do siebie** off-putting
□ **z-rażać/razić się**: **nie zrażaj się tymi drobnymi problemami** don't let these little problems discourage you
zrąb framework; (*budynku*) shell[1]
zrealizować (się) → REALIZOWAĆ (SIĘ)
zrealizowanie completion, fulfilment
zreanimować → REANIMOWAĆ
zreasumować → REASUMOWAĆ
zrecenzować → RECENZOWAĆ
zredagować → REDAGOWAĆ
zredukować → REDUKOWAĆ
zreferować → REFEROWAĆ
zreformować → REFORMOWAĆ
zregenerować → REGENEROWAĆ
zrehabilitować → REHABILITOWAĆ
zrekompensować → REKOMPENSOWAĆ
zrekonstruować → REKONSTRUOWAĆ
zrekrutować → REKRUTOWAĆ
zrelacjonować → RELACJONOWAĆ
zrelaksować się → RELAKSOWAĆ SIĘ
zrelaksowany free and easy, relaxed; **być ~m** (be/feel) at (your) ease
zremisować → REMISOWAĆ
zreorganizować → REORGANIZOWAĆ
zrepatriować → REPATRIOWAĆ
zreperować → REPEROWAĆ
zresztą: **(a) ~** anyway, but then
zrewanżować się → REWANŻOWAĆ SIĘ
zrewidować → REWIDOWAĆ
zrewolucjonizować → REWOLUCJONIZOWAĆ
zrezygnować → REZYGNOWAĆ
zrezygnowanie disclaimer
zrezygnowany discouraged, resigned (to sth/doing sth)
zręczn|y 1 (*umiejętny*) deft, dexterous, handy, practical[1], skilful; (*gra na gitarze itp.*) nifty; **~e robienie** manipulation **2** (*sprytny*) clever **3** (*reklama itp.*) slick[1]
zripostować → RIPOSTOWAĆ

zrobić (się) → ROBIĆ (SIĘ)
zrobion|y IDM **~e!** hey presto
zrodzić się: **z czegoś** spring from sth
zropieć → ROPIEĆ
zrosić → ZRASZAĆ
zrozpaczony despairing, desperate, devastated, distraught, distressed, frantic, heartbroken
zrozumiał|y comprehensible, intelligible, plain[1], understandable; **to ~e, że była zła** she was understandably angry; **~e same przez się** self-explanatory
zrozumieć → ROZUMIEĆ
zrozumieni|e appreciation, comprehension, feeling (for sb/sth), grasp[2], perception, understanding[1]; (*kłopotów itp.*) sympathy (for/towards sb); **z pełnym ~em** in hearty agreement; **dawać do ~a** hint[2], imply, insinuate, give sb to believe/understand (that), make it clear to sb; **pełen ~a** sympathetic, understanding[2]; (*spojrzenie itp.*) knowing; **sposób ~a** interpretation; **wzajemne ~e** rapport; **ze ~em** knowingly, sympathetically
zrównanie equinox
zrównoważony balanced, well balanced; (*osoba*) even-tempered, level-headed, poised, sedate[1], well adjusted
zrównoważyć → RÓWNOWAŻYĆ
zrówn(yw)ać → RÓWNAĆ (SIĘ), ZRÓWNYWAĆ (SIĘ) **1** (*usunąć różnicę*) equate sth (with sth) **2** (*teren*) even sth out **3** (*budynek itp. z ziemią*) level[3]
□ **zrówn(yw)ać się** level off/out, even out
zróżnicować (się) → RÓŻNICOWAĆ (SIĘ)
zróżnicowan|y disparate; **wyniki egzaminu były ~e** there was a lot of variation in the examination results
zrujnować → RUJNOWAĆ
zrujnowany ramshackle, ruined
zrumienić → RUMIENIĆ
zryć → RYĆ
zryw spurt noun; **~ami** spasmodically; **krótkimi ~ami** in short bursts; **podejmowany ~ami** spasmodic
zrywać/zerwać 1 (*umowę; zaręczyny*) **zerwać kontrakt** break a contract; **zerwane zaręczyny** a broken engagement **2** (*szarpnięciem*) rip[1], rupture verb, sever, tear[2] **3** (*kwiaty itp.*) break sth off, pick[1], pick sth off **4 z czymś** break with sth; **zrywać z nałogiem** break the habit, kick the habit **5 z kimś** break up (with sb), finish with sb
□ **zrywać/zerwać się 1** (*burza itp.*) break[1] **2 zerwać się ze snu** wake up with a start; **zerwać się na (równe) nogi** scramble to your feet, spring to your feet
zrywny nippy
zrzednąć → RZEDNĄĆ
zrze-kać/c się abdicate, opt out (of sth), renounce, surrender, waive; **zrzeczenie się** (*np. pretensji do czegoś*) disclaimer
zrzęda fusspot, grouch
zrzędny crusty
zrzędzić grouch, nag (at) sb
zrzu-cać/cić 1 (*upuścić*) drop, plump sb/sth down; **~ bombę atomową** nuke; **zrzucić sznur (z czegoś)** dangle a rope (from sth) **2** (*kilogramy; liście itp.*) shed[2]; (*drzewo*) **zrzucający liście** deciduous **3 na kogoś** (*obowiązki itp.*) unload sb/sth (on/onto sb); **~ odpowiedzialność** pass the buck (to sb); **~ winę** shift the blame (for sth) (onto sb) **4** (*buty itp.*) slip[1] sth off IDM **zrzucić ciężar z serca** get sth off your chest
□ **zrzucać się**: **zrzuciliśmy się po 5 funtów** we each chipped in (with) £5
zrzutka collection
z-siadać/siąść: **z czegoś** dismount, get off (sth)
□ **z-siadać/siąść się** curdle, set[1]
zsiadł|y sour; **~e mleko** curd
zsikać się wet[2]
ZSRR USSR
zsumow(yw)ać zob. też SUMOWAĆ; reckon sth up, tot sth up
zsu-wać/nąć: **~ z góry** slide down the mountain
z-sychać/eschnąć się shrivel (up)
zsyłać/zesłać exile verb
zsynchronizować → SYNCHRONIZOWAĆ
zsyntetyzować → SYNTETYZOWAĆ
zsyp chute
zszokować → SZOKOWAĆ
zszokowany appalled, shocked
zszywacz stapler
zszy(wa)ć 1 (*materiał itp.*) sew sth up **2** (*zszywaczem*) staple verb
zszywanka (*z różnych materiałów*) patchwork
zszywka staple
zu-bażać/bożyć (także **zubożać**) impoverish
zuch cub; **członkini skautowskiej drużyny dla dziewcząt** brownie; **organizacja skautowska dla młodszych chłopców** (*podobna do zuchów*) the Cubs
zuchwalstwo impudence, nerve
zuchwały audacious, bold, brash, impertinent, impudent, insolent
zupa soup; **gęsta ~** broth
zupełnie absolutely, all[2], altogether, completely, entirely, perfectly adv., plain[3], positively, purely, quite, stark[2], thoroughly, truly, utterly, well and truly, whatever, wholly
■ **zupełnoś|ć**: **w zupełności** altogether, plenty adv., quite, wholly
zużycie usage, consumption
zużytkować → UŻYTKOWAĆ
zużyty 1 gone[2]; **~ papier** waste paper **2** (*już nieciekawy*) stale
zuży(wa)ć 1 (*wykorzystać*) consume, use[1], use sth up **2** (*podeszwy itp.*) wear sth away, wear sth down **3** (*przemęczać*) drain[1] sb/sth (of sth), exhaust[2]
□ **zuży(wa)ć się 1** (*podeszwy itp.*) wear[1], wear away, wear down; **nie ~** wear well **2** (*małżeństwo itp.*) go stale
■ **zużywanie się** wear and tear
zwabić → WABIĆ
zwa-lać/lić 1 ~ na kupę pile[2] A on(to) B, B with A **2 zwalać kogoś z nóg** knock sb out **3 coś na kogoś** land sb with sth, lumber[2] sb (with sth); **zwalać brudną robotę na kogoś innego** get sb else to do your dirty work for you IDM (*przen.*) **zwalać kogoś z nóg** knock sb out
zwal-czać/czyć zob. też WALCZYĆ; combat[2], fight[1] (against sth); **kogoś/coś** fight sb/sth off
zwalić się → WALIĆ SIĘ
z-walniać/wolnić 1 kogoś release[1]; (*ze szpitala itp.*) discharge[1]; (*pracownika, ucznia z lekcji do domu*) dismiss; **zwalniać kogoś (z czegoś)** excuse[2] sb (from sth), exempt[2] sb/sth (from sth); (*np. z obowiązku*) relieve sb of sth; **zwalniać z odpowiedzialności** exonerate; **zwalniać kogoś z pracy** fire[2], lay sb off; **zwolnić kogoś, poprzestając na grzywnie** let sb off off with a fine; **został zwolniony ze względu na stan zdrowia** he was given a medical discharge **2** (*szybkość*) slacken sth (off), slow[2], slow sth down/up **3** (*mieszkanie; stanowisko*) vacate **4** (*hamulec itp.*) release[1]; **zwalniać sprzęgło** disengage the clutch
zwał pile[1]
zwałka landfill
zwany: **tak ~** so-called; **inaczej (~)** alias[1]
zwarcie[1] (*przysł.*) densely
zwarcie[2] (*rz.*) **~ elektryczne** short circuit; **powodować ~** short-circuit verb
zwariować → WARIOWAĆ
zwariowany crackpot, crazy, mad, nuts, nutty, round the bend, wacky, zany; (*na czyimś punkcie; na punkcie czegoś*) crazy about sb/sth, nuts about sb/sth, potty[1] about sb/sth; (*wydarzenia*) hectic
zwarty 1 (*tłum*) dense **2** (*grupa*) cohesive **3** (*szczelny; uścisk*) tight
zwarzyć się → WARZYĆ SIĘ
zwaśnić się → WAŚNIĆ SIĘ
zważać allow for sb/sth, heed[1]; **nie ~ na kogoś/coś** ignore; (*np. na protest*) override; **nie zważając na coś** notwithstanding; (*np. na czyjeś potrzeby, uczucia*) inconsiderately; **zważywszy (na coś)** considering
zważyć → WAŻYĆ
zwątpić → WĄTPIĆ
zwątpienie despondency
zwerbować → WERBOWAĆ
zweryfikować → WERYFIKOWAĆ
zwędzić (*ukraść*) knock sth off, lift[1] sth (from sb/sth), nick[2], pinch[1], sneak[1], whip[2]
zwęglony charred
zwęszyć zob. też WĘSZYĆ; (*usłyszeć o czymś*) get wind of sth
zwę-żać/zić narrow[2]; (*ubranie*) take sth in
■ **zwężenie**: **~ jezdni powodujące korek** bottleneck
□ **zwę-żać/zić się** narrow[2]
zwiać → ZWIEWAĆ
zwiad reconnaissance
zwiadowca scout
zwiastować foreshadow, herald
zwiastun 1 (*osoba*) (także **zwiastunka**) bearer, forerunner **2** (*znak*) forerunner **3** (*filmu*) clip[1], trailer
związan|y 1 (*mający związek z kimś/czymś*) associated, bound up with sth, pertinent, relevant; (*pociągać za sobą*) **być ~ym (z czymś)** involve

2 (*z partią itp.*) associated; **być ~ym (z czymś)** be concerned in sth
związ|ek 1 (*powiązanie z kimś/czymś*) bearing, bond[1], connection, correlation, relation, relationship, relevance; **~ek z czymś** something to do with sth; **bez ~ku** disjointed; **bez ~ku z tematem** irrelevant; **mieć ~ek z kimś/czymś** refer to sb/sth; **mieć ~ek z czymś** enter into sth; **ustalać ~ek** relate A to/with B; **w ~ku z kimś/czymś** in connection with sb/sth; **w ~ku z tym** in this/that connection **2** (*miłosny*) liaison, relationship **3** (*organizacja*) association; **~ek zawodowy** trade union, union **4** (*chemiczny*) compound[1] **5 ~ek wyrazowy** collocation
związkowiec trade unionist
związ(yw)ać → WIĄZAĆ (SIĘ); knot[2], tie sth up; (*włosy*) tie[1]; (*plik papierów, gazet itp.*) bundle sth (up)
□ **związ(yw)ać się** identify (yourself) with sb/sth
zwichnąć (*nogę, kostkę itp.*) sprain, wrench[1]; (*med.*) dislocate
zwie-dzać/dzić look around/round (sth), visit, tour verb; **zwiedzać (gruntownie)** explore
■ **zwiedzając-y/a** (*rz.*) sightseer | **zwiedzanie** sightseeing, tour
zwielokrotniać (się) multiply
zwieńczyć → WIEŃCZYĆ
zwierać/zewrzeć (*obwód itp.*) short-circuit verb
zwierz beast
zwie-rzać/rzyć się: **komuś (z czegoś)** confide in sb, confide sth to sb
zwierzak pet[1]
zwierzchnictwo dominion
zwierzchni-k/czka superior[2]
zwierzę animal, beast; **~ domowe** pet[1]; **~ mięsożerne** carnivore; **~ta stadne** social animals
zwierzęcy brute[2]
zwierzyna: **~ łowna** game[1], quarry[1]
zwieść → ZWODZIĆ
zwietrzały (*napój gazowany*) flat[1]
zwietrzyć zob. też WIETRZEĆ; (*dowiedzieć się*) get wind of sth
zwi(ew)ać 1 (*strącać*) blow[1] **2** (*uciec*) do a bunk, give sb the slip
zwiewny (*mgła*) wispy
zwiędły (*liście*) dead
zwiędnąć → WIĘDNĄĆ
zwięk-szać/szyć increase[1], raise[1]; (*głośność itp.*) turn sth up; (*prędkość*) gather; (*sprzedaż*) boost[1]; **proporcjonalnie zwiększać** scale sth up
□ **zwięk-szać/szyć się** increase[1], mount[1]; (*kapitał itp.*) accrue (to sb) (from sth)
■ **zwiększający się** (*porządek*) ascending
zwięzły brief[1], concise, pithy, succinct, terse; **błyskotliwy i ~** snappy
■ **zwięźle**: **ujmować zwięźle** compress sth (into sth)
zwi-jać/nąć roll[2] sth (up), twist[1], wind[3] IDM **zwijać interes** go out of business, wind sth down
□ **zwi-jać/nąć się** roll[2] (up), twist[1]; **zwijać się w kłębek** curl up; (*tulić się do siebie*) huddle[1] (up) (together)
zwil-żać/żyć dampen, moisten, wet[2]
■ **zwilżony** moist
□ **zwil-żać/żyć się** moisten
zwinny agile, nimble
■ **zwinność** dexterity
zwiotczały flabby
zwis-ać/nąć dangle, flop[1] down, overhang; **z kącika ust zwisał mu papieros** a cigarette hung from his lips
zwitek roll[1]
zwlekać procrastinate; (*z odejściem*) linger; **~ z odpowiedzią** be slow in replying; **nie ~/~ ze zrobieniem czegoś** be quick, slow, etc. off the mark
zwłaszcza especially, notably, particularly, primarily; **~ (że)** inasmuch as; **~ nie** (*np. ty*) least of all
zwłok|a delay[1], lag[2]; **nie cierpiący ~i** urgent
zwłoki body, corpse, remains
zwodniczy deceitful, deceptive, misleading
zwodować → WODOWAĆ
z-wodzić/wieść beguile sb (into doing sth), deceive sb (into doing sth), mislead
zwolenni-k/czka advocate[2], disciple, follower, partisan[2], protagonist, sympathizer; **grupa zwolenników** following[2]; **lojaln-y/a ~** stalwart noun; **być (wielk-im/ą) zwolenni-kiem/czką czegoś** be a (great/firm) believer in sth
zwolnić → ZWALNIAĆ
zwolnieni|e 1 (*z więzienia itp.*) release[2]; (*ze szpitala itp.*) discharge[2]; (*z pracy; ze szkoły*) dismissal; (*z pracy w wyniku redukcji*) redundancy; **~e chorobowe** sick leave; **~e od lekarza** a sick note from your doctor; **~a pracowników** staff clear-out; **~e warunkowe z więzienia** parole, probation; **~e za kaucją** bail[1] **2** (*z obowiązków, płacenia podatków itp.*) exemption
zwolnion|y 1 (*z pracy w wyniku redukcji*) redundant **2** (*spowolniony*) sluggish; **~e tempo** slow motion **3** (*z obowiązku, podatku itp.*) exempt[1] (from sth)
zwoł(yw)ać (*zebranie itp.*) convene, convoke
zwój 1 (*pętla*) coil[2]; (*liny, druta itp.*) twist[2] **2** (*banknotów*) wad; **~ papieru** scroll[1] **3** (*dymu itp.*) curl[2]
z-wracać/wrócić 1 (*oddawać*) bring sb/sth back, give sth back, hand sth back (to sb), restore sth to sb, take sth back; (*dług*) repay; **~ pieniądze** refund verb; **~ koszty/wydatki** reimburse **2 ~ uwagę (na kogoś/coś)** take heed (of sb/sth), pay heed (to sb/sth), take notice; **~ czyjąś uwagę (na coś)** catch sb's attention/eye, draw (sb's) attention to sth; **zwracający uwagę** conspicuous; **~ na siebie uwagę** adopt/keep/maintain a high profile; **nie ~ na siebie uwagi** adopt/keep/maintain a low profile **3 ~ uwagę** (*wyrażać opinię*) comment[2] (on sth) **4** (*jedzenie*) bring sth up, regurgitate, spew (sth) (up)
□ **z-wracać/wrócić się 1** (*w jakimś kierunku*) face[2], point[2] **2 ~ do kogoś/czegoś (z (oficjalną) prośbą)** make an approach to sb, put sth in, turn to sb/sth; **~ do kogoś/jakiejś instytucji** (*o pomoc*) appeal[2], approach[1], have recourse to sth/sb
zwrot 1 (*oddanie*) recovery (of sth/sb), repayment, restoration, return[2]; **~ nadpłaty** rebate; **~ pieniędzy** refund; **promocyjny ~ pieniędzy** cashback; **podlegający ~owi** repayable **2** (*ruch*) swing[2], turn[2]; **w tył ~**; **~ o 180°** about-turn **3** (*wyrażenie*) expression, phrase[1] IDM **(nieoczekiwany) ~ w wydarzeniach** twist[2]
zwrotka verse
zwrotnica point[1]
zwrotnik tropic
zwrotny 1 (*bilet; butelka itp.*) returnable; (*dług*) repayable; (*zadatek itp.*) refundable **2** (*zaimek itp.*) reflexive IDM **moment ~** watershed
zwrócić (się) → ZWRACAĆ (SIĘ)
zwycięski successful, triumphant, victorious, winning; (*mający szansę na wygraną*) prize[2]; **~ gol itp.** winner
zwycięstwo victory
zwycięz-ca/czyni victor, winner; **murowany zwycięzca** cert
zwycię-żać/żyć defeat[1], prevail, win (against/over sb/sth)
■ **zwyciężeni|e**: **nie do zwyciężenia** insuperable, insurmountable | **zwyciężon-y/a** (*rz.*) loser
zwyczaj 1 (*tradycja*) convention, custom, institution, practice, ritual, tradition **2** (*nawyk*) habit, way[1]; **zmienić ~e** change your ways; **nie miał ~u ze mną rozmawiać** he didn't use to speak to me; **jak mieli w ~u** as was their custom
zwyczajny common[1], commonplace, run-of-the-mill, simple, usual; (*ubranie*) casual
zwyczajow|y accustomed, customary, habitual, routine[2], traditional; **~a stawka (za coś)** the going rate (for sth)
zwykle commonly, in general, generally, habitually, mostly, normally, ordinarily, typically, usually; **później niż ~** later than usual; **jak ~** as usual; (*czuć się*) **tak jak ~** yourself
zwykł: **~ coś robić** (*kiedyś, ale już nie teraz*) used to
zwykły 1 (*zwyczajowy*) habitual, normal[1], standard[2], usual **2** (*dzień, osoba itp.*) ordinary **3** (*ubranie*) plain[1]
zwymiotować → WYMIOTOWAĆ
zwyrodnieni|e degeneration; **ulegać ~u** degenerate[1]; **gąbczaste ~e mózgu** BSE
zwyżkować soar
■ **zwyżkujący** (*giełda*) bullish
zwyżkow|y: **tendencja ~a** an upward trend
zygzak zigzag; **ciągnąć się/posuwać się ~iem** zigzag verb
zygzakowaty criss-cross
zysk gain[2], proceeds (of/from sth), profit[1], return[2], yield[2]; **~ całkowity** bottom line
zysk(iw)ać gain[1]; **(na czymś)** profit[2] (from/by sth), gain in sth; **~ na czasie** buy time
zyskowny lucrative, profitable
zżąć → ŻĄĆ
zżyt|y (*rodzina itp.*) **bardzo ~a** closely/tightly knit

Ź

źdźbło blade; **~ słomy** straw
źle 1 (*niedobrze*) badly, wrong[2]; (*niewłaściwie/nieodpowiednio*)

wrongly; ~ **iść** go wrong **2** (*niezdrowo*) ill[2] IDM **i tak ~, i tak niedobrze** you can't win
źrebak colt
źrebię foal
źrenica pupil
źródł|o 1 (*rzeki*) spring[1] **2** (*zła itp.*) root[1], source; **być ~em** engender; **dochodzić do ~a** trace[1] sth (back) (to sth); **mieć swoje ~o w czymś** spring from sth **3** (**źródła**) (*naukowe*) material[1] **4 ~o utrzymania** bread and butter
źródłosłów etymology

Ż

żaba frog
żabka (*styl pływacki*) breaststroke
żaden (*z rz. w zdaniach twierdzących*) no[2]; (*z wielu*) none[1] (of sb/sth); (*z rz. lub zaimkiem w przeczeniach*) any; ~ **(z dwóch)** (*z rz. lub zaimkiem w zdaniach twierdzących*) neither; (*z rz. lub zaimkiem w przeczeniach*) either[1]; **w ogóle** ~ whatever
żagiel sail[2]
żaglówka sailing boat
żal 1 (*smutek*) grief, sorrow; **ogarnął ją** ~ she was consumed by grief **2** (*pretensje*) grudge[1]; **mieć** ~ resent **3** (*ubolewanie*) regret[2], repentance, shame[1]; **pełen ~u** regretful
żaluzja blind[3]; (*zewnętrzna*) shutter; (*z poziomych listewek*) venetian blind
żałob|a bereavement, grief, mourning; **w ~ie** bereaved; **być w ~ie** grieve (for sb)
żałobnik mourner
żałosny doleful, forlorn, pathetic, piteous, pitiful, plaintive, sorrowful, wretched
żałować/po- 1 czegoś regret[1]; **mój ojciec żałuje, że nie poszedł na studia** my father wishes (that) he had gone to university **2** (*grzechu*) repent (of sth) **3 kogoś** be/feel sorry for sb **4 (komuś) czegoś** begrudge (sb) sth, grudge[2] sb sth, skimp (on sth); **nie pożałowano pieniędzy na wesele** no expense was spared at the wedding
żar 1 (*upał*) heat[1] **2** (*ogniska*) embers, glow noun **3** (*przekonań itp.*) fervour, zeal; **z ~em** heatedly
żarcie grub, nosh
żargon jargon, vernacular
żarliwy ardent, committed, devout, fervent, fervid, impassioned, passionate, zealous; **być żarliw-ym/ą zwolenni-kiem/czką kogoś/czegoś** swear by sb/sth
żarłoczny voracious
■ **żarłoczność** gluttony | **żarłocznie** ravenously, voraciously
żarłok glutton, voracious eater
żarnik filament
żarówka bulb
żart gag[1], joke[1]; (**żarty**) mockery; **bez ~ów** seriously; **na ~y** in fun; **robić (sobie) ~y z kogoś** take the mickey (out of sb)
żartobliwy facetious, jocular, playful
żartować/za- crack a joke, fool[2], joke[2], kid[2]; **z kogoś/czegoś** poke fun at sb/sth IDM **chyba żartujesz!** you must be joking, you're joking, surely not
żartowniś joker
żarzyć/roz- się glow; **żarzące się węgle** embers
żąć/z- reap
żądać/za- demand[2], require
■ **żądanie** call[2], demand[1]; **na żądanie** on demand
żądlić/u- bite[1], sting[1]
żądło sting[2]
żądny avid (for sth)
żądza appetite, lust[1], thirst
że that
żebrać/wy- beg
żebra-k/czka bum, beggar, scavenger
żebro rib; (**żebra**) ribcage
żeby: **tak,** ~ in order to do sth, so[2] (that...), so as to do sth; ~ **tylko** if only
żeglarski nautical
żeglarstwo sailing, yachting
żegla-rz/rka sailor; (*na jachcie*) yachtsman, yachtswoman; (*nawigator*) navigator
żeglować/po- cruise[2], navigate, sail[1]
■ **żeglowanie** sailing; (*jachtem*) yachting; (*nawigacja*) navigation
żeglowny navigable
żegluga 1 shipping **2** (*nawigacja*) navigation
żegnać/po- się 1 say goodbye, say your farewells; **żegnaj(cie)!** farewell **2** (*ze stanowiskiem itp.*) bow out (of sth/as sth)
żel gel
żelatyna gelatin
żelazko iron[1]
żelazn|y 1 iron[1]; (*z żeliwa*) cast-iron; **towary ~e** hardware **2** (*reguła itp.*) hard and fast; (*alibi itp.*) cast-iron; **~a ręka** a firm hand; **~a wola** an iron will IDM **~a kurtyna** the Iron Curtain
żelazo iron[1]
żelazobeton (także **żelbet**) reinforced concrete
żeliwny cast-iron
żeliwo cast iron
żenić/o- się marry
żenować/za- disconcert, embarrass, mortify, show sb up
■ **żenujący** embarrassing, mortifying; (*zachowanie*) undignified
żeński 1 (*dot. kobiet, bot.*) female[1] **2** (*szkoła itp.*) girls' **3** (*gram.*) feminine
żer prey[1]
żerdź 1 (*pal, słup*) pole, stake[1] **2** (*grzęda, np. dla kur*) perch[2]
żerować 1 na czymś feed[1] (on sth) **2 na kimś** prey on/upon sb
żeton chip[1], counter[1], token[1]
żłobek crèche, nursery
żłób manger, trough
żmija adder
żmudny heavy, laborious, uphill
żniwa harvest
żołądek insides[2], stomach[1]
żołądkowy gastric
żołądź acorn
żołnierz fighter, soldier, serviceman; (*poniżej stopnia oficerskiego*) man[1]; **kobieta** ~ servicewoman; ~ **najemny** mercenary[1]; ~ **piechoty morskiej** marine[2]; ~ **zawodowy** regular[2]
żołnierzyk toy soldier
żon|a wife; **Ewa jest ~ą Marka** Ewa's married to Mark
żonaty married (to sb)
żongler/ka juggler
żonglować 1 juggle (with sth) **2** (*przen.*) juggle sth (with sth)
żonkil daffodil
żół|ć 1 (*anat.*) bile **2** (*przen.*) **pełen ~ci** acrimonious, jaundiced
żółknąć (*od tytoniu, ze starości*) discolour
żółtaczk|a jaundice; **chory na ~ę** jaundiced
żółtawy yellowish
żółtko yolk
żółtodziób novice
żółtozielony: **kolor** ~ lime
żółt|y 1 yellow; **~y kolor** yellow noun; **~a linia** yellow line; **~a kartka** yellow card; **otrzymać ~ą kartkę** be booked for a foul **2 ~y z zazdrości** green with envy
żółw (*lądowy*) tortoise; ~ **morski** turtle
żółwi: **~e tempo** crawl[2]
żrący (*chem.*) caustic
żubr bison
żuchwa mandible
żuć chew
żuraw crane[1]
żurawina cranberry
żurawinowy cranberry
żuwaczka mandible
żużel 1 (*po wytopie rudy*) cinder, slag[1] **2** (*sport*) speedway
żwawy brisk, smart[1]
żwir gravel; **ziarnka ~u** grit[1]
żwirek (*na plaży*) shingle
żwirowaty gritty
życi|e 1 (*proces; bycie żywym*) life; (*długość życia*) lifespan, lifetime; **~e intymne** love life; **~e zawodowe** career[1]; **~e po ~u** afterlife; **utrzymać kogoś/coś przy ~u** keep sb/sth alive; **obawiać się o czyjeś ~e** fear for sb's safety; **prowadzić (np. spokojne) ~e** live[1]; **pełen ~a** lively, vivacious, full of beans/life; **bez ~a** lifeless; **na całe ~e** lifelong; **~a i śmierci** (*kwestia*) life-and-death **2** (*utrzymanie się*) living[2] **3 wchodzić w ~e** come into operation IDM **nigdy w ~u!** no fear
życiorys life, life story
życiow|y life; **~a okazja** a chance of a lifetime; **~a pasja** a consuming passion
życzeni|e 1 request[1], will[3], wish[2]; **mieć ~e** wish[1] (to do sth); **pozostawiać wiele do ~a** leave a lot to be desired **2** (**życzenia**) (*świąteczne, urodzinowe itp.*) greetings, wishes[2]
życzliw|y (*przyjacielski*) friendly, kind[2], kind-hearted, kindly adj., neighbourly, warm-hearted; (*dobry*) benevolent, charitable; (*stosunki itp.*) cordial[1]; (*przychylny*) sympathetic; **~a osoba** well-wisher; **~y słuchacz** a sympathetic ear
życzyć/po- 1 (czegoś komuś) wish[1]; (*dobrego ranka, wieczora*) bid[2] (sb) good morning, etc. **2 (sobie) (, żeby)** wish[1] (that), for sth **3** (*w pytaniach*) would you care for.../to do sth **4** (*pewnej ceny*) ask
żyć live[1]; (*z ziemi itp.*) live by doing sth, live off sb/sth, live on sth; (*o chlebie itp.*) live on sth, live off sb/sth; **dla kogoś/czegoś** live for sb/sth; **ze sobą** live together; ~ **dalej** live on; ~ **pełnią życia** live[1]; ~ **cudzym kosztem** live off sb/sth; ~ **zgodnie z czymś** live by sth, live up to sth IDM **żyli długo i szczęśliwie** they lived happily ever after | **dobrze z kimś** ~ get on/along with sb, get on/along (together)

■ **żyjący** alive, living[1]
żyd/ówka Jew
żydowski 1 Jewish **2** (*język*) Hebrew adj.
żylak varicose vein; **~i odbytu** haemorrhoids
żylast|y wiry; (*mięso*) chewy, tough
żyletka razor blade
żyła vein
żyłka: ~ **wędkarska** fishing line
żyłkowanie (*w kamieniu*) grain
żyrafa giraffe
żyrandol chandelier
żytni rye
żyto rye
żywica resin
żywiciel/ka: **żywiciel/ka rodziny** breadwinner
żywić (*uczucia*) bear[1], feel[1], have[1]; (*nadzieję itp.*) cherish, nourish, nurse[2] □ **żywić/po- się** feed[1] (on sth), live on sth
żywieniowy dietary
żywio|ł (**żywioły**) elements IDM **(nie) w swoim ~le** in/out of your element
żywiołow|y: **klęski ~e** natural disasters
żywnościowy: **artykuł** ~ foodstuff
żywność food
żywo 1 (*grać itp.*) boisterously **2** (*koncert, transmisja itp.*) **na** ~ live adv., live[2]; **komentarz na** ~ running commentary **3** (*opisać itp.*) vividly
żywopłot hedge[1], hedgerow
żywot life
żywotny vital
żywy 1 (*żyjący*) alive, animate, living[1], live[2]; **jak** ~ lifelike; **ledwie** ~ very run-down, shattered **2** (*ruchliwy*) lively; (*gra itp.*) boisterous; (*krok*) smart[1] **3** (*światło; wspomnienie; kolor itp.*) vivid; (*melodia*) snappy **4** (*osobowość*) vibrant, vivacious **5** (*miasto itp.*) alive
żyzny fertile, rich

Dodatki

DODATEK 1

Wyrażenia liczbowe

Numbers Liczebniki

	Cardinal Główne		**Ordinal** Porządkowe
1	one	**1st**	first
2	two	**2nd**	second
3	three	**3rd**	third
4	four	**4th**	fourth
5	five	**5th**	fifth
6	six	**6th**	sixth
7	seven	**7th**	seventh
8	eight	**8th**	eighth
9	nine	**9th**	ninth
10	ten	**10th**	tenth
11	eleven	**11th**	eleventh
12	twelve	**12th**	twelfth
13	thirteen	**13th**	thirteenth
14	fourteen	**14th**	fourteenth
15	fifteen	**15th**	fifteenth
16	sixteen	**16th**	sixteenth
17	seventeen	**17th**	seventeenth
18	eighteen	**18th**	eighteenth
19	nineteen	**19th**	nineteenth
20	twenty	**20th**	twentieth
21	twenty-one	**21st**	twenty-first
22	twenty-two	**22nd**	twenty-second
30	thirty	**30th**	thirtieth
40	forty	**40th**	fortieth
50	fifty	**50th**	fiftieth
60	sixty	**60th**	sixtieth
70	seventy	**70th**	seventieth
80	eighty	**80th**	eightieth
90	ninety	**90th**	ninetieth
100	a/one hundred	**100th**	hundredth
101	a/one hundred and one	**101st**	hundred and first
200	two hundred	**200th**	two hundredth
1 000	a/one thousand	**1 000th**	thousandth
10 000	ten thousand	**10 000th**	ten thousandth
100 000	a/one hundred thousand	**100 000th**	hundred thousandth
1 000 000	a/one million	**1 000 000th**	millionth

Przykłady

528 *five hundred and twenty-eight*
2 976 *two thousand, nine hundred and seventy-six*
50 439 *fifty thousand, four hundred and thirty-nine*

Uwaga! W język angielski tysiące oddziela się spacją lub przecinkiem, np. *25 000* lub *25,000*. Kropką oddziela się liczby dziesiętne, np. 7.63. Szczegółowo zagadnienie to jest wyjaśnione w punkcie „Fractions". Liczby *100, 1 000* itp. można wyrazić słowami *one hundred* lub *a hundred*, *one thousand* lub *a thousand*.

W mowie najczęściej używa się **a**, chyba że chce się podkreślić, iż chodzi właśnie o *jeden*, a nie na przykład o *dwa* lub *trzy* tysiące. **0** (zero) czyta się **nought** /nɔːt/, **zero**-/ˈzɪərəʊ/, **nothing** /ˈnʌθɪŋ/ lub /əʊ/. W dalszych punktach „Dodatku" przedstawiono najczęściej spotykane sposoby nazywania zera w różnych zwrotach.

Fractions Ułamki i liczby dziesiętne

$\frac{1}{2}$	a half	$\frac{1}{10}$	a tenth	**0.1**	(nought) point one
$\frac{1}{3}$	a third	$\frac{1}{16}$	a sixteenth	**0.25**	(nought) point two five
$\frac{1}{4}$	a quarter	$1\frac{1}{2}$	one and a half	**0.33**	(nought) point three three
$\frac{2}{5}$	two fifths	$2\frac{3}{8}$	two and three eighths	**1.75**	one point seven five
$\frac{1}{8}$	an eighth			**3.976**	three point nine seven six

Percentages and proportions Procenty i stosunki proporcjonalne

Przykłady

- *90% of all households have a television.*
- *Nine out of ten households have a television.*
- *Nine tenths of all households have a television.*

Mathematical expressions Wyrażenia matematyczne

+	plus	÷	divided by	3^2	three squared
–	minus	=	equals	5^3	five cubed
×	times *lub* multiplied by	%	per cent	6^{10}	six to the power of ten

Przykłady

- *6 + 9 = 15 Six plus nine equals* (lub *is*) *fifteen.*
- *5 × 6 = 30 Five times six equals thirty.* lub *Five sixes are thirty.* lub *Five multiplied by six is thirty.*

Weight Jednostki masy

		brytyjskie i amerykańskie			oparte na systemie metrycznym	
	=	**1 ounce**	(oz)	=	28.35 grams	(g)
16 ounces	=	**1 pound**	(lb)	=	0.454 kilogram	(kg)
14 pounds	=	**1 stone**	(st)	=	6.356 kilograms	
112 pounds	=	**1 hundredweight**	(cwt)	=	50.8 kilograms	
20 hundredweight	=	**1 ton**	(t)	=	1.016 tonnes	(t)

Przykłady

- *The baby weighed 7lb 4oz (seven pounds four ounces).*
- *For this recipe you need 500g (five hundred grams) of flour.*

Uwaga! W USA **hundredweight** równa się stu funtom, a **ton** to 2 000 funtów lub 0.907 tony metrycznej. Wyrazu **stone** nie używa się, a zatem kiedy Brytyjczyk mówi *She weighs eight stone ten.* Amerykanin powie *She weighs 122 pounds.*

Length and height Jednostki długości

		brytyjskie i amerykańskie			oparte na systemie metrycznym	
	=	**1 inch**	(in)	=	25.4 millimetres	(mm)
12 inches	=	**1 foot**	(ft)	=	30.48 centimetres	(cm)
3 feet	=	**1 yard**	(yd)	=	0.914 metre	(m)
1 760 yards	=	**1 mile**	(yd)	=	1.609 kilometres	(km)

Przykłady

- *Height: 5 ft 9 in (five foot nine* lub *five feet nine)*
- *The hotel is 30 yds (thirty yards) from the beach.*
- *The car was doing 50 mph (fifty miles per hour).*
- *The room is 11' × 9'6" (eleven feet by nine feet six* lub *eleven foot by nine foot six).*

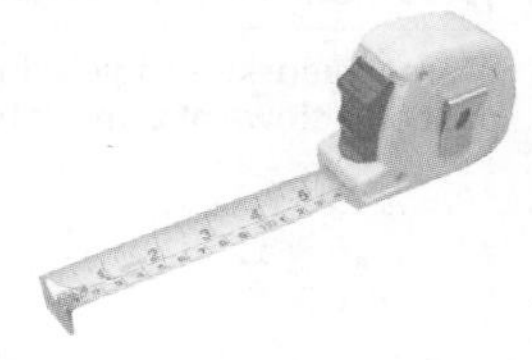

Area Jednostki powierzchni

		brytyjskie i amerykańskie		oparte na systemie metrycznym
		1 square inch	(sq in)	= 6.452 square centimetres
144 square inches	=	**1 square foot**	(sq ft)	= 929.03 square centimetres
9 square feet	=	**1 square yard**	(sq yd)	= 0.836 square metre
4 840 square yards	=	**1 acre**		= 0.405 hectare
640 acres	=	**1 square mile**		= 2.59 square kilometres *lub* 259 hectares

Przykłady

- *They have a 200-acre farm.*
- *The fire destroyed 40 square miles of woodland.*

Capacity Jednostki objętości

		brytyjskie	amerykańskie	oparte na systemie metrycznym
20 fluid ounces (fl oz)	=	**1 pint** (pt)	= 1.201 pints	= 0.568 litre (l)
2 pints	=	**1 quart** (qt)	= 1.201 quarts	= 1.136 litres
4 quarts	=	**1 gallon** (gal.)	= 1.201 gallons	= 4.546 litres

Przykłady

- *I asked the milkman to leave three pints of milk.*
- *The petrol tank holds 40 litres.*

Cubic measurements Jednostki sześcienne

		brytyjskie i amerykańskie		oparte na systemie metrycznym	
		1 cubic inch	(cu in)	= 16.39 cubic centimetres	(cc)
1 728 cubic inches	=	**1 cubic foot**	(cu ft)	= 0.028 cubic metre	
27 cubic feet	=	**1 cubic yard**	(cu yd)	= 0.765 cubic metre	

Przykład

- *The car has a 1 200 cc engine.*

Times Podawanie czasu

	w języku codziennym	w języku oficjalnym
06.00	six o'clock	(o) six hundred (hours)
06.05	five past six	(o) six o five
06.10	ten past six	(o) six o ten
06.15	(a) quarter past six	(o) six fifteen
06.20	twenty past six	(o) six twenty
06.30	half past six	(o) six thirty
06.35	twenty-five to seven	(o) six thirty-five
06.40	twenty to seven	(o) six forty
06.45	(a) quarter to seven	(o) six forty-five
06.50	ten to seven	(o) six fifty
06.55	five to seven	(o) six fifty-five
10.12	twelve minutes past ten	ten twelve
13.10	ten past one	thirteen ten
19.56	four minutes to eight	nineteen fifty-six

W amerykańskim angielskim czasem używa się słowa **after** zamiast **past** oraz słowa **of** zamiast **to**.

Uwaga! W jęz. codziennym na ogół nie używa się określeń czasu w systemie dwudziestoczterogodzinnym. Jeśli chce się podkreślić, że chodzi o godzinę 6.00, a nie o 18.00, można powiedzieć *six o'clock in the morning.* O godzinie 22.00 mówi się wówczas *ten o'clock in the evening,* a o 15.30 – *half past three in the afternoon.* W nieco bardziej formalnym języku można użyć skrótu **a.m.** w celu określenia godzin przedpołudniowych, zaś **p.m.** – godzin popołudniowych.

Przykłady

- *The train leaves at 06.56.*
- *Something woke me up at two o'clock in the morning.*
- *Office hours are 9 a.m. to 4.30 p.m.*

Dates Daty

Daty zapisuje się samymi liczbami lub liczbami i słowami:

- *15/4/07* (US *4/15/07*)
- *15 April 2007*
- *April 15th, 2007* (zwł. w amerykańskim angielskim)

czyta się:

- *April the fifteenth, two thousand and seven* lub
- *the fifteenth of April, two thousand and seven* lub (w amerykańskim angielskim) *April fifteenth, two thousand and seven*

Przykłady

- *Her birthday is 9th April (April the ninth/ the ninth of April).*
- *The restaurant will be closed May 3 – June 1* (mówi się *from May the third to June the first*).

Telephone numbers
Numery telefoniczne

Podając numer telefonu, wymawia się każdą cyfrę oddzielnie, często dzieląc długi szereg cyfr na grupy trzycyfrowe, np.:

- *295013: two nine five – o one three.*
- *59433: five nine four three three* lub *five nine four double three.*

Kiedy dzwoni się do innego miasta, należy dodać numer kierunkowy – **area code:**

- *01865 is the code for Oxford.*

Kiedy dzwoni się do osoby pracującej w dużej firmie, często należy podać telefonistce numer wewnętrzny – **extension number:**

- *(01865) 556767 x 4840 (extension 4840)*

Temperatures
Jednostki temperatury

W Wielkiej Brytanii oficjalnie mierzy się temperaturę w stopniach Celsjusza, jednak wielu ludzi nadal używa w mowie skali Fahrenheita. W USA powszechnie stosuje się skalę Fahrenheita, z wyjątkiem języka naukowego. Aby przeliczyć stopnie Fahrenheita na stopnie Celsjusza, należy od podanej temperatury odjąć 32, następnie pomnożyć wynik przez 5 i podzielić go przez 9, np.:

68°F – 32 = 36 × 5 = 180 ÷ 9 = 20°C

Przykłady

- *Water freezes at 32°F and boils at 212°F.*
- *The maximum temperature this afternoon will be 68°F.*
- *Overnight, temperatures below zero are expected, possibly reaching –10 (minus ten) before morning.*
- *He's got a temperature of 101°. I think he's got flu.*

Wlk. Br.	Suma	Moneta/Banknot
1p	a penny (one p)	a penny
2p	two pence (two p)	a two-pence piece
5p	five pence (five p)	a five-pence piece
10p	ten pence (ten p)	a ten-pence piece
20p	twenty pence (twenty p)	a twenty-pence piece
50p	fifty pence (fifty p)	a fifty-pence piece
£1	a pound	a pound (coin)
£5	five pounds	a five-pound note
£10	ten pounds	a ten-pound note

Przykłady

- *£5.75: five pounds seventy-five*
- *25p: twenty-five pence* (lub *p*)
- *The apples are 65p a pound.*
- *We pay £250 a month in rent.*

USA	Suma	Moneta/Banknot
1c	one cent	a penny
5c	five cents	a nickel
10c	ten cents	a dime
25c	twenty-five cents	a quarter
$1.00	one dollar	a dollar bill

Przykłady

- *$3.35: three dollars thirty-five*
- *59c: fifty-nine cents*
- *Do you have a quarter for the phone?*
- *The apartment costs $500 (five hundred dollars) a month.*

DODATEK 2

Nazwy geograficzne i mapy

Nazwy geograficzne

Poniższa lista zawiera angielską pisownię i wymowę nazw geograficznych oraz odpowiadające im przymiotniki. Jeśli przymiotnik nie oznacza także osoby, podane są dwie formy, np. **Denmark** (Dania); **Danish** (duński); **Dane** (Duńczyk, Dunka).

Słowa oznaczające osoby z danego kraju tworzą liczbę mnogą przez dodanie **-s.** Wyjątkiem jest słowo **Swiss** i słowa kończące się na **-ese** (np. **Japanese**), które pozostają nie zmienione, a także słowa zakończone na **-man** lub **-woman**, które zamienia się na **-men** lub **-women**, np. *three Frenchmen, two Englishwomen*.

Jeśli istnieje odrębne słowo dla całej grupy narodowościowej, jest ono podane w nawiasie: **France** (Francja); **French** (francuski); **Frenchman** (Francuz), **Frenchwoman** (Francuzka), (**the French**) (Francuzi).

Nie wszystkie wymienione tutaj kraje są niepodległymi państwami.

Kraj	*Przymiotnik/Rzeczownik*
Afghanistan /æf'gænɪstæn, -stɑ:n/	**Afghan** /'æfgæn/
Africa /'æfrɪkə/	**African** /'æfrɪkən/
Albania /æl'beɪniə/	**Albanian** /æl'beɪniən/
Algeria /æl'dʒɪəriə/	**Algerian** /æl'dʒɪəriən/
America /ə'merɪkə/	**American** /ə'merɪkən/
Andorra /æn'dɔ:rə/	**Andorran** /æn'dɔ:rən/
Angola /æŋ'gəʊlə/	**Angolan** /æŋ'gəʊlən/
Antarctica /æn'tɑ:ktɪkə/	**Antarctic** /æn'tɑ:ktɪk/
(the) Arctic /'ɑ:ktɪk/	**Arctic** /'ɑ:ktɪk/
Argentina /ˌɑ:dʒən'ti:nə/	**Argentinian** /ˌɑ:dʒən'tɪniən/, **Argentine** /'ɑ:dʒəntaɪn/
Armenia /ɑ:'mi:niə/	**Armenian** /ɑ:'mi:niən/
Asia /'eɪʃə, 'eɪʒə/	**Asian** /'eɪʃn, 'eɪʒn/
Australia /ɒ'streɪliə/	**Australian** /ɒ'streɪliən/
Austria /'ɒstriə/	**Austrian** /'ɒstriən/
Azerbaijan /ˌæzəbaɪ'dʒɑ:n/	**Azerbaijani** /ˌæzəbaɪ'dʒɑ:ni/, **Azeri** /ə'zeəri/
(the) Bahamas /bə'hɑ:məz/	**Bahamian** /bə'heɪmiən/
Bahrain /bɑ:'reɪn/	**Bahraini** /bɑ:'reɪni/
Bangladesh /ˌbæŋglə'deʃ/	**Bangladeshi** /ˌbæŋglə'deʃi/
Barbados /bɑ:'beɪdɒs; US -dəʊs/	**Barbadian** /bɑ:'beɪdiən/
Belarus /ˌbelə'ru:s/	**Belarusian** /ˌbelə'ru:siən/ **Belorussian** /ˌbelə'rʌʃn/
Belgium /'beldʒəm/	**Belgian** /'beldʒən/
Benin /be'ni:n/	**Beninese** /ˌbenɪ'ni:z/
Bolivia /bə'lɪviə/	**Bolivian** /bə'lɪviən/
Bosnia and Herzegovina /ˌbɒzniə ən ˌhɜ:tsəgə'vi:nə/	**Bosnian** /'bɒzniən/, **Herzegovinian** /ˌhɜ:tsegə'vi:niən/

Kraj	*Przymiotnik/Rzeczownik*
Botswana /bɒt'swɑ:nə/	**Botswanan** /bɒt'swɑ:nən/
Brazil /brə'zɪl/	**Brazilian** /brə'zɪliən/
Brunei /'bru:naɪ/	**Bruneian** /bru:'naɪən/
Bulgaria /bʌl'geəriə/	**Bulgarian** /bʌl'geəriən/
Burkina /bɜ:'ki:nə/	**Burkinese** /ˌbɜ:kɪ'ni:z/
Burma /'bɜ:mə/	**Burmese** /bɜ:'mi:z/
Burundi /bʊ'rʊndi/	**Burundian** /bʊ'rʊndiən/
Cambodia /kæm'bəʊdiə/	**Cambodian** /kæm'bəʊdiən/
Cameroon /ˌkæmə'ru:n/	**Cameroonian** /ˌkæmə'ru:niən/
Canada /'kænədə/	**Canadian** /kə'neɪdiən/
Cape Verde /ˌkeɪp 'vɜ:d/	**Cape Verdean** /ˌkeɪp 'vɜ:diən/
Central African Republic (CAR) /ˌsentrəl ˌæfrɪkən rɪ'pʌblɪk/	**Central African** /ˌsentrəl 'æfrɪkən/
Chad /tʃæd/	**Chadian** /'tʃædiən/
Chile /'tʃɪli/	**Chilean** /'tʃɪliən/
China /'tʃaɪnə/	**Chinese** /tʃaɪ'ni:z/
Colombia /kə'lɒmbiə, -'lʌm-/	**Colombian** /kə'lɒmbiən, -'lʌm-/
Congo /'kɒŋgəʊ/	**Congolese** /ˌkɒŋgə'li:z/
the Democratic Republic of the Congo (DROC) /deməˌkrætɪk rɪˌpʌblɪk əv ðə 'kɒŋgəʊ/	**Congolese** /ˌkɒŋgə'li:z/
Costa Rica /ˌkɒstə 'ri:kə/	**Costa Rican** /ˌkɒstə 'ri:kən/
Côte d'Ivoire /ˌkəʊt di:'vwɑ:/	**Ivorian** /aɪ'vɔ:riən/
Croatia /krəʊ'eɪʃə/	**Croatian** /krəʊ'eɪʃn/
Cuba /'kju:bə/	**Cuban** /'kju:bən/
Cyprus /'saɪprəs/	**Cypriot** /'sɪpriət/

Kraj	Przymiotnik/Rzeczownik
(the) Czech Republic /ˌtʃek rɪˈpʌblɪk/	**Czech** /tʃek/
Denmark /ˈdenmɑːk/	**Danish** /ˈdeɪnɪʃ/, **a Dane** /deɪn/
Djibouti /dʒɪˈbuːti/	**Djiboutian** /dʒɪˈbuːtiən/
(the) Dominican Republic /dəˈmɪnɪkən rɪˈpʌblɪk/	**Dominican** /dəˈmɪnɪkən/
East Timor /ˌiːst ˈtiːmɔː(r)/	**East Timorese** /ˌiːst tɪməˈriːz/
Ecuador /ˈekwədɔː(r)/	**Ecuadorian, Ecuadorean** /ˌekwəˈdɔːriən/
Egypt /ˈiːdʒɪpt/	**Egyptian** /iˈdʒɪpʃn/
El Salvador /el ˈsælvədɔː(r)/	**Salvadorean** /ˌsælvəˈdɔːriən/
England /ˈɪŋglənd/	**English** /ˈɪŋglɪʃ/, **an Englishman** /ˈɪŋglɪʃmən/, **an Englishwoman** /ˈɪŋglɪʃwʊmən/ **(the English)**
Eritrea /ˌerɪˈtreɪə; US -ˈtriːə/	**Eritrean** /ˌerɪˈtreɪən; US -ˈtriːən/
Estonia /eˈstəʊniə/	**Estonian** /eˈstəʊniən/
Ethiopia /ˌiːθiˈəʊpiə/	**Ethiopian** /ˌiːθiˈəʊpiən/
Europe /ˈjʊərəp/	**European** /ˌjʊərəˈpiːən/
Fiji /ˈfiːdʒiː/	**Fijian** /fiːˈdʒiːən/
Finland /ˈfɪnlənd/	**Finnish** /ˈfɪnɪʃ/, **a Finn** /fɪn/
(the) Former Yugoslav Republic of Macedonia (FYROM) /ˌfɔːmə ˌjuːgəslɑːv rɪˌpʌblɪk əvˌmæsəˈdəʊniə/	**Macedonian** /ˌmæsəˈdəʊniən/
France /frɑːns; US fræns/	**French** /frentʃ/, **a Frenchman** /ˈfrentʃmən/, **a Frenchwoman** /ˈfrentʃwʊmən/ **(the French)**
Gabon /gæˈbɒn; US gæˈbəʊn/	**Gabonese** /ˌgæbəˈniːz/
(the) Gambia /ˈgæmbiə/	**Gambian** /ˈgæmbiən/
Georgia /ˈdʒɔːdʒə/	**Georgian** /ˈdʒɔːdʒən/
Germany /ˈdʒɜːməni/	**German** /ˈdʒɜːmən/
Ghana /ˈgɑːnə/	**Ghanaian** /gɑːˈneɪən/
Great Britain /ˌgreɪt ˈbrɪtn/	**British** /ˈbrɪtɪʃ/, **a Briton** /ˈbrɪtn/ **(the British)**
Greece /griːs/	**Greek** /griːk/
Guatemala /ˌgwɑːtəˈmɑːlə/	**Guatemalan** /ˌgwɑːtəˈmɑːlən/
Guinea /ˈgɪni/	**Guinean** /ˈgɪniən/
Guyana /gaɪˈænə/	**Guyanese** /ˌgaɪəˈniːz/
Haiti /ˈheɪti/	**Haitian** /ˈheɪʃn/

Kraj	Przymiotnik/Rzeczownik
Holland /ˈhɒlənd/	→ (THE) NETHERLANDS
Honduras /hɒnˈdjʊərəs; US -ˈdʊər-/	**Honduran** /hɒnˈdjʊərən; US -ˈdʊər-/
Hungary /ˈhʌŋgəri/	**Hungarian** /hʌŋˈgeəriən/
Iceland /ˈaɪslənd/	**Icelandic** /aɪsˈlændɪk/, **an Icelander** /ˈaɪsləndə(r)/
India /ˈɪndiə/	**Indian** /ˈɪndiən/
Indonesia /ˌɪndəˈniːʒə/	**Indonesian** /ˌɪndəˈniːʒn/
Iran /ɪˈrɑːn, ɪˈræn/	**Iranian** /ɪˈreɪniən/
Iraq /ɪˈrɑːk, ɪˈræk/	**Iraqi** /ɪˈrɑːki, ɪˈræki/
Ireland /ˈaɪələnd/	**Irish** /ˈaɪrɪʃ/, **an Irishman** /ˈaɪrɪʃmən/, **an Irishwoman** /ˈaɪrɪʃwʊmən/ **(the Irish)**
Israel /ˈɪzreɪl/	**Israeli** /ɪzˈreɪli/
Italy /ˈɪtəli/	**Italian** /ɪˈtæliən/
(the) Ivory Coast /ˌaɪvəri ˈkəʊst/	→ CÔTE D'IVOIRE
Jamaica /dʒəˈmeɪkə/	**Jamaican** / dʒəˈmeɪkən/
Japan /dʒəˈpæn/	**Japanese** /ˌdʒæpəˈniːz/
Jordan /ˈdʒɔːdn/	**Jordanian** /dʒɔːˈdeɪniən/
Kazakhstan /ˌkæzækˈstæn, -ˈstɑːn/	**Kazakh** /ˈkæzæk, kəˈzæk/
Kenya /ˈkenjə/	**Kenyan** /ˈkenjən/
Korea, North /ˌnɔːθ kəˈriə/	**North Korean** /ˌnɔːθ kəˈriən/
Korea, South /ˌsaʊθ kəˈriə/	**South Korean** /ˌsaʊθ kəˈriən/
Kuwait /kʊˈweɪt/	**Kuwaiti** /kʊˈweɪti/
Kyrgyzstan /ˌkɜːgɪˈstæn, ˌkɪə-, -ˈstɑːn/	**Kyrgyz** /ˈkɜːgɪz, ˈkɪəgɪz/
Laos /laʊs/	**Laotian** /ˈlaʊʃn; US leɪˈəʊʃn/
Latvia /ˈlætviə/	**Latvian** /ˈlætviən/
Lebanon /ˈlebənən/	**Lebanese** /ˌlebəˈniːz/
Lesotho /ləˈsuːtuː/	**Sotho** /ˈsuːtuː/
Liberia /laɪˈbɪəriə/	**Liberian** /laɪˈbɪəriən/
Libya /ˈlɪbiə/	**Libyan** /ˈlɪbiən/
Liechtenstein /ˈlɪktənstaɪn, ˈlɪx-/	**Liechtenstein, a Liechtensteiner** /ˈlɪktənstaɪnə(r), ˈlɪx-/
Lithuania /ˌlɪθjuˈeɪniə/	**Lithuanian** /ˌlɪθjuˈeɪniən/
Luxembourg /ˈlʌksəmbɜːg/	**Luxembourg, a Luxembourger** /ˈlʌksəmbɜːgə(r)/
Madagascar /ˌmædəˈgæskə(r)/	**Madagascan** /ˌmædəˈgæskən/ **Malagasy** /ˌmæləˈgæsi/
Malawi /məˈlɑːwi/	**Malawian** /məˈlɑːwiən/
Malaysia /məˈleɪʒə/	**Malaysian** /məˈleɪʒn/
(the) Maldives /ˈmɔːldiːvz/	**Maldivian** /mɔːlˈdɪviən/
Mali /ˈmɑːli/	**Malian** /ˈmɑːliən/

Kraj	*Przymiotnik/Rzeczownik*
Malta /'mɔ:ltə/	**Maltese** /mɔ:l'ti:z/
Mauritania /ˌmɒrɪ'teɪniə; US ˌmɔ:r-/	**Mauritanian** /ˌmɒrɪ'teɪniən; US ˌmɔ:r-/
Mauritius /mə'rɪʃəs; US mɔ:'r-/	**Mauritian** /mə'rɪʃn; US mɔ:'r-/
Mexico /'meksɪkəʊ/	**Mexican** /'meksɪkən/
Moldova /mɒl'dəʊvə/	**Moldovian** /mɒl'dəʊvən/
Mongolia /mɒŋ'gəʊliə/	**Mongolian** /mɒŋ'gəʊliən/, **a Mongol** /'mɒŋgl/
Montenegro /ˌmɒntɪ'ni:grəʊ; US -tə'ne-/	**Montenegrin** /ˌmɒntɪ'ni:grɪn; US -tə'ne-/
Morocco /mə'rɒkəʊ/	**Moroccan** /mə'rɒkən/
Mozambique /ˌməʊzæm'bi:k/	**Mozambican** /ˌməʊzæm'bi:kən/
Myanmar /miˌæn'mɑ:(r)/	→ BURMA
Namibia /nə'mɪbiə/	**Namibian** /nə'mɪbiən/
Nauru /'naʊru:/	**Nauruan** /ˌnaʊ'ru:ən/
Nepal /nɪ'pɔ:l/	**Nepalese** /ˌnepə'li:z/
(the) Netherlands /'neðələndz/	**Dutch** /dʌtʃ/, **a Dutchman** /'dʌtʃmən/, **a Dutchwoman** /'dʌtʃwʊmən/
New Zealand /ˌnju: 'zi:lənd; US ˌnu:/	**New Zealand**, **a New Zealander** /ˌnju: 'zi:ləndə(r); US ˌnu:/
Nicaragua /ˌnɪkə'rægjuə; US -gwə/	**Nicaraguan** /ˌnɪkə'rægjuən; US -gwən/
Niger /ni:'ʒeə(r)/	**Nigerien** /ni:'ʒeəriən/
Nigeria /naɪ'dʒɪəriə/	**Nigerian** /naɪ'dʒɪəriən/
Northern Ireland /ˌnɔ:ðən 'aɪələnd/	**Northern Irish** /ˌnɔ:ðən 'aɪrɪʃ/, **a Northern Irishman** /ˌnɔ:ðən 'aɪrɪʃmən/, **a Northern Irishwoman** /ˌnɔ:ðən 'aɪrɪʃwʊmən/
Norway /'nɔ:weɪ/	**Norwegian** /nɔ:'wi:dʒən/
Oman /əʊ'mɑ:n/	**Omani** /əʊ'mɑ:ni/
Pakistan /ˌpækɪ'stæn, ˌpɑ:kɪ-, -'stɑ:n/	**Pakistani** /ˌpækɪ'stæni, ˌpɑ:kɪ-, -'stɑ:ni/
Panama /'pænəmɑ:/	**Panamanian** /ˌpænə'meɪniən/
Papua New Guinea (PNG) /ˌpæpjuə ˌnju: 'gɪni; Brit. also ˌpæpuə; US ˌnu:/	**Papua New Guinean** /ˌpæpjuə ˌnju: 'gɪniən; Brit. also ˌpæpuə; US ˌnu:/
Paraguay /'pærəgwaɪ/	**Paraguayan** /ˌpærə'gwaɪən/
Peru /pə'ru:/	**Peruvian** /pə'ru:viən/
(the) Philippines /'fɪlɪpi:nz/	**Philippine** /'fɪlɪpi:n/, **a Filipino** /ˌfɪlɪ'pi:nəʊ/, **a Filipina** /ˌfɪlɪ'pi:nə/
Poland /'pəʊlənd/	**Polish** /'pəʊlɪʃ/, **a Pole** /pəʊl/
Portugal /'pɔ:tʃʊgl/	**Portuguese** /ˌpɔ:tʃʊ'gi:z/
Qatar /'kʌtɑ:(r), kæ'tɑ:(r)/	**Qatari** /kʌ'tɑ:ri, kæ't-/
Romania /ru'meɪniə/	**Romanian** /ru'meɪniən/
Russia /'rʌʃə/	**Russian** /'rʌʃn/
Rwanda /ru'ændə/	**Rwandan** /ru'ændən/
Samoa /sə'məʊə/	**Samoan** /sə'məʊən/
Saudi Arabia /ˌsaʊdi ə'reɪbiə/	**Saudi** /'saʊdi/, **Saudi Arabian** /ˌsaʊdi ə'reɪbiən/
Scotland /'skɒtlənd/	**Scottish** /'skɒtɪʃ/, **Scots** /skɒts/, **a Scot** /skɒt/, **a Scotsman** /'skɒtsmən/, **a Scotswoman** /'skɒtswʊmən/ **(the Scots)**
Senegal /ˌsenɪ'gɔ:l/	**Senegalese** /ˌsenɪgə'li:z/
Serbia /'sɜ:biə/	**Serbian** /'sɜ:biən/
(the) Seychelles /seɪ'ʃelz/	**Seychellois** /ˌseɪʃel'wɑ:/
Sierra Leone /siˌerə li'əʊn/	**Sierra Leonean** /siˌerə li'əʊniən/
Singapore /ˌsɪŋə'pɔ:(r); US 'sɪŋəpɔ:r/	**Singaporean** /ˌsɪŋə'pɔ:riən/
Slovakia /slə'vækiə; US sləʊ-/	**Slovak** /'sləʊvæk/, **Slovakian** /slə'vækiən; US sləʊ-/
Slovenia /slə'vi:niə; US sləʊ-/	**Slovene** /'sləʊvi:n/, **Slovenian** /slə'vi:niən; US sləʊ-/
(the) Solomon Islands /'sɒləmən aɪləndz/	**Solomon Islander** /'sɒləmən aɪləndə(r)/
Somalia /sə'mɑ:liə/	**Somali** /sə'mɑ:li/
South Africa /ˌsaʊθ 'æfrɪkə/	**South African** /ˌsaʊθ 'æfrɪkən/
South Sudan /ˌsaʊθ su'dɑ:n; su'dæn/	**South Sudanese** /ˌsaʊθ ˌsudə'nɪ:z/
Spain /speɪn/	**Spanish** /'spænɪʃ/, **a Spaniard** /'spænɪəd/
Sri Lanka /ˌsri 'læŋkə/	**Sri Lankan** /ˌsri 'læŋkən/
St Lucia /ˌsnt 'lu:ʃə; US ˌseɪnt/	**St Lucian** /ˌsnt 'lu:ʃən; US ˌseɪnt/
Sudan /su'dɑ:n/	**Sudanese** /ˌsu:də'ni:z/
Suriname /ˌsʊərɪ'nɑ:m, -'næm/	**Surinamese** /ˌsʊərɪnə'mi:z/
Swaziland /'swɑ:zilænd/	**Swazi** /'swɑ:zi/
Sweden /'swi:dn/	**Swedish** /'swi:dɪʃ/, **a Swede** /swi:d/
Switzerland /'swɪtsələnd/	**Swiss** /swɪs/
Syria /'sɪriə/	**Syrian** /'sɪriən/
Tajikistan /tæˌdʒi:kɪ'stæn, -'stɑ:n/	**Tajik** /tæ'dʒi:k/
Tanzania /ˌtænzə'ni:ə/	**Tanzanian** /ˌtænzə'ni:ən/

Kraj	Przymiotnik/Rzeczownik
Thailand /'taɪlænd/	**Thai** /taɪ/
Tonga /'tɒŋə, 'tɒŋgə/	**Tongan** /'tɒŋən, 'tɒŋgən/
Togo /'təʊgəʊ/	**Togolese** /ˌtəʊgə'li:z/
Trinidad and Tobago /ˌtrɪnɪdæd ən tə'beɪgəʊ/	**Trinidadian** /ˌtrɪnɪ'dædiən/, **Tobagan** /tə'beɪgən/, **Tobagonian** /ˌtəʊbə'gəʊniən/
Tunisia /tju'nɪziə; US tu:'ni:ʒə/	**Tunisian** /tju'nɪziən; US tu:'ni:ʒn/
Turkey /'tɜ:ki/	**Turkish** /'tɜ:kɪʃ/, **a Turk** /tɜ:k/
Turkmenistan /tɜ:kˌmenɪ'stæn, -'stɑ:n/	**Turkmen** /'tɜ:kmen/
Uganda /ju'gændə/	**Ugandan** /ju'gændən/
Ukraine /ju'kreɪn/	**Ukrainian** /ju'kreɪniən/
(the) United Arab Emirates /juˌnaɪtɪd ˌærəb 'emɪrəts/	**Emirati** /ˌemɪ'rɑ:ti/
(the) United Kingdom /juˌnaɪtɪd 'kɪŋdəm/	**British** /'brɪtɪʃ/, **a Briton** /'brɪtn/ **(the British)**
(the) United States of America /juˌnaɪtɪd ˌsteɪts əv ə'merɪkə/	**American** /ə'merɪkən/
Uruguay /'jʊərəgwaɪ/	**Uruguayan** /ˌjʊərə'gwaɪən/
Uzbekistan /ʊzˌbekɪ'stæn, -'stɑ:n/	**Uzbek** /'ʊzbek/
Vanuatu /ˌvænu'ɑ:tu:, ˌvænwɑ:'tu:/	**Vanuatuan** /ˌvænwɑ:'tu:ən/
Venezuela /ˌvenə'zweɪlə/	**Venezuelan** /ˌvenə'zweɪlən/
Vietnam /ˌvjet'næm, ˌvi:et-, -'nɑ:m/	**Vietnamese** /ˌvjetnə'mi:z, vi:ˌet-/
Wales /weɪlz/	**Welsh** /welʃ/, **a Welshman** /'welʃmən/, **a Welshwoman** /'welʃwʊmən/ **(the Welsh)**
(the) West Indies /ˌwest 'ɪndiz/	**West Indian** /ˌwest 'ɪndiən/
Yemen /'jemən/	**Yemeni** /'jeməni/
Zambia /'zæmbiə/	**Zambian** /'zæmbiən/
Zimbabwe /zɪm'bɑ:bwi, -bweɪ/	**Zimbabwean** /zɪm'bɑ:bwɪən/

Cities of the world
Wielkie miasta świata

Amsterdam /'æmstədæm/
Athens /'æθənz/
Baghdad /bæg'dæd; US 'bægdæd/
Bangkok /bæŋ'kɒk; US 'bæŋkɒk/
Barcelona /ˌbɑ:sə'ləʊnə/
Beijing /beɪ'ʒɪŋ, -'dʒɪŋ/
Beirut /beɪ'ru:t/
Belgrade /bel'greɪd; US 'belgreɪd/
Berlin /bɜ:'lɪn/
Bratislava /ˌbrætɪ'slɑ:və; US -'slævə/
Brussels /'brʌslz/ (Bruksela)
Bucharest /'bu:kərest/
Budapest /'bu:dəpest/
Cairo /'kaɪrəʊ/
Cape Town /'keɪp taʊn/
Frankfurt /'fræŋkfət/
Geneva /dʒə'ni:və/
The Hague /ˌðə 'heɪg/
Helsinki /hel'sɪŋki/
Istanbul /ˌɪstæn'bʊl/
Jakarta /dʒə'kɑ:tə/
Jerusalem /dʒə'ru:sələm/
Johannesburg /dʒə'hænəzbɜ:g/
Kabul /'kɑ:bʊl/
Lagos /'leɪgɒs/
Lisbon /'lɪzbən/
Madrid /mə'drɪd/
Mexico City /ˌmeksɪkəʊ 'sɪti/
Milan /mɪ'læn/
Moscow /'mɒskəʊ; US -kaʊ/
Munich /'mju:nɪk/ (Monachium)
Nairobi /naɪ'rəʊbi/
New Delhi /ˌnju: 'deli; US ˌnu:/
Paris /'pærɪs; US 'perəs/
Prague /prɑ:g/
Rio de Janeiro /ˌriəʊ də dʒə'nɪərəʊ/
Rome /rəʊm/ (Rzym)
Sao Paulo /ˌsaʊ 'paʊləʊ/
Seoul /səʊl/
Shanghai /ʃæŋ'haɪ/
Stockholm /'stɒkhəʊm/
St. Petersburg /ˌsnt 'pi:təzbɜ:g; US ˌseɪnt/
Tokyo /'təʊkɪəʊ/
Venice /'vənɪs/ (Wenecja)
Vienna /vi'enə/ (Wiedeń)
Vilnius /'vɪlniəs/
Warsaw /'wɔ:sɔ:/
Zurich /'zjʊərɪk/

The British Isles
Wyspy Brytyjskie

Wielka Brytania – **Britain** lub **Great Britain** /ˌgreɪt 'brɪtn/ **(GB)** – jest wyspą, składającą się z Anglii – **England** /'ɪŋglənd/, Szkocji – **Scotland** /'skɒtlənd/ i Walii – **Wales** /weɪlz/ (ale bez Irlandii – **Ireland** /'aɪələnd/).

Nazwa **Britain** jest czasem nieprawidłowo stosowana w odniesieniu do politycznej nazwy państwa, formalnie zwanego **the United Kingdom of Great Britain and Northern Ireland** (Zjednoczone Królestwo Wielkiej Brytanii i Irlandii Północnej). Nazwę tę pisze się skrótowo **the United Kingdom** lub **UK**.

The British Isles to grupa wysp, do której należy Irlandia i kilka mniejszych wysp. **The Republic of Ireland** (także zwana **the Irish Republic**, dawniej **Eire** /'eərə/) jest niepodległym państwem, zajmującym większą część wyspy Irlandii.

Specjalne przymiotniki lub rzeczowniki opisują ludzi pochodzących z niektórych miast, np. osoba z Londynu zwana jest **Londoner** /'lʌndənə(r)/, z Dublina – **Dubliner** /'dʌblɪnə(r)/, z Glasgow – **Glaswegian** /glɑːz'wiːdʒən; US glæs-/, z Manchesteru – **Mancunian** /mæn'kjuːniən/, a z Liverpoolu – **Liverpudlian** /ˌlɪvə'pʌdliən/. Rdzenni Londyńczycy o charakterystycznej miejscowej wymowie są też nazywani **Cockney** /'kɒkni/. Zaś **Brummie** /'brʌmi/ to potoczna nazwa osoby pochodzącej z Birmingham.

The United Kingdom dzieli się na **counties** (okręgi administracyjne), a od stycznia 1995 także na **unitary authorities** (zarządy jednostkowe). Niektóre **counties** i ich nazwy, np. **Devon** i **Cumbria**, pozostają bez zmian. Inne dawne **counties** dzieli się teraz na kilka mniejszych **unitary authorities.** Wiele osób nadal używa nazw byłych **counties**.

Towns and cities in the British Isles
Miasta Wysp Brytyjskich

Aberdeen /ˌæbə'diːn/
Bath /bɑːθ; US bæθ/
Belfast /'belfɑːst, ˌbel'fɑːst; US 'belfæst/
Berwick-upon-Tweed /ˌberɪk əpɒn 'twiːd/
Birmingham /'bɜːmɪŋəm; US 'bɜːrmɪŋhæm/
Blackpool /'blækpuːl/
Bournemouth /'bɔːnməθ/
Bradford /'brædfəd/
Brighton /'braɪtn/
Bristol /'brɪstl/
Caernarfon /kə'nɑːvn/
Cambridge /'keɪmbrɪdʒ/
Canterbury /'kæntəbəri; US -beri/
Cardiff /'kɑːdɪf/
Carlisle /kɑː'laɪl; US 'kɑːrlaɪl/
Chester /'tʃestə(r)/
Colchester /'kəʊltʃestə(r)/
Cork /kɔːk/
Coventry /'kɒvəntri/
Derby /'dɑːbi/
Douglas /'dʌgləs/
Dover /'dəʊvə(r)/
Dublin /'dʌblɪn/
Dundee /dʌn'diː/
Durham /'dʌrəm/
Eastbourne /'iːstbɔːn/
Edinburgh /'edɪnbrə, -bərə/
Ely /'iːli/
Exeter /'eksɪtə(r)/
Galway /'gɔːlweɪ/
Glasgow /'glɑːzgəʊ; US 'glæz-/
Gloucester /'glɒstə(r)/
Hastings /'heɪstɪŋz/
Hereford /'herɪfəd/
Holyhead /'hɒlihed/
Inverness /ˌɪnvə'nes/
Ipswich /'ɪpswɪtʃ/
Keswick /'kezɪk/
Kingston upon Hull /ˌkɪŋstən əpɒn 'hʌl/
Leeds /liːdz/
Leicester /'lestə(r)/
Limerick /'lɪmərɪk/
Lincoln /'lɪŋkən/
Liverpool /'lɪvəpuːl/
London /'lʌndən/
Londonderry /'lʌndənderi/
Luton /'luːtn/
Manchester /'mæntʃɪstə(r)/
Middlesbrough /'mɪdlzbrə/
Newcastle upon Tyne /ˌnjuːkɑːsl əpɒn 'taɪn; US ˌnuːkæsl/
Norwich /'nɒrɪdʒ/
Nottingham /'nɒtɪŋəm; US 'nɒtɪŋhæm/
Oxford /'ɒksfəd/
Plymouth /'plɪməθ/
Poole /puːl/
Portsmouth /'pɔːtsməθ/
Ramsgate /'ræmzgeɪt/
Reading /'redɪŋ/
Salisbury /'sɔːlzbəri; US -beri/
Sheffield /'ʃefiːld/
Shrewsbury /'ʃrəʊzbəri; US -beri/
Southampton /saʊ'θæmptən/
St Andrews /ˌsnt 'ændruːz; US ˌseɪnt/
St David's /ˌsnt 'deɪvɪdz; US ˌseɪnt/
Stirling /'stɜːlɪŋ/
Stoke-on-Trent /ˌstəʊk ɒn'trent/
Stratford-upon-Avon /ˌstrætfəd əpɒn 'eɪvn/
Swansea /'swɒnzi/
Taunton /'tɔːntən/
Warwick /'wɒrɪk/
Worcester /'wʊstə(r)/
York /jɔːk/

international boundary
national boundary
capital city
city or town
0
50
100 km
Shetland Islands
Orkney Islands
Outer Hebrides
Inner Hebrides
Atlantic Ocean
SCOTLAND
Inverness
Aberdeen
Dundee
St Andrews
Stirling
Glasgow
Edinburgh
Berwick-upon-Tweed
North Sea
NORTHERN IRELAND
Londonderry
Belfast
ISLE OF MAN
Douglas
Carlisle
Newcastle upon Tyne
Durham
Keswick
Middlesbrough
Irish Sea
York
Blackpool
Leeds
Bradford
Kingston upon Hull
Galway
Dublin
Anglesey
Holyhead
Liverpool
Manchester
Sheffield
Chester
Caernarfon
Stoke-on-Trent
Lincoln
ENGLAND
Limerick
Nottingham
Shrewsbury
Derby
Birmingham
Leicester
WALES
Norwich
Coventry
Cork
Worcester
Warwick
Cambridge
Hereford
Stratford-upon-Avon
Ipswich
Gloucester
Luton
REPUBLIC OF IRELAND
Swansea
Colchester
Cardiff
Oxford
Bristol
London
Bath
Reading
Ramsgate
Canterbury
Taunton
Salisbury
Dover
Strait of Dover
Southampton
Brighton
Hastings
Exeter
Bournemouth
Poole
Portsmouth
Eastbourne
Isle of Wight
Plymouth
Isles of Scilly
English Channel

The United States and Canada
Stany Zjednoczone i Kanada

The states of the United States of America
Stany USA

Alabama /ˌæləˈbæmə/
Alaska /əˈlæskə/
Arizona /ˌærɪˈzəʊnə/
Arkansas /ˈɑːkənsɔː/
California /ˌkæləˈfɔːniə/
Colorado /ˌkɒləˈrɑːdəʊ; US -ˈrædəʊ/
Connecticut /kəˈnetɪkət/
Delaware /ˈdeləweə(r)/
Florida /ˈflɒrɪdə/
Georgia /ˈdʒɔːdʒə/
Hawaii /həˈwaɪi/
Idaho /ˈaɪdəhəʊ/
Illinois /ˌɪləˈnɔɪ/
Indiana /ˌɪndiˈænə/
Iowa /ˈaɪəwə/
Kansas /ˈkænzəs/
Kentucky /kenˈtʌki/
Louisiana /luˌiːziˈænə/
Maine /meɪn/
Maryland /ˈmeərilənd; US ˈmerə-/
Massachusetts /ˌmæsəˈtʃuːsɪts/
Michigan /ˈmɪʃɪgən/
Minnesota /ˌmɪnɪˈsəʊtə/
Mississippi /ˌmɪsɪˈsɪpi/
Missouri /mɪˈzʊəri; US məˈz-/
Montana /mɒnˈtænə/
Nebraska /nəˈbræskə/
Nevada /nəˈvɑːdə; US nəˈvædə/
New Hampshire /ˌnjuː ˈhæmpʃə(r); US ˌnuː/
New Jersey /ˌnjuː ˈdʒɜːzi; US ˌnuː/
New Mexico /ˌnjuː ˈmeksɪkəʊ; US ˌnuː/
New York /ˌnjuː ˈjɔːk; US ˌnuː/
North Carolina /ˌnɔːθ kærəˈlaɪnə/
North Dakota /ˌnɔːθ dəˈkəʊtə/
Ohio /əʊˈhaɪəʊ/
Oklahoma /ˌəʊkləˈhəʊmə/
Oregon /ˈɒrɪgən/
Pennsylvania /ˌpenslˈveɪniə/
Rhode Island /ˌrəʊd ˈaɪlənd/
South Carolina /ˌsaʊθ kærəˈlaɪnə/
South Dakota /ˌsaʊθ dəˈkəʊtə/
Tennessee /ˌtenəˈsiː/
Texas /ˈteksəs/
Utah /ˈjuːtɑː/
Vermont /vəˈmɒnt/
Virginia /vəˈdʒɪniə/
Washington /ˈwɒʃɪŋtən/
West Virginia /ˌwest vəˈdʒɪniə/
Wisconsin /wɪsˈkɒnsɪn/
Wyoming /waɪˈəʊmɪŋ/

The provinces and territories of Canada
Podział administracyjny Kanady

Alberta /ælˈbɜːtə/
British Columbia /ˌbrɪtɪʃ kəˈlʌmbiə/
Manitoba /ˌmænɪˈtəʊbə/
New Brunswick /ˌnjuː ˈbrʌnzwɪk; US ˌnuː/
Newfoundland /ˈnjuːfəndlənd; US ˈnuː-/
Northwest Territories /ˌnɔːθwest ˈterətriz; US ˈterətɔːriz/
Nova Scotia /ˌnəʊvə ˈskəʊʃə/
Nunavut /ˈnʊnəvʊt/
Ontario /ɒnˈteəriəʊ/
Prince Edward Island /ˌprɪns ˈedwəd aɪlənd/
Quebec /kwɪˈbek/
Saskatchewan /səˈskætʃəwən/
Yukon Territory /ˈjuːkɒn terətri; US terətɔːri/

Towns and cities
Miasta

Atlanta /ətˈlæntə/
Anchorage /ˈæŋkərɪdʒ/
Baltimore /ˈbɔːltɪmɔː(r)/
Boston /ˈbɒstən/
Chicago /ʃɪˈkɑːgəʊ/
Cincinnati /ˌsɪnsɪˈnæti/
Cleveland /ˈkliːvlənd/
Dallas /ˈdæləs/
Denver /ˈdenvə(r)/
Detroit /dɪˈtrɔɪt/
Honolulu /ˌhɒnəˈluːluː/
Houston /ˈhjuːstən/
Indianapolis /ˌɪndiəˈnæpəlɪs/
Kansas City /ˌkænzəs ˈsɪti/
Los Angeles /ˌlɒs ˈændʒəliːz; US ˈændʒələs/
Miami /maɪˈæmi/
Milwaukee /mɪlˈwɔːkɪ/
Minneapolis /ˌmɪniˈæpəlɪs/
Montreal /ˌmɒntriˈɔːl/
New Orleans /ˌnjuː ɔːˈliːənz; US ˌnuː ˈɔːrliənz/
New York /ˌnjuː ˈjɔːk; US ˌnuː/
Ottawa /ˈɒtəwə/
Philadelphia /ˌfɪləˈdelfiə/
Pittsburgh /ˈpɪtsbɜːg/
Quebec City /kwɪˌbek ˈsɪti/
San Diego /ˌsæn diˈeɪgəʊ/
San Francisco /ˌsæn frənˈsɪskəʊ/
Seattle /siˈætl/
St Louis /ˌsnt ˈluːɪs; US ˌseɪnt/
Toronto /təˈrɒntəʊ/
Vancouver /vænˈkuːvə(r)/
Washington D.C. /ˈwɒʃɪŋtən diː ˈsiː/
Winnipeg /ˈwɪnɪpeg/

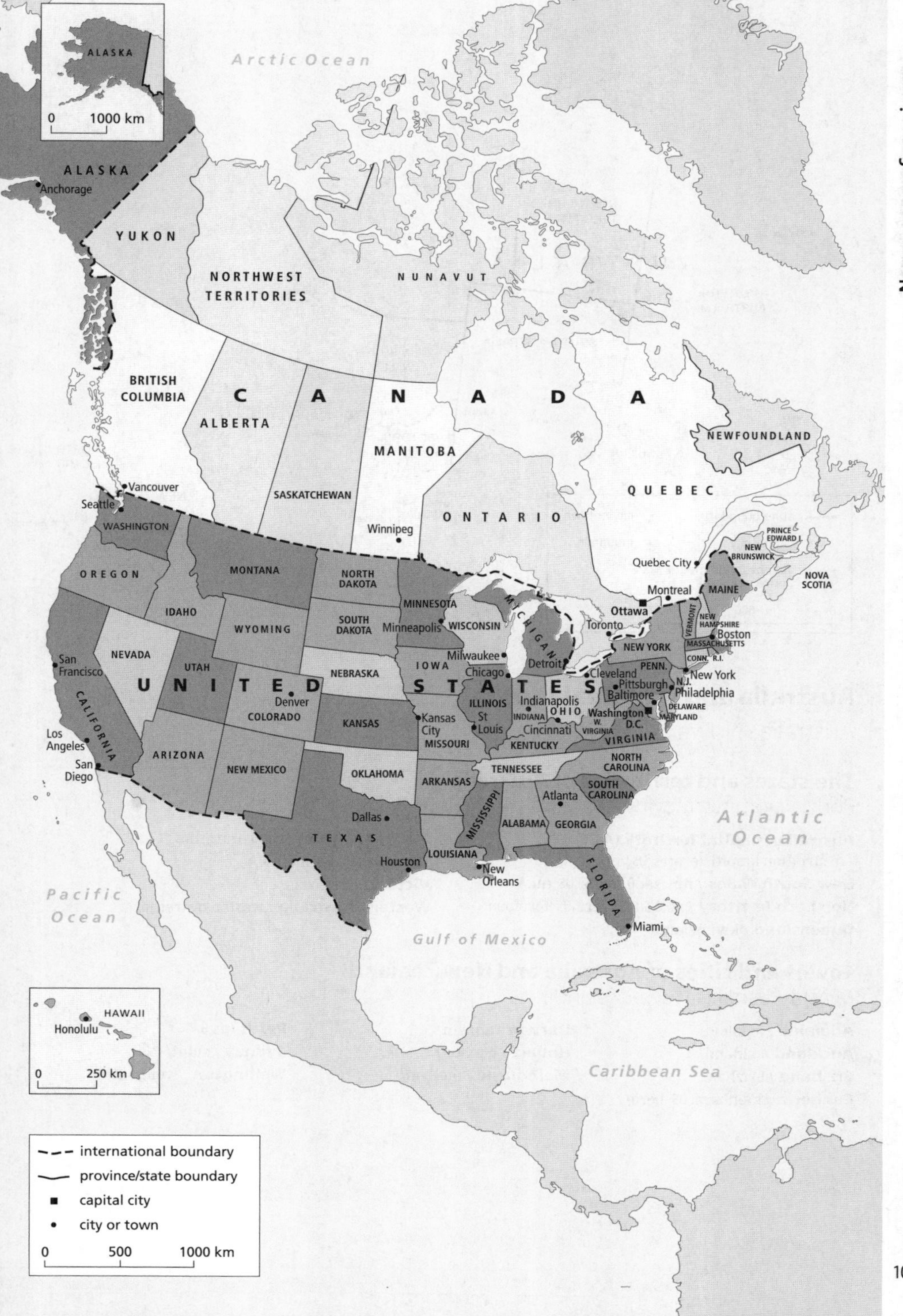
ALASKA
0 1000 km
Arctic Ocean
ALASKA
Anchorage
YUKON
NORTHWEST TERRITORIES
NUNAVUT
BRITISH COLUMBIA
C A N A D A
ALBERTA
NEWFOUNDLAND
MANITOBA
Vancouver
QUEBEC
Seattle
SASKATCHEWAN
ONTARIO
WASHINGTON
Winnipeg
PRINCE EDWARD I.
NEW BRUNSWICK
Quebec City
OREGON
MONTANA
NORTH DAKOTA
NOVA SCOTIA
Montreal
MAINE
MINNESOTA
MICHIGAN
Ottawa
IDAHO
SOUTH DAKOTA
Minneapolis
WISCONSIN
Toronto
VERMONT
NEW HAMPSHIRE
WYOMING
Boston
MASSACHUSETTS
NEVADA
Milwaukee
NEW YORK
San Francisco
CONN.
R.I.
UTAH
IOWA
Detroit
NEBRASKA
Chicago
PENN.
Cleveland
New York
U N I T E D   S T A T E S
N.J.
Pittsburgh
Philadelphia
CALIFORNIA
Denver
Indianapolis
Baltimore
ILLINOIS
DELAWARE
COLORADO
OHIO
Washington D.C.
INDIANA
KANSAS
Kansas City
St Louis
MARYLAND
W. VIRGINIA
Cincinnati
Los Angeles
VIRGINIA
MISSOURI
KENTUCKY
ARIZONA
NORTH CAROLINA
San Diego
NEW MEXICO
OKLAHOMA
TENNESSEE
ARKANSAS
SOUTH CAROLINA
Atlanta
Atlantic Ocean
MISSISSIPPI
ALABAMA
GEORGIA
Dallas
TEXAS
LOUISIANA
Houston
New Orleans
FLORIDA
Pacific Ocean
Miami
Gulf of Mexico
HAWAII
Honolulu
0 250 km
Caribbean Sea
international boundary
province/state boundary
capital city
city or town
0 500 1000 km

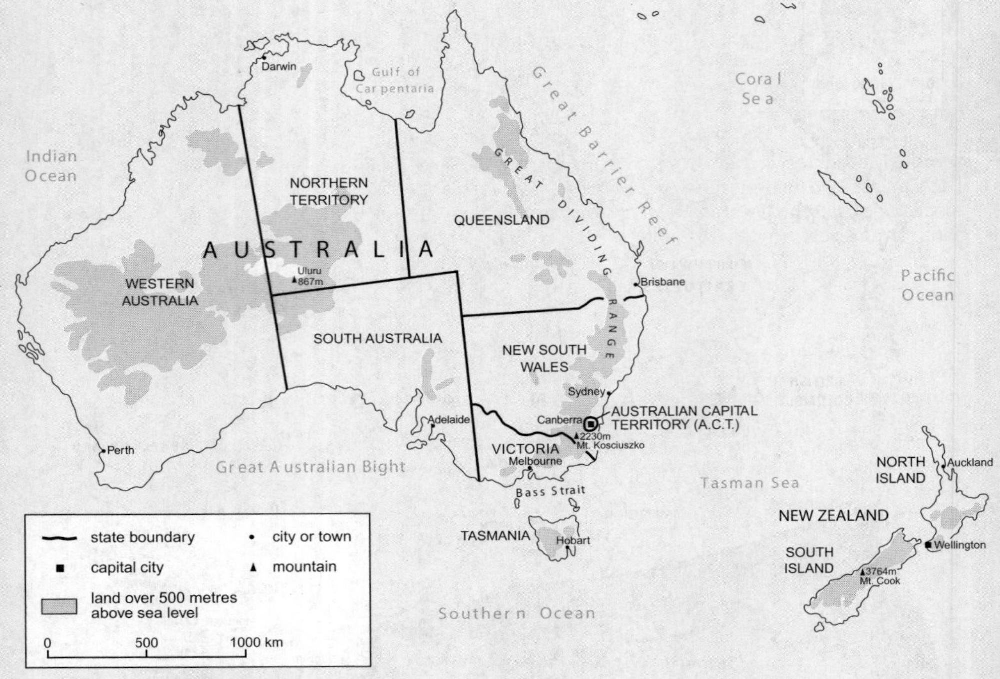

Australia and New Zealand
Australia i Nowa Zelandia

The states and territories of Australia
Podział administracyjny Australii

Australian Capital Territory (ACT) /ɒˌstreɪliən kæpɪtl 'terətri; US 'terətɔːri/
New South Wales /ˌnjuː saʊθ 'weɪlz; US ˌnuː/
Northern Territory /ˌnɔːðən 'terətri; US 'terətɔːri/
Queensland /'kwiːnzlənd/
South Australia /ˌsaʊθ ɒ'streɪliə/
Tasmania /tæz'meɪniə/
Victoria /vɪk'tɔːriə/
Western Australia /ˌwestən ɒ'streɪliə/

Towns and cities of Australia and New Zealand
Miasta Australii i Nowej Zelandii

Adelaide /'ædəleɪd/
Auckland /'ɔːklənd/
Brisbane /'brɪzbən/
Canberra /'kænbərə; US -berə/
Darwin /'dɑːwɪn/
Hobart /'həʊbɑːt/
Melbourne /'melbən/
Perth /pɜːθ/
Sydney /'sɪdni/
Wellington /'welɪŋtən/

DODATEK 3

Czasowniki nieregularne

Uwaga! Dla niektórych czasowników podano dwie możliwe formy czasu przeszłego lub imiesłowu biernego. Czasem różnią się one znaczeniem, dlatego zawsze sprawdź w słowniku, w jakich sytuacjach dana forma jest stosowana.

be

Czas teraźniejszy	Czas przeszły
I **am** (I**'m**)	I **was**
you **are** (you**'re**)	you **were**
he/she/it **is** (he**'s**/she**'s**/it**'s**)	he/she/it **was**
we **are** (we**'re**)	we **were**
you **are** (you**'re**)	you **were**
they **are** (they**'re**)	they **were**

have

Czas teraźniejszy	Czas przeszły
I **have** (I**'ve**)	I **had** (I**'d**)
you **have** (you**'ve**)	you **had** (you**'d**)
he/she/it **has** (he**'s**/she**'s**/it**'s**)	he/she/it **had** (he**'d**/she**'d**/it**'d**)
we **have** (we**'ve**)	we **had** (we**'d**)
you **have** (you**'ve**)	you **had** (you**'d**)
they **have** (they**'ve**)	they **had** (they**'d**)

do

Czas teraźniejszy	Czas przeszły
I **do**	I **did**
you **do**	you **did**
he/she/it **does**	he/she/it **did**
we **do**	we **did**
you **do**	you **did**
they **do**	they **did**

Bezokolicznik	Czas przeszły	Imiesłów bierny
arise	arose	arisen
awake	awoke	awoken
babysit	babysat	babysat
bear[1]	bore	borne
beat[1]	beat	beaten
become	became	become
befall	befell	befallen
begin	began	begun
behold	beheld	beheld
bend[1]	bent	bent
beseech	besought, beseeched	besought, beseeched
beset	beset	beset
bet	bet	bet
bid[1]	bid	bid
bid[2]	bade	bidden
bind[1]	bound	bound
bite[1]	bit	bitten
bleed	bled	bled
blow[1]	blew	blown
break[1]	broke	broken
breastfeed	breastfed	breastfed
breed[1]	bred	bred
bring	brought	brought
broadcast	broadcast	broadcast
browbeat	browbeat	browbeaten
build[1]	built	built
burn[1]	burnt, burned	burnt, burned
burst[1]	burst	burst
bust[1]	bust, busted	bust, busted
buy[1]	bought	bought
cast[1]	cast	cast
catch[1]	caught	caught
choose	chose	chosen
cling	clung	clung
come	came	come
cost[2]	cost	cost
creep[1]	crept	crept
cut[1]	cut	cut
deal[1]	dealt	dealt

Bezokolicznik	Czas przeszły	Imiesłów bierny
dig[1]	dug	dug
dive[1]	dived, US also dove	dived
draw[1]	drew	drawn
dream[2]	dreamed, dreamt	dreamed, dreamt
drink[2]	drank	drunk
drip-feed	drip-fed	drip-fed
drive[1]	drove	driven
dwell	dwelt, dwelled	dwelt, dwelled
eat	ate	eaten
fall[1]	fell	fallen
feed[1]	fed	fed
feel[1]	felt	felt
fight[1]	fought	fought
find[1]	found	found
fit[1]	fitted	fitted
flee	fled	fled
fling[1]	flung	flung
fly[1]	flew	flown
forbear	forbore	forborne
forbid	forbade, forbad	forbidden
forecast	forecast, forecasted	forecast, forecasted
foresee	foresaw	foreseen
foretell	foretold	foretold
forget	forgot	forgotten
forgive	forgave	forgiven
forgo	forwent	forgone
forsake	forsook	forsaken
freeze[1]	froze	frozen
get	got	got, US gotten
give[1]	gave	given
go[1]	went	gone
grind[1]	ground	ground
grow	grew	grown
hamstring	hamstrung	hamstrung
hang[1]	hung, hanged	hung, hanged
hear	heard	heard
hew	hewed	hewed, hewn
hide[1]	hid	hidden
hit[1]	hit	hit
hold[1]	held	held
hurt[1]	hurt	hurt
input[2]	input, inputted	input, inputted
inset	inset	inset
keep	kept	kept
kneel	knelt, kneeled	knelt, kneeled
knit	knitted, US knit	knitted, US knit
know	knew	known
lay[1]	laid	laid
lead[1]	led	led
lean[1]	leant, leaned	leant, leaned

Bezokolicznik	Czas przeszły	Imiesłów bierny
leap[1]	leapt, leaped	leapt, leaped
learn	learnt, learned	learnt, learned
leave[1]	left	left
lend	lent	lent
let	let	let
lie[2]	lay	lain
light[3]	lit, lighted	lit, lighted
lose	lost	lost
make[1]	made	made
mean[1]	meant	meant
meet	met	met
mislay	mislaid	mislaid
mislead	misled	misled
misread	misread /ˌmɪsˈred/	misread /ˌmɪsˈred/
misspell	misspelled, misspelt	misspelled, misspelt
mistake[2]	mistook	mistaken
misunderstand	misunderstood	misunderstood
mow	mowed	mown, mowed
offset	offset	offset
outdo	outdid	outdone
outgrow	outgrew	outgrown
overcome	overcame	overcome
overdo	overdid	overdone
overhang	overhung	overhung
overhear	overheard	overheard
overpay	overpaid	overpaid
override	overrode	overridden
overrun	overran	overrun
oversee	oversaw	overseen
oversleep	overslept	overslept
overtake	overtook	overtaken
overthrow	overthrew	overthrown
pay[1]	paid	paid
proofread	proofread /ˈpruːfred/	proofread /ˈpruːfred/
prove	proved	proved, US proven
put	put	put
quit	quit	quit
read[1]	read /red/	read /red/
rebuild	rebuilt	rebuilt
repay	repaid	repaid
rethink	rethought	rethought
rewind	rewound	rewound
rewrite	rewrote	rewritten
rid	rid	rid
ride[1]	rode	ridden
ring[2]	rang	rung
rise[2]	rose	risen
run[1]	ran	run
saw[2]	sawed	sawn, US sawed

Bezokolicznik	Czas przeszły	Imiesłów bierny
rise[2]	rose	risen
run[1]	ran	run
saw[2]	sawed	sawn, US sawed
say	said	said
see	saw	seen
seek	sought	sought
sell	sold	sold
send	sent	sent
set[1]	set	set
sew	sewed	sewn, sewed
shake[1]	shook	shaken
shear	sheared	sheared, shorn
shed[2]	shed	shed
shine[1]	shone	shone
shoe[2]	shod	shod
shoot[1]	shot	shot
show[1]	showed	shown, showed
shrink	shrank, shrunk	shrunk
shut[1]	shut	shut
sing	sang	sung
sink[1]	sank	sunk
sit	sat	sat
slay	slew	slain
sleep[1]	slept	slept
slide[1]	slid	slid
sling[1]	slung	slung
slink	slunk	slunk
slit[2]	slit	slit
smell[1]	smelt, smelled	smelt, smelled
sow[1]	sowed	sown, sowed
speak	spoke	spoken
speed[2]	sped, speeded	sped, speeded
spell[1]	spelled, spelt	spelled, spelt
spend	spent	spent
spill	spilt, spilled	spilt, spilled
spin[1]	spun	spun
spit[1]	spat, US also spit	spat, US also spit
split[1]	split	split
spoil	spoilt, spoiled	spoilt, spoiled
spread[1]	spread	spread
spring[2]	sprang	sprung
stand[1]	stood	stood
steal	stole	stolen
stick[1]	stuck	stuck
sting[1]	stung	stung
stink	stank, stunk	stunk
stride[1]	strode	—
strike[1]	struck	struck
string[2]	strung	strung
strive	strove	striven
sublet	sublet	sublet
swear	swore	sworn
sweep[1]	swept	swept
swell[1]	swelled	swollen, swelled
swim	swam	swum
swing[1]	swung	swung
take	took	taken
teach	taught	taught
tear[2]	tore	torn
telecast	telecast	telecast
tell	told	told
think	thought	thought
throw	threw	thrown
thrust[1]	thrust	thrust
tread[1]	trod	trodden, trod
typecast	typecast	typecast
undercut	undercut	undercut
undergo	underwent	undergone
underlie	underlay	underlain
underpay	underpaid	underpaid
understand	understood	understood
undertake	undertook	undertaken
undo	undid	undone
unwind	unwound	unwound
uphold	upheld	upheld
upset[1]	upset	upset
wake[1]	woke	woken
wear[1]	wore	worn
weave	wove, weaved	woven, weaved
weep	wept	wept
wet[2]	wet, wetted	wet, wetted
win	won	won
wind[3]	wound	wound
withdraw	withdrew	withdrawn
withhold	withheld	withheld
withstand	withstood	withstood
wring	wrung	wrung
write	wrote	written

DODATEK 4
Wymowa

Jeżeli przy jakimś słowie podano dwie wersje wymowy, oznacza to, że obie formy są poprawne oraz że pierwsza z nich jest częściej używana. Jeśli jakieś słowo wymawia się inaczej w amerykańskiej angielszczyźnie niż w brytyjskiej, wówczas podana jest wymowa amerykańska poprzedzona skrótem US.

/-/ Łącznik oznacza alternatywny sposób wymowy i jest stosowany w sytuacjach, gdy tylko część danego słowa wymawia się inaczej. Część wymawianą bez zmian zastępuje się wtedy łącznikiem.

/ˈ/ Symbol ten oznacza akcent główny padający na następną sylabę. Na przykład, w słowie *any* /ˈeni/ akcent pada na pierwszą sylabę; w *depend* /dɪˈpend/ akcent pada na drugą sylabę.

/ˌ/ Symbol ten oznacza akcent poboczny (słabszy) padający na następną sylabę. W słowie *pronunciation* /prəˌnʌnsiˈeɪʃn/ akcent główny pada na sylabę /ˈeɪʃn/, a akcent poboczny – na sylabę /ˌnʌn/.

(r) W mówionej brytyjskiej angielszczyźnie nie wymawia się litery *r* na końcu słowa lub w formie końcówki *-re* (jak w *fire*), jeżeli kolejne słowo zaczyna się na spółgłoskę. Jeśli jednak kolejne słowo zaczyna się na samogłoskę, wówczas literę *r* się wymawia. Na przykład, nie wymawia się *r* w zdaniu *His car was sold*, ale wymawia się w zdaniu *His car isn't old.* W słowniku zaznaczono to, umieszczając *r* w nawiasie okrągłym, tj. (r), w wymowie słów kończących się na *-r* lub *-re*.

W standardowej amerykańskiej angielszczyźnie literę *r* zawsze się wymawia.

Formy mocne i słabe

Niektóre często spotykane słowa, np. *an*, *as*, *that*, *of* można wymawiać na kilka sposobów: mają one tzw. formę mocną oraz jedną lub kilka form słabych. W języku mówionym częściej używa się form słabych. Na przykład, *from* wymawia się /frəm/ w *He comes from Spain*. Formę mocną stosuje się, kiedy dane słowo występuje na końcu zdania lub jeśli wymawia się je z dużą emfazą. W zdaniu *The ˌpresent's not ˈfrom John – it's ˈfor him*, słowo *from* wymawia się /frɒm/.

Wymowa wyrazów pochodnych i złożonych

Wiele wyrazów pochodnych tworzy się przez dodanie przyrostka. W wyrazach takich przyrostek wymawia się po prostu po wymówieniu danego słowa. Na przykład *slowly* /ˈsləʊli/ wymawia się, łącząc przyrostek *-ly* /li/ ze słowem *slow-*/sləʊ/.

Jeżeli jednak istnieje wątpliwość co do wymowy danego wyrazu pochodnego, to słownik podaje wymowę. Część wyrazu wymawiana bez zmian zostaje wtedy zastąpiona łącznikiem.

W wyrazach złożonych nie powtarza się wymowy poszczególnych słów. Słownik pokazuje, jak należy akcentować dany wyraz złożony za pomocą symboli /ˈ/ i /ˌ/. W ˈ*bus stop* akcent pada na pierwsze słowo. W ˌ*jacket poˈtato*, akcent poboczny pada na pierwszą sylabę słowa *jacket*, a akcent główny na drugą sylabę słowa *potato*.